W9-BKQ-478

The New Grove Dictionary of

Jazz

Second Edition

Volume Three

The New Grove Dictionary of

Jazz

Second Edition

Volume Three
Nightclubs–Zwingenberger

Edited by
Barry Kernfeld

MACMILLAN PUBLISHERS LIMITED, LONDON
GROVE'S DICTIONARIES INC., NEW YORK, NY

The New Grove Dictionary of Jazz, second edition
edited by Barry Kernfeld, in three volumes, 2002

First edition published 1988 by Macmillan Publishers Limited, London. This edition is distributed within the United Kingdom and Europe by Macmillan Publishers Limited London, and within the United States and Canada by Grove's Dictionaries Inc., New York.

Parts of this dictionary were first published in
The New Grove Dictionary of Music and Musicians®
edited by Stanley Sadie, in twenty volumes, 1980
© Macmillan Publishers Limited, 1980
and
The New Grove Dictionary of Musical Instruments
edited by Stanley Sadie, in three volumes, 1984
© Macmillan Publishers Limited, 1984
and
The New Grove Dictionary of American Music
edited by H. Wiley Hitchcock and Stanley Sadie, in four volumes, 1986
© Macmillan Publishers Limited, 1986

Parts of this dictionary were first published in *The New Grove Dictionary of Music and Musicians®. second edition* edited by Stanley Sadie, in twenty-nine volumes, 2001
© Macmillan Publishers Limited, 2001

British Library Cataloguing in Publication Data

The new Grove dictionary of jazz.—2nd ed.
1. Jazz—Dictionaries
I. Kernfeld, Barry II. Grove dictionary of jazz
III. Dictionary of jazz
781.6′5′03

ISBN 033369189X

Library of Congress Cataloguing in Publication Data

The new Grove dictionary of jazz/edited by Barry Kernfeld–2nd ed.
p. cm.
Includes bibliographical references and discographies.
ISBN 1-56159-284-6 (alk. paper)
1. Jazz–Encyclopedias. 2. Jazz–Bio-bibliography. I. Kernfeld, Barry Dean, 1950-

ML102J3 N48 2001
781.65′03–dc21

2001040794

Typeset by YHT Ltd, London, England
Music examples processed by Halstan & Co. Ltd, Amersham, England
Printed and bound by Quebecor World, Taunton, Massachusetts, USA

Contents

General Abbreviations

a	alto
AA	Associates in Arts
AAS	Associates in Arts and Sciences
AB	Bachelor of Arts
ABC	American Broadcasting Company
acc.	accompaniment, accompanied by
addn	addition
AFM	American Federation of Musicians
AFRS	Armed Forces Radio Service
AFR&TS	Armed Forces Radio & Television Service
AK	Alaska
AL	Alabama
AM	Associates in Music
a.m.	ante meridiem (Lat.: before noon)
appx	appendix
AR	Arkansas
arr.	arrangement, arranged (by/for)
ARSC	Association for Recorded Sound Collections
AS	American Samoa
ASCAP	American Society of Composers, Authors, and Publishers
Assn	Association
Aug	August
AZ	Arizona
b	bass
b	born
BA	Bachelor of Arts
bar	baritone
BBC	British Broadcasting Corporation
BFA	Bachelor of Fine Arts
BM	Bachelor of Music
BME; BMEd	Bachelor of Music Education
BMI	Broadcast Music, Inc.
BMus	Bachelor of Music
Bros.	Brothers
BS	Bachelor of Science
c	cent(s)
c	circa
CA	California
CBC	Canadian Broadcasting Corporation
CBE	Commander of the Order of the British Empire
CCNY	City College of New York
cf	confer (Lat.: compare)
chap.	chapter
cl	clarinet
CM	Northern Mariana Islands (US Trust Territory of the Pacific
cm	centimeter(s)
CO	Colorado
Co.	Company; County
c/o	care of
collab.	collaborator, collaborated (with)
colln	collection
comp.	compiler, compiled (by)
conc.	concerto
contd	continued
Corp.	Corporation
CT	Connecticut
CUNY	City University of New York
Cz	Czech
d	died
Dan.	Danish
db	double bass
DC	District of Columbia
DE	Delaware
Dec	December
Den.	Denmark
dir.	director, directed (by)
diss.	dissertation
DMA	Doctor of Musical Arts
Dr.	Doctor
ed.	editor, edited (by)
edn	edition
e.g.	exempli gratia (Lat.: for example)
elec	electric
Eng.	English
ens	ensemble
EP	extended-play (record)
esp.	especially
etc.	et cetera (Lat.: and so on)
ex(x).	example, examples
f	following (page)

f	forte
facs.	facsimile
Feb	February
ff	following (pages)
ff	fortissimo
fff	fortississimo
fig.	figure [illustration]
fl.	flourished
FL	Florida
Fr.	French
GA	Georgia
Ger.	German
GU	Guam
HI	Hawaii
hpd	harpsichord
Hung.	Hungarian
IA	Iowa
ibid.	ibidem (Lat.: in the same place)
ID	Idaho
i.e.	id est (Lat.: that is)
IL	Illinois
IN	Indiana
Inc.	Incorporated
inc.	incomplete
incl.	includes, including
inst.	instrument, instrumental
intl	international
It.	Italian
Jan	January
Jap.	Japanese
Jr.	Junior
km	kilometer(s)
KS	Kansas
KY	Kentucky
LA	Louisiana
LP	Long-play (record)
Ltd.	Limited
MA	Massachusetts; Master of Arts
MB	Bachelor of Music
MBE	Member of the Order of the British Empire
MD	Maryland
ME	Maine
MEd	Master of Education
mf	mezzo-forte
MFA	Master of Fine Arts
MGM	Metro–Goldwyn–Mayer
MI	Michigan
MIDI	Musical Instrument Digital Interface
MM; MMus	Master of Music
Mme	Madame
MN	Minnesota
MO	Missouri
mp	mezzo-piano
MPhil	Master of Philosophy
Mr.	Mister
MS	Mississippi; manuscript; Master of Science
MT	Montana
MusB	Bachelor of Music
nar	narrator
NBC	National Broadcasting Company
NC	North Carolina
ND	North Dakota
n.d.	no date (of publication)
NE	Nebraska
NEA	National Endowment for the Arts
NH	New Hampshire
NJ	New Jersey
NM	New Mexico
no.	number
Nor.	Norwegian
Nov	November
n.p.	no place (of publication)
NPR	National Public Radio
n.pub.	no publisher
nr	near
NV	Nevada
NY	New York (state)
OBE	Officer of the Order of the British Empire
Oct	October
OH	Ohio
OK	Oklahoma
op. cit.	opere citato (Lat.: in the work cited)
OR	Oregon
orch	orchestra
orig.	original
ORTF	Office de Radiodiffusion-Télévision Française
p	piano
p.	page
PA	Pennsylvania
PBS	Public Broadcasting System
perc.	percussion
pf	piano(forte)
PhD	Doctor of Philosophy
p.m.	post meridiem (Lat.: after noon)
Pol.	Polish
Port.	Portuguese
pp	pianissimo
pp.	pages
ppp	pianississimo
PR	Puerto Rico
pseud.	pseudonym
pt	part
pubd	published (by)
pubn	publication
qnt	quintet
qt	quartet
R	(editorial) revision [in signature]
R	photographic reprint
RAAF	Royal Australian Air Force
RAF	Royal Air Force
RAI	Radio Audizioni Italiane (Italy)
repr.	reprinted
Rev.	Reverend
rev.	revision, revised (by)
RI	Rhode Island

RIAS	Rundfunk im amerikanischen Sektor
RKO	Radio–Keith–Orpheum
Rom.	Romanian
r.p.m.	revolution(s) per minute
Russ.	Russian
S.	San, Santa, Santo
$	dollar(s)
sax	saxophone
SC	South Carolina
SD	South Dakota
Sept	September
ser.	series
sf, sfz	sforzando, sforzato
SFSR	Soviet Federated Socialist Republic
Sp.	Spanish
Sr.	Senior
SS	steamship
SSR	Soviet Socialist Republic
St.; Ste.	Saint, Sainte
str	string(s)
SUNY	State University of New York
suppl.	supplement, supplementary
Swed.	Swedish
sym.	symphony
t	tenor
TN	Tennessee
tpt	trumpet
trans.	translation, translated (by)
transcr.	transcription, transcribed (by/for)
trbn	trombone
TV	television
TX	Texas
U.	University
UCLA	University of California, Los Angeles
UHF	ultra-high frequency
UK	United Kingdom of Great Britain and Northern Ireland
unacc.	unaccompanied
UNESCO	United Nations Educational, Scientific, and Cultural Organization
unpubd	unpublished
US	United States [adjective]
USA	United States of America
USO	United Service Organizations
USSR	Union of Soviet Socialist Republics
UT	Utah
v	voice
VA	Virginia
VHF	very high frequency
VI	Virgin Islands
vol.	volume
VT	Vermont
vv	voices
WA	Washington
WI	Wisconsin
WPA	Works Progress Administration
WV	West Virginia
WY	Wyoming

Discographical Abbreviations

This list contains all abbreviations devised editorially for recording citations; acronyms adopted by companies for use as label names are not included.

AAFS	Archive of American Folksong (Library of Congress)
A&M Hor.	A&M Horizon
ABC-Para.	ABC-Paramount
AH	Artists House
Ala.	Aladdin
AM	American Music
Amer.	America
AN	Arista Novus
Ant.	Antilles
Ari.	Arista
Asy.	Asylum
Atl.	Atlantic
Aut.	Autograph
Bak.	Bakton
Ban.	Banner
Bay.	Baystate
BB	Black and Blue
Bb	Bluebird
Beth.	Bethlehem
BH	Bee Hive
BL	Black Lion
BN	Blue Note
Bruns.	Brunswick
BS	Black Saint
BStar	Blue Star
Can.	Candid
Cap.	Capitol
Car.	Caroline
Cat.	Catalyst
Cen.	Century
Chi.	Chiaroscuro
Cir.	Circle
CJ	Classic Jazz
Cob.	Cobblestone
Col.	Columbia
Com.	Commodore
Conc.	Concord
Cont.	Contemporary
Contl	Continental
CP	Charlie Parker
CW	Creative World
Del.	Delmark
Dis.	Discovery
Dra.	Dragon
EB	Electric Bird
Elec.	Electrola
Elek.	Elektra
Elek. Mus.	Elektra Musician
EmA	EmArcy
ES	Elite Special
Eso.	Esoteric
Ev.	Everest
EW	East Wind
Ewd	Eastworld
Fan.	Fantasy
FaD	Famous Door
FD	Flying Dutchman
FDisk	Flying Disk
Fel.	Felsted
Fon.	Fontana
Fre.	Freedom
FW	Folkways
Gal.	Galaxy
Gen.	Gennett
GrM	Groove Merchant
Gram.	Gramavision
GTJ	Good Time Jazz
HA	Hat Art
Hal.	Halcyon
Har.	Harmony
Harl.	Harlequin
HH	Hat Hut

ImA	Improvising Artists
IC	Inner City
Imp.	Impulse!
IndN	India Navigation
Isl.	Island
JAM	Jazz America Marketing
Jlgy	Jazzology
Jlnd	Jazzland
Jub.	Jubilee
Jwl	Jewell
Jzt.	Jazztone
Key.	Keynote
Kt.	Keytone
Lib.	Liberty
Lml.	Limelight
Lon.	London
Mdsv.	Moodsville
Mel.	Melodiya
Mer.	Mercury
Met.	Metronome
Metro.	Metrojazz
MJR	Master Jazz Recordings
Mlst.	Milestone
Mlt.	Melotone
Moers	Moers Music
MonE	Monmouth–Evergreen
Mstr.	Mainstream
Musi.	Musicraft
Nat.	National
NewJ	New Jazz
Norg.	Norgran
OK	OKeh
Omni.	Omnisound
PAct	Pathé Actuelle
PAlt	Palo Alto
Para.	Paramount
Parl.	Parlophone
Per.	Perfect
Phi.	Philips
Phon.	Phontastic
PJ	Pacific Jazz
PL	Pablo Live
Pol.	Polydor
Prog.	Progressive
Prst.	Prestige
PT	Pablo Today
PW	Paddle Wheel
Qual.	Qualiton
Reg.	Regent
Rep.	Reprise
Rev.	Revelation
Riv.	Riverside
Roul.	Roulette
RR	Red Records
RT	Real Time
Sack.	Sackville
Sat.	Saturn
SE	Strata-East
Sig.	Signature
Slnd	Southland
SN	Soul Note
SolS	Solid State
Son.	Sonora
Spot.	Spotlite
Ste.	Steeplechase
Sto.	Storyville
Sup.	Supraphon
Tei.	Teichiku
Tel.	Telefunken
The.	Theresa
Tim.	Timeless
TL	Time–Life
Tran.	Transition
20C	20th Century
20CF	20th CenturyFox
UA	United Artists
Upt.	Uptown
Van.	Vanguard
Var.	Variety
Vars.	Varsity
Vic.	Victor
VJ	Vee-Jay
Voc.	Vocalion
WB	Warner Bros.
WP	World Pacific
Xan.	Xanadu

Bibliographical Abbreviations

AllenH — W. C. Allen: *Hendersonia: the Music of Fletcher Henderson and his Musicians: a Bio-discography* (Highland Park, NJ, 1973)

ARJS — Annual Review of Jazz Studies

ARSCJ — Association for Recorded Sound Collections Journal

BallietA (1986) — W. Balliett: *American Musicians: Fifty-six Portraits in Jazz* (New York, and Oxford, England, 1986)

BallietA (1996) — W. Balliett: *American Musicians II: Seventy-two Portraits in Jazz* (New York, and Oxford, England, 1996)

BHcF — Bulletin du Hot Club de France

CarrJ — I. Carr, D. Fairweather, and B. Priestley: *Jazz: the Rough Guide* (London, 1995, rev. and enlarged 2/2000)

CBY — Current Biography Yearbook (New York, 1940–)

ChartersJ — S. B. Charters: *Jazz: New Orleans, 1885–1957: an Index to the Negro Musicians of New Orleans* (Belleville, NJ, 1958, rev. 2/1963/*R*1983 as *Jazz: New Orleans, 1885–1963: an Index to the Negro Musicians of New Orleans*)

ChiltonB — J. Chilton: *Who's Who of British Jazz* (London and New York, 1997)

ChiltonW — J. Chilton: *Who's Who of Jazz: Storyville to Swing Street* (London, 1970, rev. and enlarged 4/1985)

CI — Crescendo International

CK — Contemporary Keyboard

ConnorBG — D. R. Connor: *BG off the Record: a Bio-discography of Benny Goodman* (Fairless Hills, PA, 1958, rev. and enlarged [4]/1988 as *Benny Goodman: Listen to his Legacy*, addns and corrections, 1996, as *Benny Goodman: Wrappin' it up*)

DB — Down Beat

DF — Discographical Forum

EMC1, EMC2 — H. Kallmann, G. Potvin, and K. Winters, eds.: *Encyclopedia of Music in Canada* (Toronto, Buffalo, and London, 1981, rev. 2/1992, ed. H. Kallmann, G. Potvin, K. Winters, and M. Miller)

FeatherE — L. Feather: *The Encyclopedia of Jazz* (New York, 1955, rev. and enlarged 2/1960/*R*1984)

Feather '60s — L. Feather: *The Encyclopedia of Jazz in the Sixties* (New York, 1966/*R*1986)

Feather–Gitler '70s — L. Feather and I. Gitler: *The Encyclopedia of Jazz in the Seventies* (New York, 1976/*R*1987)

Feather–Gitler BEJ — L. Feather and I. Gitler: *The Biographical Encyclopedia of Jazz* (New York, and Oxford, England, 1999)

Fn — Footnote

GoldJL — R. S. Gold: *A Jazz Lexicon: an A–Z Directory of Jazz Terms* (New York, 1964, rev. 2/1975 as *Jazz Talk*)

GP — Guitar Player

GrayF — J. Gray: *Fire Music: a Bibliography of the New Jazz, 1959–1990* (New York, 1991)

GroveI — S. Sadie, ed.: *The New Grove Dictionary of Musical Instruments* (London, 1984)

Grove6 — S. Sadie, ed.: *The New Grove Dictionary of Music and Musicians* (London, 1980)

Grove7 — S. Sadie and J. Tyrell, eds.: *The New Grove Dictionary of Music and Musicians* (2/London, 2001)

GroveAM — S. Sadie and H. W. Hitchcock, eds.: *The New Grove Dictionary of American Music* (New York, 1986)

IAJRCJ — International Association of Jazz Record Collectors Journal

IM — International Musician

IMSCR — International Musicological Society Congress Report (1930–)

JB — Jazz Beat

J&B — Jazz & Blues

J&P — Jazz and Pop

JF [intl edn] — Jazz Forum [international edition]

JF [Pol. edn] — Jazz Forum [Polish edition]

Jf — Jazzforschung/Jazz Research

Jh — Jazz hot, Jazz-hot

JJ — Jazz Journal

JJI — Jazz Journal International

JJS — Journal of Jazz Studies

JM — Jazz Monthly

Jm	Jazz magazine (Paris)
JP	Jazz-Podium
JR	The Jazz Review
JSN	Jazz Spotlite News
JT	Jazz Times (Washington, 1980–)
McCarthyB	A. McCarthy: *Big Band Jazz* (London, 1974)
MD	Modern Drummer
MM	Melody Maker
MR	The Mississippi Rag
Pj	Le point du jazz
ReclamsJ	C. Bohländer and K. H. Holler: *Reclams Jazzführer* (Stuttgart, Germany, 1970, rev. and enlarged 2/1977)
RS	Rolling Stone
SchullerS	G. Schuller: *The Swing Era: the Development of Jazz, 1930–1945* (New York, and Oxford, England, 1989)
SheridanCB	C. Sheridan: *Count Basie: a Bio-discography* (Westport, CT, and London, 1986)
SJ	Swing Journal
SL	Second Line
Sv	Storyville
TuckerDE	M. Tucker, ed.: *The Duke Ellington Reader* (New York, and Oxford, England, 1993)
VV	Village Voice
WickesIBJ, i	J. Wickes: *Innovations in British Jazz*, i: *1900–1980* (Chelmsford, England, 1999)

Library Abbreviations

The abbreviations used in this dictionary for the names of American libraries are those established by the Catalog Publication Division of the Library of Congress and published in *Symbols of American Libraries* (Washington, rev. 12/1980). Only those abbreviations that appear in the dictionary (where they are always printed in italic type) are listed here.

ATaT USA, Talladega, AL, Talladega College
CaQMG Canada, Montreal, Quebec, Concordia University, Sir George Williams Campus
CHW (JdA) Switzerland, Wallbach, Jazzdocumentation Archive
CLU USA, Los Angeles, CA, University of California, Los Angeles
CtY USA, New Haven, CT, Yale University
DDS (JI) Germany, Darmstadt, Jazz-Institut Darmstadt
DLC USA, Washington, DC, Library of Congress
DSI (JOHP) USA, Washington, DC, Smithsonian Institution: Jazz Oral History Program
FiHJ Finland, Helsinki, Jazz & Pop Arkisto [Archive]
GBLnsa Great Britain, London, National Sound Archive of the British Library
ICJic USA, Chicago, IL, Jazz Institute of Chicago
ICU USA, Chicago, IL, University of Chicago
InUAtm USA, Bloomington, IN, Indiana University Archives of Traditional Music
LNT USA, New Orleans, LA, Tulane University [transcripts of interviews held at LNT were published on microfilm as *New York Times Oral History Program: New Orleans Jazz Oral History Collection* (1978-9)]
MoKmh Kansas City, MO, Kansas City Museum of History
MoUSt USA, St. Louis, MO, University of Missouri
NCH (HCJA) USA, Clinton, NY, Hamilton College: Hamilton College Jazz Archive
NjR USA, Newark, NJ, Rutgers, the State University of New Jersey
NjR (JOHP) USA, Newark, NJ, Rutgers, the State University of New Jersey: Jazz Oral History Project
NNC USA, New York, NY, Columbia University
NNSc USA, New York, NY, Schomburg Collection, New York Public Library
NNSc (HBc) USA, New York, NY, Schomburg Collection, New York Public Library, Hatch-Billops Collection
NNSc (LA JOHP) USA, New York, NY, Schomburg Collection, New York Public Library, Louis Armstrong Jazz Oral History Project
NOnj Norway, Oslo, Norsk Jazzarkiv
SSsv Sweden, Stockholm, Svenskt Visarkiv, Centralinstitution för Vis och Folkmusikforskning
TNF USA, Nashville, TN, Fisk University
TxU USA, Austin, TX, University of Texas

A Note on the Use of the Dictionary

This note is intended as a short guide to the basic procedures and organization of the dictionary. A fuller account will be found in the Introduction, Vol. 1, pp. x–xviii.

Alphabetization of headings is based on the principle that words are read continuously, ignoring spaces, hyphens, accents, parenthesized and bracketed matter, etc., up to the first comma; the same principle applies thereafter. "Mc" and "Mac" are alphabetized as "Mac"; "St." and "Mr." are alphabetized as though spelled out ("Saint" and "Mister").

Cross-references are shown in small capitals, with a large capital at the beginning of the first word of the entry referred to. Thus "Band formed in Oklahoma City in 1925 by WALTER PAGE," means that information on the band will be found in the entry "**Page, Walter**."

Abbreviations used in the dictionary are listed on pp.vii–xiv, in the order General (beginning on p.vii), Discographical (p.x), Bibliographical (p.xii), and Library (p.xiv).

Recording-lists are ordered strictly chronologically according to the date of recording. The main elements of a citation are: the name of the leader(s); the title; the year of recording; the name of the record label; the issue number. Abbreviations standing for record labels are explained on pp.x–xi.

Bibliographies are arranged chronologically (within section, where divided), in order of year of first publication, and alphabetically by author within years. Abbreviations standing for periodicals and reference works are explained on p.xii.

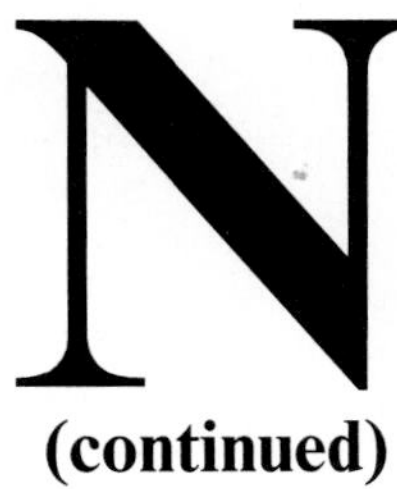

N (continued)

Nightclubs and other venues. The history of jazz in terms of the venues that have fostered it is the history of nightlife in different cities, and thus has as much to do with social, general cultural, commercial, and political history as it does with musical history. The following list, organized geographically, represents the only published comprehensive international and historical catalogue of these venues.

The list is arranged alphabetically by country, by city within country, and by name of venue (the definite article in all languages is ignored for purposes of alphabetical ordering); the only exception to this arrangement is the category of cruise ships and riverboats, which are entered under the names of the ocean or river on which they traveled. Addresses are given where possible, and the dates between which a certain address was current are supplied if they are known. Where the nature of a venue is not evident from its title, an effort has been made to supply a definition. Dates of operation are supplied when they are known, but if they are not available some indication is usually given of the period during which the venue is known to have flourished: this should not be taken to mean that it was in existence at no other time, simply that the sources consulted contain information only on the period indicated.

Many venues change performers constantly, and thus any attempt at full listings, even if that were possible, would be of questionable value; this is especially true of large cities, where the number of venues and the community of resident musicians are sufficiently large to allow owners and bandleaders to change programs and players, sometimes even on a daily basis. The list therefore aims primarily to identify extended residencies and isolated performances of particular importance or at least to offer selective lists of musicians who worked at a venue so as to give a sense of its stylistic orientation. Whenever possible, dates of performances are provided, but the appearance of such a date by no means excludes the possibility that the musician concerned performed at the venue on other occasions as well.

Items of bibliography are cited at the ends of individual entries, after a group of entries on venues in a particular city, or after a group of entries for a country, as appropriate; a general bibliography listing sources of relevance to more than one country appears at the end of the list. An alphabetical index of venues by name follows the list.

The scholars and specialists named below have contributed significant material to the sections indicated: Bruce Johnson and Peter Newton (Australia), Klaus Schulz (Austria), Robert Pernet and Howard Rye (Belgium), Mark Miller (Canada), Jaroslav Pašmik (Czech Republic), Frank Büchmann-Møller (Denmark), Wolfram Knauer (Germany), Simon Adams, Howard Rye, Alyn Shipton, and Val Wilmer (England, London), Pekka Gronow (Finland), André Clergeat and Howard Rye (France), Stefano Zenni (Italy), Alyn Shipton, Erik van den Berg, and Wim van Eyle (Netherlands), Johs Bergh (Norway), José Duarte (Portugal), Kenny Mathieson (Scotland), Alfredo Papo, Michel Rolland, and Howard Rye (Spain), Åke W. Edfeldt and Bengt Nyquist (Sweden), Bob Blumenthal, BK, Howard Rye, and Andrew Scott (USA, Boston metropolitan area), James Patrick (USA, Buffalo), Deborah Gillaspie and Howard Rye (USA, Chicago), William E. Anderson (USA, Cleveland), Herb Boyd and Kenn Cox (USA, Detroit), Anthony Bushard, BK, and Howard Rye (USA, Kansas City), Thomas Owens (USA, Los Angeles metropolitan area), Bill Russell (USA, Mississippi River), Mike Hazeldine and Bill Russell (USA, New Orleans), GK, BK, Dan Morgenstern, and Howard Rye (USA, New York), BK, Harrison Ridley, Jr., and Howard Rye (USA, Philadelphia), and BK and Erik Schwab (USA, Seattle). Other areas have been covered by BK and Howard Rye together (Morocco, Singapore, Sri Lanka, Switzerland, and USA, Atlanta, Baltimore, Cincinnati, Dallas, Indianapolis, and Pittsburgh), by BK alone (Chile, China, India, and USA, Houston, Minneapolis, Newark, Portland, St. Paul, San Antonio, San Francisco Bay area, and Washington), and by Howard Rye alone (Egypt, Greece, Hungary, and Malta).

ARGENTINA

Buenos Aires. **La Chaumière.** This club presented jazz from at least the mid-1930s. Booker Pitman, whose influence on Argentine players was considerable, performed there during the time he led his own big band, the Swing Stars, in Buenos Aires (1939–42).

——. **The Jazz Club.** Corrientes 1660, Paseo la Plaza. It has presented many styles of jazz.

——. **Novelty Club.** In operation from the early 1930s, it offered performances by a number of visiting American musicians. Herb Flemming and his International Rhythm

Aces, which included Crickett Smith and Roy Butler, were resident there in 1933. Flemming himself (in E. Biagioni: *Herb Flemming: a Jazz Pioneer around the World*, Alphen aan de Rijn, Netherlands, n.d. [?1977]) mentioned that his band played in Buenos Aires at the Ta-Ba-Ris Club, where it was "a novelty for the aristocracy"; it appears that this might be the same venue.

——. **Oliverio Jazz & Blues.** Avda Callao 360. Located in the Bauen Hotel in the city center, this venue was founded in 1986, since when it has presented many internationally known jazz and blues artists.

——. **La Oreja.** Paraná 330. One of several nightclubs run by Jorge Gonzalez (others include La Trastienda, El Fonografo, and Jazz & Pop), it is the principal venue in the city for modern jazz.

——. **Ta-Ba-Ris Club.** See Novelty Club.

Mar del Plata. **Jazz Club Mar del Plata.** Boulevard Maritimo 4017. Founded in 1981, this club has presented Harry James's orchestra, the quartet Swing 39, Hernán Oliva, Carlos Franzetti, the trumpeter Roberto "Fats" Fernandez, and many other musicians and bands; the cocktail pianist Hebert "Chiche" Gallet has performed for 20 years in the club's piano bar.
(<http://www.jazzbar.com.ar> (2000))

AUSTRALIA

Adelaide **Jazz Cellar.** Grote Street. This coffee shop operated from 1961 to 1968 and was Adelaide's main outlet for contemporary jazz during that time. Among those who made early appearances at the Jazz Cellar were the pianists Bobby Gebert, Roger Frampton, and Ted Nettlebeck, and the reed players Sylvan "Schmoe" Elhay and Bob Bertles.

——. **Tivoli Theatre.** In the 1950s Bill Holyoak, the owner of the Memphis Record Company, organized a series of jazz concerts at the theater; the music presented was mainly traditional, dixieland, and mainstream jazz. The venue was later known as Her Majesty's Theatre.

Melbourne. **Bennetts Lane.** 25 Bennetts Lane. This club was opened in November 1992 by Michael Tortoni to provide a forum for the best Australian and visiting jazz talent; although the club's policy is to support all genres of jazz, program guides indicate a preference for musicians playing in modern jazz styles, and Bennetts Lane has become Melbourne's principal venue for the music. Many of the city's finest players may be heard there, among them Ted Vining and Bob Sedergreen, and leading interstate artists appear regularly. Visiting guests from overseas have included Kenny Kirkland, Mark Levine, Harry Connick, Jr., Wynton Marsalis, and Ernie Watts. In the late 1990s the club expanded to incorporate another room, the Jazz Lab, which is able to accommodate such large events as the Melbourne Women's Jazz Festival. (<http://www.bennettslane.com> (2001))

——. **The Embers.** Toorak Road, South Yarra. This well-appointed nightclub opened in August 1959, burnt down under suspicious circumstances a few months later, and was rebuilt in 1960. In its very short operating life the Embers featured significant players, including Frank Smith and Mike Nock. American expatriates also worked there, as did Oscar Peterson's trio. The club closed in 1961.

——. **Fat Black Pussycat.** 90 Toorak Road, South Yarra. It was founded in 1963 by Ali Sugerman and functioned as a jazz club (under the ownership of Adrian Rawlins from 1965) until 1966, when it became a discothèque. The club opened with a group led by Barry McMinn and Heinz Mendelson and went on to engage other important musicians of the younger generation of modernists, including Brian Brown and Bernie McGann. The Fat Black Pussycat was the most important center in Melbourne for contemporary and experimental jazz after Jazz Centre 44 (see below) began to present mainly traditional jazz.

——. **Fawkner Park Kiosk.** Fawkner Park. Built as the pavilion for the adjacent tennis courts, it became in 1936 the venue for Sunday afternoon jam sessions. It provided a forum for the most important prewar jazz musicians, including Bob and Ern Tough and Benny Featherstone, whose performances inspired younger musicians such as Roger and Graeme Bell. It ceased to be used for jazz performances around 1941.

——. **Frank Traynor's Jazz Cellar.** Exhibition Street. Traynor, then an important traditional-jazz musician in Melbourne, opened this club in 1961 to cater for his own and other traditional-jazz bands and also for the highly popular folk revival. Among important local musicians who played at the club were Keith Hounslow, Ade Monsbourgh, and the singer Judith Durham (before she became famous as the lead singer in the popular group The Seekers).

——. **Glass House Theatre.** Swanston Street. This venue was the first regular home of the Melbourne Jazz Cooperative, a government-funded body formed in late 1982 by the jazz critic Martin Jackson and the pianist Jamie Fielding to present the best of local and interstate contemporary jazz.

——. **Jazz Centre 44.** Ackland Street, St. Kilda. It was founded by Horst Liepolt in 1957 and was managed by him until he moved to Sydney in 1960. Particularly during the late 1950s, it was the most important jazz venue in Melbourne and presented performances in a wide range of styles: among the prominent Australian groups and musicians who performed there were the Yarra Yarra Jazz Band (playing traditional jazz) and important modernists such as Brian Brown. Many of the jazz musicians active in Melbourne into the 1980s first became known through their appearances at Jazz Centre 44. After Liepolt left Melbourne the club's repertory increasingly emphasized traditional jazz, and it ceased operation around 1966.

BIBLIOGRAPHY

M. Murphy: "Mike Murphy Recalls Jazz Centre 44," *Jazz Down Under* (Nov 1975)

"Australian Jazz Today: Jazz Centre 44," *Jazz Australia* [Sydney], no.1 (1976)

——. **Jazz Lab.** See Bennetts Lane.

——. **Limerick Arms Hotel.** 364 Clarendon Street, South Melbourne. This hotel pursued a very active modern jazz policy in the 1980s. It hosted the Melbourne Jazz Cooperative, and it presented the dynamic pianist and composer Paul Grabowsky with various groups and the singer and trumpeter Vince Jones, both of whom have received international acclaim. Although jazz continues to be presented at the Limerick, the hotel is no longer regarded as a major jazz venue.

——. **Peter Gaudion's Jazz Lane.** Situated off Little Lonsdale Street, this jazz cellar and restaurant was opened by the trumpeter Peter Gaudion in the mid-1990s and survived for three or four years. In essence, the club provided an outlet for Gaudion's own traditional and mainstream bands, which appeared in the first session of each evening, together with other jazz groups; blues and funk bands were presented later at night. Overseas and interstate musicians also appeared there from time to time.

——. **Royal Terminus Hotel.** Brighton. Frank Johnson's Fabulous Dixielanders were among the musicians to perform there.

——. **Uptown Club.** Queensbury Road, North Melbourne. It was founded in 1946 by Roger and Graeme Bell and continued until 1947. Although relatively short-lived, the Uptown was active at a time when the jazz movement in Melbourne was becoming firmly established, and it rapidly developed into a center for musicians, painters, and writers who valued jazz as a legitimate modern art form.

PERTH. **Hyde Park Hotel.** 331 Bulwer Street. This suburban hotel has for some years been the main jazz venue in Perth. Both the Perth Jazz Society (PJS; supporting mainstream and contemporary styles) and the Jazz Club of Western Australia (JCWA; for traditional jazz) present regular concerts there. The PJS (founded in 1972) not only draws on an excellent pool of skilled interstate and local artists, including such expatriates as Danny Moss, but also engages many overseas musicians and groups in the course of their festival and concert tours, mainly in eastern Australia. The JCWA (founded in 1983) fulfills a similar function for its members.

——. **Railway Hotel.** 44 Tydeman Street, North Fremantle. This pub has presented traditional jazz on Saturdays for more than 20 years. The Corner House Jazz Band has been there for much of that time. Overseas traditional jazz musicians on tour and those visiting from the eastern part of Australia appear frequently, either as featured guests or sitting in informally.

SYDNEY. **The Basement.** 29 Reiby Place, Circular Quay. The club was established in 1973 by a group that included Bruce Viles and Tom Hare. In its early years it provided an important venue for contemporary and experimental jazz and featured several of the main contemporary jazz groups of the 1970s, among them the Last Straw and Jazz Co-op; it also ran a public workshop to explore ideas raised by the newly established course in jazz at the New South Wales Conservatorium. Later it gave increasing exposure to fusion groups and became the best-known jazz venue in Australia. From its opening its house band was Galapagos Duck.

The Basement closed in mid-1988 to allow major rebuilding in the area and reopened in December 1992. The programming policy remained much the same (though there was no house band), and improved conditions made the club popular as a venue for CD launches, benefit concerts to raise funds for sick musicians, and other one-off concerts of importance. Many visiting American and European musicians have appeared, notably Martin Taylor, Roy Haynes, Neils-Henning Ørsted Pedersen, John Scofield, Andy Sheppard, and Joe Zawinul.

BIBLIOGRAPHY

G. Gilbert: "Jazz on a High Note," *Jazz Australia* [Sydney], no.1 (1976)
P. Tripp: "Ten Years of the Basement," *Jazz: the Australasian Contemporary Music Magazine* (1983), spring
<http://www.basement.com.au> (2001)

——. **Don Burrows Supper Club.** Regent Hotel, George Street. Named in recognition of one of Sydney's most respected jazzmen, the club was in operation from the mid-1980s to the mid-1990s and endeavored to emulate the plush after-hours clubs of New York and London. Opening late on most nights of the week, the Supper Club presented some of the city's major traditional, mainstream, and modern groups, including bands featuring Burrows, James Morrison, Roger Frampton, and Bob Barnard, as well as singers and the occasional big band. Some performances were recorded. A large number of leading American jazz musicians appeared there while on tour, notably Lee Konitz, Red Rodney, Art Hodes, Dave McKenna, and Ralph Sutton. Despite the high quality of the music the club rarely attracted large audiences, and it closed when management refurbished the hotel and dropped jazz from its entertainment program.

——. **Jenny's Wine Bar.** Pitt Street; Goulburn Street. A major venue for contemporary jazz in the early 1980s, this small bar played host to some of the types of music to be found later in the energetic program promoted by SIMA. Bernie McGann and Eddie Bronson were regular performers, and Peter Rechniewski, a prime mover of the SIMA project, was responsible for organizing the programs. Originally on Pitt Street, it later relocated to Goulburn.

——. **Old Push.** See Rocks Push.

——. **Paradise Jazz Cellar.** 37 Darlinghurst Road, Kings Cross. An important but short-lived late-night venue which operated in Sydney's most raffish suburb during the early 1980s, this club featured some of the young and highly skilled jazz musicians then emerging from excellent high-school bands and the jazz studies program at the New South Wales Conservatorium. Several of these performers, including Dale Barlow and James Morrison, have since achieved high profiles both at home and abroad.

——. **El Rocco.** 160 Brougham Street, Kings Cross. The club was opened in 1955 by Arthur James and began to present jazz in October 1957; from then until it closed in 1969 it was the main venue for the various forms of progressive jazz performed in Australia. It saw many early experiments in free jazz and provided a meeting place for the new generation of musicians who were to carry the music into the 1980s. Many musicians from abroad and from other places in Australia played there, and the club's success inspired the founding of similar establishments elsewhere in the country. El Rocco was in its time the most important club in Australia.

In 1987 SIMA sought to revive El Rocco in the original building, but despite the high quality of the music provided the revival was short-lived. Concurrently, work was commenced on the production of the award-winning documentary film *Beyond El Rocco* (1990). This film celebrated the historical significance of the original venue and, through performances at the new venue and in concert, marked its continuing influence on musicians of another generation.

BIBLIOGRAPHY

D. Fisher: "Modern Jazz or . . . ," *Music Maker* (Sept 1963)
B. Johnson: "The El Rocco: an Era in Sydney Jazz," *Jazz: the Australasian Contemporary Music Magazine* (Jan–Feb, March–April, May–June 1983)

——. **Rocks Push** [Old Push]. It flourished as a center for jazz during the 1980s, when Graeme Bell was among the notable resident musicians. Later known as the Old Push, its house band was Bob Barnard's quartet.

——. **Side On Café.** 83 Parramatta Road, Annandale. Following the closure of the venue at the Strawberry Hills Hotel (see below) SIMA relocated to this small restaurant in 1999. It has increased its commitment to contemporary jazz, usually presenting performances three nights per week. With grant assistance, SIMA continues to present many of Australia's best contemporary jazz artists. Leading jazz educators also perform there, and reputable jazz artists from around the world are frequently engaged. Some sessions are recorded and broadcast.
(<http://www.side-on.com.au> (2001))

——. **Soup Plus Restaurant.** 383 George Street. It was founded in 1974 by James Dupree, who introduced jazz in 1975 with a performance by Bill Haesler's Washboard Band. With performances on six nights of the week and resident groups that changed monthly, it became one of the best-known and most consistent jazz venues in Sydney; while other clubs concentrated on a narrow range of styles, it offered a broad cross-section of all kinds of jazz. Performances at the club have frequently been recorded for later broadcast. A change of ownership in the 1990s saw some narrowing of programming policy and the introduction of a regular big-band swing session. From the late 1990s the venue has been attracting much younger audiences who, despite limited interests in jazz, have found it to be an attractive mid-city meeting place.
(<http://www.megazite.com.au/soupplus> (2001))

——. **Strawberry Hills Hotel.** 453 Elizabeth Street, Surry Hills. During the 1980s and 1990s this was one of Sydney's major inner-city venues, both for traditional jazz (weekends) and for contemporary jazz (weekdays). Initially it was a regular weekend home for some of the city's best traditional-jazz groups, including the New Zenith New Orleans Jazz Band and bands led by Geoff Bull and the trumpeter Tom Baker. SIMA moved into the hotel in 1989, encouraged the licensee to upgrade the performance space, and presented a much-expanded program of challenging music performed by Australian and overseas artists. Of particular importance were bands led by Mike Nock, Dale Barlow, and Bernie McGann, innovative touring bands such as Clarion Fracture Zone and Ten Part Invention, and groups led by the American expatriates Gordon Brisker, Don Rader, and Mickey Tucker. Changes in state licensing laws in the late 1990s allowed the introduction of more gaming machines into the hotel, which proved to be the death knell for music; the jazz programs were curtailed in 1998. David Perry's excellent film *Dr Jazz* (1998) celebrates the jazz life and times of the venue and captures, through performance and interview, its significance for some of its key players. However, the hotel's management had a change of heart in the year 2000: with a restructured performance space, it is once more promoting a limited weekend jazz program with established local mainstream bands.

——. **Unity Hall Hotel.** 292 Darling Street, Balmain. A short distance from the city, this pub has been presenting jazz on several nights a week for almost 30 years. Some of Sydney's best-known traditional-jazz bands, including those led by the trombonist Roger Janes and Geoff Bull, as well as the Café Society Jazz Orchestra, have held lengthy residencies. Blues and mainstream bands (most notably the All Hat Jazz Band, led by the guitarist Tony Barnard) and occasional modern groups have also been featured. Because sitting in is encouraged at Friday-night sessions, visiting interstate and overseas artists frequently make unexpected appearances.
(<http://sydney.citysearch.com.au/E/V/SYDNE/0017/18/82/1.html> (2001))

——. **Vanity Fair Hotel.** Goulburn Street and Wentworth Street. Pub. Jim Hourigan first put on jazz performances there in 1970 and later licensees continued his policy. The Vanity Fair was the most stable venue in Sydney for traditional and mainstream jazz and its durability gave it an international reputation. In addition to presenting different resident bands on various nights of the week, the club employed the Eclipse Alley Five for Saturday afternoon performances from 1970 until it closed in 1986 (this constituted the longest band residency in the history of Australian jazz, to that time). The pub also served as the unofficial headquarters for the Sydney Jazz Club. (C. Lindley: *Goodbye Vanity Fair*, Sydney, 1986)

BIBLIOGRAPHY

Australia

J. Whiteoak: *Early Modern Jazz in Australia: the Introduction of Bop* (diss., LaTrobe U., 1986)

B. Johnson and others: *The Oxford Companion to Australian Jazz* (Melbourne, Australia, 1987)

J. Clare [G. Brennan, pseud.]: *Bodgie Dada and the Cult of Cool* (Sydney, 1995)

R. Farbach: *Cleftomania: a Disease that Attacks Musicians and Makes Them Do Strange Things* (Montville, Queensland, Australia, 1999)

E. Myers, ed.: *Australian Jazz Directory 1998* (Sydney, 1998)

AUSTRIA

VIENNA. **Fatty's Jazz Casino.** It was established in 1955 by Fatty George as a venue for his Two Sounds Band, which included Joe Zawinul and Carl Drewo. In February 1956 Lionel Hampton visited the club and an album was recorded there (*Fatty George Meets Lionel Hampton*, Mastertone 013). It closed in 1958, when George opened new premises as Fatty's Saloon.

——. **Fatty's Saloon.** Petersplatz. It was opened in 1958 by Fatty George, whose new band at the time included the trumpeter Fred Wallisch and Heinz Bigler. Among the major American and European jazz musicians to have played there are Hans Koller, Oscar Pettiford, Attila Zoller, George Maycock, Ella Fitzgerald, Cat Anderson, Jimmy Hamilton, John Lewis, Art Blakey, Curtis Fuller, Freddie Hubbard, and Herb Ellis; Friedrich Gulda often performed and rehearsed at the saloon.

——. **Jazzland.** 29 Franz Josephs Kai. Built into the catacombs of a medieval church, this jazz club was founded by Axel Melhardt and Klaus Schulz; on 4 March 1972 Albert Nicholas appeared at its opening as a guest soloist with the Austrian traditional-jazz group the Red Hot Pods. Under Melhardt's management from 1973, it became the most important jazz venue in Austria. By the late 1990s more than 300 notable American and European jazz and blues musicians had appeared there, among them Max Kaminsky, Wild Bill Davison, Eddie "Lockjaw" Davis, Jay McShann, Al Grey, Roy Eldridge, Peanuts Hucko, Kai Winding, Harry Edison, Joe Newman, Dexter Gordon, Cecil Payne, Hal Singer, Lee Konitz, Shelly Manne, Art Hodes,

Ralph Sutton, Bob Wilber, Warren Vaché, Ken Peplowski, Lew Tabackin, Barbara Dennerlein, Albert Mangelsdorff, Attila Zoller, Guy Lafitte, Danny Moss, and Dusko Goykovich; for many years Art Farmer appeared with his European quintet three times annually. The most important Austrian traditional and mainstream jazz groups, such as Together, Just Friends, Jazzclusive, the Barrelhouse Jazzband, the Original Storyville Jazzband, and Oscar Klein's band, also play there often. (A. Melhardt: *Geschichte und G'schictln: 20 Jahre Jazzland*, Vienna, 1992).

——. **Porgy & Bess.** 2 Spiegelgasse. It was founded by Mathias Rüegg, Renald Deppe, and Christof Huber in 1992 as a venue for jazz projects. Many American, European, and Austrian avant-garde and bop musicians have performed there, including Charles Lloyd, Michel Portal, Herbert Joos, Dieter Glawischnig, Albert Mangelsdorff, Tommy Flanagan, Wolfgang Muthspiel, his brother the trombonist Christian Muthspiel, Karl Ratzer, the Vienna Art Orchestra, the Upper Austrian Jazz Orchestra, the NDR Big Band, Lee Konitz, and Attila Zoller. In May 1998 it closed; however, it reopened, with financial help from the Austrian government, at a new location on Riemergasse on 28 December 2000. (<http://www.porgy.or.at> (2001))

——. **WeihburgBar.** It presented jazz from at least the 1920s. Among the jazz musicians who performed there were Arthur Briggs with the Savoy Sycops Orchestra (three times between 1925 and 1927), which was one of the first jazz ensembles to play arrangements by Spike Hughes. Eddie South performed there in 1930.

——. **Wiener Metropol.** Hernalser Hauptstrasse 55. Theater. It opened as a general arts center early in 1981 under the artistic direction of Alf Krauliz. As part of its highly varied program of events the Wiener Metropol has offered performances of many kinds of music, among them jazz, rock, and pop; among its other activities are theater, dance, and cabaret, and the center emphasizes entertainment for children and young people. Many notable American and European jazz musicians have performed there, including Bireli Lagrene, Jan Garbarek, Chet Baker, Art Blakey, Lester Bowie, Aladár Pege, Carla Bley, Charlie Mariano, and Baden Powell. The Wiener Metropol publishes a youth magazine, *Metropol.* (<http://www.wiener-metropol.at> (2001))

Wiesen. **Jazz-Pub-Wiesen.** Hauptstrasse 140. It was founded as a discothèque in the early 1970s by Franz Bogner and took the name Jazz-Pub-Wiesen in 1976, when it staged the first International Jazzfest Wiesen (*see* Festivals). One of the first discothèques to encompass jazz in its program, the club has favored fusion (particularly jazz-rock and jazz-funk) though all styles of jazz are presented (including, occasionally, avant-garde improvised music). Among notable jazz musicians who have appeared there are Barbara Thompson, Jon Hiseman, Jasper van 't Hof, and Larry Coryell.

BELGIUM

Antwerp. **Desingel Concerthall.** Desguinlei 22. Arts center. From 1982 Desingel has presented concerts in various genres in its three halls, a chamber music room and two much larger rooms; the emphasis is on avant-garde arts and music. Cecil Taylor, John Zorn, and Mal Waldron performed there in the 1980s, and a regular series of concerts of jazz and improvised music commenced in autumn 1990. The quartet led by Connie Crothers and Lenny Popkin, Lee Konitz with Steve Lacy (in various settings), Misha Mengelberg's trio, and Derek Bailey are among those who have appeared. (<http://www.desingel.be> (2001))

——. **King-Kong.** Keizerstraat 38. This nightclub was active from at least the early 1970s. From 1974 into the late 1980s it played host to the festival Free Music Antwerpen, which presents avant-garde improvised and composed music and free jazz (*see* Festivals).

——. **Zuidpool Theatre.** By the late 1990s it was hosting the festival Free Music Antwerpen.

Brussels. **L'Abbaye.** 3a rue du Bastion/Bolwerkstraat 3a. It opened around 1923 and after an unknown period reopened in September 1927. The house band was Arthur Briggs's Savoy Sycop's Orchestra, and many jazz bands performed there. This venue later became Le Boeuf sur le Toit (see below).

——. **Alhambra.** Boulevard de la Seine (now 20–22 boulevard Emile Jacqmain/Emile Jacqmainlaan 20–22). The Alhambra presented revues; a bar and nightclub, Le Perroquet, was added when the theater reopened after World War I, in January 1920. Jazz bands that appeared there included Louis Mitchell's Jazz Kings (24 January 1920 – April 1921), Mitchell's Jazz Friends, Frank Guarente's Georgians, and a group led by the drummer Hughes Pollard (1922). (R. Pernet and H. Rye: "Visiting Firemen 18: Louis Mitchell," *Storyville 2000–2001*, ed. L. Wright (Chigwell, England, 2001), 221).

——. **L'Archiduc.** 6 rue Antoine Dansaert/Antoine Dansaert Straat 6. This art-deco café, built in 1937, offers concerts on Sunday afternoons by leading Belgian and international jazz artists; occasionally there are performances on other days as well. Among those who appeared in the late 1990s were Mark Helias, Eric Legnini, Philip Catherine, and Toots Thielemans. (<http://www.archiduc.com> (2001))

——. **Blue Note.** Rue de la Montagne/Bergstraat (14 July 1958 – summer 1960); 11 galerie des Princes/Prinsengalerij 11 (from 20 October 1960). Founded by Benoit Quersin with financial help from the saxophonist Jean-Pierre Gebler, it presented mainly Belgian and European jazz musicians. After opening at its new site in October 1960 it became perhaps the most important Belgian jazz club of its time, featuring Ben Webster, Philip Catherine (accompanied, on drums, by the noted Belgian jazz historian and discographer Robert Pernet), Lou Bennett, Roland Kirk, Fats Sadi, Toots Thielemans, Clark Terry, Martial Solal, Oliver Jackson, Lucky Thompson, and many others. The trumpeter Léon "Podoum" Demol took over the club's operation on 21 May 1965; it closed in 1968.

——. **Le Boeuf sur le Toit.** 3a rue du Bastion/Bolwerkstraat 3a. Formerly l'Abbaye, this cabaret was named for the famous nightclub in Paris; it was opened by Jean Omer in 1937. Regular performers in 1937 and 1938 included Coleman Hawkins and Benny Carter, the singer Joan "Babe" Daniels, and various Belgian and Dutch soloists accompanied by the house band, which was led by Omer. The club became an important center for jazz performance by Belgian musicians. Omer himself recorded there with his group, which he led into the early 1960s. Le Boeuf sur le Toit closed around 1964.

——. **Brussels Jazz Club.** Grand Place/Grote Markt. It opened in the 1980s and presented many European and American jazz musicians.

——. **Corso.** Boulevard Adolphe Max/Adolphe Max Laan. Jazz was performed at this café from at least the early 1940s by many Belgian bands, including those of Fud Candrix (1942) and Gus Deloof.

——. **Le Gaity.** 18 rue Fosse-aux-Loups/Wolvengracht 18. This dance hall opened beneath the Gaieté Théâtre in 1920. Among the bands that held residencies there were the Jazz Imperators, led by the drummer Dooley Wilson and including the trumpeter Bobby Jones and the trombonist Frank Withers (1921–2), and Johnny Dunn's New Yorkers (1932). Many other bands and soloists appeared as well.

——. **Merry Grill.** Place du Samedi/Zaterdagplein. Restaurant. It offered performances of jazz from at least the early 1930s. Sam Wooding's group played there in 1931, then, when it disbanded (November), Willie Lewis took over as the resident bandleader, forming a group that consisted of several of Wooding's American sidemen and Belgian musicians.

——. **Marcus Mingus.** 17–19 rue de la Fourche/Greepstraat 17–19. In the new century it has been presenting Belgian jazz musicians. (<http://www.marcusmingus.com> (2001))

——. **Music Village.** 50 rue des Pierres/Steenstraat 50. This venue, which opened in the late 1990s, has featured local, national, and international artists. (<http://www.themusicvillage.com> (2001))

——. **Palais des Beaux-Arts/Paleis voor Schone Kunsten.** 5–23 rue Ravenstein/Ravensteinstraat 5–23. Arts complex. It contains facilities for music, theater, cinema, and art exhibitions. One of the earliest rhythm clubs, the Sweet and Hot Club, founded in 1932, met in a lecture room there. It continued to be used for jazz, and most of the concerts organized by the Hot Club de Belgique were presented there; these involved many of the great names in jazz (Duke Ellington, Louis Armstrong, Count Basie, the Modern Jazz Quartet, Dizzy Gillespie, Gerry Mulligan, Coleman Hawkins, Ben Webster, Art Blakey, Jazz at the Philharmonic, Ella Fitzgerald, Oscar Peterson, and so forth), as well as numerous Belgian and European jazz musicians.

——. **Le Perroquet.** See Alhambra.

——. **Pol's (Jazz Club)** [Pol's Jazz Place]. Rue du Marché-au-Charbon/Kolenmarkt; rue de Stassart/Stassartstraat. Founded by and named for the entrepreneur Pol (Léopold Lenders), it flourished from the 1960s into the 1980s, presenting jazz from one to four nights per week. Most Belgian and many European and American jazz musicians appeared there. Its second location (the dates unknown) was in the same building as the former postwar Victory Club.

——. **Rose Noire.** 30 petite rue des Bouchers/Korte Beenhouwersstraat 30. Managed by Louis Laydu, it operated from the early 1950s to 1960 and was for a period the only jazz venue in the city. American and European jazz musicians variously went to the club following a concert to take part in jam sessions or appeared there regularly.

——. **Théâtre des Galeries.** It was used for jazz performances from at least the 1940s when, under the auspices of the Hot Club de Belgique and its president Willy de Cort, weekly jazz concerts were given there.

——. **Victory Club.** Rue de Stassart/Stassartstraat. Managed by Félix Faecq and Jack Kluger from 1945 to 1946, the club had a house band led by Gus Deloof and featured American and British jazz musicians who were in town with the allied forces. It operated its own record label, Victory.

BIBLIOGRAPHY

Brussels

Archives d'Architecture Moderne: *Lieux de plaisir: Bruxelles, 1900–2000* (Brussels, 1998)

DENDERMONDE. **Jazzclub Honky Tonk.** Bastion V, Leopold II Laan. It was founded and is managed by Piet Heuvinck. While it originally specialized in traditional jazz, later it incorporated various other styles into its repertory; the club has its own swing big band. In 1971 Heuvinck and others founded the Dendermonde jazz festival (*see* FESTIVALS). (<http://www.honkytonk.be> (2001))

GHENT. **Lazy River Jazz Club.** Stadhuissteeg 5. Established in cellar premises in nearby Gentbrugge in 1966, it at first presented jazz on Friday evenings; it became more active after moving to the premises in Stadhuissteeg. Although it is best known for traditional jazz, the club also offers most other styles (except free jazz) as well as ragtime, blues, and rhythm-and-blues. From 1969 it mounted an annual jazz festival (*see* FESTIVALS) and it publishes a monthly newsletter, *Lazy River News*.

HEIST OP DEN BERG. **Hnita Jazz Club.** Lostraat 106. By the late 1990s it was presenting nationally and internationally known musicians and groups.

KNOKKE. **Casino.** The casino at Knokke presented jazz during its summer season from at least the mid-1930s. Notable appearances in later decades were made by Hot Lips Page (summer 1952) and Sidney Bechet (May 1953, April and August 1956). In July 1958 it hosted the Festival Mondiale de Jazz.

KORTRIJK. The town's jazz club was a center for traditional and mainstream jazz from the early 1970s. It engaged many of Belgium's leading bands, including the Cotton City Jazz Band (under the leadership of Rudy Balliu and later Jacques Cruyt) and the Jegg Papp Jazz Band, and also offered performances by other leading European musicians.

LEUVEN. **At the Bebop.** Vismarkt 4/5. By the late 1990s it was presenting nationally and internationally known musicians and groups.

OOSTAKKER. **Cotton Fields Jazzclub.** Pegasus-Hoeve, Nieuwstraat 11. It flourished during the mid-1970s, when it was an important venue for visiting American and European artists. Most of the music performed was traditional or mainstream jazz.

OSTEND. **Pan** [Chez Pan]. Boulevard Van Iseghemlaan. Opened on 3 July 1920, it was operated by the Schneyder brothers and fell partly under the management of London's Murray Club; some of the bands from that English venue (including the Continental Five) transferred there. Among other featured artists and bands were Arthur Briggs and the Jazz Imperators, led by the drummer Dooley Wilson (who later became famous as the pianist in the film *Casablanca*).

Ruiselede. **Banana Peel Club.** Minitheater voor Jazz en Blues, Bruggestraat. Founded in 1966 by the discographer Erik Karette, this club has been devoted principally to blues but has also offered jazz. In addition to visiting American musicians, it has presented European players such as Sammy Rimington. (<http://www.bananapeel.freeservers.com> (2001))

Willebroek. **Jazzclub het Veerhuis.** Hoofd 2. The club was founded by Camiel van Breedam, Johnny van Breedam, and Marc Vandevelde in 1970 and opened on 1 June. It specialized in New Orleans jazz and regularly engaged American musicians who developed the style early in the century, including Kid Thomas Valentine and Emanuel Sayles. The resident band was the Fondy Riverside Bullet Band. The club had its own record label, Fondy, on which Alvin Alcorn recorded the album *Alvin Alcorn Meets his Friends in Belgium* (1976, Fondy 7771).

Zaventem. **Sheraton Brussels Airport.** Zaventem Airport. From at least the late 1990s a weekly Sunday brunch has been held at this hotel, at which leading local players and international groups and guest soloists have performed. (<http://www.sheraton.com/property.taf?prop=295&lc=en> (2001))

CANADA

Edmonton. **Yardbird Suite.** A venue of this name, run by a musicians' cooperative, functioned at several addresses for a decade from 1957. The name was revived by the Edmonton Jazz Society in 1984 for a nightclub at 1023 86th Street. It remained active in the late 1990s.

Montreal. **L'air du Temps.** 101 St. Paul Street West. It opened in 1978 and for the most part has presented local musicians. It remained active in the late 1990s.

——. **Alberta Lounge.** 1061–1063 Windsor. It was home to Oscar Peterson's first trio from 1947 to 1949. The venue presented music into the 1950s.

——. **Black Bottom.** 1350 St. Antoine Street (1963–8); 22 St. Paul Street East (from 1968). It featured Nelson Symonds until 1968. After moving to a new site it presented mixed jazz (including the bands of Art Blakey, Miles Davis, and Thelonious Monk) with other bookings at least until 1972.

——. **Café St.-Michel.** 770 Mountain Street. This venue, a show bar rather than a jazz club, flourished under several names from 1934 to around 1954. Louis Metcalf's International Band appeared there from 1947 to 1950.

——. **Rising Sun.** 236 St. Catherine Street West. One of the principal nightclubs in the city, it pursued a policy of presenting visiting American groups. It was operated from 1974 to 1991 on St. Catherine Street West and briefly at two other addresses by Roué-Doudou Boiçel, who offered major American jazz and blues artists and, latterly, reggae.

——. **Rockhead's Paradise.** 1252 St. Antoine Street, on the corner of Mountain Street. It was opened by Rufus Rockhead around 1928 and became Canada's longest-running club, remaining active until 1981. Like the Café St.-Michel, which was directly across the street, it was a show bar, not a jazz club, though it employed jazz musicians to play in its house band. Its heyday was the 1940s. Later, in the 1970s, jazz groups performed in its lower lounge.

Toronto. **Basin Street.** 180 Queen Street West. It occupied premises upstairs in the same building as Bourbon Street (see below) and similarly favored visiting American musicians. It presented mainly jazz-blues revues and occasionally jazz: in a short period in the spring of 1980, for example, players of the standing of Benny Carter, Stan Getz, and Joe Williams appeared.

——. **Bourbon Street.** 180 Queen Street West. This nightclub was opened in 1971 by Doug Cole, who had long owned George's Spaghetti House (see below). Under the management of Jim Galloway briefly and Paul Grosney for much of its existence, it gained international renown as a venue for solo and small-group jazz performed by both Canadian and visiting foreign musicians. Many American players, in particular, appeared there, usually performing as guest soloists with Canadian rhythm sections; among them were Benny Carter (1973), Junior Cook (1974), Flip Phillips (1975), and Zoot Sims and Herb Ellis (both 1980). Notable recordings were made at the club by Jim Hall (June 1975), Paul Desmond (October–November 1975), Frank Rosolino (April 1976), and Lenny Breau (an album released posthumously). A second nightclub, Basin Street (see above), operated intermittently in the same building. Bourbon Street closed in 1986.

——. **Café des Copains.** 50 Wellington Street East. Piano bar. It was operated by Jim Galloway and John Norris and was active from 1983 to 1991. Canadian, American, and European pianists appeared there, several of whom, including Art Hodes, Jay McShann, and Ralph Sutton, were recorded for Sackville (the company run by Norris and Bill Smith (ii)).

——. **Colonial Tavern.** 201 Yonge Street. It operated from the 1950s until 1984; in the early 1960s its activities were in the hands of Goodie Lichtenstein. It was on the touring circuit for visiting jazzmen and thus presented performances by many internationally known soloists and groups, including those of Duke Ellington and Ornette Coleman.

——. **George's Spaghetti House.** 290 Dundas Street East. Restaurant. It was opened in 1956 by Doug Cole and at first offered jazz at weekends only; from 1960 the program was extended to cover six evenings a week. American musicians appeared there for only a few months in 1968, but George's was known as the principal venue in the city for hearing Canadian jazz musicians. Among the bands that played there regularly was that of Moe Koffman, who served as booking agent and music director for the venue from 1960 to 1990; Ed Bickert recorded there in 1975, and broadcasts were frequently made from the restaurant. In 1984 it moved from a downstairs to an upstairs room in the same building, and it continued to offer jazz until its closure in 1994.

——. **Massey Hall.** 178 Victoria Street, on the corner of Shuter Street. Concert hall. Opened in 1894 as Massey Music Hall (the name changed in 1933), it was for many years the only purpose-built concert hall in the country. It has been the venue for numerous popular-music performances and recording sessions. The most important jazz event to take place there was the concert given on 15 May 1953, under the auspices of the New Jazz Society, by a quintet consisting of Charlie Parker, Dizzy Gillespie, Bud Powell, Charles Mingus, and Max Roach; a landmark in the history of bop, the performance was preserved on record though the recording quality is poor.

——. **Montreal Bistro.** 65 Sherbourne Street. Under the same ownership as the Café des Copains, it assumed that venue's jazz policy in 1991 but also expanded piano bookings to include Canadian, American, and European bands. It has also hosted recordings for Sackville, notably sessions by Dave McMurdo's Jazz Orchestra, Geoff Keezer, and the pianist Barbara Sutton-Curtis (the sister of Ralph Sutton), and for Justin Time, by Oliver Jones and the quintet of Sonny Greenwich and Kenny Wheeler.

——. **Music Gallery.** 30 St. Patrick Street; 1087 Queen Street (from 1984); 179 Richmond Street (from 1993). It was opened in warehouse premises in 1975 by the Canadian Creative Music Collective (CCMC), an improvising ensemble formed in 1974, some of whose music is close to free jazz. The group played at the Music Gallery twice a week, and the venue also mounted performances in other avant-garde areas of music. In 1976 the record company Music Gallery Editions was launched; 27 albums of folk music, avant-garde improvised music, and jazz were issued before the label's demise in 1981. From 1978 the venue produced a quarterly newsletter, *Musicworks.* Around 1984 the Music Gallery moved to a building formerly occupied by the YMCA, and in 1993 it relocated to Richmond Street West, where it flourished in the late 1990s.

——. **Top o' the Senator.** 235 Victoria Street. Opened in 1990, it has presented both American and Canadian bands. This venue and the Montreal Bistro were the two main jazz clubs in the city in the late 1990s.

——. **Town Tavern.** 16 Queen Street East. Opened in 1949, it presented both Canadian and American jazz musicians consistently from 1955 to 1971. Oscar Peterson recorded there in 1958.

VANCOUVER. **Blue Horn Jazz Workshop.** 3623 West Broadway. It opened in April 1965 shortly after its predecessor at this location, the Flat Five, had closed. It engaged several American bands, including the Mastersounds and Charles Mingus's Jazz Workshop, but closed in March 1966.

——. **The Cellar.** 222 East Broadway, at Main and the Kingsway. Managed by musicians, it was in operation from 1956 until 1964. It regularly engaged visiting American players.

——. **Classical Joint.** 231 Carrall Street. This coffee house opened in the late 1960s. From the early 1970s until 1989 it was an important forum for Vancouver musicians playing in a variety of contemporary jazz styles. It also offered classical music and music of the folk revival.

——. **Flat Five.** 3623 West Broadway. It opened in December 1962 and presented local modern jazz players. It closed in March 1965, but re-opened the following month as the Blue Horn Jazz Workshop.

BIBLIOGRAPHY

Canada

EMC2

J. Litchfield: *The Canadian Jazz Discography, 1916–1980* (Toronto, Buffalo, and London, 1982)

CHILE

SANTIAGO **Club de Jazz de Santiago.** José Pedro Alessandri 85, Ñuñoa. The club was founded in the early 1940s; owned and operated by jazz musicians, it has presented dixieland and, in later years, modern mainstream musicians and bands, in an old mansion in the Ñuñoa area of Santiago. Louis Armstrong, Elvin Jones, Wynton Marsalis, James Moody, Paquito D'Rivera, Herbie Hancock, and Lew Tabackin are among the many famous players who have appeared there. (<http://www.clubdejazz.cl> (2001))

——. **Santiago Hyatt Regency Santiago.** Avda Kennedy 4601. From time to time this hotel has hosted series of jazz concerts; Joe Zawinul appeared there in 2000.

CHINA

BEIJING **Big Easy.** Chao Yang Gong Yuan. By the late 1990s this venue was presenting modern jazz and blues, played by both local musicians and Western visitors.

——. **Moon Shanghai.** 4 Gongti Beilu. By the late 1990s, on Thursday through Saturday nights, musicians from Beijing performed in this restaurant in a style of traditional jazz which incorporated elements of traditional Chinese music.

HONG KONG. **The Jazz Club.** 2nd floor, 34–36 D'Aguilar Street, Central. Located within the entertainment district Lan Kwai Fong, the Jazz Club opened in 1989 and became a major venue during the last decade of British rule in Hong Kong, presenting such American artists as Anita O'Day (at its opening), Jon Hendricks, Mose Allison, James Moody, and Wynton Marsalis, as well as numerous English players, including Stan and Clark Tracey, Peter King, Ronnie Scott, Guy Barker, Don Weller, and Dick Pearce. Herbie Hancock sat in with the house band there. The club has continued its musical policy into the new century, under Chinese authority, and in 2001 it presented live music five nights per week, Tuesday through Saturday. (<http://www.lkfgroup.com/jazzclub> (2001))

——. **Swing.** 14 Wo On Lane. By the late 1990s this club featured local and international artists and groups.

SHANGHAI. **Astor House Hotel.** In 1925 to 1926, during the course of an engagement at the Plaza Hotel (see below), the New York Singing Syncopators also played at the Astor House Hotel; the band included Darnell Howard. Later Teddy Weatherford and Herb Flemming performed there.

——. **Canidrome Ballroom.** Situated in the French settlement, this was the largest room in a building situated next to a greyhound racetrack which contained several other ballrooms. From 1929 to 1933 Teddy Weatherford led bands there. He then returned to the USA as a representative for the ballroom, and in Los Angeles in 1934 he engaged Buck Clayton to take a band to the Canidrome. Clayton's group worked there until November 1934, with Teddy Buckner, Caughey Roberts, Bumps Myers, and Eddie Beal among his sidemen; during this period Weatherford served as intermission pianist and gave concerts on Sundays, though otherwise he worked at several other local venues.

——. **Carlton Palais de Dance.** Teddy Weatherford played in this two-room ballroom around 1928 as a member of a dance orchestra led by a Russian composer named Bakaleinikoff.

——. **Casa Nova Ballroom.** Buck Clayton led the band there from November 1934 into 1935.

——. **Peace Hotel Jazz Bar.** 20 Nanjing East Road. Late in 1980, soon after Deng Xiaoping came to power, jazz was again allowed to be played at Shanghai hotels, beginning with this venue; in 1987 foreigners were admitted to jazz performances for the first time during the communist era.

——. **Plaza Hotel.** The hotel featured jazz in the mid-1920s, at a time when it was under Chinese ownership and managed by an Englishman; it was run by an American after the manner of an American hotel. The New York Singing Syncopators, with Jack Carter on drums, were resident in summer 1924 and again from May 1925; Darnell Howard joined them there from October 1925 until June 1926, when he returned to Chicago. Carter's band, which included Valaida Snow, Albert Nicholas, and Teddy Weatherford, played there for nearly a year, beginning in September 1926. (J. T. Schenck: "The Colourful Saga of Darnell Howard," *Jazz Session* (1945), March–April, 2)

BIBLIOGRAPHY

China

P. Darke and R. Gulliver: "Teddy Weatherford," *Sv*, no.65 (1976), 175
——: "Roy Butler's Story," *Sv*, no.71 (1977), 178
B. Clayton and N. M. Elliott: *Buck Clayton's Jazz World* (London and New York, 1986)
J. Pomfret: "Jazz Making a Comeback in Post-Mao China," *Sunday Star-Ledger* [Newark, NJ] (28 April 1988), 35
R. Lynam: "Swingapore and All Points South East," *Jazz FM*, no.5 (1991), 26

CZECH REPUBLIC

Prague. **Agharta Jazz Center.** Krakovská 5. This venue was founded in 1991 by Michal Heina and Jan Hála as part of a larger project involving the establishment of a new record company and label, Arta, and the launch of a year-round Agharta Jazz Festival, the latter bringing major international artists to various of Prague's large concert halls. The jazz center itself features mainly Czech musicians playing in modern mainstream and fusion styles.
(<http://www.arta.cz> (2001))

——. **Delux.** Vaclavske Námesti 4. This restaurant and nightclub was founded in 1999 by the American businessman and jazz drummer Glen D. Spicker along the same stylistic lines as those involved at his club U Malého Glena (see below). At the Delux jazz performances end around 10 p.m. and are dance parties.
(<http://www. delux.cz> (2001))

——. **Jazz Art Club.** Vinohradská 40. The Jazz Art Club was founded in 1990 by two jazz musicians, Aleš Charvát and Milan Svoboda, at a time of great enthusiasm following the toppling of the totalitarian regime. It became well known as part of the European jazz milieu and featured such musicians as Alphonse Mouzon, Richard Beirach, Lonnie Plaxico, Ronnie Burrage, and George Mraz. The club was equipped to serve as a recording studio, and the duo of Jasper Van 't Hof and Bob Malach recorded there, as did Gerd's Dudek quartet. But in 1992, when the building's ownership changed, the club was obliged to close.

——. **Jazz Club u Staré Paní.** Michalská 9. The Jazz Club u Staré Paní [Jazz club at the old lady's] opened in 1995 within the newly renovated U Staré Paní hotel. It presents mainstream jazz, singers, and Latin jazz. Among notable musicians who have performed there are Philip Catherine, Hal Galper, and Gregory Hutchinson. Jam sessions are frequently held at the club. (<http://www.ustarepani.cz> (2001))

——. **Jazz Club Železná.** Železná 16. This jazz club opened in 1996 in a gothic cellar in the city center near the Old Town Square. Its owner, Petr Hrubeš, presents local artists as well as musicians and groups from Eastern Europe. The club houses an art cinema theater and features poetry readings. In June 2000 it hosted the Prague International Jazz Conference. The venue is a favorite of young jazz musicians who play fusion, modern mainstream, and world music. (<http://www.jazzclub.cz> (2000))

——. **Reduta.** Národní 20. The club dates back to the late 1950s, but it is not clear whether it became a regular jazz club as early as 1958, as some sources claim. In any event, Reduta is the oldest jazz club in the former Czechoslovakia. It features dixieland and mainstream bands and often presents big bands; in the 1990s it began to host an annual big-band festival. It is especially important as a venue for the older generation of Czech jazz musicians.

——. **U Malého Gleno.** Karmelitská 23. The music club U Malého Glena [At Little Glen's] was founded in 1995 by the American businessman and jazz drummer Glen D. Spicker. The club's activities are centered on young musicians, and it is mainly modern mainstream jazz bands that are featured; however, rock, funk, folk, and country bands also perform there. It is a favorite venue for jam sessions, and one of the most memorable such events in 1998 involved Brad Mehldau with local players. (<http://www.malyglen.cz> (2001))

DENMARK

Århus. **Jazzbar Bent J.** Nørre Alle 66. It was opened in 1973 by Bent J. Jensen and features mainly bop and other contemporary jazz styles.

Copenhagen. **Blue Heaven.** Vesterport. It was opened in September 1941 by Svend Asmussen and his brother-in-law Jens Dennow. Asmussen appeared as its main attraction and was also instrumental in arranging jam sessions on Saturday afternoons. The venue closed in spring 1943.

——. **Copenhagen JazzHouse.** Managed by Lars Thorborg, it opened on 2 Oct 1991. The club offers 200 performances a year, mainly in modern jazz styles, and it has become by far the most prominent jazz venue in Denmark. Important performances are broadcast almost weekly by Danish Radio, most often featuring the Danish Radio Big Band with or without guest soloists. (<http://www.jazzhouse.dk> (2000))

——. **La Fontaine.** Kompagnistrade 11. It presented mainly small-group jazz and performances by unaccompanied soloists.

——. **Hollaenderbyen.** Restaurant. From 1935 until 1960 it was managed by Thorkild and Agnete Larsen, and it offered jazz performances from at least the late 1930s, when Richard Stangerup's Jazzband was the resident group. A large venue, with seating for more than 700, it was regularly packed during the residency held there by Leon Abbey's band in October 1938, when among the Danish musicians who heard the visitors was Svend Asmussen. Abbey and his group made a triumphant return visit the following year for a residency of six weeks, during which they also broadcast on Danish Radio.

——. **Jazzhus Slukefter.** Tivoli Gardens. Principally a summer venue (it was open only occasionally between September and May), it engaged many visiting American musicians, including Count Basie, Benny Carter, Benny Goodman, Buddy Rich, Teddy Wilson, and Milt Jackson. The house band, led by Papa Bue, played traditional jazz. Its management changed in the 1990s, as did its name, which became first Tivoleans and then the Tivoli JazzHouse. The venue stopped presenting jazz in 1998, when new management changed its name again, to Mantra, and it became known for techno-oriented pop music.

——. **Loppen Christiania.** Baadmandsstraede 43. Nightclub and discothèque. Its repertory covers a broad range of styles, from blues and jazz to rock and funk. (<http://www.loppen/dk> (2000))

——. **Montmartre (Jazzhus).** Dahlerupsgade; Store Regnegade; Nørregade 41 (1976–93). The venue developed out of a non-profit jazz society, the Club Montmartre, founded in 1954 by Anders Dyrup, and began activities in 1959 under Dyrup at premises on Dahlerupsgade. It moved under Herluf Kamp-Larsen and Per Svensson to Store Regnegade before opening at Nørregade 41 on 15 September 1976. George Lewis (i) and his band were the first musicians to appear at the club, playing there for two weeks in 1959, and were followed by Stan Getz, who took on a regular weekly residency of Monday through Thursday nights. The Montmartre soon became the foremost jazz club in Scandinavia, presenting all kinds of jazz from bop and Latin jazz to fusion, and has made a point of fostering experimental styles; it also functions as a discothèque. It has engaged many Scandinavian and visiting foreign musicians. Niels-Henning Ørsted Pedersen and other Danish players began their careers there, and among those who held long residencies were the Americans Dexter Gordon, Idrees Sulieman, Horace Parlan, and Thad Jones, all of whom settled for some time in or near Copenhagen. Many performers recorded at the club, including Jackie McLean and Gordon, Ben Webster, Charles Lloyd, Getz, Cedar Walton, and Tania Maria; Danish Radio made numerous broadcasts of important performances. Notable house players have been Alex Riel and Kenny Drew. The club published a bi-monthly newsletter, *Jazz & Rock*, and in 1986 issued a book to mark the club's ten years in the Nørregade premises, *Montmartre gennem 10 år*, written by the jazz journalist Jens Jørn Gjedsted with the assistance of Montmartre's music directors Niels Christensen and Lars Thorborg. However, during its last years there were changes in management which resulted in the music policy being altered to accommodate rock rather than jazz.

BIBLIOGRAPHY

D. L. Maggin: *Stan Getz: a Life in Jazz* (New York, 1996), 182
E. Wiedemann: "The Montmartre, 1959–76: Toward a history of a Copenhagen jazz house," *Musik & Forskning*, xxi (1996), 274

——. **De Tre Musketerer.** Nikolaj Plads 25. Owned and managed by Bodil and Hans-Henrick Humleback, this club presented dixieland jazz, played mostly by Danish musicians. It closed on 20 November 1993.

——. **Tivoleans; Tivoli JazzHouse.** See Jazzhus Slukefter.

ODENSE. **Jazzhus Dexter.** Vindegade 65. It was opened on 31 August 1991 by Poul Falck after major restoration and enlargement of the original venue, a bar called Kabyssen. The club, which each year presents about 120 performances of mainstream and modern jazz, established itself in the 1990s as the most important Danish jazz venue outside Copenhagen.

EGYPT

ALEXANDRIA. **Monseigneur.** Willie Lewis and his band were resident there from January to March 1938.

CAIRO. **Continental Cabaret.** Arthur Briggs, leading his American Cubano Boys, played for the 1937 winter season at this venue.

——. **Shepheard's Hotel.** El-Alfi Street. This famous hotel of the colonial era presented Herb Flemming's band in 1934. It was destroyed by fire in 1952.

ENGLAND

BARNEHURST **Red Barn.** Barnehurst Road, Barnehurst, Kent. It was founded in 1943 by the Bexleyheath and District Rhythm Club. The first important postwar British revival jazz club, it flourished until around 1950. The performances given there in the mid-1940s by the resident band, George Webb's Dixielanders, are usually regarded as having sparked off the traditional revival in Britain; a plaque commemorating their association with the Red Barn was unveiled there on 4 July 1985.

BIRMINGHAM. **The Bear.** Bearwood Road. From 1987 through the 1990s Andy Hamilton had a regular Monday-night residency at this pub, which has a capacity of 160; guests included Art Farmer, Harry Edison, and Scott Hamilton.

——. **Palais de Dance.** Monument Road. Dance hall. It opened on 21 December 1920 with a performance by the Frisco Jazz Band. After the summer recess in 1921 Benny Peyton's Jazz Kings, which included Sidney Bechet, played there (1–10 September); the band returned for a residency of a month in February 1922, and during that year the Paramount Six also appeared. Emile Christian was a member of the house band in late 1921 and early 1922. (E. S. Walker: "Saturday Night at the Palais, '21," *Sv*, no.105 (1983), 108)

——. **Ronnie Scott's.** 258 Broad Street. Opened in 1991, the 300-capacity club presents live music seven nights a week, concentrating on mainstream and modern jazz. A resident trio – Steve Palmer on double bass, Tubby Dunne on drums, and John Andrews on piano – performs nightly.

LONDON. **Bag o' Nails.** 9 Kingly Street. It flourished as a venue for jazz in the 1930s, when Gerry Moore was among the important musicians who performed there. Towards the end of the decade it was the meeting place of the No.1 Rhythm Club.

——. **Barbican.** Arts complex. It opened in 1982 and has developed a lively program of pop and jazz performance, both in the concert hall and in the foyer and public areas. Among the jazz musicians who have appeared in concert are Keith Jarrett, Buddy Rich, Louie Bellson, John Dankworth, Cleo Laine, Carmen McRae, Billy Eckstine, Sarah Vaughan, Oscar Peterson, Stephane Grappelli, George Shearing, Marian Montgomery, Clark Terry, the Preservation Hall Jazz Band, Cab Calloway, and Wynton Marsalis. Free performances take place in the foyer at lunchtime on Sundays. In the 1980s and 1990s the hall was a regular venue for concerts under the name "A Night at the Cotton Club," which sought to re-create the music of the Cotton Club in the 1930s using the big band Harlem and such guest soloists as Benny Waters and Doc Cheatham.

——. **Bass Clef.** 1 Hoxton Square. It was founded by Peter Ind around 1984 and rapidly became one of the city's most popular clubs; it presented mostly a modern repertory, including free improvised music, and from the late 1980s it was an important venue for acid jazz. In another part of the same building were the Tenor Clef club, which offered more mainstream fare, and the studios for Ind's record company, Wave; these were linked to the club, and performances were sometimes recorded. Both clubs closed in 1994, and the venue became the Blue Note, which briefly continued to offer acid-jazz groups before abandoning live music.

——. **Blanchard's Club.** See Murray's Club.

——. **Bull's Head. Lonsdale Road, Barnes.** Pub. The manager, Albert Tolley, began presenting jazz in 1960; performances continued nightly through the 1990s, leading to the venue becoming one of the most renowned in Britain. As well as engaging some of the country's most important players (Tony Lee's trio was resident from the early 1960s, and Humphrey Lyttelton's band and Bill Le Sage's trio appeared regularly), the Bull's Head booked important visiting musicians, including Jimmy Witherspoon, Al Casey, Snub Mosley, Don Ewell, Benny Waters, George Coleman, Lanny Morgan, Hal Singer, and Mundell Lowe.

——. **Café de Paris.** 3 Coventry Street. One of the fashionable establishments for dining and dancing in London, it presented jazz from at least the late 1920s; Ethel Waters was resident there in 1929-30. It became known especially as a center for Afro-Caribbean bands, among them the West Indian Swing Band, led by Ken "Snake Hips" Johnson, which opened in October 1939; Johnson was killed when the premises were destroyed by a bomb on 8 March 1941.

——. **Carlton Dance Hall.** See Rector's.

——. **Casino de Danse.** 160 Finchley Road. The premises operated as a dance hall from 1919 (as Valhalla Dancing Hall or O'Dett's Dancing Hall) and took the name Casino de Danse around 1922. Jazz was played for dancing from at least the mid-1930s, when bands led by Cyril Blake and others appeared there.

——. **Ciro's.** 39 Orange Street. It was opened in April 1915 by the French entrepreneur Ciro and was modeled on his sophisticated and expensive restaurant club in Paris; later he set up other such clubs in Deauville and Monte Carlo. Although he insisted (perhaps for licensing reasons) that his establishments were restaurants, they offered musical entertainment from the start; the London Ciro's opened with Dan Kildare's Clef Club Orchestra as the resident band. The club was frequented by the *haut monde*, and among its patrons were members of the British royal family. It closed between 1917 and 1919, then reopened, and continued until 1939. Among the musicians to perform there were Noble Sissle, with a band that included Arthur Briggs and Tommy Ladnier (1930), and Art Tatum (March 1938). The club reopened again at an unknown date after 1939 and finally closed on 27 March 1954. (H. Rye and T. Brooks: "Visiting Firemen, 16: Dan Kildare," *Storyville 1996/7*, ed. L. Wright (Chigwell, England, 1997), 30)

——. **Club Eleven.** 41 Great Windmill Street (1948–50); 50 Carnaby Street (1950). It was established in 1948, and its 11 founders were, apart from the business manager Harry Morris, all bop musicians. They included Ronnie Scott and John Dankworth, each of whom led a resident band, with such players as Tony Crombie, Lennie Bush, Hank Shaw, and others. The club became an important center for early experiments with the bop style in London, but it closed only months after moving to new premises in 1950. (J. Fordham: *Let's Join Hands and Contact the Living: Ronnie Scott and his Club*, London, 1986, rev. 2/1995, as *Jazz Man: the Amazing Story of Ronnie Scott and his Club*)

——. **Cook's Ferry Inn.** Angel Road, Edmonton. Pub. It was one of the principal venues for traditional jazz in London in the late 1940s and 1950s. Rex Stewart performed there in 1949, and the resident band was led for some time by Freddy Randall. It was the home of the Cleveland Jazz Club.

——. **Cossack.** 39–40 Jermyn Street. Restaurant. In the early 1930s the orchestra African Polyphony, led by the conductor and clarinetist Rudolph Dunbar, appeared there and also made broadcasts for the BBC; among the jazz musicians who played in Dunbar's orchestra was Cyril Blake.

——. **Cuba Club.** 44 Gerrard Street. This club was a regular venue for Afro-Caribbean jazz groups from the mid-1930s. In 1935 the drummer Happy Blake led a band that included Jiver Hutchinson and Bertie King. In 1938 the expatriate American singer Ike Hatch was host for a period during which the club was temporarily renamed the Hell Club and the band was led by Al Craig.

——. **Downbeat.** Old Compton Street. It was established in 1958 by Jack Sharpe and Mike Senn, co-leaders from 1957 of the Downbeaters, a group which in 1958 became known as the Downbeat Big Band. The club continued until the mid-1960s.

——. **Embassy Club.** 6–8 Old Bond Street. It was one of the first nightclubs to be established in London, and from December 1919 to August 1920 Benny Peyton's group the Jazz Kings (made up of former members of Will Marion Cook's Southern Syncopated Orchestra, and at first including Sidney Bechet) was the resident band. Jazz and dance bands continued to play there into the 1950s; Bert Ambrose was music director from 1920 to 1926 and again from 1933 to 1936, and Reginald Foresythe led the resident band in 1940. The premises later served principally as a discothèque.

——. **Feldman Swing Club.** See 100 Oxford Street.

——. **'51 Club.** See Studio 51.

——. **Flamingo.** Beneath Mapleton Restaurant, Leicester Square (1953); Café Anglais, Leicester Square (early 1950s); Wardour Street (from mid-1950s). Under the management of Sam Kruger it became one of the better-known venues for bop in London, employing as resident musicians Tony Kinsey, Dizzy Reece, Bill Le Sage, Wilton "Bogey" Gaynair, Tommy Whittle, and Ronnie Ross, among others. In the early 1950s the club operated at both venues in Leicester Square, but its most important activities began with the move to Wardour Street, where it flourished until the mid-1960s.

——. **Florida Club** [Old Florida Club; New Florida Club]. 5 South Bruton Mews; 23 Bruton Mews (from *c* late 1930s [from 1940, Bruton Lane]); 23 Kingly Street (1944–6). One of London's most luxurious and exclusive clubs, it opened in the mid-1920s. Ronnie Monroe led the first resident band (with Ben Davis, saxophones, Frank Wilson, trumpet, and Max Bacon, drums), which played hot dance music. The club quickly became important for the presentation of Afro-Caribbean jazz and was the venue at which Ken "Snake Hips" Johnson and his Rhythm Swingers undertook their first London residency in 1936–8. Adelaide Hall sang there for several years: she was accompanied first by Fela Sowande's band (1938–40), during which period the club, renamed the New Florida Club, moved to 23 Bruton Mews (as the street had by then become); she then continued accompanied by the bandleader Gerry Moore (1940–42). There was a later Florida Club at 23 Kingly Street, in the premises formerly occupied by the Nest Club (1944–6).

——. **Grafton Galleries.** 8 Grafton Street. A dance club which operated at these premises was an early venue for African-American bands in London, among them Dan Kildare's in 1916. Like other London dance clubs it was soon closed "for the duration," but it had reopened by October 1919 and in 1921 featured the International Five, another African-American group.

——. **Hammersmith Palais (de Danse).** Brook Green Road. Dance hall. It opened in 1919, and from that October to June 1920 the Original Dixieland Jazz Band played there, giving some of the first jazz performances in London. Another early jazz band to appear was Benny Peyton's Jazz Kings, whose first residency began on 3 October 1920. For a time in the 1930s the venue was used as an ice-rink. In 1950 the National Federation of Jazz Organizations hired the hall for a special event, the Jazz Band Ball. After several years as a discothèque and a venue for rock concerts, the Hammersmith Palais began to promote jazz again on an occasional basis following a concert given in 1984 by Kid Thomas Valentine and the Preservation Hall Jazz Band.

——. **Havana Club.** 6 New Compton Street (1938); 4 Denman Street (1938–?1940; 1942–3). It was associated chiefly with Afro-Caribbean jazz bands, including that led by the double bass player Jack Davis, though it engaged Una Mae Carlisle and Mabel Scott during their visits to Europe in 1938. In 1936–7 the club was at 25 Oxendon Street, but it is not established that any jazz groups were featured during this period. It closed after a police raid on 6 May 1943.

——. **Hell Club.** See Cuba Club.

——. **Hippodrome.** Charing Cross Road at Cranbourn Street. Theater and ballroom. It was the site of the first performance by a jazz band in Britain, when the Original Dixieland Jazz Band played in the revue *Joy Bells* on 7 April 1919, and it continued to promote jazz throughout the 1920s, engaging Paul Whiteman's orchestra in 1923 and 1926. In the 1930s the Hippodrome functioned as a theater, and concerts of jazz were given there on Sundays: Garland Wilson appeared at one of these in 1935 and Benny Carter in 1937. From 1958 until the mid-1980s the premises housed a nightclub, the Talk of the Town, where a number of jazz musicians, including Louie Bellson, performed. Thereafter the entrepreneur Peter Stringfellow opened a discothèque there, using the building's original name.

——. **Humphrey Lyttelton Club.** See 100 Oxford Street.

——. **Jazz Café.** 56 Newington Green (1987–90); 5 Parkway (1990–). Founded by Jon Dabner in August 1987, the café moved to a larger venue (holding 350 people) in December 1990, when its opening set was by David Murray. It was owned from September 1992 by Vince Power's Mean Fiddler Organization, Britain's largest music and festival promoter, and programmed by Adrian Gibson. The Jazz Café presents one-night performances and residencies by leading American musicians, who have included Gene Harris, Stanley Jordan, Pharoah Sanders, McCoy Tyner, the Art Ensemble of Chicago, and Jimmy Smith, and by British musicians, such as Courtney Pine, as well as jazz dance and Latin club nights.

——. **Jazzshows.** See 100 Oxford Street.

——. **Jig's Club.** 124–6 Wardour Street. It flourished as a center for jazz from at least the early 1930s, when it was managed by Alec and Rose Ward. Its name derived from an American slang word for black, and its clientèle was mostly West Indian. In the early 1940s the club band included Cyril Blake; four recordings were made by the band for the Regal-Zonophone label in December 1941. Jig's Club closed soon afterwards. The Coloured People's Club, which operated in 1943 at 23 Frith Street, is described in contemporary sources as it successor.

——. **Ken Colyer's.** Great Newport Street. A small cellar nightclub on the fringes of Soho, it was an important venue for traditional jazz in the early 1960s. Colyer's own band, the New Orleans Jazzmen, playing a faithful form of classic jazz, was joined there by a dixieland band, the Original Downtown Syncopators, and the Delta Jazzmen.

——. **Kit Kat.** 47–9 Haymarket. Its name was taken from an 18th-century Whig club founded by Christopher Catt. The club opened on 11 May 1925 with Vincent Lopez's orchestra, and it presented jazz from the mid-1920s, when Noble Sissle and Eubie Blake appeared there. It was a favorite haunt of Duke Ellington and his bandmembers during their visit to London in 1933. Cab Calloway performed at the Kit Kat in 1934, and other musicians to play there included Léo Vauchant and Jack Hylton. The club closed about 1935 and the premises later became a cinema. Another club of the same name operated on Regent Street around the turn of the decade; among the musicians it engaged were the reed player and bandleader Teddy Joyce and Al Jennings, in whose band Joe Appleton was a sideman.

——. **Leicester Square Jazz Club.** Above Café de l'Europe, Leicester Square. It operated on Monday nights in 1947–8 in premises rented from the National Society for the Prevention of Cruelty to Children and was the first jazz club in London to offer traditional jazz for dancing. Humphrey Lyttelton's band played regularly and Graeme Bell's Australian Jazz Band was also resident for a time.

——. **Little Theatre Club.** Great Newport Street. Established in 1965 by Paul Rutherford, John Stevens, and Trevor Watts to promote free improvised music, the club saw the first performances of the Spontaneous Music Ensemble and Watts's group Amalgam, as well as sessions from a wide pool of free improvisers. It closed in 1968.

——. **London Jazz Club.** Great Windmill Street (1948–?1951); 100 Oxford Street (?1951–1958). At first the club operated twice weekly in a large rehearsal room beneath a gymnasium in Great Windmill Street. Among the musicians who performed there was Humphrey Lyttelton, whose band (including Wally Fawkes) was resident from around 1949 and played with guest musicians such as Rex Stewart and Jimmy McPartland. In 1950 or 1951 the club moved to 100 Oxford Street (see below), where it coexisted for a time with the Humphrey Lyttelton Club. It closed in 1958.

——. **London Palladium** [Palladium Theatre]. 7–8 Argyll Street. Variety theater. An important venue for concert performances of popular music, the Palladium first presented jazz in April 1919, when the Original Dixieland Jazz Band played there during its first visit to London. Will Marion Cook's Southern Syncopated Orchestra gave performances in the following year. From the 1930s many eminent musicians and big bands held short residencies at the theater, among them Ethel Waters and Wilton Crawley (both 1930), Duke Ellington (1933), Cab Calloway (1934), Coleman Hawkins (1934), Garland Wilson (1936), Teddy Hill (1937), and Fats Waller (1938); Louis Armstrong led his group there in 1932 and 1933, and Joe Venuti and the guitarist Frank Victor appeared in August 1934. Many notable performances also took place in the 1940s and 1950s, such as those of Ellington with Ray Nance and Kay Davis (1948), Benny Goodman (1949), Ellington with his orchestra (1957), Count Basie's orchestra (November 1957), and Bob Crosby (1958). From 1944 Ted Heath gave regular monthly concerts.

——. **Lyons Corner House.** Shaftesbury Avenue at Coventry Street. Café. Jazz was played there from at least the early 1920s; the Georgians, led by Paul Specht and including Chauncey Morehouse and Arthur Schutt as sidemen, was the resident band in 1923.

——. **Lyttelton Club.** See 100 Oxford Street.

——. **Mack's.** See 100 Oxford Street.

——. **Marquee Club.** 165 Oxford Street (at Poland Street) (1958–64); Wardour Street (from 1964). It was established by the National Jazz Federation and opened early in 1958 with a performance by Kenny Baker. The club espoused a fairly broad programming policy, offering mainly traditional and mainstream jazz together with blues and rhythm-and-blues; indeed, it made an important contribution to the development of blues in London. Among the bands that performed were those of Chris Barber, Humphrey Lyttelton, John Dankworth, Joe Harriott, and Harold McNair; Alexis Korner's Blues Incorporated was resident there in 1962, often accompanying guest singers. After the club moved in 1964 to premises owned by Harold Pendleton it concentrated on blues and rock music, and by the late 1960s it was no longer thought of as a jazz venue. In 1995 it became a restaurant, Mezzo's. ("Mainstream at the Marquee," *Jazz News*, iii (1958), March, 4)

——. **Mayfair Hotel.** Berkeley Street. Music was played for dancing from at least the 1920s. Bert Ambrose's band was resident there from 1927 to 1933 and from 1928 made fortnightly broadcasts from the hotel's ballroom; Ambrose returned to the Mayfair in 1937–8 and again in 1939–40.

——. **Moody's Club.** 71 Tottenham Court Road and 40 Whitfield Street. It flourished from about 1922 to about 1927; many black groups performed there regularly, and of particular importance were the several ensembles that grew out of Will Marion Cook's Southern Syncopated Orchestra. Ellis Jackson was bandleader from 1921 to 1925, and his band may be seen there with the club's dancers in the silent short film *Moody's Club Follies* (1923).

——. **Murray's Club.** 9 Beak Street. The club, which opened on 6 November 1913, was the London home until 1917 of the pioneering African-American ragtime group the Versatile Four, who played a major part in introducing syncopated music to London. It later featured the Five Musical Dragons with Arthur Briggs (1921–2) and then Noble Sissle and Eubie Blake (November 1925). By that time it was known as Blanchard's Club, in succession to a club of that name which had been active at the same address in 1911–13.

——. **Nest Club.** 12 Little Pulteney Street (now Brewer Street); 23 Kingly Street (by mid-1930s). The Nest Club at Kingly Street was an important venue before World War II for visiting American jazzmen, among them Coleman Hawkins, Fats Waller, and Benny Carter. In 1937 Dizzy Gillespie sat in at the club with local musicians; at that time the house band included the trumpeter Duncan Whyte and George Chisholm.

——. **New Florida Club.** See Florida Club.

——. **Ocean.** Mare Street, Hackney. This complex, which opened in March 2001, has three performance spaces designed to accommodate a full spectrum of music. It has an overall capacity of 2700. David Mossman, who had previously run the Vortex club (see below), moved his jazz program to the new venue to take advantage of the increased capacities, improved technical infrastructure, and high quality accommodation.

——. **Old Florida Club.** See Florida Club.

——. **Olympia Ballroom.** Dance hall. It was active from at least the 1920s. Leon Abbey and his band performed there in 1927–8, and Joe Appleton led his Hot Maniacs there in December 1931.

——. **100 Club.** See 100 Oxford Street.

——. **100 Oxford Street.** In the 1930s the premises housed a dance hall. From the early 1940s a succession of clubs operated at this address, making 100 Oxford Street the longest-running venue for traditional and mainstream jazz in London; a number of broadcasts were made from the club and many musicians recorded there.

In 1942 Joseph Feldman took over the premises and started a Sunday jazz club to promote the work of his sons Robert (clarinet), Monty (accordion), and Victor (drums). The club presented traditional jazz and swing, and the bands of Vic Lewis and Jack Parnell, Freddy Randall, and others played there, as did several American forces ensembles. The Feldman Swing Club continued until 1954. By 1951 the London Jazz Club (see above) and the Humphrey Lyttelton Club were also offering sessions, on different nights of the week, at 100 Oxford Street. By 1953 Lyttelton was appearing twice weekly, and the number of evenings on which jazz was presented gradually increased until 1955 (by which time the venue itself was known as Mack's); Lyttelton's organization issued a regular newsletter called the *Humphrey Lyttelton*

Club Bulletin. The London Jazz Club ceased to function in 1958 and from December of that year the premises were called The 100.

In September 1959 Ted Morton opened the Jazzshows Jazz Club at 100 Oxford Street with Don Kingswell as his manager (Morton also presented jazz at other locations under the name Jazzshows). In 1964 the venue became the 100 Club, and the following year Roger Horton replaced Don Kingswell. Horton and Morton together continued to run the club into the new century, continuing with a mix of traditional jazz, swing groups, blues, and rhythm-and-blues. Until 1983 they published a bimonthly newsletter, *Jazz at the 100 Club*.

——. **Palais de Danse.** East Ham. Dance hall. It was active during the 1920s; Victor Vorzanger's Broadway Band, which included the trombonist Ellis Jackson, was resident there in 1922–3.

——. **Palladium Theatre.** See London Palladium.

——. **Palm Beach.** 46 Frith Street. A number of visiting American jazz musicians performed at this Soho club, including Fats Waller (1938) and Coleman Hawkins (1939). The banjoist Ike Hatch was the principal resident musician there at that time, and the house band was led by the pianist Hettie Booth (1938–40).

——. **Pizza Express.** 10 Dean Street. Restaurant. In the mid-1970s Peter Boizot began to engage jazz musicians to play in the restaurant, which under his direction (and later that of K. C. Sulkin and Dave Bennett) became an important location for small-group jazz of all traditions and styles. A number of visiting American and European musicians appeared there, including Bob Wilber and Bud Freeman. Around 1978 Boizot began to publish the news sheet *Jazz at the Pizza Express*, which developed into a monthly journal (from 1984 *Jazz Express*). In 1994 the new manager, Peter Wallis, refurbished and extended the club and reopened it in 1996 as a venue capable of attracting high-profile international players, among themg Joey Calderazzo, Kenny Garrett, Steve Grossman, Dave Liebman, Kirk Lightsey, and T. S. Monk. Many new young contemporary artists also appeared there, although the traditional mainstream policy of the old club was not abandoned: such artists as Scott Hamilton and Warren Vaché were booked at regular intervals, notably during August and over Christmas.

——. **Pizza on the Park.** Knightsbridge. Restaurant. It was established in the mid-1970s and its manager, Peter Boizot, presents mostly solo and duo performances. The venue has two pianos; among the resident pianists have been Ralph Sutton and Eddie Thompson.

——. **Purcell Room.** See South Bank.

——. **Queen Elizabeth Hall.** See South Bank.

——. **Rainbow Roof.** See Shim Sham Club.

——. **Rector's.** 31 Tottenham Court Road. It was one of the London venues at which the Original Dixieland Jazz Band performed during its visit to the city in 1919. In the 1920s it was a fashionable nightspot and was associated with several of the small ensembles to grow out of Will Marion Cook's Southern Syncopated Orchestra. Among the resident groups at the club between 1920 and 1922 were Benny Peyton's Jazz Kings and the Red Devils; the personnel of both of these bands originated from Cook's ensembles, and the first included Sidney Bechet. In 1928 the Tottenham Court Road premises became the Carlton Dance Hall. A later club under the name Rector's operated from the late 1930s at 207 Regent Street; Al Jennings led a band there in which Joe Appleton was a sideman.

——. **Red Barn.** See England, Barnehurst.

——. **Rhythmic.** 88–91 Chapel Market. It opened on 1 December 1995 as a venue to present a wide range of jazz, blues, and related music by both British and visiting American artists, including Andy Hamilton, Jimmy Smith, and Hank Crawford. Despite its adventurous policy the club did not succeed as a jazz venue, and it closed in autumn 1996.

——. **Ronnie Scott's.** 39 Gerrard Street (1959 – mid-December 1965); 47 Frith Street (from mid-December 1965; see fig.1). It was founded in 1959 by Ronnie Scott, who managed it until his death in 1996 with Peter King, under whose control the club continued to flourish. (The clubowner King should not be confused with the British saxophonist of the same name, who played in the club's house band from its opening night in 1959.) It became the most important venue for jazz performance in London, especially after it moved to Frith Street, and is frequently used for recordings and broadcasts. Numerous eminent performers have appeared there: the club accommodated big bands such as those of Count Basie, Buddy Rich, Gil Evans, and Maynard Ferguson, but it was equally suited to solo performers and small groups: Monty Alexander, Earl Hines, Dizzy Gillespie, Dexter Gordon, McCoy Tyner, Wynton Marsalis, Stanley Jordan, Regina Carter, Frank Foster, and Jimmy McGriff are among those who have given memorable performances in the club. For many years it had a house rhythm section led by Stan Tracey, who worked with visiting soloists such as Sonny Rollins and Ben Webster; other Americans to play there included Illinois Jacquet and Panama Francis. During the 1980s the club formed a link with promoters of Cuban music, and many Cuban musicians, notably Arturo Sandoval, performed there. The Brazilian musicians Airto Moreira and Flora Purim also held monthly residencies at Ronnie Scott's from 1986 into the 1990s. However, the club's promotion of British jazz was of supreme significance, and many British musicians appeared regularly, among them Ronnie Scott's own trio.

In 1978 the club established its own record company and label, Ronnie Scott's Jazz House, and initially produced an album by Scott's own quintet. The label became more prominent in the late 1980s and the 1990s, when it issued historic recordings from club performances in the 1960s and new recordings by such diverse groups and artists as Irakere, the National Youth Jazz Orchestra, Al Cohn, Marian Montgomery, Roy Ayers, Peter King, and Art Themen. The club's magazine *Jazz at Ronnie Scott's* has appeared on a bimonthly basis from 1979.

BIBLIOGRAPHY

K. Grime: *Jazz at Ronnie Scott's* (London, 1979)

R. Ottaway: "Scott's London Roost Swings into 3d Decade as Leading Jazz Joint," *Variety* (9 Jan 1980), 195

J. Fordham: *Let's Join Hands and Contact the Living: Ronnie Scott and his Club* (London, 1986, rev. 2/1995, as *Jazz Man: the Amazing Story of Ronnie Scott and his Club*)

<http://www.bigbearmusic.com/ronniescotts> (2001)

——. **Royal Festival Hall.** See South Bank.

——. **Savoy Hotel.** The Strand. To celebrate the armistice that ended World War I, in 1919 the hotel gave a ball, the Peace Ball, at which the Original Dixieland Jazz Band played. During the first two decades of the 20th century the resident dance bands in the hotel ballroom at times included notable jazz musicians: the Savoy Quartet (1915–20) and the Savoy Orpheans (from mid-1920s) made numerous recordings, some of which contain points of jazz interest. In 1927–9 Fred Elizalde led the Savoy Hotel Band, among the members of which were Adrian Rollini and Fud Livingston. Zinky Cohn appeared there in 1931.

——. **Shim Sham Club.** 37 Wardour Street. It opened in March 1935, and by late 1936 Garland Wilson was leader of the resident band. Benny Carter performed there in 1936 and Una Mae Carlisle the following year; such jazz-oriented dance-band players as the trumpeter Duncan Whyte, the guitarists Alan Ferguson and Ivor Mairants, the drummer Maurice Burman, and the trombonist Edgar Jackson also appeared during the 1930s. In 1937 Joe Appleton became the bandleader, and late that year the club's name was changed to the Rainbow Roof; it had reverted to the original name by April 1938. (R. Dunbar: "Harlem in London," *MM*, xii (7 March 1936), 2)

——. **Six Bells.** King's Road, Chelsea. Pub. A large upstairs room was used for jazz performances and jam sessions from the 1930s until the early 1960s. Spike Hughes's composition *Six Bells Stampede* (1932, Decca F2844) was dedicated to the venue. In the 1950s and 1960s it was used as a recording studio by Decca, and sessions led by such musicians as Ken Colyer and Mick Mulligan took place there. In 1961 Bruce Turner's Jump Band, which included John Chilton and John Mumford, which was then resident, used the pub as a location in Jack Gold's film *Living Jazz*. Among other notable British bands to appear was Wally Fawkes's Troglodytes, who also recorded there for Decca.

——. **606 Club.** 606 Kings Road (mid-1960s – October 1987); 90 Lots Road (from October 1987). The original 606 Club opened in a small basement venue in the mid-1960s. Owned and managed from 1976 by Steve Rubie, it moved to larger basement premises in Lots Road in October 1987 and opened for business as a jazz club and restaurant on 28 May 1988. The club presents two bands a night from Monday through Wednesday, a headline performer or band on Thursday through Saturday, and a singer every Sunday evening, and has a policy of booking local British musicians as well as encouraging younger players.

——. **South Bank.** Arts complex. The Royal Festival Hall, the Queen Elizabeth Hall, and the Purcell Room, which form part of the complex, are among the principal concert halls in London. The first major jazz concert at the Royal Festival Hall took place on 14 July 1951 under the auspices of the National Federation of Jazz Organizations. By the 1980s jazz was part of the program in all three halls, and free performances were given regularly in the Royal Festival Hall foyer. Particularly important is the series of jazz events held in association with festivals (*see* Festivals).

——. **Streatham Locarno.** 158 Streatham Hill. This ballroom was open at least by 1931, when Joe Appleton led the band there. The mid-1930s brought engagements by many visiting American jazzmen, including Duke Ellington (1933), Cab Calloway and Coleman Hawkins (both 1934), Benny Carter (1937), and Fats Waller (1938).

——. **Studio 51** ['51 Club]. Founded around 1956 by Ken Colyer, it was an important venue for traditional jazz in the

1. Ronnie Scott with his quartet playing at Ronnie Scott's, London, October 1979: (left to right) John Critchinson (keyboards), Scott (tenor saxophone), Ron Mathewson (double bass), and Martin Drew (drums)

1950s and 1960s. Parts of the film *West 11* (1963), with a soundtrack played by Colyer, Acker Bilk, and Tony Kinsey, were set in the club.

——. **Suzi-Q.** Gerrard Street. It was run by the banjoist Ike Hatch and was active in the late 1930s.

——. **Talk of the Town.** See Hippodrome.

——. **Tenor Club.** 1 Hoxton Square. Club operated by Peter Ind on the same premises as the Bass Clef (see above).

——. **The Vortex.** 139–141 Stoke Newington Church Street (to 2001); Mare Street, Hackney (from 2001). Originally an art gallery with space for live music performances, the Vortex Jazz Bar was launched in 1986 under the management of David Mossman. The first-floor venue had a seating capacity of 100 and standing room at the bar. It catered for and promoted a wide range of music falling broadly within the definition of jazz, from unaccompanied soloists to performances by big bands; special guest club nights were devoted to international music, cabaret, women musicians, and young contemporary artists. The club also presented occasional visiting musicians from the USA and mainland Europe. On 18 March 2001 Mossman moved the club to become part of the Ocean music complex in Mare Street, Hackney (see above).

BIBLIOGRAPHY

London

A. Gray: "London's After-dark Swing Spots," *MM*, xiii (17 April–10 July 1937, 24 July 1937, 17 Sept 1937) [series of 14 articles]

H. Lyttelton: *I Play as I Please: the Memoirs of an Old Etonian Trumpeter* (London, 1954)

——: *Second Chorus* (London, 1958)

P. Green: "Jazz in London, June 1962," *Sixth Form Opinion*, no.5 (1962), 11

J. Godbolt: *A History of Jazz in Britain, 1919–1950* (London, Melbourne, Australia, and New York, 1984)

MILTON KEYNES. **The Stables.** Wavendon, Milton Keynes. The Stables grew out of the Wavendon Allmusic Plan, a charity founded in December 1969 by John Dankworth and his wife, Cleo Laine, "to break down the perceived barriers which exist between jazz, classical, and other forms of music through education and the presentation of public concerts featuring leading exponents of diverse musical forms." Its buildings consist of the stable block of the Victorian rectory (the Dankworth's home) and the next-door converted factory unit, which contains a 300-seat auditorium, although Dankworth and Laine intend to demolish this and construct a new 400-seat auditorium. The Stables presents about 170 concerts annually, covering the range of jazz, classical, and other musics, as well as 30 workshops and courses and a month of residential courses for young people during the summer.

ESTONIA

TALLINN. **Eeslitall.** Dunkri 4. This restaurant was opened in 1999 by Jens Moust-Tallinn. Jazz, primarily in mainstream styles, is heard on Fridays and Saturdays from September to April, and on Thursdays as well from May to August, when the summer courtyard is open.

——. **Kiko.** 12 Vaike-Karja Street. This café and bar, which was part of the publishing house Valgus, began to present jazz in 1981. Music took place on every second and fourth Monday of the month and featured mainstream and modern jazz, including jam sessions with visiting musicians.

TARTU. **Illegaard.** Ülikooli 5. Founded by Sirje Ginter in 1993, this art gallery and jazz club offers live jazz performances once or twice weekly.

FINLAND

HELSINKI. **Down Beat Club.** Olavinkatu. Situated in a former factory building (and on the site of the present-day Hotel Ramada President) in downtown Helsinski, this short-lived successor to the Old House Jazz Club opened in 1965. It hosted some remarkable visiting musicians, including Dexter Gordon, but went out of business within a few months.

——. **Groovy.** Ruoholahdenkatu. Groovy opened in 1977 within a restaurant, Kantakrouvi. On some nights there was a cover charge and musicians would be paid by the establishment, but most nights were run as jam sessions. This concept carried the club for ten years, and there were even attempts to expand the idea: at one time Ted Curson toured a dozen restaurants belonging to the same chain throughout Finland, but by 1987 interest had waned and Kantakrouvi abandoned live music.

——. **Jumo Club.** Kaivokatu. This small cellar studio opened in the business center of Helsinki in 1988. The home of UMO, it was used to present concerts featuring UMO and guest artists, as well as other performers. The project was subsidized by the city but survived for only a few years, partly because there were other businesses interested in the site.

——. **Kulttuuritalo.** Sturenkatu 4. Designed by the famous architect Alvar Aalto, this concert hall was the home of the Finnish Radio Symphony Orchestra, and in the 1960s and 1970s it was the main venue in Helsinki for jazz concerts. The promoter Paavo Einiö's concert agency Rytmi presented many of the major jazz groups touring Europe during these decades, including the orchestras of Count Basie and Duke Ellington, John Coltrane, Sonny Rollins, Roland Kirk, Dizzy Gillespie, and the Modern Jazz Quartet. Among other events was the American Folk Blues Festival. From the 1980s jazz concerts have been dispersed to several other locations in Helsinki and the main focus of activity at Kulttuuritalo has been festivals.

——. **Old House Jazz Club.** Albertinkatu 20. The first jazz club in Helsinki, the Old House Jazz Club opened in 1957 in a condemned two-story wooden house. It was a club in both senses of the term – a venue for nighttime performances and an organization of jazz fans; its operations were financed by membership fees and by the sale of soft drinks, and musicians performed for free. During the day the club served as a rehearsal studio. Practically all Finnish jazz musicians of the era performed there during its lifetime, and visiting American jazz musicians would also sit in after concerts. The club closed in 1964 to make way for a new apartment building, but it is documented in two short films, *Jazzia vanhassa talossa* (Jazz at the Old House), which was made for Finnish television in 1961, and *I'll Remember Old House* (1991), produced by Pentti Teirikari.

——. **Storyville Jazz Club.** Museokatu 8. This nightclub, which opened in 1993, is situated next to the Finnish parliament house, and many of the clientele appear more interested in drinks and conversation than listening to music. Nonetheless, Storyville Jazz Club has been supporting live jazz regularly into the new century, with an emphasis on lesser-known traditional-jazz groups. (<http://www.storyville.fi> (2001))

BIBLIOGRAPHY

Finland

J. Haavisto: *Puuvillapelloilta kaskimaille* [From the cotton fields (of the USA) to the backwoods (of Finland)] (Helsinki, 1991)

FRANCE

Biarritz. **Bricktop's.** At the Merry Sol (near the Grand Casino). One of several clubs set up by the singer Bricktop (Ada Smith) in different cities (others were in Paris, Mexico City, and Rome), it operated only for the 1932 season. Among the resident artists were Charlie Lewis and his band, Mabel Mercer, and Bricktop herself. The following year Bricktop took new premises for the season, which were less successful. An attempt to run a similar club during the 1950 season lasted only four nights. (Bricktop and J. Haskins: *Bricktop*, New York, 1983).

Cannes. **Palm Beach Casino.** It was opened in April 1929, and its cabaret mounted performances of jazz from that time; Django Reinhardt appeared in the early 1930s, and in 1953 Big Chief Moore led a band there, which included Geo Daly, Raymond Fol, and the singer Anita Love. Among the club's managers was the impresario Leon Voltera. (J. Duclos-Arkilovitch: *Jazzin' Riviera: 70 ans de jazz sur la Côte-d'Azur*, Nice, France, 1997)

Juan-les-Pins. **Le Vieux Colombier.** Boulevard de la Pinède (near the casino). It was owned and managed by Annet Badel and modeled on his Parisian club of the same name. Claude Luter's band, featuring Sidney Bechet, was resident there for several seasons in the 1950s. (J. Duclos-Arkilovitch: *Jazzin' Riviera: 70 ans de jazz sur la Côte-d'Azur*, Nice, France, 1997)

Levallois-Perret. **La Toque Blanche.** 115 rue Paul Vaillant-Couturier. Restaurant. Opened in 1995 as a traditional-jazz venue, it gradually adopted a policy oriented towards bop. Among the musicians featured have been Maurice Vander, Michel Legrand, and Georges Arvanitas.

BIBLIOGRAPHY

F. Moulin: "La Toque Blanche," *Jh*, no.572 (2000), 10
<http://www.toque-blanche.com> (2001)

Montreuil. **Les Instants Chavirés.** 7 rue Richard Lenoir. Situated on the outskirts of Paris in Montreuil (where Kenny Clarke lived and died), this little club holds about 100 people and constitutes a type of workshop generally open to all musicians of the French and European avant garde.

BIBLIOGRAPHY

A. Merlin: "Philippe Bacchetta: le dernier détricheur," *Jazzman*, no.160 (1992), 11
——: "Les Instants Chavirés: touchés mais pas coulés," *Jazzman*, no.177 (1994), 10
<http://www.instantschavires.fr.st> (2001)

Nice. **Negresco Hotel.** Among the jazz musicians who played in resident bands there were Dave Tough and the baritone saxophonist Spencer Clark (both in the late 1920s). Sam Wooding's band played there for the winter season 1928–9. (J. Duclos-Arkilovitch: *Jazzin' Riviera: 70 ans de jazz sur la Côte-d'Azur*, Nice, France, 1997)

——. **Palais de la Méditerranée.** Jazz musicians played there for dancing during the venue's heyday in the 1920s and 1930s. Among them were Benny Peyton and his band, which for its residency in Nice in 1929 included June Cole and Tommy Ladnier. (J. Duclos-Arkilovitch: *Jazzin' Riviera: 70 ans de jazz sur la Côte-d'Azur*, Nice, France, 1997)

Paris. **Abbaye de Thélème.** 1 place Pigalle. It offered performances by European and American jazz musicians from 1924 to 1934, when it closed. Among those who appeared there were Léo Vauchant (1925), the pianist Jack O'Brien with Dave Tough (1929), and the Plantation Orchestra (1929–30), led at first by Joe Hayman and Edwin Swayze and later by Herb Flemming.

——. **ABC Music Hall.** 11 Boulevard Poissonnière, Montmartre. One of the leading variety venues in Paris, its presentations included performances by jazz musicians. Django Reinhardt appeared there intermittently from 1938 for a decade, and the recording *ABC*, which he made with his orchestra in 1942 (Swing 180), is named after the theater. It operated as the ABC Music Hall until 1962 and was later converted to a cinema.

——. **Ad Lib.** Rue Fontaine. It flourished as a center for jazz until at least 1930; during the period of its greatest importance it was managed by Joe Zelli, who was manager of several clubs in the city (see Royal Box, Tempo Club, and Zelli's below).

——. **Les Ambassadeurs.** 1 avenue Gabriel, off avenue des Champs-Elysées. This large venue, which had several rooms, presented variety acts, revues, and the like, as well as performances by jazz and popular musicians. In its heyday in the late 1920s it was one of the most fashionable and exclusive venues in Paris, attracting a clientèle that included foreign royalty and the "international set." Among the jazzmen who appeared there were Leon Abbey (mid-1920s, 1929), Sam Wooding (*c*1925), Paul Whiteman (1928, with the Rhythm Boys, a vocal group led by Bing Crosby), Noble Sissle (1928–31, at first with the pianist Harry Revel, then with his own band, in which Sidney Bechet, Johnny Dunn, and the pianist Charlie Lewis were sidemen), and Fred Elizalde (1928); George Gershwin was also to be heard playing his own music there, both as a solo pianist and with duo partners. The club continued to offer jazz after the war: in the late 1950s André Ekyan and his orchestra made regular appearances on Sundays.

——. **Apollo.** 20 rue de Clichy. An early venue for jazz in Paris, the club hosted a lengthy residency by Louis Mitchell's Jazz Kings, who opened there on 6 July 1919, two days after beginning to play at the Casino de Paris (which was next to the Apollo); the Jazz Kings worked concurrently at both venues until 20 January 1920. Dizzy Gillespie's big band played there in February 1948, and the club continued to operate until 1955. Another Apollo Club later operated in the premises of the Blue Note (see below).

——. **La Bagatelle.** 20 rue de Clichy (next to the Casino de Paris). It presented jazz from 1937 to 1946; Eddie Brunner performed there around 1938.

——. **Barclay's Club.** 83–85 avenue de la Grand Armée. Barclay's Club was a musicians' rehearsal room owned by the French jazz pianist and entrepreneur Eddie Barclay, who also ran the record companies Blue Star and Barclay and edited the journals *Jazz News: Blue Star Revue* (1948–50) and *Jazz magazine* (from 1954). It was active from 1947 to 1955.

——. **Bar Gaya.** This small nightclub was in operation in the years following World War I, when the pianist Jean Wiener played American music – ragtime and Broadway songs, which were at that time spoken of as jazz – to a bohemian clientele. Its management took larger premises in 1921 and opened Le Boeuf sur le Toit (see below).

——. **Le Bilboquet.** 13 rue Saint-Benoît. On the same site as the former Club Saint-Germain, this club and restaurant has entertained a clientele with a jazz ambiance; it opened in 1967 and remains active in the new century. From 1973 to 1987 its house pianist was Marc Hemmeler; later, Maurice Vander, René Urtreger, Olivier Hutman, and others filled this role. The organist Rhoda Scott appeared there in 1989, and Sacha Distel performed in the club the following year. (<http://www.jazzvalley.com/bilboquet> (2001))

——. **Blue Note.** 27 rue d'Artois. It opened in the former premises of the Ringside (see below) in autumn 1958, with Zoot Sims accompanied by Floris Nico Bunink, the Canadian double bass player Lloyd Thompson, and Al Levitt. It was managed first by Ben Benjamin and later by George Gainford (the former manager of the boxer Sugar Ray Robinson). Jimmy Gourley joined a house band alongside Henri Renaud in November 1958 before the club entered into a longstanding association with Kenny Clarke (1959 – November 1966); his resident rhythm section at times comprised Bud Powell and Pierre Michelot (known as the Three Bosses). Thereafter many visiting American musicians appeared at the club, including Stan Getz, Buck Clayton, Don Byas, Dexter Gordon, Kenny Drew, and Nathan Davis. Lester Young played his final engagements there between January and March 1959, and Lou Bennett and René Thomas were also members of Clarke's house band. The club closed in May 1968. The Blue Note reopened in February 1970 as the Apollo Club, with Jimmy McGriff's trio performing; Groove Holmes and Annie Ross later played there. The original Blue Note was reconstituted for the film *Round Midnight*, featuring Dexter Gordon (1986). (M. Hennessey: *Klook: the Story of Kenny Clarke* (London, 1990), 133)

——. **Le Boeuf sur le Toit.** 28 rue Boissy-d'Anglas (1921–8); rue de Penthièvre (1928–?); 43bis avenue Pierre-1er-de-Serbie (by 1934); 34 rue du Colisée (16 September 1941–). The club occupied a succession of premises in the seventh and eighth arrondissements. Having begun as Le Gaya in rue Duphot in 1919 or 1920, it was reopened on 21 December 1921 by Louis Moyses and named after a popular Brazilian song, *Le Boeuf sur le Toit* (on which the composer Darius Milhaud later based a work). In its early days the club was the haunt of French writers, artists, and musicians, notably Jean Cocteau, Erik Satie, René Clair, and Maurice Ravel, and the influence of jazz on the music of Parisian composers at this time was in some part a result of what they heard there. The first resident pianist was Jean Wiener, who performed both as an unaccompanied soloist and with other musicians, including Clément Doucet. Among the many French and visiting musicians who performed there were Léo Vauchant (1924), Leon Abbey (before 1935), Una Mae Carlisle (1937, 1939), Bobby Martin (1937–8), Benny Carter (15 October 1937 – April 1938), and Django Reinhardt (late 1930s, 1944, 1947, 1948). Carter's residency, as the leader of the seven-piece band that played for dancing in a downstairs room, coincided with performances by Reinhardt, who played upstairs in the dining room and often joined Carter for jam sessions between sets. In the 1930s and again in the 1950s Le Boeuf sur le Toit was the Parisian home of Garland Wilson: he led the resident band there from July 1937 to December 1938 and was host in his own room in the club from January to May 1954. Mary Lou Williams played there in 1954, just before her retirement. From 1956 Le Boeuf sur le Toit operated as the Spaghetti Service and offered programs devoted to traditional jazz; the trombonist Mowgli Jospin and Raymond Fonsèque were among the leading revivalists who performed there. In 1962 it again assumed its old name. The club may be seen in the film *Quartet* (1981). (J. Chastenait: *Quand le boeuf montait sur le toit*, Paris, 1958)

——. **Bricktop's.** 1 rue Fontaine (1925– ?1939); ?66 rue Pigalle (1930s); 26 rue Fontaine (from 1950). The singer Bricktop (Ada Smith) first sang in Paris in 1924 at Le Grand Duc (see below), owned by George Jamerson and his wife. Stories of her activities as a club owner are confusing and contradictory. By one account, she opened Bricktop's on rue Pigalle in 1928 after running the Music Box (see below) from November 1924 and then Le Grand Duc from 1926; another source gives the opening date of Bricktop's as 1925, at 1 rue Fontaine (at the corner of rue Pigalle, opposite from Le Grand Duc); yet another situates Bricktop's at 66 rue Pigalle in the 1930s. In any event, Bricktop's became one of the most fashionable clubs in Paris. From November 1931 her partner was Mabel Mercer. Bricktop fled Paris in 1939. She opened a new club on the rue Fontaine in May 1950. Many important musicians performed for Bricktop, and her patrons included the cream of Parisian society. She also opened clubs at different times in Biarritz, Mexico City, and Rome. (Bricktop and J. Haskins: *Bricktop*, New York, 1983).

——. **La Calavados.** 40 avenue Pierre-1er-de-Serbie. From 1947 to 1950 it was an important venue for solo pianists, notably Joe Turner (i).

——. **Le Caméléon.** 57 rue Saint-André-des-Arts. Henri Renaud and his quartet played at the opening of this cellar of Saint-Germain-des-Prés in 1955. Among the important soloists to follow him during the 1950s were Chet Baker, Allen Eager, Jean-Claude Fohrenbach, Guy Lafitte, and Jean-Louis Chautemps. It closed in late 1969.

——. **Casanova Club.** Rue Fromentin. A fashionable venue for jazz in Paris before the war, in the 1930s it offered performances by the Quintette du Hot Club de France (for illustration *see* Jazz (i), fig.4).

——. **Casino de Paris.** 16 rue de Clichy. Jazz formed part of the entertainment from summer 1918, when Louis Mitchell appeared there as a solo drummer. He returned from 4 July 1919 to 20 January 1920 with his septet the Jazz Kings, again from 26 March 1921 until 8 May 1922, when the club was destroyed by fire, and yet again from December 1922, when it reopened, until the following summer. Crickett Smith's Real Jazz Kings replaced Mitchell's group from 20 August 1920. In the spring of 1933 the singer and actress Josephine Baker performed in a revue at the casino. (Le Perroquet (see below) occupied part of the same building.)

——. **Caveau de la Huchette.** 5 rue de la Huchette. One of the older jazz "caves" (cellars) on the Left Bank, it opened in 1946. In the mid-1960s it offered traditional jazz by musicians such as Raymond Fonsèque. It was later owned by the vibraphonist Dany Doriz, who presented a range of styles there; Hal Singer and Benny Waters both appeared often from the late 1970s, and other important performers in that period included Bill Coleman (1979), Gene Conners (1981), Wild Bill Davis (1982), and Maxim Saury (1983). The big band of Roger Guérin was resident in the mid-1980s. The club, which celebrated its 50th anniversary in 1996, continued in the new century to present its established repertory of traditional jazz, jump, and rhythm-and-blues, with regular appearances by such expatriate and visiting Americans as Connors, Bob Wilber, and Alvin Queen. (<http://www.jazzvalley.com/venue/caveaudelahuchette> (2001))

——. **Cave du Hot Club de France.** 9 rue Pavée. The premises, which were acquired in late 1969 and were initially used for concerts, form the Paris home of the Hot club de France. Following renovations in December 1970, regular jazz performances were given there; among the French and resident American musicians to appear were Benny Waters and Joe Turner (i). The club was also used as a rehearsal room and for record recitals; it closed in 1989.

——. **La Chapelle des Lombards.** 62 rue des Lombards (1978–80); 19 rue de Lappe (from 1980). From 1978 this club near the Pompidou Center presented both avant-garde jazz (Don Cherry, Henry Threadgill, Alan Silva's Celestrial Communication Orchestra, Dave Burrell) and blues (Luther Allison). It relocated to Rue de Lappe in 1980 and later became an Antillean dance club.

——. **Le Chat qui Pêche.** Rue du Chat qui Pêche (4 rue de la Huchette). This cellar nightclub on the Left Bank flourished from 1957 to 1969, when the owner Madame Ricard sold her license. Among those who appeared there were Jackie McLean (1961), Woody Shaw, Nathan Davis, Eric Dolphy, Larry Young, Don Cherry, and Steve Lacy (all 1965), Noah Howard (1969), and Dexter Gordon and Johnny Griffin.

——. **Chez André Ekyan.** See Swing Time.

——. **Chez Boudon.** Rue Fontaine and rue Mansart. Restaurant and bar. Open day and night, it was a favorite haunt of local and visiting musicians, though in all likelihood no jazz was performed there. In 1937 Dicky Wells recorded a number (*Hangin' around Boudon*, Swing 16) named for the bar.

——. **Chez Django Reinhardt.** 62 rue Pigalle. In the spring of 1944 the nightclub La Roulotte was temporarily given this name for a residency by Reinhardt under the management of Lulu de Montmartre. It was frequented, after the curfew, both by members of the Gestapo and by British agents, and Reinhardt's band was often requested (and permitted) to play *God Save the King*. The engagement apparently ended before the Liberation, but the name remained over the door for some time afterwards.

——. **Chez Florence.** Rue Pigalle (? to 1926); 61 rue Blanche (? from *c*1927). It was founded by Louis Mitchell in the 1920s as Mitchell's, but renamed for the singer and hostess Florence Embry Jones (*d* New York, early January 1932). The original premises were closed in autumn 1926 but the club was in operation again by 1928, when the International Five played there. Among the musicians who performed at the club from the 1930s were Willie Lewis (1935–6, with a band that included Benny Carter), Wilson Myers (1937, in a band led by Roger Devereaux), the Quintette du Hot Club de France (1938), and a number of others, notably a group led by Bobby Martin (1937); after the war Arthur Briggs led the house band from 1946 to 1951. It closed the following year.

——. **Chez Jane Stick.** 70 rue de Ponthieu. It operated from 1941 to 1943 and is known chiefly for a series of performances given in 1941 by Django Reinhardt with the drummer Pierre Fouad, Hubert Rostaing, and others.

——. **Chez Joséphine.** Rue Fontaine. It was opened in December 1926 by the singer and actress Josephine Baker, who continued to run nightclubs in Paris through the 1930s. Her establishments were favored by the haut monde, whose darling Baker became through her own colorful and exotic performances. (L. Haney: *Naked at the Feast: a Biography of Josephine Baker*, London, 1981)

——. **Chez Sidney Bechet.** 67 rue Pierre-Charron. The club, which was large enough for dancing, was opened on 23 December 1953 by Bechet with the band led by the clarinetist and soprano saxophonist André Réwéliotty. For a short time early in 1954 Bechet performed as resident musician both in his own club and at Métro Jazz (see below), but his operation on the rue Pierre-Charron was short-lived and closed after a few months.

——. **(Brasserie de) La Cigale.** 124 boulevard Rochechouart, near place Pigalle. Café. It was named after a nearby music hall. In the early 1940s it flourished as a venue for West Indian and Madagascan music, and in June 1942 the Cameroonian drummer Freddy Jumbo obtained a permit from the German authorities to present an Antillean jazz band, which included Robert Mavounzy; Harry Cooper later joined this group. After the war the café became a meeting place for jazz musicians (particularly American servicemen), who regularly played jam sessions. Among the musicians to perform there in the 1950s and 1960s were Benny Waters and Jacques Butler, who was resident from 1951 until he returned to the USA in 1968. Mavounzy continued to work at La Cigale until 1974, but thereafter it ceased to offer jazz.

BIBLIOGRAPHY

"Au coeur de Pigalle, La Cigale chante toujours," *Jm*, no.26 (1957), 14
P. Vacher: "Montmartre Mainstream," *JJ*, xvi/2 (1963), 15
——: "La Cigale, 1963," *JM*, ix/11 (1964), 10
J.-P. Meuner: liner notes, *Swing Caraïbe* (Frémeaux & Associés FA069, 1997)

——. **Ciro's.** 6 rue Daunou (1930–49) [other addresses and years are unknown]. The entrepreneur Ciro founded a number of exclusive restaurant clubs from the 1910s, notably those in Paris, London, Deauville, and Monte Carlo, which were frequented by the cream of society, including the British royal family. His establishments were first and foremost restaurants, but they were important jazz venues and Ciro built up a longstanding association with black-American musicians. The Paris club was in existence before April 1915, when Ciro opened in London; among the musicians who led bands there were Noble Sissle (summer 1930), the British violinist James Boucher (1931), the double bass player Louis Vola (1932), Django Reinhardt (1940), and Nat Gonella.

——. **Club l'Arlequin.** Angle 1 rue du Four/113bis boulevard St. Germain. Thanks to the lively artistic and student community centered on the Sorbonne, this club flourished from 1951 to 1953, at the period (from the early 1950s) when the Left Bank enjoyed a renaissance. Native and visiting musicians played there, including Don Byas and his quintet (1951), Claude Bolling (1953), and Jef Gilson.

——. **Club Saint-Germain.** 13 rue Saint-Benoît. This nightclub on the Left Bank opened on 11 June 1948, run initially by Boris Vian and his associates, and continued as a center for jazz during the 1950s and 1960s. During its early days it typified the intense, sophisticated atmosphere of the area, where a highly intellectual café society flourished. It was at first the club where the clarinetist and soprano saxophonist André Réwéliotty was based, and in 1951 Django Reinhardt staged a brief comeback there, performing with Hubert Fol; Claude Bolling's band (which included Bill Coleman) played lengthy engagements in 1951 and 1952, and in April 1954 Stephane Grappelli began a residency there, establishing an association with the club that lasted for many years. Other notable musicians to perform in the 1950s were Lester Young (1956), Miles Davis, J. J. Johnson, and Bud Powell (all 1957), and Kenny Clarke, who was resident from spring 1957 through 1958 and again through much of 1963. The club was later renamed Le Bilboquet.

BIBLIOGRAPHY

"After hours à St-Germain," *Jm*, no.28 (1957), 22
P. Cressant: "De nouveau sur la Rive Gauche: un Birdland à Paris," *Jh*, no.116 (1956), 31
M. Hennessey: *Klook: the Story of Kenny Clarke* (London, 1990)

——. **Club des Trois Mailletz.** See Les Trois Mailletz.

——. **Club du Vieux-Colombier.** See Le Vieux-Colombier.

——. **La Croix du Sud.** 3 boulevard Montparnasse. It may have presented jazz as early as 1918, when the pianist Alain Romans was the resident musician for a year, but one source gives its years of operation as 1927 to 1932. During this period the club became a lively bohemian haunt, popular with the more exotic elements of Parisian society. It was also a favorite of visiting musicians – Jimmy Dorsey and Muggsy Spanier were among those who in the early 1930s occasionally jammed there with the resident band. André Ekyan led the house ensemble at that time, with Stephane Grappelli among his sidemen, and it was supposedly there that Grappelli first met Django Reinhardt late in 1931.

——. **Le Doyen** [L'Impératrice]. Champs-Elysées gardens. Restaurant. It offered musical entertainment from at least the early 1940s. In the spring of 1941 Django Reinhardt performed there daily for the afternoon *thé dansant* (before going on to perform in the evenings at Chez Jane Stick).

——. **Le Dreher.** 1 rue Saint-Denis. In the basement of a large Parisian brasserie in the Halles quarter, this cellar was opened by Mal Waldron on 26 October 1979; it became a place where such free-jazz musicians as Jimmy Lyons (ii), Sunny Murray, Frank Wright, and Archie Shepp alternated with Chet Baker, Pepper Adams, and other bop-oriented players.

——. **Duc des Lombards.** 42 rue des Lombards. Near the Pompidou Center, in the ancient Halles quarter, this ground-floor club opened in 1988; Didier Nouyrigat has served as its manager from 1990. Although the programs have been rich and varied, involving such musicians as Aldo Romano, Paolo Fresu, Kirk Lightsey, and Stefano di Battista, the clientele (a maximum of about one hundred people) has had difficulty both hearing and seeing the performers. It remains in operation in the new century.

BIBLIOGRAPHY

S. Siclier: "Lombards sur jazz," *Jazzman*, no.180 (1994), 9
<http://www.jazzvalley.com/duc> (2001)

——. **Dunois (Théâtre).** 28 rue Dunois (1977–90); 108 rue du Chevaleret (from 1990). Under the direction of Sylvain Torikian from 1977, this venue played host to a varied artistic program in which jazz appeared alongside dance, theater, and ethnic musics. After its move in 1990 to a 200-seat theater in the same quarter, it continued the same policy of political audaciousness.

——. **Ecole Normale de Musique.** 78 rue Cardinet, at boulevard Malesherbes. The hall of the school was used by the Hot Club de France for many of its concerts from the 1930s to 1954, beginning with the first performance by the Quintette du Hot Club de France (2 December 1934). Among the musicians whom the club presented were Garland Wilson (1935, 1937), Bill Coleman (1935, 1938), Benny Carter (1937), and Eddie South (1937, 1938), and during the Nazi occupation it promoted afternoon concerts by Harry Cooper and Antillean jazz musicians. In November 1944 Arthur Briggs appeared at a special performance there to celebrate his release from internment. Further jazz concerts were given there in 1962, 1966, and 1968.

——. **Embassy Club.** 136 avenue des Champs-Elysées. It was a prominent venue for jazz from 1927 to 1934, when the bands of Sam Wooding and Leon Abbey (both 1929), and Paul Whiteman, among others, played there. The double bass player Louis Vola led a group there in late 1932, standing in for Arthur Briggs, the current resident, while he played a winter season elsewhere.

——. **L'Ermitage Moscovite.** 24 rue Caumartin. It operated from 1925 to 1934 and then continued for one more year (to 1935) as L'Ermitage Caumartin. Jazz was performed there from at least the late 1920s; Mezz Mezzrow's quartet appeared in March 1929.

——. **Espace Cardin.** 1 rue Gabriel. In the 1980s this famous fashion house, located in a chic theater (near the Champs-Elysées and facing the American embassy), entered into an agreement with Radio Française which permitted the latter to organize many afternoon concerts under the direction of the producer André Francis. These events were enlivened by the presence of such major American performers as Gary Burton, Dexter Gordon, Bobby Hutcherson, and Anthony Braxton.

——. **Florida Night Club.** 20 rue Clichy. The Florida was an exclusive club which flourished from 1928 to 1929; Leon Abbey led a resident group in the latter year and Benny Peyton's band also appeared there.

——. **Le Furstemberg.** 25 rue de Buci. After spending a long period in the USA, André Persiany was resident in this restaurant and club in Saint-Germain-des-Prés from 1970 to 1988, leading a trio consisting of the double bass player Roland Lobligeois and the drummer Roger Paraboschi; they recorded the album *Every Night at Furstemberg* (1979, Open 06).

——. **Gill's Club.** 7 rue Sainte-Croix-de-la-Bretonnerie. Active from 1964 until at least 1972, it presented various French and visiting traditional musicians, such as Irakli.

——. **Le Grand Duc** [Mitchell's]. 52 rue Pigalle, at rue Fontaine. A small nightclub, barely bigger than a bar, it was opened in the early 1920s by George Jamerson and his wife. It was known as Mitchell's from 22 November 1923, when Louis Mitchell reopened it, and became Le Grand Duc later that year or early in 1924. Le Grand Duc was closed from July to September 1924, when it reopened again; Mitchell remained involved in the enterprise, but had left by November of that same year. Among the club's managers was Gene Bullard, who worked for the Jamersons and then for the singer Bricktop; the latter, having performed there from 1924, ran the club for about a year from 1926 (see also Bricktop's).

——. **Le Grand Ecart.** 7 rue Fromentin. Cabaret. It was in operation from 1929 to 1934, and in 1931 the house band there was led by the double bass player Dan Parrish. The same premises later housed the club Les Nuits Bleues (see below).

——. **Harlem Club.** 58 rue Notre-Dame-de-Lorette. Although it was short-lived, the Harlem was an important venue while it lasted. It was opened in 1937 by the trumpeter, singer, guitarist, and dancer Freddy Taylor and was run by Taylor (who led the house band) with James Monroe (later the first husband of Billie Holiday). It closed the following year.

——. **Hôtel Claridge.** 74 avenue des Champs-Elysées. Jazz was played there from at least 1923, when the Georgians under the leadership of Frank Guarente were the resident band. Among the other groups that played at the hotel were those led by Paul Gason (1928–9) and the double bass player Louis Vola (1934). Vola's orchestra accompanied the daily *thé dansant* between 5 and 7 in the evening; Django Reinhardt and Stephane Grappelli, who were members of Vola's ensemble, spent time between sets jamming backstage, and it was out of this activity that the Quintette du Hot Club de France was born. Grappelli returned to the hotel 20 years later to play a long season in 1956.

——. **Hôtel Hilton.** See Le Toit de Paris.

——. **Hôtel Méridien.** 81 boulevard Gouvion-Saint-Cyr. The club opened in 1976 and jazz was promoted there by the entrepreneur Moustache Galépides, who was earlier active as a jazz drummer; it was reputed to be one of the most expensive jazz venues in Europe. His successor was Vivian Sicnasi, who presented blues as well as swing. Among those who appeared there were Buddy Tate (1982, 1983, 1986), Eddie "Lockjaw" Davis (1983, 1984, 1986), John Collins's trio, Al Grey, Arnett Cobb, and Buck Clayton (all 1983), Panama Francis and his Savoy Sultans (1986, 1987), Joe Newman and Jimmy Witherspoon (both 1986), and Doc Cheatham and Jimmy Smith (both 1987). In the mid-1980s the orchestra of Claude Bolling performed regularly at Sunday brunch. Following the opening of other Méridien hotels in the late 1980s it became known as the Hôtel Méridien Paris-Etoile and the musicians performed in the Lionel Hampton Bar. In 1995 Linda Hopkins and Mulgrew Miller were among those who performed here. The club closed in February 2000 for renovation and reopened that September with two new programmers, Didier Tricard and Jean-Pierre Vignola, who continued the policy of mixing blues and swing.

BIBLIOGRAPHY

F. Bergerot: "Méridien de Paris: nouvelle latitude," *Jazzman*, no.62 (2000), 26
<http://www.france-hotel-online.com> (2001)

——. **Hot Feet.** Rue Notre-Dame-de-Lorette. It opened in 1939 with performances by Django Reinhardt, and in the late summer of that year Duke Ellington played informally with him there.

——. **L'Impératrice.** See Le Doyen.

——. **Jimmy's Bar.** 4 rue Huyghens, angle 206, boulevard Raspail. The club was operated by an English barman, Jimmy Charles, from late 1935 until 1948, and offered jazz from at least the late 1930s. A band that included Django Reinhardt, Alix Combelle, the pianist Charlie Lewis, and Philippe Brun held a residency there in the winter of 1939–40. By one account the club later reopened as New-Jimmy's in more prominent premises a short distance away, at 124 boulevard du Montparnasse, but another source has no mention of a relocation.

——. **Latitudes Saint-Germain.** 7, 11 rue Saint-Benoît. From 1984 to 1999 this club in a hotel on Paris's "swing street" offered a training ground and springboard to wider success for a number of young instrumentalists and singers.

——. **Living-Room.** 25 rue du Colisée. Located near the Champs-Elysées, this club operated from 1963 to 1969; its resident performer was Aaron Bridgers, at times seconded by a singer.

——. **Le Lorientais.** 5 rue des Carmes. Le Lorientais was situated in the cellar of the Hotel des Carmes and named for its proprietors, who were Bretons from Lorient. It was from this early-evening club (open only from 5 to 8 p.m.) that Claude Luter et ses Lorientais launched the traditional-jazz revival in France in April 1946; the group continued to play there until the venue closed in December 1948. Jacques Becker's film *Rendez-vous de juillet* (1949), set in a studio facsimile of the club and featuring Rex Stewart, became the seminal document of the contemporary youth culture of the Latin Quarter, dubbed "le Désordre."

——. **Mars Club.** 6 rue Robert-Estienne. In a cul-de-sac near the Champs-Elysées, this club was active from the late 1940s. Open from 11 p.m. until 4 a.m., it served as a sanctuary for night people. With a house band led by Art Simmons on piano, which drew on Pierre Cullaz and Elek Bacsik on guitar and Michel Gaudry on double bass, it became over the years a constant gathering place for Americans passing through Paris – members of the Ellington and Basie orchestras, members of Jazz at the Philharmonic, John Lewis, and Billy Strayhorn, as well as such singers as Ella Fitzgerald, Sarah Vaughan, and Billie Holiday (who sang there on 5 February 1954 and again on 12 November 1958).

BIBLIOGRAPHY

M.-C. Jalard: "Les plaisirs du Mars Club," *Jm*, no.145 (1959), 27
M. Hennessey: *Klook: the Story of Kenny Clarke* (London, 1990)

——. **Métro Jazz.** 56 rue Galande (to 1953); beneath the Théâtre du Quartier Latin, 9 rue Champollion (from 1953). The earlier club, though it had presented musicians of the stature of Lil Armstrong and Peanuts Holland, was eclipsed by the new establishment, which opened in autumn 1953 in cellar premises dating back to the 12th century. The house ensemble was led by Michel Attenoux and accompanied such important visiting musicians as Sidney Bechet, who played there in 1953–4. The premises on the rue Galande were taken over by Les Trois Mailletz (see below).

——. **Mitchell's.** Louis Mitchell's involvement in two different Parisian clubs in the early 1920s led to these being temporarily named after him; see Chez Florence and Le Grand Duc.

——. **Le Montana.** 28 rue Saint-Benoît. Opened in 1985 in a hotel on the street made famous by the Club Saint-Germain, this tiny venue was the domain of René Urtreger for many years.

——. **Musée d'Art Moderne de la Ville de Paris.** 11 avenue du Président-Wilson. Under the auspices of l'ARC (Animation-Recherche-Confrontation) from 1967 to 1972 Daniel Humair organized a series of jazz concerts at the museum on Monday afternoons. All styles of jazz were presented and among the principal performers were Maxim Saury and Sunny Murray; others who appeared included Tony Scott, Gato Barbieri, Jimmy Owens, and Karl Berger. An important retrospective exhibition covering l'ARC's activities was mounted at the museum in 1972.

——. **Music Box.** 41 rue Pigalle. A short-lived but successful nightclub run by the singer Bricktop with the help of Louis Mitchell, it opened in November 1924 and closed soon afterwards, since the authorities refused to grant it a permanent license. A second club of this name, also in Montmartre, operated in the 1930s and closed in 1935; among the jazz musicians to perform there were Herb Flemming (autumn 1930), the cabaret singer Zaidee Jackson (1931), and Fats Waller, whose band included Spencer Williams.

——. **New-Jimmy's.** See Jimmy's Bar.

——. **Le New Morning.** 7, 9 rue des Petites Ecuries. Located in a Parisian quarter which is still not normally a place for shows, this somewhat hastily laid-out loft is one of the largest clubs in the capital, accommodating nearly 500 people. Under the direction of Eglal Fahri, who had opened the first New Morning in Geneva in 1972, it presents many genres (salsa, rock, popular song, ethnic music), but jazz predominates. It was opened on 14 April 1981 by Art Blakey's Jazz Messengers (including the older Marsalis brothers), since when it has welcomed many important modern and contemporary jazz musicians, from George Russell to Archie Shepp, by way of Betty Carter, Stan Getz, Chet Baker, and others.

BIBLIOGRAPHY

J.-P. Julien: *Escale au New Morning* (Paris, 1993) [photos of artists performing]

A. Dutilh: "Eglal Fahri: la dame du New Morning," *Jazzman*, no.1 (1995), 27

J. Szlamowicz: "New Morning," *Jh*, no.572 (2000), 12

<http://www.jazzvalley.com/newmorning> (2001)

——. **Les Nuits Bleues.** 7 rue Fromentin. It was opened in late summer 1935 under the direction of Mme. Moises in the premises formerly occupied by Le Grand Ecart. The resident bands included the Quintette du Hot Club de France, with which Bill Coleman occasionally played informally. It closed that same year.

——. **Olympia.** 28 boulevard des Capucines. Music hall, later theater. In 1929 Gregor and his Gregorians appeared there, and during the war it offered performances by the Quintette du Hot Club de France (1941, 1944). But it was most important as a venue for jazz from the 1950s, when its director, the musician and impresario Bruno Coquatrix, began to present concerts of jazz, many of them by visiting American musicians. A successful performance by Sidney Bechet with Claude Luter's band in December 1954 was recorded on the Vogue label, and Bechet appeared there again at a concert in March 1955 to celebrate the 20th anniversary of the founding of the journal *Jazz hot*. Among other musicians who performed at the Olympia were Lionel Hampton (1954, 1961), Louis Armstrong and his All Stars and Mezz Mezzrow (both 1955), Jack Teagarden, Earl Hines, Cozy Cole, and Erroll Garner (all 1957), Count Basie (1957, 1959, 1960), Art Blakey (1958, 1965) and Johnny Hodges, Ella Fitzgerald, Ruby Braff, John Coltrane, and Dizzy Gillespie (all 1961). Buck Clayton made well-known recordings there in 1959 with Jimmy Rushing and in 1961 with Jimmy Witherspoon. The venue lost its importance for jazz after the mid-1960s, and concerts took place there only occasionally thereafter. (The Ten Gallons (see below) operates in a cellar beneath the theater.) (A. Tercinet: "50 ans de jazz à l'Olympia," *Jazzman*, no.61 (2000), 41)

——. **Le Perroquet.** 16 rue de Clichy. It occupied premises behind the Casino de Paris (see above). Among the bands that held residencies there were Louis Mitchell's Jazz Kings (March 1921 – mid-1923), which became the Real Jazz Kings under Crickett Smith when Mitchell left in 1923, André Ekyan's band, and Lud Gluskin's orchestra, which was the house ensemble in the last few years of the decade.

——. **Le Petit Journal.** 71 boulevard Saint-Michel. Managed by André Damon, it was one of the principal venues in the city for traditional jazz from 1972 into the mid-1980s, though its repertory ranged somewhat more widely. Claude Bolling appeared regularly at the club, which also engaged many prominent Americans, including Bill Coleman and Benny Waters (1981), the pianist Champion Jack Dupree (1982), Kenny Burrell, Joe Turner (i), Carrie Smith, Buddy Tate, and Harry Edison (all 1983), Sam Woodyard (1984), and Benny Bailey (1986). It remained active into the 21st century. (<http://www.jazzvalley.com/venue/petitjournal-saint-michel> (2001))

——. **Le Petit Journal Montparnasse.** 13 rue de Commandant-Mouchotte. It was founded by André Damon, who had been the proprietor of Le Petit Journal on boulevard Saint-Michel and who followed the same format in his new club. In a room holding more than 250 people, he presented such French and American musicians as Eddy Louiss, Michel Petrucciani, Clark Terry, Johnny Griffin, Mal Waldron, and Jon Hendricks. The venue was sufficiently large to accommodate big bands, and Gerard Badini's group played at the opening performance on 22 September 1985. (<http://www.jazzvalley.com/pjm> (2001))

——. **Le Petit Opportun.** 15 rue des Lavandières-Sainte-Opportune. This tiny 14th-century cellar, holding 40 people, is familiarly known as Le Petit Op. It was opened by a pianist, Bernard Rabaud, in the Halles quarter near the Pompidou Center, in September 1977, and presented Georges Arvanitas, Jimmy Gourley, and Pierre Michelot, among others. The size of the cellar prevented ensembles larger than a quartet from appearing, but the soloists heard there were always first-rate. It has continued to present a full program of jazz into the new century.

BIBLIOGRAPHY

S. Siclier: "Bernard Rabaud: Petit Op, grand patron," *Jazzman*, no.6 (1995), 19

<http://www.jazzvalley.com/petitopportun> (2001)

——. **Ringside.** 81 rue Marbeuf (from 1949); 27 rue d'Artois (by 1953). It was founded in 1949 by the boxer Sugar Ray Robinson. James Moody and Henri Renaud played at the opening, and Art Simmons was the house pianist for three and a half years, probably in the early 1950s. In 1951 Nelson Williams appeared there. Don Byas, accompanied by a rhythm section that included Pierre Michelot and Simmons, gave a series of after-hours performances that same year and returned to the club after it moved to new premises, when he played with Buck Clayton and a rhythm section. The Ringside had closed by 1957; in 1958 the Blue Note (see above) opened at the 27 rue d'Artois address.

——. **Riverboat.** 67 rue Saint-André-des-Arts. In the 1960s this club operated only on weekends. It presented numerous traditional-jazz groups, often semi-professional, including the High Society Jazz Band. It closed in mid-1977 and then re-opened the following year as Riverbop (see immediately below).

——. **Riverbop.** 67 rue Saint-André-des-Arts. This club succeeded the Riverboat at the same location in 1978 and presented modern and avant-garde musicians, including Cesarius Alvim, Aldo Romano, Michel Portal, and Bernard Lubat.

——. **Riverside.** 13 rue du Petit-Pont. During its brief existence from 1953 to 1957 this club in the Latin quarter presented traditional jazz (Albert Nicholas, Maxim Saury) as well as modern jazz (Barney Wilen, René Urtreger).

——. **La Rose Rouge.** 76 rue de Rennes. From 1948 this little club, situated in the basement of a brasserie in Saint-Germain-des-Prés, presented cabaret shows (Les Frères Jacques), theater (Compagnie Grenier-Hussenot), and jazz. Among those who appeared there were Michel de Villers, Geo Daly, and the Grand Orchestre de la Rose Rouge directed by Fats Sadi, with Roger Guérin, Bobby Jaspar, and David Amram, as well as numerous soloists such as Martial Solal.

——. **La Roulotte.** See Chez Django Reinhardt.

——. **Royal Box.** 16 rue Fontaine. It flourished as a center for jazz performance during the 1920s and 1930s, when it was directed by Joe Zelli (the manager of several Parisian nightclubs at this period – see Ad Lib, Tempo Club, and Zelli's). The house band was led for many years by the ragtime pianist J. Glover Compton and included Crickett Smith, Frank "Big Boy" Goudie, and the drummer Gene Bullard (see fig.2), who had earlier worked as the manager of Le Grand Duc (see above).

——. **Salle Gaveau.** 45 rue La Boëtie. Concert hall. It was regularly used for jazz concerts. Willie Lewis and Arthur Briggs appeared at the hall on 21 March 1935. Pierre Nourry organized an appearance by the Quintette du Hot Club de France there on 20 October 1937, and the group performed again in March the following year. The hall was also the venue for an important concert on 19 December 1940, at which many notable French jazz musicians, including Django Reinhardt and Hubert Rostaing, performed. Later Martial Solal made the notable album *Jazz à Gaveau* (1963, Col. FPX221); Jef Gilson recorded at a festival of French jazz held there on 3 April 1965.

——. **Salle Pleyel.** 252 rue du Faubourg-Saint-Honoré. One of several concert halls in the same building (the others are the Salles Chopin, Rameau, and Debussy), it has been the

2. The Royal Box, Paris, 1927: (the band, left to right) J. Glover Compton (piano), Ferdie Allen (banjo), Crickett Smith (trumpet), Frank "Big Boy" Goudie (tenor saxophone), unidentified trombonist, and Gene Bullard (drums); the proprietor, Joe Zelli, is seated immediately in front of the piano

venue for many important jazz performances from before World War II. Among those who played there in the prewar period were Cab Calloway (1934), Louis Armstrong (two concerts, November 1934), Duke Ellington (two concerts), and the Quintette du Hot Club de France. (Coleman Hawkins appeared at the Salle Rameau in 1935.) During and after the war the hall presented performances by Fud Candrix (1942), André Ekyan, Eddie Barclay, and others (1942), the reunited Quintette du Hot Club de France (1947), Dizzy Gillespie (1948), Mezz Mezzrow (1951, 1952), Bill Coleman (1952), Sidney Bechet (1952), Sammy Price (1956), Kid Ory (1956, 1959), and Duke Ellington (1958). In 1949, 1952, and 1954 the Festival International de Jazz (popularly known as the Paris Jazz Fair), organized by Charles Delaunay, was held in the hall; Charlie Parker, Miles Davis, and Tadd Dameron, among others, appeared at the festival in 1949 (*see* FESTIVALS). In 1954 Gerry Mulligan gave an electrifying performance there, which was recorded and released as a double album ([*Paris Concert*], Vogue 7381, 7383). A gala evening to celebrate Stephane Grappelli's 75th birthday was held at the Salle Pleyel on 29 March 1983.

——. **Slow Club** [Swingtime]. 130 rue de Rivoli. It was opened by Pierre Braslawsky as Swingtime in 1954 and took its longstanding name the following year. The Slow Club presented various French jazz musicians, including Claude Luter, and in the mid-1980s a sextet led by Dany Doriz appeared there. It remained active into the new century. (<http://www.jazzvalley.com/slowclub> (2001))

——. **Spaghetti Service.** See Le Boeuf sur le Toit.

——. **Le Stadium.** See Totem Bar.

——. **Sunset.** 60 rue des Lombards. Located underneath a restaurant near the Pompidou Center, this cellar opened in 1980 and accommodates 80 people. It offered a training ground for young French musicians but also welcomed experienced performers who volunteered to play at after-hours jam sessions. It was still presenting a full program of jazz in the year 2000.

BIBLIOGRAPHY

V. Bessières: "Sunset, Sunside: jazz à tous les étages," *Jazzman*, no.62 (2000), 26
J. Szlamowicz: "Le Sunset," *Jh*, no.572 (2000), 8
<http://www.jazzvalley.com/sunset> (2001)

——. **Swing Time** [Chez André Ekyan]. 7 rue Fromentin. This club was the base for André Ekyan and his band in the late 1930s. Many French and American musicians dropped in to play in jam sessions with Ekyan, among them Benny Carter, Coleman Hawkins, Bill Coleman, and Django Reinhardt.

——. **Swingtime.** See Slow Club.

——. **Le Tabou.** 33 rue Dauphine. Second, after Le Lorientais, among the clubs opened after the war, and located under a bistro in the heart of Saint-Germain-des-Prés, it initiated the fashion for ancient vaulted cellars. From 11 April 1947 it welcomed poets, painters, writers (Raymond Queneau, Jean-Paul Sartre, Maurice Merleau-Ponty), and then Boris Vian's musicians. In 1951, at the instigation of Henri Renaud, Le Tabou became the stronghold of the cool-jazz movement in Paris, presenting Bobby Jaspar and Jimmy Gourley. Lester Young (1952) and Clifford Brown (1953) participated in memorable jam sessions there. The venue remained active until the late 1950s.

BIBLIOGRAPHY

H. Renaud: "La période du Tabou," *Les cahiers du jazz*, no.5 (1995), 21
P. Fréchet: "Paris: les clubs à travers la littérature," *Les cahiers du jazz*, no.1 (2001), 19

——. **Tempo Club.** Rue Caumartin. It occupied premises above Zelli's (see below) and was probably an after-hours club. It was active in the 1920s, and among the groups that appeared there was Louis Mitchell's band the Jazz Kings. (P. Soupault: *Le nègre*, Paris, 1927/*R*1975)

——. **Ten Gallons.** 28 boulevard des Capucines. Cellar bar and nightclub in premises beneath the Olympia theater (see above). The pianist Bob Vatel, active for many years in Parisian clubs and bars, made it his base; his connection with the club is honored in Jaki Byard's *Dedicated to Bob Vatel of the "Ten Gallons"*, on his solo album *Parisian Solos* (Futura Swing 05).

——. **Le Toit de Paris.** Hôtel Hilton, 18 avenue de Suffren. The bar and restaurant of the Paris Hilton has presented notable performances of jazz on an occasional basis from the mid-1960s. Stephane Grappelli led a resident quintet there for five years from 1967 and in January 1969 recorded the album *Sur le Toit de Paris* (RCA 740038).

——. **Totem Bar** [Le Stadium]. 66 avenue d'Ivry. A free-jazz venue in the late 1970s, it presented Sam Rivers and Chris McGregor in 1977, Archie Shepp, David Murray, and the Art Ensemble of Chicago in 1978, and Shepp again in 1979.

——. **Les Trois Mailletz.** 56 rue Galande. It opened in 1953 in the premises on the Left Bank that had formerly housed Métro Jazz (see above) and was managed by Mme. Calvet. Bill Coleman held a notable residency there from 1955 to 1960 (with occasional absences), and other important musicians to appear included Mezz Mezzrow (with Nelson Williams and André Persiany, 1959), Stephane Grappelli (with a band led by Michel Attenoux, 1960), Peanuts Holland (again with Attenoux, 1961), Sonny Criss (with Henri Renaud, 1963), and Buck Clayton (*c*1967). It was still open in 1975, but had closed by the mid-1980s. (C. Roby: "Blue Stomping at the Trois Mailletz," *JB*, ii/11 (1965), 4)

——. **Le Vieux-Colombier** [Vieux-Co]. 21 rue du Vieux-Colombier. In existence from January 1949, this cellar club, owned and managed by Annet Badel, was an important venue for jazz. Badel operated a second club of this name, modeled on his Paris operation, at Juan-les-Pins, near Antibes. At both venues his most important performers were Sidney Bechet with Claude Luter's orchestra. Among the other musicians who appeared at the Paris club were Mezz Mezzrow, Hot Lips Page, Lionel Hampton, the clarinetist and soprano saxophonist André Réwéliotty, and Big Chief Moore. It closed in 1962. ("A Night at the Vieux Colombier," *Jazz Illustrated*, i/3 (1950), 6)

——. **La Villa.** 29 rue Jacob. The club, managed by Danny Michel, opened in 1990 in the basement of a hotel in Saint-Germain-des-Prés. In an elegant 100-seat room, a French rhythm section accompanied such soloists as Joshua Redman, Teddy Edwards, Hank Jones, Kenny Barron, Brad Mehldau, and Diana Krall. It closed in 1999.

——. **La Villa d'Este.** 4 rue Arsène-Houssaye. With Sacha de Horn as its director, the club was active as a center for jazz performance from 1934 to 1951. Freddy Taylor's Swing Men from Harlem, which included Billy Taylor (i) and

Fletcher Allen and featured Bill Coleman, played there in 1935. The resident band in the mid-1940s was the Jazz de Paris, led by the drummer Jerry Mengo.

——. **Zelli's.** 16 bis rue Fontaine. It was one of several Parisian clubs owned and run by Joe Zelli and was in operation from 1919 to 1932. Among the musicians who played there were Crickett Smith, the pianist and accordionist Tom Waltham, and the African-American trumpeter Bobby Jones.

BIBLIOGRAPHY

Paris

T. Wolfram: "Coloured Bands in Paris," *MM* (1931), Nov, 907

——: "French News," *MM* (1931), Dec, 964

L. Feather: "Vive le hot! Snapshots of Paris and its Dance Music," *MM*, x (17 Nov 1934)

G. Wilson: "Whatcha Say, Folks?," *Hot News and Rhythm Record Review*, i/1 (1935), 15

——: "Tempo di Jazz," *Radio Times* (23 July 1937)

H. Panassié: *Douze années de jazz (1927–1928): souvenirs* (Paris, 1946)

C. Delaunay: *Django Reinhardt: souvenirs* (Paris, 1954; Eng. trans., London, 1961, rev. 2/1981/*R*1993)

M. Dorigné: "Petite chronique du jazz New Orleans en France," *Jazz*, i: *Les origines du jazz, le style Nouvelle-Orléans et ses prolongements* (Paris, 1968), 140

P. Lafargue: Liner notes, *Le jazz parisien . . . libéré* (Barclay 81004–5, 1976)

K. Henriques: "Jazz sur Seine," *Jazz Express*, no.80 (1987), 7

——: "Jazz sur Seine," *Jazz Express*, no.103 (1989), 7

——: "Paris in the Swing," *Jazz Express*, no.119 (1990), 21

M. Fabre: *Way Back There: a Street Guide to African-Americans in Paris* (New York, 1992, rev. 2/Paris, 1996, by Fabre and J. A. Williams, as *A Street Guide to African-Americans in Paris*)

J. Abbott: "Art Existentialism & all that Jazz: Sights and Sounds of Paris in the Fifties," *Jazz on CD*, i/4 (1993), 55

F. Ténot: *Boris Vian, le jazz et Saint-Germain* (Paris, 1993)

——: *Boris Vian, le jazz à Saint-Germain* (Paris, 1999)

L. Tournès: *New Orleans sur Seine: histoire du jazz en France* (Paris, 1999)

J.-D. Brierre: *La jazz français de 1900 à aujourd'hui* (Paris, 2000)

L. Gourse: "Jazz Liberates Paris," *American Heritage*, li/2 (2000), 42

P. Fréchet: "Paris: les clubs à travers la littérature," *Les cahiers du jazz*, no.1 (2001), 19

R. Pernet and H. Rye: "Visiting Firemen 18: Louis Mitchell," *Storyville 2000–2001*, ed. L. Wright (Chigwell, England, 2001), 221

J. Rousseau: "Lieux Parisiens du jazz: répertoire historique," *Les cahiers du jazz*, no.1 (2001), 207

Sceaux. **Sceaux What.** 49 Avenue Georges Clémenceau. This very comfortable and elegant club, holding about 100 people, was active from 1984 to 1991 underneath Les Gémeaux, a theater managed by the adjacent Parisian suburbs of Sceaux and Bourg-la-Reine. In 1995, after being dormant for four years, the club was reactivated by its promoter, Françoise Letellier, though the programs were now limited to French (or French-based) musicians of a modern tendency, such as Martial Solal, Daniel Humair, Michel Portal, and Patrice Caratini. Performances took place only two or three evenings per month. (<http://www.jazzfrance.com> (2001)>)

GERMANY

Berlin. **A-Trane.** Bleibtreustrasse 1, Charlottenberg. This club presents nationally and internationally known musicians in various modern-jazz formats. (<http://www.a-trane.de> (2001))

——. **Badenscher Hof.** Badensche Strasse 29, Wilmersdorf. Jazz club and restaurant. It presents German and American jazz musicians on weekends and serves as a venue for jazz festivals in Berlin. Ed Schuller, Benny Bailey, and Charles Owens are among those who appeared there in 2001. (<http://www.badenscher-hof.de> (2001))

——. **Badewanne.** This was an important club in the 1950s and 1960s, when it presented both German and visiting American musicians.

——. **Barbarina Cabaret.** Hardenbergstrasse 18, Charlottenberg. Its program included jazz from at least 1927, when an all-star group, the New Yorkers (i), led by the guitarist and banjoist George Carhart, played at the club; among Carhart's players were Danny Polo and Dave Tough.

——. **Delphi** [Delphi-Palast]. Kantstrasse 12. The Delphi flourished as an important venue for jazz from the 1920s and was particularly noted for its jam sessions during the 1930s and 1940s; it continued to present jazz, under other guises, throughout the period of Nazi rule. By the 1980s the building had become a cinema that was used occasionally as a concert hall; jazz performances took place there only during the Jazzfest Berlin (*see* Festivals).

——. **Eierschale.** Like the Badewanne, this was an important club in the 1950s and 1960s; many American musicians on tour met there and played with their German colleagues. Lionel Hampton and Louis Armstrong were among those who participated in jam sessions there. Eierschale remained active into the late 1980s.

——. **Haus der Jungen Talente.** Klosterstrasse 68–70. Youth club. Its various programs included modern, mainstream, and free jazz and free improvised music; jazz was normally presented on Monday evenings. In 1992 it became known as Podewil (see below).

——. **Haus Germania.** Hardenbergstrasse 29a–e, Charlottenberg. It offered performances of jazz from at least 1929, when Lud Gluskin's band performed there.

——. **Haus Vaterland.** Potsdamer Platz (Köthenerstrasse 1–5, Schöneberg). Entertainment complex. This vast establishment was built on six floors and offered entertainment of many different kinds. At any one time at least six bands were playing in its various restaurants and nightclubs. One of the jazz musicians to perform there (mainly in the Wild West Bar) was Sidney Bechet, who in 1930–31 was engaged as the principal soloist in small bands that played for dancing and cabaret acts; one of its venues, the Palmengarten, was re-created (it is assumed) at Berlin-Babelsberg film studios for the scene featuring Bechet in *Einbrecher* (1930), although it is possible (if unlikely) that the scene was actually filmed on location. The Haus Vaterland issued its own magazine, *Berolina*.

——. **Podewil.** Klosterstrasse 68–70. Formerly known as the Haus der Jungen Talente, this concert hall and café was established in 1992. It presents avant-garde and experimental music, as well as theater, art, dance, and other media oriented towards the avant garde and experimentation. (<http://www.podewil.de> (2001))

——. **Quasimodo.** Kantstrasse 12a. Founded in 1975, it presents internationally known jazz performers. Tuesdays are reserved for musicians from Berlin, and jam sessions take place on Wednesdays. (<http://www.quasimodo.de> (2001))

BIBLIOGRAPHY

Berlin

W. Jansen: *Glanzrevuen der zwanziger Jahre* (Berlin, 1987)

K. Wolffram: *Tanzdielen und Vergnügungspaläste: Berliner Nachtleben in den dreissiger und vierziger Jahren, von der Friedrichstrasse bis Berlin W., vom Moka Efti bis zum Delphi* (Berlin, 1992)

Bonn. **Harmonie.** Frongasse 28–30. Jazz club and restaurant. While it also presents blues, folk, and world music, several jazz performances are featured per month with internationally known artists, presented by Jazz Zirkel Bonn, an organization founded in 1995 by Harry Lintzmeyer. (<http://www.harmonie-bonn.de> (2001))

Cologne. **Stadtgarten.** Venloer Strasse 40. From the mid-1980s to the mid-1990s this was one of the most important jazz venues in Germany, with a range of offerings extending from performances by students from the Musikhochschule to those by visiting Americans, as well as American expatriates living in Cologne. The Initiative Kölner Jazzhaus, formed in 1978, hosted concerts in various locations in the city until 1986, when it moved its activities to the Stadtgarten, which had both a large concert hall and a small club, Schmuckkästchen. WDR radio produced and broadcast many concerts there during this period. By the late 1990s, however, jazz was no longer the focus of activities at the Stadtgarten, although it continued to be presented on an occasional basis. (<http://www.stadtgarten.de> (2001))

——. **Subway.** Aachener Strasse 82. Subway opened in 1970 as a jazz club featuring music in styles ranging from the traditional to the avant garde. From the 1970s onwards WDR radio produced and broadcast many jazz concerts there, and from 1984 these were also shown on television.

BIBLIOGRAPHY

Cologne

R. von Zahn: *Jazz in Köln nach 1945: Konzertkultur und Kellerkunst* (Cologne, 1997)
——, ed.: *Jazz in Nordrhein-Westfalen seit 1946* (Cologne, 1999)

Dortmund. **Domicil.** Güntherstrasse 65. This jazz club, founded in 1969, became a cultural center in 1996 and has been partially supported by the city of Dortmund from 1998. It books many well-known German jazz performers as well as the occasional international musician. Although concerts are predominantly of jazz, Domicil also presents other genres, chiefly techno. (<http://www.kulturnetz.de/domicil/club.html> (2001))

Dresden. **Jazzclub Tonne.** Tzschirnerplatz 3 (1981–*c*1998); Am Brauhaus 3 (from *c*1998). It opened in 1981 as the premises for the jazz club IG Jazz Dresden, founded in 1977, and presents all styles of jazz, from dixieland to free improvised music.

BIBLIOGRAPHY

M. Creutziger: "Happy Birthday Tonne Dresdner Jazzclub: Tonne feiert 15 jähriges Jubiläum," *JP*, xlv/4 (1996), 32
M. Bäumel: "Vom Inspirator zur Bedürfnisanstalt? Zur Situation des Jazzclubs Dresdner 'Tonne'," *JP*, lxvii/11 (1998), 59
<http://www.jazzclub-tonne.de> (2001)

Erfurt. **Jazzclub Erfurt.** Fischmarkt 13–16. Founded in 1982, it began presenting touring American musicians (while continuing to feature many German artists) around 1990, following the reunification of Germany. (<http://www.jazzclub-erfurt.de> (2001))

Frankfurt am Main. **Brotfabrik.** Bachmannstrasse 2–4. This cultural center presents regular concerts of jazz and African music. (<http://www.brotfabrik.de> (2001))

——. **Der Jazzkeller** [Domicile]. Bockenheimer Landstrasse (1947–52); Kleine Bockenheimer Strasse 18a (1952–). The club was founded (as Der Jazzkeller) in cellar premises on Bockenheimer Landstrasse in 1947 by the trumpeter and writer Carlo Bohländer; later known for a time as the Domicile, it eventually reverted to its original name. At first it specialized in traditional and contemporary styles of jazz, though little live jazz was presented at the earlier of the two locations. After it moved, however, the club became the venue in which the most important Frankfurt musicians, who have been among the foremost German jazzmen, met and played together. Under the ownership of Willi Geipel in the late 1980s Der Jazzkeller was known mostly for modern styles, from mainstream to avant-garde jazz; by the early 1990s ownership had transferred to Eugen Hahn. The club, which is known as "Frankfurt's Village Vanguard," continues to host well-known American performers as well as many German musicians.

BIBLIOGRAPHY

W. Liefland: "Das Loch in der Szene," *Jazzaz: Texte zur Jazzmusik*, ed. J. Oehlmann (Giessen, Germany, 1982), 9
V. Kriegel: "Der Jazzkeller: eine Frankfurter Institution," *Jazzrock: Tendenzen einer modernen Musik*, ed. B. König (Reinbek, Germany, 1983), 44
<http://www.jazzkeller.com> (2001)

——. **Schumann Café.** In spite of the restrictions imposed under Nazi rule, jazz performances continued at the café during World War II, when the trumpeter and writer Carlo Bohländer was among the musicians who played there.

BIBLIOGRAPHY

Frankfurt am Main

W. Schwörer: *Jazzszene Frankfurt: eine musiksoziologische Untersuchung zur Situation anfangs der achtziger Jahre* (Mainz, Germany, 1989)
W. Sandner, ed.: *Jazz in Frankfurt* (Frankfurt am Main, 1990)

Freiburg. **Jazzhaus.** Schnewlinstrasse 1. The Jazzhaus opened in 1987 and over the course of the next decade became one of the major German venues for jazz, with Miles Davis and other famous artists appearing. The club also published the *Freiburger Jazzhaus Journal*, offering information about jazz and culture in the region. Programming policies changed in 1998, and thereafter jazz has been presented only a few times per month.

BIBLIOGRAPHY

J.-E. Berendt: "10 Jahre Freiburger Jazzhaus," *Freiburger Jazzhaus Journal*, xii/1 (1998), 38
<http://www.jazzhaus.de> (2001)

Hamburg. **Birdland.** Gärtnerstrasse 122. This jazz club features swing and bop musicians from around Germany, with pre-eminent American musicians appearing monthly.

BIBLIOGRAPHY

L. Jurgeit: "Zehn Jahre Hamburger Birdland," *JP*, xliv/12 (1995), 41
<http://hamburg-jazz.de/birdland> (2001)

——. **Cotton Club** [Vat's Tube Jazzclub]. Tiefbunker Grindelhof 89b (to 1965); Spaldingstrasse (*c*1965); Paul-Toosen-Strasse (*c*1966); Hochbunker Pölchaukamp 10 (1967–71); Alter Steinweg 10 (1971–). Founded in 1959 as Vat's Tube Jazzclub, it was taken over in 1961 by W. Dieter Roloff, who changed its name to Cotton Club in 1963. Following a number of moves the club settled in the former Jailhouse Taverne at Alter Steinweg in 1971. Although Sammy Rimington had appeared in the early years, it was only after 1971 that other well-known traditional-jazz and swing musicians and groups began to perform there consistently, among them the Barrelhouse Jazz Band, Monty Sunshine, Peanuts Hucko, Ken Colyer, Benny Waters, Gene Conners, and others. The Cotton Club has continued to present jazz on a nearly daily basis into the new century.

BIBLIOGRAPHY

<http://www.cotton-club-hamburg.de> (2001)
<http://www.gohamburg.de/Nightlive/LiveMusik/Jazz/cotton_club/ShowIndex.cgi> (2001)

——. **Fabrik.** Barnerstrasse 36. This venue, which was an arms factory during World War II, became a cultural center in 1971. Among many other activities it has offered regular presentations of well-known mainstream and fusion artists, including the Crusaders, Sonny Rollins, Michel Petrucciani, John Lurie, Miles Davis, Gil Evans, Herbie Hancock, Dizzy Gillespie, Chet Baker, Lee Ritenour, and Al Di Meola. (<http://www.fabrik.de> (2001))

——. **Onkel Pö's Carnegie Hall** [Onkel Pö]. Lehmweg 44 (?1970–1985). It was founded in 1968 by Peter Marxen under the name Onkel Peu à Peu; Marxen managed the club until 1979, when Holger Jass took over. One of the principal jazz clubs in Germany during the 1970s, Onkel Pö presented mainly modern jazz and popular music; Al Jarreau, Pat Metheny, and other Americans performed there early in their careers, and Dizzy Gillespie's birthday was celebrated in a performance broadcast on NDR television. However, the repertory became increasingly popular, and by the time the club closed in 1985 little jazz was being performed. (K. Berger: "Pö à Pö abwärts," *JP*, xxxv/2 (1986), 18)

BIBLIOGRAPHY

Hamburg

K. Neumeister: *And our Hearts in New Orleans: die Geschichte des Hot-Jazz in Hamburg ab 1950* (Schacht-Audorf, Germany, 1998)

Heidelberg. **Cave 54.** Krämergasse 2. From the end of World War II Heidelberg was the German headquarters of the US Army, and, from the time of its founding in February 1954, Cave 54 attracted many jazz musicians to its Sunday-night jam sessions. Around 1957 Leo Wright led a band there, with Don Ellis, Eddie Harris, Cedar Walton, and Lex Humphries among his sidemen. Cave 54 was thus a significant venue for German musicians interested in a career in jazz, and the pianist Wolfgang Lauth, the Mangelsdorff brothers, and Karl Berger played there; Berger was its house pianist when Wright's band was in residence. The Sunday jam sessions ceased for many years, but they resumed in the late 1980s. Steve Coleman was among the American musicians who played there in later decades.

BIBLIOGRAPHY

K. Brigl and S. Schmidt-Joos: *Fritz Rau: Buchhalter der Träume* (Berlin 1985), 57
<http://www.nadir.org/nadir/periodika/contraste/cave54> (2001)

Heilbronn. **Jazzclub Cave 61.** Hafenstrasse 76. For several decades this was a club in both senses of the term – a venue for jazz and an organization of jazz fans – but it has continued into the new century only in the latter form.

Karlsruhe. **Jazzclub Karlsruhe.** Am Kronenplatz 1. As was the case in Heilbronn, the jazz club in Karlsruhe is both a specific venue and an organization of jazz fans. From the 1980s into the new century it has presented modern and avant-garde jazz.

BIBLIOGRAPHY

<http://www.jazzclub.de> (2001)
<http://www.karlsruhe.de/Kultur/Jazzclub> (2001)

Munich. **Bayerischer Hof.** Promenadeplatz 2–6. This luxury hotel, first built in 1841, has been in the Volkhardt family from 1897. It was destroyed in an air raid in April 1944, but restoration was completed in 1959. By the 1990s it was run by Innegrit Volkhardt, a jazz fan who instituted a nightclub within the hotel. Robben Ford first performed there in the spring of 1992, and Monty Alexander, Terence Blanchard, Lee Konitz, Roy Haynes, John Scofield, Steve Coleman, Dave Holland, Ray Brown's trio, the Gil Evans Orchestra, the quintet led by Albert Mangelsdorff and Wolfgang Dauner, Wynton Marsalis, and many other leading musicians and groups have appeared there. The club hosts a yearly jazz festival, Munich Klaviersommer, which (as the name indicates) places an emphasis on prominent jazz pianists, but other major instrumentalists also participate.

BIBLIOGRAPHY

M. Hennessey: "Jazz is Where You Find it," *CJM*, xxxvi/5 (1999), 18
<http://www.bayerischerhof.de> (2001)

——. **Domicile.** Siegesstrasse 19/1 (to late 1970s); Leopoldstrasse 19 (late 1970s–). Joe Haider was house pianist at the Domicile in the 1960s and owned the venue for a period in the 1970s. It played an important role in the jazz life of Munich and was a favorite venue for visiting American musicians; the Thad Jones–Mel Lewis Orchestra played a noted engagement there in the mid-1970s. In the 1980s the club became better known for the performance of rock music. (W. Thoma: "Nach 16 Jahren: ab Oktober ist das Domicile kein Jazzclub mehr," *Jazz Zeitung* (1981), Sept, 1)

——. **Jazzclub Unterfahrt.** Kirchenstrasse 96; Einsteinstrasse 42. Founded in 1978 by the Förderkreis für Jazz und Malerei, it presents mostly modern styles of jazz (mainstream and free jazz and Latin music) under the direction of the program manager Josef M. Dachsel. Different performers, regularly including musicians of international standing, appear every evening; an open jam session takes place on Sundays. (<http://www.jazzrecords.com/unterfahrt> (2001))

Nuremberg. **Jazz-Studio Nürnberg.** Paniersplatz 27–9. Jazz-Studio Nürnberg was founded by a group of 13 people as a nonprofit organization on 4 April 1954; it is run by a council elected annually. The studio promotes the performance of all styles of jazz, and musicians from all over the world have appeared there; another aspect of its activities is to support local jazz musicians by providing rehearsal facilities and devoting one night per week to performances by local players. It sponsors the festival Jazz Ost-West (*see* Festivals) and presents a weekly radio program, "Jazztime Nürnberg," in cooperation with a private station, Radio Franken.

BIBLIOGRAPHY

W. Schätzlein, ed.: Vierzig Jahre Jazz Studio Nürnberg: ein Kellerloch als Tor der Welt (Regensburg, Germany, 1994)
<http://www.jazzstudio.de> (2001)

Villingen. **Jazzclub Villingen e.V.** [Jazzkeller]. Webergasse 5. Founded in 1961, this is one of the oldest continuing clubs in Germany. It presents jazz mainly in traditional, swing, and the more moderate side of modern styles. Among those who appeared there in 2001 were Gary Barone, Eberhard Weber, and Rob van den Broeck.

BIBLIOGRAPHY

F. Schulz, ed.: *Jazz im Gässle: 20 Jahre Jazzclub Villingen e. V.* (Villingen, 1981)
<http://www.jazzclub-villingen.de> (2001)

BIBLIOGRAPHY
Germany

H. H. Lange: *Jazz in Deutschland: die deutsche Jazz-Chronik, 1900–1960* (Berlin, 1966)
J.-E. Berendt: *Ein Fenster aus Jazz: Essays, Portraits, Reflexionen* (Frankfurt am Main, Germany, 1977), 163
W. Knauer, ed.: *Wegweiser Jazz 2000: Clubs, Festivals, Initiativen und mehr* ... (Darmstadt, Germany, 1999); updated at "Wegweiser Jazz," <http:www.jazzinstitut.de> (2001)

GREAT BRITAIN. See England and Scotland.

GREECE

ATHENS. **Half-Note.** Trivonianoú 17, Ambelókipi. From the 1990s it has been the principal venue for foreign jazz musicians in Greece. The premises were formerly a stonemason's workshop.

HUNGARY

BUDAPEST. **Benkó Dixieland Club.** Török Pál Utca 3. Organized in 1966 by Barnabás Sentényi, Sándor Benkó, and Katalin Majsik, the club serves as the home base of the Benkó Dixieland Band. Other European traditional-jazz bands have also appeared there, as have occasional American guests, including Al Grey and Buddy Tate.

——. **Dália Jazz-Klub.** Bajcsy-Zsilinsky út 72. For 18 months from 25 October 1962 the Dália bar housed sessions promoted by the Ifjúsági Jazz-Klub (the Budapest Youth Jazz Club), the first officially organized jazz club in the Hungarian People's Republic. It provided opportunites for many young Hungarian jazz musicians.

——. **Merlin Jazz-Klub.** Gerlóczy Utca 4. This was one of the most prominent of the clubs which sprang up in the late 1980s and early 1990s to provide performance opportunities for Hungary's growing number of jazz musicians.

——. **Parisien Grill.** Paulay Ede Utca 35. An African-American group led by the pianist James Shaw appeared there in 1924–5. In September 1927 Withers' Jazz Stompers, led by the trombonist Frank Withers, were in residence; their singer Madge Coffie stayed on in Budapest, and the venue adopted a policy of employing Hungarian jazz musicians, initially to accompany her. For much of 1933 Chappy was the bandleader, with the African-American singer Rosie Poindexter, and in March 1934 Garland Wilson appeared accompanying the singer Nina Mae McKinney. Jazz continued to be presented there in the later 1930s.

——. **Royal Revű Varieté.** Erzsébet korut 31. Joe Turner (i) played there for six months in 1948, being fitted into successive variety bills. The premises were later occupied by the Madách Theatre.

BIBLIOGRAPHY
Budapest

G. G. Simon: *The Book of Hungarian Jazz* (Budapest, 1992)

INDIA

BOMBAY **Taj Mahal Hotel.** Jazz bands played there from 1934 to 1942. Late in 1935 Crickett Smith's Symphonians, in which Rudy Jackson and Sterling Conaway were sidemen, began to play for dancing in the ballroom located on the second floor of the hotel; Teddy Weatherford joined the band during this engagement. Over the next two years the Symphonians alternated residencies with Leon Abbey's band, which included not only Bill Coleman, Fletcher Allen, and Emile Christian, but also, from November 1936, Smith and Jackson. Weatherford led a trio involving Christian at the Tavern of the Taj (downstairs from the ballroom) in 1936. In September 1937 Weatherford appeared at another venue, the Harbour Bar (on the hotel's ground floor), and took over Smith's band in the ballroom.

CALCUTTA. **Grand Hotel.** 15 Chowringhee. Herb Flemming's band, which included Crickett Smith, played at the Grand Hotel from around mid-December 1933 to April 1934. Teddy Weatherford performed there from September 1941 and recorded three sessions at the hotel in mid-1942; the last of these involved Cedric West, who, together with Reuben Solomon, had left Burma in advance of the Japanese invasion and joined Weatherford at the Grand Hotel. While serving in the Merchant Marine, Jimmy Witherspoon sat in and sang with Weatherford's band The pianist continued to perform at the hotel until his death in 1945.

BIBLIOGRAPHY
India

P. Darke and R. Gulliver: "Teddy Weatherford," *Sv*, no.65 (1976), 175
——: "Roy Butler's Story," *Sv*, no.71 (1977), 178

IRELAND

DUBLIN. **Alfie Byrne's Pub.** Conrad International Dublin, Earlsfort Terrace. In the year 2000 Louis Stewart was leading a quartet at this hotel pub on Saturday nights. (<http://www.conrad-international.ie> (2001))

ITALY

BOLOGNA. **Cantina Bentivoglio.** Via Mascarella 4. From the 1980s it has been a meeting place for young and adventurous local musicians, often playing with the most venturesome American musicians.
(<http://www.affari.com/bentivoglio/home-uk.html> (2001))

GENOVA. **Lousiana Jazz Club.** Via di S. Sebastiano. This nightclub opened in 1964 and was managed by Giorgio Lombardi; it hosted swing and mainstream musicians.
(<http://utenti.tripod.it/clublouisiana> (2001))

MILAN. **Arethusa.** Opened in the 1950s, it was devoted to dixieland.

——. **Capolinea.** Via Ludovico il Moro 119. Founded in 1969 by the amateur drummer Giorgio Vanni, this club was the most important venue for jazz in Milan in the 1970s: many young italian musicians met American masters there and developed their style. In the 1980s, following Vanni's death, the club lost its central role.
(<http://www.geocities.com/BourbonStreet/Delta/1538> (2001))

——. **Intra's al Corso.** Galleria del Corso. This venue operated under the same circumstances at its companion club (see above).

——. **Intra's Derby Club.** Via Monterosa. Active in the 1960s and managed by the pianist Enrico Intra, it hosted Italian and American musicians, among them Lennie Tristano.

——. **Jazz Power.** Piazza del Duomo. Active in the 1970s under the management of Franco Fayenz, it presented the best Italian, European, and American jazzmen in styles ranging from mainstream to the avant garde.

——. **Santa Tecla.** Piazzetta Santa Tecla. Active in the 1950s, it featured the best Italian musicians, including Gianni Basso, performing with their groups and in jam sessions with important American musicians.

——. **Taverna Messicana.** Piazza Dal Verme. Active in the 1950s, this nightclub provided a venue for Italian jazz musicians to perform and jam with leading American players.

Rome. **Alexander's Platz.** Via Ostia 9. Opened in 1983 and managed by Giampiero Rubei, it has been the only Italian club to feature jazz every night – from Italian groups to international jazz stars.

——. **Big Mama.** Vicolo S. Francesco a Ripa 18. Managed by Marco Tirienni, it is devoted mainly to blues but also hosts jazz concerts. (<http://www.bigmama.it> (2001))

——. **Bricktop's.** Via Veneto. It was opened early in 1951 by the singer Bricktop (Ada Smith), who also founded nightclubs of the same name in Paris, Biarritz, New York, and Mexico City. Charlie Lewis's band was resident at the club's opening and Ralph Burns was the house pianist; Bricktop herself performed often. The club closed in March 1964.

BIBLIOGRAPHY

"Bricktop, Queen of Night Clubs, Abdicates," *New York Daily News* (6 March 1964)

Bricktop and J. Haskins: *Bricktop* (New York, 1983)

——. **Fonclea.** Via Crescenzio 82A. It was founded in 1978, and from 1979 was directed by Claude Mage, Francesco Ghidoli, Massimo Altano, and Marco Caroni. The club presented not only many styles of jazz (swing, dixieland, and fusion), but also funk, easy listening, and Latin music. It was used for two years as the venue for a drum school directed by Marvin Boogaloo Smith. Among the musicians who have played at the club are Chet Baker, Tony Esposito, Joe Bonner, and Massimo Urbani.

——. **Manuia.** Vicolo del Cinque 54–6. Restaurant and bar. It was opened on 1 April 1971 by owner-managers Sandro and Tony Melaranci and soon became a favorite meeting place for players specializing in Brazilian music and jazz. Among the jazz musicians who have appeared there are Chet Baker and Pat Metheny; the pianist and singer Jim Porto was engaged as the resident performer in 1979.

——. **Mississippi Jazz Club.** Borgo Angelico 16. Founded in 1979 by the trumpeter Luigi Toth, Roberto Toth, and Rodi Adele, it specialized in traditional and mainstream jazz but often presented modern jazz as well: prominent visiting musicians included John Lewis, Chet Baker, Elvin Jones, Max Roach, Archie Shepp, Barney Kessel, Attila Zoller, Abbey Lincoln, Buck Clayton, Wild Bill Davison, and Abdullah Ibrahim; Luigi Toth and his Old Time Jazz Band performed as the house band. The club closed in the late 1980s but reopened under new management in 1998 as the New Mississippi Jazz Club. (<http://www.mississippi.8m.com> (2001))

——. **Music Inn.** Largo dei Fiorentini 3. Founded in 1974 by the amateur drummer Pepito Pignatelli, it was the most important club in Rome until his death in 1981. Many major jazzmen, from Teddy Wilson to Ornette Coleman, played there. Thereafter Pignatelli's wife, Picchi, managed the club for few years until her own death.

——. **New Mississippi Jazz Club.** See Mississippi Jazz Club.

——. **Open Gate.** This exclusive nightspot offered jazz from around 1950, when it was regarded as a fashionable form of entertainment in Rome. In 1950 Svend Asmussen held a residency, and he was followed into the club by Django Reinhardt and André Ekyan; Reinhardt's services were secured by Christian Livorness, a jazz enthusiast and founding member of the Open Gate. In 1953 the singer Thelma Carpenter appeared there.

——. **Rupe Tarpea.** Restaurant. It had a dance floor and presented jazz from at least the late 1940s; Django Reinhardt performed there in 1948.

LATVIA

Riga. **Do-re-mi.** 1 Sverdlov Street. Café. It operated as a venue for jazz performance from 1984 into the late 1980s and specialized in mainstream jazz. The house duo consisted of the pianist Ilga Berzinya and the double bass player Boris Bannykh.

——. **Dizzi Mŭzikas Klubs** [Dizzi Music Club]. Marstalu Iela 10. This club opened in 2000 on the first floor of the old Reformatu church, which in the soviet era had been partitioned for various uses. Leading jazz, blues, and rhythm-and-blues musicians appear there. (<http://www.zagars.lv/dizzi/dizzi_lv.htm> (2001))

——. **Hamlets.** Jana Seta 5. Raimond Raubiško founded this club in 1998; he died two years later, but the theater, café, and bar continue his jazz policy, hosting jam sessions and presenting jazz groups on Friday, Sunday, and Monday nights.

LITHUANIA

Vilnius. **Brodvejus Pub.** Mesiniu Gatve 4. From around 1999 the Lithuania organization Jazz Gallery has presented concerts on Thursday nights at this pub in mainstream and modern styles. The concerts involve bands not only from Lithuania, but also from Finland, Sweden, Switzerland, and elsewhere in Europe. (<http://www.geocities.com/brodvejus> (2001))

——. **Music Club Langas.** Asmenos Gatve 8. In the late 1990s this was the country's principal venue for avant-garde jazz and free improvisation. (<http://mail.delfi.lt/langas/index_en.html> (2001))

——. **Prie Universiteto.** Dominikonu Gatve 9. This pub hosts the Jazz Gallery's concerts on Wednesday nights. (<http://www.pub.lt/index_lt.html> (2001))

——. **Uzsuk.** Vienuolio Gatve 2. This restaurant hosts the Jazz Gallery's concerts on Friday nights.

MALTA

Sliema. **Cairo Bar.** Juice Wilson led a trio there for several years from 1939 until the premises were bombed.

MOROCCO

Tangier. **African Rhythms Club.** In 1968 Randy Weston took his trio to Morocco and not long thereafter he founded the African Rhythms Club. When his sidemen Vishnu Wood and Ed Blackwell returned to the USA, Weston remained to run the club and played there until 1972, often accompanied by his son, the drummer Azzedin (Niles) Weston, and sometimes joined by Moroccan musicians.

——. **Safari Club.** Juice Wilson held a long residency at this club from the mid-1950s until after 1960. Among those who sat in on visits to Tangiers were Idrees Sulieman and Jamil Nasser.

NETHERLANDS

Amsterdam. **Bimhuis.** Oude Schans 73–7. The Bimhuis is the principal jazzclub of the Netherlands. It opened on 1 October 1974 in a former warehouse on the initiative of a group of musicians that included Willem Breuker, Misha Mengelberg, and Hans Dulfer. The club was extensively renovated in 1985, when capacity was doubled (to 400) and a bar was constructed which can be shut off from the stage by a flexible wall. There are three to five concerts per week, plus workshops and sessions. Huub van Riel, who became artistic manager in 1977, organized two week-long October Meetings in 1987 and 1991; both festivals spread out to venues in other Dutch cities and focused on impromptu combinations of some fifty participants, from Cecil Taylor to Paul Bley. Concert recordings from both October Meetings were issued on the Bimhuis label. From 1996 the bandleader and arranger Henk Meutgeert and his New Concert Big Band (from 1999, Jazz Orchestra of the Concertgebouw) have performed and recorded there every other Sunday night, together with a string of soloists of international renown. Among musicians who have played at the Bimhuis are Charles Mingus, Arnett Cobb, Von Freeman, Sun Ra, Anthony Braxton, John Zorn, and many Dutch and European luminaries. In 2002 the club will move to a new location at the harbor, shared with the new music center De Ijsbreker.

BIBLIOGRAPHY

K. Whitehead, ed.: *Bimhuis 25: Stories of Twenty-five Years at the Bimhuis* (Amsterdam, 1999)

<http://www.bimhuis.nl> (2001)

H. van Riel: "Dove abita il jazz: Bim Huis," *Musica Jazz*, lvii/4 (2001), 24

——. **Carlton Hotel.** Vijzelstraat. Jazz was played there for the entertainment of guests from the late 1920s. Edwin Swayze and the Plantation Band played at the hotel in the summer of 1930, during a tour of Europe, and in November 1933 Louis Armstrong appeared there for four nights when making his first tour of the continent.

——. **Concertgebouw.** Concertgebouwplein 2–6. From 1952 until the mid-1960s the competing impresarios Lou van Rees and Paul Acket organized a long-running series of nighttime concerts in this temple of classical music, presenting such musicians as Louis Armstrong, Duke Ellington, Count Basie, Coleman Hawkins, Stan Kenton, Miles Davis, John Coltrane, and several editions of Norman Granz's Jazz at the Philharmonic. From October 1996 jazz regained its place in the Concertgebouw's program, since when Wynton Marsalis, Sonny Rollins, the Mingus Big Band, Joshua Redman, Ahmad Jamal, and many others have played there. Photographs from these events have been published by E. van der Elsken: *Jazz* (Amsterdam, 1959, rev. 3/1991, as *Jazz, 1955–61*).

——. **La Gaîté.** See Tuschinski Theater.

——. **Joseph Lam Jazz Club.** Laagte Kadijk 35 (1976–85); Van Diemenstraat 242 (1984–96). Originally based in a spacious warehouse on the waterfront, it was the principal venue in Amsterdam for traditional jazz. The allusion to the ragtime composer Joseph Lamb was unintentional – "lam" being a Dutch equivalent for the expression "dead drunk."

——. **Negro Palace.** Thorbecke Plein. Coleman Hawkins and Freddy Johnson formed a trio with the Dutch drummer Maurice van Kleef for a residency at this venue from September to November 1937 and again from March to August 1938. Johnson returned without Hawkins for a further engagement in September 1938. (J. Chilton: *The Song of the Hawk: the Life and Recordings of Coleman Hawkins*, London and New York, 1990)

——. **Paradiso.** Weteringschans 6–8. In March 1968 a century-old congregation hall of a Dutch protestant sect was converted into the hippie center Paradiso, and in September of that same year Hans Dulfer organized his first "Jazz in Paradiso," thereby initiating a series of Monday-night concerts presenting such improvising musicians as Han Bennink, Willem Breuker, Willem van Manen, Peter Brötzmann, and John Tchicai. Dulfer's admiration for the tenor saxophone also resulted in appearances by Don Byas, Clifford Jordan, J. R. Monterose, Ben Webster, Hal Singer, Dexter Gordon, Lucky Thompson, Johnny Griffin, and Frank Wright. The series ended in August 1971 with a performance by Sunny Murray and resumed briefly in 1973. Thereafter Paradiso occasionally presented jazz, but it has served mainly as a venue for pop music.

——. **Sheherazade.** Waagstraat 3–7. It opened in 1942 on the site of the former Kit Kat Negro Club (which had opened in 1936), but the Germans closed it in 1943. It reopened as a bar and dance club in June 1945, and in the late 1950s and early 1960s the club became Amsterdam's foremost venue for jazz; its house band, the Diamond Five (including the tenor saxophonist Harry Verbeke and Cees Slinger), performed six nights per week from 1958 to 1962. Among visiting soloists were Don Byas, Thelonious Monk, Kenny Clarke, Lars Gullin, Stan Getz, and Johnny Griffin, and Louis Armstrong, Lionel Hampton, and Zoot Sims participated in jam sessions there after performing at the Concertgebouw. After 1964, in which year Albert Ayler's free-jazz quartet shocked the audience, the importance of Sheherazade dwindled.

——. **Tuschinski Theater.** Reguliersbreestraat. La Gaîté, a club for dancing, was active in this art deco theater from around 1923 to 1940 with Max Tak as its director of music; it offered hot dance music and small-group jazz. In 1934 it featured a band led by the Surinamese saxophonist Lex Van Spall. Eddie South performed there in 1938. A half-century later Hans Loonstijn organized a series of nighttime concerts in the Tuschinski's luxurious main theater, presenting, between 1988 and 1991, the Modern Jazz Quartet, Oscar Peterson, Hank Jones, J. J. Johnson, Benny Golson, Dizzy Gillespie, Tony Williams, and others.

Arnhem. **Storyville Jazz Club.** It flourished in the 1980s, when it engaged many American and British musicians.

Breda. **Roaring Twenties Jazzclub.** In the 1980s the club was one of the main venues for traditional jazz in the Netherlands.

Dordrecht. **Dordtse Jazz Sociëteit** (1947–92); **Jazzpodium DJS** (from 1992). Groenmarkt (1947–76); Grote Kerksplein 1 (from 1976). A club in both senses of the term (a venue, and an organization of jazz fans), it opened in 1947 as the Dordtse Jazz Sociëteit. In 1976 it moved from Groenmarkt to an intimate club in the shadow of the city's monumental church tower. In 1989 the Dordtse Jazz Sociëteit began presenting the Jazzdagen Dordrecht, an annual festival which takes place on many stages in town, and from 1991 it has offered the Dordtse Jazzprijs, involving a national contest for new bands. It took a new name, Jazzpodium DJS, in 1992. All styles of jazz are presented, as are blues and world music.

BIBLIOGRAPHY

<http://www.dordtnl/djs> (2001)
<http://www.xs4all.nl/~adwit> (2001)

Eindhoven. **Wilhelmina.** Wilhelminaplein 6. From 1977 this traditional pub has been an important center for modern jazz and avant-garde music. Stichting Jazzpower presents concerts there on Monday nights (some 35 each year). (<http://www.dse.nl/jazzpower> (2001))

Enschede. **Jazzpodium de Tor.** Walstraat 21. Opened in 1970 and under the artistic management of Peter Huijts from 1975, Jazzpodium de Tor has become the most important jazz venue in the eastern part of the country, presenting all modern styles of jazz. (<http://www.jazzpodiumdetor.nl> (2001))

Groningen. **De Oosterpoort.** Trompsingel 27. Inaugurated in 1974 and since then home of the Jazz Marathon, an annual festival devoted to avant-garde jazz, this cultural center has also presented mainstream jazz, blues, and other genres on its two stages. Charles Mingus, Milt Buckner, Arnett Cobb, the Thad Jones–Mel Lewis Orchestra, Sonny Rollins, and Wayne Shorter are among those who have appeared there.

——. **De Spieghel.** Peperstraat 11. This café has offered concerts from 1979. Arnett Cobb, Dorothy Donegan, Von Freeman, Red Holloway, Sonny Stitt, Jimmy Raney, Frank Foster, Buddy Tate, and many others performed there. (R. in 't Hof and R. Zijlstra: *The Saddest Place: jazzcafé De Spieghel 1979–1994* (Groningen, 1994) [with photographs by A. C. Wieringa])

Haarlem. **Haarlemse Jazz Club** [Zanderzaal]. Groot Heiligland 37. Known to locals as Zanderzaal, the Haarlemse Jazz Club was founded by Han Baas, John Easton, and Cas Jeekel and opened on 24 September 1949. It was run by the Stichting Haarlemse Jazz Club and was one of the oldest jazz clubs in the Netherlands; its Friday-night concerts offered traditional, mainstream, and avant-garde jazz, and blues. The Haarlemse Jazz Club regarded itself as the direct descendant of the Haarlemse Hot Club, established in 1932 by Eddie C. Commelin. In 1934 the club promoted a recording session by Freddy Johnson and the Surinamese saxophonist Lex Van Spall at the Casino Hamdorff in Laren (see below); one of the numbers recorded was *Haarlem Hot Club Stomp*, on which Rosy Poindexter was the singer (Decca F42045). The club closed in December 1994.

BIBLIOGRAPHY

J. Trabsky: Liner notes, F. Johnson and L. Van Spall: *Haarlem Hot Club: 20 Years Haarlemse Jazz Club* (Cat 3, 1969) [commemorative EP]
H. Openeer: Liner notes, B. Carter, C. Hawkins, and F. Johnson: *Made in Holland, 1934–'37* (Panachord H2005, 1982)

The Hague. **Kurhaus Hotel.** Gevers Deynootplein. This hotel in the popular seaside resort of Scheveningen (in The Hague) engaged jazz musicians from at least the mid-1930s. In July 1933 Duke Ellington made his Netherlands début there. Benny Carter held two notable residencies at the hotel, in 1936 and 1937; for the latter he was supported by a band of internationally known musicians, including George Chisholm and Bertie King. These performances received extensive coverage in *De jazzwereld*, the leading jazz journal in the Netherlands at the time. In the 1950s and early 1960s many American stars performed in the Kurhaus, often before participating in a second (nighttime) concert a few hours later at the Concertgebouw in Amsterdam.

——. **Netherlands Congress Centre.** Churchillplein 10. This huge building, which opened in 1969, has played host to the North Sea Jazz Festival from the latter's inception in 1976. Over the years the capacity of the venue has gradually increased to fifteen stages, the largest of which – the Statenhal – accommodates an audience of approximately 10,000. The Prins Willem Alexander Zaal has also been used for concerts of symphonic music by the Residentie Orchestra. Both of these halls present jazz and pop concerts throughout the year.

——. **Tabaris.** Wagenstraat. This dance hall was a major venue for American jazz musicians in the 1930s. Among the ensembles that played there were Freddy Johnson's Harlemites (1934) and the bands led by Willie Lewis (1933, 1936) and Leon Abbey (1938). Between visits by foreign bands the club featured European groups playing hot dance music. The hall closed probably in 1940.

BIBLIOGRAPHY

The Hague

R. Z.: "How they Swing at The Hague," *MM*, x (12 May 1934), 3
J. P. Holloway: "Cross-channel Coloured Rhythm," *MM*, xii (17 Oct 1936), 2

Laren. **Casino Hamdorff.** Associated with the Hotel Hamdorff, the casino flourished from about 1913 until 1950. The repertory it offered was chiefly hot dance music, and one of the ensembles that performed there regularly was the Ramblers; the group recorded at the casino with Coleman Hawkins in 1935 and 1937. The Dutch Decca company set up another recording session at the casino in 1934, with a band led by Freddy Johnson and the Surinamese saxophonist Lex Van Spall. A number of visiting American and European musicians were engaged to play at the Hamdorff, including Benny Carter in 1936.

——. **Nick Vollebregt's Jazzcafé.** Naarderstraat 42. This café was run by the jazz drummer Nick Vollebregt, who produced concerts and jam sessions on Sunday afternoons from 1973 until his death in 1977. From September 1978 a continuous series of weekly concerts has been broadcast from the café on the show "Sesjun," produced by the Dutch radio company TROS. Musicians who have performed there include Dizzy Gillespie, Chet Baker, Art Blakey, Bill Evans (ii), Jimmy Smith, Tony Williams, and Joshua Redman. Transcriptions of the concerts have been broadcast in the USA on the NPR program "World Wide Jazz"; Radio Netherlands has also issued compact discs of some of this material.

Leeuwarden. **Brouwershoeck.** Poststraat 21. Ben Scheper and his Stichting Hothouse Redbad presented modern jazz and improvised music on Sunday afternoons in this traditional pub from January 1976 to November 1997. The Brouwershoeck then closed, and Scheper's Sunday-afternoon series continued at a theater, De Harmonie. (<http://www.harmonie.nl> (2001))

——. **De Harmonie.** See Brouwershoeck.

NIJMEGEN. **O'42.** Oranjesingel 42. The Werkgroep Improvisatie Muziek (WIM) presented weekly workshops and concerts of improvised and avant-garde music in this cultural center from 1975 until it closed in March 2000.

ROTTERDAM. **De Doelen.** Kruisstraat 2. The impresario Paul Acket presented a series of festivals in this large concert hall from its opening in 1966. A touring Newport Jazz Festival, produced in collaboration with George Wein, continued until 1972 and involved, among many others, Joe Venuti, Duke Ellington, Miles Davis, Cecil Taylor, Thelonious Monk, and Archie Shepp. From 1972 festivals carrying different names presented such musicians as Roland Kirk and Sonny Rollins. This tradition was carried on by the Heineken Jazz Festival, held at De Doelen from 1983 to 1992.

——. **Harbour Jazz Club.** One of the largest jazz clubs in the Netherlands, it flourished in the 1970s and early 1980s, regularly presenting traditional and mainstream jazz; among the groups that performed there was Chris Barber's band.

——. **Mephisto** [Thelonious]. Lijnbaan 120 (March 1984 – November 1992); Witte de Withstraat 16 (November 1992 – December 1993). Mephisto opened in March 1984 in a former underground cinema. It was run by the double bass player Ed de Vos and named after a Rotterdam club where Coleman Hawkins and Benny Carter played in the mid-1930s (and which burned down in 1938). It closed in May 1985 on account of financial problems, but in September of that year the colorful Rotterdam jazz entrepreneur Willem van Empel took over the premises as a squatter. Operating under a new name, Thelonious, the club survived in semi-illegality until July 1988, presenting such musicians as Frank Wright, Pharoah Sanders, Gato Barbieri, and Egberto Gismonti. In April 1989 it reopened under the management of Cyriel Pluimakers. Thelonious moved to a new location in November 1992 but closed permanently in December 1993.

——. **Nighttown.** Westkruiskade 28. While Nighttown is principally a venue for pop music, following the closing of Thelonious at the end of 1993, prominent jazz concerts in Rotterdam have taken place there from May 1994. (<http://www.nighttown.nl> (2001))

——. **Pschorr.** Restaurant and dance hall. The music played for dancing there from around 1924 until 1940 included hot dance music and small-group jazz. During this period the establishment was directed by Dick Reese, and among the notable jazz musicians who performed were Louis Armstrong (for two nights during his tour of November 1933) and Freddy Johnson (1934). In 1936 the Ramblers recorded there with the Dutch "lady crooner" Topy Glerum.

——. **Thelonious.** See Mephisto.

TERNEUZEN. **Porgy & Bess.** Noordstraat 52. It was founded in 1957 by the Surinam-born entrepreneur Hans Koulen (1922–85). Many Americans have played there, notably Don Byas, Lee Konitz, Mel Lewis, Arnett Cobb, Art Blakey, Chet Baker, and Roy Hargrove. From 1972 the club has produced the yearly Schelde jazz festival. Because of its proximity to the Belgian border, Porgy & Bess has also presented many Belgian musicians.

BIBLIOGRAPHY

W. Bareman, ed: *40 jaar Porgy & Bess* (Terneuzen, 1997)
<http://www.porgyenbess.nl> (2001)

TILBURG. **Paradox.** Telegraafstraat 62. Opened in December 1985, this club offers four to five concerts, workshops, and sessions per week in styles ranging from mainstream to avant-garde jazz, blues, salsa, and alternative rock. In 1993 it began hosting Stranger than Paranoia, a yearly festival of jazz, world music, and contemporary art music held during the last days of December. (<http://www.xs4all.nl/~paradox> (2001))

UTRECHT. **Muziekcentrum Vredenburg.** Vredenburgpassage 77. This architecturally striking concert hall opened in 1979, and its general manager, Peter Smids, has engaged many jazz and blues artists, including Sun Ra's Arkestra and Pat Metheny. The main hall (1700 seats) is the home of the annual Blues Estafette. From 1987 Rein de Graaff organized his own concert series in the second hall (300 seats), accompanying such neglected veterans such as Bill Perkins, Sal Nistico (ii), James Clay, Ted Brown, and the trumpeter Webster Young. From 1989 the SJU Jazz Festival has taken place on this smaller stage.

——. **SJU-huis.** Vark Kroonstraat 9. The home of the Stichting Jazz in Utrecht (SJU; founded in 1977), it opened in November 1983 on the ground floor of a parking garage and operated under the management of Cyriel Pluimakers (1985–9) and Marcel Kranendonk (from 1989); in 1989 the club became one of the producers of the annual SJU Jazzfestival. It closed in 1992 and reopened in January 1994 as the SJU Jazzpodium.

——. **SJU Jazzpodium.** Varkenmarkt 2. The club opened in January 1994 as the successor to the SJU-huis; it has continued under the management of Marcel Kranendonk and in its role as a producer of the SJU Jazzfestival. (<http://www.sjujazz.nl> (2001))

BIBLIOGRAPHY

Netherlands

J. van de Klomp, ed.: *One Night Stand: jazzconcerten in Nederland, 1947–1967* (Amsterdam, 1999)

NORWAY

BERGEN **Bergen Jazz Forum.** Sardinen, USF. The club, which is situated in an old fishing factory at the seaside, has presented local and visiting jazz musicians once a week from 1972 into the new century; it focuses on modern jazz. The club also hosts the two-week-long Nattjazz (Night jazz) festival every year in late May to early June. (<http://www.bergenjazzforum.no> (2001))

——. **Hotel Neptun.** Valkendorfsgt. 8. This well-known hotel and restaurant in Bergen presented jazz from 1961 to 1966; at this time its operators, Gunnar and Inni-Carine Holm, were a couple deeply interested in jazz. A local rhythm section accompanied an array of Norwegian and international soloists for week-long engagements; Dexter Gordon, Kenny Dorham, Don Byas, and Idrees Sulieman are among the many important players who appeared there.

OSLO. **Amalienborg Jazzhus.** Arbeidergata 2. Run by the Oslo Jazz Circle, this small venue functioned as a restaurant and pub during the day and in the evenings presented Norwegian and foreign jazz musicians of all styles, six days a week, from 1973 to 1984. It was the main meeting place during that period for the jazz community in Oslo.

——. **Big Chief Jazz Club.** Valkyriegate 8. Jazz was presented here every Sunday evening from 1953 to 1965 in a cellar room used as a dancing school on the other days of the week. While those playing were mainly traditional-jazz musicians, from 1960 many of the more modern soloists appearing at Metropol Jazz Center performed here (the Metropol was closed on Sundays). It was extremely popular for a period, and during its 12 years had more than 11,000 members; no alcohol was served.

——. **Herr Nilsen.** C. J. Hambros plass. A small bar and pub with a good stage, it opened in 1993 and for three to four days a week presents mainly local musicians playing in contemporary jazz styles.

——. **Hot House.** Pilestredet 15b. A small bar and restaurant, it was run by the pianist Christian Reim and the actor Kjell Kjær, who presented jazz seven days per week from 1979 to 1984. With a focus on modern jazz, it brought in such visiting soloists as Chet Baker, Hal Singer, and Clifford Jordan, among others.

——. **Jazz Alive.** Observatoriegata 2b (formerly a gourmet restaurant) (1980–83); Rådhusgaten 6 (formerly a state liquor store) (1985–6). Run by the saxophonist Bernt Brinck-Johnsen and the drummer Ole Jacob Hansen, it offered mainly modern jazz from 10 p.m. until 4 a.m. six nights per week; Chet Baker and Philly Joe Jones were among the leading players who appeared there.

——. **Metropol Jazz Center.** Akersgata 8. Probably the finest jazz club in Norwegian history, it presented jazz six days per week from 1960 to 1965. During the day it operated as a restaurant. The venue became enormously popular and hosted local bands of all styles, as well as a number of international bands and soloists, including J. C. Higginbotham, Coleman Hawkins, Don Byas, Dexter Gordon, Bud Powell, Cecil Taylor, and Don Ellis.

——. **New Orleans Workshop.** Pløensgate 8 (1972–82); Rådhusgaten 2 (1982–90); Grensen 1 (from 1990). Established in 1972 by two local groups, the Christiania Jazzband and the Magnolia Jazzband, this venue presented traditional jazz each Thursday, initially in Bergums Kafé, a very small lunch restaurant. In 1982 it moved to Restaurant Gullfisken, where it remained until this traditional building burned down in 1990; it then moved to Stortorgets Gjæstgiveri, another very old Oslo restaurant.

——. **Oslo Jazzhus.** Toftesgate 69. This small and charming venue was the canteen of the Musikken Hus (House of music), where many music organizations had their offices. From 1985 to 1996 it offered jazz three nights per week; focusing on contemporary styles, it served as a base for young local players but also hosted many international musicians.

——. **Oslo Swing Club.** Kronprinsens gate 1. The home of the Oslo seamen's association, it presented jazz once a week from 1939 to 1941, when it was the premier jazz venue in Oslo. Jacques Butler, Svend Asmussen, and Nat Gonella are among those who appeared there.

——. **Penguin Club.** Pilestredet 75c (1952–60); Universitetsgaten 26 (1960–65). Run by the pianist Terje Kjær, the club originally operated in a large room with a small stage and then in 1960 moved to the Restaurant Humlen. Both venues had jazz every Sunday, beginning with a popular jam session from 6 p.m. to 8 p.m. and afterwards presenting a dance, with Kjær's quintet supplying jazz in styles modeled after those of Svend Asmussen's group and George Shearing's quintet. The jam session was often visited by foreign musicians, including members of Jazz at the Philharmonic, Louis Armstrong's All Stars, and the orchestras of Lionel Hampton and Count Basie.

——. **Stortorvet Gjæstgiveri Jazz Club.** Grensen 1. Located in a charming old restaurant building with many rooms, from 1982 into the new century this club has presented mainly local bands playing traditional jazz and swing on Fridays and Saturdays. It serves as a kind of spiritual center for the annual Oslo Jazz Festival.

——. **Studentbyens Jazzklubb.** Sognsveien 85. Established in a rather austere restaurant and canteen in a university area by Steinar Kristiansen, a student and jazz fan, it presented jazz every Sunday from 1967 to 1978. It focused on young Norwegian groups, including such musicians as Karin Krog and Jan Garbarek, but also hosted visiting soloists, among them Don Cherry, Keith Jarrett, and Hampton Hawes.

POLAND

KATOWICE. **Half-Note.** Gugalander. Ulica Jagiellońska 17a. Founded in 1989, this cultural center has presented films, theater, music, and other arts. Maciej Sikała, Tomasz Szukalski, and Piotr Wojtasik are among those who have performed there. (<http://www.gugalander.art.pl> (2001))

POZŃAN. **Blue Note.** Located in central Pozńan, the Blue Note has been presenting major jazz artists from at least the late 1990s, including, among many others, John Abercrombie, Lynne Arriale, Lee Konitz, Steve Lacy, Tony Lakatos, Dave Liebman, Pat Metheny, Paul Motian, Idris Muhammad, Tony Oxley, Mike Stern, and Steve Swallow. (<http://www.bluenote.info.poznan.pl> (2001))

WARSAW. **Akwarium.** Ulica Emilii Plater 49. It was founded in April 1977 and was supported by sponsorship from the Polskie Stowarzyszenie Jazzowe. The Akwarium presented performances by such Polish players and groups as Henryk Majewski's Old Timers (who recorded there in that first year), Swing Session (recording in 1979), and Tomasz Stańko, while also engaging visiting foreign musicians, including the L. A. Four, Sheila Jordan, the Thad Jones–Mel Lewis Orchestra, and the Toshiko Akiyoshi–Lew Tabackin Big Band. It closed in 2000.

——. **Café Bodega.** Between Chmienla and Nowy Świat streets. This venue flourished as a center for jazz during World War II, when among the musicians who performed there was the big band led by George Scott.

——. **Contemporary Music Club.** See U Wandy Warskiej.

——. **Hybrydy.** Ulica Mokotowska 48. It opened as a student club in 1957; Jan Borkowski was one of its founders and its first president. Zbigniew Namysłowski, Krzysztof Komeda, Krzysztof Sadowski, Andrzej Trzaskowski, Jerzy Matuszkiewicz, and Urszula Dudziak and Michal Urbaniak are among the many leading Polish musicians who played there. Hybrydy closed in the early 1970s.

——. **Jazz Club Remont.** Warynskiego 12. A student club under the direction of Waldemar Deska, among others, it flourished in the 1970s and 1980s and offered performances by European and American groups and musicians, including Gunter Hampel, Manhattan Transfer, and Buddy Rich.

——. **Latawiec.** Ulica Stanow Zjednoczonych 26. In the 1980s it was one of several venues in the city to offer principally a traditional-jazz repertory.

——. **Rio Rita.** Krakowskie Przedmieście Street. Café. Among the jazz musicians to be resident performers there were the pianists Marek Cybulski and Stefan Kisielewski, who both played at the café during the period of German occupation.

——. **Stodoła.** Ulica Trebacka 7; Batorego 10. This student club was founded in 1957 and has presented mostly traditional and mainstream jazz. Among the Polish musicians to have appeared with the resident big band (which made a number of recordings) are Zbigniew Jaremko and Sławomir Kulpowicz; Henryk Majewski's group the Old Timers played there regularly.

——. **U Wandy Warskiej** [Contemporary Music Club]. Rynek Staromiejski 19. Jazz was played there from the time of its opening in 1967 by Andrzej Kurylewicz and his wife, the singer and painter Wanda Warska.

PORTUGAL

Lisbon. **Hot Clube de Portugal.** Praça da Alegria 38, 1250 Lisbon. Founded in 1948, it is the most important and longest-lived nightclub in Portugal and has presented jazz nightly from its opening. Besides Portuguese musicians it has engaged numerous visiting jazz performers; Dexter Gordon, Count Basie, Charlie Mariano, Charlie Haden, Enrico Rava, Atilla Zoller, and Tete Montoliu, among others, appeared there. In 1978 Zé Eduardo founded and became the director of a jazz school run by the Hot Clube; this school, which remains active under other teachers, has helped young Portuguese musicians to make their way in the international world of jazz. In 1998 the clube acquired the collection of its first and then oldest member, Luís Villas-Boas, who had produced the jazz festival at Cascais; this collection comprises 78 r.p.m. and LP recordings, Portuguese, French, British, and American periodicals, newspaper clippings, posters, and videos, and photographs dating from the mid-1940s.

RUSSIA

Moscow. **Dmitrovka Cinema.** One of the earliest performances of jazz in the USSR was given there on 22 February 1926 by an African-American band organized by the trombonist Frank Withers; among the musicians were Sidney Bechet, Benny Peyton, and Crickett Smith.

——. **Le Klub.** Tanganka. Located within a theater, Le Klub is owned and operated by Igor Butman. It is one of the leading venues for jazz in Moscow in the 21st century. (<http://www.jazz.ru.clubs/mosclubs/default.htm#leclub> (2001))

——. **Sinyaya Ptitsa** [Bluebird]. 23 Chekhov Street. Café. A club of this name was first active there in the 1960s. In the mid-1980s the Sinyaya Ptitsa operated in the workshop of the sculptor Sergey Gadjukov. The journalist Vartan Tonoyan established the club as a publicly owned operation in its premises on Chekhov Street in 1986, and it was officially opened on 5 April 1987 with Eric Avagimov as its commercial director. It has offered a wide range of styles, from traditional to avant-garde jazz and jazz-rock, and celebrates the birthdays of prominent musicians with special programs. Among the visiting Americans who have appeared at the club are Grover Washington, Jr., Dave Brubeck, Pat Metheny, and Billy Taylor (ii); the Sinyaya Ptitsa has also been a center for musicians from other Russian cities, and it has run regular jam sessions. (<http://www.sinyayaptitsa.narod.ru> (2001))

St. Petersburg. **Café in the Cultural Palace of Seamen.** 2 Vindavskaya Street. Active as a center for jazz from 1986, it presented principally mainstream jazz; the house band was led by David Goloshchokin. Important Western musicians such as Dave Brubeck, who visited the club with his quartet in April 1987, have worked with local musicians there.

——. **Kvadrat** [Chorus]. Leningrad Palace of Culture (1965–86); 47 Professor Popov Street (1986–?); Bolshoi Prospekt Vasilievskogo, o-va 83 (by 2001). Founded by the city's Komsomol committee in January 1965, this club operated without interruption into the late 1980s, when the president was N. Leites. It presented mostly dixieland and mainstream jazz and bop, though occasionally free-jazz performances have taken place. All the leading Russian jazz musicians have appeared there, and it is the major venue for St. Petersburg players; the Leningrad Dixieland Band was the resident ensemble for the first year of the club's existence. Kvadrat was associated with the first two jazz festivals to take place in the city, in 1965 and 1966 (*see* Festivals), and in 1986 it organized a festival of traditional jazz, Jazz on the Neva. Between 1965 and 1985 about 40 lectures were given there on jazz-related topics, and the club also issued its own journal. It remains active in the post-Soviet era.

——. **Vostok.** 10 Pravda Street. Café. It opened in the Leningrad Palace of Culture in September 1985, under the management of Anatoly Popov and Yakov Zeitlin. The resident band, playing mainstream jazz, was led by the drummer Valery Myssovsky. The venue also ran the only jazz workshop in Leningrad.

SCOTLAND

Edinburgh. **Henry's Cellar Bar.** Morrison Street. This basement bar below a Chinese restaurant has been Scotland's only all-week jazz venue since the eponymous owner allowed Kulu, a photographer and jazz fan from Hong Kong, to begin presenting groups there in 1996. Kulu ran the venue principally for young local musicians and fostered a notable ambience of jazz meets hip-hop, with disc jockeys taking over from live bands in the early-morning hours. Henry's became a popular spot, albeit often a noisy one, despite its inadequate technical facilities. After Kulu returned to Hong Kong the organization Assembly Direct became involved in helping to promote the venue in the summer of 2000; it installed a better piano and sound system and increased the number of visiting musicians from England and abroad. Their intention was to develop the venue into more of a listening environment, where serious international musicians could perform, while retaining its crucial role in encouraging local players. Edinburgh Jazz Projects, a smaller-scale promoting organization, moved its operations to Henry's in January 2001.

BIBLIOGRAPHY

<http://members/theglobe.com/jazzjoint> (2001)
<http://www.jazzmusic.co.uk> (2001)

——. **Queen's Hall.** Clerk Street. The Queen's Hall was opened in 1979 in a former church in the center of Edinburgh and quickly became established as Scotland's most important jazz concert venue. The rather hard pews in the downstairs stalls have never been replaced, but the open area in front of the stage can be laid out in more formal concert seating or in the style of a cabaret, with tables, to give some of the flavor of a jazz club. The huge painting *Jazz Giants*, by the Glasgow artist Dominic Snyder, has provided a backdrop for jazz concerts since it was commissioned in 1989 by Platform Jazz, an organization whose role at the venue was taken over by Assembly Direct, Scotland's main jazz promoters, shortly afterwards. The first jazz concert in the hall, on 5 April 1980, featured Bruce Turner. Among the hundreds of major artists who have played there over the years are the Modern Jazz Quartet, the Art Ensemble of Chicago, Sonny Rollins, Jan Garbarek, Jimmy Smith, Gil Evans's orchestra, Ornette Coleman, Wynton Marsalis, and John Zorn. The venue is used regularly by the Edinburgh International Jazz Festival and occasionally by other festivals and promoters.
<http://www.queenshalledinburgh.co.uk> (2001)

——. **West End Café.** Shandwick Place. The West End Café entered Scottish jazz lore through its association with the most famous Scottish jazzmen of the day, Sandy Brown and Al Fairweather, but it was also a model for much that came after. Sunday-night jazz sessions were begun around 1949 by the guitarist Pete Chilvers, whose family owned the bar and restaurant business, and it became a focal point for jazz in Edinburgh until the mid-1950s. The West End also played host to such visiting musicians and groups as John Dankworth and Kenny Graham's Afro-Cubists from London and Graeme Bell from Australia.

Glasgow. **Society of Musicians.** 73 Berkeley Street. The Society of Musicians was formed in 1884 and acquired its premises (celebrated by Martin Taylor, once a regular at the venue, in a composition entitled *73 Berkeley Street*) in 1905. The club was open only to members, and the original emphasis was on classical music, but the society's membership also included many jazz and dance-band musicians. It became a more public forum for jazz in the early 1980s, when the constitution was changed to allow nonmembers to be charged for entry, and jazz concerts featuring mainstream artists from the UK and America became a regular feature, alongside local musicians. Don Menza inaugurated the new series, and Barney Kessel, Scott Hamilton, Mundell Lowe, Warren Vaché, and Kenny Davern were among other artists who appeared there. A shrinking membership base and mounting financial pressures finally forced the society to sell its premises and disband in 1994; Ken Peplowski played the last concert there. The organizers, led by the guitarist Lex Kelly and his wife, Anne Kelly, continued to run occasional concerts in various venues under the name the Jazz Co-op.

SINGAPORE

Singapore. **Adelphi Hotel.** In 1926 a band of eight Filipino musicians was led there by Ted Lewis, an African-American drummer who should not be confused with the contemporary white clarinetist of the same name. The band led by the drummer Jack Carter, which included Valaida Snow, Albert Nicholas, and Teddy Weatherford, performed at the Adelphi in 1928.

——. **Saxophone Bar & Restaurant.** 23 Cuppage Terrace. This small bistro was active as a jazz venue during the early 1990s.

BIBLIOGRAPHY

Singapore

P. Darke and R. Gulliver: "Teddy Weatherford," *Sv*, no.65 (1976), 175
R. Lynam: "Swingapore and All Points South East," *Jazz FM*, no.5 (1991), 26

SPAIN

Almería. **Georgia Jazz Club.** Padre Lugue 17. The club was founded in 1978 and remains active in the new century. Jazz concerts are given monthly or fortnightly, and the club participates in Jornadas de Jazz de Almería, an annual season of jazz.

Barcelona. **Amaya.** George Johnson's group played there after leaving the Lamaga club early in February 1947.

——. **La Cova del Drac.** Carrer Tuset; Carrer Vallmajor 33. This basement club opened in 1966 as a venue devoted to *nova cançó*; it began to feature jazz in 1968–9 when the Yerba Mate Jazz Band, an Argentinian traditional-jazz group, appeared. In 1970 Joaquim Gili began to present sessions under the name La Locomotora Negra, and his brothers Ricard, Carles, and Toni Gili formed the band of that name shortly afterwards. Joaquim Gili soon persuaded the club's director, Ramon Tordera, to devote more and more time to jazz, with such guest soloists (usually accompanied by La Locomotora Negra) as Hal Singer and Albert Nicholas (both 1972), Benny Waters (1972, 1978), Bill Coleman (1972, 1979), Guy Lafitte (1972–6, 1978–9), Tete Montoliu (1973–6, 1978), Gene Conners (1973–8, 1980), Wallace Davenport (1977), Buddy Tate (1979), and Joe Newman, Oliver Jackson, Harry Edison, Wild Bill Davis, Carrie Smith, and Red Richards (all 1980). The club remained wholly devoted to jazz from this early period into the 1990s; at some point after the mid-1980s it relocated from Carrer Tuset to Carrer Vallmajor. In the new century La Cova del Drac has presented mainly local jazz, rock, and pop groups. The venue hosts concerts organized by the AMJC (Associatió de Músicos de Jazz i Música Moderna de Catalunya).
(<http://www.atiza.com/bar.asp?Bar=LACOVADELDRAC> (2001))

——. **Harlem Jazz Club.** Carrer Comtessa de Sobradiel 8. An intimate club which flourished in the mid-1990s, it featured local musicians, but international guests who were performing at nearby festivals also participated in jam sessions there.

——. **Jamboree.** Plaça Reial 17. Owned by Ana and Juan Mas, it opened on 1 October 1959 and in its first two years employed only Catalan players. Jamboree was most important during its first period of operation, when it presented such diverse musicians and groups as Duke Ellington, Ella Fitzgerald, Elvin Jones, Lionel Hampton, Art Farmer, Chet Baker, Lucky Thompson, Peanuts Holland, Ornette Coleman, Stephane Grappelli, Guy Lafitte, and the Double Six. It closed around 1969. The club was operating again by the 1990s, when it regularly presented jazz groups and blues singers, including Peter King, Danilo Pérez, Jacky Terrasson, Lou Bennett, Tete Montoliu, and Art Farmer. Brad Mehldau played there with one of his first groups, a quartet consisting of Perico Sambeat, Jorge Rossy, and the latter's brother, the double bass player Mario Rossy.
(http://www.masimas.com/jamboree> (2000))

——. **Lamaga.** Plaça Calvo Sotelo [Plaça Francèsc Marià]. George Johnson's group made its début in Barcelona at this club late in 1946.

——. **Oasis.** Carrer de Canuda. Hot Club de Barcelona jam sessions were transferred from the Saratoga to the Oasis in 1948 and continued until 1950. Participants included Josep Puertas, George Johnson, and Don Byas.

——. **Pipa Club.** Plaça Reial 3. In 1992 this friendly and cozy club opened in an apartment on the first floor of one of the buildings in the famous Plaça Reial. Apart from its central role as a club for pipe smokers, it organized conferences, pool championships, and various cultural events, including important jazz concerts. But in 2000, after eight years of activity, the club was obliged to close because of problems associated with holding live performances in such premises. It has continued to present jazz (in the lobby of Hotel Oriente in 2000, and elsewhere), but no longer at its own venue.
(<http://www. bpipaclub.com> (2001))

——. **Saratoga Club.** Galerias Malda. From spring 1947 the Hot Club de Barcelona hosted jam sessions at the Saratoga whose participants included Josep Puertas, Joe Farreras, George Johnson and his band, Don Byas, and the young Tete Montoliu.

——. **Zeleste.** Carrer de la Plateria. Opened in 1973 by Victor Zou, this club was not wholly devoted to jazz, but among visiting Americans who appeared were Lou Bennett, Gerry Mulligan, Pharaoh Sanders, Johnny Griffin, Dexter Gordon, and Joe Newman.

BIBLIOGRAPHY

Barcelona

A. Papo: *El jazz a Catalunya* (Barcelona, 1985)

DONOSTIA. **Altxerri Pub-Galería.** Reina Regente 2. This two-story venue presents art and photographic exhibitions upstairs and blues, folk revival, and jazz concerts downstairs, mainly with Spanish musicians. Important international visitors are involved during the annual Donostiako Jazzaldía (Festival de Jazz de San Sebastián).
(<http://sansebastianhoy.com/recomienda/rec_loc_13.htm> (2001))

——. **Bebop Bar.** Paseo de Salamanca 3. Located just around the corner from the Altxerri Pub-Galería, this smaller and more modest club has a reputation for hosting jam sessions during the annual Donostiako Jazzaldía (Festival de Jazz de San Sebastián). The sessions last almost until daybreak and involve participants from all of the festival events, with musicians literally playing elbow-to-elbow in front of a crowd of standing listeners.

MADRID. **Balboa Club.** One of the three most important jazz clubs in Madrid, it presented musicians playing mainly in modern styles, but by the 1990s it was no longer in operation.

——. **Bourbon Street.** Together with the Balboa Club and the Whiskey Jazz Club, it was one Madrid's most important jazz clubs, presenting dixieland. It had closed by the 1990s.

——. **Café Berlin.** Jacometrezo 4. This club opened in the 1990s and became important as a venue for new local musicians and visiting artists to get together for very late-night jam sessions.

——. **Café Central.** Plaza de Angel 10. This venue has operated from 1983, presenting mainly Spanish musicians, but occasionally visiting Americans, performing in jazz, rock, folk revival, and Latin styles. Tete Montoliu played there throughout the month of August for many years, and during the 1990s Café Central hosted such artists as Lou Bennett, Barry Harris, George Cables, Ben Sidran, Brad Mehldau, Lew Tabackin, Jeanne Lee, and Paolo Fresu, among others.

——. **Café Jazz Populart.** Huertas 28. The café was in operation by the late 1990s. It offers groups in blues, country, and modern-jazz styles; rock, salsa, and folk revival bands are also featured. Visiting American and European players appear from time to time: Gary Bartz, Eddie Henderson, Wallace Roney, Sonny Fortune, Bob Mover, Jimmy Ponder, and Frank Lacy have performed as featured artists, and Paquito D'Rivera, Arturo Sandoval, and members of Lester Bowie's Brass Fantasy and of Lionel Hampton's big band are among those who have participated in jam sessions at the café. Many Spanish jazz musicians have also appeared, including Perico Sambeat, Jorge Pardo, Ximo Tebar, and Jorge Rossy. (<http://www.populart.es/historia.htm> (2001))

——. **Clamores Jazz y otras Músicas.** Albuquerque 14. This venue has operated contemporaneously with the Café Jazz Populart and follows a similar music policy. Among visitors during the 1990s were Tete Montoliu, Lou Bennett, Paul Motian, Roy Haynes, Benny Green, and Ben Sidran.

——. **Dizzy Jazz.** La Luz 8. Situated in Las Matas, a residential area on the outskirts of Madrid, Dizzy Jazz was in operation by the late 1990s, presenting mainly local jazz musicians on weekends.
(<http://www.musicaactual.com/dizzyjazz> (2001))

——. **Segundo Jazz.** Comandante Zorita 8. Spanish musicians, and occasionally visiting Americans, were performing there by the 1980s, but in the 1990s jazz was no longer featured.
(<http://www.madridhoy.net/recomienda/rec_ loc_13.htm> (2001))

——. **Whiskey Jazz Club.** The first jazz club in Madrid, it presented local musicians in alternation with visiting Americans, mainly in modern-jazz styles. Tete Montoliu held a lengthy residency there in the late 1960s. It had closed by the 1990s.

Ourense. **Café Latino.** Coronel Ceano 7. Café Latino was founded in 1986, and it has been devoted exclusively to jazz from at least the 1990s. Many leading American musicians have appeared there, including, in April 2001, Benny Green's trio. (<http://www.cedinor.net/latino/latino.htm> (2001))

San Sebastián. See Donostia.

Santiago de Compostela. **Dado-Dadá.** Alfredo Brañas 19. From the late 1990s this club has presented Spanish jazz musicians, though leading international players appear during the annual Festival de Jazz de Santiago de Compostela.

Seville. **Teatro Central.** Isla de la Cartuja. This beautiful and modern theater space was created during the international exposition in 1992 and thereafter has served as one of the most important venues for jazz in Spain. In November it hosts the festival Jazz en el Central, and in March a full weekend of concerts. Among those who appeared in the 1990s were Dave Douglas, John Zorn, Randy Weston, Lester Bowie, Ran Blake, Steve Coleman, Uri Caine, Abdullah Ibrahim, and Roscoe Mitchell. (<http://www.teatrocentral.com> (2001)

Terrassa. **Jazz Cava.** Carrer de Sant Quirze. Situated in a suburb of Barcelona (though outside the city limits), the Jazz Cava opened on 17 March 1971 and shared international guests with La Cova del Drac and the Zeleste (see above, Barcelona), notably Dizzy Reese, Art Farmer, Bill Coleman, Benny Waters, Ben Webster, Gene Conners, Johnny Griffin, Hal Singer, Slide Hampton, Buddy Tate, and Al Grey. Tete Montoliu also appeared there, as did various traditional-jazz groups. It operated into at least the mid-1980s. (A. Papo: *El jazz a Catalunya*, Barcelona, 1985)

——. **Nova Jazz Cava de Terrassa.** Passatge Tete Montoliu. On the site of a ballroom, l'Ateneu Terrassenc, built in 1896, the new Jazz Cava opened in 1994. Various styles of music are presented on the stage in this octagonally shaped auditorium, and it is a principal site for the annual Festival de Jazz de Terrassa. (<http://www.jazzterrassa.org> (2000))

Valencia. **Black Note Club.** Polo y Peyrolo 15. The principal venue for jazz in Valencia, this basement club has a reputation along the eastern Spanish coast for its bohemian flavor and as a refuge for jazz aficionados in the city. The Black Note has hosted many Spanish musicians and visiting international artists. (<http://www.resident.cc/wempre/sectores/cv/valencia/gastronomia/otros/CafeConcBlackNdefault.htm> (2001))

Valladolid. **Café Espana.** Plaza de la Fuente Dorada 8. Devoted exclusively to jazz, by the late 1990s the Café Espana was presenting many leading American and Spanish musicians.

SRI LANKA

Colombo. **Galle Face Hotel.** Herb Flemming led a band at this hotel in Ceylon (as Sri Lanka was then known) in 1934. Teddy Weatherford and Rudy Jackson played there from late July through August 1939, and in September 1940 Weatherford returned for a year-long engagement.

——. **Saxophone Jazz Club.** 46 Galle Road. By the year 2000 this was the principal jazz venue in Colombo.

BIBLIOGRAPHY

Colombo

P. Darke and R. Gulliver: "Teddy Weatherford," *Sv*, no.65 (1976), 175
——: "Roy Butler's Story," *Sv*, no.71 (1977), 178

SWEDEN

Gothenburg. **Art-dur.** See Nefertiti.

——. **The Jazz.** See Liseberg.

——. **Kungsgillet.** Kungstorget. Larger and more elegant than Kungshall, this dance hall featured the ten-piece orchestra led by the saxophonist Malte Johnson. The trumpeter Sven Sjöholm and the drummer Kenneth Fagerlund were among other bandleaders who performed at Kungsgillet before it closed in the 1960s.

——. **Kungshall.** Kungstorget. The saxophonist Sonny Persson led a band in this old, rather shabby dance hall; among his sidemen were the trumpeter Sture Dahlander, the pianist Gösta Bredberg, and, briefly, Bengt Hallberg.

——. **Liseberg.** This amusement park opened in 1923, mainly for summer seasons, but its theater and restaurant and some other activities operated in winter as well. The Jernås Collegians was the first orchestra to play modern dance music at Liseberg. From 1931 the band led by the pianist Åke Fagerlund played at the outdoor dance pavilion, commonly called The Jazz, and from 1940 he performed at the newly inaugurated indoor dance pavilion, Rotundan, an elegant hall with a flower-decked fountain and expensive light fixtures which accommodated more than 1200 people. In 1944 Fagerlund was succeeded by the saxophonist Malte Johnson, whose group over the next 14 years included at various times the trumpeters Bengt-Arne Wallin, Lasse Samuelsson, Gösta Nilsson, Putte Björn, and Arnold Johansson, the trombonists Rickard Brodén, Bror Skogehall, and Andreas Skjold, the saxophonists Börje Fredriksson, Georg Björklund, Rolf Bäckman, and Rolf Lindell, the drummers Bert Dahlander and Arne Milefors, and the singer Sonya Hedenbratt.

In 1953 the old Rotunda was rebuilt as a modern dance restaurant, Rondo, licensed to serve wine, spirits, and beer on the premises; Johnson's 14-piece orchestra continued as the house band. He was followed by the bandleader Sören Ahrnot (1959–60), whose group featured the tenor saxophonist Erik Norström. From 1961 into the new century the Danish violinist Ronnie Hartley has led his Light Music Orchestra at the amusement park, and there is no longer a specific resident dance or jazz band.

——. **Nefertiti.** Originally named Art-dur, the Nefertiti is a licensed jazz club and restaurant and hence (under Swedish regulations) offers jazz for listening and not for dancing. Founded in 1978 by the nonprofit organization Jazz i Göteborg, it presents more than 220 concerts every year in a range of genres, including jazz, improvised music, blues, soul, funk, and ethnic styles. Many Swedish and international jazz stars have played there.

BIBLIOGRAPHY

<http://www.ejn.it/promo/nefertiti.htm> (2000)
<http://www.nefertiti.se/sv/flash/index.html> (2000)

——. **Wauxhall.** Första Långgatan. This public dance hall is often called the Gothenburg Nalen because of its similar interior decoration to the Nalen in Stockholm and its presentation of jazz-inspired dance music. In the 1920s the bandleader Åke Fagerlund appeared there. In 1932 the Stockholm jazz bandleader Sam Samson took over, and in 1935 a new saxophonist, Malte Johnson, became a member of the band. Johnson and his Swinging Septet were engaged to play at the club from 1936 to 1943, when he transferred to Kungsgillet. Thereafter the trumpeter Sven Sjöholm led the resident orchestra, and Wauxhall became a gathering point for visiting jazz stars; its nocturnal jam sessions were legendary among a whole generation of Swedish jazzmen. Bengt Hallberg and Jan Johansson are among those artists who started their careers playing there in a West Coast jazz style.

——. **Rondo.** See Liseberg.

——. **Rotundan.** See Liseberg.

Malmö. **Amiralen.** From 1939 Malmö's Folkets Park (People's Park) housed the Amiralen, a dance palace accommodating more than 1250 dancers. Count Basie and Duke Ellington are among those visiting Americans whose bands gave concerts and then played for the nightly dancing at the venue. The best-known Swedish bandleader in residency there was Harry Arnold. The Amiralen is now used more for conferences and expositions than for jazz or dance music.

——. **Arena.** This dance hall was open nightly to the public. In residence from 1939 to 1948 was the ten-piece band led by the trumpeter Gösta Tönne, whose sidemen included the saxophonists Carl-Henrik Norin, Rolf Blomqvist, and Lasse Schöning, the pianist Gunnar Svensson, and the drummer Gunnar Ohlsson.

Stockholm. **Bern's Restaurant.** Berzelli Park. This restaurant, the largest in Stockholm, opened in the city center in 1863, and from the 1930s to 1943 it regularly presented jazz for dancing, played by the orchestras of Håkan von Eichwald, Charles Redland, and Arne Hülphers, among others; Jimmie Lunceford's orchestra alternated with von Eichwald's during one night in 1937. In 1955, after a ban (introduced in 1896) on allowing variety artists to perform in venues where spirits were consumed was finally lifted, it again became profitable to present jazz in restaurants, and the music was played regularly at Bern's in the 1960s. A performance there by Count Basie in July 1968 was recorded by Swedish Radio and transmitted later in that year under the title "We go to the Jazz Concert," and Swedish public television broadcast Woody Herman's performance at the restaurant during one of Herman's many tours of Sweden in the 1970s. Among others who appeared at Bern's during this second period of jazz activity were Nancy Wilson, Cab Calloway, the Swed-Danes (Alice Babs, Svend Asmussen, and the guitarist Ulrik Neumann), Bengt Hallberg, Arne Domnérus, and Putte Wickman. By the early 1980s all types of dance music and jazz had ceased to be presented.

——. **Bal Palais.** Kungsgatan 65. This public dance hall, which opened as Bal Tabarin in 1924, changed ownership and took the name Bal Palais in 1931 and thereafter presented the orchestras led by Sune Lundwall (1932–44), Thore Ehrling (1944–55), and Simon Brehm (1955–61). The venue has continued to present dance music into the new century, but not in a jazz vein.

——. **China Theatre.** Berzelli Park. This summer variety theater was in operation from 1937 to 1964. Both Swedish and international jazz artists gave stage performances there, and Svend Asmussen's quintet played as the resident band in 1942. By the late 1990s it was again open as a theater all year round.

——. **Embassy.** See Salle de Paris.

——. **Fasching.** Kungsgatan 63. On the site of a theater café and a dance hall which operated under various owners and names, Fasching opened in 1975 and engaged many internationally known jazz musicians, playing mostly free jazz, fusion, and Latin jazz. Among those who have performed there are Ornette Coleman, the Art Ensemble of Chicago, Don Pullen and George Adams, Tomasz Stańko, Steve Lacy, James Moody, John Tchicai, Bobo Stenson, Joe Henderson, Carla Bley, Wayne Shorter, and Rena Rama. (<http://www.fasching.se> (2001))

——. **Fenix-Kronprinsen.** Adolf Fredriks Kyrkogata 10. This venue was inaugurated in 1912 as the Grand Palais Phoenix and was intended to serve as an indoor sports arena, but during construction the plans changed and instead it became an entertainment complex comprising a concert hall, a winter garden, a restaurant with bar, a music café, and an oyster bar. From the late 1920s the restaurant, named Kaos (Chaos), served wine, and in 1930 Håkan von Eichwald began to lead the first big band in Sweden there; Louis Armstrong (1933) and Coleman Hawkins (1934) appeared as his guest soloists. In 1934 the restaurant won the right to serve spirits on the premises, and it took a new name, Fenix-Kronprinsen (the Phoenix Crown Prince Room); Arne Hülphers's orchestra became the resident band. Profits declined during the war, and in 1941 the whole complex was offered for sale. A group from the Pentecostal movement was the only interested buyer, and Fenix-Kronprinsen became a free church with a coffee room attached.

——. **Gamlingen.** See Stampen.

——. **Gazell Club.** Österlånggatan. In 1950 the premises, which had been used as stock rooms for linens and as a potato cellar, took the name of Dag Haeggqvist's record label, Gazell, and promoted traditional jazz. It became an important center for this style in Stockholm. The club closed in 1971.

——. **Gröna Lund.** Djurgården Island. This summertime amusement park, situated on one of the many small islands on which the center of Stockholm was built, has several bandstands and dance pavilions where the orchestras led by Seymour Österwall, Carl-Henrik Norin, Arne Domnérus, Putte Wickman, and others appeared. The big bands of Duke Ellington, Count Basie, and Maynard Ferguson were among those who performed on the park's outdoor bandstands; portions of Basie's performances from summer 1962 are preserved on the album *Basie in Sweden* (Roul. 52099).

——. **Gyllene Cirkeln** [Golden Circle]. The best-known nightclub in the city, it presented performances by both Scandinavian and visiting American musicians, among them Coleman Hawkins, Bud Powell, George Russell, Sonny Rollins, Bill Evans (ii), Albert Ayler, Johnny Griffin, Lucky Thompson, Ben Webster, and Cecil Taylor. During this period Sveriges Radio AB (the Swedish Radio Corporation) broadcast every Friday night from the club. A number of recordings were made there, notably by Lars Gullin, as well as *The Ornette Coleman Trio at the Golden Circle* (1965, BN 84224-5). Gyllene Cirkeln closed around 1967.

——. **Kaos** [Chaos]. See Fenix-Kronprinsen.

——. **Maxim.** In the 1940s and 1950s this small but popular ballroom presented jazz a couple of nights per week for members only. The accordionist and trumpeter Lill-Arne Söderberg was among the bandleaders who performed at Maxim, and the pianist Gunnar Svensson, the saxophonist Rolf Blomqvist, Putte Wickman, and Gunnar Nilsson appeared as sidemen. In autumn 1946 and spring 1947 Thore Jederby led a quartet with Jack Norén on drums and either Bjarne Nerem on tenor saxophone or Ingmar Glanzelius on clarinet or alto saxophone; the quartet was somewhat controversial because of the extent of its allegiance to the bop style. After the Jederby period, a smoother style of dance music followed. Like so many other ballrooms, in the 1960s Maxim was turned into business premises.

——. **Nalen** [Grand National]. Regeringsgatan 74. The building in which Nalen is situated was constructed in 1886 to house a fraternal order, but by the turn of the 20th century it had transferred into more worldly hands. Around World War I, when public dancing became popular in Sweden, crowds danced to ragtime favorites, traditional folk waltzes, and polkas. From the 1920s, the first "jazz decade" in Sweden, the dance tunes were predominantly jazz standards played by the legendary Paramountorkestern, the first real jazz group in Sweden. The early gold and glitter of the premises, however, had obviously worn off, and in the mid-1930s Gustaf "Topsy" Lindblom purchased the whole establishment for a symbolic sum, one Swedish crown. Lindblom wanted to give the young generation healthy leisure-time entertainment at low cost, and at Nalen they could dance to the music of the best national orchestras and international soloists; the only refreshments (which were also included in the admission fee) were non-alcoholic beverages, sandwiches, and cookies.

Seymour Österwall's orchestra was resident at Nalen for 14 years (1935–48); his group was followed by those led by Putte Wickman (1948–60), Carl-Henrik Norin (1948-62), Arne Domnérus (1951–64), and Hacke Björksten (1954–9). Among other Swedish jazz stars to appear were Lars Gullin, Jan Johansson, Rune Gustafsson, Bengt Hallberg, and Åke Persson, and nightly jam sessions attracted such famous artists as Stan Getz, Jack Teagarden, Charlie Parker, and Sonny Rollins. Nalen also offered all sorts of stage performances, bringing professionals together with amateurs from the venue's young crowd.

Following a short period as a rallying-point for Stockholm's rock musicians, the whole quarter where Nalen was situated was scheduled to be demolished. But (as was the case with the Fenix-Kronprinsen) the venue was saved by the Pentecostal movement. After around thirty years as a free church, Nalen once again came into the hands of Swedish musicians: Svenska Artisters och Musikers Intersseorganisation (Swedish Artists' and Musicians Interest Association) purchased the building and completely restored its original interior. The club reopened in November 1998 offering a varied program, though jazz is still a main component. (<http://www.sami.se/nalen2/index.html> (2001))

——. **Nöjesfältet.** Djurgården Island. This amusement park, smaller and in all respects less sophisticated than Gröna Lund, operated from 1924 to 1957. It was of greatest importance to the first generation of Swedish jazz musicians: Charles Redland and Thore Ehrling were among those who held engagements there at the beginning of their careers in the 1920s. International guests were not so usual at Nöjesfältet, but in the summer of 1938, during a period when the park was under the direction and ownership of J. E. Lindgren, Leon Abbey's orchestra played at the outdoor dancing pavilion.

——. **Salle de Paris.** Sturegatan 10. One of many venues at which a legal dance hall (offering teas and fruit cobblers) operated in conjunction with an illegal nightclub (serving spirits), the Salle de Paris presented a swing group in the 1930s, when it was known as the Embassy. Later Simon Brehm played there with the first bop group in Sweden, consisting of the trumpeter Leppe Sundewall, Arne Domnérus, Gösta Theselius, Thore Swanerud, and the drummer Sven Bollhem.

——. **Stampen.** Stora Nygatan 5. Stampen (the Pawn Shop) took its name from a pawn shop which had formerly operated in the adjoining building, at Stora Gråmunkegränd 7. From 1968 until 1981 this nightclub hosted jam sessions in traditional and modern styles for Swedish jazz musicians and visiting stars from Europe and the USA. In 1981 its premises were taken over by another club, the Gamlingen (the Old One), which has been of less importance to jazz.

——. **Vinterpalatset.** Norra Bantorget. The Vinterpalatset building was remodeled as a hotel for the Stockholm Olympic Games in 1912 and then transformed into a concert hall, virtually the only one of the kind until the city's concert hall was completed in 1926. Thus many Swedish and foreign soloists performed there, irrespective of the style in which they played; Louis Armstrong appeared in 1933 and Fats Waller in 1938. The Vinterpalatset was inaugurated as a dance palace on Boxing day 1943, to the vexation of the Swedish clergy. It was immense by comparison with other Swedish dance floors, offering room for 1500 participants, and thus acquired an informal name, Snö-vidden (in English, literally "snow-width," and in Swedish a pun on the snow-covered high plateaus, called snövidder). Lulle Ellboj led a youthful and progressive 16-piece big band from the opening in 1943 to spring 1947, with Gösta Theselius and Gunnar Lundén-Welden serving as arrangers and music directors. Ellboj's trumpeters Nisse Skoog, Anders Swärd, and Rolf Ericson became legendary among the Swedish jazz-loving public for their solos and ensemble playing, which featured a vigorous brass vibrato; Arne Domnérus and Theselius were also among Ellboj's sidemen. Charles Redland's semi-professional band succeeded Ellboj's group. Redland's band played three nights per week, but for decreasing numbers of dancers. Vinterpalatset was then transformed into a wide-screen cinema, but was demolished within a few years.

——. **La Visite.** A restaurant providing music for dancers, La Visite encouraged young jazz musicians in the 1940s and 1950s. Miff Görling led an eight- to 11-piece band there, with Arne Domnérus, Putte Wickman, Gösta Törner, and Thore Swanerud among his sidemen.

STRÖMSHOLM. **Jazz Museum.** The museum was founded in 1998 with the reed player Rolf Carvenius as its director. In addition to offering exhibits and a restaurant serving Cajun food, it hosts, every night from late May through August, outdoor concerts featuring Swedish, Scandinavian, and (occasionally) international jazz artists. (<http://www.jazz-museum.com> (2000))

SUNDSVALL. **Wivex.** During the 1940s and 1950s this privately run dance hall in a small town on the Baltic coast brought in professional leaders, including Arne Domnérus and Charles Redland, to direct semiprofessional and amateur orchestras.

SWITZERLAND

BASEL. **Bird's Eye Jazz Club.** Elsässerstrasse 184 (summer 1994 – May 1998); Kohlenberg 20 (from 18 Feb 1999). This club and restaurant opened in summer 1994 in conjunction with the founding of the organization Jazz-Live Basel, and except for a period of reorganization during the latter part of 1998 (when it relocated to the Kohlenberg premises) it has presented small groups from three to five nights per week. (<http://www.birdseye.ch> (2001))

——. **Chicago Hotel.** Aeschengraben 31. Located within the Hilton Hotel, this has been, along with the Bird's Eye Jazz Club, the only jazz club operating in Basel on a regular basis into the new century.

BERNE. **Chikito.** Coleman Hawkins played with a Swiss band at this long-standing jazz venue in summer 1936. In 1950 the club was described as "a regular hang-out for jazz musicians and enthusiasts": Bill Coleman led bands there for a series of residencies in 1949, 1950–51, and 1952, with Benny Waters as a sideman in this last year. Coleman, who met his Swiss wife, Lily, at the club, made many return visits, and in May 1965 appeared with Stuff Smith. Buck Clayton also played at the Chikito, in 1950 with Coleman and in 1967 with Guy Lafitte.

BIBLIOGRAPHY

A. Goepfert: "The 'Lion' and others in Switzerland," *JJ*, iii/5 (1950), 5
B. Coleman: *Trumpet Story: souvenirs d'un grand du jazz* (Paris, 1981; Eng. orig., London and Boston, 1990, as *Trumpet Story*)

——. **Mahogany Hall.** Klösterlistutz 18. Mahogany Hall opened in 1968 in association with the Longstreet Jazzclub and presented traditional jazz and swing. By 1987 it had hosted more than 1800 concerts, with Oscar Klein, Bill Coleman, Barney Bigard, Albert Nicholas, Claude Luter, and Clark Terry among those who appeared. After undergoing renovation for 27 months, it reopened in February 1990 and has continued its activities into the new century, presenting both jazz and folk groups. (<http://www.mahogany.ch> (2001))

——. **Marian's Jazzroom.** Engestrasse 54. It opened in the Hotel Innere Enge on 8 December 1992 and thereafter presented Jon Hendricks, Abbey Lincoln, Lillian Boutté, Carrie Smith, Harry Edison, Randy Sandke, Clark Terry, Roy Hargrove, Nicholas Payton, Lew Tabackin, John Scofield, Paul Bollenback, and dozens of other internationally known artists. (<http://www.mariansjazzroom.ch> (2001))

GENEVA. **Blue Note.** Chris McGregor's Blue Notes played there at some point during their time in Switzerland in the years 1964–5.

——. **Maxim's.** 2 avenue Thalberg and Place des Alpes. Dance hall. The music played for dancing included jazz from at least the early 1940s. From time to time between 1941 and 1955 the French trumpeter Philippe Brun led his bands there.

——. **Palladium.** Rue du Stand. Sidney Bechet held a month's residency there with the band of the Swiss soprano saxophonist Claude Aubert in spring 1954 and returned to the club in December for a performance in which he was reunited with another New Orleans clarinetist, Albert Nicholas.

——. **Sud des Alpes.** 10 rue des Alpes. This modest venue of just over 100 seats has engaged leading musicians from 1975, when Charles Mingus, Elvin Jones, Archie Shepp, Steve Lacy, and Steve McCall appeared. From 1981 the organization AMR (Association pour l'Encouragement de la Musique Improvisée; founded 1973) has presented about 90 concerts per year there, involving local, national, and international performers.

BIBLIOGRAPHY

<http://www.amr-geneve.ch> (2000)
<http://www.ejn.it/promo/sud.htm> (2000)
<http://www.fusions.ch/sud-des-alpes.html> (2000)

USTER. **Music-Container.** Asylstrasse 10. By the late 1990s this was the venue for the activities of the Jazzclub Uster (founded in 1963), which presents approximately 30 concerts each year. George Gruntz, Charlie Byrd, Nat Adderley, Daniel Humair, John Abercrombie, Lou Donaldson, and Pierre Favre are among those who have performed there. (<http://www.jcuster.ch> (2000))

ZURICH. **Club Africana.** In 1962 Abdullah Ibrahim was contracted to play there for 20 weeks a year for three years; later that year his South African trio members Johnny Gertze and Makaya Ntshoko played with him. Chris McGregor's Blue Notes held a residency at the club in 1964–5.

——. **Casa Bar.** Münster-Gasse 30. This nightclub, owned by Maurice Berger, has concentrated chiefly on presenting traditional jazz. Bill Coleman, Albert Nicholas, and Wallace Bishop are among the musicians who performed there; the groups most often engaged to play are the British bands Piccadilly Six and Bob Wallis's Storyville Jazzmen.

——. **Embassy Club.** Active from at least the mid-1950s, in 1957 it presented performances by Sammy Price with the band of George Johnson.

——. **Moods.** Schiffbaustrasse 6. The club, which holds a maximum of 150 people, opened in August 1992 and thereafter has presented concerts from Tuesday through Saturday in most weeks of the year. Hundreds of leading musicians have appeared at the venue.

BIBLIOGRAPHY

<http://www.ejn.it/promo/moods.htm> (2000)
<http://www.music.ch/moods/Sites/veranstalter.html> (2000)
<http://www.moods.ch> (2001)

——. **Rote Fabrik.** Seestrasse 395. The Rote Fabrik (Red Factory) is just that, a red-brick industrial plant built in 1892 and converted into a cultural and community center during the latter part of the 1970s. From the 1990s it has hosted concerts of jazz and avant-garde art music, including the Taktlos Festival. (<http://www.rotefabrik.ch/homepage_de.html> (2001))

——. **Widder-Bar.** Widdergasse 6. Active at least from the early 1980s, it has presented jazz in various styles; among the American visitors who appeared there were Wild Bill Davis and Oliver Jackson, each of whom held a short residency in 1983. From 1995 it continued within the newly renovated Widder Hotel. Abbey Lincoln, Hank Jones, and Phil Woods are among those who have appeared at the bar in the new century.

BIBLIOGRAPHY

J. Simmen: "Jazz au Widder-Bar," *BHcF*, no.306 (1983), 9
<http://www.widderhotel.ch/de/bar> (2001)

UNITED KINGDOM See England and Scotland.

USA

Acton, MA. **Acton Jazz Café.** 452 Great Road (Route 2A Acton). Opened in 1996, the Acton Jazz Café features a rotating schedule of thirty-six bands from the Boston area. Jerry Bergonzi leads a group at the café every Tuesday evening; Billy Pierce, Bruce Gertz, and Adam Nussbaum have also performed there, mainly for listeners having dinner. It regularly hosts well-attended jazz jam sessions. (<http://www.actonjazzcafe.com> (2001))

Akron, OH. **The Bank.** 316 South Main Street. In 1978 it brought in Art Blakey, Red Garland, Yusef Lateef, Gary Burton, and others.

——. **East Market Gardens.** In the late 1930s it featured, among others, Fats Waller, Jimmie Lunceford, Earl Hines, Fletcher Henderson, Count Basie, Andy Kirk, Don Albert, Lucky Millinder, and Roy Eldridge.

——. **The Nite Club.** 289 Darrow Road. In 1978 McCoy Tyner, Lionel Hampton, Sonny Rollins, Woody Shaw, Joe Williams, Dexter Gordon, and others played here.

Alhambra, CA. See Los Angeles (metropolitan area).

Anaheim, CA. See Los Angeles (metropolitan area).

Annapolis, MD. **King of France Tavern.** 16 Church Circle. This tavern, located within the Maryland Inn and dating from 1784, is best known as the principal venue where Charlie Byrd played for many years. The Left Bank Jazz Society, in addition to its regular activities in Baltimore, has organized concerts by major jazz musicians at the King of France Tavern, and occasionally these have been broadcast on the Baltimore station WBJC-FM.

Arkansas River. **SS *J.S.*** This steamer, owned by the Streckfus Line, was purpose built for the excursion trade and named after Captain John Streckfus, who had founded the line in 1884. The boat was launched in 1901 and plied out of Little Rock; 175 feet long, it had a ballroom with a dance floor 100 feet by 27 feet and could carry 2000 passengers. It was the first riverboat on which Fate Marable performed – he joined the band led by the violinist Emil Flindt (or Flint) around 1907, and by 1910 he was leading his own small ragtime band. The *J.S.* was destroyed by fire in 1910; its namesake, the *J.S. Deluxe* (often, confusingly, referred to simply as the *J.S.*) traveled on the Mississippi River (see below) from 1919.

Asbury Park, NJ. **Smile-a-While Café.** One of many resorts near Atlantic City, Asbury Park was sometimes included on the itinerary of touring jazz musicians. Claude Hopkins's band worked at the Smile-a-While Café around 1924.

Aspen, CO. **Sunnie's Rendezvous.** This supper club, owned by Sunnie Anderson, presented Ralph Sutton from September 1964 to 1969, both as an unaccompanied soloist and as the leader of distinguished groups involving such musicians as Edmond Hall, Ruby Braff, Bob Wilber, and Milt Hinton, among many others. Sutton and Anderson married in June 1965, and in December of that year they relocated within Aspen, moving Sunnie's Rendezvous to the patio of the Gallun Building. They sold the club in October 1969. (D. Shacter: *Piano Man: the Story of Ralph Sutton*, Chicago, 1975, rev. and enlarged [2]/1994, as *Loose Shoes: the Story of Ralph Sutton*)

Astoria, NY. **Momart Café.** In 1939 Sidney Bechet played there in a trio with Willie "the Lion" Smith and the drummer Dinah Taylor.

Atlanta. **La Carrousel.** 830 Martin Luther King, Jr., Drive, SW. This nightclub is located within the Paschal Motor Hotel in an African-American district of Atlanta; the venue opened as a restaurant in 1947 and expanded into a hotel and club in the 1950s. In the 1960s and 1970s such musicians as Ramsey Lewis, Dizzy Gillespie, Jimmy Smith, Count Basie, and Cannonball Adderley appeared at La Carrousel. The club remained open into the 1990s, and continued to offer jazz on weekend nights, but was no longer a significant venue for the music.

——. **Churchill Grounds.** 660 Peachtree Street. From around the late 1990s this small café has been the principal venue for jazz in Atlanta. Cedar Walton, Chico Freeman, Donald Harrison, Marcus Printup, and Philip Harper are among those who have performed there.
(<http://churchillgrounds.com> (2001))

——. **Dante's Down the Hatch.** 3380 Peachtree Road. This multi-level restaurant, owned by Dante Stephenson, is meant to resemble various aspects of shipping, and the jazz area is built on the theme of a 19th-century wharf and ship. The pianist Paul Mitchell has led a trio there from 1970 into the new century, and from time to time visiting artists have appeared, including Max Roach, Keith Jarrett, and Chuck Mangione. Around the late 1980s to early 1990s there was also a second Dante's Down the Hatch in the Underground Atlanta shopping and entertainment complex.
(<http://www.dantesdownthehatch.com> (2001))

——. **81.** 81 Decatur Street. The larger of two theaters on Decatur Street, it was the principal venue for African-American artists in Atlanta in the 1920s and 1930s, notably Bessie Smith.

——. **Just Jazz.** 2101 Tula Street, NW. For a few years in the early 1990s this lounge presented such artists as Ramsey Lewis, Freddie Hubbard, and Lionel Hampton.

——. **Royal Peacock.** 186 Auburn Avenue. Opened in 1949, this two-story venue (with a theater on the upper floor) presented jazz, pop, and rhythm-and-blues artists, including Lucky Millinder, Cab Calloway, and Nat "King" Cole.

——. **Sambuca Jazz Café.** 3102 Piedmont Road, NE. Arising from a successful enterprise begun in Dallas in 1991, this was the third Sambuca Jazz Café to be established in the 1990s. It offers Mediterranean cuisine.
(<http://www.sambucajazzcafe.com/atlanta.html> (2001))

——. **Waluhaje.** West Lake Avenue. In the 1950s this was a luxury hotel which hosted dances and concerts, with music at times being provided by such well-known artists as Dinah Washington, Tony Bennett, Ella Fitzgerald, and, in December 1956, Dizzy Gillespie.

Atlantic City, NJ. **Cotton Club.** 15–17 Illinois Avenue. This club presented Dinah Washington in 1958 and Louie Bellson's band with Pearl Bailey in 1959.

——. **Paradise Club.** In operation by at least the early 1930s, the Paradise Club engaged important jazz musicians to perform during the summer season. Lucille Hegamin worked there in 1933-4, and Count Basie was resident from June to August 1947.

——. **Silver Slipper.** One of the earlier clubs in Atlantic City, it was open by the early 1920s. Joe Venuti and Eddie Lang regularly led a band there for summer seasons through the decade.

Baltimore. **Al-Ho Club.** Frederick Avenue. It served for about six months from 8 August 1964 as the first venue for performances organized by the city's Left Bank Jazz Society.

——. **Carlin's Park.** Tommy Ladnier played there in the band led by Billy Fowler in 1926, and Cuba Austin's Original Cotton-Pickers, which toured widely in the USA, played one of its last engagements there in 1934.

——. **Club Astoria.** 1309–11 Edmonson Avenue. This club was in existence by December 1935, when Lucky Millinder and the Mills Blue Rhythm Band played there. In August–September 1936 it presented Blanche Calloway's band and from late 1938 into 1939 the Harlem Dictators, the first band to record for the Savoy label.

——. **Famous Ballroom.** 1717 North Charles Street. After two fires severely damaged the Madison Club, the Left Bank Jazz Society transferred its activities to this ballroom in central Baltimore. In April 1968 Joe Henderson recorded the album *Four!* there accompanied by Wynton Kelly's trio (Verve 314-523657-2). Later the ballroom closed and the society relocated to the Teamsters Union Hall. The society taped all of its concerts at the Famous Ballroom, but owing to a dispute over the rights these (other than the Henderson album) began to be issued only with the establishment of a new label, M, around the year 2000.

——. **Madison Club.** Madison Street and Chester Street. Located in East Baltimore, this large room replaced the Al-Ho Club in 1965 as the site for Sunday concerts sponsored by the Left Bank Jazz Society.

——. **New Albert Auditorium** [New Albert Hall; New Albert Casino]. 1234 Pennsylvania Avenue. This venue was presenting jazz by 1923. The Baltimore-based band of Ike Dixon appeared there frequently, along with many other local bands. The hall was a regular stopping point for name bands and bandleaders, including the 10 Cotton Pickers, led by the pianist Bobby Lee (1924), the saxophonist Billy Fowler and his Club Alabam Orchestra (1926, billed as "better than Fletcher Henderson"), Horace Henderson (1926, 1930), Chick Webb (1927), Fletcher Henderson (annually, 1928–31), Jelly Roll Morton (1929), McKinney's Cotton Pickers, Zack Whyte, Johnson's Happy Pals (led by the drummer Roy Johnson), and Fess Williams (all 1929, 1930), Louis Armstrong, Cecil Scott, and Charlie Johnson (all 1930), Cab Calloway (1931, 1933), Don Redman, Claude Hopkins, and Duke Ellington (all 1932), and Blanche Calloway (1933); in later years Edgar Hayes (1941) and Noble Sissle (1945) appeared there. The auditorium was a regular venue for functions organized by Baltimore's African-American musicians' local.

——. **New Haven Lounge.** 1552 Havenwood Road. From the early 1990s this restaurant and nightclub has been the leading venue for jazz in Baltimore. Gary Bartz, Ralph Moore, Steve Wilson, Joey DeFrancesco, Paul Bollenback, and Sonny Fortune were among those who appeared early in the decade.

——. **Regent Theatre.** Pennsylvania Avenue at Pitcher Street. The Regent was frequently visited by African-American revues, in one of which Perry Bradford appeared in 1919. It regularly presented singers working on the vaudeville circuits, including Mamie Smith (September 1921, November 1923, July 1927), Ethel Waters (November 1921, December 1925, April 1926), Eva Taylor with Clarence Williams (July 1922), and Lucille Hegamin (December 1926). By mid-1928 it had become a cinema.

——. **Royal.** 1329 Pennsylvania Avenue. This venue was built as the Douglass, "the finest colored theatre in America, owned and controlled by colored people," but the venture under that name failed. It reopened on 30 November 1925 as the Royal and featured traveling African-American revues. Bills in 1926 include the names Bessie Smith (January, March), *Bamville Dandies* and the bandleader Edwin Swayze (both February), Ma Rainey (April), *Tan Town Topics*, with Fats Waller's band (April), *Go Get 'em*, with Gus Aiken's band (May, July), Clara Smith (May), Ethel Waters (July), Sara Martin and Mamie Smith (both September), and *Desires of 1927* with Adelaide Hall (October). January 1927 brought *Neath the Southern Moon* with Lovey [*sic*] Austin and Hazel Meyers. This pattern of presentation continued until the mid-1930s. In June 1934 *Dixie Follies* featured Wilton Crawley. The theater was refurbished in summer 1936 and it reopened on 25 September, with Fats Waller, under white management. Over the next two decades it served as one of the major concert halls for touring African-American artists. The building was demolished in 1971.

——. **Sportsmen's Lounge.** 4723 Gwynn Oak Avenue. This handsome nightclub with a large stage flourished as a jazz venue in the 1960s, when it was owned by the football player Lenny Moore; Count Basie's orchestra, Dexter Gordon, Sonny Stitt, and Gene Ammons were among those who appeared. The lounge has held Monday night jam sessions, usually led by the tenor saxophonist Mickey Fields, for more than two decades and extending into the new century. It is known for supporting emerging local artists; Cyrus Chestnut, for example, played there early in his career.
(<http://www.citypaper.com/2000-07-12/music4.html> (2001))

——. **Teamsters Union Hall.** 6000 Erdman Avenue. This has been the site for weekly Sunday concerts organized by the Left Bank Jazz Society into the new century.

——. **Wonderland Park.** Billed as "the Colored Coney Island of America" and "the Coney Island of the South," this was a regular open-air venue during the 1920s for presentations involving jazz by both local and visiting groups. Elmer Snowden's Jazz Kings appeared in June 1923, Cliff Jackson's Krazy Kats in September 1923, Fletcher Henderson's orchestra in August 1925, July 1926, and August 1929, Horace Henderson and his 10 Collegians in July 1927, and King Oliver and his Dixie Syncopators in June 1928. Jazz-band contests, often pitting Ike Dixon's locally based group against out-of-town bands, were a regular feature of the programming. Dixon's band battled in June 1930 against Johnson's Happy Pals (led by the drummer Roy Johnson) and a fortnight later against Duke Ellington.

BIBLIOGRAPHY

Baltimore

<http://www.baltimoremd.com/leftbank/lbhist.html> (2001)

For another venue in the Baltimore metropolitan area see Catonsville, MD.

Baton Rouge, LA. **Bernard Hall.** Dance hall. It was used as a venue for minstrel shows and was on the Theater Owners' Booking Association circuit. The hall did not employ a permanent music director but relied on each group that played there to administer the running of the establishment during its residency. Among the musicians who appeared at the hall were Joe Darensbourg and Kid Ory with his band.

Bel Air, CA. See Los Angeles (metropolitan area).

Berkeley, CA. **Big Bear Tavern.** Redwood Canyon, in the Berkeley Hills, near Oakland. Roadhouse. Jazz was presented there from at least the late 1930s and the management developed a policy of mounting all-night jam sessions. The musicians who regularly took part included Lu Watters and some of the sidemen from his big band, with whom in 1940 he formed his Yerba Buena Jazz Band.

——. **Maybeck Recital Hall.** 1537 Euclid Street. Located in a house designed by the architect Bernard Maybeck in 1914, and owned and operated by the jazz pianist Dick Whittington, it has been the site of unaccompanied solo concerts given by many of the leading jazz pianists on Sunday afternoons. These events have been captured periodically on a lengthy series of CDs recorded by Concord from 1989, when JoAnne Brackeen played there; a parallel series of concerts by distinguished duos has followed from the early 1990s.

Berwyn, IL. **Red Arrow Club.** 6927 Pershing Road. This nightclub in the metropolitan area of Chicago was active from at least the mid-1950s under the ownership of Otto Kubik. Franz Jackson's Original Jass All Stars, which included Bob Shoffner, Al Wynn, and Lawrence Dixon, held a ten-year residency there from 1957.

Beverly Hills, CA. See Los Angeles (metropolitan area).

Boston. **Berklee Performance Center.** 136 Massachusetts Avenue. Built in 1945, the center adjoins the Berklee College of Music. It handles multiple functions, including graduation ceremonies, educational clinics, student recitals, and occasional concerts in a variety of musical styles. Gary Burton, Pat Metheny, Jeff "Tain" Watts, and many others have performed there. (<http://www.berkleebpc.com> (2001))

——. **Bob the Chef's.** 604 Columbus Avenue. Although Bob the Chef's had been in existence as a diner since the early 1960s, it did not become a jazz venue until Daryl Settles, who bought the club in 1989, initiated a music policy in 1994. It is now a community restaurant serving exclusively New Orleans Cajun food and hosting jazz regularly during the week. Ensembles are led mainly by student groups, but professional musicians have performed there. The club sees a mixture of mainstream and smooth-jazz artists. (<http://www.bobthechefs.com> (2001))

——. **Copley Square Hotel.** See Mahogany Hall and Storyville.

——. **Crescent Club.** This nightclub was in existence from at least the early 1930s. During an extended stay in Massachusetts in the winter of 1933–4 Pee Wee Russell held a residency at the Crescent with Bobby Hackett and Teddy Roy.

——. **Good Life.** Milk Street. The Good Life was opened by Brian O'Neill in January 1997 in the leather district of downtown Boston, and it continues to offer jazz five nights per week in its "Velvet Basement." It proved to be a great success, and three years later O'Neill opened a second venue of the same name in Cambridge (see below, Cambridge, MA). (<http://www.the-goodlife-us.com> (2001))

——. **Hi Hat.** Columbus Avenue and Massachusetts Avenue. Nightclub. Situated at the intersection of the two avenues, it was in operation from the late 1940s into the 1950s and was the first club to offer bop to Boston audiences. In 1953 Charlie Parker made a number of broadcasts from the club, selections from which were later issued as the album *New Bird: Hi Hat Broadcasts, 1953* (Phoenix Jazz 10).

——. **Howard Johnson's Motor Inn.** See Starlight Roof.

——. **Izzy Ort's.** Tremont Street. This was a favorite venue for local musicians, who gathered there to listen to and take part in jam sessions. Quincy Jones was among those who played there around 1950.

——. **Jazz at 76.** 76 Warrenton Street. Late in October 1950 Steve Connolly, the former manager of the Savoy Café, opened this venue as the New Rathskeller Room, with Vic Dickenson's Dixieland Stompers featuring Buster Bailey. They were soon followed by Jimmy McPartland and his Chicago Five, including Marian Page (Marian McPartland), and then (into 1951) by Bobby Hackett's group. By December 1950 Connolly had renamed the club Jazz at 76.

——. **Jazz Workshop.** 733 Boylston Street. The Jazz Workshop opened in 1964, managed by Fred Taylor and Tony Mauriello. In an adjacent room in the same basement premises, and also under the direction of Taylor and Mauriello, was a separate club, Paul's Mall. The two venues offered similar repertories, though the Jazz Workshop leaned more towards jazz and Paul's Mall towards jazz-rock and popular music. Among the many prominent musicians to appear at the Workshop were Charles Mingus, Roland Kirk, Elvin Jones, Miles Davis, and Ted Curson; Davis also played at the Mall. Both clubs closed in 1978.

——. **Jordan Hall.** 30 Gainsborough Street. Jordan Hall is one of the performance spaces of the New England Conservatory; seating 1013 people, it opened in October 1903. Classical music makes up the majority of the hall's programming, but student jazz recitals are also featured there, and it has hosted jazz concerts by such musicians as Stan Getz, Benny Goodman, and Fred Hersch (whose performance was recorded and issued on CD). Jordan Hall underwent extensive renovations in 1995.

——. **Ken Club.** Warrenton Street. It was in operation from at least the early 1940s. Henry "Red" Allen and his band were resident there during 1942, when among the guest musicians who appeared with them was Sidney Bechet.

——. **Lizard Lounge.** 1667 Massachusetts Avenue. Opened in 1998, the Lizard Lounge is located in the basement of the Cambridge Common restaurant. George Garzone's group the Fringe performs there at a popular weekly session, and Bob Moses appears with various groups.

——. **Lulu White's.** 3 Appleton Street. Although it was in operation for only three years (1977–80), it presented performances by many well-known musicians, including Dizzy Gillespie, Illinois Jacquet, Lionel Hampton, the Art Ensemble of Chicago, Harry Edison, Eddie "Lockjaw" Davis, Clifford Jordan, Zoot Sims and Al Cohn, and Henry Threadgill's group Air.

——. **Mahogany Hall.** 47 Huntington Avenue (*c*1952 – spring 1953; September 1953 – spring 1954; from September 1954). Situated in the basement of the Copley Square Hotel, where George Wein had first operated the club Storyville in 1950, this venue was opened by Wein around 1952. It specialized in the presentation of dixieland and swing. Bobby Hackett and Muggsy Spanier performed there in late November and early December 1952 respectively. Shortly before the end of that year the new house band, Vic Dickenson's Mahogany All Stars, began a two-year-long residency. This six-piece group included Doc Cheatham, Wein, and Buzzy Drootin; Jimmy Woode and Al Drootin were also among its members by the time that the group began to broadcast on WBZ, in February 1953. Mahogany Hall closed temporarily during the summer, while Wein operated Storyville in the Oceanside Hotel on route 127 in Magnolia, Massachusetts. Then, from 21 September 1953, Wein opened Storyville at the Copley Square Hotel, upstairs from Mahogany Hall, which resumed its activities, featuring the Mahogany All Stars; 1954 brought a repetition of the previous year, with a summer closing and Storyville located at the Oceanside Hotel.

——. **Michael's.** 52 Gainsborough Street. It was active as a jazz venue from the 1970s. Among the players who performed there were Miroslav Vitous, Ricky Ford, and Jaki Byard.

——. **Music Inn.** 47 Huntington Avenue at Exeter Street. By March 1951, not long after the Storyville club had left the Copley Square Hotel, this venue had taken its place. Bobby Hackett's group appeared there and broadcast from the inn on station WMEX.

——. **New Rathskeller Room.** See Jazz at 76.

——. **Paul's Mall.** See Jazz Workshop.

——. **Pioneer Club.** 3 Westfield Street. In the 1940s and 1950s it was a popular after-hours site for jam sessions, often involving major jazz artists.

——. **Roof Restaurant.** 15 Arlington Street. Situated within the Ritz-Carlton Hotel, the Roof Restaurant hosted major bands of the swing era, notably those of Benny Goodman, Tommy Dorsey, and Artie Shaw. It closed in 1946 but reopened in 1993 for dining and dancing, with music provided by Shaw's reconstituted orchestra under the direction of Dick Johnson.

——. **Roseland State Ballroom.** Massachusetts Avenue. This venue was presenting jazz by January 1940, when both Duke Ellington and Cab Calloway appeared there. It remained a regular stopping place for well-known bands up to at least 1944.

——. **Savoy Café.** 441 Columbus Avenue (early 1940s); 410 Massachusetts Avenue (by mid-1943). It began advertising in the *Baltimore African-American* in 1940, when it was at the Columbus Avenue address. After March 1941 performances by Frankie Newton and Sabby Lewis were announced, with no address given; the first mention of the Massachusetts Avenue address was in July 1943, by which time Lewis and Pete Brown were appearing. In 1945, through the intervention of Dick Schmidt, the president of the Boston Jazz Society, the venue's manager, Steve Connolly, engaged Sidney Bechet's New Orleans Rhythm Kings to play there; this group consisted of Bechet, Pops Foster, Ray Parker (piano), George Thompson (drums), and (perhaps the greatest attraction) Bunk Johnson, lately rediscovered in Louisiana and taken to the East Coast by Bechet. In spite of difficult relationships among the players and the ultimate failure of Bechet's intention to re-create authentic New Orleans jazz, the residency (which began on 12 March and continued through the spring) was a success, and the group made a number of broadcasts and recordings. Among others who played at the club was a band led by Bob Wilber and later by Jimmy Archey, which held a long residency starting in December 1948 and extending into the spring of 1950. George Wein, who was just beginning to be active in Boston at this time, organized some of the performances there in 1950, and Jimmy McPartland's group appeared late in 1951.

——. **Scotch and Soda.** In the mid-1970s the Drootin brothers were resident in a house band at this club. Many notable guest soloists appeared with them, including Bobby Hackett, Roy Eldridge, Zoot Sims, Ruby Braff, and Joe Venuti.

——. **Scullers Jazz Club.** 400 Soldiers Field Road. Scullers Jazz Club opened in the Double Tree Guest Suites Hotel in 1990. It has played host to some of the finest jazz musicians, usually for week-long engagements. Dakota Staton, Jimmy McGriff, Herb Ellis, Jimmy Witherspoon, Phil Woods, Earl Klugh, Pat Martino, John Patitucci, Randy Brecker, Joey DeFrancesco, and Abbey Lincoln have all performed there. Concert recordings have been made at Scullers by such artists as Garrison Fewell (1992), Ray Brown (1996), and Roy Haynes (*The Roy Haynes Trio featuring Danilo Perez & John Patitucci*, 1999, Verve 314-543534-2). Although the audience consists largely of tourists, the layout of the club gives prominence to the performers, encouraging listening rather than socializing. (<http://www.scullersjazz.com> (2001))

——. **Slades.** 958 Tremont Street. One of the oldest African-American-owned bars in Massachusetts, Slades has been in existence since the 1920s. The venue features jazz three nights per week, when it presents both visiting artists and local players.

——. **Southland Casino.** 76 Warrenton Street. It opened in the 1930s and flourished into the next decade. Blanche Calloway's last big band (which included Ray Perry and Frank Wess) played at the casino in early autumn 1940 during a short tour of East Coast cities. Charlie Barnet's recording *Southland Shuffle* (1940, Bb 10602) was named for the venue.

——. **The Stable(s).** Huntington Avenue. Located not far from the Storyville club, it opened in 1953 and remained active until 1962 as a venue for swing and bop played by local musicians. Herb Pomeroy and the saxophonist Varty Haroutunian led a big band there for a protracted residency from 1956 until 1960; Benny Golson's number *Stablemates* was written for the band. Other performers to appear there were Jaki Byard and Dick Twardzik, who played solo piano during intermissions.

——. **Starlight Roof.** Howard Johnson's Motor Inn, Kenmore Square. During its short period of activity (1984–6) this nightclub within the motel engaged several prominent jazz musicians; among those who appeared there were Art Farmer, Kenny Burrell, Jay McShann, James Moody, Jimmy Smith, Phil Woods, and Sheila Jordan.

——. **Storyville.** 47 Huntington Avenue (late 1950); Kenmore Square (early 1951 – spring 1953); Oceanside Hotel, route 127, Magnolia, MA (summer 1953, summer 1954); 47 Huntington Avenue (September 1953 – spring 1954; from September 1954). Storyville specialized in dixieland and swing. It was opened by George Wein in October 1950 in the basement of the Copley Square Hotel, with Bob Wilber and his band playing. However, that venture lasted only six weeks, and early in 1951 Wein reopened Storyville in the Hotel Buckminster at Kenmore Square. During the summer of 1953 he closed both this club and his other venue, Mahogany Hall, and instead operated Storyville at the Oceanside Hotel on Route 127 in Magnolia, Massachusetts, near Boston. Late in summer the club moved back to the Copley Square Hotel, but was now situated upstairs from Mahogany Hall (which occupied its original position in the hotel's basement); George Shearing's quintet played at the opening, and soon afterwards Charlie Parker appeared. In summer 1954 Wein again temporarily transferred his activities to the Oceanside Hotel location. Storyville remained in operation, featuring dixieland and swing, until at least 1956.

During the early 1950s Sidney Bechet established an association with the club, performing there in October and December 1951 and again in October 1953. The first of these engagements was shared with a quartet led by Jo Jones, and for the second Bechet was accompanied by a trio led by Wein. Wein made a number of recordings at his clubs – with Wild Bill Davison (1951), as a replacement for Claude Hopkins in a session with Bechet (25 October 1953), and with Jones (*c*1953) – as did Ruby Braff, Pee Wee Russell, Vic Dickenson, and others; several of the resulting albums were released under the title *Jazz at Storyville*. Among other important musicians to appear at Storyville were Duke Ellington, Count Basie, and Billie Holiday.

——. **Tic-Toc Club.** Jazz was played there from at least the early 1940s. In Boston for his last important show, *Early to Bed*, which opened in May 1943, Fats Waller also held a residency at the Tic-Toc. Among other bandleaders to appear at the club was Lionel Hampton, who led a group there that included Joe Williams.

——. **Wally's Paradise** [Wally's Café]. 428 Massachusetts Avenue (to 1979); 427 Massachusetts Avenue (from 1979). One of the oldest African-American-owned businesses in Massachusetts, Wally's Paradise was opened in 1947 by Joseph L. Walcott. Although the club enjoyed its greatest popularity during the 1940s and 1950s, it remains active, under the management of Walcott's granddaughter and her three sons. Known chiefly as a venue for local musicians, it first focused on big bands, and later emphasized for many years soul jazz, especially performances by organ trios. The club moved across the street, to smaller premises, in 1979, and took the name Wally's Café. By the late 1990s it was hosting a funk night, a blues night, jazz nights, and a highly competitive Sunday-afternoon jazz jam session. Wally's Café has provided many fine players with opportunities to perform early in their careers; Darren Barrett, Roy Hargrove, Donald Harrison, Antonio Hart, Javon Jackson, Branford and Delfeayo Marsalis, Sam Newsome, Greg Osby, Danilo Pérez, Joshua Redman, and Mark Whitfield are among those who played there. Some of these artists, when in Boston, have returned to Wally's later in their careers, and others, including Wynton Marsalis, have appeared on occasion for impromptu performances.

BIBLIOGRAPHY

<http://www.wallyscafe.com> (2001)
L. Pellegrinelli: "A Guided Tour of America's Most Fascinating Jazz Clubs," <http://www.newmusicbox.org/third-person/jan00/home.html> (2001)

——. **Wonderbar.** 186 Harvard Street. Frequented by students from neighboring Boston University, the bar features jazz every night of the week. Many student bands from the Berklee College of Music and the New England Conservatory hold weekly jobs at the club, and pianists like to play there because there is a grand piano. Although the Wonderbar does not host an official jam session, because of the absence of a stage, and because of the informality of student-led bands, many guest artists sit in. Darren Barrett is among the artists who have performed there early in their careers.

For other venues in the metropolitan area of Boston see Acton, Cambridge, Everett, Gloucester, Natick, Peabody, and Somerville, MA.

BIBLIOGRAPHY

Boston

M. Hazeldine: "Dear Wynne: a Review of the Events of 1945–6 Concerning Bunk Johnson, Sidney Bechet, Boston and Beyond," *Fn*, xv/5 (1984), 4
M. Selchow: *Profoundly Blue: a Bio-discographical Scrapbook on Edmond Hall* (Lübbecke, Germany, 1988)
——: *Ding! Ding!: a Bio-discographical Sketchbook on Vic Dickenson* (Westoverledingen, Germany, 1998)

Brentwood, CA. See Los Angeles (metropolitan area).

Buffalo. **Anchor Bar.** Main Street. Successive owners of this bar and club, from the 1930s into the 1980s, have pursued a policy of presenting jazz. From 1942 to 1954 George Clarke's band was resident there. Latterly the club engaged renowned musicians to play as guest soloists with a house band of local professionals.

——. **Casino.** Main Street. This became an important venue for jazz in the 1950s, when such major bop musicians as Charlie Parker played there.

——. **Colored Musicians' Club.** Broadway Street. The premises housed the African-American local of the AFM until 1969 (when black and white branches of the union amalgamated), and jazz musicians had played in jam sessions there for decades. When the AFM had no further use for the building a social club opened and more formal jazz performances were given. Among the leading visiting artists to appear there were Sarah Vaughan, Art Tatum, and Zoot Sims; rehearsal bands also play at the club.

——. **Davio's.** Sheridan Drive. The club flourished in the late 1970s and early 1980s as a venue for bop. Among the musicians who have played there are Sonny Stitt, Phil Woods, and Mark Murphy.

——. **Downtown Room.** Statler Hotel. Jazz was performed there from at least the 1970s. The first programs in the "Jazz Alive" series broadcast on National Public Radio were made there.

——. **Eduardo's.** Bailey Avenue. Restaurant. It offered jazz for the entertainment of patrons from the 1970s and sometimes engaged big bands; the bands of Maynard Ferguson and Woody Herman were among those that played there.

——. **Joe Rico's Milestones.** Main Street and Fillmore Street. Around 1986 the disc jockey Joe Rico opened this nightclub in the premises formerly occupied by the Tralfamadore Café (see below).

——. **Little Harlem Club.** This was in operation by around 1930. In 1931 Stuff Smith was resident, during which time Jonah Jones joined the band.

——. **Lloyd's Lounge.** Ferry Street. It flourished in the 1950s and 1960s, presenting a repertory that focused on soul jazz.

——. **Memorial Auditorium.** This downtown venue, on the lakeside, was an important location for major bands visiting Buffalo from the 1930s to the 1960s.

——. **Milestones.** See Joe Rico's Milestones.

——. **Moonglow.** Williams Street. This was a prominent venue for jazz in the city during the swing era. From the 1930s to the 1950s most of the leading African-American bands appeared there.

——. **Nietzsche's.** Allen Street. It opened around 1985 and offered a repertory of jazz and blues; by the 1990s jazz was no longer featured there.

——. **Paradise Ballroom.** Jazz big bands and dance bands played there from at least the late 1920s. Bennie Moten's was among the resident ensembles there at that period.

——. **Pine Grill.** Restaurant. Active in the 1970s, it presented performances mostly by soul-jazz players.

——. **Rainbow Ballroom.** Dance hall. Jazz was played for dancing there from at least the 1930s.

——. **Rebelot.** This flourished in the 1970s as a venue for soul jazz.

——. **Renaissance II.** Bailey Avenue. Owned by Sam Noto, it operated for about two years in the early 1980s. Among the musicians who played there were Chet Baker, Scott Hamilton, Sal Nistico (ii), and David Schnitter.

——. **Royal Arms.** Main Street and West Utica Street. This was an important venue for bop in the 1950s and 1960s. Miles Davis and many other prominent musicians appeared there.

——. **Shea's Buffalo Theater.** Main Street. Built in 1926, this opulent theater presented variety performances into the 1940s; leading jazz bands occasionally played for the stage acts that formed part of these programs – Jimmie Lunceford's orchestra appeared there in 1935. The theater continues to be used for jazz concerts and other musical performances.

——. **Silver Grill.** Restaurant. Jazz was played there during the 1930s; among the groups who performed at that period was Stuff Smith's band, which included Jonah Jones.

——. **Statler Hotel.** See Downtown Room.

——. **Tralfamadore Café.** Main Street and Fillmore Street (to 1980); Main Street at Theater Place (from 1983). Opened by Ed Lawson in the 1970s, this cellar club became the principal venue for jazz in the city, presenting renowned bop, free-jazz, and jazz-rock musicians. (Its programs also occasionally included poetry and comedy acts.) In 1980 Lawson sold the name to a corporation, which after an interval opened a new Tralfamadore, where the repertory was broadened to include other kinds of music besides jazz. In 1997 the club was purchased by Bobby Militello, who has been presenting a mixture of funk, fusion, pop, and jazz. (<http://www.tralf.com> (2001))

——. **Vendome Hotel.** Among the musicians who performed at this venue were Stuff Smith's group (early 1930s) and Count Basie's orchestra (*c*1936).

BURBANK, CA. See Los Angeles (metropolitan area).

CAMBRIDGE, MA. **Charles Hotel.** See Regattabar.

——. **Charlie's Tap.** Green Street. During its short existence (1985–6) this club presented a large number of performances by nationally known figures. Among those who appeared there were Dave Holland, Lester Bowie's Brass Fantasy, Henry Threadgill, Oliver Lake, Jaki Byard, Abbey Lincoln, David Murray, Hamiet Bluiett, Stanley Cowell, Ran Blake, Kenny Barron and Bill Barron, Amina Claudine Myers, Ricky Ford, and Frank Lowe.

——. **Dante Alighieri Society Cultural Center.** 41 Hampshire Street. The center is the principal venue of the Boston Creative Music Alliance. Dedicated to providing a listening environment for avant-garde music, the center may be thought of as Boston's equivalent (in programming policy) to New York's Knitting Factory. Artists such as Chris Speed, Uri Caine, and Dave Douglas have performed there. (<http://www.dantealighieri.net/cambridge/info_mass.html> (2001))

——. **Elk's Ballroom.** Central Square. By 1940 this venue was presenting leading big bands, including that of Cab

Calloway (May 1940). In 1941–2 Sabby Lewis's band made frequent appearances, sometimes in battles of music with visiting groups, such as that of Hot Lips Page in July 1942.

——. **Good Life.** Massachusetts Avenue, in Central Square. Following upon the success of his Boston location of the Good Life (see above, Boston), Brian O'Neill opened a second Good Life in Cambridge in April 2000. This location offers jazz every Tuesday through Saturday. Mainly local student players perform there, but occasionally such prominent local professionals as Jerry Bergonzi make an appearance. The club hosts weekly jam sessions, and impromptu guest performances are encouraged. (<http://www.the-goodlife-us.com> (2001))

——. **Middle East Restaurant.** 472 and 480 Massachusetts Avenue. The Middle East consists of four rooms, three of which – Upstairs, Downstairs, and the Corner (also known as the Bakery) – have live entertainment nightly. The restaurant portion of the club opened in the 1970s. Rock musicians began performing in the Upstairs club (actually at ground level) in the early 1980s; the Corner (the Bakery) is a small room, also on the ground floor, which has presented everything from jazz guitarists to belly dancers. In 1993 the owners, Nabil and Joseph Sater, opened the larger Downstairs room (formerly a bowling alley, situated at basement level) in an effort to attract well-known artists representing many diverse styles of music, including jazz. Tony Bennett, Hamiet Bluiett, JoAnne Brackeen, Gil Scott-Heron, Lew Tabackin, Henry Threadgill, the World Saxophone Quartet, Bob Moses, and John Medeski are among those who have performed in one of the rooms at the club, as has the local Either/Orchestra. (<http://www.mideastclub.com> (2001))

——. **Nightstage.** Central Square, Main Street. This club, which opened in 1985, presented a varied repertory of African-American music – blues, reggae, and African music in addition to jazz. In the latter part of the decade jazz performances were given there by Dizzy Gillespie, Wynton Marsalis, the World Saxophone Quartet, Steve Lacy's sextet, Lacy and Mal Waldron, Archie Shepp and Horace Parlan, Sun Ra, Abdullah Ibrahim, Tal Farlow, Jan Garbarek, Gato Barbieri, Carla Bley, Gil Evans, Vyacheslav Ganelin's trio, Art Blakey, and Ran Blake. Nightstage, which had a dance floor, was also known for presenting new rock groups. It had closed by the mid-1990s.

——. **Regattabar.** Charles Hotel, 1 Bennett Street, Harvard Square. The nightclub of the hotel opened in 1985 and has engaged many notable jazz musicians, including Stan Getz, J. J. Johnson, Branford Marsalis, Milt Jackson, McCoy Tyner, Ahmad Jamal, Sphere, Phil Woods, Tommy Flanagan, Astrud Gilberto, the Jazztet, the Timeless All Stars, Bobby Hutcherson, Donald Harrison and Terence Blanchard, Tony Williams, Art Blakey, Gary Burton, James Moody, Richie Cole, Morgana King, and Cedar Walton. Jazz is also played in the hotel's ballroom, where Sonny Rollins and the Modern Jazz Quartet, among others, have appeared. The club offers multiple-night engagements to out-of-town performers and hires local musicians to complete the schedule. The Regattabar is notable for its good sound, and concert recordings have been made there, notably an album by Jim Hall and Joe Lovano's group Grand Slam (*Live at the Regattabar, Cambridge, Massachusetts*, 2000, Telarc 83485). Because of its proximity to the Charles Hotel and Harvard Square, the club is frequented largely by tourists and students. (<http://www.regattabar.com> (2001))

——. **Ryles.** 212 Hampshire Street, in Inman Square. Ryles is an intimate club, seating approximately one hundred people. Formerly an Italian restaurant, it has been active as a jazz club from the mid-1980s into the new century. There are two rooms: the smaller, windowless one tends to present lesser-known groups (often a trio led by a guitarist); the main room has a huge classic jukebox stocked with vintage jazz singles. Ryles has engaged such musicians as Pat Metheny, Mal Waldron, Julius Hemphill, Charlie Haden, Paul Motian, Dewey Redman, Robben Ford, and Grover Washington, Jr. Students and professors from the Berklee College of Music often perform there: Metheny's first trio with Jaco Pastorius and Bob Moses had an early job as the house band at Ryles when the guitarist taught at Berklee, and Tiger Okoshi's band Tiger's Baku appears regularly. (<http://www.rylesjazz.com> (2001))

——. **1369 Club.** 1369 Cambridge Street. Jazz was performed in this venue from 1980 until it closed in 1989. Among those who played at the club were Archie Shepp, New Air, Kenny Burrell, Barry Harris, Mark Helias, Lew Tabackin, Clifford Jordan, George Adams and Don Pullen, Jack Walrath, Mulgrew Miller, Gary Bartz, Steve Lacy, Roscoe Mitchell, Bill Frisell, JoAnne Brackeen, Paul Motian, Dave Liebman, Bobby Watson, Roswell Rudd, and a number of organists, including Brother Jack McDuff, Lonnie Smith, Charles Earland, and Don Patterson.

——. **University Lutheran Church.** 66 Winthrop Street, in Harvard Square. The church offers a "Jazz at the Church" concert series, often with no admission charge. An emphasis is placed on free-jazz concerts, and Laszlo Gardony and Garrison Fewell are among those who have performed there. (<http://www.unilu.org> (2001))

Canoga Park, CA. See Los Angeles (metropolitan area).

Carson, CA. See Los Angeles (metropolitan area).

Catalina island, CA. See Los Angeles (metropolitan area).

Catonsville, MD. **Greenwood Electric Park.** Winters Avenue. From 1919 to 1930 this was a regular venue for dances and functions at which Baltimore-based African-American bands appeared, notably Ike Dixon's Orchestra from 1922. There were occasional appearances by out-of-town visitors, including Elmer Snowden's band in 1922. In July 1930 Eddie White and his 12 Kings of Jazz were advertised as "the band Duke Ellington refused to meet in a war of jazz."

Cedar Grove, NJ. **Meadowbrook Inn.** Pompton Turnpike. Ballroom. Owned by Frank Dailey, this was an important venue during the swing era. Numerous bands, both African-American and white, played there between 1935 and 1945, including Fats Waller's big band (1935) and the orchestras of Charlie Barnet and Count Basie. The ballroom was later converted into a restaurant and theater performance space and was known variously as the Meadowbrook Lounge and Meadowbrook Theater.

Century City, CA. See Los Angeles (metropolitan area).

Chicago. *Note.* Addresses are given as precisely as possible, though sources do not consistently use the locations "North," "South," "East," and "West." The names of a number of streets in Chicago were changed during the 20th century. For the purposes of this list the following changes are important: a roughly 3 mile-long portion of 55th Street, extending from 400 East 55th to 2400 West 55th, became Garfield Boulevard; and Grand Boulevard became South Parkway Boulevard (1926) and later Dr. Martin Luther King Drive (31 July 1968).

——. **Ace of Clubs.** See Dave's Café.

——. **Alabam.** See Club Alabam.

——. **Alexander's Steak House.** 3010 East 79th Street. Open from at least 1991, this restaurant was the long-time home of the Jazz Unites Jazz Masters (a septet including Eddie Johnson and John Young), who played on Thursday nights, ran jam sessions, and provided young players with a chance to sit in. It closed in 1999.

——. **Al Turner's Café.** See Plantation Café.

——. **Alvadere.** See Club Alvadere.

——. **Ambassador.** See Club Ambassador.

——. **Ambassador Hotel.** See Pump Room.

——. **Andy's.** 11 East Hubbard Street. This restaurant began to present jazz in 1977 when, under Penny Tyler's management, it absorbed the weekly "Jazz at Noon" program of concerts which had begun at Marina Towers. In 1981 it assimilated the similar "Jazz at Five" series, also begun at Marina Towers. Tyler expanded both and began presenting music every weekday as well as on Saturday nights and Sunday afternoons, in styles ranging from early jazz and swing (for example, Truck Parham and Franz Jackson) to bop. Cy Touff is a member of the resident band, Ears. Among "Jazz at Noon" regulars are the guitarist Pat Fleming and the double bass player Steve Hashimoto, while those who have taken part in evening performances include Chuck Hedges's Swingtet, Paul Wertico's trio, Von Freeman, and other notable locals.

——. **The Annex.** 2840 South State Street; 2300 South State Street (from October 1934). Entertainment center. It flourished in the 1930s. Among the bands that played there were Chippie Hill's, which was resident from 1934 (at both locations) until 1936, Jimmy Cobb's Annex Syncopators, which held a residency in the café from April to October 1936, Jack Ellis's Musical Wildcats, in June 1937, and a band led by Zinky Cohn, also in 1937. The venue may have closed in the late 1930s since in 1939 the opening was announced of the New Annex on South Parkway Boulevard (see below).

——. **Apex Café.** See Apex Tavern.

——. **Apex Chateau.** See Robbins, IL.

——. **Apex Club.** East 35th Street between South Prairie Avenue and South Calumet Avenue. The first owner of the Apex Club was Julian Black, who was a close friend of the politician Dan Jackson. The premises, which had earlier operated as the Club Alvadere and the Nest Club (see below), were bought by Black in 1926, renovated, and opened in the autumn as a luxurious supper club. The most important residency was that of Jimmie Noone, who had led a small group at the venue before Black's time; his Apex Club Orchestra, which at different times included Earl Hines, Johnny St. Cyr, Dave Nelson, Joe Poston, and Johnny Wells, was the resident band from 1926 until the club closed in the spring of 1928.

——. **Apex Grill and Road House.** See Robbins, IL.

——. **Apex Tavern.** 354½ East 51st Street. It was in operation at least from 1934, as it advertised in June that year that it was lately refurbished; at this time the club was owned by Doc Jennings and managed by Harry Boyd. The resident band was Duke Patterson and his Syncopators, with Art Campbell on piano and the singer Lil Christian. By October the Apex Café, owned by Jennings (presumably the same venue), was under the direction of Charles Christian, with the Apex Continental Syncopators as the house band. The New Apex Café (see below) opened in 1935.

——. **Apollo Theater.** 526 East 47th Street. During the 1920s it presented shows in which the music was sometimes provided by jazz musicians. Frankie "Half Pint" Jaxon, for example, played there in March 1927. By 1930 the theater had become a cinema.

——. **Aragon Ballroom.** 1100 West Lawrence Avenue. Jazz began to be played for dancing there in the mid-1920s; the first jazz-oriented group to appear was one led by Wingy Manone, which included Art Hodes, Bud Freeman, Floyd O'Brien, and Gene Krupa. During the swing era the ballroom regularly engaged big bands, and live broadcasts were frequently made on Chicago radio stations. The Aragon still exists, but it hosts touring rock bands rather than jazz groups.

——. **Arcadia Ballroom.** This venue, on the West Side, was owned (like the later Dreamland Ballroom, see below) by Paddy Harmon and offered jazz from at least 1917, when Darnell Howard led a band there. Among the resident bands during the 1920s was one from St. Louis led by Joe Kayser and including Jess Stacy among its sidemen (1926), the Creole Orchestra led by Charlie Elgar (early 1926; September 1926 – February 1927), and Walter Barnes's Royal Creolians (April 1928 into 1929).

——. **Archway Lounge** [Archway Supper Club]. 356 East 61st Street. Opened on 24 April 1947, with a group led by the guitarist Ike Perkins resident, it was known as the Archway Supper Club by 1960. Dorothy Donegan performed at the club in March 1962, and that same year there were appearances by Jimmy Witherspoon, Ben Webster, and Carmen McRae.

——. **Arie Crown Theatre.** McCormick Place. A prominent concert venue in the mid-1960s, it presented, among others, Nancy Wilson with Cannonball Adderley (1963), Jimmy Smith and Ray Charles (both 1964), Louis Armstrong (1964, 1966), and a "World Series of Jazz" (1966), with Count Basie, Hank Crawford, Jimmy Smith, and Groove Holmes.

——. **Arsonia Café.** Around 1915 it engaged Charlie Elgar's band, which included the trombonist George Filhe and a number of New Orleans players, among them Manuel Perez, Lorenzo Tio, Jr., and Louis Cottrell, Sr. Small groups made up of these and other players continued to be resident for several years at the club under different leaders; for example, around 1917 Perez led a quintet there in which Alphonse Picou was a sideman.

——. **Ascher's Metropolitan Theater.** See Metropolitan Theater.

——. **Athenia Café.** Around the beginning of 1917 the management booked the Louisiana Five, a New Orleans band led by the drummer Anton Lada, to play a six-month engagement there; this was among the first residencies by a jazz-oriented ensemble in the city.

——. **Avenue Theater.** 3108 South Indiana Avenue, at East 31st Street. Variety theater. It opened in August 1913 and, like several theaters in the city, maintained separate seating areas for African-Americans and Whites. Its revues, vaudeville shows, and other theatrical productions provided work for a number of musicians. Many of the great singers of the vaudeville tradition appeared there in touring companies, including Lucille Hegamin and Ethel Waters (both December 1923), Bessie Smith (May 1924, October 1932), and Sara Martin (February 1925). In the mid-1920s the resident orchestra was directed by Hugh Swift. The venue was still active in the mid-1930s.

——. **Bacon's Casino.** East 49th Street and South Wabash Avenue. It occupied premises on the northeast corner of the intersection which had been built as a garage. In 1927 the Bacon brothers, Robert and Ernest, opened a dance hall in the building, which came in time to be used for functions of many kinds, such as lectures, public meetings, and charity events. The venue flourished until 1945, and a number of jazz musicians performed there; Jimmie Noone's orchestra played for a cabaret party in 1935, and the singer Joe Williams appeared with Floyd Campbell's orchestra (of which Scoops Carry was also a member) during the late 1930s and early 1940s. Bacon's Casino had closed by the late 1940s.

——. **Bamboo Room.** 936 North Rush Street. It opened in May 1959 with Georg Brunis and his dixieland band.

——. **Band Box.** Randolph Street and Dearborn Street. In the early 1940s Boyd Raeburn's band performed for servicemen in this basement dance hall; during the course of its residency Johnny Bothwell and the singer Shirley Luster (later to become famous as June Christy) joined the group. By the mid-1940s the Band Box had evidently become an African-American venue, and in 1946 there were appearances by Louis Armstrong (July), Andy Kirk and Stuff Smith (on the same bill through August and September), and Kirk again (December); at this time Red Saunders was playing at the club on a weekly basis.

——. **Basin Street.** 6312 Cottage Grove. Managed for the proprietor, Allyne Nixon, by the singer and dancer Dr. Jo Jo Adams, and initially sharing acts with the Flame Show Lounge, this was the venue for residencies by Eddie "Cleanhead" Vinson (with Johnny Griffin, October 1954 – June 1955) and King Kolax (February–March 1955). In July 1955 Griffin became the leader of the house band, with Junior Mance on piano. The band led by the tenor saxophonist Melvin Scott transferred from the Flame later that year, but Griffin had returned by the following January as a member of the group led by the drummer Buddy Smith. Later the club's musical offerings were oriented towards contemporary Chicago blues.

——. **Beale Street Blues Café.** 1550 Rand Road. Owned by Joe Barrutia, it was originally known as the Chicago Blue Note, but a lawsuit by the Blue Note in New York resulted in the name change in October 1997. (<http://www.bealestreetbluescafe.com> (2001))

——. **Bee Hive Club.** 1503 East 55th Street. This nightclub opened in 1948 at a time when jazz was flourishing in the city. It engaged a number of older musicians, including Chippie Hill, Art Hodes, Doc Evans, Baby Dodds, Miff Mole, and Darnell Howard. Lester Young also performed there during the month he spent in Chicago in 1949 (February–March), and over the course of the next year he was followed by Louis Armstrong with Earl Hines (April), Dizzy Gillespie (April), Slim Gaillard (May–June, August), Duke Ellington (October), Lionel Hampton (November), and Erroll Garner with Hodes, Pee Wee Russell, and Hill (February 1950). Norman Simmons was the house pianist from 1953 to 1956. Before the club closed in April of the latter year it featured many famous soloists, notably, in 1953, Coleman Hawkins, Sonny Stitt accompanied by Junior Mance, Israel Crosby, Buddy Smith, Eddie "Lockjaw" Davis, Young, and Charlie Parker (who played his last engagement in Chicago in November); in 1954, Candy Johnson, Mance, Tom Archia, Johnny Griffin, Gene Ammons, Hawkins, Howard McGhee, Wardell Grey, Stitt, Young, and Sonny Rollins; in 1955, J. J. Johnson, Paul Quinichette, Johnson and Kai Winding, Stitt, Clifford Brown, Young, Milt Jackson, and Art Blakey; and, in 1956, Roy Eldridge, a "battle" featuring Stitt versus Ammons, and Dexter Gordon. In 1977 the record producer Jim Neumann adopted the club's name for a newly founded record label (*see* Bee hive).

——. **Bert Kelly's Stables.** See Kelly's Stables.

——. **Big House.** See New Apex Café.

——. **Blackhawk Restaurant.** 139 North Wabash Avenue, south of East Randolph Street. It presented jazz performances from the 1920s. In 1924 Joe Sanders and Carleton Coon took their band, the Coon–Sanders Nighthawks, to Chicago, and from 1926 it was resident at the Blackhawk; the group continued to appear regularly through the 1930s, and Sanders occasionally returned there in the 1940s. Other important bands to hold residencies at the venue were those of Ben Pollack (from May 1927), Red Norvo, Bob Crosby (1938; for illustration *see* Crosby, bob), Jack Teagarden (1939), and Raymond Scott (1940).

——. **Blatz Palm Gardens.** Ballroom. Jazz was played there from at least the end of World War I. From 1919 Elmer Schoebel led a resident group that included Paul Mares, Georg Brunis, and Jack Pettis, who later formed the nucleus of the New Orleans Rhythm Kings. Schoebel was still at the ballroom in 1921, when Muggsy Spanier joined his band.

——. **Blue Note Club.** 3 North Clark Street, at West Randolph Street. The club flourished in the 1940s and early 1950s under the direction of Frank Holzfeind. Among the notable jazzmen who led resident bands there were Doc Evans (1940s), Muggsy Spanier (1947), Paul Mares (1948), Miff Mole (around the turn of the decade), and Sidney Bechet (during a tour of America in 1951); Count Basie regarded the Blue Note as his Chicago headquarters and played there regularly from 1949 to 1958, Gene Ammons performed his last engagement with Woody Herman's Herd there in 1949, and Duke Ellington's orchestra was there in 1952, 1953, and 1959. The venue also engaged a number of important singers, including Billie Holiday, who appeared in December 1949, Chippie Hill, who gave her last Chicago performance at the club in 1950, and Mildred Bailey, who performed there with Joe Marsala in 1950.

——. **Bop Shop.** 1807 West Division Street (1990 – January 1997); 5419 North Clark Street (May–June 1997); 1146 South Wabash (July–October 1997). Owned by Kate Smith, this venue featured mainly avant-garde jazz, and it also hosted the annual Asian-American Jazz Festival. It closed in October 1997.

——. **The Bottom.** See Dusty Bottom.

——. **Brass Rail.** 329 East 47th Street (*c*1939–42); Dearborn Street and Randolph Street (1950s). In July 1940 Lonnie Johnson's swing trio appeared at the 47th Street club, which was run by Nelson Sykes. The better-known downtown venue, at Dearborn and Randolph, was in existence from at least 1950; Count Basie and Joe Williams held short residencies there from February to March of that year and from December to January the following winter. Later in the decade Art Hodes held lengthy residencies at the club (July–November 1955, February–September 1956). Jack Teagarden, Joe Venuti, and Wingy Manone were among those who appeared in the late 1950s.

——. **Breakfast Club.** See Liberty Inn.

——. **Butch Webb's Strand Lounge.** See Strand Show Lounge.

——. **Cabin Inn.** See Cozy Cabin Inn.

——. **Café de Paris.** See Lincoln Gardens.

——. **Café de Society.** 309 East 55th Street (Garfield Boulevard). The Chicago "Café Society" was in existence by March 1944, when a trio led by Raymond Scott (not the well-known musician of this name) was playing there. In July 1944 the singer Scatman Crothers was leading the band. King Perry appeared in August, Saunders King in September, and Tab Smith in February 1945. Café de Society continued to operate until at least April 1946.

——. **Camel Gardens.** It offered performances of jazz from around 1920. Georg Brunis and Paul Mares played in the resident band, led by the drummer Ragbaby Stevens, in 1920–21, and in 1922 Eddie Condon appeared there as a member of a sextet.

——. **Capitol Lounge.** It flourished from at least 1940 as a venue for small groups and soloists. Roy Eldridge led an ensemble there in late 1940, and in 1951 Dizzy Gillespie and Count Basie both held residencies with small groups.

——. **Cascade Gardens** [Cascades Ballroom]. North Sheridan Road and West Argyle Street. Owned by Palmer Cody, this dance hall on an upper floor of a building on the north side of the intersection was in operation from the early 1920s. The Wolverines played there early in 1924.

——. **Casino Gardens.** North Clark Street, north of West Kinzie Street. Dance hall. It was part-owned by the promoter Harry James, who also managed the Schiller Café (see below) at the time when Johnny Stein led his band of New Orleans musicians there in 1916. The Original Dixieland Jazz Band, which grew out of Stein's group, opened at the Casino Gardens on 6 July 1916, following a residency at the Del'Abe Café (see below), and continued to play there for the rest of the year.

——. **Casino Moderne.** 913 East 63rd Street. Among those who played there in 1957 were Bud Powell, Buddy De Franco, and Kai Winding; on 29 December there was a saxophone "battle" between Gene Ammons and Johnny Griffin, with the All Girl Combo of Birdie (Bert Etta) Davis also appearing.

——. **The Cellar** [My Cellar]. 222 North State Street. During the late 1920s Wingy Manone led a band (which included Joe Marsala) at this nightclub; the musicians associated with the so-called Austin High School Gang, notably Frank Teschemacher, Bud Freeman, and Bix Beiderbecke, often dropped into the club to play in jam sessions with Manone's group. The premises were later the site of the Three Deuces (see below).

——. **Chicago Blue Note.** See Beale Street Blues Café.

——. **Chicago Cultural Center.** 78 East Washington Street. Formerly the main branch of the Chicago Public Library, the Cultural Center became a major venue for jazz in 1997. The Chicago Jazz Institute's annual January Jazz Fair is held there, and the center offers free and low-cost jazz events featuring local and visiting musicians year-round. (<http://www.ci.chi.il.us/Tourism/CulturalCenter> (2001))

——. **Chin Chow Café.** South Parkway at 47th Street. Fess Williams and his Joy Boys appeared in February 1929 at this South Side Chinese restaurant, which advertised jazz throughout that year. Bud Byron's Chin Chow Orchestra was the resident band.

——. **Cinderella Ballroom.** It offered jazz for dancing from at least the mid-1920s. Among the bands that performed there were those led by Joe Sullivan (1927) and George Wettling (1928).

——. **Circle Inn.** East 63rd Street and South Cottage Grove Avenue. Junie Cobb appeared there in June 1943, and Buster Bennett from October 1944 to April 1946, when the group led by the trumpeter George Dixon began a long residency; among the notable musicians who played with Dixon was Roy Eldridge. Horace Henderson and his Great Hollywood Combo performed at the Circle Inn from September 1949 to August 1950, and they were followed by Oett Mallard's band in September 1950.

——. **Civic Opera House.** 20 North Wacker Drive. Opened in 1929, the theater seats 3500. It hosted many jazz concerts. Duke Ellington's orchestra and members of Jazz at the Philharmonic performed there a number of times from the mid-1940s into the 1960s. Other notable appearances were by Coleman Hawkins, in a "battle" with Lester Young (22 June 1946), Paul Eduard Miller's "Operations Jazz" (in which Dizzy Gillespie, Sidney Bechet, Gene Sedric, Jimmy McPartland, and Bud Freeman, among others, took part; October 1946), Lionel Hampton, Art Tatum, and Nat "King" Cole's trio (all 1947); Illinois Jacquet and Ella Fitzgerald (30 January 1948), and Gerry Mulligan, Dave Brubeck, and Stan Getz (all on the same bill in April 1964).

——. **Claremont.** East 39th Street and South Indiana Avenue. This nightclub occupied premises in a building on the northwest corner of the intersection. It was opened around 1922 by the trumpeter and pianist Jimmy Wade and provided a platform for numerous bands. Although it closed in 1938 following a performance by Albert Ammons, it reopened briefly in April the following year, when the blues singer Kokomo Arnold appeared.

——. **Club Alabam.** 747 North Rush Street, at West Chicago Avenue. A small venue downtown, it was in existence from at least the mid-1920s. Eddie South's Alabamians played there in 1927.

——. **Club Algiers.** 3933 Drexel Boulevard. This club, located in the Morocco Hotel, was flourishing in 1948, when, among other attractions, it presented the bands of Buster Bennett and the tenor saxophonist Dick Davis.

——. **Club Alvadere.** East 35th Street between South Prairie Avenue and South Calumet Avenue. This was the first of at least three clubs to operate in premises on an upper floor of the building (which was two doors away from the Plantation Café, see below); it was in existence by the turn of the 1920s, when Junie Cobb led a band there (1920–21). By 1922 the venue was known as the Nest Club (see below) and by autumn 1926 as the Apex Club (see above).

——. **Club Ambassador.** Situated on Chicago's North Side, it was offering jazz by the late 1920s. Musicians who performed there at that period were Darnell Howard (summer 1928), Jimmie Noone (1928–31), Junie Cobb, and Jerome Don Pasquall, who led a quintet at the club (1929–30).

——. **Club Congo.** 35th Street and South State Street. It was active at least around 1930; in 1931 bands led by Dave Peyton (September) and Walter Barnes (December) appeared there. Another Club Congo was at 4733 South Parkway Avenue from December 1940 until at least November 1944, but it seems not to have been a significant venue.

——. **Club DeLisa.** 5516 South State Street (1933–41); 5521 South State Street (1941–58). This nightclub was opened during the 1933 World's Fair by the brothers Mike, Louie, and Jim DeLisa. After the original premises were destroyed by fire on 11 February 1941 the club opened again on Sunday 27 April at a large new location (with seating for more than a 1000) on South State Street under the name the New Club DeLisa; its activities were under the direction of the producer and choreographer Sam Dyer. Many bands held long residencies at the DeLisa, including Junie Cobb's (early 1930s), the Rhythm Kings led by Albert Ammons and later by Red Saunders (1935–6), and ensembles led by Saunders (1937–45, 1947–57), Billy Eckstine (1938), Jimmie Noone (1939), and Fletcher Henderson (1946–7). Among other musicians who worked there were a number of singers; Chippie Hill was resident for a long period in the early 1940s, and it was at the DeLisa that Count Basie first heard Joe Williams sing in the 1950s. The club closed in 1958. (D. J. Travis: "Club DeLisa," *An Autobiography of Black Jazz* (Chicago, 1983), 123)

——. **Club Deluxe.** See Joe's Deluxe Club.

——. **Club Dixie.** Jazz was played there from at least the early 1930s. The club was one of the many venues where Jimmie Noone performed during his years in Chicago; he was resident there in 1932.

——. **Club Evergreen.** 1322 North Clyburn Avenue. It flourished from 1950; artists holding residencies there included Johnny Griffin (1951), Buster Bennett (1952), and Red Holloway and Eddie Chamblee (both 1954). A Jazz Jamboree in September 1960 featured King Kolax.

——. **Club Metropole.** It was active as a venue for jazz from the end of the 1920s; among the musicians who led bands there in the following decade was Junie Cobb.

——. **Club Morocco.** 66 East 55th Street (Garfield Boulevard). Managed by Sam Rifas, this club presented, among others, Jimmie Noone and his orchestra (late December 1933) and Carroll Dickerson and his Syncopators (September 1934).

——. **Club 65.** 65 East 55th Street (Garfield Boulevard). It presented, among others, Dave Peyton and the violinist Willie Tyler with the 65 Club Orchestra (August 1933), Tiny Parham's orchestra (December 1933), and Fat Walker and his Jazz Hounds (June 1934). Another (and less important) Club 65 operated at 5507 South Michigan Avenue from 1936 to 1941.

——. **Club Tally-Ho.** 4753 South Parkway Boulevard. Stuff Smith's trio was resident there for a year from June 1951 and played with such guests as Billie Holiday, Horace Henderson, and Gene Ammons. Ammons made a further appearance in September 1952 with his own band.

——. **Club 29.** It flourished in the 1930s, when Albert Ammons and his Rhythm Kings and a small band led by Johnny Dodds appeared there.

——. **Coach Club.** It was in existence by 1940, in the winter of which year Jimmie Noone began a residency there with a band that included Baby Dodds; the engagement ended in spring 1941.

——. **Coliseum.** East 15th Street and South Wabash Avenue. Theater. This large venue was the site of two sensational events in 1926, when, under the auspices of the record company OKeh, numerous prominent jazz musicians were brought together to entertain audiences of several thousands. On 27 February Clarence Williams, Louis Armstrong, Sara Martin, Chippie Hill, Doc Cook, Blanche Calloway, Sippie Wallace, and Bennie Moten, among others, performed at a concert billed as "OKeh Race Records Artists Night." On 12 June a great battle of bands was staged between many of the most notable ensembles of the day, including those led by Charlie Elgar, Carroll Dickerson, Dave Peyton, Cook, King Oliver, Armstrong, Al Wynn, and Erskine Tate, all of which were then based in the city.

The Coliseum Annex (at the same address) engaged Tate's orchestra to appear in October 1923 and that of Ollie Powers in December of that year. 1 May 1924 saw a competition between Honore Dutrey's Creole Jazz Band, which was playing at Lincoln Gardens at the time, and the bands of Cook, Sammy Stewart, Dickerson, and Jimmy Wade. Fletcher Henderson's orchestra gave an acclaimed performance for a dance there on 17 September 1927.

——. **College Inn.** See Sherman Hotel.

——. **Colosimo's.** 2126 South Wabash Avenue. This café was one of the numerous venues where Billie Holiday performed as a soloist in the last decade of her career; she appeared there at its opening in April 1947 on a bill which also featured Louis Armstrong, and in May she worked with Henry "Red" Allen and J. C. Higginbotham; their group was then held over (i.e., without the singer). John Kirby's band succeeded that of Allen and Higginbotham, and Una Mae Carlisle appeared in May and June of that same year.

——. **Congress Hotel.** South Michigan Avenue north of East 22nd Street. The hotel engaged jazz and dance bands from at least the mid-1920s. An orchestra led by Fletcher Henderson played there in the summer of 1927, making nightly broadcasts on radio station KYW. Eddie South led a group there in 1932, playing in the hotel lobby to entertain the members of the Democratic National Convention. Benny Goodman's band was resident from 6 November 1935 to May 1936, and it was followed by Duke Ellington's in May–June 1936; Henderson played at the hotel again in the same year.

——. **Cotton Club.** 6249 Cottage Grove Avenue. As in other cities, a number of venues in Chicago borrowed the name Cotton Club from the famous New York venue; at least four clubs of this name (or, at their début, under the name New Cotton Club) have been reported, and sometimes conflated, in accounts of Chicago nightlife. The most important of these as far as jazz was concerned was the (New) Cotton Club which opened on Cottage Grove Avenue in May 1951 with Red Simms's group, which included Buster Bennett. Among the musicians who appeared there in 1953 were Roy Eldridge (August) and Henry "Red" Allen (September). By 1956 the Cotton Club was focusing on blues groups.

——. **Cotton Club Ballroom.** 35th Street and South State Street. This venue on the top floor of the Arcade Building opened on 9 September 1933 with Walter Barnes's band playing for the dancing. Erskine Tate led a 12-piece group in a long residency there in the 1930s.

——. **Cozy Cabin Inn** [Cozy Cabin Club, Cabin Inn]. 3119 Cottage Grove Avenue (*c*1934 – May 1935); 3353 South State Street (August 1935–1938); 3520 South State Street (October 1938–1940). Billed as "the South Side's Oddest Nite Club," it specialized in floor shows by female impersonators, it had a transvestite chorus line, and it allowed homosexual and interracial dancing. The venue was renamed the Cabin Inn in August 1935, when it moved to South State Street; Jimmie Noone was resident there in 1938–9, at the time of its second relocation, across the street. The club closed in 1940.

——. **Crown Propeller Lounge.** 868 East 63rd Street. It flourished in the 1950s, engaging small groups and also dancers and entertainers. Leon Abbey's trio played for the opening on 3 August 1951 and then remained there; by September it was alternating sets with Oett Mallard's quartet. Mallard's group appeared alone from November 1951 and was followed in 1952 by King Kolax and, later, Tiny Davis and her Hell Divers. Abbey and Davis were both there again in 1953. Among others who appeared at the club were Wynonie Harris (1954), Johnny Hodges, Sonny Stitt, Jimmy Rushing, T-Bone Walker, Eddie Chamblee, and Erskine Hawkins (1955), Willis Jackson (January 1956), Nancy Wilson, with a band led by Rusty Bryant (1956), and Louis Jordan (November 1956). In 1957 Johnny Griffin, Gene Ammons, and Lester Young held a residency. The club continued to be active until at least 1959.

——. **Dave's Café.** East 51st Street and South Michigan Avenue (to 1934); 343 East 55th Street (Garfield Boulevard) (from 16 July 1934). It was one of several nightclubs to occupy premises in the Ritz Building on the northwest corner of the intersection; earlier the Ace of Clubs had operated there. Owned by Dave Heighly, Dave's Café opened in the early 1930s, but it was burned out by gangsters and Heighly moved into a new venue close by in 1934. In 1933 a band led by George McClennon and Ray Nance's sextet were simultaneously in residence; Nance and his Rhythm Barons were still playing for Heighly in April 1934, and in the same year May Alix (ii), Carroll Dickerson, and Fletcher Henderson (with Coleman Hawkins in his band) all appeared. Other bands to perform at the club included François' Louisianians (1935–6). Under new management the venue was renamed the Swingland Café in August 1936 (see below).

——. **Del'Abe Café** [De Labbie Café]. Hotel Normandy, North Clark Street and West Randolph Street. In the mid-1910s it was managed by Sam Rothschild, who presented the first performances by the Original Dixieland Jazz Band; the group was resident there from 2 June 1916 until the beginning of July, when it moved on to the Casino Gardens (see above).

——. **De Lisa Club.** See Club DeLisa.

——. **De Luxe Café.** 3503 State Street. Under the management of Isidore Schorr, it flourished before the 1920s and was among the first venues in Chicago to offer jazz consistently; the club had a billiard hall, bar, and dance hall. A number of important early jazz musicians played there, notably Jelly Roll Morton, King Oliver, Manuel Perez, and Lawrence Duhé, whose band included Wellman Braud, Sidney Bechet, Louis Keppard, Roy Palmer, Minor Hall (who replaced his brother Tubby Hall), and Lil Hardin. At the turn of the decade Freddie Keppard brought a group to the De Luxe, which remained there for some time under the leadership successively of Perez, the trombonist George Filhe, Lorenzo Tio, Jr., and Bechet. This venue should not be confused with Joe's Deluxe Club (see below).

——. **DeLuxe 400 Lounge.** 715 East 63rd Street. May Alix (ii) sang here in 1948–9.

——. **Disc Jockey Lounge.** See McKee's Disc Jockey Show Lounge.

——. **Downbeat Room.** See Garrick Stage Bar.

——. **Downtown** [Down Town]. State Street at Van Buren Street. It was an important venue for visiting bands in winter 1944–5, when the orchestras of Lionel Hampton, Billy Eckstine, Charlie Barnet, Benny Carter, Eddie Heywood, Andy Kirk, Jimmie Lunceford, Fletcher Henderson, and Noble Sissle, as well as the International Sweethearts of Rhythm, all played week-long engagements. Nat "King" Cole's trio and Lil Green also appeared.

——. **Dreamland Ballroom** [Harmon's Dreamland Ballroom]. South Ashland Avenue and West Van Buren Street. This venue on the city's North Side was active by at least 1915 and offered dancing for a white clientèle accompanied by African-American bands. Under the management of Paddy Harmon a number of prominent early jazz musicians played there, including Charlie Elgar, with a 15-piece band (1916–22), and Doc Cook, who led the resident group for about six years (from 1922); among Cook's sidemen at different times were Freddie Keppard, Jimmie Noone, and Johnny St. Cyr. Jerome Don Pasquall led a band there in 1929.

For the other venue active under this name during the same period see Dreamland Café.

——. **Dreamland Café** [Dreamland Gardens]. 3518–20 South State Street (to 1928); 4700 South State Street (1933–46). A venue known as the Dreamland Ballroom was opened at 3518–20 South State Street in 1912 by Elijah Johnson. For a time in the mid-1910s the managers and dance instructors were Robert and Ernest Bacon, who later opened Bacon's Casino (see above); the manager late in the decade was Bill Bottoms. Among the bands that played there was one in 1918 led by Lawrence Duhé (which included King Oliver and Sidney Bechet). In the 1920s the premises were renovated and reopened as the Dreamland Café, an opulent nightclub with a mirror-hung dance floor. It was managed during its heyday by J. H. Carlis (1923–4), Walter J. Burton (1924), Bill Bottoms (1924), and Warren La Rue (by 1928). The club was closed in October 1928 for violating the prohibition laws but reopened further down South State Street on 25 November 1933 under the proprietorship of Saul Ruben, with Raymond "Sheeny" Barnett as its manager; Barnett was succeeded by Billy Page and Fess Wade (both 1934) and Joe Peterson (1935). Among the jazz musicians to appear there were Mae Bradley (1921), Ollie Powers and his Harmony Syncopators, in which Louis Armstrong was a sideman (1924), Honore Dutrey, whose band included Baby and Johnny Dodds (1924), Lil Armstrong (1925–6), Cab Calloway, Freddie Keppard, and Tiny Parham (all 1928).

——. **Dusty Bottom.** South Wabash Avenue and East 33rd Street. Open-air café. It had a freestanding wooden dance floor, the dust from which gave the venue its name. Among the jazz musicians who held residencies there in the 1930s was Albert Ammons.

——. **Elbo Room.** 2871 North Lincoln Street. By the 1990s this club frequently offered jazz. Barrett Deems and his big band were resident on Tuesday nights for more than six years, and George Freeman and Bernard Purdie were among others who appeared. By the turn of the century the venue's musical policy had changed, and it now offers everything from swing dancing and jazz to alternative rock, hip-hop disc jockeys, grunge bands, and acid-jazz groups.
(<http://www.elboroomchicago.com> (2001))

——. **Elite Club** [Elite Café]. 3030 South State Street; State Street between 26th Street and 31st Street. An early venue for jazz in Chicago, the club flourished between around 1910 and 1928 at two locations on State Street (usually referred to as Elite #1 and Elite #2), where the managers were (respectively) Dan Gain and Teenon Jones. The pianists J. Glover Compton and Tony Jackson played in a duo there around 1912, and Jelly Roll Morton was the resident pianist when he first arrived in Chicago around 1914.

——. **Empty Bottle.** 1035 North Western Street. From the 1990s this venue has presented avant-garde jazz, blues, country music, and rock, as well as strange and stylistically unidentifiable performances. Among the regular performers have been Ken Vandermark and various of his ensembles, Brad Mehldau, and Hamid Drake. Local musicians have played there with such European free-jazz musicians as Peter Brötzmann, Evan Parker, Paul Lytton, and Mats Gustafsson; Andrew Cyrille and Steve Lacy have also appeared. In 1997 the club began to host the Empty Bottle Festival of Jazz and Improvised Music.
(<http://www.emptybottle.com> (2001))

——. **Entertainers' Café** [Entertainers' Club]. East 35th Street and Michigan Avenue; East 35th Street between South Indiana Avenue and South Prairie Avenue. This club functioned at two locations close to each other on 35th Street. Freddie Keppard led a band of New Orleans musicians there before 1920, and Carroll Dickerson performed regularly from 1921 with an ensemble that included Natty Dominique. Earl Hines played in the resident band (led by the violinist Vernie Robinson) in 1924 and later returned to the club with a group of his own.

——. **5th Jack Show Lounge.** 3340 West Jackson Boulevard. In 1961 Gene Ammons (February) and the Sun Ra Arkestra (May) were among attractions there. The venue was still operating in mid-1962, when weekly jam sessions were advertised.

——. **Fiume Café.** State Street north of 35th Street. It engaged jazz musicians from at least 1919, when a band led by Freddie Keppard and including Buster Bailey played there.

——. **Flame Show Lounge.** 809 East Oakwood Boulevard. Advertised in January 1952 as "Chicago's Newest Nite Spot," when Tom Archia's band was featured, the venue was owned by Allyne Nixon and for a long period was managed by the singer and dancer Dr. Jo Jo Adams. By May 1952 Adams was appearing in a revue that also involved the trumpeter Melvin Moore and his band, in which Archia played in December of that year. In January 1954 the Joe Williams Show was billed, again with Moore's band. From late 1954 the venue shared acts for a time with Basin Street. Eddie "Cleanhead" Vinson performed in February 1955 with Johnny Griffin in his band, and the group led by the tenor saxophonist Melvin Scott was resident for several months after this. The Flame Show Lounge came under new management from mid-1956, at which time Griffin's band was again resident, and in October–November that year the group was billed in "Jazz vs the Blues" promotions opposite Jo Jo Adams. An earlier Flame Lounge which operated at 3020 Indiana Avenue in the mid-1940s was mainly a blues venue.

——. **Fountain Inn.** West 63rd Street and South Halsted Street. It was one of many venues in the city to engage New Orleans musicians in the 1910s. Charlie Elgar led a quintet there in 1914 and the trombonist George Filhe a sextet in 1916.

——. **411 Club.** 411 East 63rd Street. A trio led by the guitarist and banjoist Mike McKendrick was featured at this club in November 1941, and Preston Jackson's Victor Recording Orchestra was resident at 411 Club's Annex, which opened on 16 December 1946 at 411½ East 63rd Street. The club continued to book local acts until at least 1969.

——. **Friar's Inn.** South Wabash Avenue and East Van Buren Street. This nightclub on the North Side is remembered chiefly because of its connection with the white jazz band that became known as the New Orleans Rhythm Kings. The nucleus of this group played at the club for 17 months from autumn 1921 and recorded in 1922 as the Friars Society Orchestra; their performances and recordings provided a model for a generation of white jazz musicians in Chicago. Merritt Brunies followed the New Orleans Rhythm Kings into the club, holding a long residency from 1923 to 1926. Among other bands to appear there was Bill Paley's Rhythm Kings (*c*1926), whose members included Jimmy McPartland and Jim Lanigan.

——. **Gaffer's Jazz Club.** 60 East South Water Street. Bud Freeman and his band held a residency there in September 1949, and Danny Alvin's Alley Cats followed in October 1949.

——. **Gallo's 29 Club.** See Peven's 29 Club.

——. **Garfield Hotel.** See El Rado Café.

——. **Garrick Stage Bar** [Garrick Showbar, Garrick (Stage) Lounge]. West Randolph Street and North Clark Street. Situated next door to the Garrick Theater, the bar was owned from the 1940s by Joe Sherman. Henry "Red" Allen's band was resident in the venue's Downbeat Room from 15 August 1942 to August 1945; Billie Holiday shared top billing with Allen into 1943, and Ben Webster played with the group as a guest soloist in 1944. In 1942 Jimmie Noone performed in another area of the venue, upstairs from the Downbeat Room, and Louis Jordan, Hot Lips Page, Stuff Smith, and Al Casey all led small groups there in 1943, as did Webster in the mid-1940s. Lil Armstrong and Eddie South held long residencies at the Garrick. Other notable performers who appeared included Alberta Hunter and Ethel Waters. The venue is variously referred to as the Garrick Stage Bar, Garrick Showbar, Garrick Lounge, and Garrick Show Lounge. (J. Chilton: *Ride, Red, Ride: the Life of Henry "Red" Allen* (London, 1999), 120)

——. **Gaslight Club.** Marty Grosz played in a trio at this club intermittently for five years from 1957.

——. **George's.** 230 West Kinzie Street. Dinner club. Jazz has been played in the club from the early 1980s. Following the policy established at London House (see below) and then at Rick's Café Americain (see below), George's presented such musicians as the pianists George Shearing and Ahmad Jamal and the singer Joe Williams, and, less often, noted performers on other instruments, among them the saxophonist Eddie Harris.

——. **Goat's Nest.** See Three Deuces.

——. **Golden Lily (Tavern).** 309 East 55th Street (Garfield Boulevard). A Chinese restaurant opened on the second floor of the building in September 1926 and jazz was offered there from the start: on the opening night Tiny Parham and Ikey Robinson led a performance by the Victor Recording Orchestra. From 1929 to at least 1935 a band led by the drummer François Moseley (known variously as Frankie Franko and his Louisianians, the Louisiana Stompers, and François' Louisianians) held a long residency there; among the sidemen were Teddy Wilson, Albert Ammons, and Punch Miller. The venue was sold in 1939 and its name was changed to White's Emporium (see below).

——. **Golden Pumpkin.** This venue presented jazz from the late 1920s. The double bass player Thelma Terry and her Playboys, which included Gene Krupa, was resident there in 1929–30.

——. **Gold Star Sardine Bar.** 680 North Lake Shore Drive. Co-owned by the grocery magnate William Allen and the cabaret pianist Bobby Short, this venue specialized in cabaret pianists and singers and the occasional small group, and it booked both national and local musicians. Patricia Barber was artist-in-residence there from 1984 to 1995. The bar closed in 1997.

——. **Grand Terrace** [New Grand Terrace]. 3955 South Parkway Boulevard (28 December 1928–24 January 1937); 315–17 East 35th Street (from 19 June 1937). Ballroom. It opened on 28 December 1928 in a building that from 1917 had been the Peerless Theater, a movie theater where jazz was played during intermissions (Dave Peyton bought partial control of the Peerless in April 1926 and led an orchestra there, but the venue failed that summer); these premises were reconverted to a theater when the Grand Terrace closed, and were renamed The Park. The ballroom's second location was in premises formerly occupied by the Sunset Cafe (see below). Its change of name clearly did not coincide with the move, since it was known as the New Grand Terrace by at least 1932.

Activities at the Grand Terrace were directed by Edward Fox and the producer of the musical shows was Ralph Cooper, but the venue is supposed to have been controlled for some time by Joe Fusco, a henchman of the gangster Al Capone. Among the resident performers were Tiny Parham (*c*1931), Earl Hines (1928–38), Carroll Dickerson (1934), Fletcher Henderson (1936–9, 1941–2), Count Basie (from 1936), and Horace Henderson (from January 1939); Billie Holiday appeared in the summer revue there in 1936. The ballroom was the site of Hines's first real success as a bandleader, and the long residencies by his band throughout the 1930s, together with his many radio broadcasts made from there, gained him a large following. Other musicians who performed at the Grand Terrace included George Dixon, Walter Fuller, Reginald Foresythe, Chu Berry, and, in the mid-1950s, Sun Ra's big band.

——. **Grand Theater.** 3110–12 South State Street. Vaudeville theater. In the heart of the city's vaudeville district, it was opened in the early days of the 20th century. Although it presented mostly variety acts until at least 1914, some early jazz bands played there: Wilbur Sweatman's trio, of which Dave Peyton was a member, was resident between 1908 and 1912, and in February 1915 the theater was on the itinerary of a tour by the Original Creole Band. Peyton was directing the pit band by late November 1914, and he continued to do so for about 12 years; latterly his groups included, at different times, Charlie Allen, George Mitchell, Bob Shoffner, Reuben Reeves, Kid Ory, Bud Scott, Jimmy Bertrand, Zue Robertson, and Baby Dodds. *Plantation Days*, one of the most successful musical shows of the 1920s, played to ecstatic receptions at the Grand in August 1927; among the cast were Blanche and Cab Calloway. In the 1920s the theater was often used for performances by singers, and almost all the prominent vocalists who recorded in that decade appeared there, notably Clara Smith and Bessie Smith. The theater's fortunes declined with the shifting of the African-American entertainment center downtown in the late 1920s; it seems to have ceased to operate as a venue for jazz in 1930, and the building was eventually demolished to make way for a program of urban renewal.

——. **Green Dolphin Street.** 2200 North Ashland Street. It opened on 17 August 1995 and has presented jazz, acid jazz, blues, rhythm-and-blues, and Latin music. Among those who have appeared are Ari Brown, Wynton Marsalis, Jimmy Smith, William Russo's Chicago Jazz Ensemble, and Buddy DeFranco. (<http://www.jazzitup.com> (2001))

——. **Green Mill Ballroom.** 4802 North Broadway Street. The Green Mill engaged jazz musicians to play for dancing from around 1920, and Isham Jones (*c*1920) and Charlie Elgar (1922) both led orchestras there. The venue continued to be active into at least the 1940s. It reopened in the 1980s under the ownership of Dave Jemilo, who retained the original decor from the 1920s. Among local musicians who have appeared there on a regular basis are Von Freeman, Willie Pickens, Robert Shy, Jodie Christian, Patricia Barber, and Kurt Elling; visitors have included Nat Adderley and the group Astral Project, led by Tony Dagradi.

——. **El Grotto.** 6412 South Cottage Grove Avenue. Supper club. It occupied a large room with a dance floor in the basement of the Pershing Hotel (see below). Charlie Cole and Harry Fields took out a lease on the club in autumn 1944, then, after entering into part-ownership, Earl Hines finally bought it in April 1947. Tiny Bradshaw's band performed at El Grotto from its opening on 22 December 1944 until February 1945, and Hines played there himself from March 1945. Among other prominent musicians who appeared were Johnny Otis and his Hollywood Orchestra (August 1946), Johnny Griffin, a band led by T-Bone Walker, and Roy Eldridge and Eddie "Lockjaw" Davis (1947).

——. **Harlem Café.** 346 East 31st Street. It was active as a venue for jazz from the 1930s until at least March 1942. Sammy Price was among the musicians who played there.

——. **Harmon's Dreamland Ballroom.** See Dreamland Ballroom.

——. **Harry's Cocktail Lounge** [Harry's Show Lounge]. 432 East 63rd Street. It opened on 3 June 1947 with Lonnie Simmons and the pianist and singer Beverley White, and from 1947 to 1950 it was home to Leon Abbey and his trio. The venue changed its name to Harry's Show Lounge in late 1950. Stuff Smith's Combo with Floyd Smith appeared in November that year and were followed by Abbey. The harpist Olivette Miller was resident in late 1951. Abbey returned once again in March 1953 and remained until summer. Jazz was featured at Harry's at least until 1963.

——. **Hi Note.** 450 North Clark Street. It presented Anita O'Day and Miles Davis (November 1949), Billie Holiday (December 1950 – January 1951, June 1951), Coleman Hawkins (April 1951), Red Norvo (June 1951), Mary Lou Williams (October 1951), and Duke Groner's trio (November 1952).

——. **Hotel Normandy.** See Del'Abe Café.

——. **Hot House.** 1565 North Milwaukee Street (1989–95); 31 East Balbo Street (from May 1998). This nonprofit performing and visual arts center operated in a storefront in Wicker Park from 1989 to 1995 and then two years later reopened downtown. Owned by Marguerite Horberg, Hot House has presented an eclectic mix of styles, but with an emphasis on avant-garde jazz. Tatsu Aoki is among those who appear regularly, and the club has presented Irakere, Ernest Dawkins's New Horizons Ensemble, the 8 Bold Souls, led by Ed Wilkerson, Jr., Mwata Bowden and Sound Spectrum, Roscoe Mitchell, Malachi Favors, Kahil El'Zabar, Ari Brown, Malachi Thompson, and Hamiet Bluiett's Baritone Nation. Special events have included a series sponsored by the Association for the Advancement of Creative Musicians, a South African Jazz Festival, the Women Hold up the Sound Jazz Festival, and a World Music Festival. (<http://www.hothouse.net/history.html> (2001))

——. **Hurricane Show Lounge.** 347–51 East 55th Street (Garfield Boulevard). Buster Bennett led the house band there in September 1945, and Rosetta Howard and Lester Young appeared in 1946. The jazz harmonica player Rhythm Willie (Willie Hood) also took part in several shows in the latter year.

——. **It Club.** 5450 South Michigan Avenue. This basement nightclub, which flourished in the 1930s, was in the middle of a lively area of Chicago's nightlife at the intersection of Michigan Avenue and East 55th Street (Garfield Boulevard). A small group led by Albert Ammons held a residency there in the mid-decade, and Tommy Powell and his Hi-de-ho Boys appeared from December 1938. A new It Club operated in the early 1950s.

——. **Jazz Buffet.** 2556 West Diversey Street. Owned by Suzanne and John Dubiel, it opened in late October 1993. Initially it presented major national and local jazz musicians, including McCoy Tyner's trio, Paquito D'Rivera, Johnny Frigo's quartet, Paul Wertico's trio, and Jimmy Smith, but by 1996 it had ended this policy and instead was presenting a musical written by the owners, *The [Rat] Pack is Back!*.

——. **Jazz Ltd.** 11 East Grand Avenue. Founded by Bill Reinhardt and his wife Ruth Reinhardt, this nightclub on the North Side opened in June 1947. It flourished until at least the late 1960s. Reinhardt led the five-piece house band, which at different times included Munn Ware, Danny Alvin, Sidney Bechet, Floyd Bean, Big Chief Moore, Sid Catlett, and Barrett Deems. In order to avoid tax regulations singers were not engaged. Among the guest musicians who played at Jazz Ltd. were Doc Evans, Miff Mole, and Muggsy Spanier with Georg Brunis (all in the late 1940s), Art Hodes (1950s and 1960s), Zinky Cohn (who had a regular engagement on Monday evenings from 1950 to 1952), and Marty Marsala (1962). (S. S. Reinhardt: "Jazz Ltd. Owner Tells Tavern's Tale," *DB*, xv/8 (1948), 17)

——. **Jazz Showcase.** See Joe Segal's Jazz Showcase.

——. **Jeffrey's Tavern.** Nightclub on the South Side. In the mid-1920s a band, fronted by Hugh Swift, was featured in nightly broadcasts from the club on radio station WBJC. The saxophonist Vernon Roulette held a residency there in 1926 with a group that included Zutty Singleton (substituting for Baby Dodds) and George Mitchell.

——. **Joe's Bebop Café.** Navy Pier. Opened in 1997 by the Segals of Joe Segal's Jazz Showcase and a restauranteur, Joe's Bebop Café presents Chicago musicians and good barbecue. Franz Jackson performs there on Monday and Tuesday nights, and the trumpeter Sonny Turner on Sundays. The music presented on other nights varies from month to month. (<http://www.joesbebop.com> (2001))

——. **Joe's Deluxe Club** [Joe's De Luxe Café]. 6323 South Parkway Boulevard. It opened in April 1939 under the direction of its owner Joe Hughes. By December of that year Hughes was advertising a weekly "Swing Session" with a different band every week. The club's principal attraction became its celebrity night on Monday, to which many famous jazz musicians came, among them Duke Ellington,

Earl Hines, Cab Calloway, Nat "King" Cole, Sarah Vaughan, and Dizzy Gillespie. Others who appeared at the club included the bandleader Ted Weems, Joe Williams, Johnny Letman, Johnny Griffin, Ray Nance, and the dancer and producer Joe "Ziggy" Johnson. Joe's Deluxe Club should not be confused with the Deluxe Café (see above).

——. **Joe Segal's Jazz Showcase.** North Clark Street; Rust Street; 636 South Michigan Avenue, in the Blackstone Hotel (1970s – November 1995); 59 West Grand Street (from January 1996). Owned and managed by Joe Segal, it was established in the late 1940s and has been the most important club in Chicago since the demise of the Bee Hive Club in 1956. Many leading bop musicians have played there over the years, and the Art Ensemble of Chicago and Dizzy Gillespie appear in videos filmed at the Blackstone location. (<http://www.jazz-showcase.com> (2001))
Oral history material in *ICU* [Joe Segal].

——. **Joe's Paradise.** East 35th Street and South Prairie Avenue. The club was situated on the southeast corner of the intersection and was active in the 1920s. Among the jazz musicians who led bands there were Jimmie Noone and Jimmy O'Bryant.

——. **Kelly's Stables** [Bert Kelly's Stables]. 431 North Rush Street. A small, intimate venue, it was opened by Bert Kelly during the first heyday of Chicago jazz in the 1920s. Several musicians had long associations with the club: from 1924 Freddie Keppard, Johnny Dodds, and Baby Dodds worked there together in a group which Johnny Dodds took over and led as the house band for six years; Dodds's sidemen included his brother, Honore Dutrey, and Charlie Alexander, and Keppard returned frequently as a guest soloist. The venue was destroyed by fire in the late 1920s.

——. **Kimball Hall.** Concert hall. Jazz concerts were given in this small hall (capacity 450) from at least the mid-1940s. On 11 or 12 May 1946 a "Gold Award Jazzmen" concert involved Red Norvo, Chubby Jackson, Bill Harris, Flip Phillips, Ralph Burns, Sonny Berman, Billy Bauer, and Don Lamond, while on 1 December 1946 the author and raconteur Studs Terkel acted as compère at a concert that included performances by Mezz Mezzrow and Sidney Bechet backed by local musicians. Bechet returned on 26 January 1947, when the program also featured Bill Harris (i), Fletcher Henderson, and the tenor saxophonist Otis Finch, and he made further appearances in May and June 1947, the latter with Max Kaminsky.

——. **Lamb's Café.** North Clark Street and West Randolph Street. It was an early venue for jazz-oriented music in the city, and among the groups to play there before 1920 was Tom Brown's Ragtime Band, which was resident from May to September 1915; Brown's was probably the first white jazz band to appear in Chicago. The club came into its own during the first flowering of jazz in Chicago in the 1920s and continued to flourish into the 1930s. In the mid-1930s Jabbo Smith held a brief residency and Johnny Dodds led his small band there.

——. **Liberty Inn.** North Clark Street and West Erie Street. Owned by the Irish-American Johnny McGovern, it was known as the Breakfast Club during the Prohibition era. Boyce Brown formed a connection with the venue, leading his own trio there for a long period from the late 1930s and returning intermittently until the early 1950s. The Liberty Inn was a favorite venue for jam sessions, and among the musicians who took part in these was Art Hodes.

——. **Lincoln Gardens** [Royal Gardens]. 459 East 31st Street. Dance hall. A huge venue, it could accommodate around 1000 dancers and was open from the early years of the 20th century. It was originally known as the Royal Gardens, but the name was changed to Lincoln Gardens between February and July 1921. Following a fire late in 1924 the hall was magnificently refurbished for its reopening on 28 October 1925, when the name was again changed, to the New Charleston Café; the venue later became known as the Café de Paris. Dave Peyton led a band there from late November 1926, but in June 1927 it was bombed – perhaps in gang warfare – and closed.

The residency at the Royal Gardens in 1918 of the Original Creole Band, led by Bill Johnson (i), established the dance hall's reputation as a venue for jazz and initiated a series of appearances by New Orleans musicians that were of great significance for the development of the music in Chicago. King Oliver's Creole Jazz Band held a residency from 17 June 1922 until February 1924, when Oliver left and his former sidemen Johnny Dodds, Baby Dodds, and Honore Dutrey formed a new resident group with Bob Shoffner on trumpet; Oliver returned in June, with different personnel, and remained until the fire closed the hall at the end of the year.

——. **London House.** 360 North Michigan Avenue. Dinner club. It opened in 1951 and flourished into the 1970s. The owner, George Marianthal, presented for the most part piano trios, sometimes together with a singer. Oscar Peterson and George Shearing performed there regularly, and the house band included such distinguished local musicians as the pianist Norman Simmons. Erroll Garner appeared in 1956, 1962–3, and 1965–6, and Cannonball Adderley's quintet in December of that last year.

——. **Lucky Spot.** See Roberts Show Club.

——. **McKee's Disc Jockey Lounge.** East 63rd Street and South Cottage Grove Avenue. It was directed around 1950 by the dance promoter McKee Fitzhugh, who had been associated in the 1940s with several of the major ballrooms in Chicago. He engaged the saxophonist Johnny Board as the house bandleader, and Board formed an organ trio, which accompanied various visiting artists, among them Gene Ammons and Sonny Stitt. The club became well known for the exciting jam sessions that developed when such players were in residence. It remained active at least into the early 1960s, presenting Ammons and Dexter Gordon in 1961 and Ammons and Stitt the following year.

——. **The Macomba.** East 39th Street and South Cottage Grove Avenue. It was owned by the brothers Leonard and Philip Chess of Chess Records and flourished in the 1940s. In addition to various local bands, it engaged guest soloists such as Louis Armstrong, Lionel Hampton, and Ella Fitzgerald.

——. **Mark Twain Lounge.** Active in the 1940s and 1950s, this was one of the clubs where Lil Armstrong held long residencies as an unaccompanied soloist.

——. **Merry Gardens.** It was in operation by the mid-1920s. In 1927 Detroit Shannon's band, of which Walter Barnes was a member, was in residence; Barnes took over the band, and under the name the Royal Creolians it returned to the Merry

Gardens the following year. Other groups to appear were Joe Kayser's (1928), which included Muggsy Spanier and Jess Stacy, the Alabamians, with Cab Calloway as master of ceremonies (from April 1929), and Tiny Parham's big band (1931–2).

——. **Metropolitan Theater** [Ascher's Metropolitan Theater]. 4644 South Grand Boulevard. It flourished as a venue for jazz performance from 1917 until around 1930, when it fell victim to the enormous popularity of the Regal Theater and Savoy Ballroom and the consequent removal downtown of the African-American entertainment area; the building then became a movie theater, and it was eventually demolished to make way for a program of urban renewal. The managers of the Metropolitan when its jazz activities were at their height in the late 1920s were Cary Lewis (1927) and Matt Taylor, Jr. (1928). Among the musicians who played there were Sammy Stewart (who appeared regularly in the late 1920s), Fats Waller (1927), Erskine Tate (1928–30), whose orchestra included Bob Shoffner, Omer Simeon, Quinn Wilson, and Wallace Bishop, and Clarence Jones's Syncopators (February 1928), in which Louis Armstrong was featured.

——. **Michigan Theater.** East 55th Street (Garfield Boulevard) and South Michigan Avenue. It became known for its presentation of jazz late in the 1920s. Sammy Stewart performed there in November 1929 (when his sidemen included Chu Berry and Sid Catlett) and Boyd Atkins in 1930; Erskine Tate was music director from 1930 to 1932. In the 1930s the venue functioned mainly as a movie theater.

——. **Midnite Club.** 3140 South Indiana Avenue. It was in operation by at least the mid-1930s. Among the musicians who appeared there at that period were Jimmie Noone (1934), Ray Nance and his Rhythm Boys (March 1935), and Frankie "Half Pint" Jaxon (June 1935).

——. **Midway Garden Ballroom** [Midway Gardens]. South Cottage Grove Avenue between East 55th Street and East 63rd Street. Active as a jazz venue from at least the early 1920s, it engaged a number of prominent musicians. Elmer Schoebel's band played there around 1923, and the Air Kings, led by the tenor saxophonist Floyd Town and including Muggsy Spanier, Frank Teschemacher, Jess Stacy, and George Wettling, performed in 1926. The following year the reed player Art Kassel led a resident group with Benny Goodman, Schoebel, and Teschemacher among his sidemen. The ballroom became renowned for the staging of battles of bands in which as many as 15 ensembles might take part on a single night.

——. **Mister Kelly's.** Larry Novak played there from 1963 to 1975.

——. **Monogram Theater.** 3435–40 South State Street. Vaudeville theater. One of the foremost variety venues in the city, it was located in the heart of the African-American nightlife area and flourished from the early years of the 20th century. Besides important vaudeville singers such as Ma Rainey and Ethel Waters, a number of jazz musicians appeared there, including a band from New Orleans (1917) of which Sidney Bechet was a member. Lovie Austin was music director at the theater for 20 years from the mid-1920s.

——. **El Morocco.** 55th Street. This nightclub was active from at least the 1930s. It was among the several venues where Jesse Stone led residencies with his band the Cyclones in the mid-decade.

——. **Moulin Rouge Café.** South Wabash Avenue north of East Van Buren Street. It offered jazz from at least the early 1920s, when among the resident performers were the pianist Clarence Jones and his Wonder Orchestra (1922), a band led by Jimmy Wade (1923–6) with Eddie South as front man and music director, and Izzy Friedman's group (*c*1923).

——. **My Cellar.** See The Cellar.

——. **Nest Club.** East 35th Street between South Prairie Avenue and South Calumet Avenue. A club functioned on an upper floor of a building at this location from at least 1920 (see Club Alvadere above) and by 1922 had become a luxurious supper club under the name of the Nest Club. Jimmie Noone led a small band there from summer 1926 and continued to be associated with the venue when it became the Apex Club (see above) in autumn of that year.

——. **New Annex.** 6323 South Parkway Boulevard. Its opening, in premises that also housed Joe's Deluxe Club (see above), was announced in April 1939. The club's management may have been connected with that of the Annex (see above).

——. **New Apartment Lounge.** 504 East 75th Street. The venue flourished in the 1980s presenting soul-jazz groups, including those of Hank Crawford and Jimmy McGriff. Von Freeman also appeared there.

——. **New Apex Café.** 4311–17 South Indiana Avenue. It occupied premises where a venue called the Big House had operated earlier. Managed by Doc Jennings, it opened in January 1935, by which time his Apex Café (see Apex Tavern above) may have closed. At the opening the resident band was Georgia Gorham and her Syncopators, with the singer Dan Grisson and the guitarist John Collins; by the end of January Elbert Topps and his Famous Orchestra had begun a residency there.

——. **New Charleston Café.** See Lincoln Gardens.

——. **New Club DeLisa.** See Club DeLisa.

——. **New Deal Tavern.** West 55th Place at the Loop. Active by at least the mid-1930s, it was owned by Warren La Rue, who was associated with a number of clubs in Chicago. The resident pianist from March 1936 until at least the end of 1939 was Laura Rucker.

——. **New Grand Terrace.** See Grand Terrace.

——. **New Pekin Theater.** See Pekin Theater.

——. **New Plantation Café.** 5060 South Michigan Avenue. Nightclub. It flourished in the mid-1930s and may have been connected with the Plantation Café, active earlier on East 35th Street (see below). In 1934 the Rhythm Kings, led by Johnny Dodds and Natty Dominique, held a residency at the New Plantation.

——. **New Regal Theater.** 79th Street and Stony Island Street. The old Avalon Theater was renovated and reopened in 1987 as the New Regal Theater. Performers have included Count Basie's orchestra under the direction of Frank Foster, and Bobby McFerrin.

——. **New Trianon Ballroom.** See Trianon Ballroom.

——. **Nob-Hill Club.** 5228 Lake Park Avenue. In May 1953 Gene Ammons's performances there were followed by a "battle" pitting Harold Ashby against Tom Archia; Ammons returned the following month. Miles Davis was a guest soloist in November 1953, and Ben Webster was billed as an additional attraction later in the month. It is not clear whether this is the same venue at which Lil Armstrong appeared as an unaccompanied soloist during the 1940s and early 1950s.

——. **North American Restaurant.** North State Street and West Monroe Street, on the northwest corner of the intersection. The performances given there around 1914 by the Original Creole Band, led by Bill Johnson (i), were among the first by African-American jazz musicians in the city.

——. **The Note.** Armitage Street; 1565 North Milwaukee Street (from 1997). Barrett Deems's big band ended its longstanding Tuesday-night residency at the Elbo Room to play on Wednesday nights at the North Milwaukee Street location of The Note, where it appeared from 1997 until Deems's death the follow year. The club has presented Latin music, acid jazz, swing, and mainstream jazz styles; Von Freeman, Kurt Elling, Fareed Haque, Hamid Drake, and Ken Vandermark are among those who have appeared there.

——. **Off Beat Room.** See Three Deuces.

——. **100 Club.** It offered performances of jazz from at least 1930. Danny Alvin led the resident band from around 1930 until 1933.

——. **Orchestra Hall.** 216 South Michigan Avenue. Concert hall. It was used from time to time as a venue for jazz, beginning in the late 1910s with a concert by Charlie Elgar's band. Other musicians who appeared there included Will Marion Cook's New York Syncopated Orchestra (1919), Chippie Hill, and Kid Ory and Joe Darensbourg (late 1940s).

——. **Oriental Café.** 3532 State Street. It appears to have occupied premises where the Panama Club (see below) functioned earlier. In the mid-1920s resident musicians included the pianist J. Glover Compton with his band the Syncopators (1924–5) and Reuben Reeves (1925).

——. **Oriental Theater.** This downtown venue engaged a number of prominent big bands in the 1930s. Duke Ellington's orchestra appeared there in 1930 and 1934, Erskine Hawkins's band in 1938, and Earl Hines's in 1939.

——. **Owl Theater.** 4653 South State Street. It was used as a movie theater and also as a venue for other kinds of performance, including vaudeville acts, from around 1914; jazz formed part of many of the presentations. From about 1919 to 1927 the pianist Clarence Jones directed a small band there with Clarence Williams and the drummer Jasper Taylor among his sidemen. Others to appear there later were Williams's protégée Sara Martin and (in 1927) George Mitchell.

——. **Panama Café (Nite Club).** 307 East 58th Street. Nightclub. It was opened by Ben Tolliver after Prohibition was repealed in February 1933; he had previously run a gambling house on the premises, which he renovated when he converted them to a nightclub. The club was initially known as the Panama Tavern, but in December 1933 the name was changed to Panama Café Nite Club. The saxophonist Billy Paige, who had earlier worked with King Oliver, ran the Panama's activities. Jabbo Smith and the drummer and singer Floyd Campbell were resident musicians for two years from shortly after the club opened, and Budd Johnson also performed there in 1933. Nat "King" Cole appeared in a band led by his brother Eddie in 1935, then returned for a six-month period the following year.

——. **Panama Club.** 3532 State Street. Around 1914 it was owned and directed by Isadore Levine, who engaged a number of prominent singers to perform there, including Bricktop (Ada Smith), Florence Mills, Cora Green, and the young Alberta Hunter. Tony Jackson appeared around 1919. In the 1920s the Oriental Café (see above) seems to have operated from the same premises.

——. **Panther Room.** See Sherman Hotel.

——. **The Park.** See Grand Terrace.

——. **Park City Bowl.** 345 South 63rd Street. In late 1947 the "largest roller rink in the Midwest" presented one-night stands by traveling bands, including the International Sweethearts of Rhythm, Dinah Washington, and Gene Ammons on a triple bill on 10 August, Luis Russell on 17 August, Henry "Red" Allen in a battle of the bands with Flip Phillips and Ammons on 24 August, Dizzy Gillespie on 31 August, Johnny Griffin on 7 September, and Lucky Millinder on 19 October. Following this intensive activity there were at least occasional jazz performances in later years, notably by Lionel Hampton's band on 30 May 1950 and Paul Bascomb's on 21 April 1957.

——. **Parkway Ballroom.** 4459 South Parkway Boulevard. It opened on 9 March 1940 under African-American ownership with performances by Floyd Campbell's orchestra, which played there regularly; a second "grand opening" featured Horace Henderson's orchestra on 9 September 1940. In 1941 Gene Ammons appeared as the star attraction in a band led by the trumpeter King Kolax. During the 1940s the dances at the Parkway were promoted by McKee Fitzhugh, who was associated with a number of ballrooms in the city. It remained in operation at least through 1954.

——. **Paul Mares Barbecue.** 935 North State Street. Restaurant and bar. It was owned and run by Paul Mares, formerly a member of the New Orleans Rhythm Kings, and was in operation from at least the late 1930s. Among its activities were after-hours jam sessions. Mares sold the restaurant when he embarked on war work in the 1940s.

——. **Peerless Theater.** See Grand Terrace.

——. **Pekin Theater.** 2700 South State Street. Early in the century Robert T. Motts, an African-American entrepreneur, ran a saloon and gambling house in the building. On 18 June 1905 he opened the Pekin Temple of Music for variety performances in an upstairs room at the north end of the premises, and barely a year later he refurbished the venue and reopened it as the New Pekin Theater. The shows presented consisted essentially of vaudeville and cabaret acts, but a number of early jazz musicians appeared there. Manuel Perez led a quintet there before 1920, and Tony Jackson's band (which included Sidney Bechet) performed regularly until shortly before Jackson's death in 1921. King

Oliver was also a resident bandleader around 1920. The venue is variously referred to as the Pekin Theater, the Pekin Café, the Pekin Inn, and the Pekin Cabaret.

——. **Pershing Hotel.** East 64th Street west of South Cottage Grove Avenue. The hotel offered music for the entertainment of its patrons in at least three venues – the Pershing Lounge (the hotel's main bar), the Pershing Ballroom (where Muggsy Spanier played in the orchestra around 1925), and the El Grotto supper club (see above). Among the musicians to appear in the lounge were the tenor saxophonist and organist Lonnie Simmons, whose ten-piece band was resident for long periods in the mid-1940s, and the pianist Ahmad Jamal. Around this time the dance promoter McKee Fitzhugh was responsible for the activities of the ballroom, which began to admit African-American patrons when the lease of the hotel was taken over by African-American owners in 1944. Private recordings survive of Charlie Parker's group performing there in 1949 and ?1950, and the Freeman brothers played in the house band in the late 1940s to early 1950s.

——. **Peven's 29 Club.** 29 West 47th Street. In operation by June 1935, when Albert Ammons and his Rhythm Kings appeared, this club was featuring Joe Lindsay and his orchestra early in 1936. By October that year it had become Gallo's 29 Club, and it continued until at least December 1938, when Rosetta Howard was performing.

——. **Pioneer Lounge.** 57–9 East 51st Street. It was open by June 1938, when Junie Cobb's band was featured. In February 1939 a Girls Novelty Band [*sic*], led by "Doll Amera" (Dolly Jones) on trumpet, was advertised. The jive group the Cats and the Fiddle was resident in mid-1940, Monette Moore appeared that August, and Alberta Hunter began an "indefinite engagement" in November. Johnny Letman was featured in May 1941. This venue remained open until 1946, but there was also a later Pioneer Lounge in the 1960s at 1200 East 71st Street.

——. **Plantation Café.** 338 East 35th Street. Nightclub. It was opened on 29 October 1924 under the ownership of Edward Fox and Al Turner in premises formerly occupied by Al Turner's Café; like other clubs in which Fox had an interest, it was controlled by the Capone syndicate. One of the most popular "black and tan" venues in Chicago in the 1920s, it offered all-night dancing and drinking. A dance orchestra led by Dave Peyton opened the club, and King Oliver's Dixie Syncopators held a long residency from February 1925 until spring 1927. The club may have ceased operations in the 1930s, since a New Plantation Café (see above) had opened by 1934.

——. **Platinum Lounge.** 601 East 36th Street. A room in the basement of the Vincennes Hotel, it was run by Pops Lewis, a prominent gambling operator on the South Side who was the husband of the hotel's owner, Elizabeth B. Lewis. The lounge opened on 3 December 1936, and the following year Jimmie Noone took a band there for a residency; among his sidemen were Franz Jackson and Joe Williams. Broadcasts were made frequently from the club in the late 1930s. The hotel was demolished in the course of a program of urban renewal.

——. **Plugged Nickel.** North Wells Street. Many leading musicians played at the Plugged Nickel, which featured mainly modern-jazz styles, though swing and blues performers were also presented. Miles Davis's quintet made a series of acclaimed recordings (portions of which were first issued in Japan in 1976) during the beginning of a two-week residency from 21 December 1965 to 2 January 1966. Among others who appeared between October 1965 and October 1967 were Jimmy Smith, Brother Jack McDuff, Art Blakey, Dizzy Gillespie, Sonny Stitt, Wes Montgomery, Groove Holmes, Willis Jackson, Thelonious Monk, Lionel Hampton, and Mose Allison. In 1969 Gene Ammons returned to public performance leading a quintet there. The club closed in the 1970s.

——. **Pops for Champagne.** 2934 North Sheffield Street. Owned by Tom Verhey, Pops for Champagne began to present jazz on Thursday through Saturday nights in September 1986. Among the local artists who have appeared are Willie Pickens, Von Freeman, and Fareed Haque. (<http://www.popschampagne.com> (2001))

——. **Premier Studio.** See Rhumboogie Club.

——. **Pump Room.** Ambassador Hotel. It was active in the 1930s and offered performances mostly by soloists and small groups. Among the musicians to appear there were Maxine Sullivan with John Kirby's sextet (for illustration *see* Kirby, John), Teddy Wilson, and Caspar Reardon, who held a residency in the mid-1930s.

——. **El Rado Café.** 231 East 55th Street (Garfield Boulevard). The café was in the basement of the Garfield Hotel, which was in the area at the hub of Chicago's South Side nightlife in the 1920s. Following the closure of the Apex Club (1928) Jimmie Noone led his Apex Recording Orchestra in a residency at the El Rado (1928–31).

——. **Rainbow Café** [Rainbow Gardens]. It flourished around 1920. Among the jazz musicians who played there were Isham Jones and his orchestra and Art Hodes (1924).

——. **Red Mill Café.** East 39th Street between South Parkway Boulevard and South Cottage Grove Avenue. It was active as a venue for jazz in the early 1920s, when the resident bandleaders included Roy Palmer and Tommy Ladnier.

——. **Regal Theater.** 4719 South Parkway Boulevard. Variety theater. Built in a Moorish style and opulently, even garishly, decorated, with chandeliers, rhinestone-studded stage curtains, and silk and velvet drapery, the theater itself could seat 3500 and the spacious foyer could accommodate 1500. With the Savoy Ballroom, it occupied the block on the east side of 47th Street and the boulevard.

The Regal opened on 4 February 1928, and its glitter and glamor soon lured audiences away from the older Chicago theaters. The resident band for more than a year after the opening was conducted by Fess Williams, who also served as master of ceremonies for the shows. In the early years the programs consisted of variety acts and musical numbers, and the Regal engaged famous singers and dancers such as Blanche Calloway, Josephine Baker, Buck and Bubbles, and the Mills Brothers; the show producer at that time was Percy Venable, an uncle of Lucky Millinder. The numerous famous jazz musicians to appear in the 1930s and 1940s included Louis Armstrong, Duke Ellington, Count Basie, Jimmie Lunceford, Millinder, Lionel Hampton, Woody Herman, and Jay McShann. Later the theater offered jazz concerts among its other events, and in the 1950s and 1960s leading bop and cool-jazz players appeared, notably Miles Davis, Dizzy Gillespie, and Sonny Stitt. The manager of the Regal for 20 years (1939–59) was Ken Blewett, whose successful operation did much to maintain live entertainment on Chicago's South Side. the theater closed in 1968 and was demolished in 1973. The New Regal Theater (see above), which opened in 1987, is not connected with this venue.

BIBLIOGRAPHY

S. Tomashefsky: "Farewell to the Regal," *Living Blues*, no.15 (1973), 20
D. J. Travis: "The Regal Theater that I Remember," "Ken 'Mr. Regal' Blewett," *An Autobiography of Black Jazz* (Chicago, 1983), 145, 157

——. **Rendezvous.** 622 West Diversey Avenue. It was active in the mid-1920s, when bands led by Charlie Straight (with Bix Beiderbecke among the members) and Ben Pollack played there.

——. **Rhumboogie Club.** 343 East 55th Street (Garfield Boulevard). It occupied premises on the first floor of the Ritz Building, where the Swingland Café (see below) had been located in the 1930s; its principal feature was its balcony bar. The venue was owned by Joe Louis and managed by Leonard Reed and Pat Brooks, and the show producer was Joe "Ziggy" Johnson. It was active from the early 1940s until April 1947, when it was closed by the revenue service for nonpayment of taxes. Among the jazz musicians who appeared at the Rhumboogie were Milt Larkin (as leader of the house band in 1941–2, and resident bandleader in 1946), Fletcher Henderson (1945), the drummer and singer Floyd Campbell (1946–7), Walter Fuller, Horace Henderson, Sarah Vaughan, and George Dixon.

A new club, the Premier Studio, opened in the Rhumboogie's place in August 1949; aided financially by a number of jazz musicians (among them Joe Dixon, Chester Lewis, and George Johnson), it functioned for three nights a week for 15 months before it closed.

——. **Rick's Café Americain.** 910 North Lakeshore Drive. Situated in the Holiday Inn, it was modeled after the club of the same name in the film *Casablanca* and opened in 1976 after the demise of London House (see above); it presented pianists who would have worked at the earlier venue and soon became the major competition for Joe Segal's Jazz Showcase. The excellent quality of its piano elicited memorable performances from such players as Oscar Peterson, Teddy Wilson, Hank Jones, and Bill Evans (ii). Benny Carter, Red Norvo, Joe Williams, and Clark Terry were among other musicians who worked there. It closed in the early 1980s.

——. **Rituals.** 537 South Dearborn Street. A tiny club featuring free jazz, this venue is especially well attended by members of the Association for the Advancement of Creative Musicians. Performers have included Ed Wilkerson's quartet, the Ethnic Heritage Ensemble, and Ari Brown's quartet.

——. **Riverview Park Ballroom.** Western Avenue and West Madison Street. Dance hall. Active from before 1920, it presented jazz-oriented bands to accompany the dancing. Doc Cook was the music director for three years from 1918 to 1921. The hall is of jazz interest mainly for the staging of battles of bands: a notable event of this kind took place on 11 September 1927, when 12 groups assembled to compete with one another.

——. **Roberts Show Club.** 6222 South Parkway Boulevard. It was owned and managed by Herman Roberts, who began his career as the owner of a fleet of taxi cabs. He first ran a nightclub called the Lucky Spot (renamed the Roberettes) at 605 East 71st Street, which was so successful that it soon outgrew its premises. Roberts decided to relocate his club to the garage on South Parkway Boulevard from which his cab company functioned, and after completely renovating the building he opened a large dance hall there, which shortly afterwards he refurbished as a nightclub, able to seat 1000 people, under the name Roberts Lounge and Liquor. In 1957 Roberts sold his cab franchise to devote himself to his club, which by now was known as Roberts Show Club. Among the many prominent performers he engaged were Dinah Washington, who appeared regularly three times a year, Sarah Vaughan, Count Basie, Sammy Davis, Jr., Billy Eckstine, Ray Charles, and Louis Jordan; Red Saunders directed the house band. (D. J. Travis: "Roberts Show Club," *An Autobiography of Black Jazz* (Chicago, 1983), 191)

——. **Royal Gardens** [Royal Garden Café]. See Lincoln Gardens.

——. **Rupneck's.** 5900 North ?Thorndale and Broadway. Art Hodes led bands at this dixieland venue in the early 1950s.

——. **Savoy Ballroom.** South Parkway Boulevard and East 47th Street. The opening of the Savoy on 23 November 1927 and of the Regal Theater (see above) on the same block in 1928 marked the removal downtown of Chicago's center of African-American entertainment and commerce, and the consequent decline of the area around 35th Street and State Street. The Savoy's fortunes rose and fell several times in its 20-year existence. Until the collapse of the New York stock exchange in 1929 the ballroom flourished, offering music and dancing seven nights a week; thereafter it was found expedient to introduce such activities as boxing and skating. The ballroom was partly refurbished in 1938, and when it reopened its policy was to present dances on four nights; however, this lasted no more than a year before the management decided that it could afford only one dance night – Sunday. The ballroom closed in summer 1948 and the building was later demolished.

Despite its checkered commercial history, the Savoy was a major center for jazz in Chicago for two decades. Among the bands that appeared there in its first few sensational years were those led by Carroll Dickerson (which included Louis Armstrong and Zutty Singleton), Charlie Elgar, Fletcher Henderson, and the violinist Clarence Black. From the 1930s virtually all the prominent bandleaders of the day were engaged by the Savoy, notably Henderson (1936–9, 1941, 1943–5), Duke Ellington, Count Basie, Horace Henderson, Andy Kirk, Jimmie Lunceford, Chick Webb, Earl Hines, Erskine Tate, Tiny Parham, and Willie Bryant. After the renovation in 1938 the ballroom reopened on 16 May with a gala performance by 25 swing bands, and from that time live broadcasts were regularly made. In its later years the Savoy continued to present the greatest jazz performers: among those who appeared were Basie, Ellington, Stan Kenton, Dizzy Gillespie, Ella Fitzgerald, Gene Krupa, Woody Herman, Louis Jordan, and the International Sweethearts of Rhythm. (D. J. Travis: "Jumping at the Savoy," "The Many Faces of Lady Savoy, 1927 to 1948," *An Autobiography of Black Jazz* (Chicago, 1983), 77, 93)

——. **Schiller Café.** 318 East 31st Street. Like the Casino Gardens (see above), this venue was managed by the promoter Harry James and offered some of the earliest performances by New Orleans players in Chicago. In March 1916 a band consisting of Johnny Stein, Alcide "Yellow" Nunez, Eddie Edwards, Henry Ragas, and Nick LaRocca began a long engagement there (first as Stein's Band from Dixie and later as Stein's Dixie Jass Band); Edwards, Ragas, and LaRocca left on 26 May to form the Original Dixieland Jazz Band, and Stein was obliged to form a new group to fulfill his contract at the club.

——. **Sherman Hotel.** West Randolph Street and North Clark Street. Jazz was played for the entertainment of patrons in several rooms in the hotel. Paul Whiteman's band was resident in the College Inn in 1933, and in the late 1930s the Old Town Room engaged a number of important performers. The Panther Room, lavishly decorated with panther-skin patterning (for illustration *see* Spanier, muggsy), was the hotel's principal venue for the presentation of jazz and a fashionable nightspot. Count Basie's orchestra undertook an engagement in June 1939, and most of the best-known big bands of the 1940s played there, but it also offered performances by small groups led by Bud Freeman, Fats Waller, Hot Lips Page, and Muggsy Spanier. Other prominent jazzmen who played at the Sherman included Jimmy McPartland, Joe Sullivan in a duo with Meade "Lux" Lewis, and Caspar Reardon. Radio broadcasts were frequently made from its various venues.

——. **Showboat Cabaret.** North Clark Street. A speakeasy on the Chicago Loop, it was owned in the early 1930s by Sam Beers and controlled by the Capone syndicate. Bands led by Jabbo Smith and Cassino Simpson held residencies there, and Louis Armstrong appeared in 1931.

——. **El Sid's Trianon Ballroom.** See Trianon Ballroom.

——. **65 Club.** See Club 65.

——. **Southmoor Hotel.** See Venetian Room.

——. **Square's Boulevard Lounge** [Square's Lounge, Square's Steak House]. 104 East 51st Street. Owned by Earl "Square" Washington, this venue was in existence by March 1940, when Lonnie Johnson was leading a quartet there, though the pianist Wilbur Hobbs was appearing at the same time; Johnson's residency continued until December 1942. Known as Square's Lounge from mid-1943, the club featured a band including John Lindsay and the tenor saxophonist Johnny Board from August to December of that year. From January 1944 it was called Square's Steak House, and in March of that year Buster Bennett's trio became the resident band. In September Johnson returned, advertising "Swing tunes you'll like," and he was still playing there in February 1946, when he was billed as "Mr. Blues Himself."

——. **Stage Lounge.** 1524 East 63rd Street. The Stage Lounge was a new venue in April 1955, when Eddie Chamblee and his novelty jazz all stars were billed. Roy Eldridge, Milt Buckner, Sonny Stitt, Jimmy Rushing, Art Blakey, Charles Mingus, Lou Donaldson, Bud Powell, Gene Ammons, Lester Young, and Howard McGhee were among those who appeared there during the next three years. Jump Jackson's band was resident for a time in 1957.

——. **Strand Show Lounge** [Strand Lounge]. 6325 South Cottage Grove Avenue. Situated in the Strand Hotel, it opened in August 1951 under the management of Bernie Skoller, formerly of the Circle Inn, with a residency by Horace Henderson and his Hollywood Band (which continued until April 1953). In summer 1953 Oett Mallard appeared. Henderson returned that autumn, to be followed by Roy Eldridge in January 1954; Henderson took over again in May, and later in 1954 Duke Groner's group was resident. Leon Abbey's trio appeared in June 1955, and there was a further residency by Henderson at the end of the year. In 1955–6 the club advertised as Butch Webb's Strand Lounge. The Strand Show Lounge was still or again featuring jazz in August 1966, when Mallard was leading the band there.

——. **Studio Club.** One of several Chicago nightclubs owned and run at different times by Earl Hines, it opened in the spring of 1940; the operation lasted only until October, when Hines reorganized his band for engagements in California.

——. **Sunset Café.** 315–17 East 35th Street. Nightclub. It was opened on 3 August 1921 by Edward Fox and Sam Dreyfus, though it was under the control of Al Capone's gangster syndicate. Situated at the center of Chicago nightlife in the 1920s, close to the Apex Club and the Plantation Café, it was soon one of the most popular "black and tan" clubs on the South Side. It came into its own as a jazz venue when Carroll Dickerson became the resident leader in 1922; following a residency by Sammy Stewart's band from 1924 to 1926 Dickerson returned for another long period in 1926–7. His band, which latterly included Louis Armstrong and Earl Hines, was a phenomenal success and drew jazz musicians from all over Chicago to hear it. When Dickerson left the club in February 1927 Armstrong led the Sunset Stompers there, with Hines as music director; it is supposed to have been at the Sunset that he first met Joe Glaser, who later became his manager. The club continued to flourish for the remainder of the decade, engaging bands led by Charlie Elgar (1929–30), Boyd Atkins (1929–30), and Tiny Parham (1930). Dickerson returned in the mid-1930s for a further residency, but the Sunset was by that time in financial difficulty, and it closed in 1937. The premises were taken over by the Grand Terrace, which was also owned and run by Fox (see above).

——. **Sutherland Show Lounge.** South Drexel Boulevard and East 47th Street. The nightclub and bar of the Sutherland Hotel offered jazz performances from at least the late 1950s. It engaged mainly soloists and small groups, and among those who appeared there were Cannonball Adderley, Nancy Wilson, John Coltrane, Miles Davis, Jaki Byard, Count Basie, and Dinah Washington. The club was one of the first to be officially desegregated, in 1952. Decades later Malachi Thompson began working to restore the club; in the 1990s he was booking Thursday-night jazz under the auspices of the Sutherland Community Arts Initiative, and the Hyde Park Kenwood Jazz Festival has been held there several times. In September 1997 the club was celebrated at Chicago's Victory Gardens Theater in the world première of Charles Smith's play *The Sutherland.*

——. **Swingland Café.** 343 East 55th Street (Garfield Boulevard) (late 1930s); 6249 South Cottage Grove Avenue (late 1950s). In August 1936 Benny Skoller took over these premises in the Ritz Building from Dave Heighly, who had run them as Dave's Café (see above). Among the prominent musicians to perform at the Swingland were Horace Henderson's orchestra (1937–8) with the singer Viola Jefferson. From the 1940s the same building housed the

Rhumboogie Club (see above). A later Swingland presented "Jazz for Moderns," featuring Johnny Griffin, in 1958.

——. **Swing Room.** See Three Deuces.

——. **Tejar's Slipper Lounge.** 1321 South Michigan Avenue. It was active in the 1960s under the ownership of Ahmad Jamal. Besides Jamal himself, a number of soloists and small groups played there. It had closed by March 1971, when the blues club Pepper's Lounge opened in its place.

——. **Three Deuces.** 222 North State Street. Nightclub. It occupied premises that formerly housed clubs called the Goat's Nest and The Cellar (see above) and was in operation by the mid-1930s; by 1936 it was owned and managed by Sam Beers. Zutty Singleton led a sextet at the club from May 1935 and stayed to play in Roy Eldridge's band, which began a long and highly successful residency in September 1936; among Eldridge's other sidemen were Dave Young, Scoops Carry, and Tiny Parham. During this period the club enjoyed enormous popularity; simultaneously with Eldridge's residency, Art Tatum was the pianist in the Swing Room, a small venue downstairs from the main club. Among other important musicians to play at the Three Deuces in the late 1930s were Art Hodes, Jimmy McPartland (*c*1937), Baby Dodds (who was the house drummer, 1936–9), Johnny Dodds (late 1930s), Lonnie Johnson (*c*1937–1939), Julia Lee (1939), and Anita O'Day (with Max Miller's band, 1939–40); Muggsy Spanier's group and Billie Holiday shared a booking at the Off Beat Room, another downstairs section of the Three Deuces, in autumn 1939. Broadcasts were frequently made from the club.

——. **Tiny and Ruby's Gay Spot.** 2711 South Wentworth Street. Opened about 1954, "The Nite Spot that Jumps," operated by Tiny Davis and the double bass player Ruby Lucas, featured the all-female band led by Davis. Other musicians who appeared included Paul Bascomb and Vi Burnside (April to June 1955).

——. **Tivoli.** 43rd Street and Cottage Grove Avenue. This cinema resumed presenting stage shows in March 1959 with Pearl Bailey's all-star revue featuring Louie Bellson's orchestra. In the ensuing months packages involving the bands of Sonny Thompson, Red Prysock, Paul Williams, and Louis Jordan appeared, and in January 1960 Ahmad Jamal and Duke Ellington were on the bill. The policy of presenting jazz continued there until at least 1963.

——. **Toulouse Cognac Bar.** 2140 North Lincoln Park West. Owned by Bob Djahanguiri, this tiny venue opened in 1979 and began specializing in jazz singers and cabaret; among those who have appeared there are Dave McKenna, Blossom Dearie, Patricia Barber, and Johnny Frigo.

——. **Tradesmen's Exclusive Club.** 6240 Cottage Grove Avenue. This club flourished from May 1945, when Buster Bennett's band was resident. In February 1947 Sonny Thompson was appearing with the group led by the tenor saxophonist Dick Davis, and in November 1947 a "Silhouette Show" was presented with Louis Jordan. In January 1948 the club reopened under new management as the Tradesman's Lounge, with the band led by the double bass player Al Smith performing.

——. **Trianon Ballroom.** 6201 South Cottage Grove Avenue. Like other ballrooms in the city, it enjoyed its greatest celebrity in the 1930s, when major swing bands played for dancing there and broadcasts brought a wide audience for the music it offered. The dance promoter McKee Fitzhugh organized its activities in the mid-1930s. It operated a strict segregationist policy until 1950, admitting Whites only.

The ballroom closed early in 1954, but quickly returned as the New Trianon; Count Basie was featured at the opening on 28 May 1954, and the segregationist policy was abandoned. Horace Henderson and Louis Jordan were announced as forthcoming attractions. Among the many famous musicians to play there over the course of the next six years were Lil Armstrong, Earl Bostic, Dinah Washington, and Lionel Hampton (all 1954), Illinois Jacquet (1955), Bill Doggett (1956), and Hampton again (early in 1959). After another hiatus the venue was operating as El Sid's Trianon Ballroom by March 1963, when Doggett, Roy Eldridge, and Ben Webster appeared; Lou Donaldson and Sonny Stitt performed in April of that same year, and Milt Buckner's trio in May; rhythm-and-blues and soul acts were also booked, and El Sid's Trianon Ballroom remained active until at least 1965. The building was demolished in the late 1960s.

——. **Twin Terrace Café.** 3 North Clark Street. Among those who appeared at this venue in 1947 were Lee Collins, Preston Jackson, Bill Johnson (i), Little Brother Montgomery, Chippie Hill, Lil Armstrong, Bunk Johnson and his Dixieland Band, and Art Hodes and his Blue Note Jazzmen (October).

——. **Velvet Lounge.** 2128 South Indiana Street. Owned by Fred Anderson from 1982, the Velvet Lounge presents free jazz. Local ensembles from the Association for the Advancement of Creative Musicians perform there, as do returning members visiting for the Chicago Jazz Festival and other events. (<http://www.velvetlounge.net> (2001))

——. **Vendome Theater.** 3145 South State Street. Built in 1909, it was one of many vaudeville theaters in the area where Chicago's nightlife was busiest early in the century. By the time jazz emerged in the city in the 1910s the Vendome was directed by the Hammond brothers and was offering silent films with musical accompaniment and an hour-long floor show during the intermissions. The venue is of jazz interest principally for its association with Erskine Tate, whose Vendome Theater Symphony Orchestra opened there in 1919 and remained the resident band until 1928; Tate returned to the theater in the 1930s. The most important of his sidemen was Louis Armstrong, who was a member of the band in 1926. Among the other jazz musicians to appear there was Fats Waller, who was the house organist in 1927. In the late 1920s, when the success of the Regal Theater was threatening older theaters on the South Side, the pianist Clarence Jones and Armstrong moved from the Metropolitan to the Vendome in an attempt to restore audiences there, but the ploy failed and the decline continued. The theater was eventually demolished in 1949.

——. **Venetian Room.** Southmoor Hotel. Jazz was offered in the hotel's nightclub from at least 1926, when Ben Pollack and his Sunkist Serenaders (later renamed the Californians) began a residency that lasted a year; among Pollack's sidemen was Benny Goodman.

——. **Victory Club.** 644 North Clark Street. It was founded and directed by Werlie Catanese and flourished during the 1940s and 1950s, when it became known as a venue for traditional and mainstream jazz. Among the resident performers employed by the club was Lee Collins, who worked there in 1945 and again from November 1951.

——. **Vincennes Hotel.** See Platinum Lounge.

——. **White City Ballroom.** East 63rd Street and South Parkway Boulevard. It was situated in the White City Amusement Park at 6300 South Parkway Boulevard and offered jazz for dancing from at least the early 1920s. Among the resident groups during that decade were Sig Meyers's band, in which Muggsy Spanier gained his first professional experience (1922), the Wolverines (1925), and Doc Cook's band (spring 1927 – spring 1930). The ballroom was still in operation in the mid-1930s, when McKee Fitzhugh promoted the dances there. Sometime afterwards the ethnic composition of the area changed, and the White City Ballroom became an African-American venue. Between March 1942 and March 1945 there were performances by King Kolax, Duke Ellington, Count Basie, Louis Jordan, the International Sweethearts of Rhythm, Lionel Hampton, Jimmie Lunceford, Nat "King" Cole's trio, Benny Carter, and other leading musicians and groups.

——. **White's Emporium.** 309 East 55th Street (Garfield Boulevard). It opened in 1939 under the ownership of Ed White in the premises that had formerly been occupied by the Golden Lily and began presenting live music late in 1941. Coleman Hawkins appeared there as a guest soloist in January 1942 and then held a residency with his own band from February to May. Al Cooper's Savoy Sultans performed in July 1942.

——. **Yvette Wintergarden.** 311 South Wacker Street. This venue was opened in 1990 by Bob Djahanguiri, who presents mainly cabaret acts and jazz pianists; Dorothy Donegan and George Shearing are among those who have appeared.

——. **Zeppelin Inn.** South Indiana Avenue and East 31st Street. It was a small venue and flourished only briefly, around 1930, under the management of Big Boy Mills. Frankie "Half Pint" Jaxon's quintet was in residence in 1930, and Freddie Keppard's band played there as a guest attraction.

For other venues in the metropolitan area of Chicago see Berwyn, Cicero, and Robbins.

Materials on Chicago venues appear in the Robert Peck Collection at the Chicago Jazz Archive (see Libraries and archives, §2).

BIBLIOGRAPHY

Chicago

P. E. Miller: "Thirty Years of Chicago Jazz," with G. Hoefer: "Chicago Jazz History," *Esquire's Jazz Book*, ed. P. E. Miller and R. Venables (London, 1947) [abridged edn of three vols., previously pubd (New York, 1944–6)]

C. Sengstock: "Chicago Jazz Landmarks Crumble," *SL*, xi/5–6 (1961), 3

T. J. Hennessey: "The Black Chicago Establishment 1919–1930," *JJS*, ii/1 (1974), 15-45

S. Dance: *The World of Earl Hines* (New York, 1977)

D. J. Travis: *An Autobiography of Black Chicago* (Chicago, 1981)

——: *An Autobiography of Black Jazz* (Chicago, 1983)

——: "Chicago's Jazz Trail: 1893–1950," *Black Music Research Newsletter*, ix/2 (1987), 1

JazzGram (1989–)

B. Koester "Koester's Guide to Chicago's on and off the Beaten Path Nightclubs," *Rhythm & News*, no.963 ([*c*1995]), 9

S. Dirks: "Standing on the Corner, 47th and South Parkway," *Blues & Rhythm* (1996), no.112, p.4; no.113, p.4; no.115, p.4

Cicero, IL. **Cotton Club.** One of several establishments named after the famous nightclub in New York, it was owned by Ralph Capone, the brother of Al Capone. Among the jazz musicians to play there were Lucky Millinder (then working as Lucius Venable), who was probably connected with the club around 1928, and Walter Barnes, whose band was resident from late 1929; Barnes's band became a favorite with radio listeners as a result of its broadcasts from the club. The venue closed in July 1930 when the federal authorities prosecuted Ralph Capone.

Cincinnati. **Babe Baker's.** 3128 Reading Road. Named for its owner, this bar and restaurant was the leading jazz venue in Cincinnati from the mid-1950s into the 1960s, when it presented, among others, Miles Davis's group and John Coltrane's quartet.

——. **Blue Wisp.** Founded by Marjean and Paul Wisby, it operated for 16 years in the O'Bryonville section of Cincinnati and then around the early 1990s moved to 19 Garfield Place, where it began presenting jazz six nights per week. In both its locations the Blue Wisp has supported the careers of a number of important local jazz players as well as bringing in major visiting artists. From 1979 to the mid-1980s John Von Ohlen led the Blue Wisp Big Band, which recorded several highly acclaimed albums in Cincinnati; this big band has continued to appear at the club on Wednesday nights into the new century.
(<http://www.cincynights.com/Bars/BlueWisp.asp> (2001))

——. **Cotton Club.** The family band of the Hamptons, led by the tenor saxophonist Duke Hampton and featuring other family members, including Duke's brother Slide Hampton, was in residence there in 1953 when the group recorded for King.

——. **Doyle's Dance Hall** [Dancing Academy]. Court Avenue and Central Avenue. It occupied premises on the third floor of the building on the northwest corner of the intersection. Jazz was played there for dancing from at least the early 1920s; the Wolverines with Bix Beiderbecke held a three-month residency in 1924 which attracted as many local musicians as it did dancers.

——. **Greenwich Tavern.** 2440 Gilbert Ave. This restaurant and nightclub, built around 1910, presented such musicians as James Moody and Kenny Burrell.

——. **Kaldi's Coffeehouse and Bookstore.** 1204 Main Street. From the early 1990s this second-hand bookstore has presented jazz and bluegrass music; Cal Collins and Joshua Breakstone were among those jazz musicians who appeared during the venue's first years.
(<http://keycincinnati.com/0600/hotspot.htm> (2001))

——. **Moonlight Gardens Ballroom.** 6201 Kellog Avenue. In 1936 Noble Sissle's band, which included Sidney Bechet, Billy Banks, and the singer Lena Horne, was engaged to perform there; it was the first African-American band to do so. In the event Sissle himself was unable to appear, owing to an automobile accident on the journey to Cincinnati, and Horne fronted the band in his place. The ballroom still exists within Coney Island, an amusement park on the Ohio River.

——. **Sungarden Lounge.** 151 West Fifth Street. Situated on the second floor of a four-story atrium in the Hyatt Regency Hotel, this lounge hosted a number of free monthly series of jazz concerts in autumn and winter in the 1980s and 1990s. From 1986 to 1990 portions of these concerts were broadcast on the NPR radio show "Jazz: Live from the Hyatt."

City of Industry, CA. See Los Angeles (metropolitan area).

Cleveland. **Adelbert Gym.** See Case Western Reserve University.

——. **Agora Ballroom.** 1730 East 24th Street. It featured many types of popular music in the 1970s and 1980s. Jazz artists appearing here between 1976 and 1982 included Dave Brubeck, Anthony Braxton, Tony Williams, Oregon, Dizzy Gillespie with Sonny Stitt, the Thad Jones–Mel Lewis Orchestra, Herbie Hancock, Larry Coryell, Pat Martino, Weather Report, Charlie Rouse, Freddie Hubbard, and Pat Metheny.

——. **Algiers Lounge** [Algerian Lounge]. 10309 Euclid Avenue. It operated from 1959 to 1964, and in a brief period in 1960–61 featured, among others, Betty Carter, James Moody, Chico Hamilton, Horace Silver, Cannonball Adderley, John Coltrane, Miles Davis, and Lambert, Hendricks, and Ross.

——. **Alma Theater.** See Cain Park.

——. **Bop Stop.** 4001 St. Clair Avenue (1991–5); 1216 West 6th Street (1996–2000). It was opened by the vibraphonist Ron Busch, principally to provide a home for local performers, including the Jack Schantz Jazz Unit and Dan Wall. After moving to a more spacious and inviting location in 1996, the club began to bring in such artists as John Abercrombie, Tom Harrell, Dave Liebman, Hal Galper, Ray Brown, and a former Clevelander, Joe Lovano. It closed in 2000. (<http://www.clevelandbopstop.com> (2000))

——. **Cafe Tia Juana.** 1045 East 105th Street. Owned by the Hoge Family, Cafe Tia Juana began presenting jazz and blues in 1947 and continued this mix, involving both national and local artists, into the early 1970s. Among performers in the late 1940s were Gene Ammons, Ella Fitzgerald, Nat "King" Cole, Erroll Garner, Roy Eldridge, Dinah Washington, and Charlie Parker (second on a bill to Paul Gayten's band). The house band of this period was led by the pianist Jimmy Saunders. In the 1950s performers included the singers Carmen McRae, Sarah Vaughan, and Billie Holiday, as well as the regional favorites Roland Kirk, Johnny (later Hammond) Smith, Johnny Lytle, Rusty Bryant, and Joe Alexander (a tenor saxophonist). Sonny Stitt, Betty Carter, the Three Sounds, and the local East Jazz Trio, featuring Bobby Few, appeared in the early 1960s.

——. **Cain Park.** Superior Road between Lee Road and Taylor Road, in Cleveland Heights. Cain Park, built in 1938 and the earliest municipally owned outdoor theater in the United States, has featured summer jazz concerts at its Evans Amphitheater (3000 seats) from 1986, presenting Kenny Burrell, Jimmy Smith, Sonny Rollins, McCoy Tyner, and Don Byron, among others. In 1984 the smaller Alma Theater (300 seats) became the site of the free summer Sunday Jazz Series featuring local artists. (<http://cainpark.citysearch.com> (2001))

——. **Case Western Reserve University.** The university's Adelbert Gym was the site of concerts by Duke Ellington, Weather Report, and Oregon in 1973. Harkness Chapel, with its excellent acoustics, was used by the Northeast Ohio Jazz Society for concerts by James Moody, Ernestine Anderson, Steve Lacy, the World Saxophone Quartet, and others in 1985 and 1986, and by radio station WRUW-FM for concerts by Oregon in the 1970s and by the Ethnic Heritage Ensemble, Matthew Shipp, Myra Melford, and others in the 1990s. Strosacker Auditorium, on the same campus, hosted an exceptional concert by Old and New Dreams in 1982.

——. **Cedar Gardens.** 9706 Cedar Avenue. Opened in 1934, it featured floor shows in the 1930s and 1940s and was similar in many ways to the Cotton Club in Harlem. The house band of the mid-1930s was led by Marion Sears, brother of Al Sears, and included at times Buster Harding, Earle Warren, Freddie Webster, Tadd Dameron, and Bullmoose Jackson. A later band was led by Tadd Dameron's brother Caesar Dameron. From the mid-1940s until the late 1960s the club featured local jazz groups.

——. **Chatterbox.** 5123 Woodland Avenue. Open from 1949 to 1959, it featured mostly rhythm-and-blues, but in the mid- to late 1950s it presented James Moody and a number of jazz singers: Jimmy Rushing, Betty Carter, Carmen McRae, Billie Holiday, and Dinah Washington.

——. **China Casino.** See Towne Casino.

——. **Chung's Restaurant.** 21080 Lorain Avenue. Opened by Albert Chan as a Chinese restaurant in the early 1960s, it booked mainstream jazz from the late 1970s to the late 1980s; Art Hodes, Ray Bryant, Dave McKenna, Dick Wellstood, Kenny Davern, Dick Hyman, Marty Grosz, and Maxine Sullivan are among those who appeared. Larry Booty was the house pianist during these years.

——. **Circle Theatre** [Circle Ballroom]. East 105th Street and Euclid Avenue. Opened in 1920 as the Hoffman Theater, the building, on the edge of University Circle, was expanded in 1927 to form an entertainment complex, the Circle Theatre and Ballroom. The theater featured mostly rhythm-and-blues from 1951 to 1959. Jazz artists included Sarah Vaughan, Count Basie, and Erroll Garner, as well as Leo Parker, Lucky Thompson, and James Moody on package shows with rhythm-and-blues acts. The buildings continued to be used sporadically for African-American popular music and occasional jazz performances until the mid-1970s, when, along with all the other clubs around East 105th Street and Euclid Avenue, they were demolished to make room for urban renewal developments.

——. **Cleveland Convention Center.** East 6th Street and Lakeside Avenue. Music Hall is a 2800-seat auditorium opened in 1929 as part of the Cleveland Convention Center complex. It was the site of Jazz at the Philharmonic concerts from 1946 through 1954 (and again in 1957 and 1967). Among other tour packages to play there were the Festival of Modern Jazz (1953–4), the Birdland Stars (1955–7), and the Newport All Stars (1959). Music Hall also featured concerts by Duke Ellington (1939, 1968), Nat "King" Cole (1947), Dizzy Gillespie (1949, 1973), Louis Armstrong (1956, 1960), Weather Report (1978, 1982), and many others. Public Auditorium, built in 1922, is a much larger performance space which is also used for circuses and conventions. It hosted concerts by many big bands in the 1930s and 1940s, including those of Andy Kirk, Count Basie, Buddy Johnson, Lionel Hampton, and Lucky Millinder. From 1967, when the Ohio Valley Jazz Festival presented Ramsey Lewis, Jimmy Smith, Dizzy Gillespie, Cannonball Adderley, Herbie Mann, and Nina Simone, Public Auditorium has been used for occasional jazz concerts.

——. **Cleveland State University.** 1983 East 24th Street. The Main Classroom Auditorium was used by the Northeast Ohio Jazz Society from 1979 to 1982 for concerts by Woody Shaw, Bobby Hutcherson, Sonny Fortune, Johnny Griffin, Arthur Blythe, and Red Rodney and Ira Sullivan. The music department presented Cedar Walton (1975) and the Art Ensemble of Chicago (1980), as well as other concerts and clinics. In 1978 the university initiated Sundown Jazz, a continuing free series featuring local artists, and in 1979 annual concerts by the saxophonist and composer Howie Smith; these events moved to the new Drinko Recital Hall in 1989.

——. **Club Congo** [Congo Club]. 4410 Woodland Avenue. From 1951 to 1957 it mainly featured local players, including Sir Charles Thompson and the young Frank(ie) Wright. In 1955 the members of Jack's Town Criers included Tadd Dameron and Joe Lovano's father, the tenor saxophonist Tony Lovano.

——. **Club One Hundred** [Club 100]. 10020 Euclid Avenue. Local players, including Roland Kirk, performed here from 1959 until a fire destroyed the venue in 1966.

——. **Club Trinidad.** 10607 Superior Road. Having opened in 1955 with such artists as Barbara Carroll, Bill De Arango, the Modern Jazz Quartet, Eddie "Lockjaw" Davis, and Marian McPartland, it turned to local players in 1956 and remained active until 1958. It reopened in 1962 as the Playhouse.

——. **Congo Club.** See Club Congo.

——. **Corner Tavern.** 7800 Cedar Avenue. It operated from 1953 until it burned down in 1965. After featuring local players until 1963, it thereafter presented such musicians as Jimmy McGriff, J. J. Johnson, Ramsey Lewis, the Three Sounds, Lou Donaldson, Jack McDuff, Shirley Scott, and Stanley Turrentine.

——. **Cotton Club (i).** 2226 East 55th Street. In 1934 it featured Don Redman and Fletcher Henderson.

——. **Cotton Club (ii).** See Modern Jazz Room.

——. **Crystal Slipper.** See Trianon Ballroom.

——. **Cuyahoga Community College.** 2900 Community College Avenue. It has hosted the Tri-C Jazzfest from 1980. Among the performers and clinicians at Metro Auditorium and other venues have been the Heath Brothers, Dexter Gordon, Art Blakey, Betty Carter, Sonny Rollins, Max Roach, Johnny Griffin, Clark Terry, Jaki Byard, Billy Taylor (ii), Alvin Batiste, Red Rodney, Jane Ira Bloom, Sun Ra, Lee Konitz, George Adams and Don Pullen, Art Farmer, Buddy DeFranco, James Williams, Marcus Belgrave, James Moody, Benny Carter, Sheila Jordan, Bobby Watson, Richard Davis, Vanessa Rubin, Joe Lovano, Ernie Krivda, Benny Golson, Steve Coleman, and James Newton.
(<http://www.tri-c.cc.oh.us/jazz> (2001))

——. **Domino Lounge.** See Loop Lounge.

——. **Eastown Motor Hotel** [Jazz Emporium Lounge]. 15103 Euclid Avenue. Intermittently from 1971 to 1978 the club in this motel booked various artists, including Rusty Bryant, Dizzy Gillespie, Jimmy Smith, Johnny Hartman, James Moody, Joe Williams, Betty Carter, Kenny Burrell, Gene Ammons, Charles Earland, Groove Holmes, Roland Kirk, Freddie Hubbard, Lou Donaldson, Art Blakey, Grant Green, George Benson, Sonny Stitt, Stanley Turrentine, Shirley Scott, and Houston Person with Etta Jones; at some point during the same period it became known as the Jazz Emporium Lounge. Later, under the name Schatzi's, it continued a similar jazz policy into the 1980s.

——. **Ebony Lounge.** 6916 Cedar Avenue. From 1949 until 1959 this club featured mainly rhythm-and-blues but also presented such artists as Gene Ammons and Sonny Stitt, Illinois Jacquet, Oscar Peterson, James Moody, Ella Fitzgerald, Babs Gonzales, Johnny Hodges, and an all-star group organized by the disc jockey Symphony Sid and comprising J. J. Johnson, Miles Davis, Milt Jackson, Zoot Sims, Percy Heath, and Kenny Clarke.

——. **Evans Amphitheater.** See Cain Park.

——. **Front Row.** Wilson Mills Road at interstate freeway 271. This theater with a revolving stage presented a variety of popular music styles from 1974 to 1993. Among jazz performers were Weather Report, Herbie Hancock and Wayne Shorter, Sarah Vaughan, Chick Corea, Count Basie, Miles Davis, and Wynton Marsalis.

——. **Gleason's Musical Bar.** 5219 Woodland Avenue. Opened in 1944 as a bar and restaurant by William A. (Jap) Gleason, it booked local jazz musicians in the late 1940s and continued in the 1950s to be a place for younger jazz musicians to sit in and learn from older players and visiting stars. Gleason's was known mainly as a rhythm-and-blues venue until 1964, when it continued as the House of Blues, but between 1951 and 1955 the club booked some jazz artists, notably Dizzy Gillespie, Johnny Hodges, James Moody, Illinois Jacquet, Sonny Stitt, Benny Green, Jimmy Rushing, Snooky Young, and Rusty Bryant.

——. **Globe Theatre.** Woodland Avenue and East 55th Street. In the 1920s and 1930s this African-American vaudeville theater featured such classic blues singers as Bessie Smith, Mamie Smith, Sarah Martin, and Lucille Hegamin, as well as Sam Wooding, Ethel Waters, the Norfolk Jazz Quartet, Butterbeans & Susie, and Cheatham's Jazz Syncopators.

——. **Greystone Ballroom.** See Marcane Ballroom.

——. **Harkness Chapel.** See Case Western Reserve University.

——. **Heat Wave Bar.** See Majestic Hotel.

——. **The House of Blues.** 5219 Woodland Avenue. Formerly Gleason's Musical Bar, from 1964 to 1967 it presented jazz musicians, among them Brother Jack McDuff, Jimmy McGriff, Hank Crawford, Charles Earland, Willis Jackson, Groove Holmes, Lou Donaldson, the Jazz Crusaders, Johnny Lytle, and Sonny Stitt with Don Patterson. In 1966, as reported in the *Call and Post*, Miles Davis was observed after hours at the club's piano.

——. **Jazz Emporium Lounge.** See Eastown Motor Hotel.

——. **Jazz Temple.** 11339 Euclid Avenue. This club, opened in late 1962 by Winston E. Willis and others, was exceptional for the emphasis it placed on the audience listening to the music and for its hip ambiance. In its short lifespan it presented Art Blakey, Philly Joe Jones, Sonny Rollins, Horace Silver, John Coltrane, Herbie Hancock with Donald Byrd and Jimmy Heath, Miles Davis, Jimmy Smith and Stan

Getz, Dinah Washington, and Lambert, Hendricks, and Bavan. It closed not long after a bomb explosion on 13 August 1963.

——. **Leo's Casino.** East 49th Street and Central Avenue (1954–62); 7500 Euclid Avenue (1962–71). Founded by Leo Frank, it first presented mainly local musicians, but among those who appeared from 1961 were Gene Ammons, Betty Carter, Jimmy Smith, Ramsey Lewis, Etta Jones, Art Blakey, John Coltrane, Dizzy Gillespie, and Cannonball Adderley. A fire destroyed the venue in 1962. With a new partner, Jules Berger, Frank reopened the club on a new site in the Quad Hall Hotel with space for 725 people. The new casino booked jazz, blues, soul, and other African-American acts until it closed in 1971. Jazz performers from this period included many of the foregoing, as well as Oscar Peterson, Joe Williams, Carmen McRae, Count Basie, Ahmad Jamal, Thelonious Monk, Roland Kirk, and Wes Montgomery.

——. **Lindsay's Sky Bar.** See Sky Bar.

——. **Loop Lounge** [Ted's Loop Lounge]. 614 Prospect Avenue. Operated initially by Teddy Blackmon, it offered a mixture of jazz and rhythm-and-blues from 1948 until 1958. From 1953 to 1957 it brought in many of the best-known jazz artists. Frequent visitors included Gene Ammons, Roy Eldridge, Ben Webster, Lester Young, Chet Baker, Johnny Hodges, Milt Buckner, Terry Gibbs, Illinois Jacquet, James Moody, Max Roach, and Sonny Stitt. Many visiting soloists, notably Charlie Parker in 1954, used the house rhythm section of Jimmy Saunders, Rodney Richardson, and Lawrence Jackson (Jacktown). The Domino Lounge operated on this site from 1959, booking local jazz performances.

——. **Lucky Bar.** 9812 Cedar Avenue. Gay Crosse led the house band here in the 1940s. Later it presented Johnny Coles and other local artists. It closed in 1969.

——. **Majestic Hotel.** 2291 East 55th Street and Central Avenue. From around 1922 this was the primary hotel for African-American visitors to Cleveland, including many musicians. In the 1930s in its Heat Wave Bar and from the 1940s in the Rose Room, the hotel presented live music, and many visiting artists sat in at the "Blue Monday Party" jam sessions in the early 1950s. In 1952 Gay Crosse's band at the Rose Room included John Coltrane, in 1957 Rusty Bryant brought in Nancy Wilson, and throughout much of the 1950s the house band was led by Duke Jenkins.

——. **Marcane Ballroom** [Ritz Ballroom; Greystone Ballroom]. 3705 Euclid Avenue. A roller-skating rink in the 1930s, in the 1940s and early 1950s it featured big bands, including those of Stan Kenton, Claude Thornhill, Gene Krupa, Woody Herman, Artie Shaw, Charlie Barnet, Buddy DeFranco, and Elliott Lawrence.

——. **Metropolitan Theatre** [WHK Auditorium]. 5012 Euclid Avenue. The Metropolitan, a 1400-seat venue originally opened as the Gayety Theatre in 1913, hosted the touring shows of *Shuffle Along* (1923) and *Running Wild* (1924). Jim Vaughan and his Jazz Hounds played there in 1927. In the 1940s the theater featured bands led by Lucky Millinder, Earl Hines, Fletcher Henderson, and Billy Eckstine. The International Sweethearts of Rhythm also played there, as did a trio consisting of Albert Ammons, Pete Johnson, and Joe Turner (ii). From 1950 to 1975 the building was renamed the WHK Auditorium; it was used occasionally for jazz in the 1960s, notably for concerts by Cannonball Adderley, Thelonious Monk, and Albert Ayler, as well as by local musicians.

——. **Mirror Show Bar.** 12376 Superior Avenue. This bar featured local players from 1956, including the Jazz Angels with Roland Kirk (1957), Tony Lovano (father of Joe), Bobby Few, and Johnny Coles. It continued from 1962 to 1969 as the Kit-Kat Lounge.

——. **Modern Jazz Room** [Cotton Club]. 2230 East 4th Street. Located near the Central Market, this venue opened in 1954 as the Cotton Club and the following year gained a reputation as the "jazz corner of Cleveland" (*Call and Post*). In 1957 the drummer Fats Heard bought the club and renamed it the Modern Jazz Room. It featured week-long engagements until 1960. Among frequent visitors were Erroll Garner, J. J. Johnson, the Australian Jazz Quintet, Miles Davis, Dizzy Gillespie, Carmen McRae, the Modern Jazz Quartet, George Shearing, and Horace Silver; Randy Weston, Bill De Arango, Jimmy Giuffre, Toshiko Akiyoshi, Bud Shank, and Abbey Lincoln also appeared, as did local players, including Bobby Few in 1961.

——. **Musicarnival.** 4401 Warrensville Road. This 1500-seat summer tent theater operated from 1954 until 1975. Erroll Garner, Duke Ellington, Louis Armstrong, and Pharoah Sanders are among those who appeared there.

——. **Music Box.** 10616 Euclid Avenue. From 1960 until 1967 it featured primarily rhythm-and-blues and soul musicians, a few exceptions being Jimmy Rushing, Milt Buckner, Jimmy Smith, and, in December 1962, Miles Davis with Hank Mobley, J. J. Johnson, Wynton Kelly, Paul Chambers, and Jimmy Cobb.

——. **Music Hall.** See Cleveland Convention Center.

——. **Nighttown.** 12383 Cedar Avenue, in Cleveland Heights. From 1978 this restaurant has featured such local traditional and mainstream players as Bill Gidney, Sam Finger, Joe Howard, George Foley, Ted Witt, and Larry Booty. Beginning in 1988 internationally known musicians were booked periodically, among them Keith Ingham, Marty Grosz, Art Hodes, Dave McKenna, Ralph Sutton, Randy Weston, and Scott Hamilton with Bucky Pizzarelli. In the new century Nightown has become the major jazz club in Cleveland, and it has ventured into modern styles more often, bringing in such players as Joshua Redman, Ray Brown, McCoy Tyner, Jimmy Smith, and Joe Chambers.

——. **Palace Theatre** [RKO Palace]. Euclid Avenue at East 17th Street. The venue, built in 1922, has featured jazz along with other American music, though it also served as a major film theater until the 1960s. Early performers included Ted Lewis, Ethel Waters, Paul Whiteman, the Boswell Sisters, Louis Armstrong, Don Redman, and Noble Sissle with Sidney Bechet. Among the big bands that played there in the 1930s and 1940s were those of Duke Ellington, Benny Goodman, Cab Calloway, Jimmy Dorsey, Red Norvo with Mildred Bailey, Woody Herman, and Charlie Barnet. The Palace and the adjacent State Theatre have been used since 1978 by the Tri-C Jazz Fest.
(<http://www.playhousesquare.com> (2001))

——. **Peabody's Café.** 2140 South Taylor Road. From 1978 into the 1990s this two-level club presented such groups and musicians as Spyro Gyra, Yusef Lateef, Steve Kuhn, Phil Woods, Lew Tabackin, and Henry Threadgill. It later continued as the Rhythm Room.

——. **Peabody's Downunder.** 1059 Old River Road. Formerly a rock club known as the Pirate's Cove, Peabody's Downunder reopened as a jazz club with Stan Getz in 1983 and continued to offer jazz frequently into the early 1990s. Jimmy Smith with Kenny Burrell, Maynard Ferguson, Milt Jackson with Ray Brown, Flora Purim and Airto Moreira, David Murray, Jaco Pastorius, Stanley Jordan, Dave Holland, Betty Carter, Elvin Jones, Emily Remler, John Scofield, Bennie Wallace, and Craig Harris were among those who appeared there.

——. **Public Auditorium.** See Cleveland Convention Center.

——. **Rhythm Room.** 2140 South Taylor Road. Formerly Peabody's Café, it occasionally presented jazz in the late 1990s, bringing in Greg Osby and Stefon Harris in 1999.

——. **Ritz Ballroom.** See Marcane Ballroom.

——. **RKO Palace.** See Palace Theatre.

——. **Rose Room.** See Majestic Hotel.

——. **Severance Hall.** 11001 Euclid Avenue. Opened in 1931 as the home of the Cleveland Orchestra, the hall has occasionally offered concerts by jazz artists over the years, most notably Louis Armstrong (1947), Dizzy Gillespie and the Modern Jazz Quartet (1971), and the Thad Jones–Mel Lewis Orchestra (1972). In 1990 it was the setting for the Cleveland première of Charles Mingus's posthumously reconstructed symphony *Epitaph*. Together with the Cleveland Museum of Art, beginning in the late 1990s it hosted the series Jazz in the Circle.

——. **Sir Rah's.** 4170 Lee Road. This club featured jazz from 1966 until 1986, presenting Sonny Stitt, Johnny Lytle, Gene Ammons, Grant Green, and Lou Donaldson, as well as many organists and local players.

——. **Sky Bar** [Lindsay's Sky Bar]. 10625 Euclid Avenue. It featured local players from 1948 until 1952, among them Benny Bailey, Tadd Dameron, and his brother Caesar Dameron; jam sessions took place on Sundays. In 1951 and the beginning of 1952 the club brought in Gene Ammons and Sonny Stitt, Charlie Parker, Art Tatum with Slam Stewart, Erroll Garner, Johnny Hodges, Billie Holiday, Dizzy Gillespie, Stan Getz, Mary Lou Williams, Oscar Peterson, and many others.

——. **Smiling Dog Saloon.** 3447 West 25th Street. From 1971 to 1975 this club, run by Rodger Bohn, offered blues, folk-rock, and jazz. Among its many performers were McCoy Tyner, Weather Report, Oregon, Cannonball Adderley, Herbie Hancock, Roland Kirk, Bill Evans (ii), Gil Evans, Charles Mingus, Pharoah Sanders, Keith Jarrett, Miles Davis, and Sun Ra, as well as local players Bill De Arango and Ernie Krivda.

——. **Strosacker Auditorium.** *See* Case Western Reserve University.

——. **Ted's Loop Lounge.** See Loop Lounge.

——. **Theatrical Grill.** 711 Vincent Avenue [Short Vincent]. Run by Morris "Mushy" Wexler and his family, this restaurant was a favorite haunt for politicians, gamblers, and entertainers from 1937 until 1990; it was completely rebuilt after a fire in 1960. Over the years it featured a variety of artists, including Dorothy Donegan, Jonah Jones, Muggsy Spanier, Marian and Jimmy McPartland, Jack Teagarden, Bobby Hackett, Wild Bill Davison, Joe Venuti, Henry "Red" Allen, Gene Krupa, Dizzy Gillespie, Red Norvo, Earl Hines, Bill Doggett, and the house pianist Hank Kahout. Later it became an "upscale gentlemen's club."

——. **Towne Casino** [China Casino]. 10613 Euclid Avenue. Although it opened as the China Casino in February 1951, it was reopened in July of that same year as the Towne Casino. The club remained in operation until 1953 and brought in many big bands, notably those led by Lionel Hampton, Stan Kenton, Count Basie, and Duke Ellington. Other jazz performers included Coleman Hawkins, Howard McGhee with J. J. Johnson, Sarah Vaughan, George Shearing, and Louis Armstrong.

——. **Trianon Ballroom** [Crystal Slipper]. 9802 Euclid Avenue. It operated from 1934 until 1956 and featured big bands, including those of the Dorsey Brothers, Duke Ellington, Bob Crosby, Andy Kirk, Jimmie Lunceford, Benny Goodman, Count Basie, Benny Carter, and Ella Fitzgerald. In the mid-1950s it became the Trianon Bowling Lanes.

——. **Val's in the Alley.** East 87th Street and Cedar Avenue. From around 1928 until 1935 this legendary after-hours club was frequently home to Art Tatum. Its hours in 1934 were 2 p.m. to 6 a.m., and it was referred to in a *Call and Post* advertisement as "Ye Rhythm Club in the Alley by the Greasy Spoon."

——. **Welcome Inn.** 3344 East 116 Street. Known briefly as "Cleveland's jazz corner" (*Call and Post*), the club opened in 1961, when it brought in Roland Kirk, John Coltrane, Sonny Stitt, Donald Byrd, Art Blakey, Bill Hardman, Philly Joe Jones, and Slide Hampton. As the Hound Dog's Den the club had booked blues from 1959, and it continued to feature blues and local jazz into 1962.

——. **WHK Auditorium.** See Metropolitan Theatre.

BIBLIOGRAPHY

J. Prohaska: "Cleveland: Jazz Town: a Brief History of Jazz Artists, Recordings, and Venues," *IAJRC Journal*, xxiii/3 (1990), 2
J. Mosbrook: *Cleveland Jazz History* (Cleveland, 1993, 2/forthcoming)
G. L. Reece: *Jazzkeepers: a Pictorial Tribute and Memoir: Cleveland, Ohio* (Winter Park, FL, 1996)
J. Mosbrook: "Jagged in Cleveland," <http://www.cleveland.oh.us/wmy_news.jazzhome.htm> (2001)
<http://www.nojs.org> (2001)

Compton, CA. See Los Angeles (metropolitan area).

Covington, KY. **Look Out House.** This sophisticated nightclub was active from at least the mid-1930s. In the autumn of 1937 Noble Sissle's band, which at that time included Sidney Bechet and Erskine Butterfield, was engaged to appear there for a month.

Culver City, CA. See Los Angeles (metropolitan area).

Dallas. **Adolphus Hotel.** 1321 Commerce Street. The hotel was built in 1912, jazz and dance music was played for the entertainment of patrons from at least the mid-1920s, and bands continued to perform there through the 1930s.

Alphonso Trent's orchestra held a long residency of 16 months from 1925, during which time it made highly successful broadcasts from the hotel on radio station WFAA, and it returned to the hotel in 1928. The orchestras of Benny Goodman, Artie Shaw, Harry James, and other famous bandleaders performed there during the swing era.

——. **American Woodmen's Hall.** Southwest corner of Oakland Avenue and Carpenter Street. It became well known in the 1950s for weekend jam sessions, some of which were hosted by James Clay and the pianist and saxophonist Claude Johnson; David "Fathead" Newman and Red Garland were among the participants.

——. **Cain's Hitching Post.** This club was in existence by around 1950 as a venue for jazz and blues. Sammy Price held a long residency there in the early 1950s.

——. **Central Dance Hall.** See Tip Top Inn.

——. **Empire Room.** See Rose Room.

——. **Rose Room** [Rose Ballroom]. Hall Street. This venue was opened by T. H. Smith as the Rose Ballroom in March 1942 with a performance by Buster Smith and his band and was renamed in 1943. It became a major showcase for touring rhythm-and-blues acts, including jump bands. King Kolax and Eddie "Cleanhead" Vinson were among those who appeared there, as did Ray Charles in 1951, after it became known as the Empire Room.

——. **Royal Social and Amusement Club.** See Tip Top Inn.

——. **Sambuca Jazz Café.** 2618 Elm Street (from 1991) and 15207 Addison Road (from the mid-1990s). The downtown location of the Sambuca Jazz Café opened in 1991 as a restaurant offering Mediterranean food and live jazz every night. The combination proved highly successful, and thereafter cafés of the same name opened on Addison Road in North Dallas, in Atlanta, in Houston, and in Denver. (<http://www.sambucajazzcafe.com/TooCool.html> (2001))

——. **Tip Top Inn** [Central Dance Hall; Royal Social and Amusement Club]. Central Avenue and Pacific Street. Situated on the second floor of a former railroad hotel, the club took its name from the Tip Top tailor shop downstairs. It featured jazz from around 1925, when the resident group was Lee Collins's band. New Orleans musicians were in great demand at that time, and the Tip Top was regarded as the principal venue for African-American bands in Dallas.

BIBLIOGRAPHY

Dallas

A. B. Govenar: *Deep Ellum and Central Track: Where the Black and White Worlds of Dallas Converged* (Denton, TX, 1998), 27

Dayton, OH. **Cotton Club.** This was a regular venue for territory bands in the 1930s. Between January and May 1937 presentations by the Paramount Amusement Club included the bands of Andy Kirk, Blanche Calloway, Fats Waller, and Claude Hopkins.

——. **Gilly's.** 132 South Jefferson Street. Situated next to a bus station, this club, owned by Jerry Gilliotti, has been one of the principal venues for jazz in Ohio from the 1970s into the new century; Wynton Marsalis, Woody Herman, Stanley Jordan, Elvin Jones, and Wayne Shorter are among those who have appeared there. Gilly's has also presented rock groups.

Delaware Water Gap, PA. **Deer Head Inn.** 5 Main Street. John Coates has played piano at this club for nearly a half century, from 1956. Al Cohn, Keith Jarrett (who played drums), Zoot Sims, and Phil Woods were among those who appeared there with Coates in the 1960s and 1970s, and from around 1973 Woods was a regular performer, having settled in Delaware Water Gap. From 1977 to 1980 Coates made a series of recordings there, both as an unaccompanied soloist and as the leader of groups, and in 1978 Woods was the key figure in the founding of a yearly festival, the Delaware Water Gap Celebration of the Arts, which has continued into the new century. In 1993 Jarrett's trio recorded the album *At the Deer Head Inn* (ECM 1531) and Mike Melillo became the inn's house pianist. (<http://www.deerheadinn.com> (2001))

Denver. **Navarre.** Built as a school in 1879, the premises were used for various purposes before becoming a restaurant in the 1920s. Navarre flourished as a venue for jazz performance during the 1960s and early 1970s, when among the musicians who played there were the World's Greatest Jazz Band, Peanuts Hucko, and Ralph Sutton. It closed in January 1974.

——. **Sambuca Jazz Café.** 1320 15th Street. The fifth venue in the chain of cafés under this name (originating in Dallas), it opened in the late 1990s. It offers live jazz nightly and a Mediterranean cuisine.
(<http://www.sambucadenver.citysearch.com> (2001))

——. **Tivoli Terrace.** West 32nd Street and Shoshone Street. It featured jazz from at least the mid-1930s, when Hymie Hirschorn was the manager and an engagement at the club was regarded by musicians as the best in the city. From 1934 to 1940 the drummer Kenney "Sticks" McVey led the house band, which made regular broadcasts on local radio and gained a high reputation for its supple swing playing.

——. **Trocadero Ballroom.** The venue was managed by Jack Gurtler, who put on jazz performances there from at least the 1960s. In collaboration with the businessman Dick Gibson he engaged a band organized by Gibson, which with varying personnel played at the Trocadero every year between 1965 and 1971. In 1968 it crystallized into the World's Greatest Jazz Band of Yank Lawson and Bob Haggart, and the following year it recorded the album *Jazz in the Troc* (WCS 3330).

Des Moines, IA. **Riverview Park.** Jazz musicians held summer engagements in the park from at least the mid-1920s. Husk O'Hare's Wolverines, which was led by Jimmy McPartland and included Frank Teschemacher, Bud Freeman, and Dave Tough, played there in 1926.

Detroit. **Arcadia Ballroom.** Dance hall. Touring jazz groups performed there from at least the mid-1920s. Among the bands that appeared were McKinney's Cotton Pickers in 1926, Paul Whiteman's orchestra in 1928, and Benny Carter's band, which played for a Thanksgiving Day ball on 29 November 1934.

——. **Artists Workshop.** West Forest Street, near the John C. Lodge Expressway. Formed by community activists and progressive artists in the mid-1960s, the workshop was a veritable clearing-house for lively discourse, poetry recitals, light shows, and concerts. John Sinclair organized its events and a number of established and promising musicians called the workshop their second home. The guitarist Ron English, the double bass player John Dana, the drummer Danny Spencer, the saxophonist Larry Nozero, Don Moye, and the brass player Charles Moore were among the musicians who were regularly featured. The workshop ceased operation in the early 1970s when the Strata Concert Gallery came into existence.

——. **Baker's Keyboard Lounge.** 20510 Livernois Street at Eight Mile Road. It was opened in 1934 by Chris Baker and was managed for 45 years by his son Clarence before coming under new direction late in 1985. Despite its name, it has presented not only pianists and organists but also other leading instrumentalists and singers. Among the diverse performers who have worked there are John Coltrane, Art Pepper, Yusef Lateef, Kenny Burrell, Groove Holmes, Jimmy McGriff, the Modern Jazz Quartet, George Benson, Gene Krupa, Eddie "Lockjaw" Davis and Harry "Sweets" Edison, Bobby Hutcherson, Woody Shaw, and Herb Ellis.

——. **Bert's Market Place.** 2727 Russell Street. This club was active in the 1990s. Located on the rim of the city's major outdoor marketplace, it superbly balances local and well-known touring groups. The owner of the club is the impresario Bert Dearing, who has two other locations, among them his "jazz on the river" site on Belle Isle Park.

——. **Bluebird Inn.** 5021 Tireman Street. Clarence Eddins was the owner of the club, which opened in the early 1940s. By the end of the decade, during the heyday of bop, it had become the most important venue in Detroit, presenting groups every week from Tuesday to Sunday. In the late 1940s Billy Mitchell's group, with Tommy Flanagan, Barry Harris, Thad and Elvin Jones, and Pepper Adams, was the resident band. Charlie Parker, Miles Davis, Wardell Gray, and Sonny Stitt were among the notable guest artists who made the spot popular for many aspiring musicians. After a score of years when the club was closed, in the late 1980s Kenn Cox led a number of concerned residents in reviving it. From 1993 there has been an annual "Blue Bird Reunion" dinner-concert organized by the Societie for the Culturally Concerned. Sheila Jordan, Kirk Lightsey, and George Bohanon were saluted in 1995 and Louis Hayes, Curtis Fuller, and the double bass player Herman Wright, the long-time core of Yusef Lateef's band, were honored in 1996. Another such celebration, featuring Charles McPherson and Harris, took place in 1997.

——. **Bomac's.** 281 Gratiot Street. Bar. For several years the quintet led bythe pianist and saxophonist Teddy Harris was the house band at this bar, which attempts to keep the city's blues and bop tradition current. It opened in the late 1980s and has presented such local musicians as the pianist and singer Pamela Wise, Wendell Harrison, and the guitarist Robert Lowe. The hostess Lottie the Body adds to the bar's ambience.

——. **Bowl-o-Drome.** See Drome.

——. **Chocolate Bar.** 632 Livingstone Street. Slim Jones bought the bar from two white men in 1935 and immediately hired Sunnie Wilson to run it. Wilson started a cocktail hour and Blue Monday parties, giving the bar a name and profits. The saxophonist Cecil Lee, formerly a member of McKinneys Cotton Pickers and the band led by the tenor saxophonist Lanky Bowman, was in charge of the music. He and Wilson were instrumental in launching the career of Herb Jeffries.

——. **Club Plantation.** See Plantation.

——. **Club 12.** See Klein's Showbar.

——. **Cozy Corner.** Hastings Street and Alfred Street. In 1933 Sam Ivey became the only African-American man to own a bar on Hastings Street. Ivey hired Sunnie Wilson to manage the bar upstairs, while he watched over the gambling downstairs. Musical revues, booked by Wilson, were the club's staple, and the bands often consisted of the top musicians in the city.

——. **Detroit Jazz Center.** 2100 Park Avenue. The center was opened in August 1979 and was the outgrowth of a merger of several local organizations, including Allied Artists Associates, Strata Associates, the Jazz Research Institute, the Pioneer Jazz Orchestra, and the Friends of Jazz. Herb Boyd was executive director and John Sinclair president. For more than four years the center was a focal point of jazz in the city, presenting workshops, seminars, jam sessions, and concerts. Archie Shepp, Jackie McLean, Dave Wilborn, Sun Ra, the Art Ensemble of Chicago, Marion Brown, and the Pioneer Jazz Orchestra, led by the saxophonist Sam Sanders, were among artists who performed there.

——. **El Dorado.** Woodward Avenue. Nightclub. Johnny Trafton led the band there during the 1930s. Whereas in Detroit at that time African-American musicians typically performed for white cabaret audiences at venues located within the African-American community, El Dorado, as a top nightclub on the city's major thoroughfare, had integrated audiences. Trafton stayed at El Dorado for about four years and became music director of its floor show.

——. **Drome** [Bowl-o-Drome]. Dexter Boulevard and Buena Vista Street. Owned by Irv Hellman, the club opened in the late 1940s and was often called the Bowl-o-Drome. It featured such important performers as John Coltrane, Eddie Harris, Frank Rosolino, Pepper Adams, Wes Montgomery, and Rufus Harley. Among the local artists who accompanied these guests and led their own groups were Dorothy Ashby, the pianist Boo Boo Turner, Yusef Lateef, the double bass player Will Davis, the pianist Kenn Cox, and Terry Pollard.

——. **Flame Show Bar.** 4264 John R. Street. Morris Wasserman opened the bar in 1949, and for over a decade, along with its talented house band led by the pianist Maurice King, the Flame featured such noted performers as Billie Holiday, Sarah Vaughan, Dinah Washington, Erroll Garner, and the singer Savannah Churchill. Later it beame a lively rhythm-and-blues venue, where Clyde McPhatter and his Dominoes and Jackie Wilson gained popularity. In the mid-1950s Berry Gordy, the founder of Motown Records, was the club's enterprising photographer.

——. **Forest Club.** 710 East Forest Street. Cocktail lounge and bar. It was owned by Sunnie Wilson, who bought it in 1941 from Leo Adler. Wilson – who had managed the Harlem Cave before purchasing the Forest – was one of two African-American proprietors to own a bar at this time on Hastings Street. The club, noted for its bar – at 107 feet the longest in Detroit – had a meeting hall, roller rink, and bowling alley attached to the building, making it larger than the old Madison Square Garden. Earl "Fatha" Hines, Cab Calloway, Louis Jordan, Jay McShann, and Lionel Hampton were among the musicians featured, and it was here that Nat "King" Cole's trio made its Detroit début. Unable to renew his lease, Wilson sold the club in 1951.

——. **Graystone** [Greystone] **Ballroom.** 4237 Woodward Avenue. Dance hall. It was built by the bandleader and entrepreneur Jean Goldkette in the mid-1920s. Goldkette managed the ballroom and directed the resident band, the Jean Goldkette Victor Recording Orchestra, which made numerous radio broadcasts; among his sidemen were Bix Beiderbecke and Frankie Trumbauer. After a successful residency at the ballroom by the Fletcher Henderson Orchestra, Goldkette wished to engage an African-American band that would play in a style reminiscent of Henderson's; he chose McKinney's Cotton Pickers, who established a close association with the ballroom from 1926 until they disbanded (for illustration *see* MCKINNEY'S COTTON PICKERS). A number of "battles" between bands were staged at the Graystone, including one between McKinney's Cotton Pickers and Benny Carter's band in 1928 and another between bands led by Count Basie and Stan Kenton in 1955. At one point in the late 1940s several of the finest young bop musicians in the city had their first opportunity to play with Charlie Parker there. The Graystone was eventually closed down and the building began a long, sad, slow decline; it was finally demolished in 1980. However, the spirit of the venue has been preserved through the efforts of James Jenkins, who devoted some 20 years to gathering artifacts and acquiring resources to keep the glory of the ballroom alive. (L. Wright, comp.: "They've Torn the Old Place Down," *Sv*, no.94 (1981), 127)

——. **Klein's Showbar.** 12th Street (Rosa Parks Boulevard) and Pingree Street. George Klein was the proprietor and the club was made famous by the extended stay of Yusef Lateef's band, featuring at various times Hugh Lawson, Terry Pollard, the double bass player Will Austin, Curtis Fuller, Frank Gant, Louis Hayes, Wilbur Harden, and Bernard McKinney (Kiane Zawadi). Pepper Adams, Kenny Burrell, Tommy Flanagan, Paul Chambers, Ernie Farrow, and Elvin Jones were among frequent guests, particularly at the Monday night jam sessions. In the late 1950s, after Lateef ended his tenure there, Klein sold the bar to Al Mendolsohn, who continued the jazz policy for a time and changed the name to the Club 12.

——. **The Minor Key.** Dexter Boulevard and Burlingame Street. Micki and Sam Garmo were the owners of the club, which had a brief but distinguished existence from the late 1950s to the early 1960s. An old, refurbished grocery store, it was the city's premier "coffeehouse," and presented prominent artists such as John Coltrane, Ornette Coleman, Art Blakey and the Jazz Messengers, Miles Davis, and Sonny Stitt on the weekends and local players (organized into sets of one hour per group) on weekday nights.

——. **Odum's Cave.** Woodrow Wilson Street, near Elmhurst Street. Owned by Mary Odum, the club was a leading spot for local musicians to develop their skills. It began featuring local jazz artists in the late 1950s and remained open through the late 1970s. The drummer Bill Hyde and the pianist and saxophonist Teddy Harris led the house band, which included Bennie Maupin, the guitarist Rod Hicks, and George Bohanon.

——. **Paradise Theater** [Orchestra Hall]. Woodward Avenue, near Mack Avenue. From 1920 to 1939 Orchestra Hall was home to the Detroit Symphony Orchestra, but the orchestra was forced to move out after the hall incurred financial difficulties and jazz began to flourish there, with concerts in the newly named theater by the big bands of Duke Ellington, Lionel Hampton, and Dizzy Gillespie. During its heyday from 1943 to 1952 the Paradise was second to none in the city in presenting the very best in African-American entertainment. The theater fell into disrepair in the mid-1950s, and when the building was threatened with demolition a group of concerned citizens salvaged it through a series of benefit performances, featuring McCoy Tyner, Gillespie, Yusef Lateef, Donald Byrd, and a host of local musicians. It is now the centerpiece in the city's revitalization movement.

——. **Parrot Lounge.** East Canfield Street at St. Antoine Street. It was in operation from the mid-1940s through the early 1960s. The club was a key spot for many noted touring performers but also featured local musicians. The tenor saxophonist and clarinetist Lamont Hamilton, the saxophonist Moon Mullins, and the pianist and singer Detroit Count were among a few local players to hold long engagements there.

——. **Plantation** [Club Plantation]. 550 E. Adams. This venue was located in the basement of the Norwood Hotel, owned by Walter Norwood, and was one the most prominent of the black-and-tans during the 1930s. Andrew "Jap" Sneed, who later owned the Three Sixes, was its manager, and his partner, Stutz Anderson, provided the music at the opening of the club in the autumn of 1933. Bands led by the violinist Earl Walton and the alto saxophonist Cecil Lee played there before the Plantation closed in 1939. Lee's band included a number of musicians who started their careers in Detroit during the 1930s and later moved on to jobs with well-known bands.

——. **Rouge Lounge.** Bar and bowling alley. In the 1950s it was run by Ed Sarkesian, who presented both local and touring musicians. As the house pianist, Barry Harris accompanied Lester Young and Flip Phillips there, and, after leaving his job at the Bluebird Inn (see above) late in 1954, Elvin Jones joined Kenny Burrell as an accompanist to Carmen McRae. A number of local artists took part in competitive jam sessions with the reed player Dezie McCullers leading the house band.

——. **El Sino.** St. Antoine Street. This downtown club was opened in 1947. Paul Bascomb led a group there for seven years from the early 1950s; other notable bands to appear were those led by Andy Kirk, Dizzy Gillespie, Henry "Red" Allen, and Illinois Jacquet. The club acquired a wider reputation after a sterling performance by Charlie Parker.

——. **Strata Concert Gallery.** Selden Street and Woodward Avenue. An outgrowth of a merger between musicians and community activists in the early 1970s, the gallery was a venue for concerts and workshops. With the Contemporary Jazz Quintet acting as a resident band, the visits of such renowned artists and groups as Herbie Hancock, Elvin Jones, Joe Henderson, Charles Mingus, Archie Shepp, Ornette Coleman, Weather Report, and Sam Rivers placed the gallery at the center of the city's avant-garde musical activity.

——. **Three Sixes.** 666 East Adams Street. Theater and cabaret. It was owned by Andrew "Jap" Sneed and managed by Richard King, and took its name from its address. In the late 1930s it was one of the most elegant clubs in the city. Entertainment included a fifteen-piece band and a dozen chorus girls, and steak dinners were priced at 6 dollars.

——. **West End Hotel.** Located near the Cadillac Fleetwood automobile plant. It was a venue noted around the late 1940s and early 1950s for its exciting, and extensive, jam sessions on Saturdays and Sundays. Kenny Burrell, Pepper Adams, Donald Byrd, Harold McKinney, the saxophonist Donald Walden, Wendell Harrison, and the trumpeter Donald Townes were among a few of the notable participants.

——. **World Stage.** Woodward Street, near Davidson Street. Theater. In the mid-1950s concerts were presented there on Tuesday nights under the auspices of the New Music Society, for which Kenny Burrell served as both president and concert manager. The society's members, which at times numbered more than 5000, heard performances by many leading young bop musicians, including Pepper Adams, Roy Brooks, Burrell, Donald Byrd, Barry Harris, Lonnie Hillyer, Yusef Lateef, Charles McPherson, Bernard McKinney (Kiane Zawadi), and Lucky Thompson; some of these were recorded for the label Transition. In the mid-1980s a new World Stage was opened in Harmonie Park by the saxophonist Donald Walden. Tommy Flanagan, Brooks, Sun Ra, and McPherson are among the musicians who have been featured at the loft.

BIBLIOGRAPHY

Detroit

H. Boyd and L. Sinclair: *Detroit Jazz Who's Who* (Detroit, 1984)
H. Boyd: "Cookin' in the Motor City," pts i–iii, *Metro Times* [Detroit] (17–23 Sept 1997), 22; (24–30 Sept 1997), 24; (1–7 Oct 1997), 24

El Cerrito, CA. **Hambone Kelly's.** 204 San Pablo Avenue. Restaurant, bar, and dance hall. Located in a building that had been previously occupied by Sally Rand's Nude Dancers, it was opened in mid-June 1947 under the cooperative ownership of the members of Lu Watters's Yerba Buena Jazz Band, with Watters himself serving as both cook and bandleader. Its ceiling decor retained the wild frescoes which had been commissioned by Rand; the bar was 100 feet long, and the dance floor held as many as 400 people. Mutt Carey, Kid Ory, and James P. Johnson appeared at Hambone Kelly's as guest soloists in 1949. The club failed the following year.

El Segundo, CA. See Los Angeles (metropolitan area).

Emeryville, CA. **Kimball's East.** 5800 Shellmound. Owned by Kimball Allen and Jan Allen, it opened in 1989, and in its first years groups were booked by Chuck LaPaglia. Herbie Hancock was the first of many internationally known musicians to appear. By 1994, with Kimball's (his companion venue in San Francisco) having failed, Allen was presenting such artists as Wynton Marsalis and Elvin Jones less often and was concentrating instead on presenting soul bands and jazz groups which played in a more pop-influenced style.

BIBLIOGRAPHY

P. Elwood: "Elegant Jazz Venue Debuts," *San Francisco Examiner* (29 March 1989)
D. Richardson: "Out on a Limb in Emeryville," *San Francisco Bay Guardian* (22 March 1989)
<http://www.kimballs.com> (2001)

Eunice, LA. **Berro's Club.** This club, owned by Berro Picou, operated from 1951 into New Year's Day 1955. Although it was a club for white patrons, African-American acts were booked from time to time. Louis Armstrong and his All Stars appeared on 11 May 1952, despite threats from a local racist on account of the presence in the trumpeter's band of the white pianist Marty Napoleon. (S. C. Picou: "Louis Armstrong and his All Stars, Berro's Club, Eunice, Louisiana," <http://www.louisianamusic.org/SCPSatchmo1. html> (2001))

Everett, MA. **Arcanum Ballroom.** 423 Broadway, Everett Square. In 1939–41 the Afro-American Association promoted a series of dances featuring nationally known bands. There was a battle of music between Count Basie and Artie Shaw on 27 October 1939 and appearances by the bands of Jimmie Lunceford, Louis Armstrong, and Benny Carter.

Fonda, NY. **Log Cabin.** Route 5, 6 miles west of Fonda. Roadhouse. The proprietor of this establishment, Allen Armstrong, presented jazz performances from at least the late 1930s. Sidney Bechet performed there from 8 September 1939 to January 1940 with a group that latterly included Sonny White, Kenny Clarke, and Wilson Myers. In spite of difficulties with Armstrong, Bechet returned to the Log Cabin in October 1940 for a further three-month engagement; among his sidemen on this occasion were Wellman Braud and Cliff Jackson.

Ft. Lauderdale, FL. **Bread of Life Natural Food Market and Restaurant.** 2388 North Federal Highway. Owned by a saxophonist, Richie Gerber, in the early 1990s this natural food store and restaurant brought in weekly guest artists, including Melton Mustafa, Ira Sullivan, and Eddie Higgins, to play with his group, the Nutrients.

——. **O'Hara's Jazz Café.** 722 East Las Olas Boulevard. This venue combines a sidewalk café with a brick interior, mahogany bars, and 18th-century chandeliers. By the 1980s it was presenting jazz and rhythm-and-blues groups, and at the turn of the 21st century Lonnie Smith was appearing regularly as the house pianist. Turk Mauro, Duffy Jackson, and Melton Mustafa have also played there. (<http://www.oharasjazzcafe.com> (2001))

Fort Worth, TX. **Caravan of Dreams.** 312 Houston Street. This large club was designed to evoke the Middle-Eastern flavor of a sultan's pavilion. Directed by Ed Bass, it was active from the 1970s as a venue for avant-garde performances of dance, theater, and music, including jazz. Ornette Coleman first recorded for its label, Caravan of Dreams Productions, in 1985. It also presented jazz in mainstream styles, with Herbie Hancock, Stanley Turrentine, Carmen McRae, Billy Eckstine, and Grover Washington, Jr., among those who appeared there. (<http://www.caravanofdreams.com> (2001))

Frederick, MD. **Dancing Pavilion** [Waltz Dream]. 400 block of West Patrick Street. In 1930–31 it hosted weekly dances featuring mainly locally based African-American bands, including Ike Dixon's orchestra from Baltimore and the Trenton Night Hawks. In January 1931 Speed Webb and his 12-piece orchestra were described as one of many special features booked for that year by the "New Waltz Dream."

Fullerton, CA. See Los Angeles (metropolitan area).

Gary, IN. **Miramar Ballroom.** 1401 Madison Street. It was in operation by January 1948, when it presented a one-night stand by Lionel Hampton's band. This was followed by appearances by the bands of Charlie Ventura (March 1948), Roy Milton (May 1948, July 1949), Lucky Millinder (April 1949), and Dizzy Gillespie (September 1949).

Glendale, CA. See Los Angeles (metropolitan area).

Gloucester, MA. **Café Beaujolais.** 284 Main Street. Opened in 1994 by David Amaral, Café Beaujolais is best known as a restaurant serving traditional French cuisine. It hosts many jazz trios, especially those featuring guitar. Herb Pomeroy, who has lived in Gloucester for some time, performs weekly at the restaurant, and in 1999 he recorded the album *Live at Café Beaujolais* there (independently released without label name or issue number).

Half Moon Bay, CA. **Bach Dancing and Dynamite Society.** Douglas Beach House, Miramar Beach. It was established by Pete Douglas in the mid-1960s and remained under his direction in the 1990s. In the course of holding engagements at San Francisco Bay area clubs, many leading jazz musicians and groups, including Max Roach, Dexter Gordon, and the World Saxophone Quartet, organized their touring schedules to include a Sunday afternoon performance at this society's venue. (<http://www.bachddsoc.org> (2001))

Harrisburg, PA. **Hilton Harrisburg & Towers.** North 2nd Street. The hotel's rather drab ballroom, located on the second floor, has been the principal site for concerts hosted by the Central Pennsylvania Friends of Jazz from at least the 1980s into the new century, as well as for that organization's annual Central Pennsylvania Mellon Jazz Festival. A far more satisfying venue is the hotel's bar on the ground floor, where Steve Rudolph has played for many years.

Hermosa Beach, CA. See Los Angeles (metropolitan area).

Hollywood, CA. See Los Angeles (metropolitan area).

Houston. **Blue Moon.** 1010 Banks Street. The Blue Moon had a restaurant on the ground floor and a nightclub upstairs. In the 1980s it was the principal venue for jazz in Houston, presenting such artists as Freddie Hubbard, Doc Cheatham, Emily Remler, Mose Allison, and Herb Ellis. By the mid-1990s it had closed and the premises were taken by a non-jazz venue, Ernie's on Banks.

——. **Eldorado Ballroom.** Elgin Street and Dowling Street. This dance hall and nightclub was the principal venue for jazz and rhythm-and-blues in Houston from the 1930s into the 1960s. Count Basie's orchestra with Jimmy Rushing, Lionel Hampton's orchestra, Arnett Cobb, Ray Charles, and Bullmoose Jackson were among those who appeared there. By 1970 the venue had closed, but efforts were underway to renovate it in the new century.

BIBLIOGRAPHY

A. Govenar and B. Joseph: *The Early Years of Rhythm & Blues: Focus on Houston* (Houston, 1990)

A. Turner: "'Home of Happy Feet': Eldorado's Rebirth will Showcase Music of Past, Present," *Houston Chronicle* (24 Feb 2001), repr. at <http://www.chron.com/cs/CDA/printstory.hts/metropolitan/832645> (2001)

——. **Rockefeller's.** 3620 Washington Avenue. Opened in 1979 in an old and monumental building that had formerly been a bank, this plush nightclub hosted major touring blues, rhythm-and-blues, and jazz musicians and groups.

——. **Sambuca Jazz Café.** 909 Texas Avenue. The fourth venue in the chain of cafés under this name (originating in Dallas), it opened in the late 1990s. It offers live jazz nightly and a Mediterranean cuisine.

Hudson Lake, IN. **Blue Lantern Inn.** Roadhouse. It was built by Victor Smith on Hudson Lake, between South Bend and Michigan City, and opened in 1922 as the Hudson Lake Casino. Following Smith's death in 1926 it was taken over by Jean Goldkette, who renamed it the Blue Lantern Inn (he ran a similar establishment under the same name at Island Lake, near Detroit). Goldkette continued Smith's policy of opening only in spring and summer; in 1926 a unit from his Victor Recording Orchestra, led by Frankie Trumbauer and including Bix Beiderbecke, alternated with Joe Dockstader's Indianans at the Blue Lantern.

Hudson River. From at least the 1930s jazz was played on the steamers that plied the Hudson between New York and Albany during the summer season. Among the famous musicians who played in the bands from time to time was Lorenzo Tio, Jr.

Indianapolis. **Indiana Roof Ballroom.** 140 West Washington Street. Built in 1927, it hosted many leading bands of the swing era and continued as a venue into the early 1970s; following extensive renovation it had reopened by the 1990s.

——. **Jazz Kitchen.** 3377 North College Avenue. From the 1990s this restaurant and bar (which serves New Orleans food) has been the principal venue for jazz in Indianapolis, presenting local artists and touring players; John Abercrombie's quartet appeared there in February 2001. (<http://www.thejazzkitchen.com> (2001))

——. **Jim & Hi's.** See Stein's.

——. **Missile Room.** West Street. In 1959 this after-hours club provided Wes Montgomery with his third job (see below, Turf Bar); Cannonball Adderley heard Montgomery there and recommended him to the Riverside company.

——. **Nick & Jerry's.** See Stein's.

——. **Stein's.** 1110 North Meridien Street. The Hampton band, led by the tenor saxophonist Duke Hampton and featuring other family members, including his brother Slide Hampton, was resident for 15 years in the 1940s and 1950s at the club at this location, which was also known from time to time as Nick & Jerry's and Jim & Hi's. (D. Schiedt: *The Jazz State of Indiana* (Pittsboro, nr Lebanon, IN, 1977), 190)

——. **Sunset Terrace.** 400 block of Indiana Avenue. This large dance hall hosted Count Basie, Billy Eckstine, Ella Fitzgerald, Charlie Parker, and other leading artists in the 1940s and 1950s; J. J. Johnson played there in 1941 as a member of a band which accompanied Pha Terrell.

——. **Tropics Club.** 10th Street. In 1955 the Montgomery–Johnson quintet (comprising the three Montgomery brothers together with the reed player Alonzo "Pookie" Johnson and the drummer Sonny Johnson) played at the club in a style modeled after that of George Shearing's famous quintet.

They continued at the venue until 1957, when Buddy and Monk Montgomery left Indianapolis for the West Coast. In later years the building became the Snug Harbor Club.

——. **Turf Bar.** In February 1957 Art Hodes began an 11-week engagement in a dixieland band at the club. In 1959, having worked the day shift (from 7 a.m. to 3 p.m.) as a welder at a factory, Wes Montgomery performed at the Turf Club from 9 p.m. until 2 a.m. and then rushed off to the Missile Room to play from 2:30 a.m. until 5 a.m.

Inglewood, CA. See Los Angeles (metropolitan area).

Island Lake, MI. **Blue Lantern Inn.** It offered jazz for dancing from at least 1925, when Jean Goldkette's Breeze Blowers (the nucleus of what became his Victor Recording Orchestra) played there for the summer season. Bix Beiderbecke joined the band during that period. Goldkette later organized further residencies at the Blue Lantern for his musicians, dividing his band between the Island Lake venue and its namesake in Hudson Lake, Indiana (see above).

Jefferson Parish, LA. **Club Forrest.** 407 Jefferson Highway. Supper and gambling club. Situated just outside the boundaries of New Orleans, this club was active by the late 1920s. Among the jazz bands that played there were those of A. J. Piron, Papa Celestin, Louis Prima and Sharkey Bonano (1928), and Abbie Brunies; Louis Armstrong also performed at Club Forrest.

——. **Suburban Gardens.** Jefferson Highway, near the Huey Long Bridge. Supper and gambling club. It was probably controlled by the mafia. In 1931 Louis Armstrong held his only extended engagement in the New Orleans area at the Suburban Gardens after leaving the city in 1922 to join King Oliver in Chicago. He performed there through the summer, broadcasting regularly. The club was called the Beverly Gardens or the Embassy Club in other years, but neither of these venues was known for jazz performances.

Kansas City, KS. **Buffalo Club.** 544 State Street. This club, formerly known as Del Ray Gardens, opened under its new name in September 1932, with Julia Lee and her orchestra supplying music for the opening night festivities. In December 1932 Thamon Hayes's orchestra became the house band. As often happened with clubs, the Buffalo was renovated and redecorated to stay current with the most "modernistic" fashions: a drape ceiling of black was added, "forming a mystic background for huge clusters of silver stars." Radio station WLBF broadcast from the club every Monday through Saturday from 10:30 p.m. to 11 p.m.

——. **Cotton Club.** Fifth Street and Richmond Street. Formerly the Royal Gardens, it became the Cotton Club in September 1934; the Kansas City Rockets continued there as the house band.

——. **Memorial Hall.** Seventh Street and Barnett Street. This was probably the major jazz venue on the Kansas side of Kansas City. In the 1930s Bennie Moten's orchestra was the most popular of the bands that played there, though Harlan Leonard and his Kansas City Rockets and Thamon Hayes's orchestra were also frequent performers. The hall continues to present concerts in all genres of music.

——. **Royal Gardens.** Fifth Street and Richmond Street. Bands such as the Kansas City Rockets and Gene Todd and his Rhythm Aces (from Denver) played at this venue. It was renamed the Cotton Club after a change in ownership in September 1934.

Kansas City, MO. **Band Box.** See Lucille's Band Box.

——. **Beau Brummels.** 1731 Lydia Street. Formerly the Lyric Hall (see below), in the mid-1950s this social club employed Joe Thomas (iii) to lead its house band.

——. **Birdland.** See Club Mardi Gras.

——. **Blue Room.** 1510 East 18th Street. It opened in 1933 as the Crystal Palace (see below) and then reopened in 1939 as the Blue Room at Street's Hotel, with Harlan Leonard's Kansas City Rockets as the house band. In memory of this venue, a club called the Blue Room serves as both a museum exhibit and a nightclub at the 18th and Vine Museum in Kansas City.
(<http://www.americanjazzmuseum.com/blueroom.html> (2001))

——. **El Capitan.** 1610 East 18th Street. Charlie Parker and Dizzy Gillespie played at this neighborhood bar and nightclub in the early 1940s.

——. **Castle Theater.** 1500 East 12th Street. From July 1939 the theater played host to a variety show, *The 12th Street Revue*. Among the prominent performers at this show were Julia Lee, and the Rocket Swing Unit, led by the reed player Woodie Walder and including Pete Johnson and Baby Lovett. An interesting edition of the show took place on "Get Together Night" (18 November 1939), when both whites and African-Americans competed together in a talent show.

——. **Cherry Blossom.** 1822 Vine Street. It was opened in April 1933 on the site of the old Eblon Theatre, where Bill Basie (not yet known as Count Basie) had played for silent pictures; the seats were removed to make room for a dance floor, and the floor was lined with "chromium posts with gold-plated ropes connecting the posts." As was the case in several other Kansas City clubs, it was fashionable at that time to use the Orient as a theme for decoration; the Cherry Blossom offered pictures of the Japanese countryside, and the orchestra platform was decorated with vivid colors and "emblems of dragons and other characteristic Japanese monsters." During the mid-1930s the club presented performances by the most eminent Kansas City bands catering to an African-American audience: in 1933 Count Basie's first band was known as Count Basie and his Cherry Blossom Victor Recording Orchestra, and that same year the merged bands of George E. Lee and Bennie Moten were resident. The Cherry Blossom was also the venue of a spectacular cutting contest between Coleman Hawkins, Ben Webster, Herschel Evans, and Lester Young on 18 December 1933. In the 1940s the club became Chez Paree and continued to host jam sessions; in the 1950s it was renovated and reopened as a bowling alley, the Monarch Bowl.

——. **City Light.** 7425 Broadway (to early 1990s); 4749 Penn Avenue (from early 1990s). In the 1980s and 1990s this was one of the principal venues for jazz in Kansas City. Claude Williams, Sheila Jordan, Jay McShann, and Kevin Mahogany are among those who appeared there.

——. **Club Mardi Gras.** 1600 East 19th Street. Under various owners, this nightclub was in operation from the 1930s into the 1960s and then again for a period in the 1980s; it reopened under a new name, Birdland, from the late 1980s into the early 1990s and yet again, as Club Mardi Gras, from the late 1990s until 1 October 2000, when it finally closed. In the 1950s and 1960s Club Mardi Gras hosted such musicians as Charlie Parker, Count Basie, Miles Davis, Thelonious Monk, Dexter Gordon, and John Coltrane.

——. **College Inn.** It offered jazz probably from the 1930s. Milt Larkin was the resident bandleader there at the turn of the decade, and the tenor saxophonist and clarinetist Jimmy Keith led his sextet at the club in 1945.

——. **Convention Hall.** 13th Street and Central Street. In the early 1930s large dance halls hosted performances by both local artists and established nationally known bands; thus for example, between 1931 and 1933 Convention Hall presented the bands of Bennie Moten and Cab Calloway, among others. Thereafter local musicians thrived in the city's smaller clubs and the large dance halls booked famous bands.

——. **Crystal Palace.** 1510 East 18th Street. This club opened in April 1933 in the Blue Room of Street's Hotel. It was decorated with multi-colored lights and mirrors, giving the effect of a "genuine palace of crystal." Bennie Moten's big band, featuring Jimmy Rushing, played at its opening. In 1939 a new club opened in this same location as the Blue Room (see above).

——. **Cuban Room.** See Milton's Tap Room.

——. **Dreamland Hall.** Cottage Street and Vine Street. Harlan Leonard's Kansas City Rockets served as the house band at Dreamland Hall for several years in the late 1930s. The group played for weekly Sunday-night dances; at one such event, in September 1938, Lionel Hampton and Teddy Wilson sat in with the Rockets.

——. **East Side Musicians Club.** See Sunset Club

——. **Elk's Rest.** 1606 East 18th Street. This club first came to prominence in 1933 when the saxophonist LaForest Dent (formerly a member of Bennie Moten's band) appeared with his Swinging Gents. In 1935 Pete Johnson and his orchestra played at a cabaret dance. George E. Lee's orchestra and Harlan Leonard and his Rockets were among other bands which performed at Elk's Rest. In December 1939 the Recreation Club, which hosted Thursday-night dances, posted a sign that stated "No jitterbugs allowed," and this put an end to jazz at the venue.

——. **Fairyland Park.** 75th Street and Prospect. During summer seasons from at least the 1930s jazz was played for dancing in a pavilion in the park, located in the southernmost portion of Kansas City. Among the African-American jazz bands that performed for white dancers were Bennie Moten's (resident in 1930–31), the Kansas City Rockets (1932), and Andy Kirk's Twelve Clouds of Joy (1935). Earl Hines presented a show in the park in September 1939. From 1940 Jay McShann's big band often performed at Fairyland Park between tours.

——. **Gem Theater.** 1615 East 18th Street. This 500-seat theater opened in the center of Kansas City's African-American community in 1912 and hosted concerts into the 1960s, although it was not one of the area's most important venues for jazz. After being derelict for a period, it reopened in September 1997 and since that time has hosted performances by Tony Bennett, Ellis Marsalis, Pat Metheny, Kevin Mahogany, the Dizzy Gillespie Alumni All Stars (including Clark Terry and Slide Hampton), Venessa Rubin, Roy Haynes, Kenny Barron, and many other leading players and groups. (R. Trussell: "Gem will Glow Again within the Glory of 18th Street," *Kansas City Star* (28 Aug 1997); repr. at <http://www.kcstar.com/jazz/stories/jazgem.htm> (2001))

——. **Gold Crown Tap Room.** 1702 East 12th Street. Formerly the Monarch BBQ Inn and Tavern, the Gold Crown Tap Room opened in July 1938 as a club attached to the Gold Crown Liquor Store (which became the Royal Crown Cut Rate Liquor Store with a change in management in February 1939). Harlan Leonard's Kansas City Rockets were frequent performers, as was Jay McShann and a very young Charlie Parker.

——. **Harlem Night Club.** See Paseo Recreational Hall.

——. **Hawaiian Garden.** 801 Independence Street. This club opened in July 1932 on the site of the short-lived Black and Tan Cotton Club Cabaret (which had opened in January 1931). It held 500 people comfortably and presented a thematic décor in which "tropical effects are heightened by a profusion of gorgeous palms." Later that year, at an early point in his career, the singing bartender Joe Turner (ii) appeared there.

——. **Hi-Hat Inn.** 22nd Street and Vine Street. This club opened in December 1935, with George Stewart and his Collegians as the house band. The Hi-Hat Inn achieved its fame as the site where Charlie Parker first honed his skills at cutting contests; on one legendary occasion Parker played so ineptly that he was obliged to leave the stage, and this experience is said to have provided one of his strongest motivations for achieving success.

——. **Hymie's Tap Room.** 1523 East 18th Street. The club, which opened in October 1935, was owned by Hymie Hurst but managed by a former club owner, Frank Banks. George E. Lee's orchestra played there on Thursday and Saturday nights.

——. **Jack's Place.** 1600 East 12th Street. Also known as Jack's Café, it was owned by Jack Johnson, who opened the club in October 1936 after redecorating the premises; pea-green walls served as the backdrop for paintings and mahogany fixtures. Julia Lee was the featured attraction. Several months later the venue became Piney's Tavern (see below).

——. **Kentucky Barbecue.** 2331 Forest Street (1937–mid-1938); 1516 East 19th Street (from July 1938). This club opened in the southern part of town before relocating to the more prominent jazz center around 18th Street and Vine in July 1938. The new venue offered a large dance floor and a mezzanine floor, with 125 tables in the main room and an additional 50 tables in a private room. Patrons could sit at their tables and use coin-operated jukeboxes. Given the popularity in the late 1930s of jukeboxes, many clubs used them for entertainment instead of live bands; indeed, in several advertisements for the Kentucky Barbecue, nothing other than "dining and dancing" is mentioned. However, there was also live entertainment there, with the Rocket Swing Unit, led by the reed player Woodie Walder, and Harlan Leonard's Kansas City Rockets appearing frequently.

——. **Labor Temple.** 14th Street and Woodland Street. This was an important dance hall throughout the 1930s and hosted several major artists, who often performed at "Break 'o Day Dances" similar to the "spook breakfasts" held at Piney's Tavern; Bennie Moten played at several such events early in the decade. When Moten was touring, Andy Kirk, the trombonist Thamon Hayes, and George E. Lee were among those who appeared at the Labor Temple. In 1936 nationally known performers began to play there: Jimmie Lunceford was booked in March 1936 and again in 1937, and Fletcher Henderson performed in November 1936.

——. **Liberty Park.** 34th Street at Raytown Road. In the late 1930s Hot Lips Page appeared at this park, which operated only during the summer months.

——. **Lincoln Hall.** 1601 East 18th Street. This large dance hall, which could accommodate more than 1700 people, flourished from the early 1930s. It presented mainly local groups, and Andy Kirk's orchestra, including Mary Lou Williams, gained its first fame there. Cab Calloway appeared for one night in 1937, and the following year Kirk's band, with Williams, returned there to play for a homecoming dance. The Deans of Swing, of which Charlie Parker was a member, began an extended engagement at Lincoln Hall late in 1938.

——. **Lincoln Theatre.** 18th Street and Lydia Street. This was primarily a movie theater, but Bessie Smith performed there in 1932, and in 1938 a series of *Vine Street Varieties* began. Broadcast over station WHB on Saturday afternoons at 3 p.m., these shows presented both aspiring local artists and well-known performers; Julia Lee, Joe Turner (ii), Pete Johnson, Lionel Hampton, Teddy Wilson, Jay McShann, and Count Basie were among the latter.

——. **Lone Star.** 1708 East 12th Street. This club opened in 1933 but did not come to prominence until about 1936, when it was redecorated in a Spanish style, with walls painted blue and gray to give the appearance of stone and hand-painted murals of trees, lakes, and mountains; it could comfortably seat 250. Jimmy Ruffin was hired from the Cherry Blossom to run the club, and Julia Lee was the first major artist to appear under his management. Later in 1936 Jimmie Lunceford's group played there. Jay McShann, Andy Kirk, Pete Johnson, and Joe Turner (ii) all performed frequently at the Lone Star, often at its "spook breakfast," beginning at 4:30 a.m.

——. **Lucille's Band Box.** 1713 East 18th Street. The club was owned by a Miss Lucille and was in operation by the late 1920s. It offered performances by Kansas City musicians, notably Bennie Moten's band, whose *Band Box Shuffle* (1929, Vic. 23007) was named for it.

——. **Lucille's Paradise.** 1711 East 18th Street. It was operated by Lucille Webb. Having previously offered music provided by a Wurlitzer jukebox, Lucille's Paradise became popular in 1936 when it began to present live bands; performances were broadcast nightly over radio station KXBY. Decorations were in the latest "modernistic" fashion, with rust, gold, and silver against a black enamel background, which contrasted with booths of green with red borders. The first band was the 3 Giants of Swing, featuring Claude Williams, which continued to be a popular attraction at Lucille's. The Rocket Swing Unit, led by the reed player Woodie Walder, became the house band in 1939.

——. **Lyric Hall.** 1731 Lydia Street. Jazz was regularly presented there from at least the early 1920s, when, at the beginning of his career, the prominent Kansas City musician George E. Lee led his own trio at the hall for a long residency. Later it became a social club, Beau Brummels (see above.)

——. **Main Street Theatre.** 14th Street and Main Street. Like the Lincoln, this was primarily a movie theater, but jazz musicians played there occasionally, most notably Bennie Moten's orchestra, featuring Jimmy Rushing, which performed for the all-white audiences. An account of what the theater was like offstage for African-American performers appears in the *Kansas City Call* (16 Jan 1931).

——. **Milton's Tap Room.** It was active from the early 1930s. Julia Lee formed a long association with the club, opening there in 1934 and continuing to perform as the resident artist until 1948. She moved from Milton's to the Cuban Room, where she began a residency in late 1950.

——. **Municipal Auditorium.** 1323 Highland Street. The Municipal Auditorium was the site of several major jazz concerts. The first of these was in July 1936, when Louis Armstrong took the stage; the advertisement for the concert stated that approximately 10,000 people could dance comfortably at the auditorium. In 1938 Count Basie's orchestra, with Jimmy Rushing, played a homecoming dance attended by 3100 people. Later that year the Municipal Auditorium hosted Cab Calloway, Ella Fitzgerald, Chick Webb, and Jimmie Lunceford.

——. **Paseo Recreational Hall.** 1414 East 15th Street. The Paseo Recreational Hall was the most popular jazz venue for African-American audiences, if not all audiences, in Kansas City. It was a large dance hall, often catering for 1500 to 2500 people. Built in 1918, it hosted dances until 1938. All of the major Kansas City-based bandleaders played at the Paseo in the early 1930s, including Bennie Moten, Andy Kirk, George E. Lee, and Thamon Hayes; touring artists such as McKinney's Cotton Pickers, Earl Hines, Noble Sissle, Duke Ellington, and Cab Calloway also appeared there. Many dances were sponsored by African-American social clubs.

The most popular events at the Paseo Recreational Hall were the semi-annual "battles of the bands" sponsored by the Musicians' Union Local 627. These contests usually presented eight to ten bands, with the winner decided by the applause of the fans; for example, in the 1931 Labor Day edition of one of these battles, bands led by Moten, Kirk, Walter Page, and several others competed against each other before an audience of 2400 people.

Following a change in management, in July 1933 the Harlem Night Club opened at the hall. The new owners catered to white audiences, but with the result that fewer big-name bands performed there, and the popular battles of the bands transferred to other establishments. Around this time the amalgamated bands of Bennie Moten and George E. Lee moved to the club after playing at the Cherry Blossom (see above) and remained resident until 1934. Then, in March 1935 (when an advertisement stated that the hall was being "turned over to Negro patronage again"), the Paseo Recreational Hall resumed its previous approach with the spring Musicians' Ball. Thereafter Harlan Leonard, Pete Johnson, Count Basie, Fats Waller, Don Redman, Fletcher Henderson, Ellington, and Jimmie Lunceford were among the many major bandleaders who played at the Paseo; the orchestras of Basie and Ellington engaged in a battle of the bands there on 31 October 1936. This policy came to an end in 1938, when St. Stephen's Baptist Church purchased the premises, its previous building having been destroyed in a fire. St. Stephen's still occupies the site.

——. **Phoenix Piano Bar & Grill.** 302 West 8th Street. From around 1988 this has been a leading venue for local players, with such famous artists as Jay McShann appearing on occasion.

——. **Piney's Tavern.** 1600 East 12th Street. In April 1937 Piney Brown acquired Jack's Place and renamed it Piney's Tavern. Brown, immortalized in Joe Turner (ii)'s hit *Piney Brown Blues*, was famous for hosting "spook breakfasts" from 5 a.m. to 9 a.m.; Julia Lee and Turner were frequent performers.

——. **Playmates Club.** It was in existence from at least the 1950s. The tenor saxophonist and clarinetist Jimmy Keith was the resident leader there for many years into the 1960s.

——. **Reno Club.** 602 East 12th Street. The club flourished during the 1930s but was closed in 1938 after the owners had been indicted for tax evasion. The club's activities, directed by Papa Sol Epstein, were segregated, and separate dance floors, bars, and dining areas were reserved for African-American and white patrons. Bennie Moten played there in the early 1930s, and in 1935 Count Basie formed a nine-piece group, the Barons of Rhythm, for a residency; it was at this venue that Basie was discovered by John Hammond in 1936. Nightly broadcasts from the club were relayed on radio station W9XBY. In 1938 Jesse Price's big band played there, and the following year George E. Lee, whose career passed through a decline in the mid-1930s, took his new band (formed the preceding year for a residency at the Brookside Club) to play an engagement at the Reno. The club was as important for after-hours jam sessions by the many jazz musicians playing in the city at that time as it was for the music that was performed to entertain the clientele.

——. **Roscoe Hall.** 18th Street and Prospect Street. Among the jazz musicians who were resident performers at this venue in its heyday in the 1930s was Tommy Douglas.

——. **Roseland Ballroom.** 14th Street and Troost Street. Until about 1933 this large dance hall catered to white audiences, but that year an article was placed in the *Kansas City Call* stating that it was under "negro patronage." Locally based bands, including those of Bennie Moten, Andy Kirk, and Count Basie, played at the Roseland, as did such visitors as Fletcher Henderson, Jimmie Lunceford, and Duke Ellington; indeed, when Ellington performed in Kansas City it was most often at this venue. Coleman Hawkins was with Henderson's band at the ballroom on 18 December 1933 before going over to the Cherry Blossom to engage in a now legendary competition with the Kansas City tenor saxophone masters.

——. **Subway Club.** 1516 East 18th Street. In the 1930s the Subway was owned by Felix Payne and managed by Piney Brown. It was noted for its all-star jam sessions, which attracted the important musicians playing at other clubs in the city in the bands of leaders such as Fletcher Henderson, Benny Goodman, and Count Basie.

——. **Sunset Club** [East Side Musicians Club; Sunset Crystal Palace]. 1715 East 12th Street. Like the Subway Club, the Sunset was owned by Felix Payne and managed by Piney Brown, who presented many of the stars of Kansas City jazz and blues; it, too, was a favorite after-hours venue for musicians, and it was the site of many cutting contests among such players as Irving "Mouse" Randolph, Ben Webster, Herschel Evans, Dick Wilson, Lester Young, Chu Berry, and Coleman Hawkins. Joe Turner (ii) had one of his first jobs at this club, where he was engaged as a barman and singer; Turner, Pete Johnson, Eddie Durham, and Hot Lips Page all played on one particular evening, and George E. Lee and Julia Lee were joined on another by Count Basie and his orchestra. In an advertisement for the latter event, patrons were urged to "come out and hear all the musicians of the city, including the whites, swing out"; this suggests that white performers were welcomed at the establishment. In May 1935 Piney Brown arranged to have shows broadcast from the club on radio station W9XBY on Sunday nights from 11:30 p.m. to midnight; in its first installment listeners heard both Turner and Andy Kirk's orchestra featuring Pha Terrell. During the mid-1930s Pete Johnson was a resident performer. In July 1937 the name of the club changed to Sunset Crystal Palace. The Rocket Swing Unit, led by the reed player Woodie Walder, which included Johnson and Baby Lovett, was often a featured attraction. It is the Sunset Club which is celebrated in the film *Kansas City* (1996), directed by Robert Altman.

——. **El Torreon Ballroom.** 31st Street and Gillham Street. Phil Baxter's Texas Tommies opened this venue and became the house band. Among those who led ensembles for dancing there during the 1920s was Bennie Moten.

——. **Troost Avenue Ballroom.** 1413 Troost Street. George E. Lee and his Thirteen Piece Syncopated Band performed at the grand opening of the Troost Avenue Ballroom on 11 July 1938. The advertisement for this event made special mention of the dance floor, which was of maple and covered 10,000 square feet. This occasion also marked the first time in three years that Lee had played before an African-American audience.

——. **Wolf's Buffet.** 1522 East 18th Street; 21st Street and Harrison Street (from May 1939). This was another prominent club in the 18th and Vine district. Its grand opening took place on 21 September 1935 after the owner, Wolf Binkowitz, redecorated the club. Among those who performed there were George E. Lee, Pete Johnson, Joe Turner (ii), and Jay McShann, who was the featured attraction at Wolf's Buffet starting in 1938. In May 1939 the club moved several blocks south from the center of Kansas City's African-American entertainment district, as Binkowitz hoped to attract a racially mixed clientele.

——. **Yellow Front Café.** Jazz was played there from at least 1930. During his stay in Kansas City from 1930 to 1933 Sammy Price held a long residency at the Yellow Front, and for a brief time he performed with Bunk Johnson.

BIBLIOGRAPHY

Kansas City

D. Schiedt: "Kansas City Still Stomps," *Jazz Notes*, vii/3, n.d. [*c*1962], 2

R. Russell: *Jazz Style in Kansas City and the Southwest* (Berkeley, CA, Los Angeles, and London, 1971, rev. 2/1973/*R*1997)
N. W. Pearson, Jr.: *Goin' to Kansas City* (Urbana, IL, and London, 1988)
Kansas City Jazz Museum: *Kansas City and All that Jazz* (Kansas City, MO, 1999)
A. J. Bushard: *The Jazz and Blues Club Scene in Kansas City as Portrayed in the "Kansas City Call," 1930–1939* (thesis, U. of Kansas, 2000)
C. Haddix: "18th and Vine: Streets of Dreams," <http://www.kcjazz.com/jazztext/18thvine.htm> (2001)
<http://home.kc.rr.com/kcjazz> (2001)

Las Vegas. **Blue Room.** Hotel Tropicana. Like many of the hotels, casinos, and supper clubs in the city, the Blue Room offered popular music and jazz for the entertainment of its patrons. Among the important bands that played there was Count Basie's orchestra, which appeared frequently in the late 1960s and early 1970s.

——. **Cinderella Club.** It flourished in the 1960s, when Charlie Teagarden, who lived in Las Vegas for the last 25 years of his life, led his band for several long residencies there.

Lenox, MA. **Music Inn** [Berkshire Music Barn]. Adjoining Tanglewood, the summer home of the Boston Symphony Orchestra, the Music Inn hosted summer jazz workshops organized by Marshall Stearns from 1950 to around 1960; the most famous of these events occurred in the 1959 concert season, when Ornette Coleman and Don Cherry were among the workshop's students. From 1957 to 1961 this venue also served as the site for concerts billed annually as a summer-long jazz and folk festival; among those who appeared were Ella Fitzgerald (1957), Duke Ellington, Wilbur De Paris, Lionel Hampton, Anita O'Day, Oscar Peterson, and Max Roach (all 1958), and Dizzy Gillespie (1961); by 1961 hotel accommodation was offered with free access to concerts.

Long Beach, CA. See Los Angeles (metropolitan area).

Los Angeles (metropolitan area). **Alex Lovejoy's Breakfast Club.** $4416\frac{3}{4}$ South Central Avenue. An upstairs after-hours club located near the Club Alabam, it flourished in the 1930s and 1940s. Art Tatum, Charlie Parker, Dizzy Gillespie, and others played there, though the piano was in poor condition.

——. **Alfonse's.** 10057 Riverside Drive, Toluca Lake. In the 1980s Charlie Chiarenza's club was a favorite place for studio musicians needing an outlet to play jazz. Usually there was no cover charge and only a semi-enforced minimum charge for drinks; generally different groups played almost every night, with big bands on Mondays. It closed on 31 January 1990, then reopened later that year as POV, or M.K.P.O.V. (an acronym for Martha K. Hanson's Point of View – Hanson being the owner). The pianist Marty Harris served as music director. The venue's policy of presenting jazz ended in 1992.

——. **Alleycat Bistro.** 3865 Overland Avenue, Culver City. This pleasant neighborhood club, located in a small shopping center, operated during the 1980s. The International Association of Jazz Appreciation sponsored jazz concerts and jam sessions on Sunday afternoons; during the evenings the club featured bop, and occasionally free-jazz, groups.

——. **Alligator Lounge.** 3321 Pico Boulevard, Santa Monica. From 1993 to 1997 this club was an important venue for free-jazz players on Monday nights.

——. **Ambassador Auditorium.** Ambassador College, 300 West Green Street, Pasadena. This opulent concert hall was the site of many expensive jazz concerts given by well-known swing and bop groups from the 1970s to 1995, when it closed.

——. **Ambassador Hotel.** 3400 Wilshire Boulevard. Jazz musicians played from at least the early 1920s for dancing in the hotel's main ballroom/showroom, the Cocoanut Grove; the drummer Abe Lyman led a band there from 1924 to 1927, and Benny Goodman's band broadcast from the room in spring 1940. From the 1950s into the 1970s many jazz and pop singers appeared there. The name changed to the Now Grove around 1970, and the entertainer Sammy Davis, Jr., accompanied by a band that included Marshal Royal, was resident for about a year. Other rooms that sometimes featured jazz were the Circus Room, the Ambassador Room, and the Embassy Room. The hotel closed in 1989.

——. **American Federation of Musicians, Local 47.** Georgia Street at Pico Boulevard; 817 North Vine Street, Hollywood (from the late 1940s). The Vine Street auditorium at Local 47 has periodically hosted long benefit concerts for jazz musicians in medical distress or for the families of recently deceased members. Also from time to time Jazz Central sponsors a concert there, featuring some of Los Angeles's best-known jazz musicians.

——. **Apex Nite Club.** 4015 South Central Avenue (1928–31); 1063 East 55th Street (1935–?). It was founded in August 1928 by Esvan and Curtis Mosby, the "honorary mayor" of Central Avenue. A large, luxurious room with a spacious dance floor, a balcony, and a bar, it featured dancing and musical entertainment nightly for an almost entirely white audience. Marshal Royal, Lionel Hampton, and Lawrence Brown were in Mosby's Dixieland Blue Blowers there in the late 1920s, and Duke Ellington first heard Ivie Anderson singing there in 1928. The club was shut after a police raid in November 1929, but its owners were acquitted and it soon reopened. Around 1930 Curtis Mosby opened a second Apex club in San Francisco, and bands alternated between the two venues on a fortnightly basis. In 1931 he filed for bankruptcy and the Apex Nite Club closed; it reopened later that year as the Club Alabam (see below). Mosby opened a new Apex club on 55th Street in 1935, with Buck Clayton leading the house band; it closed later that decade, or even in the same year.

——. **Aragon Ballroom.** Lick Pier, Ocean Park, Venice. This large ballroom, located south of Santa Monica, was called Bon Ton or Lick Pier Ballroom until the 1940s. Count Basie (summer 1943), Louis Armstrong, and others played there. During the 1950s it was the home of Lawrence Welk's band. It burned down on 27 May 1970.

——. **Arion Hall.** $116\frac{1}{2}$ East 3rd Street. This was an early jazz venue (*c*1919–27) where the Black and Tan Orchestra, the Sunnyland Jazz Orchestra, and Sonny Clay played.

——. **Arlequin Club.** 13730 Ventura Boulevard. Formerly the Moonlight Tango (which by 1999 had largely abandoned jazz), the Arlequin Club opened in 2001 and resumed the policy of presenting jazz groups at this venue.

——. **Armand Hammer Cultural Museum.** 10899 Wilshire Boulevard, Westwood. From 1996, on Friday evenings in summer, major bop musicians based in Los Angeles have given free jazz concerts on the patio.

——. **Artworks 4.** 3436 West 43rd Street. Carl Burnett operated this performance space near Leimert Park from 1982 to 1989. After it closed its furniture and stage were moved to the nearby World Stage (see below).

——. **Assembly Auditorium.** 833 South Central Avenue. In the mid-1920s this was a skating rink by day and a dance hall by night, where the Sunnyland Jazz Orchestra, Morrison's World Famous Orchestra, and Paul Howard's Quality Four played.

——. **Atlas Bar & Grill.** 3760 Wilshire Boulevard, next to the Wiltern Theater. This large restaurant with a high ceiling was an important venue for bop in the 1990s. (<http://www.clubatlas.com> (2001))

——. **At my Place.** 1026 Wilshire Boulevard, Santa Monica. This large club presented fusion, and some bop, from the 1980s. In 1993 its name was changed to Night Winds, and soon afterwards it ceased to present jazz.

——. **Avodon.** 843 South Spring Street, behind the Orpheum Theater. This "ballroom-cafe" opened in April 1946 and presented leading swing bands. It was called the Rhumba Palace for a short time in 1949 and then renamed the Avodon. It held its last dance on New Year's Eve 1951 and not long thereafter made way for a garage.

——. **Baked Potato.** 3787 Cahuenga Boulevard, North Hollywood. A restaurant and club, it features mostly fusion groups, such as the bands of Don Randi (owner of the club), Lee Ritenour, Larry Carlton, and Brandon Fields. In 1992 a second Baked Potato opened at 26 East Colorado Boulevard, in the Old Town section of Pasadena; this was an important venue for Latin jazz until it closed in 1997. In 1999 the New Baked Potato (Baked Potato Hollywood) opened at 6266½ Sunset Boulevard; like the original club, it is largely a venue for fusion groups. (<http://www.thebakedpotatojazz.com> (2001))

——. **Bal Tabarin.** Western Avenue. A large showroom south of the center of the city, it was active in the 1930s and presented Jack Teagarden, Louis Armstrong, and Billie Holiday in the 1940s.

——. **Basin Street West.** See Strip City.

——. **Bel-Age Hotel** [Wyndam Bel-Age Hotel]. 1020 North San Vicente Boulevard, West Hollywood. The hotel's important Club Brasserie, which offers a stunning view of Hollywood's city lights, opened in the early 1990s. The excellent jazz musicians who appeared there during the club's first years had to contend with one of the worst grand pianos in Los Angeles. Late in 2000 the club ended its music policy, but a few months later, and under a new name, Club Thelonious, it became a weekend venue for student jazz groups. (<http://www.wyndham.com/BelAge> (2001))

——. **Beverly Cavern.** Northeast corner of Beverly Boulevard and Ardmore Avenue, Hollywood. It flourished from the 1940s into the 1970s. At first its repertory emphasized dixieland – the club opened with performances by a dixieland band led by the trombonist Ted Vesely. In the late 1940s it was owned by Sam Rittenberg and Rose Stanman. Among the jazzmen who played there were Jim Robinson, Kid Ory's band (which broadcast nightly in 1949), Ward Kimball's Firehouse Five Plus Two, a sextet led by Ben Pollack (*c*1950), and Teddy Buckner, whose band played there in 1965 and then was resident for a long period in the 1970s. The venue became a Korean restaurant.

——. **Big Apple.** 4311–13 South Central Avenue. Curtis Mosby managed this 1930s jazz club where Mutt Carey and others played.

——. **Bill Whistling's (Modern Jazz).** See Whistling's.

——. **Billy Berg's Swing Club.** 1356 North Vine Street, Hollywood. In the mid-1940s Billy Berg sold the Waldorf Cellar, the Trouville, and the Swing Club (see below) and bought this club. It opened on 13 February 1945 with Coleman Hawkins's band, and that December Dizzy Gillespie and Charlie Parker made their first appearance on the West Coast there. From 1945–6 bands broadcast nightly from the club. In 1947 Parker and Erroll Garner's trio battled Pete Dailey's Chicagoans on Sundays, and on 13 August that year Louis Armstrong's All Stars made their official début. In 1948 the venue became Billy Berg's Restaurant, but it closed in 1949. Two other clubs run by Berg also existed in the 1940s and 1950s – Billy Berg's Front Room (next door to the Swing Club) and Billy Berg's (1841 North Cahuenga).

——. **Biltmore Hotel.** 506 North Grand Avenue and 515 South Olive (there are entrances on both streets). An opulent hotel that opened on 2 October 1923, it contains several banqueting halls and lounges. In 1996, having come under the ownership of the Hong Kong-based Regal Hotels International, it became the Regal Biltmore Hotel. In the late 1980s its large Grand Avenue Bar presented early evening jazz concerts during the week produced by the pop singer Diane Varga. The club had no cover charge and served a free buffet of appetizers while the top jazz musicians of Los Angeles performed. Thirty-minute live broadcasts on KKGO originated from there on Tuesday nights in 1988–9. From April 1990 one night each week became big-band night and a cover charge was instituted; Nancy Wilson also taped her syndicated television show, "Red Hot & Cool," there. From 1991 to 1994 Bill and Betty Berry's International Jazz Party took place one weekend of each year, with many Japanese and American musicians participating. The policy of presenting jazz at the Grand Avenue Bar ended in 1994. The hotel's Biltmore Bowl is a large, ornate performance space offering occasional concerts, and from 1990 it has been the site of tributes by major stars, organized by the Los Angeles Jazz Society, to Ray Brown, Benny Carter, Louie Bellson, Buddy Collette, and others. Local jazz pianists and trios often perform in the Rendezvous Court, a high-ceilinged foyer inside the Olive Street entrance. (<http://www.thebiltmore.com/grandhotel.html> (2001))

——. **Bird in the Basket.** See Jack's Basket.

——. **Birdland West.** 105 West Broadway (second floor), Long Beach. The drummer Al Williams operated this important bop-oriented club from 1986 to 1994. Carmen McRae recorded there. Later it reopened as the Beach Palace and featured occasional jazz events.

——. **Bjlauzezs News Café.** 14502 Ventura Boulevard Sherman Oaks. Pronounced "blauzes," it was open from autumn 1995 to November 1996, and during that year presented bop groups three nights per week.

——. **Black Orchid.** See Hillcrest Club.

——. **Blain** [Blaine] **Nell Country Club** [Blaine-Nell Chateau; The Chateau; Chateau Nite Club]. Wilmington Avenue and 118th Street. Weekend dances took place there from at least 1928 to the early 1930s, featuring the Kansas City Stomper Syncopators, Pep Prince, the Blaine Nell Superior Six Orchestra, and Johnnie Mitch-hell's Chateau Orchestra. It was renamed Blainell's New Deal Club in 1933.

——. **Blanchard Hall** [Blanchard's Hall]. 233 (232?) South Broadway. This dance hall operated from about 1919 until at least the early 1930s and featured the Hightower Orchestra, Spikes Celebrated Orchestra, Wood Wilson, Colen's Famous Jazzers, Seven Southern Syncopators, Kid Ory's Creole Band, and Mitchell's Darktown Syncopators.

——. **Blossom Room.** See Hollywood Roosevelt Hotel.

——. **Blue Bird Inn.** South Central Avenue at 12th Street. Paul Howard's Quality Serenaders played at this high-priced club in the 1920s.

——. **Bob Burns Restaurant.** 202 Wilshire Boulevard, Santa Monica. The pianist, singer, and composer Howlett Smith has been resident in the lounge continuously from 1977, usually with a double bass player. On his nights off, Betty Bryant, Dwight Dickerson, and other pianists have performed.

——. **Bon Appetit.** 1061 Broxton Avenue, Westwood. In the 1980s and early 1990s Don Gimpel's club usually presented fusion bands. It closed in October 1991.

——. **Bonaventure Hotel.** 401 South Flower Street. In 1976 a series of free noon-time summer concerts by bop bands began on the roof of this spectacular hotel. The Bonaventure Brewery and Restaurant, on the fourth floor, began presenting jazz in 1998.

——. **Bon Ton.** See Aragon Ballroom.

——. **Bovard Auditorium.** See University of Southern California.

——. **Breakfast Club.** See Alex Lovejoy's Breakfast Club.

——. **Bronx Palm Garden.** Bronx Hotel, 423 East 7th Street. The hotel opened in 1924 and closed late in 1927. Curtis Mosby's Dixieland Blue Blowers played in its showroom, the Palm Garden.

——. **Ca' del Sole.** 4100 Cahuenga Boulevard, North Hollywood. Located on the site of the old Maison Gerard, this restaurant opened in 1996 with jazz presented five nights per week. Initially pianists and guitarists were featured, but later singers accompanied by pianists were the norm. (<http://www.cadelsoleristorante.com> (2001))

——. **Cadillac Café.** 553 Central Avenue. One of the first venues in the city to present hot music, it featured Jelly Roll Morton and the singer Bricktop (Ada Smith) around 1917. Paul Howard's Quality Serenaders played there in 1923.

——. **Le Café.** 14633 Ventura Boulevard, Sherman Oaks. While downstairs there was a fashionable restaurant, upstairs there was a small club with a grand piano in excellent condition. In the early and middle 1980s the typical group was bop-oriented; later the venue leaned towards fusion. It presented music seven nights per week until 1995 and then ceased to offer jazz.

——. **Café Intime.** See Dynamite Jackson's Club.

——. **Calabassas Inn.** A large venue in northwest Los Angeles County, it was active in the 1960s and 1970s. Joe Darensbourg led his own trio for a residency there in 1970, when the group was often joined for jam sessions by other musicians, including Barney Bigard, Matty Matlock, and Eddie Miller.

——. **Caldwell's Recreation Garden.** Santa Monica. In 1921 the Black and Tan Orchestra, the Westside Jazz Band, and Wood Wilson's Satisfied Vendome Band played there.

——. **California(n) Club.** 1759 (1756?) West Santa Barbara Avenue (now Martin Luther King Boulevard) at St. Andrew. The Max Roach–Clifford Brown quintet made its début there in 1953. During the 1950s and 1960s the club presented bop groups and revues.

——. **Capri Club** [Club Capri]. 374 South La Cienega Boulevard, Hollywood. Billy Berg owned this club before establishing Billy Berg's on North Vine Street (see above). The club hosted radio broadcasts on KHJ twice a week. Slim and Slam, Lee and Lester Young, and Barney Bigard appeared there in 1941–2. Berg closed this club in 1942 and later opened the Trouville (see below).

——. **Carmelo's.** 4449 Van Nuys Boulevard, Sherman Oaks. This restaurant opened in June 1979. In August jazz was presented there three nights a week, and by 1980 it was an important nightly venue. Shelly Manne recorded there in 1980, Don Menza in 1981, and the Blue Wisp Big Band in 1984. Thereafter it changed ownership and name and was no longer a significant jazz venue.

——. **Casablanca.** 2801 South San Pedro Street. An after-hours club, it was owned and run by the guitarist Stanley Morgan (the father of Frank Morgan) or by Elihu "Black Dot" McGee (sources disagree); it was in existence at least by the mid-1940s. Charlie Parker was a frequent attraction there during his stay in California from 1945; Ernie Andrews and Art Tatum also appeared there.

——. **Casa Mañana.** See Sebastian's Cotton Club.

——. **Casino Ballroom** [Avalon Casino]. 100 St. Catherine Way, at the Avalon harbor, Catalina Island. This large hall has hosted jazz intermittently from at least 1940, when it presented Benny Goodman. In 1987 the Trax Festival began there, and in 1996 Terry Gibbs's big band and the memorial Woody Herman big band appeared.

——. **Casino Gardens Ballroom.** 2946 Ocean Front, Ocean Park, Venice. Located across from the Aragon, it presented Tommy Dorsey, Jimmy Dorsey, Harry James, and Woody Herman in the 1940s. Tommy Dorsey leased the ballroom and played there for several years; it was closed from Spring 1950 to June 1951, when he returned, and later it closed and reopened several more times. In autumn 1954 the country star Spade Cooley took over its operation.

——. **Catalina Bar and Grill.** 1640 North Cahuenga, Hollywood. Catalina Popescu opened this restaurant and jazz club in 1986, and soon it was one of the principal jazz venues in Los Angeles. Located a few yards north of the site of Shelly's Manne Hole, it seats 150 people and features a well-maintained Steinway Model B piano. Typically a small bop group visits and plays Tuesday through Sunday nights, while a local band appears on Monday nights. Sometimes fusion or free jazz groups also perform. The club was remodeled in the late 1980s and again in 1997. (<http://www.catalinajazzclub.com> (2001))

——. **Central Park West.** 11604 San Vicente Boulevard, West Los Angeles. This club presented bop players and singers from 1990 to 1992.

——. **Century Plaza Hotel.** 2025 Avenue of the Stars, Century City. Jazz musicians, including Louis Armstrong and Lionel Hampton, have played in the ballrooms of this hotel from the 1960s. The Hong Kong Bar was an excellent venue for major jazz artists in the 1960s and 1970s. Later, in 1991, the Lobby Court Bar presented a local trio three nights per week. The Westside Room has been the site of the annual International Jazz Party from 1995, when it moved from the Grand Avenue Bar of the Biltmore Hotel.

——. **Chadney's.** 3000 West Olive Avenue, Burbank (to late 1998); 3575 Cahuenga Boulevard, Studio City (from late 1998). This restaurant is located across the street from NBC studios. In the 1980s its lounge area began hosting a jam session on Tuesdays and various local and traveling bop groups on other nights; Earl Palmer ran the jam sessions for years. In December 1998 it closed and reopened about 2 miles southwest, at the site of Mallory's. Jazz groups continued to appear for a few months, but the lounge area was poorly designed for music and the piano was in poor condition; by mid-1999 the policy of presenting jazz had all but ended.

——. **Charlie O's**. 13725 Victory Boulevard, Van Nuys. This restaurant has offered jazz six nights per week from the year 2000.

——. **The Chateau** [Chateau Nite Club]. See Blain Nell Country Club.

——. **La Chris.** See Club La Chris.

——. **Chubby's Jazz Estate.** Lankershim Boulevard, near Vanowen Street, North Hollywood. The owner, Chubby Jackson, led a band at this club in the 1970s.

——. **Cinegrill.** See Hollywood Roosevelt Hotel.

——. **Circus Room.** See Ambassador Hotel.

——. **Ciro's** [Ciro's Living Room]. 8433 West Sunset Boulevard, West Hollywood. This famous nightclub sometimes featured Duke Ellington, Cab Calloway, Nat "King" Cole, Cal Tjader, and others during the 1940s and 1950s. It closed for a period during World War II, reopened in July 1944, then it closed and reopened two or more times in the next few years. In 1965 the owners renamed it the Living Room and featured bop-oriented Sunday jam sessions. Later it became The Comedy Store.

——. **Civic Auditorium.** See Pasadena Civic Auditorium.

——. **Clark Hotel.** 1820–24 South Central Avenue. This African-American-owned hotel opened in 1911. Lee Young played there in 1935, and other jazz players appeared from time to time until at least the late 1950s.

——. **Classic Bar and Grill.** 4253 South Central Avenue. Herb Jeffries hosted this jazz club, owned by Curtis Mosby, in the late 1930s.

——. **Clef Club.** 1841 North Cahuenga Boulevard, Hollywood. Before becoming a jazz venue it was known as the Hollywood 1841 Club. Dexter Gordon and Wardell Gray recorded there in March 1952, and it continued as a jazz venue until it closed in 1955.

——. **Club Alabam.** 4015 South Central Avenue (from the late 1930s, remaining at the same location, but renumbered as 4215 South Central Avenue). Formerly the Apex Nite Club (see above), this luxurious room was reopened on 4 September 1931, with the same policy of presenting dancing and musical entertainment nightly, almost exclusively for white audiences. An important venue, located next door to the Dunbar Hotel, it was at the center of the hot jazz activity in Los Angeles during the 1930s and 1940s; generally the focus was on variety shows, but leading jazz bands accompanied singers and dancers and were featured as well. Late in 1940 the Apex's former owners, Esvan and Curtis Mosby, took it over; Curtis's Blue Blowers played there, and in mid-decade the house bands were successively those of Harlan Leonard (1943 – mid-1944), Roy Milton (from mid-1944), and Johnny Otis (1945). The club closed from 1947 to 1949, while Curtis Mosby was engaged in problems with the Internal Revenue Service and subsequently served a jail term, then reopened briefly as the New Club Alabam. The building had been demolished by the mid-1980s.

——. **Club Araby** [New Apex Nite Club]. 5326 South Central Avenue or 1063 East 55th Street. This venue, located upstairs from the Savoy Ballroom (see below) or the Savoy Theater, opened on 28 March 1935 with a big band and continued to operate in the 1940s; in the 1930s it was called the New Apex Nite Club. Lionel Hampton, Buck Clayton, Curtis Mosby, and others led bands there.

——. **Club Brasserie.** See Bel-Age Hotel.

——. **Club Capri.** Pico and La Cienega boulevards, near Beverly Hills. This was Billy Berg's first club. In 1941, shortly after he left Count Basie's band, Lester Young led a sextet there.

——. **Club Caprice.** See The Strand.

——. **Club Ebony.** See Dunbar Hotel.

——. **Club Finale.** See Finale Club.

——. **Club 47.** 12319 Ventura Boulevard, Studio City. Nappy Lamare and Doc Rondo opened this club in the late 1940s. It became popular with dixieland and swing musicians, who went there to listen and to take part in frequent jam sessions. The many musicians who played there included Eddie Miller, Matty Matlock, Sharkey Bonano, Zutty Singleton, Joe Darensbourg, and the owners themselves.

——. **Club La Chris.** 4154 South Avalon Boulevard. Owned by Ollie Jackson, this club presented jazz seven nights a week in 1957 and continued as a bop venue well into the 1960s. It was a popular site for after-hours jam sessions.

——. **Club Memo.** See Memo Club.

——. **Club Oasis.** See Oasis.

——. **Club Plantation.** See Jazzland Café and Plantation Club.

——. **Club Renaissance.** See The Mocambo.

——. **Club Sirocco.** 4269 Lankershim Boulevard, North Hollywood. Roy Porter and Joe Liggins worked there in the mid-1950s. The venue later became famous as Donte's (see below).

——. **Club Sorrento.** See Zanzibar Club.

——. **Club Thelonious.** See Bel-Age Hotel; see also Music Center.

——. **Club 331.** See Three-Thirty-One Club.

——. **Club Tropicana** [The Tropicana]. 247 East Manchester Avenue. The owners of this major jazz club called it the "Birdland of the West Coast" in the late 1960s; many leading bop musicians played there.

——. **Cocoanut Grove.** See Ambassador Hotel.

——. **Comeback Inn.** 1633 West Washington Boulevard, Venice. This was a small vegetarian restaurant where Los Angeles-based bop and free-jazz musicians often played in the 1980s; it closed in 1990.

——. **Compton Lazben Hotel.** 111 East Artesia Boulevard, Compton. Ozzie Cadena booked excellent bop jazz groups when the hotel and its Indigo Jazz Club first opened in December 1988. In 1989 the room became the Count Basie Ballroom, with jazz continuing twice a week. The hotel, which was absorbed into the Ramada chain and renamed, closed in 1994 and reopened in 1997, but no longer offered jazz.

——. **Concerts by the Sea.** 100 Fisherman's Wharf (under the pier), Redondo Beach. Howard Rumsey, who had formerly managed the Lighthouse Café, 2 miles north (see below), opened Concerts by the Sea in 1972. Its semicircular theater seating, its well-maintained Steinway Model B piano, and its isolated area for drink preparation made it a favorite venue for performing musicians and serious listeners. It became one of the leading jazz clubs in Los Angeles County, and most of the world-class bop and fusion bands of the era performed there, among them Herbie Hancock and his Headhunters band and Toshiko Akiyoshi and her West Coast big band (both of which were first appearances). Bob Florence, Rob McConnell, Dizzy Gillespie, and others recorded albums and videos in the club. Rumsey retired in 1985, and Concerts by the Sea closed about three years later.

——. **Copacabana.** West Sunset Boulevard, between The Mocambo and Ciro's, West Hollywood. This fashionable nightclub, which contained two rooms, sometimes featured Billy Eckstine, Dave Brubeck, and other jazz artists in the early 1950s.

——. **Cosmo's Alley.** 1608 North Cosmo Street, Hollywood. In the late 1950s this venue operated as an after-hours jazz club and also presented jazz and poetry sessions on Tuesdays. Les McCann appeared there, as did the comedian Lenny Bruce (accompanied by jazz musicians). Later it became successively the Gaslight, the Streets of Paris, and, from 1992, Cosmo's, which offered jazz occasionally.

——. **Cotton Club.** See Florentine Gardens, Last Word, and Sebastian's Cotton Club.

——. **Count Basie Ballroom.** See Compton Lazben Hotel.

——. **The Crescendo.** 8572 West Sunset Boulevard, West Hollywood. This large club opened in mid-1952 with Billy Eckstine (an owner at the time) and Dave Brubeck; it closed the following year, then reopened in 1954, when Gene Norman and Chuck Landis purchased it. Often the attractions were in genres other than jazz, but in the years 1955–62 Duke Ellington, Louis Armstrong, and others jazz musicians appeared there and Count Basie and Ella Fitzgerald recorded excellent albums in the club.

——. **Cricket Club Café.** 1571 West Washington Boulevard. It was an important club in the late 1940s, when Dizzy Gillespie, Horace Henderson, and others appeared there.

——. **Deauville Country Club.** 1525 Ocean Front, Santa Monica. Dances and bop concerts took place there in the late 1950s and early 1960s. It was renamed the Deauville-Bayview in 1962.

——. **Dino's Italian Inn.** 2055 East Colorado Boulevard, Pasadena. In the early 1980s this venue featured major Los Angeles-based bop players.

——. **Disneyland.** 1313 South Harbor Boulevard, Anaheim. Amusement park. Walt Disney opened his famous amusement park in 1955. From the beginning dixieland bands performed there, especially on a replica of a Mississippi riverboat, the *Mark Twain*; the original resident band, the Young Men from New Orleans, included Joe Darensbourg and Johnny St. Cyr. Teddy Buckner's band played there intermittently from 1955 into the 1980s. During summer seasons in the 1960s, 1970s, and 1980s the park booked well-known swing and bop big bands for the Carnation Plaza, an outdoor dance area. Among the numerous important musicians who appeared at Disneyland were Benny Goodman, Kid Ory, Earl Hines, Jack McVea, and Louie Bellson.

——. **Dodsworth Bar & Grill.** 2 West Colorado Boulevard, in the Old Town section of Pasadena. This restaurant booked bop musicians four nights per week from 1987 until it closed in August 1996.

——. **Donte's.** 4269 Lankershim Boulevard, North Hollywood. Formerly the Club Sirocco, it was opened by Carey Leverette as Donte's in June 1966 with the trio of Hampton Hawes, Red Mitchell, and Donald Bailey; Pete Jolly's trio appeared on a regular basis. It became a favorite meeting place for musicians living in the San Fernando Valley. Carmen McRae recorded there in 1972, but usually the bandstand was occupied by Los Angeles studio musicians who accepted the club's low pay for the chance to play jazz. Donte's closed on 2 April 1988 with a performance by Bob Florence's big band and was demolished soon afterwards.

——. **Dorothy Chandler Pavilion.** See Music Center.

——. **Down Beat Room Café.** 4201 South Central Avenue. Black Dot McGee owned, and Hal Stanley operated, this club, located two doors away from the Club Alabam. It was an important venue, especially from 1945 to 1948, which offered swing and bop every night and jam sessions on Sunday afternoons. The Stars of Swing (including Lucky Thompson, Buddy Collette, Britt Woodman, and Charles Mingus) are among those who appeared.

——. **Drakes.** 330 North Brand Boulevard, Glendale. From autumn 1989 to 1993 this club presented bop singers and instrumentalists two or three nights per week.

——. **Dreamland Café** (East 4th Street). See Waldorf Café.

——. **Dreamland Café** (South Central Avenue). See Jazzland Café.

——. **Dunbar Hotel** [Hotel Dunbar]. 4025 South Central Avenue; renumbered 4225 South Central Avenue in the late 1930s. In 1929 Louis Lomax purchased the Somerville Hotel (built the previous year) and renamed it after Paul Lawrence Dunbar. It was the preferred Los Angeles hotel for African-American entertainers during the 1930s and 1940s. Leon Rene's orchestra played for dances there as early as 1928, and the Woodman family band (Britt, his brothers, and his father) appeared in the Gold Room (Golding Room) in the late 1930s. Jack Johnson's Show-Boat Café showroom opened on 9 October 1931; in 1932 it was renamed the Harlem Show Boat Café and featured Sunny Clay's band, and later it was named Club Ebony and the Black Derby Rathskellar. Nellie Lutcher began her singing career at this venue, and Nat "King" Cole, Billy Eckstine, Count Basie, Fats Waller, Sarah Vaughan, Lionel Hampton, Duke Ellington, Herb Jeffries, Louis Armstrong, Cab Calloway, and others performed in the hotel lounge. The hotel was vandalized during the Watts riots of 1965. In 1988 the owners began refurbishing it, and in the early 1990s it hosted occasional jazz concerts. From 1996 there have been annual street festivals outside the hotel on one weekend of each summer.

——. **Dynamite Jackson's Club.** 4701 South Central Avenue. Jackson, an ex-fighter, owned this upstairs jazz club in the 1930s and 1940s; the Café Intime was downstairs.

——. **Dynamite Jackson's Cocktail Lounge.** 4456 or 4460? West Adams Boulevard. Jackson owned this venue in the 1950s and 1960s; Bill Douglass (i), Curtis Amy, and Groove Holmes are among those who played there. In 1962 the new proprietor, Isadore Bailey, changed the name to Mr. Adams and continued to present jazz.

——. **Eddie Spivak's.** 6315 Hollywood Boulevard, Hollywood. This was a dixieland club, located during the late 1940s in the same building as Sardi's.

——. **Elk's Hall** [Elk's Auditorium]. Washington Boulevard and South Central Avenue; later 3416, 3616, or 4016 South Central Avenue (sources vary). Initially called the Washington and Central Avenue Hall, in the 1920s it presented most of the jazz bands based in Los Angeles, and in the following decade many traveling big bands played there. In August 1946 Lucky Thompson rented the hall for concerts with Miles Davis and Charles Mingus. Howard McGhee, Dexter Gordon, Wardell Gray and others recorded there in a concert held on 6 July 1947. Jazz events continued until at least 1960. The building was later demolished.

——. **Embassy Auditorium** [Embassy Theater]. 847 South Grand Avenue. This 2400-seat hall was formerly the Trinity Auditorium, but by 1946, when Count Basie played there, it had been renamed the Embassy Auditorium (or Embassy Theater). A Jazz at the Philharmonic concert took place there on 22 April of that year, and in the mid-1950s Irving Granz (brother of Norman) produced the series "Jazz a La Carte" in the hall. Jazz concerts continued until at least the 1980s.

——. **Empire.** See Hollywood Empire.

——. **5th Street Dick's Coffee Company.** 3347½ West 43rd Place (to 1998); 3335 West 43rd Place (from 1998). Owned by Richard Fulton, this tiny coffeehouse became part of the World Stage jazz community (see below) around 1992. The performance area upstairs seated only a handful of people, but it was an important playing venue for such young Los Angeles bop musicians as Ronald Muldrow, the pianist Nate Morgan, and Willie Jones III. Fulton presented jazz five nights per week and held after-hours jam sessions on weekends. After the coffeehouse moved to a nearby site in January 1998 he continued the jazz policy until his death in 2000.

——. **Fifty-Four Ballroom.** 5409 South Broadway. This second-floor dance hall was built in 1922 and hosted Count Basie, Nat "King" Cole, and others during the swing era. Billy Berg bought the ballroom in the early 1950s. Usually Latin and pop bands played there, but major jazz musicians appeared as well. Jam sessions took place two nights per week.

——. **Finale Club.** 115 South San Pedro Street (or 230½ 1st Street). This was an after-hours "bottle" club (that is, a club to which the patrons brought their own drinks) in the Little Tokyo area of downtown Los Angeles, a neighborhood that became known as Bronzeville when the government forced West Coast Japanese-Americans into concentration camps during World War II. The club was opened in 1945 by the dancer and vaudevillian Foster Johnson, who sometimes gave impromptu performances to the jazz played there. For a brief time it was a hotbed of young bop players: Charlie Parker and Miles Davis were resident in spring 1946, and many of the most prominent West Coast musicians dropped by to hear them and sometimes to join them in jam sessions. Johnson closed the club abruptly in the middle of Parker's engagement, but it was reopened shortly afterwards, on March 16, by Howard McGhee and his wife, with a broadcast on KXLA by Parker, Erroll Garner, and others. Parker continued to appear into the summer of that year. Bronzeville and its jazz clubs gradually disappeared, as the newly released Japanese-Americans returned to their homes and businesses.

——. **First Lutheran Church.** 1300 East Colorado Street, Glendale. The church presented bop groups in jazz vespers on occasional Sunday evenings from September 1993.

——. **Florentine Gardens.** 5955 Hollywood Boulevard, Hollywood. Hal Stanley, the husband of the singer Kay Starr, and Lew LeRoy opened this club in 1946 and brought in well-known jazz bands and singers. In 1947 it was renamed the Cotton Club; it closed in April 1949.

——. **400 Club.** 3330 West 8th Street. Larry Shields led a band there in the early 1920s. Later Teddy Buckner (1954–7), Andy Blakeney, Rosy McHargue, and other dixieland players worked there. It began presenting strip shows in 1958, though Buckner returned for a further residency in the 1970s.

——. **Gene Norman's Interlude Room.** See Interlude Room.

——. **The Gig.** 11637 Pico Boulevard, Sawtelle. In late 1997 free-jazz concerts began on Monday evenings (they formerly

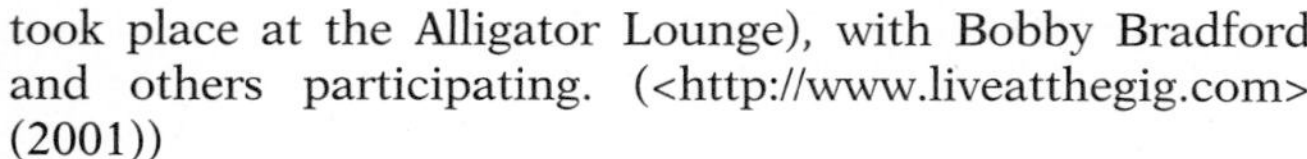
took place at the Alligator Lounge), with Bobby Bradford and others participating. (<http://www.liveatthegig.com> (2001))

——. **Glendale Grill.** 200 Burchett Street, Glendale. In 1990 this club presented bop four nights per week, though later this was cut to three nights per week; it closed in April 1992.

——. **Grand Avenue Bar.** See Biltmore Hotel.

——. **Greek Theater.** 2700 North Vermont Avenue. This outdoor theater, located near Griffith Park, presented jazz concerts occasionally from at least the 1960s, when Nat "King" Cole, Nancy Wilson, Ella Fitzgerald, Duke Ellington, and Ramsey Lewis played there. Numerous fusion bands appeared in later years.

——. **Hacienda Hotel.** 525 Sepulveda Boulevard, El Segundo. Roy Porter played in a variety-show band there for three years in the 1960s, while in the 1980s and 1990s it was the chosen venue of the Jazz Forum, a monthly jam session of dixieland and swing players.

——. **The Haig.** Wilshire Boulevard, across the street from the Ambassador Hotel. In the 1930s this club was called the Haig Cocktail Lounge. Erroll Garner and other unaccompanied solo pianists played there in the 1940s, and during the 1950s it became a leading venue for West Coast jazz. Its publicity officer was Richard Bock, of the record company Pacific Jazz. It was small – a converted bungalow – and suited only to performances by small groups; many important jazz musicians active in Los Angeles at that time appeared, including Red Norvo's trio, Wardell Gray, Gerry Mulligan's pianoless quartet, and Curtis Counce's quintet (making its début). Hampton Hawes, Warne Marsh, Mulligan and Lee Konitz, Bud Shank, and others recorded there. Jam sessions were held on Monday nights. The club closed on 4 April 1956.

——. **Hal's Bar and Grill.** 1349 Abbot Kinney Boulevard, Venice. From 1996 this venue has offered bop groups, initially one night per week, and later, two nights per week.

——. **Hangover Club.** 1456 Vine Street, Hollywood. This was an important dixieland club in the 1940s and 1950s. Bob Zurke and his band held a long residency from 1942 until the leader's death in 1944, and Pete Daily was the house bandleader for many years, playing dixieland jazz. The building was demolished early in 1957.

——. **Harbor Inn.** 1326 Pico Boulevard, Santa Monica. Red Norvo owned this club and opened it with his trio in mid-1956; Shelly Manne also appeared there.

——. **Hiawatha Dancing Academy.** 1824 South Central Avenue. Mamie Smith and her Jazz Hounds and Kid Ory's band appeared there in 1923.

——. **Hideaway Supper Club.** 5775 West Adams Boulevard. In the early 1960s this club featured revues in which the performers included Plas Johnson, Arthur Prysock, Ernestine Anderson, Jimmy Witherspoon, Coleman Hawkins, Gildo Mahones, and the group Lambert, Hendricks, and Bavan.

——. **Hi-De-Ho.** South Western Avenue and West 50th Street. Early in 1947 Howard McGhee, Hampton Hawes, Charlie Parker, and others performed in this club after Parker was released from Camarillo Hospital; Nappy Lamare also played there.

——. **Hillcrest Club** [Hilcrest Club]. 4557 West Washington Boulevard. Paul Bley led a band there with Dave Pike, Charlie Haden and Billy Higgins in 1957, playing six nights per week. Early in 1958 Don Cherry and Ornette Coleman replaced Pike (a concert recording of that quintet exists), but they were fired soon afterwards. During that time Les McCann was the house pianist for Monday-night jam sessions which were frequented by leading players. The club was renamed the Black Orchid in 1960 and continued as a jazz venue for a time.

——. **Holiday Inn.** 1755 North Highland Avenue, Hollywood. The hotel was built in 1972. Windows on Hollywood, a restaurant on the top floor that rotates 360° every hour, began a Sunday jazz brunch in 1988 and continued it through much of the 1990s. Many of the city's leading players appeared.

——. **Holly Street Bar & Grill.** 175 East Holly Street, Pasadena. This restaurant, near the Old Town redeveloped area, began to present jazz in 1991. It occupies a picturesque brick building that was originally a mortuary. (<http://www.larestaurant.com/Eclectic/HollyStreet/HollyStreet.htm> (2001))

——. **Hollywood Bowl.** 2301 North Highland Avenue, Hollywood. This 18,000-seat open-air concert arena was built around 1921 and has been the site of summer jazz concerts from at least the late 1930s, when Benny Goodman's band appeared. In 1956 and 1957 Norman Granz booked Ella Fitzgerald, Art Tatum, and other Jazz at the Philharmonic musicians into the amphitheater, and Fitzgerald performed there many times thereafter, making her last appearance in 1992. In 1959 the Hollywood Bowl hosted the first Los Angeles Jazz Festival, and in 1973 it was one of the venues for the annual Newport Jazz Festival West; the two-day Playboy Jazz Festival takes place there each June. In August 1997 many musicians took part in a 90th-birthday tribute to Benny Carter, and in the summer of 1999 the Clayton–Hamilton big band became the arena's jazz band in residence.

——. **Hollywood Canteen.** Cahuenga Boulevard, near West Sunset Boulevard, Hollywood. Duke Ellington's big band opened this servicemen's club in October 1942, and it operated seven nights per week from around 1942 to 1946; the musicians – including the singer Lena Horne, Count Basie, Horace Henderson, Lucky Millinder, and Gerald Wilson – played for free.

——. **Hollywood Empire (Room).** 1539 Vine Street, Hollywood. Located within Tom Breneman's restaurant, this club, owned in part by Gene Norman, opened in December 1948 but closed four months later. During that short time Duke Ellington, Louis Armstrong, Slim Gaillard, Art Tatum, and other prominent swing musicians worked there and Woody Herman's group broadcast from the club. Its official greeter, Pee Wee Marquette, later gained some notoriety as a master of ceremonies at venues in New York.

——. **Hollywood Palladium** [Palladium]. 6215 Hollywood Boulevard, Hollywood. Leading swing big bands played in and broadcast from this famous dance hall from its opening in 1940, and in 1950 Claude Thornhill and others played for televised dances. The hall's management reduced operations from seven to five nights per week in 1955, and then to two nights per week in 1959. Lawrence Welk bought the venue in the 1960s and moved his popular group into it, but jazz concerts continued to be held occasionally over the years. In 1995 it was the site of the first annual Hollywood Jazz Festival.

——. **Hollywood Park Casino.** 3883 West Century Boulevard, Inglewood. In 1997 this gambling casino at the Hollywood Park race track began presenting bop every Tuesday evening.

——. **Hollywood Roosevelt Hotel.** 7000 Hollywood Boulevard, Hollywood. This hotel was built in 1927 and the Cinegrill opened three years later. Turk Murphy appeared there in 1956, but more commonly it hosts jazz singers (among them Shirley Horn and Little Jimmy Scott) and cabaret singers. Another venue is the Blossom Room, where on Monday evenings in 1991–2 the pop singer Diane Varga, who had earlier produced concerts in the Grand Avenue Bar at the Biltmore Hotel, continued her work with a series of big-band concerts.

——. **Honey Murphy's.** South Central Avenue and 93rd Street. This after-hours jazz club was active from the 1930s to the mid-1940s; Zoot Sims, Art Tatum, Illinois Jacquet, Lester Young, Charlie Parker, and Ben Webster played there.

——. **Hong Kong Bar.** See Century Plaza Hotel.

——. **Hop Singh's.** 4110 Lincoln Boulevard, Marina del Rey. Rudy Underweiser (who had previously owned the Lighthouse Café) ran this large club during the 1980s, bringing in major groups and big bands in the bop and free-jazz idioms.

——. **Hotel Dunbar.** See Dunbar Hotel.

——. **Humming Bird Café.** 1143 East 12th Street. Formerly the Quality Café (see below), it was renamed the Humming Bird Café in 1924; late in 1925 the American Legion took it over and renamed it the Legion Club (Legion Hall). However, it became known as the Humming Bird again in the 1930s, when it was one of the principal venues in the city for African-American performers. Curtis Mosby led a band there.

——. **Hyatt on Sunset.** 8401 West Sunset Boulevard, West Hollywood. Jazz musicians played in the Sunset Lounge from around 1982 to 1986. Later Ozzie Cadena brought major national figures into the Silver Screen Room, but after 1992 jazz was no longer presented.

——. **Indigo Jazz Club.** See Compton Lazben Hotel.

——. **Inn Arty's.** 36 East Holly Street, Pasadena. This was one of several restaurants in Old Town, the redeveloped area of Pasadena; it featured bop from the 1980s until 1994.

——. **Interlude Room** [Gene Norman's Interlude Room]. 8568 West Sunset Boulevard, West Hollywood. Located upstairs from the Crescendo, in the 1950s this smaller club featured Jess Stacy, Cal Tjader, Shelly Manne, Chico Hamilton, and the Modern Jazz Quartet.

——. **It Club.** 4731 West Washington Boulevard. John T. McClain's club was an important bop venue from the late 1950s until about 1970. Thelonious Monk and the Three Sounds recorded there.

——. **Ivie's Chicken Shack.** 1105½ Vernon Avenue, near South Central. This popular jam-session site, owned by Ivie Anderson, was active when Central Avenue was the major area for jazz in Los Angeles.

——. **Jack's Basket (Room)** [Bird in the Basket]. 3219 South Central Avenue. This restaurant was a popular after-hours venue from the late 1930s for high-level jam sessions.

——. **Jackson's Cafe.** 1271 East 33rd Street. This was active as a venue for jazz from at least the 1940s. Teddy Bunn and his group, which included Pony Poindexter and Curtis Counce, were in residence there at the time they recorded *Jackson's Nook* (Selective 114) in 1949.

——. **Jade Palace.** 6619 Hollywood Boulevard, Hollywood. A luxurious club with beautiful décor, it was a favorite haunt of jazz musicians, who went there to listen to the playing of the resident dixieland bands. Jimmie Noone led a small group there in the early 1940s, and Kid Ory's band performed there in 1945. Howard McGhee, Teddy Edwards, Roy Porter, and other bop players played there, but did not meet with success.

——. **Jax.** 339 North Brand Boulevard, Glendale. From 1984, when this noisy restaurant opened, it has presented many well-known Los Angeles bop bands. It remains active in the new century.

——. **Jazz Bakery.** 3221 Hutchison Avenue, Culver City (to 1994); 3233 Helms Drive (from 1994). In 1991 the singer Ruth Price and the photographer Jim Britt converted part of the garage at the defunct Helms Bakery complex (near the former location of Sebastian's Cotton Club) into a modest-sized performance space and provided the audience with complimentary soft drinks, coffee, and cake. At first they presented local musicians, especially singers, on weekends, but later they expanded to five nights a week and began booking traveling groups as well as local musicians. In 1994 the club moved one block west, to a much larger venue in the main Helms Bakery building. This major jazz club offered bop groups and occasionally free-jazz bands seven nights a week, as well as in matinées on Sundays.

BIBLIOGRAPHY

L. Pellegrinelli: "A Guided Tour of America's Most Fascinating Jazz Clubs," <http:www.newmusicbox.com/thirdperson/jan00/index.html> (2000)
<http://thejazzbakery.com> (2001)

——. **Jazz Cabaret.** See Jazz City.

——. **Jazz Cellar.** 1708 North Las Palmas Avenue (or 6685 Hollywood Boulevard), Hollywood. Terri Lester opened this club in the basement of the Vermillion Hotel in mid-December 1957. Mel Lewis and Bill Holman worked there until they were fired for letting Ornette Coleman sit in. An important venue for bop during its short life, the club was renamed Vermillion's Jazz Room in 1958 and closed that September.

——. **Jazz City.** 5510 Hollywood Boulevard, Hollywood. Maynard Sloate owned this important bop venue from 1954 to 1957, but a new proprietor ended the jazz policy on 21 March 1957. Early the following year yet another owner, Carl Green, reopened the venue as the Jazz Cabaret and restored its policy of presenting major bop bands. It was the home of Jazz International, a group of fans headed by Howard Lucraft which sponsored jazz concerts at the club. By 1961 it was again called Jazz City.

——. **Jazz Concert Hall.** See Los Angeles Jazz Concert Hall.

——. **Jazz, Etc. Club.** 64 Santa Barbara Plaza. Isaac Suthers opened this club in 1991 and presented organized bands and jam sessions. It burned down during the Los Angeles riots of 1992.

——. **Jazzland Café.** 10718 South Central Avenue. This large club had a complicated history, as it closed and reopened several times under different names. Known from around 1914 as Byron (or Baron) Long's Tavern, it first opened as the Jazzland Café in 1926. In 1927 it was renamed the Dreamland Café, then in autumn 1928, when Alton Redd's 8 Pards [*sic*] of Pepper played there, became the Jazzland. In 1933 it was called the New Jazzland Night Club. Joe Morris, who also owned the Club Alabam, opened it in 1942 as the Club Plantation (or Plantation Club, or New Plantation); many leading swing players appeared there until 1945.

——. **Jazz Safari.** 1119 Queen's Way, London Towne, Long Beach. In spring 1978 the drummer Al Williams acquired this club, situated next to the *Queen Mary.* While he often led his own house band, at other times he brought in bop bands. Around 1986 he closed this harbor site and opened Birdland West.

——. **The Jazz Spot.** 2138 Hillhurst Avenue. In January 2000 Jim Britt, one of the founders of the Jazz Bakery (see above), renamed the venue which had formerly been Pierre's Los Feliz Inn (see below) and the Primavera Restaurant, and remodeled its lounge; with an excellent sound system and a concert grand piano, The Jazz Spot quickly became one of the city's principal sites for hearing major bop groups.

——. **Jimmy Smith's (Jazz) Supper Club.** 12910 Victory Boulevard at Coldwater Canyon, North Hollywood. This club was opened by Smith and his wife, Lola, in January 1976, and he and his trio played on Friday through Sunday nights; the group recorded an album there in 1977. Kenny Burrell, Blue Mitchell, and others also appeared at the club. Jam sessions took place on Monday nights. The venue closed around 1980.

——. **Jitterbug House.** In the 800 block of Vine Street, Hollywood. Louis Prima owned this small club and played there in the 1930s. The club was demolished long ago, and the site is now part of the parking lot for the musicians' union building.

——. **Jockey Club.** 2220 South Central Avenue. In 1930 the Kentucky Club was remodeled and renamed the Jockey Club; it offered revues involving Les Hite's band. Other venues operated on the same site from 1931.

——. **John Anson Ford Theater.** See Pilgrimage Theater.

——. **Joseph's.** 6531 Sepulveda Boulevard, Westchester. In 1994 the bar of this large restaurant began featuring Sunday-afternoon jazz concerts by local bands, sponsored by the International Association of Jazz Appreciation; the club also presented jazz nightly, with the double bass player James Leary, Billy Higgins, Charles Owens, and others appearing. In April 1996 the owners opened a companion venue, Joseph's at the Plaza (at 3791 Santa Rosalia Drive, north of Leimert Park), and presented jazz groups at this newer club five or six nights per week. Both venues closed in 1998.

——. **J. P.'s Lounge.** 3718 Magnolia Boulevard, Burbank. This club offered jazz from at least 1990; it often shared its musicians with its sister club, the Money Tree (see below). In the early 1990s it presented a Thursday jam session, but the jazz offerings dwindled in 1994.

——. **J. P.'s Money Tree.** See Money Tree.

——. **J. P.'s Restaurant & Lounge.** 1333 North Hollywood Way, Burbank. This venue offered jazz several nights per week from late 1994; in 1998 its name changed to Mr. B.

——. **Kentucky Club.** 2220 South Central Avenue. This club opened on 14 March 1929 with Paul Howard's Quality Serenaders in residence. It closed and then reopened in 1930 as the Jockey Club.

——. **Keyboard Club.** 453 North Canon Drive, Beverly Hills. Art Tatum, Benny Carter's trio, and others appeared there in 1953–4. In 1957 it became the Keyboard Supper Club.

——. **Kid Ory's Club.** See Morocco.

——. **King Arthur's.** 6510 Platt Avenue, Canoga Park. This was an important venue for big bands in the 1970s. The Capp–Pierce Juggernaut recorded there in 1976.

——. **King Cole Room.** See El Trocadero.

——. **Knitting Factory Hollywood.** 7021 Hollywood Boulevard. It opened in the Hollywood Galaxy building as the West Coast cousin of the Knitting Factory, New York, in late summer 2000. The memorial Sun Ra Arkestra, Charles Lloyd, Elvin Jones, and Danilo Pérez are among those jazz artists who have appeared here, but many of the club's musical offerings are in other genres.

——. **Labor Temple Hall** [Union Labor Temple]. Maple Avenue, between 5th and 6th streets. From around 1921 to 1925 most of the city's jazz bands played at this venue.

——. **L.A. Court.** See Westin Hotel.

——. **L.A. Jazz Concert Hall.** See Los Angeles Jazz Concert Hall.

——. **Last Word. 4206 South Central Avenue.** One of the Central Avenue venues near the Club Alabam, in the 1930s it was an after-hours club owned by Curtis Mosby and open to members only. Nat "King" Cole played there in December 1943. In 1947 it opened for regular nightclub hours and many important bop musicians worked there. It was renamed the Cotton Club in the 1950s and eventually presented non-jazz floor shows.

——. **La Vé Lee.** 12514 Ventura Boulevard, Studio City. This club opened in 1990 and featured a variety of fusion, Latin jazz, and rock on different nights of the week. (<http://www.laveleejazzclub.com> (2001))

——. **Leaks Lake.** Off South Central Avenue, near 116th Street (or Abila), Carson. In the early 1920s there was a large ballroom at this site, and the Spikes Brothers' Novelty Orchestra, the Black and Tan Orchestra, Mamie Smith, and Jelly Roll Morton (with a ten-piece group) played there. It was sometimes called Wayside Park.

——. **Legends of Hollywood.** 6555 Hollywood Boulevard, Hollywood (to autumn 1994); 11720 Ventura Boulevard, Studio City (from autumn 1994). Bob Marks owned the club and led the house band, which set up next to the front window by the entrance; they used a battered Fender-Rhodes keyboard instead of a piano. In 1990 the club presented jazz five nights per week, including a Sunday-night jam session, but by the following year jazz offerings were reduced to three nights per week. In autumn 1994 the club moved to the former St. Moritz restaurant in Studio City, where there was a new grand piano; bop bands played there regularly. Late in 1995 the club's name changed to Smokin' Johnny's.

——. **Leimert Park.** Crenshaw Boulevard at 43rd Street. In 1995 the summer Leimert Park Jazz Festival began here, featuring Billy Higgins, Horace Tapscott, Black/Note, and other musicians and groups with strong ties to the local community. The business district adjoining the park includes (or has included) several jazz venues (Artworks 4, 5th Street Dick's, Shabazz R50K Restaurant, the World Stage, and the blues club Babe and Ricky's Inn).

——. **Liberty Dance Hall.** East 3rd Street. Mutt Carey's Liberty Syncopators, including Joe Darensbourg and Minor Hall, played at this taxi-dance hall (where the clientele paid for each dance) in the 1920s.

——. **Lighthouse Café.** 30 Pier Avenue, Hermosa Beach. Originally a restaurant, Verpilate's, built in 1934, this site became the Lighthouse, a neighborhood bar, around 1940. Jazz began to be presented on 29 May 1949, when the owner, John Levine, engaged Howard Rumsey to lead jam sessions on Sunday afternoons. Soon Rumsey became the manager, and in 1951 he assembled a house band, the Lighthouse All Stars. Other bands appeared as well, and by the mid-1950s the club had become a major jazz venue: the Lighthouse All Stars, Art Pepper, Lee Morgan, Cannonball Adderley, Don Ellis, Mose Allison, Ramsey Lewis, the Modern Jazz Quartet, the Three Sounds, the Jazz Crusaders, Joe Henderson, and Lee Morgan all recorded there. In the late 1950s the club sponsored inter-collegiate jazz festivals; winners included Mike Melvoin, Pete Jolly's drummer Nick Martinis, and Les McCann. In 1970 Levine died and ownership reverted to his family; eventually they sold the club to Rudy Underweiser, the former manager of Shelly's Manne Hole. Meanwhile, Rumsey left and opened Concerts by the Sea in neighboring Redondo Beach. Underweiser sold the club in 1981, and the new owner remodeled and largely abandoned the jazz policy of the preceding three decades. But in the mid-1990s Bobby White's band began playing for Sunday brunch, and in 1997 jazz expanded to involve Saturday brunches as well, with Ray Pizzi and others participating. In 1999 Ozzie Cadena began to bring in jazz groups on Wednesday evenings.

——. **Lincoln Theater.** 2300 South Central Avenue. This vaudeville and movie theater opened on 7 October 1926 and was the first African-American theater on the West Coast; Curtis Mosby's Dixie Blues Blowers was the first band to play there and was followed by Les Hite. In the 1930s and 1940s many major African-American swing bands appeared, and Melba Liston began her career in 1942 playing in the house band. In 1943 weekly amateur contests began, hosted by Bardu Ali and broadcast on KMTR. Ernie Andrews, an usher there in 1945, won the talent show once. From the 1960s, however, the building has served as the Church of God in Christ.

——. **Linda's.** 6715 Melrose Avenue. In the 1980s Jimmie Rowles and Stacy Rowles, Gerald Wiggins, Lou Levy, Alan Broadbent, and others bravely performed in this noisy restaurant, where high, bare walls accentuated the din of dishes and conversation.

——. **Little Harlem.** South Central Avenue, in the Watts area. Jelly Roll Morton played there around 1917–19. In the 1930s it was a venue for T-Bone Walker and other blues performers, and in the early 1940s it was once again a jazz venue.

——. **Living Room.** See Ciro's.

——. **The Loa.** 3321 Pico Boulevard, Santa Monica. Mariko Omura opened this club in 1987, when Ray Brown functioned as its music director. Brown's trio and numerous other important bop bands played there until the club closed early in 1990.

——. **Loews Santa Monica Beach Hotel.** 1700 Ocean Avenue, Santa Monica. In the 1990s this was largely a venue for singers, though Joe Pass, Dave McKenna, Walter Norris, Ron Eschete, and other instrumentalists also appeared. (<http://www.santamonica.com/hotel/lowes/ext/lowes_ext.html> (2001))

——. **Los Angeles County Museum of Art.** 5905 Wilshire Boulevard. From the 1960s a large covered area between buildings has served as a venue for free Sunday-afternoon or early Friday-evening jazz concerts; occasionally jazz concerts also took place in Bing Auditorium. In the 1990s the Friday concert series became year-round.

——. **Los Angeles Jazz Concert Hall** [L.A. Jazz Concert Hall]. 3020 Crenshaw Boulevard. This theater, run by Benny Carter and Jack Hampton, opened on 14 June 1957 with weekend concerts. It closed after a brief run, but reopened in November 1958 and featured major bop groups six nights per week.

——. **Lovejoy's.** See Alex Lovejoy's Breakfast Club.

——. **Lucky Seven.** 1610 North Vine Street, Hollywood. Formerly the Vine Street Bar and Grill, this club presented jazz, mainly in a bop style, from 1998.

——. **Luna Park.** See Seelig Zoo.

——. **LunaPark** [Luna Park]. 665 North Robertson Boulevard, West Hollywood. This large club, which seats 400, opened in January 1994; although at first it was not a jazz venue, it soon housed occasional jazz concerts. From 1995 Sun Ra, Billy Childs, and others appeared there. In March 1998 it replaced the Alligator Lounge as Los Angeles's main Monday night free-jazz venue, but this policy had ended before November 2000, when LunaPark closed.

——. **Lunaria.** 10351 Santa Monica Boulevard, West Los Angeles. In the 1980s Bernard Jacoupy's club, with its living-room ambiance (couches, easy chairs, and coffee tables surrounding the performance area), began featuring a mix of pop and jazz involving such musicians as Jack Sheldon, Conrad Janis, the singer Stephanie Haynes, and Dave Mackay. (<http://www.lunariajazzscene.com> (2001))

——. **Maiden Voyage.** 2424 Wilshire Boulevard. This club opened in December 1979 with the big band of Toshiko Akiyoshi and Lew Tabackin and for a few years was an important bop and free-jazz venue. Art Pepper recorded there in 1981.

——. **Majestic Dancing Academy.** 15th and South Main streets. Between 1923 and 1929 most of Los Angeles's jazz bands played at this dance venue.

——. **Marla's Memory Lane.** 2323 Martin Luther King Jr. Boulevard. In 1981 the actress Marla Gibbs bought Memory Lane (Supper Club) and changed the name to Marla's Memory Lane. Often she presented the comedian Renaldo Rey and a major bop group, such as that of Horace Silver, Harold Land, Billy Higgins, or Teddy Edwards. Nat Adderley recorded an album there, and hundreds of major jazz musicians appeared until the jazz policy ended in 1995. Jazz resumed at the venue in 1998–9, when the pianist Rose Gales (Larry Gales's widow) led her band there for Sunday jazz brunches.
(<http://www.seeing-stars.com/Dine/Marlas.shtml> (2001))

——. **Marty's.** 5735 South Broadway (to the 1960s); 5005 South La Brea Avenue (from the 1960s). From 1954 to 1959 Plas Johnson, the organists Louis Rivera and Charles Kynard, and others played here six nights per week. In the 1960s the club closed and then reopened as Marty's on the Hill about 5 miles west of the original site. This new club also played an important role in the jazz life of Los Angeles, but it closed in the 1970s.

——. **Masonic Hall.** 1050 East 50th Street at South Central Avenue. The Black and Tan Orchestra played for dances there as early as 1918, and other bands appeared at least through the 1940s.

——. **M Bar & Grill.** 213A Pine Avenue, Long Beach. In 1995 it became noted as a venue for bop, free jazz, and related modern styles, though from 1997 it presented mainly blues performers.

——. **Meadowbrook Club.** See Sebastian's Cotton Club.

——. **Melody Room.** West Sunset Boulevard, West Hollywood. Georgie Auld ran this club in the mid-1950s and brought in such players as Red Norvo, Tal Farlow, Benny Carter, Chico Hamilton, Buddy Rich, Slim Gaillard, and Gerry Wiggins.

——. **Memo Club** [Club Memo]. 4264 South Central Avenue. Located across the street from Club Alabam and the Dunbar Hotel, this after-hours club began operation in the 1930s. In the 1940s the owners usually employed one to three musicians; Art Tatum played there in 1943.

——. **Miceli's.** 1646 North Las Palmas, Hollywood. Carmine Miceli opened this Italian restaurant in 1949. Bill Berry played there often into the late 1990s, as did many bop groups, and the club continues to present jazz in the new century.

——. **Mike Lyman's Playroom** [Mike Lyman's Hollywood Grill]. 1623 North Vine Street, Hollywood. This was a dixieland venue in the early 1950s, when Kid Ory, Joe Venuti, Red Nichols, and others played there.

——. **Mike's Waikiki Inn** [Waikiki]. 3743 South Western Avenue. This cocktail lounge offered jazz from the late 1930s. Later it became the Tiki Island (Tiki Room), and Ray Crawford, Willie Jones, Charles Kynard, and others played there.

——. **Million Dollar Theater.** 307 South Broadway. This downtown theater often presented leading big bands along with feature films; Horace Henderson led the house band in the 1930s. Later that decade Al Adams's house band included Buddy Collette, Jackie Kelso, Charles Mingus, and Chico Hamilton. In the 1940s prominent bands continued to play there, though some time afterwards it became the city's main venue for Spanish-language variety shows and feature films.

——. **Milomó Cocktail Lounge.** 2829 South Western Avenue. Helen Humes sang in this small cocktail lounge in the 1940s. In the mid-1950s Clora Bryant led Monday-night sessions in which Max Roach, Dizzy Gillespie, Art Blakey, and Ben Webster participated; Coleman Hawkins, Carl Perkins, Curtis Counce, Frank Butler, and Harold Land also played there.

——. **Mr. Adams.** See Dynamite Jackson's Cocktail Lounge.

——. **M.K.P.O.V.** See Alfonse's.

——. **The Mocambo.** 8588 West Sunset Boulevard, West Hollywood. Eddie South performed in this famous supper club as early as 1943. In the 1950s the Firehouse Five Plus Two, Ella Fitzgerald, Dinah Washington, and Sarah Vaughan appeared; during the same period this large facility also contained the Club Renaissance (later the New Renaissance), where major bop groups performed.

——. **Money Tree.** 10149 Riverside Drive, Toluca Lake. This club presented jazz duos and trios at its piano bar from the 1980s. In 1990 it became J. P.'s Money Tree for a short time, and its schedule of performers dovetailed with that of J. P.'s Lounge.

——. **Montmartre Café.** 6757 Hollywood Boulevard, Hollywood. Owned by Eddie Brandstatter, this was an exclusive venue for jazz in the late 1920s. Paul Howard's Quality Serenaders played there in 1930, after they had completed their engagement at the Kentucky Club; by this time the band included Lawrence Brown and Lionel Hampton. The club closed later that year.

——. **Moonlight Tango.** 13730 Ventura Boulevard, Sherman Oaks. This club offered a mix of jazz, swing-style dance bands, and Latin jazz. From early in 1992 Tuesday nights featured most of Los Angeles's big bands. The pop singer Diane Varga booked the concerts until her death in December 1992, when Lenetta Kidd took over. In 1997 the club was remodeled and renamed Moonlight. The jazz policy all but ended in 1999. The venue re-opened in 2001 as the Arlequin Club (see above).

——. **Morocco** [Club Morocco]. On the west side of Vine Street, north of Sunset Boulevard, Hollywood. From 1945 this club presented a variety of dixieland, swing, and bop groups (including that of Charlie Parker's legendary devotee Dean Benedetti, who was apparently a failure). Late in 1949 Kid Ory took over the club, with financial help from Billy Berg; Sidney Desvigne, who by then was no longer playing full-time, was in charge of catering. The venue, renamed Kid Ory's New Orleans Club, closed after only a month.

——. **Morocco Club.** South Western Avenue and 46th Street. Boyd Raeburn's big band played there in 1945–6. During the 1950s it was a venue for swing and bop groups. In 1953 Dorothy Donegan operated the club, and in 1957 its new owner, Wild Bill Davis, renamed it the New Morocco.

——. **Mulberry Street.** 12067 Ventura Place, Studio City. In the early 1980s this club, operated by the drummer Allan Goodman, presented leading Latin and bop groups.

——. **Museum of Contemporary Art.** 250 South Grand Avenue (Museum of Contemporary Art at California Plaza) and 152 North Central Avenue, Little Tokyo (The Geffen Contemporary at Museum of Contemporary Art). The museum is split between two locations, both of which, from the mid-1990s, offered free concerts by major bop groups on Thursday evenings. (<http://www.artcom.com/museums/nv/mr/90012-b.htm> (2001))

——. **Music Art Hall** [Music Art Auditorium]. 233 South Broadway. From 1923 to 1927 Sonny Clay's Jazz Band, the Black and Tan Orchestra, the Harmony Kings, and the Jazz Fiends played there.

——. **Music Center.** 135 North Grand Avenue. Three performance halls open onto a public plaza in this handsome central-city location. The Dorothy Chandler Pavilion is a beautiful, 3200-seat concert hall which opened in December 1964, when it became the home of the Los Angeles Philharmonic Orchestra. Jazz events occurred there sporadically, such as Stan Kenton's Neophonic Orchestra concerts (1965–7), a duo recital by Chick Corea and Herbie Hancock (1978, partly recorded), performances by the Orchestra (later called the New American Orchestra, 1979–1980s), a presentation of Wynton Marsalis's oratorio *Blood in the Fields* (1996), and some concerts sponsored by the Thelonious Monk Institute. In late 1998 the Impresario Ristorante e Bar, on the fifth floor of the pavilion, began presenting jazz on weekends, using the name Club Thelonious. In 1999 it moved to Otto's Grill (at street level). A smaller hall, Ahmanson Theater, is mostly a site for musical theater, though there have been jazz concerts there as well. (<http://www.performingartscenterla.org/lead.html> (2001))

——. **Nap Moore's.** Named for its owner, this café was open 24 hours a day; it became a meeting place for musicians, who jammed informally round the café's piano. Among those who spent their off-hours there in the late 1920s were Lionel Hampton, Alex Hill, and Joe Darensbourg, who were all engaged to play elsewhere in the city.

——. **New Apex Nite Club.** See Club Araby.

——. **New Deal Club.** See Blain Nell Country Club.

——. **New Jazzland Night Club.** See Jazzland Café.

——. **New Morocco.** See Morocco Club.

——. **New Oasis.** See Oasis.

——. **New Plantation.** See Jazzland Café.

——. **New Renaissance.** See The Mocambo.

——. **Night Winds.** See At my Place.

——. **Normandie Hall.** 1445 West Jefferson Boulevard. Around 1920–22 the West Side Jazz Orchestra and Kid Ory's Creole Band played there. In the 1950s it was an important weekend venue for a wide variety of players, from Art Tatum and Nat "King" Cole to Eric Dolphy and Ornette Coleman.

——. **Nucleus Nuance.** 7267 Melrose Avenue, Hollywood. This club was an active bop venue in the 1980s and early 1990s. Late in 1993 its new owners changed the name to Nucleus but maintained the jazz policy; it closed early in 1994.

——. **Oasis.** 3801 South Western Avenue. Originally owned by Eddie DeSure, it was a dixieland club, and in the late 1940s it was called the Oasis & Camel Room. In 1949 DeSure and his new partner, Curtis Mosby, renamed it the Crewcut Room and presented shows. Bill Robinson and Joe Abrams then bought the club, changed its music policy, and restored its name to Oasis (or New Oasis); in the 1950s many swing and bop ensembles played there. The club presented revues as well as jazz.

——. **111 Dance Hall.** 111 West 3rd Street. The Black and Tan Orchestra played there for dancing from the 1910s. In 1922 Kid Ory and Pops Foster appeared, from around 1927 Ed Garland's band was resident for a long period, and in 1930 Paul Howard joined the band after the breakup of his Quality Serenaders.

——. **Orpheum Theater.** 842 South Broadway. During the 1930s and 1940s this ornate downtown theater, dating from the 1920s, often presented leading big bands and groups along with feature films. In June 1946 live shows ceased to be presented there and transferred instead to the Million Dollar Theater, owned by the same company.

——. **Palladium.** See Hollywood Palladium.

——. **Palomar Ballroom.** South Vermont Street, at 2nd Street. In 1935 this ballroom was the scene of the sensational success of Benny Goodman's big band, which returned there in later years; a number of films were made there, including Goodman's *The Big Broadcast of 1937*, filmed during his residency in 1936, and *Dancing Coed* (1939), which starred Artie Shaw. During Charlie Barnet's engagement in October 1939 a fire destroyed the ballroom, along with the band's instruments and music.

——. **Papashon Restaurant.** 91 North Raymond Avenue, Pasadena; 8635 Wilshire Boulevard, Beverly Hills; 15910 Ventura Boulevard, Encino; and 200 Pine Avenue, Long Beach. The Pasadena restaurant, located on the site of the former Tra Fiore, began presenting jazz five nights per week in 1996, the Beverly Hills and Encino restaurants started to offer jazz in 1997, and the Long Beach one followed suit in 1999. By 1998, however, the Encino venue was the main jazz site. The management preferred guitarists, such as John Pisano, Ron Eschete, Larry Koonse, and Phil Upchurch, but also employed a varied mix of singers and instrumentalists. Legal problems led to the closing of all four restaurants in 1999.

——. **Paradise Tavern** [Paradise Club]. 6100 South Main Street. This club presented jazz from at least the mid-1930s. The big band of Lionel Hampton – later taken over by one of his sidemen, Teddy Buckner – played there in 1936, and Benny Goodman's quartet was formed there one evening, when the clarinetist's trio sat in with Hampton. After Hampton broke up his orchestra, Cee Pee Johnson's band, which included Ernie Royal and Marshal Royal, replaced him. Buckner's band broadcast nightly for a half hour on KFVD in 1936–7.

——. **Paramount Theater.** 323 West 6th Street. This downtown theater often presented leading bands along with feature films during the 1930s and 1940s. The policy of presenting jazz had ended by the mid-1950s.

——. **Parisian Room.** 4960 West Washington Boulevard. Owned by Ernie France, this was an important jazz club for bop groups and singers from the 1950s to the 1980s. The club closed in 1983 and was replaced by a post office.

——. **Pasadena Civic Auditorium.** 300 East Green Street, Pasadena. One of the city's main performance venues, the civic auditorium was the site of occasional jazz concerts from at least the 1940s. Stan Kenton recorded there in 1944. In 1947 Gene Norman's "Just Jazz" concerts began, with jazz star attractions rivaling those of the Jazz at the Philharmonic (notably a performance by Lionel Hampton which was recorded). Other recordings were made by André Previn (1947), Dizzy Gillespie's big band (1948), Charlie Ventura (1949), and Wardell Gray and Dexter Gordon (1952). The venue also staged a performance in June 1956 by Kid Ory and Louis Armstrong. Major concerts continued into the 1990s.

——. **Pasquale's.** 22724 Pacific Coast Highway, Malibu. Owned by the double bass player Pat Senatore (who led the house band), this seaside club operated from February 1978 to 1983 and featured many fine bop groups.

——. **Pauley Pavilion.** See University of California at Los Angeles.

——. **Peacock Lane.** 5501 Hollywood Boulevard at Western Avenue, Hollywood. Situated across the street from Jazz City, this club presented jazz from at least the mid-1940s, but blossomed as a major jazz venue in the years 1955–8 with appearances by many important swing and bop players. Woody Herman's band made a recording there.

——. **Pedrini Music.** 230 West Main Street, Alhambra. Adjoining this music store, established in 1938, the Pedrini family established a small concert space. From 1991 to 1998 they presented Los Angeles-based bop musicians in free concerts each Saturday afternoon.

——. **Philharmonic Hall.** 427 West 5th Street. This venue, which seated 2600, was inaugurated in 1906 as The Auditorium. From 1915 it was known as the Clune Auditorium, and in 1920 it took its current name. Jazz was performed there as early as 1924, in a vaudeville show, *Steppin' High*. Norman Granz launched his concert series Jazz at the Philharmonic there on 2 July 1944 and continued to use the auditorium until early in 1946, when its administration banned the concerts because of audience disturbances. The performances given under JATP's banner are preserved on scores of recordings. In 1945 an Esquire jazz concert featured Duke Ellington and Billie Holiday, and in the next few years there were concerts by Count Basie, Ethel Waters with Fletcher Henderson, and Stan Kenton. The hall was the home of the Los Angeles Philharmonic Orchestra until 1964, when the larger Dorothy Chandler Pavilion opened a few blocks away. It was demolished in 1985 to make way for a parking lot.

——. **Pied Piper.** 4325 South Crenshaw Boulevard. This club was a half-block north of Leimert Park; owned by Freddie Jet, it was open by at least 1948. From 1967 to 1971 it was an important venue for bop.

——. **Pierre's Los Felix Inn.** 2138 Hillhurst Avenue. This restaurant presented bop groups in its cocktail lounge in the early 1990s, and then continued this policy later in the decade under a new name, the Primavera Restaurant, but it has been more important from the year 2000, when it became the Jazz Spot (see above.)

——. **Pilgrimage Theater.** 2580 Cahuenga Boulevard East, Hollywood. An outdoor theater located across the Hollywood Freeway from the Hollywood Bowl, its original function was to serve as a site for Easter sunrise services. In the mid-1960s the city of Los Angeles and the American Federation of Musicians' Trust Fund began sponsoring free concerts by many leading bop groups on Sunday afternoons during the spring and summer months. In the mid-1970s it was renamed the John Anson Ford Theater.

——. **Plantation Club** [Club Plantation]. 1831 North Vine Street, Hollywood. Throughout the 1940s Sarah Vaughan, Billy Eckstine, Count Basie, Horace Henderson, Helen Humes, and others appeared at what was largely a venue for big bands, located in the Hollywood Plantation Hotel.

——. **Plantation Club** (Central Avenue). See Jazzland Café.

——. **Playboy Club.** 8560 West Sunset Boulevard, West Hollywood (to 1973); 2020 Avenue of the Stars (from 1973). In 1966 the singer Della Reese, Stan Kenton, and Clare Fischer appeared at this fashionable club, located between the Crescendo and the Renaissance. In 1973 it moved to the Schubert theater building. In 1974 the first Playboy Festival lasted for weeks there, and the following year this festival extended throughout the summer. Jazz continued to be presented intermittently in the early 1980s.

——. **POV.** See Alfonse's.

——. **Primavera Restaurant.** See Pierre's Los Felix Inn.

——. **Purple Onion.** 7290 West Sunset Boulevard, Hollywood. In 1957 the Jazz Society sponsored Monday-night jam sessions in this club, owned by James Kidd. From that same year to 1963 it served as a venue for bop.

——. **Quality Café** [Quality Club]. 1143 East 12th Street. Frank Nelson and Eugene Nelson opened this club on 31 December 1923. The following year Paul Howard formed a quartet to play there which soon became known as the Quality Serenaders. Jimmy Rushing sang with the group as a guest artist, and several other Los Angeles bands also played in the club in the 1920s. It later flourished as the Humming Bird Café (see above).

——. **Queen Mary.** Queens Highway, at the harbor, Long Beach. This opulent cruise ship docked permanently at this site in the late 1960s. Occasionally there is a jazz event in one of its ballrooms or showrooms. The annual Queen Mary Jazz Festival, held in the parking lot adjacent to the ship, began on an autumn weekend in 1978 and ran until 1988, presenting mainly jazz fusion.

——. **Randini's.** 600 South Western Avenue. During the 1940s it was active as a venue for unaccompanied solo pianists, such as Meade "Lux" Lewis, and small groups, such as Al Casey's trio.

——. **Redd Foxx Night Club.** 339 North La Cienega Boulevard. In the late 1960s the club, owned by the comedian Redd Foxx, usually featured variety shows, but it also booked jazz singers and bop groups. In 1970 Bill Cosby became the owner and presented Les McCann and the Modern Jazz Quartet.

——. **Red Feather.** West Manchester Avenue and South Figueroa Street. In 1947 the band led by the saxophonist Butch Stone (with Shorty Rogers, Stan Getz, and Herbie Stewart) and Herb Jeffries appeared there, and the following year Gene Norman began running Sunday jam sessions. Jazz continued for a few more years, but the club became a burlesque house in 1951.

——. **Renaissance Club.** 8428 West Sunset Boulevard, West Hollywood. In 1958 this club on Sunset Strip featured Sunday jam sessions with Bob Dorough. Ben Webster played there into the early 1960s, with Jimmie Rowles, Jim Hall, Leroy Vinnegar, Red Mitchell, and Frank Butler among his sidemen; Webster and Mitchell both recorded there in 1960 and Art Blakey in 1962. In 1995 it was remodeled, renamed the House of Blues (with a new address of 8430 West Sunset Boulevard), and became a blues and rock venue, but some bop and Latin bands continued to play there.

——. **Rhumba Palace.** See Avodon.

——. **Ritz Club.** 1105 East Vernon Avenue. Next to Ivie's Chicken Shack in the Central Avenue area, this was an after-hours venue where Charles Mingus, Gerald Wiggins, and Dexter Gordon played during the 1940s.

——. **Rix Restaurant.** 1413 Fifth Street, Santa Monica. In 1999 Earl Palmer and George Gaffney began to host jam sessions on Tuesdays (Palmer had done the same thing at Chadney's for years).

——. **Rocco Ristorante.** 2930 Beverly Glen Circle, Bel Air. Formerly known as Adriano's, this venue in the Hollywood hills was renamed by its owner, Rocco Somazzi, in July 1998. Having started with Ronald Muldrow's quartet on Thursdays, Somazzi expanded the jazz offerings and by the following year was presenting bop five nights a week. It closed on 23 December 2000. (<http://www.roccoinla.com> (2001))

——. **Royal Room.** 6700 Hollywood Boulevard, Hollywood. Formerly Susie-Q, it became the Royal Room in the late 1940s. In the 1950s, under the ownership of Abe Bush, it was known principally for jam sessions, in which as many as 30 musicians might play together; Louis Armstrong took part in one of the Sunday sessions by invitation in 1950. The Royal Room also offered more formal performances – Kid Ory led a band there for a 12-week residency in 1950, and he was followed into the club by Pete Daily; other musicians who appeared there included Zutty Singleton. It closed in mid-1958.

——. **Royce Hall.** See University of California at Los Angeles.

——. **Rubaiyat Cocktail Lounge.** 1400 South Western Avenue. The successor to the Rubaiyat Room, it presented jazz in the late 1970s.

——. **Rubaiyat Room.** 2022 West Adams Boulevard. The Watkins Hotel opened under African-American ownership in 1946, and its nightclub, the Rubaiyat Room, in 1952. During the 1950s and 1960s many bop musicians worked there. It later became an apartment house.

——. **St. Marks.** 23 Windward Avenue, Venice. In 1990 this restaurant (which Orson Welles had used as a location for his film *A Touch of Evil* in 1958) presented leading bop groups seven nights per week, but by 1996 jazz was rarely heard there.

——. **Santa Monica Civic Auditorium.** 1855 Main Street, Santa Monica. Major jazz groups appeared there occasionally in the 1950s and 1960s. In 1972 a Jazz at the Philharmonic concert took place, and in the following year the auditorium hosted a portion of the first annual Newport Jazz Festival West, featuring Chick Corea, Gil Evans, and Cecil Taylor (see also Hollywood Bowl). Jazz concerts continued over the years.

——. **Sardi's (Chi Chi)** [Zardi's (Jazzland)]. 6315 Hollywood Boulevard, Hollywood. This popular jazz venue was called Sardi's Chi Chi around 1948, Zardi's through the early to mid-1950s, and Zardi's Jazzland in its final year. It was a popular jazz venue from the late 1940s. Among the musicians who played there were Benny Carter and his big band, Anita O'Day, Red Nichols, Eddie Miller, Pete Fountain, and Joe Darensbourg, who led a band there on Sundays during the time he held an engagement at the Beverly Cavern. In the 1950s many other dixieland, swing, and bop players performed there, including perhaps most notably Stan Getz's quintet from July to August 1953. The club closed in 1957, after appearances by Shorty Rogers (1954), Louis Jordan (1956), Dinah Washington (1957), and Lizzie Miles with Bob Scobey's band (1957).

——. **Savoy Ballroom** [Savoy Dance Hall]. 5326 South Central Avenue. Situated upstairs from the Savoy Theater, this ballroom opened in 1929; in its early years Les Hite and Paul Howard were among those who played there. Earl Bostic and Benny Carter appeared as late as 1954. (There is some confusion in the literature as to the locations of this venue and the Club Araby; see above.)

——. **Sebastian's Cotton Club.** 8781 West Washington Boulevard, Culver City. This barn-like venue opened in 1926 as the Green Mill Club, but Frank Sebastian bought it in 1927 and renamed it, making it one of the many clubs in the USA called after the famous establishment in New York. A large, beautiful club, it presented not only jazz but (like the New York venue) all-black floor shows to all-white audiences. Paul Howard's Quality Serenaders, which included Lionel Hampton, played there in the late 1920s, and when that group disbanded Hampton returned to join the house band, led at first by the trumpeter Vernon Elkins and then by Les Hite. Hite continued as the bandleader at the club, except for tours during the summers, until its temporary closure in 1939; among the members of his band in the early 1930s were Lawrence Brown and Marshal Royal. Louis Armstrong performed with the band as a guest soloist, first in July 1930 and again for three months in 1932. From the mid-1920s to the late 1940s many of the nation's leading orchestras appeared there (notably McKinney's Cotton Pickers from May 1931 and Fats Waller's band in June 1935), and early in his career Buck Clayton led a group there after returning from the Orient (1936). Radio broadcasts from the club were frequent in the 1930s and 1940s. The venue was also called Casa Mañana (in 1940, when the Zucca brothers owned it and ended the whites-only policy), the Meadowbrook Club (beginning in September

1945), and Zucca's Opera House (1948, when they tried an ice show briefly). It remained a jazz venue until it burned down on 20 February 1950.

——. **Seelig Zoo.** *c*2800 North Mission Road (later, Avenue), opposite Lincoln Park, Boyle Heights. Reb Spikes played there once for the making of a silent film in 1914. In the mid-1920s the Black and Tan Orchestra, Kid Ory's orchestra, and Sonny Clay played for picnics there; during that time the name changed to Luna Park, but by 1933, when the Harlem Dukes appeared, it was called Seelig Zoo again.

——. **Shabazz R50K Restaurant.** 3405 West 43rd Street. This restaurant, in a mini-mall about a block and a half away from the World Stage, opened in 1996. It presented jazz groups on weekends and a jam session hosted by the pianist Rose Gales (Larry Gales's widow) on Sunday evenings. It closed in mid-1998, and Gales continued the jazz brunches at the newly reopened Marla's Memory Lane (see above).

——. **Shelly's Manne-Hole.** 1608 North Cahuenga Boulevard, Hollywood (to 3 September 1972); 6420 Wilshire Boulevard (from 15 October 1973). Shelly Manne's famous club opened on 3 November 1960, and Manne's own groups appeared there often, in alternation with other well-known bop groups. Terry Gibbs, Manne and his Men, Bill Evans (ii), the Adderley brothers, Les McCann, Don Ellis's big band, Buddy Rich, Keith Jarrett, Michel Legrand, Milt Jackson and Lenny Breau, and others recorded there. On 3 September 1972, following a performance by the quintet led by Jackson and Ray Brown, Manne closed the club at its original site (now marked by a commemorative miniature manhole cover embedded in the sidewalk outside the door) because the music was disrupting the work at Wally Heider's recording studio in the adjacent building. On 15 October 1973 he reopened the Manne-Hole at the Wilshire Boulevard address, sharing the premises with Tetou's Restaurant. However, the new operation was unsuccessful, and Manne closed the club permanently on 7 April 1974, after a set by the Stan Getz Quartet. (H. Siders: "The Manne-Hole Chronicles," *Down Beat Music '73* (1972), 11)

——. **Shepp's Playhouse.** 204½ First Street. This club was one of the principal jazz venues in the Little Tokyo area of Los Angeles, which became known as Bronzeville during World War II (see Finale Club above). There was a large nightclub upstairs and a lounge downstairs, both offering music. Herb Jeffries, Red Callender, Gerald Wilson's big band, Eddie Heywood, Harlan Leonard, Coleman Hawkins, Helen Humes, and Valaida Snow appeared; some of these musicians broadcast from the club, which closed soon after the war ended.

——. **Sheraton San Pedro Hotel.** 601 South Palos Verdes Street, San Pedro. Ozzie Cadena booked bop and Latin groups into the Stingaree Gulch lounge from mid-1990 to 1993. The hotel then became the Radisson Los Angeles Harbor Hotel and no longer offered jazz.

——. **Sherry's Lounge** [Sherry's Bar, Sherry's on the Strip]. 8106 West Sunset Boulevard, West Hollywood. This was a piano bar in the 1930s. It gained unwanted publicity on 19 July 1949 when an organized crime mob attacked the mobster Mickey Cohen. In the late 1950s the duos of Carl Perkins and Leroy Vinnegar, Claude Williamson and Curtis Counce, and Pete Jolly and Ralph Peña played there. The policy of presenting jazz continued until at least the early 1970s.

——. **Shrine Auditorium.** 644 West 32nd Street and 649 West Jefferson Boulevard (it extends between both streets). Built in 1926, this enormous auditorium seats about 6300 people. That same year the Sunnyland Orchestra played there "with amplifiers." Among jazz musicians who appeared later were Fletcher Henderson (1937), those taking part in Gene Norman's "Just Jazz" concerts (December 1946–1947), Dizzy Gillespie's big band (which recorded there in 1948 and gave several concerts in the 1950s), Jazz at the Philharmonic (1948 and again in the 1950s), and Stan Getz (who recorded *Stan Getz at the Shrine Auditorium*, 1954, Norg. 2000). The Dixieland Jubilee (*see* FESTIVALS) took place there from 1948 to 1960. In the mid-1970s one of the last jazz concerts in the auditorium featured Miles Davis, and in November 1978 the hall presented Scott Joplin's opera *Treemonisha*.

——. **Shrine Ballroom.** 700 West 32nd Street. This ballroom is ancillary to the auditorium. John C. Spikes played there in 1926, Fats Waller in 1935, and Jimmie Lunceford in 1937. In the early 1940s the big bands which performed at the Shrine (Glenn Miller, Lunceford, Lionel Hampton, and others) usually appeared at the ballroom rather than in the auditorium. As late as 1960 Miles Davis, the Modern Jazz Quartet, Paul Horn, and the Adderley brothers performed there.

——. **Silver Screen Room.** See Hyatt on Sunset.

——. **Smokin' Johnny's.** See Legends of Hollywood.

——. **Solomon's Penny Dance Hall** [Solomon's Pavilion De Luxe]. South Grand Avenue and 9th Street. The owner, Fred Solomon, presented Curtis Mosby's Dixieland Blue Blowers in 1924–6 and Les Hite around 1927. Later the name changed to the Vogue Ballroom, and in the 1930s and early 1940s it served as a venue for big bands.

——. **Spaghettini.** 3005 Old Ranch Parkway, Seal Beach. In 1995 this club began presenting bop groups six nights per week.

——. **Spazio.** 14755 Ventura Boulevard, Sherman Oaks. Originally named the Signature Grill, this upscale restaurant opened in 2000 and presented jazz, initially two nights per week, and then by year's end, nightly.

——. **Steamer's Café.** 138 West Commonwealth Avenue, Fullerton. Opened in 1994, Terence Love's club, with its unusually good piano and sound system, quickly became the best-known jazz club in Orange County; the club presented important bop and Latin groups six nights a week and local big bands on Mondays.
(<http://www.jazzqwest.com/STEAMERS> (2001))

——. **Sterling's.** 1535 Ocean Avenue, Santa Monica. Rosy McHargue played there regularly in the mid-1980s.

——. **Stevie G's.** 11996 Ventura Boulevard, Studio City. Eddie Beal worked there in the 1940s; later, between 1980 and 1985, Buddy Collette and Dick Cathcart were among those who appeared.

——. **Stingaree Gulch.** See Sheraton San Pedro Hotel.

——. **The Strand.** 1700 South Pacific Coast Highway, Redondo Beach. This large restaurant and nightclub was built in the 1960s and originally named the Plush Horse; in the 1980s it became a singles bar, Annabelle's. As the Strand, beginning in 1988, it usually presented popular or blues artists, but it sometimes booked well-known fusion, Latin, and bop groups as well. It closed in 1996 but reopened in April 1997 as the Club Caprice with a similar music policy. It closed permanently in 1999.

——. **Streets of Paris.** Hollywood Boulevard near Highland Avenue, Hollywood. This venue specialized mainly in unaccompanied and small-group dixieland and swing in the 1930s, 1940s, and 1950s. Jimmie Noone played there in 1943 with a small ensemble, Monette Moore was the resident singer from 1945, and Zutty Singleton led a group at the club after 1945.

——. **Strip City.** 1304 South Western Avenue. In the mid-1950s Dizzy Gillespie, Clora Bryant, and others played in this African-American burlesque house. Sunday-afternoon jam sessions began in 1959. The following year it was renamed Basin Street West, and during the 1960s it became one of the main jazz clubs in Los Angeles; Woody Herman recorded two excellent albums there in 1963.

——. **Strollers.** Locust Avenue, near Ocean Boulevard, Long Beach. Harry Rubin, who had owned several clubs in and around Los Angeles, founded this club around 1955. Shortly after it opened Rubin engaged Chico Hamilton's newly formed quintet, who made a concert recording there in August 1955 and broadcast twice a week on KFOX. Other bop players appeared in 1955–6.

——. **The Summit.** 6507 West Sunset Boulevard, Hollywood. Formerly Whisling's, in October 1960 the club was renamed The Summit by its new owner, Bob Gefaell, who began to bring in many well-known groups. The big bands of Terry Gibbs and Louie Bellson recorded there in the early 1960s.

——. **Surf Club.** 3981 West 6th Street, Hollywood. This small club, actually located miles inland from the surf, presented bop groups in the early 1950s; Hampton Hawes recorded there in 1952.

——. **Susie-Q.** 6700 Hollywood Boulevard, Hollywood. This club was open from at least the late 1930s, when it usually featured small swing groups. In the late 1940s it was renamed the Royal Room (see above).

——. **Suzi-Q.** Hollywood. It was in operation from at least the late 1930s and featured performances mainly by small groups. Red Callender's trio appeared there around the turn of the decade and Charlie Teagarden led a band for a short residency in December 1946. In the late 1940s, when there was a vogue in Los Angeles for blues-oriented styles, Jimmy Witherspoon appeared at the Suzi-Q with a group that included Benny Bailey, Addison Farmer, and the drummer Pete McShann.

——. **Swanee Inn.** 143 North La Brea Avenue. This little restaurant-bar was opened in 1937 by Bob Lewis, who presented unaccompanied solo pianists and small groups. It was one of Nat "King" Cole's earliest venues in Los Angeles. Cole played there for six months with Oscar Moore, the double bass player Wesley Prince, and Lee Young and formed his longstanding trio in 1939 after Young left to join Les Hite's orchestra. Among the pianists who played at the club were Joe Turner (ii), Lorenzo Flennoy, Gladys Bentley, Meade "Lux" Lewis, Eddie Beal, and Art Tatum. Oscar Pettiford's trio appeared in the early 1950s.

——. **Swing Club.** 1710 North Las Palmas Avenue, Hollywood. Billy Berg owned this club in the early 1940s, before he opened Billy Berg's on North Vine Street (see above). Among the first to play there were a small group led by Lester Young and Lee Young (1941) and Benny Carter's band – the first big band that Berg engaged. In 1943 Norman Granz produced all-star sessions there on Tuesday nights.

——. **Tail o' the Cock.** 12950 Ventura Boulevard, Studio City. Johnny Guarnieri played, often six nights per week, in the piano bar of this restaurant from 1971 until 1982.

——. **Terrace.** See Zucca's Terrace.

——. **Three-Thirty-One Club** [Club 331]. 3361 West 8th Street. Herb Rose's club flourished from around the late 1930s, when Nat "King" Cole performed there. Art Tatum appeared in 1941, and Cole returned for eight months in 1942–3. In 1943 Norman Granz produced all-star jam sessions on Monday nights (and soon afterwards followed suit at Billy Berg's on Tuesday nights). The club remained a jazz venue until at least the early 1950s, when Kid Ory played there.

——. **Tiffany Club.** 3260 West 8th Street. This club, owned at various times by Chuck Landis, Jack Tucker, and Max Factor, offered jazz from at least the late 1940s, when Sharkey Bonano played there. Stan Getz and Chet Baker recorded there, and Gene Norman produced Sunday-afternoon jam sessions in the early to mid-1950s, when leading players took part. In 1956 Shelly Manne's newly formed quintet became the house band for a few months.

——. **Tiki Island.** See Mike's Waikiki Inn.

——. **Times Restaurant.** 12749 Ventura Boulevard, Studio City. This restaurant opened in 1974 and for a few years was a venue for Jimmie Rowles, Warne Marsh, Anita O'Day, Victor Feldman, and others.

——. **Tip Toe Inn.** 3971 Whittier Boulevard. In late 1943 Kid Ory led a quartet drawn from his band for a residency there; Bunk Johnson sat in with the group occasionally. The Tip Toe was frequented by the record producer Nesuhi Ertegun and others who were prominent in the Los Angeles jazz industry. Among the celebrity visitors was Orson Welles, on whose radio show Ory's band played in 1944.

——. **Top o' the Brae Lounge.** One Industry Hills Parkway, City of Industry. In 1989 this lounge in the Sheraton Resort Hotel began offering jazz on Sunday evenings, and over the years many leading Los Angeles players appeared there. In 1992 its name changed to Winston's Lounge.

——. **Tra Fiore.** 91 North Raymond Avenue, Pasadena. From 1992 this restaurant in Pasadena's Old Town presented bop groups on Sundays; it closed early in 1994, but later reopened as a Papashon restaurant.

——. **Trianon Ballroom.** 2800 Firestone Boulevard, South Gate. In 1941 the big bands of Duke Ellington and Ella Fitzgerald performed at this ballroom. Horace Heidt bought it in 1943, and that same year Count Basie's band appeared and recorded its part in the film *Reveille with Beverly.* As late as the mid-1940s the ballroom often presented leading African-American bands (including Basie again around 1945) but restricted the customers to whites. In 1946 Ike Carpenter's band began a long residency.

——. **Trinidad.** Beverly Boulevard and Fairfax Avenue. Formerly the Trouville, it became the Trinidad in mid-1943. It was a Latin venue at first, but Avery Parrish, Slim Gaillard, Slam Stewart, Joe Turner (ii), and Zutty Singleton also played there. It closed in the mid-1940s.

——. **El Trocadero.** 8600 West Sunset Boulevard, West Hollywood. This club, located two doors west of the Mocambo, was a jazz and blues venue in the 1940s. T-Bone Walker held a long residency there early in the decade, when Charlie Barnet (1942), Duke Ellington, Matty Malneck, Dorothy Donegan, and Louis Jordan also appeared. In 1945 Benny Carter and his band were booked but were fired after one week for playing too loudly and refusing to present Latin dance music. In 1946 Eddie South's group held an extended engagement. The site also contained the King Cole Room, named for the man who played there in 1945.

——. **The Tropicana.** See Club Tropicana.

——. **The Troubadour.** 9081 Santa Monica Boulevard, West Hollywood. It opened in 1957. The Troubadour was mostly a folk club, but Oscar Brown, Jr., appeared there in 1963, and several jazz groups held engagements in the 1970s, including the Adderley brothers, who recorded an album at the club in 1972. It remained an occasional venue for bop and fusion groups as late as the mid-1990s.

——. **Trouville.** Beverly Boulevard and Fairfax Avenue. Formerly called the Century Club, it became the Trouville when its new owner, Billy Berg, opened it in the 1940s. The early attractions were Lee Young and Lester Young, Billie Holiday, and some proto-Jazz at the Philharmonic jam sessions started by Norman Granz on Sunday afternoons.

——. **Tudor Inn.** Norwalk. It was in operation by the 1960s. Among longtime residents there was the duo of Al Morgan and the pianist Buddy Banks, who played throughout the latter part of the decade.

——. **Turban Room** [Turban Lounge]. 4217 South Central Avenue. This small 1940s club, owned by Harry Weiss, was in the basement of the Dunbar Hotel (though remembrances of its location differ). Gerald Wiggins, Art Tatum, and others played there, though the small upright piano was in poor condition.

——. **Union Labor Temple.** See Labor Temple Hall.

——. **Universal Amphitheater.** 100 Universal City Plaza, Universal City. From the mid-1970s this 6200-seat pop-music venue has occasionally offered jazz concerts by well-known bop and fusion artists.

——. **University of California at Los Angeles.** 405 Hilgard Avenue, Westwood. Royce Hall, its 1800-seat concert hall built in the 1920s, was one of the first permanent buildings on the Westwood campus. Among jazz artists who appeared there were Duke Ellington (21 January 1937), Count Basie, Nat "King" Cole, and Benny Carter (1940s), and numerous famous dixieland, swing, and bop bands thereafter. The building was damaged by an earthquake early in 1994 and remained closed for repairs until 1998. In 1965 Louis Armstrong gave the first jazz concert at the basketball arena, Pauley Pavilion, in May 1967 the Los Angeles Jazz Festival (including Miles Davis, Ornette Coleman, Stan Getz, and Carmen McRae) took place there, and in 1975 Les McCann appeared. The 525-seat Schoenberg Hall, in the Music Building, was an occasional site for jazz concerts, some of which, in the late 1990s, involved Kenny Burrell, director of the jazz studies program. From 1986 the university has presented a two-day jazz and reggae festival at its outdoor athletic field.

——. **University of Southern California.** 3551 University Avenue. The university's Community Service Center and Bovard Auditorium presented occasional jazz concerts from at least 1973; a variety of bop and Latin ensembles appeared. From the late 1990s the campus has hosted a free week-long jazz festival each spring.

——. **Velvet Turtle.** 1701 South Catalina Avenue, Redondo Beach. From 1977 to 1991 Paul Smith's duo (or a substitute when he was on tour with Ella Fitzgerald) played on weekends in the lounge of this restaurant.

——. **Venice Ballroom.** Venice Pier. Ben Pollack's band played at this dance hall from 1924 to 1946; Benny Goodman and Glenn Miller joined the band in 1925. Later the ballroom was renamed the Villa Venice. Stan Kenton played there in 1938.

——. **Veterans Wadsworth Theater.** See Wadsworth Theater.

——. **Victor Hugo's Restaurant.** North of the 9800 block of Wilshire Boulevard, Beverly Hills. This large, luxurious showroom presented the Harry James Orchestra with Frank Sinatra in 1939. Benny Goodman appeared in August of that same year, when John Hammond introduced Charlie Christian to him; James returned in 1942.

——. **Villa Venice.** See Venice Ballroom.

——. **Vine Street Bar and Grill.** 1610 North Vine Street, Hollywood. Ron Bernstein's club was located two blocks east of the Catalina Bar and Grill and offered similar jazz attractions in the 1980s and early 1990s. The policy of presenting jazz ended in 1994 but resumed briefly in 1998 under a new name, Lucky Seven.

——. **Vogue.** Vine Street, Hollywood. Gene Norman operated this large club for a short time in the mid-1940s and presented Duke Ellington, Georgie Auld, and others.

——. **Vogue Ballroom.** See Solomon's Penny Dance Hall.

——. **Wadsworth Theater** [Veterans Wadsworth Theater]. 226 Eisenhower Avenue, Brentwood. A 1450-seat theater on the grounds of the Veterans Administration, it was the site of bop, free-jazz, and Latin concerts on the first Sunday of the month from 1983 to 1998. The American Federation of Musicians' Trust Fund and the Associated Students of University of California at Los Angeles sponsored these free events (the university campus is a few blocks away, to the northeast). The second half of many concerts were broadcast on KKGO in the 1980s. When UCLA's Royce Hall suffered earthquake damage in 1994, most of the university's major concert events were transferred to the Wadsworth.

——. **Waikiki.** See Mike's Waikiki Inn.

——. **Waldorf Café** [Dreamland Café]. 620 East 4th Street. Opened in 1908 or earlier, by 1913 it was the only club in Los Angeles owned by African-Americans. Reb Spikes (1914), Kid Ory (1919), and the Black and Tan Orchestra (1919) were among the early groups who played there.

——. **Waldorf Cellar.** 521 South Main Street. This downtown club opened in the 1920s or early 1930s. In the early 1940s it was owned by Billy Berg and booked jazz groups, but it stopped offering jazz when Berg opened his successful club on North Vine Street (see Billy Berg's Swing Club). Jay McNeely played there in 1952.

——. **Washington and Central Avenue Hall.** See Elk's Hall.

——. **Watkins Hotel.** See Rubaiyat Room.

——. **Watts Towers State Historic Park.** 1765 East 107th Street. Adjoining the bizarre but indestructible towers built single-handedly by the eccentric Simon Rodia, this park hosts music festivals two or three times a year. The Watts Towers Jazz Festival, which takes place over a Sunday afternoon and evening, began in 1976; the Watts Towers Day of the Drum Festival, a Saturday afternoon and evening affair, began in 1982. Both feature leading bop and free-jazz bands from the African-American community. Usually the bands play on outdoor stages, but occasionally they perform inside the Watts Towers Art Center – a gallery at the park.

——. **Wayside Park.** See Leaks Lake.

——. **Westin Hotel.** 5400 Century Boulevard. This hotel began a jazz series in its L.A. Court on Wednesday evenings in the late 1990s, and by 2001 the series was offered year-round, two evenings per week.

——. **Westside Room.** See Century Plaza Hotel.

——. **Westwood Playhouse.** 10886 Le Conte Avenue, Westwood. This 500-seat theater across the street from the southern edge of the University of California at Los Angeles presented jazz events on occasion. Jon Hendricks's show *Evolution of the Blues* ran there in 1978–9, and in later years there were concerts by, among others, Oscar Peterson, Ella Fitzgerald, the Jazz Tap Ensemble, and Wynton Marsalis (whose performances there, filmed around 1987, appear in the video documentary *Wynton Marsalis: Blues & Swing*, *c*1997). In 1993 UCLA purchased the theater and in 1995, following a large donation by the David Geffen Foundation, renamed it the Geffen Playhouse.

——. **Whisling's** [Bill Whisling's (Modern Jazz), Whisling's Hawaii]. 6507 West Sunset Boulevard, Hollywood. Sunday-afternoon jam sessions took place there in the 1940s, and in 1956–7 bop musicians played on weekends and in jam sessions that lasted into the early hours of Sunday morning. In October 1960 it became The Summit (see above).

——. **Wilshire Ebell Theatre.** 4401 West 8th Street. There was jazz occasionally in this concert hall from at least 1938, when the African-American musical *Dixie Goes Hi-hat* played there with the band led by the pianist Phil Moore. Over the years a variety of bop bands appeared, and in 1992 the Coltrane Festival was held there.

——. **Wiltern Theater.** 3790 Wilshire Boulevard. This 2200-seat art deco theater, renovated in 1985, occasionally featured jazz concerts. Most of the annual Coltrane festivals from the late 1980s were held there; in addition, well-known singers, bop groups, and big bands often appear at the theater while on tour.

——. **Windows on Hollywood.** See Holiday Inn.

——. **Winston's Lounge.** See Top o' the Brae Lounge.

——. **World Stage.** 4344 Degnan Boulevard. In 1989 Billy Higgins and the poet Kamau Daa'ood opened this store-front performance space. Soon there were drummers' workshops on Mondays, singers' workshops on Tuesdays, poets' workshops on Wednesdays, jam sessions on Thursdays, performances by both major groups and unknown bands on weekends, and workshops on Saturday afternoons by Elvin Jones, Ron Carter, Higgins, Max Roach, Barry Harris, and others. Higgins and the World Stage managers also made the space available for rehearsals during the day and late at night. Through their encouragement Black Note, B Sharp, and other young groups honed their skills and became nationally known. The World Stage has developed into the cornerstone of the vibrant jazz community in the Leimert Park area. (<http://www.jps.net/seker/stage/index.html> (2001))

——. **Zanzibar Club** [?Zamboango]. ? Next door to the Florentine Gardens on Hollywood Boulevard. This club was in operation by the early 1940s; Fats Waller held his last residency there from early autumn to December 1943. Later it became the Club Sorrento. Around 1954 Vido Musso purchased the club and played there.

——. **Zardi's (Jazzland).** See Sardi's.

——. **Zebra Lounge.** 8505 South Central Avenue. From 1959 to 1961 this club was an important venue for bop.

——. **Zucca's Cottage.** 1770 East Foothill Boulevard, Pasadena. In the mid-1950s a variety of swing and bop bands played at this venue in the San Gabriel Valley; it became Zucca's Ranch House in 1961.

——. **Zucca's Opera House.** See Sebastian's Cotton Club.

——. **Zucca's Terrace** [Terrace]. Pier Avenue, Hermosa Beach. In the early 1940s the Zucca brothers owned this upstairs venue, located across the street from the Lighthouse Café; they brought in a variety of big bands.

BIBLIOGRAPHY

Los Angeles

AllenH

C. Emge: "West Coast: Whiteman to Welk," *DB*, xx/8 (1953), 35

W. Claxton: *Jazz West Coast: a Portfolio of Photographs* (Hollywood, CA, 1954, 2/1980/*R*1996, as *Jazz*)

R. Russell: *Bird Lives: the High Life and Hard Times of Charlie "Yardbird" Parker* (New York, 1973/*R*1994)

P. Willard: liner notes, [various artists:] *Black California* (Savoy 2215, 1976)

L. Feather: "Where the Gigs Are – Southland Jazz Clubs," *Los Angeles Times* (9 Nov 1980)

P. Willard (continued by F. Nemko): "West Coast Notes," *JT* (1984–91)

E. Andrews: *Ernie Andrews on Central Avenue* (1986) [video]

R. Gordon: *Jazz West Coast: the Los Angeles Jazz Scene of the 1950s* (London and New York, 1986)

J. Roberts: "The Lighthouse, Then and Now," *Daily Breeze* [Torrance, CA] (5 Sept 1986)

Jazz Link (San Diego, 1988–91)

L.A. Jazz Scene (Los Angeles, 1988–)

C. Bird: *The Jazz and Blues Lover's Guide to the US* (Reading, MA, 1991)

R. Porter: *There and Back*, ed. D. Keller (Wheatley, Oxford, England, and Baton Rouge, LA, 1991)

T. Gioia: *West Coast Jazz: Modern Jazz in California, 1945–1960* (New York, and Oxford, England 1992)

T. Reed: *The Black Music History of Los Angeles: its Roots: a Classical Pictorial History of Black Music in Los Angeles from 1920–1970* (Los Angeles, 1992)
M. Royal and C. P. Gordon: *Marshal Royal: Jazz Survivor* (London and New York, 1996)
B. Y. Cox: *Central Avenue: its Rise and Fall, 1890–c1955* (Los Angeles, 1997)
M. Bakan: "Way out West on Central: Jazz in the African-American Community of Los Angeles before 1930," *California Soul: Music of African Americans in the West*, ed. J. C. DjeDje and E. S. Meadows (Berkeley, CA, Los Angeles, and London, 1998), 23
C. Bryant and others, eds.: *Central Avenue Sounds: Jazz in Los Angeles* (Berkeley, CA, Los Angeles, and London, 1998)
R. Eastman: "'Pitchin' up a Boogie': African-American Musicians, Nightlife, and Music Venues in Los Angeles, 1930–45," *California Soul: Music of African Americans in the West*, ed. J. C. DjeDje and E. S. Meadows, eds (Berkeley, CA, Los Angeles, and London, 1998), 79

MAGNOLIA, MA. **Storyville.** Oceanside Hotel, route 127. In the summers of 1953 and 1954 (and perhaps later as well) George Wein closed his clubs Mahogany Hall and Storyville (see Boston) and transferred the activities of the Storyville to this seaside location.

MANDEVILLE, LA. **Dew Drop Social Hall.** Lamarque Street. This country dance hall was built in 1895 as a venue for the activities of the Dew Drop Social Club, formed a decade earlier. Buddy Petit's band, which included Edmond Hall and Chester Zardis, played there around 1922. In 2000 the city of Mandeville purchased the building with the aim of creating a museum and possibly reviving jazz performance there.

BIBLIOGRAPHY

K. Koenig: "Mandeville," *SL* (1986), winter, 10
<http://www.ci.mandeville.la.us/dewdrop.html> (2001)

MARINA DEL RAY, CA. See Los Angeles (metropolitan area).

MILNEBURG, NEW ORLEANS. An incorporated village on Lake Pontchartrain, it was an active resort from the 19th century. Until 1984 it was the site of the Pontchartrain Amusement Park, and during its heyday (to the mid-1930s) it boasted numerous venues, both public and private, which engaged jazz bands for residencies or for individual functions. On the pier, for example, were Morgan's Saloon, the Joy Club, Romer's Café, The Inn, Quarelles, Nick's Restaurant, and The Lighthouse, and there were 100 more such venues close by. Its memory is preserved (though its name is misspelled) in the often performed and recorded tune *Milenberg Joys*.

MILWAUKEE. **Crystal Ballroom.** This was one of the many venues in the city where Jabbo Smith played from the mid-1940s, mostly as a part-time musician; he led a sextet there for a residency late in the decade.

——. **Down Under.** This nightclub was in existence from at least the mid-1950s; Jabbo Smith held a residency there in 1958.

——. **Eagle Ballroom.** Jazz was played there for dancing from at least the mid-1920s. Charlie Elgar's band, which included Omer Simeon, was resident in the summer of 1927.

——. **East Town Bar.** It flourished as a venue for jazz in the 1940s. Lil Armstrong held a long residency there as an unaccompanied soloist during the time she was based in Chicago (1940s to early 1950s).

——. **Roof Ballroom.** Wisconsin Theater. The resident bands in the 1920s, which included the Creole Roof Orchestra led first by Arthur Sims and later (as the Wisconsin Roof Orchestra) by Bernie Young, numbered several jazz-oriented musicians among their personnel: such players as Cassino Simpson, Preston Jackson, and Zilner T. Randolph played in the band between 1926 and the early 1930s, and Buster Bailey, Wallace Bishop, and Quinn Wilson all spent short periods as members under Young.

——. **Tina's Lounge.** It offered jazz performances from the 1960s at least. Jabbo Smith held a residency there as a trombonist (playing the valve instrument) and pianist in 1966.

——. **Wisconsin Theater.** See Roof Ballroom.

MINNEAPOLIS. **Cotton Club.** Named after the famous venue in New York, it was open by at least the late 1930s, when Boyd Atkins's band held a long residency there.

——. **Fine Line Café.** 318 North First Avenue. From its opening late in 1987 it has presented fusion groups (including those of John Scofield and Al Di Meola), blues, ethnic music, and a Sunday gospel brunch. Branford Marsalis is just one of the jazz musicians who has appeared there on occasion.
(<http://www.finelinemusic.com> (2001))

——. **Nest Club.** It was in existence by 1930. In 1931–2 Lester Young played there in bands led by Frank Hines, Eddie Barefield, and Leroy White; during the same period he also worked with Paul Cephas at the South Side Club.

——. **White House Restaurant.** Jazz was offered for the entertainment of the diners from at least the 1960s. The performances were often given by a solo pianist: Meade "Lux" Lewis was resident there at the time of his death.
For other venues in the Twin Cities see St. Paul, MN.

MISSISSIPPI RIVER. The Streckfus Line of Mississippi steamboats was started in 1884 by Captain John Streckfus, and for a time its activities were restricted to the carrying of freight. With the launching of the SS *J.S.* in 1901 (see Arkansas River, above) the line entered the excursion trade for which its name is now remembered. After the death of John Streckfus, Sr. (1925), his sons Joe (*d* 1959), Roy (*d* 1967), John, Jr., and Verne directed the business, which was still active in the 1970s; in 1980 the family dissolved the Streckfus business, selling it to the New Orleans Steamboat Company and an agency in St. Louis. The Streckfus boats traveled mainly on the Mississippi, but their routes also took them onto the Illinois, the Ohio, and the Arkansas rivers, and some were based in cities not on the Mississippi. Others appear not to have traveled at all but were moored for use as floating clubs or ballrooms. The excursion season lasted from Memorial Day (late in May) until Labor Day (in early September).

Musicians were employed on the pleasure craft from the beginning, though Joe Streckfus apparently promoted this aspect of the entertainment with particular zeal; he engaged the individual players himself, insisting that they be able to read music. Many early jazz musicians gained invaluable experience playing in riverboat bands, and the name most strongly associated with the Mississippi vessels is that of Fate Marable, who spent all his professional life in the employ of the Streckfus line and directed bands that at different times included such musicians as Louis Armstrong, Henry "Red" Allen, Jimmy Blanton, Pops Foster, and the Dodds brothers. Other bandleaders to work for Streckfus were A. J. Piron, who played for long periods on the

3. *Fate Marable's riverboat band aboard the SS Capitol, New Orleans, 1919: (left to right) Henry Kimball (double bass), Boyd Atkins (violin), Marable (piano), Johnny St. Cyr (banjo), David Jones (C-melody saxophone), unidentified saxophonist, Louis Armstrong (cornet), James Brashear (trombone), and Baby Dodds (drums)*

riverboats from 1934 until his death in 1943, Alphonso Trent, Sidney Desvigne, Carlisle Evans, Dewey Jackson, and Charlie Creath.

Streckfus Steamers was not the only concern to be active in the pleasure-boat business. Another company that ran a similar service was General Excursion, which was based in St. Louis. It was generally acknowledged by musicians, however, that the Streckfus boats were the more notable for their presentation of jazz.

——. **SS *Admiral*.** Launched around 1940, this was reputed to be the largest inland steamer in the world. It worked out of St. Louis for more than 30 years, and in October 1971 it carried the "Jazz on the River" excursion, at which bands based in St. Louis played to audiences of about 3000. It was later moored at the waterfront in St. Louis, and in 1984 it was converted into a floating mall of shops and restaurants.

——. **SS *Capitol*.** Perhaps the Streckfus boat most celebrated in jazz history, the *Capitol* was launched as a pleasure steamer in 1920 after conversion from the sternwheel packet boat the *Dubuque*. It spent summers in St. Paul, Minnesota, and winters in New Orleans. Among the bandleaders associated with the *Capitol* were Fate Marable (from 1917; see fig.3), Carlisle Evans (*c*1919), Albert "Doc" Wrixon (*c*1921), Tony Catalano (early 1920s), Dewey Jackson (1924–6, 1935), and Fats Pichon (1930s). Bix Beiderbecke played briefly with Wrixon in 1921, and Marable's sidemen included Johnny Dodds, Al Morgan, Amos White, Emanuel Sayles, and Charlie Creath. The steamer was dismantled in 1945.

——. **SS *Island Queen*.** The *Island Queen* was owned by General Excursion and traveled between St. Louis and Cincinnati. By way of music on board there was usually a large orchestra that played band arrangements for dancing. Sidney Desvigne led the Southern Syncopators for a long period from the mid-1920s, numbering among his sidemen at different times Al Morgan and the reed player Warner A. Seals.

——. **SS *J.S. Deluxe*.** This was named for Captain John Streckfus in 1919 on its conversion from the sternwheel packet boat the *Quincy*. It worked out of St. Louis throughout the 1920s and was finally taken out of commission and dismantled in 1938. Fate Marable, Dewey Jackson, Charlie Creath, and Harry Dial were among the jazz musicians who entertained on board the boat. It should not be confused with the earlier steamer of the Streckfus line, the SS *J.S.*, which sailed on the Arkansas River.

——. **SS *Majestic*.** This was a large sternwheeler with five decks, capable of accommodating as many as 2500 passengers. Its route took it out of St. Louis and along the upper Mississippi to Winona, Minnesota. Among the jazz musicians who played on board the *Majestic* was Bix Beiderbecke, who served as a temporary member of the resident band in 1921.

——. **SS *President*.** A sidewheeler, the *President* cruised out of New Orleans from at least the 1910s. Beginning around 1918, jazz bands played for its moonlight river excursions; Fate Marable led a group which at different times included Louis Armstrong, Baby Dodds, Pops Foster, and Johnny St. Cyr. The steamer continued to offer performances of jazz until about 1970, when the repertory changed to rock music. It was still in operation in the late 1980s, when it was docked on the river at Canal Street in New Orleans.

——. **SS *St. Paul*.** Converted from a sidewheel packet boat of the same name, it was put into service as a pleasure steamer in 1917 and was based in St. Louis. In 1939 it went out of commission and was refitted before starting work again in 1940 as the SS *Senator* (see below). Fate Marable played on the boat as a solo pianist in 1918 and the following year led a band that involved Louis Armstrong, Joe Howard, David Jones, Johnny St. Cyr, and Baby Dodds. Marable maintained his connection with the *St. Paul*, playing every spring during the 1930s on a cruise up the Ohio to Pittsburgh. Charlie Creath formed his association with the vessel in the 1920s, when his Jazz-o-Maniacs was the resident band; he too returned regularly to the boat in the following decade. Other bandleaders on the *St. Paul* included Dewey Jackson and Sidney Desvigne.

——. **SS *Senator*.** Formerly the SS *St. Paul*, it was renamed after being rebuilt in 1939–40. In its new guise it had a short career as an excursion craft: in 1942 it was put to use in the coast guard service, and it was scuttled in 1953. Fate Marable was the bandleader on board in 1942, when his sidemen included Dewey Jackson.

——. **SS *Sidney*.** This sidewheeler was in operation from at least 1918, by which time Fate Marable was the bandleader on board; he remained with the vessel until 1921, when it was withdrawn from service, rebuilt, and renamed the SS *George Washington* (see Ohio River). Tony Catalano also played on the *Sidney*, probably in 1919 or 1920. Marable's sidemen included Baby Dodds, and Emmett Hardy worked with Catalano.

BIBLIOGRAPHY

Mississippi River

W. Dobie: "Remembering Fate Marable," *Sv*, no.38 (1971), 44

P. Foster, T. Stoddard, and R. Russell: "On the Boats," *Pops Foster: the Autobiography of a New Orleans Jazzman* (Berkeley, CA, Los Angeles, and London, 1971), 105

D. Coller: "Jazz on the Mississippi River," *Fn*, vi/6 (1975), 4

C. Landrum: "From Quincy's Past: when the Excursion Boat was Queen of the Mississippi," *Quincy Herald-Whig* (14 Oct 1984), 4E

"Operator of Steamship Fleet, Capt. [Verne Walter] Streckfus, Dies at 89," *New Orleans Times-Picayune* (16 Oct 1984)

D. Chevan: "Riverboat Music from St. Louis and the Streckfus Steamboat Line," *Black Music Research Journal*, ix/2 (1989), 153

MONROEVILLE, PA. **Town House.** Route 22, Monroeville. In the 1950s this restaurant and nightclub presented, among others, Dizzy Gillespie, and Red Nichols and his Five Pennies.

NATCHEZ, MS. **Rhythm Club.** This dance hall, which occupied premises that had once been a church, was in operation by the early 1920s and was one of the better venues in the South on the regular circuit for touring bands. Walter Barnes's big band was playing an engagement there on 23 April 1940 when fire destroyed the building, killing most of the people inside.

NATICK, MA. **Center for Performing and Visual Arts.** The center is a converted storefront/art gallery that hosts jazz concerts in the evenings. It is community run, serves no alcohol, and attracts a largely local clientele who encourage listening rather than socializing. Performances have often involved Jerry Bergonzi, Dave Samuels, and other members of the faculties of the Berklee College of Music and the New England Conservatory. (<http://www.natickarts.org> (2001))

NEWARK, NJ. **Adams Theater.** 26–30 Branford Place. Formerly Kinney's (built in 1913) and then the Shubert, it was renamed the Adams Theater in 1939. Over roughly the next dozen years it presented prominent bands of the swing era, such as those of Duke Ellington, Jimmie Lunceford, Fats Waller, Count Basie, Woody Herman, and Stan Kenton.

——. **Alcazar.** 72 Waverley Avenue. This venue had a huge double horseshoe-shaped bar, and it presented music nightly from at least the late 1930s, when it was run by Pop Durham; at that time the trumpeter and singer Leon Eason led a band there. Jabbo Smith held a long residency from around 1940, first with his own trio and then, in 1944, with the band of the saxophonist, trumpeter, and pianist Larry Ringold. In the 1980s the guitarist Bill Johnson owned and managed the New Alcazar (on 16th Avenue), where Ringold also played.

——. **Caravan Club.** 8 Bedford Street. Formerly Dodger's Bar and Grill, it was redecorated and reopened late in 1949 as the Caravan Club and briefly presented such leading musicians as Buddy Johnson, Sarah Vaughan, Illinois Jacquet, and George Shearing.

——. **Front Room.** Active in the 1950s, this was an important venue for contemporary jazz. Among the musicians who appeared both there and at other similar clubs in the city were Miles Davis, Art Blakey, and John Coltrane. In the 1960s, however, it fell victim to a general decline in interest in jazz, and by the middle of the decade it had closed.

——. **Johnson's Cafe.** 296–8 Plane Street (now University Avenue). In the 1920s Willie "the Lion" Smith was the pianist at this whites-only venue.

——. **Key Club.** Corner of William Street and Halsey Street. It was founded on West Street in the 1930s by an uncle of Walter Dawkins, who moved it to its location at William and Halsey when he inherited it in the 1950s. The organists Rhoda Scott and Jimmy McGriff played there early in their careers, and George Benson also appeared regularly. The Key Club weathered the lean years of the 1960s, and by the middle of the decade it was the only important nightclub in Newark still open. In the 1970s it became the center for the revival of jazz in the city, but following Dawkins's death his wife ended the musical policy and used the venue to run a flea market.

——. **Krueger's Auditorium.** Charlton Street and Belmont Avenue. This was another of the large Newark venues where big bands appeared in the 1940s, notably those of Jay McShann, Les Hite, and Lucky Millinder.

——. **Laurel Garden.** 457 Springfield Avenue. The Laurel Garden hosted major big bands of the swing era, including those of Duke Ellington and Count Basie.

——. **Lloyd's Manor.** 42–8 Beacon Street. Owned by Bill Lloyd, this spacious club was located above a bowling alley. While it had a large ballroom, where the big bands of Willie Bryant, Luis Russell, Billy Eckstine (1946), Dizzy Gillespie (1947) and Lionel Hampton (1949) appeared, there was also a lounge, which served for roughly a decade from around 1946 as Newark's principal venue for emerging bop musicians. Among those who played there were James Moody, Babs Gonzales, Hank Mobley, Charli Persip, Jimmy Ponder, and George Benson. In addition such famous artists of the swing era as Nat "King" Cole and Billie Holiday performed in the lounge. Lloyd's Manor was sold in 1956 and renamed the Penguin Club.

——. **Lynn & Lynn's.** In the early 1960s it mounted regular jam sessions on Tuesday nights; among the musicians to play on these occasions was Johnny Griffin. The club closed around the middle of the decade.

——. **New Alcazar.** See Alcazar.

——. **Paramount Theater.** 193–5 Market Street. Built in 1896, it was remodeled in 1916, converted to a movie theater, and renamed the Paramount. One of several large halls in the city, it came into its own as a jazz venue in the swing era, when notable big bands performed there. It closed in the 1980s.

——. **Pere's East.** It was active as a jazz venue from at least the 1970s, when its weekly jam sessions formed an important element in the jazz revival in Newark.

——. **Pitt's Place.** It was open by the mid-1950s. The trumpeter and singer Leon Eason, whose career was intimately bound up with Newark's nightclubs – in the late 1930s he played at the Park Rest, the Miami Club, and the Alcazar (see above) – led his trio in a long residency there from 1956 to 1967.

——. **Powell's Lounge.** This was one of many flourishing small venues in the 1950s. Some of the most prominent American musicians of the period, including Miles Davis and John Coltrane, appeared there. It was closed some time in the 1960s.

——. **Savoy Ballroom.** Springfield Avenue and Belmont Avenue. Jazz was played there for dancing from at least the 1930s. Besides visiting bands, two local groups, the Savoy Dictators (of which Bobby Plater was a member) and Gil Fuller's Barons of Rhythm, played there regularly.

——. **Sparky J's.** It opened in the 1970s at a time when jazz began to re-establish itself in the city. Along with those of the Key Club and Pere's East (see above), its activities made an important contribution to the revival of the music during that decade.

——. **Terrace Ballroom.** 1020 Broad Street. Located within the Mosque Theater complex, it hosted fashion shows and dances in the late 1940s to early 1950s. During that period such artists as Duke Ellington, Sarah Vaughan, and Count Basie were featured.

BIBLIOGRAPHY

Newark

K. D. Wright: "Jazz in Newark, 1930–1970," *JSN*, ii/1 (1980), 14

B. J. Kukla: *Swing City: Newark Nightlife, 1925–50* (Philadelphia, 1991)

New Orleans. *Note*. Addresses are given as precisely as possible in the historically correct form. The names of a number of streets were changed during the 20th century. For the purposes of this list the following changes are important: Basin Street became Saratoga Street for a period, then in 1945 reverted to its original name; Customhouse Street became Iberville Street (*c*1912); Franklin Street became Crozat Street (*c*1912); Howard Street became LaSalle Street; and Liberty Street became Treme Street.

——. **Abadie's.** 1501 Bienville Street, at Marais Street. Cabaret. Owned by Eloise Blankenstein and Louis Abadie, it was active between 1906 and 1917. Richard M. Jones led his Four Hot Hounds in a residency there around 1912, when King Oliver and Wooden Joe Nicholas were among his sidemen.

——. **Absinthe House.** See Old Absinthe House.

——. **Amis de l'Espérance Hall.** See Hopes Hall.

——. **Anderson's Annex** [Tom Anderson's Annex]. 201 North Basin Street, at Iberville Street. Saloon. From 1901 to around 1925 it was the headquarters from where Tom Anderson controlled the brothel district of New Orleans. The venue was managed by Billy Struve, who also produced the famous Blue Book (a guidebook to the district), which advertised it somewhat misleadingly as a "café and restaurant." From about 1905 it was sometimes known as the Arlington Annex, after Josie Arlington's whorehouse, one of the three largest and most popular on Basin Street. The saloon offered music on a modest scale, presenting small bands, such as string trios (mandolin or violin, guitar, and double bass); among the musicians who worked there were Bill Johnson (i) (before 1908), the African-American guitarist Tom Brown, and Wellman Braud, playing violin. In published accounts such famous musicians as Louis Armstrong and Albert Nicholas are said to have appeared at Anderson's Annex, but they actually worked at Tom Anderson's New Cabaret and Restaurant (see below).

——. **Anderson's Café.** 110–12 North Rampart Street. Owned by Tom Anderson, it presented music during the early years of the 20th century until some time after 1912, when the original venue was closed and Tom Anderson's New Cabaret and Restaurant was opened in premises further down the street (see below).

——. **Anderson's Saloon.** See Tom Anderson's New Cabaret and Restaurant.

——. **Antoine's.** 713 St. Louis Street. Probably the most famous French restaurant in the city (because of the novel *Dinner at Antoine's* by Frances Parkinson Keyes), it has several private dining-rooms, where jazz bands have often performed at functions and parties. John Robichaux' orchestra played there as early as about 1906, and jazz groups continued to be engaged on such occasions into the 1980s.

——. **Arlington Annex.** See Anderson's Annex.

——. **Artisan Hall.** 1460 North Derbigny Street. It served regularly as a venue for dances and banquets, at which jazz musicians often performed; those who appeared there early in the 20th century included Chris Kelly, Sidney Bechet, Manuel Perez, Big Eye Louis Nelson, and Johnny St. Cyr. On at least two occasions recordings were made at the hall: Wooden Joe Nicholas recorded for the American Music label in 1945 and George Lewis (i) for Decca in 1952.

——. **Astoria.** 235–43 South Rampart Street. Dance hall. It flourished during the 1920s and 1930s and often engaged jazz musicians to accompany the dancing. Among the bands that played there were Kid Rena's and one led by David Jones and Lee Collins, which recorded as the Jones and Collins Astoria Hot Eight in 1929. The venue is variously referred to as the Astoria Dance Hall, the Astoria Ballroom, and the Astoria Gardens.

——. **Autocrat (Social and Pleasure) Club.** 1725 St. Bernard Avenue. Once one of many clubs of its kind, by the 1980s the Autocrat was among the very few remaining active in the city. It was not often used for public dances, but private functions and Mardi Gras balls were held there at which musicians were engaged to play.

——. **Betsy Cole's.** Josephine Street and Willow Street. For many years in the 1910s and 1920s Betsy Cole held lawn parties in the yard behind her house. Jazz bands played there regularly for dancing.

——. **Bienville Roof Gardens.** Bienville Hotel, St. Charles Avenue at Lee Circle. This venue, on the roof of a large hotel, offered jazz for dancing during the 1920s and 1930s. Monk Hazel led the Bienville Roof Orchestra there in the late 1920s and early 1930s, and in December 1928 the band, directed by Sharkey Bonano, recorded four sides for Brunswick.

——. **Big 25** [The 25, Johnny Lala's]. Near the intersection of North Franklin Street and Customhouse Street. Gambling house and bar. Established by the beginning of the 20th century, its activities were directed by Johnny (John T.) Lala. It served exclusively an African-American clientele and became the most popular meeting place for musicians in the red-light district. Big Eye Louis Nelson stated that he played there in Buddy Bolden's band around 1900, and among those who at different times performed or rehearsed in a small room separating the gambling house from the bar were Bunk Johnson and Tony Jackson, and Manuel Manetta and Jelly Roll Morton. By 1940 musicians were no longer hired to perform there, and the building was demolished in the mid-1950s.

——. **Blue Angel.** 225 Bourbon Street. Nightclub. It was presenting jazz by at least the early 1970s, since Pud Brown appeared there in 1973. For several years it employed more than one band, offering both afternoon and evening performances, but by the mid-1980s the afternoon sessions had been discontinued. It often engaged the city's younger jazz musicians.

——. **Blue Room.** 123 Baronne Street. The Blue Room was opened in the 1930s, when the bands that performed included one led by Sharkey Bonano. At its opening it was situated in the Roosevelt Hotel; this hotel was formerly known as the Grunewald and its nightclub as The Cave (see below). At some stage in its existence the club became known as the New Blue Room, and it continued to present jazz into the 1980s, engaging leading musicians such as Lionel Hampton, who appeared there in December 1987.

——. **Buddy Bartley's Club.** See Toodlum's Bar.

——. **Budweiser Dance Hall.** See Fern Dance Hall.

——. **Bulls Club.** 1913 8th Street, at Danneel Street. One of the more important uptown venues during the early part of the 20th century, it numbered among its members many butchers, and the name of the club probably derives from their practice of leading a bull around in their parades. Music was presented both indoors and in an adjacent vacant lot on the corner of the two streets; the latter served as an outdoor beer garden, at which two bands played, one at each end. The club's programs included jazz from at least 1918, when Chris Kelly and Mutt Carey played there, and in the 1920s Kid Rena's band appeared regularly. By around the 1940s the venue had been taken over by the Elks Club, and music was no longer presented.

——. **Cadillac Café** [Cadillac Club]. 342 Rampart Street. It was active from at least the 1910s. Willie Hightower led his band the American Stars there in 1914–15, and in the early 1920s the orchestra of Arnold Du Pas, which included Luis Russell and Albert Nicholas, held a residency.

——. **Café Brasil.** 1200 Chartres Street. By the 1990s it was offering a wide cross-section of all styles of New Orleans music, including jazz, blues, rhythm-and-blues, Cajun, and folk.

——. **Can Can Café.** 300 block of Bourbon Street. This venue is situated on the corner of the Royal Sonesta Hotel. Although the personnel often changes, its resident five-piece band consistently offers high quality interpretations of the classic repertory of early jazz.
(<http://www.sonesta.com/neworleans_royal> (2001))

——. **The Cave.** Hotel Grunewald, University Place. This nightspot within the hotel was suitably dimly lit and decorated with imitation stalagmites and stalactites. It was an important jazz venue from around 1912 until 1926. A band led by the cornetist Johnny De Droit, which included Tony Parenti, played there about 1916. The Fountain Lounge (see below) was also in the Grunewald. The hotel's name was later changed successively to the Roosevelt and the Fairmount, and the nightclub became known as the Blue Room (see above).

——. **Claiborne Theatre.** Claiborne Avenue and St. Louis Street. It was one of several venues owned by Pete Lala that was used for jazz performances. Sidney Bechet and King Oliver played there regularly around 1916, and according to Bechet it was in use as a movie house in 1917. Manuel Manetta stated that at some point Kid Ory had a controlling interest in the theater.

——. **Club Lavida.** See La Vida Dance Hall.

——. **Cooperators Hall.** See Hopes Hall.

——. **Dew Drop Inn.** 2836 La Salle Street. It was opened in April 1939 by Frank G. Painia, who began featuring live music in August 1945, and from that time into the 1960s it was the most popular uptown venue for African-Americans. Its favored repertory was rhythm-and-blues, and many bands and popular entertainers played there, including Dave Bartholomew, Joe Turner (ii), Cecil Gant, the International Sweethearts of Rhythm, and Ray Charles. By 1967, when Turner made another appearance, the club was losing prominence. Musicians had ceased to be employed by 1969, and Painia died in 1972. The adjacent hotel was still in the family in 1986. (J. Hannusch: "The South's Swankiest Night Spot: Jumpin' at the Dew Drop Inn," *Blues Unlimited*, no.147 (1986), 10; repr. at <http://www.ikoiko.com/jh9704a.html> (1997))

——. **Dixieland Hall.** 522 Bourbon Street; 616 Bourbon Street. Concert hall. The first of the two venues to use this name opened in 1962. Both presented commercial dixieland jazz, performances of which provided a popular tourist attraction. Kid Howard played regularly at Dixieland Hall in the 1960s.

——. **Donna's Bar & Grill.** 800 North Rampart Street. Donna's Bar & Grill presents music from Thursday through Monday nights, and it has been probably the most exciting of all New Orleans jazz venues since it began to feature new brass bands in 1987. A generation of young African-Americans formed bands there, the best known of which is the Rebirth Brass Band. Donna's has its own record label, which records local musicians.
(<http://www.donnasbarandgrill.com> (2001))

——. **Eagle Saloon.** 401 South Rampart Street. This was a favorite haunt of the many musicians who played at the Masonic Hall next door on Perdido Street. While it gave its name to Frankie Dusen's Eagle Band, it was not itself a venue for jazz performance.

——. **Economy Hall.** 1422 Ursuline Street. Dance hall. It flourished from perhaps as early as 1885 until about 1942; the building was then used as a church, and it was finally demolished after being damaged severely by Hurricane Betsy in 1965. Kid Ory played there regularly, and at one time he held a lease on the hall so that no other band could perform without his agreement. Among other musicians who appeared there were King Oliver, who was a member of Ory's band, and Johnny Dodds (both before World War I) and George Lewis (i) and Chris Kelly (both 1920s). The name was revived during the 1970s for a nightclub in the basement of the Royal Sonesta Hotel, at the downtown end of the 300 block on Bourbon Street; it was associated with the New Orleans Jazz Club Museum, which was located in the hotel at that time.

——. **Entertainers Club.** 206 Franklin Street. It occupied premises known variously in the early years of the 20th century as the 101 Ranch (see below), the 102 Ranch, and Phillips Café. The name seems to have been changed to the Entertainers Club by the mid-1920s, by which time the venue was under new management. Around this time Lee Collins's quartet played there and Capt. John Handy led a resident band.

——. **Espérance Hall.** See Hopes Hall.

——. **Fairgrounds.** See New Orleans Fairgrounds Race Track.

——. **Fairmount Hotel.** See Blue Room.

——. **Famous Door.** 339 Bourbon Street. An important venue for dixieland jazz, it was in existence by the 1940s and continued to be active into the 1980s; among its managers was Hyp Guinle. In the early 1940s Alton Purnell played there, and later in the decade Sharkey Bonano; Pete Fountain worked at the club in 1953, and around 1960 the bandleader for several years was Santo Pecora.

——. **Fern Dance Hall.** 1017 Iberville Street. In the mid-1920s Armand Hug made his professional début there at the age of 15. The hall was in operation until at least 1940, when Kid Rena led a resident band; by that time it was known officially as the Budweiser Dance Hall, a name derived from the beer advertisement outside the door. It was also known as the Fern Café and Dance Hall.

——. **Fewclothes Cabaret.** 135 North Basin Street. Its name was probably a corruption of that of its owner, George Foycault. Opened in about 1902, it flourished as a center for jazz performance until 1917. Many of the leading New Orleans musicians performed there, among them Big Eye Louis Nelson, Freddie Keppard, King Oliver, and Baby Dodds. Sidney Bechet appeared at the club both in a group led by Richard M. Jones, which also included Keppard and Oliver on occasions, and in the Eagle Band (*c*1917).

——. **501 Club.** See Tipitina's.

——. **Fountain Lounge.** Hotel Grunewald, University Place. It offered jazz performances from at least 1923, when the New Orleans Owls played there. Its activities complemented those of The Cave (see above), another nightclub in the hotel.

——. **Francs Amis Hall.** 1820 North Robertson Street. The hall was owned by an exclusive creole social, aid, and pleasure club; its social activities included dances, organized strictly by invitation only. From about 1940 the building was used as a church.

——. **The Frenchman's.** Villere Street and Bienville Street. In the early years of the 20th century it was a lively venue where the best pianists and entertainers of the brothel district gathered after hours to perform.

——. **French Quarter Inn.** 800 Bourbon Street. It was purchased by Pete Fountain in 1959 and opened with his trio the following year.

——. **Friends of Hope Hall.** See Hopes Hall.

——. **Funky Butt at Congo Square.** 714 North Rampart Street. Named in honor of its famous predecessor (see immediately below), it opened around 1997 and began presenting a full schedule of jazz, funk, and blues performances involving, among many others, the Marsalis brothers Wynton, Delfeayo, and Jason (each featured separately), Nicholas Payton, the Dirty Dozen Brass Band, Henry Butler, and the group Astral Project (including Tony Dagradi, Steve Masakowski, and John Vidacovich). (<http://www.funkybutt.com> (2001))

——. **Funky Butt Hall.** 1319 Perdido Street. From 1866 it was owned by the Union Sons Relief Association of Louisiana and was properly known as Union Sons Hall; it was popularly referred to as Funky Butt Hall from the 1890s, when Buddy Bolden played there, though it was also known as Kenna's or Kinney's Hall. It played an important part in the development of jazz in the city from the 1890s until about 1910. Besides Bolden, the musicians who played there included the Eagle Band (with Sidney Bechet) and Louis Armstrong. On Sunday mornings the hall was used for Baptist services and in the 1920s it became exclusively a church; it was demolished in the 1950s to make way for new civic buildings.

——. **Globe Hall.** St. Claude Street and St. Peter Street. Dance hall. Situated at the end of the old Basin Canal, near Basin Street, it was active until about 1920. In the period from 1900 to 1906 Buddy Bolden's band frequently played there for dances.

——. **Grunewald Hotel.** See The Cave; Fountain Lounge.

——. **Guidrey and Allen's Upstairs Club.** Perdido Street. It flourished in the 1910s, when among the musicians who played there were Minor Hall and Sidney Bechet.

——. **Gypsy Tea Room.** 1432 St. Ann Street. The premises consisted of a large bar room in the front, and a room behind which was advertised as "the largest nightclub in the South." Jazz was played there from at least 1936, when Kid Rena's band appeared; George Lewis (i) led his band for a residency at the club in 1943.

——. **Halfway House.** City Park Avenue and Pontchartrain Boulevard. It was active as a venue for jazz performance from at least 1914 until 1930. The cornetist Abbie Brunies had a long connection with the club; among the bands he led there was the Halfway House Orchestra, which made a number of recordings from 1925 to 1928.

——. **Hopes Hall** [Friends of Hope Hall, Amis de l'Espérance Hall, Cooperators Hall]. 922 North Liberty Street. It was named after the Society of Friends of Hope, one of many early African-American social and benevolent clubs in New Orleans. Jazz regularly formed part of the activities there from around the beginning of the 20th century. It should not be confused with Hopes Hall at Burgundy Street and Spain Street.

——. **Hotel Grunewald.** See The Cave; Fountain Lounge.

——. **Italian Hall.** 1020 Esplanade Avenue, near North Rampart Street. A handsome building, it was later converted into an apartment house. The New Orleans Rhythm Kings played for a dance there in the early 1920s, and the recording session by the Jones and Collins Astoria Hot Eight for Victor took place in the hall in 1929.

——. **Jackson Hall.** See Longshoremen's Hall.

——. **Jazz Alley.** See Storyville District.

——. **Jazz Parlor.** See Storyville District.

——. **Johnny Lala's.** See Big 25.

——. **Johnson Park.** Adjacent to Lincoln Park (see below). One of several outdoor sites in New Orleans where jazz was played, it presented performances by Buddy Bolden's band from around 1902.

——. **Kenna's Hall** [Kinney's Hall]. See Funky Butt Hall.

——. **Kolb's Restaurant.** 125 St. Charles Avenue. A well-known German restaurant, it was open from at least the early years of the 20th century. In the 1910s and 1920s the cornetist Johnny De Droit fulfilled a long engagement there; in May 1983 the restaurant's managers mounted a night of music by the group Tulane Hot Jazz Classic to honor De Droit as a special guest.

——. **La Vida Dance Hall.** 1014 Iberville Street; 66 St. Charles Avenue at Canal Street; Burgundy Street. The premises on Iberville Street formerly housed Pup's Café. A number of jazz musicians played for dancing at this establishment, including Lee Collins (mid-1920s), Tony Parenti (1924), and Capt. John Handy, Jim Robinson, and Kid Howard, all of whom led resident bands for long periods in the 1930s. The venue has sometimes been referred to as the Club Lavida.

——. **Liberty Hall.** Dance hall. The promoter of dances at this establishment was the trombonist Frankie Dusen, whose Eagle Band played there three times a week in the 1910s.

——. **Lincoln Park.** Carrollton Avenue at Oleander Street. A popular African-American resort, in the early years of the 20th century it presented performances by the bands of John Robichaux and Buddy Bolden.

——. **Little Club.** Rampart Street near Common Street. Under the direction of Tony Dinapolis, it presented jazz from at least the late 1920s, when the Prima–Sharkey Orchestra, led by Leon Prima and Sharkey Bonano, performed there.

——. **Longshoremen's Hall** [Jackson Hall]. 2059 Jackson Avenue. It was one of the most important halls in the uptown area of the city. Although its function was principally that of headquarters for the Musicians' Union, many dances were given there from the time of Buddy Bolden, and jazz bands played there regularly. The building was demolished in the late 1970s.

——. **Luthjens'.** 2527 Marais Street (to January 1960); 2300 Charters Street (mid-1970s). Owned by Mrs. Luthjens, this small venue flourished from the late 1930s. The clarinetist Big Eye Louis Nelson formed a long and important association with the club, leading a quartet for a residency that lasted from 1939 to 1948. The duo of Billie and De De Pierce performed there from around 1949 into the 1950s and in 1953 recorded for the documentary series on New Orleans clubs made by Center Records (*Billie and De De Pierce at Luthjens'*, 1953, Center 15). The original premises were destroyed by fire in January 1960, but the name was revived in the mid-1970s for a bar and bistro. (H. Friedwald: Liner notes, B. Pierce and D. D. Pierce: *Vocal Blues & Cornet in the Classic Tradition*, Riv. 9390, 1961)

——. **Lyric Theater.** 201 Burgundy Street. It was one of the establishments on the Theater Owners' Booking Association circuit and presented performances by a number of jazz musicians; Bessie Smith sang there in 1921. A band led by John Robichaux was in residence from 1918 until 1927, when the theater was destroyed by fire. From the 1970s Vernal Bagneris had huge success with his show *One Mo' Time*, which sought to re-create an evening at the Lyric Theater in 1927.

——. **Mahogany Hall.** 235 Basin Street, at Bienville Street. Brothel. It functioned from at least the beginning of the 20th century until 1917, when legal prostitution was abolished in the Storyville district; the building was demolished in the 1950s. The name was revived in the mid-1980s, when it was taken up by the venue formerly known as the Paddock Lounge (see below). The establishment's musical and other activities were directed by Lulu White, known variously as "the Queen of the Demi-monde" and "the Queen of Diamonds"; she was the aunt of the composer Spencer Williams. By way of providing background music White employed pianists: Kid Ross appeared regularly, and of the others she engaged the finest were Tony Jackson, Jelly Roll Morton, and Manuel Manetta; Richard M. Jones and Clarence Williams also played there.

——. **Maison Bourbon.** 641 Bourbon Street. It was in existence by at least the 1960s; Danny Barker began a residency there in autumn 1969, and among others who played there was Wallace Davenport.

——. **Mama Lou's.** Off Little Woods Road. It was a wooden building erected on piles and set about 75 feet out from the shore of Lake Pontchartrain. Jazz was played there from at least the 1940s: Herb Morand led his band in a residency that lasted for much of the decade, and the trumpeter Louis "Kid Shots" Madison appeared in the mid-1940s. The club remained in operation until at least 1961 but had closed by the time that Hurricane Betsy damaged the area in 1965.

——. **Manny's Tavern.** 3129 St. Roch Avenue. George Lewis (i) played there intermittently between 1946 and 1952.

——. **Maple Leaf Bar.** 8316 Oak Street. It opened around 1970 and became one of the most important venues in the city, presenting music on five or six nights each week. Its programs cover a wide range of styles, including jazz, folk music, and Cajun music. (<http://commerce.prodigybiz.com/customer/m/mapleleafclub> (2001))

——. **Mardi Gras Lounge.** 333 Bourbon Street. This nightclub was owned by the clarinetist Sid Davilla. Among the jazz musicians who appeared there were Alphonse Picou and Paul Barbarin. The Mardi Gras was probably the only venue in New Orleans at which Lizzie Miles worked in the 1950s, during her last active years.

——. **Masonic Hall** [Odd Fellows Hall]. 1116 Perdido Street. One of several Masonic halls in the city, it was located uptown, in the heart of the African-American prostitution district; a number of published photographs mistakenly represent other halls as the Perdido Street venue. It was built in 1850 and consisted of a dance hall, a dining area, and a pool room. Because it was used (and may have been partly owned) by the Odd Fellows Lodge, it was also known as Odd Fellows Hall, but it should not be confused with the Odd Fellows Hall on Camp Street, a white venue where the Carnival French Balls, sponsored in part by Tom Anderson, were held. Masonic Hall was a flourishing venue for jazz from the early days of the 20th century, in particular in its function as a dance hall; music for dancing was supplied by Buddy Bolden's band between 1900 and 1906 and later by the Eagle Band, formed by Bolden's sideman Frankie Dusen.

——. **Matranga's.** Franklin Street and Perdido Street. This club, named after its owner, presented jazz from at least 1915; Louis Armstrong, who made his professional début there, was one of its resident performers around that date.

——. **El Morocco.** 200 Bourbon Street. It was active in the 1940s, when it played a part in the revival of New Orleans jazz. Among the musicians who performed there was George Lewis (i), who appeared frequently in the period 1949–51. The club was featured in the 20-minute film documentary *Night Clubs Boom* (1946), in Louis de Rochemont's series *The March of Time* (made by Time and RKO Radio).

——. **Moulin Rouge.** Bourbon Street and Bienville Street. Jazz musicians were engaged to play at the Moulin Rouge from at least 1923, when the resident band was led by the tuba and double bass player Octave Gaspard. Sharkey Bonano performed there late in 1939 and from that year until around 1941 Percy Gabriel led small groups at the club. Around 1954 Kid Thomas recorded there for a documentary series on New Orleans venues made by Center Records (*Kid Thomas at Moulin Rouge*, *c*1954, Center 14).

——. **Municipal Auditorium.** Saratoga Street (formerly and later Basin Street). Concert hall. It has been used for jazz performances from at least December 1944, when the National Jazz Foundation arranged a concert by Benny Goodman and various New Orleans musicians. The same local organization, which flourished before the founding of the New Orleans Jazz Club, staged an event there on 17 January 1945, which was broadcast live; the concert presented stars from *Esquire* magazine's 1945 All-American Band, including Louis Armstrong, Paul Barbarin, Sidney Bechet, J. C. Higginbotham, Bunk Johnson, and James P. Johnson. (It was at this time that the name of the street reverted to Basin Street.) From the 1950s to the early 1970s the auditorium was used for jazz festivals sponsored by several local organizations and then for the New Orleans International Jazz Festival (during its early years), which became the New Orleans Jazz and Heritage Festival. It was also used for concerts by Armstrong, the gospel singer Mahalia Jackson, and others.

——. **New Blue Room.** See Blue Room.

——. **New Orleans Fairgrounds Race Track.** Near City Park. In the early years of the 20th century bands played there for picnics and special events, as well as at the horse races. In 1972 it became the principal site of the New Orleans Jazz and Heritage Festival.

——. **New Slipper Night Club** [Silver Slipper]. 426 Bourbon Street. Active in the 1930s, it was one of several clubs at which Abbie Brunies, one of the city's more successful bandleaders during the lean years of the Depression, held residencies.

——. **Odd Fellows Hall.** The name of two venues in New Orleans: see Masonic Hall.

——. **Old Absinthe House** [Absinthe House]. 238 Bourbon Street, at Bienville Street. This venue (which remains open in the new century) presented jazz performances from the 1920s into the 1950s. It specialized in solo and small-group jazz and engaged many outstanding pianists among its resident musicians. Jazz performers who played there included Ray Bauduc (before 1924), the Creole Serenaders (during most of the 1930s), Fats Pichon (regularly in the 1940s and 1950s), and various four- or five-piece bands often numbering Sweet Emma Barrett and the Humphrey brothers among their members (1950s).

——. **101 Ranch.** 206 Franklin Street. Dance hall. Under the ownership of Billy Phillips and Harry Parker, it was one of the largest and most popular dance halls in the red-light district early in the 20th century. In 1909 Phillips bought out his partner and changed the name of the hall to the 102 Ranch (it was also known as Phillips Café and the Entertainers Club; see above); Parker opened the Tuxedo Dance Hall across the street (see below). Jazz was played for dancing and entertainment at this venue under its different guises from 1902 until the early 1930s; among the musicians who performed there in the early period were Freddie Keppard, Kid Ory, Mutt Carey, and King Oliver.

——. **Paddock Lounge.** 309 Bourbon Street. It flourished from at least the 1940s as a venue for jazz. Papa Celestin led a band in a long residency there from 1949 into the 1950s; following his death the group continued to be connected with the club into the 1960s under the leadership (successively) of the trombonist Bill Matthews and the pianist Octave Crosby. Alphonse Picou, who played with Celestin for a year at the turn of the decade, led his own small group at the Paddock in the 1950s, with Johnny St. Cyr among his sidemen. In the mid-1980s the venue took the name of a former brothel in the Storyville district, Mahogany Hall (see above).

——. **Palm Court Café.** 1204 Decatur Street. From its opening in 1989 by Nina Buck and her husband, the record producer George H. Buck, Jr. (of GHB, Jazzology, and other labels), this restaurant presented all of the remaining veterans of the New Orleans jazz revival, including Percy Humphrey, Danny Barker, Louis Nelson, and Pud Brown. Early in 2001 the Palm Court Café was offering jazz from Wednesday through Sunday nights; only the 90-year-old trumpeter Lionel Ferbos was still active at this point, leading a band there twice a week, and younger traditional-jazz bands perform on the other three nights.

——. **Parisian Room.** 124 Royal Street. Nightclub. Occupying premises above Gluck's Restaurant, it was opened by Tony Almerico in 1948 and remained active as a jazz venue until his death in 1961. Weekly coast-to-coast radio broadcasts were made from the club in the 1950s.

——. **Pelican Roof Ballroom** [Pelican Club Roof Garden]. 407 South Rampart Street. It flourished from the 1920s. Among the jazz groups that played there were one led by Manuel Perez, Sam Morgan's Jazz Band, Sidney Desvigne's Southern Syncopators, and Papa Celestin's band (1939).

The owners of the ballroom ran other venues in New Orleans. References occur in the literature to the Pelican Annex (where Alton Purnell appeared in the late 1920s), the Pelican Café (where Fats Pichon led a band in 1927), and the Pelican Dance Hall at the intersection of Rampart Street and Gravier Street; it is not clear whether different venues or alternative names for one or more venues are involved.

——. **Perseverance Hall.** 1642 North Villere Street. The hall was the headquarters of the Benevolent Mutual Aid Association (founded 13 November 1853). Much fine jazz was presented there in the early decades of the 20th century. The venue was later used as a church. It should not be confused with the Perseverance Hall (a Masonic hall) at 907 St. Claude Avenue and Dumaine Street (now in Louis Armstrong Park).

——. **Pete Lala's.** 1300 Customhouse Street, at Marais Street. The premises included a bar room in front and a dance hall behind and operated variously as a nightclub, café, and dance hall. Named after its owner (whose real name was Pete Ciaccio), it flourished from 1906 until 1917, and according to the Blue Book (the guidebook to the African-American brothel district) operated a non-segregationist policy. Among the musicians who played there were Freddie Keppard, Kid Ory, King Oliver, Sidney Bechet, Manuel Manetta, Zue Robertson, and Big Eye Louis Nelson.

——. **Pete's Place.** 231 Bourbon Street (1968–77); 2 Poydras Street (from 1977). Pete Fountain opened this venue with his ten-piece band in 1968. In 1977 it moved to the third floor of the New Orleans Hilton Riverside, where Fountain led smaller bands into the new century.

——. **Phillips Café.** See 101 Ranch.

——. **Poodle Dog.** Liberty Street and Bienville Street. Cabaret. Active in the 1910s, it provided an early engagement for Buddy Petit around 1916; Sidney Bechet played with Petit's band during its residency.

——. **Preservation Hall.** 726 St. Peter Street. It opened in June 1961 in premises adjacent to Larry Borenstein's art gallery (for illustration *see* Humphrey), where Borenstein had been mounting informal performances by veteran jazz musicians during the 1950s. Its activities were directed variously by Borenstein and Grayson Mills, and Allan and Sandra Jaffe, and its presentation of New Orleans jazz quickly became internationally renowned. The resident band, known as the Preservation Hall Jazz Band, has been led by such musicians as Punch Miller, Kid Thomas Valentine, and George Lewis (i); it remains active in the new century.

BIBLIOGRAPHY

L. Borenstein and B. Russell: *Preservation Hall Portraits* (Baton Rouge, LA, 1968) [photographs by N. Rockmore]

W. Carter: *Preservation Hall: Music from the Heart* (Wheatley, Oxford, England, and New York, 1991, rev. 2/1999)

<http://www.preservationhall.com> (2001)

——. **Providence Hall.** 2241 South Liberty Street. It was probably in existence by the 1890s and offered jazz performances from an early period: it was one of the venues where Buddy Bolden led his band. The building was demolished in 1937 and a church built in its place.

——. **Puppy House.** Jazz was performed there from at least 1939, when Sidney Arodin was resident for a year's engagement.

——. **Pup's Café.** See La Vida Dance Hall.

——. **Red Onion.** 762 South Rampart Street. This low-class nightclub was situated in a dangerous area and was regarded by musicians as an unpleasant venue in which to work. Jelly Roll Morton, Louis Armstrong, Johnny Dodds, Sidney Bechet, and Lee Collins were among those who played there. Later, in New York in 1924, Armstrong recorded in several groups called the Red Onion Jazz Babies, the last of which included Bechet.

——. **Rhythm Club.** 3000 Jackson Avenue. A large venue in the uptown area, it offered jazz from at least the late 1930s. Joseph Robichaux' New Orleans Rhythm Boys appeared there in 1938.

——. **Rice's Café.** Marais Street and Customhouse Street (1501 Iberville Street). Cabaret. It was situated on the downtown side of the intersection, opposite Pete Lala's, and it catered for an exclusively white clientèle. Manuel Perez played there regularly.

——. **Ringside Club** [Ringside Café]. Dauphine Street and Bienville Street. In existence by the early 1920s, it was run by the bantamweight champion prizefighter Pete Herman. The New Orleans Rhythm Kings played there in 1927, and among others who appeared during the 1920s were Sidney Arodin and Wingy Manone.

——. **Roosevelt Hotel.** See Blue Room.

——. **St. Katherine's Hall.** South Liberty Street near Tulane Avenue. It was around the corner from St. Katherine's Church (which was at 1509 Tulane Avenue) and was probably connected with the church. The hall was an important venue for dancing, and many jazz groups played there, including those of Kid Ory, Bunk Johnson, King Oliver, and John Robichaux, as well as the Crescent Band, led by Mutt Carey's brother the trombonist Jack Carey. The entire block was demolished in the 1960s to make way for the Tulane University Medical Center.

——. **San Jacinto Hall.** 1422 Dumaine Street. It was one of a score of halls in the city that were hired by social clubs for their dances, and jazz was played there from at least the early 1920s until the 1960s; it was destroyed by fire on 9 January 1967. The hall became noted for the presentation of battles of bands between such groups as Sidney Desvigne's Southern Syncopators (which was resident around 1928) and those led by Papa Celestin and Joseph Robichaux. Other musicians to appear there included Bunk Johnson. It was also used for a number of recordings made by Bill Russell's American Music label; the last of these sessions took place in December 1965.

——. **Silver Slipper.** See New Slipper Night Club.

——. **Snug Harbor.** 626 Frenchmen Street. Nightclub and restaurant. Opened in the 1980s, it presents live music every night and has become one of the city's most important venues for the presentation for jazz in modern styles, both by local and by visiting musicians; Ellis Marsalis played there on a regular basis, as did Nicholas Payton, and the group Astral Project (including Tony Dagradi, Steve Masakowski, and John Vidacovich). Steve Lacy, Peter Bernstein, Peter Martin, JoAnne Brackeen, Herman Riley, and Donald Harrison are among those who were appearing there early in 2001. (<http://www.snugjazz.com> (2001))

——. **Storyville District.** 125 Bourbon Street. Opened in 1999 as a long-term venture between the Brennan restauranteur family and the jazz festival organizer Quint Davis, the Storyville District presents jazz daily in three adjoining venues – Jazz Alley, the Jazz Parlor, and the Storyville Jazz Café – with performances ranging in style from traditional New Orleans bands to modern Latin-based groups. Sunday brunch often features the New Orleans Ragtime Orchestra. (<http://www.thestoryvilledistrict.com> (2001))

——. **Storyville Jazz Café.** See Storyville District.

——. **Storyville Jazz Hall.** 1104 Decatur Street. Situated near the French Market, this hall opened in the mid-1980s. It presented music on almost every night of the week and offered a wide repertory of jazz and rock styles.

——. **Tin Roof Café** [Tin Roof Dance Hall]. There are conflicting accounts of both the name and the location of this venue. According to Abbie Brunies and other musicians, it was situated at Washington Avenue and Claiborne Avenue in a large old building which by the mid-1950s had become a vinegar factory; Brunies's identification is probably correct, but others give Tchoupitoulas Street and Napoleon Avenue as the address. The Tin Roof was active as a venue for jazz performance until 1910 and later lent its name to the *Tin Roof Blues*, which became a standard after being recorded by the New Orleans Rhythm Kings in 1923 (Gen. 5105).

——. **Tipitina's.** 501 Napoleon Street. Nightclub. It was formerly the 501 Club, founded as a venue for the rhythm-and-blues musician Professor Longhair in his declining years, and took the name Tipitina's in 1977. It has presented both local and visiting musicians playing in a variety of styles, including rock, blues, and rhythm-and-blues, with jazz featured on occasion.

——. **Tokyo Gardens.** Ballroom. It was situated in the resort at Spanish Fort, near where the Bayou St. John runs into Lake Pontchartrain. Among the jazz groups that performed there was a band led by the cornetist Johnny Bayersdorffer, which was resident in the summer of 1924.

——. **Tom Anderson's Annex.** See Anderson's Annex.

——. **Tom Anderson's New Cabaret and Restaurant** [Tom Anderson's Saloon]. 122–6 North Rampart Street. It opened some time after 1912 as a successor to Anderson's Café (see above); owned by Tom Anderson, who controlled the African-American brothel district of the city, it was run by his son-in-law George Delsa. Among the leading jazz musicians who worked there were Louis Armstrong, who was associated with the club in the early 1920s before he left New Orleans to join King Oliver in Chicago, and Albert Nicholas (1923–4), whose six-piece resident band included Luis Russell, Paul Barbarin, and Barney Bigard.

——. **Toodlum's Bar.** It occupied premises near Perdido Street in the Storyville district, which had formerly housed Buddy Bartley's Club. Its owner, Toodlum, also organized lawn parties, and he engaged jazz musicians for these as well as for work in the bar. Among the performers he booked in the 1910s were Sidney Bechet and King Oliver.

——. **Tranchina's Restaurant.** It was situated in the resort at Spanish Fort, near where the Bayou St. John runs into Lake Pontchartrain. Jazz was performed there from at least 1918, when A. J. Piron formed an orchestra to begin an engagement at the restaurant that continued intermittently until 1923 (for illustration *see* Bands, fig.1).

——. **Tuxedo Dance Hall.** 219 Franklin Street. It was opened in 1909 by Harry Parker, who had been the partner of Billy Phillips at the 101 Ranch (see above). A band led by Papa Celestin, which included Peter Bocage, accompanied the dancing there from 1910 until 1913. On the day after Easter that year Parker and Phillips were murdered in a brawl arising from their business rivalry and the hall was closed by the police. The Villa Café (see below) opened shortly afterwards in the same building.

——. **The 25.** See Big 25.

——. **Tyler's.** 5234 Magazine Street. Active from at least the 1980s, it became one of the most thriving venues in the city for the performance of modern styles of jazz.

——. **Villa Café** [Villa Cabaret]. 221 Franklin Street. Situated in the same building as the Tuxedo Dance Hall (see above), it opened some time shortly after the Tuxedo's activities were discontinued in 1913. The jazz musicians who appeared there in its early years included Papa Celestin and Manuel Manetta.

For other venues in the New Orleans area see Jefferson Parish and Milneburg. For riverboats that plied into and out of the city see Mississippi River.

BIBLIOGRAPHY

New Orleans

P. E. Miller: "Fifty Years of New Orleans Jazz," *Esquire's Jazz Book* (New York, 1944–6) [three vols., pubd annually; abridged P. Miller and R. Venables (London, 1947)]

A. Rose and E. Souchon: *New Orleans Jazz: a Family Album* (Baton Rouge, LA, 1967, rev. and enlarged 3/1984)

R. J. Martinez, ed.: *Portraits of New Orleans Jazz: its People and Places* (Jefferson, LA, 1971)

A. Rose: *Storyville, New Orleans: being an Authentic Illustrated Account of the Notorious Red-light District* (Tuscaloosa, AL, and London, 1974/*R*1989)

R. Spedale, Jr.: *A Guide to Jazz in New Orleans* (New Orleans, 1984)

J. Hannusch: *I Hear You Knockin': the Sound of New Orleans Rhythm and Blues* (Ville Platte, LA, 1985)

K. Koenig: *Jazz Map of New Orleans* (New Orleans, 1985) [annotated map]

——: *"Just a Closer Walk": the Walker's Guide to Jazz's History in the French Quarter* (New Orleans, 1988)

E. Wengel: "Music Spots in the Downtown New Orleans Red Light District," *New Orleans Music*, iv/5 (1994), 16

New Rochelle, NY. **Armory.** 270 Main Street. The Os-We-Go Club presented the bands of Don Redman and Claude Hopkins for one-night stands at the Armory in April and May 1934. A later one-night stand, on 26 April 1948, was by the Jimmie Lunceford Orchestra directed by Eddie Wilcox and Joe Thomas (iii).

——. **Glen Island Casino.** Shore Road. Dance hall. It offered jazz for dancing by the late 1920s. The Casa Loma Orchestra was resident there in 1931, and during the 1930s numerous swing bands appeared, including those led by Tommy Dorsey, Jimmy Dorsey, Benny Goodman, Glenn Miller, and Alberto Socarras.

New York. **Adrian's Tap Room.** President Hotel. It was opened, probably in November 1934, by Adrian Rollini, who also directed its activities; it was situated in a basement room in the hotel and quickly became a fashionable venue, both with New York society and with musicians. Throughout the 1930s Rollini engaged numerous prominent swing performers to play there, including Fats Waller, Willie "the Lion" Smith, John Kirby's quartet, Wingy Manone, Joe Marsala, and Albert Nicholas.

——. **Alamo Café.** 253 West 125th Street. Situated in Harlem, in the basement of the Hurtig and Seamon burlesque house, this rowdy club presented dixieland bands for white audiences. Jimmy Durante served as house pianist from 1915 to 1917, the dancer and singer Eddie Jackson performed from 1917 to 1921, and Durante's New Orleans Jazz Band, comprising Achille Baquet, the trombonist Frank Lhotak, Frank Christian, and Johnny Stein, was resident there from 1919 to November 1921. In 1925 it became an African-American venue, the Swanee Club (see below).

——. **Alhambra Ballroom.** 2100 Seventh Avenue. Located above the Alhambra Theater, it opened on 13 September 1929 with the bands of Benny Carter, Luis Russell, and Zach Whyte, the Missourians, and Johnson's Happy Pals playing alternately for dancers. The Gene Rodgers Revellers, which included Otis Johnson and Rudy Powell, served as intermission band for one year. The ballroom was a venue for leading Harlem-based African-American bands into the mid-1940s.

——. **Alhambra Theater.** 2100 Seventh Avenue. It was built by Percy G. Williams around 1905 and later sold to the B. F. Keith chain of theaters. Until 1926 African-Americans were allowed only in the second balcony, but thereafter advertisements read "sit where you please." Under the direction of Milton Gosdorfer, the Alhambra Theater became an important circuit venue, rivaling the Lafayette Theatre in popularity. Gosdorfer staged variety shows that often included musical acts, and among the musicians who performed for him were Bessie Smith (1927) and Cab Calloway (1931); Edgar Hayes led the resident orchestra there from August 1927 until 1930, when a band led by Emmett Mathews took over. It later became a motion picture theater.

——. **Ali Baba.** 400 East 59th Street. From 1963 until at least 1967 Louis Metcalf led a band there, with Sonny White among his sidemen.

——. **Ali's Alley.** North Greene Street between Spring Street and Broome Street. It was opened by Rashied Ali in 1972 in a village loft under the name Studio 77, which he changed in 1974 to Ali's Alley. It presented mainly free jazz, and to begin with Ali was the principal performer; once the club became established, however, other major free-jazz musicians led groups there, among them Gunter Hampel, Archie Shepp, and Perry Robinson. By 1976 Ali had converted the premises into a bar, restaurant, and club. The venue closed in summer 1979.

——. **Alt. Coffee.** 137 Avenue A. A Monday-night jazz series at this venue featured Andrew D'Angelo and the drummer Matt Hollenbeck, among others. The club has also presented jazz on Friday nights.

——. **Angry Squire** [The Squire]. 216 Seventh Avenue. Bar and restaurant. It opened in 1981 in premises that had formerly been used as a factory and has presented performances by many prominent contemporary-jazz musicians, including Junior Mance (1981), Hal Galper, Walter Bishop (1983), Barry Harris and Jaki Byard (1984), Scott Hamilton and Harold Ousley (1985), and Dakota Staton (1987). The Angry Squire appears to have closed in the late 1980s; it reopened as The Squire shortly afterwards and continued with a similar music policy into the early 1990s before closing once again.

——. **Apollo Theatre.** 253 West 125th Street. Variety theater. It was opened in 1913 under the direction of Frank Schiffman and Leo Brecher, who had earlier owned the Lafayette Theatre. In the 1920s it staged various shows in which jazz played some part, but it came into its own as a venue for jazz only in the 1930s. The building was bought by Sidney Cohen late in 1933, and structural renovations were set in train. The theater reopened on 26 January 1934 under the management of Morris Sussman and quickly became the center of Harlem entertainment and an internationally known venue.

During the 1930s and 1940s, particularly, the Apollo offered performances by all the leading jazz musicians, and an engagement there was regarded as an important landmark in a musician's career. The great swing bands (among them those of Duke Ellington, Fletcher Henderson, Chick Webb (for illustration *see* Webb, chick), Count Basie, Cab Calloway, and Benny Carter), singers (Bessie Smith, Lena Horne, Ella Fitzgerald, and Sarah Vaughan), pianists (James P. Johnson, Lil Armstrong, and Fats Waller), and jazz dancers and entertainers (Buck and Bubbles and Bill Robinson) all appeared on the Apollo's stage. The theater also played an important role in the discovery of new talent; it mounted competitions and weekly sessions specifically for amateur musicians. Although it continued to be active after the 1940s, its heyday as a jazz venue was over and it later specialized in presenting rhythm-and-blues, gospel, and soul music.

The Apollo Theatre on 125th Street should not be confused with that on 42nd Street, usually referred to as the old Apollo, which flourished in the 1920s.

BIBLIOGRAPHY

J. Schiffman: *Uptown: the Story of Harlem's Apollo Theatre* (New York, 1971)

T. Fox: *Showtime at the Apollo* (New York, 1983/*R*1993)

J. Schiffman: *Harlem Heyday: a Pictorial History of Modern Black Show Business and the Apollo Theatre* (Buffalo, 1984)

——. **Arcadia Ballroom.** Broadway and West 53rd Street. It was opened in 1924 by the brothers Jay and John Faggin (or Fagin) and flourished until at least the late 1930s. By 1929 the manager was H. M. Corrigan. Among the numerous jazz musicians and groups who worked there were the Mound City Blue Blowers, Frankie Trumbauer and Bix Beiderbecke (1925), Isham Jones, Benny Carter (from 1928),

4. 52nd street at night

Luis Russell (late 1920s), Sammy Stewart (1930), Sam Wooding (early 1930s), Charlie Turner (1934), and Roy Eldridge (1939). Coleman Hawkins formed a big band for a residency there beginning in November 1939. Jay Faggin also owned the Golden Gate Ballroom and the Harlem Uproar House (see below).

——. **Arthur's Tavern.** 57 Grove Street. In the 1950s this club in Greenwich Village presented trios of piano, double bass, and drums, notably a lengthy residency by the pianist Loumell Morgan; modern-jazz players such as Brew Moore frequently sat in. From the 1960s into the new century the repertory has centered on traditional jazz, and the resident band is the Grove Street Stompers. (<http://www.arthurstavernnyc.com> (2001))

——. **Audubon Ballroom.** Broadway at 166th Street. A small venue, it offered bop performances in the 1940s. In January 1949 or January 1950 (sources differ) a sextet that included Sonny Rollins, Art Blakey, J. J. Johnson, and Miles Davis played there. The club is celebrated in the title of Rollins's composition *Audubon*, recorded by Johnson in 1949 (Savoy 947).

——. **Audubon Bar and Grill.** 3956 Broadway. Located in a business complex on the site of Harlem's former Audubon Ballroom, the Audubon Bar and Grill opened in March 1996. Jazz is offered on Monday nights, and among the performers who have appeared there are Gary Bartz, Hamiet Bluiett, James Carter, Hilton Ruiz, and Dakota Staton. (<http://cait.cpmc.columbia.edu:88/news/reporter/archives/repo_v08n04_0005.html> (2001))

——. **Augie's.** 2751 Broadway. Active from the 1970s, it regularly presented jazz until its closure in August 1998. Eddie Henderson, Cecil Payne, and Peter Bernstein were among those who appeared there. In April 1999 Augie's former manager, Paul Stache, opened a new jazz club, Smoke (see below), at this location.

BIBLIOGRAPHY

L. Williams: "Neighborhood Report: Upper West Side: Jazz Spot Escapes Auction Hammer," *New York Times* (22 Sept 1996)

C. Kilgannon: "Neighborhood Report: Upper West Side: Broadway Stores' Revolving Doors," *New York Times* (28 Feb 1999)

——. **Bamboo Inn.** 2389 Seventh Avenue. It was opened late in 1926 by Honey Brown as a combined Chinese restaurant and taxi dance (i.e., dime-a-dance) hall; the Palace Garden Club (see below) had previously occupied the building, but it was closed by the police and the Bamboo Inn opened in its place. Early in 1927 it was renovated and made into an expensive supper club, but after suffering a fire in summer of that year it resumed its existence as a Chinese restaurant and dance hall. Brown played at the club in his own band, which was led by the pianist Willie Wilkins and included the banjoist John Marrero and the trombonist Clyde Bernhardt. Among other jazz musicians who performed there were Jimmy Archey in a band led by the reed player Edgar Campbell (1926–7); Archey, Greeley Walton, Harry Carney, Russell Procope, Charlie Holmes, and the pianist Joe Steele in a band led by Henri Saparo (1927); Archey, Langston Curl, Ward Pinkett, Holmes, and Manzie Johnson in a band led by Steele (1927–8); and Elmer Snowden, who worked there before moving to Smalls' Paradise. The Bamboo Inn closed in late 1929 and a new club, the Dunbar Palace (see below), took over the premises.

——. **Bamville Club.** 65 West 129th Street. It opened in October 1924 in premises that had formerly housed the Rendezvous Cabaret (see below) and took its name from the title of the successful show *In Bamville*, by Noble Sissle and Eubie Blake. Horace Henderson's Collegians played there in 1924. Following a temporary closure the club was reopened in November 1926 by the orchestras of Fletcher Henderson, Jimmy Wade, and Fess Williams. In mid-1927 it became Club Ebony. Sources are unclear, but Elmer Snowden seems to have held residencies at both the Bamville Club and Club Ebony.

——. **Band Box.** 161 West 131st Street. The club was active from the 1920s to around 1935 on the second floor of a building that contained several rehearsal rooms; it was managed by the cornet player Addington Major, who had earlier played with Mamie Smith. The Band Box became a popular after-hours venue with musicians playing engagements elsewhere in the city; among those who took part in the impromptu jam sessions there was Jabbo Smith. By the 1960s the premises had become a funeral home.

——. **Bandbox.** Near Broadway north of 52nd Street. A basement venue close to Birdland, it was opened in summer 1953. During its short existence (it lasted only a matter of months) it engaged a number of prominent jazz musicians to lead bands for short residencies; they included Sidney Bechet (with Herb Flemming, Panama Francis, and Dick Wellstood), Earl Hines, Muggsy Spanier, Count Basie, and Machito. Art Tatum also played there.

——. **Barron's Club** [Barron Wilkins' Club]. 2259 Seventh Avenue/198 West 134th Street. One of the first large clubs in Harlem, it was opened by Barron Wilkins around 1915 in the basement of a building at the corner of Seventh Avenue and 134th Street. In its first years it featured leading stride pianists, including James P. Johnson and Willie "the Lion" Smith. Mamie Smith sang there before 1920. Among the musicians whom Wilkins engaged in the early to mid-1920s were Sam Wooding and his Society Syncopators (early 1920s), Duke Ellington (as a solo pianist, 1923), the Washingtonians, led by Elmer Snowden (1923), and Joe Turner (i) with Hilton Jefferson. The club's activities seem to have ceased around the time of Wilkins's death in 1926. Venues at the same location in later years – notably the Theatrical Grill and Monroe's Uptown House – used the 134th Street address rather than Wilkins's Seventh Avenue address.

——. **Basement Brownie's.** 152 West 133rd Street. From around 1930 to 1935 this was an after-hours venue for pianists, notably Fats Waller, James P. Johnson, Willie "the Lion" Smith, and Art Tatum.

——. **Basin Street.** Broadway and West 51st Street. Situated in the Roseland Theater building, it was active in the early 1950s under the direction of Ralph Watkins. Buck Clayton (1953–4) and Erroll Garner (1954–5) were among the musicians who played there. The club had closed by 1959 and the building was eventually demolished to make way for the City Squire Motel.

——. **Basin Street East.** 137 East 48th Street. It was founded as the Casa Cugat in 1959, after the closure of Basin Street, and was managed by Ralph Watkins. It flourished into the 1960s, engaging some of the most important names in jazz of the day, including Lionel Hampton, Dicky Wells, and Rex Stewart (all 1959), Erroll Garner (1960–61), Count Basie (1962, 1964), and Duke Ellington (1965); Louis Armstrong was also frequently heard there.

——. **Bechet's.** 1319 Third Avenue. It was active for a short period in the early 1980s as a venue for traditional jazz and swing. Among the musicians who played there were Kenny Davern and Warren Vaché.

——. **Bemelmans Bar.** Madison Avenue at East 76th Street. One of the several venues within the Hotel Carlyle to offer music for the entertainment of patrons, it has been active as a jazz lounge from at least the early 1970s. It has presented mostly solo performers, notably Marian McPartland (from 1974) and Barbara Carroll (from 1976) – both of whom formed lasting connections – and George Shearing (from 1984). Carroll has continued to play there into the new century.

——. **Birdland.** 1678 Broadway (to 1965); 2745 Broadway (1988–96); 315 West 44th Street (from November 1996). The original club occupied premises that had earlier housed clubs called the Ebony (in the late 1920s), the Ubangi, and the Clique (1948–9). It took its name from Charlie Parker's nickname "Bird" and opened on 15 December 1949 with Parker playing. Under the direction of Morris Levy it became known as one of the foremost venues for bop, and it offered performances by all the leading players in the style; Parker appeared there regularly (for illustration *see* Parker, Charlie, fig.2), and the club also became Count Basie's New York headquarters during the 1950s. From the early days Birdland maintained its own radio wire and booth (nationwide broadcasts were later made from the club in conjunction with NBC); the resident disc jockey was the renowned Symphony Sid (Torin), and the master of ceremonies was Pee Wee Marquette, who became notorious for hassling the musicians. Many of the broadcasts were also recorded and later issued on record labels owned by Boris Rose. Numerous other recordings were made at the club, including one in 1955 at which Basie recorded George Shearing's composition *Lullaby of Birdland*. By this time the club was managed by Oscar Goodstein. Later, performances given in 1963 by John Coltrane's quartet, which was resident at the club for several periods from 1963 to 1965, were recorded and issued as the highly acclaimed album *Live at Birdland* (Imp. 50).

Birdland's fortunes declined immediately thereafter. It closed in 1965 and the premises were eventually taken over by the rhythm-and-blues and rock-and-roll singer Lloyd Price, who opened the Turntable there. But the venue's old name continued to be celebrated, largely through the enormous popularity of Joe Zawinul's composition *Birdland*, which was recorded by Weather Report (1976) as an instrumental piece and was later supplied with lyrics by Manhattan Transfer, and then through the establishment of a new club of the same name at 2745 Broadway. According to its website, this opened in 1986, though Watrous gives

1988. In any event jazz performances began only in the latter year, from which time it focused on bop and related styles, although at first such avant-garde performers as Anthony Davis, Mark Helias, Gerry Hemingway, and Dewey Redman appeared as well. In 1996 Birdland relocated to West 44th Street, where on Sundays, Mondays, and Tuesdays performances are reserved respectively for Chico O'Farrill's Afro-Cuban Jazz Big Band, Toshiko Akiyoshi's Jazz Orchestra featuring Lew Tabackin, and the Famous Duke Ellington Orchestra directed by Paul Ellington or Jack Jeffers; the remaining evenings are usually held as three- or four-day residencies, involving, for example, groups led by Cedar Walton and Peter Bernstein (both March 2001) and James Moody (April 2001), and the trio of Paul Bley, Gary Peacock, and Paul Motian (April 2001).

BIBLIOGRAPHY

B. Rusch: "Eddie Lockjaw Davis," *Cadence*, xiv/1 (1988), 16

P. Watrous: "Pop/jazz: Jazz for Dessert in Club-restaurants where Music is on the Menu," *New York Times* (9 Sept 1988)

J. Pareles: "New Night Life in Midtown Manhattan," *New York Times* (13 Dec 1996)

E. Louie: "Another Chance at Flight for a Venerable Jazz Club," *New York Times* (6 March 1997)

<http://www.birdlandjazz.com/history.html> (2001)

——. **Black Cat.** West Broadway, in Greenwich Village. It was active during the 1930s and presented jazz performances by leading bands and musicians. A quintet led by the tenor saxophonist Lonnie Simmons, the members of which included Freddie Green and Kenny Clarke, played there in 1937. (M. Hennessey: *Klook: the Story of Kenny Clarke* (London, 1990), 18)

——. **Blue Note.** 131 West 3rd Street. It was founded by Dan Bensusan in 1981 and quickly established itself as an important venue for mainstream jazz and bop, offering major musicians the opportunity to hold residencies in a club ambience. Numerous well-known players have appeared there, including Dizzy Gillespie, Tal Farlow, Oscar Peterson, Gerry Mulligan, Johnny Griffin and Eddie "Lockjaw" Davis, Toshiko Akiyoshi, Jaco Pastorius, the Modern Jazz Quartet, Phil Woods, Illinois Jacquet, Herbie Hancock, Cassandra Wilson, Tito Puente, McCoy Tyner, Max Roach, Ray Brown, and Jimmy Smith. Keith Jarrett and Chick Corea both recorded sets of albums at the club. The Blue Note also broadcasts performances over the Internet on Monday and Thursday nights, on which lesser-known artists are usually featured. In addition to its regular evening shows, the club holds after-hours sessions.

Bensusan runs the parent company Blue Note International, Inc., which has established jazz club franchises; as of 2001 there were three Blue Note clubs in Japan (Tokyo, Osaka, and Fukuoka) and one in Las Vegas. The parent company is also a partner in the B. B. King Blues Club, located in Times Square in New York, and in the late 1990s it established the record company and label Half Note, on which it has released recordings made at the 3rd Street venue, mainly by lesser-known performers.

BIBLIOGRAPHY

L. Pellegrinelli: "A Guided Tour of America's Most Fascinating Jazz Clubs," <http://www.newmusicbox.org/third-person/jan00/bluenote.html> (2000)

J. Woodard: "Label Watch: in the House: Half Note," *JT*, xxx/1 (2000), 81

<http://www.bluenote.net> (2001)

<http://www.halfnote.net> (2001)

<http://www.webcom.com/%7Einotes/bluenot2.html> (2001)

——. **Blue Room.** Eighth Avenue at West 44th Street. This small venue within the Lincoln Hotel engaged small groups, solo performers, and big bands; Count Basie played three extended engagements there between 1943 and 1945.

——. **Blue Water Grill.** See Downstairs at the Metropolis.

——. **Boomer's.** 340 Bleecker Street. Established in 1971, it specialized in the presentation of bop and soul jazz, offering performances by Barry Harris, Junior Mance, Joe Newman, Junior Cook, Cedar Walton, and Woody Shaw, among others; Walton recorded there in 1973 (*A Night at Boomer's*, Muse 5010, 5022). The club closed in 1977.

——. **Bop City.** 1619 Broadway. It opened in 1948, but it was soon overshadowed by the nearby Birdland, which was founded the following year, and it survived only into the early 1950s. The club's activities were directed briefly by Ralph Watkins, who promoted programs of bop, swing, traditional jazz, rhythm-and-blues, and pop music there; among the jazz musicians to appear were Fletcher Henderson (1948), Artie Shaw (1949), Mary Lou Williams (early 1950s), and Louis Armstrong's All Stars, who gave a number of successful performances.

——. **Bottom Line.** 15 West 4th Street. In spacious premises in Greenwich Village, it was opened in 1974 as a rock and folk club, though jazz was occasionally presented there from the beginning – Grover Washington, Jr., appeared in 1974 and Charles Mingus also worked there in the mid-1970s. In the 1980s jazz formed a small but constant element of the repertory, and performers included Sun Ra and Dexter Gordon (both 1980), Andrew Cyrille and Lester Bowie (both 1983), Sonny Rollins (1984), Ralph Towner, John Abercrombie and Makoto Ozone (1985), and John Scofield (1987). By the 1990s jazz offerings were much more infrequent. (<http://www.bottomlinecabaret.com/index.html> (2001))

——. **Bowman's Grill.** 92 St. Nicholas Place. Overlooking the Polo Grounds (where the New York Giants baseball team played), this lounge presented jazz trios and organists from 1955 to 1958, when Bowman's Grill became Branker's Lounge (and, perhaps coincidentally, when the Giants abandoned New York for San Francisco).

——. **Bradley's.** 70 University Place. Piano bar. Named for its owner, Bradley Cunningham, it flourished as a venue for mainstream jazz and bop from the 1970s into the mid-1990s. It specialized in the presentation of duos, usually consisting of piano and double bass, piano and guitar, or guitar and double bass. Among those who appeared there were the pianists John Hicks, Cedar Walton, Duke Jordan, Barry Harris, Jimmie Rowles, Tommy Flanagan, JoAnne Brackeen, Hank Jones, and Kirk Lightsey, and the double bass players Red Mitchell, George Mraz, Rufus Reid, and Calvin Hill. Following Cunningham's death (1988) Bradley's was run by his wife, Wendy Cunningham, whose bookings, while continuing to present piano and double bass duos, extended to small bop groups (i.e., incorporating reeds, brass, and drums), including notably those led by Roy Hargrove (1991), Stephen Scott, Jacky Terrasson, and Bruce Barth. The club closed in October 1996.

BIBLIOGRAPHY

W. Balliett: *Barney, Bradley, and Max: 16 Portraits in Jazz* (New York, 1989), 53

P. Watrous: "Quietly, Sorrowfully, a Jazz Club Dies," *New York Times* (19 Oct 1996)

——. **Branker's Lounge.** 92 St. Nicholas Place. It succeeded Bowman's Grill (see above) in 1958. Kenny Burrell and Sonny Red were among those who appeared there into the mid-1960s.

——. **Breakfast Club.** See Lenox Club.

——. **Brittwood.** 594 Lenox Avenue. Bar and grill. It offered jazz from around 1932 to 1942. Among the musicians who held residencies there were the pianist Willie Gant, Frankie Newton, Pete Brown, and Clyde Hart; the house pianist for a considerable period was Don Frye.

——. **Broadway Joe's.** 315 West 46th Street. Bar. It offered jazz performances from around 1980; Warren Vaché held a residency there in 1983.

——. **Café Bohemia.** 15 Barrow Street. Located in premises formerly occupied by the Pied Piper (see below), it was owned by Jimmy Giarofolo and opened in the spring of 1955 with Oscar Pettiford as director of music. Pettiford himself led a band there, and it was the site of Cannonball Adderley's New York début in 1955. The name of the club is commemorated in Kenny Clarke's tune *Bohemia after Dark*, recorded on the album of the same name (1955, Savoy 12017) with Adderley among the sidemen.

——. **Café Carlyle.** Madison Avenue at East 76th Street. Like the rather less well-known Bemelmans Bar in the Hotel Carlyle (see above), the Café Carlyle specializes in presenting solo pianists, duos, and small groups. The performer most closely associated with the club is the pianist Bobby Short, who first appeared there in the 1970s and continued to do so into the new century; others who have held extended residencies are Marian McPartland (1979–82, recording an album there in her first year), George Shearing and Brian Torff (1979–81), and Joe Bushkin (1983). The Modern Jazz Quartet played at the café in the early 1990s, and Barbara Carroll recorded there in 1991, as did Short in 1993.

——. **Café Pierre.** Pierre Hotel, Fifth Avenue at East 61st Street. Restaurant. This venue within the hotel offered jazz from at least the late 1970s – Bucky Pizzarelli played there regularly between 1979 and 1983, as did Hank Jones – but by the 1990s jazz was rarely presented.

——. **Café Society.** (Downtown): 2 Sheridan Square; (Uptown): 128 East 58th Street. The downtown venue of Café Society opened on 18 (or, by another account, on 22) December 1938 under the direction of Barney Josephson, who presented Billie Holiday (in one of her most important engagements), Frankie Newton's band, and the Boogie-Woogie Trio, consisting of Albert Ammons, Pete Johnson, and Meade "Lux" Lewis (making their New York nightclub début). Lena Horne followed Holiday into the club and remained until 1941. Among other jazz musicians who appeared there were Joe Sullivan (October 1939–1940), James P. Johnson (June 1940), Kenny Kersey (*c*1940), Teddy Wilson (1941), Lee Young's sextet (September 1942), Eddie Heywood's sextet (mid-1940s), John Kirby (1945), J. C. Heard (1946), and Hayes Alvis, Buck Clayton, Art Tatum, and Sarah Vaughan (all *c*1947). Fletcher Henderson played his last engagement there, leading a sextet in 1950, and Hot Lips Page led one of his last groups at the café in 1953. The club also staged jam sessions in 1941, directed by George Simon and Leonard Feather.

Following the success of his downtown venue, on 8 October 1940 Barney Josephson opened a second club uptown, between Lexington and Third avenues on East 58th Street. A number of the musicians mentioned directly above played at both of Josephson's clubs, as did Edmond Hall, who led a sextet (1944–6), and Mary Lou Williams (1944–7). Those who apparently appeared only at the uptown venue, which closed in December 1947, include Mildred Bailey and Count Basie.

A third club named Café Society, unrelated to the two famous earlier venues, opened at 915 Broadway around July 1987 and featured swing music for dancing. It had closed by 1993; later Metronome (see below) was located there.

BIBLIOGRAPHY

G. Hoefer: "Cafe Society Downtown and Uptown: the Wrong Place for the Right People," *Down Beat Music '67* (Chicago, 1966), 73
D. W. Stowe: "The Politics of Café Society," *Journal of American History*, lxxxiv/4 (1998), 1384
R. Alexander: "A Step Back to Supper Clubs and Swing," *New York Times* (15 Dec 1991)

——. **Café Zanzibar.** See Zanzibar.

——. **Cajun.** 129 Eighth Avenue. Open from the mid-1980s, this restaurant has regularly presented dixieland and swing bands.

——. **Capitol Palace.** 575 Lenox Avenue. Owned by Johnny Powell, it was opened in 1922 under the management of Rudolph Brown. Among the musicians who played there were Fats Waller (early 1920s), Willie "the Lion" Smith (1920s), the Broadway Syncopators, led by the reed player Billy Paige (1924), Lloyd and Cecil Scott (1925–8), Lizzie Miles (1926), Cliff Jackson (late 1920s), and the banjoist Bernie Robinson (1927). The Capitol Palace closed in 1929 and the venue reopened as the Saratoga Club (see below).

——. **Carlos I.** 432 Sixth Avenue. Restaurant. From the 1980s it offered jazz performances for the entertainment of diners. Musicians who appeared there include Chico Freeman, Bobby Watson, Benny Carter, David Murray, Clark Terry, and, in 1989, Hank Jones. Hamiet Bluiett recorded an album there (1986), as did Billy Bang (1987) and Carter (1988). The club appears to have closed in 1990.

——. **Carlyle Hotel.** See Bemelmans Bar; Café Carlyle.

——. **Carnegie Hall.** West 57th Street and Seventh Avenue. Concert hall. It opened on 5 May 1891 and has offered performances in all styles of music by musicians from all over the world to audiences that can number nearly 3000. Concerts related to jazz and its origins have been given there from the first years of the 20th century. From around 1912 to 1914 James Reese Europe organized events in aid of the Clef Club, which aimed to promote African-American performers. A number of commemorative and celebratory concerts have taken place in the hall. In 1928 a tribute to W. C. Handy featured James P. Johnson and Fats Waller. The most notable event of this kind was the first "From Spirituals to Swing" concert (23 December 1938), organized by John Hammond in memory of Bessie Smith. Among the musicians who participated were Sidney Bechet, who played in a sextet with James P. Johnson, Jo Jones, Tommy Ladnier, Walter Page, and Dan Minor; appearances by the boogie-woogie pianists Meade "Lux" Lewis, Albert Ammons, and Pete Johnson inspired a general kindling of interest in the boogie-woogie style. The great impact made by Hammond's first venture led to the staging of a second event in 1939 (24 December), and in 1955 Count Basie adapted Hammond's title for his concert "Spirituals to Jazz Hour" on 6 May; Hammond presented a further "From Spirituals to Swing" concert in 1967. The hall was also used regularly between 1949 and 1953 for performances in Norman Granz's Jazz at the Philharmonic series.

Many of the greatest jazz musicians have appeared at Carnegie Hall, which has been at the center of the presentation of jazz as a concert music. Benny Goodman's first performance there (16 January 1938) was highly acclaimed and was brought to a wide audience through the later release of a number of recordings; Goodman returned to the hall on 17 January 1978 to celebrate the 40th anniversary of the original concert, and in 1988 its 50th anniversary was marked by a re-creation of the first program by a big band led by Bob Wilber. Duke Ellington's orchestra played his suite *Black, Brown and Beige* on 23 January 1943, and gave six further concerts between 1943 and 1948. In March 1946 Woody Herman and his Herd gave the first performance of the *Ebony Concerto*, written for Herman by Igor Stravinsky. Charlie Parker established a link with the venue in the late 1940s, and his numerous performances between 1949 and 1954 were often broadcast. Important events from the 1960s onwards include a concert given by Miles Davis on 19 May 1961 in which his quintet was accompanied by Gil Evans's orchestra (recorded and issued as *Miles Davis at Carnegie Hall*, Col. CS8612), a performance by John Coltrane's quartet (1961), and Charles Mingus's concert on 19 January 1974. The presentation of leading figures of the jazz world continued in the 1980s, when Jean-Luc Ponty was among those who played in the hall. Carnegie Hall has also been one of the principal venues for the Newport Jazz Festival (and its continuation under other names) from its move to New York in 1972 into the new century (*see* FESTIVALS). From 1991 it has been the home of the Carnegie Hall Jazz Band (for details and bibliography *see* CARNEGIE HALL JAZZ BAND).

——. **Carnegie Tavern.** 165 West 56th Street. Restaurant. It was in existence by the late 1970s. Ellis Larkins performed there regularly from 1979 to August or September 1985, when its name was changed to the Chinese Tea Room; the venue closed in April 1986. (B. Miller: "Diner's Journal," *New York Times*, 25 April 1986)

——. **Carousel.** See Downbeat.

——. **Casa Cugat.** See Basin Street East.

——. **Celebrity Club.** 35 East 125th Street. This Harlem social club was open from around the mid-1930s and housed two venues, one at street level and another in the basement. Art Simms served as house pianist in 1945; much more significantly, Buddy Tate led the band (usually a septet) in the basement room from 1953 to 1971.

BIBLIOGRAPHY

F. Driggs: "The Buddy Tate Story," *JM*, v/2 (1959), 2

J. Norris and B. Smith: "Buddy Tate: the Texas Tenor," *Coda*, no.195 (1984), 4

——. **Central Plaza.** 111 Second Avenue. Dance hall complex. The building, owned by Bernie Birns, contained five separate ballrooms on five floors, the largest of which was used for jam sessions and held an audience of 700. Regular jazz concerts were staged at this establishment every Friday and Saturday night under the direction of Jack Crystal (the manager of Milt Gabler's Commodore Music Shop), and from the late 1940s into the 1960s Central Plaza was an important venue for traditional and mainstream jazz in the city. Numerous prominent jazz musicians appeared there, among them Willie "the Lion" Smith, Roy Eldridge, Jo Jones, and Sidney Bechet, who played at a jam session organized by Gabler on 21 January 1949 and from December of that year gave a series of weekly performances. Bechet was also one of the many players who made guest appearances in the 1950s and 1960s; others included Wild Bill Davison, J. C. Higginbotham, Dick Wellstood, Zutty Singleton, Panama Francis, Buck Clayton, Eldridge, Charlie Shavers, Hot Lips Page, Coleman Hawkins, James P. Johnson, Henry "Red" Allen, Vic Dickenson, Herb Flemming, Russell Moore, Ralph Sutton, and Sammy Price. Central Plaza was used by the producer Roger Tilton as the location for the film *Jazz Dance* (1954), which features performances by Smith, Pops Foster, George Wettling, Jimmy McPartland, Pee Wee Russell, and Jimmy Archey.

——. **Chestnut Room.** See Tavern on the Green.

——. **Childs' Paramount.** Times Square at Broadway and West 48th Street. It occupied premises earlier used as the Cinderella Ballroom (see below) and was active as a venue for jazz in the late 1940s and early 1950s. Wilbur De Paris's band, which included Buster Bailey and Sidney De Paris, was resident there in 1948–9.

——. **Chinese Tea Room.** See Carnegie Tavern.

——. **Cinderella Ballroom.** Times Square at Broadway and West 48th Street. It was established in September 1923 by Robert Blum and the Joseph brothers. Between September and November 1924 the Wolverines (with Bix Beiderbecke) played there, and from early 1925 Tony Sbarbaro led the Original Dixieland Jazz Band in a residency. The premises later housed a club known as Childs' Paramount (see above).

——. **Cinderella Club.** 83 West 3rd Street. Among the jazz musicians who appeared there were Cliff Jackson, who led his own trio in the early 1940s, Shirley Clay, in 1944, and the trumpeter Harvey Davis, whose band (which included Sonny White and Herb Hall) held a long residency from 1947 to 1954.

——. **Ciro's Club.** Probably named for the prestigious restaurant clubs established in London and Paris in the 1910s, it was in operation from the early 1920s. At the mid-decade it engaged a number of important jazz musicians, including Blanche Calloway and Duke Ellington's Washingtonians.

——. **Cleopatra's Needle.** 2485 Broadway. Restaurant. Open from 1990, it held a nightly after-hours jam session, beginning at 1 a.m.

——. **Clique.** 1678 Broadway. It was opened in December 1948 by Sammy Kay and Irving Alexander (owners of the Three Deuces; see below) in premises earlier occupied by the Ebony club (see below). During its short existence it engaged some notable performers, among them a sextet led by Lennie Tristano and an ostensibly all-star band under Oscar Pettiford's leadership, including Fats Navarro, Miles Davis, Dexter Gordon, Lucky Thompson, and Bud Powell, whose performances reportedly fell well below expectations. The operation failed in July 1949, and Birdland opened at the location late that year (see above). (J. Chambers: *Milestones*, i: *The Music and Times of Miles Davis to 1960* (Toronto, Buffalo, and London, 1983), 108)

——. **Club Alabam.** 216 West 44th Street. It was situated beneath the Nora Baye Theater in basement premises that had formerly housed the Little Club (from at least 1921 until April 1923) and the Club Balagan, which specialized in the presentation of Russian music. It opened in 1923 or 1924, and in the first few years of its existence offered performances by notable jazz musicians, including Fletcher Henderson, whose ten-piece band accompanied the singer Edith Wilson (1924), Lovie Austin, Sam Wooding and Garvin Bushell (early 1925), and Jimmy Wade (1927).

——. **Club Balagan.** See Club Alabam.

——. **Club Baron.** West 132nd Street and Lenox Avenue. It opened in the early 1940s, during which period Sabby Lewis's big band appeared, as did Valaida Snow. A photograph dating from 1964 shows that the club was still in existence then, but jazz was evidently no longer featured after 1946, when Leonard Ware performed there.

——. **Club Basha.** 2493 Seventh Avenue. Owned and run by Sidney Bechet and a partner, its name was derived from Bechet's surname (in the corrupt pronunciation used by his New York friends). The club opened in summer 1925 in basement premises that in the preceding year had housed a venue called Hermit's End. Bechet led the house band, which included Johnny Hodges and Tommy Benford, and his enterprise quickly became a success; however, owing to a quarrel with his fellow manager, Bechet withdrew and by September 1925 was on his way to Europe. The club continued to prosper at least into 1926.

——. **Club Condon.** See Eddie Condon's.

——. **Club Deluxe.** See Cotton Club.

——. **Club Ebony.** 65 West 129th Street. In mid-1927 the Bamville Club (see above) was renovated and reopened as Club Ebony, under the management of Gardner Pickett and Lloyd C. Thomas. Sources are unclear, but Elmer Snowden seems to have held residencies at both the Bamville Club and Club Ebony. By the 1960s the premises had become a laundry.

——. **Club 18.** 18 West 52nd Street; 20 West 52nd Street. Owned by Jack White, it flourished as a venue for burlesque shows and comedy acts. Jack Purvis led a quartet there in 1935, but the club is principally of jazz interest for the long residency (1935–44) held by Frank Froeba's band.

——. **Club 845.** 845 Prospect Street. In 1945 and 1946 Johnny Jackson organized a series of jam sessions at this club on the corner of 160th Street in the Bronx. Among those who participated were Henry "Red" Allen, Ray Nance, Harry Edison, J. C. Higginbotham, Gene Ammons, Dexter Gordon, Marlowe Morris, Ray Perry, Tiny Grimes, Al Hall, and Gene Ramey; a "battle of the alto saxes" pitted Earl Bostic against Don Stovall.

——. **Club Flamingo.** See Flamingo Club.

——. **Club Harlem.** West 130th Street and Lenox Avenue. Luis Russell led his band there from November 1928 into early 1929, when it moved to the Saratoga Club. Club Harlem later became a restaurant, the Harlem Grill.

——. **Club Riviera.** See Riviera Club.

——. **Club Samoa.** 62 West 52nd Street. It was situated in the building where the Onyx club had premises between 1937 and 1939 (see below). Active as a venue for jazz in the early 1940s, it was owned by Leo Bernstein and directed by Henry Fink. Elmer Snowden led a trio there around 1940. From 1943 into the 1950s it operated as a striptease club.

——. **Club Sudan.** 644 Lenox Avenue. After having been vacant for nearly a decade, the former Cotton Club opened as the Club Sudan in November 1945, with Andy Kirk's band featured. Billy Eckstine performed there in 1946, after which the venture failed. The building was later demolished and replaced by an apartment house.

——. **Club Zanzibar.** See Zanzibar.

——. **Cocoanut Grove.** 253 West 125th Street. It operated for a period around 1930 in a room in the basement of the Apollo Theatre; its owner and manager was Joe Ward. Louis Armstrong performed there from February 1930. The venue was later known as the Rathskeller, and eventually it reverted to use as a rehearsal room.

——. **College Arms Cabaret.** See College Inn.

——. **College Inn.** Coney Island. Situated in a popular resort in Brooklyn, it was an early venue for jazz in the area. George Baquet worked there between 1916 and 1923. In 1915 Ted Lewis played at the College Arms Cabaret, which may be the same venue.

——. **Composer Room.** Situated in the Park Chambers Hotel, it presented George Wallington's trio for several engagements in 1954 and 1955. John Mehegan's trio, consisting of Eddie Costa and Vinnie Burke, appeared in autumn of the latter year, and Wallington returned to the club in 1956.

——. **Condon's.** 117 East 15th Street. It was not named after Eddie Condon (for whose club see Eddie Condon's below), but for its owner, Jim Condon; it opened in 1990 and quickly established itself as a jazz venue, despite its owner's contention that it was principally a restaurant. Clifford Jordan led a big band there from January 1990. It appears to have closed in late 1992.

——. **Connie's Inn.** 2221 Seventh Avenue (to 1933); 200 West 48th Street (1933–6). The Seventh Avenue venue, which consisted of basement premises next door to the Lafayette Theatre, had earlier functioned as the Shuffle Inn, at 165 West 131st Street. In June 1923 Connie and George Immerman opened Connie's Inn there, with a new entrance on Seventh Avenue (and consequently a new address). Wilbur Sweatman's band, which included Coleman Hawkins, played at the opening. From September 1923 until February 1926 the house band was led by the violinist Leroy Smith, and thereafter until late 1927 by the clarinetist and saxophonist Allie Ross, with whom Zutty Singleton later played; in 1929 the pianist Leroy Tibbs was in residence there.

Connie's Inn enjoyed its greatest success in the 1920s and early 1930s and established a strong rivalry with the Cotton Club for audiences and performers. Among the numerous important groups engaged to play at the club were Horace Henderson's Dixie Stompers (late 1920s) and bands led by

Luis Russell (late 1920s, 1932), Louis Armstrong (1929–30), Fletcher Henderson (November 1930 into 1931), Fats Waller (1931), and Don Redman (1932–*c*1935); in the early 1930s a number of performances were broadcast from the club on radio station WBC. In 1933 Connie's Inn moved downtown to 200 West 48th Street, a building formerly occupied by the Palais Royal, with the Seventh Avenue venue becoming first the Harlem Club and then, more successfully, the Ubangi Club (see below). In 1935–6 the revue *Stars over Broadway*, which featured Fats Waller and Billie Holiday among others, was staged at the new location of Connie's Inn. It apparently continued in operation until sometime in 1936, since the Cotton Club took over the premises in September of that year (see below).

——. **Connor's Café.** 71 West 135th Street. Owned by J. W. Connor, this café was an important venue during the blossoming of African-American music in Harlem from the 1910s. Its repertory turned towards jazz around 1922, when June Clark, Willie "the Lion" Smith, and Buddy Christian worked in a band there. Connor's Café had closed by 1927, in which year Murray's Roseland operated briefly at the same site (see below).

——. **Cookery.** 21 University Place. It was owned by Barney Josephson, who had formerly run the celebrated Café Society clubs (see above). Originally opened as a restaurant, it offered music from the early 1970s and quickly became a flourishing venue for jazz performance. It specialized in solo and small-group jazz, and among the important performers to appear there were Mary Lou Williams (1970–71, 1976), Blossom Dearie, Helen Humes, Jimmie Rowles, Sammy Price (1971), Teddy Wilson (1973, 1983), Alberta Hunter (1977), and Carrie Smith (1984).

——. **Cornelia Street Café.** 29 Cornelia Street. Open from July 1977, it presented poetry readings and music from its early years. In the late 1990s it began to offer jazz regularly in a basement-level room. Notable performers have included Michael Formanek, Wolfgang Muthspiel, and Tony Malaby. (<http://www.corneliastcafe.com/about.htm> (2001))

——. **Cotton Club.** 644 Lenox Avenue (to 16 February 1936); 200 West 48th Street (September 1936–10 June 1940); 656 West 125th Street (from *c*1978). The venue on Lenox Avenue was first opened within the Douglas Casino building in 1920 as the Club Deluxe, under the ownership of the former heavyweight boxing champion Jack Johnson. Owney Madden took it over and in 1922 changed its name to the Cotton Club; the club's manager in the early 1920s was Don Healy and the stage manager was Herman Stark. Following race riots in Harlem in 1935 the area was considered unsafe for whites (who formed the Cotton Club's clientele) and the club was forced to close (16 February 1936). It reopened in September 1936 downtown on West 48th Street, in premises that had formerly housed the Palais Royal and Connie's Inn (1933–6) and continued to operate at this location until June 1940.

The Cotton Club was the most famous of the city's nightclubs in the 1920s and 1930s, attracting a clientele that often included the cream of New York society. Its glittering revues provided a medium for performances by the most prominent jazz musicians of the day, and the club's activities were brought to a wide audience by frequent broadcasts. The house band when the venue first opened was Andy Preer's Cotton Club Syncopators; after Preer's death in 1927 Duke Ellington's orchestra was engaged, and its residency became the most celebrated in the club's history, lasting until 1931. Cab Calloway and his Missourians, who had first appeared with great success in 1931, then took over, and Calloway's time as the Cotton Club's bandleader (which extended to 1934, when Jimmie Lunceford succeeded him) was to make his reputation. Both Ellington and Calloway returned after the club moved downtown; the Lenox Avenue premises remained vacant until November 1945, when the Club Sudan opened (see above). Most of the principal jazz musicians, singers, and dancers of the period appeared at the Cotton Club at some stage, notably Louis Armstrong, Ethel Waters, Ivie Anderson, Bill Robinson, and the Nicholas Brothers. The heyday of the club's existence was re-created in Francis Ford Coppola's film *The Cotton Club* (1984).

A new club of the same name had opened at 656 West 125th Street by at least 1978. In the late 1990s it offered swing bands on Monday nights and various jazz groups on Thursday through Saturday nights.

BIBLIOGRAPHY

G. Hoefer: "Cotton Club Parade, 1923–1936," *Down Beat Music '65* (Chicago, 1964), 68

J. Haskins: *The Cotton Club* (New York, 1977/*R*1994)

N. Siegal: "Harlem after Dark is Cooking Again," *New York Times* (28 March 1999)

——. **Count Basie's (Club)** [Count Basie's Lounge]. 2245 Seventh Avenue. A small, comfortable venue, it was opened by Count Basie. Although it was not his primary purpose to create a club where he could play, he sat in from time to time; in October 1956, shortly after it opened, he recorded there as a member of a mainstream sextet, with Emmett Berry, Vic Dickenson, Aaron Bell, Bobby Donaldson, and Joe Williams. The club operated into the mid-1960s; among the other musicians who played there were Eddie "Lockjaw" Davis and Shirley Scott, Lou Donaldson, Marlowe Morris, Wild Bill Davis, Sir Charles Thompson, and Joe Newman.

——. **Crawdaddy.** Vanderbilt Avenue at East 45th Street. Situated in the Roosevelt Hotel, it was active from around the mid-1970s. Among the musicians who held residencies there were Buddy Tate and Vic Dickenson (both 1978) and Warren Vaché (1979-80). Walter Bishop performed there in June 1980, but soon thereafter it ceased to offer jazz.

——. **Dan Shaku.** 300 East 41st Street. Open from 1993 to 1994, this karaoke bar offered jazz at the weekends; Gary Bartz, accompanied by Michael Weiss's trio, appeared there in the former year. Later a wine and spirits shop was located at this address.

——. **Delmonico's.** See Harlem Uproar House.

——. **Detour.** 349 East 13th Street. It opened in the mid-1990s and by 1997 was presenting jazz every night of the week. Matt Wilson, George Schuller, and the pianist David Berkman are among those who have made regular appearances there. (<http://www.jazzatdetour.com> (2001))

——. **Diamond Horseshoe.** It was owned and managed by Billy Rose and was opened in the 1930s. Among the musicians who worked there were Billy Banks, who played an unbroken series of more than 7000 performances between December 1938 and June 1948, and Noble Sissle, whose orchestra was resident at the club from 1938 to 1942 and again from 1945 to the mid-1950s.

——. **Dickie Wells's Shim Sham Club.** 169 West 133rd Street. It was opened by Wells (who should not be confused with the famous trombonist of the same name) in 1933 in premises that had previously housed the Nest Club (see below) and operated successfully for several years. Among the musicians who performed there was Billie Holiday (1936).

——. **Downbeat.** 66 West 52nd Street (1944–8); West 54th Street (from 1952); Lexington Avenue at East 42nd Street (by the late 1960s); 101 Seventh Avenue (from late 1993). At least four different clubs in New York have used this name. The first opened on 52nd Street in premises that had earlier been occupied by the Yacht Club (see below). It was managed to begin with by Morris Levy and then (when he moved to the Royal Roost) by his brother Irving Levy. It became one of the most flourishing venues in the city, engaging many major musicians. Dizzy Gillespie, who had played at the Yacht Club, appeared regularly at the Downbeat, as did Coleman Hawkins from its early days. Others who worked there were Red Norvo and the Bascomb brothers (both 1944), Art Tatum, Tiny Grimes, and Sid Catlett (all 1944–6), Jay McShann (1945), Billie Holiday (1945, 1947), Sarah Vaughan (*c*1946), and Eddie Heywood, Gillespie, Ella Fitzgerald, and Lester Young (all 1947). In 1948 the 52nd Street venue became a striptease club called the Carousel. In 1952 a new club, known as Le Downbeat, opened on West 54th Street, and it remained active until at least 1954; Mary Lou Williams, Billy Taylor (ii), and Terry Gibbs were among those who played there. The third Downbeat was opened in the late 1960s on Lexington Avenue at 42nd Street and engaged such musicians as Maxine Sullivan with the World's Greatest Jazz Band, Roy Eldridge (1969), and Anita O'Day (1970). The venue became a rock club in 1970. The fourth Downbeat opened in December 1993 and early on featured Jerry Gonzalez's Fort Apache Band and Roy Hargrove, but it appears to have failed within one or two years.

——. **Downstairs at the Metropolis.** 31 Union Square West. Located in the basement of the Metropolis Café in the former Bank of the Metropolis building, it offered jazz from April 1994 into 1995. Elvin Jones, Lee Konitz, Jimmy Heath, Milt Hinton, and Art Taylor were among those who worked there. In May 1996 the Blue Water Grill, a seafood restaurant which presents jazz as background for its diners, opened at this location.

——. **Dunbar Palace.** 2389 Seventh Avenue. Formerly the Bamboo Inn (see above), this venue opened as the Dunbar Palace in October 1930 with a battle of the bands pitting Fletcher Henderson's group against that of his brother Horace Henderson. During the 1930s the Dunbar Palace presented dances hosted by Harlem social clubs. It later became the Dawn Casino.

——. **East.** 10 Claver Place, Brooklyn. It was active from at least the 1970s as a venue for free jazz.

——. **Ebony.** 1678 Broadway. Owned by Dickie Wells (who should not be confused with the trombonist of the same name), it was opened around 1944 and was run by Wells with the help of John Levy and Al Martin. In December 1948 the Clique opened in the same premises, and a year later Birdland took its place (see above).

——. **Eddie Condon's.** 47 West 3rd Street (20 December 1945–1957); 330 East 56th Street (1958 – mid-1967); 144 West 54th Street (March 1975 – 31 July 1985). It was opened

5. Eddie Condon's, New York, June 1954: (on stage, left to right) Condon (guitar), Urbie Green (trombone), Dick Cary (trumpet), Bobby Donaldson (drums), Ernie Caceres (clarinet), Al Hall (double bass), and Gene Schroeder (piano)

by Eddie Condon in December 1945 and managed by him in association with Pete Pesci. The club remained on West 3rd Street until 1957, then the following year Condon took new premises uptown on East 56th Street. This second venue closed in mid-1967. In 1975, after Condon's death, a new club on West 54th Street (next to Jimmy Ryan's) was opened by Red Balaban, who led its house band, Balaban and Cats, from that time; their playing was recorded and issued on the LP *A Night at the New Eddie Condon's* (1975, CJ 17). It closed on 31 July 1985. The original Eddie Condon's was one of the clubs featured in the 20-minute film documentary *Night Clubs Boom* (1946), in Louis de Rochemont's series "The March of Time" (made by Time and RKO Radio).

Condon's specialized in the presentation of Chicago jazz, and all the principal players in the style appeared there. The club's resident band (see fig.5) always bore Condon's name during his lifetime, even during those periods when he seldom played with it. Among his regular sidemen were Sammy Price (1940s), George Wettling (1940s–1950s), Walter Page (early 1950s), Pee Wee Russell (1955–6), Herb Hall (for several years in the mid-1950s), Tony Parenti (1962–3), and Yank Lawson; Wild Bill Davison was resident at the West 3rd Street location for much of its existence and played again at the club in its uptown venue in 1983. James P. Johnson worked there as an intermission pianist (1946), as did Ralph Sutton and Dick Wellstood.

Eddie Condon's should not be confused with the early 1990s venue called Condon's, owned by Jim Condon (see above).

BIBLIOGRAPHY

E. Condon and T. Sugrue: *We Called it Music: a Generation of Jazz* (New York, 1947/*R*1988)

E. Condon and H. O'Neal: *The Eddie Condon Scrapbook of Jazz* (New York, 1973)

——. **Edwardian Room.** Fifth Avenue at 59th Street. Jazz was played in this venue within the Plaza Hotel from at least the 1980s. Bucky Pizzarelli performed there regularly in 1984–5.

——. **Embers.** East 54th Street. This flourished as a venue for soloists and small groups from the late 1940s into the 1960s. Its activities were directed briefly by Ralph Watkins, who worked there between his appointments at Bop City and Basin Street. Among the musicians who played at the club were Roy Eldridge, Louis Metcalf, Charlie Shavers, Mary Lou Williams, Buck Clayton, Joe Bushkin (who was the house pianist in the early 1950s), Art Tatum, Stuff Smith, and Tyree Glenn. Earl Hines and Eddie Heywood were resident in 1959–60, and they were succeeded by a quartet led by Jonah Jones (from 3 January 1960); Jones's group formed a lasting association with the Embers, playing there again in 1961, opposite a quartet led by Erskine Hawkins, and in 1963.

——. **Empire Ballroom.** West 48th Street and Broadway. Jazz bands were engaged to accompany the dancing from at least the 1930s. Among the prominent orchestras that appeared there were those of Fletcher Henderson (1933), Benny Carter (1933), and Rex Stewart (1933–4). A number of performances by the Henderson band were broadcast on radio stations WINS and WMCA.

——. **Empire Room.** See Waldorf Astoria.

——. **Enduro Restaurant.** Brooklyn. It presented jazz for the entertainment of the diners from at least 1940, when Sidney Bechet and Sidney De Paris both played there every Monday night throughout the summer. Bechet returned between August and November of the same year as the leader of a quintet.

——. **Essex House Hotel.** 160 Central Park South. It was in operation from at least the early 1930s. The Casa Loma Orchestra held a residency of almost two years in the hotel in 1933–4 (for illustration *see* CASA LOMA ORCHESTRA) and during that time made pioneering broadcasts on radio.

——. **Famous Door.** 35 West 52nd Street (1 March 1935–10 May 1936); 66 West 52nd Street (December 1937 – November 1943); 201 West 52nd Street (November 1943 – early 1944); 56 West 52nd Street (1947–50); West 52nd Street, between Sixth and Seventh avenues (1960s). The club was opened at the first of its many locations on 1 March 1935 as a cooperative venture financed by, among others, Lennie Hayton and his manager Jack Colt, Glenn Miller, and Jimmy Dorsey. Its name derived from an autographed door, which was set on a dais next to the bar; it bore the signatures of the original investors and, in time, of many celebrities who visited or played at the club. Founded principally as a venue where musicians employed by other New York clubs could meet to eat, drink, and play together, it rapidly gained popularity with theater and film actors as well. On its opening night Louis Prima and his New Orleans Gang (which included Pee Wee Russell) played at the Famous Door; following Prima, Georg Brunis, Max Kaminsky, Bobby Hackett, Billie Holiday, Red Norvo, and Wingy Manone (all 1935) and Bunny Berigan (1935–6) were among the various musicians who established its reputation as a venue for dixieland jazz and swing. It was the club chosen by Bessie Smith in February 1936 for her only performance on 52nd Street. The original purpose of the Famous Door was not neglected, however, and regular jam sessions were held in an upstairs room. Despite its successful beginning it ran into financial difficulties and was forced to close on 10 May 1936.

The second club of the name was opened in December 1937 at 66 West 52nd Street (premises that were later used by the Downbeat (see above)); it was directed initially by Al Felshin and Jerry Brooks and later by various other managers, including Arthur Jarwood (1940–43). Prima was again engaged as the first resident bandleader, and Art Tatum played solo piano between sets. Although its bandstand was small, the club presented some of the leading bands of the period, notably those of Count Basie (1938, 1939; for illustration *see* BASIE, COUNT), Red Norvo (regularly from 1938 into the 1940s), Mildred Bailey (1938), John Kirby, Charlie Barnet, Red Nichols, and Ella Fitzgerald (all 1939), Teddy Powell (1939–40), Woody Herman (1939, *c*1941), Joe Sullivan (1940–41), Benny Carter (1940–42), Andy Kirk (1941), and Hot Lips Page (1943); CBS made regular broadcasts from the venue during the late 1930s. The club was closed temporarily from June 1940 because of failure to pay the musicians' wages, but it reopened on 25 September.

In November 1943 the Famous Door moved to another location on 52nd Street, where it operated for little more than a month. During this time John Kirby and Lionel Hampton were among the musicians who played there. A fresh start was made in 1947, when a new venue was opened at 56 West 52nd Street; the Famous Door at this location was active until 1950. It featured a repertory of swing and bop, as before staging performances by the most prominent musicians of the day, among them Henry "Red" Allen, Ella Fitzgerald, Lester Young, Sid Catlett, Art Tatum, Roy Eldridge, Dizzy Gillespie, Ben Webster, and Jack Teagarden. After the closure of the club in 1950 this venue became a striptease club. The last of the locations to take the illustrious name of the Famous Door was active on 52nd Street in the 1960s; clubs in other American cities have also used the name, including one in New Orleans.

BIBLIOGRAPHY

G. Hoefer: "Tales of 52nd Street: The Famous Door," *Down Beat Music '68* (Chicago, 1967), 72

A. Shaw: "Swingin' at the Famous Door," "The Big Bands and the Famous Door," "Cracks in the Door," *The Street that Never Slept: New York's Fabled 52nd Street* (New York, 1971/*R*1983 as *52nd Street: the Street that Never Slept*), 105, 125, 312

——. **Fat Tuesday.** 190 Third Avenue. It was founded in 1979 and flourished as a venue for bop, blues, and mainstream jazz during the 1980s. Among the many important musicians who played there were Gerry Mulligan, Jack DeJohnette, Eddie Gomez, and Hilton Ruiz (all 1980), Helen Merrill and Sheila Jordan (both 1983), McCoy Tyner and Joe Henderson (1987), and Jay McShann, Zoot Sims, Joe Turner (ii), Stan Getz, Dexter Gordon, Buddy DeFranco, Ahmad Jamal, Freddie Hubbard, and the Jazztet. From the mid-1980s until it closed in September 1995 the guitarist Les Paul played a regular engagement on Monday nights; thereafter he continued at Iridium (see below).

BIBLIOGRAPHY

N. Strauss: "The Pop Life: a Difficult Year for Clubs and Those who Love Them," *New York Times* (28 Dec 1995)

J. Pareles: "Pop Review: Les Paul Has a New Home and Time for a Little Chat," *New York Times* (24 April 1996)

——. **Fez.** 380 Lafayette Street. A basement performance space situated beneath Time Café, Fez presents music every night of the week. Jazz became a regular feature in 1992, when the Mingus Big Band began to play every Thursday night. Anita O'Day and Chris Connor performed there in March 2001. (<http://www.feznyc.com> (2001))

——. **Fiesta Danceteria.** West 42nd Street and Broadway. Restaurant. This venue, which opened in November 1939, was situated on the second floor of the Rialto Theater and consisted of a self-service restaurant, a glass-covered roof garden, and a dance floor. Joe Marsala led a big band there late in 1939 and Jimmie Lunceford's orchestra was resident in 1940 (for illustration *see* LUNCEFORD, JIMMIE).

——. **55 Bar.** 55 Christopher Street. Opened in 1965, this tiny club has a jazz jukebox, and from at least the early 1990s it has regularly featured Mike Stern (usually on Monday and Wednesday nights), Leni Stern, and Wayne Krantz, all of whom were still performing there in 2001.
(<http://barcrawler.com/55bar.html> (2001))

——. **Five Spot (Café).** 5 Cooper Square (to 1962); Third Avenue and East 7th Street (1962–72); 2 St. Marks Place (from 1972). It was owned by Joe and Iggy Termini and opened at its first location on the edge of the Bowery by the mid-1950s. From the start it was noted for the uncompromising presentation of the latest styles of music. In 1956 an all-star sextet, including Phil Woods, Duke Jordan, Art Taylor, and Cecil Payne, recorded a tribute to Charlie Parker at the club (released on the Signal label). Landmarks in the Five Spot's history were the long residencies held from 1956 by Cecil Taylor and in 1957–9 by Thelonious Monk as the leader of a quartet of changing personnel, involving, most notably, John Coltrane (1957). Ornette Coleman made his controversial New York début there and held a series of residencies at the club between 1959 and 1961. In the latter year Eric Dolphy gave important performances that were recorded and issued as *Live! at the Five Spot* (NewJ 8260; Prst. 7294). Monk returned to the club in 1963 after it had moved to its new location on the West side. Another influential connection was that with Charles Mingus, who first appeared at the Five Spot in its early days and played for an extended period in 1964–5.

In 1972 the club's management took a new direction, opening premises on St. Marks Place under the name the Two Saints and presenting a repertory that emphasized jazz-rock. The original name was resumed, however, in 1975 and the Five Spot reopened with Art Blakey's Jazz Messengers. Among others who performed there were Coleman (1975) and Jackie McLean. The club was forced to close after losing its cabaret license. The Termini brothers also ran the Jazz Gallery in Greenwich Village (see below).

A new club named the Five Spot was open from at least 1993 at 4 West 31st Street. It presented David Sanborn, the Brecker Brothers, and McCoy Tyner's big band early on before changing its music policy to contemporary rhythm-and-blues.

——. **Flamingo Club** [Club Flamingo]. 38 West 52nd Street. It was active in the 1940s, when among the resident leaders was the cornetist Johnny Bayersdorffer. The venue became a striptease club in the 1950s.

——. **Fortune Garden Pavilion.** 209 East 49th Street. This Chinese restaurant, which opened in 1985, presented leading jazz musicians from early in 1988, when the trio led by the stride pianist Judy Carmichael, consisting of Michael Hashim and Chris Flory, took up an engagement on Thursday, Friday, and Saturday nights. Thereafter the restaurant usually presented duos or trios led by pianists, although Harry Edison and Al Grey also led trios there. The venue had closed by mid-1991. (P. Watrous: "Brave New Spaces: Music: Jazz Menus: Two from Column A," *New York Times*, 11 Sept 1988)

——. **Freddy's Restaurant and Supper Club.** 308 East 49th Street. In February 1982 it began hosting a lunchtime jazz series, Jazz at Noon, and in the mid-1980s it presented such performers as John Bunch, Carol Sloane, and Frank Tate. It appears to have closed in 1987.

——. **Garden of Joy.** Seventh Avenue between 138th and 139th streets. This open-air cabaret, which catered for white audiences only, occupied an entire block on Seventh Avenue; the site had a dance floor, illuminated at night by Japanese lanterns. It was in operation from at least 1920, when Willie "the Lion" Smith held the first of a series of long residencies there. During the early 1920s Sidney Bechet, James P. Johnson, Bubber Miley, and Coleman Hawkins played at the Garden of Joy as sidemen with Mamie Smith, and in the middle of the decade Hawkins was a member of a band led by the pianist Ginger Jones. Other jazzmen to appear there included Charlie Gaines, who played with several different leaders.

——. **Garvin's Café Lido.** 15 Waverly Place. It was active as a venue from at least July 1986, when a trio comprising Chris

Flory, Phil Flanigan, and Chuck Riggs performed there; James Williams appeared in August 1987 as the leader of a trio consisting of Harvie Swartz and Eliot Zigmund.

——. **Gaslight (Club).** It flourished in the 1950s and 1960s. Clarence Hutchenrider's successful trio held a long residency (from 1958), and one of his sidemen, George Wettling, led a trio of his own there in the mid-1960s. Sol Yaged's quintet, which included Ray Nance, also appeared at the Gaslight in the mid-1960s.

——. **Ginger Man.** 51 West 64th Street. Restaurant. Open from 1964 into the early 1990s, it presented the Harlem Blues and Jazz Band for a year-long engagement beginning in February 1981.

——. **Golden Gate Ballroom.** Lenox Avenue and 142nd Street. Founded in October 1939 by Jay Faggin (or Fagin) (who had earlier owned the Arcadia Ballroom and the Harlem Uproar House), it was situated in the auditorium of the Douglas Theater. Meant to compete with the Savoy Ballroom (two blocks south on Lenox Avenue), it could hold 6500 people, but the venue failed in less than a year. During this brief period Coleman Hawkins, Hot Lips Page, Count Basie, Teddy Wilson, Harlan Leonard, and Les Hite led big bands there, and Sammy Stewart played organ.

——. **Golden Triangle.** See Village Vanguard.

——. **Greene Street.** 101 Greene Street. Bar and restaurant. Occupying premises that had been converted from a sanitation truck garage, it opened in 1980. It was known particularly for presenting drummerless ensembles (most often duos consisting of piano and double bass) in its downstairs restaurant. Musicians who played there included Lee Konitz, John Hicks, Mal Waldron, Hilton Ruiz, Art Davis, John Abercrombie, Andy LaVerne, Rufus Reid, Amina Claudine Myers, and, in 1991, Walter Norris. It also occasionally presented singers in its upstairs (street-level) room. Greene Street closed around July 1992.

——. **Gregory's.** 1149 First Avenue. It was established in 1972. Ellis Larkins, Brooks Kerr, Lee Konitz, Jimmy Raney, Don Friedman, Chuck Wayne, Mike Longo, and Bob Dorough, among others, performed there. It closed on 28 February 1988.

——. **Griff's (Plaza Café).** Third Avenue and East 37th Street. Restaurant. Jazz was performed to entertain the diners from at least the early 1980s. John Bunch, Major Holley, and Junior Mance appeared there around 1981–2.

——. **Half Note.** 289 Hudson Street (1957–72); 149 West 54th Street (October 1972–1974). The venue in Greenwich Village, operated by the Canterino family, was active from 1957 to 1972 and quickly established a name as a center for contemporary styles of jazz. Many of the most prominent musicians of the 1950s and 1960s performed there, notably Charles Mingus (1957–8), Lennie Tristano (1958–9), John Coltrane with his quartet (1960–65), and the Modern Jazz Quartet (1966); Al Cohn and Zoot Sims appeared there together throughout the 1960s, and each returned with his own group during the 1970s. Others who played at the Half Note were Ben Webster (1962), Jimmy Rushing (1965–6, 1971), and Anita O'Day (1969).

In October 1972 the Half Note opened in larger premises at 149 West 54th Street, across the street from Jimmy Ryan's. Those who played there included Woody Herman, Dizzy Gillespie, Bill Evans (ii), and Zoot Sims. The club closed in late 1974.

——. **Hanratty's.** 1754 Second Avenue. Bar. Opened in 1979, it presented jazz from that time until September 1986, when its musical policy changed. Dick Wellstood played there regularly in 1979–80 and 1983–4 and was responsible for booking other pianists, including John Coates (1980), Don Ewell (1981), Ralph Sutton (1982), Roland Hanna (1985), Dick Hyman (1986), Dave McKenna, Tommy Flanagan, and Judy Carmichael.

——. **Harlem Club.** 2221 Seventh Avenue. Formerly Connie's Inn (see above), this nightclub operated briefly in the mid-1930s. It was succeeded at the same location by the Ubangi Club (see below).

——. **Harlem Opera House.** 211 West 125th Street. It was opened in 1889 as an opera house, but by the early years of the 20th century it was used for variety performances. Its most active period as a jazz venue occurred in the mid-1930s but was short-lived: on 9 June 1934 Frank Schiffman and Leo Brecher, the owners of the rival Apollo Theatre, took over the opera house and in the late spring of 1935 discontinued its stage policy, converting it to a movie theater. After the cessation of jazz performances at the Harlem Opera House the Apollo was the only theater in Harlem presenting variety acts. The building was demolished in December 1959 and a bowling alley was constructed on the site.

Among the jazz musicians who appeared at the Harlem Opera House during its brief golden era were Tiny Bradshaw, Don Redman, Teddy Hill, Chick Webb, Benny Carter, Fletcher Henderson, and Charlie Turner's Arcadians. Ella Fitzgerald won an amateur contest there early in 1935, before her success at a similar competition staged at the Apollo Theatre, which launched her career.

——. **Harlem Uproar House.** 52nd Street. It was at least the third club to occupy the premises, which had earlier housed Delmonico's and then the Uptown Lowdown Club. The dates at which the name of the venue changed are not clear, but it was known as the Harlem Uproar House by 1937. At that time the club was owned by Jay Faggin (or Fagin), who also owned the Arcadia Ballroom (see above), and it offered an elaborate floor show every night. Among the bands that appeared there were those led by Lucky Millinder (1932), Kaiser Marshall (1935), Coleman Hawkins (1937), Alberto Socarras (1937), and Mezz Mezzrow (1937); Mezzrow's 14-piece ensemble included Zutty Singleton, Dicky Wells, Frankie Newton, and Sidney De Paris. During the same period Hazel Scott played piano during intermissions and the club presented a trio led by the violinist Emilio Caceres (brother of Ernie Caceres).

——. **Heat Wave.** 266 West 145th Street. The club was active in the 1930s and 1940s under the direction of Louis Metcalf, who also played there until 1946. Hot Lips Page, Dizzy Gillespie, Charlie Parker, Ben Webster, and Lester Young are among those who performed at the Heat Wave; Marlowe Morris was house pianist.

——. **Hermit's End.** 2493 Seventh Avenue. It was in operation by the early 1920s. Cecil Scott and Lloyd Scott led the resident band there in 1924. The premises were taken over in 1925 by the Club Basha (see above).

——. **Hickory House.** 144 West 52nd Street. Restaurant and club. One of the longest-lived jazz venues on 52nd Street, it was opened in 1933 and under the direction of John Popkin soon became known for the presentation of dixieland jazz and swing; later it was also a major venue for bop. Wingy Manone was the resident leader from late 1934, and when he left the club in 1936 one of his sidemen, Joe Marsala, took his place, establishing a connection with the Hickory House that lasted on and off to the mid-1940s. Other notable residencies were held by Art Hodes (1938, 1944), John Kirby's sextet (late 1930s), Hot Lips Page (1940), Eddie South (1942), Red Norvo (intermittently until 1944), Billy Taylor (ii), Marian McPartland (1952–60), and Mary Lou Williams. The club mounted regular jam sessions on Sunday afternoons, and Sidney Bechet played as a guest soloist at a number of these in the late 1930s. Its various activities featured in a number of broadcasts. The Hickory House closed in 1968.

BIBLIOGRAPHY

A. Shaw: "Hickory-broiled Steaks and Jazz," *The Street that Never Slept: New York's Fabled 52nd Street* (New York, 1971/*R*1983 as *52nd Street: the Street that Never Slept*), 141

M. McPartland: "Halcyon Days: Remembering the Hickory House," *All in Good Time* (New York, and Oxford, England, 1987), 19

——. **Hickory Log.** It was in operation by the late 1940s. Ernie Caceres led his own quartet there in 1949 and John Kirby worked at the club with Henry "Red" Allen in the 1950s.

——. **Hollywood Club.** 203 West 49th Street. It was opened in 1923 by Leonard Bernstein (not the composer, conductor, and pianist of that name), but was active under this name only until the following year, when the premises were renamed the Kentucky Club (see below). The Washingtonians, first led by Elmer Snowden, then by Duke Ellington, formed the resident band from 1923, and in spring 1924 James P. Johnson led a band at the Hollywood with Benny Carter and Sidney Bechet among his sidemen.

——. **Hollywood Restaurant.** 2262 Seventh Avenue. From around 1943 to 1952 this was a venue for jazz pianists, including Don Lambert, Marlowe Morris, and Billy Taylor (ii).

——. **Homefront.** 236 West 54th Street. A performance space situated on the lower floor of a bed and breakfast establishment, it featured jazz from summer 1997 into early 1998; Ray Anderson, the pianist Orrin Evans, Donald Harrison, and Dave Liebman were among those who appeared. (A. Ramirez: "Neighborhood Report: Midtown: B & B Opens where Bawdy Once Reigned," *New York Times*, 10 Aug 1997)

——. **Hoofer's Club.** 2235 Seventh Avenue. Situated in the basement of the Lafayette Theatre, where the Rhythm Club had originally been, the Hoofer's Club opened in 1932. It was a gathering place for the leading African-American dancers of that era, including Bill Robinson, Honi Coles, Bunny Briggs, Baby Lawrence, Chuck Green, and Cholly Atkins; Willie "the Lion" Smith, Benny Carter, and Bernard Addison were among those jazz musicians who played there. Remembrances of legendary tap-dancing cutting contests at the Hoofer's Club are celebrated in a re-creation of the venue in the film *The Cotton Club* (1984).

——. **Hot-Cha Bar and Grill.** 2280 Seventh Avenue. In the mid-1930s this Harlem nightclub and restaurant presented musical revues, one of which featured Billie Holiday early in her career (1934), and Garland Wilson served as intermission pianist on its second-floor balcony. Don Frye was house pianist, and the venue also hosted jam sessions, with Roy Eldridge, Cecil Scott, and Chu Berry among those who participated. The jazz policy was discontinued soon afterwards, but a photograph from 1964 shows the building's façade unchanged.

——. **Hotel Carlyle.** See Bemelmans Bar; Café Carlyle.

——. **Hotel Cecil.** 210 West 118th Street. Brooks Kerr was resident there in 1996–7.

——. **Hot Feet Club.** West Houston Street. The principal bandleaders at this downtown venue, which flourished in the late 1920s and 1930s, were Otto Hardwick and Elmer Snowden; among the musicians who played with them there were Al Morgan and Fats Waller.

——. **Hurricane Club.** Broadway and West 51st Street. It was in operation by the early 1940s. In 1943 Duke Ellington's orchestra played there from April to September, and in the spring of that year Sidney Bechet led a small group at the club on the orchestra's nights off.

——. **Indigo Blues.** 221 West 46th Street. Located in the Edison Hotel, this stylish room could accommodate more than 200 people. It opened on 16 December 1988 with a performance by Miles Davis and presented jazz regularly for approximately a year and a half before abandoning that policy. The Dirty Dozen Jazz Band appeared there in January 1989 and was followed by the groups of Joe Henderson, Toshiko Akiyoshi, Jack Walrath, Phil Woods, Ahmad Jamal, Randy Weston, Tommy Flanagan, Hank Jones, and Eddie Harris. Indigo Blues appears to have closed in early 1994. ("The Newest Arrivals for the New Year," *New York Times*, 6 Jan 1989)

——. **International.** Broadway. It was active from at least 1960, when Doc Cheatham began the first of a series of residencies there. He continued to be connected with the club until 1965.

——. **Internet Café.** 82 East 3rd Street. It opened early in 1995 and began to feature avant-garde jazz the following year, six nights per week. Tony Malaby and Mark Helias have regularly led groups; Tim Berne and George Schuller's group Schulldogs have also appeared. (<http://www.bigmagic.com> (2001))

——. **Iridium.** 48 West 63rd Street. Restaurant and club. Located across from the Lincoln Center, the jazz club is situated in the basement below the restaurant; this performance space has expanded three times since it opened in December 1993 or January 1994. Iridium broadcasts performances on WBGO radio; in April 1996 (i.e., after Fat Tuesday closed) the guitarist Les Paul began performing there on Monday nights. The repertory presented at the club is varied and a number of important jazz musicians have appeared.

BIBLIOGRAPHY

J. Pareles: "Pop Review: Les Paul Has a New Home and Time for a Little Chat," *New York Times* (24 April 1996)

<http://www.iridiumjazzclub.com> (2001)

——. **Jasmine.** 168 West 96th Street. A short-lived nightclub on the upper West side, it functioned in the mid-1980s. Among the musicians engaged to play there in 1984 were John Hicks and Steve Grossman.

——. **Jazz Forum.** 50 Cooper Square (*c*1979–81); 648 Broadway (1981–3). The club's second premises, on the fifth floor, was a large loft run by the trumpeter Mark Morganelli, who presented jazz there seven nights a week. Its repertory was varied, incorporating tap-dance performances, quartets with the unusual instrumentation of two pianos, double bass, and drums, and groups playing in hard-bop and free-jazz styles. Performers who appeared there in the early 1980s included Walter Bishop, Jr., Warne Marsh, Dewey Redman, Michele Rosewoman, Woody Shaw, Jimmy Slyde, and Reggie Workman. In 1982 Barry Harris conducted workshops on Monday nights and the club held a week-long film festival. Jazz Forum closed in mid-1983.

BIBLIOGRAPHY

J. S. Wilson: "Jazz: Berg and Harrell," *New York Times* (15 Feb 1981)
R. F. Shepard: "Going Out Guide," *New York Times* (20 March 1982)
——: "Going Out Guide," *New York Times* (28 May 1984)

——. **Jazz Gallery.** 80 St. Marks Place; 290 Hudson Street. The original club was founded around December 1959 by Joe and Iggy Termini (who also owned the Five Spot, see above); among the groups that played there in its early days were the Jazztet (1959–60) and John Coltrane's first quartet (May–June 1960). In 1961 the club featured an orchestra led by Gil Evans whose sidemen included Budd Johnson, Keg Johnson, and Ray Crawford. During the same year the singer Joe Williams appeared, accompanied by Harry Edison, and in 1962 Charles Mingus performed there.

A new Jazz Gallery at a museum in Hudson Street was founded in 1995 and regularly presents evening jazz performances. Frank Lacy leads an ensemble every Monday night, and many younger lesser-known musicians have appeared there. (<http://www.jazzgallery.org/about.html> (2001))

——. **Jazzmania Society.** 14 East 23rd Street; 40 West 27th Street. It was opened in 1978 as Jazzmania, but by late the following year, when it was owned by the saxophonist Mike Morgenstern, it was known as Jazzmania Society. It originally occupied a room on the fourth floor of the 23rd Street building but later moved to a more spacious loft on West 27th Street. Lee Konitz played regularly at the club in 1980 and 1982, and Sun Ra appeared there in the latter year.

——. **Jazz Standard.** 116 East 27th Street. Basement club and restaurant. It is situated below its sister restaurant, 27 Standard. Since its opening on 28 October 1997 it has become one of the pre-eminent jazz venues in New York. The club has presented musicians as varied as Gary Bartz, Jane Ira Bloom, Jonny King, David "Fathead" Newman, Ralph Peterson, Jr., Steve Turre, Bennie Wallace, Benny Waters, and Denny Zeitlin, and many other leading players. (<http://www.jazzstandard.com> (2001))

——. **Jimmy Ryan's (Club).** 53 West 52nd Street (1940–62); 154 West 54th Street (from 1962). Named for its owner, it was opened in 1940 and became one of the most celebrated of all New York clubs. Ryan managed the venue in collaboration with Matty Walsh, and Milt Gabler was responsible for organizing its jam sessions, which formed an important part of its activities. Following Ryan's death in 1963 the club continued to be active until December 1983.

Many of the most famous musicians in dixieland and swing styles played at Jimmy Ryan's at one time or another; resident musicians from the 1940s included Mezz Mezzrow (*c*1943), James P. Johnson (1943), Art Hodes (1945–9), J. C. Higginbotham (1946), Henry "Red" Allen (1946), Sidney De Paris (1947–57), Sidney Bechet (1948), Max Kaminsky (1948–9), Wilbur De Paris (1951–62), Zutty Singleton (1963–70), and Roy Eldridge (1970–80). Among the prominent participants in the jam sessions were Bechet, Pops Foster, Hot Lips Page, Pee Wee Russell, Eddie Condon, Mezzrow, Kaiser Marshall, Hank Duncan, Sandy Williams, Brad Gowans, Ben Webster, Chu Berry, and Coleman Hawkins.

——. **Joanna.** See Whippoorwill.

——. **Jock's Place.** See Yeah Man.

——. **Johnson's Tavern.** St. Nicholas Avenue at 130th Street. From around 1935 to 1945 the drummer Theodore "Puss" Johnson hosted jam sessions at his tavern; Milt Hinton recalled Coleman Hawkins, Roy Eldridge, Lester Young, and Ray Perry as being among those who participated. The venue later became a grocery store.

——. **J's.** 2581 Broadway. Bar and restaurant. It occupied premises on the second floor of the building and was active from the mid-1980s, favoring a repertory of mainstream jazz. Those who played there in 1987 included John Pizzarelli, Dick Hyman, and a duo consisting of Jay Leonhart and Joe Beck.

——. **K'av'eh'az.** 123 Mercer Street. Coffee house and art gallery. K'av'eh'az (Hungarian for "coffee house") offers jazz nightly, with Joe Locke appearing on Thursdays, and also presents afternoon performances on Saturdays and Sundays. Among those who performed there in 2001 were Steve Khan, and Jack Walrath and his group the Masters of Suspense. (<http://www.kavehaz.com> (2001))

——. **Kelly's Stable.** 141 West 51st Street (to 1940); 137 West 52nd Street (1940–47). Named for Bert Kelly's club in Chicago (see Chicago, Kelly's Stables), it was opened during the 1930s by Ralph Watkins, who directed its activities himself; Watkins's interest in the venue waned in the mid-1940s when he opened the Royal Roost (see below) with Morris Levy, and he sold Kelly's Stable in 1947.

At its first location the club presented such musicians as Hot Lips Page, Bud Freeman, Coleman Hawkins, Stuff Smith, the Spirits of Rhythm, and Baby Laurence; it was at Kelly's that Hawkins worked up his famous rendering of *Body and Soul* (1939). After the removal to new premises in 1940, Watkins engaged a stream of notable players, including Roy Eldridge and Slam Stewart (both 1940), Henry "Red" Allen, Benny Carter, Lester Young, and Benny Waters (all 1941), Kenny Clarke (1942, with Thelonious Monk in his band), Mezz Mezzrow (1943), Nat "King" Cole, Art Tatum, J. C. Higginbotham, Billie Holiday, Una Mae Carlisle, Dizzy Gillespie, and Dinah Washington. A particular feature of the club's programs were the all-star jam sessions staged there, in which such musicians as Young, Chu Berry, and Hawkins took part. (A. Shaw: "Cats in a Stable," *The Street that Never Slept: New York's Fabled 52nd Street* (New York, 1971/*R*1983 as *52nd Street: the Street that Never Slept*), 200)

——. **Kentucky Club.** 203 West 49th Street. This venue, formerly known as the Hollywood Club (see above), had taken the name Kentucky Club by the summer of 1924. The new venue continued to present Duke Ellington and his Washingtonians, who had been in residence at the Hollywood, until 1927. Other bandleaders to work at the Kentucky were Red Nichols (1929), Jimmy Reynolds, who remained for many years in the 1930s and 1940s, and Lester Boone, who led a quartet there in 1940.

——. **King Cole Room.** See St. Regis Hotel.

——. **Knickerbocker Saloon.** 33 University Place. Restaurant and bar. It was opened in 1978 and has continued to be active into the new century, presenting a veritable who's who of jazz pianists, mainly in duos with a double bass player and on occasion in trios. Among those who have appeared are Billy Taylor (ii), Junior Mance, Tommy Flanagan, Roland Hanna, Bill Mays, Fred Hersch, Kirk Lightsey, and James Williams; the stride pianist Judy Carmichael has also appeared regularly, often working in a duo with Michael Hashim. In 2001 the Knickerbocker Saloon presented jazz on Wednesday through Saturday nights.

——. **Knitting Factory.** 47 East Houston Street (February 1987 – November 1994); 74 Leonard Street (from November 1994). For a detailed history of its interlocking activities as a jazz venue, a record company, a sponsor of international jazz tours, and a festival host *see* Knitting factory.

——. **Ladies Fort.** 2 Bond Street. Located near Studio Rivbea and situated in a basement, Ladies Fort was owned and operated by Joe Lee Wilson from 1973 to 1978, when it was sold to the bass player Hakim Jami. David Murray recorded there in June 1976. ("Joe Lee Wilson Leaves the Fort," *JF* [intl edn], no.53 (1978), 16)

——. **Lafayette Theatre.** 2227 Seventh Avenue. Variety theater. This 2000-seat theater opened around 1915 under the ownership of the Coleman brothers and became one of the principal venues of its kind in Harlem. In the 1920s it was taken over by Frank Schiffman and Leo Brecher, who by the mid-1930s also owned the Apollo Theatre and the Harlem Opera House; as was the case with the opera house, the Lafayette's activities as a variety theater were discontinued by its owners in 1935 and it became a movie theater.

The Lafayette flourished as a venue for jazz performance in the 1920s and 1930s, when many of the most important musicians of the day played in the bands that accompanied its shows. Wilbur Sweatman topped the bill there in 1923, with Duke Ellington, Otto Hardwick, and Sonny Greer in his band; Ellington later returned with the Washingtonians (*c*1927). Other prominent bandleaders who appeared included Fletcher Henderson (intermittently 1928–34), Zutty Singleton (1929), Louis Armstrong fronting Carroll Dickerson's band (June 1930), Blanche Calloway and Noble Sissle (both 1931), Bennie Moten (1931–4), and Chick Webb (1933). Fats Waller worked there as an organist with James P. Johnson in the show *Fireworks of 1930*. The basement of this theater housed the Rhythm Club (see below) and its successor, the Hoofer's Club (see above).

——. **Lenox Club.** 652 Lenox Avenue. Owned by Caspar Holstein, it was opened in the 1920s; it was located in Harlem next door to the Cotton Club (see above). The main feature of the Lenox's programs was its Sunday-morning breakfast dances, beginning at 7 a.m. and continuing until 11; the popularity of these events led to the venue's informal adoption of the name Breakfast Club. Among the jazz musicians who played there during the early 1930s were Cliff Jackson and Johnny Russell. In addition to nightly floor shows the Lenox hosted jam sessions, often involving members of Duke Ellington's orchestra; other of its jam sessions featured Louis Armstrong in a battle with Rex Stewart, and Chu Berry. In the mid-1930s it became the Radium Club and then a dance venue, the Continental Hall.

——. **Lenox Lounge.** 288 Lenox Avenue. It opened in either 1939 or 1942 (sources disagree) and offered jazz, among other genres, in its Zebra Room. In 1988 it was taken over by Alvin Reed, Sr., who in 1999 restored the club's original art-deco interior. It has continued to offer jazz into the new century, with bookings being handled by Mickey Bass; in the late 1990s such notables as Johnny Coles, Charles Davis, Hamiet Bluiett, Chico Freeman, John Hicks, and James Spaulding appeared there on Friday and Saturday nights.

BIBLIOGRAPHY

W. L. Hamilton: "A Legendary Harlem Club Preens for its Second Act," *New York Times* (30 March 2000)

L. Richardson: "Longing for Authenticity: Is the Jazz Really Jazz in Harlem without the Locals?," *New York Times* (16 Nov 2000)

<http://www.harlemlive.org/community/bidness/lenoxlounge> (2001)

<http://www.Lenoxlounge.com/index1.html> (2001)

——. **Leroy's.** 2220 Fifth Avenue. This basement club was founded around 1910 by Leroy Wilkins, the elder brother of Barron Wilkins (see Barron's Club, above), and was one of the earliest jazz venues in the city. It frequently presented pianists, among them James P. Johnson (*c*1918), Willie "the Lion" Smith (from 1920), and Fats Waller (early 1920s). Other musicians who appeared included Mamie Smith (before 1920) and Cyrus St. Clair (*c*1925). The building was later demolished.

——. **Lickety Split Lounge and Restaurant.** 2361 Adam Clayton Powell Jr. Boulevard. Makanda Ken McIntyre performed there in the late 1990s; the venue also held a weekly jam session beginning at 11 p.m.

——. **Lido Ballroom.** 160 West 146th Street. Active from at least the early 1930s, it offered music for both dancing and concerts. Jelly Roll Morton led a band there in October 1932, and on 19 August 1944 Mamie Smith (singing one of her last engagements), Billie Holiday, and others gave a benefit concert in the ballroom.

——. **Lincoln Hotel.** See Blue Room.

——. **Lincoln Theater.** 58 West 135th Street. Variety theater. A small theater was opened at this address by Marie Downs in 1909; it was later demolished and the Lincoln was built in its place in 1915. The theater was run for a short time by Frank Schiffman and Leo Brecher (see also Apollo Theatre, Harlem Opera House, and Lafayette Theatre, above). The Lincoln Theater was a member of the Theater Owners' Booking Association circuit and presented many jazz performances as part of its variety programs. Fats Waller was the house organist there in the mid-1920s, doubling at the same time at the Lafayette. In 1927 Victoria Spivey held a highly successful residency there. It later became a church.

——. **Little Club.** A number of venues in New York, apparently unconnected, have gone by this name. Between 1921 and 1923 the premises later occupied by the Club Alabam (see above) were known as the Little Club. The venue at which Ben Pollack played in 1928 was probably the speakeasy on West 44th Street, between Broadway and Seventh Avenue, run by John Popkin, who later directed activities at the Hickory House (see above). During the 1950s a Little Club was in operation at 70 East 55th Street; although this was not essentially a jazz venue, Bud Freeman played there on 31 December 1959.

——. **Log Cabin.** See Pods' and Jerry's.

——. **Lou Terrassi's.** West 47th Street. This dark nightclub was a popular venue for swing and dixieland groups in the early 1950s, and in 1952 it served as the site for the seven-month radio series "Dr. Jazz," broadcast on WMGM, with Aime Gauvin (the Doctor) as disc jockey. Recordings of Bobby Hackett's participation in the series (leading a band from 7 February to 17 April 1952) were later issued on the Storyville label. Henry "Red" Allen, Billy Butterfield, Buck Clayton (in a band which included Herb Flemming, Sol Yaged, and Kenny Kersey), Pee Wee Erwin, Charlie Shavers, Buster Bailey, and Willie "the Lion" Smith were among other leading musicians who played at Lou Terrassi's.

——. **Luckey's Rendezvous** [Rendezvous Inn, Rendezvous Club]. 773 St. Nicholas Avenue. It was opened by Luckey Roberts in 1940 and was active as a venue for many styles of music, from opera (sung by the waiters) to jazz, until around 1954, when Roberts gave up its ownership. The high point of each evening's entertainment was Roberts's own solo piano spot.

——. **Lush Life.** 184 Thompson Street. It was opened on 26 December 1982 by Horst Liepolt and Mel Litoff, the managers of Sweet Basil (see below), and was active until 1985. During its brief existence it presented performances by, among numerous others, Bob Moses, Muhal Richard Abrams, Cecil Taylor (who led a big band there), and Don Cherry (all 1982), Red Garland, Charlie Rouse, and Paquito D'Rivera (all 1983), the Toshiko Akiyoshi–Lew Tabackin Big Band (1984), and Paul Bley (1985).

——. **Makor.** 35 West 67th Street. Opened in the late 1990s as a Jewish community center, Makor has regularly presented jazz among its various activities. Among those who have performed there are Steve Bernstein, Ron Affif, Anthony Coleman, Avishai Cohen, and James "Blood" Ulmer. (<http://www.makor.org> (2001))

——. **Manhattan Casino.** 280 West 155th Street. This Harlem amusement hall, holding 6000 people, operated from around 1910. In 1920 and 1921 it hosted all-star concerts featuring, among others, Lucille Hegamin. Around the late 1920s it became the Rockland Palace (see below).

——. **Mark Twain Riverboat.** Empire State Building, Fifth Avenue at 34th Street. Situated in the basement of the building, this nightclub was open by the early 1960s. It was a venue for big bands, including those of Woody Herman and Harry James. Count Basie held a number of short residencies there between 1964 and 1968 and returned to the club in 1978.

——. **Martin's Tavern.** See Saratoga Club.

——. **Marty's.** 1265 Third Avenue. It flourished from the late 1970s into the early 1980s and presented performances principally by jazz and popular singers. The jazz-oriented performers who appeared there included Joe Williams (1980) and Mel Tormé (1982).

——. **Metronome.** 915 Broadway. This restaurant and lounge, which opened in late 1993 or early 1994, has occasionally presented jazz; Ron Affif, the pianist Orrin Evans, Eddie Henderson, Judy Niemack, Cecil Payne, Ralph Peterson, Jr., and the organist Reuben Wilson are among those who have led groups there.
(<http://www. metronomenyc.com/ns/index.html> (2001))

——. **Metropole.** Seventh Avenue and West 48th Street. Although it was active as a cabaret, the Metropole did not offer jazz until the early 1950s, when it began to put on afternoon sessions, at which Tony Scott, Max Kaminsky, and Sol Yaged, among others, appeared. Henry "Red" Allen introduced evening performances and was resident there himself from 1954 until shortly before his death in 1967 (for illustration *see* Allen, Henry "Red"). In its heyday from the late 1950s until the mid-1960s the club featured trios in the afternoons (Zutty Singleton and Tony Parenti each led groups for long periods) and two bands, alternating, in the evenings (Allen's was one, the other was often led by Roy Eldridge or Coleman Hawkins). Resident players included Cozy Cole, Claude Hopkins, Buster Bailey, J. C. Higginbotham, and Charlie Shavers. Occasionally the Metropole presented single performances by such musicians as Louis Armstrong and Gene Krupa, and it also engaged big bands from time to time, notably those of Lionel Hampton and Woody Herman. While the club's repertory was essentially mainstream jazz, for a short period during the 1960s it offered modern jazz in an upstairs room; among the musicians to play in this venue was Sonny Rollins.

——. **Metropolis Café.** See Downstairs at the Metropolis.

——. **Michael's Pub.** 211 East 55th Street (1972–96); 118 West 57th Street (1996); 119 West 56th Street (1996); 57 East 54th Street (October 1997 – June 1998); 109 or 111 East 56th Street (September 1998 – January 1999); 714 Seventh Avenue (2000). Restaurant and club. This venue was established in 1972 and flourished during the 1970s and 1980s. It presented swing and traditional jazz from 9 p.m. to 1 a.m., specializing in small groups. Among the many well-known musicians to have held residencies there were Benny Carter, Ray Bryant, George Melly, Dave McKenna, Ruby Braff, Teddy Wilson, Terry Gibbs, George Shearing, Dick Hyman, Pee Wee Erwin, Bob Rosengarden, Milt Hinton, and Dick Wellstood. By the late 1980s the venue was better known for the presentation of Broadway show music than jazz. It closed at its original location in late April 1996 and reopened one week later (still late April) in the Café Montparnasse at the Parker Meridien Hotel; over the next several years it continued to operate, but frequently moved premises (jazz was no longer offered). In October 2000 Michael's Pub was located in the Renaissance New York Hotel on Seventh Avenue, but it appears to have closed shortly afterwards. (C. Kilgannon: "Neighborhood Report: Midtown: Woody Allen's Gigs: Blowing Westward," *New York Times*, 28 April 1996)

——. **Mikell's.** 760 Columbus Avenue. It was active in the 1970s and 1980s and engaged such musicians as McCoy Tyner (1985); both Art Blakey and Randy Weston played there regularly. John Tropea recorded at the club in the early 1980s. Mikell's appears to have closed around mid-1989.

6. *Thelonious Monk, Howard McGhee, Roy Eldridge, and Teddy Hill outside Minton's Playhouse, New York*

——. **Mimo Club.** 2237 Seventh Avenue. It was partly owned by the dancer Bill Robinson and was in operation from around 1937. Eddie Barefield and Frankie Newton led bands there; Sidney Bechet appeared in 1941 as the leader of a quartet and then continued with a nine-piece band. From 1942 the club operated under new management as the Murrain Restaurant, Cabaret and Lounge.

——. **Minton's Playhouse.** 210 West 118th Street. It was opened in 1938 by the tenor saxophonist Henry Minton. In 1940 the club's management was taken over by the former bandleader Teddy Hill (see fig.6), who concentrated much of his energy on the regular Monday-night jam sessions, in which visiting musicians took part; among the guest performers who played there often were Dizzy Gillespie, Hot Lips Page, Roy Eldridge, Charlie Christian, and Don Byas. The resident musicians included Thelonious Monk (from 1939), Kenny Clarke, Joe Guy (who led the house band), and Rudy Williams (1945). The weekly jam session and after-hours playing at Minton's provided an opportunity for musicians such as Gillespie and Monk to explore new ideas together, and their experiments played an important part in the development of bop. In the 1950s Tony Scott and Jerome Richardson held long engagements there. In 1997 ambitious plans to renovate and reopen Minton's Playhouse were initiated, but the venture appears to have failed.

BIBLIOGRAPHY

E. Holley: "Reopening Planned for Bebop's Holy Ground," *DB*, lxiv/12 (1997), 15

N. Siegal: "Neighborhood Report: Harlem: at Birthplace of Be-bop, Revival Blues," *New York Times* (24 Jan 1999)

——: "Neighborhood Report: Harlem: Minton's, Cradle of Be-bop Draws Closer to Rebirth," *New York Times* (14 Nov 1999)

——. **Monette's Supper Club.** 133rd Street. This short-lived nightclub was named after Monette Moore, who sang there. It was at Monette's that John Hammond first heard Billie Holiday in 1933.

——. **Monroe's Uptown House.** 198 West 134th Street; 52nd Street (from 1943). It was opened by Clark Monroe in the 1930s in premises formerly occupied by Barron's Club and the Theatrical Grill and became known for the presentation of swing (Billie Holiday sang there for three months early in 1937) and (from the mid-1940s) bop. The club staged jam sessions that rivaled those at Minton's Playhouse (see above); Charlie Parker was the featured soloist in 1943. In December 1944 Monroe opened a second club on 52nd Street, the Spotlite (see below). (*See also* Tinney, Al.)

——. **Murrain Restaurant, Cabaret and Lounge.** 2237 Seventh Avenue (formerly West 135th Street). Formerly the Mimo Club, it came under new management and was renamed in 1942. Hot Lips Page was the resident bandleader, and Earl Bostic, who first played at the Mimo Club with Page, also led a group there. It closed in 1945.

——. **Murray's Roseland.** 71 West 135th Street. Formerly J. W. Connor's Café, it had a brief existence in 1927 as Harlem's parallel to the famous Roseland Ballroom downtown on Broadway. The entire block of buildings had been demolished by the 1960s.

——. **Music Hall.** Broadway. This club was owned by Billy Rose and presented jazz from at least 1934, when Benny Goodman's big band played its first engagement there.

——. **Nest Club.** 169 West 133rd Street. It was opened in the early 1920s by John Carey and Mel Frazier and managed by Johnnie Cobb (1923) and Jeff Blood (1927). Among the jazz musicians who led bands there were Sam Wooding (*c*1923), Elmer Snowden (mid-1920s to early 1930s), George Howe (1927–8), Luis Russell (1928), and Lorenzo Tio, Jr. (1933). In 1932 the Rhythm Club (see below), which had functioned at 168 West 132nd Street, closed at that venue and began to operate in a room behind the Nest Club. The Nest Club itself closed in 1933, and Dickie Wells's Shim Sham Club (see above) took over the venue. By the 1960s the premises were being used as a loft and warehouse.

——. **New Garden Ballroom** [New Gardens]. Jazz was played there from at least the 1940s. The venue is chiefly of interest for the long residency of a band led by the pianist Benton Heath (from the early 1940s to the mid-1960s). Heath's sidemen at different times included Abe Bolar, Ed Allen, Floyd Casey, and Rudy Powell.

——. **Nick's (Tavern).** 140 Seventh Avenue South (?1936–1937); West 10th Street and Seventh Avenue (from 1937). Steak restaurant. It was opened by Nick Rongetti, probably in 1936, and quickly became known for the presentation of dixieland jazz. By late 1938 the term "Nixieland" (or "Nicksieland") was used to refer to music heard at the club, which was one of the main haunts of major jazz musicians during the 1930s. In the early years of the club's existence the resident band was led by Bobby Hackett and featured Eddie Condon, Pee Wee Russell, and Zutty Singleton; Russell and Singleton continued to play there with their own groups – Singleton leading a trio in 1939 and Russell several ensembles throughout the 1940s. Sidney Bechet, who first appeared as a guest musician with the venue's intermission group, the Spirits of Rhythm, remained at the club as the leader of a quartet until 1940. The numerous important resident performers there also included Georg Brunis (1936–8, 1941–2), Meade "Lux" Lewis (as intermission pianist, *c*1936), Muggsy Spanier (1939, mid-1940s to 1948), Wild Bill Davison (1941), Brad Gowans and Bob Casey (both 1942–3), Miff Mole (1943–7), Billy Butterfield (from late 1947), Hank Duncan (1947–63), Phil Napoleon (1949–55, alternating with Pee Wee Erwin during the early 1950s), and Kenny Davern (1961). Others who played less regularly at Nick's were Cliff Jackson and Buster Harding (both as intermission pianists) and Sidney De Paris. The club closed in 1963.

BIBLIOGRAPHY

G. Hoefer: "The Saga of Nick's," *Down Beat Music '64* (Chicago, 1963), 55
J. Harris: "Bobby Hackett at Nick's," *Jazz Session*, no.9 (1945), 11
M. Peart: "Home of Dixieland Jazz," *Jazz Session*, no.9 (1945), 3

——. **One Fifth Avenue.** Fifth Avenue and 8th Street. Lounge. In the late 1970s and early 1980s it offered jazz performances by such musicians as Al Haig and Freddie Moore.

——. **Onyx.** 35 West 52nd Street (1927–34); 72 West 52nd Street (4 February 1934 – spring 1937); 62 West 52nd Street (April 1937 – December 1939); 57 West 52nd Street (1942–*c*1949). The first club of this name was a speakeasy which opened in 1927 and was managed by Joe Helbock; among those who performed there were Joe Sullivan (as an unaccompanied soloist, 1933) and the Spirits of Rhythm. After the repeal of Prohibition in 1933, a new Onyx opened on 4 February 1934 as a legitimate nightclub at 72 West 52nd Street, still under Helbock's direction. Art Tatum was employed there as the club's intermission pianist and the Spirits of Rhythm returned; other jazz musicians to appear were Stuff Smith and Billie Holiday (both 1936) and the participants in the Onyx's organized jam sessions, who included Jack Teagarden, the Dorsey brothers, and Bud Freeman. A fire on 28 February 1935 closed the premises until 23 July, but the club resumed its activities at the same address and remained there until 1937. In that year the Onyx moved along West 52nd Street to no.62, where it was managed by Helbock in association with Carl Kress. The most notable performances at this location were those of John Kirby's sextet with Maxine Sullivan. This venue closed in its turn in the final week of 1939, but in 1942 Irving Alexander opened another Onyx club, the last to bear the name, at 57 West 52nd Street, which was active under various managers until around 1949; it then became a striptease club.

At its last address, the Onyx became well known for the presentation of swing, bop, and dixieland jazz, offering performances by many illustrious musicians and groups. Among them were a trio led by Al Casey (1943), Dizzy Gillespie's small group, which included Lester Young, Oscar Pettiford, and Budd Johnson (winter 1943–4), Billie Holiday (1943–4), Cozy Cole (to 1944), Barney Bigard (1944), Hot Lips Page (1944–5), Roy Eldridge, Ben Webster, Sarah Vaughan (1946), and Gillespie and Charlie Parker (both 1948).

BIBLIOGRAPHY

G. Hoefer: "Father of the Street: Onyx Club Days Recalled," *Down Beat Music '66* (Chicago, 1965), 90
A. Shaw: "Tape 4: the Onyx Club Review," "Onyx III," *The Street that Never Slept: New York's Fabled 52nd Street* (New York, 1971/*R*1983 as *52nd Street: the Street that Never Slept*), 75, 296

——. **Opaline.** 85 Avenue A. This restaurant, which opened in summer 1996, offered jazz on Sunday nights. Among the performers who appeared there were Larry Ridley's All Stars, which included Benny Powell. It closed in 2001.

——. **Open Door.** West 3rd Street and Washington Square South. Saloon. In spring 1953 Robert Reisner, assisted by Dave Lambert, began to present bop sessions on Sunday nights in the spacious room behind the bar; among the illustrious players they engaged were Charlie Parker, Bud Powell, Charles Mingus, Max Roach, Sonny Rollins, Milt Jackson, and Brew Moore. In October 1953 Reisner introduced a more extensive program of jazz, running from Sunday to Thursday, but this proved short-lived, even though he presented fine groups led by Jackson, Roach, and others. After Reisner left the Open Door it became a venue for jam sessions: Moore, the trumpeter Tony Fruscella, the guitarist Ronnie Singer, and the drummer Freddie Gruber formed the resident band and such players as Cecil Taylor sat in. Fruscella and Moore recorded the album *Fru 'n Brew* at the club in 1953 (Spot. 151). By early 1954 jazz was no longer offered there.

——. **Palace Garden Club.** 2389 Seventh Avenue. At its grand opening on 14 March 1925 Fletcher Henderson's band and June Clark's Creole Orchestra played there. The club was closed by federal agents one year after it opened; late in 1926 the Bamboo Inn took over the premises (see above).

——. **Palais Royal.** 200 West 48th Street, at Broadway. It was in operation from at least 1920: Paul Whiteman led a nine-piece orchestra there from 1 October of that year. The venue was later used first by Connie's Inn and then by the Cotton Club (see above). There was apparently another Palais Royal in operation about a decade later, since the Dorsey Brothers Orchestra played at a club of that name in 1934.

——. **Palsson's.** 158 West 72nd Street. Bar. The venue consisted of a bar room and a separate room for performances. Its second floor was converted into a theater around 1980. In 1981 Anthony Davis, Chico Freeman, and Rita Reys appeared at Palsson's, and Emily Remler first worked as a leader there, but the club abandoned its jazz policy in mid-1981. Later it became the cabaret and supper club Steve McGraw's, which closed in 1994. (R. Kennedy: "Neighborhood Report: Upper West Side: Curtain to Fall on Old-time Cabaret," *New York Times*, 26 June 1994)

——. **Paradise Club.** Eighth Avenue and 110th Street. Big Nick Nicholas led jam sessions there in 1950 to 1951, with Charlie Parker, Dizzy Gillespie, Sonny Stitt, Sonny Rollins, Gene Ammons, Hot Lips Page, Shorty Baker, Joe Newman, Ike Quebec, and Charli Persip among the participants.

——. **Paramount Hotel Grill.** This restaurant within the hotel offered jazz performances from at least the early 1930s. Charlie Barnet led a band there in 1933 and 1939.

——. **Paramount Theater.** Situated on Broadway downtown, by the time it became known in the 1930s as the mecca of swing bands in New York it had a dual function as a theater for films and stage shows. All the best-known big-band leaders appeared there, including Artie Shaw and Glen Gray (both December 1936), Ray Noble (January 1937), Benny Goodman (March 1937), and Cab Calloway.

——. **Park Central Hotel.** Seventh Avenue and West 55th Street. Jazz was offered for the diversion of the hotel's clients from at least the late 1920s. Ben Pollack appeared there in 1928, and in 1931 Noble Sissle and Red Nichols were both resident bandleaders (Artie Shaw was one of the latter's sidemen); Nichols continued to be associated with the hotel during the early years of the 1930s.

——. **Park Lane Hotel.** Regular jam sessions, organized by Paul Smith, Ernie Anderson, and Eddie Condon, took place in a venue in the hotel in the late 1930s. Among the musicians who took part in them was Sidney Bechet (early 1939).

——. **Patagonia.** See Pods' and Jerry's.

——. **Peacock Alley.** See Waldorf Astoria.

——. **Pied Piper.** 15 Barrow Street. This venue in Greenwich Village was active during the war years. James P. Johnson held an extended residency there in 1944–5, engaging Pee Wee Russell and Frankie Newton, among others, as members of his band. Ensembles led by Max Kaminsky and Willie "the Lion" Smith also performed at the club. On 26 December 1944 Wilbur De Paris presented a public jam session there, in which, besides De Paris himself, Sidney Bechet, Hank Duncan, Eddie Dougherty, Bob Wilber, Mary Lou Williams, Al Hall, and Bill Coleman took part; it was billed as a "Swing Soiree." The premises were later taken by the Café Bohemia (see above).

——. **The Plantation.** 50th Street and Broadway. The name Plantation was used at various times for venues in different parts of New York. It is not always possible to distinguish from references in the literature which of them is meant. The Plantation at which Duke Ellington's orchestra played between April and June 1926 seems likely to be the Plantation Theater Restaurant (see below).

——. **Plantation Café.** Winter Garden Theater. The restaurant above the theater offered jazz performances from at least 1927, when Duke Ellington's orchestra appeared there in the revue *Messin' Around.* It may or may not be the same venue as those referred to in different sources as the Plantation (see above) and the Plantation Theater Restaurant (see below).

——. **Plantation Club.** Two major venues in the city were known by this name. The principal Plantation Club opened at 644 Lenox Avenue (at West 142nd Street) in the premises occupied until February 1936 by the Cotton Club; it flourished until the early 1940s. Among the bands that appeared there were those led by Willie Bryant (1937), Ovie Alston (1937), and Hot Lips Page (1938). Una Mae Carlisle performed at the club in the early 1940s, after her return from Europe.

Around 1930 Connie and George Immerman (who also owned and ran Connie's Inn, see above) took over a venue on Lenox Avenue and West 126th Street, intending to extend the rivalry that Connie's Inn already posed to the Cotton Club; Cab Calloway was to have been the resident bandleader. But their Plantation Club was destroyed, probably on its opening night, by gangsters hired by the Cotton Club's proprietor Owney Madden.

——. **Plantation Theater Restaurant** [Plantation Room]. Broadway. This venue was opened in 1922 by Sam Salvin for the express purpose of staging *The Plantation Revue*, starring the singer Florence Mills. Salvin's first venture was so successful that the theater restaurant continued to flourish for several years (to at least 1926).

——. **Pods' and Jerry's.** 168 West 133rd Street. Its formal name was the Patagonia, but it was known by the nicknames of its owners, Pods (Charles) Hollingsworth and Jerry (Jeremiah) Preston; after the repeal of Prohibition in 1933 it was renamed the Log Cabin. It flourished as a venue for small groups from 1932 and featured such musicians as Willie "the Lion" Smith, Jelly Roll Morton, Fats Waller, Sidney Bechet, and Billie Holiday. By the 1960s the premises had become a church.

——. **Prelude.** 3219 Broadway. It was active from the late 1950s into at least the mid-1960s. Mary Lou Williams played there in December 1959; Stuff Smith, Billy Taylor (ii), Gene Rodgers, and Ramsey Lewis all led trios at the Prelude.

——. **President Hotel.** See Adrian's Tap Room.

——. **Primrose Dancehall.** 125th Street. This Harlem venue engaged jazz bands to play for dancing during the 1930s. Cozy Cole and his Hot Cinders were among the groups that worked there. In 1935–6 Ray Noble led a band at the Primrose that included Charlie Spivak, Pee Wee Erwin, Bud Freeman, Glenn Miller, and Claude Thornhill.

——. **Pyles's.** Fifth Avenue at 138th Street. This Harlem saloon, run by Harry Pyles, hosted informal piano cutting contests from around 1918 to 1920, with James P. Johnson, Willie "the Lion" Smith, and other leading stride players participating.

——. **Rainbow Room.** RCA Building, 30 Rockefeller Plaza, Sixth Avenue. At the top of the RCA Building, the club consists of a bar, restaurant, and dance floor. It offered jazz performances from at least the late 1930s and continued to flourish through the 1980s. Landmarks in its history as a jazz venue included residencies by the Casa Loma Orchestra (1937), Sy Oliver's band (1970s and 1980s), and Panama Francis and his Savoy Sultans (1980–85). Other musicians who played there were Jonah Jones (1950s), Bob Wilber, Woody Herman, Bob Haggart (1984), and Bob Rosengarden (1985). It closed for remodeling in the mid-1980s and after reopening presented dance bands; John Pizzarelli led a big band there during this time. An adjacent supper club, Rainbow and Stars, presented cabaret singers.

——. **Rathskeller.** See Cocoanut Grove.

——. **Red Blazer Too.** 1576 Third Avenue (to 1984); 349 West 46th Street (1987–96); 32 West 37th Street (from *c*1998). It began its jazz policy in spring 1977 and by summer 1980 was presenting jazz for dancing every night of the week, with big bands appearing from Monday to Wednesday and small groups from Thursday through Sunday. Its repertory focused on early jazz and dance music; Vince Giordano and the Nighthawks held a residency from the late 1970s, and Sol Yaged led small groups for Sunday brunch and evening appearances. The Third Avenue location closed after celebrating New Year's Eve in 1984, at which point a related older venue, Red Blazer (a restaurant and bar at 1571 Second Avenue), undertook to continue the music policy, although in a greatly diminished capacity.

Red Blazer Too reopened at West 46th Street in early 1987, and over the course of the next decade it continued to present music nightly, as before. It appears to have closed at this location in December 1996. In January 1998 the club moved to West 37th Street, in premises which were once the home of John Barrymore and also the former club the

Hideaway (37th Street Hideaway). It continues to operate in the new century.

BIBLIOGRAPHY

J. S. Wilson: "Jazz: John Bucher Group is Fixture at Red Blazer," *New York Times* (8 Sept 1980)
——: "Smoke Filled Rooms – Comics, Bands, and All that Jazz," *New York Times* (8 Aug 1980)
R. F. Shepard: "Going Out Guide," *New York Times* (18 April 1985)
J. S. Wilson: "The Pop Life: Traditional Jazz: a Flicker of Life," *New York Times* (22 Oct 1986)
——: "Jazz: Pete Compo Quartet," *New York Times* (20 April 1987)

——. **Reisenweber's Restaurant.** West 58th Street and Eighth Avenue, south of Columbus Circle. It was open by the mid-1910s, when its activities were directed by Max Hart. It is of jazz interest chiefly because it was the scene of the first sensational success of the Original Dixieland Jazz Band in January 1917. It continued to engage jazz musicians now and again into the 1920s; Bubber Miley played for cabaret acts there around 1923.

——. **Renaissance Ballroom and Casino.** 150 West 138th Street. It was active from the early 1920s into the 1960s in large premises in a two-story red-brick building; the entertainment it offered, besides gambling and dancing, included cabaret acts, and there was always a call for jazz musicians. Vernon Andrade was resident at the Renaissance for a period of 15 years from around 1923, and among his sidemen at different times were Happy Caldwell, George Washington, Zutty Singleton, and Al Sears. Fletcher Henderson led his band there regularly in the late 1920s, Chick Webb's orchestra played in 1928–9, and Edgar Hayes's in 1937–8. In the early 1940s Sears led a big band, of which Lester Young was a member early in 1943.

——. **Rendezvous Cabaret.** 65 West 129th Street, near Lenox Avenue. It opened on 11 September 1923 under the direction of Broadway Jones. Fletcher Henderson's group may have played there shortly before beginning a residency at the Club Alabam, but sources are unclear. In October 1924 the Bamville Club opened at the same location (see above).

——. **Rendezvous Inn** [Rendezvous Club]. See Luckey's Rendezvous.

——. **Reno Sweeney.** See Zinno's.

——. **Reuben's.** 262 West 130th Street (*c*1930–38); 242 West 130th Street (*c*1938–45). Run by Reuben Harris, it offered yet another venue in Harlem where stride and swing pianists could play, and compete, informally. Fats Waller and Clarence Profit are among those who appeared there. By the 1960s both buildings had been incorporated into a housing project.

——. **Rhythm Club.** 168 West 132nd Street/2235 Seventh Avenue (to 1932); 169 West 133rd Street (from 1932). It was opened in the early 1920s and managed by Bert Hall, a trombonist from Chicago. An informal venue in a basement room below the Lafayette Theatre, it is identified by both the 132nd Street and the Seventh Avenue addresses. The Rhythm Club became a favorite haunt of musicians, who often jammed with the house band there. Sidney Bechet, Buddy Christian, Tommy Benford, and Louis Metcalf worked together at the club in 1924, and Bechet returned as resident bandleader the following year. The Rhythm Club was apparently still active in the early 1930s, for in 1932 it moved to a room at the back of the Nest Club on 133rd Street and the old venue was renamed the Hoofer's Club (see above). For a time the Rhythm Club published its own newsletter, the *Rhythm Club News*. In later decades the 133rd Street venue was converted into a loft and warehouse.

——. **Riviera Club** [Club Riviera]. There appear to have been a number of venues of this name in the New York area at different times. The first, which may have been some way out of the city, was managed by Ben Marden and presented jazz from at least the mid-1930s. In 1934 the short-lived Dorsey Brothers Orchestra appeared there, and the following year the violinist Eddie South led a big band opposite Paul Whiteman's orchestra; among South's sidemen were Everett Barksdale, Milt Hinton, and Tommy Benford. In March 1939 a Riviera club at St. John's Place and Kingston in Brooklyn advertised "4 Big Swing Days" with Bunny Berigan and Bob Howard.

Somewhat later a Riviera Club was active in Greenwich Village on Seventh Avenue South. Pee Wee Russell, Art Hodes, and Willie "the Lion" Smith appeared there in 1949, and between that time and 1951 other performers included Hot Lips Page, Vic Dickenson, Jonah Jones, Gene Roland, and Frank Orchard. The club later engaged a resident trio of lesser-known players led by the clarinetist Ben Parrish and became a venue for informal jam sessions.

——. **Rockland Palace.** 280 West 155th Street. This dance hall, which held 6000 people, was formerly the Manhattan Casino (see above); it took its new name around 1928, when the Royal Garden Orchestra, led by the drummer Herbert Cowens, played there. In late 1930 Noble Sissle's band, with Sidney Bechet, undertook its first New York engagement at the Rockland. Other groups to perform at the dance hall during its long existence were Horace Henderson's Dixie Stompers (1931), Fletcher Henderson's Orchestra (1932), and a band led by Happy Caldwell (1957).

——. **Rose Danceland.** 309 West 125th Street. A small venue, established in a former dancing school on the second floor of a corner building, it was in operation from at least 1927. In that year Tony Sbarbaro and Chick Webb played there and Jelly Roll Morton began a residency that lasted into 1928, with a group that included at various times Lee Blair, Russell Procope, Omer Simeon, and Ed Anderson. In the early 1930s Bingie Madison (1931) and the pianist Earle Howard (1932) were both resident at the club. By the 1960s the premises had been converted into an office building.

——. **Roseland Ballroom.** Several venues in the New York area used this name. Following the success of his Roseland Ballroom in Philadelphia (see below) Louis J. Brecker opened the New York Roseland Ballroom at 1658 Broadway (at West 51st Street) on New Year's Day 1919. One of the largest ballrooms in New York, it was sumptuously decorated and beautifully maintained (it was thoroughly refurbished in 1930) and became the center for hot music and jazz dancing in the downtown area.

Early in its existence it began to engage African-American bands (the clientele was exclusively white): in 1924 A. J. Piron's orchestra appeared there and Fletcher Henderson started his long and influential association with the ballroom, which was to last intermittently until 1942. Jean Goldkette's band (with Bix Beiderbecke) also played at the Roseland (1926–31), and in 1926 it engaged in a battle of bands with the Henderson ensemble (the two groups also played in alternation at the Graystone Ballroom in Detroit, see above).

From the late 1920s all the major swing bands took their turn at the Roseland, including McKinney's Cotton Pickers (1928), the Casa Loma Orchestra (1929), Marion Hardy's Alabamians (1931), and ensembles led by Claude Hopkins (late 1920s, 1931–4), Andy Kirk (1930), Chick Webb (intermittently 1930–31), Cab Calloway (1932), Luis Russell (1933), Count Basie (1936–9), Benny Carter (1939), and Ovie Alston (1942–7). Broadcasts took place regularly from the venue by landline and were transmitted throughout the USA. The ballroom closed on 27 December 1956 and the magnificent building was demolished shortly afterwards. A new and even larger ballroom, Roseland Dance City, opened in the same year at 239 West 52nd Street. Among the bands that worked there was Count Basie's, which appeared several times in the 1970s (1972, 1973, 1979). From 1981 Roseland Dance City has offered music for dancing (including ballroom dancing), but most of its activities fall outside the scope of this dictionary.

The success of the main Roseland Ballroom in mid-town Manhattan led to the opening in Harlem of the short-lived Murray's Roseland in 1927 (see above) and in Brooklyn of another Roseland around 1930. Woody Herman's band made its official début there in 1936.

——. **Roseland Dance City.** See Roseland Ballroom.

——. **Ross Tavern.** West 51st Street and Sixth Avenue. After-hours club. This basement venue, active in the 1930s, was a favorite meeting place for jazz musicians. Among those who played there was Art Hodes (1939).

——. **Roundtable.** 151 East 50th Street. It was in operation by at least the late 1950s. Tyree Glenn played there from late 1958 into the late 1960s. Muggsy Spanier appeared in 1959, as did Jimmy Rushing and Cootie Williams, and in December of that year Jack Teagarden played with Don Goldie; a quintet led by Cootie Williams was resident in 1960–61.

——. **Royal Roost.** 1674 Broadway. It was owned by Ralph Watkins (who had earlier run Kelly's Stable, see above) and Morris Levy (later the proprietor of Birdland (see above) and director of the record company Roulette) and was managed by Monte Kay; it probably opened in 1945. While it originated as a chicken restaurant, by 1946 it was known principally as a venue for jazz. Following an initial residency by Jimmie Lunceford's orchestra, the club's repertory turned increasingly to bop and cool jazz. This tradition was well established by the late 1940s, when among the musicians featured at the Royal Roost were Miles Davis, Lester Young, Charlie Parker, and Lennie Tristano. Watkins left the club in 1948 to open a new club called Bop City (see above), but the Royal Roost continued to be active into the 1950s; Buck Clayton was among the resident players around 1953.

——. **Royston's Rhythm.** 63 Lafayette Street. Located near the Brooklyn Academy of Music, Royston's Rhythm was open from around 1992 to 1998. It often presented jazz on weekends, with such performers as Donald Harrison and Cassandra Wilson appearing. ("Neighborhood Report: Fort Greene/Bedford-Stuyvesant: 'It's Getting Pretty Snazzy': a Brownstone Enclave," *New York Times*, 4 June 1995)

——. **Ryan's.** See Jimmy Ryan's.

——. **St. James Infirmary.** 22 Seventh Avenue South. Opened by Hod O'Brien and Roswell Rudd around 1974, the club operated into late 1975 before closing. It presented various guest musicians accompanied by a house band which initially included O'Brien, Rudd, and Sheila Jordan; a later group consisted of Bob Mover, O'Brien, Cameron Brown or Richie Youngsteen on double bass, and Beaver Harris or Jimmy Madison on drums.

——. **St. Nick's Pub.** 773 St. Nicholas Ave. This venue, run by Berta Alloway, is perhaps best known for its Monday-night jam sessions, which began in the mid-1990s and are led by Patience Higgins and the Sugar Hill Jazz Quartet. St. Nick's Pub also presents jazz on at least five other nights of the week, featuring mostly house bands. Brooks Kerr played there in 1996. (T. Souter: "Neighborhood Report: Harlem: Major Sax Appeal: on Mondays, the Joint is Jumping. Guess Where," *New York Times*, 22 Feb 1998)

——. **St. Regis Hotel.** Fifth Avenue and 55th Street. Its name was later changed to the St. Regis-Sheraton Hotel. Jazz was performed in various parts of the hotel from at least the late 1930s. In 1938 a jam session involving Sidney Bechet, Max Kaminsky, Yank Lawson, Hot Lips Page, Bobby Hackett, Mezz Mezzrow, Pee Wee Russell, Tommy Dorsey, Bud Freeman, Eddie Condon, Zutty Singleton, Dave Tough, and others was organized in the Viennese Roof Room by Joe Marsala; it was broadcast in both the USA and the UK. The venue was still in operation in 1973, when Count Basie appeared there. Jazz was occasionally presented in the King Cole Room in the 1980s, when Doc Cheatham (1984), Woody Herman (1985), and Joe Bushkin (1986) were among those who played there. The hotel closed for remodeling in 1988 and after reopening in 1992 rarely offered jazz.

——. **Salt Peanuts.** 399 Greenwich Street. Opened in March 1980 by Betty Rodgers, her daughter Constance Rodgers, and Nancy Nathan-Amborn, Salt Peanuts presented mainly bop; it appears to have closed after approximately one year. Musicians and groups who appeared there included Red Garland, Randy Weston, Clifford Jordan, Barry Harris, Charlie Rouse, Hugh Lawson, Dizzy Reece, Sheila Jordan, Louis Hayes and Ben Riley, and the quintet led by Junior Cook and Bill Hardman.

BIBLIOGRAPHY

"Salt Peanuts Giving Itself a Benefit," *New York Times* (29 Oct 1980)
R. F. Shepard: "Going Out Guide," *New York Times* (25 Dec 1980)

——. **Saratoga Club.** 575 Lenox Avenue. Opened in 1929 in premises formerly occupied by the Capitol Palace (see above), it was managed by Johnny Carey and Sandy Thompson. It was one of the earliest cabarets in Harlem to adopt a jazz policy; Sidney Bechet's New Orleans Feetwarmers and a band led by Luis Russell both appeared there before the turn of the decade. Among resident musicians in the 1930s were Charlie Green and the pianist Earle Howard (both 1930) and Reggie Johnson, whose band included Cedric Wallace (1932). The venue was renamed Martin's Tavern in 1933.

——. **Savoy Ballroom.** 596 Lenox Avenue. It was opened on 12 March 1926 by Moe Gale (Moses Galewski), Charles Galewski, and a Harlem real-estate businessman called Charles Buchanan, who functioned as the ballroom's manager. The Savoy, which occupied the second floor of a building that extended along the whole block between 140th and 141st streets, was billed as the world's most beautiful ballroom; it had a large dance floor (200 feet by 50 feet), two bandstands, and a retractable stage. It swiftly became the most popular dance venue in Harlem, and many of the jazz dance crazes of the 1920s and 1930s originated there; the ballroom enjoyed a long and glittering career that lasted well into the 1950s before a decline in its fortunes set in.

On its opening night the Savoy featured Fess Williams and his Royal Flush Orchestra, the Charleston Bearcats, fronted by Leon Abbey, and, as a guest band, Fletcher Henderson's Roseland Orchestra; the Charleston Bearcats formed a lasting connection with the venue and later changed its name to the Savoy Bearcats. Except on special occasions, the ballroom engaged two bands, which played alternate sets, and this policy led to its becoming a famous venue for battles of bands. Elaborate events of this kind were also organized by the management: on 15 May 1927 the Savoy presented a "Battle of Jazz," which featured King Oliver's Dixie Syncopators, a band led by Williams, Chick Webb's Harlem Stompers, and Henderson's Roseland Orchestra; other battles were fought between bands led by Lloyd Scott, Webb, Alex Johnson, Charlie Johnson, Williams, and Henderson (6 May 1928) and between Cab Calloway's Missourians and groups led by Duke Ellington, Henderson, Cecil Scott, Lockwood Lewis, and Webb (14 May 1930).

From the 1930s a number of bandleaders formed long and influential associations with the ballroom. By the mid-1930s Chick Webb's name was inextricably linked with that of the Savoy, and he continued to lead his band there through the decade; his singer from 1934 was Ella Fitzgerald, who took over leadership of the ensemble after Webb's untimely death in 1939. Al Cooper's Savoy Sultans first appeared at the ballroom in 1937 and remained for many years. The Erskine Hawkins Orchestra enjoyed a similar connection with the venue, holding extended residencies from the 1940s through the 1950s. Besides those who played there regularly, most of the important bands and musicians of the swing era appeared at the Savoy at some time: Andy Kirk, the Mills Brothers, Sidney Bechet, Count Basie, Coleman Hawkins, Roy Eldridge, and many others appeared for single engagements or held short residencies there. Benny Carter's big band made its début in the ballroom in March 1939 and Carter continued to work there intermittently until January 1941. As was the case with several of the city's most famous nightspots, the Savoy was connected by landline with a New York radio station, which allowed its music to be broadcast throughout the nation. The building was demolished in 1958, and the grounds were absorbed into a housing project.

——. **Savoy Lounge.** 355 West 41st Street. It opened in June 1997, with John Webber both assisting with its bookings and leading groups there. Etta Jones and Claude Williams were among others who appeared at the club. A house band performed on Monday nights. It had closed by 2001. (C. C. Ray: "New Yorkers & Co.: in Clinton, Monday Night is the Jazziest Night of the Week," *New York Times*, 20 July 1997)

——. **Seventh Avenue South.** 21 Seventh Avenue South. This small venue was opened in 1978 and remained active until 1985. It was owned by Mike and Randy Brecker, whose band, the Brecker Brothers, often played there. Until the early 1980s it offered a repertory that emphasized jazz-rock, but the range of styles gradually broadened; in 1984, for example, Lew Soloff and Gil Evans's big band appeared there. Videos of performances at the club have been released, including *Art Blakey: Jazz Live*, ii: *From Seventh Avenue South* (*c*1985 [filmed January 1982]) and *Mike Mainieri: the Jazz Life* (*c*1985), which captures the vibraphonist leading a sextet whose members were Bob Mintzer, Warren Bernhardt, Marcus Miller, Eddie Gomez, and Omar Hakim.

——. **721 Club.** 721 St. Nicholas Avenue. Formerly the Silver Dollar Café (see below), it was renamed the 721 Club following the repeal of Prohibition in 1933 and thereafter presented small jazz groups, including, in 1941, that of Ernie Henry. By the 1960s it had become a neighborhood bar, the Spot, and was no longer featuring jazz.

——. **Shalimar.** 2065 Seventh Avenue. This Harlem nightclub, operated by Red Randolph, flourished from around 1940 to 1960, presenting such artists as Ben Webster, Marlowe Morris, and Julian Dash.

——. **Sherwood Inn.** It was active from at least the late 1950s, when Billy Bauer first played there; his connections with the club continued into the next decade. Other musicians who performed at the Sherwood included Miff Mole and Pee Wee Russell (1960).

——. **Showman's Café.** 125th Street (mid-1940s–1985); 2321 Frederick Douglass Boulevard (1985–98); 375 West 125th Street (Dr. Martin Luther King Jr. Boulevard) (from August 1998). Open from the 1940s, the Showman's Café was originally situated next door to the Apollo Theatre and served as a post-show gathering spot for the Apollo's patrons. It began to offer soul jazz in 1978, when its new owner purchased a Hammond B-3 organ for the club. In 1985, after a fire destroyed the premises, it moved to Frederick Douglass Boulevard. Its specialty continued to be soul jazz – Danny Mixon and Reuben Wilson are but two of the organists who have graced its stage – but for many years it has also featured tap-dancing on Thursday nights. The club moved to 125th Street in August 1998, during a period of gentrification of that area of Harlem. It is a frequent stop for numerous Japanese and other non-American tourists.
(<http://www.bigapplejazz.com/nycjazzclubs.html> (2001))

——. **Showplace.** 146 West 4th Street. Bill Evans (ii) played with Tony Scott there in August 1959, and soon thereafter the pianist held a lengthy engagement with his new trio, consisting of Scott LaFaro and Paul Motian. Charles Mingus performed at the Showplace between December 1959 and October 1960. After Mingus left the club his former sidemen Lonnie Hillyer and Charles McPherson led a band there.

——. **Shuffle Inn.** 165 West 131st Street. Named for the hit musical revue *Shuffle Along*, by Noble Sissle and Eubie Blake, this venue opened in November 1921 and was managed by Jack Goldberg; the orchestra was directed by Luckey Roberts. In 1923 it became Connie's Inn (see above), with a new entrance, and consequent new address, on Seventh Avenue.

——. **Silver Dollar Café.** 721 St. Nicholas Avenue. The club flourished from the mid-1920s until the repeal of Prohibition. At some point in the early 1930s Kaiser Marshall's trio, which included Rudy Powell, played there.

——. **Slugs.** 242 East 3rd Street. It was opened early in 1966 and specialized in (but was not restricted to) the presentation of hard bop. During its first year of operation the performers who appeared there included Jackie McLean,

Joe Henderson, Philly Joe Jones, Yusef Lateef, Stanley Turrentine, Charles Lloyd, and Ornette Coleman (who led a trio in September 1966). The club later engaged such other prominent players as Freddie Hubbard (1967), Sun Ra (1967–8), Art Blakey (1969), McCoy Tyner (1969), Elvin Jones (1970–71), Lee Morgan (1971–2), and Gato Barbieri (1972). Performances given by Charles Tolliver at Slugs in 1970 were recorded and issued on the LP *Live at Slugs* (SE 1972). The club closed shortly after Lee Morgan was murdered there in 1972.

——. **Smalls.** 183 West 10th Street. Situated in a basement, this small, highly informal club (which seats about 50 people) was opened in autumn 1994 by Mitch Borden, who from that time has offered jazz every night. Groups are presented from 10 p.m. to 2 a.m., and then jam sessions (usually) run well into the next morning (i.e., to around 9 a.m.). Most of the programming at Smalls involves lesser-known musicians, such as the double bass player Omer Avital, the pianist Jason Lindner (who regularly led a big band there for much of the late 1990s), and the organist Sam Yahel. Avishai Cohen has also appeared frequently. In 1998 a recording of groups that regularly performed at the club was released by Impulse! on the album *Jazz Underground: Live at Smalls* (1997, 245).

BIBLIOGRAPHY

J. Macnie: Liner notes, *Jazz Underground: Live at Smalls* (Imp. 245, 1997); repr. at <http://www.smallsjazz.com/about/article2.html> (2001)
C. Wilson: "Refrain: Notes from the Underground: a Basement Bar in Manhattan Offers a Window on the Scene," *Jazziz*, xv/5 (1998), 94
M. Zwerin: "All Hail the World's First Self-service Jazz Club," *International Herald Tribune* (8 April 1998), 20
A. Sinnreich: "Where the Solos Last Till Dawn: with Endless Music and Open Jams, Smalls Stands Out among Jazz Clubs like a Blue Note in a Major Scale," *New York Times* (16 Jan 2000)
<http://www.smallsjazz.com/home.html> (2001)

——. **Smalls' Paradise.** $2294\frac{1}{2}$ Seventh Avenue. Soon after closing his venue on Fifth Avenue (see immediately below) Ed Smalls opened Smalls' Paradise (on 22 October 1925) in basement premises, where he offered music and dancing. It became one of the most successful clubs in Harlem, surviving the Depression and then the difficult postwar years, when most venues in the area felt the pinch and many closed.

Smalls' enjoyed its heyday in the 1920s and early 1930s, when many of the most important groups and musicians of the period occupied its bandstand. Charlie Johnson (whose band was heard at the opening), Willie "the Lion" Smith, Jimmy Archey, and Fletcher Henderson all first played there in the mid- to late 1920s, and Smith and Johnson both returned to the club for long residencies; Elmer Snowden led the Smalls' Paradise Orchestra there during the early 1930s, and the group made the film *Smash your Baggage* in 1932. During the Depression Smalls cut back his operation, and in 1934–5 James P. Johnson led a band of reduced size; after 1935, however, the club's resources were restored, and by 1937 Hot Lips Page was leading a big band there. In the 1940s and 1950s resident bandleaders included Chris Columbus (1944), Gene Sedric (late 1940s), Harry Dial (1947–55), Happy Caldwell (1950–53), and Gus Aitken (1950).

At some point Smalls sold the venue and operated a liquor store on 154th Street. In the mid-1960s, when Red Prysock and Ray Charles were among those who appeared, Smalls' Paradise was owned by the basketball star Wilt Chamberlain. It continued to be active into the 1980s and ceased operations only in 1986.

——. **Smalls' Sugar Cane Club.** 2212 Fifth Avenue. From around 1917 to 1925, before he established his famous Smalls' Paradise (see immediately above), Ed Smalls ran Smalls' Sugar Cane Club, which was said to be the first such venue to cater to affluent white audiences who went "slumming" (i.e., traveled uptown to Harlem for an evening of entertainment). The club initially featured the pianist Paul Seminole, as well as waiters who sang and danced while serving and during floor shows. From 1923 the club's house band was led first by the pianist Charlie Smith and then by June Clark, whose sidemen in 1924 included Benny Carter. By the 1960s the premises had been absorbed into a housing project.

——. **Smoke.** 2751 Broadway. It was opened in early April 1999 by Paul Stache and Frank Christopher in the former location of Augie's (see above), and since that time has presented mainly bop and related styles. Among those who have appeared there are Eric Alexander, the pianist David Berkman, George Coleman, Larry Goldings's trio (with Peter Bernstein and Bill Stewart), Benny Golson, Eddie Henderson, Joe Locke, Harold Mabern, Cecil Payne, and Michael Weiss. The group One for All recorded at Smoke in 2001.

BIBLIOGRAPHY

C. Kilgannon: "New Yorkers & Co.: the Restaurant as Leading Economic Indicator," *New York Times* (19 Dec 1999)
<http://www.smokejazz.com> (2001)

——. **Soundscape.** 500 West 52nd Street. This loft was opened in June 1979 by the ethnomusicologist Verna Gillis, who presented mainly free jazz and Afro-Cuban jazz into the mid-1980s. Soundscape featured a broad scope of musical talent, including notably Steve Lacy (1980), the quartet of Ernst-Ludwig Petrowsky, Hans Reichel, Rüdiger Carl, and Sven-Åke Johansson (1981), Bob Moses and David Murray (both 1982), and Marilyn Crispell and Odean Pope (both 1983). On Tuesdays Cuban and Latin jazz musicians appeared; among those who performed were Jerry Gonzalez, Paquito D'Rivera, and Claudio Roditi. During the Kool Jazz Festival in 1983 the club hosted the series "New Music at Soundscape," which featured groups led by, among others, Michele Rosewoman, Andrew Cyrille, Jimmy Lyons (ii), Billy Bang, and D'Rivera. Gillis closed the venue in 1987.

BIBLIOGRAPHY

R. Palmer: "Music is Living in a Loft on 10th Avenue," *New York Times* (28 Nov 1980)
——: "Pop Jazz: Cuban Jazz Finds Home in 52nd St. Loft," *New York Times* (12 June 1981)
S. G. Freedman: "What Really Makes New York Work: Secret Powers: Verna Gillis: the Muse of the Melting Pot," *New York Times* (8 April 1990)

——. **Spotlite (Club).** 56 West 52nd Street. It was opened in December 1944 by Clark Monroe (also the proprietor of Monroe's Uptown House, see above) and operated for about three years as a venue for swing and bop. Among the leading musicians he engaged were Coleman Hawkins, Hot Lips Page, Billie Holiday, Ben Webster, Charlie Ventura, Charlie Parker, Dizzy Gillespie, and Oscar Pettiford; Baby Laurence danced at the Spotlite Club around 1947, trading fours with Parker, Miles Davis, Bud Powell, and other famous players.

——. **The Squire.** See Angry Squire.

——. **Star and Garter.** 105 West 13th Street. Bar and restaurant. Active around 1980, it presented jazz at weekends and specialized in piano and double bass duos. The musicians who appeared there included Tommy Flanagan and Cedar Walton.

——. **Storytowne.** See Storyville.

——. **Storyville.** 41 East 58th Street. Named, like the club he founded earlier in Boston (see above), for the red-light district of New Orleans, it was opened by George Wein in 1976. By 1979 it had been renamed Storytowne. The musicians who played there included the quintet led by Harry Edison and Eddie "Lockjaw" Davis, Joe Newman, and Gerry Mulligan.

——. **Stryker's.** 103 West 86th Street. Bar. It was established in 1972 and offered performances by some notable musicians, among them Jimmy Garrison, Warren Chiasson, Chet Baker, Lee Konitz, and the duo of Chuck Wayne and Joe Puma. It had closed by 1982.

——. **Studio Rivbea.** Situated on Bond Street in the SoHo district, it was opened in 1970 by Sam and Bea Rivers and specialized in free jazz. It remained active throughout the decade.

——. **Studio 77.** See Ali's Alley.

——. **Stuyvesant Casino.** 140 Second Avenue. Ballroom. This large venue flourished during the 1940s and 1950s, offering dancing, jazz performances, and jam sessions. Bunk Johnson's New Orleans band (for illustrations *see* Johnson, bunk) made its New York début there on 28 September 1945, a performance that precipitated an upsurge of interest in New Orleans jazz. Later the promoter Bob Maltz rented the venue on Friday and Saturday nights to present traditional and mainstream jazz; he engaged, among others, Sidney Bechet, Art Hodes (1945–9), Henry "Red" Allen (1950), Zutty Singleton, and Buck Clayton.

——. **Swanee Club.** 253 West 125th Street. Formerly the Alamo Café (see above), a Harlem venue for whites, it became the Swanee Club, an African-American club managed by Joe Ward, in 1925 and operated as such for approximately a decade. The trombonist Bill Brown and his Brownies initially served as the house band and broadcast from the club twice weekly.

——. **Sweet Basil.** 88 Seventh Avenue. It was opened in January 1975 by Horst Liepolt and Mel Litoff and flourished for a quarter of a century, offering a wide-ranging repertory. Musicians who appeared there included Gil Evans, Bucky Pizzarelli, John Abercrombie, Ron Carter, Junior Mance, Lester Bowie, Pharoah Sanders, David Murray, Doc Cheatham, Jim Hall and Red Mitchell (as a duo), Abdullah Ibrahim, George Russell, and the Leaders, among countless others. Until shortly before his death Evans led a band at the club on Mondays, and performances by his ensemble were recorded in 1984 and issued on the Japanese label Electric Bird as *The Monday Night Orchestra Live at Sweet Basil*. From 1980 to 1997 Cheatham's band played there regularly for Sunday brunch; following the trumpeter's death the band continued from 1997 to 2001 as Chuck Folds and Friends. From 1983 Liepolt's Music is . . . an Open Sky festival took place at the club (*see* Festivals). Sweet Basil closed on 1 May 2001.

BIBLIOGRAPHY

"Sweet Basil to Close this Month: New Club Planned on Site," *New York Times* (7 April 2001)

<http://www.sweetbasil.com/about.html> (2001)

——. **Sweetwaters.** 170 Amsterdam Avenue. Open from at least 1980, Sweetwaters offered music for many years, with appearances variously by jazz, pop, and soul singers, including Chris Connor, Ruth Brown, and Dakota Staton. Stanley Turrentine performed there in 1988 and 1991.

——. **Syncopation.** 15 Waverly Place. Loft. It was briefly active as a venue for bop around 1980, when John Lewis appeared there. By March 1981 a roller skating rink (i.e., roller discotheque) was located at this address, and in the mid-1980s Garvin's Café Lido (see above) opened there.

——. **Tango Gardens.** Ballroom. It was active from the late 1920s, when a band led by June Clark, with at different times Jimmy Harrison and Charlie Green among its members, played there. From 1947 to 1953 Bingie Madison led a small group at the Tango Palace, which may or may not be the same venue as the Tango Gardens.

——. **Tap Room.** See Adrian's Tap Room.

——. **Tavern on the Green.** Central Park at West 67th Street. Originally built in 1870 to house sheep in Central Park, the building in which the club is situated became a restaurant in 1934. Following new ownership in 1974 and subsequent extensive renovations, it reopened in August 1976 as Tavern on the Green. From the 1990s it has presented in its Chestnut Room both pianists, including Mike LeDonne, Warren Bernhardt, Dave McKenna, Cyrus Chestnut, and Hank Jones, and big bands, notably those of Lionel Hampton and Illinois Jacquet.

——. **Theresa Hotel Bar and Grill.** 2090 Seventh Avenue. Una Mae Carlisle was the house pianist there in the late 1940s.

——. **Three Deuces.** 72 West 52nd Street. It opened in premises vacated in 1937 by the Onyx club (see above) and was active as a jazz venue until around 1950. Among the managers were Sammy Kay and Irving Alexander. The club presented a range of styles and, in the 1940s particularly, engaged many notable musicians, including Art Tatum, the Spirits of Rhythm, John Kirby, Maxine Sullivan, Slim Gaillard, Ben Webster, Eddie Heywood, Johnny Guarnieri, Billy Taylor (ii), Georgie Auld, Slam Stewart, Sid Catlett, Lennie Tristano, Erroll Garner, Don Byas, Shelly Manne, Charlie Parker, Dizzy Gillespie, Ella Fitzgerald, George Shearing, and Kai Winding. In 1950 the venue became a striptease club, and it closed around 1954. (A. Shaw: "The Three Deuces," *The Street that Never Slept: New York's Fabled 52nd Street* (New York, 1971/*R*1983 as *52nd Street: the Street that Never Slept*), 284)

——. **Tillie's Chicken Shack.** 2134 West 133rd Street (*c*1928–33); Lenox Avenue between 121st and 122nd streets (1933–5). Another of the Harlem venues dedicated to stride and swing pianists, Tillie's Chicken Shack featured Bob Howard, Fats Waller, and others from around 1928 until 1933, when Prohibition ended. After moving to larger premises on Lenox Avenue the club no longer offered any significant music.

——. **Tin Palace.** 325 Bowery. This jazz room was opened in 1979, in which year Art Davis, Hilton Ruiz, and Gary Bartz played there.

——. **Tonic.** 107 Norfolk Street. Located in an old winery, Tonic opened in March 1998. It houses a street-level café and a basement lounge and bar. From mid-1998 the club has presented avant-garde jazz, with month-long programs organized by a series of "curators," notably John Zorn (who organized its first series in summer 1998), Susie Ibarra, Eugene Chadbourne, Misha Mengelberg, and Derek Bailey. It also offers a Klezmer music series (on Sunday afternoons), a Songwriter series (on Sunday nights), and a film night (on Mondays).

BIBLIOGRAPHY

"New Yorkers & Co.: There's a Comedian and a Sax in my Hair," *New York Times* (3 May 1998)

L. Pellegrinelli: "A Guided Tour of America's Most Fascinating Jazz Clubs," <http://www.newmusicbox.com/thirdperson/jan00/tonic.html> (2000)

<http://www.tonic107.com> (2001)

——. **Top of the Gate.** See Village Gate.

——. **Town Hall.** 123 West 43rd Street. It opened in 1921 as a public meeting house, seating nearly 1500 people (for illustration *see* JAZZ (i), fig.5). The hall was acquired by New York University in 1958 and closed temporarily between 1978 and 1980. Eddie Condon presented organized jam sessions there from April 1942 to 1946. Among other important events held at Town Hall during the mid-1940s were a gala performance staged by the Blue Note record label (15 December 1945), a series of midnight concerts of blues (1947), an appearance by Louis Armstrong (17 May 1947), and an all-star concert in which Bunk Johnson, Muggsy Spanier, Albert Nicholas, James P. Johnson, and other New Orleans jazz musicians took part (4 October 1947). Among the promoters who used the venue at this time was "Symphony Sid" Torin.

A number of important recordings were made at Town Hall. Condon's concerts were transcribed for radio broadcasts, and many were subsequently issued on commercial discs. A performance given on 9 June 1945 by Don Byas with Slam Stewart, Teddy Wilson, Red Norvo, and Stuff Smith was recorded in its entirety. Concerts given by Charlie Ventura in 1945, and by an all-star group that included Sidney Bechet, James P. Johnson, and Baby Dodds in 1946, were also recorded, as were two given later by Charles Mingus (12 October 1962 and 4 February 1972).

——. **Two Saints.** See Five Spot.

——. **Ubangi Club.** 2221 Seventh Avenue (1936 or later – early 1940s); 1678 Broadway (early 1940s–*c*1948). It opened some time after 1936 in the premises formerly occupied by Connie's Inn and the short-lived Harlem Club (see above); Connie's Inn and the Ubangi were the only clubs to succeed at the location. Some time in the early 1940s the Ubangi moved downtown to a building on Broadway that later housed the Clique and Birdland (see above). Before the move bands led by Teddy Hill, Kaiser Marshall (1935), and Ovie Alston played at the club, while in the 1940s resident bandleaders included Leon Abbey, Cecil Scott (1942–3), and Erskine Hawkins. The successful floor shows at the downtown venue were written by Chappie Willett.

——. **Upover Jazz Café.** 351 Flatbush Avenue. It appears to have opened in the late 1990s, from which time it has held regular Monday-night jam sessions (led by either Vincent Herring or Eddie Allen) and presented Latin jazz on Wednesdays. Performances on Friday and Saturday nights and Sunday afternoons have featured such musicians as Gary Bartz, John Hicks, Billy Harper, Harold Mabern, Benny Powell, and James Spaulding, as well as the pianist Orrin Evans. (<http://www.upoverjazz.com/about2.htm> (2001))

——. **Uptown Lowdown Club.** See Harlem Uproar House.

——. **Victoria Café.** West 141st Street and Seventh Avenue. It presented jazz from at least the 1930s, when among the groups to perform there was a trio led by Freddie Moore (1933–6). Don Frye was the house pianist. Edgar Hayes and Kaiser Marshall also led bands at the café, and Moore returned there in November 1940, when Louis Metcalf was among his sidemen. The club closed around 1945.

——. **Viennese Roof Room.** See St. Regis Hotel.

——. **Village Fair.** See Village Vanguard.

——. **Village Gate.** 160 Bleecker Street (1958 – February 1994); 240 West 52nd Street (October 1996–*c* September 1997). It opened in 1958 and continued to be active through the mid-1990s. The Bleecker Street club contained three separate venues: the basement club, also known as the Gate, opened first, with seats for more than 400 people; in 1964 Art D'Lugoff opened the street-level Terrace Bar, which seated around 90; later he opened the Top of the Gate, which seated around 300 and functioned mainly as a venue for cabaret, musical revues, and comedians.

Among the numerous internationally known musicians who performed at the Village Gate during the 1960s and 1970s were Miles Davis, Erroll Garner, Cecil Taylor, Horace Silver, Gerry Mulligan, Earl Hines, Jaki Byard, Bill Evans (ii), Lee Konitz, Ahmad Jamal, Roland Kirk, McCoy Tyner, and Art Blakey. Numerous recordings were made there during that time, most notably by Blue Mitchell (1961), Herbie Mann (1961, 1965), Coleman Hawkins (1962), Thelonious Monk (1963), Charles Mingus (1965), John Handy (1967), and Eddie Harris (1969). From October 1979 to 1982 or 1983 the off-Broadway musical *One Mo' Time* was given at the club, and its sequel, *Further Mo'*, opened in May 1990 and ran through the following autumn.

During the 1980s the stylistic emphasis at the Village Gate changed from swing and bop to jazz-rock and salsa. Sherrie Maricle led a regular jam session there from 1987. Among performers in the Terrace Bar in the late 1980s were Patti Bown, and the duos of Bill Mays and Michael Formanek and Allan Botschinsky and Niels-Henning Ørsted Pedersen. The Bleecker Street club closed in February 1994. In October 1996 D'Lugoff (and several partners) opened a new Village Gate on 52nd Street. Jazz was offered nightly at this location from 10 p.m., and during earlier hours it operated as a restaurant and supper club. The Village Gate closed at this location around September 1997.

BIBLIOGRAPHY

F. Ferretti: "Top of the Gate is Renamed, for Laughs," *New York Times* (21 Oct 1983)

M. Quint: "New Yorkers & Co.: a Village Club's Long Lease on Success," *New York Times* (5 Sept 1988)

B. Lambert: "Neighborhood Report: Greenwich Village: New Gig for the Old Gate?," *New York Times* (6 March 1994)

D. Martin: "It's All Over for the Village Gate, but its Ex-owner Looks Ahead," *New York Times* (8 July 1994)

J. Pareles: "New Night Life in Midtown Manhattan," *New York Times* (13 Dec 1996)

A. Ramirez: "New Yorkers & Co.: Art D'Lugoff Lands on his Feet," *New York Times* (27 Oct 1996)

——. **Village Vanguard.** Charles Street and Greenwich Avenue (26 February 1934–1935); 178 Seventh Avenue (from 1935). In 1932 Max Gordon opened a club, the Village Fair, on Sullivan Street in Greenwich Village, which provided a forum for poets to meet and read their work. The first Village Vanguard, opened in a basement on Charles Street at Greenwich Avenue, also functioned as a meeting place for local poets; when he wanted to introduce music at the club, Gordon was refused a cabaret license because of the shortcomings of the premises and was therefore obliged to move again. He opened a third club early in 1935 in another basement on Seventh Avenue, where a speakeasy called the Golden Triangle had operated earlier. The new Village Vanguard offered poetry and jazz, but it was not until the mid-1950s that it became known mainly as a jazz venue.

During its long and distinguished career the Village Vanguard has offered jazz in many styles, as well as popular music, folk music, dancing, cabaret acts, and performances by comedians. In the 1930s and 1940s, though not yet fully established as a jazz venue, it engaged performers of the standing of Sidney Bechet, Una Mae Carlisle, Art Hodes, and Mary Lou Williams; during the 1940s Eddie Heywood, Zutty Singleton, and Jimmy Hamilton formed the resident trio, playing for dancing and accompanying visiting musicians. After it made its name as one of New York's main jazz venues, such musicians as Dizzy Gillespie, Art Blakey, Miles Davis, Sonny Rollins, Coleman Hawkins, Charles Mingus, Gerry Mulligan, the Modern Jazz Quartet, Thelonious Monk, Keith Jarrett, Chick Corea, J. J. Johnson, Frank Morgan, and Sphere played at the Village Vanguard. The most significant of the venue's events were perhaps the many performances given by John Coltrane's groups, which resulted in some of his finest recordings, among them *Live at the Village Vanguard* (1961, Imp. 10) and *Live at the Village Vanguard Again* (1966, Imp. 9124); the club's web page offers an archive which lists more than 95 albums made there. The Thad Jones–Mel Lewis Orchestra (from 1979 the Mel Lewis Orchestra; from 1990 the Vanguard Jazz Orchestra) has played there on Monday nights from February 1966 into the new century.

The club marked its 50th anniversary in 1985 with a year of celebratory performances by musicians who included Gillespie, Wynton Marsalis, and Annie Ross. Following Gordon's death in 1989, his wife Lorraine Gordon took over the management of the Village Vanguard. Probably the world's most famous club, and certainly a landmark – indeed a shrine – for visiting tourists who love jazz, it has continued to prosper, and in February 2000 it celebrated its 65th anniversary. While in recent decades many clubs have processed the music offered through fancy sound systems and in-house video equipment, the Vanguard has maintained its basic approach, which continues to make it one of the best places to hear jazz.

BIBLIOGRAPHY

M. Gordon: *Live at the Village Vanguard* (New York, 1980)
R. Blumenthal: "A Jazz Club Turns 65: No Retirement Planned," *New York Times* (21 Feb 2000)
L. Pellegrinelli: "A Guided Tour of America's Most Fascinating Jazz Clubs," <http://www.newmusicbox.com/thirdperson/jan00/index.html> (2000)

——. **Village West.** 577 Hudson Street. It was active for a short time around 1982–4. Among the soloists and small groups who performed there were Jaki Byard, Barney Kessel, JoAnne Brackeen, and the duo of Ron Carter and Jim Hall, which appeared regularly and recorded there in 1984.

——. **Visiones.** 125 Macdougal Street. Restaurant. Open from the 1940s, Visiones began presenting jazz in the mid-1980s, when Jay Hoggard, Pheeroan akLaff, Bobby Previte, and Andy LaVerne were among those who appeared. Maria Schneider's orchestra played there weekly for five years until January 1998, when the club's ownership changed.

——. **Vo-de-do Club.** 2110 Seventh Avenue. William "Dude" Adams ran this club, which opened in June 1927 above the Alhambra Theater. Cliff Jackson led the band there before he took up a long residency at the Lenox Club.

——. **Waldorf Astoria.** Park Avenue at East 49th and East 50th streets. The hotel opened on this site, occupying the entire block between Park Avenue and Lexington Avenue, in November 1931, and jazz was performed in its various venues from the mid-1930s. The violinist Leo Reisman led a popular orchestra in the hotel for long periods in the 1930s and 1940s, during which time residencies were also held by major big bands, including Benny Goodman's, which fulfilled an engagement in the Empire Room from October 1939 until New Year's Day 1940 (for illustration *see* Bands, fig.4). On 23 February 1949 Rudi Blesh organized a battle of bands there, and Charlie Parker and Sidney Bechet played for a youth conference; a performance by Parker on 5 March of the same year was broadcast. Among the other musicians who performed at the Waldorf was Count Basie, who worked there in June 1957, June 1959, and June 1960. During the 1970s jazz pianists played regularly at Peacock Alley, a lounge in the hotel.

——. **Wells' Upstairs Room.** 2249 Seventh Avenue. It was opened by Joe Wells around 1946 and presented music from late in that decade into the 1960s; among those to appear were the trios of Mary Lou Williams and Patti Bown, Eubie Blake and Noble Sissle, Marlowe Morris, Wild Bill Davis, Willie Lewis, Ram Ramirez, and Dizzy Reece, who made his début in the USA at Wells' Upstairs Room in 1960.

——. **West Boondock.** 114 Tenth Avenue. Restaurant. It was in existence from around the late 1970s until the mid-1980s and regularly engaged solo pianists. Among those who appeared there was Sadik Hakim (1981, 1983).

——. **West End** [West End Café, West End Gate, West End Gate Café]. 2911 Broadway, at West 113th Street. Restaurant. Situated near Columbia University, it opened in 1973 and was active as a jazz venue into the 1990s. Until the early 1980s its musical activities were directed by Phil Schaap, who engaged numerous veteran swing musicians; among those who appeared there were the Countsmen, Jo Jones, Sonny Greer, Russell Procope, Eddie Durham, Sammy Price, Harold Ashby, Franc Williams, and George Kelly. Later its repertory expanded to include bop and other more modern jazz styles; among those who performed there in the 1980s were Geri Allen, Connie Crothers, Dizzy Gillespie, Benny Carter, Oliver Lake, David Murray, David "Fathead" Newman, and Jabbo Smith. The West End appears to have abandoned its jazz policy in the mid-1990s, by which time it was presenting programs for children; from October 1997 it was known as the West End Children's Theater.

——. **Whippoorwill.** 18 East 18th Street. This venue consisted of the main nightclub on the ground floor and an upstairs restaurant named Joanna. Stan Getz, Doc Cheatham, Roland Hanna, Jack Walrath, Donald Byrd, and Jimmy Owens were among the many musicians who appeared there during 1986, its only year of operation.

——. **Wonderland.** 519 Second Avenue. Restaurant. In 1990 music was provided by jazz and blues bands, including those of David "Fathead" Newman, Hilton Ruiz, and Arnie Lawrence.

——. **Yacht Club.** 38 West 52nd Street (1934–8); 150 West 52nd Street (1938–44); 66 West 52nd Street (1944). The first club with this name was a speakeasy, which operated in the 1920s at an unknown address. After the repeal of Prohibition a supper club of this name opened at 38 West 52nd Street in 1934; it moved to no.150 in 1938. Early in 1944 it took over premises (at no.66) vacated in November 1943 by the Famous Door (see above). However, it lasted only a few months at this location and closed in May 1944; the venue was taken over by the Downbeat club (see above). The Yacht Club was noted for the presentation of popular music, swing, and bop. During its ten years' existence it featured such musicians as Red McKenzie (1936), Fats Waller (1938), Trummy Young, Billy Eckstine (1944), and Coleman Hawkins. The quintet led by Dizzy Gillespie and Oscar Pettiford was resident in 1944, and when the group disbanded Gillespie remained at the club; he continued to play there when it opened as the Downbeat.

——. **Yardbird Suite.** 35 Cooper Square. Open only from May 1993 to late that same year, this club featured Brazilian jazz on Mondays and big bands on Wednesdays. Performers who appeared there included Geoff Keezer, Pete La Roca, Charli Persip, and Claudio Roditi. The Sun Ra Arkestra also performed there.

——. **Yeah Man.** 2456 Seventh Avenue (1925–33); 2350 Seventh Avenue (from 1933). It began as a speakeasy, then after the repeal of Prohibition it opened as a legitimate club in new premises nearby. The house pianist at the second location was Don Lambert, and from the late 1930s the club featured a number of small groups, including the trio led by Clarence Profit. Yeah Man was taken over in the mid-1940s by John Velasco and began to advertise under a new name, Jock's Place, in April 1946. Al Casey appeared there in June that year, and Lambert, Maxine Sullivan, and Leonard Ware performed in July. Jock's Place remained active at least until early 1948.

——. **Ye Old Nest.** This club in Harlem was active in the 1930s, when it was a noted venue for jam sessions.

——. **Zanzibar** [Club Zanzibar, Café Zanzibar]. West 49th Street and Broadway. It was opened in July 1943 and became an important venue during and after World War II for African-American shows and performances by big bands. Many of the most important ensembles of the period played there, including those led by Don Redman (1943), Sabby Lewis (1944), Claude Hopkins (1944–6), Duke Ellington (1945), and Sy Oliver (1946).

A new club of the same name opened at 73 Eighth Avenue in 1993 and was closed less than a year later, following appearances by, among others, Steve Coleman and Jerry Gonzalez's Fort Apache Band.

——. **Zanzibar and Grill.** 550 Third Avenue. Restaurant. In the years 1988 to 1991 Marty Napoleon, Tal Farlow, C. Sharpe, Ben Aronov, Bill Mays, the Microscopic Septet, Lew Soloff's All Stars, and Hiram Bullock were among those who appeared there. (P. Watrous: "Pop/Jazz: Jazz for Dessert in Club-restaurants where Music is on the Menu," *New York Times*, 9 Sept 1988)

——. **Zebra Room.** See Lenox Lounge.

——. **Zinc Bar.** 90 West Houston Street. Ron Affif's trio, with Essiet Essiet and Jeff "Tain" Watts, has performed there regularly on Monday nights from the mid-1990s. On Sunday evenings poetry readings take place as a prelude to nighttime performances devoted to Brazilian jazz. Tuesday and Wednesday nights feature bop and bop-related jazz, while Thursdays are dedicated to Latin Jazz, Fridays to African music, and Saturdays again to Brazilian jazz. Ravi Coltrane is one of many young musicians who have performed there. (<http://www.zincbar.com> (2001))

——. **Zinno's.** 126 West 13th Street. Bar and restaurant. It was opened in 1982 in premises that housed a speakeasy in the 1920s and a club called Reno Sweeney in the 1970s; it continued to be active throughout the decade. Performers who appeared there included George Mraz, Michael Moore, Hilton Ruiz, and Major Holley (all 1982), Ray Bryant, Jimmy Rowser, and Milt Hinton (all 1986), and Ruby Braff (1987). The club specialized in the presentation of duos consisting of piano or guitar and double bass: Junior Mance and Marty Rivera, Walter Norris and Brian Torff, Ruiz and Rowser, Kirk Lightsey and Cecil McBee, and Gene Bertoncini and Moore were among numerous other combinations who played there. Early in 1999 Ruiz led a trio consisting of Lew Soloff and Lisle Atkinson. Zinno's appears to have closed shortly afterwards, and by late 2000 an Italian restaurant occupied the site. (J. S. Wilson: "Jazz: Bertoncini and Moore," *New York Times*, 28 May 1982)

——. **Zombie.** Flushing Meadows. Bar and restaurant. It was one of the stands at the World's Fair in 1940. Among the jazz ensembles that played there was John Kirby's sextet.

See also Hudson River.

BIBLIOGRAPHY

New York

AllenH
S. B. Charters and L. Kunstadt: *Jazz: a History of the New York Scene* (Garden City, NY, 1962/R1981)
J. H. Clarke, ed.: *Harlem, U.S.A.* (Berlin, 1964)
G. Hoefer: Liner notes, *Jazz Odyssey*, i: *The Sound of Harlem* (Col. C3L 33, 1964)
A. Shaw: *The Street that Never Slept: New York's Fabled 52nd Street* (New York, 1971/R1983 as *52nd Street: the Street that Never Slept*)
R. Palmer: "Jazz Thriving in the City in Biggest Surge Since 40's," *New York Times* (29 Jan 1982)
T. Fox: *Showtime at the Apollo* (New York, 1983/R1993)
J. Schiffman: *Harlem Heyday: a Pictorial History of Modern Black Show Business and the Apollo Theatre* (Buffalo, 1984)
W. Balliett: *Barney, Bradley, and Max: 16 Portraits in Jazz* (New York, 1989)
L. Blumenfeld: "Riffs: New Kids on the Block," *DB*, lxi/10 (1994), 10
P. Watrous: "Critic's Notebook: Jazz with Pizazz: a New Generation of Clubs," *New York Times* (15 April 1994)
K. L. Williams: "The Best Places to Play Jazz in America," *DB*, lxii/2 (1995), 30
J. Pareles: "New Night Life in Midtown Manhattan," *New York Times* (13 Dec 1996)
B. Ratliff: "Syncopated Homecoming: Jazz Swings Back Uptown," *New York Times* (18 April 1997)
——: "Welcome to the Club: Jazz Swings in New Spots," *New York Times* (31 Oct 1997)
J. Chilton: *Ride, Red, Ride: the Life of Henry "Red" Allen* (London, 1999)
<http://www.bigapplejazz.com/nycjazzclubs.html> (2001)

<http://www.jazz-clubs-worldwide.com/docs/newyork.htm> (2001)
<http://www.jazzpages.com/JazzinNewYork> (2001)
<http://www.ny.com/clubs/jazz> (2001)

Norwalk, CA. See Los Angeles (metropolitan area).

Oakland, CA. **Koncepts Cultural Gallery.** Jenny Lind Hall, 2267 Telegraph Avenue (1984–7); 480 Third Street (at Washington Street) (1987–92); James Mason Theater, Oakland Museum (1992–). It was opened in June 1984 by Edsel Matthews and Kimathe Asante for the performance of rhythm-and-blues, jazz (styles from bop to free jazz), and blues. Art Sato directed its "Masters of Jazz" series, which included concerts by such musicians as Sun Ra, Teddy Edwards, Joe Henderson, and Randy Weston. The club moved to new premises, formerly the Western Pacific railway station in Jack London Square, in 1987, and opened on 5 November with a performance by James Newton and his group, with Bobby Hutcherson as a guest soloist. Early in 1992 this building was donated to a Chinese senior citizens center, and Koncepts Cultural Gallery programs recommenced that autumn at the Oakland Museum.

BIBLIOGRAPHY

D. Richardson: "The Grass Roots of Jazz," *San Francisco Bay Guardian* (11 Nov 1987), 21
<http://www.sirius.com/~koncepts> (2001)

——. **Sweet's Ballroom.** It was owned by Bill Sweet, who in 1938 engaged Lu Watters's swing orchestra to play fox trots, waltzes, and slow ballads for dancing. Whenever possible Watters slotted traditional jazz pieces into his repertory, until finally in the autumn of 1939 Sweet fired the bandleader for insubordination.

——. **Yoshi's (Night Spot).** 6030 Claremont Avenue (late 1970s to 1993); 510 Embarcadero West, at Jack London Square (1994–). Japanese restaurant. It was founded by Yoshi Akiba, her husband Kaz Kajimura, and Hiro Hori, and from 1986 to 1988 presented internationally known jazz musicians engaged by its first music director, Chuck LaPaglia. The favored repertory was bop, and the restaurant became the principal venue in the San Francisco Bay area following the demise of Keystone Korner in San Francisco. It engaged numerous important players in different styles, including Jimmy Smith, Joe Henderson, Steve Lacy, Phil Woods, Ray Brown and Milt Jackson, Horace Silver, Randy Weston, Stan Getz, McCoy Tyner, Toots Thielemans, Chico and Von Freeman, Art Blakey, and Tommy Flanagan. In 1989 LaPaglia transferred his activities to a new venue, Kimball's East, in Emeryville, CA, and in 1990 an annual festival dedicated to the memory of a local drummer, Eddie Moore, was initiated at Yoshi's. The venue struggled to maintain business in the early 1990s, and from 1992 to July 1993 it operated as Keystone Korner Yoshi's, under the direction of the former Keystone owner, Todd Barkan, and, again, LaPaglia; Barkan's former New Year's Eve event, discontinued in 1982, was revived as the Keystone All-Star Holiday Festival in 1992. In 1994 the club was revitalized under the management of Kajimura and Jason Olaine. It moved to new premises in Jack London Square early in 1997 and continued that year to host the Eddie Moore Jazz Festival.

BIBLIOGRAPHY

J. Hamlin: "Jazz Club Ready to Open in New and Improved Oakland Home," *San Francisco Chronicle* (4 May 1997)
<http://www.yoshis.com> (2001)

Oberlin, OH. **Finney Chapel.** Oberlin College. Known for its wonderful acoustics, this venue has welcomed many jazz musicians, including Dave Brubeck (1953, recorded by Fantasy), Dizzy Gillespie (1957), and Miles Davis (1965). Among later performers were Sam Rivers (1978), Betty Carter (1978, 1984), Art Blakey (1978, 1985), Sonny Rollins (1979, 1981, 1990), Anthony Braxton (1982), the World Saxophone Quartet (1983), Willem Breuker (1985), Henry Threadgill (1988), and Leroy Jenkins (1990, 1992).

Ocean Park, CA. See Los Angeles (metropolitan area).

Ohio River. **SS *George Washington*.** This pleasure steamer, formerly named the SS *Sidney* (see Mississippi River, above), belonged to the Streckfus line and became the *George Washington* in 1921 after major refitting. It plied the Ohio River throughout the 1920s and for much of the 1930s until it was removed from service and dismantled in 1938. In 1922 Clarence W. Elder joined the boat's band to play calliope and banjo, and he later became the *Washington*'s bandleader and ultimately its captain; Claude Thornhill played with him in 1925.

Orange, NJ. **Orange Armory.** Center and William streets. This large venue staged dances in the 1940s and early 1950s; Benny Carter, Lionel Hampton and Dinah Washington, Luis Russell, and Nat "King" Cole were among those who appeared.

Pasadena, CA. See Los Angeles (metropolitan area).

Peabody, MA. **Lennie's-on-the-Turnpike.** It was active from 1963 to 1971, during which time it presented performances by some of the most important American jazz musicians of the period. Among those who appeared there were Miles Davis, Charles Mingus, Thelonious Monk, Buddy Rich, Weather Report, Cannonball Adderley, Stan Getz, Zoot Sims and Al Cohn, and Henry "Red" Allen. Jaki Byard and Alan Dawson were members of the house rhythm section, and as a leader Byard recorded the two-volume album *Live at Lennie's* (1965, Prst. 7419, 7477).

BIBLIOGRAPHY

D. Morgenstern: "The Poll Winner as Teacher: Alan Dawson," *DB*, xxxiii/19 (1966), 27
M. Gardner: "Alan Dawson," pt ii, *JJ*, xxiv/5 (1971), 18

Philadelphia. **Alex's Jazz Underground.** 27 South 21st Street. Opened in September 2000 on premises that had been J. J.'s Grotto (see below), it is owned and operated by Alex Bartlett, a jazz guitarist who has brought in such major artists as John Abercrombie, Rick Margitza, Sonny Fortune, Eric Alexander, Jimmy Bruno, Steve Slagle, Bob Dorough, Wayne Krantz, Jack Wilkins, Howard Alden, and Paul Bollenback. (<http://www.jazzunderground.net> (2001))

——. **Aqua Lounge.** 52nd Street and Chancellor Street, West Philadelphia. It was active as a venue for jazz for about eight years in the 1960s.

——. **Benny the Bum.** 53rd Street and Market Street. It was in operation from the mid-1970s until the early 1980s and mounted performances by both local groups and nationally known musicians.

——. **Blue Note.** 15th Street and Ridge Avenue; 7400 Limekiln Pike. At least two venues in Philadelphia have been known as the Blue Note. The first was the city's principal nightclub in the 1950s and offered performances of bop and related styles. The resident pianist for a period from

1953 was Ray Bryant, and Jimmy Bond was the resident double bass player around the same time; among other musicians who appeared there were Charlie Parker, Miles Davis, Lester Young, Clifford Brown, Dizzy Gillespie, Sonny Rollins, Kenny Dorham, Eddie Jefferson, and James Moody. The club was destroyed by fire. The new Blue Note, in a different location and under different management, engaged such performers in the 1980s as Donald Byrd, Moody, Dakota Staton, and Oscar Brown, Jr., and featured open jam sessions on Monday evenings.

——. **Borgia Café.** 406 South 2nd Street. Principally a venue for local musicians, this nightclub has presented a wide range of jazz styles from the early 1980s.

——. **Broad Street Tavern.** 4638 North Broad Street. Active in the 1980s, the tavern featured bop, played mostly by local performers.

——. **Carl Drew's Lounge.** 52nd Street and Media Street. Among the players who have appeared there are many local bands and such nationally known musicians as Cat Anderson.

——. **Chestnut Cabaret.** 38th Street and Chestnut Street. It offered jazz, blues, and folk music from the mid-1970s. Jon Faddis, Jimmy Heath, Slide Hampton, Eddie "Lockjaw" Davis, and Clark Terry have performed there. In the late 1980s the house big band was led by the baritone saxophonist Joe Sudler.

——. **Chris' Jazz Café.** 1421 Sansom Street. Opened in the early 1990s, this restaurant was initially operated, and in part owned, by Alex Bartlett. The tenor saxophonist Larry McKenna led the house band and from time to time brought in such guest soloists as Randy Brecker and Danny Turner. Bartlett left in 2000 to found Alex's Jazz Underground (see above), but Chris' Jazz Café has continued to feature jazz. Among the major artists appearing on weekends in 2001 were Charles Fambrough, John Swana, James Moody, Larry Goldings, and Marc Copland. (<http://www.chrisjazz.com> (2001))

——. **Downbeat Club.** 11th Street and Market Street. It was in existence by at least the early 1940s. Dizzy Gillespie led his own small group there in 1942, and Red Garland was the house pianist from 1947 to 1949, during which time he accompanied Fats Navarro. Charlie Parker's quintet, which included Miles Davis and Max Roach, played there in December 1947.

——. **Dunbar Theatre.** South Street near 15th Street. Its programs involved jazz from at least the early 1920s. In 1923 the show *How Come*, which starred Sidney Bechet and also included Bessie Smith in the cast, was staged there, and Eubie Blake performed frequently in the theater during the decade. In the early 1930s the Dunbar was converted into a movie house.

——. **Earle Theater.** Southeast corner of 11th Street and Market Street. It was the principal venue in Philadelphia for swing bands, including those led by Jack Teagarden, Louis Armstrong, and Lucky Millinder. The theater was later demolished and replaced by a Woolworth's Five and Dime store.

——. **George Wilson's Café.** See Wilson's Café.

——. **Gibson's New Dunbar Theater** [Gibson's Theater]. Broad Street at Lombard Street. Owned and managed by John T. Gibson, this was a regular stopping place for touring African-American shows from the early 1920s. Among those who appeared there were Mamie Smith (1923–4), Noble Sissle and Eubie Blake (in *The Chocolate Dandies*, 1924), Ethel Waters (in *The Plantation Revue*, 1925, and *Africana*, over New Year 1927–8), and Claude Hopkins's band (in *Ginger Snaps of 1928*). From 1927 it was called Gibson's Theater.

——. **Gibson's Standard Theater.** South Street at 12th Street. Presenting vaudeville from the early 1920s, it regularly booked touring African-American shows (for example, *A Royal Flush Revue*, New Year 1927–8), and such stars as Ethel Waters (June 1928). It operated until at least 1932.

——. **Gino's Empty Foxhole.** 40th Street and Locust Walk. This nightclub was in existence for about ten years from the early 1970s. It presented leading bop and free-jazz musicians, such as Sunny Murray, Cecil Taylor, Sun Ra, and Byard Lancaster.

——. **Gleason's Musical Bar.** A small venue, it was active by the mid-1940s. Herman Autrey led a group there for a residency of several years from 1945.

——. **Hotel Senator.** See Swing Rendezvous.

——. **International House.** 36th Street and Chestnut Street. Established in the 1960s, it presented a broad-based repertory, including blues, folk music, and jazz. Among the jazz musicians who appeared there was Jimmy Heath.

——. **Jewel's.** 679 North Broad Street. It was opened around 1980 and offered performances by Clark Terry, Frank Wess, Joe Newman, Dakota Staton, and Etta Jones, among others.

——. **J. J.'s Grotto.** 27 South 21st Street. This Italian restaurant operated from around 1987 to 2000 and presented jazz groups and unaccompanied soloists, often featuring guitarists. Tal Farlow, Herb Ellis, Jimmy Bruno, Dave Liebman, Chris Potter, and the tenor saxophonist Larry McKenna were among those who appeared there. In September 2000 the premises became Alex's Jazz Underground (see above).

——. **Just Jazz.** 2121 Arch Street. It operated under this name for a short time from the late 1960s into the early 1970s. Its repertory was mainly hard bop, and among the musicians who performed there were Elvin Jones, Milt Jackson, and Art Blakey. A new club, named the Memphis, later opened in the same premises.

——. **Lincoln Theater.** South Broad Street and Lombard Street. One of many theaters in the city to present jazz performances as part of its variety programs, it flourished in the 1930s. Fletcher Henderson (1934–6) and Noble Sissle were regularly engaged there, and Duke Ellington, Don Redman, and Jimmie Lunceford also appeared.

——. **Memphis.** See Just Jazz.

——. **Morgan's.** 17 East Price Street. Morgan's consists of two main rooms – a discothèque on the ground floor and a jazz nightclub upstairs. For a few years, from its opening in 1985 to late in that same decade, it was a major African-

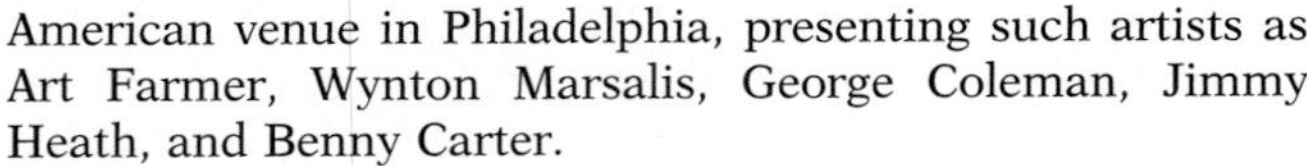

American venue in Philadelphia, presenting such artists as Art Farmer, Wynton Marsalis, George Coleman, Jimmy Heath, and Benny Carter.

——. **Natalie's Lounge.** 4003 Market Street. This nightclub was opened in the late 1960s and included jazz in its repertory from the early 1980s. Philly Joe Jones and Johnny Coles are among the musicians to have played there. Open jam sessions are held on Saturday afternoons.

——. **Night Owl.** Temple University. A nightspot on the university campus, it offers all styles of jazz as well as Latin music. Performances are often broadcast on radio station WRTI.

——. **Ortlieb's Jazz Haus.** 847 North 3rd Street. Formerly a small bowling alley, this long and narrow bar and restaurant was opened in the mid-1980s by the tenor saxophonist Pete Souders, who has presented mainly local musicians. Mickey Roker has often appeared on drums, and Shirley Scott has served as the house pianist for several years.
(<http://www.astecsoft.com/phillyjazz/ortliebs.html> (2001))

——. **Painted Bride.** 4th Street and Arch Street; Vine Street, between 2nd and 3rd streets. The Painted Bride is an arts center which hosts many types of events, both public and private. It opened in the late 1970s and has flourished into the new century. Among the musicians to have appeared there are Mal Waldron, Odean Pope, Sun Ra, Dave Douglas, Uri Caine, and Michele Rosewoman.
(<http://www.paintedbride.org> (2001))

——. **P & T Club.** Broad Street and Arch Street. Active from the early 1980s, the club has featured Donald Byrd and Philly Joe Jones, among others.

——. **Pearl Theater.** Ridge Avenue near 23rd Street. Jazz was performed there from at least the late 1920s and appears to have formed part of the entertainment until well into the 1940s. Wilbur De Paris was manager of the resident orchestra in 1927–8. In 1930 Noble Sissle's band appeared, and the following year Andy Kirk's Clouds of Joy held a residency there under the leadership of Blanche Calloway. Other important bands to visit the Pearl were those of Bennie Moten (for illustration *see* Moten, bennie) and Count Basie.

——. **Pep's Musical Bar.** Broad Street and South Street. The bar was in existence from the 1940s until the mid-1960s and offered performances by many of the principal musicians of the period. Herman Autrey led his own group for a long residency there from 1945; among the other jazz players who performed there were John Coltrane, Dizzy Gillespie (as the leader of a small group), Sonny Rollins, Max Roach, Clifford Brown, Dinah Washington, and Benny Golson. A performance by Yusef Lateef was recorded at the club in 1964 (*Live at Pep's,* Imp. 69).

——. **Prince Total Experience Lounge.** 1410 Hunting Park Avenue. This nightclub was opened in the mid-1980s and offered jazz on Sunday and Monday nights. Among the performers who have appeared there are McCoy Tyner and Ray Bryant.

——. **Roseland Ballroom.** 12th Street and Chestnut Street. It was opened in 1918 by Louis J. Brecker. Its successful operation led to his opening a second ballroom of that name in New York the following year.

——. **Showboat.** 1409 Lombard Street. Among the many famous jazz musicians to play at this venue in the 1950s were John Coltrane, Thelonious Monk, Ahmad Jamal, Horace Silver, Miles Davis, J. J. Johnson, Stan Getz, and Sonny Rollins. It later became a mental health clinic.

——. **Spider Kelly's.** It was active from at least the 1950s as a venue for solo and small-group jazz. Among the musicians who worked there was Ray Bryant, who appeared at the club in 1958.

——. **Sterling's Place at Dino's.** 135 South 46th Street. This nightclub has presented a repertory that emphasizes bop and related styles. Milt Jackson, Art Blakey, Dakota Staton, and Junior Cook, among others, have performed there.

——. **Strand Ballroom.** From 1928 to 1930 Fletcher Henderson's orchestra played there several times for dances, sharing the bandstand with the Ten Arcadians (1928–9) and Wilbur De Paris's orchestra (1928). The venue was active at least to the end of 1938, when Henderson returned.

——. **Swing Rendezvous.** This nightspot within the Hotel Senator was in existence by the 1950s, employing solo performers and small groups. Sidney Bechet led a group there regularly around 1950, and Dick Wellstood was the resident pianist for a time.

——. **Watusi Club.** 46th Street and Walnut Street. Although it opened in the 1950s, it first offered performances of jazz in the mid-1980s.

——. **Wilson's Café.** Named for its owner, George Wilson, it was a venue for jazz performances from at least the 1920s. George Baquet led a band there for more than 14 years during the 1920s and 1930s.

——. **Zanzibar Blue.** 301–5 South 11th Street. This restaurant was an important venue for jazz in the early 1990s, when it presented local groups and such visiting artists as Joshua Redman, Don Pullen, and Joey DeFrancesco. It consisted of a dining room, the small Jazz Café, where jazz musicians usually appeared, and, upstairs, the Blue Bar, which was modeled after Harlem nightclubs of the 1920s and which hosted jazz on weekend nights.
(<http://www.zanzibarblue.com> (2001))

Phoenix, AZ. **Bud Brown's Barn.** Situated on the outskirts of Phoenix, this venue, owned by Bud Brown, specialized in country music and was used for barn dances and barbecues. Its musical programs often included dixieland jazz, and Kid Ory's band performed there regularly.

Pittsburgh. **Balcony.** 520 Walnut Street. Originally a restaurant called the Shadyside Balcony, it offered jazz performances from the 1990s; among those who appeared were Pat Martino, Jacky Terrasson with Ugonna Okegwo and Leon Parker, Mark Murphy, and Mose Allison.

——. **Bill Green's.** Route 51, Carrick. This nightclub presented such artists as Charlie Spivak in the 1940s.

——. **Carnegie Music Hall.** This theater was the site of many of the University of Pittsburgh jazz seminar concerts organized by Nathan Davis. It also hosted festivals in the 1990s, including Spring into Jazz; featured performers included Roy Hargrove, Danilo Pérez, Patrice Rushen, Abe Laboriel, Tal Farlow with Art Farmer, and Jon Faddis. (<http://www.carnegiehall.org> (2001))

——. **Carousel.** 815 Liberty Avenue. It was operated by Jackie Heller in the 1940s.

——. **Charlie Ray's Club.** Owned and operated by Charlie Ray, it presented such artists as Erroll Garner and Billy Strayhorn in the 1930s and 1940s.

——. **Civic Arena.** In the 1960s this performing arts center presented Sy Oliver and other jazz artists.

——. **Clearwater.** 5401 Walnut Street. In the late 1980s and 1990s this bar, café, and restaurant offered jazz on a regular basis; Jimmy Ponder was among those who appeared monthly.

——. **Collins Inn.** Wylie Avenue. In the 1920s Earl Hines performed at this hotel, which was owned and operated by Harry Collins.

——. **Copa Club.** 818 Liberty. Owned and operated by Lenny Litman, it offered jazz during the 1940s and 1950s, including artists such as Sarah Vaughan, Dakota Staton, and Erroll Garner's trio.

——. **Crawford Grill #1.** 2141 Wylie Avenue. This nightclub and restaurant was owned during the 1940s and 1950s by Gus Greenlee and later by William "Buzzy" Robinson. Local musicians George Benson and Stanley Turrentine played there early in their careers, and over the years the venue brought in such artists as Charles Mingus, Clifford Brown, Nat "King" Cole, Maynard Ferguson, Thelonious Monk, Max Roach, and Erroll Garner. It remained in operation in the 1990s.

——. **Crawford Grill #2.** Wylie Avenue and Elmore Street. Under the same ownership as its companion venue, the second Crawford Grill flourished from the 1940s into the early 1970s, presenting many of the same artists.

——. **Duquesne Garden Ballroom.** Occasional presentations of African-American jazz groups in the 1920s and 1930s included those of Fletcher Henderson (22 September 1927, when it was specified that "Guests will use front entrance for this night") and Earl Hines (23 June 1930) and the Blue Rhythm Band (17 November 1931).

——. **Eileen's Zebra Room.** 708 North Dallas Avenue. Located in a basement beneath Eileen's Bar, this nightclub operated in the 1970s. The quartet led by Roger Humphries appeared there regularly.

——. **Elk's Club.** Lincoln Avenue. During the 1930s and 1940s many jazz artists performed there, notably Erroll Garner and Ray Brown.

——. **Elmore Theatre.** 2312 Center Avenue. The theater served as a venue for touring African-American shows from the 1920s into the early 1930s. Among those who appeared were Mamie Smith (January and May 1925, April and September 1926, February 1928), Clara Smith (March and October 1925, August 1927), Ida Cox (November 1925, December 1928, June 1929, this last in the show *Raisin' Cain*), Ethel Waters (March and July 1926), Ma Rainey (June 1926, October 1927), Adelaide Hall (November 1926, in *Desires of 1927*), Bessie Smith (January and September 1928, October 1929 in *Midnight Steppers*, and February 1930), and Gladys Bentley (November 1929).

——. **Flower Garden.** Babcock Boulevard. This nightclub presented such artists as Erroll Garner and Billy May during the 1930s.

——. **Fort Pitt Hotel.** Erroll Garner is among those who performed there during the 1930s and 1940s.

——. **Foster's Bar & Grill.** 100 Lytton Avenue. From 1987 into the new century the Pittsburgh Jazz Society has presented weekly concerts on Sunday evenings in this large, drab room within the local Holiday Inn. (<http://www.fosterselect.com/entertainment.htm> (2001))

——. **Gayety.** 6th Street and Duquesne Way. This venue presented African-American touring revues from 1924 to 1927, including the show *Black and White* in August 1925. In October 1927 the mixed company of Jimmie Cooper and his Original Black and White Revue appeared with the band of Eddie Heywood, Sr.

——. **Graffiti.** This nightclub presented jazz and popular music in the 1980s and 1990s. Among the jazz and jazz-fusion artists who appeared were Vyacheslav Ganelin's trio, Jack DeJohnette, Greg Osby and Gary Thomas, Branford Marsalis, the Lounge Lizards, and Béla Fleck and the Flecktones.

——. **Grand Theatre.** See Lando Theatre.

——. **Harlem Bar.** Wylie Avenue and Townsend Street. In the 1930s it presented such artists as Billy Eckstine and Erroll Garner.

——. **Harlem Casino.** Centre Avenue and Roberts Street. It was owned and operated by Gus Greenlee in the 1940s, when Erroll Garner was among those who played there.

——. **Heinz Hall.** 600 Penn Avenue. The hall has hosted numerous jazz events and concerts, from Erroll Garner in the 1940s to Wynton Marsalis in the 1990s.

——. **Hurricane.** Wylie Avenue. It began presenting jazz in the 1930s and remained in operation in the 1990s, when it was managed by Ferdie Dunlap; Jimmy Smith was among those who appeared there.

——. **James Street Tavern.** 422 Foreland Street. Once a sports bar, this restaurant and bar has presented such jazz musicians as David "Fathead" Newman, Roger Humphries, Gary Bartz, Dwayne Dolphin, and Jimmy Ponder from 1987 into the new century. (<http://jamesstreet.citysearch.com> (2001))

——. **Lando Theatre** [Grand Theater]. 1851 Center Avenue. In 1930 this cinema presented live shows involving both touring African-American companies and one-night stands, the latter including an appearance by McKinney's Cotton Pickers on 6 April; the show *Midnight Steppers of 1930* in October featured the Washboard Serenaders with Teddy Bunn. The following year the Lando became the Grand Theater. Mamie Smith appeared there that September and Bessie Smith in January 1932.

——. **Leader House.** 1401 Wylie Avenue. Originally called Liederhouse, this nightclub was operating as the Leader House by September 1923, when the male impersonator

Teddy Peters performed there. Earl Hines played at the club early in his career; advertisements from 1924 place his band at the club on a Sunday in May, and Ida Cox followed on 20 June.

——. **Lincoln Theatre** [New Lincoln Theatre]. 2424 Wylie Avenue. "The home of clean colored vaudeville," the Lincoln presented Bessie Smith in *Blues as They Should be Sung*, with Irving Johns at the piano, in March 1924; over the course of the next year the featured blues and vaudeville singers included Clara Smith in May, Ida Cox in June, Ma Rainey with her Georgia Jazz Orchestra in October, Margaret Johnson in February 1925, and both Edmonia Henderson and Sara Martin in March.

——. **Manchester Craftsmen's Guild.** 1815 Metropolitan Street. Opened in 1968, this arts and crafts school has offered an annual series of jazz concerts from 1986 into the new century. In the 1990s it presented such artists as Slide Hampton, Johnny Griffin, Jimmy Heath, Louie Bellson, Dwayne Dolphin, Joe Henderson, Nilson Matta, Duduka da Fonseca, Roger Humphries and Mulgrew Miller, Don Braden, Ravi Coltrane, Jimmy Ponder, Charles Earland, McCoy Tyner, Joe Sample, Michael Brecker, James Genus, Joey Calderazzo, George Coleman with Harold Mabern, Ray Brown's trio with Stanley Turrentine, Ernie Wilkins, and Toots Thielemans. Max Roach recorded an album there. (<http://manchesterguild.org> (2001))

——. **Melody Bar.** Centre Avenue and Arthur Street. Operating in the late 1930s and 1940s, it presented Erroll Garner, Charlie Shavers, Count Basie, and Lionel Hampton, among others.

——. **Mercur's Music Bar.** Wylie Avenue. Erroll Garner and Ray Brown are among those who played at this bar, which was owned and operated by Lew and Al Mercur, in the 1940s.

——. **Musician's Club.** Wylie Avenue. Gus Greenlee owned and operated this nightclub and restaurant, which had previously been the Paramount Inn. A central spot for jazz artists in the 1930s, it offered performances by Erroll Garner, Ray Brown, Duke Ellington, Cab Calloway, Woody Herman, Illinois Jacquet, Ben Webster, Lester Young, Nat "King" Cole, and Art Tatum, among others

——. **New Lincoln Theatre.** See Lincoln Theatre.

——. **Nixon Theatre.** Sixth Avenue and William Penn Way. Noble Sissle and Eubie Blake's show *In Bamville* was presented at this theater in March 1924, Miller and Lyles's *Runnin' Wild* in March 1925, Lew Leslie's *Blackbirds* in October 1929, *Connie's Hot Chocolates*, with Edith Wilson and Fats Waller, in March 1930, and *Brown Buddies*, with Bill Robinson and Adelaide Hall, in September 1930.

——. **Penn–Sheraton Hotel.** Quincy Jones performed in the ballroom of this hotel in the 1960s.

——. **Pittsburgh Hilton and Towers.** From the 1980s jazz performers were occasionally featured at the Pittsburgh Hilton, notably the memorial Tommy Dorsey Orchestra under Buddy Morrow and, later, McCoy Tyner and Geri Allen.

——. **Ramsey's II.** 7310 Frankstown Avenue. Run by John and Christina Brewer, this restaurant was functioning in the early 1990s as a sort of informal cultural center for Pittsburgh's large African-American community, with poetry, drama, fashion shows, and various other special events during the week, and jazz on weekends. Jimmy Ponder and other less well-known local players performed there.

——. **Regent Theatre.** It opened in 1995. Sonny Rollins is among the jazz musicians who performed there.

——. **Ritz Café.** Fullerton Street. This nightclub presented such jazzmen as Erroll Garner and Art Blakey.

——. **Roosevelt Theatre.** 1862 Centre Avenue. This cinema regularly presented touring African-American shows from 1929; Clara Smith's *Black Bottom Revue* was billed in February 1930. Duke Ellington played a one-night stand in June 1931, and Baron Lee and his Aristocrats of Rhythm Orchestra appeared with the *Cotton Club Revue* in May 1935.

——. **Savoy Ballroom.** Centre Avenue, near Devilliers Street. Owned by Harry Hendel and under the management of Lee Mathews, this club presented major jazz performers, including Woody Herman, Billy Eckstine, Duke Ellington, Cab Calloway, and Erroll Garner. It was situated on the second floor of the four-story New Granada Theater, which closed permanently following riots in the aftermath of the assassination of Martin Luther King in 1968. (T. Barnes: "Arts Revival for Hill?," *Pittsburgh Post Gazette*, 6 Sept 1993)

——. **Shadyside Balcony.** See Balcony.

——. **Stanley Theater.** 7th Street and Penn Avenue. From the 1930s this venue presented Erroll Garner and the bands of Gene Krupa, Benny Goodman, and Cab Calloway.

——. **Syria Mosque.** 4423 Bigelow Boulevard. Leading big bands played there in the early years of the swing era, notably McKinney's Cotton Pickers (11 April 1932) and the orchestras of Cab Calloway (18 April 1933) and Duke Ellington (31 August 1934). From the 1960s through the 1980s jazz events were again offered occasionally at this performing arts center; Art Blakey and his Jazz Messengers (13 April 1964), Ella Fitzgerald, Oscar Peterson, Clark Terry, Roy Eldridge, Dave Brubeck, and Pat Metheny were among those who appeared.

——. **Too Sweet Lounge.** 7101 Frankstown Avenue. In the 1990s a stage was brought out in this bar for jazz performances by Roger Humphries and others.

——. **William Penn Hotel.** 530 William Place. Count Basie played there in 1936. His was the first African-American band to be presented there, and Basie himself was the first African-American patron in the lounge, where Erroll Garner also performed in the 1930s. The hotel later became the Westin William Penn.

PORTLAND, OR. **Atwater's.** 111 SW Fifth Avenue. This restaurant, located at the top of a downtown skyscraper, began to present jazz in the early 1990s, when Leroy Vinnegar and the drummer Mel Brown transferred from The Hobbit (see below).

——. **Brasserie Montmartre.** 626 SW Park Avenue. Situated within the Calumet Hotel, this elegant restaurant has presented jazz every night from at least the 1980s. Among those who appeared there from the late 1990s into the new century were John Stowell, Jerry Hahn, and David Friesen.

BIBLIOGRAPHY
<http://members.home.net/magic01/brasserie> (2001)
<http://www.brasseriemontmartre.com> (2001)

——. **The Hobbit.** 4420 SE 39th Avenue. This nightclub presented jazz from the early 1980s into the early 1990s; the drummer Mel Brown was a longstanding member of the house band, and Leroy Vinnegar joined him after moving to Portland in 1986. Visiting artists included Ray Brown, Tommy Flanagan, and Mark Murphy. A weekly Sunday-afternoon jam session was broadcast on radio station KKEY.

——. **Jazz de Opus.** 33 NW Second Avenue. This opened in 1972 as a small beer and wine bar which presented such leading musicians as Sonny Rollins, Nat Adderley, Roy Eldridge, and Oscar Peterson. It expanded to become a large restaurant, and then for roughly a decade stopped presenting jazz. Music activities resumed in the early 1990s, with Leroy Vinnegar, David Friesen, and Nancy King among those appearing in a small bar area situated near the door; Friesen and King have continued to perform there into the new century. (<http://www.jazzdeopus.com> (2001))

Potomac River. Jazz formed part of the entertainment offered on the pleasure craft that worked the river during the summer season. Around 1920 Rex Stewart gained his first professional experience playing in one of the riverboat bands.

Redondo Beach, CA. See Los Angeles (metropolitan area).

Robbins, IL. **Apex Chateau** [Apex Grill and Road House, New Apex Country Club, Apex Club]. West 136th Street and South Kedzie Avenue (1936–*c*1940); 13614 Claire Boulevard (from *c*1940). On the extreme south side of Chicago, the location of this venue testifies to the steady drift of the African-American population from the center of the city to the suburbs, starting in the 1930s. It was in operation by June 1936 and by spring 1940 had moved its premises and changed its name to the Apex Grill and Road House. In May 1940 the pianist Sonny Thompson and his Swingsters formed the resident band, and the following summer Rosetta Howard appeared there. The proprietors at that time were Jesse "Fats" Robinson and Walter Flowers. On 8 August 1943 the venue reopened as the Apex Chateau, under the management of Mr. and Mrs. George Richards, but by 1946 it was the Apex Grill again. In December 1949, again under new management, it became the New Apex Country Club, with the double bass player Al Smith's band performing from that time into at least summer 1950. From April 1952 it was the Apex Club, with James C. Davis its proprietor, and during that decade it presented blues artists. In 1959 the comedian Dick Gregory opened a club on the site and appeared in a revue which included Paul Bascomb's band.

St. Louis. **Arcadia Ballroom.** 3515–23 Olive Street. It was built before World War I as the Dreamland Ballroom and took its new name shortly after the war, when Joe Ternes became the owner. A six-piece New Orleans group played there in the mid-1920s; originally using the name Crescent City Jazzers, it soon became the Arcadian Serenaders and recorded under that name in St. Louis, with Wingy Manone as the trumpeter in 1924 and Sterling Bose in 1925. In the ballroom the Arcadian Serenaders played alongside a group led by Frankie Trumbauer (resident from 8 September 1925 to 3 May 1926), which included Bix Beiderbecke and Pee Wee Russell. The Arcadia continued to be active in the 1930s: Charlie Creath led a band there in 1933. The venue was later known as the Tune Town Ballroom. It was demolished in 1966.

——. **Chauffeur's Club.** 3133 Pine Boulevard. It offered performances of jazz from at least 1918, when De Priest Wheeler played in the resident band. In the 1920s Charlie Creath, Ed Allen (1923–4), and Dewey Jackson (*c*1927) all led bands there.

——. **Club Plantation.** See Plantation Club.

——. **Club Riviera.** Billy Eckstine's orchestra, which included Dizzy Gillespie and Charlie Parker, performed there in 1944.

——. **Dreamland Ballroom.** See Arcadia Ballroom.

——. **Elk's Club.** It was used during the 1930s and 1940s for after-hours jam sessions. Although he had met Miles Davis earlier, it was there that Clark Terry first appreciated the latter's talent as an improviser.

——. **Jazzland.** 22nd Street and Market Street. It may have been owned by Charlie Creath, who from the mid-1920s held a long residency there which lasted into the 1930s. In the summer of 1925 he led a pickup band at the club in a recording session for OKeh.

——. **Just Jazz.** 1019 Pine Street. Situated on the ground floor of the Hotel Majestic, Just Jazz had an elegant restaurant on one side and a lounge on the other, with a stage in between. It was an important venue for jazz in St. Louis in the early 1990s, with Ray Brown, Benny Green, Roy Hargrove, and Mulgrew Miller among those who appeared. A New Year's Eve celebration from the club on 31 Dec 1992 was broadcast on PBS television, and WSIE produced the radio show "Just Jazz," syndicated on NPR.

——. **Moose Lounge.** 4571 Pope Street. This nightclub, which opened in the 1960s, presented mainly local artists (including, early in his career, David Sanborn), though nationally known artists such as Sonny Stitt passed through on occasion. The venue remains in operation in the new century, but it is no longer significant from a jazz perspective.

——. **Plantation Club.** Active from at least the early 1930s, it appears to have opened only during the winter. In 1932–3 the house band was led by the trumpeter Walter Stanley; his ensemble was followed into the club by the Jeter–Pillars Orchestra, which held an extended residency from 1934 until the mid-1940s.

——. **Red Inn.** Jimmy Blanton played there in the late 1930s.

——. **Rhumboogie Club.** It flourished at least during the early 1940s, when Tiny Bradshaw's orchestra, in which Sonny Stitt was a sideman, performed there.

——. **Tune Town Ballroom.** See Arcadia Ballroom.

See also Mississippi River.

St. Paul, MN. **Artists' Quarter.** 366 Jackson Street. In 2001 it presented such artists as Paul Bollenback, the trio led by the pianist Rick DellaRatta (with Eddie Gomez and Lenny White), Lew Tabackin, David Friedman, and JoAnne Brackeen. (<http://www.mnjazz.com/aq> (2001))

——. **Dakota Bar & Grill.** 1021 Bandana, Bandana Square. From the late 1980s this restaurant has been the principal venue for jazz in the Twin Cities (Minneapolis and St. Paul). It has presented local jazz groups as well as such touring artists as Betty Carter, Ahmad Jamal, Carmen McRae, Max Roach, Toots Thielemans, McCoy Tyner, Chucho Valdés, and Joe Williams; Makoto Ozone, Steve Lacy, John Scofield, Jerry Gonzalez, Avishai Cohen, and David Sanchez were among those who appeared there early in 2001. (<http://www.dakotacooks.com> (2001))

For other venues in the Twin Cities see Minneapolis.

San Antonio. **Cameo Theater.** 1123 E. Commerce Street. The theater is located in the center of St. Paul Square, which was the heart of the city's African-American entertainment district from the 1930s into the 1950s; in the 1990s it was one of the few venues still standing. The big bands of Cab Calloway and Dizzy Gillespie were among those who appeared there.

——. **Jim Cullum's Landing** [The Landing]. River Walk (1963–?); 123 Losoya Street. Founded by Jim Cullum, Sr., and continued by his son, this venue has been the home of the Jim Cullum Jazz Band, and San Antonio's principal venue for jazz, from 1963. It was originally located in a basement on the city's River Walk and later moved 150 yards south to a plush site within the River Walk's Hyatt Regency Hotel. In 1988 the band began a series of broadcasts from the club on NPR. (<http://www.landing.com> (2001))

San Diego. **Club Royal.** It was in existence from at least the mid-1940s. The trumpeter and singer Walter Fuller led his own band there for a 12-year residency from 1946.

——. **Honeybucket Club.** It was active from the 1950s. Late in the decade and into the 1960s Johnny Best played there five nights a week.

——. **Juke Joint Cafe.** 427 4th Avenue. By the late 1990s this restaurant was presenting jazz several nights per week in its two rooms, the Bistro and the Kinda Blue Room. (<http://jukejointcafe.com/index.htm> (2001))

San Francisco. **Ace Café.** 1539 Folsom Street. In the 1990s it was a venue for bop, fusion, and avant-garde jazz.

——. **Basin Street West.** Broadway Street and Montgomery Street. Named after the club Basin Street East in New York, it flourished in the 1960s. Its policy was to engage major musicians for short residencies: Duke Ellington, Count Basie, Woody Herman, Oscar Peterson, and Erroll Garner played there when the club's activities were at their height in the mid- to late decade.

——. **Bimbo's 365 Club.** 1025 Columbus Avenue. Nightclub and restaurant. Founded in the 1950s, it has sometimes presented jazz; in the 1990s it served as a venue for the San Francisco Jazz Festival. (<http://www.bimbos365club.com> (2001))

——. **Blackhawk.** Along with the Jazz Workshop, this was the principal jazz club in the city in the 1950s and early 1960s. Vernon Alley served as its music director, and the repertory it offered was mainly bop, although Art Tatum held one of his last residencies there in 1955. Miles Davis recorded an album with his quintet there in 1961 (*In Person: Friday and Saturday Nights at the Blackhawk*, Col. C2S820).

——. **Blanco's Cotton Club.** 859 O'Farrell Street. Nightclub. Owned by Barney Deasy, it was opened in June 1948 on the site which became the Great American Music Hall. Unlike its Harlem namesake, it was opened with the specific intent of being a racially integrated club. It failed financially a few months later, after bringing in Lionel Hampton's orchestra at a time when big bands were becoming prohibitively expensive to engage.

——. **Bop City.** See Jimbo's Bop City.

——. **Both/And.** Divisadero Street. It was active in the 1950s and 1960s as a venue chiefly for bop and (later) free jazz. Dexter Gordon, John Handy, and Ornette Coleman were among the prominent musicians who performed there.

——. **Café du Nord.** 2170 Market Street. In the 1990s it presented local Latin jazz, bop, fusion, and big bands. (<http://www.cafedunord.com> (2001))

——. **The Cellar.** See Jazz Cellar.

——. **Citro's.** Geary Street. Nightclub. Inspired by the example of the failed Blanco's Cotton Club, in the late 1940s it presented jazz to a racially integrated audience.

——. **Club Hangover.** 729 Bush Street. It was in operation from at least the 1940s, when it was owned by Doc Dougherty. Ted Buckner's band made weekly broadcasts from the club on Saturday evenings and Kid Ory also led a band there (until 1949). In the early 1950s notable residencies were held by George Lewis (i) with Lizzie Miles (1952), Don Ewell, and Earl Hines (1952); Hines also returned for a long period beginning in September 1955. Among other musicians who performed at the Hangover were Joe Sullivan (who played solo piano between band sets, from 1955), Jimmy Rushing, Joe Darensbourg (who led an all-star sextet there in 1960), Marty Marsala (1962), and Muggsy Spanier (early 1960s). The club closed in the 1960s and the premises were taken over by a Japanese restaurant called Ginza West.

——. **Club 36.** 345 Stockton Street. Located in the Mandarin Lounge at the top of the Hyatt Union Square Hotel, in the 1990s it featured a house band led by Larry Vuckovich. It also has served as one of the venues for the San Francisco Jazz Festival.

——. **Coffee Gallery.** Grant Street at Green Street. Coffeehouse. It opened in 1950 and was directed by Leo Riegler. At first its activities centered on poetry, but its programs soon included, and later concentrated exclusively on, jazz. Pony Poindexter led the house band there after leaving the Jazz Cellar. It survived for a time the decline of jazz in San Francisco in the late 1960s but closed in 1971.

——. **Cotton Club.** See Blanco's Cotton Club.

——. **Dawn Club.** 20 Annie Street. It was active in the 1940s in the basement of the Monadnock Building. Lu Watters's Yerba Buena Jazz Band held a residency there from August 1940 to August 1942 and again from March through December 1946 (for illustration *see* Watters, Lu). In the interim the traditional-jazz band led by the trumpeter Benny Stricker (to November 1942) and other such groups appeared, and around 1947 Kid Ory's band performed at the venue. The Front Page club (see below) later opened in the same premises. (J. Buchanan: *Emperor Norton's Hunch: the Story of Lu Watters' Yerba Buena Jazz Band*, Sausalito, CA, 1996)

——. **Down Beat Club.** 90 Market Street. Open from at least 1950, it became an important venue for modern jazz. Among the musicians who appeared there were Buddy DeFranco (around 1951) and, later, Miles Davis.

——. **Earthquake McGoon's.** 99 Broadway (29 September 1960–1962); William Tell Hotel, 630 Clay Street (1962–79); Pier 39, Embarcadero (1979 – early 1980s). Turk Murphy's Jazz Band was resident throughout the life of the club. Murphy was responsible for the music policy, and his pianist, Pete Clute, managed the venue. (J. O. Goggin and P. Clute: *The Great Jazz Revival: a Pictorial Celebration of Traditional Jazz*, San Rafael, CA, 1994)

——. **Easy Street.** 2215 Powell Street. This nightclub was managed by Turk Murphy's pianist, Pete Clute, and Murphy's band was resident there from 31 December 1957 through 1958. Ralph Sutton was the intermission pianist. Louis Armstrong's All Stars and the bands of Red Norvo and Louis Jordan also appeared during this period.

——. **Elbo Room.** 647 Valencia Street. In the 1990s it sometimes presented fusion and avant-garde groups, including Charlie Hunter's band. (<http://www.elbo.com> (2001))

——. **Fairmont Hotel.** See New Orleans Room.

——. **Front Page.** 20 Annie Street. It opened in the 1980s in the premises that formerly housed the Dawn Club (see above). In 1986 Turk Murphy opened his Traditional Jazz Museum there.

——. **Great American Music Hall.** 859 O'Farrell Street. Built the year after the earthquake and fire of 1906 (and originally called Blanco's), it flourished as a jazz venue in the 1970s and 1980s, and in 1987 founded its own record label, on which recordings of performances given at the club were issued. It offered a great variety of performances in jazz and popular styles; among the numerous jazz musicians who appeared there were Lee Konitz, Bobby McFerrin, the Preservation Hall Jazz Band, Maynard Ferguson, Art Blakey, Woody Herman, John Scofield, Stan Getz, Count Basie, Sarah Vaughan, Jan Garbarek, Pharoah Sanders, Annie Ross, Betty Carter, Oregon, Flora Purim and Airto Moreira, the World Saxophone Quartet, Branford Marsalis, and J. J. Johnson. It remains an active venue but almost entirely in genres other than jazz. (<http://www. musichallsf.com> (2001))

——. **Half Note Club.** Divisadero Street. It flourished during the 1960s, when it specialized in the presentation of bop.

——. **Hangover Club.** See Club Hangover.

——. **Hotel Utah.** 4th Street and Bryant Street. In the 1990s it sometimes presented fusion and avant-garde groups. (<http://www.hotelutahsaloon.com> (2001))

——. **Hungry i.** Jackson Street. It was an important venue for bop in the 1950s and 1960s. Among the musicians who played there was Vince Guaraldi.

——. **Italian Village.** Columbus Avenue at Lombard Street. Big bands, including that of Ted Lewis, played in the supper club upstairs in the 1940s, and Turk Murphy's band appeared for weekly sessions at the Venetian Room there from 1952 to 1954. It was managed by Charles Campbell, commemorated in Murphy's composition *Duff Campbell's Revenge*.

——. **Jack's Tavern.** Sutter Street, between Fillmore Street and Webster Street. It flourished in the 1940s and was an early venue for bop in the city. Pony Poindexter, who was to be closely connected with a number of San Francisco clubs, played an engagement there early in his career.

——. **Jazz Cellar.** It was known familiarly to musicians as The Cellar and became known for the performance of bop. One of its founders (in the 1950s) was the drummer Willy Carson. The house band was led by Leo Wright until 1959 (when he joined Dizzy Gillespie) and then by Pony Poindexter, who later moved on to the Coffee Gallery (see above). Like those of many clubs in the city, its fortunes waned in the 1960s when rock music diverted the attention of audiences away from jazz.

——. **Jazz Workshop.** 473 Broadway. One of the principal jazz venues on the West Coast, it engaged the most important bop and free-jazz musicians in the 1950s and 1960s. Among those who played there were Cannonball Adderley, who recorded *The Cannonball Adderley Quintet in San Francisco* (1959, Riv. 311) at the club, Ornette Coleman (1960, 1967), John Coltrane (with his quartet in 1961 and his quintet in July–August 1966), and Charles Mingus (1964), whose performance was recorded and issued as *Right Now* (Fan. 86017). Other notable performances were given by Brew Moore, Wes Montgomery, Jackie McLean, Kenny Dorham, and Roland Kirk.

——. **Jimbo's Bop City.** Post Street at Buchanan Street. An after-hours club owned by Jimbo Edwards, with financial backing from the used-car salesman "Horsetrader Ed" Shapiro, it was located on the site of the former club Vout City, at the back of Jimbo's Waffleshop. It was an important venue for jam sessions, in which many leading swing and bop musicians took part. Between 1949 and 1953 Dexter Gordon, Sonny Criss, Hampton Hawes, Roy Porter, and Pony Poindexter were regularly heard there.

——. **Kennel Club.** 628 Divisadero Street. In the 1990s it sometimes presented fusion groups, and early in the decade Don Cherry's group Multikulti appeared there.

——. **Keystone Korner.** Vallejo Street at Stockton Street. Situated on the northeast corner of the intersection, the club was opened around 1972 and its activities were directed by Todd Barkan. In the 1970s and early 1980s it was one of the most important jazz venues in the USA. Aided by its fine acoustics, comfortable performing conditions, and appreciative audiences, it attracted internationally renowned bop musicians. A number of recordings were made there, including *In this Korner* (1978, Conc. 68), by Art Blakey and his Jazz Messengers, and Tete Montoliu's *Live at Keystone Corner* (1979, Tim. 138). National Public Radio broadcast performances from the club on New Year's Eve as part of a coast-to-coast celebration which took place annually until the club closed in 1982; the Keystone name was later revived, with Barkan's participation, for events at Yoshi's (Oakland, California) from 1992 to 1993.

——. **Kimball's.** 300 Grove Street. Nightclub. Owned by Kimball Allen and Jan Allen, it was active as a venue for jazz performance from the mid-1980s. Among the notable players in various styles who appeared there were Cedar Walton, Bireli Lagrene, George Coleman, Jimmy Heath, Dewey Redman, Art Farmer, Eddie Harris, Johnny Griffin, Charlie Rouse, Toshiko Akiyoshi, JoAnne Brackeen, Chet Baker, Freddie Hubbard, Joe Henderson, Anita O'Day, Paquito D'Rivera, the Timeless All Stars, and Stan Getz. The club closed on 1 January 1992, reopened under Allen's ownership in September of that year, and was sold the following year.

——. **Mark Hopkins Hotel.** See Top of the Mark.

——. **El Matador.** Another of the city's many venues specializing in bop in the 1950s and early 1960s, it presented performances by such prominent musicians as Eddie Duran, Kenny Burrell, and Cal Tjader.

——. **Milestones.** 376 5th Street. It flourished from the mid-1980s, when the proprietor was Sonny Buxton. Performances were given there by Teddy Edwards, John Handy, Harold Land, Johnny Coles, and Freddie Hubbard. It failed in the early 1990s.

——. **New Orleans Room.** Located in the Fairmont Hotel, it offered jazz for the entertainment of patrons from at least the 1950s. Notable jazz musicians who appeared there include Louis Armstrong, who brought a group to the hotel for a residency (early 1962), and Ella Fitzgerald. Turk Murphy's band was resident in 1984. It presented many important jazz bands in the early 1990s and Terence Blanchard and Charlie Hunter in mid-decade, but thereafter it was no longer a jazz venue.

——. **New Orleans Swing House.** Post Street, near Fillmore. Louis Armstrong's All Stars performed there in the early 1950s.

——. **Off Planet.** See Storyville.

——. **On the Levee.** This nightclub was owned and managed from at least the mid-1950s by Kid Ory, whose band was the resident ensemble from 1954 to 1961. Others who led groups there included Joe Sullivan (1961) and Muggsy Spanier (early 1960s).

——. **Pearl's Jazz Restaurant and Bar.** 256 Columbus Avenue. Run by Pearl Wong, this Italian restaurant has been a major venue for jazz from the 1990s, with Bruce Forman's group appearing on a regular basis. (<http://www.sfstation.com/live/pearls.htm> (2001))

——. **Pergola Dancing Pavilion.** 949 Market Street. Dance hall. Among the bands to have been resident at this venue was King Oliver's Creole Jazz Band, which performed there from 12 June 1921.

——. **Pier 23.** On the Embarcadero. Nightclub. It began operating as a jazz venue in at least the early 1950s. Burt Bales held a long residency there from 1954 to 1966, and jazz musicians continued to appear there into the 1990s. (<http://www.sfstation.com/live/pier23.htm> (2001))

——. **Rasselas Ethiopian Cuisine and Jazz Club.** 2801 California Street. Restaurant and nightclub. In the 1990s it presented local bop and fusion musicians.

——. **Rasselas on Fillmore.** 1534 Fillmore Street. It opened in 1999 as part of the city's Jazz Preservation District project and presented jazz, blues, salsa, rhythm-and-blues, and reggae groups. (V. Wagner: "New Jazz Club Augers Return to a Great Era," *San Francisco Examiner* (15 Oct 1999))

——. **Say When.** Bush Street. Inspired by the example of Blanco's Cotton Club, it was a racially integrated club which operated from *c*1949 into the 1950s. Charlie Parker and Billie Holiday appeared there.

——. **Storyville.** Fulton Street at Masonic Street. Nightclub and restaurant. It was opened in 1996 by the big-band reed player Don Pender and the ceramic artist Katherine Hoffman on the site of what had formerly been a rock club, Brave New World, and before that, a soul-jazz club, Off Planet, which had featured organ trios. Named, with George Wein's permission, after the latter's famous club in Boston, it presented Pender's house band in alternation with such musicians as Chico Freeman, George Cables, Ernie Watts, and Phil Woods.

——. **Top of the Mark.** Mark Hopkins Hotel, Nob Hill, at California Street and Jones Street. Though in no sense strictly a jazz venue, from at least the mid-1970s solo and small-group jazz has been played for the entertainment of patrons in the revolving restaurant and bar on the top floor of the hotel. (<http://www.sfstation.com/live/topmark.htm> (2001))

——. **Tropics Club.** It operated as a venue for jazz from at least the 1950s. Brew Moore performed there in 1958.

——. **Up and Down Club.** 1151 Folsom Street. Nightclub. Located on the former site of the club Eddie Jack's, it was founded by Tim Dale and J. J. Morgan in December 1992. It has become an important venue for local jazz bands, including that of Charlie Hunter.

BIBLIOGRAPHY

C. Robbins: "Jazz Clubs: a Presence of the Past," *San Francisco Examiner* (23 May 1993)
<http://www.sfstation.com/live/updown.htm> (2001)

——. **Venus Club.** It was active in the late 1940s under the direction of its Greek proprietor. Among the resident bands at that period was Kid Ory's (at that time including Joe Darensbourg and Bob Scobey), which appeared there in 1948.

——. **Vout City.** Post Street at Buchanan Street. Run by Slim Gaillard around 1948, it abruptly became Jimbo's Bop City when Gaillard (who had been selling alcohol without a license) forgot to pay his police bribe and, to avoid imprisonment, handed the keys to Jimbo Edwards and left for Los Angeles.

——. **Washington Street Bar and Grill.** 1707 Powell Street. Burt Bales was its resident pianist through the 1980s.

For other venues in the San Francisco Bay area see Berkeley, El Cerrito, Emeryville, Half Moon Bay, Oakland, San Jose, and Santa Clara.

BIBLIOGRAPHY

San Francisco

J. Lind: "When Jazz was King," *North Beach Magazine*, i/2 (1985), 6
D. Richardson: "Jazz on the Rebound," *San Francisco Bay Guardian* (30 Sept 1992)
D. Ouellette: "Jazz Junctions: Where to Bop by the Bay," *San Francisco Examiner Image* (24 October 1993)
J. Hamlin: "The Club Scene," *San Francisco Chronicle Datebook* (17 July 1994)

D. Ouellette: "Clubs: New Jazz Blows into Town," *San Francisco Examiner Magazine* (23 Oct 1994)
S. Stolder: "Young Turks Jazz up the City: Graybeards and Greenhorns Make New Music at Local Clubs," *San Francisco Examiner* (19 July 1995)
J. Hamlin: "Jazz Helped Break the Color Barrier," *San Francisco Chronicle* (8 Feb 1998)
V. Wagner: "New Jazz Club Augers Return of a Great Era," *San Francisco Examiner* (13 Oct 1999)

San Jose, CA. **Ajax Lounge.** 374 South 1st Street. In the 1990s it presented local and San Francisco-based musicians performing in various jazz styles.

——. **Gordon Biersch Brewery Restaurant.** 33 East San Fernando Street. Fusion groups, bop groups, and big bands appeared there in the 1990s. (<http://www.gordon biersch.com/restaurants/index.html> (2001))

San Pedro, CA. See Los Angeles (metropolitan area).

Santa Clara, CA. **Kuumbwa Jazz Center.** 320–22 Cedar Street. It was founded in the 1980s by Tim Jackson, who became the general manager of the Monterey Jazz Festival in the mid-1990s. Well before securing this prestigious position he brought in leading jazz musicians for local performances. He also presented a weekly jam session on Tuesday nights. (<http://www.jazzqwest.com/KUUMBWA> (2001))

Santa Monica, CA. See Los Angeles (metropolitan area).

Sawtelle, CA. See Los Angeles (metropolitan area).

Seal Beach, CA. See Los Angeles (metropolitan area).

Seattle. **Alhambra** [Black and Tan]. 1201 Jackson Street. It was founded in 1922 as the Alhambra by Noodles Smith in the basement of the Entertainers Club (also owned by Smith) and was one of Seattle's top nightclubs from that time into the 1930s; around 1932 it was renamed the Black and Tan. Among those who held residencies were the pianist Phil Moore (1931) and Eubie Blake (1934). The club was on the touring circuit for leading bands of the swing era, and many important musicians played engagements there, including Duke Ellington, Lucky Millinder, and Louis Jordan.

——. **Dimitriou's Jazz Alley.** NE 41st Street and University Avenue NE (1979–85); 315 Second Avenue S (1984–5); 2033 Sixth Avenue (from 1985). Dimitriou's Jazz Alley opened in November 1979 in Seattle's University District, with Ahmad Jamal's trio playing at the opening and appearing soon thereafter. John Dimitriou set up a second Jazz Alley downtown in the Duncan Building on Second Avenue South in 1984, but within a year this venture failed, and he consolidated his clubs and moved into a new location on Sixth Avenue; this venue was renovated in 1990. Currently Seattle's pre-eminent jazz club, the Jazz Alley presents nationally and internationally renowned musicians for four to six nights at a time, as well as one-night stands by local artists in association with such nonprofit organizations as Earshot Jazz or the Pacific Jazz Institute.

BIBLIOGRAPHY

<http://www.jazzalley.com> (2001)
L. Pellegrinelli: "A Guided Tour of America's Most Fascinating Jazz Clubs," <http://www.newmusicbox.org/third-person/jan00/home.html> (2001)
K. Raether: "Pop Music: Jazz Alley at 20: Not Just a Business, it's a Labor of Love," *Seattle Post-Intelligencer* (1 Nov 1999); repr. at <http://seattlepi.nwsource.com/pop/ally01.html> (2001)

——. **Elk's Club.** Madison Street; 662 Jackson Street. The local African-American chapter of the well-known fraternal order (often referred to as "the black Elks Club"), it was active from at least 1938. In early 1948 Ray Charles made his début in Seattle at the Jackson Street location of the Elk's, in a duo with the guitarist Garcia McKee.

——. **Entertainers Club.** 1238 Main Street (1920); 12th Avenue South and Jackson (by 1921). Founded in 1920 by Noodles Smith and Jimmy Woodland, it was first located on Main Street (Jelly Roll Morton performed at this location in August 1920) but quickly moved into a small upstairs venue in premises next door to the Alhambra (later, the Black and Tan) on 12th and Jackson. Its activities were managed by George Moore. Among the jazz musicians who performed there in the early 1930s were Joe Darensbourg and Bumps Myers.

——. **Jungle Temple.** Everett Highway. Roadhouse. Under the direction of Fred Owens, it presented jazz from the late 1920s. Joe Darensbourg played there around 1929 with his Jungle Temple Syncopators.

——. **Trianon Ballroom.** Third Avenue and Wall. It was built in 1927 by John Savage, and in the late 1930s and early 1940s became the principal venue in Seattle for swing music and dancing. Duke Ellington, Jimmie Lunceford, and other nationally known bandleaders performed there (for white audiences) in the 1940s, and Quincy Jones appeared on a bill with Lionel Hampton in 1951.

——. **Washington Social Club.** 23rd Avenue and Madison. It was founded in 1944 by Sy Groves; such prominent Seattle musicians as Ernestine Anderson, Ray Charles, and Quincy Jones performed there, as did the touring groups of B. B. King, Henry "Red" Allen, and Wardell Gray. It was closed in 1951.

BIBLIOGRAPHY

Seattle

P. De Barros and E. Calderon: *Jackson Street After Hours: the Roots of Jazz in Seattle* (Seattle, 1993)

Sherman Oaks, CA. See Los Angeles (metropolitan area).

Silver Spring, MD. **Showboat Lounge.** Active at least by the 1970s, it was directed at that time by Pete Lambrose. In 1976 a performance given there by Phil Woods's sextet was recorded and released as *"Live" from the Showboat* (1976, RCA BGL22202), which confirmed Woods's reputation as one of the finest mainstream saxophonists of that era.

Somerville, MA. **Johnny D's Uptown Restaurant and Music Club.** 17 Holland Street, in Davis Square. Mainly a rock and blues nightclub, Johnny D's occasionally books jazz or fusion acts that have commercial appeal. John Abercrombie, Bill Frisell, and Ralph Towner are among those who have performed there. (<http://www.johnnyds.com> (2001))

——. **The Willow.** 699 Broadway. This nightclub, in the metropolitan area of Boston, opened in 1980, with the local pianist Brian Walkley serving as its booking agent. Among the jazz musicians to appear there were John Scofield, Charles McPherson, Steve Turre, Kenny Werner, Kevin Eubanks, Joshua Redman, Alan Dawson, George Garzone and the Fringe, Freddie Redd, James Williams, Mal Waldron and Chico Freeman, Horace Tapscott, Andrew Hill, Sonny Fortune, Bill Evans (iii), Mike Stern, James Williams, and

Tiger Okoshi. After the Willow closed in 1997, many of its regular performers began to work at the Lizard Lounge in Boston.

South Gate, CA. See Los Angeles (metropolitan area).

Springfield, IL. **Club Rio.** West Grand Avenue. Restaurant. It was owned by Vito Impastato and featured jazz from at least the 1940s. Among the musicians who performed at this venue were the Brown Cats led by the guitarist Adam Lambert (1942), Paul Barbarin's band (September–December 1943), Sidney Bechet (two residencies in 1944), and Punch Miller (early autumn 1944).

Squaw Valley, CA. **Squaw Valley Lodge.** Situated high in the Californian Sierras, around 200 miles northeast of San Francisco, Squaw Valley was the site of the Winter Olympics in 1959–60. Alex Cushing, the owner of the lodge, engaged Ralph Sutton to perform there for four winter seasons from 1958 to 1961.

Studio City, CA. See Los Angeles (metropolitan area).

Taunton, MA. **Roseland Ballroom.** This was a regular venue for one-night stands by touring bands in the 1940s. Those announced included the orchestras of Count Basie (10 November 1940, 17 January 1941, and 7 May 1942), Andy Kirk (1 January 1941), Jimmie Lunceford (4 December 1941), Roy Eldridge (21 February 1942), Sabby Lewis (several times in 1943–4), Duke Ellington (11 November 1943), and Benny Carter (14 February 1944).

Toluca Lake, CA. See Los Angeles (metropolitan area).

Universal City, CA. See Los Angeles (metropolitan area).

Venice, CA. See Los Angeles (metropolitan area).

Washington, DC. **Blues Alley.** 1073 Rear Wisconsin Avenue NW, Georgetown. It opened, literally in an alley, in 1965 under the direction of Tommy Gwaltney, who sold his interest in the club in 1969 but continued to lead the house band there. Despite its name, Blues Alley features jazz – principally dixieland in its early years, when Gwaltney was involved, and latterly (from 1975) modern mainstream jazz, when John Dimitriou took over the management of the club and for the first time brought in such artists as Betty Carter, Ahmad Jamal, and Art Blakey's Jazz Messengers. (Dimitriou moved to Seattle in 1977 and in 1979 founded Dimitriou's Jazz Alley there; see above, Seattle.) Countless renowned performers have appeared at Blues Alley since that time. (<http://www.bluesalley.com> (2001))

——. **Bohemian Caverns.** 2001 11th Street NW. Formerly the Crystal Caverns (see below), it was opened in the early 1960s by Tony Taylor and Angelo Alvino, who presented such innovative artists as John Coltrane and Eric Dolphy. Andrew White led his JFK Quintet there during this same period, and Ramsey Lewis's hit recording *The In Crowd* was made at the club in 1965. After being derelict for nearly 30 years the venue was renovated, and it reopened in 2001. The elegant restaurant, situated on the ground floor, features a memorial to Duke Ellington and a panoramic photograph of U Street from early in the 20th century; downstairs, the revived jazz venue has been redecorated after the manner of the Crystal Caverns, with a *faux-cave* interior (including stalactites) and furniture made from petrified wood. The new owners plan to present major jazz groups and to host a Sunday gospel jazz brunch. (<http://bohemiancaverns.com> (2001))

——. **Constitution Hall.** 18th Street, between C Street and D Street. The hall was opened and originally run by the Daughters of the American Revolution. It has long been used for jazz concerts and in the 1980s was one of the most important auditoriums in the city for large events of this kind.

——. **Crystal Caverns.** 2001 11th Street NW. Jazz was played in this cellar club from at least the mid-1920s, when Claude Hopkins and his band appeared for an extended engagement; around the turn of the decade Elmer Calloway led a group (which included Jimmy Mundy) there. In the 1940s it was operated by Benny Caldwell, who presented leading swing and bop players. Later it became the Bohemian Caverns (see above). Ruth Brown sang there in the early 1950s, before her rise to fame as a rhythm-and-blues singer.

——. **d.c. space.** Founded in 1977, this performance center was presenting jazz roughly once a week in the late 1980s, when among those who appeared were Sun Ra's Arkestra and the World Saxophone Quartet. It closed in December 1991.

——. **Evening Star Jazz Bar.** 1200 19th Street NW. In the 1990s it presented jazz. Ron Holloway appeared on a regular basis.

——. **Howard Theater.** 620 T Street NW. Opened in 1915, it became the principal African-American theater in Washington, presenting popular entertainers and musicians, including such artists as Ethel Waters, Alberta Hunter, Duke Ellington, Billy Eckstine, Dinah Washington, and Ella Fitzgerald. On occasion white bands appeared, notably those of Artie Shaw, Woody Herman, and Stan Kenton. The Howard had become a venue for rock-and-roll by the late 1950s, and a decade later, in 1968, it closed.

——. **Jungle Inn.** 1211 U Street NW. This small second-floor club, with a dozen tables, a jukebox, and a battered upright piano, was owned by C. Rice Lyle and managed by Jelly Roll Morton from 1935 until December 1938. Morton tended the bar, played unaccompanied solo piano, and, according to local advertisements, occasionally featured his Red Hot Peppers. The club's name was later changed to the Music Box and then to the Casbah. The building was demolished in 1989 during subway installation.

——. **Lincoln Theater.** 1215–19 U Street NW. Built in 1921, it showed films and also presented jazz and blues groups.

——. **One Step Down.** 2517 Pennsylvania Avenue NW. In the 1970s this nightclub began presenting local artists, including Steve Novosel, and, on weekends, such musicians as Benny Carter, Art Farmer, Carmen McRae, David "Fathead" Newman, and Joe Locke, among many others. In summer 2000 the building was sold to a developer for conversion into an apartment building, and the club closed.

——. **Rogue and Jar.** Dottie Dodgion served as music director at this club in *c*1976–8.

——. **Twins Lounge.** 5516 Colorado Avenue NW. Serving Ethiopian and American cuisines, this small restaurant and nightclub opened around 1987. It has presented local jazz artists, including Buck Hill, as well as groups led by such touring musicians as Harold Mabern and Frank Lacy, and remains active as a jazz venue in the new century. (<http://www.dcjazz.com/twins> (2001))

BIBLIOGRAPHY

Washington

"Hot Spots for Jazz," <http://yp.washingtonpost.com/E/E/WASDC/0002/40/27/cs1.html> (2001)

<http://www.dcjazz.com> (2001)

WESTCHESTER, CA. See Los Angeles (metropolitan area).

WESTFIELD, NJ. **Shady Rest Country Club** [Shady Rest Golf Club]. In existence by 1927, it presented both residencies and one-night stands by jazz groups. Among those who appeared there were Johnson's Happy Pals, led by the drummer Roy Johnson (November 1929 and March 1930), Ike Dixon's Orchestra from Baltimore (January 1930), the Missourians, under the direction of Cab Calloway (May 1930), Claude Hopkins (September 1933), and Earl Hines (April 1934).

WESTWOOD, CA. See Los Angeles (metropolitan area).

WHITE PLAINS, NY. **Westchester County Center.** Bronx River Parkway. Among the functions promoted there in the 1930s by the Os-We-Go Club were performances by Fletcher Henderson (31 March 1932), Claude Hopkins (27 May 1933), Duke Ellington (4 September 1933), Luis Russell (26 April 1934 and 2 September 1935), Lucky Millinder (22 April 1935), Cab Calloway (3 September 1936), Fess Williams (29 March 1937), and Count Basie (2 January 1939). On 3 September 1934 there was a battle of the bands between Tiny Bradshaw and Hopkins. Occasional jazz presentations continued in later decades, notably a "Battle of Swing" between the bands of Illinois Jacquet and Dizzy Gillespie on 15 May 1947, a concert by Duke Ellington's orchestra on 28 November 1948, and a concert featuring Charlie Parker and George Shearing on 4 January 1952.

BIBLIOGRAPHY

USA

J. Durante and J. Kofoed: *Nightclubs* (New York, London, and Toronto, 1931)

G. Fernett: *Swing Out: Great Negro Jazz Bands* (Midland, MI, 1970/*R*1993)

R. Russell: *Jazz Style in Kansas City and the Southwest* (Berkeley, CA, Los Angeles, and London, 1971, rev. 2/1973/*R*1997)

R. M. Sudhalter, P. R. Evans, and W. Dean-Myatt: *Bix: Man and Legend* (New Rochelle, NY, and London, 1974)

J. Darensbourg: *Telling it Like it is*, ed. P. Vacher (London, 1987, Baton Rouge, LA, 1987, as *Jazz Odyssey: the Autobiography of Joe Darensbourg*)

C. Bird: *The Jazz and Blues Lover's Guide to the US* (Reading, MS, and elsewhere, 1991, rev. 2/1994)

J. Ephland: "The Best Places to Play Jazz in America," *DB*, lxvii/2 (1995), 30

L. Pellegrinelli: "A Guided Tour of America's Most Fascinating Jazz Clubs," <http://www.newmusicbox.org/third-person/jan00/home.html> (2001)

GENERAL BIBLIOGRAPHY

ChiltonW; *McCarthyB*; *SheridanCB*

P. E. Miller, ed.: *Esquire's Jazz Book* (New York, 1944-6) [three vols., pubd annually; abridged P. Miller and R. Venables (London, 1947)]

O. Keepnews and B. Grauer, Jr.: *A Pictorial History of Jazz: People and Places from New Orleans to Modern Jazz* (New York, 1956, rev. 2/1966)

D. Morgenstern: *Jazz People* (New York, 1976)

E. Townley: *Tell your Story: a Dictionary of Jazz and Blues Recordings* (Chigwell, England, 1976-87)

C. Goddard: *Jazz away from Home* (London and New York, 1979)

M. Berger, E. Berger, and J. Patrick: *Benny Carter: a Life in American Music* (Metuchen, NJ, and London, 1982)

F. Driggs and H. Lewine: *Black Beauty, White Heat: a Pictorial History of Classic Jazz, 1920–1950* (New York, 1982/*R*1996)

M. Zwerin: *La tristesse de Saint Louis: Swing under the Nazis* (London, 1985/*R*2000)

P. Clayton and P. Gammond: *Jazz: A–Z* (Enfield, England, 1986)

J. Chilton: *Sidney Bechet: the Wizard of Jazz* (London, 1987/*R*1996)

F. Hoffmann and I. Buckley, comp.: *Jazz Advertised, 1910–1967: a Documentation*, i–iii: *The Negro Newspapers of New England, 1910–1967*; iv–vi: *The Chicago Defender, 1910–1967*; vii: *The New York Times, 1929–1950*; viii: *Index* (Berlin, [1997])

<http://www.jazz-clubs-worldwide.com> (2001)

INDEX

A

D

S

T

Nighthawk Orchestra. Shortened form of the name Coon–Sanders Original Nighthawk Orchestra, taken in 1924 by the band led by Carleton Coon and JOE SANDERS; the band was established (with fewer members) as the Coon–Sanders Novelty Orchestra in 1920 and became known as the Nighthawks from 1922 as a result of playing on late-night radio programs.

Night Hawks. Name used in the late 1950s by the CRUSADERS.

Nightingale, Mark (Daryl) (*b* Evesham, England, 29 May 1967). English trombonist. He began learning trombone at the age of nine and played with the Midland Youth Jazz Orchestra and National Youth Jazz Orchestra before studying at Trinity College of Music in London (1985–8). Following a performance at the 1989 International Trombone Workshop with his five-trombone ensemble Bonestructure he was invited to play as a soloist at the organization's workshops in Germany (1992), the USA (1994), and Austria (1996). He has played with John Dankworth, Cleo Laine, Urbie Green, Carl Fontana, Jiggs Whigham, Clark Terry, Slide Hampton, Thilo Berg (including recordings, 1991, 1993), Alan Barnes, Bill Holman, Clark Tracey, and Stan Tracey, and from 1994 to 1997 he recorded and played extensively in Europe with the Australian multi-instrumentalist James Morrison. He is a well-respected composer and arranger, and has also published two trombone tutors, *20 Jazz Etudes* (Warwick, England, 1995) and *Multiplicity* (Warwick, 1996). Influenced in particular by Frank Rosolino and Fontana, Nightingale has become a leading exponent of mainstream and bop trombone.

SELECTED RECORDINGS

As leader: *What I Wanted to Say* (1994, Mons 874763); *Destiny* (1996, Mons 874793)

As sideman: C. Terry: *Remember the Time* (1994, Mons 874762); C. Tracey: *Full Speed Sideways* (1994, 33 Records 018); C. Martin: *Old Boyfriends* (1994, Linn 028)

BIBLIOGRAPHY

ChiltonB
"Rising Star: Mark Nightingale," *JP*, xlvi/5 (1997), 20

MARK GILBERT

Nilson, Gunnar [Siljabloo] (*b* Luleå, Sweden, 2 Sept 1925; *d* Örebro, Sweden, 12 Dec 1989). Swedish singer and clarinetist. He played in amateur bands in northern Sweden before moving in the 1940s to Stockholm, where he was a member of a professional singing group, the Flickery Flies (1947–51). From 1952 to 1955 he was associated with Carl-Henrik Norin's band at Nalen, where he became known as Siljabloo, from one of his bop-inspired vocal improvisations on the blues *Sil-ja-bloo*, recorded by Norin in 1953 (Roul. [Swed.] 30). He later worked for many years as a freelance and made several fine recordings as a singer and clarinetist, including his own albums *Siljabloo is Back* (1969, Odeon E062-34072) and *That's my Desire* (1971, Odeon E062-34446). Nilson was one of few male jazz singers to have emerged in Sweden; he was effective at both bop improvisation and singing standards. He is also well represented as a singer on *If You Could See Me Now*, on Åke Johansson's album *Monday Date* (1979, Odeon EO62-35147).

Oral history material in *SSsv*.

BIBLIOGRAPHY

"På omslaget" [On the cover], *Orkester journalen*, xxii/1 (1954), 4
A. von Konow: "Gunnar: en genuin jazzmusikant" [Gunnar: a genuine jazz man], *Orkester journalen*, lviii/2 (1990), 29

ERIK KJELLBERG/LARS WESTIN

Nilva. Record label established in Geneva by ALVIN QUEEN around 1980. Issues featured Queen and his associates in a wide range of contexts.

Nimbus. Record label formed in the late 1970s to record HORACE TAPSCOTT's music.

Nimitz, Jack (Jerome) [the Admiral] (*b* Washington, DC, 11 Jan 1930). Baritone saxophonist. He learned clarinet at the age of 13 and later played alto saxophone in local bands. He continued to play in Washington for a time, and worked in Willis Conover's orchestra from 1952 to late 1953, when he became Woody Herman's baritone saxophonist. He recorded as a soloist with Herman and toured Europe with the band in spring 1954. After leaving Herman in mid-1955 he joined Stan Kenton (1956), with whom he recorded and made another European tour. As a freelance in 1957–8 he performed in a quintet at the Savoy Ballroom and recorded with Herbie Mann (1957). In 1959 he rejoined Kenton to record and make appearances at several important jazz festivals. In the 1960s he worked in films (Johnny Mandel and David Amram were among the composers with whom he collaborated), but he also played and recorded in big bands under Terry Gibbs and Gerald Wilson, performed with orchestras accompanying Charles Mingus (at the Monterey Jazz Festival in 1964) and Thelonious Monk, and again worked with Kenton (1965). In Los Angeles in 1964 he led a quintet with Bill Hood, which was made up of various combinations of saxophones and clarinets (besides his principal instrument Nimitz plays other saxophones, soprano and bass clarinets, and flute).

Nimitz continued to work as a studio musician in the 1970s and played on the soundtrack to the film *Lady Sings the Blues* (1972). He appeared at festivals on the West Coast in bands led by Louie Bellson (1973) and Chuck Mangione (1974). One of the founders of Supersax, he toured and recorded with the group from 1972 through the 1990s. He was also associated with the big bands of Oliver Nelson (recording in 1966–7) and Bill Berry (recording in 1974 and 1976), continued to play with Berry and Wilson's big bands in the 1980s and 1990s, and recorded with the latter's ensemble in 1981 and *c*1994. In the 1990s he was also a member of Frank Strazzeri's sextet Woodwinds West, which recorded (1992, 1994) and made a self-titled video (1992). He recorded with Bud Shank's sextet (1993, *c*1995) and Frank Capp's big band (*c*1994), in which he sometimes deputizes, and in 1995 he made his first recording as a leader. In April 1997 he performed with Buddy Childers at the Pizza Express in London. Nimitz is best known for the secure foundation he provides in big-band performances, but he is a capable instrumentalist in all the styles and settings in which he plays.

SELECTED RECORDINGS

As leader: *Confirmation* (1995, Fresh Sound 5008)
As sideman: S. Kenton: *Stan Kenton in Hi-fi* (1956, Cap. W724), incl. The Peanut Vendor; H. Mann: *Sultry Serenade* (1957, Riv. 234); Supersax: *Supersax Plays Bird* (1972, Cap. ST11177); F. Strazzeri: *Woodwinds West* (1992, Jazz Mark 111); B. Shank: *New Gold!* (1993, Can. 79707); F. Strazzeri: *Somebody Loves Me* (1994, Fresh Sound 5003); B. Shank: *Bud Shank Sextet Plays Harold Arlen* (*c*1995, Jimco 9502)

SELECTED FILMS AND VIDEOS

The Swingin' Singin' Years (1960); Gerald Wilson All-Star Orchestra (1962); Woodwinds West (1992)

BIBLIOGRAPHY

FeatherE; *Feather '60s*; *Feather–Gitler '70s*
W. D. Clancy with A. C. Kenton: *Woody Herman: Chronicles of the Herds* (New York and elsewhere, 1995)
G. Jack: "Jack Nimitz," *JJI*, l/12 (1997), 6

LAWRENCE KOCH/BK

Nimmons, Phil(ip Rista) (*b* Kamloops, Canada, 3 June 1923). Canadian composer, bandleader, and clarinetist. He played in dance bands and with Ray Norris and others on radio in Vancouver (1940–45), then studied at the Juilliard School in New York (1945–7) and the Royal Conservatory of Music in Toronto (1948–50). He began a long association with the CBC in Toronto in 1950, first as a composer of incidental music for radio and television and then as the leader of a jazz band formed in 1953, dubbed Nimmons 'n' Nine in 1957, and expanded to Nimmons 'n' Nine Plus Six in 1965. The band, which changed its approach from a cooly lyrical, West Coast style to one that was rougher and more vividly orchestral before it broke up in 1980, broadcast frequently and toured widely in Canada. It made several albums, including *Take 10* (1963, RCA LCPS1066) and a recording of one of Nimmons's major compositions, *The Atlantic Suite* (1975, Sack. 2008, reissued on a CD of the same title with other material from the 1970s, Sack. 2-5003). Nimmons taught at the Advanced School of Contemporary Music in Toronto with Oscar Peterson and others (1960–63) and was later instrumental in establishing jazz programs at the Banff School of Fine Arts, the University of Toronto, and elsewhere.

BIBLIOGRAPHY

EMC2
J. Batten: "Anybody wanta Pay Attention!," *The Canadian* (23 June 1979)
——: "Phil Nimmons," *Boogie, Pete & the Senator: Canadian Musicians in Jazz: the Eighties* (Toronto, 1987), 181

MARK MILLER

Nine Winds. Record company and label founded in 1977 by VINNY GOLIA.

Niosi, Bert [Bartolo] (*b* London, Canada, 10 Feb 1909; *d* Toronto, 3 Aug 1987). Canadian bandleader, clarinetist, alto saxophonist, trumpeter, and arranger. As a teenager he briefly played clarinet with Guy Lombardo in Cleveland. In 1931 he formed a dance band and soon after began a long series of engagements (which lasted through 1950) at the Palais Royale in Toronto. He was known as Canada's King of Swing during this period and enjoyed considerable renown for his skill as a multi-instrumentalist. His orchestra was heard frequently on CBC radio, as was a small group drawn from its personnel and styled after the John Kirby Sextet. Three airchecks of the big band from 1946 were first issued on the anthology *Swing Canada*, ii (Cowtown 04); the small band, in which Niosi played clarinet and alto saxophone, recorded ten titles in 1947, including *The World is Waiting for the Sunrise* (Vic. 56-0021). In later years Niosi was active as a CBC studio musician. He was a member from 1952 to 1959 of the Happy Gang, on the daily radio series of the same name, and he served as a composer, arranger, and conductor for several other radio and television variety shows. His brothers Joe and Johnnie were also musicians: Joe (*b* London, 26 May 1906; *d* Toronto, 14 May 1977) played double bass with Trump Davidson and the Happy Gang, and Johnnie (*b* London, 26 Sept 1914; *d* Toronto, 21 Nov 1965) was the drummer with the Niosi band for many years.

BIBLIOGRAPHY

EMC2
J. Buller: "Bert Niosi," *Metronome*, lxii/10 (1946), 48
J. Litchfield: *The Canadian Jazz Discography, 1916–1980* (Toronto, Buffalo, and London, 1982)
M. Miller: *Such Melodious Racket: the Lost History of Jazz in Canada, 1914–1949* (Toronto, 1997)

JACK LITCHFIELD/MARK MILLER

Nippon Columbia. Japanese record company and label. The company was founded in 1910 as Nippon Chikuonki Shōkai (Japan Phonograph Company) by the American businessman Frederick Whitney Horne; it immediately undertook a recording program, one of the first Japanese companies to do so, and specialized in classical music. In 1927 it began to manufacture and distribute in Japan recordings made by the British Columbia company, and in the following year it changed its name to Nippon Columbia Chikuonki Kabushiki Kaisha. In 1935 it became a wholly Japanese-owned company, and in 1946 it changed its trading name to Nippon Columbia Kabushiki Kaisha. While continuing its affiliation with British Columbia (to 1962), Nippon Columbia began in 1948 to manufacture and distribute recordings from American Columbia; its affiliation with American Columbia ended in 1968, when the CBS/Sony company was created, but Nippon Columbia retained the right to use the name Columbia in Japan. It first issued LPs in 1951 and stereo recordings in 1958. From that time Nippon Columbia releases in Japan have featured either the Nippon Columbia or the Denon label, which is the name of Nippon Columbia's audio equipment manufacturing company; because of conflicts over the Columbia trademark, international issues have been on Denon.

Nippon Columbia recorded jazz in Japan before the 1970s, but in the mid-1970s it recorded various American and international jazz musicians, including Billy Harper, Reggie Workman (who served as his own producer), Walter Davis, Archie Shepp, Abdullah Ibrahim, Frank Foster, Jo Jones, Mickey Tucker, Stan Getz, and Tommy Flanagan. Around 1983 Denon began operations in the USA as a division of Nippon Columbia, and in the years 1986–8 it recorded Bob Berg, Eliane Elias, McCoy Tyner, Bennie Wallace, Phil Woods, and the Count Basie Orchestra under the direction of Foster. In 1991 Nippon Columbia purchased the Savoy label and shortly afterwards began a comprehensive reissue program of the latter's material on CD; it also revived the label for new issues by Marc Copland, Ralph Moore, and others. Its initial program, which extended to more than 250 items issued on CD as facsimiles of the original Savoy LPs, received much criticism for the brief playing time of the discs (routinely filling less than half of the time available on a CD) and, in comparison with the models for facsimile reissues established earlier by Blue Note and Fantasy, for the lack of proper discographical information. Around 1998

Nippon Columbia embarked on a new reissue program of the Savoy material, which was overseen by Steve Backer and produced by Orrin Keepnews and which made fuller use of the CD format. Denon has also re-released material from the Groove Merchant and LRC catalogues. In the late 1990s the activities of the Denon and Savoy labels were operating as a division of Denon Active Media in Georgia, USA.

BIBLIOGRAPHY

J. Nash: "Label Watch: Denon Records Purchases the Savoy Record Label," *JT*, xi/5 (1991), 38
I. Horowitz: "Keeping Score (Denon Records to Move to Allegro Imports from A&M for Distribution)," *Billboard*, civ (15 Aug 1992)
B. Shoemaker: "Label Watch: Remastering the Masters," *JT*, xxiii/3 (1993), 20
<http://www.denon.com/denonrecords/welcome.htm> (2000)

GK

Nistico, Sal (i). *See* Nestico, sammy.

Nistico, Sal(vatore) (ii) (*b* Syracuse, NY, 12 April 1940; *d* Berne, Switzerland, 3 March 1991). Tenor saxophonist. He took up alto saxophone in 1949, then changed to the tenor instrument in 1956 and spent three years playing with local rhythm-and-blues bands. He first gained recognition in 1959–61 as a member of the Jazz Brothers, a group led by Chuck and Gap Mangione, with which he made his first recordings. From April 1962 through summer 1964 he played with Woody Herman, an association he maintained intermittently into the early 1980s; Nistico's driving solos and virile sound made him an important asset to Herman's groups. After playing with Count Basie for a few months from September 1964 he resumed touring and recording with Herman, lived in Sweden, then in 1966 returned to Herman's band for a tour of Africa. During these years he appeared as a soloist in episodes of the television shows "Jazz Casual" and "Big Band Series," respectively "Woody Herman and the Swinging Herd" (1964) and "Count Basie and his Orchestra" (1965). A further period with Basie (for several months from March 1967) was followed by two more stints with Herman (1968–70 and 1971), between which he worked in Los Angeles, briefly with Don Ellis, and in Boston.

From 1972, apart from a tour of Europe with Slide Hampton, Nistico lived in New York. His work as a freelance included periods with Buddy Rich's band in 1974 and the National Jazz Ensemble under Chuck Israels in the mid- and late 1970s; he also led his own groups. On occasion from 1981 to 1983 he again toured internationally and recorded with Herman. He recorded infrequently as a leader. A live concert in Half Moon Bay, California, with some excellent playing was rather poorly recorded (1981), but after settling in Europe he took part in a few studio recordings: a tenor saxophone "battle" with Johnny Griffin and Roman Schwaller (Munich, 1985), a quartet session (Rome, 1988), and a quintet session (Zagreb, 1989). Nistico fused elements of the styles of Charlie Parker, Sonny Stitt, Gene Ammons, and Sonny Rollins into a powerful bop idiom of his own, which is best displayed on Herman's *Northwest Passage* (1965).

SELECTED RECORDINGS

As leader: *Heavyweights* (1961, Jlnd 966); *Neo/Nistico* (1978, BH 7006); with J. Griffin and R. Schwaller: *Three Generations of Tenor Saxophone* (1985, JHM 3611); *Empty Room* (1988, Red 123222-2)
As sideman with W. Herman: *Woody Herman, 1963* (1962, Phi. 600065); *Encore, 1963* (1963, Phi. 600092); *Woody's Winners* (1965, Col. CS9236), incl. Northwest Passage
As sideman with others: Jazz Brothers: *Hey Baby!* (1961, Riv. 9371); B. Rich: *The Buddy Rich Septet* (1974, GrM 3301); C. Israels: *National Jazz Ensemble* (1975, Chi. 140)

BIBLIOGRAPHY

Feather '60s; *Feather–Gitler '70s*; *SheridanCB*
L. Tompkins: "Personally Speaking: Sal Nistico," *Crescendo*, iii/6 (1965), 27
——: "Sal Nistico," *CI*, xiii/5 (1974), 12
Obituary, S. Woolley, *JJI*, xlii/5 (1991), 19
J. Simmen: "Sal Nistico," *BHcF*, no.392 (1991), 38
W. D. Clancy with A. C. Kenton: *Woody Herman: Chronicles of the Herds* (New York and elsewhere, 1995), 242

SCOTT YANOW/BK

Nix, Bern (Maynard) (*b* Toledo, OH, 21 Sept 1947). Electric guitarist. He was initially influenced by rock and pop guitarists and began playing jazz at the age of 14 after hearing a recording of Charlie Christian. Later he moved to Boston, where he attended the Berklee College of Music and worked locally. After graduating in 1975 he continued to perform in Boston and taught briefly, but later that year he joined Ornette Coleman's Prime Time, with which he worked until 1987. During the same period he played with Julius Hemphill (1976) and Ronald Shannon Jackson's Decoding Society (1977–80), accompanied Jayne Cortez with the Firespitters (from 1980), and was a member of the group Divine Monochord (1980–87). In 1985 Nix joined Jemeel Moondoc and formed his own trio, in which he played at first with William Parker and the drummer David Cappello, although his sidemen later included Fred Hopkins and Newman Taylor Baker; it performed at the Toronto Du Maurier Ltd. Downtown Jazz festival in 1996. In the early 1990s he worked in the cooperative sextet String Faced alongside Jim Nolet, Hopkins, Diedre Murray, the keyboard player Nick Balaban, and Baker. Thereafter he co-led various groups with Nolet, notably a double quartet that appeared at the Earshot World Jazz Festival in 1994; the following year the two men performed at the Knitting Factory with a sextet consisting of Carlos Ward, Bob Stewart, Brad Jones, and the drummer Calvin Weston. Nix has also collaborated with the avant-garde guitarist Elliott Sharp and recorded with Kip Hanrahan (1981). He continued to lead his trio in the late 1990s.

SELECTED RECORDINGS

As leader: *Alarms and Excursions* (1993, New World 80437)
As sideman: on [various artists]: *Wildflowers*, iv: *The New York City Loft Sessions* (1976, Douglas 7048), J. Hemphill: Pensive; O. Coleman: *Body Meta* (1976, AH 1); J. Moondoc: *Nostalgia in Times Square* (1985, SN 1141); O. Coleman: *In All Languages* (1987, Caravan of Dreams 85008); J. Nolet: on *With You* (*c*1993, Knitting Factory Works 150), Madoka's Organic Jam; J. Cortez: *Cheerful & Optimistic* (1994, Bola Press 9401), incl. War Devoted to War

BIBLIOGRAPHY

J. Pareles: "Pop in Review," *New York Times* (29 Aug 1991)
R. Hicks: "Profile: Bern Nix," *GP*, xvii/11 (1993), 25
K. L. Williams: "Riffs: Bern Nix," *DB*, lx/9 (1993), 14
O. McNally: "Nix, Veteran of Coleman's Prime Time, Charting his own Path," *Hartford Courant* (5 June 1997)

GK

NJF. *See* Norsk jazzforbund.

NJSO. *See* National jazz service organization.

Nkosi, Zacks [Isaac Ben; Zakes] (*b* Ingogo, near Newcastle, South Africa, 1918; *d* Johannesburg, 1980). South African alto saxophonist and clarinetist. His family moved to Alexandra township and he attended Holy Cross Catholic School. Having received basic instruction in piano and organ at the age of nine, by the time he was 15 he was playing accordion, violin, and clarinet, and he soon took up alto saxophone to play with such local bands as the Blue Diamonds, the Jazz Havanas (also known as the Havana Swingsters), and, eventually, the well-known Jazz maniacs, top-rated interpreters of American swing whose playing moved towards a township jazz style in the 1940s. During the golden era of South African jazz, from the 1950s into the 1960s, Nkosi made many recordings as a freelance with the African Swingsters (including *Swazi Stomp*, 1952, HMV JP133) and as the leader of the City Jazz Nine and Zacks and the Sextet. His first album, *Our Kind of Jazz* (*c*1957–*c*1962, HMV JCLP52) – actually a compilation of singles made during the period by the City Jazz Nine and his sextet – is considered the benchmark album of African jazz.

Nkosi's son, the keyboard player and composer (Patrick) Jabu Nkosi (*b* Alexandra township, 26 June 1952; *d* 1999), was a jazz musician who also accompanied such singers as Miriam Makeba and Harry Belafonte. In 1997 he made the award-winning and best-selling album *Remembering Bra' Zacks* (Gallo 40718), which reworked some of his father's hits.

DARIUS BRUBECK

Noble, Ray(mond Stanley) (*b* Brighton, England, 17 Dec 1903; *d* London, 2 April 1978). English bandleader, arranger, and composer. He studied classical piano but became interested in dance music. From 1929 he served as house conductor for HMV records, and attracted attention with the recordings of his New Mayfair Dance Orchestra (1930–34), particularly those with the singer Al Bowlly. He moved to the USA to direct his own orchestra at the Rainbow Room in New York (1935–7), then went to Los Angeles and worked into the 1950s as a bandleader and radio personality. In the jazz field Noble's significance was as a catalyst rather than as a performer. His own arrangements and performances were generally of "sweet" dance music, and his major compositions were highly successful romantic ballads such as *Goodnight, sweetheart* (1931), *Love is the sweetest thing* (1932), *The very thought of you* (1934), *The touch of your lips* (1936), and *I hadn't anyone till you* (1938). However, his New York band, assembled by Glenn Miller (who also provided its more jazz-oriented arrangements, and thereby discovered his own distinctive way of writing), included such musicians as Pee Wee Erwin, Charlie Spivak, Sterling Bose, Johnny Mince, Bud Freeman, Will Bradley, and Claude Thornhill. Noble's instrumental composition *Cherokee* became the theme tune of Charlie Barnet's band (1938, Bruns. 8247); as a familiar test piece for jazz musicians in the early bop style, it was also associated with Charlie Parker.

BIBLIOGRAPHY

FeatherE

G. T. Simon: *The Big Bands* (New York and London, 1967, rev. 4/1981)

J. H. Klee: "Noble American, 1935–37," *MR*, iv/1 (1976), 1

C. Garrod: *Ray Noble and his Orchestra* (Zephyrhills, FL, 1991) [discography]

W. W. Vaché: *Jazz Gentry: Aristocrats of the Music World* (Landham, MD, and London, 1999), 227

ANDREW LAMB

Nock, Mike [Michael Anthony] (*b* Christchurch, New Zealand, 27 Sept 1940). New Zealand keyboard player. He grew up in the towns of Ngaruawahia and Nelson and began taking piano lessons at the age of 11; four years later he became a professional musician, doubling on alto saxophone. When he was 18 he moved to Australia and worked first in Melbourne with Frank Smith and then in Sydney, where he formed the influential hard-bop Three Out Trio and played at El Rocco. The trio traveled to England in 1961, but Nock left and went to the USA to attend the Berklee School of Music; while in Boston he played with Herb Pomeroy, Tony Williams, and Sam Rivers. A year later he left school to become the house pianist at Lennie's-on-the-Turnpike in Peabody, Massachusetts, and, with John Neves or Kent Carter on double bass and Alan Dawson on drums, accompanied Coleman Hawkins, Pee Wee Russell, Benny Golson, Phil Woods, Sonny Stitt, Zoot Sims, and many other important soloists. After touring with Yusef Lateef (1963–5) he replaced Keith Jarrett in Art Blakey's Jazz Messengers (briefly in 1966). He worked as a freelance with Stanley Turrentine and Booker Ervin, then moved to San Francisco, where in 1967 he joined John Handy, with whom he recorded the following year. In 1968 he established the Fourth Way, a pioneering jazz-rock group. This disbanded in 1970, and Nock composed and recorded film soundtracks on synthesizer for a while before returning to New York in 1975 to work as a studio musician; he also played with the Thad Jones–Mel Lewis Orchestra, toured Germany with Jeremy Steig and the Far East with Rivers, performed with Howard Roberts at the Showboat in Washington, DC, and appeared in New York in a trio with John Abercrombie and Rick Laird (all *c*1976).

Early in 1985 Nock went back to Australia, where he composed (for the groups Synergy and Ten Part Invention and many others) and taught improvisation at New South Wales Conservatorium of Music in Sydney (from 1990, the Sydney Conservatorium of Music), though he continued to tour regularly in the USA and Europe. In 1989 he performed in a duo with Helen Merrill and played with Jon Faddis in Vancouver, Canada, and in the 1990s he returned to New Zealand for festivals and workshops. In 1992 he toured in a band which included the New Zealand trumpeter Kim Patterson, Billy Harper, and the drummer Malcolm Pinson, and which performed in New York. Nock appeared in the film *Beyond El Rocco* (1990), which documented the development of jazz in Sydney, and he may also be seen in the video *Dr. Jazz* (1998). In the 1990s he led his own groups, which featured many of the best younger players emerging from the conservatorium and elsewhere, among them a long-term colleague, the saxophonist Tim Hopkins. He also accompanied many visiting musicians during their tours of Australia. In 1995 he took charge of artists and repertory for Naxos jazz, and he has made several recordings for that label.

SELECTED RECORDINGS

As unaccompanied soloist: *Piano Solos* (1978, Tim. 134); *Talisman* (1978, Enja 3071); *Touch* (1993, Birdland 001)

Duos with M. Ehrlich: *The Waiting Game* (1999, Naxos Jazz 86048-2)

As leader: (of Three Out Trio): *Move* (1960, Col. 330SX7639); *Almanac* (1967, ImA 373851); *Magic Mansions* (1977, Laurie 6001); *In, Out, and Around* (1978, Tim. 119); *Climbing* (1979, Tomato 8009); *Ondas* (1981, ECM 1220); *Dark & Curious* (1990, Australian Broadcasting Corporation 846873)

As sideman: Y. Lateef: *Live at Pep's* (1964, Imp. 69); J. Handy: *Projections* (1968, Col. CS9689); Fourth Way: *The Fourth Way* (1969, Cap. ST317); D. Barlow: *Horn* (1989, Spiral Scratch 0003); AtmaSphere: *Flying* (1992–3, Tall Poppies 038)

BIBLIOGRAPHY

CarrJ

M. Rozek: "Profile: Mike Nock," *DB*, xliv/7 (1977), 35

P. Hinely: Liner notes, *In, Out, and Around* (Tim. 119, 1978)

B. Blumenthal: Liner notes, *Climbing* (Tomato 8009, 1979)

L. Means and B. Primack: "Mike Nock, Journeyman Keyboardist Rediscovers Acoustic Jazz," *Keyboard*, v/9 (1979), 18 [incl. discography]
B. Smith: "Mike Nock: Jazz Down Under," *Coda*, no.214 (1987), 17
G. Brien: "Mike Nock," *Music in New Zealand*, no.12 (1991), 32
A. Lewis and L. Lewis: "Mike Nock: Interview," *Cadence*, xviii/7 (1992), 11
J. McLeod: *Jazztrack* (Sydney, 1994), 134
J. Pressing, ed.: *Compositions for Improvisers: an Australian Perspective* (Melbourne, Australia, 1994)
J. Clare [G. Brennan, pseud.]: *Bodgie Dada and the Cult of Cool* (Sydney, 1995)
W. Bebbington, ed.: *The Oxford Companion to Australian Music* (Melbourne, Australia, 1997)

ROBERT L. DOERSCHUK/ROGER T. DEAN, BK

Nocturne. Record company and label. The company was established around 1953 in Los Angeles by Roy Harte and Harry Babasin. It was devoted to West Coast jazz, and its catalogue included recordings by Bud Shank, Babasin, and Bob Gordon (all 1954), but it was only short-lived.

BIBLIOGRAPHY

R. Gordon: *Jazz West Coast: the Los Angeles Jazz Scene of the 1950s* (London and New York, 1986), 98
A. Morgun: "The Nocturne Label," *DF*, no.1 (1960), 13

BK

NOJC. *See* New orleans jazz club.

NOJCC [NOJCOC]. *See* New orleans jazz club of california.

Nolet, Jim [James Michael] (*b* Dallas, 11 Dec 1961). Violinist and violist. He took up classical violin at the age of seven and began to play professionally and improvise when he was 13. Later he studied at the Cornish Institute of the Arts and the Juilliard School and had private lessons with Gary Peacock. He became involved with jazz in New York in the mid-1980s, when he performed with such artists as JoAnne Brackeen and John Hicks. From 1985 to 1991 he was a member of Fred Hopkins and Diedre Murray's band Stringfaced, and in 1987 he founded the Composers Improvisers Workshop, with which he remained active until 1995. Around the same period he recorded seven albums as a member of the Jazz passengers (late 1980s – mid-1990s). During the 1990s Nolet performed and recorded with Ed Blackwell, Peacock, Steve Turre, Marc Ribot, and Joseph Jarman, co-led the Double Quintet with Bern Nix (1994–5), and performed with Cecil Taylor (1995–6) and David Murray's big band (1995–7). In 1998 he founded the record company and label Cathexis, on which he has released his own albums as well as those by other artists. Three lead sheets to Nolet's compositions were published as an appendix to Barnett's interview in *Fable Bulletin* (pp.21–4).

SELECTED RECORDINGS

As leader: *With You* (1993, Knitting Factory Works 150); *Syzygy* (1998, Cathexis 930003-2); *Arco voz* (2000, Cathexis 930010-2)
As sideman with Jazz Passengers: *Deranged and Decomposed* (1988, Crepuscule 846); *Implement Yourself* (*c*1990, New World 398); *In Love* (*c*1994, High Street 10328-2)

BIBLIOGRAPHY

A. Barnett: "Jim Nolet," *Fable Bulletin: Violin Improvisation Studies*, xi/4 (1999), 4
<http://www.knittingfactory.com/Persons/JimNolet.html> (1999)

STEVE SMITH

Nonesuch. Record company and label founded in 1964 by Elektra as a subsidiary devoted to classical and world music. Around 1970 Elektra was purchased by Kinney National Services Corporation (which approximately three years earlier had purchased Warner Brothers). Nonesuch continued its affiliation with Elektra until around 1994, when, following the restructuring of Time-Warner's music division, it became part of the Warner Music Group. While it continues to concentrate on classical music, it has issued important jazz and jazz-related recordings by the World Saxophone Quartet (1986–*c*1993), John Zorn (late 1980s – early 1990s), Don Byron (1990–96), Bill Frisell (from 1992), and Fred Hersch (from *c*1995).

BIBLIOGRAPHY

Grove7
H. Waleson: "Nonesuch Gives Modern Classics Room to Grow," *Billboard*, cvii (26 Aug 1995), 10
<http://www.nonesuch.com> (2000)
<http://www.warner-classics.com/nonesuch/home.htm> (2000)

GK

Noone, Jimmie(, Sr.) [Jimmy] (*b* Cut Off, nr New Orleans, 23 April 1895; *d* Los Angeles, 19 April 1944). Clarinetist and leader, father of Jimmy Noone, Jr. He first played guitar, took up clarinet at the age of 15, and after the Noone family moved to New Orleans in 1910 studied casually with Sidney Bechet (who was two years his junior). In 1913–14 he substituted for and then replaced Bechet in Freddie Keppard's Olympia Orchestra. When Keppard left the city in 1914 Noone and Buddy Petit founded the Young Olympia Band. Noone also performed with Kid Ory and Papa Celestin and led his own trio for two summer seasons (1916, 1917). He went to Chicago in 1917 and toured the Midwest with Keppard's Original Creole Band until it broke up in spring 1918. After returning briefly to New Orleans he left the city permanently in autumn 1918, traveling with King Oliver to Chicago, where they joined the band led by Bill Johnson (i) at the Royal Gardens. Noone quit the Royal Gardens in 1920 to join Doc Cook's Dreamland Orchestra, with which he played until 1926 and again in 1927. During this period he made his first recordings, with Ollie Powers (September 1923) and as a substitute for Johnny Dodds in Oliver's band (October 1923), as well as others for Gennett, Okeh, and Columbia. He also took lessons from the renowned classical clarinetist Franz Schoepp.

Noone's most important and influential period began after he left Cook in autumn 1926 to take up residence at the Apex Club in Chicago. Here he led his own group, Jimmie Noone's Apex Club Orchestra, which eventually included Joe Poston (alto saxophone), Earl Hines (piano), Bud Scott (banjo), and Johnny Wells (drums). With this group he made a classic series of recordings for Vocalion in spring and summer of 1928. During the 1930s, except for an engagement at the Savoy Ballroom in New York in 1931 and a failed attempt to start a new venue, the Vodvil Club, in Harlem in 1935, Noone remained in Chicago leading small groups at various clubs and broadcasting; Teddy Wilson was among his sidemen in 1933, and Budd Johnson at some point before mid-1935. His band toured the South and Midwest from 1938. Noone was taken up by the New Orleans revival movement in the early 1940s and from 1943 joined Ory, Zutty Singleton, Jack Teagarden, and others in club work and recording sessions in San Francisco and Los Angeles. Shortly before his death he performed in the film *Block Busters* (1944) and joined Ory's all-star revival band, organized for Orson Welles's CBS variety show.

Noone, along with Bechet and Johnny Dodds, was one of the most significant New Orleans reed players, and a vital link between the older New Orleans style of clarinet playing and the Chicago swing manner. His musical style was influenced by his teachers and colleagues in New Orleans, especially Bechet. Later, in Chicago, his formal study with Franz Schoepp helped give him a secure command of all three clarinet registers. His expressive performance of blue notes and solo breaks is nowhere better illustrated than in his four recordings with Oliver's band from October 1923. His later Apex Club recordings of *I Know that You Know*, *Four or Five Times*, and *Apex Blues* set a new standard for post-New Orleans ensemble playing. These recordings use the New Orleans ensemble style with a revised orchestration: alto saxophone as lead instrument, clarinet providing embellishments, and a three-piece rhythm section, with Hines often supplying a third independent line with his "trumpet-style" right hand. Noone's manner influenced many of his contemporaries as well as later generations of jazz musicians, including the clarinetists Buster Bailey, Barney Bigard, Joe Marsala, Omer Simeon, and, in particular, Benny Goodman; saxophonists as varied as Bud Freeman and Eric Dolphy also admitted to being influenced by him. Especially impressive and widely copied (though not always with his dexterity and sumptuous tone) was his manner of articulating rapid, syncopated figures, mainly in the clarinet's low register, as heard in the latter part of *I Know that You Know*.

See also Blues, §2; for illustrations *see* Clarinet, fig.3, and Drum set, fig.4.

SELECTED RECORDINGS

As leader: I Know that You Know/Sweet Sue – Just You (1928, Voc. 1184); Four or Five Times/Every Evening (1928, Voc. 1185); Apex Blues/Sweet Lorraine (1928, Voc. 1207); A Monday Date (1928, Voc. 1229); It's tight like that (1928, Voc. 1238); 'Way Down Yonder in New Orleans (1936, Parl. R2281); The blues jumped a rabbit (1936, Parl. R2303)

As sideman: O. Powers: Play that thing (1923, Para. 12059); K. Oliver: Chattanooga Stomp/New Orleans Stomp (1923, Col. 13003D); Camp Meeting Blues (1923, Col. 14003D); Capitol Jazzmen: Clambake in B Flat (1943, Cap. 10009)

BIBLIOGRAPHY

ChiltonW; *McCarthyJ*; *WrightK*
W. M. Neff: "New Orleans Clarinets 5: Jimmie Noone," *Jazz Information*, ii/6 (1940), 6
H. Panassie: "Jimmie Noone," *Jazz Information*, ii/15 (1941), 10
A. J. McCarthy: "Jimmy Noone," *Hot Notes*, ii/3 (1947), 13
N. Shapiro and N. Hentoff, eds.: *Hear me Talkin' to ya: the Story of Jazz by the Men who Made it* (New York and London, 1955/*R*1966)
J. G. Jepsen: "Discographie de Jimmie Noone," *Cahiers du jazz*, no.8 (1963), 93
A. J. McCarthy: "Jimmie Noone," *JM*, x/4 (1964), 10
M. Williams: *Jazz Masters of New Orleans* (New York and London, 1967/*R*1978), 188
G. Schuller: *Early Jazz: its Roots and Musical Development* (New York, 1968), 203
B. McRae: "A B Basics, no.36: Jimmie Noone," *JJ*, xxii/12 (1969), 16
S. Dance: *The World of Earl Hines* (New York, 1977), 55
V. McHugh: "The Blues for Jimmie," *Selections from the Gutter: Jazz Portraits from "The Jazz Record,"* ed. A. Hodes and C. Hansen (Berkeley, CA, Los Angeles, and London, 1977), 105
W. H. Kenney, III: "Jimmie Noone: Chicago's Classic Jazz Clarinetist," *American Music*, iv (1986), 145
L. Wright: "Jimmie Noone," *Sv*, no.153 (1993), 84 [discography]
——: "Jimmie Noone (the Vocalion Recordings)," *Sv*, no.154 (1993), 124; no.155 (1993), 188; no.157 (1994), 28; no.158 (1994), 68; no.159 (1994), 90
B. H. Behncke and K.-U. Dürr: *Jimmie Noone* (Hamburg, Germany, 1996) [discography]

RICHARD WANG/BK

Noone, Jimmy [Jimmie; James Fleming], **Jr.** (*b* Chicago, 21 April 1938; *d* San Diego, CA, 29 March 1991). Clarinetist and soprano and alto saxophonist, son of Jimmie Noone. His full name is taken from the California death index. After spending much of his career in obscurity in San Diego, playing alto saxophone and organ, he began working on clarinet with Jeannie and Jimmy Cheatham in the 1980s and had an active recording and international touring schedule. His blues playing may be heard on the Cheathams' album *Homeward Bound* (1987, Conc. 4321), especially *Goin' Down Slow* and *Trouble in Mind*. He also played traditional jazz with Cottonmouth Darcy's Jazz Vipers and Hal Smith's Creole Sunshine Orchestra, working in a lyrical style based on that of his father; this is exemplified by *Jimmy Remembers Jimmie* (1985, Stomp Off 1121), where the co-leader, John R. T. Davies, plays the role of Joe Poston, while Jimmy takes that of his father, Jimmie Noone.

BIBLIOGRAPHY

J. Simmen: "Jimmy Noone Junior," *BHcF*, no.320 (1984), 9
S. Dance: "Jimmie Noone Junior," *JJI*, xxxviii/7 (1985), 18
J. Simmen:: "Jimmy Noone," *BHcF*, no.329 (1985), 1
——: "A Note on Jimmy Noone," *Sv*, no.127 (1986), 19
Obituaries: S. Dance, *BHcF*, no.392 (1991), 5; J. Simmen, *BHcF*, no.393 (1991), 32; J. Trageser, *Living Blues*, no.98 (1991), 40

HOWARD RYE

Noordijk, Piet (*b* Rotterdam, Netherlands, 25 May 1932). Dutch alto saxophonist and clarinetist. He attended the Rotterdam Conservatory (1950–54) and taught himself to play alto and soprano saxophones. From 1957 to 1962 he led a group with his brother, the tenor saxophonist Kees Noordijk, and worked on radio with Pia Beck, the pianist Ger van Leeuwen, and the violinist Frans Poptie. With Misha Mengelberg he led a quartet from 1963 to 1967 that appeared at the Newport Jazz Festival in 1966; later he performed on radio broadcasts with the Skymasters, the Ramblers, the accordionist and bandleader Malando, and the pianists Tony Nolte and Ruud Bos. He played with many American musicians, including Thad Jones, Mel Lewis, Johnny Griffin, Ben Webster, Lee Konitz, Oliver Nelson, Kenny Clarke, Herb Geller, Dexter Gordon, Teddy Edwards, Hank Mobley, Benny Carter, and Wynton Marsalis; he also performed with Toots Thielemans and accompanied such singers as Tony Bennett, Billy Eckstine, Mark Murphy, and Betty Carter. From 1978 to 1992 he played lead alto saxophone in the Metropole Orchestra. Thereafter he has toured with his quartet, which appears regularly at the North Sea Jazz Festival. Noordijk is a versatile alto saxophonist who has played dixieland with the Storktown Dixie Kids, Latin jazz with Malando and the guitarist Tom Kelling, bop with a big band led by the pianist Boy Edgar, and free jazz with Mengelberg and Willem Breuker. His playing may be heard to advantage on his albums *Loverman* (1980, VR 22112) and *Plays Bird!* (1997, Via Jazz 922030-2).

WIM VAN EYLE

Norby, Cæcilie (*b* Frederiksberg, Denmark, 9 Sept 1964). Danish singer. Her father is Erik Norby, a classical composer, and her mother, Solveig Lumholt, is a renowned opera singer. She was a co-founder of the group Street Beat (1982) and a member of Jørgen Emborg's jazz-funk group Frontline (1984–5) before beginning what became a lengthy collaboration with the singer Nina Forsberg in the popular rock group One-Two (1985–93). However, from the mid-1990s she has concentrated entirely on jazz, touring extensively with her own quartet and performing as a soloist with local quartets and big bands at clubs and festivals in Europe, the Far East, and the USA. She has been much in demand in studios and has recorded with both rock and jazz bands, including those of Børge Roger Henrichsen (1985), Emborg (1994), and Thomas Clausen and Ib Glindemann (both 1997). Norby's voice is lyrical and supple, she improvises elegantly, and she displays a great variety of emotion in her interpretations.

SELECTED RECORDINGS

As leader: *Cæcilie Norby* (1994, BN 32222-2); *My Corner of the Sky* (1996, BN 53422-2); *Queen of Bad Excuses* (1999, BN 522342-2)
As sideman: Frontline: *Frontline* (1985, Tuba 310); J. Emborg: *A Circle of Songs* (1994, Stunt 19403)

BIBLIOGRAPHY

M. W. Keller: "Ærlighed og spilleglæde" [Honesty and joy of playing], *MM: tidsskrift for rytmisk music m.m.*, xvii/6 (1984), 25
K. Frandsen: *Politikens jazzleksikon* (Copenhagen, 1987)
K. Brinkeby: "Dansk dynamit," *Jazz Stage*, ii/1 (1996), 4

FRANK BÜCHMANN-MØLLER

Nordskog. Record company and label. The company was established in 1921 in Santa Monica, California, by Andrae Nordskog. Its records were at first pressed by Arto in New Jersey, and the two companies released pressings of each other's masters. Nordskog is particularly notable for having been the first company to issue recordings of an African-American band from New Orleans; three titles by Kid Ory's band were put out on the Nordskog label under the pseudonym Spikes' Seven Pods of Pepper (they were also released on SUNSHINE).

BIBLIOGRAPHY

J. Bentley and R. W. Miller: "Andrae Nordskog," *JM*, v/3 (1959), 8
C. Kendziora: "Behind the Cobwebs: Nordskog," *Record Research*, no.91 (1968), 6
F. Owen: "A Glimpse of the Past, 12: Sunshine and Nordskog," *Sv*, no.21 (1969), 94

HOWARD RYE

Noren [Norén], **Jack** (*b* Chicago, 19 Oct 1929; *d* Chicago, 17 March 1990). Drummer. His parents were Swedish, and after playing briefly with Gene Ammons, among others, he moved with his family to Sweden in 1946. While working as a lumberjack in summer 1947 he joined a touring Swedish jazz band, the drummer of which had been taken ill. By the following November he had become a member of Thor Jederby's group, with which he performed and recorded into 1950. During the same period he worked with the trumpeter Nisse Skoog (1948) and the band led by Seymour Österwall (1949). He joined Arne Domnérus in 1949 and performed in a group led by Domnérus and Rolf Ericson at the National Ballroom in Stockholm from 1950 until Ericson's departure in 1952; between 1951 and 1953 he also worked with Lars Gullin. Around this time Noren was considered the best modern-jazz drummer in Sweden, and he toured and recorded with such visiting American musicians as James Moody (1949, 1951), Charlie Parker and Zoot Sims (both 1950), Stan Getz and Lee Konitz (both 1951), and Clifford Brown and George Wallington (both 1953). He also played drums on numerous recordings with Swedish musicians and groups, notably Reinhold Svensson and Gösta Törner (both 1949), Swede Starband (1950), Expressens Elitorkester (1950, 1952), Leonard Feather's Swinging Swedes and Jazzkritikerorkestern 1951 (both 1951), Jazzkritikernas Elitorkester, Bengt Hallberg, and Putte Wickman (all 1952), and Åke Persson, the Scandia All Stars, and the Swinging Swedes (all 1953); as a singer he recorded with Jederby (1949), Domnérus and Ericson (both 1951), and the drummer Anders Burman (1952).

From 1954 Noren spent a period in Chicago, where he worked locally, performing in the trios of Eddie Higgins (recording in 1958) and the pianist Marty Rubenstein (1959–60). Once more in Sweden, he played with Monica Zetterlund (1960) and then in Nisse Sandström's quartet, accompanied such visiting Americans as Coleman Hawkins and Nat Adderley, and recorded with Zetterlund and Harry Arnold's radio band. Noren returned to the USA in the early 1960s, after which nothing is known of his career.

SELECTED RECORDINGS

As leader: Yvette/You go to my head (1953, Karusell 38)
As sideman: A. Domnérus: Conversation (1949, Met. 103); L. Gullin: That's it (1951, Met. 180); A. Domnérus: You can count on me (1951, HMV X7757); Lady Estelle's Dream (1951, HMV X7759); B. Hallberg: Flying Saucer (1952, Met. 242); Zig-zag (1952, Met. 247); C. Brown: Stockholm Sweetnin'/'Cuse these Blues (1953, Met. 18) [EP]; Falling in love with love/Lover come back to me (1953, Met. 19) [EP]

BIBLIOGRAPHY

FeatherE
L. Feather: "Bouquet to Sweden: Meet Some of the Swinging Swedes," *DB*, xviii/23 (1951), 2
Obituary, A. von Konow, *Orkester journalen*, lviii/5 (1990), 33

GK

Norgran. Record label. It was founded in Los Angeles in 1953 by Norman Granz and used to issue new recordings by swing and bop musicians as well as a considerable amount of material that had previously been put out on CLEF. Along with the latter label it was absorbed in 1956 into Granz's new company, VERVE. (M. Ruppli: *The Clef/Verve Labels*, Westport, CT, 1986)

Noriki, Soichi (*b* Kyoto, Japan, 20 Oct 1957). Japanese pianist, leader, and arranger. He took piano lessons from the ages of four to 12, joined his father's group, the Kyoto Bel-Ami All Stars, in 1974, and in 1977 moved to Tokyo. There he joined George Kawaguchi's band and performed with Toshiyuki Honda's group Burning Waves, Sadao Watanabe, a band co-led by Motohiko Hino and Joe Henderson (1988), Terumasa Hino, Yoshio Suzuki, Kimiko Itoh, Shunzo Ohno, and others. He recorded frequently with musicians in Los Angeles. His own groups included Noriki (1983–6), Pole Pole I's (1988–90), and a trio (from 1998). Noriki maintains an active career as a studio musician and arranges music for films and television.

SELECTED RECORDINGS

As leader: *Noriki* (1983, Toshiba–EMI 9290); *Dream Cruise* (1984, Toshiba–EMI 5004); *Just!* (1987, Toshiba–EMI CD32-5014)
As sideman: Y. Suzuki: *The East Bounce Collection* (1997, Video Arts 1015); N. Terai: *Thinking of You* (1999, Video Arts 1031)

KAZUNORI SUGIYAMA

Norin, Carl-Henrik (*b* Västerås, Sweden, 27 March 1920; *d* Stockholm, 23 May 1967). Swedish tenor saxophonist, bandleader, composer, and arranger. He became a professional musician in 1940 and first played with the bandleader Gösta Tönne in Malmö. In 1941 he joined Thore Ehrling's orchestra in Stockholm, remaining there until 1948 as one of its main soloists and arrangers; his blues composition *Mississippi Mood*, recorded with Ehrling in 1944 (HMV X7089), is considered a classic of Swedish jazz. He then formed his own six-piece group, with which he worked at Nalen in Stockholm until 1962 and made a number of tours both during and after this time; by the early 1960s the band was focusing largely on popular music rather than jazz. Norin was elected to most Swedish all-star jazz groups from

1942 onwards. He played at the Paris Jazz Fair (1949), was a member of Harry Arnold's Radiobandet (1956–8, and occasionally thereafter until 1964), and recorded with many Swedish and foreign musicians, including Peanuts Holland (1948), Roy Eldridge (1951), and Lars Gullin (1953). His work as soloist, arranger, and bandleader is well represented on two albums consisting mainly of previously unissued tracks from 1949 to 1964, *Jazz Sessions*, ii (Tenor 9401, 9501).

BIBLIOGRAPHY

"Svenskt stjärnalbum" [Swedish star-album], *Orkester journalen*, x/9 (1942), 5
"På omslaget" [On the cover], *Orkester journalen*, xxiii/11 (1955), 4
C.-E. Lindgren: Untitled article, *Estrad*, xxiv/1 (1962), 4
Obituary, R. Dahlgren, *Orkester journalen*, xxxv/6 (1967), 5

ERIK KJELLBERG/LARS WESTIN

Norman, Charlie [Karl-Erik Albert] (*b* Ludvika, Sweden, 4 Oct 1910). Swedish pianist, singer, and entertainer. He worked professionally from the mid-1930s, was a member of Håkan von Eichwald's big band, and performed in Seymour Österwall's orchestra (1939–41); he also played boogie-woogie as an unaccompanied soloist. During World War II he worked with Alice Babs, and from 1943 he led his own groups, with which he made many recordings, including *AFN-boogie* (1946, Col. DS1610) and *Anitra Dance Boogie* (1949, Met. 115); the latter aroused harshly expressed anger from the Norwegian Edvard Grieg Foundation, as Norman had turned the famous melody from Grieg's *Peer Gynt* into a boogie-woogie piece. In the 1950s Norman was a popular disc jockey and at the same time was active in Sweden and abroad as the leader of a quartet. He continued his career as an entertainer into the new century, and in the 1990s he resumed his collaboration with Babs for concert tours and recordings. His autobiography, *Musikant med brutet gehör* (Musician with broken ear), was published in Stockholm in 1980. ("Svenskt stjärnalbum" [Swedish star-album], *Orkester journalen*, ix/4 (1941), 3)

ERIK KJELLBERG/LARS WESTIN

Norman, Fred (*b* Leesburg, FL, 5 Oct 1910; *d* New York, 19 Feb 1993). Arranger. He took up trombone while in school in Fessenden (near Ocala), Florida, and later followed one of his teachers to Washington, DC; while attending high school there he met Claude Hopkins, whose orchestra was on tour. He began to send arrangements to Hopkins's band in New York, and late in 1932, after spending a period at Howard University, he joined the group as a trombonist and singer; he may be heard as a trombone soloist on a recording of one of his own compositions, *Church Street Sobbin' Blues* (Decca 1286), made by Hopkins in 1937, and he appeared with the group in the short films *Barbershop Blues* (1934) and *By Request* (1936). After leaving Hopkins Norman worked full-time as an arranger for Benny Goodman (for whom he wrote *Smoke House Rhythm*, 1938, Vic. 26107), Gene Krupa (1938–40), Lionel Hampton, Teddy Powell, and Jack Teagarden (all 1939), Artie Shaw (1941), and others, including Bunny Berigan and Tommy Dorsey. He was a staff arranger for Gene Krupa from 1940 to 1943, and he also worked with Tommy Dorsey in 1945 and with Charlie Spivak. In the 1950s he was employed by record companies as a music director for such musicians as Sarah Vaughan and Dinah Washington. He continued to write arrangements into the 1970s.

BIBLIOGRAPHY

ChiltonW; *FeatherE*; *McCarthyB*; *SchullerS*
J. Simmen: "Fred Norman," *BHcF*, no.181 (1968), 6
S. Dance: *The World of Swing* (New York, 1974), 232
M. Selchow: *Profoundly Blue: a Bio-discographical Scrapbook on Edmond Hall* (Lübbecke, Germany, 1988)
W. Vaché, Sr.: "Fred Norman: He Makes Them All Sound Good!," *MR*, xvi/1 (1988), 11
W. W. Vaché: *Crazy Fingers: Claude Hopkins' Life in Jazz* (Washington, DC, and London, 1992)

BK

Normann, Robert (*b* Sarpsborg, Norway, 27 June 1916; *d* Skjeberg, Norway, 20 May 1998). Norwegian guitarist. He played accordion and tenor saxophone before taking up guitar and performing in the swing style from 1937. His first engagement was with the guitarist and singer Freddie Valier (1938), after which he worked with the group String Swing (1939–42) and the bandleader Gunnar Due (1939–41); he also led his own quartet, and in 1945 he joined a big band led by the drummer Pete Brown. In the early 1950s he played with the violinist Frank Ottersen and the pianist Willy Andresen. While he was seldom active in jazz after 1955 he remained busy as a musician on radio, in recording studios, and in theater orchestras. In 1989 Hot Club Records reissued a four-volume retrospective of Normann's work in its Vintage Guitar series; he broadcast again with some of his old colleagues that same year and again in 1991. A leading performer in Europe, Normann was little known elsewhere owing largely to his avoidance of publicity. A good example of his work is String Swing's recording *Farewell Blues/ Swingtime in the Rockies* (1940, Col. GN5067).
Oral history material in *NOnj*.

BIBLIOGRAPHY

K. Sandregen and others: *Boken om jazz* (Oslo, 1954)
O. Angell, J. E. Vold, and E. Økland: *Jazz i Norge* (Oslo, 1975)
J. Evensmo: *The Guitars of Charlie Christian, Robert Normann, Oscar Aleman (in Europe)* (n.p. [Oslo], n.d. [?1976]) [discography]
K. Michelsen, ed.: *Cappelens musikkleksikon* (Oslo, 1978)
B. Stendahl: *Jazz, Hot & Swing: jazz i Norge, 1920–1940* (n.p. [Oslo], 1987) [incl. discography]
B. Stendahl and J. Bergh: *Sigarett Stomp: jazz i Norge, 1940–1950* (Oslo, 1991) [incl. discography]
——: *Cool, Kløver and Dixie: jazz i Norge, 1950–1960* (Oslo, 1997) [incl. discography]
J. Bergh: *Norwegian Jazz Discography, 1905–1998* (Oslo, 1999)

VIDAR VANBERG

Normaphone. A valved brass instrument of conical bore, shaped like a saxophone, but played with a brass mouthpiece. The family of instruments, which are believed to have been manufactured in Germany during the early twentieth century, ranges from soprano (in B♭ and using a trumpet mouthpiece) to contrabass (also in B♭, but employing a tuba mouthpiece). In 1960 William Kelly recorded on the tenor instrument (in B♭, using a trombone mouthpiece) as a member of the group Modern Jazz Disciples on the album *Right Down Front* (1959–60, NewJ 8240), but the principal exponent in jazz is Scott Robinson, who began playing the tenor normaphone occasionally in the late 1970s; he may be heard as a soloist on *If I Were a Bell*, on his LP *Multiple Instruments* (1984, Multijazz 101), the cover of which shows a picture of the instrument.

GK

Nørregaard, Svend-Erik (*b* Frederiksberg, Denmark, 6 Feb 1941). Danish drummer. He first performed with the tenor saxophonist Frank Jensen in Sweden (1960–63) and then with the violinist and vibraphonist Finn Ziegler and the guitarist Jørn Grauengaard (1965–75). Thereafter he worked as a freelance, playing in shows, theatre bands, and jazz groups, notably with the Kansas City Stompers, Papa Bue's Viking Jazz Band, Ole Kock Hansen, the singer Etta Cameron (recording in 1980), Jesper Thilo (with whom he made several recordings as a sideman from 1980 into the 1990s), the pianist Atli Bjørn, Richard Boone, Kenny Drew, Horace Parlan, Bob Rockwell, and the pianist, composer, and arranger Niels Jørgen Steen (recording in 1991). Among the visiting musicians he accompanied were Pepper Adams, Nat Adderley, Benny Carter, Al Cohn and Zoot Sims, Eddie "Lockjaw" Davis, Wild Bill Davison (recording in 1977), Buddy DeFranco and Terry Gibbs, Dizzy Gillespie, Harry Edison, Dexter Gordon, Johnny Griffin, Roland Hanna, Hank Jones, Warne Marsh and Lee Konitz, Red Mitchell, Tete Montoliu, James Moody, Joe Newman, Ralph Sutton, Buddy Tate, Clark Terry, Putte Wickman, and Teddy Wilson.

SELECTED RECORDINGS

As sideman: A. Cohn and Z. Sims: *Motoring Along* (1974, Sonet 684); W. Marsh: *Warne Marsh Quintet Jazz Exchange*, i (1975, Sto. 4001); E. Davis: *Eddie "Lockjaw" Davis–Harry "Sweets" Edison–John Darville Quartet with Kenny Drew* (1976, Sto. 276); R. Sutton: *Ralph Sutton Quartet* (1977, Sto. 275); A. Bjørn: *Atlicity* (1979, 1982–3, Stunt 8705); J. Thilo: *Jesper Thilo Quintet Featuring Hank Jones* (1991, Sto. 4178)

BIBLIOGRAPHY

K. Frandsen: *Politikens jazzleksikon* (Copenhagen, 1987)
N. J. Steen: "Musikerstafet" [Relay musician], *Jazz Special*, no.14 (1994), 24
F. Fryd: "Jazzens håndværker" [Craftsman of jazz], *Jazz Special*, no.34 (1997), 22

FRANK BÜCHMANN-MØLLER

Norris, Al(bert Everett) (*b* Kane, PA, 4 Sept 1908; *d* New York, 26 Dec 1974). Guitarist. He played banjo with territory bands in Buffalo from 1927 and in 1932 joined Jimmie Lunceford; the following year he changed to guitar, though he also occasionally played violin (for illustration *see* LUNCEFORD, JIMMIE). Norris took solos on several of Lunceford's recordings, including *Organ Grinder's Swing* (1936, Decca 908), *Pigeon Walk* (1937, Decca 1659), which is believed to be his longest recorded solo, and *Put on your old grey bonnet* (1937, Decca 1506), on which his powerful rhythm work may be heard to particular advantage within the context of a reduced instrumentation; in 1936 he appeared in the short film *Jimmie Lunceford and his Orchestra*. Apart from a period in the army during World War II he remained with Lunceford's band until it broke up in 1949. He then played and recorded with Eddie Wilcox (1949–50) before ceasing to work as a musician.

BIBLIOGRAPHY

ChiltonW; *FeatherE*
B. Elliott and J. Aldam: "Collector's Corner, Great Unrecogniseds, no.33: Albert Norris," *MM*, xix (1 May 1943), 4

HOWARD RYE, BK

Norris, Ray (*b* Saskatoon, Canada, 1916; *d* Toronto, 21 Dec 1958). Canadian guitarist and bandleader. He worked during the late 1930s on Vancouver radio with country-swing bands, then in 1941 formed the Ray Norris Quintet. Influenced by Nat "King" Cole, Raymond Scott, and others, the quintet had its own CBC program, "Serenade in Rhythm," until 1950; latterly it broadcast from Toronto, where it recorded four lightly boppish original titles in 1949. A sextet led by Norris made CBC radio transcriptions in Vancouver in 1951. Norris continued to work in Vancouver on CBC radio and television during the 1950s, but returned to Toronto with a country group, the Rhythm Pals, just months before his death.

MARK MILLER

Norris, Walter (Metcalf) (*b* Little Rock, AR, 27 Dec 1931). Pianist. He learned piano in Little Rock from the age of five, and later at the Manhattan School of Music (1964–9) and privately (until 1974) in New York, where he also studied conducting (1970–72). His first work was in Little Rock with the big band of Howard Williams (1944–50), in Houston with Jimmy Ford (1952–3), and in Las Vegas with his own trio (1953–4). In 1954 he moved to Los Angeles, where he served as house pianist at the Haig and the Tiffany clubs (1955–6), accompanying such soloists as Howard McGhee, Teddy Edwards, Charlie Ventura, Herb Geller, and Zoot Sims. He recorded there with Jack Sheldon (1954, 1956) and Frank Rosolino (1955) before joining the quintet led by Shorty Rogers and Bill Holman for performances in Los Angeles and on tour (1957). In San Francisco he played at the Blackhawk with the quintet of Rogers and Eric Dolphy (1957), with Stan Getz and Edwards (both 1958), and at the Jazz Gallery with Johnny Griffin (1959), this last after having spent a further period in Los Angeles, when he recorded with Herb Geller and Ornette Coleman (both 1958).

From 1963 to 1970 Norris worked in New York as the music director of the Playboy Club, where he led a trio, consisting of Bill Crow and Ronnie Bedford, and a quartet, with Joe Farrell, Crow, and Bobby Donaldson. He joined the Thad Jones–Mel Lewis Orchestra in 1974, with which he played at the Village Vanguard in New York and toured Europe (where he recorded with Klaus Weiss, 1974, and Pepper Adams, 1975) and Japan (where he recorded with Frank Foster, 1975). Also in 1974 he formed a duo with George Mraz in New York which recorded in Germany. After leaving the Jones–Lewis Orchestra in 1976 he played for seven months in Scandinavia with Red Mitchell and the quartets led by Dexter Gordon and Red Rodney, and in autumn 1976 he returned to New York and worked for a brief period in Charles Mingus's quintet. In Berlin he was a member of the orchestra of Sender Freies Berlin from 1977 to 1980; at the same time he performed throughout Europe with Aladár Pege (1978–80) and made annual visits to the USA. From 1984 to 1994 he was on the faculty of the Hochschule der Kunste-Berlin, where he taught piano improvisation. In 1988 he joined the NDR big band for a recording led by Chet Baker and recorded as a sideman with Geller, and in 1994 he traveled to Japan for the Fujitsu-Concord Jazz Festival. He has made several recordings under his own name, as an unaccompanied soloist, in duos, in a cooperative trio with Heinz von Hermann and Mads Vinding, and as the leader of small groups; in 1998 he formed his own company, Sunburst Recordings, whose first issue was a duo album by Norris and Mike Richmond. Norris is proficient in many styles, including bop, cool jazz, and free jazz; he has been influenced not only by Art Tatum and Bud Powell but also by such classical composers as Chopin, Debussy, and Bartók. He has recorded several of his own compositions, among them *Space Maker*, *Drifting*, *Stepping on Cracks*, and *Synchronicity*.

SELECTED RECORDINGS

As unaccompanied soloist: *Live at Maybeck Recital Hall*, iv (1990, Conc. 4425)

Duos: with G. Mraz: *Drifting* (1974, Enja 2044), incl. Drifting, Space Maker; with A. Pege: *Synchronicity* (1978, Enja 3035); with Phillip Wilson: *Live at the Berklee Performance Center* (1985, Shiah 117); with G. Mraz: *Hues of Blues* (1995, Conc. 4671)
As leader: *Stepping on Cracks* (1978, Prog. 7039); with H. von Hermann and M. Vinding: *2nd Trio* (1989, Koala 23); *Lush Life* (1990, Conc. 4457); *Sunburst* (1991, Conc. 4486); *Love Every Moment* (1992, Conc. 4534)
As sideman: O. Coleman: *Something Else!!!! The Music of Ornette Coleman* (1958, Cont. 3551); K. Weiss: *The Git Go* (1974, BASF 20224066)

BIBLIOGRAPHY

FeatherE; *Feather–Gitler '70s*
J. S. Wilson: "And Now, Walter Norris," *Hi Fidelity/Musical America*, xxv/5 (1975), 64
C. J. Safane: Review of *Synchronicity* (1978), *DB*, xlvii/9 (1980), 39
F. Bouchard: "Waxing On: Triology," *DB*, l/12 (1983), 45 [review of *Stepping on Cracks* (1978)]
W. Balliett: "Herr Professor," *New Yorker*, lxii (12 Jan 1987), 88; repr. in *Bradley, Barney, and Max: 16 Portraits in Jazz* (New York, 1989); repr. in *BalliettA (1996)*
Z. Stewart: "Riffs: Walter Norris," *DB*, lx/3 (1993), 13
F. Krieger: "Jazz-Solopiano: zum Stilwandel am Beispiel ausgewaehlter *Body and Soul*: Aufnahmen von 1938–1992," *Jf*, xxvii (1995), 5
S. Burlingame: "Walter Norris: Renegade Romantic," *5/4 Magazine* (1996), Feb
J. Engels: "Walter Norris," *JP*, xlv/6 (1996), 19
A. LaVerne: "Part 3: Shop Talk," *Piano Today* (1996), May–June, 38
F. Krieger: "*I Got Rhythm*? Walter Norris und die Kunst der irritierenden Akzentuierung," *Jf*, xxxi (1999), 119

GREGORY E. SMITH/BK

Norsk Jazzarkiv. Archive founded in Oslo in 1981; *see* LIBRARIES AND ARCHIVES, §2.

Norsk Jazzforbund [Norwegian Jazz Federation, NJF]. Norwegian national jazz organization founded in 1953 in Trondheim. Its objectives are to promote interest in and knowledge of jazz in Norway, to support amateur activity and local clubs, and to establish national and international contacts with other organizations. From 1960 it published the journal *Jazznytt* (Jazz News) and in 1967 it produced its first LP, which was also Jan Garbarek's first recording; in 1981 it set up the Odin record company. NJF is a member of the International Jazz Federation and has links with the other Nordic countries through Nordjazz (established in 1974). From 1978 it received a small amount of funding from the Norwegian government, and the following year it participated in the formation of the Foreningen Norske Jazzmusikere (Association of Norwegian Jazz Musicians); it is also associated with the Norsk Jazzarkiv (Norwegian Jazz Archive), established in 1981. (*The Norwegian Jazz Scene*, Paris, 1985)

Norsk Jazzforum [Norwegian Jazz Forum] **(i).** Organization of Norwegian jazz musicians. It was established in Oslo in 1965 on the initiative of Karin Krog. The early 1960s was a slow period for jazz in Oslo, and the forum's members organized a succession of concerts – with huge success – until 1970, when a number of new clubs began to flourish. Similar organizations appeared in the late 1960s in other Norwegian cities and regions, including Bergen, Trondheim, and northern Norway.

JOHS BERGH

Norsk Jazzforum [Norwegian Jazz Forum] **(ii).** Organization for the coordination of jazz activity in Norway. It was formed in Oslo in 1997 through the amalgamation of Norsk Jazzforbund (the Norwegian Jazz Federation), Den Norske Jazzscene (the Norwegian Jazz Scene), and Foreningen Norske Jazzmusikere (the Association of Norwegian Jazz Musicians).

JOHS BERGH

North Sea Jazz Festival. Festival held annually from 1976 in The Hague. It was founded by Paul Acket, who served as its director until 1992 and was succeeded by Paul Dankmeijer in 1993 and then by Theo van den Hoek in 1997. The festival takes place over three days in July (four days in 1990–91) at the Congresgebouw, where simultaneous performances are offered at 15 venues; there are also screenings of jazz films and videos. From 1990 there have been additional outdoor and indoor events under the title North Sea Jazz Heats the Hague. Over the years many leading musicians and groups have appeared and the festival has grown substantially: the first event had an audience of 9000, and in 1999 there was a total of 1200 musicians performing before a combined audience of 70,000. From 1985 the festival has presented three Bird awards each year: a prestigious international award given to an active and famous musician, a Netherlands award for one of the country's best musicians, and a special appreciation award for record producers and other nonmusicians who have contributed to jazz. In 2000 and 2001 the Dutch staff also produced a North Sea Jazz Festival in Cape Town, South Africa.

BIBLIOGRAPHY

R. D'Rozario: *North Sea Jazz Festival, 1976–1985* (The Hague, 1985) [photographs]
<http://www.northseajazz.nl> (1999)

PAUL R. LAIRD

Norvo, Red [Norville, Joseph Kenneth] (*b* Beardstown, IL, 31 March 1908; *d* Santa Monica, CA, 6 April 1999). Xylophonist, vibraphonist, and leader. He took piano lessons at around the age of eight, but at that early point he was so skilled at (and so dependent upon) playing by ear that the lessons were soon discontinued. When he was about 13 he took up marimba, and not long afterwards he learned to play xylophone; he was self-taught on both instruments. He began his professional career (as Red Norville) in 1925, touring across the nation with a marimba band, the Collegians, then was active in the Chicago area as a xylophone soloist in vaudeville; in the course of work under the orchestra leader Paul Ash at the Oriental Theater his name was persistently garbled – as Norvin, Norvick, Norwath, and, among other such distortions, the name which stuck, Norvo.

Norvo continued as a soloist in vaudeville for a few years. His featured number involved his playing xylophone with the now-standard four-mallet technique while tap-dancing at the same time. Having tired of this, he instead began to lead bands in Milwaukee (summer 1929) and then in Minneapolis (1930), where he also began to work in radio. This in turn led to theater and radio work in Chicago, where he joined Paul Whiteman's orchestra (1931); Mildred Bailey, the singer in the band, became his first wife (see illustration). With Whiteman's orchestra Norvo played xylophone, marimba, and a newly emerging instrument, the vibraphone; he used this last instrument only occasionally, as a novelty, in part because a damper pedal for the vibraphone had not yet been developed, and the layered ringing of overlapping pitches thus rendered it rather impractical for the sort of fast, intricate, and florid two- (not four-) mallet melodic lines which Norvo favored throughout his career.

From 1933 Norvo worked as a freelance in New York, and that year he recorded his first solos as a leader, on xylophone in April and on marimba in October; Benny Goodman played bass clarinet at this latter session, in which Norvo's composition *Octopus* was recorded. In 1934 Norvo began working with Charlie Barnet, with one or the other man serving as leader; as Barnet's sideman he played piano rather than xylophone, and in November that year he appeared under Barnet in the first white band to perform at the Apollo Theatre in Harlem. Later he made race records for Decca as a pianist accompanying blues singers. Barnet's group worked in New Orleans in January 1935 and then returned to New York, where it disbanded. That summer Norvo formed a band for an engagement in Bar Harbor, Maine, which included Chris Griffin, Eddie Sauter (on trumpet), Herbie Haymer, and Dave Barbour. After returning to New York, in the autumn he began to play at the Famous Door with a small group of unusual instrumentation, and without piano or drums: trumpet (Stew Pletcher), clarinet, tenor saxophone (Haymer), guitar (Barbour), xylophone, and double bass, with Sauter supplying arrangements and sometimes playing mellophone. The group then continued at the Hickory House and at a restaurant on Broadway. In summer 1936 it expanded to 13 pieces (with piano and drums, and additional brass and reeds) for an engagement at the Commodore Hotel, following which it began to tour. When Bailey traveled to the Midwest for a residency at the Blackhawk in Chicago (late 1936 – early 1937, involving nightly broadcasts over radio station WGN), she and Norvo were nicknamed "Mr. and Mrs. Swing" by the writer George Simon. The big band continued to tour until it disbanded in spring 1939. Earlier that year Norvo ceased working regularly with Bailey, and they divorced in 1945; however, they continued to record and broadcast together on an occasional basis until her death in 1951.

Norvo led other big bands from 1939, and then, between 1942 and 1944, small groups which were based in clubs on 52nd Street; he also toured to Boston, Chicago, and elsewhere on the East Coast and in Canada. The first of these small groups consisted of Shorty Rogers, Eddie Bert, Aaron Sachs, the pianist Hank Kahout, Clyde Lombardi, and Specs Powell; later members were Flip Phillips, Ralph Burns, and Conrad Gozzo. Norvo ended his activities as a bandleader to join Benny Goodman's quintet in October 1944, at which time he changed permanently to vibraphone; he remained with Goodman through 1945. Given carte blanche for a recording session in June 1945, he organized an octet which involved Charlie Parker, Dizzy Gillespie, and Teddy Wilson. Having already recommended to Woody Herman some of the sidemen from his small groups of the early 1940s, he recorded as a guest soloist with Herman's First Herd in September 1945 and then performed in the group from December 1945 until it disbanded a year later. In 1947 he settled in Santa Monica, California, and worked mainly in the Los Angeles area.

In spring 1949 Norvo toured the West Coast as the leader of a band accompanying Billie Holiday; Charles Mingus joined this group in San Francisco, but soon aftewards Holiday quit, and the remainder of the tour was canceled. Later that same year Norvo formed a trio with guitar (Mundell Lowe) and double bass (Red Kelly) for engagements in Philadelphia and New York; Tal Farlow replaced Lowe for a tour across the country and to Honolulu, and the group then returned to Los Angeles, where it became one of the outstanding cool-jazz ensembles, with Mingus in place of Kelly (1950–51; for illustration *see* MINGUS, CHARLES). The trio continued with Lombardi (September 1951), Red Mitchell (1952–4), Jimmy Raney (March 1953–1954), and others until it disbanded (summer 1956). Norvo then led further small groups, often quintets, mainly in lounges at hotels in Las Vegas. In January 1957 he was leader of a recording session with Ben Webster as his guest soloist. In autumn 1959, for a European tour, and again in spring and summer 1960, for touring, recording, and broadcasting in the USA, Goodman took over the leadership of Norvo's band, adding Bill Harris (i) (or Urbie Green), Phillips, and (for the European tour) Anita O'Day to the core personnel of Jack Sheldon, Jerry Dodgion, Russ Freeman (or Gene Di Novi or John Bunch), Jimmy Wyble, Red Wootten or John Mosher on double bass, and John Markham.

Thereafter hearing problems severely disrupted Norvo's career. Following a serious ear operation he toured Europe as a soloist (1968) and with George Wein's Newport All Stars (1969), but during the 1960s and 1970s he worked mainly in Nevada and California. Several albums with famous swing musicians in the mid- to late 1970s announced his return to the international arena. In the 1980s he toured Europe with regularity, led another trio with Farlow and Steve Novosel (*c*1980–85), and joined Benny Carter, Louie Bellson, and others for a swing concert in New York which received considerable acclaim (1985). He ceased playing in 1986 after suffering a serious stroke. His papers are held at the Irving S. Gilmore Music Library at Yale University (*see* LIBRARIES AND ARCHIVES, §2).

In the early 1930s, with Whiteman and later with his own ensembles, Norvo proved himself an exceptional improviser on xylophone, a previously neglected instrument in jazz. He usually played vibraphone without vibrato, producing a sharply articulated sound, almost like a xylophone; by contrast he was occasionally heard using a shimmering sound, with the instrument's motorized vibrato rotating at full speed, as for example in the four-mallet chordal accompaniment during the opening chorus of his recording

Red Norvo and Mildred Bailey, New York, 1935

of *The Man I Love* (1944). His improvising, strongly influenced by Teddy Wilson's piano style, suffered an occasional rhythmic stiffness at fast tempos (taking on a cute, sing-song quality in, for instance, his solo on Wilson's version of *Bugle Call Rag*, 1945), but was outstanding on such jazz ballads as *Ghost of a Chance* (1945), recorded during a concert at Town Hall in New York. As a bandleader Norvo preferred delicate sounds, and in the 1930s his orchestra was noted for its subtle approach to swing; in 1936–7 it specialized in the performance of highly praised arrangements by Eddie Sauter, particularly *Remember*, which has an outstanding solo by Norvo. Having transferred his concern for clarity and restraint to the trio with Farlow and Mingus, Norvo became, through this association, a leading figure in cool jazz, although his own playing remained firmly grounded in the swing style.

Oral history material in *NjR* (JOHP) and *DSI* (JOHP).

SELECTED RECORDINGS

(on xylophone to 1943 and on vibraphone from 1944 unless otherwise indicated)

AS LEADER

Knockin' on Wood/Hole in the Wall (1933, Bruns. 6562); In a Mist/Dance of the Octopus (1933, Bruns. 6906) [marimba]; Old Fashioned Love/Honeysuckle Rose (1934–5, Col. 3059D); Bughouse/Blues in E Flat (1935, Col. 3079D); Decca Stomp (1936, Decca 691); I got rhythm/Lady be Good (1936, Decca 779); A Porter's Love Song to a Chambermaid (1936, Bruns. 7744); Smoke Dreams (1937, Bruns. 7815); Remember (1937, Bruns. 7896); I would do anything for you (1937, Bruns. 7868); first issued on *Giants of Jazz: Red Norvo* (1933–57, T-L STL-J14), Ain't Misbehavin' (take B) (1937) [vibraphone]; Ain't Misbehavin' (take C) (1937, Bruns. 7964); Russian Lullaby (1938, Bruns. 7975); Just You, Just Me (1938, Bruns. 8240)

Subtle Sextology/Russian Lullaby (1944, Key. 1310); Blues à la Red (1944, Key. 1319); The Man I Love (1944, Key. 1314); Hallelujah/Slim Slam Blues (1945, Dial 1045); Get Happy (1945, Comet T7); Ghost of a Chance (1945, Baronet 47103); Ghost of a Chance (1947, Cap. 10188) [xylophone]; September Song (1950, Dis. 147); Move (1950, Dis. 145); I've got you under my skin (1950, Dis. 144); I'll Remember April (1950, Dis. 146); Godchild (1950, Dis. 167); *Red Norvo Trio* (1953, Fan. 3-12); *Red Plays the Blues* (1957, RCA LPM1792); *Vibes à la Red* (1974–5, FaD 105); with R. Tompkins: *Red and Ross* (1979, Conc. 90)

AS SIDEMAN

H. Carmichael: Moon Country (1934, Vic. 24627); T. Wilson: Just a Mood (1937, Bruns. 7973); Honeysuckle Rose (1937, Bruns. 7964); E. Hall: Rompin' in 44/Smooth Sailing (1944, BN 30); Blue Interval/Seein' Red (1944, BN 31); T. Wilson: Bugle Call Rag (1945, Mus. 318); B. Goodman: After You've Gone (1945, Col. 36781); Slipped Disc (1945, Col. 36817); W. Herman: *At Carnegie Hall* (1946, MGM 30601-8); Igor/Nero's Conception (1946, Col. 37228); I surrender dear (1946, Col. 37226); G. Wein: *Newport All Stars* (1969, Atl. 1533); [no leader]: *Swing Reunion* (1985, Book-of-the-Month 717627)

SELECTED FILMS AND VIDEOS

Hit Parade of 1947 [High and Happy] (1947); Disc Jockey (1951); Eddie Peabody and Sonny Burke's Orchestra (1951); Texas Carnival (1951); Jimmy Dorsey's Varieties (1952); Keep it Cool (1954); Kings Go Forth (1958); Swing into Spring (1958); Jazz at the Smithsonian (1982)

BIBLIOGRAPHY

ConnorBG; *SchullerS*

L. Feather: "The Vibraharp," *The Book of Jazz: a Guide to the Entire Field* (New York, 1957, rev. 2/1965)

G. T. Simon: *The Big Bands* (New York, 1967, rev. 4/1981)

W. Balliett: "The Music is More Important," *Ecstasy at the Onion* (New York and Indianapolis, 1971), 194; repr. in *Improvising: Sixteen Jazz Musicians and their Art* (New York, 1977), 113; *BallietA (1986)*; *BallietA (1996)*

A. Shaw: *The Street that Never Slept: New York's Fabled 52nd Street* (New York, 1971/R1977 as *52nd Street: the Street of Jazz*)

R. Stewart: "Red Norvo: a Tale of a Pioneer," *Jazz Masters of the Thirties* (New York and London, n.d. [1972]), 71

S. Woolley: "Red Norvo: Interview," *Cadence*, ii/1 (1976), 3

D. H. Kraner: "The Red Norvo Trio with Tal Farlow and Charlie Mingus," *Journal of Jazz Discography*, no.2 (1977), 6

J. McDonough: "Red Norvo: a Man for All Eras," *DB*, xliv/18 (1977), 16

S. Klett: "Red Norvo: Interview," *Cadence*, v/7 (1979), 5

D. DiMicheal: Liner notes, *Giants of Jazz: Red Norvo* (T-L STL-J14, 1980)

L. Tomkins: "Happy Again with the Trio: Red Norvo," *CI*, xx/4 (1981), 22

D. Chamberlain and R. Wilson, eds.: *The Otis Ferguson Reader* (Highland Park, IL, 1982), 111

B. Priestley: *Mingus: a Critical Biography* (London, Melbourne, Australia, and New York, 1982)

J. Réda: "Un thé avec Norvo," *Jm*, no.313 (1982), 22

J. L. Anderson: "Mr. & Mrs. Swing," *MR*, xix/6 (1992), 1

B. Lylloff: "An Interview with Red Norvo," *Percussive Notes*, xxxi/1 (1992), 42

P. B. Matthews: "Eddie Bert Interview," pt 1, *Cadence*, xviii/1 (1992), 11 (esp. 14–15)

S. Klett: "Celebrating Red Norvo: 1908–1999," *IAJRC Journal*, xxxii/3 (1999), 8 [incl. discography]

Obituaries: M. Oliver, *Los Angeles Times* (8 April 1999); P. Watrous, *New York Times* (8 April 1999); S. Voce, *The Independent* (9 April 1999); B. Crowther, *JJI*, lii/5 (1999), 18

BK

Norwegian Jazz Archive. *See* LIBRARIES AND ARCHIVES, §2.

Norwegian Jazz Federation. *See* NORSK JAZZFORBUND.

Norwegian Jazz Forum. *See* NORSK JAZZFORUM (i) and (ii).

Nose flute. Any kind of flute that is sounded by nasal breath; of non-Western origin, nose flutes are occasionally used by jazz musicians whose work includes elements of so-called world music. Roland Kirk also played nose flutes. *See* FLUTE, §6.

Nosov, Konstantin (Georgyevich) (*b* Leningrad [now St. Petersburg], 24 July 1938; *d* Sofia, 29 June 1984). Russian trumpeter and composer. He studied trumpet at the N. A. Rimsky-Korsakov music school in Leningrad (graduating in 1956), was a member of a group led by the alto saxophonist Orest Kandat, and performed at the Leningrad Jazz Club (from 1958). While playing under the bandleader Yosif Vainstein (1959–66) he gained considerable recognition, and, with Gennady Golstain, he led a quintet composed of members of Vainstein's orchestra. Later he toured with Ady Rosner, and in 1968 he joined the Kontsertny Estradny Orkestr Tsentral'novo TV i Vsesoyuznovo Radio (Concert variety orchestra of central TV and all-union radio). From 1969 to 1973 he was a sideman in the big band at the restaurant Vecherny Arbat in Moscow, and he also worked with the ensemble Melodiya and took part in concerts with Oleg Lundstrem's orchestra. In 1980 he settled in Sofia, where he played in the groups Sofia and Dinamit Brass Band. Nosov never recorded as a leader, but he may be heard as a guest soloist on about a dozen albums, including Georgy Garanian's *Labirint* (1974, Mel. C60 052778), on which he plays his composition *Ognennaya reka* (Fiery river); among his other compositions is *Skoree k Dul'sinee Tobosskoy* (Faster to Dulcinea of Toboso). (S. F. Starr: *Red and Hot: the Fate of Jazz in the Soviet Union, 1917–1980*, New York, and Oxford, England, 1983, rev. 2/1994, as *Red and Hot: the Fate of Jazz in the Soviet Union, 1917–1990*)

WALTER OJAKÄÄR

Notation. Any means, graphic or (more loosely) verbal, of representing musical sounds, either by symbolizing them or by giving instructions for producing them. This article deals with notations used in jazz, some of which originated in and remain specific to jazz, while others are borrowed from or shared with other musical traditions.

1. Introduction. 2. Notation for performance. 3. Notation for teaching and learning. 4. Notation for transcription. 5. Notational symbols: (i) Introduction (ii) Pitch and melody (iii) Harmony (iv) Rhythm, duration, and tempo (v) Timbre and articulation.

1. Introduction. Aural tradition and improvisation are central to the practice of jazz, and their importance has given rise to the common misconception that jazz is an unwritten music. It is true that notation plays no part in many great jazz performances and that a number of prominent jazz musicians, being unable to read music, learned their art entirely from recordings and through performance with others. But throughout its history much jazz has been notated and most of its practitioners have been musically literate, at least to some degree.

The association of musical notation and jazz falls into three main categories: prescriptive notation for performance; prescriptive notation for the teaching and learning of jazz; and descriptive notation for transcription and analysis. (A subcategory, which overlaps with the first and last of these, is notation for the purpose of preserving copyright in music not originally written down.) The problems and conventions of notation in each area are to some extent peculiar to it, and each is therefore treated somewhat separately in the following discussion.

By and large, composers, arrangers, performers, teachers, and scholars of jazz use conventional Western staff notation, supplemented by symbols and usages to convey information not adequately expressed by the standard means. Western staff notation efficiently transmits equal-tempered pitch, rational subdivisions of individual beats, and local or large-scale changes in tempo and dynamics; but the essence of jazz lies precisely in the characteristics that standard notation cannot easily show, such as subtle and intricate rhythmic play, expressive nuances of accent and timbre, and pitches and pitch complexes outside equal temperament. Many and various attempts have been made to capture such elements in notation, but no standard solutions to the problems they pose have been reached.

2. Notation for performance. Notated versions of jazz pieces for the purpose of performance may take any form, from the sketchiest of cue sheets to a fully written-out composition or arrangement. The term "chart," which in jazz parlance means a score, part, or any item of written music, accurately indicates the relationship of most notated instructions for jazz performance to the performance itself; the notation is only a map to guide musicians while playing, and many essential elements of the music are prescribed only vaguely, if at all. (Although this is true for any kind of music that employs notation, the extent to which the written source and its realization differ seems particularly marked in jazz.)

The notational vehicle most favored in small-group jazz is the "lead sheet." A lead sheet typically presents only the melody of a composition, written in the treble clef, with the lyrics if any, and the essential harmonic changes, shown by chord symbols (see §5(iii) below) placed above or below the staff. Additional information, such as cues for essential accompanimental figures (fills, ostinatos, inner lines, etc.) and elements of the arrangement, may also be included (ex.1). This format is ubiquitous in the manuscript and (often illegally) printed tune books known as fake books (*see* Fake book), which are widely used by jazz musicians.

Ex.1 Excerpt from O. Nelson: *111–44*, in lead-sheet format

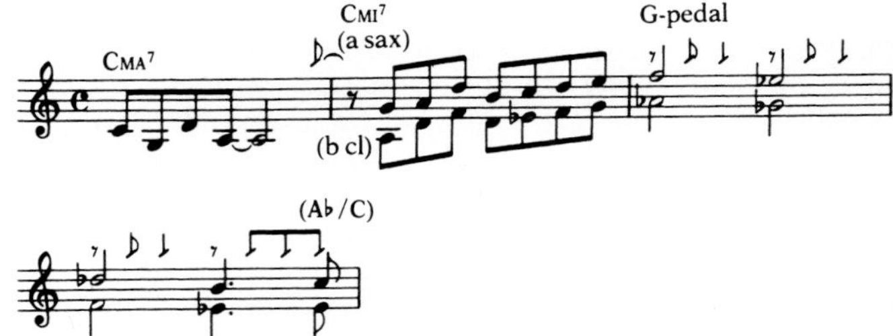

Somewhat more elaborate than the lead sheet is the "master rhythm part," which is often produced as the result of a sketchy transcription from a recording. It is typically written on two staves; on the upper one is shown the melody, on the lower the bass line or bass cues and cues for accompanimental rhythms and figures. Other elements, such as chord symbols (sometimes with specific voicings), lyrics, and dynamic markings, are distributed between the staves (ex.2*a*). In more elaborate form the master rhythm part may resemble a fully notated piano score and could be played as a solo piano version of the piece (ex.2*b*); however, the pianist playing from such a part in an ensemble context would ignore some components and at the same time might cover lines implied by the notation that were not being taken by other members of the group.

Ex.2
(a) Excerpt from the master rhythm part for M. Tyner: *In Search of my Heart*

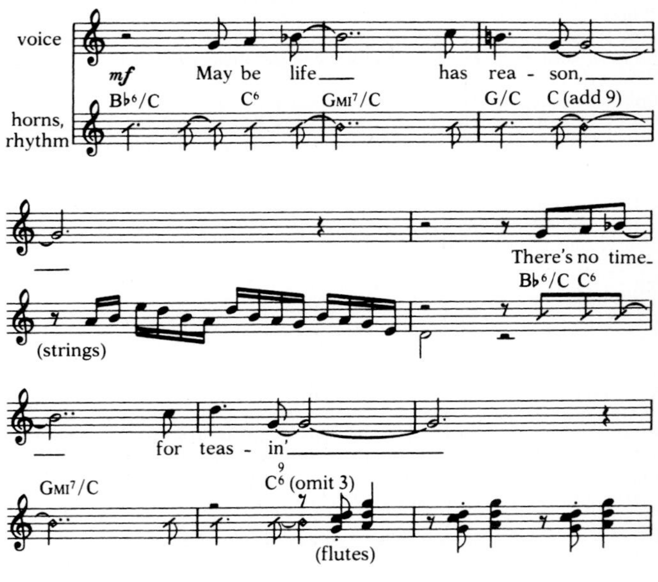

(b) Excerpt from the master rhythm part for H. Silver: *Ecaroh*

Ex.3 Excerpt from the sheet music for *Detour Ahead!*, by John Frigo, Lou Carter, and Herb Ellis

• chord symbols for guitar, tablature for ukulele tuned *g′–c′–e′–a′*

Jazz musicians also occasionally use the sheet music for a popular song as the source for a performance based on it. In this form, songs are normally printed on three staves; the uppermost shows the melody, lyrics, and chord symbols (often with guitar or ukulele tablature), while the lower two are occupied by a fully written-out piano arrangement (ex.3). The notated piano parts and tablature in sheet music are generally unidiomatic to jazz and are therefore ignored by jazz musicians, who treat the sheet music as if it were a lead sheet and indeed may well transcribe the music into lead-sheet form rather than play from the printed copy (this not only eliminates superfluous piano and guitar parts but also allows the musician to reposition awkward page turns and enlarge chord symbols that are too small to be easily read).

Where lead sheets, master rhythm parts, or sheet music are used, all the musicians usually work from identical parts, extracting what they need from the notation and relying on their experience, custom and usage, their own creativity, and visual cues for the other ingredients of the performance. Occasionally in such a situation some musicians may have parts of their own that differ from those used by the other members of the ensemble: the players of transposing instruments sometimes use parts written out at the relevant pitch (though a professional player is usually expected to play from an untransposed part); the drummer may be given, or may be required to create, a more elaborate part than the others, including cues for specific events which he must accompany and written instructions for the deployment of the various elements of the drum set.

In the majority of cases the overall form, structure, and organization of the performance are not specified in scores of the types discussed above. The order, number, and length of choruses and improvised solos, the presence or absence of an introduction, coda, and interludes, and often changes in instrumentation, texture, and dynamics, are decided on during rehearsal or established during the performance itself by means of various visual or aural cues. The notation gives only the form and structure of the tune upon which the performance is to be based.

A more detailed form of notation is used by many big bands, as well as by ensembles of medium size (such as Miles Davis's nonet, which made the recordings later issued as *Birth of the Cool*), ensembles playing third-stream music, some groups that use arranged themes and interludes (such as Horace Silver's quintet), and even some free-jazz groups (particularly those, such as Anthony Braxton's, that draw on elements of the European classical tradition). Large segments of a piece may be fully written out as individual parts. The rhythm section generally plays from less formally notated parts, but these may still contain cues for specific rhythmic events. In pieces of this level of elaboration the overall form may be fully indicated; nevertheless some flexibility as regards the order, number, nature, and length of improvised sections is generally retained.

In all but the most fully composed works (see below) room is allowed for improvisation. While accompanimental figures in these passages may be fully notated for wind instruments (often with cues showing specific events in other voices), for the soloists only the harmonic basis and duration of the improvisation are notated (in the form of a lead sheet). Exceptionally, in performances of extremely famous pieces, the soloist may have both a lead sheet and a transcription of an existing solo and may choose whether to improvise something fresh or re-create the famous original version.

Fully notated pieces that leave practically no opportunity for improvisation, such as Ellington's *Ko-Ko* (1940), occur much more rarely. But even in this instance the rhythm parts would probably take the form of a lead sheet; Ellington himself usually improvised the piano rhythm part, adding obbligato figures in the background. It should be noted that until perhaps the 1960s it was not always customary to make full scores even for pieces notated to this degree of precision, and composers and arrangers sometimes learned and practiced their craft using only individual parts. Benny Carter, for example, began by studying and writing in this manner, and only later discovered how to use stock arrangements and full scores. Furthermore, the individual parts are often unavailable to any but the musicians who use them, being (except for stock arrangements) largely unpublished; in the case of *Ko-Ko*, for instance, the original parts became available to the public only in the 1990s, in the Duke Ellington Collection at the Smithsonian Institution, and before that time any version of the piece was attainable only through transcription from the recording (this is true of the extract from a full score printed in ELLINGTON, DUKE, ex.1, as well as of the full score and parts transcribed by David Berger and Alan Campbell for performance by the National Jazz Ensemble and then published around 1980 by United Artists Music). From the 1960s the advent of the third-stream and jazz education movements brought greater ties with the publishing traditions of Western art music, and scores (in either full or short form) by such composers as John La Barbera, Sammy Nestico, Hank Levy, Thad Jones, Toshiko

Akiyoshi, and Oliver Nelson became widely available. Since the 1970s a large amount of excellent band music from the swing era has become accessible, not through publication, but through the donation of manuscripts formerly in private hands to public collections; for important holdings of such material *see* Libraries and archives.

See also Arrangement.

3. Notation for teaching and learning. Notation for pedagogical purposes, such as may be found in method books and arrangements for student ensembles, is frequently more detailed than that intended for professional performers. Because they assume a certain level of familiarity with the conventions of jazz, parts for professionals are largely unencumbered with detailed instructions for phrasing, articulation, and ornamentation, whereas those for student players are deemed to need prescriptions of this kind. Jazz method books, which have appeared in increasing numbers since the 1960s, exhibit a variety of notational techniques. Pedagogical texts on jazz theory differ widely in their approach to the notation of harmony, variously using chord symbols, figured-bass notation, and roman-numeral notation, and defining chordal and scalar relationships in terms of modes. Likewise method and exercise books for specific instruments often include ad hoc notations that show optimum fingerings, systems of counting for rhythms, and other elements. All these differences underline the lack of standard practice in the notation of jazz, particularly in the field of education.

4. Notation for transcription. In that they are used to explain to the performers what should be played and in what way, the notations discussed above are prescriptive. Notations used in jazz research and scholarship, by contrast, are descriptive, and aim to represent and document existing recorded performances by rendering them in written form. The systems used for this purpose tend to be more complex and detailed than those used by teachers, and more complex still than those used by performers. (This is not to say, however, that teachers and performers do not on occasion use the descriptive transcriptions made by researchers; indeed, such material has become an important resource in the teaching of the intricacies of jazz practice to aspiring musicians.) To represent on paper the nuances of jazz in sufficient detail to make meaningful study possible, a large collection of notational symbols is required in addition to the repertory of the Western staff system; some of these are discussed and illustrated in §5 below.

Certain mechanical, electrical, or electronic devices have been invented for, or adapted to, the task of transcription. Each of these produces its own machine-generated notation which must be learned before the information thus presented can be properly comprehended. One of the earliest mechanical transcription devices, the melograph model C, was devised to assist ethnomusicologists but has been applied to recorded jazz with interesting results. With advances in computer and synthesizer technologies it has become possible to obtain a computer-generated transcription of material played on a suitably equipped synthesizer. This is a valuable means of recording the working practices of living musicians. Data created by such methods is most efficient as a descriptive notation, however, and can rarely be used for prescriptive purposes. (For the principles, history, and methodology of written versions of recorded jazz *see* Transcription (i).)

5. Notational symbols.

(i) Introduction. The basis of jazz notation is the standard Western system with its symbols for elements such as dynamics, phrasing, accentuation, attack, etc. Those signs and symbols used in jazz with their established meanings are not dealt with extensively here. Instead the discussion focuses on signs from the standard system that have acquired peculiar meanings in jazz, and on new symbols and usages devised by jazz notators (or borrowed from ethnomusicology) to indicate aspects of the performance. As well as symbols, verbal instructions are often added to musicians' parts: for example, to indicate to a trumpeter that a certain mute should be used an arranger may simply name the mute in the part; in a drum part the word "fill" indicates that the drummer should insert a fill at that point.

Composers, arrangers, teachers, and transcribers have all devised their own ways of representing the sounds of jazz; although there have been attempts at standardization (particularly in the field of education by such groups as the International Association of Jazz Educators) there exists no agreed practice in the use of notational symbols nor has any systematic survey been made of the many and disparate methods adopted. The following discussion offers selected examples of the many symbols employed to notate various elements of the music.

(ii) Pitch and melody. While standard notation is easily adapted to represent melody in jazz, it has only limited ability to convey such deviations from standard pitch as vibrato, blue notes, bends, and various other microtonal and intonational nuances. Often such effects go unnotated since musicians may be expected to inflect notes, according to convention and personal style, without being specifically instructed to do so. Where the microtonal alteration of a pitch must be indicated, an arrow is sometimes placed above the note head, pointing upwards if the note is to be raised, downwards if it is to be lowered; the degree of adjustment may be indicated by the number of arrow heads. Verbal instructions are also sometimes used, keyed by means of asterisks or crosses to the notes to be inflected; the cross, particularly, is employed to indicate a blue note.

Symbols for the various types of Gliss vary according to context; many scribes simply write "gliss" (or one of the names denoting a specific type of gliss) above the note or between the notes concerned. Graphic marks, placed above or beside the note or notes, take the form of straight or curved, thin or thick, wavy or sawtoothed lines. These may or may not indicate the extent of the deviation from the given pitch, but they do generally prescribe its direction (inferred from the angle of the line) and show whether the gliss precedes or follows the note. Some examples of the many markings used to notate glisses are shown in ex.4.

In parts for wind players Overblowing and Multiphonics are requested by means of verbal instructions. Brass parts carry the instruction Half-valve or the symbol ∅ above or below the staff when that technique is required.

Vibrato may be indicated verbally, or by means of a wavy line placed above the note or beside it on the staff (ex.5*a*, 5*b*); the dip is shown by a U-shaped symbol above the staff (ex.5*c*). Although the degree of pitch fluctuation is rarely specified, certain transcribers (notably André Hodeir) have

Ex.4 Symbols for various types of gliss

devised symbols that indicate approximately the point during the note at which the vibrato begins. The gradual introduction of vibrato into a note (*see* TERMINAL VIBRATO) is indicated by the symbols shown in ex.5*d*; the notation sometimes used for vibrato executed with a certain rhythm is shown in ex.5*e*.

Ex.5 Symbols for various types of vibrato

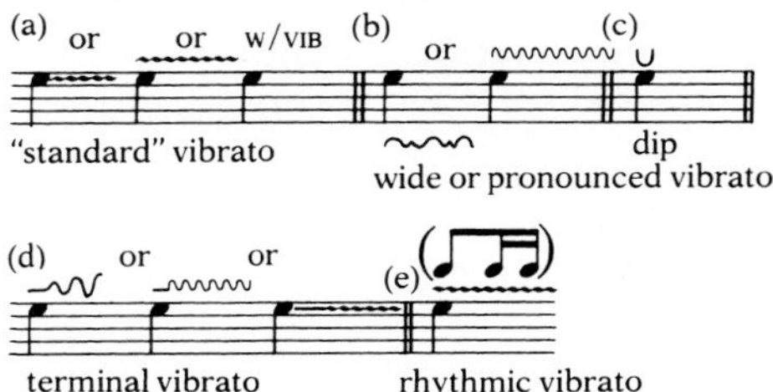

Wider variations of pitch, such as the trill and SHAKE, are also indicated by means of lines above the note, often wavy for the lip trill and sawtoothed for the shake (ex.6), though some scribes use the wavy line for both, simply writing "shake" above the staff to distinguish that effect from a lip trill.

Ex.6 Symbols for wider fluctuations of pitch

Vague or indeterminate pitches such as the GHOST NOTE are indicated variously by placing the note head in parentheses, using a cross-shaped note head, or combining both symbols (ex.7); some transcribers employ both parentheses and cross-shaped note heads, using the first to indicate a note that, though indistinct, is more definitely pitched than one shown by the second. It is also common practice in transcription to enclose in brackets any passage or line that is too indistinct to be rendered accurately.

Ex.7 Symbols for the ghost note

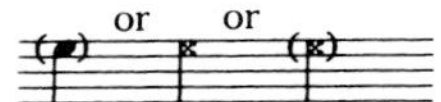

(iii) Harmony. Whereas in much classical music harmonic elements (chords, their voicing and rhythmic articulation, etc.) are fully specified by staff notation, in jazz they are typically conveyed by various types of shorthand. The most commonly used and universally applicable of these is the system of chord symbols based on the letter names of the notes. These symbols designate the root and, either implicitly or explicitly, the other members of a chord, but generally leave other factors (inversion, range, voicing, and rhythmic articulation) to the discretion of the player. As well as providing information for the rhythm section, chord symbols indicate to soloists the harmonic structure to keep in mind while improvising. (It should be noted that, whereas performers and practitioners always use chord-symbol notation, analysts and transcribers often employ roman numerals to define chords in their harmonic relationships to one another.)

The chord-symbol system is by no means a standardized notational language, but certain conventions pertain. The following discussion presents symbols and abbreviations in general use: those given in parentheses are less common.
See also HARMONY (i), esp. §1(v) (a).

(a) Triads. The root of a chord is shown by a capital letter. The quality of a chord is indicated by letters, symbols, or numerals (or combinations of these), which follow the root designation.

A major triad is most often indicated by a capital letter standing alone. The major triad is seen to be the most common chord; thus an unmodified root symbol is taken, by default, to mean the major triad. Abbreviations for the word "major" may be added.

C (CMA Cma Cmaj)

There is also a symbol for the major triad that instructs the performer (who might otherwise expand the chord by enriching the harmony) to play only the notes of the triad itself:

C tri

Here the abbreviation "tri" refers to triad, not triangle (the latter symbol indicates a major seventh chord).

The minor triad is notated by any of the following symbols:

CMI Cm C– (Cmi Cmin)

The minus sign may also be used to inflect an individual element of a chord (see §(c) below). Although this is a potential cause of ambiguity, performers generally infer what is intended by drawing on prior knowledge, custom, and convention.

The augmented triad is generally indicated by a plus sign, more rarely by other means:

C+ (CAUG $C^{(\sharp5)}$ $C^{5\sharp}$ $C^{(+5)}$)

The sharp and plus signs (as in the last three symbols above) may also be used to inflect other elements of a chord (see §(c) below).

The diminished triad is a special case, interpreted according to jazz convention rather than traditional systems. It is commonly indicated by the symbols:

C° CDIM

Strictly these simply indicate a diminished triad with pitches a minor 3rd and a diminished 5th from the root. In practice, however, jazz musicians render this triad as a tetrad, adding a diminished seventh above the root, for which strictly the symbols would be:

$C^{\circ7}$ CDIM^{7}

Thus the symbols ° and DIM apparently serve a double function, indicating that both the triad and the added seventh are diminished. Should the diminished triad without the seventh be required the triad is notated as an inflected minor triad (see also §(c) below):

CMI$^{(\flat5)}$

The half-diminished chord, that is a diminished triad with an added minor seventh, is indicated by an adaptation of the symbol for the diminished chord, though in this case the seventh is specified:

C^{ø7}

This chord is also commonly referred to as a minor seventh chord with a flatted fifth:

CMI$^{7(\flat5)}$

The commonly occurring chord in which the fourth is substituted for the third (generally called in jazz, misleadingly, a suspension, whether or not it is technically suspended from the preceding chord or ultimately resolves to the third) is shown by the following symbol:

Csus

(b) Extended chords. To indicate more complex chords, numerals are appended to the root designation. These are understood to indicate diatonic degrees added to a major triad treated as though it were built on the dominant of the key: the upper elements therefore produce the following intervals from the root: minor 7th, major 9th, perfect 11th, and major 13th. Thus it is understood that the addition of the figure 7 to a chord symbol indicates that the pitch a minor 7th from the root is to be added to the triad in question, whether or not that interval results in a diatonic scale degree. This applies equally to the major, minor, and augmented triads (ex.8*a*). Should the pitch a major 7th from the root be

required it is indicated by the figure 7 preceded by the abbreviation for "major" (ex.8*b*). The chord symbols for common forms of the seventh chord, together with the intervals they indicate, are shown in Table 1.

Chords of the ninth, 11th, and 13th are similarly indicated.

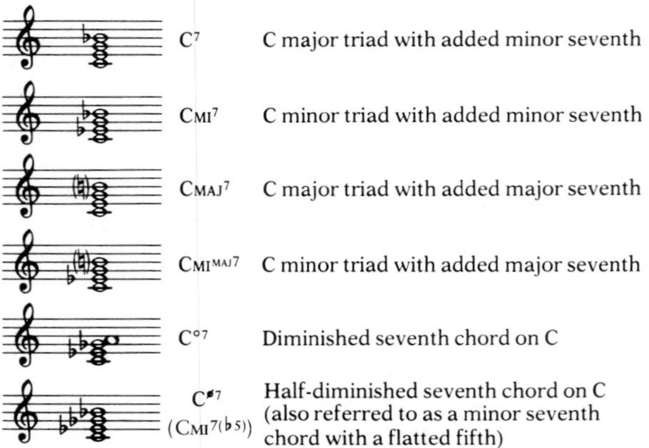

TABLE 1: Chord symbols for seventh chords

Symbol	Description
C^{7}	C major triad with added minor seventh
CMI^{7}	C minor triad with added minor seventh
CMAJ^{7}	C major triad with added major seventh
CMI$^{\text{MAJ}7}$	C minor triad with added major seventh
C$^{\circ7}$	Diminished seventh chord on C
C^{ø7} (CMI$^{7(\flat5)}$)	Half-diminished seventh chord on C (also referred to as a minor seventh chord with a flatted fifth)

In expressing chords made up entirely of diatonic elements, it is common to indicate only the uppermost extension, the presence of the intermediate elements being assumed. For example, the chord of the ninth is expected also to include the seventh and the figure 7 need not appear; similarly the chord of the 11th is assumed to include the seventh and ninth. In practice musicians voice these chords according to taste and custom and may omit certain elements or rearrange them. For example, certain conventions apply to the chord of the 11th. The symbol

C^{11}

indicates the chord shown in ex.9*a*, but generally a jazz musician would omit the third degree of this chord, as in ex.9*b*, to eliminate the interval of a minor 9th between it and the top note. Another such omission is standard when the

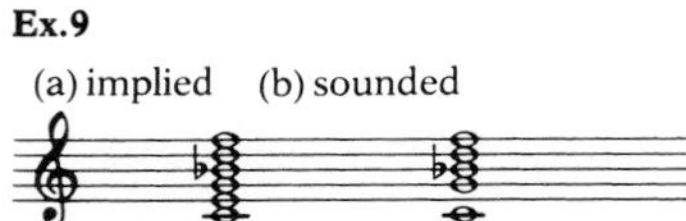

major dominant chord of the 13th is indicated: instead of the full chord (ex.10*a*) a jazz player would generally omit the 11th (to avoid the minor 9th between it and the third) and often the fifth as well (ex.10*b*). The most characteristic voicings of the chord of the 13th in jazz are shown in ex.10*c*.

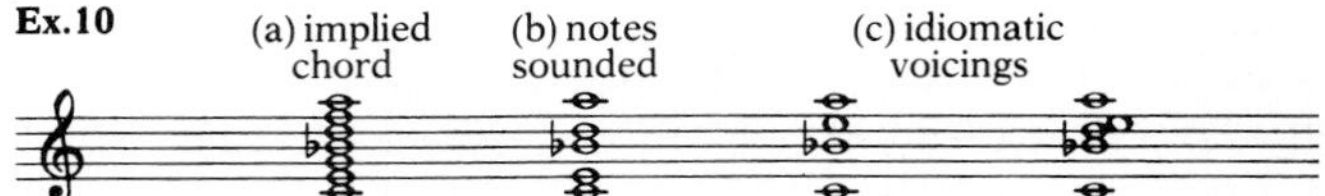

Musicians realize the symbol in this manner according to unwritten "rules," which they absorb as they learn jazz; indeed, it has all but lost its function as an index to the elements of the chord and has come instead to represent a particular aggregate.

(c) Altered chords. Chromatic alterations to the upper elements of a chord are indicated by sharps and flats (or plus and minus signs), which precede the arabic numerals. Where more than one element is designated, the numerals are stacked (or may be placed one after the other to the right of the capital letter), and altered elements are sometimes placed in parentheses (ex.11). An exception to the use of

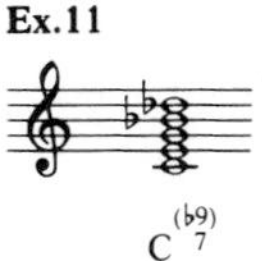

sharps and flats to inflect the elements of a chord is often made in the case of the seventh; as shown in Table 1 the note a major 7th above the root is normally inflected by means of the abbreviation "MAJ" (or "MA") and not by the sharp sign. The chord comprising the pitches C E G B is expressed as:

CMAJ^{7} (C△ C^{⑦})

The chord comprising the pitches C E♭ G B D is expressed as:

CMI$^{(\text{MAJ}7)\,9}$

The convention of using sharp and flat signs to specify inflected chord elements is also applied to the fifth, so that the diminished and augmented triads may be indicated respectively by the symbols ♭5 and ♯5 added to the root (as shown in §(a) above).

Complex chords are expressed by combining the principles for notating extensions and alterations. For example, should the chord shown in ex.12 be required, the scribe would simply build up a symbol showing altered extensions as necessary, using the sign for an augmented chord on C with an added (minor) seventh, raised ninth, and raised 11th.

Ex.12

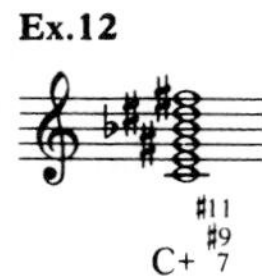

C+ $^{\sharp 11}_{\sharp 9}{}_{7}$

As in expressing all extended chords, only the uppermost extension of an altered chord need be specified, provided the intervening elements are unaltered. All altered elements must, however, be specified. Some scribes use a notational shorthand for extended altered chords on the dominant. The symbols

C^7(ALT) CALT

indicate (among others) the chord given in ex.12.

Chords are usually spelled according to their context and tonal function. But notational practice favors the expression of upper elements in terms of odd-numbered intervals above the root. Thus, for example, the following notation is used for a chord of the seventh based on C to which a raised ninth degree is to be added:

This obscures harmonic and tonal function, since the uppermost note is equivalent to a flatted 10th (which clashes with the major third of the chord, creating the effect of a blue note). In jazz that scale degree is notated as a raised ninth so as to preserve the odd-numbered naming of the degrees.

(d) Omission and addition of individual notes. If an individual pitch is to be left out of a chord a specific instruction to this effect may be given, usually in parentheses:

C^7 (omit 3)

If an individual pitch is to be added, the verbal instruction "add" followed by the relevant numeral is used, indicating that this pitch alone, and not all the other partials otherwise implied by the numeral, be included in the chord:

C (add 9)

(e) Other chordal symbols and annotations. Should two chords be required simultaneously they are set above and below a horizontal line, showing the upper and lower sonorities:

$\frac{\text{C}}{\text{F}\sharp}$ $\frac{\text{C triad}}{\text{F}\sharp\text{ triad}}$

The annotation "triad" (or "tri") is sometimes used to prevent confusion with the similar symbol shown below, in which the slash (solidus) indicates that the triad (shown to the left) should be played over a "foreign" bass note (shown to the right). Further clarification in this case may be achieved by the addition of the word "bass" to the bass note.

C/F♯ (C/F♯ bass)

The notation using a slash is also used to express inversions of simple chords: for example, a second inversion of the chord of C major could be indicated thus:

C/G (C/G bass)

If the harmonic accompaniment is to be discontinued during a certain passage various written indications are used: "NC" (no chord), "harmony tacet," or "break." A line of dashes above the staff normally indicates the duration of the passage, though this may also be shown by the symbol for a full bar's rest annotated with the requisite number of bars.

(f) Conclusion. Theoretically chord-symbol notation is capable of expressing precisely almost any vertical aggregate. However, most arrangers, composers, and music copyists use symbols that specify only the bare essentials of the chordal progression, assuming that individual players will enrich the harmony and voice the chords according to context, usage, and their own preference. Many of the refined notational details described above have been evolved for the purposes of teaching jazz or making descriptive transcriptions, and they would not normally be found in parts for professional musicians.

(iv) Rhythm, duration, and tempo. Rhythm is one of the most elusive elements of jazz to represent in notated form, because, by its very nature, jazz relies on rhythmic subtleties and complexities not accurately shown by standard notation. The principal rhythmic subtleties characteristic of jazz are the largely undefinable element of swing (*see* SWING (i)) and the highly refined and complex rhythmic play achieved by manipulation of the placement of the BEAT. The jazz composer and arranger use standard durational signs and expect the performer to introduce his own rhythmic adjustments. Many transcribers, however, being concerned with the accurate representation of a particular performance, have devised methods of indicating the nuances of rhythmic and durational variation. Ex.13 shows some of the solutions that transcribers have found for the notation of such refinements.

Ex.13 Methods of denoting deviation from prevailing pulse

(a)

← = note slightly anticipated
→ = note slightly delayed

(b)

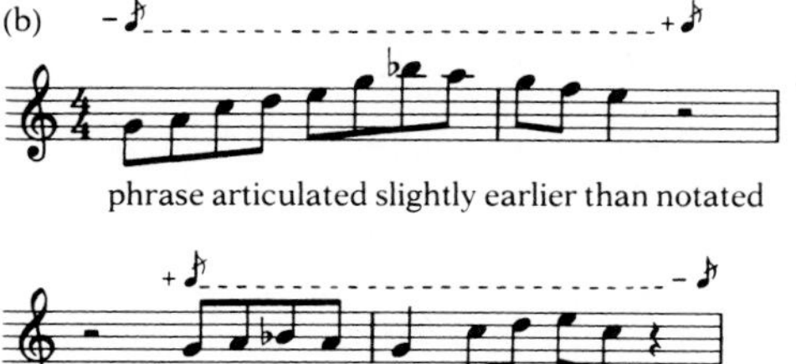

phrase articulated slightly earlier than notated

phrase articulated slightly later than notated

To make their rhythmic notation easy to read jazz composers and arrangers generally restrict themselves to a grid based on a minimum note value, making no attempt to notate rhythmic subtleties that cannot be expressed by that value. For example, if the grid is based on 16th-notes, in any one 4/4 bar there are only 16 possible durational positions. In practice, because of the speed at which much jazz moves, a grid based on the eighth-note is more appropriate, giving eight possible durational positions in the 4/4 bar. This simplistic representation of rhythm and duration will be variously rendered in performance depending on the tempo of the piece and the "time feel" of the players. At extremely slow or fast tempos and in certain styles of jazz (such as LATIN JAZZ and JAZZ-ROCK) the notated rhythms are usually rendered much as they are written; but in the broad range of more moderate tempos the notated rhythms are freely and inventively manipulated.

A prevalent aspect of jazz rhythm is the triplet lilt known as "swing," which varies in degree according to context. By common consent most composers and arrangers and even transcribers assume that, in jazz that swings, rhythms notated as regular duple subdivisions of the beat are performed as if they were based on a triple subdivision (ex.14); any player who rendered them as written would be

Ex.14

written — or, less frequently — played

guilty of a performance that lacked one of the most basic attributes of jazz. A number of scribes have attempted a more accurate representation of swing rhythms as they are performed, using dotted notes or compound meter (the use of compound meter for the notation of jazz was advocated by Hoke Roberts as early as 1939); generally, however, only the most scholarly transcriptions attempt to present swing rhythms as they are actually played.

Tempo indications are normally given (if at all) in English and are placed at the head of the piece in the conventional way. These range from simple indications of speed (e.g., "medium fast") to descriptions of the style of music (e.g., "fast funk" or "slow ballad").

Arrangers and composers commonly observe certain conventions when notating rhythm-section parts. If a certain rhythmic articulation is required it is indicated on a staff by means of slash marks and, if necessary, rests. The slashes for quarter-note pulses do not take stems and indicate simply that the performer should maintain the pulse, though not necessarily by articulating every quarter-note. Diamond-shaped note heads are used for half-notes and longer values; slashes with stems, tails, and beams are used to show shorter durations (ex.15). The symbol commonly employed in classical music to specify that a bar should be repeated is also used in jazz, as shown in the fourth bar of ex.15.

Ex.15

Drum and percussion parts are generally shown on the standard five-line staff and use the slash-mark notation shown above. Different styles and patterns, instructions as to which components of the drum set should be used, particular requests for sticks, brushes, or mallets, and other sorts of cues may be indicated verbally (e.g., "Latin," "two beat," "cym.," "brushes") rather than by special symbols. More fully notated parts, with written-out lines for each component of the drum set, are less common but by no means unknown.

A proposal to standardize the notation for the drum set (see Weinberg, 1994) has been widely adopted by music publishers and arrangers. Under these guidelines the individual components of the set are notated on a single staff, with a neutral clef (two vertical lines) indicating instruments of indeterminate pitch. The bass-drum part is notated in the lowest space, that for the snare drum in the third space up, those for hi-hat and ride cymbal above the staff and on the top line respectively, and those for high- and low-pitched tom-toms in the top space and second space up; cymbal sounds are further distinguished from drum sounds by the use of cross-shaped note heads. When cue notes appear above the staff, the drummer is invited (but not required) to reinforce a rhythmic figure played by the ensemble; when such a figure appears as slash-mark notation, the drummer is expected to realize it using appropriate elements of the drum set (ex.16).

Ex. 16

(ride) (tom) (hi-hat) (crash) (cowbell)

The terms "time" and "figure" are sometimes used in notating drum parts. "Time" may appear in lieu of a specific notated pattern when the drummer is expected to maintain a repetitive and conventional timekeeping pattern (i.e., swing rhythm; bossa nova; funk); "figure" refers to the specifically notated rhythmic figure which the drummer should play in support of the ensemble.

(v) Timbre and articulation. In jazz, as in most other types of music, timbre and articulation (attack and release) lend themselves least easily to representation by notation. Customarily they are not meticulously prescribed by jazz composers and arrangers: they are held to be elements of a player's individual style, or of a collective style transmitted by aural (and oral) tradition, or they are regarded as matters to be decided by discussion during rehearsal. Nevertheless some symbols have gained wide currency.

Among the most important standard signs, which are applicable to many instruments, are those that mean "closed" (i.e., choked, stopped, damped, muted) and "open" (i.e., sounding freely, unmuted, etc.) (ex.17). These symbols

Ex.17 Symbols for "open" and "closed"

may be used to indicate the DU WAH on brass instruments; stopped and open strings; closed and open hi-hat; or, even more generally, the application or removal of a mute (though these instructions are more commonly given verbally, the particular kind of mute normally being specified).

More specific signs are used for different instrumental groups: the most common of these are for wind and brass. Thomas Owens uses phonetic syllables to denote different types of tonguing on wind instruments: "TA" for a sharp attack, "DA" and "TH" for softer ones, and, for the HONK, the symbol shown in ex.18. FALSE FINGERING is most often denoted

Ex.18 Symbol for the honk

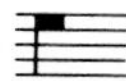

by the placement of a written direction, sometimes specifying that a side key should be used. Timbral or articulatory directions specific to brass instruments include the symbol used by Gunther Schuller in *Early Jazz* for the GROWL, shown in ex.19.

Ex.19 Symbol for the growl

Generally symbols for accents have been borrowed from the Western classical tradition, as have dynamic markings where they are needed.

BIBLIOGRAPHY

H. Roberts: "Jazz Should be Written in Six-eight Time," *DB*, vi/6 (1939), 9
J. Coker: *Improvising Jazz* (Englewood Cliffs, NJ, 1964/R1986)
G. Read: *Music Notation: a Manual of Modern Practice* (Boston, 1964, rev. 3/1971)
J. LaPorta: *Developing the School Jazz Ensemble* (Boston, 1965)
J. Giuffre: *Jazz Phrasing and Interpretation: Aspects of Jazz Performance, Analyzed for the Player ... a Personal Approach* (New York, 1969)
D. Baker: *Arranging and Composing for the Small Ensemble: Jazz, R & B, Jazz-rock* (Chicago, 1970)
R. Kowal: "New Jazz and Some Problems of its Notation," *Jf*, iii–iv (1971–2), 180
C. Roemer: *The Art of Music Copying: the Preparation of Music for Performance* (Sherman Oaks, CA, 1973, rev. 2/1985)
C. Brandt and C. Roemer: *Standardized Chord Symbol Notation: a Uniform System for the Music Profession* (Sherman Oaks, CA, 1976)
K. Stone: *Music Notation in the Twentieth Century: a Practical Guidebook* (New York, London, and Toronto, 1980)
M. S. Haywood: "Melodic Notation in Jazz Transcription," *ARJS*, vi (1993), 271
N. Weinberg: "Guidelines for Drumset Notation," *Percussive Notes*, xxxii/3 (1994), 15
——: *Guide to Standardized Drumset Notation* (Lawton, OK, 1998)

ROBERT WITMER/RICK FINLAY (5, (iv))

Notes. Nickname of RICHARD WILLIAMS.

Noto, Sam (*b* Buffalo, 17 April 1930). Trumpeter and flugelhorn player. His first important associations were with Stan Kenton (November 1953 – spring 1958, 1960), Louie Bellson (1959), Woody Herman (for four months, 1959), and Count Basie (September 1964 – January 1965), with whom he appeared in "Count Basie and his Orchestra," an episode of the television series "The Big Bands" (1965); he also led his own quintet, including Don Menza and Wade Legge (1958–60). After leaving Basie he formed another quintet with Joe Romano; it toured regionally and appeared for about a year at Noto's own venue, the Renaissance, a coffee shop in Buffalo. During this same period he was briefly with Basie again in New York (October to early November 1967). From 1968 to 1975 he worked as a freelance in Las Vegas. He was recommended to the producer Don Schlitten by Red Rodney, with whom he recorded (1974); Schlitten produced several recordings for Noto, most of which were released on the former's label, Xanadu. In 1975 Noto moved to Toronto and worked in studios and at clubs; from 1975 to 1982 he played for Rob McConnell's group Boss Brass. He also recorded in 1978 with Blue Mitchell, Al Cohn, and Dexter Gordon in an all-star group at the Montreux International Jazz Festival. In the early 1980s he operated the Renaissance II club in Buffalo. Around 1983 he began playing frequently with show bands in Toronto, where he has continued to work as a freelance. In 1994 he formed a new quintet and began working as a sideman in Peter Appleyard's group. Noto is recognized for his assertive, virtuoso style of improvisation; his playing reflects the influence of Clifford Brown and Dizzy Gillespie, but he also draws on other sources. He may be seen in the video *Don Menza Quintet: Live in New Orleans* (1991).

Video oral history material in *NCH* (HCJA).

SELECTED RECORDINGS

As leader: *Entrance!* (1975, Xan. 103); *Act One* (1975, Xan. 127); *Notes to You* (1977, Xan. 144); *Noto-riety* (1978, Xan. 168)
As sideman: R. Rodney: *Superbop* (1974, Muse 5046); R. McConnell: *The Jazz Album* (1976, Attic 1015); *Again!* (1978, Umbrella 1-12)

BIBLIOGRAPHY

FeatherE; *Feather '60s*; *Feather–Gitler '70s*

ROBERT DICKOW

Notte, Flavius (*b* Martinique, ?1890s; *d* ? Paris, after 1931). Martinique drummer and bandleader. He performed with Bertin Salnave's band in France in 1925 and during the 1930s he worked in Paris, notably at the club La Coupole. In 1931 he made recordings as a leader for Ultraphone with such Caribbean musicians as Salnave and the trumpeter Abel Beauregard (including *'Tain't no Sin*, AP121, and *I've found a wonderful girl*, AP144).

BIBLIOGRAPHY

A. Boulanger: Liner notes, *Jazz and Hot Dance in Martinique* (Harl. 2018, 1985)
J.-C. Averty: "A Note on Notte," *Sv*, no.134 (1988), 59

RAINER E. LOTZ

Nottingham, Jimmy [James Edward, Jr.; Sir James] (*b* New York, 15 Dec 1925; *d* New York, 16 Nov 1978). Trumpeter and flugelhorn player. His professional career began in 1943 when he performed in Brooklyn with Cecil Payne and Max Roach. Having served in Willie Smith's navy band (1944–5), he gained a reputation as a high-note player while he was with Lionel Hampton (1945–7). Always in demand, he spent periods with Charlie Barnet and Lucky Millinder (both 1947), Count Basie (September 1948 – late 1949), Millinder again (*c*1950), and Herbie Fields (1951); he then played with several Latin bands (1951–3). In 1954 he joined the staff of CBS; he worked with the company for 20 years, dividing his time between jazz and popular music. He also led a group with Budd Johnson (1962) and performed as a sideman with many orchestras, including those of Dizzy Gillespie (with whom he played in France in 1962), Oliver Nelson, Quincy Jones, Ray Charles, Benny Goodman, Thad Jones and Mel Lewis (1966–70), Benny Carter (at the Newport Jazz Festival New York, 1973 and 1975), and Clark Terry (1974–5). In 1970 he ran a nightclub, Sir James Pub, in New York. A versatile lead trumpeter and an expert with the plunger mute, Nottingham was a player of great taste and sensitivity.

SELECTED RECORDINGS

As sideman: L. Hampton: on *Rarities* (*c*1946, MCA 1351), Cobb's Idea (1946); first issued on [no leader]: *Wardell Gray, Featuring Stan Hasselgard and his Orchestra* (1947–8, Spot. 134), C. Basie: The King; E. Sampson: *Swing Softly Sweet Sampson* (1956, Coral 57049); T. Jones and M. Lewis: *Thad Jones–Mel Lewis Live at the Village Vanguard* (1967,

SolS 18016); L. Hampton: *Newport Uproar* (1967, RCA LSP3891), incl. Misunderstood Blues; T. Jones and M. Lewis: *Central Park North* (1969, SolS 18058)

BIBLIOGRAPHY

FeatherE; *Feather–Gitler '70s*; *SheridanCB*
R. Horricks: *Count Basie and his Orchestra: its Music and its Musicians* (London and New York, 1957), 165
Obituaries: M. Hennessey, *JJI*, xxxii/2 (1979), 22; *DB*, xlvi/1 (1979), 10

SCOTT YANOW

Novak, Gary (Laurence) (*b* Chicago, 6 Aug 1969). Drummer, son of Larry Novak. His mother, Carol Novak, is also a pianist. He played drums at the age of eight and began working with his father's trio at Mr. Kelly's and other Chicago clubs when he was ten. During his high school years he played with Buddy DeFranco, Joe Williams, Milt Hinton, Kenny Burrell, Barney Kessel, and others. He took a general music course at De Paul University (1987–8) but found himself occupied in Chicago mainly by studio work. In 1988 he moved to the Los Angeles area in search of wider opportunities. After one semester of liberal arts studies at California State University, Northridge, he toured with Maynard Ferguson and worked with Brandon Fields (1989), Lee Ritenour (1989–90), and George Benson and David Sanborn (both 1990–91). In 1992 he joined Chick Corea, playing in both the latter's acoustic quartet and Elektric Band II; he may be seen with the acoustic group in the video *Chick Corea Quartet: Time Warp, One World Over* (*c*1996, filmed 1995). From the mid-1990s he toured and recorded with Bob Berg and Allan Holdsworth, and around 1996, with Billy Childs, the electric bass guitarist Les King, and the poet Paul Calderon, he formed the group Prophecy, which performs a mixture of rap, funk, and rock.

SELECTED RECORDINGS

As sideman: C. Corea: *Paint the World* (1993, GRP 9731); *Time Warp* (1995, Stretch 0015); B. Berg: *Another Standard* (1997, Stretch 9013)

BIBLIOGRAPHY

"Auditions," *DB*, lii/8 (1985), 61
L. Birnbaum: "Up and Drumming: the Next Generation of Percussion," *DB*, lx/11 (1993), 27
K. Micallef: "Chick Corea's Gary Novak: the Right Touch," *MD*, xxi/4 (1997), 72 [incl. discography]

MARK GILBERT

Novak, Larry [Lawrence R.] (*b* Chicago, 18 May 1933). Pianist, father of Gary Novak. He learned piano from the age of five and started playing jazz when he was 14. After attending Loyola University in Chicago and the University of Minnesota he played in an army special services band (1959–60). Back in Chicago he led a trio at the London House (1961–3) and then at Mr. Kelly's (1963–75). He conducted and arranged for Peggy Lee, spent four years with Pearl Bailey, and also worked with other singers, including Mel Tormé, Frank Sinatra, Joe Williams, Sarah Vaughan, and Carmen McRae. Among many others, he has worked with instrumentalists as diverse as Dizzy Gillespie, Al Hirt, Charlie Shavers, Barney Kessel, Scott LaFaro, Sonny Stitt, Louie Bellson, Terry Gibbs, Buddy DeFranco, Phil Woods, and Scott Hamilton. Novak began teaching at DePaul University in 1984.

SELECTED RECORDINGS

As sideman: L. Bellson: *Live at Joe Segal's Jazz Showcase* (1988, Conc. 350); *Air Bellson* (1996, Conc. 4742); T. Gibbs, B. DeFranco, and H. Ellis: *Memories of You* (1991, Cont. 14066); *Kings of Swing* (1991, Cont. 14067); B. DeFranco: *Chip Off the Old Bop* (1992, Conc. 4527)

DEBORAH GILLASPIE

Novi Singers. Polish vocal group. It was formed around 1965 by Bernard Kawka with the singers Aleksander Głuch, Janusz Mych, Waldemar Parzyński, and Ewa Wanat; when Głuch left the group around 1968 it continued as a quartet. Kawka went to the USA in 1974, and the ensemble performed briefly as a trio; later Kawka's place was taken by the pianist and singer Tomasz Ochalski. In the tradition of such groups as Lambert, Hendricks, and Ross and the Double Six, the members sang closely arranged music with little opportunity for individual improvisation; in later years elements of rock music were incorporated into performances. In the early 1970s an album of vocal arrangements of compositions by Chopin, *Novi Sings Chopin* (1971, Muza 0755), became a popular hit. The group was accompanied by many notable Polish jazz musicians, including Adam Makowicz, Michal Urbaniak, Zbigniew Namysłowski, and Tomasz Stańko. It disbanded soon after recording in 1980.

BIBLIOGRAPHY

J. Byrczek: "Eurojazz Personalities: Poland," *JF* [intl edn], no.17 (1972), 85
J. Fest: "Whatever Happened to Bernard Kawka?," *JF* [intl edn], no.37 (1975), 40
——: "Ad lib with the Novi Singers," *JF* [intl edn], no.39 (1976), 42
<http://compost-records.com/sections/jcr/jcr_arti/novis.htm> (2000)

WOLFRAM KNAUER

Novosel, Steve [Stephen John, Jr.] (*b* Farrell, PA, 17 Feb 1940). Double bass player. His grandfather was an amateur pianist, and as a youngster Novosel briefly played that instrument. In his early teens he took up trumpet, which he studied for two years in New York in the late 1950s. During the first six months of his army service (1961–4) he attended the Navy School of Music in Washington, DC, and while there he played double bass in a military big band. He continued as a trumpeter at Fort Belvoir (near Washington), and played valve trombone as well, but following his discharge he suffered an infection of the gums and abandoned both instruments. Novosel began his professional career as a double bass player in the mid-1960s in Bobby Timmons's trio. In 1967 he joined Roland Kirk, with whom he toured internationally, performed at the Jazz Jamboree in Warsaw (*c*1968), and recorded. In 1969 he toured Europe as a member of Charles Tolliver's group Music Inc. and recorded with both Tolliver and Stanley Cowell, and the following year he recorded with David "Fathead" Newman.

After returning to Washington, Novosel maintained an affiliation with Andrew White from the early 1970s, and he took part in numerous of the saxophonist's recording sessions into the 1980s. During the same period he worked with the trumpeter Allen Houser (recording in 1973 and 1977), toured Europe again and recorded there with Tolliver's Music Inc. (1977), and performed with, among others, Pepper Adams, Milt Jackson, and Philly Joe Jones. In 1979 he played alongside Howard Alden in Red Norvo's trio in Atlantic City, New Jersey, then from 1980 to 1985 he was the regular bass player in Norvo's trio (with Tal Farlow); this latter group may be seen performing in the video *Jazz at the Smithsonian* (1982). Later Novosel worked extensively as a freelance, performing with, among others, Anita O'Day, Billy Eckstine, Teddy Wilson's trio (with Jake Hanna on drums), Buddy Tate, and Eddie Harris, serving as a house double bass player at Blues Alley in Washington, and appearing regularly at the Manassas Jazz Festival with Norma Teagarden, Soprano Summit, and others. In 1990, as a member of Al Grey's quartet, he toured Europe and performed and recorded on a jazz cruise; he remained in the trombonist's small group during the early 1990s. He also led his own groups, mainly in the Washington area, formed a duo with the pianist Reuben Brown, and recorded for Mapleshade, notably as a sideman with Jack Walrath and Larry Willis (1992), Warren Smith (ii) (1995), and John Hicks (1997). From the mid-1990s Novosel worked regularly with Willis, Newman (with whom he recorded again in 1996 and 1998), and Shirley Horn.

SELECTED RECORDINGS

Duo with W. Smith: on Smith: *Cats are Stealing my Shit* (1995, Mapleshade 05332), Jitterbug Waltz

As sideman: R. Kirk: *The Inflated Tear* (1967, Atl. 1502); C. Tolliver: *The Ringer* (1969, Pol. 583750); S. Cowell: *Blues for the Viet Cong* (1969, Pol. 583740); S. Horn: on *the Main Ingredient* (1995, Verve 314-529555-2), All or nothing at all, Blues for Sarge, Come in from the rain; D. Newman: *Chillin'* (1998, HighNote 7036)

BIBLIOGRAPHY

M. Richards: "Steve Novosel," *JJI*, xliv/6 (1991), 6

GK

Novus. Record label. Operated by Arista and run by Steve Backer, from around 1978 to 1980 it issued approximately 25 albums by Muhal Richard Abrams, Air, Warren Bernhardt, Oliver Lake, Larry Coryell, and others. The label was revived by Backer when he began working for BMG in the mid-1980s. It recorded anew from that time and issued both jazz and new-age recordings from late 1986; later it focused primarily on jazz. Its first recordings from this period featured, among others, Steve Lacy, James Moody, Adam Makowicz, Hilton Ruiz, and Henry Threadgill, and from 1990 Steve Coleman recorded for the label. However, from around 1989 Novus began to feature younger musicians, including Roy Hargrove, Antonio Hart, Christopher Hollyday, and Marcus Roberts. It also reissued material that Backer had originally produced for the Arista label in the 1970s. By the mid-1990s, as BMG reorganized its music division, it had ceased operations.

BIBLIOGRAPHY

"Arista Unveils Novus Label," *DB*, xlv/13 (1978), 11

B. McRae: "Avant Courier: India Navigation/Novus," *JJI*, xxxii/4 (1979), 22

R. D. Laing and C. Sheridan: *Jazz Records: the Specialist Labels* (Copenhagen, 1981), 50

J. Levenson: "RCA Revitalizes Jazz Rosters, Imprints," *Billboard*, cvii (25 Feb 1995), 12

GK

NOW. *See* New orchestra workshop.

NRG Ensemble. Group formed in 1978 by Hal Russell.

Ntoni, (Mhleli) Victor [Bra' Vic] (*b* Cape Town, 21 June 1947). Double bass player and composer. Having taught himself to play guitar, he moved to Johannesburg and took up double bass, learning to read music and to understand music theory with the help of musicians frequenting the legendary Dorkay House, a cooperative cum rehearsal complex cum music school in a run-down industrial neighborhood. In 1976 he toured South Africa as a guest double bass player with the New Brubeck Quartet (Dave, Darius, Chris, and Dan Brubeck). He then studied composition and arranging at the Berklee College of Music, and while he was in the USA he worked with Hugh Masekela. He returned to South Africa in 1983, and in 1988 co-founded, with Darius Brubeck, the Brubeck/Ntoni Afro Cool Concept, which played at festivals in South Africa and also at the New Orleans Jazz and Heritage Festival in 1990. In addition Ntoni worked as a freelance producer and for the South African Broadcasting Corporation, for which in the late 1980s he hosted the series "Jazz, Jazz, Jazz." Other highlights of his career include international tours with Abdullah Ibrahim, leading and arranging for big bands specially formed for festivals and television shows, and a recording in 1990 with his Xhosa "brothers" (i.e., members of the Xhosa nation) Duke Makasi, Ezra Ngcukana, Tete Mbambisa, and Lulu Gontsana. In the late 1990s he was playing regularly with the group Iconoclast.

Ntoni has been involved extensively with the theater. He wrote music for the film *Shout at the Devil* (1973), composed a musical, *Meropa* (1975), and composed and arranged music for the director and playwright Barney Simon and others at the Market Theatre. Another musical, *Nebo's Daughter* (1993), was produced at the Standard Bank National Arts Festival in Grahamstown and at the Brooklyn Academy of Music in New York.

SELECTED RECORDINGS

As leader with Darius Brubeck: *Afro Cool Concept: Live at New Orleans Jazz & Heritage Festival 1990* (1990, African Echoes 7865)

As sideman: A. Ibrahim: *Peace* (1971, Soultown 110); D. Pukwana: on *Diamond Express* (1975, Arista 1041), Tete and Barbs in Mind; H. Masekela: *Home* (Moonshine 5574, 1982); [no leader]: *The Brothers* (1990, Roots 137)

BIBLIOGRAPHY

K. Shippey: "A Black and White Production in Living Color: Theater History Made in South Africa," *Christian Science Monitor* (8 May 1975)

M. Gevisser: "St. Louis Whites," *VV* (28 Nov 1989), 65

DARIUS BRUBECK

Ntshoko, Makaya [Makhaya] (*b* Cape Town, 29 Oct 1939). South African drummer. In Cape Town in 1958 he was a member of the trio led by Dollar Brand (later known as Abdullah Ibrahim). He recorded in Johannesburg in September 1959 in a sextet, alongside Hugh Masekela, Jonas Gwangwa, Kippie Moeketsi, and the double bass player Johnny Gertze, under the leadership of the visiting American pianist John Mehegan. Later that same month, or in the next, he joined the Jazz Epistles, in which Brand replaced Mehegan (who had returned to the USA), and early in 1960 the group recorded the seminal South African hard-bop album *Jazz Epistle: Verse I*. It disbanded soon thereafter, and Ntshoko returned home to Cape Town, where he formed his own group, the Jazz Giants. In 1962 he recorded the album *Jazz Fantasia* in a quintet consisting of Moeketsi, Dudu Pukwana, the pianist Gideon Nxumalo, and the double bass player Martin Mgijima.

In autumn 1962 Ntshoko and Gertze left South Africa, Gertze traveling via Sweden to join Brand in Zurich in September, at which time they started playing in a duo; Ntshoko followed directly to Switzerland in late November or early December. From 1963 to 1965, for four and a half months each year, the musicians served as the resident trio at the Club Africana in Zurich. The trio also appeared at the Festival Mondial du Jazz Antibes–Juan-les-Pins in 1963 and 1964, recording there in the former year, and it may be seen performing in the Danish documentary short film *Portrait of a Bushman* (1966). Ntshoko recorded with Sathima Bea Benjamin in 1963. After Brand moved to New York (1965) Ntshoko spent periods in the house band at the Montmartre in Copenhagen (1966, 1969–70) and recorded with Stuff Smith (1967), Benny Bailey (1968, while performing at the Domicile in Munich), Dexter Gordon (at the Domicile, 1968 or 1969), and Ben Webster (1969); he may be seen with Gordon in the video *Tenor Legends* (*c*1995 [filmed 1969]).

In the early 1970s Ntshoko toured the USA and the Bahamas and recorded in London (1972) with Masekela and appeared at the Berliner Jazztage in Karl Berger's group Creative Music Studio (1973). In 1974 he formed the group Makaya and the Tsotsis, consisting of Heinz Sauer, Bob Degen (with whom he recorded independently of this group in 1976), and Isla Eckinger (later replaced on double bass by Jürgen Wuchner). Around the same time, with the trombonist Nick Evans and Radu Malfatti, he co-founded the ensemble Nicra, which recorded in 1975; their sidemen included Keith Tippett and Buschi Niebergall. In 1975 Ntshoko performed and recorded with Joe McPhee and Pepper Adams and recorded at the first Willisau Jazz Festival in a quartet with John Tchicai, Irène Schweizer, and Niebergall. Two years later he recorded in Hannibal Peterson's group at the Festival International du Jazz Antibes–Juan-les-Pins and performed with Pukwana at an NDR workshop in Germany. Ntshoko worked regularly with Mal Waldron from around 1977 to 1979, and during the 1970s he performed in a duo with Ibrahim. Nothing is known of his career during the 1980s, but in the early 1990s he was a member of the group led by the double bass player Stephan Kurmann, whose work in 1991 involved a recording date and an appearance at the Montreux International Jazz festival – the latter preserved on the video *Stephan Kurmann Strings: Alive in Montreux* (1991). From around 1993 he was no longer active as a musician.

SELECTED RECORDINGS

As leader: *Jazz Fantasia* (1962, Renown 233); *Makaya and the Tsotsis* (1974, Enja 2042)

As sideman: Jazz Epistles: *Jazz Epistle: Verse 1* (1960, Gallo Continental 14); D. Brand (A. Ibrahim): *Anatomy of a South African Village* (1965, Fon. 888314); P. Adams: *Julian* (1975, Enja 2060); J. McPhee: *The Willisau Concert* (1975, HH B); Nicra: *Listen/Hear* (1975, Ogun 010); M. Waldron and S. Lacy: *One-upmanship* (1977, Enja 2092); J. Dyani: *Song for Biko* (1978, Ste. 1109); S. Kurmann: *Alive* (1991, TCB 96152)

BIBLIOGRAPHY

M. Kunzler: *Jazz-Lexicon* (Reinbek, nr Hamburg, Germany, 1988)
L. Rasmussen: *Abdullah Ibrahim: a Discography* (Copenhagen, 1999)

LARS RASMUSSEN, GK

Nucleus. Group founded in 1969 by IAN CARR.

Nueva Manteca. Dutch Latin-jazz ensemble founded late in 1987 by the pianist Jan Laurens Hartong as an outgrowth of his former ten-piece salsa band, Manteca. Among its founding members were Jarmo Hoogendijk and the tenor saxophonist Ben van den Dungen. The group has performed mainly in the Netherlands, although it has also toured Britain and North America, and in 1997 it appeared at the Eddie Moore Jazz Festival in Oakland, California. Nueva Manteca's blend of salsa and jazz is well represented on its recordings *Varadero Blues* (1988, Tim. 318) and *Afrodisia* (1990, Tim. 355).

BIBLIOGRAPHY

L. Birnbaum: "Latin Lovers Go Dutch," *DB*, lxiii/2 (1996), 37
<http://www.iahev.nl/users/flxy/latin/nueva.html> (1999)
<http://www.westnet.nl/jwajazz/engels/nueva.htm> (1999) [incl. discography]

GK

Nugetre. Pseudonym of AHMET ERTEGUN.

Nunez, Alcide "Yellow" (*b* New Orleans, 17 March 1884; *d* New Orleans, 2 Sept 1934). Clarinetist. He began playing professionally as a guitarist, but from 1902 concentrated entirely on the clarinet and played in many New Orleans groups, including Papa Jack Laine's Reliance Brass Band and Tom Brown's band. He was also a member of a trio at the 101 Ranch in Storyville. After journeying to Chicago in March 1916 with Johnny Stein's group, Nunez and three other band members (Nick LaRocca, Eddie Edwards, and Henry Ragas) formed a group that later became the Original Dixieland Jazz Band. Disagreements between Nunez and LaRocca, however, caused the clarinetist to leave the group at the end of October. He toured briefly on the vaudeville circuit, then performed with Anton Lada's LOUISIANA FIVE (1918–19), with whom he made his most representative recordings. In the mid-1920s he toured with his own quartet, but after 1927 worked for various leaders in New Orleans.

Nunez's tone was harsh and brittle and he was skilled in the production of "barnyard" effects. Although he had a talent for improvisation, his vaudevillian approach to the music sometimes detracted from his performances.

SELECTED RECORDINGS

As sideman with Louisiana Five: I ain't-en got-en no time to have the blues (1919, Col. A2775); Ringtail Blues/ Blues my naughty sweetie gives to me (1919, Emerson 1083)

BIBLIOGRAPHY

ChiltonW
H. O. Brunn: *The Story of the Original Dixieland Jazz Band* (Baton Rouge, LA, 1960/*R*1977)
S. B. Charters and L. Kunstadt: *Jazz: a History of the New York Scene* (Garden City, NY, 1962/*R*1981)
F. Ramsey, Jr.: Liner notes, *Jazz Odyssey*, i: *The Sound of New Orleans (1917–1947)* (Col. C3L30, *c*1964)
G. Schuller: *Early Jazz: its Roots and Musical Development* (New York, 1968)

LAWRENCE KOCH

Nussbaum, Adam (*b* New York, 29 Nov 1955). Drummer. He grew up in Norwalk, Connecticut, and took up drums before his fifth birthday; having studied piano for five years, he acquired a drum set at around the age of 12. He took lessons with Charli Persip in New York, and from 1975, while studying music at the City College of New York, played at local clubs with Monty Waters, Al Dailey, and the pianist Nina Sheldon, as well as in Washington, DC, with Dave Liebman. From 1978 to 1981 he worked with John Scofield, performing and recording with him in Europe in 1978–9 and playing alongside him in sessions led by Hal Galper in 1979. Nussbaum and Scofield also worked with Liebman (1980) and toured and recorded in a trio with Steve Swallow (1980–81). Nussbaum then performed with Bob Brookmeyer (1982–3), Stan Getz (1982–4), Gil Evans's orchestra (1983–6, touring Europe and Japan in 1985), and the quintet of Randy Brecker and Eliane Elias (1984–5), and recorded with Bill Evans (iii) (1983), Art Farmer and Slide Hampton (1984), and Bobby Watson (1984); he also worked briefly with Eddie Gomez (1984) and Gary Burton, Jeff Palmer, and Lew Soloff (all 1985).

Nussbaum was a member of George Gruntz's Concert Jazz Band and trio (1984–90 and intermittently thereafter into the late 1990s) and of trios led by Mike Stern (1985–8), Richie Beirach and Ron McClure (1985–94), Elias (1988–94), John Abercrombie (his organ trio with Dan Wall, from 1991), and Niels-Henning Ørsted Pedersen (1992–6). Through these same years he played with Michael Brecker's band (1987–

90), the Doky brothers (1989–93), Carla Bley's Very Big Band (1992), the quartets of Toots Thielemans (1986–95), Jerry Bergonzi (from 1989), Kenny Wheeler (from 1996), and James Moody (from 1996), and Swallow's quintet (from 1996); he may be seen in the videos *Newport Jazz '87* (in Michael Brecker's band, 1987) and *Toots Thielemans in New Orleans* (1988). In 1992 he played with Don Grolnick at a festival in Israel. Nussbaum recorded with most of these musicians, and he served as a freelance with many others – with, for example, Liebman (1987), Palmer (1987, in a trio with Abercrombie), Conrad Herwig (from *c*1987), Lee Konitz (1987–8), Herb Geller and Mike Richmond (both 1988), Tom Harrell (1989), Chris Hunter (1989–90), Eddie Daniels (1989, 1994), Salvatore Bonafede and Joey Calderazzo (both 1990), Bruce Gertz (from 1991), Dave Stryker (1991, 1994), Paul Bley, George Cables, and Doug Raney (all 1993), Stefan Bauer (in Montreal, 1994), Lars Danielsson (in yet another trio with Abercrombie, 1994), Dave O'Higgins (1994), Karlheinz Miklin (in concert in Graz, Austria, 1995), Anders Bergcrantz (1995–6), Steve Slagle (1997), and Christian Jacob (1998).

SELECTED RECORDINGS

As sideman: J. Scofield: *Shinola* (1981, Enja 4004); *Out like a Light* (1981, Enja 4038); G. Gruntz: *Serious Fun* (1989, Enja 6038); J. McNeely: *East Coast Blowout* (1989, Lipstick 8907); J. Bergonzi: *Standard Gonz* (1989–90, BN B21Z-96256); M. Brecker: *Now You See it ... (Now You Don't)* (*c*1990, GRP 9622); R. McClure: *Inspiration* (1991, Ken 015); J. Abercrombie: *While We're Young* (1992, ECM 1489); P. Bley: *If We May* (1993, Ste. 31334); J. Abercrombie: *Tactics* (1996, ECM 1623); S. Swallow: *Deconstructed* (1996, XtraWatt 9)

BIBLIOGRAPHY

J. Woodard: "Adam Nussbaum: New York Dues," *MD*, x/6 (1986), 22

T. Saccone: "Update," *MD*, xii/4 (1988), 6

H. Pinksterboer: "Update: Adam Nussbaum," *MD*, xiv/11 (1990), 8

K. Franckling: "John Abercrombie: Low-cholesterol Organ Trio," *JT*, xxiii/6 (1993), 28

J. Milder: "Att vara musiker är en strävan som aldrig tar slut" [To be a musician means forever yearning], *Orkester journalen*, lxi/1 (1993), 2

W. F. Miller: "Adam Nussbaum: I am Third," *MD*, xviii/1 (1994), 18

——: "Adam Nussbaum: Finally," *MD Hot Trax* (1998), 63

BK

NYC. Record company and label founded in 1992 by MIKE MAINIERI.

N.Y. Hardbop Quintet. Quintet formed by the pianist Keith Saunders in summer 1991. A group formed with the trumpeter Joe Magnarelli, the double bass player Bim (Erik) Strasberg, and the drummer Eddie Ornowski had toured Japan in autumn 1990, and with the addition of the tenor saxophonist Jerry Weldon it became the N.Y. Hardbop Quintet in summer 1991; in 1995 Cliff Barbaro replaced Ornowski. It initially worked only in New York but from 1994 began to perform on the West Coast and in other American cities; Mickey Roker plays drums with the group when it appears in Philadelphia. From 1996 Strasberg served as co-leader with Saunders.

SELECTED RECORDINGS

The Clincher (1994, TCB 9520-2); *Rokermotion* (1996, TCB 9635-2); *A Whisper Away* (1997, TCB 9870-2)

BIBLIOGRAPHY

Z. Stewart: "Tradin' Fours: Hard Bop Lives up to its Name," *DB*, lxiii/1 (1996), 38

<http://www.users.interport.net/~commish/players.html> (1999) [incl. discography]

GK

NYJO. Acronym for the National Youth Jazz Orchestra, founded by BILL ASHTON.

NYJRC. *See* NEW YORK JAZZ REPERTORY COMPANY.

NYRL. *See* NEW YORK RECORDING LABORATORIES.

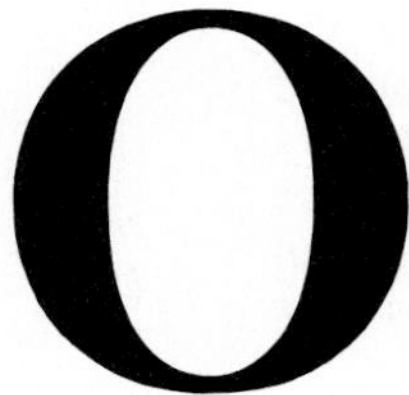

Oatts, Dick [Richard Dennis] (*b* Des Moines, IA, 2 April 1953). Alto saxophonist. His father, a saxophonist and high-school band director, was his first teacher, and he attended Drake University briefly (1971–2). After moving to New York in 1977 he immediately joined the Thad Jones–Mel Lewis Orchestra (continued from 1979 as the Mel Lewis Orchestra); he appears in the video *Jazz at the Smithsonian: Mel Lewis and the Orchestra* (1982). He also worked in Lewis's small groups from 1979 until the drummer's death in 1990. Lewis's orchestra then became the Vanguard Jazz Orchestra, of which Oatts was nominated co-leader, with John Mosca, in 1991. He was a member of the fusion group Flim & the BB's (1980–92), Ray Mantilla's Space Station (1981–6), Bob Brookmeyer's sextet (1983–4), and Joe Haider's Euro Jazz Orchestra (1983–6), and he played with Armen Donelian's small groups, recording and touring in Europe and Turkey (1983–90), Red Rodney's quintet, with which he also recorded and toured internationally (1986–92), Eddie Gomez (1988–93), and the Carnegie Hall Jazz Band (from 1995). In 1987, with Garry Dial, he formed Dial + Oatts; their sidemen have included Jay Anderson and Joey Baron or Jeff Hirshfield, all members of Rodney's quintet. From 1993 Oatts has led or co-led ensembles with the bass player Dave Santoro. He taught at New York University (1981–4) and the Manhattan School (1989). He also plays soprano and tenor saxophone, clarinet, and flute.

SELECTED RECORDINGS

As leader with G. Dial: of Dial + Oatts: *Dial and Oatts* (1988, DMP 465); *Brassworks* (1990, DMP 477)

As sideman: M. Lewis: *Naturally!* (1979, Telarc 10044); R. Rodney: *No Turn on Red* (1986, Denon CY-73149); *One for Bird* (1988, Ste. 1238); M. Lewis: *The Lost Art* (1989, Musicmasters 6022-2); A. Farnham: *Playcation* (1992, Conc. 4521); T. Rosenthal: *Images of Monk* (1992, Jazz Alliance 10023)

BIBLIOGRAPHY

G. Lees and J. Reeves: *Jazz Lives: 100 Portraits in Jazz* (Toronto, 1992), 174

GK

Obendorfer, Jenő. *See* CHAPPY.

Oboe. A double-reed woodwind instrument of narrow, conoidal bore, terminating in a moderately flared bell. Its basic scale begins on *c′* and its compass generally extends from *b♭* to about *a‴*. There are several larger versions of the Western orchestral instrument, of which the english horn (or cor anglais), the tenor member of the family, is pitched in F (a 5th below the oboe) and has a distinguishing feature in its bulb-shaped bell. Jazz musicians have also been drawn increasingly to the numerous types of non-Western oboe, notably the *nāgasvaram* of south India and the *zūrnā* of the Arab world (which has many derivatives elsewhere).

The oboe is quite rare in jazz. It first appeared in the 1920s, when it was included, for the sake of its tone-color, in the reed section of the band; its use was prompted by the influence of symphonic jazz. Don Redman played oboe in his arrangement of *Shanghai Shuffle*, recorded by Fletcher Henderson in 1924 (PAct 036157), and oboe parts were also written for Paul Whiteman's orchestra. In these contexts the oboist was a section member, playing from written parts, and had the opportunity neither to improvise nor to play solos. The oboe continued to be used in this way: Alec Wilder wrote for the instrument in a series of light, jazzlike octets composed in 1939, and from that year Mitch Miller played oboe and english horn in Wilder's orchestra accompanying Mildred Bailey on several recordings of Wilder's songs; Miller also performed as a member of a group (otherwise consisting mostly of string players) that accompanied Charlie Parker on a recording in 1949; and George Barnes's octet recorded jazz-flavored chamber pieces that included oboe (1946).

The oboe was first employed as a solo instrument and for improvisations during the 1950s when jazz musicians began to explore orchestral instrumentation and classical compositional forms. Several examples of the use of oboe and english horn in cool jazz and West Coast jazz include the work of Bob Cooper (principally a tenor saxophonist), who played both instruments on several of his recordings. In the later 1950s YUSEF LATEEF began to play oboe (as well as other wind instruments), adopting a soulful, bluesy style and a rich tone; an example of his work may be heard on the track *In the Evening* from the album *The Complete Yusef Lateef* (1967, Atl. 1499). Marshall Allen plays a solo on oboe on *Thither and Yon* on Sun Ra's album *Cosmic Tones for Mental Therapy* (1963, Sat. 408). Paul McCandless, who came to prominence as a member of the group Oregon (formed 1970), is most highly regarded for his extraordinary playing of jazz oboe and english horn, though he also played soprano saxophone and other wind instruments; Oregon's repertory incorporates elements of ethnic music and is not always identified with jazz, but McCandless's solos (well represented by the album *Together*, 1976, Van. 79377) clearly draw on the tradition of John Coltrane's soprano saxophone playing and reveal the influence of the *nāgasvaram*, which Coltrane also admired. Another musician to synthesize the style of Coltrane with ethnic traditions is Charlie Mariano, who studied the *nāgasvaram* in South Asia and has been deeply influenced by Carnatic music. Use of the oboe in jazz-rock includes the work of Andrew White, who plays a solo on english horn on the track *Unknown Soldier* (1971) from Weather Report's album *I Sing the Body Electric* (1971–2, Col. KC31352). The oboe has also occasionally been used by the Art Ensemble of Chicago. Dewey Redman plays an instrument related to the oboe, which he calls the musette.

BIBLIOGRAPHY

P. A. T. Bate: *The Oboe* (London, 1956, rev. 3/1975)
P. Bate and N. O'Loughlin: "Oboe," *GroveI*

LEWIS PORTER

O'Brien, Floyd (W.) (*b* Chicago, 7 May 1904; *d* Chicago, 26 Nov 1968). Trombonist. He first played professionally in the early 1920s with local bands in Chicago and with many of the Austin High School Gang, though he also sat in with many leading African-American players in the city. After working in a pit band in Des Moines, Iowa (1930–31), he returned to Chicago and performed with a number of bandleaders, including Floyd Town (1932), Joe Venuti, and Mal Hallett. In New York he played with the trombonist Mike Durso (1933–4) and recorded with Fats Waller (1934). He was in demand for recording dates, and his warm playing, inspired by the great New Orleans musicians, may be heard on *Tennessee Twilight*, recorded with Eddie Condon (1933), and *Old Fashioned Love*, recorded with Mezz Mezzrow (1934). O'Brien then worked with the drummer and singer Phil Harris (1935–9), Gene Krupa (1939–40), and Bob Crosby (May 1940–1942); *Tin Roof Blues*, recorded with Crosby in 1942, shows him in a robust mood. He also appeared in a soundie from this period, *Lazybones* (1941). In Los Angeles he played with Eddie Miller (1943), Jack Teagarden (*c* late 1943 – early 1944), Freddy Slack (1944), Shorty Sherock (1945), and as a freelance musician, and recorded with Wingy Manone, the Chicago Loopers, led by the pianist Charles La Vere, and Bunk Johnson (all 1944). In 1948 he returned to Chicago, where he worked with Bud Freeman and performed and recorded with Art Hodes (1954–6), Danny Alvin (1957–8), and the trumpeter Smokey Stover (1959–60); he also recorded with Natty Dominique (1954) and Albert Nicholas (1959), and he was active as a brass teacher and piano tuner. In 1965 he appeared with members of the Austin High School Gang in a festival organized by *Down Beat*.

SELECTED RECORDINGS

As sideman: B. Freeman: Can't help lovin' dat man (1928, OK 41168); E. Condon: Tennessee Twilight/Madame Dynamite (1933, Bruns. 01690); The Eel/Home Cooking (1933, Bruns. 6743); M. Mezzrow: Old Fashioned Love (1934, Vic. 25202); Sendin' the Vipers (1934, Vic. 25019); G. Wettling: I wish I could shimmy like my sister Kate (1940, Decca 18044); B. Crosby: Tin Roof Blues (1942, Bruns. 04003); C. LaVere: Baby won't you please come home (1944, Jump 1); A. Nicholas: *All Star Stompers* (1959, Del. 209)

BIBLIOGRAPHY

ChiltonW; *FeatherE*; *Feather–Gitler '70s*
G. Avakian: "Why Bury O'Brien," *Jazz Information*, ii/3 (1940), 12
W. H. Miller: "Floyd O'Brien," *Three Brass*, v (Melbourne, Australia, 1945)
M. Mezzrow and B. Wolfe: *Really the Blues* (New York, 1946/*R*1990), 268, 345
A. Shaw: *The Trouble with Cinderella: an Outline of Identity* (New York, 1952/*R*1992), 146
L. Wright: *"Fats" in Fact* (Chigwell, England, 1992)

BRIAN PEERLESS

O'Brien, Hod [Walter Howard] (*b* Chicago, 19 Jan 1936). Pianist. He grew up in Salisbury, Connecticut, where his mother taught him piano from the age of six, and he made his professional début in the state in 1950. Having briefly attended Oberlin College (1954) and the Manhattan School of Music, he led a trio at Avaloch, a club in Lennox, Massachusetts (1956–7), and recorded in New York as a sideman with Art Farmer, Donald Byrd, and Idrees Sulieman (January 1957). Shortly afterwards he worked in Oscar Pettiford's quintet (1957–8) and alongside Wilbur Ware and Elvin Jones in J. R. Monterose's small group (late 1958). From 1959 he performed at the Cork 'n Bib and the Jazz Gallery, and towards the end of that year he began working with Teddy Kotick in the house rhythm section of a club in Staten Island; they usually accompanied a different soloist each week, among them such leading saxophonists as Zoot Sims, Stan Getz, Charlie Rouse, and Lee Konitz. In the early 1960s O'Brien gave up music to study mathematics at Columbia University, and later in the decade he earned a degree in psychology.

O'Brien resumed his musical career in the early 1970s and joined Roswell Rudd's quintet (*c*1973). Around 1974 he and Rudd opened a club, the St. James Infirmary, and with Sheila Jordan they formed the nucleus of its house band. Upon Rudd's departure from the business O'Brien formed a quartet with Bob Mover; among their sidemen were Cameron Brown or Richie Youngsteen on double bass and Beaver Harris or Jimmy Madison on drums; this group also served as the St. James Infirmary's house band, and it accompanied various guest musicians until the club closed (? late 1975). O'Brien then performed as a freelance and recorded with, among others, Allen Eager (1982), Chet Baker and Warne Marsh (1984), Joe Puma (1984), Ted Brown (1987), and Danny D'Imperio (1991). In 1980 he began working with the singer Stephanie Nakasian, both in a duo and in larger groups; they toured internationally and performed frequently on the East Coast and in Europe, and maintained their association into the late 1990s. From December 1984 to January 1986 O'Brien worked in New York with Baker, after which he moved to the Poconos.

SELECTED RECORDINGS

As leader: *Opalessence* (1985, Criss Cross 1012); *Hod & Cole* (*c*1992, Jazzmania 6005); *So That's How it Is* (*c*1998, Reservoir 155)
As sideman: [no leader]: *Three Trumpets* (1957, Prst. 7092); R. Thomas: *Guitar Groove* (1960, Jlnd 27); R. Rudd: *Flexible Flyer* (1974, Ari. 1006); C. Baker: *Blues for a Reason* (1984, Criss Cross 1010); T. Brown: *Free Spirit* (1987, Criss Cross 1031); S. Nakasian: *French Cookin'* (1990, V.S.O.P. 79); D. D'Imperio: *Blues for Philly Joe* (1991, V.S.O.P. 81)

BIBLIOGRAPHY

FeatherE
M. Cuscuna: Liner notes, *Flexible Flyer* (1975, Ari. 1006)
"Interview with Hod O'Brien," *The Note*, iv/2 (1992), 7
<http://www.jazzcanadiana.on.ca/_obrien.htm> (1999)

GK

O'Bryant, Jimmy [Jimmie] (*b* Arkansas, *c*1896; *d* Chicago, 24 June 1928). Clarinetist and alto saxophonist. He toured with a vaudeville troupe, the Tennessee Ten (*c*1920–1921), and in early 1923 he was a member of the short-lived band led by Jelly Roll Morton and W. C. Handy in Chicago. During the same year he began recording for Paramount, working as the regular clarinetist with the studio's house band, Lovie Austin's Blues Serenaders (1923–6). After playing briefly with King Oliver (1924) he made a number of recordings under his own name with the Washboard Band (1925–6). In 1927 he was a member of Paul Stuart's Wee Hours Serenaders in Terre Haute, Indiana, but early the following year he returned to Chicago.

O'Bryant's tone was sweet and plaintive in the upper register (notably when he accompanied singers), though his fast vibrato and characteristic edge caused his playing to stand out in ensemble work. In the chalumeau register of the instrument his tone was full-bodied and warm, and he often made judicious use of feather tonguing for dramatic effect – a legacy of his years on the vaudeville circuit. During his brief career at Paramount he made more recordings than any other Chicago jazz clarinetist; a tribute to the quality of these performances is that his playing has often been mistaken for that of Johnny Dodds or Junie Cobb.

SELECTED RECORDINGS

(all recorded for Paramount)

As leader: Red Hot Mama/Drunk Man's Strut (1924, 12246); Georgia Break Down (1925, 12277); Three J Blues/Steppin' on the Gas (1925, 12294); Clarinet Get Away/Back Alley Rub (1925, 12287); The Joys/Switch it, Miss Mitchell (1925, 12297); Down to the Bricks/I found a good man after all (1925, 12308); Chicago Skiffle (1925, 12339)

As sideman: I. Cox: Graveyard Dream Blues/Weary Way Blues (1923, 12044); L. Austin: Peepin' Blues (1925, 12277)

BIBLIOGRAPHY

C. Hillman: "Paramount Serenaders, 1923–1926," *Sv*, no.67 (1976), 8; no.70 (1977), 149; no.72 (1977), 226 [incl. discography]

D. M. Bakker: "Jimmie O'Bryant, 1923–26," *Micrography*, no.44 (1977), 14

MICHAEL TOVEY/HOWARD RYE (recording-list)

Ochs, Larry (*b* New York, 1949). Tenor saxophonist, member of Rova.

Octave divider. An electronic device that takes as input a pitch played on an instrument and adds to it a replica one or more octaves lower. The result is an instrumental line in parallel octaves; often some modification of the original timbre also takes place. Commercially available effects units that exploit this principle include the Multivider, the Octivider, and the Varitone. The device was used by several jazz musicians, most notably Eddie Harris.

Octobans. A set of eight single-headed drums; *see* Drum set, §I, 4.

October Revolution in Jazz. A series of free-jazz concerts organized in 1964 by Bill Dixon.

Oda, Satoru (*b* Fukuoka, Japan, 27 Sept 1927). Japanese tenor saxophonist and leader. He played piano from the age of 13, took up alto saxophone in a navy band in 1943, and changed to the tenor instrument two years later to play jazz. Having been a member of the groups Tokyo Jive and Gay Septet, he launched his own Prez Six (later Prez Nine as well) in 1956. In the 1960s he composed a few Japanese pop hits. He formed the Great Jazz Quintet with Hank Jones in 1989 and performed at the Monterey Jazz Festival several times. Oda was known throughout his career as "Japanese Prez" because of his devotion to Lester Young's style.

SELECTED RECORDINGS

As leader: *Live Session* (1971, AMJ 34); *Live at the New Five Spot* (1976, Toho YX6103); *All of Me* (1982, Lob 1036); *Lover Man* (1989, King K32Y6288)

As sideman with Jun Sugihara: *Full Swing* (1981, Toshiba–EMI 5812)

KAZUNORI SUGIYAMA

O'Day, Anita [Colton, Anita Belle] (*b* Kansas City, MO, 18 Oct 1919). Singer. Having left home at the age of 12, she took the stage name O'Day while working as a contestant in dance marathons, and when she was about 19 she sang professionally in nightclubs in Chicago. From 1941 to 1943 she was a member of Gene Krupa's big band (see illustration), with which she recorded her biggest hit, *Let me off uptown*. After singing in Stan Kenton's band (1944–5) and again with

Anita O'Day (front) with Gene Krupa's big band at the Hotel Pennsylvania, New York, 1941; the trumpet soloist (standing) is Roy Eldridge and the guitarist is Ray Biondi

Krupa (1945–6) she embarked on a solo career that was interrupted periodically by problems stemming from heroin addiction. In the mid-1950s O'Day recorded several albums for Verve which were very well received. She made a sensational appearance at the Newport Jazz Festival in 1958 (captured in the film *Jazz on a Summer's Day*) and thereafter worked regularly in clubs both in the USA and elsewhere. In 1964 she made the first of several tours of Japan, and around 1970 she first toured Europe. In 1972 she established Anita O'Day Records. By the middle of the decade her career was again floundering, but a successful residency at Hopper's in New York (1976) helped to re-establish her popularity, as did her autobiography (co-written with G. Eells), *High Times, Hard Times* (New York, 1981, rev. 2/1989), which vividly chronicles the harsh experiences of her life and her sense for the outrageous.

In the early 1980s O'Day formed another recording company and label, Emily, in partnership with Elaine Poole and John Poole (who played drums with her from the late 1950s through the 1980s). In 1985 she gave a concert at Carnegie Hall to celebrate her fiftieth year in jazz. Later she made new recordings (1989, 1991) and further tours of both Europe (1988, when she appeared at the New Morning in Paris) and Japan. She continued to perform in clubs in the USA (most notably for a residency at Michael's Pub in New York from May into July 1989) until December 1996, when severe consequences from the mistreatment of a broken arm led to her being hospitalized for more than two years. O'Day resumed working in May 1999, singing in Los Angeles at the Jazz Bakery and the Atlas Supper Club before giving a successful performance at the JVC Jazz Festival in New York. Later that year she celebrated her eightieth birthday with a concert at the Palladium in Hollywood.

O'Day excels at improvisation; whether scat singing or skillfully interpreting a song text, she allows herself all the liberties of instrumental jazz performance in refashioning a popular song. Her performance of *Tea for Two* in *Jazz on a Summer's Day* is one of the greatest moments of jazz on film, as she dances vocally around the melody, conveying an irrepressible sense of swing and somehow remaining utterly relaxed even in the face of a furiously fast tempo.

SELECTED RECORDINGS

As leader: *Anita* (1955, Verve 2000); *Pick Yourself Up* (1956, Verve 2043); *Anita O'Day Sings the Winners* (1958, Verve 8283); *Anita O'Day Swings Cole Porter with Billy May* (1959, Verve 2118); *Cool Heat* (1959, Verve 8312); *All the Sad Young Men* (1961, Verve 68442); *Live at Mingos* (1976, Emily 11579); *Mello'Day* (1979, GNP 2126); *Live at the City* (1979, Emily 102479); *A Song for You* (c1984, Emily 83084); *Anita O'Day at Vine Street Live* (1991, DRG 8435)

As sideman with G. Krupa: Let me off uptown (1941, OK 6210)

SELECTED FILMS AND VIDEOS

Let Me off Uptown (1942); Thanks for the Boogie Ride (1942); Artistry in Rhythm (1944); Cool and Groovy (1956); The Gene Krupa Story [Drum Crazy: the Gene Krupa Story] (1959); Jazz on a Summer's Day (1960); Zigzag [False Witness] (1970); The Outfit (1973); Anita O'Day in Tokyo '63 (1985)

BIBLIOGRAPHY

D. Cerulli: "Anita's Back," *DB*, xxiii/18 (1956), 13

H. Lucraft: "Anita Admits: I'm a Nut," *MM* (1 July 1961), 7

A. Surpin: "Dawn of a New O'Day," *DB*, xxxvi/23 (1969), 16

L. Feather: *The Pleasures of Jazz: Leading Performers on their Lives, their Music, their Contemporaries* (New York, 1976), 120

H. Howard: "Anita O'Day," *JP*, xxx/6 (1980), 4

L. Gourse: *Louis' Children: American Jazz Singers* (New York, 1984), 234

A. Duncan: "Anita O'Day Can Still Command a Band – and an Audience," *Christian Science Monitor* (18 June 1985), 29

W. Friedwald: "Anita O'Day: What a Difference a Day Makes," *The Wire*, no.23 (1986), 28

C. Deffaa: "At 70, and in her Prime: Anita O'Day," *JT* (1989), Nov, 19

A. Duncan: "Better-than-ever Comeback for Anita O'Day," *Christian Science Monitor* (3 July 1989)

S. Holden: "From Anita O'Day, Hints of Many Hurdles," *New York Times* (8 June 1989)

J. Wolfer: *Anita O'Day: an Exploratory Discography* (Zephyrhills, FL, 1990)

A. Defosse: "Anita O'Day," *Revue d'esthétique*, no.19 (1991), 36

H. Reich: "At 73, Anita O'Day Keeps Busy on the Road," *Chicago Tribune* (12 Nov 1992)

C. M. Peyton: "Jazz Legend Anita O'Day: a Portrait of Perseverance," *Chicago Tribune* (2 July 1999)

B. Donaldson: "Interview with Alan Eichler," *Marge Hofacre's Jazz News* (2000), spring, sec.II, 32

——: "Interview with Anita O'Day," *Marge Hofacre's Jazz News* (2000), spring, sec.II, 32

BK

Odeon. Record label. Named after a theater in Paris, it was established for issue in France and Germany by the International Talking Machine Company, then acquired in 1910 by Carl Lindström. From the early 1920s Odeon was used to release much important jazz (drawn mostly from OKeh) in France, Belgium, Germany, Spain, Italy, Scandinavia, and parts of South America; this role was maintained after 1925, when Lindström sold his interests to Columbia International, Ltd., and after 1931, when the latter company merged with the Gramophone Company to form EMI. Among Odeon's most notable material were two recordings by Carroll Dickerson on which Louis Armstrong played; these were released in Argentina, though never put out by OKeh in the USA. The Odeon Swing Music Series, first issued on German Odeon in 1937–9 and later sold throughout occupied Europe during World War II, ran to 92 discs and contained much fine jazz. There was also a designated swing series on Italian Odeon. After 1945 the label remained in use for jazz reissues in France, Japan, and Germany, and in 1978 a scheme was set up to re-release material from the Swing Music Series.

In the USA the label name was used by the General Phonograph Corporation, at first for classical music, then, in 1929, for a series intended for sale on the West Coast. This contained material by many of OKeh's most important musicians (including the Casa Loma Orchestra), often in versions specially recorded without the vocal part; these were presumably aimed at the Spanish-speaking community. This series was discontinued in 1931.

BIBLIOGRAPHY

H. Avery: "The American Parlophone–Odeon Series," *The Jazzfinder*, i/12 (1948), 13

H. Sagawe: "A Glimpse of the Past, 14: the German Odeon Swing Series, 1937–39," *Sv*, no.25 (1969), 14

B. Rust: *The American Record Label Book* (New Rochelle, NY, 1978), 210

A. Sutton: *Directory of American Disc Record Brands and Manufacturers, 1891–1943* (Westport, CT, and London, 1994), 106

P. Martland: *Since Records Began: EMI, the First 100 Years* (London, and Portland, OR, 1997)

H. Rye: "Italian Rhythm Style," *Names & Numbers*, no.9 (1999), 9; "Additional Notes," no.10 (1999), 15

P. Vernon: "Odeon Records: their Ethnic Output," *Musical Traditions Internet Magazine CD-ROM* (Stroud, England, 2000 [*recte* 1999]), article MT003

HOWARD RYE

Odin. Record company and label. It was established in May 1981 by the Norsk jazzforbund to produce recordings of Norwegian jazz, in particular music that would not be issued by a commercial record company.

O'Farrill, Chico [Arturo, Sr.] (*b* Havana, 28 Oct 1921; *d* New York, 27 June 2001). Cuban composer, arranger, and trumpeter. He discovered big-band jazz at boarding school in Florida (1936–9). Later he studied composition in Havana, and in the mid-1940s he played with a band led by Armando Romeu and with his own group. In 1948 he moved to New York, where he wrote music for Benny Goodman, Stan Kenton, Machito and Charlie Parker, and Dizzy Gillespie; in the early 1950s he formed his own band – which played at Birdland – toured the USA, and recorded as a leader the album *Jazz* (1951–2, Clef 132). In 1957 O'Farrill moved to Mexico. He wrote a suite for Art Farmer (1959), and in 1962-3 he gave concerts in Mexico City. After returning to the USA in 1965 he settled in New York and worked as an arranger and music director for CBS on the television program "Festival of the Lively Arts"; among the musicians who took part were Count Basie, Gillespie, Gerry Mulligan, and Stan Getz. In 1965–6 O'Farrill wrote arrangements of pop songs for albums by Basie, and in the latter year Clark Terry recorded an album of his Latin-jazz scores. From the 1970s he was less active in jazz, but he wrote pieces for Gato Barbieri and Kenton (both 1974) and a band led by Gillespie and Machito (1975). Later he participated in a concert by "Dizzy's Dream Band" broadcast on television as "Jazz in America: Lincoln Center, New York" (1982). After years of studio work, he led a 17-piece Afro-Cuban orchestra at the Blue Note, New York, in August 1994. The following year he made a new recording as a leader, *Pure Emotion*, and was commissioned by Wynton Marsalis to write a trumpet concerto. From 1998 until his retirement in March 2001 O'Farrill conducted his big band for a weekly engagement at Birdland in New York.

His son, the pianist Arturo O'Farrill, Jr. (*b* Mexico City, 22 June 1960), performed with Carla Bley (1979–82), Earl McIntyre (1980–91), Tony Dagradi (1981), Lester Bowie (1990–91), and Howard Johnson's Gravity (1990–91), among others. He was pianist and musical director for his father's big band from 1991 (recording with it in 1995), and he also deputized for Larry Willis in Jerry Gonzalez's Fort Apache Band.

Oral history material in *DSI* (JOHP).

Principal publisher: Camerica.

RECORDED COMPOSITIONS

(all arranged by O'Farrill)

As leader: on *Pure Emotion* (1995, Mlst. 9239-2), Campina

Recorded by others: B. Goodman: Undercurrent Blues (1949, Cap. 15409); S. Kenton: Cuban Episode (1950, Cap. 28000); Machito: *Afro-Cuban Jazz Suite* (1950, Clef 505); on D. Gillespie: *Afro* (1954, Norg. 1003), Manteca Suite; on D. Gillespie and Machito: *Afro-Cuban Jazz Moods* (1975, Pablo 2310771), Oro, incienso y mirra

BIBLIOGRAPHY

FeatherE; *Feather '60s*; *Feather-Gitler '70s*

S. Woolley: "The Spanish Tinge," *JJI*, xxxviii/7 (1985), 8

D. Gordon: "Fanning the Cubop Flame," *JT*, xxv/10 (1995), 46

J. Macnie: "Tradin' Fours: Thirty Years in the Making," *DB*, lxii/12 (1995), 48

Obituary, B. Ratliff, *New York Times* (29 June 2001)

CRISTÓBAL DÍAZ AYALA/BK

Offbeat. Any beat of the bar other than the first or downbeat; *see* Beat, esp. §4(i).

Off-note. A note played slightly out of tune (usually flat) for expressive effect; the term is sometimes used as a synonym for "blue note" (*see* Blue note (i)).

Oganesyan, Tatevik. *See* Hovanesian, datevik.

Ogerman, Claus [Ogermann, Claus [Klaus]] (*b* Ratibor, Germany [now Racibórz, Poland], 29 April 1930). Composer, conductor, and pianist. After studying classical piano, theory, and conducting in Nuremberg he played with Kurt Edelhagen (1952) and performed and recorded with Max Greger (1952–7). In 1955 he began to write arrangements for recordings. He went to the USA in 1959, settling permanently in New York (and later taking Amercan citizenship), and established himself as a successful commercial arranger who also composed classical music; he earned some critical acclaim for his work on jazz albums, notably those with Antonio Carlos Jobim (1963), Bill Evans (ii) (1965), and Oscar Peterson (1969). Ogerman formed two music publishing companies and also produced albums for such popular performers as Caterina Valente. In the 1970s he turned away from commercial writing and began to compose more classical and jazz music, including *Symbiosis* for jazz piano and orchestra (1975). After 1979 he ceased altogether to work as an arranger and devoted himself exclusively to his own compositions in the European art music tradition, but he has occasionally written scores for recordings by Michael Brecker (1982, early 1990s). A collection of his complete printed works is in the music division of the Deutsche Bibliothek in Berlin (*see* Libraries and archives, §2); the principal publishers of his works are CJC, Ebony, Glamorous Music, Helios, and Kendor.

SELECTED ARRANGEMENTS

Recorded by others: A. C. Jobim: *Antonio Carlos Jobim, the Composer of "Desafinado," Plays* (1963, Verve 68547); B. Evans: *Bill Evans Trio with Symphony Orchestra* (1965, Verve 68640); O. Peterson: *Motions and Emotions* (1969, MPS 15251); M. Brecker: *Cityscape* (1982, WB 23698)

BIBLIOGRAPHY

Feather '60s; *Feather–Gitler '70s*

G. Lees: "The Real Claus Ogerman Stands up," *High Fidelity/Musical America*, xxv/10 (1975), 19

STEVEN STRUNK

Ogun. Record company and label. The company was established in London in 1973 by Harry Miller, his wife Hazel Miller, and Keith Beal. By 1998 it had issued 30 LPs and 13 CDs. The repertory consists mainly of free jazz and improvised music. Much of the material is by expatriate South Africans, notably by members of the Brotherhood of Breath and the Blue Notes, but the company has also recorded British musicians such as Trevor Watts, Evan Parker, and SOS and the work of some European players (including Irène Schweizer) and Americans. In 1977 Ogun released the only album Miller made as the leader of his own group, Isipingo, which featured the playing of Louis Moholo and Keith Tippett. In 1992 the label recorded *Spirits Rejoice* (Ogun 101), a 20-piece ensemble celebration by two generations of British-based improvisers – among them Kenny Wheeler, Paul Rutherford, Parker, Tippett, Moholo, and Django Bates – of the massive contribution made to jazz by such expatriate South African musicians as Chris McGregor and Johnny Dyani, who were forced into exile in the early 1960s. Proceeds from the sale of the album went to the Spirits Rejoice Trust, a fund to help support and nurture young musical talent in South Africa.

SIMON ADAMS

O'Higgins, Dave [David Charles] (*b* Birmingham, England, 1 Sept 1964). English saxophonist. As a child he played classical trumpet and piano and rock drums, and when he was 16 he took up alto saxophone. He was first inspired by cross-over players such as Wilton Felder and Grover Washington, but later discovered Charlie Parker, who became a major and continuing influence on his playing. He moved to London in 1983 and studied music at City University, though he left in 1985 without a degree. From 1983 to 1986 he played and recorded with the National Youth Jazz Orchestra. He went on to lead his own small bands, and played regularly with Cleo Laine and John Dankworth (from 1986), Roadside Picnic (1987–92), Gang of Three (1988–9), Sax Appeal (1988–96), Jason Rebello (1990), Clark Tracey (1994–6), Itchy Fingers (1993–5), and Jim Mullen (1992–6). Although he came to notice as a fluent post-Coltrane tenor player, in the 1990s O'Higgins has worked in a number of mainstream situations, including, from 1995, Martin Taylor's bands. He also co-led the South African quintet Short Attention Span with Johnny Fourie and his son the pianist Sean Fourie.

SELECTED RECORDINGS

(recorded for EFZ unless otherwise indicated)

As leader: *All Good Things* (1992, 1002); *Beats Working for a Living* (1994, 1009); *Under the Stone* (1995, 1016); *The Secret Ingredient* (1996, 1020); *The Grinder's Monkey* (1999, Short Fuse 001)

As sideman: J. Mullen: *Soundbites* (1992, 1003); M. Taylor: *Spirit of Django* (1994, Linn 030); J. Siegel and P. Robson: *Partisans* (1996, 1021)

BIBLIOGRAPHY

CarrJ; ChiltonB

T. Herrington: "Dave O'Higgins: Three's a Gang," *Wire*, no.58–9 (1988), 46

M. Hrebeniak: "After the Picnic," *Jazz: the Magazine*, no.17 (1993), 14

S. Bowerman: "Dave O'Higgins: Straight Ahead," *Straight No Chaser*, no.36 (1996), 46

MARK GILBERT

Ohno [Ono], **Shunzo** (*b* Gifu, Japan, 22 March 1949). Japanese trumpeter. After moving to Tokyo he worked with the alto saxophonist Keiichiro Ebihara and his Lobsters (from 1968), Takeshi Inomata's group Sound Limited, and the group Soul Media, led by the tenor saxophonist Jiro Inagaki. From 1971 to 1973 he performed in George Otsuka's quintet, and in New York from 1973 to 1975 he was a member of Art Blakey's Jazz Messengers. He then played with Roy Haynes and Norman Connors, recorded as a leader (from 1975), and with Machito recorded two albums (1982) and performed at the North Sea Jazz Festival in The Hague. In 1983 he became a sideman in Gil Evans's orchestra, and between 1985 and 1987 he made tours of Japan with Herbie Hancock, Wayne Shorter, and Larry Coryell in the band Super Sounds. After injuring his lips in an automobile accident in 1989 he was obliged to retire for more than a year. However, he appeared in Buster Williams's quintet at the Village Vanguard, New York, in late summer 1990 and early summer 1991. Ohno continued to work with Williams until 1994, but from 1995 he was again forced into retirement, as he fought against throat cancer. He played with Junko Onishi at the club Body and Soul in Tokyo in December 1997, toured with Shorter and the Fantastic Five in November 1998, and toured Europe and the USA as a member of Coryell's re-formed Eleventh House in 1999. The following year he toured Japan as a leader and continued to play with Shorter in the USA. Ohno has a rich, warm, brilliant tone; he is perhaps best known for his recording of his own composition *Bubbles*.

SELECTED RECORDINGS

As leader: *Something's Coming* (1975, EW 7011); *Bubbles* (1975, EW 8028); *Quarter Moon* (1979, EB SKS8008); *Anteress* (1980, EB K28P6013); *Manhattan Blue* (1986, EB K32Y6168); *Maya* (1991, Three Blind Mice 5037); *Live '94 – Take Off* (1994, Crown CRCJ9128)

As sideman with G. Evans: *Live at Sweet Basil*, i–ii (1984, EB K23P6355–6, K19P6421–2); *Bud and Bird* (1986, EB K32Y6171)

BIBLIOGRAPHY

<http://www.btinternet.com/~didcot/Biography.htm> (2000) [incl. discography]

YOZO IWANAMI/BK

Oida, Toshio (*b* Berlin, 21 Feb 1925). Japanese singer. The first Japanese jazz singer after World War II, he rose to popularity after joining the Blue Coats orchestra in 1949. He also acted and sang in films and the musical theater. In 1962 he performed with Chico Hamilton, and in 1989 he recorded with Al Grey and Bobby Tucker among his sidemen. Oida remained active in the 1990s, when he led the Japan Just Jazz All Stars in New York (1994) and sang in Los Angeles (1997).

SELECTED RECORDINGS

It Was a Very Good Year (1976, Three Blind Mice 64); *The Longest Dream* (1981, Express ETJ85020); *Goodnight Sweetheart* (1989, King 292E6047)

KAZUNORI SUGIYAMA

Oishi, Manabu (*b* Yokohama, Japan, 2 April 1963). Japanese pianist and keyboard player. He began on electronic organ at the age of eight and changed to piano when he was 18. Later he performed and recorded with numerous groups, including those of the alto saxophonist Hidefumi Toki (from 1990), Motohiko Hino (1994–6), Yoshio Suzuki (from 1995), Kimiko Itoh, the singer Yasuko Agawa, and the Brazilian singer Joyce, among others. In 1996 Oishi formed his own trio.

SELECTED RECORDINGS

As leader: *Tears Rained Down* (1997, Meldac 30105)

As sideman: H. Toki: *The Good Life* (1993, Fun House 2150); M. Hino: *Hip Bone* (1994, Fun House 2190); Y. Suzuki: *The East Bounce Collection* (1997, Video Arts 1015)

KAZUNORI SUGIYAMA

Okegwo, Ugonna (*b* London, 15 March 1962). British double bass player. He studied privately with the double bass player Jay Oliver and Walter Norris (1987–8). In 1988 he performed and recorded with Charles Tolliver in Berlin. While attending Long Island University, New York (BFA 1994), he began working with Leon Parker (from 1990), Jacky Terrasson (from 1992), with whom he toured internationally, and Tom Harrell (from 1996). He also played with Tolliver again (1991) and with Jon Hendricks (1992–4).

SELECTED RECORDINGS

As sideman: J. Hendricks: *Boppin' at the Blue Note* (1993, Telarc Jazz 83320); J. Terrasson: *Jacky Terrasson* (1994, BN B21Z-29531); *Reach* (1995, BN B21Z-35739)

GK

OKeh. Record company and label. The label was established by the General Phonograph Corporation, an enterprise set up in New York in 1916 (as the Otto Heinemann Phonograph Corporation) to manage the American operations of Carl Lindström's German company Odeon; it was launched in September 1918. Jazz recordings commenced around two months later with items by the New Orleans Jazz Band; these discs were vertically cut. Issue of laterally cut records began in February 1920, and that same month Perry Bradford persuaded OKeh's agent for artists and repertory, Fred Hagar, to organize sessions by Mamie Smith. The resulting

Label for "Cake-walking Babies from Home," recorded by Clarence Williams's Blue Five for OKeh (1925)

recordings established OKeh's primacy in the field, which was reinforced in summer 1921 by the setting up of a specific race series, the 8000s (until 1923 called the Colored Catalog). With Clarence Williams supervising artists and repertory in New York and Richard M. Jones undertaking the same role in Chicago, this became an extremely important jazz catalogue. It included material by Williams himself (from 1921, notably many important recordings with the Blue Five from 1923), King Oliver (1923), Louis Armstrong's Hot Five and Hot Seven (1925–9), Lonnie Johnson (1925–32), and many others. Searches for talent in other cities brought to the label such ensembles as Bennie Moten's band, which recorded several times for OKeh between 1923 and 1925. Items by Frankie Trumbauer, Bix Beiderbecke, and Eddie Lang were issued in a general popular series.

The company's activities were little affected when it was taken over by Columbia in 1926; Heinemann ran OKeh as a new subsidiary, the OKeh Phonograph Corporation, and maintained a largely independent program of recording. Control ultimately passed to ARC–BRC in August 1934. Later that year the 8000 series was discontinued; of the many race series inaugurated in the 1920s this was one of the most prolific and the longest lasting, having run to almost a thousand issues. ARC–BRC then dropped the name OKeh, but CBS, which acquired the company in 1938, revived it and continued the numerical series of the Vocalion label, pressing early issues anew with OKeh labels. In the early 1950s, when artists and repertory were directed by Danny Kessler, the label became CBS's main outlet for rhythm-and-blues, but a jazz catalogue was maintained that included work by Wild Bill Davis and Red Saunders. In later years the label has occasionally been used by CBS's successors for reissues.

BIBLIOGRAPHY

Okeh Race Records (New York, n.d. [?1924]/*R*1976) [*R*1976 is a facs. of Clarence Williams's annotated copy]
Okeh Race Records: the Blue Book of Blues (New York, n.d. [?1927]/*R*1976)
R. M. W. Dixon and J. Godrich: *Recording the Blues* (London, 1970)
R. D. Kinkle: "Okeh Numerical List," "Vocalion–Okeh Numerical List," *The Complete Encyclopedia of Popular Music and Jazz, 1900–1950* (New Rochelle, NY, and Westport, CT, 1974), iv, 2123, 2255
B. Rust: *The American Record Label Book* (New Rochelle, NY, 1978), 212
A. Shaw: "Groove 20: Danny Kessler and Okeh Records," *Honkers and Shouters: the Golden Years of Rhythm and Blues* (New York, 1978), 445
A. Sutton: *Directory of American Disc Record Brands and Manufacturers, 1891–1943* (Westport, CT, and London, 1994), 107, 201, 217
W. Agenant: *Columbia 78 rpm Record Listing 20001 thru 21571: plus OKeh Records 18001 thru 18059* (Zephyrhills, FL, 1996)
R. M. W. Dixon, J. Godrich, and H. Rye: *Blues & Gospel Records, 1890–1943* (Oxford, England, rev. and enlarged 4/1997), xxvii
P. Martland: *Since Records Began: EMI, the First 100 Years* (London, and Portland, OR, 1997)

HOWARD RYE

Oki, Itaru (*b* Kobe, Japan, 10 Sept 1941). Japanese trumpeter and flugelhorn player. He grew up in a musical family and learned *koto* from the age of ten; his mother was a master teacher of that traditional instrument. In 1955 he began to study trumpet in a brass band in high school, and some time afterwards he took lessons from Fumio Nanri. From 1959 he played in a dixieland band while studying architecture at Osaka Industrial University. Around 1956, when Kenny Dorham was performing in Osaka, Oki discovered bop and briefly studied with Dorham; later he went to Tokyo to study with Sadao Watanabe. He played in groups led by the double bass player Nobusuke Miyamoto (1965), the pianist Yoku Tamura (1965–8), Kosuke Mine (1968–70), and the tenor saxophonist Akio Nishimura (1970–73), and formed the group ESSG with Masahiko Togashi, Masahiko Sato, and the saxophonist Mototeru Takagi (1966). During the same period he wrote music for films and the theater, and in 1969 he performed at the International Jazz Festival Ljubljana.

Oki settled in Paris in 1974. He played free jazz with Takashi Kako and others in the group Message from Japan (1974–6), with Kako's quintet (which recorded in 1976), with Noah Howard's quartet (1975–8, recording in 1977), in Michel Pilz's small groups (recording in 1978 and 1983), and in Alan Silva's Celestrial Communication Orchestra (from as early as 1978, when Oki recorded with the orchestra, to 1990). Elsewhere in Europe he worked with such musicians as Art Farmer, Maynard Ferguson, Lee Konitz, Sam Rivers, and Steve Lacy. He formed a duo with the pianist Thangodeï in 1987, toured Germany with Sato and the dancer Tadashi Endo in 1989, and joined the group World Residents in 1992. Oki doubles on various Japanese, Indian, and African flutes, and in 1982 he began designing and playing fanciful brass instruments (e.g., a trumpet with three bells and a hybrid trumpet-flugelhorn).

SELECTED RECORDINGS

As leader: *Satsujin kyoshitsu* (Homicidal classroom; 1970, Mobys 13); *Genso note* (Fantasy note; 1975, Offbeat 1010); *One Year: Afternoon and Evening* (1978, FMP 0720); *Concert with Strings* (1999, What's New 1004)

BIBLIOGRAPHY

P. Carles, A. Clergeat, and J.-L. Comolli: *Dictionnaire du jazz* (Paris, 1988, rev. and enlarged 2/1994)
"Itaru Oki: Surrealist of the Trumpet," *Brass Bulletin*, no.68 (1989), 75
H. Kumpf: "Japanisches Tanztheater mit Trompete," *JP*, xlii/4 (1993), 33

KAZUNORI SUGIYAMA, BK

Okka Disk. Record company and label founded in Chicago in 1993 or 1994 by Bruno Johnson. Its first issue was a recording of duos by Fred Anderson and Steve McCall made in January 1980. Thereafter it made and issued new recordings of numerous musicians involved in or affiliated with the Chicago free-jazz community, including Anderson, Peter Brötzmann, Hamid Drake, Georg Gräwe, Mats Gustafsson, and Ken Vandermark. It also released a recording by Evan Parker as an unaccompanied soloist.

BIBLIOGRAPHY

A. Cohen: "Okka Disk Recognizes Chicago's Free-jazz Gems," *DB*, lxi/12 (1994), 11
<http://www.dpo.uab.edu/~moudry/discog/okkadisk.htm> (2000)
<http://www.okkadisk.com/> (2000)
<http://www.shef.ac.uk/misc/rec/ps/efi/labels/okka/cokka.html> (2000)

GK

Oklahoma. Nickname of HAL SINGER.

Okoshi, Tiger [Toru] (*b* Ashita, Japan, 21 March 1950). Japanese trumpeter and leader. Self-taught, he took up trumpet at the age of 11. While attending Kansei Gakuin University he performed with Terumasa Hino and Sadao Watanabe, among others. He led a quintet at a number of clubs in 1971, and then following his graduation he married in 1972 and traveled across the USA on his honeymoon; having arrived on the East Coast he chose to remain in Boston to attend the Berklee College of Music. Graduating in 1975, he toured the USA with Buddy Rich's orchestra later that same year and in 1976 began teaching at Berklee. Okoshi accompanied Tony Bennett (1976), toured worldwide and recorded (1978) with Gary Burton, and played with George Russell and Dave Liebman. During the same period he founded his own group, Tiger's Baku, which made its first recording in 1980; his sidemen at various times included Mike Stern, Bill Frisell, Vinnie Colaiuta, Tommy Campbell, and Kermit Driscoll. In 1983 he performed and recorded with Bob Moses, and later, while continuing to lead Tiger's Baku and to teach at Berklee, he worked with Dave Grusin (1985) and Pat Metheny (1990–92).

SELECTED RECORDINGS

(recorded for JVC unless otherwise indicated)

As leader: *Tiger's Baku* (1980–81, VICJ28009); *Echoes of a Note: Tribute to Louis Armstrong* (1993, VICJ166); *Two Sides to Every Story* (1993, VICJ204); *Color of Soil* (1998, VICJ60209)
As sideman with G. Burton: *Times Square* (1978, ECM 1111)

BIBLIOGRAPHY

H. Grey: "Hearsay: Echoes of a Big Fat Note," *JT*, xxiii/7 (1993), 11
<http://www.impr.com/tiger/index_e.html> (2000)
<http://www.yamaha.com/band/ARTIST/trumpet/okoshi.htm> (2000)

KAZUNORI SUGIYAMA, BK

Okoun, Mikhail (Moiseevich) (*b* Moscow, 4 April 1946). Russian pianist, leader, and educator. He trained as a mechanical engineer at the Moscow Textile Institute, completing his studies in 1969, and a decade later he graduated from a music college in the city of Elektrostal, near Moscow. Having first led a student group (1964–7), he participated in the activities of the Moscow Association of Musical Ensembles (1967–75), played in German Luk'yanov's jazz studio (1970–71), and gave concerts at the Moscow Studio of Musical Improvisations as the co-leader of a quartet with Nikolay Panov (1971–7). From 1975 to 1978 he worked in the State Variety Orchestra of the Russian Federation under the leadership of Leonid Utyosov, after which he served as a member of Luk'yanov's ensemble Kadans (1978–82). In 1983 Okoun began teaching at the Gnesin Institute and joined Oleg Lundstrem's orchestra; he also appeared as an unaccompanied soloist, and, from the 1990s, as the leader of a trio.

SELECTED RECORDINGS

Duos with E. Gomez: on *Live in Moscow* (1992, B&W Music 038), Alice in Wonderland, Stella by Starlight, Someday my prince will come
As leader: *Jazz at the Old Fortress '94* (Mel. 60-00523)
As sideman: G. Luk'yanov: *Ivanushka-durachok* (1982, Mel. 17435004); *Way to Olymp* (1984, Mel. 20875003); O. Lundstrem: *V stile sving* (1986, Mel. C60 23709006)

SERGEY BELICHENKO

Okuchi, Junichiro (*b* Tokyo, 5 July 1949). Japanese pianist and leader. He took piano lessons from the ages of five to 19, began to play jazz and Brazilian music, and turned professional in 1974 after graduating from Tokyo Institute of Technology. In 1979 he made his first recording as a leader, with a quartet featuring Frank Wess. Later he led a quintet (1989–90) whose members included Issei Igarashi and Atsushi Ikeda. In 1992 Okuchi established his own trio and joined Kosuke Mine's quintet. He also serves as accompanist and arranger for the Brazilian-Japanese singer Lisa Ohno.

KAZUNORI SUGIYAMA

Okudaira, Shingo (*b* Tokyo, 11 Aug 1966). Japanese drummer and leader. He started playing drums at the age of three, when he was given a miniature set as a birthday gift. While living in Kenya from ages five to eight he worked professionally as a musician at the Nairobi National Theater for a month. After returning to Japan he studied drums privately (1975–8). He was featured on various radio and TV programs as a child prodigy and gave his first recital in Tokyo when he was 11; that same year he recorded his first album as a leader. In 1978 he accompanied Dizzy Gillespie and Sonny Stitt at the Monterey Jazz Festival in Japan. He then worked with Toshiyuki Honda (1978–84), Mikio Masuda (1984–7), and Fumio Karashima (1987–91). Having graduated from Hosei University in 1987, he moved in 1991 to New York, where he later performed with Kenny Garrett, Don Friedman, and Ron McClure, among many others. Okudaira became a member of Carlos Garnett's quartet in 1995 and the group led by the saxophonist Tim Armacost in 1996, and in the latter year he formed his own quartet, Shungo.

SELECTED RECORDINGS

As leader: *Kilifi* (1995, King KICJ252); *Maconde* (1996, King KICJ292); *Alisema* (1998, Mediaring 1011)
As sideman: F. Karashima: *Transparent* (1987, Pol. H33P20149); M. Masuda: *Smokin' Night* (1987, JVC 1111); K. Fujiwara: *Modern Bass* (1996, King KICJ284); C. Garnett: *Fuego en mi alma (Fire in my soul)* (1996, HighNote 7001)

KAZUNORI SUGIYAMA

Old and New Dreams. Quartet formed in 1976 by Don Cherry (trumpet), Dewey Redman (tenor saxophone), Charlie Haden (double bass), and Ed Blackwell (drums), all of whom had been sidemen with Ornette Coleman. In an era when jazz fusion was the predominant style, they came together to celebrate and re-create the style of Coleman's classic acoustic groups. The quartet toured and recorded into the early 1980s and reunited in 1987 in Atlanta at a festival in Blackwell's honor.

BIBLIOGRAPHY

B. Blumenthal: "Children of Ornette Coleman: Cross Country Tour of Old and New Dreams," *RS* (31 May 1979), 24
G. Giddins: "Riffs: Old and New Dreams Change the Century," *VV* (2 April 1979), 57
C. Silvert: "Old and New Dreams," *DB*, xlvii/6 (1980), 16
V. Wilmer: "The Discreet Charm of Blowing Free," *Time Out* (9–15 May 1980), 14

BK

Oleszkiewicz [Oles], **Darek** (*b* Wrocław, Poland, 20 Feb 1963). Polish double bass player. After working in Poland with Jan Wróblewski, Zbigniew Namysłowski, and Tomasz Szukalski he moved in 1988 to Los Angeles, where his surname came to be known in abbreviated form, as Oles. He studied from 1989 at the California Institute of the Arts and remained there as a faculty member after graduating in 1992. The following year he became a founding member of a cooperative group, the L.A. Jazz Quartet, which mainly performed locally but toured France in 1998. He also joined James Newton's quartet and groups led by Kei Akagi and by the drummer Gerry Gibbs. As a freelance Oleszkiewicz appeared in the studio, in concert, and at clubs with such musicians as Joe Lovano, Bennie Maupin, Ravi Coltrane, Scott Hamilton, Marcus Printup, Brian Lynch, Tim Hagans, Art Farmer, Arturo Sandoval, Billy Childs, Joe LaBarbera, Larance Marable, Terri Lyne Carrington, and Albert "Tootie" Heath; he was reunited with Wróblewski for a performance in West Hollywood in January 1999. He toured Europe and the USA in a duo or trio with Brad Mehldau from 1997 to 1999 and in Charles Lloyd's quartet (with John Abercrombie and Billy Higgins) from 1998 to 2000; in this last year he appeared with Lloyd's quartet on PBS television. As of 2000, Oleszkiewicz had recorded more than 40 albums.

SELECTED RECORDINGS

As sideman with L.A. Jazz Quartet: *Astarte* (1994, Gowi 13); *Look to the East* (1995, Naxos Jazz 86009-2); *Family Song* (1998, Not Two 705-2); *Conversation Piece* (1999, Naxos Jazz 86045-2)

As sideman with others: James Carney: *Fables from the Aqueduct* (1993, Jacaranda 71001); Traveling Birds: *Traveling Birds Quintet* (1993, Polonia 030); J. Newton: *Suite for Frida Kahlo* (1994, Audioquest 1023); P. Baron: *Take One* (1995, Polonia 049); G. Gibbs: *The Thrasher* (1995, Qwest 9-46228-2); P. Baron: *Bogurodzica* (1999, Universal Music Polska 159220-2)

BIBLIOGRAPHY

<http://www.calarts.edu/music/faculty_fr_cnt.htm> (2000)
<http://www.hnh.com/intro/186045.htm> (2000)

BK

Oliva, Hernán (*b* Valparaíso, Chile, 4 July 1913; *d* Buenos Aires, 17 June 1988). Chilean violinist. A self-taught musician, he played popular music in Chile before moving in 1935 to Argentina. While a member of René Cóspito's orchestra (1935–40) he studied violin with Jascha Bergosky (1937), and during the following years he worked with Enrique Villegas (1940), Oscar Alemán (recording to 1943), and Ray Ventura's orchestra (1944). In 1945 he performed and recorded in a group led by Louis Vola that was modeled after the Quintette du Hot Club de France. Later he worked as a sideman (to 1955), as a leader (to 1967), and as a member of a swing quintet that made several recordings in the 1970s (including *El paso del tigre*, 1975, Redondel 10510, and *El violin del jazz*, 1978, Redondel 10523). He continued to perform into the late 1980s.

LAUREANO FERNÁNDEZ, OMAR GARCÍA BRUNELLI

Oliver, King [Joe] (*b* in or nr New Orleans, 11 May 1885; *d* Savannah, GA, 8/10 April 1938). Cornetist and bandleader. From about 1909 he played in brass bands and dance bands and in various small groups in New Orleans bars and cabarets; among these affiliations and venues were the Eagle Band (his first professional job), the Magnolia Band, the Original Superior Orchestra (in which he deputized for Bunk Johnson, *c*1910–12), Richard M. Jones's Four Hot Hounds (at the Abadie Cabaret), the band at Pete Lala's saloon (which at various times included Sidney Bechet and Lorenzo Tio, Jr.), the Olympia Band, Kid Ory's group, also at Pete Lala's (from 1914), and Ory's brass band. Early in 1918 he moved to Chicago (at which time he may have acquired his nickname), where he joined bands led by Bill Johnson (i) at the Royal Gardens and Lawrence Duhé at the Dreamland Café; the latter group served as the White Sox Booster Band at the infamous "Black Sox" baseball World Series of October 1919.

In January 1920 Oliver began to lead his own band, consisting of Honore Dutrey, Johnny Dodds, Lil Hardin, Ed

King Oliver's Creole Jazz Band, Chicago, 1923: (back, left to right) Honore Dutrey (trombone), Baby Dodds (drums), Oliver (cornet), and Bill Johnson (i) (banjo); (front) Louis Armstrong (soprano trombone; also known as the slide cornet), Lil Hardin (piano), and Johnny Dodds (clarinet)

Garland, and Minor Hall; they worked at the Dreamland Café (to 1 a.m.) and then continued through the night at the Pekin Cabaret (to 6 a.m.). The group left Chicago late in May 1921 and two weeks later began an engagement at the Pergola Dance Pavilion in San Francisco. While playing also at the California Theater and elsewhere, David Jones (i) and the violinist Jimmy Palao joined the band; Baby Dodds replaced Hall in September. Following a period when he struggled to obtain work, during which he appeared with Jelly Roll Morton's band in Los Angeles (April 1922), Oliver returned to Chicago and, with some of the same musicians, embarked on an engagement at Lincoln Gardens as King Oliver's Creole Jazz Band (June 1922). This group was joined a month later by the 20-year-old Louis Armstrong as second cornetist. With two cornets (Oliver and Armstrong), clarinet (Johnny Dodds), trombone (Dutrey), piano (Hardin), drums (Baby Dodds), and double bass and banjo (Bill Johnson (i)), Oliver began recording in April 1923 (see illustration) for Gennett in Richmond, Indiana, either during or shortly after a brief midwestern tour. Bud Scott had joined during the tour, but the band's first three historic sessions involved seven pieces, not eight (i.e., without Scott, and then with Scott in place of Johnson). After some further changes in membership the Creole Jazz Band disbanded, probably in December 1923. That year many young white jazz musicians had the opportunity to hear Oliver and his influential group, either on recordings or in person at Lincoln Gardens.

By late 1924, following a tour of the Midwest and Pennsylvania, Oliver's new band included two or three saxophones. In Chicago it played as the Dixie syncopators (February 1925 to March 1927), with Bob Shoffner, Ory, Barney Bigard, Albert Nicholas, Darnell Howard, Omer Simeon, Luis Russell, Scott, and Paul Barbarin among its sidemen. Soon after a brief but successful engagement at the Savoy Ballroom in New York (from May 1927) the members began to disperse and by autumn the group had disbanded, but Oliver stayed in New York, recording frequently with ad hoc orchestras. From 1930 to 1936 he toured widely, chiefly in the Midwest and upper South, with various ten- to 12-piece bands; he himself seldom performed during this period, and he made no further recordings after April 1931. He spent the final months of his life in Savannah retired from music.

Oliver is generally considered one of the most important musicians in the New Orleans style. Like other early New Orleans cornetists, he played in a relatively foursquare rhythm and clipped melodic style (contrasting with the deliberate irregularity of the younger Armstrong and his imitators) and had a repertory of expressive deviations of rhythm and pitch, some verging on theatrical novelty effects and others derived from blues vocal style (*see* Blues, §2). He frequently used timbre modifiers of various sorts and was especially renowned for his wa-wa effects, as in his famous three-chorus solo on *Dipper Mouth Blues* (1923), which was learned by rote by many trumpeters of the 1920s and 1930s and which, as *Sugar Foot Stomp*, became a jazz standard. (For a partial transcription of *Dipper Mouth Blues see* Harmony (i), ex.21.) As a soloist he may best be heard in a number of blues accompaniments, notably with Sippie Wallace.

In contrast to his near-contemporaries Freddie Keppard and Bunk Johnson, Oliver integrated his playing superbly with his ensemble and was an excellent leader; the Creole Jazz Band may have been successful largely because of the discipline he imposed on his musicians. Indeed, of the earlier New Orleans cornetists, only Oliver was extensively recorded in the 1920s with an outstanding ensemble, and the revival of New Orleans style, which began shortly after his death, owed much to the rediscovery of his early three dozen Creole Band recordings, which were internationally known by the 1940s. After 1924 the quality of his recordings declined, partly because of his recurrent tooth and gum ailments and partly because his style was at odds with that of his younger sidemen; but with a good orchestra he was capable of coherent and energetic playing even as late as 1930. Almost all of his recorded performances have been reissued.

Oliver's influence is difficult to assess: his playing during his New Orleans period (his best years, according to Souchon, 1960) was not recorded, and by 1925 his style had been largely superseded by Armstrong's. He had an obvious formative impact on Ellington's sideman Bubber Miley and perhaps on such white musicians as Muggsy Spanier; his mute tricks were copied by Johnny Dunn; and trumpeters such as Natty Dominique and Tommy Ladnier, who remained apart from Armstrong's influence, may have derived their styles in part from Oliver. The extent of Oliver's influence on Armstrong himself, though clearly audible and significant, has yet to be examined properly. Oliver is credited with many melodies on record labels and in copyright registrations, but it is not known how many of these he actually composed.

Oral history material in *LNT* [his wife Stella Oliver].

See also Trumpet, §3.

SELECTED RECORDINGS

Duos with J. R. Morton: King Porter/Tom Cat (1924, Aut. 617)

As leader of the Creole Jazz Band (all 1923): Just Gone/Canal Street Blues (Gen. 5133); Mandy Lee Blues/I'm going away to wear you off my mind (Gen. 5134); Chimes Blues/Froggie Moore (Gen. 5135); Weather Bird Rag/Dipper Mouth Blues (Gen. 5132); Snake Rag/High Society Rag (OK 4933); Sweet Lovin' Man/Sobbin' Blues (OK 4906); Where did you stay last night?/Dipper Mouth Blues (OK 4918); Alligator Hop/Krooked Blues (Gen. 5274); Zulu's Ball/ Working Man's Blues (Gen. 5275); Chattanooga Stomp/New Orleans Stomp (Col. 13003D); London Cafe Blues/Camp Meeting Blues (Col. 14003D); Buddy's Habit/Tears (Col. 40000); Riverside Blues/Working Man Blues (OK 40034); Sweet Baby Doll/Mabel's Dream (OK 8235)

As leader of other groups: Deep Henderson/Jackass Blues (1926, Voc. 1014); Someday, Sweetheart/Dead Man Blues (1926, Voc. 1059); Call of the Freaks/The Trumpet's Prayer (1929, Vic. 38039); St. James Infirmary/When you're smiling (1930, Vic. 22298)

As sideman: Butterbeans and Susie: Kiss Me Sweet (1924, OK 8182); S. Wallace: Morning Dove Blues/Every dog has his day (1925, OK 8205); Devil Dance Blues (1925, OK 8206); L. Miles: You're such a cruel papa to me/My Dif'rent Kind of Man (1928, Col. 14335D); V. Spivey: My Handy Man/Organ Grinder Blues (1928, OK 8615); Texas Alexander: 'Frisco Train Blues (1928, OK 8658)

BIBLIOGRAPHY

ChartersJ; *ChiltonW*

P. Jackson: "King Oliver: Daddy of the Trumpet," *Hot News*, i (1935), no.2, p.5; no.3, p.3

F. Ramsey, Jr.: "King Oliver," *Jazzmen*, ed. F. Ramsey, Jr., and C. E. Smith (New York, 1939/*R*1977)

E. Williams: "King Oliver and his Dixie Syncopators: Notes for a Discography," *Record Changer* (1944), Sept, 49

F. Moore: "King Oliver's Last Tour," *Jazz Record*, no.31 (1945), 10; repr. in *Selections from the Gutter: Jazz Portraits from "The Jazz Record"*, ed. A. Hodes and C. Hansen (Berkeley, CA, Los Angeles, and London, 1977), 86

R. Blesh: *Shining Trumpets: a History of Jazz* (New York, 1946, rev. and enlarged 2/1958/*R*1975)

L. Armstrong: "Joe Oliver is Still King," *Record Changer*, ix/6 (1950), 10; repr. in *Louis Armstrong in his own Words: Selected Writings*, ed. T. Brothers (New York and Oxford, England, 1999), 37

W. C. Allen and B. A. L. Rust: *King Joe Oliver* (Belleville, NJ, 1955)

E. Souchon: "King Oliver: a Very Personal Memoir," *JR*, iii/4 (1960), 6; repr. in *Jazz Panorama*, ed. M. Williams (New York and London, 1962/*R*1979)

M. Williams: *King Oliver* (London, 1960); repr. in *Kings of Jazz*, ed. S. Green (South Brunswick, NJ, and New York, 1978)
K. Kramer: "MCA Booked Oliver in 1924," *SL*, xi/11–12 (1961), 13
L. Gushee: "King Oliver," *Jazz Panorama*, ed. M. Williams (New York and London, 1962/*R*1979)
G. Schuller: *Early Jazz: its Roots and Musical Development* (New York, 1968)
"Ladies and Gentlemen . . .: the King," *Sv*, no.46 (1973), 136
L. O. Koch: "Structural Aspects of King Oliver's 1923 Okeh Recordings," *JJS*, iii/2 (1976), 36
W. Balliett: "For the Comfort of the People," *Improvising: Sixteen Jazz Musicians and their Art* (New York, 1977), 21; repr. in *BalliettA (1986)*; *BalliettA (1996)*
J. L. Collier: *Louis Armstrong: an American Genius* (New York, 1983, London, 1984 as *Louis Armstrong: a Biography*)
B. Bigard: *With Louis and the Duke*, ed. B. Martyn (London, 1985)
C. E. B. Bernhardt and S. Harris: *I Remember: Eighty Years of Black Entertainment, Big Bands, and the Blues* (Philadelphia, 1986), 90
H. S. Kaye: "Some Observations on King Oliver's Death," *IAJRCJ*, xix/4 (1986), 18
L. Wright and others: *Walter C. Allen & Brian A. L. Rust's "King" Oliver* (Chigwell, England, 1987) [completely rev. version of Allen and Rust: *King Joe Oliver* (Belleville, NJ, 1955)]
L. Wright: "Additional information on King Oliver," *Sv* (1988), no.134, p.49; no.136, p.139; (1992), no.149, p.190; (1994), no.160, p.143
C. Hillman: "Bunk Johnson and King Oliver," *Sv*, no.141 (1990), 91
L. Wright: "Pieces of the Jigsaw: King Oliver," *Storyville 1996/7*, ed. L. Wright (Chigwell, England, 1997), 217
T. Brothers, ed.: *Louis Armstrong in his own Words: Selected Writings* (New York and Oxford, England, 1999)
P. Carr: *Jimmy Archey: the Little Giant of the Trombone* (New Orleans, 1999)

LAWRENCE GUSHEE/HOWARD RYE, BK

Oliver, Paul (Hereford) (*b* Nottingham, England, 25 May 1927). English writer. He first wrote about jazz in the early 1950s. In the following decades he wrote articles and reviews for *Jazz Journal* (1952–*c*1960), *Music Mirror* (1954–9), and *Jazz Monthly* (1956–70), columns for *Jazz Beat* (1960s) and *Hi-fi News and Record Review* (1960s–1980), and many liner notes, and became particularly well known for his writings on early jazz and the blues; he first broadcast over the BBC in 1954. Oliver successfully brought the techniques of ethnomusicology to the study of blues: he made field visits to Africa and the American South, and challenged many of the assumptions of such earlier writers on jazz as Rudi Blesh by finding a stronger kinship with the blues and early jazz in the music of the savannahs than in that of West Africa. He also conducted important research into the influence of the songster and sermon traditions on race records. In addition to his work as a writer he has given lectures on jazz at Cambridge University, and his drawings of jazz and blues musicians have appeared in *Jazz Journal* and *Radio Times*. He is well known as an architectural historian and critic, having written many books and articles on the subject and taught architecture and design at universities in England, the USA, and Africa.

WRITINGS

(selective list)

Bessie Smith (London, 1959); repr. in *Kings of Jazz*, ed. S. Green (South Brunswick, NJ, and New York, 1978)
Blues Fell this Morning: the Meaning of the Blues (London, 1960, New York, 1961, as *The Meaning of the Blues*, rev. 2/1990)
Conversation with the Blues (London, 1965, rev. 2/1997)
Screening the Blues (London, 1968, New York, 1970/*R*1989, as *Aspects of the Blues Tradition*)
The Story of the Blues (London, 1969/*R*1982, rev. 2/1997)
Savannah Syncopators: African Retentions in the Blues (London, 1970)
"Blues," "Gospel Music," §II, *Grove6*; rev. and enlarged in P. Oliver, M. Harrison, and W. Bolcom: *The New Grove Gospel, Blues and Jazz* (London and New York, 1986 [*recte* 1987])
Blues off the Record: Thirty Years of Blues Commentary (New York, and Tunbridge Wells, England, 1984)
Songsters and Saints: Vocal Traditions on Race Records (Cambridge, England, and elsewhere, 1984)
ed.: *Black Music in Britain: Essays on the Afro-Asian Contribution to Popular Music* (Milton Keynes, England, and Philadelphia, 1990)

BIBLIOGRAPHY

T. Mazzolini: "A Conversation with Paul Oliver," *Living Blues*, no.84 (1982), 24
"Long May your Banjo Ring – 70 – Birthday Greetings to Paul Oliver," *Blues Access*, no.30 (1997), 44

ROBERT GANNON

Oliver, Sy [Melvin James] (*b* Battle Creek, MI, 17 Dec 1910; *d* New York, 27 May 1988). Arranger, trumpeter, singer, and leader. His father was a singer, his mother an organist, and both taught music. He was brought up in Zanesville, Ohio, where he learned trumpet and performed in local bands as a teenager, helping to support the family after his father suffered a stroke. From 1927 to 1930 he played with and wrote arrangements for Zack Whyte's Chocolate Beau Brummels; while with Whyte he acquired his nickname, Sy (for psychology), "for no reason," he recalled, "except that it was a big word and sounded ridiculous" (Jones, 1974). He spent a short period with Alphonso Trent (late 1930 – early 1931) helping Trent rebuild the orchestra's notated instrumental parts after a disastrous nightclub fire, then settled in Columbus, Ohio, and worked as a teacher and freelance arranger, though he also played again with Whyte intermittently and was briefly a member of Speed Webb's band.

In 1933 Oliver joined Jimmie Lunceford's orchestra, for which he wrote arrangements and compositions, played, and occasionally sang (*see* LUNCEFORD, JIMMIE); he also appeared in the short film *Jimmie Lunceford and his Dance Orchestra* (1936). From 1934 until 1939 he regularly wrote arrangements for Benny Goodman. He remained with Lunceford until 1939, when he ceased performing on trumpet and became a member of Tommy Dorsey's orchestra as an arranger and singer; after army service he again worked as a freelance arranger and received regular commissions from Dorsey. He led his own band in New York from at least November 1946 (at the Club Zanzibar) to June 1947, and thereafter worked as a music director and supervisor for various record companies, often recording with his own bands. He toured frequently during the 1960s and 1970s, and in 1974 visited Europe with the Dorsey ghost band under Warren Covington's direction. After directing a band in Paris (1968 – February 1969) he resumed playing trumpet and led a nonet, which was resident at several clubs in New York; among his sidemen were Money Johnson, Britt Woodman, Cliff Smalls, Bobby Jones, Haywood Henry, Mousey Alexander, and Chris Woods. This group, which played Oliver's well-known arrangements for big band, newly orchestrated for a smaller ensemble, continued to perform into the 1980s. In the mid-1970s Oliver also served as music director for the New York Jazz Repertory Orchestra.

Oliver achieved widespread fame during his association with Lunceford, mainly because of his arrangements, but also on account of his fine trumpet playing and pleasant singing. His scores for Lunceford invariably inspired the band to swing; they combine surface charm and simplicity with an inner variety and richness. Oliver donated a few manuscript scores to the BMI Archives in New York, but the vast majority, together with sheet music, clippings, photos, and other memorabilia, are held at the Performing Arts division of the New York Public Library at Lincoln Center (see LIBRARIES AND ARCHIVES, §2).

See also ARRANGEMENT, §3, Table 4, and ex.2.

RECORDED COMPOSITIONS

* – with Oliver as sideman

Recorded by J. Lunceford: *For Dancers Only (1937, Decca 1340); *Le jazz hot (1939, Voc. 4595)
Recorded by T. Dorsey: Opus no.1 (1944, Vic. 201608)

SELECTED ARRANGEMENTS

* – with Oliver as singer

† – with Oliver as singer and trumpeter

As leader: †*Yes, Indeed* (1973, BB 33048)
Recorded by J. Lunceford: Stomp it off/My Blue Heaven (1934, 1935, Decca 712); Organ Grinder's Swing (1936, Decca 908); *On the Beach at Bali-Bali (1936, Decca 915); Slumming on Park Avenue (1937, Decca 1128); Margie (1938, Decca 1617); 'Tain't what you do (it's the way that you do it) (1939, Voc. 4582)
Recorded by T. Dorsey: On the Sunny Side of the Street (1944, Vic. 20-1648)

BIBLIOGRAPHY

McCarthyB; *SchullerS*
G. Simon: "Sy Oliver: the Most Surprised Party is Me!" *Metronome*, lxii/2 (1946), 23
B. Coss: "Triple Play," *Metronome*, lxxvii/11 (1960), 40
H. Renaud: "Sy Oliver à Paris," *Jh*, no.245 (1968), 41
S. Dance: "The Return of Sy Oliver," *JJ*, xxiii/9 (1970), 2; repr. in *The World of Swing* (New York, 1974), 125
J. S. Wilson: "Sy Oliver's 9-Piece Band at Riverboat," *New York Times* (3 July 1970)
——: "Sy Oliver," *International Musician*, lxix/7 (1971), 7
C. Carrière: "Welcome, Sy Oliver," *Jh*, no.294 (1973), 16
L. Verdeaux and D. Brigaud: "Sy Oliver," *BHcF*, no.229 (1973), 7
M. Jones: "Oliver: the Insider," *MM* (27 April 1974), 58; repr. in Jones, *Talking Jazz* (London, 1987), 170
B. Priestley: "Sy Oliver," *Into Jazz*, i/7 (1974), 11
Z. Knauss: *Conversations with Jazz Musicians* (Detroit, 1977), 150
D. J. Travis: *An Autobiography of Black Jazz* (Chicago, 1983), 435 [incl. interviews]
J. Pareles: "Oliver Donates Notes to Jazz Archive," *New York Times* (22 April 1984)
Obituary, *New York Times* (28 May 1988)
J. Simmen: "Sy Oliver," *BHcF*, no.364 (1988), 6; no.365 (1989), 4
E. Berger: *Bassically Speaking: an Oral History of George Duvivier* (Metuchen, NJ, and London, 1993), 72
C. Garrod: *Sy Oliver and his Orchestra* (Zephyrhills, FL, 1993) [discography]

EDDIE LAMBERT/BK

Olu Dara [Jones, Charles, III] (*b* Louisville, MS, 12 Jan 1941). Trumpeter, cornetist, singer, and bandleader. He was brought up in Natchez, Mississippi, and took up trumpet at the age of seven. Following navy service, in 1963 he moved to New York, where in 1969 he adopted his Yoruba name and resumed playing. As a sideman he worked with Art Blakey's Jazz Messengers (*c*1973) and various reed players belonging to the Black Artists Group (such as Oliver Lake), as well as with David Murray, Henry Threadgill, Bill Laswell (in the group Material), and others. He performed and recorded with Hamiet Bluiett in New York (1976) and with Phillip Wilson in a duo in Paris (1977) and in a quartet at the Moers festival, Germany (1978); he also recorded with Lake (1975), Murray (1976), James "Blood" Ulmer (1980), Julius Hemphill (in Milan, Italy, 1980), Tim Berne and Material (both 1981), Cecil McBee (1982), Threadgill's Sextett (1983), Craig Harris, James Newton, and Don Pullen (all 1985), and Charles Brackeen (1987). In the early 1980s he was a member of Murray's octet and big band.

Around 1980 Olu Dara began to sing on a regular basis, and not long afterwards he abandoned trumpet in favor of the cornet, though he also played a wooden African side-blown trumpet and harmonica. From this time he led his Natchezsippi Band and Okra Orchestra, with the guitarist Kwatei Jones-Quartey, the bass player Alonzo Gardner, the drummer Greg Bandy, and the conga player Acosta Musama as longstanding members. In this setting he cultivated an entertainment-oriented style which emphasized dance rhythms but incorporated elements of West African music, the blues, marches by John Philip Sousa, and soul ballads; improvisations were lyrical but energetic and sometimes stark in character. Olu Dara acted in Robert Altman's film *Kansas City* (1996) and took part in the resulting soundtrack recording (1995) and video (1997). In 1997 he made his first album as a leader, playing and singing in a style inclined towards downhome blues. He also recorded as an accompanist to Cassandra Wilson (1987, *c*1993, 1999) and as a sideman with his son, the popular rap singer Nas(ir Jones) (1994).

Olu Dara frequently drawls sexually suggestive monologues over a vamp; his solos are highly melodic and cover a wide dynamic range (he often uses mutes).

SELECTED RECORDINGS

As sideman: O. Lake: *Heavy Spirits* (1975, Ari. 1008); H. Bluiett: *Endangered Species* (1976, IndN 1025); D. Murray: *Home* (1981, BS 0055); H. Threadgill: *Just the Facts and Pass the Bucket* (*c*1983, About Time 1005); D. Murray: *Live at Sweet Basil*, i–ii (1984, BS 0085, 0095); J. Newton: *The African Flower* (1985, BN 85109); D. Pullen: *The Sixth Sense* (1985, BS 0088); C. Brackeen: *Attainment* (1987, Silkheart 110); *Worshippers Come Nigh* (1987, Silkheart 111); C. Wilson: on *Blue Light 'Til Dawn* (*c*1993, BN B21Z-81357), Hellhound on my Trail

BIBLIOGRAPHY

R. Woessner: "Profile: Olu Dara," *DB*, xlix/8 (1982), 52
S. McElfresh: "A Taste of Okra Every Day," *Ear: Magazine of New Music*, xi/2 (1986)
Touré: "One Son Learns Lessons from a Father," *New York Times* (6 Oct 1996)
T. Lepin: "Interview: Eclipses: Olu Dara: Back to the Blues," *Jazzman*, no.41 (1998), 10
A. Nahigian: "Olu Dara: Looking for Blues," *DB*, lxv/5 (1998), 36 [incl. discography]
D. Palmer: "Profile: Olu Dara: Meandering like the Mississippi," *Jazziz*, xv/4 (1998), 54

HOWARD MANDEL/BK

Olympia. Theater in Paris; *see* NIGHTCLUBS AND OTHER VENUES.

Olympia Brass Band. New Orleans group founded in March 1962 by Harold Dejan, who over the previous several years had begun leading a brass band, the Eureka Number Two, to take on jobs when the Eureka Brass Band was overbooked. The Olympia Brass Band performed and recorded frequently in New Orleans with a typical instrumentation of three trumpets, two trombones, two saxophones, tuba, snare drum, and bass drum, although it toured and made recordings in Europe (including *Dejan's Olympia Brass Band in Europe*, 1968, 77 LEU31) as a smaller ensemble. Its regular sidemen included the trumpeters Andy Anderson (i), Milton Batiste, and Kid Sheik Cola, the trombonists Paul Crawford and Gerald Joseph, the tenor saxophonist Emanuel Paul, the snare drummer Andrew Jefferson, and the bass drummers John Smith, Henry "Booker T" Glass, and Glass's son Nowell "Papa" Glass. Cag Cagnolatti, Kid Thomas Valentine, Louis Nelson, Louis Cottrell, Jr., Cié Frazier, and Emanuel Sayles were also among those who played with the group. The Olympia Brass Band became closely associated with Preservation Hall: some of its members played there on Sundays, while until his death in 1987 the hall's owner, Allan Jaffe, appeared regularly as the group's sousaphone or helicon player. Among the band's later recordings is the album *Here Come da Great Olympia Band* (*c*1978, VPS 4); it may be seen in the James Bond film *Live and Let Die* (1973).

BIBLIOGRAPHY

J. Roberts: "Talking to Harold Dejan," *JB*, ii/7 (1965), 19
B. Martyn: Liner notes, *Dejan's Olympia Brass Band in Europe* (77 LEU31, 1969)
G. Valentin: "Harold 'Duke' Dejan," *Fn*, vi/5 (1975), 4
M. Joly: "Everything's Lovely: the Life and Times of Harold 'Duke' Dejan," *SL*, xxxv (1983), autumn, 24
——: "New Orleans '89: the Brass Bands," *New Orleans Music*, i/1 (1989), 18
R. H. Knowles: *Fallen Heroes: a History of New Orleans Brass Bands* (New Orleans, 1996), 238

WILLIAM J. SCHAFER/BK

Olympia Orchestra. New Orleans dance band active from about 1906 to 1914. It was formed by Freddie Keppard and consisted of between five and seven musicians, a typical instrumentation being cornet, trombone, clarinet, guitar or banjo, piano, double bass or tuba, and drums. As leader of the group Keppard gained a reputation as one of the finest early jazz cornetists; when he left in spring 1914 the leadership of the orchestra passed to A. J. Piron, who replaced Keppard with King Oliver. Among the sidemen at various times under Keppard were Joseph Petit, Alphonse Picou, Sidney Bechet, Louis Keppard, and the drummer Ernest Trepagnier, while those under Piron included Zue Robertson, Clarence Williams, Billy Marrero, John Lindsay, and Louis Cottrell, Sr.

WILLIAM J. SCHAFER

OM. Swiss quartet. It was formed in 1972 by Urs Leimgruber (saxophone), Christy Doran (guitar), Bobby Burri (double bass), and Fredy Studer (drums) and took its name from the title of one of John Coltrane's albums of modal and free jazz. The following year the quartet appeared at festivals throughout Europe. OM was inspired by the psychedelic music of Pink Floyd and Jimi Hendrix, as well as by Coltrane, and the resulting brand of fusion was influential in Europe. The group was sometimes joined by the percussionist Dom Um Romão, with whom it recorded an album in 1977 (*OM with Dom Um Romão*, Japo 60022). By 1982, when it played its last concert in Willisau, the group had recorded five albums; its members later collaborated on different projects. (J. Solothurnmann: Liner notes, *Jazz in Switzerland 1930–75*, Elite Special 9544002/1–4, 1997).

ARMIN BÜTTNER

Oma. Nickname of ISAO SUZUKI.

O'Mara, Peter (*b* Sydney, 9 Dec 1957). Australian guitarist. He studied at the Academy of Guitar and at the New South Wales Conservatorium of Music. Having worked professionally from 1976, he traveled in 1981 to New York, where he studied variously with Dave Liebman, John Scofield, Roland Hanna, Jimmy Raney, and Atilla Zoller. Late in 1981 he moved to Munich and worked with many important musicians, notably Kenny Wheeler, Uli Beckerhoff, John Marshall, John Taylor, Adelhard Roidinger, Benny Bailey, Charlie Mariano, and Johnny Griffin. From 1982 to 1990 he led the trio Sundial, consisting of Wayne Darling (double bass) and Billy Elgart (drums), with which he recorded and toured Europe. In 1990 he joined Klaus Doldinger's group Passport, and from 1991 he led the Munich-based quartet Cross Rhythms; he also worked in Wolfgang Haffner's small groups. In 1995 O'Mara performed in Australia in a trio with the double bass player Adam Armstrong and the drummer Andrew Gander, and the following year he formed a quartet with his fellow Australian expatriate Adrian Mears (trombone), and a trio with Henning Sieverts (double bass) and Guido May (drums). Late in 1997, with the saxophonist Johannes Enders, he formed a quintet. O'Mara is also a member of the jazz-rock group Travellers, consisting of Tony Lakatos, the keyboard player Robert Di Gioia, Anthony Jackson, Haffner, and the percussionist Ernst Ströer, and in 1999 he joined the United Jazz and Rock Ensemble. He has taught at the Bruckner Conservatorium in Linz, Austria, and in Germany at the Musikhochschule in Hamburg and the Richard Strauss Conservatorium in Munich; he has published instructional books.

SELECTED RECORDINGS

As leader: with W. Darling and B. Elgart: *O'Mara–Darling–Elgart* (1987, Core 9.00670); *Avenue U* (1989, Enja 6046-2); *Cross Rhythms* (1991, Jazz4ever 4720); *Symmetry* (1994, Edition Collage 484); *Spirits* (1994, Acoustic Music 319.1068.242); *Back Seat Driver* (*c*1999, Enja 9126-2)
As sideman: D. Barlow: *Horn* (1989, Spiral Scratch 0003); Carlo Mombelli and C. Mariano: *Happy/Sad* (1990, ITM-Pacific 970057)

BIBLIOGRAPHY

<http://www.jazzrecords.com/musicians/omara.htm> (2000) [incl. discography]

GK

Omer, Jean (*b* Nivelles, Belgium, 9 Sept 1912; *d* Brussels, 30 May 1994). Belgian clarinetist and alto saxophonist. He first played violin in an amateur orchestra and began his professional career with a band in Strasbourg, France. After performing in Brussels he returned to France for a six-month engagement with the bandleader Billy Smith. He then replaced André Ekyan in the Golden Stars and played in a group led by René Compère. Later he toured Europe as a soloist with the Carolina Stomp Chasers, but as a result of problems with his work permit he was forced to return to Belgium. In Brussels Omer attempted to establish his own band and worked with Robert De Kers in the orchestra accompanying the cabaret singer Josephine Baker (until 1936), then toured as a member of the quartet the Four Notes, which included Ernst van 't Hoff. Thereafter he played in Brussels at the Cotton Club and performed regularly at le Boeuf sur le Toit, where he continued to lead his own band until the early 1960s. Omer recorded with Gus Deloof (1931), Rudy Bruder (1941), and as a leader (1937, 1940–43, 1951, and 1958).

BIBLIOGRAPHY

R. Pernet, J.-P. Schroeder, and others: *Dictionnaire du jazz à Bruxelles et en Wallonie* (Liège, Belgium, 1991)
R. Pernet: *Belgian Jazz Discography (1897–1999)* (Brussels, 1999)

ROBERT PERNET

O'Neal, Johnny (*b* Detroit, 10 Oct 1956). Pianist. His father, John O'Neal, was a blues and rhythm-and-blues pianist who worked in Erskine Hawkins's band. He took up piano at the age of 13 and was largely self-taught; initially he was involved in gospel music in a local Baptist church, but he preferred to play the blues at home. In 1976 he began playing jazz locally and the following year performed further afield. In 1978, while working in Toledo, Ohio, he sat in with Ray Brown, whose influence helped to secure him a recording session with Concord. Again through Brown's influence he joined Milt Jackson's small group, with which he remained until Jackson re-joined the Modern Jazz Quartet and it disbanded. O'Neal then worked with Lionel Hampton (1980) and as a freelance. In Atlanta he led a house trio that accompanied such visiting musicians as Eddie "Lockjaw" Davis, Jackson, Urbie Green, Scott Hamilton, Harry Edison, Nat Adderley, and Clark Terry (all *c*1981). In 1982 he moved to New York, where he immediately began working with Terry at the Blue Note. He was heard there by Art Blakey, and shortly afterwards he joined the Jazz Messengers; he toured internationally with the group until autumn 1983.

After leaving Blakey's ensemble O'Neal led a trio, performed as an unaccompanied soloist, and formed a duo with the stride pianist Judy Carmichael. In 1984 he appeared at the JVC Grande Parade du Jazz Nice in various small groups with, among others, Al Grey, Georgie Auld, Edison, Joe Newman, Buddy Tate, George Duvivier, Benny Carter, J. J. Johnson, and Dizzy Gillespie; that same year he gave a solo concert at Carnegie Hall. He established his own trio in 1985, with Dave Young and Terry Clarke as his sidemen, and he performed and recorded around 1988 with the group the Murphys. Later he returned to Detroit before settling in Atlanta, where he worked locally through the late 1990s. In 1995 he recorded as a leader in Montreal.

SELECTED RECORDINGS

As leader: *Coming Out* (1979, Conc. 228); with D. Young: *Soulful Swinging* (1985, Parkwood 110); *Live at Baker's Keyboard Lounge* (1985, Parkwood 105); with the Murphys: *Reunion* (*c*1988, Sophia 003); *On the Montreal Scene* (1995, Justin Time 85)

BIBLIOGRAPHY

Feather–GitlerBEJ
R. Horricks: "New Natural Primitive of Jazz: Johnny O'Neal," *CI*, xxii/7 (1985), 16
<http://homepages.go.com/~fitzgera/chron.htm> (1999)
<http://www.justin-time.com/hiband/> (1999)
<http://www3.sympatico.ca/villagejazz/scandals.htm> (1999)

GK

One for All. Cooperative sextet formed in 1995 by the trumpeter Jim Rotondi, the trombonist Steve Davis (iii), the tenor saxophonist Eric Alexander, the pianist David Hazeltine, the double bass player Peter Washington, and the drummer Joe Farnsworth; later, Washington alternated in the bass chair with John Webber. One of the finer small groups performing in the hard-bop idiom in the late 1990s, its work is characterized by an energetic, yet refined sense of improvisation and swing, which may be heard to advantage on its recordings *Too Soon to Tell* (1997, Sharp Nine 1006) and *Upward and Onward* (1999, Criss Cross 1172).

GK

100 Club. One of the several venues to have occupied premises at 100 Oxford Street, London; *see* Nightclubs and other venues.

101 Ranch. Dance hall in New Orleans; *see* Nightclubs and other venues.

Ones. Single bars, as in the expression "to trade ones"; *see* Forms, §1(ii).

Onishi, Junko (*b* Kyoto, Japan, 16 April 1967). Japanese pianist and leader. She learned piano from the age of four. While attending the Berklee College of Music (from 1986) she played in jam sessions with Delfeayo Marsalis, Roy Hargrove, Geoff Keezer, and others, and she made her professional début with Slide Hampton in France (1988). After graduating in 1989 and moving to New York she became the pianist in Jesse Davis's quintet, which served as the house band at Augie's. She toured the USA, Japan, and Europe with Gary Thomas (1990), Europe and the USA with Joe Henderson, and the USA and Japan with Kenny Garrett (1991), and during the same period she worked with Terence Blanchard, Greg Osby, the Mingus Big Band, and Mingus Dynasty. On moving back to Japan in 1992 Onishi joined Shigeharu Mukai's quintet and formed her own trio, whose first recordings were highly successful; Rodney Whitaker and Billy Higgins were the sidemen on her second album. In May 1994 her trio, with Reginald Veal and Herlin Riley, held a week-long engagement at the Village Vanguard, New York, and afterwards she toured Europe and North America. In 1996 she recorded with Jackie McLean and Joe Lovano.

SELECTED RECORDINGS

(recorded for Somethin' Else unless otherwise indicated)

As leader: *Wow* (1993, 5547); *Cruisin'* (1994, 5555); *Live at the Village Vanguard* (1994, 5570); *Piano Quintet Suite* (1995, 5576); *Play Piano Play* (1996, 5583); with J. Lovano: *Tenor Time* (1996, 5584); *The Sextet* (1997, 5586); *Fragile* (1998, 8008); with P. Woods: *Cool Woods* (1999, 68041)
As sideman: J. McLean: *Hat Trick* (1996, BN 38363-2); Jazz Workshop: *Pandora* (1998, 5597–9)

BIBLIOGRAPHY

K. Micallef: "Hearsay: Junko Onishi," *JT*, xxiv/7 (1994), 10
C. Gauffre: "Junko Onishi," *Jm*, no.455 (1996), 6
E. Sato: Liner notes, *Fragile* (BN 98108-1, 1998)

KAZUNORI SUGIYAMA

ONJ. *See* Orchestre national de jazz.

Ono, Shunzo. *See* Ohno, shunzo.

Onward Brass Band [Imperial Brass Band] **(i).** New Orleans group active from *c*1886 to 1930. It performed for picnics, excursions, parades, and baseball games, and by 1887, under the leadership of the cornetist Joseph Othello Lainez (1836–*c*1904), rivaled the older Excelsior and Pickwick bands in popularity. An affiliated Onward String Band supplied music for dances and parties. The group was led from 1903 by Manuel Perez and became closely identified with his dignified and classical style of playing; it was considered by important contemporary jazz musicians to be the most consistent and exciting of the early brass bands. It comprised ten to 12 players, with an instrumentation of three cornets (trumpets), two trombones, two clarinets, alto horn, baritone horn, tuba, snare drum, and bass drum. Members of the band at various times included Isidore Barbarin, the trombonist George Filhe, Lorenzo Tio, Jr., Peter Bocage and, occasionally, George Baquet and King Oliver. At some point in the mid-1920s Perez changed the Onward's name to the Imperial Brass Band.

For illustration *see* Brass band, fig.1.

BIBLIOGRAPHY

C. Kinzer: *The Tio Family: Four Generations of New Orleans Musicians, 1814–1922* (diss., Louisiana State U., 1993)
R. H. Knowles: *Fallen Heroes: a History of New Orleans Brass Bands* (New Orleans, 1996), 44

WILLIAM J. SCHAFER/CHARLES KINZER

Onward Brass Band (ii). New Orleans group active from 1960 to 1978. Modeled on its predecessor the Onward Brass Band (i), it was founded and led until 1969 by Paul Barbarin and directed thereafter by Louis Cottrell, Jr.; after Cottrell's death in 1978 it appeared into at least the late 1980s under the leadership of the snare drummer Placide Adams. The group consisted of eight to ten players and had a typical instrumentation of two trumpets, two trombones, clarinet, tuba, snare drum, and bass drum. It toured widely in the late 1960s, presenting early brass-band practices in an authoritative manner. Among the sidemen who recorded with the band were Cag Cagnolatti, Kid Howard, Andrew Morgan, Joe Thomas (i), and Louis Barbarin (all 1965) and Alvin Alcorn, Cagnolatti, Danny Barker, and Freddie Kohlman (all 1968).

BIBLIOGRAPHY

C. Bolton: "Summer Concerts Begin: Onward Band Jazzes it up," *SL*, xx/7–8 (1968), 77
J. V. Buerkle and D. Barker: *Bourbon Street Black: the New Orleans Black Jazzman* (New York, 1973)
M. Joly: "New Orleans '89: the Brass Bands," *New Orleans Music*, i/1 (1989), 18
R. H. Knowles: *Fallen Heroes: a History of New Orleans Brass Bands* (New Orleans, 1996), 242

WILLIAM J. SCHAFER

Onyx (i). Nightclub in New York; *see* NIGHTCLUBS AND OTHER VENUES.

Onyx (ii). Record company and label. The company was established in 1973 by Don Schlitten (the organization's president) and Joe Fields. The label was devoted to reissues and to the release of material that had previously been confined to archives (including items taken from the collection of Jerry Newman, who made recordings at clubs in Harlem during the early 1940s). Schlitten collected much valuable and obscure music that had never before been available on LPs; items were issued by, among others, Art Tatum, Coleman Hawkins, Louis Armstrong, Johnny Hodges, Hot Lips Page, Charlie Shavers, Teddy Edwards, Wardell Gray, and Charlie Parker. Not two years after its inception, however, Onyx was placed in receivership. From that time the catalogue and some 18 albums issued by the owners' other company, Muse (*see* MUSE (ii)), were the subject of litigation that was not settled until 1988, when Schlitten received the rights to some of the masters that he had produced; these, together with some previously unissued recordings by Terry Gibbs, were transferred to Schlitten's Xanadu catalogue and distributed internationally via licensing to other labels.

MARK GARDNER/BK

Open. (1) Unstopped or unmuted. The word is used in jazz principally of the trumpet and trombone to distinguish the full tone produced when a mute is not used from the muffled sound of the muted instrument (*see also* MUTE and DU WAH). It is also applied to the hi-hat, the two cymbals of which stand apart until the controlling pedal is fully depressed (when they are brought into contact and thus stop each other) (*see* DRUM SET, §I, 5). The symbol commonly used for open in these cases is shown in NOTATION, ex.17.

(2) To alter an arrangment informally, making room for additional solos on an ad hoc basis, as for example when stretching out a performance to accommodate dancers.

Orange Blossoms. Name by which the CASA LOMA ORCHESTRA was originally known.

Orange then Blue. Group formed in Boston by George Schuller in 1984. A small big band, averaging 12 pieces, it is devoted to performing original compositions and historical material arranged from a contemporary perspective. Members have included Bruce Barth, Tim Hagans, Chris Speed, Dave Douglas, Mark Taylor (i), Tom Varner, Herb Robertson, and Andrew D'Angelo. The group performed at the Jazzfest Berlin and the 11th Music Meeting in Nijmegen, the Netherlands (both 1995), and has released several albums under its own name; it also appears on Gunther Schuller's album of compositions and arrangements *Jumpin' in the Future*.

SELECTED RECORDINGS

(all recorded for GM)

Orange then Blue (1985–6, 3006); *Where Were You* (1987–8, 3012); [G. Schuller]: *Jumpin' in the Future* (1988, 3010); *Funkallero* (1989, 3023); *While You Were Out* (1992, 3028)

BIBLIOGRAPHY

F. Bouchard: "Orange then Blue," *DB*, lx/12 (1993), 15

GK

Orchard, Frank [Francis H.] (*b* Chicago, IL, 21 Sept 1914; *d* New York, 27 Dec 1983). Trombonist. He studied from 1932 to 1933 at the Institute of Musical Art, New York, then worked as a salesman until 1941, when he joined Jimmy McPartland. After playing with Bobby Hackett (1942) he performed and recorded with Max Kaminsky, Wingy Manone, and Joe Marsala (all 1944). As a freelance he worked with dixieland groups in New York until the mid-1950s; he then moved to Dayton, Ohio, and later to St. Louis, where he occasionally organized jam sessions. Having returned to New York in the 1960s, he performed with Billy Butterfield (1969) and often appeared informally at Jimmy Ryan's (1970–71). A typical example of his playing may be heard on *Muskrat Ramble/Bugle Call Rag* (Black & White 24), which he recorded with Kaminsky's band (under the name the Lion's Band) in 1944. (*ChiltonW*; *FeatherE*)

Orchestra U.S.A. Large ensemble that combined the instrumentation of a big band with orchestral woodwind and string sections. It was formed in the autumn of 1962 by John Lewis, and led by Lewis, Gunther Schuller, and the percussionist Harold Farberman. It included jazz and classical musicians and devoted its performances largely to third-stream works; among those who wrote compositions for the orchestra were Lewis, Schuller, Gary McFarland, Miljenko Prohaska, Hall Overton, Jimmy Giuffre, Teo Macero, and Benny Golson. Although the quality of the orchestra's repertory was uneven, its performances were of a high standard; Eric Dolphy, Phil Woods, Jim Hall, and Richard Davis were regular members, and Golson, Gerry Mulligan, and Ornette Coleman appeared occasionally as guest soloists. The orchestra disbanded in 1965, after recording three albums; six of its members recorded another album in 1964. During its brief existence the group played an influential role in the development of third-stream music.

SELECTED RECORDINGS

Orchestra U.S.A.: *Debut* (1963, Colpix 448); *Jazz Journey* (1964, Col. CS9047); *Sonorities* (1965, Col. CS9195)
Sextet of Orchestra U.S.A.: *Mack the Knife* (1964, RCA LSP3498)

BIBLIOGRAPHY

B. Coss: "John Lewis and the Orchestra," *DB*, xxx/4 (1963), 20
G. Lees: "View of the Third Stream," *DB*, xxxi/4 (1964), 16

WOLFRAM KNAUER

Orchestre National de Jazz [ONJ]. French big band. It was created in January 1986 on the initiative of the French ministry of culture, which granted a subvention covering the better half of its budget. At its head is a music director who carries out the artistic project for which he has been chosen; to prevent stagnation, the director's term is limited to two years. While he composes and arranges the majority of the repertory performed under his direction, he has leave also to call upon other writers and to invite guest soloists. Thus Gil Evans, McCoy Tyner, Martial Solal, Carla Bley, Quincy Jones, Johnny Griffin, and others have worked with the group. Often controversial ("Can jazz be official?"), the orchestra had, as of the late 1990s, given about 40 concerts in France and abroad and recorded 13 albums. Its music directors have been François Jeanneau (1986), Antoine Hervé (1987–9), Claude Barthélémy (1989–91), Denis Badault (1992–4), Laurent Cugny (1995–7), Didier Levallet (1997–9), and Paolo Damiani (2000–).

SELECTED RECORDINGS

Orchestre National de Jazz 1986 (1986, Label Bleu 6503–04); *African Dream* (1988–9, Label Bleu 6521); *Jack Line* (1991, Label Bleu 6538); *Monk Mingus Ellington* (1993, Label Bleu 6562); *Reminiscing* (1995, Verve 532457-2); *ONJ Express* (1997, Evidence [Fr.] 825); *Sequences* (1998, Evidence [Fr.] 928); *Deep Feelings* (2000, Evidence [Fr.] 2030)

BIBLIOGRAPHY

D. Aronson: "On the Scene: the French National Jazz Orchestra," *JF* [intl edn], no.99 (1986), 8
P. Carles: "L'Afrique de l'ONJ par Chautemps," *Jm*, no.351 (1986), 26
F. Jeanneau: "Enfin l'O.N.J. grave . . .," *Jm*, no.355 (1986), 26
X. Prévost: "L'Orchestre National . . . de Jazz!," *Diapason-harmonie*, no.313 (1986), 12
N. Sokolowski: "ONJ: on jazze français," *Jh*, no.428 (1986), 12
J. Sorano: "L'ONJ fait ses comptes," *Jm*, no.356 (1986), 37
——: "L'O.N.J. casse la cabane au Canada," *Jm*, no.364 (1987), 34
J. Hatot-Sorano: "Claude Barthélémy: 'nous ne pousserons pas mémé dans l'escalier'," *Jm*, no.378 (1989), 23
X. Matthyssens and F. Marmande: "L'ONJ nouveau est arrivé," *Jm*, no.387 (1989), 24
X. Matthyssens: "ONJ: cher Claude, par six qui te veulent du bien," *Jm*, no.397 (1990), 28
X. Prévost and S. Ollivier: "ONJ: le changement dans la continuité," *Jm*, no.393 (1990), 24
X. Matthyssens: "ONJ: Guitar Words," *Jm*, no.406 (1991), 42
R. Grosman and P. Richard: "Laurent Cugny: Lumière à l'ONJ," *Jh*, no.520 (1995), 31
F. Goaty: "Laurent Cugny Lumières sur l'ONJ," *Jm*, no.460 (1996), 50
X. Prévost: "ONJ: cinq chefs à table," *Jm*, no.461 (1996), 38
S. Siclier: "ONJ, dix ans: l'heure du bilan," *Jazzman*, no.15 (1996), 5
J. Noémaurane: "Laurent Cugny," *Jm*, no.471 (1997), 6
<http://www.onj.org> (2001)

ANDRÉ CLERGEAT

Ore, John (Thomas) (*b* Philadelphia, 17 Dec 1933). Double bass player. After studying cello at the New School of Music, Philadelphia (1943–6), then double bass at the Juilliard School (1952) he played with Tiny Grimes (briefly in 1953), George Wallington and Lester Young (both 1954), Ben Webster, Coleman Hawkins, and Elmo Hope (all 1955), and Bud Powell (1955, 1957). In 1958 he led his own group, and for the next two years worked as a freelance in and around New York. Ore joined Thelonious Monk's quartet in spring 1960, and remained with the group until spring 1963, making two tours of Europe. After performing in Canada with the Double Six (1964) he worked in the trios led by Bud Powell (whose skills had deteriorated severely at the time of their recording in September 1964) and Teddy Wilson (1964–5). He recorded with Earl Hines in 1977.

SELECTED RECORDINGS

As sideman: L. Young: *Somebody Loves Me* (1954, Norg. 1022); E. Hope: *Meditations* (1955, Prst. 7010); T. Monk: *Monk's Dream* (1962, Col. CS8765); *Criss Cross* (1963, Col. CS8838); E. Hope: *Last Sessions* (1966, IC 1018, 1037); E. Hines: *Jazz is his Old Lady and my Old Man* (1977, Cat. 7622)

BIBLIOGRAPHY

FeatherE; *Feather '60s*
J.-L. Ginibre and P. Carles: "Dictionnaire de la contrebasse," *Jm*, no.166 (1969), 51

DIANNA RHYAN

Oregon. Jazzchamber ensemble. Its original members, Paul McCandless (oboe, english horn, bass clarinet), Glen Moore (double bass, violin, piano, flute), Ralph Towner (acoustic guitar, piano, french horn, trumpet, flugelhorn), and Collin Walcott (tablā, sitar, clarinet, percussion), all played in the Paul Winter Consort before forming their own group in 1970; Walcott died in 1984 and was replaced by Trilok Gurtu. The group appeared in the video *Live at the 1987 Freiburg Arts Festival* (*c*1988), and continued to tour and record into the 1990s. Oregon's eclectic but integrated style combines elements of classical music, modern jazz, and ethnic music, and reveals the influence of composers and musicians as diverse as John Dowland, Bach, Stravinsky, Bartók, the serialists, John Coltrane, Bill Evans (ii), and Scott LaFaro. The sensitive interaction of the players in performance allows them to improvise collectively without assuming rigidly defined roles. Their recordings include pieces based upon complex harmonies, such as *Yellow Bell*, and others based on a drone or totally free improvisation. While the soaring oboe in *Icarus* is characteristic, the fact that the musicians play 60 to 80 different instruments gives the group a wide palette of sounds. Oregon's pioneering work set the stage for the emergence of the popular easy-listening genres which came to be known as "new age" and "world music," but its own music-making was far more substantial and complex than much of what followed in this vein.

SELECTED RECORDINGS

Our First Record (1970, Van. 79432); *Together* (1976, Van. 79377); *Friends* (1977, Van. 79370); *Violin* (1978, Van. 79397); *Out of the Woods* (1978, Elek. 154), incl. Yellow Bell; *Oregon in Performance* (1979, Elek. 304), incl. Icarus; *Oregon* (1983, ECM 1258); *Crossing* (1984, ECM 1291); *45th Parallel* (1988, Portrait 44465); *Always, Never, and Forever* (1990, VeraBra 2073-2)

BIBLIOGRAPHY

M. Bourne: "The Natural Timbre of Oregon," *DB*, xli/16 (1974), 14
C. Mitchell: "Ralph Towner: a Chorus of Inner Voices," *DB*, xlii/12 (1975), 16
R. Henschen: "The Musical Worlds Meet in Oregon," *Music Journal*, xxxvii/2 (1979), 5
M. Zipkin: "Oregon: Out of the Woods, Into the World," *DB*, xlvi/5 (1979), 13
L. Lyons: "Goodbye Oregon," *Musician*, no.29 (1981), 56
S. Larson: *Some Aspects of the Album "Out of the Woods" by the Chamber Ensemble "Oregon"* (thesis, U. of Oregon, 1981)
——: "Yellow Bell and a Jazz Paradigm," *In Theory Only*, vi/2 (1982), 31
H. U. Werner and K. Bettermann: "Oregon: Acoustic State of Music: eine dokumentarisch-analytische Annäherung," *Jf*, xviii (1986), 87
J. Diliberto: "Oregon: Beauty, and the Beat," *DB*, lv/2 (1988), 24 [incl. discography and interviews]
A. Gilbert: "Oregon Still Giant of its Genre," *San Jose Mercury News* (11 May 2000)

STEVE LARSON/BK

Orendorff, George (Robert) (*b* Atlanta, 18 March 1906; *d* Los Angeles Co., 28 June 1984). Trumpeter. He moved with his family to Chicago in 1915, and first played guitar before taking up cornet. After working in Chicago (from 1923) he traveled to Los Angeles in a show band (1925). He performed and recorded on trumpet with Paul Howard (1925–30) and as a member of Les Hite's band (1930–38), which also made recordings with Louis Armstrong (1930–31) and performed in several films. Orendorff played with the guitarist Ceele Burke until 1943 and again in 1945 after military service.

Although he ceased full-time performing from the mid-1940s, he continued to play regularly and recorded with such musicians as Maxwell Davis. Like many trumpeters of his generation he had a distinct and passionate style of blues accompaniment, which may be heard on his recordings with T-Bone Walker. Details of his death are taken from the California death index.

SELECTED RECORDINGS

As sideman: P. Howard: The Ramble/Moonlight Blues (1929, Vic. 38068); Overnight Blues (1929, Vic. 38070); Quality Shout (1929, Vic. 38122); I. Anderson: Play Me the Blues (1946, Exclusive 3114); Kay Thomas: Raise up (1946, Black & White 784); T. Walker: First Love Blues/T-Bone Shuffle (1947, Comet T53); Lonesome Woman Blues (1947, Comet T50); Inspiration Blues (1947, Comet T51); Peppy Prince: *Dance Party* (1956, Dooto 240)

SELECTED FILMS AND VIDEOS

Taxi (1931); I'm No Angel (1933); Sing, Sinner, Sing (1933); The Music Goes 'Round (1936); Murder in Swingtime (1937); Imitation of Life (1959)

BIBLIOGRAPHY

ChiltonW; *McCarthyB*

B. Wood: "George Orendorff: Quality Serenader," *JJ*, x (1957), no.1, p.4; no.2, p.4

J. Simmen: "Carnet de notes, 9: Un trompette-poète: George Orendorff," *BHcF*, no.172 (1967), 8

M. Royal and C. P. Gordon: *Marshal Royal: Jazz Survivor* (London and New York, 1996)

Organ. A keyboard instrument, which in jazz is commonly one of two types: a pipe organ or an electric (or electronic) organ. The former consists of one or more scale-like rows of individual pipes, which are made to sound by air under pressure from a wind-raising device and admitted to the pipes by means of valves operated by the keyboard. In the latter, sounds emulating those of the pipe organ are generated electronically. The Reed organ has also been used in jazz.

1. The pipe organ. 2. The electronic organ.

1. The pipe organ. By the early part of the 20th century two distinct types of pipe organ were available to jazzmen: neither was portable, and both were governed by their location. The first type was the church or concert organ, which in the 1920s generally had two or three manuals (keyboards), operating, in effect, three separate organs – great, choir, and swell; each of these could also be brought into action by a pedalboard (which sometimes governed an additional set of pipes of its own). The individual organs each contained several sets or "ranks" of pipes, and by selecting particular combinations or "registrations" of these by means of "stops," an extremely large range of tone colors and timbres was available. Since organ keyboards are not touch sensitive, and open or close valves to the pipes by means of mechanical, electric, or hydraulic linkage, the only means of regulating the volume is to change the number of pipes sounding at any one time; on the swell organ, however, the pipes are enclosed in a case with shutters, which may be used to control volume.

The second type of organ used in jazz was the theater organ, which was a greatly expanded version of the church or concert instrument introduced at the beginning of the 20th century by the Wurlitzer company of Chicago. It was developed by Robert Hope-Jones (1859–1914) to provide the perfect accompaniment to silent films and had a wide range of stops designed to imitate various instruments. Theater organs were installed in cinemas and theaters throughout the USA and in many parts of Europe. An innovation of Hope-Jones's, fitted to many of these instruments, was "second touch" – additional ranks of pipes which could be brought into action by pressing the keys beyond their normal resting point.

The first significant jazz organist was Fats Waller, whose experience playing the church instrument and as organist at the Lincoln and Lafayette theaters in New York gave him a unique command of the expressive possibilities of the pipe organ. He performed on the instrument with all sizes of ensemble: in duos with singers, in trios, quartets, and his swing sextet, and in Fletcher Henderson's orchestra. In all contexts he showed mastery of the possibilities of registration afforded by the organ to vary the timbre of a performance, and of a number of strategies designed to overcome the difficulty of making what was often a cumbersome instrument conform to the rhythmic needs of jazz.

Waller's recordings were made largely on two instruments: the modified Estey church organ in the Victor studios in Camden, New Jersey, and the Compton theater organ at the HMV studios in London. He adopted the same technique on both organs, achieving momentum by employing pedal-operated notes on the first and third beats of the bar, playing sustained chords or comping gently with his left hand, and providing melodic and rhythmic impetus (using a great variety of registration) with his right. In his analysis of the musician's organ work (1985), Machlin suggests that Waller used changes in registration as a deliberate extension of the possibilities available to him for improvisation, and argues that his choice of stops in his performance on *Rusty Pail* (1927, Vic. 20492) was based on the compositional framework of the piece.

In ensemble work, Waller frequently relied on the other instrumentalists to provide rhythmic impetus (the very reverse of his technique on piano) and used the organ for tonal and melodic effects. This is evident on his recordings with the Louisiana Sugar Babes (1929), on which he allows the rhythmic momentum to be furnished by James P. Johnson on piano, Jabbo Smith on cornet, or Garvin Bushell on reed instruments. He also used this technique with Henderson's group on *The Chant* (1926, Col. 817D), where he plays sustained chords on the organ against the movement of the whole big band.

The scarcity of church and theater organs in the venues where jazz was usually performed restricted their use, though a small number of organists came to prominence in New York; in addition to Waller, such musicians as Milt Herth and Count Basie played in the theaters of Broadway and Harlem. Basie's recording activity was limited to the availability of suitably equipped studios. Like Waller (his tutor on the organ), he employed changes in registration to highlight parts of his solos and to shade the accompaniment to other soloists in the band, and he used the pedals to emphasize the first and third beats of the bar. His recording of *Live and love tonight* (1939, first issued on the album *The Complete Count Basie*, i–x, 1936–41, Col. 66101), made with a reduced version of his band on the organ at United Studios in Chicago – an instrument which had not been in use for some time – demonstrates another drawback of the pipe organ in jazz: mechanical noise almost drowns Basie's right-hand trills on a 4′ flute stop, which initially caused the takes to be rejected.

The pipe organ has not been widely employed as a jazz instrument since the 1940s. Isolated experiments in its use

1. Count Basie playing the pipe organ at radio station WHAS, Louisville, KY, February 1947

continued, however, in particular during the 1960s in the work of Michael Garrick, who followed an exploration of the integration of jazz and the spoken word with a series of devotional pieces. On *Jazz Praises at St. Paul's* (1968, Airborne 0021), for full choir and bop jazz ensemble, he played the organ of St. Paul's Cathedral, London. Garrick's settings from the mass and of other texts, including Psalm 73, integrated formal composed passages for choir with sections in which organ and ensemble improvise. He exploited the reverberation and echo effects of the building as an integral part of his compositions, contrasting the sharp rhythms from bass and drums with sustained chords from the choir and organ. A similar intention lay behind John Surman's Salisbury Festival commission *Proverbs and Songs* (1996, ECM 1639), in which John Taylor, playing the cathedral organ, interpolated freely improvised passages between fully scored extracts for choral singers and, in contrast to the sharply defined rhythmic drive of Surman's soprano and baritone saxophone solos, used sustained organ chords in a variety of registrations to employ the reverberant acoustics of the nave.

In 1979 Fred van Hove recorded in a free-jazz style on pipe organ (*Church Organ*, FMP SAJ25). The following decade the Austrian organist Wolfgang Mitterer recorded a sequence of free-jazz duos with the saxophonist Wolfgang Puschnig in the church of St. Andra in Leinz, East Tyrol, which made a comparable use of the building's acoustics to that of the British organists mentioned above, notably on *Hollidi jodldijo* (from the album *Obsoderso*, 1985, Moers Music 02044).

In the 1970s and 1980s Dick Hyman performed and recorded on Wurlitzer theater organs (notably in a duo with the cornetist Ruby Braff on the album *Fats Waller's Heavenly Jive*, 1976, Chi. 162), making use of the immense tonal possibilities of the instrument to complement his own eclectic style, which draws on many periods of jazz. The 1990s saw a number of attempts to look wider than the jazz repertory and back to early and baroque organ music as a basis for pipe-organ improvisation. Particularly notable in Britain is the duo of Steve Lodder and Mark Ramsden (on the album *Above the Clouds*, 1991–5, Breathe 001), which draws on source material by Albinoni, Fiocco, and Stanley. Similar in spirit, but consisting largely of original compositions, which range from funk to neoclassicism and from minimalism to impressionist abstraction, is the album *Un mondo illusorio* (1998, Challenge 70059) by Jasper Van 't Hof, recorded on an Italian baroque organ in the town of Bonefro.

2. The electronic organ. The first electronic organ to be widely used in jazz was the Hammond organ (manufactured from 1935), the relative portability of which led to its adoption on a much wider scale than the pipe organ. On the earliest models the sound was generated by a system of rotating steel "tone wheels" and an electromagnetic pickup, but developments from about 1960 led to a considerable degree of sophistication and the introduction of frequency division and crystal oscillators in the sound generation process, which eventually supplanted the use of tone wheels. It was not possible for players to control the attack of notes on the tone-wheel models, and in order to overcome this rhythmic shortcoming they developed a somewhat staccato style. The innovation of the "percussion" stop greatly increased the definition of attack, and this, together with the use of the rotating Leslie speaker, which produces a tremulant effect, characterized the sound of the Hammond organ (compared with that of other types of electric organ) and made it particularly suitable for jazz as well as for gospel and soul music.

The Hammond organ was immediately adopted by Waller, who recorded a series of spirituals in 1939; these contrast directly with his recordings of the same pieces on pipe organ the previous year. Since the electronic instrument was capable of more rhythmic definition than the pipe organ, he tended to return to a style more akin to that of his piano playing and made fewer changes in registration. Waller took a Hammond organ with him on tour in the late 1930s and made more frequent use of it in performance than his relatively few recordings on the instrument would suggest.

The recordings made in 1939 by Glenn Hardman with a contingent from Basie's orchestra are some of the earliest to include the Hammond organ in an ensemble context. On *Upright Organ Blues* (1939, Col. 35263) Hardman comps firmly on the beat; there is little evidence of the use of pedals, and only in his solo does his right hand escape the attempt to define the tempo in an emulation of a swing trumpet or saxophone solo. On the faster *Who?* (1939, Voc. 4971), from the same session, he relies on Freddie Green on guitar and Jo Jones on drums to maintain the beat; he then uses the organ to play riff patterns behind the soloists and to punctuate the ensemble passages with occasional, but effective, chords, while sustaining root harmonies in his left hand. In this, Hardman's technique is the precursor of that adopted in the late 1940s by Wild Bill Davis and from 1952 by Milt Buckner. Milt Herth, who transferred from the theater organ to the Hammond in the late 1930s, adopted a different solution to

2. *Members of Bill Doggett's band during a recording session for Columbia, New York, February 1962: (left to right) Wilmer Snakesnider and Clifford Davis (tenor saxophones), Les Taylor (baritone saxophone), and Doggett (Hammond B-3 electronic organ; the lever on the left below the keyboards operates the Leslie speaker)*

this rhythmic problem, comparable to that chosen by the Louisiana Sugar Babes, by including a pianist (generally a stride player such as Willie "the Lion" Smith or Ralph Sutton) in his quartet.

Having taken up Hammond organ in 1951, Jimmy Smith formed his first trio in 1955, the same year in which the Hammond company introduced its now classic model B-3 (the last B-3 was manufactured in 1973). Smith brought together the pipe-organ styles of Waller and Basie and the later swing approach, with its rhythm-and-blues overtones, of Davis and Buckner and quickly became one of the most significant figures in jazz. He also introduced to the secular bop idiom elements of the style associated with the Hammond organ in sacred African-American gospel music (which was developing as a consequence of the widespread adoption of the instrument in African-American churches during the early 1950s). His mature improvisational style, combining these three features, was coupled with a prodigious technique, which in itself would have made him worthy of critical attention. Smith developed his skill on pedals to a point where he played full walking bass lines with his feet, together with chordal accompaniment with his left hand and everything from fast bop lines to stabbing punctuating chords with his right. A good example of his work is the album *New Sounds on the Organ* (1956, BN 1514). Since Smith's style allowed him to take on most of the work of a conventional rhythm section, the sidemen in his trios tended to be a drummer and a saxophonist. However, he often incorporated a guitarist such as Kenny Burrell in his small groups, and organists who played bass lines on the keys rather than employing a pedalboard followed this example, using the guitarist to comp chords and leaving their own left hand free to play walking bass and other linear figures.

Smith's success owed much to the enthusiasm of Francis Wolff at Blue Note. Wolff first heard him at Smalls' Paradise in January 1956 and went on to manage that portion of the label's output which dealt with organ jazz and funk; the players he recorded included Billy Gardner (with George Braith and Grant Green), Brother Jack McDuff, Jimmy McGriff, Big John Patton, Emmanuel Riggins (with Grant Green), Freddie Roach, Lonnie Smith, Earl Van Dyke (with the saxophonist Fred Jackson), Baby Face Willette, and Larry Young. Shirley Scott also recorded for the label, notably with her then husband, Stanley Turrentine. Although Blue Note did not hold a monopoly on Hammond organ players, with Prestige serving as its principal rival, Wolff's devoted stewardship of the Philadelphia school of players created a sub-genre of organ jazz. In due course several of his roster moved on to other record labels, and through them the style was carried forward, as well as in the work of such players as Groove Holmes and (in the UK) Mike Carr (particularly in his work with Ronnie Scott).

The Hammond organ, through its promotion by Smith and its assimilation into rock music (in the work of Billy Preston and others), made a vital contribution to the development of jazz in the 1960s and 1970s. In the mid-1960s Jacques Loussier extended his experiments on piano with the trio Play Bach to the organ, using a Hammond instrument set to replicate the sound of a Baroque church organ. On *Play Bach*, iv (1963, Lon. 3365), Loussier may be heard on organ and piano simultaneously, an effect achieved by means of double tracking, and within the self-imposed limitations of his genre the results add tonal variety to his work.

In the late 1960s, after a fruitful collaboration with Johnny Hodges, Wild Bill Davis joined Duke Ellington's orchestra, adding yet another texture to those available to Ellington for his compositions. On *Blues for New Orleans*, from *New Orleans Suite* (1970, Atl. 1580), Davis and Ellington tackle the same problems of integrating the organ into the big band that Waller and Henderson faced 44 years previously. For Davis's solo, Ellington adopts the solution of reinforcing the organist's sustained chords with a rhythmic piano accompaniment, just as Waller relied for this support on the playing of James P. Johnson.

Also in the late 1960s Larry Young brought the language of modal free jazz to the Hammond organ. Although the encroachment of other electronic keyboards threatened the survival of the instrument in jazz in the early 1980s (*see also* SYNTHESIZER), it has enjoyed a gradual and successful rehabilitation ever since. Free-jazz ideas have been as significant in the oeuvre of Alice Coltrane as her preoccupations with non-Western scales and harmonies, and her idiosyncratic organ playing is in many ways more personal and distinctive than her piano work. That this remained true for over three decades was reinforced by her appearance on organ with her son Ravi Coltrane at the 1998 Knitting Factory Festival in New York. Don Pullen, certainly better known as a pianist, spent considerable periods of his early career as a soul-jazz organist, and on occasion transferred his Ayleresque technique of sweeping countercurrents of glissandos from the piano to the organ; later he played the instrument with John Scofield, Maceo Parker, and Kip Hanrahan, but an outstanding example of his playing is on David Murray's *Shakill's Warrior* (1991, DIW 850).

Technically the Hammond organ has not remained beached in the 1930s: in addition to continual refinements of its design and modifications to the Leslie speaker, some players have experimented with sampling and other electronics. Principal among these is Barbara Dennerlein, who coupled a MIDI system to her instrument so that the synthesizer tone and the woody sound of her bass lines on her album *Hot Stuff!* (1990, Enja 6050-2) are actually generated by the Hammond keyboard and pedals. Another player who incorporated modifications to the Hammond into his work is Joey DeFrancesco, who plays an upgraded C-3, but who essentially employs a style that assimilates much of the funk-based organ-trio jazz of the 1960s. This is evident on his numerous recordings for Columbia, including *Live at the Five Spot* (1993, Col. CK53805). Larry Goldings also plays in a style that owes much to the 1960s tradition, but he has equally effectively absorbed the freer improvisational vocabulary of Larry Young, and, like Young, has arrived at a distinctive individual tone (not least through disabling the slow spin speed of his Leslie speakers). He shared Pullen's talent for collective and group improvisation, especially in a fruitful collaboration with John Scofield, starting with *Hand Jive* (1993, BN B21Z-27327) and continuing through the 1990s in both recordings and international tours.

Whereas Goldings's collaborations with Scofield kept a discernible connection with the 1960s style of organ ensemble, the similar instrumentation of John Abercrombie's groups with organ and guitar tended to inhabit a more fluid musical landscape, using the tone of Dan Wall's Hammond B-3 to complement the open, spacey sound of his guitar, a characteristic example being the trio album (with the drummer Adam Nussbaum) *Speak of the Devil* (1993, ECM 1511). Through the work of DeFrancesco, Dennerlein, Goldings, and Wall there was a worldwide renewal of interest in the electronic organ at the end of the 20th century, involving such international players as James Taylor, Gary Baldwin, and Ed Bentley in Britain, and Andy Emler and Eddy Louiss in France.

BIBLIOGRAPHY

J.-E. Berendt: *Das Jazzbuch: Entwicklung und Bedeutung der Jazzmusik* (Frankfurt am Main, Germany, 1953, rev. 2/1959 as *Das neue Jazzbuch*, Eng. trans., New York, 1962; rev. and enlarged 5/1981 as *Das grosse Jazzbuch: von New Orleans bis Jazz Rock*, Eng. trans. as *The Jazz Book: from New Orleans to Fusion and Beyond*, Westport, CT, 1982)
M. Brooks: Liner notes, *Superchief: Count Basie, 1936–1942* (CBS M67205, 1972)
H. Davies: "Hammond organ," *GroveI*
P. Williams and B. Owen: "Organ," *GroveI*
E. Peterson: "The Rich History of the Electronic Organ," *Keyboard*, ix/11 (1983), 32
C. Basie and A. Murray: *Good Morning Blues: the Autobiography of Count Basie* (New York, 1985)
P. S. Machlin: *Stride: the Music of Fats Waller* (Boston and London, 1985), 41
H. C. Boyer: "Gospel music, §II," *GroveAM*
F. Wolff: Liner notes, *The Best of Jimmy Smith* (BN B1-91140, 1988)
G. X. Alexander: "Jazz Organ: Burnin' on the Big Bad B-3," *Keyboard*, xv/5 (1989), 42
B. Watson: "The Beast Bites Back: Jimmy McGriff," *Wire*, no.65 (1989), 26
B. Morton: "Barbara Dennerlein: Hammonds are a Girl's Best Friend," *Wire*, no.90 (1991), 34
K. Shadwick: "Hammond Organ Heroes," *Jazz FM*, no.11 (1992), 20
P. Watson: "Don Pullen: Invisible Jukebox," *Wire*, no.109 (1993), 44
A. Shipton: "Let There be Jazz: John Surman, Salisbury Cathedral," *The Times* (5 June 1996)
J. Lacomme, comp.: *Jazz Organ: a Discography* (Paris, 1997)
R. Palmer: "Jimmy Smith on Record," *JJI*, l/11 (1997), 6

ALYN SHIPTON

Original Creole Band [Original Creole Orchestra, Original Creole Jass Band]. Early jazz band. It grew from a five-piece group formed by BILL JOHNSON (i) to tour the Southwest around 1908. Johnson, principally a double bass player, was performing on mandolin at the time; the other members of the group were the cornetist Ernest Coycault, the trombonist H. Pattio or Albert Paddio, the guitarist Charles Washington, and the double bass player Alphonse Ferzand. When the tour was over the musicians settled in Los Angeles. The name Original Creole Band may have been employed from around 1912 and was certainly in use from the time, in 1913, when the pianist and drummer Dink Johnson, the guitarist Norwood Williams (*c*1880–1943), and the violinist Jimmy Palao (*c*1885–*c*1925), all of whom had been working in New Orleans, joined the ensemble. When in 1914 the band was invited to tour, Johnson sent to New Orleans for the cornetist Freddie Keppard, the clarinetist George Baquet, and the trombonist Eddie Vincent (Venson; *b c*1885). The band toured on the Pantages, Loew, and Orpheum circuits (without Dink Johnson, who decided to remain in Los Angeles), and during the next three years appeared throughout North America and held long-term engagements in Chicago and New York. Although Johnson was the leader and Williams the manager, Keppard was the dominant personality, and it was he who refused Victor's offer in 1916 to become the first jazz band to record. The group disbanded in Boston in the spring of 1917 but re-formed in New York in the autumn of that year, when Baquet's place was taken by Big Eye Louis Nelson and, after a few months, Jimmie Noone; the trombonist George Filhe (1872–1954) replaced Vincent for a brief period. Back in Chicago, Keppard continued to work occasionally with the band until 1918, when he was succeeded by Joe (not yet King) Oliver, who eventually took over its leadership. It is therefore thought unlikely that this is the same "Creole Band" which recorded for Victor in New York in December 1918.

A photograph of the band taken around 1914 shows the name Original Creole Orchestra on the bass drum, but the group later appeared on the East Coast as the Original Creole Jass Band. Sometimes billed as "the Famous Creole Band from New Orleans," it was also known simply as the Creole Band, the Creole Orchestra, or the Creole Jass Band.

BIBLIOGRAPHY

S. B. Charters and L. Kunstadt: *Jazz: a History of the New York Scene* (Garden City, NY, 1962/*R*1981), 55
A. Rose and E. Souchon: *New Orleans Jazz: a Family Album* (Baton Rouge, LA, 1967, rev. and enlarged 3/1984)
A. Barrell: "B is for . . . Baquet," *Fn*, xvii/3 (1986), 4
L. Gushee: "How the Creole Band Came to Be," *Black Music Research Journal*, viii/1 (1988), 83

MIKE HAZELDINE

Original Dixieland Jazz [Jass] **Band** [ODJB]. Five-piece jazz band. Its original members, all from New Orleans, were Nick LaRocca (leader and cornet), Larry Shields (clarinet), Eddie Edwards (trombone), Tony Sbarbaro (drums), and Henry Ragas (who was replaced by J. Russel Robinson, piano). After playing in Chicago in 1916, the five musicians moved to New York, where they enjoyed sensational receptions during their residency at Reisenweber's Restaurant from January 1917. During the same year the group became the first jazz band to make phonograph recordings, and in doing so the

The Original Dixieland Jazz Band, New York, 1917: (left to right) Tony Sbarbaro (drums), Eddie Edwards (trombone), Nick LaRocca (cornet), Larry Shields (clarinet), and Henry Ragas (piano)

musicians achieved a degree of eminence that was out of proportion to their musical skills. The group was based in London from April 1919 to July 1920, when it returned to New York. During the mid-1920s, when the vogue for dancing to jazz temporarily subsided, the group disbanded; it re-formed again in 1936, but the reunion was brief and only moderately successful.

No member of the Original Dixieland Jazz Band was particularly talented as an improviser, and the group's phrasing was rhythmically stilted; but, even so, its collective vigor had an infectious spirit. When African-American jazz bands began to record regularly it soon became apparent that many of them were more adept at jazz improvising and phrasing than was the Original Dixieland Jazz Band. Detractors of the band maintain that it merely simplified the music of African-American New Orleans groups, and cite specific antecedents for its compositions *Tiger Rag* and *Sensation Rag*. Casual listeners were intrigued by its repertory, however, which was unlike anything else then on record. The group presented a new sound rather than a new music; this sound, and the rhythms in which it was couched, appealed to young dancers, who were eager to break away from the rigidly formal dance steps of the era.

The most passionate advocate of the Original Dixieland Jazz Band's importance to jazz history was LaRocca himself, who never ceased claiming that his band had played a vital role in the "invention" of jazz in New Orleans during the early years of the 20th century. The fact that there is no evidence to support LaRocca's contention has caused many jazz devotees to ignore the merits of the band's music. But it is indisputable that the group played a major part in popularizing the dixieland style of jazz throughout the USA and Europe.

SELECTED RECORDINGS

(all recorded for Victor)

Livery Stable Blues (1917, 18255); Tiger Rag (1918, 18472); Sensation Rag (1918, 18483); Clarinet Marmalade Blues (1918, 18513); Jazz Me Blues (1921, 18722); Royal Garden Blues (1921, 18798); Skeleton Jangle/Tiger Rag (1936, 25524)

SELECTED FILMS AND VIDEOS

The Good-for-nothing (1917); It's on the Record (1937); March of Time, iii/7 (1937); March of Time, x/12 (1944)

BIBLIOGRAPHY

SL, vi/9–10 (1955) [special issue]
H. H. Lange: *The Fabulous Fives* (Lübbecke, Germany, 1959, rev. 2/1978, by R. Jewson, D. Hamilton-Smith, and R. Webb) [discography]
H. O. Brunn: *The Story of the Original Dixieland Jazz Band* (Baton Rouge, LA, 1960/*R*1977)
H. H. Lange: *Nick LaRocca: ein Porträt* (Wetzlar, Germany, 1960)
R. Blesh: Liner notes, *The Original Dixieland Jazz Band* (RCA LPV547, 1967)
B. Rust: "Grateful for the Warning," *Sv*, no.9 (1967), 24
D. Morgenstern: Liner notes, *The Original Dixieland Jazz Band* (GHB 100, 1983)
B. Rust: *My Kind of Jazz* (London, 1990)
H. H. Lange: *Als der Jazz begann, 1916–1923: von der Original Dixieland Jazz Band bis zu King Olivers Creole Jazz Band* (Berlin, 1991)

JOHN CHILTON

Original Jazz Classics [OJC]. Record label founded in 1983 by the Fantasy company.

Original Memphis Five. Dixieland quintet. Its formation in 1917 has been credited in some sources to the trumpeter Phil Napoleon (who became its leader) and in others to the pianist Frank Signorelli; it disbanded temporarily around 1920, but then re-formed. Regular sidemen were the clarinetist Jimmy Lytell (1922–5), the drummer Jack Roth, and either Miff Mole or Charlie Panelli on trombone;

numerous other players recorded with the group occasionally, among them many of the best session and dance-band musicians of the period. Between 1921 and 1931 it made hundreds of titles, recording for almost every label in the USA, and appeared regularly at the Balconades, a club on Broadway.

Although the repertory of the Original Memphis Five included much contemporary popular music, it consisted mainly of New Orleans and dixieland standards, blues, and original material. The group's performance routine was fairly inflexible: pieces were made up of opening and closing ensemble choruses and a series of solos for the members of the front line and sometimes the pianist. The recordings reveal that the soloists played with energy and power, though their style had something of the jerkiness of ragtime. Lytell's solos are lyrical and he makes use of the chalumeau register as a means of expression; Mole plays ruggedly, but with splendid control and melodic flair; and Napoleon, often criticized for a preoccupation with technique, gives a firm lead. On the early tracks, which were made before the development of electric techniques in 1925, the drums were often silenced and the quintet had to rely on the piano alone for rhythmic support, thereby forfeiting some depth and immediacy. In the 1940s and 1950s the name Original Memphis Five was used again by both Napoleon and Signorelli for occasional performances and recordings.

SELECTED RECORDINGS

My Honey's Lovin' Arms (1922, Arto 9140); I wish I could shimmy like my sister Kate (1922, Para. 20161); Aggravatin' Poppa (1923, Voc. 14506); Sweet Lovin' Mama (1923, PAct 020921); Great White Way Blues/ Shufflin' Mose (1923, Edison 51204); Jazz Me Blues (1931, Col. 2588D)

BIBLIOGRAPHY

R. Harris and B. Rust: *Recorded Jazz: a Critical Guide* (Harmondsworth, England, 1958), 161
H. H. Lange: *The Fabulous Fives* (Lübbecke, Germany, 1959, rev. 2/1978, by R. Jewson, D. Hamilton-Smith, and R. Webb) [discography]
B. Morris: "Busiest Band in the Land," *SL*, xlii (1990), summer, 8

KEN RATTENBURY

Original New Orleans Jazz Band (i). New Orleans jazz band. It was active from around 1916 in Chicago under the leadership of the cornetist and trombonist Merritt Brunies; its other members were the trombonist and cornetist Emile Christian, the clarinetist Johnny Fischer, the pianist Freddie Rose, and the drummer Freddie Williams. The band did not record, and it ceased to be active in 1918. (A. Rose and E. Souchon: *New Orleans Jazz: a Family Album*, Baton Rouge, LA, 1967, rev. and enlarged 3/1984)

MIKE HAZELDINE

Original New Orleans Jazz Band (ii). New Orleans jazz band. It was formed as the New Orleans Jazz Band in New York in 1918 by the comedian and pianist Jimmy Durante and was modeled on the Original Dixieland Jazz Band, which Durante had heard at Reisenweber's Restaurant; the other members were Frank Christian (cornet), Achille Baquet (clarinet), Frank L'Hotak (trombone), and Johnny Stein (drums). Stein was replaced later in 1918 by Arnold Loyacano, but had returned by 1920. As the Original New Orleans Jazz Band the group recorded *Ole Miss/Ja-da* (1918, OK 1156) and *Ja-da/He's had no lovin' for a long, long time* (1919, Gen. 4508). In 1920 it performed and recorded as Jimmy Durante's Jazz Band.

BIBLIOGRAPHY

H. H. Lange: *The Fabulous Fives* (Lübbecke, Germany, 1959, rev. 2/1978, by R. Jewson, D. Hamilton-Smith, and R. Webb) [discography]
H. R. Rookmaaker: Liner notes, *New Orleans Boys, 1918–1927* (Riv. 8818, 1966)
A. Rose and E. Souchon: *New Orleans Jazz: a Family Album* (Baton Rouge, LA, 1967, rev. and enlarged 3/1984)

MIKE HAZELDINE

Original Nighthawk Orchestra. Shortened form of the name Coon-Sanders Original Nighthawk Orchestra, taken in 1924 by the band led by Carleton Coon and JOE SANDERS.

Original Teddies [International Teddies, Teddies]. Swiss swing band. It was led by TEDDY STAUFFER from 1929 and was re-formed by him in 1939; when he left in 1941 the leadership was assumed by the former sideman EDDIE BRUNNER. Among the group's principal soloists were Kurt Hohenberger, Ernst Höllerhagen, Walter Dobschinski, and Brunner.

Original Tuxedo Orchestra [Tuxedo Brass Band, Tuxedo Jazz Orchestra]. New Orleans group active as a brass band and a dance orchestra. Although Papa Celestin's group, which played at the Tuxedo Dance Hall from 1910, was sometimes known as the Tuxedo Brass Band, the Original Tuxedo Orchestra was founded in 1917 by Celestin and the trombonist William "Bebe" Ridgley. It served as an important training ground for several musicians and included such players as Lorenzo Tio, Jr. (who had already worked with Celestin and Ridgley at the Tuxedo Dance Hall, *c*1913–14), Mutt Carey, Willie Pajeaud, Louis Armstrong, Alphonse Picou, Sam Dutrey, Sr., Isidore Barbarin, and Louis Keppard. In 1925 divisions within the ensemble led to a breakup of the group, with Ridgley taking many of the sidemen and keeping the original name and Celestin forming a new band called the Tuxedo Jazz Orchestra. Celestin made a number of recordings with his new group (1926–7). (R. H. Knowles: *Fallen Heroes: a History of New Orleans Brass Bands* (New Orleans, 1996), 106)

See also CELESTIN, PAPA; for illustration *see* BANJO.

WILLIAM J. SCHAFER

Oriole (i). Record label. It was established by McCrory's stores in 1921 and at first drew its catalogue from those of Emerson and Grey Gull. From the mid-1920s the label belonged to the Plaza group, and is of interest in that it occasionally issued takes of recordings that were not put out on Plaza's other labels; these included items by Clarence Williams's groups. The label was continued after the formation of the AMERICAN RECORD CORPORATION, becoming one of that organization's "dime-store" labels with its own important race series. With the other dime-store labels, Oriole was discontinued in April 1938.

BIBLIOGRAPHY

R. M. W. Dixon and J. Godrich: *Recording the Blues* (London, 1970)
B. Rust: *The American Record Label Book* (New Rochelle, NY, 1978), 220
A. Sutton: *Directory of American Disc Record Brands and Manufacturers, 1891–1943* (Westport, CT, and London, 1994), 112
R. M. W. Dixon, J. Godrich, and H. Rye: *Blues & Gospel Records, 1890–1943* (Oxford, England, rev. and enlarged 4/1997), xxxii

HOWARD RYE

Oriole (ii). Record label. It was owned by Levy's of London and made issues only intermittently. The 1000 series, which contained 13 discs released from 1927, is commonly known as Oriole's race series because all but one of its titles were drawn from Vocalion's race repertory. In 1931 issue began of the P100 series, which consisted of recordings made in Britain, including some by Adelaide Hall accompanied by the pianists Francis Carter and Joe Turner (i). The LV100 series of 1934 drew its repertory from the French label Ultraphon and contained discs by the Quintette du Hot Club de France and an excellent item by the trumpeter Freddy Taylor and his group. Levy's revived the label again in 1950, taking material from several American labels, most notably Mercury. In the early 1960s a related company, Oriole Records Ltd., embarked on a major program of reissues of jazz LPs from Savoy, which they released on the Realm label. After 1965 Realm was maintained by CBS.

BIBLIOGRAPHY

L. Wright: "A Glimpse into the Past, 5: the Oriole 1000 Series," *Sv*, i/6 (1966), 26

R. Jewson, D. Smith, and R. Webb: "Arthur Gainsbury's Guide to Junkshoppers: Oriole," *Sv*, no.34 (1971), 148

B. Rust: *The American Record Label Book* (New Rochelle, NY, 1978), 221

H. Rye: "Visiting Firemen, 10(a): Adelaide Hall, Joe Turner, and Francis J. Carter," *Sv*, no.114 (1984), 211

HOWARD RYE

Orlay, Jenő [Orlay-Obendorfer, Chappy]. *See* Chappy.

Orquesta Cubana de Música Moderna. Cuban group. It was founded in 1967 by the alto saxophonist Paquito D'Rivera, the trumpeter Arturo Sandoval, and the pianist Chucho Valdés; its name was intended to disguise the fact that it played jazz, which was not officially tolerated by the Cuban government in the 1960s and 1970s. Around 1973 the three founders and other members of the group formed Irakere.

Ørsted Pedersen, Niels-Henning [NHOP] (*b* Osted, Denmark, 27 May 1946). Danish double bass player. He learned piano at around the age of seven and took up double bass to play in a family band when he was 13. Quickly becoming a virtuoso on the instrument, he joined the house band at the Montmartre Jazzhus in Copenhagen on New Year's Eve 1961, and there over the next several years he played in a rhythm section with Kenny Drew, Bent Axen, or Tete Montoliu on piano, and Alex Riel, Makaya Ntshoko, or Albert "Tootie" Heath on drums. He refused offers to join Count Basie's orchestra in the USA in order to finish his studies. While at the Montmartre, and in the years that followed, he performed and recorded with Bud Powell, Brew Moore, Don Byas, Roland Kirk, Kenny Dorham, Sahib Shihab, Drew, Ben Webster, Johnny Griffin, Karin Krog, and scores of other leading jazz musicians; he toured Europe for a week in mid-autumn 1965 as a member of a quartet led by Bill Evans (ii), and he was associated with Dexter Gordon on a regular basis until 1976, when Gordon returned to the USA. From 1972 he toured and recorded with Oscar Peterson (see illustration); he also worked frequently with Joe Pass (for further illustration *see* Pass, Joe) and Drew, and he was much in demand in the studios (he had recorded about 400 albums by the time he left Peterson in 1987). Thereafter he performed as the leader of his own groups, which from the 1990s have been mainly trios, with Ulf Wakenius on guitar and either Lennart Gruvstedt or Jonas Johansen on drums, though he also worked extensively as a freelance. In the late 1980s Ørsted Pedersen formed a trio with Palle Mikkelborg and the keyboard player Kenneth Knudsen and recorded an album of duos with Allan Botschinsky (1987). Later he performed and recorded in a trio with Maria João and Aki Takase (1990) and in duos with Philip Catherine (1991) and Michel Petrucciani (1994). He has taught at the Rytmiske Musikkonservatorium in Copenhagen.

Oscar Peterson (piano) and Niels-Henning Ørsted Pedersen (double bass) at the BBC television studios, London, c1982

Although Ørsted Pedersen has performed in swing and free-jazz ensembles, he is at his best as a sideman in bop groups. His perfect sense of rhythm, compelling walking bass lines, and deep, roaring timbre are particularly evident on the album *Catalonian Fire* (1974), recorded with Montoliu. He is especially talented in the manipulation of rapid solo lines in the higher register of the instrument and at playing pizzicato with three or four fingers of his right hand, and he is accomplished in the use of the bow.

SELECTED RECORDINGS

Duos: with K. Drew: *Duo* (1973, Ste. 1002); with J. Pass: *Chops* (1978, Pablo 2310830); with A. Shepp: *Looking at Bird* (1980, Ste. 1149); with P. Catherine: *The Viking* (1983, Pablo 2310894)

As leader: *Jaywalkin'* (1975, Ste. 1041); *Double Bass* (1976, Ste. 1055); *Live at Montmartre*, i (1976, Ste. 1083); *To a Brother* (1993, Pladekompagniet 481362-2); *Friends Forever* (1995, Mlst. 9269); *This is All I Ask* (1997, Verve 539695-2)

As sideman: D. Byas: *Anthropology* (1963, Debut 142); D. Gordon: *One Flight Up* (1964, BN 84176); T. Montoliu: *Catalonian Fire* (1974, Ste. 1017); O. Peterson: *Oscar Peterson at the Montreux Jazz Festival 1975* (1975, Pablo 2310747); S. Getz: *Live at Montmartre* (1977, Ste. 1073–4); O. Peterson: *The Paris Concert* (1978, PL 2620112); C. Basie: *Kansas City Six* (1981, Pablo 2310871); Per Goldschmidt: *Frankly: a Tribute to Sinatra* (1993, Mlst. 9224)

SELECTED FILMS AND VIDEOS

The South Bank Show: Oscar Peterson (1984); Svend Asmussen Quartet (1986); Kenny Drew Trio (*c* late 1980s)

BIBLIOGRAPHY

J. Lind: "Danish Modern: Niels-Henning Ørsted Pedersen," *DB*, xxxii/12 (1965), 18

D. C. Hunt: "Definitive Bass Artistry: Niels-Henning Ørsted Pedersen and Charles 'Buster' Williams," *J&P*, ix/10 (1970), 43

I. S. Petersen: "NHOP," *Jh*, no.316 (1975), 16; Eng. trans. in *Coda*, xii/6 (1975), 2

J. Solothurnman: "The Life and Experiences of Niels-Henning Oersted Pedersen," *JF* [intl edn], no.39 (1976), 34

D. Grisman: "Niels-Henning Ørsted Pedersen: Jazz's European Bass," *Musician*, no.48 (1982), 26
P. Carles: "NHOP ou la basse eclairée," *Jm*, no.347 (1986), 28
A. Astrup: "Niels-Henning Ørsted Pedersen," *JJI*, xli/6 (1988), 6
G. Endress: "Melodische Dialoge: Niels-Henning Ørsted Pedersen und Allan Botschinsky," *JP*, xxxvii/1 (1988), 8
P. H. Larsen: NHOP for the Record," *Nordic Sounds*, no.1 (1991), 2
M. Jansson: "Niels-Henning Ørsted Pedersen," *Bass Player*, vii/5 (1996), 36
P. Pettinger: *Bill Evans: How my Heart Sings* (New Haven, CT, and London, 1998)
J. Woodard: "Niels-Henning Ørsted Pedersen: the Great Dane's Low Tones and Highlights," *JT*, xxviii/3 (1998), 34

FRANK BÜCHMANN-MØLLER, BK

Orszaczky, Jackie [Miklos Jozsef] (*b* Budapest, 8 May 1948). Hungarian and Australian composer, arranger, electric bass guitarist, and singer. He studied classical piano and violin. By the time he was in his early twenties he was a significant influence in Hungarian rock music, though his band Syrius, which toured Europe and then Australia in 1970–71, incorporated jazz concepts. In 1974 he returned to Australia and recorded his first jazz album. He took dual citizenship in 1979. While he worked mainly within the soul genre, Orszaczky regularly used jazz musicians in his bands, and thereby proved an enormous influence on the composing, arranging, producing and bandleading skills of a generation of Sydney-based musicians. Some of his bands, such as the Hungarian Rap Sadists and Industrial Accident, were more unclassifiable and experimental in nature. In the late 1990s his Orszaczky Budget Orchestra performed compositions by Albert Ayler and Eddie Harris alongside those of the soul singer James Brown and Orszaczky himself.

SELECTED RECORDINGS

As leader: *Beramiada* (1974, Real 322); *100%* (1994, Gong 37759); of Orszaczky Budget Orchestra: *Deep Down and Out* (1997, LK 001)
As sideman with David Addes: *Bird on a Head* (1991, RooArt 84811-2)

BIBLIOGRAPHY

J. Shand: "The Grandmaster Himself," *Australasian Jazz 'n' Blues*, ii/4 (1995), 22

JOHN SHAND

Ortega, Anthony (Robert) [Tony] (*b* Los Angeles, 7 June 1928). Alto and tenor saxophonist, clarinetist, and flutist. His early professional work included performances and recordings with the bandleader Earle Spencer (1947). After three years in the army (1948–51) he joined Lionel Hampton's big band, and recorded with Hampton, Gigi Gryce, and Art Farmer in Paris (1953). He played briefly with Milt Buckner (late 1953), performed and recorded with Norwegian players in Oslo (mid-1954), then formed his own group in Los Angeles. In 1955 he moved to New York, where he worked with Nat Pierce from 1956 to 1958. He then returned to Los Angeles and played with Paul Bley, the Lighthouse All Stars, and Claude Williamson; he also recorded the album *Jazz for Young Moderns* with Jimmy Cleveland and other former members of Hampton's band. This received extremely unfavorable reviews and Ortega had difficulty finding significant work during the next few years; he played in hotels, theaters, and desert nightclubs in California and Nevada. From 1964, however, he performed as a soloist on soundtracks for several films, most notably *The Pawnbroker* (1964), on which he plays soprano saxophone. In 1965 he was engaged by Don Ellis and Gerald Wilson, and the following year he began to perform and record once more as a leader. Together with Dizzy Gillespie he was a soloist in Lalo Schifrin's band for a concert at the Hollywood Bowl in 1968. He toured Japan with Quincy Jones in 1971, played flute and alto saxophone in the Los Angeles area with Wilson's big band into the mid-1980s, and returned to Japan with Benny Carter in 1994. From 1992 he toured France annually, and he recorded three albums there (1992–4). Although he is essentially a bop musician, Ortega incorporated some aspects of free playing in his style, as may be heard on his albums for the Revelation label in the mid-1960s, in a duo with Chuck Domanico and in a trio with Bill Goodwin and the double bass player Bill West.

Oral history material in *CLU*.

SELECTED RECORDINGS

Duos with C. Domanico: on *New Dance!* (1966–7, Rev. 3), The Shadow of your Smile, Sentimentalize, Conversation Piece (1966); on *Permutations* (1966–7, Rev. 7), I Love You, Pizzicato, Arco (1966)
As leader: Blues for Ortega/I can't get started (1954, Musica 9006); *Jazz for Young Moderns* (1958–9, Beth. 79); on *New Dance!* (1966–7, Rev. 3), New Dance (1967); on *Permutations* (1966–7, Rev. 7), My Buddy, G, the Key, 'Tis Autumn (1967); *Rain Dance* (1978, Dis. 788); *On Evidence* (1992, Evidence 213); *Neuf* (1994, Evidence 620)
As sideman: M. Ferguson: *Boy with Lots of Brass* (1957, EmA 36114); N. Pierce: *Chamber Music for Moderns* (1957, Coral 57128); M. Wofford: *Mike Wofford Plays Jerome Kern* (*c*1980, Dis. 808)

BIBLIOGRAPHY

FeatherE
J. Delmas: "Comment Anthony Ortega fait sa musique avec un jugement circonstancié sur la relation Konitz/Ortega/Braxton," *Jh*, no.311 (1974), 14
F. Billard and M. Gourgues: "Quand le silence est d'Ortega," *Jm*, no.304 (1982), 20

BRENDA PENNELL/BK

Ory, Kid [Edouard, Edward] (*b* La Place, LA, 25 Dec 1886; *d* Honolulu, 23 Jan 1973). Trombonist and bandleader. His baptismal certificate, dated 7 May 1887, gives his birth name, Edouard, and confirms his birthday as 25 December; while not giving the year of birth, the certificate nonetheless implies most strongly that it must have been 1886 (lest the parents leave their Catholic son unbaptized), and certainly rules out the year 1890, which has appeared in many sources. He made various informal instruments before acquiring a banjo at the age of ten and a trombone – first with valves and then the slide instrument – about four years later; by this time he was a laborer supporting the family, his mother having died and his father having become an invalid. Between 1912 and 1919 he led one of the most prominent bands in New Orleans, with Mutt Carey, King Oliver, Louis Armstrong, Johnny Dodds, Sidney Bechet, Big Eye Louis Nelson, Jimmie Noone, and Ed Garland among his sidemen. He then moved to California, taking with him Carey and Garland, and led a group known first as Kid Ory's Brownskinned Babies and later as Kid Ory's Original Creole Jazz Band, or, occasionally, Sunshine Orchestra; in Los Angeles, as SPIKES' SEVEN PODS OF PEPPER, it became the first of the African-American New Orleans style jazz bands to issue a recording, *Ory's Creole Trombone/Society Blues*. (The session has long been dated spring 1922, but Floyd Levin asserts that the record firm's files give 1921.) Late in 1925 Ory went to Chicago, where he joined King Oliver's Dixie Syncopators and participated in some of the period's most important jazz recording sessions, with Oliver, Louis Armstrong's Hot Five (for illustration *see* ARMSTRONG, LOUIS, fig.1), Jelly Roll Morton's Red Hot Peppers, and the NEW ORLEANS WANDERERS. Having begun to tour to New York with Oliver in May 1927, he instead returned to Chicago to work with Dave Peyton and lesser-known bandleaders.

Ory returned to Los Angeles in 1930, where he worked initially with Carey's Jeffersonians. After performing in the show *Lucky Day* in San Francisco, in 1933 he abandoned music to work on a poultry farm, in a railroad post office, as a cook, and as a custodian; he resumed playing in Barney Bigard's group in Los Angeles in 1942, however, and regained prominence through his performances with Bunk Johnson in San Francisco in 1943 and more significantly on Orson Welles's radio broadcasts in 1944, with Noone (replaced by Bigard, Omer Simeon, and then Darnell Howard), Carey, Garland, and Zutty Singleton as fellow bandmembers. With Howard, Joe Darensbourg, Bigard, and Minor Hall among his sidemen, Ory then held long residencies at the Jade Room in Hollywood (April 1945–1949), the Beverly Cavern in Los Angeles (1949–53), his own club, On the Levee, in San Francisco (1954–61), the Beverly Cavern again, and the riverboat at Disneyland. In 1966 he retired to Hawaii.

Ory's playing was highly rhythmic; he made full use of slurs and glissandos in the early tailgate trombone style, of which he was the most famous exponent, and was also notable for his use of mutes (*see* Mute, §3). Ory is widely believed to have composed the well-known *Muskrat Ramble*. However, on a Voice of America broadcast (a tape of which is held at the Louis Armstrong House and Archives), Armstrong explains in detail that he wrote *Muskrat Ramble* but Ory took credit for it; Armstrong – ever the *laissez-faire* personality in regard to questions such as this – simply let Ory's claim go unchallenged.

Oral history material in *LNT*.

SELECTED RECORDINGS

As leader: of Spikes' Seven Pods of Pepper: Ory's Creole Trombone/Society Blues (1921/1922, Nordskog 3009); Get out of Here/Blues for Jimmie (1944, Crescent 2); Maryland, my Maryland (1945, Crescent 3); Down Home Rag (1945, Crescent 4); Maple Leaf Rag (1945, Crescent 8); *Kid Ory's Creole Jazz Band, 1954* (1954, GTJ 12004)

As sideman: Louis Armstrong: Muskrat Ramble (1926, OK 8300); Lil Armstrong: Drop that Sack (1926, Voc. 1037); New Orleans Wanderers: Perdido Street Blues/Gate Mouth (1926, Col. 698D); J. R. Morton: Smoke-house Blues (1926, Vic. 20296); Dead Man Blues (1926, Vic. 20252); Doctor Jazz (1926, Vic. 20415); K. Oliver: Every Tub (1927, Voc. 1114); Louis Armstrong: Potato Head Blues (1927, OK 8503); S.O.L. Blues (1927, Col. 35661); Ory's Creole Trombone (1927, Col. 35838)

SELECTED FILMS AND VIDEOS

Crossfire (1947); New Orleans (1947); Sarah Vaughan and Herb Jeffries/Kid Ory and his Creole Jazz Band/Mahogany Magic (1950); Tailgate Man from New Orleans (1956); L'Homme de la Nouvelle-Orléans (1958); L'INA présente Kid Ory (1959); Disneyland after Dark (1962)

BIBLIOGRAPHY

ChartersJ; *WrightK*
R. Blesh: "Listen to What Ory Says," *Jazz Record*, no.37 (1945), 8
A. Hubner: "Ory: That New Orleans Trombone," *Jazz Notes*, no.60 (1946), 4
J. Greenough: "What Did Ory Say?," *Record Changer*, vi/9 (1947), 5
O. Keepnews: "Ory Rhythm," *Record Changer*, viii/1 (1949), 12
M. Ertegun: "Just Playing Music I Love, Says Kid Ory," *DB*, xviii/16 (1951), 2
K. Mohr: "Kid Ory," *Jh*, no. 113 (1956), 16
A. Nicholas: "Parle de Kid Ory," *Jh*, no. 113 (1956), 16
N. Ertegun: "The Ory Story," *Kid Ory's Creole Jazz Band, 1954* (GTJ 12004, 1957) [liner notes]
J. G. Jepsen: *Kid Ory* (Copenhagen, 1957) [discography]
Giltrap and Dixon: *Kid Ory* (London, n.d. [?1958])
T. Standish: "Ory & Co.," *JJ*, xii/12 (1959), 3
"The Legend that is Kid Ory," *Jazz News* (15 Jan 1960), 6
J. Hubbart: "Kid Ory: Ageless as his Music," *Jazz Report*, i/12 (1961), [3]
G. Probert: "Blowing with the Kid," *Jazz Report*, i/10 (1961), [3]
G. Marne: "The Kid Ory Story," *IM*, lxii/6 (1964), 18
E. Lambert: "Quality Jazz, no.4: Kid Ory," *JJ*, xviii/11 (1965), 19
J. Lucas: "Kid StOry," *JJ*, xviii/1 (1965), 6
M. Williams: "The Kid," *Jazz Masters of New Orleans* (New York and London, 1967/*R*1978), 205
L. Feather: "Kid's Place in the Sun," *MM* (16 Jan 1971), 14
M. Jones: "The New Orleans Kid," *MM* (3 Feb 1973), 18
H. Panassié: "Kid Ory," *BHcF*, no.225 (1973), 3
P. Vacher: "Andrew Blakeney: a Lifetime in Music," *Sv*, no.58 (1975), 124
A. Hubner: "Kid Ory," *Selections from the Gutter: Jazz Portraits from "The Jazz Record"*, ed. A. Hodes and C. Hansen (Berkeley, CA, Los Angeles, and London, 1977), 112
D. Marquis: *In Search of Buddy Bolden, First Man of Jazz* (Baton Rouge, LA, and London, 1978/*R*1993)
B. Bigard: *With Louis and the Duke*, ed. B. Martyn (London, 1985)
J. Darensbourg: *Telling it Like it is*, ed. P. Vacher (London, 1987; Baton Rouge, LA, 1987, as *Jazz Odyssey: the Autobiography of Joe Darensbourg*)
S. Bailey: *Greatest Slideman Ever Born* (Southwick, England, n.d. [1988]) [discography]
Gene Anderson: "Johnny Dodds in New Orleans," *American Music*, viii (1990), 405
F. H. Hüger: "Ory's Creole Trombone: Transkription und Analyse der ersten Schallplattenaufnahme einer schwarzen New Orleans Jazzband," *Jf*, xxiii (1991), 9
F. Krieger: "*Society Blues*: zur Geschichte und Analyse der ersten schwarzen Jazz-Schallplattenaufnahmen," *Jf*, xxiv (1992), 99 [incl. transcrs.]
H. Rye: Liner notes, *Kid Ory and his Creole Jazz Band, 1922–1947* (Document 1002, 1996)
S. Bailey: *Greatest Slide Man Ever Born: a Discography of Edward "Kid" Ory* (Southwick, England, 1997)
J. McCusker: "Kid Ory's Baptismal Certificate," *New Orleans Music*, vii/4 (1998), 17

JOSÉ HOSIASSON

Osaka, Masahiko (*b* Akita, Japan, 28 Sept 1966). Japanese drummer and leader. He took up drums at the age of ten and in 1986 enrolled at the Berklee College of Music. In 1990 he returned to Japan to start a professional career, and his participation that same year in Roy Hargrove's quartet with Yutaka Shiina led to the formation, in 1991, of the quintet Jazz Networks (with the addition of Antonio Hart); the group made several successful recordings. In 1992, with Tomonao Hara, Osaka formed a quintet. He teaches part-time at Senzoku Junior College.

SELECTED RECORDINGS

As leader (all recorded for King): *Twelve Colors* (1994, KIJC371); *Black Box* (1996, KICJ280); *Walkin' Down Lexington* (1998, KICJ351); with T. Hara: *def* (1994, KICJ203), *Street and Avenue* (1996, KICJ305), *Quintuplets* (1996, KICJ3506)

As sideman with Jazz Networks (all recorded for Novus J): *Straight to the Standards* (1991, 117); *Beauty and the Beast* (1992, 601); *Blues 'n Ballads* (1993, 616); *In the Movies* (1995, 37056)

KAZUNORI SUGIYAMA

Osamu, Koichi (*b* Osaka, Japan, 24 Oct 1960). Japanese double bass player and leader. He received piano lessons from the age of three, took up guitar at age 13 and electric bass guitar the following year, and changed to double bass when he was 19. Later he performed with Sadao Watanabe, Motohiko Hino, the pianist and keyboard player Makoto Kuriya, and the guitarist Toshiki Nunokawa, with whom he recorded the album *DuoRama* (1999, Jizo 0001). In 1994 Osamu set up his own orchestra, which in 1996 recorded *Three Colored Rainbow* (1996, P-Vine 9403).

KAZUNORI SUGIYAMA

Osborne, Mary [née Orsborn, Mary Estella; Scaffidi, Mary Estella] (*b* Minot, ND, 17 or 18 July 1921; *d* Bakersfield, CA, 4 March 1992). Guitarist and singer. Wilson's obituary (1992) states that the family name was Orsborn; details of the change to Osborne are unknown. Her birthdate appears in standard sources as 17 July, but 18 July appears in both the social security and California death indexes; the latter also confirms her birthname as Orsborn and gives her full married name, Mary Estella Scaffidi. She grew up in a musical family, played ukulele from the age of four, took up violin in elementary school, and changed to guitar when she was nine; a year later she joined her father's ragtime and country string band as a banjoist. From the ages of 11 to 14 she broadcast twice weekly on radio station KLPM in Minot, and when she was 12 she led an all-girl trio in Bismarck, North Dakota, which performed hillbilly music, popular songs, and light classical pieces. At the age of 15 Osborne joined the trio of the pianist Winifred McDonnell (or, as some sources give it, McDonald) as a singer, guitarist, and double bass player; on hearing Charlie Christian perform locally two years later, she immediately acquired an electric instrument and began to imitate his pioneering single-note style. McDonnell's trio broadcast on radio station KDKA, Pittsburgh, before being absorbed into the group led by the bandleader Buddy Rogers, with which Osborne traveled to New York. She then worked on radio, in recording studios, and on 52nd Street, and around 1941 she performed with Joe Venuti.

While working as a freelance in Chicago in 1942 Osborne recorded with Stuff Smith. She performed in concert with Coleman Hawkins and Art Tatum in Philadelphia in 1944 and recorded in concert in New Orleans in January 1945. After moving to New York she recorded with Mary Lou Williams (1945), Coleman Hawkins, Mercer Ellington, and Beryl Booker (all 1946) and led her own swing trio for club work (including a year-long engagement at Kelly's Stable, 1945–6) and several recordings (1945–8). From 1952 to 1962 she played with Elliot Lawrence's quartet on Jack Sterling's radio program on CBS, and she recorded with Tyree Glenn (1957–8) and again as a leader (1959); she may reportedly be seen playing an excellent version of *The Man I Love* in a film clip from a 1958 television show, but exact details are unknown. Osborne settled in 1968 in Bakersfield, California, where she operated the Osborne Guitar Company with her husband, the trumpeter Ralph Scaffidi, taught music, and played locally and in Los Angeles. She performed at the Newport and Concord festivals (early 1970s) and the Kool Jazz Festival in New York (1981) and recorded with Marion McPartland's quintet (1977). Later she appeared in Los Angeles at the Classic Jazz Festival (1989, 1990), the Playboy Jazz Marathon (1990), and the Airport Hilton (1991). She returned to New York in 1990 to play at the Village Vanguard.

SELECTED RECORDINGS

As leader: The one I love belongs to someone else/Mary's Guitar Boogie (1946, Signature 15077); *Now and Then* (1959, ?1981, Stash 215)

As sideman: C. Hawkins: Spotlite (1946, Vic. 40-0131); Low Flame/Allen's Alley (1946, Vic. 40-0133); B. Booker: Low Ceiling (1946, Vic. 40-0147); M. McPartland: *Now's the Time* (1977, Hal. 115)

BIBLIOGRAPHY

L. Feather: "Girls in Jazz: Mary Osborne: a TV Natural," *DB*, xviii/10 (18 May 1951), 4

L. Ferris: "Mary Osborne: a Unique Role in Jazz Guitar History," *GP*, viii/2 (1974), 10

S. Placksin: *American Women in Jazz, 1900 to the Present: their Words, Lives, and Music* (New York, 1982, London, 1985, as *Jazzwomen, 1900 to the Present: their Words, Lives, and Music*), 184

L. Dahl: *Stormy Weather: the Music and Lives of a Century of Jazzwomen* (London, Melbourne, Australia, and New York, 1984), 259

K. Schoemer: "Pop/Jazz: Mary Osborne Makes a Return after 10 Years," *New York Times* (30 Aug 1991)

Obituaries: B. A. Folkart, *Los Angeles Times* (5 March 1992); J. S. Wilson, *New York Times* (6 March 1992); M. Gilbert, *JJI*, xlv/9 (1992), 17; J. Simmen, *BHcF*, no.406 (1992), 28

BK

Osborne, Mike [Michael Evans; Ossie] (*b* Hereford, England, 28 Sept 1941). English alto saxophonist and clarinetist. After moving to London in 1959 to study clarinet, piano, and harmony at the Guildhall School of Music and Drama he quickly developed associations with leading British players. He worked with Mike Westbrook (1959–63, 1967–71), Chris McGregor (1961–75), Stan Tracey (1972, 1975–80), SOS (a trio with Alan Skidmore and John Surman, 1973–5), and Keith Tippett (1980). Between 1961 and 1977 he led his own trios (including one in the mid-1970s with Harry Miller and Louis Moholo), and from 1970 he made several recordings as a leader, notably *Marcel's Muse* (1977, Ogun 810). Osborne ceased to perform in public in 1982, but played occasionally with friends in the late 1990s. In 1999 the label FMR released *Shapes* (FMR 10), an album of previously unissued material which he recorded in 1972 with Surman, Skidmore, Miller, Moholo, and the double bass player Earl Freeman.

BIBLIOGRAPHY

CarrJ; *ChiltonB*; *WickesIBJ*, i

R. Williams: "Mike: Underrated but Undefeated," *MM* (3 Jan 1970), 8

M. Walters: "Fresh Music from Osborne," *Sounds* (6 Feb 1971), 12

C. Fox and V. Wilmer: *The Jazz Scene* (London, 1972), 40

R. Cotterrell, ed.: *Jazz Now: the Jazz Centre Society Guide* (London, 1976)

E. Parker: "Evan Parker Talks to Mike Osborne," *Avant*, no.1 (1997), 48

MARK GILBERT

Osby, Greg(ory Thomas) (*b* St. Louis, MO, 3 Aug 1960). Alto and soprano saxophonist and leader. He began playing clarinet at the age of 12 and took up alto saxophone a year later. He was a professional player by the time he was 15, working in rhythm-and-blues bands around St. Louis. In 1978 he was awarded a scholarship to study at Howard University in Washington, where he met Gary Thomas and Geri Allen. He then attended the Berklee College of Music (1980–83), but left before graduation to tour with Jon Faddis and Dizzy Gillespie. He moved in 1983 to New York, where he played with Woody Shaw, the World Saxophone Quartet, Lester Bowie, and others.

In 1985 Osby began collaborating with Steve Coleman, Dave Holland, Marvin "Smitty" Smith, Thomas, and others in M-BASE, a self-help collective designed to further its members' musical and business interests. Dismissive of the exclusive revivalism of other young musicians centered around Wynton Marsalis, the group's members consciously pursued a modernist agenda and employed numerous resources from beyond the jazz mainstream, including electronics and vernacular idioms such as funk, as well as devising their own ways of organizing pitch and rhythm. Osby devised a method he called "shifting melodic order" and applied this to both composition and improvisation. In essence this involved taking familiar phrases and systematically displacing them melodically and rhythmically, creating a disjunct, off-kilter effect. In some respects the resulting music sounded like an extension of the fusion produced by Miles Davis's groups of the 1980s, but the totality was far more dissonant and abstract. As his recordings as a leader demonstrate, Osby applied his method to a wide range of music, including sombre quasi-operatic performances with the singer Cassandra Wilson, funk vamps, adaptations of hip-hop and rap, and, in the late 1990s, swing with a traditional acoustic jazz group. Despite the chromaticism and angularity of his musical language, Osby maintains that, rather than Parker or Coltrane, his primary influences have been pre-bop players such as Earl Bostic, Johnny Hodges, Louis Jordan, and Don Byas – a measure of the modernizing effect of his method.

Although he is best known for his work as a leader and co-leader in groups variously called Sound Theatre (1985–91), Street Jazz (1992–5), No-Tet (from 1996), and Strata Institute (from 1989), Osby also played with Jack DeJohnette (in his group Special Edition, 1985–91), Herbie Hancock (1988), Muhal Richard Abrams (from 1988), Andrew Hill (from 1988), Michael Formanek (in the group Wide Open Spaces, 1990 – October 1992), and Jaki Byard (1997). He may be seen in the video *M-BASE Jams at BAM* (*c*1989 [filmed 1988]).

SELECTED RECORDINGS

As leader: *Season of Renewal* (1989, JMT 834 435-2); *Man-Talk for Moderns Vol. X* (1991, BN B21Z-95414); *Further Ado* (1996, BN 56543-2)

As sideman: M. Helias: on *The Current Set* (1987, Enja 5041), The Current Set; J. DeJohnette: *Audiovisual Scapes* (1988, MCA/Imp. 8029); A. Hill: *Eternal Spirit* (1989, BN B21S-92051); M. Formanek: *Wide Open Spaces* (1990, Enja 6032-2); J. DeJohnette: *Earth Walk* (1991, BN B21S-96690); J. Hall: *Panorama: Live at the Village Vanguard* (1996, Telarc 83408)

BIBLIOGRAPHY

CarrJ
D. Helland: "Greg Osby: Open on all Sides," *DB*, lvi/10 (1989), 26
E. T. Louis: "Jazz Makes a New Sound with Soul, Pop and Computers," *Smithsonian*, xx/7 (1989), 176
X. Daverat: "Osby et Plaxico: First Exit to Brooklyn," *Jm*, no.390 (1990), 28
R. Cook: "I Will Stand Out . . .," *Wire*, no. 89 (1991), 14
C. Gauffre: "Greg Osby: 'On m'a tiré dessus: il etait temps que je me range . . .'," *Jm*, no.405 (1991), 66
W. Jenkins: "Greg Osby: Restless, Provocative and Now," *JT*, xxi/9 (1991), 27
D. Block: "Greg Osby," *JJI*, xlv/6 (1992), 16
F. Goaty: "Greg Osby, ou, Le meilleur des deux mondes," *Jm*, no.429 (1993), 24
K. Whitehead: "Jazz rebels: Lester Bowie & Greg Osby," *DB*, lx/8 (1993), 17 [incl. discography]
W. Jenkins: "Greg Osby: Taking it all in," *JT*, xxv/10 (1995), 54
K. Vonna: "Greg Osby," *Jh*, no.545 (1997), 14
B. Ratliff: "The Moves of a Jazz Contrarian," *New York Times* (6 Dec 1998)
T. Moon: "In Osby's Orbit," *Jazziz*, xvii/3 (2000), 38
L. Nai: "Greg Osby Interview," *Cadence*, xxvi/5 (2000), 5

MARK GILBERT

Osterwald, Hazy [Osterwälder, Rolf] (*b* Berne, 18 Feb 1922). Swiss trumpeter, vibraphonist, and bandleader. He studied piano in Berne. At the age of 17 he wrote an arrangement of *Rosetta* for a recording by Fred Böhler, which was coupled with his own composition *Fred's Jump* (1939, Col. ZZ1006). He performed as a trumpeter with Böhler (1941), Edmond Cohanier, Philippe Brun, and Teddy Stauffer's Original Teddies. In 1944 he formed his own band, with which he made a large number of recordings (1946–78); among his soloists were Ernst Höllerhagen and Werner Dies. He also recorded as a sideman with the bandleader Bob Huber (1942), the Original Teddies under Eddie Brunner (1944), and Gil Cuppini (1949). Osterwald performed and recorded on vibraphone at the Paris Jazz Fair (1949) with various American musicians, including Sidney Bechet and Charlie Parker, and he toured Europe, Latin America, Israel, and the USA. His band's recordings of modern jazz are well represented by *Boppin' at the Dodge* (1950, Musica 3135), while it may be heard playing swing on *Tired Cats* (1955, Col. ESFD1181). Osterwald's life was the subject of the film *Musik ist Trumpf (Die Hazy Osterwald Story)* (1961).

BIBLIOGRAPHY

ReclamsJ
W. Grieder: *Hazy Osterwald Story: Musik ist Trumpf* (Zurich, 1961)
J.-R. Hippenmeyer: *Le jazz en Suisse, 1930–1970* (Yverdon, Switzerland, 1971)

RAINER E. LOTZ

Österwall, Seymour (*b* Stockholm, 20 Feb 1908; *d* Stockholm, 3 Aug 1981). Swedish bandleader and tenor saxophonist. He played banjo before taking up tenor saxophone. In 1935 his six-piece amateur orchestra, Astoria, was engaged to play at the newly reopened Nalen in Stockholm. A few years later it had developed into Seymour Österwall's (or just Seymour's) Orchestra, a professional, full-time big band; it recorded extensively from 1938 (notably *Margie*, 1941, Son. 3783) and took part in numerous sessions in which it provided accompaniments to popular singers. The group remained at Nalen until 1948, though it also played for summer seasons at the Gröna Lund Tivoli in Stockholm from 1940 to 1957. During this time Österwall's band was one of the best known in Sweden, having several excellent jazz soloists among its members, including at various times the guitarist Sven Stiberg, Gösta Theselius, Charlie Norman, and Lars Gullin. Österwall remained a bandleader until 1959 and then served from 1960 to 1975 as the artistic director at Folkparkerna, a chain of outdoor amusement parks and dance venues. His sister, the singer Irmgard Österwall, and his brother, the double bass player Arthur Österwall, were also well known to Swedish audiences.

BIBLIOGRAPHY

"Svenskt stjärnalbum" [Swedish star-album], *Orkester journalen*, xi/11 (1943), 5
Obituary, R. Dahlgren, *Orkester journalen*, xlix/9 (1981), 6

ERIK KJELLBERG/LARS WESTIN

Ostinato. An accompanimental pattern, usually of one, two, or four bars, repeated continuously beneath precomposed or improvised lines; *see* FORMS, §§1(i)(e) and 7.

OTB [Out of the Blue]. Bop-revival group organized by Blue Note in 1985 on the strength of numerous auditions of emerging players. The band's founding members were the trumpeter Michael Philip Mossman, the alto saxophonist Kenny Garrett (replaced in 1986 by Steve Wilson), the tenor saxophonist Ralph Bowen, the pianist Harry Pickens, the double bass player Robert Hurst (replaced in 1986 by Kenny Davis), and the drummer Ralph Peterson, Jr. Later Renee Rosnes succeeded Pickens (1987), both Kenny Drew, Jr., and Jonny King deputized for Rosnes, and Billy Drummond succeeded Peterson (1988). The group disbanded in 1989. At its best OTB played bop-revival jazz with just enough reckless abandon to lend a hint of freshness to the proceedings.

SELECTED RECORDINGS

(all recorded for Blue Note)

Out of the Blue (1985, 85118); *Inside Track* (1986, 85128); *Live at Mt. Fuji* (1986, 85141); *Spiral Staircase* (1989, B21S-93006)

BIBLIOGRAPHY

P. Keepnews: "They Still Make 'em that Way Anymore," *Musician*, no.95 (1986), 29
J. Levenson: "Riffs: Out of the Blue," *DB*, liii/3 (1986), 15
P. Lawson: "Ralph Bowen: Out of the Blue," *Coda*, no.214 (1987), 16

GK

Otic. Record company and label founded in 1969 by BOBBY NAUGHTON.

Otis, Johnny [Veliotes, John] (*b* Vallejo, CA, 28 Dec 1921). Drummer, vibraphonist, pianist, singer, and bandleader. His father was a grocer in the African-American community in Berkeley, California, and, although he is of Greek ancestry,

Otis adopted an African-American identity as a teenager. He received his first drum set in 1940 and began his career with the pianist Count Otis Matthews and his West Oakland House Rockers. The following year he worked with Matthews and the double bass player Bob Johnson in Reno, Nevada, then joined the violinist and bandleader George Morrison in Denver. In 1942 he transferred to the territory band of Lloyd Hunter, with whom he toured the Midwest. Late in 1943 he formed a band with Preston Love for an engagement at the Barrel House in Omaha, Nebraska. Otis then went to Los Angeles to join Harlan Leonard's band at the Club Alabam. Following a stint with a band led by Bardu Ali, he began leading his own big band at the Club Alabam (1945). His group achieved some success with the recording of *Harlem Nocturne* made at its first session in 1945 and went out on tour, but it soon fell victim to contemporary trends and Otis was obliged in 1947 to reduce it to a jump band.

Later in 1949 an accident which severed three of his fingers interfered with his drumming and led him to concentrate on piano and vibraphone. In that same year, 1949, Otis discovered the singer Little Esther Phillips at a talent show and began featuring her at the Barrel House, a club he had opened in 1948 with Ali. Phillips made a major contribution to the renewed success that followed the band's recording contract with Savoy (1949–51) and the group began touring as the Johnny Otis Rhythm and Blues Caravan. Similar recordings followed for the labels Mercury (1951–2) and Peacock (1953–5). Late in 1955 Otis formed his own record company and label, initially called Ultra and later Dig, for which he recorded through 1957, often as a non-playing leader. In August 1957 he signed a contract with Capitol, aiming at commercial success in the new rock-and-roll market.

In the 1960s, like many who had taken this road, Otis was somewhat eclipsed, but in 1968 he returned to his roots with a blues album, *Cold Shot*, which introduced his son Shuggie Otis (Johnny, Jr.; *b* Los Angeles, 30 Nov 1953) on guitar and which received some acclaim. A new band including Gene Conners, Preston Love, and, from 1970, Clifford Solomon made appearances at the Monterey Jazz Festival; it may be seen in the film *Play Misty for Me* (1971). Tours followed to the Far East (1971), Great Britain (1972), and Africa and Europe (1974). Otis continued to lead bands in California and on tour, making many festival appearances and working across the whole spectrum of jazz, blues, and rhythm-and-blues.

For ten years in the 1970s and 1980s Otis was pastor of his own Landmark Community Church. He also devoted his energies to painting, sculpture, wood-carving, and various entrepreneurial activities outside music. He has published a number of autobiographical memoirs, including two books. From the mid-1990s he has taught a course in black music at Vista College in Berkeley, California, and in 1999 he established the Center for Bay Area Black Music in conjunction with his course.

Another of his sons, Nicky Otis, plays drums, and may be heard on Johnny Otis's album *Spirit of the Black Territory Bands* (1990). A grandson, the electric bass guitarist Lucky Otis, has worked with the Johnny Otis Show.

SELECTED RECORDINGS

As leader: My Baby's Business/Preston's Love Mansion (1945, Excelsior 141) [drums]; Jimmy's Round-the-Clock Blues/Harlem Nocturne (1945, Excelsior 142) [drums]; I'm not falling in love with you (1949, Savoy 749) [vibraphone]; New Orleans Shuffle/Blues Nocturne (1949, Savoy 743) [drums]; Cool and Easy (1950, Savoy 724) [vibraphone]; Dreamin' Blues (1950, Savoy 748) [vibraphone]; first issued on *The Original Johnny Otis Show* (1949–51, Savoy 2230), Honky Tonk Boogie (1951) [vibraphone]; first issued on *Creeping with the Cats* (1955–7, Ace 325), Sleepy Shines Butt Shuffle/Sadie (*c*1955–7); *Cold Shot* (1968, Kent 534); *The Johnny Otis Show Live at Monterey!* (1970, Epic 30473) [pf and vibraphone]; *Spirit of the Black Territory Bands* (1990, Arhoolie 384) [pf and vibraphone]

As sideman: I. Jacquet: Uptown Boogie (1945, Philo 102); Ladies Lullaby/Illinois Stomp (1945, ARA 144); W. Harris: Cock-a-doodle doo/Yonder goes my baby (1945, Philo 104) [all drums]

WRITINGS

Listen to the Lambs (New York, 1968)
"Midnight in the Barrelhouse," *Blues Unlimited* (1970), no.75, p.12; no.76, p.11; no.77, p.13; no.78, p.12
"I Posed as Negro for 18 Years," *Blues Unlimited*, no.129 (1978), 8
Upside your Head! Rhythm and Blues on Central Avenue (Hanover, NH, and London, 1993)

BIBLIOGRAPHY

FeatherE; *Feather–Gitler '70s*; *Feather–GitlerBEJ*
D. Stevens: "Focus on the Johnny Otis Show," *Pop Music Mirror* (1958), Feb, 9
R. Williams: "The Godfather of R and B," *MM* (5 Aug 1972), 21
J. Broven: "A Rap with Johnny Otis," *Blues Unlimited*, no.100 (1973), 11
B. Day, C. Battestini, and J.-P. Battestini: "Johnny Otis," *BHcF*, no.337 (1986), 3
D. Penny: "Johnny Otis Discography, 1945–1952," *Blues & Rhythm* (1986), no.21, p.22; no.22, p.16; no.23, p.17
A. Fonteyne: "Johnny Otis: That TV Screen has Created an Homogenized Culture that is Diluted and No Longer has the Rich Black Beauty of Blues and Jazz," *Soul Bag*, no.122 (1991), 8
S. Stolder: "Nobody Said I was a White Man - I was Just There," *Blues & Rhythm*, no.101 (1995), 4
J. Selvin: "A Life in R&B: Johnny Otis Looks Back on his Remarkable Career, and at the End of an Era," *San Francisco Chronicle* (4 April 2000) <http://www.johnnyotisworld.com/biography/index.html> (2001)
J. J. Perry: "Johnny Otis Pioneering Rhythm and Blues Legend," *Herald Times* [Bloomington, IN] (23 Oct 1998); repr. <http://home.bluemarble.net/~jjperry/features/otis.html> (2001)

HOWARD RYE

Otsuka, George [Keiji] (*b* Tokyo, 6 April 1937). Japanese drummer. Self-taught, he took up drums while working as an assistant for bands, made his professional début with Sadao Watanabe's Cozy Quartet in the late 1950s, and rose to popularity as a member of Hidehiko Matsumoto's quartet (1961–4). In 1965 he formed a successful trio featuring the pianist Hideo Ichikawa and recorded with Roy Haynes as guest drummer; in 1970 he toured Japan in the group Four Drums, consisting of Haynes, Jack DeJohnette, and Mel Lewis. He led a quintet from 1971 and various units under the name of Maracaibo from the late 1970s, and he toured Japan with many visiting musicians, including Elvin Jones, Phil Woods, Reggie Workman, Kenny Kirkland, John Scofield, Richard Beirach, Miroslav Vitous, and Nana Vasconcelos. From the late 1980s he led the group We Three (not to be confused with another Japanese group, We 3), with Hiroyuki Takimoto on piano and Hideaki Kanazawa on double bass. Otsuka has been one of the busiest modern-jazz musicians in Japan, and his group is known for providing a stepping stone for developing young musicians.

SELECTED RECORDINGS

As leader: *Page Two* (1968, Col. XMS10002); *Groovin' with my Soul Brother* (1968, JVC SMJ7506); *Go On* (1972, Three Blind Mice 13); *You are my Sunshine* (1974, Three Blind Mice 35); *Guardian Angels* (1978, Art Union 58); *Maracaibo Cornpone* (1978, Apollon BY30-5142)

KAZUNORI SUGIYAMA

Ottaviano, Roberto (*b* Bari, Italy, 21 Dec 1957). Italian soprano saxophonist and leader. He first played jazz with Pino Minafra in the group Praxis (1980–82), after which he was a member of the Jazz Studio Orchestra (1982–5). During the same period he worked with the drummer Andrea Centazzo (1980–86), led a sextet (1983) and a quartet (1984–5), both with Paolo Fresu, and joined Franz Koglmann's Pipetet (1984). In 1986 he founded Six Mobiles, a sextet of woodwinds and brass, though he also led a conventional quartet with Stefano Battaglia (1986–91). Ottaviano played in the group Similado with Albert Mangelsdorff, Franco D'Andrea, and Trilok Gurtu (1988–90) and in Giorgio Gaslini's groups (1987–93). From 1994 he worked with Mal Waldron, mainly in a duo, and from 1995 in Pierre Favre's groups. He led his own quintet, Koiné, consisting of soprano saxophone, brass, and drums, and Trio Veloce, with Favre and either Irène Schweitzer or Marilyn Crispell (1996). From the early 1990s he also performed as an unaccompanied soloist; the album *Otto* involved eight layers of overdubbing.

Influenced by Steve Lacy, Ottaviano has an individual, edgy sound and plays in a cool manner; he makes use of short, fragmented phrases with a strong rhythmic component. In his compositions he favors contrapuntal writing and modal forms, into which he inserts passages of free jazz.

SELECTED RECORDINGS

As unaccompanied soloist: *Otto* (1991, Splasc(h) 340)

Duos with M. Waldron: *Black Spirits are Here Again* (1996, DIW 917)

As leader: *Aspects* (1983, Tactus 0010); *The Leap* (1987, Red 213); *Sotto il sole giaguaro* (1989, Solstice 1000); of Six Mobiles: *Mingus: Portrait in Six Colours* (1988, Splasc(h) 169); *Above Us* (1991, Splasc(h) 330); of Koiné: *Hybrid and Hot* (1996, Splasc(h) 453)

As sideman: G. Gaslini: *Multipli* (1987, SN 1220); G. Gräwe: *Songs and Variations* (1989, HA 6028); Similado: *Capriccio a Milano* (1989, LMJ 3341); F. Koglmann: *Cantos I–IV* (1992, HA 6123); K. Wheeler: *Window Steps* (1995, ECM 1584); P. Favre: *Souffles* (1997, Intakt 049)

BIBLIOGRAPHY

A. Bazzurro: "Roberto Ottaviano, uno scultore di suoni," *Musica jazz*, lv/11 (1999), 10

<http://www.ijm.it/enartists.html> (1999)

STEFANO ZENNI

Ottersen, Frank (*b* Oslo, 14 March 1921; *d* Kolding, Denmark, 22 May 1971). Norwegian violinist and saxophonist. He played violin from the age of ten and studied with Arvid Fladmo before beginning his career in jazz in Oslo in 1938. Ottersen led orchestras at the Chat Noir and the Grand Hotel, toured Norway, and made recordings as a leader (1942–5, including *Ding dong dang/Skumring* (Twilight), 1942, Odeon N3893), with Alf Søgaard's big band, and with the accordionist Rolf Syversen (1945); later he worked in Denmark with Stuff Smith. His style as a violinist was influenced by that of Stephane Grappelli and Svend Asmussen.

BIBLIOGRAPHY

K. Sandegren and others: *Boken om jazz* (Oslo, 1954)

O. Angell, J. E. Vold, and E. Økland: *Jazz i Norge* (Oslo, 1975)

K. Michelsen, ed.: *Cappelens musikkleksikon* (Oslo, 1978)

B. Stendahl and J. Bergh: *Sigarett Stomp: jazz i Norge, 1940–1950* (Oslo, 1991) [incl. discography]

J. Bergh: *Norwegian Jazz Discography, 1905–1998* (Oslo, 1999)

VIDAR VANBERG

Ousley, Harold (Lomax) (*b* Chicago, 23 Jan 1929). Tenor saxophonist and composer. He first played piano and then clarinet, took up tenor saxophone while in high school, and began playing professionally in the 1940s; at one point he accompanied Billie Holiday. From 1949 to 1956 he performed with circus bands, and in King Kolax's band with Gene Ammons, who strongly influenced his playing; he also was a member of Sun Ra's band in 1952. While with Kolax he made a number of recordings (1954–6), initially accompanying the singer Danny Overbea, and then under Kolax's leadership, including *Right Now* (1954, first issued on *Jazzville Chicago*, ii, 1954–8, Top Rank 111) and *Goodnite Blues* (1954, Vee-Jay 136). He then joined a rock-and-roll group that traveled to New York (1957). In 1958 he performed and recorded as a member of the band accompanying Dinah Washington at the Newport Jazz Festival, and the following year he went to Paris with a song revue; after returning to the USA he played with Clark Terry, Howard McGhee, Joe Newman, Machito, Lionel Hampton (1970), and Count Basie (1973–4). From the 1960s he also led groups of his own. In his later career Ousley became known chiefly as a performer of soul jazz; he made recordings with Brother Jack McDuff (1966) and as a leader (including *The People's Groove*, 1972, Cob. 9017). In 1990 he recorded with Jimmy Witherspoon, and he may be seen performing on New York streets in the video documentary *Jazz Corner* (1991).

BIBLIOGRAPHY

P. Brodowski: "Harold Ousley: Jazz Crusader," *JF* [intl edn], no.61 (1979), 24

<http://hubcap.clemson.edu/~campber/saunders.html> (2000)

HOWARD RYE, BK

Out chorus. The final chorus of a piece (*see* Forms, §2). The term is used generally to mean the repetition of the theme (or "head") at the end of a piece; it is applied more specifically to early styles of jazz where it is used of the final, collectively improvised chorus of a lively number, played in a loud spirited manner.

Outline. Record company and label founded around 1977 by Jane Ira Bloom.

Out of the Blue. *See* Otb.

Outside [out]. To play "outside" or "out" is to depart, in improvisation, from the harmonic structure of the theme. The term came into use in the early 1960s, in conjunction with its antonym, "inside," to describe the playing of musicians who brought into performances of hard bop and modal jazz some of the harmonic license of free jazz; the outstanding exponent of playing outside was Eric Dolphy. The term is cleverly used in the title of Yusef Lateef's album *The Doctor is In . . . and Out* (1976, Atl. 1685).

Ouwerx, John [Jean] (*b* Nivelles, Belgium, 8 March 1903; *d* Brussels, 13 Jan 1983). Belgian pianist. A classically trained musician, he moved in August 1925 to New York and for about four months played organ at the Strand Palace. On his return to Belgium he gave the first performance in the country of George Gershwin's *Rhapsody in Blue* (18 Nov 1927), worked with the group Bistrouille ADO, and lectured on jazz. From 1928 he toured the Netherlands, Switzerland, Italy, and Egypt, and, as a member of the band led by the violinist Marek Weber, Hungary, Switzerland, and Germany; he also arranged film music. After making his first recording, with Gus Deloof in 1931, he worked in 1934 with Robert De Kers in Antwerp and in the same year performed with Stan Brenders. While playing in Brenders's big band (1936–44) he toured with Jean Omer (1941). In the following years he took part in concerts of music for two pianos and four pianos (with, among others, Johnny Jack and Egide Van Gils), worked with Fud Candrix (1945), and played at the

Continental in Brussels. He opened a piano bar on the Belgian coast and then played for eight years in the Belgian Congo (now Zaire). Ouwerx returned to Brussels for the World's Fair of 1958; later he ran another piano bar in Brussels which continued for 14 years.

BIBLIOGRAPHY

H. Ray: *John Ouwerx: sa carrière, ses oeuvres, ses souvenirs* (Brussels, 1945)
R. Pernet, J.-P. Schroeder, and others: *Dictionnaire du jazz à Bruxelles et en Wallonie* (Liège, Belgium, 1991)
R. Pernet: *Belgian Jazz Discography (1897–1999)* (Brussels, 1999)

ROBERT PERNET

Overblowing. A term applied to the technique by means of which the player of a wind instrument produces the octave, 12th, 15th, and further partials above the fundamental in place of the fundamental itself. The technique involves increasing the air pressure and making minute adjustments to the embouchure. Overblowing is a basic facet of wind technique, providing as it does the principal ranges of brass instruments (on some of which the fundamentals or pedal notes are too low to be much used) and the higher octaves in the ranges of woodwinds. Woodwind instruments are often said to "overblow" at a certain interval (the flute and saxophone at the octave, for example, the clarinet at the 12th).

In jazz overblowing is used not only to produce the normal instrumental range, but also to create particular effects. Using False fingering and adjusting the embouchure as required a player overblows to produce pitches above the instrument's normal range and unusual timbres. The exponents in jazz of such unconventional forms of overblowing are principally saxophonists, including Coleman Hawkins, Illinois Jacquet, John Coltrane, Albert Ayler, John Gilmore, Pharoah Sanders, Richie Cole, Joseph Jarman, Roscoe Mitchell, and Anthony Braxton, but such techniques have also been practiced by the bass clarinetist Eric Dolphy (in the early 1960s), the clarinetist John Carter, and the flutist James Newton.

Overton, Hall (F.) (*b* Bangor, MI, 23 Feb 1920; *d* New York, 24 Nov 1972). Composer and pianist. He began composing while still in high school and later studied at the Juilliard School (1947–51) and took private lessons with Wallingford Riegger and Darius Milhaud. While serving in the army (1942–5) he developed great skill as a jazz improviser, and later played with such musicians as Stan Getz, Oscar Pettiford, Teddy Charles, and Jimmy Raney. He also wrote arrangements for Thelonious Monk's orchestra (*The Thelonious Monk Orchestra at Town Hall*, 1959, Riv. 1138) and contributed articles to *Down Beat* and *Jazz Today*. His own music was deeply influenced by jazz, but without his trying to make jazz "respectable" through the unnatural imposition of classical forms or materials.

OLIVER DANIEL/R

Overwater, Tony (*b* Rotterdam, Netherlands, 24 March 1965). Dutch double bass player and composer. Having taken up double bass when he was 17, he studied with John Clayton at the Royal Conservatory in The Hague and received private lessons from Ray Brown, Niels-Henning Ørsted Pedersen, Dave Holland, and Charlie Haden, among others. At the age of 24 he formed his own group, Scapes, and began touring. He joined David Murray and Sunny Murray on a tour of Europe in 1989, and in 1992 toured and recorded with the former and toured further with the latter; he also wrote music for Fritz Lang's classic film *Metropolis* for a performance at a festival in the Netherlands. In 1993 he initiated the Joris Ivens Project and the Cinema Pur Project, each of which combined avant-garde silent films from early in the century with performances by his quartet. During this same period he worked with Michel Godard, Yuri Honing's trio (recording from 1992, including the albums *Gagarin*, 1995, A Records 73025, and *Star Track*, 1996, Jazz in Motion 992010-2), Sylvie Courvoisier, Marc van Roon, Ack van Rooyen, Misha Mengelberg, Dave Liebman, Dave Burrell, Idris Muhammad, and the percussionist Joshua Samson. Overwater composed works for performances at two festivals in the Netherlands (1995), toured Finland, Canada, and Malta with Honing's trio (1996), wrote ballet music (1997), and performed at the opening of the European Film Festival in Nairobi (also 1997). In 1998 he toured China and the Middle East. His group, V, appeared at the Holland Festival, the North Sea Jazz Festival, and the Jazz Marathon in Groningen, playing the music of the popular singer and songwriter Joni Mitchell. He is a co-founder and the director of Jazz in Motion, a foundation which promotes jazz in the Netherlands and issues recordings, notably his own *Motion Music* (1994, Jazz in Motion 0001).
(<http://www.netcetera.nl/jazzfacts/muze/tony.html> (1999))

WIM VAN EYLE

Ovesen, Thomas (*b* Glostrup, Denmark, 4 Dec 1965). Danish double bass player. Self-taught, he began playing professionally in 1984, when he was chosen to represent Denmark in the European youth big band Eurojazz. He became a member of the Radioens Big Band in 1991 and joined Lars Møller's group in 1994. Ovesen, whose playing was inspired by that of Niels-Henning Ørsted Pedersen, has accompanied and recorded with a large number of Danish and visiting jazz musicians, including John Abercrombie, Benny Bailey, Django Bates, the singer Marie Bergman (recording in 1994), Jerry Bergonzi, Bob Brookmeyer, the singer Etta Cameron, Tony Coe, Eliane Elias, Jørgen Emborg, Art Farmer, Benny Golson, Al Grey, Jim Hall, Tom Harrell, Joe Henderson, Abdullah Ibrahim, Jimmy Knepper, Lee Konitz, Joe Lovano, Rob McConnell, Jim McNeely, Hermeto Pascoal, Enrico Pieranunzi, Chris Potter, David Sanborn, Maria Schneider, Jack Sheldon, Clark Terry, Toots Thielemans, Jesper Thilo, McCoy Tyner, Kenny Werner, Putte Wickmann, Jens Winther, and the violinist and vibraphonist Finn Ziegler.

SELECTED RECORDINGS

As sideman: N. Bentzon: *Nexus* (1994, Olufsen 5327); T. Coe and B. Brookmeyer: *Captain Coe's Famous Raceabout* (1995, Sto. 4206); L. Møller: *Colours* (1996, Stunt 19711); D. Bates and Radioens Big Band: *Like Life* (1997, Sto. 4221); Radioens Big Band: *Ways of Seeing* (1997, Sto. 4224)

BIBLIOGRAPHY

K. Frandsen: *Politikens jazzleksikon* (Copenhagen, 1987)
B. Noglik: "On the Scene," *JF* [intl edn], no.122 (1990), 7
K. Vogel: "Thomas Ovesen," *Jazz Special*, no.11 (1993), 20
I. Rod: "Kontrabassister og kæpheste" [Double bass players and hobbies], *Jazz Special*, no.41 (1998), 26

FRANK BÜCHMANN-MØLLER

Owens, Charles [Brown, Charles M.] (*b* Phoenix, AZ, 4 May 1939). Saxophonist. He began to learn saxophone while a student at the University of San Diego, and after military service attended the Berklee School of Music, where he studied alto saxophone with Joe Viola. In 1967–8 he was a member of Buddy Rich's band (he arranged *Ode to Billy Joe* for Rich's album *Mercy, Mercy*), after which he was with Mongo Santamaria's group for two years. During the 1970s he played principally tenor saxophone, though he also worked on the soprano instrument. Following appearances with Bobby Bryant, Paul Humphrey, and the group accompanying the pop and soul singer Diana Ross he toured with the blues-rock musician John Mayall (1971) and with Frank Zappa (1972) and recorded with Bryant (1971) and Henry Franklin (1971, 1974). Later he worked with Patrice Rushen and Gerald Wilson on the West Coast. In 1978 and 1980 Owens made recordings as a leader, including compositions of his own such as *Night Cry*. He also recorded with Lorez Alexandria (1978), James Newton (1979, 1985), and John Carter (1982), from the late 1970s doubling frequently on oboe, english horn, and flute. In the 1980s he worked with Horace Tapscott, with whose band he toured Europe in 1987, and held the baritone saxophone chair in Mercer Ellington's orchestra. He is the leader of the Jazz Winds, a group made up of four wind players. He continued to be active in Los Angeles in the 1990s, and recorded with Carmen Bradford (1993), Jeannie and Jimmy Cheatham (1993, 1995), and Buddy Childers's big band (*c*1996).

SELECTED RECORDINGS

As leader: *The Two Quartets* (1978, Dis. 787), incl. Night Cry; *Charles Owens Plays the Music of Harry Warren* (1980, Dis. 811)

As sideman: B. Rich: *Mercy, Mercy* (1968, PJ 20133), incl. Ode to Billy Joe; H. Franklin: *The Skipper* (1971, Black Jazz 7); *The Skipper at Home* (1974, Black Jazz 17); L. Alexandria: *How Will I Remember You?* (1978, Dis. 782)

BIBLIOGRAPHY

Feather–Gitler '70s

J. A. Simon: "Charles Owens: the Two Quartets," *DB*, xlvi/6 (1979), 24 [record review]

<http://www.gallery41.com/artists/c_owens1.htm> (1999)

DAVID WILD

Owens, Jimmy [James Robert, Jr.] (*b* New York, 9 Dec 1943). Trumpeter, flugelhorn player, composer, and educator. He played informally with Miles Davis's band in 1958 and studied trumpet with Donald Byrd and Carmine Caruso; in 1959–60 he was a member of Marshall Brown's Newport Youth Band. Later he performed with Slide Hampton (1962–3), Lionel Hampton (1963–4), Maynard Ferguson and Gerry Mulligan (both 1964), Charles Mingus and Hank Crawford (both 1964–5), Herbie Mann (1965–6), and Max Roach. He was a founding member of the Thad Jones–Mel Lewis Orchestra in 1966, then played with the New York Jazz Sextet (1966–8) and Clark Terry's big band (from 1967) and toured Europe with Dizzy Gillespie (1968). In 1969 he performed and recorded with Duke Ellington, and at some point he worked with Count Basie (?1968). From 1969 to 1972 he performed in a band led by Billy Taylor (ii) on the "David Frost Show." Also from 1969 he toured and recorded with his own group, the Jimmy Owens Quartet Plus One. He toured Europe with the Young Giants of Jazz (1973), recorded jazz-rock with Billy Cobham's group Spectrum (also 1973), worked with radio orchestras in Germany and Holland, and played in the USA with Chuck Israels's National Jazz Ensemble. Later he recorded with Mingus Dynasty (1979) and Errol Parker (1980).

Owens has been involved in education and business administration and holds a degree from the University of Massachusetts (MEd, 1975); in 1969 he was one of the founders of Collective Black Artists, an organization dedicated to teaching and performing jazz. He has taught and played with Jazzmobile and has toured internationally giving lectures, workshops, and master classes at colleges. He served on the faculties of SUNY, Old Westbury (1962–6), Queensborough Community College, Bayside, New York (1985–7), and Oberlin College Conservatory of Music, Oberlin, Ohio (1992–3), and in 1991 joined the faculty of the Jazz and Contemporary Music Program at the New School for Social Research, New York (from 1996 at the Mannes/New School; from autumn 1999 at the New School University).

Owens may be seen in the television show "Great Performances: Wolf Trap Salutes Dizzy Gillespie: an All-Star Tribute to the Jazz Master" (1988) and the documentary "Jazz-n-Detroit" (1990). In 1989 he performed in a duo with Oliver Jones at the JVC Jazz Festival New York and recorded with Taylor's Jazzmobile Allstars, and in 1992 he worked with Joe Henderson's big band at Lincoln Center. He continued to lead his own quintet into the 1990s; over the years his sidemen have included the pianists Kenny Barron and Stanley Cowell, the guitarists Ted Dunbar, Jimmy Ponder, Eric Johnson, and Michael Howell, the bass players Chris White, Jerry Jemmott, and Kenny Davis, and the drummers Freddie Waits, Billy Cobham, Billy Hart, Charli Persip, Brian Brake, Warren Benbow, and Giulio Capiozzo. He is at his best when improvising fast, deftly articulated hard-bop melodies. His compositions include *Complicity* and *Milan is Love* (both written in 1968).

Oral history material in *NN-Sc* (HBc).

SELECTED RECORDINGS

As leader: with K. Barron: *You had Better Listen* (1967, Atl. 1491); *No Escaping it!* (1970, Pol. 2425031), incl. Complicity, Milan is Love; *Young Man on the Move* (1976, A&M Hor. 712)

As sideman: H. Mann: *Herbie Mann Today* (1965, Atl. 1454); J. Byard: *On the Spot* (1965, 1967, Prst. 7524); on Newport in New York '72: *The Jam Sessions* (1972, Cob. 9025), Lo-slo-bluze; B. Cobham: *Spectrum* (1973, Atl. 7268); Mingus Dynasty: *Chair in the Sky* (1979, Elek. 248); B. Taylor: *Billy Taylor and the Jazzmobile Allstars* (1989, Taylor Made 1003)

BIBLIOGRAPHY

Feather–Gitler '70s

G. Hoefer: "Marshall Brown's Talent Incubator," *DB*, xxxiv/19 (1967), 19

I. Gitler: "Jimmy Owens: Going up," *DB*, xxxv/2 (1968), 20

L. Underwood: "Creating the Business Legacy," *DB*, xlv/17 (1978), 15

E. Jost: *Jazzmusiker: Materialen zur Soziologie der afro-amerikanischen Musik* (Frankfurt am Main, Germany, Berlin, and Vienna, 1981), 97

M. Richards: "Jimmy Owens," *JJI*, xxxix/8 (1986), 6

FREDERICK A. BECK/BK

Owl. Record company and label. The company was founded in 1975 in Paris by Jean-Jacques Pussiau. It remained in operation through the 1990s, and issued new recordings by such artists as Randy Weston, Dave Liebman, Michel Petrucciani and Lee Konitz, Gil Evans and Steve Lacy, Helen Merrill, Ran Blake, the trio of Jimmy Giuffre, Paul Bley, and Steve Swallow, Paolo Fresu, Aldo Romano, and Linda Sharrock and Eric Watson.

BIBLIOGRAPHY

S. Loupien: "Deux stratégies phonographiques en France: Owl par Jean-Jacques Pussiau," *Jm*, nos.266–7 (1978), 25

B. McRae: "The Wise Owl," *JJI*, xxxiii/6 (1980), 26

X. Matthyssens: "Jean-Jacques Pussiau: histoire d'Owl," *Jm*, no.437 (1994), 38

"Owl Records," *Jm*, no.455 (1996), suppl., p.xxiv

BK

Oxley, Tony [Oxo] (*b* Sheffield, England, 15 June 1938). English drummer and percussionist. After playing in military bands he collaborated with Derek Bailey and the double bass player Gavin Bryars in Joseph Holbrooke (1963–6), a group that played jazz before turning to free improvisation. In 1967 he moved to London and became the house drummer at Ronnie Scott's, where he accompanied numerous American visitors. As a result of winning a readers' poll in *Melody Maker* in 1968 he was invited to record, and his first album, *The Baptised Traveller* (1969), illustrated his growing commitment to free improvisation. In the late 1960s he played with, among others, Gordon Beck, Alan Skidmore, John Surman, John McLaughlin, Rolf Kühn, and Mike Gibbs. Oxley began experimenting with amplified percussion in 1970; in the same year, with Evan Parker and Derek Bailey, he founded a record company, Incus, which promoted music of limited commercial appeal. In the 1970s he continued to work as a leader and played with the London Jazz Composers' Orchestra, Parker, Bailey, Kenny Wheeler, Howard Riley, and Paul Rutherford; he also performed in a duo with the multi-instrumentalist Alan Davie and formed the trio SOH with Skidmore and Ali Haurand (1978). During this decade his music was more readily accepted on the Continent than in Britain, and in 1979 he settled in Germany.

In 1984 Oxley formed the Celebration Orchestra, a 14-piece group which underlined his particularly European style of jazz. In broadcasts for Westdeutsche Rundfunk the group sometimes performed in unusual contexts; in 1986–7 it gave concerts with the Glasgow Skye Pipers, and in 1989 it was accompanied by the recorded sounds of the Ruhr Valley steel complex. From 1988 to 1991 Oxley played with Cecil Taylor, performing in groups which ranged in size from duo to orchestra, notably the Feel Trio (alongside William Parker). In the 1980s he also worked with Radu Malfatti, Peter Brötzmann, and Anthony Braxton's trio (with Adelhard Roidinger), and in a quartet with Miroslav Vitous, Joe Lovano, and Enrico Rava; he toured with both Braxton's trio and the cooperative quartet in 1989 and recorded with the trio that same year. While he continued to run the Celebration Orchestra, in the 1990s he led his own quartet, recorded with Tomasz Stańko, and played in duos with Alex Schlippenbach and Bailey. After recording in a quartet with Surman, Paul Bley, and Gary Peacock in 1991, he was a member of a trio with Bley and Furio Di Castri. The following year he began collaborating with Bill Dixon, both in small groups and in the Celebration Orchestra. Oxley's 60th birthday (1998) was marked by two days of concerts in Cologne that were funded by WDR and featured the Celebration Orchestra, Dixon, and the original Joseph Holbrooke group. In 2000 he was again involved with Taylor in various projects, among them a duo.

Although he has always championed rhythmic freedom, Oxley has never rejected the notion of the drummer as a timekeeper and has worked consistently with both approaches; his achievements in the field of free jazz have made him one of the most respected contemporary percussionists. He has generally used an unorthodox set, with a small, incisive hi-hat, an extra large horn-like cowbell, and a collection of drums and cymbals with a wide timbral range. In 1954 he began playing a theater drum set and he retained its variety in his subsequent sets, which have included skulls, blocks, saucepans, home-made electronics, and proprietary signal processors. These he arranges so that striking one instrument will cause its neighbors to resonate in sympathy; his playing has been referred to as "rainforest percussion" because of the rich, showering sound that he creates. In order to reach a wider range of instruments Oxley sometimes performs standing up. He is also a painter and has exhibited his work at multi-media performances which feature his music.

Tony Oxley at the Bath International Music Festival, England, 1997

SELECTED RECORDINGS

Duos with C. Taylor: *Leaf Palm Hand* (1988, FMP CD6)

As leader: of Joseph Holbrooke (with D. Bailey and G. Bryars): Rehearsal Extract (1965, Incus CD Single 01); *The Baptised Traveller* (1969, CBS 52664); *Four Compositions for Sextet* (1970, CBS 64071); *Ichnos* (1971, RCA SF8215); *February Papers* (1977, Incus 18); of SOH (with A. Haurand and A. Skidmore): *SOH* (1981, View 0018); of Celebration Orchestra: *Tomorrow is Here* (1985, Dossier 7507); with P. Bley and F. Di Castri: *Chaos* (1994, SN 121285-2); of Celebration Orchestra: *The Enchanted Messenger* (1994, SN 121284-2)

As sideman: J. McLaughlin: *Extrapolation* (1969, Marmalade 608007); P. Brötzmann: *Berlin Djungle* (1984, FMP 1120); A. Braxton: *Seven Compositions (Trio) (1989)* (1989, HA 6025); Feel Trio: *Looking (Berlin Version)* (1989, FMP CD25); C. Taylor: *Melancholy* (1990, FMP CD104); J. Surman: *Adventure Playground* (1991, ECM 1463); P. Bley: on *In the Evenings Out There* (1991, ECM 1488), Article Four, Interface; B. Dixon: *Vade mecum*, i–ii (1993, SN 121208-2, 121211-2); T. Stańko: *Leosia* (1996, ECM 1603)

BIBLIOGRAPHY

CarrJ; *ChiltonB*; *GrayF*; *WickesIBJ*, i

B. Dawbarn: "Oxley, Drummer at the Storm Centre," *MM* (10 Aug 1968), 8

B. Houston: "Tony's Big Break, at Last," *MM* (26 April 1969), 8

R Williams: "Riley, Oxley and the New Music," *MM* (29 Nov 1969), 10

——: "Electric Tony Oxley," *MM* (7 March 1970), 12

——: "Forget the Thick Drummer Myth," *MM* (5 Sept 1970), 14

K. Hyder: "Oxley in Control," *MM* (16 Feb 1974), 56

B. McRae: "Dying with my Boots on," *JJI*, xxxi/6 (1978), 41

D. Bailey: *Improvisation: its Nature and Practice in Music* (Ashbourne, England, 1980, Englewood Cliffs, NJ, as *Musical Improvisation: its Nature and Practice in Music*, rev. 2/1992)

B. Noglik: "Tony Oxley," *Jazzwerkstatt international* (Berlin, 1981), 447 [incl. interview, discography]

P. Renaud: *La discographie du jazz anglais* (Chaumont, France, 1985)

G. Endress: "Tony Oxley," *JP*, xxxv/4 (1986), 10

B. Priestley: "Tony Oxley: a Drum Celebration," *Wire*, no.32 (1986), 22

E. Jost: *Europas Jazz, 1960–1980* (Frankfurt am Main, Germany, 1987), 289

S. Goodwin: "Tony Oxley," *MD*, xiv/4 (1990), 28

T. Taylor: "A Different Kind of Swing," *Avant*, no.2 (1997), 46

H. Eisenstadt: "Tony Oxley: the Medicine Man Turns 60," *Coda*, no.286 (1999), 2

B. Watson: "Exiled in Time," *Wire*, no.186 (1999), 18

<http://www.shef.ac.uk/misc/rec/ps/efi/moxley.html> (2000) [incl. discography]

MARK GILBERT

Ozone. Record label established in the early 1970s by BORIS ROSE.

Ozone, Makoto (*b* Kōbe, Japan, 25 March 1961). Japanese pianist. The son of a jazz pianist and organist, he was a reluctant student of classical piano as a child. At first, under the influence of Jimmy Smith, he would only play jazz on the Hammond organ, but after attending a concert by Oscar Peterson at the age of 12 he took up jazz piano and transcribed some of Peterson's solos. From 1980 he attended the Berklee College of Music, where he quickly assimilated new ideas through his work with Gary Burton and from the playing of such musicians as Chick Corea. Ozone recorded albums in a duo with Phil Wilson (1982), a faculty member at Berklee, and in a quartet led by Bobby Shew. More significantly, after graduating he joined Burton's band and in 1983 made a world tour; he also began to give performances as an unaccompanied soloist. In 1984, with Burton and Eddie Gomez, he recorded the album *Makoto Ozone*, which demonstrates the versatility and skill that led by the mid-1980s to his being recognized, despite his youth, as an important jazz musician. In 1985 Ozone performed at several international jazz festivals and recorded with Burton for ECM, and in the mid- to late 1980s he occasionally led a trio with Marc Johnson and the drummer Dan Gross; he recorded again with Burton (1987), with Chuck Loeb (1988), and with Johnson (1989).

In 1989 the expiration of Ozone's US work permit forced him to return to Japan, where he hosted the radio show "Ozmic Notes" on KISS-FM in Kōbe (1990–99), playing jazz and other music. During this period he maintained his international connections, performing at the JVC festival in New York with Burton and Eddie Daniels (1992), recording with Johnson and Peter Erskine (1992), and appearing at European festivals (1994). In 1995 he recorded and toured worldwide with Burton and recorded with John Patitucci and Erskine. The following year he played Mozart's Double Piano Concerto in E♭ with Corea and toured in South America. He then formed a trio with Kyoshi Kitagawa and Clarence Penn, which in 1997 recorded with John Scofield as guest soloist and twice on its own. In 1999, inspired by the work of his trio and by the musical environment of New York, Ozone returned to the USA; that same year he performed his symphonic composition *Aguascalientes* with the trio and the Symphony Orchestra of Aguascalientes in Mexico.

SELECTED RECORDINGS

Duos: with P. Wilson: *Live!! at the Berklee Performance Center* (1982, Shiah 113); with M. Johnson: on Johnson: *2 x 4* (1989, EmA 849153-2), Dinner for one please, James, Miss Teri, One Finger Snap; with G. Burton: *Face to Face* (1994, GRP 98052)

As leader: *Makoto Ozone* (1984, Col. FC39624); *Now You Know* (*c*1987, Col. C40676); *The Trio* (1997, Verve 314-537503-2); *Three Wishes* (1997, Verve 314-557562-2); *No Strings Attached* (1999, Verve/Pol. 1450)

As sideman: G. Burton: *Real Life Hits* (1984, ECM 1293); C. Loeb: *My Shining Hour* (1988, Jazz City D22Y-03447)

BIBLIOGRAPHY

F. Bouchard: "Profile: Makoto Ozone," *DB*, lii/9 (1985), 48

R. Hershon and B. Doerschuk: "The Future of Jazz Piano Rests Secure in the Hands of Makoto Ozone," *Keyboard*, xi/11 (1985), 22

K. Franckling: "The Artistry of Makoto Ozone," *JT* (1988), March, 18

B. Donaldson: "An Interview with Makoto Ozone," *Marge Hofacre's Jazz News* (2000), spring, section 2, p.1

ROBERT L. DOERSCHUK/MARK GILBERT, BK

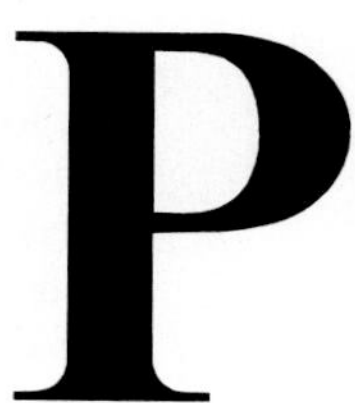

Paakkunainen, Seppo [Baron, Paroni] (*b* Tuusula, nr Kerava, Finland, 24 Oct 1943). Finnish baritone saxophonist, flutist, and composer. He studied flute at the Sibelius Academy in Helsinki (1962–6) and composition at the Berklee College of Music (1975–6). Paakkunainen is a versatile studio musician, but is best known for his unusual fusions of jazz with ethnic music. In the 1970s his group Karelia successfully combined jazz and Finnish folk music and his Conjunto Baron introduced Latin jazz in Finland. With the Lapp singer Nils-Aslak Valkeapää he forged an amalgam of jazz and traditional *joiku* singing. Later he was a co-founder of Saxperiment, a quartet including three saxophonists. His style is well illustrated by his album *Nunnu* (1971, Blue Master 301). He has also written film and theater music.

Oral history material in *FiHJ*.

BIBLIOGRAPHY

A. Granholm: *Finnish Jazz* (Helsinki, 1974, rev. and enlarged 5/1997, by M. Huuskonen, J. Muikku, and T. Vähäsilta)

J. Sermila: "Seppo Paakkunainen: Baron's Beat," *JF* [intl edn], no.36 (1975), 42 [incl. discography]

J. Muikku: "Traditional Values in a Modern Light," *Finnish Music Quarterly* (1989), no.1, p.44

G. Olson: "Seppo: suit paa finska graatkväden" [Seppo: suite on Finnish dirges], *Orkester journalen*, lvii (1989), Feb, 11

T. Tammivuori: "Baron Seppo Paakkunainen: shameneras ättling" [Baron Seppo Paakkunainen: a successor of the shamans], *Musikrevy*, xliv/4 (1989), 17

PEKKA GRONOW

Pablo. Record company and label. The company was established in Los Angeles in 1973 by NORMAN GRANZ and named after the artist Pablo Picasso. It rapidly became extremely successful, continuing the recording policies that Granz had pursued during his association with Verve. Material by such well-known performers as Oscar Peterson, Count Basie, Joe Pass, and Ella Fitzgerald predominated in the catalogue. Granz also set up two subsidiary labels. One of these, Pablo Live (established in 1977), was used to issue recordings of concert performances; the first 14 albums were made at the Montreux International Jazz Festival of 1977, and later recordings were taken at various venues throughout the world. On the other, Pablo Today (founded in 1979), albums were released in much the same styles as those on Pablo itself. By the late 1980s the three labels had been used to issue hundreds of albums, some by previously existing groups, others by all-star ensembles specially organized for the occasion by Granz. The company issued mainly new recordings, but the catalogue also included reissues of material Granz produced for his earlier labels Clef, Norgran, and Verve, as well as a few albums by Jazz at the Philharmonic groups and an LP recorded by John Coltrane in 1963. In 1987 Granz sold Pablo to Fantasy.

BIBLIOGRAPHY

E. Tiegel: "Granz Gamble: Veteran Producer Says Plenty Material Exists for Two Labels," *Billboard*, lxxxix (15 Jan 1977), 29

M. Jones: "Granz: the Prolific Patron," *MM* (30 Dec 1978), 11

E. Tiegel: "Granz will Introduce New Label," *Billboard*, xci (21 April 1979), 3

C. Morris: "Kaffel's Fantasy Buys out Granz's Pablo Jazz Label," *Billboard*, xcix (31 Jan 1987), 6

BK

Pace, Sal(vatore Frank) (*b* White Plains, NY, 10 Aug 1906; *d* New York state, May 1982). Clarinetist and saxophonist. His year of birth has been published as 1910, but Pace gave 1906 in his application for social security. He studied clarinet from 1918 and played dixieland with the Crescent City Five in New York between 1924 and 1928. During the 1930s he was a member of Joe Haymes's swing band (1936) and later he played with the bandleader Al Donahue (1940), Bunny Berigan (1941), and Charlie Spivak (1942–5). At the height of the dixieland revival Pace was performing this style again. After joining Phil Napoleon (1949) he worked with Billy Butterfield, Yank Lawson, and Jimmy McPartland (1951–3). Pace recorded three albums with Pee Wee Erwin (1953, 1955, 1956) and one with Billy Maxted (1955–6). He also played at Nick's in New York with Maxted (1956 – early 1958) and Napoleon (January–April 1959). The track *After You've Gone*, from Erwin's album *Dixieland at the Grandview Inn* (1956, Cadence 1011), offers an example of Pace's style. The social security death index gives his last known residence as Flushing, New York. (*FeatherE*)

BK

Pacific Jazz. Record company and label. The company was founded in Los Angeles in 1952 by Richard Bock and the drummer Roy Harte; Bock later became the sole owner. Its most important early recordings were of the quartet led by Gerry Mulligan and Chet Baker, which were extremely successful and contributed to the formation of the West

Coast jazz style. Under Bock's astute artistic direction Pacific Jazz became one of the most dynamic independent companies on the West Coast in the 1950s, building an impressive catalogue that included the work of some of the most famous instrumentalists in California. Although many later signed contracts with larger organizations, the company captured the finest early work of several musicians, among them Chet Baker, Clare Fischer, Jim Hall, Groove Holmes, Les McCann, Art Pepper, Wes Montgomery, Chico Hamilton, Curtis Amy, Joe Pass, and Don Ellis, all of whom recorded their first sessions as leaders for the label. Bock said that he felt this documentation to have been his most satisfying achievement; he also instituted a Jazz West Coast label for the release of a series of anthologies of the company's recordings.

In 1958 Bock first recorded the work of the Indian sitarist Ravi Shankar. Feeling that Pacific Jazz was an inappropriate label for this music, he founded a subsidiary, World Pacific, to issue Shankar's recordings. This was used to put out several different kinds of music, including some jazz, but was only short-lived. However, the use and seeming interchangeability of the names Pacific Jazz and World Pacific in record catalogues was longstanding and confusing; additionally, some of the Jazz West Coast albums have the World Pacific name at the head of the label. Disillusioned by trends in jazz of the 1960s Bock sold the enterprise to Liberty in 1965; he continued nevertheless to work in an advisory capacity until 1970, when he became a film producer. EMI purchased Liberty in 1980, and control of Pacific Jazz passed to Capitol, which had become a division of EMI in the previous year. In the late 1980s reissue of portions of the catalogue was undertaken by Mosaic (ii), via a licensing agreement; material was also put out on compact disc under leasing arrangements with Japanese companies. By the 1990s control of the Pacific Jazz catalogue had come within the domain of Blue Note, which retained the Pacific Jazz name for reissues. In 1990 Capitol reactivated World Pacific, but not as a jazz label, though among its issues are jazz-tinged recordings by the composer and arranger Vince Mendoza and Gil Goldstein.

BIBLIOGRAPHY

N. Hentoff: "In the Mainstream," *New Yorker*, xxxv (21 March 1959), 51

R. Gordon: *Jazz West Coast: the Los Angeles Jazz Scene of the 1950s* (London and New York, 1986)

J. A. Harrod: "Pacific Jazz: a Discography in Progress," *IAJRC Journal*, xxxi/1 (1998), 9

MARK GARDNER/BK

Packay, Peter [Paquet, Pierre] (*b* Brussels, 8 Aug 1904; *d* Westende, Belgium, 26 Dec 1965). Belgian trumpeter, composer, and arranger. With his family he moved at an early age to China, where he first studied music. He returned in 1912 to Brussels, and despite an accident that left him without the use of one arm took up trumpet in 1924. In the following years he was a member of the Varsity Ramblers and, with David Bee, of the group Bistrouille ADO, as a member of which he wrote such compositions as *Alabama Mamma*, *The Blue Duke*, and *Dixie Melody*; the last named was recorded by the band in 1930 (Col. DF319). After Bee's departure from the group early in 1927 Packay became its leader and devoted greater attention to composition. With several members of Bistrouille ADO he later formed a band called Packay's Swing Academy, which accompanied Coleman Hawkins in Brussels; he also wrote arrangements for the American bandleader Billy Arnold. Packay recorded his piece *Lullaby for a Mexican Alligator* with his own group in 1939 (Jazz Club 4200), but after World War II he abandoned the trumpet and worked exclusively as a composer and arranger. (R. Pernet: *Jazz in Little Belgium, 1881–1966*, Brussels, 1967)

ROBERT PERNET

Padovani, Jean-Marc (*b* Villeneuve-les-Avignon, France, 2 Feb 1956). French saxophonist and composer. After conservatory training in piano and guitar he took up saxophone and made his professional début in 1977. In 1981 he joined Jef Gilson's group Europamérica and the Orchestre Franco-Allemand, directed by Albert Mangelsdorff and Jean-Louis Chautemps. He then turned to composition and worked in theater and films. In 1982 he formed a quartet which included Claude Barthélémy, and the following year he recorded his first album, with Henri Texier and Siegfried Kessler among his sidemen. His association with Barthélémy continued in 1985–6 with some compositions which were recorded in a trio on the album *Sax Blues* for the label Big Noise, which he founded. After giving a concert of flamenco jazz, "Tres horas de sol" (1987), he formed a quartet with the pianist Stéphane Kochoyan, Hélène Labarrière, and the drummer François Verly (1989) and gave several concerts with the writer Enzo Cormann (1989–95). In 1996 he recorded with Paul Motian, Jean-François Jenny-Clark, and Jean-Marie Machado, composed for the flamenco singer Carmen Linares, and toured Africa with a saxophone quartet, l'Echappée Belle. In 1997 he discovered Cambodian music and recorded *Jazz Angkor!*. In his compositions for theater, dance, and film Padovani has continued to bring together jazz and ethnic musics.

SELECTED RECORDINGS

As leader: *Sax Blues* (1985, Big Noise 001); with M. Godard: *Comedy* (1986, Big Noise 113); *Tres horas de sol* (1988, CELP 5); *Nimeno* (1990, Label Bleu 6534); *Mingus, Cuernavaca* (1992, Label Bleu 6549); *Nocturne* (1994, Label Bleu 6566); *Takiya! Takiya!* (1996, Hopi 200014); *Jazz Angkor!* (1997, Hopi 200019); *Chants du Monde* (1998, Hopi 200022)

BIBLIOGRAPHY

C. Gauffre: "Voix nouvelles: ils ont l'âge de *Jazz Mag*: Jean-Marc Padovani," *Jm*, no.334 (1984), 65

——: "Barthélémy et Padovani à grand bruit," *Jm*, no.354 (1986), 19

X. Prévost: "Les personnages de Comedy," *Jm*, no.362 (1987), 28

F. Marmande: "Padovani et le jen de paumes: disque et spectacle, *Tres horas de sol*," *Jm*, no.380 (1989), 22

C. Gauffre: "Ou rode Padovani," *Jm*, no.401 (1991), 50

——: "Jean-Marc Padovani," *Jm*, no.441 (1994), 36

A. Merlin: "Jean-Marc Padovani," *Jazzman*, no.6 (1995), 26

S. Siclier: "Jean-Marc Padovani: dramaturge du jazz," *Le Monde* (18–19 Oct 1998), 25

JACQUES ABOUCAYA

Page, Hot Lips [Oran Thaddeus] (*b* Dallas, 27 Jan 1908; *d* New York, 5 Nov 1954). Trumpeter and singer. Having received his first music lessons from his mother, Page tried his hand at piano, clarinet, and saxophone before finally changing to trumpet at the age of 12. He worked as a professional musician in his home state of Texas during the 1920s, and maintained that he learned to play authentic blues by listening to the local performers there. He toured on the Theater Owners' Booking Association circuit, accompanying such singers as Bessie Smith and Ida Cox, and also toured to New York as a member of the band that accompanied Ma Rainey. From 1928 to 1930 he played with Walter Page's Blue Devils, but by October of the latter year he had joined Bennie Moten's band in Kansas City (for illustration *see* MOTEN, BENNIE). He remained with the band until 1933, when Moten had few jobs and Page transferred into the new band of his fellow sideman Count Basie for work in Little Rock, Arkansas, and elsewhere in the Southwest. In 1934 Page returned to Kansas City and again worked with Moten. Following the leader's death in April 1935 he led a quintet including Herschel Evans and Pete Johnson and also worked occasionally with Basie, whose new band he finally joined at the Reno Club the following year. Page was a featured soloist, as he had been with Moten, but that same summer he left at the behest of Louis Armstrong's manager Joe Glaser to become a solo artist (a move generally regarded as having crippled a potentially illustrious career).

Page's story thereafter is one of failed to only modestly successful attempts at bandleading, brief periods as a featured soloist with other bandleaders, and a continuing, irrepressible enthusiasm for jam sessions. Based in New York, he played in the big band of Louis Metcalf (autumn 1936) before forming his own group for residencies at Smalls' Paradise (August 1937) and the Plantation Club (May 1938). He was a soloist in the first Spirituals to Swing concert at Carnegie Hall (23 December 1938) and in June 1939 recorded with Joe Turner (ii) and Pete Johnson. After leading a new band at Kelly's Stable and the Golden Gate Ballroom he left New York temporarily to tour with Bud Freeman's big band (July 1940). He joined Joe Marsala's group in October 1940, briefly led another big band at the West End Theater Club in November, and that same month recorded with Turner again.

Having led a septet at Kelly's Stable (May–*c* August 1941) Page spent a period in Artie Shaw's band (mid-August 1941–January 1942), during which time he attracted much publicity and made several important recordings as a singer and trumpeter; while with Shaw he suffered from racist reactions to his still uncommon position as an African-American starring in an otherwise white band. In February 1942 he participated in Eddie Condon's first concert at Town Hall, again in a racially integrated band. After forming yet another big band without success, he concentrated on playing in smaller groups from 1943 to 1949. He appeared in some of Condon's Town Hall concerts during 1944, worked in Don Redman's band at the Apollo Theatre in the summer of 1945, and the following spring accompanied Ethel Waters, all while regularly making his presence felt at jam sessions on 52nd Street. From March to August 1949 he was occasionally on the television program "Eddie Condon's Floor Show"; that May he went to Paris to play at the first Festival International de Jazz. He made a recording with Pearl Bailey in 1949, but the resulting hit songs did much more for her career than for his. During the 1950s he appeared mainly as a soloist, twice touring Europe (July–October 1951, summer 1952) and working at Café Society (May–June 1953).

Page made many fine recordings under his own name (1938–54), often leading bands made up of some of the finest swing musicians, among them Earl Bostic, Don Byas, J. C. Higginbotham, and Ben Webster. His purposeful, exciting trumpet playing and his deeply felt blues singing were probably too rugged to gain widespread favor, however. Throughout his career he thrived on the atmosphere of impromptu jam sessions, in which his searing tone, dramatic phrasing, and improvised blues lyrics were a source of considerable inspiration to his fellow musicians.

SELECTED RECORDINGS

As leader: Feelin' High and Happy/Skull Duggery (1938, Bb 7583); I would do anything for you (1940, Decca 7699); Gone with the Gin (1940, Decca 7714); Lafayette/South (1940, Decca 18124); Harlem Rhumbain' the Blues (1940, Decca 8531); Do it if You Wanna (1940, Bb 8634); Pagin' Mr. Page (1944, Savoy 520); I Keep Rollin' on (1944, Savoy 521); Lips' Blues (1944, Savoy 529); The Sheik of Araby (1944, V-disc 418); *Hot Lips Page, 1944–1950: Plays the Blues in B* (1944–5, 1950, Jazz Archives 17), incl. The Blues in "B" (1950) [1944 tracks misattributed to Page; actually E. Berry]; They Raided the Joint (1945, Contl 6017); St. James Infirmary (1947, Har. 1069); with P. Bailey: Baby, It's Cold Outside/The Hucklebuck (1949, Har. 1049)

As sideman: W. Page: Blue Devil Blues/Squabblin' (1929, Voc. 1463); B. Moten: That Too, Do (1930, Vic. 22793); The Blue Room/Milenberg Joys (1932, Vic. 24381); Pete Johnson: Cherry Red (1939, Voc. 4997); J. Turner: Piney Brown Blues (1940, Decca 18121); C. Berry: Gee, ain't I good to you? (1941, Com. 1508); A. Shaw: Blues in the Night (1941, Vic. 27609); St. James Infirmary (1941, Vic. 27895); E. Condon: Uncle Sam Blues (1944, V-disc 191)

BIBLIOGRAPHY

ChiltonW; *McCarthyB*; *SchullerS*; *SheridanC*

L. Page and P. E. Miller: "Forget High Ones and Stick to Melody, Advice of Lips to Trumpeters," *DB*, x/13 (1943), 15

A. Hodeir: "Notes sur Hot Lips Page," *Jh*, no.33 (1949), 11

K. C. Thompson: "Kansas City Man: Hot Lips Page," *Record Changer*, vii/12 (1949), 9

H. Kahn: "That's How Mr. Page Swings – Like a Pendulum," *MM*, xxvii (28 July 1951), 3

Obituaries: *New York Times* (7 Nov 1954); E. Anderson, *MM*, xxx (20 Nov 1954), 7

H. Panassié: "Lips Page," *BHcF*, no.93 (1959), 3

J. G. Jepsen and K. Mohr: *Hot Lips Page* (Basel, Switzerland, 1961) [discography]

D. Morgenstern: "Hot Lips Page," *JJ*, xv (1962), no.7, p.4; no.8, p.2

D. Morgenstern and others: "Hot Lips Page on Record," *JJ*, xv (1962), no.11, p.13; no.12, p.17

D. Morgenstern: "Three Forgotten Giants," *Down Beat Music '65* (Chicago, 1964), 80

G. Schuller: *Early Jazz: its Roots and Musical Development* (New York, 1968)

R. Russell: *Jazz Style in Kansas City and the Southwest* (Berkeley, CA, Los Angeles, and London, 1971, rev. 2/1973/*R*1997)

A. Shaw: *The Street that Never Slept: New York's Fabled 52nd Street* (New York, 1971/*R*1977 as *52nd Street: the Street of Jazz*)

S. Dance: *The World of Count Basie* (New York and London, 1980)

G. Murphy: "The Forgotten Ones: Hot Lips Page," *JJI*, xxxiv/8 (1981), 12

J. Chilton: *Sidney Bechet: the Wizard of Jazz* (London and New York, 1987/*R*1996)

T. Farmerie: "The Sheiky Man from Araby: Hot Lips Page," *Whisky, Women and*, no.17 (1988), [18] [incl. discography by Dave Penny]

N. W. Pearson, Jr.: *Goin' to Kansas City* (Urbana, IL, and London, 1988)

M. Selchow: *Profoundly Blue: a Bio-discographical Scrapbook on Edmond Hall* (Lübbecke, Germany, 1988)

D. Morgenstern: "Oran Hot Lips Page: a Trumpet King in Harlem," *VV* (28 Aug 1990), 73

A.V[asset]: "Notes discographiques: Hot Lips Page et l'orchestre de Bennie Moten," *BHcF*, no.377 (1990), 27

JOHN CHILTON/BK

Page, Marian. Stage name of MARIAN MCPARTLAND early in her career.

Page, Nathen (*b* Leetown, WV, 23 Aug 1937). Electric guitarist. He is self-taught as a guitarist, and was not exposed to jazz until he served in the army. Following his discharge he moved to Washington, DC, where he worked locally with rock bands and in 1965 joined Jimmy Smith's band, replacing Quentin Warren; he stayed with the organist until 1970, touring the USA and Europe, but made only one album, *The Boss* (1969, Verve 68770). After leaving Smith he worked with Herbie Mann and the singer Roberta Flack. He later played with Jackie McLean at the Five Spot and then with Sonny Rollins from 1975 to 1977, including an appearance at the Newport Jazz Festival New York in 1975. He also worked with Tony Williams, and recorded and toured with Rene McLean (1975), Kenny Barron, and

Charles Tolliver, with whom he made an album in Paris (1977). In 1980 Page moved to Orlando, Florida, where he learned to play piano and electric bass guitar. He leads his own quartet, works as a jazz radio announcer, and promotes local concerts. He toured Europe with Lonnie Smith in 1990 and with Alvin Queen in 1991.

BIBLIOGRAPHY

Feather–Gitler '70s
G. Henderson: "Nathen Page: a Short Talk," *Cadence*, xii/11 (1986), 19
M. Baillie: "Nathen Page," *JJI*, xliv/4 (1991), 12

GK

Page, Walter (Sylvester) (*b* Gallatin, MO, 9 Feb 1900; *d* New York, 20 Dec 1957). Double bass player and bandleader. He began on brass bass and bass drum in brass bands and took up double bass in high school in Kansas City. As both a brass bass and double bass player, he worked occasionally with Bennie Moten's band in the early 1920s, and in 1925 founded his own band, the Blue Devils, in Oklahoma City. At various times this group included Hot Lips Page (no relation), Buster Smith, Count Basie, Jimmy Rushing, Lester Young, Eddie Durham, Dan Minor, Alvin Burroughs, and A. G. Godley, making the Blue Devils, along with Moten's group, the most influential jazz band in the area. In 1931 Page was forced for financial reasons to give up leadership of the Blue Devils, and he joined Moten until 1933, during which period he evidently abandoned tuba to concentrate exclusively on double bass. After playing with Basie's Cherry Blossom Orchestra in Kansas City and Little Rock, Arkansas (1933–4), in autumn 1934 he joined the Jeter–Pillars Orchestra in St. Louis. In 1935 he began a fruitful association with Basie's band, with which he remained until August 1943, when he was drafted; following his army service and a tenure in the bands of Nat Towles (spring 1945) and Jesse Price, he worked again with Basie from July 1946 to August 1948 (*see* Basie, count, §2). He was a mainstay of Basie's celebrated rhythm section (for illustrations *see* Films, fig.3, and Jones, jo), where the solidity and swing of his playing enabled the leader to dispense with stride left-hand patterns and Jo Jones to transfer the pulse to the hi-hat cymbals. *Pagin' the Devil*, recorded with the Kansas City Six, a unit from Basie's band, includes one of the earliest jazz solos on double bass. These and other performances established Page as the leading jazz bass player of the late 1930s, and a creator of the walking bass style. In the late 1930s, while with Basie, he also recorded in small groups accompanying Billie Holiday (under her name and that of Teddy Wilson) and Harry James.

After leaving Basie, Page performed and recorded with Sidney Bechet and in 1949 joined Hot Lips Page. In the 1950s he worked mostly in swing and dixieland groups, mainly in New York, with Jimmy Rushing (intermittently from 1951), Jimmy McPartland, Eddie Condon (on television, in recordings, and at Condon's club, 1953–6), and Ruby Braff. However, he was also involved as a freelance in the emerging mainstream jazz movement, notably in the seminal recording sessions led by Vic Dickenson (1953–4) and Buck Clayton (1953–6). He also recorded again with Bechet and with Mel Powell (both 1954), performed with Clayton and Dickenson on the NBC television show "Excursions in Jazz" (February 1954), and, with Clayton, accompanied Holiday at Carnegie Hall (May 1955). He toured with Wild Bill Davison (summer 1956), worked with Roy Eldridge (late 1956), and rejoined Clayton one last time to accompany Rushing at the Great South Bay Jazz Festival in Great River, New York (July 1957).

In the years around 1940, Basie's recording engineers were no match for those at Victor when it came to capturing the sound of a double bass, and so, by comparison with Jimmy Blanton in Duke Ellington's orchestra, Page was ineptly recorded. That such a muddy-sounding bass (nothing of which should be inferred about Basie's contemporary live performances, or Page's ability) could nonetheless be a component of the greatest rhythm section of the swing era in itself says something interesting about the nature of swing: sometimes in the classic Basie recordings the pitches Page is playing can barely be discerned, but the notes are in the right place, and that is what matters most. A dozen or so years later, when Page became a rhythmic anchor of dixie-swing groups and the mainstream jazz movement, he was well captured on recordings. Those who wish to appreciate his pitch selection in bass lines and his melodic sense as a soloist may find numerous examples, including *Beale Street Blues* with Condon.

SELECTED RECORDINGS

As leader: Blue Devil Blues/Squabblin' (1929, Voc. 1463)
As sideman: B. Moten: Toby/Moten Swing (1932, Vic. 23384); Jones–Smith, Inc. [C.Basie]: Shoe-shine Boy/Evenin' (1936, Voc. 3441); C. Basie: Swinging at the Daisy Chain (1937, Decca 1121); One o'Clock Jump (1937, Decca 1363); Jumpin' at the Woodside (1938, Decca 2212); Kansas City Six: Pagin' the Devil (1938, Com. 512); C. Basie: Oh! Red/Fare thee honey, fare thee well (1939, Decca 2780); Dickie's Dream/Lester leaps in (1939, Voc. 5118); E. Condon: *Jam Session Coast to Coast* (1953, Col. CL547), incl. Beale Street Blues; B. Clayton: *A Buck Clayton Jam Session: the Huckle-buck and Robbins' Nest* (1953, Col. CL548); V. Dickenson: *The Vic Dickenson Septet*, i–ii (1953, Van. 8001–2); *The Vic Dickenson Septet*, iii–iv (1954, Van. 8012–13)

BIBLIOGRAPHY

ChiltonW; *McCarthyB*; *SchullerS*; *SheridanCB*
R. Horricks: *Count Basie and his Orchestra: its Music and its Musicians* (London and New York, 1957), 132
Y. Bruynoghe, L. Vaes, and O. Keller: "Le 20 décembre 1957, décédait à New York Walter Page," *Jazz 58*, no.2 (1958), 14
W. Page and F. Driggs: "About my Life in Music," *JR*, i/1 (1958), 12
G. Schuller: *Early Jazz: its Roots and Musical Development* (New York, 1968), 293
R. Russell: *Jazz Style in Kansas City and the Southwest* (Berkeley, CA, Los Angeles, and London, 1971/*R*1983, rev. 2/1973/*R*1997)
M. L. Hester: *Going to Kansas City* (Sherman, TX, 1980), 27
N. W. Pearson, Jr.: *Goin' to Kansas City* (Urbana, IL, and London, 1988)

J. BRADFORD ROBINSON/BK

Paich, Marty [Martin Louis] (*b* Oakland, CA, 23 Jan 1925; *d* Santa Ynez, CA, 12 Aug 1995). Arranger, composer, pianist, and bandleader. He began playing and writing arrangements in Oakland at the age of 16, and from 1943 to 1946 served as arranger for the US Army Air Force Band. He then studied composition with Mario Castelnuovo-Tedesco (1946–50) and gained bachelor's and master's degrees from the Los Angeles Conservatory of Music and Arts. After touring with Jerry Gray (1951) he provided a repertory of compositions for Dan Terry's orchestra (1952), played with Shelly Manne, worked as pianist and conductor for Peggy Lee (1953), and performed with Shorty Rogers's Giants (1954). He became well known in the 1950s for his arrangements for Mel Tormé (which he recorded with his own group, the Marty Paich Dek-tette), as well as work for the Dave Pell Octet (1957), for Art Pepper (1959), and for his own 12- to 13-piece band, which recorded three albums (1957, 1959) with Pepper, Jack Sheldon, Bob Cooper, Jimmy Giuffre, Bill Perkins, Victor Feldman, Scott LaFaro, and Mel Lewis among his sidemen. Paich wrote music for several other artists, including Ella Fitzgerald,

Anita O'Day, Chet Baker, Ray Brown, Buddy Rich, and Stan Kenton, as well as for films and television. In his last decades his activities had little connection to jazz, apart from a visit to Britain in 1988 to conduct the English Neophonic Jazz Orchestra (in a revival of his mid-1960s compositions for Stan Kenton's Los Angeles Neophonic Orchestra) and a revival of his Dek-tette, also in 1988, accompanying Tormé in the USA and Japan. He may be seen in the video documentary *Sarah Vaughan: the Divine One* (1987), taken from the television series "American Masters." The principal publishers of his works are Creative World, Drum City, Kendor, and WIM.

SELECTED RECORDINGS

As leader: *What's New* (1957, Cadence 3010); *The Broadway Bit* (1959, WB 1296); *I Get a Boot out of You* (1959, WB 1349); with M. Tormé: *Reunion* (1988, Conc. 4360)

SELECTED ARRANGEMENTS

(all recorded by others with Paich as sideman)

M. Tormé: *Mel Tormé with the Marty Paich Dek-tette* (1956, Beth. 52); A. O'Day: *Anita O'Day Sings the Winners* (1958, Verve 8283); A. Pepper: *Art Pepper + Eleven* (1959, Cont. 3568); E. Fitzgerald: *Whisper Not* (1966, Verve 64071)

BIBLIOGRAPHY

FeatherE
R. Horricks: "American in London," *MM*, xxxi (26 May 1956), 5
J. Tynan: "Marty Paich," *DB*, xxv/18 (1958), 18
P. Gowers: "Modern Jazz," *Musical Times*, ciii (1962), 389
M. Jones: "Marty Paich," *MM* (8 July 1967), 6
P. Carles, A. Clergeat, and J.-L. Comolli: *Dictionnaire du jazz* (Paris, 1988, rev. and enlarged 2/1994)
R. Horricks: "Marty Paich," *CI*, xxv/11 (1988), 8
T. Gioia: *West Coast Jazz: Modern Jazz in California, 1945–1960* (New York, and Oxford, England, 1992)
Obituaries: *Los Angeles Times* (17 Aug 1995); *New York Times* (18 Aug 1995)

STEVEN STRUNK/BK

Pairing. *See* Coupling.

Pallemaerts, Dré (*b* Anvers, Belgium, 1964). Belgian drummer. He began playing drums at the age of five and studied percussion from 1975. After turning to jazz and then forming a bop group with Erwin Vann he studied with Jeff Hamilton in Los Angeles (1984), performed at a festival in Singapore (1985), and joined Hein Van de Geyn in the trio led by the pianist Jack van Poll. He accompanied such soloists as Arnett Cobb, Spike Robinson, Dave Pike, Dee Dee Bridgewater, and another singer, Dee Daniels, with whom he toured Europe and North Africa. Having played with Buddy Catlett at Jazz Alley in Seattle, he was engaged to remain on at the club as accompanist to Art Farmer and James Williams; he also appeared with Ernestine Anderson at a festival in Bellevue, Washington. On returning to Belgium he formed a trio with Van de Geyn and Michel Herr; the group accompanied Slide Hampton, the trumpeter Bert Joris, and others, and recorded in a quartet under Joris and in a quintet, including Joris, under the leadership of Joe Lovano (both 1986). In 1986 he joined Steve Houben's quartet and worked with Toots Thielemans in Paris, and the following year he toured and recorded with Jarmo Hoogendijk in the Netherlands. Pallemaerts performed with John Campbell and Junior Cook in New York and then returned to Belgium to record with Philip Catherine in advance of a tour of Europe and Africa as a member of the guitarist's trio (1988). He then joined other groups, including a trio with Vann (recording in 1990) and the quartet of the guitarist Serge Lazarevitch (recording in 1989 and 1993), and recorded with Charles Loos (1992, 1996–7).

SELECTED RECORDINGS

As sideman: B. Joris: *Sweet Seventina* (1986, Jazz Cats 6985012); J. Lovano: *Solid Steps* (1986, Jazz Club de Belgique 6011); J. Hoogendijk: *Heart of the Matter* (1987, Tim. 269)

BIBLIOGRAPHY

R. Pernet, J.-P. Schroeder, and others: *Dictionnaire du jazz à Bruxelles et en Wallonie* (Liège, Belgium, 1991)
R. Pernet: *Belgian Jazz Discography (1897–1999)* (Brussels, 1999)
<http://www.jazzinbelgium.org/mus/dre.htm> (2000) [incl. discography]

BK

Palmer, Earl (C., Sr.) (*b* New Orleans, 25 Oct 1924). Drummer. From childhood he performed in vaudeville as a singer and dancer, in which context he toured widely with Ida Cox, among others. After serving in the army (1942–5) he took up drums (*c*1947) and became involved in the groundbreaking rhythm-and-blues style that was emerging at the time in New Orleans; he made his first recordings as a member of Dave Bartholomew's group, with which he may be heard on *Messy Bessy* (*c*1950, first issued on the album *Dave Bartholomew 1949–52*, Charly CD273) and *Stormy Weather* (1952, King 4585). Although he was smitten by bop, he made his mark as the drummer on a number of now classic rhythm-and-blues recordings made in the 1950s by Fats Domino and Little Richard. In 1957 he moved to Los Angeles, where he continued in this vein. Although he recorded for various labels, notably Capitol and Aladdin (1957–61), with his own pop bands, more significantly he supplied the drum parts on definitive hits by such popular artists as Sam Cooke, Ray Charles, and the Righteous Brothers.

As a studio and freelance musician Palmer pursued his interest in jazz whenever circumstances allowed, and his playing is well represented by *Honeysuckle Rose*, on Earl Bostic's *Hits of the Swing Age* (1957, King 571). From 1958 to 1960 he recorded extensively as a member of Ernie Fields's orchestra, the output of which comprised mostly simplified versions of jazz standards aimed at the teenage market. He also played with Red Callender (1959) and Buddy Collette and recorded at the Monterey Jazz Festival with Dizzy Gillespie (1965); later he toured the Middle East as a member of Benny Carter's quintet (December 1975 – January 1976). Palmer performed occasionally with his own band and continued to work regularly as a studio musician until electronic devices began to replace drummers in pop styles in the 1980s. In 1983 he served as the secretary of the Musicians' Union in Los Angeles. Palmer ran jam sessions for many years at Chadney's in Burbank, California; after Chadney's relocated in 1998 to Studio City he led sessions at the Rix Restaurant in Santa Monica. In 1994 he performed in a tribute to Ed Blackwell at the New Orleans Jazz and Heritage Festival. Around 1998 he made an instructional video, *New Orleans Drumming: from R&B to Funk*, and the following year he recorded a ferociously swinging album alongside former members of Charles's band accompanying the blues musician B. B. King (*Let the Good Times Roll: the Music of Louis Jordan*, MCA 112042).

BIBLIOGRAPHY

J. Broven: "Earl Palmer," *Blues Unlimited*, no.115 (1975), 4
R. Flans: "Earl Palmer," *MD*, vii/5 (1983), 8
T. Scherman: "Earl Palmer the Rhythm Bomber, the Funk Machine from New Orleans," *Musician*, no.159 (1992), 62

S. Aiges: "The Peak of Percussion," *New Orleans Times-Picayune* (5 Feb 1993)
W. Thompson: "The Rhythm & Blues Drummers of New Orleans," *Percussive Notes*, xxxiv/4 (1996), 28
T. Scherman: *Backbeat: Earl Palmer's Story* (Washington, DC, and London, 1999)

HOWARD RYE, BK

Palmer, Jeff (*b* Jackson Heights, NY, 1 June 1948). Organist. His father was a professional guitarist. As an accordionist he learned classical music from the age of four, though he was self-taught on organ, which he took up when he was 15. After graduating from high school he worked extensively on the African-American club circuit (although he is white), playing blues and soul jazz. He recorded as an unaccompanied soloist in 1981, toured Europe with Paul Bley in 1982 and 1984, and from 1987 recorded regularly as the leader of a quartet which included Arthur Blythe and John Abercrombie. In 1996 he performed and recorded with Phil Haynes.

SELECTED RECORDINGS

As leader: *Laser Wizard* (1985, Statiras 8081); *Ease On* (1992, Audioquest 1014); *Island Universe* (1994, SN 121301-2); *Shades of the Pine* (1994, Reservoir 137)
As sideman with P. Haynes: *Live Insurgency – Set 1* (1996, SN 121302-2)

BIBLIOGRAPHY

<http://theatreorgans.com/grounds/doodlin/index.html> (2000) [incl. discography]

GK

Palmer, Robert (*b* Little Rock, AR, 19 June 1945; *d* Valhalla, NY, 20 Nov 1997). Writer. As a youth he played reed instruments with rock, country, and soul bands, and later performed as a member of an eclectic group called the Insect Trust, with which he recorded two albums. He was a co-founder of the Memphis Blues Festival in 1966, and the following year graduated from the University of Arkansas. In New York thereafter he became a widely published freelance writer on jazz, rock, and the avant garde. From 1975 he was a regular reviewer for the *New York Times* and in 1981 he was appointed to its staff of jazz and pop critics. Palmer wrote four books, the most important of which was a study of the Delta blues (*Deep Blues*, New York and London, 1981). He held teaching positions at Bowdoin College, Memphis State University, Brooklyn College, CUNY, Yale University, Carnegie Mellon University, and the University of Mississippi, where he worked after leaving the *New York Times* in 1988. He suffered liver and kidney failure in 1996 and returned to the New York area, but died while awaiting a liver transplant. Palmer collaborated musically on informal projects with Ornette Coleman, among others, and wrote and served as music director for two documentaries, "The World According to Coltrane" (1991) and "Deep Blues." He was rare among jazz writers of his and earlier generations in maintaining an unembarrassed interest in a range of music that extended far beyond the traditional boundaries of jazz. (Obituaries: J. Pareles, *New York Times* (21 Nov 1997); K. Mathieson, *The Scotsman* (23 Dec 1997))

JOHN ROCKWELL

Palmer, Roy (*b* New Orleans, 2 April ?1892; *d* Chicago, 22 Dec 1963). Trombonist. His year of birth has been given variously from 1887 to 1896; in an untaped interview with Russell in Chicago in 1940, Palmer gave 1892, and Russell felt that this fitted best the chronology of his career, though the social security death index gives 1887. He first played guitar and worked in New Orleans in the Rozele Orchestra (1906). After taking up trombone he played with Richard M. Jones, Freddie Keppard (1911), Willie Hightower (*c*1914–15), and the Tuxedo and Onward brass bands (1915–16). He toured in 1917, then settled in Chicago, where he played with Lawrence Duhé, King Oliver, and Keppard. Later he played with Doc Cook's orchestra and in a band at the Red Mill Café which included Tommy Ladnier and Teddy Weatherford (*c*1923). Palmer also made recordings with Jelly Roll Morton (1924), Johnny Dodds (1927), Jones and Ida Cox (both 1929), the State Street Ramblers (1931), and the Alabama Rascals (pseudonymously, as the Memphis Night Hawks, 1932). After 1932 he worked mostly in factories, but also taught music; among his pupils were Preston Jackson and Albert Wynn.

SELECTED RECORDINGS

Duos with Bob Hudson: first issued on *State Street Ramblers*, ii (1931–6, RST 1513-2), The Trombone Slide (1932)
As sideman: J. R. Morton: Fish Tail Blues/High Society (1924, Aut. 606); I. Cox: I'm so glad/Jail House Blues (1929, Para. 12965); State Street Ramblers: Georgia Grind/South African Blues (1931, Champion 16279); Sic 'em, Tige' (1931, Champion 16464); first issued on *The Memphis Night Hawks and Chicago Rhythm Kings featuring Roy Palmer* (1932–6, Cygnet CYG1001), Memphis Night Hawks: Beedle-um-bum (1932); Alabama Rascals: Dirty Dozen's Cousins (1932, Per. 0246); Stomp That Thing (1932, Ban. 32760); Memphis Night Hawks: Sweet Feet (1932, Voc. 1736); first issued on [various artists]: B. Crosby: *Bing Crosby and the Rhythm Boys* (1930–35, Arcadia 5001), C. Bullock: My Gal Sal

BIBLIOGRAPHY

W. C. Allen: "Trombone Giants, 1: Roy Palmer," *Hot Notes*, no.13 (n.d. [1948]), 2
P. Van Vorst: "Roy Palmer's Story," *MR*, v/5 (1978), 1
C. Hillman: "The Forgotten Ones: Roy Palmer & Honore Dutrey," *JJI*, xxxix/5 (1986), 12
B. Russell: *New Orleans Style*, comp. and ed. B. Martyn and M. Hazeldine (New Orleans, 1994), 182
C. Hillman: Liner notes, *The Memphis Night Hawks and Chicago Rhythm Kings featuring Roy Palmer* (Cygnet CYG1001, 1997)

BILL RUSSELL/BK

Palmer, Singleton [William] (*b* St. Louis, 13 Nov 1912; *d* St. Louis, 8 March 1993). Double bass and tuba player. Chilton, in *Who's Who of Jazz*, gives his name as Singleton Nathaniel Palmer, but, according to Palmer's own account, on applying for social security payments he discovered that he was born William Palmer. By the time that he enrolled in school his family had somehow dropped the name William in favor of his uncle's name, Singleton; his father was named Nathaniel. He performed and recorded on tuba with the cornetist and singer Oliver Cobb (1929–31) and on double bass with the pianist Eddie Johnson (1931–?1934), then worked with Dewey Jackson (?1934–1941) and George Hudson (1942–8), recorded with Clark Terry (1947), and played with Jimmy Forrest (1948). In September 1948 he joined Count Basie, and when Basie disbanded in January 1950 he left to form his own group, the Dixieland Band, which worked regularly in St. Louis into the early 1990s. Despite suffering from bone cancer in his last years, Palmer played tuba in the band until a few months before his death. A good example of his playing may be heard on *I can't believe that you're in love with me*, on the album *At the Opera House* (1961, Norman 206).
Oral history material in *MoU-St*.

BIBLIOGRAPHY

ChiltonW; *McCarthyB*; *SheridanCB*
S. Dance: "Lightly & Politely: 834: Gaslight Square, St. Louis," *JJ*, xv/9 (1962), 12
B. Rusch: "Singleton Palmer," *Cadence*, xiii/2 (1987), 5
Obituary, *New York Times* (13 March 1993)

J.-P. Battestini: "Singleton 'Cocky' Palmer, 13 nov. 1912 – 8 mars 1993," *BHcF*, no.433 (1995), 5

FRANK DRIGGS

Palmetto. Record company and label formed in New York in 1990 by the guitarist Matt Balitsaris. It recorded in its year of inception and began to issue compact discs about a year later. The only jazz-related material in its first ten recordings was by Balitsaris, but in 1993 Palmetto began recording the organist Greg Hatza, and from 1995 it recorded jazz extensively. By late 2000 it had issued more than 65 recordings, with its catalogue featuring, among others, Ben Allison, the tenor saxophonist Joel Frahm, Larry Goldings's trio with Peter Bernstein and Bill Stewart, Andrew Hill, Cecil McBee, the guitarist Pete McCann, the pianist Steve Million, Dewey Redman, and Matt Wilson.
(<http://www.palmettorecords.com> (2000))

GK

Palmier(i), Remo (*b* New York, 29 March 1923). Guitarist. His first professional work was with the Nat Jaffe Trio in New York (December 1942). He then played with Coleman Hawkins (April–May 1943), but contracted scarlet fever while with the band in Toronto and to his severe disappointment was obliged to quit and remain in an isolation hospital to recover. In 1944 he worked with Red Norvo and led a group accompanying Billie Holiday on 52nd Street. He was with the pianist Phil Moore (November 1944 – February 1945) and recorded with Barney Bigard (1944), Teddy Wilson (1944–5), and, with Charlie Parker, in Dizzy Gillespie's sextet (1945). Although Palmier's primary influences were Django Reinhardt and Charlie Christian, he later adopted the melodic and harmonic concepts of Hawkins and Parker. In 1945 he received the "new star" award from *Esquire* magazine and began a 27-year period as guitarist for the "Arthur Godfrey Show" on television, and the following year he made further recordings with Wilson in a group accompanying Sarah Vaughan. Later, around 1972, he played in a band co-led by Bobby Hackett and Vic Dickenson, and in 1974–5 he occasionally deputized for Bucky Pizzarelli in Benny Goodman's small group. He performed in California at the Concord Jazz Festival's "Guitar Explosion" with Herb Ellis, Emily Remler, Howard Roberts, Tal Farlow, and Barney Kessel in 1975, and during the 1970s also played with Dick Hyman. In 1985 he appeared with Norvo, Louie Bellson, Wilson, and others at an acclaimed concert in New York. In the 1990s he recorded with Bellson's big band (1990) and Joe Wilder's small group (1991) and participated in a concert given by Benny Carter's big band (1992).

SELECTED RECORDINGS

As leader: with H. Ellis: *Windflower* (1978, Conc. 56); *Remo Palmier* (1978, Conc. 76)

As sideman: D. Gillespie: Groovin' High (1945, Guild 1001); All the things you are (1945, Musi. 488); [no leader]: *Swing Reunion* (1985, Book-of-the-Month 717627); J. Wilder: *Alone with my Dreams* (1991, Evening Star 101)

BIBLIOGRAPHY

ConnorBG; *FeatherE*

A. Berle and J. Obrecht: "Remo Palmieri: from Jamming with Jazz Greats on 52nd Street to 27 Years with CBS," *GP*, xii/8 (1978), 38

J. Chilton: *The Song of the Hawk: the Life and Recordings of Coleman Hawkins* (London and New York, 1990)

JIM FERGUSON/BK

Palmieri, Eddie [the Latin Monk] (*b* New York, 15 Dec 1936). Pianist, arranger, and leader. He studied piano from the age of eight, but began his career playing timbales in his uncle's Afro-Cuban band when he was 13. Around this time he learned classical piano and in the mid-1960s he studied arranging. Having worked for Johnny Segui (1955) and the singers Vincentino Valdes (1956) and Tito Rodriguez (1958–60), he formed Conjunto la Perfecta (1961), in which he employed two trombones and a flute rather than a conventional Afro-Cuban front line of several trumpets. By the time the group accompanied Cal Tjader on the album *El sonido nuevo* (1966) Palmieri had added another two trombones, one of which was played by Julian Priester. However, the group disbanded because of financial difficulties in 1968. During the early 1970s Palmieri worked with the Tico All Stars and the Fania All Stars, recorded with Cachao, and continued to lead various groups which played in the Afro-Cuban style that came to be known as salsa. In the remainder of the 1970s and 1980s he incorporated elements of rhythm-and-blues and rock into his recordings, but failed to achieve commercial success. Later he recruited the jazz musicians Bryan Lynch (1988) and Conrad Herwig (1987), and by the early 1990s he had dispensed with a singer and added the alto saxophonist Donald Harrison. With a front line of Herwig, Lynch, and Harrison, and a rhythm section consisting of piano, double bass, timbales, congas, percussion, and drums, his performances and recordings from that time combined energetic salsa rhythms with jazz-influenced improvisation. In the late 1990s Palmieri toured and recorded as a member of the TropiJazz All Stars. Willie Bobo named Palmieri the Latin Monk, after Thelonious Monk, for his use of jazz harmonies and phrasing within the salsa idiom. His brother Charlie Palmieri (*c*1925–1988) was a pianist who led the Afro-Cuban band Orchestra Charanga.

SELECTED RECORDINGS

As leader: with C. Tjader: *El sonido nuevo* (1966, Verve 68651); *Palmas* (1993, Elek. Nonesuch 9-61649-2); *Arrete* (*c*1994, Tropijazz 81657); *Vortex* (*c*1995, Tropijazz 82043)

BIBLIOGRAPHY

CarrJ

J. S. Roberts: "Salsa's Prodigal Sun: Eddie Palmieri," *DB*, xliii/8 (1976), 21

T. Sabournin and E. Fernandez: "Eddie Palmieri: the Times & Temper of Salsa's Space Man," *Musician*, no.54 (1983), 38

F.-M. Coudert: "Eddie Palmieri: le Monk Latin," *Jm*, no.342 (1985), 34

C. Santiago: "The Latin Monk," *JJI*, xlii/5 (1989), 20

F. Gonzalez: "Avant-gardist with a Traditionalist's Heart," *Boston Globe* (17 Feb 1990)

——: "Palmieri's Jazz that Makes You Dance," *Boston Globe* (30 July 1993)

H. Mandel: "Fire on the Clavé: Eddie Palmieri," *DB*, lxi/8 (1994), 28 [incl. discography]

B. Milkowski: "Eddie Palmieri: Burning Down the House," *JT*, xiv/8 (1994), 41

A. Valdés: "Eddie Palmieri Raps on Music and Life," *Boston Globe* (1 Oct 1994)

R. Grosman: "Eddie Palmieri: Mister Latin Jazz," *Jh*, no.519 (1995), 31

D. Heckman: "Music for the Millennium," *Los Angeles Times* (28 April 1996)

GK

Palo Alto. Record company and label. The company was founded in Palo Alto, California, in 1981 by Jim (James) Benham (*b* Joliet, IL, 24 Nov 1935), chairman of the Benham Capital Management Group and a big-band trumpeter. Until 1985 it operated in Palo Alto under the artistic direction of its executive director, Herb Wong, who was well respected in the San Francisco Bay area as a jazz educator and disc jockey. At first it concentrated on issuing new bop recordings, but, after a shift in its emphasis towards insubstantial jazz-rock, Wong left the company and the office in Palo Alto closed. In a different stylistic vein Palo Alto also recorded a session by Linda Hopkins accompanied by a notable group of principally swing-oriented musicians (1982). The organization later moved to Studio City, California.

BIBLIOGRAPHY

L. Feather: "Jim Benham: He Has Full Faith in his Jazz and Business Credits," *San Francisco Chronicle Datebook* (6 Jan 1985), 18

M. Langton: "Jazz Label Closes Bay Area Office, Fires Executive," *San Francisco Examiner* (10 Oct 1985), §C, p.5

BK

Palomar Ballroom. Ballroom in Los Angeles; *see* NIGHTCLUBS AND OTHER VENUES.

Panachord. Record label. It was established in 1931 by Warner Brothers as a British counterpart to American Brunswick's subsidiary Melotone. After 1932 it was administered by Decca, and issue continued until 1939; the jazz catalogue was drawn first from Brunswick, then from the American Record Corporation, and later from Decca. Dutch Decca also used a Panachord label to release cheap recordings in the Netherlands, including important items by such Americans resident in Europe as Coleman Hawkins. The label was revived in the 1980s (by the company Stichting Granny's Records) for a series of reissues on LP of these and of contemporary Dutch jazz recordings.

BIBLIOGRAPHY

J. Hayes: "Date that Disc!, no.4: Panachord 25000 Series," *Gunn Report* (June 1972), 42

B. Rust: *The American Record Label Book* (New Rochelle, NY, 1978), 224

HOWARD RYE

Panassié, Hugues (*b* Paris, 27 Feb 1912; *d* Montauban, France, 8 Dec 1974). French writer. He studied saxophone and first wrote about jazz at the age of 18. In 1932 he was one of the founders of the HOT CLUB DE FRANCE, of which he served as president, and from 1935 to 1939 and, after the war, from 1945 to 1946 he was the editor of the journal *Jazz hot*. With his unrivaled enthusiasm for communication, Panassié wrote hundreds of articles for this and other periodicals (in particular *Bulletin du Hot Club de France*) and was the author of several books, notably *Le jazz hot* (1934), an important study that was among the first to treat jazz seriously. In 1937, with Charles Delaunay, he established the label SWING (ii). In 1938 Count Basie dedicated to him and recorded a composition called *Panassié Stomp*. The same year, in New York, Panassié organized a series of small-group recording sessions with Mezz Mezzrow which also included (at various times) Tommy Ladnier and Sidney Bechet; these were highly influential and contributed considerably to the New Orleans revival movement. In 1939 he recorded a swing septet under the leadership of Frankie Newton. However, Panassié's reputation as an articulate advocate of jazz has to some extent been tarnished by his extreme conservatism: from the mid-1940s he expressed the opinion that bop was not a valid evolution of jazz. His private collection is now in the Discothèque Municipale at Villefranche-de-Rouergue (*see* LIBRARIES AND ARCHIVES, §2).

For illustration *see* MEZZROW, MEZZ.

WRITINGS
(selective list)

Le jazz hot (Paris, 1934; Eng. trans., rev. Panassié, London and New York, 1936/*R*1970)

The Real Jazz (New York and Toronto, 1942 [in Eng. trans.], rev. and enlarged by Panassié 2/1960/*R*1973)

La musique de jazz et le swing (Paris, 1943, [2]/1945)

Douze années de jazz (1927–1938): souvenirs (Paris, 1946)

Cinq mois à New-York (Paris, 1947)

Louis Armstrong (Paris, 1947)

Jazz Panorama (Paris, 1950)

with M. Gautier: *Dictionnaire du jazz* (Paris, 1954; Eng. trans., London, 1956, rev. A. A. Gurwitch as *Guide to Jazz*, Boston, 1956)

Petit guide pour une discothèque de jazz (Paris, 1955)

Discographie critique des meilleurs disques de jazz (Paris, 1958)

Histoire du vrai jazz (Paris, 1959)

La bataille du jazz (Paris, 1965)

The Panassié Sessions (RCA RD7887, 1967) [liner notes]

Louis Armstrong (Paris, 1969; Eng. trans., New York, 1971/*R*1980)

Monsieur Jazz (Paris, 1975)

BIBLIOGRAPHY

BalliettA (1986); *BalliettA (1996)*

"Témoignages recueillis à l'occasion du vingtième anniversaire de la disparition d'Hugues Panassié," *Jazz Dixie/Swing: du Ragtime au Big Band*, no.5 (1994), 24

C. Senn: *Hugues Panassié* (Lutry, Switzerland, 1996)

ANDRÉ CLERGEAT

Panayi, Andy (*b* London, 18 Jan 1964). English tenor saxophonist. His father, a Greek Cypriot, was a professional musician. He learned to play flute and baritone and alto saxophones before settling on the tenor instrument, and studied at Trinity College of Music. Having toured with the National Youth Jazz Orchestra, he played in various jazz groups, in theater orchestras, and with the pop group the Blow Monkeys. In the 1990s he worked with Alec Dankworth's quartet, the Dankworth Generation band, Tommy Smith, and Stan Tracey, and in 1996 he formed his own quartet.

SELECTED RECORDINGS

As leader: *Blown Away* (1996, Ronnie Scott's Jazz House 057); of Flux: *Uschi's House* (1997, M Records 010)

As sideman with A. Barnes: *Thirsty Work* (1995, Fret 106)

BIBLIOGRAPHY

ChiltonB

GK

Pannon Jazz. Hungarian record company and label. Established in 1994 by the Foundation for Jazz Education and Research in Hungary, it is the successor of the labels Pannonton, Hotelinfo-Ferdinandus, and Tandem-Ferdinandus, all co-owned by Géza Gábor Simon. From 1997 it has operated in conjunction with the affiliated label Pannon Classic, and from 2000 with the affiliated label Pannon Archiv. It has issued approximately ten to 12 CDs per year in all periods and all styles of Hungarian jazz, notably by such groups and musicians as the Benkó Dixieland Band, the Trio Acoustic, the Trio Midnight, Lajos Dudás, Laszlo Gardony, Yochkó Seffer, and Tony Lakatos, as well as historical reissues of Hungarian gypsy ragtime and Hungarian swing and some previously unissued and rare recordings. (G. G. Simon: *Magyar jazztőrtéret* [Hungarian jazz history] (Budapest, 1999))

GÉZA GÁBOR SIMON

Panov, Nikolay (Alexandrovich) (*b* Bogorodsk, Russian SFSR [now Russia], 30 Aug 1945). Russian tenor and soprano saxophonist, flutist, clarinetist, and leader. After studying accordion he played clarinet in a brass band and then alto saxophone in a variety orchestra. He learned instrument making at Bauman's Moscow Higher Technical College (to 1968), and while there formed his first quartet. In 1969 he joined the group led by the alto saxophonist Vitaly Shemankov. From 1971 to 1973 he played saxophone and clarinet in the orchestra led by Alexander Gorbatyh, and from 1971 to 1977 he co-led a quartet with Mikhail Okoun. The following year he completed studies at the Third Music College in the city of Elektrostal, near Moscow. Panov then worked in German Luk'yanov's group Kadans (1978–84), which greatly influenced his creative work; the ensemble performed in Warsaw (1980), Székesfehérvár (Hungary) (1981), and The Hague (1984). In 1984 he became a soloist on tenor saxophone and flute and an arranger for Oleg Lundstrem's orchestra. By 1996 he had organized Jazz Gallery, a joint project involving Russian and foreign musicians, particularly singers, but also such instrumentalists as Phil Abraham and Hervé Sellin. Panov moved to the USA in 1999.

SELECTED RECORDINGS

As leader: *Virgo Constellation* (1993, Qualitet 003); *Indian Project* (1994, Qualitet 004); *Jazz Gallery* (1996, PMP 002)

As sideman: G. Luk'yanov: *Ivanushka-durachok* (1982, Mel. 17435004); *Way to Olymp* (1984, Mel. 20875003); O. Lundstrem: *V stile sving* (1986, Mel. C60 23709006)

SERGEY BELICHENKO

Papa Bue [Jensen, Arne Bue] (*b* Copenhagen, 8 May 1930). Danish trombonist and bandleader. In the mid-1950s he performed and recorded with the Bonanza Jazz Band, Chris Barber, the pianist Adrian Bentzon, and the clarinetist Henrik Johansen. From 1956 he led the New Orleans Jazz Band, a septet based in Copenhagen, which in 1958 he renamed the Viking Jazz Band. The group remained in existence, with only infrequent changes of personnel, through the 1990s; among those who recorded with it were George Lewis (i) (1959), the pianist Champion Jack Dupree (1962), Art Hodes (1970), and Wild Bill Davison (1970, 1974). Papa Bue appeared with the group at the Newport Jazz Festival New York in 1972 and later made a video, *Papa Bue's Viking Jazzband: the 40 Years Jubilee Concert* (*c*1998 [filmed 1996]). His playing is well represented on his albums *Papa Bue's Viking Jazz Band with Wingy Manone and Edmond Hall* (1966, Sto. 192) and *On Stage* (1982, Tim. 511).

BIBLIOGRAPHY

ReclamsJ

O. Bendix: *Papa Bue* (Copenhagen, 1962)

G. Bielderman and E. Elvers: *Papa Bue Discography* (Zwolle, Netherlands, 1989, rev. 2/1994)

<http://www.jazz-sargans.ch/papa.htm> (2000)

Papadimitriou, Sakis (*b* Kavala, Greece, 1 May 1940). Greek pianist and writer. He was self-taught on piano, and in 1960 he formed a trio to perform his own compositions. Early in his career he worked as a literary critic and writer: he published the first two Greek-language books on jazz, served as a correspondent for *Jazz Forum* (contributing, among other articles, "Chance Music, Performers and Improvisation" to the international edition [no.29 (1974), 48]), and was editor-in-chief of *Jazz* (Thessaloniki, Greece) from 1977 to 1981. He founded a magazine and publishing house, Plus and Minus, devoted to jazz and improvised music, and in 1980 he created a record company and label, Improvisation Series. In 1982 Papadimitriou performed at Jazzbühne Berlin and the following year in Paris and in Lyons, where he appeared with the musicians of ARFI. In 1984 he co-founded, with André Jaume, a festival in Greece. He performed as an unaccompanied soloist at the Europa Jazz Festival in LeMans in 1985, and at the same festival, in 1993, he participated in the creation of Jaume's *Mare nostrum*; he also performed at the Druga Godba festival in Ljubljana, Slovenia, in 1985 and 1990. In 1993 he recorded in the group Periferia, consisting of Daunik Lazro, Carlos Zingaro, and the double bass player Jean Bolcato. That same year he wrote new music for the reissue of the 1928 film *Lulu – Pandora's Box*, by George Pabst, which he recorded in 1996 in a duo with the singer Georgia Sylleou.

While sometimes playing in a conventional manner, Papadimitriou has consistently used the inner workings of the piano for musical explorations, stifling, rubbing, or striking the strings to create new timbres and sounds. He often sets up repetitive figures, and through liberal use of the sustaining pedal he allows the resonance of the piano to prolong his unusual sounds.

SELECTED RECORDINGS

As unaccompanied soloist: *Piano Contacts* (1980, Improvisation Series 3); *Piano Plays* (1983, Leo 111); *First Move* (1984–5, Leo 128); *Piano Oracles* (1985, 1987, Leo 163); *In situ* (1986, Adda 590010)

Duos: with Floros Floridis: *Improvising at Barakos* (1979, Improvisation Series 1–2); with Lefteris Agouridakis: *Plus and Minus* (1995, Leo 246)

As leader with D. Lazro, J. Bolcato, and C. Zingaro: *Periferia* (1993, In Situ 164)

BIBLIOGRAPHY

GrayF

A. Jaume: "Sakis's Moods," *Jm*, no.330 (1984), 10

P. Carles, A. Clergeat, and J.-L. Comolli: *Dictionnaire du jazz* (Paris, 1988, rev. and enlarged 2/1994)

P. Carles: "In situ(ables)," *Jm*, no.427 (1993), 13

A. Dümling: "Postmoderne Musik ist nicht neokonservativ: zu einem Komponisten-Symposium beim Patras-Festival – schwierige Begriffsbestimmung," *Neue Musikzeitung*, xxxv (1986), Oct–Nov, 50

GK

Paque, (Eric) Glyn (*b* Poplar Bluff, MO, 29 Aug 1907; *d* Basel, Switzerland, 29 Aug 1953). Alto saxophonist and clarinetist. He started on piccolo at the age of eight and changed to clarinet two years later. In 1926 he moved to New York, and he began working professionally in January 1927, when he joined the trumpeter Dave Alford. After leading his own trio in Albany, New York (1927), he toured with the Missourians (late 1928–1929) and played with the saxophonist Gene Kennedy (based in New England), the violinist Warren Adams (again in Albany, at Powell's Inn), and the bandleader Charley Skeete (in New York). He was a member of the White Brothers Orchestra (1929–30) and was in Emmett Matthews's band at the Alhambra Theater (spring 1930). Paque recorded (from autumn 1929) and toured (mid-1930) with King Oliver and then joined Dave Nelson. During the early 1930s he worked with Jelly Roll Morton, Benny Carter, the Savoy Bearcats, Claude Hopkins, Elmer Snowden, and Luis Russell, and from late 1934 to 1937 he was a sideman in Willie Bryant's band. In June 1937 he traveled to Europe with Bobby Martin's band. At the beginning of the war Martin returned to the USA and Paque took over the group, which he renamed the Cotton Club; in autumn 1939 the band, at that time including Johnny Russell and Ram Ramirez, was at the Odeon in Basel. Having settled in Switzerland, Paque played with Fred Böhler (1940 – summer 1945) and with other Swiss bands (to 1949), among them that of Philippe Brun. He formed a group for an engagement at the Chikito, Berne, beginning in February 1949 (with Frank "Big Boy" Goudie among his sidemen until April), then in May returned to the Odeon in Basel; from June 1949 to February 1950 he continued with his band at Johnny's Bar in Zurich. Paque recorded in the USA with Oliver, Carter, and Bryant and in Europe with Martin, Böhler, and Eddie Brunner.

SELECTED RECORDINGS

As sideman: K. Oliver: Boogie Woogie/Mule Face Blues (1930, Vic. 38134); W. Bryant: The Sheik (1935, Vic. 25038); Jerry the Junker (1935, Vic. 25045)

BIBLIOGRAPHY

ChiltonW; *McCarthyB*
A. Schwaninger and A. Gurwitsch: *Swing discographie* (Geneva, 1945)
L. Choquart: "Le saxophoniste alto Glyn Paque," *Hot Revue* (1947), no.3, p.14; no.5, p.13
K. Mohr: "Glyn Paque," *Jazz Music*, v/1 (n.d.[*c*1952]), 8
L. Wright and others: *Walter C. Allen & Brian A. L. Rust's "King" Oliver* (Chigwell, England, 1987)

OTTO FLÜCKIGER, HOWARD RYE

Pâques, Jean (*b* Liège, Belgium, 16 Sept 1901; *d* Liège, 19 April 1974). Belgian pianist and composer. From the end of World War I he worked as an unaccompanied soloist and in small groups, and in 1923–6 he led the Five Merry Kids, which played mainly in Liège. He then performed in the Netherlands and Germany in the Russian North Star Orchestra (recording in 1928), a dixieland septet led by the reed player Grégoire Nakchounian, and worked with Sid Phillips in England, where he also made more than 200 recordings as the house pianist of the Edison Bell Company. Pâques made five tours of Italy with the singer Lydia Johnson, and in Belgium he played at the Carlton in Blankenberge and the Barclay in Liège. After World War II he worked mostly in piano bars and made many recordings in a distinctive "sweet" style. A good example of his work is his recording of his own composition *Hot Piano* (1928, EBR 804). (R. Pernet: *Belgian Jazz Discography (1897–1999)*, Brussels, 1999)

ROBERT PERNET

Paquet, Pierre. *See* Packay, peter.

Paquinet, André (*b* Arcueil, France, 1 Oct 1926). French trombonist, son of Guy Paquinet. He played first with his father (1944), then with the saxophonist Tony Proteau (1946–8), under the bandleader Jacques Hélian (1951–2), again with Proteau (1953), and with Claude Bolling (1954–7), Michel Legrand (1956–7), and Fred Gerard (1957). From 1957 to 1970, with the trombonist Benny Vasseur, he co-led a group modeled after Jay and Kai (J. J. Johnson and Kai Winding); its recordings include *The Man I Love*, *Mood Indigo*, and *Sonny Boy* (*c*1959, Festival 2183). He also played with Dany Doriz (1966), André Hodeir (1963, 1966), Jean-Claude Naude (1967, 1971, 1975), François Guin's group Four Bones (1968), Slide Hampton, Ivan Jullien (1970–71), and Roy Eldridge (1970), and under Paul Kuntz in Berlin (1973–7). From 1990 he worked regularly with the group Swing Locomotive led by the bass trombonist Emile Vilain. At the height of his career Paquinet was noted for his breath control and his production of a good sound over the full compass of the instrument. (F. W. Sportis: "André Paquinet," *Jh*, no.538 (1997), 12)

MICHEL LAPLACE

Paquinet, Guy [Patrick] (*b* Tours, France, 13 Aug 1903; *d* Selle-sur-le-Bied, France, 5 Jan 1981). French trombonist, father of André Paquinet. After first playing in a military band he worked with the group Melody Six, Paul Gason's band (1925, 1928), Lud Gluskin (1926, 1932), the bandleader and percussionist Fred Mélé (1926–8), the alto saxophonist Don Parker, and Gregor (1930). From 1934 to 1936, using the pseudonym Patrick, he led an orchestra in performances and recordings; he then played with Ray Ventura (1937–40), Django Reinhardt (1940), and Alix Combelle (1940), and again with Ventura (1945–9). He led his own groups from time to time in the 1940s, in one of which (1944) his son André Paquinet, also a trombonist, gained his first professional experience; from 1949 to 1951 he was leader of a seven-piece orchestra. In the latter part of his career he played with the saxophonist Tony Proteau, Dizzy Gillespie, and Sidney Bechet (1953). Paquinet was a pioneer of jazz trombone in France; his playing is well represented on recordings made by the group Jazz Dixit in 1940 (*Strictement pour les persans/Saut d'une heure*, Col. DF2819). (M. Laplace: *Portraits of French Jazz Musicians* (Menden, Germany, 1985), 14)

MICHEL LAPLACE

Parachute. Record label founded around 1975 by Eugene Chadbourne.

Paradiddle. One of the drumstrokes collectively known as Rudiments.

Paradox. Record label. It was launched in September 1948 by Globe Industries of New York and managed by Dante Bollettino. The catalogue consisted mainly of recordings by such traditional-jazz performers as Ray Burke and Knocky Parker. Both 78 r.p.m. discs and LPs were issued. Operations ceased in February 1952 at the same time as those of Bollettino's label British Rhythm Society, and the catalogue was acquired by Chimes Music Shop, which that same year began reissuing the material on the label Pax. This arrangement ceased in 1956, and Paradox's repertory was later made available to Jazztone. (D. Mahony and others: "The Dante Bolletino [*sic*] Labels," *Matrix*, no.58 (1965), 3)

HOWARD RYE

Paramount. Record label. The main label of the New York Recording Laboratories of Port Washington, Wisconsin, it was established in 1916. The first issues were of $9\frac{1}{2}$-inch vertical-cut discs; lateral-cut discs were first put out in 1919. A race series, the 12000s, commenced in August 1922 and proved extremely successful; it ran into the 13000s, and by the time it was discontinued in 1932 more than 1100 releases had been made. The work of singers predominated, among them Ma Rainey (the label's most famous musician), Ida Cox, and Alberta Hunter. Many items in the race catalogue are now acknowledged to be classics, including recordings by King Oliver and Freddie Keppard and longer series by such small groups based in Chicago as Lovie Austin's Blues Serenaders and Jimmy O'Bryant's Original Washboard Band. Artists and repertory were directed by Art Satherley (who later worked for the American Record Corporation) and by J. Mayo Williams, who supervised the race series until 1927. Williams also managed an associated music publisher, Chicago Music, which published many of the compositions released on the label. Paramount's General Series, the 20000s, contained a smaller proportion of jazz, but incorporated some discs by Fletcher Henderson and the Original Memphis Five, as well as a considerable amount of hot dance music.

For much of its history Paramount's activities were linked with those of other companies. During the early 1920s it was closely associated with the Bridgeport Die & Machine Company, and it also exchanged many masters with Plaza (later part of ARC). As well as its own recording studios in New York, which closed in 1926, Paramount used the recording facilities of Marsh Laboratories in Chicago in 1924–7 and of the Starr Piano Company (owners of Gennett) at Richmond, Indiana, in 1929. That year it transferred its business, which was steadily declining, to Grafton, Wisconsin. Operations ceased in 1932. Thereafter, however, a small number of race issues appeared (under circumstances not yet fully understood) in a Paramount 9000 series produced by ARC. The collector John Steiner revived the label in the late 1940s, putting out in a 14000 series both new material and reissues dubbed from early Paramount discs. LPs of the new material were released until the early 1950s.

BIBLIOGRAPHY

M. Wyler: *A Glimpse of the Past: an Illustrated History of some Early Record Companies that Made Jazz History* (West Moors, England, 1957)
R. M. W. Dixon and J. Godrich: *Recording the Blues* (London, 1970)
M. E. Vreede: *Paramount 12/13000 Series* (London, 1971) [discography]
C. Hillman: "Paramount Serenaders 1923–1926," *Sv*, no.67 (1976), 8; no.68 (1976), 52; no.69 (1977), 91; no.70 (1977), 149; no.72 (1977), 226; no.73 (1977), 29; no.74 (1977), 67; no.75 (1978), 84 [incl. discography]
B. Rust: *The American Record Label Book* (New Rochelle, NY, 1978), 226
D. M. Bakker: "Duke Ellington and the Paramount Re-issue Series," *Names & Numbers*, no.3 (1986), 10
S. Calt: "Paramount: the Anatomy of a 'Race' Label," *78 Quarterly*, no.3 (1988), 9; no.4 (1989), 9
S. Calt and G. Wardlow: "The Buying and Selling of Paramounts," *78 Quarterly*, no.5 (1990), 7; contd as "Paramount, pt 4 (the Advent of Arthur Laibley)," no.6 (1991), 9; contd as "Paramount's Decline and Fall (pt 5)," no.7 (1992), 7
M. Vreede and G. van Rijn: "The Paramount L Master Series," *78 Quarterly*, no.9 (n.d.), 67
A. Sutton: *Directory of American Disc Record Brands and Manufacturers, 1891–1943* (Westport, CT, and London, 1994), 115, 211
R. M. W. Dixon, J. Godrich, and H. Rye: *Blues & Gospel Records, 1890–1943* (Oxford, England, rev. and enlarged 4/1997), xxxvi
L. Wright: "Dating Paramount's Chicago Recordings 1923–1926", *Storyville 1996/7* (Chigwell, England, 1997), 58
G. D. Wardlow: *Chasin' that Devil Music: Searching for the Blues* (San Francisco, 1998)
L. Wright: "Dating Paramount's Chicago Recordings – Concluded", *Storyville 1998–99* (Chigwell, England, 1999), 80
R. Kennedy and R. McNutt, eds.: *Little Labels – Big Sound: Small Record Companies and the Rise of American Music* (Bloomington, IN, and Indianapolis, 1999)

HOWARD RYE

Paramountorkestern. Swedish band. Formed in 1926 by the violinist Folke "Göken" Andersson (1902–76), it had from six to nine members at various times. Among those who were members of the band were the trumpeters Gösta "Smyget" Redlig, Gösta "Chicken" Törnblad, and Ragge Läth; the saxophonists Sam Jacobsson, Tony Mason, and Olle Henricson; the pianists Nils Lind and Nils Soderman; the banjoists Curt Ljunggren and Jean Paban; and the drummer Anders Soldén. The Paramountorkestern was the first important jazz band in Sweden; it gave many performances on radio and made about 100 recordings (including *Tambou*, 1928, Col. 8629), most of which had a commercial orientation. The group disbanded about 1930. (B. Englund: "Paramountorkestern: Sveriges första egentliga jazzorkester" [Paramountorkestern: Sweden's first real jazz orchestra], *Orkester journalen*, xxxvi/12 (1968), 8)

ERIK KJELLBERG

Paraphernalia. British jazz-rock group formed by BARBARA THOMPSON around 1972.

Pardo, Jorge (*b* Madrid, 12 Dec 1956). Spanish flute player and tenor and soprano saxophonist. He studied flute and piano at the conservatory in Madrid for three years, during which time he began playing jazz on the flute. He worked professionally from 1974, and appeared at the club Balboa Jazz with Slide Hampton, Pony Poindexter, Steve McCall, Tete Montoliu, Vlady Bas, and others, and at Whisky Jazz with Lou Bennett and the Brazilian guitarist Jayme Marques. Pardo took up the tenor and soprano saxophones in 1975. The following year, together with the singer and drummer Pedro Ruy Blas, he formed the group Dolores, which included his brother Jesus Pardo, a pianist, and the percussionist Ruben Dantas. This group brought the flamenco guitarist Paco de Lucia into jazz; he recorded an homage to the composer Manuel de Falla with Dolores in 1978. In 1981 Pardo performed in Paris with Chet Baker and with the Brazilian musicians José Boto and Tania Maria. During the 1980s he continued to play with Tania Maria, while also appearing with Chick Corea (at a festival in Tokyo), Astrud Gilberto, and the guitarist Pepe de Lucia (brother of Paco). In the 1990s he worked often with Carles Benavent and with such Latin-jazz musicians as Alex Acuña, Gil Goldstein, and the Brazilian pianist and composer Wagner Tiso.

SELECTED RECORDINGS

As leader: *Las cigarras son quinzà sordas* (1991, Mlst. 9206); *Veloz hacia su sino* (1993, Mlst. 9223); *2332* (1996, Nuevos Medios 15712)
As sideman with P. de Lucia: *Paco de Lucia interpreta a Manuel de Falla* (1978, Phi. 8360322)

BIBLIOGRAPHY

"Seven Spanish Jazz Musicians the World Should Know About: Jorge Pardo," *Jazz Changes*, vi/2 (1999), 14

ALFREDO PAPO

Parenti, Tony [Anthony] (*b* New Orleans, 6 Aug 1900; *d* New York, 17 April 1972). Clarinetist and saxophonist. His father was a musician. Parenti studied violin before taking up the clarinet. He first played jazz in 1914 in a band led by Alfred "Baby" Laine, and by the age of 15 he was working frequently at the Pup Cabaret. From 1917 he led his own band in New Orleans, with which he recorded in 1925–6 and 1928. In 1927 he went to New York, where he often deputized for Benny Goodman in Ben Pollack's band. He joined the staff orchestra at CBS in 1930, and also led a saxophone quartet for radio broadcasts; he then played for four years with the orchestra at Radio City Music Hall. From 1939 until summer 1945 Parenti traveled with Ted Lewis's orchestra. On his return to New York he recorded with Georg Brunis (January 1946), performed and recorded with Eddie Condon (January–June 1946), and joined Brunis's group (June–November 1946). He led his own band at Jimmy Ryan's and Nick's before rejoining Condon. After working in Chicago with Muggsy Spanier at the Blue Note for ten weeks (November 1947 – February 1948) and then with Miff Mole (1948 – January 1949) he moved to Miami (1950), where he played with Preacher Rollo and the Five Saints and briefly with the Dukes of Dixieland (1952). He also led his own group before returning in 1954 to New York, where he worked at the

Metropole (initially in a trio with Joe Sullivan and Zutty Singleton, 1954) and the Central Plaza. After further touring as a leader he led house bands at Condon's (1962–3) and Ryan's (1963–9). He appeared at the New Orleans Jazz Festival in 1969 and the Manassas Jazz Festival in 1970, and was still performing and recording in New York in 1971. Parenti was a master of ragtime and dixieland jazz, and was also comfortable in classical ensembles. Although he greatly admired the playing of Leon Roppolo, he developed his own distinctive, swinging style.

Oral history material in *LNT*.

SELECTED RECORDINGS

As leader: That's a Plenty/Cabaret Echoes (1925, OK 40308); Old Man Rhythm (1929, Ban. 0580); Crawfish Crawl/Lily Rag (1949, Cir. [USA] 1056); Blues for Faz/Bugle Call Rag (1949, Jlgy 2); *Jazz, that's all* (1955, Jzt. 1215), incl. City of the Blues, Vieux Carré

As sideman with Preacher Rollo: Ostrich Walk (1951, MGM 30446)

BIBLIOGRAPHY

ChiltonW

B. Aurthur: "That's a Parenti," *Jazz Record*, no.49 (1946), 7

B. Rust: "A Study of Anthony Parenti," *Hot Notes*, ii/4 (1947), 15

B. Grauer: "Dixieland Clarinet: the Odyssey of New Orleans' Tony Parenti," *Record Changer*, vii/8 (1948), 11

K. C. Thompson: "Selections from Tony Parenti's Dixieland Scrapbook," *JJ*, iii/10 (1950), 10

T. Parenti: "Early Years in New Orleans," *SL*, ii (1951), no.9, p.6; no.10, p.7; no.11, p.5

T. Parenti (as told to R. Morser): "Early Years in New Orleans," *Jazz Music*, iv/8 (1952), 3

N. Shapiro and N. Hentoff, eds.: *Hear me Talkin' to ya: the Story of Jazz by the Men who Made it* (New York and London, 1955/*R*1966)

F. Gillis and R. Morser: "Tony Parenti's Story: the Years in New York 1928–1950," *Record Research*, no.28 (1960), 4

Obituary, T. Piazza, *DB*, xxxix/11 (1972), 10

B. Whyatt: *Muggsy Spanier: the Lonesome Road: a Biography and Discography* (New Orleans, 1995)

RAYMOND J. GARIGLIO/BK

Parham, Tiny [Hartzell Strathdene] (*b* Winnipeg, Canada, 25 Feb 1900; *d* Milwaukee, 4 April 1943). Pianist, bandleader, and organist. He grew up in Kansas City, where he worked in a theater in 1923. After touring the Southwest with a big band (1925) he moved to Chicago and led a group with the violinist Leroy Pickett (1926–7). From 1926 to 1930 he made more than 30 recordings, mainly accompanying blues singers, but also collaborating with the Paramount Pickers and Johnny Dodds. In addition he led his own recording groups, which at times included Punch Miller. Parham led big bands until 1936 and then worked as a solo organist until his death. He recorded again in 1940 as the leader of a five-piece band with Darnell Howard among his sidemen.

SELECTED RECORDINGS

(recorded for Victor unless otherwise indicated)

As leader: with L. Pickett: Alexander, where's that band/Mojo Strut (1926, Para. 12441); with J. Dodds: Loveless Love/19th Street Blues (1927, Para. 12483); Cuckoo Blues (1928, 21553); Stompin' on Down/Tiny's Stomp (Oriental Blues) (1929, 38060); Blue Melody Blues (1929, 38047); Jungle Crawl/Lucky "3–6–9" (1929, 38082); Fat Man Blues/Black Cat Moan (1929, 38126); Cathedral Blues (1929, 38111); Doin' the Jug-jug/Blue Moon Blues (1930, 23027); Nervous Tension/Memphis Mamie (1930, 23386)

As sideman: Hattie McDaniel: I thought I'd do it/Just One Sorrowing Heart (1927, OK 8569); Bertha Henderson: So Sorry Blues (1928, Para. 12645)

BIBLIOGRAPHY

ChiltonW; *McCarthyB*

Obituary, *Chicago Defender* (24 April 1943)

C. Strachwitz: Liner notes, *Tiny Parham and his Musicians* (Folklyric 9028, *c*1981)

B. Rust: Liner notes, *Tiny Parham and his Musicians*, i–iv (Swaggie 831–4, 1985)

E. Grossmann: *Tiny Parham's Victor Recordings and Toad's Krazy Kats' Golden Lily* (Menden, Germany, 1989)

HOWARD RYE

Parham, Truck [Charles Valdez] (*b* Chicago, 25 Jan 1911). Double bass player. His year of birth has been published as 1913, but when interviewed in 1986 for the first edition of this dictionary, and the following year for *Cadence*, he confirmed 1911. In the early 1930s he was a professional football player and boxer. Having first played drums, he began his musical career playing tuba with regional bands in western Ohio (before 1932). As a member of Zack Whyte's band (1932–4) in Cincinnati, he worked mainly as a singer and as a valet, helping to "truck" around the instruments (hence his nickname); he then changed to double bass and took lessons with Walter Page in exchange for his services as a bodyguard. After returning to Chicago he worked at the Three Deuces with Zutty Singleton (summer 1935) and Art Tatum (late 1935 – early 1936), studied classical double bass, performed and recorded with Roy Eldridge (late 1936–1938), and recorded with Mildred Bailey (1937). Later he played briefly with Fletcher Henderson (1939) and in the band led by the drummer Floyd Campbell, which included Bob Shoffner (1940). From around December 1940 to September 1942 Parham toured as a member of Earl Hines's orchestra, providing the rhythmic impetus for such recordings as *Jelly Jelly* (1940). With Hines, and later on tour with Jimmie Lunceford (*c* October 1942–1947), he developed the powerful yet buoyant swing style that had been established by Page. He returned in 1947 to Chicago, where he recorded with the singer and pianist Nellie Lutcher. In the 1950s he performed and recorded with Muggsy Spanier (1950–55) and Louie Bellson (1957–9) and played with Gigi Gryce (1954) and Herbie Fields (late 1956 – June 1957), and in 1960 he toured Canada with Spanier. He was associated with Art Hodes intermittently from 1957 through the 1970s, and may be seen on videos from several episodes of Hodes's television show of 1979. Parham continued to work in Chicago clubs, and in the 1980s he held a lengthy residency at Andy's. In 2000 he was a member of Franz Jackson's band.

Oral history material in *ICU*.

SELECTED RECORDINGS

Duos with A. Hodes: *Plain Old Blues* (1962, EmA 26005), incl. Buddy Bolden's Blues

As sideman: M. Bailey: Where are You?/You're Laughin' at Me (1937, Voc. 3456); R. Eldridge: Florida Stomp (1937, Voc. 3479); Heckler's Hop (1937, Voc. 3577); E. Hines: Jelly Jelly (1940, Bb 11065); On the Sunny Side of the Street/My Melancholy Baby (1941, Vic. 27562); J. Lunceford: Strictly Instrumental/Knock Me a Kiss (1942, Decca 18463); J. Thomas (iii): Don't blame me/For Boobs Only (1945, Melodisc 113); N. Lutcher: *Fine Brown Frame* (1947, Cap. 15032); M. Spanier: *Live at Club Hangover*, ii (1953, Sto. 249); L. Bellson: *Louis Bellson at the Flamingo* (1957, Verve 8256); A Hodes: *Hodes' Art* (1968, Del. 213)

BIBLIOGRAPHY

ChiltonW; *FeatherE*

B. Rusch: "Truck Parham," *Cadence*, xiii (1987), no.11, p.17; no.12, p.19

JOHN CURRY

Paris, Jackie (*b* Nutley, NJ, 20 Sept 1927). Singer. In Rusch (1996) he states that his year of birth was 1927 and not 1926, as had appeared in all sources. He worked as a vaudeville singer and dancer from early childhood, then during the early 1940s played guitar in New York. After serving in the army (1944–6) he returned to New York, where he performed, principally as a singer, with groups on 52nd Street; in 1948 he toured with Charlie Parker. As a leader he recorded intermittently from 1947 to 1962 (he is best known for his recording of *Skylark*, 1947), and as a sideman he sang, but did not record, with Lionel Hampton in 1949–50. Although he was named "best new male vocalist" by *Down Beat* in 1953, he had difficulty securing steady work as a jazz musician; nevertheless, he performed at nightclubs and resorts in the 1950s and 1960s, sometimes, as a guitarist, accompanying the singer Anne Marie Moss (they married in 1961, but had divorced by the 1970s). A recording made with Donald Byrd and Gigi Gryce in 1957 features his scat singing in swing and bop styles. Having performed with Charles Mingus's group for a few months at some point in the early 1960s, he recorded with him in 1974. He continued to record as a leader into the 1990s, concentrating on luxuriously slow ballad singing, and at a session in 1981 he was accompanied by Carlos Franzetti, Marc Johnson, and Joe LaBarbera. Paris taught guitar and singing at the New School for Social Research in New York into the 1990s.

SELECTED RECORDINGS

As leader: Skylark (1947, MGM 10114); *Jackie Paris* (1981, Audiophile 158)
As sideman: D. Byrd and G. Gryce: *Modern Jazz Perspective* (1957, Col. CL1058); C. Mingus: on *Changes Two* (1974, Atl. 1678), Duke Ellington's Sound of Love

BIBLIOGRAPHY

W. Friedwald: "Music: Paris when He Sizzles," *VV* (17 Jan 1995), 61
B. Rusch: "Jackie Paris Interview," *Cadence*, xxii/4 (1996), 5

BK

Paris Reunion Band. Group originally conceived in autumn 1984 to pay tribute to Kenny Clarke and his involvement with jazz in Paris; however, Clarke died in January 1985, before it could be organized. The saxophonist Nathan Davis served as its leader and music director, and its other founding members were the trumpeters Woody Shaw and Dizzy Reece, the trombonist Slide Hampton, the saxophonist Johnny Griffin, the pianist Kenny Drew, the double bass player Jimmy Woode, and the drummer Billy Brooks. The group first performed in public on 30 June 1985 at the Kongsberg Festival in Norway, and three days later it recorded the album *French Cooking* (Sonet 945); it toured throughout Europe in summer and autumn that year and appeared at a number of European festivals. Brooks left shortly into this tour and was succeeded by Victor Jones, who was in turn replaced by Alvin Queen; Reece left soon after Brooks, and the group continued with one trumpeter until 15 August 1985, when Benny Bailey joined. Later members included the cornetist Nat Adderley (who replaced Bailey in 1986), the trombonists Glenn Ferris (March 1986), Grachan Moncur III (1986–8), and Curtis Fuller (1988), the tenor saxophonist Joe Henderson (who replaced Griffin in 1986), and the drummer Idris Muhammad (from 1986). Walter Bishop, Jr., also worked with the group, and he performs on the album *Jazz Buhne Berlin* (1988, Amiga 856 418). The Paris Reunion Band, with Shaw, Adderley, Henderson, Walter Davis, Woode, and Muhammad (1988), may be seen in an eponymous video.

BIBLIOGRAPHY

I. Dittke: "Honoring Kenny Clarke: the PRB Plays On," *JT* (1985), April, 11
M. Hennessey: "Paris Reunion Band," *JF* [intl edn], no.102 (1986), 33; repr. as "Parisian Heyday Recreated," *CI*, xxiv/2 (1987), 26
"Nathan Davis und die Paris Reunion Band," *JP*, xxxvi/10 (1987), 20

GK

Paris Washboard. French traditional-jazz band, established in 1987, comprising clarinet, trombone, piano, and washboard. This unusual instrumentation was heard as early as 1970 when Gilbert Leroux, as the leader of a group called the Luteciens, recorded the album *Planche à laver* (AZ 76). From 1978 to 1986, during which period Louis Mazetier and the clarinetist Alain Marquet joined the band, it was known as the Gilbert Leroux Washboard Group, and in 1987, when it took the name by which it has become well known, Paris Washboard, the personnel consisted of Leroux, Marquet, Mazetier, and Daniel Barda. Gérard Bagot replaced Leroux in 1990, and occasionally from 1993 Michel Marcheteaux or Gérard Gervois has been added on tuba. The band toured California in 1993, 1994, and 1995, and appeared at the Santa Rosa festival and in concerts at San Diego, Los Angeles, Santa Monica, San Francisco, and Concord. Its first American album was *When We're Smiling* (1988, Stomp Off 1182). (G. A. Borgman: "Le jazz hot from Paris Washboard," *MR*, xxiv/5 (1997), 1)

MICHEL LAPLACE

Parker, Bradley. *See* PARKER-SPARROW, BRADLEY.

Parker, Charlie [Charles, Jr.; Bird; Chan, Charlie; Yardbird] (*b* Kansas City, KS, 29 Aug 1920; *d* New York, 12 March 1955). Alto saxophonist. He was one of the most important and influential improvising soloists in jazz, and a central figure in the development of bop in the 1940s. A legendary figure in his own lifetime, he was idolized by those who

1. Charlie Parker at a Dial recording session, Los Angeles, February 1947

worked with him, and he inspired a generation of jazz performers and composers.

1. Life. 2. Style. 3. Influence.

1. Life. He was the only child of Charles and Addie Parker. In 1927 the family moved to Kansas City, Missouri, an important center of African-American music in the 1920s and 1930s. Parker had his first music lessons in the local public schools; he began playing alto saxophone in 1933 and worked occasionally in semiprofessional groups before leaving school in 1935 to become a full-time musician. From 1935 to 1939 he worked mainly in Kansas City with a wide variety of local blues and jazz groups. Like most jazz musicians of his time, he developed his craft largely through practical experience: listening to older local jazz masters, acquiring a traditional repertory, and learning through the process of trial and error in the competitive Kansas City bands and jam sessions.

In 1939 Parker first visited New York (then the principal center of jazz musical and business activity), and stayed for nearly a year. Although he worked only sporadically as a professional musician, he often participated in jam sessions. By his own later account (see Levin and Wilson, 1949), he was bored with the stereotyped changes that were being used then: "I kept thinking there's bound to be something else . . . I could hear it sometimes, but I couldn't play it." While working over *Cherokee* in a jam session with the guitarist Biddy Fleet, Parker suddenly found that by using the higher intervals of a chord as a melody line and backing them with appropriately related changes, he could play what he had been "hearing." Yet it was not until 1944–5 that his conceptions of rhythm and phrasing had evolved sufficiently to form his mature style.

Parker's name first appeared in the music press in 1940; from this date his career is more fully documented. From 1940 to 1942 he played in Jay McShann's band, with which he toured the Southwest, Chicago, and New York, and took part in his first recording sessions in Dallas (1941). These recordings, and several made for broadcasting from the same period, document his early, swing-based style, and at the same time reveal his extraordinary gift for improvisation. In December 1942 he joined Earl Hines's big band, which then included several other young modernists such as Dizzy Gillespie. By May 1944 they, with Parker, formed the nucleus of Billy Eckstine's band; Parker quit the group in late August.

During these years Parker regularly participated in after-hours jam sessions at Minton's Playhouse and Monroe's Uptown House in New York, where the informal atmosphere and small groups favored the development of his personal style, and of the new bop music generally. Unfortunately a strike by the American Federation of Musicians silenced most of the recording industry from August 1942, causing this crucial stage in Parker's musical evolution to remain poorly documented (there are nine privately recorded acetates of Parker playing tenor saxophone in February 1943 and four more from late 1943 to early 1944, with Parker on alto saxophone). When the recording ban ended, Parker recorded as a sideman (from 15 September 1944) and as a leader (from 26 November 1945), which introduced his music to a wider public and to other musicians.

The year 1945 marked a turning-point in Parker's career: in New York he led his own group for the first time and worked extensively with Gillespie in small ensembles. In December 1945 he and Gillespie took the new jazz style to Hollywood, where they fulfilled a six-week nightclub engagement. Parker continued to work in Los Angeles, recording and performing in concerts and nightclubs, until 29 June 1946, when a nervous breakdown and addiction to heroin and alcohol caused his confinement at the Camarillo State Hospital. He was released in January 1947 and resumed work in Los Angeles.

Parker returned to New York in April 1947. He formed a quintet (with Miles Davis, Duke Jordan, Tommy Potter, and Max Roach), which recorded many of his most famous pieces. The years from 1947 to 1951 were Parker's most fertile period. He worked in a wide variety of settings (nightclubs, concerts, radio, and recording studios) with his own small ensembles, a string group, and Afro-Cuban bands, and as a guest soloist with local musicians when traveling without his own group. He visited Europe (1949 and 1950) and recorded slightly over half his surviving work. Though still beset by problems associated with drugs and alcohol, he attracted a very large following in the jazz world, and enjoyed a measure of financial success.

In July 1951 Parker's New York cabaret license was revoked at the request of the narcotics squad: this banned him from nightclub employment in the city and forced him to adopt a more peripatetic life until the license was reinstated (probably in autumn 1953). Sporadically employed, badly in debt, and in failing physical and mental health, he twice attempted suicide in 1954 and voluntarily committed himself to Bellevue Hospital, New York. His last public engagement was on 5 March 1955 at Birdland, a New York nightclub named in his honor. He died seven days later in the Manhattan apartment of his friend the Baroness Pannonica de Koenigswarter, sister of Lord Rothschild.

Films of Parker are rare. He may be seen playing *Hot House* with Gillespie in the short film *Stage Entrance*, from the *Down Beat* awards show in 1951, and he performs in a duo with Coleman Hawkins and in a quartet consisting of Hank Jones, Ray Brown, and Buddy Rich in the video *Norman Granz présente improvisation: documents exceptionnels et inédits des plus grands noms de jazz* (n.d.).

2. Style. Parker was among the supremely creative improvisers in jazz, one whose performances, like Armstrong's before him, changed the nature of the music. The force and originality of his style was such that many listeners rejected his music as no longer part of the jazz tradition, and as other jazz musicians took up and elaborated his innovations the music sank to what was then its lowest ebb in popular acceptance. Only decades after his death did Parker shed the élite aura attached to him by fellow musicians and admiring jazz fans and begin to assume a classical status in the popular imagination.

Although Parker was an innovator, his music is rooted firmly in tradition. Like the Kansas City music he heard when young, Parker's repertory was built on a very limited number of models: the 12-bar blues, a number of popular songs, several jazz standards, and newly invented jazz melodies using the underlying harmonies of popular songs. A clear sense of this may be gained from a brief statistical summary of his 427 studio recordings, made mainly for Dial, Savoy, and Verve (and its associated labels). These represent about 30% of his roughly 1450 surviving recordings (including all of the incomplete and low-fidelity tracks preserved "live" and by amateur enthusiasts) and reflect trends pertaining to this entire discography. The 427 tracks contain

Ex.1 Parker's opening thematic statement on *Out of Nowhere* (1948, Le Jazz Cool 102); transcr. J. Patrick

202 individual pieces, of which 94 are original, and 108 are based on borrowed chord progressions; within the latter category, 49 are 12-bar blues, 24 are from *I got rhythm*, 9 are built upon a combination of *I got rhythm* and *Honeysuckle Rose* (*see* FORMS, §8,), and 29 are from other chord plans.

A few general conclusions are unmistakable. Parker's repertory and the harmonic substratum that fueled his melodic and improvisatory imagination was surprisingly limited. Only 32 borrowed chord schemes generate 108 pieces, well over half of the total studio repertory. What is astonishing is that only three harmonic models – the 12-bar blues, and the George Gershwin and Fats Waller songs *I got rhythm* and *Honeysuckle Rose* – underlie 79 pieces, or nearly 40% of the total. Although the device of composing new melodic themes to borrowed chord progressions was not new to jazz, bop musicians of the 1940s employed this technique much more extensively, partly for financial reasons (to avoid paying copyright royalties) and partly to frighten the uninitiated (who could not always recognize the underlying chord patterns), but also to invent themes that were more consistent with the new jazz style than the original melodies. Thus, by restricting himself to a few harmonic sources, Parker was able to improvise over a few familiar patterns, against which he constantly tested his ingenuity and powers of imagination. A number of Parker's newly composed melodic themes (based on existing harmonic and metric structures) themselves became jazz standards, among them *Anthropology* (based on the chord progressions of *I got rhythm*, and written in collaboration with Gillespie), *Now's the Time* (blues), *Ornithology* (based on Morgan Lewis's *How High the Moon*, probably written in collaboration with Little Benny Harris, and incorporating a melodic phrase improvised by Parker on Jay McShann's *Jumpin' the Blues* in 1942), and *Scrapple from the Apple* (the *a* section from *I got rhythm* and the bridge from *Honeysuckle Rose*).

Parker's outstanding achievement was not his composition but his brilliant improvisation. His improvised line combined drive and a complex organization of pitch and rhythm with a clarity rarely achieved by earlier soloists. In contrast to the rich timbres of Johnny Hodges and Benny Carter, the two most important predecessors on his instrument, Parker developed a penetrating tone with a slow, narrow vibrato. This suited the aggressive nature of the new music, and allowed him to concentrate on line and rhythm. Parker's improvisations usually ignore the original melody, being based instead on its harmonic structure. Melodic ornamentation or paraphrase occasionally occur, but characteristically these are reserved for thematic statements of popular

Ex.2 Parker's improvisation on D. Gillespie, *Groovin' High* (1945, Guild 1001); transcr. J. Patrick

melodies in the opening or closing chorus (ex.1). However, his use of rhythm and pitch is sometimes subtly linked to the pulse and the chord progressions of the original. In *Groovin' High* (ex.2) Parker maintained the prominent descending 3rds of Dizzy Gillespie's theme, but distorted them by inversion and elision (bar 1), compression (bar 5), and displacement (bar 10), the last two being ornamented as well. Other portions of the solo (bars 4, 7–8, 11–15) likewise follow the theme in pitch and contour, with bar 12 reducing the corresponding bar of the theme at the same time that it foreshadows the broken chords of the succeeding bar. In contrast to Gillespie's theme, Parker's solo breaks the quarter-note pulse, steadfastly maintained by the accompanying double bass, into a succession of varied and discontinuous subdivisions; this rhythmic variety is one of the foremost features of his style. The pulse, meter, and harmonic rhythm are further obscured by syncopation and the persistently contrasting accents and phrase lengths.

Parker's line typically includes pitches outside the given harmony: in addition to those produced by passing notes, suspensions, and other familiar devices, these result from free use of chord extensions beyond the 7th (particularly the flatted 9th and raised 11th), chromatic interpolations suggesting passing chords, the interchange of triads with others on the same root, and the anticipation or prolongation of chords within the given progression. Despite this harmonic complexity, Parker's best work has a clear and coherent line. Sometimes this is achieved by motivic development, as in the first ten bars of his solo on *Klactoveedsedstene* (ex.3), based on the chord progressions

Ex.3 *Klactoveedsedstene* (1947, Dial 1040); transcr. J. Patrick

of Juan Tizol's *Perdido*. This passage is constructed almost entirely of three very short ideas, developed and combined (bars 4 and 8), with silences of subtly varied length throughout.

Parker most often used a technique of improvisation known in musicology as the *cento* (or patchwork) method, where the performer draws from a corpus of formulae and arranges them into ever-new patterns. This aspect of Parker's art has been exhaustively investigated by Owens (*Charlie Parker*, 1974), who codified Parker's improvisational work according to about 100 formulae. Many of these are specific to certain keys (where they may be easier to finger) or to particular pieces. Some occur in earlier swing music, particularly in the work of Lester Young, but others originated with Parker himself, and later became common property among musicians working in the bop style. Ex.4 shows a few of Parker's favorite and most characteristic formulae. Ex.5*a–f*, all drawn from his solos on two takes of *Klactoveedsedstene*, offer some sense of how he works with this approach: ex.5*a* presents a basic formula, the simple first inversion arpeggiation of a G dominant seventh chord, and ex.5*b* offers variants thereof, some incorporating – or ending on – the minor ninth, *a♭*; ex.5*c* illustrates common approaches to the first note of the arpeggiation, *b*, and ex.5*d–e* show common departures from the last note, whether *a♭* or *g*; finally, ex.5*f* shows how these generalized formulaic lines are in fact combined in three phrases from *Klacktoveedsedstene*.

Ex.4 Some characteristic Parker formulae

Although it is based on a limited number of such formulae, Parker's work is neither haphazard nor "formulaic" in a restricted sense: the arrangement of the formulae was subject to constant variation and redisposition, and his performances of a piece were never identical. The overriding criterion was always the coherence and expressiveness of the musical line.

Closely related to this "formulaic" approach is Parker's use of musical quotations. Probably no jazz musician before him was as fond of this device, or as wide-ranging in his choice of material, as Parker, particularly in private performances in a relaxed atmosphere. His improvisations contain snatches of melody from Wagner, Bizet, and Stravinsky; from popular songs and light classics; from earlier jazz performances such as Armstrong's *West End Blues*; and even quotations from his own jazz compositions. He retained this device throughout his career, and it is another measure of his authority in jazz that witty quotations became characteristic of the bop style as a whole.

3. Influence. Although Parker was not solely responsible for the development of the bop style, he was its most important representative and a source of inspiration to all musicians who took part in its early growth. His influence was not limited to performers on his own instrument: his lines, rhythmic devices, and favorite motifs were transferred to instruments other than reeds, such as the trombone, vibraphone, piano, and guitar, and many innovations of bop drummers were made in response to the increased rhythmic complexity of his music.

Parker's influence was immediate and intense. His most famous early solos were learned note-for-note by thousands of aspiring young bop musicians on all instruments; as early as 1948 published transcriptions of them were available for study purposes. Some were even given texts by bop singers and performed as independent pieces. Parker's impact was naturally strongest on alto saxophonists such as Sonny Stitt, Cannonball Adderley, Phil Woods, and many others; only Lee Konitz and West Coast musicians such as Paul Desmond managed to create viable independent styles on alto saxophone. Despite the differences in timbre and mobility of the lower-pitched, bulkier instrument, many tenor saxophonists also came under Parker's sway, most notably Sonny Rollins and John Coltrane. Only in the early 1960s did Parker's influence gradually wane as the modal style led to the abandonment of bop's formulaic approach and the

Ex.5 Parker's use of formulae in two takes of *Klacktoveedsedstene* (both 1947, respectively Dial matrix no. D1112-A [K1] and D1112-B [K2])

(a) A basic formula, the arpeggiation of a G dominant seventh chord

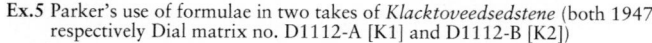

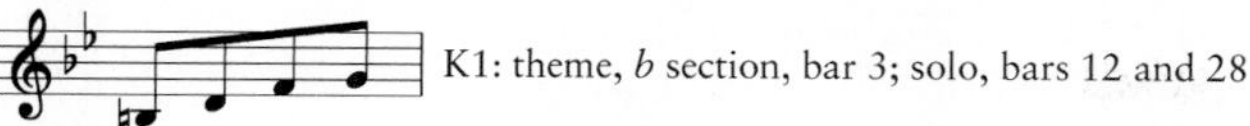
K1: theme, *b* section, bar 3; solo, bars 12 and 28

(b) Variants of this same arpeggiation

K1: solo, bar 32
K2: solo, bars 4, 12, and 20

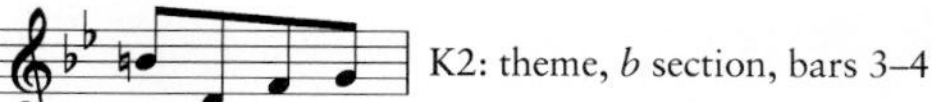
K2: theme, *b* section, bars 3–4

K1: solo, bar 20

K2: solo, pickup to bar 1

(c) Connecting formulae approaching the note *b*

K2: solo, bars 11–12

K2: solo, bars 19–20

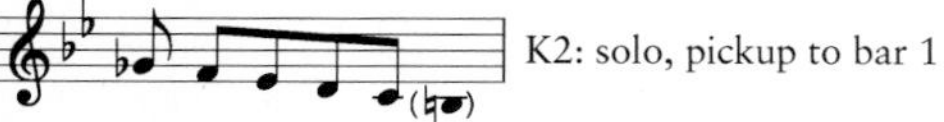
K2: solo, pickup to bar 1

K2: solo, bars 3–4

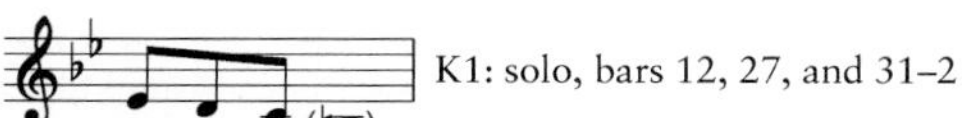
K1: solo, bars 12, 27, and 31–2

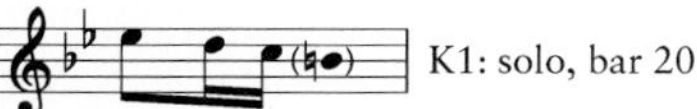
K1: solo, bar 20

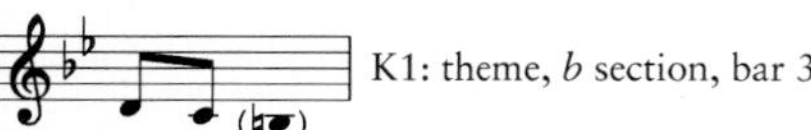
K1: theme, *b* section, bar 3

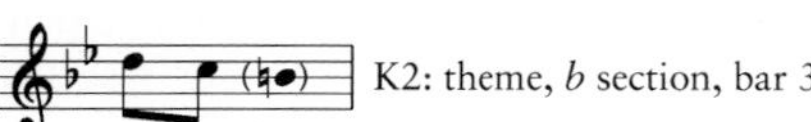
K2: theme, *b* section, bar 3

(d) Connecting formulae leaving the note *g*

K1: solo, bars 13 and 28
K2: theme, *b* section, bar 4

K1: theme, *b* section, bar 4

Ex.5 *continued...*

(e) Connecting formulae leaving the note *a*♭

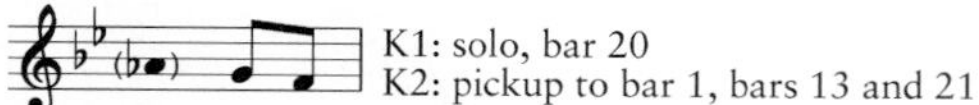
K1: solo, bar 20
K2: pickup to bar 1, bars 13 and 21

K2: solo, bar 4

K1: solo, bar 32

(f) Formulae combined

K1: solo, bars 12–13

K2: solo, bars 11–13

K1: solo, bar 20

smoothing out of its erratic rhythms, and the free-jazz style dispensed with preset harmonic patterns; nor did Parker's music play a role in the emergence of jazz-rock in the early 1970s. Nevertheless, his work remained available on disc in more or less complete reissue series, and recordings of his performances were discovered on private tapes, matrices, or radio recordings, and issued posthumously.

One of the fascinating subtexts of the Parker legend concerns Dean Benedetti. Benedetti, it was said, was a dance-band saxophonist who quit performing when he came under the spell of Parker and devoted himself to traveling around the country making surreptitious wire recordings of Parker's improvisations at club dates – only to vanish, die in Sicily, and leave no clues about the wire spools. In fact, Benedetti was a talented West Coast musician who diligently studied Parker and recorded him in Los Angeles and New York. When his career stalled late in 1948, Benedetti returned to California. He discovered that he had myasthenia gravis, an autoimmune disorder causing weakness of muscles, and he stopped playing as the disease progressed. With his parents and sister he moved to Torre del Lago, Italy, in 1953, and left his recordings of Parker in the care of his aunt and uncle in California. When Benedetti died in 1957, his brother inherited the collection; it remained in his home in Burbank, California, for the next three decades. These recordings were rediscovered in 1980 and acquired by Mosaic (ii) in 1988. They comprise 222 individual items recorded on disc in Los Angeles in March 1947, with Parker performing as a member of Howard McGhee's quintet, and 65 further items recorded on tape in New York while Parker led his classic quintet in March and July 1948. The tapes and discs together form the largest discrete block of recordings in Parker's discography. Most of these items capture only his

2. *Charlie Parker and Dizzy Gillespie at Birdland, New York, 1951: (left to right) Tommy Potter (double bass), Parker (alto saxophone), Gillespie (trumpet), and John Coltrane (tenor saxophone)*

improvisations, with themes and other solos excluded. The repertory consists of jazz and early bop classics and favorite popular songs, as described above, though the material recorded in New York is more bop-oriented, current, and focused on Parker's own compositions and material from his then recent studio sessions for Dial and Savoy; of special interest are performances which preserve his only known interpretations of 18 different pieces. Not surprisingly, there are many first-rate solos; among them are an untitled blues in B♭ (4 April 1947), *The Man I Love*, *Bird Lore* (*Ornithology*), and *A Night in Tunisia* (all 9 April 1947), and *All the Things You Are* (1 March 1948).

With the revival of bop in the mid-1970s Parker's music once again became a vital force in the evolution and teaching of jazz. The Fine Arts Library at the University of Texas, Austin, holds the world's largest collection of recordings by Parker, and hundreds of his solos are now available to the student in published transcriptions. The group Supersax, based in Los Angeles, achieved some popular success playing Parker's solos in harmonized arrangements for saxophone chorus. His work has been the subject of several university dissertations. Although the evanescent, hieratic, and emotionally disturbing nature of Parker's music precludes popularity on a par with that of Armstrong or Ellington, his place alongside them as a creative force in jazz history is assured.

Oral history material in *TxU*.

See also Blues, §11; Improvisation, §§4(iii), 5(ii), and ex.2; Jazz (i), §§V, 2, 3, and fig.5; and Saxophone, esp. §3.

SELECTED RECORDINGS

EARLY STYLE

As sideman with J. McShann: on C. Parker: *First Recordings!* (1940–45, Onyx 221), Lady be Good (1940); Swingmatism (1941, Decca 8570); The Jumpin' Blues (1942, Decca 4418); Sepian Bounce (1942, Decca 4387)

Others: on C. Parker: *First Recordings!* (1940–45, Onyx 221), [no leader]: Cherokee (1942 or 1943); first issued on *Birth of the Bebop* (Stash 260), Boogie Woogie, Embraceable You, Indiana, Sweet Georgia Brown, Three Guesses (1943)

MATURE STYLE

As sideman: T. Grimes: Tiny's Tempo (1944, Savoy 526); Red Cross (1944, Savoy 532); D. Gillespie: Groovin' High (1945, Guild 1001); Dizzy Atmosphere (1945, Musi. 488); Shaw 'Nuff (1945, Guild 1002); Salt Peanuts/Hot House (1945, Guild 1003); R. Norvo: Slam Slam Blues (1945, Dial 1045); C. Thompson: 20th-century Blues/The Street Beat (1945, Apollo 759)

As leader (all recorded for Savoy): Billie's Bounce/Now's the Time (1945, 573); Thriving from a Riff (1945, 903); Koko (1945, 597); Donna Lee (1947, 652); Chasin' the Bird (1947, 977); Cheryl (1947, 952); Bluebird (1948, 961); Klaunstance (1948, 967); Barbados (1948, 936); Ah-leu-cha (1948, 939); Parker's Mood (1948, 936); Perhaps (1948, 938)

As leader (all recorded for Dial): Moose the Mooche/Yardbird Suite (1946, 1003); Ornithology/A Night in Tunisia (1946, 1002); Lover Man (1946, 1007); Cool Blues (1947, 1015); Relaxin' at Camarillo (1947, 1012); Carvin' the Bird (1947, 1013); Dexterity (1947, 1032); Embraceable You (1947, 1024); Klactoveedsedstene (1947, 1040); Scrapple from the Apple (1947, 1021); Crazeology (1947, 1034)

As leader (recorded for Mercury/Clef unless otherwise indicated): The Closer (1949, Mer. 35013); Bloomdido (1950, 11058); An Oscar for Treadwell (1950, 10082); Relaxin' with Lee (1950, 11076); Au Privave (1951, 11087); Charlie Parker (1951–3, Clef 287) [EP], incl. Blues for Alice (1951); Swedish Schnapps (1951, 11103); Chi Chi (1953, Clef 89138)

Others: first issued on *Charlie Parker in Historical Recordings*, ii (1948–50, Le Jazz Cool 102), Out of Nowhere (1948); on *Charlie Parker and the Swedish All Stars* (1950, Sonet 27), Anthropology; Jazz at Massey Hall: *Quintet of the Year* (1953, Debut 2, 4), incl. All the Things you Are, Perdido, Salt Peanuts

TRANSCRIPTIONS

[M. Feldman, ed.]: *Charles Parker's Bebop for Alto Sax: 4 Solos* (New York, 1948)

P. Pinkerton, ed.: *Charlie Parker: Nine Solos Transcribed from Historic Recordings* (New York, 1961)

W. D. Stuart: *Famous Transcribed Recorded Jazz Solos: Charlie "Bird" Parker* (New York, 1961)

Charlie Parker: Sketch Orks, Designed for Small Groups (New York, 1967)

T. Owens: *Charlie Parker: Techniques of Improvisation*, ii (diss., UCLA, 1974) [190 pieces]

S. Watanabe, ed.: *Jazz Improvisation: Transcriptions of Charlie Parker's Great Alto Solos* (Tokyo, *c*1975) [25 pieces]

J. Aebersbold and K. Slone, eds.: *Charlie Parker Omnibook* (New York, 1978) [60 pieces]

A. White, ed.: *The Charlie Parker Collection: 308 Transcribed Alto Saxophone and Tenor Saxophone Solos* (Washington, 1978–9)

BIBLIOGRAPHY

DOCUMENTS AND SOURCES

N. Hentoff and R. Sanjek: *Charlie Parker* (New York, 1960) [list of compositions]
R. Reisner: *Bird: the Legend of Charlie Parker* (New York, 1962/*R*1975)
J. G. Jepsen: *A Discography of Charlie Parker* (Copenhagen, 1968)
T. Williams: "Charlie Parker Discography," *Discographical Forum* (Sept 1968 – Sept 1970)
G. R. Davies: "Charlie Parker Chronology," *Discographical Forum*, nos.17–26 (1970–71)
D. Morgenstern and others: *Bird and Diz: a Bibliography* (New York, 1973)
P. Koster and D. M. Bakker: *Charlie Parker*, i: *1940–1947* (Alphen aan de Rijn, Netherlands, 1974); ii: *1948–1950* (Alphen aan de Rijn, 1975); iii: *1951–1954* (Alphen aan de Rijn, 1975); iv: *1940–1955* (Alphen aan de Rijn, 1976) [addns and corrections] [discography]
C. Parker and F. Paudras: *To Bird with Love* (Antigny, France, 1981) [photographs]
N. Saks and L. Bukowski: *Yardbird Inc.: the Charlie Parker Discography* (Port Jefferson, NY, 1989)
R. Bregman, L. Bukowski, and N. Saks: *The Charlie Parker Discography* (Redwood, NY, 1993)
T. Hirschmann: *Charlie Parker: kritische Beiträge zur Bibliographie sowie zu Leben und Werk* (Tutzing, Germany, 1994)
E. Bubley and H. O'Neal: *Charlie Parker, Ray Brown, Benny Carter, J. C. Heard, Johnny Hodges, Barney Kessel, Oscar Peterson, Flip Phillips, Charlie Shavers, Ben Webster (Norman Granz Jam Sessions)* (Levallois-Perret, France, 1995) [album of photos of 1952 jam session]
Bird: the Chan Parker Collection (London, 1996) [auction catalogue from Christie's, South Kensington]
K. Vail: *Bird's Diary: the Life of Charlie Parker, 1945–1955* (Chessington, England, 1996)
J. Burton: *Charlie Parker Discography* <http://www.wam.umd.edu/~losinp/music/bird.html> (1997)
E. M. Komara: *The Dial recordings of Charlie Parker: a Discography* (Westport, CT, and London, 1998)

BIOGRAPHICAL STUDIES

BalliettA (1996)
L. Feather: *Inside Be-bop* (New York, 1949/*R*1977 as *Inside Jazz*), 11
M. Levin and J. S. Wilson: "'No Bop Roots in Jazz': Parker," *DB*, xvi/17 (1949), 1; rev. as "The Chili Parlor Interview," *DB*, xxxii/6 (1965), 13
N. Shapiro and N. Hentoff, eds.: *Hear me Talkin' to ya: the Story of Jazz by the Men who Made it* (New York and London, 1955/*R*1966), esp. 312
M. Harrison: *Charlie Parker* (London, 1960); repr. in *Kings of Jazz*, ed. S. Green (New York, 1978)
R. G. Reisner: "Charlie Parker: a Biography in Interviews," *JR*, iii (1960), no.8, p.6; no.9, p.8; iv/1 (1961), 12
I. Gitler: "Charlie Parker and the Alto and Baritone Saxophonists," *Jazz Masters of the Forties* (New York, 1966/*R*1983 with discography)
J. Burns: "Bird in California," *JJ*, xxii/7 (1969), 10
D. Amram: "Bird in Washington," *JJ*, xxiii/8 (1970), 4
M. Williams: *The Jazz Tradition* (New York, 1970, rev. 2/1983)
R. Russell: *Jazz Style in Kansas City and the Southwest* (Berkeley, CA, Los Angeles, and London, 1971, rev. 2/1973/*R*1997)
——: *Bird Lives: the High Life and Hard Times of Charlie "Yardbird" Parker* (New York, 1973/*R*1994)
——: "West Coast Bop," *J&B*, iii/2 (1973), 9
N. T. Davis: *Charlie Parker's Kansas City Environment and its Effects on his Later Life* (diss., Wesleyan U., 1974)
J. Patrick: "Al Tinney, Monroe's Uptown House, and the Emergence of Modern Jazz in Harlem," *ARJS*, ii (1983), 150
B. Priestley: *Charlie Parker* (Tunbridge Wells, England, and New York, 1984) [incl. discography]
I. Gitler: *Swing to Bop: an Oral History of the Transition in Jazz in the 1940s* (New York, and Oxford, England, 1985)
G. Giddins: *Celebrating Bird: the Triumph of Charlie Parker* (New York, 1987)
P. N. Wilson and U. Goeman: *Charlie Parker: sein Leben, seine Musik, seine Schallplatten* (Schaftlach, Germany, 1988)
M. Miller: *Cool Blues: Charlie Parker in Canada, 1953* (London, Ontario, 1989)
Chan Parker: *Ma vie en si bémol* (Paris, 1993; Eng. trans., Columbia, SC, as *My Life in E-flat*)
E. Komara: "The Dial Recordings of Charlie Parker," in *The Bebop Revolution in Words and Music*, ed. D. Oliphant (Austin, TX, 1994)
H. O'Neal: *Charlie Parker: Norman Granz Jam Session Series* (Paris, 1995)
C. Woideck: *Charlie Parker: his Music and Life* (Ann Arbor, MI, 1996)
C. Gauffre and J.-L. Chautemps: *Charlie Parker* (Paris, 1997)
A. Tercinet: *Charlie Parker* (Marseilles, France, 1997)

ANALYTICAL STUDIES

A. Hodeir: *Hommes et problèmes du jazz, suivi de La religion du jazz* (Paris, 1954; Eng. trans., rev. Hodeir, as *Jazz: its Evolution and Essence*, New York, 1956/*R*1975), 99
A. Morgan: "Charlie Parker: the Dial Recordings," *JM*, i/7 (1955), 7
L. Feather: *The Book of Jazz: a Guide to the Entire Field* (New York, 1957, rev. 2/1965), 231
R. Russell: "The Evolutionary Position of Bop," *The Art of Jazz: Essays on the Nature and Development of Jazz*, ed. M. Williams (New York, 1959/*R*1979), 195
M. James: *Ten Modern Jazzmen: an Appraisal of the Recorded Work of Ten Modern Jazzmen* (London, 1960), 111
J. F. Mehegan: *Jazz Improvisation*, ii (New York, 1962), 101
D. Heckman: "Bird in Flight: Parker the Improviser," *DB*, xxxii/6 (1965), 22
J. Siddons: "Parker's Mood," *DB*, xxxii/6 (1965), 25
F. Tirro: "The Silent Theme Tradition in Jazz," *Musical Quarterly*, lii (1967), 313
D. Baker: "Charlie Parker's 'Now's the Time' Solo," *DB*, xxxviii/19 (1971), 32
O. Peterson: "Early Bird," *JJ*, xxiv/4 (1971), 34
R. Wang: "Jazz Circa 1945: a Confluence of Styles," *Musical Quarterly*, lix (1973), 531
T. Owens: "Applying the Melograph to 'Parker's Mood'," *Selected Reports in Ethnomusicology*, ii/1 (1974), 167
——: *Charlie Parker: Techniques of Improvisation* (diss., UCLA, 1974)
L. Koch: "Ornithology: a Study of Charlie Parker's Music," *JJS*, ii/1 (1974), 61; ii/12 (1975), 61
——: "A Numerical Listing of Charlie Parker's Recordings," *JJS*, ii/2 (1975), 86
J. Patrick: "Charlie Parker and Harmonic Sources of Bebop Composition: Thoughts on the Repertory of New Jazz in the 1940's," *JJS*, ii/2 (1975), 3
——: Liner notes, *Charlie Parker: the Complete Savoy Studio Recordings* (Savoy 5501, 1978)
T. Hirschmann: *Untersuchungen zu den Kompositionen von Charlie Parker* (diss., U. of Mainz, Germany, 1982)
L. O. Koch: *Yardbird Suite: a Compendium of the Music and Work of Charlie Parker* (Bowling Green, OH, 1988)
J. Patrick: Liner notes, *The Complete Dean Benedetti Recordings of Charlie Parker* (Mosaic 129, 1990)
S. Sandvik: "Polyharmony, Polyrhythm, and Motivic Development in Charlie Parker's *Klack-Oveedseds-Tene* (Take 1) Solo," *Jf*, xxiv (1992), 83
T. Owens: *Bebop: the Music and its Players* (New York, and Oxford, England, 1995), 28
S. Larson: "The Art of Charlie Parker's Rhetoric," *ARJS*, viii (1996), 141
H. Martin: *Charlie Parker and Thematic Improvisation* (Lanham, MD, and London, 1996)
J. Henriksson: *Chasing the Bird: Functional Harmony in Charlie Parker's Bebop Themes* (Helsinki, 1998)
T. Owens: "Bird's Children and Grandchildren: the Spread of Charlie Parker's Musical Language," *Jf*, xxxi (1999), 75
J. Patrick: "Charlie Parker," in *The Oxford Companion to Jazz*, ed. B. Kirchner (New York, and Oxford, England, 2000), 316
J. Patrick, I. Gitler, and B. Kirchner: Liner notes, *Charlie Parker: The Complete Savoy and Dial Studio Recordings, 1944–1948* (Savoy Jazz 92911-2, 2000)

OTHER STUDIES

DB, xxxii/6 (1965) [Parker issue]
J. Patrick: "The Uses of Jazz Discography," *Notes*, xxix (1972–3), 17
——: "Discography as a Tool for Musical Research and Vice Versa," *JJS*, i/1 (1973), 65
——: "Musical Sources for the History of Jazz," *Black Perspective in Music*, iv (1976), 46
Coda, no.181 (1981) [Parker issue]
B. Priestley and others: "Charlie Parker: Thirty 'Bird' Years Away," *The Wire*, no.13 (1985), 25
C. Woideck, ed.: *The Charlie Parker Companion: Six Decades of Commentary* (New York, 1998)

JAMES PATRICK

Parker, Erik (*b* Århus, Denmark, 13 July 1918). Danish trumpeter. He grew up in Copenhagen and became a leading jazz soloist, playing with Svend Asmussen (1938) and Leo Mathisen (1939–45); he made many recordings with Mathisen (including *I don't want to walk without you, baby*, 1944, Tono Z18014) and with others. Later he worked as a club manager, as an actor (1945–51), and as a trumpet teacher and restaurant manager in the Los Angeles area (from 1953). (E. Wiedemann: *Jazz i Danmark i tyverne, trediverne og* *fyrrerne: en musikkulturel undersøgelse* [Jazz in Denmark in the twenties, thirties, and forties: a study of musical culture] (Copenhagen, 1982))

ERIK WIEDEMANN

Parker, Errol [Schecroun, Ralph [Raph(aël)]] (*b* Oran, Algeria, 30 Oct 1930; *d* New York, 2 July 1998). Drummer and pianist. He took up piano at the age of 14. In 1947 he moved to Paris to study sculpture and soon became involved in the local jazz scene, winning an amateur contest sponsored by *Jazz hot* magazine. The following year, as Ralph Schecroun, he recorded with Kenny Clarke, James Moody, and Django Reinhardt, but in 1951 he abandoned music and returned to college, graduating in 1955. From 1956 to 1958 he performed and recorded as a member of Don Byas's group. To avoid a conflict with his recording company, Ricordi, Schecroun changed his name in 1960 to Errol Parker; he also recorded for Decca, Phillips, and Brunswick, and in 1963 had a hit with *Lorré* for Brunswick. An automobile accident that year permanently damaged his right shoulder, causing him to modify his piano playing. He moved to New York in February 1968 and appeared regularly as an unaccompanied soloist at La Bohème or in a trio with Reggie Workman and Billy Hart at the Top of the Gate. In 1969 he worked with rhythm-and-blues bands, and around this time he began to focus on drumming. He founded a record label, Sahara, in 1971. In January 1973 he led a group for eight Sunday afternoon concerts at the New York Jazz Museum, and later that year he appeared at the Festival of Tabarka, in Tunisia. Thereafter he led groups, including the Errol Parker Experience (1976–80) and a tentet (from 1982), in which he served as drummer; his tentet made several albums in the 1980s and 1990s, most notably *Live at the Wollman Auditorium* (1987, Sahara 1014). He also recorded as an unaccompanied pianist in 1990.

Parker worked with a modified drum set in which a conga replaced the snare drum and in which there were more tom-toms and fewer cymbals than usual. His music was a blend of quirky rhythmic textures underpinning traditional jazz instruments. His recordings always held up to the critics, but he never achieved the popular success that he felt was his due. In 1984, in an effort to help advance his career, he wrote an autobiography, *A Flat Tire on my Ass*, but it was published only later (Redwood, NY, 1995).

BIBLIOGRAPHY

GrayF
W. Wood: "Errol Parker: Interview," *Cadence*, vi/8 (1980), 8
L. Jeske: "Profile: Errol Parker," *DB*, xlviii/8 (1981), 53
B. Rusch: "Errol Parker: Interview," *Cadence*, xi/12 (1985), 8
P. Carles, A. Clergeat, and J.-L. Comolli: *Dictionnaire du jazz* (Paris, 1988, rev. and enlarged 2/1994)
D. Franklin: "An Original . . . Errol Parker," *JT* (1989), May, 12
"Ah! Sahara, Sahara, Sahara, ou, la revolution d'Errol Parker," *Jm*, no.390 (1990), 44
F. Davis: *Outcats: Jazz Composers, Instrumentalists, and Singers* (New York, and Oxford, England, 1990), 53
G. Futrick: "The Errol Parker Experience," *Coda*, no.232 (1990), 8
B. McRae: "Errol Parker," *JJI*, xliii/8 (1990), 8
D. Palmer: "Riffs: Errol Parker," *DB*, lix/8 (1992), 14
S. Stein: "Hearsay: Parker's Novel Notions," *JT*, xxii/9 (1992), 14
J. Weiss: "Errol Parker: North African Jazz," *JF* [intl edn] nos.136–7 (1992), 40
R. Schecroun: "Parker: l'Errol de composition," *Jm*, no.448 (1995), 38
Obituary, *New York Times* (6 July 1998)

GK

Parker, Evan (Shaw) (*b* Bristol, England, 5 April 1944). English tenor and soprano saxophonist. At first, inspired by Paul Desmond, he played alto saxophone, but after discovering John Coltrane's music in 1960 he changed to the tenor and soprano instruments. In the early 1960s he studied botany at Birmingham University and played with Howard Riley and in a Coltrane-inspired quartet. Late in 1966 he moved to London, where he became involved in the free-jazz movement centered around the Little Theatre Club and played in the Spontaneous Music Ensemble, led by John Stevens (1967–8). While with this group he met Derek Bailey, with whom he formed the Music Improvisation Company (1968); around the same time he was a member of Tony Oxley's groups, and in 1970 Parker, Bailey, and Oxley founded the record label Incus. Like many of his colleagues, Parker found a sympathetic response to his playing in continental Europe; he made several connections there in the late 1960s, working with Peter Brötzmann (1968), Manfred Schoof (1969), and two groups led by Alex Schlippenbach (from 1970) – a trio with Paul Lovens and the Globe Unity Orchestra. In addition he played in Pierre Favre's quartet (alongside Irène Schweizer and Peter Kowald) and with Misha Mengelberg, Han Bennink, and Willem Breuker in ICP (in the Netherlands). During the 1970s he worked in England with Chris McGregor's Brotherhood of Breath and Barry Guy's London Jazz Composers' Orchestra, as well as in big bands and small groups led by Kenny Wheeler, in various ensembles with Bailey, notably Company (for illustration *see* Jazz (i), fig.9), and in duos with Stevens and Paul Lytton (from 1971). In 1980 he formed a trio with Guy and Lytton, and activities with this group and the Schlippenbach trio remained important for him through the late 1990s.

In 1974, uncertain of the purity of free improvisation in ensembles (where the improviser's work is inevitably modulated by interaction with others), Parker began improvising alone on soprano saxophone. Working in an austere free atonal context, he developed a range of virtuoso techniques such as circular breathing, split tonguing (in which an up and down motion of the tongue facilitates rapid successions of short notes), overblowing, multiphonics, and broken air columns (so-called cross-fingering); these enabled him to create a pseudo-polyphonic sound in which fragments of real and implied patterns suggest that several independent lines are being played at once. One way in which Parker achieves this effect is to establish a low-pitched drone using circular breathing and simultaneously interpose overtone fingerings derived from *Top Tones for Saxophone*, a method book by the classical saxophonist Sigurd Rascher.

Parker's solo improvisations typically progress through the mutation of repeated motifs, accomplished by the addition and subtraction of notes, and by rhythmic, timbral, and dynamic variation. This quality of repetition with variation led some observers to liken Parker's music to that of the minimalist composer Steve Reich and to draw comparisons between the mathematics behind his improvisations and those of fractal patterns. However, despite the similarities, Parker's work differs at least in the respect that, as an improviser, he is able to change direction at will, in response to his imagination or external factors. Taken together, the techniques and aesthetic that he displays as a solo improviser create a strikingly individual syntax for his instrument.

Although unaccompanied improvisation has been Parker's primary focus since the mid-1970s, he has also played in tonal, relatively conventional contexts, such as the big bands of Wheeler and Charlie Watts. Among those avant-garde musicians and groups with which he has been associated are Cecil Taylor, Rashied Ali, Anthony Braxton, Steve Lacy, George Lewis (ii), Paul Bley, Louis Moholo, Lol Coxhill, the Dedication Orchestra (which celebrates South African jazz in Britain), and the Berlin Contemporary Jazz Orchestra. In the 1990s he renewed his interest in improvising with live electronics, and in 1995 he formed the Evan Parker Electro-Acoustic Ensemble, which combined the trio of Parker, Guy, and Lytton with electronics processed by Phil Wachsmann (who also played violin and viola), Walter Prati, Marco Vecchi, and Lawrence Casserley.

SELECTED RECORDINGS

As unaccompanied soloist: *Saxophone Solos* (1975, Incus 19); *Monoceros* (1978, Incus 27); *Six of One* (1980, Incus 39); *Conic Sections* (1989, Ah Um 015); *Process and Reality* (1991, FMP CD37)

Duos: with P. Lytton: *Collective Calls (Urban)* (1972, Incus 5); with D. Bailey: *The London Concert* (1975, Incus 16); *Compatibles* (1985, Incus 50); with S. Lacy: *Chirps* (1985, FMP CD29); with A. Braxton: *Duo (London) 1993* (1993, Leo 193)

As leader: with B. Guy and P. Lytton: *Imaginary Values* (1993, Maya 9401); *50th Birthday Concert* (1994, Leo 212–13); of Electro-Acoustic Ensemble: *Drawn Inward* (1998, ECM 1693)

As sideman: Spontaneous Music Ensemble: *Karyöbin* (1968, Isl. 9079); P. Brötzmann: *Machine Gun* (1968, FMP 0090); T. Oxley: *The Baptised Traveller* (1969, CBS 52664); Music Improvisation Company: *The Music Improvisation Company 1968–71* (1969–70, Incus 17); D. Bailey: *Company 1* (1976, Incus 21); C. McGregor: *Procession* (1977, Ogun 524); Globe Unity Orchestra: *Intergalactic Blow* (1982, Japo 60039); A. Schlippenbach: *Anticlockwise* (1982, FMP 1020); C. Taylor: *The Hearth* (1988, FMP CD11); *Elf Bagatellen* (1990, FMP CD27); K. Wheeler: *Music for Large and Small Ensembles* (1990, ECM 1415–16); Dedication Orchestra: *Spirits Rejoice* (1992, Ogun 101); London Jazz Composers' Orchestra: *Portraits* (1993, Intakt 035); P. Bley: *Time Will Tell* (1994, ECM 1537)

BIBLIOGRAPHY

GrayF; *WickesIBJ*, i
W. Schonfield: "Evan, from Time to Time," *MM* (29 March 1969), 12
——: "Total Improvisation," *It* [London], no.53 (1969), 15
I. Carr: "Evan Parker," *Music Outside: Contemporary Jazz in Britain* (London, 1973), 68
K. Hyder: "Evan for Free," *MM* (20 Oct 1973), 59
K. Dallas: "Improvisations," *MM* (26 June 1976), 41
L. Goddet: "Une musique de l'éclatement: Evan Parker/Paul Lytton," *Jh*, no.327 (1976), 16
K. Ansell: "Evan Parker," *Impetus*, no.6 (1977), 255
B. Case: "If it's too Easy it ain't Music," *New Musical Express* (12 Nov 1977), 58
M. Patton: "Jazzscene: Solo Parker," *MM* (19 Nov 1977), 50
S. Lake: "Evan Parker," *JF* [intl edn], no.51 (1978), 38
P. Riley: "Incus Records," *Coda*, no.167 (1979), 3
B. Rusch: "Evan Parker: Interview," *Cadence*, v/4 (1979), 8
R. Terlizzi: "Evan Parker," *Coda*, no.167 (1979), 2
D. Bailey: *Improvisation: its Nature and Practice in Music* (Ashbourne, England, 1980, Englewood Cliffs, NJ, 1980, as *Musical Improvisation: its Nature and Practice in Music*, rev. 2/1992)
T. Johnson: "Evan Parker's Free Sax," *VV* (19 Nov 1980), 82
G. Rouy: "Evan Parker: le message des anches," *Jm*, no.282 (1980), 22; contd as "Evan Parker d'une musique à l'autre," no.284 (1980), 32
G. Cerutti and R. Bergerone: *Discographie: Evan Parker* (Sierre, Switzerland, n.d. [?1981]; rev. and enlarged 2/n.d. [?1985] as *Evan Parker Discography (on Records and Cassettes), 1968–1983*)
B. Noglik: "Evan Parker," *Jazzwerkstatt international* (Berlin, 1981), 9 [incl. interview, discography]
B. McRae: "Evan Parker: Moving Forward with Tradition," *JJI*, xxxviii/1 (1985), 10
P. Renaud: *La discographie du jazz anglais* (Chaumont, France, 1985)
E. Jost: *Europas Jazz, 1960–1980* (Frankfurt am Main, Germany, 1987), 289
P. Keegan: "Evan Parker: the Breath and Breadth of the Saxophone," *DB*, liv/4 (1987), 26 [incl. discography]
R. Summers: "Sax Obsessed: Evan Parker's 'Obscure Hobby'," *Option*, no.32 (1990), 58
G. Lock: "Speaking of the Essence," *Wire*, no.85 (1991), 30
L. Svirchev: "Evan Parker: an Intensity of Purpose," *Coda*, no.250 (1993), 4
F. Martinelli: *Evan Parker Discography* (Pontedera, Italy, 1994)
J. Shiurba: "Evan Parker: Interview," *Cadence*, xxii/9 (1996), 5
M. Greenaway: "Evan Parker: Recorded Delivery," *Avant*, no.4 (1997), 9
S. Beresford: "Process and Reality: Evan Parker in Conversation," *Gramophone Explorations*, no.3 (1998), 86
<http://www.shef.ac.uk/misc/rec/ps/efi/mparker.html> (2000) [incl. discography]

MARK GILBERT

Parker, Frank (*b* New Orleans, 18 Aug 1919; *d* New Orleans, 24 Jan 2001). Drummer. He first played in the band led by the trumpeter Kid Clayton, then in 1941 moved to the West Coast and worked with, among others, Horace Henderson. By 1948 he was back in New Orleans, where he played with the rhythm-and-blues singer and pianist Fats Domino and the trumpeter Joe Phillips. In the 1950s Parker performed with several rhythm-and-blues groups, and in 1958 he toured with Ray Charles. He spent a further period in California from 1959 to 1970, but thereafter he worked in his home town with such musicians as the trumpeters Wallace Davenport, Thomas Jefferson, and Kid Sheik Cola; he also played with his wife, the pianist and singer Lavergne Smith (1975–9). From 1980 he worked regularly at Preservation Hall and made several tours of the USA and Europe with the band under the leadership of Percy Humphrey; he ceased to perform after suffering a stroke in 1990. Parker was a solid drummer who was capable of playing traditional music as well as in more modern styles; in 1981 he recorded an album, *Shake it & Break it* (Nola 22), with Michael White (ii).

BIBLIOGRAPHY

M. Joly: "Frank Parker: Beating my Way through the World," *Fn*, xv/1 (1983), 15
D. Dudine: "Portraits: Preservation Hall's Frank Parker," *MD*, x/12 (1986), 34

MARCEL JOLY

Parker, Johnny [John Robert] (*b* Beckenham, England, 6 Nov 1929). English pianist. Although he took piano lessons as a young child he was largely self-taught. He began his career in the late 1940s with Beryl Bryden, the trumpeter Mike Daniels, and others, and worked with Mick Mulligan for a year from May 1950 before joining Humphrey Lyttelton's band. With this ensemble he performed, broadcast, made recordings (including *Bad Penny Blues*, 1956, Parl. R4184), and accompanied Sidney Bechet and Eddie Condon; he also played in the supporting band to Louis Armstrong's All Stars (1956). After leaving Lyttelton in September 1957 he formed his own band and, for a year from July 1958, played with the trombonist Graham Stewart, recording in Denmark. During the following decade Parker was active only intermittently as a musician, but he worked with Monty Sunshine (February 1961 – August 1962), Alexis Korner (August 1962 – August 1963), Diz Disley and Bryden (on a tour of the Far East, late 1963), and blues-rock groups (1964). In 1967 he joined Kenny Ball's Jazzmen, initially on a temporary basis. He led a group which included Wally Fawkes and then returned to Ball's band, with which he remained, except for a brief period of illness, from March 1969 through 1978. In 1979 he played with Sammy Rimington for a few months. Through the 1970s and 1980s Parker worked as a freelance, led his own bands, and appeared as an unaccompanied soloist. His performances with such American musicians as Wild Bill Davison, Buddy Tate, Doc Cheatham, and Eddie Miller confirmed his reputation as one of Britain's leading stride pianists. He also played with Pat Halcox, Keith Smith's group Hefty Jazz (1979–80), Rimington again (1983–6), and the Harlem Blues and Jazz Band (in Denmark and Germany). In the 1990s he worked less regularly on account of ill-health, but he continued to appear in London as an unaccompanied soloist and as the leader of a trio. He wrote several pieces for piano, one of which, *Feline Stomp*, he recorded in 1958 (Sto. 366 [EP]).

BIBLIOGRAPHY

CarrJ; *ChiltonB*
M. Jones: "Johnny Parker: Having a Ball," *MM* (24 Oct 1970), 32
G. Bielderman: *Johnny Parker Discography* (Zwolle, Netherlands, 1987, rev. 2/1994)

SALLY-ANN WORSFOLD/BK

Parker, Kim [Ibeko, Kim] (*b* New York, 22 Aug 1946). Singer. She is the daughter of Chan Richardson, the common-law wife of Charlie Parker, whose surname she took; following Parker's death she was brought up by her mother and Phil Woods. She began singing at an early age and was appearing in local theatrical performances when she was nine. In 1968 she moved to France, where she began her professional career in 1978. In September 1979 she sang at the Delaware Water Gap Jazz Festival, Pennsylvania, and around the same time, under the name Kim Ibeko, she recorded the first of two albums with the pianist Larry Gelb. She toured through the mid-1980s, recorded with Woods, and appeared in the PBS television special "Jazz at the Delaware Water Gap" (1983) and in "Jazz-In" (1986) on Swiss and German television. She has also performed on a number of soundtracks for films, notably *La mémoire tatouée* (1985), in which she provided the singing voice of Julie Christie. Parker continued to sing in the 1990s.

SELECTED RECORDINGS

As leader: with L. Gelb: *The Language of Blue* (1980–81, Cadence 1012); with K. Drew: *Havin' myself a Time* (1981, SN 1033); with T. Flanagan: *Good Girl* (1982, SN 1063); with M. Waldron: *Sometimes I'm Blue* (1985, SN 1133)
As sideman with L. Gelb: *New Souls* (*c*1979, Essence 7001)

BIBLIOGRAPHY

M. Isherwood: "Kim Parker: Interview," *Cadence*, xii/3 (1986), 5; repr. in *CI*, xxvi/1 (1989), 18
C. Nilsson: "Kim Parker – sig själv nog!" [The self-sufficient Kim Parker], *Orkester journalen*, lvi/5 (1988), 16

GK

Parker, Knocky [John William, Jr.] (*b* Palmer, TX, 8 Aug 1918; *d* Los Angeles, 3 Sept 1986). Pianist. His middle name is taken from the California death index. He began his career playing in Texas with western swing bands, including the Wanderers (with whom he played and recorded in 1935) and the Light Crust Doughboys (1937–9). After his military service in World War II he worked with Zutty Singleton and Albert Nicholas. He gained a PhD in American studies from the University of Kentucky, and thereafter he taught at Kentucky Wesleyan College and, from 1963, the University of South Florida. During the same period he performed and recorded with Omer Simeon, Doc Evans (intermittently, 1954–65), Tony Parenti, the singer Carol Leigh, and others. Parker remained active into the 1980s, appearing at the New Orleans Jazz and Heritage Festival in 1983 and the Sacramento Dixieland Jubilee in 1984. In addition to piano he played harpsichord and celeste. He made the first recordings of the majority of the piano rags of Scott Joplin and James Scott, and with these he helped to familiarize specialist audiences with much little-known music. In 1986 a recording he made with Joe Turner (ii) was nominated for a Grammy Award. His papers are held at the William Ransom Hogan Jazz Archive at Tulane University in New Orleans (*see* LIBRARIES AND ARCHIVES, §2).
Oral history material in *LNT*.

SELECTED RECORDINGS

As unaccompanied soloist: *The Complete Piano Works of Scott Joplin* (*c*1960, Audiophile 71–2); *The Complete Piano Works of James Scott* (*c*1962, Audiophile 76–7); *Golden Treasury of Ragtime* (*c*1968, Audiophile 89–92); *Complete Piano Works of Jelly Roll Morton* (*c*1970, Audiophile 102–5)
As sideman with J. Turner: *Big Joe Turner with Knocky Parker and his Houserockers* (1983, Slnd 13)

BIBLIOGRAPHY

ChiltonW; *FeatherE*
C. Richards: "Knocky-Knocky," *Record Changer*, vi/6 (1947), 11
T. Cundall: "'The Strenuous Life': Knocky Parker," *JJ*, v/9 (1952), 1
J. Daugherty: "Ragtime Revival Makes Sense to Knocky," *St. Petersburg Times* (6 Nov 1974)
B. Mitchell: "Knocky Parker Interview," *Jazz Report*, ix/4 [1978], [9]; ix/5 [1978], [21]; ix/6 [?1979], [4]; x/1 [1980], [8]
Obituary, R. Rhodes and T. Wyndham, *MR*, xiii/12 (1986), 5
D. Phillips and L. Phillips: "Knocky Parker, Professor of Blues Piano," *Grit* (22 June 1986), 3

JOHN EDWARD HASSE

Parker, Leo (*b* Washington, DC, 18 April 1925; *d* New York, 11 Feb 1962). Baritone saxophonist. He first recorded on alto saxophone with Coleman Hawkins in 1944. During his tenure with Billy Eckstine's orchestra (1944–5, 1946) he changed to baritone saxophone, and he became known as one of the finest performers in the bop style on that instrument, modeling his playing on that of Charlie Parker. (By other accounts he spent some period of this time apart from Eckstine, touring instead with Benny Carter's big band from December 1944 into 1945; or he may have joined Carter in 1946.) He worked on 52nd Street with a small group led by Dizzy Gillespie in 1946, and performed briefly in Gillespie's big band. His recording with Sir Charles Thompson of *Mad Lad* (1947), which gained him wider public attention, demonstrates a style of improvisation combining elements of bop with an extroverted rhythm-and-blues idiom. In 1947 Parker joined the group led by Illinois Jacquet, with whom he worked intermittently into the 1950s; he also toured with Fats Navarro in 1948, and appeared at the Pershing Hotel, Chicago, and El Sino club, Detroit. He recorded two albums as a leader shortly before his death.

SELECTED RECORDINGS

As leader: Wee Dot (1947, Savoy 950); *Leo Parker's All Stars* (1948, Savoy 9009), incl. Sweet Talkin' Leo; Woody/Rolling with Parker (1950, Gotham 262); on [various leaders]: *Back to Back Baritones* (1948–50, Krazy Kat 849), Solitude, Leo Leaps In (1950); Leo's Boogie/Cool Leo (1952, United 141); *Let Me Tell You 'bout it* (1961, BN 84087)
As sideman: C. Hawkins: Woody 'n You (1944, Apollo 751); I. Jacquet: Jivin' with Jack the Bellboy (1947, Ala. 179); F. Navarro: Fat Girl (1947, Savoy 906); I. Jacquet: Robbins' Nest (1947, Apollo 769); C. Thompson: Mad Lad (1947, Apollo 773); D. Gordon: Settin' the Pace (1947, Savoy 913)

BIBLIOGRAPHY

L. Feather: *Inside Be-bop* (New York, 1949/*R*1977 as *Inside Jazz*)
J. Burns: "Leo Parker," *JJ*, xviii/4 (1965), 16
I. Gitler: *Jazz Masters of the Forties* (New York, 1966/*R*1983 with discography), 38
M. Berger, E. Berger, and J. Patrick: *Benny Carter: a Life in American Music* (Metuchen, NJ, and London, 1982)
D. Stewart: "The Forgotten Ones: Leo Parker," *JJI*, xxxviii/3 (1985), 12
L. Bukowski: "Rollin' with Leo Parker," *Whisky, Women and*, no.17 (1988), 59 [incl. discography by D. Penny and J. Burns]

SCOTT DEVEAUX

Parker, Leon (Evans, Jr.) (*b* White Plains, NY, 21 Aug 1965). Drummer and percussionist. He taught himself drums from the age of three and studied classical percussion during his senior year of high school. In the mid- to late 1980s he played with the Mighty Zippers, Carmen Leggio, Melvin Sparks, Harvie Swartz, Sheila Jordan, and Kenny Barron, and in 1989 he toured Spain and Portugal in a duo with his wife, the flutist Lisa Parker. He led various groups, with Steve Wilson and Ugonna Okegwo among his sidemen, at clubs in New York from 1987 into the 1990s, and attracted widespread attention with a series of sparsely textured, percussion-oriented recordings. These typically combined Parker's own compositions with minimalist interpretations of jazz standards and featured the leader on the greatly reduced drum kit which has become his trademark. From 1996 he worked in a duo with Wilson, and in the late 1990s he began giving unaccompanied solo performances. He has also played as a sideman with Dewey Redman (performing in Switzerland and recording), Tom Harrell, Jesse Davis, David Sanchez, Jacky Terrasson (from 1993), Virginia Mayhew, and James Carter (recording in 1994).

SELECTED RECORDINGS

As leader: *Above & Below* (1994, Epicure EK66144); *Belief* (1996, Col. CK67457)

As sideman: H. Swartz: on *In a Different Light* (1990, Blue Moon 79153), As Calm as the Eye, Equilibrium, Watson, pt ii; J. Davis: *As We Speak* (1992, Conc. 4512); U. Caine: *Sphere Music* (1992, JMT 514007-2); D. Redman: *Choices* (1992, Enja 7073-2); G. Keezer: *Other Spheres* (1992, DIW 871); J. Davis: *Young at Art* (1993, Conc. 4565); B. Barth: *Morning Call* (1994, Enja 8084-2); J. Terrasson: *Jacky Terrasson* (1994, BN B21Z-29351); D. Sanchez: *Sketches of Dreams* (1994, Col. CK67021); J. Terrasson: *Reach* (*c*1995, BN B21Z-35739); D. Kikoski: *Inner Trust* (1997, Criss Cross 1148)

BIBLIOGRAPHY

L. Birnbaum: "The Nonconformists: Leon Parker and Graham Haynes," *DB*, lxii/8 (1995), 34 [incl. discography]
C. Gauffre: "Leon Parker," *Jm*, no.448 (1995), 36
R. Grosman: "Leon Parker," *Jh*, no.522 (1995), 31
D. Heckman: "Drumming Up a Different Sound," *Los Angeles Times* (12 Feb 1995)
B. Milkowski: "Portraits: Leon Parker: Seeking the Essence of Rhythm," *MD*, xix/7 (1995), 112
F. Goaty and R. Grosman: "Quand Leon Parker écoute ses pairs avec le coeur," *Jm*, no.464 (1996), 30
K. Micallef: "Rough Mix: Private Lesson: Leon Parker: Single Cymbal Swing," *Musician*, no.213 (1996), 18
G. Robinson: "Hearsay: Leon Parker," *JT*, xxvi/7 (1996), 22
K. Le Gendre: "Wake-up Call!," *Jazzwise*, no.15 (1998), 11
A. Shatz: "Through his Hands, the Healing Power of Rhythm," *New York Times* (2 Aug 1998)

MARK GILBERT

Parker, Maceo (*b* Kinston, NC, 14 Feb 1943). Alto saxophonist. He was born into a musical family, and by the age of eight he was playing in a rhythm-and-blues band with his brothers. He began working with the soul singer James Brown as a baritone saxophonist (1964–5) and then as a tenor saxophonist (1967–70), the break in his tenure being due to military service. He led his own group, Maceo and All the King's Men (1970–73), before returning to Brown's band as its alto saxophonist (1973–6). Next he worked with the singer George Clinton and Brown's former electric bass guitarist Bootsy Collins (1976–80), but again returned to Brown (1984–90). He also performed and toured with the tenor saxophonist (Alfred) Pee Wee Ellis and the trombonist Fred Wesley (fellow bandmates from his days with Brown) under various group names – the J.B.'s, the Horny Horns, and Pee Wee Ellis's All-Stars – and he recorded under Wesley's leadership. Parker, the definitive soul saxophonist, made an acclaimed foray into jazz on his recording *Roots Revisited* (*c*1990, Minor Music 1015), which offered a fresh perspective on the possibilities of soul-jazz fusion by stressing the soul component of this stylistic hybrid. He has made further recordings in this vein.

BIBLIOGRAPHY

CarrJ
R. S. Ginell: "Maceo Parker," *Windplayer*, vii/3 (1990), 14
B. Milkowski: "Maceo Parker: Everything's Coming up Maceo!," *DB*, lviii/3 (1991), 22
T. Moon: "Maceo Parker's Got a Brand New Bag," *Musician*, no.147 (1991), 26
D. Rubien: "Funky Sax Player Makes Jazz with Pizzazz," *San Francisco Chronicle Datebook* (3 Feb 1991)
S. Dollar: "It's a New Groove for Maceo," *Atlanta Constitution* (5 Feb 1993)
"Maceo Parker," *JP*, xliii/10 (1994), 16
A. Stinshoff: "Soul Brother," *Stereoplay*, no.3 (1995), 135
J. Sullivan: "Maceo Parker Shows What He Knows: Alto Saxophonist to Funk Legends has Created a Following for his Sound," *San Francisco Chronicle Datebook* (7 Sept 1997)

GK

Parker, Sonny [Sonnie] (*b* Youngstown, OH, 5 May 1925; *d* New York, 7 Feb 1957). Singer, dancer, and drummer. He was brought up in Chicago by the vaudeville duo Butterbeans and Susie (Joe and Susie Edwards). In 1948 he was the drummer and leader of the band at the Cincinnati Cotton Club; among his sidemen was King Kolax, with whom he first recorded in December in Los Angeles. In 1949 he joined Lionel Hampton, in whose band he worked for the remainder of his professional career. He can be seen performing *Hamp's Gumbo* in the short film *Lionel Hampton and his Orchestra* (1949), and his passionate blues shouting is heard to good effect in *Money Ain't Everything/Worried Life Blues* (1952, Peacock 1595) with a small group nominally led by Gladys Hampton. Parker toured Europe with Hampton in late 1953 and again in 1954–5. He suffered a cerebral haemorrhage during a concert at Valenciennes, France, in May 1955, from which he never fully recovered, and he died of the effects of a second stroke.

BIBLIOGRAPHY

Y. Bruynoghe: "Sonny Parker," *Jazz 57*, no.4 (1957), 6
J. D[emetre]: "Sonny Parker est mort," *Jh*, no.120 (1957), 12 [incl. discography by K. Mohr]
H. P[anassié]: "Sonny Parker," *BHcF*, no.67 (1957), 7
T. Burke and D. Penny: "Sonny Parker," *Blues & Rhythm*, no.19 (1986), 4 [incl. discography]
J. Morgantini: Liner notes, *The Complete Sonny Parker, 1948–1953* (Blue Moon 6003, 1995)

HOWARD RYE

Parker, William (*b* New York, 10 Jan 1952). Double bass player. As a child he listened to his father's jazz albums and, after hearing Ornette Coleman's recordings for Atlantic, developed an interest in the free jazz of the early 1960s. He began playing cello in his early teens and took up double bass in his final year at school, then studied with Richard Davis, Milt Hinton, Art Davis and Paul West on the Jazzmobile and took private lessons with Wilbur Ware and Jimmy Garrison. From the early 1970s he was involved with such free-jazz musicians as Charles Brackeen, Sunny Murray, and Frank Lowe, often performing at Studio Rivbea and the Creative Music Studio. In 1973 he played at Carnegie Hall as a member of Cecil Taylor's group, and the following year he made his first album as a leader. From around 1973 to 1980 he was a member of Jemeel Moondoc's group Muntu, and during the same period he worked with Gunter Hampel's big band, Sam Rivers's orchestra, and Ted Daniel's Energy Band. In addition he wrote music for and performed with a local theater company (1976–81), played with Don Cherry at the Five Spot (*c*1980), and formed a trio with Butch Morris and Wayne Horvitz (recording in 1982).

From December 1980 into the 1990s Parker performed and recorded regularly with Taylor; he was a member of the Feel Trio with Taylor and Tony Oxley (1989–90) and appeared with the pianist in the video *Burning Poles* (*c*1991). In the early 1980s he began playing with Roy Campbell, Daniel Carter, and Rashid Bakr in the collaborative ensemble Other Dimensions in Music; the group later appeared at the Vision Festival in New York (1998). At the same time he worked regularly with Bill Dixon, performing in a quartet with Mario Pavone and the drummer Lawrence Cook, and in a seven-piece ensemble which recorded in 1985 and included the alto saxophonist Marco Eneidi and Peter Kowald. Parker first performed and recorded with David S. Ware in the early to mid-1980s and with Charles Gayle around 1987; initially he worked with Gayle in a duo but later often played cello or violin in his quartets while Vattel Cherry played double bass – as may be heard on the album *Consecration* (1993). In 1994 he performed at the JVC Jazz Festival with Gayle in Rashied Ali's group By Any Means.

Parker worked in a cooperative trio with Eneidi and Dennis Charles which recorded in Vermont in 1986, and in 1989 he recorded with Charles in Rob Brown's trio. In 1992 he performed and recorded with Roscoe Mitchell's group, and in the same year he began working regularly with Peter Brötzmann; he toured the USA in Brötzmann's trio alongside the drummer Gregg Bendian and performed in the USA and Europe with a number of his other ensembles, including a quartet, Die like a Dog, with Toshinori Kondo and Hamid Drake. From the late 1980s he worked with Matthew Shipp, often in a duo, and the two men toured the USA together in 1997 and performed at the Monterey Jazz Festival the following year. In 1993 he formed the quartet In Order to Survive, with Brown among his sidemen, and presented a concert series under the same name, and in 1994 he began leading a free-jazz big band, the Little Huey Creative Music Orchestra. He has also recorded with the multi-instrumentalist Steve Cohn (1986) and the alto saxophonist Christopher Cauley (1996), and he took part in a documentary of the New York avant-garde movement, *Rising Tones Cross* (1984).

As well as performing, Parker has been involved in a number of community arts projects. In 1975 he and his wife, the dancer and choreographer Patricia Nicholson-Parker, founded the Centering Music Dance Ensemble, which includes Ellen Christi and Bakr among its members. He organized the Sound Unity Festival with Peter Kowald in 1984 and presented a second festival in 1988. Between 1994 and 1995 he helped to run the Improviser's Collective, and in 1996, with his wife and the Israeli saxophonist Assif Tsahar, he founded the Vision Festival, which promotes jazz and other kinds of music, as well as poetry and dance. Nicholson-Parker and Tsahar are the festival's producers and Parker is its resident bass player, in which capacity he played in most of the jazz groups that performed at the event in 1998.

Parker has a ferocious free-jazz style. His pizzicato is highly percussive, but perhaps the most impressive aspect of his playing is the rich and intense sound he creates with the bow. He usually plays a half-sized double bass which has a much brighter timbre than the standard instrument.

SELECTED RECORDINGS

As unaccompanied soloist: on C. Taylor: *In Florescence* (1989, A&M 75021-5286-1), Anast in Crisis, Mouthful of Fresh Flowers; *Testimony* (1994, Zero In 301581-2)

Duos with M. Shipp: *Zo* (*c*1994, Rise 126-2)

As leader: *Through Acceptance of the Mystery Peace* (1974, Centering 1001); with M. Eneidi and D. Charles: *Vermont Spring 1986* (1986, Botticelli 1001); with G. Spearman and Paul Murphy: *Trio Hurricane* (1986, BS 120102-2); *In Order to Survive* (1993, BS 120159); of Little Huey Creative Music Orchestra: *Flowers Grow in my Room* (1994, Centering 1002); *Compassion Seizes Bed-Stuy* (1995, Homestead 231); with R. Bakr and Frode Gjerstad: *Seeing New York from the Ear* (1996, Cadence Jazz 1069)

As sideman with C. Taylor: *Calling it the 8th* (1981, Hat Music 3508); *Olu Iwa* (1986, SN 121139-2); *Looking (Berlin Version)* (1989, FMP CD25); *Looking (Berlin Version) Corona* (1989, FMP CD31)

As sideman with others: J. Moondoc: *The Evening of the Blue Men* (*c*1979, Muntu 1002); *Konstanze's Delight* (1981, SN 1041); E. Christi: *Live at Irving Plaza* (1984, SN 1097), incl. Frightened of Feeling; B. Bang: *The Fire from Within* (1984, SN 1086); P. Brötzmann: *Berlin Djungle* (1984, FMP 1120); J. Moondoc: *Nostalgia in Times Square* (1985, SN 1141); D. S. Ware: *Passage to Music* (1988, Silkheart 113); R. Brown: *Breath Rhyme* (1989, Silkheart 122); M. Marcus: *Under the Wire* (1990, Enja 6064-2); Feel Trio: *Celebrated Blazons* (1990, FMP CD58); M. Shipp: *Circular Temple* (1990, Quinton 1); C. Gayle: *Touchin' on Trane* (1991, FMP CD48); D. S. Ware: *The Flight of I* (1991, DIW 856); P. Brötzmann: *The März Combo* (1992, FMP CD47); M. Shipp: *Prism* (1993, Brinkman 058/Röv 009-2); C. Gayle: *Consecration* (1993, BS 120138-2); B. Dixon: *Vade mecum* (1993, SN 121208-2); P. Brötzmann: *Die Like a Dog (Fragments of Music, Life and Death of Albert Ayler)* (1993, FMP CD64); C. Gayle: *Kingdom Come* (1994, Knitting Factory Works 157); M. Shipp: *Critical Mass* (1994, 2.13.61 Records 213CD003-2); *By the Law of Music* (1996, HA 6200)

BIBLIOGRAPHY

E. Hazell: "William Parker: Sound Unity," *Coda*, no.206 (1986), 24

R. Riggins: "The Avantgarde Today: an Interview with William Parker," *New Observations*, no.65 (1989), 21

B. Rusch: "William Parker," *Cadence*, xvi/12 (1990), 5

R. Hicks: "Bass Notes: William Parker: Sound & Light," *Bass Player*, iv/5 (1993), 10

——: "William Parker: in Order to Survive," *Coda*, no.270 (1996), 10

R. D. Sawyer: "The 4th Quarter of the Circle," *Jazziz*, xiv/10 (1997), 54

H. Mandel: "William Parker: Beneath the Underdog," *DB*, lxv/7 (1998), 32

R. Lopez: "The William Parker Sessionography," <http://www.velocity.net/~bb10k/PARKER.disc.html> (2000)

R. D. Sawyer: "Where I was standing, it didn't rain," *Jazziz*, xvii/8 (2000), 40

GK

Parker-Sparrow, Bradley [Parker, Bradley; Sparrow] (*b* Chicago, 9 Sept 1954). Pianist, composer, and record producer. He opened his own recording studio in Chicago in 1977 and later formed the jazz label Southport Records, which recorded primarily Chicago-based musicians. That same year he began scoring music for film, theater, and ballet. He was an artist-in-residence for the city of Chicago in 1979–80. Parker-Sparrow has led the groups Sparrow, Sparrow AM/FM, and Sparrow Shortwave. In addition he has worked with his wife, the singer Joanie Pallato (from 1982), Von Freeman (from 1990), Hal Russell (1994), Tatsu Aoki (1990s), among others. He may be heard to advantage on his recording *If It Wasn't for Paul* (1994, Southport 34).

BIBLIOGRAPHY

J. Hevrdejs: "New Nightclub Entices Singer Out of Studio," *Chicago Tribune* (13 Oct 1989)

H. Hart: "Hanging Out: Getting Needled is all Part of the Job for this Chicago Jazz Composer," *Chicago Tribune* (21 Aug 1991)

A. Obejas: "Sparrow Takes Wing as Soundtrack Composer," *Chicago Tribune* (27 Sept 1996)

GK

Parlan, Horace (Lumont) (*b* Pittsburgh, 19 Jan 1931). Pianist. His middle name appears incorrectly as Louis in a number of reference books; Parlan himself confirmed Lumont. He studied piano from the age of 12 and developed a strong left-hand technique after suffering from polio. He played in Pittsburgh (1952–7) and briefly with Sonny Stitt in Washington, DC. In October 1957 he moved to New York, where he performed and recorded with Charles Mingus's Jazz Workshop (to mid-1959), Lou Donaldson (1959–60), the Playhouse Four, with Booker Ervin, George Tucker, and Al Harewood (1960–61), a quintet led by Eddie "Lockjaw" Davis and Johnny Griffin (1961 – July 1962), and Roland Kirk (November 1963 – March 1966). During the early 1960s he made several albums as a leader for Blue Note and recorded as a sideman with Tommy Turrentine, Stanley Turrentine, Dexter Gordon, Slide Hampton, Ervin, and Babs Gonzales (this last in performance at Small's Paradise in 1963).

In 1973 Parlan moved to Copenhagen. He recorded as a sideman with Gene Ammons (1973), Gordon (1975), Howard McGhee, Red Mitchell, and Claude Williams (all 1976), Idrees Sulieman (1976, 1985), Clark Terry (1978), Davis (1981), Johnny Coles and Frank Foster (both 1982), Bernt Rosengren (1983), Red Holloway and Michal Urbaniak (both 1984), Benny Bailey and Tony Coe (both in London, 1988), and David Murray with Pierre Dørge's Jungle Orchestra (1991); he also recorded in a quartet (1986) and duo (1988) with the tenor saxophonist Joe van Enkhuizen, as a co-leader (1989) and in a duo (1994) with the saxophonist Rainer Pusch, in a piano duo with Jan Kaspersen (1994), as a co-leader with the guitarist Peter Almqvist (1996), and as a leader. Parlan toured Japan with Griffin in 1976, co-led a quintet with Doug Raney (with whom he recorded in 1978 and 1982–3), and in the early 1980s played with the tribute band Mingus Dynasty – though he felt that, without Mingus as catalyst, the group was somehow lacking. He toured Scandinavia with Bjørn Johansen, accompanied such visiting players as Dizzy Gillespie, Teddy Edwards, Leon Thomas, Eddie "Cleanhead" Vinson, and Jimmy Witherspoon in Copenhagen, and at times played with Sal Nistico (ii) while the saxophonist was based in Germany. In addition he led his own trio, wrote arrangements for Rosengren's big band, and toured throughout Western Europe. He often worked with Archie Shepp, with whom he made a number of recordings, both in a duo (from 1977 into the 1990s) and in the saxophonist's quartet (from 1987 into the 1990s), and in 1997 he accompanied Ray Charles. Parlan's album *Us Three* (1960) provided the inspiration for the seminal jazz and hip-hop group of the early 1990s, Us3.

SELECTED RECORDINGS

As unaccompanied soloist: *Musically Yours* (1979, Ste. 1141); *Voyage of Rediscovery* (1999, Sto. 4233)

Duos: with A. Shepp: *Trouble in Mind* (1980, Ste. 1139); with J. van Enkhuizen: *Ellington Ballads* (1988, Tim. 288); with J. Kaspersen: *Joinin' Forces* (1994, Olufsen 1584)

As leader: *Movin' and Groovin'* (1960, BN 84028); *Us Three* (1960, BN 84037); *Speakin' my Piece* (1960, BN 84043); *Headin' South* (1960, BN 84062); *On the Spur of the Moment* (1961, BN 84074); *Up and Down* (1961, BN 84082); *Happy Frame of Mind* (1963, BN 84134); *Arrival* (1973, Ste. 1012); *No Blues* (1975, Ste. 1056); *Frank-ly Speaking* (1977, Ste. 1076); *Glad I Found You* (1984, Ste. 1194); *Keep your Hands Wide Open* (1988, Olufsen 5050); with P. Almqvist: *Peter Almqvist with Horace Parlan* (1996, Sto. 4201); *Hi-fly* (1997, Ste. 31417)

As sideman: C. Mingus: *Blues and Roots* (1959, Atl. 1305); *Mingus Ah Um* (1959, Col. CL1370); L. Donaldson: *Sunny Side Up* (1960, BN 84036); S. Turrentine: *Look Out!* (1960, BN 84039); B. Ervin: *Cookin'* (1960, Savoy 12154); *That's it!* (1961, Can. 9014); S. Turrentine: *Up at Minton's* (1961, BN 84069–70); D. Gordon: *Doin' Allright* (1961, BN 84077); B. Ervin: *Exultation!* (1963, Prst. 7293); R. Kirk: *I Talk to the Spirits* (1964, Lml. 86008); D. Gordon: *Stable Mable* (1975, Ste. 1040); J. Griffin: *Live in Tokyo* (1976, Phi. [Jap.] RJ7160); T. Coe: *Canterbury Song* (1988, Hot House 1005); D. Murray and P. Dørge: *The Jazzpar Prize* (1991, Enja 7031-2); A. Shepp: *Black Ballad* (1992, Tim. 386)

BIBLIOGRAPHY

FeatherE; *Feather '60s*

D. Morgenstern: "Horace Parlan," *Jazz*, ii/4 (New York, 1963), 7

H. E. Philip and I. S. Petersen: "Horace Parlan," *Coda*, xi/3 (1973), 6

J. Jeremy: "Parlan: a Happy Exile," *MM*, xlix (27 April 1974), 24

A. Levitt: "San cinema Parlan," *Jm*, no.256 (1986), 48

P. Howell: "Jazz Pirates who Topped the Charts," *Toronto Star* (5 Aug 1994)

PAUL RINZLER/BK

Parlato, David (Charles) (*b* Los Angeles, 31 Oct 1945). Bass player. While attending Valley City (North Dakota) State College (1966–8) he performed and recorded with Don Ellis. He was then associated for several years with Paul Horn (1968–71) and Gil Melle (1969–74). In addition he performed and recorded with Warne Marsh and Frank Strazzeri (both 1969) and John Klemmer (1972–4), and played with Frank Zappa (1972), in a quintet which consisted of sitar, tablā, vibraphone, and keyboards (1973), and with Gábor Szabó (1974–5). Parlato may be heard to advantage on Ellis's *Electric Bath* (1967, Col. CS9585). (*Feather–Gitler '70s*)

Parlophone. Record company and label. The company was established in Britain after World War I as a subsidiary of the German company Lindström, and the label became the British outlet for the catalogue of jazz and race recordings produced by Lindström's American affiliate OKeh; it retained this role after Lindström's company was acquired by Columbia International, Ltd., in October 1925, and also after Columbia's merger into EMI in March 1931. Parlophone's artists and repertory were supervised by Ted Sommerfield, and issues of jazz were initially made as part of the company's general popular-music catalogues. In November 1929, however, the New Rhythm Style Series was launched, specifically for jazz; this was superseded in May 1932 by the Second New Rhythm Style Series. From 1934 into the 1950s issue took place annually in a Super Rhythm Style Series. Although these discs bore catalogue numbers taken from the main sequence, they were distinguished by series numbers on the labels. At first repertory was drawn from OKeh, then after 1934 also from the American Record Company and Brunswick, until rights to this material were lost in the 1950s.

From the mid-1930s Parlophone became important for its British recordings, both of American expatriates such as Coleman Hawkins (1934) and Valaida Snow (1935–7) and of such British musicians as Harry Parry and Humphrey Lyttelton. EMI also used the label Parlophone (or, where linguistically more appropriate, Parlophon) in other territories, including Australia, Switzerland, Scandinavia, and Germany, issuing similar material in each country. In 1929 the Spanish company Parlophon made notable recordings of Sam Wooding and his Chocolate Kiddies when the group visited Barcelona. In addition a Parlophone label was used briefly in the USA (1929–32) to issue pseudonymously on the West Coast some 200 items drawn from OKeh's catalogue; among these were instrumental versions of songs previously issued with a vocal part.

In the 1950s Parlophone was employed in Britain and Italy to put out recordings made by the American company King, but its importance as a jazz label declined from the mid-1960s. Nevertheless from that time an important series of chronological reissues was made on LPs of material made for OKeh before 1931, the rights to which EMI held until the copyrights expired.

BIBLIOGRAPHY

E. Jackson: *The Parlophone "Rhythm-Style" Series: the Complete List of Records up to and Including December, 1935, Arranged Alphabetically and Numerically Together with the Personnels of the Orchestras and Index to Artistes* (London, n.d. [?1936], rev. and enlarged 6/n.d. [1948])
H. Avery: "The American Parlophone–Odeon Series," *The Jazzfinder*, i/12 (1948), 13
H. H. Lange: *Die Deutsche Jazz-Discographie: eine Geschichte des Jazz auf Schallplatten von 1902 bis 1955* (Berlin, 1955), 26
C. Ellis: "The Programming of Re-issue LPs," *Sv*, no.32 (1970), 44
B. Englund: "Sam Wooding's Parlophons," *Sv*, no.49 (1973), 13
B. Rust: *The American Record Label Book* (New Rochelle, NY, 1978), 212
P. Pelletier: "The Columbia and Parlophone Labels," *Record Information*, no.5 (1985), 6
B. Englund: "A Glimpse into the Past: Parlophon B12500 Series," *Sv*, no.124 (1986), 132
A. Badrock: *The Parlophone Red Label Popular Series E5000–E6428* (Cupar, Scotland, 1994)
A. Sutton: *Directory of American Disc Record Brands and Manufacturers, 1891–1943* (Westport, CT, and London, 1994), 118
P. Martland: *Since Records Began: EMI, the First 100 Years* (London, and Portland, OR, 1997)
H. Rye: "Italian Rhythm Style," *Names & Numbers* (1999), no.9, p.9; "Additional Notes," no.10, p.15

HOWARD RYE

Parnell, Jack [John Russell] (*b* London, 6 Aug 1923). English drummer. He studied piano as a child and took up drums at the age of 14. While in the RAF he played and recorded with Buddy Featherstonhaugh (1943–4), after which he led a group with Vic Lewis (1944 – summer 1945) and recorded with Kenny Baker (1946–7). From 1944 to spring 1951 he worked with Ted Heath's orchestra, then until 1955 led his own band, which at various times included Jimmy Deuchar, Ronnie Scott, Phil Seamen, Hank Shaw, and Joe Temperley; he may be heard to good effect in a drum duet with Seamen on *The Champ* (1952, Parl. R3607). Having studied conducting (1956) Parnell led the Associated Television staff orchestra for more than 20 years. From the mid-1970s into the 1990s he played in the Best of British Jazz with Baker, Don Lusher, and Betty Smith, and from 1976 he was a member of Tommy Whittle's quartet; he also played in Danny Moss's quartet in the late 1970s and appeared with the Ted Heath Tribute Band. In the 1980s he worked at the Pizza Express in London with, among others, Ruby Braff, performed with Bob Wilber, continued leading groups, one of which recorded at Scott's club, and played with Keith Smith's shows. He continued to work on a part-time basis in the 1990s, when he appeared with Martin Taylor in David Newton's trio (1994), directed the BBC Big Band (1994), and accompanied Annie Ross in London (1995, 1996).

SELECTED FILMS AND VIDEOS

The Small Back Room [Hour of Glory] (1948); Uneasy Terms (1948); The Blue Lamp (1949); All that Jazz (1964)

BIBLIOGRAPHY

CarrJ; *ChiltonB*; *FeatherE*; *Feather–Gitler '70s*
J. Parnell: "I'm Really Only a Mildly Frustrated Drummer," *Crescendo*, i/1 (1962), 16
L. Tomkins: "Looking Back, and Forward with Jack Parnell," *CI*, xiv/11 (1976), 20
D. Matthews: "In Conversation with Jack Parnell," *CJM*, xxxi/3 (1994), 16

NEVIL SKRIMSHIRE/BK

Parran, J(ohn) D(avis) (*b* St. Louis, 16 Dec 1947). Clarinetist and educator. As a child he sang in his church choir. His father was a saxophonist, and at around the age of 11 Parran took up the tenor instrument; later he studied saxophone and clarinet at Washington University and Webster College. In the late 1960s he was a founding member of the Black Artists Group and worked in the Human Arts Ensemble. In 1971, after gaining a masters degree in music, he moved to New York, where he joined the big bands of Frank Foster and the arranger James Jabbo Ware and worked extensively as a freelance studio musician; during the same period he received some tuition from George Coleman. Back in St. Louis he recorded two albums with the Human Arts Ensemble (1972–3). Following studies in Africa, Parran settled again in St. Louis (1974) and joined the faculty of Southern Illinois University (located across the river from St. Louis, in Edwardsville, Illinois); he sang in and directed the university's gospel choir, collaborated with local poets and comedians, formed a trio with the electronic music composer Thomas Hamilton and the classical percussionist Rich O'Donnell, and founded, with the trumpeter Floyd LeFlore, the group Third Circuit 'n' Spirit, which merged bop, funk, electronic music, and free jazz. In the late 1970s he recorded as a leader (1977) and as a sideman with the alto saxophonist Luther Thomas (1977) and Leroy Jenkins (1979), and he toured Europe with George Lewis (ii).

In 1981 Parran was a founding member of the cooperative trio New winds, and he remained with the group until 1996. From the early 1980s he worked regularly in Anthony Davis's various groups, including Episteme, performed with Tony Coe, Louis Sclavis, Ernst-Ludwig Petrowsky, and John Zorn in Peter Brötzmann's Clarinet Project (1984), and participated in the Clarinet Family reunion of Hamiet Bluiett (recording in 1984); he also recorded with Edward Vesala (1980), John Lindberg (1984), and Julius Hemphill's big band (1988). In 1990 he performed and recorded in Don Byron's klezmer group Don Byron Plays the Music of Mickey Katz and worked in Byron's twentieth-century music group Semaphore. Later he played in Gerry Hemingway's Mixed Quintet (consisting of Marilyn Crispell, Mark Helias, and Erik Friedlander), Ware's We, Me & Them Orchestra (with which he recorded from *c*1991), Anthony Braxton's large ensembles, and James Emery's Iliad Quartet (from the late 1990s). In 1997 he recorded with Ken Peplowski. In addition to his principal instrument he plays alto and bass clarinet, soprano, alto, tenor, and baritone saxophone, various flutes, and *nāgasvaram*.

SELECTED RECORDINGS

Duo with N. Rothenberg: on [no leader]: *Dix improvisations, Victoriaville 1989* (1989, Victo 009), Mookie
As leader: *J. D. Parran & Spirit Stage* (1995, Y'All 02)
As sideman: A. Davis: *Variations in Dream-time* (*c*1982, IndN 1056); *Hemispheres* (1983, Gram. 8303); P. Brötzmann Clarinet Project: *Berlin Djungle* (1984, FMP 1120); on [no leader]: *Live at the Knitting Factory*, iii (1989–90, Knitting Factory Works 75021-5299), D. Byron: Wedding March (1990); J. J. Ware: *Today's Move* (*c*1992, Y'All [unnumbered]), incl. Emotions [cl], The Devil at Work [a cl]

For further recordings *see* New winds.

BIBLIOGRAPHY

G. J. Marshall: "Profile: Some People Behind the Music: J. D. Parran," *DB*, xliv/13 (1977), 23
T. Johnson: "The Kitchen Improvises," *VV* (24 Sept 1980), 72
J. La Barbara: "The Kitchen Center," *High Fidelity/Musical America Edition*, xxxi/1 (1981), 16
K. Silsbee: "New Winds: Interesting Overtones," *Windplayer*, iii/3 (1986), 24
P. Carles, A. Clergeat, and J.-L. Comolli: *Dictionnaire du jazz* (Paris, 1988, rev. and enlarged 2/1994)
B. Bernotas: "Air Time: J. D. Parran," *Windplayer*, x/2 (1993), 8

GK

Parricelli, John [Giovanni Antonio] (*b* Evesham, England, 5 April 1959). English guitarist. After learning classical violin as a child, he took up guitar at the age of 15, inspired at first by rock and blues players and later by Larry Carlton in Steely Dan. He studied social science at City University, London (1977–80), and after graduation took guitar lessons with Dave Cliff (1981–2). He then played with Let's Eat (1982–4), Loose Tubes (1984–9), Annie Whitehead (1984–7), the saxophonist Tim Whitehead (1984–8), Martin Speake (1985–98), John Dankworth (1993–4), Matheran (1994), Paul Motian (1995), Julian Argüelles (1995), Norma Winstone (1995–7), the flutist Eddie Parker (1995–8), Stan Sulzmann (1996), Lee Konitz (1996), Iain Ballamy (1996–8), Kenny Wheeler (from 1996), Gerard Presencer (1997–8), the composer Colin Towns, Andy Sheppard, and others. Parricelli's predominantly fluid, lyrical style owes much to the influence of Pat Metheny as well as that of Mark Wood, a lesser-known English guitarist, but he also draws on the work of blues-rock players and the textural approach developed by Bill Frisell.

SELECTED RECORDINGS

As leader: *Alba* (1999, Provocateur 1021)
As sideman: Loose Tubes: *Delightful Precipice* (1986, Loose Tubes 003); Matheran: *Matheran* (1993, Isis 02); M. Speake: *In our Time* (1994, Jazz Label 005); I. Ballamy: *Acme* (1996, B+W 101); G. Presencer: *Platypus* (1997, Linn 079); K. Wheeler: *Music for Brass Ensemble and Soloists* (1997–8, ECM 1691)

MARK GILBERT

Parrish, Avery (*b* Birmingham, AL, 24 Jan 1917; *d* New York, 10 Dec 1959). Pianist. He attended Alabama State Teachers College and was a member of the 'Bama State Collegians, which was directed by Erskine Hawkins. Following a performance by the band in New York (1934) Parrish chose to stay there to work professionally with Hawkins; among the recordings he made with the group was one of his own compositions, the blues solo *After Hours* (1940), which became extremely popular. After leaving Hawkins in 1941 Parrish worked in California until the following year, when injuries sustained in a fight left him partially paralyzed.

SELECTED RECORDINGS

(all recorded for Bluebird)

* – arranged by Parrish

As sideman with E. Hawkins: *Strictly Swing (1938, 10012); *Swing Out (1939, 10224); *After Hours Out (1940, 10879); *Put yourself in my place (1940, 10932); *Rifftime (1940, 11161); Blackout (1941, 11192)

BIBLIOGRAPHY

ChiltonW; *FeatherE*; *McCarthyB*
S. Dance: *The World of Swing* (New York, 1974)

HOWARD RYE

Parry, Harry (Owen) (*b* Bangor, Wales, 22 Jan 1912; *d* London, 18 Oct 1956). Welsh clarinetist and bandleader. He was playing cornet, tenor horn, and flugelhorn in a brass band by the age of ten, and tried drums and violin before taking up clarinet and alto saxophone in 1927. Five years later he moved to London, where he worked with dance bands led by the pianist Percival Mackey and others before forming his own sextet. A residency at the St. Regis Hotel in 1940 led to his being selected by the BBC as the resident leader for a series of radio programs, "Radio Rhythm Club." With his sextet, which included George Shearing and the singer Doreen Villiers, he later made more than a hundred recordings for Parlophone, including *Blues for Eight/Thrust and Parry* (1942, R2832). After World War II he began working in television and radio as a compère and disc jockey, and in 1947 he made the first of several tours as a leader, which included engagments in the Netherlands and Egypt (both 1949), the Middle East (1950), and India (October 1952 – October 1953). Parry's fluent, technically proficient playing was often likened to that of Benny Goodman in the 1940s.

BIBLIOGRAPHY

CarrJ; *ChiltonB*
T. Middleton: *A Harry Parry Bio-discography* (London, 1995)

CLARRIE HENLEY

Parson, Dion (Gary) (*b* St. Thomas, US Virgin Islands, 11 June 1967). Virgin Island drummer. He first played trombone and changed to drums at the age of 15. Under a grant from the Virgin Islands Council of the Arts he attended Interlochen Arts Academy in Michigan, and he later returned to the USA to study at the campus of Rutgers in Newark, New Jersey (BMEd 1990), where Keith Copeland was one of his teachers. He then moved to New York, where he worked with, among others, Ray Anderson (1990–91), Donald Harrison (1993–7), Marc Cary and Dwayne Burno (both from 1994), Monty Alexander (1994–5), David Sanchez (1995–6), Don Byron (1995–7), Laurent de Wilde (from 1996), and Ernest Ranglin (late 1990s). In the late 1990s, with Ron Blake, he co-founded 21st Century; he recorded with this group, as well as with Justin Robinson (*c*1998) and in a quartet led by the guitarists Peter Bernstein and Helmut Kagerer. Parson has taught at Cheyney University in Pennsylvania and the Harlem School of the Arts, and in 1992 he was appointed to the faculty of Rutgers in Newark.

SELECTED RECORDINGS

As leader with R. Blake: *21st Century* (1997, Tahmun 2100)
As sideman: M. Cary: *Listen* (1996, Arabesque 0125); L. de Wilde: *Spoon-a-rhythm* (1996, Col. CK68635); E. Ranglin: *In Search of the Lost Riddim* (*c*1998, Palm Pictures 2001); J. Robinson: *Challenge* (*c*1998, Arabesque 0137)

BIBLIOGRAPHY

Feather–GitlerBEJ
E. Holley: "Jazzed Up Virgin Grooves," *DB*, lxvi/5 (1999), 39
<http://www.21st-centurymusic.com/> (1999)

GK

Pascoal, Hermeto (*b* Lagoa da Canoa, Brazil, 22 June 1936). Brazilian multi-instrumentalist and arranger. He grew up in a musical family, played accordion from the age of seven, and began performing in bands with his father and brother when he was 11. In 1950 the family moved to Recife, where until 1958 he worked with his brother in groups that broadcast on radio. He then played in a small band in southern Brazil. In 1960, in São Paulo, he took up flute and saxophone and formed the ensemble Som Quatro. While continuing to perform with various bands, in 1964 he joined Airto Moreira's Quarteto Novo. This quartet became popular and was acclaimed for its use of rhythms from northeastern Brazil; it recorded Pascoal's first composition, *O ovo.* Late in 1969, at the invitation of Moreira, Pascoal went to New York, and in 1970 he recorded with Miles Davis, Donald Byrd, and Duke Pearson, as well as with Moreira; his own début recording, *Hermeto*, was made with a large group of leading jazz players. After living in California for a brief period he returned to Brazil in 1972, and from the mid-1970s he recorded and performed with Flora Purim's small groups. In the late 1970s he organized a sextet consisting of younger Brazilian musicians, with which he toured internationally, and thereafter he was active principally with this group. Pascoal's work has inspired a generation of Brazilian musicians, including Moreira, Purim, Milton Nascimento, and Dom Um Romão. He plays flutes, percussion, keyboards, guitar, and soprano saxophone.

SELECTED RECORDINGS

As unaccompanied soloist: *Zabumbê-bum-á* (*c*1978, WB BR36.104)

As leader: *Hermeto* (*c*1972, Cob. 9000); *Slaves Mass* (1977, WB BS2980); *Cérebro magnético* (1980, WB BR30.127); *Hermeto Pascoal e grupo* (1982, Som da Gente 014); *Lagao de Canoa, Municipio de Arapiraca* (1984, Som da Gente 021); *Só não toca quem não quer* (1987, Som da Gente 001/87); *Fest dos deuses* (1992, Phi. 510407-2)

As sideman: M. Davis: on *Live-Evil* (1970, Col. G30954), Nem um talvez, Selim; A. Moreira: *The Natural Sound of Airto* (*c*1970, Buddha 5085); F. Purim: *Encounter* (1976–7, Mlst. 9077)

BIBLIOGRAPHY

CarrJ; *Feather–GitlerBEJ*

M. Zwerin: "Hermeto Pascoal," *Jazz Echo*, no.42 (1979), 5

D. Dreyfus: "Les grands airs d'Hermeto," *Jm*, no.327 (1984), 28

H. Mandel: " Riffs: Hermeto," *DB*, liv/4 (1987), 15

——: "Rio on the Hudson,"*Ear*, xi/5–xii/1 (1987), 8

K. Brodacki: "Hermeto Pascoal," *JF* [intl edn], no.113 (1988), 33

P. Carles, A. Clergeat, and J.-L. Comolli: *Dictionnaire du jazz* (Paris, 1988, rev. and enlarged 2/1994)

J. Levenson: "Blue Notes: Hermeto Pascoal: the Sound of Brazil's People," *Billboard*, ci (4 March 1989), 71

E. M. Raymond: "Vore jag kvinna skulle jag vara gravidast i världen" [If I were a woman, I would be the most pregnant one in the world!], *Orkester journalen*, lix/1 (1991), 18

"Hermeto Pascoal: bruxo dos sons," *Jh*, no.517 (1995), 34 [incl. discography]

<http://www.dystopia.fi/~arvnik/PASCOAL.HTM> (1999) [incl. discography]

GK

Pasquall, Jerome Don (*b* Fulton, KY, 20 Sept 1902; *d* New York, 18 Oct 1971). Saxophonist and clarinetist. In 1903 his family moved to St. Louis, where he played mellophone in brass bands as a child and in his teens before changing to clarinet. Around 1919 he worked with Ed Allen, and in 1921 he played with Charlie Creath and with Fate Marable on the Mississippi riverboats; later that year he began studying at the American Conservatory in Chicago, where he performed and recorded with Doc Cook's Dreamland Orchestra for two years, mainly on tenor saxophone. His primitive playing at this time may be heard on Cook's *The Memphis Maybe Man* (1924, Gen. 5374). While in Chicago Pasquall also worked with Charlie Elgar (1922). He performed under the bandleader Will Vodery in the revue *Dixie to Broadway* (1924–5), studied at the New England Conservatory (to 1927), and then served as lead alto saxophonist with Fletcher Henderson (July 1927 – October 1928). *There's a rickety rackety shack* (1927, Ban. 6129) offers an example of his work on solo soprano saxophone, and he plays bass saxophone, both in the rhythm section and as a soloist, on *Feeling Good* (Har. 636H) and *I'm feeling devilish* (Har. 974H), recorded in 1928 with Henderson's Dixie Stompers. He led his own band in Chicago (after 1928) and worked with Freddie Keppard, Dave Peyton (1930), Jabbo Smith (1931), Tiny Parham (1931–2), Fess Williams (1934, 1936), the violinist Leroy Smith (1935), and Eddie South (1935–6). From around April to October 1936 he was with Henderson once more, and he spent several years with Noble Sissle (1937–44) before settling in New York, where he continued to work as a freelance musician. A photograph in McCarthy's *Big Band Jazz* (1974) shows him with Sissle again in 1950.

BIBLIOGRAPHY

AllenH; *ChiltonW*; *McCarthyB*

F. Driggs and T. Hagert: "Jerome Don Pasquall," *JJ*, xvii (1964), no.4, p.22; no.5, p.19

T. J. Hennessey: "The Black Chicago Establishment, 1919–1930," *JJS*, ii/1 (1974), 15

J. Evensmo: *History of Jazz Tenor Saxophone: Black Artists*, i: *1917–1934* (Oslo, 1996); ii: *1935–1939* (Oslo, 1997); iii: *1940–1944* (Oslo, 1997)

HOWARD RYE

Pass, Joe [Passalaqua, Joseph Anthony Jacobi] (*b* New Brunswick, NJ, 13 Jan 1929; *d* Los Angeles, 23 May 1994). Guitarist and leader. He started playing at the age of nine. Four years later he performed in a group patterned after the Quintette du Hot Club de France, and in summer 1943 he toured in Tony Pastor's band. He left school early to play professionally. After arriving in New York in 1948 or 1949 he played with Brew Moore. At this point he became addicted to heroin and consequently spent many years in prisons, hospitals, and halfway houses. In 1961, together with other jazz musicians in Synanon, a self-help organization for drug addicts, he issued a collective album which attracted some critical attention to his easy-going manner and astounding technical prowess. He recorded with Johnny Griffin, Groove Holmes (1962), Gerald Wilson (1962–3, 1965), Les McCann, and Bud Shank (1963), and played at Shelly's Manne-Hole in Hollywood in a quartet with Shank, Ralph Peña, and Donald Dean (1963). From 1965 to 1967 he toured in George Shearing's group. Pass then worked for several years in studios in Los Angeles and toured Australia with Benny Goodman (March 1973), but remained more or less in obscurity until December 1973, when he was retained for the Pablo label and recorded his first solo album, *Virtuoso.* The success of this catapulted him to fame, and he immediately began to dominate jazz popularity polls for his instrument. From that time on he was greatly in demand for concerts, festivals, and recording sessions, notably as an accompanist to Ella Fitzgerald and Sarah Vaughan, and as a member of Oscar Peterson's groups. Probably the most widely recorded jazz guitarist of the 1980s, he also made many albums as an unaccompanied soloist, in duos, and as a sideman with Milt Jackson and in Count Basie's reconstituted "Kansas City" ensembles. In 1987, while continuing his affiliation with Pablo, Pass co-founded Polytone Records with Tommy Gumina. He continued his international touring until shortly before his death, appearing in ad hoc all-star groups with Peterson, Lee Konitz, Niels-Henning Ørsted Pedersen, Benny Carter, Herb Ellis, and Ray Brown, or giving performances as an unaccompanied soloist or with his quartet, which for many years consisted of John Pisano, Jim Hughart, and Colin Bailey.

Pass was one of the few jazz guitarists to master the technique of finger picking, which allowed him to give fully satisfying performances as an unaccompanied soloist. Like Art Tatum, with whom he is often compared because of his comprehensive grasp of instrumental technique, Pass is heard to best advantage in his elaborate solo paraphrases of popular songs, where he reveals a refined sense of harmony and an uncommonly wide array of accompaniment textures. His playing is the subject of numerous instructional books, including *The Joe Pass Guitar Method* (New York, *c*1977), *Joe Pass Guitar Style* (Van Nuys, CA, 1985), and *Mel Bay Presents Joe Pass Improvising Ideas* (Pacific, MO, *c*1994), and many volumes of transcriptions.

SELECTED RECORDINGS

(recorded for Pablo unless otherwise indicated)

As unaccompanied soloist: *Virtuoso* (1973, 2310708); *At the Montreux Jazz Festival* (1975, 2310752); *Virtuoso*, ii (1976, 2310788); *Virtuoso*, iii (1977, 2310805); *I Remember Charlie Parker* (1979, PT 2312109)

Duos: with E. Fitzgerald: *Take Love Easy* (1973, 2310702); with O.

Joe Pass and Niels-Henning Ørsted Pedersen at Jazz à Vienne, France, 1990

Peterson: *Porgy & Bess* (1976, 2310779); with N.-H. Ørsted Pedersen: *Chops* (1978, 2310830); with Z. Sims: *Blues for Two* (1982, 2310879)
As leader: with R. Brown and M. Jackson: *The Big Three* (1975, 2310757); *Eximious* (1982, 2310877); *Whitestone* (1985, 2310912); *Appassionato* (1990, 2310946-2)
As sideman: Sounds of Synanon: *Sounds of Synanon* (1961, PJ 48); C. Basie: *Kansas City Six* (1981, 2310871)

SELECTED FILMS AND VIDEOS

Guitars: from Flamenco to Jazz (1962); Joe Pass Solo Jazz Guitar (1986); Legends of Jazz Guitar, i–ii (?early 1990s); Joe Pass in Concert (1991); The Genius of Joe Pass (*c*1998)

TRANSCRIPTIONS

Jazz Guitar Solos (Englewood, CO, *c*1971/*R*1986)
Joe Pass Chord Solos (Englewood, CO, 1972)
Chops (Boston, n.d.)
Intercontinental (Brookline, MA, 1979)
Portraits of Duke Ellington (Brookline, MA, 1981)
Virtuoso (Brookline, MA, 1981)
A. De Mause: *Mel Bay Presents Joe Pass Virtuoso #3* (Pacific, MO, 1985)
Mel Bay Presents Joe Pass and Herb Ellis Duets (Pacific, MO, *c*1986)
R. Leone: *Mel Bay Presents Joe Pass Plays the Blues* (Pacific, MO, 1987)
——: *Mel Bay Presents Joe Pass Live* (Pacific, MO, 1990)
——: *Mel Bay Presents Joe Pass Note for Note* (Pacific, MO, 1993)
——: *Mel Bay Presents Joe Pass Off the Record* (Pacific, MO, 1993)

BIBLIOGRAPHY

J. Tynan: "Joe Pass: Building a New Life," *DB*, xxx/17 (1963), 18
L. Henshaw: "Success Comes to Pass," *MM* (13 April 1974), 48
L. Tomkins: "The Guitaristry of Joe Pass," *CI*, xii/10 (1974), 6
"Joe Pass Discography," *SJ*, xxix/6 (1975), 238
M. Jones: "Pass: Serious Guitar Maestro," *MM* (19 April 1975), 58
L. Underwood: "Joe Pass: Life on the Far Side of the Hour Glass," *DB*, xlii/5 (1975), 14
B. James: "Joe Pass: Interview," *JJ*, xxix (1976), no.5, p.12; no.6, p.24
L. Tomkins: "The Challenge of the Solo Guitar," *CI*, xiv/10 (1976), 16
J. Sievert: "Joe Pass," *The Guitar Player Book* (Saratoga, CA, and New York, 1978, 2/1979)
L. Underwood: "Joe Pass: Virtuoso Revisited," *DB*, xlv/7 (1978), 16
J. Ferguson: "Joe Pass: Reflections of a Jazz Virtuoso," *GP*, xviii/9 (1984), 51 [incl. discography]
T. Schneckloth: "Joe Pass on Guitar," *DB*, li/3 (1984), 21
J. Pass: "One on One with Joe Pass: Learn Solo Jazz from the Master," *GP*, xx/8 (1986), 78 [incl. discography]
L. Feather: "Top Guitarist's Jazz New Plans," *San Francisco Chronicle Datebook* (17 July 1988)
J. Ferguson: "Joe Pass' Guide to Walking Bass Lines & Beyond," *GP*, xxiv/2 (1990), 54
W. Enstice and P. Rubin: *Jazz Spoken Here: Conversations with Twenty-two Musicians* (Baton Rouge, LA, and London, 1992), 226

J. BRADFORD ROBINSON/BK

Passport. German group, formed in 1970 by Klaus Doldinger; it was known as Passport from 1971. Its principal members in the mid-1970s were Doldinger, the keyboard player Kristian Schulze, the electric bass guitarist Wolfgang Schmid, and the drummer Curt Cress. The group was the first jazz-rock ensemble in Germany, and in the 1970s its recordings had considerable success; in the middle of the decade it made annual tours of the USA and also toured South America. It reached a still larger audience in the 1980s by emphasizing simple melodies and dance rhythms rather than improvisation.

For recordings and bibliography *see* Doldinger, Klaus.

WOLFRAM KNAUER

Pastor, Tony [Pestritto, Antonio] (*b* Middletown, CT, 26 Oct 1907; *d* Old Lyme, CT, 31 Oct 1969). Bandleader, singer, and saxophonist. He began his career as a sideman in the orchestras of the bandleaders John Cavallaro, Irving Aaronson, and Vincent Lopez, and was a tenor saxophone soloist and singer in that of Artie Shaw from 1936 until the group disbanded in 1940. Pastor then formed his own band, which included some of Shaw's former sidemen. Many of the arrangements played by this group were written by the guitarist Al Avola; others were contributed by Budd Johnson, Walter Fuller, and the pianist and arranger Ralph Flanagan. In the late 1940s Pastor performed with Rosemary Clooney and her sister Betty. Having disbanded his orchestra in 1959, he formed with his two sons a small group which performed at nightclubs until his retirement in 1968. Pastor acknowledged the strong influence of Louis Armstrong's singing style on his own, which was throaty and somewhat gruff; a good example may be heard on Shaw's recording of *Indian Love Call* (1938).

SELECTED RECORDINGS

(recorded for Bluebird unless otherwise indicated)

As leader: Dance with a Dolly with a Hole in her Stocking (1940, B10582); Let's do it (1940, B10902); Confessin' (1940, B11105); I Wonder, I Wonder, I Wonder (1947, Col. 37353)

As sideman with A. Shaw: Indian Love Call (1938, B7746); Rosalie (1939, B10126)

BIBLIOGRAPHY

G. T. Simon: *The Big Bands* (New York, 1967, rev. 4/1981)

C. Garrod: *Tony Pastor and his Orchestra* (Zephyrhills, FL, 1973, rev. 3/1997) [discography]

L. Walker: *The Big Band Almanac* (Hollywood, CA, 1978, rev. 2/1989)

MARK TUCKER

Pastorius, Jaco [John Francis, III] (*b* Norristown, PA, 1 Dec 1951; *d* Fort Lauderdale, FL, 12 Sept 1987). Electric bass guitarist. From 1958 he lived in Fort Lauderdale. His father was a drummer and singer, and Pastorius played drums until he injured his left arm in a football game. He then took up electric bass guitar, and while still a teenager accompanied visiting rhythm-and-blues and pop musicians on guitar and piano. After coming to the attention of jazz musicians, he spent four months in 1974 with Paul Bley, played locally with Ira Sullivan, and in 1975 worked with Pat Metheny in Boston. The following year he attracted widespread notice with his performances on the album *Heavy Weather* by Weather Report, with whom he had a long association (for illustration *see* ZAWINUL, JOE). From that time he was much in demand as a bass player and producer in a wide variety of settings. Unlike many jazz and rock bass guitarists, Pastorius used a fretless instrument, and played with immaculate intonation and melodic clarity (*Donna Lee*). Although sometimes faulted for his flamboyant stage personality and eclecticism, he won the admiration of jazz and rock bass players for his fleet technique, incorporating among other features an unprecedented facility for producing artificial harmonics on the instrument (*Portrait of Tracy*) and the imaginative fusion of styles in his solos. From 1980 to about 1983 he toured with his own group, Word of Mouth, with which he recorded in 1980 (together with many leading jazz musicians) and 1982 (as a big band); in this setting he often preferred not to incorporate a chordal instrument, leaving instead the space for his own chords and the implied chords that were very much a part of his style. In 1983-4 he recorded an album with the drummer Brian Melvin. He died as a result of injuries sustained during a brawl at the Midnight Club in Fort Lauderdale.

Jaco Pastorius playing at the Grande Parade du Jazz, Nice, France, 1983

From a strictly chronological point of view, Stanley Clarke should be credited with pioneering a new melodic role for the electric bass guitar in jazz fusion, but Pastorius soon proved to be the greater player, pursuing creative new paths even as Clarke settled into a lightweight fusion style. His performances set the standard for this style of bass playing. A recording, video, and accompanying volume of transcriptions were published by J. Jemmott: *Jaco Pastorius: Modern Electric Bass* (New York, *c*1985); further transcriptions have been issued by L. Moore: *Solo Transcriptions of Jaco Pastorius* (Los Angeles, *c*1988).

SELECTED RECORDINGS

As leader: *Jaco Pastorius* (*c*1975, Epic 33949) , incl. Donna Lee, Portrait of Tracy; *Word of Mouth* (1980, WB 3535); *Invitation* (1982, WB 3876), incl. The Chicken

As sideman: P. Metheny: *Bright Size Life* (1975, ECM 1073); Weather Report: *Heavy Weather* (1976, Col. PC34418); A. Mangelsdorff: *Trilogue* (1976, MPS 15424); Joni Mitchell: *Hejira* (1976, Asy. 7E1087), *Shadows and Light* (1979, Asy. 704); Weather Report: *Night Passage* (*c*1980, Col. JC36793)

BIBLIOGRAPHY

CarrJ

J.-E. Berendt: "Jaco Pastorius: the Human Sound on the Bass Guitar," *JF* [intl edn], no.48 (1977), 35

N. Tesser: "Jaco Pastorius: the Florida Flash," *DB*, xliv/2 (1977), 12

D. Roerich: "Jaco Pastorius: the Musician Interviewed," *Musician*, no.26 (1980), 38

R. Allen: "Jaco Pastorius' Solo on 'Havona'," *DB*, xlviii (1981), 60 [transcr.]

C. Silvert: "Jaco Pastorius: the Word is Out," *DB*, xlviii/12 (1981), 17

B. Milkowski: "Jaco Pastorius: Bass Revolutionary," *GP*, xviii/8 (1984), 58 [incl. discography]

——: "Portrait of Jaco: a Genius Emerges: 1967–1972," *Bass Player*, ii/1 (1991), 46 [incl. transcr. by J. Goodwin]

J. Mitchell: "Jaco," *The Jazz Musician*, ed. M. Rowland and T. Scherman (New York, 1994), 191

B. Milkowski: *Jaco: the Extraordinary and Tragic Life of Jaco Pastorius, "the World's Greatest Bass Player"* (San Francisco, 1995)

J. BRADFORD ROBINSON/BK

Pastre, Michel (*b* Nîmes, France, 7 April 1966). French tenor saxophonist. He took up drums and alto saxophone, then at the age of 16 changed to the tenor instrument. He moved to Toulouse and played with Paul Chéron's group Banana Jazz (1991–8) and also as a soloist with the Tuxedo Big Band (from 1991) and Gérard Badini's Super Swing Machine (from 1995). From 1997 to July 1999 he co-led a quintet with Alain Bouchet. In that same year he sat in with the Harlem Blues and Jazz Band on a visit to New York, and in 1998 he joined Marc Richard's Paris Swing Orchestra and formed his own Basie-oriented big band. He toured France with Al Casey and Bubba Brooks in 1999. His style, situated among those of Lester Young, Don Byas, and Illinois Jacquet, is well represented on such recordings as *What a Dream*, by Banana Jazz (1993, Banana Jazz 04), and *Siesta at the Fiesta*, by the Tuxedo Big Band (1996, TBB 102).

BIBLIOGRAPHY

A. Vasset: "Brève rencontre," *BHcF*, no.453 (1996), 3
M. Laplace: "Michel Pastre: Blue Michel," *Jh*, no.564 (1999), 36
A. Tomas: "Michel Pastre: le swing sans frontières," *Jazzman*, no.60 (2000), 24

MICHEL LAPLACE

Pathé(–Frères–Pathéphone). Recording company and record label. The company was established by the brothers Charles and Emile Pathé in France in 1894. Shortly thereafter it began manufacturing cylinders, and by 1906, when it started issuing vertical-cut discs (in various sizes up to 20 inches in diameter, and playing at 90 r.p.m.), it also had branches in Britain, Italy, and Russia. Cylinders were discontinued in 1914, but the discs (albeit by this time in standard sizes and playing at 80 r.p.m.) were manufactured into the 1920s and remained extremely popular in France. Recordings made in Paris by Mitchell's Jazz Kings (1921–3) were issued in this form; lateral-cut records were not released in France until the mid-1920s.

In 1914 the company established an American branch, managed by Russell Hunting, which made notable recordings in New York of early jazz by the bands of Noble Sissle (1917–20) and James Reese Europe (1919). Lateral-cut discs, at first bearing the label Actuelle, later Pathé Actuelle, were introduced in the USA in September 1920 and in Britain 12 months later. A parallel series of vertical-cut issues was maintained until November 1925 in the USA, and later in some other territories. A subsidiary label, PERFECT, was established in 1922 to issue cheaper records in the USA. All the company's discs were made in a unique manner whereby the music was recorded onto vast master cylinders, then dubbed onto records of the required size and format.

Though not notable for the quantity of jazz it recorded, Pathé issued some items of excellent quality. These included material by Fletcher Henderson and a series of recordings by white musicians based in New York; the series contained important discs by the Original Memphis Five and by the Redheads, a group led by Red Nichols. The 7500 race series, which began in 1926, was most notable for the work of Rosa Henderson, Buddy Christian, the Dixie Jassers Washboard Band, and early material by Duke Ellington. The company also exchanged masters with Ajax and various members of the Plaza group.

In 1928, the American branch, by that time called the Pathé Phonograph and Record Corporation, merged with the Cameo Record Corporation; the two companies pooled their repertory and maintained their labels. The following year the new organization merged with Plaza to form the AMERICAN RECORD CORPORATION, and the label Pathé was dropped in March 1930. The European sections of the company, and Pathé Orient, Ltd., which traded in the Far East, were purchased in 1928 by Columbia International, Ltd. The label was terminated in Britain but continued in France (where Sam Wooding's band was recorded in 1929) and elsewhere. Thereafter issue was sporadic but remained widespread; jazz items were released on Pathé in China in the 1930s. From 1960 to the end of the LP era the French branch of EMI, trading as Pathé–Marconi–EMI, used the label Pathé for reissues of early jazz.

BIBLIOGRAPHY

R. M. W. Dixon and J. Godrich: *Recording the Blues* (London, 1970), 10, 67
B. Rust: *The American Record Label Book* (New Rochelle, NY, 1978), 236
A. Badrock: *English Pathé Perfect: a Catalogue and History* (Hayes, England, 1983)
A. Sutton: *Directory of American Disc Record Brands and Manufacturers, 1891–1943* (Westport, CT, and London, 1994), 118, 220
R. M. W. Dixon, J. Godrich, and H. Rye: *Blues & Gospel Records, 1890–1943* (Oxford, England, rev. and enlarged 4/1997), xxxii

HOWARD RYE

Patitucci, John (James) (*b* New York, 22 Dec 1959). Bass player. He began playing pop music on electric bass guitar at the age of ten and took up double bass five years later. After his family had settled in California (1972) he studied the acoustic instrument at San Francisco State University (1977–8) and Long Beach State University (1978–80). In 1980 he moved to Los Angeles, where he made important contacts in studios and with those involved with jazz, working with the popular composer Henry Mancini, Mark Isham, Tom Scott, and Dave Grusin, among others. As a jazz player he was a member of groups led by Joe Farrell (1982–3), and Victor Feldman and Hubert Laws (both 1983–5). However, he came to international notice playing the electric instrument in Chick Corea's Elektric Band (from April 1985); during his time with Corea he worked intermittently with Freddie Hubbard (to 1988). Later he was the double bass player in the MANHATTAN JAZZ QUINTET (*c*1988–9) and in various other groups led by Corea, notably his Akoustic Band (from *c*1988)

John Patitucci at Jazz in Marciac, France, 1993

and his acoustic quartet (1994–5). In 1991 Patitucci led a trio comprised of Joey Calderazzo and Peter Erskine, and from 1992 to 1994 he was the leader of an acoustic fusion quartet with the keyboard player John Beasley, Steve Tavaglione, and Vinnie Colaiuta; from 1994 his sidemen were Chris Potter, either Beasley, Bruce Barth, or Alan Pasqua on piano, and Paul Motian or Billy Hart on drums. After leaving Corea (1995) he concentrated on working as a leader and as a freelance, and he played with Roy Haynes, among others, and recorded with the pianist Helio Alves (1997). He also collaborated on an occasional basis with Herbie Hancock and with Wayne Shorter (1992–7). In 1996 Patitucci was appointed artistic director of the Bass Collective School in New York, where he returned to live.

SELECTED RECORDINGS

As leader: *Sketchbook* (1990, GRP 9617); *Heart of the Bass* (1992, Stretch 1101); *Another World* (1993, GRP 9725); *One More Angel* (1995–6, Conc. 4753); *Now* (1998, Conc. 4806)

As sideman: B. Shew: *Playing with Fire* (1986, MAMA Foundation 1017), incl. Cloud Dance; C. Corea: *The Chick Corea Elektric Band* (1986, GRP 1026); *Light Years* (1987, GRP 1036); *Eye of the Beholder* (1988, GRP 1053); *Chick Corea Akoustic Band* (1989, GRP 9582); G. Goldstein: *City of Dreams* (1989, BN B21S-98393); G. Rubalcaba: *Images: Live at Mt. Fuji* (1991, BN B21Z-99492); B. Berg: *Riddles* (1994, Stretch 1111); C. Corea: *Time Warp* (1995, Stretch 1115); H. Alves: *Trios* (1997, Reservoir 156); M. Stern: *Give and Take* (1997, Atl. 83036-2); D. Pérez: *Central Avenue* (1998, Imp. 279)

SELECTED FILMS AND VIDEOS

Chick Corea Elektric Band: Live in Madrid (n.d. [filmed 1986]); Chick Corea Elektric Band: Inside Out (n.d.); Jazzvisions: All Strings Attached (1988); Chick Corea Quartet: Time Warp, One World Over (*c*1995)

BIBLIOGRAPHY

T. Mulhern: "John Patitucci: on Bass with Chick Corea," *GP*, xx/5 (1986), 56
P. Booth: "Profile: John Patitucci," *DB*, lv/7 (1988), 50
L. Feather: "Touching All Basses: John Patitucci," *JT* (1988), May, 14
T. Mulhern: "John Patitucci & the Art of the 6-string Bass," *GP*, xxii/6 (1988), 46
P. Braybrooke: "Fine Lines . . . John Patitucci," *Guitarist*, vii/1 (1990), 40
Z. Stewart: "John Patitucci: Way Beyond Basics," *DB*, lvii/10 (1990), 19 [incl. discography]
P. Cole: "Bass Player Steps Out on his Own," *Los Angeles Times* (21 April 1992)
R. Johnston: "Bridging the Gap between Jazz & the Classics," *Bass Player*, iii/7 (1992), 51
T. Quénum: "Les bas(s)es de Patitucci," *Jm*, no.413 (1992), 32
J. Roberts: "Now's the Time: John Patitucci: to Everything there is a Season," *Bass Player*, iii/4 (1992), 30
P. Cole: "Defending the Bottom Line: Robert Hurst & John Patitucci," *DB*, lxii/4 (1995), 28 [incl. discography]
J. Ferguson: "John Patitucci: Brazilian Double Bass," *JT*, xxv/3 (1995), 37
D. Koehler: "John Patitucci: the Jazz from Ipanema," *International Society of Bassists*, xx/2 (1995), 16
R. Johnson: "Meeting of the Minds: Bi-coastal Brain-picking with Manring & Patitucci," *Bass Player*, ix/12 (1998), 46
B. Milkowski: "John Patitucci," *JT*, xxix/3 (1999), 38

MARK GILBERT

Patrick. Pseudonym of GUY PAQUINET.

Patrick, Pat [Laurdine Kenneth, Jr.] (*b* 23 Nov 1929; *d* Moline, IL, 31 Dec 1991). Saxophonist. As a child he studied piano and drums and took trumpet lessons from his father and Clark Terry; while at Du Sable High School in Chicago he met John Gilmore, Clifford Jordan, and Richard Davis and served as baritone saxophonist in the house band at the Regal Theater, accompanying such singers as Nat "King" Cole and Pearl Bailey. In 1949 he enrolled at Florida Agricultural and Mechanical University, but he soon returned to the Chicago area to study at Wilson Junior College. Around 1950 he joined Sun Ra's trio, which was playing at local striptease clubs. He continued in Sun Ra's newly formed Arkestra intermittently in the early 1950s and regularly from 1954, after returning to Florida to get married. Apart from a brief period in New York in the late 1950s he remained with Sun Ra, and moved to New York with the Arkestra in 1961; he figured prominently on the group's radical free-jazz recordings. While in New York Patrick also worked with Ted Curson, Mongo Santamaria (for whom he served as music director in 1963 and composed a hit song, *Yeh, Yeh*), Willie Bobo, James Moody, John Coltrane, Cootie Williams, and Duke Ellington; in 1970 he was a member of Thelonious Monk's quartet and later he played with the Jazz Composer's Orchestra under Clifford Thornton and Grachan Moncur III. In 1972, with Charles Davis, he co-founded the group Baritone Saxophone Retinue, which in 1977 made one of the two albums recorded by Saturn not involving Sun Ra as a performer. Although he toured Europe with Sun Ra in 1970 and 1976 and participated in several of the Arkestra's other activities during the 1970s, he became involved in teaching at SUNY, Old Westbury, and was with the group again on a regular basis only from 1986 to 1988. Patrick was a well-schooled, versatile soloist and ensemble player and made an important contribution to Sun Ra's music. Besides his principal instrument, which was baritone saxophone, he played flutes, bass, and percussion.

Oral history material in *NjR*.

SELECTED RECORDINGS

(recorded for Saturn unless otherwise indicated)

As leader of Baritone Saxophone Retinue (with C. Davis): *Sound Advice* (1977, 770)

As sideman with Sun Ra: *Super Sonic Sounds* (1956, 216); *Angels and Demons at Play* (1956, 1960, 9956-2-O/P); *Jazz by Sun Ra* (1956, Tran. 10); *Sound of Joy* (1957, Del. 414); *Sun Ra Visits Planet Earth* (1958, 9956-11-A/B); *Jazz in Silhouette* (1958, K70P3590-91); *The Lady with the Golden Stockings* (*The Nubians of Plutonia*) (1958–9, 9956-11-E/F), incl. The Nubians of Plutonia; *Bad and Beautiful/Art Forms of Dimensions Tomorrow* (1961, 532), incl. Ankh, On the Blue Side; *Secrets of the Sun* (1962, GH9954-E/F), incl. Space Aura; *When the Sun Comes Out* (*c*1962, 2066), incl. Calling Planet Earth; *Cosmic Tones for Mental Therapy* (1963, 408); *Other Planes of There* (1964, KH98766), incl. Pleasure; *The Heliocentric Worlds of Sun Ra*, i (1965, ESP 1014); *The Magic City* (1965, 711); *The Heliocentric Worlds of Sun Ra*, ii (1965, ESP 1017); *Live at Montreux* (1976, IC 1039); *Reflections in Blue* (1986, BS 0101), incl. Nothin' from Nothin'

As sideman with others: J. Coltrane: *Africa/Brass* (1961, Imp. 6); C. Thornton: *The Gardens of Harlem* (1974, JCOA 1008); G. Moncur III: *Echoes of Prayer* (1974, JCOA 1009)

BIBLIOGRAPHY

T. Fiofori: "Pat's Rhythm Thing," *MM* (10 April 1971), 28
M. Cullaz: "Pat Patrick," *Jh*, no.330 (1976), 34
V. Wilmer: *As Serious as your Life: the Story of the New Jazz* (London, 1977, rev. [3]/1987)
P. Schaap: "Pat Patrick," *Jm*, no.306 (1982), 18
R. L. Campbell: *The Earthly Recordings of Sun Ra* (Redwood, NY, 1994)
H. Geerken and B. Hefele: *Omniverse Sun Ra* (Wartaweil, Germany, 1994)
J. F. Szwed: *Space is the Place: the Lives and Times of Sun Ra* (New York, 1997)

ED HAZELL/BK

Patterson, Ann (Estelle) (*b* Snyder, TX, 30 July 1946). Saxophonist and leader. She began piano lessons at the age of seven, but took up saxophone when she was 11 and played oboe while in junior high school. Following studies in oboe at the University of North Texas, Denton (BA, 1968), and the University of Illinois, Urbana (MA 1971), she returned to the latter institution (MME 1973); she became involved in jazz after teaching for a short time at the University of Wisconsin, Stevens Point. In 1974 she moved to the Los Angeles area, where she studied saxophone with Bill Green and improvisation with Charlie Shoemake and at Dick Grove's school (1976–80). Soon she was a busy as a freelance, working in big bands led by Don Ellis (1976–8), the vibraphonist and drummer Tommy Vig, the tenor saxophonist and arranger Roger Neumann, Bill Holman, Bill Berry, Frank Capp and Nat Pierce, Jack Sheldon, Buddy Childers, and James Newton, and in small groups led by Buddy Collette, Plas Johnson, Marshal Royal, Shelly Manne, and Art Pepper. She also accompanied the singers Cleo Laine, Joe Williams, Sammy Davis, Jr., Etta James, and Ray Charles and played for a variety of other pop singers and on television and film soundtracks.

In 1980 Patterson and the drummer Bonnie Janofsky organized a women's big band; it made its début at Donte's and gave a concert at the Women's Jazz Festival in Kansas City. Patterson named the band Maiden Voyage in 1981, and the following year Mel Powell composed a three-movement suite, *Settings for Jazz Band*, for it. The group appeared at the Monterey, Playboy, Sedona, and Mary Lou Williams Women in Jazz festivals, toured Japan three times, and recorded *Now's the Time* (1996, Panda [unnumbered]). Longstanding band members included Stacy Rowles (trumpet and flugelhorn) and Betty O'Hara (trombone); Janofsky left the band early on.

Patterson is an excellent lead player and a strongly swinging soloist with a rich tone and a lyrical sense of melody; she doubles on oboe, flute, and clarinet. She taught at Cerritos College, the Dominguez Hills campus of California State University, and the University of Southern California.

BIBLIOGRAPHY

L. Feather: "Women's Band Gets a Strong Send-off," *Los Angeles Times* (20 March 1980)

——: "Revamped Maiden Voyage at Donte's," *Los Angeles Times* (21 Jan 1981)

A. J. Liska: "Maiden Voyage," *DB*, xlviii/11 (1981), 53

——: "Patterson: a Musical Voyage," *Los Angeles Times* (7 March 1982)

S. Placksin: *American Women in Jazz, 1900 to the Present: their Words, Lives, and Music* (New York, 1982, London, 1985, as *Jazzwomen, 1900 to the Present: their Words, Lives, and Music*)

L. Dahl: *Stormy Weather: the Music and Lives of a Century of Jazzwomen* (London, Melbourne, Australia, and New York, 1984)

L. Feather: "Maiden Voyage – Rough Sailing," *Los Angeles Times* (15 June 1986)

R. Lewis: "Women in Jazz: an Upbeat Attitude," *Los Angeles Times* (14 Jan 1986)

L. Feather: "Female Musicians Still Struggle for Acceptance," *Los Angeles Times* (26 Aug 1990)

F. Nemko: "Maiden Voyage: Ann Patterson," *JT* (1990), Aug, 25

D. L. Stein Hunt: *Women who Play Jazz: A Study of the Experiences of Three Los Angeles Musicians* (thesis, U. of California, Los Angeles, 1994)

L. Gourse: *Madame Jazz: Contemporary Women Instrumentalists* (New York, and Oxford, England, 1995)

G. Gibson: "Women's Jazz Band Breaks Through Barriers," *Third Age* (31 May 1997), <http://www.thirdage.com/news/archive/970531-01.html>

D. Heckman: "Brass Ceiling," *Los Angeles Times* (24 Aug 1997)

B. Agnew: "Be my Guest," *L. A. Jazz Scene*, no.130 (1998), 26

F. Nemko: "Ann Patterson: Still on a Maiden Voyage," *Jazz Now*, viii/6 (1998), 13

THOMAS OWENS

Patterson, Don(ald B.) [Duck] (*b* Columbus, OH, 22 July 1936; *d* Philadelphia, 10 Feb 1988). Organist. He played piano as a youth, but decided to change to Hammond organ after hearing Jimmy Smith. Having made his professional début as an organist in 1959 he performed with such musicians as Sonny Stitt (at intervals, 1962–9), Eddie "Lockjaw" Davis (1963), Gene Ammons, and Wes Montgomery, and recorded with Ammons and Davis (both 1962), Stitt (1964–5, 1968, 1971), and Eric Kloss (1965–6). During the 1960s he played frequently in a duo with Billy James, and in the 1960s and 1970s he made a number of recordings as a leader. In 1980 he recorded with Al Grey and Jimmy Forrest; he worked with Grey intermittently to 1986.

SELECTED RECORDINGS

(recorded for Prestige unless otherwise indicated)

As leader: *Goin' Down Home* (1963, Cadet 787); *The Exciting New Organ of Don Patterson* (1964, 7331); with B. Ervin: *Hip Cake Walk* (1964, 7349); *Patterson's People* (1964, 7381); *Tune-up!* (1964, 1969, 7852); with S. Stitt: *The Boss Men* (1965, 7466); with D. Newman: *Mellow Soul* (1965, 7510); *Four Dimensions* (1967, 7533); *Boppin' & Burnin'* (1968, 7563); *Funk You* (1969, 7613); *Brothers-4* (1969, 7738); *The Return of Don Patterson* (1972, Muse 5005); *Why Not?* (1978, Muse 5148)

As sideman: E. Kloss: *Introducing Eric Kloss* (1965, 7442); A. Grey and J. Forrest: *O.D. (Out 'Dere)* (1980, Grey-Forrest 1001)

BIBLIOGRAPHY

Feather '60s

J. Lacomme, comp.: *Jazz Organ: a Discography* (Paris, 1997), 78

PAUL RINZLER/JOSH FERKO (recording-list)

Patterson, (Anna-)Ottilie (*b* Comber, Ireland, 31 Jan 1932). Irish singer. She learned piano from the age of nine, began singing the blues during her early teens, and worked with local bands before moving to England in 1954. Thereafter she performed, recorded, and participated in broadcasts for some 15 years with Chris Barber, who was then her husband (for illustration *see* Barber, chris). Her early style may be heard to advantage on *I Hate a Man like You/Reckless Blues* (1955, Decca DFE6303), and her later work is well represented by *Squeeze Me* and *Too Many Drivers*, from the album *Chris Barber at the London Palladium* (1961, Col. 33SX1436); she also appeared with the group on such television shows as "All that Jazz" (1964) and in films, including *Chris Barber Jazz Band* (1956) and *Momma Don't Allow* (1965). Patterson began incorporating Irish folk songs into her repertory in the late 1950s and wrote music to texts by Shakespeare and the poet Louis MacNeice. Illness forced her to retire in the 1970s, but she resumed performing with Barber on a part-time basis in the 1980s and toured with him in 1991, after which time she withdrew from public performance.

BIBLIOGRAPHY

ChiltonB; *FeatherE*

B. Matthew: *Trad Mad* (London, 1962)

SALLY-ANN WORSFOLD

Patton, Big John (*b* Kansas City, MO, 12 July 1935). Organist. He played piano from 1948 and received his first lessons from his mother, a church pianist; however, he was mainly self-taught. His early career was spent touring with the rhythm-and-blues singer Lloyd Price (1954–9). After taking up Hammond organ he made his first recordings, with Lou Donaldson (1962–4), Johnny Griffin, Red Holloway, and Harold Vick (all 1963), Grant Green (1963, 1967), and George Braith and Clifford Jordan (both 1966). From 1963 to 1969 he led his own soul-jazz trio, in which Braith, Clifford Jarvis, and James "Blood" Ulmer were among his sidemen; the group recorded with such guest soloists as Vick, Junior Cook, Bobby Hutcherson, Blue Mitchell, and Richard Williams. Patton later recorded as a sideman with Johnny Lytle (1977), John Zorn (1986), and Jimmy Ponder (1987–8) and again as a leader (1983, 1994–5). He continued to tour, and in 1997 he renewed his affiliation with Braith. Two years later he appeared in London in an organ duo with Reuben Wilson.

SELECTED RECORDINGS

(recorded for Blue Note unless otherwise indicated)

As leader: *Along Came John* (1963, 84130); *The Way I Feel* (1964, 84174); *Oh Baby!* (1965, 84192); *Let 'em Roll* (1965, 84239); *Accent on the Blues* (1969, 84340); *Soul Connection* (Nilva 3406); *Minor Swing* (1994, DIW 896)

As sideman: L. Donaldson: *Good Gracious!* (1963, 84125); G. Green: *Blues for Lou* (1963, 21438-2)

BIBLIOGRAPHY

CarrJ; *Feather '60s*

HOWARD RYE, BK

Pauer, Fritz [Friedrich] (*b* Vienna, 14 Oct 1943). Austrian pianist, composer, and leader. He played with Hans Koller from 1960 to 1962, and then, leading his own groups, accompanied Dexter Gordon, Don Byas, Booker Ervin, Art Farmer, and other American jazzmen in clubs in Berlin (1962–8). In 1966 he recorded with Friedrich Gulda in Vienna and with Annie Ross in Frankfurt am Main, Germany. He taught jazz at the conservatory in Vienna in 1968, and two years later he joined the dance orchestra of Österreichischer Rundfunk, with which he recorded in 1973 and 1979. He made recordings as a leader (from 1970, including *Live at the Berlin "Jazz Galerie"*, 1970, MPS 15268), again with Gulda (1971), and with Klaus Weiss (1971–2), Peter Herbolzheimer (1979), and Koller (1980), as well as accompanying Farmer on four albums (1970–81). After spending a year in Peru (1985–6) he settled in Switzerland and resumed playing. In the late 1980s he returned to Austria to become a teacher at the jazz department of the Hochschule für Musik und Darstellende Kunst in Graz. A regular member of Farmer's European quintet, for which he provided small-group arrangements, he also performed and recorded with Karl Ratzer (including *Gumbo Dive*, 1991, RST 91540-2) and his own trio (with the double bass player Hannes Strasser and the drummer Christian Salfellner). Pauer likes to collaborate with musicians from many jazz styles, and he has absorbed influences from several different cultures.

BIBLIOGRAPHY

Feather–Gitler '70s

H. Weber: "Plattentest mit Fritz Pauer," *JP*, xxvii/6 (1978), 12

KLAUS SCHULZ

Paul, Emanuel (*b* New Orleans, 2 Feb 1904; *d* New Orleans, 23 May 1988). Tenor saxophonist. He first played violin when he was 18, then, after working as a banjoist from around 1928 to 1935, took up saxophone; he played the soprano and alto instruments before settling on the tenor in 1940. From that year he played with the Eureka Brass Band (for illustration *see* Brass band, fig.2), and he was largely responsible for initiating the role of the tenor saxophone in place of the baritone horn in such ensembles. On fast-tempo pieces his brass-band style was arpeggio based – he often moved in octaves with the brass bass and broke into eighth-notes on final choruses – while on slow funerary numbers his role varied according to the instrumentation of the band. When he recorded *West Lawn Dirge* with the full 11-piece Eureka band in 1951, his solos were limited to simple obbligatos behind the trumpet melody during the second theme; by the late 1960s, with Harold Dejan's smaller nine-piece Olympia Brass Band, he played this theme himself in place of the trumpet, something he was later often to do with similarly sized bands or when the number of New Orleans musicians familiar with or able to read parts for the traditional burial dirges was limited.

Around 1943 Paul began an association with Kid Thomas Valentine that continued into the 1980s and produced many notable recordings. In a dance-band context he modified his ensemble and solo style little over the years. In common with Capt. John Handy he had much to do with establishing the place of the saxophone in the New Orleans revival bands of the 1960s. He also recorded with Papa Celestin (1953), Emanuel Sayles (1961), and as a member of the Olympia Brass Band (1966–71), with which he made two tours of Europe (1967, 1968). He appeared briefly in the film *The Cincinnati Kid* (1965) and took a featured role with the bands of Valentine and Dejan in the documentary film *'Til the Butcher Cuts Him Down* (1971).

Oral history material in *LNT*.

SELECTED RECORDINGS

As sideman: Eureka Brass Band: *New Orleans Parade* (1951, Pax 9001), incl. West Lawn Dirge; K. T. Valentine: *New Orleans Today: a Jazz Document* (1957, 77 LP11); *Kid Thomas Valentine's Creole Jazz Band* (1959, 77 LA9); Eureka Brass Band: *Jazz at Preservation Hall*, i: *The Eureka Brass Band of New Orleans* (1962, Atl. 1408); Olympia Brass Band: *Dejan's Olympia Brass Band in Europe* (1968, 77 LEU31); K. T. Valentine: *Kid Thomas Valentine and his Algiers Stompers in Lugano* (1983, Picayune 1)

BIBLIOGRAPHY

CarrJ; *ChartersJ*

L. Borenstein and B. Russell: *Preservation Hall Portraits* (Baton Rouge, LA, 1968) [photographs by N. Rockmore]

T. Stagg and C. Crump: *New Orleans, the Revival: a Tape and Discography of Negro Traditional Jazz Recorded in New Orleans or by New Orleans Bands, 1937–1972* (n.p. [London], 1973)

Obituaries: *New York Times* (23 May 1988); P. van Vorst, *MR*, xv/9 (1988), 9; *Fn*, xix/6 (1988), 2

W. Carter: *Preservation Hall: Music from the Heart* (Wheatley, Oxford, England, and New York, 1991, rev. 2/1999)

R. H. Knowles: *Fallen Heroes: a History of New Orleans Brass Bands* (New Orleans, 1996)

ALYN SHIPTON, BK

Paulo, João (*b* Lisbon, 17 May 1961). Portuguese pianist and composer. He studied in Lisbon at the Conservatório Nacional and in 1979 played at the Cascais International Jazz Festival. He toured with Hal Singer in 1980 and studied with Zé Eduardo from 1980 to 1983. He also played in Paris and New York and recorded with the most important Portuguese folk musicians. Paulo spent eight years in France. After returning to Portugal he recorded *Serra sem fim* (*c*1994, Farol 005) and an album with Mário Laginha. In 1996 he began recording for the company MA, notably *Exílio* (1998, MA 045), with Peter Epstein on alto saxophone and Carlos Bica on double bass; he also toured Japan with and composed songs for the singer Maria Ana Bobone. Later he recorded in duos and trios with Epstein, Bica, and Mark Feldman. He usually works with Portuguese folk and jazz musicians, including Laginha, Maria João, and Carlos Barretto.

JOSÉ DUARTE

Pauls, Raimonds (*b* Riga, Latvian SSR [now Latvia], 12 Jan 1936). Latvian pianist, composer, and bandleader. He attended the Latvian SSR Yazep Vitol State Conservatory in Riga (graduating in piano, 1958) and studied composition (1962–5). From 1964 to 1971 he led the Rīgas Estrādes Orkestris (REO; Riga variety orchestra), in which he played piano and with which he made recordings (including *REO* *džeza ritmā* (1970, Mel. CM020456). In 1973 he formed the jazz-rock group Modo; he played with the group until 1978, when he became the music director and conductor of the Latvian television and radio orchestra. Among Pauls's compositions are many jazz pieces, a ballet, two musicals, television and film scores, and more than 300 popular songs. He is a fine jazz pianist, but in the 1980s he turned from jazz to songwriting and then in the 1990s became involved in politics; he was minister of culture and ran for the Latvian presidency in 1999.

WALTER OJAKÄÄR

Paulus, Tiit (*b* Tallinn, Estonian SSR [now Estonia], 14 June 1945). Estonian guitarist, composer, and educator. A self-taught musician, he played in dance bands and jazz groups from the age of 16, in the Estonian Philharmonic Society from 1966, and in the variety orchestra of Estonian Television and Radio from 1974 to 1989. He performed at concerts and festivals in the USSR, Europe, Cuba, Syria, Iraq, Lebanon, and Sudan and recorded several albums, including *Tiit Paulus ja sõbrad* (1981, Mel. C60 154578) and *Basic Concept featuring Tiit Paulus* (1998, Elwood Music 0156-00141). In 1989 Paulus moved to Kuressaare, on the island of Saaremaa, where he taught young guitarists at the local music school; he continued to perform and also taught every year in Finland at a summer camp in Nilsiä and at the Oulunkylä Pop-Jazz Conservatory. In 1996 he published an instructional manual, *Improvisatsioon ja harmoonia kitarril* (Improvisation and harmony on the guitar). Among his compositions are a song cycle, *Eino ja Leino* (Eino and Leino), based on lyrics by Hando Runnel, *Sunday*, *Melanhoolne valss* (Melancholy waltz), *Simmanilugu* (Tune from a village dance), and the excellent *Bluus kahele* (Blues for two), this last recorded in a duo with the tenor saxophonist Arvo Pilliroog (1981, Mel. C62 12371-2).

WALTER OJAKÄÄR

Pavageau, Alcide "Slow Drag" [Drag] (*b* New Orleans, 7 March 1888; *d* New Orleans, 19 Jan 1969). Double bass player. He taught himself to play guitar at an early age and became celebrated as a dancer, taking his sobriquet "Slow Drag" from the dance of that name. About 1927 he learned to play a homemade three-string double bass, and in the following years he performed with Buddy Petit, Herb Morand, and Emile Barnes. In 1943 he was engaged by George Lewis (i), with whom he was associated for the rest of his career. Pavageau recorded extensively with Lewis in 1944–5, notably in a trio (alongside Lawrence Marrero), as a member of Bunk Johnson's band, and at sessions under the leadership of Jim Robinson and the trumpeter Kid Shots Madison in 1944; in 1945–6 he performed with Johnson's group in New York. He continued to work with Lewis in New Orleans, at Manny's Tavern and El Morocco in the late 1940s and early 1950s and at Preservation Hall during the late 1950s and early 1960s. Apart from his work with Lewis, Pavageau recorded further with Robinson (1961–4), as well as with Kid Thomas Valentine (1959), Louis Cottrell, Jr. (1961), Kid Sheik Cola (1961, 1963), Kid Howard (1963), Sweet Emma Barrett (1964), and Percy Humphrey (1965). In his later years he was active as a grand marshal with brass bands.

Pavageau was a key member of Lewis's band, commonly providing a consistent and heavy 4/4 beat and outlining the fundamental notes of each chord. Although he could play lightly under intimate circumstances, his characteristic timbre was, like that of Pops Foster, intensely percussive; he made use of a low string action and employed a slapping technique to great effect, especially in final choruses.

Oral history material in *LNT*.

For illustrations *see* HUMPHREY and JOHNSON, BUNK.

SELECTED RECORDINGS

As sideman: B. Johnson: Tiger Rag/See See Rider (1944, AM 251); G. Lewis: *American Music by George Lewis* (1944–5, AM 639), incl. Burgundy Street Blues; *Jazz at Vespers* (1954, Riv. 230); *George Lewis and his New Orleans Stompers*, i (1955, BN 1205); on *George Lewis & Turk Murphy at Newport* (1957, Verve 8232), That's a plenty

BIBLIOGRAPHY

ChartersJ; *ChiltonW*
L. Borenstein and B. Russell: *Preservation Hall Portraits* (Baton Rouge, LA, 1968) [pictures by N. Rockmore]
Obituary, D. M. Marquis, *Jazz Report*, vi/5 [1969], [28]
G. Russell: "Magee String Band," *Sv*, no.49 (1973), 14
A. Shipton: "Styles of New Orleans Bass Playing," *Fn*, vii/1 (1976), 18

ALDEN ASHFORTH

Pavone, Mario(, Jr.) (*b* Waterbury, CT, 11 Nov 1940). Double bass player. He began playing double bass at the age of 24. After earning a degree in engineering from the University of Connecticut he moved to New York (1966) and played in Paul Bley's trio (late 1968–1969) and synthesizer group (recording in 1971); around the same time he led his own trio, with Mark Whitecage and the drummer Lawrence Cook; in 1969, 1971, and 1974 he recorded with Bobby Naughton. Collaborations with Bill Dixon and Archie Shepp led Pavone to set up his own record label, Alacra, for which he made three albums between 1979 and the early 1980s. He worked further with Dixon from 1981 to 1990, most often alongside Cook in a trio or a quartet, and then held a fruitful association with Thomas Chapin that lasted from 1990 until the saxophonist's death in 1998. In addition Pavone worked with Anthony Braxton (1993–5) and made further recordings as a leader.

SELECTED RECORDINGS

(recorded for Knitting Factory Works unless otherwise indicated)

Duos with A. Braxton: *Duets (1993)* (1993, Music & Arts 786)
As leader: *Digit* (1979, Alacra 1002); *Toulon Days* (1991, New World 80420); *Song for (Septet)* (1993, New World 80452); with A. Braxton: *Seven Standards 1995 Quintet* (1995, 168); *Dancers Tales* (1996, 205); *Remembering Thomas* (1999, 257)
As sideman: B. Dixon: *Thoughts* (1985, SN 1111); *Son of Sisyphus* (1988, SN 1138); T. Chapin: *Insomnia* (1992, 132); *Haywire* (1996, 176); *Sky Piece* (1997, 208)

BIBLIOGRAPHY

V. Frazer: "Mario Pavone," *Coda*, no.190 (1983), 14
——: "Master of his own Music," *Hartford Advocate* [Connecticut] (19 June 1989)
S. Gribetz: "Hearsay: Mario Pavone," *JT*, xxiv/3 (1994), 16
L. Blumenfeld: "Traditions: Building a Better Bridge," *Jazziz*, xiv/7 (1997), 28
B. Young: *Dixonia: a Bio-discography of Bill Dixon* (Westport, CT, and London, 1998)

STEVE SMITH

Pawlik, Włodek (*b* Kielce, Poland, 4 Oct 1958). Polish pianist. He attended the academy of music in Warsaw (1979–84), where he gained a master's degree in classical piano, and then continued his studies at the Hochschule für Musik und Darstellende Kunst in Hamburg, Germany (1986–9), graduating from its jazz department. In 1986 he began leading a trio; Wolfgang Haffner was a member in its early years, and around 1991 it became established with the double bass player Zbigniew Wegehaupt and the drummer Cezary Konrad. The group recorded in 1988 as a quartet with Richie Cole as a guest soloist. Pawlik also recorded as an unaccompanied soloist, as co-leader with Billy Hart of a quartet including the double bass player Thomas Kniffic (1993), and as leader of a quartet consisting of Randy Brecker, Kniffic, and Konrad (1995).

SELECTED RECORDINGS

As unaccompanied soloist: *Four Seasons* (1993, Polonia 012)
As leader: *Live at Birdland* (1988, Polonia 004); with B. Hart: *Live at Aquarium* (1993, Koch Int. 3811-2); *Turtles* (1995, Polonia 095)

ADAM CEGIELSKI, BK

Payne, Bennie [Benjamin E.] (*b* Philadelphia, 18 June 1907; *d* Los Angeles, 2 Sept 1986). Pianist and singer. His professional career began in 1926 at the Philadelphia Cotton Club, and he worked with various groups before joining Wilbur Sweatman in 1928. He studied with Fats Waller, then (1929–30) played in revues in Europe and New York; he also worked as an accompanist for singers and recorded with Waller (in a duo, 1929) and Duke Ellington (1930–31). His principal association was with Cab Calloway's band (November 1931–1943; for illustration *see* CALLOWAY, CAB), but he seldom played solos for Calloway and may be heard to greater advantage on Chu Berry's *Ebb Tide* (1937, Var. 657), one of the few recordings he made in a small group; the pairing on this disc, *My Secret Love Affair*, provides an example of his singing. During his time with Calloway Payne took part in the band's many films; he returned to Calloway after war service, and left finally in August 1946. He then worked with Pearl Bailey and led his own trio, and from 1949 he was accompanist and music director for the singer Billy Daniels. In 1955 he recorded an album as leader, *Sunny Side Up* (Kapp 1004). After settling in Los Angeles in the mid-1950s Payne continued to perform with Daniels at least until the end of the decade.

BIBLIOGRAPHY

C. Calloway and B. Rollins: *Of Minnie the Moocher and Me* (New York, 1976)
Obituary, J. Simmen, *BHcF*, no.348 (1987), 29
M. Hinton and D. G. Berger: *Bass Lines: the Stories and Photographs of Milt Hinton* (Philadelphia, 1988)

based on *ChiltonW*

Payne, Cecil (McKenzie) (*b* New York, 14 Dec 1922). Baritone saxophonist. He grew up in a musical family, where he learned guitar and then alto saxophone. Later he was a clarinetist in army bands (1943–6). He first played baritone saxophone in 1946 in Clarence Briggs's band, and his last recorded work on the alto instrument was later the same year in a bop session with J. J. Johnson. Although he worked briefly (on baritone) with Roy Eldridge, he established his reputation as a fine bop saxophonist with a weighty timbre while a member of Dizzy Gillespie's big band (1946–9); his inventive solos on *Ow!* and *Stay on it* are good examples of his style. Payne worked in New York for James Moody and Tadd Dameron, then as a freelance (1949–52), before touring with Illinois Jacquet (1952–4). By the mid-1950s his approach had softened, and he produced a lighter, more breathy sound. Despite the many fine recordings he made during this period, notably those with Duke Jordan and Randy Weston, he left music temporarily. With Kenny Drew he acted in and composed songs for Jack Gelber's play *The Connection* (1961–2). He was a soloist with Machito's Afro-Cubans (1963–4) and a member of Lucky Thompson's octet, and he toured Europe with Lionel Hampton (1964); however, he then left music again. Later he worked with Weston (1966), Woody Herman (*c* September 1966–1968), and Gillespie (1968), after which he spent two periods with Count Basie (December 1969 – May 1970; November 1970 – August 1971).

Payne led his own groups intermittently from the 1970s. In 1974 he played with the New York Jazz Repertory Orchestra and toured Europe as a member of a jazz show, "The Musical Life of Charlie Parker." He worked with Benny Carter from 1977 to 1979, when he recorded with Nick Brignola. From the early 1980s he was a member of DAMERONIA. Later he appeared at Jazzfest Berlin for a set featuring baritone saxophonists (1985), performed alongside Bill Hardman in Richard Wyands's trio in San Francisco (1986), and took part in the television show "Great Performances" in an episode devoted to Gillespie ("Wolf Trap Salutes Dizzy Gillespie: An All-star Tribute to the Jazz Master," 1988). Having rejoined Jacquet during the late 1980s, as a member of the tenor saxophonist's big band, he figured prominently in the documentary film *Texas Tenor: the Illinois Jacquet Story* (1991). He continued to lead small groups, mainly in Philadelphia and New York, and in 1990 he toured the USA as the co-leader of a quintet with Junior Cook. In the 1990s he worked with Eric Alexander, recorded new albums for Delmark, and led the group Bebop Generation, which in 1996 consisted of Dizzy Reece, Alexander, Wyands, John Webber, and Joe Farnsworth.

Oral history material in *GBLnsa* and *NjR*.

SELECTED RECORDINGS

As leader: *Cecil Payne and his Quartet/Quintet* (1956, Signal 1203); *Patterns of Jazz* (1957, Signal 1204); *Charlie Parker Music* (1961, CP 801); *The Connection* (1962, CP 806); *Bird Gets the Worm* (1976, Muse 5061); *Bright Moments* (1979, Spot. 21); *Scotch and Milk* (1996, Del. 494)
As sideman: J. J. Johnson: Coppin' the Bop/Jay Jay (1946, Savoy 615); D. Gillespie: Ow! (1947, Vic. 20-2480); Stay on it (1947, Vic. 20-2603); K. Dorham: *Afro Cuban* (1955, BN 1535); D. Jordan: *Duke Jordan Trio and Quintet* (1955, Signal 1202); R. Weston: *Jazz à la Bohemia* (1956, Riv. 232); J. Coltrane: *Dakar* (1957, Prst. 7280); on D. Jordan and S. Hakim: *East and West of Jazz* (1962, CP 805), D. Jordan: Yes, He's Gone; Dameronia: *Live at the Theatre Boulogne-Billancourt, Paris* (1989, SN 121202-2); E. Alexander: *Two of a Kind* (1996, Criss Cross 1133)

BIBLIOGRAPHY

Feather–GitlerBEJ
B. Coss: "Cecil Payne: Baritonist by Choice," *DB*, xxx/13 (1963), 22
M. Gardner: "Discography: Cecil Payne," *JM*, x (1964), no.3, p.5; no.4, p.5; no.5, p.7
"Payne: One of the Few," *MM*, xli (12 Nov 1966), 6
S. Woolley: "Cecil Payne: Interview," *Cadence*, iii/8 (1977), 14
D. Gillespie and A. Fraser: *To be, nor not . . . to Bop: Memoirs* (Garden City, NY, 1979, London, 1980, as *Dizzy: the Autobiography of Dizzy Gillespie*)
S. Krasinsky: "Baritone Saxophonist: Cecil Payne," *Rhythm & News*, no.964 (n.d. [1995]), 3
B. Blumenthal: "Payne Blows Life into Bebop Generation," *Boston Globe* (3 Aug 1996)
H. Boyd: "Brooklyn Celebrates Jazz Luminaries," *Amsterdam News* (18 March 1999)

BK

Payne, Don(ald Ray) (*b* Wellington, TX, 7 Jan 1933). Bass player. In a questionnaire for the first edition of this dictionary he gave his place of birth as Wellington, rather than Amarillo, as has been published elsewhere. He grew up in southern California and took up trumpet at the age of ten, then changed to double bass when he was 16. From 1955 to 1958 he played with Art Pepper, Joe Maini, Calvin Jackson, Georgie Auld, and Maynard Ferguson; during the same period he performed on Ornette Coleman's first album (*Something Else!!!! The Music of Ornette Coleman*, 1958,

Cont. 3551), though his bop-based conception was not well suited to Coleman's vision of free jazz. After moving to New York (1958) Payne worked with Mundell Lowe, Chris Connor, and Tony Bennett (1959). In December 1959 he joined Herbie Mann, with whom he toured Africa early the following year. He performed in South America and Japan with Astrud Gilberto in 1961 and recorded bossa nova albums with Gilberto and Stan Getz in 1963; in addition he continued to work with Mann (to 1962) and Bennett (to 1963) and led a trio in New York, which at different times included Gene Bertoncini, Mike Abene, and Joe Beck. In 1964 he took up electric bass guitar, on which he played rhythm-and-blues, pop, and jazz-rock. From 1966 Payne worked as a studio musician in New York, though he continued to tour occasionally with jazz players and appear at festivals; he also recorded with Ferguson (1967) and Bobby Hackett (1968) and, on electric bass guitar, with Jackie Cain and Roy Kral (1966). Based in Nyack, New York, he continued to be active as a studio musician into the 1990s.

BIBLIOGRAPHY

FeatherE; *Feather '60s*
R. Gordon: *Jazz West Coast: the Los Angeles Jazz Scene of the 1950s* (London and New York, 1986)

Payne, Sonny [Percival] (*b* New York, 4 May 1926; *d* Los Angeles, 29 Jan 1979). Drummer, son of Chris Columbus. He studied with Vic Berton in 1936. After playing with the band led by Dud and Paul Bascomb and that of Hot Lips Page (both 1944) he worked with Earl Bostic (1945-7) and performed and recorded with Tiny Grimes (1947, 1949-50) and Erskine Hawkins (1950-53). From 1953 through 1954 he led his own band, then early in 1955 joined Count Basie's orchestra as a replacement for Gus Johnson. A forceful generator of swing rhythms, Payne provided the band with an exciting impetus; this is evident on the album *Count Basie Swings, Joe Williams Sings*, which also includes *In the Evening*, an example of his softer, more sensitive playing. Magnificent examples of his solo playing may be witnessed on *Old Man River* and *Rule Brittania* from the 1963 television show "Sarah Sings and Basie Swings." Payne remained with Basie until 1965, when he formed his own trio and also worked as an accompanist to Frank Sinatra, in which capacity he was reunited with Basie; later that year he rejoined the orchestra (with which he remained until July 1966). He then played with Harry James's orchestra (December 1966–*c*1973) before spending another period with Basie (February 1973 – May 1974). He toured and recorded in Europe with Illinois Jacquet and Milt Buckner in 1976, and performed again with James shortly before his death.

SELECTED RECORDINGS

As leader: on *More Drums on Fire* (1959, WP 1261), Clap hands, here comes Charlie

As sideman: J. Dash: Holiday in Cuba (1951, SiW 619); Fire Water/Deacon Dash (1953, Mer. 70087); C. Basie: *Count Basie Swings, Joe Williams Sings* (1955, Clef 678), incl. In the Evening; *April in Paris* (1955–6, Verve 8012), incl. April in Paris, Shiny Stockings; P. Quinichette: *The Kid from Denver* (1956, Dawn 1109); C. Basie: *Chairman of the Board* (1958, Roul. 52032), incl. Segue in C; Lambert, Hendricks, and Ross: *The Swingers* (1959, WP 1264); C. Basie: *Breakfast Dance and Barbecue* (1959, Roul. 52028); *The Count Basie Story* (1960, Roul. 1); *Basie at Birdland* (1961, Roul. 52065)

SELECTED FILMS AND VIDEOS

Jamboree [Disc Jockey Jamboree] (1957); Sarah Sings and Basie Swings (1963); Sex and the Single Girl (1964); Count Basie and his Orchestra (1965); Count Basie Live at the Hollywood Palladium (1984 [filmed 1970s])

BIBLIOGRAPHY

FeatherE; *Feather '60s*; *Feather–Gitler '70s*; *SheridanCB*
J. Tynan: "Sonny Payne: Count Basie's Swinger," *DB*, xxiii/13 (1956), 14
R. Horricks: *Count Basie and his Orchestra: its Music and its Musicians* (London and New York, 1957), 280
M. Laverdure: "L'explosif Sonny Payne," *Jm*, no.186 (1971), 18
S. Payne: "You've Got to Study All Forms of Music," *CI*, ix/12 (1971), 15
Obituary, *DB*, xlvi/6 (1979), 9
B. Korall: "The Great Drummers of Count Basie," *MD*, xviii/4 (1994), 30
M. Royal and C. P. Gordon: *Marshal Royal: Jazz Survivor* (London and New York, 1996), 102

LEROY OSTRANSKY/BK

Payton, Nicholas (Anthony) (*b* New Orleans, 26 Sept 1973). Trumpeter and leader. His father, Walter Payton, Jr., is a double bass player and tuba player who worked at Preservation Hall, and his mother is a classical pianist. He took up trumpet at the age of four and began learning to read music with his father when he was about eight. At the age of 12 he joined a brass band that performed locally and at festivals in Europe, and as a teenager he played trombone on a jazz cruise. He had lessons with Clyde Kerr, Jr., and then studied for one semester at the University of New Orleans with Ellis Marsalis, the saxophonist Harold Battiste, Alvin Batiste, and Victor Goines. Payton played locally, often with Peter Martin, the double bass player Christopher Thomas, and Brian Blade, and with the Louisiana Repertory Orchestra, Leroy Jones's group New Orleans' Finest, and Alvin "Red" Tyler. In 1990 he performed with Marcus Roberts at the Bottom Line in New York. The following year he appeared with Roberts at Carnegie Hall, recorded with Teresa Brewer (September), and began working with Carl Allen, both in a small group and in Manhattan Projects. He then performed and recorded alongside Wessell Anderson, Martin, Thomas, and Blade in the New Orleans Collective (1992) and was a member of Elvin Jones's Jazz Machine (March 1992–1994), of which he served as music director (from *c*1993).

In the mid-1990s Payton recorded in New Orleans with Doc Cheatham (1994, 1996), with whom he toured until the latter's death in 1997. In addition he was a member of the Lincoln Center Jazz Orchestra (recording in 1994), the Carnegie Hall Jazz Band, and George Wein's Newport Jazz Festival All Stars. In 1997 he was featured with Randy Sandke in the tribute concert "The Re-discovered Music of Louis (Armstrong) & Bix (Beiderbecke)" during the JVC Jazz Festival New York. As a freelance he performed with Marsalis (1989) and Roberts (1990–91), and recorded with Mark Whitfield (1994), Jesse Davis (1994, 1996), Milt Jackson, Renee Rosnes, Jimmy Smith, Rodney Whitaker, and Black/Note (all 1995), Joe Henderson's big band and Eric Reed (both 1996), and Mark Elf (1996–7). From 1996 Payton has toured extensively as the leader of his own band, with one or two of the saxophonists Jesse Davis, Donald Harrison, Tim Warfield, and Greg Tardy, and a rhythm section consisting of Anthony Wonsey, Reuben Rogers, and the drummer Adonis Rose. He appears as a musician in and plays on the soundtrack for Robert Altman's film *Kansas City* (1996), and he may be seen in the associated video *Jazz '34: Remembrances of Kansas City Swing* (1997) and in the German- and English-language versions of the documentary video *New Orleans: City of Jazz* (*c*1998). He also plays piano, double bass, and drums.

Payton is an assured and mature trumpeter whose style and concept have grown considerably in a short time. Like a number of young musicians who emerged during the late 1980s and 1990s, he has received much attention from the jazz industry and the press. Hamlin (1998) describes him as "a sensational young player whose vocabulary encompasses the clarion tones and bluesy growls of Louis Armstrong and the fluidity and fire of modern masters like Clifford Brown and Freddie Hubbard."

SELECTED RECORDINGS

As leader: *Gumbo nouveau* (1995, Verve 314-531199-2), incl. Wildman Blues; with D. Cheatham: *Doc Cheatham & Nicholas Payton* (1996, Verve 314-537062-2); with C. McBride and M. Whitfield: *Fingerpainting: the Music of Herbie Hancock* (1997, Verve 314-537856-2); *Payton's Place* (1997–8, Verve 314-557327-2)

As sideman: E. Jones: *It don't Mean a Thing...* (1993, Enja 8066-2); Manhattan Projects: *We Remember Cannonball* (1994, Alfa Jazz 3029); J. Smith: *Damn!* (1995, Verve 314-527631-2); [no leader]: *Kansas City* (1995, Verve 314-529554-2) [film soundtrack]; R. Rosnes: *Ancestors* (1995, BN B21Z-34634); P. Yellin: *It's You or No One* (1995, Mons 874772-2); Kansas City Band: *Kansas City after Dark* (1996, Verve 314-537322-2); J. Davis: *From Within* (1996, Conc. 4727)

BIBLIOGRAPHY

G. Wycoff: "Hearsay: Payton's Place," *JT*, xxii/3 (1992), 9
B. Beuttler: "Riffs: Nicholas Payton," *DB*, lx/6 (1993), 15
S. Aiges: "A Young Lion Roars," *New Orleans Times-Picayune* (26 March 1995)
B. Milkowski: "Nicholas Payton: the Next Great New Orleans Trumpeter?," *DB*, lxii/3 (1995), 40 [incl. discography]
J. D'Souza: "Nicholas Payton," *Coda*, no.266 (1996), 8
G. Endress: "Die Trompete symbolisiert Power: Nicholas Payton," *JP*, xlv/7–8 (1996), 20
H. Reich: "Jazz: New Orleans is Payton's Place," *Chicago Tribune* (19 May 1996)
C. Stern: "Braggin' in Brass: Doc Cheatham, Nicholas Payton," *Musician*, no.213 (1996), 50
I. Gitler: "Peers Beyond his Years: Nicholas Payton," *DB*, lxiv/11 (1997), 24
R. D. Johnson: "Nicholas Payton: He Could be Another Budding Louis Armstrong," *Jazzbeat*, ix/2 (1997), 30
H. Reich: "Jazz: the Ascent of Nicholas Payton," *Chicago Tribune* (23 Nov 1997)
G. Wycoff: "Doc Cheatham & Nicholas Payton: Trumpets for 2," *JT*, xxvii/4 (1997), 40
J. Hamlin: "Payton Adds Real Heat to Concord Festival," *San Francisco Chronicle Datebook* (27 July 1998)

GK

Paz. English group. It was formed in 1972 by the vibraphonist and composer Dick Crouch; other members have included the alto saxophonist and flutist Ray Warleigh, the alto saxophonists Phil Todd and Matt Wates, the keyboard player Geoff Castle, the electric bass guitarists Ron Mathewson, Henry Thomas, and Rob Statham, the guitarists Phil Lee, Jim Mullen, and Adam Salkeld, and the percussionists Simon Morton, Chris Fletcher, and Frank Holder. The group blends jazz, rock, funk, classical, folk, and ethnic music and makes extensive use of Brazilian percussion instruments. Exciting rhythms, skillful jazz solos, and imaginative writing have won the group both popular and critical acclaim, and it has recorded numerous albums, among them *Look Inside* (1983, Paladin 001), which included the disco hit *AC/DC*, and *Dancing in the Park* (1997, Turret 2). Castle took over the leadership of Paz when Crouch became ill in 1995 and continued to lead it after Crouch's death in 1999. (R. Tee: "Paz Jazz," *Blues and Soul*, no.398 (1984), 16)

MARK GILBERT

Pazuza. Nickname of STAFFORD SIMON.

Peacock, Annette (*b* New York, 1941). Singer, composer, pianist, and synthesizer player. She grew up in California and was self-taught as a pianist. In 1960 she eloped to New York to marry Gary Peacock, and soon afterwards she became associated with Timothy Leary's psychedelic community at Millbrook. In 1962 she befriended Albert Ayler and accompanied him on his European tour, but she left midway and returned to New York to concentrate on her own music. From 1965 she worked closely with her new partner, Paul Bley, and began writing "environments," sparsely detailed structures which his band used as a basis for improvisation; Bley's *Ballads* (1967–8, ECM 1010) is comprised entirely of her compositions, of which he has recorded more than 30 in total. In 1968 Peacock acquired a synthesizer from Robert Moog and toured in the Synthesizer Show (1968–71) with Bley and others, including Gary Peacock, Barry Altschul, and Han Bennink; she became one of the first performers to use a synthesizer in jazz fusion, merging electronics with her earlier acoustic approach. The group recorded three albums, the first of which, *Revenge*, included *I belong to a world that's destroying itself*, a track which augured the later African-American pop style rap. In 1971 she recorded *I'm the One*, which made use of unaccompanied piano and voice processed through a Moog. In 1972 she turned down an offer to work with the rock musician David Bowie, and instead spent a period at the Juilliard School of Music (1972–4).

Peacock moved in 1974 to Britain, where she later worked in more of a rock idiom with Bill Bruford (1978–9), who may be heard on *X-Dreams*. In 1980 she founded her own record label, Ironic, and released a series of semi-abstract introspective albums, beginning with the entirely unaccompanied concert recording *Sky-skating* (*c*1981) and culminating in the sparsely arranged, poignant *Abstract-contact* (1988). She performed only infrequently in the 1980s and early 1990s, playing at the WOMAD festival and at other British and European venues in 1983, appearing as an unaccompanied soloist in London in 1986 and 1990, and touring Europe and performing with Karlheinz Stockhausen in 1987; she occasionally played in a duo with the free-improvising drummer Roger Turner, as heard on *I Have No Feelings* (1986), and in the 1990s she performed with the electric bass guitarist Mike Mondesir. In 1995 she led a trio with Evan Parker before returning to the USA to live and work. Accompanied by the Cikada String Quartet, she recorded a new collection of her songs in 2000.

Peacock is a versatile musician with a distinctively dark voice whose work foreshadowed many later musical developments. Her early acoustic compositions with Bley helped to establish the style now most associated with ECM Records, while her synthesized-treated voice and the elements of poetry and performance art in her work predate similar experiments by such musicians as Brian Eno (with whom she also declined to work), Laurie Anderson, and Cabaret Voltaire. In the mid-1970s her experiments with rock music, notably on *X-Dreams*, prefigured much of the punk style, while *The Perfect Release* stretched the AOR (album-orientated rock) medium to breaking point. An album of her music, *Nothing Ever Was, Anyway: the Music of Annette Peacock*, was recorded by Marilyn Crispell's trio with Gary Peacock and Paul Motian in 1996 (ECM 1626-7).

SELECTED RECORDINGS

As leader: *Revenge* (1969, Pol. 244046), incl. I belong to a world that's destroying itself; *I'm the One* (1971, RCA LSP4578); *Been in the Streets Too Long* (1974–83, Ironic 3); *X-Dreams* (1978, Aura 702); *The Perfect Release* (1979, Aura 707); *Sky-skating* (*c*1981, Ironic 2); *I Have No Feelings* (1986, Ironic 4); *Abstract-contact* (1988, Ironic 5); *An Acrobats' Heart* (2000, ECM 1733)

As sideman with P. Bley: *Improvise* (1971, Amer. 6121); *Dual Unity* (1971, Fre. 40109)

BIBLIOGRAPHY

WickesIBJ, i

K. Ansell: "Annette Peacock," *Impetus*, no.8 (1978), 324
——: "Annette Peacock," *The Wire*, no.5 (1983), 24
L. Barber: "X-Dreams & Extremes," *MM* (20 Aug 1983), 28
J. Coe: "Irony in the Soul," *Wire*, no.75 (1990), 22

SIMON ADAMS

Peacock, Burnie [Bernie; Burney; Bernard L.] (*b* Columbia, TN, 2 June 1921). Alto saxophonist. All three spellings of his forename can be found in contemporary sources; his own recordings give it as Burnie. He took up clarinet when he was 11 and studied saxophone from the age of 14. After attending college in Tennessee (from 1936) he made his professional début in 1938, and from 1938 to 1942 he worked in Detroit and Chicago, latterly with the bandleader Jimmy Raschel. He then played in navy bands (1942–5). In 1945–6 he performed with Don Redman and Lucky Millinder, recording with both, as well as with groups drawn from Millinder's band under the leadership of Bullmoose Jackson and Panama Francis; he may be heard on Jackson's *Honeydripper* (1945, Queen 4100). Peacock remained with Millinder until 1947 but is believed to have worked briefly also with Jimmie Lunceford, Lionel Hampton, and Cab Calloway, in whose band he deputized for Hilton Jefferson that year. From September 1948 to January 1949 he was with Count Basie, and around the same time he made recordings with Buddy Tate, notably *Swingin' away with Willie and Ray* (late 1948 or early 1949, Supreme 1514). He worked with Calloway and Millinder again in 1949–50 and recorded with Jackson again in 1951–2. In late 1951 he took over leadership of Earl Bostic's band for six months after Bostic was incapacitated in a road accident, and he led two recording sessions in an idiom similar to that which had brought Bostic success, though with less distinction; *Charmaine* (1951, King 4506) is representative. Peacock toured with a band of his own in March 1952, undertook a USO tour for Far East Command late that year, and made further recordings with Millinder and Jackson through 1952–3. He continued touring into the late 1950s.

BIBLIOGRAPHY

FeatherE
P. Carles, A. Clergeat, and J.-L. Comolli: *Dictionnaire du jazz* (Paris, 1988, rev. and enlarged 2/1994)

HOWARD RYE

Peacock, Gary (*b* Burley, ID, 12 May 1935). Double bass player. He grew up in Idaho, Washington, and Oregon, and played piano in elementary school and drums from around the age of 14 in junior-high and high-school jazz bands. When he was 17 he went to Los Angeles and studied drums and vibraphone at the Westlake School of Music. In 1954 he entered the army; while stationed in Germany he played for two years in military bands and as a pianist in his own jazz band. In 1956, when his bass player was demobilized, Peacock took up double bass and played with Albert Mangelsdorff, Hans Koller, and Attila Zoller. After moving to Los Angeles later that year he toured with Terry Gibbs and then played locally with Harold Land, Art Pepper, Dexter Gordon, Bud Shank, Bob Cooper, and Paul Bley, and performed and recorded with Barney Kessel, Clare Fischer (including his first album, 1962), and Don Ellis.

In December 1962 Peacock settled in New York. He deputized for Steve Swallow in Jimmy Giuffre's group, performed with George Russell and Archie Shepp, and was a member of Bley's quartet, alongside Don Cherry and Pete La Roca. From mid-1963 to around March 1964 he belonged to the trio led by Bill Evans (ii), and during this same period he recorded with Evans's drummer Paul Motian in a trio under Bley's leadership. He deputized for Ron Carter in Miles Davis's quintet (April–May 1964), but his preference was for playing the most radical free jazz with Albert Ayler, with whom he made several adventurous recordings and toured Europe in 1964 in a quartet with Cherry and Sunny Murray.

These performances established Peacock as one of the most accomplished double bass players in jazz. But he suffered a perforated ulcer before that European tour and soon afterwards largely withdrew from music, apart from a period with Bley in 1967–8. He studied Eastern philosophy and medicine and in 1969 moved to Japan, where he recorded with Sadao Watanabe, Masabumi Kikuchi, and several visiting Americans. After two and a half years he returned to the USA (1972) and studied biology at the University of Washington (1972–6). In the summer of 1976 he returned to Japan for a tour with Bley and Barry Altschul and from 1977 he made several recordings (and wrote a number of compositions) for the ECM label as a leader, notably an album by a trio consisting of Keith Jarrett and Jack DeJohnette. From 1983 they worked under Jarrett's name, performing stylistically updated versions of jazz standards; over the next dozen years Jarrett's trio was one of the most popular groups in jazz, touring internationally and recording frequently. In 1989 Peacock recorded in a duo with Bley and in the trio of Niels Lan Doky, and in 1992 he played with Bley in trios at the Festival International de Jazz de Montreal and recorded with him in Germany (this last for the album *Annette*, named after the ex-wife of Peacock, and later, of Bley). He also worked in a trio, Tethered Moon, with Kikuchi and Motian in the 1990s, and from 1994 he led a group including Vic Juris. From 1979 he taught at the Cornish Institute of the Allied Arts in Seattle, and in the mid-1990s he gave master classes at the Royal Academy of Music in London.

SELECTED RECORDINGS

(recorded for ECM unless otherwise indicated)

As unaccompanied soloist: *December Poems* (1977, 1119) [incl. duos with J. Garbarek]

Duos: with P. Bley: *Partners* (1989, Owl 058); with R. Towner: *Oracle* (1993, 1490); with B. Frisell: *Just So Happens* (1994, Postcards 1005)

As leader: with M. Waldron: *First Encounter* (1971, Cat. 7906); *Tales of Another* (1977, 1101); *Shift in the Wind* (1980, 1165); *Voice from the Past–Paradigm* (1981, 1210); with M. Kikuchi and P. Motian: *Tethered Moon (Play Kurt Weill)* (1991, PW K1CJ93); with P. Bley and F. Koglmann: *Annette* (1992, HA 6118)

As sideman: B. Evans: *Trio '64* (1963, Verve 68578); P. Bley: *Paul Bley with Gary Peacock* (1963, 1968, 1003); A. Ayler: *New York Eye and Ear Control* (1964, ESP 1016); T. Williams: *Spring* (1965, BN 84216); P. Bley: *Ballads* (1967–8, 1010); K. Jarrett: *Standards*, i (1983, 1255); *Changes* (1983, 1276); *Standards*, ii (1983, 1289); *Still Live* (1986, 1360–61); D. Pullen: *New Beginnings* (1988, BN B1-91785); *The Cure* (1990, 1440); J. Surman: *Adventure Playground* (1991, 1463); K. Jarrett: *Tokyo '96* (1996, 1666)

SELECTED FILMS AND VIDEOS

Bud Shank–Clare Fischer Bossa-Nova Show (1962); Frankly Jazz: Guitars from Flamenco to Jazz (1962); Jazz Scene USA: Shorty Rogers and his Giants (1962); Keith Jarrett: Trio Standards (1985); Keith Jarrett: Trio Standards, ii (*c*1987); Trio Live at Open Theater East, 1993 (*c*1995)

BIBLIOGRAPHY

GrayF
M. Williams: "Gary Peacock: the Beauties of Intuition," *DB*, xxx/13 (1963), 16
B. Quersin: "Les Horizons de Peacock," *Jm*, no.114 (1965), 24
M. Lequime: "Gary Peacock," *Jh*, no.290 (1973), 14
L. Goddet: "Gary le Magnifique," *Jh*, no.338 (1977), 8
M. Solomon: "Bassist Peacock into Zen, Est and ECM," *DB*, xlvi/10 (1979), 9

G. Endress: *Jazz Podium: Musiker über sich selbst* (Stuttgart, Germany, 1980), 196
I. Carr: *Keith Jarrett: the Man and his Music* (New York, 1991) [incl. discography]
J. Rosenbaum: "Gary Peacock: the Experience of Music," *Bass Player*, iv/4 (1993), 54
K. Micallef: "Hearsay: Gary Peacock," *JT*, xxv/3 (1995), 14
J. Ephland: "Why Play Standards?" *DB*, lxiii/2 (1996), 16 [incl. discography]
P. Pettinger: *Bill Evans: How my Heart Sings* (New Haven, CT, and London, 1998)

MICHAEL ULLMAN/BK

Peacock's Progressive Jazz. Record label. It was founded in 1958 by Peacock, a long-established record company based in Houston that specialized in rhythm-and-blues and country music. The jazz division existed for less than twelve months, and the catalogue contained only two items; however, these were notable LPs by Sonny Criss and Betty Carter which remained in Peacock's catalogues for many years and which were reissued in the UK in the 1980s. (G. Gart and R. C. Ames: *Duke/Peacock Records: an Illustrated History with Discography*, Milford, NH, 1990)

MARK GARDNER

Peagler, Curtis (Gregory) (*b* Cincinnati, 17 Sept 1934; *d* Los Angeles, 19 Dec 1992). Saxophonist. His first professional work – accompanying the singers Pinocchio James and Big Maybelle at clubs in Cincinnati – led to a lifelong predilection for the blues. He was initially drawn to alto saxophone by Louis Jordan's music and later fell under the influence of Charlie Parker. After working with territory groups he served in the army (from 1953), where he met Junior Mance and Cannonball Adderley. Peagler then enrolled at Cincinnati Conservatory but left to tour as a musician. Later he co-led the Modern Jazz Disciples, which recorded and held a residency at Count Basie's club in Harlem. In 1964 he moved to Los Angeles, and from 1965 to 1969 he was a member of Ray Charles's orchestra. While traveling with Basie's band (February 1971 – May 1975) he earned critical attention for his impassioned solo work. From the 1980s he recorded regularly and toured internationally with the hard-swinging Sweet Baby Blues Band, led by Jeannie and Jimmy Cheatham. In addition he performed with Jimmy Smith and Jimmy McGriff and toured Japan with Frank Wess's big band. He founded Sea Pea Records in 1980. Peagler was an exceptional soloist whose blues-based style merited greater prominence.

SELECTED RECORDINGS

As leader: *For Basie and Duke* (1981, Sea Pea 5001); *I'll be Around* (1986, Pablo 2310930)
As sideman with J. and J. Cheatham: *Sweet Baby Blues* (1984, Conc. 258); *Homeward Bound* (1987, Conc. 4321); *Back to the Neighborhood* (1988, Conc. 4373); *Luv in the Afternoon* (1990, Conc. 4429); *Basket Full of Blues* (1991, Conc. 4501)
As sideman with others: Modern Jazz Disciples: *Modern Jazz Disciples* (1959, NewJ 8222); *Right Down Front* (1959–60, NewJ 8240); L. Winchester: *Lem's Beat* (1960, NewJ 8239); R. Charles: *Jazz Number II* (*c*1969, Tangerine 1512); on [various artists]: *Jazz at the Santa Monica Civic '72* (1972, Pablo 2625701), C. Basie: The Meeting; H. Edison: *For my Pals* (1988, Pablo 2310934); F. Wess: *Dear Mr. Basie* (1989, Conc. 4420); F. Redd: *Everybody Loves a Winner* (1990, Mlst. 9187); F. Wess: *Entre nous* (1990, Conc. 4456)

BIBLIOGRAPHY

Feather–GitlerBEJ; *SheridanCB*
P. Vacher: "Raw Edge of Basie," *MM* (3 Nov 1973), 65
Obituary, P. Vacher, *JJI*, xlvi/4 (1993), 16
P.Vacher: "In Honor of Curtis," *MR*, xxiv/4 (1997), 43

PETER VACHER

Pearce, Dick [Richard] (*b* London, 19 April 1951). English trumpeter and flugelhorn player. A cousin of the pianist and arranger John Pearce, he took up trumpet at the age of 13, served as a musician with the Horse Guards (1968–71), and played in the National Youth Jazz Orchestra (1969–72). During the 1970s he collaborated with, among others, Graham Collier, Chris Biscoe, Dudu Pukwana, Don Rendell, Keith Tippett, Mike Westbrook, and Michael Garrick. Pearce is best known for his work with Ronnie Scott's quintet (1980–90) and sextet (1991–3). He played with various others in the 1980s, notably John Williams (iii) and Peter King, and during the same period he was a member of Gil Evans's British Orchestra. Later he re-joined Westbrook, and in the mid-1990s he led his own quartet, which included the pianist John Donaldson and the drummer Mike Bradley.

SELECTED RECORDINGS

As leader: *Big Hit* (1994, FMR 17)
As sideman: G. Collier: *Portraits* (1972, Saydisc 244); M. Westbrook: *The Cortege* (1982, Original 309); P. King: *New Beginning* (1982, Spot. 520); R. Scott: *Never Pat a Burning Dog* (1990, Ronnie Scott's Jazz House 012)

BIBLIOGRAPHY

CarrJ; *ChiltonB*

MARK GILBERT

Pearson, Duke [Columbus Calvin, Jr.] (*b* Atlanta, 17 Aug 1932; *d* Atlanta, 4 Aug 1980). Pianist, composer, arranger, and bandleader. He was nicknamed by an uncle who admired Duke Ellington's music. As a youth he learned piano and several brass instruments. He studied trumpet under Waymon Carver at Clark College and performed with Wynton Kelly, Phineas Newborn, Jamil Nasser (then known as George Joyner), and Louis Smith in an army special services show (1953–4). Dental problems prevented his becoming a professional trumpeter, and after being discharged he worked as a pianist in Florida and Georgia (1954–9). He then moved to New York, where he played most often with Pepper Adams and Donald Byrd (Byrd recorded his best-known compositions, *Jeannine* and *Cristo Redentor*). He also joined the Jazztet briefly (1960) and toured North and South America as the accompanist to Nancy Wilson (1961). From 1963 to 1970 Pearson worked as a producer for Blue Note records and made a few outstanding albums as a leader of small groups, with Adams, Joe Henderson, Bob Cranshaw, Mickey Roker, James Spaulding, Jerry Dodgion, Garnett Brown, Stanley Turrentine, and Freddie Hubbard among his sidemen. During this period he formed a big band, initially led also by Byrd. As the Duke Pearson Band (1967-70), it rivaled the Thad Jones-Mel Lewis Orchestra, which also shared some of the same personnel; at various times it included most of the aforementioned players from his Blue Note sessions (although not Henderson or Hubbard), as well as such soloists as Julian Priester, Benny Powell, George Coleman, Frank Foster, Lew Tabackin, Randy Brecker, and the trumpeter Joe Shepley. The ensemble provided a forum for the performance of Pearson's lyrical, swing-oriented compositions. In 1971 Pearson taught at Clark College, and the following year he re-formed his band with virtually the same musicians as before. He toured with Carmen McRae and Joe Williams from 1972 to 1973; in the late 1970s his ability to play was impaired by the onset of multiple sclerosis.

SELECTED RECORDINGS

As leader: *Wahoo!* (1964, BN 84191); *Honeybuns* (1965, Atl. 3002); *Sweet Honey Bee* (1966, BN 84252); *The Right Touch* (1967, BN 84267);

Introducing Duke Pearson's Big Band (1967, BN 84276); *Now Hear This* (1968, BN 84308); *It Could only Happen to You* (1970, BN LA317)
As sideman: D. Byrd: *Byrd in Flight* (1960, BN 4048); *Donald Byrd at the Half Note Cafe* (1960, BN 84061), incl. Jeannine; *A New Perspective* (1963, BN 84124), incl. Cristo Redentor; J. Coles: *Little Johnny C.* (1963, BN 84144)

BIBLIOGRAPHY

M. Gardner: "Duke Pearson," *JM*, xiii/8 (1967), 11
——: "The Duke Pearson Big Band," *JJ*, xxi/7 (1968), 12
I. Gitler: "The Other Duchy: Duke Pearson's New Big Band," *DB*, xxxv/8 (1968), 25
M. Gardner: "Discography: Duke Pearson," *JM*, no.175 (1969), 29 [incl. list of compositions]
B. Rusch: "Duke Pearson: Interview," *Cadence*, vi/9 (1980), 12

BK

Peck, Nat (*b* New York, 13 Jan 1925). Trombonist. He first played with Glenn Miller (1943–5) and Don Redman (1947). While living in France (1947–51) he performed and recorded with Coleman Hawkins (1949), James Moody (1949–50), Roy Eldridge, Don Byas, and Kenny Clarke (1950) and studied at the Paris Conservatoire (1949–51). After returning to New York (1951) he was active in television, but he continued to appear intermittently in Paris; his work in the 1950s is well represented by a number of recordings that he made with Dizzy Gillespie for the Vogue label (22 February 1953). By the early 1960s Peck had again settled in France, where he played and recorded with Michel Legrand, André Hodeir (1963), and Duke Ellington, though he spent periods in England and in Germany, as a staff musician at Sender Freies Berlin; he was also a member of Quincy Jones's group, the Clarke–Boland Big Band (he played on all its recordings between 1963 and 1969 and may be heard as a soloist on *Bei mir war es immer so schön*, on the album *More Smiles*, 1969, MPS 15287), and the Norddeutscher Rundfunk Jazz Workshop (1964). From 1965 he was based in London and worked as a studio musician and in television; he played on the soundtracks of more than 100 films. In the 1970s he recorded with Benny Goodman (1970–72) and Peter Herbolzheimer (1979). While he worked rarely as a trombonist by the 1990s, he continued to be involved in music as a contractor, organizing bands for various different jobs.

BIBLIOGRAPHY

Feather '60s
B. Dawson: "New Trombone Man in Town: Nat Peck," *Crescendo*, v/3 (1966), 23
"Nat Peck from London," *The Note*, iv/1 (1992), 4

Peck horn. A colloquial American term for the E♭ alto or tenor horn; *see* Saxhorn.

Pecora(ro), Santo (Joseph) [Mr. Tailgate] (*b* New Orleans, 31 March 1902; *d* New Orleans, 29 May 1984). Trombonist. He first studied french horn but changed to trombone for commercial work when in his teens. He was a member of the New Orleans Rhythm Kings (1924–5), and his recordings with the group, including versions of his own compositions *I never knew what a gal could do* and *She's Crying for Me Blues*, show him to have been a strong exponent of the tailgate ensemble style. During the late 1920s he worked in theaters in Chicago. Pecora was a good reader and spent the early 1930s in big bands, including those of Buddy Rogers, Will Osborne, and Ben Pollack, but returned to small groups with Paul Mares (1935), Sharkey Bonano (1936), and Wingy Manone (1938). He then became a studio musician in Hollywood and appeared in the soundie *Rhythm on the River* (1940, with Manone) and on the soundtrack of the film *Blues in the Night* (1941). After returning to New Orleans he led his own group and worked again with Bonano (1948–late 1950s). He took his band to Chicago (1959), and from 1960 to the mid-1970s played at the Famous Door and the Dream Room in New Orleans.

Pecora's nephew Santo Pecoraro (*b* 1906) was a drummer who worked frequently with Johnny Wiggs.

Oral history material in *LNT*.

SELECTED RECORDINGS

As leader: Rose of the Rio Grande/Canal Street Stomp (1950, Clef 8914); *Dixieland Mardi Gras* (1956, Vik 1081)
As sideman: New Orleans Rhythm Kings: I never knew what a gal could do (1925, OK 40422); She's Crying for Me Blues (1925, OK 40327); P. Mares: Reincarnation/The Land of Dreams (1935, OK 41575); S. Bonano: Mudhole Blues/Swing in, swing out (1936, Voc. 3353)

BIBLIOGRAPHY

ChiltonW; *FeatherE*
Obituary, *MR*, xi/9 (1984), 4

LAWRENCE KOCH

Pedersen, Guy (*b* Grand-Fort-Philippe, nr Dunkerque, France, 10 June 1930). French double bass player. After studying at the conservatoire in Roubaix he moved in 1952 to Paris, where he worked with Henri Renaud, Sacha Distel, and Jean-Louis Viale at the clubs Tabou and Ringside (1954). He played for one year in a commercially oriented band led by Jacques Hélian and at the same time worked as a studio musician, and he was a member of Michel Legrand's big band, with which he appeared in Moscow, André Hodeir's Jazz Groupe de Paris, and Stephane Grappelli's quintet. From 1960 to 1965 he worked with Martial Solal; he also played with Roland Kirk and in 1963 toured with Dexter Gordon. For the next three years Pedersen toured the world with the Swingle Singers, and after returning to France he recorded with Grappelli (at intervals, 1972–6), played in Baden Powell's group (from around 1974 to around 1977), and recorded with Noah Howard (1977).

SELECTED RECORDINGS

As sideman: J. Archey: *Jimmy Archey et l'orchestre Michel Attenoux* (1955, Barclay 84001); L. Hampton: *Hamp and his French New Sound* (1955, Barclay 84004–5); S. Grappelli: *Django* (1962, Barclay 84089); M. Solal: *Suite pour une frise* (1962, Col. ESDF1430); *Jazz à Gaveau* (1963, Col. FPX221); J.-L. Ponty: on *Jazz Long Playing* (1964, Phi. 77810), Manoir de mes rêves; C. Bolling: *Toot Suite* (1981, CBS 73999)

BIBLIOGRAPHY

J.-L. Ginibre: "Le troisième homme," *Jm*, no.115 (1965), 16

ANDRÉ CLERGEAT

Peer, Beverly (A.) (*b* New York, 7 Oct 1912; *d* New York, 16 Jan 1997). Double bass player. He began working as a pianist, but later changed to double bass. In summer 1936 he joined Chick Webb's orchestra (for illustration *see* Webb, Chick), which frequently accompanied Ella Fitzgerald; she assumed its leadership following Webb's death in 1939. Peer made many recordings with the band. After leaving in 1942 he played with Taft Jordan at Small's Paradise (1942), Sabby Lewis (from 1944), and Lucky Millinder, and in the 1950s and 1960s he worked briefly with Harry Dial, Barbara Carroll, and Sarah Vaughan. Among the jazz musicians with whom he recorded were Mildred Bailey (1946–7), Chris Connor (1954), and Ellis Larkins (*c*1955, 1956). However, he spent the second half of his career mainly accompanying popular singers and cabaret artists, and he worked for 14 years at the Blue Angel, a supper club in New York. Having begun to play with the cabaret singer and pianist Bobby

Short in 1962, he was resident with Short at the Café Carlyle from 1968 until ill-health forced his retirement in December 1996.

SELECTED RECORDINGS

(all recorded for Decca)

As sideman with C. Webb: Rusty Hinge (1937, 1273); In a little Spanish town/I ain't got nobody (1937, 1513); Strictly Jive (1937, 1586); Sweet Sue, Just You (1937, 1759); Undecided (1939, 2323)

BIBLIOGRAPHY

ChiltonW

C. Battestini and J.-P. Battestini: "Interview: Beverly Peer," *BhcF*, no.459 (1997), 3

Obituaries: S. Holden, *New York Times* (27 Jan 1997); I. Crosbie, *JJI*, l/3 (1997), 19

HOWARD RYE, BK

Peet, Wayne (Edward) (*b* Dallas, 12 June 1954). Pianist and keyboard player. Fascinated by the pianist in his church, he had lessons from the age of six and played piano at churches in Washington, Oregon, and Idaho before settling in 1969 in Imperial, California. From 1973 to 1978 he studied music at Westmont College in Santa Barbara, where in 1977 he formed his own piano trio. From grade school through college he had also played trombone, but he gave it up following graduation. In 1978 he moved to Los Angeles to join John Rapson, with whom he had first played at Westmont in 1975. Peet quickly became a key player in the city and worked in the bands of Alex Cline and Vinny Golia (both from 1981) and with Nels Cline (from 1983). In the mid-1980s he co-led with Nels Cline and the electric bass guitarist Steuart Liebig an improvising trio, Rhythm Plague (1983–6), and led a septet, Doppler Funk (1983–7), in which the Cline brothers, Liebig, and Golia were among his sidemen. He has also been active as a producer and engineer for various record labels, notably Golia's Nine Winds, and has performed and composed prolifically for television and film; in 1992 he began collaborating with Bennie Wallace on film scores. In addition he wrote arrangements for the guitarist Brian Setzer's swing revival big band (1992–4), formed an organ trio (1993), and played in Bobby Bradford's quintet (2000).

SELECTED RECORDINGS

(recorded for Nine Winds unless otherwise indicated)

Duos with V. Golia: *No Reverse* (1984, 0114)

As leader: *Down-in/Ness* (1981, 0111); *Blasto!* (1988, 0126); *Fully Engulfed* (1994, 0165)

As sideman: V. Golia: *The Gift of Fury* (1981, 0109); *Out for Blood* (1988, 0127); A. Cline: *Montsalvat* (1992, 0174); J. Rapson: *Dances & Orations* (1994, Music & Arts 923); A. Cline: *Sparks Fly Upward* (1998, Cryptogramophone 102)

BIBLIOGRAPHY

T. Levi: "Discoveries: Wayne Peet," *Keyboard*, xiii/2 (1987), 16

D. Snowden: "Keyboardist Peet Plans Daring 'Day of Music'," *Los Angeles Times* (23 Sept 1989)

STEVE SMITH

Peeters, Joep (*b* Breda, Netherlands, 18 Feb 1949). Dutch multi-instrumentalist. His father and brothers gave him his first music lessons, but otherwise he was self-taught on piano, vibraphone, alto saxophone, trombone, and tuba. Although he formed his own trio in 1965, he also worked with the Hot Cat Rhythm Kings (1965–8), the Original Dixieland Heebie Jeebie Jazzband (1968–76), the Brassband Ochtendchloor (1971–6), the Original Victoria Band (1972–81, recording in 1974), and the Polka Dots (1976–81, recording in 1979). From 1981 he performed and made recordings with the Jojo Swingband (including the albums *Oop-pop-a-da*, 1985, Spronk 581; *Airmail Special*, 1996, Feel the Jazz 41; and *Still Going Jojo!!*, 1998, Feel the Jazz 49). His later recording work was with the tenor saxophonist Joop Hendriks (1982), the group Fried Potatoes (1986–7), De Nootenraaksters (1990–91), and the alto saxophonist Robert Veen (1996). Peeters has often performed with such musicians as Benny Waters, Scott Hamilton, Marty Grosz, Howard Alden, Wallace Davenport, Beryl Bryden, Mannie Klein, Roy Williams, George Masso, and Jake Hanna at the Breda Jazz Festival, of which he was a founder in 1971; he is one of the festival's concert programmers and, in addition to playing, may be seen there as a humorous master of ceremonies.

WIM VAN EYLE

Pege, Aladár(, Jr.) [Ali] (*b* Budapest, 8 Oct 1939). Hungarian double bass player. His father, Aladár Pege(, Sr.), also a double bass player, was a pioneer of Hungarian swing in the 1940s. Pege took up double bass at the age of 15 and studied classical music at the Béla Bartók Musical Training College. He first worked in dance orchestras, then in 1963 formed a jazz quartet, which performed in Yugoslavia at the Bled Jazz Festival. From the early 1960s he performed at Hungarian jazz festivals, and in 1964 he performed at jazz festivals in Frankfurt am Main, Prague, and Warsaw. While attending the Franz Liszt Academy he worked in commercial recording studios, and following his graduation (1969) remained to teach double bass. He then re-formed his jazz quartet, which took part in a jazz competition sponsored by Magyar Rádió (where he won the first prize) and appeared at the International Jazz Jamboree in Warsaw (1969), the Montreux International Jazz Festival (1970), the International Jazz Festival Zürich and the Berliner Jazztage (1971), and the International Jazz Festival Ljubljana (Yugoslavia) (1974); Pege's prodigious technique greatly impressed audiences. From 1975 to 1978 he lived in Berlin, where he found greater opportunities to play bop and free jazz, but he later returned to his teaching post and commercial work in Budapest. His talents became more widely known through recordings with Walter Norris (1978, 1980) and concerts with Mingus Dynasty; the latter included a performance at the Jazzyatra in Bombay (1980), which moved Mingus's widow to give Pege one of her husband's instruments. In 1982 Pege played at the Kool Jazz Festival in New York with Herbie Hancock and Tony Williams, and in the 1980s and 1990s he performed at all of the Hungarian jazz festivals. He often includes arrangements of Hungarian folksongs in his performances.

SELECTED RECORDINGS

As unaccompanied soloist: *Solo Bass* (1982, RST 120472); *Solo Bass, ii: Live* (1984, RST 130472)

Duos with W. Norris: *Synchronicity* (1978, Enja 3035); *Winter Rose* (1980, Enja 3067)

As leader: *Montreux Inventions* (1970, Hungaroton 17418); *Live* (1981–2, Krém 17742); *Hungarian Jazz Workshop* (1991, Krém 37519)

As sideman: B. Petrovic: *Swinging East* (1971, MPS 15332); Mingus Dynasty: *Live at Montreux* (1980, Atl. 16031); C. Antolini: *Bop Dance* (1981, Jazz Publications 8202); R. Wilfer: *Rudi Wilfer Trio* (1982, RST 91574-2)

BIBLIOGRAPHY

G. Noël and M. Noël: "Aladár Pege," *Jh*, no.266 (1970), 25

B. Noglik: "Aladár Pege," *Jazzwerkstatt international* (Berlin, 1981), 212 [incl. discography]

L. Jeske: "Profile: Aladár Pege," *DB*, l/1 (1983), 47

G. Riskó: *Pege Aladár* (Budapest, 1985)

G. G. Simon: *The Book of Hungarian Jazz* (Budapest, 1992)

——: *Magyar jazzdiszkografia, 1905–1994* (Budapest, 1994)

BK, GÉZA GÁBOR SIMON

Peiffer, Bernard (*b* Epinal, France, 23 Oct 1922; *d* Philadelphia, 7 Sept 1976). French pianist. He studied classical piano at the conservatory in Marseilles and the Ecole Normale in Paris and began to play jazz at the age of 17; he worked professionally from 1943 and first played with André Ekyan. In 1944 he performed with Django Reinhardt and Hubert Rostaing, and after army service in 1946 worked again with Ekyan. He recorded in Basel with Rex Stewart (1948), with whom he also appeared in the film *Rendez-vous de juillet* (1949), and made further recordings in Paris with Bill Coleman, Don Byas, Sidney Bechet, and James Moody (all 1949). In the 1950s he played with Reinhardt and Hubert Fol, but during this period was best known for his work in Paris as a soloist and the leader of a trio; his elaborately ornamented, swinging performances earned him strong support from the American writers Barry Ulanov and Leonard Feather. Peiffer went to the USA in 1954 and first worked in New York the following year, but his career suffered, perhaps because he was frequently compared with Art Tatum. After settling in Philadelphia he worked mainly in clubs there, though he recorded in New York (1956–60), performed at the Newport festival (1957, 1958), made several concert tours of universities (1959–65), and played in France (1966). He made his last appearances in 1974.

SELECTED RECORDINGS

As unaccompanied soloist: Jealousy/Caravan (1952, BStar 260)

As leader: Jeepers Creepers/Slow Burn (1952, BStar 263); *Bernie's Tunes* (1956, EmA 36080); *Modern Jazz for People who Like Original Music* (1960, Laurie 1006)

As sideman with R. Stewart: Jug Blues/Vernon's Story (1948, Elite 8192)

BIBLIOGRAPHY

L. Feather: "Bernard Peiffer Proves to be France's Loss, America's Gain," *DB*, xxii/15 (1955), 36

F. Manskleid: "Un musicien français peut-il réussir en Amérique?" *Jh*, no.164 (1961), 22

J.-L. Ginibre: "Antibes 007: Bernard Peiffer," *Jm*, no.134 (1966), 40

BARRY KERNFELD (with MICHEL LAPLACE)

Pell, Dave [David] (*b* New York, 26 Feb 1925). Tenor and baritone saxophonist and bandleader. He toured with Tony Pastor (1944–5) and then settled on the West Coast, where he played and recorded with Bob Crosby (1946) and Les Brown (1947–55). From 1953 he led his own groups (often an octet), which he organized from former members of Brown's band. Although his recordings were oriented towards a pop music audience (as may be heard, for example, on his first album, *The Dave Pell Octet Plays Irving Berlin*, 1953, Trend 1003), he employed such sidemen as Pepper Adams, Benny Carter, Don Fagerquist, Mel Lewis, Red Mitchell, Marty Paich, Art Pepper, and Ray Sims. He also recorded with Shorty Rogers (1953), John Graas (1955–6), Pete Rugolo (1956, 1958), Benny Goodman (1958), and Gene Krupa (1959). From 1955 Pell worked as a producer for Tops Records, and by the following decade production had become his principal occupation; he formed associations with Liberty Records (from 1961) and Uni Records (from 1966), and again with Liberty (from 1967), and published *The Producer's Handbook*. For many years he was involved in the activities of NARAS (National Academy of Recording Arts & Sciences), and he spent a period as the president of its influential branch in Los Angeles.

From 1978 to 1983 Pell led the group Prez Conference, which aimed to treat Lester Young's legacy in the same way that the better-known group Supersax approached that of Charlie Parker. In 1984 he made a further recording as a leader, *The Dave Pell Octet Plays Again* (Fresh Sound 101); among his sidemen were Med Flory, Buddy Clark, and Frank Capp, who had played with Pell in the 1950s. In addition he founded a small company, Headfirst Records (1982), and made a recording of his octet for the label (*Live at Alfonse's*, 1988, Headfirst 715). In 1994 he led a group at a festival in the Los Angeles area.

Video oral history material in *NCH* (HCJA).

SELECTED FILMS AND VIDEOS

Les Brown and the Band of Renown (1949); Connee Boswell and Les Brown's Orchestra (1950); Crazy Frolic (1953)

BIBLIOGRAPHY

FeatherE

L. Feather and F. Nemko: "Back in Business: Dave Pell," *JT* (1988), Nov, 15

BK

Pelzer, Jacques (*b* Liège, Belgium, 24 June 1924; *d* Liège, 6 Aug 1994). Belgian alto saxophonist, flutist, and composer. As a member of the Bob Shots he played in France, the Netherlands, and Czechoslovakia (1945–6) and occasionally during the following years in Belgium and at festivals in Nice and Paris. After the group disbanded he worked with René Thomas in Liège and at monthly intervals in Paris and made 14 visits to the Belgian Congo (now Congo). In 1959 he met Chet Baker, with whom he performed in Italy, at clubs in the USA, and at Carnegie Hall in New York. Later he played briefly in the Open Sky Unit, a jazz-rock group, and he remained active throughout Europe into the late 1980s.

BIBLIOGRAPHY

R. Pernet, J.-P. Schroeder, and others: *Dictionnaire du jazz à Bruxelles et en Wallonie* (Liège, Belgium, 1991)

R. Pernet: *Belgian Jazz Discography (1897–1999)* (Brussels, 1999)

ROBERT PERNET

Pemberton, Bill [William McLane] (*b* New York, 5 March 1918; *d* New York, 13 Dec 1984). Double bass player. After studying violin as a youth he changed to double bass and worked in New York with Frankie Newton (1941–5), Herman "Ivory" Chittison (1945–7), Mercer Ellington and Eddie Barefield (both 1946), and Billy Kyle (1948). Later he performed and recorded with Art Tatum (1956) and recorded with Rex Stewart in the Fletcher Henderson reunion band (1957–8), although he had never actually worked with Henderson. His association with Earl Hines (1966–9) included several recordings, a tour of the USSR (1966), performances throughout North America, and appearances at the Monterey and Newport jazz festivals (1967). In 1967 he toured Europe with Buck Clayton's group in the show *Jazz from a Swinging Era*. Pemberton was a member of the JPJ Quartet, with Budd Johnson, Oliver Jackson, and Dill Jones, from 1969 to 1975; in 1972 this ensemble undertook a tour of high schools in 24 cities as part of the educational project "New Communications in Jazz." During the same period Pemberton worked with Ruby Braff (1972), Max Kaminsky (1973), and Vic Dickenson, with whom he recorded in New York (1974) and France (1975). In 1977 he worked again with Hines and performed at the Grande Parade du Jazz, Nice, with Benny Carter, and from 1979 to 1983 he played with Panama Francis and the Savoy Sultans (ii). He was with Bill Coleman in France in 1980 and made his last recording, with Doc Cheatham, in November 1983.

SELECTED RECORDINGS

As leader of JPJ Quartet (with O. Jackson, B. Johnson, and D. Jones): *Montreux '71* (1971, MJR 8111)

As sideman with E. Hines: *Blues in Thirds* (1967, Jazz and Jazz 611); *Blues and Things* (1967, MJR 8101), incl. Louisiana; *Fatha Blows Best* (1968, Decca DL75048); *A Night at Johnnies* (1968, BB 33300–01); *Father of Modern Jazz Piano* (1977, MF 203–05)

As sideman: M. Ellington: Metronome All Out/Pass me by (1946, Musi. 379); L. Wiley: *Lee Wiley Sings Rogers and Hart* (1954, Sto. 312); R. Stewart: *The Big Reunion* (1957, Jzt. 1285); Jazz from a Swinging Era: *Trumpet Summit* (1967, Pumpkin 101); V. Dickenson: *Gentleman of the Trombone* (1975, Mahogany 558105); P. Francis: *Gettin' in the Groove* (1979, BB 33320–21); *Everything Swings* (1983, Stash 233); D. Cheatham: *The Fabulous Doc Cheatham* (1983, Parkwood 104)

BIBLIOGRAPHY

ChiltonW; *FeatherE*; *Feather '60s*

E. Schocket: "News: JPJ Quartet Turns on High School Kids," *DB*, xxxix/4 (1972), 9

S. Dance: *The World of Earl Hines* (New York, 1977), 117

[C. and/or J.-P.] Battestini: "Bill Pemberton," *BHcF*, no.279 (1980), 8

Obituary, *DB*, lii/4 (1985), 14

M. Selchow: *Ding! Ding!: a Bio-discographical Sketchbook on Vic Dickenson* (Westoverledingen, Germany, 1998)

JOHN CURRY

Peña, Ralph (Raymond) (*b* Jarbidge, NV, 24 Feb 1927; *d* Mexico City, 20 May 1969). Double bass player. He studied baritone horn and tuba as a child and worked professionally from the age of 15. After attending college in San Francisco he played on the West Coast with Art Pepper, Vido Musso, and Cal Tjader (all 1950), Barney Kessel (intermittently 1953–5), and Stan Getz (briefly in 1954), and was a member of the big bands of Billy May (*c*1951–3, recording in the last year) and Charlie Barnet (also briefly in 1954). In the following years he made recordings with Shorty Rogers (1955–8) and Jimmy Giuffre (1955, 1956) and in a duo with Pete Jolly (February 1958 – January 1962), and sometimes played with all three musicians in the same group; he may be seen with Rogers and Frank Sinatra in the film *The Man with the Golden Arm* (1955), and he was a member of Giuffre's trio with Jim Hall. He also recorded with the arranger Duane Tatro (1954–5) and Jack Montrose (1955). Peña worked intermittently with Buddy DeFranco from 1956 to 1959 and led his own groups in the Los Angeles Area; he traveled east in 1957 for performances at the Newport and Great South Bay festivals. Later he worked with Ben Webster (1960), Sinatra (from 1960, including a world tour in 1962), and George Shearing (touring Europe in 1962). He performed and recorded with Joe Pass (1963) and also recorded with Bud Shank (1962–3), Dick Grove (1963), Nancy Wilson, Ella Fitzgerald, and Anita O'Day (all *c* early 1960s). Occasionally he worked as the leader of a group that played his own compositions. He died after being hit by an automobile while working on a film score in Mexico. Peña's playing was marked by a rich sound in the lower register of his instrument and a strong drive; his style is particularly well represented by his recordings with Jolly and as a member of Giuffre's trio. He was adept in his use of the bow, as may be heard on the track *Slow Freight* from the album *Bob Brookmeyer* (1957).

SELECTED RECORDINGS

Duos with P. Jolly: *Impossible* (1959, Metro. 1014)

As sideman: J. Giuffre: *Tangents in Jazz* (1955, Cap. T634); on *The Jimmy Giuffre Clarinet* (1956, Atl. 1238), Quiet Cook; *The Jimmy Giuffre 3* (1956, Atl. 1254); B. Brookmeyer: on *Bob Brookmeyer* (1957, Crown 5318), Brook's Blues, Slow Freight

BIBLIOGRAPHY

FeatherE; *Feather '60s*; *Feather–Gitler '70s*

T. Gioia: *West Coast Jazz: Modern Jazz in California, 1945–1960* (New York, and Oxford, England, 1992)

LAWRENCE KOCH

Penland, Ralph (Morris) (*b* Cincinnati, 15 Feb 1953). Drummer and leader. He began playing a friend's drum set at the age of eight, but had to wait seven years before he was able to acquire his own; from 1969 to 1971 he had formal lessons at high school and in his teens he performed as a percussionist with the Cincinnati Symphony Orchestra. After leaving school he moved to Boston, where he studied and later taught at the New England Conservatory; he also worked locally with Gil Scott-Heron and the pianist Webster Lewis (1971–3), with whom he toured Europe. During the same period he traveled frequently to New York to sit in with bands, and on one occasion he performed with Freddie Hubbard, in whose group he subsequently worked (1973–4). Around 1975 he settled in Los Angeles, and in that year he formed the group Penland Polygon. As a studio musician and a freelance jazz drummer he performed with numerous important musicians, among them Charles Lloyd, Eddie Harris, Kenny Burrell, Harold Land, Nancy Wilson (with whom he toured Europe in 1978), Chet Baker (with whom he appears in the trumpeter's film biography, *Let's Get Lost*), and Ronnie Mathews; he accompanied both Hubbard and Jeanie Bryson as a member of Mathews's trio at the Warsaw Jazz Festival in 1991.

In the 1990s Penland toured with Frank Sinatra and the Latin-rock guitarist Carlos Santana (both 1991), and with Herbie Hancock (1993–4), and while a member of Don Menza's quintet he made a video in New Orleans. He is one of several drummers of his generation whose versatility in contemporary jazz styles is highly regarded, and he has recorded with artists as varied as George Cables (1982–3, 1987), Diane Reeves (1987), Buddy Montgomery, Charlie Rouse, and Jimmie Rowles (all 1988), the guitarist Rick Zunigar (*c*1988), Andy Simpkins and Dave Mackay (both *c*1989), Bunky Green, the french horn player Richard Todd, and the vibraphonist John Nagourney (all 1989), Bob Cooper (1990), Eddie Daniels (1990–92), the double bass player James Leary (1991–2), a trio led by Marc Copland and Dieter Ilg (1991–2), Lou Levy (1992), Hubbard and the singer Carmen Bradford (both 1993), the singer Janis Siegel and Fred Hersch (*c*1994), Rickey Woodard and Carmen Lundy (both 1994), Joe Sample (*c*1995), and the singer Miki Coltrane (1996). He also continued to lead his group Polygon, with such sidemen as the saxophonist Gerald Pinter and either Robert Hurst or Tony Dumas on double bass. Penland's polyrhythmic style derives from those of Tony Williams and Lenny White.

SELECTED RECORDINGS

As sideman: G. Cables: *By George* (1987, Cont. 14030); C. Rouse: *Epistrophy* (1988, Landmark 1521); J. Nagourney: *Second Flight Up* (1989, Trend 560); B. Green: *Healing the Pain* (1989, Delos 4020); M. Copland and D. Ilg: *Two Way Street* (1992, Jazzline 1133); R. Woodard: *Yazoo* (1994, Conc. 4629)

SELECTED FILMS AND VIDEOS

Let's Get Lost (1989); Don Menza Quintet: Live in New Orleans (1991); Jeanie Bryson: Live at Warsaw Jazz Festival 1991 (*c*1993); Freddie Hubbard: Live at Warsaw Jazz Festival 1991 (*c*1993)

BIBLIOGRAPHY

Feather–Gitler '70s

Z. Stewart: "Sounds: Penland Plays to the Beat of his own Drum," *Los Angeles Times* (23 Nov 1995)

<http://daddario.com/Evans_endorsees/penland.htm> (1999)

GK

Penn, Clarence (Lacquese) (*b* Detroit, 2 March 1968). Drummer. He began playing drums when he was about eight and performed professionally from around the age of 15. During his senior year of high school he attended the Interlochen Arts Academy (1986), and he spent a year at the University of Miami in Florida (1986–7) before transferring to Virginia Commonwealth University, where he received a degree in classical percussion (1991) and studied with Ellis Marsalis – in whose trio he also worked (1987–91). In summer 1989 he had private lessons from Alan Dawson in Boston, and in 1990, while touring Japan with Marsalis, he met Lewis Nash, who recommended him to Betty Carter. Penn served as a member of Carter's trio (*c*1990–93), toured Europe with Stanley Clarke (1993), and then joined the trios of both Cyrus Chestnut and Stephen Scott (his former bandmates with Carter). From around this time he worked in Tim Warfield's quintet. He performed with Bob Berg (1994), the band co-led by Clarke and George Duke (1995), Diana Krall (1995), Steps Ahead (with which he recorded from 1995), David Sanchez (recording in 1996), the singer Melissa Walker (recording in 1997), Slide Hampton's big band, Jimmy Smith, and the organist Greg Hatza, among others. Around 1997 he became a member of Makoto Ozone's trio, alongside Kiyoshi Kitagawa. Penn also recorded with Joshua Redman (1992), Javon Jackson (1993), Roseanna Vitro (*c*1994–5), Joey Calderazzo (1995), the singer and pianist Loston Harris (*c*1997), and Nnenna Freelon (1997).

Penn is well versed in funk, popular, and jazz drumming styles. In jazz settings he maintains a dexterous, polyrhythmic style that reveals a strong sense of swing and remarkable sensitivity, and he can maintain the power to drive an organ trio.

SELECTED RECORDINGS

As leader: *Penn's Landing* (1996, Criss Cross 1134)

As sideman: J. Redman: on *Joshua Redman* (1992, WB 45242-2), Trinkle Tinkle; C. Chestnut: *Revelation* (1993, Atl. 82518-2); S. Scott: *Renaissance* (1994, Verve 314-523863-2); T. Warfield: *A Cool Blue* (1994, Criss Cross 1102); *Gentle Warrior* (1997, Criss Cross 1149); M. Ozone: *Three Wishes* (1998, Verve 314-557562-2); *No Strings Attached* (1999, Verve/Pol. 1450)

BIBLIOGRAPHY

Feather–GitlerBEJ

C. Levin: "Update," *MD*, xvii/4 (1993), 9

K. Micallef: "Jazz Up & Comers: Gregory Hutchinson, Yoron Israel, and Clarence Penn: a Trio to Swing By," *MD*, xix/7 (1995), 64

R. Grosman: "Recontre: Clarence Penn," *Jh*, no.527 (1996), 16

<http://209.143.147.190/asp/newpage1.htm> (1999)

GK

Pépé. Nickname of ANDRÉ PERSIANY.

Peplowski, Ken(neth Joseph) (*b* Cleveland, 23 May 1959). Clarinetist and alto and tenor saxophonist. He was born into a musical family, and started on a clarinet given to him by his father. By the age of nine he had helped to form a polka band and was performing locally; he acquired a tenor saxophone when he was about 11 and later learned the alto instrument. He spent two years at Cleveland State University, studying performance and music education, but left to tour England and the USA as an alto saxophonist with the memorial Tommy Dorsey Orchestra under the direction of Buddy Morrow (1978–80). While in Chicago with the band he met Sonny Stitt, with whom he studied informally over the years. He joined the touring company for the musical *Annie* (*c*1980), then moved to New York (*c*1981), where he worked as a clarinetist in dixieland groups, joined Jimmy McPartland on a jazz cruise, and played with Max Kaminsky and as a substitute in groups at Eddie Condon's club; he also toured with the popular singer Leon Redbone. He was a member of Loren Schoenberg's big band, which in turn became Benny Goodman's band (1985–6), led a group at the JVC Grande Parade du Jazz Nice (1990), and recorded duos with Howard Alden (1992). His own band, consisting of Alden, Ben Aronov, the bass player Murray Wall, and the drummer Tom Melito, appears together with guest soloist Harry Edison in the video *Ken Peplowski Quintet: Live at Ambassador Auditorium* (*c*1995 [filmed 1994]). A later group, with Aronov, Greg Cohen, and Chuck Riggs, toured Europe in 1997. Peplowski has been a prominent performer at many jazz parties, involving such players as Ralph Sutton, Kenny Davern, and Milt Hinton. He has toured Europe and Japan with a variety of bands, including George Wein's Newport All Stars, and has worked extensively with Alden, Dan Barrett, and Warren Vaché in contemporary swing settings. Although not as fiery a performer on saxophone as his fellow swing musician Scott Hamilton, Peplowski is held in high regard for his clarinet work.

Oral history material in *PES* (ACMJC); video oral history material in *NCH* (HCJA).

SELECTED RECORDINGS

(recorded for Concord unless otherwise indicated)

Duos with H. Alden: *Concord Duo Series*, iii (1992, 4556)

As leader: *Double Exposure* (1987, 344); *Sunny Side* (1989, 376); *Mr. Gentle and Mr. Cool* (1990, 4419); *Illumination* (1990, 4449); with S. Hamilton and Spike Robinson: *Groovin' High* (1991, 4509); *Steppin' with Peps* (1993, 4569); *The Other Portrait* (1995, Conc. Concierto 42043); *A Good Reed* (1996, 4767)

As sideman: D. Barrett: *Strictly Instrumental* (1987, 331); S. McCorkle: *No More Blues* (1988, 370); H. Alden: on *The Howard Alden Trio Plus Special Guests* (1989, 378), Douce Ambiance, Back Home Blues, Reflections; Hank Jones: *Lazy Afternoon* (1989, 391); M. Grosz: *Songs I Learned at my Mother's Knee and other Lowdown Places* (1992, Jlgy 220); F. Vignola: *Let it Happen* (1994, 4625)

BIBLIOGRAPHY

G. Endress: "Ken Peplowski," *JP*, xxxviii/12 (1989), 3

C. Deffaa: "Ken Peplowski," *JT* (1990), Oct, 17

M. Richards: "Ken Peplowski," *JJI*, xliii/10 (1990), 6

B. Scherman: "Melodioest swingspel," *Orkester journalen*, lviii/5 (1990), 14

C. Deffaa: "The Natural Approach of Ken Peplowski," *MR*, xviii/7 (1991), 13

——: *In the Mainstream: 18 Portraits in Jazz* (Metuchen, NJ, and London, 1992), 289

J. D. Shacter: *Loose Shoes: the Story of Ralph Sutton* (Chicago, 1994) [incl. discography]

J. Snavely: "Ken Peplowski," *Saxophone Journal*, xix/3 (1994), 17

"Interview with Ken Peplowski," *The Note*, viii/1 (1996), 4

D. Zych: "Ken Peplowski: Spin Control," *JT*, xxvii/5 (1997), 68

GK

Pepper, Art(hur Edward, Jr.) (*b* Gardena, CA, 1 Sept 1925; *d* Panorama, CA, 15 June 1982). Alto saxophonist. He took up clarinet at the age of nine and switched to alto saxophone three years later. In 1943 he played with Dexter Gordon and Charles Mingus in Lee Young's band at the Ritz and then joined the big bands of Benny Carter (April–September) and Stan Kenton (September 1943 – February 1944). After serving in the US Army he worked as a freelance in Los Angeles and became absorbed in the new style, bop. He toured with Kenton as the band's outstanding soloist (autumn 1947–1951; see illustration) and then resumed his freelancing. He became addicted to heroin around 1950 and from 1953 his career was hampered by a series of jail terms for drug abuse. He attempted several times to resume

Soloists with Stan Kenton's band, ?Los Angeles, December 1947: (left to right) Conte Candoli (trumpet), Art Pepper (alto saxophone), and Bob Cooper (tenor saxophone)

playing, joining a quintet with Jack Montrose (1956), issuing several acclaimed recordings for the Contemporary label (1957–60), and performing with Howard Rumsey's Lighthouse All Stars (1960). In 1964 he adopted the tenor saxophone and began to play free jazz; during this period his quartet included Frank Strazzeri and Bill Goodwin. Then in 1968 he returned to mainstream jazz by joining Buddy Rich's band, but serious ailments forced his departure in the following year. Pepper spent three years in a rehabilitation center and worked as a bookkeeper before returning to music as a demonstrator for Buffet instruments (1973) and as a saxophonist in Don Ellis's orchestra (1975). From 1977 until his sudden death he gave a series of sensational bop performances in Japan and also in New York at the Newport Jazz Festival and the Village Vanguard, which brought him increasing recognition and popularity; George Cables, Milcho Leviev, Bob Magnusson, Tony Dumas, David Williams, Carl Burnett, and Billy Higgins were among the members of the rhythm section in his quartets of these last years. Pepper made some impressive contributions to film soundtracks, notably those of *The Enforcer* (1976) and *Heart Beat* (1979). He performed *Roll 'em Pete* with Jimmy Witherspoon on the television show "L. A. Jazz" (1981), and he was the subject of a documentary, *Art Pepper: Notes from a Jazz Survivor* (1982).

Pepper was a leading figure in West coast jazz, a movement with which he was associated not only because of his choice of location and musical colleagues but also because of his light, clear, precise sound on alto saxophone; he took part in the earliest recordings in this style under the leadership of Shorty Rogers in 1951. However, Pepper was a stronger, more fiery improviser than his fellow West Coast musicians, as is amply demonstrated by his recordings in 1957 and 1960 with Miles Davis's rhythm section. His album *Art Pepper + Eleven* (1959), with Marty Paich's harmonized recasting of a solo by Charlie Parker, foreshadowed by 15 years the popular recordings of the Los Angeles group Supersax. In the mid-1960s, under the overwhelming influence of John Coltrane, he took up tenor saxophone, on which his playing stressed intense and expressive noise elements. Eventually, having returned to the alto instrument, he combined the two approaches in performances such as *Cherokee* (1977), in which traditional bop lines erupt at explosive moments into squeals, growls, and flurries of notes.

Collections of transcriptions of Pepper's solos include *The Genius of Art Pepper* (North Sydney, Australia, 1989) and *The Art Pepper Collection: Artist Transcriptions, Saxophone* (Milwaukee, 1995).

Oral history material in *NjR*.

SELECTED RECORDINGS

As leader: *The Early Show* (1952, Xan. 108); *Art Pepper Quartet* (1956, Tampa 20); with C. Baker: *Playboys* (1956, WP 1234); with R. Kamuca and B. Perkins: *Just Friends* (1956, PJ 401); *The Way it Was* (1956–7, 1960, Cont. 7630); *Art Pepper Meets the Rhythm Section* (1957, Cont. 3532); *The Omega Man* (1957, Omega Tape 7020); *Art Pepper + Eleven* (1959, Cont. 3568); *Gettin' Together* (1960, Cont. 3573); *Smack Up* (1960, Cont. 7602); *Intensity* (1960, Cont. 7607); *Living Legend* (1975, Cont. 7633); *The Trip* (1976, Cont. 7638); *Saturday Night at the Village Vanguard* (1977, Cont. 7644), incl. Cherokee; *Art Pepper Today* (1978, Gal. 5119); *Straight Life* (1979, Gal. 5127); *Winter Moon* (1980, Gal. 5140); *Roadgame* (1981, Gal. 5142)

As sideman: S. Kenton: Art Pepper (1950, Cap. 28008); Jump for Joe (1951, Cap. 1704); Street of Dreams (1951, Cap. 1823); S. Rogers: Over the Rainbow (1951, Cap. 15764); B. Rich: *Mercy, Mercy* (1968, PJ 20133); [various artists:] on *Ballads by Four* (1978, Gal. 5133), Over the Rainbow; M. Leviev: *Blues for the Fisherman* (1980, Mole Jazz 1)

SELECTED FILMS AND VIDEOS

Jazz Casual: Art Pepper Quartet (1964); L.A. Jazz, no.1 (1981); Art Pepper: Notes from a Jazz Survivor (1982)

BIBLIOGRAPHY

J. McKinney: "Art Pepper: Profile of a Comeback," *Metronome*, lxxvii (1960), Sept, 26

J. Tynan: "The Return of Art Pepper," *DB*, xxvii/8 (1960), 17

——: "End of the Road," *DB*, xxvii/25 (1960), 13

——: "Art Pepper's not the Same," *DB*, xxxi/22 (1964), 18

C. Marra: "Art Pepper: 'I'm Here to Stay!'," *DB*, xl/4 (1973), 16

L. Underwood: "Pepper's Painful Road to Pure Art," *DB*, xlii/11 (1975), 16

A. Pepper and L. Pepper: *Straight Life: the Story of Art Pepper* (New York and London, 1979, rev. 2/1994) [incl. discography by T. Selbert]

P. Welding: "Art Pepper: Rewards of the Straight Life," *DB*, xlvi/18 (1979), 16 [incl. discography]

"Art Pepper," *SJ*, xxxiv/1 (1980), 162 [discography]

G. Giddins: *Riding on a Blue Note: Jazz and American Pop* (New York, and Oxford, England, 1981)

B. Priestley: *Mingus: a Critical Biography* (London, Melbourne, Australia, and New York, 1982)

R. Gordon: *Jazz West Coast: the Los Angeles Jazz Scene of the 1950s* (London and New York, 1986/*R*1990), 165

D. N. Pepperell: "Art Pepper: I Want to Play so Bad," *Wire*, no.28 (1986), 26

T. Gioia: *West Coast Jazz: Modern Jazz in California, 1945–1960* (New York, and Oxford, England, 1992), 283

R. A. Luckey, ed.: *West Coast Jazz Saxophone Solos: Fifteen Recorded Solos from 1952–1961* (Lafayette, LA, *c*1996) [incl. transcrs.]

BK

Pepper, Jim [Hung-a-che-eda [Flying Eagle]] (*b* Portland, OR, 17 June 1941; *d* Portland, 10 Feb 1992). Tenor and soprano saxophonist. His mother was a Creek indian and his father, a Kaw indian, played saxophone. He learned to tap-dance as a child and was primarily self-taught on tenor saxophone and clarinet. In 1964 he moved to New York and worked in the early jazz-rock group Free Spirits, with which he recorded around 1967. In the late 1960s he played in the group Everything is Everything and was encouraged by Don

Cherry and Ornette Coleman to express his native American heritage in his music. In 1971 Pepper began working as a salmon fisherman in Alaska and returned to playing only in 1979, when he toured Africa with Cherry. In 1982 he was a member of Charlie Haden's Liberation Music Orchestra and around the same time he joined Paul Motian's quintet, with which he toured internationally and recorded. From the mid-1980s he worked with Marty Cook and Mal Waldron. He is the subject of the documentary film *Pepper's Pow-wow* (*c*1995).

Pepper is best known for his version of the Peyote chant *Witchi-tai-to*, which he recorded on his albums *Pow Wow* (1971, Embryo 731) and *Comin' and Goin'* (1983, Europa 2014); it was also recorded as an instrumental by Jan Garbarek and Bobo Stenson on their album *Witchi-tai-to* (1973, ECM 1041) and by Oregon on *Out of the Woods* (1978, Elek. 154). Pepper's style was based on bop, although the influence of Albert Ayler led him to incorporate a wide, sentimental vibrato and elements of free jazz, notably vocal-like bursts of sound.

SELECTED RECORDINGS

Duos with M. Waldron: *Art of the Duo* (1988, Tutu 888006)
As leader: *Dakota Song* (1987, Enja 5043); *The Path* (1988, Enja 5087); *West End Avenue* (1989, Nabel 4633); *Camargue* (1989, Pan Music 1106)
As sideman: C. Haden: *The Ballad of the Fallen* (1982, ECM 1248); P. Motian: *The Story of Maryam* (1983, SN 1074); *Jack of Clubs* (1984, SN 1124); Nana Simopoulos: *Wings and Air* (1986, Enja 5031); P. Motian: *Misterioso* (1986, SN 1174); M. Cook: *Nightwork* (1986–7, Enja 5033); *Red, White, Black, and Blue* (1987, Enja 5067); M. Waldron: *Quadrologue at Utopia*, i (1989, Tutu 888118-2)

BIBLIOGRAPHY

D. Heckman: "Jim Pepper Talks to Don Heckman," *J&P*, viii/4–5 (1969), 41
W. Gschwendner: "Marty Cook's New Jazz and Jim Pepper," *JP*, xxxv/5 (1986), 24
——: "Ungeahnte Höhenflüge: Mal Waldron, Jim Pepper," *JP*, xxxix/4 (1990), 36
G. Harris: "Jim Pepper," *Windplayer*, vii/5 (1990), 16
J. Kaliss: "Music: Jazz Saxophonist: Jim Pepper Returns for Bay Powwow," *San Francisco Chronicle Datebook* (7 July 1991)
Obituaries: D. Lands, *JJI*, xlv/4 (1992), 16; *Jm*, no.414 (1992), 4
<http://www.rojac.co.at/rojac/pepper_j> (1999) [discography]

GK

Peraza, Armando (*b* Havana, 30 May 1924). Cuban percussionist. From 1943 he worked with leading Cuban bands. After moving to the USA as a member of Mongo Santamaria's group (1948) he played and recorded with Machito. Peraza performed on the West Coast with Slim Gaillard (1950) and then played with Cal Tjader, the bandleader Perez Prado, and Dave Brubeck. From 1953 to 1962 he was a soloist in George Shearing's quintet, with which he made a number of recordings. He also worked with Stan Kenton and Wes Montgomery and performed and recorded with Tjader (1964–70). Following a period touring and recording with Santamaria he joined the Latin-rock group Azteca in San Francisco (1970). During the 1970s he played with the Latin-rock guitarist Carlos Santana (1971) and recorded with several rock groups; he continued to work regularly with Santana until 1990 and was a member of the band led by the guitarist and Wayne Shorter in 1988. In the 1990s a diabetic condition forced Peraza to restrict his activities. However, he toured the Netherlands and Germany with the Latin-jazz group Nueva Manteca around 1992 and performed with Santana occasionally into the mid-1990s, when he retired. His principal percussion instruments were bongos and conga.

SELECTED RECORDINGS

As sideman: Machito: Cu-bop City (1949, Roost 502); G. Shearing and the Montgomery Brothers: *Love Walked In* (1961, Jlnd 955); C. Tjader: *Along Comes Cal* (1967, Verve 68671)

BIBLIOGRAPHY

FeatherE; *Feather '60s*; *Feather–Gitler '70s*
R. Tolleson: "Santana's Percussion: a Profile in Latin Artistry," *MD*, vi/7 (1982), 12
<http://www.lpmusic.com/armandoperaza.html> (1996) [biography by B. Sanabria and R. Wilson]
R. Tolleson: "The Righteous Rhythm of Armando Peraza," *MD*, xxiii/1 (1999), 98

RICK MATTINGLY/BK

Perciful, Jack (T.) (*b* Moscow, ID, 26 Nov 1925). Pianist. His mother played piano for silent films. He was a member of an army band in Japan (1945–6), and after graduating from the University of Idaho (BME 1951) he performed with groups in Los Angeles and Las Vegas (early 1950s). From April 1957 he recorded and toured widely with Harry James, appearing at jazz festivals on several occasions; his playing may be heard on the album *In a Relaxed Mood* (1964, MGM 4274), which he made as a member of James's septet. Perciful also recorded with Charlie Barnet (1959) and Corky Corcoran (1972). He left James in 1974 and the following year played with Red Kelly in Tumwater, Washington.

BIBLIOGRAPHY

FeatherE; *Feather '60s*; *Feather–Gitler '70s*
J. Perciful: "A Sideman's Story," *CI*, x/3 (1971), 14

Percussion. In jazz, the term is used to refer to the equipment of the drummer (*see* Drum set) and a number of additional instruments (*see* Agogo, Berimbau, Bongos, Cabaca, Caxixi, Claves, Conga, Cuíca, Darabukka, Frame drum, Ganzá, Güiro, Marimba, Reco-reco, Sekere, Steel drum, Tablā, Timbales, Vibraphone, and Xylophone).

Perelman, Ivo (*b* São Paulo, 12 Jan 1961). Brazilian tenor saxophonist and cellist. His father was Polish, and his mother, a pianist and music teacher, a Brazilian of Russian descent. He studied classical guitar before playing cello in a school orchestra, then took up piano, clarinet, and, briefly, trombone. In March 1981 he went to the USA to study at the Berklee College of Music in Boston, where he began on tenor saxophone, and the following year he was in Montreal, playing bossa nova guitar in nightclubs. He then moved to Los Angeles, where he studied composing and arranging at the Dick Grove School of Music (1984). After a year in Italy in 1986, he returned in 1987 to Los Angeles and in 1989 recorded his first album, *Ivo*, a collection of Brazilian children's songs, with Airto, Flora Purim, John Patitucci, and Peter Erskine. Having moved to New York, in October 1990 he was filmed in performance with Geri Allen, Fred Hopkins, Andrew Cyrille, Mino Cinélu, the percussionist Elson Nascimento, and Purim at the Knitting Factory, released on video as *Live in New York* (1991). In 1991 he spent another period in Brazil, where he investigated the plight of homeless children pursued by paramilitary forces. There followed two further collections, *Children of Ibeji* (1991), again with Purim in New York, and *Tapeba Songs* (1995), recorded in Brazil; these completed the children's trilogy.

Perelman established his own record label, Ibeji, in 1994 to record his work. In 1996 he recorded with Marilyn Crispell, William Parker, and Gerry Hemingway (the improvised

Sound Hierarchy and *En Adir*, an album of traditional Jewish songs) and with Parker and Rashied Ali (*Sad Life* and *Live*). In September that year he set up a regular trio, consisting of the double bass player Dominic Duval and the drummer Jay Rosen, as heard on *Seeds, Vision and Counterpoint*. In 1996-7 he returned to the cello to record in a string duo with Joe Morris (ii), and in 1998 he played tenor saxophone with Duval's CT String Quartet on *The Alexander Suite*.

Influenced by the music of his native Brazil and by John Coltrane, Perelman is a free-jazz musician who uses Brazilian and other traditional songs in his work. His playing is both microtonal and melodic; despite similarities in style, he developed independently of both Ayler and Gato Barbieri, with whom he is often wrongly compared.

SELECTED RECORDINGS

Duos with J. Morris: *Strings* (1996–7, Leo 249)
As leader: *Ivo* (1989, K2B2 2769); *Children of Ibeji* (1991, Enja 7005-2); *Soccer Land* (1994, Ibeji 0959); *Tapeba Songs* (1995, Ibeji 2599); *Sad Life* (1996, Leo Lab 027); *En Adir* (1996, Music & Arts 996); with W. Parker and R. Ali: *Live* (1996, Zero In 2); *Seeds, Vision and Counterpoint* (1996, Leo 252); *Sound Hierarchy* (1996, Music & Arts 997); *The Alexander Suite* (1998, Leo 258)

BIBLIOGRAPHY

R. Somarriba: "Air Time: Ivo Perelman," *Windplayer*, ix/5 (1992), 9
J. Lloyd: "Jazz: Turbulent Saxophone from Brazil," *Philadelphia Inquirer* (7 Jan 1994)
J. Corbett: "Tradin' fours: a New Kind of Samba," *DB*, lxii/12 (1995), 51
T. Owen: "Ivo Perelman: Unlocking the Beast," *Wire*, no.173 (1998), 12
B. Rusch: "Ivo Perelman: Interview," *Cadence*, xxiv/10 (1998), 5

SIMON ADAMS

Pérez, Danilo (Enrico, Jr.) (*b* nr Panama City, Panama, 29 Dec 1965). Panamanian pianist and leader. Some sources have published his year of birth as 1966, but Pérez gave 1965 in a questionnaire for this dictionary. His father, a mambo singer, gave him a pair of bongos when he was only three. He took up classical piano at the age of seven or eight and later attended the national conservatory of Panama (1978–81); to appease his mother, he also studied electronics. In 1984 he emigrated to the United States and attended Indiana University of Pennsylvania; the following year he transferred to the Berklee College of Music, from which he graduated in 1988. During this time Pérez played for Jon Hendricks (1987–8), but he left the singer to work with Paquito D'Rivera (1988–93). While with D'Rivera he performed briefly with Claudio Roditi and with Dizzy Gillespie (1989–92), both in the latter's quintet and as a member of the United Nation Orchestra. In 1990 he contributed to the score of the film *Winter in Lisbon* (in which Gillespie acted), and in 1995 he toured as a member of the Diamond Jubilee group, a posthumous tribute to Gillespie. During the early 1990s he worked regularly at Bradley's in New York as an unaccompanied soloist and from 1990 to 1997 he was a member of Tom Harrell's group; he also joined Slide Hampton's Jazzmasters (1993) and recorded regularly with David Sanchez (1993–6). In 1995 Pérez toured Poland with Wynton Marsalis's band and performed with the Panamanian Symphony Orchestra, presenting a program of original material and the music of George Gershwin. In the same year he moved back to Boston and joined the faculty of the New England Conservatory. He formed a duo with Gary Burton, which toured Argentina in 1996 and Italy the following year, and in late 1996 he joined Joe Lovano's quartet.

Pérez has led a number of his own bands, and in 1992 he formed the Afro-Cuban Explosion, in which he has worked with Charlie Sepulveda, Sanchez, Oscar Stagnaro, and Adam Cruz. From 1993 to 1995 he led a quartet, with Sanchez or George Garzone (saxophone), Larry Grenadier (bass), and Ignacio Berroa or Cruz (drums), and in 1996 he formed a trio which has included the double bass players Avishai Cohen, Reuben Rogers, and Charles Fambrough and the drummers Jeff "Tain" Watts, Terri Lyne Carrington, and Jeff Ballard. He is an impressive player, whether pounding out an ostinato in a Latin-jazz group, interpreting (simultanously and independently in each hand) the melodies of Thelonious Monk's compositions *Evidence* and *Four in One* with his trio, or embarking on an extended and rhapsodic unaccompanied free improvisation. However, like Sanchez, he stands apart from other virtuoso Afro-Cuban and Afro-Puerto Rican soloists of his generation, as he has a comprehensive command of jazz styles and seldom allows his technical skill to dictate the music.

SELECTED RECORDINGS

As leader: *Danilo Pérez* (1992, Novus 63148-2); *The Journey* (1993, Novus 63166-2); *PanaMonk* (1996, Imp. 190), incl. Evidence, Four in One; *Central Avenue* (1998, Imp. 279)
As sideman: D. Gillespie: *Dizzy Gillespie and the United Nation Orchestra: Live at the Royal Festival Hall* (1989, Enja 6044); T. Harrell: *Form* (1990, Cont. 14059); C. Roditi: *Two of Swords* (1990, Can. 79504-2); P. D'Rivera: *Who's Smoking?* (1991, Can. 79523-2); *Havana Café* (1991, Chesky 60); T. Harrell: *Passage* (1991, Chesky 64); R. Drummond: *Excursions* (1992, Arabesque 0106); C. Sepulveda: *Algo Nuestro (Our Thing)* (1992, Ant. 314-512768-2); T. Harrell: *Upswing* (1993, Chesky 103); D. Sanchez: *The Departure* (1993, Col. CK57848); *Street Scenes* (1996, Col. CK67627)

SELECTED FILMS AND VIDEOS

Jazzvisions: Rio Revisited (1988); Dizzy Gillespie and the United Nation Orchestra: Live at the Royal Festival Hall, London (*c*1990 [filmed 1989]); Ignacio Berroa: Mastering the Art of Afro-Cuban Drumming (1993)

BIBLIOGRAPHY

B. Blumenthal: "Two Voices of Jazz to be Featured at Festival," *Boston Globe* (14 June 1992)
L. Birnbaum: "Riffs: Danilo Pérez," *DB*, lx/5 (1993), 14
P. Benkimoun: "Danilo Pérez," *Jm*, no.439 (1994), 34
D. Helland: "World View: Danilo Pérez," *Keyboard*, xx/6 (1994), 14
E. Holley: "Danilo Pérez & David Sanchez: Import Duties," *DB*, lxiii/11 (1996), 32 [incl. discography]
W. Jenkins: "Danilo Pérez: Brilliant Sphere," *JT*, xxvi/8 (1996), 42
R. Reynard: "Danilo Pérez," *Jh*, no.528 (1996), 12
F. W. Sportis: "Danilo Pérez: Panamonk," *Jh*, no.550 (1998), 19 [incl. discography]

GK

Perez, Manuel [(Emile) Emanuel] (*b* New Orleans, 28 Dec 1878; *d* New Orleans, 1946). Cornetist and bandleader. In a revision of an earlier article, De Donder (1993) confirms that Perez was born in 1878; 1871, which he had given earlier, is instead the year of birth of another man of the same name (who was white, and not a musician). A cigar maker by trade, Perez received classical training on cornet from the age of 12 and was active in brass and dance bands in New Orleans; by his own account he was playing ragtime on cornet in 1898. He joined the Onward Brass Band (*see* Onward brass band (i)) in 1900 and led it from 1903 until it disbanded in 1930; he was also the leader of the of the Imperial orchestra (*c*1901–1912). In the mid 1910s he spent two years in Chicago, where remembrances of his activites are confusing and contradictory. The most likely account places him there from 1916 to 1918, leading a five-piece band at the Arsonia Café that included Lorenzo Tio, Jr., the trombonist Eddie Atkins, and Louis Cottrell, Sr. Despite other reports, he evidently did not work there with the trombonist George Filhe and Charlie Elgar, who may simply have secured the job for him; Elgar seems to have led his own band at the Arsonia, alternating with Perez during this period. After returning to New Orleans in 1918 Perez performed that summer on the SS *Capitol* and from the 1920s led dance orchestras in clubs and dance halls in the city, including the Oasis Cabaret (1921–2) and the Pythian Temple Roof Gardens (from 1924). He is also said to have rejoined Elgar in Chicago in 1928, but in his interview with Goffin (1946) he denied this: "Depuis lors [the earlier period in Chicago], je n'ai plus bougé du quartier créole!" He retired from music in 1937; details of his death are unknown.

Perez was regarded as one of the finest parade cornetists; he played wide-ranging melodies with a sharp, clear attack and beautiful tone. He believed that playing in a brass band tested a musician's sight-reading skill and technical execution and was generally more demanding than playing jazz. While he prided himself on the ability of the members of his brass bands to play from written arrangements, when such bands began to include improvisation in their work he was prepared to engage good improvisers, including the young Joe (later King) Oliver. As a dance-band musician he proved that he too could improvise competently. He was also a highly respected teacher whose private students included Sidney Desvigne, Willie Pajeaud, Alvin Alcorn, and Natty Dominique.

Oral history material in *LNT* [interviews of Barney Bigard, Peter Bocage, Albert Burbank, Louis Cottrell, Jr., Natty Dominique, Jack Laine, and Alphonse Picou].

BIBLIOGRAPHY

ChiltonW
R. Goffin: *La Nouvelle-Orléans: capitale du jazz* (New York, 1946), 67
D. M. Marquis: *In Search of Buddy Bolden, First Man of Jazz* (Baton Rouge, LA, and London, 1978/*R*1993)
D. Barker: *A Life in Jazz*, ed. A. Shipton (London and New York, 1986)
J. De Donder: "Emanuel Perez," *Fn*, xvii/6 (1986), 4
R. Wang: "Researching the New Orleans–Chicago Jazz Connection: Tools and Methods," *Black Music Research Journal*, viii/1 (1988), 101
A. W. Barrell: "Nightmare, a Sudden Awakening, or Dreams of Manuel Perez," *New Orleans Music*, i/3 (1990), 21
J. De Donder: "Manuel Perez," *New Orleans Music*, iv/3 (1993), 14
R. H. Knowles: *Fallen Heroes: a History of New Orleans Brass Bands* (New Orleans, 1996)

KARL KOENIG/BK

Perfect. Record label. It was established in June 1922 by American Pathé and was used to issue cheap records, most of which were also released at full price on Pathé. A race series, the Perfect 100s, equivalent to Pathé's 7500s, was started in 1926. There was also a British label Perfect, which ran for a year from December 1927 and was used mostly to issue items first put out on American Perfect and Pathé; these, however, are of little jazz interest. American Perfect survived the incorporation of its parent into the AMERICAN RECORD CORPORATION and became one of the new organization's "dime-store" labels. The race series was continued until around July 1935; its issues were also put out on the other dime-store labels. From September 1935 Perfect's numerical sequence was aligned with ARC's, and a popular series was maintained in addition to the race material. With the other dime-store labels, Perfect was discontinued in April 1938.

BIBLIOGRAPHY

C. Kendziora, Jr., and P. Armagnac: "Perfect Dance-series and Race-series Catalog, 1922–1930," *Record Research*, nos.51–2 (1963), 13
J. Godrich: "The Pefect 100 Race Series," *78 Quarterly*, no.1 (1967), 56; no.2 (1968), [p. unknown]
R. M. W. Dixon and J. Godrich: *Recording the Blues* (London, 1970)
R. D. Kinkle: "Perfect Numerical List," *The Complete Encyclopedia of Popular Music and Jazz* (New Rochelle, NY, and Westport, CT, 1974), iv, 2236
B. Rust: *The American Record Label Book* (New Rochelle, NY, 1978), 236
A. Badrock: *English Pathe Perfect: a Catalogue and History* (Hayes, England, 1983)
A. Sutton: *Directory of American Disc Record Brands and Manufacturers, 1891–1943* (Westport, CT, and London, 1994), 121
R. M. W. Dixon, J. Godrich, and H. Rye: *Blues & Gospel Records, 1890–1943* (Oxford, England, rev. and enlarged 4/1997), xxxii

HOWARD RYE

Perkins, Bill [William Reese] (*b* San Francisco, 22 July 1924). Tenor and baritone saxophonist, flutist, and clarinetist. The son of a mining engineer, he grew up in Chile, then in Santa Barbara, California. He took up clarinet and piano, but lacked interest in these instruments and changed to the tenor saxophone. After serving in the armed forces during World War II he earned degrees in music and engineering at the University of California, Santa Barbara. He then studied at the Westlake School of Music in Los Angeles (1949 – early 1951), belonged to the big band of the clarinetist Jerry Wald (1950–51), and worked with Woody Herman (late May 1951 – August 1953). While playing with Stan Kenton (November 1953 – March 1954), again with Herman (March 1954 – February 1955), and once more with Kenton (spring 1955 – mid-January 1959) he figured prominently as a soloist. He recorded in 1956 with John Lewis, and in the same year recorded an album as a leader with Richie Kamuca and Art Pepper, for which he also wrote arrangements and a blues.

In the 1960s Perkins worked in studios both as a performer and as a recording engineer, though he was once again in Herman's band for a brief period in May 1963. By 1969 he chose to abandon his engineering duties to work exclusively as a studio musician. He played in the orchestra of the "Tonight Show" under Doc Severinsen from around 1968 to 1992, and from 1974 to 1977 he performed and recorded (usually as a baritone saxophonist) with the Toshiko Akiyoshi–Lew Tabackin Big Band. He also appeared as a guest soloist with Herman in July 1981 and July 1983, toured Europe and Japan and recorded with Shorty Rogers throughout the mid-1980s, and performed in Britain as the co-leader of a quintet with Tommy Whittle in 1986. At home in the Los Angeles area he often worked at night and at weekends in groups apart from Severinsen, with Frank Strazzeri or Alan Broadbent on piano, Putter Smith or Gene Cherico on double bass, and John Terry on drums; one such quartet, including Broadbent and Cherico, recorded in 1986.

In 1987 Perkins was the co-leader of an intriguing recording session with the more extroverted tenor saxophonist James Clay. Later he recorded duos with Strazzeri (1990–91) and with a big band, with which he strove to re-create the musical spirit rather than the letter of Herman's Herds (1991); he also recorded with Strazzeri's group Woodwinds West and the reconstituted Lighthouse All Stars. In 1992, at around the same time that Severinsen's longstanding group gave way to a new and younger "Tonight Show" band under Branford Marsalis, Perkins was forced to retire and undergo an operation for lung cancer. He recorded with Bud Shank's group in December 1993 and resumed working with Severinsen's big band once again.

In his early career Perkins favored a light style of playing influenced by Lester Young, which is well represented by his work on John Lewis's album *Two Degrees East, Three Degrees West* (1956). His later style is exemplified by his own recording *Journey to the East* (1984), which displays the influence of John Coltrane (on the track *From the Hip*) and

Sonny Rollins (on *I'm an Old Cowhand*), as well as Perkins's fine sense of structure.

For illustration *see* MULLIGAN, GERRY.

SELECTED RECORDINGS

Duos with F. Strazzeri: *Two as One* (1990, Interplay 8611); *Warm Moods* (1991, Fresh Sound 191)

As leader: *On Stage: the Bill Perkins Octet* (1956, PJ 1221); with R. Kamuca and A. Pepper: *Just Friends* (1956, PJ 401); with P. Adams: *Confluence* (1978, Interplay 7721); *Journey to the East* (1984, Cont. 14011), incl. From the Hip, I'm an Old Cowhand; with B. Shank: *Serious Swingers* (1986, Cont. 14031); with J. Clay: *The Right Chemistry* (1987, Jazz Mark 108); with H. Harper: *Two Brothers* (1989, V.S.O.P. 80); *Our Man Woody: in Remembrance of Woody Herman* (1991, Jazz Mark 110)

As sideman: S. Kenton: *Music of Bill Russo and Bill Holman* (1954, Cap. H526), incl. King Fish; W. Herman: *The Woody Herman Band!* (1954, Cap. T560), incl. Autobahn Blues, Hittin' the Bottle, Sleep, Wild Apple Honey; S. Kenton: Opus in Chartreuse (1955, Cap. 3243); J. Lewis: *Two Degrees East, Three Degrees West* (1956, PJ 1217); S. Rogers and B. Shank: *America the Beautiful* (1991, Can. 79510-2); B. Shank: *New Gold!* (1993, Can. 79707)

SELECTED FILMS AND VIDEOS

Woody Herman's Varieties (1951); The Subterraneans (1960); The Swingin' Singin' Years (1960); Woodwinds West (early 1990s [filmed 1992])

BIBLIOGRAPHY

B. Korall: "Bill Perkins," *Metronome*, lxxii/2 (1956), 21
J. Tynan: "From Slipstick to Jazz Horn," *DB*, xxiii/9 (1956), 13
D. Ioakimidis: "Kings of the Tenor Sax: Bill Perkins," *Jh*, no.133 (1958), 15
J. Tynan: "Two Tenor Conversation," *DB*, xxv/10 (1958), 14
A. Morgan: "Woody's Tenors," *JM*, vi (1960–61), no.7, p.4; no.8, p.13; no.12, p.9
S. Voce: "Bill Perkins," *JJI*, xxxix (1986), no.2, p.16; no.3, p.8
L. Tomkins: "I'd Never Trade what I've Done . . .: Bill Perkins," *CI*, xxiv/6 (1987), 20; contd as "Bill Perkins is Given a New Pulsation," xxiv/7 (1987), 22
W. D. Clancy with A. C. Kenton: *Woody Herman: Chronicles of the Herds* (New York and elsewhere, 1995)
B. Rusch: "Bill Perkins Interview," *Cadence*, xxi/11 (1995), 5
K. Richmond: "Bill Perkins," *Saxophone Journal*, xxii/6 (1998), 16 [incl. discography]

MICHAEL ULLMAN/BK

Perkins, Carl (*b* Indianapolis, 16 Aug 1928; *d* Los Angeles, 17 March 1958). Pianist. He took up piano at the age of nine and, although he grew up in a musical family, was largely self-taught; he often played with his left arm parallel to the keyboard, using his elbow to strike low notes. In 1948–9 he performed rhythm-and-blues with Big Jay McNeely in California, where he settled in 1949. The following year he played with Miles Davis, and in 1951 he recorded with Illinois Jacquet. After serving in the US Army (1951 – November 1952) he re-joined Davis and performed and recorded with Oscar Moore (1953, summer 1954). From the mid-1950s he worked with bop groups, playing with Jim Hall, Teddy Edwards, and Red Mitchell, and recording with Clifford Brown and Max Roach (1954), Dexter Gordon (1955), Chet Baker (1956), Art Pepper (1956–7), and Pepper Adams, Buddy DeFranco, Victor Feldman, Hall, Stuff Smith, and Richie Kamuca (all 1957). He was also a member of Curtis Counce's band (1956–8), and he led his own bop trios and recorded two albums as a leader (1956, 1957). Perkins's career was severely disrupted by the consequences of drug addiction.

SELECTED RECORDINGS

As leader: *Introducing Carl Perkins* (1956, Dootone 211)

As sideman with C. Counce: *The Curtis Counce Group* (1956, Cont. 3526); *You Get More Bounce with Curtis Counce* (1957, Cont. 3539); *Carl's Blues* (1957–8, Cont. 3574);

As sideman with others: D. Gordon: *Dexter Blows Hot and Cold* (1955, Dootone 207); S. Smith: *Have Violin, Will Travel* (1957, Verve 8282); A. Pepper: *The Omega Man* (1957, Omega Tape 7020); L. Vinnegar: *Leroy Walks* (1957, Cont. 3542); H. Land: *Harold in the Land of Jazz* (1958, Cont. 3550)

BIBLIOGRAPHY

L. Grigson and A. Morgan: "Carl Perkins," *JM*, viii/5 (1962), 11 [incl. discography]
R. Gordon: *Jazz West Coast: the Los Angeles Jazz Scene of the 1950s* (London and New York, 1986)
B. Charlesworth: "The Forgotten Ones: Carl Perkins," *JJI*, xli/5 (1988), 16
T. Gioia: *West Coast Jazz: Modern Jazz in California, 1945–1960* (New York and Oxford, England, 1992), 320
A. Balalas: "Carl Perkins: Piano," *BHcF*, no 469 (1998), 3

BK

Perkins, Walter (*b* Chicago, 10 Feb 1932). Drummer. He performed in the Chicago area with Ahmad Jamal (1956–7) and at the Playboy Jazz Festival with Coleman Hawkins (1959), and then formed the group MJT + 3, whose members consisted of the trumpeter Paul Serrano, the tenor saxophonist Nicky Hill, Muhal Richard Abrams, and Bob Cranshaw. Booker Little and George Coleman played with the group around 1958, and their fellow Memphis-based musicians Frank Strozier and Harold Mabern recorded with it, as did the trumpeter Willie Thomas. Perkins moved with the MJT + 3 to New York in 1960. After the group disbanded in 1962 he remained in New York, where he performed with Carmen McRae (1961–3), Sonny Rollins (1962), Art Farmer (1963), and Teddy Wilson (1964) and made many recordings, including albums with George Shearing, McRae, Gene Ammons (1961, 1962), Billy Taylor (ii) (1962), Booker Ervin, Farmer, and Charles Mingus (all 1963), Clark Terry and Jaki Byard (both 1964), and Lucky Thompson (1965). Later he recorded with Pat Martino (1967), Mabern (1968), and Charles Earland (1977). In 1981 he performed and recorded in Paris as a member of Hilton Ruiz's trio. Perkins's drumming is notable for its drive and swing; he plays to support the soloist rather than to display his own technique.

SELECTED RECORDINGS

As leader: *MJT + 3* (1959, VJ 1013)

As sideman: A. Jamal: *Count 'em 88* (1956, Argo 610); G. Shearing and Montgomery Brothers: *Love Walked in* (1961, Jlnd 955); C. Mingus: *Mingus, Mingus, Mingus, Mingus, Mingus* (1963, Imp. 54); B. Ervin: *Exultation!* (1963, Prst. 7293); J. Byard: *Out Front* (1964, Prst. 7397); L. Thompson: *Happy Days are Here Again* (1965, Prst. 7394)

BIBLIOGRAPHY

Feather '60s
J. Litweiler: "Chicago's Richard Abrams: a Man with an Idea," *DB*, xxxiv/20 (1967), 23

J. KENT WILLIAMS/BK

Perkiömäki, Jari (*b* Pori, Finland, 13 April 1961). Finnish alto saxophonist, clarinetist and flutist. He studied jazz at the Sibelius Academy, Helsinki, and taught there after graduating in 1989. In 1985 he recorded his début album (*Jari Perkiömäki Quartet*, Kompass 64) to much acclaim, and in the 1990s he became the leading young Finnish saxophonist, appearing with his own group (which recorded the album *Shades*, 1996, Jazzweaver 97001) and with UMO in both Finland and Europe.

Oral history material in *FiHJ*.

BIBLIOGRAPHY

M. Kontinnen: "Finland's First Master of Jazz," *Finnish Music Quarterly* no.1 (1990), 66
M. Huuskonen, J. Muikku and T. Vähäsilta: *Finnish Jazz* (Helsinki, 5/1997)

PEKKA GRONOW

Perko, Jukka (*b* Huittinen, Finland, 8 Feb 1968). Finnish alto saxophonist. He played with Dizzy Gillespie's big band (1987–8) and with his own quartet in Europe and the USA. In the 1990s he formed, with Severi Pyysalo, the group Perko-Pyysalo Poppoo, which may be heard to advantage on their recording *Varia* (1998, Porijazz 110).

BIBLIOGRAPHY

M. Konttinen: "Young Talents in Finnish Jazz," *Finnish Music Quarterly* no.2 (1991), 42

M. Huuskonen, J. Muikku and T. Vähäsilta: *Finnish Jazz* (Helsinki, 5/1997)

PEKKA GRONOW

Perla, Gene (August) (*b* Hackensack, NJ, 1 March 1940). Bass player. He grew up in Woodcliff Lake, New Jersey, and learned classical piano from the age of five; he played jazz piano after the manner of Nat "King" Cole and while at high school he took up trombone and sang. After studying engineering and business for four years at the University of Toronto he attended the Berklee School of Music (1962–4), where he recorded as a pianist with the college band, and the Boston Conservatory of Music (1962–4). Having changed to double bass he returned to the New York area in 1966 and joined Willie Bobo. Later he played in lofts in New York (late 1960s) and performed with Woody Herman (1969–70), Sarah Vaughan (1970), Elvin Jones (1971–3), and Sonny Rollins (1974–5); he also recorded with Herman and Jones. Around 1971 he often played with the Thad Jones–Mel Lewis Orchestra and Quartet. As a studio musician he recorded with Jeremy Steig (1970–71), Steve Grossman (1973–6), Dave Liebman and Frank Foster (both 1974), Jones (1975), and Charlie Mariano (1979). In 1975 he formed Stone Alliance with Grossman and Don Alias; among the group's recordings is *Stone Alliance* (1975–6, PM 013). Perla was the head of a financial corporation and founded a music publishing company (Perla Music Company) and two record companies, PM Records (1973) and Plug Records (1983); PM issued recordings by Liebman, Grossman, Jones, Bernie Senensky, Don Thompson, Pat LaBarbera, and Ed Bickert. Stone Alliance disbanded in 1983, after which Perla worked as an educator, a theater sound designer, a record producer, and a computer consultant. In 1996 he re-formed the group as a trio with Alias among his sideman.

BIBLIOGRAPHY

Feather–Gitler '70s

P. Brodowski: "Gene Perla: a Musician with a Business Sense," *JF* [intl edn], no.24 (1973), 37

B. Rusch: "Gene Perla: Interview," *Cadence*, vii/6 (1982), 10

<http://www.ccinyc.com/pmrecords/stone/> (2000)

<http://www.finewinetrio.com/bioperla.htm> (2000)

BK

Perowsky, Ben(jamin Arthur) (*b* New York, 12 May 1966). Drummer. His father played saxophone and worked with Woody Herman and Roland Hanna. He took up drums at the age of five and later attended the High School of Music and Art (1980–84), the Berklee College of Music (1984–6), and the Manhattan School of Music (1986–7). In 1986 he played briefly with James Moody at the Village Vanguard and in 1988 he was a founding member of the cooperative group Lost Tribe, with which he has toured and recorded. Perowksy recorded and performed internationally with Roy Ayers between 1988 and 1989, during which time he made a video at Ronnie Scott's in London. In the 1990s he played in Mike Stern's group (1990–95), toured Japan with Eliane Elias (1991), and worked with Spanish Fly (from 1992), Pat Martino (1996), Dave Douglas (from 1996), and Don Byron (1997); in 1996 he formed a trio with Chris Speed and Scott Colley. He has also worked with pop musicians, notably Rickie Lee Jones (1987) and John Cale.

SELECTED RECORDINGS

As sideman: M. Stern: on *Odds and Evens* (*c*1990, Atl. 82297-2), Keys, Seven Thirty, Walkie Talkie; on *Standards (and other Songs)* (*c*1991, Atl. 82419-2), Lost Time, Nardis; Lost Tribe: *Lost Tribe* (*c*1992, Windham Hill 10143-2); R. Cuber: *Airplay* (1992, Ste. 31309); R. Bowen: *Movin' on* (1992, Criss Cross 1066); Lost Tribe: *Soulfish* (*c*1993, High Street 10327-2); Spanish Fly: on *Rags to Britches* (1993, Knitting Factory Works 114), Baby, Folk Song, Hoe cheez

BIBLIOGRAPHY

G. Antonopoulos: "Up & Coming: Ben Perowsky: the Proof is in the Musician," *MD*, xvi/7 (1992), 56

GK

Perrilliat, Nat(haniel Leonard) (*b* New Orleans, 29 Nov 1936; *d* Sacramento, CA, 26 Jan 1971). Tenor saxophonist. He played alto and baritone saxophones in high school and was a regular accompanist for talent shows at the Caffin Theater in New Orleans; he also played piano. In 1952 he joined the blues pianist Professor Longhair and became a professional musician. Two years later he formed a working relationship with the guitarist Roy Montrell, and their group, featuring the young James Black, began to undertake session work in rhythm-and-blues. Perrilliat's playing reached maturity during his years with Ellis Marsalis's quartet (to 1963), yet he continued to study, learning from Alvin Batiste and from performing with Ed Blackwell. A strong, vital musician with a broad tone, Perrilliatt was equally at home playing jazz or rhythm-and-blues; his booting sound, incorporating a substantial vibrato, inspired the singer and pianist Fats Domino, and on *But I do* (1960), by the singer Clarence "Frogman" Henry, provided a classic of the genre. In 1962 he formed a big band consisting of the city's pioneering jazz musicians, but it was not intended as a commercial venture and he returned to touring with the singers Junior Parker and Joe Tex and to driving a taxi. He was touring with Domino again when he suffered a cerebral haemorrhage.

SELECTED RECORDINGS

As sideman: C. Henry: But I do (1960, Argo 5378); N. Adderley: *In the Bag* (1962, Jlnd 75); Willie T (Wilson Turbinton): All for One/Always Accused (1962, A.F.O. 307); first issued on [no leader]: *New Orleans Heritage – Jazz: 1956–1966* (1956–66, Opus 43 4302–05), E. Marsalis: Little Joy, Round 'bout Midnight, Swinging at the Haven (1963)

BIBLIOGRAPHY

M. Vernon: "Domino Men: Nat Perrilliat and Wallace Davenport," *JM*, xiii/6 (1967), 11

J. Broven: *Walking to New Orleans: the Story of New Orleans Rhythm and Blues* (Bexhill-on-Sea, England, 1974; Gretna, LA, 1983, as *Rhythm & Blues in New Orleans*)

H. Battiste: Liner notes, *New Orleans Heritage – Jazz: 1956–1966* (Opus 43 4302–05, 1976)

C. Suhor: "Jazz in New Orleans in the 1960s," *Jazz Archivist*, x/1–2 (1995), 1

VAL WILMER

Perrin, Mimi [Jeannine] (*b* Paris, 2 Feb 1926). French pianist, singer, and arranger. She began her career as the leader of a trio and in 1956 recorded as a pianist and singer. Around the same year she joined the Blue Stars, of which she remained a member until 1958; she also recorded with the pianist Christian Chevallier (1959). She is best known for having led the DOUBLE SIX (1959–66), with which she made recordings (including *Dizzy Gillespie et les Double Six*, 1963, Phi. 200106); she also appeared in Martin Ritt's film *Paris*

Blues (1961). From 1968 she lived in the USA. Perrin's style was strongly influenced by the work of King Pleasure and Lambert, Hendricks, and Ross.

BIBLIOGRAPHY

Feather '60s
J. Tronchot: "Ce chant qui jouent, cette musique que chantent les Double Six . . . cette bande de copains terribles," *Jh*, no.171 (1961), 16
M. Cullaz: "Mimi Perrin," *Jh*, no.346 (1978), 53

MICHEL LAPLACE

Perry, King [Oliver Hazard] (*b* Forest City, AR, 10 Oct 1914; *d* Bakersfield, CA, 5 Feb 1990). Alto saxophonist, clarinetist, arranger, and leader. He first learned violin, and took up alto saxophone when a local band would not accept him as a violinist. A report of his joining AFM local 627 in Kansas City was published in April 1937, and that same month he made an application for a social security number (in which his full name and details of his birth appear). Later he studied piano at a college in West Virginia, and by early 1940 he was leading his own band, based in Gary, Indiana. In mid-1945 he traveled to Los Angeles with a show that involved Dorothy Donegan and Nat "King" Cole, and he made his first recordings there in July. He continued to lead a jump band, sometimes called the Pied Pipers, until the mid-1950s, recording extensively and making several cross-country tours, including one to Canada in late 1951. The band was resident at the Longbar, San Francisco, for four weeks around August 1950. Following a period of retirement Perry resumed his musical career in 1967 when he moved to Bakersfield, California, where he worked in the 1970s as a one-man band, playing organ, alto saxophone, and percussion; he also recorded comedy albums for his own Octive label. Details of his death appear in the social security death index.

SELECTED RECORDINGS

As leader: King Perry Blues/The Man I Love (1945, Melodisc 107); Keep a dollar in your pocket/Rocks in my Bed (1948, Excelsior 522); Perry's Wiggle Woogie (1948, Excelsior 532); Going to California Blues (1949, De Luxe 3216); Christopher Columbus/Things ain't what they used to be (1954, Lucky 45-003)
As sideman with Duke Henderson: Leona's Boogie (1947, UA 507); San Quentin Quail (1947, UA 505)

BIBLIOGRAPHY

Professor Hi-Jinx: Liner notes, *King Perry* (Krazy Kat 7438, 1986)

HOWARD RYE

Perry (Guloien), P(aul) J(ohn) (*b* Calgary, Canada, 2 Dec 1941). Canadian alto and tenor saxophonist. His father, Paul Perry (Guloien) (1916–92), a tenor saxophonist, led dance bands throughout Western Canada (1939–44) and operated his own summer dance hall at Sylvan Lake, near Edmonton (1947–65). Perry began playing with his father's band at the age of 14 and thereafter divided his time mostly between Vancouver (1956–9, 1963–75) and Edmonton (1975–81, from 1984), while spending shorter periods in Toronto, Montreal, Berlin, and London during the early 1960s and in Toronto again from 1981 to 1984. In Vancouver he worked with Fraser MacPherson, the trumpeter Bobby Hales, and the trombonist Dave Robbins; he was also a member of the jazz-rock band Pacific Salt (1972–5). In Toronto he appeared with Rob McConnell and the Boss Brass, Dizzy Gillespie, Woody Shaw, and others, and in Edmonton he has worked with the pianist Tommy Banks, performed as a soloist with the Edmonton Symphony Orchestra, and led his own bands. A vivacious bop stylist, Perry has recorded with Banks, Hugh Fraser, Pacific Salt, and others; his own recordings include *Worth Waiting For* (1990, Jazz Alliance 10007).

BIBLIOGRAPHY

EMC2
M. Miller: "A Blow in the Afternoon," *Jazz in Canada: Fourteen Lives* (Toronto, 1982), 41
B. Turner: "P. J. Perry: a Canadian legend," *Coda*, no.202 (1985), 14
S. Husain: "P. J. Perry: Worth Waiting For," *Coda*, no.253 (1994), 4

MARK MILLER

Perry, Ray (*b* Boston, 25 Feb 1915; *d* New York, aut. 1950). Violinist and alto saxophonist. He began performing on violin and became known for singing in unison with his playing; from 1935 he also worked as an alto saxophonist. He was a member of Blanche Calloway's big band from January to September 1940 before joining Lionel Hampton, with whom he remained until October 1943. While with Hampton he made a number of recordings, including *Fiddle-dee-dee* (1940, Vic. 27364), which was designed as a vehicle for his solo violin playing. He also recorded with Sabby Lewis (*Sweet Georgia Brown*, *I surrender dear*, and *Undecided*, all 1944, first issued on Lewis's *Boston Bounce*, 1944–7, Phoenix Jazz 9), as well as with Ethel Waters (as a member of J. C. Heard's orchestra, early 1946), and Illinois Jacquet (1946, 1947); later he played again with Lewis (1948) and Jacquet (1950). Perry briefly led his own bands in 1946, 1947, and 1948. (A. Barnett: "Ray Perry, the Rosenkrantz Transcriptions and other Violin Recordings," *Fable Bulletin: Violin Improvisation Studies*, no.2 (1993))

based on *ChiltonW*/HOWARD RYE

Perry, Rich(ard) (*b* Cleveland, 22 July 1955). Tenor saxophonist. He joined the Thad Jones–Mel Lewis Orchestra in 1977 (continued from 1979 as the Mel Lewis Orchestra), left the band in 1981, but rejoined in 1988 (continued from 1990 as the Vanguard Jazz Orchestra). In 1991 he became a member of Maria Schneider's orchestra and John Fedchock's New York big band. He has worked in small groups led by Harold Danko (from 1990), Fred Hersch (1991–6), George Mraz (from 1995), and Dave Stryker (from 1996), and he recorded with Joe Henderson's big band (1992), Ron McClure (1992, 1997), Paul Bley (1994), and Lee Konitz (1997). Perry has been active as a leader for recording purposes only. He also plays flute.

SELECTED RECORDINGS

As leader: *To Start Again* (1993, Ste. 31331); *Beautiful Love* (1994, Ste. 31360); *What Is This?* (1995, Ste. 31374)
As sideman: F. Hersch: *Forward Motion* (1991, Chesky 55); R. McClure: *Inner Account* (1992, Ste. 31329); P. Bley: *Speachless* (1994, Ste. 31363); F. Hersch: *Point in Time* (1995, Enja 9035-2); H. Danko: *New Autumn* (1995, Ste. 31377)

GK

Persiany, André [Persiani, André Paul Stephane; Pépé] (*b* Paris, 19 Nov 1927). French pianist. He studied violin and then piano with his father. From 1945 he led his own group, though he also played with the BeBop Minstrels (1947–8) and in a duo with the pianist Eddie Bernard. He recorded as a sideman with Bill Coleman (1949, 1955–6), Buck Clayton (1949, 1953), Mezz Mezzrow (1951), and Lionel Hampton (1953), and performed with the saxophonist Tony Proteau, Raymond Fonsèque's group T4, and Michel Attenoux (all 1953) and Guy Lafitte (1954–5). He may be seen in the film shorts *Jam Session* (1951) and *Bill Coleman from Boogie to*

Funk (1961). In New York he worked at the Metropole and Birdland from 1956 to 1957, and from 1961 to April 1969 he was a member of Jonah Jones's quartet. After returning to France Persiany was the house pianist at Le Furstemberg in Paris from 1970 to 1988, leading a trio consisting of the double bass player Roland Lobligeois and the drummer Roger Paraboschi; they recorded there in 1979. He performed with Charlie Shavers and Budd Johnson (1970), Milt Buckner (1973, 1975–6), Arnett Cobb and Eddie Chamblee (1976), Al Grey (1977), and Cat Anderson (1978). In the 1980s he led his own groups and accompanied the singer Jan Harrington (1989). Persiany is an able swing player, influenced by Buckner, who employs block chords in his playing; he has written several arrangements. His son Stéphane Persiani (*b* 1959) is a double bass player.

SELECTED RECORDINGS

As leader: *Swinging Here and There* (1956–8, Pathé 05411721); *The Real Me* (1970, BB 333024); *As Time Goes By* (1975, BB 33147); *Every Night at Furstemberg* (1979, Open 06)

As sideman: L. Hampton: *Lionel Hampton Jam Session* (1953, Barclay 6839), incl. Blues for the Hot Club de France; Jonah Jones: *Blowin' up a Storm* (1963, Cap. T2087), incl. Sleepy Time Gal; C. Shavers: *Live!* (1970, BB 33302), incl. Prelude to a Kiss [unaccompanied solo]

BIBLIOGRAPHY

FeatherE

H. Panassié and M. Gautier: *Dictionnaire du jazz* (Paris, 1954, enlarged 3/1980; Eng. trans., London, 1956, rev. A. A. Gurwitch as *Guide to Jazz*, Boston, 1956)

A. Clergeat: *Dictionnaire du jazz* (Paris, 1966)

F. W. Sportis: "Pépé," *Jh*, no.501 (1993), 28 [incl. discography]

MICHEL LAPLACE

Persip, Charli(e) [Charles Lawrence] (*b* Morristown, NJ, 26 July 1929). Drummer. His family moved to East Orange and then to Newark before leaving New Jersey to settle in Springfield, Massachusetts, when he was four years old. He took up drums when he was seven and learned the instrument for one and a half years, but at that time had only a casual interest in it; he became seriously devoted to drums only later, when at the age of 13 he and his mother moved back to Newark and he began to go to theaters to hear big bands, especially that of Lionel Hampton. After graduating from high school (1945), shortly before his 16th birthday, he began working professionally in local bands in the emerging rhythm-and-blues field, accompanying such musicians as James Moody, Dave Burns, Hank Mobley, and Walter Davis. Later he worked with the blues musician Brownie McGhee, a vocal group, the Four Keys, Hal Singer, and others, but he was devoted to bop, and whenever circumstances allowed he went to Harlem to listen to or to participate in jam sessions at Minton's and at the Paradise Club (where the sessions were hosted by Big Nick Nicholas). He played with Tadd Dameron in a band in Atlantic City, New Jersey (1953), then toured and recorded with Dizzy Gillespie (1953–8), with whom he may be seen in the short film *Date with Dizzy* (1956). Persip worked with Johnny Richards's orchestra and Phil Woods and joined Harry Edison's quintet and the Harry James Orchestra (for six weeks in spring 1959) before forming his own group, the Jazz Statesmen, with Freddie Hubbard and Ron Carter (1960). During this period, from his last years with Gillespie through his first attempt at bandleader, he achieved his highest level of prominence. Much in demand in the studios, he recorded with dozens of leading swing and bop musicians, including Frank Rehak (1956), Lee Morgan (1956–7), Mobley (1956, 1958), Jimmy Cleveland and Art Farmer (1957), Dinah Washington (1957), Benny Golson (1957, 1962), Kenny Dorham, Edison, Melba Liston, Joe Newman, Gene Quill, and Zoot Sims (all 1958), Jerome Richardson (1958–9), Randy Weston (1958, 1960), Red Garland (1958, 1960–61), Ray Charles and Quincy Jones, Curtis Fuller, Hampton, and Kai Winding (all 1959), Bob Brookmeyer and George Russell (both 1959–60), Farmer (1959, 1962), Gil Evans, Johnny Griffin, Budd Johnson, David "Fathead" Newman, and Sal Salvador (all 1960), Don Ellis (1960–61), and Cannonball Adderley, Carter and Eric Dolphy, Johnny Coles, Taft Jordan, Roland Kirk, Oliver Nelson, Cecil Payne, Clark Terry, and Mal Waldron (all 1961); he was also involved in an excellent all-star recording of *Porgy and Bess*, arranged and conducted by Bill Potts.

Over the next few years Persip took part in a few more significant studio sessions, with Gene Ammons, Pony Poindexter, and Dizzy Reece (all 1962), Milt Jackson (1963), and Kenny Burrell (1964), but his career declined somewhat. He accompanied the popular singer Yves Montand (1962), drummed for dance classes, and joined the house band at the Apollo Theatre in Harlem (1963), where he played for funk and soul artists, notably James Brown. From 1966 to 1973 he toured as a drummer and conductor with Billy Eckstine, and in 1974 he became the principal drum instructor for the Jazzmobile in New York, though he continued to perform and record, with Archie Shepp (1975, 1977), Kirk (1976), and Frank Foster (1977–8). With the trumpeter Gary La Furn, he led a big band, Superband, which recorded in New York in 1980; two years later Persip took over sole leadership of the group. In 1984 he formed a trio with Jack DeJohnette (who played piano) and Eddie Gomez and recorded an outstanding album, *In Case You Missed it*, with his Superband. In the 1990s he continued to teach on the Jazzmobile and to lead the Superband, for which Jack Walrath supplied many arrangements. He performed at festivals in Europe with Clifford Jordan and Al Jarreau (both 1991), founded a quintet, Persipitation (1992), recorded with Weston and Liston (1993), and taught in the Jazz and Contemporary Music Program at the New School for Social Research and in its continuation at the Mannes/New School (1996–9) and (from autumn 1999) the New School University.

Persip is one of the foremost bop big-band drummers and prefers the big-band setting to that of the small group; however, his work is heard to great advantage on *We Free Kings*, made in 1961 by Kirk's quartet, on which the drums are prominently recorded. He displays his command of a wide variety of modern styles on *How Time Passes*, which he recorded as a member of Ellis's quartet (1960). Persip is the author of a clever instructional book, *How Not to Play Drums: Not for Drummers Only* (New York, *c*1987).

SELECTED RECORDINGS

As leader: *The Jazz Statesmen* (1960, Beth. 6046); with G. La Furn: *Charli Persip and Gary La Furn's 17-piece Superband* (1980, Stash 209); *In Case You Missed it* (1984, SN 1079)

As sideman: D. Gillespie: *World Statesman* (1956, Norg. 1084): *Duets with Sonny Rollins and Sonny Stitt* (1957, Verve 8260); B. Potts: *The Jazz Soul of Porgy and Bess* (1959, UA 4032); D. Ellis: *How Time Passes* (1960, Can. 9004); G. Evans: *Out of the Cool* (1960, Imp. 4); R. Carter: *Where?* (1961, NewJ 8265); M. Waldron: *The Quest* (1961, NewJ 8269); R. Kirk: *We Free Kings* (1961, Mer. 60679); R. Weston and M. Liston: *Volcano Blues* (1993, Ant. 314-519269-2)

BIBLIOGRAPHY

M. Jones: "Persip: All the Way from Dizzy to Eckstine," *MM* (16 Dec 1967), 6

J. B. Litweiler: "Profile: Charlie Persip," *DB*, xlii/3 (1975), 28

B. Primack: "Blindfold Test: Charli Persip," *DB*, xlvi/16 (1979), 61
——: "Charli Persip: the Art of Creative Accompaniment," *JT*, xxi/8 (1991), 56
B. Korall: "Charli Persip: his own Man," *MD*, xviii/12 (1994), 26

BK

Person, Eric (Anthony) (*b* St. Louis, 2 May 1963). Alto and soprano saxophonist. His father, an amateur saxophonist, inspired him to start playing when he was seven and took him to see Count Basie's orchestra, in which he was particularly impressed by Jimmy Forrest. He studied privately and attended the St. Louis Conservatory of Music in 1980. Two years later he moved to New York, where he worked in John Hicks's big band until 1984; in August of that year he performed in Ronny Burrage's quintet in Washington, DC. Person began playing regularly in Chico Hamilton's small groups in 1983. He also spent periods in Ronald Shannon Jackson's Decoding Society (1984–7), Kelvyn Bell's Kelvynator (1988–93), the World Saxophone Quartet (1993–5), McCoy Tyner's big band (1994–6), and Dave Holland's quartet (1994–7), as well as with David Murray's big band, Woody Shaw, Michele Rosewoman, Onaje Allen Gumbs, Jean-Paul Bourelly, and the pianist John Esposito. In February 1990 he played with the New York Symphony Orchestra in a performance of Duke Ellington's *Three Black Kings* at the Apollo Theatre, and in the same year he worked with the pop singer Ofra Haza and the rock group Living Colour. While continuing his association with Hamilton (throughout the 1990s) he recorded with Franklin Kiermyer (1995), played with the slide guitarist and singer Ben Harper (from 1996), toured Europe with Michiel Borstlap (1997), and appeared in the television documentary "Blue Note: a Story of Modern Jazz" (1997). Person has led a number of his own groups, notably a quartet with the guitarist Cary Denigris, Kevin Bruce Harris, and Burrage, a duo with the tablā player Bob Coke (1987–91), and an eponymous quartet in which he played alongside Esposito, Kenny Davis, and Gene Jackson (1994–98); in 1999 he formed the group Meta-Four, which included Esposito and the drummer E. J. Strickland. In 1988 he joined the faculty of the New School for Social Research (from 1996 the Mannes/New School; from autumn 1999 the Jazz and Contemporary Music Program at the New School University), and in 1995–6 he taught at the Harlem School for the Arts and on the Jazzmobile.

SELECTED RECORDINGS

As leader: *Arrival* (1992, SN 121237-2); *Prophecy* (1992, SN 121287-2)
As sideman: C. Hamilton: *Arroyo* (1990, SN 121241-2); *Trio!* (1992, SN 121246-2); World Saxophone Quartet: *Moving Right Along* (1993, BS 120127-2); F. Kiermyer: *Kairos* (1995, Evidence 22144); D. Holland: *Dream of the Elders* (1995, ECM 1572)

BIBLIOGRAPHY

M. Tapley: "Eric Person is Sax-sational with New York Symphony at Apollo," *Amsterdam News* (3 March 1990)
S. Gribetz: "Hearsay: Eric Person," *JT*, xxiv/5 (1994), 15
M. J. Renner: "Dad's Sunday Jazz Lit Up Saxophonist Eric Person," *St. Louis Post-Dispatch* (15 May 1998)
<http://www.joyousshout.com> (1999)

GK

Person, Houston (Stafford, Jr.) (*b* Florence, SC, 10 Nov 1934). Tenor saxophonist. Although he was taught piano by his mother as a child, he took little interest in music until he began collecting jazz recordings and playing tenor saxophone at the age of 17. He studied for three years at South Carolina State College (in Orangeburg) and then during military service in Germany played in groups that included Eddie Harris, Lanny Morgan, Leo Wright, Cedar Walton, and Lex Humphries. He attended the Hartt School of Music in Hartford, Connecticut, and then toured with Johnny Hammond; from that time he showed a liking for working with organists. After leaving Hammond he formed his own group, which, with changing personnel, has made a number of recordings. He performed intermittently with Etta Jones from 1968 and from 1973 they worked together regularly, making nightclub and concert appearances. His touring group continued in the late 1980s and 1990s, with the pianist Stan Hope, the double bass player Peter Martin Weiss, and the drummer Cecil Brooks, III (replaced by Michael Carvin), among his longstanding sidemen. Besides his recordings as a leader, Person took part in many sessions as a sideman with Groove Holmes's quintet, Charles Earland, Shirley Scott, Jimmy McGriff, Jimmy Ponder, Johnny Lytle, Warren Vaché, Joey DeFrancesco, Junior Mance (for the Enja label), and others, and in duos with Ran Blake (for Soul Note) and Ron Carter. From the mid-1970s into the mid-1990s the vast majority of these recordings were on the Muse label, for which Person also served as a producer, usually in collaboration with Rudy van Gelder. The influence of rhythm-and-blues is evident in Person's direct, swinging style and full-toned sound; he performs blues and ballads with particular skill.

Video oral history material in *NCH* (HCJA).

SELECTED RECORDINGS

(recorded for Muse unless otherwise indicated)

Duos: with R. Blake: on *Suffield Gothic* (1983, SN 1077), Curtis, Vanguard, Midnight Local to Tate County; with R. Carter: *Something in Common* (1989, 5376); *Now's the Time* (1990, 5421)
As leader: *The Nearness of You* (1977, 5178); *Wild Flower* (1977, 5161); *Very Personal* (1980, 5231); *Basics* (1987, 5344); *The Party* (1989, 5451); with B. Tate and N. Simkins: *Just Friends* (1990, 5418); *Why Not!* (1990, 5433)
As sideman: E. Jones: *Love Me with All your Heart* (1983, 5262); G. Holmes: *Blues All Day Long* (1988, 5358)

BIBLIOGRAPHY

Feather–Gitler '70s
E. Cook: "'I Just Like People who Swing': Houston Person," *JJI*, xxxviii/1 (1985), 13
B. Franklin, V: "Houston Person: Interview," *Cadence*, xvi/8 (1990), 24
S. McElfresh: "Houston Person: Rehearsing for Tomorrow," *DB*, lviii/7 (1991), 27
J. Kaliss: "In Tune with Each Other: Vocalist Etta Jones, Instrumentalist Houston Person," *San Francisco Chronicle Datebook* (25 April 1993)

EDDIE COOK/BK

Persson, Åke [Kometen] (*b* Hässleholm, Sweden, 25 Feb 1932; *d* Stockholm, 5 Feb 1975). Swedish trombonist. Rich in imagination, with a virtuoso command of his instrument and an ever-present rhythmic spark, Persson was the first modern jazz trombonist in Sweden and immediately became a sought-after sideman and soloist. Early on he received the nickname Kometen (the Comet), referring both to his immediate rise to stardom at the age of 19 and to his confident style of playing. He worked with Simon Brehm (1951–2, recording in 1951–4), Arne Domnérus (1952–3, recording at intervals from 1952 to 1960), and Hacke Björksten (recording in 1955–7, performing in 1957) and was a member of Harry Arnold's Radiobandet (1956–9, recording in 1956–61). In 1953 he recorded two tracks with a sextet co-led by Frank Rosolino (who was then on tour with Stan Kenton); he also recorded as a co-leader with Gullin (1957) and with Benny Bailey and Joe Harris (ii) (1959), and as a sideman with Gullin (1951–7), Clifford Brown and Art Farmer (1953), George Wallington (1953), the Modern

Swedes and Roy Haynes (both 1954), and Stan Getz (1958). After playing in Quincy Jones's orchestra, in 1961 he joined the band of RIAS, Berlin, with which he remained until 1975; at the same time he played in the Clarke–Boland Big Band (recording in 1963 and 1967–71) and occasionally with Count Basie (recording in 1962), Duke Ellington, and Dizzy Gillespie.

SELECTED RECORDINGS

As leader: with F. Rosolino: Monotones/Don't Blame Me (1953, Karusell 33); with L. Gullin: *Lars Gullin & Åke Persson* (1957, Phi. P08202L); B. Bailey and J. Harris (ii): *Quincy, Here We Come* (1959, Met. 15030), incl. The Golden Touch

As sideman: C. Brown and A. Farmer: Cliff Brown & Art Farmer with the Swedish All Stars, i–ii (1953, Met. 18, 19) [EP]; L. Gullin: Piano Holiday (1953, Met. 34) [EP]; Modern Swedes: The Modern Swedes, i (1954, Met. 66) [EP]; R. Haynes: Little Leona (1954, Met. 90) [EP]; H. Björksten: Woodpecker's Groove/Gromek/On the Alamo (1955, Met. 167) [EP]; S. Getz: *Imported from Europe* (1958, Verve 8331); Clarke–Boland Big Band: *Sax No End* (1967, Saba 15138), incl. New Box

BIBLIOGRAPHY

FeatherE; *Feather–Gitler '70s*

C.-E. Lindgren: "Mannen med unikaboxen" [The man with the lunch-box], *Orkester journalen*, xliii/4 (1975), 10

Obituary, R. Dahlgren, *Orkester journalen*, xliii/3 (1975), 5

ERIK KJELLBERG/LARS WESTIN

Persson, Bent (*b* Blekinge, Sweden, 6 Sept 1947). Swedish cornetist. In the 1970s he played traditional jazz with Maggie's Blue Five and the Weatherbird Jazzband. He has been a member of Kustbandet (from 1974), with which he recorded *On Revival Day*, 1992–4, Stomp Off 1294), the Harlem Jazz Camels (from 1978), recording in 1986, 1993, and 1996, and the Swedish Jazz Kings (from 1985), which recorded with Roy Williams as guest soloist in 1994–6; he also worked in the 1980s as the leader of Bent's Blue Rhythm Band and collaborated with such American visitors as Maxine Sullivan, Doc Cheatham, Kenny Davern, Benny Carter, and Benny Waters. Persson is best known for his recording *Louis Armstrong's 50 Hot Choruses for Cornet* (i–ii, 1976–9, Kenneth 2044–5; iii–iv, 1986–92, Kenneth 3413), on which he performs recreations of solos by Armstrong.

BIBLIOGRAPHY

<http://www.mic.stim.se/engelsk/11/facts/perssonb.html> (1998)

L. Westin: "Bent Persson: Trogen tratitionen" [Bent Persson: Faithful to the tradition], *Orkester journalism*, lxviii/4 (2000), 2

PEKKA GRONOW

Petersen, Edward (Allen, III) (*b* Evanston, IL, 20 May 1952). Tenor saxophonist. His father was a musician. He learned clarinet from around the age of nine and then took up saxophone, on which he had classical lessons before he became interested in jazz. From 1970 to 1974 he studied at the University of Illinois, and during this period he toured with various big bands; later he completed his education at the Chicago campus of the university (BA 1978), where he then worked as a music teacher (1978–91). Petersen played locally in a quintet led by the pianist Art Hoyle (1978–94) and with the Jazz Members Big Band of Chicago (recording from 1983 to 1992) and Frank Mantooth's big band (*c*1990–91); in addition he worked with Wilbur Campbell's Jazz Express (1988–94), an educational group sponsored by the Chicago Institute of Jazz. In the 1990s he performed internationally and recorded with Kurt Elling (from 1991) and with the rhythm-and-blues singer Johnny Adams (1996–8, recording in 1996). Between 1986 and 1994 Petersen appeared weekly at the Green Mill as the leader of a small group, which at various times included Willie Pickens, Fareed Haque, and the double bass player Rob Amster; from 1987 to 1994 he led the Green Mill All Stars, and in 1991 he took his small group to the Red Sea Jazz Festival, where he also played with Eddie Harris. Later he formed the group Edward Petersen and the Test (1997). As a freelance he has performed extensively with Dizzy Gillespie, J. J. Johnson, Von Freeman, Johnny Griffin, Clifford Jordan, and Ellis Marsalis, and he has recorded with numerous local musicians, including the trumpeter Guy Fricano (1987), the pianist Don Bennett (1990), and Larry Gray and the pianist Larry Luchowski (both 1993).

In 1994 Peterson was awarded a master's degree in jazz pedagogy from Northwestern University, and in autumn of that year he began teaching music at the University of New Orleans. He has written chamber pieces for saxophone quartet and string quartet, and his company, Roving Bovine Music, has published a book of his compositions and two books of studies. He doubles on soprano saxophone and at times has played clarinet and flute.

SELECTED RECORDINGS

As leader: *Upward Spiral* (1989, Del. 445); *The Haint* (1994, Del. 474); with V. Freeman: *Von and Ed* (1998, Del. 508)

As sideman: D. Bennett: *Sleeping Giant* (1990, Southport 0012); L. Gray: *Solo + Quartet* (1993, Premonition 66917-7736); L. Luchowski: *Shadowplay* (1993, Lake Shore Jazz 006); K. Elling: on *Close your Eyes* (1994, BN B21Z-30645), Hurricane

BIBLIOGRAPHY

S. Aiges: "New Horn in Town Packs a Punch," *New Orleans Times-Picayune* (20 Jan 1995)

G. Wyckoff: "Jazz All-Stars: Contemporary," *New Orleans Magazine*, xxxii/7 (1998), 63

<http://www.uno.edu/~music/bios/petersen.htm> (1999)

GK

Peterson, Chuck [Charles Horace] (*b* Detroit, 18 Nov 1915; *d* Michigan, 21 Jan 1978). Trumpeter. His full name and date of birth appear in his application for social security. He played horn and trombone in his high school band, then changed to trumpet and worked with several local ensembles before joining a band led by Hank Biagini. In 1937 he became a member of Artie Shaw's band, with which he made several recordings (including *One Foot in the Groove*, 1939, Bb 10202) and appeared as a soloist on *I Have Eyes* in the short film *Artie Shaw's Class in Swing* (1939). After leaving Shaw he performed and recorded with Tony Pastor (1939–41), Tommy Dorsey (1939–42; for illustration *see* DORSEY, TOMMY), and Woody Herman (1941–2). Peterson served in the army, then returned to live and work in Detroit, though he took part in a Just Jazz concert in Pasadena, California (April 1947), and recorded with Herman's First Herd in Chicago (1946) and possibly with Benny Carter in Los Angeles (1949).

based on *ChiltonW*

Peterson, Hannibal (Marvin) [Marvin (Charles); Lokumbe, Hannibal; Hannibal] (*b* Smithville, TX, 11 Nov 1948). Trumpeter and composer. He learned drums and cornet in his youth and at the age of 14 formed a group, the Soul Masters, which accompanied such guest singers as Jackie Wilson, Etta James, and T-Bone Walker. While studying at North Texas State University (1967–9) he played trumpet in the college's renowned big band. In 1970 he moved to New York; he sat in with the Thad Jones–Mel Lewis orchestra (at Jones's invitation) and then made a tour of the East Coast with Roland Kirk. The following year he began playing with the Gil Evans Orchestra, an association that continued slightly beyond Evans's death early in 1988 in order to record a memorial album later that year. He performed and recorded with Pharoah Sanders (1971), Roy Haynes (*c*1972), and Elvin Jones (1973) and recorded with Richard Davis (1972, 1977), Eric Kloss (1973), Frank Foster and Grachan Moncur III (both 1974), and Billy Hart and Don Pullen (both 1977). In 1974 he formed his own band to present his composition *Children of the Fire*. From that time he played trumpet and *koto* as leader of the Sunrise Orchestra (a quintet or sextet with Diedre Murray and a conventional rhythm section) and other small ensembles, among them a free-jazz group with Enrico Rava, Roswell Rudd, Ken McIntyre, and Pat Patrick (1976). In 1977, at the festival in Antibes, France, his group included George Adams. Peterson was extremely ill in 1979 and traveled to Africa, where he was healed. He returned to the USA, resumed his career, and made further recordings as a leader in 1981. In 1983 he began working with John Hicks, and in 1984 he toured Britain in a quintet co-led by Don Weller and Bryan Spring and recorded with Adams as the co-leader of a sextet at a club in Zurich.

During the late 1980s and early 1990s Peterson performed in churches, prisons, and schools more often than in conventional jazz venues. Around the same time he took the name Hannibal Lokumbe, although he continues to appear as Hannibal Peterson or Hannibal Marvin Peterson in many sources. His composition *African Portraits*, for soloists, chorus, jazz group, and orchestra, was given its première at Carnegie Hall in 1990 and was performed and recorded at Orchestra Hall, Chicago, in May 1995. In 1991 Peterson served as a sideman in sessions led by Adams and by Andrew Cyrille, and in 1992 he played in Cyrille's band and performed and recorded in Japan as a member of the New York Unit, a quartet led by the drummer Tatsuya Nakamura, with Hicks and Davis as fellow sidemen. He left New York temporarily around 1993, visited South Dakota to gain permission from the Lakota tribe to write a piece, *Dance Chief Crazy Horse Dance*, for the Kronos String Quartet, and then spent a period in Texas. In August 1994 he again performed and recorded with the New York Unit in Japan. His play *Diary of an African-American* was given its first performance at the World Jazz Festival in Washington, DC, in July 1995, and the following year he acted in *Portrait of the Artist as a Soul Man Dead* in St. Paul, Minnesota. In 1999 he began a three-year stint in New Orleans as composer-in-residence in the "Pathways to Connections" concert series, involving the Contemporary Arts Center and the Louisiana Philharmonic Orchestra; his tenure began early that year with a combined concert of classical chamber music and jazz. Peterson is the subject of a video documentary, *Kiss on the Bridge*, released in 1990.

As a trumpet soloist, Peterson sometimes interrupts carefully articulated hard-bop melodies with piercing sweeps through the upper register of the instrument. His preference for combining aspects of hard bop, modal jazz, and free jazz extends also to his choice of repertory and sidemen: on the album *Naima*, for example (recorded with Kenny Barron, Cecil McBee, Billy Hart, and David Murray in 1978), the musicians improvise in a bop manner on the standard *In a Sentimental Mood*, whereas the title track involves them in freer playing. From the 1990s his principal creations have been large-scale works, but during this period he made perhaps his finest recordings centered in the hard-bop tradition (and, as before, incorporating elements of later styles), as a sideman on Cyrille's album *My Friend Louis* (1991).

SELECTED RECORDINGS

As leader: *Children of the Fire* (1974, Sunrise 1944); *Hannibal* (1975, MPS 15444); *Naima* (1978, EMI 98004); *The Angels of Atlanta* (1981, Enja 3085); with G. Adams: *More Sightings* (1984, Enja 4084); [as Hannibal Lokumbe] *African Portraits* (1995, Teldec 4509-98802)

As sideman: P. Sanders: *Black Unity* (1971, Imp. 9219); R. Davis: *Epistrophy and Now's the Time* (1972, Muse 5002); R. Haynes: *Senyah* (*c*1972, Mstr. 351); A. Cyrille: *My Friend Louis* (1991, DIW 858)

BIBLIOGRAPHY

Feather–GitlerBEJ

P. Carles and F. Marmande: "Six vois dans la ville: Marvin Peterson," *Jm*, no.215 (1973), 36

L. Goddet: "Interview: Hannibal," *Jh*, no.304 (1974), 11

G. Endress: "Hannibal Marvin Peterson," *JP*, xxiv/5 (1975), 14

B. J. Primack: "Hannibal," *DB*, xliv/15 (1977), 24

B. Höhne: "Hannibal Marvin Peterson: Visionen einer neuen Welt," *JP*, xxxix/9 (1990), 22

G. Endress: "Hannibal: die Geschichte der Schwarzen in Amerika, dargestellt in grenzüberschreitender Musik," *JP*, xliv/12 (1995), 12

J. Mischke: "Hannibal Lokumbe," *Jazzthetik*, ix/12–x/1 (1995–6), 30

L. Van Trikt: "Marvin 'Hannibal' Peterson," *Cadence*, xxii/3 (1996), 5

T. P. Mahne: "Music: Establishing Roots," *New Orleans Times-Picayune* (14 Jan 1999)

<http://www.rojac.co.at/hannibal> (2000) [incl. discography, bibliography]

BK

Peterson, Oscar (Emmanuel) (*b* Montreal, 15 Aug 1925). Canadian pianist and leader. He took up trumpet and piano at the age of five, and three years later, after overcoming tuberculosis, he commenced classical piano lessons. When he was 14 he won a local talent contest. A high school classmate of Maynard Ferguson, he played on a weekly Montreal radio show during his late teens and from 1944 to 1947 was heard with Canada's well-known Johnny Holmes Orchestra, playing in a style that blended elements from the styles of Teddy Wilson, Art Tatum, Nat "King" Cole, Erroll Garner, and others. In 1948–9 he led a trio in Montreal. Norman Granz invited him to appear at Carnegie Hall in September 1949 in a Jazz at the Philharmonic concert and

Oscar Peterson's trio playing at Basin Street, Toronto: Peterson (piano), Herb Ellis (guitar), and Ray Brown (double bass)

from that time onwards managed Peterson's career. Peterson toured regularly with Jazz at the Philharmonic during the early 1950s, initially working in a duo with Ray Brown. In 1952 he formed his own trio using the combination popularized by Cole of piano, guitar (Irving Ashby), and double bass (Brown). Soon afterwards Ashby gave way to Barney Kessel, who disliked touring but agreed to stay for one year. Peterson's most popular trio, the other members of which were Herb Ellis (guitar) and Brown, remained together from 1953 until 1958 (see illustration), apart from a period in the spring of 1955 when Ellis was ill and Kenny Burrell took his place. Ellis was eventually replaced by a drummer, Gene Gammage, in November 1958. Ed Thigpen replaced Gammage at the new year, and in this form the group, considered by many to have been the ideal vehicle for Peterson's unique talents, remained intact from 1959 until 1965. Louis Hayes took over the drum chair from 1965 to 1967 and not long afterwards Brown left; Sam Jones succeeded Brown from February 1966 to 1970 and Bobby Durham replaced Hayes in 1967.

In 1960, with Brown, Thigpen, and Phil Nimmons, Peterson established the Advanced School of Contemporary Music in Toronto, which he ran for three years. He sang for the first time since the mid-1950s on the album *With Respect to Nat* (1965), dedicated to Cole. Peterson turned his attention to solo performances in the mid-1960s, when he began to record unaccompanied for the SABA label in Germany, and in the early 1970s he proved incontestably that he was one of the greatest solo pianists in the history of jazz. From the mid-1970s he played with symphony orchestras throughout North America and joined established jazz musicians such as Dizzy Gillespie, Clark Terry, Joe Pass, and Niels-Henning Ørsted Pedersen for a number of memorable duo performances (for illustration *see* ØRSTED PEDERSEN, NIELS-HENNING), many of them recorded by Granz for Pablo Records; from the mid-1970s his touring group often included Martin Drew. In 1980 he hosted the television series "Oscar Peterson and Friends," featuring such guests as Mary Lou Williams, Roy Eldridge, Eddie "Cleanhead" Vinson, and Gillespie. In 1985 he joined the faculty of York University as an adjunct professor of music and in 1991 became chancellor of the university. However, serious illness, including a severe stroke in 1993, greatly reduced his activities. Although he sometimes found it difficult to sustain his usual exuberance and was largely unable to use his left hand, he nonetheless continued performing, making new recordings, and touring Europe. In May 1995 he gave a concert at Carnegie Hall. By that time he had recovered considerable use of his left hand, and he performed with increasing flexibility into the late 1990s, making tours as the leader of a quartet comprising Ulf Wakenius, Ørsted Pedersen, and Drew.

Peterson was a prolific recording artist, having issued as many as five or six albums a year. He was also active as a jazz composer (his *Canadiana Suite* was nominated by the National Academy of Recording Arts and Sciences as one of the best jazz compositions of 1965; his principal publisher was Hansen). Because of his extraordinary technique and his comprehensive grasp of jazz piano history, he is often compared with Art Tatum, with whom he shares an exceptional gift for inspiring awe from musicians, critics, and listeners alike, but this oft-cited relationship is perhaps exaggerated. Tatum, the more original player and a true genius of jazz harmony, was often rhythmically four-square or unswinging, and so self-centered that he was almost incapable of working well in a group and especially unwilling to support other soloists when their turn came. By contrast, Peterson spent much of his career playing quite comfortably in duos and trios, and, despite his potentially intimidating individual skills, he was fully capable of subsuming his role to that of accompanist, as may be heard in numerous sessions which he made as the virtual house pianist for Granz's recording companies. Never a pathbreaker stylistically, he also differed drastically from Tatum in his ongoing concern for generating a sense of continuous, hard-driving swing.

Oral history material in *DSI* (JOHP); video oral history material in *NCH* (HCJA).

SELECTED RECORDINGS

As unaccompanied soloist: *My Favorite Instrument* (1968, MPS 15181); *Tracks* (1970, MPS 15306); *Live At Salle Pleyel, Paris* (1975, Pablo 2625705) [incl. duos with J. Pass]

Duos: with R. Brown: Tenderly (1950, Clef 8917); with D. Gillespie: *Oscar Peterson and Dizzy Gillespie* (1974, Pablo 2310740)

As leader: *The Oscar Peterson Trio at the Stratford Shakespearean Festival* (1956, Verve 8024); *The Oscar Peterson Trio at the Concertgebouw* (1958, Verve 8268); *Affinity* (1962, Verve 68516); *Night Train* (1962, Verve 68538); *Live in Tokyo* (1964, Pablo [Jap.] 9055–6); *The Oscar Peterson Trio Plus One: Clark Terry* (1964, Mer. 60975); *With Respect to Nat* (1965, Lml. 86029); *The Way I Really Play* (1968, MPS 15180); *Oscar Peterson in Russia* (1974, Pablo 2625711); *Face to Face* (1982, Pablo 2310876); *If You Could See Me Now* (1983, Pablo 2310918); *Live at the Blue Note* (1989, Telarc 83304); *Fallin' in Love with Oscar* (1994, Jazz Door 1276)

As sideman: B. Carter: *Cosmopolite* (1952, Clef 141); D. Gillespie and S. Getz: *Diz and Getz* (1953, Norg. 1050); B. Webster: *Soulville* (1957, Verve 8274); S. Getz and J. J. Johnson: *Stan Getz and J. J. Johnson at the Opera House* (1957, Verve 8265); S. Stitt: *Sonny Stitt Sits in with the Oscar Peterson Trio* (1959, Verve 8344); B Webster: *Ben Webster Meets Oscar Peterson and his Trio* (1959, Verve 8349)

SELECTED FILMS AND VIDEOS

The Nat King Cole Show (n.d. [filmed *c*1956]); Oscar Peterson Trio (1958); The Performer (1959); Jazz USA, no. 5 (1960); Newport Jazz Festival 1962 (1962); Jazz 625 (*c*1964); Jazz at the Maltings (*c*1969); Jazz Scene at Ronnie Scott's (*c*1969); The South Bank Show: Oscar Peterson (1984); Music in the Key of Oscar (1992); Norman Granz présente improvisation: documents exceptionnels et inédits des plus grands noms de jazz (n.d.)

BIBLIOGRAPHY

EMC2

B. James: "Oscar Peterson," *Essays on Jazz* (London, 1961/*R*1990, with new foreword and index), 134

D. Ioakmidis: "Oscar Peterson: une lente maturation?," *Jh*, no.177 (1962), 20

A. Johnson and L. Tomkins: "Oscar Peterson: my Approach to Playing," *Crescendo*, ii/9 (1964), 10

R. Palmer: "Oscar Peterson," *JJ*, xxi/3 (1968), 4

L. Feather: *From Satchmo to Miles* (New York, 1972/*R*1987), 187

L. Lyons: "Oscar Peterson: Piano Worship," *DB*, xlii/21 (1975), 12

S. Quaver: "Oscar Peterson: the History of an Artist," *CI*, xiii (1975), no.8, p.17; no.9, p.17; no.10, p.16

L. Feather: "Piano Giants of Jazz: Oscar Peterson," *CK*, iv/7 (1978), 53

L. Lyons: "Oscar Peterson," *CK*, iv/3 (1978), 30

R. Palmer: "Oscar Peterson: Genesis and Revelation," *JJI*, xxxiv (1981), no.7, p.8; no.8, p.6; no.10, p.6

J. Litchfield: *The Canadian Jazz Discography, 1916–1980* (Toronto, Buffalo, and London, 1982), 552–640

G. Armbruster: "Oscar Peterson: a Jazz Piano Giant Talks about his Synthesizer Debut," *Keyboard*, ix/10 (1983), 56 [incl. discography]

L. Lyons: *The Great Jazz Pianists, Speaking of their Lives and Music* (New York, 1983), 130

R. Palmer: *Oscar Peterson* (Tunbridge Wells, England, 1984) [incl. discography]

S. L. Larson: *Schenkerian Analysis of Modern Jazz*, i–iii (diss., U. of Michigan, 1987) [incl. transcrs.]

M. Miller: *Boogie, Pete & the Senator: Canadian Musicians in Jazz: the Eighties* (Toronto, 1987)

G. Lees: *Oscar Peterson: the Will to Swing* (Toronto, 1988)

F. Postif: *Les grandes interviews de Jazz hot* (Paris, 1989)

J. McDonough: "Oscar Peterson: the Best Of Intentions," *DB*, lviii/1 (1991), 26 [incl. discography]

F. Fini and L. Rigazio: *The Oscar Peterson Discography* (Imola, Italy, 1992)

R. Palmer: "Oscar Peterson: the Surviving Titan," *Jazz CD*, i/2 (n.d [1992]), 11

M. Haywood: "Force, Mass and Acceleration in Oscar Peterson," *Jf*, xxvi (1994), 109
B. Blumenthal: "Recovery & Renewal: Oscar," *JT*, xxv/4 (1995), 26
F. Krieger: "Jazz-Solopiano: zum Stilwandel am Beispiel ausgewaehlter *Body and Soul*: Aufnehmen von 1938–1992," *Jf*, xxvii (1995), 5 [incl. transcrs.]
K. Grosen: *In the Key of Oscar: Oscar Peterson on LP/CD* (Lunderskov, Denmark, 1996)
M. Miller: *Such Melodious Racket: the Lost History of Jazz in Canada, 1914–1949* (Toronto, n.d. [1997]), 241
D. Ouellette: "Oscar Winner: Even a Stroke Couldn't Keep Jazz Pianist Peterson from the Keys," *San Francisco Chronicle Datebook* (16 Aug 1998)
A. Shipton: "Oscar Winning," *Piano*, viii/2 (2000), 22

BILL DOBBINS/BK

Peterson, Ralph, Jr. (*b* Pleasantville, NJ, 20 May 1962). Drummer and leader. His father and his uncles were drummers. He grew up in Atlantic City and began playing drums when he was about three; he is primarily self-taught. From around the age of nine he had trumpet lessons in order to learn to read music, and later he played the instrument in high school bands. As a drummer he performed mainly in local funk bands, but in 1975, after seeing Sonny Payne with Count Basie's orchestra, he became interested in jazz, and he began playing in jazz groups when he was about 18. Having failed an entrance examination on drums he enrolled in a trumpet performance course at the Livingston College campus of Rutgers, but in his second year he changed to study both percussion and trumpet; he received tuition from Kenny Barron, Paul Jeffrey (composition), and Michael Carvin (drums). In 1983 he was selected by Art Blakey to be the second drummer in the Jazz Messengers' big band, and he subsequently performed with the group at the Boston Globe Jazz Festival and in 1988 at the Mt. Fuji Jazz Festival in Japan. Peterson recorded with the quintet of Terence Blanchard and Donald Harrison in December 1984, and the following year he began working with Walter Davis, with whom he recorded in 1989. From 1985 to 1988 he was a member of OTB. In addition he worked regularly with David Murray's quartet, octet, and big band, Craig Harris's Tailgater band (recording in 1987), and Jon Faddis's small group (recording in 1989), and deputized in Wynton Marsalis's group (for Jeff "Tain" Watts) and in the Basie ghost band. After performing in a trio with Dewey Redman and Mark Helias (1989), in the early 1990s he worked with Jack Walrath (*c*1990), Craig Handy (*c*1991–3), and Charles Lloyd (recording in 1992), and toured North America with Courtney Pine (spring 1990). Later he performed in Europe as a member of Steve Coleman's Renegade Way (August 1995) and spent seven months in Betty Carter's group (*c*1997).

Peterson has also been active as a leader. He led the quintet V (also known as Volition) from 1988 to around 1992, with Blanchard, Steve Wilson, Geri Allen, and Phil Bowler as his sidemen, and toured Scandinavia with the group in 1991. During the late 1980s he worked with Allen and Bowler in the trio Triangular, although Essiett Essiett replaced Bowler when the group recorded in 1988. In late 1989 he established his Fo'tet, a quartet with Don Byron, Steve Wilson or Bobby Franchesini, Melissa Slocum or Belden Bullock, and Bryan Carrott. Having moved from Edmonton, Canada, to Philadelphia (*c*1992) he continued to lead his Fo'tet and formed the group Triangular Too (mid-1990s), with Uri Caine and Slocum, and the quartet Hip Pocket, in which he plays trumpet. He has recorded with Tom Harrell (1985), Branford Marsalis (1986), James Spaulding (1988), Roy Hargrove (1989), Byron (1990–91), Kip Hanrahan (1992), Caine (1992, 1995), Bheki Mseleku, the pianist George Colligan, and Stanley Cowell (all 1995), and Mark Shim (1997). He has taught at the University of the Arts in Philadelphia.

For illustration *see* RECORDING, fig.6.

SELECTED RECORDINGS

As leader: *V* (1988, BN B21Y-91730); *Triangular* (1988, BN B21Z-92750); *Volition* (1989, BN B21Y-93894); *Ralph Peterson Presents the Fo'tet* (1989, BN B21Z-95475); *Ornettology* (1990, BN B21Z-98290); *Art* (1992, BN B21Z-27645); *The Reclamation Project* (1994, Evidence 22113); *The Fo'tet Plays Thelonious Monk* (1995, Evidence 22174)
As sideman: D. Murray: *New Life* (1985, BS 0100); T. Harrell: *Moon Alley* (1985, Criss Cross 1018); D. Harrison and T. Blanchard: *Nascence* (1986, Col. BFC40335); D. Murray: *Ballads* (1988, DIW 8040); *Tenors* (1988, DIW 881); J. Spaulding: *Gotstabe a Better Way* (1988, Muse 5413); W. Davis: *Scorpio Rising* (1989, Ste. 31255); R. Hargrove: *Diamond in the Rough* (1989, Novus 3082-2-N); M. Rosewoman: *Occasion to Rise* (1990, Evidence 22042); A. Cox: *Factor of Faces* (1992, Minor Music 801035); C. Handy: *Introducing Three for All + One* (1993, Arabesque 0109); U. Caine: *Toys* (1995, JMT 514022-2); G. Colligan: *Activism* (1995, Ste. 31382); M. Shim: *Mind over Matter* (1997, BN 37628-2)

For further recordings *see* OTB.

BIBLIOGRAPHY

GrayF
W. F. Miller: "Up and Coming: Ralph Peterson, Jr.," *MD*, x/5 (1986), 58
C. Deffaa: "Ralph Peterson, Jr.: the Drummer as a Leader," *JT* (1988), Oct, 18
J. Macnie: "V is for Volcano: Ralph Peterson Plays More than One Roll," *Musician*, no.138 (1990), 20
K. Whitehead: "Ralph Peterson: Man and his Cymbals," *DB*, lvii/7 (1990), 22 [incl. discography]
S. Gribetz: "Ralph Peterson: Eyes and Ears on the Past and Future," *JT*, xxi/8 (1991), 20
K. Micallef: "Ralph Peterson: Pushing the Limits of Bop," *MD*, xv/2 (1991), 28
M. Smith: "Ralph Peterson Interview," *Cadence*, xvii/8 (1991), 5
J. Pareles: "Drumming with Muscle and Wit," *New York Times* (24 July 1992)
L. Van Trikt: "Ralph Peterson Interview," *Cadence*, xxii/7 (1996), 22
K. Kean: "Riffs: Lessons Borrowed from Hip-hop," *DB*, lxiv/2 (1997), 39
K. Micallef: "Profile: Ralph Peterson: Filling the Hole," *Jazziz*, xiv/10 (1997), 76
<http://www.allaboutjazz.com/iviews/ralphp.htm> (1998)

GK

Pethman, Esa (*b* Kouvola, Finland, 17 May 1938). Finnish tenor saxophonist, flutist, and composer. He played with Erkki Melakoski's band (1959–63), and in 1962 formed a quartet with his brother, the drummer Anssi Pethman, and Heikki Sarmanto. He performed at the Landskrona (1963) and Montreux (1967) jazz festivals. Pethman combines a flowing style of playing with an ability to create original jazz compositions using unusual forms and instrumental colors. His work is well represented by the album *The Modern Sound of Finland* (1964, RCA LSP10040).

Oral history material in *FiHJ*.

PEKKA GRONOW

Petit, Buddy [Buddie; Crawford, Joseph] (*b* White Castle, LA, *c*1897; *d* New Orleans, 4 July 1931). Cornetist and bandleader. His original name was Joseph Crawford, but he took the surname of his stepfather, the trombonist Joseph Petit. He began attracting favorable attention with his cornet playing in New Orleans while he was still a teenager. Having formed the Young Olympians, which included Sidney Bechet, in 1914, upon the departure of Freddie Keppard from the city, he became joint leader of the Young Olympia Band with Jimmie Noone (whose place was later taken by Albert Nicholas). In February 1918 he played briefly in San Diego, California, with Jelly Roll Morton; he then returned to New Orleans and formed his own band, which worked in Texas and for the next ten years had long-term engagements in several Louisiana towns, among them Mandeville and Covington. The band also worked regularly in New Orleans and occasionally in Florida. Edmond Hall was Petit's clarinetist from 1920 to 1922, when Hall left and George Lewis (i) joined. Petit himself paid another short visit to California around 1922 as a member of Frankie Dusen's band. By the late 1920s he was working aboard the SS *Madison.*

There are no recorded examples of Petit's playing, which over the years has taken on legendary qualities. From the testimony of his colleagues there can be no doubt that he was an exceptional musician, remembered even more for his tone and expressive ideal than for his range. Several New Orleans trumpeters, including Punch Miller, Herb Morand, and Wingy Manone, cited Petit as an influence.

For illustration *see* Bands, fig.2.

BIBLIOGRAPHY

J. De Donder: "My Buddy," *Fn*, xiv/3 (1983), 24; xiv/4 (1983), 4

L. Gushee: "A Preliminary Chronology of the Early Career of Ferd 'Jelly Roll' Morton," *American Music*, iii (1985), 389; repr. in *Sv*, no.127 (1986), 11

M. Selchow: *Profoundly Blue: a Bio-discographical Scrapbook on Edmond Hall* (Lübbecke, Germany, 1988), 23

R. H. Knowles: *Fallen Heroes: a History of New Orleans Brass Bands* (New Orleans, 1996)

JOHN CHILTON/BK

Petit, Joseph (*b* New Orleans, 1873; *d* New Orleans, 1946). Trombonist, stepfather of Buddy Petit. Before World War I he led the Security and Terminal brass bands, then in the early 1920s worked with Wooden Joe Nicholas's Camellia Orchestra and Brass Band. He recorded, with Nicholas, as a member of the Original Creole Stompers for the American Music label in 1945. (*ChartersJ*)

MARCEL JOLY

Petrahn, Sean. Nom de plume of Jack Reilly.

Petrin, Umberto (*b* Broni, nr Pavia, Italy, 15 May 1960). Italian pianist. He learned piano from the age of six and when he was 18 began to write poetry and literary reviews – his main creative work until he discovered jazz; he published several books of poetry and from 1980 was employed in the field of contemporary visual arts as a writer and critic. In 1984 he formed a jazz trio, and in 1986 his involvement in the music grew as he played with a quartet and occasionally with the RAI Big Band in Milan. He recorded his first album of music and poetry in 1987. In 1989 he played with Tiziana Ghiglioni and formed a duo with the trumpeter Guido Mazzon. As a sideman he appeared with Steve Lacy, Paul Lovens, and Paul Rutherford. In 1993 he played in a duo with the guitarist Lanfranco Malaguti and in Ghiglioni's Tenco project. From 1995 he played the music of Alexander Scriabin and Richard Strauss in a duo with Lee Konitz, and that same year he formed a trio with Tiziano Tononi. Petrin replaced Giorgio Gaslini as the pianist in the Italian Instabile Orchestra in 1997, and the following year he worked on north Italian folk music in the theater and as a poet. He also joined Stefano Maltese's Open Music Orchestra and formed a duo with the singer Gioconda Cilio.

Influenced by Lennie Tristano's late style, and by his involvement in literary genres, Petrin's improvising has a strong structural coherence, based on persistent motivic development, angular sounds (after the manner of Thelonious Monk), and harmonic freedom. In trio settings his playing shows the influence of John Coltrane.

SELECTED RECORDINGS

(recorded for Splasc(h) unless otherwise indicated)

As unaccompanied soloist: *Ooze* (1992, 384); *Monk's World* (1997, 619)

Duos: with L. Malaguti: *Percorsi* (1993, 419); with L. Konitz: *Breaths and Whispers* (1995, Philology 75); with T. Berne: *Ellissi* (1999, 806)

As leader: with G. Mazzon: *Other Line* (1990, 317); *Wirrwarr* (1996, 481)

As sideman: T. Ghiglioni: *S.O.N.B.* (1992, 370); *Canta Luigi Tenco* (1993, Philology 60); Italian Instabile Orchestra: *Italian Instabile Festival* (1997, Leo 262–3); [various artists]: *A Night in Italy* (1997, Musica Jazz 1117)

BIBLIOGRAPHY

<http://www.ijm.it/enartists.html> (1999)

<http://www.shef.ac.uk/misc/rec/ps/efi/minstab.html> (1999)

STEFANO ZENNI

Petrovic, Boško (*b* Bjelovar, Yugoslavia, 18 Feb 1935). Yugoslav vibraphonist. He started on violin at the age of seven and later played accordion, piano, and, at the age of 15, drums. In 1950 he formed his first group, in which he played violin. Around 1956 he took up vibraphone, and in 1959 he formed the Zagreb Jazz Quartet, which interpreted the music of his homeland; the group continued as a quintet in 1968–9, after a one-year hiatus, and in 1970 again became a quartet, which through the decade was regarded as the best jazz group in Yugoslavia. In 1970 Petrovic formed the group B. P. Convention, with which he toured internationally, and from around the same time he led the Nonconvertible All Stars (recording in 1971), which at times included Michal Urbaniak, Zbigniew Seifert, and Ernst-Ludwig Petrowsky. As a sideman he performed with John Lewis, Stan Getz, Gerry Mulligan, Art Farmer, Albert Mangelsdorff, and Svend Asmussen, among many others, and from mid-1985 he worked in a duo with the Croatian pianist Neven Franges. In 1991 his quartet performed and recorded with Clark Terry in Austria. Petrovic also hosted jazz shows on radio and television. In the late 1990s he was living in Zagreb, Croatia, where he ran the record company Jazzette and led the B. P. All Stars, which served as the house band at his own jazz venue, the B. P. Club.

SELECTED RECORDINGS

Duos with N. Franges: *Un chien andalou* (1986, Jazzette 003)

As leader: of Zagreb Jazz Quartet: *In Concert* (1965, Jazzette 002); *With Pain I Was Born* (1965, Fon. 900); of Non-Convertible Eastern All Stars: *From Europe with Jazz* (1971, MPS 15369); of Convention Big Band: *Blue Sunset* (1975, Jugoton 63041)

As sideman: [no leader]: *After Midnight*, i (*c*1991, Jazzette 012); [no leader]: *Loverman: Ballads for Dreamers* (1991–2, Jazzette 013)

BIBLIOGRAPHY

Feather–Gitler '70s

J.-L. Ginibre and P. Carles: "Dictionnaire du vibraphone," *Jm*, no.151 (1968), 44

M. Kunzler: *Jazz-Lexicon* (Reinbek, nr Hamburg, Germany, 1988)

<http://jazz.ring.net/bpclub/bosko.html> (1999) [incl. discography]

GK

Petrowsky, Ernst-Ludwig (*b* Güstrow, Germany, 10 Dec 1933). German reed player, flutist, and leader. Having learned violin as a child, in the 1950s he took up reed instruments and played dance music and music for the theater. He first played jazz in a small group (1955–7) and a big band (1957–60), both led by the pianist Eberhard Weise, after which he worked in Max Reichelt's Tanz- und Showorchester (1960–61). In 1962, with Manfred Schulze, he formed a hard-bop group, the Manfred Ludwig Sextet; it recorded in 1963 and 1964, and in 1964 accompanied and recorded with the singer Dorothy Ellison. In the mid-1960s Petrowsky was a sideman in the big band led by Klaus Lenz and played with Joachim Kühn, whom he names as an important influence. In 1966 he was a founding member of the jazz ensemble Studio IV, which mainly broadcast on radio, but it also recorded in 1966, 1969, and 1979; Klaus Koch was also in this group. Throughout the 1970s Petrowsky played in the Radio Big-Band Berlin (which again included Koch). He worked in Ulrich Gumpert's jazz-rock group SOK, (1971–3, alongside Günter Sommer), in Boško Petrovic's group the Nonconvertible All Stars (recording in 1971), and again in big bands led by Lenz (recording in 1974). In 1973, with Conrad Bauer, Gumpert, and Sommer, he founded the cooperative group Synopsis; it was active until 1979 and then, under Sommer's impetus, re-formed in 1984 as the Zentral-Quartett. In the late 1970s Petrowsky also worked in Gumpert's Workshop Band (recording in 1978–9) and performed and recorded (1979) in Europe as a member of John Carter's group Clarinet Summit.

Petrowsky led various trios with Koch on double bass, in which they were joined by Sommer (1972–9), the church organist Hans-Günter Wauer (from 1976), the flugelhorn player Heinz Becker (1979–83), and Helmut "Joe" Sachse (from 1983); the first trio, with Sommer, performed on occasion as a quartet with the addition of Becker (it recorded in 1979), and the third, with Becker, as a quartet with the addition of Sachse. In 1979 he led an octet at the International New Jazz Festival Moers, and from 1980 until 1988 (shortly before it disbanded) he was a member of the Globe Unity Orchestra. In the early 1980s he formed a duo with his wife, Uschi Brüning, joined George Gruntz's Concert Jazz Band, and (together with Rüdiger Carl, Hans Reichel, and Sven-Åke Johansson) toured internationally (including performances in Japan and the USA in 1982, when they recorded as the Bergisch–Brandenburgisches Quartett). He joined the European Jazz Ensemble in 1982 and performed in a large ensemble led by George Lewis (ii) at the International New Jazz Festival Moers the following year. In the late 1980s he was a founding member of the successor to the Globe Unity Orchestra, the Berlin Contemporary Jazz Orchestra. From the early 1990s Petrowsky concentrated on his duo with Brüning, and he continued to work with her and with the Zentral-Quartett into the new century. In 1999 he appeared at Jazzfest Berlin in the trio Alliance, with the saxophonist Thomas Borgmann, and in Gumpert's Workshop Band, and in 2000 he performed at the Total Music Meeting in the Preussisches Trio, consisting of Alex Schlippenbach and the drummer Achim Trampenau.

Petrowsky plays clarinet, flute, and soprano, alto, and tenor saxophones, and in his duos with Brüning he has recorded on zither. His work on saxophone suggests the influence of Ornette Coleman but is tempered by the cool-jazz style of both Chet Baker and Lee Konitz; he is one of the finest free-jazz flute players.

SELECTED RECORDINGS

(recorded for FMP unless otherwise indicated)

Duos with U. Brüning: *Das neue Usel* (1986, S18); *Features of Usel* (1992, OWN90001)

As leader: on [various artists]: *Snapshot Jazz Now: Jazz aud der DDR* (1979, SP1), Enfant, Talar; *Selb-Viert* (1979, 0760); *Selb-Dritt* (1980, 0890); *Bergisch-Brandenburgisches Quartett* (1982, Amiga 856031)

As sideman: U. Gumpert: *Echoes von Karolinenhof* (1979, 0710); H. Becker: *Pan-vielleicht Tau* (1982, 1010); European Jazz Ensemble: *European Jazz Ensemble at the Philharmonic Cologne* (1989, MA Music 800-2); Zentral-Quartett: *Plie* (1994, Intakt 037); *Careless Love* (1997, Intakt 050)

SELECTED FILMS AND VIDEOS

European Jazz Ensemble: Jazz vor Mitternacht (n.d.); Festival de Viersen 87 (n.d.); European Jazz Ensemble: 10th Leverkusener Jazztage '89 (n.d.)

BIBLIOGRAPHY

CarrJ; *GrayF*; *ReclamsJ*

"Swinging News," *JF* [intl edn], no.20 (1972), 23

"Eurojazz Personalities," *JF* [intl edn], no.27 (1974), 67

J. Kalwa: "Die Jazz-Musiker sind keine Aussenseiter," *Neue Musikzeitung*, xxvii/5 (1978), 12

H. Kumpf: "Ernst Ludwig Petrowsky," *JP*, xxx/1 (1981), 14

B. Noglik: "Ernst-Ludwig Petrowsky, Günter Sommer," *Jazzwerkstatt international* (Berlin, 1981, 2/1983) [incl. discography]

——: "Ernst Ludwig Petrowsky," *JP*, xxxiii/1 (1984), 33

E. Jost: *Europas Jazz, 1960–1980* (Frankfurt am Main, Germany, 1987)

P. Carles, A. Clergeat, and J.-L. Comolli: *Dictionnaire du jazz* (Paris, 1988, rev. and enlarged 2/1994)

M. Kunzler: *Jazz-Lexicon* (Reinbek, nr Hamburg, Germany, 1988)

J. Corbett: "Ernst-Ludwig Petrowsky: Interview," *Cadence*, xv/9 (1989), 16

BERT NOGLIK/GK

Petrucciani, Michel (*b* Orange, France, 28 Dec 1962; *d* New York, 5 Jan 1999). French pianist. His father, Antoine Petrucciani, is a jazz guitarist, and his elder brothers Philippe and Louis play, respectively, guitar and double bass. He learned classical piano from the age of four and was playing with the family band at around the age of nine; he gave his first concert with this group at the age of 13 and played with Kenny Clarke in 1977 and Clark Terry in 1978. When he was 17 he moved to Paris, where he recorded his first album. Around the same time he began working with Lee Konitz. In 1981 he traveled to California and became associated with Charles Lloyd, who was encouraged to come out of retirement by the strength of Petrucciani's playing and his irrepressible exuberance; their performance at the Montreux International Jazz Festival won the *prix d'excellence* in 1982. Petrucciani began receiving acclaim in the USA after his appearance at Carnegie Recital Hall in 1983 as part of the Kool Jazz Festival. He led a trio, which in the 1980s consisted first of Jean-François Jenny-Clark and Aldo Romano (this group recorded in the Netherlands in 1981), then of Palle Danielsson and Eliot Zigmund (with whom he recorded in 1984–5 and made a videotape in a quartet, with the addition of Jim Hall, at the Village Vanguard in 1986). These sidemen were succeeded by Andy McKee and Zigmund, Gary Peacock and Roy Haynes, and Eddie Gomez and Al Foster; an album was recorded in 1987 by these last two trios. Petrucciani was celebrated in 1985 in a five-day festival in Paris, where he performed with his first two trios, as well as with guest artists Hall and John Abercrombie; the following year he appeared at the Montreux festival with Hall and Wayne Shorter. From 1989 to 1992 he led a quartet (or quintet) that included Adam Holzman on synthesizer. While continuing to tour internationally through the 1990s, mainly as an unaccompanied soloist and freelance trio leader, Petrucciani made New York his home. He also led a group which brought a string quartet together with his trio, then made up of his brother Louis on double bass and Lenny White on drums, and another band oriented towards electronic funk and African percussion. In 1995 he recorded in a trio with his father and Louis. The lifelong debilitating effects of the congential disease osteogenesis imperfecta ("glass bones") led to his death from pneumonia at the age of 37.

Petrucciani's style combined the lyricism and thoughtful harmonic approach of Bill Evans (ii) with a technical

Charles Lloyd carrying Michel Petrucciani at the Grande Parade du Jazz, Nice, France, 1983

assurance comparable with that of Oscar Peterson. During performances he often extemporized medleys of standards and his own compositions linked by freely improvised transitional passages. Seven of his pieces appear, as recorded, in *Michel Petrucciani: Original Transcription* (Milwaukee, *c*1992).

SELECTED RECORDINGS

As unaccompanied soloist: *Oracle's Destiny* (1983, Owl 032); *100 Hearts* (1984, Conc. 3001)

Duos: with L. Konitz: *Toot Sweet* (1982, Owl 028); with E. Louiss: *Conférence de presse*, i–ii (1994, Dreyfus 36568, 36573)

As leader: *Michel Petrucciani Trio* (1981, Owl 925); *Pianism* (1985, BN 85124); *Power of Three* (1986, BN 85133); *Michel Plays Petrucciani* (1987, BN B11E-48679)

As sideman: C. Lloyd: *Montreux '82* (1982, Elek. Mus. 960220); [no leader]: *One Night with Blue Note*, iv (1985, BN BT85116); J. Lovano: *From the Soul* (1991, BN B21S-98636)

SELECTED FILMS AND VIDEOS

One Night with Blue Note (n.d.); The Michel Petrucciani Trio (1982); Jazz Comes Home to Newport (1984); Michel Petrucciani: Live at the Village Vanguard, ii (*c*1989 [filmed 1986]); Michel Petrucciani: Power of 3 (*c*1990 [filmed 1986]); The Manhattan Project (*c*1990 [filmed 1989]); Non Stop: eine Reise mit Michel Petrucciani (1995)

BIBLIOGRAPHY

M. Zwerin: "Michel Petrucciani," *Jm*, no.295 (1981), 44
P. Carles: "Michel Petrucciani," *Jm*, no.330 (1984), 42
L. Gourse: "Profile: Michel Petrucciani," *DB*, li/1 (1984), 49
K. Brodacki: "Michel Petrucciani," *JF* [intl edn], no.99 (1986), 26
B. Doerschuk: "Michel Petrucciani," *Keyboard*, xii/11 (1986), 34 [incl. discography]
W. Goode: Liner notes, *Pianism* (BN 85124, 1986)
K. Franckling: "Michel Petrucciani: a Stand-out Style," *JT* (1987), March, 10
G. Endress: "Musik ist mein Leben: Michel Petrucciani," *JP*, xxxvii/9 (1988), 3
G. Peacock: "L'harmonie Petrucciani," *Jm*, no.373 (1988), 35
T. Pérémarti: "Michel Petrucciani: 'Music'," *Jh*, no.468 (1989), 24
A. Romano: "Michel Petrucciani," *Jm*, no.406 (1991), 34
T. Pérémarti: "Rencontres," *Jh*, no.498 (1993), 8
X. Prevost: "Michel Petrucciani: même dans l'improvisation le risque est réfléchi," *Jm*, no.437 (1994), 34
R. Grosman: "Michel Petrucciani: the Entertainer," *Jh*, no.516 (1994–5), 42
D. Ansell: "Michel Petrucciani," *JJI*, xlviii/12 (1995), 12
P. Anquetil and A. Merlin: "School Days: Michel Petrucciani, le bonheur à la clé," *Jazzman*, no.38 (1998), 5
B. Maury: "Michel Petrucciani: l'interview," *Jazzman*, no.44 (1999), 6
Obituaries: S. Holden, *New York Times* (7 Jan 1999); M. Zwerin, *International Herald Tribune* (12 Jan 1999)

ROBERT L. DOERSCHUK/BK

Pettiford, Oscar (*b* Okmulgee, OK, 30 Sept 1922; *d* Copenhagen, 8 Sept 1960). Double bass player, cellist, and bandleader. Of mixed African- and native-American extraction, he was born into a large, musical family and learned many instruments in the family's touring band, which was based in Minneapolis. In January 1943 he was engaged as a double bass player for Charlie Barnet's band (see illustration), with which he traveled to New York in the same year; at that time Barnet employed two bass players, and Pettiford shared his duties with Chubby Jackson. After leaving Barnet in May 1943 he found a place in the emerging bop scene, working with Thelonious Monk at Minton's. At the Onyx he joined Budd Johnson, Sir Charles Thompson, and Doc West in a quintet led by Roy Eldridge. He remained at the Onyx as co-leader with Dizzy Gillespie of a quintet with Lester Young, George Wallington, and West (winter 1943–4); Don Byas soon replaced Young, and Max Roach succeeded West. Personal differences caused this pioneering bop group to disband, with Gillespie moving to the Yacht Club and Pettiford continuing at the Onyx with his own quintet, including Joe Guy and West; one year later, however, he and Gillespie recorded together.

Pettiford toured to California with Coleman Hawkins's band, which included Howard McGhee, Thompson, and Denzil Best; he may be seen playing with them in the film *The Crimson Canary* (1945), but perversely the soundtrack was dubbed by the unknown double bass player Budd Hatch. After leading a trio, Pettiford worked with Duke Ellington (mid-November 1945 – March 1948). He played alongside J. C. Heard in Erroll Garner's trio at the Three Deuces in April

Members of Charlie Barnet's band, spring 1943: (left to right) Howard McGhee (trumpet), Trummy Young (trombone), Oscar Pettiford (double bass), Peanuts Holland (trumpet) and Barnet (leader)

1948; shortly thereafter George Shearing replaced Garner. At the end of the year he continued at the Three Deuces with Kai Winding and Miles Davis in his band, and then transferred to the Clique in an all-star bop ensemble that soon failed owing to clashes among the leader and his sidemen – Davis, Fats Navarro, Lucky Thompson, Dexter Gordon, Milt Jackson, Bud Powell, and Kenny Clarke.

In February 1949 Pettiford joined Woody Herman's Second Herd. While playing baseball with Herman's men he broke his arm, and consequently his activites were greatly reduced over the next year, during which time he focused on playing cello. He joined a sextet co-led by Louis Bellson and Charlie Shavers (1950) and Bud Powell's trio at Birdland (1953), then led a quintet including Jimmy Cleveland, Jerome Richardson (replaced by Cannonball Adderley), Horace Silver, and Clarke at the Café Bohemia (mid-1955) and a trio with Phineas Newborn and Clarke at Basin Street West (March 1956). In 1956–7 he led his own big band which, though highly regarded for its inventive arrangements and instrumentation, suffered from instability of personnel, owing in part to Pettiford's difficult temperament; Art Farmer, Donald Byrd, Cleveland, David Amram, Gigi Gryce, Bennie Golson, Sahib Shihab, Dick Katz, and Gus Johnson were among his sidemen. During this period he also recorded prolifically.

Having traveled to Europe with a Jazz from Carnegie Hall show in September 1958, Pettiford toured France and Germany and then in June 1959 settled in Copenhagen. In the last years of his life he often performed with Hans Koller, Atilla Zoller, and Clarke or Jimmy Pratt on drums. Despite fracturing his skull in a car crash in 1959, he continued recording, held an engagement at the Montmartre club in Getz's quartet (including Joe Harris, 1959 – early 1960), and performed in Getz's band in the film *Soldaterkammerater* (1959).

Pettiford was the first jazz bass player to adapt and elaborate the innovations of Jimmy Blanton within a bop context, and his ideas and discoveries had a lasting influence on the bop style as a whole. His earliest recorded solos, such as *The man I love* (1943), were learned by rote by many aspiring bop bass players, though few could approach his penetrating tone and clear projection of ideas. Later, from about 1950, he transferred his solo style to amplified cello, which he played in a bouncy, dexterous style, reminiscent of Charlie Christian. Together with Ray Brown and Charles Mingus, who owed much to his influence, Pettiford was influential in establishing the double bass as a jazz solo instrument equal in importance to the winds. For transcriptions of his solos, see V. Nahmann: *The Music of Oscar Pettiford*, i: *80 Bass Solos* (Billerica, MA, 1988).

SELECTED RECORDINGS

As leader: *Basically Duke* (1954, Beth. 1019); *The Oscar Pettiford Orchestra in Hi-fi* (1956–7, ABC-Para. 135, 227)

As sideman: C. Hawkins: The man I love (1943, Sig. 9001); Woody 'n' You (1944, Apollo 751); B. Webster: Honeysuckle Rose (1944, Savoy 553); D. Gillespie: Good Bait (1945, Manor 1042); W. Harris: Everybody's Boogie/ Time to Change your Town (1945, Apollo 378); D. Ellington: Swamp Fire (1946, Vic. 20-1992); M. Davis: *The Musings of Miles* (1955, Prst. 7007), incl. Green Haze; L. Konitz and W. Marsh: *Lee Konitz with Warne Marsh* (1955, Atl. 1217); P. Newborn: *Here is Phineas* (1956, Atl. 1235); L. Thompson: *Lucky Thompson Featuring Oscar Pettiford* (1956, ABC-Para. 111, 171); T. Monk: *Brilliant Corners* (1956, Riv. 226); S. Rollins: *The Freedom Suite* (1958, Riv. 258)

BIBLIOGRAPHY

FeatherE

P. Harris: "Oscar Pettiford now on Cello Kick," *DB*, xvii/26 (1950), 20

F. Appel, Jr.: "À New York City: le Grand Orchestre Oscar Pettiford," *Jh*, no.125 (1957), 15

N. Hentoff: "An Oscar," *DB*, xxiv/6 (1957), 17; Fr. trans. as "Un Oscar Pour Pettiford," *Jh*, no.121 (1957), 11

G. Hoefer: "Oscar Pettiford," *DB*, xxxiii/11 (1966), 25

I. Gitler: *Jazz Masters of the Forties* (New York, 1966/*R*1983 with discography), 150

D. C. Hunt: "Oscar Pettiford: Absolute Artistic Clarity," *JJ*, xxvi/8 (1973), 6

C. Carrière: "Pitter Panther Patter: les bassistes de Duke Ellington," *Jh*, no.316 (1975), 10
J.-E. Berendt: "Thank You, Oscar Pettiford," *Ein Fenster aus Jazz: Essays, Portraits, Reflexionen* (Frankfurt am Main, Germany, 1977), 135
J. Chambers: *Milestones*, i: *the Music and Times of Miles Davis to 1960* (Toronto, Buffalo, and London, 1983)
M. Hennessey: *Klook: the Story of Kenny Clarke* (London, 1990)
C. Gazdar: *First Bass: the Oscar Pettiford Discography* (Bangalore, India, 1991)

J. BRADFORD ROBINSON/BK

Pettis, Jack (*b* Danville, IL, 1902). Saxophonist, clarinetist, and bandleader. He taught himself to play C-melody saxophone at the age of 16 and first worked in Chicago with Elmer Schoebel and Paul Mares in 1919; he was a member of Mares's Friars Society Orchestra, which first recorded in 1922 and the following year was renamed the New Orleans Rhythm Kings. Having moved to New York, in 1924 he joined the orchestra led by the violinist Ben Bernie, in which he played tenor and C-melody saxophone and clarinet. From 1926 he made a number of recordings as a leader, some of which were issued under pseudonyms; his bands contained many well-known musicians, including Jack Teagarden and Benny Goodman. Pettis, who continued performing into the 1930s, played with a distinctive tone in the hot style.

SELECTED RECORDINGS

As leader: Dry Martini/Hot Heels (1928, Voc. 15703); Spanish Dream/Doin' the New Low Down (1928, Vic. 21559); Freshman Hop/Sweetest Melody (1929, OK 41411)
As sideman: I. Mills: St. Louis Blues (1929, Ban. 32701); I wonder what my gal is doin'?/What a Night! (1929, 1930, Bruns. 4998); Crazy 'bout my Gal/Railroad Man (1930, Bruns. 4838)

BIBLIOGRAPHY

W. W. Vaché, Sr.: "The Piquant Puzzle of Jack Pettis," *MR*, xiii/2 (1985), 7 [incl. discography]
S. Ashcroft and D. Coller: "More on Jack Pettis," *MR*, xx/6 (1993), 24

WARREN VACHÉ, SR.

Peyton, Benny [Benton Ellsworth] (*b* Washington, DC, 20 July 1888; *d* New York, 24 Jan 1965). Drummer. His full name and the details concerning his birth are taken from his application for social security. After traveling to Europe as a member of Will Marion Cook's Southern Syncopated Orchestra in 1919 he formed his own group from members of the band and led the Jazz Kings in London; it was resident at the Hammersmith Palais in 1921. In the 1920s and 1930s he continued to perform with his own band throughout Europe; among his sidemen were Tommy Ladnier and June Cole (both 1929). He also toured the USSR with the trombonist Frank Withers and Sidney Bechet (1926) and with Joe Turner (i) accompanied Adelaide Hall in Zurich (1935). Peyton returned to New York in 1939 and became closely involved in the AFM (Local 802); during the 1950s he played regularly as a percussionist.

BIBLIOGRAPHY

ChiltonW; *McCarthyB*
B. E. Peyton: "The Jazz Kings are Welcomed in a New Country," *Dancing World*, i/6 (1920), 4
C. Goddard: *Jazz away from Home* (London and New York, 1979)
F. Driggs and H. Lewine: *Black Beauty, White Heat: a Pictorial History of Classic Jazz, 1920–1950* (New York, 1982)
J. Chilton: *Sidney Bechet: the Wizard of Jazz* (London and New York, 1987/*R*1996)
H. Rye: "Visiting Firemen 15: The Southern Syncopated Orchestra," *Sv* (1990), no.142, p.137; no.143, p.165; no.144, p.227

HOWARD RYE

Peyton, Dave (*b c*1885; *d* Chicago, May 1955). Bandleader and pianist. After playing in Wilbur Sweatman's trio in Chicago from around 1908 to 1912 he led his own band in the city; among his sidemen in the late 1920s were Charlie Allen, George Mitchell, Bob Shoffner, Reuben Reeves, Kid Ory, Bud Scott, Jasper Taylor, Jimmy Bertrand, and Baby Dodds, and in the early 1930s Preston Jackson, Darnell Howard, Jerome Don Pasquall, and Lee Collins. He also worked as a band contractor and supplied musicians for other engagements. In the mid-1930s his orchestra was resident at the Regal Theatre, after which he performed mainly as a soloist until the late 1940s. Peyton was best known for his abilities as a leader and organizer. He took part in only one recording session, with Richard M. Jones, though his band recorded in 1928 under the titular leadership of Fess Williams (*Dixie Stomp/Drifting and Dreaming*, Voc. 15690); his participation in the session with Jones is disputed, standard discographies placing him on *Baby o' Mine* (1935, Decca 7115), but Jones by his own account (in Hoefer, 1945) identified Peyton as the pianist on the other item recorded on the day, *Joe Louis Chant*. From 10 October 1925 to 24 August 1929 Peyton wrote a weekly column on music for the *Chicago Defender*.

BIBLIOGRAPHY

ChiltonW; *McCarthyB*
G. Hoefer, Jr.: "The Hot Box," *DB*, xii/19 (1945), 11
C. Hansen: "Social Influences on Jazz Style: Chicago, 1920–32," *American Quarterly*, xii (1960), 493
T. J. Hennessey: "The Black Chicago Establishment, 1919–1930," *JJS*, ii/1 (1974), 15–45
D. J. Travis: *An Autobiography of Black Jazz* (Chicago, 1983)

based on *ChiltonW*

Phalanx. Small group formed in April 1984 by George Adams (saxophone, flute), Billy Bang (violin), James "Blood" Ulmer (electric guitar, flute), Sirone (double bass), and Rashied Ali (drums). It gave its first performance at the Public Theater in New York and later appeared as a quartet without Bang. For a recording made in September 1985 and a performance in Düsseldorf, Germany, the following February, Adams and Ulmer played with the electric bass guitarist Amin Ali and the drummer Calvin Weston. However, Sirone and Rashied Ali returned to record in 1987–8 and performed with the group at the Knitting Factory in 1988, soon after which Phalanx appears to have disbanded.

SELECTED RECORDINGS

Got Something Good for You (1985, Moers Music 2046); *Original Phalanx* (1987, DIW 8013); *In Touch* (1988, DIW 8026)

BIBLIOGRAPHY

GrayF
G. Giddins: "First Phalanx and Other Naturals," *VV* (22 May 1984), 77
J. Eipasch: "Jazz aktuell: Mangelsdorff–Surman, Phalanx," *JP*, xxxv/5 (1986), 21
R. J. Smith: "Swing Shift: Hardscrabble," *VV* (5 July 1988), 70
M. Joyce: "Electric Ensemble Powers Up Phalanx," *Washington Post* (12 April 1991)

GK

Phase shifter. An electronic device that transforms the timbre of an instrument or a voice by superimposing on the original sound a copy of it, the phase patterns of which are altered. It is closely akin to a Flanger, and can produce a similar effect.

Philburn, (Michael) Al(oysius) (*b* Newark, NJ, 24 Aug 1902; *d* Glen Cove, NY, 29 Feb 1972). Trombonist. He learned trombone from the age of 14 and first performed locally. In the 1920s he played and recorded in the orchestras of Paul Specht (1925–7) and Cass Hagen (1927–8), and performed frequently with the singer Ed Kirkeby (1927–30), with whom, as a member of the California Ramblers, he made several recordings (1927). After serving as a member of Bert Lown's orchestra for some years (from 1929) he worked in studios, recording with many musicians, among them Chick Bullock (1933), Adrian Rollini (1933, 1934), and Red McKenzie and Bob Howard (both 1936); he may be heard as a soloist on Louis Armstrong's *Yes! Yes! My! My!* (1936, Decca 698). Philburn was a staff musician at radio station WNGW and NBC (1936–48), and in the 1950s he concentrated on session work. Following a brief period with Tony Parenti in 1962 he led his own dixieland band until 1964. He continued performing until the late 1960s.

based on *ChiltonW*

Phillips, Barre (*b* San Francisco, 27 Oct 1934). Double bass player. He took up double bass at the age of 13, first in school orchestras, then in dixieland and bop groups. After meeting Ornette Coleman, in 1962 he moved to New York, where he played free jazz with Don Heckman and Don Ellis (1962) and with Archie Shepp, Bill Dixon, and Paul Bley (1963); he also performed in the première of Larry Austin's *Improvisations for Orchestra and Jazz Soloists* with the New York Philharmonic Orchestra under Leonard Bernstein (1962). From 1963 to 1965 he was a member of Jimmy Giuffre's trio, and in 1964 he toured Europe with George Russell's big band. The following year he began playing with the trio led by the pianist Peter Nero, recorded with Bob James, and appeared with Shepp at the Newport Jazz Festival; he was a member of Atilla Zoller's trio from around 1965 to 1967.

Having found European audiences more receptive to his playing than American ones, Phillips moved to London, where by 1967 he was working with John Stevens and Evan Parker; after two years there he moved to Paris, and then settled permanently in the south of France. He performed in France with Marion Brown and in Germany with Gunter Hampel, and in 1968 he recorded a solo album, *Journal violone*, which was the first LP to consist entirely of improvised music for unaccompanied double bass. After working in The Trio, with John Surman and the drummer Stu Martin (1969–72), and in Mumps, a quartet consisting of Surman, Martin, and Albert Mangelsdorff (1976–7), he formed the sextet Music By (1979) and led a trio consisting of Beb Guérin and Léon Francioli. In 1984 he was musician-in-residence at the Music Gallery in Toronto. However, he continued to play frequently in Europe, collaborating to various degrees with film-makers, painters, sculptors, and dramatists. In 1988 he played with Company, and around the same time he worked in a duo with Peter Kowald. Phillips performed with Maarten Altena and Pierre Dørge in Vancouver, Canada, in 1990, and from early in the decade he worked with the percussionist Alain Joule, both in a duo and in a trio with Michel Doneda (the latter recording in 1992); he also recorded in a duo with Barry Guy (1989) and in a cooperative trio with André Jaume and Barry Altschul (1992). In the mid-1990s he recorded (1994) and then toured in a trio with Bley and Parker, and he toured France and the US West Coast as co-leader of a quartet with Ken Filiano, with Vinny Golia among their sidemen. In 1997 he recorded in Sweden in a cooperative group with the wind player Biggie Vinkeloe and the drummer Peeter Uuskyla.

For illustration, *see* John Tchicai.

SELECTED RECORDINGS

As unaccompanied soloist: *Journal violone* (1968, Music Man 601)
Duos with D. Holland: *Music for Two Basses* (1971, ECM 1011)
As leader: *Journal violone*, ii (1979, ECM 1149); *Music By* (1980, ECM 1178); with A. Jaume and B. Altschul: *Giacobazzi, autour de la rade* (1992, CELP 25); with E. Parker and P. Bley: *Time Will Tell* (1994, ECM 1537); with B. Vinkeloe and P. Uuskyla: *One Way Out* (1997, Slask 8433).
As sideman: B. James: *Explosions* (1965, ESP 1009); L. Austin: *Improvisations for Orchestra and Jazz Soloists* (1967, Col. MS6733); M. Portal: *Alors!* (1970, Futura 12); G. Hampel: *Jubilation* (1983, Birth 0038)

BIBLIOGRAPHY

GrayF
J.-L. Ginibre: "Phillips c'est plus pur," *Jm*, no.166 (1969), 63
V. Wilmer: "Barre Blasts off at 'Cold' British," *MM* (12 April 1969), 8
M. Cullaz: "John Surman, Barre Phillips, Stu Martin: Interview," *Jh*, no.259 (1970), 16
G. Terrones: "Barre Phillips," *Jh*, no.260 (1970), 20
R. Williams: "Barre: Playing his Birth," *MM* (21 March 1970), 8
P. Carles: "Barre Phillips: la basse et le reste," *Jm*, no.239 (1975), 34
G. Schoukroun: "Phillips à la barre," *Jm*, no.296 (1981), 26
B. Smith: "Barre Phillips," *Coda*, no.198 (1984), 19
E. Jost: *Europas Jazz, 1960–1980* (Frankfurt am Main, Germany, 1987)
U. Buhrdorf: "Barre Phillips," *Jazzthetik*, ix/11 (1990), 12
E.-L. Petrowsky: "Barre Phillips Trio," *JP*, xlii/ (1993), 36
J. Solothurnmann: "Barre Phillips: Wahrhaftigkeit und inneres Ohr," *JP*, xliii/12 (1994), 22

JOHN VOIGT/BK

Phillips, Flip [Filipelli, Joseph Edward] (*b* New York, 26 March 1915). Tenor saxophonist. After experimenting with chords on the piano from the age of five he took up clarinet when he was 11, and he received his first lessons from a cousin who was a professional musician. Like many others of his generation, in 1927 he was smitten by jazz, and the saxophone, upon hearing Frankie Trumbauer's recording *Singin' the Blues*. He played clarinet in a band at Schneider's Lobster House in Brooklyn (1934–9) and with Frankie Newton (1940–41), and he worked with Benny Goodman (briefly in late 1942), Wingy Manone, and Red Norvo (late in 1943). In spring 1944 he replaced Vido Musso as tenor saxophonist in Woody Herman's First Herd (for illustration *see* Herman, Woody, fig.1*a*). While with Herman (to 1946), and later, on tours with Jazz at the Philharmonic (1946–57), he acquired a reputation for his energetic improvisations (notably on *Perdido*); despite his rather tasteless, honking tone, these performances were popular with audiences but unfortunately tended to overshadow his sumptuous ballad playing (as on *Sweet and Lovely*), his feeling for the blues (as heard on recordings with Norvo in 1945), and the many swinging, melodic solos he recorded as the leader of small groups.

Late in 1959 Phillips toured Europe with Goodman (alongside Norvo) and then settled in Pompano Beach, Florida, where he played part-time and managed an apartment building. He appeared at the Colorado Jazz Party in 1970 and with Herman at the Newport Jazz Festival in 1972. Having resumed full-time playing in 1975, he continued to appear at the Colorado event, participating in Herman's 40th anniversary concert in 1976 and recording with Herman's Thundering Herd as a guest soloist for an album of ballads in January 1978. From July 1978 until the venue was sold in 1981 he led a quartet at Beowulf's Restaurant and Lounge at Lighthouse Point in Pompano Beach. He recorded yet again as a guest soloist with Herman in 1981, and the following year he toured Europe and Japan, the latter with Herman's group. In 1985 he worked with Norvo one last time at the first Minneapolis Jazz Party, and in 1987 he sailed with Kenny Davern on the SS *Norway*, playing for a four-week cruise to Oslo and back, and worked with Scott Hamilton; the two men performed at Fat Tuesday in New York and also recorded together. Phillips again toured Europe in 1988. He continued to perform into the 1990s, recording as a leader in 1993 and making a video with an all-star group in 1995 in celebration of his 80th birthday.

Phillips is a masterful saxophonist, and his recordings from the 1970s onwards consistently exhibit the control, imagination, and warmth of his playing. He should not be confused with the vibraphonist Flip Phillips, who recorded in Austria with the group Yacazu in 1996–7.

Video oral history material in *NCH* (HCJA).

SELECTED RECORDINGS

As leader: Skyscraper/Pappiloma (1944, Sig. 28106); A Melody in the Sky (1944, Sig. 28119); Sweet and Lovely (1944, Sig. 90003); *Flip Phillips Quintet* (1954, Clef 260–62); *Phillips' Head* (1975, Choice 1013); *Flipenstein* (1981, Prog. 7063); *A Real Swinger* (1988, Conc. 358); with B. Nerem and K. Davern: *Mood Indigo* (1987, Gemini 59); *Try a Little Tenderness* (1993, Chi. 321)

As sideman: R. Norvo: Get Happy/Congo Blues (1945, Comet T7); Slim Slam Blues (1945, Dial 1045); W. Herman: Apple Honey (1945, Col. 36803); Sweet and Lovely (1946, MGM 30602); Igor (1946, Col. 37228); Jazz at the Philharmonic: Perdido (1947, Mer./Clef 11000–02); The Opener (1949, Mer./Clef 11054–6); Jam Session: *Jam Session no.2* (1952, Clef 4002), incl. Funky Blues, What is this thing called love?

SELECTED FILMS AND VIDEOS

Wintertime (1943); Earl Carroll Vanities (1945); Hit Parade of 1947 [High and Happy] (1947); Flip Phillips' 80th Birthday Party Featuring the All-Stars (*c*1996 [filmed 1995]); Norman Granz présente improvisation: documents exceptionnels et inédits des plus grands noms de jazz (n.d.)

BIBLIOGRAPHY

A. Morgan: "Woody's Tenors," *JM*, vi/8 (1960), 13
J. Burns: "Swing Tenors," *JJ*, xix/12 (1966), 13
B. Rusch and S. Miller: "Flip Phillips," *Cadence*, ii/12 (1977), 6
E. Cook: "Flip Phillips," *JJI*, xxxv/6 (1982), 8
M. Jones: "Jazz: on the Flip Side," *MM* (30 Jan 1982), 23; repr. in *Talking Jazz* (London, 1987), 63
M. L. Hester: "Flip: Past and Present," *MR*, xv/4 (1988), 1
M. Bourne: "Riffs: Flip Phillips," *DB*, lvi/3 (1989), 14
W. D. Clancy with A. C. Kenton: *Woody Herman: Chronicles of the Herds* (New York and elsewhere, 1995)
G. Lees: *Leader of the Band: the Life of Woody Herman* (New York, and Oxford, England, 1995)

BK

Phillips, Gene [Eugene Floyd] (*b* St. Louis, 25 May 1915; *d* Lakewood, CA, 20 April 1992). Guitarist, singer, and leader. The month of his birth has been published erroneously as July rather than May. He took up ukulele at the age of ten and changed to guitar two years later. In St. Louis he worked in the bands of Dewey Jackson and the reed player Jimmy Powell and was taught by Floyd Smith to play lap steel guitar, which he later used to great effect on such recordings as *Gene's Guitar Blues* (1950). In 1937 he traveled to Georgia to join the Atlanta Troubadors. He was a member of the Miami-based band of Hartley Toots before returning to St. Louis in 1939 to form his own group, the Rhythm Aces, a trio in which he played electric guitar; his sidemen were Ray Agee on rhythm guitar and Smith on banjo. He also briefly led another group, the College Troubadors or Collegians, then in 1941 joined the popular singing act the Mills Brothers as their guitarist. Phillips left the Mills Brothers in Los Angeles in 1943 because his draft status prevented him from undertaking a tour of Canada; he was briefly with Eddie Beal, then became a member of the trio led by the pianist Lorenzo Flennoy, with whom he recorded (1944–5) and held a long residency at the Casablanca Breakfast Club. He recorded with Jack McVea in 1945 and 1946, and in 1947 he began a series of recordings with his Rhythm Aces. Until 1950 this group, which featured Jake Porter and Maxwell Davis and which also recorded under Lloyd Glenn's name, was one of the most consistently creative of the recorded jump bands. Phillips worked with the bandleader Sammy Franklin in the early 1950s and recorded again with McVea in 1954 and 1956, but soon thereafter he seems to have retired from music to run a junkyard.

SELECTED RECORDINGS

As leader: I could make you love me/Boogie Everywhere (1947, Modern 148); Big Legs (1947, Modern 20-527); Punkin' Head Woman (1947, Modern 20-559); I wonder what the poor folks are doin' (1950, Modern 20-743); first issued on *Gene Phillips and his Rhythm Aces*, 1947–50, Ace 169), Gene Jumps the Blues, Gene's Guitar Blues (1950); first issued on *I Like 'em Fat* (1947–50, Ace 245), My baby's mistreatin' me (1950); first issued on *Rock Bottom Blues* (1947–50, Crown 5375), Broke and Disgusted, Crying won't help you (1950)

As sideman with L. Glenn: That other woman's got to go/Rampart Street Jump (1947, Imperial 5022); Jumpin' with Lloyd (1948, RPM 332); Levee Blues/Brazos Bottom (1949, Swing Time 199)

BIBLIOGRAPHY

G. Richards: "Jump with Me Baby (Second Chorus), 2: Gene Phillips," *Alley Music*, i/3 (1968), 6
Slim, Slam & Bam: "Boogie in the Dark: Gene Phillips & his Rhythm Aces," *Pickin' the Blues*, no.14 (1983), 8
J. Simmen: "Maxwell Davis," *BHcF*, no.323 (1985), 3
J. Dawson: Liner notes, *Gene Phillips and his Rhythm Aces* (Ace 169, 1986)

HOWARD RYE

Phillips, Sid [Isador Simon] (*b* London, 14 June 1907; *d* Chertsey, England, 24 May 1973). English clarinetist and arranger. As a child he studied violin and piano and taught himself theory and harmony, and in his late teens he began playing saxophone and clarinet and performed with his brothers' band in Europe. He first worked as staff arranger for a music publisher and as music director for the Edison–Bell Gramophone Company, then from 1930 he wrote arrangements for Bert Ambrose and led his own quintet. Later he joined Ambrose's band (1933), with which he recorded on clarinet and alto and baritone saxophones (1933–7). In 1937 Phillips visited the USA, where he broadcast and recorded with American musicians. After serving in the RAF he formed another quintet (1946) and composed several classical works for the BBC Symphony Orchestra. From 1949 until his death he led his own dixieland band; among his sidemen were George Shearing, Colin Bailey, Tommy Whittle, and Kenny Ball. Phillips made several recordings as a leader from 1928 into the 1970s, including *Royal Garden Blues* (1941, Decca F7972). Reference sources give his date of death variously as 23, 25, and 26 May 1973, but the date on his death certificate is 24 May.

BIBLIOGRAPHY

CarrJ; *ChiltonB*
J. Godbolt: *A History of Jazz in Britain, 1919–50* (London, Melbourne, Australia, and New York, 1984)
E. S. Walker: "Sid Phillips: the Early Years," *Sv*, no.130 (1987), 143
T. Middleton: *Sid Phillips Discography* (London, 1997)

NEVIL SKRIMSHIRE

Phillips, Sonny [Roosevelt; Rushdan, Jalal Sabir] (*b* Mobile, AL, 7 Dec 1936). Organist and pianist. He grew up in a musical family, though he did not concentrate on studying music until 1959, when he took some lessons on piano with Ahmad Jamal. He soon changed to organ after hearing Jimmy Smith, and, listening to Thelonious Monk, Bud

Powell, and Oscar Peterson, developed an individual style in the blues tradition. In the 1960s and 1970s he traveled in the Northeast with Eddie Harris, Gene Ammons, and Lou Donaldson. After settling in New York in 1967 Phillips converted to Islam (which he had studied since 1959) and, with the Congolese drummer Titos Sompa, began to operate the Tanawa Art Center. From 1969 to 1970, and again from 1974, he played and recorded with, and also wrote arrangements for, Houston Person's group. Illness curtailed his activities in 1980, but the following year he moved to Los Angeles, where he performed as a pianist and organist and worked as a teacher.

SELECTED RECORDINGS

As leader: *Sure 'nuff* (1970, Prst. 7737); *Black Magic* (1971, Prst. 7799); *My Black Flower* (1976, Muse 5118); *I Concentrate on You* (1977, Muse 5157)
As sideman with H. Person: *Wild Flower* (1977, Muse 5161)

BIBLIOGRAPHY

S. Freedman: "Profile: Sonny Phillips," *DB*, xlvi/14 (1979), 46

STEVEN STRUNK

Philo. Original name of the record company and label which was founded in 1944 but changed its name in March 1946 to ALADDIN.

Philology. Italian record company and label, named in homage to Phil Woods. It was founded in Macerata in 1987 by its manager, Paolo Piangiarelli, and first issued recordings by such touring American artists as Woods, Mike Melillo, and Lee Konitz. Piangiarelli then recorded many Italian musicians, among them such established players as Enrico Pieranunzi and Franco D'Andrea (often with Woods or Konitz) as well as younger ones such as Massimo Urbani, Tiziana Ghiglioni, and Umberto Petrin. The company also produced previously unissued recordings by Clifford Brown, Lester Young, and Wardell Gray and a 22-disc series of live recordings by Charlie Parker.

STEFANO ZENNI

Phineas Newborn Project. *See* CONTEMPORARY PIANO ENSEMBLE.

Phoemipol Aduldej. *See* BHUMIBOL ADULYADEJ.

Phoenix Jazz. Record company and label. The company was established by Bob Porter in Kingston, New Jersey, in 1972; its policy was to reissue historic jazz. The first album in the catalogue was a collection of all the material recorded by Cootie Williams with Bud Powell for Hit and Majestic. Later releases presented small-group and big-band material by Dizzy Gillespie and rare items by Nat "King" Cole, Charlie Ventura, Coleman Hawkins, Roy Eldridge, Billie Holiday, and Sabby Lewis. Perhaps the most important issues, however, were two LPs that contained recordings made in 1953–4 (for broadcasting purposes) of performances given by Charlie Parker in Boston. To celebrate the fifth anniversary of its formation, the company issued in 1977 a compilation of obscure but enlightening material by Gillespie, Hawkins, Benny Golson, and Bill Harris (i). Thereafter its activities declined, but the company remained in existence into the 1990s.

MARK GARDNER

Phontastic. Record company and label founded in Stockholm in 1975 by the attorney, critic, and jazz record collector Anders R. Öhman. It has won international acclaim for a large number of albums centered on the swing style, involving new recordings by artists such as Bob Wilber, Arne Domnérus, Bengt Hallberg, and Ove Lind, as well as reissues and original releases of older material by Benny Goodman and others (the "Nostalgia" series). Phontastic also offers the series "Portrait of a year in music," where albums with jazz or jazz-derived music reflect a specific year (the first being 1929), and another series reissuing the best recordings of individual artists, for example *The Permanent Benny Goodman*. A subsidiary label, Artemis, specializes in classical music.

LARS WESTIN

Piana, Dino (*b* Refrancore, nr Asti, Italy, 3 July 1930). Italian valve trombonist. After studying trumpet and accordion, at the age of 15 he changed to trombone. He began to play jazz around 1958 in the Turin area with the Quintetto di Torino, then performed throughout Italy with Romano Mussolini (1960–62), Gil Cuppini's big band (1964–9), and Giorgio Gaslini (1968–9). He was a member of the sextet led by Gianni Basso and Oscar Valdambrini (1962–74) and served as co-leader of the Piana–Valdambrini quintet (1975–8) and sextet (from 1978). He also played with Chet Baker and Gato Barbieri (both 1960), Gerry Mulligan (1974), and, most often, Kai Winding, with whom he toured in 1978 and 1981. From 1969 he was a soloist in the Italian television orchestra, in which setting he worked with Frank Rosolino, Conte Candoli, Dusko Goykovic, Mel Lewis, and many others. In 1976 he recorded with Charles Mingus. He retired from music in the mid-1980s. Piana produced a lithe, warm sound with shades and ripples, and favored long, agile, boppish phrases.

SELECTED RECORDINGS

As leader: *Così con Dino Piana* (1962, Ricordi 6120); with O. Valdambrini: *Oscar Valdambrini & Dino Piana* (1976, Horo 34), *Afrodite* (1976, Vedette 8337); with K. Winding: *Duo Bones* (1978, Red 143)
As sideman: G. Basso and O. Valdambrini: *Gianni Basso & Oscar Valdambrini plus Dino Piana* (1960, Jolly 5010); *The Best Modern Jazz in Italy 1962* (1962, RCA PML10326); C. Mingus: on *Cumbia and Jazz Fusion* (1976, Atl. 8801), Music for "Todo Modo"

STEFANO ZENNI

Piano [pianoforte]. A keyboard instrument distinguished by the fact that its strings are struck by rebounding hammers. From the end of the 18th century it has been the principal domestic keyboard instrument in Europe and the USA. The modern piano has a range of a little over seven octaves, from *A''* to *c'''''*; the player can sound a large number of notes simultaneously and vary their loudness by changing the force with which the keys are struck. The present article covers the history and use of the piano in jazz.

1. Development of early jazz piano. 2. The stride school and Art Tatum. 3. Swing and boogie-woogie. 4. The transition to bop. 5. After 1950: the acoustic piano. 6. After 1950: the electric and electronic piano.

1. DEVELOPMENT OF EARLY JAZZ PIANO. The piano, both as a solo instrument and in ensembles of various sizes, was important in the development of early jazz. During the first two decades of the 20th century (before the arrival of radio and television) piano playing was a major form of domestic entertainment. Player pianos, which reproduced performances mechanically from punched paper rolls, served to disseminate RAGTIME (the immediate predecessor of jazz) to a wide public, and during the same period pianists in New Orleans, as well

as those in other southern cities, developed the playing and harmonization of the Blues.

The piano was the major performance medium for ragtime, the percussive nature of the instrument being perfect for the clipped syncopations of the music; in addition it was possible for the piano to imitate an entire group. While the player's left hand kept strict time, alternating pedal notes with chords in the "oompah" manner of the marching band, the right hand played syncopated "raggy" figures, often derived from chordal hand positions, in the treble. The general left-hand approach, with its repeated leap from bass note to chord, formed the basis of the later jazz style known as stride (see §2 below). Scott Joplin's *Maple Leaf Rag* was one of the best known and most typical examples of the characteristics of ragtime piano (ex.1).

Ex.1 From Scott Joplin's *Maple Leaf Rag*, as recorded on a piano roll in 1916; transcr. L. Koch

In the development from ragtime to jazz the major transforming element was an increased sense of freedom, in which the left hand gradually took on more linear aspects – walking 10ths and octaves and melodic runs – as well as a greater feeling of movement. At the same time the right hand was liberated from a literal reading of composed ragtime melodies by several distinct innovations: a growing use of swinging eighth-notes; a freer approach to rhythm by playing ahead of or behind the beat set up by the left hand; and a more liberal treatment of the melody in a tendency towards paraphrase and a gradual increase in other, freer, procedures of improvisation. Joplin's *Maple Leaf Rag* played as composed (as on the piano roll made in 1916 from which ex.1 was transcribed) compares strikingly with the recording made by Jelly Roll Morton for the Library of Congress (1938, Cir. [USA] 22), which was a conscious attempt to re-create the innovations of early jazz performers (ex.2). Not only does Morton illustrate some of the points already mentioned, he also injects a true jazz rhythmic feeling into his playing with four beats to the bar, completely obliterating the stiff, march-like rhythms of ragtime.

Ex.2 From Jelly Roll Morton's version of *Maple Leaf Rag* (1938, Circle [USA] 22); transcr. L. Koch

An investigation of Morton's solo piano recordings from 1923–4 reveals many elements of early jazz piano techniques, some of them within the fashion for using the piano in "orchestral imitation." Among these was the "Spanish tinge," an early instance of Latin jazz, in which the left hand created a tango-influenced rhythm within the basic stride style; good examples may be heard on *New Orleans Joys* (1923, Gen. 5486) and *Mamanita* (1924, Gen. 5632).

The early jazz piano style was developed to its full potential by Earl Hines, who displayed great originality both as an unaccompanied soloist and as a band pianist. His solo on *Save it, pretty mama* (1928, OK 8657), with Louis Armstrong's Savoy Ballroom Five, illustrates, in the left hand, strings of walking 10ths, a suspension of the stride rhythm at climactic points, and a melodic use of eighth-notes; and, in the right, virtuoso 16th-notes runs and arpeggios which genuinely further his musical ideas rather than being solely decorative. The overall performance gives a sense of unbridled swing coupled with stark originality.

In ensembles, however, the early jazz pianist changed roles to suit the varying needs of the group. The percussive nature of the piano made it an ideal accompanying instrument, along with the banjo and drums, for wind and brass players, but the pianist could be freer than the other instrumentalists in the rhythm section and add embellishments to the ensemble sound. Because of its ability to maintain a strongly rhythmic bass line, the piano was sometimes employed as a solo instrument to provide contrast to the group sound; it was also occasionally used in a lone capacity to accompany an improvised solo. Lil Hardin provides a good example of the latter in her own composition *Sweet Lovin' Man* (1923, OK 4906), recorded with King Oliver's Creole Jazz Band, in which she alone accompanies Johnny Dodds's blues improvisations, using tasteful ornamental figures; during the rest of the piece, however, she plays in a strict ensemble style, even being charged with keeping a firm bass. Along the same lines, but with stronger emphasis on musical interchange and on the piano and pianistic techniques, is *Weather Bird* (1928, OK 41454), the classic duet between Earl Hines and Louis Armstrong. While maintaining a relentless drive, Hines varies his approaches to accompaniment. In general Hines and other early pianists adopted such devices as dividing the stride bass pattern between the hands, playing four chords to a bar, and adding right-hand embellishments over a stride left hand. Hines's performance on *Weather Bird* also gives ample evidence of his "trumpet" style, in which he played octaves instead of full chords in the right hand; his octave attack was sharp, like that of a brass instrument, and he used tremolos on long notes to simulate vibrato and/or a breath crescendo.

A similar variety of approaches to accompaniment and to solo playing within an ensemble may be heard on almost any of the recordings made by Morton with his Red Hot Peppers for Victor between 15 September 1926 and 11 June 1928. *Cannonball Blues* (1926, Vic. 20431) offers some excellent examples of his use of embellishment, such as the passages in double-time over each phrase-ending of a low guitar solo; he also plays a beautiful piano solo, using treble notes only, over the sustained chords of the brass and wind instruments.

2. The stride school and Art Tatum. The style most directly associated with ragtime, and which grew out of it by way of the so-called East Coast ragtimers, was that of the Harlem stride piano school, which had its origins around the time of World War I. Its main practitioners were Luckey Roberts, Willie "the Lion" Smith, and James P. Johnson. When playing as soloists, Count Basie and Duke Ellington were also formidable exponents of stride. The distinctive "stride bass" (ex.3), adapted from left-hand patterns of ragtime,

Ex.3 A typical stride bass

represents only one of the increased virtuoso demands of the style, which in general called for fast tempos, a full use of the piano's range, and a wide array of pianistic devices – some from the classical repertory in which many of the Harlem pianists were trained. While the pieces performed by the stride pianists were fully composed (Johnson's *Carolina Shout* (1921, OK 4495) is perhaps the most famous early example), they were nevertheless seen as a basis for improvisation. Paul Machlin's analysis of the music of Johnson's pupil, Fats Waller, discusses at length the latter's improvisational approach, notably in an examination of different takes of some of his solo recordings made in 1929.

The culmination of stride piano is probably the work of Art Tatum, where dazzling ornamental runs and arpeggios and a sophisticated harmonic vocabulary are fused to the basic style. The approaches that influenced Tatum, and the growth of the stride style, may be heard in such recordings as Hines's *Save it, pretty mama*, Waller's *Numb Fumblin'* (1929, Vic. 38508), and Johnson's *You've got to be modernistic* (1930, Bruns. 4762). Later, Tatum's prodigious technique, use of advanced harmonies, and sympathy for popular-song material resulted in some refinement of the style, but his individual approach was a direct development of stride. His recordings set a standard for solo jazz piano in terms of virtuosity: *Tiger Rag* (1940, Decca 18051), in particular, demonstrates both his debt to the true stride style and his personal refinement of it.

1. Art Tatum, c1942

2. Teddy Wilson, 1942

3. Swing and boogie-woogie. Generally speaking, the solo piano style became more refined during the swing period. In order for players to deal with the faster tempos they made more use of single bass notes and simple chords (sometimes merely broken 10ths or seventh chords used in an "oompah" fashion), thus lightening the left-hand part; walking 10ths remained an important device for connecting chord progressions. The right-hand part was treated in a similar fashion, so that it often carried only single notes. Teddy Wilson's recording of *Between the devil and the deep blue sea* (1937, Bruns. 8025) exemplifies these qualities (ex.4).

Ex.4 From the fourth chorus of Teddy Wilson: *Between the Devil and the Deep Blue Sea* (1937, Bruns. 8025); transcr. H. Martin (Martin, 1986)

Wilson carried his lightness of touch into his group playing, as may be heard on *China Boy* (1936, Vic. 25333) and many other titles he recorded between 1935 and 1938 as a member of Benny Goodman's small groups.

Perhaps the varied approaches to the use of the piano as an ensemble instrument in the swing period are best illustrated by the four tunes with which Count Basie began his recording career in 1936. *Shoe Shine Boy* (Voc. 3441) has an introduction of pure stride piano and passages of "oompah" comping; the embellished accompaniment to the melody instruments on *Evenin'* (also Voc. 3441) is light and swinging; on *Boogie Woogie* (Voc. 3459) Basie comps in a rhythmically free manner behind the soloists, placing isolated chords in the manner echoed later by bop pianists; and *Lady Be Good* (also Voc. 3459) offers an example of a spare solo introduction in the right hand and quietly jabbed random left-hand chords (there are also moments when Basie's four-beat accompaniment of Lester Young's solo resembles the playing of a guitar). Basie employed the same techniques when playing in larger ensembles, and his recordings of the late 1930s provide good examples of band piano.

There was an important exception to the move towards refinement, however, in the resurgence during the late 1930s and early 1940s of the more earthy blues style known as BOOGIE-WOOGIE, which had developed in the 1920s and is typified by Pine Top Smith's *Pine Top's Boogie Woogie* (1928, Voc. 1245). Its reappearance resulted in a renewed interest in the work of such pianists as Pete Johnson, Meade "Lux" Lewis, and Jimmy Yancey. Boogie-woogie is characterized by a repetitive pounding bass pattern, usually in eighth-notes, on a simple 12-bar blues progression, and examples of widely used patterns are shown in ex.5. Johnson's *Lone Star Blues* (1939, first issued on *Riverside History of Classic Jazz*, 1924–39, Riv. 114; ex.5*a*) shows a typical walking line with a rocking motion; this type of bass generally became more even as the tempo of the piece increased. Memphis Slim's pattern on *44 Blues* (from the album *The Real Boogie Woogie*, 1959, FW 3524; ex.5*b*) is also common, either in straight eighth-notes or in the more rocking fashion created by triplets. The term "honky-tonk" became associated with the figure (and its variants) in Lewis's *Honky Tonk Train Blues* (1927, Para. 12896; ex.5*c*); Bill Doggett's rhythm-and-blues hit *Honky Tonk* (1956, King 4950) gained its name from this type of accompaniment. Yancey's bass line in *Yancey Stomp* (1939, Vic. 26589; ex.5*d*) is an interesting pattern sometimes referred to as "the fives," and is best played keeping the eighth-notes slightly uneven (a tenuto mark has been used in the transcription to indicate this). The final example, from Johnson's *Let 'em jump* (1939, Solo Art 12005; ex.5*e*), shows the honky-tonk pattern with an even subdivision of the beat (usually played at a faster tempo than the figures in ex.5*a–d*). The blues improvisations played in the right hand above these ostinatos could contain riff-like passages in the high treble, tremolos, single-line melodies, and punctuated chords. Often interesting cross-rhythms were created. Lewis contributes a characteristic "bluesy" flavor to *Honky Tonk Train Blues* by striking adjacent pitches to produce the effect of blue notes and makes deliberate use of dissonance.

4. THE TRANSITION TO BOP. The 1940s was a decade in which jazz pianists began to liberate the left hand from the tyranny of timekeeping. This was at first a subtle movement, but later, with the advent of bop, it became more blatant. On *Fly Right* (*Epistrophy*) (1942, first issued on *Jazz Odyssey*, iii: *The Sound of Harlem*, Col. C3L33), recorded with Cootie Williams's big band, Kenny Kersey plays the first half of his solo in a "swing stride" style, after the manner of Teddy Wilson; at the bridge, however, he strikes a low pedal note, breaks the stride, and proceeds in a more "modern" fashion, with no steady left-hand pulse. There are short passages of block chords and unison playing with a single note in each hand, as well as angular uses of rhythm.

Examples of another technique of the period – comping – may be heard on recordings made by Kersey and Thelonious Monk in jam sessions in 1941. Kersey's approach seems to be governed by the harmony of the piece; on *Kerouac* (*Exactly Like You*) and *Stardust* (on the album *The Harlem Jazz Scene*, 1941, Eso. 4), both with Dizzy Gillespie, he freely plays two-handed chord voicings at times. Monk, however, shows a greater concern with rhythm: on *Swing to Bop* (*Topsy*; on the album *Jazz Immortal*, 1941, Eso. 1), with Charlie Christian, he jabs chords in between, and sometimes with, Kenny Clarke's drum kicks.

The new concepts of harmony and rhythm that were developed by these musicians during informal jam sessions in the early 1940s were the main elements that transformed the jazz piano style. Because of a dispute between the musicians' union and the recording industry, however, no commercial recordings were made between August 1942 and late 1943, and an important formative year in the development of bop remains undocumented.

Two pieces recorded by Stan Kenton's orchestra just after the ban was lifted in 1943 illustrate the influence of this group on the development of jazz piano, particularly with regard to chord voicing for comping and in the use of orchestral imitation. *Artistry in Rhythm* (first issued as *Production on Theme*) and *Eager Beaver* (both Cap. 159) have melodies that are derived from a right-hand distribution of a chord – just as were many ragtime melodies. In these examples, however, the right-hand structures emphasize higher partials of chords: sixths, sevenths, and ninths (ex.6). It would appear that Kenton worked these voicings out at the piano and then transferred them to the format of the big band. His orchestra's early popularity (despite, or because of, controversy) ensured that his music was heard

Ex.5 Typical left-hand boogie patterns

Ex.6
(a) Opening of Stan Kenton: *Artistry in Rhythm* (first issued as *Production on Theme*, 1943, Cap. 159); transcr. L. Koch

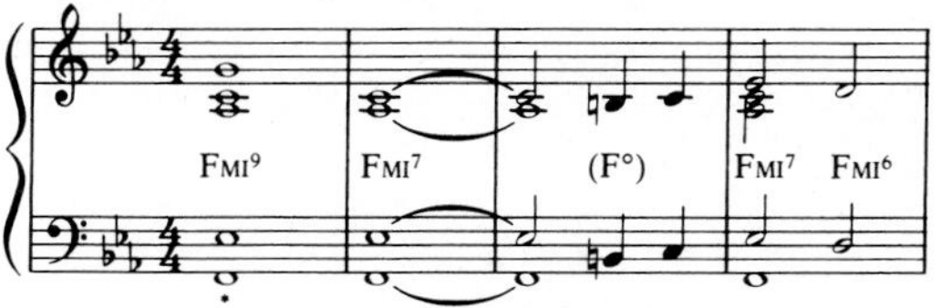

• = basic chord from which melody is derived

(b) Opening of Kenton: *Eager Beaver* (1943, Cap. 159); transcr. L. Koch

• = basic chord from which melody is derived

throughout the USA, and many pianists began to transfer his voicings back to the keyboard.

A comparison between ex.6*b* and ex.1 shows how both compositions are pianistically related: Joplin's melody is derived from the position of the chord of A♭, with C as the pivotal note; Kenton's has its origins in the right-hand part of a two-handed band voicing of an A♭ major seventh chord, where the major seventh (G) is the pivot. (Morton's jazz version of Joplin's piece (ex.2) also contains the major seventh.)

Both Kenton's works illustrate (at the end of the *a* section) the distinct chromaticism often apparent in band voicing which helped shape the melody. Further examples of influential features are the chord voicings in the bridge of the opening theme of *Eager Beaver*, where each phrase ends on a diminished fifth (later a bop trademark), and the rubato statement of the melody by the piano in *Artistry in Rhythm*.

Jazz musicians whose major instrument is other than the piano have always used the keyboard as a self-teaching tool, to formulate interesting voicings and to understand harmonic principles for the creation of solos on their main instrument. (As early as 1927 Bix Beiderbecke was using his piano composition *In a Mist* (*Bixology*) (1927, OK 40916) to explore impressionistic seventh chords (incorporating diminished fifths) combined with a bluesy stride style.) During the 1940s, when harmony was the basis of so many new concepts in jazz, an ability to play the piano at a fairly basic level was almost a prerequisite for any instrumentalist. An example of a figure better known for his work on another instrument is Milt Jackson, whose piano accompaniments with the Boptet led by Howard McGhee and Fats Navarro may be heard on *The Skunk/Boperation* (1948, BN 558); Jackson's style also gives an insight into the rhythmic nature of comping.

Similarly, two pianists who could more correctly be defined as composers used the piano in an experimental fashion and were highly influential in the area of chord voicing. The works of Thelonious Monk and Tadd Dameron, like those of Kenton, were often built directly from piano voicings of new chord sequences. In addition, both the melodies in ex.7 are derived from the principle of voice

Ex.7 Melodies derived from voice leading
(a) From Thelonious Monk's *'Round Midnight*

(b) From Tadd Dameron's *If you could see me now*

leading: in Monk's *'Round Midnight*, for example, the seventh of one chord resolves onto the third of the next – A (7th of BMI7) to A♭ (enharmonic 3rd of E); A♭ (7th of B♭MI7) to G (3rd of E♭7). Monk's approach to the piano – a jagged use of seconds, sevenths, and other dissonant intervals and much feeling of space – is a study in itself. When playing unaccompanied he often employed a disjointed stride style, and his pieces usually involved unpredictable rhythmic displacement.

Indeed, rhythm was also a strong factor in the development of bop piano, and much stylistic modification arose through the changing function of the rhythm section. With the coming of amplification, the guitar began to be used as a solo instrument, and its new-found power often upset the delicate balance of the section. The recordings issued on the album *The Harlem Jazz Scene* also illustrate this aspect: the new rhythmic feel and the accents played by Monk may be heard quite well during Christian's solos, but are obliterated when the latter strums an accompaniment. A performance by Tiny Grimes of Charlie Parker's *Red Cross* (1944, Savoy 532) is also instructive: the guitarist is effective when doubling the melody with Parker, taking a solo, or playing background licks, but he impedes the rhythm when he strums squarely on all four beats. The pianist, Clyde Hart, had already mastered the new comping style and sounds comfortable; his solo, however, is still of the swing type. On a further recording by the same group, *Tiny's Tempo* (1944, Savoy 526), Grimes strums a four-beat rhythm almost throughout, and Hart, unsure where to place his chords so as not to cause conflict, plays in the high treble register after the manner of Count Basie.

A comparison of this last performance with one made by Gillespie and Parker only eight months later – Gillespie's *Salt Peanuts* (1945, Guild 1003) – shows in the later recording the complete transition of the jazz piano style and the new role of the instrument in the rhythm section. There is no guitar, and the pianist, Al Haig, provides perfect examples of pure bop comping, complete with extended chord voicings jabbed in a rhythmically free manner during gaps in the melodic lines. Haig's improvised solo is also pure bop: his right hand plays running figures in imitation of Gillespie and Parker, and his left performs the comping function exactly as in his role as accompanist, but with spare chords or intervals (often only a root and a 7th) so as not to limit his choice of notes in the melodic line.

Pure bop piano reached its apotheosis in the work of Bud Powell. The statement of the theme in his trio performance of *All God's Chillun Got Rhythm* (1949, Mer./Clef 11046) provides excellent examples of bop chord voicings. His linear right-hand improvisation shows supreme creativity and technique, and his left hand also exhibits a number of interesting devices: ostinato octave leaps on the dominant against tonic harmony; spare intervals such as 10ths and 7ths; and occasional single notes in the bass moving in half-notes (mostly when the chord progression follows a succession of fifths). Powell's hammer-like approach to the piano lent great drive to his performances, and such solos as that on Parker's *Ornithology* (1950; on the album *Charlie Parker in Historical Recordings*, i, 1948, 1950, Le Jazz Cool 101) had a great influence on other bop pianists.

In his solo work Powell treated the instrument in a similar fashion, simply allowing the feeling of a rhythm section to be implied. In *Hallucinations* (1951) on the album *Bud Powell Moods* (1950–51, Clef 610) (ex.8) he derives his melody from

Ex.8 From the second improvised chorus of Bud Powell: *Hallucinations,* (1951), from the album *Bud Powell Moods* (1950–51, Clef 610); transcr. L. Feather (Feather, 1957)

successive hand positions of ninth chords played alternately up and down in an arpeggiated manner, while his left hand shows the use of spare intervals and single notes.

Even as many bop pianists were relieving the emphasis on the left hand and lightening the instrument's role in the rhythm section, an alternative approach was being developed by Erroll Garner. Garner sometimes created the effect of continuous strumming in his left hand, articulated by occasional accents in the lower register, thus recalling the impression of a swing rhythm section. His right-hand playing, with its use of treble chords and/or octaves, also drew on earlier styles, but Garner's harmonic vocabulary was close to that of bop musicians. His playing is most effective when unaccompanied, though it is also successful in trios and in solos within an ensemble. On the slowest take of Parker's *Cool Blues* (1947, Dial 1015), for instance, Garner plays a full chorus before the closing theme in this manner; in all other solos in the piece, however, he adopts a blend of swing and bop elements. Garner's mature style is well represented by the album *Concert by the Sea* (1955, Col. CL883).

Certain elements of swing era big-band music were also transformed and carried over into bop piano. One of these was the "locked hands" block-chord style, which derived from the voicing of big-band saxophone sections. The pianist harmonized each note of the melody with a four-note chord in the right hand, while the left hand doubled the melody an octave lower (*see* Harmony (i), §1(iv)). Phil Moore is credited with developing this style as early as 1939 and Milt Buckner made use of it in Lionel Hampton's band during the early 1940s. Lennie Tristano, on *Blue Boy* (*Fine and Dandy*) (1947, Key. 681), shows a strong understanding of its potential, using block chords when comping, in solo passages, and in simultaneous improvisation with the guitarist Billy Bauer. But the true popularizer of the technique was George Shearing (ex.9); Shearing added vibraphone to the upper

Ex.9 Beginning of the bridge section in the first chorus of George Shearing: *Bop, Look, and Listen* (1949, MGM 10426); transcr. L. Koch

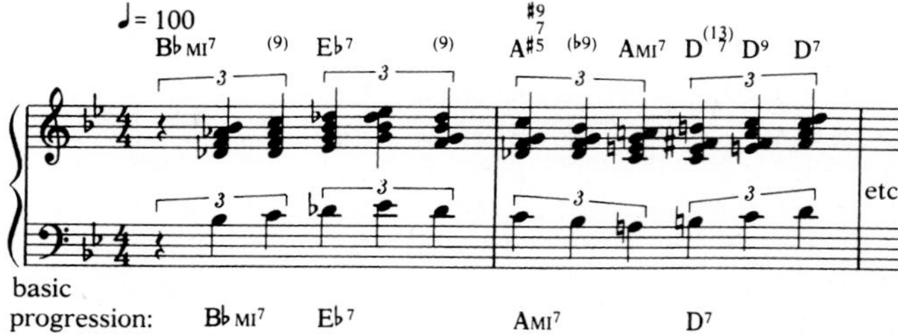

melody line of the piano and guitar to the lower, creating a distinctive ensemble sound that brought him much commercial success.

The nature of the locked hands style generates nonharmonic tones in every voice, producing in effect "passing chords" and "neighbor chords" within the basic progression. Although very effective in a group setting, this approach was generally not satisfactory in solo playing unless it was interspersed with other styles; the lack of steady rhythm and bass roots was too difficult to overcome by implication. Furthermore, the use of such a block-chord texture can tend to become monotonous. Shearing usually played his improvisations in a single-line manner and reserved the locked hands style mainly for melody statements, which created a balanced performance.

Later pianists who made exemplary use of block chords in improvisation include Dick Hyman (for example, Charlie Parker's *Hot House* (1952) on the album *New Bird*, ii, 1951–4, Phoenix 12); Lennie Tristano (*Ghost of a Chance*, on *Lennie Tristano*, 1955, Atl. 1224); Bill Evans (ii) (*Green Dolphin Street* (1959) on *Peace Piece and other Pieces*, 1959, 1962, Mlst. 47024); and Oscar Peterson (*Give me the simple life*, on *Tracks*, 1970, MPS 15306).

5. After 1950: the acoustic piano. During the 1950s a number of pianists expanded the block-chord style by adopting a two-handed full-chord approach, imitating more closely the orchestral sound of a big-band brass section. The effect created also bore some resemblance to the voicings (though not, of course, the rhythms) used in Afro-Cuban jazz in the late 1940s. An early use of expanded block chords may be heard played by Red Garland with the Miles Davis Quintet on *Bye Bye Blackbird* (on the album *'Round about Midnight*, 1955–6, Col. CL949).

Another approach, which derived, more or less, from the Latin style, was that of playing a single-note melody simultaneously in both hands, one or more octaves apart. An example may be heard on *Barbados* (on the album *Here is Phineas*, 1956, Atl. 1235), recorded by Phineas Newborn, and many instances of the technique used in improvisation are performed by Eddie Costa on Clark Terry's *The Jazz Version of All American* (1962, Mdsv. 26).

The basic bop piano style received a healthy injection of the blues during the 1950s through the funky work of Horace Silver. By his witty use of short bluesy licks (usually involving a simple two-note chord with the addition of sliding grace notes to give the effect of blue notes), Silver restored some of the earthiness which the bop musicians had deliberately destroyed. His approach is well represented by *Doodlin'* (on the album *Horace Silver and the Jazz Messengers*, 1954, BN 5058) (ex.10) and *The Preacher* (on *Horace Silver and the Jazz Messengers*, 1955, BN 5062).

Ex.10 Bars 10–11 of the first improvised chorus of Horace Silver: *Doodlin'*, from the album *Horace Silver and the Jazz Messengers* (1954, BN 5058); transcr. L. Koch

An interesting comparison can be made by examining the work of John Lewis in the early 1950s (for example, any of his recordings with the Modern Jazz Quartet between 1952 and 1957) and that of Wynton Kelly at the beginning of the next decade (in particular his recordings with Miles Davis in 1961). Both pianists follow in the footsteps of Bud Powell, but Lewis's spare style was strongly influenced by the cool-jazz movement, while Kelly's more funky approach exhibits the use of expanded block chords and a number of impressionistic touches.

The impressionistic aspect of jazz piano was unveiled in the late 1950s by Bill Evans (ii), who used in his left hand rootless voicings which implied chord roots (sometimes a choice of several); an effect of unabated tension was created by the progression of ambiguous chords that never seemed to resolve (ex.11). This method resulted in a new sound for

Ex.11 From Bill Evans (ii): *Blue in Green*, on the album *Portrait in Jazz* (1959, Riv. 1162); transcr. L. Koch

the pianist and gave much freedom of choice to the double bass player. In *Blue in Green* (on the album *Portrait in Jazz*, 1959, Riv. 1162), when he reaches a climactic point in his solo, Evans makes use of this type of voicing in rhythm with his right-hand ideas; this produces the same feeling as the older block-chord technique, but, since the left-hand voicing does not move with the melody, gives a more hammer-like effect. For comping within an ensemble, the rootless voicings could be used in the left hand while the right hand played contrasting chords, sometimes setting up dual harmonic implications; they could also be transferred to the right hand so that the left could provide a bass line. For a solo performance, however, this style is usually best when modified with the addition of some bass notes and an injection of rhythmic vitality, and/or melded with earlier jazz styles, as in Evans's performance in *Alone* (1969, Verve 68792).

Other pianists also began using rootless voicings in a more blues-based manner, sometimes employing fuller chords. With the advent of modal and free jazz at the end of the 1950s, the left hand soon became preoccupied with voicings in fourths in order to accommodate the nonharmonic nature of the music. In the modal style pianists often played

3. Cecil Taylor at Ronnie Scott's in London, 1985

improvisatory patterns in the right hand against the fourths, using the pentatonic or other modal scales, or, particularly when comping, added to the structure by playing block chords; the same approach was used in freer performances, but more random tonalities were employed. Another technique of modal jazz was to derive a melodic improvisation from the position of fourths in the right hand (just as the bop pianists had done with right-hand chord voicings – see ex.8).

In the 1960s pianists had to adjust to nonharmonic thinking. Before that time, most melodies (both composed and improvised) were harmonically derived. The best examples as to how this adjustment was achieved may be found in the work of McCoy Tyner, a pianist of equivalent standing in a more modern era to that of Bud Powell in the bop period. Tyner's recorded performances are infused with an underlying blues feeling and jazz vitality whatever approach he chooses to take – bop, modal, or freer style. On *Village Blues* (on the album *Coltrane Jazz*, 1959–60, Atl. 1354), an early recording with Coltrane, he shows a bluesy type of voicing used by Evans, in which chords seem to be built from the elements of mixolydian scales; at several points in his improvisations on *Blue Monk* (ex.12*a*) (on his own LP *Nights of Ballads and Blues*, 1963, Imp. 39) he combines this type of voicing (in which chords derive from a C mixolydian scale – C–D–E–F–G–A–B♭) with chords voiced in fourths. On *Tunji* (on the album *Coltrane*, 1962, Imp. 21) Tyner accompanies Coltrane with one open chord in a repeated pattern (ex.12*b*), but for his solo he reverts to the blues form, using rootless structures in seventh-chord mixolydian voicings (ex. 12*c*). *The night has a thousand eyes* (on his own LP *Song for my Lady*, 1972, Mlst. 9044) gives (in the right hand) countless examples of phrases derived from

Ex.12 Some elements of McCoy Tyner's style: (a) and (d) transcr. P. Rinzler (Rinzler, 1983); (b) and (c) transcr. L. Koch

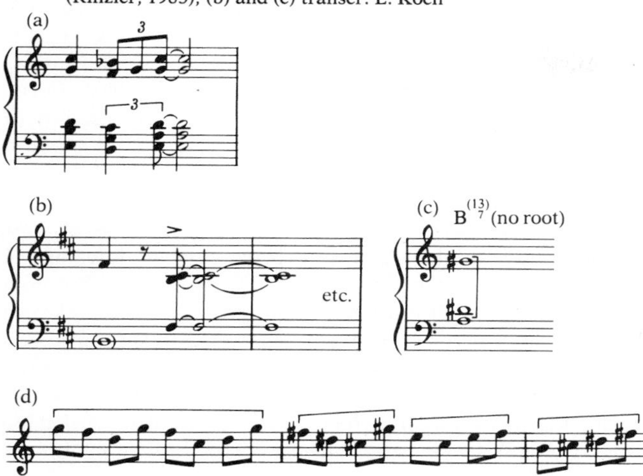

pentatonic scales (ex. 12*d*), while the album *Expansions* (1968, BN 84338) includes a modern approach to ballad form; Tyner exhibits a surprisingly gentle though crystal clear touch on *I thought I'd let you know* and engages in a "free" exchange with the drummer on *Smitty's Place*.

Other pianists departed more radically from the bop style, applying such free-jazz techniques as "gesture-derived" figures (i.e., passages originating through a physical gesture), tone clusters, atonal motivic development, and unusual attacks (with the palm or fist, etc.), and ignoring a steady rhythmic pulse. Lennie Tristano experimented with atonal music, mostly in a linear fashion, in the late 1940s (notably on *Intuition*, 1949, Cap. 1224), but the most exemplary musician in this style is Cecil Taylor, who began recording in 1956. *Enter Evening* (on the album *Unit Structures*, 1966, BN 84237) (ex.13) shows the use of gesture-derived figures, fourths, and a final tone cluster.

Ex.13 "Gesture-derived" figures from Cecil Taylor: *Enter Evening* on the album *Unit Structures* (1966, BN 84237); transcr. H. Martin (Martin, 1986)

In the 1970s free-jazz procedures were ingeniously fused with diatonic harmonies and a lyrical approach to the piano in the work of Keith Jarrett, as may be heard on his album *Eyes of the Heart* (1976, ECM 1150), while the synthesis of "modern" and bop techniques that evolved in the 1980s is exemplified by the playing of Michel Petrucciani, notably on the album *Pianism* (1985, BN 85124).

A healthy eclecticism may be seen most clearly in the evolution of the piano as a solo instrument. In the hands of a technician such as Oscar Peterson, a variety of styles and approaches are evident on a single album (*Tracks*, 1970, MPS 15306). The development from the 1950s of a single-note walking bass or rock ostinato in the left hand to imitate a bass player gave new scope to the solo pianist. Dave McKenna adopted a "rolling" approach to a walking bass on his album *Dancing in the Dark and other Music of Arthur Schwartz* (1985, Conc. 292), while on *Have you Met Miss Jones* (on the LP *Music for Perla*, 1974, Ste. 1021) Tete Montoliu exhibits a driving use of the technique at a fast tempo. Roland Hanna's album *Sir Elf* (1973, Choice 1003) shows various left-hand formulas, including some derived from Erroll Garner's personal style, a humorous stride after Thelonious Monk, and a rock-influenced line. A good example of a pianist assimilating new techniques into an older jazz style in a creative manner is Earl Hines (*Hines Does Hoagy*, *c*1973, Audiophile 113), and a masterful approach to the piano as a lone accompanying instrument is demonstrated by Jimmie Rowles in his duets with Stan Getz on the album *The Peacocks* (1977, Col. JC34873). A fine overview may be gained from the album *A Jazz Piano Anthology* (Col. KG32355), on which the featured pianists range from Eubie Blake to Cecil Taylor (details of dates and supporting players may be found in a review by Dan Morgenstern in *Down Beat*, xli/1, 1974).

But perhaps the best medium for hearing any jazz pianist's work is the trio of piano, double bass, and drums, and most players since the 1940s have recorded in that format at some time during their careers. The early trios, however, often used guitar instead of drums: the strummed rhythm was lighter and softer, and the guitar could also add melodic relief to the basic sound. The trios of Nat "King" Cole and Art Tatum were exemplary.

As for the future, jazz pianists will probably continue to develop a command of *all* styles and draw from them, as well as from classical techniques, for their inspiration. Dave Brubeck, who used this type of approach in the past, created a body of work that, while not always even in quality, was spontaneously conceived and cliché-free. In an earthier sense, the same broad conception is found in the work of Mary Lou Williams – for example, on her album *A Keyboard History* (1955, Jzt. 1206). From the mid-1960s Jaki Byard began to gain recognition for his pan-stylistic approach to the instrument, and in later decades this sort of eclecticism has become the norm.

6. After 1950: the electric and electronic piano. With the advent of electronically amplified instruments, many musicians felt that the volume of the acoustic piano was not adequate. (More practically, there was a need for a portable instrument which could be taken to venues that had either no piano or, more commonly, a piano that was out of tune and ill cared for.) As early as 1940 Earl Hines recorded two titles, *Body and Soul/Child of a Disordered Brain* (Bb 10642), on the Storytone piano, which relied on vacuum tubes and sounded like a fuzz-toned harpsichord. Hines also took the instrument on tour until its unwieldiness (it weighed one and a half tons) became overwhelming.

The earliest electric piano used to any extent in jazz, however, was developed in 1954 by Benjamin F. Miessner (whose early patent was also responsible for the manufacture of the Storytone) and marketed by Wurlitzer. Miessner's instrument was based on struck tuned reeds of steel, with individual electronic pickups for amplification affixed near each reed. Many musicians used this piano for practical purposes (it weighed only about 75 pounds), but most were disgruntled because of the touch and sound. A pianist's touch is a mark of individuality, and one which the use of an electric or electronic instrument, where the sound is not generated purely by the striking power of the player, threatened to obliterate. The later models of Miessner's piano, however, made with a plastic case, were more touch sensitive than the metal prototype. Some pianists, such as Joe Zawinul, found the tone of the instrument extremely pleasing: he played it when touring with Ray Charles in 1959 and again in the 1960s, as a member of Cannonball Adderley's group. Sun Ra recorded with it on *Medicine for a Nightmare* and *A Call for all Demons* (on the album *Angels and Demons at Play*, 1955–7, Saturn 407).

The electric piano that eventually found favor in the eyes of jazz musicians was that designed by Harold Rhodes and Leo Fender (who invented the electric bass guitar) and manufactured from 1965. It has lengths of tunable thin steel wire which are struck by rubber hammers; the wire forms one tine of a structure resembling a tuning-fork, the other tine of which is a longer, flat "tone bar" tuned to reinforce and sustain the vibrations of the wire. The sound of the Fender-Rhodes piano is more bell-like than that of the acoustic piano, and certain voicings tend to blur more than others. Pianists therefore had to revise their approach to playing when using the instrument (Bill Evans, for instance, never found it very satisfactory), and it took well over a decade of experimentation before musicians ascertained that the Fender-Rhodes piano was an instrument in its own right and not just a replacement for the acoustic piano.

The Fender-Rhodes piano was very effective in jazz-rock groups during the 1970s, when triadic voicings were formulated and pianists began to use it in a guitar-like manner. Herbie Hancock, who at the urging of Miles Davis played it on *Miles in the Sky* (1968, Col. CS9628), went on to employ the instrument to great artistic and commercial success on his album *Headhunters* (1973, Col. KC32731). Zawinul may be heard playing a creative solo on *American Tango* on Weather Report's album *Mysterious Traveler* (*c*1974, Col. KC32494).

The perfect union of artist and instrument, however, and one which has set the standard for performance on the Fender-Rhodes piano, is probably that demonstrated by Chick Corea. Whether it is the balance between volume setting and finger force, the regulation of volume, or his general sensitivity to the instrument that allows penetration of Corea's personality remains unknown, but nevertheless he plays with true expression. His long, clean right-hand lines (often derived from pentatonic scales) ring out over clipped figures comped in the left hand; he gives the impression that each note is being treated to a different level of force. Surprisingly, Corea (who, like Hancock, was introduced to the Fender-Rhodes piano by Davis) claims that at first he disliked the feel of the instrument, and he had many adjustments to make to it. The fruits of these adjustments may readily be heard on the album *Light as a Feather* (1972, Pol. 5525), recorded with his band Return to Forever, which shows a highly effective use of the piano in a jazz context. Corea's solo on the title track is particularly well suited to the instrument; there is a passage in *Five Hundred Miles High* where he plays a repeated note with rapid changes of fingering, the execution of which shows his intuitive knowledge of its capabilities; and his use of rubato in the introduction to *Spain* demonstrates its lyrical quality.

Many musicians have found problems with the electric piano when using it for comping to back acoustic instruments, and have had to take account of different soloists when making volume adjustments. Bob James, for example, almost buries Paul Desmond with his accompaniment on *Autumn Leaves* and *Tangerine* on Chet Baker's album *She Was Too Good to Me* (1975, CTI 6050); moreover, the instrument seems constantly to intrude on Desmond's ideas – although it sounds effective behind Baker's solos. Corea achieves a perfect balance, however, in his accompaniment of Stan Getz on the title track of the latter's LP *Captain Marvel* (1972, Col. KC32706).

Later advances in the development of electric and electronic technology have resulted in the manufacture of new instruments, as makers aspire to produce the equivalent of the acoustic piano. One of the first of these was the Yamaha CP70, an electric grand piano that sounds much like an acoustic instrument with pickups attached to it, and which was admired by many jazz pianists for its touch and sound. With the emergence of such instruments in the 1980s, the Fender-Rhodes fell completely out of the picture. A decade later, in the 1990s, the quality of these instruments continued to improve. Nonetheless, in an intimate setting, where one can hear timbre clearly, the electronic piano remains no match for a good acoustic instrument, and it is inconceivable that anyone would choose to use one for a studio recording (though – a different matter altogether – some fusion pianists use acoustic instruments with a synthesizer attached to create new timbral effects). The distinction holds in live performance as well: even though an electronic piano is far more convenient to transport and to keep in tune, nearly any jazz musician would prefer to use a venue's acoustic instrument, amplified through a public address system, rather than an electronic one.

The use of the piano in jazz is explored deeply in the multimedia CD-ROM *Dick Hyman's Century of Jazz Piano*, recorded by Hyman and created by J. Simpson (New Orleans, 1999).

For further illustrations *see* Basie, count; Evans, bill (ii); Herman, woody, fig. 1a; Jazz (i), fig.8; Jones, fig.1a; Monk, thelonious; Shearing, george; Sullivan, joe; and Taylor, billy (ii).

BIBLIOGRAPHY

H. Panassié: "The Pianists," *The Real Jazz* (New York and Toronto, 1942 [in Eng. trans.], rev. and enlarged by Panassié, 2/1960/*R*1973)

R. Blesh and H. Janis: *They All Played Ragtime* (New York, 1950, rev. 4/1971)

L. Feather: "The Piano," *The Book of Jazz: a Guide to the Entire Field* (New York, 1957, 2/1965 as *The Book of Jazz from Then till Now: a Guide to the Entire Field*)

J. Mehegan: *The Jazz Pianist: Studies in the Art and Practice of Jazz Improvisation*, i–iii (New York, n.d. [?1960-61])

——: *Contemporary Styles for the Jazz Pianist* (New York, n.d. [?1964-70], 2/n.d. [?1980])

I. Gitler: "Bud Powell and the Pianists," *Jazz Masters of the Forties* (New York 1966/*R*1983 with discography), 110

G. Schuller: *Early Jazz: its Roots and Musical Development* (New York, 1968), 214

W. Bishop, Jr.: *A Study in Fourths* (New York, 1976)

E. H. Newberger: "The Transition from Ragtime to Improvised Piano Style," *JJS*, iii/2 (1976), 3

——: "Archetypes and Antecedents of Piano Blues and Boogie Woogie Style," *JJS*, iv/1 (1977), 84

——: "The Development of New Orleans and Stride Piano Styles," *JJS*, iv/2 (1977), 43

B. Dobbins: *The Contemporary Jazz Pianist: a Comprehensive Approach to Keyboard Improvisation* (Jamestown, RI, 1978, 2/1984)

J. M. Wildman: "The Function of the Left Hand in the Evolution of Jazz Piano," *JJS*, v/2 (1979), 23

E. H. Newberger: "Refinement of Melody and Accompaniment in the Evolution of Swing Piano Styles," *ARJS*, i (1982), 85

B. Taylor: *Jazz Piano: History and Development* (Dubuque, IA, 1982)

M. Weiss: *Jazz Styles and Analysis: Piano* (Chicago, *c*1982)

L. Koch: "Thelonious Monk: Compositional Techniques," *ARJS*, ii (1983), 67

P. Rintzler: "McCoy Tyner: Style and Syntax," *ARJS*, ii (1983), 109–49

M. Williams: "Jelly Roll Morton," "Art Tatum," "Thelonious Monk," *The Jazz Tradition* (New York, rev. 2/1983), 16–46, 92, 154

J. Jeckovich: "The Forms and Orchestration of Five Jelly Roll Morton Piano Solos," *ARJS*, iii (1985), 1
P. S. Machlin: *Stride: the Music of Fats Waller* (Boston and London, 1985)
T. Rhea: "The Electric Piano," *The Art of Electronic Music*, ed. T. Dorter and G. Armbruster (New York, 1985), 16
H. Martin: "Piano Styles," *Enjoying Jazz* (New York, 1986), 156
F. Krieger: *Jazz-Solopiano: zum Stilwandel am Beispeiel ausgewählter "Body and Soul": Aufnahmen von 1938–1992* (Graz, Austria, 1995 [*recte* 1996])
R. Laird: *Tantalizing Tingles: a Discography of early Ragtime, Jazz, and Novelty Syncopated Piano Recordings, 1889–1934* (Westport, CT, and London, 1995)

LAWRENCE KOCH

Piano(la) roll. A roll, usually of paper, on which music is preserved in the form of perforations; it is recorded and played back mechanically on a player piano or pianola. *See* Recording, §I, 1(ii).

Picard, John (Francis) (*b* London, 17 May 1934). English trombonist. He studied piano from the age of six but was self-taught on trombone. After his military service he performed and recorded with Cy Laurie (1953–4), then with Humphrey Lyttelton (November 1954 – September 1960), the trumpeter and reed player Mike Daniels (from October 1960), Bruce Turner (February–July 1961), Wally Fawkes (briefly, early 1962), Tony Coe (as co-leader of groups, 1962–1970s), and Kathy Stobart (as co-leader of a quintet, late 1960s). During the 1970s and 1980s the style of his work became more catholic. He recorded with Brian Lemon (1970) and Phil Seamen (1971), led a septet which included Colin Smith, Don Weller, and Coe (1970s), wrote for and played with Stan Greig's London Jazz Big Band (1975–83), and worked with the group Rocket 88 (with the pianist Ian Stewart and the rock drummer Charlie Watts, 1978–) and the Charlie Watts Big Band (1985–); Art Themen and Trevor Tompkins were among those who also played in Picard's own groups. He continued to work as a freelance and a leader into the early 1990s. His playing may be heard to advantage on Lyttelton's *Triple Exposure* (1959, Parl. PMC1110) and Tubby Hayes's album *Jazz tête à tête* (1966, Prog. 7079). Picard's son, Simon Picard, has played tenor saxophone in several small groups and performed and recorded with the London Jazz Composers Orchestra from 1989 into the late 1990s.

BIBLIOGRAPHY

CarrJ; ChiltonB
R. Cotterrell, ed.: *Jazz Now: the Jazz Centre Society Guide* (London, 1976)

DIGBY FAIRWEATHER/SIMON ADAMS, BK

Piccolo. The highest-pitched member of the orchestral flute family, sounding an octave higher than the flute itself; *see* Flute, §§1 and 3.

Piccolo bass. A small Double bass with sloping shoulders (like those of a viol) and four strings tuned in 4ths (usually *E–A–d–g*); it should not be confused with the half- and three-quarter-size double basses, which have the characteristics of the full-size instrument. The piccolo bass was developed for double bass players who wished to extend the solo opportunities offered by the cello to an instrument constructed and played like a double bass. The cello has several advantages over the double bass as a solo instrument: its higher range enables it to be better heard when pitted against an accompanying rhythm section, and the closer spacing of the fingerings means that shifts in position of the left hand are necessary less often and are smaller than on the double bass, so that greater mobility and speed of execution are possible. A few double bass players took up cello, among them Oscar Pettiford, Ray Brown, and Percy Heath, who among them developed a pizzicato technique for solo work on the instrument. But many players who might have wished to double on the cello did not do so because the instrument was tuned in 5ths instead of 4ths, and because it had tuning pegs instead of machine heads, making quick retuning difficult.

In 1960, in collaboration with the Kay Company of Chicago, Brown developed a hybrid instrument combining features of the cello and the double bass; it had machine-head tuning and a modified bridge, which, together with its thin, flexible strings, made the instrument peculiarly suitable for solo pizzicato playing. In time this was developed into the piccolo bass. The instrument is not widely used, but Ron Carter regularly doubles on it, and in the early 1970s he had made for him a piccolo bass tuned *A–d–g–c′*. (Frederick Lyman, who has built instruments for Carter, is one of the principal makers of piccolo basses.) The first albums on which Carter played piccolo bass were those he made for the label CTI in 1973–6; on *Piccolo* (1977, Mlst. 55004) and *Parfait* (1980, Mlst. 9107) he plays only piccolo bass, accompanied by a rhythm section.

BIBLIOGRAPHY

M. Jones: "Down the Poll: Ray Brown," *MM*, xl (25 March 1961), 12
L. Tomkins: "The Bass in the Foreground: Ron Carter," *CI*, xix/10 (1981), 6

ALYN SHIPTON

Pichon, Fats [Walter] (*b* New Orleans, 1906; *d* Chicago, 26 Feb 1967). Pianist, singer, and arranger. He began playing piano as a child, moved to New York in his teens, and later studied in Boston at the New England Conservatory. In the 1920s he returned intermittently to New Orleans, where he performed in the Tulane Orchestra, led his own band at the Pelican Café, and worked with Sidney Desvigne on the SS *Island Queen* (for riverboat jobs he sometimes played calliope). During the same period he toured Mexico and Texas, worked in New York for various bands (notably that of Luis Russell), and recorded both as the leader of a trio with Henry "Red" Allen and Teddy Bunn (*Doggin' that Thing/ Yo Yo*, 1929, Vic. 38544) and as a singer with King Oliver (*I've got that thing*, 1929, Vic. 38521). At the beginning of 1929 Pichon took part in an early "fusion" session when he recorded with the Hawaiian guitarist Benny Nawahi; the recordings, which include *Dad Blame Blues/Black Boy Blues* (QRS R7067), are credited to the QRS Boys. Later his band accompanied Mamie Smith on tour (1932–4). After returning to New Orleans Pichon collaborated further with Desvigne, played in A. J. Piron's big band, and led his own band on the SS *Capitol* (to 1941). Throughout the 1940s and 1950s he worked regularly as a soloist and continued to tour outside New Orleans. Although troubled by failing eyesight, he continued to play intermittently in the 1960s.

BIBLIOGRAPHY

ChiltonW; FeatherE
Obituaries: D. Marquis, *Jazz Report*, v/v [1967], [36]; *SL*, xviii (1967), 40
A. Rose and E. Souchon: *New Orleans Jazz: a Family Album* (Baton Rouge, LA, 1967, rev. and enlarged 3/1984), 100
R. H. Knowles: *Fallen Heroes: a History of New Orleans Brass Bands* (New Orleans, 1996)

ALDEN ASHFORTH/HOWARD RYE

Pickens, Willie (L.) (*b* Milwaukee, 18 April 1931). Pianist, composer, and arranger. He began formal piano study at the age of 14 and attended the Wisconsin Conservatory of Music before entering the army in 1951. Later he studied music education at the University of Wisconsin, Milwaukee (BS 1958). After moving to Chicago in 1958 he taught music in public schools (1966–90) and at the American Conservatory (1971–87); in 1997 he joined the faculty of Northern Illinois University. He is best known outside Chicago for his work with Eddie Harris (1961–6) and, later, Elvin Jones (1990–97), with whom he appears in the video *Elvin Jones Jazz Machine* (n.d. [filmed 1991]). A powerful and harmonically sophisticated pianist, he formed a short-lived trio with Muhal Richard Abrams and Amina Claudine Myers (December 1975) and appeared with many leading players, among them Roy Eldridge, Art Farmer, Dexter Gordon, Johnny Griffin, Roy Haynes, Milt Jackson, Roscoe Mitchell, Red Norvo, Max Roach, and Joe Williams; his trio consisting of Larry Gray on double bass and Robert Shy on drums is one of the finest modern-jazz rhythm sections in Chicago. Pickens appeared regularly at international jazz festivals and performed at Chicago Jazz Festival almost yearly from its inception. He was interviewed by Marian McPartland for her NPR radio show "Piano Jazz" in 1996, and again at the Chicago Jazz Festival in 1999. In 1998 he recorded his jazz arrangements of Christmas carols, the annual performance of which has become a Chicago jazz tradition.

SELECTED RECORDINGS

As leader: *It's About Time* (1981, 1986–7, Southport 8); *A Jazz Christmas* (1998, Southport 0056)

As sideman: E. Harris: *Exodus to Jazz* (1961, VJ 3016); *Mighty Like a Rose* (1961, VJ 3025); Elvin Jones: *Going Home* (1992, Enja 7095-2); *It Don't Mean a Thing* (1993, Enja 8066-2); L. Bellson: *Salute* (1994, Chi. 329); C. Terry: *Top and Bottom* (1995, Chi. 347)

BIBLIOGRAPHY

T. Schneckloth: "Willie Pickens," *DB*, xliv/13 (1977), 32

DEBORAH GILLASPIE

Pickering, Tom [Thomas Mansergh] (*b* Burra, Australia, 8 Aug 1921). Australian clarinetist, tenor saxophonist, bandleader, and composer. He grew up in Hobart, Tasmania, where he played clarinet from 1936 and helped to form a dixieland group, the Barrelhouse Four. Following wartime dance-band work he reconstituted the Barrelhouse Four (1945), which played at the first Australian Jazz Convention (Melbourne, 1946). From 1949 until the late 1950s Pickering led a group which held important residencies at the 7HT Theatrette and the Town Hall in Hobart; in that first year it recorded *What makes me love you so* (first issued on *Jazz Notes (1949) Fourth Australian Jazz Convention*, NFSA TA003). The release of his first recording on the Swaggie label (1970) revitalized his jazz activity and, except in 1979 when he was traveling on a Churchill Fellowship, he continued to lead his own group; he may be heard to advantage on the albums *Sweet, Soft, Plenty Rhythm* (1979–83, Swaggie 1404) and *Red Hot & Blue* (1983, Candle 122), both of which he recorded as co-leader with the pianist Ian Pearce. In 1982 he was made a Member of the Order of Australia.

BIBLIOGRAPHY

A. Bisset: *Black Roots, White Flowers: a History of Jazz in Australia* (Sydney, 1979, rev. 2/1987)

B. Johnson: *The Oxford Companion to Australian Jazz* (Melbourne, Australia, 1987)

W. Bebbington, ed: *The Oxford Companion to Australian Music* (Melbourne, Australia, 1997)

BRUCE JOHNSON

Pickup group. A group assembled for a particular engagement, consisting of musicians who do not normally play together.

Picou, Alphonse (Floristan) (*b* New Orleans, 19 Oct 1878; *d* New Orleans, 4 Feb 1961). Clarinetist. From the age of 16 he played regularly with "reading" bands and orchestras in New Orleans, including the Excelsior Brass Band (occasionally in the late 1890s and regularly from 1904 to the mid-1920s) and the Bloom Philharmonic Orchestra (which he joined in 1903), but his improvising skills also allowed him to work successfully with smaller jazz groups. He was a member of Freddie Keppard's Olympia Orchestra (1907–10) and Louis Keppard's Magnolia Orchestra (1909), in which King Oliver and Pops Foster were also sidemen; Foster recalled Picou doubling as a soprano saxophonist at this time. Picou then performed with Manuel Perez (1910–12) and was a founding member of Papa Celestin's Tuxedo Orchestra and Tuxedo Brass Band, in which he played both B♭ and E♭ clarinet. While with the latter ensemble he is said to have adapted to the clarinet a piccolo solo on *High Society* from a written arrangement by Robert Recker, and his adaptation has since become a traditional part of the tune's performance. From 1912 to 1915 he led a band, and then spent a brief period in Chicago.

Soon back in New Orleans, Picou played with A. J. Piron, Perez, and Buddy Petit (1918) and held long affiliations with John Robichaux (until 1927) and Wooden Joe Nicholas's Camelia Brass Band and Dance Orchestra (1917–1920s). In 1923 he made another brief visit to Chicago, where Oliver's band recorded two of his compositions, *Olympia Rag* and *Onzaga* (which Oliver retitled *Chattanooga Stomp* and *New Orleans Stomp* for their pairing on Col. 14003D). Once more in New Orleans, in addition to his continuing work with the Excelsior, Tuxedo, and Camelia bands and Robichaux, he played with Lee Collins from 1923 to 1924.

In 1932 Picou reduced his musical activities and devoted more time to his occupation as a tinsmith; but, with the revival of interest in traditional jazz, he re-emerged to record with Kid Rena in 1940. He worked from the late 1940s to 1954 in a small group with Celestin in a residency at the Paddock; leadership of the band transferred from Celestin to the double bass player Ricard Alexis and finally to the pianist Octave Crosby. Picou became a doyen of New Orleans music, recording with the Eureka Brass Band in 1956 and playing at Picou's Bar and Restaurant fairly regularly until just before his death. His recorded work lacks the fire and the passionate flow of the great New Orleans clarinetists, but his tone and graceful articulation won him admirers.

Oral history material in *LNT*.

SELECTED RECORDINGS

As sideman: K. Rena: Low Down Blues (1940, Delta 803); High Society Rag (1940, Delta 804); Weary Blues (1940, Delta 806); Ricard Alexis: Clarinet Marmalade (1951, Palm 3020); Paddock Jazz Band: *Paddock Jazz Band, 1953* (1953, Center 10), incl. Eh la bas

BIBLIOGRAPHY

WrightK

G. Hoefer: "The Hot Box: Re-recording Etched of Picou 'High Society' Ride," *DB*, xvii/19 (1950), 6

A. Lomax: *Mister Jelly Roll: the Fortunes of Jelly Roll Morton, New Orleans Creole and "Inventor of Jazz"* (New York, 1950, 2/1973/*R*1993)

K. G. Mills: "Discography of Alphonse Picou," *Jazz Report*, i/8 (1961), 3; "Alphonse Picou: an Appreciation," i/8 (1961), 4
Obituaries: *New York Times* (5 Feb 1961); *SL*, xi/3–4 (1961), 3
"2 Jazz Bands March at Picou's Funeral," *New York Times* (10 Feb 1961)
J. St. Cyr: "Jazz as I Remember it, pt 2: Storyville Days," *JJ*, xix/10 (1966), 22
P. Foster, T. Stoddard, and R. Russell: *Pops Foster: the Autobiography of a New Orleans Jazzman* (Berkeley, CA, Los Angeles, and London, 1971)
T. Stagg and C. Crump: *New Orleans, the Revival: a Tape and Discography of Negro Traditional Jazz Recorded in New Orleans or by New Orleans Bands, 1937–1972* (n.p. [London], 1973)
F. J. Gillis and J. W. Miner, eds.: *Oh, didn't he Ramble: the Life Story of Lee Collins* (Urbana, IL, Chicago, and London, 1974/*R*1989) [incl. discography]
W. J. Schafer: "Breaking into 'High Society': Musical Metamorphoses in Early Jazz," *JJS*, ii/2 (1975), 53
P. Haby: "Alphonse Picou: New Orleans Creole," *Fn*, xi/5 (1980), 4
H. H. Broun: Liner notes, *Prelude to the Revival*, ii (American Music CD41, 1992)
R. H. Knowles: *Fallen Heroes: a History of New Orleans Brass Bands* (New Orleans, 1996)

JOHN CHILTON/BK

Pieces of Time. Percussion ensemble formed in 1983 by Andrew Cyrille. Kenny Clarke, Milford Graves, and Don Moye were its other members, and Philly Joe Jones joined the group following Clarke's death early in 1985. Its only album, *Pieces of Time* (1983, SN 1078), is a marvelous showcase for the group and an even stronger example of the flexibility of the talented Clarke, who fits in well with his avant-garde bandmates. Pieces of Time disbanded in 1986.

GK

Pieranunzi, Enrico (*b* Rome, 5 Dec 1949). Italian pianist, composer, and leader. Having studied jazz with his father, a guitarist, and classical piano at the conservatory in Reggio Calabria, he began his professional career in 1968 with the trombonist Marcello Rosa, whom he rejoined in 1972–3. From 1974 to 1975 he worked as a freelance pianist at the Music Inn in Rome, where he played with Kenny Clarke and Johnny Griffin, among others. He toured with Art Farmer (1975–81), Bill Smith (ii) (1977–8), and Kai Winding (1978–9). During the same period he recorded with Chet Baker (1979–80) and as an unaccompanied soloist and led several groups of his own, including a trio consisting of Bruno Tommaso and Roberto Gatto (1975–9), a quartet with the addition of Maurizio Giammarco (1979–80), and another trio consisting of Riccardo Del Fra and Gatto (1980–81). In 1984 he founded the long-lived SPACE JAZZ TRIO, with Enzo Pietropaoli on double bass and Fabrizio Sferra on drums, and he began to work with Marc Johnson, Joey Baron, and Paul Motian; he recorded duos with Lee Konitz, Baker, Phil Woods, Johnson, and Motian.

Pieranunzi's trios present a style of group interplay drawn from trios of Paul Bley and Bill Evans (ii). Some of his later recordings have been in a more conservative vein but are also more lyrical. His pieces *Don't forget the poet* and *Dee Song* (from the album *Deep Down*) are the only Italian jazz compositions included in a volume of the renowned fake book the *Real Book* (vol. ii, *c*1986). Pieranunzi is the author of *Bill Evans: ritratto di artista con pianoforte* (Rome, 1994).

SELECTED RECORDINGS

As unaccompanied soloist: *The Day after the Silence* (1976, Edi-Pan 800); *Parisian Portraits* (1990, Ida 026); *Un'alba dipinta sui muri* (1998, Egea 070)
Duos: with C. Baker: *The Heart of the Ballad* (1988, Philology 20); with L. Konitz: *Solitudes* (1988, Philology 28); with M. Johnson: *The Dream before Us* (1990, Ida 028)
As leader: *Enrico Pieranunzi* (1975, Horo 24); with C. Baker: *Soft Journey* (1979–80, Edi-Pan 805); *Isis* (1980, SN 1021); *New Lands* (1984, Tim. 211); *Autumn Song* (1984, Enja 4094); *Deep Down* (1986, SN 1121), incl. Dee Song, Don't forget the poet; with C. Haden and B. Higgins: *First Song* (1990, SN 121222-2); *Triologues*, iii (1991, Yvp 3026); *The Untold Story* (1993, IDA 036); *Trioscape* (1995, Yvp 3050); *Seaward* (1995, SN 121272-2); *The Night Gone By* (1996, Alfa Jazz 3906); *The Chant of Time* (1997, Alfa Jazz 3915)
As sideman: D. Piana and K. Winding: *Duo Bones* (1978, Red 143); B. Smith (ii): *Colours* (1978, 1980, Edi-Pan 807); C. Haden: *Silence* (1987, SN 121172-2); P. Woods and Space Jazz Trio: *Phil's Mood* (1988, Philology 27)

BIBLIOGRAPHY

"Enrico Pieranunzi," *JP*, xxxv/3 (1986), 12
P. Carles, A. Clergeat, and J.-L. Comolli: *Dictionnaire du jazz* (Paris, 1988, rev. and enlarged 2/1994)
P. Benkimoun: "Un duo arc-en-ciel," *Jm*, no.410 (1991), 56
M. Franco: "Enrico Pieranunzi," *Musica jazz*, xlix/10 (1993), 35
——: "Discografia completa," *Musica jazz*, xlix (1993), no.10, p.49; no.11, p.34
"Ten Italian Musicians the World Should Know about . . .," *Jazz Changes*, iv/2 (1997), 16
<http://www.ijm.it/enartists.html> (1999)

STEFANO ZENNI

Pierce, Billie [née Goodson, Wilhelmina] (*b* Marianna, FL, 8 June 1907; *d* New Orleans, 29 Sept 1974). Pianist and singer. She grew up in a musical family and during the early 1920s danced in theaters in Pensacola, Florida, in which setting she worked with Ma Rainey; she also deputized for Clarence Williams for two weeks as Bessie Smith's pianist at the Belmont Theater (1922). At this same venue she accompanied Ida Cox, but not Rainey, as some accounts claim. Thereafter Goodson toured as a singer, dancer, and pianist, initially in Florida only, but more widely into the early 1930s with such obscure groups as the Mighty Wiggle Carnival, Joe Jesse's orchestra, and her own touring revue. Around 1929 she may have replaced her elder sister Sadie Goodson in Buddy Petit's band on the riverboat SS *Madison*, but accounts of his bandmembers are contradictory. After settling in New Orleans she worked with A. J. Piron and then at the Rialto with Alphonse Picou (1932). She began performing with De De Pierce when they were both members of the band led by George Lewis (i) at a dime-a-dance hall, the Kingfish (1933–4). The couple were married in March 1935, and thereafter their careers ran in parallel. Billie Pierce first recorded with Emile Barnes in 1946 (issued in 1997) and under her own name in 1953.

Oral history material in *LNT.*

SELECTED RECORDINGS

As unaccompanied soloist: on [no leader:] *Primitive Piano* (1956, Tone 1), Got a Working Man, Panama Rag, In the Racket
As sideman with E. Barnes: on *Emile Barnes 1946: the Very First Recordings* (1946–53, AM CD102), Strolling in the Moonlight, St. Louis Blues (both 1946)

BIBLIOGRAPHY

P. Oliver: *Conversation with the Blues* (London, 1965, rev. 2/1997)
S. Harris: *Blues Who's Who: a Biographical Dictionary of Blues Singers* (New Rochelle, NY, 1979/*R*1994)
Obituaries: *New Orleans Times-Picayune* (2 Oct 1974); *New York Times* (3 Oct 1974); P. van Vorst, *DB*, xli/19 (1974), 10

For details of the principal part of her career, recordings, and further bibliography, *see* PIERCE, DE DE.

BK

Pierce, Billy [Bill; William Watson, III] (*b* Hampton, VA, 25 Sept 1948). Tenor and soprano saxophonist. He grew up in Florida, both in and near Jacksonville, and started on tenor saxophone; later he took up alto saxophone, clarinet, and bass clarinet as well. After completing high school in Miami he enrolled at Tennessee State University (Nashville), where he learned to play oboe; during the same period he worked professionally in local funk and soul bands. While studying at the Berklee School of Music in Boston he performed in bands at various clubs, accompanying such visiting soul musicians as Marvin Gaye and Stevie Wonder; he toured the Americas with Wonder for about six months in 1970 and then returned to Boston. After touring with obscure variety bands he taught at Berklee between 1975 and 1979. He performed and recorded with James Williams (1979–80, 1984–5) in a duo, a big band, and various small groups, notably Alan Dawson's quartet. From 1980 to 1982 Pierce toured the USA and Europe with Art Blakey, with whom he made several recordings on tenor saxophone, and from 1983 he was again based in Boston, where he continued to perform and resumed teaching at Berklee. As a member of Tony Williams's quintet he toured internationally from the group's formation in spring 1986 until it disbanded early in 1993. Pierce made further recordings with James Williams through the 1990s and took part in sessions led by Gary Burton (in Tokyo, 1985), Makoto Ozone (*c*1986), Geoff Keezer (1988, 1992), John Swana (1990–91), Antonio Hart (1991), and Jeff Palmer (1994).

SELECTED RECORDINGS

As leader: *William the Conqueror* (1985, Sunnyside 1013); *One for Chuck* (1991, Sunnyside 1053); with J. Jackson: *Burnin'* (1991, Criss Cross 1139); *Epistrophy* (1992, Evidence 22126); *Rio (Ballads & bossa nova)* (1994, Sunnyside 1065); with Chris McCann: *Froggin' Around* (1996, CIMP 107)

As sideman: A. Blakey: *Album of the Year* (1981, Tim. 155); J. Williams: *James Williams Meets the Saxophone Masters* (1991, DIW 868); T. Williams: *Tokyo Live* (1992, BN B22V-99031); J. Williams: *Talkin' Trash* (1993, DIW 887)

SELECTED FILMS AND VIDEOS

Art Blakey & the Jazz Messengers (n.d. [filmed *c*1980]); Jazz at the Smithsonian: Art Blakey and the Jazz Messengers (1982); Tony Williams: New York Live (*c*1993 [filmed 1989])

BIBLIOGRAPHY

S. Vandermark: "Bill Pierce: Interview," *Cadence*, xi/11 (1985), 5
M. Martin: "Bill Pierce," *Saxophone Journal*, xv/4 (1991), 14

BK

Pierce, De De [Joseph De Lacrois [De Lacroix]] (*b* New Orleans, 18 Feb 1904; *d* New Orleans, 23 Nov 1973). Cornetist and singer. He was largely self-taught. Although he worked principally as a brick mason, he played with several dance bands in New Orleans (including that of Arnold De Pass in 1924) and was in demand as a member of brass bands for parades. During the 1930s he worked in riverfront honky-tonks. In 1933–4 he became acquainted with Billie Goodson during the course of their membership in the band led by George Lewis (i) at the Kingfish, a jitney (dime-a-dance) hall, and they were married in March 1935. After their marriage Billie and De De Pierce usually worked together, mostly in obscure neighborhood dance halls in New Orleans; they held engagements, most notably at Luthjen's between 1936 until 1960, when the building burned down. They also toured with Ida Cox in 1935 (possibly again in the early 1940s) and with Alphonse Picou in the late 1940s, and they spent periods working in rough venues in Florida. De De's sight failed in the 1950s and Billie suffered from cancer, and the couple retired from music in 1954. However, they later resumed their residency at Luthjen's and made a number of recordings. From 1961 the Pierces led one of the principal Preservation Hall bands, which toured the USA and Europe. The group appeared on NBC television (late 1961), the PBS television show "New Orleans Jazz" (*c*1963), and in the television documentary "Anatomy of Pop: the Music Explosion" (1969; issued on film as *American Music: from Folk to Jazz to Pop*). It toured from 1965, appearing at the Newport Folk Festival (1966) and in Europe (1967), Mexico (1968), and Israel and Italy (1971). From summer 1967 the Pierces and their Preservation Hall band held annual residencies at Stanford University in Palo Alto, California, and from 1968 to 1973 they gave concerts at Philharmonic Hall in New York. De De was recognized as the leading interpreter of songs in Creole patois, while Billie was a forceful and energetic pianist and blues singer.

Oral history material in *LNT*.

SELECTED RECORDINGS

As leader with B. Pierce: *Billie and De De Pierce at Luthjen's* (1953, Center 15); *New Orleans Jazz* (1959, Folk Lyric 110); *Blues in the Classic Tradition* (1961, Riv. 9370); *Jazz at Preservation Hall*, ii (1962, Atl. 1409); *Billie and De De* (1966, Preservation Hall 3)

As sideman (together with B. Pierce): E. Barnes: on *Emile Barnes 1946: the Very First Recordings* (1946–53, AM CD102), High Society, Walking the Dog (both 1946); *American Music* (1951, AM 641), incl. Tout de moi, De De and Billie's Blues

BIBLIOGRAPHY

ChartersJ
P. Oliver: *Conversation with the Blues* (London, 1965, rev. 2/1997)
L. Borenstein and B. Russell: *Preservation Hall Portraits* (Baton Rouge, LA, 1968)
C. Strachwitz: Liner notes, *Billie and De De* (Arhoolie 2016, *c*1971)
Obituaries: *New York Times* (24 Nov 1973); M. Jones, *MM* (11 Dec 1973), 18
D. Pawson: "De De Pierce: Romance and Reality," *Fn*, v/1 (1973), 4
T. Stagg and C. Crump: *New Orleans, the Revival: a Tape and Discography of Negro Traditional Jazz Recorded in New Orleans or by New Orleans Bands, 1937–1972* (n.p. [London], 1973)
J. De Donder: "Billie and De De," *MR*, viii (1981), no.7, p.1; no.8, p.7
W. Carter: *Preservation Hall: Music from the Heart* (Wheatley, Oxford, England, and New York, 1991)

BILL RUSSELL/BK

Pierce, Nat(haniel) (*b* Somerville, MA, 16 July 1925; *d* Los Angeles, 10 June 1992). Pianist, arranger, and bandleader. He took piano lessons for a few years as a child, but hated the experience and abandoned the instrument; however, he returned to it to perform at high school as an unaccompanied boogie-woogie soloist and in dance bands. Having finished high school early to work professionally in 1943, he played mainly with bands in Boston, including one led by Shorty Sherock. In the years that followed he participated in local jam sessions with many established and future stars of swing and bop, and he studied classical music at the New England Conservatory for about one year. Later he worked with Larry Clinton (1948) and others and led his own bop-oriented big band in Boston. In 1951 he joined Woody Herman's band and at various times served as its pianist (September 1951–1955, June 1961 – mid-1966), arranger, and road manager (1960s); during the same period he led a group with Dick Collins (1954), worked as an arranger for Count Basie (from 1950), Ella Fitzgerald, Quincy Jones, and others, and took part in several recording sessions, notably that by Al Cohn's Natural Seven (1955). When apart from Herman he wrote all the arrangements for the television show "The Sound of Jazz" (1957), including that of his own composition, *Open all Night*, which was performed as the program's opening number by an all-star band under Basie's direction; he also took Basie's role on Lambert, Hendricks, and Ross's first album, *Sing a Song of Basie* (1957). Pierce performed and recorded with Ruby Braff (1955–7), accompanied Lester Young for an evening at Birdland, New York (1956), and directed his own big band at various venues in the city (1957–9), playing the last engagement at the Savoy

Ballroom before it was razed. In addition he accompanied Emmett Berry, toured Sweden with Joe Newman and the Basie All Stars for two weeks (October 1958), led a trio (1959), and recorded in small groups led by Paul Quinichette (1956), Eddie "Cleanhead" Vinson and Phil Woods (both 1957), Lambert, Hendricks, and Ross (1957), Bob Brookmeyer, Gene Quill, and Pee Wee Russell (all 1958), and Coleman Hawkins (1960). Later, after his second tenure with Herman, he recorded with Charlie Barnet's big band (in concert at Basin Street East, 1966), Johnny Hodges (1967), and Roy Eldridge (1970). In 1970 he toured Europe with Buddy Tate.

While serving as accompanist to Carmen McRae in 1971, Pierce went to Los Angeles, where he settled. He remained active as an arranger, working further with McRae, as well as with Anita O'Day, Earl Hines, and others, and he undertook much freelance work, including engagements with Zoot Sims (early 1970s), and international tours and recordings with Louie Bellson and reunions with Herman (both intermittently into the 1980s); he deputized for Stan Kenton for two months when the bandleader was ill in 1972. Pierce led his own groups (1972, 1974–5) and appeared in the film *New York, New York* (1977). In 1975, with FRANK CAPP, he formed the Capp–Pierce Orchestra (later known as the Capp–Pierce Juggernaut), and the following year he toured with Basie's band during the latter's illness. In the 1970s and 1980s he was a regular sideman for recordings on the Concord label, notably several by Scott Hamilton and by Rosemary Clooney, and others with Jake Hanna, Eiji Kitamura, Marshal Royal, and Warren Vaché. In 1978 he recorded for the Realtime label with Bill Berry's Ellington All Stars and Wild Bill Davison, and in the early 1980s he toured Europe with the Countsmen and with Keith Smith's band in the show "The Wonderful World of Louis Armstrong."

Pierce was a talented swing pianist who often attenuated his own musical personality to imitate Basie, notably in his association with Capp. His ability to propel a rhythm section was particularly evident on his recordings for Concord.

SELECTED RECORDINGS

As leader: with D. Collins: *Herdsman* (1954, Fan. 3-14); *Kansas City Memories* (1956, Coral 57091); *Nat Pierce Orchestra with Buck Clayton* (1957, Vic. LPM2543); *The Ballad of Jazz Street* (1961, Hep 2009); with F. Capp: *Juggernaut* (1977, Conc. 40), *Live at the Century Plaza* (1978, Conc. 72), *Juggernaut Strikes Again* (1981, Conc. 183)

As sideman with W. Herman: Beau Jazz (1953, Mars 900); *Swing Low, Sweet Clarinet* (1962, Phi. 600004); *Woody's Winners* (1965, Col. CS9236)

As sideman with others: A. Cohn: *The Natural Seven* (1955, RCA LPM1116); Lambert, Hendricks, and Ross: *Sing a Song of Basie* (1957, ABC-Para. 223); B. Brookmeyer: *Kansas City Revisited* (1958, UA 4008); R. Eldridge: *The Nifty Cat* (1970, MJR 8110); J. Hanna: *Kansas City Express* (1976, Conc. 22)

SELECTED ARRANGEMENTS

As leader with F. Capp: on *Juggernaut* (1977, CJ 40), Dickie's Dream

Recorded by others: C. Basie: New Basie Blues (1952, Clef 8964); W. Herman: Blue Lou (1953, Mars 700); Opus de funk, on Herman: *Road Band* (1955, Cap. T658)

BIBLIOGRAPHY

FeatherE; *Feather '60s*; *Feather–Gitler '70s*; *SheridanCB*

L. Tomkins: "The Nat Pierce Story," *Crescendo*, iv (1966), no.10, p.16; no.11, p.35

"The Benefits of Maturity: Nat Pierce," *CI*, xviii/6 (1980), 20

S. Dance: *The World of Count Basie* (New York and London, 1980), 236

S. Voce: "In Deep with Nat Pierce," *JJI*, xxxiv/10 (1981), 19

C. Deffaa: "Profile: Jazz Veteran Nat Pierce Grooves on the Music not on the Business," *Keyboard*, xii/6 (1986), 19

G. Endress: "Nat Pierce," *JP*, xxxv/2 (1986), 6

F. Büchmann-Møller: *You Just Fight for your Life: the Story of Lester Young* (New York, Westport, CT, and London, 1990), 206

Obituaries: *Los Angeles Times* (11 June 1992); *New York Times* (13 June 1992)

J. Simmen: "Johnny Simmen Reports," *BHcF*, no.407 (1992), 22

W. D. Clancy with A. C. Kenton: *Woody Herman: Chronicles of the Herds* (New York and elsewhere, 1995)

B. Crowther: "Nat Pierce: Monster Jazzman," *JJI*, xlix/4 (1996), 6

SCOTT YANOW/BK

Pierończyk, Adam (*b* Elblag, Poland, 24 Jan 1970). Polish saxophonist. After studying at a music school in Braniewo, Poland, he continued his education in Germany and Austria, taking private lessions from 1990 to 1992 and then attending the Folkwang-Hochschule in Essen (graduating in 1996). While still a student he led the trio (or quartet) Temathe (1992–6) and the quartet Gutter Music (1994–5). Thereafter he played in a duo with Leszek Możdżer (from 1996), led a trio (from 1997), co-led another trio with Ed Schuller and Jacek Kochan (from 1999), and led the group Digivooco, which included Gary Thomas (from 2000). As a sideman Pierończyk worked with Archie Shepp (1996), Możdżer (from 1996), Ted Curson, Joey Calderazzo, and Vitold Rek (all 1997), Thomas (from 1998), Schuller (1999–2000), and others. He has performed throughout Europe as well as in Israel and the USA.

SELECTED RECORDINGS

Duos with L. Możdżer: *Live in Sofia* (1997, Not Two 701-2)

As leader: *A Few Minutes in the Space* (1997, Gowi 43); with E. Schuller and J. Kochan: *Plastinated Black Sheep* (1999, Not Two 710-2); with Interzone: *Interzone Plays with Adam Pierończyk* (1999, Not Two 716-2); *Digivooco* (2000, PAO 10230)

BK

Pifarély, Dominique (Yves Michel) (Bègles, France, 26 Dec 1957). French violinist. He began playing violin at the age of six and was classically trained at the Montreuil Conservatoire, from which he graduated in 1977. When he was 13 he developed an interest pop, folk, and jazz, and thereafter he concentrated on jazz and improvised music. From 1978 he held a long association with Didier Levallet, manifest in such groups as Trio Levallet-Marais-Pifarély and Swing Strings System. In the 1980s he began leading his own ensembles and played as a sideman with, among others, François Jeanneau, Martial Solal, Eddy Louiss, Jean-Paul Céléa, the pianist François Couturier, Patrice Caratini, Mathias Rüegg, and Günter Sommer; he also worked with Mike Westbrook, recording in 1984 and 1992. Pifarély collaborated regularly with Louis Sclavis from 1985, and the two men formed the Acoustic Quartet in 1992, with Marc Ducret and the double bass player Bruno Chevillon as their sidemen. Around 1993 he established the trio Triplicity with Stefano Battaglia and Paolino Dalla Porta, and in the late 1990s he began working in a duo with Couturier; during the same period he played with Joachim Kühn, Daniel Humair, and Tim Berne and recorded with Rabih Abou-Khalil (1998).

SELECTED RECORDINGS

Duos with F. Couturier: *Poros* (1997, ECM 1647); with C. Zingaro: on [various artists]: *Icis* (1996, In Situ 167–9), *Pifarély/Zingaro* (In Situ 167)

As leader: *Insula Dulcamara* (1988, Nocturne 104); *Oblique* (1992, Ida 034); with L. Sclavis: *Acoustic Quartet* (1993, ECM 1526)

As sideman: M. Westbrook: *On Duke's Birthday* (1984, HA 6021); L. Sclavis: *Rouge* (1991, ECM 1458); *Les violences de Rameau* (1995–6, ECM 1588); R. Abou-Khalil: *Yara* (1998, Enja 9360-2)

BIBLIOGRAPHY

C. Gauffre: "Tête à tête," *Jm*, no.331 (1984), 34

P. Carles, A. Clergeat, and J.-L. Comolli: *Dictionnaire du jazz* (Paris, 1988, rev. and enlarged 2/1994)

F. Marmande and F. M. Coudert: "Doux-amer Pifarély?," *Jm*, no.380 (1989), 42

P. Carles and G. Le Querrec: "Je sais ce que je ne vais pas jouer," *Jm*, no.431 (1993), 30
F. Goaty: "Quand parle le quartette dont on parle," *Jm*, no.435 (1994), 22
H. Taylor: "French Jazz," *Strings*, no.50 (1995), 30
M. Gammel: "Dominique Pifarély," *JP*, xlv/2 (1996), 27
D. C. Martin: "Dominique Pifarély," *Jm*, no.458 (1996), 10
D. Levallet: "Signés ECM: Pifarély-Couturier: à trajectoire naturelle," *Jazzman*, no.33 (1998), 10
X. Prévost: "Un outil d'extraction d'une singularité," *Jm*, no.479 (1998), 29

MARK GILBERT

Pike, Dave [David Samuel] (*b* Detroit, 23 March 1938). Vibraphonist. He played drums from the age of eight and taught himself vibraphone, on which he was influenced from an early age by the work of Milt Jackson and Lionel Hampton. Having moved with his family to Los Angeles in 1953 he worked professionally from the following year and soon afterwards played hard bop with Curtis Counce, Harold Land, Elmo Hope, and Dexter Gordon; he often appeared at the Hillcrest club in a rhythm section, as the Jazz Couriers, with Hal Gaylor (double bass) and Lennie McBrowne (drums). He worked for two years at the Hillcrest with Paul Bley (recording in 1958) and for a brief period led a quartet that played in the San Francisco area (1959); by this time he had begun to play marimba in addition to his principal instrument. In 1960 he moved to New York and began to use amplification in his performances. From 1961 to 1965 he toured with Herbie Mann's group, as a member of which he played a repertory consisting largely of bossa nova, and he then led his own band, which played nightly for a year at the Top of the Gate, New York.

After moving to Berlin, Pike worked on radio and in a house band at a jazz club. He remained in Europe and in 1967 formed the Dave Pike Set, comprising Volker Kriegel (guitar), J. A. Rettenbacher or Eberhard Weber (double bass), and Peter Baumeister (drums); this group performed at clubs and festivals during the next five years. In 1968 Pike also gave a performance at the Berliner Jazztage that was well received, joined Kenny Clarke's band, and toured and recorded with the Clarke–Boland Big Band. Later he returned to the USA and settled in southern California, where he formed a group that from 1975 to 1980 played regularly at his own venue, Hungry Joe's Club in Huntington Beach; Ron Eschete and Tom Ranier were among his sidemen. He worked with Buddy DeFranco at Donte's club and joined Ray Anthony's big band. In 1980 he moved to New York, where he shattered his arm in an accident; after a lengthy period of rehabilitation he led a group for two and a half years at the Bonaventure Hotel in Los Angeles. He was again in Europe during the late 1980s, running his own club, Pike's Groove, in Ghent, Belgium, playing variously in Belgium, the Netherlands (where he recorded as a co-leader with Charles McPherson in 1988), and Germany, and occasionally working with Rein de Graaff's trio. He played first in Florida and then with Ben Tucker in Savannah, Georgia, spent a period working as an unaccompanied pianist, and appeared as an actor in Wilmington, North Carolina, before returning to Los Angeles to take up employment as a piano salesman. From June 1996 he resumed playing vibraphone in clubs throughout southern California; he recorded again as a leader in 1997.

SELECTED RECORDINGS

As leader: *It's Time for Dave Pike* (1961, Riv. 9360); *Times out of Mind* (1975, Muse 5092); *Let the Minstrels Play On* (1979, Muse 5203); *Moon Bird* (1981, Muse 5261); *Pike's Groove* (1986, Criss Cross 1021); with C. McPherson: *Bluebird* (1988, Tim. 302); *Bophead* (1997, Ubiquity Jazz 033)
As sideman with H. Mann: *Live at Newport* (1963, Atl. 1413)

BIBLIOGRAPHY

FeatherE; *Feather '60s*; *Feather–Gitler '70s*
M. Barker: "Dave Pike," *Crescendo*, ii/3 (1963), 18
M. Hennessey: "Europajazz," *JT* (1987), Jan, 23
T. Gioia: *West Coast Jazz: Modern Jazz in California, 1945–1960* (New York, and Oxford, England, 1992), 355
R. Simon: "Dave Pike," *Bird*, no.1 (1998), 32

GARY THEROUX/BK

Pilc, Jean-Michel (*b* Paris, 19 Oct 1960). French pianist and composer. He studied piano from the age of ten. In 1987 he abandoned his career as an engineer, formed his first trio, and joined Christian Escoudé's quartet; he also made his début as an arranger with the group Electrochoc. He then accompanied such musicians as Eric Le Lann, Enrico Rava, Marc Ducret, and the singer Elizabeth Kontomanou, who helped him reveal a more passionate temperament in his playing and discover an interest in the rhythmic possibilities of the piano. Pilc wrote compositions and arrangements for Michel Portal, Aldo Romano, and André Ceccarelli, performed with Roy Haynes, recorded with Martial Solal, Le Lann (1989), and Jean Toussaint (1995), and headed both a trio and a big band which he established in 1993. Based in New York from 1995, he formed the Big Apple Three with the double bass player Darryl Hall and the drummer Dave Gibson (replaced by François Moutin and Ari Hoenig respectively). While directing the tentet Big One, which performed his compositions, he launched the project Cardinal Points, involving Rick Margitza, Stephano di Battista, the guitarist Nelson Veras, Toussaint, and Mark Mondesir. Initially influenced by Bud Powell, Herbie Hancock, and Keith Jarrett, Pilc later created a more personal language.

SELECTED RECORDINGS

As leader: *Funambule* (1990, Blue Line 051); *Big One* (1992, EMP 890); *Together: Live at Sweet Basil*, i (1999, Challenge 73195-2)
As sideman with A. Ceccarelli: *From the Heart* (1996, Verve 529851-2)

BIBLIOGRAPHY

X. Matthyssens: "Jean-Marie Pilc," *Jm*, no.407 (1991), 49
A. Merlin: "Jean-Michel Pilc: zones de turbulences," *Jazzman*, no.174 (1994), 9
T. Pérémarti: "Les jeunes Français à New York: pourquoi?," *Jazzman*, no.12 (1996), 11
A. Merlin: "Guide des nouveaux talents," *Jazzman*, no.24 (1997), 11
Fara C.: "About Pilc," *Jazzman*, no.44 (1999), 28
T. Pérémarti: "As de Pilc," *Jazzman*, no.56 (2000), 4

JACQUES ABOUCAYA

Piliso, Ntemi [Edmund Mthuthuzeli] (*b* Alexandra township, South Africa, 16 Dec 1925; *d* Johannesburg, 18 Dec 2000). South African alto saxophonist. Self-taught, he played in the army during World War II, then in 1947 he joined the Casablanca Orchestra and learned to read music. In the late 1940s he was a member of the Harlem Swingsters, and by the early 1950s he had founded and was leading the Alexandra All Star Band. In the middle of the decade he performed with the African jazz and variety shows promoted by Alfred Herbert, and in the late 1950s he worked alongside Kippie Moeketsi, the pianist Todd Matshikiza, and others in the musical *King Kong*. Piliso was active as a studio musician in the 1970s. In 1982 he became the leader of the African Jazz Pioneers, which brought together a group of veteran South African jazz musicians and aimed to revive the big-band township jazz sounds of the 1950s.

SELECTED RECORDINGS

As leader: African Jazz Pioneers: *The African Jazz Pioneers* (Gallo 40186, 1989); *Live at the Montreux Jazz Festival 1991* (1991, Mélodie 66904-2); *Sip 'n fly* (Mélodie 66927-2, 1993); *Shufflin' Joe* (Mélodie 66988-2, 1996)

NISHLYN RAMANA

Pillars, Hayes (*b* North Little Rock, AR, 30 April 1906; *d* Richmond Heights, MO, 11 Aug 1992). Tenor saxophonist and bandleader. After playing with bands based in Little Rock, Arkansas, and Jackson, Tennessee, he worked with Alphonso Trent's orchestra (1927–8), then became a leader of the JETER–PILLARS ORCHESTRA. He continued to perform in the St. Louis area from the 1950s into the mid-1980s. Pillars may be heard performing solos with Trent on *I've found a new baby* (1933, Champion 16587) and with the Jeter–Pillars Orchestra on *Make Believe* (1937, Voc. 3973)

Oral history material in *NjR* (JOHP).

BIBLIOGRAPHY

S. Floyd: "An Oral History: the Great Lakes Experience," *Black Perspective in Music*, xi/1 (1983), 41
B. Rusch: "Hayes Pillars," *Cadence*, xii/12 (1986), 17
Obituary, *St. Louis Post-Dispatch* (15 Aug 1992)
J. Evensmo: *History of Jazz Tenor Saxophone: Black Artists*, i: *1917–1934* (Oslo, 1996); ii: *1935–1939* (Oslo, 1997)

HOWARD RYE, BK

Pilz, Michel (*b* Bad Neustadt an der Saale, Germany, 28 Oct 1945). German bass clarinetist. After studying classical clarinet at the conservatory in Luxembourg he was a member from 1968 into the 1980s of Manfred Schoof's quintet. At the same time he played with the German All Stars (touring Asia in 1971), in Alex Schlippenbach's trio, and in Schlippenbach's Globe Unity Orchestra (until 1982). From 1972 he led groups which at times included Peter Kowald, Buschi Niebergall, and Paul Lovens, and from 1978 he often played with Itaru Oki, with whom he toured Japan the following year. Pilz's style is more lyrical and less intellectual than that of other European free-jazz players; one can discern in his playing the influence of Eric Dolphy, of Ornette Coleman's later compositions, and of Eastern music, with which he became familiar while touring Asia.

SELECTED RECORDINGS

As leader: *Carpathes* (1975, FMP 0250); with I. Oki and R. Hübner: *One Year: Afternoon & Evening* (1978, FMP 0720); *Jamabiko* (1983, MP 841); *Melusina* (1991, Nabel 16)
As sideman: M. Schoof: *Scales* (1976, Japo 60013); Globe Unity Orchestra: *Improvisations* (1977, Japo 60021); M. Schoof: *Light Lines* (1977, Japo 60019); Globe Unity Orchestra: *Compositions* (1979, Japo 60027)

BIBLIOGRAPHY

P. Schmid: "Michel Pilz: Europas Jazz: Bassklarinettist der ersten Stunde," *Jazz Live*, no.125 (1999), suppl., p.10

WOLFRAM KNAUER

Pine, Courtney (*b* London, 18 March 1964). English tenor and soprano saxophonist and bass clarinetist. Having first played recorder at the age of eight, he took up clarinet when he was 13 and changed to saxophone two years later. In his teens he formed a hard-bop group, Dwarf Steps, then worked with various reggae and funk bands; in the early 1980s he began to concentrate on playing jazz, though continuing to keep an interest in West Indian and African music, hip-hop, and soul. After taking part in John Stevens's workshops he occasionally performed with the latter's group Freebop, and in 1984 he formed the Abibi Jazz Arts (TAJA); this organization, intended to promote interest in jazz among black British musicians, gave rise in 1986 to the all-black big band JAZZ WARRIORS, which fused jazz with other styles of black music. From 1985 Pine led his own small groups, among them the World's First Saxophone Posse (a saxophone quartet). His first album as leader, *Journey to the Urge Within* (1986), one of the best-selling British jazz albums of all time, was recorded with some of the most promising of young British jazz musicians, including Julian Joseph and Gary Crosby, with whom he has continued to work sporadically. From that time he also recorded with some important American musicians, notably Ellis Marsalis (1989), Jeff "Tain" Watts (1989, 1990, 1997), Kenny Kirkland (1990), Charnett Moffett (1990, 1995), and Geri Allen and Cassandra Wilson (1995). He also worked with the big band led by the drummer Charlie Watts (1985–6), toured with George Russell's orchestra (1986), played with Art Blakey's Jazz Messengers and Elvin Jones's Jazz Machine (in London, the USA, and Japan, 1986), toured with Marsalis, and worked with Marvin "Smitty" Smith (1991). He took part in recording the soundtrack of Alan Parker's film *Angel Heart* (1987) and played at Nelson Mandela's 70th birthday concert at London's Wembley Stadium (1988). The first black British musician of his generation to make a strong impact on jazz in Britain, Pine is an inspiration to many young musicians. He is a virtuoso performer with a restless musical curiosity and a willingness to integrate styles of music outside jazz into his work.

SELECTED RECORDINGS

Journey to the Urge Within (1986, Isl. 9846); *Destiny's Song + The Image of Pursuance* (1987, Isl. 842772-2); *The Vision's Tale* (1989, Isl. 842373-2); *To the Eyes of Creation* (1992, Isl. 524044-2); *Modern Day Jazz Stories* (1995, Ant./Talkin' Loud 529028-2); *Underground* (1997, Ant./Talkin' Loud 537745-2)

BIBLIOGRAPHY

CarrJ; *ChiltonB*; *GrayF*
B. Case: "A Cool Blast of Pine," *Sunday Times Magazine* (3 Aug 1986)
J. Laret: "Courtney Pine: une voix nouvelle," *Jm*, no.354 (1986), 39
S. Nicholson: "Young Turks: Courtney Pine," *Wire*, no.25 (1986), 31
"Shrink Rap," *MM* (13 Dec 1986), 12
D. Stubbs: "Blowing Hot," *MM* (15 Nov 1986), 12
C. Gauffre: "Pas trop star Courtney Pine," *Jm*, no.361 (1987), 22
R. Cook: "The Main Man: Courtney Pine," *Wire*, nos.46–7 (1987–8), 40
M. Hennessey: "The Ascent of Courtney Pine," *JT* (1988), June, 20
J. Levinson: "Courtney Pine: Pursuing a Song of Destiny," *DB*, lv/9 (1988), 25
T. Herrington: "Locking Horns," *Wire* (1989), Nov, 33
B. Emerson: "Courtney Pine Has all the Chops, Now He's Learning to Blow American-style," *Atlanta Constitution* (23 March 1990)
N. Tesser: "Splendid Isolation: Courtney Pine Charts a New Course for British Jazz," *Chicago Tribune* (25 March 1990)
F. Bouchard: "Jazz–Reggae Fusion: Ska's the Limit: Courtney Pine," *DB*, lix/5 (1992), 24
J. Fordham: "Reborn from Loss," *The Guardian* (19 Oct 1992)
D. Freeman: "Stripping Pine," *Jazz on CD*, i/2 (1993), 81
M. Sinker: "Pining for the Future," *Wire*, nos.106–7 (1993), 48
T. Green: "Courtney Pine: Moving Target," *JT*, xxvi/2 (1996), 42
K. Micallef: "Creation Stepper," *Jazziz*, xiii/3 (1996), 48
D. Cohen: "On the Trail of the Homesome Pine," *The Guardian* (12 Sept 1997)
R. Cook: "The Sax Factor," *South Bank Magazine* (Nov 2000), 10

SIMON ADAMS

Pinecone. Nickname of WYCLIFFE GORDON.

Pinkett, (William) Ward (*b* Newport News, VA, 29 April 1906; *d* New York, 15 March 1937). Trumpeter. He grew up in a musical family and took up trumpet at the age of ten; later he studied the instrument at the Hampton Institute in Virginia and the New Haven Conservatory of Music in Meridian, Mississippi. In 1926 he moved to New York, where he played with several musicians, notably Jelly Roll Morton

(1928, 1930) and Chick Webb (1929), and recorded with Bubber Miley and Clarence Williams (both 1930) and King Oliver and James P. Johnson (both 1931). Later he performed with Rex Stewart (1933), Teddy Hill (1934), and Bernard Addison and Louis Metcalf (both 1935). In 1935 he replaced Freddie Jenkins in a quartet led by Albert Nicholas that appeared at Adrian's Tap Room; as a sextet this group recorded six tracks in 1935 using the name the Little Ramblers. By this time, however, the consequences of Pinkett's alcoholism were beginning to impair his playing.

SELECTED RECORDINGS

As sideman: J. R. Morton: Kansas City Stomps (1928, Vic. 38010); Shoe Shiner's Drag (1928, Vic. 21658); Little Lawrence (1930, Vic. 38135) [second t solo]; Blue Blood Blues (1930, Vic. 22681); K. Oliver: Stop Crying (1931, Bruns. 6053)

BIBLIOGRAPHY

ChiltonW
A. J. McCarthy: "Ward Pinkett," *Jazz Forum*, no.2 (1946), 24; repr. in *Record Changer*, viii/2 (1949), 13; *Jazz Reprints*, no.2 (1963), 39
M. Boujut: "Un certain Ward Pinkett: portrait," *Jm*, no.136 (1966), 62
D. Barker: *A Life in Jazz*, ed. A. Shipton (London and New York, 1986)
E. Townley: "The Forgotten Ones: Ward Pinkett," *JJI*, xl/1 (1987), 15
L. Wright and others: *Walter C. Allen & Brian A. L. Rust's "King" Oliver* (Chigwell, England, 1987)

BK

Pirchner, Werner (Preisegott) (*b* Hall in Tirol, Austria, 13 Feb 1940). Austrian vibraphonist and composer. He played dance music as a teenager and again after army service (1958–62). In 1963 he joined Oscar Klein's quartet in Innsbruck. After leaving Klein he led his own ensembles and composed for radio and films. He was influenced by modern jazz, especially by the work of Milt Jackson, and also by the theories of the twelve-tone composer Arnold Schoenberg. In 1973 he recorded *Ein halbes Doppelalbum* (Original LP 1), a mixture of jazz, cabaret, and musical theater. One year later he composed the music to the film *Der Untergang des Alpenlandes*. Together with the Austrian guitarist Harry Pepl he formed the duo Pepl–Pirchner-Jazz-Zwio, which recorded the album *Gegenwind* (1979, Mood 23999) and performed for ten years (1975–85) at European festivals, including those at Montreux (where the duo recorded in 1981), Vienna, and Velden, Austria; with the addition of Jack DeJohnette it also recorded as a trio, *Werner Pirchner/Harry Pepl/Jack DeJohnette* (1982, ECM 1237). Pirchner was a member of Hip Jargon (a group formed in Austria by the American bass player Wayne Darling), the trio Austria Drei (together with Adelhard Roidinger and Alvin Queen), and the Vienna Art Orchestra. In the 1970s and 1980s he performed and recorded with Marc Johnson, Leszek Żądło, Michael Di Pasqua, Steve Swallow, Vocal Summit and Bobby McFerrin, Herbert Joos, Daniel Humair, Charlie Mariano, Frank Rosolino, Lee Konitz, the Family of Percussion, Lauren Newton, and Tommy Flanagan. In 1988 he gave his last concert as a performing musician, at the Deutsches Jazzfestival in Frankfurt, with Albert Mangelsdorff and the Austrian double bass player Robert Riegler. From the late 1980s he composed contemporary music variously influenced by such composers as Mozart, Bartók, Schoenberg, Theolonious Monk, and Gil Evans, and in 1994 he designed the sound for the Austrian radio program Ö1. He has received many prizes from international cultural organizations. (W. Szmolyan: "Werner Pirchner," *Österreichische Musikzeitschrift*, xliii/5 (1988), 257)

KLAUS SCHULZ

Piron, A(rmand) J(ohn) (*b* New Orleans, 16 Aug 1888; *d* New Orleans, 17 Feb 1943). Violinist and composer. He received training in music from his father, a professional teacher, whose dance orchestra he joined sometime after 1900; he also became a member of the Bloom Philharmonia Orchestra (1903) and the Peerless Orchestra (*c*1910). In spring 1914 he succeeded Freddie Keppard as the leader of the Olympia Orchestra, in which Clarence Williams was a sideman. In New Orleans the following year he and Williams established the Piron and Williams Publishing Company, which published many of Piron's compositions, including his commercially successful song *I wish I could shimmy like my sister Kate*. In 1918, with Peter Bocage, Piron formed a "sweet" society band, the Piron Orchestra, to play regularly at Tranchina's restaurant at Spanish Fort on Lake Pontchartrain (for illustration *see* Bands, fig.1); among the orchestra's personnel were Lorenzo Tio, Jr., Louis Cottrell, Sr., and the gifted pianist Steve Lewis, with whom Piron wrote his theme song, *The Purple Rose of Cairo*. The band performed in New York, at the Cotton Club late in 1923 and at the Roseland Ballroom early the following year, and made a number of recordings for Victor, Columbia, and OKeh. After returning to New Orleans it continued to play at Tranchina's until it disbanded in 1928. Thereafter Piron led the Moonlight Serenaders aboard the SS *Pelican* and continued to work on other river steamers until his death.

The recordings of the Piron Orchestra have been assumed to represent uniquely a more polite strain of New Orleans jazz that was intended for traditional social dancing at country clubs and dinner dances, often for white audiences; the style of its arrangements may represent a bridge between ragtime and jazz practices.

SELECTED RECORDINGS

Bouncing Around/Kiss Me Sweet (1923, OK 40021); New Orleans Wiggle/Mama's Gone, Goodbye (1923, Vic. 19233); Sud Bustin' Blues/West Indies Blues (1923, Col. 14007D)

BIBLIOGRAPHY

ChartersJ; *ChiltonW*
E. S[ouchon]: "Armand J. Piron," *SL*, iii/1 (1952), 4 [incl. discography and list of compositions]
G. Schuller: *Early Jazz: its Roots and Musical Development* (New York, 1968), 255
F. Driggs and H. Lewine: *Black Beauty, White Heat: a Pictorial History of Classic Jazz, 1920–1950* (New York, 1982/*R*1996), 24
C. E. Kinzer: *The Tio Family: Four Generations of New Orleans Musicians, 1814–1922* (diss., Louisiana State U., 1993)

ALDEN ASHFORTH/HOWARD RYE

Pisano, John (*b* New York, 6 Feb 1931). Guitarist. His month and date of birth were inverted in the first edition of this dictionary: 2 June is incorrect – his questionaire, press kit, and published sources confirm 6 February. He studied piano from the age of ten and started playing guitar when he was 14. After touring with an air force band (1952–5) he played in Chico Hamilton's quintet (1956–8), with which he appeared in the film *The Sweet Smell of Success* (1957). He then settled in Los Angeles, where he played with Buddy DeFranco and Jimmy Giuffre and recorded some excellent duets with Billy Bean; he also recorded with Fred Katz and Joe Pass, among others. From 1960 to 1969 he worked as an accompanist for Peggy Lee, and from 1965 to 1969 he toured the world as a member of Herb Alpert's band, the Tijuana Brass. Pisano collaborated with the songwriter Burt Bacharach and wrote some material for Sergio Mendes's group Brazil '66. In the early 1970s he performed with the guitarists

Lee Ritenour and Tony Rizzi in Los Angeles. From 1976 to 1983 he taught at Valley College in North Hollywood, and in the 1980s he worked with Oscar Castro-Neves. He made further recordings with Pass in 1981 and 1985, and from December 1989 until Pass's death in 1994 helped re-create the latter's small group of the mid-1960s. He led the Brazilian jazz group Velas from 1983 to 1993. In 1989 he participated in a reunion of Hamilton's original quintet; the group recorded in Milan. In the 1990s Pisano played in Frank Capp's Juggernaut, and from 1991 he has led the Flying Pisanos with his wife, the singer Jeanne Pisano. From 1997 he hosted a weekly guitar night at Papashon's club in Encino, California; he has also performed at the Zinc Bar in New York. Pisano's agile playing is influenced by the styles of Chuck Wayne, Jimmy Raney, and Tal Farlow, but is laced with the more assertive timbre and rhythmic vitality of jazz-rock.

SELECTED RECORDINGS

Duos with J. Pass: *Duets* (1991, Pablo 2310959)

As leader with B. Bean: *Makin' it* (1958, Decca 9206); *Take your Pick* (1958, Decca 9212); *Among Friends* (1994, Pablo 2310956); *Conversation Pieces* (1994–5, Pablo 2310963)

As sideman: C. Hamilton: *The Chico Hamilton Quintet* (1956, PJ 1225); F. Katz: *Fred Katz and his Jammers* (1958, Decca 9217); J. Pass: *For Django* (1964, PJ 85); *Appassionato* (1990, Pablo 2310946); *My Song* (1993, Telarc 83326)

BIBLIOGRAPHY

Feather '60s
F. R. Nemko: "John Pisano," *GP*, viii/11 (1974), 18
"John Pisano," *Just Jazz Guitar*, no.13 (1997)

NORMAN MONGAN/BK

Pitman, Booker (T.) (*b* Fairmont Heights, MD, 3 Oct 1909; *d* São Paulo, 13 Oct 1969). Alto saxophonist and clarinetist. His name is sometimes misspelled Pittman. He probably made his professional début with Jap Allen in summer 1930 before working in Philadelphia with Blanche Calloway, with whom he recorded in 1931; he also played as a sideman with Bennie Moten. After a short time as the leader of his own group, the Blue Moon Chasers, he joined the orchestras of Count Basie (Kansas City, Missouri) and Ralph Cooper (Chicago). In 1933 he toured Europe as a member of Lucky Millinder's band; while in Europe he worked with the Brazilian bandleader Romeu Silva, with whom he later toured in Brazil (1935). For the next 15 years Pitman worked in South America, where in the late 1940s he recorded with the Cotton Pickers led by Ahmed Ratip. In 1950 he retired from music, but in 1959 made his first recordings as a leader, working with trios, quartets, big bands, and the São Paulo Dixielanders; he also accompanied his daughter, the singer Eliana Pitman. During the 1950s and 1960s he again toured Latin America. His playing during this period may be heard to advantage on *Booker Pitman Plays Again* (1959, RCA BBL1028) and *The Fabulous Booker Pitman* (1959, Hi-Fi Jazz 111). Pitman's preferred instrument was the alto saxophone, on which he was strongly influenced by the swing style of Johnny Hodges; he also occasionally played in bop and dixieland styles.

BIBLIOGRAPHY

E. Vidossich: "Booker Pittman au Brésil," *Jazz 57*, no. 2 (1957), 6
S. Fonseca: Liner notes, *The Fabulous Booker Pitman* (Hi-Fi Jazz 111, 1959)
J. Guinle, L. Rangel, and N. R. Ortíz Oderigo: Liner notes, *Booker Pitman Plays Again* (RCA BBL1028, 1959)
F. Driggs: [untitled], *Coda*, vi/3 (1963), 2
F. Manskleid: "Booker Pittman returns to the US," *JM*, x/11 (1965), 12
J. Duprat: Liner notes, *The Rhythmakers of Buenos Aires* (Harlequin 2064, 1988)

RAINER E. LOTZ

Pitterson, Pete [Egbert George] (*b* Kingston, Jamaica, 8 March 1921; *d* Southend-on-Sea, England, 2 Nov 1994). Jamaican trumpeter. He played cornet in a boys' band, took up trumpet at the age of 14, and continued his music studies while playing for countryside dances. His army service took him to the USA in 1942, and while stationed in Florida he formed a band to play on weekends. He worked in a quintet at a club in Connecticut and traveled to New York before returning to Jamaica in 1945. In Kingston he was a member of the dance band led by the pianist Milton McPherson and formed his own big band. In 1946 he went to England and worked with big bands in the London area, including that of Vic Lewis, and in 1949 he toured Sweden with Jiver Hutchinson. In London he took part in early broadcasts, led quartets at the Sunset Club and Club Eleven, and worked with Denis Rose and Eddie Thompson and with musicians associated with John Dankworth. In 1952 he moved to Birmingham to take up a residency with the bandleader Sonny Rose and jobs with Andy Hamilton. In 1955 Pitterson joined Bert Ambrose, in whose band he played alongside Tubby Hayes, and he continued thereafter to mix big-band and theater work with jazz dates. He took a band to Turkey and, in England, accompanied the singers Georgie Fame, Long John Baldry, and Jimmy Witherspoon. Later he left music to work as a truck driver, but he played with local bands in the Ilford area until glaucoma forced his retirement. Influenced by Dizzy Gillespie, Pitterson is best heard on two tracks by the singer and conga drummer Buddy Pipp (1954).

SELECTED RECORDINGS

As leader: Let's go a'huntin'/Mango Time (1951, Esquire 5-053); Ball Game/West Indian Folk Music (1951, Esquire 5-058)

As sideman: B. Pipp: Positive Action/Akee Blues (1954, Lyragon 730); Rupert Nurse: Lord Kitchener "Birth of Ghana" (1956, Melodisc 1390)

BIBLIOGRAPHY

ChiltonB
V. Wilmer: "Musicians of the Caribbean, no.6: Pete Pitterson – a Jazzman First," *Flamingo* [London], iii/10 (1964), 41
Obituaries: V. Wilmer, *The Guardian* (25 Jan 1995); V. Wilmer, *JJI*, xlviii/4 (1995), 20

VAL WILMER

Pizza Express. Two restaurants in London belonging to this chain regularly offer performances of jazz; *see* NIGHTCLUBS AND OTHER VENUES.

Pizza Man. Nickname of RAY PIZZI.

Pizzarelli, Bucky [John (Paul, Sr.)] (*b* Paterson, NJ, 9 Jan 1926). Guitarist, father of John Pizzarelli. He learned to play banjo and guitar when he was young. At the age of 17 he toured with Vaughn Monroe's dance band, which he rejoined (after military service) in 1946; he made recordings with the band for RCA and also played on radio. In 1951 he recorded with Joe Mooney, and the following year he joined the staff of NBC. After touring for two years (1956–7) with the Three Suns trio he returned to New York to work as a freelance and in studios, when he recorded with Toots Thielemans (1958, *c*1967–8). He first played with Benny Goodman's small group in New York in 1966, thus beginning an association that lasted until Goodman's death and included four European tours in the early 1970s. Pizzarelli formed a duo with George Barnes and another with Les Paul (the latter in 1973). In 1977 he toured Japan with Zoot Sims and appeared in an all-star group alongside Lionel Hampton, Dexter Gordon, and Hank Jones. He performed at the Grande Parade du Jazz in Nice, France, yearly from 1976 to 1979 and led his own trio; he recorded in duos with Eddie Daniels (1973), Joe Venuti (*c*1974), Sims (1976), Slam Stewart (1978), Stephane Grappelli (1979), and his son John, with whom he worked frequently from 1980.

Pizzarelli participated regularly in Dick Gibson's Colorado Jazz Party and many other such events, as well as in major festivals, including that of Umbria, Italy (1989, 1991–4); he may be seen in the film *The Great Rocky Mountain Jazz Party* (1977) and the video *Flip Phillips' 80th Birthday Party featuring the All-Stars* (*c*1996 [filmed 1995]). From the 1980s he recorded with Ruby Braff (1981, 1996), Svend Asmussen and Red Norvo (both 1983), Yank Lawson and Bob Haggart (1989–91), George Masso and Ken Peplowski (both 1990), the Basie Alumni (1992), Flip Phillips (from 1992), Bob Wilber, Summit Reunion, and Haggart (all 1995), Kenny Davern (1995–6), Roland Hanna and Jon Burr (1996), and the violinist Richard Carr (1997). He toured Canada with Peter Appleyard annually from 1985 to 1988. During the same period he performed in Berne, Switzerland (1986), Japan (with Benny Carter, 1987), and London (1988). Later he toured the USA with Howard Alden (1991), Barney Kessell and Charlie Byrd (1991), and, on a regular basis, Grappelli (1991–5). While he continued to work in his duo with John, in the 1990s they sometimes played together in a trio or quartet with his younger son, the double bass player Martin Pizzarelli.

Pizzarelli plays a seven-string electric guitar; the extra string (tuned to *A'*) allows him to play a bass line to his own solos. He is known not only for his exceptional solo performances on the electric instrument but also for his proficiency as a classical guitarist. His publications include *Power Guitar* (1979, Norwich, England, *c*1982) and *A Pro's Approach to Melody and Chord Playing* (n.d.).

SELECTED RECORDINGS

Duos: with E. Daniels: *A Flower for All Seasons* (1973, Choice 1002); with R. Carr: *String Thing* (1997, Savant 2010)

As leader: *Bix Beiderbecke Arrangements by Bill Challis* (1974, MonE 7066); *Bucky's Bunch* (1975, MonE 7082); *Nightwings* (1975, FD 1120); *The Café Pierre Trio* (1982, MonE 7093); with R. Hanna and J. Burr: *3 for All* (1996, CEI 806)

As sideman: J. Venuti: *Blue Four* (1974, Chi. 134); J. Frigo: *With Bucky & John Pizzarelli* (1988, Chesky 1); K. Peplowski: *Mr. Gentle and Mr. Cool* (1990, Conc. 4419); K. Davern: *Breezin' Along* (1996, Arbors 19170)

BIBLIOGRAPHY

Feather–Gitler '70s

M. Jones: "An Extra String to his Bow," *MM* (8 Sept 1979), 34

L. Tomkins: "'Some of my Best Things are Duos,' Says Bucky Pizzarelli," *CI*, xviii/4 (1979), 18

C. Deffaa: "Bucky and John Pizzarelli: Like Father, Like Son," *MR*, xi/12 (1984), 1, repr. with update in *In the Mainstream: 18 Portraits in Jazz* (Metuchen, NJ, and London, 1992), 275

M. Bourne: "Profile: Bucky Pizzarelli," *DB*, lvi/10 (1989), 47

"Interview with Bucky Pizzerelli," *The Note*, vii/3 (1995), 2

H. Glatzer: "They Got Rhythm: Father and Son Jazz Masters Bucky and John Pizzarelli," *Acoustic Guitar*, vii (1996), Aug, 68

T. M. Ripmaster: *Bucky Pizzarelli: a Life in Music* (Pacific, MO, 1998)

G. Lees: "Master's Touch: Bucky Pizzarelli," *JT*, xxix/6 (1999), 54

WARREN VACHÉ, SR./BK

Pizzarelli, John (Paul, Jr.) (*b* Paterson, NJ, 6 April 1960). Electric guitarist, singer, and leader, son of Bucky Pizzarelli. Although he grew up in the environment of his father's music and musical friends, he first played guitar in rock bands, and he spent a period as a trumpeter before returning to the guitar and a repertory of swing and American popular song. Through the 1980s he played and sang in a duo with his father, with whom he made several recordings. In 1986 he joined the trio led by the pianist Tony Monte, with which he performed on radio station WNEW in New York. He also performed and recorded as a leader, and in the 1990s he began to gain considerable fame, independent of his father, as a pianist, singer, and leader of a trio which consisted of his younger brother, the double bass player Martin Pizzarelli, and the pianist Ray Kennedy; this group toured and recorded and appeared in the television series "Melrose Place" and, in 1997, the Broadway musical *Dream*. Pizzarelli also formed a big band which made its debut at the Blue Note, New York, early in 1997, with Don Sebesky as arranger and conductor.

Like his father, Pizzarelli plays the seven-string electric guitar, and the resemblance between their styles is sometimes uncanny; his approach to singing is strongly influenced by that of Nat "King" Cole.

Video oral history material in *NCH* (HCJA).

SELECTED RECORDINGS

Duos with B. Pizzarelli: *At the Vineyard Theater* (1987, Challenge 70025)

As leader: *I'm Hip* (1983, Stash 226); *Naturally* (*c*1992, Novus 63151-2); *Dear Mr. Cole* (1994, Novus 63182-2); *After Hours* (*c*1995, Novus 63191-2); *Our Love is Here to Stay* (*c*1996, RCA 67501-2)

As sideman with J. Frigo: *With Bucky & John Pizzarelli* (1988, Chesky 1)

BIBLIOGRAPHY

C. Deffaa: "Bucky and John Pizzarelli: Like Father, Like Son," *MR*, xi/12 (1984), 1, repr. with update in *In the Mainstream: 18 Portraits in Jazz* (Metuchen, NJ, and London, 1992), 275

M. Bourne: "Riffs: John Pizzarelli," *DB*, lix/4 (1992), 15

D. Gelly: "John Pizzarelli," *Jazz: the Magazine*, no.20 (1993), 9

G. Endress: "Der Swingende, singende Siebensaiter: John Pizzarelli," *JP*, xliv/4 (1995), 30

H. Glatzer: "They Got Rhythm: Father and Son Jazz Masters Bucky and John Pizzarelli," *Acoustic Guitar*, vii (1996), Aug, 68

J. Hamlin: "Pizzarelli's at Home with Saloon Swing," *San Francisco Chronicle Datebook* (9 March 1996)

C. Deffaa: "Out and About in New York: John Pizzarelli, Jnr, Don Sebesky, Ralph Burns, Ellington Broadway Musicals," *CJM*, xxxiv/2 (1997), 14

J. Ferguson: "John Pizzarelli: Like Father, Like Swing," *JT*, xxvii/6 (1997), 44

J. Kaufman: "John Pizzarelli: Jazz Man Living a 'Dream'," *Wall Street Journal* (13 March 1997)

J. Steinberg: "Stepping out of his Father's Long Shadow," *New York Times* (21 Sept 1997)

D. Toroian: "John Pizzarelli Brings Jazz Classics to a New Generation of Fans," *St. Louis Post-Dispatch* (11 Nov 1997)

M. Zwerin: "John Pizzarelli: out of his Father's Shadow," *International Herald Tribune* (23 Sept 1997)

WARREN VACHÉ, SR./BK

Pizzi, Ray(mond Michael) [Pizza Man] (*b* Everett, MA, 19 Jan 1943). Tenor and soprano saxophonist, bassoonist, and flutist. He began clarinet lessons as a child and from 1960 to 1966 studied at the Boston Conservatory and the Berklee School of Music. He taught for five years in the public schools of Randolph, Massachusetts (1964–9), during which period he toured with Woody Herman (*c*1966). In 1969 he moved to California, where he worked with a wide variety of groups and musicians, including the Thad Jones–Mel Lewis Orchestra, Frank Zappa (1977), Shelly Manne (1978), Willie Bobo (1979), Nancy Wilson (1982), and Milcho Leviev (1986). He recorded with a number of these leaders and with the baritone saxophonist Moacir Santos (*c*1972–5), Mark Levine (1975), and Dizzy Gillespie (1976); this last session was organized by Gillespie after he heard Pizzi play in the band of the "Dinah Shore Show." Pizzi also made recordings as a leader (from 1975), some of which involved his own compositions. Later he recorded with Bob Florence's big band (1979, 1981), acted and played in a short film, *End of the Rainbow* (1984), and performed with the American Jazz Orchestra (late 1980s – early 1990s). In 1988 he formed the quintet Windrider and began to play in a woodwind trio, the Wind Syndicate, and in 1994 he joined the group Jazz Adventure, led by the bass player Bobby Rodriguez. In 1997 he became a member of the faculty of the Mancini Institute. Pizzi's work draws on a range of contemporary musical styles; he has been influenced by guitarists as well as saxophonists and this has led to his exploring vibrato, bends, slides, and glisses in his playing. He is one of the few reed players in jazz to feature the bassoon as a main instrument.

SELECTED RECORDINGS

As leader: *Appassionato* (1975, P.Z. 333); *Conception* (1976, Pablo 2310795); *The Love Letter* (1979, Dis. 801); *Expressivo* (1981, Dis. 853)
As sideman: M. Santos: *Maestro* (*c*1972, BN LA007F); D. Gillespie: *Dizzy's Party* (1976, Pablo 2310784)

BIBLIOGRAPHY

F. R. Nemko: "Profile: Ray Pizzi," *DB*, xliii/8 (1976), 38
L. Underwood: "Ray Pizzi: West Coast Breakthrough," *DB*, xliv/17 (1977), 18 [incl. discography]
A. J. Liska: "Versatile Jazzman, and Not a Bad Actor Either," *Los Angeles Times* (15 April 1986), 2
F. Nemko: "Ray Pizzi," *Windplayer*, v/2 (1988), 22
T. Fitterling: "Ray Pizzi auf Tour mit dem Götz Tangerding Trio," *JP*, xxxviii/7 (1989), 28
U. Dörges: "Ray Pizzi," *JP*, xlv/1 (1996), 30

PAUL RINZLER/BK

Plantation. The name of several venues, notably ones in Chicago, Los Angeles, and New York; *see* NIGHTCLUBS AND OTHER VENUES.

Plater, Bobby [Robert] (*b* Newark, NJ, 13 May 1914; *d* Lake Tahoe, NV, 20 Nov 1982). Alto saxophonist and flutist. He took up alto saxophone at the age of 12, played with Donald Lambert in his early teens, and worked professionally from 1937, when he joined the Savoy Dictators. Later he played with Tiny Bradshaw (1940), served in the armed forces (1942–5), and was briefly with Cootie Williams. In 1946 he joined Lionel Hampton's band, and two years later he became one of its principal soloists; he also wrote arrangements for the group, most of which were intended specifically for Sonny Parker. In September 1964 Plater left Hampton's ensemble to replace Frank Wess in Count Basie's orchestra; he became the principal alto saxophonist in this group in 1970 and, eventually, Basie's music director. Although he seldom took solos in recordings he did so frequently in concert, usually on such ballads as *Soft as Velvet*. Plater had a rich, mellifluous style that was influenced first by Earle Warren and Willie Smith and later by Benny Carter and Johnny Hodges. A fine example of his work as an arranger is his version of *Lonesome Nights*, which was recorded in 1960 (*The Many Sides of Lionel Hampton*, Gladhamp 1001).

SELECTED RECORDINGS

As sideman: Savoy Dictators: Rhythm & Bugs/Tricks (1939, Savoy 100); L. Hampton: *Apollo Hall Concert, 1954* (1954, Phi. 10157), incl. The Nearness of You; *Hamp's Big Band* (1959, Audio-Fidelity 1913), incl. Elaine and Daffy, Red Top; C. Basie: *Basie Big Band* (1975, Pablo 2310756), incl. Soft as Velvet; *Farmers Market Barbecue* (1982, Pablo 2310874), incl. Blues for the Barbecue, Lester Leaps In

SELECTED FILMS AND VIDEOS

Lionel Hampton and his Orchestra (1949); Air Mail Special (1950), Cobb's Idea (1950); Mister Rock and Roll (1957); Count Basie and his Orchestra (1965); The Last of the Blue Devils (1979)

BIBLIOGRAPHY

ChiltonW; *FeatherE*; *Feather '60s*
J. Morgantini: "Bobby Plater: musicien trop méconnu," *BHcF*, no.54 (1956), 3
J. Dawson: "Bobby Plater: Basie's Right-hand Man," *MM* (23 Dec 1972), 42
S. Dance: *The World of Count Basie* (New York and London, 1980), 223

CHRIS SHERIDAN

Plaxico, Lonnie (Luvell) (*b* Chicago, 4 Sept 1960). Double bass player. He played professionally from the age of 14, and after working with Junior Cook, Sonny Stitt, and Chet Baker he joined Wynton Marsalis's group (1982). In 1983 he played with Dexter Gordon and Hank Jones, and in June of that year he became a member of Art Blakey's Jazz Messengers; he appeared with the regular group and also with an all-star ensemble of the same name which performed and recorded in Japan that year (Blakey disbanded this version of the Jazz Messengers in 1986). During the same period Plaxico recorded with Dizzy Gillespie and David Murray (both 1984) and worked alongside Blakey's sidemen Terence Blanchard and Donald Harrison in the group New York Second Line. Through his involvement in the activities of M-Base he expanded his stylistic compass, moving from hard bop into the realms of soul music and the avant garde and playing both double bass and electric bass guitar in collaborations with, among others, Steve Coleman, Greg Osby, and Cassandra Wilson. After leaving Blakey he served as a member of Jack DeJohnette's Special Edition from 1987 into the early 1990s, during which period he took up five- and then six-string electric bass guitar. Plaxico also recorded with Marvin "Smitty" Smith (1987), Michele Rosewoman (1988), Steve Williamson (1989), Cecil Brooks III (1989, 1993), Cindy Blackman and Andrew Hill (both 1990), Bud Shank (in performance at Birdland) and Carola Grey (both 1992), Hannibal Peterson and Gust William Tsilis (both 1993), Talib Kibwe (1994), Robin Eubanks and Graham Haynes (both 1995), Barbara Dennerlein (1996), Ravi Coltrane (1997), Ray Anderson (1998), and Osby (regularly through the 1990s); as a leader he made a series of albums in a pop-jazz vein for Muse in the early 1990s. His command of the electric bass guitar is captured especially well on the title track of DeJohnette's *Earth Walk* (1991).

SELECTED RECORDINGS

As sideman: T. Blanchard and D. Harrison: *New York Second Line* (1983, Conc. 3002); S. Coleman: *Motherland Pulse* (1985, JMT 850001); A. Blakey: *Blue Night* (1985, Tim. 217); J. DeJohnette: *Irresistible Forces* (1987, MCA/Imp. 5992); *Audio-visual Scapes* (1988, MCA/Imp. 8029); C. Wilson: *Blue Skies* (1988, JMT 834419-1); A. Hill: *But Not Farewell* (1990, BN B21Z-94971); C. Blackman: *Code Red* (1990, Muse 5365); J. DeJohnette: *Earth Walk* (1991, BN B21S-96690); B. Shank: *I Told You So!* (1992, Can. 79533); C. Wilson: *New Moon Daughter* (*c*1995, BN 32861-2), incl. Strange Fruit; G. Osby: *Zero* (1998, BN 93760-2); J. Moran: *Soundtrack to Human Motion* (1998, BN 97431-2)

BIBLIOGRAPHY

I. Gitler: Liner notes, A. Blakey: *Art Blakey Live at Sweet Basil* (PW 6357, 1985)
X. Daverat: "Osby et Plaxico: First Exit to Brooklyn," *Jm*, no.390 (1990), 28
B. Milkowski: "Bass Notes: Lonnie Plaxico: New Mission," *Bass Player*, i/1 (1990), 9

BK

Plaza Music Company. Record company. It established the label Banner in January 1922, and at the end of the same year opened its own recording studios. During the mid- and late 1920s the company either founded or supplied with discs the labels Regal, Domino, Oriole (i), Conqueror, Jewel, and Homestead; in August 1929 it joined Cameo and Pathé to form the American record corporation. The matrix series started by Plaza in 1922 was continued by ARC and survived to become CBS's main numerical sequence for material recorded in New York; the same matrix series was used in the 1950s and 1960s for 45 r.p.m. singles taken from tape masters.

BIBLIOGRAPHY

W. Allen, P. Armagnac, and C. Kendziora: "Plaza–American Record Corporation, a Clarification," *Matrix*, no.70 (1967), 3

B. Rust: *The American Record Label Book* (New Rochelle, NY, 1978)

A. Sutton: *Directory of American Disc Record Brands and Manufacturers, 1891–1943* (Westport, CT, and London, 1994), 222

R. M. W. Dixon, J. Godrich, and H. Rye: *Blues & Gospel Records, 1890–1943* (Oxford, England, rev. and enlarged 4/1997), xxxii

HOWARD RYE

Pleasure, King [Beeks, Clarence] (*b* Oakdale, nr Harriman, TN, 24 March 1922; *d* Los Angeles, 21 March 1981). Singer. He grew up in Cincinnati, and became inspired to write original lyrics to famous instrumental solos after hearing Lester Young's recording of *DB Blues* (1945). Having moved to Hartford, Connecticut, he later he won a talent contest at the Apollo Theatre, New York, singing Eddie Jefferson's lyrics to James Moody's *I'm in the mood for love* (1949). This success resulted in a contract with Prestige, and his version of the song, *Moody's Mood for Love*, became a substantial hit in 1952. The following year he achieved some success with *Parker's Mood*, but thereafter, apart from occasionally taking part in recording sessions, he receded into obscurity. He spent much of his later life in California. Pleasure was responsible for popularizing Jefferson's invention, vocalese; as such he instigated a trend for this style that boosted the career of the group Lambert, Hendricks, and Ross. Other singers and ensembles such as Al Jarreau and Manhattan Transfer owe much to his innovations.

SELECTED RECORDINGS

Moody's Mood for Love (1952, Prst. 924); Parker's Mood (1953, Prst. 880); *Golden Days* (1960, HiFi 425)

BIBLIOGRAPHY

FeatherE

D. Halperin: Liner notes, *Golden Days* (Vogue LAE12258, 1961)

K. Pleasure: Liner notes, *Golden Days* (HiFi 425, 1961)

I. Gitler: Liner notes, *Original Moody's Mood* (Prst. 7586, 1968)

R. Russell: *Bird Lives: the High Life and Hard Times of Charlie "Yardbird" Parker* (New York, 1973/*R*1994), 322

MARK GARDNER

Pletcher, Stew(art Francis) (*b* Chicago, 21 Feb 1907; *d* Michigan, 29 Nov 1978). Trumpeter. His full name and place of birth appear in his application for social security. He studied at Yale University and played trumpet and sang with the Yale Collegians. In the early to mid-1930s he led his own band and recorded as a leader (1930, 1936) and with Ben Pollack (1934). Pletcher is best known for his association with Red Norvo (1935 – July 1937, September–December 1937), with whom he made several recordings (including *Remember*, 1937, Bruns. 7896). He also worked with Tony Pastor (1939) and Jack Teagarden (1945, 1955) and performed and recorded with Nappy Lamare (late 1949). The social security death index gives his last known residence as Whitehall, Michigan. His son Tom Pletcher is a cornetist. (F. Levin: "The Forgotten Ones: Stew Pletcher," *JJI*, xli/7 (1988), 19)

based on *ChiltonW*

Plimley, Paul (Horace) (*b* Vancouver, Canada, 16 March 1953). Canadian pianist. Following a classical training he turned to improvised music in the mid-1970s and began a longstanding affiliation with Lisle Ellis. He studied briefly with Karl Berger in Vancouver (1978–9) and Cecil Taylor in Woodstock, New York (1979), and later with Taylor in Berlin (1988). He was a founder of the New Orchestra Workshop (NOW) in Vancouver in 1977 and has remained associated with several of its myriad groups, including the NOW Orchestra. He has also performed internationally and recorded with Ellis, both in a duo (notably on their tribute to Ornette Coleman, *Kaleidoscopes*, 1992) and in trios together with Joe McPhee (1994) and the drummers Andrew Cyrille (1990), Gregg Bendian, Donald Robinson (1994), and Scott Amendola (1999). His album *Everything in Stages* (1995), which he recorded as an unaccompanied piano soloist, suggests Taylor's influence leavened by a sense of whimsy, romanticism, touch, and scale that is entirely Plimley's own.

SELECTED RECORDINGS

As unaccompanied soloist: *Everything in Stages* (1995, Songlines 1503)

Duos: with L. Ellis: *Both Sides of the Same Mirror* (1989, Nine Winds 0135); *Kaleidoscopes* (1992, HA 6117); with B. Guy: *Sensology* (1995, Maya 9701)

As leader: with L. Ellis and A. Cyrille: *When Silence Pulls* (1990, Music & Arts 692); with L. Ellis and J. McPhee: *Sweet Freedom: Now What?* (1994, HA 6162)

BIBLIOGRAPHY

EMC2

M. Miller: "Paul Plimley," *Boogie, Pete & the Senator: Canadian Musicians in Jazz, the Eighties* (Toronto 1987), 217

S. Lewis: "Paul Plimley: Out into the World," *Coda*, no.231 (1990), 10

D. Rubien: "Paul Plimley Brings Jazz Wizardry to S. F.," *San Francisco Chronicle Datebook* (6 Feb 1994)

L. M. Svirchev: "Kaleidoscopes: the Music of Paul Plimley & Lisle Ellis," *Coda*, no.255 (1994), 4

B. Rusch: "The Questionnaire," *Cadence*, xx/1 (1995), 75

MARK MILLER

Plop. A rapid Gliss falling to the beginning of a note; the gliss precedes the beat.

Plunger (mute). *See* Mute, §2(i).

PM. Record company and label founded in 1973 by gene Perla.

Pochée, John (Kenneth) (*b* Sydney, 21 Sept 1940). Australian drummer and leader. He plays left handed on a normal drum set. He began working with the pianist Dave Levy in 1956 and appeared at El Rocco from 1957. Between 1959 and 1962 he was in Melbourne, working with the reed player Graeme Lyall, Tony Gould, and Joe Lane. Later he lived mainly in Sydney, where he performed with Bobby Gebert, Judy Bailey, Bernie McGann, and others. He also formed the group Last Straw, worked frequently as music director for touring popular artists, and accompanied a number of visiting musicians. From 1986 he concentrated particularly on leading Ten Part Invention, which played compositions written by its members, notably Roger Frampton (co-leader and music director), Mike Bukovsky, and

Sandy Evans. The rhythm section of this group, known as the Engine Room, often worked independently under the leadership of Frampton and Pochée. Pochée was also a member of McGann's trio.

SELECTED RECORDINGS

As leader with R. Frampton: of Ten Part Invention: *Ten Part Invention* (1987, ABC 846729), *Tall Stories* (1993, Rufus 006); of Engine Room: *Full Steam Ahead* (1996, ABC 489270-2)

As sideman: J. Bailey: *One Moment* (1974, Phi. 6357018); *Colours* (1976, Eureka 103); *At Long Last* (1983, Emanem 3601); Last Straw: *The Last Straw* (1990, Spiral Scratch 0005); B. McGann: *Ugly Beauty* (1991, Spiral Scratch 0010); *McGann McGann* (1994, Rufus 011); *Playground* (1996, Rufus 023)

BIBLIOGRAPHY

A. Bissett: *Black Roots, White Flowers: a History of Jazz in Australia* (Sydney, 1979, rev. 2/1987)

G. Brennan: "John Pochée: Not the Bitter End," *Jazz: the Australasian Contemporary Music Magazine*, no.21 (1986), 4

B. Johnson: *The Oxford Companion to Australian Jazz* (Melbourne, Australia, 1987)

J. Clare [G. Brennan, pseud.]: *Bodgie Dada and the Cult of Cool* (Sydney, 1995)

W. Bebbington, ed: *The Oxford Companion to Australian Music* (Melbourne, Australia, 1997)

ROGER T. DEAN

Pocket cornet. A miniature Cornet with closely coiled tubing, having a range equivalent to the cornet of usual size. Don Cherry played a pocket cornet, which he termed a pocket trumpet.

Pocket trumpet. Name used by Don Cherry for the pocket cornet he played (*see* Cherry, Don); pitched in B♭, the instrument was built in the first half of the century by the French company Besson.

Poetry. Jazz has influenced the history of 20th-century poetry more than any other form of music. But defining "jazz poetry" has caused a good deal of contention among poets and critics. Some writers feel passionately that a jazz poem must emulate the rhythmic pulse of the music; others claim that "jazziness" is an arbitrary term at best and that allusions to jazz might be the only sure way to know if poems have been informed by the music. Neither viewpoint, however, should negate the other, for the range of influence varies in the extreme and, for that matter, extends far beyond the stereotypical images of hipsters from the 1950s.

One reason for this diversity concerns the poets' depth of musical knowledge. The works of some writers, for example, cannot be fully evaluated without discussing the influence of jazz; others are not known for their jazz poems but have nevertheless written a few excellent responses to the music. The thousands of jazz-related poems published by a diverse, international collection of poets present a remarkable variety of styles and sensibilities: portraits of and homages to famous musicians, poems meant for performance with live accompaniment, images of nightclubs and concert halls, meditations on the nature of improvisation, verse written in blues form, and so on. The associations seem unlimited and ongoing.

1. Early works. 2. Poetry and jazz in performance. 3. Bird and Trane poems. 4. Contemporary work.

1. Early works. In a situation somewhat parallel to that of the premier jazz recordings, the first published jazz poems were written by white writers. Carl Sandburg's "Jazz Fantasia" (*Smoke and Steel*, New York, 1920), a fairly trite yet exuberant response to dixieland, was one of the first to appear in print:

Drum on your drums, batter on your banjoes,
sob on the long cool winding saxophones.
Go to it, O jazzmen.

Sling your knuckles on the bottoms of the happy
tin pans, let your trombones ooze, and go husha-
husha-hush with the slippery sand-paper.

Moan like an autumn wind high in the lonesome tree-
tops, moan soft like you wanted somebody terrible,
cry like a racing car slipping away from a motorcycle
cop, bang-bang! you jazzmen, bang altogether drums,
traps, banjos, horns, tin cans – make two people fight
on the top of a stairway and scratch each other's eyes
in a clinch tumbling down the stairs.

Can the rough stuff . . . now a Mississippi steamboat
pushes up the night river with a hoo-hoo-hoo-oo . . .
and the green lanterns calling to the high soft stars
. . . a red moon rides on the humps of the low river
hills . . . go to it, O jazzmen.

Some of Sandburg's contemporaries, particularly Hart Crane ("For the Marriage of Faustus and Helen," *White Buildings*, New York, 1924) and Mina Loy ("The Widow's Jazz," *Pagany*, no.2, 1931), wrote still more engaging verse about the music. Books by less gifted writers, such as DuBose Heyward's *Jasbo Brown & Other Poems* (New York, 1924) and Maxwell Bodenheim's *Bringing Jazz!* (New York, 1930), expressed an appreciation for African-American music, despite shortcomings in the verse itself. Vachel Lindsay's "The Daniel Jazz" (*The Golden Whales of California*, New York, 1920) invoked the sounds of early jazz and caused critics to label him a "jazz poet"; many still consider him to be a pioneer in the field, even though he knew nothing about the music and actually spent a good deal of energy attacking jazz on grounds that it was both hysterical and blasphemous. Other writers from the 1920s also associated racial and sexual anxieties with jazz, as seen in "The Jazz Cannibal" (*Punch*, 10 Dec 1924), a shockingly racist poem published anonymously in Britain, or "[god pity me whom (god distinctly has)]" (*&*, New York: privately printed, 1925), a poem by e. e. cummings that equates jazz with sexual promiscuity. Other poems, such as Amy Lowell's "Jazz Dance" (*Ballads for Sale*, New York, 1927) or Clement Wood's book-length poem *Greenwich Village Blues* (New York, 1926), seem less hostile but equally condescending.

The landmark publication for jazz poetry, however, must be Langston Hughes's first collection, *The Weary Blues* (New York, 1926). In this book, and virtually all the other publications by Hughes, jazz and the blues clearly inform a wealth of poems, both thematically and formally. For the first time a poet presented jazz as an art form integral to American and African-American culture. Hughes's critics (of both races) attacked his jazz poems as degrading portraits of African-American society. But Hughes maintained his belief that poetry could offer respectability to jazz and that the music would in turn give poetry a larger audience. His considerable body of work pulses with references to cabaret and street musicians, with exotic dancers and silver horns, with the joy of swing rhythms and the complex emotional qualities of the blues. *The Weary Blues* included several exceptional pieces, among them the title poem and "Jazzonia":

Oh, silver tree!

Oh, shining rivers of the soul!

In a Harlem cabaret
Six long-headed jazzers play.
A dancing girl whose eyes are bold
Lifts high a dress of silken gold.

Oh, singing tree!
Oh, shining rivers of the soul!

Were Eve's eyes
In the first garden
Just a bit too bold?
Was Cleopatra gorgeous
In a gown of gold?

Oh, shining tree!
Oh, silver rivers of the soul!

In a whirling cabaret
Six long-headed jazzers play.

Through 1950 Hughes published many other important poems, such as "Song for Billie Holiday" (*One-way Ticket*, New York, 1949), probably the first homage to that singer. In general his writing career reflects an increasing interest in the jazz aesthetic, and his early efforts laid the groundwork for two exceptional jazz-related poetry collections (*Montage of a Dream Deferred*, New York, 1951; and *Ask your Mama: 12 Moods for Jazz*, New York, 1961), several books of prose about jazz (notably *The First Book of Jazz*, New York, 1955), and a career within a career as a poet performing with live jazz accompaniment. His contributions to jazz poetry outweigh the efforts of any other writer from the first half of the 20th century.

Several writers from the 1930s and 1940s, however, must be mentioned for their substantial contributions, especially Sterling A. Brown, whose *Southern Road* (New York, 1932) brilliantly explored the structure and meter of the blues. Brown heard the blues as a representative sound of African-American speech and embraced the politics of the music as well. Like a musician, he altered the repeated phrases in his blues lines and wrote memorable refrains that hold up very well decades later. Many poems from *Southern Road* deserve close attention ("New St. Louis Blues," "Strong Men," "When de Saints Go Ma'ching in"), and "Ma Rainey," the first poem to celebrate a major blues or jazz artist, is one of the most significant jazz poems of the 1930s. It concludes:

I talked to a fellow, an' the fellow say,
"She jes' catch hold of us, somekindaway.
She sang Backwater Blues one day:

> *It rained fo' days an' de skies was dark as night,*
> *Trouble taken place in de lowlands at night.*
>
> *Thundered an' lightened an' the storm begin to roll*
> *Thousan's of people ain't got no place to go.*
>
> *Den I went an' stood upon some high ol' lonesome hill,*
> *An' looked down on the place where I used to live.*

An' den de folks, dey natchally bowed dey heads an' cried,
Bowed dey heavy heads, shet dey moufs up tight an' cried,
An' Ma lef' de stage, an' followed some de folks outside."

Dere wasn't much more de fellow say:
She jes' gits hold of us dataway.

The poem simultaneously characterizes the magnificence of this blues singer and admits to the limitations of language when describing music. In that respect "Ma Rainey" pays homage to all of the best blues and jazz musicians.

Two other poets, Melvin Tolson and Frank Marshall Davis, also wrote important works. Tolson began *A Gallery of Harlem Portraits* (Columbia, MO, 1979) in 1932, and his passion for the blues courses throughout the collection. Much later he published *Harlem Gallery: Book I, The Curator* (New York, 1965), which incorporated the principles of modernism to approximate the syncopated feel of jazz and included many references to the music. Davis's first jazz poems ("Jazz Band," "Cabaret," "Lynched") appeared in *Black Man's Verse* (Chicago, 1935), and his last collection, *Jazz Interlude* (Chicago, 1985), featured a series of jazz portraits. Gwendolyn Brooks published some blues-related poems in *A Street in Bronzeville* (New York, 1945) and Langston Hughes published several books of poems during the 1940s. But the dance bands and the commercial values of the swing era, shallow and superficial when compared to the horrors of World War II, did not, for obvious reasons, inspire poets. Few jazz poems appeared during this decade, and the exceptions proved to be primarily of historical interest: Ethel Jacobson's "Air de Barrelhouse" (*New York Times Magazine*, 18 Aug 1940) and Anderson Scruggs's "Meditation on Swing" (*Hygeia*, no.19, March 1941), both overtly racist poems; Peter Bowman's *Beach Red* (New York, 1945), a meditation on war with passing references to jazz; and William Carlos Williams's "Ol' Bunk's Band" from 1945 (*Selected Poems*, New York, 1969), a spirited but banal portrait of Bunk Johnson, somewhat akin to Sandburg's "Jazz Fantasia."

2. Poetry and jazz in performance. The popularity of bop, particularly among beat poets, generated a stunning number of jazz poems in the late 1950s. Bop became an integral part of being hip – part of the jargon, the image – and poets began to popularize readings with live musical accompaniment. In 1957 Kenneth Rexroth and Lawrence Ferlinghetti performed their work with a jazz band in San Francisco's The Cellar. From coast to coast this reading spurred a series of performances of poetry read to jazz, as well as a number of jazz poetry recordings.

Rexroth and Ferlinghetti released *Poetry Reading in "The Cellar"* (1957, Fan. 7002), featuring Rexroth's political attack against corporate America ("Thou Shalt Not Kill") and Ferlinghetti's dixieland-influenced "Autobiography," later published in *A Coney Island of the Mind* (New York, 1958). Within two years many writers had recorded poetry with musical accompaniment. Kenneth Patchen's first professional recording, *Kenneth Patchen Reads with the Chamber Jazz Sextet* (1958, Cadence 3004), set pre-recorded poetry to pleasant background music, but his more significant achievement appeared the following year on the album *Kenneth Patchen Reads with Jazz in Canada* (Folkways 9718), recorded together with a quartet.

In 1959 World Pacific released *Jazz Canto: an Anthology of Poetry and Jazz* (WP 1244), a wildly uneven collection highlighted by Bob Dorough's interpretation of Ferlinghetti's "Dog." That same year Jack Kerouac made three recordings. The first, *Poetry for the Beat Generation* (1959, Hanover 5000), presented Steve Allen playing cocktail jazz in the background. For the second, *Blues and Haikus* (1959, Hanover 5006), Kerouac requested his two favorite tenor saxophonists, Al Cohn and Zoot Sims, but, despite Kerouac's diction and solid delivery, this recording often sounds disjointed and awkward. On *Readings by Jack Kerouac on the Beat Generation* (Verve 15005, 1960), however, he relied entirely on his own voice to create rhythm, and this recording outshines the other two.

The surging interest in jazz poetry readings sparked a renewed appreciation for Langston Hughes. Leonard Feather produced *Weary Blues with Langston Hughes* (MGM E3697) in 1958, Hughes's most prolific year in terms of reading poetry to jazz, and his popularity swelled exponentially. Although Hughes's voice often sounds thin, the recording itself, which involved such outstanding musicians as Charles Mingus, surpasses the other efforts from that time.

The pretentiousness of many jazz poetry performances inspired parodies, most notably Lenny Bruce's "Psychopathia Sexualis" (*The Sick Humor of Lenny Bruce*, 1959, Fan. 7003), and by 1960 the craze for jazz poetry had dissipated almost to the point of extinction. Ironically, the stereotypes linked with the least successful jazz poetry performances from the late 1950s still constitute the general image of this genre. For more than 30 years the most ostentatious qualities of jazz poetry have remained representative and have hurt rather than helped the diverse efforts by poets from the 1960s to the present who have been interested in the union between poetry and jazz.

While the poetry and jazz movement in the United States had virtually ended by 1960, a similar movement flourished in Britain from 1961 to 1969, and many of the concerts from this decade have been chronicled in Jeremy Robson's *Poetry from Poetry and Jazz in Performance* (London, 1969). Among the central figures from these concerts were Pete Brown, Anselm Hollo, Christopher Logue, and Adrian Mitchell. Robson's *Poems for Jazz* (Leicester) appeared in 1963.

A number of poets and musicians since 1960 have worked with jazz and poetry as a performance art, and many of these efforts, unlike those from the late 1950s, achieve a greater union between the poet and the instrumentalists. These include recordings by famous musicians who incorporated some poetry into their recordings (Mingus, Archie Shepp, Jackie McLean), more contemporary musicians who have done the same (Charlie Haden, David Murray, Don Byron), and other jazz musicians who have written and recorded their own poetry (Sun Ra, Ahmad Jamal, Cecil Taylor). A few jazz poetry recordings collect the voices of numerous writers (*New Jazz Poets*, Folkways BR461, 1967; *JazzSpeak*, New Alliance 054, 1991) and many others present individuals, such as Wanda Coleman, Quincy Troupe, Nathaniel Mackey, the Last Poets, Barry Wallenstein, Ntozake Shange, and, most successfully, Amiri Baraka and Jayne Cortez.

3. Bird and trane poems. Although poets have celebrated hundreds of jazz musicians, two saxophonists dominate the list: Charlie Parker and John Coltrane. Poets in the late 1950s, predominantly white writers from the West Coast, repeatedly found inspiration in Parker's artistic innovations, as well as his self-destructive lifestyle. In the late 1960s African-American poets began to equate Coltrane's music with the civil rights movement, and for many writers these two musicians inspired their work as much as, if not more than, the literary figures from those decades.

While jazz musicians copied Parker's technique and studied his solos, poets struggled to capture the vitality of his music and presence, and their attempts tended to emphasize either the formal elements of the music or, even more, the biographical aspects of Parker himself. On the one hand there was the relationship between music and the poetic line, and several poets, principally Robert Creeley, insisted that Bird's music directly informed their sense of method. On the other there were portraits written by poets who were eager – perhaps desperately so – to share in Parker's magnificence. More often than not, poets projected a God-like status on Parker and, in doing so, lost the humanness of the man.

Jack Kerouac's most famous jazz poem, "Charlie Parker," first appeared in *Mexico City Blues* (New York, 1959) as three consecutive poems. The choruses are part biography and part hero worship, with frequent parallels between Parker and Buddha. Kerouac wrote the poems in this collection in the spirit of improvisation – without revision – and they typify his passion for jazz. Although uneven in quality, the volume holds up fairly well against similar collections, such as Kenneth Ford's *Poetry for Jazz* (Carmel, CA, 1959).

One of the better poems for Parker is Jack Spicer's "Song for Bird and Myself" (*Collected Books of Jack Spicer*, Santa Barbara, CA, 1975), written in 1956. The poem recognizes the dignity of bop and implicitly rejects the contemptuous, belittling criticisms of those who did not understand modern music. The Bird poems by Howard Hart, a poet and jazz drummer, are also stronger than many others, for they fuse evocative nightclub and street scenes with engaging abstractions. Ted Joans's career has been inextricably linked to jazz, as suggested by his title *Black Pow-wow: Jazz Poems* (New York, 1969). His best-known pieces from that collection, "Jazz is my Religion" and "Jazz Must be a Woman," mention numerous musicians, but overall Parker, more than anyone else, emerges as a luminary.

Bob Kaufman, known by some as the "original bebop man," worked diligently to make words sound like jazz. Consumed by the magnificent presence of Parker, Kaufman lived much like a jazz musician's stereotype: addicted to nightlife, to drugs, and to the avowedly non-academic, non-self-promoting world of the arts. In poems such as "Walking Parker Home" (*Solitudes Crowded with Loneliness*, New York, 1959) he consciously avoids a dramatic narrative and re-creates a series of emotive, sensory images that combine parts of Bird's life with the imagistic collision of beauty and horror:

Sweet beats of jazz impaled on slivers of wind
Kansas Black Morning/ First Horn Eyes/
Historical sound pictures on New Bird wings
People shouts/ boy alto dreams/ Tomorrow's
Gold belled pipe of stops and future Blues Times
Lurking Hawkins/ shadows of Lester/ realization
Bronze fingers – brain extensions seeking trapped sounds
Ghetto thoughts/ bandstand courage/ solo flight
Nerve-wracked suspicions of newer songs and doubts
New York altar city/ black tears/ secret disciples
Hammer horn pounding soul marks on unswinging gates
Culture gods/ mob sounds/ visions of spikes
Panic excursions to tribal Jazz wombs and transfusions
Heroin nights of birth/ and soaring/ over boppy new ground.
Smothered rage covering pyramids of notes spontaneously exploding
Cool revelations/ shrill hopes/ beauty speared into greedy ears
Birdland nights on bop mountains, windy saxophone revolutions
Dayrooms of junk/ and melting walls and circling vultures/
Money cancer/ remembered pain/ terror flights/
Death and indestructible existence

In that Jazz corner of life
Wrapped in a mist of sound
His legacy, our Jazz-tinted dawn
Wailing his triumphs of oddly begotten dreams
Inviting the nerveless to feel once more
That fierce dying of humans consumed
In raging fires of Love.

Here, and in other works, Kaufman suggests the spontaneity of jazz, and he presents the music not as an invisible art form but as something to be touched, embraced, ingested. Few poets have equaled Kaufman's passion for the physicality of Parker as a man and a musician.

John Coltrane's premature death in 1967 became immediately identifiable with the profound losses of other African-American leaders, most notably Martin Luther King, Jr., and Malcolm X. Some of the most explosive poetry from that period is steeped in his music, and a remarkable number of Coltrane poems appeared between 1967 and 1969, as posthumous reflections. Notable exceptions include John Sinclair's "Homage to John Coltrane" (*This is our Music*, Detroit) and A. B. Spellman's "John Coltrane" (*The Beautiful Days*, New York), both from 1965. Coltrane himself rarely discussed politics, but many poets from the late 1960s felt entirely comfortable interpreting his tenor solos as statements for African-American nationalism.

In 1969 John Taggart edited *Maps #3: Poems for John Coltrane* (Syracuse, NY), which offered a range of international voices responding to Coltrane's music, and in 1972 Stephen Henderson published his groundbreaking collection *Understanding the New Black Poetry* (New York), which discussed and anthologized many examples of the powerful connection between African-American poetry and jazz – particularly Coltrane's music. "Don't Cry, Scream" (*Don't Cry, Scream*, Detroit, 1969) by Haki Madhubuti, then known as Don L. Lee, became a signature poem, but there were many others, among them Larry Neal's "Orishas" (*Black Boogaloo*, San Francisco, 1969), Carolyn M. Rodgers's "Me, in Kulu Se, & Karma" (*Songs of a Black Bird*, Chicago, 1969), Askia Muhammad Touré's "Ju Ju" (*Ju Ju*, Chicago, 1970), David Henderson's "A Coltrane Memorial" (*De Mayor of Harlem*, Chicago, 1970), Sonia Sanchez's "a/coltrane/poem" (*We a BaddDDD People*, Detroit, 1970), and Sam Greenlee's "Memorial for Trane" (*Blues for an African Princess*, Chicago, 1971).

During this time Amiri Baraka emerged as a central figure in both the literary and jazz communities, and his political interpretations of modern jazz can be found in many works, notably the poem "Black Art," which he read on Sunny Murray's album *Sunny's Time Now* (1965, Jihad 663). Baraka's most ambitious Coltrane poem, "AM/TRAK" (*Selected Poetry and Amiri Baraka/LeRoi Jones*, New York, 1979), sketches the musician's career and presents him as a *"black blower of the now."* For Baraka, Coltrane articulated the passion of a decade remembered for extreme expressions of and attacks against racism: "Trane was the spirit of the 60's/ He was Malcolm X in New Super Bop Fire."

In the 1970s Michael S. Harper established himself as the best-known jazz poet, and since the publication of his first book, *Dear John, Dear Coltrane* (Pittsburgh, 1970), his career has been saturated by the music and memory of Coltrane. In general Harper's poetry requires an intimate knowledge of jazz history, and his references to musicians and songs demand complex and well-informed associative responses. Many poems from *Dear John, Dear Coltrane* and later volumes invoke Coltrane in order to address the politics of race, as seen in "Here Where Coltrane Is" (*History is your Own Heartbeat*, Urbana, IL, 1971), which concludes:

Dreaming on a train from New York
to Philly, you hand out six
notes which become an anthem
to our memories of you:
oak, birch, maple,
apple, cocoa, rubber.
For this reason Martin is dead;
for this reason Malcolm is dead;
for this reason Coltrane is dead;
in the eyes of my first son are the browns
of these men and their music.

In the center of Joy Harjo's "Healing Animal" (*In Mad Love and War*, Middletown, CT, 1990) Coltrane's music becomes "the collected heartbeat of" a Papago Indian tribe:

And I ask you
what bitter words are ruining your soft-skinned village,
because I want to make a poem that will cup
the inside of your throat
like the fire in the palm of a healing animal. Like
the way Coltrane knew love in the fluid shape
of a saxophone
that could change into the wings of a blue angel.

Indeed, the contemporary poets who have turned to Coltrane as a musical, if not spiritual, leader represent a vast range of social and literary backgrounds: Edward Kamau Brathwaite, Lawson Fusao Inada, Kazuko Shiraishi, Garrett Hongo, and Akua Lezli Hope, to name a few. Like Coltrane's personal interest in music from around the world, his music sustains a cross-cultural influence.

4. Contemporary work. Frank O'Hara's "The Day Lady Died" (*Lunch Poems*, San Francisco, 1964), an elegy for Billie Holiday, may be included in more anthologies than any other jazz poem. Curiously, his created persona consciously avoids mentioning Holiday until the final lines, after the speaker sees her photograph on a newspaper:

and I am sweating a lot by now and thinking of
leaning on the john door in the FIVE SPOT
while she whispered a song along the keyboard
to Mal Waldron and everyone and I stopped breathing

While this may not be a representative jazz poem in terms of its approach, the gesture is similar to a great many tributes from the 1970s: urgent expressions of loss for the passing of major jazz figures and, in some cases, entire eras. Many poems from the 1970s describe tragic deaths (the list is long) and tragic lives (including the expatriation of many great players). Perhaps in response a few jazz poems have consciously adopted an anti-elegiac stance, and Larry Neal's "Don't Say Goodbye to the Pork-pie Hat" (*Black Boogaloo*, San Francisco, 1969) might be the first to do so.

Compared with the work from the 1950s and 1960s, jazz poems since 1970 have been rather quiet in tone and strongly narrative, in keeping with William Matthews's "Mingus in Shadow" (*After All*, Boston, 1998):

What you see in his face in the last
photograph, when ALS had whittled
his body to fit a wheelchair, is how much
stark work it took to fend death off, and fail.
The famous rage got eaten cell by cell.

His eyes are drawn to slits against the glare
of the blanched landscape. The day he died,
the story goes, a swash of dead whales
washed up on the Baja beach. Great nature grieved
for him, the story means, but it was great

nature that skewed his cells and siphoned
his force and melted his fat like tallow
and beached him in a wheelchair under
a sombrero. It was human nature,
tiny nature, to take the photograph,

to fuss with the aperture and speed, to let
in the right blare of light just long enough
to etch pale Mingus to the negative.
In the small, memorial world of that
negative, he's all the light there is.

Matthews's other Mingus poems portray the bass player fully in command – characteristically explosive – and generally the most recent jazz poems tend to celebrate rather than mourn jazz musicians and their music. Among the many highlights are the "paragraphs" for swing musicians by Hayden Carruth (*Brothers, I Loved You All*, New York, 1978); "Testimony," a libretto for Parker by Yusef Komunyakaa (*Thieves of Paradise*, Middletown, CT, 1998); blues poems by Raymond R. Patterson (*Elemental Blues*, Merrick, NY, 1983); reflections on 1950s jazz in Detroit by Philip Levine (*Brilliant Corners*, summer 1997); the Bessie Smith narratives by Sherley Anne Williams (*Some One Sweet Angel Chile*, New York, 1982); elegies for Chet Baker by Ai, Mark Doty, and Lynda Hull (anthologized in *The Second Set*, Bloomington, IN, 1996); and the many publications and recordings by such enduring poets as Amiri Baraka, Jayne Cortez, and Al Young.

Several jazz poetry anthologies appeared in the 1990s, as did *Brilliant Corners: a Journal of Jazz & Literature* and a few critical books on the subject. The recently published work suggests an unfailing fascination with the nature of jazz as well as with the lives of jazz musicians, and it implies that poets will turn to jazz for inspiration long into the 21st century.

BIBLIOGRAPHY

C. Johnson: "Jazz Poetry and Blues," *Carolina Magazine* (1928), May, 16
O. Jemie: *Langston Hughes: an Introduction to the Poetry* (New York, 1965)
S. Henderson, ed.: *Understanding the New Black Poetry* (New York, 1972)
L. Smith: "The Poetry-and-Jazz Movement in the United States," *Essays on California Writers*, ed. C. Crow (Bowling Green, OH, 1978)
W. Harris: *The Jazz Aesthetic: the Poetry and Poetics of Amiri Baraka* (Columbia, SC, 1985)
S. Feinstein and Y. Komunyakaa, eds.: *The Jazz Poetry Anthology* (Bloomington, IN, 1991)
A. Lange and N. Mackey, eds.: *Moment's Notice* (Minneapolis, 1993)
S. Feinstein and Y. Komunyakaa, eds.: *The Second Set: the Jazz Poetry Anthology, Volume 2* (Bloomington, IN, 1996)
S. Feinstein: *Jazz Poetry: from the 1920s to the Present* (Westport, CT, 1997)
A. Nielsen: *Black Chant* (Cambridge, MA, 1997)
S. Feinstein: *A Bibliographic Guide to Jazz Poetry* (Westport, CT, 1998)

SASCHA FEINSTEIN

Pohjola, Pekka (*b* Finland, 13 Jan 1952). Finnish electric bass guitarist and composer. He originally studied violin and piano, but became an electric bass guitarist with the progressive rock group Wigwam in 1970. After leaving the group in 1974 he made an album as a leader which featured Eero Koivistoinen, Seppo Paakkunainen, and the Swedish guitarist Costa Apetrea (*Harakka Bialoipokku* [The magpie Bialoipokku], 1974, Love 118). He played with the group Made in Sweden (1975–7) and with the guitarist and multi-instrumentalist Mike Oldfield (1979), and led the Pekka Pohjola Group, which may be heard to advantage on the album *Urban Tango* (1982, Pohjola 1). From 1992 he has led the group Classic Pohjola. Pohjola is a remarkable bass player in both jazz and rock genres, but he has increasingly presented himself as a self-taught composer of a personal brand of "heavy jazz," freely mixing influences from pop and classical music and jazz.

BIBLIOGRAPHY

E. Lehtonen: *Suomalaisen rockin tietosanakirja* [Encyclopedia of Finnish rock] (Tampere, Finland, 1983)
J. Muikku: "Broadening out: Finnish Jazz Breaks down Barriers," *Nordic Sounds* (1989), June, 12
V. Siren: "Pekka Pohjola: Music Speaks without Words," *Finnish Music Quarterly* no.3 (1994), 29
M. Huuskonen, J. Muikku and T. Vähäsilta: *Finnish Jazz* (Helsinki, 5/1997)

PEKKA GRONOW

Poindexter, Pony [Norwood Eugene] (*b* New Orleans, 8 Feb 1926; *d* Oakland, CA, 14 April 1988). Alto saxophonist. His middle name is taken from the California death index. He studied clarinet in elementary school, and began playing alto saxophone at the age of 12 and the soprano instrument four years later. When he was 15 his family moved to Oakland, California, where he quickly found work in nightclubs even though he was a minor. On graduating from high school he was drafted into the army; he played for a brief time with Tiny Bradshaw in New York, but was absent without leave at the time and his arrest cut short the engagement. After being discharged (*c* January 1946) he returned to Oakland, where he studied at the Candell Conservatory of Music and worked in Ernie Henry's group for about two years. He then joined Billy Eckstine's big band and toured with Jack McVea's small group. In March 1951 he returned to the San Francisco area, where he worked with Vernon Alley's quartet. Late in 1951 he joined Lionel Hampton's band, replacing Jerome Richardson, who at that time joined Alley. From 1952 Poindexter led his own groups in San Francisco, though he also worked briefly with Nat "King" Cole, Billie Holiday, T-Bone Walker, and Joe Turner (ii). In autumn 1953 he moved to Portland, Oregon, and one year later settled in Seattle. He played with Cal Tjader early in 1957, then resumed his role as a leader. In mid-1960 he joined the ensemble that accompanied Lambert, Hendricks, and Ross to play in Hendricks's show *The Evolution of the Blues*, and remained with this group (which later became Lambert, Hendricks, and Bavan) until 1963. From 1964 to 1979 he lived and worked in Europe, and he may be seen in *Appunti per un film sul jazz* (1965); he then returned to the USA and settled once more in Oakland. After an illness in 1979 forced him to cease playing saxophone he began performing as a singer. Although Poindexter's early work favored the styles of Jimmy Dorsey and Johnny Hodges, his recordings show clearly that the principal influence upon his playing was that of Charlie Parker. He published an autobiography, *The Pony Express: Memoirs of a Jazz Musician* (Frankfurt am Main, Germany, 1985)

SELECTED RECORDINGS

As leader: *Pony's Express* (1962, Epic 17035); *Gumbo!* (1962, Prst. 16001)
As sideman: W. Montgomery: on *Montgomeryland* (1958–9, PJ 5), Monk's Shop, Summertime, Falling in Love with Love, Renie (1958); J. Hendricks: *A Good Git Together* (1959, WP 1283); *Evolution of the Blues* (1960, Col. CS8383); Lambert, Hendricks, and Bavan: *Lambert, Hendricks, and Bavan at Basin Street East* (1962, RCA LSP2635)

BIBLIOGRAPHY

"Pony Poindexter Joins Hampton," *DB*, xviii/26 (1951), 19
P. Koechlin: "Little Pony: croyez-moi, le jazz est plus français qu'américain," *Jh*, no.202 (1964), 7
J. Howard: "Pony Poindexter: the European Circuit," *Radio Free Jazz*, xvii/2 (1976), 7
M. Hennessey: "Europajazz," *JT* (1985), Aug, 8

THOMAS OWENS

Pokorný, Roman (*b* Moravský Krumlov, Czechoslovakia [now Czech Republic], 2 April 1966). Czech electric guitarist, leader, and composer. His grandfather was an accordionist, and his father, a trumpeter, led a brass band in which the young Pokorný served as drummer from the age of six. Later he also played bass guitar, but when he moved to Prague at the age of 15 for training in stucco masonry he changed to acoustic guitar and then to electric guitar; at that time he listened mainly to hard rock and folk music. Following his studies he returned to Brno. In 1985 he enrolled in the Frýdlant summer jazz workshop in northern Bohemia, and this experience prompted him to focus on jazz guitar. Pokorný formed his first jazz trio in 1989, quit his daytime job to became a professional guitarist in 1991, and formed a quartet in 1994 with which he recorded his first album as a leader the following year; he also played in rock, fusion, and pop bands and recorded with the Czech fusion group Tutu (1995–6). In 1997 he recorded with the Czech jazz pianist and composer Emil Viklický, and he formed a septet and a trio which recorded respectively in 1998 and 1999.

SELECTED RECORDINGS

(all recorded for Arta)

As leader: *Magic Holidays* (1995, 0067-2); *Jazz Perception* (1998, 0087-2); *Blue Point* (1999, 0097-2)

As sideman: Tutu: *Sundance* (1995–6, 0068-2); E. Viklický: *UV Drive* (1997, 0081-2)

JAROSLAV PAŠMIK

Polcer, Ed(ward Joseph) (*b* Paterson, NJ, 10 Feb 1937). Cornetist. He learned cornet from the age of eight, formed a dixieland group in his teens, and played with local groups while studying at Princeton University (1954–8). From 1958 to 1969, at the same time as he pursued a career in business, he performed traditional jazz at various clubs in and around New York, notably Ryan's. In 1969 he joined Red Balaban's group, with which he worked intermittently until 1985, as joint leader from 1975 and as co-owner of Eddie Condon's club from 1979. In addition he toured North America with Benny Goodman (1972) and made recordings with swing groups led by the singer Jane Harvey and Dick Wellstood and by the singer Cathy Chamberlain (1976). From 1970 he led sextets and quintets which accompanied many prominent jazz musicians, and his group Midtown North played at Condon's from 1983 until the venue closed in July 1985. Polcer appeared regularly at American jazz parties and made annual trips to play in Britain. He performed and recorded as a member of an all-star group in Germany (*A Salute to Eddie Condon*, 1993, Nagel-Heyer 040) and with the singer Terry Blaine (1995, 1997, the latter recorded in Germany). Among his own recordings, which he made in 1982 and regularly during the early 1990s, are *In the Condon Tradition* (1982, Jazzology 150) and *The Magic of Swing Street* (1993, BlewZ Manor [unnumbered]).

Video oral history material in *NCH* (HCJA).

BIBLIOGRAPHY

Feather–Gitler '70s

M. L. Hester: "He Fights to Keep Jazz Flame Alive in New York City," *MR*, xvii/7 (1990), 18

C. Deffaa: *Traditionalists and Revivalists in Jazz* (Metuchen, NJ, and London, 1993), 218

BK

Polish Jazz Society. *See* POLSKIE STOWARZYSZENIE JAZZOWE.

Pollack, Ben (*b* Chicago, 22 June 1903; *d* Palm Springs, CA, 7 June 1971). Drummer and bandleader. By 1923 he was playing with the NEW ORLEANS RHYTHM KINGS, where he

Ben Pollack's band outside the MGM studios in Culver City, CA, summer 1927: (left to right) Larry Binyon (tenor saxophone), Benny Goodman (clarinet), Gil Rodin (alto saxophone), Al Lasker (tuba), Pollack (drums, leader), Al Gifford (banjo), Wayne Allen (piano, arranger), Al Harris and Harry Greenberg (trumpets), and Glenn Miller (trombone)

established himself as the leading drummer in the early Chicago style of white jazz, particularly on account of his innovative cymbal technique. In 1926 he founded the first of several jazz-oriented dance bands for which he is largely remembered today. From 1928 he only directed the band, and Ray Bauduc took over the drumming. Although commercially only moderately successful, these bands were highly regarded by contemporary jazz musicians, and provided valuable exposure early in their careers for such important players as Benny Goodman, Glenn Miller, Bud Freeman, Jimmy McPartland, and Jack Teagarden, as well as Fud Livingston, Steve Brown, Gil Rodin, Matty Matlock, Yank Lawson, and Eddie Miller. In 1934 Pollack's band broke up in California, and most of its members subsequently formed the nucleus of Bob Crosby's band. Pollack's later groups included Harry James and Dave Matthews (both 1935–6), Muggsy Spanier (1936–8), and Irving Fazola (1938). From the 1940s he occasionally organized groups in California in the dixieland revival style, but was active chiefly as a restaurateur.

SELECTED RECORDINGS

As leader: 'Deed I do (1926, Vic. 20408); My Kinda Love (1929, Vic. 21944); Two Tickets to Georgia (1933, Vic. 24284); Song of the Islands (1937, Decca 1424)

As sideman with New Orleans Rhythm Kings: Sweet Lovin' Man (1923, Gen. 5104); Shimmeshawabble (1923, Gen. 5106); Tin Roof Blues (1923, Gen. 5105)

SELECTED FILMS AND VIDEOS

Ben Pollack and his Park Central Orchestra (1929); Ben Pollack and his Orchestra (1934); The Benny Goodman Story (1955); Ben Pollack and his Pick-a-Rib Boys (1962)

BIBLIOGRAPHY

CarrJ; *McCarthyB*; *SchullerS*

S. B. Charters and L. Kunstadt: *Jazz: a History of the New York Scene* (Garden City, NY, 1962/*R*1981), chap.13

A. Napoleon: "May it Please You: Thoughts on Ben Pollack," *JJ*, xxiv/9 (1971), 10

A. Napoleon and J. R. T. Davies: "A Discography," *Sv*, no.36 (1971), 222

T. D. Brown: *A History and Analysis of Jazz Drumming to 1942* (diss., U. of Michigan, 1976), 282, 560

G. Collins: "Sweet and Hot: the Ben Pollack Story," *Memory Lane*, ix/34 (1979)

J. Chilton: *Stomp Off, Let's Go! The Story of Bob Crosby's Bob Cats & Big Band* (London, 1983)

J. L. Collier: *Benny Goodman and the Swing Era* (New York, and Oxford, England, 1989), 45

J. BRADFORD ROBINSON

Pollard, Terry (Jean) (*b* Detroit, 15 Aug 1931). Pianist and vibraphonist. She first performed and recorded in Detroit alongside Thad and Elvin Jones in Billy Mitchell's quintet (1952–3), playing both piano and vibraphone. From 1953 to 1957 she toured and made recordings (notably *Terry Gibbs Quartet*, 1953, Bruns. BL58055) as the pianist and second vibraphonist in Terry Gibbs's groups; she also recorded with her own quintet in Los Angeles and with Dick Garcia in New York (1955). After returning to Detroit (1957) Pollard played piano in clubs and took part in recording sessions with Yusef Lateef (1958–9). She recorded with Dorothy Ashby in 1961. (*FeatherE*)

Polo, Danny (*b* Toluca, IL, 22 Dec 1901; *d* Chicago, 11 July 1949). Clarinetist and saxophonist. He grew up in Clinton, Indiana, played clarinet in a local marching band, and while still a child formed a duo with Claude Thornhill. His first professional engagements were with Elmer Schoebel in Chicago (*c*1923) and Merritt Brunies. During the winter of 1926–7 he deputized for Don Murray in Jean Goldkette's orchestra, and the following summer he toured Europe with Dave Tough. He also worked with the banjoist George Carhart throughout Europe, recording with his New Yorkers in Berlin (*see* New Yorkers (i)) before leading his own band in Paris. He remained in France until 1929, playing with Arthur Briggs, Lud Gluskin, and Ray Ventura, then moved to London, where he performed and recorded with Bert Ambrose's orchestra (intermittently, 1929–35); while in London he made numerous jazz and "hot dance" recordings, notably with Philip Lewis and his Dance Orchestra, Spike Hughes and his Dance Orchestra, Ray Noble's Night Club Kings, the Embassy (Rhythm) Eight, the Rhythmic Eight, and the Rhythm Rascals. He worked again with Gluskin in 1932. After a period in the USA (1935–7) Polo returned to Europe; in London he recorded as a leader (October 1937 and January 1938) and rejoined Ambrose (1938), and in Paris he rejoined Ventura and again recorded as a leader (January 1939). He resettled in the USA in 1939 and from November that year played with Joe Sullivan at Café Society, New York: Edmond Hall was the principal clarinet soloist and Polo played mainly tenor saxophone, on which he was less accomplished. He recorded with Sullivan, and also with the Sextet of the Rhythm Club of London (in New York), the Varsity Seven (including Benny Carter, Coleman Hawkins, Sullivan, and Joe Turner (ii)), Hawkins's octet, and George Wettling's Chicago Rhythm Kings. When Sullivan abruptly left Café Society and disbanded in June 1940, Polo became a member of Jack Teagarden's band (July 1940 – January 1942). In February 1942 he joined Thornhill's band. He led his own groups in the mid-1940s, during Thornhill's years of military service, then worked again with Thornhill from May 1947 to March 1949, and from June 1949 until his death; he was regularly featured with the band.

Polo was often credited with popularizing jazz in Britain. His playing was smooth, gentle, and restrained. Among jazz musicians who had come to prominence in the 1920s, he showed in his later work with Thornhill (as did his friend Tough with Woody Herman's First Herd) an unusual ability to slot comfortably into a stylistic context oriented towards modern jazz.

SELECTED RECORDINGS

As leader: Stratton Street Strut/More than Somewhat (1937, Decca F6518); Money for Jam/Mr. Polo Takes a Solo (1937, Decca F6578); You made me love you/Montmartre Moan (1939, Decca F7039); Doing the Gorgonzola/Montparnasse Jump (1939, Decca F6989)

As sideman: J. Goldkette: My Pretty Girl (1927, Vic. 20588); Clementine (1927, Vic. 20994); Rhythmic Eight: Kansas City Kitty/Louise (1929, Zonophone 5437); Night Club Kings: In The Moonlight/Someone (1930, HMV B5776); B. Ambrose: Cotton Pickers' Congregation/Caravan (1937, Decca F6458); Varsity Seven: It's Tight Like That/Easy Rider (1939, Vars. 8147); C. Hawkins: The Sheik of Araby (1940, Bb 10770); Bouncing with Bean (1940, Bb 10693); Varsity Seven: Shake it and break it (1940, Vars. 8179); C. Thornhill: Robbin's Nest (1947, Col. 38136); first issued on *The Uncollected Claude Thornhill* (1947, Hindsight 108), 'Deed I do

BIBLIOGRAPHY

ChiltonW

J. Burns: "The Forgotten Boppers," *J&B*, ii/3 (1972), 4

D. Schiedt: *The Jazz State of Indiana* (Pittsboro, IN, 1977)

J. Godbolt: *A History of Jazz in Britain, 1919–50* (London, Melbourne, Australia, and New York, 1984)

M. Selchow: *Profoundly Blue: a Bio-discographical Scrapbook on Edmond Hall* (Lübbecke, Germany, 1988)

B. Amstell: "The Forgotten Ones: Danny Polo," *JJI*, xlvii/10 (1994), 14

H. S. Kaye: "Dave Tough with the New Yorkers in Europe," in *Storyville 1998/9*, ed. L. Wright (Chigwell, England, 1999), 5

RAYMOND J. GARIGLIO/BK

Polskie Stowarzyszenie Jazzowe [Polish Jazz Society]. A Polish jazz organization which sponsored and arranged concerts and festivals and issued records and periodicals. It evolved from the Federacja Polskich Klubów Jazzowych (Federation of Polish Jazz Clubs), formed in 1956 by Jan Byrczek, Roman Waschko, and others. After this organization disbanded the Polska Federacja Jazzowa (Polish Jazz Federation) was formed in March 1963; this had become the Polskie Stowarzyszenie Jazzowe by 1967 and was led by Byrczek until December 1975, when Zbigniew Namysłowski became the society's president and Byrczek and Jan Wróblewski its vice-presidents. Andrezej Jaroszewski succeeded Namysłowski in December 1977, and Tomasz Tluczkiewicz became president in 1980.

The society sponsored and organized a piano competition and workshop in Kalisz; workshops in Radost (near Warsaw) and Chodziez; and a festival, the Pomorian Jazz Autumn, in Toruń and Bydgoszcz. It also founded the journal *Jazz Forum* and in 1972 became affiliated with the record label Poljazz. It played an important role in establishing the International Jazz Federation. In 1982 it established a jazz archive (*see* LIBRARIES AND ARCHIVES, §2).

Pomeroy, (Irving) Herb(ert, III) (*b* Gloucester, MA, 15 April 1930). Bandleader, trumpeter, and teacher. After studying at the Schillinger House of Music (1950–52) and playing in Boston with Charlie Parker (for one week in June 1953) and Charlie Mariano (later that same year) he toured as a trumpeter with Lionel Hampton (December 1953 – April 1954) and Stan Kenton (September 1954). He then returned to Boston and worked with Serge Chaloff (1954–5). In 1955 he began teaching at Schillinger, which the previous year had taken a new name, the Berklee School of Music. While establishing himself as the cornerstone of this school's growing jazz program he led a 16-piece swing and bop ensemble that performed regularly at The Stables (1956–60); among its sidemen were Joe Gordon, Jaki Byard (who was then playing tenor saxophone), Boots Mussulli, and later, Mariano and Bill Berry. He was also the leader of another band (1960–62), which played some of his own arrangements; its 13 members included Dusko Goykovich, Mike Gibbs, Sam Rivers, Hal Galper, and Alan Dawson. Pomeroy was in Orchestra USA from 1962 to 1963, and in addition to his duties at Berklee he directed jazz bands at the Massachusetts Institute of Technology from 1963; he took one such group to the Montreux Jazz Festival in 1976. In 1975 he organized a third group, bringing together students, members of his original band, and such well-known jazzmen as John LaPorta and Phil Wilson, and around the same time he worked in musical theater, playing in pit orchestras for Broadway shows visiting Boston. Pomeroy led his own orchestra until 1993. He retired from the Berklee faculty in 1995, and thereafter worked as a freelance trumpeter; in 1996 his small group, in which Dave McKenna and Gray Sargent were sidemen, recorded on its own and as accompanists to the singer Donna Byrne. From 1987 through the 1990s he also appeared as a guest conductor of big bands, among them UMO, the Stockholm Jazz Orchestra, the NDR Big Band, and other such ensembles, in Denmark, Israel, and Finland.

SELECTED RECORDINGS

As leader: *Jazz in a Stable* (1955, Tran. 1); *Band in Boston* (1958, UA 4015); *Pramlatta's Hips* (*c*1980, Shiah 1); with D. Byrne: *Walking on Air* (1996, Arbors 19176)

As sideman: C. Mariano: *Boston All Stars* (1953, Prst. 153); S. Chaloff: *The Fable of Mable* (1954, Sto. 317)

BIBLIOGRAPHY

FeatherE; *Feather '60s*
L. Feather: "Herb Pomeroy Orchestra," *DB*, xxiv/13 (1957), 35
"The New Herb Pomeroy," *DB*, xxvii/11 (1960), 14
K. C. Sulkin: "Herb Pomeroy," *DB*, xliv/17 (1977), 32
F.-J. Hadley: "Herb Pomeroy: Maverick of Music Education," *DB*, lv/6 (1988), 56
P. Dorian: "Bill Chase, the Early Years in Boston: an Interview with Herb Pomeroy," *Jazz Research Papers*, xiv (1994), 65
B. Blumenthal: "Jazzman Herb Pomeroy Retires from Teaching but Not from Music," *Boston Globe* (28 April 1995)
"6th Annual Down Beat Achievement Awards for Jazz Education: Hall of Fame: Herb Pomeroy," *DB*, lxiv/5 (1997), 50

BK

Ponce, Daniel (*b* Havana, Cuba, 21 July 1953). Cuban percussionist and bandleader. He received early musical training from his grandfather and began playing with local Cuban bands at the age of 11, eventually performing as a bata drummer with the band Watusi. In 1980, having been exiled from Cuba, he arrived in the USA and settled in New York, where he began working with such local Latin musicians as José Fajardo and Andy and Jerry Gonzalez, and later with Paquito D'Rivera and Eddie Palmieri. Ponce played frequently for studio recordings as well as live performances, working with a diverse roster of artists, among them Yoko Ono, Mick Jagger, McCoy Tyner, Dizzy Gillespie, and Laurie Anderson, with whom he may be seen in the video *Home of the Brave* (1986). He received critical and popular attention for his recordings with Herbie Hancock (1984) and performances with Bobby McFerrin. In 1983 Ponce recorded an album in collaboration with Bill Laswell; this and later recordings as a leader combined Cuban rhythms with American pop and jazz influences. He also recorded with Hilton Ruiz in 1989 and 1991.

SELECTED RECORDINGS

As leader: *New York Now!* (1983, Celluloid 5005); *Arawe* (1987, Ant./New Directions 90631-2); *Chango te llama* (1990, Mango 162-539877-2)

As sideman with H. Ruiz: *Doin' it Right* (1989, Novus 3085-2-N)

BIBLIOGRAPHY

L. Gourse: "Ignacio Berroa and Daniel Ponce," *MD*, viii/1 (1984), 57
J. Camacho: "Les deux faces des tambours," *Jm*, no.340 (1985), 26
R. Prince: "Afro-Cuban," *Folk Roots*, no.67 (1989), 17
L. Birnbaum: "Daniel Ponce: an Undesirable Percussionist Becomes a Wanted Man," *Musician*, no.112 (1988), 22
C. Larkin, ed.: *The Guinness Encyclopedia of Popular Music* (Enfield, England, 1995)

RUSS GIRSBERGER

Ponder, Jimmy [James Willis] (*b* Pittsburgh, 10 May 1946). Electric guitarist. He joined soul bands as a teenager, but was fired for playing in too jazz-oriented a manner. In 1966 he began an association with Charles Earland that continued until 1969. On recordings made in 1967–8 with Lou Donaldson he is identified as Jimmy "Fats" Ponder, a nickname which refers to his full-bodied guitar timbre and which appears not to have stayed with him (unlike Waller and other jazz "Fats," he is not fat); he also recorded in 1968 with Big John Patton, Stanley Turrentine, and Johnny Hodges and played briefly with David "Fathead" Newman in New York. After moving to Newark, New Jersey, he performed in a group led by Joe Thomas (v) from 1969 to 1972. He performed and recorded with Jimmy McGriff (intermittently from *c*1975), led a band, Final Edition, with the drummer Grassella Oliphant (1975), and continued to lead his own ensembles. He also recorded with Mickey

Tucker (1975) and, for the Muse label, with Willis "Gator" Jackson and Sonny Phillips (both 1976), Houston Person (1976–7), Etta Jones (1977), and Earland (1977–8). Later he recorded with Turrentine when the saxophonist ceased to make pop-oriented albums and recorded again in a soul-jazz style (1984). He made a series of albums under his own name for Muse from 1987, and during the same period took part as a sideman in sessions with Hank Crawford (1984, 1991), Crawford and McGriff (1987, 1989), Groove Holmes (1988–9), the alto saxophonist Louis Keel (1990), and Ernie Andrews and Chris White (both 1992). At some point Ponder also worked with Andrew White, Sonny Stitt, and Gary Bartz before returning in 1990 to Pittsburgh, where he led a trio including Roger Humphries. Ponder's playing combines aggressive rhythm-and-blues figurations with swift and lucid bop lines. His choice of material is influenced by a keen ear for chromaticism, which gives his performances an emotionally volatile yet distanced, astringent quality.

SELECTED RECORDINGS

(recorded for Muse unless otherwise indicated)

As leader: *Mean Streets: No Bridges* (1987, 5324); *Jump* (1988, 5347); *To Reach a Dream* (1988–9, 5394); *Come on Down* (1990, 5375); *Soul Eyes* (1991, 5514); *Something to Ponder* (1994, 5541); *James Street* (1997, HighNote 7017)

As sideman: J. Patton: *That Certain Feeling* (1968, BN 84281); L. Donaldson: *Say it Loud!* (1968, BN 84299); C. Earland: *Soul Crib* (1969, Choice 520); *Infant Eyes* (1979, 5181); S. Turrentine: *Straight Ahead* (1984, BN 85105); G. Holmes: *Blues All Day Long* (1988, 5358)

BIBLIOGRAPHY

Feather–Gitler '70s

L. Birnbaum: "Profile: Jimmy Ponder," *GP*, xxvii/10 (1992), 31

ANDREW WAGGONER/BK

Ponomarev, Valery (*b* Moscow, 20 Jan 1943). Trumpeter. He studied music in Moscow and became interested in jazz after hearing a recording by Clifford Brown. He performed at the Youth Club in Moscow (1965–9) and at jazz festivals in the USSR and recorded for the Melodiya label with a hard-bop group led by the pianist Vadim Sakun. In 1973 he defected to the West, and in 1977 he joined Art Blakey's Jazz Messengers, with which he toured Europe, Brazil, and Japan and took part in a number of recording sessions; he was granted Amercian citizenship in 1979. The following year he organized his own band, Universal Language, which remained active through the 1990s. He also performed internationally as a freelance soloist (recording as a guest soloist with Roger Kellaway in Japan in 1986 and touring Europe and Australia), and appeared in the USA in Lee Konitz's nonet, the big bands of Mercer Ellington, Frank Foster, and Lionel Hampton, the orchestra which performed Charles Mingus's reconstructed symphony *Epitaph*, and numerous small groups under Joe Morello and Pepper Adams, among others. After the fall of communism Ponomarev first returned to Russia in 1990; in the course of the following decade he made further visits, during which he performed at a festival in Moscow and toured with Benny Golson, Curtis Fuller and Bobby Watson, and Bob Berg. In 1991 he recorded with Junior Cook's hard-bop group and collaborated with Max Roach, Harold Land, the pianist Sam Dockery, and George Morrow in a re-creation of the Brown–Roach quintet at a concert in Wilmington, Delaware; he later toured with Land, performing a repertory associated with Brown.

SELECTED RECORDINGS

As leader: *Means of Identification* (1985, Reservoir 101); *Trip to Moscow* (1988, Reservoir 107); *Profile* (1991, Reservoir 120); *A Star for You* (1997, Reservoir 150)

As sideman: A. Blakey: *In my Prime* (1977–8, Tim. 114, 118); J. Cook: *You Leave Me Breathless* (1991, Ste. 31304)

BIBLIOGRAPHY

Feather–Gitler '70s

L. Birnbaum: "Profile: Valery Ponomarev," *DB*, xlvi/12 (1979), 46

"Ein Gespräch mit dem Exil-Russen Valery Ponomarev," *JP*, xxix/10 (1980), 22

B. Rusch: "Valery Ponomarev: Interview," *Cadence*, xi/2 (1985), 10

R. Baranello: "Riffs: Valery Ponomarev," *DB*, lix/4 (1992), 13

D. Briggs: "Valery Ponomarev," *CJM*, xxx/2 (1993), 9

J. Bradley: "Moscow Jazz: Music his International Language," *Denver Post* (18 July 1994)

BK

Ponta. Nickname of SHUICHI MURAKAMI.

Ponty, Jean-Luc (*b* Avranches, France, 29 Sept 1942). French violinist. His father was a violin teacher and the director of the school of music in Avranches, and his mother taught piano. He played violin and piano from the age of five and clarinet from the age of 11. When he was 13 he left school to concentrate on becoming a concert violinist; he studied for two years at the Paris Conservatoire, winning the *premier prix* when he was 17. He then played with the Concerts Lamoureux orchestra for three years, during which time he was introduced to jazz; he first played jazz as an amateur clarinetist and tenor saxophonist, but by 1962 he was performing and recording on violin with Jef Gilson, with whom he continued to be associated for some time.

Following his military service (1962–4) Ponty devoted himself exclusively to jazz. He led a quartet with René Urtreger and in 1964 performed at the Festival Mondial du Jazz Antibes–Juan-les-Pins. He then played and recorded in

Jean-Luc Ponty playing at the Newport Jazz Saratoga Festival, 1978

quartets and trios with Eddy Louiss and Daniel Humair (1964–7) and as the leader of a quartet with Wolfgang Dauner, Niels-Henning Ørsted Pedersen, and Humair (1967). In 1967 he made his first visit to the USA to play in a violin workshop at the Monterey Jazz Festival; he may be seen in two film documentaries from this event, *Monterey Jazz Festival* (1967) and *Monterey Jazz* (1968). His quartet first played in England in February 1969, and the following month he went to Los Angeles, where he performed and recorded with Frank Zappa and made an album that included some of Zappa's compositions (*King Kong*); in the same year he joined George Duke's trio. After returning to France he led a free-jazz group, the Jean-Luc Ponty Experience (*c*1970–72). He settled in the USA in 1973 and toured with Zappa's Mothers of Invention, then with the second Mahavishnu Orchestra (1974–5). From 1975 he led fusion bands, touring extensively and reaching a large audience with his recordings; the title track of one of his most popular albums, *Individual Choice*, was made into a video (1984). Ponty toured worldwide with his band in 1987–8, and while in Europe in the latter year he became involved in the burgeoning "world music" movement: later, for his album *Tchokola* (1991), he traveled back to Paris to work with African musicians based there and recorded compositions and improvisations based on traditional musics of West and Central Africa; he made a similar album in Paris and Los Angeles (December 1992 – March 1993). In 1995, with Al Di Meola and Stanley Clarke, he formed the trio Rites of Strings, which recorded and toured internationally. He toured with his American fusion band in 1996 and with his group of Western and African musicians from 1997 into the new century.

By developing a range of new sounds, grounded in electronic effects, Ponty made a place for the violin in a number of modern jazz styles. At first he simply amplified his acoustic violin in order to be heard, but from 1969 he used mainly electric violin and violectra (an electric instrument tuned an octave below the violin), which he played through distortion, Echoplex, phase shifter, and wa-wa devices, sometimes combining these with the conventional mute. In 1977 he replaced the two instruments with a five-string electric violin, the lowest string on which (tuned to *c*) offered part of the violectra's range. With his own bands he also plays synthesizer, and in the 1980s he often reverted from electric to acoustic violin, using the synthesizer to create electronic effects. The broad spectrum of sounds he produces and the contrast between them and conventional jazz timbres may be heard on the swing album *Violin Summit* (1966), recorded with Svend Asmussen, Stephane Grappelli, and Stuff Smith, and the jazz-rock album *Jean-Luc Ponty–Stephane Grappelli* (1973).

Ponty is equally at home in swing, bop, modal jazz, free jazz, and fusion and plays distinguished improvisations in every style. One of the most creative European jazz musicians, he is a supreme exponent of jazz fusion. *Upon the Wings of Music* (1975) marked his move away from the raucous styles of Zappa and the Mahavishnu Orchestra; instead he developed a style in which his imaginative themes and improvisations – at times soaring and lyrical, at times bluesy, biting, and rhythmically complex – are accompanied by rich, highly polished ostinatos based on soul and rock rhythms.

See also Improvisation, §§4(iii) and 4(vi), and ex.6.

SELECTED RECORDINGS

As leader: *Jazz Long Playing* (1964, Phi. B77810L); with S. Asmussen, S. Grappelli, and S. Smith: *Violin Summit* (1966, Saba 15099); *Sunday Walk* (1967, Saba 15139); *King Kong* (1969, PJ 20172); *Jean-Luc Ponty–Stephane Grappelli* (1973, Amer. 6139); *Upon the Wings of Music* (1975, Atl. 18138); *Imaginary Voyage* (1976, Atl. 19136); *Individual Choice* (*c*1983, Atl. 80098); *Tchokola* (1991, Epic 47378)

As sideman: J. Gilson: *Enfin!* (1962–3, Club de l'Echiquier 30J1002); *Oeil vision* (1962, 1965, Club de l'Echiquier AF1); W. Dauner: *Free Action* (1967, Saba 15095); Mahavishnu Orchestra: *Visions of the Emerald Beyond* (1974, Col. PC33411)

BIBLIOGRAPHY

J. Tronchot: "Jean-Luc Ponty: de Jef Gilson à la gloire," *Jh*, no.198 (1964), 8
M. Delorme: "Notre prodige du violon en constante évolution: souverain Ponty," *Jh*, no.221 (1966), 20
M. Hennessey: "French Cookin': Jean-Luc Ponty," *DB*, xxxiii/22 (1966), 24
M. Gardner: "Jean-Luc Ponty: Violin Virtuoso," *JJ*, xxii/3 (1969), 5 [incl. discography]
P. Senoff: "Jean-Luc Ponty," *J&P*, ix/3 (1970), 26
R. Palmer: "Soaring with the Frenchman Jean-Luc Ponty," *DB*, xlii/20 (1975), 17 [incl. discography]
L. Magee and E. F. von Bergen: "The Jazz-rock Violin of Jean-Luc Ponty," *The Instrumentalist*, xxx/6 (1976), 62
T. Schneckloth: "Jean-Luc Ponty: Synthesis for the Strings," *DB*, xliv/20 (1977), 12 [incl. discography]
G. Endress: "Pionier des Elektro-Geige: Jean-Luc Ponty," *JP*, xxviii/8 (1979), 4
M. Glaser and S. Grappelli: *Jazz Violin* (New York and elsewhere, 1981) [incl. transcrs.]
H. Mandel: "Jean-Luc Ponty's Electronic Muse," *DB*, li/1 (1984), 20 [incl. discography]
B. Doerschuk: "Jean-Luc Ponty, No Strings Attached: a Violinist Turns to Synthesizers," *Keyboard*, xii/4 (1986), 38
M. Glaser: "*Violin Summit*: Great Solos by Stephane Grappelli, Svend Asmussen, and Jean-Luc Ponty, Transcribed with Commentary and Advice on Playing Jazz Violin," *Strings*, ii/1 (1987), 20
J. Nash: "Jean-Luc Ponty," *JT* (1989), Oct, 11
W. F. Miller: "A Different View: Jean-Luc Ponty: a Leader's Perspective," *MD*, xiv/5 (1990), 60
P. Polkow: "Fiddler at the Roots," *Chicago Tribune* (19 July 1990)
T. Cheney: "Jean-Luc Ponty's Excellent Adventure," *Musician*, no.157 (1991), 22
J. Diliberto: "Violin Juju: Jean Luc Ponty," *DB*, lviii/9 (1991), 28
"Jean-Luc Ponty: retour en Afrique," *Jm*, no.410 (1991), 38
A. Romano: "Jean-Luc Ponty," *Jm*, no.430 (1993), 24
G. Endress: "Jean-Luc Ponty," *JP*, xliii/8 (1994), 43
R. L. Doerschuk: "Life after Fusion: Jean-Luc Ponty, Stanley Clarke, & Al Di Meola Unplugged and Proud of it," *Musician*, no.205 (1995), 60
J. Woodard: "Rite of Strings: from Return to Return," *JT*, xxv/8 (1995), 56
M. Gilbert: "Jean-Luc Ponty," *JJI*, l/7 (1997), 6
<http://www.ponty.com> (2000) [incl. biography, discography]

BK

Poo(-sun). Nickname of Masabumi Kikuchi.

Pope, Odean (*b* Ninety Six, SC, 24 Oct 1938). Tenor saxophonist and bandleader. His mother was a pianist and organist and his father played trombone and drums. When he was ten his family moved to Philadelphia, where he learned saxophone and studied harmony with Ray Bryant. In 1955 he appeared for a week in Jimmy Smith's group, when Smith's saxophonist John Coltrane left suddenly to join Miles Davis's quintet. Having been introduced by Jymie Merritt to Max Roach, he served as a member of Roach's quartet from June 1967 to April 1968; as such he toured Europe and accompanied Vi Redd in a recording session in London (1967). In 1971 he formed the cooperative group Catalyst, which recorded four albums between 1972 and 1975, and in 1977 he organized the Saxophone Choir, a group with eight saxophones and a rhythm section. Later he collaborated with Roach for another tour of Europe (1979) and was artist-in-residence at Amherst College in Massachusetts (1979–83). Pope continued to play with Roach (he took part in the video

Jazz in America: Max Roach Quartet, 1983) and to lead a trio and the Saxophone Choir through the 1980s and 1990s. For several years his trio, with Gerald Veasley and Cornell Rochester, performed in a fusion vein; however his recordings of the mid-1990s, with Roach's sideman Tyrone Brown on double bass and either Mickey Roker or Craig McIver on drums, are oriented more towards hard-bop and avant-garde styles. In 1996 Pope toured Europe with David Murray.

SELECTED RECORDINGS

As leader: of Saxophone Choir: *The Saxophone Shop* (1985, SN 1129), *The Ponderer* (1990, SN 121229-2), *Epitome* (1993, SN 121279-2); of trio: *Ninety-six* (1995, Enja 9091-2), *Collective Voices* (1996, CIMP 124)
As sideman with M. Roach: *Pictures in a Frame* (1979, SN 1003); *Chattahoochee Red* (1980, Col. FC37367); *Scott Free* (1984, SN 1103)

BIBLIOGRAPHY

R. Woessner: "Profile: Odean Pope," *DB*, l/3 (1983), 46
C. Stern: "Odean Pope: Students & Teachers: Tracing Forgotten Tenor Traditions," *Musician*, no.65 (1984), 26
L. Van Trikt: "Odean Pope: Interview," *Cadence*, xv/2 (1989), 5
F. Davis: *Outcats: Jazz Composers, Instrumentalists, and Singers* (New York, and Oxford, England, 1990), 107
J. Diliberto: "Riffs: Odean Pope," *DB*, lix/4 (1992), 13
K. Kean: "Tradin' Fours: the Pope Gets Serious," *DB*, lxiii/6 (1996), 39
<http://www.powerup.com.au/~msafier/odean/OdeanPope.html> (2000) [incl. discography]

BK

Popek, Krzysztof (*b* Rybnik, Poland, 27 Jan 1957). Polish flutist and record producer. While he led the groups Pick Up and D-Box (1985–7) and recorded as a member of Kazimierz Jonkisz's sextet (1986), as a performer he is best known as the leader of and principal composer for the large ensemble Young Power; its members have included, among many others, Bernard Maseli, Grzegorz Nagórski, Janusz Skowron, Piotr Wojtasik, the trombonist Bronisław Duży, and the electric bass guitarist Marcin Pospieszalski. In 1992 he founded the record company and label Power Bros., which has issued albums by such musicians as Joe Lovano, Billy Harper, Buster Williams, Billy Hart, and David Friesen, as well as a multimedia edition of the music of Krzysztof Komeda.

SELECTED RECORDINGS

As leader: of Young Power: *Young Power* (1987, Muza 2525), *The Man of Tra* (1990, Power Bros. 00111); with Volker Greve: *Places* (1993, Power Bros. 00115); *Letters and Leaves* (*c*1995, Power Bros. 00139)
As sideman: K. Jonkisz: *Outsider* (1986, Muza SX2453); P. Wojtasik: *Lonely Town* (1995, Power Bros. 00137)

BIBLIOGRAPHY

P. Brodowski: "Young Power: New Sensitivity," *JF* [intl edn], no.100 (1988), 36
K. Brodacki and S. Graham: "What's Goin' on: Poland," *JF* [intl edn], no.131 (1991), 10
"What's Goin' on: Poland," *JF* [intl edn], nos.136–7 (1992), 13
A. Chodkowski, ed.: *Encyklopedia muzyki* (Warsaw, 1995)
<http://www.powerbros.com.pl> (2001)

ADAM CEGIELSKI, BK

Popkin, Lenny [Leonard] (*b* New York, 30 May 1941). Tenor saxophonist and leader. At various times he played piano, ukulele, harmonica, accordion, and drums. He took up violin at the age of ten, changed to alto saxophone when he was about 17, and later settled on the tenor instrument. While at Brandeis University (BA 1963, MFA 1966) he led a trio in the Boston area. After completing his graduate work he moved to New York, where he studied with Lennie Tristano. He worked in a duo with Sal Mosca (1967), performed as a member of Tristano's quartet (1968), and formed new trios, in which setting he continued to work into the 1990s. In 1979, with Connie Crothers, he co-produced the Lennie Tristano Memorial Concert at Town Hall, New York, and co-founded the Lennie Tristano Jazz Foundation. From around 1980 he and Crothers have led a quartet; he also played in a duo with Eddie Gomez (1981–2) and with Crothers (1981–3), and in a trio with Gomez and the pianist Liz Gorrill. In 1983 he worked with Tristano's associate Warne Marsh. Popkin has taught privately from the 1960s and composed music for film shorts (1963–72). He was co-founder, again with Crothers, of New Artists records.

SELECTED RECORDINGS

As leader: *Falling Free* (1979, Choice 1027); with L. Gorrill and E. Gomez: *True Fun* (1984, Jazz 7); with C. Crothers: *Love Energy* (1988, New Artists 1005); *Jazz Spring* (1993, New Artists 1017)

BIBLIOGRAPHY

I. Gitler: Liner notes, *Falling Free* (Choice 1027, 1981)
F. Billard: "Lenny Popkin: ma Tristano Story," *Jm*, no.313 (1982), 32; no.314 (1983), 40

GK

Popular song form. A term applied to the forms common in the refrains of popular songs and therefore in the jazz pieces based on them; *see* FORMS, esp. §1(i)(a).

Porcino, Al (*b* New York, 14 May 1925). Trumpeter. He briefly played drums before changing to trumpet. After studying in New York with Charles Colin he played with Louis Prima (1943), Tommy Dorsey, Georgie Auld (*c* mid-1945 – mid-1946), Gene Krupa (*c* September–November 1946), and Woody Herman (November–December 1946), and then with Stan Kenton (1947–8), Chubby Jackson (at the Royal Roost, early 1949), and Herman again (*c* March–November 1949, mid-1950). He participated in Count Basie's first effort to re-form a big band (late March–early April 1950) and was a member of Charlie Parker's orchestra with strings (intermittently, early 1950s). He then worked with Pete Rugolo, Elliot Lawrence (*c*1951–2), and Charlie Barnet (1952) before rejoining Herman (February 1954 – February 1955, including a European tour) and Kenton (1955). Between 1945 and 1955 he recorded with nearly all of these leaders.

In 1957 Porcino settled in Los Angeles, where he formed the Jazz Wave Orchestra with Med Flory; it performed and made recordings until 1959. He spent the next three years working with Terry Gibbs, with whom he also recorded. He played in big bands at the Monterey Jazz Festival in 1958 (with Flory), 1959 (with Herman), and 1962. In the 1960s he toured with popular singers, worked in studios, and played with Buddy Rich in London (1968) and the Thad Jones–Mel Lewis Orchestra (1969–70). He then worked with Chuck Mangione (1970–72), playing in the premières of three of his compositions, and again toured with Herman (1972). He formed his own big band in 1974, which accompanied various popular singers, among them Mel Tormé. By January 1976 Porcino had rejoined the Jones–Lewis Orchestra, with which he toured Europe later that year; the band recorded in Sopot, Poland, and then in Munich, where Porcino chose to settle permanently. He recorded again with Jones in 1977, accompanying the singer Aura, and continued to tour widely, performing and giving jazz workshops, but also founded a big band of European players. This ensemble played classic scores by Johnny Mandel, Neal Hefti, Gerry Mulligan, Bob Brookmeyer, Bill Holman, and others, and in 1987 it recorded an album of arrangements by Al Cohn, with

Cohn as principal soloist. Porcino's big band celebrated the fiftieth anniversary of his joining Prima with a concert in Munich in 1993; for his seventieth birthday there in May 1995 it made a video in concert with Charlie Mariano as guest soloist. Porcino is an experienced big-band lead trumpeter, well known for the brilliance and forcefulness of his sound.

SELECTED RECORDINGS

As leader: with M. Flory: *Jazz Wave Orchestra* (1957, Jub. 1066); *In Oblivion* (1986, Jazz Mark 106); with A. Cohn: *The Final Performance* (1987, Razmataz Jazz 44003)

As sideman: G. Auld: Stompin' at the Savoy (1945, Guild 135); C. Jackson: Tiny's Blues (1949, Col. 38623); T. Gibbs: *The Exciting Big Band of Terry Gibbs* (1961, Verve 62151); W. Herman: *The Raven Speaks* (1972, Fan. 9416); C. Mangione: *Together* (1973, Mer. 2-7501); M. Tormé: *Live at the Maisonette* (1974, Atl. 18129); T. Jones and A. Rully: *Thad and Aura* (1977, Four Leaf Clover 5020)

SELECTED FILMS AND VIDEOS

Herman's Herd (1949); Stars of Jazz (1957); Frankly Jazz: Gerald Wilson All-Star Orchestra (1962); Al Porcino Big Band (*c*1996)

BIBLIOGRAPHY

McCarthyB; *SheridanCB*

R. Williams: "Al Porcino," *MM* (22 Nov 1969), 18

W. Whiteworth: "Al Porcino: the Art of Playing Lead," *DB*, xxxix/8 (1972), 14

T. Baron: "The Peripatetic Al Porcino," *Cadence*, ii/5 (1977), 8

M. Wangler: "Al Porcino Big Band," *JP*, xxxvi/4 (1987), 26

G. Lutz: "Al Porcino," *JP*, xlii/6 (1993), 36

L. T. Petruzzi: *Lead Trumpet Performance in the Thad Jones–Mel Lewis Jazz Orchestra: an Analysis of Style and Performance Practices* (diss., New York University, 1993)

W. D. Clancy with A. C. Kenton: *Woody Herman: Chronicles of the Herds* (New York and elsewhere, 1995)

R. Köchl: "'Play Lead, Mr. Leader ...': Al Porcino wird 70," *JP*, xliv/5 (1995), 10

FREDERICK A. BECK/BK

Pori (International) Jazz (Festival). Festival held annually from 1966 in Pori, Finland. It takes place in July at several venues, particularly on outdoor stages along the banks of the River Kokemaenjoki and in the Kirjurinluoto Concert Park; it was originally held over an extended weekend, but in 1985 it lasted nine days and in 2000 it continued for ten days. In the 1980s and 1990s the festival was directed by Jyrki Kangas. Pori Jazz is among Europe's oldest jazz festivals; all styles of jazz are offered, as well as blues and rock. In 1988 its concerts drew a combined audience of more than 40,000 at 12 separate venues, and by 1999 it had 14 stages and attracted 150,000 people. In 1982 Soviet musicians performed for the first time and Benny Goodman appeared. Among other artists who participated in the 1980s were the Dirty Dozen Brass Band, Steps Ahead, and groups led by Lou Donaldson, Bob Moses, and Flora Purim and Airto Moreira. Freddie Hubbard performed in 2000.

(<http://www.porijazz.fi/> (1999))

PAUL R. LAIRD

Portal, Michel (*b* Bayonne, France, 27 Nov 1935). French saxophonist, clarinetist, and composer. He studied clarinet at the Paris Conservatoire and became noted as a virtuoso player of classical and contemporary art music who received international prizes in Geneva (1963) and Budapest (1965). He gained experience in light music with the bandleaders Henri Rossotti and (in Spain in 1958) Perez Prado, as well as with the drummer Benny Bennett (1960), Raymond Fonsèque (1963), Aimé Barelli, and, for many years, the singer Claude Nougaro, undertook studio work with Boulou Ferré (1964), and performed with André Hodeir and with the Paris Jazz All Stars (both in 1966). Portal was a pioneer of free jazz in France and played with Don Cherry, Jef Gilson (1963, 1965), Enrico Rava, Sunny Murray (1968), Anthony Braxton, Alan Silva (1969–70), Joachim Kühn (1969), Kenny Wheeler, and John Surman (1970). He made recordings as a leader in 1969–71, including the LP *Alors!* (1970, Futura 12), then in 1972 formed the Portal Unit, which in that same year recorded a celebrated free-jazz album, *Michel Portal Unit à Châteauvallon* (Chant du Monde 74526). He also played with Derek Bailey (1974) and Eddy Louiss (1979), in a trio with Pierre Favre and Léon Francioli (1980), and with Albert Mangelsdorff and Steve Lacy (both 1981), George Lewis (ii) (1984), Mino Cinélu (1985), and Jack DeJohnette (1986). He performed in duos with Martial Solal (1988, 1992) and Richard Galliano (from 1995), and appeared as a guest soloist with Charlie Haden (1989) and with a trio led by his main disciple, Louis Sclavis (1995–6). Portal has also written film scores. His playing is well represented on the recording *Musiques de cinéma déjouées avec des amis jazzmen* (1995, Label Bleu 6574).

BIBLIOGRAPHY

P. L. Rossi: "Michel polyvalent Portal," *Jm*, no.142 (1967), 24

P. Carles and F. Marmande: "Michel Portal ou la parole au présent," *Jm*, no.210 (1973), 10

D. Soutif: "Michel Portal: le prix de la musique," *Jm*, no.329 (1984), 51

E. Jost: *Europas Jazz, 1960–1980* (Frankfurt am Main, Germany, 1987), 384

M. Zwerin: "Michel Portal: Proud Eurojazzer," *International Herald Tribune* (29 July 1998)

MICHEL LAPLACE

Portamento. A continuous slide in pitch over a given interval without the sounding of discrete intermediate steps. In jazz no distinction in terminology is made between the portamento and the glissando (a slide in which intermediate steps may be heard): *see* Gliss.

Porteña Jazz Band. Argentine band. Formed in 1964 under the leadership of the pianist Ignacio Romero, its other original members were the cornetist Norberto Gandini, the trombonist Sergio Tamburri, the saxophonists Horacio Schere and Alfredo Espinosa, the clarinetist Ernesto Carrizo, the banjoists Alfredo Carozzi and Ricardo Scarremberg, the tuba player Carlos Balmaceda, the double bass player Alberto Mazza, and the drummer Daniel Passero. The band made several recordings during the following decades and in 1985–6 toured the USSR, Germany, the Netherlands, and Belgium. It was among the best-known traditional-jazz bands in Argentina, and may be heard to advantage on the album *Porteña Jazz Band* (1972–3, Trova 80073).

LAUREANO FERNÁNDEZ, OMAR GARCÍA BRUNELLI

Porter, Art(hur Lee, Jr.) (*b* Little Rock, AR, 3 Aug 1961; *d* Bangkok, 23 Nov 1996). Alto and soprano saxophonist. At first he played drums, then when he was 15 took up saxophone. The following year he spent a semester at the Berklee College of Music in Boston before returning to Little Rock where, because of his age, he was barred from playing in clubs with his father, the pianist Art Porter, Sr. His case was adopted by the state attorney-general at the time, Bill Clinton, and the result was Act 321 (known as the "Art Porter Bill"), which allows minors to play in clubs if accompanied by a supervising parent or guardian. After graduating in music education from Northeastern Illinois University, Porter toured with Brother Jack McDuff, Pharoah Sanders, the popular singer Gene Chandler, and the rhythm-and-blues vocal group After 7. In 1990 he recorded with the pianist Don Bennett. From 1992, in partnership with Jeff Lorber, he made a series of jazz-funk recordings which brought considerable character and invention to a genre more often noted for its vapidity. In April 1994 he performed in a concert sponsored by Verve, which was recorded on the video *Carnegie Hall Salutes the Jazz Masters.* He died in a boating accident following an appearance at the Golden Jubilee Jazz Festival in Bangkok.

SELECTED RECORDINGS

As leader: *Pocket City* (1992, Verve Forecast 314-511877-2); *Straight to the Point* (1993, Verve Forecast 314-517997-2); *Undercover* (1994, Verve Forecast 314-523356-2); *Lay your Hands on Me* (1996, Verve Forecast 314-533119-2)

As sideman with D. Bennett: *Sleeping Giant* (1990, Southport 0012)

BIBLIOGRAPHY

J. Gower: "Oh! Mr Porter," *Jazz Express*, no.145 (1992), 11

T. S. Taylor: "Room for Everyone: Saxophonist Plays on Both Sides of the Jazz Tracks," *Chicago Tribune* (11 Sept 1992)

M. Ervin: "Riffs: Art Porter," *DB*, lx/8 (1993), 13

D. Kasrel: "Hearsay: Art Porter," *JT*, xxvi/10 (1996), 26

Obituaries: *DB*, lxiv/2 (1997), 15; *JT*, xxvii/2 (1997), 20; M. Gilbert, *JJI*, l/3 (1997), 19

MARK GILBERT

Porter, Gene [Eugene] (*b* Pocahontas, nr Jackson, MS, 7 June 1910; *d* San Diego Co., CA, 24 Feb 1993). Saxophonist and clarinetist. He first played cornet, but when that instrument was stolen acquired a C-melody saxophone; he began his career as an alto saxophonist and later studied clarinet with Omer Simeon (*c*1929). Having worked in New Orleans and on Mississippi riverboats with various musicians, including Papa Celestin, Joseph Robichaux (1933, with whom he recorded), and Sidney Desvigne (1935), he joined the Jeter–Pillars Orchestra (1935). He left the band in 1937 to work with Don Redman, but was again with the Jeter–Pillars Orchestra from later that year until 1942. After spending some months with Jimmie Lunceford (1942) he performed, recorded, and made several films with Benny Carter (1942–4), whose assistant leader he became; he may be seen in the film *Thousands Cheer* (1943) with Carter and in *Stormy Weather* (1943) with Fats Waller's group. Following army service (1944–5) Porter rejoined Carter and recorded with Dinah Washington (1945), Charles Mingus (1946), and Lloyd Glenn (1947), among others. He then settled in San Diego, where he played with Walter Fuller (1948–60) and led his own small group, which played at the Bronze Room in La Mesa, California (from 1967). His date of death is taken from the social security death index, which gives his last known residence as San Diego. He recorded variously as a soloist on tenor saxophone, clarinet, or both of these instruments, and he also played flute and sang.

SELECTED RECORDINGS

As sideman: J. Robechaux [*sic*]: Ring dem Bells/Forty Second Street (1933, Voc. 2575); King Kong Stomp (1933, Voc. 2539); Stormy Weather (1933, Voc. 2540); Every Tub (1933, Voc. 2827); Jig Music (1933, Voc. 2545); Just Like a Falling Star (1933, Voc. 2881); D. Redman: first issued on *Don Redman* (1932–7, CBS 52539), Swingin' with the Fat Man (1937); B. Carter: first issued on *Sleep* (1943–5, Alamac 2449), Sleep (1943); L. Glenn: That other woman's gotta go/Rampart St. Jump (1947, Imperial 5022)

BIBLIOGRAPHY

K. Gert zur Heide: "Eugene Porter," *Fn*, vii (1976), no.5, p.11; no.6, p.17

J. Evensmo: *History of Jazz Tenor Saxophone: Black Artists*, i: *1917–1934* (Oslo, 1996); ii: *1935–1939* (Oslo, 1997); iii: *1940–1944* (Oslo, 1997)

based on *ChiltonW*/HOWARD RYE (recording-list)

Porter, Jake [Vernon Haven] (*b* Oakland, CA, 3 Aug 1916; *d* Los Angeles, 25 March 1993). Trumpeter and record producer. He began playing violin in 1923 and changed to cornet in 1925. Between 1931 and 1939 he worked with bands in the San Francisco Bay area; in 1938–9 he was with Saunders King. Porter moved in 1940 to Los Angeles, where he performed with Cee Pee Johnson and Slim Gaillard, among others. In 1942–3 he served in the 10th Cavalry Band at Camp Lockett near San Diego, and following his discharge in May 1943 he played with Benny Carter and Fats Waller. During 1944 he worked with Noble Sissle, Fletcher Henderson, with whom he made a tour of the Southwest in the spring, Lionel Hampton, with whom he played trombone from around June until October (during which time he took part in a recording session), and, from November, Horace Henderson, with whose band he recorded accompanying the singer Lena Horne. While a member of Fletcher Henderson's band (1945–6) he recorded as a leader. From 1947 he was one of a pool of musicians who recorded in the jump style under various bandleaders; on recordings credited to Gene Phillips and Lloyd Glenn he may be heard playing both in a contemporary style and in a traditional blues-obbligato style. It is probable that he is the King Porter under whose name a similar band recorded for Imperial, though he is not otherwise known to have used this sobriquet. During 1947 he also recorded with Benny Goodman and Mel Powell, and in December of that year he was leading the band at the Down Beat Room Café in Los Angeles. In late 1949 he fronted a nine-piece female group on a tour of the South, after which he returned to Los Angeles. By June 1950 he held a weekend residency at the Norbo Grill.

In autumn 1951 Porter founded the Combo record company and label, which lasted for ten years and presented a full spectrum of African-American music, though latterly there was a heavy concentration on doo-wop vocal groups in its output. He continued to lead his own band, which held residencies at the Tailspin Club and Club Alimony in Los Angeles during 1954 and at the Largo on Sunset Boulevard during the late 1950s. After Combo ceased operations, Porter worked in Canada with Mike Riley (1964) but remained based mainly in California as a freelance. He became an official of the Los Angeles AFM Local 47, toured Europe in 1978, and was still working regularly in the 1980s. Although he may be seen in the Palm Club Band accompanying the singer Diahnne Abbott in the film *New York, New York* (1977), he did not play on the soundtrack. He has been confused in the past with both James Porter and King Porter, and he is evidently not the Jake Porter who recorded with James Reese Europe in 1919.

SELECTED RECORDINGS

As sideman (all recorded in 1947): G. Phillips: Boogie Everywhere (Modern Music 148); Hey Lawdy Mama (Modern 20-572); Punkin' Head Woman (Modern 20-559); Rock Bottom (Modern 20-546); L. Glenn: Joymaker's Boogie (Imperial 5031); Rampart Street Jump (Imperial 5022); B. Goodman: Henderson Stomp (Cap. 15766)

BIBLIOGRAPHY

AllenH; *ChiltonW*

D. Penny: Liner notes, *King Porter and his Orchestra Special Request* (Official 6056, 1989)

J. Dawson: Liner notes, *Honk! Honk! Honk!* (Ace 781, 2000)

R. Topping: Liner notes, *Gene Phillips: Swinging the Blues* (Ace 746, 2000)

HOWARD RYE

Porter, James (F.) [Porter, King; the King of the Coast] (*fl.* 1920–1945). Trumpeter. He first came to notice when he went to Los Angeles from Chicago to replace the trumpeter Ernest "Nenny" Coycault in the Black and Tan Orchestra. In 1924–5 he was a member of the Sunnyland Jazz Orchestra, and in late 1924 he also worked with Harvey Brooks accompanying the show *Steppin' High*. Porter joined Curtis Mosby's Blue Blowers at Solomon's Dance Pavilion DeLuxe in 1925 and remained with the band until 1931, taking part in its recordings; at the end of 1930 he played in the band Mosby took to San Francisco to appear at Mosby's new club. In mid-1931 he was with Sonny Clay's band at the Hartford Ballroom in San Bernardino, California, but he played again with Mosby in San Francisco later in the year. From then until 1938 he was a sideman in Les Hite's band (possibly not continuously). He is believed to appear in the band's films and to have taken part in its 1935 recording sessions, from which nothing has been issued; he is confirmed as having toured with Hite's band from mid-1936 to the end of 1938. Porter is known to have been a member of a committee of AFM Local 767 in 1945. There is a slight possibility he may be the King Porter who recorded for Imperial in 1947, but this was more likely Jake Porter; he was not the King Porter for whom Jelly Roll Morton titled *King Porter Stomp*, who was a Florida pianist named Porter King.

SELECTED RECORDINGS

As sideman: C. Mosby: Whoop 'em up Blues/Tiger Stomp (1927, Col. 1192-D); Blue Blowers' Blues (1928, Col. 1442-D); S. Clay (as the Dixie Serenaders): Cho-King (1931, Champion 16365)

SELECTED FILMS AND VIDEOS

Thunderbolt (1929); Hallelujah (1929); Taxi (1932); Cabin in the Cotton (1933); Cavalcade (1933); Murder in Swingtime (1937)

BIBLIOGRAPHY

McCarthyB

M. B. Bakan: "Way out West on Central: Jazz in the African-American Community of Los Angeles before 1930," *California Soul: Music of African-Americans in the West*, ed. J. C. DjeDje and E. S. Meadows (Berkeley, CA, Los Angeles, and London, 1998), 47

HOWARD RYE

Porter, King [Pope [Poe], James A.] (*b* Bessemer, AL, 23 Nov 1916; *d* Lynn, MA, 24 Sept 1983). Trumpeter and leader. He was active in Detroit by late 1943, when he joined AFM Local 5. The name King Porter was used certainly by James Porter and possibly by Jake Porter, both of whom were also trumpeters. James Pope is almost certainly not the King Porter who recorded in Los Angeles for Imperial in 1947, but his band did record in Detroit for the Paradise label around 1948 and soon afterwards for King, and he also recorded extensively as a member of groups led by Paul Williams. In 1950 his band was resident at the Royal Blue Bar in Detroit, and it may well be the group that recorded for the 4-Star label in 1951 as King Porter and his Orchestra. Although his Detroit bands recorded some fine tracks in the contemporary jump idiom, these contain no solo work by the leader; however, he may be heard playing a weak obbligato to the blues singer and pianist Detroit Count (Robert White) on the pairing *Little Tillie Willie/My Last Call* (1948).

SELECTED RECORDINGS

As leader: Russel St. Hussel/Porter's Ball (1948, Paradise 124); Russell Street Hustle (1948, King 4295); King Porter Special (1948, King 4267); Come on in/Battle Ax (1949, King 4333)

As sideman with Detroit Count: Little Tillie Willie/My Last Call (1948, King 4279)

BIBLIOGRAPHY

D. Penny: Liner notes, *King Porter and his Orchestra Special Request* (Official 6056, 1989)

J. Gallert: "Oh! Mr. Porter," *Blues & Rhythm*, no.52 (1990), 9

HOWARD RYE

Porter [Portnoff]**, Lewis (Robert)** (*b* Scranton, PA, 14 May 1951). Musicologist and educator. His family changed its surname from Portnoff to Porter around 1952, after moving to Decatur, Georgia; from 1958 Porter grew up in New York, where he learned violin from the ages of ten to 12 and took up piano. While studying psychology at the University of Rochester (1968–72) he took music courses at the Eastman School, led his own jazz trio, and began on alto saxophone (1972). Following graduate work in counseling at Northeastern University in Boston (MEd 1976) he taught jazz history (1977–9) and studied music theory at Tufts University (MA 1979). Later he completed a doctoral degree in musicology at Brandeis University (1983) and spent another period teaching at Tufts (1982–6). In 1986 he joined the faculty at Rutgers in Newark, New Jersey. Having performed as an alto saxophonist and pianist from the early 1970s, he abandoned the saxophone in 1993.

Porter has contributed to numerous professional journals and music books and has served as an editor for the Institute of Jazz Studies's monographs series; he was the jazz editor for *Black Perspective in Music* from 1979 to 1990 and edited the *Annual Review of Jazz Studies* during the first half of the 1990s. He has published two well-regarded books on Lester Young, a jazz history, and a biography of John Coltrane.

WRITINGS

(selective list)

John Coltrane's Music of 1960 through 1967: Jazz Improvisation as Composition (diss., Brandeis U., 1983)

Lester Young (Boston and London, 1985)

A Lester Young Reader (Washington, DC, and London, 1991)

with M. Ullman and E. Hazell: *Jazz: from its Origins to the Present* (Englewood Cliffs, NJ, 1993)

with Y. Fujioka and Y. Hamada: *John Coltrane: a Discography and Musical Biography* (Metuchen, NJ, and London, 1995)

ed., *Jazz, a Century of Change: Readings and New Essays* (New York and elsewhere, 1997)

John Coltrane: his Life and Music (Ann Arbor, MI, 1998)

BIBLIOGRAPHY

<http://www.furious.com/perfect/coltrane.html> (2000)

<http://www.galenet.com/servlet/GLD/form?l=2> (2000)

GK

Porter, Roy (*b* Walsenburg, CO, 30 July 1923; *d* Los Angeles, 25 Jan 1998). Drummer and bandleader. He grew up in Colorado Springs from the age of eight and studied at Wiley College in Marshall, Texas, between 1941 and 1943; while he was there he met Kenny Dorham and toured with the college dance band, but he left to help support his mother. From April 1943 he toured east to New York with Milt Larkin. Following his military service (August 1943 – February 1944) he moved to Los Angeles and worked with Teddy Bunn's Spirits of Rhythm (1944) and Howard McGhee (1945–7); in addition he participated in Charlie Parker's first sessions for Dial (1946), and he may be heard to advantage on *Ornithology/A Night in Tunisia* (Dial 1002). Thereafter he performed and recorded with Teddy Edwards (1947) and in New York with Dexter Gordon (1947–8). After leading a big band (until 1949) that included Eric Dolphy, Art and Addison Farmer, Jimmy Knepper, and Chet Baker, Porter played at various clubs in San Francisco, notably Bop City, with Sonny

Criss, Hampton Hawes, Edwards, and Gordon, among others. From June 1953 through 1956 he was imprisoned for narcotics possession, and during this period he appeared in the film *Unchained*, performing in a band alongside Gordon and Hadley Caliman (though the soundtrack was actually recorded by studio musicians).

Porter then returned to Los Angeles and worked with Earl Bostic, Louis Jordan, and the Latin bandleader Perez Prado (all 1957). During the 1960s he was active as a session musician outside jazz, but in 1970 he organized and led his own group. He recorded several times as a leader and as a sideman before illness caused him to give up drumming in 1978. Porter was the subject of three lengthy periodical surveys, and in 1993 he wrote an autobiography, *There and Back* (ed. D. Keller, Wheatley, Oxford, England, and Baton Rouge, LA, incl. discography). He was interviewed in the PBS television documentary "American Masters: Celebrating Bird: the Triumph of Charlie Parker" (1987).

BIBLIOGRAPHY

M. Gardner: "It's All Happening for Roy," *MM* (19 Dec 1970), 12
——: "Roy Porter," *J&B*, i (1971), no.4, p.10; no.5, p.26
G. Mack and H. Mansfield, Jr.: "Roy Porter," *Be-bop and Beyond*, iii (1985), no.4, p.10; no.5, p.17
S. Klett: "Roy Porter: Interview," *Cadence*, xii (1986), no.9, p.5; no.10, p.5
Obituaries: P. Vacher, *The Guardian* (26 Feb 1998); M. Gardner, *JJI*, li/3 (1998), 17

BK

Porter, Yank [Allen] (*b* Norfolk, VA, *c*1895; *d* New York, 22 March 1944). Drummer. In 1926 he settled in New York and worked mainly with Cliff Jackson until 1930. Later he played in a band led by the pianist and arranger Charlie Matson (1932) and with Louis Armstrong (January–February 1933), Bud Harris (1933), and James P. Johnson (1934). He then performed and recorded with Fats Waller (autumn 1935 – spring 1936) and played with the pianist Dave Martin (1936). After working with Johnson again late in 1939 and with Joe Sullivan at Café Society from March to early June 1940, Porter was a member of Teddy Wilson's small band through the remainder of 1940; he appeared with the group at the opening of Café Society Uptown in October of that year. As a freelance he recorded with Benny Carter (1940) and Art Tatum (1941). His mature style was highly discreet, and is well represented on Waller's *Oooh! Look-a there, ain't she pretty?* (1936, Vic. 25255) and Wilson's *I never knew* (1940, Col. 35905), while his earlier, more assertive work may be heard on Armstrong's *Basin Street Blues* (1933, Vic. 24351).

BIBLIOGRAPHY

McCarthyB
M. Selchow: *Profoundly Blue: a Bio-discographical Scrapbook on Edmond Hall* (Lübbecke, Germany, 1988)
L. Wright: *"Fats" in Fact* (Chigwell, England, 1992)

based on *ChiltonW*

Port Jackson Jazz Band. Australian jazz group. It was founded in 1944 by the trombonist Jack Parkes, who invited the trumpeter Ken Flannery to serve as leader; it first recorded in 1945. Despite sparking an era of jazz concerts in 1948, by 1950 the group had disbanded. There were brief revivals in 1952 and 1954 under the leadership of the guitarist and banjoist Ray Price, and by October of the following year it had regained its place as Sydney's leading jazz band; among its recordings from these years are the albums *Jazzin' at the Con* (1957, Jazz Incorporated 001) and *Ray Price and his Port Jackson Jazz Band* (1961, Pix 001–002). In 1965 personal differences between Price and his musicians caused the group to disband yet again, though it reformed periodically thereafter. In addition to Flannery, notable members included Bob Barnard, the clarinetist Johnny McCarthy, the pianists Jimmy Somerville and Dick Hughes, and the drummer Alan Geddes. The Port Jackson Jazz Band took a hot, free-wheeling approach inspired by the Chicago-jazz style of Eddie Condon's numerous groups. On 24 March 1994 it gave a concert in Sydney to mark its 50th anniversary.

BIBLIOGRAPHY

D. Hughes: *Daddy's Practising Again: an Australian Jazzman Looks Back and Around* (Melbourne, Australia, 1977)
A. Bissett: *Black Roots, White Flowers: a History of Jazz in Australia* (Sydney, 1979, rev. 2/1987)
B. Johnson: *The Oxford Companion to Australian Jazz* (Melbourne, Australia, 1987)
J. Clare [G. Brennan, pseud.]: *Bodgie Dada and the Cult of Cool* (Sydney, 1995)
J. Mitchell: *Back Together Again: the Story of the Port Jackson Jazz Band* (Sydney, 1995)
W. Bebbington, ed: *The Oxford Companion to Australian Music* (Melbourne, Australia, 1997)

KEVIN JONES

Post-bop. A vague term, used either stylistically or chronologically (with divergent results) to describe any continuation or amalgamation of bop, modal jazz, and free jazz; its meaning sometimes extends into swing and earlier styles or into fusion and third-world styles. It emerged as an attempt to circumscribe the eclecticism which has characterized jazz from the 1980s onwards.

BK

Postcards. Record company and label. It was established in 1993 by the saxophonist Ralph Simon and Sybil R. Golden. Through early 1997 it had produced 16 albums, including Paul Bley's first recording on synthesizer since the early 1970s, two recordings by Reggie Workman's groups, and work by duos consisting of Sam Rivers and Julian Priester and Gary Peacock and Bill Frisell. In June 1999 Postcards was purchased by Arkadia, which reissued all the label's original recordings and in early 2000 began to release new recordings.

BIBLIOGRAPHY

R. D. Sawyer: "Coda: Postcards," *Jazziz*, xiii/5 (1996), 92
R. Hicks: "Timbre: a New Frontier," *DB*, lxiv/1 (1997), 43
<http://www.pstcds.com> (1999)
<http://www.view.com/home-postcards.html> (2000)

GK

Poston, Joe [Doc; Joseph E.] (*b* Alexandria, LA, *c*1895; *d* Illinois, May 1942). After working with Doc Cook (1922–4) he played with Fate Marable on riverboats. In 1927 he returned briefly to Cook's band, then from 1928 to 1930 he performed and made recordings with Jimmie Noone. He spent a further period with Cook before illness forced him to retire.

SELECTED RECORDINGS

As sideman with J. Noone: I know that you know (1928, Voc. 1184); Four or Five Times/Every Evening (1928, Voc. 1185); Chicago Rhythm (1929, Voc. 1267); My Daddy Rocks Me (1929, Bruns. 7096)

based on *ChiltonW*/HOWARD RYE (recording-list)

Po Torch. Record company and label founded in the mid-1970s by PAUL LOVENS and Paul Lytton; Lovens later took over its operation.

Potter, (Joseph) Chris(topher) (*b* Chicago, 1 Jan 1971). Tenor and soprano saxophonist. His family settled in Charleston, South Carolina, when he was an infant. He first played piano and around the age of ten took up saxophone, on which he soon revealed great potential. After performing locally he moved to New York, where he attended the Manhattan School of Music (graduating in 1993) and worked with Red Rodney (1989–93) and John Hart (from 1989, recording in 1995); while with Rodney he played mainly alto saxophone, although he was featured occasionally on piano. In 1993 he joined Paul Motian's Electric Bebop Band, and from 1997 he worked alongside Steve Swallow in Motian's Trio 2000. In addition he played with the rock group Steely Dan and the Mingus Big Band and formed a cooperative trio with Scott Colley and Bill Stewart, which made its first recording in 1996; around 1994 he joined Jim Hall's quartet. In 1995–6 he worked with Renee Rosnes, with whose group he appeared at the Du Maurier International Jazz Festival Vancouver in 1996; that same year he joined Dave Douglas's quartet Magic Triangle and John Patitucci, and from June 1998 he was a member of Dave Holland's quintet. During the 1990s he also performed with Joe Henderson's big band and Ron Vincent's quintet (1997) and toured with Mike Mainieri (summer 1998).

From 1992 Potter has led various small groups which have regularly included Colley and Stewart, and in 1994 he performed and recorded in a duo with Kenny Werner; with Larry Goldings, Colley, and Billy Drummond as his sidemen, he performed as the leader of a quartet at the Texaco Jazz Festival in summer 1998. As a freelance he has recorded extensively, with the singer Laverne Butler and Peter Madsen (both 1992), Greg Gisbert (1992, 1994), Marian McPartland and the drummer Owen Howard (both 1993), Ryan Kisor (*c*1993), Randy Sandke and John Swana (both 1994), the singer Eden Atwood (1994, 1996), Ray Drummond (1995), Susannah McCorkle (from 1995), the pianist Steve Million (1995–6), Swallow, Al Foster, the trumpeter Alexander Sipiagin, Allen Farnham and the RIAS big band, and Brother Jack McDuff (all 1996), and Billy Hart, Rosnes, and the drummer Jochen Rückert (all 1997).

Potter first gained recognition as Rodney's protégé, and his early work as an alto saxophonist showed a remarkable understanding of the bop idiom. However, from around 1993 he began to explore freer styles and to concentrate on tenor saxophone; although his voice on this instrument is not fully developed, his assertive style reveals, particularly when performing in concert, a more sophisticated use of harmony and rhythm than that of many of his more heralded contemporaries. He often doubles on soprano saxophone and bass clarinet, and he also plays flute.

SELECTED RECORDINGS

Duos with K. Werner: *Concord Duo Series*, x (1994, Conc. 4695)

Chris Potter's quartet at the Cheltenham International Jazz Festival, England, 1999: (left to right) Jim Hall, Terry Clarke, Potter, Scott Colley

As leader: *Presenting Chris Potter* (1992, Criss Cross 1067); *Sundiata* (1993, Criss Cross 1107); *Concentric Circles* (1993, Conc. 4595); *Pure* (1994, Conc. 4637); *Moving In* (1996, Conc. 4723); *Unspoken* (1997, Conc. 4775)

As sideman: P. Madsen: *Snuggling Snakes* (1992, Minor Music 801030); M. McPartland: *In my Life* (1993, Conc. 4561); R. Drummond: *Vignettes* (1995, Arabesque 0122); B. Drummond: *Dubai* (1995, Criss Cross 1120); S. Colley: *Portable Universe* (1996, Freelance 027); J. Patitucci: on *One More Angel* (1996, Conc. 4753), Quasimodo; S. Swallow: *Deconstructed* (1996, Xtrawatt 9); R. Rosnes: *As We Are Now* (1997, BN 56810-2); D. Douglas: *Magic Triangle* (1997, Arabesque 0139); P. Motian: *Trio 2000 + One* (1997, Winter & Winter 910032-2); S. Colley: *Subliminal...* (1997, Criss Cross 1157)

BIBLIOGRAPHY

"Audition: Chris Potter," *DB*, liii/4 (1986), 62

C. Deffaa: "Hearsay: Saxaphonist [*sic*] Chris Potter ... 20 Going on 35 ...," *JT*, xix/5 (1991), 51

G. Lees and J. Reeves: *Jazz Lives: 100 Portraits in Jazz* (Toronto, 1992), 198

B. Milkowski: "Chris Potter: Raising the Bar," *JT*, xxvii/10 (1997), 82

H. Reich: "Deeper Concepts," *DB*, lxiv/12 (1997), 66

B. Blumenthal: "Chris Potter Reaches Out with Reeds," *Boston Globe* (30 Oct 1998)

<http://www.aent.com/concord/bios/potterbio.html> (1999)

GK

Potter, Tommy [Charles Thomas] (*b* Philadelphia, 21 Sept 1918; *d* ?New York, 15 March 1988). Double bass player. He first studied piano and guitar, and did not take up double bass until 1940. After early associations with John Malachi and Trummy Young he played with Billy Eckstine's big band (1944–5) and then with John Hardee, Max Roach, and others in New York (1946–7). He is best known for his work from 1947 to 1950 when he was a member of Charlie Parker's quintet; the recordings he made with Parker for Savoy and Dial demonstrate his clear tone and ability to create varied and interesting lines while maintaining a strong, reliable pulse, even at extreme tempos. As a result of his association with Parker, Potter was, after Oscar Pettiford, one of the best-respected double bass players of the bop era, and in the late 1940s he recorded prolifically with such musicians as Fats Navarro, Wardell Gray, and Bud Powell. In 1950 he performed with Stan Getz (who at that time was using Parker's rhythm section), and he accompanied Eckstine (until 1951), recording apart from the singer under Sonny Criss's nominal leadership. He then worked with Earl Hines (1952–3), Artie Shaw (September 1953 – July 1954), Eddie Heywood (1955), Powell (1956), and Rolf Ericson, with whom he toured Sweden (summer 1956), and recorded with Cecil Payne (1956). Potter led his own trio in 1957. He was with Tyree Glenn at the Roundtable in New York (1958–*c*1959), was a member of Harry Edison's quintet (*c*1959-61), joined Dizzy Reece (1961) and Buck Clayton (in Toronto, 1963), toured Europe with a Newport Jazz Festival show (1965), and performed and recorded with the sextet of Al Cohn, Zoot Sims, and Richie Kamuca (1965). Thereafter he worked mainly outside music, returning to jazz only occasionally. In the late 1960s he performed with Buddy Tate and Jimmy McPartland, and in 1975 he led his own group and participated in a television show devoted to Parker's legacy. In 1980 he appeared at Carnegie Hall. His place and date of death are taken from the social security death index, which gives his last known residence as Brooklyn, New York.

For illustration *see* Parker, Charlie, fig.2.

SELECTED RECORDINGS

As sideman with C. Parker (all recorded in 1947): Donna Lee/Buzzy (Savoy 652); Cheryl/Bird Gets the Worm (Savoy 952); Bongo Bop/Embraceable You (Dial 1024); The Hymn/Drifting on a Reed (Dial 1056)

As sideman with others: B. Eckstine: Blowin' the Blues Away (1944, De Luxe 2001); B. Powell: Bouncing with Bud/Wail (1949, BN 1567); D. Lanphere: Wailing Wall (1949, NewJ 819); Go (1949, NewJ 812); W. Gray: Twisted (1949, NewJ 817); M. Davis: Conception (1951, Prst. 868); S. Rollins: *Sonny Rollins Quartet* (1954, Prst. 190); H. Edison: *Patented by Edison* (1960, Roul. 52041)

BIBLIOGRAPHY

FeatherE; *Feather '60s*; *Feather–Gitler '70s*

R. G. Reisner: *Bird: the Legend of Charlie Parker* (New York, 1962/*R*1975)

M. Jones: "Tommy Potter, a Baby Bass Checker," *MM*, xxxix (31 Oct 1964), 6

S. Dance: *The World of Earl Hines* (New York, 1977)

SCOTT DeVEAUX/BK

Potts, Bill [William Orie] (*b* Arlington, VA, 3 April 1928). Arranger, pianist, and conductor. In his youth he took up Hawaiian guitar and then accordion. During his army service in Washington, DC (1949–54), he played in military ensembles and wrote arrangements for the Orchestra (the radio band of the broadcaster Willis Conover, from 1951). In 1954–5 he provided arrangements for Tony Pastor, Stan Kenton, and Woody Herman. Among his engagements as a pianist in Washington were performances with Lester Young (1956), which were recorded and later released as *Lester Young in Washington, DC* (PL 2308219, 2308225, 2308228, 2308230). After touring with Herman (1957–9) Potts arranged the music for and conducted *The Jazz Soul of Porgy and Bess* (1959, UA 4032), an interpretation of Gershwin's opera that featured solos by Zoot Sims, Al Cohn, Bob Brookmeyer, Art Farmer, and Harry Edison, and which received critical acclaim. He recorded with his own studio band in 1963 and again in 1967 when he also worked as an arranger for Buddy Rich. From the early 1970s he taught arranging at Montgomery College.

BIBLIOGRAPHY

FeatherE

A. Scott: "Jazz Composer Calls the Tunes in Washington," *Metronome*, lxxv/10 (1958), 16

——: "Bill Potts is Back!," *Radio Free Jazz*, xx (1979), Jan, 9

Potts, Steve (*b* Columbus, OH, 21 Jan 1945). Soprano and alto saxophonist. A nephew of Buddy Tate, he studied saxophone with Charles Lloyd in Los Angeles at the beginning of 1957 and then with Eric Dolphy in New York. There he played with Chick Corea, Sam Rivers, and Joe Henderson, and with rhythm-and-blues and rock groups, before joining Chico Hamilton, in whose group he replaced Arnie Lawrence. He left for Spain in 1970, then settled in France, which thereafter he left only for tours of Europe and America as a member of Steve Lacy's group between 1972 and 1996; he may be seen with the group in the video *Steve Lacy: Lift the Bandstand* (*c*1985 [filmed 1983]). Based in Paris, he led the group Recent History from 1975, played with Georges Arvanitas, Christian Escoudé, the Art Ensemble of Chicago, Alan Silva, and others, and accompanied the singer Jessye Norman in her show *Great Day in the Morning* (1982).

SELECTED RECORDINGS

As leader: *Pearl* (1990, Caravan 002); *Wet Spot* (1999, SP 01)

As sideman: S. Lacy: *Futurities* (1984, HA 2022); *The Gleam* (1986, Silkheart 102); *Live in Budapest* (1987, ITM 2011); *The Door* (1988, Novus 3049-1-N); *Anthem* (1989, Novus 3079-2-N); *Wee See* (1992, HA 6127); Peter Gritz: *Thank You to Be* (1995, Charlotte 170)

BIBLIOGRAPHY

J. J. Pussiau: "Steve Potts: 'ma récente histoire'," *Jm*, no.229 (1975), 19

P. Carles, A. Clergeat, and J.-L. Comolli: *Dictionnaire du jazz* (Paris, 1988, rev. and enlarged 2/1994)

"Encyclopédie permanente *Jazzmag*," *Jm*, no.389 (1990), 43

T. Quénum: "Steve Potts," *Jm*, no.407 (1991), 48

<http://www.stevepotts.net> (2001)

ANDRÉ CLERGEAT

Povel, Ferdinand (*b* Haarlem, Netherlands, 13 Feb 1947). Dutch tenor saxophonist and flutist. He is self-taught as a musician. As a freelance he played with Dusko Goykovich, Kurt Edelhagen, Kenny Clarke, Francy Boland, Slide Hampton, Maynard Ferguson, Peter Herbolzheimer, the Skymasters, Just in Case, Loek Dikker, Jiggs Whigham, Doug Raney, Cees Slinger's octet, the singer Roland Douglas, and others. He recorded with the pianist Martin Haak (1964), Goykovich (1970–71), Ferguson (1973), Herbolzheimer (from 1973), Hampton (1974), Benny Bailey (1976), Whigham, Toots Thielemans, and Jan Morks (all 1977), the arranger and conductor Rogier Van Otterloo (1978), and Raney's sextet and the singer Soesja Citroen (both 1983). Povel has frequently appeared as a featured soloist with Dutch and German bands. In addition to his principal instruments he is an adept player of the soprano and alto saxophones. He teaches at the Hilversum Conservatory.

SELECTED RECORDINGS

As leader: *Beboppin'* (1983, Limetree 198403); *Quintet* (1983, Varajazz 4212)

As sideman: D. Goykovich: *Live at the Domicile* (1970, Session 102851-6); *It's About Blues Time* (1971, Ensayo 48); D. Raney: *Meeting the Tenors* (1983, Criss Cross 1006)

WIM VAN EYLE

Powell, Baden. *See* Baden Powell.

Powell, Benny [Benjamin Gordon, Jr.] (*b* New Orleans, 1 March 1930). Trombonist. He studied music with local teachers, and played drums from the age of nine and trombone from the age of 12; he made his professional début on New Year's Day 1944. After playing with the 'Bama State Collegians and various bands in Texas and Oklahoma in the mid-1940s he toured with Lionel Hampton (1948–51), with whom he may be seen in several short films. In October 1951 he joined Count Basie's band, and some months later began to share the trombone solo work with Henry Coker; in 1956 he won the critic's poll in *Down Beat.* During the 1950s he also recorded frequently with smaller ensembles, including sessions with Buck Clayton and Sir Charles Thompson (both 1953), Frank Foster (1954, 1956), Joe Newman (1955), Frank Wess (1956), Thad Jones (1957), and J. C. Heard (1958).

In August 1963 Powell left Basie to lead his own groups in New York, but also recorded with Pepper Adams and worked with Roland Kirk and Grant Green. He played for Merv Griffin's television show and Broadway musicals, took part in studio sessions, and worked as an administrator for Billy Taylor (ii) and Jazzmobile and Joe Newman and Jazz Interactions; at the same time he performed and recorded with the Thad Jones-Mel Lewis Orchestra (1966–70) and Duke Pearson's big band (1967–70). In 1970 he moved with Griffin's show to Los Angeles, where he played with Bill Holman (1974) and Terry Gibbs and performed thoughout the decade with Bill Berry's big band (including recordings). He was in the band with Basie that may be seen (but not heard) in the film *Blazing Saddles* (1974), and he also returned to New York for reunions with Basie (1973, 1976) and Hampton (1978).

Powell left Los Angeles in 1980 as a member of the orchestra for the touring musical *Ain't Misbehavin',* which visited Europe in 1981. Thereafter he joined Dameronia, worked on John Carter's series of sessions for the Gramavision label in an avant-garde musical interpretation of African-American history (1985–9), played at a memorial concert for Louis Armstrong in New York (1986), recorded with Abdullah Ibrahim (1988), and led groups from time to time, recording under his own name in 1982 and 1991; throughout these years he was a freelance in all-star swing and bop groups, including the American Jazz Orchestra and the Smithsonian Jazz Masterworks Orchestra, and he toured and recorded with Randy Weston. He teaches privately and at the New School for Social Research, New York. In the late 1990s he was a member of the Statesmen of Jazz, and in 1998 he worked at Zinno's in New York as a member of a trio with Jane Jarvis and Earl May. Powell's style owes much to the influence of J. J. Johnson; he has a fluent technique, the ability to enunciate rapid notes clearly, and a strong sense of melodic line.

Video oral history material in *NCH* (HCJA).

SELECTED RECORDINGS

As leader: *Coast to Coast* (1982, Trident 507); *Why Don't You Say "Yes" Sometime?!* (1991, Inspire 0002)

As sideman: C. Basie: *Dance Session no.1* (1953, Clef 626); B. Clayton: on *How High the Fi* (1953, Col. CL567), Moten Swing, Sentimental Journey; F. Wess: *Frank Wess Quintet* (1964, Com. 20031), incl. Basie ain't Here, You're my Thrill; *North, South, East . . . Wess* (1956, Savoy 12072); C. Basie: *Basie–Eckstine, Inc.* (1959, Roul. 52029); L. Hampton: *Newport Uproar!* (1967, RCA LSP3891); *Newport '78* (1978, Tim. 142); J. Carter: *Castles of Ghana* (1985, Gram. 8603); *Dance of the Love Ghosts* (1986, Gram. 8704); A. Ibrahim: *Mindif* (1988, Enja 5073); J. Carter: *Fields* (1988, Gram. 8809); *Shadows on a Wall* (1989, Gram. R2-79422); R. Weston: *The Spirits of our Ancestors* (1991, Ant. 314-511896-2), incl. The Healers, African Sunrise; *Saga* (1995, Verve 314-529237-2), incl. F. E. W. Blues

SELECTED FILMS AND VIDEOS

Air Mail Special (1950); Bongo Interlude (1951); Vibe Boogie (1951); Who Cares? (1951); A Man Called Adam (1966); Blazing Saddles (1974); Quartet (1981); Jazz in America: Lincoln Center, New York (1982)

BIBLIOGRAPHY

FeatherE; *Feather '60s*; *Feather–Gitler '70s*

L. Feather: "More Gen on Basie's Men," *MM*, xxx (3 April 1954), 13

R. Horricks: *Count Basie and his Orchestra: its Music and its Musicians* (London and New York, 1957), 268

S. Voce: "Benny Powell and the Count Basie Trombone Team," *JJ*, x/11 (1957), 1

H. Siders: "Spendour in the Brass," *DB*, xl/2 (1973), 13

A. Levitt: "Benny, Dixie, Basie," *Jm*, no.299 (1981), 36

——: "Benny Powell accords en coulisse," *Jm*, no.300 (1981), 58

D. Minger: "Two Profiles of Basieites," *Coda*, no.236 (1991), 12

LEROY OSTRANSKY/BK

Powell, Bud [Earl] (*b* New York, 27 Sept 1924; *d* New York, 1 Aug 1966). Pianist and leader, brother of Richie Powell. Born into a musical family, he studied classical piano from the age of six. Between late 1940 and early 1942 he occasionally took part in informal jam sessions at Minton's Playhouse, New York, where he came under the tutelage and protection of Thelonious Monk and contributed to the emerging bop style. By 1943–5, when he played in the band of his guardian Cootie Williams, he had already developed his individual style in most of its essentials. After sustaining a head injury during a racial incident in 1945, he suffered the first of many nervous collapses which were to confine him to sanatoriums for much of his adult life. Thereafter he appeared intermittently with leading bop musicians or in his own trio. He was a member of Dizzy Gillespie's quintets at the Three Deuces late in 1945 and at the Spotlite briefly in 1946, after which he recorded with Kenny Clarke, Sonny Stitt, and the Bebop Boys (August–September 1946), as a

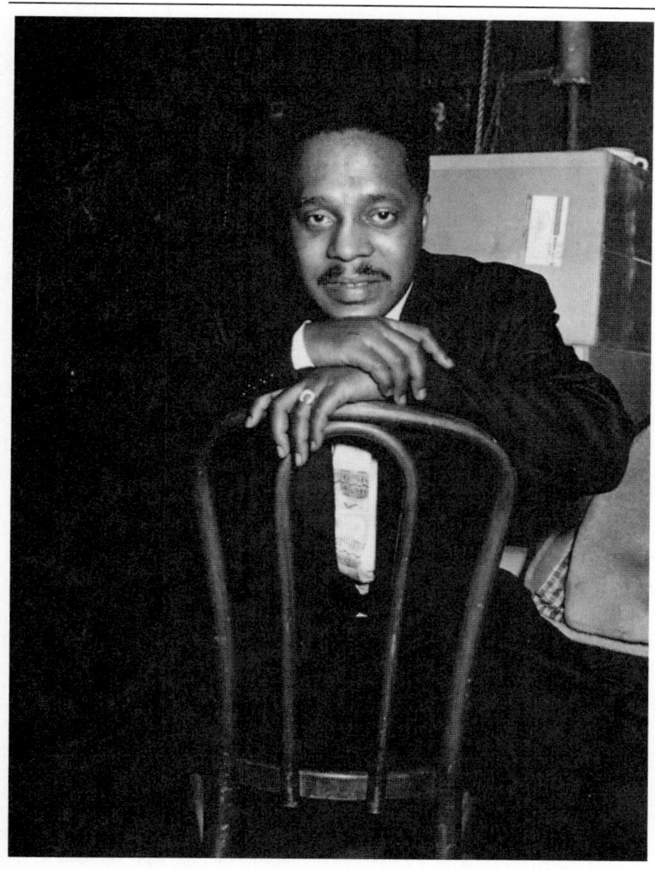

Bud Powell, 1965

leader (January 1947), and with Charlie Parker (May 1947). He played at such clubs as the Royal Roost and the Clique (soon renamed Birdland) and from 1949 made classic recordings with his trio, usually with Curley Russell or Ray Brown on double bass and Max Roach serving as his drummer. From 1953 to 1956 his trios included Oscar Pettiford, Roy Haynes, Charles Mingus, Art Taylor, and George Duvivier.

During this period, as his mental health and musical powers deteriorated, Powell gradually restricted his public appearances. Having first performed in Europe in autumn 1956, he moved in 1959 to Paris, where he led a trio (1959-62) with Kenny Clarke, the third member of which was usually Pierre Michelot, and enjoyed a certain celebrity status. With interruptions for further illnesses, he continued at the Blue Note with Gilbert Rovère and the drummer Larry Ritchie (1963), and then with Michel Gaudry and Ritchie or Taylor (1964). After returning to the USA in August 1964, he made a disastrous appearance at Carnegie Hall (1965) and was soon obliged to abandon music altogether. His experiences provided the central material for the film *Round Midnight* (1986).

Powell was the most important pianist in the early bop style, and his innovations transformed the jazz pianism of his time. A prodigious technician, he was able at will to reproduce the demanding styles of Art Tatum and Teddy Wilson, echoes of which can sometimes be heard in his ballad performances. At fast and medium tempos, however, he preferred the spare manner that he devised in the early 1940s: rapid melodic lines in the right hand punctuated by irregularly spaced, dissonant chords in the left. This almost antipianistic style (which was adopted by most bop pianists of the time) left him free to pursue linear melody in the manner of bop wind players, and it was as a melodist that Powell stood apart from his many imitators. At its best, Powell's playing was sustained by a free unfolding of rapid and unpredictable melodic invention, to which he brought a brittle, precise touch and great creative intensity. Except in his later years, when his virtuosity flagged and he self-consciously adopted a primitivism resembling Monk's, Powell never altered this basic approach, but worked ceaselessly within it to devise new melodic ideas, harmonies, and ways of coupling the hands. He greatly extended the range of jazz harmony by reducing his chordal underpinning to compounds of 2nds and 7ths, and achieved an extraordinary variety in his phrase lengths, which range from brief flurries to seemingly inexhaustible lines that ignore the structure of the original.

Although most at ease in a trio setting, Powell was stimulated to his best work in competition with other leading bop soloists such as Charlie Parker, Dizzy Gillespie, J. J. Johnson, Sonny Stitt, and especially Fats Navarro. Powell also composed a number of excellent jazz tunes, among them *Hallucinations* (recorded by Miles Davis as *Budo*), *Dance of the Infidels*, *Tempus Fugue-it*, and *Bouncing with Bud*, as well as the remarkable *The Glass Enclosure*, a musical impression of his experiences in mental asylums, which points to a talent for composition that was unfortunately left undeveloped. Transcriptions of six of his solos have been published by C. J. Safane (*Bud Powell*, New York, 1978).

See also Jazz (i), §V, 4; and Piano, §4.

SELECTED RECORDINGS

As leader: Bud's Bubble (1947, Roost 509); Tempus Fugue-it (1949, Clef 11045); All God's chillun got rhythm (1949, Clef 11046); Bouncing with Bud (1949, BN 1567); Dance of the Infidels (1949, BN 1568); *Bud Powell Moods* (1950–51, Clef 610), incl. Parisian Thoroughfare, Hallucinations, Just One of Those Things; Hallucinations (1950, Clef 610); Un poco loco (1951, BN 1577); Night in Tunisia (1951, BN 1576); The Glass Enclosure (1953, BN 1628)

As sideman: C. Williams: Floogie boo (1944, Hit 8089); J. J. Johnson: Jay Bird (1946, Savoy 975); Bebop Boys: Webb City (1946, Savoy 585); S. Stitt: Fine and Dandy (1950, Prst. 706); Jazz at Massey Hall: *Quintet of the Year* (1953, Debut 2, 4), incl. All the things you are, Perdido, Salt Peanuts

SELECTED FILMS AND VIDEOS

Cootie Williams and his Orchestra (1944); Bud Powell, Paris 1959 (1959); Stopforbud (1962)

BIBLIOGRAPHY

S. Pease: "Bud Powell's Style," *DB*, xviii/12 (1951), 16

L. Feather: *The Book of Jazz: a Guide to the Entire Field* (New York, 1957, rev. 2/1965), 238

M. James: *Ten Modern Jazzmen: an Appraisal of the Recorded Work of Ten Modern Jazzmen* (London, 1960), 125

L. Ostransky: *The Anatomy of Jazz* (Seattle, 1960), 238

M. Harrison: "Bud Powell," *Jazz Era: the 'Forties*, ed. S. Dance and others (London, 1961/*R*1985), 200

M. Hennessey: "Bud Powell Today," *MM* (29 July 1961), 7

I. Gitler: *Jazz Masters of the Forties* (New York, 1966/*R*1983 with discography), 110

J. G. Jepsen: *A Discography of Thelonious Monk & Bud Powell* (Copenhagen, 1969)

R. Johnson: "Bud Powell on Blue Note," *JM*, no.188 (1970), 8

"Bud Powell," *SJ*, xxxi/13 (1977), 298 [discography]

J. Réda: "La force de Bud Powell," *L'improviste: une lecture de jazz* (Paris, 1980), 158

C. Schlouch: *Once upon a Time: Bud Powell: a Discography* (Marseilles, France, 1983, rev. 2/1993)

B. Doerschuk: "Bud Powell," *Keyboard*, x/6 (1984), 26 [incl. discography]

F. Paudras: *La danse des infidèles: Bud Powell* (Paris, 1986)

M. Hennessey: *Klook: the Story of Kenny Clarke* (London, 1990)

E. Berger: *Bassically Speaking: an Oral History of George Duvivier* (Metuchen, NJ, and London, 1993), 90
A. Groves and A. Shipton: *The Glass Enclosure: the Life of Bud Powell* (Tunbridge Wells, England, 1993)
S. Carini: "Bud Powell: dix doigts de génie," *Jazzman*, no.62 (2000), 18

J. BRADFORD ROBINSON/BK

Powell, Jesse (Benny) [Tex] (*b* Smithville, TX, 27 Feb 1924; *d* New York, 19 Oct 1982). Tenor saxophonist. Following formal music studies he became a professional musician at the age of 18 and toured with Hot Lips Page (1942–3), Louis Armstrong (1943–4), and Luis Russell (1944–5). He replaced Illinois Jacquet in Count Basie's band in September 1946 for a tour in California, and he first recorded that same year accompanying the blues singer and pianist Champion Jack Dupree and the blues singer and guitarist Brownie McGhee. In November 1947 he recorded in Curly Russell's band accompanying the singer Doc Pomus. Having led his own band in New York early in 1948, he traveled to France to play with Howard McGhee's sextet in May of that year at the Festival International de Jazz; while in Paris he recorded with both Howard McGhee and Kenny Clarke. In 1949–50 Powell was a member of Dizzy Gillespie's big band, after which he formed a jump/rhythm-and-blues group which recorded from 1953 into the early 1960s. In 1964 he led a quintet at Birdland, New York.

SELECTED RECORDINGS

As leader: first issued on *Saxophony!* (1951–7, Sequel 648), Jesse's Blues (1953); Love to Spare/Rear Bumper (1953, Federal 12159); Turnpike (1957, Josie 834); *Blow, Man, Blow* (1959/1960, Jub. 1113)
As sideman: D. Pomus: Doc's Boogie/My Good Pott (1947, Savoy 5545) [1st t sax solo on both]; K. Clarke: I'm in the mood for love (1948, Swing 289); D. Gillespie: Coast to Coast (1950, Cap. 15852)

BIBLIOGRAPHY

FeatherE; *Feather–GitlerBEJ*
P. Carles, A. Clergeat, and J.-L. Comolli: *Dictionnaire du jazz* (Paris, 1988, rev. and enlarged 2/1994)
D. Penny: Liner notes, *Saxophony!* (Sequel 648, 1995)
J. Evensmo: *History of Jazz Tenor Saxophone: Black Artists*, iv: *1945–1949* (Oslo, 1999)

HOWARD RYE

Powell, Jimmie [James Theodore] (*b* New York, 24 Oct 1914; *d* 16 Feb 1994). Alto saxophonist. He worked in New York with Frankie Newton in 1931 and various bandleaders during the mid-1930s. Between 1938 and 1941 he played with Edgar Hayes and Sidney Bechet (briefly in February 1940), recorded with Gene Sedric and Hot Lips Page, and performed and recorded with with Benny Carter (*c* March 1939 – early 1940) and Fats Waller. In the 1940s he was a member of Count Basie's band (February 1943 – May 1945, late autumn 1945 – mid-summer 1946; for illustration *see* Films, fig.3), with which he made a number of recordings, among them *Taps Miller* (1944, Col. 36831); he also performed with Don Redman, Eddie Heywood, Sid Catlett, and Page and recorded with Lester Young (1944). Later he worked with Lucky Millinder (1952) and Lucky Thompson (1953). Powell toured the Middle East and Latin America with Dizzy Gillespie (1956) and Machito (1958) and worked with rhythm-and-blues and soul musicians (1960s – early 1970s), notably at the Apollo Theatre in Harlem and as a member of the band accompanying Aretha Franklin. In 1975 he joined Sy Oliver's band. He recorded with Oliver Jackson and Haywood Henry in New York (the album *Real Jazz Express*, 1977, BB 33126) and in Brignoles, France (1978), and as the leader of a quartet, consisting of Cliff Smalls, Leonard Gaskin, and Jackson, in Paris (1978, *Midnight Slows*, ii, BB 19188-2). The social security death index gives his last known residence as Mount Vernon, New York.

BIBLIOGRAPHY

ChiltonW; *FeatherE*; *SheridanCB*
C. Battestini and J.-P. Battestini: "Jimmy Powell," *BHcF*, no.270 (1979), 3

Powell, Mel [Epstein, Melvin] (*b* New York, 12 Feb 1923; *d* Los Angeles, 24 April 1998). Pianist and arranger. He began learning classical piano at the age of four, but by his early teens, having heard Teddy Wilson, he had turned to jazz; he also played baseball on a semi-professional basis, but after seriously injuring his finger he had to choose between sport and music. In New York he worked with Bobby Hackett, Georg Brunis, and Zutty Singleton (1939), performed and recorded with Wingy Manone (1941), joined Muggsy Spanier (April 1941), and wrote arrangements for Earl Hines. At this point he changed his name to Mel Powell, and as such he performed and recorded as a pianist and arranger for Benny Goodman (May 1941 – August 1942) and was briefly a member of the CBS orchestra under Raymond Scott (1942). During his military service he toured and recorded with Glenn Miller's band (1943) and recorded in Paris with the Jazz Club American Hot Band (1944, 1945), which included Django Reinhardt, with Ray McKinley (1945), and as an unaccompanied soloist (1945). Following his discharge he was again a member of Goodman's group (August 1945 – June 1946), with which he visited Los Angeles (early 1946). Back in Los Angeles he worked in studios, recorded with Jazz at the Philharmonic (1946), and spent a further period with Goodman (July 1947 – March 1948), with whom he may be seen in the film *A Song is Born* (1948); he recorded as a leader in 1947 and 1949.

Powell studied composition at Yale University (BM 1952) with Paul Hindemith, and thereafter he pursued a career as a classical composer in the serial tradition; his activities as a jazz musician largely ceased, although between 1953 and 1955 he worked again with Goodman and recorded as a leader. From 1957 he was a professor at Yale, and in 1969 he was appointed professor and founding dean of music at the California Institute for the Arts, where he worked for nearly thirty years. He performed again as a jazz soloist in 1986 with all-star swing and bop groups on the cruise ship SS *Norway*; thereafter a rare neuro-muscular disorder forced him to stop playing. His papers are held at the Irving S. Gilmore Music Library, Yale University (*see* Libraries and archives, §2).

SELECTED RECORDINGS

* – arranged by Powell

As unaccompanied soloist: Homage à Fats Waller (1945, Jazz Club Français 140); Don't blame me (1945, Jazz Club Français 141)
As leader: When did you leave heaven?/Blue Skies (1943, Com. 543); The world is waiting for the sunrise (1944, Com. 544); *Glenn Miller's Uptown Hall Gang* (1944–5, Esquire 302); *Out on a Limb* (1955, Van. 8506), incl. Gone with the Wind, Pennies from Heaven; *The Return of Mel Powell* (1986, Chi. 301)
As sideman: B. Goodman: *The Count (1941, Col. 36379); *The Earl (1941, OK 6474); Tiger Rag (1945, Col. 36922); *Clarinade (1945, Col. 36823); I got rhythm (1945, Col. 36923); Liza (1945, Col. 35234); China Boy (1945, Col. 36924); Jazz at the Philharmonic: Sweet Georgia Brown (1946, Disc 2004); B. Goodman: The world is waiting for the sunrise (1947, Cap. 15069)

BIBLIOGRAPHY

ConnorBG; *FeatherE*; *Feather–Gitler '70s*; *SchullerS*
L. Feather: "Mel Powell, the Rip Van Winkle of Jazz," *San Francisco Chronicle* (16 Nov 1986)

R. Swift: "Powell, Mel," *GroveAM*
W. Balliett: "Profiles: What Ever Happened to Mel Powell?" *New Yorker*, lxiii (25 May 1987), 37; repr. in Balliett: *Bradley, Barney, and Max: 16 Portraits in Jazz* (New York, 1989), 102; *BalliettA* (1996)
A. Kozinn: "Mel Powell's Musical Journey to a Pulitzer Prize," *New York Times* (24 April 1990)
J. McDonough: "Riffs: Mel Powell," *DB*, lvii/7 (1990), 13
H. Reich: "Music Man: Mel Powell Makes his Mark in Jazz and Classics," *Chicago Tribune* (15 April 1990)
Obituaries: M. Oliver, *Los Angeles Times* (25 April 1998); A. Kozinn, *New York Times* (27 April 1998); M. Swed, *Los Angeles Times* (27 April 1998)
T. Teachout: "Making a Case for an Overlooked Swing Pianist," *New York Times* (26 July 1998)

BK

Powell, Richie [Richard] (*b* New York, 5 Sept 1931; *d* Pennsylvania, 26 June 1956). Pianist, brother of Bud Powell. He studied music at City College, New York, and learned to improvise while practicing at the home of Mary Lou Williams in New York, where musicians often met. After playing with the saxophonists Paul Williams in 1951–2 and Johnny Hodges from 1952 to 1954 he was the pianist and arranger for Clifford Brown's and Max Roach's group from 1954 to mid-1956, when he and Brown died in an automobile accident. Powell made a brief appearance with Roach in the film *Carmen Jones* (1954).

SELECTED RECORDINGS

As sideman: J. Hodges: on *More of Johnny Hodges* (1951–4, Norg. 1009), Autumn in New York (1954); C. Brown and M. Roach: *Clifford Brown with Max Roach* (1954–5, EmA 36036); *Study in Brown* (1955, EmA 36037); S. Rollins: *Sonny Rollins plus Four* (1956, Prst. 7038)

BIBLIOGRAPHY

FeatherE

PAUL RINZLER

Powell, Roy (Temple) (*b* Langham, England, 2 Oct 1965). English pianist and composer. He studied composition at the Royal Northern College of Music in Manchester (1984–7) with Harrison Birtwistle and others, but left without a degree in order to play jazz. He led the fusion band Some Other Country (1989–93) before forming the Roy Powell Group and recording the highly acclaimed *A Big Sky* (1994, Totem 101). He also toured Britain in the Creative Jazz Orchestra with guest leaders Vince Mendoza (1993) and Anthony Braxton (1994). In 1995 he began teaching in Kristiansund, Norway, but returned to the UK in 1997 to play at Ronnie Scott's and other venues in a quartet comprising the guitarist Mike Walker, the double bass player Arild Andersen, and the drummer John Marshall. Later that year, while resident in Oslo, he set up a group with the double bass player Terje Gewelt and the drummer Jarle Vespestad to play free improvisation. Powell is a fluent pianist in the post-Hancock style, but is most notable for the skilled writing evident on his début recording.

MARK GILBERT

Powell, Rudy [Everard Stephen, Sr.; Root; Karweem, Musheed] (*b* New York, 28 Oct 1907; *d* New York, 30 Oct 1976). Clarinetist and alto saxophonist. As a child he played piano, violin, and saxophone. From 1928 to 1930 he was at the Lenox Club in New York with Cliff Jackson, in whose band he remained until summer 1931. He then worked with Elmer Snowden, Dave Nelson, Sam Wooding, Kaiser Marshall, and Rex Stewart (this last at the Empire Ballroom in 1933). Although best known for his work with Fats Waller (at intervals, 1935 – January 1937) Powell also toured Europe while with Edgar Hayes (1937–8) and enjoyed a successful career as a sideman in many other bands, including those led by Claude Hopkins (for four months in 1938–9), Teddy Wilson (April 1939 – spring 1940), Andy Kirk (June 1940 – January 1941), and Fletcher Henderson (January 1941 – March 1942). He joined Eddie South for a lengthy residency at Café Society and for a few further months at the Hickory House (1942–3), played with Don Redman (June 1943) and Chris Columbus (briefly in 1944), and worked with Hopkins at the Zanzibar (late 1944). Later he was a member of bands led by Cab Calloway (April 1945 – May 1948), Lucky Millinder (June 1948–1951, except for a brief period with Charlie Ventura), Jimmy Rushing (his Kansas City Seven, 1951–2), Buddy Tate (1953), the pianist Benton Heath (for eight years to 1961), Ray Charles (1961–2), and Buddy Johnson. In 1960 he recorded with Al Casey, who had also worked as a sideman with Waller, and he appeared in the documentary film *Jazz on a Summer's Day*, made at the Newport festival two years earlier. From 1965 to 1969 he toured internationally with the Saints and Sinners. Although he played less frequently from 1969 on account of illness, he continued to work occasionally around New York until his death. Powell played conventional swing alto saxophone, but his clarinet work (particularly with Waller) was more distinctive; Lyttelton (1981) characterizes it as having "a persistently rasping tone . . . geared, like his restless, angular phrasing, to generating heat."

SELECTED RECORDINGS

As sideman: F. Waller: Louisiana Fairy Tale (1935, Vic. 24898); 12th Street Rag/Sweet Sue (1935, Vic. 25087); Truckin' (1935, Vic. 25116); H. Allen: When Did You Leave Heaven?/Algiers Stomp (1936, Voc. 3302); E. Hayes: Blue Skies/Sweetheart (1937, Decca 1684); Saints and Sinners: *Sugar: the Saints and Sinners in Europe* (1968, MPS 15174)

BIBLIOGRAPHY

AllenH; *ChiltonW*; *FeatherE*; *Feather '60s*; *McCarthyB*
D. Hague: "Rudy Powell and Jimmy Rushing," *JJ*, x/7 (1957), 3
E. Smith: "Saga of a Sideman," *Record Research*, no.20 (1958), 3
A. Close: "Rudy Powell: an Appreciation," *Coda*, v/4 (1962), 2
A. Lawrie: "The Big Names: Rudy Powell Reminisces," *Toronto Globe and Mail* (11 Nov 1967)
J. Norris: "Biographies of 'The Saints and Sinners'," *Jazz Notes* (1968), spring, 2
F. Owens: "Rudy Powell," *JJ*, xxiii/6 (1970), 20
H. Lyttelton: *The Best of Jazz*, ii: *Enter the Giants* (London, 1981), 57
M. Hinton and D. G. Berger: *Bass Line: the Stories and Photographs of Milt Hinton* (Philadelphia, 1988), 133
L. Wright: *"Fats" in Fact* (Chigwell, England, 1992)
M. Selchow: *Ding! Ding!: a Bio-discographical Sketchbook on Vic Dickenson* (Westoverledingen, Germany, 1998)

WARREN VACHÉ, SR.

Powell, Seldon (*b* Lawrenceville, VA, 15 Nov 1928; *d* Hempstead, NY, 25 Jan 1997). Tenor saxophonist and flutist. In an interview with *Cadence* (1989) Powell is reported to have given his birth month as September, but all other sources, including social security records, give November. He grew up in New York, where he received classical music training, and in 1949 he worked briefly with Tab Smith. In late December 1949 he joined Lucky Millinder as tenor saxophone soloist, and the following year recorded with him – though not as a soloist. He continued his playing career during his military service (1951–2), and after receiving his discharge established himself in New York as a freelance and studio musician. At this time he studied at the Juilliard School (1953–7), formed associations with Sy Oliver and Erskine Hawkins, led a group at Birdland, and recorded as a leader and with Neal Hefti (1955), Louie Bellson (1955), Friedrich Gulda (with whom he also performed at Birdland

and the Newport Jazz Festival, 1956), Johnny Richards and the composer Billy Ver Planck (both 1957–8), and the arranger A. K. Salim (1958). In 1958 he traveled to Europe with Benny Goodman's band, and he then played briefly with Woody Herman. In the 1960s he worked chiefly for ABC TV, but he also played and recorded with Buddy Rich (1960), Bellson (1962–4), Clark Terry (1963), and Ahmed Abdul-Malik (1964). In 1968 he spent a year with the Thad Jones–Mel Lewis Orchestra, replacing Joe Farrell. His numerous recordings as a studio musician include many made in the late 1960s and early 1970s with soul and soul-jazz musicians, including Groove Holmes (*c*1973), and sessions in the big bands that accompanied Gato Barbieri (1974) and Anthony Braxton and Dizzy Gillespie (both 1976). Powell played in many Broadway musicals and then, through much of the 1980s, was on the staff of the Westbury (Connecticut) Music Fair. He performed as a principal soloist in Gerry Mulligan's 16-piece orchestra at the JVC Jazz Festival, New York, in 1987, and he recorded with the Basie Alumni in 1992.

SELECTED RECORDINGS

As leader: *Seldon Powell Plays* (1955, Roost 2205); *Seldon Powell Sextet* (1956, Roost 2220); on *We Paid our Dues* (1961, Epic 17018), Bowl of Soul, For Lester, Two for One

As sideman: H. L. Page and Sylvia Vanderpool: Chocolate Candy Blues/ Pacifying Blues (1950, Col. 30220); L. Bellson: on *The Driving Louis Bellson* (1955, Norg. 1020), All right jump it man, Basie, Charlie-o, Greetings; B. Ver Planck: *Jazz for Play Girls* (1957, Savoy 12121); Basie Alumni: *Swing for the Count* (1992, Can. 79724)

BIBLIOGRAPHY

ConnorBG; *FeatherE*; *Feather '60s*

B. Ulanov: Untitled review, *DB*, xxii/21 (1955), 14

B. Rusch: "Seldon Powell: Interview," *Cadence*, xv/11 (1989), 5

Obituaries: M. Gardner, *JJI*, l/8 (1997), 15; E. LeBlanc, *Blues & Rhythm*, no.119 (1997), 10

LAWRENCE KOCH/BK

Powell, Specs [Gordon] (*b* New York, 5 June 1922). Drummer. After achieving recognition in the late 1930s as a pianist and drummer with his own small group he played drums exclusively for the rest of his career, principally with swing groups. He played with Edgar Hayes (1939), Eddie South (1939–40), John Kirby (1941–2), Benny Carter (1942), and Ben Webster (in New York in the early 1940s), then worked at CBS with Raymond Scott; as a staff musician at CBS (from 1943) he played both popular and symphonic works. During the following years he performed and recorded with Benny Goodman (1944) and Red Norvo (1944–5) and also recorded with Sidney and Wilbur De Paris (1944), Joe Bushkin (1944), Mildred Bailey (1944–6), and Clyde Hart, Foots Thomas, and Billie Holiday (all 1945); later he made recordings with Erroll Garner (1956), with Gerry Mulligan and Teddy Wilson at the Newport Jazz Festival (1957), as a member of Monday Night at Birdland (1958), an all-star group that also included Lee Morgan, Curtis Fuller, and Hank Mobley, and with the guitarist Billy Butler (1969).

SELECTED RECORDINGS

As leader: *Movin' In with Specs Powell* (1957, Roul. 52004)

As sideman: E. South: Oh! Lady be Good (1941, Col. 36193); S. Benskin: Cherry/When all the World is Waiting for the Sunrise (1945, BN 522); E. Garner: *The Most Happy Piano* (1956, Col. CL939); B. Butler: *Guitar Soul* (1969, Prst. 7734)

BIBLIOGRAPHY

ConnorBG; *FeatherE*

J. M. Doran: *Erroll Garner: the Most Happy Piano* (Metuchen, NJ, and London, 1985), 80 [incl. discography]

EDDIE LAMBERT

Power Bros. Record company and label founded in 1992 by KRZYSZTOF POPEK.

Pöyry, Pekka (*b* Pori, Finland, 10 Dec 1939; *d* Helsinki, 4 Aug 1980). Finnish saxophonist and flutist. He studied law but his admiration for Charlie Parker led him to take up a career in jazz. He joined Juhani Vilkki's sextet in the mid-1960s and was soon a leading soloist in Finnish jazz. Of a retiring disposition, Pöyry shunned the responsibilities of a bandleader and played with a number of different groups. In the early 1970s he was a member, with Jukka Tolonen, of the jazz-rock group Tasavallan Presidentti, and in the mid- and late 1970s he performed and recorded with UMO. He also recorded with Eero Koivistoinen, Erik Lindström, Seppo Paakkunainen, Esa Pethman, Heikki Sarmanto, and Dexter Gordon. Pöyry may be heard to advantage on the album *Sunweb* (Love 156), which he recorded with Mike Koskinen in 1975. (A. Granholm: *Finnish Jazz*, Helsinki, 1974, rev. and enlarged 5/1997, by M. Huuskonen, J. Muikku, and T. Vähäsilta)

PEKKA GRONOW

Pozo, Chano [Pozo y Gonzales, Luciano] (*b* Havana, 7 Jan 1915; *d* New York, 2 Dec 1948). Cuban drummer, singer, and dancer. His drumming and singing were rooted in the Cuban *lucumí* faith, derived from West African rituals. On 29 September 1947 he and the bongo player Chiquitico performed in a concert at Carnegie Hall with Dizzy Gillespie – this was the first time an attempt had been made to fuse elements of jazz and Latin music at a serious artistic level. Pozo was murdered before he could fully develop his ideas with Gillespie, but during his brief career in the USA he provided the starting point for much popular music of the late 1940s and the 1950s. The collaboration between the two men supplied the initiative for American musicians, and some of the listening public, to appreciate fully the tradition of Latin music. Pozo was a cousin of Chino Pozo.

For illustration *see* GILLESPIE, DIZZY.

SELECTED RECORDINGS

As sideman with D. Gillespie: *Dizzy Goes to College* (1947, Jazz Showcase 5000, 5002); Algo bueno/Minor Walk (1947, Vic. 20-3186); Cool Breeze/ Cubana Be/Cubana Bop (1947, Vic. 20-3145); Manteca (1947, Vic. 20-3023); Good Bait/Ool-ya-koo (1947, Vic. 20-2878); *Afro-Cuban Suite* (1948, Swing 33301); *Melodic Revolution* (1948, Alto 703)

As sideman with M. Jackson: Boppin' with Robin (1948, Sensation 19)

BIBLIOGRAPHY

D. Gillespie and A. Fraser: *To be, or not . . . to Bop: Memoirs* (Garden City, NY, 1979, London, 1980, as *Dizzy: the Autobiography of Dizzy Gillespie*)

J. S. Roberts: *The Latin Tinge: the Impact of Latin American Music on the United States* (New York, and Oxford, England, 1979)

JOHN STORM ROBERTS/R

Pozo, Chino [Valdés, Francisco] (*b* Havana, 4 Oct 1915; *d* New York, March 1979). Cuban percussionist, cousin of Chano Pozo. He taught himself to play piano and double bass. After moving to the USA (1937) he worked with Machito (1941–3) and accompanied a dance troupe (1943–9). In 1948 he performed with Tadd Dameron and Fats Navarro, and with Dameron's sextet (of which Navarro was also a member) he recorded the single *Jahbero* (1948, BN 559). While working in various Latin groups he recorded with Dizzy Gillespie and with Machito and Charlie Parker (both 1950). Thereafter he toured with Peggy Lee (1954–5), performed with Stan Kenton (1955) and Herbie Mann (1956), and recorded with Illinois Jacquet (1954), Phineas

Newborn (1957), Billy Taylor (ii) (1959), and Gábor Szabó (1965). From the 1960s he worked as a percussionist for the popular singer Paul Anka. The social security death index gives only the month and year of his death and has his last known residence, Las Vegas, Nevada. (*FeatherE*)

Practice mute. *See* Mute, §1.

Preacher. Nickname of Wardell Jones.

Preissac, Ludovic de (*b* Ancenis, France, 8 Sept 1962). French pianist. His mother played harp and his father, Philippe de Preissac (*b* 1936), is a clarinetist and bandleader in the Benny Goodman mold. Ludovic de Preissac studied at the conservatory in Sèvres and the Schola Cantorum in Paris. He was influenced by Teddy Wilson, Bud Powell, and Phineas Newborn. From 1979 to 1990 he played with the clarinetist Stéphane Guérault, Maxim Saury, Gérard Badini, Jean-Loup Longnon, and Turk Mauro. His ability to play stride piano is evident on *Honeysuckle Rose*, on *Manda Djinn et le 78 All Stars avec en guest star Ludovic de Preissac* (1988, Jazz Trade 4022). From 1990 he has made his name as a bop virtuoso and leader. His quintets have included such French players as the trumpeters Stéphane Belmondo (1991) and Michel Delakian (1992), and the saxophonist Guillaume Naturel; his recording *American Quintet* features Scott Wendholt and Ted Nash (ii) (1997, DOC 037). (F. W. Sportis: "Ludovic de Preissac," *Jh*, no.508 (1994), 13)

MICHEL LAPLACE

Pres. Nickname of Lester Young.

Presencer, Gerard (*b* London, 12 Sept 1972). English flugelhorn player and trumpeter. Inspired at first by Roy Eldridge, he took up trumpet at the age of ten. He played with the National Youth Jazz Orchestra (1983–9) and gained valuable experience in Ziggy's, a jazz club run by his father in central London. He made his recording début in Barcelona at the age of 15 with Tete Montoliu and Peter King, and thereafter played frequently in King's bands. From 1991 he toured worldwide and recorded with the jazz quintet led by Charlie Watts (the drummer of the Rolling Stones). In his late teens he was much involved in acid jazz; he played the trumpet solo on *Cantaloop*, a single on the biggest-selling album in Blue Note's history, Us3's *Hand on the Torch* (1992). In the mid-1990s he played with the Dankworth Generation Band and Stan Tracey's Quartet and worked widely as a freelance, notably on a tour of Europe with Evan Parker and as a member of Tracey's group playing freely improvised music. In autumn 1999 he succeeded Graham Collier as head of the jazz department at the Royal Academy of Music in London. In the same year he was made a full professor at the Hochschule für Musik in Berlin. Although influenced by leading trumpeters from the 1960s and 1970s, Presencer cites Herbie Hancock's work from the mid-1970s as his chief inspiration.

SELECTED RECORDINGS

As leader: *Platypus* (1997, Linn 079)

As sideman: T. Montoliu and P. King: *New Year's Morning '89* (1989, Fresh Sound 117); Us3: *Hand on the Torch* (1992, BN B1NR-80883); T. Garland: *Enter the Fire* (1995, 1997, Linn 074); C. Martin: *Make this City Ours* (1996, Linn 066)

BIBLIOGRAPHY

D. Gelly: "Growing up," *Jazzwise*, no.15 (1998), 12

MARK GILBERT

Preservation Hall. Venue in New Orleans; *see* Nightclubs and other venues.

Preservation Hall Jazz Band. New Orleans jazz band. In the 1950s the art dealer Larry Borenstein engaged veteran jazz musicians to play at his art gallery on St. Peter Street, New Orleans, and from 1961 the performances took place in part of an adjacent building, which Borenstein opened as Preservation Hall. Allan Jaffe (i) and his wife, Sandra, took over the administration of the hall and began to organize tours for the musicians who regularly played there, calling the group the Preservation Hall Jazz Band. In early 1963 Kid Thomas Valentine and George Lewis (i) led the band on a tour of the USA; then, under Lewis's leadership, Punch Miller (trumpet), Louis Nelson (trombone), Joseph Robichaux (piano), Emanuel Sayles (banjo), John Joseph (double bass), and Joe Watkins (drums) visited Japan, where the band returned in 1964 and 1965. For a tour of Europe in 1967 the members of the band were De De Pierce (trumpet), Nelson, Willie Humphrey (clarinet), Billie Pierce (piano), Chester Zardis (double bass), and Cié Frazier (drums); a similar group performed at the Newport Jazz Festival in 1970. On a tour of Japan, Australia, Canada, and Europe the following year the personnel consisted of Nelson, Emanuel Paul (saxophone), Albert Burbank (clarinet), Charlie Hamilton (piano), Joseph Butler (double bass), and Alonzo Stewart (drums), with Valentine again acting as leader; later, in 1979, Valentine took a Preservation Hall band on a State-Department sponsored tour of the USSR. From the mid-1970s Percy Humphrey led the main touring band, which consisted of Humphrey himself (occasionally replaced by Valentine), Willie Humphrey, Jim Robinson (trombone; replaced after his death by Frank Demond), Sing Miller (piano), Narvin Kimball (banjo), Jaffe (until his death in 1987; tuba), and Frank Parker (drums). Another group often toured with Kid Sheik Cola as its leader. A Preservation Hall Jazz Band including Valentine and Willie Humphrey appeared in a documentary broadcast on television as "American Patchwork: Songs and Stories of America, no.101: Jazz Parades: Feet Don't Fail Me Now" (1990).

As many as 20 different bands, drawn from a pool of about 150 local musicians, had played at Preservation Hall in the 1960s, but by 1999 virtually all of the older generation of musicians had died and the bandmembers were a mixture of younger African-American players and white musicians from overseas. Most notable among the former were Michael White (ii), Wendell Brunious (who gradually took over the leadership of Valentine's band in the elder trumpeter's final years), Freddy Lonzo, and the tuba player Walter Payton; Europeans included the Swedish pianist Lars Edegran, the English trumpeter Clive Wilson, Orange Kellin, and Jacques Gauthé. In 1994 the Jaffes' son, the double bass player Ben Jaffe, joined. The band continues to perform for tourists in New Orleans and makes annual tours.

For illustration *see* Humphrey.

SELECTED RECORDINGS

Billie and De De Pierce and their Preservation Hall Jazz Band (1966, Preservation Hall 3); *New Orleans*, i–iii (1977, 1981, 1983, Col. M34549, FM37780, FM38650)

BIBLIOGRAPHY

T. Dash: "Kid Thomas in Europe," *Fn*, iii/2 (1971), 16
B. Byler: "Dancing in the Aisles," *MR*, iv/10 (1977), 1
N. Thimmesch: "Jazzmen Deserve a Medal," *Philadelphia Inquirer* (2 Aug 1979), §A, p.11
"Veterans Unleashed," *MM*, lv (20 Sept 1980), 24
W. Carter: *Preservation Hall: Music from the Heart* (Wheatley, Oxford, England, and New York, 1991)
B. Kohlhaase: "To Preserve and Protect," *Los Angeles Times* (23 Feb 1995)
Z. Stewart: "Proudly Declaring New Orleans his Home Bass," *Los Angeles Times* (6 July 1995)

MIKE HAZELDINE/BK

Pressing. The process whereby a recording in its original form is converted into a marketable commodity in the shape of a disc (*see* Recording, §I, 1(i)), hence a synonym for a commercial disc.

Press roll. A type of roll, one of the drumstrokes collectively known as Rudiments.

Prestige. Record company and label. The company was established in 1949 in New York by Bob Weinstock and quickly embarked upon an ambitious program of recording many famous young musicians of the day. Its catalogue included mainstream jazz, bop, cool jazz, and hard bop by such musicians as Gene Ammons, Wardell Gray, Miles Davis, Thelonious Monk, Sonny Rollins, Stan Getz, John Coltrane, and many others; some recordings were issued on a subsidiary label, New Jazz. In the 1950s many sessions were recorded by Rudy Van Gelder at his studio in Hackensack (later in Englewood Cliffs), New Jersey. In 1960 the company began to diversify, setting up new labels: Swingville (to put out material from a growing catalogue of mainstream jazz by older musicians); Moodsville (to release muted, atmospheric recordings by swing and bop musicians); and Bluesville (a blues label). Artists and repertory were supervised by Weinstock, though others, including Chris Albertson, Ozzie Cadena, Ira Gitler, Bob Porter, and Don Schlitten, were also involved with the catalogue at various times. From the late 1960s until the late 1970s Prestige was associated chiefly with soul jazz, issuing recordings by Brother Jack McDuff, Groove Holmes, Shirley Scott, and Johnny Hammond with various tenor saxophonists. In 1967 the company transferred its headquarters to Bergenfield, New Jersey, but in May 1971 it was acquired by Fantasy, which ran the catalogue and label from its base in Berkeley, California. The label name was revived around 1995 for new recordings.

Label for "Strike up the Band," recorded by the quartet led by Sonny Stitt and Bud Powell for Prestige (New York, 26 January 1950)

BIBLIOGRAPHY

A. Morgan: "The Prestige–Swingville Series," *JM*, xiii (1967), no.1, p.19; no.2, p.15; no.3, p.17; [no.7], p.21
M. Ruppli: *Prestige Jazz Records, 1949–1969* [*recte* 1971]*: a Discography* (n.p. [Copenhagen], 1972; rev. and enlarged 2/1980, with B. Porter, as *The Prestige Label: a Discography*)
G. Marsh and G. Callingham, eds.: *East Coasting: the Cover Art of New York's Prestige, Riverside and Atlantic Records* (Zurich, 1993)

HOWARD RYE, BK

Preston, Don(ald Ward) (*b* Flint, MI, 21 Sept 1932). Synthesizer player and pianist. He studied and played piano with Herbie Mann while in the army, and following his discharge (early 1950s) he worked in Detroit with Tommy Flanagan and Elvin Jones and in Los Angeles with Carla Bley (1957–8) and Charlie Haden (1959). At some point in the 1960s he collaborated with Don Ellis. An interest in experimental music and theater prompted him to establish a number of mixed-media groups, notably Aha! (1963). Preston joined Frank Zappa and the Mothers of Invention in 1967 and worked intermittently with the group until 1974. During the same period he toured and recorded with Gil Evans and organized an ensemble with Buell Neidlinger (both 1971); later he recorded with Neidlinger (1973). From 1975 through the 1990s he was involved in many genres: he wrote and played music for films (notably *Apocalypse Now*) and theater, performed concerts of electronic music, sang in avant-garde operas (1996–7), and gave the première of his piano concerto as part of a mixed-media performance that involved glass sculpture (1997); he was also a founding member of an outgrowth of Zappa's Mothers of Invention, the Grandmothers, which was active from the 1980s into the 1990s.

At the same time Preston retained a connection to jazz. He played synthesizer, piano, and various keyboards and electronic devices on the last three parts (1986–9) of John Carter's five-volume series of albums *Roots and Folklore: Episodes in the Development of American Folk Music*, performed and recorded on synthesizer and piano with a small group co-led by Carter and Bobby Bradford (1988), and took part in Ivo Perelman's first session as a leader (1989). In addition he formed jazz trios with Art Davis and Albert "Tootie" Heath (*c* late 1980s) and with the double bass player Joel Hamilton and Alex Cline (late 1990s). In 1996 he recorded as an unaccompanied solo pianist. Having maintained an interest in the unusual throughout his career, in 1999 Preston gave a concert together with a cornetist (Bradford), an electric guitarist, and a tuba player, at which he played keyboard instruments, as well as "wood of the piano, desk, and iron grate."

SELECTED RECORDINGS

Duos with M. Mantler: *Alien* (1985, Watt 15)
As sideman: J. Carter: *Dance of the Love Ghosts* (1986, Gram. 8704); *Fields* (1988, Gram. 8809); J. Carter and B. Bradford: *Comin' On* (1988, HA 6016); I. Perelman: *Ivo* (1989, K2B2 2769), incl. O cravo e a rosa; J. Carter: *Shadows on a Wall* (1989, Gram. R2-79422)

BIBLIOGRAPHY

Feather–Gitler '70s
L. Underwood: "Profile: Buell Neidlinger & Don Preston," *DB*, xlii/7 (1975), 28

J. Woodward: "Don Preston: Synthesizer from Apocalypse Now to Zappa," *DB*, liv/8 (1987), 25 [incl. discography]
<http://www.echograph.com/donbio.html> (2000)
<http://www.jps.net/dwpreston/> (2000)

BK

Preston, Eddie [Edward L.] (*b* Dallas, 5 Sept 1925). Trumpeter. His year of birth was published erroneously as 1928 in the first edition of this dictionary; Preston gave 1925 in his questionnaire for the second edition. He studied music at Wiley College in Marshall, Texas (1941–2), took trumpet lessons in New York (1944), and then studied in Los Angeles, both privately (1944, 1946) and at the University of California (1946). Having gained early experience in big bands (from 1945), notably that of Johnny Otis, with which he toured the USA (1945–7), he joined Lionel Hampton, with whom he recorded in Los Angeles (1955) and, while touring Europe, in Paris and Madrid (both 1956); he may be heard as a soloist in a small group led by Hampton on *Baby don't love me no more*, from the rather misleadingly titled album *Lionel Hampton Big Band* (1955, Clef 670). He toured with Ray Charles (1959) and Louis Jordan (1960–61), then played briefly and recorded in New York with Duke Ellington (1962) and Count Basie (1963, as a temporary replacement for Thad Jones). In 1963 Preston worked for the first time with Charles Mingus, performing at the Village Gate in New York and recording; he continued to play with the group in 1964 and 1965. This association with Mingus was renewed in the 1970s, when he toured Europe (1970) and Japan (1971) and took part in recording sessions (1971–2); his playing is well represented by *Blue Bird* (1970, Amer. 6110), which was recorded at a concert in Paris. He also recorded with Sonny Stitt (1966), played with Frank Foster, and toured and recorded in the USA and Europe with Ellington (1971); later he recorded with Roland Kirk (1977) and toured with Archie Shepp (1979). In 1973 Preston formed his own quintet, which took part in the Jazzmobile's work and performed at young people's concerts into the 1980s; among his his sidemen was Walter Perkins. He recorded again in 1993 in a big band led by the arranger James Jabbo Ware.

BIBLIOGRAPHY

V. Wilmer: "Eddie: a Chance to be Heard," *MM* (21 Nov 1970), 10
M. Jones: "Preston: a Leading Question," *MM* (6 Nov 1971), 24
B. Priestley: *Mingus: a Critical Biography* (London, Melbourne, Australia, and New York, 1982)

BK

Previn, André (George) [Priwin, Andreas Ludwig] (*b* Berlin, 6 April 1929). Pianist, conductor, and composer of Russian descent. As a child he took piano lessons at the Berlin Hochschule für Musik. In 1938 his family moved to Paris, where he studied at the conservatoire, and the following year they emigrated to the USA and settled in Los Angeles; Previn continued his musical training there, studying piano, theory, and composition. He became an American citizen in 1943. Influenced by Art Tatum, he worked professionally as a jazz pianist and as an arranger for MGM while he was still in high school. In 1945 he made his first recording, for the Sunset label; his early recordings for RCA in 1947 were substantial hits and brought him considerable success. Although he was not immediately sympathetic to bop when he first heard it in 1950 he eventually embraced the style. Following his army service (during which he studied conducting in San Francisco with Pierre Monteux) he settled in Los Angeles and became extremely active as a pianist. He played with the acclaimed Jazz at the Philharmonic All Stars in Los Angeles (1952), and his collaboration with Shelly Manne, *My Fair Lady* (1956), started a fashion for jazz albums based on Broadway musicals and continued to be popular for many years. Previn worked with such musicians as Benny Goodman, Herb Ellis, Shorty Rogers, Pete Rugolo, Jackie Cain and Roy Kral, and Ella Fitzgerald. In 1961 he received a Grammy Award for the album *André Previn Plays Harold Arlen*. During the 1960s and 1970s he devoted his time to conducting and composing classical and popular music. However, he revived his career in jazz with his album *After Hours* (1989), as the leader of a trio consisting of Joe Pass and Ray Brown. He made further jazz recordings in the 1990s, initially with Mundell Lowe in place of Pass (1990–91), gave occasional concerts with a jazz trio, and continued to use elements of jazz in his classical compositions. He published an autobiography, *No Minor Chords: my Days in Hollywood* (New York, 1991).

For illustration *see* Mulligan, Gerry.

SELECTED RECORDINGS

(recorded for Contemporary unless otherwise indicated)

As leader: *André Previn All Stars* (1946, Monarch 203); *André Previn* (1947, Vic. 20-3040, 20-3041, 20-3042, 20-3043) [album of 78 r.p.m. discs]; with R. Freeman (i): *Double Play!* (1957, 3537); *André Previn Plays Vernon Duke* (1958, 3558); *Like Previn!* (1960, 7575); *André Previn Plays Harold Arlen* (1960, 7586); *A Different Kind of Blues* (1980, HMV ASD3965); *After Hours* (1989, Telarc 83302); *Old Friends* (1991, Telarc 83309); *What Headphones?* (1993, Angel 54917-2); *Jazz at the Musikverein* (1995, Verve 314-537704-2)

As sideman: S. Manne: *My Fair Lady* (1956, 3527); B. Goodman: on *Happy Session* (1958, Col. CL1324), You'd be so nice to come home to

BIBLIOGRAPHY

FeatherE; *Feather '60s*; *Feather–Gitler '70s*
E. Greenfield: *André Previn* (London, 1973)
M. Bookspan and R. Yockey: *André Previn: a Biography* (Garden City, NY, 1981)
H. D. Ruttencutter: *Previn* (New York, 1985)
L. Feather: "André Previn Returns to his Roots," *Los Angeles Times* (13 May 1990)
S. Stein: "André Previn: After Hours, After All," *DB*, lvii/1 (1990), 25
R. L. Doerschuk: "There & Back Again: Conductor/Composer André Previn Rediscovers Jazz," *Keyboard*, xvii/1 (1991), 52
M. Freedland: *André Previn* (London, 1991)
R. Hershenson: "André Previn, Joyful about Playing Jazz for the Neighbors," *New York Times* (7 July 1991)

PAUL RINZLER

Previte, Bobby [Robert] (*b* Niagara Falls, NY, 16 July 1957). Drummer and leader. He first played guitar and took up drums in his early teens; he used home-made instruments until his parents realized how serious he was and bought him a professional set, which he continued to play into the 1990s. While studying classical percussion at the University of Buffalo he was exposed to the avant-garde music of John Cage and Lou Harrison, and he began to focus on jazz drumming after hearing Tony Williams on Miles Davis's album *Filles de Kilimanjaro*. In 1980 Previte moved to New York and worked with the electric guitarist Elliott Sharp. By the mid-1980s he had formed a trio with Wayne Horvitz and Butch Morris and was collaborating with John Zorn. Later he joined the New York Composers Orchestra and played with Horvitz in a rock group, The President; he also worked with the blues musician Bobby Radcliffe (mid-1980s), Tim Berne's group Caos Totale, Billy Bang, Tom Waits, Ray Anderson, Christy Doran, and Jane Ira Bloom (regularly from 1994).

In the early 1990s Previte formed the electric and acoustic band Empty Suits (*c*1990) and the acoustic group Weather

Clear, Track Fast (c1991); he toured Europe with these ensembles in winter 1994 and in 1995 respectively. From around 1996 he led Latin for Travelers, with which he recorded while on tour in Australia (January 1997) and Europe. About the same time he formed an 11-piece ensemble, The Horse (You Rode in on), with which he toured Europe and Canada (1997) and performed at the Knitting Factory (from 1997); this group explores the jazz-rock style of Miles Davis from the late 1960s and that of Weather Report from the early 1970s. The pianist and keyboard player Steve Gaboury and Jerome Harris are among his regular sidemen, and Robin Eubanks, Marty Ehrlich, Don Byron, Andrew D'Angelo, Anthony Davis, and Anthony Cox have taken part in his recordings. In 1997 Previte founded the record company and label Depth of Field, which released an album of duos he recorded with Zorn in the same year, and in October 1998 he presented a week of concerts in a retrospective of his career. He may be seen performing in Robert Altman's film *Short Cuts* (1993).

Previte also works as a composer: he has been commissioned to write music for the String Trio of New York, the chamber ensemble Relâche (1989), and the International Puppet Festival (1992) and has devised the scores to various films. In 1991 he traveled to Russia to rehearse the music he had composed for the Moscow Circus; the circus's American première was held in New York in November 1991, after which Previte continued to perform the music with his own group. While he has been involved with rock and the avant garde, Previte has an energetic, bop-oriented style which reflects the polyrhythmic approach of Tony Williams. His compositions, which often feature characteristically dense textures, draw from a variety of musical sources, including minimalism, film music, and rock, yet are consistently permeated by jazz.

SELECTED RECORDINGS

Duos with J. Zorn: *Euclid's Nightmare* (1997, Depth of Field 1-2)

As leader: *Bump the Renaissance* (1985, Sound Aspects 008); with W. Horvitz and B. Morris: *Nine below Zero* (1986, Sound Aspects 014); *Pushing the Envelope* (1987, Gram. 18-8711-1); *Claude's Late Morning* (1988, Gram. 18-8811-1); *Empty Suits* (1990, Gram. R2-79447); *Weather Clear, Track Fast* (1991, Enja 6082-2); *Music for the Moscow Circus* (1991, Gram. R2-79446); *Slay the Suitors* (1993, Avant 036); *Hue and Cry* (1994, Enja 8064-2); *My Man in Sydney* (1997, Enja 9348-2)

As sideman: Sonny Clark Memorial Quartet: *Voodoo* (1985, BS 0109); T. Varner: *Covert Action* (1987, New Note 1009); M. Ehrlich: *Pliant Plaint* (1987, Enja 5065); *The Traveller's Tale* (1989, Enja 6024-2); T. Berne: *Pace Yourself* (1990, JMT 834442-2); W. Horvitz: *Miracle Mile* (1991, Elek. Mus. 79278-2); C. Doran: *Corporate Art* (1991, JMT 849155-2); M. Ehrlich: *Can You Hear a Motion?* (1993, Enja 8052-2); T. Berne: *Nice View* (1993, JMT 314-514013-2); J. I. Bloom: *The Nearness* (1995, Arabesque 0120)

BIBLIOGRAPHY

CarrJ

B. Milkowski: "Profile: Bobby Previte," *DB*, liv/12 (1987), 54

J. Macnie: "Pen as Mighty as the Stick," *Musician*, no.122 (1988), 12

A. Budofsky: "Bobby Previte," *MD*, xiii/9 (1989), 28

B. Milkowski: "3-Ring Circus: Bobby's Excellent Adventure: Bobby Previte," *DB*, lix/3 (1992), 25 [incl. discography]

<http://members.aol.com/previte/biography.html> (1998)

P. Watrous: "A Drummer, Different and yet in the Groove," *New York Times* (1 Oct 1998)

K. Micallef: "Bobby Previte: Trailblazer," *MD*, xxiii/10 (1999), 70

T. Panken: "Bobby Previte: Assimilation Man," *DB*, lxvi/2 (1999), 34

GK

Prévost, Eddie [Edwin] (*b* Hitchin, England, 22 June 1942). English drummer. In 1965 he was a founding member of the free-jazz group AMM, with which he has remained throughout his career. In the second half of the 1970s he formed a quartet with the trumpeter Gerry Gold, the tenor saxophonist Geoff Hawkins, and the double bass player Marcio Mattos, and in the early 1980s he formed a free-jazz quartet with the saxophonist Larry Stabbins, Veryan Weston, and Mattos, as well as a duo with Weston. He also worked during the 1980s in the trio Resoundings (alongside the saxophonist Pete McPhail and the double bass player Tony Moore), in the group Supersession (with the guitarist Keith Rowe, Evan Parker, and Barry Guy), in a free-jazz quartet (with Paul Rutherford, the reed player Harrison Smith, and Moore, on cello), and in a trio (with the pianist Akemi Kunishoshi-Kuhn and Mattos). While performing with AMM in the 1990s he formed a duo with Marilyn Crispell (1991), recorded in a duo with Evan Parker, worked with EAR (Experimental Audio Research, a loose association consisting mostly of rock musicians), and formed a trio with two younger musicians, the soprano saxophonist Tom Chant and the double bass player John Edwards. Prévost has written in magazines about improvised music and has lectured and led workshops in his own right as well as with AMM. His book *No Sound is Innocent* (Matching Tye, England, 1996), a study of what he calls meta-music, contains a history of AMM. Prévost takes an unconventional approach to drums: he bows cymbals, uses his drums as amplifiers for other sounds, and plays a stringed contra-bass drum.

SELECTED RECORDINGS

(recorded for Matchless unless otherwise indicated)

As unaccompanied soloist: *Loci of Change: Sounds and Sensibility* (1996, 32)

Duos: with K. Rowe (as AMM3): *It Had Been an Ordinary Enough Day in Pueblo, Colorado* (1979, Japo 60031); with E. Parker: *Most Materiall* (1997, 33)

As leader: *Live*, i–ii (1977, 1–2); *Continuum* (1983, 07); *Touch: the Weight, Measure and Feel of Things* (1997, 34)

As sideman: AMM: *The Crypt – 12th June 1968* (1968, 5); Supersession: *Supersession* (1984, 17); AMM: *The Nameless Uncarved Block* (1990, 20); *Newfoundland* (1992, 23)

BIBLIOGRAPHY

V. Schonfield: "We're not Interested in Music," *MM* (5 June 1971), 28

P. Renaud: *La discographie du jazz anglais* (Chaumont, France, 1985)

For further recordings and bibliography *see* AMM.

MARK GILBERT

Prez. Nickname of LESTER YOUNG.

Price, Jesse (*b* Memphis, 1 May 1909; *d* Los Angeles, 19 April 1974). Drummer, bandleader, and singer. He took up drums at the age of 14 and first performed in the pit orchestra at the Palace Theater, Memphis. After touring extensively with major blues singers, in 1934 he moved to Kansas City, where he played with territory bands led by George E. Lee, Thamon Hayes, and Count Basie (this last in 1936). In addition he led his own big band and spent some time in 1938–9 with the trumpeter Dee "Prince" Stewart and briefly on tour with Ida Cox. Price worked with Harlan Leonard (late 1939 – mid-1941) and performed and recorded in Los Angeles with Ella Fitzgerald (briefly in summer 1941). Thereafter he led his own groups, often supporting blues singers, though he also appeared with Walter Fuller (in Chicago, August 1942), Louis Armstrong (for a few months from July 1943), Stan Kenton (May 1944), Basie (October–November 1944), Benny Carter (1948), Slim Gaillard (spring 1949), and Jay McShann (in Kansas City, c1949). In the 1950s and 1960s he worked regularly as a bandleader on the West Coast. Illness ended his career in 1969, but he returned to lead a band at the Monterey Jazz Festival in 1971. Price helped to develop the smooth, understated, but always swinging style of playing that was particularly characteristic of Basie's drummers, and which is well illustrated by his performance on Leonard's *Rock and Ride* (1940). He may be seen in the documentary film *The Last of the Blue Devils* (1979).

Oral history material in *TxU*.

SELECTED RECORDINGS

As leader: Kansas City Mama/You Satisfy (1946, Cap. 295); Sleepy Baby Blues (1946, Cap. 326); Kansas City Boogie (1946, AFRS Jubilee 291)

As sideman: H. Leonard: Rockin' with the Rockets (1940, Bb 10586); Rock and Ride (1940, Bb 10883); first issued on *Harlan Leonard and his Rockets* (1940, RCA LPV531), Take 'em; J. McShann: Bucktown Boogie/ Voodoo Woman Blues (1946, Mer. 8020); I want a little girl/Jimtown Boogie (1946, Mer. 8026)

BIBLIOGRAPHY

ChiltonW

R. Russell: "Master Drummer: Jesse Price," *J&B*, iii/4 (1973), 14

D. Penny: Liner notes, *Jump it with a Shuffle* (Jukebox Lil 620, 1987)

BOB WEIR/HOWARD RYE (recording-list)

Price, Ray (*b* Sydney, 20 Nov 1921; *d* Sydney, 5 Aug 1990). Australian bandleader, banjoist, and guitarist. He gained early experience playing with his family's band, then during his army service (1940–43) worked at the Booker T. Washington Club in Sydney. From at least 1947 he played intermittently with the Port Jackson Jazz Band, a dixieland band of which he was the leader from 1955 to 1965; among its albums during this period were *Jazzin' at the Con* (1957, Jazz Incorporated 001) and *Ray Price and his Port Jackson Jazz Band* (1961, Pix 001–002). In 1949 Price began to play double bass, and later he was a member of the orchestra of the Australian Broadcasting Commission and of the Sydney Symphony Orchestra (from which he was dismissed in 1956 because of his jazz activities). He led a series of groups which toured with government support, and from the mid-1950s to 1980 he presented jazz education programs in schools. Among the numerous Australian jazz musicians who played in his groups were John Sangster, Bob Barnard, and Dick Hughes. He made many recordings as a leader, including *Jazz Party no.1* (1975, Dixie 001). Price retired in 1982 but from 1985 occasionally played at reunions of the Port Jackson Jazz Band.

BIBLIOGRAPHY

D. Hughes: *Daddy's Practising Again: an Australian Jazzman Looks Back and Around* (Melbourne, Australia, 1977)

A. Bissett: *Black Roots, White Flowers: a History of Jazz in Australia* (Sydney, 1979, rev. 2/1987)

B. Johnson: *The Oxford Companion to Australian Jazz* (Melbourne, Australia, 1987)

J. Clare [G. Brennan, pseud.]: *Bodgie Dada and the Cult of Cool* (Sydney, 1995)

J. Mitchell: *Back Together Again: the Story of the Port Jackson Jazz Band* (Sydney, 1995)

W. Bebbington, ed: *The Oxford Companion to Australian Music* (Melbourne, Australia, 1997)

BRUCE JOHNSON/ROGER T. DEAN

Price, Sammy [Sam, Samuel Blythe] (*b* Honey Grove, TX, 6 Oct 1908; *d* New York, 14 April 1992). Pianist and singer. He first toured as a dancer with Alphonso Trent's band and led his own band in Athens, Texas. Later he formed a big band in Dallas and played with theater bands and touring revues. In 1929 he broadcast on radio with Lem Johnson and the trumpeter Leonard Chadwick in Oklahoma City, Oklahoma, and made his first recordings in Dallas, where he was active until 1933. He then worked in Chicago and Detroit (1934–7). In 1937 he became a staff musician for Decca in New York, accompanying many well-known blues and gospel singers, among them Blue Lu Barker. He also led his own group, the Texas Blusicians, which included at various times Lester Young, Emmett Berry, Ike Quebec, J. C. Heard, and Sid Catlett. During the 1940s Price worked mainly as a soloist at clubs in New York. He made an influential series of unaccompanied solo boogie-woogie recordings for Mezz Mezzrow's King Jazz label (1945) and recorded with Mezzrow and Sidney Bechet (1945, 1947). In 1948 he played at the Nice Jazz Festival and toured France. In the early 1950s he lived in Dallas, where he owned two clubs, but thereafter he was based in New York. He toured Europe as the leader of the Blusicians (1955–6) and worked at the Metropole with Henry "Red" Allen (late 1950s and early 1960s) and at Eddie Condon's with Tony Parenti (1962–3). From the 1960s he visited Europe frequently; as well as undertaking several tours he performed at the festivals in Antibes, France (1963), and Lugano, Switzerland (1986). He continued to work in New York, both unaccompanied and with the group Two Tenor Boogie (which involved two tenor saxophonists and a drummer), at such venues as the West End Café and the Cookery, and played until shortly before his death; early in 1992 he appeared with Haywood Henry and Vernel Fournier in a trio at Condon's. Price may be seen with fellow blues musicians in episode 22 of the television show "Jazz USA" (1960) and in the documentary film *Swingmen in Europe* (1977). With C. Richmond he published *What do they Want? A Jazz Autobiography* (Oxford, England, and Chicago, 1989) [incl. discography by B. Weir].

Oral history material in *MoKmh*, *NjR* (JOHP), and *NjR*.

SELECTED RECORDINGS

As unaccompanied soloist: I Finally Gotcha/Boogin' with Mezz (1945, King Jazz 145); *Midnight Boogie* (1969, BB 33025); *Blues and Boogies*, ii (1969, BB 33040)

Duos: with S. Catlett: Boogin' with Big Sid (1945, Dudan 204); with J. C. Heard: *Boogie and Jazz Classics* (1975, BB 33111)

As leader: Sweepin' the Blues Away (1940, Decca 7781); Jumpin' the Blues (1940, Decca 8515); The Goon Drag (1941, Decca 8547); Do you dig my jive? (1941, Decca 8575); Harlem Gin Blues (1941, Decca 8609); *The Price is Right* (1956, Jzt. 1260); *Blues and Boogie Woogie* (1959, World Wide 20016); *The New Sammy Price: King of Boogie-woogie* (1975, Mahogany 558102); with D. Cheatham: *Black Beauty: a Salute to Black American Songwriters* (1979, Sack. 3029)

As sideman: Cow Cow Davenport: The Mess is Here (1938, Decca 7813); B. L. Barker: That made him mad (1938, Decca 7538); J. Rushing: *Going to Chicago* (1954, Van. 8011); S. Bechet: *Sidney Bechet with Sammy Price's Blusicians* (1956, Swing 30041)

BIBLIOGRAPHY

ChiltonW

J. Bradley: "Sammy Price Goes to Church," *Coda*, iii/11 (1961), 22; iv/2 (1961), 25

M. Jones: "Call it Sam's Song," *MM* (20 Dec 1969), 12

J. Simmen: "Samuel B. Price," *BHcF*, no.196 (1970), 3; no.197 (1970), 6; no.198 (1970), 5

B. Rusch: "Sammy Price: Oral History," *Cadence*, ii/10–11 (1977), 3

V. Montgomery: "Texas Bluesician Sammy Price," *JJI*, xxxv (1982), no.10, p.9; no.11, p.6 [incl. discography]

D. Kochakian: "The Legacy of Sam Price," *Whiskey, Women, and . . .*, nos.12–13 (1983), 8 [incl. discography]

B. Osgood: "Sam Price," *MR*, x/9 (1983), 6

H. Bordowitz: "World View: Sammy Price: Witness to the Birth of Boogie-woogie," *Keyboard*, xvi/1 (1990), 27

J. Demêtre: "Sammy Price," *Soul Bag*, no.127 (1992), 22

Obituaries: P. Watrous, *New York Times* (16 April 1992); D. Penny, *Blues & Rhythm*, no.70 (1992), 16

J. Simmen: "Personality Galore: Sammy Price," *BHcF*, no.405 (1992), 27

J. Demêtre and M. Chauvard: *Voyage au pays du blues/Land of the Blues* (Levallois-Perret, France, 1994) [Fr. and Eng. text]

MICHAEL TOVEY/HOWARD RYE (recording-list)

Priester, Julian (Anthony) [Mtoto, Pepo] (*b* Chicago, 29 June 1935). Trombonist. He studied piano as a child, took up euphonium while in his teens, and changed to trombone two years later. Having first played blues with Muddy Waters and rhythm-and-blues with Bo Diddley, in 1954 he joined Sun Ra's ensemble, for which he supplied arrangements (among them his own composition *Urnack*) and with which he recorded; he left after two years to tour with Lionel Hampton. After working for a year with Dinah Washington he moved to New York, and in 1958 he joined a group led by Max Roach that at various times included Booker Little, Clifford Jordan, and Eric Dolphy; he also recorded with Philly Joe Jones (1959), Johnny Griffin (1959–60), Tommy Turrentine (1960), and Freddie Hubbard, Abbey Lincoln, Little, and Harold Ousley (all 1961). Priester retired from Roach's group to work as a freelance in recording studios and pit orchestras in New York, and he made further recordings as a sideman in sessions led by Clifford Jordan (1965–9), Blue Mitchell and Stanley Turrentine (both 1966–7), Duke Pearson's big band, Sam Rivers, and McCoy Tyner (all 1967), and Lee Morgan and Lonnie Smith (both 1969). In 1965 he played with Clark Terry's big band, late in 1969 he toured Europe with the Thad Jones–Mel Lewis Orchestra, and for six months in 1969–70 he was a member of Duke Ellington's orchestra. From 1970 to 1973 he was with Herbie Hancock's sextet, during which time he took the Swahili name Pepo Mtoto. Later he worked in the San Francisco area, where he made recordings with Stanley Cowell (1977–8) and Red Garland's quintet (1979); in the 1980s he recorded with Dave Holland (1983, 1984) and George Gruntz's big band (1983).

After settling in Seattle, Priester joined the faculty of the Cornish College of the Arts, where he remained through the 1990s. He recorded in Portland with David Friesen (in concert in 1987), in Seattle with Jay Clayton (also in concert in 1987) and Jerry Granelli (from 1990), and on the East Coast with Jordan and Ran Blake (1989), Reggie Workman (1993, 1995), and Jane Ira Bloom (1995); he took a major role as a soloist on Granelli's album of blues pieces in various jazz styles, *A Song I Thought I Heard Buddy Sing* (1992). In 1994, at Yoshi's in Oakland, California, an evening of the Eddie Moore Jazz Festival was devoted to Priester's compositions, performed by a sextet under the leadership of the guitarist John Schott and by Priester's own quartet, consisting of Bobby Hutcherson, Anthony Cox, and Billy Hart.

SELECTED RECORDINGS

As leader: *Spiritsville* (1958, Jlnd 25); *Polarization* (1977, ECM 1098)

As sideman: Sun Ra: *Angels and Demons at Play* (1956, 1960, Sat. 9956-2-O/P), incl. Urnack (1956); *Super-sonic Jazz* (*c*1955, Sat. H70P0216); *Jazz by Sun Ra* (1956, Tran. 10); M. Roach: *Percussion Bitter Sweet* (1961, Imp. 8); H. Hancock: *Mwandishi* (1970, WB 1898); B. Harper: *Capra-black* (1973, SE 19739); R. Garland: *Strike up the Band* (1979, Gal. 5135); J. Granelli: *A Song I Thought I Heard Buddy Sing* (1992, ITM-Pacific 970066)

BIBLIOGRAPHY

E. Chadbourne: "Wandering Spirit Song: Pepo's Interview," *Coda*, xii/2 (1974), 2

M. Crooks: "Julian Priester: Interview," *Cadence*, iv/1 (1978), 12

H. Geerken and B. Hefele: *Omniverse Sun Ra* (Wartaweil, Germany, 1994)

J. F. Szwed: *Space is the Place: the Lives and Times of Sun Ra* (New York, 1997)

DAVID WILD/BK

Priestley, Brian (*b* Manchester, England, 10 July 1946). English pianist and writer. After private piano tuition he led college groups at Leeds University (BA French), played with Roy Bower's sextet in Manchester (1964), and, having moved to Oxford, arranged for the National Youth Jazz Orchestra (late 1960s). He settled in London in 1969 and played in bands led by the drummer Tony Faulkner and by Alan Cohen, the latter an association which continued into the 1980s. He led his own trio in the early 1970s, played with the quintet of the tenor saxophonists Dave Gelly and Jeff Scott in the mid-1970s, and with Gelly and the drummer Ken Hyder led Stylus (1979–80). In 1980 he formed a group with Don Rendell that was variously a sextet or septet; it remained active in the 1990s. An accomplished solo pianist, often performing at Kettner's Restaurant, London, Priestley recorded an album of unaccompanied performances, and duos with Don Rendell, in 1994 (*You Taught my Heart to Sing*, Spirit of Jazz 09-0995). He taught jazz piano at Goldsmith's College from 1977 to 1993, and has held jazz workshops there and at other colleges, as well as jazz history classes.

With Cohen, Priestley recorded the first complete transcription of Duke Ellington's composition *Black, Brown, and Beige* (1972, Argo 159). He has made many transcriptions of the works of Ellington, including *Creole Rhapsody* for the New York Jazz Repertory Company (1977), *In the Beginning, God* (1982), and *Cottontail*, *C-jam Blues*, and *Caravan* (all 1984). He has also prepared transcriptions for the Midnite Follies Orchestra and Stan Tracey, and has published six anthologies of piano transcriptions (1982–90). He is a frequent broadcaster, and from 1971 to 1988 presented the weekly program "All that Jazz" for BBC Radio London; later he broadcast on London's Jazz FM. Priestley writes prolifically: he has contributed regularly to the journals *Melody Maker*, *Down Beat*, *Jazz Journal International*, *Jazz Express*, and *The Wire*, and has published several books, among them a major biography of Charles Mingus, a history of recorded jazz, and, with Ian Carr and Digby Fairweather, one of the central reference sources in the field, *Jazz: the Essential Companion* (updated as *Jazz: the Rough Guide*).

WRITINGS

(selective list)

Mingus: a Critical Biography (London, Melbourne, Australia, and New York, 1982)

Charlie Parker (Tunbridge Wells, England, and New York, 1984) [incl. discography]

John Coltrane (London, 1987) [incl. discography]

with I. Carr and D. Fairweather: *Jazz: the Essential Companion* (London, 1987)

Jazz on Record: a History (London, 1988)

with I. Carr and D. Fairweather: *Jazz: the Essential Companion* (London, 1987, rev. 2/1995, as *Jazz: the Rough Guide*, 3/2000) [*CarrJ*]

DIGBY FAIRWEATHER/SIMON ADAMS

Prima, Leon (*b* New Orleans, 28 July 1907; *d* Mississippi, Aug 1985). Trumpeter, brother of Louis Prima. He began studying piano but later learned trumpet. After working with Leon Roppolo, Ray Bauduc, and Jack Teagarden he joined Peck Kelley's Bad Boys in Texas (1925), then returned to New Orleans, where he led the Melody Masters with Sharkey Bonano (*c*1928–1930). From 1940 to 1946 he played with his brother's orchestra in New York, following which he led his own small band in New Orleans until 1955, when he ceased full-time performing. His recordings as a leader include *Leon Prima and his New Orleans Jazz Band* (1954, Slnd 210). The social security death index gives his last known residence as Bay Saint Louis, Mississippi. (*FeatherE*)

MIKE HAZELDINE

Prima, Louis [Loui, Louie] (*b* New Orleans, 7 Dec 1911; *d* New Orleans, 24 Aug 1978). Trumpeter and singer, brother of Leon Prima. He studied violin from 1918. After teaching himself trumpet in 1925 he performed locally, and he remained in New Orleans until 1935 except for brief spells with Red Nichols in Cleveland (*c*1932) and in New York (1934), where he made a number of recordings for Brunswick. His residency at the Famous Door, New York, in 1935 was followed by long-term engagements in Chicago and Los Angeles. In the 1940s he led a big band, but in the 1950s and 1960s he again worked with small groups. He was married for a time (1952–61) to the singer Keely Smith (*b* Norfolk, VA, 9 March 1932), and together they achieved great commercial success with recordings in a popular style. Prima also appeared in many films, including *The Benny Goodman Story* (1955), and undertook lengthy engagements in Las Vegas. His hoarse singing and extrovert trumpet playing were influenced by Louis Armstrong, but both his diction and his fingering technique displayed a more flashy approach. After 1940 his style became overtly commercialized and closer to cabaret than to jazz; except for those made for Brunswick in the 1930s, his recordings are not generally representative of his qualities as a jazz musician.

SELECTED RECORDINGS

(all recorded for Brunswick)

Let's Have a Jubilee (1934, 7394); It's the Rhythm in Me (1934, 7471); Dinah (1936, 7666); Let's Get Together and Swing (1936, 7740)

SELECTED FILMS AND VIDEOS

Swing it (1936); Vitaphone Variété (1936); Manhattan Merry-go-round [Manhattan Music Box] (1937); Swing Cats Jamboree (1938); New Orleans Blues (1943)

BIBLIOGRAPHY

ChiltonW
"Backstage with Louis Prima and Keely Smith," *DB*, xxvi/4 (1959), 14
A. Shaw: *The Street that Never Slept: New York's Fabled 52nd Street* (New York, 1971/*R*1977 as *52nd Street: the Street of Jazz*)
C. Garrod: *Louis Prima and his Orchestra* (Zephyrhills, FL, 1991) [discography]

MIKE HAZELDINE

Prima Materia. Quintet formed around 1994 by Rashied Ali in an effort to re-create the style of classic free jazz of the mid-1960s, principally the works of John Coltrane and Albert Ayler. It originally comprised Allan Chase (alto saxophone), Louie Belogenis (tenor saxophone), Joe Gallant and William Parker (both on double bass), and Ali (drums); in 1995 Parker was replaced by the pianist Greg Murphy. The group performed at the North Sea Jazz Festival that year and at the Knitting Factory's Heineken What is Jazz? Festival in 1996. Its first two recordings re-created works associated with Coltrane, and its third, *Bells* (1996, Knitting Factory Works 190), which best represents the group's oeuvre, pays tribute to Ayler. Prima Materia should not be confused with a quartet of the same name from Boston that recorded around 1992.

GK

Prime Time. Band formed in 1975 by ORNETTE COLEMAN.

Prina, Curt (*b* Zurich, 31 Aug 1928). Swiss pianist, organist, and keyboard player. He took up accordion at the age of six and piano when he was ten, and later added trumpet, trombone, double bass, vibraphone, organ, and other keyboards to his instrumentarium. At the age of 16 he formed a big band which performed his own arrangements. In 1946 he toured Spain with the bandleader Bob Huber, and in 1948 he joined Fred Böhler's sextet as vibraphonist, pianist, organist, and arranger. He left Böhler in 1950, formed his own sextet, then in 1952 replaced Pierre Cavalli in Hazy Osterwald's sextet, with which he toured internationally until it disbanded in 1978; he may be heard on the album *Hazy Osterwald Show* (1954, Ex Libris 603). Prina also appeared on television and played for films. From 1978 he served as an adviser and a touring demonstrator for the company WERSI, which builds pianos and organs. (T. Gulz: "Curt Prina: Kosmopolit, Musik- und Sprachengenie," *Okey!*, no.12 (1996), 4)

OTTO FLÜCKIGER

Prince, Roland (Don Matthew) (*b* St. John's, Antigua, 27 Aug 1946). Antiguan guitarist. After living in Toronto (mid-1960s), where he played with local musicians, he moved to New York (1969). There he performed with Brother Jack McDuff (1969–70), Billy Mitchell (from 1970), Wynton Kelly, Art Blakey (1971), Stanley Turrentine, and Jimmy Smith (1974) and also led his own trio. Prince toured Europe and Japan and made recordings with Elvin Jones (1974–8, including *New Agenda*, 1975, Van. 79362) and took part in sessions with Roy Haynes (*c*1972), James Moody (1975), Frank Foster (1976), and Don Pullen (1976–7). (*Feather–Gitler '70s*)

Prince of Darkness. Nickname of MILES DAVIS.

Pring, Bobby [Robert Edward, Jr.] (*b* New Bedford, MA, 28 Nov 1924). Trombonist. After playing in an army air force band (1943–6) he settled on the West Coast and worked briefly with Tony Pastor and Herbie Fields (1946). He played first trombone in the orchestras of Tex Beneke (1946–9) and Les Brown (1950–56) and also performed with Pee Wee Russell (1950). From 1958 to 1976 he was active primarily as a studio musician and freelance; he played with Benny Goodman in 1960–61 at Disneyland and led his own band from 1971 to 1977, when he moved to New York. There he worked at Eddie Condon's and Jimmy Ryan's, playing small group jazz with Max Kaminsky and Roy Eldridge (both 1978–83), and was a member of Vince Giordano's Nighthawks (1979–83). Pring has also appeared with Loren Schoenberg's big band (from 1981), Marty Grosz (from 1981), the Goodman big band (1985), Buck Clayton's big band (1986–91), the Harlem Blues and Jazz Band (from 1993), and the Smithsonian Jazz Masterworks Orchestra.

SELECTED RECORDINGS

As sideman: D. Meldonian: *'S Wonderful* (1982, Cir. 150); B. Clayton: *A Swingin' Dream* (1988, Stash 281); L. Schoenberg: *Just a-Settin' and a-Rockin'* (1989, Musicmasters 5039-2)

BIBLIOGRAPHY

ConnorBG

GK

Printup, Marcus (Edward) (*b* Conyers, GA, 24 Jan 1967). Trumpeter. He played in a funk band while at school and later studied music at the University of North Florida (BM 1992). In 1992 he began working with Marcus Roberts and the following year he joined the Lincoln Center Jazz Orchestra. He also performed with Billy Taylor (ii), Betty Carter, and Wynton Marsalis, with whom he may be seen in the video *Accent on the Offbeat* (*c*1994), and formed his own quartet (1994). Printup moved in November 1997 to Los

Angeles, where he worked in the Clayton–Hamilton Jazz Orchestra and continued to lead a quartet in 1998, with Billy Childs, Darek Oleszkiewicz, and Gregory Hutchinson as his sidemen. In addition, as co-leader with Tim Hagans, he recorded (1997) and toured (1998) with a Freddie Hubbard tribute group.

SELECTED RECORDINGS

As leader: *Song for the Beautiful Woman* (1994, BN B21Z-30790); *Unveiled* (1996, BN 37302-2); with T. Hagans: *Hubsongs* (1997, BN 56509-2)
As sideman: Carl Allen: *The Pursuer* (1993, Atl. 82572-2); M. Roberts: *Blues for the New Millenium* (1996–7, Col. CK68637)

BIBLIOGRAPHY

"Auditions," *DB*, lix/4 (1992), 62
O. Cordle: "Tradin' Fours: all the Right Grooves," *DB*, lxii/6 (1995), 37
S. Dollar: "Printup Lends Updated Slant to Old-school Swing," *Atlanta Journal Constitution* (10 Sept 1995)
N. Hentoff: "Heralding the Trumpeter," *Wall Street Journal* (18 Dec 1996)
B. Kohlhaase: "No Pianist? No Problem for Trumpeter Marcus Printup," *Los Angeles Times* (9 May 1998)

GK

Privin, Bernie [Bernard] (*b* New York, 12 Feb 1919; *d* New York, 8 Oct 1999). Trumpeter. He was self-taught and performed locally from the age of 16. In 1937 he joined Harry Reser, after which he played with Bunny Berigan and Tommy Dorsey. He worked in 1938–9 with Artie Shaw, who gave him considerable prominence. In 1940–41 he was a member of Charlie Barnet's band, which he rejoined in 1943 after working with the clarinetist Mal Hallett (1941) and Benny Goodman (December 1941 – June 1942). During his military service Privin was the trumpet soloist in Glenn Miller's Army Air Force Band (June 1943 – January 1946), with which he worked in Europe. Following his discharge he returned to Goodman's band for several months, worked for NBC, then spent 22 years as a staff musician for CBS. During this period he also took part in many recording sessions, mostly with big bands, including those of Sy Oliver (1949–51), and Goodman (intermittently 1951–61), and he recorded as a soloist with the guitarist Al Caiola (1955). In the 1960s he achieved popularity in Sweden, where he performed several times, and during the 1970s he worked as a freelance: he toured Europe with the Tommy Dorsey Orchestra under Warren Covington and with Pee Wee Erwin (both 1974) and visited Russia with the New York Jazz Repertory Company (1975). Privin remained active into the early 1990s.

SELECTED RECORDINGS

As leader: *Dancing and Dreaming* (1956, Regent 6027); When did you leave heaven?/East of the Sun (1969, HMT 7BD-268)
As sideman: A. Shaw: *In the Blue Room/In the Cafe Rouge* (1938–9, RCA LPT6000); C. Barnet: Lois (1941, Bb 11265); G. Miller: I can't give you anything but love (1944, V-disc 482); Jazz Club Mystery Hot Band: If Dreams Come True (1944, JCF 121); M. Powell: Avalon (1946, Com. 1522); V. Giordano: *New Orleans Night Hawks* (1980, GHB 98)

BIBLIOGRAPHY

ChiltonW; *ConnorBG*; *FeatherE*
L. Karlsson: "Bernie Privin," *JJ*, xxvii/4 (1974), 4
A. Stevens: "Privin Blows on Strong," *MM* (21 Dec 1974), 22
L. Tomkins: "The Bernie Privin Story," *CI*, xii/12 (1974), 9
B. Korall: Liner notes, A. Shaw: *The Complete Artie Shaw*, ii: *1939* (RCA AXM2-5533, 1977)
G. Butcher: *Next to a Letter from Home: Major Glenn Miller's Wartime Band* (Edinburgh, 1986, rev. 2/1994) [incl. discography]
Obituary, B. Peerless, *JJI*, liii/1 (2000), 19

BRIAN PEERLESS

Probert, George (Arthur, Jr.) (*b* Los Angeles, 5 March 1927). Soprano saxophonist, clarinetist, and bandleader. He performed and made recordings with Bob Scobey (1950–53) and with Kid Ory (notably, *Creole Jazz Band 1954*, 1954, GTJ 12004). From 1954 to 1969 he played and recorded with the FIREHOUSE FIVE PLUS TWO, a traditional-jazz band formed from employees of the Walt Disney studio, and in 1955 he became the music director of the studio. During the same period he recorded with Georg Brunis (1957, 1968). From 1973 Probert led bands that performed traditional jazz on the West Coast and in Europe: he appeared frequently in the Netherlands at the Oude Stijl Jazz Festival Breda and recorded at the Manassas Jazz Festival (1973) and in Budapest with the Benkó Dixieland Band (1978). While continuing to tour extensively and to perform at jazz festivals, in the mid-1990s he recorded as a leader (notably the album *By George! It's Probert in England*, 1995, Jazz Crusade 3021) and with Bob Helm as a member of the small group Reed Renaissance (1996). In May 2000 he was one of the featured performers at the Sacramento Jazz Jubilee. (R. Cremer: "George Probert and his Happy Riff Machine," *6e internationale Oude stijl Jazz Festival: Breda, 27–30 May 1976* (Breda, Netherlands, 1976), 34 [program book])

Procope, Russell (*b* New York, 11 Aug 1908; *d* New York, 21 Jan 1981). Alto saxophonist and clarinetist. He learned violin for eight years before taking up clarinet and alto saxophone as a teenager. He performed and recorded as a clarinetist with Jelly Roll Morton (June 1928 – April 1929), then played alto saxophone and clarinet in the big bands of Benny Carter, with whom he was at the Arcadia Ballroom in autumn 1929, and Chick Webb, whom he joined by the end of that year. He remained with Webb until March 1931, when in a celebrated exchange Procope and Benny Morton went to Fletcher Henderson's band in return for Carter and Jimmy Harrison. Procope's big-band experiences continued with Henderson (to November 1934), Tiny Bradshaw, Teddy Hill (1935–7), with whom he toured Europe in 1937, and Willie Bryant. From 1938 to 1943 he was the alto saxophonist in John Kirby's sextet. During his army service he was stationed in New York, where he continued to play, mainly in shows. He rejoined Kirby for a brief period in 1945 before becoming a member of Duke Ellington's orchestra the following year, and he remained with Ellington until 1974, except for a spell with Wilbur De Paris in 1961. After Ellington's death he played in New York, where he worked with Sonny Greer in Brooks Kerr's trio, performed in the musical *Ain't Misbehavin'*, and led the group Ellingtonia. Although he recorded as a soloist with Morton, Henderson, Hill, and Kirby, early in his career Procope was not an innovative improviser and was valued chiefly as a reliable section player. His reading of *Mood Indigo* (1950) established his later reputation as a bluesy, warm-toned clarinetist.

Oral history material in *CtY*, *NjR*, *NjR* (JOHP).

For illustrations *see* BAILEY, BUSTER, ELLINGTON, DUKE, fig.2, HENDERSON, FLETCHER, and KIRBY, JOHN.

SELECTED RECORDINGS

As sideman: J. R. Morton: Red Hot Pepper/Deep Creek (1928, Vic. 38055); F. Henderson: I'm crazy 'bout my baby (1931, Mlt. 12145); Blue Rhythm (1931, Crown 3180); T. Hill: Blue Rhythm Fantasy (1936, Voc. 3247); The Harlem Twister (1937, Bb 6908); J. Kirby: It's only a Paper Moon/Fifi's Rhapsody (1941, Vic. 27598); D. Ellington: *Masterpieces* (1950, Col. ML4418), incl. Mood Indigo; The Mooche (1952, Col. B1629); C. Anderson: *Cat Anderson Plays at 4 a.m.* (1958, Col. FPX116); D. Ellington: *Duke Ellington's Seventieth Birthday Concert* (1969, SolS 19000), incl. 4.30 Blues

SELECTED FILMS AND VIDEOS

Mood Indigo (1952); Anatomy of a Murder (1959); Duke Ellington and his

Orchestra (1962); Duke Ellington: Love You Madly (1967); On the Road with Duke Ellington (1974); Memories of Duke (1980)

BIBLIOGRAPHY

AllenH; *ChiltonW*
J. Armitage: "Russell Procope," *Jazz Music Mirror*, v/7 (1958), 5
S. Dance: "Russell Procope," *JJ*, xvi (1963), no.1, p.14; no.2, p.4
R. Procope: "Wonderful, Wonderful Jazz," *JJ*, xx/5 (1967), 6
J. R. T. Davies and L. Wright: *Morton's Music* (London, 1968)
S. Dance: *The World of Duke Ellington* (London and New York, 1970/*R* 1981)
G. Colombé: "Russell Procope," *JJI*, xxxiv/4 (1981), 10
M. Berger, E. Berger, and J. Patrick: *Benny Carter: a Life in American Music* (Metuchen, NJ, and London, 1982)
J. Armitage: "Russell Procope," *BHcF*, no.331 (1985), 7
T. T. Reed: *Jimmy Hamilton and Russell Procope: The Clarinet Soloists of the Duke Ellington Orchestra, 1943–1974* (diss., Ohio State U., 1995)

BK

Profit, Clarence (*b* New York, 26 June 1912; *d* New York, 22 Oct 1944). Pianist and leader. He began playing at the age of three, and during his teens he performed with local dance bands, broadcast with Edgar Sampson, and held a number of engagements in New York as the leader of his own ten-piece band. In 1930-31 he was a member of Teddy Bunn's Washboard Serenaders. After visiting Antigua in the West Indies he led an octet there and also worked in Bermuda and St. Kitts. In 1936 he returned to New York and formed his own trio, which was resident at several well-known clubs, including Kelly's Stable (1940–43). By the time he made his first recordings Profit was already an able and energetic stride pianist, as may be heard on the Washboard Serenaders' *Teddy's Blues/Tappin' the Time Away* (1930, Vic. 38610). In his maturity he achieved a greater delicacy of touch and originality of melodic and harmonic ideas (evident on his own trio's *Times Square Blues/Hot and Bothered*, 1940, Decca 8503); his playing was widely influential and he became a favorite opponent of Art Tatum's in cutting contests.

BIBLIOGRAPHY

ChiltonW; *FeatherE*
J. Simmen: "Clarence Profit," *JM*, no.180 (1970), 14; Fr. version, as "Un grand pianiste peu remarqué: Clarence Profit," *BHcF*, no.204 (1971), 7

HOWARD RYE

Progressive. Record company and label. The company was established in New York in 1950 by Gus Statiras, but it has functioned only sporadically from that time. Its first recordings were by Al Cohn, who later recorded twice more for the label (1953, 1954); the catalogue also contained two albums by George Wallington (1951, 1955). In the late 1950s, however, operations declined for several years, and much of the material was later sold to and reissued by Savoy. In 1970 some items recorded by Cohn for Progressive in 1954 but never released were issued on Prestige. The company became active again in the late 1970s, cooperating with the Japanese company Baybridge to reissue the excellent album *George Wallington Quartet at Cafe Bohemia* (1955) in a new format that included some previously unreleased material. This was followed by newly recorded albums by J. R. Monterose, Al Haig, and Tommy Flanagan, among others; the sessions were supervised by Statiras, who also took photographs and wrote notes for the liners. All new material was issued with facsimiles of the label of the 1950s. In the mid-1980s the company was purchased by Jazzology, which continued to offer LP and CD reissues of its material.

MARK GARDNER

Progressive jazz. A term applied, mainly in the 1940s and 1950s, to continuations and extensions of the jazz orchestral tradition. It is associated chiefly with the more ambitious parts of the output of Stan Kenton's large band, though it is also applied to shorter-lived ensembles of Boyd Raeburn and, less importantly, Earle Spencer; it is used, too, in connection with a few bands whose main activity lay elsewhere, for example, the group with which Charlie Barnet recorded some excellent pieces for Capitol in 1949, such as *Cu-ba* (Cap. 15417).

The music of these bands grew directly out of that of the big swing groups of the 1930s and early 1940s – Kenton's *Intermission Riff* (1946, Cap. 298), for instance, using the same theme as Jimmie Lunceford's *Yard Dog Mazurka* (1941, Decca 4032). In pieces such as *Chorale for Brass, Piano and Bongos* (1947, Cap. 10183) and *Fugue for Rhythm Section* (1947, Cap. 10127), however, Kenton and, more particularly, Pete Rugolo (Kenton's chief composer and arranger during this period) arrived at a significant further development of orchestral jazz. This was consolidated by later recordings by Kenton, such as Bill Holman's *Invention for Guitar and Trumpet* (1952, Cap. EAP2-383). In partial contrast, Bob Graettinger's music for the Kenton band made additional use of a medium-sized string section and a considerably more dissonant harmonic vocabulary, and conveyed a dark emotional turbulence that almost invoked the Second Viennese School. An example is the four-movement *City of Glass* (1951, Cap. 28062–3).

Boyd Raeburn's output during the same period was also self-consciously modernistic, as is suggested by titles such as *Boyd meets Stravinsky* (1946, Jwl 10002). Yet the scores, by George Handy (a pupil of Aaron Copland), Ed Finckel and others, retain their interest; their characteristically complex textures and dissonant harmony were qualified by the exhilaratingly full-throated power of the band's performance. Raeburn also performed works in a quieter, pastel-toned vein, exemplified by Handy and Hal McKusick's *Yerxa* (1945, Jwl 10001).

In the late 1950s the term "progressive jazz" was also used as a synonym for "modern jazz."

See also Forms, §4, and Jazz (i), §V, 6.

BIBLIOGRAPHY

A. Jackson: "Boyd Raeburn," *JM*, xii/11 (1966), 5
M. Sparke and P. Venudor with J. Hartley: *Kenton on Capitol and Creative World: a Discography* (Lake Geneva, WI, 1994)
A. Morgan: "The Progressives," *Jazz on Record: a Critical Guide to the First 50 Years: 1917–1967*, ed. A. McCarthy and others (London, 1968), 361
M. Harrison: "Stan Kenton: the 'Innovations' Band," *JJI*, xxxii (1979), no.4, p.4; no.5, p.18
W. F. Lee: *Stan Kenton: Artistry in Rhythm* (Los Angeles, 1980/*R*1994) [incl. discography; *R* without discography]

MAX HARRISON

Projazz. Record company and label founded in the late 1980s by Al Hirt.

Prowizorka Jazz Band. Polish traditional-jazz and swing quintet formed in 1983 by Tomasz Sacha, who plays the "gobophone" (consisting of a kazoo blown into a beerglass). Its members have included the clarinetist, soprano saxophonist, and arranger Ryszard Kwaśniewski, the tenor and soprano saxophonist Piotr Cieślikowski, the guitarist Jacek Korohoda, the banjoists Paweł Tartanus and Henryk Stefański (or, instead of banjo, a second guitarist, Jan Kalinowski), and the double bass player Stanisław Piotrowski;

unusually for this sort of group, there is no drummer. Among its recordings are *Moonlighting* (1985, Tim. 526) and *Prowizorka Jazz Band* (1989, Tim. 558), as well as an album made in the late 1990s with a seven-piece Russian traditional-jazz group, the Uralsky All Stars (i.e., together forming a 12-piece band with drums).

BIBLIOGRAPHY

<http://www.timelessjazz.com/prowizorka_jazzband.html> (2000)
<http://www.wwmusic.com/timeless/rel/d617.html> (2000)

BK

Pruitt, Carl (Briggs) (*b* Birmingham, AL, 3 June 1918; *d* June 1977). Double bass player. He took up piano in 1934 and changed to double bass in 1937, by which time he was living in Pittsburgh. After leaving Pittsburgh he performed and made recordings with Cootie Williams (to June 1945), Roy Eldridge, Maxine Sullivan (to September 1945), the Jeter–Pillars Orchestra (with which he toured Japan and various military bases in the Pacific, 1945–6), Lucky Millinder (1946–8), and Mary Lou Williams (from 1948). From 1953 he played intermittently in concerts and clubs and at recording sessions as a member of Earl Hines's group; while with the band he made national tours (into 1954) and appeared at the Embers in New York (late in 1959). In 1955 he performed briefly with the Sauter–Finegan Orchestra. His principal work, however, was as a studio musician, and from 1949 into the mid-1950s he recorded with a number of blues and rhythm-and-blues musicians, among them Bullmoose Jackson, Wynonie Harris, Arnett Cobb, and Bill Doggett; he later took part in sessions with Sahib Shihab and Roland Kirk (both 1956), Eddie "Lockjaw" Davis and Hal Singer (both 1957), and Shorty Baker and George Shearing (both 1958). Although he was less active after 1960, Pruitt recorded at the Monterey Jazz Festival with Woody Herman in 1967, in New York with Ray Nance in 1969, and, while performing in France, with both Sammy Price and Doc Cheatham in 1975. The social security death index gives his last known residence as Pittsburgh.

SELECTED RECORDINGS

As sideman: C. Williams: Somebody's gotta go/'Round Midnight (1944, Hit 7119); *Cootie Williams with Charlie Parker* (1945, Alamac 2440), incl. Floogie boo; W. Harris: Tremblin' (1951, King 4448); M. L. Williams: *Piano Panorama* (1951, Atl. 114); B. Jackson: Cherokee Boogie (1951, King 4472); B. Doggett: on *Dance Awhile with Doggett* (1953–8, King 585), Smoochie (1957); S. Price: *Fire* (1975, BB 33079); D. Cheatham: *Hey Doc* (1975, BB 30090)

BIBLIOGRAPHY

FeatherE
S. Dance: "Earl's Four," *JJ*, xiii/7 (1960), 9
——: *The World of Earl Hines* (New York, 1977)

HOWARD RYE, BK

Prysock, Red [Wilburt] (*b* Pomona, NC, 2 Feb 1925; *d* New York, 19 July 1993). Tenor saxophonist and leader. His given name is generally quoted as Wilbert, but his own social security application has the spelling Wilburt and also his place and date of birth, which differ from previous accounts. After starring in a military band during army service (1944–7) he joined Tiny Grimes, with whom he recorded (1948–9). In 1950 he was with Roy Milton for about a month and then traveled with a show to Tulsa, Oklahoma; he returned to New York as a member of the Sweethearts of Rhythm. From January 1951 to early 1953 he played with Tiny Bradshaw. Following a period with Cootie Williams he formed his own band (1954), which recorded for Mercury (to 1960). In 1955–6 he was extensively featured by the rock-and-roll disc jockey Alan Freed on his shows and tours. Prysock's simple rhythmic phrasing and overt emotionalism, heard at its apogee on *Wiggles/Cryin' my Heart Out* (1952, Red Robin 107), typifies the transition from jump to rhythm-and-blues. He was capable of the more sober approach heard on *Body and Soul* (1954, Mer. 70367) but was among the most successful of those who made the crossover to rock-and-roll by simplifying their music. When the craze passed Prysock led a smaller group, and in the 1960s he was employed mainly as an accompanist for soul singers. After 1971 he worked in clubs with his brother, the singer Arthur Prysock (*b* Greensboro, NC, 2 Jan 1924), and in July 1990 they appeared together at the North Sea Jazz Festival.

BIBLIOGRAPHY

B. Niquet: "Deux précurseurs: Red Prysock, Al Sears," *Soul Bag*, no.65 (1978), 7 [incl. discography]
J. Bernholm: Liner notes, *Cryin' my Heart Out* (Saxophonograph 502, 1983)
Obituaries: S. McGarvey, *Juke Blues*, no.30 (1994), 27; M. Redenac, *Soul Bag*, no.135 (1994), 27
C. B. Wirtz: "Backside: Double Visionaries," *Musician*, no.211 (1997), 98

HOWARD RYE

Ptaszyn [Ptak]. Nickname of JAN WRÓBLEWSKI.

Puente, Tito [Ernest Anthony, Jr.; El Rey] (*b* New York, 20 April 1923; *d* New York, 31 May 2000). Timbales player and leader. He grew up in Spanish Harlem and as a child studied piano, sang in a street corner group, and took tap-dance lessons. He gave up piano to study the drum set, and at the age of 13 took up timbales to work professionally in Afro-Cuban bands. Around 1938 he left school and moved to Miami to play during the winter with José Curbelo's orchestra. When he returned to New York he worked with the pianist Noro Morales at the Stork Club, with Curbelo, and briefly in Machito's Afro-Cubans (1941). He then spent three years in the navy, during which time he taught himself saxophone and led a band. Later he studied composition and orchestration at the Juilliard School, played and wrote arrangements for Machito, Curbelo, and others, and served as music director for Pupi Campo's band.

In 1949 Puente formed his own group, the Picadilly Boys, which had a heavy brass sound influenced by that of Stan Kenton's orchestra. During the 1950s and early 1960s the orchestra worked regularly at the Palladium and occasionally at Birdland and the Royal Roost. Although his albums of this period focused on Afro-Cuban dance music, Puente recorded *Puente Goes Jazz* (1956) and *Night Beat* (1957) as crossovers into the jazz market; the latter features Doc Severinsen on trumpet. Puente continued to record and perform, often accompanying singers such as Celia Cruz, but by the late 1960s his popularity had declined. However, his career was resuscitated by Carlos Santana's rock recording of Puente's composition *Oye como va* (1970), and he subsequently became a leading figure in the revival of Afro-Cuban dance music which in the 1970s came to be known as salsa.

Around 1980 Puente initiated a scholarship fund at the Juilliard School. The following year he disbanded his orchestra to form the Latin Percussion Jazz Ensemble, which he organized on behalf of the instrument company Latin Percussion, Inc., to direct workshops in Europe and Japan. It was initially conceived as a trio with Carlos "Patato" Valdez and the percussionist Johnny Rodriguez, but Puente suggested adding a pianist and bass player, and thus formed a touring quintet under his leadership. It performed internationally at various festivals, notably those in Montreux, Switzerland, and Monterey, and, later, in Japan. The group grew in size, to eight and then 12 pieces, and by 1988, when it recorded with Phil Woods as a guest soloist, Puente had reestablished an 18-piece big band that included singers – a standard in salsa bands. In the 1990s it became known as the Latin Jazz Ensemble. Among its members were Mario Rivera, Jerry Gonzalez, Jorge Pardo, and Ignacio Berroa. In 1992 Puente recorded as leader of the Golden Latin Jazz All Stars. He also played vibraphone, marimba, and piano.

SELECTED RECORDINGS

Puente Goes Jazz (1956, RCA LPM1312); *Night Beat* (1957, RCA LPM1447); *On Broadway* (1982, Conc. 207); *Mambo Diablo* (1985, Conc. 283); *Un poco loco* (1987, Conc. 329); *In Session* (1992, RMM 660.58.037)

SELECTED FILMS AND VIDEOS

Salsa (*c*1979); Live at the Montreux Jazz Festival 1980 (1980); Images/Imagenes (*c*1986); Machito (*c*1987); A Bailar! (*c*1988); Jazzvisions: Latin Jazz (1988); Newport Jazz '90 (1990); Tito Puente: the Mambo King (1992)

BIBLIOGRAPHY

CarrJ
A. J. Smith: "Sounds from the Salsa Source: Tito and Machito," *DB*, xliii/8 (1976), 16
A. Levitt: "Tito Puente," *Jm*, no.300 (1981), 30
L. Birnbaum: "Tito Puente: Timbales' Titan," *DB*, li/1 (1984), 27
W. J. Stock: "Interview mit Tito Puente," *JP*, xxxiv/2 (1985), 12
J. Nash: "Tito Puente," *JT* (1988), Oct, 33
D. Gordon: "Tito Puente: Polyrhythm Pioneer," *MD*, xiv/4 (1990), 24
F. Bouchard: "Tito Puente: King of the Middle World," *DB*, lviii/5 (1991), 20
M. Breton: "Tito Puente: Championing the Latin Jazz Cause," *JT*, xxi/8 (1991), 29
P. Watrous: "Tito Puente Celebrates 100 Albums," *New York Times* (14 Feb 1992)
L. Birnbaum: "That's Entertainment: Tito Puente, Lionel Hampton," *DB*, lxii/11 (1995), 16
D. Richardson: "The King of Cool," *San Francisco Bay Guardian* (10 Jan 1996)
Obituaries: J. Wadler, *New York Times* (2 June 2000); S. Voce, *The Independent* (2 June 2000)

GK

Puertas, Josep (*b* Spain, *c*1910; *d* after 1947). Spanish trumpeter and violinist. After the Spanish Civil War he played with many important big bands in Barcelona, and also led his own groups, sometimes with his sister Cecilia Melé, a singer. During the 1940s he recorded prolifically, although his output was predominantly highly commercialized music. In 1947 he took part in a session with Don Byas and George Johnson that was organized in Barcelona under the auspices of the jazz magazine *Ritmo y melodía*; Puertas's trumpet playing may be heard to advantage on *Janine/Byas Jump* (Gramophone 738). His style as a trumpeter was in the tradition of Louis Armstrong, and his violin playing had a ferocity reminiscent of Stuff Smith's work.

ALFREDO PAPO

Pugh, Jim [James Edward] (*b* Butler, PA, 12 Nov 1950). Trombonist. He took up trombone around the age of ten, after his family had moved from Butler to Atlanta, and later he studied at the Eastman School (1968–72), where he played in a jazz ensemble under Chuck Mangione. In October 1972 he joined Woody Herman's band, with which he toured Europe and the USA and recorded several albums (including *Giant Steps*, 1973, Fan. 9432), both as lead trombonist and as a soloist; he left the band after Herman's fortieth anniversary concert in 1976. The following year he performed at a concert in New York with Chick Corea's group Return to Forever. Thereafter Pugh worked extensively as a studio musician: he recorded with various jazz and popular musicians, with big bands led by Marvin Stamm (1983), Bob Mintzer (1989), Louie Bellson (1990), George Gruntz (1991), Joe Roccisano (1992, 1995), Paquito D'Rivera (1996), and Jon Faddis and Carlos Franzetti (1997), as well as with the Manhattan Jazz Orchestra (1990–91), and in small brass sections accompanying John Scofield and Bill Frisell (1991) and Daniel Schnyder (*c*1995). In 1984 he recorded an album as a co-leader with Dave Taylor (*The Pugh–Taylor Project*, DMP 448).

BIBLIOGRAPHY

Feather–Gitler '70s
J. Pugh: "I've Settled into the Suitcase Lifestyle," *CI*, xiv/9 (1976), 19
W. D. Clancy with A. C. Kenton: *Woody Herman: Chronicles of the Herds* (New York and elsewhere, 1995), 286

BK

Puíta. *See* CUÍCA.

Pukwana, Dudu [Mtutuzel] (*b* Port Elizabeth, South Africa, 18 July 1938; *d* London, 30 June 1990). South African alto saxophonist. He grew up in a musical family. Having first played piano in Port Elizabeth (late 1950s), he took up alto saxophone and worked with his own group, the Jazz Giants (1962), and then joined Chris McGregor's Blue Notes (1963); with the latter group he traveled to France for an appearance at the Festival Mondial du Jazz Antibes–Juan-les-Pins (1964), worked in Zurich and Geneva (1964–5), and moved to London (1965). He was a member of McGregor's Brotherhood of Breath through the 1970s, but he also played in reggae bands and performed with such musicians as Han Bennink, Misha Mengelberg, John Surman, and Mike Osborne. At the same time he led his own groups – Spear (which toured South Africa briefly in 1969), Assagai (which recorded in 1971–2), a new version of Spear (from 1973; which also toured Africa, 1977–8), and Zila (with which he toured and recorded from 1978 until his death). Pukwana, a seasoned session musician, was a vibrant player influenced by the music of the South African townships, the melodies of Ben Webster, and the free forms of Ornette Coleman.

SELECTED RECORDINGS

As leader: of Spear: *In the Townships* (1973, Car. 1504), *Flute Music* (1974, Car. 1512); of Jabula/Spear (with J. Bahula): *Thunder in our Hearts* (1977, Car. 2009); with J. Dyani and J. Tchicai: *Witchdoctor's Son* (1978, Ste. 1098); of Zila: *Zila* (*c*1982, Zila 1), *Live in Bracknell & Willisau* (1983, Jika 2), *Zila '86* (1986, Jika 3); with C. McGregor and L. Moholo: *Blue Notes for Johnny* (1987, Ogun 532)
As sideman: C. McGregor: *The Blue Notes Legacy: Live in South Africa 1964* (1964, Ogun CD007); *Very Urgent* (1967, Pol. 184137); H. Masekela: *Home is where the Music is* (1972, Chisa 6003); C. McGregor: *Live at Willisau* (1974, Ogun 100); J. Dyani: *Witchdoctor's Son* (1978, Ste. 1098), incl. Magwaza [2nd a sax solo]; *Song for Biko* (1978, Ste. 1109)

BIBLIOGRAPHY

CarrJ; *ChiltonB*; *GrayF*
V. Wilmer: "Pukwana," *MM* (26 Sept 1970), 32
——: "Assegai: Spearhead of the African Sound," *MM* (6 Feb 1971), 35
B. Okonedo: "I'll Never Return to South Africa until Liberation Day," *Black Music and Jazz Review*, i/4 (1974), 39
R. Cotterrell, ed.: *Jazz Now: the Jazz Centre Society Guide* (London, 1976)
C. May: "Dudu Pukwana: King of Afro Rock," *Black Music*, no.27 (1976), 40
——: "Home is where the Music is," *Black Music and Jazz Review* (1981), April, 16
R. Latxaque: "Dudu: change de cap," *Jm*, no.319 (1983), 30 [incl. discography]
C. de Ledesma: "Afro Jazz: Evolution and Revolution," *The Wire*, no.12 (1985), 26, esp. 30f

Dudu Pukwana at the Seen on the Green Festival, London, 1989

P. Renaud: *La discographie du jazz anglais* (Chaumont, France, 1985)
Obituaries: J. Fordham, *The Guardian* (3 July 1990); *The Times* (4 July 1990); M. Gilbert, *JJI*, xliii/10 (1990), 25

CHARLES DE LEDESMA/BK

Pullen, Don (Gabriel) (*b* Roanoke, VA, 25 Dec 1941; *d* East Orange, NJ, 22 April 1995). Pianist, organist, and leader. For some time he gave his year of birth as 1944, but 1941 appears in his own questionnaire for the first edition of this dictionary, as well as in obituaries; this earlier year places him in college just before his eighteenth birthday, as would be the norm. He was born into a musical family and took up piano at about the age of ten; the son of a preacher, he gained his first experience by playing gospel music in church and rhythm-and-blues in local groups. In his late teens he became interested in jazz, initially through the work of Art Tatum, and then that of Eric Dolphy and Ornette Coleman. He was a pre-med student at Johnson C. Smith University in Charlotte, North Carolina, from 1959 to 1963, but left his studies to devote himself to performance.

Pullen's important early associations were with Muhal Richard Abrams's Experimental Band in Chicago (*c*1964) and Giuseppi Logan's quartet in New York (1964–5). But work in free-jazz ensembles was scarce, and he supported himself by accompanying rhythm-and-blues singers, such as Big Maybelle, Ruth Brown, and Arthur Prysock, and by playing organ in soul-jazz groups. Between 1965 and 1972 he led such a group, sometimes of three, sometimes of four members, his sidemen including Roland Prince, Tina Brooks, and Al Dreares. He also played in a duo with Milford Graves (1966). After serving as accompanist to Nina Simone (1970–71), continuing his organ trio, and sitting in with Art Blakey's Jazz Messengers for a few days, he worked from 1973 to 1975 with Charles Mingus, whose eclectic approach enabled Pullen to exploit the diverse styles in which he practiced.

Pullen first gave concerts and recorded as an unaccompanied soloist in 1975. He also recorded several albums with free-jazz musicians, including Sam Rivers (1975), David Murray, and Hamiet Bluiett (both 1977). With Chico Freeman, Fred Hopkins, and the drummer Bobby Battle he toured Europe, and in 1978 they recorded the album *Warriors* under Pullen's leadership. Having recorded that same year under the name of the Magic Triangle with two members of the Art Ensemble of Chicago, Joseph Jarman and Don Moye, Pullen performed with this trio occasionally into the early 1980s, appearing mainly in New York when their schedules allowed. He worked intermittently as a leader with Beaver Harris of 360 Degree Music Experience. In 1979 he recorded with this ensemble and with Mingus Dynasty, but his principal activity from that year to 1988 was as co-leader with George Adams of a quartet including Cameron Brown and Dannie Richmond. For practice and relaxation, Pullen continued to play organ in soul-jazz groups in small clubs in Harlem, other New York boroughs, and New Jersey.

In 1988, after Richmond's death, Lewis Nash joined the quartet, but it disbanded several months later. Thereafter Pullen led trios and worked as an unaccompanied soloist. Additionally, while in residence at the Yellow Springs Institute, Chester Springs, Ohio, in 1990, he founded the African Brazilian Connection, including Carlos Ward, the Senegalese percussionist Mor Thiam, and two Brazilian musicians, the bass player Nilson Matta and the percussionist Guiherme Franco. Nearly all of his recorded work was as a pianist, but late in his career he appeared as the organist in John Scofield's trio in the film *John Scofield: Live 3 Ways* (made in 1990); he also recorded sessions as a soul-jazz organist with Maceo Parker (*c*1990) and with Murray's quartet (1991, 1993).

Pullen's playing drew on his varied musical experience: melodic lines in the style of bop were underpinned by rhythms and harmonies characteristic of soul jazz and decorated with devices often associated with free jazz. Most

Don Pullen at the Grande Parade du Jazz, Nice, France, 1982

significant was his manner of forming highly charged melodies from a rapidly changing series of glissandos and tone clusters. Although the essential idea may be traced back to Cecil Taylor's work, Pullen's use of the device became a personalized musical signature. At the time, no one else was so successful in integrating these washes of sound into a conventional jazz setting; later, from the 1990s, his sweeping keyboard gestures were taken up by younger pianists, including Craig Taborn. A less common facet of Pullen's playing comes across strongly in the unaccompanied solo *Ode to Life* (1990), in which his introspective improvisation on a brief, cyclic pop-gospel progression alternates between rhapsodic lyricism and a bitingly rhythmic approach.

Oral history material in *DSI* (JOHP).

SELECTED RECORDINGS

As unaccompanied soloist: *Solo Piano Album* (1975, Sack. 3008); *Healing Force* (1976, BS 0010); *Evidence of Things Unseen* (1983, BS 0080); on *New Beginnings* (1988, BN B1-91785), Silence = Death; on *Random Thoughts* (1990, BN 94347), Ode to Life

Duos: with M. Graves: *Nommo* (1966, SRP 290); with D. Moye: *Milano Strut* (1978, BS 0028)

As leader: with S. Rivers: *Capricorn Rising* (1975, BS 0004); *Warriors* (1978, BS 0019); with J. Jarman and D. Moye: *The Magic Triangle* (1979, BS 0038); with G. Adams: *Don't Lose Control* (1979, SN 1004), *Earth Beams* (1980, Tim. 147), *Melodic Excursions* (1982, Tim. 166); *The Sixth Sense* (1985, BS 0088); of African-Brazilian Connection: *Kele Mou Bana* (1991, BN B21S-98166)

As sideman: G. Logan: *The Giuseppi Logan Quartet* (1964, ESP 1007); C. Mingus: *Mingus Moves* (1973, Atl. 1653); S. Murray: *Apple Cores* (1978, Philly Jazz 1004); Mingus Dynasty: *Chair in the Sky* (1979, Elek. 248); M. Parker: *Roots Revisited* (*c*1990, Minor Music 1015); D. Murray: *Shakill's Warrior* (1991, DIW 850); *Shakill's II* (1993, DIW 884)

BIBLIOGRAPHY

GrayF
B. Smith, "Don Pullen," *Coda*, ix/10 (1970), 40
V. Frazer: "Don Pullen: an Interview," *Coda*, no.151 (1976), 2
L. Goddet: "Free Blues: Don Pullen," *Jh*, no.331 (1976), 15
A. J. Smith: "Don Pullen," *DB*, xliv/13 (1977), 17
P. Gamble: "Don Pullen," *JJI*, xxxiii/6 (1980), 28
M. Davis: "Don Pullen: Mingus Sideman, Club Organist, Solo Pianist," *Keyboard*, viii/9 (1982), 42 [incl. discography]
H. Mandel: "Don Pullen: Piano Inside and Out," *DB*, lii/6 (1985), 20 [incl. discography]
J. Macnie: "Don Pullen: a Romantic Avant-gardist Plays the Whole Piano," *Musician*, no.96 (1986), 19
K. Whitehead: "Don Pullen: Reconciling Opposites," *DB*, lvi/11 (1989), 28
Obituary, H. Mandel, *DB*, lxii/7 (1995), 12
M. Bond: "Don Pullen: a Song Everlasting," *JJI*, xlix/11 (1996), 14

BK

Pull-off. A technique on string instruments, and in the realm of jazz, particularly on guitar, electric bass guitar, and double bass, whereby the player plucks or picks the higher of two notes and then pulls his left hand sideways off the string, leaving the lower pitch sounding; this can be either an open string or a note which has been held with a different finger. For a recorded example of Ray Brown's use of the pull-off in alternation with the device known as hammer-on, *see* Hammer-on; two illustrations, played by Marc Johnson, may be seen in the video *The Bill Evans Trio: Jazz at the Maintenance Shop*, i–ii (*c*1992 [filmed 1979]), the first at approximately the 53-minute mark and the second at around 54:40.

BIBLIOGRAPHY

T. Greene: *Jazz Guitar: Single Note Soloing*, i (Miami, 1978), 30
M. Richmond: *Modern Walking Bass Technique*, i (Englewood, NJ, 1983), 24
T. Coolman: *The Bottom Line: the Ultimate Bass Line Book* (New Albany, IN, 1990), 37

JOHN CURRY

Puma, Joe [Joseph J.] (*b* New York, 13 Aug 1927; *d* New York, 31 May 2000). Electric guitarist. He came from a family of guitarists, and he began his professional career performing and recording with Joe Roland (1949–50, 1953) and Louie Bellson, Don Elliott, and Artie Shaw (all 1954). He then recorded with Eddie Bert and Dick Garcia (both 1955), Herbie Mann (1955, 1957), Mat Mathews, Bernard Peiffer, and Chris Connor (all 1956), Candido Camero (1956–8), and

Paul Quinichette (1957), and as a leader. After playing with Lee Konitz and Dick Hyman (1958), Puma accompanied Morgana King for two years. During the 1960s he recorded with Sir Charles Thompson (1961), Bobby Hackett (1963), Gary Burton (1964), and Carmen McRae (1965). In 1972 he formed a duo with Chuck Wayne, which appeared at the Newport Jazz Festival in New York in 1973; when the duo broke up after five years Puma led his own trio. He also taught at Housatonic College in Bridgeport, Connecticut, and later, while at the Purchase campus of SUNY, recorded with King (1992) and one track in a duo with Warren Vaché (1993). A versatile guitarist, Puma had a light, restrained sound and a jaunty playing style.

SELECTED RECORDINGS

Duos with C. Wayne: *Interactions* (1973, Choice 1004); W. Vaché: on *Horn of Plenty* (1993, Muse 5524), Bix Fix

As leader: *Joe Puma Quintet* (1954, Beth. 1012); *Like Tweet* (1961, Col. CS8418)

As sideman: H. Mann and S. Most: *Herbie Mann–Sam Most Quintet* (1955, Beth. 40); H. Mann: *Salute to the Flute* (1957, Epic 3395); G. Burton: *Groove Sound* (1964, RCA LSP3360)

BIBLIOGRAPHY

Feather '60s; *Feather–Gitler '70s*

R. Gogerty: "Chuck Wayne/Joe Puma: a Magical Jazz Duo," *GP*, viii/3 (1974), 20

Obituary, *New York Times* (10 June 2000)

GARY CARNER/BK

Purbrook, Colin (Thomas) (*b* Seaford, England, 26 Feb 1936; *d* London, 5 Feb 1999). English pianist. His father played piano professionally, and Purbrook took up the instrument at the age of six. He first joined Sandy Brown in 1958, and from July of that year spent a period in the (Al) Fairweather–Brown All Stars; by September he was working with Kenny Ball, with whom he also played double bass and trumpet. After performing in the Jazzmakers, led by Alan Ganley and Ronnie Ross, he worked with the quintet of Ronnie Scott and Jimmy Deuchar (August–December 1960), the Jazzmakers again, Wally Fawkes (1961), the trumpeter Bert Courtley (1961, in Germany), the Jazzmakers yet again (October 1961 – March 1962), and Kenny Baker (on tour, March 1962). From 1961 to 1963 he led a group with Tony Coe, and in 1962 he recorded under Coe's leadership; he also played on cruise ships (summer 1962), broadcast on radio with his own trio and octet, and appeared on television and in the film *All Night Long* (1961). Purbrook played double bass in Dudley Moore's trio, and then, as pianist, led the trio in *Beyond the Fringe* at the Mayfair Theatre, London, after Moore, who was pianist, co-star, and co-author of the show, went with the original cast to New York (1963). He was a member of the quintets led by Don Rendell (1964), Rendell and Ian Carr (1964), and Coe and John Picard (1965–6), and recorded again under Coe (1966). Having rejoined Brown (1966), he worked with his own quartet (1967–8) and that of Phil Seamen (1968), briefly played with Humphrey Lyttelton (1968), and then once again appeared as a double bass player, this time in Brian Lemon's trio (1969). In the late 1960s he held engagements as a pianist in Spain.

From the mid-1960s into the 1980s Purbrook accompanied such visiting American musicians as Benny Goodman, Benny Carter, Dexter Gordon, Chet Baker, Art Farmer, Barney Kessel, Eddie "Lockjaw" Davis, Ruby Braff, Zoot Sims, Howard McGhee, James Moody, Buddy Tate, and Doc Cheatham, and worked for many years as accompanist to Annie Ross. He performed and recorded with Lyttelton (1972) and was music director for the shows *Bubbling Brown Sugar* (1977) and *One Mo' Time* (1981). In the 1980s and 1990s he continued to lead his own small groups; he performed with Coe again in the London production of *Lady Day*, featuring Dee Dee Bridgewater, and then worked in the shows *Rent Party* (1989) and *The Cotton Club* (1992). His trio appeared with Ross in March 1996, and in his last years it held a residency at Pizza on the Park in London. Despite suffering from cancer, Purbrook continued to play through 1998, and he accompanied Scott Hamilton just before the end of that year. His playing may be heard to advantage on the album *Shades of Blue* (1964, Col. 33SX1733), which he recorded in a sextet led by Rendell and Carr.

BIBLIOGRAPHY

ChiltonB

M. Creese: "Colin Purbrook, an Appreciation," *Just Jazz*, no.12 (1999), 27

Obituaries: S. Voce, *The Independent* (8 Feb 1999); [A. Shipton,] *The Times* (1 March 1999); P. Vacher, *JJI*, lii/4 (1999), 19

NEVIL SKRIMSHIRE/BK

Purcell, John (Raymond) (*b* New York, 8 May 1952). Saxello player and saxophonist. He grew up in Westchester, New York, and studied french horn while attending a summer music program at the Westchester Conservatory; he then began playing saxophone because his school had no french horn. During summer vacations he continued on french horn and also took up trombone, though he studied saxophone in school and privately and began playing it in bands. With his twin brother he founded the Modern Jazz Messengers. He played in classical and jazz settings while at the Manhattan School of Music (BM 1974, MA 1978), and he formed a 22-piece band in Westchester, the leadership of which he shared at one point with Frank Foster. He also began playing in salsa bands based in New York. Around 1975 he was diagnosed with a tumor on his larynx; the ensuing operation kept him from playing for a year, during which time he studied education and developed an in-depth understanding of the workings of reed instruments in an effort to understand better the physical requirements that face musicians. Since that time he has been active as a consultant, adjusting players' instruments to suit their needs; he has also worked on the design of mouthpieces and on the acoustics involved in recording reed instruments.

After returning to playing, Purcell joined Chico Hamilton's group, then worked as a freelance, performing in Latin, funk, and jazz bands, recording jingles, and playing in pit orchestras for Broadway musicals. He toured with Sam Rivers's big band, then replaced Arthur Blythe in Jack DeJohnette's group Special Edition (*c*1980–85), with which he played flute and alto and baritone saxophones. Around the same time he began deputizing for David Murray and Julius Hemphill on an ad hoc basis in the World Saxophone Quartet. In 1982 he performed in the Young Lions group at the Kool Jazz Festival in New York. Purcell was a member of Onaje Allen Gumbs's quartet (*c*1983), Muhal Richard Abrams's large and small groups (*c*1983–90), Murray's large ensembles (*c*1984–8), the American Jazz Orchestra (1985–91), and the cooperative Third Kind of Blue with Anthony Cox and Ronnie Burrage (1984–7), which reunited for a tour in 1997. He recorded as co-leader of an octet with Dennis Gonzalez and as a sideman with Tania Maria and Chico Freeman (both 1984), Henry Butler (1987), and David Sanborn (1990s), among others. In the 1980s and 1990s he occasionally worked in film and television, serving as a music consultant for Sanborn's show "Night Music" and occasionally performing, notably in the film *The Cotton Club* (1985).

Purcell taught at the Westchester Conservatory (1970–80), Dwight Morrow High School (1976–9), Lehman College (1985–9), Rutgers University (1987–90), and the Manhattan School of Music (1987–94). In the mid-1990s he joined the World Saxophone Quartet as a permanent member, having at one time or another filled every chair in the group, and in the late 1990s he became a member of Andrew Cyrille's quintet. Although he claims the saxello is his main instrument, he has performed or recorded on all of the single-reed instruments and on all sizes of flute (including piccolo), as well as on the oboe and english horn.

SELECTED RECORDINGS

As leader with D. Gonzalez: *Little Toot* (1985, Daagnim 13)
As sideman: J. DeJohnette: *Tin Can Alley* (1980, ECM 1189); *Inflation Blues* (1982, ECM 1244); C. Freeman: *The Pied Piper* (1984, Black Hawk 50801); J. DeJohnette: *Album Album* (1984, ECM 1280); D. Gonzalez: *Stefan* (1986, Silkheart 101); M. R. Abrams: *Colors in Thirty-third* (1986, BS 0091); H. Butler: *The Village* (1987, MCA/Imp. 2-8023)

BIBLIOGRAPHY

L. Jeske: "Profile: John Purcell," *DB*, l/12 (1983), 54
W. Jenkins: "World Saxophone Quartet: Higher Ground," *JT*, xxvii/3 (1997), 38

GK

Purdie, Bernard [Pretty] (*b* Elkton, MD, 11 June 1939). Drummer. After moving to New York in 1960 he worked as a studio musician, recording with, among others, the soul singer James Brown and King Curtis. As the drummer for the recording company CTI (1968–74) he recorded with various musicians, notably Grover Washington, Jr. In addition he toured with Curtis in 1970–71 and Aretha Franklin from 1970, and during the next five years he served as Franklin's music director. Purdie continued to work in studios in the 1970s and recorded with a number of jazz performers, among them Louis Armstrong (1970) and Gato Barbieri (1971, *c*1973), as well as with many rock and pop musicians. In 1980 he recorded at the Montreux International Jazz Festival with Dizzy Gillespie, with whom he toured in 1982–3. From 1983 through the 1990s he was associated with Hank Crawford, with whom he made numerous albums and tours, often in groups co-led by Crawford and Jimmy McGriff.

Purdie continued recording throughout the 1980s and 1990s with a variety of blues and popular musicians. In addition he worked intermittently with Houston Person (from 1990) and Bucky Pizzarelli (from 1994) and alongside the pianist Bross Townsend and Bob Cunningham as a member of the Dynamic 3 B's (early 1990s); with the addition of Person and Carrie Smith the group recorded an album around 1992. Later Purdie made a video, *Groove Master* (*c*1994), performed and recorded with Jimmy Smith (1995–6), toured and recorded with Junior Mance (from 1995), and recorded with Eddie Harris and Nils Landgren (both 1996); he appeared with the WDR Big Band (1997–8), performed and recorded with Brother Jack McDuff (1998–9), and gave concerts with Max Roach (1999). In 2000 he toured Europe in a trio, the Masters of Groove. Purdie is best known for his work with soul musicians in the 1960s and as an innovator in the funk style of drumming in the 1970s. His playing is characterized by a reliance on precise, syncopated ostinatos rather than busy technique, and he is especially famous for his shuffle feel.

SELECTED RECORDINGS

As leader: *Soul is...Pretty Purdie* (1972, FD 10154); *Soul to Jazz* (1996, ACT 9242); *Soul to Jazz*, ii (1997, ACT 9253)
As sideman: J. Brown: It's a man's, man's, man's world (1966, King 6035); K. Curtis: *King Curtis Live at the Fillmore West* (1971, Atco 359); A. Franklin: *Aretha Franklin Live at the Fillmore West* (1971, Atl. 7205); H. Person: *Houston Express* (1971, Prst. 10007); D. Gillespie: *Dizzy Gillespie at Montreux, 1980* (1980, PL 2308226); H. Crawford: *Roadhouse Symphony* (1985, Mlst. 9140); B. Lagrene: on *Inferno* (1987, BN 48016), Hips, Rock it; J. Faddis: on *Hornucopia* (1990, Epic 46958), Rapartee; J. Smith: on *Damn!* (1995, Verve 314-527631-2), Papa's got a brand new bag, Watermelon Man; E. Harris: *The Last Concert* (1996, ACT 9249); N. Landgren: *Paint it Blue: a Tribute to Cannonball Adderley* (1996, ACT 9243)

BIBLIOGRAPHY

Feather–Gitler '70s
G. Gray: "Bernard Purdie: Soul Beat Mavin," *DB*, xxxviii/2 (1971), 18
B. Niquet: "Bernard Purdie," *Pj*, no.7 (1972), 4 [incl. discography]
C. Iero: "The New York Scene: Bernard Purdie," *MD*, iii/3 (1979), 20
M. Weinberg: "Pretty Purdie," *The Big Beat* (Chicago, 1984), 60
C. Fisher: "Pretty Purdie," *MD*, ix/11 (1985), 8
C. Atkins: "'After Hours with 3 B's' Called so Good Money Can't Buy," *Amsterdam News* (24 July 1993)
G. Endress: "Bernard 'Pretty' Purdie," *JP*, xlv/12 (1996), 12
M. Griffith: "Artist on Track: Bernard Purdie," *MD*, xxii/11 (1998), 158 [incl. discography]

RICK MATTINGLY

Puretone. Record label. It was established by the Bridgeport Die & Machine Company after the latter ceased to issue records on its label Puritan. Many issues first made on Puritan were re-pressed with Puretone labels, and the catalogue drew on the same sources as that of its predecessor. The repertory included recordings by Jelly Roll Morton (drawn from Paramount) and a reissue of one side of Duke Ellington's first recording (originally put out on Bludisc). Production ceased in mid-1925.

BIBLIOGRAPHY

B. Rust: *The American Record Label Book* (New Rochelle, NY, 1978), 255
M. E. Vreede: "Puritanism in Discography," *Sv*, no.89 (1980), 178
A. Sutton: *Directory of American Disc Record Brands and Manufacturers, 1891–1943* (Westport, CT, and London, 1994), 127

HOWARD RYE

Purim, Flora (*b* Rio de Janeiro, 6 March 1942). Brazilian singer. The daughter of professional classical musicians, she studied piano and guitar. She first performed in São Paulo and Rio de Janeiro with AIRTO MOREIRA (*c*1966–1967), whom she later married (1972). After moving to Los Angeles and then to New York she joined Stan Getz's Latin jazz group in 1968. She recorded with Duke Pearson (1969–70) and Moreira (from 1971), worked with Gil Evans (1971), and gained considerable renown as a member of Chick Corea's quintet RETURN TO FOREVER (with Moreira, Stanley Clarke, and Joe Farrell, 1971–3). Purim's high-pitched voice and soft, airy tone may be heard to advantage on Corea's recording of *Five Hundred Miles High*, on which she sings dreamy lyrics in English with a strong Portuguese accent; *Spain* provides an example of her deft skill as a scat singer. Purim and Moreira left Corea in 1973 to form their own group, but from 1974 to 1975 Purim was imprisoned for possessing cocaine. Following her release from jail she continued to work as a jazz singer but aimed at more commercial markets on her recordings as a leader (1976–8). In 1978 she formed another group, but without Moreira, as the two had begun to attract different audiences. In the mid-1980s she resumed working with Moreira; they toured worldwide, and each year from 1986 they held month-long residencies at Ronnie Scott's in London. In the 1990s their group, Fourth World, consisted of the saxophonist Gary Meek and the guitarist José Neto. Purim also sang with Ivo Perelman in New York (1990–91). She is the author, with E. Bunker, of *Freedom Song: the Story of Flora Purim* (New York, 1982).

SELECTED RECORDINGS

As leader: *Butterfly Dreams* (1973, Mlst. 9052); *500 Miles High at Montreux* (1974, Mlst. 9070); *That's What She Said* (1976, Mlst. 9081); *Nothing Will Be as it Was . . . Tomorrow* (*c*1976, WB 2985); with A. Moreira: *The Colours of Life* (1980, 1987, In + Out 001); of Fourth World (with A. Moreira): *Fourth World* (1992, Ronnie Scott's Jazz House 026)

As sideman: D. Pearson: *It Could only Happen to You* (1970, BN LA317); C. Corea: *Return to Forever* (1972, ECM 1022); *Light as a Feather* (1972, Pol. 5525), incl. Five Hundred Miles High, Spain; D. Gillespie: on *Dizzy Gillespie and the United Nation Orchestra: Live at the Royal Festival Hall* (1989, Enja 6044-2), Tanga; I. Perelman: *Children of Ibeji* (1991, Enja 7005-2)

SELECTED FILMS AND VIDEOS

Rio Monterey Jam (*c*1981); Harvest Jazz (1986 [filmed 1985]); Jacksonville Jazz Festival VII (1987); Airto and Flora Purim: the Latin Jazz All-Stars Live at the Queen Mary Jazz Festival (*c*1988 [filmed 1985]); Great Performances: Wolf Trap Salutes Dizzy Gillespie: An All-star Tribute to the Jazz Master (1988); Dizzy Gillespie and the United Nation Orchestra: Live at the Royal Festival Hall, London (*c*1990 [filmed 1989]); Ivo Perelman: Live in New York (1991 [filmed 1990])

BIBLIOGRAPHY

J.-E. Berendt: "Flora Purim: eine Stimme der Freiheit," *Ein Fenster aus Jazz: Essays, Portraits, Reflexionen* (Frankfurt am Main, Germany, 1978), 89

H. Nolan: "Flora Purim: Flying High on Freedom," *DB*, xlv/16 (1978), 23

L. Underwood: "Airto and his Incredible Gong Show," *DB*, xlv/8 (1978), 15

J. Williams: "New Music and Direction for Flora Purim," *Billboard*, xc (27 May 1978), 46

S. Marriott: "Fabulous Flora," *Jazz on CD*, no.15 (1995), 46

S. Rawles: "Jazz: Flora Purim," *Jazz on CD*, no.18 (1995), 62

BK

Puritan. Record label. It was established before 1920 and was used to issue discs produced by three different companies – the United Phonographs Corporation (UPC), the New York Recording Laboratories (NYRL) (both subsidiaries of the Wisconsin Chair Company), and the Bridgeport Die & Machine Company (BD&M). The organizations pooled their masters for this purpose, though the most important jazz material (including items by King Oliver and Jelly Roll Morton) came from NYRL and was often issued on Paramount as well; the catalogue also contained recordings by the Original Memphis Five and the California Ramblers. Each company manufactured and distributed the discs in its own territory (UPC and NYRL in the Midwest, BD&M in the North); until 1923 the catalogue numbers in each company's series were the same. Thereafter, however, the sequences began to diverge, and BD&M left the scheme and established the label Puretone. NYRL continued to issue discs on Puritan until 1927, using both its own repertory and material leased from Plaza.

BIBLIOGRAPHY

B. Rust: *The American Record Label Book* (New Rochelle, NY, 1978), 256

M. E. Vreede: "Puritanism in Discography," *Sv*, no.89 (1980), 178

A. Sutton: *Directory of American Disc Record Brands and Manufacturers, 1891–1943* (Westport, CT, and London, 1994), 127

HOWARD RYE

Purnell, Alton (*b* New Orleans, 16 April 1911; *d* Inglewood, CA, 14 Jan 1987). Pianist and singer. After studying piano with Burnell Santiago and Fats Pichon he worked from around 1928 at the Pelican Annex. He toured in the mid-1930s with Isaiah Morgan, worked with Kid Howard, Big Eye Louis Nelson, Alphonse Picou, and George Lewis (i), was a member in late 1930 of Sidney Desvigne's big band, and in the early 1940s performed at the Famous Door with the singer Cousin Joe. In 1945 he moved to New York to join Bunk Johnson's band, with which he remained when the group's leadership was assumed by Lewis. Purnell moved in 1957 to California, where he worked as a soloist and with Joe Darensborg, Andrew Blakeney, Teddy Buckner, Ben Pollack, Barney Bigard, the Young Men from New Orleans, and Kid Ory's last band. He toured the world as a guest soloist from 1964 and later as a member of the Legends of Jazz. Purnell's driving style made him the most influential traditional-jazz pianist of the postwar era. His brother was the reed player Theodore Purnell (1908–74).

Oral history material in *LNT*.

SELECTED RECORDINGS

As leader: *Alton Purnell Quartet* (1958, WB 1228)

As sideman: B. Johnson: One Sweet Letter from You/Franklin Street Blues (1945, Vic. 40-0129); G. Lewis: *George Lewis and his New Orleans Stompers*, i (1955, BN 1205); New Orleans All Stars: *New Orleans All Stars* (1966, GHB 35); *It's the Talk of the Town* (1972, 77 SEU44); Legends of Jazz: [untitled album] (1973, Crescent 1); K. T. Valentine: *Kid Thomas* (1975, Smoky Mary 1975T)

BIBLIOGRAPHY

ChiltonW

G. Boatfield: Liner notes, *Live with Keith Smith's Climax Jazz Band* (77 LEU13, 1965)

T. Stagg: Liner notes, *It's the Talk of the Town* (77 SEU44, 1972)

J. Darensbourg: *Telling it Like it is*, ed. P. Vacher (London, 1987, Baton Rouge, LA, 1987, as *Jazz Odyssey: the Autobiography of Joe Darensbourg*)

Obituary, F. Levin, *Fn*, xviii/4 (1987), 4

MARCEL JOLY

Purnell, Keg [William] (*b* Charleston, WV, 7 Jan 1915; *d* New York, 25 June 1965). Drummer. While attending West Virginia State College (1932–4) he played with the Campus Revellers, led by the pianist Chappie Willett, after which he worked with King Oliver (late December 1934 – autumn 1935). In addition to leading his own trio (late 1930s) he played with Thelonious Monk (1939), Benny Carter (1939–40), and Claude Hopkins (1941–2). Between late 1942 and 1948, and again in 1951–2, his principal association was with Eddie Heywood, with whom he had recorded in the Quintones in 1940; he also recorded with Rex Stewart (1945), Teddy Wilson (1947), and Willie "the Lion" Smith (1953). From 1957 Purnell worked with Snub Mosley at the Sands Beach Hotel in Howard Beach, New York.

SELECTED RECORDINGS

As sideman: B. Carter: Shufflebug Shuffle/More than You Know (1939, Voc. 5508); Sleep/Slow Freight (1940, Voc. 5399); Quintones: Honey Bunny Boo/Harmony in Harlem (1940, Voc. 5596); E. Heywood: Blue Lou/Please don't talk about me when I'm gone (1944, Decca 23427); S. Mosley: on *Cascade of Quartets*, i (1959, Col. 33SX1191), So Sad Blues

BIBLIOGRAPHY

ChiltonW; *FeatherE*; *Feather '60s*

L. Wright and others: *Walter C. Allen & Brian A. L. Rust's "King" Oliver* (Chigwell, England, 1987), 168

AL VOLLMER

Purrone, Tony [Anthony Michael; Tony the Tiger] (*b* Bridgeport, CT, 18 Oct 1954). Guitarist. He began playing guitar at the age of nine and joined the University of Bridgeport Jazz Ensemble as a teenager; he studied at the university in the mid-1970s, during which time he performed with Don Elliot and Gerry Mulligan. After transferring to New York University (BS music 1976) he worked in the Heath Brothers band (1978–82), with which he recorded and toured internationally, and with Jimmy Heath's small and large groups (1978–95, from 1997). In addition he performed with the group Five Guitars Play Mingus and in a trio with Pete Levin and Lenny White, and toured Europe as a member of the group Urbanator, alongside Michal Urbaniak and the trumpeter Tom Browne. He recorded with Ed Thigpen (1989, 1991), Hod O'Brien (1993), White (*c*1994), and the Essence All Stars (1996). His extensive list of freelance associations includes performances with Count Basie's orchestra (under Frank Foster), Jerome Richardson, Lee Konitz, Al Cohn, Pepper Adams, Paquito D'Rivera, Sal Nistico (ii), Nick Brignola, Bill Barron, Dave Liebman, Freddie Hubbard, Dizzy Gillespie, Randy Brecker, Lew Soloff, Jon Faddis, Donald Byrd, Lionel Hampton, Stanley Cowell, Billy Eckstine, Johnny Hartman, and Lyn Christie. Purrone has also led his own trios and quartets (from 1970), which have involved a number of distinguished sidemen, and has recorded as a leader (1979, 1986, and from 1993). He has taught at Housatonic Community College in Bridgeport (late 1970s), Wesleyan University (from 1985), and Queens College, New York (1990–97).

SELECTED RECORDINGS

As leader: with Joe Fonda and Steve McCraven: *Up from the Sky* (1986, Kaleidoscope 46125); *Set 'em Up* (1996, Ste. 31389)

As sideman: Heath Brothers: *Passin' Thru* (1978, Col. JC35573); *Brotherly Love* (1981, Ant. 1003); J. Heath: *Peer Pleasure* (1987, Landmark 1514); E. Thigpen: *Mr. Taste* (1991, Justin Time 43-2); J. Heath: *You've Changed* (1991, Ste. 31292), incl. Bluesville; H. O'Brien: *Hod & Cole* (1993, Jazzmania 6005); J. Heath: *You or Me* (1995, Ste. 31370)

BIBLIOGRAPHY

J. Obrecht: "A Once Mellow Jazzman Goes for Blood," *GP*, xxvii/12 (1993), 15

<http://www.geocities.com/~tonypurrone> (1998)

GK

Purtill, Moe [Maurice Benny] (*b* Huntington, NY, 4 May 1916; *d* New York, 9 March 1994). Drummer. He worked with lesser-known bandleaders in New York (mid-1930s), then performed and made recordings with Red Norvo (notably *I got rhythm*, 1936, Decca 779), Mildred Bailey (1936–7), Glenn Miller (1937, spring 1939 – September 1942), and Tommy Dorsey (1938–9); he may be seen with Miller in the films *Sun Valley Serenade* (1941) and *Orchestra Wives* (1942). While serving in the navy he played in a dance band. After a short period as a member of the memorial Glenn Miller Orchestra under Tex Beneke, Purtill worked mostly as a session musician in New York. Around 1958 he recorded as a sideman with Billy Maxted. In 1973 he moved to Sarasota, Florida, where he played in Jerry Jerome's quartet; five years later he retired and returned to the New York area.

For illustrations *see* Miller, glenn, and Mute, fig.3.

BIBLIOGRAPHY

ChiltonW

G. T. Simon: *Glenn Miller and his Orchestra* (New York, 1974/*R*1980)

C. Deffaa: *Swing Legacy* (Metuchen, NJ, and London, 1989), 118

B. Korall: "From the Past: Maurice Purtill," *MD*, xix/1 (1995), 130

BK

Purvis, Jack (*b* Kokomo, IN, 11 Dec 1906; *d* San Francisco, 30 March 1962). Trumpeter and trombonist. After playing in Lexington, Kentucky, with the Original Kentucky Night Hawks he worked as a freelance trumpeter and arranger (1926) and played briefly in Europe (1928). He joined Hal Kemp's band as a trombonist in 1929, then changed to trumpet before leaving the band the following year. During the same period he made recordings with his own band, including *Poor Richard/Down Georgia Way* (1929, OK 8782). In 1930 he played with the California Ramblers in New York. Later he worked in radio orchestras, and he also recorded as a freelance with the Dorsey Brothers and other bands. Occasionally he served as the fourth trumpeter with Fletcher Henderson, and in 1933 he played briefly with Charlie Barnet. Following a short period in California as an arranger in film studios, Purvis led his own quartet in New York and recorded with Frank Froeba (1935). He then toured briefly with Joe Haymes, but thereafter he played only sporadically.

BIBLIOGRAPHY

P. Kelley: "Poor Jack Purvis," *JJ*, xx/10 (1967), 17 [incl. discography]

P. A. Larson: "Final Curtain," *Sv*, no.39 (1972), 83

S. A. Worsfold: "The Forgotten Ones: Jack Purvis," *JJI*, xxxv/3 (1982), 20

H. S. Kaye: "Dave Tough with the New Yorkers in Europe, 1927–1929," *Storyville 1998–9*, ed. L. Wright (Chigwell, England, 1999), 5

based on *ChiltonW*

Puschnig, Wolfgang (*b* Klagenfurt, Austria, 21 May 1956). Austrian saxophonist, flutist, and composer. He formed his first band, Sokrates, at the age of 14, with which he pursued an early interest in jazz and Asiatic music. He studied classical music and jazz saxophone at the conservatory in Vienna. In 1977 he was a co-founder of the Vienna Art Orchestra, and he remained active in nearly all of its projects until 1989. From 1980 he worked for several years with Hans Koller's saxophone ensembles, but he also led his own bands and performed with such groups as Part of Art (with Herbert Joos, Uli Scherer, and the German double bass player Jürgen Wuchner, 1981), Air Mail (with the Austrian guitarist Harry Pepl, Mike Richmond, and the Austrian drummer Wolfgang Reisinger, 1982–4), and Pat Brothers (with Linda Sharrock, Reisinger, and the synthesizer player Wolfgang Mitterer, 1984). In the mid-1980s he became a member of Carla Bley's Very Big Band, in which he has been a featured soloist, and he also performed with the Austrian writer and poet Ernst Jandl. From 1986 Puschnig collaborated with Samul Nori, a group of Korean master drummers. In this setting he recorded as a member of Red Sun, a small group with Scherer, Jamaaladeen Tacuma, and Sharrock; Red Sun and Samul Nori recorded in 1989, again in 1993, with the guitarist Rick Iannacone in place of Scherer, and in 1996, with both Iannacone and Scherer. In 1988 Puschnig formed the trio AM4 (A Monastic Quartet) with Scherer and Sharrock. Two years later he established Alpine Aspects, his first large ensemble, including the trumpeter Karl "Bumi" Fian, Tacuma, and the drummer Thomas Alkier, and also incorporating the Austrian folklore band Amstetten Blasmusik; Alpine Aspects also recorded with Samul Nori in 1996. In the 1990s he often appeared in a quartet with Christof Lauer, Bob Stewart, and Alkier. In celebration of his fortieth birthday he performed and recorded all of his projects of the previous decade during three days of concerts in mid-August 1997. Puschnig is equally at home in bop, modal jazz, free jazz, and funk, and plays outstanding improvisations in these styles.

SELECTED RECORDINGS

Duos with J. Tacuma: *Gemini-Gemini* (1991, ITM 970063), incl. Caravan

As leader: *Mixed Metaphors* (1994, Amadeo 527266-2); *Roots and Fruits* (1996, Amadeo 537495-2)

As sideman: Vienna Art Orchestra: *Tango from Obango* (1979, Art 1002); C. Bley: *The Very Big Carla Bley Band* (1990, Watt 23); Red Sun and Samul Nori: *Then Comes the White Tiger* (1993, ECM 1499); C. Bley: *Big Band Theory* (1993, Watt 25)

BIBLIOGRAPHY

K. Schulz: "Wolfgang Puschnig," *JP*, xxxviii/3 (1989), 3

KLAUS SCHULZ

Pyne, (Norman) Chris(topher) (*b* Bridlington, England, 14 Feb 1939; *d* London, 12 April 1995). English trombonist, brother of Mick Pyne. He was taught piano as a child but later changed to trombone. In the 1960s he worked with the drummer Fat John Cox (1963), Alexis Korner's Blues Incorporated (1964–5), John Stevens's Spontaneous Music Ensemble (1965–6), and the London Jazz Orchestra. During his association with Humphrey Lyttelton (summer 1966–70) he recorded with John Dankworth (1967), Ronnie Scott (1968), and Stan Tracey (1968–70), and performed with Tubby Hayes. Pyne was associated with Mike Gibbs from 1967 to 1979, toured Europe with groups accompanying Frank Sinatra between 1970 and 1983, and was a member of John Taylor's sextet from 1971 to 1981. In the 1970s he also worked in the sextet led by his brother Mick and as a freelance with Kenny Wheeler (recording in 1969 and 1973), John Surman (recording in 1970), Philly Joe Jones, Maynard Ferguson, Tony Coe, the band led by the trombonists Bobby Lamb and Ray Premru (1971), Ronnie Ross, Barbara Thompson's group Jubiaba, and many others, including orchestras accompanying Ella Fitzgerald, Sarah Vaughan, and Tony Bennett; during the same period he recorded with Stevens (1970–71), Norma Winstone (1971), Dankworth again (1972), Alan Cohen (1972), and Tony Coe (1976). Later he toured with Gordon Beck (1982) and performed in Surman's Brass Project (1984–92, recording in 1992 under the leadership of Surman and John Warren), and in the big band led by the drummer Charlie Watts. He also worked further with Wheeler and Gibbs and appeared in theater orchestras and studio bands.

SELECTED RECORDINGS

As sideman: M. Gibbs: *Michael Gibbs* (1969, Deram 1063), incl. And on the third day; K. Wheeler: *Music for Large & Small Ensembles* (1990, ECM 1415–16), incl. Sophie; *Kyack* (*c*1992, Ah-Um 012); J. Surman and J. Warren: *The Brass Project* (1992, ECM 1478)

BIBLIOGRAPHY

CarrJ; *ChiltonB*

R. Cotterrell, ed.: *Jazz Now: the Jazz Centre Society Guide* (London, 1976)

P. Renaud: *La discographie du jazz anglais* (Chaumont, France, 1985)

Obituaries: R. Atkins, *The Guardian* (27 April 1995); B. McRae, *JJI*, xlviii/7 (1995), 21

NEVIL SKRIMSHIRE/BK

Pyne, Mick [Michael John] (*b* Thornton Dale, England, 2 Sept 1940; *d* London, 23 May 1995). English pianist, brother of Chris Pyne. He was taught piano from the age of three and later learned violin; when he was 13 he began playing cornet. Around 1957 he formed a band with his brother. He moved to London as a freelance in 1959 and returned in 1961, initially to work as an unaccompanied soloist at the Down Beat Club, but from May 1962 he was with Tony Kinsey. From mid-1962 into 1963 he performed principally as a tenor saxophonist on American military bases in France and as a sideman with Alexis Korner. After returning home for a period to practice he settled in London late in 1963, and in January 1964 he joined John Stevens's septet. He toured Europe with Stan Getz, Hank Mobley, Joe Williams, Lee Konitz, Roland Kirk, and others, and in 1966 he played in Phil Seamen's quartet. Pyne made many recordings during his associations with Tubby Hayes (1966–73) and Humphrey Lyttelton (autumn 1972 – summer 1985); he also performed with Amalgam, the Spontaneous Music Ensemble, and Ronnie Scott's sextet (all 1970), Stevens's dance orchestra (1974), and Scott's quintet (1978), and recorded in duos with Lyttelton (1974, 1976) and John Eardley (1977) and in Cecil Payne's quintet (1979). After 1985 he performed with the rhythm-and-blues singer Georgie Fame, the group Hefty Jazz, led by Keith Smith, and the drummer Charlie Watts, and accompanied visiting American musicians in London and Europe; in the late 1980s his trio accompanied Adelaide Hall. Chilton, in *Who's Who of British Jazz*, gives his death date as 24 May, but an obituary in *The Times* gives 23 May.

SELECTED RECORDINGS

As unaccompanied soloist: *Alone Together* (1977, Spot. 506)

Duos with H. Lyttelton: *Once in a While* (1974, 1976, BL 12149)

As sideman: T. Hayes: *Mexican Green* (1967, Fon. 911); *For Members Only* (1967, Miles Music 079); *Live 1969* (1969, Harlequin 3006); H. Lyttelton: *Movin' and Groovin'* (1983, BL 760504)

BIBLIOGRAPHY

CarrJ; *ChiltonB*

R. Cotterrell, ed.: *Jazz Now: the Jazz Centre Society Guide* (London, 1976)

P. Renaud: *La discographie du jazz anglais* (Chaumont, France, 1985)

Obituaries: *The Times* (1 June 1995); P. Hawes, *JJI*, xlviii/8 (1995), 18

NEVIL SKRIMSHIRE/BK

Pyysalo, Severi (*b* Pori, Finland, 18 Oct 1967). Finnish vibraphonist. He made a sensational début at the Pori Jazz Festival at the age of 15. From 1986 he studied at the Sibelius Academy in Helsinki, and later he led a group, the Front, which gave an acclaimed performance at the Nordic Radio Jazz Days in 1989. In the 1990s he played mainly with the group Perko–Pyysalo Poppoo, which he formed with Jukka Perko and which may be heard to advantage on the album *Varia* (1998, Porijazz 110).

Oral history material in *FiHJ*.

BIBLIOGRAPHY

M. Konttinen: "Young Talents in Finnish Jazz," *Finnish Music Quarterly*, no.2 (1991), 42

M. Huuskonen, J. Muikku and T. Vähäsilta: *Finnish Jazz* (Helsinki, 5/1997)

PEKKA GRONOW

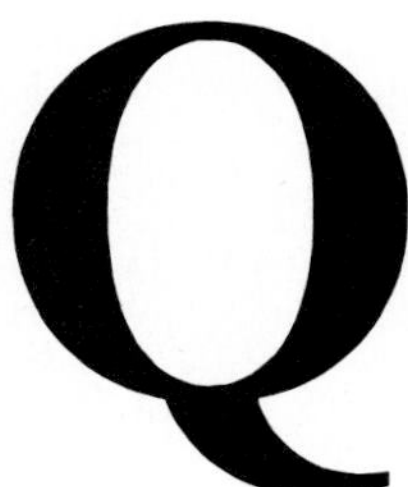

Q. Nickname of both QUINCY JONES and HISAO ISHIKAWA.

QED. Record label on which material was issued temporarily by EMANEM after it moved in 1979 from New Jersey to Massachusetts.

QRS. Manufacturer of piano rolls. The company was established in Chicago before 1916 by Melville Clark, the inventor of the "marking piano." This machine made possible the cutting of piano rolls that accurately captured performances. Involved at an early stage in the recording of ragtime, QRS soon also turned to jazz, especially after Max Kortlander joined its staff and it transferred its premises to New York around 1921. Among the notable musicians who cut rolls for the company were James P. Johnson (1921–7) and Fats Waller (1923–43); in 1926 some 11 million rolls were cut.

The company established a record label of the same name, on which it put out three series of discs. The first of these, during the early 1920s, was of items previously put out on Gennett. The second, the 7000 race series of 1928–9, was more notable: it included recordings made especially for the company under the supervision of Arthur E. Satherley, who had earlier worked in Paramount's artists and repertory department. In 1929, shortly after QRS merged with a film company, the DeVry Corporation, a third series of records appeared, made by the Cova Record Corporation of New York. This continued until mid-1930 but contained very little important jazz.

By this time the market for piano rolls had severely declined, and in 1931 Kortlander bought the company. For many years its existence was frequently precarious, and its employees often worked only part-time. Among these was the stride pianist J. Lawrence Cook, who made many rolls, some under the pseudonym Sid Laney. By the 1950s production had dropped to around 20,000 rolls per year, although thereafter interest revived among collectors. Kortlander died in 1961, and the company was acquired by Ramsi P. Tick, who moved production to Buffalo in 1966. Earl Hines cut some rolls for QRS in the 1970s, and operations continued in Buffalo through the 1990s; in 1993 QRS acquired a company, based in Seneca, Pennsylvania, which manufactured player-pianos. The meaning of the acronym is unknown; the initials have been interpreted as standing for "Quality Reigns Supreme" and "Quality, Reliability, Service."

BIBLIOGRAPHY

M. Wyler and B. Kumm: "QRS Past and Present," *Sv*, ii/7 (1966), 19 [incl. discography]

B. Kumm: "Mr. Piano Roll: J. Lawrence Cook," *Sv*, no.10 (1967), 14

R. M. W. Dixon and J. Godrich: *Recording the Blues* (London, 1970), 58

T. Magnusson: "The Piano Rolls by Thomas Waller and by 'Fats' Waller," *Matrix*, no.106 (1975), 3

B. Rust: *The American Record Label Book* (New Rochelle, NY, 1978), 259

M. Montgomery: "James P. Johnson Rollography," in F. H. Trolle: *James P. Johnson, Father of the Stride Piano* (Alphen aan de Rijn, Netherlands, 1981), 25

L. Wright: "QRS," *Sv*, no.114 (1984), 218

M. E. Ruane: "A One-man Band Keeps Player Pianos Rolling on," *Philadelphia Inquirer* (21 Nov 1993)

A. Sutton: *Directory of American Disc Record Brands and Manufacturers, 1891–1943* (Westport, CT, and London, 1994), 127

HOWARD RYE

Quark. Record label under which material was issued temporarily by EMANEM after it moved in 1979 from New York to New Jersey.

Quaye, Terri [Theresa; Naa-koshie] (*b* Bodmin, England, 8 Nov 1940). English singer, pianist, and percussionist, daughter of Cab Kaye. She began singing professionally in 1962 with the Latin jazz band led by the Filipino pianist and vibraphonist Ido Martin, then sang with the pianists Colin Purbrook, Leon Cohen, and Brian Lemon (with John Stevens on drums). Following a nightclub residency with the Guyanese singer and percussionist Frank Holder she joined a Trinidadian band, the Merrymakers, in Germany. She continued to alternate nightclub work with jazz, playing congas and singing. In Berlin she worked with Carmell Jones, Dave Pike, and Leo Wright. Quaye traveled to Ghana, and in Paris she played with the Cameroonian saxophonist Manu Dibango. At this point she reclaimed her Ga name Naa-koshie, which she used professionally for some years. In New York in the early 1970s she played congas for Syvilla Forte's dance troupe, sang with Harold Mabern, Jiunie Booth, Richard Davis, and Art "Shaki" Lewis, took part in jam sessions with Billy Higgins and others, and recorded on congas with Archie Shepp (*The Cry of my People*, 1972, Imp. 9231); she then played this instrument, mainly in the UK, with Dudu Pukwana's groups Spear and Assagai (including the album *Zimbabwe*, 1972, Phi. 6308079), Trevor Stevens's Amalgam (*Innovation*, 1974, Tangent 121), John Stevens's Away, Jabula, and the keyboard player and singer Dr. John, and she led her own trio, Moonspirit. Having become involved in education, she taught African percussion in London before moving to Washington, DC, to serve as artist-in-residence at the Capital Children's Museum and the Smithsonian Museum of African Art. Quaye gave ethnomusicological lecture-recitals through the 1980s and composed and played percussion for theatrical productions; in 1988 she graduated from London University with an MMus in ethnomusicology. In the 1990s she concentrated on performing as an unaccompanied solo pianist and singer, and she opened the London music bar Jazzers.

BIBLIOGRAPHY

[?D. Nelson:] "People," *West Africa* [London] (9 April 1971), 390

T. Quaye: "Hello, We're your Family," *Drum* [Ghana] (1971), Jan

V. Wilmer: "Caught in the Act," *MM* (30 Jan 1971), 14

M. Fudger: "Women in Music," *Spare Rib* [London], no.26 (1974), 44

B. Case: "The Drums Say: 'Women Get a Raw Deal'," *New Musical Express* (8 Oct 1977), 26

V. Wilmer: *Mama Said There'd be Days Like This* (London, 1989, rev. 2/1991)

VAL WILMER

Quealey, Chelsea (*b* Hartford, CT, 1905; *d* Las Vegas, NV, 6 May 1950). Trumpeter. He first played saxophone, then took up trumpet and worked with the bandleader Jan Garber (*c*1925) and the California Ramblers (1926–7). In December 1927 he sailed to England, where he performed and made recordings (including *Singapore Sorrows*, 1929, Parl. R1201) with Fred Elizalde until he was forced by illness to return to the USA (June 1929). After working again with the California Ramblers he played briefly with Paul Whiteman, then joined Ben Pollack in Chicago and traveled with him to California. In 1935–6 he was a member of Isham Jones's band. Having returned to the East Coast, he undertook a residency with Red McKenzie and Joe Marsala on Coney Island (summer 1936) and with Marsala in New York (autumn 1936) and played with Frankie Trumbauer (1937). Thereafter he worked as a freelance, though he performed with Bob Zurke's big band from September 1939 to early 1940. In the early 1940s Quealey played regularly at Nick's, New York, with Georg Brunis, Brad Gowans, Miff Mole, and others. He went back to California around 1946.

based on *ChiltonW*

Quebec, Ike (Abrams) (*b* Newark, NJ, 17 Aug 1918; *d* New York, 16 Jan 1963). Tenor saxophonist. He began his career as a pianist and dancer, but in 1940 he changed to tenor saxophone and played with the Barons of Rhythm. During the early 1940s he performed with various small bands in the New York area, including those led by Benny Carter, Kenny Clarke, Roy Eldridge, Coleman Hawkins, Frankie Newton, Hot Lips Page, and Trummy Young. He was a member of Cab Calloway's orchestra from 1944 to 1951 and he also played in the Cab Jivers, Calloway's small group within the band. Concurrently from 1944 he recorded several sessions for Blue Note as a leader of a swing quintet and a seven-piece "swingtet"; during the late 1940s he served as artists and repertory agent for Blue Note records and took an active part in promoting bop recordings, bringing, among others, Bud Powell, Thelonious Monk, and Tadd Dameron to the label. He led his own small band until the late 1950s, when he ceased working as a full-time musician, but in 1959 he renewed his relationship with Blue Note, recording, acting as a music director and assistant producer for many sessions, and once again serving as an A&R man, in which capacity he brought renewed attention to Dexter Gordon and Leo Parker. He performed again in the early 1960s and achieved some success, but soon after he became seriously ill, and he died of lung cancer in 1963. Quebec's style was modeled after that of Hawkins, though he was also influenced by Herschel Evans and Joe Thomas (iii). A strong and direct performer, he was particularly impressive when playing slow blues.

SELECTED RECORDINGS

As leader: Blue Harlem (1944, BN 37); Mad about you (1944, BN 42); I. Q. Blues (1945, Savoy 570); *Heavy Soul* (1961, BN 84093); *It Might as Well be Spring* (1961, BN 84105); *Blue and Sentimental* (1961, BN 84098); *Easy Living* (1962, BN 84103); *Soul Samba* (1962, BN 84114)

As sideman with C. Calloway: first issued on *Cab Calloway 1943–1946* (1943–6, Spot. 148), Cruisin' with Cab (1944), Dawn Time (1945), We the cats (1945)

BIBLIOGRAPHY

FeatherE

Obituary, D. Ioakimidis, *Jh*, no.186 (1963), 19

C. Schlouch: *In Memory of Ike Quebec: a Discography* (Marseilles, France, 1983, rev. 3/1985)

M. Cuscuna: "Ike Quebec," *The Complete Blue Note Recordings of Ike Quebec and John Hardee* (Mosaic 107, 1984; repr. in *The Complete Blue Note 45 Sessions of Ike Quebec and John Hardee*, Mosaic 121, 1990) [liner notes]

——: "The Blue Note Story," in M. Cuscuna and M. Ruppli: *The Blue Note Label: a Discography* (New York, Westport, CT, and London, 1988), xi

EDDIE LAMBERT/BK

Queen, Alvin (*b* New York, 16 Aug 1950). Drummer. He grew up from the age of two in Mount Vernon, New York, and when he was seven he began to practice with his older brother's drum sticks. A few years later he joined the school marching band and embarked on private lessons in drumming; before his teenage years he was befriended by many leading jazz musicians, who informally helped him learn to play. At the age of 16 he worked with the singer Ruth Brown and with Don Pullen. He then replaced Billy Cobham in Horace Silver's group, with which he remained for two years, touring the USA (1968–9). After periods with George Benson and Stanley Turrentine he traveled to Europe with Charles Tolliver's quartet Music Inc. (1970). While working in Tolliver's group (until around 1978) he recorded gospel music, performed with Pharoah Sanders and Leon Thomas (both *c* early 1970s), and worked as a freelance with Big John Patton, George Braith, and others (late 1970s). Also during this association he spent two years living in Montreal, where he worked mainly with Sadik Hakim and the tenor saxophonist Billy Robertson.

In 1979 Queen settled in Geneva, where he established his own record label, Nilva, and thereafter he was active mainly in Switzerland and France. He alternated with Dannie Richmond as the drummer in Bennie Wallace's group from 1979 to 1982, though at that time he did not take part in the saxophonist's recordings. From 1980 to 1985 he recorded for Nilva as a leader (including a trio session in 1982, with Junior Mance as his pianist) and as a sideman with John Collins (1982); Patton, Ray Drummond, and Charles Davis are among others who served as leaders for the label in the early 1980s. In 1982 Queen toured France with Plas Johnson and Harry Edison, and in 1983 he worked in Zurich with Wild Bill Davis's trio. In the 1990s he again played with Wallace, with whom he recorded in 1993 and 1998. He also recorded with Horace Parlan (at the Domicile in Munich, 1981), Dusko Goykovich (1981, 1983), Terence Blanchard

(1985), Niels Lan Doky (1986), George Coleman and Kenny Drew (both 1989), Christian Escoudé (1991), Frank Wess (1992), the baritone saxophonist Per Goldschmidt (1993), Mance (1995), Pierre Boussaguet and Tommy Flanagan (both 1998), and the trumpeter Stepko Gut (1999), appeared in the video *Kenny Drew Trio* (*c* late 1980s), and accompanied numerous other leading jazz musicians. *Lenox and Seventh* (1985), recorded by a trio led by Queen and Lonnie Smith, perfectly captures Queen's commitment to a powerful and varied swing style; Goldschmidt's album offers an especially well-recorded example of Queen's playing in a bop context, both as an accompanist and in brief and tasteful solos.

Video oral history material in *NCH* (HCJA).

SELECTED RECORDINGS

As leader: *Glidin' and Stridin'* (1982, Nilva 3403); with L. Smith: *Lenox and Seventh* (1985, BB 33178)

As sideman: J. Collins: *The Incredible John Collins* (1982, Nilva 3412); N. L. Doky: *Here or There* (1986, Sto. 4117); B. Wallace: *The Old Songs* (1993, Audioquest 1017); P. Goldschmidt: *Frankly: a Tribute to Sinatra* (1993, Mlst. 9224); *Bennie Wallace* (1998, Audioquest 1051)

BIBLIOGRAPHY

H. Ruland: "Ein 'Aussteiger' auf dem Weg zum Erfolg: Alvin Queen," *JP*, xxxii/4 (1983), 15
J. Simmen: "Jazz au Widder-Bar," *BHcF*, no.306 (1983), 9
M. Richards: "Alvin Queen," *JJI*, xxxviii/11 (1985), 8
S. Crouch: "Alvin Queen," *VV* (13 May 1986), 85
H. Panassié and M. Gautier: *Dictionnaire du jazz* (Paris, rev. and enlarged 3/1987 by A. Vasset and J. Pescheux), 379
J. Simmen: "Trois disques avec Alvin Queen," *BHcF*, no.345 (1987), 24
<http://www.jazzchronicles.com/jc_queen.htm> (2000)
<http://www.jazzcorner.com/queen/index.html> (2000)
F. W. Sportis: "Alvin Queen," *Jh*, no. 572 (2000), 50

HOWARD RYE, BK

Queener, Charlie [Charles Conant] (*b* Pineville, KY, 27 July 1921; *d* 25 Feb 1997). Pianist. His year of birth has been published as 1923, but in his application for social security he gave 1921. From around the age of six he grew up in Knoxville, Tennessee, where he took piano lessons reluctantly; he was mainly self-taught. After graduating from high school at the age of 16 he began touring with a college dance band. He studied business at the University of Tennessee, again reluctantly, but left when the opportunity arose and moved to New York. Early in his career he performed and made recordings with Muggsy Spanier (1942), Harry James (briefly on the West Coast, 1944), Glen Gray (*c*1944), Joe Marsala (1944–5, notably *Southern Comfort/Gotta be this or that*, 1945, Musi. 328), and Benny Goodman (February–November 1945). From 1946 he worked for four years at Nick's in New York, although in 1947 he traveled with Spanier to Chicago for the opening of the Blue Note club; during the same period he was associated with Billy Butterfield (1947–9). Later, after a brief return to his home town, Queener played swing and dixieland as a freelance at such venues as the Metropole with, among others, Bobby Hackett (with whom he recorded the album *Jazz Session*, 1950, Col. CL6156), Wingy Manone (intermittently, *c*1950–60), Max Kaminsky (1951–2), Jimmy McPartland (1954), Ruby Braff, and Pee Wee Erwin; his longest association was with Clarence Hutchenrider, with whom he played from 1958 to 1973 at the Gaslight and then at Bill's Gay Nineties. In 1963–4 he led a trio with Carl Kress and Bob Wilber. In addition he recorded with Hackett (1948), Jerry Gray (1951), Manone (1954–60), Wild Bill Davison (*c*1958), Sidney De Paris (1962), and the drummer Merrill Morris (1970). Having studied with the composer Paul Creston, he wrote orchestral works from the mid-1960s. Queener continued to be active as a performer in the late 1980s. His date of death is taken from the social security death index, which gives his last known residence as Rangeley, Maine.

BIBLIOGRAPHY

FeatherE
W. W. Vaché, Sr.: "Quiet Queener," *MR*, xiv/5 (1988), 18

BK

Quersin, Benoit (*b* Brussels, 24 July 1927; *d* Vaison-la-Romaine, France, 31 May 1992). Belgian double bass player. He learned classical piano from the age of six and first played jazz with Toots Thielemans when he was 16. Soon afterwards he took up double bass and performed in the Big John Trio and with Francis Coppieters at the Versailles in Brussels; with Thielemans he appeared at the first Paris Jazz Fair (1949). Quersin was a member of the Jump College (1950–51) and worked for eight years in Paris, during which time he accompanied French musicians and visiting soloists and made many recordings. After returning in 1957 to Belgium he spent three months in Africa. He then moved back to Brussels, where he wrote four film scores and opened the Blue Note Club. In 1961 he joined the staff of Belgian Radio, where he formed a jazz department. During the following decades he made several more trips to Africa, wrote articles for various periodicals, and worked as the director of the Art Museum of Central Africa, Kinshasa, Zaire. Quersin made recordings in Belgium, France, and Italy with Thielemans, the Jump College, and many other musicians, including Chet Baker (notably *Chet is Back*, 1962, RCA LPM10307), Sidney Bechet, Billy Byers, Jay Cameron, Blossom Dearie, Jack Diéval, Stephane Grappelli, Lionel Hampton, Bobby Jaspar, Jonah Jones, Helen Merrill, Jacques Pelzer, André Persiany, Jack Sels, Zoot Sims, Martial Solal, René Thomas, Lucky Thompson, René Urtreger, and Maurice Vander.

BIBLIOGRAPHY

R. Pernet, J.-P. Schroeder, and others: *Dictionnaire du jazz à Bruxelles et en Wallonie* (Liège, Belgium, 1991)
R. Pernet: *Belgian Jazz Discography (1897–1999)* (Brussels, 1999)

ROBERT PERNET

Quest. Quartet formed late in 1981 by the soprano saxophonist Dave Liebman and the pianist Richard Beirach; the original rhythm section consisted of the double bass player George Mraz and the drummer Al Foster. On account of the busy schedules of all concerned, the group did not work as a full-time unit until 1984, when Ron McClure and Billy Hart replaced Mraz and Foster respectively. Quest toured internationally and recorded steadily from that time until 1991, when it disbanded.

SELECTED RECORDINGS

Quest (1981, Trio 25027); *Quest II* (1986, Sto. 4132); *Midpoint: Quest III: Live at the Montmartre Café Copenhagen Denmark* (1987, Sto. 4121); *Natural Selection* (1988, Pathfinder 8839); *Of One Mind* (1990, CMP 47)

BIBLIOGRAPHY

L. Gourse: "Richie Beirach and Dave Liebman's 'Quest': What's in a Name?," *JT* (1985), Feb, 5
C. Berg: "A Band of Survivors: Quest," *JT* (1988), Sept, 15
J. Y. Le Bec: "En quête de Quest," *Jm*, no.378 (1989), 36
<http://www.upbeat.com/lieb/bio.htm> (2000)

GK

Quíca. *See* Cuíca.

Quicksell, Howdy [Howard] (*b* 1901; *d* Pontiac, MI, 30 Oct 1953). Banjoist. From 1922 to 1927 he was a member of Jean Goldkette's orchestra (for illustration *see* BEIDERBECKE, BIX), though he also recorded with Bix Beiderbecke (1925) and Frankie Trumbauer. Beiderbecke made a recording of Quicksell's composition and arrangement *Sorry* (1927, OK 41001). Quicksell ceased to work as a musician in the 1930s.

BIBLIOGRAPHY

O. G. Dwight: "Bix's Pal Howdy," *Des Moines Register and Tribune* (24 April 1952); repr. in *SL*, vii/9–10 (1956), 1

R. M. Sudhalter, P. R. Evans, and W. Dean-Myatt: *Bix: Man & Legend* (New Rochelle, NY, and London, 1974)

based on *ChiltonW*

Quill, Gene [Daniel Eugene] (*b* Atlantic City, NJ, 15 Dec 1927; *d* 8 Dec 1988). Alto saxophonist and clarinetist. He started playing saxophone as a child and began working professionally at the age of 13. For many years his activities centered on big bands; in the 1950s and early 1960s he performed and recorded in the dance and jazz bands of Buddy DeFranco, Claude Thornhill, Gene Krupa, Quincy Jones, Johnny Richards, Manny Albam, Johnny Carisi, Bill Potts, Gerry Mulligan (1960-62), and others. He also played in the small groups of Mundell Lowe and Jimmy Knepper, led his own ensembles, and appeared as a guest soloist in "The Future of Jazz," episode 13 of the television series "The Subject is Jazz" (1958). He is best known for his association with Phil Woods in the late 1950s. He later worked as a session musician, but his career was cut short in the late 1970s by partial paralysis following brain damage. The social security death index gives no place of death for Quill, but his last known residence appears therein as Atlantic City.

In the 1950s Quill was among the best of Charlie Parker's imitators, but in the following decade, influenced perhaps by Lee Konitz or Paul Desmond, he tempered his fluent style with a mellower tone quality and more relaxed rhythms.

SELECTED RECORDINGS

As leader: *Jazzville '56* (1955, Dawn 1101); *Three Bones and a Quill* (1958, Roost 2229)

As sideman: P. Woods: *Pairing Off* (1956, Prst. 7046); M. Lowe: *A Grand Night for Swinging* (1957, Riv. 238); P. Woods: *Phil Talks with Quill* (1957, Epic 3521); J. Knepper: *A Swinging Introduction to Jimmy Knepper* (1957, Beth. 77)

BIBLIOGRAPHY

FeatherE; *Feather '60s*

I. Gitler: Liner notes, *Pairing Off* (Prst. 7046, 1957)

M. Goode: Liner notes, *Phil Talks with Quill* (Odyssey PC36806, 1980)

B. Crow: *From Birdland to Broadway: Scenes from a Jazz Life* (New York, and Oxford, England, 1992), 104

P. Woods: "Reflections in E Flat . . . Quill," *Saxophone Journal*, xix/3 (1994), 43

THOMAS OWENS

Quinichette, Paul [Vice Pres] (*b* Denver, 17 May 1916; *d* New York, 25 May 1983). Tenor saxophonist. He was taught clarinet and alto saxophone as a child, but later changed to tenor saxophone. In 1928 or 1930, while Lester Young was with Art Bronson, Quinichette practiced with and received informal lessons from Young. He attended Denver University, transferred to Tennessee State College, and then returned to Denver University, from which he graduated in music. While in college he played with local bands, and during summer vacations he toured with Nat Towles and the trumpeter Lloyd Hunter. In the late 1930s he worked with Shorty Sherock, and in the early 1940s he played with Ernie Fields (1942), Jay McShann (1942–3), Johnny Otis, Benny Carter, and Sid Catlett. He moved to New York in the late 1940s and performed there with several musicians, including Louis Jordan (recording in 1948), Ed Wilcox, Lucky Millinder (1948 – early 1949), Joe Thomas (i), J. C. Heard, Henry "Red" Allen, and Hot Lips Page (1951). At the time of his association with Count Basie (May 1951 – February 1953) Quinichette was nicknamed the Vice Pres because his playing was heavily influenced by that of Lester Young. With the success of some recordings made under his own name for the EmArcy label he left Basie to lead his own groups; he also recorded in small groups accompanying Dinah Washington for EmArcy's parent label, Mercury (1953–4), and played with Benny Goodman and Nat Pierce (both 1955), John Coltrane (1957), and Billie Holiday. In the 1960s he worked as an electrical engineer and, although he performed again from 1973 with Brooks Kerr, Sammy Price, Buddy Tate, Goodman (1974), McShann, and others, his activities were restricted by ill-health. Quinichette's style displayed a sense of swing unequaled among those musicians who followed Young.

SELECTED RECORDINGS

As leader: *The Vice Pres* (1952, EmA 36027); *Paul Quinichette's New Stars* (1957, Prst. 7103); with J. Coltrane: *Cattin' with John Coltrane and Paul Quinichette* (1957, Prst. 7158); *For Basie* (1957, Prst. 7127)

As sideman: D. Washington: Cold, Cold Heart (1951, Mer. 5728); New Blowtop Blues (1951, Mer. 8269); C. Basie: New Basie Blues/Sure Thing (1952, Clef 8964)

SELECTED FILMS AND VIDEOS

Look Out Sister (1948); The Subject is Jazz (1958); The Last of the Blue Devils (1979)

BIBLIOGRAPHY

ChiltonW; *ConnorBG*

Len: "'More like Pres than Pres himself': Meet Mr. Quinichette," *DB*, xix/18 (1952), 7

R. Horricks: *Count Basie and his Orchestra: its Music and its Musicians* (London and New York, 1957), 272

B. Rusch: "Paul Quinichette, Jazz Master," *Cadence*, i/4 (1976), 3

S. Dance: *The World of Count Basie* (New York and London, 1980), 298

M. L. Hester: *Going to Kansas City* (Sherman, TX, 1980), 153

F. Büchmann-Møller: *You Just Fight for your Life: the Story of Lester Young* (New York, Westport, CT, and London, 1990)

D. Clarke: *Wishing on the Moon: the Life and Times of Billie Holiday* (London and New York, 1994)

EDDIE LAMBERT/BK

Quinn, Snoozer [Edwin McIntosh] (*b* McComb, MS, 18 Oct 1906; *d* New Orleans, 1949 or 1952). Guitarist. He grew up in a musical family, played mandolin and violin before turning to the guitar at the age of seven, and performed professionally before his teens; when he was 17 he toured with the Paul English Traveling Shows. Following work in lesser-known jazz groups, in 1925 he joined the Bad Boys, led by Peck Kelley and featuring Johnny Wiggs, then from autumn 1928 to mid-1929 performed and recorded as a rhythm guitarist with Paul Whiteman. He later recorded with the hillbilly singer Jimmy Davis (1931) and worked with the drummer Earl Crumb. Shortly after appearing at the New Orleans National Jazz Foundation concert in 1948 he underwent hospitalization for tuberculosis; at this late point in his career he recorded as an unaccompanied soloist and in duos with Wiggs (*The Legendary Snoozer Quinn with Johnny Wiggs*, ?1948, Fat Cat Jazz 104). Quinn was highly regarded by such colleagues as Bix Beiderbecke, Jimmy McPartland, and Jack Teagarden. His instrumental work was based on a fluid chord-melody approach that in its day rivaled that of George Van Eps.

BIBLIOGRAPHY

G. W. Kay: "The Legendary 'Snoozer' Quinn," *SL*, xxiii (1970), March–April, 293

T. Russell: Liner notes, Jimmie Davis: *Nobody's Darlin' but Mine* (Bear Family 15943, 1998)

JIM FERGUSON

Quintette du Hot Club de France. French quintet. It was formed in Paris in 1934 in connection with the Hot club de France, founded two years earlier. It grew out of informal sessions in which the guitarists Django Reinhardt and Roger Chaput, the violinist Stephane Grappelli, and the double bass player Louis Vola, all members of Vola's band, played together backstage during breaks in their performances at the Hôtel Claridge. After a third guitarist, Joseph Reinhardt, was added, the quintet gave its first concert at the Ecole Normale de Musique on 2 December 1934. Soon afterwards it made its first recordings, which were highly acclaimed: the public was immediately drawn by the unfamiliar style of the music, and by the mixture of seductiveness and exuberance that Grappelli and Django Reinhardt brought to the group's playing. Between 1934 and 1939 Chaput was replaced successively by Pierre Ferret, Marcel Bianchi, and Eugene Vees, and Vola's place was taken by Lucien Simoens, Roger Grasset, and finally Emmanuel Soudieux. The group performed widely in the late 1930s and soon became established as a major force in French jazz. Grappelli moved to England during World War II and was replaced by the clarinetist Hubert Rostaing; at the same time the drummer Pierre Fouad was substituted for the third guitarist. On Grappelli's return to France in 1946 the group was re-formed with its original members, but it disbanded in 1949. The original quintet recorded almost 200 titles, which continue to fascinate listeners by Grappelli's weaving of delicate traceries around the improvised guitar lines of great genius produced by Reinhardt.

See also String band; for illustrations *see* Guitar, fig.1, and Jazz (i), fig.4.

SELECTED RECORDINGS

Dinah (1934, Ultraphone 1422); Djangology (1935, Ultraphone 1548); Sweet Chorus (1936, HMV K7843); Minor Swing (1937, Swing 23); My Sweet (1938, Decca F6769); Hungaria (1939, Decca F7198); Swing 39 (1939, Decca F7027); Echoes of France (1946, Swing 229)

BIBLIOGRAPHY

H. Panassié: *Douze années de jazz (1927–1938): souvenirs* (Paris, 1946), 139, 189

C. Delaunay: *Django Reinhardt: souvenirs* (Paris, 1954; Eng. trans., London, 1961, 1982, rev. 2/1981/*R*1993) [incl. discography]

——: *Django, mon frère* (Paris, 1968)

F. Murphy: "*Liebestraum* Cast in a Transatlantic Mould: Liszt and the Hot Club Quintet," *Jf*, xxvi (1994), 123

ANDRÉ CLERGEAT

Rabbit. Nickname of both GEORGE HUNT and JOHNNY HODGES.

Rabold, Frederic (*b* Paris, 23 Nov 1944). German trumpeter. Having moved to Karlsruhe, Germany (1956), he studied trumpet at the Musikhochschule there (1961–4). In the 1960s he played with several bands in Stuttgart and founded his first band, the Frederic Rabold Crew (1968); among its numerous albums are *Flair* (1972, Calig 30608) and *Balance* (1976–7, Calig 30616). Over the years his ensembles have included musicians such as Herbert Joos, Joki Freund, Eberhard Weber, and Lauren Newton. Rabold also organized other bands, notably the Jazz Inspiration Orchestra. In the 1970s he was a member of Gunter Hampel's Galaxie Dream Band and became active in jazz education. His playing is influenced by that of Clifford Brown and Chet Baker, while his compositions make use of sudden changes, in which composed static passages are contrasted with free solo statements and modern jazz and free jazz are fused with elements from jazz-rock, West Indian, or Eastern European music.

WOLFRAM KNAUER

Race, Steve [Stephen Russell] (*b* Lincoln, England, 1 April 1921). English pianist and broadcaster. After studying at the Royal Academy of Music in London he worked in the early 1940s as an arranger for Ted Heath and in 1949 recorded with his own bop group. During the early 1950s he worked as a freelance and began to develop a reputation as a propagandist for jazz. From 1955 to 1960 he was the adviser on light music to the television company Associated–Rediffusion. He presented various programs for BBC radio, notably "Jazz Record Requests," "My Music" (1966–90), and "Steve Race" (1984–90), the last of which featured the BBC Radio Orchestra and Big Band; "My Music" was transferred to BBC television in the 1980s. Race published an autobiography, *Musician at Large* (London, 1979), and continued to write books after he retired from broadcasting in 1995. His abilities as a pianist and arranger may be heard on the album *Take One* (World Record Club 453), which he recorded with a big band in 1965.

BIBLIOGRAPHY

ChiltonB; *FeatherE*

J. Godbolt: *A History of Jazz in Britain, 1919–50* (London, Melbourne, Australia, and New York, 1984)

MARK GILBERT

Race record. A term applied between 1921 and 1942 to phonograph recordings made especially for African-American listeners. It was coined by Ralph Peer of Okeh, the first company to have a "race series"; he adapted the generic term "the Race," which was employed at that time in the African-American press. Okeh commenced its 8000 series in 1921; other race series included, from 1922, the Paramount 12000s; from 1923, Columbia's 14000s; from 1926, Vocalion's 1000s; and from 1927, the Victor 21000s and 38000s (among others). Many smaller companies had race series and by 1927 some 500 race records were being issued each year. Sales declined with the Depression and many concerns closed. But in 1933 Victor's Bluebird subsidiary began issuing race records to compete with the issues of the American Record Corporation labels, and the English Decca company started its successful American Decca 7000 race series in 1934.

Although a number of instrumental jazz recordings were issued in the race series, jazz titles were often circulated on general lists that did not differentiate between African-American and white performers. The appeal of jazz was broader than that of blues or gospel, and the large number of white jazz bands made any distinction on grounds of color invalid. While instrumental jazz recordings were, and are, often loosely categorized in the race series proper as race records, vocal recordings predominated. Between 1921 and 1925 these were mainly by professional "classic" blues singers and spiritual and gospel quartets. Self-accompanied blues singers became popular in 1926, and field trips to record new talent in the South were undertaken by several companies. Recordings by preachers, either as soloists or accompanied by their congregations (and sometimes musicians), sold well, but were less popular after 1930. By that time performances by "classic" blues singers and vocal duets were also losing their popularity, but quartets became increasingly sophisticated, and small groups accompanied blues singers to boost sales of their recordings in the 1930s.

After World War II the term "race records" was dropped and "rhythm-and-blues" was used in its stead, until the latter assumed a more specific stylistic meaning. To collectors, "race record" is applied generally to 78 r.p.m. discs intended for the African-American market; with their increasing rarity, many such records are much prized.

See also Recording, §II, 2.

BIBLIOGRAPHY

D. Mahony: *The Columbia 13/14000-D Series: a Numerical Listing* (Stanhope, NJ, 1961, rev. 2/1966/R1973 with addns)

R. C. Foreman, Jr.: *Jazz and Race Records, 1920–1932: their Origins and their Significance for the Record Industry and Society* (diss., U. of Illinois, 1968)

R. M. W. Dixon and J. Godrich: *Recording the Blues* (London, 1970)

M. E. Vreede: *Paramount 12/13000* (London, 1971)

P. Oliver: *Songsters and Saints: Vocal Traditions on Race Records* (Cambridge, England, and elsewhere, 1984)

R. M. W. Dixon, J. Godrich, and H. Rye, *Blues & Gospel Records, 1890–1943* (rev. and enlarged 4/1997), "The Race Labels," xxiii

PAUL OLIVER

Rachabane, (Joel) Barney (*b* Alexandra township, South Africa, 2 March 1946). South African alto and soprano saxophonist, flutist, and penny whistle player. In a career that typifies the history of jazz in South Africa in the second half of the twentieth century, from the age of 11 he played penny whistle on street corners in a group called the Little Bunnies, then continued in the same vein with the Kwela Kids. He was self-taught, but passed Royal Schools exams through Grade VI in music theory and flute. In the 1960s and 1970s he played saxophone with Abdullah Ibrahim, and he may be heard on albums that are now considered to be classic. He also performed in Chris McGregor's Castle Lager Big Band (1963) and such groups of the 1960s as the Big Five (alongside Johnny Mekoa and the drummer Early Mabuza) and the Soul Giants (which included the trumpeter Dennis Mpali). Two of his compositions from this era, *Barney's Way* and *Kwela Mama*, represent his fluency in bop and in township jazz respectively.

Affiliations with Hugh Masekela (1982–6) and Paul Simon (1986–92) brought Rachabane international recognition. Other important associations from the 1970s into the 1990s were with Allen Kwela, the Brazilian pianist Izio Gross, and the group Conversations (with Bruce Cassidy on trumpet and Denzil Weale or Rashid Lani on piano). He appeared with Darius Brubeck and Victor Ntoni's Afro Cool Concept in New Orleans, Rome, Bangkok, and Grahamstown, South Africa. Outside of jazz he collaborated with Cassidy on music for a television drama series and toured with the musical *The Buddy Holly Story*; the South African Broadcasting Corporation made a television documentary on his life.

Rachabane's playing exemplifies "the African sound," characterized by a special musical vocabulary developed during his apprenticeship with the township players Zacks Nkosi and Kippie Moeketsi. Regarded as South Africa's foremost alto saxophonist, because of his dazzling technique he has also been likened to Sonny Stitt. He is proud of saying that he is one of the few South African jazz musicians who has never held any other job.

SELECTED RECORDINGS

As leader: *Blow Barney Blow* (1985, Jive Africa 8002); *Barney's Way* (Jive 9001, 1989)

As sideman: C. McGregor and Castle Lager Big Band: *Jazz the African Sound* (1963, [original issue unknown]); P. Matshikiza and others: *Castle Lager Jazz Festival* (EMI JPL(M)4019, 1964); A. Ibrahim: *African Herbs/ Soweto* (1975, The Sun 786135); H. Singer: *Blue Stompin'* (Gallo 1912, 1977); D. Brubeck: *Tugela Rail* (RPM 609, 1984); P. Simon: *Graceland* (WB 1602, 1986); D. Brubeck and V. Ntoni: *Brubeck/Ntoni Afro Cool Concept Live at New Orleans Jazz & Heritage Festival, 1990* (1990, African Echoes 7865)

BIBLIOGRAPHY

L. Rasmussen: *Abdullah Ibrahim: a Discography* (Copenhagen, 1999)

<http://www.music.org.za/artists/rachabane/> (2000)

DARIUS BRUBECK

Rader, Don(ald Arthur) (*b* Rochester, PA, 21 Oct 1935). Trumpeter, flugelhorn player, teacher, arranger, and composer. He began playing at the age of five, studying with his father and later at the US Naval School of Music and Sam Houston State University. He played with Woody Herman (October 1959–1961, 1965, including a tour of Europe), Maynard Ferguson (1961–3, 1964), and Count Basie (replacing Thad Jones, April 1963 – July 1964) and wrote arrangements for all three bands. He also performed with Harry James, Terry Gibbs (with whom he recorded in 1965), and Frank Foster's quintet. In the period 1967–72 he played with Les Brown on three world tours and began working with Louie Bellson (from 1968). As a member of Stan Kenton's band he appeared as a principal soloist in a special program on PBS television in 1969; he also taught in Kenton's jazz workshops (1968–70). In 1972 he formed his own quintet, with which he gave numerous concerts and classes throughout the country. In the 1980s and 1990s his quintet included such sidemen as Lanny Morgan, Joe Roccisano, Alan Broadbent, and Ron Eschete; it recorded in 1990. As a freelance musician in and around Los Angeles Rader continued his associations with Gibbs (to 1983) and Bellson (to 1988), worked again with Brown (1986–94), performed at Herman's fiftieth anniversary concert (1986), played with Benny Carter (1988–92), and recorded with Bill Holman's big band (1986–7). He also worked in Germany, performing and recording with Peter Herbolzheimer (1981–96) and others and playing in several radio orchestras, including the SDR big band (1980s–1990s). In June 1992 he toured Europe. Rader has been active in the field of jazz education, performing and adjudicating at many college jazz festivals; he has written a number of articles for the *Jazz Educators Journal*. Among his compositions is *Polluted Tears*, which he recorded with his own band.

SELECTED RECORDINGS

As leader: *Polluted Tears* (1972, DRM 3236); *Wallflower* (1978, Dis. 796); *A Foreign Affair* (1990, L+R 45034)

As sideman: M. Ferguson: *Maynard '62* (1962, Roul. 52083); E. Fitzgerald: *Ella and Basie* (1963, Verve 64061); W. Herman: *Woody's Winners* (1965, Col. CS9236); T. Gibbs: *Terry Gibbs Quartet* (1965, Dot 3683); D. Menza: *Burnin'* (1980, RT 301)

SELECTED ARRANGEMENTS

* – with Rader as sideman

Recorded by M. Ferguson: *Sin Blues, on *Maynard '63* (1963, Roul. 52090)

Recorded by W. Herman: Greasy Sack Blues, *My Funny Valentine, *Poor Butterfly, on *Woody's Winners* (1965, Col. CS9236)

BIBLIOGRAPHY

Feather '60s; *Feather–Gitler '70s*

"Don Rader," *JP*, xli/6 (1992), 17

W. D. Clancy with A. C. Kenton: *Woody Herman: Chronicles of the Herds* (New York and elsewhere, 1995)

FREDERICK A. BECK/BK

Radiobandet. Group led from 1956 to 1965 by Harry Arnold.

Radioens Big Band [Danish Radio Big Band; Danish Radio Jazz Orchestra]. Danish big band. Formed in 1964 in affiliation with Danmarks Radio, it was known during its first three years as the Ny Radiodanseorkester; during this period it was led by Ib Glindemann, who was influenced chiefly by Stan Kenton. From 1968 the band's repertory was more diverse, and several European and American musicians worked with it as guest soloists and leaders. Among the band's full-time leaders were the saxophonist Ray Pitts, Palle Mikkelborg, Ole Kock Hansen, and, from 1977 to 1978, Thad Jones. Thereafter the Radioens Big Band resumed using guest conductors, with Hansen appearing most frequently among a plethora of international conductors, including (from 1964) Oliver Nelson, Kenton, Dizzy Gillespie, Frank Foster, Mary Lou Williams, Mike Gibbs, Jimmy Heath, Bengt-Arne Wallin, Ernie Wilkins, Butch Lacy, George Russell, Bob Brookmeyer, Helge Hurum, and Maria Schneider. The band toured extensively from 1984 in Europe, the USA, Australia, and China.

SELECTED RECORDINGS

Brownsville Trolley Line (1969, Sonet 1520); *No Fool, No Fun* (1970, Spot. 142); *By Jones, I Think We've Got it* (1978, Met. 15629); *A Good Time was Had by All* (1978, Met. 15644); *Crackdown* (1987, Hep 2041); *Suite for Jazz Band* (1991, Hep 2051); with Marie Bergman: *But Beautiful* (1994, Stunt 19404); *Ways of Seeing* (1997, Sto. 4224)

BIBLIOGRAPHY

L. Malone: *The Danish Radio Big Band, 1964–1984* (Copenhagen, 1984)
"Reaching other Parts: the Danish Radio Big Band," *CI*, xxiv/2 (1987), 6

ERIK WIEDEMANN/FRANK BÜCHMANN-MØLLER

Radiojazzgruppen [Danish Radio Jazz Group] **(i).** Danish big band. It was formed in 1961 as a nine-piece workshop group and later acquired additional members. The band was led from its inception by Erik Moseholm (who may be heard as its leader on the album *The Radio Jazz Group*, 1965, Debut 1145), then by the saxophonist Ray Pitts (1966–7) and by Palle Mikkelborg (1967–72), under whose direction it was known by the name Opportunity. In 1973 the group reverted to its original name and from this time had several leaders, including the trumpeter Lars Togeby, under whom it also performed as the Crème Fraîche Big Band in the 1970s. After a period of relative inactivity the group was formally disbanded in 1986. Most members of the Radioens Big Band played first in the Radiojazzgruppen, which was less closely associated with Danmarks Radio and had a more adventurous programming policy.

ERIK WIEDEMANN

Radiojazzgruppen [Swedish Radio Jazz Group] **(ii).** Swedish group. Formed in 1967 as a studio ensemble, its leaders have been Arne Domnérus (1967–78) and Lennart Åberg (from the early 1980s); its regular members have included Jan Johansson, Bengt Hallberg, and Georg Riedel. The group has performed works by George Russell, Carla Bley, Anthony Braxton, Gil Evans, Thad Jones, and several Swedish jazz composers, and made about 15 recordings of compositions by Russell (1977), Jones (*Greetings and Salutations*, 1975, Four Leaf Clover 5001), and others. After a reorganization in the early 1980s the group comprised a smaller number of permanent members whose ranks were supplemented by visiting soloists. (S. Boija: "Två sidor av Guy" [Two sides of Guy], *Orkester journalen*, lxiv/3 (1996), 17)

PEKKA GRONOW

Rae, Johnny [John; Pompeo, John Anthony] (*b* Boston, 11 Aug 1934; *d* San Francisco, 4 Sept 1993). Drummer, vibraphonist, and percussionist. He grew up in a musical family and studied piano at the New England Conservatory, timpani at the Boston Conservatory, and drums at the Berklee School of Music. After performing in Boston with such leaders as the pianist Al Vega (August–December 1953, July 1954 – January 1955), Herb Pomeroy (December 1953 – July 1954), and Jay Migliori (April–July 1954) he moved to New York (1955), where he worked as a vibraphonist with George Shearing (1955 – October 1956), Johnny Smith (1956 – early 1957), Ralph Sharon (1957), Cozy Cole (for six months in 1958), Herbie Mann (1959–60, touring Africa in 1960), and Peter Appleyard (1960–61). From May 1961 he played drums in San Francisco for five years with Cal Tjader, during which time he recorded with Stan Getz (1962), led his own group in Aspen, Colorado (1963), and performed with Vince Guaraldi (summer 1964). Having left Tjader in March 1966, he joined Gábor Szabó as a drummer, though later he played vibraphone. During another period with Tjader (August 1968 – March 1970) he worked as a freelance with Herb Ellis and Joe Pass. From 1973 to 1975 Rae was with Charlie Byrd and served as a member of Great Guitars. Thereafter he performed in show bands and concentrated on playing Latin jazz. From 1982 he was a member of the quintet Radcliffe (named after Tjader's middle name), in which he appeared alongside three other former members of Tjader's band, the drummer Vince Lateano, Mark Levine, and the percussionist Willie Colon, as well as lesser-known musicians from the San Francisco Bay area. At the same time he played in local dixieland bands and big bands, accompanied singers, and continued to work in pit bands and orchestras for musical theater. Rae wrote two books, *Jazz Phrasing for Mallets, Vibes, Marimba, Xylophone* (New York, 1961) and *Latin Guide for Jazz Drummers* (late 1960s), and contributed a number of articles to *Modern Drummer* (1981–2).

SELECTED RECORDINGS

As leader: *Opus de jazz*, ii (1960, Savoy 12156); *Afro-jazz Septet* (1961–2, UA 4042)
As sideman: G. Shearing: *The Shearing Spell* (1955, Cap. T648); C. Tjader: *Cal Tjader Plugs In* (1969, Skye 10); Great Guitars (C. Byrd, H. Ellis, and B. Kessel): *Three Guitars* (1974, Conc. 4)

BIBLIOGRAPHY

FeatherE; *Feather '60s*; *Feather–Gitler '70s*
C. M. Bernstein: "John Rae: Total Musicality," *MD*, ix/3 (1985), 25
P. Elwood: "The Spirit and Music of Cal Tjader," *San Francisco Examiner* (26 July 1988)

RICK MATTINGLY/BK

Raeburn, Boyd (Albert) [Raben, Boyd(e) Albert)] (*b* Faith, SD, 27 Oct 1913; *d* Lafayette, LA, 2 Aug 1966). Bandleader and tenor and bass saxophonist. Raeburn's son notes that he was born Raben (not Raden, as it appears in many sources) and that primary sources give his first name as both Boyd and Boyde. He led various types of commercial dance bands from 1933 but began to take a substantial turn towards jazz during an engagement at the Arcadia Ballroom in New York in November 1942, when Budd Johnson and Jerry Valentine contributed arrangements to his orchestra. For nine months in 1943 he was resident at the Band Box in Chicago with a band that included Johnny Bothwell and the singers Ginnie Powell and Shirley Luster (soon to be famous as June Christy). He is important for his jazz groups of 1944–6, which played advanced arrangements influenced by both bop and European concert music. During this period his band was initially based in New York, and among its sidemen were Bothwell, the arranger Eddie Finckel, and three future members of Woody Herman's orchestra – Sonny Berman, Earl Swope, and Don Lamond. George Handy

Boyd Raeburn's band at the Virginia Polytechnic Institute, Blacksburg, Virginia, 12 April 1947: (back row, left to right) Ray Rossi (piano), Joe Burriece (double bass), Irv Kluger (drums), Wes Hensel, Pete Candoli, Bernie Glow, and Gordon Boswell (trumpets); (middle row, left to right) Steve Jordan (guitar), Leon Cox, Dick Noel, and Hal Smith (trombones); (front row, left to right) Jay Johnson and Ginnie Powell (voice), Lloyd Otto and Vince DeMino (french horns), Sam Spumberg (clarinet), Shirley Thompson (tenor saxophone), Raeburn (bass saxophone), Buddy DeFranco (clarinet), Jerry Sanfino (alto saxophone), Frank Socolow (tenor saxophone), and Hy Mandel (baritone saxophone)

replaced Finckel in May 1944 and also served as the group's pianist, and important African-American swing and bop musicians began to be associated with it. Little Benny Harris and Oscar Pettiford toured until the band reached the South, where a racially mixed big band was unacceptable; Roy Eldridge, Trummy Young, and Dizzy Gillespie sat in in New York, and Gillespie introduced one of his finest pieces, recorded as *Night in Tunisia* for the V-Disc label in 1944 and again, but retitled *Interlude*, for Guild in 1945. The incorporation of more talented guest sidemen for the latter session (Gillespie, Harris, Al Cohn, Serge Chaloff, Pettiford, and Shelly Manne) improved both the band's section work and the quality of the improvised solos. Dodo Marmarosa joined as pianist around 1946.

Raeburn began to play baritone saxophone in 1945, then from 1946 concentrated on the bass instrument. His arrangements were commissioned from important modernists of the day, including Gillespie, Handy, who rejoined the band in San Francisco in summer 1945 after spending six months writing for films in Hollywood, and Johnny Richards, who replaced Handy in 1946 following the revelation that Raeburn had appropriated rights to Finckel's and Handy's compositions. The music was characterized by harmonic ideas drawn from the French impressionist composers and, especially, Stravinsky (*see* PROGRESSIVE JAZZ). Although Raeburn's bands were greatly admired by musicians, the music puzzled ordinary dance-band enthusiasts. In 1947 a short film, *Boyd Raeburn and his Orchestra*, was issued, but Raeburn continued to struggle to find an audience for his music. By 1950 he had returned to more commercial styles and later in that decade he finally left music altogether.

SELECTED RECORDINGS

Interlude (1945, Guild 107); March of the Boyds (1945, Guild 111); Tonsilectomy (1945, Jwl 10000); Yerxa (1945, Jwl 10001); Dalvatore Sally (1946, Jwl 1-1); Boyd Meets Stravinsky (1946, Jwl 10002); Over the Rainbow (1946, Jwl 1-2)

BIBLIOGRAPHY

G. Hoefer: "Boyd Raeburn," *DB*, xxix/9 (1962), 24
A. Jackson: "Boyd Raeburn: 'the Successful Failure'," *JM*, xii/9 (1966), 5
Obituaries: *New York Times* (4 Aug 1966); *DB*, xxxiii/18 (1966), 14
G. T. Simon: *The Big Bands* (New York and London, 1967, rev. 4/1981), 398
G. Hall: *Boyd Raeburn and his Orchestra: a Complete Discography* (Laurel, MD, 1972)
J. McKinney: Liner notes, B. Raeburn: *Jewells* (1980, Savoy 2250)
S. Woolley: "The Forgotten Ones: Boyd Raeburn," *JJI*, xxxvii/2 (1984), 18
C. Garrod and B. Korst: *Boyd Raeburn and his Orchestra plus Johnny Bothwell and George Handy* (Zephyrhills, FL, 1985, rev. 2/1997) [discography]

JAMES LINCOLN COLLIER/BK

Raecox. Record company and label founded by Teddy McRae and EDDIE WILCOX.

Ragas, Henry (W.) (*b* New Orleans, 1891; *d* New York, 18 Feb 1919). Pianist. After working as an unaccompanied solo pianist from 1910 to 1913 he joined Johnny Stein's band, with which he moved to Chicago in 1916. A few months later Ragas, Nick LaRocca, and Eddie Edwards left Stein to form the Original Dixieland Jass Band, which in 1917 began playing at Reisenweber's Restaurant in New York and made the first recordings of jazz (*see* ORIGINAL DIXIELAND JAZZ BAND). Ragas composed *Bluin' the Blues*, which was recorded by the band in 1918 (Vic. 18483). Weakened by alcoholism, he died during an influenza epidemic.

BIBLIOGRAPHY

"Henry Ragas," *SL*, vi/9–10 (1955), 29
H. O. Brunn: *The Story of the Original Dixieland Jazz Band* (Baton Rouge, LA, 1960/*R*1977)

MIKE HAZELDINE

Ragin, Hugh (*b* Houston, 9 April 1951). Trumpeter. He took up trumpet at the age of 13 and soon made up his mind to become a professional performer and teacher. While attending the University of Houston he played in local rhythm-and-blues bands. He later studied at Colorado State University in Fort Collins, where he led the group Corner Culture with the tenor saxophonist Mars Williams. In late 1978 Ragin attended a workshop at the Creative Music Studios and met Lester Bowie, Joseph Jarman, and Malachi Favors. The following year he toured Europe with the Creative Orchestra of Leo Smith and Roscoe Mitchell and in a duo with Anthony Braxton, and performed in Braxton's quartet; he continued to perform and record with Mitchell into the late 1980s. In 1983 he toured the USA and Japan with Maynard Ferguson's band, and while the group was in New York he met David Murray; he subsequently performed and recorded with a number of Murray's groups, including his Octet, his chamber jazz quartet with Fred Hopkins and Abdul Wadud, his big band, and his funk ensemble Fo Deuk Revue. He has also recorded with John Lindberg (1981–4), A. Spencer Barefield (1987), Fred Wesley (1991–4), and D. D. Jackson (*c*1996). In 1998 Ragin was teaching and performing in Colorado. He also plays piccolo trumpet and flugelhorn.

SELECTED RECORDINGS

Duos with J. Lindberg: *Team Work* (1982, Cecma 1004)
As leader: *Metaphysical Question* (1984, Cecma 1007)
As sideman: R. Mitchell: *Snurdy McGurdy and her Dancing Shoes* (1980, Nessa 20); *More Cutouts* (1981, Cecma 1003); *Live at the Knitting Factory* (1987, BS 120120-2); D. Murray: *The People's Choice* (*c*1987, Cecma 1009); F. Wesley: *Comme ci comme ça* (1991, Ant. 314-512002-2)

BIBLIOGRAPHY

E. Hazell: "Hugh Ragin: the Metaphysical Question," *Coda*, no.215 (1987), 24

GK

Raglin, Junior [Alvin Redrick] (*b* Omaha, NE, 16 March 1917; *d* Boston, 10 Nov 1955). Double bass player. From 1938 to 1941 he played with Eugene Coy's Happy Black Aces, a territory band based in Amarillo, Texas. Later in 1941, while a member of Wilbert Baranco's trio in San Francisco, he came to the attention of Duke Ellington, whose double bass player, Jimmy Blanton, was seriously ill. Raglin deputized for Blanton in Ellington's orchestra in Los Angeles and by November 1941 had replaced him; he remained with the band until 1945. Blanton's influence had caused Ellington to expand the role of the double bass in his arrangements to include demanding ensemble parts and solo passages, with which Raglin coped admirably. He played on many of the great recordings of this era, among them *Raincheck* and *Chelsea Bridge* (both 1941) and *The "C" Jam Blues*, *Perdido*, and *Main Stem* (all 1942), made soundies and appeared briefly in the feature-length films *Cabin in the Sky* (1942) and *Reveille with Beverley* (1943), and participated in concerts in Carnegie Hall (1943, 1944). His playing is also well represented on *Emancipation Celebration*, from the suite *Black, Brown and Beige* (1943), and on *Carnegie Blues* (1945). In addition Raglin recorded with Edmond Hall (1944), Rex Stewart (1945), Ella Fitzgerald (1946), and Al Hibbler (1947). In 1946 he won the "new star" award from *Down Beat*. In December 1947 he rejoined Ellington to deputize for, and eventually replace, Oscar Pettiford, but he left the band again in September the following year and thereafter fell into obscurity.

SELECTED RECORDINGS

As sideman with D. Ellington: Chelsea Bridge (1941, Vic. 27740); Raincheck/Perdido (1941–2, Vic. 27880); The "C" Jam Blues/Moon Mist (1942, Vic. 27856); Main Stem/Johnny Come Lately (1942, Vic. 20-1556); *Carnegie Hall Concert* (1943, Jazz Panorama 1), incl. Emancipation Celebration; *Black, Brown and Beige* (1944, Vic. 28-0040–01), incl. Emancipation Celebration; Carnegie Blues (1945, Vic. 20-1644); Diminuendo in Blue/Crescendo in Blue (1945, V-Disc 534A)
As sideman with others: E. Hall: Big City Blues/ Steamin' and Beamin' (1944, BN 36); R. Stewart: Dutch Treat/Rexercise (1945, Cap. 10035); Three-horn Parlay (1945, Parl. R3108); Dreamer's Blues (1945, Parl. R3102); E. Fitzgerald: I'm a lucky so and so (1946, Decca 18814)

BIBLIOGRAPHY

ChiltonW; *SchullerS*
Obituary, *DB*, xxiii/1 (1956), 9
C. Carrière: "Pitter panther patter: les bassistes de Duke Ellington," *Jh*, no.316 (1975), 10

JOHN CURRY

Ragtime. A style of American popular music that flourished from about 1890 to World War I.

1. Definition and origins. 2. Piano ragtime. 3. Band and orchestral ragtime.

1. Definition and origins. The term "ragged time" came to be used in the late 19th century to describe the idiomatic syncopation characteristic of a style of popular music, predominantly for the piano, that emanated from the South and Midwest. The word "ragtime" was a corruption of this; the practice of syncopation was described as "ragging," and typical pieces, in which an internally syncopated melodic line was set against a rhythmically straightforward bass, as "rags." Although ragtime was primarily a written genre, ragtime tunes and performance practices were influential in shaping the direction of solo and collective improvisation in early jazz. In the early decades of the 20th century the term "ragtime" was used synonymously with "jazz" by many performers, particularly in New Orleans (*see* New orleans jazz), and, even later, jazz musicians referred to the characteristic syncopation of a melody as "ragging a tune." Whereas it began as a style for solo piano, ragtime subsequently encompassed popular songs, and, towards the end of the era, broadened to include band and orchestral repertory.

2. Piano ragtime. During the 1890s itinerant black pianists such as Scott Joplin, Tom Turpin, James Scott, and Artie Matthews composed and notated works that formalized practices hitherto improvisatory and irregular. Early published rags resembled cakewalks but adopted the word "rag" in their titles – for example, William H. Krell's *Mississippi Rag* (1897). In 1899 Joplin's *Original Rags* and *Maple Leaf Rag* appeared, the latter achieving nationwide success.

Piano ragtime as conceived by midwestern pianist-composers was a multithematic form with three or four discrete 16-bar strains (*see* Forms, esp. §1(d)). The music was melodically inventive and rhythmically lively, built on a bright, steady duple pulse and making use of strong tonal progressions. The multithematic structure of ragtime compositions became incorporated into many early jazz pieces, both for solo piano and for ensemble, but while in ragtime performances the themes were repeated literally as written, in jazz improvised variations were introduced. Solo pianists began to make use of more sophisticated rhythms, and, in particular, introduced syncopation in the duple subdivision of the beats in the left hand.

As the term "ragtime" came to be applied indiscriminately to many forms of popular music, and indeed to the age itself, availability of piano scores and player-piano rolls disseminated the music widely to middle-class Americans, and, as the repertory expanded, so too did the variety of more jazz-oriented performance styles associated with it. "Novelty" piano pieces and rags less identifiable as "classic," such as Charles Johnson's *Dill Pickles Rag* (1906), George Botsford's *Black and White Rag* (1908), Adeline Shepherd's *Pickles and Peppers* (1908), and Henry Lodge's *Temptation Rag* (1909), were widely performed by parlor pianists. Meanwhile the more jazz-oriented aspects of ragtime were incorporated in the compositions of Eubie Blake and Jelly Roll Morton. Ragtime subsequently formed the basis of the stride piano style (*see* Piano, §2), whose exponents possessed a consummate technical command of the keyboard, made more extensive use of improvisation, and employed a much broader range of expressive devices. Composers such as James P. Johnson, Fats Waller, Willie "the Lion" Smith, and Luckey Roberts used the multithematic forms of ragtime as the foundation for their works.

From the late 1940s there has been a revival of piano ragtime. Performers such as Max Morath and Ralph Sutton integrated elements of stride piano with the purer ragtime style, while the musicologist Joshua Rifkin has endeavored, in his recordings and concert appearances, to preserve a relatively unsyncopated form of the music, adhering more closely to the notated scores.

3. Band and orchestral ragtime. From the late 1890s, when the first ragtime pieces were published, arrangements of the more popular pieces were made available for dance or theater orchestras, whose instrumentation predated that of the earliest jazz bands. Accompanying or rhythmic parts were taken by piano, guitar, double bass, and drums, and the melodic parts were assigned to one or two violins, one or two cornets or trumpets, flute, clarinet, trombone, and cello. Composers added tonal color to the repetition of each strain of the music by making use of alternate combinations of strings, brass, or woodwind. An early collection of orchestral pieces for such forces, *The Red Back Book of Rags* (*c*1915), which consisted principally of works by Joplin (notably *Maple Leaf Rag* and the more accomplished *Sugar Cane Rag*), set the standard for orchestration, although string bands and spasm bands in New Orleans and elsewhere in the South performed ragtime tunes on a variety of instruments, usually including mandolins and guitars. The multithematic element of most of the compositions in *The Red Back Book* also influenced early jazz, and pieces such as *High Society* and W. H. Tyers's *Panama* were adopted as staple items in the jazz repertory. Ragtime was later transcribed for the large concert bands of John Philip Sousa and Arthur Pryor, but the instrumentation of earlier arrangements was preserved by the society orchestras of New Orleans, such as that led by A. J. Piron, that flourished in the early 1920s.

In the late 1940s some musicians, notably Tony Parenti's Ragtimers and Mutt Carey's New Yorkers (both 1947), attempted to re-create the sound of early ragtime orchestras. Perhaps the most influential recordings of the period, however, have been those collectively issued as *The Last Testament of Bunk Johnson* (1947, Col. GL520), on which the New Orleans trumpeter plays with a group of New York session musicians. Later ensembles dedicated to the music have included the Love–Jiles Ragtime Orchestra of New Orleans, which endeavored to reproduce the orchestral sound of works from *The Red Back Book*, and the more formal New Orleans Ragtime Orchestra and the New England Conservatory group led by Gunther Schuller. Schuller attempts, in his arrangements of compositions from *The Red Back Book*, to convey in notated form some of the likely variety of tone color and texture of the early performances.

The relation of ragtime to jazz is explored deeply in the multi-media CD-ROM *Dick Hyman's Century of Jazz Piano*, recorded by Hyman and created by J. Simpson (New Orleans, 1999).

BIBLIOGRAPHY

R. Blesh and H. Janis: *They all Played Ragtime* (New York, 1950, rev. 4/1971)
R. J. Carew: "Reminiscing in Ragtime," *JJ*, xvii/11 (1964), 8
D. A. Jasen: "Ragtime: a Re-evaluation," *JJ*, xxi/4 (1968), 22
G. Schuller: *Early Jazz: its Roots and Musical Development* (New York, 1968)
B. Rust: "Ragtime on Records," *Sv*, no.27 (1970), 110
D. Flowitt: "Ragtime in Retrospect," *Sv*, no.36 (1971), 203
D. A. Jasen: "Ragtime Explained," *Sv*, no.37 (1971), 4
——: *Recorded Ragtime, 1897–1958* (Hamden, CT, 1973) [incl. 78 r.p.m. recordings of jazz versions of ragtime pieces]
W. J. Schafer and J. Riedel: *The Art of Ragtime* (Baton Rouge, LA, 1973)
T. Waldo: *This is Ragtime* (New York, 1976) [incl. discography]
D. A. Jasen and T. J. Tichenor: *Rags and Ragtime: a Musical History* (New York, 1978)
E. A. Berlin: *Ragtime: a Musical and Cultural History* (Berkeley, CA, Los Angeles, and London, 1980/*R*1984 with addns)
E. S. Walker: "The Spread of Ragtime in England," *Sv*, no.88 (1980), 123
J. E. Hasse, ed.: *Ragtime: its History, Composers, and Music* (New York and London, 1985)
R. E. Lotz: *German Ragtime and the Prehistory of Jazz*, i: *The Sound Documents* (Chigwell, England, 1985)
L. Fisher: "What is Ragtime? Is it Really Jazz?," *Jazz Research Papers*, vii (1987), 65
P. Köhler and M. Schubert, eds.: *Vom Ragtime endlich auch dem Swing: zur frühen Geschichte des Jazz in Deutschland* (Neu-Isenberg, Germany, 1991)
G. J. Haydon: *A Study of the Exchange of Influences between the Music of Early Twentieth-century Parisian Composers and Ragtime, Blues, and Early Jazz* (diss., U. of Texas, Austin, 1992)
E. A. Berlin: *King of Ragtime: Scott Joplin and his Era* (New York, and Oxford, England, 1994)
R. Badger: *A Life in Ragtime: a Biography of James Reese Europe* (New York, and Oxford, England, 1995)
R. Laird: *Tantalizing Tingles: a Discography of early Ragtime, Jazz, and Novelty Syncopated Piano Recordings, 1889–1934* (Westport, CT, and London, 1995)
W. H. Tallmadge: "Ben Harney: the Middlesborough Years, 1890–93," *American Music*, xiii/2 (1995), 167
T. Frew: *Scott Joplin and the Age of Ragtime* (New York, 1996)

WILLIAM J. SCHAFER

Rainey, Chuck [Charles Walter, III] (*b* Cleveland, 17 June 1940). Electric bass guitarist. His place of birth has been published as Youngstown, but in an interview (Jisi, 1997) he stated that he was born in Cleveland and grew up in nearby Youngstown. As a youth he studied violin, piano, and trumpet. He briefly played double bass while in high school and sang bass parts in a vocal group; in college he played baritone horn, and he took up electric guitar while on duty in the military reserves. At the age of 21 he moved to Cleveland, where he played electric guitar and electric bass guitar with rhythm-and-blues groups. Later he joined King Curtis's group in New York (1964). From this time he took part in hundreds of recording sessions with soul, pop, and jazz musicians, including Jerome Richardson (1967), Grady Tate (1968), and Mose Allison, Gato Barbieri, and Gene Ammons (all 1971). He also performed with Eddie "Cleanhead" Vinson at the Montreux International Jazz Festival (1971) and toured and recorded with Aretha Franklin. After moving to Los Angeles (June 1972) he performed with the Crusaders (1972–3) and Hampton Hawes (1974–5) and recorded with Donald Byrd (1973–5), Sonny Rollins (1975), and John Handy (1976). Later he recorded with Hiroshi Fukumura in Japan (1978). From 1984 he led his own groups, among them the Rainey/Walker Band, with the guitarist David T. Walker, Herman Riley, and Ndugu Chancler, playing what he described as a smooth jazz-pop fusion. Having moved between Dallas and Los Angeles, in the late 1980s he settled in Dallas and from 1992 to 1997 worked with Herbie Mann. Rainey's versatility and professionalism are highly regarded by critics and musicians alike. He has been active in education in both academic workshops and as a private teacher, was a columnist for *Guitar Player* (1975–6), *Bass Player* (1990–93), and other journals, and has written a number of instructional books, including *The Complete Electric Bass Player* (New York, *c*1985–6) and *Time Signature Studies for Bass* (Pacific, MO, *c*1995); he has also made several instructional videos, notably *Fusion Bass Styles* and *The Legendary Bass of Chuck Rainey* (both *c*1993).

SELECTED RECORDINGS

The Chuck Rainey Coalition (*c*1971, Cob. 9008); *Born Again* (1981, Hammer n' Nails 1949)

BIBLIOGRAPHY

M. Cuscuna: "Dreams," *J&P*, x/3 (1971), 32
M. Cullaz: "Chuck Rainey et Cornell Dupree," *Jh*, no.293 (1973), 12
R. Williams: "King Bass," *MM* (3 Feb 1973), 37
C. Jisi: "Groove Convergence: Will Lee interviews Chuck Rainey, the 'Godfather of the Groove'," *Bass Player*, viii/2 (1997), 42

BILL MILKOWSKI/BK

Rainey, Ma [Pridgett, Gertrude] (*b* Columbus, GA, 26 April 1886; *d* Rome, GA, 22 Dec 1939). Singer. Her career began in a talent show in Columbus when she was 13, and soon afterwards she appeared as a cabaret singer. She married Will "Pa" Rainey in 1904, and toured with him in F. S. Wolcott's Rabbit Foot Minstrels and other shows until 1916, when they formed their own company. By the time she first recorded (1923) she had become famous throughout the South. In five years she made more than 100 recordings. These did little justice to her vocal powers, but a majestic phrasing and "moaning" style close to folk tradition are evident from two of her first titles (and most celebrated compositions), *Bo-weavil Blues* and *Moonshine Blues*. She also recorded with Louis Armstrong and with her Georgia Jazz Band, which at various times included Tommy Ladnier, Joe Smith, and Coleman Hawkins. Although she recorded under the name of Ma Rainey, she was known as "Madame" on tour with the Georgia Jazz Band during the 1920s, when she played to large audiences throughout the South and in Mexico and established a lasting reputation as the most significant early female blues singer (for illustration *see* BLUES, fig.1). Her rambunctious disposition is rarely evident in her recordings, and *Ma Rainey's Black Bottom* is one of the few to demonstrate her humor. In the early 1930s Rainey was still touring, sometimes as a featured entertainer. Her attempts to recapture her popularity were unsuccessful, however, and in 1935 she retired to Columbus, where she was active in the Baptist church.

SELECTED RECORDINGS

(all recorded for Paramount)

Bo-weavil Blues (1923, 12080); Moonshine Blues (1923, 12083); See See Rider (1924, 12252); Jelly Bean Blues (1924, 12238); Yonder come the blues (1926, 12357); Soon this morning (1927, 12438); Ma Rainey's Black Bottom (1927, 12590)

BIBLIOGRAPHY

T. Pridgett: "The Life of Ma Rainey," *Jazz Information*, ii/4 (1940), 8
T. Fulbright: "Ma Rainey and I," *JJ*, ix/3 (1956), 1
D. Stewart-Baxter: *Ma Rainey and the Classic Blues Singers* (New York and London, 1970)
J. Godrich: "'Ma' Rainey," *Sv*, no.35 (1971), 173
S. Harris: *Blues Who's Who: a Biographical Dictionary of Blues Singers* (New Rochelle, NY, 1979/*R*1994)
S. R. Lieb: *Mother of the Blues: a Study of Ma Rainey* (Amherst, MA, 1981) [incl. discography]
D. Seroff: "Blues Itineraries: Ma Rainey on the Road," *Whiskey, Women, and . . .*, nos.12–13 (1983), [58]
L. Wright: "Pieces of the Jigsaw: Ma Rainey," in *Storyville 1996/7*, ed. Wright (Chigwell, England, 1997), 220; cont. in *Storyville 1998/9*, (Chigwell, 1999), 198

PAUL OLIVER

Rainey, Tom [Thomas Gaines] (*b* Los Angeles, 17 Sept 1957). Drummer. After studying at the Berklee College of Music (1975–8) he moved to New York (1979), where he served as a longstanding member of Kenny Werner's trio (1981–95). During the same period he worked in Jane Ira Bloom's small groups (1980s), with Carla White (from 1985), in Neal Kirkwood's Chromatic Persuaders and alongside Phil Haynes in Tom Varner's quintet (both from 1989), in Ben Monder's trio (1989–91), in Scott Lee's quartet (1990–93), with Klaus König (recording in 1991–2), and in Kirkwood's octet (from 1991). From 1990 to 1995 he played with the quintet NEW AND USED. Rainey was a member of various groups led by Mark Helias, most notably the quintet Attack the Future and the trio Open Loose (from around 1990). From 1991 to 1996 he worked in Fred Hersch's quintet, and from 1992 he played alongside Drew Gress in Hersch's trio. He joined Andy Laster's ensemble Hydra (1994), was a founding member with Gress of Tim Berne's trio Paraphrase (1996), and, with Berne and Marc Ducret, formed the group Big Satan (1998). In 1999 he toured in Joe Lovano's quintet Symbiosis. As a leader he took part in a concert of drums and percussion with Dave Samuels and Arto Tuncboyaçiyan. Rainey has recorded as a freelance with, among others, Roseanna Vitro (1991, *c*1993), Simon Nabatov (1992), the pianist Janice Friedman (*c*1993), Matthias Schubert, the trombonist Christoph Schweizer, and Ray Anderson (all 1994), and Rich Perry (1995).

SELECTED RECORDINGS

As leader with T. Berne and M. Ducret: *Big Satan* (1996, Winter & Winter 91005-2)

As sideman: J. I. Bloom: *Modern Drama* (1987, Col. FC40755); *Slalom* (1988, Col. FC44415); K. Werner: *Introducing the Trio* (1989, Sunnyside 1038); S. Nabatov: *Tough Customer* (1992, Enja 7063-2); T. Varner: *The Mystery of Compassion* (1992, SN 121217-2); F. Hersch: *Dancing in the Dark* (1992, Chesky 90); New and Used: *Consensus* (1993, Knitting Factory Works 163); J. Friedman: *Finger Paintings* (*c*1993, Jazzmania 6008); M. Helias: *Loopin' the Cool* (1994, Enja 9049-2); A. Laster: *Polyogue* (1995, Songlines 1507); F. Hersch: *Point in Time* (1995, Enja 9035-2); K. Werner: *Live at Visiones* (1995, Conc. 4675); Paraphrase: *Visitation Rites* (1996, Screwgun 70002)

BIBLIOGRAPHY

P. Watrous: "3 Uncategorizable Bands in Corner Store Festival," *New York Times* (29 April 1990)
<http://www.screwgunrecords.com/rainey.htm> (1999) [incl. discography]
T. Panken: "Players: Tom Rainey," *DB*, lxvi/9 (1999), 47

GK

Raja, Mario (*b* Naples, 20 April 1956). Italian tenor saxophonist, composer, arranger, and leader. He gained a degree in saxophone in 1979, but had already begun his professional career in 1977 in Rome working in big bands, including the RAI Orchestra (1983). In 1983 he founded, with Baldo Maestri, the saxophone quartet Arundo Donax, which played jazz, classical, and third stream music; it remained active in the late 1990s, but with a different personnel, including Pietro Tonolo. In 1988 Raja founded his Big Bang, a jazz orchestra featuring some of the foremost Italian modern-jazz soloists, among them Tonolo, Maurizio Giammarco, Roberto Gatto, the trumpeter Marco Tamburini, the trombonists Danilo Terenzi and Roberto Rossi, the tenor and baritone saxophonist Piero Leveratto, and the pianist Danilo Rea; it recorded an album of pieces by Duke Ellington (1997) and at the end of the 1990s worked on a project of Herbie Nichols's music. Raja assisted Gunther Schuller in the European première of Charles Mingus's posthumously reconstructed symphony *Epitaph* in 1991. He directed the Grande Orchestra Nazionale di Jazz from 1996 to 1998 and thereafter played in the Eliseo Big Band, led by the arranger and composer Tommaso Vittorini. In 1998 he founded the Orchestra Giovanile Valdostana di Jazz. Raja has written compositions and arrangements for many jazz orchestras, notably the Mingus Big Band and the Pekin Big Band, and he performed with Mel Lewis, Bob Brookmeyer, Sal Nistico (ii), Gary Smulyan, and several Italian symphony orchestras.

Raja plays tenor saxophone after the manner of Sonny Rollins. His writing for big band is inspired by that of Ellington, Mingus, Thad Jones, and Brookmeyer. An effective conductor of both orchestras and small groups, he is also a respected teacher.

SELECTED RECORDINGS

As leader of Big Bang: with P. Woods: *Embraceable You* (1988, Philology 25); *Ellington* (1994, Splasc(h) 427); *Dodici storie* (1997, Splasc(h) 626)
As sideman: R. Gatto: *L'avventura* (1993–4, Urlo 4509-97375); Arundo Donax: *C'era una volta* (1996, Splasc(h) 459); Gabriele Mirabassi: *Cambaluc* (1997, Egea 064); Arundo Donax: *Arundo Donax* (1999, BMG 74321-68585-2)

STEFANO ZENNI

RAM. Record company and label. It was established in Italy in the early 1990s by Raimondo Meli Lupi. Its most frequently recorded artist is Joe Diorio (with eight albums as of July 2000), but its catalogue of more than 30 items also includes recordings by Claudio Fasoli, Mick Goodrick, Hal Crook, and Bruce Gertz. RAM should not be confused with several rock and rhythm-and-blues labels of the same name.

GK

Ramblers. Dutch big band. It was formed in September 1926 by Theo Uden Masman and achieved great popularity in the Netherlands with a repertory of jazz, popular tunes, and nonsense songs. It acquired an international following after recording with Coleman Hawkins (1935, 1937), Benny Carter (1937), and Freddy Johnson (1937–8); it was sometimes known as the Ramblers Dance Orchestra. The group continued to be led by Masman until 1964, when it changed its name to the VARA Dance Orchestra (after the Verenigde Arbeiders Radio, on which it played) and its repertory to one consisting entirely of popular music. In the mid-1980s it was led by Marcel Thielemans, who had played trombone under Masman. In the 1990s, when Thielemans retired, the double bass player Jacques Schols became its new leader. Thereafter the band played mainly at special occasions organized by its active fan club.

SELECTED RECORDINGS

Decca Stomp (1933, Decca F3588); White Heat/Farewell Blues (1934, Decca F42029); Steeplechase (1937, Panachord H1020); Zuiderzee Blues (1938, Panachord H1056); Darktown Strutter's Ball/Jitterbug's Nightmare (1939, Panachord H1077); Pork and Beans (1939, Panachord H1076); Bouncin' in Bavaria/Rue de Radis (1946, Decca M32107)

BIBLIOGRAPHY

"Dutch Ramblers Reinstated," *MM*, xxi (24 Nov 1945), 5
J. Bulterman: *The Ramblers Story* (Bussum, Netherlands, 1973)
C. de Kloet and G. de Wagt: *Mooi Holland: de woelige jaren van de Ramblers* (Hilversum, 1981)
R. Braunberg: "The Ramblers," *JP*, xxxviii/10 (1989), 14

WIM VAN EYLE

Ramboy. Record company and label founded by MICHAEL MOORE (ii).

Ramey, Gene [Eugene Glasco] (*b* Austin, TX, 4 April 1913; *d* Austin, 8 Dec 1984). Double bass player. He grew up in a musical family and received piano lessons from his grandmother. From the age of eight through high school he played ukulele, and in his youth he took up temple blocks, trumpet, snare drum, baritone horn, and tuba; after graduating from high school (1930) he began working professionally on this last instrument. While attending Western University in Kansas City (from late summer 1932) he continued to work as a tuba player, though he also acquired a double bass and began lessons with Walter Page. In the mid-1930s he changed permanently to double bass, led his own band, and performed with various local groups, notably those of the pianist Countess (Margaret) Johnson and the accordionist Buster Moten. From April 1938 to 1943 he worked with Jay McShann.

After McShann joined the army Ramey toured with Luis Russell (*c* January–October 1944) and then traveled to New York, where he worked as a freelance with many important musicians, notably Ben Webster, Coleman Hawkins, Sid Catlett, Charlie Parker, Eddie "Lockjaw" Davis, Miles Davis, and Lester Young; he first joined Young's small group early in 1951. Following a period as a member of Count Basie's orchestra (November 1952 – spring 1953) he appeared intermittently with Young (to 1958) and played with Art Blakey (1954). Among those with whom he recorded in the 1940s and 1950s were John Hardee (1946), Thelonious Monk (1947), Clyde Bernhardt and Stan Getz (both 1949), Flip Phillips (1951), Young (1951, 1953, 1956), Lou Donaldson and Horace Silver (both 1952), Duke Jordan (1954), and Sonny Rollins and Teddy Wilson (both 1956). Towards the end of the 1950s he played with Roy Eldridge, Sol Yaged, and Cozy Cole at the Metropole in New York. Thereafter he continued to perform and record extensively on a freelance basis with such musicians as Buck Clayton (touring Europe in 1959 and 1961), Muggsy Spanier (1962), Wilson (1963), Cootie Williams, Earl Hines, Dick Wellstood, Jimmy Rushing, Peanuts Hucko, Nat Pierce, and Lem Johnson. He toured Europe with McShann (1969, 1977, 1979) and Lloyd Glenn (1980) and recorded with both in France. In 1976, having worked for ten years as a security officer at a bank, he retired to Austin, and he continued to play in Texas regularly into the early 1980s with Jim Cullum, Jr., and Herb Hall, among others. Ramey's playing was indebted to Page and the rhythmic propulsion of the Kansas City style.

Oral history material in *MoKmh* and *NjR* (JOHP).

SELECTED RECORDINGS

As sideman: J. McShann: Swingmatism (1941, Decca 8570); Red River Blues (1941, Decca 8595); The Jumpin' Blues (1942, Decca 4418); Sepian Bounce (1942, Decca 4387); J. Hardee: Nervous from the Service (1946, BN 520); River Edge Rock (1946, BN 521); T. Monk: Humph (1947, BN 560); Nice work if you can get it (1947, BN 1575); Well You Needn't (1947, BN 543); C. Bernhardt: Meet me on the corner (1949, BN 1202); C. Basie: *The Count Basie Sextet* (1952, Clef 146); S. C. Thompson: *Sir Charles Thompson Sextet* (1953, Van. 8003); L. Young: *Pres and Teddy* (1956, Verve 8205)

SELECTED FILMS AND VIDEOS

Buck Clayton and his All Stars (1961); Born to Swing (1973); The Last of the Blue Devils (1979)

BIBLIOGRAPHY

ChiltonW; *SheridanCB*
F. Postif: "Gene Ramey: j'ai été chaperon de Charlie Parker et l'un des rares amis de Lester Young, une interview," *Jh*, no.174 (1962), 20; repr. in *Jazz Me Blues: interviews et portraits de musiciens de jazz et de blues* (Paris, 1998), 133
G. Reisner: *Bird: the Legend of Charlie Parker* (New York, 1962/*R*1975)
A. Hope: "You can Bank on Gene," *MM* (6 May 1972), 50
R. Morris: "Kansas City Man on Bass," *MR*, iii/10 (1976), 1
S. Dance: *The World of Count Basie* (New York and London, 1980), 257
M. L. Hester: *Going to Kansas City* (Sherman, TX, 1980), 173
D. K. Ramsey: *Jazz Matters: Reflections on the Music and Some of its Makers* (Fayetteville, AR, 1989), 112
F. Büchmann-Møller: *You just Fight for your Life: the Story of Lester Young* (New York, Westport, CT, and London, 1990)

BK

Ramirez, Ram [Roger] (*b* Puerto Rico, 15 Sept 1913; *d* New York, 11 Jan 1994). Pianist, organist, and composer. He grew up in New York and was a child prodigy as a pianist. At the age of 13 he joined the musicians' union, and his first engagements followed in the early 1930s with the Louisiana Stompers, an amateur band. In 1933 he accompanied Monette Moore and, that summer, performed with Rex Stewart and Sid Catlett at the Empire Ballroom in New York. The following year he joined the Spirits of Rhythm, and early in 1935 he became a member of Willie Bryant's band; he traveled to Europe with Bobby Martin in June 1937. After returning to the USA (1940) he led his own groups in Asbury Park, New Jersey, then played with Ella Fitzgerald and Frankie Newton (1940–42), with Charlie Barnet (1942), again with Newton (1943), and for two years with John Kirby's sextet, and performed with Catlett at the Downbeat club in New York (1945). From 1945 to 1953 Ramirez was active as a freelance, both as an unaccompanied soloist and in a trio. While fulfilling an engagement at the Senator Hotel in Atlantic City, New Jersey (1953), he was inspired by the example of Wild Bill Davis to take up electronic organ, which he played at several clubs in New York. He toured Europe with the blues singer and guitarist T-Bone Walker in 1968 and in the summers of 1979 and 1980 played piano in the Harlem Blues and Jazz Band, with which he appeared at the Tenth Anniversary Dixieland Festival in Dresden, Germany (the band was the first American ensemble to be invited to this event). Later he worked again as a freelance pianist, and in 1987 he rejoined the Harlem Blues and Jazz Band for a cruise of the Caribbean. As a pianist and organist Ramirez had an exceptional sense of time, swing, and melody. Among his compositions is the ballad *Lover Man*, which became a jazz standard; perhaps the best known of many recordings of the song is by Billie Holiday (1944, Decca 23391).

Oral history material in *NjR* (JOHP).

SELECTED RECORDINGS

As unaccompanied soloist: *Rampant Ram* (1973–4, MJR 8122)
As leader: *Lover Man* (1966–7, RCA LPM3616)
As sideman: R. Stewart: Stingaree/Baby, Ain't You Satisfied? (1934, Voc. 2880); W. Bryant: Is it True what They Say about Dixie?/Moonrise on the Lowlands (1936, Bb 6362); B. Martin: Crazy Rhythm/Let's Dance (1938, Bruns. 81578); E. Fitzgerald: If it weren't for you/Sing Song Swing (1940, Decca 3126); Harlem Blues and Jazz Band: *Harlem Blues & Jazz, 1973–1980* (1973–80, Barron 403)

BIBLIOGRAPHY

ChiltonW
P. LaFargue: Liner notes, *Lover Man* (RCA PM42419, *c*1967)
S. Dance: *The World of Swing* (New York, 1974), 325
Obituary, *New York Times* (17 Jan 1994)
J. Simmen: "Roger 'Ram' Ramirez," *BHcF*, no.425 (1994), 1
——: "Roger 'Ram' Ramirez: After All these Years," *IAJRC Journal*, xxvii/2 (1994), 1

ALBERT VOLLMER

Rampart. Record label. It was operated by Harry Crawford between 1948 and 1950. The catalogue included some of the first recordings by Bob Wilber and Dick Wellstood and contained American issues of material by European and Australian traditional-jazz bands. The records remained available until 1952. Crawford also managed another label, Mouldie Fygge (1947–9), dedicated to reissuing jazz of the 1920s. (D. Mahony: "The Mouldie Fygge and Rampart Labels," *Matrix*, no.40 (1962), 17)

HOWARD RYE

Ramsey, (Charles) Fred(eric, Jr.) (*b* Pittsburgh, 29 Jan 1915; *d* Paterson, NJ, 18 March 1995). Writer and record producer. He attended Princeton University (BA 1936), then worked as an editor for the publisher Harcourt, Brace (1936–9) and as a writer for the US Department of Agriculture (1941–2) and the Voice of America (from 1942); at the same time, with Charles Edward Smith, he edited the anthology *Jazzmen* (1939), an influential early study of jazz that includes a moving account by Ramsey of King Oliver's career. In 1953 and 1955 he made visits to the South sponsored by Guggenheim fellowships, during which he made field recordings of musical performances and interviews; he later used these recordings to produce a series of commercial discs issued by Folkways, *Music from the South* (1954), and a television documentary of the same name (1957). For Folkways he also produced a series of recordings entitled *Jazz*, a historical anthology of recordings made in the 1920s and 1930s. Among his published writings are *Been Here and Gone* (1960), a treatment of traditional black music of the South that combines photographs and oral history. In 1970 Ramsey became a consultant on educational programs to the Institute of Jazz Studies, Rutgers, which in the same year published his book *Where the Music Started*. Later he undertook research into the life and music of Buddy Bolden with grants from the National Endowment for the Humanities (1974–5) and the Ford Foundation (1975–6). In 1987 he presented a series of five interviews on early jazz entitled "Been Here and Gone" for National Public Radio.

WRITINGS

(selective list)

ed. with C. E. Smith: *Jazzmen: the Story of Hot Jazz Told in the Lives of the Men who Created it* (New York, 1939/*R*1977)
with C. E. Smith and others: *The Jazz Record Book* (New York, 1942/*R*1978) [listeners' guide with discography]
Chicago Documentary: Portrait of a Jazz Era (London, 1944)
A Guide to Longplay Jazz Records (New York, n.d. [1954]/*R*1977) [listeners' guide]
Been Here and Gone (New Brunswick, NJ, and London, 1960)
Where the Music Started: a Photographic Essay (New Brunswick, NJ, 1970)

BIBLIOGRAPHY

P. Whelen: "Fred Ramsey Speaks Out: an Interview with the Historian, Writer, Photographer," *78 Quarterly*, no.4 (1989), 31; repr. as "Fred Ramsey Speaks: a Conversation with Pete Whelen," *New Orleans Music*, ii/2 (1990), 14

DANIEL ZAGER

Rand, Odell (*b c*1905; *d* Chicago, 22 June 1960). Clarinetist. During the late 1930s he played E♭ clarinet on recordings by the Harlem Hamfats, and he recorded with a number of blues singers, both as a member of the Hamfats and as a freelance. During much of the same period he worked at the Rock Cellar in Chicago, but he was known to tour local clubs, playing for tips. Rand continued to work around Chicago in the 1940s and thereafter led his own band, the Ebonites, for many years, which held several residencies in the city. He also worked with Natty Dominique (1952), Baby Dodds (1957) and Lil Armstrong (1959).

See also Clarinet, §2.

SELECTED RECORDINGS

(recorded for Decca to 1938 and for Vocalion from 1939)

As sideman: Harlem Hamfats: Sales Tax on It (1936, 7206); Little Girl/ Weed Smoker's Dream (1936, 7234); We gonna pitch a boogie woogie (1936, 7326); Hamfat Swing (1936, 7262); Growling Dog (1936, 7283); It was Red/Jam Jamboree (1937, 7312); You got to be satisfied/Toodle oo Blues (1937, 7406); Rosetta Howard: Stomp it out gate (1938, 7640); Stay Away from my Door (1938, 7551); All on Account of You (1938, 7531); Harlem Hamfats: You've had your last good time with me/Something wrong with my mind (1939, 04925); Big Bill Broonzy: Just Wondering (1939, 05043); Woodie Woodie (1939, 04938); Harlem Hamfats: Business is gone away/Take me in your alley (1939, 02587)

BIBLIOGRAPHY

P. Van Vorst: "The Harlem Hamfats," *MR*, iv (1977), no.4, p.5; no.5, p.8

based on *ChiltonW*/HOWARD RYE (recording-list)

Randall, Freddy [Frederick James] (*b* London, 6 May 1921; *d* Teignmouth, England, 18 May 1999). English trumpeter and cornetist. He took up trumpet in 1937 and formed the St. Louis Four in 1939 and a dixieland band in 1943; from 1944 he played traditional jazz with the Garbage Men, led by the drummer Freddy Mirfield. After performing on the radio series "BBC Jazz Club" he worked again as a leader. Among the members of his band in the late 1940s to mid-1950s were Eddie Thompson, Lennie Hastings, Dave Shepherd, Bruce Turner, Roy Crimmins, Al Gay, Lennie Felix, and Archie Semple; the group appeared in the film short *Parade of the Bands* (1955). Randall performed in New Orleans and toured the southern USA in 1956, and he appeared as a guest soloist with such British musicians as Ted Heath, the bandleaders Henry Hall, Harry Parry, and Bert Ambrose, and with such American visitors as Pee Wee Russell, Wild Bill Davison, Bud Freeman, Teddy Wilson, Sidney Bechet, Bill Coleman, and Jimmy and Marian McPartland. Owing to a lung ailment he retired from music in 1958; however, he resumed playing part-time in May 1963 and toured Britain with Davison two years later. Following another period of retirement (1966 through late 1960s) he collaborated with Shepherd for a recording (1971) and as a member of Britain's Greatest Jazz Band (from 1972). From summer 1972 through 1973 this group was known as the Freddy Randall–Dave Shepherd Jazz All Stars, and Danny Moss and Brian Lemon were among its sidemen; in the latter year it broadcast on radio and television (notably the television program "That's Jazz") and gave a successful performance at the Montreux International Jazz Festival. Randall toured into the late 1970s, after which he confined his work to the Essex area until his retirement in 1993. In 1982 he recorded as a co-leader with Benny Waters. He was a technically accomplished musician who was capable of performing in both a lyrical and a boisterous manner.

SELECTED RECORDINGS

As leader: Hurry on Down/Cook's Ferry Parade (1948, Cleveland 5–6); That's a-plenty/Since my best gal turned me down (1951, Parl. R3382); I'm Coming Virginia/Professor Jazz (1953, Parl. R3709); with W. B. Davison: *Wild Bill Davison with Freddy Randall's Band* (1965, BL 30187), incl. Ghost of a Chance, Memories of You; with D. Shepherd: *Freddy Randall–Dave Shepherd Jazz All Stars* (1972, BL 194),*"Live" at Montreux Jazz Festival* (1973, BL 214)

As sideman with F. Mirfield: Good Old Wagon Blues/Miss Annabelle Blues (1944, Decca F8526)

BIBLIOGRAPHY

CarrJ; *ChiltonB*; *FeatherE*

"Focus on Freddy," *JJ*, i/7 (1948), 6

B. Dawbarn: "Randall," *MM*, xxxi (14 April 1956), 3

——: "I Never Went for Gimmick Uniforms, Says Freddy Randall," *MM* (5 Oct 1963), 8

——: "Of Course Trad isn't Dead!, Says Freddy Randall," *MM*, xxxviii (11 May 1963), 5

E. Lambert: "Wild Bill Davison with Freddy Randall's Band," *JJ*, xviii/3 (1965), 24

A. Napoleon [R. Sudhalter]: "Randall: Creating Chicago in Clapton," *MM* (28 July 1973), 48

B. Turner: *Hot Air, Cool Music* (London, Melbourne, Australia, and New York, 1984)

G. Bielderman and R. Stansby: *Freddy Randall Discography* (Zwolle, Netherlands, and Hornchurch, England, 1987, rev. 3/1995)

Obituaries: *Daily Telegraph* (10 June 1999); H. Rainey, *JJI*, lii/7 (1999), 17; S. Voce, *The Independent* (26 May 1999)

KEN RATTENBURY/BK

Randolph, Irving "Mouse" (*b* St. Louis, 22 Jan 1909). Trumpeter. He began playing in the bands of Walt Farrington (1923–4), Willie Austin (1925–6), Art Sims and Norman Mason (both 1926), Fate Marable (1927), Floyd Campbell (1927–8), Alphonso Trent (1928), and J. Frank Terry (1929–30). From 1931 to spring 1934 he worked with Andy Kirk, and perhaps at this time acquired his nickname, "Mouse," which he said Ben Webster gave him because he never talked much. He continued in big bands with Fletcher Henderson (*c* May–November 1934), Benny Carter (November–December 1934), Cab Calloway (1935–9), Ella Fitzgerald (1939–42), Don Redman (1943), and Sabby Lewis (late 1943–1944), recording as a soloist with all but Russell, Fitzgerald, and Lewis; while with Calloway he appeared in the film short *Hi-de-ho* (1937), and he was a soloist in Teddy Wilson's small swing group accompanying Billie Holiday at two studio sessions late in 1936. From September 1944 to 1948 Randolph was a member of Edmond Hall's sextet, after which he played with Eddie Barefield (1950). During the 1950s he toured with Marcellino Guerra's Latin American Orchestra, and from 1958 into the 1970s he worked regularly with Chick Morrison in New York; he recorded with Harry Dial in 1961. Initially, Randolph's playing resembled that of Henry "Red" Allen, but he later settled into a simpler and more individual style: he had a big tone and his solo lines tended to follow the melody.

SELECTED RECORDINGS

As sideman: F. Henderson: Shanghai Shuffle (1934, Decca 158); B. Carter: Shoot the Works (1934, Voc. 2898); C. Calloway: Are you in love with me again? (1936, Bruns. 7685); T. Wilson: Tea for Two/I'll see you in my dreams (1936, Bruns. 7816); C. Calloway: Rustle of Swing (1938, Voc. 4144); I Like Music (1938, Voc. 3995); Skrontch (1938, Voc. 4045); Afraid of Love (1939, Voc. 4905)

BIBLIOGRAPHY

AllenH; *ChiltonW*; *McCarthyB*

J. Evensmo: *The Trumpets of Dizzy Gillespie, 1937–43, Irving Randolph, Joe Thomas* (n.p. [Oslo], n.d. [?1982]) [discography]

M. Selchow: *Profoundly Blue: a Bio-discographical Scrapbook on Edmond Hall* (Lübbecke, Germany, 1988)

FRANK DRIGGS/BK

Randolph, Zilner T(renton) (*b* Dermott, AR, 28 Jan 1899; *d* Chicago, 2 Feb 1994). Trumpeter and arranger. In the early 1920s he played at clubs in St. Louis, and from 1927 to 1930 he performed in Milwaukee with a band led by the trumpeter Bernie Young. After moving to Chicago (1931) he worked as a trumpeter and arranger with Louis Armstrong, with whom he toured and recorded intermittently (March 1931 – March 1932, 1933, July–October 1935); he arranged and played on *Swing You Cats* (1933, Bb 10225) and Armstrong recorded his composition *Old Man Mose* (1935, Decca 622). In addition Randolph worked with Carroll Dickerson (1934) and formed his own big band (1936). Towards the end of the 1930s he was a staff arranger for Woody Herman and wrote arrangements for Earl Hines, Duke Ellington, Fletcher Henderson, and Blanche Calloway. During the following decade he led his own quartet, taught, and performed in a musical act with his children; he continued to teach into the 1970s. Randolph is interviewed in the television documentary "American Masters: Satchmo: the Life of Louis Armstrong" (1989).

Oral history material in *NjR* (JOHP).

BIBLIOGRAPHY

ChiltonW; *FeatherE*

P. Van Vorst: "Z. T. & Old Man Mose," *MR*, ii/6 (1975), 1

J. L. Collier: *Louis Armstrong: an American Genius* (New York, 1983, London, 1984, as *Louis Armstrong: a Biography*)

Random Acoustics. Record company and label founded in 1993 by GEORG GRÄWE.

Raney, Doug(las) (*b* New York, 29 Aug 1956). Guitarist, son of Jimmy Raney. He was first inspired by the rock guitarists Jeff Beck, Jimi Hendrix, and Eric Clapton, but after listening to his father's recordings he took lessons with Barry Galbraith; he decided to become a jazz musician after he was invited to play with Al Haig at Gregory's in New York. In 1977 he worked in duo with his father for club and concert dates in New York, after which the two men toured Europe. Raney remained there, first spending a year in The Hague, where he played with Ferdinand Povel, and then moving to Copenhagen, where he settled permanently. He became a member of the European Jazz Guitar Orchestra, but otherwise has worked as a freelance, touring constantly. Among those with whom he has performed are Chet Baker, George Cables, Kenny Drew, Tal Farlow, Dexter Gordon, Johnny Griffin, Hank Jones, Clifford Jordan, Duke Jordan, Adam Nussbaum, Horace Parlan, Bernt Rosengren, and Jesper Thilo. Raney, who plays in a subdued and lyrical style not unlike that of Jim Hall, has recorded with his own groups, in a duo with his father, and as a sideman with Haig (1975), Parlan (1978), Baker (1979), his father (1981), Red Mitchell (1982), Rosengren (1983), and Thilo (1991).

SELECTED RECORDINGS

(recorded for Steeplechase unless otherwise indicated)

Duos with J. Raney: *Duets* (1979, 1134); *Nardis* (1983, 1184)

As leader: *Introducing Doug Raney* (1977, 1082); *Meeting the Tenors* (1983, Criss Cross 1006); *Guitar Guitar Guitar* (1985, 1212); *The Doug Raney Quintet* (1988, 1249); *Raney '96* (1996, 31397); *You Go to my Head* (1998, 31474)

As sideman with J. Cohn: *Two Funky People* (1996, Double-Time 126)

BIBLIOGRAPHY

M. J. Summerfield: *The Jazz Guitar: its Evolution and its Players* (Gateshead, England, 1978, 4/1998, as *The Jazz Guitar: its Evolution, Players and Personalities since 1900*)

B. Olson: "Bernt & Doug," *Orkester journalen*, liv/11 (1986), 12

K. Frandsen: *Politikens jazzleksikon* (Copenhagen, 1987)

J. Seidel: "Tal Farlow–Doug Raney," *JP*, xliv/2 (1995), 34

J. R. K. Keller: "Doug Raney," *Jazz Special*, no.26 (1996), 18

FRANK BÜCHMANN-MØLLER

Raney, Jimmy [James Elbert] (*b* Louisville, KY, 20 Aug 1927; *d* Louisville, 9 May 1995). Guitarist, father of Doug Raney. His mother played guitar, and he studied with the guitarist Hayden Causey, whom he replaced at the Hotel New Yorker, New York, in 1944 in the band led by Jerry Wald; among Wald's sidemen was Al Haig, who introduced Raney to the emerging new style, bop. He returned to Louisville to practice, then in June 1945 moved to Chicago, where he worked with Lou Levy, both in the big band of Jay Burkhart and in a trio; he also played in jam sessions which Sonny Stitt directed at the Yes Yes Club. In 1948 he returned to New York to join Woody Herman's orchestra, and in the same year recorded with Stan Getz. After leaving Herman he played with Haig, Buddy DeFranco, Artie Shaw (1949–50), and Terry Gibbs, then joined Getz's quintet; he became internationally known for his playing on several of Getz's important albums (1951–3). He also recorded as a sideman with Herbie Steward (1950) and Teddy Charles (1952), and in 1953 took part in his first session as a leader, with Getz appearing under the pseudonym Sven Coolson. From March 1953 to 1954 he worked with Red Mitchell in the trio led by Red Norvo, with whom he toured Europe; while there he made further recordings under his own name in January–February 1954 in Stockholm (with Gösta Theselius, Putte Wickman, Bengt Hallberg, Sonny Clark, and Mitchell among his sidemen) and in Paris (including Clark, Mitchell, Bobby Jaspar, and others). He joined the trumpeter Les Elgart and played for several years (1955–60) at the Blue Angel, New York, in a trio led by the pianist Jimmy Lyon; during this period he continued to record as a leader, and as a sideman with Ralph Burns (*c*1954–5), Bob Brookmeyer, Al Cohn (1955), and Edmond Hall (1959).

In 1960 Raney played on stage with Don Elliott's band in the Broadway show *A Thurber Carnival*. He accompanied singers, notably Anita O'Day, and in March 1961 led a group including Jaspar. He rejoined Getz in 1962 but remained with him only until the following year; in the mid-1960s he was active in New York as a studio musician in radio and television, and in 1968 he returned to Louisville. Later he played at clubs in New York (1972), gave a recital at Carnegie Hall with Al Haig (1974), and toured internationally with Haig and with his son Doug Raney, with whom he also recorded guitar duos. In April 1976 he performed in Japan, where he was recorded as a member of Barry Harris's quintet and as the leader of a trio which consisted of Harris's rhythm section of Sam Jones and Leroy Williams; later that same month he appeared at a club in Belgium as co-leader with Lee Konitz of a quartet. In 1979–80 he performed and recorded in New York and Germany in a duo with Attila Zoller. From the 1980s he toured internationally and recorded as the leader of his own groups, which included his son. Raney suffered a paralyzing stroke in 1994; published obituaries are in disagreement over the exact date of his death, in May the following year at a Louisville nursing home; however, Kentucky death records give his date of death as 9 May.

Raney was first influenced by Charlie Christian, but adapted his style to accommodate elements of bop; his flawless technique enabled him successfully to transfer the bop vocabulary to the guitar. As a soloist he emphasized lines inspired by those of Lester Young. He compensated for the emotional coolness of his improvisations by employing long melodic lines, cleanly articulated. One of the true innovators on his instrument, he exercised a profound influence upon guitarists of the 1950s. A collection of lead sheets for pieces associated with Raney was published by J. Aebersold: *A New Approach to Jazz Improvisation*, xx: *Jimmy Raney* (New Albany, IN, 1979).

SELECTED RECORDINGS

As unaccompanied soloist: *Solo* (1976, Xan. 140)
Duos: with D. Raney: *Duets* (1979, Ste. 1134); with M. Solal: *The Date* (1981, Stil 0703S81); with D. Raney: *Nardis* (1983, Ste. 1184)
As leader: *Jimmy Raney Plays* (1953, Prst. 156), incl. Round Midnight; *Jimmy Raney Quartet* (1954, NewJ 1101); *Jimmy Raney Quintet* (1954, NewJ 1103); *Jimmy Raney Quintet* (1955, Prst. 199); *Two Jims and a Zoot* (1964, Mstr. 56013); with A. Haig: *Special Brew* (1974, Spot. 8); *The Influence* (1975, Xan. 116); *Live in Tokyo* (1976, Xan. 132); *Stolen Moments* (1979, Ste. 1118); *Raney '81* (1981, Criss Cross 1001); *The Master* (1983, Criss Cross 1009); *Wisteria* (1985, Criss Cross 1019); *But Beautiful* (1990, Criss Cross 1065)
As sideman: S. Getz: *Jazz at Storyville* (1951, Roost 407, 411); R. Norvo: *Red Norvo Trio* (1953, Fan. 3-12); Project G5 [with T. Farlow, H. Ellis, C. Collins, and Royce Campbell]: on *A Tribute to Wes Montgomery* (1992, Evidence 22101), Wes, West Coast Blues, Yesterdays, The End of a Love Affair

BIBLIOGRAPHY

I. Gitler: "Jimmy Raney," *DB*, xxviii/15 (1961), 19
A. Morgan: "Jimmy Raney," *JM*, ix/8 (1963), 16
J. Gourley: "Jimmy Raney," *Jh*, no.283 (1972), 26
A. Berle: "Jimmy Raney: a Legend in Jazz Guitar," *GP*, xi/3 (1977), 29
L. Tomkins: "The Jimmy Raney Story," *CI*, xv/11 (1977), 14
J. Hughes: "Intro: Reflections of a Jazz Survivor," *GP*, xxii/2 (1988), 10
M. Selchow: *Profoundly Blue: a Bio-discographical Scrapbook on Edmond Hall* (Lübbecke, Germany, 1988), 445
G. Lees: *Leader of the Band: the Life of Woody Herman* (New York, and Oxford, England, 1995), 163
Obituaries: P. Watrous, *New York Times* (16 May 1995); M. Gilbert, *JJI*, xlviii/7 (1995), 48

NORMAN MONGAN/BK

Ranger, Claude (*b* Montreal, 3 Feb 1941). Canadian drummer. In Montreal he worked in show bands and played jazz with the saxophonists Lee Gagnon and Brian Barley, the trumpeter Ron Proby, and the pianist Pierre Leduc. He moved in 1972 to Toronto, where he appeared as a sideman in local clubs with Canadian musicians (including Lenny Breau, Sonny Greenwich, Moe Koffman, and Don Thompson) and visiting Americans (notably James Moody and Phil Woods). He also recorded there with Greenwich, Koffman, Dave Liebman, and others before moving in 1987 to Vancouver. He led small bands of younger musicians in Montreal and Toronto and during the early 1990s organized the youthful Jade Orchestra (with 15 to 19 members) in Vancouver. Ranger, whose combative style was originally influenced by Max Roach, can be heard to advantage on Barley's album *1970* (1970, Just a Memory 9502) and P. J. Perry's *Quintet* (1993, Unity 142).
Oral history material in *CaQMG*.

BIBLIOGRAPHY

EMC2
M. Miller: "Claude Ranger," *DB*, xxxxv/16 (1978), 48
——: "Crazy," *Jazz in Canada: Fourteen Lives* (Toronto, Buffalo, and London, 1982), 166
——: "Claude Ranger," *Boogie, Pete & the Senator: Canadian Musicians in Jazz: the Eighties* (Toronto, 1987), 226

MARK MILLER

Ranglin, Ernest (Adair) (*b* Manchester, Jamaica, 19 June 1932). Jamaican guitarist, arranger, and composer. Self-taught, he started on ukulele and became interested in recordings by Charlie Christian, Django Reinhardt, Les Paul, and Barney Kessel. His professional career began in 1947 with the tenor saxophonist Val Bennett, then continued in hotel bands in Haiti and the Bahamas and with the pianist Baba Motta and the saxophonist Eric Deans. Working with the record producers Duke Reid, Clement "Coxsone" Dodd, and Lee "Scratch" Perry, he accompanied and arranged music for most Jamaican singers, including Bob Marley and Jimmy Cliff, and played a key role in creating ska – but with a backbeat sounded on the bass drum. A prolific popular composer, Ranglin went to London in 1963 as an artists and repertory director for Island Records and returned the following year for an extended period; he appeared regularly at Ronnie Scott's club and toured and broadcast. Based in Jamaica, he played jazz in Bertie King's radio band, with Randy Weston, Melba Liston, Paul Desmond, and sidemen from Count Basie's orchestra, and on trips to the USA, but his major chance to develop harmonic complexity came in 1973 when he began to work with Monty Alexander. The two men recorded together in Jamaica and Germany, and the album they made in 1980 shows his technique to advantage. Ranglin lived in the USA from 1978 to 1981 and again from 1984 to 1990, performing with Alexander and others and leading his own group. An earlier visit with Cliff to Senegal (1976) inspired his collaborations at the end of the 1990s with African musicians. His association as a guest soloist with Jazz Jamaica emphasizes equally the jazz, ska, and reggae elements that characterize his open, relaxed, and swinging style.
Oral history material in *GBLnsa*.

SELECTED RECORDINGS

Duos with M. Alexander: *Monty Alexander–Ernest Ranglin* (1980, MPS 15570)
As leader: *Guitar in Ernest* (1962, Island 23); *Wranglin'* (1963, Island 909); *Soul D'Ern* (1963–4, Ronnie Scott's Jazz House 611); *Reflections* (1964, Island 915); *Ranglypso* (1974, MPS 15440); *Ranglin Roots* (1976, Water Lily 004); *Below the Bassline* (1996, Island Jamaica Jazz 4002); *Memories of Barber Mack* (1997, Island Jamaica Jazz 4004); *In Search of the Lost Riddim* (1997, Palm Pictures 2001)
As sideman: R. Scott: on *When I Want your Opinion, I'll Give it to You* (1963–5, Ronnie Scott's Jazz House 610), Ronnie's Blues (1963); S. Stitt: *Sonny's Blues* (1964, Ronnie Scott's Jazz House 603); M. Alexander: *Jamento* (1978, Pablo 2310826); *Yard Movement* (1995, Island Jamaica Jazz 4001); Skatalites: *Ball of Fire* (1997, Island Jamaica Jazz 4005)

BIBLIOGRAPHY

ChiltonB
B. Dawbarn: "Hold on to your Hats! Ernest Ranglin is Heading your Way," *MM* (9 May 1964), 13
C. Spedding: "Ernest Ranglin," *BMG* [London], lxi (1964), 157
——: "Cover Artist," *BMG* [London], lxi (1964), 314
V. Wilmer: "Ernest Ranglin: an Important 'Find' Talks about Jazz and Blues," *Jazz Beat*, no.5 (1964), June, 9
S. Clarke: *Jah Music: the Evolution of the Popular Jamaican Song* (London, 1980), 203
S. Barrow: Liner notes, *Below the Bassline* (Island Jamaica Jazz 4002, 1996)
T. Green: "Ernest Ranglin: Jamaica's Ska/Bop Giant," *GP*, xxx/12 (1996), 31
——: "Hear Say: Ernest Ranglin," *JT*, xxvi/9 (1996), 22
R. Grosman: "Entrevues: Ernest Ranglin," *Jm*, no.462 (1996), 7
J. D'Souza: "Ernest Ranglin: the Jamaican Jazz Guitarist," *Coda*, no.271 (1997), 28
H. Bordowitz: "Ernest Ranglin: Afro-Cuban King," *GP*, xxxii/10 (1998), 35
T. Snow: "Interview: Ernest Ranglin: Master Craftsman," *The Voice* [London] (27 July 1998), 51
V. Wilmer: "The Ten Bob Special," *Mojo* [London], no.58 (1998), 24

VAL WILMER

Ranier, Tom [Thomas John] (*b* Chicago, 13 July 1949). Pianist, clarinetist, and saxophonist. His father played clarinet and saxophone, and his mother was a singer. At the age of six he moved with his family to Garden Grove, California. He began learning classical piano when he was ten, took up clarinet about two years later, and studied composition at California State University, Fullerton (BA), and classical piano at the University of Southern California and the California Instute of the Arts. As a member of Dave Pike's group (*c*1973–81) he performed regularly at Hungry Joe's in Huntington Beach (1973–5) and made recordings. During the mid- to late 1970s he also worked with Don Ellis,

Carmen McRae, Dexter Gordon, Joe Farrell, and Harold Land and recorded with Monty Budwig (1978). Later he played with Milt Jackson (*c*1980–83) and co-led a trio with John Heard and Sherman Ferguson (*c*1982–4); he spent the remainder of the 1980s working as a studio musician.

In 1989 Ranier performed in Clora Bryant's Central Avenue All Stars and joined small groups led by Frank Capp and John Leitham; he worked with the latter until 1996. From 1993 he performed and recorded with Herb Geller, and in 1995 he began leading his own trio. In the 1990s he recorded with, among others, the Rather Large Band, led by the arranger Roger Neumann (1993), Joe Pass (1993), Rosemary Clooney (1994), Lanny Morgan (1996), the singer Barbara Morrison (*c*1997), and a group led by the trombonist Andy Martin and the tenor saxophonist Bill Liston. Ranier taught at the University of California, Los Angeles, and released an instructional video, *The Contemporary Rhythm Section*.

SELECTED RECORDINGS

As leader: with J. Heard and S. Ferguson: *Back to Back* (1983, ITJ 003); *In the Still of the Night* (1997, Cont. 14087), incl. Excuse Me

As sideman: D. Pike: *Times out of Mind* (1975, Muse 5092); *Let the Minstrels Play* (1978, Muse 5203), incl. Groovin' High [as, p]; M. Jackson: *Jackson, Johnson, Brown and Company* (1983, Pablo 2310897); F. Capp: *Frank Capp Trio Presents Rickey Woodard* (1991, Conc. 4469), incl. Sweet Lorraine [p]; J. Pass: *My Song* (1993, Telarc 83326), incl. I can't Kick [ts]; R. Neumann: on *Instant Heat* (1993, Sea Breeze 2053), Sweden in the Rain [p]; F. Capp: *Quality Time* (1993–4, Conc. 4677), incl. 9:20 Special [p]; H. Geller: *Playing Jazz: the Musical Autobiography of Herb Geller* (1995, Fresh Sound CD5011)

BIBLIOGRAPHY

Feather–GitlerBEJ

Z. Stewart: "An Ideal Outing for a Ranier Day," *Los Angeles Times* (23 Sept 1995)

——: "For Noted Pianist, Jazz is Addictive Art Form," *Los Angeles Times* (30 Jan 1997)

B. Kohlhaase: "Variations on a Tune: Odessa Supper Club in Laguna Beach is a Distinguished, Intimate Venue for Fine Jazz Seven Nights a Week," *Los Angeles Times* (11 Aug 1999)

<http://www.carsproductions.com/ranierb.html> (2000)

GK

Rank, Bill [William C.] (*b* Lafayette, IN, 8 June 1904; *d* Cincinnati, 20 May 1979). Trombonist. He worked in Florida and Indiana, then from 1923 to summer 1927 played with Jean Goldkette's band in Detroit; during this period he recorded frequently with his colleague Bix Beiderbecke. Later in 1927 he played with Adrian Rollini and worked as a freelance before joining Paul Whiteman's band, with which he played until 1938; he may be heard to advantage on *Walkin' the Dog* (OK 41344), which he recorded with Eddie Lang and a group drawn from Whiteman's orchestra in 1929. After working as a studio musician in Hollywood in the late 1930s and early 1940s he moved to Cincinnati, where he led a ten-piece band through the rest of the decade. Although he then ceased to play full-time, he worked steadily until shortly before his death, performing (1968, 1969) and recording (1968) in Europe, playing with Gene Mayl (1971), recording as a leader in Vancouver (1973), and appearing at numerous jazz festivals. (L. Wright: "Bill Rank," *Sv*, no.19 (1968), 18; no.20 (1968–9), 44)

based on *ChiltonW*

Rantala, Iiro (*b* Helsinki, 19 Jan 1970). Finnish pianist. After studies at the Sibelius Academy, Helsinki (1988), and the Manhattan School of Music (1989–90) he formed the Trio Töykeät [the Brusque Trio], which has performed extensively worldwide. Rantala is known both for his technically brilliant piano work and for his blunt sense of musical humor, which may be heard on the trio's début album, *Päivää* [Hello] (1990, Sonet 1038).

BIBLIOGRAPHY

M. Konttinen: "Young Talents in Finnish Jazz," *Finnish Music Quarterly* no.2 (1991), 42

H. Lahtonen: "Iiro Rantala: Jazz Pianist from the Sunny Side of the Street," *Finnish Music Quarterly* no.3 (1995), 33

PEKKA GRONOW

Rap. A spoken rhyme, often improvised and usually delivered over a background derived from recordings in the funk or soul style. As part of the Hip-hop movement which emerged in the Bronx area of New York in the late 1970s it made a considerable impact on jazz players. (D. Toop: "Rap," *Grove7*)

MARK GILBERT

Rappolo, Leon. Name by which leon Roppolo has often (and incorrectly) been identified.

Rapson, (Ira) John(, III) (*b* Gary, IN, 4 Feb 1953). Trombonist and educator. He took up piano at the age of five and later changed to trombone, and he studied music at Westmont College in Santa Barbara, California (BA 1976), and composition at California State University, Northridge (MA 1981). From autumn 1980 to 1990 he taught at Westmont, although he lived in Los Angeles, where he could play with more adventurous musicans such as Vinny Golia; he played in the latter's quintet (1979–83), large ensemble (1980–90), and chamber trio (1982–6). Other musicians with whom he collaborated include Tim Berne (recording in New York in 1980, performing in 1986), the alto saxophonist Walter Thompson (recording in 1980), Bobby Bradford (1986–90), and John Carter (1988–90). Rapson also led his own sextet (1982–5), with Golia, Wayne Peet, Roberto Miguel Miranda, and Alex Cline among its members, an octet (1985–90), with Golia, Cline, Ken Filiano, the trumpeter John Fumo, the saxophonist Steve Fowler or Kim Richmond, and the tuba player Bill Roper, and a trio (1986–7) with Golia and Miranda.

In late 1990 Rapson moved east, and from 1991 to 1993 he studied ethnomusicology at Wesleyan University. During the same period he joined Anthony Braxton's large ensemble (recording in 1992), performed with Ed Blackwell (1990–91) and Jay Hoggard (1990–92), and recorded with Allen Lowe (1991–2). Between 1992 and 1999 he was the leader of another sextet, in which he played alongside Braxton, Bradford, Peet, Bill Roper, and Cline, and in autumn 1993 he joined the faculty of the University of Iowa. In addition he led a big band, OftENsemble (from 1994), and worked with Charlie Kohlhase and Matt Wilson. In 1996 he formed the Oddbar Trio plus Trombone, which included the saxophonist Steve Grismore, and toured Brazil with a group of his graduate students.

SELECTED RECORDINGS

As leader: *Deebadah dwee* (1984, Nine Winds 0112); *Bu wah* (1986, Nine Winds 0118); *Dances and Orations* (*c*1996, Music & Arts 923)

As sideman with A. Lowe: *Mental Strain at Dawn: a Modern Portrait of Louis Armstrong* (1992, Stash 563)

BIBLIOGRAPHY

S. Lester: "Associate Professor Moonlights in Local Jazz Band OftENsemble," *Daily Iowan* (19 March 1997); repr. in <http://www.uiowa.edu/~dlyiowan/issue/v128/il62/stories/a0201m.html> (1998)

<http://members.aol.com/ninewinds/bios/rapson.html> (1999)

GK

Rare Silk. Vocal group. It was formed in Boulder, Colorado, in 1979, and consisted of four singers: Gaile Gillespie (*b* San Fernando, CA, 22 Aug 1949); Marylynn Gillespie (*b* San Fernando, 1 Feb 1951); Todd Buffa (*b* Beloit, WI, 27 Nov 1952); and Barbara Reeves. Among its recordings were songs as diverse as *Up from the Skies* by the rock guitarist Jimi Hendrix, Thelonious Monk's *'Round Midnight*, and Spyro Gyra's *Hello*. Most of the group's vocal arrangements were written by Buffa. Rare Silk seems to have disbanded not long after appearing in a concert captured on the video *Jacksonville Jazz Festival VII* (1987).

SELECTED RECORDINGS

New Weave (1983, Pol. 810028-1); *American Eyes* (1985, PAlt 8086), incl. Hello, 'Round Midnight, Up from the Skies; *Black and Blue* (1986, PAlt-TBA 214)

BIBLIOGRAPHY

R. Robbins: "Rare Silk: New Weave," *CI*, xxii/2 (1984), 28
S. Yanow: "Hodgepodge and Shorties," *Cadence*, xi/7 (1985), 29

PAUL RINZLER

Raskin, Jon (*b* Heppner, OR, 1954). Alto saxophonist, member of Rova.

Raskin, Milt(on William) (*b* Boston, 27 Jan 1916; *d* Los Angeles, 16 Oct 1977). Pianist. He studied at the New England Conservatory in the early 1930s and by 1937 had moved to New York, where he performed with Wingy Manone and recorded with Ziggy Elman; Elman's *Love is the sweetest thing* (1939, Bb 10741) offers a good example of Raskin's early style. He went on to play in the big bands of Gene Krupa (early 1938 – late 1939, 1941–2), Teddy Powell (late 1939 – mid-1940), Alvino Rey (summer 1940), and Tommy Dorsey (1942–4), and recorded with all but Rey; he may be heard to advantage as a soloist on Dorsey's *Well, Git it* (1942, Vic. 27887). After settling in Los Angeles he recorded with Artie Shaw and Billie Holiday (both 1946), Woody Herman and Manone (both 1947), Sarah Vaughan (1951), Georgie Auld (1952), B. B. King (1959), and Stan Kenton (1963, 1965). In addition he worked as a music director, conductor, and arranger for studio orchestras and wrote lyrics occasionally for pop songs. (*ChiltonW*; *FeatherE*; *Feather '60s*)

Rasmussen, Hugo (Finn) (*b* Bagsvaerd, Denmark, 22 March 1941). Danish double bass player. He played banjo in dixieland bands from the age of 16 and began teaching himself double bass when he was 18. One of his first professional jobs on double bass was with the group Jazz Incorporated, in which he worked alongside Jesper Thilo and Palle Mikkelborg. He was then a member of a band led by the trumpeter Arnved Meyer (mid-1960s – early 1970s) and of Beat Kapel, under the pianist Niels Jørgen Steen (1970s). In these groups and later as a freelance he accompanied numerous American musicians, notably Coleman Hawkins, Ben Webster, Roy Eldridge, Dexter Gordon, Jimmy Raney, Stuff Smith, Horace Parlan, Al Cohn and Zoot Sims, Oliver Nelson, Joe Albany, Wild Bill Davison, Harry Edison, Ralph Sutton, Al Grey, Kenny Drew, Red Rodney, Ed Thigpen, and Duke Jordan. From the mid-1980s Rasmussen played frequently with Pierre Dørge's Jungle Orchestra, and in 2000 he worked regularly with younger Danish musicians.

SELECTED RECORDINGS

As sideman: B. Webster: on *Atmosphere for Lovers and Thieves* (1965, BL 30105), My Romance; on *Duke's in Bed* (1965, BL 30137), Stompy Jones; W. B. Davison: *But Beautiful* (1974, Sto. 248); A. Cohn and Z. Sims: *Motoring Along* (1974, Sonet 684); P. Dørge: *Brikama* (1984, Ste. 1188)

MARK GILBERT

Rasmussen, Peter (Christian Hans) (*b* Hørsholm, Denmark, 16 Dec 1906; *d* Copenhagen, 27 Sept 1992). Danish trombonist and bandleader. He played with Valdemar Eiberg (1925–6) and Kai Ewans (1927–8), then was a principal soloist with Bernard Etté in Germany (1928–31). After returning to Denmark he was a prominent member of the bands of Kai Julian (1931–2), Erik Tuxen (1932–6), and Ewans (1936–43). In 1943 he assumed leadership of Svend Asmussen's group and until the early 1950s he led small groups that played in a style influenced partly by bop; his work is represented on several recordings (including *Fine and Dandy*, 1951, Odeon DK1128). Rasmussen led big bands in the mid- and late 1950s, then worked for several years as a freelance radio producer.

ERIK WIEDEMANN

Rassinfosse, Jean-Louis (*b* Brussels, 9 Jan 1952). Belgian double bass player. After playing guitar in the 1960s he took up double bass and worked in dixieland bands. In 1975 he joined Charles Loos. He accompanied Bill Coleman, Slide Hampton, Sal Nistico (ii), and Carmell Jones, and served as the double bass player at jam sessions at the Festival Mondial du Jazz Antibes–Juan-les-Pins, where he played with such musicians as Martial Solal and Sam Rivers. In 1976 he recorded with Loos and toured with Chet Baker in a drummerless trio. One of the busiest double bass players in Belgium, he worked with Fats Sadi, Jacques Pelzer, Philip Catherine, Michel Herr, Richard Rousselet, and Bruno Castellucci, among others, and accompanied such visiting soloists as Baker (with whom he recorded late in 1978), Tete Montoliu, Pepper Adams, and Kai Winding. In 1979 he toured Europe with Baker, Horace Parlan, and Doug Raney, then back in Belgium he performed or recorded with Félix Simtaine's Act Big Band (1981), Rousselet (1984), Steve Houben, and Toots Thielemans.

In 1983 Rassinfosse formed his own trio and embarked on a long series of concerts throughout Europe in a trio with Baker and Catherine (with which he recorded that year and again in 1985) and in another trio with Catherine and Aldo Romano. He played further with Rousselet and Herr (1984, 1986), appeared at a jazz festival in Singapore (1985), and toured Europe with Clifford Jordan and Philly Joe Jones (?1985). With the singer Deborah Brown he recorded in Brussels (1986) and visited Spain (1987). As a freelance in the latter part of the 1980s he accompanied such visiting musicians as Michel Petrucciani, George Coleman, Joe Lovano, Bob Mover, and Nistico, and played with Pelzer, Phil Abraham, Dré Pallemaerts, and Diederik Wissels. In 1988 Rassinfosse joined Houben and then, in the mid-1990s, Castellucci, to form the rhythm section of Eric Legnini's trio and quintet; around the same time he began what became another longstanding affiliation, with Klaus Ignatzek, with whom he made a number of recordings from 1989 to 1993. He also recorded with Abraham (from 1991) and again with Rousselet (1994), and toured and recorded extensively in the trio L'âme des Poètes, which interpreted French chansons. He joined Rousselet's Ecaroh Quintet in 1998. Rassinfosse has taught at the conservatories in Liège and Brussels.

SELECTED RECORDINGS

As leader with C. Baker and P. Catherine: *Chet Baker–Philip Catherine–Jean-Louis Rassinfosse* (1983, Les Lundis d'Hortense 1009)

As sideman: C. Baker: *Chet Baker in Bologna* (1985, Dreyfus 191133-2); *Chet's Choice* (1985, Criss Cross 1016); *Strollin'* (1985, Enja 5005); E. Legnini: *Essentiels* (1989, Igloo 080); *Natural Balance* (1991, Jazz Club de Belgique 6013); K. Ignatzek: *The Answer* (1992, Can. 79534); E. Legnini: *Rhythm Sphere* (1994, Igloo 117); P. Abraham: *En public* (1996, Lyrae 9703007)

BIBLIOGRAPHY

R. Pernet, J.-P. Schroeder, and others: *Dictionnaire du jazz à Bruxelles et en Wallonie* (Liège, Belgium, 1991)
R. Pernet: *Belgian Jazz Discography (1897–1999)* (Brussels, 1999) <http://www.jazzinbelgium.org/jlrass.htm> (2000) [incl. discography]

BK

Ratamacue. One of the drumstrokes collectively known as Rudiments.

Ratip, Ahmed [Mike; Muhiddin, Ahmed] (*b* Constantinople [now Istanbul], 24 Sept 1905). Argentine bandleader, banjoist, guitarist, and singer of Turkish birth. While attending the University of Michigan he played banjo under the name Ahmed Muhiddin in student bands (1924–31) and in an orchestra led by Jean Goldkette (1927). He worked as a newspaper correspondent in Uruguay and at the same time played in and around Montevideo in a trio led by the pianist Luis Rolero, with which he later moved to Buenos Aires; after this group disbanded in 1934 he joined the Dixie Pals, led by the violinist Paul Wyer, with which he recorded several tracks for Victor, including a version of his own composition *Africa* (1934, 37642). From 1936 to the early 1940s he played with the pianist Rene Cospito and his Orquesta Argentina de Jazz, with the drummer Mario D'Alo's Rhythm Kings, and in a group modeled after the Quintette du Hot Club de France that included Hernán Oliva (violin), Dave Washington (second guitar), and Louis Vola (double bass). In the late 1930s, by which time he had taken the name Ahmed Ratip, he studied harmony with the bandleader Russ Goudy. Early in 1943 he formed the Cotton Pickers, as the leader of which he made several recordings between 1946 and 1952 for Victor (notably *El boogie de los platillos*, 1950, 60-1857), and until his retirement in 1960 performed at clubs, at concerts, and on radio in Argentina, Chile, Brazil, and Uruguay; he also operated a nightclub from 1944. He should not be confused with the pianist Arman Ratip (*b* Cyprus), who worked as a journalist in London (where in 1970 he recorded two albums, the second with Marc Charig and Harry Miller) and played with Maggie Nichols and Mongezi Feza. (G. Olliver: Liner notes, *Jazz and Hot Dance in Argentina*, Harl. 2010, 1984)

GUILLERMO I. OLLIVER, RAINER E. LOTZ

Ratzer, Karl (Alfred) (*b* Vienna, 4 July 1950). Austrian electric guitarist. He began playing rock and rhythm-and-blues at the age of 15. After becoming interested in jazz he went in 1972 to the USA and toured with the soul-funk band High Voltage. In late 1973 he moved to Atlanta and met Dan Wall, with whom he toured in Europe the following year. In 1977 he left Atlanta for New York, where he led his own groups and played with Jeremy Steig, Bob Mintzer, Bob Berg, Steve Grossman, and others. In 1980 he toured Europe and recorded three albums with Chet Baker. In Vienna from the early 1980s, he led bands such as Unity and Beat the Heat and accompanied such visiting Americans as Clark Terry, Johnny Griffin, James Moody, Eddie "Lockjaw" Davis, and Lee Konitz. His style has ranged convincingly from bop to funk, the former exemplified by his *Waltz for Ann* (1991, L+R 45078), with Art Farmer (also resident in Vienna), the latter by his *Saturn Returning* (1996, Enja 9315-2).

BIBLIOGRAPHY

J. Seidel: "Schöopft aus der Quelle des Bebop," *JP*, xl/11 (1991), 29
B. Milkowski: Liner notes, *Saturn Returning* (Enja 9315-2, 1997)
A. Felber: "Die zweite Rückkehr des Karl Ratzer," *JP*, xlvii/6 (1998), 16 [incl. discography]

MARK GILBERT

RAU. Acronym of Reform art unit; also the name of a record label formed by that group.

Raubiško, Raimonds (*b* Riga, Latvian SSR [now Latvia], 28 May 1939; *d* Riga, 27 Sept 2000). Latvian tenor saxophonist and composer. He began his career in an orchestra led by the pianist Ivan Mazur and in 1964 became a principal soloist in the Rīas Estrādes Orkestris (REO; Riga variety orchestra) under Raimond Pauls. After studying clarinet at the Latvian SSR Yazep Vitol State Conservatory in Riga (graduating in 1968) he performed at the International Jazz Festival Prague (1970) under the bandleader Václav Zahradník. From 1974 he was a member of the dance orchestra of Riga Radio and Television, led his own groups, and worked as a freelance musician in concerts and in studios. He remained active into the year of his death, playing, teaching, and organizing jazz events, including a competition for saxophonists (2000). His first recording, *Kartinï drevnevo Egipta* (1984, Mel. C60 20651000), features a cycle of four pieces of his own composition. (H. J. Schaal: "Perestroyka Blues: Who is Who im sowjetischen Jazz der 80er Jahre," *JP*, xxxix/4 (1990), 28)

WALTER OJAKÄÄR

Rava, Enrico (*b* Trieste, Italy, 20 Aug 1939). Italian trumpeter. His year of birth, 1939, appears incorrectly in some sources as 1943. He was brought up in Turin, and was given piano lessons by his mother, a conservatory graduate. A self-taught brass player, he played traditional jazz on trombone from the age of 16, and when he was 18, inspired by Miles Davis, he changed to trumpet. He played in Rome, first working with Gato Barbieri (*c*1965) and Mal Waldron, recorded with Giorgio Gaslini (1966), and then toured and recorded in Europe and the Americas with Steve Lacy (1966–9); he also recorded with Lee Konitz (1968) and Manfred Schoof (1969). Having visited New York with Lacy in 1967, he returned in 1969 to work with Roswell Rudd, with whom he later recorded (from 1973) and toured (1977–8). He settled in the city but began in 1972 to tour and record regularly as a leader in Europe and South America; his wife, a film maker, resided in Buenos Aires. Rava also recorded with Gunter Hampel (1972) and Abdullah Ibrahim (1973), and in 1975 performed as a guest soloist with the Globe Unity Orchestra, of which he later became a member.

For his early recordings as a leader, made in various European locations and in New York, Rava made use of such sidemen as John Abercrombie and Massimo Urbani. His working quartets consisted successively of Urbani, Jean-François Jenny-Clark, and Aldo Romano (*c*1976–7); Rudd, Giovanni Tommaso, and Bruce Ditmas (*c*1978–9); and Franco D'Andrea and Furio di Castri, with Romano (*c*1980–83) or Tony Oxley (*c*1984–5) on drums. He continued to form groups with several of these players, as well as with John Taylor and others, in the mid- to late 1980s; with Tommaso, Oxley, the guitarist Augusto Mancineli, Nana Vasconcelos, and a string quartet, he recorded in 1984 as the Rava String Band.

Having returned to Italy around 1977, Rava toured widely. He worked with Gil Evans (1982), toured with Cecil Taylor (1984), performed with a number of French groups, and recorded as a sideman with Barry Altschul (1983), Jimmy Lyons (ii) and Archie Shepp (both 1985), Dino Saluzzi (1986), George Gruntz's Concert Jazz Band (1987), the singer Tiziana Simona (with Waldron's quartet, including Lacy, 1988), Enrico Pieranunzi's Space Trio (1990), and Tiziana Ghiglioni (1992), as well as in a duo with Pieranunzi (1993); in 1998–9 he played with the Italian Instabile Orchestra. From 1989 to 1991 he was a member of the cooperative group Quatre, with D'Andrea (piano), Miroslav Vitous, and Daniel Humair; it recorded in 1989 and 1991 and performed at the Chicago Jazz Festival shortly before disbanding. In many of his groups, however, Rava has preferred the sound of the electric guitar to the piano; he has used two such instruments in the Electric Five, his group from 1994.

Rava's work with Lacy in the late 1960s familiarized him with free jazz, elements of which have persisted in his style, although from the 1970s he preferred to play and compose lyrical melodies; a free-jazz gesture he often employs is to bring an improvisation to a climax with rapid, blurred, sweeping lines of imprecise pitch. His timbre, warm and clear in the trumpet's middle register, becomes nasal in the high register, and at this extreme his attack becomes noticeably coarse; these qualities suggest similarities between Rava's playing and that of Davis. His compositions have a singing, lyrical, and harmonically circular quality.

SELECTED RECORDINGS

As leader: *Quotation Marks* (1973–4, Japo 60010); *The Plot* (1976, ECM 1078); *Enrico Rava Quartet* (1978, ECM 1122); *Opening Night* (1981, ECM 1224); *Rava String Band* (1984, SN 1114); *Secrets* (1986, SN 1164); *Enrico Rava Quintet* (1989, Nabel 4632); *Rava l'opéra va* (1993, Label Bleu 6559); *Chansons* (1994, Gala 91048); *Electric Five* (1994, SN 121214-2); *Carmen* (1995, Label Bleu 6579); with P. Fresu: *Shades of Chet* (1999, Via Venuto Jazz 023)

As sideman: S. Lacy: *The Forest and the Zoo* (1966, ESP 1060); M. Schoof: *European Echoes* (1969, FMP 0010); G. Hampel: *Angel* (1972, Birth 009); A. Ibrahim: *African Space Program* (1973, Enja 2032); R. Rudd: *Inside Job* (1976, Ari. 1029); Globe Unity Orchestra: *Pearls* (1977, FMP 0380); J. Lyons: *Give it up* (1985, BS 0087); Quatre: *Quatre* (1989, Gala 91030); *Earth Cake* (1991, Label Bleu 6539)

BIBLIOGRAPHY

CarrJ
G. Rouy: "Enrico Rava," *Jm*, no.215 (1973), 44 [incl. discography]
M. Cuscuna: "Enrico Rava," *DB*, xli/7 (1974), 15
D. Soutif: "Enrico Rava entre New York et l'Italie," *Jm*, no.252 (1977), 14 [incl. discography]
H. Mandel: "Enrico Rava: Italian on the Upswing," *DB*, xlv/3 (1978), 16 [incl. discography]
L. Jeske: "Free Players from Many Lands Form Globe Unity Orchestra," *DB*, xlvii/9 (1980), 28
P. Carles: "Pièges pour Enrico Rava," *Jm*, no.293 (1981), 42
E. Jost: *Jazzmusiker: Materialen zur Soziologie der afro-amerikanischen Musik* (Frankfurt am Main, Germany, Berlin, and Vienna, 1981), 155
R. Urmann: "Enrico Rava," *JP*, xxxii/7 (1983), 29
P. Carles: "Ravis du nouveau Rava," *Jm*, no.333 (1984), 24
K. Brodacki: "Enrico Rava Update," *JF* [intl edn], no.92 (1985), 41
J. Solothurnmann: "Enrico Rava: Jazz is Everywhere," *JF* [intl edn], no.92 (1985), 36
P. Carles, A. Clergeat, and J.-L. Comolli: *Dictionnaire du jazz* (Paris, 1988, rev. and enlarged 2/1994)
G. Endress: "Enrico Rava," *JP*, xxxvii/7 (1988), 12
J.-Y. Le Bec: "Enrico Rava: maintenant je joue pour . . . ," *Jm*, no.388 (1989), 22
L. Jurgeit and W. Klimaschewski: "Enrico Rava," *JP*, xliv/3 (1995), 26
"Ten Italian Musicians the World Should Know about . . . ," *Jazz Changes*, iv/2 (1997), 16
A. Leonardi: "Enrico Rava," *Musica jazz*, liv/10 (1998), 35
<http://www.ijm.it/enartists.html> (1999)

STEFANO ZENNI, BK

Rawls, Lou(is Allen) (*b* Chicago, 1 Dec 1935). Singer. His year of birth has been published variously as 1935, 1936, and 1937; an inquiry, via his manager, confirmed 1935 as the correct year. Rawls began singing gospel in his church choir around the age of seven, but in his teens he became strongly influenced by the singing of Billy Eckstine, Arthur Prysock, and Joe Williams. He also sang in various high-school vocal groups with a classmate, Sam Cooke. Around the mid-1950s he moved to Los Angeles and toured in Cooke's accompanying group, the Pilgrim Travelers. After army service (1955–*c*1957) he worked again with the Pilgrim Travelers until he was seriously injured in a car accident in November 1958. He resumed performing in Los Angeles in 1959 and in 1962 recorded with a trio of Les McCann, Leroy Vinnegar, and the drummer Ron Jefferson; the resulting LP, *Stormy Monday* (1962, Cap. T1714), was his crossover into the realm of jazz and blues singing. He continued to record in this vein, though usually accompanied by a large studio orchestra, until around 1966, when he released the pop recording *Love is a Hurting Thing* (1966, Cap. ST2566); the following year he won a Grammy Award for rhythm-and-blues vocal performance. By the late 1960s Rawls's repertory was oriented towards soul music, and he continued to perform and record as a soul and pop singer until the late 1980s; of his later recordings, the album *Portrait of the Blues* (1992, Manhattan 99548) offers the best example of his return to jazz-tinged work. Rawls also appeared extensively on television and in films, and in his own Broadway show.

BIBLIOGRAPHY

FeatherE
L. Feather: "Is He Blue? Lou Rawls Back to his Roots," *Los Angeles Times* (10 Sept 1989)
S. Holden: "Lou Rawls: Back in Club, Back to Blues," *New York Times* (7 July 1989)
J. Bradley: "Lou Rawls Sticks with Tried, True," *Denver Post* (19 June 1994)
P. Smith: "Your Basic Lou Rawls," *Boston Globe* (12 June 1994)
"This Week in Black History," *Jet* (2 Dec 1996), 19
<http://www.bayfest.com/lourawls.htm> (1998)
A. Martin: "Lou Rawls Center, Blues Mecca Proposed," *Chicago Tribune* (11 Feb 1998)

SCOTT FREDRICKSON, GK

Ray (Russell), Carline (*b* New York, 21 April 1925). Bass player, guitarist, pianist, and singer. Her father played with James Reese Europe's 369th Infantry Band. She began studies at the Institute of Musical Art in September 1941, first studying piano, and graduated in 1946 (the year in which it was renamed the Juilliard School), majoring in composition. While still there she worked with the double bass player Edna Smith, with whom she started playing guitar. In May 1946 both women joined the International Sweethearts of Rhythm, with which Ray sang and played rhythm guitar; she may be seen in the group's short films *How About that Jive* and *Harlem Jam Session* (both 1946) and is a member of the rhythm section on the pairing *Don't get it twisted/Vi Vigor* (1946, Vic. 40-0106). She left the International Sweethearts in March 1947 and in June was appearing with Earl Bostic's band in a revue at Club 845 in the Bronx. In February 1948 she joined Erskine Hawkins's band as a singer, though occasionally she also played rhythm guitar. In the early 1950s, as a pianist, she co-led a trio with Smith and Pauline Braddy which held a six-month engagement at Town Hall, New York. (It was around this time that she met Luis Russell, whom she married in 1956.) Ray first played electric bass guitar with this trio, when at times she and Smith would swap instruments. From 1954 to 1956 she also majored in voice at the Manhattan School of Music (MMus).

From 1956 Ray has been active primarily as a bass player; she worked around New York with Skitch Henderson (early 1970s), Mary Lou Williams (with whom she recorded in 1970), Marian McPartland (1974–5), and Sy Oliver (in the house band at the Rainbow, mid- to late 1970s), and made a tour of the USA, Canada, and Japan with Mercer Ellington (mid-1970s). She took part in the first two years of the Women's Jazz Festival in Kansas City in 1978 and 1979, when she led the 17-piece Big Apple Jazz Women. In the early 1980s Ray studied acoustic bass with Major Holley, and in 1985–6 she taught guitar at Hunter College, New York. At the same time she held affiliations with Melba Liston (1980–83), Carrie Smith (1983–8), Tiny Grimes (1987–9), and the singer Ruth Brown (1989–95); she may be heard on Brown's album *Live in London* (1994, Ronnie Scott's Jazz House 046). In 1995, with the pianist Bertha Hope and drummer Paula Hampton, she formed the group Jazzberry Jam, which continues to perform in the new century; it made a privately issued recording, *Jazzberry Jam! Live*, in 1997. Ray deputized for Earl May in Doc Cheatham's group at Sweet Basil in 1996–7, and in 1998 she became a member of the Harlem Blues and Jazz Band. In 1999 she recorded the album *In Your Eyes* with the pianist Linda Presgrave (Metropolitan 1119). In 2000 she appeared in presentations of Cab Calloway's music by his grandson Chris Calloway Brooks.

BIBLIOGRAPHY

D. A. Handy: *Black Women in American Bands and Orchestras* (Metuchen, NJ, 1981, rev. and enlarged 2/1998), 93

——: *The International Sweethearts of Rhythm* (Metuchen, NJ, and London, 1983, rev. 2/1996), 196

S. Placksin: *American Women in Jazz, 1900 to the Present: their Words, Lives, and Music* (New York, 1982, London, 1985, as *Jazzwomen, 1900 to the Present: their Words, Lives, and Music*), 187

U. Schlicht: "It's Gotta be Music First," *Zur Bedeutung, Rezeption und Arbeitssituation von Musikerinnen* (Karben, Germany, 2001)

HOWARD RYE

Ray, Michael (Arthur) (*b* Trenton, NJ, 24 Dec 1952). Trumpeter and leader. Around October 1977 he joined Sun Ra, with whom he worked through 1992. As a member of the band he toured Italy, where he recorded in Sun Ra's quartet (alongside John Gilmore and the drummer Luqman Ali, January 1978), and he appeared with the Arkestra in the film *A Joyful Noise* (1980) and the video *Sun Ra: in Time and Space* (1994 [filmed 1986–91]). From 1979 to 1990 he also toured and recorded with the soul group Kool and the Gang. In 1989 Ray moved to New Orleans and formed his own large ensemble, Cosmic Krewe, in which he incorporates much of Sun Ra's philosophy regarding the merging of theatricality and music. While an artist-in-residence at Dartmouth College, New Hampshire (1990–91), he formed a second Cosmic Krewe with musicians from the New England area. Both of these ensembles continued through the late 1990s. In addition Ray worked with the alternative-rock group Phish and in multi-media performances with the neon-light artist Jerry Therio.

SELECTED RECORDINGS

As leader: *Michael Ray and the Cosmic Krewe* (1993, Evidence 22084)

As sideman with Sun Ra: *Taking a Chance on Chances* (1977, Saturn 772), incl. Untitled improvisation, What's New?; *New Steps* (1978, Horo 25–26); *Other Voices, Other Blues* (1978, Horo 23–24); *Media Dream* (1978, Saturn 1978); *Omniverse* (1979, Saturn 91379); *On Jupiter* (1979, Saturn 101679); *Sleeping Beauty* (1979, Saturn 79); *Live from Soundscape* (1979, DIW 388); *Sunrise in Different Dimensions* (1980, HH 17); *Voice of the Eternal Tomorrow* (*The Rose Hue Mansions of the Sun*) (1980, Saturn 91780); *Dance of Innocent Passion* (1980, Sun Ra 1981); *Hidden Fire*, i–ii (1988, Saturn Sun Ra 12988II, 12988B); *Cosmo Omnibus Imagiable Illusion: Live at Pit-Inn* (1988, DIW 8024); *Mayan Temples* (1990, BS 120121-1); *Destination Unknown* (1992, Enja 7071-2)

BIBLIOGRAPHY

R. L. Campbell: *The Earthly Recordings of Sun Ra* (Redwood, NY, 1994)

J. Koransky: "Let the Sun Ra Shine," *DB*, lxv/10 (1998), 46

K. Spera: "Funk for the Millennium and Jazz into the Cosmos," *New Orleans Times-Picayune* (23 Oct 1998)

<http://www.satchmo.com/CosmicRay/> (1999)

GK

Rayner, Alison (*b* Bromley, England, 7 Sept 1952). English bass player. Her uncle was the pianist Harry Rayner. She played in the pioneering women's rock band Jam Today before joining the Guest stars, with which she appeared at festivals, recorded, and toured the USA, Europe, and the Middle East; she worked with the other members of the Guest Stars in the Lydia D'Ustebyn Swing Orchestra and played in other big bands, including Gale Force 17, led by the french horn player Sharon Freeman. Rayner wrote for her own group, the Jazz Garden (1990–92), taught extensively, and played with Jayne Cortez, Tal Farlow, Peter King, Jim Mullen, and Jean Toussaint. A long association with Deirdre Cartwright involved her in small groups and in a duo. In 1989 the two women set up Blow the Fuse, an umbrella organization involving a record label and a venue for regular sessions, especially (from 1994) at the Vortex in London; their recordings together for the label include *One Night Stands: Live at Blow the Fuse* (1994, 9402) and Cartwright's albums *Debut* (1994, 9401) and *Play* (1997, 9703). An adherent of the freewheeling electric bass guitar style championed by Jaco Pastorius, Rayner has also played double bass from 1993. In 1997 she took part in the London Jazz Festival with the group Giant Steppes, led by the saxophonist Diane McLaughlin. (*CarrJ*)

For further recordings *see* Guest stars.

VAL WILMER

RBT-Orchester [Radio Berlin Tanzorchester]. German big band. It was founded in late May 1945 and first conducted by the composer Michael Jary. The first big band founded in Germany after World War II, it played many styles of music, including jazz. At the end of 1945 Horst Kudritzki became its new leader. The orchestra included such German and Italian musicians as the trombonist Rudi Arndt, the reed players Omar Lamparter and Baldo Maestri, and the pianist and vibraphonist Erwin Lehn, who became its co-leader in spring 1948. Its recordings for the Amiga label in 1947 include *Skyliner* (1105) and *Airmail Special* (1124). At the end of the decade the East German communist party increasingly placed restrictions on the group, and consequently Kudritzki and Lehn gave up its leadership and went to West Berlin. It disbanded in 1950. (J. Schütte: *Discographie des RBT-Orchesters und der anderen Formationen des Berliner Rundfunks* (Menden, Germany, 1977))

GERHARD CONRAD

RCA Victor. Record company and label. On 4 January 1929 the Victor company became the Radio–Victor Company of America, and from 1930 it was known as RCA (Radio Corporation of America) Victor. Through January 1946 the company's principal label retained the name Victor (for a history of its jazz recordings to this point *see* Victor). RCA also made several attempts to establish a subsidiary label to issue cheap discs, starting in April 1931 with Timely tunes;

this was quickly succeeded by the short-lived Elektradisk, and later by Sunrise and Bluebird.

February 1946 brought a regularization of the longstanding corporate change, with the name RCA Victor beginning to appear on record labels in place of Victor. The company started pressing discs out of vinyl in October 1946, and in February 1949 it issued the first 45 r.p.m. single. In the decades which followed it remained one of the most important jazz record companies, making new recordings and re-releasing large sections of the back catalogue. In the early 1950s it established a subsidiary label, X, which it used for the systematic reissue of early jazz; this was one of the first schemes of its kind. Later it issued albums by such musicians as Sonny Rollins (1962–4), Joe Williams (1962–5), J. J. Johnson (1964–6), and Phil Woods (1975–6).

From 1913 much of Victor's material in territories other than the USA had been put out on His Master's Voice (HMV); this policy continued in the RCA Victor era until 1957, when the company terminated its arrangements with HMV. Thereafter in territories formerly covered by that contract it issued much of its material (including the highly regarded Vintage Series of the 1960s and 1970s) either by agreement with other companies (such as British Decca, 1959–71), or, later, by establishing autonomous subsidiaries. French RCA was particularly notable for its reissue schemes Treasury of Jazz (1960s), Black & White (1970s; one of the largest single reissue programs ever undertaken, and not to be confused with the label of the same name of the 1940s), and Jazz Tribune (1980s). RCA also made use throughout the world of the label Camden, established in the 1950s for the issue of cheap records, the catalogue of which contained important jazz recordings. By 1976 the albums on the Flying Dutchman label were manufactured and distributed by RCA Victor.

In May 1983 the RCA Corporation acquired from BMG a 50 percent interest in Arista (the parent company of the Novus label); then, in a higher level transaction which unfolded over the course of more than two years and was finalized in 1986, BMG purchased portions of the RCA Corporation, including its recording division, from the corporation's owner, General Electric. From May 1986, when Novus was reactivated as a subsidiary of BMG, until around 1996 new recordings in this reactivated series appeared under the combined names of Novus, RCA Victor, and BMG (for further details *see* Novus). Following a reorganization in the mid-1990s, new material by such artists as Don Braden, Steve Coleman, Tom Harrell, and Kenny Werner appeared under the combined names of BMG and RCA Victor. Extensive reissue programs have continued into the new century, variously on Bluebird, RCA Bluebird, RCA, and Victor Jazz.

BIBLIOGRAPHY

A. J. McCarthy: "German RCA 'Jazz Star Series'," *JM*, xiii (1967), no.4, p.13; no.6, p.15

"Reissue Series, 1: French Treasury of Jazz," *JM*, xii (1967), no.11, p.29; no.12, p.23

"Reissue Listing: RCA 'Vintage' Series," *JM*, no.156 (1968), 30

"International Record Scene," *J&B*, i (1971), no.5, p.29; no.8, p.34; ii/2 (1972), 28

T. Russell: "Rock and Romance," *J&B*, ii/4 (1972), 14

K. Terry: "RCA Purchases Half of Arista Records," *Variety*, cccx (30 March 1983), 115

B. Korst: *RCA Victor Record Listing, 20-1500 thru 20-7300*, ed. C. Garrod (Zephyrhills, FL, 1986)

K. Terry: "Bertelsmann Set to Buy up Rest of RCA Records," *Variety*, cccxxiv (10 Sept 1986), 1

B. Primack: "Label Watch: RCA Victor Goes All Out," *JT*, xxv/6 (1995), 90

E. Holley: "RCA Victor Reissues Oldies, Signs up New Jazz Roster," *DB*, lxiii/7 (1996), 15

M. Stryker: "RCA Starts to Respect its Jazz Treasures," *Detroit News & Free Press* (2 June 1996)

S. Jones: "RCA Compiles Ellington's Jazz," *USA Today* (29 April 1999)

HOWARD RYE, BK

Reardon, Casper [Glissandi, Arpeggio] (*b* Little Falls, NY, 15 April 1907; *d* New York, 9 March 1941). Harpist. He was first a member of the Philadelphia Orchestra. While the principal harpist of the Cincinnati Symphony Orchestra he played jazz on the radio under the pseudonym Arpeggio Glissandi. As well as recording with Jack Teagarden (notably *Junk Man*, 1934, Bruns. 7652) and Paul Whiteman, he worked in Hollywood and led his own small groups in New York and Chicago.

BIBLIOGRAPHY

H. Mückenberger: *Meet Me where They Play the Blues: Jack Teagarden und seine Musik* (Gauting, Germany, 1986), 97

E. R. Deveau and others: "Casper Reardon: a Retrospective Portrait," *American Harp Journal*, xii/4 (1990), 52

T. Middleton: *Caspar Reardon* (London, 1994) [discography]

Rebello, Jason (Matthew) (*b* Carshalton, England, 29 March 1969). English pianist. He learned classical piano from the age of eight and discovered jazz as a teenager; he was particularly inspired by a concert given in London by Herbie Hancock's band Rockit. While attending the Guildhall School of Music (1987–90) he recorded with Alan Skidmore, Jean Toussaint, Tommy Smith, Steve Williamson, and the singer Cleveland Watkiss; he played often with Smith, and also performed in quartets led by Skidmore and Dave O'Higgins. In 1990 he made his recording début as a leader (produced by Wayne Shorter), and early the following year he toured Japan with Shorter. He continued to lead and record with his bands through the early 1990s, as well as playing with Courtney Pine, Branford Marsalis, Bud Shank, Julian Joseph, and others. In 1996 he retreated to a Buddhist monastery in Bradford-on-Avon, where he stayed for two months before taking an office job. He returned to playing jazz in May 1997 and went on to record with Tim Garland, Gerard Presencer, the guitarist Tony Rémy, and others. In 1999–2000 he toured worldwide with the pop singer Sting. His own recordings have tended to focus on skillfully crafted fusion and soul jazz, but he is also a highly accomplished straight-ahead pianist whose work is reminiscent of that of Hancock and Chick Corea.

SELECTED RECORDINGS

As leader: *A Clearer View* (1990, Novus 63000-2); *Make it Real* (1994, BMG 74321-22408-2)

As sideman: T. Smith: *Paris* (1992, BN International 80612-2); T. Garland: *Enter the Fire* (1995, 1997, Linn 074); G. Presencer: *Platypus* (1997, Linn 079)

BIBLIOGRAPHY

CarrJ

M. Sinker: "Step Forward Youth," *Wire*, no.54 (1988), 26

R. Cook: "Rebello with a Cause," *Wire*, no.81 (1990), 12

N. Hadsley: "Jason Rebello," *Jazz FM*, no.3 (1990), 9

K. Grimes: "Jason Rebello," *Jazz Express*, no.134 (1991), 11

D. Kasrel: "Hearsay: Jason Rebello's Forward March," *JT*, xxii/1 (1992), 12

S. Graham: "Mellow Rebello," *Jazz on CD*, i/1 (1993), 68

S. Rawles: "Scale Change," *The Guardian* (24 June 1995)

D. Skan: "Jazz's New Monk," *Sunday Times* (25 June 1995)

D. Gelly: "Mini-Interview: Jason Rebello," *The Observer* (29 June 1997)

C. Duncan: *Structure and Design Considerations in the Melodic Improvising of Jason Rebello* (thesis, U. of Kingston, England, 1998)

MARK GILBERT

Rebillot, Pat(rick Earl) (*b* Louisville, OH, 21 April 1935). Keyboard player. He was classically trained and served as a church organist during his teens while studying both piano and organ at Mt. Union College; in 1957 he graduated from Cincinnati College-Conservatory with a degree in music education. During his military service (1958–60) he performed with a variety of musicians and entertainers, and following his discharge he worked as a freelance in New York, playing both jazz and commercially oriented music. His better-known associations at this time were with Jeremy Steig, Benny Goodman, Paul Winter (with whom he toured Brazil in 1965), Sarah Vaughan, Zoot Sims, and Roy Eldridge. Thereafter he was a member of groups led by Gary Burton (1971–2) and Herbie Mann (1972–6), and he recorded with John Klemmer (1977). In the 1980s and 1990s, as well as working intermittently with Mann, Rebillot continued to play jazz, Latin-American music, and pop; he recorded with Bob Belden (*c*1990), Mark Murphy (1990–91), and Nnenna Freelon (1992).

SELECTED RECORDINGS

As leader: *Free Fall* (1973, Atl. 1663)

As sideman: F. Foster: *Soul Outing* (1966, Prst. 7479); C. O'Farrill: *Nine Flags* (1966, Imp. 9175); P. Desmond: *Crystal Illusions* (1969, A&M 3024); H. Mann: *Hold on, I'm Comin'* (1972, Atl. 1632); M. Murphy: *Bridging a Gap* (1972, Muse 5009); D. Newman: *Newmanism* (1973, Atl. 1662); David Friedman: *Futures Passed* (1976, Enja 2068); J. Klemmer: *Arabesque* (1977, ABC 1068); H. Mann: *Brazil, Once Again* (1978, Atl. 19169)

BIBLIOGRAPHY

Feather–Gitler '70s

SCOTT YANOW

Re-Birth Brass Band. Septet formed in New Orleans around summer 1982 by the brothers Philip and Keith Frazier (respectively tuba and bass drum), John Gilbert (saxophone), and Kermit Ruffins (trumpet), all of whom were teenagers at the time. After playing in the French Quarter during the summers, from the mid-1980s it gained an international reputation and toured and recorded extensively; it performed in West Africa (spring 1993), Istanbul (summer 1994), and Japan (May 1998). Ruffins left the group in 1994. Among later notable soloists was the tenor saxophonist Roderick "Claude" Paulin. The band may be seen in *The JVC/Smithsonian Folkways Video Anthology of Music and Dance of the Americas*, i (*c*1995 [filmed 1986]), and it also appeared during the 1990s in the short-lived cable television series "The Big Easy." Strongly influenced by the Dirty Dozen Brass Band, the Re-Birth Brass Band blends aspects of New Orleans brass-band music with contemporary funk rhythms; it may be heard at its best on a remarkably effective version of Herbie Hancock's *Chameleon*, on *Take it to the Street* (*c*1992, Rounder 2115), and on its album *Rollin'* (1994, Rounder 2132).

BIBLIOGRAPHY

J. Berry: "Echoes of the Beat of the Streets," *New Orleans Times-Picayune* (19 Dec 1989)

M. Joly: "New Orleans '89: the Brass Bands," *New Orleans Music*, i/1 (1989), 24

D. Sutro: "Rebirth Band Livens up New Orleans-style Jazz," *Los Angeles Times* [San Diego County edn] (6 Sept 1990)

P. Watrous: "New Orleans in New York as 2 Bands Share a Stage," *New York Times* (17 Aug 1990)

B. Sandmel: Rocking the Cradle of Jazz," *Musician*, no.154 (1991), 14

S. Aiges: "Kermit Ruffins Leaves Rebirth to give Solo Career New Life," *New Orleans Times-Picayune* (1 July 1994)

J. Berry: "ReBirth Revisited," *New Orleans Magazine*, xxix/2 (1994), 26

C. Flake: "Re-Birth," *Boston Globe* (10 April 1994)

G. Wyckoff: "N'Awlins Brass Bands: Rebirth of the School," *JT*, xxiv/8 (1994), 34

P. A. Harris: "Rebirth of the Brass Band: New Look for Old Tradition," *St. Louis Post-Dispatch* (13 Jan 1995)

R. Grosman and G. Boudry: "L'esprit New Orleans: Re-Birth Brass Band," *Jh* [special issue] (1996), 24

T. Terrell: "Hearsay: ReBirth Brass Band," *JT*, xxvii/8 (1997), 25

K. Spera: "Rebirth Hits 15 with Energy and Roots Still Intact" *New Orleans Times-Picayune* (29 May 1998)

GK

Rebop. *See* Bop.

Recording. A term applied to any of the various means by which sound and visual images are stored, and to the storage medium. This article concerns the general developments in sound-recording technology and their applications in jazz; for a discussion of recordings involving visual images with sound *see* Films. The systematic study of sound recordings as documents and as physical objects is the subject of the article Discography.

I. Technological developments. II. History of jazz recording.

I. Technological developments

1. The acoustical era: 1877–1925: (i) Cylinders and discs (ii) Piano rolls. 2. The electrical era: 1925–47 (i) Recordings for commercial distribution (ii) Private recordings. 3. New techniques of recording and playback after 1947: (i) Magnetic tape (ii) Microgroove discs (iii) Stereophonic sound on tape and disc (iv) Other developments. 4. The digital era.

1. The acoustical era: 1877–1925

(i) Cylinders and discs. The earliest methods of sound recording are described as "acoustical" and employ only mechanical means for both recording and playback. The sounds to be preserved are directed into a large horn, which at its tapered end is connected to a cutting stylus. In response to the vibrations of air in the horn, the stylus cuts a spiral groove in the thick wax coating of a cylinder or disc, rotated steadily by means of a crank. The cutting process creates variations in the groove analogous to the varying frequency and amplitude of the vibrations; the stylus moves up and down in "hill-and-dale" or "vertical cut" recording and from side to side in "lateral cut" recording.

To convert a disc from its original form into a marketable commodity, a process known as "pressing" is employed. It involves several stages during which alternately negative and positive images are made of the master version. The procedure as it is described here in terms of disc recording remained essentially unchanged until the advent of digital technology in the 1980s, though an additional stage was added once master recordings began to be made on magnetic tape instead of disc (see §3(i) below). The grooved master disc (sometimes called a wax (*see* Wax (i)) in the early recording era, later sometimes a "lacquer" – in both cases owing to the material with which it is coated) is electroplated; from this is formed a ridged negative (also called a master), which is stronger than the original positive; a further, sturdy positive, the "mother" (also known as the "matrix"), is made from the second master, and a metal negative stamper from the mother; from the stamper (which can withstand heat) the final discs are pressed. Roughly 1000 to 1500 discs can be produced before the stamper wears out and a new one must be made. A "master pressing" is one created from a master cut directly from a microphone or recording horn; the term thus applies to all recordings made before the introduction of magnetic tape recording (and also to those produced in the 1970s by the direct-to-disc method, see §3(iv) below). A "dub pressing" is one made from a master cut from a pre-existing pressing, a process adopted when all master material is lost or otherwise unavailable.

Mechanical playback of acoustical recordings involves a reversal of the recording process: a stylus tracks along the groove, following its contours, the variations of which are converted into analogous vibrations of the air inside the horn. (Acoustical recordings may also be played back on electrical equipment; see §2 below.)

The principal deficiencies of the acoustical recording process were the limitations and variability of its "fidelity." (Fidelity is the accuracy with which the original sound is reproduced by recording and playback, and depends on the range of frequencies reproduced and on the degree of distortion caused by the recording, pressing, and playback processes.) Acoustical recording never yielded high fidelity, its dynamic range was limited, and, because of the sensitivity of the technology, it required a high degree of skill in the recording engineer. The quality of acoustical recordings varied greatly, depending on the equipment used and on the ability of the engineer to position the performers correctly in relation to the horn. The quality of the equipment and the technical expertise available to some companies was so low that they were unable to use standard instrumentation; bass instruments were particularly problematical (see §II, 2, below).

The first sound-recording mechanism practical for commercial use was invented in 1877 by Thomas Edison (1847–1931) as an adjunct to his experiments with a telegraphic repeater. Edison's "phonograph" used a wax cylinder about five to six inches long and utilized the hill-and-dale recording technique. In the first decade after the invention of the phonograph, other important inventors in the USA received patents for recording devices; they included Alexander Graham Bell (1847–1922), who shared a patent with his cousin Chichester A. Bell and Charles S. Tainter in 1886 for a flat recording disc of wax-coated cardboard, and Emile Berliner (1851–1929), who received a patent for a disc phonograph in 1888. The duration of both cylinder and disc recordings was typically two to four minutes. Berliner's machine employed lateral cut recording, which became the standard method of commercial disc recording until the introduction of stereophonic recording in the 1950s (see §3(iii) below).

The principal uses that Edison and other early inventors envisioned for recording were communications, business stenography, telegraphy, and to some extent entertainment; Berliner appears to have been the first to look upon recording primarily as an entertainment and cultural medium. Venture capital was obtained for the manufacture of sound recorders from investors who were attracted by the apparent security of the patents and the likelihood of substantial returns. In spite of continuing patent litigation, the financial rewards of the recording industry on the whole justified their confidence. In 1889 the first playback device was produced for sale by a German toy factory, Kammerer & Reinhardt of Waltershausen, and in 1893 machines of the same kind became available in the USA.

Other developments in the late 19th century were also of great importance to the future of sound recording. Patents for recording sound in synchronization with moving film were established by Georges Demeny in 1892 and Edison in 1894, and a patent for the "telegraphone," a magnetic recording device, was issued in 1898 to Valdemar Poulsen (1869–1942). A number of patents for "wireless" devices for radio broadcasting were secured by Guglielmo Marconi (1874–1937), beginning in 1896, and other radio equipment was soon under development by the international firms of Marconi (1897) and Telefunken (1899).

1. The Gramophone Company's HMV Model 125 table gramophone, 1922

By the turn of the century several companies had been set up to manufacture recordings and playback equipment based on the patents of Edison, the Bells and Tainter, and Berliner and his associate Eldridge Johnson. The phonograph and gramophone industry expanded rapidly in the USA, England, and Europe; among the important firms were American Graphophone, Berliner Gramophone, and Columbia Phonograph. Patent-pool agreements in 1902 between Columbia and the Victor Talking Machine Company (which had grown out of the Berliner firm and taken over its patents) helped to establish the dominance of these two companies in the USA during the first half of the 20th century. Between 1900 and the outbreak of World War I the cultural and entertainment applications of recording came to surpass other uses in commercial significance.

In 1914 several basic patents expired, which led to a diversification in the manufacture of records and record-playing equipment by new companies such as Brunswick–Balke–Collender. In the same year the American Society of Composers, Authors and Publishers (ASCAP) was organized to collect fees for the use of published music, and General Electric began the manufacture of vacuum tubes for electronic amplification (Lee de Forest's patent on this process had been granted in 1907).

By this time flat discs were the predominant medium for sound recording. (Although Edison continued to manufacture recorded cylinders until 1929, and blank cylinders continued to be used for business stenography and portable recording equipment, it was, by 1930, many years since any repertory had been recorded only on cylinders.) In the early period of sound recording the characteristics of discs varied from one manufacturer to another. Until the mid-1930s sizes varied greatly: discs of diameters of between 5 and 20 inches were made, and although the standard sizes became 10 and 12 inches, 8-inch discs continued to be produced in large numbers into the 1930s. The playing time of the standard disc was between three and four minutes per side. Recording and playing speeds ranged from 72 to 86 r.p.m. before the standard settled at 78 (though Columbia, for example, issued 80 r.p.m. discs for some time after 1920). The materials of which discs were made and with which they were coated were also various; shellac eventually became the commonest material. By around 1920 lateral cut recording was the norm; a less exacting technique than vertical cut, it produced a level of fidelity adequate to the standard of the equipment the general public could afford to buy.

(ii) Piano rolls. Another mechanical recording medium was developed during the acoustical era – the piano (or pianola) roll. This is a roll, usually of paper, on which music is encoded in the form of perforations. The roll is marked mechanically as a player performs the piece on a recording piano; the marks are then cut by hand by an operator. The recording is played back on a mechanical instrument, known as a player piano or pianola, by means of a pneumatic system that automatically operates the keys of the instrument in response to the perforations in the roll.

Player-piano devices were first developed in the 1890s, in the form of separate cabinets that were moved up to the keyboard and played it mechanically; they gave a range of 65 notes at first, later the full 88. Around the turn of the century the apparatus was built into the piano itself. The first instruments to record faithfully all the nuances of a performance were built in Germany, by Edwin Welte in Freiburg in 1904 and by the firm Hupfeld of Leipzig in 1905. By 1913 two American reproducing player-piano mechanisms had been developed, the Duo-Art, made by the Aeolian Company, and the Ampico, made by the American Piano Company (which became the Ampico Corporation in 1915). At their best, reproducing player pianos could re-create the style of the original artist to a remarkably accurate degree.

2. The electrical era: 1925–47

(i) Recordings for commercial distribution. In electrical recording the sounds to be preserved are gathered by a transducer (a microphone) and the vibrations converted into an analogously varying electrical signal, which is amplified and applied to another transducer (a stylus), which cuts a spiral groove in a waxed or (later) lacquered disc; the deviations of the incised groove from the regular path correspond to the variations in the electrical signal. In playback the process is reversed, the signal being converted through a phonograph cartridge, an amplifier, and a loudspeaker into sound. The term "electrical recording" is normally used in contradistinction to "acoustical recording" (in the preceding era) and "magnetic tape recording" and "microgroove recording" (in the succeeding era); even though the process described here continued, broadly, to be standard until the advent of digital recording in the 1980s, and electricity, of course, has remained essential to recording and playback processes of all kinds, the term "electrical recording" is not customarily used after the introduction of magnetic tape in 1947.

The first electrical recording was issued in 1925, and from that time electronic amplification became the principal technological factor in the development of recording. The physical format of electrical recordings remained the same as that of the many acoustical ones utilizing the lateral cut technique; thus acoustical and electrical recordings were usually compatible and could be played on the same equipment. Electronic amplification made possible a dramatic improvement in fidelity. Other developments of importance to the recording industry during this period were the growth of commercial radio broadcasting, the standardization of synchronized sound-film recording, and the invention of the coin-operated jukebox; connected with the increase in the number of radio stations was the making and marketing of recordings designed specifically for broadcasting, so-called broadcast transcriptions (*see* Transcription (iii)), which employed a technology superior to that of commercially available recordings, based on a 16-inch disc that played at $33\frac{1}{3}$ r.p.m. and offered about 15 minutes of playing time.

(ii) Private recordings. A great many sound recordings survive from the pre-tape era which are not commercial pressings, transcriptions, film soundtracks, or part of the process by which such material was prepared for issue and distribution. Many such sound documents have later been issued commercially, particularly in the microgroove and CD eras.

The largest class of private recordings is test pressings, which may be of unissued material or of material that was later released. Although their name implies that they were made for assessment purposes – and this forms the greatest proportion – pressings with similar characteristics were also made as favors for artists and staff members, and some companies maintained matrix series whose sole purpose was to catalogue recordings of this character (for example, the TO- series at ARC). Before tape duplication was possible there was no reason for record companies to restrict the circulation of such material, since it could not be copied in sufficiently good sound quality for commercial release, and some enthusiasts who assisted in early reissue programs were actually "paid" in test pressings of their own choice. This, coupled with the large number of such pressings given to artists and staff, accounts for the quantity of such material that has survived in private hands to appear in reissue programs (which have always been so called, even when the material has not in fact been available to the public before). From the late 1930s many companies also recorded whole sessions, including breakdowns and studio chatter, onto "safeties," which provided some back-up if those takes mastered conventionally became unusable. Many of these have survived and have been used for comprehensive "reissues" of important works. Safeties, which became the main system of recording for many smaller companies as techniques for duplication improved in the 1940s, are often referred to as "acetates."

The term "acetate" is loosely used to describe any standard-grooved recording which is not a pressing, but was directly cut, and thus embraces not only safeties and the acetate masters of the immediate pre-tape period, but also private recordings made on the recording machines available before the introduction of tape. While these used various systems, all had in common that the resulting records were not very durable. Strictly speaking, an acetate is a metal disc coated with cellulose nitrate lacquer on which an instantaneous recording has been made; from the mid-1930s into the tape era these discs were actually used for radio recording and even to distribute programs on a more limited basis than broadcast transcriptions (*see* Transcription (iii)). Such acetates often had an extra hole, situated off-center, which engaged a driving pin on the turntable to keep the disc from dragging under the weight of the cutting head. Most coated discs employed this driving-pin technique, but at an earlier period uncoated aluminum discs, which were held in place by a weight, were used for instantaneous recording.

Although many of the broadcast recordings which have survived to be issued in later years derive from issued transcriptions, acetates, whether made by broadcasting organizations themselves or by enthusiasts using their own recording machines, are the source of many of the off-air recordings from the 1930s and 1940s known as "air-checks" (or "air-shots"). It is often forgotten that contemporary listeners were not necessarily aware whether a broadcast was being made live or was a transmission of a published transcription; privately made air-checks may therefore survive of commercial transcriptions, thus accounting for the wide variation in fidelity that may be encountered in different issues of the same "broadcast."

3. New techniques of recording and playback after 1947

(i) Magnetic tape. The process of recording on magnetic tape involves the conversion of sound signals, by means of a transducer (a microphone), into electrical impulses, which are recorded analogously as variations of magnetic flux along the tape. To make discs from tape masters the recording is first cut on a master disc before the normal series of operations that constitute the pressing process can begin.

Although Poulsen's magnetic recording patent was granted in 1898, it was not until the advent of electronic amplification that the musical potential of the technique could be realized. And because of complex economic and political factors a practical method of recording music magnetically, which required a reliable and inexpensive medium, was not arrived at until around 1950.

Poulsen's magnetic recorder used steel wire, and solid steel tape was used for magnetic recorders developed in Europe by both Kurt Stille and Ludwig Blattner in the 1920s, and by S. J. Begun and C. Lorenz in 1935. Work on paper and plastic recording tape coated with magnetic oxides was carried out in the 1930s by BASF in Germany and TDK in Japan, and by 1936 these companies were producing a limited amount of coated paper and plastic tape. The German company AEG demonstrated its Magnetophon tape recorder in 1935. In the USA magnetic recording techniques were being developed by such firms as Bell Laboratories (1937) and Brush Soundmirror (1938). Development (by Brush and the Webster–Chicago Corporation) of magnetic wire recorders for American military applications continued throughout World War II on a limited basis, but major work took place in Germany between 1935 and 1945. In September 1944 an improved version of the AEG Magnetophon was obtained by American forces as war booty from Radio Luxembourg, which had been occupied by the Germans. That machine provided the model for the first high-quality magnetic recorder for studio use in the USA, produced by the Ampex Corporation in 1947; the Brush and Magnecord companies also had tape recorders in production by 1947. By that time, too, oxide-coated recording tape with a paper or plastic base, which had been under development in the USA by the Minnesota Mining and Manufacturing Company (3M) from 1944, was available commercially.

After 1947 the recording, broadcasting, and film industries in the USA achieved general agreement on standards for magnetic recording. The main advantages of tape over the

2. Disc-cutting lathe on which the signals from the master tape are transcribed as a microgroove spiral on the disc

disc were the relative ease of editing and the substantially lower cost. Magnetic tape was also reusable and seemingly less fragile. (In some cases, though, it has proved disastrously fragile: in the 1980s it was discovered that after 20 or 30 years some types of adhesive used to bind the oxide to the plastic base, notably that produced by 3M for the recording industry's standard tape in the 1950s and 1960s, had disintegrated, transforming irreplaceable master recordings into useless boxes of blank tape and magnetic dust.) By 1950 magnetic tape had become the predominant medium for making sound recordings.

(ii) Microgroove discs. Changes of parallel importance took place in the area of disc recording in the postwar period; these arose principally from the development of polyester plastics, called polyvinyl chloride (PVC) or "vinyl," a comparatively unbreakable material, with a smaller grain structure than shellac (of which 78 r.p.m. discs were commonly made) and thus capable of receiving more refined impressions. The introduction of vinyl discs made possible a new standard "pitch" (or groove spacing) of around 100 grooves to the centimeter (superseding the old standard on shellac and other discs of fewer than 40); these "microgroove" discs allowed the recording of a broader range of frequencies and dynamics than their predecessors and suffered considerably less from surface noise. An incidental advantage of vinyl was its ready availability: since it is made from petroleum it could be obtained from sources within the USA, whereas shellac had to be imported (principally from India and Southeast Asia).

The advent of the microgroove disc led to the fixing of new standard speeds for recording and playback, longer playing times, and new physical formats for records. The $33\frac{1}{3}$ r.p.m. "long-playing" disc, introduced by Columbia in 1948, eventually allowed for about 25 minutes of music per side (although its duration was initially limited, for technical reasons, to that of a broadcast transcription – about 15 minutes); though by no means the first disc of its kind (there were experiments with long-playing discs in the 1920s and 1930s, see §II, 3, below), the 12-inch (less often 10-inch or 7-inch) $33\frac{1}{3}$ r.p.m. disc quickly became standard, replacing multiple-disc albums of 78s. The 45 r.p.m., 7-inch "single," first marketed by RCA Victor in 1949, ultimately replaced the single 78 r.p.m. disc (having a similar playing time of three to four minutes per side) and continued to account for many new issues. In due course two notable variants of the 45 r.p.m. disc were devised: the 7-inch EP (extended-play disc), which normally has two tracks on each side and runs for twice as long as a single, and the 12-inch single, which normally runs for up to 12 minutes per side.

A combination of factors accounts for the volatile expansion of the recording industry after 1950. The new discs gave better fidelity and were less fragile than their predecessors; a decrease in the cost of materials, manufacturing, and distribution also made them more affordable than recordings had been in the past. The use of easily edited magnetic tape improved the efficiency of the record companies' operations, and this, together with the favorable economic conditions of the 1950s, encouraged new companies to compete with established larger firms. Finally the record-buying public was larger, more affluent, and, as a result of wartime travel and radio broadcasting, more catholic in its musical taste than it had ever been.

(iii) Stereophonic sound on tape and disc. The technique of stereophonic (or stereo) recording and playback produces the effect of sound coming from different directions in three-dimensional space. It is achieved by means of two channels, recorded and played back independently, and relied for its development on the invention of two-track magnetic tape. The principal manifestation of the technique is the stereophonic, long-playing, microgroove disc made from two-track master tapes (later from multitrack master tapes mixed down to two channels, see below). (Other formats in which stereophonic recordings are issued are the cassette tape and the compact disc, see respectively §(iv) and §4 below.) On a microgroove disc the two channels are recorded as independent variations in the left and right walls of a V-shaped groove (the stylus moving vertically and laterally at the same time). The introduction of stereophonic sound thus gives higher fidelity than a process involving only lateral cutting. Although stereo recordings were made as early as the 1930s, it was only with the advent of high-fidelity microgroove discs that the technique gained importance.

Spurred on by the use of stereophonic sound in both broadcasting and films, the recording industry introduced stereophonic discs in 1957. Stereo recordings rapidly supplanted monophonic ones in the 1960s, and for newly made recordings this represented a significant improvement in every way. But the market forces set in motion by the introduction of the new technology proved disastrous in the area of reissues of recordings made earlier. Monophonic recordings were quickly relegated to a separate section of standard record listings, such as Schwann's *Long Playing Record Catalog*, and then disappeared entirely. In order to continue selling established material, record companies needed to adapt it so that it qualified for inclusion in the catalogues and satisfied public demand for stereo sound. Many (not all) companies added a false and muddled second track to monophonic recordings, marketing them as "enhanced for stereo effect" or "simulated stereo." Unfortunately such "improvements" were commercially successful. Only from the 1970s were substantial collections of classic monophonic recordings issued in their original form, with identical signals recorded on each channel.

Two-track tape was the first step in what became known as "multitrack recording," which made possible not only stereophonic sound but also new and complex editing techniques in the recording studio; introduced in the late 1950s, it was standard practice by 1970. Multitrack recording involves the synchronized recording, either simultaneously or consecutively, of multiple tracks (each normally carrying a single voice or line), which are then mixed and remixed until the desired result is obtained; up to 24 tracks may be recorded on tape up to two inches wide. (Some analogue studios can offer extended facilities by linking two 24-track consoles. This technique is commonly referred to as "48-track" recording, though in fact only 46 are available because, to enable the two recorders to be synchronized, a time pulse is recorded onto one track of each console. Techniques using digital technology – also referred to as "multitrack recording" – follow related procedures, but there are fewer limitations as to the track capacity; see §4 below.)

(iv) Other developments. A number of other experiments with recording formats and techniques were made possible by the technological advances of the postwar era; some produced

results that proved short-lived, others were commercially highly successful.

In the early 1960s an attempt was made to introduce long-playing discs recorded at $16\frac{2}{3}$ r.p.m., but by that time the $33\frac{1}{3}$ and 45 r.p.m. discs were well established and the slower speed attracted little interest. A decade later a similar failure attended quadraphonic sound, which extended the stereo principle to the use of four channels. In the mid-1970s direct-to-disc recording enjoyed a brief vogue. This technique combines the high fidelity made possible by contemporary equipment with the simplicity of the electrical recording process, whereby the signal is recorded directly onto the disc; although it gives higher fidelity than conventional tape-transfer methods (in which a subtle loss of quality results from the transference of the signal from tape to disc), the direct-to-disc process means that recordings cannot be edited, since each sound is irrevocably etched on the disc as the performance proceeds.

The commercial exploitation of magnetic tape was revolutionized by the introduction by Philips in 1966 of the stereophonic compact cassette (a sealed case containing a miniature reel-to-reel tape), and the machine on which it could be used. By 1980 the cassette had become competitive with the disc, and albums were usually issued in both forms. Cassette recorders have the additonal advantage of portability. From 1965 electronic devices for reducing unwanted noise were developed and applied by the recording industry for studio use, and later included in domestic equipment; one of these, Dolby-B (1970), markedly improved the sound quality of cassette tapes and contributed substantially to their success. The level of fidelity on cassettes was further improved by Dolby-C, Dolby-SR, and the studio system DBX, as well as variations in the materials used for tape coating – cobalt, chrome, and combinations of these with iron.

4. The digital era. Digital technology had been in use in computers for a quarter of a century before it began to be employed by the recording industry. Until the mid-1970s most advances in recording technology were refinements or extensions of basic analogue principles established in the 19th century.

So-called digital recording techniques use digital technology either in combination with or in place of the analogue techniques based on the continuously varying signals that characterize electrical and stereophonic recording. In 1976 the process of "digital mastering," which combines digital and analogue techniques, was introduced. It involves the initial preservation of sound on magnetic tape by encoding the continuously varying characteristics of sound waves as a sequence of discrete numbers, stored in the form of magnetic pulses; the digital master tapes are then decoded to produce analogue discs (sometimes described, misleadingly, as "digital recordings"). An important application of such hybrid techniques, particularly in jazz, is the potential they offer for subtle manipulation of the recorded sound: using "digital remastering" – that is, the making of a new digital master on magnetic tape – recordings of the acoustical and electrical eras can be re-recorded while in digitally encoded form for the purpose of improving clarity and balance and minimizing undesired noise.

In the early 1980s a medium based entirely on digital recording and playback technology – the compact disc – was introduced. The fidelity of discs recorded by analogue methods is affected by the inability of the medium to reproduce the sound signal in its entirety with sufficient accuracy at the extremes of the frequency range, and by the surface noise produced in playback by the physical contact between the stylus and the disc. Digital methods of recording and playback aimed to solve both these difficulties. A digital recorder "samples" the sound signal 44,100 times per second, and assigns each sample a binary number, thus creating multimillion-character streams of numbers. This digital representation of the sound is encoded by a process known as pulse-code manipulation (PCM) and recorded optically as a sequence of microscopic pits in the surface of a plastic disc (approximately eight billion pits are needed to record the hour or so of music that can be carried by the $4\frac{3}{4}$-inch disc). The stored signal never loses its original quality and can be copied many times with no audible change. A small semiconductor laser is used to play back the recording from the disc so that there is no loss of definition in the sound and no surface noise; compact discs revolve at a constant linear speed rather than at a constant angular speed, as do conventional discs. The industry standard for maximum playing time is 74 minutes, but discs are sometimes issued with as much as 81 minutes of music; far more often, however, this capacity is underutilized.

The first applications of digital technology in recording appeared in the late 1970s in the form of electronic equipment used in the studio in multitrack recording; the public first encountered its results in the sound-modification devices used in rock and electroacoustic music. At the turn of the decade the more affluent recording companies installed expensive digital magnetic tape recorders for making master tapes. By the mid-1980s marketing decisions about the format in which recorded music was issued indicated that the compact disc would supersede the 12-inch microgroove album, just as the album superseded the 78 r.p.m. single; within a few years this changeover was fully in place.

Other developments in digital recording took place during the late 1980s, notably a system on magnetic tape called "DAT." One implementation of DAT, known as RDAT, followed standards of compatibility reached by international agreement. The RDAT system uses a special cassette to hold the recording medium and, in contrast to the compact disc, enables digital recordings to be copied. The RDAT format can record both stereophonic and quadraphonic music, as well as computer data; intended to replace the conventional cassette tape, just as the CD supplanted the LP, it has had useful applications in the recording studio, but it has never become a significant commercial product.

In its first years the compact disc utilized 16-digit codes for both recording and playback. This "16-bit" technology allowed for nearly 66,000 possible timbres, but that number proved too small for audiophiles, who sought a greater sonic palette. The industry thus introduced 20-bit recording (with more than 1 million timbral possibilities), 24-bit recording (exponentially increasing this timbral palette into the millions), and other non-linear methods (some imitating analogue recording), each of which was then translated into a 16-bit format for playback.

In 1999 two new formats emerged, both endeavoring to supplant the CD and thus generate another boom in sales. Following on the success of the digital video disc (which aimed to supersede home videotape), DVD audio utilizes the technology of compact discs, including the same maximum playing time, but offers a sampling rate as high as 192,000 times per second and the capacity for disseminating a six-channel signal ("surround sound"). Its competitor, Super Audio CD, utilizes a faster and simplified type of sampling which more closely approximates an analogue soundwave, and offers a playing time of up to 110 minutes; early models produced stereophonic, not multi-channel sound.

II. History of jazz recording

1. Introduction. The relationship between jazz and sound recording is of paramount importance. Most jazz has the property of spontaneity, its creativity being concentrated in the act of improvisation – a form of impromptu composition. As a result, any recording of improvised or partly improvised jazz acts as a snapshot, freezing a single creative moment which can never be repeated without subconscious change. Because it is impossible for such a performance to be repeated exactly, each recording acquires a unique value, and it is this that has made the recording of jazz so vitally important: no other genre rivals jazz in its preoccupation with issues of alternative and multiple takes of individual titles.

In addition, jazz quickly came to rely for its geographical expansion, and hence its continued existence, on documentation by means of recordings. At first it spread locally by aural experience; its dissemination beyond the immediate locality of its origins was achieved through demonstrations given by itinerant musicians plying their trade. Economically generated migrations carried it further afield, but it was the advent of sound recordings that transmitted it fastest and gave rise to further musical development.

2. Early recordings. Initially the paths of jazz and recording did not cross, even though they originated in the same period. Nothing more frivolous than telegraphy and communications was at first seen as the object of the fledgling technology, so it is unsurprising that the musical movement then growing up in New Orleans and elsewhere, at that time also in its infancy, went largely undocumented. No recorded evidence survives of the manner in which jazz developed from its roots in blues, spirituals, folk music, African rhythm and harmony, marches, dance music, and creole music. A persistent but unsubstantiated claim exists that Buddy Bolden, who is generally credited with taking important steps in the shaping of the music, was recorded on cylinder in 1894 improvising the instrumental blues *Make me a pallet on the floor*.

While Bolden's cylinder remains part of the music's colorful mythology, there is a surprisingly large number of extant recordings of ragtime, one of the principal roots of early jazz. They serve to highlight a major problem of early recording techniques: although ragtime was essentially piano music, it proved difficult to register the sound of the piano on recordings, so banjo and small ensembles were often substituted for it. The characteristics of ragtime were diluted by the use of saxophone, accordion, and trombone (by Arthur Pryor, among others), and xylophone, the piano appearing only rarely before World War I; Charles H. H. Booth's unaccompanied piano solo *Creole Belles* (1901, Vic. 1079) is a notable exception.

Because of these technical difficulties almost all early piano recordings, especially those by the composers themselves, including Scott Joplin, were made on piano rolls. The crucial drawback of this medium was that the rolls could very easily be "doctored" by the cutting of additional holes, and this has caused the accuracy of some surviving recordings to be questioned. The piano roll, the most important producer of which was QRS, flourished into the 1920s and has continued. It provides an essential source for early recordings of the Harlem stride pianists, such as James P. Johnson (who made nearly 60 piano rolls as a freelance player in 1917–18 and exclusively for QRS from 1921 to 1927) and Fats Waller. In the 1970s QRS made many recordings on piano roll of the work of Earl Hines.

Identification of the first jazz recording is of course dependent on the permanently contentious question "what is jazz?" Some listeners credit James Reese Europe with the earliest, in 1914, but there is general agreement that it was not until 1917 that the first jazz records were made and released – ironically by several different companies; after ignoring the music for 30 years, record companies began to compete for jazz, and the race commenced, albeit with a stuttering start. The immense popularity of ragtime, boosted by sheet-music sales and spurred on by early recordings, provided the commercial bedrock for the infant recording industry. It is hardly surprising, then, that late in 1916 two leading companies, Columbia and Victor (both founded at the turn of the century), began casting about for a fresh novelty. Early the following year that need was satisfied when the Original Dixieland Jazz Band opened at the chic Reisenweber's Restaurant in New York. By mid-January the group had become a sensation, and on the penultimate day of the month it recorded for Columbia the tunes *Darktown Strutters' Ball* and *Indiana*. Columbia was slow to issue its recordings, however, and, as the ODJB's phenomenal success at Reisenweber's continued, Victor stepped in. On 26 February 1917 the group recorded *Livery Stable Blues* and *Dixie Jass Band One-step*, and Victor rushed the first pressing into the shops a week later, on Monday 5 March. The first jazz release was numbered 18255, cost 75 cents, and sold many copies (but not, as is often claimed, a million).

However, it has been realized recently that these recordings are not in fact the first on which jazz improvisation occurs. This honor belongs to Wilbur Sweatman's two versions of *Down Home Rag*, recorded in December 1916 (6-inch version, Emerson 5163; 7-inch version, Emerson 7161) with the Emerson String Trio; the latter is not a jazz group and provides what is largely an inappropriate accompaniment, which helps to account for the general indifference to the recording's claim to stylistic precedence. Sweatman's *Joe Turner Blues* (April 1917, Pathé 20167), and others recorded at the same session, has the curious characteristic of being performed by six reed players with no rhythm section, but the resulting music is unambiguously jazz. These recordings by Sweatman are probably the earliest by African-Americans of which this can be said. It is to be noted that they were made for companies with poor distribution and are vertical cut discs, which many later students of the music have been unable to play.

Despite the commercial success of the Original Dixieland Jazz Band, recording companies' interest in jazz remained low. A number of lesser-known bands modeled on the ODJB, including the Louisiana Five, recorded between 1917 and 1920. Mention should also be made of W. C. Handy's

Orchestra of Memphis, whose recordings, made in September 1917, offer some insight into the sound of an African-American territory band at this early date. On the whole, before 1920 the companies grossly underestimated the possible market for jazz, especially among the African-American population, none of whom, it was erroneously believed, could afford the equipment to play back records. Even when this view was modified, the companies still failed to grasp the extent of the jazz market.

Their second chance to exploit the untapped resources of the record-buying public – which again they failed spectacularly to realize – arose with the arrival in New York in 1919 of the African-American songwriter Perry Bradford, a shrewd southern businessman, who had identified the possibilities offered by the market. After unsuccessful attempts to interest the prominent Columbia and Victor companies in his work, Bradford eventually persuaded Fred Hager, a director of the General Phonograph Corporation, to record two of his songs in February 1920, using Mamie Smith. Issued on the General Phonograph Corporation's label OKeh, the pairing *That Thing Called Love* and *You can't keep a good man down* (OK 4119), though not a resounding success, sold well enough to justify a further venture. *Crazy Blues* and *It's right here for you* (OK 4169) were recorded on 10 August 1920 and 100,000 copies were sold in the last month of summer, sparking off interest in the neglected black market.

Thus so-called race records were born. At this time of the Harlem renaissance, with its emphasis on African-American virtues, the word "race" was not regarded as pejorative. The term RACE RECORD was subsequently assigned to many (though by no means all) recordings by black artists, and it indicates a segregationist attitude that led to what has been perceived as the second great mistake made by many record companies. Assuming that white buyers would have no interest in blues, gospel, and, later, some jazz, companies issued recordings by African-Americans in special series, often on separate labels (Victor even scratched the word "colored" in the record's wax). In the populous North, race records were advertised only in the black media and distributed only to African-American areas; in the rural South they were marketed by mail order, which accounts for the extensive race catalogues maintained by Sears Roebuck and Montgomery Ward.

Now, swept along in the wake of a tide of classic blues recordings by such singers as Ma Rainey, Clara Smith, Mamie Smith, and, most notably, Bessie Smith – who often included among their accompanists distinguished jazzmen such as Fletcher Henderson, Charlie Green, Louis Armstrong, and Jabbo Smith – and with not a little commercial impetus from the hyperbole of such musicians as Paul Whiteman, the record companies discovered jazz. Their activities baptized the "jazz age."

The development of jazz through recording was initially, and has continued to be, fostered not only by the major recording companies but also (except during the 1930s) by numerous independent labels. Among the earliest and most important of the latter were Gennett, Paramount, and OKeh.

Gennett not only established the noteworthy claim of being the first recording concern west of the Allegheny Mountains but also served as a model for similar companies. Formed by the famous Starr Piano Company in 1917, the recording side of the business was named after the Starr directors, Harry, Fred, and Clarence Gennett. Gennett operated two studios, one in New York, the other in Richmond, Indiana (see fig.3); the latter especially carved a niche in jazz history for turning out important early recordings, yet the company entered the jazz field almost by accident. As the result of a chance call at the neighboring Friar's Inn, Fred Wiggens, the manager of Starr's Chicago music store, strongly recommended the resident band to the Gennett executives. The success of the recordings made in

3. The Wolverines at Gennett's recording studio in Richmond, Indiana, 18 February 1924: (left to right) Min Leibrook (sousaphone), Jimmy Hartwell (clarinet), George Johnson (tenor saxophone), Bob Gillette (banjo), Vic Moore (drums), Dick Voynow (piano), Bix Beiderbecke (cornet), and Al Gandee (trombone)

1922 by the New Orleans Rhythm Kings (under the name Friars Society Orchestra) gained for Wiggens a free hand in deciding whom the label would record. His musical judgment, allied with his liberal attitude towards jazzmen, white or black, enabled Gennett to attract many of the seminal artists and bands of early jazz. Besides the New Orleans Rhythm Kings, these included King Oliver's Creole Jazz Band, Bix Beiderbecke and the Wolverines, Jelly Roll Morton, and Alphonso Trent.

However, recording jazz in the acoustic era was a taxing business. Gennett's Richmond studio was especially notorious, consisting of a wood-paneled room, capable of squeezing in eight musicians; they were asked to play into (or at) two large horns suspended on the wall at one end. Interruptions were frequent: if cold weather did not cause grease to clog the recording machinery, then steam locomotives clanked past on the line running alongside the studio. Even playing caused problems. Georg Brunis, the trombonist on Gennett's first recordings by the Friars Society Orchestra, recalled being made to face the side wall of the studio because when he played directly into the horn the cutting needle jumped about on the wax master disc. George Wettling, a white Chicagoan drummer, noted that the first great percussionist in jazz, Baby Dodds playing with King Oliver, was confined by the limitations of early recording technology to playing on woodblocks and the rims of snare and bass drums, and struck the cymbals only sparingly. The recordings therefore obscured more than they revealed of his work. If a bass instrument was used, similar problems of balance and audibility meant that it was more often a tuba or bass saxophone, or the pianist's left hand, than a double bass.

Compared with the major companies, Gennett undoubtedly produced low-fidelity recordings, but at least the documentation of jazz was under way. Other race-music specialists included Paramount, which began recording jazz, hillbilly music, and foreign-language discs as an adjunct to the manufacture of phonograph cabinets. Centered in Chicago, Paramount built the foundations of its catalogue with classic blues recordings by singers such as Ma Rainey and Ida Cox, but also recorded important instrumentalists, including Johnny Dodds. In 1924 it reached a leasing agreement with the first, and for a time the only, African-American recording company, Black Swan.

Other important small labels were Banner, Brunswick, Columbia's subsidiary Harmony, and OKeh, which swiftly outpaced Gennett in the astute ability to select fine musicians. OKeh contracted such luminaries of jazz as Oliver, Beiderbecke, the duo of Joe Venuti and Eddie Lang, James P. Johnson, Clarence Williams, and, most notably, Louis Armstrong, whose Hot Five and Hot Seven recordings for the company would prove to be among the most influential and enduring of all jazz.

The series of sessions Armstrong led for OKeh (1925–8) straddled the next great step forward in recording techniques, the first electrical recording, issued in 1925. Electronic amplification dramatically improved the fidelity of recordings, but it was a measure of the low status of jazz and the relative poverty of the smaller labels that the breakthrough, patented by the company Western Electric, did not have an impact on jazz for another two years. When it finally arrived, electrical recording emancipated drummers, pianists, and double bass players from the shadowy position imposed on them by more primitive recording techniques. It also facilitated the carriage of recording equipment into the field, though some acoustic recordings had already been made in temporary studios on location: OKeh recorded Bennie Moten's orchestra in St. Louis (1923–4) and Kansas City (1925) and Papa Celestin in New Orleans (1925). But electrical recording increasingly opened up these fresh areas of development to listeners, notably the territory bands, which were a barometer of the burgeoning of jazz in Kansas City and the Southwest. Recordists also moved properly into the birthplace of jazz, New Orleans, and captured elements of the music's prehistory through distinguished recordings made *en locale*; Papa Celestin (1926) and Sam Morgan (1927) recorded for Columbia, and the cornetist Louis Dumaine's Jazzola Eight (1927) and the Jones and Collins Astoria Hot Eight (1929) for Victor.

3. Major companies and the big bands. Other significant technical advances – the growth of radio and sound films – began to affect jazz in the 1930s. Allied with the economic depression, radio, films, and later the jukebox had far-reaching effects on the recording industry and the music profession as a whole. During the 1920s many musicians, including those in jazz, had been regularly employed in performing for silent films, but moving pictures with synchronized sound removed some of their job opportunities. Musicians who worked in cafés, taverns, and clubs were similarly replaced by jukeboxes. Radio became a popular diversion, rivaling phonograph recordings; from the late 1920s, and especially from 1935 until the late 1940s, many broadcasting organizations installed land lines to clubs and ballrooms to allow them to make remote broadcasts of performances.

Of greater immediate consequence was the onset of the Depression following the 1929 Wall Street crash. Between 1927 and 1932 annual sales of records in the USA dropped from a flood to a trickle – from nearly 100 million to 6 million – and annual sales of phonographs fell from nearly 1 million to 40,000. This caused a sharp cut in recording activity and wiped out almost all of the independent labels. Most disappeared altogether. Gennett stopped making commercial discs but continued in business as a custom-recording concern. Paramount went bankrupt. Others of the best, such as Brunswick, OKeh, and Vocalion, were taken over by major companies. Furthermore the major companies realigned. Symptomatic of the growing symbiotic relationship between radio and recording was the merger in 1929 of Victor and RCA (Radio Corporation of America), which had been formed from the Marconi Company in 1919. Other important changes included the mergers of the Plaza Music Company, Pathé Phonograph and Radio Corporation, and Cameo Record Corporation with the American Record Corporation (ARC) in 1929, the further merger of ARC with the Brunswick Record Corporation (BRC) in 1931, and the acquisition by the Columbia Broadcasting System (CBS) of American Columbia and ARC–BRC in 1938.

1932 may have marked the recording industry's nadir in one respect; in another it saw a technical advance – stereo recording – the earliest examples of which were to remain, paradoxically, a secret for 55 years. Why these first examples were made is uncertain; it may have been simply a matter of chance. At that time jazz was becoming increasingly constrained by the three-minute time limit imposed on recordings by 78 technology. In informal clubs and jam sessions musicians were improvising quite lengthy performances (Kansas City was noted for jam sessions that continued all night on a single tune), and the formal theaters, where big bands would evolve the swing style, also required elaborate, extended performances.

Chief among those trying to break out of the straitjacket of the three-minute piece was the music's principal composer, Duke Ellington, who had already produced his first formally extended work, *Creole Rhapsody* (1931), which spread over two sides of a 78. At this time Ellington was recording largely (but not exclusively) for Victor, who in 1931–2 began to experiment with recording at a speed of 33⅓ r.p.m. as a means of extending the playing time of a record. The process was expensive, and it is thought that, to avoid any possibility of failure, two cutting turntables, each with its own microphone, were used; the result was a pair of masters, which, played simultaneously, reproduced a performance in true stereo. But this was not discovered until 1981, when a collector in California obtained a pair of masters of one of the two recordings now known to have been made – full-length versions of *Black and Tan Fantasy* and *Creole Love Call*. Whether Victor's stereo recordings were simply a lucky by-product of an experiment directed towards other ends or a deliberate attempt to obtain stereo sound remains open to conjecture. In either case their discovery sparked off speculation that many other stereo recordings were made.

But the Victor experiment fizzled out and Ellington was left to create extended works that divided in a way that coincided with the duration of the 78, notably *Reminiscing in Tempo* (1935), which spreads over four sides. These extended works were exceptions in an output that sublimated the three-minute form.

By now jazz had also begun to be seen and heard on film. The work of a handful of makers of "shorts" has become justly celebrated, whereas Hollywood's attitude from the beginning was largely patronizing and has remained so. An interesting sidelight on the sound film (which is discussed at length in Films) is that, although optical track recording allowed extended playing time, this was rarely taken up. In addition it is worth noting that, apart from a few flimsily plotted musicals and generally embarrassing biographical features, the genre's one concession to the commercial success of swing was the series of so-called soundies recorded in the early 1940s (*see* Films, §II, 2). These productions – by RCM (Roosevelt, Coslow & Mills) – were three-minute films of a single performance for replay on a kind of jukebox in bars and clubs, each play costing 14 cents; they featured such musicians as Count Basie, Cab Calloway, Duke Ellington, and Lucky Millinder.

More significant for jazz was the continuing growth of radio broadcasting, which in the 1930s gradually took over as the leading source of entertainment for the family; by 1935 the radio set was a standard item of furniture in most homes. Once that had happened the broadcasting of jazz provided another source of unique performances for recording.

The swing era at its height saw a battle fought by the major record companies, involving price cutting and the taking of large stakes in the infant broadcasting industry with its potential for promoting their recorded product. At the same time radio itself was a voracious user of material, broadcasting nightly for hours at a time from a succession of ballroom venues where the big bands played. However, the most popular bands were not always booked by the most accessible venues, so their popularity boosted another recorded product, the broadcast transcription (*see* Transcription (iii)), a type of recording made exclusively for the purposes of broadcasting. Transcriptions were usually on 16-inch discs which allowed up to 15 minutes of playing time, but once again few bands or musicians took advantage of it, though the arrangements used in ballrooms and dance halls regularly included more instrumental parts and solo opportunities than commercial releases.

Independent of this burgeoning business were the activities of devoted amateur recordists, ever mindful that every jazz performance is unique. Using disc cutters and, later, wire recorders, they made recordings for their own pleasure on location or from radio broadcasts (the latter are known as "air checks" or "air shots"), capturing much material that would otherwise not have survived; although the sound quality was predictably inferior to that of recordings made in the studio with professional equipment, they provided material for an explosion of unofficial issues when copyrights began to expire in the 1970s. By 1938 Carnegie Hall was equipped with a recording system which was used by John Hammond to record his "From Spirituals to Swing" concerts, and an ever-growing number of jazz aficionados in the United States were equipped to make unofficial recordings of this type; the efforts of Jerry Newman at Minton's Playhouse and Monroe's Uptown House are merely among the most important documentations of this type to have come to public notice. Instantaneous recordings were also used by music publishers to facilitate notation for publication, such as the recordings of Fats Waller's *London Suite* made at Billy Higgs's London studio in 1939.

4. Developments outside the USA. Throughout the 78 r.p.m. era, and even later in some areas (for example, Japan), non-Americans learned about jazz primarily by listening to recordings and to radio broadcasts (usually themselves consisting of recordings, rather than of live transmissions). The simple reason for this is that the early history of jazz is dominated by musicians who usually performed and recorded in the USA. Certainly there were many instances of Americans touring and even living abroad (*see* Jazz (i), esp. §IV, 5), but all such events and circumstances taken together were comparatively insignificant beside the activity going on in the USA, particularly in the matter of stylistic innovation.

In the early decades of jazz, therefore, non-American record companies were important for rather different reasons from their American counterparts. Their significant contributions were, first, to issue recordings made in the USA, an activity (pursued by labels such as Brunswick, Odeon, and Panachord) that formed the bedrock of the dissemination of jazz in Europe and the rest of the world; second to document the development of the music in their own countries; and only third to make important new recordings by performers of the first rank.

Although they may have been comparatively few, noteworthy recordings of major figures were nevertheless made by European countries. Columbia recorded the Original Dixieland Jazz Band in London in 1919–20. Deutsche Grammophon recorded Arthur Briggs in Berlin in 1927–8. During his residency in Europe in the mid-1930s Benny Carter recorded for Vocalion and in the same period Coleman Hawkins, also living for a time in Europe, recorded for Parlophone. In addition Carter and Hawkins recorded for Decca, as did Duke Ellington, Stephane Grappelli, and Django Reinhardt; the Quintette du Hot Club de France for Ultraphone; Carter, Hawkins, Bill Coleman, and the Quintette du Hot Club de France for His Master's Voice; and Hawkins for Panachord. Perhaps the most important of the European organizations was the small label Swing, established in Paris in 1937 by Charles Delaunay and Hugues Panassié, which produced fine items by the Quintette du Hot Club de France, Carter, Hawkins, Coleman, Rex Stewart, Dicky Wells, and Teddy Weatherford. Weatherford also later recorded for Columbia in Calcutta (1942–3).

5. The war years and the AFM recording ban. As the 1940s began, little at first sight seemed likely to affect the enormous boom being enjoyed by those guiding the progress of the swing era. But events were combining that would forever change the face of jazz and the way it was documented on disc. The crucial event was the war. Its immediate effects on the American treasury led to several significant fiscal and other measures. Driving for pleasure was banned to save gasoline; a cabaret tax of 30 per cent (later reduced to 20 per cent) was imposed, making smaller, cheaper bands a more attractive booking proposition; and for a time a midnight curfew was introduced. In addition, the stresses of wartime, as though echoing those of the Depression, increased popular demand for the sentimental and the reassuring; this in turn boosted the standing of vocalists, who very soon began to see their names appearing in headlines at the top of the bill, before the bands' names.

At the same time the loss of employment opportunities for musicians, which the AFM put down to the new popularity of radio, caused a backlash against broadcasting. Because musicians were losing jobs as places of public entertainment closed – partly as a result of potential patrons having a ready-made source of entertainment at home in the form of broadcasting, partly because of wartime measures – the AFM called for a royalty payment to be made to the union by record companies for each commercial disc sold. When no progress was made in talks, the union demand was backed by a ban on instrumental recording from 1 August 1942, which lasted roughly two years. Decca came to an agreement with the AFM in September 1943 and Blue Note in November, but Columbia and Victor did not settle the dispute until November 1944, when they agreed to pay into a union fund a percentage of their income, amounting to between 0.25 and 5 cents for each disc sold. In the meantime singers, who were not members of the AFM, continued to be able to record, and the prominence this gave them put another nail in the coffin of the big-band business.

The strike, coupled with the dispersal of vast numbers of people into branches of wartime service, led to a need to organize the entertainment industry in new ways. Major network radio series and wholly new ones were transcribed for the Armed Forces Radio Service on 16-inch discs, which were freighted to service personnel all over the world for replay at their bases. And, in the absence of commercial record issues, the US War Department authorized the special series called V-discs exclusively for military personnel. Culled from commercial recordings, broadcasts, and transcriptions, as well as specially organized sessions, some 8 million V-discs were distributed between 1943 and 1949, on 12-inch 78s that could carry up to $6\frac{1}{2}$ minutes of sound. The AFM, having banned commercial recordings, permitted musicians to take part in the V-disc sessions on condition that the discs would be treated as army surplus at the end of hostilities and destroyed; many were, but it is believed that few, if any, titles were lost altogether.

Thus V-discs, together with the broadcast transcription products of AFRS, Associated, Lang–Worth, Standard, Thesaurus (of NBC), and World Transcriptions, form a jazz archive covering an immensely important period, which (except for "soundies") is otherwise undocumented because of the AFM ban. However, instead of providing a view of the

(a) (b)

4. (a) Label for "Way Down Yonder in New Orleans," recorded by the Kansas City Six for Commodore (1938); (b) key, identifying the types of information that may appear on a label (the matrix number is always inscribed on the disc itself close to or beneath the label)

5. Gerry Mulligan's quartet during a recording session for Columbia, December 1958 or January 1959; (left to right) Dave Bailey (drums), Mulligan (baritone saxophone), Bill Crow (double bass), and Art Farmer (trumpet)

music's continual development in the mid-1940s, these recordings effectively present a picture of jazz frozen as it was at the beginning of the decade, thus obscuring the major changes that emerged suddenly, as though they were revolutionary, when recording began again in 1944–5.

6. The re-emergence of independent labels. After the demise of many independent companies during the Depression, a certain recovery had already begun before the AFM ban. Towards the end of the 1930s, as a reaction to the commercial excesses of the swing era, a fresh group of companies emerged to record "pure" styles that their proprietors felt were being neglected.

Among the first was Milt Gabler's label Commodore, named for his record store in New York. Although it was formed to record the greatly neglected music of the white Chicago school of the 1920s led by Eddie Condon, its short existence (to the mid-1940s) resulted in highly influential recordings by small swing bands, featuring such musicians as Lester Young, Coleman Hawkins, Chu Berry and Roy Eldridge, Eddie Durham (who made some of the first recordings on electric guitar), Hot Lips Page, Don Byas, and many others. Commodore was also one of the first record companies to encourage longer performances by issuing them on 12-inch 78 r.p.m. discs, a format avoided by the major companies, who were locked in a price war and regarded 12-inch discs as uneconomic, reserving them for classical music.

Varsity was established in 1939 by Eli Oberstein, formerly a recording manager at Victor. Although it was also short-lived, the label preserved important performances by Roy Eldridge, Benny Carter, and Coleman Hawkins (each as a principal soloist in a single group), Stuff Smith, and John Kirby's sextet (under Buster Bailey's name), which together with Fats Waller and his Rhythm (on Victor and Bluebird) was the most commercially successful small group of the era. Other notable documenters of small-group swing and the transition to bop were Black & White, Continental, Musicraft, and the vital label Keynote, run by Harry Lim (who later, in 1972, established the company and label Famous Door).

Alongside these, another group of entrepreneurs was allowing the public to rediscover New Orleans styles through recordings for Jazz Man, Climax, and, most important, American Music, on which players such as Bunk Johnson, George Lewis (i), Wooden Joe Nicholas, and Baby Dodds provided a glimpse of the music's prehistory. Another label, King Jazz, partly owned by Mezz Mezzrow, recorded 56 masters in its brief existence (1945–8), the most important being quintet and septet titles featuring Sidney Bechet.

Such enterprises ensured that the past remained in the present, and from this time on the documentation of developing jazz styles would lie almost completely in the hands of the independent labels. The major companies, whose interest in jazz declined sharply with the disintegration of the big-band era, henceforth confined their jazz activities to styles and musicians of proven commercial worth or prospect.

The first major new style to be nurtured by the independents was bop, which had been rapidly developing in clubs along New York's 52nd Street during the difficult years of the war and the AFM recording ban. An avant-garde movement, its documentation was left almost exclusively to the custody of small, independent, specialist labels such as Guild, Manor, and Ross Russell's Dial, and three that were destined to become giants – Clef, Savoy, and Blue Note.

Clef, under the direction of Norman Granz, arose from the documentation of the rousing and often rowdy jam sessions given as part of his Jazz at the Philharmonic series. It grew to encompass both new and old styles and became perhaps the most important label in defining the jazz mainstream. Absorbed into Verve in 1956, it was sold to MGM late in 1960. Clef was also one of the few labels before the LP era (another was Gene Norman Presents) to break away from the restriction of commercial issues to a duration of three or four minutes: many of the jam-session recordings preserve performances of between ten and 25 minutes, and in their original form were therefore issued on three to seven sides of a set of 78 r.p.m. discs.

Savoy, founded in 1942 by Herman Lubinsky, owed its musical success to its artists and repertory men, including Ozzie Cadena, Buck Ram, and Teddy Reig. But its economic survival was due to its activities in the area of rhythm-and-blues and gospel music, though it recorded many important bop sessions, notably one by Charlie Parker's quintet in 1945.

Blue Note more than any other label gained cult status among listeners, not through following fashions but simply because of the quality of its recordings. It was founded in 1939 by Alfred Lion to provide a practical means of expressing his enthusiasm for the boogie-woogie pianists Albert Ammons and Meade "Lux" Lewis, who had impressed him at John Hammond's first "From Spirituals to Swing" concert in Carnegie Hall in 1938. 50 pressings each of the five performances could hardly secure a future for the new label, but a single performance from the next, greatly contrasting, session did: Sidney Bechet's profound interpretation of *Summertime* (1939, BN 6).

Although they suspended recording activities during the war, Lion and his partner Francis Wolff continued to sell existing recordings; Wolff noted that wartime and the AFM ban sharpened demand and allowed Blue Note to build financial reserves for its next phase of recording. This began in November 1943 and documented the first aspect of the postwar changes in jazz – the rapid growth of small swing groups that split away from the disintegrating big bands. Some of these were led by Ike Quebec, who became the talent scout for Blue Note, leading Lion and Wolff to bop and enabling them to make classic recordings by Thelonious Monk, Bud Powell, Fats Navarro, and others. In the 1950s Blue Note groomed the talents of such musicians as Art Blakey, Horace Silver, Hank Mobley, and Kenny Dorham, dominating the scene against powerful competition by means of carefully planned sessions, always preceded by sufficient rehearsal time to allow challenging material to be played with the greatest creativity.

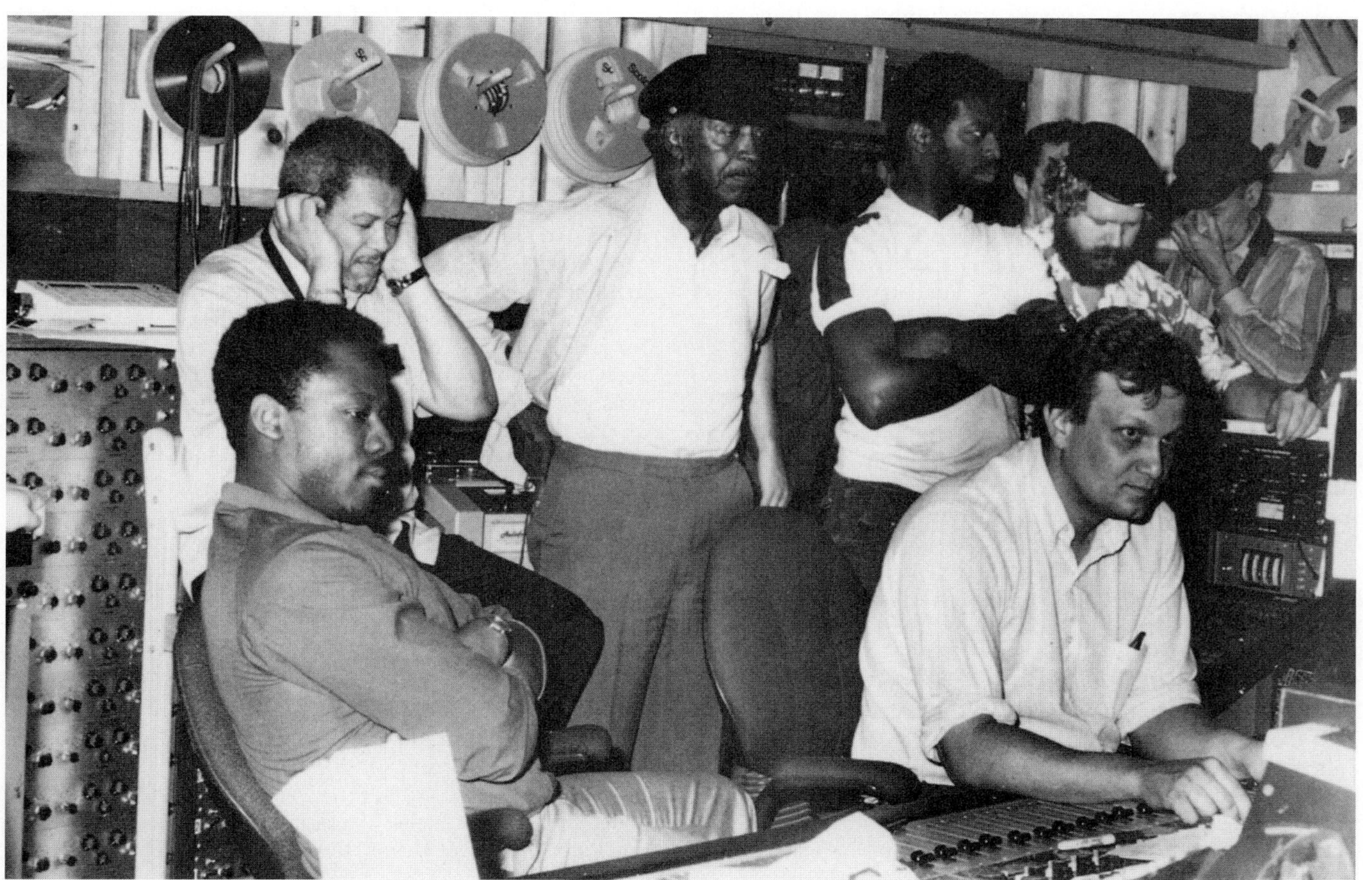

6. Members of the Count Basie Orchestra in the control room at Power Station studio, New York, during the recording of "Long Live the Chief," June 1986: (back row, left to right) Frank Foster (tenor saxophone), Freddie Green (guitar), Dennis Wilson (trombone), Lynn Seaton (bass), and John Williams (baritone saxophone); (front row) Ralph Peterson, Jr., and Malcolm Pollack (engineer)

In the middle of this period there was a second recording ban, less effective than the first. By October 1947 the AFM had announced that a strike would begin on 1 January 1948. The warning gave companies several months in which to accumulate new recordings, which they did with the cooperation of their musicians; they then issued these recordings through the period of the ban, which ended early in 1949. The ban seems to have pushed forward somewhat the demise of the big bands – even Benny Goodman concentrated on leading small groups – but it was no more than a minor factor in their decline.

In general this was a great age for jazz, witnessing the simultaneous flowering of traditional and mainstream as well as modern styles, all assiduously catered for by independent producers. Blue Note documented the entire period, stamping on it a distinctive sound so beloved of collectors that the label was able to make a comeback from 1985 under the guidance of Bruce Lundvall.

But it had important competitors, notably Bob Weinstock's labels Prestige and New Jazz, established after the ban ended in 1949, and the Riverside label of Orrin Keepnews and Bill Grauer, established in 1953, and its subsidiary Jazzland, set up in 1960. Both enterprises discovered important new stars and rediscovered important old ones: Miles Davis and John Coltrane recorded for Prestige, Monk, Bill Evans (ii), and Wes Montgomery for Riverside. As was often the case, however, these two companies lost musicians, once their reputations were firmly established, to the major companies, which tended to acquire rather than develop talent: Columbia took Davis in 1955 and Monk in 1962, Verve took Evans in 1963 and Montgomery in 1964. This was not necessarily detrimental, since Columbia recorded many of Davis's finest albums, as well as some of Charles Mingus's best work, and Verve found a proper setting for Jimmy Smith after his less notable sessions for Blue Note.

During the 1950s, with the advent of the long-playing disc, musicians finally began regularly to record extended performances. The decade also saw the rise of West Coast jazz, documented by labels of high quality such as Richard Bock's Pacific Jazz, Lester Koenig's Contemporary, and Atlantic (particularly the sectors of the catalogue supervised by Nesuhi Ertegun). In New York, Vanguard established its series Jazz Showcase under the direction of John Hammond, which presented Count Basie, Buck Clayton, Vic Dickenson, and other leading swing musicians. In the mid-decade Atlantic turned its attention to jazz, recording diverse styles and mounting sessions by Wilbur De Paris and his New New Orleans Jazz, the Modern Jazz Sextet, and Mingus; at the turn of the decade it recorded John Coltrane and Ornette Coleman, and in 1962, as part of a series called Jazz at Preservation Hall, it recorded the first technically well-made album of a New Orleans brass band, the Eureka.

In 1960 the company Impulse! was formed, whose label became one of the most important of the decade, above all for Coltrane's modal-jazz and free-jazz recordings. Ironically Coltrane's extended improvisations on individual titles, in a number of instances covering one or both sides of a long-playing disc, caused a curious reversal in critics' attitudes: those who disliked Coltrane now lamented the demise of the three-minute performance, which obliged a soloist to be concise.

7. The effects of technological change. From the late 1940s, when magnetic tape became the principal recording medium, the possibility existed of editing (cutting and splicing) recordings; the development of multitrack recording a decade later allowed the isolation and separate manipulation of individual components and voices of a recording. These advances exaggerated the distinction between performance and recording, and meant that, in theory at least, recordings could no longer be regarded as the documentation of a spontaneous act of creation. However, the facility for "improving" on a recorded performance by editing was, on the whole, used less in jazz than, for instance, in classical music, and musicians and listeners alike continued to value the indefinable effect of the element of risk that had hitherto characterized all recordings.

At first editing was used simply to remove blatant mistakes and to retrieve fine passages from otherwise flawed performances. Thus, for example, Keepnews explains that Monk's composition *Brilliant Corners* was so difficult that even such formidable players as Sonny Rollins and Oscar Pettiford were unable to make their way through a completely satisfactory take at a session on 23 December 1956; the issued track is therefore a composite, in which the final statement of the theme is part of a different take from the remainder of the performance. Similar work was done on recordings by Mingus; he was notorious for producing brand-new material at a recording session, and as a result he was obliged to rely on studio editing to eliminate mistakes.

It was only after rock musicians led the way in the mid-1960s that jazz musicians turned to editing as a means of exploring new sounds. The first important examples were the fruits of the collaboration between Miles Davis and his producer at Columbia, Teo Macero. In their work from 1968 into the 1980s the recording session itself was only the first part of making a recording: tapes of hours of improvisation provided the raw material from which they created the structure and content of an issued track. In effect Davis's producer became as important a member of his group as any individual sideman.

The technical innovations of the 1970s had, on the whole, little impact on jazz. Cassette tapes became generally available, but during this era they never replaced the LP for jazz listeners. There are several possible reasons for this: even with sophisticated recorders, equipped with music sensor devices, it proved difficult to locate individual tracks on tape; few listeners possessed the expensive equipment needed to produce a cassette tape sound that rivaled a good (not even a great) phonograph; and the extensive liner notes and handsome photographs and artwork that became an essential part of the presentation of a jazz recording could not be successfully reduced to the tiny size of a cassette-tape box. Direct-to-disc recording had small importance for jazz. Retakes were expensive and editing impossible. The discs themselves were also costly and most companies trying the process risked it only on lightweight forms of jazz. The high fidelity proved to be insufficient compensation for these shortcomings, and no label attempted more than a few direct-to-disc recordings.

8. Non-American companies and labels, and reissues. Between the end of World War II and the late 1950s there emerged in Europe and elsewhere a number of new companies, recording bop and the revived traditional styles played by touring Americans and by new, important non-American players. These enterprises included Esquire and Tempo in England,

Barclay, Blue Star, and Vogue in France, Cupol, Metronome, Sonet, and Storyville in Scandinavia, Supraphon in Czechoslovakia, Muza in Poland, and Swaggie in Australia.

From the late 1960s numerous European companies came to prominence, several in the recording of new styles of jazz – a significant development in consideration of the earlier role of the European companies as followers of the American lead. Among the most important were Black and Blue (1968–) in France; MPS (1968–83), ECM and FMP (both 1969–), Enja (1971–), and Moers Music (1974–) in Germany; Incus (1970–), Ogun (1973–), and Leo (ii) (1980–) in England; Steeplechase (1972–) in Denmark; Hat Hut (1974–) in Switzerland; Black Saint (1975–), its subsidiary Soul Note (1979–), Red (1976–), and Splasc(h) (1982–) in Italy; Timeless (1975–) and Criss Cross Jazz (1981–) in the Netherlands; and Leo (i) (*c*1978–) in Finland. Black Saint, FMP, Hat Hut, and Incus, as well as portions of the catalogues of ECM, Enja, the Leos, Moers Music, and Ogun, were devoted to free jazz, in contrast to the more conservative repertory of swing and bop offered by the principal new labels established in the same period in the USA, among them Master Jazz Recordings (1967–), Chiaroscuro (1970–), Muse (ii) (1972–), Concord (1973–), Pablo (1977–), and Palo Alto (1981–), and Canada, including Sackville (1968–).

Concurrently reissues flourished. Among noteworthy anthologies were a Time–Life series of boxed sets, each one consisting of three albums devoted to leading early jazz and swing soloists, a monumental and stylistically comprehensive series of 100 albums issued by the Franklin Mint in Philadelphia, and scholarly collections put together by the Smithsonian Institution in Washington. Fantasy issued double (and in a few cases triple) albums drawn from the catalogues of Prestige and Riverside, RCA revived the Bluebird catalogue on a series of double albums, Mosaic (ii) offered luxurious boxed sets of recordings including reissued and previously unissued material, and first Arista then (from around 1985) Muse (ii) reissued the Savoy catalogue. An important development was the revival in 1985 of the Blue Note label, both for reissues and new recordings.

By the 1980s several Japanese labels had introduced the concept of facsimile reproductions of acclaimed albums. This idea was taken up by French Verve, then, more importantly, by Fantasy, which in 1983 set up the Original Jazz Classics label, offering facsimiles of hundreds of albums from the catalogues of Contemporary, Debut, Fantasy, Jazz Workshop, Prestige, and Riverside. An even larger collection of this kind was concurrently developed by the Spanish company Fresh Sound, which has drawn material from RCA Victor, Pacific Jazz, Bethlehem, Roulette, Columbia, and other labels, both American and European.

Digital remastering techniques (see §I, 4, above) had a profound, and also controversial, effect on reissues. A notable engineer in this field was the Australian Robert Parker, whose work was broadcast and issued on tape, disc, and compact disc as the result of a collaborative venture by the Australian Broadcasting Company and the BBC. While Parker's techniques of filtering and clarifying acoustical recordings produced some remarkable results, at the time of their first appearance (in the mid-1980s) a critical storm arose about their faithfulness to the original performances in comparison with the best monaural analogue transfers of the 1960s; Parker's addition of echo effects and attempts to simulate stereophonic sound were particularly censured. But this proved to be just a minor outcry when set against the concerns raised in later years, when digital remastering began to be applied across the board to jazz reissues.

9. The CD era. Following a long period of stability in recording technology (as regards both the prevailing techniques of analogue recording and the normal distribution of music on stereo microgroove records and stereo cassettes), the 1980s witnessed an upheaval, as first digital studio recording techniques and then digital discs quickly came to prominence. By the mid-1980s the industry had wholeheartedly embraced the compact disc, which in time replaced the 12-inch long-playing album for all new recordings and reissues. This development proceeded more swiftly in genres other than jazz, many of whose fans maintained a strong connection to the LP as a physical document (with its cover art and liner notes). And, as would be expected for many such technological developments, the changeover occurred more speedily in America and Japan than elsewhere, but by the early 1990s it was in place worldwide. Even the highly popular and ongoing series of facsimile reissues were transferred to CD, with cover art and liner notes miniaturized, and sometimes with a few "bonus tracks" added, the additional available playing time of a compact disc allowing for the inclusion of rejected takes or previously unissued titles from a session. In jazz circles, the only movement of even moderate significance against the tidal wave of compact discs occurred late in 1993, when Mosaic introduced its nostalgic "Q-LP," utilizing a heavy, high-quality vinyl reminiscent of albums of the early 1950s; however, this offering attracted only a small number of audiophiles, and by 1999 few Mosaic sets were available on LP.

(i) A three-tiered system. With the arrival of CDs the industry began to operate on three different tiers; these might be characterized as the industrial giant, the jazz company, and the home operator. At the grandest level (in which context jazz sales represent a small percentage of the whole), many major corporations were absorbed and merged into other, ever-larger conglomerates controlling much of the worldwide market. Of particular relevance to jazz, RCA was absorbed into the German company BMG (Bertelsmann AG); the Japanese corporation Sony acquired the CBS Records Group (including Columbia and all of the historical labels which had come into its fold); the WEA group (the "A" in WEA being Atlantic) became a subsidiary of Time Warner; and – this is complicated – Seagram's Universal Music Group came into being through its acquisition of Polygram (whose predecessor Polydor had purchased Verve and Mercury), which it merged with Universal (which had acquired MCA, which in turn had earlier acquired GRP, Impulse!, and the American label Decca).

The second tier, that of the jazz company, remained reasonably stable. The vast majority of labels initiated in the 1970s and early 1980s (see §II, 8, above) remained active, as did the revived Blue Note label, which once again became a leader in the field. To be sure there were many changes, but none of these developments were startling within the context of the always volatile recording industry: Fantasy acquired another major catalogue in the Pablo label; Jazzology reactivated the American Music catalogue, producing CD reissues of considerable significance to fans of the New Orleans revival; Savoy transferred from Muse to the

Japanese company Nippon Columbia and its label Denon; 32 Jazz bought Muse; with the death of its dynamic owner Carl Jefferson, Concord appeared to yield its leading role in mainstream and swing to the new labels Arbors (in the USA) and Nagel-Heyer (Germany); other emerging companies, such as DIW (Japan and America), ITM and L+R (both Germany), and Arabesque, CIMP, Knitting Factory Works, and Music & Arts (all USA) provided important forums for new jazz recordings; and so forth.

The most far-reaching development in the area of reissues occurred outside of the USA, where the otherwise international limitation of copyright protection to 50 years meant that, by the end of the 20th century, the entire output from the era of 78 r.p.m. records was available for reissue by anyone. The most successful and ambitious program of this sort, numbering many hundreds of issues, was produced by the French label Classics, whose series of compact discs cut across distinctions among original labels (and their current owners) to offer reissues of master takes of titles organized chronologically by artist. The similar program of reissues of blues and gospel material by the Austrian label Document has included a great deal of related jazz, in particular the first serious attempt at making available the legacy of the many female singers of the 1920s who operated on the boundaries between jazz, blues, and popular music. Both of these programs are dependent on what collectors are able to supply and on the condition in which they supply it, with the result that sound quality, while generally acceptable, is rarely the best that can be achieved and occasionally the finished product is of documentary interest only.

By contrast, the British recording engineer John R. T. Davies has continued to make available full-frequency dubbings of jazz from the vintage and swing eras in sound quality unlikely to be improved on (unless those who may still have access to surviving masters should begin to acknowledge a responsibility to the jazz past which extends beyond the most famous musicians). Davies's unsurpassed work appears principally on such smaller labels, often owned by enthusiasts, as Frog, Gannet, Hep, and JSP (all UK), Collector's Classics (Denmark), Retrospect (Netherlands), and Jazz Oracle (Canada).

The new third tier of jazz recording has consisted of small independent operators, often the musicians themselves. While homemade recordings had been produced since the 1940s, and were commonplace with the advent of cassette tapes in the 1960s, the inferior recording equipment available outside of an expensive studio made for a clear and obvious distinction between the amateur and the professional. This situation changed in the 1990s, when reasonably priced digital recording equipment became widely available. Many people established their own studios and labels and independent recording flourished. Some sense of the extent of these activities may be gleaned from the computerized labels report held at the Institute of Jazz Studies: as of 1999 (that is to say, in little more than a decade after digital recording became firmly entrenched) the institute's collection included roughly 1900 labels on compact disc, perhaps 1700 of which emanate from small, and sometimes one-off, enterprises.

(ii) Ongoing and new concerns. As always, preservation of original recordings was a concern during the era of the compact disc, not just for jazz, but industry-wide. The CD itself was originally promoted, in 1982, as a vehicle for holding music in a "permanent" form (ironic, in light of attempts to replace it with DVD audio and Super Audio CD only 17 years after it first appeared) and, as had often been the case within the industry, archival material was neglected. Several periodical articles in the early to mid-1990s documented the deterioration and disorganization of original recorded documents.

Another concern was for the quality of sound in some jazz reissues. A number of CD reissues were carelessly produced, for various reasons, including unfamiliarity with digital equipment, but most often simply because the reissuer failed to obtain a good master of the original recording; GRP actually acknowledged this problem, and in the mid-1990s its series of reissues from the Impulse! catalogue were freshly manufactured. However, to compensate there was a flood of high-quality reissues produced by Classics, Blue Note, Fantasy, Fresh Sound, Mosaic, and others. Indeed, at no time before had so much historical recorded jazz been made available for the general public in a satisfying form.

Hand in hand with the flood of reissues on compact disc came an even more overwhelming tide of new recordings: the market became saturated. Furthermore, these new albums were longer than ever before, because the compact disc was capable of holding many more minutes of music than the LP. Unfortunately, artistic creativity could rarely keep pace with technical capacity; few jazz musicians possess the resources to create more than an hour of engaging music with each and every issue. If in earlier eras jazz fans lamented the gaps of coverage of an important player's career, now, with few exceptions, the problem was overexposure.

An even greater concern resided in the general relationship of digital sound to jazz. Trying out a new idea, making a mistake, and perhaps playing further with that mistake to make it work, has been standard procedure for players in many styles. Whereas there were improvisers such as Bobby Hackett, who had such a fully formed conception of melody that he seemingly played perfectly time after time, few jazz musicians have ever operated at that level. Instead, throughout the music's history, its exponents practiced a shift in balance between professionalism and audacious creativity, in moving between the studio and "live" performance; with the knowledge that a recording is being made, caution, conciseness, and formality come to the fore. But the essential characteristics of digital recording tipped this balance over the edge: by comparison with that of 78 r.p.m. and microgroove discs, the sound of a compact disc is so clean that the disruptive potential of a mistake is greatly exaggerated. The consequent need to avoid making any mistakes had a stultifying effect on countless jazz musicians, whose excessively restrained work on CD routinely stands in marked contrast to their ambitious playing in clubs and concerts.

THE FOLLOWING RECORD COMPANIES AND LABELS HAVE ENTRIES IN THIS DICTIONARY:

A (i), A (ii), Accurate, Ace of Hearts, ACT, Actuelle, Affinity, A.F.O., AFRS, Ajax, Alacra, Aladdin, Alpha Phonics, Alto (ii), Altsax, Ambassador, Ambiances Magnétiques, American Clavé, American Music, American Record Corporation, Antilles, Ap-Gu-Ga, Apollo, Arabesque, Arbors, Arc, ARC–BRC, Arco, Argo, Arista, Arkadia, Artists House, Arto, Asian Improv, Atco, Atlantic, Audiophile, Audioquest, Auricle, Aurora, Autograph, Ava, Avant

Bakton, Banner, Barclay, Bardo, Bassic Sound, Bee Hive, Bet-Car, Bethlehem, Big Noise, Biograph, Birth, Black and Blue, Black & White, Black Hawk, Black Jazz, Black Lion, Black Patti, Black Saint, Black Swan, Blu-disc, Bluebird, Blue Note (ii), Blue Star, BMG, Bosco,

Bridgeport Die & Machine Company, Broadway, Brownstone, Brunswick, Buddy, Buzz, Bvhaast, BYG

Cadence Jazz, Cadet, Cadillac (ii), Cameo, Candid, Capitol, Capri, Cardinal, Catalyst, Cathexis, CBS, Chabada, Challenge, Champion, Charlie Parker Records, Chesky, Chiaroscuro, Choice, CIMP, Circle (i), Circle (iii), Classic Jazz, Classics, Claxon, Claxtonola, Clef, Climax, CMP, Cobblestone, Collectors Items, Columbia, Commodore, Concord, Conqueror, Consolidated Artists, Contact, Contemporary, Continental, Creative World, Creole, Crescent, Criss Cross Jazz, Crown, CTI, Cupol

DAAGNIM, Daffodil, Dauntless, Davis & Schwegler, Dawn, Day Eight Music, Debut (i), Debut (ii), Decca, Dee Gee, Delmark, Delta, De Luxe, Denon, Depth of Field, Derby (ii), Deutsche Grammophon, Dial, Dire, Discovery, Diva, DIW, Doctor Jazz, Domino, Double-Time (ii), Dragon, Dreamstreet, Dreyfus Jazz, Dune

East: West, East Wind (i), East Wind (ii), ECM, Edison, Edison-Bell, EGO, Ekaya, Electrola, Elektra Musician, Emanem, EmArcy, Emerson, EMI, Emily, Empire, Enja, Epic, ESP-disk, Esquire, Everybody's, Evidence (i), Evidence (ii), Exclusive

Famous, Famous Door (ii), Fantasy, Fat Cat's Jazz, Felsted, Flying Dutchman, Flyright, FMP, Foolish Music, Fountain, Freedom, Fresh Sound

Galaxy, Gazell (i), Gazell (ii), General, Gennett, Geobo, GHB, Gilt-edge, GM, GNP, Good Time Jazz, Gramavision, Gramophone Company, Grey Gull, Groove, GRP, Guardsman, Guild

Halcyon, Handy Record Company, Harlequin, Harmograph, Harmony (ii), Hat Hut, Hep, Herwin (i), Herwin (ii), Hifijazz, HighNote, His Master's Voice, Hit of the Week, Hollywood, Hopscotch, Horizon, Hot Record Society

IAJRC (i), Ibeji, Imperial, Improvisation Series, Improvising Artists, Impulse!, In + Out, Incus, India Navigation, Inner City, Intakt, Interplay, Interstate Music, Intro (ii)

Japo, Jaro, JAZA, Jazz (ii), Jazz Alliance, Jazz City, Jazz Document, Jazzette, Jazz Focus, Jazz4ever, Jazz Haus Musik, Jazzland, Jazzline (i), Jazzline (ii), Jazzology, Jazzpoint, Jazz Record, Jazz Society (i), Jazz Society (ii), Jazztime, Jazztone, Jazz West, Jazz West Coast, Jazz Workshop, J Curve, Jen Bay, Jewel, JKMN, Judson, Justin Time

Ken Music, Kenneth, Keynote, Keytone, King, King Jazz, Klacto, Knitting Factory Works, Koch Jazz, Konnex, Krazy Kat, Kudu

Label Bleu, Lake Shore Jazz of Chicago, Landmark, Lang–Worth, Legacy, Legend, Leo (i), Leo (ii), Liberty Music Shop, Limelight, Limetree, Lincoln, Lindström, Lipstick, London, Love

Mad-Kat, Magpie, Mainstream, MAMA Foundation, Manhattan, Manor, Mapleshade, Marathon, Marsh Laboratories, Master (ii), Master Jazz Recordings, Maya, MCA, Meantime, Medallion, Melotone, Mercury, Meritt (i), Meritt (ii), Messidor, Metalanguage, Metrojazz, Metronome, Milestone, Minor Music, Modern, Moers Music, Mole, MONO, Mons, Montgomery Ward, Mood, Moodsville, Mosaic (i), Mosaic (ii), MPS, Muse (i), Muse (ii), Music & Arts, Musicmasters, Musicraft

Nabel, Nagel-Heyer, National (i), National (ii), National (iii), Nato, Naxos Jazz, Nessa, New Artists, New Jazz, New Note, New World, New York Recording Laboratories, Nilva, Nimbus, Nine Winds, Nippon Columbia, Nocturne, Nonesuch, Nordskog, Norgran, Novus, NYC

Odeon, Odin, Ogun, OKeh, Okka Disk, Onyx (ii), Original Jazz Classics, Oriole (i), Oriole (ii), Otic, Outline, Owl, Ozone

Pablo, Pacific Jazz, Palmetto, Palo Alto, Panachord, Pannon Jazz, Parachute, Paradox, Paramount, Parlophone, Pathé, Peacock's Progressive Jazz, Perfect, Philo, Phoenix Jazz, Phontastic, Plaza Music Company, PM, Postcards, Po Torch, Power Bros., Prestige, Progressive, Projazz, Puretone, Puritan

QED, QRS, Quark

Raecox; RAM, Ramboy, Rampart, Random Acoustics, RAU, RCA Victor, Red, Red Baron, Re-entry, Regal (i), Regal (ii), Regal (iii), Regal–Zonophone, Regina, Regis, Reprise, Reservoir, Resonant Music, Retrieval, Revelation, Rex, Rhino, Rialto, Ring, Ristic, Riti, Riverside, Romeo, Ronnie Scott's Jazz House, Rosetta, Roulette, Royal Roost (ii), Rykodisc

Saba, Sackville, Sahara, Satellites, Saturn, Savant, Savoy (i), Savoy (ii), Scala, Scepter, Score, Screwgun, SESAC, Session (ii), Session Disc, Sessoms, 77, Sharp Nine, Shih Shih Wu Ai, Signal, Signature, Silkheart, Silvertone, Sittin' in With, Solid State, Solo Art, Sonet, Songlines, Sonora, Sony, Soul Note, Southport, Spotlite (ii), Starr, Stateside, Steam, Steeplechase, Stomp Off, Storyville (ii), Storyville (iii), Strata-East, Stretch, Sun (i), Sun (ii), Sunnyside, Sunrise, Sunset (i), Sunset (ii), Sunshine, Super Disc, Superior, Supertone (i), Supertone (ii), Supreme, Swaggie, Swing (ii), Swingville, Symphonola

TCB, Teddy Wilson School for Pianists, Telarc, Tempo (ii), Theresa, Three Blind Mice, Time (ii), Timeless, Timely Tiptoe, Transition, Triangle, Tribe, Trip, Tunes, Tutu

UHCA, Unit, United, United Artists, United Phonographs Corporation, Unity, Universal Music Group

Vanguard, Variety (i), Variety (ii), Varsity, Vault, V-disc, Vee Jay, Verve, Via, Victo, Victor, Vinyl, Vocalion, Vogue, V.S.O.P. (ii), V.S.O.P. (iii)

Warner Brothers, Warwick, Waterland, Watt, Wave, Wax (ii), WenHa, World Pacific, World Wide, World Wide Jazz

Xanadu, XtraWatt

Zonophone

BIBLIOGRAPHY

R. D. Darrell: *The Gramophone Shop Encyclopedia of Recorded Music* (New York, 1936, rev. and enlarged 3/1948/*R*1970)

D. C. Black: *Matrix Numbers: their Meaning and History* (Melbourne, Australia, n.d. [*c*1946])

F. F. Clough and G. J. Cuming, eds.: *The World's Encyclopedia of Recorded Music* (London, 1952/*R*1970; suppls. 1953, 1957)

R. Gelatt: *The Fabulous Phonograph* (New York, 1954, 3/1977)

H. Lyttelton: "Introducing the Tape Surgeon," *Second Chorus* (London, 1958), 38

O. Read and W. L. Welch: *From Tin Foil to Stereo* (Indianapolis and New York, 1959/*R*1971, rev. 2/1976)

V. K. Chew: *Talking Machines, 1877–1914: some Aspects of the Early History of the Gramophone* (London, 1967, rev. 2/1973)

J. Bornoff and L. Salter: *Music and the Twentieth Century Media* (Florence, Italy, 1972)

C. Hamm: "Technology and Music: the Effect of the Phonograph," in C. Hamm, B. Nettl, and R. Byrnside: *Contemporary Music and Music Cultures* (Englewood Cliffs, NJ, 1975), 253

B. Lane: "75 Years of Magnetic Recording," *Wireless World*, lxxxi (1975), 102, 161, 222, 283, 341

E. B. Moogk: *Roll Back the Years: History of Canadian Recorded Sound and its Legacy: Genesis to 1930* (Ottawa, 1975)

R. Angus: "The History of Recording," *Modern Recording*, i (1975–6), no.1, p.22; no.2, p.18; no.3, p.22; no.4, p.22; no.5, p.28; no.6, p.26

W. R. Isom, ed.: "The Phonograph and Sound Recording after 100 Years," *Journal of the Audio Engineering Society*, xxv/10–11 (1977) [complete issue]

H. Lindsay: "Magnetic Recording," *DB: the Sound Engineering Magazine*, xi/12 (1977), 38; xii/1 (1978), 40

J. B. Smart and J. W. Newsom: *A Wonderful Invention* (Washington, DC, 1977) [catalogue of Library of Congress exhibition on the centennial of the phonograph]

B. Bastin: "Test Exists!," *Sv*, no.82 (1979), 127

H. W. Hitchcock, ed.: *The Phonograph and our Musical Life*, Institute for Studies in American Music Monographs, xiv (New York, 1980)

J. Ryan: "BG Alternate Takes Re-visited," *Meritt Rag*, i/1 (1980), 8

R. Connor: "BG Alternate Takes," *Meritt Rag*, ii/1 (1981), 9

W. F. Anderson: "The Movies, $33\frac{1}{3}$, and E.T.'s (Not Extra-terrestrials)," *Joslin's Jazz Journal* (1982), August, 4

M. Berger, E. Berger, and J. Patrick: *Benny Carter: a Life in American Music* (Metuchen, NJ, and London, 1982)

I. Carr: *Miles Davis: a Critical Biography* (London and New York, 1982)

C. Hamm: "Changing Patterns in Society and Music: the US since World War II," *Music in the New World* (New York, 1983), 35–70

P. Oliver: *Songsters and Saints: Vocal Traditions on Race Records* (Cambridge, England, and elsewhere, 1984)

S. DeVeaux: "Bebop and the Recording Industry: the 1942 AFM Recording Ban Reconsidered," *Journal of the American Musicological Society*, xli (1988), 126

B. Priestley: *Jazz on Record: a History* (London, 1988)

C. Arnat: "Vinyl Records are No Longer Groovy," *San Francisco Examiner* (12 Feb 1990)

P. Elwood: "Waking up to Need for Record Preservation," *San Francisco Examiner* (15 Jan 1992)

B. Holland: "Labels Strive to Rectify Past Archival Problems," *Billboard*, cix (12 July 1997), 1; contd as "Upgrading Labels' Vaults No Easy Archival Task" (19 July 1997), 1

M. Gerzon: "Don't Destroy the Archives," <http://www.waves.com/htmls/tech/faq/dont.html> (1998)

J. Brinkley: "A New Audio Format: Well, Make that Two," *New York Times* (8 Aug 1999)

S. Buckingham: "Technical Notes," *From Spirituals to Swing* (Van. 169/71-2, 1999) [liner notes]

R. Kennedy and R. McNutt: *Little Labels – Big Sound: Small Record Companies and the Rise of American Music* (Bloomington, IN, and Indianapolis, 1999)

G. Wheeler: *Jazz by Mail: Record Clubs and Record Labels 1936 to 1958, including Complete Discographies for Jazztone and Dial Records* (Manassas, VA, 1999)

H. Rye: "The ARC TO- 'Test Only' Series," *Names and Numbers* (2000), no.12, p.13; no.13, p.15; no.14, p.18; no.15, p.19

GORDON MUMMA/HOWARD RYE, BK (I), CHRIS SHERIDAN (II, 1–3, 5–6), BK (II, 4, 7–9)

Record label. (1) The paper disc glued to the center of a vinyl record on which details of the recorded performance and various other items of information are shown; *see* RECORDING, fig.4.

(2) The name under which a record company issues recordings; recordings are thus spoken of as appearing "on a

label." The name of the company and the label may, but need not, be the same; many companies own more than one label, often using a different name for each of their catalogues of recordings (the catalogues normally cover different styles or may be intended for different markets); any one catalogue may be subdivided into titled series (for example, the Parlophone label issued a number of series named New Rhythm Style Series, Super Rhythm Style Series, etc.). Record labels are often identified in printed form (notably on the paper disc glued to the center of a vinyl record, see (1) above) by distinctive typography or by a trademark or logo; perhaps the most famous of these is the image, used by His Master's Voice, of the dog with his ear cocked to the horn of an old-fashioned phonograph. A list of the record labels on which entries appear in this dictionary is given at the end of RECORDING.

Reco-reco. A Brazilian scraper, made of wood, used in traditional rural dances and in carnival sambas and marches. The instrument was introduced into jazz by Airto Moreira.

Red. Italian record company and label. Founded in 1976 by Sergio Veschi and Alberto Alberti, it began by documenting the music of some young avant-garde Italian musicians and such visiting American masters as Sam Rivers and the expatriate Steve Lacy. In the early 1980s the label recorded some fine work by Franco D'Andrea, Tiziano Tononi's group Nexus, Gianluigi Trovesi, Massimo Urbani, and Giovanni Tommaso. From the late 1980s Veschi, having become sole owner, began to a concentrate on the American modern mainstream, recording Bobby Watson, Joe Henderson, Jerry Bergonzi, Victor Lewis, Billy Higgins, Sphere, Cedar Walton, Phil Woods, and Steve Nelson, though he also recorded Italian musicians, such as the trumpeter and flugelhorn player Fabio Morgera and the alto saxophonist Piero Odorici, who play in similar styles. (C. M. Bailey: "Red Records: the Blue Note of Europe," <http://www.allaboutjazz.com/articles/a0599_03.htm> (1999))

STEFANO ZENNI

Red, Sonny [Kyner, Sylvester] (*b* Detroit, 17 Dec 1932; *d* Detroit, 20 March 1981). Alto saxophonist and bandleader. He first worked with Barry Harris (1949–52). In 1954 he played tenor saxophone with Frank Rosolino, but later that year he returned to the alto instrument when he joined Art Blakey. Red traveled to New York with Curtis Fuller in 1957 and settled there two years later; he recorded with Paul Quinichette and Fuller (both 1957) and made a number of albums under his own name (1958–62). During the 1960s and 1970s he worked as a freelance in hard-bop groups, performing with Donald Byrd (early 1960s) and Kenny Dorham (1966) and recording with Clifford Jordan (1961), Pony Poindexter (1962), Byrd (1966, 1967), Yusef Lateef (1968), and Howard McGhee (1978).

SELECTED RECORDINGS

Out of the Blue (1959–60, BN 4032); *The Mode* (1961, Jlnd 59); *Images* (1962, Jlnd 74)

BIBLIOGRAPHY

FeatherE; *Feather '60s*
Obituary, *DB*, xlviii/8 (1981), 13

JOSH FERKO, BK

Red Baron. Record company and label. It was formed in New York around 1991 by Bob Thiele and produced new recordings by David Murray, Steve Marcus, McCoy Tyner, John Hicks, Ali Ryerson, and others, including special projects under the appellative Bob Thiele Collective. Red Baron also reissued items by Ruby Braff, Mel Lewis, and Paul Desmond and the Modern Jazz Quartet (all originally recorded for Finesse), Earl Hines (made for Contact in 1964 and 1966), and Al Cohn with Al Porcino's big band (made for Razmataz Jazz in 1987), and released previously unissued material by Duke Ellington, Hines, and Billy Strayhorn. The label was discontinued when Thiele died in 1996.

BIBLIOGRAPHY

B. Primack: "Bob Thiele: the Red Baron Flies Again," *JT*, xxi/8 (1991), 34
K. Terry and J. Levenson: "Bob Thiele Teams with Sony on his New Red Baron Label," *Billboard*, ciii (17 Aug 1991), 6
B. Thiele and B. Golden: *What a Wonderful World: a Lifetime of Recordings* (New York, and Oxford, England, 1995)

GK

Redd, Chuck [Charles Randolph] (*b* Takoma Park, MD, 10 Sept 1958). Drummer and vibraphonist. He took up piano at the age of seven and three years later began playing drums. After working in Bill Potts's big band from 1977 to 1979 he began, in 1980, what became a longstanding association with Charlie Byrd, both in the latter's trio and in Great Guitars (Byrd died in 1999). He also performed with Tal Farlow, Emily Remler, and Red Norvo (all 1980–88), Monty Alexander (1987–9), Tommy Flanagan (1989), and Steve Novosel (*c* late 1980s – early 1990s), among others. In 1990 Redd toured Africa in Dizzy Gillespie's quintet, and the following year he performed as a vibraphonist with Mel Tormé. From the mid-1990s he worked with the Smithsonian Jazz Masterworks Orchestra and toured and recorded with Ken Peplowski; in 1997 he performed and recorded with Loren Schoenberg. He may be seen performing in the video *The Charlie Byrd Trio Live in New Orleans* (*c*1992). In 1996 he recorded on vibraphone as a sole leader, with his brother Robert Redd serving as pianist.

SELECTED RECORDINGS
(on drums unless otherwise indicated)

As leader: *Stomp, Look & Listen* (1996, Exclusive Arts 12102) [vibraphone]
As sideman: Great Guitars: *Great Guitars at Charlie's Georgetown* (1982, Conc. 209); C. Byrd: *It's a Wonderful World* (1988, Conc. 4374); *Bossa Nova Years* (1991, Conc. 4468); *My Inspiration* (1998, Conc. 4850) [vibraphone]

BIBLIOGRAPHY

Feather–GitlerBEJ
<http://www.exclusivearts.com/artists.html> (2000)

GK

Redd, Freddie (*b* New York, 29 May 1928). Pianist and composer. He received some instruction in music as a child but was largely self-taught on piano. After serving in the army (to 1949) he worked at clubs in Manhattan and in Syracuse, New York, in a small group led by the drummer Johnny Mills, and in 1951 he recorded with Tiny Grimes and toured the South in Cootie Williams's sextet. In 1952 he returned to New York, where in the following year he worked briefly with Oscar Pettiford and Charles Mingus. He was a member of the Jive Bombers with the saxophonist Earl Johnson, the double bass player Clarence Palmer, and the singer and guitarist Pee Wee Tinney (1954), recorded with Art Farmer and Gigi Gryce's quintet and Gene Ammons's All Stars (both 1955), and toured Sweden with Ernestine

Anderson and Rolf Ericson (summer 1956); while there he recorded with Ericson and Tommy Potter and as the leader of a trio. On returning to the USA he moved to San Francisco, where he played for a brief period with Mingus at the Blackhawk and worked as the house pianist at Bop City for six months. He wrote the music for Jack Gelber's play *The Connection*, in performances of which he took part in New York (1959–60) and London and Paris (1961); he performed on the soundtrack to a filmed version of the play, recorded his own album of the music for Blue Note, and participated in a second recording of music from the play under the leadership of Howard McGhee, with whom he appeared pseudonymously as I. Ching, for contractual reasons.

From the early 1960s Redd lived and performed, or held jobs outside music, in many locations: he played jazz on a television show in Guadalajara, Mexico, appeared with Tony Scott, Charlie Haden, and Philly Joe Jones at a club in New York, worked in John Handy's group in California and at a performance filmed in Vancouver, Canada (*John Handy at the Blue Horn*, 1965), recorded in London on the first album by the popular singer James Taylor (with Paul McCartney on electric bass guitar), and recorded in Paris as the leader of a jazz trio including Didier Levallet (1971). An indefatigable traveler, he spent periods in Berlin, Copenhagen, and Amsterdam. After returning to the USA in 1974 he was in Los Angeles and then in Mississippi and became progressively less active in music, although he did record an album as the leader of a trio in 1977 and appeared for 18 months as the house pianist at the Studio Grill in Hollywood, where he recorded a set in a trio alongside Al McKibbon and Billy Higgins (1988). He gave performances in New York at Barry Harris's Jazz Cultural Center (*c*1986) and at Birdland (May 1991), the latter with a group involving Junior Cook. A boxed-set reissue of his Blue Note recordings in 1989 brought him some renewed attention. Around this time he settled in Pacifica, a suburb on the coast just south of San Francisco, and he performed and recorded in the Bay area in the early 1990s.

Redd's playing has been described as a barrelhouse equivalent of that of Bud Powell; Franklin in his discographical survey (1991) takes severe exception to this description, but it seems an apt way of encapsulating Redd's refreshingly creative, unpolished, and (sometimes) "wrong-note" approach to the bop piano tradition.

SELECTED RECORDINGS

As leader: *Freddie Redd Trio* (1955, Prst. 197); *San Francisco Suite* (1957, Riv. 250); *Music from "The Connection"* (1960, BN 84027); *Under Paris Skies* (1971, Futura Swing 03); *Straight Ahead!* (1977, Inter. 7715); *Lonely City* (1985, Upt. 27.30); *Live at the Studio Grill* (1988, Triloka 182); *Everybody Loves a Winner* (1990, Mlst. 9187)

As sideman: G. Ammons: on *Gene Ammons All Star Sessions* (1950, 1955, Prst. 7050), Juggernaut, Woofin' and Tweetin' (1955); A. Farmer: *Art Farmer Quintet* (1955, Prst. 209)

BIBLIOGRAPHY

FeatherE; *Feather '60s*

V. Wilmer: "Freddie Redd," *JJ*, xiv/4 (1961), 3

F. Postif: "Freddie Redd," *Jh*, no.269 (1971), 15; repr. in *Jazz Me Blues: interviews et portraits de musiciens de jazz et de blues* (Paris, 1998), 303

J. Barr: Liner notes, *Straight Ahead!* (Inter. 7715, 1977)

W. F. Lee: "Freddie Redd," *People in Jazz: Jazz Keyboard Improvisors of the 19th and 20th Centuries* (Hialeah, FL, 1984)

W. Thornbury and B. Sidran: Liner notes, *The Complete Blue Note Recordings of Freddie Redd* (Mosaic 124, 1989)

B. Franklin V and M. Johnston: "Everybody Loves a Winner: Two Views of Freddie Redd," *Coda*, no.240 (1991), 16

J. Levenson: "Jazz: Blue Notes: Whatever Happened to Renowned Pianist Freddie Redd," *Billboard*, ciii (11 May 1991), 50

P. Watrous: "Jazz Pianist Returns to Spotlight," *New York Times* (25 May 1991)

GREGORY E. SMITH/BK

Redd, Vi [Elvira; Goldberg, Elvira; Avelino, Elvira] (*b* Los Angeles, 20 Sept 1928). Alto and soprano saxophonist, and singer. She grew up in a musical family; her father, Alton Redd (*d* 1979), played drums with Les Hite, Cee Pee Johnson, Kid Ory, Johnny St. Cyr, Dexter Gordon, and Wardell Gray. Redd took up the saxophone at the age of 13, and while in high school played in a band with Melba Liston. She began to play bop in 1948 when she enrolled at Los Angeles Community College, but she first emerged as an important soloist only in the 1960s, after graduating from Los Angeles State College of Applied Arts and Sciences and spending several years as a social worker. In 1961 she played at Shelly's Manne-Hole and in 1962 she appeared at the Las Vegas Jazz Festival and in an episode of the "Jazz Scene USA" television series, "Vi Redd Septet."

Through the mid-1960s Redd worked as a saxophonist and singer with leading bands. She toured with Earl Hines, including engagements in Chicago and New York (1964), and in 1965–6 led a bop quartet in San Francisco with her husband, the drummer Richie Goldberg (*d* 1994; Avelino is her surname from a later marriage). She performed at the Monterey Jazz Festival in 1966 and in 1967 held a lengthy engagement in London at Ronnie Scott's, where she was featured, in succession, with Ben Webster, Max Roach, Archie Shepp, and Coleman Hawkins. Following club work in the USA, in July 1968 she joined Dizzy Gillespie at the Newport Jazz Festival and then toured Africa and Europe with Count Basie. She returned to Los Angeles the following year to teach. In 1974 she was a guest performer with Roland Kirk at UCLA and in 1977 she appeared at Marian McPartland's jazz festival in Rochester, New York. She remained active in music in the 1980s and in the mid-1990s retired from a job as a teacher working with handicapped children. In 1996 she was leading a rhythm-and-blues quartet that included her son, the drummer Randall Goldberg (*b* 27 Aug 1960). As an alto saxophonist Redd was influenced chiefly by Charlie Parker. Her performances are emotionally charged and highly personal; she employs an unusual voice in the service of a strong, deeply felt blues style, which may be heard to advantage on *Dinah*, recorded in 1965 with Al Grey.

Video oral history material in *NCH* (HCJA).

SELECTED RECORDINGS

As leader: *Bird Call* (1962, UA 15016)

As sideman: A. Grey: on *Shades of Grey* (1965, Tangerine 1504), Dinah, Put it on Mellow; G. Ammons and D. Gordon: *The Chase!* (1973, Prst. 10010); M. McPartland: *Now's the Time!* (1977, Hal. 115)

BIBLIOGRAPHY

L. Feather: "Focus on Alto Saxophonist, Soprano Saxophonist, Vocalist Vi Redd," *DB*, xxix/24 (1962), 23

P. Carles and L. Feather: "Vi Redd ou le saxe fort," *Jm*, no.148 (1967), 29

S. Nurullah: "Vi Redd: Interview," *Cadence*, iii/9 (1978), 3

S. Placksin: *American Women in Jazz, 1900 to the Present: their Words, Lives and Music* (New York, 1982; London, 1985, as *Jazzwomen, 1900 to the Present: their Words, Lives and Music*), 259

L. Feather: *The Jazz Years: Earwitness to an Era* (London and New York, 1986), 160

L. Hildebrand: "Jazz's Top Horn Woman," *San Francisco Chronicle Datebook* (5 June 1988)

P. Vacher: "Vi Redd," *JJI*, xlix/5 (1996), 8

LEROY OSTRANSKY/BK

Red Heads. Recording group led in the late 1920s by RED NICHOLS.

Red Hot Peppers. Recording group led by JELLY ROLL MORTON in Chicago from 1926. It was formed to make recordings for Victor, and consisted at any one time of seven or eight of the best freelance players available: among them were the cornetist George Mitchell, the trombonist Kid Ory, the clarinetists Omer Simeon and Johnny Dodds, the banjoists Johnny St. Cyr and Bud Scott, the double bass player John Lindsay, and the drummers Andrew Hilaire and Baby Dodds. *Black Bottom Stomp*, *Smoke-House Blues*, *The Chant*, and *Doctor Jazz* (1926) set a standard for arranged jazz for small groups that has never been surpassed. After Morton moved to New York in 1928 he began to use members of his regular band for recordings under the name Red Hot Peppers, and occasionally he also borrowed players from other orchestras; only the trumpeter Ward Pinkett took part in every session in 1930, after which the name ceased to be used. (L. Wright: *Mr Jelly Lord*, Chigwell, England, 1980)

For recordings, further bibliography, and illustration *see* MORTON, JELLY ROLL.

MIKE HAZELDINE

Rediske, Johannes (*b* Berlin, 11 Aug 1926; *d* Berlin, 22 Jan 1975). German electric guitarist. He was the founder in 1947 of the group Berlin Swingsters, which performed at American clubs and on broadcasts of the Armed Forces Network. From 1948 he led a swing quartet and from 1949 a swing quintet, both of which performed on radio and television and from 1951 to 1959 made recordings (including *Moonlight in Vermont*, 1957, Amiga 550036 [EP]). Rediske appeared at festivals in Germany from 1954 and accompanied a number of visiting American musicians; in 1959 he wrote the score to the film *Begrenztes Wochenende*.

BIBLIOGRAPHY

FeatherE; *Feather-Gitler '70s*; *ReclamsJ*
Untitled item, *JP*, viii/4 (1959), 84

HEIDI BOULTON

Redland, Charles [Nilsson, Carl Gustaf Mauritz] (*b* Södertälje, Sweden, 7 July 1911; *d* Stockholm, 18 Aug 1994). Swedish saxophonist, composer, arranger, and bandleader. His father, John, was a musician, and from an early age Redland studied several wind, percussion, and string instruments. In the 1930s he was a member of many bands, in which he most often played clarinet and alto saxophone though he occasionally performed on trumpet, trombone, and other instruments. As a leader he was active from the mid-1930s and made a number of recordings (including *Atlantic Stomp*, 1935, Son. 3079, and *Blue Evening*, 1941, Son. 3738); in 1936 he recorded as a clarinetist with Benny Carter in Sweden. Redland also became highly sought after as a composer and arranger of jazz, popular music, and film scores. Scores used by his band are in the Svenskt Visarkiv, Stockholm (*see* LIBRARIES AND ARCHIVES, §2).

Oral history material in *SSsv*.

BIBLIOGRAPHY

"Svenskt stjärnalbum" [Swedish star-album], *Orkester journalen*, iv/12 (1936), 3
"Våra arrangörer" [Our arrangers], *Estrad*, iii/12 (1942), 8
"Mannen bakom orkestern" [The man behind the orchestra], *Estrad*, v/9 (1944), 11
J. Bruér and B. Nyquist: "Charles Redland: Jazzmusiker, jag?" [Charles Redland: jazz musician, me?], *Svensk jazzhistoria*, iii (Cap. 2014, 1984) [liner notes]

ERIK KJELLBERG

Red Mack [McClure, Morris] (*b* Memphis, 18 Jan 1912; *d* Los Angeles, 14 June 1993). Trumpeter and singer. His family moved to Los Angeles when he was one year old, and as a child he played piano at the Church of God in Christ; he took up trumpet in high school. He played with Sonny Clay in 1929–30, and at the end of 1930 he joined Les Hite's Sebastian's New Cotton Club Orchestra, which at the time was working with Louis Armstrong at Sebastian's Cotton Club in Culver City, California. In spring 1931 he transferred to the band led by the trumpeter Charlie Echols, but he left in late 1933 to travel with the bandleader Gene Coy to Chicago, where he also worked with Erskine Tate. Red Mack then returned to Los Angeles and rejoined Echols, initially as the band's drummer; late in 1934 they were resident at Sebastian's Cotton Club. In the late 1930s he worked in Los Angeles with the bandleader Floyd Ray, the drummer Alton Redd, and Lionel Hampton; he may be seen in the films *Every Day's a Holiday* (1937) and *Going Places* (1938), but he did not play on the soundtracks.

Red Mack was working with the pianist Lorenzo Flennoy when he was recruited to play in the dance band led by the singer Will Osborne. Despite having a very difficult time as an African-American member of a white touring band, he remained with the group until it broke up in New York at the outbreak of war in December 1941. After returning to Los Angeles he joined Lee Young at Billy Berg's. Around 1945 he accompanied several artists, including Monette Moore, for the Gilt-Edge label and worked with Barney Bigard and Kid Ory. That year he made a trip to Alaska and the Aleutian Islands with Luke Jones and recorded under his own name while leading a group at the Streets of Paris Club in Hollywood. In spring 1946 he was a member of Jimmy Mundy's band. Soon afterwards he became a regular sideman in bands led by Jones, and in the late 1950 he led his own group, with Jones among his sidemen, which held a residency at the Downbeat in Los Angeles. In 1952 he played with the band led by singer and trumpeter Calvin Boze. Red Mack appears as a member of Kid Ory's band in the film *The Benny Goodman Story* (1955), but it is Alvin Alcorn who is heard on the soundtrack. Deteriorating health led him to give up playing trumpet, but he occasionally worked in the 1960s and 1970s as a pianist and organist.

SELECTED RECORDINGS

(recorded for Atlas, c1946, unless otherwise indicated)

As sideman: M. Moore: You don't live here no more (1945, Gilt-Edge 532); L. Jones: Feeling Low Down (116); What You Bet (115); Ditch Diggin' Daddy (134); Midnight Blues (135); Say Hello to Miss Brown (143); Jump Me Some Boogie (1949, Modern 20-669)

BIBLIOGRAPHY

McCarthyB
B. Clayton and N. M. Elliott: *Buck Clayton's Jazz World* (London and New York, 1986)
Professor Hi-Jinx: Liner notes, Luke Jones/Red Mack: *West Coast R & B, 1947–1952* (Krazy Kat 7400, 1987)
J. C. DjeDje and E. S. Meadows, eds.: *California Soul: Music of African-Americans in the West* (Berkeley, CA, Los Angeles, and London, 1998)

HOWARD RYE

Redman, (Walter) Dewey (*b* Fort Worth, 17 May 1931). Tenor saxophonist and musette player, father of Joshua Redman. He studied clarinet from the age of 13, later took up alto saxophone, and finally changed to the tenor instrument at Prairie View Agricultural and Mechanical University (BS 1953). Segregation prevented his functioning as a musician during his army service. From 1956 to 1960, while attending

North Texas State University (MA 1959), he worked as a high-school teacher and also played professionally. His commitment to a career in jazz was marked by a move to San Francisco, where he played with Donald Garrett and co-led a big band with Monty Waters and Art "Shaki" Lewis. From mid-1967 to late 1974 Redman was a member of Ornette Coleman's group in New York, although he also played in Charlie Haden's Liberation Music Orchestra (1969) and Keith Jarrett's group (1971–6) and led his own bands; Eddie Moore was one of his most frequent sidemen, and Ted Daniel, Sirone, Fred Hopkins, and Beaver Harris were among others who played in his groups of the mid- to late 1970s. During this period Redman adopted a startling manner of vocalizing through, and together with, his saxophone, and took up musette as his second instrument. In 1976, with Don Cherry, Haden, and Ed Blackwell (his former associates in Coleman's band), he formed the group Old and New Dreams, with which he toured and recorded into the early 1980s. The group reunited for a concert at the Ed Blackwell Music Festival in November 1987 and gave another reunion concert in 1991.

Redman appeared with Blackwell in a duo in Germany in 1980, and he continued to lead his own small groups, performing (as, for example, on the album *The Struggle Continues*, 1982) a repertory of blues, hard bop, and free jazz, with Mark Helias and Moore among his sidemen. In 1988 he recorded with Paul Motian and formed a quartet with Joe Lovano, Henri Texier, and Aldo Romano, and the following year his own quartet consisted of Geri Allen, Cameron Brown, and Moore. His son Joshua Redman worked with him in 1991, and Allen and Brown continued in his group in the early 1990s; in 1996–7 the members were Rita Marcotulli, Brown, and Matt Wilson. He also toured as a guest soloist with Jane Bunnett's group, played in Haden's re-formed Liberation Music Orchestra, performed and recorded with Anthony Cox (1991–2) and Ed Schuller (1993–4), and recorded with Randy Weston (1991) and Wilson (1996) and as a co-leader with Cecil Taylor and Elvin Jones (1998).

SELECTED RECORDINGS

Duos with E. Blackwell: *Redman and Blackwell in Willisau* (1980, BS 0093)
As leader: *Look for the Black Star* (1966, Fon. 881311); *Ear of the Behearer* (1973, Imp. 9250); *Coincide* (1974, Imp. 9300); *Living on the Edge* (1989, BS 120123-2); *In London* (1996, Palmetto 2030); with C. Taylor and E. Jones: *Momentum Space* (1998, Verve 314-559-944-2)
As sideman in Old and New Dreams: *Old and New Dreams* (1976, BS 0013); *Soundsigns* (1978, Gal. 5130); *Old and New Dreams* (1979, ECM 1154); *The Struggle Continues* (1982, ECM 1225); *A Tribute to Blackwell* (1987, BS 0113)
As sideman with others: O. Coleman: *New York is Now* (1968, BN 84287); C. Haden: *Liberation Music Orchestra* (1969, Imp. 9183); K. Jarrett: *El juicio* (1971, Atl. 1673); P. Metheny: *80/81* (1980, ECM 1180–81); M. Benita: *Preferences* (1990, Label Bleu 6532); C. Haden: *Dream Keeper* (1990, DIW 8045); R. Weston: *The Spirits of our Ancestors* (1991, Ant. 314-511896-2), incl. African Cookbook; A. Cox: *Dark Metals* (1991, Minor Music 801019); E. Schuller: *Mu-point* (1993, Tutu 888154); Daniele Cavallanti: *Times for Peace* (1993, Splasc(h) 412); M. Wilson: *As Wave Follows Wave* (1996, Palmetto 2020), incl. Body and Soul

BIBLIOGRAPHY

GrayF
V. Wilmer: "Song of Dewey," *MM* (13 Nov 1971), 26
F. Postif: "Dewey Redman: l'homme qui chante en jouant du tenor," *Jh*, no.279 (1972), 10
J. Litweiler: "Dewey Redman: Coincidentals," *DB*, xlii/18 (1975), 14
B. Henderson: "Dewey Redman into the Spotlight," *Black Music and Jazz Review*, i/4 (1978), 10
V. Wilmer: "Singing through the Horn," *Time Out* (28 May–1 June 1978)
R. Riggins: "Dewey Redman," *Coda*, no.171 (1980), 28
C. Silvert: "Old and New Dreams," *DB*, xlvii/6 (1980), 16
J. Pareles: "Pop/Jazz: Redman, a Tenor Sax Player who Bloomed Late," *New York Times* (26 Nov 1982)
H. Mandel: "Dewey Redman: Nobody's Foil," *DB*, 1/2 (1983), 18
K. Whitehead: "Dewey Redman: Setting out on his own," *JT* (1983), Oct, 6
S. Crouch: "Dewey Redman," *VV*, xxx (13 Aug 1985), 31
K. Mathieson: "Dewey Redman: New Music, Old Dreams," *Wire*, no.32 (1986), 10
H. Mandel: "Dew Date: Cringe of the Lone Wolf: Dewey Redman," *DB*, lix/2 (1992), 22 [incl. discography]
B. Loupias: "Dewey Redman: au nom du père," *Jm*, no.432 (1993), 24
B. Primack: "Joshua & Dewey Redman: Confronting Reality and Expectations," *JT*, xxiii/4 (1993), 28
S. Bardot: "Looking: Dewey Redman," *Jh*, no.525 (1995), 30 [incl. discography]
F. Postif: *Jazz Me Blues: interviews et portraits de musiciens de jazz et de blues* (Paris, 1998), 329
B. Shoemaker: "Dewey Redman: Singular Voice, Multiple Paths," *JT*, xxviii/4 (1998), 54

BK

Redman, Don(ald Matthew) (*b* Piedmont, WV, 29 July 1900; *d* New York, 30 Nov 1964). Composer, arranger, bandleader, and alto saxophonist. He was a child prodigy from a musical family, and learned to play most conventional instruments. By the end of his years in high school he had already begun writing arrangements. At the age of 20 he graduated from Storer College in Harper's Ferry, West Virginia, with a degree in music. After working professionally for about a year in Piedmont he joined Billy Paige's Broadway Syncopators, a band based in Pittsburgh. Here he played clarinet and saxophones and also wrote some arrangements. While on tour with Paige's band Redman met FLETCHER HENDERSON in New York, and joined him in several recording sessions. When Henderson formed an orchestra shortly afterwards Redman was one of the members (for illustration *see* JAZZ (i), fig.2); besides writing

Don Redman, c1932

the band's arrangements he played clarinet, saxophones, and occasionally other instruments. The addition of Louis Armstrong in 1924–5 as jazz specialist had a deep impact on all the players and also on Redman's arrangements; the band turned increasingly from dance music to jazz, and by the mid-1920s it was the most prominent African-American jazz orchestra in the country.

Redman left Henderson in June 1927 to become music director of McKinney's Cotton Pickers, and in a few months he transformed this group from a little-known novelty ensemble into one of the major jazz orchestras of the period. The Cotton Pickers focused less attention on its soloists than Henderson's band had done and concentrated more on Redman's arrangements, which were played with precision and control. Redman's writing became more elaborate, especially in harmony and rhythm; his new sophistication is apparent in his outstanding arrangement of *Rocky Road*. Besides playing as a soloist (principally on alto saxophone) and in the reed section, Redman began to appear as a singer, performing in a high pitched, half-spoken style. He also composed his best-known popular songs with the Cotton Pickers: *Cherry* and *Gee, (baby,) ain't I good to you?*.

In October 1931 Redman formed his own band with Shirley Clay, Langston Curl, Benny Morton, Claude Jones, Fred Robinson, Edward Inge, Rupert Cole, Bob Carroll, Talcott Reeves, Bob Ysaguirre, Manzie Johnson, Harlan Lattimore, and others. In 1932 he composed *Chant of the Weed*, perhaps his most masterly work. Sidney De Paris, Horace Henderson, and Quentin Jackson joined Redman in that year, and Harold Baker, Reunald Jones, and Gene Porter were among his sidemen later in the 1930s. Although the success of his band waned in later years, it broadcast regularly on radio, made the short film *Don Redman and his Orchestra* (1934), and took part in numerous recording sessions for Brunswick, Victor, and other labels before breaking up in January 1940. Redman temporarily led another band at the end of that year.

Redman spent most of the 1940s composing and writing arrangements for radio, television, and many big bands, including those of Count Basie and Jimmy Dorsey. In 1942 Jay McShann's band temporarily worked under Redman's leadership. He led a big band at the Zanzibar in New York in 1943, and organized another big band to tour Europe from autumn 1946, at which point his sidemen included Peanuts Holland, Jackson, Tyree Glenn, Don Byas, Ray Abrams, and Billy Taylor (ii). After performing in several countries the orchestra went to Paris for a three-week residency in December 1946, but it was banned from playing at the instigation of protests by French musicians and disbanded; Redman and the others continued to work in Europe in 1947. In 1951 he became music director for Pearl Bailey, an association which lasted throughout the 1950s. At the end of the decade he once again issued a few jazz recordings. He seldom performed during his final years, but spent his time writing several extended works (which have never been performed in public). McCarthy, in *Big Band Jazz* (1974), reported that Redman's scores were still with his widow; their later fate is unknown.

The writings of Schuller and Collier have revised previous assessments of Redman, since they credited the emergence of the central concepts of big-band orchestration to white arrangers and bandleaders active in the late 1910s and early 1920s, notably Ferde Grofé, Isham Jones, Art Hickman, and Paul Whiteman. This reassessment, however, threatens to undervalue Redman's creativity: by comparison with the predominantly genteel offerings of the earlier white bands, Henderson's finest recordings of Redman's arrangements suggest that there is a chasm between a conceptualization in a pop context and a convincing execution in jazz. Redman was an outstanding jazz arranger and the first master of jazz orchestration. His early arrangements integrated solo improvisations with passages for ensemble in the style of improvised jazz, and he also incorporated certain aspects of collectively improvised jazz, such as breaks, chases, and call-and-response patterns, into his scores. His versions of *Copenhagen*, *Sugar Foot Stomp*, *Go 'long mule*, and *Shanghai Shuffle* for Henderson are important landmarks in the evolution of ensemble jazz. Some of Redman's scores are held in the Schomburg Center for Research in Black Culture, New York Public Library (*see* Libraries and archives, §2).

See also Arrangement, §2.

SELECTED RECORDINGS

(on alto saxophone unless otherwise indicated)

As leader: Down Home Rag (1938, Bb 10061) [sop sax]; Baby, won't you please come home (1939, Vic. 26266) [sop sax]

As sideman: P. Bradford: Lucy Long (1925, Voc. 15165); McKinney's Cotton Pickers: Shim-me-sha-wabble (1928, Vic 21611) [bar sax]; L. Armstrong: Save it, pretty mama (1928, OK 8657); Heah me talkin' to ya (1928, OK 8649); McKinney's Cotton Pickers: Peggy (1929, Vic. 38133)

SELECTED ARRANGEMENTS

* – composed by Redman

As leader: *Chant of the Weed/*Shakin' the African (1931, Bruns. 6211); Got the jitters (1934, Bruns. 6745); Sweet Sue (1937, Var. 605)

Recorded by F. Henderson with Redman as sideman: Go 'long mule (1924, Col. 228D); Shanghai Shuffle (1924, PAct 036157); Copenhagen (1924, Voc. 14926); Sugar Foot Stomp (1925, Col. 395D); The Stampede (1926, Col. 654D); The Henderson Stomp/The Chant (1926, Col. 817D); Rocky Mountain Blues (1927, Co. 970D); St. Louis Shuffle (1927, Vic. 20944A); Whiteman Stomp/I'm Coming Virginia (1927, Col. 1059D)

Recorded by McKinney's Cotton Pickers with Redman as sideman: *Cherry (1928, Vic. 21730); Shim-me-sha-wabble (1928, Vic. 21611); *Gee, ain't I good to you? (1929, Vic. 38097); Rocky Road (1930, Vic. 22932)

Recorded by L. Armstrong with Redman as sideman: *Save it, pretty mama (1928, OK 8657)

BIBLIOGRAPHY

AllenH; *McCarthyB*; *SchullerS*

E. A. C. Ballard: "Let us Now Praise Famous Men: an Appreciation of the Biggest Little Man in Jazz: Don Redman," *Hot News and Rhythm Record Review*, i/1 (1935), 8

B. Ulanov: "Thanks, Mr. Redman, for Modern Style," *Metronome*, lvii/6 (1941), 20

H. Grut: "Don Redman," *Jazz Music*, iii/3 (1946), 4

"Don Redman in Denmark Talks to the MM," *MM* (5 Oct 1946), 5

A. J. McCarthy: "The Redman Band in Europe: a Discography," *Jazz Forum*, no.5 (1947), 14

H. Niesen, Jr.: "The Redman Band in Holland," *Jazz Forum*, no.5 (1947), 13

H. Panassié: "An Evening with Don Redman," *Hot Notes*, no.12 (1948)

F. Driggs: "Don Redman, Composer-arranger," *JR*, ii/10 (1959), 6; repr. as "Don Redman: Jazz Composer-arranger," in *Jazz Panorama*, ed. M. Williams (New York and London, 1962/R1979), 91

C. Fox: "The Big Band Era: Don Redman," *JM*, viii/2 (1962), 8

M. Mezzrow: "Sur Don Redman," *BHcF*, no.145 (1965), 3

D. Ives: "A View of Don Redman," *JJ*, xxi/7 (1968), 14

G. Schuller: *Early Jazz: its Roots and Musical Development* (New York, 1968), 256

G. Fernett: *Swing Out: Great Negro Jazz Bands* (Midland, MI, 1970/R1993), 93

J. Chilton: *McKinney's Music: a Bio-discography of McKinney's Cotton Pickers* (London, 1978)

M. Berger, E. Berger, and J. Patrick: *Benny Carter: a Life in American Music* (Metuchen, NJ, and London, 1982), 74

F. Ferriano: "Don Redman: Pioneer Big Band Arranger," *Jazz Research Papers*, vii (1987), 54

J. L. Collier: *Jazz: the American Theme Song* (New York, 1993)

J. McGee: "Revisiting Fletcher Henderson's *Copenhagen*," *Journal of the American Musicological Society*, xlviii/1 (1995), 42

ROBERT KENSELAAR/BK

Redman [Shedroff], **Joshua** (*b* Berkeley, CA, 1 Feb 1969). Tenor saxophonist and leader, son of Dewey Redman. He grew up with his mother in Berkeley, California, and had little contact with his father during his youth. Primarily self-taught, he took up alto saxophone at the age of ten after he had played clarinet for a year. In the mid-1980s he performed with his high school's jazz band at the Monterey Jazz Festival and played occasionally with Peter Apfelbaum's Hieroglyphics Ensemble. He read urban studies at Harvard University and graduated summa cum laude in 1991; despite being offered a place at Yale University's law school, he then moved to New York to pursue a career in music. Around this time he changed his surname to Redman, to help alleviate the confusion created when he performed on the same concert billings as his father. In late 1991 he won the Thelonious Monk International Jazz Saxophone Competition, having entered only at the last moment at the suggestion of a friend. The following year he toured with Jack DeJohnette's Special Edition and the Young Masters sextet, and toured Europe and recorded with his father; in addition he performed and recorded with Elvin Jones's Jazz Machine and Paul Motian's Electric Bebop Band and, with Geoff Keezer and Christian McBride, formed the cooperative group Three Musicians.

In the mid-1990s Redman toured and recorded in a group with Pat Metheny, Charlie Haden, and Billy Higgins (1993), with the Lincoln Center Jazz Orchestra (1994), and as a member of Chick Corea's Bud Powell tribute band (1996–7). During the same period he recorded music for the one-woman show *Twilight: Los Angeles 1992* (1995) and appeared as a musician in Robert Altman's film *Kansas City* (1996); he also performed on the film's soundtrack and appeared in the resulting video, *Jazz '34: Remembrances of Kansas City Swing* (1997). In 1997 he was in Japan with Dave Liebman, Michael Brecker, and George Garzone at a festival in tribute to John Coltrane. As a freelance he recorded with Mario Pavone (1991), Eric Felten and Jimmy Knepper (1991–2), the studio group New York Stories, John Hicks, and Kenny Drew, Jr. (all 1992), Joe Lovano, Roy Hargrove, Jimmy Haslip, Mel Rhyne, and Mike LeDonne (all 1993), Milt Jackson and Larry Goldings (both 1993, 1995), Toots Thielemans, McBride, Diane Reeves, Marcus Miller, and Tyner (all 1994), Dave Brubeck, Michael Franks, Ray Brown, King, and Mark Turner (all 1995), Geoff Keezer (*c*1997), and Nicholas Payton (1997–8).

In 1992 Redman performed as a leader at the Village Vanguard, and towards the end of the year he began touring internationally and recording with his own groups; his sidemen have included the pianists Kevin Hays (to 1993), Brad Mehldau (1993–4), Jonny King (1994) and Peter Martin (1995–7), the guitarist Peter Bernstein (1995–7), the double bass players McBride (to late 1994) and Christopher Thomas (1994–7), and the drummer Brian Blade (1992–7). In 1997, with McBride and Blade, he co-founded The Trio; the group has toured extensively and in January 1998 it held a week-long engagement at Yoshi's in Oakland, California, performing as a quartet with McCoy Tyner. He formed a new quartet in late 1998 with the pianist Aaron Goldberg, Reuben Rogers, and Gregory Hutchinson, and in 2000 he was appointed to work for a year as the artistic director and artist-in-residence for SFJAZZ (the San Francisco Jazz Organization – formerly Jazz in the City).

Redman's sudden rise to fame in 1993, following his excellent début recording, is reminiscent of Wynton Marsalis's career in the early 1980s. Although Redman is perhaps better versed than Marsalis in the bop vernacular, by comparison his compositional style, particularly on later recordings, is bland and somewhat repetitive. As a hard-bop saxophonist his main influence at an early stage was Sonny Rollins; his introduction to *St. Thomas* (1995) demonstrates his ability to play in a virtuoso manner on fast-moving chord progressions. Unfortunately his concert performances as a leader and with The Trio have been marred by vulgar displays of technique, and by the late 1990s his playing had

Joshua Redman at the Brecon Jazz Festival, Wales, 1996

in some ways become a cliché of itself, with predictable altissimo smears, and bop lines often giving way to a rather "polite" soul saxophone style. By contrast his recordings as a sideman, most of which are in a hard-bop vein, have been consistently impressive.

SELECTED RECORDINGS

Duo with K. Drew: on *A Look Inside* (1992, Ant. 314-524211-2), Ugly Beauty

As leader: *Joshua Redman* (1992, WB 45242-2); *Wish* (*c*1993, WB 45365-2); *MoodSwing* (1994, WB 45643-2); *Spirit of the Moment: Live at the Village Vanguard* (1995, WB 45923-2); *Freedom in the Groove* (1996, WB 46330-2); *Timeless Tales (for Changing Times)* (*c*1998, WB 47052-2)

As sideman: M. Pavone: *Toulon Days* (1991, New World 80420-2); E. Felten and J. Knepper: *T-Bop* (1991–2, SN 121196-2), incl. Deconstruction; J. Hicks: *Friends Old and New* (1992, Novus 01241-63141-2); P. Motian: *Paul Motion and the Electric Bebop Band* (1992, JMT 514004-2); E. Jones: *Youngblood* (1992, Enja 7051-2), incl. Angel Eyes; M. Rhyne: *Boss Organ* (1993, Criss Cross 1080); M. LeDonne: *Soul Mates* (1993, Criss Cross 1074); J. Lovano: *Tenor Legacy* (1993, BN B21Z-27014); L. Goldings: on *Caminhos cruzados* (1993, Novus 41-63184-2), So danco samba, Where or When, Words; C. McBride: *Gettin' to it* (1994, Verve 314-523989-2); M. Tyner: on *Prelude and Sonata* (1994, Mlst. 9244), Contemplation; D. Brubeck: on *Young Lions and Old Tigers* (1995, Telarc 83349), Joshua Redman; R. Brown: on *Some of my Best Friends are ... the Sax Players* (1995, Telarc 83388), Just you, just me, Polka Dots and Moonbeams; J. King: *Notes from the Underground* (1995, Enja 9067-2); M. Turner: on *Mark Turner* (1995, WB 46701-2), Kathelin Gray, Mr. Brown, 317 East 32nd Street; C. Corea: *Remembering Bud Powell* (*c*1996, Stretch 9012-2); N. Payton: on *Payton's Place* (1997–8, Verve 314-557327-2), A Touch of Silver

BIBLIOGRAPHY

B. Shoemaker: "Redman Tops Tough Tenors to Take Thelonious Trophy," *DB*, lix/3 (1992), 12

P. Cole: "Joshua Redman: So, You Wanna Be a Jazz Star," *DB*, lx/12 (1993), 17 [incl. discography]

C. Gauffre and B. Loupias: "Joshua et ses pairs," *Jm*, no.432 (1993), 19

M. Hrebeniak: "Simply Redman," *Jazz: the Magazine*, no.19 (1993), 14

F. Keizer: "Joshua, 24 ans, tenor," *Jm*, no.427 (1993), 26

T. Moon: "The Joshua Reed," *Musician*, no.175 (1993), 21

B. Primack: "Joshua & Dewey Redman: Confronting Reality and Expectations," *JT*, xxiii/4 (1993), 28

Z. Stewart: "Ivy League Tenor: Joshua Redman: Believe the Hype," *DB*, lx/6 (1993), 26 [incl. discography]

G. Endress: "Das intellektuelle Naturtalent," *JP*, xliii/1 (1994), 3

M. Gilbert: "Joshua Redman," *JJI*, xlvii/4 (1994), 6

P. Keegan: "Come Blow your Horn," *Gentlemens Quarterly*, lxiv/6 (1994), 93

G. Reynard, F. W. Sportis, and R. Grosman: "Joshua Redman," *Jh*, no.512 (1994), 38

K. Bennett: "Frontman," *Musician*, no.197 (1995), 7

P. Watrous: "Jazz's New Fans Act as if it's Michael Jordan on Sax," *New York Times* (23 April 1995)

D. Ouellette: "Redman & Green: the Berkeley Boys," *DB*, lxiii/5 (1996), 16 [incl. discography]

B. Primack: "Joshua Redman: on Fame, Focus, & Freedom," *JT*, xxvi/9 (1996), 28

G. Endress: "Joshua Redman: der Jazz fordert Opfer," *JP*, xlvii/10 (1998), 3

GK

Red Onion. Nightclub in New Orleans; *see* NIGHTCLUBS AND OTHER VENUES.

Red Onion Jazz Babies. Recording group assembled for Gennett in 1924. It was based on the members of the Clarence Williams Blue Five, which had recorded for OKeh, and consisted of Louis Armstrong (cornet), Buster Bailey or Sidney Bechet (clarinet and soprano saxophone), Aaron Thompson or Charlie Irvis (trombone), Buddy Christian (banjo), and Lil Armstrong (piano). In the course of four sessions the group recorded three instrumental numbers and five titles accompanying Alberta Hunter (who, because she was contracted to Paramount, used the pseudonym Josephine Beatty for these releases). However, on its most famous title, *Cake Walking Babies from Home*, the singer is not Hunter, but rather Eva Taylor, who was joined by a second vocalist, Clarence Todd.

SELECTED RECORDINGS

(all recorded in 1924 for Gennett)

As Red Onion Jazz Babies: Of all the wrongs you done to me/Cake Walking Babies (from Home) (5627); Terrible Blues/Santa Claus Blues (5607)

As J. Beatty (A. Hunter) with Red Onion Jazz Babies: Everybody loves my baby/Texas Moaner Blues (5594); Nobody knows the way I feel 'dis mornin'/Early Every Morn (5626)

BIBLIOGRAPHY

T. Lord: *Clarence Williams* (Chigwell, England, 1976), 113, 442

J. L. Collier: *Louis Armstrong: an American Genius* (New York, 1983, London, 1984, as *Louis Armstrong: a Biography*), 141

MIKE HAZELDINE/BK

Reece, Dizzy [Alphonso Son] (*b* Kingston, Jamaica, 5 Jan 1931). Jamaican trumpeter. He grew up in a musical family and studied baritone horn from the age of 11 and trumpet from the age of 14; among his classmates were Joe Harriott and Wilton "Bogey" Gaynair. After working in Jamaica with Sonny Bradshaw's Beboppers and with the swing-band leader Jack Brown (1947) he moved to London (1948) and then to Paris, where he played with Jay Cameron and Don Byas. From 1950 he performed in the Netherlands, Germany, and Italy with Wallace Bishop, the pianist Rob Pronk, and the double bass player Buddy Banks. He was again in London in 1952–3, when he played with Cab Kaye and occasionally with Kenny Graham. Following another period on the continent, in 1954 he returned to London; there he formed a quintet (1954), worked with Kathy Stobart, Terry Shannon, and Kenny Graham's Afro-Cubists (1954–5), and made recordings as a leader (1955–7). In 1955 he spent a short time with Tony Crombie's big band, and the following year he performed in Paris with Martial Solal, Byas, and members of the Modern Jazz Quartet. Reece then recorded in London alongside, among others, Tubby Hayes, Ronnie Scott, and Jimmy Deuchar in groups led by Victor Feldman (1956–7). He led a quartet and another quintet in Britain (1957–8) and played in France with the bandleader Jacques Hélian (1958).

Reece re-formed his quintet in London and worked in Switzerland, then in October 1959 moved to New York, where he led a group at the Village Vanguard (1960) and recorded as a sideman with Duke Jordan. Later he was active as a freelance sideman and occasionally as a leader. In 1968 he toured Europe in Dizzy Gillespie's big band, and in 1969 he performed in Britain as a soloist and recorded in Copenhagen in a sextet led by Dexter Gordon and Slide Hampton. He may be seen with Johnny Griffin's group in the film *Jazz is our Religion* (1972). Reece recorded in 1978 as the leader of an all-star sextet with Clifford Jordan and Roy Haynes among his sidemen, and he toured Europe in 1985 with the Paris Reunion Band; in Jamaica he appeared as a guest soloist with Bradshaw. In the early 1990s he was a member of Clifford Jordan's big band, and in 1996 he toured as a member of Cecil Payne's group Bebop Generation. Reece is an inventive, disciplined soloist in the bop idiom and extemporizes in extended, thoughtfully developed, and melodically constructed phrases.

SELECTED RECORDINGS

As leader: *The Dizzy Reece Quintet* (1955, Tempo LAP3), incl. O Moon, Bang!; *Progress Report* (1956, Tempo TAP9), incl. Basie Line, Chorus, Out of Nowhere, Scrapple from the Apple; A Variation on Monk (1957, Tempo EXA84) [EP]; *Blues in Trinity* (1958, BN 4006); Nowhere to Go (1958, Tempo EXA86) [EP], incl. Main Title, The Search; *Star Bright*

(1959, BN 4023), incl. Groovesville, The Rake; *Soundin' Off* (1960, BN 4033); *Asia Minor* (1962, NewJ 8274); *Manhattan Project* (1978, BH 7001)
As sideman: V. Feldman: on *Victor Feldman in London* (1956, Tempo TAP8), Wilbert's Tune; D. Jordan: *Flight to Jordan* (1960, BN 84046); P. J. Jones: *'Round Midnite* (1966, Passport 11-115), incl. 'Round Midnite; C. Jordan: *Down through the Years* (1991, Mlst. 9197), incl. Don't get around much anymore, Status quo

BIBLIOGRAPHY

CarrJ; *ChiltonB*; *FeatherE*; *Feather '60s*
J. Cooke: "Dizzy Reece: an Introduction," *JM*, v/8 (1959), 25 [incl. discography]
M. James: "Out of the Bag, Number Six: Dizzy Reece," *JM*, ix/7 (1963), 14
T. Hall: Liner notes, *Progress Report* (Jasmine 2013, 1982)

KEN RATTENBURY/BK

Reed, Eric (Scott) (*b* Philadelphia, 21 June 1970). Pianist and composer. He played piano from the age of two, and in 1977 began taking piano lessons and playing in his father's Baptist church. In 1981 the family moved to Los Angeles. While in high school Reed performed locally with Clora Bryant, John Clayton, Art Hillery, Bennie Maupin, Earl Palmer, and Gerald Wilson's big band, and when he was 18 he began playing on occasion with Wynton Marsalis, who had heard him four years earlier and give him encouragement. In 1990 he joined Marsalis's septet. He left the group in 1991 and worked with Freddie Hubbard and Joe Henderson, then rejoined Marsalis in 1992; he also worked with Marlon Jordan from 1990 to 1992. In December 1994 he began leading his own groups on a regular basis, though he took part in tributes to Thelonious Monk in concerts at the Lincoln Center under Marsalis's direction from 1996 to 1998. He also accompanied Vanessa Rubin in a tribute to Billy Higgins in New York in 1998. Although Reed's playing is rooted in bop, he is skilled in the gospel piano style and in earlier jazz styles, including stride. He is a talented composer and has written most of the pieces on his own recordings.

SELECTED RECORDINGS

As leader: *Soldier's Hymn* (1990, Can. 79511); *It's All Right to Swing* (1993, MoJazz 37463-7006-2); *The Swing and I* (1994, MoJazz 314-530468-2); *Pure Imagination* (1997, Imp. 244)
As sideman: W. Marsalis: *Citi Movement (Griot New York)* (1992, C2K53324); *In this House, on this Morning* (1992–3, C2K53220); W. Anderson: *Warmdaddy in the Garden of Swing* (*c*1994, Atl. 82657-2); M. Printup: *Song for the Beautiful Woman* (1994, BN B21Z-30790); West Coast Jazz Summit: *West Coast Jazz Summit* (1995, Mons 874773)

SELECTED FILMS AND VIDEOS

Accent on the Offbeat (*c*1994); Garth Fagan's Griot New York (*c*1995); Marsalis on Music (1995); Bravo Profiles: Wynton Marsalis (1996)

BIBLIOGRAPHY

"Auditions: *Down Beat* Spotlights Deserving Young Musicians," *DB*, lv/3 (1988), 64
B. Hershon: "Eric Reed," *California Jazz Now*, i/6 (1991), 4
G. Reynard and F. W. Sportis: "Génération Marsalis: Eric Reed," *Jh*, no.505 (1993), 32
Z. Stewart: "Riffs: Eric Reed," *DB*, lx/12 (1993), 14
M. Daniels: "Talking with . . . Eric Reed," *L.A. Jazz Scene*, no.79 (1994), 3
J. Ferguson: "Eric Reed: It's All Right to Swing," *JT*, xxiv/1 (1994), 25
W. Marsalis and F. Stewart: *Sweet Swing Blues on the Road* (New York, 1994), 33
R. L. Doerschuk: "Eric Reed: Young Jazz Lion Ponders Life after Wynton," *Keyboard*, xxi/1 (1995), 15
B. Kohlhasse: "Pianist Eric Reed is Still Just 'Trying to Swing'," *Los Angeles Times* (21 Feb 1995)
J. Macnie: "Fracturing the Mainstream: Stephen Scott & Eric Reed," *DB*, xlii/6 (1995), 22
<http://www.raba.com/jazz/reed> (1998)
J. Macnie: "Eric Reed: Pure Imagination," *Cuadernos de jazz*, no.46 (1998), 33
B. Margolis: "Tradin' Fours: Eric Reed: Change Everything," *DB*, lxv/7 (1998), 47
L.-V. Mialy and F. W. Sportis: "Eric Reed," *Jh*, no.559 (1999), 8

THOMAS OWENS

Reed, Waymon (*b* Fayetteville, NC, 10 Jan 1940; *d* Nashville, 25 Nov 1983). Trumpeter. He grew up in Nashville, and played trumpet in school bands. Later he attended the Eastman School of Music for a year. After touring with carnival and rhythm-and-blues bands he settled in Miami, where he played in bands with Ira Sullivan and Pee Wee Ellis and led his own group. From 1965 to 1969 he was a member of James Brown's soul band. He then worked briefly as a freelance in New York before playing in Count Basie's orchestra (1969–73). He recorded with the big bands led by Frank Foster (1975), Thad Jones and Mel Lewis (1975–6), and Basie (1977–8), as well as with his own bop quintet (1977). From 1978 to 1980 he toured with his wife, Sarah Vaughan, as the principal soloist in her quartet and director of her orchestra; they divorced in 1981. Reed joined Buddy Rich's band in 1981 and played in the show *Sophisticated Ladies* in Los Angeles before he was forced to retire through ill-health.

SELECTED RECORDINGS

As leader: *46th and 8th* (1977, AH 10)
As sideman: E. Jefferson: *Still on the Planet* (1976, Muse 5063); C. Basie: *Count Basie Big Band, Montreux '77* (1977, Pablo 2308207); S. Vaughan: *Duke Ellington Song Book* (1979, PT 2312111, 2312116)

BIBLIOGRAPHY

S. Dance: Liner notes, *46th and 8th* (AH 10, 1978)
L. Gourse: *Sassy: the Life of Sarah Vaughan* (New York and Toronto, 1993), 176

BK

Reed organ. A generic term for those keyboard instruments whose sound is produced by freely vibrating reed tongues and activated by air under pressure or suction. Common names for such instruments include harmonium (generally used in Europe), melodeon, vocalion, seraphine, *orgue expressif*, cabinet organ, and American organ; the last of these is also a European term, used to distinguish suction from pressure instruments. Reed organs vary in size from compact single-manual instruments powered by one or two foot treadles to large models with two manuals and pedals and several sets of reeds which are operated by a separate blowing lever or electric motor. Other members of the reed-organ family include the accordion and concertina.

The reed organ is comparatively rare in jazz, and recorded examples of its use date in general from the early period. Probably the best-known instance of an early appearance of the instrument is in accompaniments to jazz-oriented songs written and orchestrated by Kurt Weill, particularly in the period 1925–9. In the USA Arthur Ray played the instrument in a series of duo recordings made with Bubber Miley (as the Texas Jazz Destroyers) in early October 1924, and it was sometimes employed to accompany blues and vaudeville singers; a notable example may be heard on Bessie Smith's *The St. Louis Blues* (1925, Col. 14064D) and *Reckless Blues* (1925, Col. 14056D), where the singer is accompanied by Fred Longshaw (and also Louis Armstrong). It is possible that the instrument played by Fats Waller with Fletcher Henderson's band on *The Chant* (1926, Col. 817D) is a reed organ.

In most conventional jazz ensembles the reed organ was supplanted from the 1950s by the electric or electronic organ (*see* Organ, §2). However, the unusual tone color of the instrument made it attractive for a number of avant-garde musicians. In particular it has been adopted by Myra Melford, who uses a single-manual harmonium from the Indian subcontinent, pumped by hand and operated from a kneeling or squatting position; its quiet and delicate sound is ideal in blending with the viola of Leroy Jenkins and the flute or bass flute of Joseph Jarman in the trio Equal Interest.

ALYN SHIPTON

Reed section. A term applied to the reed instruments (i.e., saxophones and clarinets, and, occasionally, flutes) within a big band; *see* BANDS, §§2, 4.

Reedus, Tony [Anthony Dewayne] (*b* Memphis, 22 Sept 1959). Drummer. His father was in the air force and his family moved to various bases before settling in Memphis when his father retired around 1962. He took up drums when he was 14 and began playing in church. After his uncle James Williams had introduced him to jazz he performed locally from the age of 17 with the saxophonist Herman Green. Between 1978 and 1980 he studied music at Memphis State University, where he met Mulgrew Miller, but he left school early to move to New York. There he joined Woody Shaw, with whom he toured internationally and recorded (October 1980–1984). When Shaw's group disbanded he returned to Memphis, although he left periodically to deputize for Rocky White in Mercer Ellington's band and for Ralph Peterson, Jr., in Jon Faddis's group. Reedus then returned to New York and worked as a freelance with, among others, Barbara Dennerlein, Billy Taylor (ii), Freddie Hubbard, and the Smithsonian Jazz Masterworks Orchestra. In addition he was a member Bobby Hutcherson's group (1986–8), and he performed and recorded with Williams (from *c*1984), Miller (from *c*1987), Teddy Charles (at the Verona Jazz Festival, June 1988), Kenny Garrett (late 1980s), Benny Golson (*c*1989–92), and the Contemporary Piano Ensemble and JoAnne Brackeen (both from the early 1990s); he toured Europe with Brackeen in November 1993.

Reedus made his first recording as a leader in 1988, and in 1989–90 he led a group which performed and recorded, with Gary Thomas, Steve Nelson, and either Dave Holland (recording only), Kenny Davis, or Ira Coleman on double bass. As a sideman he recorded with Bill Easley (1986), Billy Pierce (1987), Nelson (1987–8), Ronnie Mathews (1988), Benny Green (1988), Geoff Keezer (1988, 1992), Robin Eubanks and Steve Turre (1989), Brian Lynch (1990), Jim Snidero (1991, 1994), the studio group Memphis Convention (1992), Gust William Tsilis (1993), Philip Harper (1994), and Ronnie Cuber, Mike Nock, Harold Mabern, and James Spaulding (all 1996).

SELECTED RECORDINGS

As leader: *The Far Side* (1988, Jazz City 016); *Incognito* (1989, Enja 6058-2); *Minor Thang* (1994–5, Criss Cross 1117)

As sideman: W. Shaw: *Master of the Art* (1982, Elek. Mus. 60131); *Time is Right* (1983, Red 168); J. Williams: *Alter Ego* (1984, Sunnyside 1007); M. Miller: *Wingspan* (1987, Landmark 1515); G. Keezer: *Waiting in the Wings* (1988, Sunnyside 1035); B. Golson: *Live* (1989, Dreyfus 36552); M. Miller: *Time and Again* (1991, Landmark 1532-2); J. Brackeen: *Power Talk* (1994, Turnipseed 08); R. Cuber: *N.Y. Cats* (1996, Ste. 31394); M. Nock: *Not We but One* (1996, Naxos Jazz 86006-2); H. Mabern: *Mabern's Grooveyard* (1996, DIW 621); J. Spaulding: *The Smile of the Snake* (1996, HighNote 7006)

BIBLIOGRAPHY

K. Micallef: "Exploring the Far Side with Tony Reedus," *MD*, xvii/12 (1993), 26 [incl. discography]

A. Lewis and L. Lewis: "Tony Reedus Interview," *Cadence*, xxi/1 (1995), 17

<http://www.jazzcorner.com/reedus.html> (1998)

GK

Re-entry. Record label founded in 1977 by JOHN FISCHER.

Reeves, Dianne (Elizabeth) (*b* Detroit, 23 Oct 1956). Singer. Her father was a singer and her mother played trumpet; her cousin is George Duke. She grew up in Denver, where her uncle the classical double bass player Charles Burell helped to shape her musical development. She began singing and studying piano around 1971. In 1973, while performing with her high school band at the National Association of Jazz Educators' convention in Chicago, she was discovered by Clark Terry. She then sang occasionally with Terry's groups, including performances at the Colorado Jazz Party (1973) and, later, the Wichita Jazz Festival (1979). Reeves attended the University of Denver for one year before moving to Los Angeles, where as a studio singer she recorded with Alphonso Johnson, Lenny White, and Stanley Turrentine and, around 1976, as a member of the fusion group Caldera. In 1980 she founded, with Billy Childs, the fusion group Night Flight. She toured with the Brazilian pop musician Sergio Mendes (1981–3), then moved to New York, where she worked with Harry Belafonte (1983–6). After returning to Los Angeles in 1987 she sang at a concert devoted to Duke Ellington; she may be seen in the resulting video *Echoes of Ellington*, i (*c*1987). In August 1987 she performed with Art Blakey's big band at the Mt. Fuji Jazz Festival in Japan. She toured with the Philip Morris SuperBand, under Gene Harris's direction, from 1989, and after several appearances with Quincy Jones at the Montreux International Jazz Festival between 1989 and 1995 made her début there as a leader in 1995. She has also performed at the Monterey Jazz Festival.

Reeves continued to collaborate with Childs through the 1990s and led her own groups; among her regular sidemen were the pianist David Torkanowsky (who also served as her music director), the bass player Chris Severin, and the drummer Billy Kilson. In 1992 she moved to Denver, but she remained involved in activities in the Los Angeles area. She toured Europe as a leader in October–November 1997, and in this same year recorded with T. S. Monk's tentet Monk on Monk; she also performed occasionally with the band, notably in December 1997 at Yoshi's in Oakland, California. Reeves's recordings show an eclectic juxtaposition of folk, popular, soul, smooth jazz, and jazz styles, often on one album. She has a wonderfully rich voice; her overall conception, and in particular her manner of phrasing rhythms, indicates that she is more comfortable in pop settings than in jazz.

SELECTED RECORDINGS

As leader: *Dianne Reeves* (*c*1986, BN 46906); *I Remember* (*c*1989, BN B21Z-90264); *The Grand Encounter* (1996, BN 38268-2)

BIBLIOGRAPHY

CarrJ

L. Dahl: *Stormy Weather: the Music and Lives of a Century of Jazzwomen* (London, Melbourne, Australia, and New York, 1984), 181

W. Friedwald: "Dianne Reeves: She's No Purist," *JT* (1988), Jan, 7

Z. Stewart: "Variety the Spice of Reeves' Musical Life," *Los Angeles Times* (9 May 1990)

D. Baranello: "Riffs: Dianne Reeves," *DB*, lviii/9 (1991), 14

D. Kasrel: "Dianne Reeves: the Personal Touch," *JT*, xix/6 (1991), 23

J. Bradley: "Dianne Reeves is Back in Town," *Denver Post* (15 March 1994)

W. Jenkins: "Dianne Reeves' Ultimate Jazz Journey," *JT*, xxv/6 (1995), 62

M. Joyce: "Dianne Reeves: Deep and Sprawling Roots," *Washington Post* (9 June 1995)

Z. Stewart: "Dianne Reeves: Aligned with her Allies," *DB*, lxiv/2 (1997), 28 [incl. discography]

M. Zwerin: "Dianne Reeves: Uniting Cultures and Sounds," *International Herald Tribune* (16 Oct 1997)

<http://www.diannereeves.com> (2000)

SCOTT FREDRICKSON, GK

Reeves, Nat(haniel Garfield) (*b* Lynchburg, VA, 27 May 1955). Double bass player and educator. His grandfather played blues guitar, banjo, and harmonica. He taught himself electric bass guitar from the age of 16 and changed to double bass six years later. In 1979 he moved to New York, where he played with Kenny Garrett, Mulgrew Miller, Sadik Hakim, Warne Marsh, and Andy Bey, and took part in Barry Harris's workshop and jam sessions at the Jazz Forum (1979–81). Reeves toured Japan with Sonny Stitt in 1982. That same year he met Jackie McLean in Hartford, Connecticut, and he moved there to joined McLean's group and his Artists Collective; he also became a member of the faculty at the Hartt School of Music. While continuing his association with McLean (through the 1990s) he recorded with Christopher Hollyday (1984), performed with Walter Davis (1990), and toured (from 1991) and recorded (1984, 1997) with Garrett. From January to March 1995 he toured South Africa with T. S. Monk and various winners of the Thelonious Monk Institute's jazz competitions, and in 1996 he began working with Steve Davis (iii).

SELECTED RECORDINGS

As sideman: J. McLean: *Dynasty* (1988, Triloka 181); *Rites of Passage* (1991, Triloka 188); *The Jackie Mac Attack Live* (1991, Verve 314-519270-2); *Hat Trick* (1996, BN 38363-2); K. Garrett: *Songbook* (1997, WB 46551-2)

BIBLIOGRAPHY

Feather–GitlerBEJ
<http://libaxp.hartford.edu/hartt/hartt/www/faculty/musicfac/reeves_n.html> (1999)
<http://www.labella.com/home/LB_nat.html> (1999)

GK

Reeves, Reuben [Red; River] (*b* Evansville, IN, 25 Oct 1905; *d* New York, Sept 1975). Trumpeter. He learned trumpet in high school in Evansville. In February 1924 he traveled to New York, where he played at Smalls' Paradise, and in January 1925 he moved to Chicago and worked with Erskine Tate (1926, 1927–8) and Dave Peyton (1927, 1928–30); he also gained a master's degree from the American Conservatory, led his own groups for recordings, and taught music at Wendell Phillips High School. After playing with the pianist and organist Jerome Carrington (1931) he spent a period with Cab Calloway in New York (1931–2); he is introduced as Red for the second trumpet solo heard on Calloway's *Bugle Call Rag* (1931), but River was his more common nickname. Reeves worked with Fess Williams before returning to Chicago, where he led his own band (1933–5). In 1936 he toured with the show *Connie's Hot Chocolates* and then went back to New York and joined a band led by the drummer Dick Ward. From the late 1930s until the end of World War II he played with and led army bands; following his discharge he worked with Harry Dial. In 1952 he ceased to work as a full-time musician, but he continued to perform occasionally with Dial and other leaders. The trombonist Gerald Reeves, who took part in some of his recording sessions and also recorded with Jelly Roll Morton, was his brother.

SELECTED RECORDINGS

As leader (all recorded for Vocalion): River Blues/Parson Blues (1929, 1292); Papa Skag Stomp/Bugle Call Rag (1929, 1297); Low Down Rhythm (1929, 15837); Texas Special Blues (1929, 1411); Moanin' Low (1929, 1407)

As sideman with C. Calloway: Basin Street Blues (1931, Ban. 32237); Bugle Call Rag (1931, Bruns. 6196)

BIBLIOGRAPHY

ChiltonW; *McCarthyB*
F. S. Driggs: "Reuben 'Red' Reeves," *JJ*, xii/7 (1959), 6
J. S. Schneider: "Reuben Reeves," *78 Quarterly*, i/2 (1968/*R*1992), [35]
H. Dial: *All that Jazz about Jazz: the Autobiography of Harry Dial* (Chigwell, England, 1984)
D. Barker: *A Life in Jazz*, ed. A. Shipton (London, 1986), 129

HOWARD RYE

Reeves, Talcott (Walter) (*b* Little Rock, AR, 15 July 1904; *d* Sept 1980). Banjoist and guitarist. His middle name and a birthdate in July (not June, as elsewhere) appear in his application for social security. He began playing banjo at the age of 20 and studied at Wilberforce College, Ohio, where in 1925 he joined Horace Henderson; he performed regularly with Henderson until 1930 and also worked with Benny Carter in 1928–9. From 1932 until 1936 and intermittently until the early 1940s he was with Don Redman, with whom he made several recordings (including *Chant of the Weed*, 1931, Bruns. 6211, and *I got rhythm*, 1932, Bruns. 6354) and with whom he may be seen in the short film *Don Redman and his Orchestra* (1934). Reeves ceased full-time performing after 1943 but continued to work as a freelance musician. The social security death index, from which his date of death is taken, gives his last known residence as Whitsell, North Carolina. (*AllenH*)

based on *ChiltonW*/HOWARD RYE

Reform Art Unit [RAU]. Austrian free-jazz group. It was formed in Vienna in 1965 after a number of different free improvising musicians had played together in informal sessions and in such short-lived groups as the Masters of Unorthodox Jazz and the Pechoc Trio. The founding members were the saxophonist and flutist Fritz Novotny, the trumpeter Sepp Mitterbauer, and several drummers, among them Günter Grafton, Fritz Kotrba, and Marjan Pakar. From 1966 an enlarged group, including the saxophonist and drummer Walter M. Malli and the double bass player Toni Michlmayr, worked for television and radio and took part in concerts and recording sessions with such international free-jazz musicians as Don Cherry, Kent Carter, the trumpeter Ambrose Jackson, Sunny Murray, Barre Phillips, Carla Bley, and Peter Kowald, the Indian sitar player Ram Chandra, the bop saxophonist J. R. Monterose, and the Austrian jazz musicians Peter Wolf (keyboards) and Franz Koglmann. The group performed in Austria at the Musikforum Ossiach (1971), at festivals in Ljubljana, Yugoslavia, and Altena, Germany, and at the Steirischer Herbst in Graz, Austria (1974). In 1976 it performed together with Kowald, Paul Lovens, Evan Parker, and Alex Schlippenbach, and in 1978 with Clifford Thornton. Many concerts, several festival performances, recording sessions, and radio broadcasts followed in the 1980s and 1990s, variously involving Burton Greene, Louis Moholo, Andrew Cyrille, Jim Pepper, Linda Sharrock, the singer Leena Conquest, the Austrian pianist Giselher Smekal, and often, Murray. Novotny also worked in duos with Cyrille, Murray, and the Austrian violinist Paul Fields, and from 1977 a band within the band, Three Motions, existed. The Reform Art Unit's music is influenced by American free jazz, world music, and the second Viennese school (Schoenberg, Berg, and Webern), and for this reason its members would prefer to be known as the Viennese School of Free Improvisation. The group made many recordings for its own label, RAU, including the album *For John Coltrane and Pablo Picasso* (1969, RAU 1002), as well as for the labels ESP, WM, and Extraplatte. (G. Smekal: "Neue Improvisationsmusik in Österreich," *Österreichische Musikzeitschrift*, xxxv/2 (1980), 88)

KLAUS SCHULZ

Regal (i). Record label. Issue began in spring 1921, and at first most of the catalogue was drawn from Emerson. By 1923, however, the Plaza Music Company was the source; most of the material was also put out on Banner and other labels connected with Plaza, though different takes were sometimes used. The label was discontinued by the American Record Corporation in the summer of 1931 or early in 1932.

BIBLIOGRAPHY

B. Rust: *The American Record Label Book*, New Rochelle, NY, 1978), 263
A. Sutton: *Directory of American Disc Record Brands and Manufacturers, 1891–1943* (Westport, CT, and London, 1994), 131

HOWARD RYE

Regal (ii). Record label. It was established by the British branch of Columbia, and issue began in April 1914; it was used for cheap recordings. The label name was also used by Australian Columbia after its formation in 1926. American material was drawn from Columbia and Harmony and included a considerable amount of jazz. The label was maintained after British Columbia merged with the Gramophone Company to form EMI in March 1931, but around the beginning of 1933 Regal was merged with the Gramophone Company's label Zonophone to form Regal-zonophone, which was used both in Britain and Australia. The name Regal was later used by EMI for issues in territories where its other labels were not available. Thus albums of recordings by Duke Ellington, which elsewhere appeared on Columbia, were issued on Regal in Spain; an important series of jazz reissues (on LPs) of the 1970s was released under the name Regal.

BIBLIOGRAPHY

P. Burgis: "Discs from Down Under," *Sv*, no.11 (1967), 4
B. Rust: *The American Record Label Book* (New Rochelle, NY, 1978), 264

HOWARD RYE

Regal (iii). Record company and label. The company was established in July 1949 by the four Braun brothers after the termination of the arrangement whereby they operated their earlier label De Luxe as an autonomous subsidiary of King. Regal was based at Linden, New Jersey, and recorded the work of such musicians as Alberta Hunter and Cab Calloway. The last recording sessions were organized in May 1951, and the company ceased to exist around six months later. (B. Daniels: "Regal Records 1949–1951," *Whiskey, Women, and . . .*, no.10 (1982), 12)

HOWARD RYE

Regal Theater. Theater in Chicago; *see* Nightclubs and other venues.

Regal–Zonophone. Record label. It was formed by EMI in both Britain and Australia by the merger of Columbia's label Regal with the Gramophone Company's cheap label Zonophone. The Regal numerical series were continued, but some Zonophone issues were re-pressed with the new label. American repertory was drawn from Bluebird, including work by such jazz musicians as Wingy Manone and Hot Lips Page. After 1939 the label's importance waned, and it was finally discontinued in 1949.

BIBLIOGRAPHY

R. Jewson, D. Smith, and R. Webb: "Arthur Gainsbury's Guide to Junkshoppers: Regal," *Sv*, no.42 (1972), 211
B. Rust: *The American Record Label Book* (New Rochelle, NY, 1978), 265

HOWARD RYE

Reggae. A musical form that originated in Jamaica around 1968, distinguished chiefly by an emphasis on the second half of each beat in common time. This regular pattern of accentuation has remained constant even as the style has developed in other respects. Reggae is in essence a slowed-down version of ska, a Jamaican form which was conceived in the late 1950s and was in large part an adaptation of New Orleans rhythm-and-blues and the instrumentation of American swing big bands. Elements of both forms, but chiefly the rhythm, have been used by jazz players.

Perhaps the earliest meeting of ska and jazz was in the hands of one of the originators of ska, Ernest Ranglin; a founding member in the early 1960s of the seminal ska band the Skatalites, he is also a jazz player whose performances have frequently juxtaposed elements of jazz, ska, and reggae. One such example may be heard on *Sound Invasion*, from his album *Modern Answers to Old Problems* (2000, Telarc 83526), where a monochordal reggae-style accompaniment forms a modal backdrop for improvisations by Ranglin and Courtney Pine. When he emerged in the 1980s, Pine spoke of the possibility of a new, essentially British direction for jazz in its amalgamation with reggae. His recordings, along with others by such black British players as the guitarist Cameron Pierre, have occasionally reflected this idea, but no more sustained fusion of jazz and reggae has emerged. It may be an indication of the resistance of jazz to a widespread adoption of reggae that, when he arrived in America in the early 1960s, the Jamaican pianist Monty Alexander largely avoided reference to his background in reggae, only slowly integrating elements of the latter into his performances. However, in later years, in his band Ivory and Steel and on his recordings made by his small groups, he has played explicitly in a reggae style. Particularly lucid examples of the meeting of reggae and jazz are the reggae version of Herbie Hancock's *Chameleon*, on Alexander's album *Monty Meets Sly and Robbie* (2000, Telarc 83494), where over the tune's two-chord vamp he superimposes jazz phrases reminiscent of Hancock's own polytonal approach, and Lester Bowie's *Freereggaehibop*, on James Carter's album *Conversin' with the Elders* (1995–6, Atl. 82908-2).

Other jazz players with no background in Caribbean music have also found inspiration in reggae. In contrast to the idea of playing jazz solos over non-jazz rhythms, Charlie Hunter recast tunes by the reggae star Bob Marley over funk and swing rhythms and expunged all traces of the reggae beat on his album *Natty Dread* (*c*1997, BN 52420-2). In a more esoteric milieu, the integration of playfully distorted reggae into a free-jazz context may be heard on *Ja*, from the Art Ensemble of Chicago's album *Nice Guys* (1978, ECM 1126), and on *Hurry up and wait*, from the String Trio of New York's album *Blues ...?* (1993, BS 120148-2). A sparse, emphatic reggae rhythm is an essential component of Marc Johnson's composition *Mojo Highway*, on his album *Bass Desires* (1985, ECM 1299), whereas a modified reggae rhythm is evident in the accompaniment by the drummer Peter Erskine to Steps Ahead's version of Don Grolnick's piece *Pools*, on the album *Steps Ahead* (1983, Elek. Mus. 60168). By the late 1990s, and despite the recent examples cited above, the interest among jazz players in reggae had diminished considerably; except within a small circle of players who remained active and committed to the hybrid style (including Roland Alphonso, Tommy McCook, and other members of the Skatalites, the group Jazz Jamaica, and Ranglin), reggae had become a diversionary flavor for jazz players rather than spawning a specific subgenre.

BIBLIOGRAPHY

S. Davis: *Reggae Bloodlines* (London, 1977, 2/1992)
K. McKnight and J. Tobler: *Bob Marley and the Roots of Reggae* (London, 1977)
L. Backus: "An Annotated Bibliography of Selected Sources on Jamaican Music," *Black Perspective in Music*, viii/1 (1980), 35
S. Clarke: *Jah Music: the Evolution of the Popular Jamaican Song* (London, 1982)
H. Johnson and J. Pines: *Reggae: Deep Roots Music* (New York, 1982)
S. Davis and P. Simon, eds.: *Reggae International* (London, 1983)
J. A. Winders: "Reggae, Rastafarians and Revolution," *Journal of Popular Culture*, xvii/1 (1983), 61 [incl. bibliography]; repr. in *American Popular Music*, ii: *The Age of Rock*, ed. T. E. Scheurer (Bowling Green, OH, 1990), 225
M. R. Mulvaney and C. I. H. Nelson: *Rastafari and Reggae: a Dictionary and Sourcebook* (Westport, CT, 1990) [incl. bibliography and discography]
S. Bader: *Words Like Fire: Dancehall Reggae and Ragga Muffin* (London, 1993)
B. Jahn and T. Webber: *Reggae Island: Jamaican Music in the Digital Age* (Kingston, Jamaica, 1994)
S. Barrow and P. Dalton: *The Rough Guide to Reggae* (London, 1997)
K. Chang and W. Cheng: *Reggae Routes: the Story of Jamaican Music* (Philadelphia, 1998)

MARK GILBERT

Regina. Record company and label. The company was established in New York in the early 1960s, and its catalogue included albums by Charlie Mariano, Roger Kellaway, Eddie Thompson, and Dorothy Donegan.

MARK GARDNER

Regis. Record label. It was launched in 1943 by the Regis Record Company of Newark, New Jersey; the proprietor was Irving Berman. At first the catalogue consisted only of gospel music, but it was soon expanded to include the work of Tiny Bradshaw, Tab Smith, and other jazz musicians. Operations ceased at the end of 1944, and the artists and repertory were transferred to Berman's new label, Manor, which maintained Regis's matrix series. ("Regis–Manor–Arco," *Blues Research*, no.15 (n.d. [?1966]), 2)

HOWARD RYE

Regoli, Enrique [Soler, Enrique Llácer] (*b* Alcoy, Spain, 20 June 1934). Spanish drummer, percussionist, and composer. He taught himself to play drums, then undertook conservatory training in Valencia and Madrid. In 1952 he began playing jazz in Barcelona, then moved to Madrid, where he worked mostly at the club Whisky Jazz and played with many visiting American bop soloists, including Gerry Mulligan, Slide Hampton, and Pony Poindexter. In 1972 he began performing as a percussionist with the National Symphony Orchestra and became a professor of percussion at the conservatory in Madrid. Regoli has written many compositions in various styles. Among his most celebrated jazz pieces are *Blues for David* (dedicated to the double bass player David Thomas), *Spiritual*, and *Regoli's Blues*. He is one of the most versatile drummers in Spain, and continued to perform and make recordings as a leader (including the album *Fundamentos del ritmo*, 1983, Phi. 412262I) into the early 1980s. However, from the late 1980s he abandoned jazz and dedicated himself to performing and composing symphonic music.

ALFREDO PAPO

Rehak, Frank (James) (*b* New York, 7 July 1926; *d* Badger, CA, 26 June 1987). Trombonist. He studied piano, cello, and baritone horn, then while in the navy during World War II he took up trombone and played in a swing sextet in Hawaii. In 1949 he joined Gene Krupa's band, forming with Frank Rosolino and Urbie Green an outstanding trombone section. Rehak became addicted to heroin while touring as a principal soloist with Jimmy Dorsey's orchestra (1950–52); he found some commercial studio work in New York, but in 1955 left music and became a plumber. The following year he toured the Near East and South America with Dizzy Gillespie's big band, then resumed studio work, notably as a member of the Gil Evans–Miles Davis Orchestra (1957–62), and began to make a name as a bop soloist; he may be seen with Evans's group, accompanying Davis, in the television show "Theater for a Story" (1959). In the early 1960s, however, he once more became dependent on heroin, the consequences of which brought an end to his career. In 1969 he entered Synanon's drug rehabilitation center in Los Angeles, where in 1973 he established a music department. Thereafter he took a permanent position as the director of Synanon in Houston. In September 1985 he participated in the Colorado Jazz Party, but soon thereafter the effects of cancer meant he could no longer play.

SELECTED RECORDINGS

As sideman: A. Cohn: *Be Loose* (1956, Dawn 1110); on Down Beat Critic Poll Winners: *Winner's Choice* (1957, Beth. 6024), If I'm Lucky, Love and the Weather; on Prestige All Stars: *Roots* (1957, NewJ 8202), Roots; G. Quill: *3 Bones and a Quill* (1958, Roost 2229)

BIBLIOGRAPHY

M. Hohman: "Frank Rehak," *DB*, xliv/9 (1977), 36
J. Kafalos and T. Everett: "Frank Rehak: Interview," *Cadence*, x (1984), no.8, p.5; no.9, p.16
T. Everett: "An Interview with Frank Rehak," *ITA Journal*, xv/2 (1987), 36
Obituary, *ITA Journal*, xv/4 (1987), 10

BK

Reichel, Hans (*b* Hagen, Germany, 10 May 1949). German guitarist. He taught himself violin from the age of seven; when he was 15 he became interested in rock music and took up guitar and electric bass guitar. In the late 1960s he gave up music to study graphic arts and work as a typesetter, but he had returned by 1970, when he recorded a tape of guitar music. He made his first commercial recording in 1973, and thereafter performed mainly as an unaccompanied soloist, as may be heard to good effect on *The Death of the Rare Bird Ymir* (1979, FMP 0640). However, he also recorded in duos with Keith Tippett (1985), Tom Cora (1988), Fred Frith (1990–91), and Rüdiger Carl (1994, 1997), as a member of the September Band, with Carl, Shelley Hirsch, and Paul Lovens (1994), and with Butch Morris's Conduction Orchestra (1994). An inventor of instruments, Reichel has developed his own double-necked guitar and a percussion instrument, the Daxophone (originally called a dachsophon). Some of his unaccompanied solo performances on this instrument may be heard on *The Dawn of Dachsmann (Plus)* (1987, FMP CD60).

BIBLIOGRAPHY

GrayF
"Hans Reichel," *JP*, xxi/4 (1972), 114
D. H. Fröse: "Schnapsglas in der Hand: Gitarrist Hans Reichel," *JP*, xxii/2 (1973), 22
G. Rouy: "Hans Reichel ou les mains libres," *Jm*, no.253 (1977), 21
J. Buzelin and F. Buzelin: "Hans Reichel, Rüdiger Carl: deux nouvelles voix de la N.M.E.," *Jh*, no.359 (1979), 22
A. Dutilh: "Hans Reichel, Peter Kowald: pas de conversation," *Jh*, no.368 (1979–80), 51
M. Dery: "Forging a New Guitar Vocabulary: Peter Cusack, Hans Reichel, David Fulton, Davey Williams," *GP*, xxii/7 (1988), 52
C. Blackford: "Hans Reichel: Born to be Mild," *Rubberneck*, no.6 (1994), 4
B. Hopkin: *Gravikords, Whirlies & Pyrophones* (New York, 1996)

<http://www.shef.ac.uk/misc/rec/ps/efi/idax.html> (1999) [daxophone]
<http://www.shef.ac.uk.misc/rec/ps/efi/mreichel.html> (1999) [incl. discography]

SIMON ADAMS

Reichenbach, Bill [William Frank] **(i)** (*b* Washington, DC, 18 Dec 1923). Drummer, father of Bill Reichenbach (ii). He played in dance bands while in the armed forces during World War II and then worked in Tommy Dorsey's orchestra (1951). Later he accompanied the singer Georgia Gibbs (1958–9). From 1962 to 1973 he was a member of Charlie Byrd's trio, and he played with Byrd and Stan Getz on the album *Jazz Samba* (1962, Verve 68432). Reichenbach worked from 1976 as a freelance with Teddy Wilson, Hank Jones, Urbie Green, and Eddie "Lockjaw" Davis, and in 1984 he performed in New Zealand with his son. (*Feather '60s*)

Reichenbach, Bill [William Frank] **(ii)** (*b* Takoma Park, MD, 30 Nov 1949). Trombonist, son of Bill Reichenbach (i). After studying at the Eastman School (BMus 1971) he recorded as a sideman in big bands led by Buddy Rich (1972), Toshiko Akiyoshi and Lew Tabackin (1976–7), and Tom Scott (1983), among others, and in Don Menza's septet (1979). In 1980 he joined Bobby Shew's small group, with which he recorded in 1982–3. In addition he led his own bop group on the album *Quartet* (1984, Silver Seven 701) and made annual tours of New Zealand (1982–5). Reichenbach continued to record in studio big bands, and at one such session in 1987 he played bass trombone under Gene Harris's direction. Based in California, he worked extensively in television and films and collaborated with popular groups and commercial artists. He also plays euphonium.

Rufus Reid in Richmond, Surrey, England, 1996

Reid, Rufus (Lamar) (*b* Atlanta, GA, 10 Feb 1944). Double bass player and leader. His family moved to Sacramento, California, when he was about six years old; all his older siblings played instruments or sang, and both his parents played piano – his father semiprofessionally and his mother in church. Reid started on french horn and mellophone and played trumpet through his junior high school and high school years. Having joined a US Air Force band as a trumpeter he changed to double bass in 1961, at the age of 17; while stationed in Japan (1964–6) he had his first formal double bass lessons with a former member of the Tokyo Symphony Orchestra. Following his discharge he returned to Sacramento and held his first job as a jazz bass player, performing for two weeks with Buddy Montgomery and Eddie Moore. Late in 1966 he moved to Seattle to study music privately and at Olympic College (AA 1969). He continued his education at Northwestern University in Evanston, Illinois (BM 1971), and then lived in Chicago, where for about five years he served as the house bass player at Joe Segal's Jazz Showcase; in this capacity he played hard bop with Sonny Stitt, James Moody, Milt Jackson, Curtis Fuller, and Dizzy Gillespie. While in Chicago he also performed and recorded with Kenny Dorham, Dexter Gordon, Lee Konitz, and Howard McGhee (all 1970). Later he made a number of international tours, with the quintet led by Bobby Hutcherson and Harold Land (1971), with Freddie Hubbard and Nancy Wilson (1971), and with Eddie Harris (1971–4).

After moving to New York (summer 1976) Reid played and recorded with the quartet and orchestra led by Thad Jones and Mel Lewis (1976–7); he ended this association to tour internationally with Gordon (1977–9). In addition he made recordings with Konitz (1976), John McNeil (1978, 1981), Henry Threadgill and Helen Merrill (both 1979), Bob Brookmeyer (with Lewis's orchestra, 1980), Billy Mitchell (1980), Al Dailey (1981), Ricky Ford (1981, 1984), Hal Galper (1982), and Jack DeJohnette's group Special Edition (1982, 1984), in duos with Harold Danko (1982) and Kenny Burrell (1983), with a quintet led by Frank Foster and Frank Wess (1983–4), and with Joe Newman and Joe Wilder, John Stubblefield, Kenny Barron, and Art Farmer (all 1984), and Anthony Braxton, Frank Gordon, Jimmy Heath, Ralph Moore, and James Williams (all 1985). Later he toured with Stan Getz (1987), performed and recorded with J. J. Johnson (1988), and toured in an all-star group alongside Gillespie, Steve Turre, Phil Woods, Cedar Walton, Hutcherson, and Mickey Roker (*c*1989). Among his studio engagements during the latter half of the 1980s were sessions with Konitz (1986), Andrew Hill (1986, 1989), Ray Bryant and Farmer (both 1987–9), Hutcherson, Geoff Keezer, Barney Kessel, Bob Mover, and Rob Schneiderman (all 1988), Carol Sloane (1988, 1990), and Bob Rockwell, Ed Thigpen, and Mickey Tucker (all 1989).

From 1990 Reid's principal association in performance was as co-leader with AKIRA TANA of the quintet TanaReid. He appeared at festivals and played with Benny Green in Chicago (1999), and continued to work as a freelance soloist, recording with Harold Ashby, Meredith D'Ambrosio, Eddie

Higgins, Kirk Lightsey, and Michele Rosewoman (all 1990), Sumi Tonooka (1990–91), Nick Brignola (1990, 1996), Greg Abate, Jesse Davis, and Tete Montoliu (all 1991), Allen Farnham and Dave Liebman (both 1992), Jane Ira Bloom (1992, 1995), Alvin Batiste (*c*1993), the pianist Reuben Brown and Mel Martin (both 1994), Peter Leitch (1995), Conrad Herwig (1996), and Joe Locke (1996, 1998). In 1997 he recorded in a duo and made a video with Michael Moore (i). Reid recorded further as a sideman with Barron, Farmer, Johnson, Sloane, and, notably, Schneiderman, whose trio album of 1992 is filled with wonderful examples of the double bass player's style; he performs with a consistently rich tone and creates tuneful solos, in which he plays arco as well as pizzicato. He taught jazz at William Paterson College in Wayne, New Jersey (1979–99), and published two method books, *The Evolving Bassist* (1974) and *Evolving Upward: Bass Book II* (1977).

SELECTED RECORDINGS

Duos: with H. Danko: *Mirth Song* (1982, Sunnyside 1001); with M. Moore: *Doublebass Delights* (1997, Double-Time 117)

As leader: *Perpetual Stroll* (1980, The. 111); *Seven Minds* (1984, Sunnyside 1010)

As sideman: J. DeJohnette: *Album Album* (1984, ECM 1280); F. Foster and F. Wess: *Frankly Speaking* (1984, Conc. 276); A. Hill: *Shades* (1986, SN 1113), incl. Bell Square; A. Farmer: *Something to Live for: the Music of Billy Strayhorn* (1987, Cont. 14029); S. Getz: *Anniversary* (1987, EmA 38769-2); J. J. Johnson: *Quintergy: Live at the Village Vanguard* (1988, Ant. 422-848214-2), incl. Bud's Blues [duo with Johnson]; *Standards: Live at the Village Vanguard* (1988, Ant. 314-510059-2), incl. You stepped out of a dream; A. Hill: *Eternal Spirit* (1989, BN B21S-92051); C. Sloane: *The Real Thing* (1990, Cont. 14060); K. Barron: *The Moment* (1991, Reservoir 121); A. Farnham: *Play-cation* (1992, Conc. 4521), incl. Play-cation; J. I. Bloom: *Art and Aviation* (1992, Arabesque 0107), incl. Most Distant Galaxy; R. Schneiderman: *Standards* (1992, Reservoir 126)

SELECTED FILMS AND VIDEOS

Jazz in Exile (1978); Stan Getz: Live in Europe (1986); Great Performances: Wolf Trap Salutes Dizzy Gillespie: an All-Star Tribute to the Jazz Master (1988); Dexter Gordon, i (*c*1993 [filmed 1979]); Dexter Gordon, ii (*c*1994 [filmed 1979]); Bass Day with Rufus Reid and Michael Moore (n.d.)

BIBLIOGRAPHY

E. Jost: *Jazzmusiker: Materialen zur Soziologie der afro-amerikanischen Musik* (Frankfurt am Main, Germany, Berlin, and Vienna, 1981), 240

L. Gourse: "Rufus Reid, the Evolving Bassist," *JT* (1986), June, 15

S. H. Thompson: "Rufus Reid," *JT*, xxi/2 (1991), 20

J. L. Lieberman: "Rufus Reid: Tasting Each Note," *Strings*, vi/4 (1992), 13

"Talking with Rufus Reid," *The Note*, v/2 (1993), 8

L. Fischer and J. B. Bradley: "Rufus Reid: at the Pinnacle of Jazz," *The Instrumentalist*, xlix/8 (1995), 32

C. Jisi: "Meet the Advisory Board: Rufus Reid," *Bass Player*, vii/7 (1996), 26

A. Lewis and L. Lewis: "Rufus Reid: Interview," *Cadence*, xxii/11 (1996), 5

E. Holley: "Riffs: TanaReid/Hal Galper Double Tour Takes Educational Slant," *DB*, lxiv/2 (1997), 12

J. Goldsby: "Rufus Reid: Still Evolving," *Bass Player*, x/3 (1999), 50

<http://www.jazzcorner.com/reid/reidhome.html> (2000) [incl. discography]

For recordings as leader of TanaReid and further bibliography *see* Tana, Akira.

BK

Reig, Teddy [Theodore Samuel] (*b* New York, 23 Nov 1918; *d* Teaneck, NJ, 29 Sept 1984). Record producer. He grew up in Harlem, where his father ran a candy store. In the early 1940s Reig organized Sunday-afternoon jam sessions at the mid-town club Kelly's Stable. His first work as a record producer was for Continental in January 1945, and shortly afterwards he began working for Savoy, most notably on Charlie Parker's sessions as a leader. Around 1949 he became Paul Williams's manager, and later that year he was dismissed by Savoy; however, he was re-engaged, and he remained with the label through 1952. Around 1950, with Ralph Watkins, Monte Kay, and Symphony Sid, Reig founded the record company and label Royal Roost (ii). From around 1957 he worked as a promoter for rock-and-roll and rhythm-and-blues artists and as a record producer for Roulette, where he began a decade-long association with Count Basie. Reig worked for Verve from *c*1966 to 1970, and he produced his last session in 1976.

Reig's autobiography, *Reminiscing in Tempo: the Life and Times of a Jazz Hustler* (written in collaboration with E. Berger; Metuchen, NJ, and London, 1990), provides an engaging and, at times, funny look into his life. He deserves credit for his involvement in and support of bop in the mid-1940s and for his work at trying to ensure equal treatment of African-American musicians in union locals. A volatile personality, he was passionate, often to the point of excess, and candid about his beliefs and his life.

GK

Reijseger, Ernst (*b* Nardes, Netherlands, 13 Nov 1954). Dutch cellist. His mother was a pianist. He played recorder until the age of 16 and then studied classical cello at a conservatory; he left in 1972 at the advice of his teacher to focus on improvised music. Shortly afterwards he began performing: he played with Han Bennink around 1977 and with Michael Moore (ii) and Michael Vatcher in the trio Nomofo in the late 1970s. In February 1984 he recorded with Phil Minton and Tony Oxley, and from the mid-1980s he was a regular member of Gerry Hemingway's quintet; from 1989 he worked in a trio with Hemingway and Georg Gräwe. In 1987 he formed a trio with Gianni Gebbia and Pino Minafra, and the following year he performed alongside Willem Breuker in Bennink's trio at the Total Music Meeting in Berlin. Reijseger also worked with Moore and Bennink in the cooperative group Clusone 3 (from 1988), in Andy Sheppard's big band Soft on the Inside (from 1989), and in Sheppard's quartet (with Nana Vasconcelos and Orphy Robinson, 1990); he may be seen performing with Sheppard in the video *Soft on the Inside* (1990). In 1990 he also worked in the quartet MSRW with Albert Mangelsdorff, Bruno Spoerri, and Reto Weber. In addition he performed with Mario Schiano (recording in 1991 and 1995) and as a member of Misha Mengelberg's ICP Orchestra. In 1992 he replaced Hank Roberts in Arcado, and he made his first appearance with the group at the Festival International de Jazz de Montréal. In the same year he began working in a duo with Louis Sclavis, with whom he recorded in 1994 and performed at the Festival International Musique Actuelle Victoriaville in 1996, and from the mid-1990s he performed in Ettore Fioravanti's trio Belcanto. Reijseger recorded in a quintet with Mengelberg, Steve Lacy, George Lewis (ii), and Bennink (1987), with Curtis Clark (1984–8), in performance with Pino Minafra and Bennink (1990), and with Trilok Gurtu (1993).

SELECTED RECORDINGS

As unaccompanied soloist: on M. Schiano: *And so on* (1991, Splasc(h) 368), Rubber Necking; *Colla parta* (1997, Winter & Winter 910012-2)

Duos with L. Sclavis: *Et on ne parle pas du temps* (1994, FMP CD66)

As leader with G. Gräwe and G. Hemingway: *Sonic Fiction* (1989, HA 6043); *Flex 27* (1993, Random Acoustics 007); *Saturn Cycle* (1994, Music & Arts 958)

As sideman with G. Hemingway: *Outerbridge Crossing* (1985, Sound Aspects 017); *Demon Chaser* (1993, HA 6137); *The Marmalade King* (1994, HA 6164); *Perfect World* (1995, Random Acoustics 019)

As sideman with others: C. Clark: *Letter to South Africa* (*c*1987, Nimbus 501C), incl. Circumstantial Blues; M. Schiano: *Used to be Friends* (1995, Splasc(h) 452)

For further recordings *see* Arcado and Clusone 3.

BIBLIOGRAPHY

J. Böbers: "Georg Graewe/Ernst Reijseger/Gerry Hemingway," *JP*, xxxix/6 (1990), 27
B. Noglik: "Musikalische Assoziationen zu Bix Beiderbecke: das Lächeln der Legende (Wiener Musik Galerie)," *JP*, xxxix/1 (1990), 22
C. Woerner: "Der kleine Bass ganz gross: Esslinger Cello Projekt," *JP*, xxxix/4 (1990), 45
H. Kumpf: "Bennink/Moore/Reijseger," *JP*, xl/6 (1991), 32
F. van Rossum: "Ernst Reijseger: 'Improvisation is Good, Intelligent Conversation'," *Key Notes*, xxvii/1 (1993), 8
K. Whitehead: "Info: Jazz for a Weill: the Dutch Improvising Scene Revisited," *Ear*, xv/9 (1994), 16
B. Rusch: "Ernst Reijseger: Interview," *Cadence*, xxiv/1 (1998), 9
K. Whitehead: *New Dutch Swing* (New York, 1998)

GK

Reilly, Dean (Edwin) (*b* Auburn, WA, 30 June 1926). Double bass player. From 1948 to 1950 he studied music at the College of Puget Sound in Washington. He then moved to California and played swing and bop in San Francisco with Georgie Auld, Sonny Criss, and Jackie Cain and Roy Kral, performed and made recordings with Earl Hines (notably the album *Earl "Fatha" Hines Plays "Fats" Waller*, 1955–6, Fan. 3217), Vince Guaraldi (1956–7), and Eddie Duran (1957), and recorded with Mel Lewis (1956). Following a lengthy association with the folk-revival group the Kingston Trio, Reilly resumed playing jazz and recorded with George Barnes (1977), Duran (1979), Cal Tjader (1981), and the singer Dee Bell (as a member of an orchestra led by Duran and Stan Getz, 1982, 1984). *(FeatherE)*

Reilly, Jack [Petrahn, Sean] (*b* New York, 1 Jan 1932). Pianist and educator. His mother was a concert pianist and piano teacher. He learned classical piano from the ages of seven to 16 and then took up jazz. After a brief period at Brooklyn College he attended the Manhattan School of Music (BMus *c*1950), and from the early 1950s he studied with Lennie Tristano, Hall Overton, and George Russell. He served in a navy band in Puerto Rico (*c*1951–4), then returned to New York, where he undertook graduate work at the Manhattan School of Music and played with the clarinetist Jerry Wald and Warren Covington and his Commanders, among others. In July 1958 he performed at the Newport Jazz Festival with John LaPorta, and in December of that same year he recorded with the saxophonist. In 1966 he traveled to California to study Indian music. Having returned to New York in the late 1960s, he accompanied singers at a club in Greenwich Village. In 1968 he composed and performed a *Requiem Mass for Chorus and Jazz Quartet* with the tenor saxophonist Norman Marnell, Jack Six, and the drummer Jack Cocuzzo as his sidemen; Sheila Jordan also took part. In 1971 Reilly was artist-in-residence at the Molde Music School in Norway and toured that country with Ben Webster's quartet and as a classical soloist. He toured Europe in 1982 with Russell's New York Band, with which he appeared at the Village Vanguard and recorded in July of that year. Reilly may be seen performing as an unaccompanied soloist in the video *Here's What I Like* (*c*1991 [filmed 1990]). In 1995 he played at the Guinness Cork Jazz Festival.

Reilly established a jazz curriculum at the Mannes School of Music, New York, in the mid-1970s. While teaching jazz at the New School for Social Research, in 1982 he was appointed chair of the jazz studies department at the New England Conservatory. He wrote liner notes under the pseudonym Sean Petrahn, contributed articles to the periodicals *Keyboard Classics & Piano Stylist* (1994) and *Piano Today* (1996), and published an instructional book, *The Harmony of Bill Evans*, and the series *Species Blues: a Beginning Method for Jazz Piano* – the first volumes of which covered blues form, the song form, and free form, respectively.

SELECTED RECORDINGS

As unaccompanied soloist: *The Brinksman* (1981, Rev. 36)
Duos with J. Maneri: on *Masks* (1968–95, Unichrom 9001), The Conversation, Tandemonium (1989)
As leader: *Blue-Sean-Green* (1968, Carousel 1001); *November* (1981, Rev. 41)

BIBLIOGRAPHY

A. J. Smith: "Profile: Jack Reilly," *DB*, xlii/11 (1975), 30
"You Should Know: NEC Appoints Jack Reilly," *Jazz Educators Journal*, xv/1 (1982), 53
P. Hawes: "Jack Reilly," *JJI*, xlix/9 (1996), 6

GK

Reinhardt. Family of musicians.

(1) Django Reinhardt [Jean-Baptiste] (*b* Liberchies, nr Luttre, Belgium, 23 Jan 1910; *d* Fontainebleau, France, 16 May 1953). French guitarist, brother of (2) Joseph Reinhardt and father of (3) Babik Reinhardt. The son of a traveling entertainer, he grew up in a gypsy settlement outside Paris. He first played violin and later took up guitar, and began working professionally in 1922 with the accordionist Guérino. In 1928 he was badly burned in a caravan fire; the resulting mutilation of his left hand, which deprived him of the use of two fingers, led him to devise a unique fingering method to overcome his handicap. After a period of convalescence he worked in cafés in Paris and in a duo with the singer Jean Sablon. In 1934 he was a founding member, with Stephane Grappelli, of the ensemble that became known as the Quintette du Hot Club de France; in the years before World War II the group gained considerable renown through its numerous recordings, and Reinhardt became an international celebrity. He appeared throughout Europe and recorded with many important American musicians who

Django Reinhardt with the clarinetist Maurice Meunier, Bad Nauheim, Germany, 27 July 1947

visited the Continent, including Coleman Hawkins, Benny Carter, Bill Coleman, Rex Stewart, and Arthur Briggs. The Quintette's London visit of August–September 1939 was aborted by war, and Reinhardt returned to Paris to lead a group that included Alix Combelle and Charlie Lewis.

During the war, while Grappelli lived in Britain, Reinhardt remained in France. From autumn 1940 he achieved considerable success as the leader of a new quintet in which the clarinetist Hubert Rostaing took Grappelli's place. He formed a big band in autumn 1941, then returned to the quintet format early the following year. He also became interested in composition and, with André Hodeir, arranged the music for the film *Le village de la colère* (1946). In 1946 he visited England and Switzerland in a reunion with Grappelli, toured the USA as a soloist with Duke Ellington's band (playing an amplified guitar for the first time), and worked in New York. After his return to France in February 1947 he toured and recorded with his quintet, which sometimes again included Grappelli. In 1949 he resumed his gypsy life and from 1951 lived in Samois.

Reinhardt's grasp of harmony, remarkable technique, and trenchant rhythmic sense made him an excellent accompanist; his incisive support is heard to advantage on *Stardust* (1935), recorded with Coleman Hawkins. He later developed into a soloist of unique character, creating a deeply personal style out of his own cultural patrimony. By 1937, when he recorded *Chicago* with the Quintette, he was established as the first outstanding European jazz musician, a stylist with great melodic resourcefulness and a mastery of inflection. He was a gifted composer of short evocative pieces and had a flair for pacing a performance so that the maximum variety could be wrung from it without compromising its homogeneity; an excellent example is *St. Louis Blues* (1937). Endowed with remarkable sensitivity, he could work with visiting American performers without forsaking his own essentially romantic style. In the late 1940s he changed to the electric guitar, but without coarsening his playing, as he used its power with discretion. The rhythmic content of his work became more varied, as in *Minor Swing* (1947), and his improvised lines more flexible. The asymmetrical, occasionally violent playing heard in some later performances shows the continual widening of his expressive scope. A documentary film, *Django Reinhardt* (1958), was made after his death by the director Paul Paviot; it includes an introduction by Jean Cocteau, and music performed by Grappelli, Rostaing, and Joseph Reinhardt. Reinhardt's impact on guitarists is the subject of a later film documentary, *Django Legacy* (n.d.).

See also Guitar, §2, and fig.1; Jazz (i), fig.4; and String band.

SELECTED RECORDINGS

As unaccompanied soloist: Improvisation (1937, HMV B8587)

As leader with S. Grappelli of the Quintette du Hot Club de France: Lady be Good (1934, Ultraphone 1422); Confessin' (1935, Ultraphone 1443); Djangology (1935, Ultraphone 1548); Limehouse Blues (1936, HMV K7706); Tears (1937, HMV B8718); Chicago (1937, Swing 2); The Sheik of Araby (1937, HMV B8737); Montmartre/Solid Old Man (1939, Swing 56); Low Cotton (1939, Swing 203); Finesse (1939, Swing 70); Nuages (1940, Swing 88)

As leader of other groups: St. Louis Blues (1937, Swing 7); Eclats de cuivres (1942, Rythme 5024); For Sentimental Reasons (1947, BStar 30); September Song (1947, BStar 46); Nuages (1947, Swing 438); Minor Swing/Douce ambiance (1947, Swing 439); *Django Reinhardt et ses rythmes* (1953, BStar 6830), incl. Insensiblement, Manoir de mes rêves; I Cover the Waterfront (1953, Decca MF36166)

As sideman: C. Hawkins: Stardust (1935, HMV K7527); Honeysuckle Rose/Crazy Rhythm (1937, Swing 1); S. Grappelli: Sugar (1937, Swing 69); R. Stewart: Montmartre (1939, Swing 56); D. Ellington: on *Chicago Civic Opera House Concert* (1946, Prima 01-02), Blues, Honeysuckle Rose, Ride, Red, Ride

TRANSCRIPTIONS

A Treasury of Django Reinhardt Guitar Solos (New York, *c*1967/*R c*1992)
S. Averoff, ed.: *Django Reinhardt* (New York, *c*1978)
Django Reinhardt (Boston, n.d. [?late 1970s])
The Genius of Django Reinhardt (New York, n.d. [?late 1970s])
Jazz Masters: Django Reinhardt (New York, n.d. [?late 1970s])
M. Peters: *Django Reinhardt Anthology* (New York, 1984)

BIBLIOGRAPHY

BallietA (1986); *BallietA (1996)*; *SchullerS*
H. Panassié: *Douze années de jazz (1927–1938): souvenirs* (Paris, 1946), 139, 189
C. Delaunay: *Django Reinhardt: souvenirs* (Paris, 1954; Eng. trans., London, 1961, rev. 2/1981/*R*1993) [incl. discography]
G. S. McKean: "Django Reinhardt," *Jam Session: an Anthology of Jazz*, ed. R. J. Gleason (New York and London, 1958), 111
M.-C. Jalard: "Django et l'école tsigane du jazz," *Cahiers du jazz*, no.1 (1959), 54
D. Schulz-Köhn: *Django Reinhardt: ein Porträt* (Wetzlar, Germany, 1960)
A. Hodeir: *Toward Jazz* (New York, 1962/*R*1976), 186
J. J. Gaspard: "Un Blues gitan," *Jh*, no.187 (1963), 22
G. Hoefer: "The Magnificent Gypsy," *DB*, xxxiii/14 (1966), 21
C. Delaunay: *Django, mon frère* (Paris, 1968)
C. Evans: "Django Reinhardt," *JM*, no.162 (1968), 30; no.163 (1968), 31
A. Morgan: "Django Reinhardt," in A. McCarthy and others: *Jazz on Record: a Critical Guide to the First 50 Years: 1917–1967* (London, 1968), 241
——: "Collectors' Notes: Django Reinhardt," *JM*, no.171 (1969), 26; no.178 (1969), 28; no.180 (1970), 29
"'Django and I Had the First Three-guitar Group – without Electricity!,' Says Jazz Violin Virtuoso Stephane Grappelli," *CI*, ix/4 (1970), 26
C. N. Cooper: "Djangologie: an Examination of a Monument to a Jazz Master," *JJ*, xxiv/6 (1971), 10
M. Abrams: *The Book of Django* (Los Angeles, 1973) [bio-discography]
D. E. Hensley: "Remembering Django Reinhardt," *DB*, xliii/4 (1976), 15
M. Abrams: "Django Reinhardt: the Jazz Gypsy," *Sv*, no.77 (1978), 163
I. Cruickshank: *The Guitar Style of Django Reinhardt and the Gypsies* (Woodcote, nr Reading, England, 1982, rev. and enlarged 2/1985)
N. Mongan: *The History of the Guitar in Jazz* (New York, London, and Sydney, 1983) [incl. transcrs. and discography], 47
R. Spautz: *Django Reinhardt: Mythos und Realität* (Luxemburg, 1983) [incl. discography]
A. Doutart: "Django Reinhardt, mythes ou réalité?," *BHcF*, no.322 (1984), 8
A. Schmitz and P. Maier: *Django Reinhardt: sein Leben, seine Musik, seine Schallplatten* (Gauting, Germany, 1985)
M. Zwerin: *La tristesse de Saint Louis: Swing under the Nazis* (London, Melbourne, Australia, and New York, 1985)
The Complete Django Reinhardt Discography (New York, 1988)
Etudes tziganes, iii/4 (1989) [special Reinhardt issue]
R. Stewart and C. P. Gordon: *Boy Meets Horn* (Wheatley, Oxford, England, and Ann Arbor, MI, 1991), 185
P. Williams: *Django* (Montpellier, France, 1991, 2/1998) [incl. discography]
F. Billard and A. Antonietto: *Django Reinhardt: un géant sur son nuage* (Paris, 1993)
I. Cruickshank, ed.: *Django's Gypsies: the Mystique of Django Reinhardt and his People* (Newcastle upon Tyne, England, 1994)
J. Ferguson: "Django Reinhardt: the Magic beyond the Mystique," *GP*, xxviii/5 (1994), 64
P. du Petit and J. Ody: *Django Reinhardt* (Paris, 1997)
T. Cherrett, comp.: *The Genius that was Django* (Addlestone, England, 1998)
<http://members.tripod.com/~Marc_Masselin/index.html> (2000)
<http://nordi.no/music/hcr/arch3.html> (2000)
<http://pages.infinit.net/reinhard/DiscoContent.htm> (2000)
<http://www.egroups.com/group/gypsyjazzguitar> (2000)
<http://www.hotclub.co.uk/> (2000)
<http://www.multimania.com/gadjodrom/> (2000)

(2) Joseph Reinhardt [Nin Nin] (*b* Paris, 1 March 1912; *d* Paris, late February 1982). French guitarist, brother of (1) Django Reinhardt. As a member of the Quintette du Hot Club de France he accompanied his brother (whose chaotic life he helped to organize, insofar as that was possible) and made many recordings, but he never recorded a solo. Independently of Django he recorded in a small group led by Bill Coleman (1937) and joined the big band of Aimé Barelli and Alix Combelle's group Jazz de Paris. In 1943 he formed a group with André Hodeir, who was at the time playing as a violinist under the pseudonym Claude Laurence. After his brother's death in 1953 Reinhardt led a quintet, made several recordings, and appeared in three films.

For illustrations *see* GUITAR, fig.1, and JAZZ (i), fig.4.

SELECTED RECORDINGS

As leader: Un peu de rêve (1943, Decca 9133); Mon pote, le gitan (1959, Decca 450891); *Live in Paris* (1966, Hot Club 66); *Joseph Reinhardt joue pour Django* (1966–7, Simm 192)

SELECTED FILMS AND VIDEOS

Mon pote, le gitan (1958); Django Reinhardt (1958); Paris Blues (1961)

BIBLIOGRAPHY

M.-C. Jalard: "Django et l'école tsigane du jazz," *Cahiers du jazz*, no.1 (1959), 54

A. Antonietto: Liner notes, *Live in Paris* (Hot Club 66, 1992)

(3) Babik [Jean-Jacques] **Reinhardt** (*b* Paris, 8 June 1944). French guitarist, composer, and leader, son of (1) Django Reinhardt. His father put his first guitar into his hands when he was three, but he did not truly study with his fellow gypsies until around the age of 15, after his father's death. He was at first diffident about a professional career, though he worked with Jean-Luc Ponty in 1965, recorded two albums for Vogue in 1967, and evinced a passing interest in fusion and then in Brazilian music. After recording an album in homage to his father in 1974 he left music and did not return to it until the 1980s, when he played alongside Didier Lockwood, Stephane Grappelli, Larry Coryell, and others. In 1986 he founded, with Boulou Ferré and Christian Escoudé, the Trio Gitan, which appeared at many concerts and festivals, and in 1987 he formed a duo with Bireli Lagrene which performed at the festival in Freiburg. In the 1990s he wrote music for films (including *Pour le prix du silence* and *Mohamed Bertrand Duval*) and formed several small groups to perform his compositions. Despite Reinhardt's overt desire to escape the influence of his illustrious father, his writing at times expresses a romanticism and melodic verve which evokes the work of the elder man.

SELECTED RECORDINGS

Babik Reinhardt joue Sidney Bechet (1967, Vogue 213); *All Love* (1987, RDC 40001); *Live* (1989, RDC 40003); *Nuances* (1992, RDC 40018); *Vibration* (1995, RDC 40045)

BIBLIOGRAPHY

L. Sorano: "Babik Reinhardt: le troisième souffle," *Jazz Swing Journal*, no.13 (1990), 16

M. van Broekhoven: "Babik Reinhardt: un prénom qui vaut un nom," *Jh*, no.472 (1990), 18

G. Litterst: "Django's Erben: Zigeuner-Musik zwischen Traditionspflege und Fortentwicklung," *JP*, xl/2 (1991), 8

M. Maestracci: "Au nom du fils: Babik Reinhardt," *Jh*, no.541 (1997), 38

MICHAEL JAMES/HOWARD RYE, BK(1), ANDRÉ CLERGEAT (2–3)

Reis Leite, Tania Maria. *See* MARIA, TANIA.

Rek, Vitold (*b* Rzeszów, Poland, 18 Oct 1955). Polish double bass player. He grew up in a musical family, took up accordion at the age of eight, and changed to classical guitar and then to double bass when he was 14; he began to work professionally a year later, first in a folk-dance and -music group and later with his own jazz band. While playing in a local dixieland band he studied classical music at the music school in Kraków (1973–7) and at the city's conservatory (1977–82). Rek worked with Jan Wróblewski, Vładysław Sendecki's Sun Ship (1977–80), Sławomir Kulpowicz (1979–84), the band Basspace (1983–87), and Tomasz Stańko's Freelectronic (1982–90). In 1989 he moved to Germany and became in demand as a player in the Frankfurt area. He was a member of Peter Giger's Family of Percussion (1989–93) and formed a duo with John Tchicai (1989), with whom he recorded *Satisfaction* (1991, Enja 7033-2). Later he played with Karl Berger (from 1993), the pianist Elvira Plenar (with whom he recorded the album *Elvira Plenar–Vitold Rek* (1993, L+R 45089), and the Ralf Hübner–Christof Lauer Project (from 1994), led his own band East West Wind (from 1997), and performed as an unaccompanied soloist (heard on *Bassfiddle alla polacca*, *c*1998, Taso 503). Rek often makes use in his work of folk melodies and compositions from his native Poland, and he has a very melodic style. He has written music for film and the theater and has been active as a teacher.

BIBLIOGRAPHY

M. Gammel: "Vitold Rek: the Bass is the Base," *JP*, xlv/7–8 (1996), 36

<http://ourworld.compuserve.com/homepages/VITOLDREK/biograph.html> (1999)

WOLFRAM KNAUER

Release. The penultimate section in the refrain of a popular song, leading to the final repeat of the opening section (section *b* in the form *aaba*); it provides a contrast, often tonal as well as harmonic and melodic, with the opening section. *See* FORMS, esp. §1(i)(a).

Reliance Brass Band. New Orleans group formed during the 1890s by PAPA JACK LAINE.

Remler, Emily (*b* New York, 18 Sept 1957; *d* Sydney, Australia, 3 or 4 May 1990). Guitarist. She played guitar from the age of ten and was inspired first by the work of the rock guitarists Jimi Hendrix and Johnny Winter and later, while attending the Berklee College of Music, by that of the jazz guitarists Wes Montgomery, Pat Martino, and Charlie Christian. After graduating (at the age of 18) she moved to New Orleans, where as the house guitarist at the Fairmont Hotel she accompanied Nancy Wilson, Michel Legrand, and the popular singer Robert Goulet. Her career was aided by Herb Ellis, who introduced her at the Concord (California) Jazz Festival in 1978. During the following years she played with Astrud Gilberto (for three years in the early 1980s), appeared in David Friedman's quintet at the Jazzfest Berlin (1982), and spent three months in the orchestra for the musical *Sophisticated Ladies* in Los Angeles (1982). She also appeared with the group Great Guitars (with Ellis, Barney Kessel, and Charlie Byrd), performed with Hank Jones and Billy Cobham, led a quartet with John D'Earth, Eddie Gomez, and Bob Moses, and recorded an album of duos with Larry Coryell (1985), with whom she worked for about two years. She had been a member of Monty Alexander's group in the early 1980s, and married him in 1982, but they divorced in 1985. She moved to New York, and that year toured Europe with Richie Cole. She also toured the USA and Japan as an accompanist to Rosemary Clooney, and in October 1988 she led a quartet consisting of Fred Hersch, Lynn Seaton, and Terry Clarke at the Blue Note. In 1989 she toured and recorded with David Benoit, played with Ellis, and appeared at the Festival International du Jazz Antibes–Juan-les-Pins.

Remler's life was troubled by the consequences of heroin addiction, and in 1990, while touring Australia, she died of a heart attack late at night on 3 May or in the early hours of 4 May; she was found dead in bed that morning. Nearly all of her recordings were for Concord, either under her own name or with the Clayton brothers (1980), Ray Brown (1984), Clooney and Johnny Coliani (both 1986), and Susannah McCorkle (1988, 1990); she also recorded with Cole and Hank Crawford (for Milestone, 1987), Chris Hunter (for Paddle Wheel, 1988), and Benoit (for GRP, 1989). Remler was equally adept at playing with and without a pick in such diverse styles as bop, jazz-rock, and Latin music; her playing incorporated fluid eighth-note passages, doublings at the octave in the manner of Montgomery, and blues phrasing. She may be seen in the instructional videos *Advanced Jazz and Latin Improvisation with Emily Remler* and *Bebop and Swing Guitar with Emily Remler* (both 1986).

SELECTED RECORDINGS

(all recorded for Concord)

Duos with L. Coryell: *Together* (1985, 289)
As leader: *The Firefly* (1981, 162); *Take Two* (1982, 195); *Transitions* (1983, 236); *Catwalk* (1984, 265); *East to Wes* (1988, 356)

BIBLIOGRAPHY

A. Berle: "A Jazz Guitarist's Promising Debut," *GP*, xv/9 (1981), 100
A. J. Liska: "Profile: Emily Remler," *DB*, xlix/5 (1982), 49
J. Coryell: "Emily Remler: Life after Wes," *DB*, lii/5 (1985), 23 [incl. discography]
L. Gourse: "Emily Remler," *JT* (1988), Dec, 6
M. Richards: "Emily Remler," *JJI*, xli/3 (1988), 8
Obituaries: *Los Angeles Times* (7 May 1990); *New York Times* (8 May 1990)
G. Lees: *Waiting for Dizzy* (New York, and Oxford, England, 1991), 130

JIM FERGUSON/BK

Remue, Chas [Charles Achille] (*b* Brussels, 15 Oct 1903; *d* Brussels, 5 Feb 1971). Belgian alto saxophonist and clarinetist. A classically trained musician, he played in 1924 with Red Mill's Jazz and with the Bing Boys. He was a member of the White Diamonds, led by the drummer Billy Smith, and of the Royal Dance Orchestra (1926–7), after which he formed a band that recorded several tracks in London as the New Stompers Orchestra (June 1927), including *Doctor Jazz* (Edison Bell E1-0163); these were the first jazz recordings made by a group consisting entirely of Belgian musicians. At the suggestion of Frank Guarente, Remue joined the Savoy Orpheans (December 1927), then formed his own big band (recording in 1929) and worked with Bernard Etté. He joined the orchestra led by Stan Brenders in 1936 and continued to work with various groups until his death.

BIBLIOGRAPHY

R. Pernet: "The Pioneers of Jazz in Belgium, no.1: Chas. Remue," *JM*, xiii/1 (1967), 2; Fr. trans. in *Pj*, no.3 (1970), 35 [incl. discography]
——: *Belgian Jazz Discography (1897–1999)* (Brussels, 1999)

ROBERT PERNET

Remus, Alfredo (*b* Buenos Aires, 9 Nov 1938). Argentine double bass player. He made recordings with Lalo Schifrin (1957, 1970) and Enrique Villegas (1968, both in a duo and in a quintet with the visiting Americans Willie Cook and Paul Gonsalves), as a leader (1968, 1970, 1972), with Jorge López Ruiz (1971), and in the swing and bop big band of the pianist Bubby Lavecchia (1977). From 1984 he was a member of the Trío Argentina; he also recorded with Jorge Navarro (1984–5). The album *Trauma* (Ten 100), which he recorded as a leader in 1968, offers good examples of his work.

LAUREANO FERNÁNDEZ, OMAR GARCÍA BRUNELLI

Rena [René], **Joseph** (*b* New Orleans, 1 or 11 March 1897; *d* New Orleans, 26 Dec 1973). Drummer, brother of Kid Rena. His date of birth was published as 11 March in Rose and Souchon, but Rena himself said, in his *LNT* interview, "I was born on the foist day of March"; however, his application for a social security card gives 11 March. In 1920 he was a member of the Liberty Bell Orchestra led by the trumpeter Wesley Don. Thereafter he worked in bands with his brother, recording for the Delta label in 1940. He retired from music in 1945 to become a preacher. (A. Rose and E. Souchon: *New Orleans Jazz: a Family Album*, Baton Rouge, LA, 1967, rev. and enlarged 3/1984)

Oral history material in *LNT*.

MARCEL JOLY

Rena, Kid [René, Henry; Little Turk] (*b* New Orleans, 30 Aug 1898; *d* New Orleans, 25 April 1949). Trumpeter, brother of Joseph Rena. He was taught around 1912, along with Louis Armstrong, at Joseph Jones's Colored Waif's Home and later studied with Manuel Perez. In 1919 he succeeded Armstrong in Kid Ory's band, with which he remained until Ory left for California, and in 1921 he founded his own Dixieland Jazz Band, in which his sidemen included his brother Joseph and often George Lewis (i). During the 1920s he also played with the Tuxedo Brass Band, and in the 1930s he formed the Pacific Brass Band. Thereafter Rena led various groups in New Orleans until illness forced him to retire in 1947.

Rena took part in only one recording session, in 1940. However, reports of his performances of the 1920s suggest that he had a particularly strong tone and an ability to play in the upper register of the instrument for long periods; he is reputed to have developed a remarkable high obbligato for the final strain of *High Society*, which was later adapted by Sharkey Bonano. By the 1930s he was playing more in the middle register, but had retained a characteristic warm tone and considerable melodic grace. Unfortunately, by the time he recorded (alongside Big Eye Louis Nelson, Alphonse Picou, and Jim Robinson, among others) the quality of his playing had been reduced by ill-health to a cautious straightforward lead, and he exhibited only a few remnants of his former individuality.

RECORDINGS

(all recorded in 1940 for Delta)

Panama/High Society Rag (800, 804); Milenberg Joys/Clarinet Marmalade (802, 805); Gettysburg March/Lowdown Blues (801, 803); Weary Blues/Get it right (806–7)

BIBLIOGRAPHY

ChartersJ
M. Jones: "Those Kid Rena Records," *MM*, xxviii (9 Feb 1952), 9
A. Rose and E. Souchon: *New Orleans Jazz: a Family Album* (Baton Rouge, LA, 1967, rev. and enlarged 3/1984)
J. De Donder: "Henry 'Kid' Rena," *MR*, xv/8 (1988), 8
R. H. Knowles: *Fallen Heroes: a History of New Orleans Brass Bands* (New Orleans, 1996), 165
J. Sohmer: "Heywood Hale Broun, Gene Williams and the Delta Recordings of 'Kid' Rena," *IAJRC Journal*, xxxiii/3 (2000), 40

ALDEN ASHFORTH

Rena Rama. Swedish quartet. Formed in 1972, its original members were the saxophonist Lennart Åberg, the pianist Bobo Stenson, the double bass player Palle Danielsson, and the drummer Bengt Berger; Danielsson was later replaced by Anders Jormin and Berger by a succession of other drummers, among them Anders Kjellberg. The group's style is a fusion of modal jazz and other genres, including the folk music of India and Africa. It appeared at festivals in India (Jazzyatra, 1978, 1980) and several European countries and made a number of recordings, notably *Inside-outside* (1979, Caprice 1182). In the 1980s it collaborated with such guests as Marilyn Mazur, Billy Hart, Kenny Wheeler, and Don Cherry, all of whom recorded with the group. By 1990 Rena Rama was largely inactive; it disbanded in 1993, but has occasionally met for reunions in later years.

BIBLIOGRAPHY

L. Westin: "Rena Rama," *Inside-outside* (Caprice 1182, 1979) [liner notes]
E. Kjellberg: "Rena Rama and Lisa's Piano: an Essay in Jazz Analysis," *Studia musicologica upsaliensa* (Uppsala, Sweden, 1985), 323

ERIK KJELLBERG/LARS WESTIN

Renaud, Henri (*b* Villedieu-sur-Indre, France, 20 April 1925). French pianist, composer, and leader. He learned violin from the age of five and piano from the age of eight. In 1946 he formed a singing group and then, having decided to devote himself to jazz, moved to Paris; as a member of a group led by the tenor saxophonist Jean-Claude Fohrenbach he accompanied such American musicians as Don Byas (1946), James Moody (1949), and Roy Eldridge (1950). He made his first recordings as a leader in 1951. The following year he performed and recorded with his own big band, which included Nat Peck, Sandy Mosse, Jean-Louis Chautemps, Jimmy Gourley, Benoit Quersin, and Fats Sadi, and Francy Boland as arranger, at Le Boeuf sur le Toit and formed a group that played regularly at the Tabou, where it accompanied Lester Young, Sarah Vaughan, and Clifford Brown; he produced important recordings by Brown in 1953, and also recorded for Vogue as a leader and as a sideman with Zoot Sims and Lee Konitz. Renaud then spent a brief period in New York, where he produced sessions for the Swing label by Al Haig, Oscar Pettiford (for whom he also played piano), and his own small groups, in which J. J. Johnson, Al Cohn, Gigi Gryce, Curly Russell, Gene Ramey, Denzil Best, Milt Jackson, and Percy Heath appeared as sidemen (February–March 1954). He continued these activities for Vogue and Swing in Paris, recording later that same year in groups led by Frank Foster, René Thomas, Bob Brookmeyer, and Roy Haynes, and at the same time appeared with Roger Guérin, Chautemps, and Charles Saudrais at the opening of a new Parisian club, Le Caméléon.

Renaud's quintet, which included Barney Wilen and Gourley, performed at the Ringside in 1955. He recorded as a sideman with Lucky Thompson and as co-leader with Sims (both 1956), and also as a leader, with Allen Eager among his sidemen (1957). From 1957 to 1959 his quartet (with Jay Cameron) accompanied June Richmond (recording in 1957). He again visited New York, where he appeared at Birdland with Philly Joe Jones and Haynes and at the Village Gate with Sims and Cohn; on his return to Paris he played with Kenny Clarke at the Blue Note (where they may be seen accompanying Sims in the short film *Flash*, 1962) and with Buck Clayton at Les Trois Mailletz. In 1964, following an engagement at the Gyllene Cirkeln in Stockholm, he ceased full-time work as a performer to become the head of the jazz division of the CBS label in France and to produce radio and television programs. In 1985 he led a quintet which involved Mike Zwerin and Al Levitt. As a pianist Renaud has a refined, economical style that is well suited to accompaniment. He has contributed to *Jazz hot* and *Jazz magazine* and was a music consultant for Bertrand Tavernier's film *Round Midnight* (1986). A collection of his compositions was recorded in 1993 by Jimmy Rowles and Michael Moore (i) as *Profile (The Music of Henri Renaud)* (Col. 474554-2).

SELECTED RECORDINGS

As leader: *Henri Renaud–Al Cohn Quartet* (1954, Swing 33332); *Henri Renaud All Stars* (1954, Swing 33320–21); *Henri Renaud Trio* (1957, Ducretet-Thomson 052)

As sideman: L. Konitz: *Lee Konitz Plays* (1953, Vogue 169); C. Brown: *Clifford Brown Quartet* (1953, Vogue 179); Z. Sims: *Zoot Sims Sextet* (1953, Vogue 170); O. Pettiford: *Oscar Pettiford Sextet* (1954, Swing 33326); L. Thompson: *Lucky Thompson* (1956, Ducretet-Thomson 024)

BIBLIOGRAPHY

N. Hentoff: "French Jazz Fans, Musicians Come out of Basin Street, Pick up on Moderns," *DB*, xxi/12 (1954), 12
A. Morgun and N. Renaud: "Henri Renaud Discography," *JM*, iv (1958), no.2, p.23; no.3, p.26; no.6, p.32
L. Malson: "Henri Renaud ou l'épreuve de la réflexion," *Jm*, no.69 (1961), 34
H. Renaud: "Bebop Highlights," *Jh*, no.305 (1974), 18
J. Réda and P. Carles: "Henri Renaud: 'I Remember Bebop'," *Jm*, no.278 (1979), 82
P. Carles: "Quand Renaud revient," *Jm*, no.284 (1980), 34
"Le New York d' Henri Renaud," *Jm*, no.319 (1983), 29
P. Carles: "New York Renaud l'espace de trente ans," *Jm*, no.334 (1984), 72
——: "Duke a tout fait avant tout le monde ...," *Jm*, no.380 (1989), 34

ANDRÉ CLERGEAT/BK

Rendell, Don(ald Percy) (*b* Plymouth, England, 4 March 1926). English tenor saxophonist, clarinetist, and flutist. He grew up in a musical family and learned piano from the age of five; he took up alto saxophone in 1942 and changed to the tenor instrument when he turned professional the following year. Following early experience in bands led by the trumpeter Duncan Whyte (1944–5), the saxophonist George Evans (1946), and the violinist Oscar Rabin (1947–9) he played with John Dankworth's septet (March 1950–1953), one of the most important bop-influenced British groups of the period. In 1954 he formed a sextet, and in 1955 he led a band that accompanied Billie Holiday in Manchester. After working with Tony Crombie (spring 1955) and Ted Heath's band (summer 1955 – March 1956) he undertook a European tour with the Stan Kenton Orchestra (spring 1956) and played in Tony Kinsey's group (summer 1956 – January 1957), with which he performed in Cyprus. Rendell continued to demonstrate an aptitude for the West Coast style both during a tour of Europe as a member of Woody Herman's Anglo-American Herd (1959) and in his own bands: a sextet (January 1957 – June 1958), a small group co-led by the trumpeter Bert Courtley (1959), and a quartet (to November 1962). At an early stage he was influenced by the work of Lester Young, but by the late 1950s he had begun to incorporate elements of John Coltrane's style into his playing; the results may be heard on *Roarin'* (1961). In 1963, with Ian Carr, he formed a quintet, which received considerable acclaim before it disbanded in 1969.

In the 1970s Rendell co-led a band with Barbara Thompson for five years, played with Neil Ardley's orchestra, and began a long but intermittent association with Michael Garrick. Later he focused on leading his own small groups, among them a quartet (1982–mid-1990s) with the guitarist Esmond Selwyn, the bass player Mario Castronari, and the drummer Robin Jones; after Selwyn left (1992) Rendell was joined by the trumpeter Steve Waterman. In the 1990s his ensembles appeared at a number of festivals, notably in France and Britain, and during the same period he performed and recorded with, among others, Dankworth (1990), Brian Priestley, the pianist Keith Pendlebury and the singer Marcia Pendlebury, and Garrick. Rendell has earned a considerable reputation as a teacher through his work in London at the Royal Academy of Music (1974–7) and the Guildhall School of Music and Drama (from 1984); he has published the instructional books *Introduction to Flute* (London, 1972), *Advanced Flute Tutor* (London, 1972), and *Guildhall School of Music and Drama: Saxophone Selection* (London, 1990), and appears in a video, *Saxophone Skills* (1994).

Oral history material in *GBLnsa*.

SELECTED RECORDINGS

Duos with B. Priestley: on Priestley: *You Taught my Heart to Sing* (1994, Spirit of Jazz 09-0995), Dance of the Infidels, Eclypso, Heaven, In Walked Bud, Star-crossed Lovers

As leader: *Meet Don Rendell* (1955, Tempo 1); *Playtime* (1958, Decca 4265); *Roarin'* (1961, Jlnd 951); with I. Carr: *Shades of Blue* (1964, Col. SX1733), *Dusk Fire* (1966, Col. SX6064), *Live* (1968, Col. SCX6316), *Change is* (1969, Col. SCX6368); *Spacewalk* (1971, Col. SCX6491); *Earth Music* (1979, Spot. 515); *If I Should Lose You* (1990–91, Spot. 546); *What am I Here For?* (1993, 1996, Spot. 551)

As sideman: J. Dankworth: Get Happy (1950, Esquire 10103); Leon Bismarck (1951, Esquire 10173); S. Tracey: *The Latin American Caper* (1968, Col. SCX6358); N. Ardley: *Greek Variations* (1969, Col. SCX6414); K. Pendlebury and M. Pendlebury: *Fine and Mellow* (1997, PD1 008)

SELECTED FILMS AND VIDEOS

It's a Wonderful World (1956); The Golden Disc [The Inbetween Age] (1958); The 2nd Bude Jazz Festival 1989 (n.d. [filmed 1989])

BIBLIOGRAPHY

CarrJ; *ChiltonB*; *WickesIBJ*, i
B. Dawbarn: "Is Rendell the Forgotten Man?," *MM* (29 April 1961), 14
P. J. Sullivan: "Rendell/Carr," *JJ*, xxi/6 (1968), 21 [incl. discography]
M. C. King: "British Jazzmen, 1: Don Rendell," *JJ*, xxiii/7 (1970), 7 [incl. discography]
C. Fox: *The Jazz Scene* (London, 1972)
I. Carr: *Music Outside: Contemporary Jazz in Britain* (London, 1973)
R. Cotterrell, ed.: *Jazz Now: the Jazz Centre Society Guide* (London, 1976)
P. Renaud: *La discographie du jazz anglais* (Chaumont, France, 1985)
T. Middleton: *Don Rendell* (London, 1993) [bio-discography]
M. Pearson: "Don Rendell: What am I Here For?," *Jazz on CD*, no.18 (1995), 56

MARK GILBERT

Reno Club. Nightclub in Kansas City; *see* Nightclubs and other venues.

Repertory band. In jazz circles, an ensemble formed primarily to perform compositions from the repertories of past jazz bands, and secondarily to assist young musicians in acquiring skills appropriate for playing in classic jazz styles. Performances associated with repertory bands usually involve meticulous transcription and re-creation from recordings, attempting not only to capture instrumentation and voicings from historic arrangements but also in many cases to reproduce (originally improvised) solos. Repertory bands have played and recorded material ranging from the works of Jelly Roll Morton and Duke Ellington to the hard bop of Sonny Clark. From the 1990s some ensembles (most notably the Carnegie Hall Jazz Band) have routinely stepped away from carefully wrought re-creation and instead opted for imprinting performances with their own personality and arrangements.

The first great repertory band, albeit little known even in its native France, may well have been Jean-Pierre Morel's Sharkey & Co. The group's albums include magnificent re-creations of classic recordings by the Ellington and Fletcher Henderson orchestras, with new solos supplied by Morel and his sidemen; both the voicings and the spirit of the original arrangements are captured in wonderful detail, as may be heard, for example, on *East St. Louis Toodle-oo*, from the album *Jungle Crawl* (1969, AFAJNO 8), and *Shanghai Shuffle*, on the album *Kansas City Kitty* (1972, Pragmaphone 4). By the time of this second album by Sharkey & Co., a repetory movement in jazz was underway in the USA. Its beginnings have been credited to a concert series led by Gunther Schuller in 1971 at the New England Conservatory, but a more formalized effort began in 1973 when Chuck Israels formed his National Jazz Ensemble, whose spectacular re-creation of Ellington's 1940 recording of *Ko-Ko* exemplified the concept of a repertory band at its very best, capturing not only the technical details but also the spirit and intangible nuances of that classic recording, and thus affording audiences of the mid-1970s an opportunity to hear an aural facsimile of Ellington's finest band. Even though, by contrast to this *Ko-Ko*, the results would often suffer from stiffness, many similar efforts followed through the remainder of the 20th century. These included George Wein's New York Jazz Repertory Company (established in 1974) and the Smithsonian Repertory Company (formed in the late 1970s by Martin Williams).

After a brief suspension of these activities, Gary Giddins, John Lewis, and Roberta Swann (with support from Coopers Union) formed the American Jazz Orchestra, which from May 1986 to late 1992 performed both classic jazz pieces and newly commissioned works (the latter by Benny Carter, Jimmy Heath, and Lewis, among others). In 1988 Lincoln Center formed the Lincoln Center Jazz Orchestra, which from 1991 has served as the heart of Jazz at Lincoln Center, and in 1990 the Smithsonian Institution established the Smithsonian Jazz Masterworks Orchestra, which began performing in 1991; hard on the heels of this flurry of historically oriented activity, the Carnegie Hall Jazz Band was formed late in 1991. In addition to these institutional activities, from the 1970s until his retirement in 1996 Vince Giordano led his own repertory ensemble, the Nighthawks, which specialized in re-creating dance-band music from the 1920s and 1930s, and in Chicago in the late 1990s Bill Russo was leading another repertory band, the Chicago Jazz Ensemble, which performed careful transcriptions of jazz classics and in most cases re-created solos which Russo deemed historically significant or which he felt bandmembers could not improve upon.

Although the term "repertory band" may readily take on further meanings, it is probably most useful to apply it only to bands which draw from a stylistically broad-based repertory (often in association with some type of pedagogical and historical agenda) rather than using it in reference either to stylistically specific "revival" groups (such as Lu Watters's Yerba Buena Jazz Band or the bands led by T. S. Monk) or to "ghost" bands which celebrate the greatest hits of a particular leader (such as Glenn Miller or Tommy Dorsey), even though the practice of re-creation from classic recordings may play a role in any such band.

BIBLIOGRAPHY

CarrJ
G. Giddins: "Weather Bird: an Orchestra is Born," *VV* (6 May 1986), 86
I. Gitler: "The American Jazz Orchestra: Repertory Revisited," *JT* (1986), July, 7
C. Deffaa: "The American Jazz Orchestra," *JT* (1988), Dec, 20
R. B. Woodward: "The Jazz Wars: a Tale of Age, Rage, and Hash Brownies," *VV* (9 Aug 1994), 27
D. Helland: "Repertory Big Bands: Jazz's Future-Past," *DB*, lxiv/1 (1997), 34 [incl. discography]

GK

Reprise. Record company and label. The company was established by Frank Sinatra in Burbank, California, in 1961, after he ceased to record for Capitol. It immediately embarked on an extensive program of jazz recordings, encouraged partly by Sinatra's interest in jazz. The catalogue included eight albums recorded during the 1960s by Duke Ellington (who also supervised sessions for the company in Paris) and material by Count Basie, Bud Powell, Dizzy Gillespie, Ben Webster, Frank Rosolino, Barney Kessel, Chico Hamilton, Shorty Rogers, Jimmy Witherspoon, Don Ellis, Erroll Garner, Jack Sheldon, Calvin Jackson, and Al Hibbler. Sinatra himself recorded many albums for the company, on three of which he was accompanied by Basie's band and on another by Antonio Carlos Jobim. Reprise was purchased by Warner Bros. in 1963, after which it functioned mainly as a popular music label. Warner Bros. reactivated the Reprise label in 1987, but it was not involved with jazz. Classic material from Reprise began to be reissued by Discovery with the founding of its Re-Discovery label in 1993.

MARK GARDNER/BK

Reser, Harry (F.) (*b* Piqua, OH, 17 Jan 1896; *d* New York, 27 Sept 1965). Banjoist and bandleader. He performed and recorded with Paul Whiteman (1923) and worked prolifically as a studio musician, notably in sessions as an accompanist to Bessie Smith (1924) and as the leader of his own bands, which sometimes involved Red Nichols and Joe Venuti. His significance in jazz lies in his work in the 1920s as an organizer of studio bands, in which capacity he engaged many white jazz musicians. As a performer Reser was essentially a virtuoso popular instrumentalist, but he may be heard in a jazz setting on Smith's *Easy Come, Easy Go Blues* (1924, Col. 14005D), on which he provides a sympathetic (though hardly swinging) banjo accompaniment. He also composed novelty ragtime tunes and wrote methods for banjo, ukulele, and guitar.

BIBLIOGRAPHY

ReclamsJ
W. W. Triggs: *The Great Harry Reser* (London, 1978)

Reservoir. Record label. Its parent company, Reservoir Music, was established in New York in 1987 by Mark R. Feldman and Kayla Feldman. It first issued previously unreleased recordings by Valery Ponomarev, Joe Puma, Peter Leitch, and Ralph Moore, all made in the mid-1980s during Feldman's association with Uptown. Thereafter Reservoir reissued items by Tommy Flanagan and J. R. Monterose, Pepper Adams, Don Sickler, Leitch, and Buddy Tate and Al Grey, these too deriving from Feldman's work with Uptown during the same period, and began to make its own new recordings. By the late 1990s it had become one of the leading hard-bop labels. Its catalogue, which by mid-2000 numbered more than 60 albums, includes titles by Kenny Barron, Dick Berk, Nick Brignola, Steve Kuhn, Leitch, Hod O'Brien, Ponomarev, Rob Schneiderman, Andrés Boiarsky, Claudio Roditi, and the pianist Pete Malinverni; especially notable is its "New York Piano" series, which has brought exposure to such undersung pianists as Schneiderman, O'Brien, and Kuhn. Most of its recordings were made at Rudy Van Gelder's studio in Englewood Cliffs, New Jersey. It should not be confused with the rock label Reservoir.

BIBLIOGRAPHY

D. Zych: "Label Watch: Reservoir Records," *JT*, xxiii/5 (1993), 61
<http://www.reservoirmusic.com> (2000)
<http://www.rsrjazz.com> (2000)

GK

Resonant Music. Record label formed in 1998 by TERJE GEWELT.

Retrieval. Record company which in the early 1970s acquired Fountain. It maintained that label's 100, 200, and 300 series, and continued the policy of vintage jazz reissues in a 400 series on the Retrieval label; John R. T. Davies was in charge of restoring and transferring material from 78 r.p.m. discs for all of these series. The company was later purchased by Challenge, which offered vintage jazz reissues on CD under the Retrieval name.

Rettenbacher, J(ohannes) A(nton) [Hans] (*b* Vienna, 16 Sept 1939; *d* Munich, 19 Dec 1989). Austrian double bass player. He studied double bass and musicology in Austria, then attended the Berklee School of Music in Boston. After working with Gerd Dudek and Manfred Schoof (1958–9) he toured Scandinavia with Stan Getz (1960) and played in small groups and big bands with Friedrich Gulda. He then attended Oscar Peterson's Advanced School of Contemporary Music in Toronto (1963). Rettenbacher worked with Eric Dolphy and Fatty George (1964), Joe Nay (1965), and Rolf Kühn, Erwin Lehn, and Don Ellis (1967) and recorded with Oscar Klein (1964), Gulda (1969–70), Milt Buckner (1970), Eugen Cicero (*Balkan Rhapsody*, 1970, MPS 15295), and Kühn (*c*1971). From 1968 to 1971 he performed and recorded as a member of the Dave Pike Set. In the mid-1970s he became active in jazz education, teaching at Jazz School Munich, and in the 1980s he worked with Nay again and led his own quintet (*ReclamsJ*)

WOLFRAM KNAUER

Return to Forever. Jazz-rock group, formed in late 1971 (or mid-1972; accounts are conflicting) by CHICK COREA; its other original members were Stanley Clarke (electric bass guitarist), Joe Farrell (reed player), Flora Purim (singer), and Airto Moreira (percussionist). The group toured and made two recordings which exhibited the influence of Latin music and were notable for the clarity of the individual lines; the album *Light as a Feather* (1972) best exemplifies this early style. In 1973 Corea re-formed the ensemble, which from this time consisted of Corea, Clarke, the electric guitarist Bill Connors (replaced for a tour in 1974 by Earl Klugh), and the drummer Lenny White. The group adopted an amplified style, reminiscent of the work of John McLaughlin, that was strongly oriented towards rock and marked by Corea's use of the Fender-Rhodes electric piano, Hohner Clavinet, Yamaha organ, Minimoog and ARP Odyssey synthesizers, as well as various electronic gadgets and pedals. It found a wide audience among the young and became still more popular after Al Di Meola replaced Connors in 1974. By late 1975 the group's playing had begun to lose its vitality; nevertheless its album *Romantic Warrior* (1976) became its most popular recording. In the late 1970s Corea formed a third group under the name Return to Forever. This 13-piece ensemble, the instrumentation of which resembled that of a chamber orchestra and made less use of electronics, included Clarke, Farrell, the singer and keyboard player Gail Moran, and string and brass sections; it trod an uncomfortable stylistic line between third-stream jazz and light pop music and met with little favor from the critics. Between 1972 and 1979 Corea produced recordings both under the name Return to Forever and under his own name, on all of which members of the ensemble played; he then continued to use the name for various projects. In 1983 he joined Clarke, Di Meola, and White for a tour of the USA.

SELECTED RECORDINGS

Return to Forever (1972, ECM 1022); *Light as a Feather* (1972, Pol. 5525); *Where Have I Known you Before?* (1974, Pol. 6509); *Romantic Warrior* (1976, Col. PC34076); *Live: the Complete Concert* (1977, Col. C4X34350)

BIBLIOGRAPHY

C. Berg: "Professor C. C. and his Amazing Perpetual Communication Company," *DB*, xliii/6 (1976), 12 [incl. discography]
D. L. Maggin: *Stan Getz: a Life in Jazz* (New York, 1996), 263
S. Nicholson: *Jazz-Rock: a History* (Edinburgh, 1998)

PATRICK T. WILL

Reuss, Allan (John) (*b* New York, 15 June 1915; *d* Los Angeles Co., 4 June 1988). Guitarist. He took up banjo at the age of 12 and later studied guitar with George Van Eps, whom he replaced in Benny Goodman's band from April to June 1935 and for a second time from August 1935 to March 1938. He then played with Paul Whiteman, Jack Teagarden (1939–40), and Jimmy Dorsey (March – *c* summer 1942). After working for NBC (1942–3) he spent another period with Goodman (June 1943 – June 1944) and performed with Harry James (June 1944 – May 1945). Reuss was also in demand for studio recording sessions during the late 1930s and mid-1940s, and worked with such artists as Gene Krupa (1935–6), Teddy Wilson and Billie Holiday (1936–8), Lionel Hampton (1937–9), Mildred Bailey (1938), Bunny Berigan and Glenn Miller (both 1939), Coleman Hawkins (1945), and Corky Corcoran and Arnold Ross (both 1946). He participated in radio broadcasts with Goodman's big band early in 1947 and was reunited with the clarinetist for the making of the soundtrack to the film *The Benny Goodman Story* in 1955. Although he continued to play as a freelance, in later years he concentrated on teaching. His last known residence appears in the social security death index as North Hollywood, California. The California death index gives his death place as Los Angeles county; it also gives his middle name, but mis-spells his birth name as Allen. Reuss was an excellent big-band rhythm guitarist and was known for his sophisticated chordal melodies, which are often compared with those of his mentor Van Eps; he recorded notable solos with Teagarden (*Pickin' for Patsy*, 1939) and Dorsey (*Sorghum Switch*, 1942).

SELECTED RECORDINGS

As sideman: J. Teagarden: Pickin' for Patsy (1939, Bruns. 8401); J. Dorsey: Sorghum Switch (1942, Decca 18372); C. Corcoran: Minor Blues (1946, Key. 621)

SELECTED FILMS AND VIDEOS

The Big Broadcast of 1937 (1936); Hollywood Hotel (1937); Hoagy Carmichael (1939)

BIBLIOGRAPHY

ChiltonW; *ConnorBG*
B. Kessel: "Allan Reuss and Oscar Moore," *GP*, xi/7 (1977), 10
M. J. Summerfield: *The Jazz Guitar: its Evolution and its Players* (Gateshead, England, 1978, 4/1988, as *The Jazz Guitar: its Evolution, Players and Personalities since 1900*)

JIM FERGUSON/BK

Revelation. Record company and label. The company was established in 1965 in Los Angeles by John William Hardy and Jon Horwich. The first release was an album by Dennis Budimir; among the musicians who recorded regularly for the label were Clare Fischer, Gary Foster, Warne Marsh, Tony Ortega, and Joe Albany. In the late 1970s the premises were transferred to Gainesville, Florida, and from that time the repertory included albums by such leaders as Jerry Coker and Carmell Jones. By 1984 the company had issued 45 albums, most of which remained in the catalogue. Revelation is most notable for having helped to revive interest in the work of neglected players such as Marsh and Albany and for having given vital exposure to Fischer, Foster, and Budimir when they were little known outside California.

MARK GARDNER

Reverberation unit. An electroacoustic or electronic device that produces a variety of delay effects, including a simulation of natural room reverberation.

Revolutionary Ensemble. Trio. It was formed in 1971 by the violinist Leroy Jenkins, the double bass player Sirone, and the drummer Frank Clayton; all three men also sang and performed on various percussion instruments, and Jerome Cooper, who replaced Clayton in September 1971, played piano, bugle, and flute as well as drums. Each player contributed equally to the trio's wide-ranging improvisations. Years of rehearsal allowed the members to respond immediately to one another and meant that, although they played free jazz, their music was extremely well organized. But their uncompromising music never reached a substantial audience. Occasionally they performed in concert at colleges and museums, and they appeared once at the Ann Arbor Blues and Jazz Festival (1973) and made a farewell tour of Europe. The group disbanded in 1977.

SELECTED RECORDINGS

Vietnam (1972, ESP 3007); *Manhattan Cycles* (1972, IndN 1023); *The People's Republic* (1975, A&M Hor. 708); *Revolutionary Ensemble* (1977, Enja 3003)

BIBLIOGRAPHY

GrayF
R. Riggins: "The Revolutionary Ensemble," *DB*, xl/19 (1973), 15
B. McRae: "Avant Courier no.32: Manhattan Cycles," *JJ*, xxviii/1 (1975), 8
P. Occhiogrosso: "US News: End of Era as Revolutionary Ensemble Splits," *MM* (21 Jan 1978), 6
P. Williams: "Revolutionary Ensemble," *Jazz 360°*, no.28 (1980), 4 [incl. discography]

BK

Rex. Record label. It was established in England in 1937 by the record company Crystalate, and its catalogue included commercially oriented jazz drawn from the American Record Corporation. After British Decca acquired the parent company in 1937 it maintained Rex for the issue of similar material recorded by American Decca. Both owners also used the label to release items recorded in England; these included a recording by the singer and bandleader Jack Payne (1935) on which Garland Wilson performed. There were also Rex labels in other countries; Indian Rex, for example, was used to issue a notable recording made in Bombay in 1936 by Crickett Smith and his Symphonians. Rex was discontinued in 1947.

BIBLIOGRAPHY

B. Rust: *The American Record Label Book* (New Rochelle, NY, 1978), 268
J. A. Payne: "Can't We Talk it Over," *Sv*, no.102 (1982), 204

HOWARD RYE

Rey, el. Nickname of Tito Puente.

Reynolds, Jimmy [James Russel] (*b* 5 Aug 1904; *d* New York, 16 Feb 1963). Pianist. In the 1930s and 1940s he led a band at the Hollywood Café in New York, though he also performed with other leaders, including Kaiser Marshall (1935). He recorded with Henry "Red" Allen, Jabbo Smith (1938), Hot Lips Page (1938–40), Bill Dillard (1947), and the singer Larry Darnell (1952). In the 1960s he worked with Harry Dial and Lester Boone. At his best Reynolds was an effective soloist and a sensitive obbligato player, but he received few recording opportunites commensurate with his potential.

SELECTED RECORDINGS

As sideman: H. Allen: Tormented/Nothing's Blue but the Sky (1936, Voc. 3245); J. Smith: Absolutely (1938, Decca 1712); H. L. Page: Gone with the Gin (1940, Decca 7714); Walk it to Me (1940, Decca 7757); I Won't Be Here Long (1940, Decca 7699)

BIBLIOGRAPHY

ChiltonW; *McCarthyB*

HOWARD RYE

Reys, Rita [Maria Everdina] (*b* Rotterdam, Netherlands, 21 Dec 1924). Dutch singer. She sang with a Hawaiian band (from 1940), a theater orchestra led by her father (1942), the guitarist Lex Van Spall (1942–4), the double bass player Ted Powder (1945, touring Belgium and Luxembourg), and the tenor saxophonist Piet Van Dijk (1947–50, touring Spain and North Africa). In 1945 she married Wessel Ilcken, with whom she led a sextet that toured Europe and often performed on the radio stations of the American Forces Network. On tours of the USA she sang with Mat Mathews and Art Blakey in 1956 and with Chico Hamilton and Jimmy Smith the following year; in 1958 she worked with Kurt Edelhagen and Bengt Hallberg in Germany and Sweden. After the death of Ilcken (1957) she married Pim Jacobs (1960) and embarked on a career as a soloist, appearing often at festivals and making many recordings. Performing mainly a repertory of standards, she continued to record with her husband at the piano until her ill-health and his death in 1996 led her to reduce her activities.

SELECTED RECORDINGS

Our Favorite Songs (1973, CBS 65620); *That Old Feeling* (1979, CBS 83981); *Memories of you* (1983, Utopia 814273-1)

BIBLIOGRAPHY

FeatherE

WIM VAN EYLE

Rhodes, Todd (Washington) (*b* Hopkinsville, KY, 31 Aug 1900; *d* Flint, MI, 4 June 1965). Pianist and arranger. He studied at the Springfield (Ohio) School of Music (1915–17) and the Erie (Pennsylvania) Conservatory (1919–*c*1921) before joining William McKinney's Synco Jazz Band; this group was renamed McKinney's Cotton Pickers in 1926, and, apart from a brief period in 1932–3, Rhodes remained a member until 1934 (for illustration *see* MCKINNEY'S COTTON PICKERS). After settling in Detroit he played with local bands until the early 1940s. He then organized his own group (1945), which recorded under his name (1947–53) and with Dave Bartholomew (1951) and Wynonie Harris (1951–2), frequently featuring the rhapsodic alto saxophone playing of Hallie Dismukes; Rhodes may be heard to particular advantage on *Red Boy at the Mardi Gras* (1949), which he composed and probably arranged.

SELECTED RECORDINGS

As leader: Bell Boy Boogie/Flying Disc (1947, Vitacoustic 1001); Anitra's Jump (1947, Sensation 25); Sportee's jump/Blues for the Red Boy (1947, King 4240); Pot Likker/Red Boy at the Mardi Gras (1949, Sensation 15); Red Boy is Back (1952, King 4509); Thunderbolt Boogie (1952, King 4601); Specks (1954, King 4736)

As sideman with McKinney's Cotton Pickers: Selling that Stuff (1929, Vic. 38052)

BIBLIOGRAPHY

ChiltonW; *FeatherE*

T. Grove and M. Grove: "Todd Rhodes Then and Now," *JJ*, vi/2 (1953), 18

G. Richards: "Jump with Me Baby (Second Chorus): Todd Rhodes," *Alley Music*, i/3 (1968), 6

J. Chilton: *McKinney's Music: a Bio-discography of McKinney's Cotton Pickers* (London, 1978)

J. Gallert: "Blue Sensation: the Todd Rhodes Story, pt 1," *IAJRC Journal*, xxiv/3 (1991), 1; contd as "Todd Rhodes Discography," xxiv/4 (1991), 32

HOWARD RYE

Rhumboogie Club. Nightclub in Chicago; *see* NIGHTCLUBS AND OTHER VENUES.

Rhyne, Mel(vyn) (*b* Indianapolis, 12 May 1936). Organist. He first played piano, and worked in local groups and in a trio with Roland Kirk and the drummer Wilbur Jackson (1955–6). He then joined Wes Montgomery's trio, in which he played piano and then spinet organ, and around May 1958 he began using the Hammond B-3. The group recorded in New York for Riverside in October 1959, after which it toured, mainly around the Midwest, until January 1960. Following the failure of Montgomery's family band, the Montgomery Brothers, the guitarist resumed working with Rhyne; they performed locally at first in 1961 and then from 1962 toured nationally, during which time they held an engagement at the Jazz Workshop in San Francisco, with Harold Land added to the group. In autumn 1963 the difficulties of transporting the organ forced them to disband. While with Montgomery, Rhyne recorded as a leader for Riverside's subsidiary Jazzland (1960), with Blue Mitchell, Johnny Griffin, Gene Harris, Andy Simpkins, and Albert "Tootie" Heath as his sidemen; in addition, around 1961–2 he recorded with Eddie Harris, although the results were not issued until the 1990s. In the late 1960s Rhyne played in groups with his brother Ron, a drummer, and in 1969 he moved to Madison. From 1973 he lived in Milwaukee, where he was later "rediscovered" by Herb Ellis, with whom he recorded around 1991. Also in the 1990s he recorded with Brian Lynch (1991), Ronald Muldrow (1992), and Eric Alexander (1995), and as a leader for the Criss Cross label, with Peter Bernstein and Kenny Washington among his sidemen.

SELECTED RECORDINGS

(recorded for Criss Cross unless otherwise indicated)

As leader: *The Legend* (1991, 1059); *Boss Organ* (1993, 1080); with Tenor Triangle: *Tell it Like it Is* (1993, 1089), *Aztec Blues* (1994, 1143); *Mel's Spell* (1994–5, 1118); *Stick to the Kick* (1994–5, 1137)

As sideman: W. Montgomery: *The Wes Montgomery Trio* (1959, Riv. 310); E. Harris: on *The Lost Album plus the Better Half* (*c*1961–2, VJ 913), Cuttin' Out, Shakey Jake; W. Montgomery: *Boss Guitar* (1963, Riv. 9459); *Portrait of Wes* (1963, Riv. 9492); *Guitar on the Go* (1963, Riv. 9494); H. Ellis: *Roll Call* (*c*1991, Justice 81001-2); B. Lynch: *At the Main Event* (1991, 1070); R. Muldrow: *Yesterdays* (1992, Enja 8020-2); E. Alexander: *Eric Alexander in Europe* (1995, 1114)

BIBLIOGRAPHY

A. Ingram: *Wes Montgomery* (Gateshead, England, 1985/*R*1993)

<http://theatreorgans.com/grounds/doodlin/rhyne.html> (1998)

GK

Rhythm. The grouping of musical sounds, principally by means of duration and stress; for a discussion of rhythm in jazz as it depends on beat, meter, and accent *see* Beat.

Rhythmakers. Recording group. Its output, produced during four sessions in 1932, represents some of the most exciting small-group jazz ever recorded, and its existence did much to further the cause of racially mixed groups. The nine titles resulting from the first two sessions (18 April and 23 May) were issued under Billy Banks's name. The exuberant playing of Henry "Red" Allen (trumpet) found a perfect foil in Pee Wee Russell (clarinet and tenor saxophone), while Eddie Condon (banjo), Jack Bland (guitar), and Zutty Singleton (who took over from Gene Krupa on drums after the first session) formed the basis of a fine rhythm section. Joe Sullivan (piano) and Al Morgan (double bass) were replaced for the third session (26 July) by Fats Waller and Pops Foster, and Jimmy Lord (clarinet) also joined the group to record a further four outstanding numbers. For the final session (8 October) Lord, Waller, and Banks were succeeded by Happy Caldwell (tenor saxophone), Frank Froeba, and Chick Bullock, and Tommy Dorsey (trombone) was added; the four titles produced by this ensemble were recorded under Bland's leadership. The group's recordings were later reissued under a variety of names, including the Chicago Rhythm Kings.

SELECTED RECORDINGS

B. Banks: Margie/Oh, Peter (1932, Ban. 32462); Mean Old Bed Bug Blues/ Yellow Dog Blues (1932, Ban. 32502); J. Bland: Who stole the lock/ Someone stole Gabriel's horn (1932, Ban. 32605)

BIBLIOGRAPHY

M. Doyle: "The Rhythmakers," *Discographical Forum*, no.19 (1970)
B. Rust: Liner notes, *The Rhythmakers* (VJM 53, 1983)

MIKE HAZELDINE

Rhythm-and-blues. A term coined in 1949 to describe music marketed primarily to African-Americans. It was initially used by *Billboard* to replace the term "race records," which had become unacceptable (some record companies had already substituted the term "sepia series"). Labels devoted to rhythm-and-blues and the rhythm-and-blues series of the major record companies, like the race and sepia catalogues which preceded them, encompassed the whole spectrum of African-American music – blues, jazz, gospel music, popular vocal groups, and comedians. However, as there was by this time a wider market available for many types of jazz, jazz recordings in the rhythm-and-blues catalogues tended to be those aimed especially at African-American dancers and party-goers and which placed a particular stress on overt swing and blues feeling. As a catch-all term for the African-American catalogues, rhythm-and-blues was supplanted in 1969 by soul.

The term is also applied to certain characteristic African-American musical styles prominent during the late 1940s and the 1950s. Critical opinion has never coalesced as to whether rhythm-and-blues in this sense is a genre of jazz, a genre of blues, a hybrid of the two, or a separate musical idiom. Its most immediate antecedent in jazz is the music played by the blues-based big bands which came to prominence in the early 1940s, such as those of Jay McShann, Lucky Millinder, Erskine Hawkins, and Buddy Johnson, and the jump bands which flourished in the later swing era. These bands found that survival in the marketplace required increasing emphasis on an insistent beat, on blues and blues-ballad singing, and on solo work emphasizing overt emotion and rhythmic excitement. To some extent, this was a conscious reaction to the direction being taken by the jazz avant garde of the day, the creators of bop. The singer and alto saxophonist Louis Jordan later said: "I wanted to play for the people, not just a few hep cats." Bands working in this style included those already mentioned, as well as those of Roy Milton, Joe Liggins, Tiny Grimes, and Johnny Otis.

As the style developed there was a particular tendency to emphasize saxophone solos in which honking and screaming effects were used to whip up excitement. Illinois Jacquet was an early exponent and Big Jay McNeely an extreme example, but elements of this style are found in the work of many saxophonists of the period, among them Earl Bostic, Tab Smith, Eddie Chamblee, Willis "Gator" Jackson, Al Sears, and the much-recorded West Coast studio musician Maxwell Davis. In the early 1950s increasing use was made of the electric organ by practitioners such as Wild Bill Davis, Doc Bagby, and Bill Doggett. Out of these trends there developed in the later 1950s the style known as "soul jazz," which reintegrated many rhythm-and-blues instrumentalists into the mainstream of jazz. At the same time Ornette Coleman transformed an idiosyncratic approach to rhythm-and-blues saxophone playing into a seminal new style, free jazz, and soon thereafter, in the early 1960s, Albert Ayler carried this possibility to the furthest possible extreme; in the work of these musicians, and countless others who followed, the use of honking, screaming, and other noise elements came to be understand as a crucial component linking free jazz to the mainstream of African-American popular music.

A further strand in rhythm-and-blues developed from the blues shouters featured by many bands of the late swing era. Indeed, Joe Turner (ii) contrived to record for the African-American market while retaining credibility with jazz critics. Other prominent singers in this idiom, such as Jimmy Witherspoon, Wynonie Harris, Roy Hawkins, and Eddie "Cleanhead" Vinson, were more conclusively ghettoized. Vinson also played alto saxophone in a style influenced by Charlie Parker and was one of the first musicians to begin incorporating elements of bop into the swing tradition, foreshadowing the soul-jazz movement by some years.

Another style of blues-ballad singing, sometimes categorized as "club blues," developed on the West Coast; this style was influenced by the work of the King Cole Trio, though Nat "King" Cole himself had largely moved into popular music before the rhythm-and-blues era. Singers such as Cecil Gant, Roy Brown, and Charles Brown were sometimes dubbed "Sepia Sinatras," no doubt in allusion to their popularity with young women rather than to their musical idiom, which remained firmly anchored in blues. Club blues spawned a major disciple in Ray Charles Robinson (as Ray Charles was then known), who in the 1950s transformed the idiom by incorporating elements of African-American gospel music into his singing. This development was already implicit in the work of a number of female rhythm-and-blues singers, such as Dinah Washington, Ruth Brown, and LaVern Baker.

Musical conditions in New Orleans led to the development there of a distinctive local form, characterized by a swinging shuffle beat. The bands of Dave Bartholomew and Paul Gayten were the leading practitioners, and from this tradition the singer and pianist Fats Domino became one of the first and most comprehensively successful of African-American artists to make the crossover to the mass popular market.

Recordings made in the continuing southern blues traditions and down-home blues recordings made in the northern ghettos were marketed under the rhythm-and-blues umbrella, but they are not normally regarded as examples of rhythm-and-blues style – although blues singer-guitarists who worked with jazz and jump-oriented groups usually are. The key innovator in this style was T-Bone Walker, whose playing was influenced by Django Reinhardt and Charlie Christian. Later guitarists such as B. B. King and Ike Turner placed an ever-growing emphasis on solo work. The idiom continued to attract new performers into the twenty-first century, whereas most rhythm-and-blues styles are kept alive only by surviving artists and overtly revivalist groups formed by white enthusiasts.

Rhythm-and-blues is also a term sometimes applied by writers on popular music to the African-American vocal group style "doo-wop," which developed in the early 1950s. Such groups were often accompanied by instrumentalists active in other areas of rhythm-and-blues.

Many of the styles embraced by the term rhythm-and-blues played a part in the development from the mid-1950s of rock-and-roll as a new mass-market commercial idiom aimed at teenagers. In the early years of rock-and-roll many African-American artists adapted by simplifying their music and by eliminating adult themes from their lyrics. At this stage, as in the music of Chuck Berry and Little Richard, musical distinctions between the two idioms are often small. However, these distinctions became greater as rock-and-roll became more definitely a hybrid between rhythm-and-blues and country music; rock-and-roll stars were drawn from country music and performed in conformity with the values of the general popular music industry.

BIBLIOGRAPHY

C. Gillett: *The Sound of the City: the Rise of Rock and Roll* (New York,1970, rev. and enlarged 3/1996)
P. Groia: *They All Sang on the Corner: New York's Rhythm and Blues Vocal Groups of the 1950s* (New York, 1973)
S. Propes: *Those Oldies but Goodies* (New York, 1973)
J. Whitburn: *Top Rhythm and Blues Records, 1949–71* (Menomonee Falls, WI, 1973)
J. Broven: *Walking to New Orleans: the Story of New Orleans Rhythm and Blues* (Bexhill-on-Sea, England, 1974, Gretna, LA, 1983, as *Rhythm & Blues in New Orleans*)
C. Gillett: *Making Tracks: Atlantic Records and the Growth of a Multi-billion-dollar Industry* (London, 1975)
A. Shaw: *Honkers and Shouters: the Golden Years of Rhythm and Blues* (New York, 1978)
A. Pavlow: *Big Al Pavlow's The R & B Book: a Disc-History of Rhythm and Blues* (Providence, RI, 1983)
J. Hannusch: *I Hear You Knockin': the Sound of New Orleans Rhythm and Blues* (Ville Platte, LA, 1985)
J. Berry, J. Foose, and T. Jones: *Up from the Cradle of Jazz: New Orleans Music since World War II* (Athens, GA, and London, 1986)
G. Gart, ed.: *First Pressings: the History of Rhythm & Blues* (Milford, NH, 1989–95) [8 vols., each covering one year 1951–8]
——: *First Pressings: the History of Rhythm & Blues, Special 1950 Volume* (Milford, NH, 1993)
J. Otis: *Upside your Head! Rhythm and Blues on Central Avenue* (Hanover, NH, 1993)
J. Dawson: *Nervous Man Nervous: Big Jay McNeely and the Rise of the Honking Tenor Sax!* (Milford, NH, 1994)
L. Hildebrand: *Stars of Soul and R & B* (New York, 1994)
T. Collins: *Rock Mr. Blues: the Life and Music of Wynonie Harris* (Milford, NH, 1995)
P. Love: *A Thousand Honey Creeks Later: my Life in Music from Basie to Motown – and Beyond* (Hanover, NH, 1997)

HOWARD RYE

Rhythm changes. Term referring to the harmonic progression ("changes") of any piece based on George Gershwin's *I got rhythm*, but with that progression regularized from 34 to 32 bars (i.e., without the two-bar tag which occurs at the end of Gershwin's tune).

Rhythm Club. The name of several nightclubs, notably one in New York; *see* NIGHTCLUBS AND OTHER VENUES.

Rhythm section. A term applied to the rhythm, or accompanying, instruments (i.e., piano or organ, guitar or banjo, tuba or double bass (later electric bass guitar), and drums) within a band; *see* BANDS, §§2, 4.

Rialto. Record label. It was owned by the Rialto Music House of Chicago, and the discs were produced by Marsh Laboratories, Inc. Only a few issues are known, and the one of significance to jazz is the only release believed to have been made of Jelly Roll Morton's unaccompanied solo recording of *London Blues* (1924). The records were sold in the parent company's several stores at promotional prices.

BIBLIOGRAPHY

B. Rust: *The American Record Label Book* (New Rochelle, NY, 1978), 270
L. Wright: *Mr Jelly Lord* (Chigwell, England, 1980), 26
A. Sutton: *Directory of American Disc Record Brands and Manufacturers, 1891–1943* (Westport, CT, and London, 1994), 134
L. Wright: "Pieces of the Jigsaw: Rialto," *Storyville 1996/7* (Chigwell, England, 1997), 223

HOWARD RYE

Ribot, Marc (Sylvan) (*b* Newark, NJ, 21 May 1954). Acoustic and electric guitarist. He grew up in South Orange, New Jersey, played trumpet from around the age of nine, and changed to guitar about three years later; he played in garage bands and studied with the Haitian classical guitarist Frantz Casseus. Having moved to New York (1977) with the intention of becoming a jazz guitarist, he worked with Brother Jack McDuff (1979) and came to feel constrained by the jazz repertory; from 1980 he played in a group that combined punk rock and rhythm-and-blues which eventually became the house band at Tramps, where it accompanied such singers as Carla Thomas, Solomon Burke, Rufus Thomas, and Syl Johnson. Ribot toured briefly with the singer Ronnie Spector in 1982 and worked in the Lounge Lizards from summer 1984. By 1990, with several musicians from this group, he had joined the Jazz Passengers, although he continued to record with both John Lurie and the pianist Evan Lurie. In addition he toured and recorded with Tom Waits (mid- to late 1980s) and the popular singer Elvis Costello (1989–90). From 1989 he often played in John Zorn's large groups, notably the chamber ensemble Bar Kohkba, with which he recorded between 1994 and 1996.

From the late 1980s Ribot worked as an unaccompanied soloist and performed and recorded with his band Rootless Cosmopolitans, a quintet consisting of Don Byron, Anthony Coleman, Brad Jones, and the drummer Richie Schwartz. In the early 1990s he led the group Shrek (Yiddish for "horror"), which appeared at the Festival International Musique Actuelle Victoriaville (1995) and performed works inspired by Albert Ayler and punk rock. Around 1995 he began working alongside Kenny Wolleson in Ellery Eskelin's trio, which was devoted to the music of Gene Ammons. Two years later, with Coleman, Jones, and E. J. Rodriguez among his sidemen, he formed the group Los Cubanos Postizos, which explored Afro-Cuban music and toured in summer 1998. Ribot also recorded with David Sanborn (*c*1991) and Weird Nightmare (1992), a group formed by the record producer

Hal Willner to perform the works of Charles Mingus, and with various rock and pop singers, including Syd Straw, Maria McKee, Marianne Faithful, and Sam Phillips.

SELECTED RECORDINGS

As unaccompanied soloist: *Don't Blame Me* (1994–5, DIW 902)
As leader: *Rootless Cosmopolitans* (c1989, Island 422-842577-2); *Marc Ribot y los Cubanos postizos (The Prosthetic Cubans)* (c1997, Atl. 83116-2)
As sideman: Jazz Passengers: *Implement Yourself* (1990, New World 398); J. Zorn: *Bar Kohkba* (1994–6, Tzadik 7108-2)
For recordings with Lounge Lizards *see* LURIE, JOHN.

BIBLIOGRAPHY

"Intro: Marc Ribot: a Lounge Lizard's 'Neurotic Blues'," *GP*, xxi/12 (1987), 14
D. Handelman: "Leapin' Lizard," *RS* (7 Sept 1989), 25
G. P. Chapin: "Marc Ribot: Playing Oddness," *CI*, xxvii/3 (1990), 16
T. Drozdowski: "Marc Ribot: Master of the Sideways Guitar," *Musician*, no.145 (1990), 110
B. Herrmann: "Riffs: Marc Ribot," *DB*, lvii/5 (1990), 13
B. Milkowski: "Marc Ribot," *GP*, xxiv/11 (1990), 56 [incl. discography]
K. Schoemer: "With Words and Music, a Union is Forged," *New York Times* (14 Sept 1990)
R. Hicks: "Intro: Marc Ribot's Primitive Monster," *GP*, xxvii/3 (1993), 18
J. Woodard: "Jazz Guitar Mutants!," *Musician*, no.189 (1994), 62
N. Akchoté: "La marque de Ribot," *Jm*, no.464 (1996), 23
G. Giddins: "Monk with Strings," *VV* (14 May 1996), 56
H. Pekar: "Profile: Marc Ribot: Beyond Irony," *GP*, xxx/11 (1996), 35
J. Gore: "Marc Ribot: the Poetics of Scarcity," *GP*, xxx1/1 (1997), 58
<http://www.ejn.it/mus/ribot.htm> (1998)
<http://www.soulindustries.com/ribot/home.htm> (1998)
D. Ouellette: "Prosthetically Speaking," *DB*, lxv/11 (1998), 36 [incl. discography]

GK

Ricci, Paul (J.) (*b* New York, 6 April 1914). Clarinetist and saxophonist. He began playing at the age of 12 and first worked in New York in taxi-dance halls. In the early 1930s he performed with Lud Gluskin, Red McKenzie, Adrian Rollini, Joe Venuti, Red Nichols, Joe Haymes, and others. As a studio musician he was on the staff of various record companies, of NBC (from 1940), and of Paramount and Universal (1950–66); later he settled in Miami, where he continued to work in studios. Ricci's numerous recordings were made mainly with big bands, such as those of Benny Goodman (1954) and Dizzy Gillespie (1960), but he also recorded with small groups, among them the trio Three's a Crowd (1938) and a quintet led by Carl Kress (1947). His relaxed and fluent clarinet playing may be heard on Bob Howard's *If Love is Blind/The best things happen at night* (1936, Decca 862).

based on *ChiltonW*

Rich, Buddy [Bernard] (*b* New York, 30 Sept 1917; *d* Los Angeles, 2 April 1987). Drummer and bandleader. He appeared on stage in his parents' vaudeville act before his second birthday, played drums and tap-danced on Broadway when he was four, and from the age of six toured the USA and Australia; by the time he was 11 he was leading his own stage band. He joined Joe Marsala's band in October 1937 and then played briefly with Bunny Berigan (July–December 1938), Harry James, and Artie Shaw, and for somewhat longer with Tommy Dorsey (November 1939–1942; for illustration *see* DORSEY, TOMMY). From mid-November 1942 to January 1943 he was with Benny Carter's big band at Billy Berg's Swing Club in Hollywood. After serving with the US Marines he worked again with Dorsey (June 1944 – October 1945); for a two-week period beginning late in September 1944, while with Dorsey in the Los Angeles area, he doubled in Count Basie's big band as a replacement for Jo Jones, who had suddenly been drafted and inducted into the army. Rich reportedly cherished this opportunity to perform with the most swinging of all big bands, and later in his career would occasionally and willingly deputize for Basie's drummers at a moment's notice. One year later, while still with Dorsey, he filled in for the ailing drummer Dave Tough in Woody Herman's First Herd.

Rich led his own band regularly from late 1945 to January 1947, when Carl Warwick, Earl Swope, Johnny Mandel, and Aaron Sachs were among its members, and intermittently through the late 1940s, when Rob Swope, Allen Eager, Al Cohn, Terry Gibbs, Zoot Sims, and Jimmy Giuffre contributed as soloists. Concurrently he began playing with Norman Granz's Jazz at the Philharmonic, with which he participated in concerts and recordings in southern California (spring 1946) and embarked on the first of many tours (February 1947). He appeared on the "Eddie Condon Floor Show" television series late in December 1948 and regularly in spring and summer 1949 while also working with Les Brown (June–September 1949) and continuing with Jazz at the Philharmonic. Having by then acquired expertise in bop drumming, he recorded with Charlie Parker's quartet, Basie's octet, Parker and Dizzy Gillespie's quintet, and Bud Powell's trio (all 1950) and resumed leading his big band (1950–51) before working with Charlie Ventura's Big Four (to November 1951).

From spring 1953 to spring 1954 Rich spent a year with Harry James's big band. He worked again with Dorsey (to April 1955) and then returned to James (1956–7) before establishing his own small group (1957–61), when he also performed as a singer in a style resembling that of Frank Sinatra. After a final lengthy tenure with James (late 1961 to spring 1966) he organized a second big band, with which he achieved remarkable international success. At its strongest, in 1968, the band included Don Menza, Al Porcino, Art Pepper (replaced by Joe Romano), Pat and John LaBarbera, and Ernie Watts, and arrangements were contributed by Bill Holman, Oliver Nelson, Bill Potts, Don Piestrup, Don Sebesky, Joe Sample, and others; Bob Magnusson, Richie Cole, and Rick Laird joined at the end of the decade. While in Britain the band appeared once on the television show "Jazz at the Maltings" (October 1968) and several times on "Jazz Scene at Ronnie Scott's" (April–August 1970). After its dissolution in 1974 Rich played mainly in New York with a small group in his own club, Buddy's Place, before re-establishing a big band of young musicians, with Steve Marcus as its principal saxophone soloist. In June 1982 his achievements were celebrated in a special concert at Carnegie Hall during the Kool Jazz Festival. He had a long history of heart problems, having suffered a heart attack as early as 1959, and shortly after the Kool Jazz tribute he underwent quadruple heart bypass surgery. Within three months, even before fully recovering, he resumed touring internationally with his big band.

Rich's playing was characterized by phenomenal speed and dexterity. He was an extrovert performer who produced complex patterns with metronomic clarity and simpler lines with an exquisite precision.

Oral history material in *GBLnsa*.

SELECTED RECORDINGS

As leader: with L. Young: I cover the waterfront/Somebody loves me (1945, Clef 11048); I found a new baby (1945, Clef 11048); with L. Hampton and A. Tatum: *The Lionel Hampton–Art Tatum–Buddy Rich Trio* (1955, Clef 709); with G. Krupa: *Krupa and Rich* (1955, Clef 684); *This One's for Basie* (1956, Norg. 1086); *Buddy Rich vs Max Roach* (1959, Mer. 20448);

Swingin' New Big Band (1966, PJ 20113); *Mercy, Mercy* (1968, PJ 20133), incl. Channel One Suite; *Keep the Customer Satisfied* (1970, Lib. 11006); *Lionel Hampton Presents Buddy Rich* (1977, Who's Who in Jazz 21006)
As sideman: A. Shaw: Serenade to a Savage (1939, Bb 10385); T. Dorsey: Quiet Please (1940, Bb B10810); Well, Git It! (1942, Vic. 27887); The Minor Goes Muggin' (1945, Vic. 45-0002); W. Herman: Your Father's Mustache (1945, Col. 36870); C Parker: Star Eyes (1950), first issued on [various artists:] *Alto Saxes* (1947–54, Norg. 1035); C. Basie: The Golden Bullet (1950, Col. 38888); C. Parker: Bloomdido (1950, Mer./Clef 11058); B. Powell: Hallelujah/Tea for Two (1950, Clef 11069)

SELECTED FILMS AND VIDEOS

Artie Shaw's Class in Swing (1939); Artie Shaw and his Orchestra in "Symphony of Swing" (1939); Ship Ahoy! (1942); Buddy Rich and his Orchestra (1948); Thrills of Music: Buddy Rich and his Orchestra (1948); Melodies by Martin (1955); Harry James and his New Swinging Band (1965); Norman Granz présente improvisation: documents exceptionnels et inédits des plus grands noms de jazz (n.d.)

BIBLIOGRAPHY

McCarthyB; *SchullerS*
G. Hoefer: "Buddy Rich: Portrait of a Man in Conflict," *DB*, xxvii (1960), no.12, p.17; no.13, p.20
R. Kettle: "Roach vs Rich: a Notated Analysis of Two Significant Modern Jazz Drumming Styles," *DB*, xxxiii/6 (1966), 20
H. Siders: "The Nouveau Rich," *DB*, xxxiv/8 (1967), 19
G. T. Simon: *The Big Bands* (New York and London, 1967, rev. 4/1981), 404
W. Balliett: *Super Drummer: a Profile of Buddy Rich* (Indianapolis, 1968)
J. Burns: "Lesser Known Bands of the 40s: Buddy Rich and Johnny Bothwell," *JM*, no.175 (1969), 6
D. Cooper with J. Titsworth: *Buddy Rich: a Lifetime of Music* (n.p. [England], 1974, rev. Blackpool, England, 2/1991)
S. Dance: *The World of Swing* (New York, 1974)
D. Meriwether, Jr.: *The Buddy Rich Orchestra and Small Groups* (Spotswood, NJ, 1974, rev. 2/Chicago, 1984, as *We Don't Play Requests: a Musical Biography/Discography of Buddy Rich*)
S. Woolley: "Buddy Rich: Drummer, Bandleader and Wit," *JJ*, xxvii/11 (1974), 4
W. Balliett: "Super Drummer," *Improvising: Sixteen Jazz Musicians and their Art* (New York, 1977), 151; repr. in *BallietA (1986)*, 224; *BallietA (1996)*, 253
"Rich + Tormé = Wild Repartee," *DB*, xlv (1978), no.3, p.13; no.4, p.20
A. Pepper and L. Pepper: *Straight Life: the Story of Art Pepper* (New York and London, 1979, rev. 2/1994) [incl. discography by T. Selbert]
L. Tomkins: "The Drum Summit: Buddy Rich and Louie Bellson Talk to Les Tomkins on the Subject of Big Bands," *CI*, xvii/9 (1979), 12
C. Iero: "Buddy Rich: Revisited," *MD*, iv/6 (1980), 12
K. Strateman: *Buddy Rich and Gene Krupa: a Filmo-discography* (Lübbecke, Germany, 1980)
E. Tiegel: "Rich Raps," *DB*, xlix/3 (1982), 17
J. Nesbitt: *Inside Buddy Rich: a Study of the Master Drummer's Style and Technique* (Delevan, NY, 1984)
R. Mattingly: "Buddy Rich," *MD*, x/1 (1986), 15
B. Korall: "Buddy Remembered," *MD*, xi/7 (1987), 22
G. Lombardi: *Eddie Condon on Record, 1927–1971* (Milan, 1987)
J. MacSweeney: "Buddy's Classic Radio Kings," *MD*, xi/7 (1987), 29
J. Simmen: "Ceux qui s'en vont, Bernard 'Buddy' Rich," *BHcF*, no. 354 (1988), 23
B. Korall: *Drummin' Men: the Heartbeat of Jazz: the Swing Years* (New York and Toronto, 1990), 249
M. Tormé: *Traps, the Drum Wonder: the Life of Buddy Rich* (New York, and Oxford, England, 1991)
R. Dupuis: *Bunny Berigan: Elusive Legend of Jazz* (Baton Rouge, LA, 1993)
G. Nelson: *Take No Prisoners: a Drumography of Buddy Rich* (Berlin, 1996, rev. 2/1997)
F. Laudet: "Souvenir: My Buddy is Rich," *BHcF*, no.462 (1997), 8
D. Meriwether: *Mister, I am the Band!: Buddy Rich, his Life and Travels* (North Bellmore, NY, 1998) [incl. discography by C. C. Hintze]
A. Van Starrex: "Killer Force: Buddy Rich," *Coda*, no.279 (1998), 12

JOSÉ HOSIASSON/BK

Rich, Fred(eric Ephram) (*b* Warsaw, 3 Jan 1898; *d* Los Angeles Co., 8 Sept 1956). Pianist and bandleader. His full name and place of death are taken from the California death index. In the 1920s he led commercial big bands, touring Europe (1925–6, 1927–8) and performing in New York. Among the jazz musicians who played under him in studio bands were Bunny Berigan, Benny Goodman, the Dorsey brothers, Tony Parenti, and Joe Venuti. In the late 1930s he was a music director in radio, and in 1942 he joined the staff of United Artists; although partly paralyzed in 1945, he continued to work in studios into the 1950s. Rich made numerous recordings between 1925 and 1940, few of which can be classified as jazz; among them, however, is *Till we Meet Again* (1940, Voc. 5507), arranged by Benny Carter and including solos by Carter and Roy Eldridge.

based on *ChiltonW*

Richard, Marc (*b* Neuilly-sur-Seine, France, 22 Nov 1946). French cornetist, clarinetist, and alto and tenor saxophonist. He made his début on clarinet and saxophone with the band led by the drummer Dominique Obadia. In 1963 he took up cornet, which he played with the Haricots Rouges and Raymond Fonsèque's Washboard Five (1964). As a reedman he regularly played with the Jazz o'Maniacs, led by the cornetist Dan Vernhettes (1964–71), and he performed on various instruments with the Watergate Seven Plus One (1974, 1977–92) and the Melanie Jazz Band (1975). In a collaboration with Chris Woods, Jean-Claude Fohrenbach, André Villéger, and Georges Arvanitas's trio, Richard recreated Benny Carter's famous 1939 saxophone quartet arrangements (1976). In 1976 he was a co-founder of the Anachronic Jazz Band, with which he remained until 1980, and he also played in modern styles with Jef Gilson's Europamerica Band (1976–7). Later he worked with Sam Woodyard, Bill Coleman (1980), Fonsèque again (1984), Cab Calloway (1985), Irakli's Jazz Four and the François Laudet Big Band (both 1994–7), and the trumpeter Irvin Mayfield (1997). His great versatility is demonstrated on his own album *After You've Gone* (1994, BB 644-2).

BIBLIOGRAPHY

M. Laplace: "French Classic Hot Music," *Gazette des cuivres*, no.10 (1991), 37
——: "La classic hot music," *Jazz Dixie/Swing: du Ragtime au Big Band*, no.1 (1993), 24

MICHEL LAPLACE

Richards, Ann [Borden, Margaret Ann] (*b* San Diego, 1 Oct 1935; *d* Hollywood Hills, CA, on or before 1 April 1982). Singer. She played piano from the age of ten. After singing with local groups in San Francisco and Oakland, and working briefly with Charlie Barnet, she joined Stan Kenton's orchestra in early 1955. She toured and recorded with the band that year and married Kenton in October. From this time she limited her performances to occasional engagements at clubs in Los Angeles, although she undertook some recording sessions both as a leader and with Kenton. The couple were divorced in 1961, and during the 1960s Richards continued to perform at clubs in Los Angeles; she may be heard to advantage on the album *Ann, Man!* (1961, Atco 136), on which she was accompanied by Jack Sheldon, Barney Kessel, Red Callender, and Larry Bunker.

BIBLIOGRAPHY

FeatherE; *Feather '60s*
D. Hague: "Stan Kenton," *JJ*, ix/10 (1956), 11

Richards, Emil [Radocchia, Emilio Joseph] (*b* Hartford, CT, 2 Sept 1932). Vibraphonist and percussionist. He started on xylophone when he was six. While attending the Hartford School of Music (1949–52) he played percussion in several local symphony orchestras (1950–54). During his military service he played in an army band in Japan (1954–5), where he worked with Toshiko Akiyoshi, and after being discharged he became a studio musician in Los Angeles (1956). He performed and recorded as a vibraphonist with George Shearing (1956–8) and Paul Horn (1960–64), with whom he was seen in the "Paul Horn Quintet" episode of the television series "Frankly Jazz" (1962), and then played with Don Ellis (1964–9) and led his own group, the Microtonal Blues Band (1967). Having become interested in ethnic music, he began to assemble a huge collection of unusual percussion instruments, and in 1969 he went to India to study meditation. Following his return to the USA he played with Roger Kellaway and worked with the composer and inventor of instruments Harry Partch; he also performed with popular musicians and recorded soundtracks for many well-known films and television shows. His activities as a studio musician are documented in the film *The Score* (1973). He has contributed essays on percussion to *Modern Percussionist* (mid-1980s) and *Modern Drummer* (1990s–), and he is the author of *Two and Four Mallet Exercises on Vibraphone and Marimba for the Advanced Player* (Hollywood, CA, *c*1979), *Mallet Exercises: for the Drummer and Percussionist* (Ventura, CA, *c*1986), and *Studio Techniques* (San Francisco, *c*1991).

Jazz no longer has significance in Richards's career. Earlier, as a vibraphonist, he played in a swing style reminiscent of the work of Lionel Hampton and Milt Jackson. In the 1970s and 1980s he used exotic percussion instruments, such as crotales, cuíca, wind chimes, and waterphone, on recordings of jazz in several different styles.

SELECTED RECORDINGS

As sideman: P. Horn: *Something Blue* (1960, HiFi 615); G. Duke: *Liberated Fantasies* (1976, MPS 15474), incl. I can hear that; Walfredo de los Reyes and L. Bellson: *Ecue ritmos cubanos* (1977, Pablo 2310807); L. Bellson: *Prime Time* (1977, Conc. 64); Shadowfax: *Shadowfax* (1982, Windham Hill 1022)

BIBLIOGRAPHY

Feather-Gitler '70s
L. Tomkins: "James Blades of London Meets Emil Richards of Los Angeles," *CI*, xiv/12 (1976), 20
S. Bradley: "Emil Richards," *DB*, xliv/15 (1977), 46
G. Olmstead: "Interview with Emil Richards," *Percussive Notes*, xix/1 (1980), 46
D. Levine: "Show and Studio: Emil Richards," *MD*, vi/1 (1982), 50
R. Flans: "Emil Richards," *Modern Percussionist*, i/2 (1985), 6
L. V. Weiss: "Emil Richards," *Percussive Notes*, xxxii/5 (1994), 46
R. Mattingly: "Emil Richards," *Percussive Notes*, xxxii/6 (1994), 12

LEROY OSTRANSKY/BK

Richards, Johnny [Cascales, Juan Ricardo de] (*b* Querétaro, Mexico, 2 Nov 1911; *d* New York, 7 Oct 1968). Composer, arranger, and bandleader. He grew up in Schenectady, New York, and learned piano, violin, banjo, and trumpet as a child; he left home to tour in vaudeville when he was eight, and by the age of 15 he was saxophonist and house orchestrator at the Mastbaum Theater, Philadelphia. After attending Syracuse University (BA 1931) he composed film scores, first in London for Gaumont (1932–3), then in Hollywood as Victor Young's assistant at Paramount (1933–40). While there he studied with the composer Arnold Schoenberg and received a master's degree from the University of Southern California. He led a big band from 1940 to 1945, then returned to Hollywood to write arrangements for Boyd Raeburn (1946–7), Charlie Barnet, and others. In 1952 he joined Stan Kenton, for whom he composed many successful pieces. Later he moved to New York and from 1956 to 1960 led a second band, whose recordings and performances received much critical acclaim; he organized a third group in 1964–5. One of Richards's most popular compositions is *Young at Heart*, which was a hit for Frank Sinatra in 1954; he also wrote many classical works and some pieces for theater band (his works are published principally by Berklee and Southern). He is best known, however, through his writing for Kenton and his own bands. A pioneer of progressive jazz, he never compromised his standards in order to cater to commercial interests.

RECORDED COMPOSITIONS

As leader: *The Rites of Diabolo* (1958, Roul. 52008); *Aquí se habla Español* (1966, Roul. 25351)
Recorded by S. Kenton: Prologue: this is an Orchestra! (1952, Cap. 15966–7); *Cuban Fire!* (1956, Cap. T731); *Adventures in Time* (1962, Cap. ST1844)

BIBLIOGRAPHY

J. Tynan: "Johnny Richards Seeks Entry in Big Band Field," *DB*, xxiii/23 (1956), 19
B. Coss: "The Johnny Richards Orchestra," *Metronome*, lxxiv/12 (1957), 18
B. Korall: "The New Johnny Richards Band," *DB*, xxxi/13 (1964), 20
J. S. Wilson: "Return of Big Band with Jazz Sound," *New York Times* (6 Feb 1965)
J. C. Thomas: "Johnny Richards: Man with a Passion," *DB*, xxxv/4 (1968), 22
Obituaries: *New York Times* (9 Oct 1968); *DB*, xxxv/23 (1968), 10
J. Hartley and J. Wölfer: *Johnny Richards: the Definitive Bio-discography* (Lake Geneva, WI, 1999)

STEVEN STRUNK

Richards, Red [Charles Coleridge] (*b* New York, 19 Oct 1912; *d* Scarsdale, NY, 12 March 1998). Pianist. He learned piano from the age of ten and played classical music for six years before hearing Fats Waller and taking up jazz. His first major engagement was with Tab Smith at the Savoy Ballroom, New York (1945–9), after which he worked with Bob Wilber in Boston (1950, 1951) and toured with Sidney Bechet (September–November 1951). In 1953 he toured Italy and France and made several recordings as a member of Mezz Mezzrow's band, which included Buck Clayton and Big Chief Moore; he completed the tour as an accompanist to Frank Sinatra in Italy. Richards then played with Muggsy Spanier (1953/1954–1957, 1959), performed and recorded with the Fletcher Henderson reunion band (though he had never been a member of Henderson's band; 1957–8), worked as an unaccompanied soloist in Columbus, Ohio (1958), and served as a sideman with Wild Bill Davison (1958–9, 1962). In October 1960 he and Vic Dickenson formed a sextet called the SAINTS AND SINNERS, which they led together until it disbanded in 1970; it toured Europe twice and recorded several albums. In the 1970s Richards worked as an intermission pianist at Eddie Condon's club in New York (1975–7) and held two engagements with his own trio (1977–8). From 1979 he toured internationally as a soloist and in Panama Francis's Savoy Sultans (ii), performing in Spain and Japan (1986) and Australia (1987); he also recorded with Clayton (1979), Bill Coleman (1980), and Dickenson (1981). From the late 1980s to his death he continued to tour internationally and often performed and recorded in groups with George Kelly, a fellow sideman from the Savoy Sultans.
Oral history material at *DSI* (JOHP).

SELECTED RECORDINGS

As unaccompanied soloist: *Soft Buns* (1978, West 54 8000); *Lullaby in Rhythm* (1985, Sack. 2-3044); *Dreamy* (1991, Sack. 2-3053); with M. McPartland: *Marian McPartland with Guest Red Richards* (1991, Jazz Alliance 12011) [also incl. duos with McParland]; *My Romance* (1993, Jazzpoint 1042)
As leader: *In a Mellow Tone* (1979, West 54 8005); with G. Kelly: *Groove Move* (1994, Jazzpoint 1045)
As sideman: B. Coleman: *Really I Do* (1980, BB 33162); A. Casey: *A Tribute to "Fats"* (1994, Jazzpoint 1044)

BIBLIOGRAPHY

AllenH
C. Richards: "Charles 'Red' Richards," *BHcF*, no.26 (1953), 4
H. McNamara: "Jazz," *The Telegram* [Toronto] (26 Jan 1967), 68
P. Scott: "The Handwriting on a Wailing Wall," *Toronto Daily Star* (3 June 1967), 62
B. Rusch: "Red Richards: Interview," *Cadence*, i/5 (1976), 7
C. Battestini and J.-P. Battestini: "Red Richards," *BHcF*, no.279 (1980), 6
S. Dance: "Red Richards," *JJI*, xxxiii/1 (1980), 18
E. Townley: "Gentleman of Swing: an Interview with Charles 'Red' Richards," *Sv*, no.88 (1980), 149
J. Chilton: *Sidney Bechet: the Wizard of Jazz* (London and New York, 1987/*R*1996)
B. Whyatt: *Muggsy Spanier: the Lonesome Road: a Biography and Discography* (New Orleans, 1995)
Obituaries: P. Vacher, *The Guardian* (11 April 1998); G. Columbé, *JJI*, li/5 (1998), 15

JAMES M. DORAN/BK

Richards, Trevor (Hamilton Edward) (*b* Bexhill-on-Sea, England, 29 Aug 1945). English drummer. He took up drums as a child. After playing with bands in Germany from 1963 he went to the USA in 1966 and studied with Zutty Singleton in New York. He then traveled to New Orleans, where he worked with many veteran musicians. In 1967 he formed his own group. He returned to Britain, worked with Sammy Rimington, and toured Europe with Harold Dejan's Olympia Brass Band (summer 1968), recording in Germany. In March 1973 he formed a trio that often played in Germany, but also toured internationally. He made several recordings with this trio, notably with Louis Nelson, Alton Purnell (both 1973), and Freddie Kohlman (1976) as guest soloists, and as a sideman with Albert Nicholas (1970) and Benny Waters (1974). In the 1980s he toured Europe with Art Hodes; during this period he made several recordings with Hodes's International Trio (1981, 1985, 1986), including *Blues to Save the Trees* (1981, L+R 40015), as well as a tribute to Lovie Austin's Blues Serenaders, nominally as Hodes's Blues Serenaders (1988). He also toured Europe with Ralph Sutton, and in the late 1980s worked with Jacques Gauthé. In 1982 Richards returned to New Orleans, where he became co-leader with the trumpeter Clive Wilson of the Original Camelia Band. The band initially recorded under Wilson's name (1982–4), but it toured Asia from 1985 to 1989 and recorded under Richards's name in Singapore in 1986, with Leroy Jones in place of Wilson. In the 1990s Richards spent roughly half of each year in New Orleans and half in Europe. In Germany he recorded in a trio with the clarinetist Peter Müller and Butch Thompson (*New Orleans Trio*, 1990, Stomp Off 1222) and with Orange Kellin and Red Richards (1994), and with the Barrelhouse Jazz Band (*The King Oliver Heritage Band*, 1995, L+R 40033).

BIBLIOGRAPHY

ChiltonB
A. Vasset: "Trevor Richards," *BHcF*, no.460 (1997), 1

GERHARD CONRAD, BK

Richardson, Jerome (C.) (*b* Sealy, TX, 15 Nov 1920; *d* Englewood, NJ, 23 June 2000). Reed player. He explained that he was adopted, but until he was 50 was unaware of this and believed that he was born in Oakland, California, on 25 December; thereafter he tracked down the records, though he reports the adoption papers say incorrectly that he was born in Los Angeles. He grew up in California and began playing alto saxophone when he was eight, taking classical lessons for four years. After making his professional début at the age of 14 deputizing in Lionel Hampton's band at the T & B Theater in Oakland, he studied at San Francisco State College and worked until 1941 with local dance bands. Before joining the navy he served briefly as a replacement for Willie Smith in Jimmie Lunceford's band; during military service (1942–5) he played in a dance band directed by Marshal Royal. Following his discharge he re-established his career while working with Vernon Alley and then toured with Hampton from 1949 to 1951 (by most accounts) or to 4 July 1952 (Richardson, in Bernotas, 1995); he appears with Hampton's orchestra in a number of short films from this period. He recorded with Flip Phillips in San Francisco (February 1952) and after working as a freelance spent eight months with Earl Hines (1952–3). While with Hines he toured to New York, where he then led his own group at Minton's Playhouse (from 1955), worked at the Apollo Theatre and the Savoy Ballroom, and played with Oscar Pettiford (1955–7); it was Richardson who turned up late for work the night that Cannonball Adderley sat in as a substitute with Pettiford and made his legendary New York début at the Café Bohemia.

During the 1950s Richardson also worked with Lucky Millinder, Cootie Williams, Chico Hamilton, Johnny Richards, Gerry Mulligan, and Gerald Wilson and made a large number of studio recordings as a flute and saxophone soloist in small groups and as a member of wind sections in larger ensembles, notably with Adderley, Kenny Clarke, Kenny Burrell, Jimmy Cleveland, Hank Jones, the Gil Evans Orchestra accompanying Helen Merrill and Miles Davis, Johnny Hartman, Dinah Washington, Gene Ammons, Abbey Lincoln, Eddie "Lockjaw" Davis, Billy Taylor (ii), Tiny Grimes, and Charles Mingus. In the 1960s he recorded with, among many others, Adderley, Burrell, Mingus, Tadd Dameron, J. J. Johnson, Hamilton, Jimmy Smith, Wes Montgomery, Oliver Nelson, and Louis Armstrong. In 1959–60 he was a member of Quincy Jones's orchestra, which toured Europe and performed in the show *Free and Easy* in Paris. He maintained his association with Jones, but also worked with several jazz and popular singers, including Peggy Lee, Billy Eckstine, Brook Benton, and Julie London; Richardson himself also worked as a singer.

In December 1965 Richardson was a founding member of the Thad Jones–Mel Lewis Orchestra, and served as its lead alto saxophonist until 1970. After moving to Hollywood in 1971 he became active as a session musician and resumed his collaboration with Quincy Jones, touring Japan three times. In 1980 he toured Europe with Nat Adderley and worked in Thad Jones's European big band. He recorded with Jon Hendricks in 1981, but the vast majority of his studio work in the 1980s was outside jazz. In 1989 he left southern California and returned to New York, initially to play in the pit orchestra for the musical *Black and Blue*, and in the early 1990s he performed in and served as contractor for another show, *Jelly's Last Jam*. He performed and recorded with Clifford Jordan's big band (early 1990s) and Al Grey (1995) and recorded with Mario Bauzá's Afro-Cuban orchestra (1991) and in Harold Danko's quartet, accompanying the singer Giacomo Gates (1995). A member of Art Farmer's American quintet, he had begun to tour with Slide Hampton's Jazzmasters by 1995. Richardson's work in studios tended to overshadow his highly competent work as a soloist, but he was extremely versatile and adaptable, and particularly effective on tenor saxophone and flute. He is the composer of *Groove Merchant*, recorded by the Jones–Lewis Orchestra in 1969.

SELECTED RECORDINGS

As leader: *Jerome Richardson Sextet* (1958, NewJ 8205); *Roamin' with Jerome Richardson* (1959, NewJ 8226); *Going to the Movies* (1962, UA 15006); *Jazz Station Runaway* (1996–7, TCB 97402)

As sideman: O. Pettiford: *Oscar Pettiford Orchestra in Hi-fi* (1956, ABC-Para. 135); *Oscar Pettiford and his Birdland Band* (1957, Spot. 153); Q. Jones: *The Great Wide World of Quincy Jones* (1959, Mer. 60221); *The Quintessence of Quincy Jones* (1961, Imp. 11); T. Jones and M. Lewis: *Monday Night* (1968, SolS 18048); *Central Park North* (1969, SolS 18058), incl. Groove Merchant

BIBLIOGRAPHY

FeatherE; *Feather '60s*; *Feather–Gitler '70s*

B. Messinger: Liner notes, *Going to the Movies* (UA 15006, 1963)

"Jerome Richardson Talking," *CI*, ix/7 (1971), 13

L. Tomkins: "Go to New York, Young Man, Advises Jerome Richardson," *CI*, xix/7 (1981), 16

J.-L. Ginibre: "Richardson à la conquête du jazz," *Jm*, no.347 (1986), 36

B. Rusch: "Jerome Richardson," *Cadence*, xiii/12 (1987), 5

B. Bernotas: "Jerome Richardson," *Saxophone Journal*, xix/5 (1995), 30 [incl. discography]

<http://www.jazzcorner.com/richardson/bio.html> (1999)

MARK GARDNER/BK

Richardson, Rodney (V.) (*b* New Orleans, 21 Aug 1917). Double bass player. He often moved between New Orleans and Chattanooga in his youth and played ukulele and guitar before taking up double bass in his late teens. His first work was with territory bands in Tennessee during the 1930s, when he played double bass and guitar with the Georgia Boys in Chattanooga and guitar with the Royal Knights in Nashville. Having abandoned music for two years, he resumed playing in 1941 and joined Harlan Leonard in Kansas City in May 1942. The following year he traveled to California with Leonard, worked with the tenor saxophonist "Big Six" Reeves in Hollywood, and played informally with Art Tatum; late that August he returned to Kansas City to join Count Basie's group. He toured and recorded with Basie for the next three years (to July 1946), though he also made swing recordings in New York with the Kansas City Seven, Herbie Fields, and Earle Warren (all 1944), Lester Young (1944, 1947), Lucky Thompson (1945), and Roy Eldridge (1946). Richardson then worked with Eldridge in Chicago, performed with the trumpeter Eddie Mallory at the Savoy Ballroom in New York, and toured and recorded with Young's small group (*c* September 1946 – July 1947). After playing in Atlantic City, New Jersey (summer 1947 to autumn 1948), he collaborated with Charlie Rouse and Jimmy Cobb in Washington, DC. He returned to Atlantic City for another summer season (1949) and then spent nearly a year in Tiny Grimes's group (1949–50), although Ike Isaacs (i), rather than Richardson, is believed to have recorded as Grimes's double bass player during this period. Thereafter, apart from touring with Erroll Garner (1952), Richardson performed in Cleveland (to *c*1955), Detroit (to 1969), and southern California (1969–83), where he held a weekly engagement in Bakersfield (1974–8); he also played with Duke Burrell's Louisiana Shakers, which toured Europe in 1975. Later he moved to Boston and worked with Sabby Lewis (to August 1987).

SELECTED RECORDINGS

As sideman: Kansas City Seven: Lester Leaps Again (1944, Key. 1302); E. Warren: Circus in Rhythm/Tush (1944, Savoy 539); C. Basie: Taps Miller (1944, Col. 36831); Red Bank Boogie (1944, Col. 36766); L. Thompson: No Good Man Blues (1945, Excelsior 145); Phace (1945, Excelsior 146); L. Young: Jumpin' with Symphony Sid (1946, Ala. 163); Sax-o-re-bop (1946, Ala. 164)

BIBLIOGRAPHY

SheridanCB

P. Vacher: "Rodney Richardson's Story," *MR*, viii/1 (1980), 5

D. Smoak: "Rodney Richardson: Interview," *Cadence*, xv (1989), no.11, p.15; no.12, p.11

HOWARD RYE, BK

Richeson, Dane (Maxim) (*b* Columbus, OH, 17 July 1957). Drummer and percussionist. He studied classical music at Indiana University of Pennsylvania (1977–8), gained degrees in percussion from Ohio State University (BM 1982) and Ithaca College (MM 1984), and then joined the music faculty at Lawrence University in Appleton, Wisconsin. His work in jazz has included longstanding affiliations with such Wisconsin-based musicians as the trumpeter Bob Levy (from 1984, recording in 1994), the pianist John Harmon (from 1984, recording in 1995), and Joan Wildman and the double bass player Hans Sturm (both from 1985), among others; he may be heard to excellent effect in Wildman's trio (with Sturm) on the album *Inside Out* (1992, Wild 1910). Richeson has also performed regularly with the guitarist Marty Ashby (from 1982), the violinist Randy Sabien (from 1990), and Ken Schaphorst (from 1991, recording in several of the ensembles on the latter's album *Over the Rainbow: the Music of Harold Arlen*, 1996, Accurate 4204). In 1998 he recorded with the pianist Kurt Ellenberger. Richeson has worked in contemporary classical chamber ensembles in Chicago (from 1989) and Madison, Wisconsin (from 1993), and while continuing to teach at Lawrence he spent time abroad studying Ewe tribal music in Ghana (1994) and Bahia drumming styles in Brazil (1996).

(<http://www.lawrence.edu/conservatory/bios/richeson.shtml> (2000)).

GK

Richman, Boomie [Abraham Samuel] (*b* Brockton, MA, 2 April 1921). Tenor saxophonist and clarinetist. He played at clubs in Boston before moving to New York (1942), where he performed and recorded with the clarinetist Jerry Wald (1942), Muggsy Spanier (1944), Tommy Dorsey (1945–51), and Benny Goodman (1951–5). During the 1950s he was active as a freelance: he worked in radio and television and made recordings with the Sauter–Finegan Orchestra (1952), Neal Hefti and Spanier (both 1954), Ruby Braff and Billy Butterfield (who, for contractual reasons, was recording as Gus Hoo) (both 1955), Al Cohn (1956), Henry "Red" Allen and Urbie Green (both 1957), and Cootie Williams (1958). Richman worked as a studio musician in New York in the 1960s, but no longer played jazz.

SELECTED RECORDINGS

As sideman: M. Spanier: Riverside Blues/Rosetta (1944, Com. 586); That's a Plenty (1944, V-Disc 424); Jazz Me Blues (1944, V-Disc 504); B. Goodman *B. G. in Hi-fi* (1954, Cap. W565); G. Hoo (B. Butterfield): *New York Land Dixie* (1955, RCA LPM1212)

BIBLIOGRAPHY

FeatherE

J. Postgate: "The Forgotten Ones: Boomie Richman," *JJI*, xlviii/7 (1995), 10

BK

Richmond, Dannie [Charles D.] (*b* New York, 15 Dec 1931; *d* New York, 16 March 1988). Drummer. Richmond gave his year of birth as 1935, which appears widely in published sources, but his obituary in the *New York Times* gives 1931, a year which might better explain the extent of his activities before joining Charles Mingus, and his social security records confirm 1931. He grew up in both New York and Greensboro, North Carolina, and played rhythm-and-blues tenor saxophone while in his teens, doubling as a xylophone and tympani player in high school ensembles; he left high school to join Paul Williams's band, but at his mother's demand later returned and graduated. After moving north he studied reed instruments, piano, and percussion at the Music Center Conservatory in Brooklyn, then returned to Greensboro to attend the Agricultural and Technical College of North Carolina, where Jackie McLean was a fellow student; at a jam session with McLean early in 1956 he sat in for an absent drummer and played so well that he immediately bought a drum set and made this his main instrument.

Richmond was Mingus's regular drummer from October 1956, when he sat in and upstaged Willie Jones in maintaining a frenetically paced version of *Cherokee*, through the 1960s, and played on many of his albums; over the next dozen years his career paralleled that of Mingus, with whom he may be seen in the video *Charles Mingus Sextet: Mingus in Oslo* (mid-1990s [filmed 1964]) and the film documentary *Mingus* (1968). Among his occasional activities independent of Mingus were recordings with Herbie Nichols and Jimmy Knepper (both 1957) and Pepper Adams (1963), and performances with Zoot Sims, Chet Baker (intermittently 1958–9), and Freddie Redd; for a brief period in the late 1960s he was co-leader with the rhythm-and-blues singer Johnny Taylor of the group LTD. He rejoined Mingus in 1970 for an engagement at Ronnie Scott's in London, then played jazz-rock for three years with the group Mark–Almond, accompanied the rock singer Joe Cocker, and toured with the rock singer and pianist Elton John. He played for a brief period with Baker, then rejoined Mingus in 1974; after Mingus's death in 1979 he played with Mingus Dynasty and led a quintet which initially consisted of Jack Walrath, Ricky Ford, Bob Neloms, and Eddie Gomez; Cameron Brown replaced Gomez in 1980, and from 1983 the group worked as a quartet. Richmond recorded with Knepper again (1976), Duke Jordan's trio (in performance in Scandinavia, late 1978), Bennie Wallace (1978–82), Horace Parlan (1978, 1983), Walrath (1979), Mal Waldron (1981), Lew Tabackin (1984), and Ray Anderson (1985). With George Adams and Don Pullen, who also had been sidemen with Mingus, Richmond began a collaboration in 1979 that led to several outstanding albums; their quartet, which included Brown, disbanded a few months after Richmond's death in 1988.

While Richmond employed the freer elements from jazz of the 1960s, his playing was rooted in a deep understanding of swing and bop, and was occasionally further enlivened with the forcefulness of rhythm-and-blues. His drumming was emotional and unpredictable, and he could play explosively or with considerable restraint; his ability to shift from one extreme to the other is displayed to advantage on the track *Double Arc Jake* from George Adams's and Don Pullen's album *Don't Lose Control* (1979).

See also Mingus, Charles.

SELECTED RECORDINGS

As leader: *Ode to Mingus* (1979, SN 1005); *Dannie Richmond Plays Charles Mingus* (1980, Tim. 148); with G. Adams: *Gentlemen's Agreement* (1983, SN 1057)

As sideman with C. Mingus: *Mingus ah um* (1959, Col. CL1370); *Charles Mingus Presents Charles Mingus* (1960, Can. 9005); *Town Hall Concert* (1962, UA 15024); *The Black Saint and the Sinner Lady* (1963, Imp. 35); *The Great Concert of Charles Mingus* (1964, Amer. 003–5); *Changes Two* (1974, Atl. 1678); *Three or Four Shades of Blues* (1977, Atl. 1700)

As sideman with others: Mark–Almond: *Mark–Almond 2* (1972, Blue Thumb 32); D. Pullen: *Jazz a confronto 21* (1975, Horo 21); G. Adams and D. Pullen: *Don't Lose Control* (1979, SN 1004), incl. Double Arc Jake; *Earth Beams* (1980, Tim. 147); B. Wallace: *Bennie Wallace Plays Monk* (1981, Enja 3091); L. Tabackin: *Angelica* (1984, Ewd 90036)

BIBLIOGRAPHY

D. Locke: "Jazz Paradox," *JM*, xi/9 (1965), 23
D. Morgenstern: "Mingus' Man Dannie Richmond," *DB*, xxxiii/6 (1966), 18
M. Plummer: "Danny: from Mingus to Mark–Almond," *MM* (13 Nov 1971), 30
P. Senoff: "New Bands: Mark–Almond," *J&P*, x/6 (1971), 18
B. Primack: "The Gospel According to Mingus: Disciples Carry the Tune," *DB*, xlv/20 (1978), 12
B. Case: "Minus Mingus," *MM* (22 March 1980), 27
B. Shoemaker: "Danny Richmond," *Coda*, no.179 (1981), 4
B. Priestley: *Mingus: a Critical Biography* (London, Melbourne, Australia, and New York, 1982)
H. Mandel: "Dr. Dannie Richmond: Rx for Swing," *DB*, lii/11 (1985), 27 [incl. discography]
M. Mowlett and D. Roustain: "Les riches mondes de Dannie," *Jm*, no.371 (1988), 24
Obituaries: *New York Times* (18 March 1988); S. Voce, *The Independent* (30 March 1988)

JEFF POTTER/BK

Richmond, June [née Leto, Beatrice Louise; Gachon, Beatrice Louise] (*b* Chicago, 9 July 1915; *d* Gothenburg, Sweden, 14 Aug 1962). Singer. After performing with Les Hite in California she joined Jimmy Dorsey's band (1938). She recorded with Cab Calloway (1938) and as a member of Andy Kirk's band (1939–43, 1944–5), and made three soundies with Roy Milton's band (*Hey Lawdy Mama*, *Ride On, Ride On*, and *47th Street Jive*, all 1944); she also appeared in the film *Reet, Petite and Gone* (1947). From August 1948 she worked in Europe, and while there recorded as a leader in Stockholm in 1951 and with Quincy Jones's orchestra in Paris in 1957; from 1954 she had a French passport under her married name, Beatrice Louise Gachon. At the height of her powers Richmond was a powerful and effective blues shouter, but her approach to popular songs often relied on the techniques of cabaret singing rather than of jazz, and only rarely did she transcend the limitations of the material.

SELECTED RECORDINGS

(all recorded for Decca)

As sideman with A. Kirk: Then I'll be happy (1939, 2723); Please don't talk about me when I'm gone (1939, 3033); Midnight Stroll (1940, 3350); 47th Street Jive (1941, 4042); Hey Lawdy Mama (1942, 4405); Ride On, Ride On/Unlucky Blues (1942, 4436)

BIBLIOGRAPHY

ChiltonW
A. Kirk, as told to A. Lee: *Twenty Years on Wheels* (Wheatley, Oxford, England, and Ann Arbor, MI, 1989), 110

HOWARD RYE

Richmond, Kim (*b* Champaign, IL, 24 July 1940). Saxophonist, arranger, and composer. He took up piano, clarinet, and then saxophone as a child, began playing professionally in 1956, and later attended the University of Illinois (BME and BM in composition 1963). During military service (1963–7) he was a member of a US Air Force big band, the Airmen of Note, based in Washington, DC. He then moved to southern California, where he recorded and performed with the big bands of Stan Kenton (1967), Clare Fischer (1968), Louie Bellson (1969–72), Lalo Schifrin (1979), Bob Florence (from 1979), Les Brown (1989), Bill Holman (from *c*1990), Vinny Golia (1991), and others. In the 1960s he also began a career as an arranger, writing for Buddy Rich (notably *Wonderbag*, on the album *Buddy & Soul*, 1967, Cap. ST2922), Ernie Watts, Schifrin, and others. Richmond founded a large ensemble, the Concert Jazz Orchestra, which performed his compositions in the southern California area (a selection of these was recorded on *Passages* in 1992), and he played with small groups, including one co-led by the trumpeter Clay Jenkins (sheet music and a play-along CD for several of the group's pieces were published as "Kim Richmond/Clay Jenkins Ensemble," *Jazz Player*, v/5 (1998), 28). During the same period he was active in popular music as a performer, arranger, music director, and conductor, variously for concerts, recordings, and television shows. Influenced by Charlie Mariano, Richmond brings to his well-constructed jazz improvisations a technical facility after the manner of John Coltrane; he has doubled on clarinet, flute, and EWI.

SELECTED RECORDINGS

As leader: *Looking in Looking out* (1988, Nine Winds 0123); *Passages* (1992, Sea Breeze 2043); with C. Jenkins: *Range* (1994, Nine Winds 0172), *Look at the Time* (1999, Chase Music Group 8055)

As sideman with B. Florence: *State of the Art* (1988, USA Music Group 589); *Treasure Chest* (1990, USA Music Group 680); *Funupsmanship* (1993, MAMA 1006); *With All the Bells and Whistles* (1995, MAMA 1011); *Earth* (1996, MAMA 1016), incl. Straight, No Chaser; *Serendipity 18* (1999, MAMA 1025)

As sideman with others: Brad Dutz: *Railroads* (1995, Nine Winds 0178); Jim Widner: *Yesterday and Today* (1995, Chase Music 8045); *Body & Soul* (1996, Chase Music 8048); B. Dutz: *Making Ice* (1997, Truemedia 97910); *Heat the Grill Cook Lion* (1999, Household Ink 126)

BIBLIOGRAPHY

H. Siders: "Richmond Gets Break from Mother-in-law," *DB*, xxxix/12 (1972), 11

L. Underwood: "Profiles: Some People Behind the Music: Kim Richmond," *DB*, xliv/13 (1977), 24

A. Lewis and L. Lewis: "Kim Richmond Interview," *Cadence*, xxi/7 (1995), 17

S. Chamberlain: "Kim Richmond," *Saxophone Journal*, xxiii/2 (1998), 24 [incl. discography]

<http://members.aol.com/JazzKim> (1998)

THOMAS OWENS

Richmond, Mike [Michael] (*b* Philadelphia, 26 Feb 1948). Bass player. After attending Temple University (BA 1970) he studied with Jimmy Garrison (1970–72), taught high school in Philadelphia, and performed in local orchestras. In the early 1970s, while playing with Chico Hamilton, he began an association with Arnie Lawrence, with whom he later appeared at the Berliner Jazztage (1977). He toured and recorded with Stan Getz, Jack DeJohnette, Hubert Laws and Buddy DeFranco (all 1975–8), Horace Silver (1978), and Gil Evans (intermittently, 1974–9); during this period he also worked with Woody Herman and Milt Jackson (both 1975) and Sonny Stitt. In 1980 his interest in Indian music took him to Bombay, where he performed with the sitar player Ravi Shankar. His busy studio work schedule included sessions with Andy LaVerne (1977 and *c*1978, the latter as a duo), whom he had brought into Getz's group, as well as with Franco Ambrosetti (1978, 1981), Dannie Richmond (1979), Jim McNeely (1979, 1980), George Adams and Richmond (1980, 1983), Jane Ira Bloom (1981), Bennie Wallace (1984), and Wolfgang Puschnig (in the group Air Mail, 1985).

From 1980 to 1985 Richmond was music director of Mingus Dynasty and in 1980 he played with the group at the Montreux International Jazz Festival. In the following year he appeared with Ambrosetti, Christof Lauer, George Gruntz, and Daniel Humair as the Franco-German Orchestra at the festival in Frankfurt. He maintained longstanding affiliations with Lee Konitz (1976–), Gruntz's orchestra and small groups (1978–), and Tom Varner (1985–) while working with Joe Henderson (1988–95), the big band of Chris Hunter (1989–90), Miles Davis (1991), and Larry Schneider (1991–2), and recording with Herb Geller and Konitz (both 1988), McNeely (1989), Marvin Stamm (1992), the pianist Dave Berkman, Eliot Zigmund (1993), Barry Finnerty (1994), Walter Norris (in a duo, 1998), and many others; he also made some dozen albums as a leader and unaccompanied soloist. He has written a tutor, *Modern Walking Bass Technique* (Englewood, NJ, 1983); having offered workshops internationally from 1974, he has been a member of the faculty of New York University from 1985 and received its Teacher of the Year award in 1994.

Oral history material in *GBLnsa*.

SELECTED RECORDINGS

Duo with A. LaVerne: *For Us* (*c*1978, Ste. 1101)

As leader: *Dreamwaves* (1977, IC 1065); with J. McNeely and D. Humair: *East Side–West Side* (1980, Owl 024)

As sideman: J. DeJohnette: *Untitled* (1976, ECM 1074); S. Getz: *Another World* (1977, Col. JG35513); Mingus Dynasty: *Live at Montreux* (1980, Atl. 16031); A. Lawrence: *Renewal* (1981, PAlt 8033); G. Gruntz: *Serious Fun* (1989, Enja 6038-2); L. Schneider: *Just Cole Porter* (1991, Ste. 31291); T. Varner: *The Mystery of Compassion* (1992, SN 121217-2)

BIBLIOGRAPHY

A. J. Smith: "Profile: Mike Richmond," *DB*, xlv/13 (1978), 42

C. Jisi: "Working Bass Hero: a Private Lesson with Mike Richmond," *Bass Player*, v/6 (1994), 50

WILLIAM S. BROCKMAN/BK

Ricketts, Bob (*fl.* 1920s). Pianist, composer, and arranger. Around 1920 he was the bandleader at the Standard Theater in Philadelphia. With a fellow pianist and composer, Porter Grainger, he headed a race music publisher, Rainbow Music Corporation (founded in mid-1923), for Irving Berlin, Inc., and together they wrote *How to Play and Sing the Blues like the Phonograph and Stage Artists* (1926). In 1923 Ricketts supplied arrangements for Fletcher Henderson and organized accompaniments by Rickett's Stars for the singers Kitty Brown, Esther Bigeou, and Lizzie Miles and by a different band for Viola McCoy; these are thought to have involved groups of studio musicians. He also recorded on organ accompanying gospel groups. As a pianist he may be heard to advantage accompanying the singer Margaret Johnson, notably on the track *Everything that happens just pleases me* (1926, OK 8405), and especially the singer Bertha Idaho, on the pairing *Graveyard Love/You've got the right eye, but you're peeping at the wrong keyhole* (1928, Col. 14355D). Ricketts, who was well-known in his day, especially as a composer, was still active in the late 1920s, but details of his subsequent career are unknown. (*AllenH*)

HOWARD RYE

Ricotti, Frank (*b* London, 31 Jan 1949). English vibraphonist. A member of the National Youth Jazz Orchestra in his teens, he studied at Trinity College of Music, London (1967–70), and played with Neil Ardley (recording in 1968, 1969, and 1971) and the tenor saxophonist Dave Gelly. He formed his own quartet in the early 1970s, but also worked with Graham Collier, Mike Gibbs (recording in 1969–72), Stan Tracey (recording in 1970), Harry Beckett (recording in 1970–72), Norma Winstone (recording in 1971), and Gordon Beck's Gyroscope (1973–4). In the early 1980s he played with Chris Laurence and John Taylor in Paragonne (with whom he recorded *Aspects of Paragonne*, 1985, MMC 010), and also recorded with Beck (1984). Thereafter, however, he concentrated on studio and freelance work, playing and composing music for films, television, and other media.

BIBLIOGRAPHY

ChiltonB

R. Cotterell, ed.: *Jazz Now: the Jazz Centre Society Guide* (London, 1976)

P. Renaud: *La discographie du jazz anglais* (Chaumont, France, 1985)

SIMON ADAMS

Riddle, Nelson (Smock) (*b* Oradell, NJ, 1 June 1921; *d* Los Angeles, 6 Oct 1985). Composer, arranger, and leader. His middle name is taken from the California death index. In the 1940s he worked as a trombonist and arranger for big bands, including those of the clarinetist Jerry Wald, Tommy Dorsey (from May 1944), Bob Crosby, and Charlie Spivak. Later he wrote arrangements and led backup orchestras for such jazz and popular singers as Peggy Lee, Judy Garland, Nat "King" Cole, Sarah Vaughan, and Ella Fitzgerald, with whom he collaborated on the album *Ella Fitzgerald Sings the Jerome Kern Songbook* (1963, Verve 84060). He is best known for his association with Frank Sinatra, whose success in the late 1950s owed much to Riddle's arrangements; some of these were slow and introspective, others vigorous and swinging. Riddle occasionally led his own groups, and around 1957 he recorded the album *Hey, Let Yourself Go* (Cap. T814). During the 1960s and 1970s he was mostly active in films and television; towards the end of his career he recorded three albums of popular songs from the 1920s and 1930s with the singer Linda Ronstadt.

BIBLIOGRAPHY

"Nelson Riddle Talking," *CI*, vi/1 (1967), 10
N. Riddle: "Branching Out from the Sound," *CI*, vi/2 (1967), 20
H. Siders: "Nelson Riddle: Arranger, Composer, Conductor," *IM*, lxxi/12 (1973), 9
L. Tomkins: "Nelson Riddle Today," *CI*, xx/1 (1981), 20; contd as "Nelson Riddle & the Standards of Sinatra," xx/2 (1981), 24

MARK TUCKER

Ride. To improvise, or an IMPROVISATION; the word, which was current in early jazz and the swing era, carries connotations, variously, of inventiveness, freedom of delivery, and swinging rhythmic momentum. A good example of its usage occurs in the title of a recording by the Mills Blue Rhythm Band – *Ride, Red, Ride* (1935, Col. 3087D) – on which Henry "Red" Allen plays an extended solo. "To take a ride" is to improvise a solo, and a "ride man" is an improvising soloist. (*See* also RIDE-OUT.)

Ride cymbal [top cymbal]. A large cymbal used from the late 1930s to carry the regular beat; *see* DRUM SET, §§I, 5; II, 5, 6.

Ride-out. The final chorus of a lively piece, collectively improvised in a loud, spirited manner (*see* FORMS, §2); the term is associated with early styles of jazz.

Ridley, Larry [Laurence Howard, II] (*b* Indianapolis, 3 Sept 1937). Double bass player. He learned violin as a child, then after hearing Ray Brown took up double bass. Although he often played in Indianapolis with Freddie Hubbard, who was a childhood friend, his first job, at the age of 16, was with Wes Montgomery. In 1954 he was a founding member of a cooperative quintet, the Jazz Contemporaries, which included Hubbard and James Spaulding. In 1955 he entered Indiana University to study violin but soon changed to double bass. After receiving instruction from Percy Heath at the Lenox (Massachusetts) School of Jazz (summer 1959) he played briefly in New York with Hubbard and toured with Slide Hampton (1960). Apart from a period with Sun Ra in the early 1960s he performed with such hard-bop musicians as Lou Donaldson (1961), Philly Joe Jones (1961–3), Max Roach (1963, 1966), Jackie McLean and Roy Haynes (both 1963–5), Hubbard (intermittently, 1964–9), Lee Morgan (1965–6), Horace Silver (1965–7, including a tour of Scandinavia in 1966), and Sonny Rollins (in Japan, 1968). He recorded with Hampton and Bunky Green (both 1960), Hubbard, Red Garland, and Jimmy Heath (all 1961), Haynes, Jones, and McLean (all 1963), Bill Barron (1964), Hank Mobley and Morgan (both 1965), and Silver (1966). In 1968–9 he appeared at the Needle's Eye, New York, in duos with Ted Dunbar and Harold Mabern, and in 1969 he played with Mousey Alexander and toured Europe as a member of George Wein's Newport All-Stars; while with this group in France and Germany he recorded with his fellow sidemen Ruby Braff and Red Norvo, as well as with Stephane Grappelli and Joe Venuti.

In 1971 Ridley obtained a degree in music education from New York University, and subsequently he became head of the jazz program and chairman of the music department at Livingston College (Rutgers), Piscataway, New Jersey. He toured Japan in 1970 and the USA and Mexico in 1971 as a member of Thelonious Monk's group; in the latter year he also toured North America with Oscar Peterson and traveled worldwide with Kenny Burrell. During the same period he performed in duos with Kenny Barron, Burrell, Dunbar, Grimes, Roland Prince, and others. He continued to work with Monk into 1972 and again for a concert at Carnegie Hall in 1975, and in the first half of the decade he played with the Thad Jones–Mel Lewis Orchestra, Earl Hines, Duke Ellington's orchestra and its continuation under Mercer Ellington, Rollins, Milt Jackson, and Vic Dickenson, among many others, and toured further with the Newport All Stars. His quartet at the Half Note, New York, in March 1974 included Spaulding and Mabern. The following year Ridley performed in a trio with Cedar Walton and Louis Hayes in New Brunswick, New Jersey, accompanied Chet Baker and Kenny Drew and played with Zoot Sims at festivals in Italy, and toured regularly with Billy Taylor (ii), with whom he made numerous appearances on television. As a freelance in the 1970s he recorded with Dexter Gordon and Attila Zoller (both 1970), Charlie Byrd and Tiny Grimes (1971), Lucky Thompson (*c*1972), the reconstituted Jazz Contemporaries and James Moody (both 1972), Al Cohn (1975), and Teddy Edwards (1976); he also made an album as a leader (1975).

In the 1980s Ridley played in Philly Joe Jones's group Dameronia (1981–5), served on the executive committee of the National Jazz Service Organization (from 1984), and formed a new group, the Jazz Legacy Ensemble (1985), with which he continued to perform into the new century; Virgil Jones, David "Fathead" Newman, Ronnie Mathews, and Kenny Washington have served as his sidemen at various times. From 1992 he played in the Smithsonian Jazz Masterworks Orchestra. While continuing to teach at Rutgers (from which he retired as professor emeritus in 1999) he gained a masters degree in cultural policy from the Empire State College division of SUNY (1993). Ridley's driving hard-bop style may be heard to advantage on *Anthropology*, which he recorded with Moody (1973).

For illustration *see* MANGELSDORFF, ALBERT.

SELECTED RECORDINGS

As leader: *Sum of the Parts* (1975, SE 19759)

As sideman: S. Hampton: *Somethin' Sanctified* (1960, Atl. 1362); R. Haynes: *Cracklin'* (1963, NewJ 8286); L. Morgan: *Cornbread* (1965, BN 84222); H. Silver: *The Jody Grind* (1966, BN 84250); S. Grappelli and J. Venuti: *Venupelli Blues* (1969, BYG 529122); J. Moody: *Feelin' it Together* (1973, Muse 5020), incl. Anthropology; T. Edwards: *The Inimitable Teddy Edwards* (1976, Xan. 134)

BIBLIOGRAPHY

E. Meadow: "Spotlight on Larry Ridley," *DB*, xxxviii/4 (1971), 16

B. Katell: "County Resident Performed in White House with Trio," *Daily Register* [Shrewsbury, NJ] (4 March 1975)
S. Freedman: "Larry Ridley has a Bass for Jazz Studies, Thanks to Grants, Gifts, Nearby New York," *DB*, xlvi/7 (1979), 12

BK

Riedel, Georg (*b* Karlovy Vary, Czechoslovakia [now Czech Republic], 8 Nov 1934). Swedish double bass player and composer of Czechoslovakian birth. His family moved to Sweden when he was four, and he received classical training on double bass. He made his professional début in 1953 as a member of Lars Gullin's quintet, with which he recorded in 1953–6. Riedel has performed and recorded with Arne Domnérus from 1955 into the new century. He also worked with Jan Johansson, recording the albums *M* (1965–7, Megafon 24–5) and *300.000* (1967–8, Megafon 18). In the 1980s he formed Trio con Tromba with Bengt Hallberg and Jan Allan. He has composed music for many films and written for a variety of ensembles, including symphony orchestra, chamber ensembles, choirs, and many jazz combinations; in such works for big band as *Riedaglia* (1967, Sveriges Radio 1051) and *Rainbow Sketches* (1974, CAM 5906) he reveals a gift for orchestration and a strong sense of form. His children's songs are especially beloved by several generations of Swedes.

BIBLIOGRAPHY

FeatherE; *Feather–Gitler '70s*
C.-E. Lindgren: "På omslaget" [On the cover], *Orkester journalen*, xxiii/1 (1955), 4
L. Westin: "Jazzen är basen för Georg Riedel" [Jazz is the bass for Georg Riedel], *Orkester journalen*, lv/12 (1987), 15
<http://www.mic.stim.se/engelsk/11/facts/riedel.html> (2000)

ERIK KJELLBERG/LARS WESTIN

Riel, Alex (Poul) (*b* Copenhagen, 13 Sept 1940). Danish drummer. From 1957 to 1960 he played with various traditional groups, and as the house drummer from 1963 to 1965 at the Montmartre Jazzhus in Copenhagen worked with many American soloists. He was a member of Erik Moseholm's trio (1964–7) and Radiojazzgruppen (i) (1965–8), and with Palle Mikkelborg led a quintet (which performed at the Montreux and Newport festivals in 1968) and the octet V8 (1970–75); he also played with the rock group Savage Rose (1968–72). Later he worked with the Danish group Six Winds (led by Jørgen Emborg and Uffe Markussen), the quartet led by Arild Andersen and Radka Toneff, Bob Rockwell, Jesper Lundgaard's Repertory Quartet, and other groups. The most experienced of Danish drummers, Riel was much in demand as an accompanist for visiting musicians. In his impressive discography are recordings with Brew Moore, Don Byas, Stuff Smith, Archie Shepp and Lars Gullin, Kenny Dorham, Sahib Shihab, Dexter Gordon, Karin Krog, Ben Webster, Stephane Grappelli, Mikkelborg, Monica Zetterlund, Bent Jædig, Jackie McLean, Makanda Ken McIntyre, Herb Geller, Allan Botschinsky, Warne Marsh, Art Farmer, Peter Herbolzheimer, Stan Getz, Shepp, Chet Baker, Thomas Clausen, Emborg, Frans Bak, Gary Burton, Niels Lan Doky, Markussen, Jan Lundgren, Lundgaard, and Cæcilie Norby.

SELECTED RECORDINGS

As leader: *Alex Riel Trio* (1965, Fona 111), incl. In a Way; *Emergence!* (1993, Red 123263-2); *The Riel Deal* (1995, Stunt 19604); *Unriel!* (1997, Stunt 19707); *Rielatin'* (1999, Stunt 19918)

As sideman: P. Mikkelborg and Radiojazzgruppen (i): *The Mysterious Corona* (1967, Debut 150); D. Gordon: *Swiss Nights*, i (1975, Ste. 1050); T. Clausen: *Café noir* (1991, M.A. Music 004). J. Emborg: *Over the Rainbow* (1992, Sto. 4183); A. Botschinsky: *The Bench* (1995, Sto. 4207); M. Vinding: *The Kingdom (Where Nobody Dies)* (1997, Stunt 19703); *Daddio Don* (1998, Stunt 19813)

BIBLIOGRAPHY

Feather–Gitler '70s
D. Samuels: "Drums around the World: Denmark's Alex Riel," *MD*, vii/10 (1983), 25
K. Frandsen: *Politikens jazzleksikon* (Copenhagen, 1987)
L. Tømming: "The Riel Deal," *Musikeren*, no.2 (1996), 10
R. Sanborn: "Alex Riel," *Jazz Special*, no.34 (1997), 35 [incl. discography]

ERIK WIEDEMANN/FRANK BÜCHMANN-MØLLER

Riessler, Michael (*b* Ulm, Germany, 19 June 1957). German clarinetist, saxophonist, and composer. He studied clarinet at the Musikhochschulen in Cologne and Hannover. From 1978 he worked in groups that played a mixture of avant-garde jazz and contemporary composed music, notably the French Ensemble Musique Vivante and the Kölner saxophon mafia. In the mid-1980s he moved to Paris, and thereafter he was active in both France and Cologne. From 1989 to 1991 he was a member of the Orchestre National de Jazz. In 1991 Riessler founded his group Le Bucher des Silences, for which he wrote extended compositions, often requested by prestigious festivals for contemporary music. The group, which included a barrel-organ player (Valentin Clastrier) and a tambourine player (Carlo Rizzi), inspired Riessler to write CD-length compositions involving jazz, popular music, and contemporary composed music as well as medieval sources. His stunning virtuoso technique on clarinet and bass clarinet may be heard on *Suite Talk* (with Tomasz Stańko and Manfred Bründl, 1993, ITM Pacific 970081) and on *Old/New Orleans*, from the album *Momentum Mobile* (1993, Enja 9003-2); good examples of his compositional experiments with medieval music include *Héloise* (1992, Wergo 8008-2), *Tentations d'Abélard* (1994, Wergo 8009-2), and *Honig und Asche* (1997, Enja 9303-2).

BIBLIOGRAPHY

H. Lachner: "Aufbruch in eine ungewisse Vergangenheit: einige Gedanken zu Michael Riessler," *Jazz Thing*, no.1 (1993), 34
P. Renaud and P. Gentet: "Solistes: le Bucher des Silences," *Notes*, no.44 (1993), 11
A. G. Aparicio: "Michael Riessler: una estética inclusiva," *Cuadernos de jazz*, no.51 (1999), 23
W. Knauer: "Mediaeval Blues: Zu Projekten mit Jazz und mittelalterlicher Musik," *Übersetzte Zeit: Das Mittelalter und die Musik der Gegenwart* (Hofheim am Taunus, Germany, 2001), 287

WOLFRAM KNAUER

Riff. A short melodic ostinato, usually two or four bars long, which may either be repeated intact (strict riff) or varied to accommodate an underlying harmonic pattern. The riff is thought to derive from the repetitive call-and-response patterns of West African music, and appeared prominently in African-American music from the earliest times. It was an important element in New Orleans marching band music (where the word "riff" apparently originated), and from there entered jazz, where by the mid-1920s it was firmly established in background ensemble playing and as the basis for solo improvisation. Riffs also appeared in the accompaniments of many early blues, being particularly suited to their repeating structure. The conflict between an unvaried riff pattern and the changing harmonies of the blues progression became one of the most distinctive features of the blues and its derivatives.

The riff came to the fore in the early 1930s in the Southwest tradition of orchestral jazz, where the influence of rural blues musicians was notably strong. Among the innovations of these groups was the "double" or "compound" riff, in which the brass and reed sections played separate riffs in counterpoint. As exploited by Bennie Moten and, from 1936, by Count Basie's band, riffs of this sort came to dominate large-ensemble jazz, either as the accompaniment to solo improvisation or as self-sufficient sections within a score. An outstanding example of a compound riff occurs at the end of Basie's theme song *One o'Clock Jump*, where the trumpet, trombone, and saxophone sections play contrasting riffs in three distinct rhythms (ex.1).

Ex.1 Riffs from C. Basie: *One o'Clock Jump* (air-shot recording, first issued on *Shout and Feel It*, 1937, Alamac 2412); transcr. J. B. Robinson

Especially sensitive use of the riff may be found in Duke Ellington's orchestral scores from this period (e.g., *Harlem Air-shaft*, 1940, Vic. 26731). Another development of the swing era was the "riff tune," in which riff patterns were fashioned into melodies; Glenn Miller's hit *In the Mood* (1939, Bb 10416A, adapted from a stock jazz riff at least as old as Wingy Manone's *Tar Paper Stomp*, 1930, Champion 16153) is perhaps the best known, but superior examples may be found in Charlie Christian's many compositions for Benny Goodman's small groups (e.g., *Good Enough to Keep*, 1941, Col. 36099).

By the 1940s the riff had become a jazz cliché. It was taken over into rhythm-and-blues, where it became a favorite accompaniment device, and eventually entered rock-and-roll, rock, and other offshoots of rhythm-and-blues. Postwar urban blues, however, drew on a more primitive form of the riff from the rural blues tradition, a notable example being Bo Diddley's *I'm a Man* (1955, Checker 814), which consists of a simple four-note riff repeated over a tonic drone. In postwar jazz the riff was used more sparingly: bop musicians were fond of riff themes (Dizzy Gillespie's *Salt Peanuts*, 1945, Manor 5000, and *Oop-pop-a-dah*, 1947, Vic. 20-2480, are typical) but avoided riffs in their improvisations. By the 1950s the riff could be exploited for its latent nostalgia (as in Miles Davis's *All Blues*, on the album *Kind of Blue*, 1959, Col. CL1355), its comic potential (Shorty Rogers's *Martians go home*, on *The Swinging Mr. Rogers*, 1955, Atl. 1212), or its earthy connotations (for example, in the primitivist pieces of Charles Mingus). Many overlapping riffs may be heard on Ornette Coleman's avant-garde album *Free Jazz* (1960, Atl. 1364), and riffs often appear in the works of composers interested in jazz techniques, from Darius Milhaud's *La création du monde* (1923) to Leonard Bernstein's *Prelude, Fugue and Riffs* (1949). Jazz composers have continued to combine the riff with the 12-bar blues in new ways (e.g., Carla Bley's *Floater*, on the album *Social Studies*, 1980, Watt 11), and the riff still flourishes in the big-band tradition, in which composers and arrangers are constantly inventing new variants of this time-honored device.

J. BRADFORD ROBINSON

Rigby, Joe [Joseph] (*b* New York, 9 March 1940). Saxophonist and flutist. He studied at the Juilliard School and acquired a degree in music education. While working in nursery school education he played in Latin bands and for the Sounds and Motion Dance Company run by the choreographer Diane McIntyre. In 1970 he co-founded the Master Brotherhood with the drummer Steve Reid, then worked with Beaver Harris's 360 Degree Musical Experience and Carlos Garnett. In 1976 the Master Brotherhood re-formed and recorded (*Nova*, Mustevic 2001) at Studio We in New York. Later Rigby worked with Andrew Cyrille, Jeanne Lee, Ted Curson, and Norman Connors and in the world of free jazz. His most creative period was a lengthy association with former high school colleague Milford Graves, when he was often paired with Arthur Doyle or the equally intense saxophonist Hugh Glover. Although in the 1990s he was occupied mainly with teaching, he played with the blues guitarist Johnny Copeland, then in 1997 was reunited with Graves and Glover at the Vision Festival in New York. Rigby is a compelling and forceful musician who plays all of the saxophones, from sopranino to baritone, as well as flute and piccolo, and he continually explores the timbres of his extensive arsenal. (V. Wilmer: *As Serious as your Life: the Story of the New Jazz*, London, 1977, rev. [3]/1987)

VAL WILMER

Riggins, Karriem (*b* Detroit, 25 Aug 1975). Drummer. From a young age he attended rehearsals and studio sessions with his father, a professional musician. After studying jazz at high school in Southfield, Michigan, and in Detroit he moved in 1994 to New York. Soon afterwards he took part in Betty Carter's week-long workshop "Jazz Ahead" and replaced Gregory Hutchinson in her band. Later he was active as a freelance with such musicians as Roy Hargrove, Eric Reed, Stephen Scott, Rodney Whitaker, and Mulgrew Miller, and he may be heard on *The Challenge*, from Hargrove's album *Family* (1995, Verve 314-527630-2). In summer 1998 Riggins joined Ray Brown's trio, once again replacing Hutchinson, and that same year he recorded at the Blue Note with Brown, Milt Jackson, and Oscar Peterson as a member of the Very Tall Band (*The Very Tall Band*, Telarc 83443). Two years later he produced an album for the rap singer Common. Riggins's style is influenced by the soul, funk, and hip-hop of Detroit. (<http://www.hopper-management.com/kr_bio_e.htm> (2000))

LARA PELLEGRINELLI

Riggs, Chuck [Charles] (*b* Pawtucket, CT, 5 Aug 1951). Drummer. Self-taught, he took up drums at around the age of nine after seeing Gene Krupa perform. From 1976 into the late 1990s he played regularly in Scott Hamilton's small groups. During the same period he worked with Bob Wilber's various repertory groups (1978 – mid-1980s), the World's Greatest Jazz Band of Yank Lawson and Bob Haggart (and later with Haggart's small groups), Chris Flory (from the late 1970s), Benny Goodman's sextet (1978–80), the group led by Kenny Davern and Dick Wellstood (early 1980s), Flip Phillips (with whom he recorded in 1986), Ruby Braff (from *c*1985), and Jay McShann (1988–9). In 1992 he performed and recorded in Cape Cod in the Concord Jazz All-Stars, with Hamilton, Dave McKenna, Gray Sargent, and the double bass player Marshall Wood. In the 1990s he recorded with Keith Ingham and Jon-Erik Kellso (both 1993), performed and recorded in Hamburg, Germany, in Marty Grosz's Swinging Fools (1995), and toured Europe with Ken Peplowski (1997). Riggs may be seen in the video *Jazz at* *the Smithsonian: Bob Wilber and the Smithsonian Jazz Repertory: a Tribute to Sidney Bechet* (1982).

SELECTED RECORDINGS

(recorded for Concord unless otherwise indicated)

As sideman: B. Wilber: *Bob Wilber & the Scott Hamilton Quartet* (1977, 1993, Chi. 171); S. Hamilton and B. Tate: *Back to Back* (1978, 85); R. Braff and S. Hamilton: *A Sailboat in the Moonlight* (1985, 296); J. Bunch: *The Best Thing for You* (1987, 328); C. Flory: *City Life* (1993, 4589); S. Hamilton: *Organic Duke* (1994, 4623); M. Grosz: *Ring dem Bells* (1995, Nagel-Heyer 022)

BIBLIOGRAPHY

Feather–GitlerBEJ

C. Deffaa: "Portraits: Chuck Riggs," *MD*, ix/8 (1985), 34

GK

Riisnæs, Knut (*b* Oslo, 13 Nov 1945). Norwegian soprano and tenor saxophonist. His mother and sister are classical pianists, and his younger brother Odd Riisnæs (*b* 1953) is a talented jazz tenor saxophonist who first came to prominence in the mid-1970s and later made recordings as a leader, notably the album *Speak Low* (1985–6, Taurus 825). Knut Riisnæs studied at the music high school in Oslo, then from the mid-1960s worked with Karin Krog, Terje Rypdal, and others. From around 1970 he became established as a leading Norwegian soloist, playing in an agressive modern style on his main instruments; he also plays flute and writes compositions and arrangements. He was a member of the radio big band in Oslo from 1969 to 1990 and spent a year in Arild Andersen's quartet (1974–5) in addition to leading his own small groups. He recorded as a co-leader with Red Holloway in 1989 and 1992. In the 1990s he toured as co-leader of a quartet with Jon Christensen; John Scofield recorded as a member of the quartet in 1991.

SELECTED RECORDINGS

As leader: *Flukt* (1982, Odin 05); with R. Holloway: *Confessin' the Blues* (1989, Gemini 63); with J. Christensen: *Knut Riisnæs/Jon Christensen* (1991, Odin 4040); with R. Holloway: *The Gemini Twins* (1992, Gemini 75)

As sideman: A. Andersen: *Clouds in my Heart* (1975, ECM 1059): Kevin Dean: *Over at Ola's* (1997, Hot Club 104)

JOHS BERGH

Riley, Ben(jamin A.) (*b* Savannah, GA, 17 July 1933). Drummer. After studying with Cecil Scott he played in air force bands. Between 1956 and 1965 he worked with Randy Weston, Sonny Stitt, Stan Getz, Woody Herman, Junior Mance, Kenny Burrell, Eddie "Lockjaw" Davis and Johnny Griffin (1960–62, making a number of albums), Paul Winter, Jeremy Steig, Ahmad Jamal, Roland Hanna, Billy Taylor (ii), Walter Bishop, Jr., Kai Winding, and Ray Bryant, and recorded with Benny Green and Mance (both 1961), Ken McIntyre, Sonny Rollins, and Sam Jones (all 1962), Winter and Steig (both 1963), and Bryant (1964). He became best known for his work as Thelonious Monk's drummer from 1964 to 1967, during which time he traveled extensively. He recorded with Alice Coltrane (1968–75) and performed with her from 1971; the same year he joined the New York Jazz Quartet, with which he played at intervals into the 1980s. He also performed in the USSR with Toots Thielemans, Milt Jackson, and Bob James, played with Ron Carter's quartet (1975), with which he later recorded (1977), and for a brief period in 1981 with Jim Hall's trio, and recorded with Hank Jones, Charlie Rouse, Bob Mover, and Turk Mauro (all 1977), Roland Hanna (1978), Frank Wess and Muhal Richard Abrams (both 1981), Chet Baker (in performance in New York clubs, 1981–2), Bill Barron (1983, 1987), Sheila Jordan (1984–91), Maria Muldaur (1984–5), Ted Brown and Freddie Redd (both 1985), and Andrew Hill (1986, 1989).

Having worked for many years in a rhythm section with Kenny Barron and Buster Williams and recorded as a sideman with each, in the early 1980s Riley formed the group Sphere with Rouse, Barron, and Williams; it disbanded shortly before Rouse's death in 1988, but re-formed in 1998 and continued touring, with Gary Bartz as its saxophonist. From 1984 Riley also played with Abdullah Ibrahim, with whom he toured the USA and Africa, and recorded. From the late 1980s he has worked as a freelance, sometimes performing in a trio with Barron and Ray Drummond, and has recorded further with Barron, as well as with Mark Elf and Barney Kessel (both 1988), Red Mitchell and Stan Getz (both 1989), Ricky Ford (1989–91), Harold Ashby, Bartz, Larry Gales, Eddie Harris, and Claudio Roditi (all 1990), Barry Harris (1991), the trumpeter Pete Minger, Hamiet Bluiett, Dick Katz, John Blake, and Rob Schneiderman (all 1992), Larry Willis (1993), Mike Melillo (1994), Greg Abate and Valery Ponomarev (both 1996), Hank Jones again (1997), and Burrell (1998). Riley is known for his sense of swing, his command of coloristic effects, and his attention to theme and structure.

SELECTED RECORDINGS

As leader: of Sphere (with C. Rouse, B. Williams, and K. Barron): *Four in One* (1982, Elek. Mus. 60166), *Flight Path* (1983, Elek. Mus. 60313); with M. Melillo and M. Moore (i): *Moonlight on the Ganges* (1994, Red 123264-2)

As sideman with T. Monk: *It's Monk's Time* (1964, Col. CS8984); *Monk* (1964, Col. CS9091); *Live at the It Club* (1964, Col. C2-38030); *Live at the Jazz Workshop* (1964, Col. C2-38269); *Underground* (1967, Col. CS9632)

As sideman with others: A. Ibrahim: *Ekaya* (1983, Ekapa 005); M. Muldaur: *Transblucency* (1984–5, Upt. 2725); R. Mitchell: *Talking* (1989, Capri 74016); E. Harris: *There Was a Time (Echo of Harlem)* (1990, Enja 6068-2)

SELECTED FILMS AND VIDEOS

Jazz Casual: Sonny Rollins and Company with Jim Hall (1963); Jazz Casual: Paul Winter Sextet (1964); Jazz 625: Thelonious Monk Quartet (1965); Music in Monk Time (1983); Monk in Europe (*c*1990 [filmed 1965–9]); Monk in Oslo (*c*1993 [filmed 1966])

BIBLIOGRAPHY

Feather '60s; *Feather–Gitler '70s*

J. Pareles: "The Thelonious Monk Tradition, and then Some," *New York Times* (27 Aug 1982), §C, p.12

P. Watrous: "Riffs: 'Round Sphere," *VV*, xxix (31 Jan 1984), 74

J. Potter: "Ben Riley: Making History," *MD*, x/9 (1986), 26

B. Blumenthal: "Take a Bow, Ben Riley," *Boston Globe* (7 Feb 1992)

L. Gourse: "Ben Riley: around Sphere," *Jh*, no.523 (1995), 34

JEFF POTTER/BK

Riley, Herlin (*b* New Orleans, 14 Feb 1957). Drummer. He grew up in a family of musicians and had formal lessons on trumpet as a teenager and learned drums with his grandfather. After attending Mississippi Valley State College briefly he returned to New Orleans, where he worked mainly as a trumpeter. During this time he began deputizing on drums, and by the early 1980s this had become his principal instrument. He then toured with Al Hirt (*c*1981–2), in the musical *One Mo' Time* (1982), and with Ahmad Jamal (1982–7), with whom he also recorded. In February 1988 Riley began a long association with Wynton Marsalis, and around 1990 he toured with the show *Satchmo: America's Musical Legend*. In the 1990s he toured and recorded as a member of the Lincoln Center Jazz Orchestra and worked regularly with Michael White (ii), and in 1994 he performed and recorded alongside Reginald Veal in a trio led by Junko Onishi at the

Village Vanguard. Riley has recorded with various others, including Harry Connick, Jr. (1986), Marcus Roberts (1990), the trumpeter Derrick Shezbie (1993), and Diane Reeves, Wycliffe Gordon and Ron Westray, the Clayton Brothers, and Doug Raney (all 1996). He released an instructional video, *Ragtime and Beyond: Evolution of a Style* (*c*1992), and, with Johnny Vidacovich and the writer Dan Thress, published *New Orleans Jazz and Second Line Drumming* (*c*1996). He may be seen to fine effect in the video *Marsalis on Music, Tackling the Monster, Wynton on Practice* (1995), and gives an inspired performance as a washboard player on *Congo Square Rag* (1999), which was recorded in an updated New Orleans jazz style by the blues musician Corey Harris.

SELECTED RECORDINGS

As sideman: A. Jamal: *Live at the Montreal Jazz Festival 1985* (1985, Atl. 81699); M. White: *Crescent City Serenade* (1990, Ant. 422-848545-2); M. Roberts: *Deep in the Shed* (1990, Novus 3078-2-N); W. Marsalis: *Citi Movement (Griot New York)* (1992, Col. C2K-53324-2); J. Onishi: *Live at the Village Vanguard* (1994, BN B21Z-31886); C. Harris: *Greens from the Garden* (1999, Alligator 4864), incl. Congo Square Rag

SELECTED FILMS AND VIDEOS

Ragtime and Beyond: Evolution of a Style (*c*1992); Accent on the Offbeat (*c*1994); Garth Fagan's Griot New York (*c*1995); Marsalis on Music, Tackling the Monster, Wynton on Practice (1995)

BIBLIOGRAPHY

C. Bryant, Jr.: "Portrait: Herlin Riley: Working it with Wynton Marsalis," *MD*, xvi/8 (1992), 50

N. Havouis: "Wynton & Co.: Jazz for the People," *Jm*, no.428 (1993), 36

T. Scherman: "Jazzmen: Herlin Riley's Second-line Bloodline," *Musician*, no.171 (1993), 24

K. Micallef: "Herlin Riley: Wynton's Secret Ingredient," *MD*, xix/4 (1995), 40

GK

Riley, Herman(, Jr.) (*b* New Orleans, 31 Aug 1933). Tenor saxophonist. His year of birth has appeared erroneously in reference books as 1940; however, he gave 1933 to Vacher (1997) and the same date in his questionnaire for the second edition of this dictionary. His mother was a blues and gospel singer. In 1948 he took up tenor saxophone after hearing Illinois Jacquet in New Orleans, and over the next year he began playing professionally with local swing and blues bands. Around 1951–3 he studied music at Southern University in Baton Rouge. Following his military service in army bands he spent a brief period with rhythm-and-blues groups in Los Angeles (March–April 1957) and played jazz in New York (May–August 1957). He then settled temporarily in San Diego, where he continued his music education at San Diego City College. In 1963 he moved to Los Angeles, and there he joined Dolo Coker's quintet and a quartet led by the brothers Bruz and George Freeman. The following year he began working as a freelance studio musician, mainly for Motown artists. Having played in Bill Green's small groups in 1964–5, Riley worked with Green's sideman Bobby Bryant from 1965 into the 1970s. In addition he toured with the singer Della Reese (1966), performed with Count Basie, Shelly Manne, Quincy Jones, Benny Carter, Joe Williams, and Donald Byrd, and recorded with Bryant (1967, 1969, 1971), Gene Ammons (1972), and Blue Mitchell (1972–3). In 1973 he appeared at the Concord Jazz Festival with Jones and toured Japan with an all-star group, and in 1974 he toured South Africa with Monk Montgomery's band. Later he recorded as a leader and with the Capp–Pierce Juggernaut (1978), Lorez Alexandria (1980), Lionel Hampton (1980–81), and Paul Humphrey (1981).

In the 1980s and 1990s Riley was a freelance with Bill Berry's big band and small groups. He recorded (*c*1986, *c*1988) and toured Europe with Mercer Ellington's orchestra and toured with Jimmy Smith's small group (from *c*1985); he also recorded in the organist's studio big band (1989, 1993). Although he had never been a member of Woody Herman's band, in 1986 he was a featured soloist at Herman's fiftieth anniversary concert. He recorded further with Alexandria (1984, 1992) and took part in sessions led by Stacy Rowles (1984), Jimmie and Jeannie Cheatham (1988), Ernestine Anderson and the Clayton–Hamilton Orchestra (1989), the arranger and bandleader Roger Neumann (1993), and Etta Jones (*c*1994). In the 1990s he worked with Al McKibbon's trio. Riley doubles on clarinets, flutes, oboe, and english horn.

SELECTED RECORDINGS

As leader: *Herman* (*c*1983, JAM 017)

As sideman: B. Bryant: Swahili Strut (1971, Cadet 50011); J. Cheatham and J. Cheatham: on *Back to the Neighborhood* (1988, Conc. 4473), Big Bubba's Back Rub Boogie Blues, Take the wrinkles out of your birthday suit; J. Smith: *Sum Serious Blues* (1993, Mlst. 9207); E. Jones: on *Time after Time* (*c*1994, Private Music 01005-821282), The Nearness of You

BIBLIOGRAPHY

Feather–Gitler '70s

P. Vacher: "Herman Riley," *JJI*, l/2 (1997), 20

BK

Riley, (John) Howard (*b* Huddersfield, England, 16 Feb 1943). English pianist and composer. He played piano from the age of six, took an interest in jazz by the time he was 13, and studied from 1961 at the University of Wales (BA 1964, MA 1966), from 1966 at Indiana University (MMus 1967), where he was a pupil of David Baker, and from 1967 at York University in England (MPhil 1970). After belonging briefly in 1966 to Evan Parker's quartet he led a trio from 1967 to 1976 (with Barry Guy and either Alan Jackson, Jon Hiseman, or Tony Oxley on drums) with which he toured widely; in 1969 it made the first ever appearance by a jazz group in a Henry Wood Promenade Concert. Riley also worked in a duo with John McLaughlin (1968), in the London Jazz Composers Orchestra (LJCO) (1970–1990s), and in Oxley's group (1972–81). Later he played in a trio with Guy and Phil Wachsmann (1976–1980s), performed as an unaccompanied soloist in Europe, the USA, and Canada, and worked in a quartet with Guy, Trevor Watts, and John Stevens (1977–81) and in duos with Keith Tippett (from 1981), Jaki Byard (1984), and Elton Dean (from 1984). In 1985 he formed a trio with Jeff Clyne and Tony Levin.

In 1988 Riley established a new trio with the double bass player Mario Castronari and the drummer Tony Marsh. The following year he appeared with the LJCO in a piece featuring two players at one piano which involved the Globe Unity Orchestra and Alex Schlippenbach, although the recorded version (*Double Trouble*) features the LJCO and Riley only. From 1990 he worked in a group led by George Haslam and co-led a quartet with Dean; he also co-led a quartet with Art Themen from 1996. Riley has been active as a teacher in London, initially at the Guildhall School of Music and Drama (from 1969) and later at Goldsmiths' College (from 1975), as well as the Barry Summer School and other places. In 1976–7 he was the creative associate at the Center of the Creative and Performing Arts in Buffalo, New York. He contributed articles in the early 1970s to *Music Review* and *Music in Education*, and he published *The Contemporary Piano Collection* (London, *c*1982).

Riley has made a considerable reputation for himself as an unaccompanied soloist, and has recorded 13 albums in which "always the objective is to arrive at freedom through spontaneity" (web page, 1999). His recordings invariably feature his own compositions; in addition to works for jazz ensemble he has written orchestral pieces (such as *Angle* and *Overview*), duos for flute and piano, string trios and quartets, and piano music.

SELECTED RECORDINGS

As unaccompanied soloist: *Intertwine* (1975, Mosaic 771); *Toronto Concert* (1976, Vinyl 112); *Procession* (1990, Wondrous 0101); *The Heat of Moments* (1991–2, Wondrous 0103); *Making Notes* (1997, Slam 230)

Duos with K. Tippett: *The Bern Concert: Interchange* (1993, Future Music 08)

As leader: *The Howard Riley Trio* (1967, Opportunity 2499); *The Day Will Come* (1970, Col. 564077); *Flight* (1971, Turtle 301); *Synopsis* (1973, Incus 13); with J. Byard: *Live at the Royal Festival Hall* (1984, Leo 133); *Feathers* (1988, Spot. 536); with E. Dean: *All The Tradition* (1990, Slam 201), *Wishing on the Moon* (1993, FMR 14); *Descending Circles* (1995, Blueprint 221); with A. Themen: *Classics (Live)* (1996, Slam 222)

As sideman: B. Guy: *Ode for Jazz Orchestra* (1972, Incus 6–7); London Jazz Composers Orchestra: *Stringer* (1980, FMP SAJ41); *Double Trouble* (1989, Intakt 019); G. Haslam: *Level Two* (1992, Slam 303); London Jazz Composers Orchestra: *Three Pieces for Orchestra* (1996, Intakt 045)

BIBLIOGRAPHY

ChiltonB; *GrayF*; *WickesIBJ*, i
A. Walsh: "Riley: Opening up New Ideas," *MM* (4 May 1968), 8
B. Dawbarn: "The Trouble with People who Listen with their Feet," *MM* (28 June 1969), 8
R. Williams: "Riley, Oxley, and the New Music," *MM* (29 Nov 1969), 10
B. Witherdon: "Conversation Pieces," *JM*, no.170 (1969), 8
——: "Howard Helps Make Jazz Legitimate," *MM* (9 May 1970), 14
——: "Riley: Creating Despite the Establishment," *MM* (14 Aug 1971), 2
R. M. Lee: "The Music of Howard Riley: a Progress Report," *JF* [intl edn], no.15 (1972), 82
"Riley's Progress," *MM* (10 June 1972), 42
J. Fordham: "Life of Riley," *MM* (22 Dec 1973), 19
M. Barry: "Howard Riley and 'Non-jazz'," *Contact*, no.14 (1976), 12
S. Lake: "Life of Riley," *MM* (16 Oct 1976), 48
A. J. Smith: "Profile: Howard Riley," *DB*, xliv/3 (1977), 33
B. Case: "Confrontation with the Insidious Forces of Industry," *New Musical Express* (25 Feb 1978), 42
K. Ansell: "Howard Riley and his Music," *JJI*, xxxiii/10 (1980), 20
D. Ilic: "Howard Riley," *The Wire*, no.5 (1983), 7
E. Jost: *Europas Jazz, 1960–1980* (Frankfurt am Main, Germany, 1987), 318
C. Parker: "The Freedom Attitude," *Wire*, no.67 (1989), 36
——: "Howard Riley," *Jazz: the Magazine*, no.17 (1993), 9
<http://www.shef.ac.uk/misc/rec/ps/efi/mriley.html> (1999) [incl. discography]

ED HAZELL/SIMON ADAMS

Riley, John (Bernard, Jr.) (*b* Aberdeen, MD, 11 June 1954). Drummer. After studying with Joe Morello while at high school and attending North Texas State University (BM 1976) he moved to New York (September 1976). He toured with Milt Jackson in 1977 and performed and recorded with Woody Herman's big band regularly from August 1978 to January 1979 and occasionally thereafter through 1986; he also played with Marc Johnson, Toots Thielemans, and Joe Lovano (early 1980s) and toured with the composer and pianist Marvin Hamlisch (1981–3), Stan Getz and Dizzy Gillespie (1982), John Abercrombie (1983–5), and Michel Legrand (1983–6). From 1987 through the 1990s Riley maintained an association with Bob Mintzer's big band that involved both performances and recordings. In addition he toured and recorded with Red Rodney (1987–8) and toured with John Scofield (1989–90), with whom he appears in the video *Live 3 Ways* (1990). In the 1990s he toured with Gary Peacock (1991–5), John Patitucci (1995), and the Mingus Big Band (1998), and performed and recorded with George Gruntz (from 1990), the Vanguard Jazz Orchestra (from 1992), Phil Woods (1994), Gary Bartz and Eddie Henderson (1995), the Carnegie Hall Jazz Band (from 1996), and Ray Brown (1997); as a freelance he secured engagements with Bob Berg, Art Farmer, Christian McBride, John Clayton, and Bill Dobbins.

Having continued his education at the Manhattan School of Music (MM 1985), Riley became active as an educator, teaching drums at William Patterson College in Wayne, New Jersey (from 1987), the Manhattan School of Music (from 1988), New York University (from 1992), and SUNY, Purchase (from 1996); from 1995 he also taught in the Jazz and Contemporary Music program at the New School for Social Research (from 1996 at the Mannes/New School; from autumn 1999 at the New School University). He published two instructional books, *The Art of Bop Drumming* (1994) and *Beyond Bop Drumming* (1997), and contributed pedagogical articles to *Modern Drummer*. Riley's style is based firmly in bop; he is a versatile musician who is able to play with power in a big band as well as with sensitivity in a trio setting.

SELECTED RECORDINGS

As sideman with B. Mintzer: *Art of the Big Band* (1990, DMP 479); *Techno Pop: Live in the '90s* (1993, Jazz Door 1273); *Only in New York* (1993, DMP 501); *Big Band Trane* (1996, DMP 510); *Latin from Manhattan* (1998, DMP 523)

As sideman with others: W. Herman: *La fiesta* (1978, Jazz Door 1205); R. Rodney: *Red Snapper* (1988, Ste. 31252); K. Werner: *Uncovered Heart* (1990, Sunnyside 1048); John Serry: *Enchantress* (1995, Telarc 83392); Vanguard Jazz Orchestra: *Lickety Split* (1997, New World 80534-2)

BIBLIOGRAPHY

S. Bennett: "Portraits: John Riley," *MD*, xiii/6 (1989), 72
W. F. Miller: "The Art of John Riley," *MD*, xviii/7 (1994), 26 [incl. discography]

RICK MATTINGLY

Rimington, Sammy [Samuel] (*b* Paddock Wood, England, 29 April 1942). English clarinetist and alto saxophonist. He began his professional career in 1959 with Barry Martyn and from 1960 to 1965 performed with Ken Colyer; he also played guitar and mandolin in Colyer's skiffle group. After briefly touring and recording in 1964 with the International Jazz Band, which included Kid Thomas Valentine, he worked in Connecticut in casual associations with Henry "Red" Allen, J. C. Higginbotham, Zutty Singleton, Sidney De Paris, Herman Autrey, and others. In New Orleans he recorded with Valentine (1966) and in Minneapolis he replaced Butch Thompson in the Hall Brothers' Band. Having returned to Europe in 1967 he played in Belgium with Martyn and led his own bands in England (1968–9) and Denmark; he also experimented with jazz-rock as the leader of the group Armada (1971). From the mid-1970s he played with George Webb (1973), Martyn's Legends of Jazz (1974), Duke Burrell's Louisiana Shakers and his own trio (both 1974–5), Jabbo Smith (touring Europe in 1977), and his own quintet and Chris Barber (both 1977–9). He continued to lead his own bands in Europe in the 1980s and 1990s, while also appearing as a sideman with Waso (1980s) and the Ginger Pig Jazzband (1990s), and touring Japan (including a visit with Thompson in 1988) and Australia; he may be seen performing with Colin Bowden's New Orleans Hamfats in the video *Bude Jazz Festival 1990* (*c* early 1990s). Rimington was strongly influenced by George Lewis (i) and Capt. John Handy, and is widely regarded as one of the foremost European exponents of traditional New Orleans jazz. He has performed and recorded with many important New Orleans jazz musicians; his playing may be heard on *The December Band* (1966, Jazz Crusade 2007-8), a recording made by Valentine and Handy, and on his own album, *The Exciting Sax of Sammy Rimington* (1986, 1991, Prog. 7077).

BIBLIOGRAPHY

CarrJ; *ChiltonB*
M. Jones: "Sammy – Swing by the Pint!," *MM* (8 Sept 1973), 47
D. Griffiths: "World Shakers," *MR*, ii/6 (1975), 13
L. Page: "Sam: Man who Came Back," *MM* (8 Nov 1975), 49
M. Harrison, C. Fox, and E. Thacker: *The Essential Jazz Records*, i: *Ragtime to Swing* (London, and Westport, CT, 1984), 62
N. Rimington: "The Sammy Rimington 1984 European Tour," *SL* (1985), winter, 20
G. Bielderman and L. Faelt: *Sammy Rimington Discography* (Zwolle, Netherlands, 1988)
T. D[ash]: "Sammy Rimington Live," *Fn*, xx/2 (1988–9), 4
C. Deffaa: "Sammy Rimington: New Orleans Jazz and More," *MR*, xx/1 (1992), 1
B. Hooper and V. Hooper: "Sammy Rimington in Australia," *New Orleans Music*, v/4 (1995), 21
J. Richard: "Spotlight on Sammy Rimington," *Just Jazz* (1998), no.6, p.6; no.7, p.7

DEREK COLLER/BK

Rim shot. The action of striking simultaneously the rim and head of a snare drum, or of striking one stick against the other while it is resting on the drumhead.

Ring. Record label, used before the late 1970s by Moers Music Verlag; *see* Moers music.

Rip. A loud, violent Gliss rising to the beginning of a note.

Rippingtons. Group formed by russ Freeman (ii) around 1986.

Ristic. Record label. It was established by john r. t. Davies in Burnham, England; issue began in 1950. At first 10-inch 78 r.p.m. discs were used, later 10-inch EPs; the bulk of the catalogue, however, was put out on 10-inch LPs. Throughout the label's life the repertory consisted of dubbed reissues of classic early jazz from American labels no longer in operation, recordings of traditional jazz by bands resident in the UK, and unusual items from various sources. Regular issue ceased in the 1970s, though Davies's masters have been put out in several reissue series throughout the world.

HOWARD RYE

Ritenour, Lee (Mack) [Captain Fingers] (*b* Hollywood, CA, 11 Jan 1952). Guitarist. He took up guitar as a child; later he studied the instrument at the University of Southern California and took private lessons with Joe Pass and Howard Roberts. After touring Japan with Sergio Mendes's band Brasil '77 (1973) he found regular work as a studio guitarist in Los Angeles, recording with rock, disco, and jazz groups. From 1977 he recorded in Japan with Sadao Watanabe and also as the leader of his own jazz-funk ensembles. The following year he began touring with one of these bands under the name Friendship, and by the early 1980s he spent most of his time performing with the group. His album *Rit* reached a wide audience in 1982, when it appeared simultaneously on jazz and pop charts. During the mid- to late 1980s Ritenour concentrated on Brazilian styles, and recordings prove him to be an effective guitarist within that realm. He was a member of the quartet Fourplay, alongside Bob James and Harvey Mason, from 1992 until the late 1990s, when Larry Carlton took his place in the group. In 1997 he formed his own label, i.e. music [*sic*], which initially recorded interpretations of the compositions of Antonio Carlos Jobim. An irony of the continuing bop revival, though not a surprising one, is that those who are most dogmatically committed are often not as effective as those whose interests are centered elsewhere. Although Ritenour was influenced initially by Wes Montgomery, he has worked mainly in pop-fusion contexts, and yet his albums *Stolen Moments* (*c*1990) and *Wes Bound* (*c*1992) show his perfect assimilation of Montgomery's hard-bop style.

Ritenour has been a contributor to *Guitar Player*. Transcriptions of his playing have been published by R. Carter (*The Lee Ritenour Book*, Studio City, CA, 1979) and B. E. Lee and F. Sokolow (*Lee Ritenour*, Milwaukee, *c*1990).

SELECTED RECORDINGS

As leader: *First Course* (*c*1976, Epic 33947); *Gentle Thoughts* (1977, JVC 1); *Rit* (*c*1982, Elek. 6E-331); with D. Grusin: *Harlequin* (*c*1984, GRP 91015); *Festival* (*c*1988, GRP 9570); *Stolen Moments* (*c*1990, GRP 9615); *Wes Bound* (*c*1992, GRP 9697)
As sideman: P. Da Costa: *Agora* (1976, Pablo 2310785); S. Rollins: *The Way I Feel* (1976, Mlst. 9074); S. Watanabe: *Autumn Blow* (1977, FDisk 6006); J. Pisano: on *Conversation Pieces* (1994–5, Pablo 2310963), Jo-Wes, Whisper Not

SELECTED FILMS AND VIDEOS

Rit Special: Lee Ritenour Live (1984); Lee Ritenour: Guitar Secrets, i–iii (*c*1985); Lee Ritenour, Dave Grusin (*c*1985); GRP All-Stars (*c*1985); Lee Ritenour & Friends: Live from the Coconut Grove, i–ii (*c*1990)

BIBLIOGRAPHY

J. Levine: "Profile: Lee Ritenour," *DB*, xlii/5 (1975), 34
"I'm a True Product of Cross-over, Says Lee Ritenour," *CI*, xviii/4 (1979), 22
J. Sievert: "Lee Ritenour: Poll-winning Studio Guitarist, Dazzling Jazz-rock Soloist," *GP*, xiii/2 (1979), 58 [incl. discography]
Z. Stewart: "Lee Ritenour," *Musician, Player & Listener*, no.17 (1979), 46
R. Palmer: "This Guitar's for Hire," *RS*, no.321 (10 July 1980), 43
Z. Stewart: "True Rit: the Outspoken Lee Ritenour," *DB*, li/4 (1984), 24 [incl. discography]
T. Mulhern: "Allan Holdsworth, Lee Ritenour: SynthAxe," *GP*, xx/6 (1986), 109
L. Feather: "Grusin and Ritenour Plug into Future," *JF* [intl edn], no.105 (1987), 26
S. Rosen: "Lee Ritenour," *Musician*, no.99 (1987), 38
J. Woodard: "Lee Ritenour," *JT* (1988), Nov, 7
J. Ferguson: "Lee Ritenour: Rit Returns to his Jazz Roots," *GP*, xxiv/9 (1990), 80
J. Jones IV: "Lee Ritenour: Straight Ahead," *DB*, lvii/5 (1990), 16 [incl. discography]
C. Gill: "Profile: Lee Ritenour," *GP*, xxvi/5 (1992), 25
L. Kohanov: "Lee Ritenour's WES-terly Direction," *JT*, xxiii/6 (1993), 32
P. Meyers: "Parallel Bars," *JT*, xxv/6 (1995), 54
D. Heckman: "With his Label, Ritenour Calls own Tune," *Los Angeles Times* (18 April 1997)
J. Woodard: "Captain Fingers and the Fully Baked Potato: Guitarist Lee Ritenour Delivers on his Original Concept," *Jazziz*, xv/7 (1998), 46
<http://www-studbo.hit.no/~u961151/leecd.htm> (2000)

BK

Rite of Strings. Trio formed in 1994 by stanley Clarke, Al Di Meola, and Jean-Luc Ponty.

Riti. Record company and label founded in the early 1980s by joe Morris (ii).

Rivera, Mario (*b* Santo Domingo, Dominican Republic, 22 July 1939). Dominican tenor saxophonist and flutist. He played in the leading merengue bands in the Dominican Republic before moving around 1960 to New York, where he worked with the bandleader Tito Rodriguez (1963–5) and was associated with both Machito and Eddie Palmieri. His longest affliation was with Tito Puente, with whom he remained until the leader's death in 2000; in both the Latin Jazz Ensemble and the Golden Men of Jazz he played tenor saxophone and flute, taking solos mostly on saxophone. In addition he played baritone saxophone in George Coleman's octet, with which he recorded in 1977 and performed at the Lugano Estival Jazz in 1980; he recorded on the same instrument with Junior Cook in 1979 and on tenor saxophone with Jerry Gonzalez a year later. From 1988 he was a tenor saxophonist in Dizzy Gillespie's United Nation Orchestra, and he may be seen in the video *Dizzy Gillespie and the United Nation Orchestra: Live at the Royal Festival Hall, London* (*c*1990 [filmed 1989]). Following Gillespie's death (1993) Rivera continued to tour and record with the United Nation Orchestra under the direction of Paquito D'Rivera. Around 1993 he joined Slide Hampton's Jazzmasters, and in the mid-1990s he was a member of Chico O'Farrill's orchestra. He also recorded with the trombonist Papo Vazquez (1991), Dave Valentin (1993), the group Afro-Blue Impressions under the tenor saxophonist Arthur Barron (1995), and numerous Latin-music ensembles.

Rivera is a fiery jazz soloist on both his main instruments. His style on the tenor saxophone is influenced strongly by that of John Coltrane, although his rhythmic dexterity is reminiscent of Sonny Rollins's playing of the late 1950s. He doubles on soprano and baritone saxophones, piccolo, alto flute, and bass clarinet.

SELECTED RECORDINGS

As sideman: G. Coleman: *Big George* (1977, Affinity 52); J. Gonzalez: *Ya yo ma curé* (1980, American Clavé 1001); T. Puente: *Mambo diablo* (1985, Conc. 283); *Salsa Meets Jazz* (1988, Conc. 354); P. Vazquez: *Breakout* (1991, Tim. 311); T. Puente: *In Session* (*c*1993, RMM 81208); C. O'Farrill: *Pure Emotion* (1995, Mlst. 9239)

BIBLIOGRAPHY

Feather–GitlerBEJ

GK

Rivers, James (*b* New Orleans, 18 April 1937). Multi-instrumentalist. He became a prolific studio musician, deputizing around the late 1950s for the tenor saxophonist Lee Allen whenever the latter was touring, and recorded with leading rhythm-and-blues musicians, as well as with Melvin Lastie and Mel Tormé. Like many New Orleans musicians of his generation he has worked equally in rhythm-and-blues and jazz. He toured with the singers Jackie Wilson and Jerry Butler and with the group the Impressions, and he was a mainstay in the show band the Royal Dukes of Rhythm (1963–6) before forming his own group to work long, intensive sets in local clubs.

Rivers plays alto, tenor, and soprano saxophones, flute, harmonica, bagpipes, organ, and synthesizer, and he sings. His great strengths are a capacity to entertain and a tremendous feeling for the blues. The influence of Roland Kirk underlies his choice of instruments and is particularly evident in his manner of singing a melody while playing it on flute and then, by means of a harmonica attached near the flute's mouthpiece, trading fours with himself, playing harmonica and singing.

SELECTED RECORDINGS

As leader: Bird Brain (*c* mid-1960s, Eight Ball 1560); *Thrill Me* (1978, JB's 101); *Ole* (1979, JB's 103); *The Dallas Sessions* (1985, Spindletop 101); *I'm the Man* (1996, JR 5241)

As sideman: Luther Kent: *It's in the Bag* (1983, Renegade 1001); on [no leader]: *Eastwood after Hours: Live at Carnegie Hall* (1997, WB 46546-2), Tightrope [flute]

BIBLIOGRAPHY

V. Wilmer: "Dynamite Rivers," *MM* (29 July 1972), 22

J. Berry, J. Foose, and T. Jones: *Up from the Cradle of Jazz: New Orleans Music since World War II* (Athens, GA, and London, 1986)

VAL WILMER

Rivers, Sam(uel Carthorne) (*b* El Reno, OK, 25 Sept 1923). Saxophonist, pianist, and composer. Pamphlet notes to a reissue of Rivers's recordings by Mosaic (ii) revealed that he was born in 1923, not 1930 as previously believed, and with this revised date the chronology of his early career becomes reasonable – his college studies and military service ending at around the age of 24, not 17. Rivers was the grandson of a pioneering scholar of African-American hymns and plantation melodies, Marshall W. Taylor, and the son of professional musicians (he was born while his father, a gospel singer, and his mother, a pianist, were touring). He studied

Sam Rivers at a performance with Abdullah Ibrahim's group in London, 1983

piano, reed instruments, and viola in Little Rock, Arkansas, and Chicago and took up tenor saxophone at Jarvis Christian College, Hawkins, Texas. He served in the navy in the Midwest and California, and from 1947 to 1952 attended the Boston Conservatory of Music; among his musical colleagues for local performances in Boston during this period were Joe Gordon, Quincy Jones, Charlie Mariano, Gigi Gryce, Serge Chaloff, and Jaki Byard. After playing rhythm-and-blues in Florida (1955–7) and touring with Billie Holiday, he again performed regularly in the Boston area until the mid-1960s, during which time he went to great lengths to develop a personal approach, shunning imitation and creating his own exercises and practice regimen; he resumed playing with Byard and also worked with Hal Galper, Alan Dawson, and Tony Williams.

Rivers first achieved critical notice when, immediately after touring with T-Bone Walker, he received an opportunity through Miles Davis's drummer Williams to join Davis's quintet (summer 1964); he performed and recorded with the group in Japan, but soon left, because – like John Coltrane in 1960 – he found Davis's musical style too conservative. Later in 1964 Rivers made the first in a succession of recordings for the Blue Note label as a leader and as a sideman with Williams, Larry Young, Bobby Hutcherson, and Andrew Hill; on some of these sessions he doubled on flute, soprano saxophone, and bass clarinet. He joined Hill's quartet and then returned to Boston to study composition.

From about 1968 to 1970 Rivers worked intermittently with Cecil Taylor, whom he also joined as artist-in-residence at the Fondation Maeght, St. Paul de Vence, France. In 1970, with his wife Bea, Rivers established Studio Rivbea, an important forum for new music, in a loft in the SoHo district of Manhattan. Concurrently from 1968 he was also composer-in-residence for the Harlem Opera Society, and he taught at Wesleyan University (1970–73) and Connecticut College (1972). From that time he toured and recorded with his own groups (playing piano more frequently after the late 1970s), and continued to develop a highly individual musical personality, particularly in totally improvised music; he may be seen in concert at the Umbria Jazz Festival in the film *Jazz in Piazza* (1974). His late 1970s work with Dave Holland, in quartet, trio, and duo settings, was especially influential; Barry Altschul was a regular member of these groups from 1974 to 1978.

In the 1980s and 1990s Rivers was heard principally in Europe, where he found the best opportunities to work without having to compromise financial or artistic principles. He also toured during the late 1980s with Dizzy Gillespie's combo and United Nation Orchestra, with which he appears in "Wolf Trap Salutes Dizzy Gillespie: an All-Star Tribute to the Jazz Master" (1988), an episode of the television series "Great Performances." In 1989 he performed in a free-jazz trio at the Chicago Jazz Festival, and in the 1990s he settled in Orlando, Florida, where he encouraged the development of a regional avant-garde jazz scene. While continuing to focus on European tours, he also played in the USA in a quartet with Altschul in 1993. Through the mid- to late 1990s he led a trio with Doug Mathews and Anthony Cole involving a basic instrumentation of saxophone, double bass, and drums, but all three men doubled on other instruments. He also recorded with Reggie Workman (1993, *c*1995) and performed and recorded with Julian Priester (1996–7). In 1998 he assembed the Rivbea All-Star Orchestra for recordings of free jazz involving his trio from Florida (Mathews and Cole) and such New York–based musicians as Ray Anderson, Greg Osby, Steve Coleman, Gary Thomas, and Hamiet Bluiett.

SELECTED RECORDINGS

As unaccompanied soloist: *Portrait* (1995, FMP CD82)

Duos with D. Holland: *Sam Rivers/Dave Holland* (1976, ImA 373843, 373848)

As leader: *Fuchsia Swing Song* (1964, BN 84184); *Contours* (1965, BN 84206); *A New Conception* (1965, BN 84249); *Involution* (1966, 1967, BN LA453-H2) [incl. 1966 session as sideman with A. Hill]; *Hues* (1971–3, Imp. 9302); *Waves* (1978, Tomato 8002); *Colours* (1982, BS 0064); *Lazuli* (1989, Tim. 291); *Concept* (1995-6, Rivbea 50101); *Inspiration* (1998, RCA 74321-64717-2); *Culmination* (1998, RCA 74321-68311-2)

As sideman: M. Davis: *Miles in Tokyo* (1964, CBS Sony SOPL162); T. Williams: *Life Time* (1964, BN 84180); Larry Young: *Into Somethin'* (1964, BN 84187); B. Hutcherson: *Dialogue* (1965, BN 84198); C. Taylor: *Nuits de la Fondation Maeght* (1969, Shandar 83507/83508/83509); D. Holland: *Conference of the Birds* (1972, ECM 1027); D. Pullen: *Capricorn Rising* (1975, BS 0004); R. Workman: *Summit Conference* (1993, Postcards 1003)

BIBLIOGRAPHY

CarrJ; *GrayF*

B. Palmer: "Sam Rivers: an Artist on an Empty Stage," *DB*, xlii/3 (1975), 12

R. Jacchetti: "Discografia Sam Rivers," *Musica jazz*, xxxii (1976), Aug–Sept, 46

W. A. Brower: "Sam Rivers: Warlord of the Lofts," *DB*, xlv/19 (1978), 21

D. Johnson: "Play it again, Sam!," *JJI*, xxxi/12 (1978), 6

L. Lyons: "Sam Rivers: Avant-garde Jazz Pianist and Multi-instrumentalist," *CK*, iv/6 (1978), 16

B. Vuijsje: *De nieuwe jazz* (Baarn, Netherlands, 1978), 178

M. Luzzi: *Uomini e avanguardie jazz* (Milan, 1980), 53

M. Ullman: *Jazz Lives: Portraits in Words and Pictures* (Washington, DC, 1980), 131

E. Jost: Jazzmusiker: *Materialen zur Soziologie der afro-amerikanischen Musik* (Frankfurt am Main, Germany, Berlin, and Vienna, 1981), 77

M. Turner: "Sam Rivers," *Coda*, no.185 (1982), 4

J. Chambers: *Milestones*, ii: *The Music and Times of Miles Davis since 1960* (Toronto, Buffalo, and London, 1985)

W. Minor: "Sam Rivers: as Time Goes by," *Coda*, no. 224 (1989), 12

J. Cunniff: "Sam Rivers," *DB*, lvii/3 (1990), 15

D. Rubien: "Sam Rivers: Jazz Original Reappears," *San Francisco Chronicle Datebook* (7 Nov 1993)

B. Blumenthal: "Sam Rivers: Still Pushing the Bounds of Jazz," *Boston Globe* (10 Dec 1996)

B. Shoemaker: "Sam Rivers: New Streams," *JT*, xxvi/10 (1996), 76

R. D. Sawyer: "Profile: Forever Current: Sam Rivers," *Jazziz*, xiv/3 (1997), 58 [incl. discography]

S. Woodyard: "Sam Rivers: Godfather of the Avant-garde," *Windplayer*, no.58 (1998), 32

F. Davis: "At 75, a Maverick Has a Big Band 'Talking'," *New York Times* (10 Oct 1999)

R. Dante Sawyer: "The Garden of Rivers," *Jazziz*, xvi/11 (1999), 52

BILL DOBBINS/BK

Riverside. Record company and label. The company was established in New York in 1953 by Bill Grauer(, Jr.) and Orrin Keepnews. Initially it reissued famous early jazz recordings drawn principally from the catalogues of Paramount, but it also derived material from Champion, the American label Circle, Gennett, Hot Record Society, QRS, and others. In 1954, beginning with two 10-inch albums by Randy Weston, the company started recording modern jazz, and it soon became, after Blue Note and Prestige, the most important organization of its era. Most of the new sessions were produced by Keepnews. Among the musicians best represented were Thelonious Monk (1955–61), Bill Evans (ii) (1956–62), Cannonball Adderley and Johnny Griffin (both 1958–63), Wes Montgomery (1959–63), and Barry Harris (1960–62); the items by Monk rival his earlier material for Blue Note and later work for Columbia, while the sessions by Evans, Adderley, and Montgomery produced each musician's finest recordings. Riverside established the subsidiary labels Judson (late 1950s) and Jazzland (1960). The company also undertook new recordings of older styles of jazz: many of these were issued in the series Living Legends, which was recorded in New Orleans and Chicago in the early 1960s and included the work of Earl Hines, Al Wynn, Peter Bocage, and Kid Thomas. Grauer died in December 1963, and the company went bankrupt the following year. From the mid-1970s, however, Riverside's catalogue figured prominently in reissues on Fantasy's labels Milestone and Original Jazz Classics.

BIBLIOGRAPHY

S. Furusho: *Riverside Jazz Records* (Chiba, Japan, 1984)
D. Ansell: "The Riverside Story: the Independents," *Coda*, no.222 (1988), 8
G. Marsh and G. Callingham, eds.: *East Coasting: the Cover Art of New York's Prestige, Riverside and Atlantic Records* (Zurich, 1993)
T. Okajima, ed.: *Jazz Critique 1997, no.3: the Riverside Book, Discography of all series* (Tokyo, 1997)
R. Kennedy and R. McNutt, eds.: *Little Labels – Big Sound: Small Record Companies and the Rise of American Music* (Bloomington, IN, and Indianapolis, 1999)

BK

Riverside Reunion Band. Sextet formed in September 1993 by Orrin Keepnews for a tribute to Riverside at the Monterey Jazz Festival; its members were Nat Adderley, Jimmy Heath, Buddy Montgomery, Barry Harris, Ron Carter, and Albert "Tootie" Heath. The group recorded the album *Mostly Monk* (1993, Mlst. 9216) the day after its festival performance. In 1994 it toured Europe, appearing at several major festivals and recording at the Pori International Jazz Festival in July, with Tommy Flanagan replacing Harris and Bob Cranshaw in lieu of Carter. (J. Kaliss: "Riverside Ran Deep," *San Francisco Chronicle Datebook*, 12 Sept 1993)

GK

Rix, Lawrence. Pseudonym of LAUDERIC CATON.

Roach, Max(well) (*b* New Land, NC, 10 Jan 1924). Drummer and composer. His mother was a gospel singer. He played piano at the age of eight and in the following year performed in the summer Bible school of the Concord Baptist Church; this early involvement with black religious music had a significant influence on his musical development. He first played drums when he was ten, and studied formally for three years. In 1942 he became associated with Charlie Parker, Dizzy Gillespie, and others, and, as the house drummer at Monroe's Uptown House, participated in the jam sessions there and at Minton's Playhouse that led to the development of the bop style. Late in 1943 he played at Kelly's Stable and made his first recordings with Coleman Hawkins. The following year he was a member of an incipient bop band co-led by Dizzy Gillespie and Oscar Pettiford at the Onyx club, after which he transferred to the Yacht Club (soon renamed the Downbeat) in a band co-led by Gillespie and Budd Johnson (to May 1944). Roach joined Benny Carter's big band, with which he toured, with some interruptions, into 1945. He then worked briefly with the Gillespie–Parker quintet at the Three Deuces (replacing Stan Levey, *c* May 1945), toured with Gillespie's first big band (mid-1945), and spent brief periods in another version of the Gillespie–Parker quintet (again at the Three Deuces, December 1945) and in the trumpeter's second big band (mid-1946). He also worked as a freelance in clubs on 52nd Street in 1946, notably with Allen Eager, Dexter Gordon, Hawkins, and J. J. Johnson. Most significantly, he was a member of Parker's quintet from April 1947 until mid-1949, shortly after their return from performances at the Festival International de Jazz. He continued to play as a freelance while studying composition at the Manhattan School of Music. From 1951 to 1953 he was again with Parker intermittently. Throughout these years he took part in many important bop recording sessions with Miles Davis (1948–50), some of the results of which were issued as *Birth of the Cool*.

Max Roach at Massey Hall, Toronto, 1953

In 1952 Roach entered into a partnership with Charles Mingus and Mingus's wife Celia to found Debut (i) Records, and the following year he and Mingus performed in and recorded a reunion concert with Parker, Gillespie, and Bud Powell in Toronto. Late in 1953 he replaced Shelly Manne in Howard Rumsey's Lighthouse All Stars at the Lighthouse, in Hermosa Beach, California, but a few months later he left to establish his own group: he sent for Clifford Brown and Sonny Stitt from New York, and with Brown as co-leader formed an important quintet in the Los Angeles area. For a brief period their sidemen were Teddy Edwards (replacing Stitt, on saxophone), Carl Perkins (piano), and George Bledsoe (double bass), but the lasting quintet was with Harold Land, Richie Powell, and George Morrow. The group toured from summer 1954 and produced a number of seminal recordings, including *Study in Brown* and *At Basin Street*, that epitomized the style of jazz known as hard bop. At the end of 1955 Land returned to California because of his grandmother's terminal illness, and Sonny Rollins took his place. Then, tragically, in June 1956 Brown and Richie Powell were killed in an automobile accident.

Roach continued to lead small groups. Over the next few years Kenny Dorham and then Booker Little and Tommy Turrentine were his trumpet soloists, sometimes working together with the tuba player Ray Draper or the trombonist Julian Priester; Rollins remained briefly before giving way to the tenor saxophonists Hank Mobley, George Coleman, Stanley Turrentine, and Clifford Jordan; and Art Davis and lesser-known bass players replaced Morrow. At the same time Roach made a series of recordings that prefigured developments associated with free jazz: on *Max Roach Plus 4 at Newport* and *Deeds Not Words* (both 1958) he occasionally omitted the piano from his ensembles; on *We Insist! Freedom Now Suite* (1960) he utilized a wide variety of open formal structures instead of the more usual theme and variation format; and on *Drums Unlimited* (1966) he drew on his earlier innovative concept of performing solo drum improvisations as independent pieces (*Drum Conversation*, 1953).

Roach's involvement in Debut had ceased in 1957 after a dispute with Mingus, but in 1960 the two men collaborated in organizing the Cliff Walk Manor festival, held in protest and as an alternative to the Newport event. In the 1960s Roach became an articulate spokesman and activist in the African-American cultural arts movement, and the titles of many of his compositions and albums from that period – notably *We Insist! Freedom Now Suite*, on which he collaborated with Oscar Brown, Jr. – reflect his awareness of and involvement in the struggle for racial equality. Much of his work was undertaken in conjunction with the singer Abbey Lincoln, his wife at the time, and made use of solo voices and chorus as well as jazz ensemble. From that time he also composed music for Broadway musicals, films, television, and symphony orchestra.

Roach has continued to work regularly with his own quintets and quartets. Among his sidemen during the mid- to late 1960s were Jordan, Gary Bartz, Odean Pope, Charles Tolliver, Stanley Cowell, and Jymie Merritt and, in the 1970s, Cecil Bridgewater, Billy Harper, and Reggie Workman (replaced by Calvin Hill around 1978). Later colleagues were Bridgewater and Pope, with Tyrone Brown replacing Hill around 1984; they perform sometimes as Roach's Double Quartet, incorporating the Uptown String Quartet (including Roach's daughter Maxine on viola). In 1992 Roach appeared with these groups in an episode of the television show "Jazz Backstage" and in a television broadcast from the Newport Jazz Festival.

In 1970 Roach organized M' BOOM RE: PERCUSSION, an ensemble of ten percussionists that performs and records works written specifically for percussion instruments; this group, which remained active in the 1990s, has toured Europe and recorded. Roach played unaccompanied solos in an episode of the "Tonight Show" in 1982 and in a television special devoted to Martin Luther King (1986). He also recorded with such artists as Abdullah Ibrahim (1977), Anthony Braxton (1978–9), Archie Shepp (1979), and Cecil Taylor, with whom he gave concerts at Columbia University in December 1979; as a soloist with a string quartet (*Survivors*, 1984); and in a concert in a duo with Gillespie in Paris (1989). In 1998 he toured as the leader of the So What Brass 5, in which he worked with the trumpeters Rod McGaha and Eddie Henderson, the trombonist Delfeayo Marsalis, the french horn player Mark Taylor, and the tuba player Antonio Underwood. He has been an active lecturer on jazz and has held positions at the Lenox (Massachusetts) School of Jazz (late 1950s) and from 1972 at the University of Massachusetts at Amherst. He has received many awards, including two honorary doctorates and, in 1988, a MacArthur Fellowship (the first given in the field of jazz).

Roach holds a significant position in the history of jazz. Of interest is his position as perhaps the first jazz drummer to be recorded trading fours (with Tommy Potter on Parker's *Bird Gets the Worm*, 1947), the first to master a 3/4 swing beat (*Carolina Moon* with Monk, 1952, and *Valse hot* as a leader, 1957), and the first to transfer Afro-Cuban rhythms to the drum set in an idiomatic manner, without its appearing to be exotic or pretentious (the second *Bird Feathers* (*Bongo Beep*) with Parker, 1947, and *Un poco loco* with Bud Powell, 1951). These specific achievements, indicative of Roach's experimental bent, are of course not as important as his general approach to 4/4 swing patterns and his solo playing, the latter ranging in character from technical displays (on Parker's *Koko*, 1945) to drum "melodies" based on standard jazz forms (on Rollins's *Blue 7* and *St. Thomas*). With Kenny Clarke, he was particularly important in establishing the practice of setting the fixed pulse on the ride cymbal instead of the bass drum or the hi-hat; this established a flowing and continuous carpet of sound which enabled more flexible use to be made of the other parts of the drum set and allowed for greater polyrhythmic texture. His imaginative performances as a soloist and his mature technique of improvisation, which is based on the use of deft interaction of pitch and timbral variety, subtleties of silence and sound, rhythmic and metrical contrast, and a refreshingly flexible approach to the fixed pulse, establish him as one of the most outstanding and innovative drummers of his time.

Oral history material in *CtY*.

See also BLUES PROGRESSION.

SELECTED RECORDINGS

As unaccompanied soloist: Drum Conversation (1953, Debut 107); on *Drums Unlimited* (1965–6, Atl. 1467), Drums Unlimited (1966)

Duos: with C. Mingus: on *Mingus at the Bohemia* (1955, Debut 123), Percussion Discussion; with A. Braxton: *Birth and Rebirth* (1978, BS 0024); with D. Gillespie: *Max Roach + Dizzy Gillespie, Paris, 1989* (1989, A&M 6404)

As leader: Baby Sis, pts.i–ii (1949, Vogue 5010); Maximum (1949, Vogue 5012); with C. Brown: *Study in Brown* (1955, EmA 36037), *At Basin Street* (1956, EmA 36070); *Jazz in 3/4 Time* (1957, EmA 36108), incl. Valse hot; *Max Roach Plus 4 at Newport* (1958, EmA 80010); *Deeds Not Words* (1958, Riv. 1122); *We Insist! Freedom Now Suite* (1960, Can. 9002), incl. Driva' Man, Freedom Day, Tears for Johannesburg; *Percussion Bitter Sweet* (1961, Imp. 8), incl. Garvey's Ghost; *It's Time* (1962, Imp. 16); *Drums Unlimited* (1965–6, Atl. 1467); *Lift Every Voice and Sing* (1971, Atl. 1587); *Collage* (1984, SN 1059); *Survivors* (1984, SN 1093); *Easy Winners* (1985, SN 1109)

As sideman: C. Hawkins: on *Tenor Sax Stylings* (1943, Bruns. 58030), Blues Changes, Lover come back to me; Woody 'n You (1944, Apollo 751); C. Parker: Koko (1945, Savoy 597); D. Gordon: Long Tall Dexter (1946, Savoy 603); Dexter Rides Again (1946, Savoy 623); B. Powell: I'll Remember April (1947, Roost 513); C. Parker: Dexterity (1947, Dial 1032); Bird Feathers (1947, Dial 1058); Klactoveesedstene (1947, Dial 1040); Bird Feathers [Bongo Beep], first issued on *Charlie Parker Sextet* (1947, Dial 207); Crazeology (1947, Dial 1034); Bird Gets the Worm (1947, Savoy 952); M. Davis: Move/Budo (1949, Cap. 15404); J. J. Johnson: Elora (1949, NewJ/Prst. 814); Teapot (1949, NewJ/Prst. 820); S. Stitt: All God's chillun got rhythm (1949, Birdland 9001); Sonny Side (1949, Prst. 722)

I want to be happy (1949, Prst. 758); C. Parker: Au Privave/Star Eyes (1951, Mer./Clef 11087); B. Powell: Un poco loco (1951, BN 1577); Night in Tunisia (1951, BN 1576); T. Monk: Carolina Moon (1952, BN 1603); Jazz at Massey Hall: *Quintet of the Year* (1953, Debut 2, 4); C. Mingus: on *Charles Mingus Quintet* (1955, Debut 139), Work Song [Drums], I'll remember April; S. Rollins: *Worktime* (1955, Prst. 7020); *Sonny Rollins Plus 4* (1956, Prst. 7038), incl. Valse hot; *Saxophone Colossus* (1956, Prst. 7079), incl. Blue 7, St. Thomas; T. Monk: *Brilliant Corners* (1956, Riv. 226); B. Rich: *Buddy Rich vs Max Roach* (1959, Mer. 20448); D. Ellington: *Money Jungle* (1962, UA 15017)

SELECTED FILMS AND VIDEOS

Jazz on a Summer's Day (1960); Max Roach: Ciné jazz (1967); The Original Rompin' Stompin' Hot and Heavy, Cool and Groovy All Star Jazz Show (1976); Max Roach: Drummer's Drummer (1980); Jazz in America: Lincoln Center, New York (1982); Jazz in America: Max Roach Quartet (1982); Jazz in America: John Birks Dizzy Gillespie (1983); Great Performances: the Cotton Club Remembered (1985); Martin Luther

King: the Dream and the Drum (1986); Max Roach: in Concert/in Session (*c*1985)

BIBLIOGRAPHY

"Stravinsky, Bird, Vibes Gas Roach," *DB*, xvi/10 (1949), 6
Nat [N. Hentoff]: "Roach & Brown, Inc., Dealers in Jazz," *DB*, xxii/9 (1955), 7
W. Balliett: *The Sound of Surprise* (New York, 1959/*R*1978), 217
R. Horricks and others: *These Jazzmen of our Time* (London, 1959), 131
W. Balliett: *Dinosaurs in the Morning* (Philadelphia, 1962/*R*1978), 110
J. Cooke: "We Insist! The Max Roach Group Today and the Freedom Now Suite," *JM*, viii/5 (1962), 3
R. G. Reisner: *Bird: the Legend of Charlie Parker* (New York, 1962/*R*1975), 194
J. Goldberg: *Jazz Masters of the Fifties* (New York and London, 1965/*R*1980)
G. Hoefer: "Hot Box: Max Roach," *DB*, xxxii/7 (1965), 18
I. Gitler: *Jazz Masters of the Forties* (New York, 1966/*R*1983 with discography)
R. Kettle: "Max Roach vs Buddy Rich: a Notated Analysis of Two Significant Modern Jazz Drumming Styles," *DB*, xxxiii/6 (1966), 19
M. Roach: "What Jazz Means to me," *Black Scholar*, iii/2 (1972), 3
C. A. Parks: "Self-determination and the Black Aesthetic," *Black World*, xxiii (1973), Nov, 62
"Max Roach," *SJ*, xxxi/11 (1977), 288 [discography]
B. Primack: "Max Roach: There's no Stoppin' the Professor from Boppin'," *DB*, xlv/18 (1978), 20
D. Gillespie and A. Fraser: *To Be, or not . . . to Bop: Memoirs* (Garden City, NY, 1979, London, 1980, as *Dizzy: the Autobiography of Dizzy Gillespie*)
H. Howland: "Max Roach: Back on the Bandstand," *MD*, iii/1 (1979), 12
B. Rusch: "Max Roach: Interview," *Cadence*, v/6 (1979), 3
G. Endress: *Jazz Podium: Musiker über sich selbst* (Stuttgart, Germany, 1980), 104
N. Richmond: "Max Roach: an Interview," *Coda*, no.172 (1980), 4
J. Runcie: "Max Roach: Militant Black Artist," *JJI*, xxxiii/5 (1980), 20
M. Berger, E. Berger, and J. Patrick: *Benny Carter: a Life in American Music* (Metuchen, NJ, and London, 1982)
S. K. Fish: "Max Roach," *MD*, vi/4 (1982), 8
S. Laszlo: "Behind the Beat of a Different Drummer," *The Wire*, no.1 (1982), 22
B. Priestley: *Mingus: a Critical Biography* (London, Melbourne, Australia, and New York, 1982)
R. Mattingly and S. K. Fish: "M'Boom," *MD*, vii/9 (1983), 8
C. Fox: "Sit Down and Listen: the Story of Max Roach," *Repercussions: a Celebration of African American Music*, ed. G. Haydon and D. Marks (London, 1985), 80
K. Whitehead: "Max Roach: Drum Architect," *DB*, lii/10 (1985), 16
J. Ephland: "Max Roach: Mr. Maximum," *DB*, lvii/11 (1990), 16
J. T. Jones, IV: "Avoiding the Musical Rerun: Max Roach," *JT*, xxi/8 (1991), 14
T. Gioia: *West Coast Jazz: Modern Jazz in California, 1945–1960* (New York, and Oxford, England, 1992), 308
A. Groves and A. Shipton: *The Glass Enclosure: the Life of Bud Powell* (Tunbridge Wells, England, 1993)
S. McElfresh: "Max Roach: Max Attack," *DB*, lx/11 (1993), 16
R. Mattingly: "Max Roach: No Boundaries," *MD*, xvii/8 (1993), 22
K. Mathieson: "A Long Way from Minton's," *Jazz on CD*, no.11 (1994), 35
B. Kernfeld: *What to Listen for in Jazz* (New Haven, CT, and London, 1995)
L. Van Trikt: "Max Roach Interview," *Cadence*, xxii/12 (1996), 5

OLLY WILSON/BK

Road Father. Nickname of WOODY HERMAN.

Roane, Kenneth (Abraham) (*b* Hartford, CT, 26 Dec 1900; *d* New York, 3 March 1984). Trumpeter and arranger. His middle name and a birthdate of 26 December (not March, as elsewhere) appear in his application for social security. He grew up in Springfield, Massachusetts, and moved to New York in 1923, by which time he was playing trumpet, clarinet, saxophones, and oboe (he was one of the first musicians to play oboe in a jazz context). There he worked with various musicians, among them Jelly Roll Morton and Cecil Scott, and recorded with Lloyd Scott (1927) and Fess Williams (1927, 1929); he also wrote arrangements, including, for Scott, one of his own composition *Harlem Shuffle.* In the 1930s he led his own band and performed regularly with Charlie Johnson and Sam Wooding, and in 1936 he took part with Nat "King" Cole, whose first recordings these were, in a session by Eddie Cole's Solid Swingers. He was also a member of the Boston-based band of the drummer Eddie Deas. In 1939 he recorded on trumpet a selection of Creole and Haitian tunes of marginal jazz significance alongside Sidney Bechet and Willie "the Lion" Smith in a quintet called the Haitian Orchestra. Roane performed in the 1940s with Buddy Johnson (autumn 1943), Cecil Scott (at the Ubangi Club, New York, 1943–4), Claude Hopkins (1944), and Fats Waller, among others, and continued working and teaching until his death; he was also for many years an official of the AFM. He was a virtuoso performer on a type of vessel flute, the ocarina (also known in jazz parlance as a "hot sweet potato"), which he used while with Williams; he may be heard playing it with the singer Jimmy Smith and his Sepians on *Big Chump Blues* (1941). His brother was the trumpeter Eddie (Edward F.) Roane (1911–46), who is especially remembered for his work with Louis Jordan (1941–4).

SELECTED RECORDINGS

As sideman: L. Scott: Harlem Shuffle (1927, Vic. 21491); Symphonic Scronch (1927, Vic. 20495); E. Cole: Stomping at the Panama (1936, Decca 7215); Thunder (1936, Decca 7210); J. Smith: I ain't got nobody to love/Big Chump Blues (1941, Decca 8591)

BIBLIOGRAPHY

ChiltonW
L. Wright: "I'll Never Turn Back: an Interview with Nora Lee King," *Sv*, no.96 (1981), 212
C. E. B. Bernhardt and S. Harris: *I Remember: Eighty Years of Black Entertainment, Big Bands, and the Blues* (Philadelphia, 1986), 159

HOWARD RYE

Robert, George (Paul) (*b* Geneva, 15 Sept 1960). Swiss alto saxophonist and leader. He learned piano from the age of nine and soon afterwards had classical clarinet lessons at the Conservatoire Populaire de Musique in Geneva; he took up alto saxophone as a teenager. In 1980 he moved to Boston, where he studied composition and arranging at the Berklee College of Music (BA 1984) and received private tuition on saxophone from Phil Woods; during the same period he appeared on local television as the leader of the group Ashanti (1983). In 1984 he formed a quartet, with which he played at the Montreux International Jazz Festival later that year, and in 1985 he returned to Switzerland to perform at the Cully International Jazz Festival with a rhythm section consisting of Cedar Walton, Buster Williams, and Billy Higgins. Robert continued his education at the Manhattan School of Music (1985–7) as well as studying privately. From 1987 to around 1992 he co-led a quintet with Tom Harrell, in which they played alongside Dado Moroni and Reggie Johnson, with either Bill Goodwin or Byron Landham on drums. In the 1990s he performed and recorded in Europe with Clark Terry (from 1990) and toured there as a member of Woods's big band (1998), and he led a number of his own groups with Moroni and Johnson among his sidemen. He also plays soprano saxophone.

SELECTED RECORDINGS

Duos with D. Moroni: *Youngbloods* (1992, Mons 1897)
As leader: with T. Harrell: *Cape Verde* (1992, Mons 1898); with C. Terry: *The Good Things in Life* (1933, Mons 2003); *Metropole Orchestra* (1993–4, Mons 6458); *Tribute* (1994, Jazz Focus 004)

BIBLIOGRAPHY

"Auditions: George Robert," *DB*, liii/5 (1986), 62
T. Quénum: "George Robert," *Jm*, no.396 (1990), 42

GK

Robert, Jean (*b* Brussels, 25 June 1908; *d* Hilversum, Netherlands, 28 Feb 1981). Belgian tenor saxophonist. He studied piano, then played saxophone with various small groups in Brussels. In 1928 he worked in London with Peter Packay (taking part in recordings issued under the name of the Red Robins), and the following year he became a member of Gus Deloof's first professional group and performed and recorded with Chas Remue's big band. In 1930–31 he played with Deloof and with the bandleader Albert Sykes in Egypt and Ostend, Belgium. Later he led his own band at the Atlanta in Brussels (1933), played in the Netherlands with the drummer Freddie Beerman and in Belgium with Robert De Kers (1935), and led a quartet at the Cotton Club in Brussels and in Switzerland. In 1937 he met Coleman Hawkins, Benny Carter, and Freddy Johnson; he played at the Cotton Club in Johnson's trio (February 1938) and substituted for Hawkins at the Negro Palace in Amsterdam. He also worked in the Netherlands with the reed player Jascha Trabsky and others. On his return to Brussels he joined a group led by Jean Omer, with which he played at the Salle Pleyel in Paris; around 1943 he performed with Lutz Templin in Germany. Robert appeared with Omer at le Boeuf sur le Toit in Brussels until 1962 and then moved to Hilversum, where he worked principally as a composer and arranger. (R. Pernet: *Belgian Jazz Discography (1897–1999)*, Brussels, 1999)

ROBERT PERNET

Robert, Yves (*b* Chamalières, France, 17 Jan 1958). French trombonist and composer. He made his début in provincial bands, playing dixieland, then hard bop, and then free jazz, before joining ARFI (Association à la Recherche d'un Folklore Imaginaire) in Lyons (1981) and GRIM (Groupe de Recherche et d'Improvisation Musicale), founded by André Jaume in Marseilles in 1978. He worked with a French and German orchestra directed by Albert Mangelsdorff, Jean-Louis Chautemps, and Jean-François Jenny-Clark and with the group Compagnie Lubat (1984), formed a trio with the guitarist Jean-Marc Montera and the drummer Gérard Siracusa, and joined Jaume's octet (1985). In 1986 he became a member of the Orchestre National de Jazz (ONJ), under François Jeanneau, and between 1986 and 1988 he played in the quintets of Didier Levallet and Gérard Marais and performed with such musicians as Michel Portal, Daniel Humair, and Steve Lacy. He then formed another trio, with the double bass player Bruno Chevillon and the drummer Aaron Scott, and in 1990 a quartet consisting of the guitarist Philippe Deschepper, the double bass player Claude Tchamitchian, and the drummer Xavier Desandre. Robert appeared in Marc Ducret's group at the festival Banlieues Bleues (1992, 1995, 1997) and at the Festival de Jazz de Paris (1993). In 1997 he rejoined the ONJ (under Didier Levallet), and at the same time pursued his exploration of improvisation in the rock group Prohibition, Quartet Elan led by the trumpeter Andrew Crocker (recording in 1997), and the quintet Les Quatre Actifs (1998).

SELECTED RECORDINGS

As leader: *Tout de suite* (1993, Deux Z 84113); *Eté* (1998, Deux Z 84133)
As sideman: N. Akchoté: *Soundpage(s)* (1994, Deux Z 84115); L. Sclavis: *Les violences de Rameau* (1995–6, ECM 1588); *Danses et autres scènes* (1997, Label Bleu 6616); Quartet Elan: *Live* (1997, SHL 2086)

BIBLIOGRAPHY

J.-Y. Le Bec: "Yves Robert: 'Mais pourquoi font-ils ça?'," *Jm*, no.395 (1990), 42
F. Goaty: "Yves Robert: l'oreille en coulisse," *Jm*, no.413 (1992), 36
S. Siclier: "Le Robert: nouvelle édition," *Jazzman*, no.172 (1993), 7
Y. Robert: "Conversation avec mes autres," *Jm*, no.441 (1994), 22
T. Lépin: "Yves Robert: nouvelles du front," *Jazzman*, no.30 (1997), 22
J. Denis: "Yves Robert: le bel été," *Jazzman*, no.46 (1999), 26

JACQUES ABOUCAYA

Roberts, Caughey (Wesley, II) (*b* Boley, OK, 25 Aug 1912; *d* Los Angeles, 12 Dec 1990). Saxophonist and clarinetist. His middle name is taken from the California death index. He moved to Los Angeles in 1926 and learned clarinet while at high school. His first professional work was as a tenor saxophonist in taxi-dance halls. Thereafter he was associated with many bandleaders in Los Angeles, notably Buck Clayton, with whose group he traveled to China in 1934–5. He then spent a period with Cee Pee Johnson and in 1936 worked with Lionel Hampton's big band. Having been recommended by Clayton, Roberts moved to Kansas City the following year to join the Count Basie Orchestra as lead alto saxophonist, and he was present on the band's first recordings for Decca. After returning to Los Angeles he recorded with Fats Waller (1937), resumed playing with local groups, notably that of the guitarist Ceelle Burke, and was active as a music teacher. In 1942 he worked again briefly with Basie (July–August) but was then drafted into the army and served as a musician. Later Roberts joined Roy Milton's rhythm-and-blues group. He was persuaded to revert to clarinet by Teddy Buckner, in whose dixieland ensemble he performed for 19 years and made many recordings; he also recorded with Kid Ory (1959). Roberts's throaty clarinet work is reminiscent of that of Edmond Hall.

SELECTED RECORDINGS

As sideman: C. Basie: on *The Count at the Chatterbox* (1937, Jazz Archives 16), St. Louis Blues; R. Milton: Them There Eyes (1947, Roy Milton 201); K. Ory: *Kid Ory Plays W. C. Handy* (1959, Verve 1017); T. Buckner: *On the Sunset Strip* (1960, Dixieland Jubilee 510)

BIBLIOGRAPHY

SchullerS
B. Clayton and N. M. Elliott: *Buck Clayton's Jazz World* (London and New York, 1986)
Obituaries: J. Simmen, *BHcF*, no.396 (1991), 27; P. Vacher, *MR*, xviii/10 (1991), 9
C. Bryant and others, eds.: *Central Avenue Sounds: Jazz in Los Angeles* (Berkeley, CA, Los Angeles, and London, 1998)

PETER VACHER

Roberts, Hank (*b* Terre Haute, IN, 24 March 1954). Cellist. He studied classical cello from the age of ten and took up trombone in his teens with the intention of doubling as a jazz trombonist and classical cellist; he also taught himself piano and guitar, and while he was in high school he played trombone and electric guitar in local funk and rock bands. Having attended Indiana State University briefly he took part in a summer session at the Berklee College of Music (1973), where he studied improvisation with Gary Burton; he credits Burton with improving his understanding of jazz harmony and encouraging his use of cello as a jazz instrument. It was around this period that he began singing at the same time as playing in order to enrich the sound of his chordal work. Over the next few years he lived alternately in Terre Haute, Indiana, and New York, then in 1980 moved to New Jersey.

While working as a chef in 1986 Roberts began performing and recording regularly with Tim Berne, although he became a full-time musician only in October the following year; later he and Berne founded the group MINIATURE. In addition he worked with Bill Frisell (1987–91) and was a founding member of the string trio ARCADO (c1989–92); in 1990, with the cellists Ernst Reijseger, Muneer Abdul Fataah, and Tristan Honsinger, he formed the Esslinger Cello Projekt. From 1987 he has led his own groups and performed as an unaccompanied soloist, and around 1990 he formed the avant-funk group Birds of Prey, with the guitarist Mark Lampariello, Jerome Harris, the drummer Vinnie Johnson, and the singer D. K. Dyson as his sidemen; all its instrumentalists sang as well as played. Roberts became less active as a musician in 1990 in order to spend more time with his family in Ithaca, New York. In the late 1990s he worked as a cello teacher and an unaccompanied soloist and led a trio with the double bass player Peter Chwazik and the drummer Billy King, which recorded in 1997. He has also recorded with Alex Cline (1987), Henry Kaiser (1989), and Marilyn Crispell (1993).

SELECTED RECORDINGS

Duos with C. Doran: on *Christy Doran's Phoenix* (1989–90, HA 6074), Lou Yuri, Seven Shadows, Song for Sunny (1990)
As leader: *Black Pastels* (1987, JMT 880016); *Little Motor People* (1992, JMT 514005); *I'll Always Remember* (1997, Level Green 22002)
As sideman: T. Berne: *Fulton Street Maul* (1986, Col. FC40530); B. Frisell: *Lookout for Hope* (1987, ECM 1350); T. Berne: *Sanctified Dreams* (1987, Col. FC44073); M. Crispell: *Santuerio* (1993, Leo 191)

BIBLIOGRAPHY

GrayF; *ReclamsJ*
G. Endress: "Zunächst ein Fluch, dann ein Segen: das Cello: Hank Roberts," *JP*, xxxvii/11 (1988), 10
S. Lake: "Hank Roberts," *Wire*, no.52 (1988), 18
J. Rosenbaum: "Improvisations: Hank Roberts: *Revelation*," *Strings*, v/2 (1990), 36 [incl. transcr.]
C. Wörner: "Der kleine Bass ganz gross: Esslinger Cello Projekt," *JP*, xxxix/4 (1990), 45
G. Chapin: "Jazzmen: Grooves with Cellos: Hank Roberts' Music of the Spirit," *Musician*, no.160 (1992), 26
<http://www.jazzpages.com/roberts.htm> (1999)
<http://www.levelgreen.com/hank/> (1999) [incl. discography]

GK

Roberts, Howard (Mancel) (*b* Phoenix, AZ, 2 Oct 1929; *d* Seattle, 28 June 1992). Guitarist. He studied music privately and received some formal instruction in the concepts of the theorist Joseph Schillinger. In 1950 he moved to Los Angeles, where he quickly established himself as an active and versatile studio musician, and by the early 1970s he had made thousands of jazz, rock, and pop recordings. He also led his own group and worked with other West Coast bands, among them those of Wardell Gray (recording at the Haig Club in 1952), Buddy DeFranco (recording in 1956), Bud Shank (recording under Shank and Bob Cooper in 1956 and Shank alone in 1958), the Candoli brothers (recording in 1957, 1959, and 1962), Buddy Collette (recording in 1957), Shorty Rogers (recording in 1958), Lenny Niehaus, and Paul Horn. Additional jazz work from this period included recording sessions with Chico Hamilton (1953–4), Pete Rugolo (1954), John Graas (1954–6), Pete Jolly and Frank Morgan (both 1955), the West Coast Jazzmen, with whom Roberts appeared as "John Doe" (1957), and Claude Williamson (c1958). In November 1968 he was a member of a big band accompanying Thelonious Monk in Los Angeles. In the early 1970s he began teaching, writing (including, until 1989, a monthly instructional column for *Guitar Player* magazine), and giving seminars, and in 1976 he was a co-founder of the Guitar Institute of Technology (later the Musicians' Institute) in Hollywood. He made a notable recording as a leader in 1977, and he recorded as a sideman in Hank Jones's quartet that same year and with Art Pepper in 1980. Roberts's interest in 20th-century classical music and composition is reflected in his sophisticated approach to bop and fusion. This may be heard on his first recording, *Mr. Roberts Plays Guitar*, on which he made use of a string quartet, and throughout his work in his uncommonly advanced view of harmony and melody. He was the author of *Super Chops: Jazz Guitar Technique in 20 Weeks* (Port Chester, NY, c1982), and, with G. Hagberg, *The Guitar Compendium*, i–iii (Edmonds, WA, c1990).

SELECTED RECORDINGS

Mr. Roberts Plays Guitar (1956–7, Verve 8192); *Good Pickin's* (1957, Verve 8305); *H. R. is a Dirty Guitar Player* (1963, Cap. ST1961); *The Real Howard Roberts* (1977, Conc. 53)

BIBLIOGRAPHY

D. Menn: "Howard Roberts," *GP*, xiii/6 (1979), 54
L. Tomkins: "Howard Roberts," *CI*, xxii/6 (1985), 22
H. Roberts: "When I Had to Put Stardom Aside," *CI*, xxiv/10 (1987), 8
Obituaries: B. A. Folkart, *Los Angeles Times* (3 July 1992); M. Gilbert, *JJI*, xlv/9 (1992), 16

JIM FERGUSON/BK

Roberts, Luckey [Charles Luckey(e)th] (*b* Philadelphia, 7 Aug 1893; *d* New York, 5 Feb 1968). Pianist and composer. Sampson (1980), who corrects and supplements numerous published details of Roberts's career, asserts that he was born in 1893, not 1887, as has frequently been given; Roberts himself wrote 1893 in his application for a social security card. He toured with an African-American troupe while still an infant and became a child singer, dancer, juggler, and acrobat. Around 1900 he taught himself to play the piano. By about 1910 he had settled in New York, where in 1913 his first published composition, *Junk Man Rag*, appeared, and by the middle of the decade he was regarded by his colleagues James P. Johnson, Eubie Blake, and Willie "the Lion" Smith as perhaps the greatest of the Harlem pianists. While performing at Baron Wilkins's club he studied music and became involved in writing for music theater in collaboration with the lyricist Alex Rogers. In 1917 their musical comedy, *My People*, was produced in New York. A number of further comedies, none terribly distinguished, followed. From the 1920s Roberts was a popular bandleader at exclusive social functions on the East Coast, and then from 1940 to 1954 he ran a Harlem bar, Luckey's Rendezvous. He composed works for piano and orchestra which were presented in concerts at Carnegie Hall in 1939 and Town Hall in 1941. In 1946, for Rudi Blesh's Circle label, he recorded *Junk Man Rag*, and other piano compositions – *Pork and Beans* (1913), *Music Box Rag* (1914), *Railroad Blues*, and *Ripples of the Nile*; this last title had already been popularized by Glenn Miller as *Moonlight Cocktail* in 1941. Early in 1947 Roberts played in a traditional-jazz group for the first two programs in Blesh's radio series "This is Jazz."

By reputation Roberts was the most technically gifted member of the post-ragtime stride school, although he left the least trace of his work. He recorded some piano rolls in 1919 and 1923, but made only a few phonograph recordings, as an accompanist to vaudevillians early in the 1920s, and as an unaccompanied soloist late in his career; evidently the society jobs he undertook were so lucrative that he had no need to seek recording dates.

SELECTED RECORDINGS

As unaccompanied soloist: Railroad Blues (1946, Cir. [USA] 1026); Pork and Beans (1946, Cir. [USA] 1027); Ripples of the Nile/Shy and Sly (1946, Cir. [USA] 1028); *Harlem Piano Solos* (1958, GTJ 12035), incl. Nothin'

BIBLIOGRAPHY

ChiltonW
R. Blesh and H. Janis: *They All Played Ragtime* (New York, 1950, rev. 4/1971)
L. Feather: *The New Yearbook of Jazz* (New York, 1958), 145
T. Davin, "Conversations with James P. Johnson: 1912–1914," *Jazz Review*, ii/6 (July 1959): 12; repr. in J. E. Hasse, ed.: *Ragtime: its History, Composers, and Music* (New York and London, 1985)
M. Montgomery: "Luckey Roberts Rollography," *Record Research*, no.30 (1960), 2
G. Hoefer: "Luckey Roberts," *JJ*, xvi/3 (1963), 7
W. Smith and G. Hoefer: *Music on my Mind: the Memoirs of an American Pianist* (Garden City, NY, 1964/*R*1975), 33
D. Jones: "August in New York: Birdland, Charles Luckyeth 'Lucky' [*sic*] Roberts," *JB*, ii/9 (1965), 14
B. Kumm: "Charles Luckeyeth Roberts: Discovery of a Disc," *Sv*, no.14 (1967–8), 30
J. Bradley: "Luckey Roberts," *BHcF*, no.176 (1968), 4
Obituaries: B. Kumm, *Sv*, no.17 (1968), 1; *New York Times* (7 Feb 1968)
T. Vinding: "Forgotten People," *SL*, xxiii (1970), May–June, 329
S. Dance: *The World of Swing* (New York, 1974), 32
W. J. Schafer: "Fizz Water: Ragtime by Eubie Blake, Luckey Roberts and James P. Johnson," *MR*, iii/2 (1975), 1
A. Rose: *Eubie Blake* (New York, 1979)
E. A. Berlin: *Ragtime: a Musical and Cultural History* (Berkeley, CA, Los Angeles, and London, 1980/*R*1984 with addns)
H. T. Sampson: *Blacks in Blackface: a Source Book on Early Black Musical Shows* (Metuchen, NJ, 1980)

J. R. TAYLOR/BK

Roberts, Marcus [Marthaniel] (*b* Jacksonville, FL, 7 Aug 1963). Pianist and leader. He was left blind by inoperable cataracts at the age of four. Nevertheless he played organ in church and took up piano when he was eight; he began studying classical music at the age of 12 and continued at Florida State University. In June 1985 he replaced Kenny Kirkland in Wynton Marsalis's quartet and until 1991 he was a member of the trumpeter's septet; he may be seen performing in the videos *Wynton Marsalis: Blues & Swing* (*c*1987) and *Garth Fagan's Griot New York* (*c*1995). During his time with Marsalis he won the first Thelonious Monk International Piano Competition (1987). From the early 1990s Roberts has been heavily involved with the activities of Jazz at Lincoln Center: on his 30th birthday he gave the first performance of his composition *Romance, Swing and the Blues* with the Lincoln Center Jazz Orchestra and a year later he toured the USA as the music director and principal soloist of the same ensemble; in the late 1990s he gave a number of concerts as part of the Jazz at Lincoln Center program.

Around 1992 Roberts began touring as an unaccompanied soloist and as the leader of various small groups that included Marcus Printup; in addition he led a trio with the double bass player Roland Guerin and either Ali Jackson or Jason Marsalis on drums; the latter appeared with the group at the Village Vanguard in November 1998. In 1994 Roberts took part in a performance of Gershwin's *I Got Rhythm Variations* with the American Symphony Orchestra, and two years later he recorded the same work, as well as an interpretation of *Rhapsody in Blue*, for his album *Portraits in Blue* and performed some of his own compositions with a trio for another album, *Time and Circumstance*. He also recorded as a sideman with Mark Whitfield (1990), with the studio group Tough Young Tenors (1991), with Wycliffe Gordon and Ron Westray in the group Bone Structure (1996), and with Printup (1996). He has taught at Northwestern University and the University of North Florida.

Roberts's early recordings and performances revealed that he was a talented pianist, but his potential is yet to be realized. He has a brilliant technique, though the rather studied manner in which he re-creates various styles gives his later performances an air of emotional detachment.

SELECTED RECORDINGS

As unaccompanied soloist: *Alone with Three Giants* (1990, Novus 3109-2-N); *Prayer for Peace* (1990–91, Novus 01241-63124-2); *If I Could Be with You* (*c*1992, Novus 01241-63149-2)
As leader: *The Truth is Spoken Here* (1988, Novus 3051-2-N); *Deep in the Shed* (1989, Novus 3078-2-N); *Gershwin for Lovers* (*c*1994, Col. CK66437); *Time and Circumstance* (1996, Col. CK67567); *Blues for the New Millennium* (1996–7, Col. CK 68637)
As sideman: W. Marsalis: *J Mood* (1985, Col. FC40308); *Marsalis Standard Time*, i (1986, Col. FC40461); *Levee Low Moan: Soul Gestures in Southern Blue*, iii (*c*1987–8, CK47975); W. Gordon and R. Westray: *Bone Structure* (1996, Atl. 82936-2); M. Printup: *Unveiled* (1996, BN 37302-2)

BIBLIOGRAPHY

CarrJ; CBY 1994
L. Tompkins: "There are no Shortcuts to Jazz, Emphasizes Wynton Marsalis's Pianist Marcus Roberts," *CI*, xxiv/9 (1987), 26
M. Smith: "Marcus Roberts," *Cadence*, xiv/12 (1988), 15
R. L. Doerschuk: "Marcus Roberts: for Fresh Inspiration a Rising Young Jazz Force Turns to Ellington & Monk," *Keyboard*, xv/10 (1989), 51
P. Booth: "Marcus Roberts: Deep in the Groove," *DB*, lvii/4 (1990), 20
J.-Y. Le Bec: "Marcus Roberts: le clavier bien tempéré du blues," *Jm*, no.395 (1990), 36
K. Franckling: "Marcus Roberts: Reflections on Spirit, Tradition, & Purpose," *JT*, xxi/2 (1991), 13
R. Hershon: "Marcus Roberts," *JJI*, xliv/1 (1991), 14
C. Deffaa: "Marcus Roberts," *MR*, xix/5 (1992), 29
R. Mattingly: "Keyboards: Marcus Roberts Takes it in Stride," *Musician*, no.161 (1992), 82
R. L. Doerschuk: "Marcus Roberts: Salvation through Jazz: a Gospel for Savage Times," *Keyboard*, xix/9 (1993), 68 [incl. transcrs.]
B. Marantz: "Marcus Roberts: Aiming for the Core," *Jazz Educators Journal*, xxvi/2 (1993), 21
D. Ouellette: "All Together Now: Roberts' Rules of Order," *Piano & Keyboard*, no.167 (1994), 52
H. Reich: "Marcus Roberts, Piano's New Jazz Master," *Chicago Tribune* (6 Feb 1994)
D. Turner: "Music Notes: Marcus Roberts: Tradition with Vision," *American Visions*, ix/2 (1994), 46
L. Birnbaum: "Marcus Roberts: Tackling Gershwin," *DB*, lxiii/7 (1996), 19 [incl. discography]
M. Roberts: "Rough Mix – Expert Witness: True Jazz in the Culture of Disrespect," *Musician*, no.216 (1996), 15

GK

Robertson, Herb [Clarence] (*b* Plainfield, NJ, 21 Feb 1951). Trumpeter and cornetist. He took up trumpet at the age of ten and became interested in jazz in his early teens, by which time he had acquired the nickname Herb, after the pop trumpeter Herb Alpert. From 1969 to 1971 he attended the Berklee College of Music, where he studied with Charlie Mariano and played in Herb Pomeroy's big band. He briefly formed a quartet with Mark Helias in New Jersey and then performed with and wrote arrangements for a rock band in Canada, until the demands on his embouchure forced him to leave the group. Having returned to New Jersey he worked with Tim Berne from 1981 to 1993, and intermittently thereafter; he first toured Europe with Berne in 1983, and in 1998 he performed as a guest soloist with his group Big Satan. In addition he played with Helias (*c*1984–93) and was a member of Charlie Haden's Liberation Music Orchestra.

In the mid-1980s Robertson began leading his own groups, drawing on such sidemen as Berne, Lindsey Horner, Ed Schuller, Gust William Tsilis, Joey Baron, and Phil Haynes. In 1988 he toured and recorded as the leader of an ensemble, with Brian Lynch (trumpet), Robin Eubanks or Steven Swell (trombone), Vincent Chancey (french horn), Bob Stewart or Joe Daley (tuba), and Baron (drums), which performed Bud Powell's compositions. In the late 1990s he led the groups Entourage and Aboriginals and collaborated with dance and theatre companies. Much of his work has been in Europe.

Robertson has recorded with Horner (1989), the New York Composers Orchestra and The Bang (both 1990), Marc Ducret (1991), the reed player Sibylle Pomorin and the singer Terry Jenoure (1991), Ray Anderson's big band (1994), and the bass player Joe Fonda and the pianist Michael Jefrey Stevens (1993–5). He also plays pocket trumpet, flugelhorn, valve trombone, and tuba.

SELECTED RECORDINGS

(recorded for JMT unless otherwise indicated)

As leader: *Transparency* (1985, 850002); *"X"-cerpts: Live at Willisau* (1987, 834413-1); *Shades of Bud Powell* (1988, 834420-1); *Certified* (1991, 849150-2)

As sideman: T. Berne: *Mutant Variations* (1983, SN 1091); M. Helias: *Split Image* (1984, Enja 4086); Stephan F. Winter: *Die kleine Trompete/The Little Trumpet* (1986, 834407-1); M. Helias: *Desert Blue* (1989, Enja 6016-2); T. Berne: *Fractured Fairy Tales* (1989, 834431-2); M. Helias: *Attack the Future* (1990, Enja 7019-2); The Bang: *Omonimo* (1990, Nueva 3011); M. Ducret: *News from the Front* (1991, 849148-2); S. Pomorin and T. Jenoure: *Auguries of Speed* (1991, ITM 1467); T. Berne: *Nice View* (1993, 514013-2); J. Fonda and M. J. Stevens: *The Wish* (1993–5, Music & Arts 916)

BIBLIOGRAPHY

G. Endress: "Herb Robertson," *JP*, xxxvi/3 (1987), 4
P. Carles, A. Clergeat, and J.-L. Comolli: *Dictionnaire du jazz* (Paris, 1988, rev. and enlarged 2/1994)
J. Solothurnmann: "A Hipster in our Time," *JF* [intl edn], no.121 (1989), 37
K. Whitehead: "Riffs: Herb Robertson," *DB*, lix/5 (1992), 14
B. Smith: "Herb Robertson: Certified," *Coda*, no.253 (1994), 12
B. Rusch: "Herb Robertson: Interview," *Cadence*, xxiii/12 (1997), 5

GK

Robertson, Zue [C. Alvin] (*b* New Orleans, 7 March 1891; *d* Los Angeles, 1943). Trombonist. He first learned piano and took up trombone at the age of 13. Although he spent much of his career in circus and show bands, he was a member of the Olympia Band (*c*1914) and played trombone with Manuel Perez, Richard M. Jones, and John Robichaux. In 1917 he moved to Chicago to work at the De Luxe Café, and by the mid-1920s he was playing with leaders of the stature of Jelly Roll Morton, with whom he recorded *Some Day Sweetheart/London Blues* (1923, OK 8105), and King Oliver (1924). He toured extensively with W. C. Handy before returning to Chicago to join Dave Peyton at the Grand Theatre. From spring 1929 he lived in New York, where he played mainly piano and organ (in 1930 he gave up trombone entirely). After moving to California Robertson worked on piano and double bass throughout the 1930s.

BIBLIOGRAPHY

W. Russell: "Zue Robertson: King of the Trombone," *Jazz Information*, i/26 (1940), 3
L. Wright: "Who's Zue?," *Sv*, no.1 (1965), 18

based on *ChiltonW*

Robeson, Orlando [Roberson, Orlando Hurbert] (*b* Tulsa, OK, 4 Jan 1905; *d* Los Angeles, 20 April 1977). Singer. His birthdate has been published as 4 March 1909 in standard reference sources, but 4 January 1905 appears in his application for social security, together with his full given name. He recorded two items with Fats Waller in 1929. His most important association was with Claude Hopkins, with whom he worked at intervals between 1933 and 1940, making a number of recordings (including *Marie*, 1934, Col. 2904D) and appearing in the short films *Barbershop Blues* (1934) and *By Request* (1936). Robeson also performed briefly with Louis Metcalf in New York (1936), as a co-leader with Clarence Love (1936–7), and as the leader of his own band in Birmingham, Alabama. In 1943 he sang with an army group in Phoenix, Arizona, and following his discharge he moved to the West Coast. The California death index, from which his date of death is taken, gives his place of death as Los Angeles.

based on *ChiltonW*

Robichaux, John (*b* Thibodaux, LA, 16 Jan 1866; *d* New Orleans, 1939). Bandleader, drummer, and violinist, uncle of Joseph Robichaux. After moving to New Orleans in 1891 he played bass drum with the Excelsior Brass Band from 1892 to 1903. Principally as a violinist, he led various bands from 1893 until his death, including a 36-piece orchestra, formed in 1913; his ensembles, which played mainly at sight, included many of the city's best musicians. He made a large number of orchestral arrangements (now housed in the William Ransom Hogan Jazz Archive at Tulane University in New Orleans; *see* LIBRARIES AND ARCHIVES, §2) and composed more than 350 songs. Robichaux should not be confused with his nephew John Robichaux (*b* New Orleans, *c*1915), also a drummer, who was active mainly in Louisiana; he joined the New Orleans Ragtime Orchestra in 1971 and toured widely with this and with the musical show *One Mo' Time*.

BIBLIOGRAPHY

ChartersJ
J. De Donder: "Professor Robichaux," *Fn*, xx/5 (1989), 4

MIKE HAZELDINE

Robichaux, Joseph(, Jr.) [Joe] (*b* New Orleans, 8 March 1900; *d* New Orleans, 17 Jan 1965). Pianist, nephew of John Robichaux. He was taught piano by Steve Lewis. After playing as a soloist in New Orleans he went to Chicago with the trumpeter Tig Chambers (1918), then returned to New Orleans, where he worked with Papa Celestin, David Jones, and Lee Collins. In 1922–3 he toured with the Black Eagles and around 1928 he worked in the JONES AND COLLINS ASTORIA HOT EIGHT, with which he recorded in 1929. He played briefly with Willie O'Connell and Kid Rena, and in 1931 formed the New Orleans Rhythm Boys, which made recordings in New York in 1933; among its sidemen were Gene Porter, Sidney Desvigne, and Sam Dutrey, Jr. The group, by then 15 pieces, disbanded in 1939, and in the 1940s Robichaux again worked as a solo pianist in New Orleans. In the early 1950s he accompanied Lizzie Miles in California, notably during an engagement at the Hangover Club in San Francisco in 1953–4. From 1957 to 1964 he was a member of the band led by George Lewis (i), which toured Europe and Japan; he also recorded in New Orleans with Peter Bocage in 1962 and under Louis Nelson's leadership while in Japan with Lewis in 1963. Robichaux' extrovert style and stage manner masked his sensitive, shy personality.

Oral history material in *LNT*.

SELECTED RECORDINGS

As leader: Every Tub (1933, Voc. 2827); The Riff (1933, Voc. 2592)

As sideman: Jones–Collins Astoria Hot Eight: Astoria Strut/Duet Stomp (1929, Vic. 38576); Damp Weather/Tip Easy Blues (1929, Bb 10952); G. Lewis: *The Perennial George Lewis* (1958, Verve 8277)

BIBLIOGRAPHY

ChiltonW
T. Standish: "Joseph Robichaux: Those Early Days," *JJ*, xii/4 (1959), 10
M. Simpson: "Joe Robichaux, New Orleans Piano: a Biography," *Jazz Reprints*, i/3 (1963), 3
T. Stagg and C. Crump: *New Orleans, the Revival: a Tape and Discography of Negro Traditional Jazz Recorded in New Orleans or by New Orleans Bands, 1937–1972* (n.p. [London], 1973)
K. Gert zur Heide: "Eugene Porter," *Fn*, vii/6 (1976), 17

MIKE HAZELDINE

Robinson, Banjo. *See* Robinson, Ikey.

Robinson, Bill [Luther; Bojangles] (*b* Richmond, VA, 25 May 1878; *d* New York, 25 Nov 1949). Dancer. As a child he appeared in restaurants and vaudeville as a "pickaninny," the term applied to a black child entertainer with traveling troupes. Early in the century he was one of the few African-American dancers to become a star attraction on the Keith circuit, and by the 1920s he was touring on the Theater Owners' Booking Association circuit. During his routines he gave his feet anthropomorphic characteristics and commented humorously on them, and told anecdotes. He did not perform in a Broadway show until he was almost 50, when he danced and sang *Doin' the new low down* in *Blackbirds of 1928*. A good example of Robinson's recorded work may be heard on *Doin' the new low down* (1929, Bruns. 4535), accompanied by a contingent from the Duke Ellington Orchestra, billed as "Irving Mills and his Hotsy Totsy Gang." He took part in several African-American revues and musicals, including *Hot Mikado* (1939), and in *Memphis Bound* (1945), a "swing" version of *H.M.S. Pinafore*. During the 1930s he appeared in films with the child actress Shirley Temple, often performing his best-known routine, tap-dancing up and down a staircase; he also played a major role in both *Hooray for Love!* (1935) and *Stormy Weather* (1943). Robinson was obliged to invent white influences in the light of the furore which followed his incautious statement in an interview in 1928 that he "never consciously imitated a white performer," but his roots were in buck-dancing. Though he may not have invented any of his steps, he carried tap-dancing to new levels of control and percussive clarity. He pioneered tap-dancing on the toes (as opposed to the flat-footed style of his predecessors). Robinson himself said that "protracted exposure to hot jazz music" was the key to dancing, and his facility in executing complex percussive figures rivaled that of the great swing drummers.

SELECTED FILMS AND VIDEOS

Harlem is Heaven (1932); King for a Day (1934); Hooray for Love! (1935); By an Old Southern River (1942); Let's Scuffle (1942); Stormy Weather (1943)

BIBLIOGRAPHY

M. Stearns and J. Stearns: *Jazz Dance: the Story of American Vernacular Dance* (New York and London, 1968)
P. Palmore: "The King of Tap," *SL*, xxxiii (1981), winter, 42
J. Haskins and N. R. Mitgang: *Mr. Bojangles: the Biography of Bill Robinson* (New York, 1988)
D. Bogle: *Toms, Coons, Mulattoes, Mammies & Bucks: an Interpretative History of Blacks in American Films* (New York, 1973, rev. 3/1994)
S. Lasker: Liner notes, *Early Ellington: the Original Decca Recordings* (Decca Jazz 3-640, 1994)
J. Canérot and R. Carbuccia: "Bill 'Bojangles' Robinson: essai de disco-filmographie," *BHcF*, no.443 (1996), 9; no.444 (1996), 1; no.445 (1996), 5
——: "Mr. Bojangles," *BHcF*, no.456 (1997), 7

SAMUEL S. BRYLAWSKI/R

Robinson, Eli [Mr. Eli] (*b* Greenville, nr Woodbury, GA, 23 June 1908; *d* New York, 24 Dec 1972). Trombonist and arranger. He grew up in Charleston, West Virginia, took up trombone in 1925, and began playing professionally later that year. After a period in Detroit (1928) he worked in Cincinnati (from 1930) with, among others, Speed Webb (1930), Zack Whyte (1933), McKinney's Cotton Pickers, and Blanche Calloway, with whom he made his first recordings (1935). In early 1936 he settled in New York and he performed with Willie Bryant, the Mills Blue Rhythm Band under Lucky Millinder, and Teddy Hill, as well as in Millinder's own group. In Chicago during the latter half of 1939 he played with Roy Eldridge. From July 1941 to summer 1947 Robinson was a member of Count Basie's band (with which he appeared in the film *Stage Door Canteen*, 1943; for illustration *see* Films, fig.3). He then worked with various leaders, including Millinder; he may be heard to particular advantage as a blues accompanist with the singer Max "Blues" Bailey on *Rebekah* (1950, Domino 380). From 1954 Robinson played regularly with Buddy Tate's Celebrity Club Orchestra, and examples of his work as a soloist and arranger are on *Celebrity Club Orchestra*, i (1954, BB 33006), which includes some previously unreleased material, and *Swinging Like Tate* (1958, Fel. 2004).

BIBLIOGRAPHY

ChiltonW; *McCarthyB*; *SheridanCB*
S. Dance: "Skip Hall and Eli Robinson," *JM*, iv/7 (1958), 27

HOWARD RYE

Robinson, Fred(erick L.) (*b* Memphis, 20 Feb 1901; *d* New York, 11 April 1984). Trombonist. He began playing while at high school in Memphis, then studied music in Warren, Ohio. In 1927 he moved to Chicago, where he joined Carroll Dickerson's band (or Dickerson's former band under Louis Armstrong; sources are unclear). From April 1928 he worked, with Armstrong, under Dickerson at the Savoy Ballroom, and he took part in Armstrong's Hot Five and Savoy Ballroom Five recordings in June and December of that year. In May 1929 Robinson traveled to New York with Dickerson's band under Armstrong's leadership and remained with it until later that year, when he joined Edgar Hayes at the Alhambra Theater. During the 1930s he worked with Marion Hardy's Alabamians (1931) and then in other big bands, under Don Redman (1931–3), Benny Carter (1933), Charlie Turner (1934 – early 1935), Fletcher Henderson (spring 1935), and Turner once more (through 1937); from August 1935 to October 1937 this last group toured under Fats Waller's leadership. Robinson was again with Henderson from spring 1938 to spring 1939, in June 1939, and from January to March 1941 (following a period with Andy Kirk, late 1939 – August 1940). He then played with George James (1943) and Cab Calloway (1944–5), recorded with Sy Oliver (1946–50), and worked as a freelance and with Noble Sissle (1950–51). Although he ceased to work as a full-time musician in 1954, he continued to perform during the 1960s. While he was a superb trombonist in a big-band context, he is best remembered for his recordings of *West End Blues* in small groups led by Louis Armstrong (1928, OK 8597) and Jelly Roll Morton (1939, Bb 10442).

BIBLIOGRAPHY

AllenH; *ChiltonW*; *FeatherE*; *McCarthyB*
L. Wright: *"Fats" in Fact* (Chigwell, England, 1992)

MIKE HAZELDINE/BK

Robinson, Ikey [Isaac Lee; Robinson, Banjo [Ike]; Banjo Ike(y); Banjo Joe] (*b* Dublin, nr Radford, VA, 25 July 1904; *d* Chicago, 25 Oct 1990). Banjoist and guitarist. His given names, Isaac Lee, and a birthdate of 25 July (not 28 July, as elsewhere) appear in his application for social security. Both of his parents were musicians, and his brother Benny Robinson played clarinet in both circus and minstrel bands and worked for many years with groups in Newark, New Jersey. He grew up in Radford from the age of two, started on violin, and became comfortable playing many instruments, including guitar, flute, and, some time later, clarinet and piano. In his early teens he played locally with his family band for dances and on the street. He led his own band from 1918, and, having changed his main instrument from violin to banjo, began working professionally in West Virginia in 1922, and then in the upper Midwest over the next few years. After moving to Chicago (1926) he performed with Jelly Roll Morton, Clarence Moore (1928–9), and Sammy Stewart (1929), and recorded as a leader and with Jabbo Smith (1929), among others.

In 1930 Robinson traveled with Stewart to New York, where he also worked with Wilbur Sweatman and Noble Sissle, played and sang on a number of recordings with Clarence Williams (1930, 1933), performed and broadcast apart from Williams with one of the latter's sidemen, Herman Chittison, and led two groups; at this point in his career he began to play a tenor guitar with three resonators attached, enabling him to produce solos with a full-bodied sound. He returned to Chicago in 1934 and worked with Carroll Dickerson (with whom he toured the Midwest) and Erskine Tate. The following year he formed his own band, which included Scoops Carry. He continued to appear as the leader of small groups through the 1940s, mainly in Chicago, but also for 18 months in Milwaukee and for four years in Calumet City, Illinois. Later he played in a duo with Mike McKendrick (until 1960). In the 1960s Robinson was a member of the Original Jass All Stars, led by Franz Jackson, and in the 1970s he toured Europe with Little Brother Montgomery, with Red Saunders, and as a freelance soloist with German bands. From 1970 he was resident at Hackney's, a restaurant in Glenview, Illinois, where he gave a concert celebrating his 80th birthday in 1984. He may be heard as a clarinetist on *Swing it* (Champion 40011), which he recorded as a leader in 1935.

Oral history material in *ICU*.

See also Banjo.

SELECTED RECORDINGS

Duos: with Alex Hill (as Down Home Boys): It's All Gone Now (1929, Vic. 38567); with H. Chittison: Unlucky Blue/My Four Reasons (1933, Voc. 25011)

As leader: Got Butter on It (1929, Bruns. 7057); My Four Reasons/Rock Me Mama (1929, Bruns. 7059); Without a Dime (1929, Bruns. 7068)

As sideman: J. Smith: Sleepy Time Blues (1929, Bruns. 7058); Take your Time (1929, Bruns. 7061); Ace of Rhythms (1929, Bruns. 7071); Michigander Blues (1929, Bruns. 7069); Decatur Street Tutti (1929, Bruns. 7078); Hokum Trio: I'm havin' my fun/He wouldn't stop doing it (1930, Diva 6047G); Pods of Pepper: You've had your way/Get Off Stuff (1931, Col. 14590D); Gee I hate to loose that gal (1931, Col. 14664D); C. Williams: Harlem Rhythm Dance/For Sale (1933, Voc. 2602); 'Way Down Home (1933, Voc. 2778); J. Cobb: *Junie Cobb's New Hometown Band* (1961, Riv. 9415)

BIBLIOGRAPHY

ChiltonW

B. Englund: "Ikey Robinson: an Introduction and Discography," *JM*, viii/10 (1962), 10

B. Rusch: "Ikey Robinson: Interview," *Cadence*, v/4 (1979), 12

P. Van Vorst: "Banjo Ikey," *MR*, xi/9 (1984), 5

J. Simmen: "Banjo Ikey Robinson," *BHcF*, no.392 (1991), 37

J. M. Doran: *Herman Chittison: a Bio-discography* (Bel Air, MD, 1993)

HOWARD RYE, BK

Robinson, Janice (Elaine) (*b* Clairton, PA, 28 Dec 1951). Trombonist. As a teenager she played trombone in Bill Cosby's nationally broadcast television program. After graduating from the Eastman School (BME) in 1973 she moved to New York, where the following year she joined Clark Terry's big band. She visited Japan while playing with the Thad Jones–Mel Lewis Orchestra (1975–6), toured Europe with Gil Evans (1976), and returned to Japan while a member of Frank Foster's big band (1977–8). Shortly afterwards she performed with Slide Hampton (*c*1979). Robinson also worked in jazz repertory companies and free-jazz ensembles: she recorded with the Jazz Composer's Orchestra in 1974 and appeared with Sam Rivers at the Newport Jazz Festival New York in 1976. With the pianist and french horn player Sharon Freeman, she led a bop quintet that appeared at the first Kansas City Women's Jazz Festival in 1978, and she formed her own quintet, which included Buster Williams and Kenny Kirkland. Later she appeared in Dizzy Gillespie's big band on the television show "Jazz in America: Lincoln Center, New York" (1982). She continued to play with Foster until 1982 and was a member of George Gruntz's Concert Jazz Band. During the academic year 1983–4 Robinson taught at Rutgers.

SELECTED RECORDINGS

As sideman: T. Jones and M. Lewis: on *Suite for Pops* (1975, A&M Hor. 701), The Farewell; *New Life* (1975–6, A&M Hor. 707); F. Foster: *Twelve Shades of Black: for All Intents and Purposes* (1978, Leo 007)

BIBLIOGRAPHY

"Janice Robinson," *Newsletter of the International Trombone Association*, viii/3 (1981), 7

Y. A. Salaam: "Profile: Janice Robinson," *DB*, xlviii/4 (1981), 48

S. Placksin: *American Women in Jazz, 1900 to the Present: their Words, Lives, and Music* (New York, 1982; London, 1985, as *Jazzwomen, 1900 to the Present: their Words, Lives, and Music*), 285

BK

Robinson, Jim [Nathan; Big Jim, Jim Crow] (*b* Deer Range, LA, 25 Dec 1890; *d* New Orleans, 4 May 1976). Trombonist. His year of birth appears in some sources as 1892 but *ChiltonW* gives 1890 and social security records confirm this earlier year. He took up guitar as a youngster, when he became known as "Jim Crow," reportedly on account of his American Indian facial features. He began playing trombone in 1917 while stationed in France during army service and received some instruction from Willie Foster; later he had lessons with the trombonist Charles "Sunny" Henry. Robinson first worked professionally in New Orleans in 1919, with Kid Rena, and alongside Lee Collins in the Golden Leaf Band (led by the banjoist Jesse Jackson). From 1923 he was a member of the Morgan Band, working first under the leadership of Isaiah Morgan and then under Sam Morgan; he recorded with the group in 1927 and performed with it in Chicago two years later. Newsreel footage from his appearance in the Mardi Gras parade of 1928 may be seen in the documentary video *Sing On* (1999). During the mid- and late 1930s he played with Capt. John Handy and Kid Howard, and in the 1940s he recorded with Kid Rena (1940) and Bunk Johnson and George Lewis (i) (1942–6); his version of *Ice Cream* (1944), in which he leads the band without a trumpeter, is justly celebrated. Robinson later played regularly with Lewis in New Orleans and toured with him in the USA (1952–4) and Europe (1959). After 1960 he performed at Preservation Hall with Lewis and Percy Humphrey, among other leaders, and continued to tour and record frequently. He may be seen in the film *The Cincinnati Kid* (1965) and the television documentary "Anatomy of Pop: the Music Explosion" (1969; issued on film as *American Music: from Folk to Jazz to Pop*).

Robinson's highly individual style was characterized by an ebullient shouting tone and his frequent employment of tongued staccato, glottal ghost notes, and pedal notes; he also made judicious use of glissandos. Although he displayed an inventive sense of melody, he never neglected the trombone's role as the low-pitched contrapuntal voice in ensemble passages, and he was a leading exponent of the New Orleans tailgate style.

Oral history material in *LNT, NjR.*

For illustrations *see* Humphrey and Johnson, bunk.

SELECTED RECORDINGS

As leader: Ice Cream (1944, AM 254); *Robinson's Jacinto Ballroom Orchestra* (1964, GHB 28)

As sideman: S. Morgan: Short Dress Gal/Bogalusa Strut (1927, Col. 14351D); K. Rena: Weary Blues/Get it right (1940, Delta 806–7); B. Johnson: Careless Love Blues/Weary Blues (1944, AM 258); G. Lewis: *George Lewis and his New Orleans Stompers*, i (1955, BN 1205); *George Lewis at the San Jacinto Hall* (1964, San Jacinto 2); P. Humphrey: *Climax Rag* (1965, Pearl 3)

BIBLIOGRAPHY

ChiltonW

J. Robinson: "New Orleans Trombone," *Jazz Record*, no.38 (1945); repr. in *Selections from the Gutter: Jazz Portraits from "The Jazz Record"*, ed. A. Hodes and C. Hansen (Berkeley, CA, Los Angeles, and London, 1977), 124

D. Stewart-Baxter: "Jim Robinson," *Jazz Music*, iii/6 (1947), 15

M. Jones: "New Orleans Brassmen," *MM*, xxxiv (10 Jan 1959), 11; repr. in Jones: *Talking Jazz* (London, 1987/*R*2000), 175

V. Wilmer: "Robinson: Eighty Years on," *MM* (19 June 1971), 16

A. Barrell: "Jim Robinson," *Fn*, vii/2 (1975–6), 4 [incl. discography]

Obituaries: *DB*, xliii/13 (1976), 11; D. Donahoe, *Fn*, vii/5 (1976), 29; C. Hillman, *JJ*, xxix/8 (1976), 16; B. Martyn, *MM* (15 May 1976), 20

E. Kraut: "Jim Robinson," *JP*, xxxi/2 (1982), 12

F. Turner: *Remembering Song: Encounters with the New Orleans Jazz Tradition* (New York, 1982, rev. and enlarged 2/1994), 90

K. Koenig: "Nathan 'Big Jim' Robinson: Jazz Trombonist," *SL*, xxxv (1983), winter, 24

W. Carter: *Preservation Hall: Music from the Heart* (Wheatley, Oxford, England, and New York, 1991, rev. 2/1999)

R. H. Knowles: *Fallen Heroes: a History of New Orleans Brass Bands* (New Orleans, 1996)

R. Lee: *Big Jim: a Discography of Jim Robinson* (Zwolle, Netherlands, 1998)

ALDEN ASHFORTH

Robinson, J(oseph) Russel (*b* Indianapolis, 8 July 1892; *d* Palmdale, CA, 30 Sept 1963). Songwriter and pianist. He was principally self-taught as a pianist, and began his career accompanying silent films in Indianapolis when he was a teenager. Since he was crippled in his right arm by polio, he developed a distinctive left-hand style incorporating gymnastic and unorthodox passages. His playing was particularly popular with piano-roll companies, and he recorded dozens of rolls for Imperial and the United States Music Company in Chicago (1917–18) before moving under exclusive contract to the QRS company in New York to record blues songs (1918–21). From January to mid-October 1919 and again from late September 1920 to mid-April 1921 Robinson was pianist for the Original dixieland jazz band, with which he toured England; during this same period he also managed W. C. Handy's music publishing firm. He had a number of hits with his own popular songs, beginning with *Margie* (1920). Between 1923 and 1926 he accompanied a number of jazz and blues singers (notably Lizzie Miles), and during the 1930s he played on radio. From late July 1936, while affiliated with NBC radio, he participated in an effort to revive the Original Dixieland Jazz Band; the group toured, but interest in the band gradually flagged, and Robinson left it in February 1938. Later he settled in southern California, where he continued to compose songs, but with diminishing success.

Robinson broke with social tradition by collaborating extensively with African-American musicians, among them Handy, Noble Sissle, and Spencer Williams; the QRS piano roll company advertised him as "the white boy with the colored fingers," and his accompaniments to Lucille Hegamin reveal his mastery of the blues. He excelled in both the performance and the composition of blues- and jazz-influenced material, and his *That Eccentric Rag* (1912) became a staple of the traditional jazz repertory (as *Eccentric*, rev. 1923). Other well-known songs include *Singin' the blues (til my daddy comes home)* (1920), made famous in a recording by Bix Beiderbecke with Frankie Trumbauer's orchestra (1927, OK 40772), *Aggravatin' papa (don't you try to two-time me)* and *Beale Street Mama*, recorded by Bessie Smith (1923, Col. A3877), and *A Portrait of Jennie*, recorded by, among others, Donald Byrd (on the album *At the Half Note Cafe*, 1960, BN 84060).

SELECTED RECORDINGS

Duos with L. Hegamin: Down Hearted Blues/Wanna go South Again Blues (1923, Cameo 381)

As sideman: Original Dixieland Jazz Band: Ostrich Walk/Sensation Rag (1919, Col. 736); Al Bernard: Memphis Blues/Hesitation Blues (1927, Bruns. 3553); Original Dixieland Five: Barnyard Blues/Original Dixieland One-step (1938, Vic. 25502)

BIBLIOGRAPHY

J. R. Robinson: "Dixieland Piano," *Record Changer* (1947), Aug, 7

H. O. Brunn: *The Story of the Original Dixieland Jazz Band* (Baton Rouge, LA, 1960/*R*1977)

Obituary, *New York Times* (2 Oct 1963)

J. E. Hasse: *The Creation and Dissemination of Indianapolis Ragtime, 1897–1930* (diss., Indiana U., 1981), 159

B. Singer: *Black and Blue: the Life and Lyrics of Andy Razaf* (New York and Toronto, 1992)

JOHN EDWARD HASSE

Robinson, Justin (Jay) (*b* New York, 14 Aug 1968) Alto saxophonist. His father played alto saxophone and his mother, a jazz enthusiast, played clarinet in her youth. He took up alto saxophone when he was 13, learning initially with his father and later at school. From the age of 14 he had lessons with Frank Wess during the summer, and when he was 16 he began performing locally and studying with Frank Foster. He worked alongside Philip Harper in groups led by Little Jimmy Scott and Betty Carter after they had met at a jam session in about 1986; around this time he joined the Harper Brothers (*see* Harper, winard), with whom he continued to work until 1992. Robinson has performed and recorded with Stephen Scott, Cecil Brooks III, Rodney Kendrick, and Diana Ross, and has recorded with Abbey Lincoln, the Essence All Stars, and the singer Jeffrey Smith (all 1996); he recorded as a leader in 1991.

SELECTED RECORDINGS

As leader: *Justin Time* (1991, Verve 314-513254-2)

As sideman: Harper Brothers: *Remembrance: Live at the Village Vanguard* (1989, Verve 841723-2); C. Brooks: *Hangin' with Smooth* (1990, Muse 5428); S. Scott: *Something to Consider* (1991, Verve 849557-2); R. Kendrick: *Last Chance for Common Sense* (1995, Verve 314-531536-2); Essence All Stars: on *Jackie's Blues Bag* (1996, Hip Bop 8015), Bluesnik

BIBLIOGRAPHY

D. Kasrel: "Hearsay: Hyper-saxive," *JT*, xxii/5 (1992), 14

A. Lewis and L. Lewis: "Justin Robinson Interview," *Cadence*, xix/10 (1993), 5

GK

Robinson, Orphy (Everton) (*b* London, 13 Oct 1960). English vibraphonist and marimba player. He played alto saxophone, trumpet, and drums before taking up tuned percussion. In the late 1970s and 1980s he was a member of various jazz-funk bands, including Savanna. He then worked with, among others, the Jazz Warriors (1985), Courtney Pine (late 1980s, touring the USA in 1987), Andy Sheppard's big band Soft on the Inside (1988–90, including an appearance in the documentary video *Soft on the Inside*, 1990), Andy Hamilton (1992), Byron Wallen and the multi-cultural group Shiva Nova (both from 1993), David Murray (touring in May 1994), and the guitarist Alan Weekes and the reed player David Jean-Baptiste (both 1997). In the 1990s Robinson led several of his own bands, notably Annavas (named after his former group, Savanna), Nubian Vibes Ensemble, and Codefive. He has written music for television and film and composed a suite for the Balanescu String Quartet (1991).

SELECTED RECORDINGS

As leader: *When Tomorrow Comes* (1991, BN B21Z-81214); *The Vibes Describes* (1993, BN B21Z-29223)

As sideman: C. Pine: *Journey to the Urge Within* (1986, Ant. 8700); Jazz Warriors: *Out of Many, One People* (1987, Ant. 8712); A. Sheppard: *Soft on the Inside* (1989, Ant. 8751)

BIBLIOGRAPHY

CarrJ; *ChiltonB*

J. Fordham: "The Beat that's Sweet," *The Guardian* (16 June 1989)

S. S. Lwin: "Zorro of the Vibes: Orphy Robinson," *Jazz Express*, no.138 (1992), 6

L. Connelly: "Riffs: Orphy Robinson," *DB*, lx/7 (1993), 13

MARK GILBERT

Robinson, Perry (Morris) (*b* New York, 17 Sept 1938). Clarinetist. Fitzgerald's internet biography states that Robinson was born "on September 17, 1938 (not August 17, 1938, as listed in many reference works)." His family moved to Los Angeles when he was five years old. His father, the political and folk revival songwriter Earl Robinson (*d* 1991), was responsible for much of his musical background. He first studied piano, but changed to clarinet at the age of nine. Having returned to New York at the age of 12, he later attended the High School of Music and Art (1952–6) and the Manhattan School of Music (1958). His playing in a quartet alongside Chuck Israels gained him admittance to the Lenox School of Jazz in Massachusetts in 1959, and after meeting Ornette Coleman there he became interested in free jazz. His quartet with Israels traveled to Spain, where Robinson played bop with Tete Montoliu. He performed elsewhere in Europe with Don Friedman, with Archie Shepp and Bill Dixon (in Helsinki in July 1962), and further with Dixon (Stockholm, August 1962). In February 1963 he rejoined Shepp and Dixon for a radio broadcast in New York.

Robinson formed a group while playing in a band in the US Navy; following his discharge he worked with the Jazz Composers Guild in New York. He recorded with Henry Grimes (1965), played in Sunny Murray's quartet (May 1966) and with Roswell Rudd, took part in the recording of Carla Bley's *Escalator over the Hill* (1968–71), and recorded with Charlie Haden's Music Liberation Orchestra (1970). In the 1970s he played with Darius Brubeck (1973–4) and John Fischer's Interface (from 1975), recorded in a duo with the clarinetist Hans Kumpf, and joined Gunter Hampel's Galaxie Dream Band, with which he remained into the 1990s; Hampel's group worked mainly in Europe, but also appeared in the USA, and recorded at the Knitting Factory, New York, in 1991. In the 1980s Robinson was a member of John Carter's Clarinet Summit, but he did not record with the group. He led several ensembles with unusual instrumentation, including Pipe Dreams, the other members of which were two singers (Judy Niemack and Janet Lawson) and a guitarist, and Licorice Factory, consisting of up to seven clarinetists – though its album of 1984–5 utilized a somewhat more conventional instrumentation of three clarinets and a standard rhythm section; he also recorded as a sideman with Ray Anderson (1987). In the late 1980s he formed the quartet Nightmare Island, consisting of Simon Nabatov, Ed Schuller, and the drummer Ernst Bier; it recorded in 1989, 1990, and 1996, and performed mainly in Europe. Robinson then formed the Space-Time Swing Band, whose members included Mark Whitecage and Steve Swell, played in a klezmer group which Burton Greene formed in Amsterdam, and became a member of a folk-oriented trio with the guitarists David Bernz and Rande Harris.

SELECTED RECORDINGS

As leader: *Kundalini* (1978, IA 373856); *The Traveler* (*c*1978, Chi. 190); *Licorice Factory* (1985, Jazzmania 41206); *Nightmare Island: Live at the Leverkusener Jazztage* (1988, West Wind 0026); *Call to the Stars* (1990, West Wind 2052); *Angelology* (1996, Timescraper 9613)

As sideman: H. Grimes: *Henry Grimes Trio* (1965, ESP 1026); C. Bley: *Escalator over the Hill* (1968–71, JCOA EOTH); G. Hampel: *Jubilation* (1983, Birth 0038); *Celestial Glory* (1991, Birth 040)

BIBLIOGRAPHY

G. Endress: "Der Magier der Klarinette," *JP*, xxi/7 (1972), 228

B. Palmer: "Perry Robinson: Clarinet Energy," *DB*, xxxix/16 (1972), 16

"Perry Robinson: the Trailblazing Jazz Clarinetist," *OP* [Los Angeles], issue R (1983), 32

A. Kreye: "Aktiv mit drei Formationen: Perry Robinson," *JP*, xxxiii/8 (1984), 24

F. Wetzel: "Perry Robinson," *JP*, xxxviii/10 (1989), 12

B. Young: *Dixonia: a Bio-discography of Bill Dixon* (Westport, CT, and London, 1998)

J. Greene: "Still Traveling: Perry Robinson," *Coda*, no.287 (1999), 6

<http://www.eclipse.net/~fitzgera/perry/prhome.htm> (1999) [incl. biography by M. Fitzgerald, discography]

DAVID WILD/BK

Robinson, Prince (*b* Portsmouth, VA, 7 June 1902; *d* New York, 23 July 1960). Clarinetist and tenor saxophonist. At the age of 14 he taught himself to play clarinet, and he performed with local bands for three years before going to New York in 1923. There he worked with Lionel Howard's Musical Aces, Elmer Snowden, June Clark, Duke Ellington (*c* spring 1925 – summer 1926, and sporadically thereafter to spring 1927), and the saxophonist Billy Fowler, and recorded with Clara Smith, the Blue Rhythm Orchestra, and the Gulf Coast Seven (all 1925); during the same period he occasionally deputized for Coleman Hawkins in Fletcher Henderson's big band. From spring 1927 until late that same year he toured South American with Leon Abbey. On his return to New York Robinson joined McKinney's Cotton Pickers (mid-1928; for illustration *see* MCKINNEY'S COTTON PICKERS). After leaving the group he played with Blanche Calloway (summer 1935 – early 1937) and Willie Bryant (April 1937 – November 1938) and recorded with Teddy Wilson's swing groups accompanying Billie Holiday (February and November 1937) and with Lil Armstrong's small group (July 1937). He then worked with Roy Eldridge (November 1938–1940), Louis Armstrong (1940–42), Lucky Millinder (1942–3), Benny Morton (autumn 1944, at Café Society downtown), Claude Hopkins (1945–52), Henry "Red" Allen (1954, on tour), and Freddie Washington (1955 – summer 1959). He also led his own band briefly in 1953 and was a member of the Henderson reunion band in July 1958.

Robinson was one of the few reed players in jazz who regularly played solos on both clarinet and saxophone in a single tune; he preferred clarinet, but his playing of the tenor saxophone in the late 1920s and early 1930s, when he was recording with McKinney's Cotton Pickers, rivaled that of Hawkins. Thereafter, although he continued to be well regarded by his fellow musicians, he did not attain widespread recognition.

SELECTED RECORDINGS

As sideman: McKinney's Cotton Pickers: Four or Five Times (1928, Vic. 21583); I want a little girl (1930, Vic. 23000); B. Calloway: Line-a-jive (1935, Voc. 3113); T. Wilson: My Last Affair (1937, Bruns. 7840); R. Eldridge: *Roy Eldridge at the Arcadia Ballroom, August/September 1939* (1939, Jazz Archives 14), incl. Arcadia Shuffle

BIBLIOGRAPHY

AllenH; *ChiltonW*; *McCarthyB*; *SchullerS*
J. Chilton: *McKinney's Music: a Bio-discography of McKinney's Cotton Pickers* (London, 1978)
M. Selchow: *Profoundly Blue: a Bio-discographical Scrapbook on Edmond Hall* (Lübbecke, Germany, 1988)
M. Tucker: *Ellington: the Early Years* (Oxford, England, Urbana, IL, and Chicago, 1991)
J. Evensmo: *History of Jazz Tenor Saxophone: Black Artists*, i: *1917–1934* (Oslo, 1996); ii: *1935–1939* (Oslo, 1997) ; iii: *1940–1944* (Oslo, 1997)

FRANK DRIGGS/BK

Robinson, Scott (M.) (*b* Pompton Plains, NJ, 27 April 1959). Tenor and baritone saxophonist, composer, arranger, and jazz educator. He led a quartet in high school in the mid-1970s and graduated from the Berklee College of Music, Boston, in 1981. He has played in orchestras led by Illinois Jacquet (1987), Lionel Hampton (1988–9), Vince Giordano (1988–93), Buck Clayton (1990–91), Tom Harrell (1990), Frank Wess (1991), Maria Schneider (1992–), and Marty Grosz (1993–6), and small groups under the leadership of Keith Ingham and Grosz, both separately and together. His own quartet, featuring Horace Parlan, toured Europe in 1987–9 and recorded in Denmark. In 1993 he and Wess formed a two-saxophone octet and recorded. In 1998 Robinson was performing with bands led by Bob Brookmeyer, John Pizzarelli, Louie Bellson, Toshiko Akiyoshi, Randy Sandke, and Ruby Braff. In addition to his sessions with his own quartet, he has taken part in scores of recordings as a sideman. While he is primarily a tenor and baritone saxophonist, he also plays all other sizes of saxophone, clarinets, and flutes, as well as theremin, cornet, alto horn and other brass instruments. His influences range from Louis Armstrong to Sun Ra.

Video oral history material in *NCH* (HCJA).

SELECTED RECORDINGS

As leader: *Thinking Big* (1996, Arbors 19179)
As sideman: F. Wess: *Tryin' to Make my Blues Turn Green* (1993, Conc. 4592); R. Braff: *Ruby Braff Remembers Louis Armstrong* (1997, Arbors 19163)

FLOYD LEVIN

Robinson, Spike [Henry Bertholf] (*b* Kenosha, WI, 16 Jan 1930). Tenor saxophonist. He learned classical clarinet from the age of eight, took up alto saxophone when he was ten, and soon afterwards began playing in dance bands. In 1948 he joined the navy as a musician, and the following year he became a member of a band attached to the US embassy in London. While there he played with Victor Feldman, Ronnie Scott, Lennie Bush, the pianist Tommy Pollard, and John Dankworth, among others, and joined Club Eleven, with which he recorded for the label Esquire. After returning to the USA in 1952 he worked almost continuously as an engineer for 30 years; at the same time he played saxophone semi-professionally with a number of musicians, among them Dave Grusin (from 1954), Don Grusin, Johnny Smith, Gus Johnson, Benny Carter, Red Rodney, Teddy Wilson, and Milt Hinton. In 1964 he left his engineering job briefly to run a restaurant, Spike Robinson's Terrace Inn, in Boulder, Colorado, which featured jazz; however, the venture failed after a year. In the early 1980s Robinson began recording again, played for jazz parties, and toured Britain, and in 1985 he retired from engineering and returned to music full-time. He appeared in an edition of "Sidran on Record" on National Public Radio and was featured in the BBC television documentary "Club Eleven Reunion." In 1989 he moved to England.

SELECTED RECORDINGS

As leader (recorded for Capri unless otherwise indicated): Blue Bird/The Guv-nor (1951, Esquire 10-192); Spike's Choice/Spike's Delight (1951, Esquire 10-218); *Music of Harry Warren* (1981, Dis. 870); *At Chesters*, i–ii (1984, Hep 2028, 2031); *London Reprise* (1984, 44360); *Spring Can Really Hang You up the Most* (1985, 71785); *It's a Wonderful World* (1985, 72185); with A. Cohn: *Henry B. Meets Alvin G.* (1987, 61787); with Rob Mullins: *The Odd Couple* (1988, 74008); with E. Rucker: *Nice Work!* (1989, 74017); with Jim Doherty: *One Man in his Time* (1991, Cargo 001) with S. Hamilton and K. Peplowski: *Groovin' High* (1991, Conc. 4509); *A Real Corker* (1991, 74043); *Reminiscin'* (1991, 74029)
As sideman (all recorded for Esquire in 1951): T. Pollard: East of the Sun/Lover Come Back to Me (10-188); Just Friends/The Way You Look Tonight (10-142); R. Scott: Chasin' the Bird/Little Willie Leaps (10-141); El sino/Crazy Rhythm (10-154)

BIBLIOGRAPHY

CarrJ
J. Bradley: "Spike Robinson Jazzed Up for Local Concerts," *Denver Post* (3 June 1990)
——: "Jazzman Tries Fresh Breath of Air," *Denver Post* (23 April 1991)
G. Lees: *Waiting for Dizzy* (New York, and Oxford, England, 1991), 201
M. Richards: "Spike Robinson," *JJ*, xlvi/1 (1993), 6
D. Kreck: "Robinson Rediscovers Joy of Sax," *Denver Post* (16 Jan 1995)

MARK GILBERT

Roccisano, Joe(y) [Joseph Lucian] (*b* Springfield, MA, 15 Oct 1939; *d* New York, 9 Nov 1997). Alto saxophonist, bandleader, and arranger. He began on mandolin at the age of eight, took up clarinet when he was 13, and later doubled on saxophone. After touring with the Tommy Dorsey orchestra under Warren Covington (1957–9) he studied at SUNY, Potsdam (BS MusEd 1963). In 1964 he toured again with Dorsey's orchestra, this time under Sam Donahue, and in the mid-1960s he settled in Los Angeles; there he played and recorded with Don Ellis (1966–8), with whom he also appeared at the Monterey and Newport jazz festivals, and worked with Ray Charles (1967–8). As a freelance he performed with Louie Bellson, Terry Gibbs, Don Menza, and Bill Holman, and recorded with Don Rader (*c*1973). From 1976 he led a 15-piece band, Rocbop, in the Los Angeles area, with Pete Christlieb and Milcho Leviev among its principal soloists. Roccisano wrote arrangements for several jazz musicians, including Bellson, Ellis, Doc Severinsen, and Woody Herman; his score for *Green Earrings*, on Herman's album *Chick, Donald, Walter, and Woodrow* (1978, Cen. 1110), was nominated for a Grammy Award, and the album *Apogee* (1978, WB 3236), by Christlieb and Warne Marsh, for which he wrote the arrangements, includes his composition *Tenors of the Time*. In 1981 Roccisano recorded with the Capp–Pierce Juggernaut. He moved to New York in the early 1980s, and he continued to perform and record, both as a sideman with Bellson's big band and as a leader, into the mid-1990s. In December 1993 he led a group at the Zanzibar, and he recorded with his own big band in 1992 and 1994 (*Leave your Mind Behind*, Landmark 1541) and with a nonet in 1997. Roccisano died of a heart attack en route to his regular Sunday brunch job with his nonet at the Blue Note.

BIBLIOGRAPHY

Feather–Gitler '70s
L. Underwood: "Joe Roccisano," *DB*, xliii/9 (1976), 37
——: "Caught!: Joey Roccisano's Rocbop," *DB*, xlvi/8 (1979), 35
Obituary, *Saxophone Journal*, xxii/6 (1998), 32

BK

Roche, Betty [Mary Elizabeth] (*b* Wilmington, DE, 9 Jan 1920; *d* Pleasantville, NJ, 15 Feb 1999). Singer. She won an amateur contest at the Apollo Theatre in Harlem and later sang with the Savoy Sultans (1941-2) and with Hot Lips Page and Lester Young. In 1943 she joined Duke Ellington. Although she made no studio recordings with Ellington at this time, she was the first to sing the *Blues* sequence of his *Black, Brown and Beige*, performed at Carnegie Hall in January 1943; that same year she sang *Take the "A" Train* with his orchestra in the film *Reveille with Beverly*. She worked and recorded with Earl Hines (1944), then spent a period in relative obscurity before rejoining Ellington in 1952, when she recorded an acclaimed version of *Take the "A" Train*. After a period of semiretirement she recorded three solo albums (1956, 1960, 1961). Roche performed mostly blues and ballads in the 1940s, and her warm, personal style was well suited to Ellington's band. Her early work is superior to her bop singing of the 1950s.

SELECTED RECORDINGS

As leader: *Take the "A" Train* (1956, Beth. 64); *Singin' and Swingin'* (1960, Prst. 7187); *Lightly and Politely* (1961, Prst. 7198)

As sideman: D. Ellington: on *Carnegie Hall Concert: January 1943* (1943, Prst. 34004), Black, Brown and Beige; E. Hines: Blues on my Weary Mind/I'll get by (1944, Apollo 358); D. Ellington: Take the "A" Train (1952, Col. B1566)

BIBLIOGRAPHY

B. Ulanov: *Duke Ellington* (New York, 1946/*R*1975), 249
G. T. Simon: *The Big Bands* (New York and London, 1967, rev. 4/1981)
D. Ellington: *Music is my Mistress* (Garden City, NY, 1973, rev. 2/1982)
Obituary, B. Ratliff, *New York Times* (1 March 1999)

REG COOPER

Rocheman, Manuel (*b* Paris, 23 July 1964). French pianist and composer. He learned classical piano from the age of six and later took up percussion and composition; it was upon hearing Oscar Peterson that he became interested in jazz. While studying at the Paris Conservatoire he took lessons in jazz piano from Michel Sardaby and then for two years with Martial Solal. In 1984 he formed his first trio and began to perform at many concerts and jazz events, including festivals in Paris (1984, 1986, 1992), Antibes (1988), Nice (1992), Cervantino, Mexico (1993), Montreal (1996), Copenhagen, Århus, and New York (1997). Apart from leading another trio, which consisted of the twin brothers François Moutin on double bass and Louis Moutin on drums, he joined Laurent Cugny's Big Band Lumière and Didier Levallet's tentet, and collaborated with Johnny Griffin, Anthony Ortega, Aldo Romano, Christian Escoudé, and the Orchestre National de Jazz, which in 1996 performed his composition *San Felipe*.

SELECTED RECORDINGS

As leader: *Trio urbain* (1989, Nocturne 504); *White Keys* (1991, Nocturne 513); *Tropic City* (1995, A (ii) 73033); *Come Shine* (1997, Col. 491869); *I'm Old Fashioned* (1999, Col. 497620)

As sideman: A. Ortega: *On Evidence* (1992, Evidence [Fr.] 213); *Neuf* (1994, Evidence [Fr.] 620); Jacques Vidal: *Traverses* (1996, Quoi de Neuf, Docteur 038)

BIBLIOGRAPHY

S. Siclier: "Trio urbain," *Jh*, no.472 (1990), 14
P. Anquetil: "Manuel Rocheman: la métamorphose," *Jazzman*, no.159 (1992), 2
——: "Œdipe au piano," *Le Nouvel Observateur* (25 June 1992)
C. Loxhay: "Le manuel de Rocheman," *Jazz in Time*, no.44 (1993), 13

ANDRÉ CLERGEAT

Rochester, Cornell (W.) (*b* Philadelphia, *c* late 1950s). Drummer. He took up drums in his youth, and after a brief time away from playing returned to the instrument in his teens, when he studied with Sherman Ferguson and performed in local funk groups. Early in his career he played in local organ trios. In 1980 he joined Odean Pope, working initially with Gerald Veasley in the rhythm section of Pope's Saxophone Choir; during an appearance at the North Sea Jazz Festival in 1980 Pope, Veasley, and Rochester performed together in a trio, and over the course of the next decade (through *c*1991) they continued to appear together in both ensembles. In the early 1980s Rochester worked with James "Blood" Ulmer and Jamaaladeen Tacuma, and in 1985 he recorded as a co-leader with Veasley. He toured and recorded in Joe Zawinul's group Zawinul Syndicate from the late 1980s to the early 1990s. In 1990 he joined Ulmer's group the Music Revelation Ensemble, and around the same time he formed the group Cornell Rochester and the N. P. Boys, with which he toured Europe and recorded (both 1993). Having renewed his affiliation with Tacuma, throughout the 1990s he worked with the electric bass guitarist in an expanded quintet version of Wolter Wierbos's Podium Trio, with which they recorded in 1993 and 1996. In the late 1990s he joined Uri Caine's group devoted to interpreting compositions of Gustav Mahler's music and performed alongside the accordion player Zeena Parkins in the trios GTR OBLQ and Psycho Acoustic, led by the electric guitarist Elliott Sharp. Rochester maintained his association with Ulmer into the new century.

SELECTED RECORDINGS

As leader: with G. Veasley: *One Minute of Love* (1985, Gram. 8505); with J. Tacuma: *Jamaaladeen Tacuma and Cornell Rochester Meet the Podium Trio: Live in Köln* (1993, Tim. 421)

As sideman: O. Pope: *Out for a Walk* (1990, Moers Music 02072); Music Revelation Ensemble: *Elec. Jazz* (1990, DIW 839); *In the Name of . . .* (1993, DIW 885)

BIBLIOGRAPHY

R. Tolleson: "Portraits: Cornell Rochester," *MD*, xiii/9 (1989), 38

GK

Rockets. Big band formed by HARLAN LEONARD after the Kansas City Rockets disbanded in 1937.

Rockwell, Bob [Robert Neal] (*b* Miami, OK, 2 May 1945). Soprano and tenor saxophonist. He spent his early years in Nowata, Oklahoma, before moving with his family to Minneapolis, where he played clarinet from the age of 13; later he changed to tenor saxophone, on which he was self-taught. A professional from the age of 18, he worked first in rock bands, but in 1966 he joined a jazz trio with the pianist Bobby Lyle. From 1969 to 1973 he played in pit bands in Las Vegas, after which he returned to Minneapolis and formed the quartet Natural Life. Having moved to New York in 1978, he joined the Thad Jones–Mel Lewis Orchestra and also played with Tito Puente, John Hicks, Billy Hart, Marc Johnson, Ron McClure, and Freddie Hubbard, with whom he toured Australia. Rockwell then traveled to Denmark and in 1983 settled in Copenhagen. He formed his own quartet, played in the Radioens Big Band (1992–5), joined The Organizers, led by the organist Kjeld Lauritsen (1993), and served as co-leader, with Jesper Lundgaard, of the Repertory Quartet. Rockwell, whose playing is inspired by Dexter Gordon, Sonny Stitt, and Hank Mobley, has recorded with Natural Life, Tom Harrell, Duke Jordan, Jørgen Emborg, Karsten Houmark, the big band led by the conductor Jens Klüver, the pianist, arranger, and composer Niels Jørgen

Steen, Jan Kaspersen, Joe Bonner, the Jones–Lewis Orchestra, the singer Linda Peterson, Erling Kroner, Jens Winther, and Lundgaard.

SELECTED RECORDINGS

Duos: with J. Kaspersen: *Ballads and Cocktails* (1992, Olufsen 5156); *More Ballads and Cocktails . . . and the Blues* (1999, Olufsen 5393)
As leader: *No Rush* (1985–6, Ste. 1219); *The Bob Rockwell Trio* (1989, Ste. 31242); *Shades of Blue* (1995, Ste. 31378); of Repertory Quartet (with J. Lundgaard): *The Repertory Quartet Plays Ellington/Strayhorn* (1997, Music Mecca 2051-2)
As sideman: T. Harrell: *Open Air* (1986, Ste. 1220); The Organizers: *Live at Sofie's Cellar & 10'eren* (1993, Olufsen 5162); J. Kaspersen: *Live in Copenhagen JazzHouse* (1994, Olufsen 5303/04); Erik Ørum von Spreckelsen: *Need I Say More* (1999, Stunt 19907)

BIBLIOGRAPHY

K. Skaaning: "Bob Rockwell: den hårde vej" [Bob Rockwell: paying the dues], *MM: tidsskrift for rytmisk music m.m.*, xvii/5 (1984), 15
K. Frandsen: *Politikens jazzleksikon* (Copenhagen, 1987)
J. R. K. Keller: "Striptease blev hans redning" [Striptease saved him], *Jazz Special*, no.32 (1997), 14

FRANK BÜCHMANN-MØLLER

Roda, Ricard (*b* Barcelona, 13 Nov 1931). Spanish alto saxophonist. He studied music at the conservatory in Barcelona, and began playing jazz in 1947, participating in the jam sessions organized at the Hot Club de Barcelona. While working at the Jamboree Club he played with such visiting soloists as Tony Scott, Art Farmer, Tete Montoliu, Guy Lafitte, and Lucky Thompson and established a reputation as one of the finest Spanish saxophonists. In 1968 he participated in the cooperative recording *Nuits de jazz at Jamboree* (Edigsa 221). Around this time he also worked with the commercial orchestras led by Xavier Cugat and Frank Pourcel. Thereafter he concentrated on teaching and playing for television. From the late 1980s into the 1990s he played symphonic music while holding the position of professor of saxophone at the conservatory in Barcelona and at the Aula de Musica. He also led a group called Roda de Saxos and in 1988 appeared at the jazz festival in Donastia. In 1995, with the pianist Francesc Borrull, he recorded *Sinceritat* (SBD ON7-18). However, after suffering a stroke in 1996 he was no longer able to perform.

ALFREDO PAPO

Rodby, Steve(n) (*b* Joliet, IL, 9 Dec 1954). Bass player. Classically trained from the age of ten, he began playing jazz in high school; in his junior and senior years he attended jazz camps, where he met Lyle Mays, Pat Metheny, and Danny Gottlieb. After graduating from Northwestern University (BM 1977) he taught himself to play electric bass guitar, undertook studio work, and played in the house rhythm section at the Jazz Showcase in Chicago, where he accompanied many important jazz musicians. He toured with Monty Alexander and Michael Franks before replacing Mark Egan in Pat Metheny's group in 1980. While recording extensively and touring internationally with Metheny he also recorded as a freelance, worked as a record producer and an orchestra conductor, and maintained a duo with the guitarist Ross Traut (from *c*1976).

Rodby is an extremely versatile bass player on both the acoustic and the electric instrument. Together with his rhythm section partner Paul Wertico, he has expanded the rhythmic palette of Metheny's group immensely, allowing the band to explore complex polyrhythms with ease; these rhythmic changes began to show up on the album *First Circle* (1984), and the band has continued to explore denser sounds and rhythms since that time. Rodby also became involved in the production aspects of the group in the early 1990s, helping to bring a different textural sound to its recordings and live performances.

SELECTED RECORDINGS

As sideman with P. Metheny: *Offramp* (1981, ECM 1216); *Travels* (1982, ECM 1252–3); *First Circle* (1984, ECM 1278); *Still Life (Tallking)* (1987, Geffen 24145); *Letter from Home* (1989, Geffen 24245); *We Live Here* (1994, Geffen 24729); *Quartet* (1996, Geffen 24978); *Imaginary Day* (1997, WB 46791)

SELECTED FILMS AND VIDEOS

Pat Metheny Group: More Travels (1992); Pat Metheny: Secret Story: Live (*c*1993 [filmed 1992]); Pat Metheny Group: We Live Here: Live in Japan 1995 (*c*1996)

BIBLIOGRAPHY

J. Roberts: "Steve Rodby," *GP*, xxi/12 (1987), 112
G. S. Peterson: "Riffs: Steve Rodby," *DB*, lviii/2 (1991), 15

GK

Rodgers, Gene [Eugene R., Jr.] (*b* New York, 5 March 1910; *d* New York, 23 Oct 1987). Pianist and arranger. His father, a graduate of the Boston Conservatory, taught music and started Rodgers on piano when he was five. He began playing professionally in 1924, worked in New York as a leader from the age of 16 (with Rudy Powell and Elmer James among his sidemen), and then joined various bands, including those of Chick Webb and the reed player Billy Fowler; he also recorded with Clarence Williams and King Oliver. After performing with Kaiser Marshall and Teddy Hill he formed a variety act with the dancing trumpeter Frank Radcliffe, which toured the USA, Great Britain, and Australia as Radcliffe & Rodgers; while on tour he recorded as an unaccompanied soloist and with Benny Carter in London (1936). He wrote arrangements for Coleman Hawkins and Fats Waller, performed and recorded with Hawkins's small group and big band (September 1939–1940), and was a member of Zutty Singleton's trio (1940). Work as an unaccompanied soloist, mainly in Detroit and then in Los Angeles, was interrupted by a year touring with Erskine Hawkins (1943).

In 1944 Rodgers appeared in the soundies *My, My, Ain't that somethin'*, *Juke Box Boogie*, and *Big Fat Butterfly* with an all-female group, The V's; he also took part in *Sensations of 1945* (1944) and other films. He worked again in New York (1945–6, 1948), during which time he spent a period as a soloist at Café Society, then traveled widely in the USA and Canada (early 1950s) and led a trio both on tour and at the Astor Hotel, The Composer, and other venues in Manhattan (1956–1960s). Rodgers continued to perform and record during the 1960s and 1970s; he played organ in a duo with the drummer Skippy White for five years, after which he returned to the piano and solo work, mainly in Connecticut. In 1981–2 he was with the Harlem Blues and Jazz Band on a tour of Europe, and in 1987 he held a residency in Japan. His playing as a soloist is well represented by *G. R. Boogie/G. R. Blues* (1945, Joe Davis 8889), and he is heard to advantage in the setting of a small group on *Gene Rodgers/Slam Stewart/Jo Jones* (1972, BB 33047).

BIBLIOGRAPHY

ChiltonW
J. Godrich: "Margin Notes, no.33," *Vintage Jazz Mart* (1970), April, 3
J. Simmen: "Gene Rodgers: Crystal Clear," *Coda*, no.149 (1976), 21
P. Vacher: "Gene Rodgers: Looking Back, Looking Ahead," *MR*, x/3 (1983), 1
Obituary, P. Vacher, *JJI*, xli/2 (1988), 22
J. Simmen: "Ceux qui s'en vont: Gene Rodgers," *BHcF*, no.360 (1988), 20

J. Chilton: *The Song of the Hawk: the Life and Recordings of Coleman Hawkins* (London and New York, 1990)

T. Magnusson: "Gene Rodgers: an Attempted Discography and Film Listing, 1943–1987," *Skivsamlaren*, no.23 (1992), 25

HOWARD RYE

Rodin, Gil(bert A.) (*b* Russia, 9 Dec 1906; *d* Palm Springs, CA, 17 June 1974). Saxophonist and clarinetist. After working in a dance band in Chicago in the mid-1920s he moved to California, where he played briefly with Harry Bastin's orchestra, then in 1927 joined Ben Pollack's band; he also recorded as a leader with some of Pollack's sidemen (1930–31). When Pollack's group disbanded in 1934 Rodin organized a new band that recorded under the name of the singer Clark Randall in 1935; Bob Crosby assumed leadership of the group later that year. Rodin worked for Crosby as president, music director, and business manager as well as a sideman until he was drafted in 1942. After military service he led a band with Ray Bauduc (1944–5), though in the late 1940s he worked again with Crosby. During the 1950s and 1960s he was a producer for radio and television. Rodin composed *Boogie Woogie Maxixe*, which was popularized by Crosby's band in 1939. His playing was influenced by the work of Eddie Miller, Matty Matlock, Benny Goodman, and Irving Fazola, but he preferred to work as a section player and rarely took solos.

For illustrations *see* Crosby, bob, and Pollack, ben.

SELECTED RECORDINGS

As leader: Beale Street Blues (1930, Crown 3017); Ninety-nine out of a hundred wanna be loved (1931, Crown 3045)

As sideman: B. Pollack: He's the last word (1926, Vic. 20425); Memphis Blues (1927, Vic. 21184); Night on the Desert/Sleepy Head (1934, Col. 2929D); C. Randall: Jitter Bug/If you're looking for someone to love (1935, Bruns. 7466); B. Crosby: Boogie Woogie Maxixe (1939, Decca 2848)

SELECTED FILMS AND VIDEOS

Ben Pollack and his Park Central Orchestra (1929); Ben Pollack and his Orchestra (1934); Let's Make Music (1940); Presenting Lily Mars (1942)

BIBLIOGRAPHY

G. T. Simon: *The Big Bands* (New York and London, 1967, rev. 4/1981), 131

J. Chilton: "Gil Rodin," *Stomp Off, Let's Go! The Story of Bob Crosby's Bob Cats & Big Band* (London, 1983), 173

RAYMOND J. GARIGLIO

Roditi, Claudio (Braga) (*b* Rio de Janeiro, 28 May 1946). Brazilian trumpeter, flugelhorn player, and leader. He learned piano from the age of six, received his first trumpet when he was nine, and started formal lessons on the instrument at around the age of 12; later he studied briefly at the conservatory in Rio de Janeiro (*c* early 1960s) and took part in local jam sessions. In 1966 he traveled to Vienna, where he reached the finals of Friedrich Gulda's International Jazz Competition (won that year by Franco Ambrosetti). He spent several months in Graz, Austria, then toured Europe before returning to Brazil. After working mostly in commercial music from 1967 to 1970 he moved to Boston to attend the Berklee School of Music. He performed locally and co-led a big band with the trumpeter Mark Harvey, then in 1976 settled in New York. There he began working with Brazilian bands and played and recorded with Charlie Rouse (1976–7), Bob Mover (1978), and Herbie Mann (1978–81). Roditi has had longstanding affiliations with Paquito D'Rivera (1983–91) and Klaus Ignatzek (from 1987). Through D'Rivera he met Dizzy Gillespie: he was a founding member of Gillespie's United Nation Orchestra (1988–92), with which he may be seen in the video *Dizzy Gillespie and the United Nation Orchestra: Live at the Royal Festival Hall, London* (*c*1990 [filmed 1989]), and he recorded and toured internationally in Gillespie's nine-piece bop group To Diz with Love (1992–3) and its spin-off, Slide Hampton's Jazzmasters (1993–4). His activities as a freelance soloist involved recordings with Chris Connor (1986–7), Mann's Jasil Brazz (1987), Rouse (1988), Michael Carvin (1988–94), Greg Abate (*c*1989, 1992), Larry Gales and Gary Bartz (both 1990), McCoy Tyner (*c*1991), Hendrik Meurkens (1990–94), Ricky Ford (1991), and Peter Leitch (1994), among others, and a tour of Germany with Meurkens (*c*1994). From the late 1980s he has led groups which focus on a blending of bop

Claudio Roditi at Jazz à Vienne, France, 1998

and Brazilian forms; among his sidemen have been the trombonist Jay Ashby, John Lee, Duduka da Fonseca, David Sanchez, and Andrés Boiarsky. He performed at the 1994 Brecon and Nice jazz festivals. Roditi is a skilled bop trumpeter who routinely uses the instrument's mouthpiece to produce a startlingly effective imitation of the *cuíca* – as heard, for example, at the end of Gillespie's 1989 version of *A Night in Tunisia* and Bartz's *The Night Has a Thousand Eyes* (1990).

SELECTED RECORDINGS

As leader: *Claudio!* (1985, Upt. 27.27); *Slow Fire* (1989, Mlst. 9175); with P. D'Rivera, R. Moore, and J. Ashby: *Return to Ipanema* (1989, Town Crier 516); *Milestones* (1990, Can. 79515); *Jazz Turns Samba* (1993, Groovin' High 521616-2); *Free Wheelin'* (1994, Reservoir 136); *Samba: Manhattan Style* (1995, Reservoir 139)

As sideman: C. Connor: *Classic* (1986, Cont. 14023); C. Rouse: *Soul Mates* (1988, Upt. 27.34); D. Gillespie: *Dizzy Gillespie and the United Nation Orchestra: Live at the Royal Festival Hall* (1989, Enja 6044-2), incl. A Night in Tunisia; M. Carvin: *Revelation* (1989, Muse 5399); G. Bartz: *West 42nd Street* (1990, Can. 79049-2), incl. The Night Has a Thousand Eyes; P. D'Rivera: *Who's Smoking?!* (1991, Can. 79523-2); K. Ignatzek: *Son of Gaudi* (1992, Nabel 4660); N. Brignola: *Like Old Times* (1994, Reservoir 133); Chip White: *Harlem Sunset* (1994, Postcards 1006); G. Abate: *Bop Lives!* (1996, Blue Chip 878401-2)

BIBLIOGRAPHY

J.-P. Mathez: "Claudio Roditi: trompettiste brésilien flamboyant," *Brass Bulletin*, lxxiii/1 (1991), 30
G. Endress: "Eigenstandigkeit durch das brasilianische Erbe: Claudio Roditi," *JP*, xli/9 (1992), 32
F. Bouchard: "Hearsay: Claudio Roditi," *JT*, xxv/4 (1995), 12
S. Woolley: "Claudio Roditi: the Gemini Man," *JJI*, xlviii/8 (1995), 14

GK

Rodney, Red [Chudnick, Robert] (*b* Philadelphia, 27 Sept 1927; *d* Boynton Beach, FL, 27 May 1994). Trumpeter, flugelhorn player, and leader. He started on bugle, took up trumpet at the age of 13, and, with many musicians being drafted into military service, began working professionally soon thereafter, in a band which included Elliot Lawrence. At the age of 16 he left high school to tour with Benny Goodman and, for some time, with the clarinetist Jerry Wald. He then spent short periods with Tony Pastor, Jimmy Dorsey (1944), and Les Brown. Together with Gerry Mulligan, he broadcast on radio during 1945 as a member of Lawrence's band; although he was originally a swing player influenced by Harry James, Rodney modernized his style during this year after hearing Dizzy Gillespie and Charlie Parker. During associations with Gene Krupa (1946 – early 1947), with whom he appeared in the film *Beat the Band* (1947), Georgie Auld (1947), Claude Thornhill (autumn 1947), Mulligan (in a cooperative sextet, 1948), and Woody Herman (November 1948–1949) he gained recognition as one of the finest young bop trumpeters. He also recorded as a sideman with Charlie Ventura and Buddy Rich (both 1946) and with Serge Chaloff (1947, 1949), and with his own Beboppers, both as sole leader and as co-leader with Dave Lambert and Buddy Stewart (1946). The latter's version of *Perdido* introduced a new counter-melody, composed by Rodney, which became widely associated with performances of this tune.

The peak of Rodney's early career was his work in Charlie Parker's quintet (late 1949–1950), and the recording of the group's concert at Carnegie Hall demonstrates his mastery of the harmonic vocabulary of bop. While with Parker he toured the South under the pretext of being African-American (as "Albino Red"), but his appendix ruptured and he was obliged to leave the quintet. After recovering he spent a brief period with Charlie Ventura and deputized for Shorty Rogers in Stan Kenton's orchestra (December 1950), then rejoined Parker (1951). Drug addiction interrupted his career during the 1950s, though he played with local dance and society bands, recorded two jazz albums as a leader (1955, 1957, the latter in collaboration with Ira Sullivan), and worked as a booking agent in Philadelphia. In 1960 he settled in Las Vegas and played in show bands.

In 1972 Rodney suffered a paralyzing stroke. Following a year of recuperation he returned to jazz, performing at the Newport Jazz Festival New York and recording the first of several albums for Muse. Thereafter he gradually regained his former prominence. He toured Europe with "The Musical World of Charlie Parker" (1974) and played with Dexter Gordon. A chance reunion with Sullivan while he was touring in 1980 led the two men to form a group; its new material (much of it written by Garry Dial) was a challenge to Rodney and revitalized his playing. Dick Oatts, Jay Anderson, and Joey Baron are among those who also played in this group. At the end of the 1980s Rodney's quintet introduced an important emerging saxophonist, Chris Potter; others of his sidemen during this period were Dial, Chip Jackson, and Jimmy Madison. Rodney appeared regularly at the Newport event and its successors (under the Kool and JVC banners), and in 1993 he played at the Lincoln Center and the White House. He recorded as a sideman with Charlie Rouse in 1984.

During the 1980s Rodney began playing flugelhorn as often as trumpet, and late in life this became his principal instrument. In the last decade and a half of his career his solos were as creative as they were in the 1940s; a volume containing 11 transcriptions of his performances, *Red Rodney Jazz Transcriptions*, was published in New York in 1983. He may be seen in the video *Birdmen & Birdsongs: a Tribute to Charlie Parker,* i (*c* early 1990s [filmed 1990]).

SELECTED RECORDINGS

As leader: with D. Lambert and B. Stewart: Perdido (1946, Key. 668); first issued on [no leader]: *Advance Guard of the '40s* (1945–9, EmA 36016), All God's Children Got Rhythm, The Goof and I (both 1947); Honeysuckle Rose/Buckle my Shoe (1952, OK 6922); *Modern Music from Chicago* (1955, Fan. 3208); *Red Rodney, 1957* (1957, Signal 1206); *Superbop* (1974, Muse 5046); *The Three R's* (1979, Muse 5290); *No Turn on Red* (1986, Denon CY73149); *Then and Now* (1992, Chesky 79)

As leader with I. Sullivan: *Live at the Village Vanguard* (1980, Muse 5209); *Night and Day* (1981, Muse 5274); *Sprint* (1982, Elek. Mus. 60261)

As sideman with C. Parker: *Live at Carnegie Hall* (1949, CP 2); on Charlie Parker (1951–3, Clef 287) [EP], Blues for Alice (1951); Si si/Swedish Schnapps (1951, Mer./Clef 11103); Back Home Blues (1951, Mer./Clef 11095)

BIBLIOGRAPHY

J. Tracy: "Make Jazz Respectable, Asks Rodney," *DB*, xvii/11 (1950), 3
D. Cerulli: "Narcotics 'Nearly Killed Me'," *DB*, xxv/4 (1958), 13
J. Burns: "Red Rodney: an Introduction," *JJ*, xvi/10 (1963), 9
F. Gibson: "Red Rodney: a Discography," *JJ*, xvi/10 (1963), 10; addns and corrections, xvii/1 (1964), 39
M. Gardner: "Red Rodney Talks," *JM*, no.182 (1970), 2
M. James: "Red Rodney on Record," *JM*, no.187 (1970), 4
R. Russell: *Bird Lives: the High Life and Hard Times of Charlie "Yardbird" Parker* (New York, 1973/*R*1994)
R. Baggenaes: "Red Rodney," *Coda*, no.144 (1976), 13
M. Smith: "Red Rodney," *Cadence*, vi (1980), no.7, p.5; no.9, p.5
L. Birnbaum: "Red Rodney: his Bite is Back," *DB*, xlviii/2 (1981), 20
G. Giddins: *Riding on a Blue Note: Jazz and American Pop* (New York, and Oxford, England, 1981/*R*2000), 228
I. Gitler: *Swing to Bop: an Oral History of the Transition in Jazz in the 1940s* (New York, and Oxford, England, 1985)
D. Long: "Red Rodney," *Cadence*, xii/12 (1986), 5
M. Isherwood: "Red Rodney," *JJI*, xli/6 (1988), 19
L. Feather: "Red Rodney: Bebop Survivor," *DB*, lvii/12 (1990), 21
W. Herman and S. Troup: *The Woodchopper's Ball: the Autobiography of Woody Herman* (New York, 1990)

F. Bouchard: "Red Sails in the Limelight," *JT*, xxiii/10 (1993), 36
Obituary, P. Watrous, *New York Times* (28 May 1994)

SCOTT YANOW/BK

Rodowicz, Piotr (*b* Warsaw, 31 July 1954). Polish double bass player and leader. Having graduated from the Academy of Catholic Theology in Warsaw in 1980, from 1984 to 1987 he led a quartet, In Tradition. He then went to the USA to study at the Berklee College of Music, from which he graduated in 1990; while in Boston he had opportunity to accompany Joshua Redman, Geoff Keezer, Kurt Rosenwinkel, Jorge Rossy, and Walter Davis, among others. Back in Poland he led a succession of groups: the Mingus Mingus quartet (1992–7), which recorded an eponymous album (1994, Gowi 23); another quartet, Tribute to Monk (1995–8) (with Zbigniew Brzyszcz on tenor saxophone, Krzysztof Herdzin on piano, and Kazimierz Jonkisz on drums), heard on the album *We Mean Monk* (1997, Jazz Forum 005); Prophet (1997–8), which recorded in 1997; and the Grappelling Trio (from 1998), which made an album in 2000. Rodowicz was also a member of the cooperative group the Dream Seller Quartet (1996–8), which recorded in its first year. In 1997 he joined the World Strings Trio, alongside Maciej Strzelczyk and the guitarist Krzysztof Woliński, which celebrates the legacy of Stephane Grappelli and Django Reinhardt; the trio has recorded, and it has appeared at a number of European festivals. As a sideman he worked with Janusz Muniak, Tomasz Szukalski, Janusz Skowron, and others. Rodowicz teaches at the Fryderyk Chopin School of Music in Warsaw. He has contributed to *Jazz Forum*.

BIBLIOGRAPHY

K. Zalewski: "We Mean Monk," *JF*, no.183 (1998), 6
<http://www.a1artists.net/artists/worldstrings/members.html> (2001)

ADAM CEGIELSKI, BK

Rodriguez, E(dwin) J(esús) (*b* Salinas, Puerto Rico, 6 Nov 1958). Drummer and percussionist. He grew up in New York from the age of two and learned Latin percussion as a teenager; in 1978 he began to study jazz drumming with Freddie Waits. His earliest professional work was with a swing-influenced disco group, Dr. Buzzard's Original Savannah Band (1978). Between 1986 and 1988 Rodriguez was the drummer with John Lurie's group the Lounge Lizards, and in 1987 he joined the Jazz passengers. Also in the late 1980s he performed with Henry Threadgill, Cassandra Wilson, and the pianist and singer Dr. John. During the following decade he gave concerts in New York as an unaccompanied percussionist at such venues as the Knitting Factory, Harvestworks, the Alternative Museum, Roulette, and Tonic. He recorded with John Zorn in 1992. From 1997 he has played in Marc Ribot's Latin-jazz group Los Cubanos Postizos, and with Bill Ware and Brad Jones in the trio Vibes. Rodriguez has reached pop audiences as a member of the Brooklyn Funk Essentials and Tiny Universe, the latter under the leadership of the saxophonist Karl Denson.

SELECTED RECORDINGS

As sideman: J. Lurie: *No Pain for Cakes* (1986, Ant. 8714); *Voice of Chunk* (1988–9, Lagarto 003); M. Ribot: *Marc Ribot y los Cubanos postizos (The Prosthetic Cubans)* (*c*1997, Atl. 83116-2); Vibes: *Vibes* (1997, Knitting Factory Works 210); M. Ribot: *Muy divertido* (1999, Atl. 83293); Vibes: *With Drawn* (1999, Knitting Factory Works 242)

For further recordings *see* Jazz passengers.

STEVE SMITH

Rodriguez, Rod [Nicholas Goodwin] (*b* Panama Canal Zone, 10 Sept 1906; *d* July 1995). Pianist. His place of birth is given as the Canal Zone in his application for social security. He moved to New York in August 1928 and worked as an ensemble pianist with Jelly Roll Morton in 1929–30. In 1932–3 he performed and recorded with Benny Carter, and in 1933 he recorded with Carter's band under the leadership of Spike Hughes. From around March to May 1937 he toured with a band fronted by the athlete Jesse Owens, then from September 1937 to February 1939 he performed and recorded with Don Redman; after appearing with Alberto Socarras (1939) he was again with Redman (1940–43). He played with Skeets Tolbert, accompanied the singer Frances Brock on an overseas tour (1945–6), and joined the drummer Herbert Cowens (1946). In the 1950s and 1960s he taught piano and played with Johnny Coles (1953), Louis Armstrong (1961), and Doc Cheatham (mid-1960s). Rodriguez was a substitute for Billy Kyle in Louis Armstrong's All Stars in April 1961, and in the 1970s he worked with Franc Williams. *How come you do me like you do?* (1933, Decca F3972), one of the recordings he made with a small group drawn from Spike Hughes's orchestra, provides a good example of his solo style. His date of death is taken from the social security death index, which gives his last known place of residence as New York. (L. Wright: *Mr. Jelly Lord*, Chigwell, England, 1980)

based on *ChiltonW*/HOWARD RYE

Roger Henrichsen, Børge (*b* Copenhagen, 4 Oct 1915; *d* Copenhagen, 20 July 1989). Danish pianist, bandleader, composer, and trumpeter. He studied classical piano and played jazz with Svend Asmussen and others from 1937. Among the many recordings he made of his own compositions are *Dream Melody* (1938, HMV X6053), as the leader of a trio, and *Prelude in C* (1942, HMV DX6877), in a duo with Niels Foss. From 1940 to 1946 he led a quintet, and in 1950 he became director of jazz programs for Statsradiofonien (from 1959 Danmarks Radio), a position he held until 1980. He also published several volumes of jazz studies for piano, and wrote *Noget om jazz* (Something about jazz; Copenhagen, 1961), an introductory text published in conjunction with a radio series. (B. Jørgensen: *Børge Roger Henrichsen*, Copenhagen, 1963)

ERIK WIEDEMANN

Rogers, Billie (*b* Missoula, MT, *c*1919). Trumpeter and singer. Her father was a violinist, her mother was a pianist, and her older brother performed and arranged music. She grew up in Washington state and first played in vaudeville and theater bands. After moving to California she was a member of Woody Herman's big band from October 1941 to spring 1943, when she left to form her own group. Rogers recorded as a leader in 1944 and may be heard playing trumpet and singing on *I didn't know about you* (Musi. 15027) and playing trumpet on *Rogers Corner* (Musi. 15028), with Johnny Mandel and Harry Babasin among her sidemen. In the same year her band made an AFRS broadcast while appearing at the Pelham Heath Inn in the Bronx, New York; a recording of the performance was first issued on the album *One Night Stand with Billie Rogers* (Joyce 1018). Nothing is known of her later career.

BIBLIOGRAPHY

W. D. Clancy with A. C. Kenton: *Woody Herman: Chronicles of the Herds* (New York and elsewhere, 1995)

G. Lees: *Leader of the Band: the Life of Woody Herman* (New York and Oxford, England, 1995)

GK

Rogers, Paul (Leslie) (*b* Luton, England, 20 April 1956). English double bass player. After teaching himself to play the double bass he worked with Mike Osborne, John Stevens, Stan Tracey, Keith Tippett, John Etheridge, Elton Dean, Louis Moholo, Evan Parker, Dudu Pukwana, Derek Bailey, Paul Rutherford, the saxophonist Simon Picard, and others. He toured the Middle East as a member of Harry Beckett's trio (1984); Britain with Tenor Tonic, a quartet comprising Alan Skidmore, Paul Dunmall, and Tony Levin (1984–5); Europe with Parker; and South America with the group Red House (1986). From 1986 to 1988 he lived in the USA, playing on occasion with Joseph Jarman, and in 1990 he toured and recorded in Texas in a quintet featuring Dennis Gonzalez, Carlos Ward, and Moholo. Rogers moved to France in 1992 and worked with European and British musicians, including the quartet Mujician with Dunmall, Tippett, and Levin. In 1996 he recorded in Avignon in a quintet with Sam Rivers.

SELECTED RECORDINGS

As unaccompanied soloist: *Heron Moon* (1995, Rare Music 025)

Duos with P. Dunmall: *Folks* (1989, 1993, Slam 212)

As leader: with S. Picard and T. Marsh: *News from the North* (1991, Intakt 028); with M. Doneda and Lê Quan Ninh: *Open Paper Tree* (1995, FMP CD68); with S. Rivers, N. Akchoté, Tony Hymas, and J. Thollot: *Configuration* (1996, Nato 777711); *Time of Brightness* (1998, Rare Music 027)

As sideman: D. Gonzalez: *Band of Sorcerers: Hymn for the Perfect Heart of a Pearl* (1990, Konnex 5026); S. Domancich: *La part des anges* (1997, Gimini Music 1008); Mujician: *Colours Fulfilled* (1998, Cuneiform Rune 102)

BIBLIOGRAPHY

ChiltonB
A. Isham: "Everybody Digs Paul Rogers," *Avant*, no.6 (1998), 48

MARK GILBERT

Rogers, Reuben (Renwick) (*b* New York, 15 Nov 1974). Double bass player. He grew up in the Virgin Islands from the age of two. His mother was a church organist, and as a child he took up clarinet, piano, saxophone, drums, and guitar before settling on double bass when he was 14. In high school he performed with various jazz musicians in St. Thomas, among them Ron Blake. Around 1991 he studied at the Interlochen Arts Camp in Michigan and in a summer program at the Berklee College of Music in Boston; he then continued his studies at Berklee and graduated in 1997. Active professionally from around 1993, Rogers led his own trio from 1994 to 1997. He performed with Betty Carter and Marlon Jordan (both 1993), Marcus Roberts (1993–5), Teodross Avery (1993–7), and Carl Allen and Marcus Printup (both 1994–6); as a sideman he recorded with these last three, and his playing is well represented on Printup's album *Unveiled* (1996, BN 37302-2). Rogers also worked in Roy Hargrove's small and large ensembles (1995) and with those of Eric Reed (until 1996) and Wynton Marsalis (until 1997). Having recorded with Nicholas Payton he worked regularly with the trumpeter from 1996; that same year he joined Donald Harrison and worked with Terrell Stafford, Jesse Davis, and Mulgrew Miller. He was a member of Danilo Pérez's trio in the late 1990s, and from 1998 he toured in Joshua Redman's quartet. As a freelance throughout these years Rogers performed with, among others, Billy Pierce, Johnny Griffin, Doc Cheatham, Phil Woods, and Clark Terry. He plays both double bass and electric bass guitar in the group 21st Century, led by Blake and Dion Parson, with which he recorded in 1997.

BIBLIOGRAPHY

Feather–GitlerBEJ
<http://www.21st-centurymusic.com/21stcenturyreuben.html> (1999)

GK

Rogers, Shorty [Rajonsky, Milton Michael] (*b* Great Barrington, MA, 14 April 1924; *d* Van Nuys, CA, 7 Nov 1994). Trumpeter, flugelhorn player, composer, arranger, and bandleader. He studied at the High School of Music and Art, New York, and while still a teenager played professionally with Will Bradley (mid- to late 1942) and Red Norvo (late 1942 – May 1943). Following military service he was a member of Woody Herman's First Herd (September 1945 – December 1946), and after Herman disbanded he worked in the Los Angeles area. He was also in Herman's Second Herd (November 1947 – December 1949; for illustration *see* Herman, woody, fig.1*b*), where he attracted attention as an arranger of adventurous big-band scores. Later he contributed a number of important scores to the library of Stan Kenton's band (1950 – June 1951). Rogers then settled in Los Angeles, where he studied classical composition privately and led a series of big bands and groups with former Kenton sidemen: Bud Shank, Bob Cooper, Jimmy Giuffre, Maynard Ferguson, Conte Candoli, Shelly Manne, Stan Levey, Mel Lewis, and, most notably, Art Pepper. He also engaged some of the leading African-American jazz musicians in the area: Hampton Hawes joined Giuffre, Pepper, and Manne in the sessions recorded by Rogers's octet and nonet, modeled after Miles Davis's "Birth of the Cool" nonet (October 1951 and January 1953), and Curtis Counce became a member of Rogers's Giants, which he founded in 1953 while working as a member of Howard Rumsey's Lighthouse All Stars at the Lighthouse Club in Hermosa Beach, California. In a quintet with Giuffre, Russ Freeman, Counce, and Manne, Rogers performed at the Haig Club in Los Angeles from late in 1953 and then at Zardi's from mid-1954, by which time he had begun to double as a flugelhorn player. During this year duties at the piano were shared by Freeman, Marty Paich, André Previn, and Pete Jolly; among later members of the quintet were Lou Levy, Ralph Peña, and Levey.

Rogers supervised and contributed arrangements to such early jazz film scores as *The Wild One* (1953, composed by Leith Stevens) and *The Man with the Golden Arm* (1955, composed by Elmer Bernstein), and also served as an artistic director for Atlantic Records (1955) and RCA Victor (from 1954). From the 1960s he became less active in jazz as he turned increasingly to Hollywood studios, where he was in steady demand as a composer of film scores and as the supervisor of soundtrack recording sessions. He eventually stopped playing altogether and by the 1970s devoted his time to writing scores for television series; his works are published by Drum City. However, he returned to jazz work in 1982 and over the next decade toured widely with surviving colleagues from the 1950s.

Rogers was a leading figure in the West Coast style of jazz in the early 1950s, not only as an instrumentalist, composer, and arranger, but also as an organizer of concerts and teacher of young talent. His big-band scores explored irregular ostinatos (*Tale of an African Lobster*), bitonality (*I'm gonna go fishin'*), or increasing timbral densities (*Infinity Promenade*). In his own groups, and in those of

Shorty Rogers playing flugelhorn, August 1958

Jimmy Giuffre and Teddy Charles, he attempted to broaden the theoretical foundations of jazz, dispensing at times with chord progressions, improvising on modes, and, in *Three on a Row* (1954), pioneering the use in jazz of the 12-tone technique. His arrangements for small group are remarkable for their unusual variety of instrumental textures, *Martians Go Home* (1955) being a particularly intriguing and influential example. Rogers was the first jazz musician to make the flugelhorn into an important solo instrument (see illustration), and in this respect he influenced Miles Davis; conversely, on both trumpet and flugelhorn he played in a subdued manner indebted to Davis's early style and well described in Stravinsky's *Conversations*, where the composer points to Rogers as a possible influence on his use of that instrument in *Threni*. Some of his best solo playing may be heard on Teddy Charles's album *New Directions* (1953, Prst. 164), Manne's recording *The Three*, and his own *The Swinging Mr. Rogers*.

Oral history material in *DSI* (JOHP).

RECORDED COMPOSITIONS

(selective list)

As leader: *Cool and Crazy* (1953, RCA LPM3138), incl. Boar-jibu, Contours, Infinity Promenade, The Sweetheart of Sigmund Freud, Tale of an African Lobster; on *The Swinging Mr. Rogers* (1955, Atl. 1212), Martians Go Home; on *Jazz Waltz* (1962, Rep. 96060), I'm gonna go fishin', Jazz Waltz

Recorded by others: W. Herman: Keeper of the Flame (1948, Cap. 57616); S. Kenton: Art Pepper (1950, Cap. 28008); Maynard Ferguson (1950, Cap. 28009); S. Manne: on *The Three* (1954, Cont. 2516), Three on a Row

SELECTED ARRANGEMENTS

Recorded by W. Herman: That's Right (1948, Cap. 15427); Lemon Drop (1948, Cap. 15365); More Moon (1949, Cap. 15844); Lollypop (1949), on *Classics in Jazz* (1948–50, Cap. H324)

Recorded by S. Kenton: Jolly Rogers (1950, Cap. 1043); Viva Prado (1950, Cap. 1279); Round Robin (1950, Cap. 15848)

BIBLIOGRAPHY

N. Shapiro and N. Hentoff, eds.: *Hear me Talkin' to ya: the Story of Jazz by the Men who Made it* (New York and London, 1955/*R*1966), 350

I. Stravinsky and R. Craft: *Conversations with Igor Stravinsky* (London, 1959), 116

H. Lucraft: "The Gentle Giant," *JJI*, xxxii/2 (1979), 4

W. F. Lee: *Stan Kenton: Artistry in Rhythm* (Los Angeles, 1980/*R*1994) [incl. discography; *R* without discography]

S. Voce: "Cool and Crazy," *JJI*, xxxv/10 (1982), 14

C. Hofmann and E. M. Bakker: *Shorty Rogers: a Discography* (Amsterdam, 1983)

L. Tomkins: "The Shorty Rogers Story," *CI*, xxi (1983), no.5, p.20; no.7, p.12

R. Gordon: *Jazz West Coast: the Los Angeles Jazz Scene of the 1950s* (London and New York, 1986)

H. Hill: "Portrait of Shorty," *Coda*, no.235 (1990–91), 20

J. Maggs, "Shorty Rogers: an Appreciation," *CJM*, xxx/2 (1991), 23

D. Ramsey: "Shorty Rogers: Advancing the Freedom (and Fun) Principle," *JT*, xxi/9 (1991), 23

T. Gioia: *West Coast Jazz: Modern Jazz in California, 1945–1960* (New York, and Oxford, England, 1992), 245

D. Erjavec: "Transcribed Solo: Jimmy Giuffre's and Shorty Rogers' Solos on 'Martians Go Home'," *Jazz Educators Journal*, xxvii/2 (1994), 43

Obituary, *New York Times* (9 Nov 1994)

W. P. Clancy with A. C. Kenton: *Woody Herman: Chronicles of the Herds* (New York and elsewhere, 1995)

J. BRADFORD ROBINSON/BK

Rohde, Bryce (Benno) (*b* Hobart, Tasmania, Australia, 12 Sept 1923). Australian pianist and composer. He was a leading modern-jazz player in Adelaide before moving to Canada in 1953. With other Australian musicians there he founded the Australian jazz quartet, which played at many important venues, including Birdland and Carnegie Hall in New York, and recorded seven albums; latterly it worked as a quintet. After a tour of Australia in 1958 the group disbanded, and for the next six years Rohde led several quartets in Australia. He was also influential in the dissemination in Australia of the theories from George Russell's book *The Lydian Chromatic Concept of Tonal Organization* (1953). In 1962 he formed a workshop group with Charlie Munro, Bruce Cale, and drummer Mark Bowden which recorded during the following year; Rohde's mature compositional style may also be heard on his album *Just Bryce* (1965). From 1965 he lived in California and from time to time led his own groups; he recorded with Cale in 1981. Some of his compositions were published in *Turn Right at New South Wales: the Compositions of Bryce Rohde* (Mill Valley, CA, 1993) and in B. T. Hancock, ed.: *South Australian Real Book* (Adelaide, Australia, 1999).

SELECTED RECORDINGS

As leader: *More Spring* (1962, MBS Jazz 6); *Corners* (1963, CBS BP233046); *Just Bryce* (1965, CBS BP233196)

As sideman: Australian Jazz Quartet: *Australian Jazz Quartet* (1955, Beth. 1031); *Australian Jazz Quartet/Quintet* (1955, Beth. 6003); B. Cale: *A Century of Steps* (1981, Larrikin 071)

BIBLIOGRAPHY

A. Bisset: *Black Roots, White Flowers: a History of Jazz in Australia* (Sydney, 1979, rev. 2/1987)

B. Johnson: *The Oxford Companion to Australian Jazz* (Melbourne, Australia, 1987)

J. McLeod: *Jazztrack* (Sydney, 1994), 41

JEFF PRESSING (with JOHN WHITEOAK)/ROGER T. DEAN

Roidinger, Adelhard (*b* Windischgarsten, Austria, 28 Nov 1941). Austrian double bass player and composer. He learned piano from the age of five, violin from the age of nine, and double bass from when he was 15. In Graz he studied classical double bass, jazz composition, and architecture (1966–72). He played with Eje Thelin and Joachim Kühn (1970–72), Hans Koller's quartet Free Sound (1971–5), and Wolfgang Dauner (1972–8) and occasionally worked with Attila Zoller, Karl Berger, Yosuke Yamashita (with whom he recorded in 1977), Alan Skidmore, George Russell, Dusko Goykovich, Kenny Clarke, Mal Waldron, Woody Shaw, and others. In 1976 he formed the band European Jazz Consensus (renamed International Jazz Consensus in 1981). He also performed with such musicians as the guitarist Harry Pepl and Werner Pirchner (with whom he recorded as Austria Drei in 1979), Christoph Spendel and Michael Sagmeister (recording in 1984), and Anthony Braxton (in a trio with Tony Oxley which toured Europe in 1989). Roidinger has been active in jazz education, teaching workshops and clinics since the mid-1970s; he published *Der Kontrabass im Jazz* (Vienna, 1980), *Der Elektrobass im Jazz* (Vienna, 1981), and *Jazzimprovisation und Pentatonik* (Rottenburg, Baden-Württemberg, Germany, 1984), and contributed an essay, "Ist Jazz lehrbar? Ansätze zu einer effizienteren Ausbildungsmethodik," to *Blues Notes* (no.37 (1979), 31). He taught improvisation and music electronics at the Hochschule für Musik und Darstellende Kunst in Graz (1982–94) and later at the Studio for Advanced Music and Media Technology at the Bruckner-Konservatorium in Linz. In 1982 he founded his own sound studio to develop experimental multimedia projects, most notably computer composition, which he often combines with live playing. His musical activities thus comprise the broad spectrum from the modern mainstream (influenced by the trio of Bill Evans (ii)) to free jazz and experiments with computer and visual components.

SELECTED RECORDINGS

As leader: *Schattseite* (1981, ECM 1221); *Computer & Jazz Program I* (1984, Thein 100384)

Duos with Y. Yamashita: *Inner Space* (1977, Enja 3001)

As sideman: E. Thelin: *Acoustic Space* (1970, Odeon EO6234180); K. Berger: *With Silence* (1972, Enja 2022); H. Koller: *Phoenix* (1972, MPS 15315); H. Koller and W. Dauner: *Kunstkopfindianer* (1974, MPS 15422); Austria Drei: *Austria Drei* (1979, Ego 4019); International Jazz Consensus: *Beak to Beak* (1981, Nabel 8102); C. Spendel and M. Sagmeister: *Between the Moments* (1984, Teldec BS84001); A. Braxton: *Seven Compositions (Trio) 1989* (1989, HA 6025)

BIBLIOGRAPHY

W. Panke: "Adelhard Roidingers neuer Weg der Musikerziehung," *JP*, xxii/11 (1973), 10

R. Urmann: "Adelhard Roidinger,"*Blues Notes*, nos.26–7 (1975), 64

WOLFRAM KNAUER

Rojas, Marcus (*b* New York, 21 April 1962). Tuba player. After graduating from the New England Conservatory, in 1989 he founded the cooperative trio Spanish Fly with Steve Bernstein and the slide guitarist Dave Tronzo. The following year he was one of the two tuba players in Henry Threadgill's group Very Very Circus. He was a founding member of the group Plunge, with its unusual instrumentation of trombone (played by Mark McGrain), double bass (Avishai Cohen), and drums (Bob Moses), which recorded in 1995. Later he performed in Kamikaze Ground Crew, and in March 1997 he toured with Jack Walrath and Pheeroan akLaff in Ray Anderson's Pocket Brass Band. Rojas has been busy in the studios, in Broadway bands, and in various contemporary classical music settings, among them the Metropolitan and New York City ballet orchestras. He recorded, mainly as a section player in large ensembles, with Charlie Persip's Superband II and Jean-Loup Longnon's New York Big Band (both 1987), Bob Belden (1989–91), Material (*c*1991), the Jazz Passengers and the quintet led by the harpist Ann LeBaron (both 1991), Phillip Johnston, Thomas Chapin, and John Zorn (all 1992), the reed player Michael Blake (1996), and Jim Hall (1996, 1998), among others, and worked in Les Miserables Brass Band, Lester Bowie's Brass Fantasy, Howard Johnson's Gravity, and Charlie Haden's Liberation Music Orchestra. Rojas has taught at New York University.

SELECTED RECORDINGS

As sideman: H. Threadgill: *Spirit of Nuff . . . Nuff* (1990, BS 120134-2); Spanish Fly: *Fly by Night* (1994–5, Accurate 5024); Plunge: *Falling with Grace* (1995, Accurate 5016)

BIBLIOGRAPHY

H. Pekar: "Bassnotes: Marcus Rojas: Putting Brass Back on Top," *Bass Player*, ix/6 (1998), 26

<www.swr-online.de/donaueschingen/1998/komponisten/rojas.html> (1999)

GK

Roker, Mickey [Granville William] (*b* Miami, 3 Sept 1932). Drummer. He took up drums in a drum and bugle corps during military service (1953–5). In Philadelphia he worked with Jimmy Heath and in various rhythm-and-blues groups, and took part in jam sessions with local friends Lee Morgan, Reggie Workman, Kenny Barron, and McCoy Tyner. In 1959 he went to New York, where he played with Gigi Gryce at the Five Spot; he recorded with Gryce the following year, and later performed and recorded with Ray Bryant (autumn 1960–1963). As a member of Junior Mance's trio he mainly accompanied Joe Williams (1963–5), but he also recorded under Mance's own name in 1962, with the trio accompanying Irene Kral for an album in 1963, and with Ben Webster added to the trio for a club date in 1964. He performed and recorded in small groups and in the big band led by Duke Pearson (1964–70), and at the same time worked with Nancy Wilson (1965–7), Art Farmer (1966–7), and Morgan (1969–71), with whom he may be heard at length in recordings made in performance at the Lighthouse in Hermosa Beach, California. Among his freelance engagements during this period were performances with Tyner (at the Newport Jazz Festival, 1963), Webster (again with Mance's trio, 1964), Bobby Timmons (1964), Clifford Jordan, and Mary Lou Williams; he also recorded with Willis "Gator" Jackson (1961), Nat Adderley (1963), Sonny Rollins (1964–5), Harold Vick (1966), Charles Kynard and Randy Brecker (both 1969), Bobby Hutcherson (1970), Bobby Jones (1972), Gene Ammons (1972), and Ammons and Sonny Stitt (1973), and worked as a studio musician for Blue Note, in which capacity he took part in sessions with Blue Mitchell (1966), Stanley Turrentine (1966–9), Herbie Hancock (1968), Horace Silver (1968, 1970–72), Frank Foster (1968–9), and Andrew Hill (1969).

From 1971 to 1979 Roker was a member of Dizzy Gillespie's band and became especially adept at playing Latin jazz; his continuing studio work included albums with Machito (1975), Jon Faddis (1976), Hank Jones (1978), Sam Jones (1979), Bryant (1980), and the group Quadrant, comprising Joe Pass, Milt Jackson, Ray Brown, and Roker (1977, 1980). Following a tour of Europe with Ella Fitzgerald in 1979 he worked as a freelance swing and bop drummer with Oscar Peterson, Zoot Sims, and others, recording with J. J. Johnson and Al Grey (1983), Gene Harris (in performance at the Blue Note, New York, 1985), Peter Leitch (1986), Shirley Scott (from 1989), Dusko Goykovich (1993), Randy Johnston (1994, 1997), Odean Pope (1995), Joshua Breakstone, the New York Hard Bop Quintet (1996), and Hank Jones (1997). In the mid- to late 1980s he or Jeff Hamilton served as the drummer with Brown's trio, with which he toured internationally. However, Roker gradually came to abhor the rigors of touring, and avoided it whenever possible; in the 1980s and 1990s he performed mainly in Philadelphia, although he made an exception for his association with Milt Jackson: he worked in Jackson's quartet regularly, he deputized for Connie Kay in the Modern Jazz Quartet from February 1992 and April 1993, and he played with the MJQ from time to time since Kay's death in 1994. Roker may be seen performing in a sextet with Benny Carter, Johnson, and Hank Jones in "Wolf Trap Salutes Dizzy Gillespie: an All-Star Tribute to the Jazz Master" (1988), from the television series "Great Performances."

Video oral history material in *NCH* (HCJA).

SELECTED RECORDINGS

As sideman with D. Gillespie (all recorded for Pablo): *Dizzy Gillespie's Big 4* (1974, 2310719); *Jazz Maturity . . . Where it's Coming from* (1975, 2310816); *Bahiana* (1975, 2625708); *Dizzy's Party* (1976, 2310784)

As sideman with others: G. Gryce: *The Rat Race Blues* (1960, NewJ 8262); D. Pearson: *Wahoo!* (1964, BN 84191); S. Turrentine: *Rough 'n' Tumble* (1966, BN 84240); D. Pearson: *Sweet Honey Bee* (1966, BN 84252); *Introducing Duke Pearson's Big Band* (1967, BN 84276); H. Hancock: *Speak like a Child* (1968, BN 84279); L. Morgan: *Live at the Lighthouse* (1970, BN 89906); H. Silver: *United States of Mind: Phase II* (1971, BN 84368); Machito: *Afro-Cuban Jazz Moods* (1975, Pablo 2310771); R. Bryant: *Potpourri* (1980, Pablo 2310860); R. Johnston: *In A-Chord* (1994, Muse 5512)

BIBLIOGRAPHY

"Mickey Roker," *Jm*, no.247 (1976), 24
L. Tomkins: "Mickey Roker Tells his Story," *CI*, xvii/10 (1979), 12
J. Potter: "Mickey Roker: the Natural," *MD*, ix/10 (1985), 18
B. Donaldson: "Mickey Roker: Interview," *Cadence*, xxv/5 (1999), 5

JEFF POTTER/BK

Roland, Gene (*b* Dallas, 15 Sept 1921; *d* New York, 11 Aug 1982). Composer, arranger, and multi-instrumentalist. He took piano lessons at around the age of 11, and after becoming interested in big-band jazz he taught himself to play trumpet (1939). While ostensibly studying music at North Texas State College (1940–42) he spent most of his time playing jazz with his roommates Jimmy Giuffre, Herb Ellis, and Harry Babasin. He then served from 1942 to summer 1944 in the Eighth Army Air Force Band, to which he contributed dance-band arrangements. His first job was for Stan Kenton, composing songs for June Christy and playing his own new fifth trumpet parts (1944); he may be seen with Kenton in the short film *Artistry in Rhythm* (1944). Following brief periods with Lionel Hampton (as an arranger for six weeks) and Lucky Millinder (as a trumpeter and arranger, summer 1945) he rejoined Kenton as a trombonist, again on a new fifth part (1945), and writer; he contributed to the band's repertory an arrangement of *Tampico* (1945, Cap. 202) and the composition *Ain't no misery in me* (1946, Cap. 289). Roland began writing arrangements for four tenor saxophones while in New York in 1946 and continued his experiments in Los Angeles (where he played piano with Stan Getz, Giuffre, Herbie Steward, and Zoot Sims); this innovation later led to the distinctive grouping of the Four Brothers within the Woody Herman Orchestra.

In summer 1947 Roland was a member of Vido Musso's group. In the late 1940s he played trombone with Georgie Auld, bass trumpet with Count Basie, and trumpet with Charlie Barnet and Millinder; he also wrote arrangements for Claude Thornhill and Artie Shaw. In 1950 he led a 26-piece big band which included Dizzy Gillespie, Charlie Parker, and other prominent bop musicians, but it was unsuccessful and he resumed work as an arranger for Kenton (from 1951) and Herman, to whose band he contributed 65 arrangements between November 1956 and February 1958. Later, in writing for four mellophoniums he introduced a new sound to Kenton's band; he played as a soloist on both mellophonium and soprano saxophone in his compositions for Kenton's album *Adventures in Blues* (1961, Cap. ST1985). In 1963 he was a sideman on a leaderless album of his arrangements, *Swingin' Friends!* (1963, Bruns. 754114). Roland visited Copenhagen in 1967 to compose for and conduct the Radiohus Orchestra. He toured with Kenton again in 1973, but thereafter worked in New York, playing piano, tenor saxophone, and trumpet and writing arrangements for his own big bands. A fine example of his trumpet playing and an unusual instance of his singing may be heard on Jimmy Knepper's *Gee baby, ain't I good to you*, on the album *A Swinging Introduction to Jimmy Knepper* (1957, Beth. 77).

BIBLIOGRAPHY

B. Coss: "Gene Roland: the Untold Story," *DB*, xxx/24 (1963), 17
D. Nelson: "Gene Roland," *BMI: the Many Worlds of Music* (1971), Oct, 17
W. F. Lee: *Stan Kenton: Artistry in Rhythm* (Los Angeles, 1980/*R*1994) [incl. discography; *R* without discography]
S. Woolley: "Gene Roland," *JJI*, xxxv/11 (1982), 16

BK

Roland, Joe [Joseph Alfred] (*b* New York, 17 May 1920). Vibraphonist and bandleader. He began his career as a clarinetist and leader and studied at the Institute of Musical Art (1937–9); he took up xylophone in 1940. After the war he bought a vibraphone and began playing the instrument as a freelance in New York. He also organized his own bop group, which recorded in 1949 and 1950, and in 1951 he played and recorded with Oscar Pettiford. From 1951 to 1953 Roland was a member of George Shearing's quintet, with which he may be seen in five Snader telescriptions, including *Conception* and *Move* (both 1951). He then led a group with Howard McGhee and toured and recorded with Artie Shaw's Gramercy Five; his playing with this group is well represented by *Sunny Side Up*, from the album *Artie Shaw and his Gramercy Five* (1954, Clef MGC160). Roland also made several recordings under his own name, among them *Easy Living* (1955, Beth. 17). Having resumed freelance work, he recorded with Mat Mathews and Aaron Sachs (both 1956).

BIBLIOGRAPHY

FeatherE
J. Burns: "Good Vibes," *J&B*, ii/5 (1972), 7

Roll. One of the drumstrokes collectively known as RUDIMENTS.

Rollini, Adrian (*b* New York, 28 June 1903; *d* Homestead, FL, 15 May 1956). Bass saxophonist, brother of Art Rollini. His year of birth is given as 1904 in reference sources, but according to his brother's autobiography the correct year is 1903; social security records confirm this earlier year. Their father was a singer, pianist, and guitarist, and for Christmas 1925, when he was two and a half, Adrian received a toy piano. A child prodigy, gifted with perfect pitch, he gave a piano recital at the age of four, received classical lessons on the instrument for 11 years, and recorded for Republic piano rolls when he was 16. He also took up xylophone, and led his first band at the age of 14. From 1922 to 1927 he worked with the CALIFORNIA RAMBLERS, of which he assumed leadership in 1925; while with the group he made hundreds of recordings. Shortly after joining he took up bass saxophone, and he specialized on that instrument throughout the 1920s and early 1930s. He also provoked admiring astonishment among fellow musicians by playing jazz on novelty instruments such as the "hot fountain pen" (*see* CLARINET, §5) and the GOOFUS, and he recorded frequently as the leader of the Goofus Five.

On 22 September 1927 Rollini became a bandleader at the Club New Yorker; his all-star group comprised Sylvester Ahola, Bix Beiderbecke, Bill Rank, Frankie Trumbauer, Don Murray, the saxophonist Bobby Davis, Frank Signorelli, Joe Venuti, Eddie Lang, and Chauncey Morehouse; several of these distinguished sidemen had come directly from the disbanded Jean Goldkette Orchestra. But the new venue failed in less than a month, and Rollini then spent a period in London performing with Fred Elizalde (1927–9). On his return to New York he worked principally as a freelance musician. In 1934 he organized his own club, Adrian's Tap Room, at the President Hotel, where he remained into the mid-1940s (*see* NIGHTCLUBS AND OTHER VENUES), though he also continued to lead small groups at other venues. He appeared with Bunny Berigan in a short film (title unknown) made by the Lucky Strike Hit Parade Orchestra (1936) and later in the short films *Jerry Livingston and his Talk of the Town Music* and *Swing Styles* (both 1939). In the early 1950s he moved to Florida, where for the last years of his life he undertook engagements that were mainly commercial.

Rollini was one of the first outstanding white jazz musicians; his adept improvisations on the unusually cumbersome bass saxophone were melodically inventive and possessed a rhythmic vitality that made him one of the first saxophonists to swing. He is best remembered for his series of recordings with Bix Beiderbecke, wherein he displays considerable adroitness, both in the improvised ensembles and in his solos. During the 1930s he began to concentrate on playing vibraphone; he never rose above competence on that instrument, however, whereas in his by then rare performances on bass saxophone he still showed mastery.

SELECTED RECORDINGS

As leader: Davenport Blues (1934, Decca 359); Bouncin' in Rhythm (1935, Vic. 25208); Tap Room Swing (1936, Decca 787)
As sideman: California Ramblers: Stockholm Stomp (1926, Edison 51897); Crazy Words, Crazy Tune (1927, PAct 36590); M. Mole: Feelin' No Pain (1927, OK 40890); J. Venuti: Cheese and Crackers/A Mug of Ale (1927, OK 40897); F. Trumbauer: A good man is hard to find (1927, OK 40966); B. Beiderbecke: At the Jazz Band Ball/Jazz Me Blues (1927, OK 40923); Since my Best Gal Turned Me Down (1927, OK 41001); J. Venuti: Raggin' the Scale/Put and Take (1930, OK 41432); J. Purvis: Poor Richard (1930, OK 8782); J. Venuti: Jig Saw Puzzle Blues (1933, Col. 2782D) [vibraphone]

BIBLIOGRAPHY

ChiltonW
H. Taylor: "Adrian Rollini," *MM*, xiii (6 Nov 1937), 10
T. Rogers: "Adrian Rollini: the Story of that Bass Sax," *Australian Jazz Quarterly*, no.5 (1947), 10
Obituary, *DB*, xxiii/13 (1956), 9
A. Napoleon: "The Bass Sax in Jazz," *Sv*, no.8 (1966), 15; no.9 (1967), 18
T. Shoppee: "Adrian Rollini," *JJ*, xxiii (1970), no.8, p.20; no.10, p.7
R. M. Sudhalter, P. R. Evans, and W. Dean-Myatt: *Bix: Man & Legend* (New Rochelle, NY, and London, 1974)
J. Altman: "Adrian Rollini," *CI*, xiv/11 (1976), 22
S.-A. Worsfold: "The Forgotten Ones: Adrian Rollini," *JJI*, xxxiv/6 (1981), 21
Art Rollini: *Thirty Years with the Big Bands* (London, Urbana, IL, and Chicago, 1987)

JOHN CHILTON/BK

Rollini, Art(hur Francis) [Mousie, Schneeze] (*b* New York, 13 Feb 1912; *d* Florida, 30 Dec 1993). Tenor saxophonist, brother of Adrian Rollini. He began playing professionally in the late 1920s, occasionally with the California Ramblers, and in March 1929 he joined his brother in London to play with Fred Elizalde's orchestra at the Savoy Hotel. After returning to New York in December that year he began working as a freelance, playing with the re-formed California Ramblers and with Paul Whiteman. He contributed elegant, often exciting solos to many of his brother's recordings. In 1934 he joined Benny Goodman's band; he may be seen with the group in the films *The Big Broadcast of 1937* (1936) and *Hollywood Hotel* (1937). His solos from this period (such as that on *I've found a new baby*) display an appealing sense of light swing derived in part from the work of Bud Freeman. After 1936 Goodman allocated most solos to his other tenor saxophonists, and Rollini left the band in 1939. That year he participated in the first all-star recording session to be organized under the auspices of *Metronome* magazine. During the 1940s he worked as a freelance, played with the bandleaders Richard Himber (1940–41) and Will Bradley (1941–2), then joined the staff of ABC. From the 1960s he played only infrequently, but ran a rehearsal studio. He published an autobiography, *Thirty Years with the Big Bands* (London, Urbana, IL, and Chicago, 1987).

SELECTED RECORDINGS

As sideman: Adrian Rollini: Blue Prelude/Happy as the Day is Long (1933, Col. 2785D); B. Goodman: Nitwit Serenade/Bugle Call Rag (1934, Col. 2958D); Sometimes I'm Happy (1935, Vic. 25090); I've found a new baby (1936, Vic. 25355); Z. Elman: Let's fall in love (1939, Bb 10342); B. Gowans: *Brad Gowans and his New York Nine* (1946, RCA LJM3000), incl. Jazz Me Blues, Singin' the Blues

BIBLIOGRAPHY

ChiltonW; *ConnorBG*; *FeatherE*
B. M. Lytton Edwards [M. Lytton and B. Edwards]: "'Heart-Throb' Saxist," *Rhythm* (1937), Dec, 15
B. Rusch: "Art Rollini," *Cadence*, xiv/4 (1988), 5

RICHARD M. SUDHALTER

Rollins, Sonny [Theodore Walter; Newk] (*b* New York, 9 Sept 1930). Tenor saxophonist and leader.

1. Life. 2. Style.

1. LIFE. He first learned piano, studied alto saxophone from about the age of 11, and took up the tenor instrument in 1946. In high school he led a group with Jackie McLean,

Sonny Rollins, 1962

Kenny Drew, and Art Taylor. He rehearsed with Thelonious Monk for several months in 1948 and from 1949 to 1954 recorded intermittently with a number of leading bop musicians and groups, including J. J. Johnson, Charlie Parker, Fats Navarro, Bud Powell, Max Roach, Art Blakey, Monk, and the Modern Jazz Quartet. His most frequent associate during these early years was Miles Davis, with whom he performed in clubs from 1949 and recorded from 1951. In one of these recording sessions with Davis, in 1954, he introduced three compositions of his own which later became jazz standards: *Airegin*, *Doxy*, and *Oleo*. In 1955, while overcoming his dependence on drugs, he worked in Chicago and, in December, joined the Clifford Brown–Max Roach Quintet. He remained with Roach until May 1957, then performed briefly in Davis's quintet; thereafter, however, he has led his own groups.

In 1956 came the first of a series of landmark recordings issued under Rollins's own name: *Valse hot* introduced the practice, now common, of playing bop in 3/4 meter; *St. Thomas* initiated his explorations of calypso patterns; and *Blue 7* was hailed by Gunther Schuller as demonstrating a new manner of "thematic improvisation," in which the soloist develops motifs extracted from his theme. *Way Out West* (1957), Rollins's first album using a trio of saxophone, double bass, and drums, offered a solution to his long-standing difficulties with incompatible pianists and exemplified his witty ability to improvise on hackneyed material (*Wagon Wheels*, *I'm an old cowhand*). *It could happen to you* (also 1957) was the first in a long series of unaccompanied solo recordings, and *The Freedom Suite* (1958) foreshadowed the political stances taken in jazz in the 1960s. During the years 1956 to 1958 Rollins was widely regarded as the most talented and innovative tenor saxophonist in jazz. Nevertheless, he was discontented: he could not find compatible sidemen, saw shortcomings in his own playing, and suffered from poor health. For these reasons he voluntarily withdrew from public life from August 1959 to November 1961. During this period of retirement his habit of practicing on the Williamsburg Bridge in New York became legendary.

On resuming his career Rollins led a quartet consisting of Jim Hall, Bob Cranshaw, and, on drums over the course of the next year, Walter Perkins, Albert "Tootie" Heath, Ben Riley, or Billy Higgins. He had improved his already prodigious skills, but his style was now considered conservative. In an effort to rejoin the vanguard of jazz fashion he began, in mid-1962, collaborating with Don Cherry, Paul Bley, Henry Grimes, Higgins, and other musicians associated with free jazz, though he never seemed truly devoted to this path; *East Broadway Run Down* (1966) illustrates the furthest extent to which he incorporated noise elements into his playing. During these years, as Rollins continued to struggle with changing personnel and instrumentation, he focused increasingly on unaccompanied playing, and by the end of the decade he had become famous for his extended, "stream-of-consciousness" extemporizations on traditional tunes and on his own calypso songs.

Rollins has been widely and incorrectly credited for writing the film score for *Alfie* (1965) – apart from the title song (which is by Burt Bacharach) – but in fact this score is by Stan Tracey. He pursued spiritual interests in India for five months in 1968, then abandoned music altogether from September 1969 to November 1971. From 1972, when he resumed playing once more, he has led various groups of young, lesser-known musicians (but with Cranshaw on elecric bass guitar through the 1970s and again regularly from the late 1980s), performing in a commercial vein and making use of electronic instruments and contemporary African-American dance rhythms; a film made the following year, *Sonny Rollins Live*, captures the exuberance of a concert performance. Rollins has continued to experiment, recording on soprano saxophone in 1972 and on lyricon in 1979. However, touring the USA in 1978 as a member of the Milestone Jazzstars (with McCoy Tyner, Ron Carter, and Al Foster), he demonstrated that, as an individual, he remained essentially true to the bop tradition, an aspect of his playing that was again especially apparent in an acclaimed solo performance at the Museum of Modern Art, New York, in 1985. Except for a six-month hiatus in 1983, after he collapsed from exhaustion, Rollins has remained active into the new century, touring the USA, Europe, and Japan, and recording a fusion of bop, soul music, and calypso with his quintet, whose members at various times included Michael Wolff (1976–8), Mark Soskin (1978–93), Victor Bailey (1979–80, 1985), Jerome Harris (1979–81, 1984–91), Tommy Campbell (1984–8), Foster (1985), Clifton Anderson (from 1985), Billy Drummond (1994–5), and Stephen Scott (1996–8). Through the early 1990s Rollins also gave annual concerts at Carnegie Hall, each featuring a guest soloist, among them Hall, Roy Hargrove, Branford Marsalis, and Terence Blanchard.

2. Style. Rollins established himself as the outstanding jazz saxophonist between Charlie Parker and John Coltrane and a

leading figure in the hard-bop style (*see* SAXOPHONE, esp. §3). The prevailing interpretation of his method of improvisation derives from Schuller's "thematic analysis" of Rollins's celebrated solo on *Blue 7* (1956); other writers, accepting and expanding on Schuller's insights, have even declared thematic improvisation to be Rollins's greatest contribution to jazz. This view demands reconsideration: Schuller's analysis accounts for only part of Rollins's solo, and several of the motifs in that part do not derive from the theme but occur elsewhere in Rollins's earlier work (most obviously in *Vierd Blues*, which he recorded with Davis). Rollins, like most bop musicians of the period, paid little attention to composed melodies, preferring instead to improvise athematic, "formulaic" responses to underlying chord progressions. In slow ballads, of course, he often paraphrased the theme, and he sometimes developed motifs from his own calypso themes (as in ex.1, where the first two notes of the

Ex.1 From *St. Thomas*, on *Saxophone Colossus* (1956, Prst. 7079); transcr. C. Blancq

theme, inverted and rhythmically displaced, alternate with formulaic bop runs), but he rarely applied this technique to blues or popular songs. Similarly, he seldom used fragments from familiar tunes to anchor long stretches of newly improvised material; *Wagon Wheels* (1957) provides the clearest example of this technique. In essence Rollins has adhered to the bop practice of varying and elaborating a large repertory of formulas and, in a wide range of material, shows a rhythmic imagination, harmonic subtlety, and freedom of design that have perhaps been surpassed only by Charlie Parker.

The "modern" Rollins, that is to say, from the early 1970s onwards, has been something of an enigma. His studio recordings have persistently been disappointing, and in his working group he has chosen (with some exceptions) not to draw from the most talented sidemen available. But Rollins himself, in live performance, has remained, into his 70s, unceasingly brilliant, nearly bursting with energy and creative improvisational ideas as he leads his group through lengthy concerts with scarcely a pause for breath. If it makes any sense to choose a greatest living jazz saxophonist of the last quarter-century, it is almost certainly Rollins (but only in concert, not on record); and perhaps much more interestingly, in terms of general notions about this music, if ever there was an argument for conceiving of jazz group playing not as a process of democratic, interdependent, musical conversation, but as being dominated by a great individual artist, that artist is Rollins.

SELECTED RECORDINGS

As leader: *Sonny Rollins Quartet* (1954, Prst. 190); *Worktime* (1955, Prst. 7020); *Sonny Rollins Plus 4* (1956, Prst. 7038), incl. Valse hot; *Tenor Madness* (1956, Prst. 7047); *Saxophone Colossus* (1956, Prst. 7079), incl. Blue 7, St. Thomas; *Way Out West* (1957, Cont. 3530), incl. I'm an old cowhand, Wagon Wheels; *Sonny Rollins*, ii (1957, BN 1558); *The Sound of Sonny* (1957, Riv. 241), incl. It could happen to you [unaccompanied solo]; *A Night at the Village Vanguard* (1957, BN 1581); *The Freedom Suite* (1958, Riv. 258); *Newk's Time* (1958, BN 4001); *The Bridge* (1962, RCA LSP2527); *Our Man in Jazz* (1962, RCA LSP2612); *Sonny Rollins on Impulse!* (1965, Imp. 91); *Alfie* (1966, Imp. 9111); *East Broadway Run Down* (1966, Imp. 9121); *Sonny Rollins' Next Album* (1972, Mlst. 9042); *Horn Culture* (1973, Mlst. 9051); *The Cutting Edge* (1974, Mlst. 9059); *Easy Living* (1977, Mlst. 9080); *No Problem* (1981, Mlst. 9104); *Reel Life* (1982, Mlst. 9108); *Sunny Days, Starry Nights* (1984, Mlst. 9122)

As sideman: J. J. Johnson: Bee Jay (1949, Savoy 949); B. Powell: 52nd Street Theme (1949, BN 1568); M. Davis: Morpheus/Blue Room (1951, Prst. 734); *Miles Davis Quintet* (1954, Prst. 187), incl. Airegin, Doxy, Oleo; *Collector's Items* (1953, 1956, Prst. 7044), incl. Vierd Blues (1956); C. Brown and M. Roach: *At Basin Street* (1956, EmA 36070); T. Monk: *Brilliant Corners* (1956, Riv. 226); M. Roach: *Jazz in 3/4 Time* (1956–7, EmA 36108); Milestone Jazzstars: *Milestone Jazzstars in Concert* (1978, Mlst. 55006)

SELECTED FILMS AND VIDEOS

Jazz Casual: Sonny Rollins and Company with Jim Hall (1963); Sonny Rollins, Musician (1968); Sonny Rollins Live at Laren (1973); Soundstage: Down Beat Jazz Awards (1975); Saxophone Colossus (1986); Great Performances: Wolf Trap Salutes Dizzy Gillespie: An All-star Tribute to the Jazz Master (1988); Texas Tenor: the Illinois Jacquet Story (1991); Sonny Rollins and Dexter Gordon (1991 [filmed 1967–71]); A Great Day in Harlem (1995); Blue Note: a Story of Modern Jazz (*c*1997)

TRANSCRIPTIONS

J. Aebersold, ed.: *A New Approach to Jazz improvisation*, viii: *Sonny Rollins: Nine Classic Jazz Originals* (1976)
C. Gerard: *Jazz Masters: Sonny Rollins* (Chester, NY, 1988)
Sonny Rollins (Japan, n.d.)

BIBLIOGRAPHY

N. Hentoff: "Sonny Rollins," *DB*, xxiii/23 (1956), 15
R. Schecroun: "Sonny," *Jh*, no.116 (1956), 16
B. Wilen: "Sonny Rollins," *Jh*, no.117 (1957), 27
D. Cerulli: "Theodore Walter Rollins," *DB*, xxv/14 (1958), 16
G. Schuller: "Sonny Rollins and the Challenge of Thematic Improvisation," *JR*, i/1 (1958), 6; Fr. trans. *Jh*, no.164 (1961), 14
M. James: "Sonny Rollins on Record: 1949–1954," *JM*, v/8 (1959), 7
B. Korall: "Sonny Rollins: my Exile Has Paid Off," *MM* (23 Dec 1961), 7
W. Balliett: *Dinosaurs in the Morning* (Philadelphia, 1962/*R*1978)
B. Coss: "The Return of Sonny Rollins," *DB*, xxix/1 (1962), 13
D. Ioakimidis: "Sonny Rollins et John Coltrane en parallèle," *Jh* (1962), no.179, p.25; no.180, p.23; no.181, p.22; no.182, p.30
J. Goldberg: "The Further Adventures of Sonny Rollins," *DB*, xxxii/18 (1965), 19
B. McRae: "Sonny Rollins," *JJ*, xviii/3 (1965), 6
I. Gitler: "Sonny Rollins: Music is an Open Sky," *DB*, xxxvi/10 (1969), 18
M. Williams: *The Jazz Tradition* (New York, 1970, rev. 2/1983)
T. Fiofori: "Re-entry: the New Orbit of Sonny Rollins," *DB*, xxxviii/17 (1971), 14
P. Griffith: "Sonny's Back to Stay," *MM* (8 Dec 1973), 24
J. Delmas: "Traditions et contradictions de Theodore Walter 'Sonny' Rollins," *Jh*, no.307 (1974), 14
C. Berg: "Sonny Rollins: the Way Newk Feels," *DB*, xliv/7 (1977), 13 [incl. discography]
C. Blancq: *Melodic Improvisation in American Jazz: the Style of Theodore "Sonny" Rollins, 1951–1962* (diss., Tulane U., 1977); rev. as *Sonny Rollins: the Journey of a Jazzman* (Boston, 1983)
M. Ullman: "Sonny Rollins," *New Republic*, clxxviii (1 April 1978), 25
B. Blumenthal: "The Bridge: Sonny Rollins is a Tenor for All Times," *RS*, no.295 (12 July 1979), 56
M. Contat: "Sonny Rollins: des mots et des images," *Jm*, no.276 (1979), 36
I. Gitler: "Sonny Rollins," *Radio Free Jazz*, xx (1979), Nov, 14
B. Primack: "Sonny Rollins: the Way He Feels," *DB*, xlvi/2 (1979), 12
"Sonny Rollins," *SJ*, xxxiii/1 (1979), 220 [discography]
D. Baker: *The Jazz Style of Sonny Rollins: a Musical and Historical Perspective* (Lebanon, IN, 1980) [incl. transcrs.]
G. Endress: *Jazz Podium: Musiker über sich selbst* (Stuttgart, Germany, 1980), 136

D. Forte: "Sonny Rollins: Tenor Titan," *Musicians' Industry*, ii/2 (1980), 52
E. Meadow: "Rollins Reflects," *JJI*, xxxiii/6 (1980), 11
R. Zabor: "Let Us Now Praise Sonny Rollins," *Musician, Player & Listener*, no.23 (1980), 38
B. Blumenthal: "Sonny Rollins," *DB*, xlix/5 (1982), 15 [incl. discography]
C. Cioe: "Backbeat: Sonny Rollins: 'I'm Still Reaching' . . . and Still Surprising his Audiences," *Hi Fidelity*, xxxiii/5 (1983), 76 [incl. discography]
M. Isherwood: "Sonny Rollins," *JJI*, xxxvi/4 (1983), 8
T. Sjøgren: *The Sonny Rollins Discography* (Copenhagen, 1983, rev. 2/1993 as *The Discography of Sonny Rollins*)
R. Cook: "Sonny Rollins: Return of the Colossus," *The Wire*, no.18 (1985), 28
F. Davis: *In the Moment: Jazz in the 1980s* (New York, and Oxford, England, 1986), 117
B. Sidran: "Rollins des deux côtes du pont," *Jm*, no.359 (1987), 32
K. Franckling: "Sonny Rollins," *JT* (1988), Feb, 17
G. Kalbacher: "The Sonny Rollins Interview," *DB*, lv/7 (1988), 16
C. Stern: "Sonny Rollins: the Rose & the Cross," *Musician*, no.115 (1988), 82
M. Jarrett: "Sonny Rollins: Interview," *Cadence*, xvi/7 (1990), 5
G. Rouy and F. Goaty: "Sonny Rollins: à New York il n'y a plus de pont comme ça," *Jm*, no.397 (1990), 24
S. Spencer: "The Titan of Jazz," *RS*, nos.593–4 (1990), 146
Z. Stewart: "On Sonny's Side of the Street," *Los Angeles Times* (16 Sept 1990)
J.-L. Chautemps: "Pour une auscultation de Sonny Rollins," *Jm*, no.400 (1991), 26
J. Kaliss: "Sax Master Rollins Shares Improv Genius with Up-and-comers," *San Francisco Chronicle Datebook* (22 Sept 1991)
T. Moon: "Sonny Rollins: the Rigorous Art of Staying on Top," *JT*, xxi/5 (1991), 15
K. Rattenbury: "Sonny Rollins," *CJM*, xxviii (1991), no.2, p.28; no.3, p.28, no.4, p.30 [incl. transcrs.]
P. Watrous: "Sonny Rollins and Pals in a Carnegie Reunion," *New York Times* (12 April 1991)
P. N. Wilson: *Sonny Rollins: sein Leben, seine Musik, seine Schallplatten* (Schaftlach, Germany, 1991)
C. Gauffre: "Sonny Rollins, paisiblement . . .," *Jm*, no.414 (1992), 24
G. Giddins: *Faces in the Crowd: Players and Writers* (New York, and Oxford, England, 1992), 164
J. McDonough: "Sonny's Side of the Street: Sonny Rollins," *DB*, lix/12 (1992), 22 [incl. discography]
S. Nicholson: "Saxophone Colossus," *Jazz Express*, no.140 (1992), 6
H. Reich: "Storytelling by Sax: After 4 Decades Fans Still Flock to Sonny Rollins's Riveting Tenor Horn," *Chicago Tribune* (27 March 1992)
R. Palmer: "Sonny Rollins: Tenor Titan," *JJI*, xlv (1992), no.11, p.6; xlvi (1993), no.2, p.24; no.3, p.10
Fara C.: "Rollins," *Jm*, no.424 (1993), 42
G. Hines: "Brought up on Bop," *Washington Post* (5 March 1993)
H. Reich: "He's the Timeless Tenor," *Chicago Tribune* (23 May 1993)
J. Brownell: "Analytical Models of Jazz Improvisation," *Jf*, xxvi (1994), 9
B. Primack: "Sonny Rollins: Transcending the Standard," *JT*, xxiv/2 (1994), 32
M. Rowland and T. Scherman, eds.: *The Jazz Musician* (New York, 1994), 201
J. Giardullo: "Sonny Rollins: our Man in Jazz," *Coda*, no.262 (1995), 8
K. Whitehead: "Sonny Rollins: When Sonny Gets Mad," *DB*, lxii/1 (1995), 16 [incl. discography]
J. Woodard: "Sonny Rollins," *Jh*, no.518 (1995), 33
H. Gelb: "Sonny's Song," *San Francisco Chronicle* (6 Oct 1996)
G. Giddins: "The Greatest Living Jazz Musician: Sonny Rollins at 65," *VV* (2 Jan 1996), 24
B. Belden: "Jazz Artist of the Year: Sonny the Man Rollins," *DB*, lxiv/8 (1997), 18 [incl. discography]
B. Blumenthal: "Sonny Rollins," *Boston Globe* (14 June 1998)
J. Fordham: "Arts: Sax and the Over 60s: Will Jazz Legend Sonny Rollins Ever Run out of Steam? Not on his Latest Showing," *The Guardian* (20 April 1998)
R. Palmer: *Sonny Rollins: the Cutting Edge* (Hull, England, 1998)
F. Postif: *Jazz Me Blues: interviews et portraits de musiciens de jazz et de blues* (Paris, 1998), 101
B. Primack: "Summoning the Muse: Sonny Rollins," *JT*, xxviii/5 (1998), 28
D. Salemann: *Five Tenors: Ray Abrams, 1944–1949; Yusef Lateef, 1938–1949; Billy Mitchell, 1941–1950; Sonny Rollins, 1949; Charlie Rouse, 1944–1950: Solography, Discography, Bandroutes, Engagements* (Berlin, 1999)
<http://www.duke.edu/~bab7/rollins.html> (2000)
<http://www.geoities.com/BourbonStreet/Delta/4733/> (2000) [incl. discography]

BK

Rollography. A type of Discography listing piano rolls, usually those recorded by a particular performer.

Roman New Orleans Jazz Band. Italian traditional jazz band. It was formed in Rome in April 1949 and given its name by Louis Armstrong. The group's original members were the trumpeter Giovanni Borghi, the trombonist Luciano Fineschi, the clarinetist Marcello Riccio, the saxophonist Ivan Vandor, the pianist Franco Nebbia (soon replaced by Giorgio Zinzi), the banjoist Bruno Perris, the bass tuba player Pino Liberati, and the drummer Peppino d'Intino. In October 1949 the band took part in a jam session with Armstrong, Jack Teagarden, and Earl Hines, and from March of the following year made recordings (including *At the Jazz Band Ball*, 1951, HMV HN2947). The group continued to perform and record into the late 1980s.

ADRIANO MAZZOLETTI

Romano, Aldo (*b* Belluno, Italy, 16 Jan 1941). Italian drummer and leader. He moved to France while a child, studied guitar, then taught himself drums (from 1961). Often working together with Jean-François Jenny-Clark, he performed in clubs in Paris with Barney Wilen, Michel Portal, Eddy Louiss, and Jean-Luc Ponty and with such visiting Americans as Jackie McLean (1965). By this time Romano had come under the influence of Sunny Murray's new drumming style, and from 1964, when he and Jenny-Clark joined Bernard Vitet's small group, he specialized in playing free jazz. From 1965 he was a member of Don Cherry's group in Paris and on tour, and he recorded with Cherry in 1965 and 1966 (the latter date at the Gyllene Cirkeln in Stockholm). He also recorded with Steve Lacy (1965–6), Lacy and Carla Bley in Jazz Realities (1966), Giorgio Gaslini (1966), Gato Barbieri (1967), Rolf Kühn (1967), Michel Portal (1969), Karin Krog (1970), and Robin Kenyatta (1972). For several years he worked with Joachim Kühn; in 1967 he performed with Kühn and his brother Rolf at the Newport Jazz Festival. He also performed with Phil Woods and Charles Tolliver, and in 1969 he accompanied Keith Jarrett on the pianist's first European tour.

After beginning to work in a jazz-rock idiom with Barney Wilen in 1968, Romano led his own fusion group in which he sang and played drums (1971–3). He then collaborated with Philip Catherine, Charlie Mariano, Jasper van 't Hof, and Jenny-Clark in the band Pork Pie (1973–5). He accompanied Christian Escoudé, recorded with Franz Koglmann (1975), François Jeanneau (1976–7), and Enrico Rava (1978, 1981), and worked with Rava in a group where Roswell Rudd and Jenny-Clark were among his fellow sidemen (1977). In the early 1980s Romano adopted a more conventional drumming style and worked with Michel Petrucciani, again with Jenny-Clark on double bass. In 1988 he formed a quartet with Paolo Fresu, Franco d'Andrea, and Furio de Castri which performed widely throughout Europe, and in the late 1990s he led the quartet Prosodie, which included Pierre De Bethmann. He recorded two albums of compositions by Bill Evans (ii) in Stefano Battaglia's trio (1992, 1993). He has recorded as a leader from 1978 into the 1990s, and in the late 1980s he began publishing interviews in *Jazz magazine*.

SELECTED RECORDINGS

Duos with J. Lovano: *Ten Tales* (1989, Owl 53)
As leader: with J.-F. Jenny-Clark: *Divieto di santificazione* (1977, Horo 07); *Il piacere* (1978, Owl 015) [incl. duos with M. Portal and C. Barthélémy]; *Night Diary* (1980, Owl 018); *Alma Latina* (1983, Owl 031); *Ritual* (1988, Owl 050); *To be Ornette to be* (1989, Owl 057); *Dreams and Waters* (1991, Owl 63); *Non dimenticar* (1993, Verve 518264-2); *Prosodie* (1995, Verve 526854-2); *Intervista* (1996, Verve 537196-2); *Corners* (1998, Label Bleu 6615)

As sideman: D. Cherry: *Togetherness* (1965, Durium 77127); S. Lacy: *Disposability* (1965, RCA KLPV200); C. Bley: *Jazz Realities* (1966, Fon. 881010); S. Lacy: *Sortie* (1966, Pol. 423223); D. Cherry: *Live at Montmartre*, i–ii (1966, Magnetic 111–12); M. Portal: *Our Meanings and our Feelings* (1969, Pathé CO54.10525); S. Lacy: *Epistrophy* (1969, BYG 529126); E. Rava: *Enrico Rava Quartet* (1978, ECM 1122); M. Petrucciani: *Michel Petrucciani* (1981, Owl 025); *Estate* (1982, Riviera 1)

BIBLIOGRAPHY

"7 noms, 7 têtes: voici les nouveau-nés du jazz français: Aldo Romano," *Jm*, no.117 (1965), 28
P. Carles and V. Delubac: "Aldo Romano: une valeur en hausse," *Jm*, no.155 (1968), 16
D. Soutif: "Aldo Romano," *Jm*, no.286 (1980), 18; contd as "Une musique pour la rue: Aldo Romano," no.287 (1980), 40
F.-M. Coudert: "Aldo, ses rites et ses itals," *Jm*, no.374 (1988), 28
D. Soutif, "Romano, Aldo," in P. Carles, A. Clergeat, and J.-L. Comolli: *Dictionnaire du jazz* (Paris, 1988, rev. and enlarged 2/1994)
J.-Y. Le Bec: "Aldo Romano: 'pourquoi j'aime Ornette'," *Jm*, no.393 (1990), 28
G. Le Querrec: "Le tropique de concerts par le griot du trio," *Jm*, no.394 (1990), 20
C. Mulard: "Aldo Romano: Avec le temps . . .," *Jh*, no.472 (1990), 24
C. Chantoiseau: "Aldo Romano, moissonneur-batteur," *Jazzman*, no.169 (1993), 5
C. Gauffre: "Le trio du griot bis d'Afrique," *Jm*, no.429 (1993), 20
F. Médioni: "My Favorite Things," *Jm*, no.469 (1997), 12
<http://www.ijm.it/enartists.html> (1999)

ANDRÉ CLERGEAT/BK

Romano, Joe [Joseph S.] (*b* Rochester, NY, 17 April 1932). Tenor and alto saxophonist. He took up alto saxophone at the age of eight and clarinet when he was ten, and began studying tenor saxophone in his early teens; from the age of 14 he worked professionally in Rochester. After serving in the air force he played sporadically with Woody Herman's band (from 1956), recording, touring South America (1958), Europe (1964), and Britain (1968), and performing at the Monterey Jazz Festival (1967) and other festivals in Newport and Kansas City (1970s). He also recorded with the baritone horn player Gus Mancuso (1957) and worked in Rochester with Chuck Mangione (early 1960s) and in Buffalo with Sam Noto (1966–7); as a member of Mangione's quintet he recorded an album in New York in 1962 (*Recuedo*, Jlnd 84). In California he performed and recorded with Art Pepper (1968) and intermittently with Buddy Rich (1968–74) and played with Les Brown (1970–72) and Louie Bellson. Romano then returned to New York and worked with Chuck Israels's National Jazz Ensemble (1976), recorded as a soloist with Noto's bop quintet (*Act One*, 1975, Xan. 127), performed occasionally with the Thad Jones–Mel Lewis Orchestra, and toured and recorded with Bellson (1978, 1980). In the 1980s and 1990s he was once again based in southern California and worked as a studio musician. During the same period he was featured as a soloist with the Capp–Pierce Juggernaut (recording in 1987) and its successor (following Pierce's death in 1992) under Frank Capp's sole leadership, and he appeared in Capp's small groups in the Los Angeles area. He should not be confused with the jazz and popular singer Joe Romano, who is based in Houston.

BIBLIOGRAPHY

Feather–Gitler '70s
W. D. Clancy with A. C. Kenton: *Woody Herman: Chronicles of the Herds* (New York and elsewhere, 1995)

BK

Romão, Dom Um (*b* Rio de Janeiro, 3 Aug 1925). Brazilian percussionist and drummer. His father taught him to play drums, and by the age of 16 he was working professionally. During the 1960s he performed regularly with the keyboard player Sergio Mendes, notably in the latter's sextet Bossa Rio, and in 1962 he recorded with Mendes and Cannonball Adderley. He then moved to the USA and played in Chicago with Oscar Brown, Jr. (1965). From the mid-1960s he worked in Los Angeles, and from 1967 to 1970 he toured internationally as Mendes's drummer. Following the departure of Airto Moreira from Weather Report, Romão served as the group's percussionist between 1971 and 1974; his playing may be heard to advantage on *I Sing the Body Electric* (1971–2, Col. KC31352). In the early 1970s he settled in New York, where he later established a rehearsal studio. After recording in Zurich with George Gruntz in 1976 he worked regularly with the Swiss group Om from 1977; in the same year he recorded with Collin Walcott and alongside Jack DeJohnette, Gruntz, Pierre Favre, Fredy Studer, and David Friedman as a member of Percussion Profiles. Later he performed and recorded at the Donaueschingen Musiktage für Zeitgenössische Tonkunst in the group World Music (1985), which combined wind and rhythm instruments associated with jazz with others from India, the Caribbean, and Brazil. Romão remained active through the 1990s, working mainly in Switzerland, Germany, New York, and Brazil, and in 1997 he recorded as a percussionist with Peter Schärli. (F. Colon: "Dom Um Romão," *MD*, xiv/11 (1990), 58)

BK

Romeo. Record label. It was a subsidiary of the Cameo Record Corporation and was established in July 1926; the records were sold through the chain of stores of S. H. Kress. The repertory was drawn from Cameo's catalogue, though items were generally released under pseudonyms. The label was maintained after the formation of the AMERICAN RECORD CORPORATION. It became one of that company's "dime-store" labels, and its catalogue numbers were aligned with those of the others from September 1935. Issues under ARC's ownership included an important series by the Washboard Rhythm Boys (1933) and major race series. With the other dime-store labels, Romeo was discontinued in April 1938.

BIBLIOGRAPHY

R. M. W. Dixon and J. Godrich: *Recording the Blues* (London, 1970), 67, 78
B. Rust: *The American Record Label Book* (New Rochelle, NY, 1978), 272
A. Sutton: *Directory of American Disc Record Brands and Manufacturers, 1891–1943* (Westport, CT, and London, 1994), 136
R. M. W. Dixon, J. Godrich, and H. Rye: *Blues & Gospel Records,1890–1943* (Oxford, England, rev. and enlarged 4/1997), xxxii

HOWARD RYE

Roney, Antoine (*b* Philadelphia, 1 April 1963). Tenor saxophonist, brother of Wallace Roney. He grew up in a musical family and played drums until the age of six, when his grandfather, tired of the racket, destroyed the drum set; he then took up clarinet, alto saxophone, and finally tenor saxophone, and received early training from his brother Wallace. Later he studied with Jackie McLean at the Hartt School of Music in Hartford, Connecticut. In the 1980s he performed with, among others, Donald Byrd (1983), McLean (1984), Clifford Jordan, Ted Curson, and Big John Patton (all 1986), Rashied Ali (1987–8), and Art Taylor (1989). From around 1989 he worked in Jesse Davis's band at Augie's, New York, and he made his first recording in January 1991 with Davis. From the early 1990s Roney worked in his brother's small groups and also held positions in the bands led by Jacky Terrasson, Cindy Blackman, and Michael Carvin. In

1993 he performed and recorded with Ravi Coltrane in the group Grand Central. He has taught at McLean's Artists Collective in Hartford.

Roney's playing is influenced by that of Wayne Shorter, but he incorporates a rasping, almost raw-edged, blues-based approach which also draws from the spirituality associated with John Coltrane's late style. He doubles on soprano saxophone and bass clarinet.

SELECTED RECORDINGS

As leader: *Whirling* (1995, Muse 5546)

As sideman: W. Roney: *Seth Air* (1991, Muse 5441); Ricky Ford: *Tenor Madness Too!* (1992, Muse 5478); Grand Central: *Sax Storm* (1993, Alfa Jazz 9528); W. Roney: *Village* (1996, WB 46649)

BIBLIOGRAPHY

Feather–GitlerBEJ

B. Primack: "Hearsay: Conceptual Art: Antoine Roney," *JT*, xxvi/5 (1996), 23

GK

Roney, Wallace (*b* Philadelphia, 25 May 1960). Trumpeter and leader, brother of Antoine Roney. His grandmother played piano and his aunt was an organ and piano teacher, and his father, an amateur trumpeter, introduced him to recordings by Dizzy Gillespie, Clifford Brown, and Lee Morgan. He took up cornet around the age of six or seven, but by the time he was 11 he had changed to trumpet. In the mid-1970s he moved with his father to Washington, DC, where he attended the Duke Ellington School of the Arts and studied with Mickey Bass, who encouraged him to play piano in order to understand harmony; from the age of 16 he traveled to New York and sat in at clubs. While studying at Howard University (1978–9) Roney toured with Art Blakey's big band (1978) and Abdullah Ibrahim's large ensemble Ujamaah (1979) and recorded with Rodney Jones (1978). He then transferred to the Berklee College of Music, but he returned to New York in 1981, and from September of that year he played for six months in Blakey's Jazz Messengers in place of Wynton Marsalis. In addition he worked in Chico Freeman's group (1980–82) and as a freelance with, among others, Ricky Ford, McCoy Tyner, Billy Harper, Jimmy Cobb, David Murray, Cedar Walton, Walter Davis, and Philly Joe Jones; he recorded with both Freeman and Ford in 1982.

Roney was a founding member of Tony Williams's bop quintet, which was in existence from 1986 to around 1994, and in the mid- to late 1980s he spent another period in Blakey's group and recorded and performed in Kenny Barron's quintet. In 1991 he appeared with Miles Davis at the Montreux International Jazz Festival, and he may be seen in the resulting video *Miles Davis & Quincy Jones: Live at Montreux* (1991). The following year he recorded in Gerry Mulligan's Re-Birth of the Cool band, in the role originally taken by Davis, and in 1992–3 he toured with Wayne Shorter, Herbie Hancock, Ron Carter, and Williams as a member of a Miles Davis tribute band. Later he performed with Elvin Jones and Sonny Rollins (both 1995) and toured and recorded as a member of Chick Corea's Bud Powell tribute band (1996–7).

Roney became active as a leader around 1987, and in the late 1980s he performed regularly at Fat Tuesday's in New York; his sidemen have included the saxophonists Gary Thomas and his brother Antoine Roney, the pianists Mulgrew Miller, Donald Brown, Jacky Terrasson, Carlos McKinney, and Geri Allen (whom he married in May 1995), the double bass players Charnett Moffett, Reggie Hamilton, and Clarence Seay, and the drummers Cindy Blackman, Will Kennedy, Eric Allen, Lenny White, and Ralph Penland. He has recorded regularly with Bob Belden (from 1991) and Geri Allen (from 1992), and extensively as a freelance, with the pianist Andy Jaffe (1985), Marvin "Smitty" Smith (1987–9), Blackman (1987–90), Kenny Garrett and James Spaulding (both 1988), Christopher Hollyday and Don Sickler's Superblue (both 1989), Vincent Herring (1990–92), Joey DeFrancesco (1990), George Gruntz's Concert Jazz Band, Kenny Drew, Jr., and Jarmo Savolainen (all 1991), his brother Antoine (1992), Jeanie Bryson, Randy Weston, Cody Moffett, and Darrell Grant (all 1993), Helen Merrill (1994), Clifton Anderson, Lionel Hampton, the Essence All Stars, and Rodney Whitaker (all 1995), and Bill Evans (iii) (1995–6).

Roney has been maligned by the critics for imitating his idol, Davis, particularly on recordings, where this trait persisted into the late 1990s. However, he has a darker tone than Davis's, and in concert performances he is a much busier player, with an extroverted passion and rhythmic drive that departs from Davis's characteristically spare and lyrical approach.

SELECTED RECORDINGS

As leader: *Verses* (1987, Muse 5335); *Intuition* (1988, Muse 5346); *The Standard Bearer* (1989, Muse 5372); *Obsession* (1990, Muse 5423); *Munchin'* (1993, Muse 5533); *Crunchin'* (1993, Muse 5518); *Misterios* (*c*1994, WB 45641); *Village* (1996, WB 46649)

As sideman with T. Williams: *Angel Street* (1988, BN B11H-48494); *Native Heart* (1989, BN B21S-93170); *Tokyo Live* (1992, BN B22V-99031)

As sideman with others: C. Freeman: *Tradition in Transition* (1982, Elek. Mus. 52412); A. Jaffe: *Manhattan Projections* (1984, Stash 247); C. Hollyday: *Christopher Hollyday* (1989, Novus 3055-2-N); C. Blackman: *Code Red* (1990, Muse 5365); A. Roney: *The Traveler* (1992, Muse 5469); G. Allen: *Maroons* (1992, BN B21Z-99493); [no leader]: *A Tribute to Miles* (1992–3, Qwest 45059); D. Grant: *Black Art* (1993, Criss Cross 1087); C. Anderson: *Landmarks* (1995, Mlst. 9266); C. Corea: *Remembering Bud Powell* (1996, Stretch 9012); G. Allen: *Eyes in the Back of your Head* (1996, BN 38297-2)

BIBLIOGRAPHY

CarrJ

P. Carles, A. Clergeat, and J.-L. Comolli: *Dictionnaire du jazz* (Paris, 1988, rev. and enlarged 2/1994)

I. Leymarie: "Gros plan: Wallace Roney," *Jm*, no.374 (1988), 22

C. Gauffre: "New York is Now: Wallace Roney," *Jm*, no.396 (1990), 34

T. Nuccio: "Wallace Roney: a Trumpeter's Intuition," *DB*, lviii/3 (1991), 28 [incl. discography]

J. Macnie: "Wallace Roney's Fresh Prints," *Musician*, no.169 (1992), 32

B. Primack: "Wallace Roney: on Target," *JT*, xxiii/8 (1993), 28

T. Quénum: "Gros plan: Wallace Roney," *Jm*, no.440 (1994), 24

K. L. Williams: "Now That They're Gone," *DB*, lxi/3 (1994), 17 [incl. discography]

G. Reynard: "Wallace Roney: Blues, Jazz & Co.," *Jh*, no.516 (1994–5), 40

D. Block: "Wallace Roney," *JJI*, xlviii/1 (1995), 13

P. Elwood: "Roney Brothers Show How to Do it at Yoshi's," *San Francisco Examiner* (26 April 1996)

F. Shuster: "Tradin' Fours: Wallace Roney Speaks Out," *DB*, lxiii/8 (1996), 48

Z. Stewart: "Wallace Roney: his own Man," *DB*, lxiii/3 (1996), 28 [incl. discography]

P. Elwood: "Taking a Remarkable Five," *San Francisco Examiner* (14 Jan 1997)

J. LaBarbera: "Wallace Roney," *ITG Journal*, xxi/4 (1997), 50 [incl. discography and transcr.]

GK

Ronnie Scott's. Nightclub in London; *see* NIGHTCLUBS AND OTHER VENUES.

Ronnie Scott's Jazz House. Record company and label formed in 1978 by RONNIE SCOTT, the owner of the club of that name in London.

Roost. Name used on liners by the record company Royal Roost; *see* Royal roost (ii).

Root. Nickname of rudy Powell.

Root, Billy [William] (*b* Philadelphia, 6 March 1934). Tenor and baritone saxophonist. His father, a drummer, played professionally in the Philadelphia area and encouraged him to become a musician. He first worked with Roy Eldridge (1951), changed to alto saxophone temporarily when he joined Hal McIntyre (1952), and then played briefly with Red Rodney. After performing and recording with Bennie Green (1953–4) and spending about five months with Buddy Rich (*c*1955) he toured and recorded with Stan Kenton (1956, 1959). He also recorded with Clifford Brown (1956), Dizzy Gillespie's big band (1957), and alongside Lee Morgan in the septet Dizzy Atmosphere (1957). In 1958 Root performed and recorded at Birdland in New York in a hard-bop sextet that included Hank Mobley, Morgan, and Curtis Fuller; in addition he recorded with Green and with Rodney (*Red Rodney Returns*, 1958, Argo 643) and formed his own group, with which he appeared in New York and Philadelphia. Around the end of 1958 he re-joined Kenton, and from 1959 to 1960 he worked once more with Rodney. Later he played with Dakota Staton, and in 1963 he appeared with her at the Newport Jazz Festival; at some point in the mid-1960s he was a member of Al Grey's small group. Root worked regularly in Las Vegas, Nevada, from 1968 until the late 1980s, when recorded music began to replace performers in the casinos.

BIBLIOGRAPHY

FeatherE
B. Rusch: "Billy Root: Interview," *Cadence*, xvi (1990), no.11, p.5; no.12, p.7

BK

Roppolo, (Joseph) Leon (*b* Lutcher, LA, 16 March 1902; *d* Louisiana, 5 Oct 1943). Clarinetist and composer. His name is often misspelled Rappolo. He was taught to play clarinet by his father, and also learned guitar, which he played occasionally throughout his career. After working with Georg Brunis and Paul Mares at Bucktown on Lake Pontchartrain (*c*1916) and with Eddie Shields and Santo Pecora (*c*1917) he toured in a vaudeville troupe. Around 1920 he was on the Mississippi Gulf Coast with Merritt Brunies's Five Jazz Babies. He played on Mississippi riverboats, but left in Davenport, Iowa, to travel to Chicago with Brunis and Mares. Around 1921 he joined Mares's Friars Society Orchestra, remaining with the group when it became known as the New orleans rhythm kings. Roppolo went with Mares to New York in 1923 and the following year worked with Peck Kelley in Texas, then returned to New Orleans before spending a period in St. Paul, Minnesota, where he became ill. Again in New Orleans he joined Abbie Brunies's Halfway House Orchestra and played with Mares's re-formed New Orleans Rhythm Kings (spring 1925), but shortly afterwards he suffered a mental breakdown. Except for a temporary release in the early 1940s, when he played for two nights for Santo Pecora on the SS *Capitol* and sat in with Abbie Brunies's band, he spent most of the remainder of his life in a sanitorium, where he organized a band and continued to play, mainly on tenor saxophone.

Despite his short career, Roppolo was one of the most influential jazz clarinetists. He was a superb ensemble player but also, which was rare at that time, a highly imaginative soloist. He made use of subtle tonal inflections (as in *Tin Roof Blues*), and the dynamic contrast he achieved between the plaintive tone of the high register of the instrument and the full-bodied sound of its low register (*Wolverine Blues*) lent his playing an emotional quality that set him apart from his contemporaries. Among the compositions he wrote with others are such standards as *Farewell Blues*, *Milenberg Joys* (*Golden Leaf Strut*), *Sugar Babe*, and *Tin Roof Blues*.

SELECTED RECORDINGS

As sideman: New Orleans Rhythm Kings: Farewell Blues (1922, Gen. 4966); That's a Plenty/Tin Roof Blues (1923, Gen. 5105); Weary Blues/Wolverine Blues (1923, Gen. 5102); London Blues/Mad (1923, Gen. 5221); Halfway House Orchestra: Pussy Cat Rag/Barataria (1925, OK 40318); New Orleans Rhythm Kings: She's Crying for Me Blues/Golden Leaf Strut (1925, OK 40327)

BIBLIOGRAPHY

ChiltonW
D. Dexter: "Immortals of Jazz: Leon Rappolo," *DB*, vii/20 (1940), 10
P. Mares: "Leon Rappolo as I Knew Him," *Jazz Quarterly*, ii (1944), 3
M. Williams: "N. O. R. K.," *Jazz Masters of New Orleans* (New York and London, 1967/*R*1978), 121
S.-A. Worsfold: "The Forgotten Ones: Leon Roppolo," *JJI*, xxxiii/2 (1980), 21
G. W. Kay: "Joe Mares and his New Orleans Memories," *MR*, viii/3 (1981), 8
R. Sudhalter: *Lost Chords: White Musicians and their Contribution to Jazz, 1915–1945* (New York, and Oxford, England, 1999)

MICHAEL TOVEY

Rose, Boris (*b* New York, 4 Jan 1918). Record company executive. He studied chemical engineering at CUNY and began collecting records around 1938, while working during vacations in a record shop. Later he formed several dozen record labels (the most important of which were Alto (ii), Ozone, and Session (iii)), through which he issued about 400 albums; among these were acetate dubs of previously issued recordings and transcriptions of broadcast performances from the period 1936–61. The recordings feature leading swing and bop musicians from the 1940s and early 1950s (such as Charlie Christian, Count Basie, Miles Davis, Charlie Parker, Stan Getz, and Lester Young) and broadcasts from Birdland by Charles Mingus, Art Blakey, John Coltrane, and Thelonious Monk; a recording of a broadcast by Davis's jazz-rock group was issued on Session.

BIBLIOGRAPHY

B. Minor: "Sub Rosa Stuff," *Jazz Digest*, ii (1973), 263
B. Esposito: "Yes, Virginia, There is a Boris Rose," *IAJRC Journal*, xxii/1 (1989), 31

BK

Rose, Denis (David) (*b* London, 31 May 1922; *d* London, 22 Nov 1984). English pianist and trumpeter. He was active chiefly at pubs and clubs in London. In the mid-1940s he was a member of a band led by the trumpeter Johnny Claes; during World War II his activities were restricted because he evaded conscription and found it necessary to avoid being apprehended by the authorities. In the course of his work with local bands, among them Cab Kaye's Ministers of Swing (October–November 1948), he organized various informal sessions with other young British musicians, notably Ronnie Scott, and from late 1948 to 1950 was responsible for important events at Club Eleven. Rose was one of the first English players to grasp the essentials of the bop style, which he passed on to Scott and others. He participated in only two recording sessions: the second of these, led by Scott, included *Scrapple from the Apple* (1949, Esquire 10038), on which he played trumpet; this demonstrates just how well he had assimilated the bop vocabulary. He remained interested in musical developments both in London and abroad, and continued to perform, mainly as a pianist. In addition to his work as an unaccompanied soloist and a trio leader, he spent two further periods with Kaye (September 1952 – March 1953, *c*1954) and later accompanied Maggie Nicols (early 1970s).

BIBLIOGRAPHY

ChiltonB
P. Grammond, ed.: *The Decca Book of Jazz* (London, 1958)
V. Schonfield: "Denis Rose," *JJ*, xiv/10 (1961), 16
D. Fairweather: "Taking Things as they Come: the Saga of Denis Rose," *J&B*, ii/1 (1972), 20

STAN BRITT

Rose, Jon (*b* Maidstone, England, 19 Feb 1951). Australian violinist and composer of English birth. After beginning violin studies at the age of seven he played and composed in a wide variety of musical styles, firstly in England, and later in Australia, where he moved in 1976. He soon became a major figure there in free-improvisation circles, giving performances as an unaccompanied soloist at a variety of venues, often on invented instruments. In 1977 he established Fringe Benefit Records, and the following year he graduated from the jazz studies course at the New South Wales Conservatorium of Music. Rose formed an improvisation ensemble, the Relative Band, in 1980, and between that year and 1983 he conducted solo tours of the USA and Europe and performed at international festivals; he also organized an International Relative Band Festival in Australia, and at some point during this period he took Australian citizenship. In 1983 he joined the German group Slauterhaus, and in 1986 he moved to Europe to concentrate on a long-term project, the Relative Violin. In Berlin he directed the Relative Violin Festival (1989), and "Das Rosenberg Museum," commissioned for German television ZDF (1991), and he continued to tour internationally on a constant basis, performing such compositions as *The Chaotic Violin* and *Violin Music in the Age of Shopping* (1995). Rose recorded extensively with many innovators in contemporary improvised music and frequently produced extended works for radio broadcasts. He is the author of two books, *The Pink Violin* (Melbourne, 1992) and *Violin Music in the Age of Shopping* (Melbourne, n.d.). Many of his performances and books involve Dr. Johannes Rosenberg, who functions as a fictitious and highly comical reincarnation of Rose himself.

SELECTED RECORDINGS

As unaccompanied soloist: *Vivisection* (1987, AufRuhr 67013); *Paganini's Last Testament* (1989, Konnex 5021); *The Virtual Violin* (1993, Megaphone 009)
Duos with Martin Wesley-Smith: *Tango* (1983, Hot 1009)
As leader: *Towards a Relative Music* (1978, Fringe Benefit 24); *Velocity of Independent Parts* (1979, Fringe Benefit 25); *Kultural Terrorism* (1987, Dossier 7551); *Forward of Short Leg* (1980–85, Dossier 7529); *Violin Music for Restaurants* (1987, RéR BJRCD); *Violin Music for Supermarkets* (1994, Megaphone 016); *Violin Music in the Age of Shopping* (1995, Intakt 038); *Shopping.Live@Victo* (1994, RéR JR4)
As sideman: Slauterhaus: *Slauterhaus Live* (1988, 1990, Victo 013); Michael Sheridan: *Digital Jamming* (1996, Black Hole 018)

BIBLIOGRAPHY

B. Johnson: *The Oxford Companion to Australian Jazz* (Melbourne, Australia, 1987)
C. S. Russell: "Jon Rose: the Relative Violin," *Ear*, xiv/4 (1989), 24
B. Rusch: "The Questionnaire," *Cadence*, xvii/2 (1991), 67
R. T. Dean: *New Structures in Jazz and Improvised Music since 1960* (Buckingham, England, and Bristol, PA, 1992)
J. Corbett: "The Violable Tradition," *Coda*, no.249 (1993), 27
N. Saintilian, A. Schultz, and P. Stanhope: *Biographical Directory of Australian Composers* (Sydney, 1996)
H. Smith and R. T. Dean: *Improvisation, Hypermedia and the Arts since 1945* (London, 1997)

ANDREW HARRISON

Rose, Wally [Walter L.] (*b* Oakland, CA, 2 Oct 1913; *d* Walnut Creek, CA, 12 Jan 1997). Pianist. He grew up in Honolulu and San Francisco, then while in his teens returned with his family to Oakland. After graduating from high school there he worked in dance bands in the San Francisco Bay area and played on cruise ships which traveled from the West Coast to Hawaii and the orient. In 1939 he met Lu Watters and participated in the jam sessions organized by Watters at the Big Bear tavern, located in the hills behind Berkeley and Oakland. By late 1941 he had joined the Yerba Buena Jazz Band (*see* WATTERS, LU). He introduced a ragtime piano solo to the band's dance sets, and in its first recording session (19 December 1941) played, with an accompaniment of banjo, double bass, and drums, *Black and White Rag*, which became very popular in radio broadcasts. Rose's three years of service in the navy corresponded with that of Watters, but the group re-formed after their discharge. With the breakup of the Yerba Buena Jazz Band (1950) Rose joined Bob Scobey (1951) and then worked with Turk Murphy's band (until late 1954). Thereafter he performed as a solo pianist at clubs throughout the San Francisco Bay area, including the Shadow Box, the Gold Street, the Palace Hotel, the Sheraton Hotel, the Cirque Room of the Fairmont Hotel, the Tin Angel, Pier 23, L'Etoile, and Masons. During the 1950s and 1960s he appeared regularly on local television and radio shows, and he gave classical recitals, calmly moving between concert hall and saloon. He also taught classical and ragtime piano; among his students were the classical pianist Roxanna Chew Lee and Peter Clute, who played with Turk Murphy for 30 years. Later in his career Rose was a frequent performer at the Sacramento Dixieland Jubilee, and he toured internationally, appearing at jazz and ragtime festivals in Japan, Australia, Europe, and North America.

With the Yerba Buena Jazz Band, Rose was directly responsible for instigating the revival of instrumental ragtime and many early jazz pieces. His playing was characterized by a percussive touch, a loping rhythmic style, and a steady though never monotonous pulse. In his rags he generally gave a rather literal reading of the music, but often added variety by doubling certain notes at the octave.

SELECTED RECORDINGS

As unaccompanied soloist: *Ragtime Piano Masterpieces* (1953, Col. CL6260); *Wally Rose on Piano* (1970, Blackbird 12007)
As leader: *Wally Rose and the Yerba Buena Jazz Band Live from the Dawn Club* (1946, Fairmont 102)
As sideman with L. Watters: Maple Leaf Rag/Black and White Rag (1941, Jazz Man 1)

BIBLIOGRAPHY

FeatherE
T. Waldo: *This is Ragtime* (New York, 1976)
P. Martin: "Wally Rose & the West Coast Revival," *MR*, viii/1 (1980), 1 [incl. discography]
R. Stein: "Wally Rose: the Friendliest Piano Player in Town," *San Francisco Chronicle* (19 March 1980), 34
J. Goggin: *Turk Murphy: Just for the Record* (San Leandro, CA, 1982) [incl. discography]
D. Reffkin: "The Ragtime Machine," *MR*, xviii/6 (1991), 26
Obituaries: P. Elwood, *San Francisco Examiner* (17 Jan 1997); *Los Angeles Times* (18 Jan 1997); F. Levin, *JJI*, l/3 (1997), 19

JOHN EDWARD HASSE/BK

Roseland Ballroom. Name used by venues in several American cities, most notably New York; *see* NIGHTCLUBS AND OTHER VENUES.

Roseman, Josh(ua Aaron) [Mr. Bone] (*b* Boston, 27 May 1967). Trombonist. He attended the Berklee College of Music (1985) and the New England Conservatory (1985–8), during the which period he worked in the Either/Orchestra (*c*1985–6). From 1988 he played with Oliver Lake, and around 1989 he moved to New York. In the early 1990s he toured and recorded with John Gordon's Trombones Unlimited (1991–3, recording in 1991), Muhal Richard Abrams's ensembles (1991–2), and Don Byron's klezmer ensemble the Music of Mickey Katz (recording in 1992); with Byron he appeared at the International New Jazz Festival Moers in 1991. He was a member from 1992 to 1994 of Illinois Jacquet's big band and from 1993 to 1995 of the Ska-ta-lites; in 1993 he joined the jazz-funk ensemble Groove Collective and was a founding member of Ned Rothenberg's group Power Lines. From 1994 he collaborated with Lester Bowie, and in 1995 he joined Dave Douglas's sextet, Joey Baron's Barondown, and Steve Coleman. He also played with David Murray (1995–6), Uri Caine and Ben Monder (both from 1996), the sextet Honor System, led by the saxophonist Rob Reddy (late 1990s), and Peter Apfelbaum's sextet (from *c*1998). Roseman first appeared as a leader in 1995, when he performed alongside Chris Speed, Brad Jones, and Kurt Rosenwinkel, among others, in the group Xenophelia. In 1998 he formed the Exodus Ska-Jazz Ensemble, which included Apfelbaum and Kenny Wolleson, and the group Cherry, with such sidemen as Bowie, John Medeski, David Fiuczynski, Bob Stewart, and Baron. The following year he established the Josh Roseman Unit, with Apfelbaum, Fiuczynski, Jones, and Pheeroan akLaff among its members.

SELECTED RECORDINGS

As sideman: Either/Orchestra: *Dial "E"* (1986, Accurate 2222); J. Gordon: *Live in Concert* (1991, Mons 1890); B. Ware: *Long and Skinny* (*c*1993, Knitting Factory Works 131); D. Douglas: *In our Lifetime* (1994, New World/Countercurrents 80471-2); N. Rothenberg: *Power Lines* (1995, New World 80476-2)

GK

Rosenberg, Stochelo [Izaäk] (*b* Helmond, Netherlands, 19 Feb 1968). Dutch guitarist. He grew up a member of the Sinti gypsy community in the Netherlands and began to play guitar around the age of ten, inspired principally by the recordings of Django Reinhardt. Around 1980 he performed in Manouche as a member of a band led by the clarinetist Hans Meelen, but, owing to the constraints of the Pinkstergemeente religion, for the rest of the decade his appearances were confined mainly to churches and gypsy camps around Europe. In 1989 Meelen succeeded in taking Stochelo and one of his cousins, the guitarist Nous'che Rosenberg, to the gypsy jazz festival in Samois in France. As a result of their successful performances Jon Larsen of the Norwegian label Hot Club arranged to record Stochelo, Nous'che, and Nous'che's brother, the double bass player Nonnie Rosenberg, and they became known as the Rosenberg Trio. Following the group's discovery and its début recording, *Seresta*, it performed around the world throughout the 1990s; in 1993 it appeared with Stephane Grappelli at his 85th birthday concert at Carnegie Hall. It also played with Manhattan Transfer (recording *c*1997) and the Dutch Swing College Band. The trio has been featured in numerous television documentaries, notably "The Django Legacy" (1990) and "The Rosenberg Trio" (1997).

SELECTED RECORDINGS

As leader of Rosenberg Trio: *Seresta* (1989, Hot Club 59); *Gipsy Summer* (1991, Verve 531144-2); *Caravan* (1994, Verve 523030-2); *Noches calientes* (1998, Verve 557022-2)
As sideman with S. Grappelli: *85 and Still Swinging* (1993, Angel 54918)

BIBLIOGRAPHY

M. J. Summerfield: *The Jazz Guitar: its Evolution, Players and Personalities since 1900* (Blaydon on Tyne, England, 4/1998)

MARK GILBERT

Rosengarden, Bob [Bobby, Robert Marshall] (*b* Elgin, IL, 23 April 1924). Drummer and percussionist. His mother played piano for silent films, and he recalled that from a very young age he accompanied her when she was practicing, drumming with spoons. He was given a drum set as a child and began to play seriously at the age of 12. After taking up a music scholarship at the University of Michigan he performed with army and air force bands during his military service (1944–5). His first important association was with the trumpeter Henry Busse (1945–6), after which he played in New York with the tenor saxophonist Alvy West (1946–8). Thereafter he worked as a studio musician: he played a drum solo in the film *C-Man* (1949) and recorded as a percussionist with, among others, Duke Ellington (1959), Miles Davis and the orchestra led by Gil Evans (1961), and Benny Goodman's band conducted by the composer Igor Stravinsky (1965); his association with Goodman continued intermittently into the 1980s. He played in ensembles at the NBC television studios (1949–68, including a period in the band on "The Tonight Show") before leading a band at ABC for Dick Cavett's show (1969–74), when Joe Wilder, Ernie Royal, Bill Watrous, Jerome Richardson, the clarinetist Walt Levinsky, Eddie Daniels, Bucky Pizzarelli, Sir Roland Hanna, Derek Smith, George Duvivier, and Milt Hinton were among his sidemen.

Rosengarden achieved wider attention as a member of the World's Greatest Jazz Band (1974–8). His playing proved ideal for such groups as Soprano Summit (1975–8) and the Blue Three (with Kenny Davern and Dick Wellstood, 1981–3), and his versatility made him much in demand for performances with the New York Jazz Repertory Company, with which he toured to the USSR (1975) and recorded under Dick Hyman's leadership in celebrations of the music of Louis Armstrong (1974) and James P. Johnson (1975). In 1975 he recorded in a group co-led by Joe Venuti and Zoot Sims, and he played in Gerry Mulligan's sextet, with which he recorded in New York and toured Europe late in 1976. A spirited and insistent drummer, Rosengarden continued to maintain a rigorous schedule, performing at festivals and leading a band for fourteen years at the Rainbow Room, New York, where his sidemen at times included the British musicians Roy Williams, Danny Moss, and Len Skeat. He was a member of a cooperative group known as the Trio with, successively, Hank Jones and Hinton, then Smith and Duvivier (both ensembles recording in 1977), and finally Smith and Hinton (touring Europe in 1990 and recording in 1989, in 1990 as accompanists to Phil Bodner, and again as a trio in 1994). He also recorded with Pee Wee Erwin (1980), with Hinton in a trio led by Eddie Higgins (1986), and in a reformed version of Soprano Summit (also known as Soprano Reunion or Summit Reunion) (1990, 1992, 1995).

Video oral history material in *NCH* (HCJA).

SELECTED RECORDINGS

As leader: with M. Hinton and H. Jones: *The Trio* (1977, Chi. 188); with D. Smith and Hinton: *The Trio 1994* (1994, Chi. 322)

As sideman: B. Wilber and K. Davern: *Soprano Summit* (1973, World Jazz 5); D. Hyman: *Satchmo Remembered* (1974, Atl. 1671); World's Greatest Jazz Band: *The World's Greatest Jazz Band of Yank Lawson and Bob Haggart on Tour* (1975, World Jazz 8); D. Smith: *Love for Sale* (1977, Prog. 7002); K. Davern and F. Phillips: *John and Joe* (1977, Chi. 199); Blue Three: *At Hanratty's* (1981, Chaz Jazz 109); E. Higgins: *By Request* (1986, Statiras 8079); Soprano Reunion: *Yellow Dog Blues* (1995, Chi. 339)

BIBLIOGRAPHY

Feather–Gitler '70s
S. Traill: "Drums Double Bill," *JJI*, xxxi/4 (1978), 26
R. D. Johnson: "It's Fun, not Work!," *MR*, vii/3 (1980), 10
J. Buerger: "Show and Studio: Bobby Rosengarden," *MD*, v/8 (1981), 92
E. Cook: "Bobby Rosengarden," *JJI*, xliv/11 (1991), 10
H. Schade: "Was du nicht spielst, ist wichtig!" *JP*, xlv/7–8 (1996), 28

BRIAN PEERLESS

Rosengren, Bernt (Åke) (*b* Stockholm, 24 Dec 1937). Swedish tenor saxophonist, flutist, arranger, composer, and bandleader. He came to prominence in the 1950s through his performances in the Swedish hard-bop group Jazz Club '57, his membership in Marshall Brown's International Youth Band (1958), and his work in Poland (where he played with Krzysztof Komeda, 1961, and performed as a soloist on the soundtrack to Roman Polanski's film *Knife in the Water*, 1962) and in other European countries. During the following years he worked with George Russell (performing in 1965–7, recording in 1967 and 1977), Radiojazzgruppen (i) in Copenhagen (1967–8), Palle Mikkelborg (at the Montreux International Jazz Festival, 1969), Don Cherry (recording in 1968 and 1973), Lars Gullin (recording in 1969–70), and Rolf Ericson (recording in 1971). From 1959 he recorded as the leader of small groups and occasionally of a big band, in which Torbjörn Hultcrantz was among his longstanding sidemen; in 1960 he made an album as co-leader of a quartet with Lasse Werner. Rosengren toured and recorded in 1972–3 as the featured soloist in Maffy Falay's group Sevda. With Gullin he made further recordings from 1973 to 1976 and toured East Germany in 1975.

Rosengren recorded as a member of Doug Raney's bop groups from 1978 into the 1980s and with the Swedish all-star quintet Summit Meeting from 1984 into the 1990s. He rejoined Falay in various small groups which the trumpeter led from 1986 through the 1990s, and during the latter decade he appeared regularly in Falay's quintet at the Lilla Maria Restaurant in Stockholm. In the early 1990s he played in the double bass player Sture Nordin's group Summit Meeting, a quintet featuring two tenor saxophonists. In the mid-1990s he established an octet to perform and record his own instrumental arrangements of songs by George Gershwin (from *Porgy and Bess*), Kurt Weill, and the Swedish poet Evert Taube; his compositions and arrangements are straightforward, yet lucid and inventive. Later he worked in Tomasz Stańko's septet (1997) and won wide acclaim for the recordings he made (in 1999) as co-leader of a quintet with Arne Domnérus. Rosengren, who has a true command of the vocabulary of bop and associated styles, is among the finest Swedish saxophonists.

SELECTED RECORDINGS

As leader: *The Beat Generation* (1959, Sonet 2527); *Stockholm Dues* (1965, Col. SSX1013); *Improvisations* (1969, S.J.R. 1); *Notes from the Underground* (1973, Harvester E154-34958-9); *Live in Stockholm* (1974–5, Amigo 815, 818); *Big Band* (1979, Caprice 1214); *Porgy and Bess* (1996, Arietta 11); with A. Domnérus: *Face to Face* (1999, Dra. 344)

As sideman: Nannie Porres: *I Thought about You* (1971, Odeon E062-34336); D. Raney: *Meeting the Tenors* (1986, Criss Cross 1006); Summit Meeting: *Full of Life* (1991, Dra. 205); T. Stańko: *Litania* (1997, ECM 1636)

BIBLIOGRAPHY

FeatherE
B. Sundin: "Unga jazzmusiker," *Orkester journalen*, xxviii/9 (1960), 10
K. Knox: "Bernt Rosengren: en ovanlig musiker" [Bernt Rosengren: an unusual musician], *Musiktidningen*, ii/1 (1974), 25
R. Cotterell: "Bernt Rosengren," *JF* [intl edn], no.43 (1976), 24 [incl. discography]
A. von Konow: "Bernt!," *Orkester journalen*, liii/2 (1985), 9
K. Knox: "Bernt Rosengren: 'I hate amateurism'," *JF* [intl edn], no.106 (1987), 36
<http://www.mic.stim.se/engelsk/11/facts/rosengren.html> (2000)
J. Östberg: "Bernt Rosengren," *Orkester journalen*, lxviii/2–3 (2000), 4

ERIK KJELLBERG/LARS WESTIN, BK

Rosenthal, Ted [Theodore Marcus] (*b* Great Neck, NY, 15 Nov 1959). Pianist and leader. At the age of six he briefly took piano lessons. After playing electric guitar, and trumpet in his school band, he resumed piano lessons when he was 12, applying himself to both classical music and jazz; during the same period he studied briefly with Jaki Byard and Lennie Tristano. Having completed undergraduate and graduate work in piano performance at the Manhattan School of Music (BM 1981, MM 1983) he worked as a freelance in New York. In 1988 he won the second annual Thelonious Monk International Piano Competition. In 1992 he joined Gerry Mulligan's quartet, touring internationally and recording until the saxophonist's death in 1996; later he founded the Gerry Mulligan All Star Tribute Band, of which he serves as leader and music director. Rosenthal has also worked with Jon Faddis (intermittently from 1992), Art Farmer (1993 and regularly from 1997), and Greg Cohen (from 1995), performed with the Lincoln Center Jazz Orchestra (1996) and the Carnegie Hall Jazz Band (1997), and performed briefly with Benny Golson, James Moody, Phil Woods, and others. For seven years, with Joe Roccisano and Jay Leonhart, he was a member of the Sunday brunch band at the Blue Note in New York. His activities as a leader usually involve a trio; among his sidemen have been the bass players Michael Formanek and Scott Colley and the drummers Billy Drummond and Marvin "Smitty" Smith. From 1990 Rosenthal has taught in the jazz programs at the Mannes College of Music and the New School for Social Research in New York (from 1996 at the Mannes/New School; from autumn 1999 at the New School University). He is a contributing editor to and writer for *Piano and Keyboard* magazine, has published arrangements and articles in *Piano Today* and the *Piano Stylist*, and has composed a number of large-scale orchestral works.

SELECTED RECORDINGS

As unaccompanied soloist: *Ted Rosenthal at Maybeck: Maybeck Recital Hall Series*, xxxviii (1994, Conc. 4648)

As leader: *New Tunes, New Traditions* (1989, Ken 003); *Images of Monk* (1992, Jazz Alliance 10023); *Rosenthology* (1994, Conc. 4702); with B. Charlap, Dean Johnson, and R. Vincent: *Gerry Mulligan Songbook* (1996, Chi. 349)

As sideman: G. Mulligan: *Dream a Little Dream* (1994, Telarc 83364); R. Sandke: *The Chase* (1994, Conc. 4642); G. Mulligan: *Dragonfly* (1995, Telarc 83377); G. Cohen: *Way Low* (1996, DIW 918)

BIBLIOGRAPHY

<http://www.onpointpub.com/rosenthal/bio.html (1998)>

GK

Rosenwinkel, Kurt (Peter) (*b* Philadelphia, 28 Oct 1970). Electric guitarist. He played piano from the age of eight, took up guitar when he was 12, and discovered jazz on the radio in his mid-teens. During his final years at high school he learned from the alto saxophonist Tony Williams, the drummer Al Jackson, the pianist Eddie Greene, and Tyrone Brown at jam sessions at the Blue Note in Cheltenham, Philadelphia. In Boston he was a founding member of the group Human Feel in 1987 and attended the Berklee College of Music from autumn 1988 to January 1991. In the 1990s Rosenwinkel played in Paul Motian's Electric Bebop Band (from 1990) and Bruce Gertz's trio (1990–91), and with Gary Burton (1990–92), Seamus Blake (1993–4), Larry Goldings (1996), and Joe Henderson (1997). Among his own small groups were a quartet that included Mark Turner (from 1993), a quintet with Turner and the keyboard player Scott Kinsey (from 1996), and the ensembles Intuit and This (both formed in 1998).

SELECTED RECORDINGS

As leader: *East Coast Love Affair* (1996, Fresh Sound 016); *Intuit* (1998, Criss Cross 1160)

As sideman: P. Motian: *Paul Motian and the Electric Bebop Band* (1992, JMT 514002); S. Blake: *The Call* (1993, Criss Cross 1088); P. Motian: *Reincarnation of a Love Bird* (1994, JMT 514016); M. Turner: *Yam yam* (1994, Criss Cross 1094); L. Goldings: on *Big Stuff* (1996, WB 46271-2), Ida Lupino, Purple Gazelle, Where we've been; Jochen Rueckert: *Introduction* (1997, Jazzline 11152-2); M. Turner: on *In this World* (1998, WB 47074-2), Bo Brussels, In this World, She said she said; C. Potter: *Vertigo* (1998, Conc. 4843)

For further recordings *see* HUMAN FEEL.

MARK GILBERT

Rosetta. Record company and label established in New York in 1980 by Rosetta Reitz, principally to increase an awareness of early female jazz and blues singers. Its series "Independent Women's Blues" consisted of anthologies organized in a conceptual manner (for example, Rosetta 1301, *Women's Railroad Blues, 1924–4*); a separate series, "Foremothers," comprised reissues by specific artists and groups, including Ida Cox, Valaida Snow, Georgia White, Lil Green, Ethel Waters, Sister Rosetta Tharpe, Mae West, Dinah Washington, Dorothy Donegan, and the group International Sweethearts of Rhythm. By the early 1990s Rosetta had issued nearly 20 LPs and had begun to release its back catalogue on compact disc. Thereafter these were available only through direct mail order from Reitz.

BIBLIOGRAPHY

J. S. Wilson: "Blues is a Woman Tonight Explores Other Side of the Blues," *New York Times* (2 July 1980)

L. Dahl: *Stormy Weather: the Music and Lives of a Century of Jazzwomen* (London, Melbourne, Australia, and New York, 1984), 188

A. Duncan: "Female Blues Singers who Weren't So Blue," *Christian Science Monitor* (27 March 1984)

D. Langille: "Blues," *Coda*, no.201 (1985), 24

D. Snowden: "Rosetta Tracks the Women of the Blues," *Los Angeles Times* (20 July 1986)

S. Yanow: "Rosetta Records: Women in Jazz," *Coda*, no.212 (1987), 10

K. Franckling: "Hearsay: Rosetta Records: by Women Only," *JT*, xix/6 (1991), 9

D. Sutro: "Jazz: Ladies Sings the Blues," *Los Angeles Times* (12 April 1992)

GK

Rosewoman, Michele (*b* Oakland, CA, 29 March 1953). Pianist, singer, composer, and leader. She took up piano at the age of six and was exposed to jazz in her parents' record shop during her youth, although at the time she preferred to listen to Motown pop songs. She played locally in the Laney Junior College big band and had lessons with the pianist Ed Kelley; she also studied singing, percussion, Cuban music, and the traditional music of the Shona in Zimbabwe and the Yoruba in Nigeria. In 1978 she moved to New York, where she worked with various Latin dance bands, including that of the Cuban *batá* drummer Orlando "Puntilla" Rios, with whom she has continued to collaborate as both a leader and a sideman. She performed with Oliver Lake at Carnegie Hall and joined Billy Bang's quintet (recording in 1981), and later worked with Greg Osby, Baikida Carroll, Julius Hemphill, and Julian Priester. Rosewoman has led a number of her own groups, among them the quintet Quintessence (from 1986), in which she has played alongside the saxophonists Osby and Steve Coleman, Osby and Gary Thomas, and Steve Wilson and Thomas (from 1988); in addition she performed in a trio with Kenny Davis and Gene Jackson at the Festival International de Jazz de Montréal in 1994, and around 1997 she formed a cooperative quartet, FourSight, with Robin Eubanks, Rufus Reid, and Billy Hart.

Rosewoman has been awarded a number of grants for her work. In 1983 she received funding from the NEA and formed a 14-piece ensemble, New Yor-Uba, to play her music. The group, which involved *batá* drummers, conga players, female singers, and dancers, gave the first performance of her piece *New Yor-Uba: a Musical Celebration of Cuba in America* at the Astor Place Theater later that year under the direction of Butch Morris; among its members were Lake, Carroll, Reid, Bob Stewart, Howard Johnson (ii), Pheeroan akLaff, and Rios; Rosewoman led a revised version of New Yor-Uba at Sweet Basil in March 1998. In 1984 she received a Meet the Composer grant to compose for the Brooklyn Philharmonic Orchestra. She has taught at various institutions, notably New York University and the New School for Social Research, and from 1975 she has worked as a piano tuner in recording studios and concert halls. Rosewoman is a skillful pianist and composer in modern jazz and Latin styles and an accomplished scat singer, although her efforts at singing pop music have been less successful.

SELECTED RECORDINGS

As leader: *The Source* (1983, SN 1072); *Quintessence* (1987, Enja 5039); *Contrast High* (1988, Enja 5091); *Occasion to Rise* (1990, Evidence 22042); *Harvest* (1992, Enja 7069-2); *Spirit* (1994, BN 36777-2)

As sideman: B. Bang: *Rainbow Gladiator* (1981, SN 1016); G. Osby: *Greg Osby and Sound Theatre* (1987, JMT 834411)

BIBLIOGRAPHY

CarrJ; *GrayF*

J. Levenson: "Caught: Michele Rosewoman," *DB*, li/4 (1984), 61

G. Endress: "Michele Rosewoman: New Yor-uba," *JP*, xxxiv/7 (1985), 7

S. Stein: "Riffs: Michele Rosewoman," *DB*, lvi/9 (1989), 15

J. Blum: "Michele Rosewoman: Cross-cultural Consciousness," *JT* (1990), Oct, 7

F. Davis: *Outcats: Jazz Composers, Instrumentalists, and Singers* (New York, and Oxford, England, 1990), 122

L. Gourse: *Madame Jazz: Contemporary Women Instrumentalists* (New York, and Oxford, England, 1995), 156

G. Robinson: "Hearsay: Michele Rosewoman," *JT*, xxvi/10 (1996), 23

L. Gourse: "Michele Rosewoman: Getting her Due," *Keyboard*, xxiii/4 (1997), 17

<http://www.enjarecords.com/MICHELE_ROSEWOMAN.htm> (1998)

<http://www.jazzcorner.com/rosewoman/index.html> (1998)

GK

Rosner, Ady [Jack; Rozner, Adolf] (*b* Berlin, 26 May 1910; *d* Berlin, 8 Aug 1976). German trumpeter, bandleader, and violinist. After studying music at the Berlin Hochschule für Musik, he turned to jazz and dance music in 1928. He played with Willi Rosé-Petösy (1929) and performed and recorded with the Weintraub Syncopators (1930–33), then left Germany for the Netherlands (1933) and toured Belgium (1934–

5) before settling in Poland and leading his own band in Kraków (1935–6). While on tour in Europe (1938–9) he made a number of recordings in Paris (including *Midnight in Harlem*, 1938, Col. DF2404, which is a good example of his trumpet playing). On the invasion of Poland in 1939 he fled to the USSR, where he entertained troops, toured, and made recordings (notably *St. Louis Blues*, 1944, SSSR 12215). Rosner spent nine years in a labor camp (1946–55). Following his release he formed a symphony orchestra, which he continued to lead until his return to Berlin in 1973. (H. J. P. Bergmeier: *The Weintraub Story Incorporating the Ady Rosner Story* (Menden, Germany, 1982) [incl. discography])

RAINER E. LOTZ

Rosnes, Renee [Irene Louise] (*b* Regina, Canada, 24 March 1962). Canadian pianist. She grew up in Vancouver and studied classical piano there and at the University of Toronto (1980–82) before turning to jazz. After working with Oliver Gannon and others in Vancouver she moved in 1985 to New York, where she came to notice with Joe Henderson (from 1987) and OTB (1987–9). In 1988 she toured (playing electronic keyboards) with Wayne Shorter and began an extended association with J. J. Johnson that continued into the late 1990s. She has performed most often and effectively in hard-bop and post-bop settings, to which she brings her own lyricism, aversion to cliché, and sweeping sense of momentum. She was a member in the mid-1990s of two cooperative groups: Native Colours, consisting of her husband, Billy Drummond (they married in 1990), Larry Grenadier, and Ralph Moore (Chris Potter replaced Moore from 1995–6); and the all-star Canadian quintet Free Trade (with Ralph Bowen, Peter Leitch, Neil Swainson, and Terry Clarke), with which she toured and recorded in 1994. Rosnes also worked with Jon Faddis (1989–91), the Carnegie Hall and Lincoln Center jazz orchestras, James Moody (1994), and others. Her own bands have toured in the USA, Canada, Europe, and Japan. She may be seen in the video *Carnegie Hall Salutes the Jazz Masters* (1994).

SELECTED RECORDINGS

Duo with H. Alden: on Alden: *Take your Pick* (1996, Conc. 4743), You're my Thrill

As leader: *Renee Rosnes* (1988–9, Somethin' Else 511); *For the Moment* (1990, BN B21S-94859); *Without Words* (1992, BN B21Z-98168); *Ancestors* (1995, BN 34634-2); *As We Are Now* (1997, BN 56810-2)

As sideman: G. Thomas: *Seventh Quadrant* (1987, Enja 5047); OTB: *Spiral Staircase* (1989, BN B21S-93006); J. Faddis: *Into the Faddisphere* (1989, Epic EK45266); J. J. Johnson: *Let's Hang Out* (1992, Verve 314-514454-2); V. Herring: *Secret Love* (1992, Musicmasters 65092); Free Trade: *Free Trade* (1994, Justin Time 64); Native Colours: *One World* (1994, Conc. 4646); N.-H. Ørsted Pedersen: *Friends Forever* (1995, Mlst. 9269); J. J. Johnson: *Heroes* (1996, Verve 314-528864-2)

BIBLIOGRAPHY

EMC2
P. Carles: "3 femmes dans Manhattan," *Jm*, no.356 (1986), 32
L. Gourse: "Renee Rosnes: the Arrival," *JT* (1990), Aug, 14
G. Sutherland: "For the Love of it All," *Jazz Report*, iv/3 (1990), 14
G. Lees and J. Reeves: *Jazz Lives: 100 Portraits in Jazz* (Toronto, 1992), 190
L. Gourse: "Coda: Talk about Lineage," *Jazziz*, xii/8 (1996), 95
——: "World View: Renee Rosnes: JazzPiano, Past and Present," *Keyboard*, xxii/8 (1996), 17
H. Hill: "Renee Rosnes," *Performing Arts & Entertainment in Canada*, xxx/3 (1996), 9

MARK MILLER

Rosolino, Frank [the Lemon Drop Kid] (*b* Detroit, 20 Aug 1926; *d* Los Angeles, 26 Nov 1978). Trombonist. Born into a musical family, he began playing guitar when he was ten and as a teenager took up trombone, on which, by his own account, he gained his extraordinary facility by trying to imitate his elder brother's violin playing. At the age of 18 he began military service and performed with army bands in the USA and the Philippines. Following his discharge he played in the big bands of the tenor saxophonist Bob Chester (1946–7), Glen Gray (for six months in 1947), Gene Krupa (1948–9), Tony Pastor (late 1949), Herbie Fields (1950), and Georgie Auld (1951); in the course of making a film short, *Deep Purple*, while with Krupa, he acquired the nickname the Lemon Drop Kid for his zany scat singing on the tune *Lemon Drop*. Thereafter he led his own group in Detroit (1952) before working with Stan Kenton (June 1952 – May 1955). Most of his later career was spent in California. He recorded with Howard Rumsey's Lighthouse All Stars in December 1954 and was then a member of the group from May 1955 to 1960. He played with Terry Gibbs's big band from 1959 to 1962 and with Donn Trenner's band on Steve Allen's television program from summer 1962 to autumn 1964, and was active as a studio musician in Hollywood. In 1973–5 he worked at intervals in Europe with Conte Candoli, and in 1974 he toured the USA with Benny Carter. He also worked with Supersax and performed in Japan with Quincy Jones, who frequently employed him for recording sessions and film soundtracks. His demise was gruesome: hopelessly distraught over a failed family life, he shot his children, killing one and blinding the other, and then committed suicide.

As a singer Rosolino specialized in comic material, but it is as one of the most technically adroit trombonists of the bop era that he will be remembered. His large tone and staccato attack marked him as a true individual, but he was also an excellent section player.

Oral history material in *NjR*.

SELECTED RECORDINGS

As leader: Frank Rosolino Quartet (1952, Dee Gee 4012) [EP]; *Stan Kenton Presents: Frank Rosolino Sextet* (1954, Cap. T6507); *I Play Trombone* (1956, Beth. 26); *Free for All* (1958, Specialty 2161); *Turn me Loose!* (1961, Rep. 96016); *Jazz a confronto*, iv (1973, Horo 4); with C. Candoli: *Conversation* (1973, RCA APL1-1509); *Thinking about You* (1976, Sack. 2014)

As sideman: G. Auld: *Georgie Auld Quintet* (1951, Roost 403); S. Kenton: on *New Concepts of Artistry in Rhythm* (1952, Cap. H383), Frank Speaking, Twenty-three Degrees North, Eighty-two Degrees West; S. Levey: *This Time the Drum's on Me* (1955, Beth. 37); H. Rumsey: *Music for Lighthousekeeping* (1956, Cont. 3528); S. Levey: *Grand Stan* (1956, Beth. 71); B. Cooper: *Coop!: The Music of Bob Cooper* (1957, Cont. 3544); G. Auld: *Georgie Auld Plays the Winners* (1963, Phi. 600096); S. Stitt: *I Remember Bird* (1976, Cat. 7616); D. Menza: *First Flight* (1976, Cat. 7617)

SELECTED FILMS AND VIDEOS

Deep Purple [Gene Krupa and his Orchestra] (1949); Schlagerparade (1953); Jazz Scene USA: Frank Rosolino Quartet (1962); The Great Rocky Mountain Jazz Party (1977)

BIBLIOGRAPHY

J. Burns: "Bopping Bones," *J&B*, ii/7 (1972), 16
L. Tomkins: "Frank Rosolino," *CI*, xii/1 (1973), 6; contd as "Frank Rosolino: Life in Hollywood," xii/2 (1973), 24; contd as "Frank Rosolino: my Approach to Playing," xii/7 (1974), 14
L. Underwood: "Frank Rosolino: Conversation with the Master," *DB*, xliv/19 (1977), 18 [incl. discography]
Obituary, M. Hennessey, *JJI*, xxxii/2 (1979), 22
W. F. Lee: *Stan Kenton: Artistry in Rhythm* (Los Angeles, 1980/*R*1994) [incl. discography; *R* without discography]
A. Young: *Bodies and Souls: Musical Memoirs* (Berkeley, CA, 1981), 25
A. Astrup: "Frank Rosolino," *Coda*, no.187 (1982), 9; repr. in *JJI*, xlvii/8 (1994), 9
G. Lees: *Meet Me at Jim & Andy's: Jazz Musicians and their World* (New York, and Oxford, England, 1988), 111
R. L. Machado: *Basic Discography of Frank Rosolino* (n.p. [Brazil], *c*1988; rev. and enlarged 2/*c*1996)

T. Gioia: *West Coast Jazz: Modern Jazz in California, 1945–1960* (New York, and Oxford, England, 1992)
B. Rusch: "Frank Strazzeri: Interview," *Cadence*, xxi/9 (1995), 5

MARK GARDNER/BK

Ross, Annie [Lynch [née Short], Annabelle] (*b* Mitcham, England, 25 July 1930). English singer. She was taken to Los Angeles in 1933 by her aunt Ella Logan, a band and cabaret singer. She had early success there as a child film actress, then traveled to Europe in 1947 and sang in cabarets and with bands. While in Paris she had an affair with Kenny Clarke (then separated from his wife, Carmen McRae), and after the birth of their son in December 1950 she continued to work with Clarke before returning to the USA, where she created a sensation with her vocalese on *Twisted* and *Farmer's Market* (both 1952) and *Jackie* (1953). The highlight of another visit to Europe was her enormous success in the revue *Cranks*, in which she also performed in New York in 1956. She then joined Dave Lambert and Jon Hendricks to record the multitracked *Sing a Song of Basie*, in which the trio sang all the section parts and instrumental solos with only a rhythm section for support. They then began working as the trio Lambert, Hendricks, and Ross. Its successful but strenuous tours and recordings proved too much for Ross, however, and she retreated to England in 1962 to recuperate. She continued to record as a soloist and also ran her own club, Annie's Room (October 1964 to autumn 1965). During the 1960s she appeared in three episodes of the film series *Jazz USA* (1960) and in *Appunti per un film sul jazz* (1965). She began to record theme songs and dub dialogue for films, and by the 1970s was appearing on stage (in, among other things, her own show, *An Evening with Annie Ross*, 1976) and television. She also took acting roles in the films *Yanks* (1979) and *Superman III* (1983). In 1985 she returned to the USA, where she again worked as a singer. She continued to undertake roles in films (New York) and theater (London) into the 1990s, most notably as the singer Tess Trainer in the film *Short Cuts* (1993); she held residencies singing in London in 1995–6, and was reunited with Hendricks for a performance in Cambridge, Massachusetts, in January 1999.

Ross is considered one of the finest British jazz singers. She has a superb technique and is adept at performing in many styles, from ballads, such as *Skylark*, to cabaret songs and sophisticated vocalese. Although initially her range was wide, by the early 1960s her voice had deepened to a warm contralto.

See also LAMBERT, HENDRICKS, AND ROSS.

SELECTED RECORDINGS

As leader: Twisted (1952, Prst. 794); Farmer's Market (1952, Prst. 839); Jackie (1953, Met. 647); *Cranks* (1956, HMV 1082); *Annie by Candlelight* (1956, Pye 0316), incl. Skylark; *Sing a Song with Mulligan* (1958, WP 1253); *A Gasser* (1959, WP 1285); *Loguerhythms* (1962, Transatlantic 107); with P. Poindexter: *Annie Ross & Pony Poindexter* (1966, Saba 15082); with C. Laine and J. Dankworth: *Façade* (1967, Fon. 5449); with G. Fame: *In Hoagland '81* (1981, Baldeagle 181)
As sideman with C. Basie: *Sing along with Basie* (1958, Roul. 52018)

BIBLIOGRAPHY

ChiltonB
M. Jones: "Annie Ross: a Clear Case of Talent," *MM*, xxxi (21 April 1956), 13
L. Keating: "The Dave Lambert Singers," *JJ*, xv/4 (1962), 2
R. Cooper: "The Art of Annie Ross," *JJI*, xxxii/7 (1979), 9
R. Cooper and D. Tarrant: "Annie Ross Discography," *Journal of Jazz Discography* (1979), no.4; p.9; no.5, p.1
L. Gourse: *Louis' Children: American Jazz Singers* (New York, 1984), 283
M. Hennessey: *Klook: the Story of Kenny Clarke* (London, 1990)
J. Gavin: "A Free-spirited Survivor Lands on her Feet," *New York Times* (3 Oct 1993)
D. Heckman: "Annie Ross Takes a 'Short Cut' Back to High Visibility," *Los Angeles Times* (23 Oct 1993)
M. McCooey: "All About Annie," *Jazz on CD*, i/2 (1993), 28
For further recordings, films, and bibliography *see* LAMBERT, HENDRICKS, AND ROSS.

REG COOPER/BK

Ross, Arnold (*b* Boston, 29 Jan 1921; *d* Culver City, CA, 5 June 2000). Pianist. He first played violin, clarinet, and trumpet, and began learning piano at the age of 12. After working on a cruise ship that visited the West Indies and South America (1937–8) he moved to New York (1938), where he performed and recorded with Jack Jenney (1939). In the early 1940s he served as a sideman with the bandleader and singer Vaughn Monroe (1940–42) and in Glenn Miller's army band (1943–4). He recorded as a member of Harry James's band (1944–7) and with Harry Edison and Charlie Ventura (both 1945), Jazz at the Philharmonic (1946), and Charlie Parker (1947). Ross then went to California and worked as a freelance, and in 1947–8 he accompanied the popular singer Lena Horne. In the early 1950s he recorded with several leaders, among them Dizzy Gillespie, toured Europe with Horne (1952), performed, conducted, and wrote arrangements for Bob Crosby's television show (1954–6), and accompanied Billy Eckstine (1956). In the late 1950s he led his own trio in California. Having entered a Synanon house in 1960 to conquer his addiction to heroin, he succeeded and subsequently became active in the organization; he may be seen in the film *Synanon* (*Get off my Back*) (1965). From 1968 to 1976 he worked with Nelson Riddle in radio and television and occasionally toured as an accompanist to singers; he recorded as a leader in 1975–6. Ross continued performing through the 1990s and made his last appearance on 31 Dec 1999 with a memorial Harry James orchestra.

SELECTED RECORDINGS

As leader: Stairway to the Stars/Bye Bye Blues (1946, Key. 648)
As sideman: H. James: When your lover has gone/I'm Confessin' (1944, Col. 36773); C. Ventura: I don't stand a ghost of a chance/Tea for Two (1945, Sunset 10051); H. Edison: September in the Rain/Pennies from Heaven (1953, PJ 612)

BIBLIOGRAPHY

FeatherE; *Feather '60s*; *Feather–Gitler '70s*
S. Pease: "Arnold Ross Busy with James & Wax," *DB*, xiii/21 (1946), 12
Obituary, S. Voce, *The Independent* (12 June 2000)

JAMES M. DORAN

Ross, Brandon (K.) (*b* New Brunswick, NJ). Guitarist. He declines to give his birthdate. Having worked as a copyist for Leroy Jenkins, in the mid-1970s he performed and recorded in Archie Shepp's large ensemble and worked with Marion Brown, with whom he recorded (1976–7) and appeared at Jazz Festival Willisau (1977). From 1981 he was a regular member of Jenkins's ensembles, including the group Sting, with which he recorded in 1984 and performed at the Tampere Jazz Happening in Finland in 1987. In the mid-1980s he began affiliations with Oliver Lake (in the saxophonist's group Jump Up, and, together with Geri Allen, and Charles Burnham, in the short-lived quartet Blue Star) and with Butch Morris, in whose small groups and conduction ensembles he played through the 1990s. He also began leading his own groups – initially a trio with the violinist Terry Jenoure and the drummer Kamal Sabir (*c*1985–7). In the late 1980s he was a member of the cooperative quartet TenRenRen, consisting of Don Byron, Mark Dresser, and

Gerry Hemingway, performed in Wadada Leo Smith's group NDA (1987–8), and toured in John Lurie's group the Lounge Lizards (1988–9), Craig Harris's band Tailgater's Tales (1988–9), Harris's soul group Cold Sweat, and the quartet co-led by Diedre Murray and Fred Hopkins.

Ross then worked with Henry Threadgill in the saxophonist's groups Very Very Circus (1990–95) and Make a Move (from 1995) and joined Marcus Rojas and Gene Lake in the group the Sideshow, a spin-off from Very Very Circus. From 1993 to 1996 he served as music director for Cassandra Wilson, and he arranged much of the material on her first two albums for Blue Note. Among the groups he led from the early 1990s were Treasured Stranger, a trio with Melvin Gibbs and the drummer Dougie Bowne; a quintet, the Overflow, which combined aggressive jazz and poetry and consisted of Byron, Gibbs, Bowne, and the poet Sadiq; a quartet (without Sadiq) which performed at the Tampere Jazz Happening in 1991; and Harriett Tubman, a cooperative trio with Gibbs and the drummer J. T. Lewis, which combined aspects of rock, funk, and free improvisation and toured internationally and recorded from 1998. Ross may be seen performing with the dancer Erica Bornstein in the video *Chateau Avant-garde-arama: a Multi-media-mini-festival of Music, Dance, Performance and Film* (filmed 1985).

SELECTED RECORDINGS

As leader of the Overflow: on [no leader]: *Live at the Knitting Factory*, iii (1989–90, A&M 75021-5299), The Ugly Waiter (1989)

As sideman: M. Brown: *La Placita* (1977, Tim. 108); O. Lake: on *Impala* (1987, Gram. 18-8710-1), Lef' Sided; H. Threadgill: *Spirit of Nuff . . . Nuff* (1990, BS 120134-2); L. Jenkins: *Leroy Jenkins Live!* (1992, BS 120122-2); H. Threadgill: *Too Much Sugar for a Dime* (*c*1992, Axiom 314-514528-2); C. Wilson: on *Blue Light 'til Dawn* (*c*1993, BN B21Z-81357), Come on in my kitchen, Hellhound on my trail, You don't know what love is; H. Threadgill: *Where's your Cup* (1996, Col. CK67617); Harriett Tubman: *I Am a Man* (1998, Knitting Factory 228); *Prototype* (1998, Avant 078)

BIBLIOGRAPHY

S. McElfresh: "Brandon Ross: Jazz Warrior," *Ear*, xv/2 (1990), 32

J. Woodard: "Jazz Guitar Mutants!," *Musician*, no.189 (1994), 62

M. Resnicoff: "Brandon Ross: Avant-jazz High Wire," *GP*, xxx/5 (1996), 18

J. Woodard: "Fission: a Kinder, Gentler Skronk," *Jazziz*, xvi/6 (1999), 30

GK

Ross, Ronnie [Albert Ronald] (*b* Calcutta, 2 Oct 1933; *d* London, 12 Dec 1991). Scottish baritone saxophonist. He settled in the UK in 1946 and began his career as a tenor saxophonist, but changed to the baritone instrument at the request of Don Rendell, with whom he played from 1954 to early 1955 and again in 1957. After working with such musicians as Lars Gullin, Tony Crombie (from spring 1955), Tony Kinsey (August 1955 – early 1957), and Ted Heath, and appearing as a member of Phil Seamen's group in the film *The Golden Disc* (*The Inbetween Age*) (1958), he represented Britain at the Newport Jazz Festival as a member of Marshall Brown's International Youth Band (1958). In addition he recorded (1958) and toured Europe (1959) with the Modern Jazz Quartet. In 1959 he toured and recorded in the USA with the Jazz Makers, a band he led with Allan Ganley, and performed in England with Woody Herman's Anglo-American Herd. From the 1960s Ross participated in several recording sessions of popular and commercial music, an example of his work being the well-known solo on *Walk on the Wild Side*, by the rock singer Lou Reed. However, he continued to play jazz and led his own groups, notably the Jazztet (co-led by the trumpeter Bert Courtley, May 1960 – March 1961), a quartet with Bill Le Sage (1961–5), and a quintet co-led by Ray Warleigh; he worked as a sideman with a variety of musicians and recorded with John Dankworth (1961–4), the Clarke–Boland Big Band (1965–6), Friedrich Gulda (1966), Kinsey (1974), and Clark Terry (1977). In 1986 he toured Britain with his own quartet, and early the following year he led another such group with John Horler, Dave Green, and Ganley at the Bass Clef in London. Thereafter his deteriorating health limited his ability to play.

SELECTED RECORDINGS

As leader: *The Ronnie Ross Quintet* (1958, Parl. 1079); of the Jazz Makers (with A. Ganley): *Swinging Sounds of the Jazz Makers* (1959, Atl. 1333); *Cleopatra's Needle* (1968, Fon. 915)

As sideman: D. Rendell: *Meet Don Rendell* (1955, Tempo 1); John Lewis: *European Windows* (1958, RCA LPM1742); J. Dankworth: *The Zodiac Variations* (1964, Fon. 5229); L. Reed: on *Transformer* (1972, RCA LSP4807), Walk on the Wild Side

BIBLIOGRAPHY

CarrJ; *ChiltonB*; *FeatherE*; *Feather '60s*; *Feather–Gitler '70s*

P. Sullivan: "Ronnie Ross: Honest to Goodness Jazz," *JF* [intl edn], no.76 (1982), 46

R. Horricks: "The Growing Greatness of Ronnie Ross," *CI*, xxiv/4 (1987), 17

MARK GILBERT

Rossi, Aldo (*b* Milan, 1911; *d c*1980). Italian clarinetist, alto saxophonist, and leader. From the mid-1930s he played with Kramer Gorni and recorded with his orchestra; he also worked in small groups with Gorni, Cosimo Di Ceglie, and the pianist Enzo Ceragioli. After World War II he formed a big band, the Orchestra del Momento; from 1947 this was led alternately by Kramer and by Rossi, who was leader for several of the orchestra's recordings made for Fonit, including *Rhumboogie/Cow Cow Boogie* (12220), *9:20 Special* (12218), and *Diggin' for Dex/Undecided* (12219) in 1945, and *Cement Mixer* (12459) in 1947. Among Rossi's sidemen was Giorgio Gaslini.

ADRIANO MAZZOLETTI

Rossy, Jorge [Jordi] (*b* Barcelona, Spain, 21 Aug 1964). Spanish drummer. His father played accordion, his late sister Mercedes Rossy was a composer and pianist, and his brother Mario Rossy is a double bass player. He studied classical percussion from the age of 12, but the following year, having heard a recording by Weather Report, began to be interested in jazz; he first played professionally when he was about 16. From 1984 he worked with Tete Montoliu, Carles Benavent, Perico Sambeat, and the Spanish groups Beporum and Onix (recording with the latter in 1985); he also performed with such Americans as Woody Shaw and Jimmy Owens and appeared in Kenny Wheeler's ensembles at various European festivals. After moving to Boston he studied trumpet at the Berkelee College of Music (*c*1989–90) and played regularly with Joshua Redman, Billy Pierce, Paquito D'Rivera (recording in 1991), Donald Byrd, Danilo Pérez, and Antonio Hart, among others. Rossy was a member of Klaus Ignatzek's quintet (1992–4) and the small groups led by Mark Turner (recording in 1994 and 1998), Kurt Rosenwinkel, and Chris Cheek (recording in 1996–7). Most significantly, he rose to prominence touring and recording as a member of Brad Mehldau's trio from 1993; from that same year he worked in the two-drummer setting of Seamus Blake's group Bloomdaddies. In 1997–8 he occasionally worked in Spain in the group International Hashua Orchestra, and by 1999 he was again living in Spain, though he continued his associations with Mehldau and Blake. As a freelance in the 1990s he recorded with Eric Felten and Jimmy Knepper (1991–2), Sambeat (1995), the guitarist Mike Rud and Dan Faulk (both 1996), the guitarist Freddy Bryant (1997), and Avishai Cohen and the pianist Ethan Iverson (both 1998); in 1993 he recorded as the co-leader of a trio with his brother Mario and Mehldau.

SELECTED RECORDINGS

As leader with B. Mehldau and M. Rossy: *When I Fall in Love* (1993, Fresh Sound 007)

As sideman with B. Mehldau: *New York–Barcelona Connection*, ii (1993, Fresh Sound 037); *Introducing Brad Mehldau* (1995, WB 45997-2); *The Art of the Trio*, i (1996, WB 46260-2); *The Art of the Trio*, ii: *Live at the Village Vanguard* (1997, WB 46848-2); *The Art of the Trio*, iii: *Songs* (1998, WB 47051-2); *Art of the Trio*, iv: *Back at the Vanguard Again* (1999, WB, 47463-2)

As sideman with others: Onix: *Stress* (1985, Fresh Sound 104), E. Felten and J. Knepper: *T-Bop* (1991–2, SN 121196-2); S. Blake: *The Bloomdaddies* (1995, Criss Cross 1110)

BIBLIOGRAPHY

Feather–GitlerBEJ

"Seven Spanish Jazz Musicians the World Should Know About: Jordi Rossy," *Jazz Changes*, vi/2 (1999), 15

GK

Rostaing, Hubert (*b* Lyons, France, 17 Sept 1918; *d* Paris, 10 June 1990). French alto and tenor saxophonist, clarinetist, and bandleader. Influenced by Artie Shaw, Benny Goodman, and Benny Carter, he first performed with the Red Hotters in Algiers and in 1939 moved to Paris, where he performed at the Mimi Pinson club. He played and recorded as a member of the Quintette du Hot Club de France (1940–48) and from 1940 to 1962 made many recordings as a leader, including *To be bop or not to be bop* (1947, BStar 118). He also played with the bandleader and saxophonist Raymond Legrand, Aimé Barelli (recording 1940–43), Harry Cooper, Jacques Hélian's band, and Rex Stewart, and appeared in the films *Je n'aime que toi (C'est toi que j'aime)* (1949) and *La route du bonheur* (1952) and the documentary film short *Django Reinhardt* (1958). Rostaing pursued a career outside jazz as a composer of film scores and clarinetist; the composer Jean Barraqué dedicated a clarinet concerto to him, the first performance of which he gave in London in 1969.

BIBLIOGRAPHY

A. Hodeir: "Panorama du jazz français," *BHcF*, 1st ser., no.1 (1945), 9

B. Vian: "Hubert Rostaing," *Jh*, no.7 (1946), 11

C. Bellest: "Mon ami Rostaing," *Jm*, no.396 (1990), 31

MICHEL LAPLACE

Rothenberg, Ned [Edward] (*b* Boston, 15 Sept 1956). Alto saxophonist, bass clarinetist, and leader. He began playing clarinet, recorder, and saxophone when he was six and eventually took saxophone lessons from Joe Viola (1971–4). He attended Oberlin (Ohio) College (BA 1978), where he learned flute while continuing his private studies on saxophone; later he studied jazz improvisation with George Coleman (1982–3). While in college he formed the cooperative group Fall Mountain (1977–81) with the keyboard player Bob Ostertag and the violinist Jim Katzin. From 1980 he has been active as an unaccompanied soloist, primarily on alto saxophone or bass clarinet, but also on *shakuhachi* (a Japanese end-blown flute, which he took up in 1981) and ocarina. In 1981 he began a long association with the cooperative trio New winds, comprising Robert Dick and J. D. Parran (Herb Robertson replaced Parran in 1996). Rothenberg was a member of the cooperative groups Semantics (1985–91) and Odd Job (1987–9) before founding the Double Band (1988), consisting of two alto saxophonists, two electric bass guitarists, and two drummers and including Jerome Harris (who doubles on electric guitar) and Thomas Chapin (from 1998) as regular members; other members have been the bass players Kermit Driscoll, Tony Sher, and Chris Wood and the drummers Samm Bennett, Mike Sarin, Billy Martin, Jim Black, and Adam Rudolph. In 1993 he formed the group Power Lines with such sidemen as Mark Feldman, Eric Friedlander, Mark Dresser, Dave Douglas, Josh Roseman, and Sarin, and in 1996 he founded the trio SYNC, in which he plays alto saxophone, clarinet, and bass clarinet; the other members are Harris on acoustic guitar and acoustic bass guitar and Samir Chatterjee on tablā. All three groups – Double Band, Power Lines, and SYNC – remained active in the late 1990s, as did Rothenberg's duos with the *shakuhachi* player Katsuya Yokoyama (from 1985), the guitarist Paul Dresher (from 1990), Sainkho Namtchylak (from 1992), Masahiko Sato (from 1994), and Evan Parker (from 1997).

SELECTED RECORDINGS

As unaccompanied soloist: *Trials of the Argo* (1980–81, Lumina 001); *Portal* (1982–3, Lumina 006) [incl. duo with G. Hemingway]; *Trespass* (1985, Lumina 011) [incl. duo with J. Zorn]; *The Crux* (1991–2, Leo 187)

As leader: with P. Dresher: *Opposites Attract* (1990, New World 80411); *Overlays* (1991, Moers 2074); *Power Lines* (1995, New World 80476-2)

For further recordings, *see* New winds.

BIBLIOGRAPHY

J. Corbett: "At Home Alone: Ned Rothenberg's Solo Sax Obsession," *Option*, no.54 (1994), 38

B. Smith: "Ned Rothenberg: Inside & Out," *Coda*, no.257 (1994), 10

L. Farné and M. Lorrai: "Non ha frontiere il nuovo uomo dei Fiati," *Musica jazz*, li/5 (1995), 14

T. Okajima: "Ned Rothenberg is Coming Back Soon," *Jazz Critique* [Japan] (1995), no.84, p.290; contd as "Ned Rothenberg: Interview," no.85, p.225 [incl. discography]

GK

Rotondi, Jim [James Robert] (*b* Butte, MT, 28 Aug 1962). Trumpeter. His mother was a piano teacher, and he took up that instrument at the age of eight and trumpet when he was 12. After graduating from North Texas State University (BMus 1985) he worked briefly on cruise ships (1986) and toured with an off-Broadway revue (1987). Later he played with Ray Charles (1991–2), with whom he appeared on television, and with Junior Cook and Cecil Payne (both 1991–5). In 1995 he joined Lionel Hampton's Orchestra, was a founding member of the cooperative group One for All, and worked with George Coleman. Rotondi also performed in Michael Weiss's sextet (1995–7) and with Lou Donaldson (1996–7). In 1997 he joined Curtis Fuller's sextet, and in 1999 he toured in a quintet led by the double bass player Kyle Eastwood. He has recorded as a leader (1996, 1997) and as a sideman with, among others, Eric Alexander (1992, from 1997), David Hazeltine (1997), Charles Earland (1997–8), and the singer Giacomo Gates (1998).

SELECTED RECORDINGS

(recorded for Criss Cross unless otherwise indicated)

As leader: *Introducing Jim Rotondi* (1996, 1128); *Jim's Bop* (1997, 1156)

As sideman: One for All: *Too Soon to Tell* (1997, Sharp Nine 1006), incl. Stranger than Fiction; E. Alexander: *Mode for Mabes* (1997, Del. 500); D. Hazeltine: *How It Is* (1997, 1142)

BIBLIOGRAPHY

Feather–GitlerBEJ

GK

Rotondo, Nunzio (*b* Palestrina, Italy, 1924). Italian trumpeter, composer, and leader. As a child he studied piano, then trumpet. In 1948–9 he formed the sextet of the Hot Club di Roma and played in Rome with Louis Armstrong. In 1951 he took part in jam sessions with Bill Coleman, Flavio Ambrosetti, Roy Eldridge, Zoot Sims, Toots Thielemans, and Duke Ellington; during the following decade he performed and recorded as the leader of bop groups that included Gil Cuppini (from 1952), Roberto Nicolosi (1954), and Romano Mussolini (from 1954). In the 1960s he gave only two concerts – one in a big band with Albert Mangelsdorff, Martial Solal, and Niels-Henning Ørsted Pedersen (1965), the other in a quintet with Mussolini (1966) – but he performed often on radio with, among others, Gato Barbieri, Franco D'Andrea, Mal Waldron, and Pierre Favre. He led a quintet with D'Andrea from 1970 to 1973, was inactive for several years, then resumed playing publicly in 1980–81 and again in the late 1990s. Inspired by Miles Davis, Rotondo's playing has a restrained lyricism also reminiscent of that of Bix Beiderbecke and a moving sound, both full and almost frail. His singing lines are most effective in lyrical, sentimental tunes of his own composition; a good example of his style is his recording *Ten Men Blowin'* on the album *IIIrd Festival del Jazz del San Remo* (1958, Carish 15301). Among his original works are *Garineipaulus*, *Suoni lunghi*, and *Suoni flautati*. (*FeatherE*)

ADRIANO MAZZOLETTI/STEFANO ZENNI

Roto-toms. A set of shallow tunable single-headed frame drums; *see* Drum set, §I, 4.

Roulette. Record company and label. The company was founded in New York in 1957 by a group of directors headed by Morris Levy. It produced a wide variety of material, chiefly in commercially oriented styles, but it also established the Birdland Series, which was devoted to jazz. This included, most importantly, new recordings by Count Basie (1957–62), as well as material by Joe Williams (1957–62), Maynard Ferguson (1958–64), Harry Edison (1958, 1960), Jack Teagarden (1959, 1961), Randy Weston (1960), and Sarah Vaughan (1960–64). Although much of the back catalogue was no longer available, Roulette continued to exist into the late 1980s, occasionally organizing new sessions by such musicians as Betty Carter (1969, 1976), Lee Konitz (1976) and Art Blakey (1976–7) and keeping most of Basie's albums in print. Roulette later became a subsidiary of ABZ, Inc., among whose holdings were a number of labels in genres other than jazz; after Levy, then Roulette's president, was sentenced to prison in 1988 for conspiracy to extort, ABZ, Inc., was acquired jointly by Rhino and EMI (1989), with the latter corporation gaining world rights to Roulette's jazz catalogue. Numerous CD reissues followed under the direction of EMI's subsidiary company Blue Note.

BIBLIOGRAPHY

"Roulette's First Year," *Billboard*, lxx (3 Feb 1958), 14

B. Haring: "Roulette Head Sentenced for Extortion: Levy Gets 10-year Jail Term," *Billboard*, c (12 Nov 1988), 1

"Rhino, EMI Divide 'Spoils' in Buyout of Levy Labels," *Billboard*, ci (3 June 1989), 6

J. Sanchez: "Rhino Records, EMI Buy Roulette's Labels," *Los Angeles Times* (2 June 1989)

BK

Rouse, Charlie [Charles] (*b* Washington, DC, 6 April 1924; *d* Seattle, 30 Nov 1988). Tenor saxophonist. He studied clarinet and doubled on alto saxophone in high school before taking up tenor saxophone; during his senior year he worked in John Malachi's band. He played briefly in the bop big band of Billy Eckstine (June 1944), but was so taken by Charlie Parker's playing that he was unable to pay attention to his own parts and was fired, with Gene Ammons taking his place. He joined Dizzy Gillespie's big band in 1945 and took part with Thelonious Monk in jam sessions at Minton's Playhouse in New York, but made his first recordings as a soloist only in 1947, with Tadd Dameron and Fats Navarro. After playing rhythm-and-blues in Washington and New York, including brief affiliations with Louis Jordan and Eddie "Cleanhead" Vinson and his own quintet co-led by Jimmy Cobb, he became a member of the Duke Ellington Orchestra (*c* June 1949 – spring 1950), but was obliged to quit when the band embarked for Europe because he could not secure a passport, having failed to find his birth certificate. He was a member of Count Basie's octet briefly in 1950.

Rouse took part in Clifford Brown's first recordings in 1953, then worked with Bennie Green (1955) and played in Oscar Pettiford's sextet (*c*1955); with Julius Watkins, also one of Pettiford's sidemen, he led Les Modes (later the Jazz Modes), a bop quintet (1956–9). By autumn 1958, with the Jazz Modes finding few opportunties to work, Rouse was rehearsing with Monk, and in November he twice sat in with Monk's group, at the Five Spot Café and then at Town Hall, New York. He worked with Buddy Rich briefly before joining Monk's quartet formally (1959–70), the association for which he is best known; in addition to his many recordings, he may be seen in numerous films and videos with Monk (for illustration, *see* Monk, Thelonious).

During the 1970s Rouse left music for a short time to study acting. He then worked as a freelance and recorded three albums as a leader. In the early 1980s he was a member and joint leader of the quartet Sphere, and later he co-led a quartet with Mal Waldron which toured and appeared regularly at the Village Vanguard, New York. He appeared in Wynton Marsalis's group at the Concord Jazz Festival (California) in 1987 and early the following year performed compositions by Monk in San Francisco with Carmen McRae; two titles from these concerts appeared on her album *Carmen Sings Monk*. Before succumbing to lung cancer, Rouse played in tributes to Dameron at the Lincoln Center, New York (August 1988), and to Monk in San Francisco (October 1988).

In the 1960s Rouse adapted his style to Monk's work, improvising with greater deliberation than most bop tenor saxophonists, and restating melodies often. His distinctive solo playing with Monk may be heard on *Shuffle Boil* (1964), in which he alternates reiterations of the principal thematic motif with formulaic bop runs.

SELECTED RECORDINGS

As leader: with J. Watkins: *The Most Happy Fella* (1957, Atl. 1280); *Takin' Care of Business* (1960, Jlnd 919); *Yeah!* (1960, Epic 17012); *Bossa Nova Bacchanal* (1962, BN 84119); *Moment's Notice* (1977, Sto. 4079); of Sphere (with K. Barron, Buster Williams, and B. Riley): *Four in One* (1982, Elek. Mus. 60166); *Social Call* (1984, Uptown 28.17); *Epistrophy: the Last Concert* (1988, Landmark 1521)

As sideman: T. Dameron: The Chase/Dameronia (1947, BN 541); The Squirrel/Our Delight (1947, BN 540); C. Brown: *New Star on the Horizon* (1953, BN 5032); B. Green: *Benny Blows his Horn in Hi-Fi* (1955, Prst. 7052); D. Byrd: *Byrd in Hand* (1959, BN 4019); T. Monk: *5 by Monk by 5* (1959, Riv. 1150); S. Clark: *Leapin' and Lopin'* (1961, BN 84091); Benny Carter: *Further Definitions* (1961, Imp. 12); T. Monk: *Monk's Dream* (1962, Col. CS8765); *Criss Cross* (1963, Col. CS8838); *Monk Misterioso* (1963–5, Col. CS9216); on *It's Monk's Time* (1964, Col. CS8984), Shuffle Boil; *Underground* (1967–8, Col. CS9632); D. Jordan: *Duke's Delight* (1975, Ste. 1046); C. McRae: on *Carmen Sings Monk* (1988, Novus 3086-2), Get it Straight, Suddenly

SELECTED FILMS AND VIDEOS

Salute to Duke Ellington (1950); Mal Waldron and Friends: Live at the Village Vanguard (?1990s)

See also Monk, thelonious.

BIBLIOGRAPHY

D. Morgenstern: "Charlie Rouse and the Long Road to Recognition," *Metronome*, lxxvii/9 (1960), 20
D. DeMicheal: "Charlie Rouse: Artistry and Originality," *DB*, xxviii/11 (1961), 17
J.-P. Binchet: "Portrait: monsieur passe-partout," *Jm*, no.92 (1963), 24 [incl. discography]
J.-L. Ginibre: "La longue marche de Charlie," *Jm*, no.105 (1964), 20
P. Danson: "Charlie Rouse," *Coda*, no.187 (1982), 4
P. Slaughter: "Charlie Rouse: les tenors de Thelonious," *Jm*, no.306 (1982), 16
P. Elwood: "It's Not Monk, But it's Not Bad," *San Francisco Examiner* (7 Jan 1987)
A. D. Franklin: "Charlie Rouse," *Cadence*, xiii/6 (1987), 5
M. Isherwood: "Charlie Rouse," *JJI*, xli/2 (1988), 16
Obituaries: *New York Times* (2 Dec 1988); *DB*, lvi/4 (1989), 59
D. Rubien: "Charlie Rouse Comes Out of the Shadows," *San Francisco Chronicle Datebook* (12 Feb 1989)
J. Simmen: "Ceux qui s'en vont: Charlie Rouse," *BHcF*, no. 374 (1989), 30

BK

Rousselet, Richard (*b* Mons, Belgium, 1940). Belgian trumpeter. Self-taught, he played in amateur bands from his mid-teens, led a quintet that included Félix Simtaine (1960), and played at the Montreux Jazz Festival, both in a quintet alongside Philip Catherine and Simtaine and in a big band directed by Clark Terry and Ernie Wilkins (late 1960s). During the early 1970s he worked principally in jazz-rock groups (among them, from 1972, Solis Lacus, with Michel Herr), though he also appeared in swing and bop settings with such saxophonists as Johnny Griffin, Hal Singer, Pepper Adams, and Cecil Payne. He was a member of Simtaine's Act Big Band (from 1979, recording in the 1980s and 1990s), Guy Cabay's group Lemon Air (1981), and the BRT (Belgische Radio & Televisie) Big Band (1984–6), and he led his own hard-bop quintet; this group, in which Herr, Steve Houben, Jean-Louis Rassinfosse, and Erwin Vann were sidemen, recorded the albums *No Maybe . . .* (1984, B Sharp 102) and *Waitin' for You* (1993, GAM 913). Rousselet also founded a big band, West Music Club, in 1989. In 1998 he formed the Ecaroh Quintet, devoted to Horace Silver's music, and in 1999 he played in Jean Warland's sextet, which performed tributes to Duke Ellington. He has taught at the conservatories in Liège and Brussels (the latter from October 1988), as well as at other institutions.

BIBLIOGRAPHY

R. Pernet, J.-P. Schroeder, and others: *Dictionnaire du jazz à Bruxelles et en Wallonie* (Liège, Belgium, 1991)
R. Pernet: *Belgian Jazz Discography (1897–1999)* (Brussels, 1999)
<http://www.jazzinbelgium.org/mus/richard.htm> (2000) [incl. discography]

BK

ROVA. Saxophone quartet. It was founded late in 1977 by four saxophonists from the San Francisco Bay area and took its name from the initials of their surnames: Jon Raskin (alto) (*b* Heppner, OR, 1954), Larry Ochs (tenor) (*b* New York, 1949), Andrew Voigt (alto) (*b* Kentucky, *c*1956), and Bruce Ackley (tenor) (*b* Detroit, 1948); all are multi-instrumentalists who play a wide range of saxophones and other reed instruments, as well as flutes. ROVA is the most experimental of the saxophone quartets which began in the late 1970s and explores to the full the freedoms its format affords: it builds in particular on the work of Anthony Braxton, Steve Lacy, and Roscoe Mitchell. In 1978 the group gave its first performances and, together with Henry Kaiser, founded the record company and label Metalanguage to document its work. In 1983 it undertook a historic tour of the USSR, recorded on *Saxophone Diplomacy*, and was the subject of a PBS television documentary, "Jazz Summit" (released in 1987). In 1988 Steve Adams (alto) (*b* Rockville Centre, NY, 1952), a member of Boston's Your Neighbourhood Saxophone Quartet, replaced Voigt. The quartet made more than 20 European tours in the 1980s and 1990s, and in 1989 it returned to the USSR. It has collaborated with the contemporary composers Alvin Curran (1990) and Terry Riley (1994) and recorded a set of tunes by Lacy (*Favorite Street*). In December 1995, at the Great American Music Hall in San Francisco, its members investigated John Coltrane's *Ascension* in a collaboration with a fifth saxophonist, Glenn Spearman (who served as concertmaster), the trumpeters Dave Douglas and Raphé Malik, the pianist Chris Brown, the double bass players Lisle Ellis and George Cremaschi, and drummer Donald Robinson.

SELECTED RECORDINGS

As Was (1981, Metalanguage 118); *Saxophone Diplomacy* (1983, HA 6068); *Favorite Street* (1983, BS 0076); *Long on Logic* (1989, Sound Aspects 037); *The Works*, i (1994, BS 120176-2); *John Coltrane's Ascension* (1995, BS 120180-2)

BIBLIOGRAPHY

GrayF
L. Means: "The ROVA Saxophone Quartet," *Coda*, no.167 (1979), 12
H. Charlton: "There's Art in the Sax," *MM* (31 Jan 1981), 12
M. Goldberg: "ROVA Saxophone Quartet Wants to Wake You Up," *DB*, xlviii/1 (1981), 23
E. Romero and L. Pallini: "ROVA: Interview," *Cadence*, viii/2 (1982), 5
T. Gaudynski: "Rova Sax Quartet Interview," *OP* [Los Angeles] (1983), July–Aug, 48
B. Besecker: "Jazz Red Hot & Cool," *Coda*, no.196 (1984), 5
A. Kan: "ROVA on the Road," *JF* [intl edn], no.87 (1984), 50
P. Szigeti: "Bruce Ackley: Interview," *Cadence*, x/6 (1984), 19
M. Bershon: "Diversions: the Joy of Sax: Tuning into the ROVA Saxophone Quartet," *San Francisco Examiner Image* (20 July 1986)
B. Emerson: "Rova Saxophone Quartet Likes Being in 'Dangerous Territory'," *Atlanta Constitution* (14 Sept 1989)
M. M. Barelu: "Today's Consort, pt ii: is the Medium the Message?," *Chamber Music*, vii/4 (1990), 20
A. Kahn: "ROVA," *Jazzthetik*, iv/5 (1990), 12
J. Corbett: "Drove 'o' Rova," *DB*, lviii/12 (1991), 64
"ROVA Saxophone Quartet," *JP*, xli/3 (1992), 48
B. Shoemaker: "Riffs: Rova," *DB*, lix/1 (1992), 12
K. Thomas: "Airtime," *Windplayer*, no.52 (1995), 11
D. Ouellette: "Riffs: 30 Years Later, Rova rises to Coltrane's Ascension," *DB*, lxiii/3 (1996), 12

SIMON ADAMS

Rovère, Gilbert [Bibi] (*b* Toulon, France, 29 Aug 1939). French double bass player. He studied piano, then double bass, at the conservatory in Nice. In 1956 he moved to Paris and played with Jean-Claude Fohrenbach, the clarinetist Maurice Meunier, and Lionel Hampton. From 1957 to 1959 he recorded with hard-bop groups led by Barney Wilen. After performing at the Club Saint-Germain with Stephane Grappelli and Mac Kac he toured Italy with Nunzio Rotondo and played with Guy Lafitte (1961). As a sideman at the Blue Note (1962–3) he worked with Kenny Drew, Johnny Griffin, Dexter Gordon, and Kenny Clarke. He performed and recorded with Bud Powell (1963) and Duke Ellington (1963–4), and recorded with Lou Bennett (1963, 1969), Jean-Luc Ponty (1964), and Jef Gilson (1964, 1966). Rovère worked with the pianist Art Simmons in 1964–5 and joined Martial Solal in 1965. While with Solal's trio he also appeared in the film short *Max Roach (Ciné jazz)* (1967) and recorded with Ivan Jullien (1966), Bill Coleman (the album *Bill Coleman Sings and Plays 12 Negro-spirituals*, 1968, Concert Hall 1269), Tony Scott (1968), and René Urtreger (1970). He played at numerous continental jazz festivals. In 1974 he recorded the album *Invitation* (1974, Spot. 4) with Al Haig's bop trio. His brother Paul Rovère was also a professional double bass player.

BIBLIOGRAPHY

Feather '60s

J.-L. Ginibre: "Les secrets de Gilbert: entretien à coeur ouvert," *Jm*, no.106 (1964), 20

MICHEL LAPLACE

Rowles, Jimmie [Jimmy; Hunter, James George] (*b* Spokane, WA, 19 Aug 1918; *d* Burbank, CA, 28 May 1996). Pianist, father of Stacey Rowles. He took the name Rowles from his stepfather. His mother played classical music on guitar and mandolin and was a self-taught pianist; Rowles too was mainly self-taught, though he received lessons in classical piano and, while in high school, in jazz piano, and developed a taste for the style of Teddy Wilson. After attending Gonzaga University in Spokane he went to Seattle, ostensibly to study at the University of Washington, although actually he spent his time playing in jazz bands. He then moved to Los Angeles, where he first worked with Slim Gaillard and Slam Stewart, and recorded with Ben Webster as their guest soloist in April 1942. He joined Lee and Lester Young's group (with which Billie Holiday routinely sat in) before becoming a member of the big bands of Benny Goodman (September–October 1942) and Woody Herman. He was with Herman from November 1942 to June 1943, when he was drafted, and, following his discharge, from March to December 1946, when Herman disbanded the First Herd; Rowles continued to record with Herman's studio groups in 1947, while also performing and recording in Goodman's big band and small groups. In 1947 he also recorded with Dexter Gordon, worked very briefly in the orchestras of Les Brown and Tommy Dorsey, and broadcast with Bob Crosby's band.

It was as an accompanist to singers, particularly Peggy Lee (recording in 1953) and Holiday (1955–7), that Rowles became best known. In the course of his 25 years as a studio musician he also accompanied Anita O'Day (1955, 1961), Jimmy Witherspoon (1959), Jo Stafford (1960), Mel Tormé (1960–61), and June Christy (1962), and in the late 1950s he played on film and television soundtracks. In 1952 he recorded privately with the Gerry Mulligan–Chet Baker quartet and then inadvertently contributed to jazz history by reportedly failing to turn up for the subsequent studio recording, which initiated Mulligan's famous pianoless quartet. From 1953 his studio work included instrumental jazz albums with Louie Bellson (1953, 1957), Buddy Rich's small group (1953, 1955–6) and big band (1956), Stan Getz (1954), Bud Shank and Shorty Rogers (1954), Bob Brookmeyer (1955, 1960), Jimmy Giuffre and Lee Konitz (both 1956), Ray Brown's big band (1956, 1960), Buddy DeFranco (1956–8), Barney Kessel (1956–7, 1959), Pepper Adams (1957), and Sonny Stitt, Benny Carter, and the Candoli brothers (all 1959). He was involved in numerous sessions with Webster, either where the tenor saxophonist served as leader (1960; with Mulligan as co-leader, 1959; and with Carter and Barney Bigard as co-leaders, 1962) or as a fellow sideman under Harry Edison (1956), Red Norvo, Carter, Kessel, and Bill Harris (ii) (all 1957), and several of the aforementioned singers. Rowles appeared with the Mulligan–Webster group on television in December 1959 and with Carter's All Stars at a festival in Los Angeles in 1960.

After performing at the Newport Jazz Festival in 1973 Rowles settled in New York, where he worked in clubs and recorded, mainly in duos or small groups with Zoot Sims, George Mraz, and Buster Williams. He toured Europe with Carmen McRae (1973), worked with Carol Sloane, and recorded once again with Kessel (1975) and Konitz (in a duo, 1977), as well as in duos with the double bass players Rusty Gilder (1974), Brown (1978), and Red Mitchell (1978). In 1978 he performed with Konitz in several groups at the Grande Parade du Jazz in Nice, France, and while in Europe recorded as an unaccompanied soloist, as the leader of a trio including George Duvivier, and in a quintet with Jan Allan; the quintet performed in Poland the following year. In 1981 Rowles recorded with Scott Hamilton and Adams. He toured for more than two years in the early 1980s as Ella Fitzgerald's accompanist, then, having maintained his home in Burbank, returned to southern California. In 1986 he was honored in Los Angeles by the declaration of 14 September as "Jimmie Rowles Day." He worked in duos and small groups with Sims, Mitchell, Michael Moore (i), his daughter Stacey, and others, and in 1991 recorded with Gary Foster's quartet.

Rowles was a sensitive player with a swinging, mainstream style who showed a particular liking for Duke Ellington's music. He doubled as an unpretentious singer with a gruff, speak-song manner of delivery, and he composed some memorable tunes, one of which, *The Peacocks*, was included in the soundtrack to the film *Round Midnight* (1986).

Oral history material in *NjR* (JOHP).

SELECTED RECORDINGS

As unaccompanied soloist: *Jazz is a Fleeting Moment* (1974, Jazzz 103)

Duos: with Rusty Gilder: *The Special Magic of Jimmy Rowles* (1974, Hal. 110); with G. Mraz: *Music's the Only Thing that's on my Mind* (1976, Prog. 7009); with A. Cohn: *Heavy Love* (1977, Xan. 145); with E. von Essen: *Lilac Time* (1994, Kokopelli 1297)

As leader: *Rare – but Well Done* (1954, Lib. 3003); *Grandpaws* (1976, Choice 1014); with S. Getz: *The Peacocks* (1977, Col. JC34873); *Sometimes I'm Happy, Sometimes I'm Blue* (1988, Orange Blue 003); with R. Mitchell and Donald Bailey: *Trio* (1989, Capri 7409-2)

As sideman: B. Holiday: *Music for Torching* (1955, Clef 669); G. Mulligan and B. Webster: *Gerry Mulligan Meets Ben Webster* (1959, Verve 8343); C. McRae: *Great American Songbook* (1971, Atl. 2-904); S. Vaughan: *Sarah Vaughan and the Jimmy Rowles Quintet* (1972, Mstr. 404); Z. Sims: *Zoot Sims Party* (1974, Choice 1006)

SELECTED FILMS AND VIDEOS

The Powers Girl (1942); Hit Parade of 1947 [High and Happy] (1947); The Swingin' Singin' Years (1960); Jazz Scene USA: Mark Murphy (1962)

BIBLIOGRAPHY

ChiltonW; *ConnorBG*

S. A. Pease: "Jimmie Rowles Again Climbing Success Steps," *DB*, xv/23 (1948), 12

W. Balliett: "Dancing on the Carpet," *New Yorker*, l (1 April 1974), 43; repr. in *BalliettA (1996)*

L. Feather: "Piano Giants of Jazz: Jimmy Rowles," *CK*, iv/11 (1978), 93 [incl. transcr.]

L. Lyons: "Jimmy Rowles: Noted New York Jazz Pianist and Accompanist," *CK*, iv/7 (1978), 14; repr. in *The Great Jazz Pianists, Speaking of their Lives and Music* (New York, 1983), 151

L. Tomkins: "Jimmie Rowles," *CI*, xviii (1979), no.2, p.22; no.3, p.16

G. Endress: "Jimmie Rowles," *JP*, xxx/10 (1981), 3

J. Réda: "Jimmie Rowles: ou, l'épingle du jeu," *Jm*, no.308 (1982), 32

L. Tomkins: "Jimmie Rowles Reflects on Songs, Lyrics, Feelings and Ella," *CI*, xx/5 (1982), 5

J. Goldberg: "Jimmie Rowles: Beauty on a Borrowed Piano," *Musician*, no.114 (1988), 25

T. Gioia: *West Coast Jazz: Modern Jazz in California, 1945–1960* (New York, and Oxford, England, 1992)

"Jimmy Rowles," *The Note*, iv/2 (1992), 10

G. Lees and J. Reeves: *Jazz Lives: 100 Portraits in Jazz* (Toronto, 1992), 20

D. Clarke: *Wishing on the Moon: the Life and Times of Billie Holiday* (London and New York, 1994)
W. D. Clancy with A. C. Kenton: *Woody Herman: Chronicles of the Herds* (New York and elsewhere, 1995)
F. Krieger: "Jazz-Solopiano: zum Stilwandel am Beispiel ausgewaehlter *Body and Soul*: Aufnahmen von 1938–1992," *Jf*, xxvii (1995), 5
Obituaries: P. Watrous, *New York Times* (30 May 1996); M. Oliver, *Los Angeles Times* (2 June 1996)
G. P. Statiras: "Jimmy Rowles: Music's the Only Thing on my Mind," *Jazzbeat*, viii/3 (1997), 24

ROBERT L. DOERSCHUK/BK

Rowles, Stacy (Amanda) (*b* Los Angeles, 11 Sept 1955). Trumpeter, flugelhorn player, and singer, daughter of Jimmie Rowles. Her middle name, Amanda, is taken from California birth records. She studied piano for three years as a child and played percussion instruments in grammar school. When she was about 12 her father showed her how to play the chromatic scale on his old trumpet. She later studied improvisation with Charlie Shoemake. In 1973 she appeared with her father at the Monterey Jazz Festival, and two years later she performed in a women's big band led by Clark Terry at the Wichita Jazz Festival. During the 1980s she established herself in the Los Angeles jazz community as a founding member of Ann Patterson's big band, Maiden Voyage, as co-leader (with the trombonist Betty O'Hara) of the Jazz Birds quintet, in the instrumental quartet of the Jazz Tap Ensemble, and in various freelance engagements with her father, as well as with Diana Krall, Red Holloway, and others. In the 1990s she toured with the Swinging Ladies and the Jack Van Poll Trio. Rowles plays bop and sings in a lyrical, understated, but always swinging manner; her lyricism on the flugelhorn is particularly effective.

SELECTED RECORDINGS

As leader: *Tell it Like it Is* (1984, Conc. 249); with J. Rowles: *Looking Back* (1988, Delos 4009), *Me and the Moon* (1993, American Jazz Symposium 1001)

As sideman: J. Rowles and R. Mitchell: on *The Jimmie Rowles/Red Mitchell Trio* (1985, Cont. 14016), Locomotiv, The thrill is gone; N. Cline: *Angelica* (1987, Enja 5063); Swinging Ladies: *Take Two* (1998, Inakustik 9039)

BIBLIOGRAPHY

L. Feather: "Here's Why the Lady Is a Champ," *Los Angeles Times* (2 May 1982)
——: *The Jazz Years: Earwitness to an Era* (London, 1986), 159
L. Gourse: "Stacy Rowles," *JT* (1990), Aug, 23
Y. Stewart: "The Jazz Mystique: a Conversation with . . . Stacy Rowles," *L. A. Jazz Scene*, no.50 (1991), 6
G. Lees and J. Reeves: *Jazz Lives: 100 Portraits in Jazz* (Toronto, 1992), 20
L. Gourse: *Madame Jazz. Contemporary Women Instrumentalists* (New York, and Oxford, England, 1995), 106
T. S. Jenkins: "The Jazzbirds: No Compromise – Betty O'Hara and Stacy Rowles," *Marge Hofacre's Jazz News*, no.83 (1995), 14
B. Kohlhaase: "Dad's a Real Rowles Model," *Los Angeles Times* (3 June 1995)
Z. Stewart: "Jazzbirds of a Feather," *Los Angeles Times* (26 Sept 1996)

THOMAS OWENS

Rowser, Jimmy [James Edward] (*b* Philadelphia, 18 April 1926). Double bass player. He took up piano at the age of 14. From 1954 to 1956 he was a member of the house band at the Blue Note in Philadelphia, in which setting he accompanied Charlie Parker, Miles Davis, J. J. Johnson and Kai Winding, Anita O'Day, Billie Holiday, and Cannonball Adderley. He then played with Dinah Washington (1956–7, 1959–60) and performed and recorded with Maynard Ferguson (1957–9) and Red Garland and Lee Morgan (both 1959). During the 1960s he worked as a freelance in New York, recording with Junior Mance (*Big Chief*, 1961, Jlnd 953), Ray Bryant (at intervals, 1961–9), and Illinois Jacquet and Herb Ellis (both 1962). Rowser toured Mexico and recorded with Benny Goodman in 1963 and performed and recorded in Argentina with Friedrich Gulda the following year. After playing with Al Cohn and Zoot Sims he joined Les McCann (1969), with whom he worked through the 1970s; he performed in "Les McCann Trio" (1970, an episode of the television series "Jazz on Stage"), in the film *Soul to Soul* (1971), and at the Monterey Jazz Festival (1972). In 1980 he rejoined Bryant for a recording session, and he continued to work with the pianist thereafter. From 1985 he also played in a duo and a trio with Hilton Ruiz; he may be heard as a soloist on *Stella by Starlight*, from Ruiz's album *Doin' it Right* (1989, Novus 3085-2-N). Late in his career Rowser pursued a formal music education at Lehman College (BS 1985, master's 1988), and from 1989 through the 1990s he held a position teaching music in a school district in New Jersey. (*FeatherE*; *Feather '60s*; *Feather–Gitler '70s*)

BK

Roy, Badal [Choudhury, Amerendra Roy] (*b* East Pakistan [now Bangladesh], *c*1945). Pakistani tablā player. He received some lessons from his uncle but was mainly self-taught. Late in 1968 he moved to the USA to undertake graduate work in statistics at New York University and began playing jazz-rock in clubs in New York, often with John McLaughlin; he recorded two tracks on the guitarist's album *My Goal's Beyond* (1970, Douglas 9). Having gained a master's degree he began doctoral work, but he abandoned this in order to tour and record with Miles Davis (1972–*c*1974); he also recorded with Pharoah Sanders (1972) and Lonnie Liston Smith (1973). Between 1973 and 1976 Roy was a member of Dave Liebman's group Lookout Farm, with which he toured Europe, India, and Japan and made a number of recordings (including the album *Sweet Hands*, 1975, A&M Hor. 702); during the same period he performed and recorded with Frank Tusa (1975), and later he recorded with Ryo Kawasaki (1977). From 1988 through the 1990s he performed with Ornette Coleman's Prime Time, and he may be heard with the group on the album *Tone Dialing* (*c*1995, Harmolodic 314-527483-2). In addition he recorded with Leni Stern (1991) and Steve Turre (1992), formed a duo with the guitarist Amit Chatterjee, and toured and recorded alongside two Brazilian guitarists in the group Duofel (from late 1990s).

BIBLIOGRAPHY

B. Henschen: "Tabla Talk: Badal Roy," *MD*, i/4 (1977), 8
D. Liebman and others: *Lookout Farm: a Case Study of Improvisation for Small Jazz Group* (n.p., 1978)
J.-Y. Le Bec: "Prime Time une autre fois," *Jm*, no.453 (1995), 35
J. Woodward: "Out of India: the Continental Crossings of Badal Roy, Trilok Gurtu, and Zakir Hussain," *JT*, xxvii/9 (1997), 38
<http://www.harmolodic.com/bios/roy.html> (2000)
<http://www.musicoftheworld.com/MOTWPages/roy.html> (2000)

BK

Roy, Harry (*b* London, 12 Jan 1900; *d* London, 1 Feb 1971). English bandleader, clarinetist, singer, and composer. In his youth he played piano, violin, banjo, clarinet, and soprano saxophone. From 1919 he organized with his brother Syd several dance bands (notably Syd Roy's Lyricals), which performed in London at Oddenino's, Rector's, the Hammersmith Palais, and the Café de Paris, and in Paris at Rector's. The brothers toured South Africa and Australia in 1928, then played in vaudeville theaters in England before touring Germany. Later Roy formed his own band (1931), with which he toured (1933) and then held residencies in London at the Café Anglais and the Mayfair Hotel. He continued to tour extensively into the mid-1940s, but after World War II his popularity in London's clubland began to diminish. Roy was essentially a show-band leader – an energetic front man, a light, sometimes comic singer, and a clarinetist in the style of Ted Lewis. Although hardly a jazz musician himself, he employed as his sidemen a number of players who later became prominent in jazz. His signature tune, *Bugle Call Rag* (1933), set the style for compositions of his own such as *Hurricane Harry* (1933) and *The Roy Rag* (1934); another piece, *Sarawaki* (1938), was dedicated to his first wife, Elizabeth Brooke (known as Princess Pearl), the daughter of the Rajah of Sarawak. Roy and his band may been seen with the singer Mabel Mercer in the film *Everything is Rhythm* (1936) and performing in a jazz style accompanying the African-American dancer Johnny Nit in *Rhythm Racketeer* (1937).

SELECTED RECORDINGS

(all recorded for Parlophone)

* – composed by Roy

Bugle Call Rag/Stormy Weather (1933, R1526); *Hurricane Harry/Somebody Stole my Gal (1933, R1553); *The Roy Rag (1934, R1896); *Sarawaki (1938, F1178)

BIBLIOGRAPHY

ChiltonB

A. McCarthy: *The Dance Band Era: the Dancing Decades from Ragtime to Swing, 1910–1950* (London, 1971/*R*1982)

S. Colin: *And the Bands Played On* (London, 1980)

KEN RATTENBURY

Roy, Teddy [Theodore Gerald] (*b* Du Quoin, IL, 9 April 1905; *d* New York, 31 Aug 1966). Pianist. He played cornet for seven years before taking up piano, and he first worked with the Coon–Sanders Nighthawk Orchestra, Jean Goldkette, and Frankie Trumbauer. After performing in Boston with Bobby Hackett and Pee Wee Russell (both 1933) he led his own band at Cape Cod, Massachusetts (1934) and played in dance bands in New York (to early 1940s). Following army service (1943–5) he worked with Max Kaminsky (1945–6); as a member of the revived Original Dixieland Jazz Band, led by Eddie Edwards, he made such recordings as *Shake it and Break it/When you and I were Young, Maggie* (1946, Com. 612) alongside Kaminsky and Wild Bill Davison, among others. Roy then worked as a freelance in New York and on Long Island (1946–59), playing with Russell (1951), Miff Mole, Kaminsky, and Wingy Manone (1958–9), and appearing as an unaccompanied soloist. (*ChiltonW*; *FeatherE*; *Feather–Gitler '70s*)

Royal, Ernie [Ernest Andrew] (*b* Los Angeles, 2 June 1921; *d* New York, 16 March 1983). Trumpeter, brother of Marshal Royal. His birth date was given incorrectly in the first edition of this dictionary as 6 February rather than 2 June. He played with Les Hite (a summer tour, *c*1937), Britt Woodman, Cee Pee Johnson (1938–9), and Lionel Hampton (September 1940–42), then after serving in US Navy bands (1942–5) worked in Los Angeles with the pianist Phil Moore. To this point his activities paralleled those of his elder brother Marshal (except for the affiliation with Woodman), but their careers diverged when Ernie, as a member of the Second Herd, became the first African-American musician to work regularly with Woody Herman (autumn 1947 – August 1949; for illustration *see* Herman, woody, fig.1*b*). Following a period with Charlie Barnet's big band he toured Europe with Duke Ellington (April–June 1950); later that year he returned to France, where he worked with the bandleader Jacques Hélian, with whose band he is featured in the film *Musique en tête* (1951). Royal then led a band in Hollywood with Wardell Gray (1952), toured the USA with Stan Kenton (1953), and worked as a freelance in New York; from 1957 to 1972 he was a staff musician for ABC radio and television. He performed and recorded with Gil Evans intermittently from 1957 (touring Europe in 1978), joined Clark Terry's big band in 1967, and recorded prolifically under such leaders as Quincy Jones (1955–64), Oliver Nelson (1961–7), and Friedrich Gulda (1966), with whom he worked in Europe on several occasions. Royal specialized in playing high notes, and was an imaginative improviser, capable of producing fine melodic lines.

SELECTED RECORDINGS

As leader: *Accent on Trumpet* (*c*1954, Urania 1203)

As sideman: J. Lee: first issued on *Julia Lee: Kansas City Star* (1927–57, Bear Family 15770), The Curse of an Aching Heart (1947); S. Rollins: *Brass/Trio* (1958, Metro. 1002); Q. Jones: *The Birth of a Band!* (1959, Mer. 20444); C. Adderley: *African Waltz* (1961, Riv. 9377); G. Evans: on *Blues in Orbit* (1969, 1971, Ampex 10102), Blues in Orbit, Thoroughbred

SELECTED FILMS AND VIDEOS

Woody Herman and his Orchestra (1948); Herman's Herd (1949); "King" Cole and his Trio (1950); The Secret Fury [Blind Spot] (1950); Musique en tête (1951); Theater for a Story (1959)

BIBLIOGRAPHY

FeatherE; *Feather-Gitler '70s*; *SheridanCB*

J. Hélian: "Vers un grand orchestre de jazz en France? Jacques Hélian tente une grande expérience," *Jh*, no.115 (1956), 20

L. Tomkins: "Ernie Royal," *CI*, xvi (1978), no.10, p.22; no.12, p.14

J. A. Treichel: *Keeper of the Flame: Woody Herman and the Second Herd, 1947-1949* (n.p. [Zephyrhills, FL], 1978)

W. D. Clancy with A. C. Kenton: *Woody Herman: Chronicles of the Herds* (New York and elsewhere, 1995)

M. Royal and C. P. Gordon: *Marshal Royal: Jazz Survivor* (London and New York, 1996)

LEROY OSTRANSKY/BK

Royal, Marshal (Walton, Jr.) (*b* Sapulpa, OK, 5 December 1912; *d* Culver City, CA, 8 May 1995). Alto saxophonist and clarinetist, brother of Ernie Royal. His name has been persistently misspelled as Marshall, and his birth date appears in several reference books as 12 May rather than 5 December. As a child he learned piano (his mother's instrument) and violin (his father's) as well as reed instruments, and he gave his first professional performance at the age of 13; until 1929 he often worked with his family's band. Around 1929–30 he worked in bands at the Los Angeles and San Francisco locations of Curtis Mosby's Apex Club. At this time and again in the mid-1930s he also worked on a few films with Duke Ellington, but during most of the 1930s he played with Les Hite. From 1938 to 1940 he again worked in film studios and played in Cee Pee Johnson's band, and from September 1940 to 1942 he was with Lionel Hampton. After serving in a navy band he performed in the Los Angeles area (1945) and New York (January–April 1946) with Eddie Heywood, then returned to the West Coast, where he worked as a studio musician. In 1951 Royal joined Count Basie's septet, and he soon helped Basie to organize a new big band, in which he played lead alto saxophone and also took solos. He remained with the band for 20 years as its music director, and, although his responsibility for disciplining the musicians to play as a precise ensemble led to some friction, his success as a rehearsal leader was acknowledged by the other members of the group.

On 22 January 1970 Royal left Basie and settled in Los Angeles, where he performed and recorded with Bill Berry's big band (from 1972 into the 1990s) and the Capp–Pierce Juggernaut and recorded as a soloist with small groups under such leaders as Dave Frishberg (1977) and Warren Vaché (1978); he also recorded as the leader of a band with Snooky Young (1978) and with his own groups (1978, 1980). He worked with Earl Hines in 1971, toured South Africa with Monk Montgomery in 1974, and from 1980 played at the Colorado Jazz Party for ten years; later in the decade he participated in similar jazz parties in Minneapolis and San Diego. In 1983 he played for nine months in Los Angeles in the show *Sophisticated Ladies.* Royal also toured internationally: he performed regularly in France at the Nice festival (until 1987), worked in England as a soloist (late 1980s), participated in a reunion with several of Basie's sidemen for concerts in Japan (1989), and performed in Europe with Ernie Wilkins's band (1990). In 1990 he recorded with a small group led by Frank Wess at the Concord Jazz Festival. Royal had a clear, crisp tone, reminiscent of Benny Carter's; his playing remained firmly rooted in the swing style, and was both harmonically and rhythmically solid. He was highly prized as one of the finest lead alto saxophonists in jazz.

Oral history material in *CLU* (CASOHP), *DSI* (JOHP), and *NjR* (JOHP).

SELECTED RECORDINGS

As leader: with Maxwell Davis: September in the Rain/I've got the world on a string (1951, Swing Time 251), Little White Lies (1951, Swing Time 313); with S. Young: *Snooky and Marshall's Album* (1978, Conc. 55); *Royal Blue* (1980, Conc. 125)

As sideman on clarinet: A. Tatum: With Plenty of Money and You/I've got my love to keep me warm (1937, Decca 1198); first issued on [various artists:] *The Golden Swing Years*, ii (1940–42, Bruns. 87526), L. Hampton: Blues in the News (1942); J. McVea: Play it over (1946, Black & White 762); B. Mosley: Bee boogie boo (1945, BelTone 752); S. Gaillard: Santa Monica Jump (1946, BelTone 761)

As sideman on alto saxophone: L. Hampton: Bouncing at the Beacon (1940, Vic. 27364); B. Mosley: Voot Rhythm (1945, BelTone 751); D. Henderson: Get your Kicks (1945), first issued on *Get your Kicks* (1945, Del. 668); L. Glenn: Joymaker's Boogie (1947, Imperial 5031); C. Basie: *Basie* (1957, Roul. 52003), incl. Fantail; *The Count Basie Story* (1960, Roul. 1); *Back to Basie* (1962, Roul. 52113); *Basie in Sweden* (1962, Roul. 52099); D. Frishberg: *Getting Some Fun out of Life* (1977, Conc. 37); Concord All Stars: *Festival Time* (1979, Conc. 117)

SELECTED FILMS AND VIDEOS

Bundle of Blues (1933); Sing Sinner Sing (1933); Belle of the Nineties [It Ain't No Sin] (1934); Every Day's a Holiday (1938); "King" Cole and his Trio (1950); Sugar Chile Robinson–Billie Holiday–Count Basie and his Sextet (1950); Double Dynamite [It's Only Money] (1951); Jamboree [Disc Jockey Jamboree] (1957); Newport Jazz Festival 1962 (1962); Sex and the Single Girl (1964); Count Basie and his Orchestra (1965); Made in Paris (1966); Lepke (1974); To the Count of Basie (1979); Noni Bernardi Big Band: the Way it Was: the Big Band Swing Era Revisited (*c* early 1990s)

BIBLIOGRAPHY

ChiltonW; *FeatherE*; *Feather–Gitler '70s*; *McCarthyB*; *SheridanCB*

J. Hélian: "Vers un grand orchestre de jazz en France? Jacques Hélian tente une grande expérience," *Jh*, no.115 (1956), 20

R. Horricks: *Count Basie and his Orchestra: its Music and its Musicians* (London and New York, 1957), 214

S. Dance: "Marshall Royal," *JJ*, xv/3 (1962), 2

P. Hughes: "Anglo-American Exchange: the Basie Band's Marshall Royal," *Crescendo*, ii/7 (1962), 22

C. Battestini and J.-P. Battestini: "Marshall Royal: allons à l'essential," *BHcF*, no.284 (1980), 10

S. Dance: *The World of Count Basie* (New York and London, 1980), 164

L. D. Holmes and J. W. Thomson: *Jazz Greats: Getting Better with Age* (New York, 1986)

M. L. Hester: "Royal Touch," *MR*, xv/8 (1988), 1

Karrah: "Marshall Royal," *Cadence*, xiv/3 (1988) 20

Obituaries: *Los Angeles Times* (13 May 1995); *New York Times* (20 May 1995); T. Burke, *Blues & Rhythm*, no.100 (1995), 33

M. Royal and C. P. Gordon: *Marshall Royal: Jazz Survivor* (London and New York, 1996) [incl. discography by H. Rye]

LEROY OSTRANSKY/BK, HOWARD RYE

Royal Gardens. Ballroom in Chicago; *see* NIGHTCLUBS AND OTHER VENUES.

Royal Roost (i). Nightclub in New York; *see* NIGHTCLUBS AND OTHER VENUES.

Royal Roost [Roost] **(ii).** Record company and label. The company was established by Teddy Reig in New York around 1950. Named after the nightclub in the city, it used the full name on the discs themselves but only the word "Roost" on liners. It organized important sessions by Stan Getz in 1950–51 and reissued many of the tracks recorded by Charlie Parker for Dial in 1947. The company's principal artists were Johnny Smith (1952–62) and Sonny Stitt (1952–*c*1965), though the catalogue also included material by Bud Powell (made for De Luxe in 1947 but not issued), Coleman Hawkins (1950), Billy Taylor (ii) (1951–2), Seldon Powell (1955–6), and Gene Quill (1958). From the late 1950s the catalogue was distributed by Roulette, and Royal Roost soon became a division of that company, which continued to market albums under the label's name until 1971.

BIBLIOGRAPHY

P. van Engelen: "Roost Records," *Names & Numbers* (1985), no.1, p.23; no.2, p.4

T. Reig and E. Berger: *Reminiscing in Tempo: the Life and Times of a Jazz Hustler* (Metuchen, NJ, and London, 1990)

BK

Rozenbergs, Gunārs (*b* Riga, Latvian SSR [now Latvia], 23 March 1947). Latvian trumpeter, composer, and arranger. He began playing jazz in 1965 and in 1967 led a quartet at the Tallinn International Jazz Festival. During the following years he continued to lead small groups, as well as a big band that performed in Riga, Tallinn, and Moscow. In 1984 he became the conductor of the orchestra of Latvian TV and Radio, and in 1986 he graduated from the Latvian SSR Yazep Vitol State Conservatory in Riga with a degree in trumpet. Rozenbergs's playing is well illustrated by his album *Laura* (1979, Mel. C60 1122930). His best-known composition is *Limping Blues*, which is in 11/8 time (i.e., 3/8 + 3/8 + 3/8 + 2/8). He wrote many arrangements of pieces by Latvian composers, especially Raimonds Pauls.

WALTER OJAKÄÄR

Rubalcaba, Gonzalo (Julio Gonzales Fonseca) (*b* Havana, 27 May 1963). Cuban pianist. He grew up in a musical family: his grandfather was a conductor, composer, and educator who composed the Cuban danzon *El cadete constitucional*, his father was a classical pianist who also played tenor saxophone, and his three brothers played bass, piano, and percussion. Exposed to jazz through his father's record collection, Rubalcaba began on piano when he was eight and took classical lessons at the Amadeo Roldan Conservatory in Havana; he learned percussion from the age of 13, and later he studied composition at Havana's Institute of Fine Arts. He began working professionally, as both a drummer and a pianist, in his teens, and from 1980 he toured internationally in the Cuban dance band Orquesta Aragon. In 1984 he formed a fusion band, Grupo Proyecto, with which he again toured internationally. At the Jazz Plaza festival in Havana in 1985 he met Dizzy Gillespie, with whom he recorded and appeared in the video *A Night in Havana: Dizzy Gillespie in Cuba* (1987). In 1989 he performed and recorded in Charlie Haden's trio, alongside Paul Motian, at the Festival International de Jazz de Montréal. That same year a scheduled performance with Gillespie in New York was cancelled after Rubalcaba and his Grupo Proyecto bandmembers were denied performance visas by the American government, which banned all Cuban employees. Rubalcaba continued to appear elsewhere with his own groups; he performed and recorded with Haden and Motian at the Montreux International Jazz Festival (1990), recorded with Haden and Jack DeJohnette (1991), and performed and recorded with John Patitucci and DeJohnette at the Mt. Fuji Jazz Festival (1991).

In 1992 Rubalcaba was granted a departure visa by the Cuban government and moved to Santo Domingo in the Dominican Republic. In May 1993 he performed at Alice Tully Hall in New York as an unaccompanied soloist, in a trio with Haden and DeJohnette, and with his own Cuban quartet (but with the stipulation that the Cubans perform for free); in September of the same year he appeared with Joe Henderson at the Free Jazz Festival in São Paulo. In 1994 the diplomatic battle finally ended: having established residence in the Dominican Republic, Rubalcaba was allowed to perform in the USA without prior governmental approval, even though he remained a Cuban citizen. That year he appeared twice with his quartet, and he played on television in "An All-star Tribute to Antonio Carlos Jobim." He performed in a duo with Joe Lovano in San Francisco (1995), and the two men later recorded in New York (1997). In 1996 he toured the USA with his quartet, and that August he performed at Yoshi's in Oakland in a trio consisting of Brian Bromberg and Tony Williams. Around 1997, again with the approval of the Cuban government, Rubalcaba moved to Miami, where he formed a trio consisting of the double bass player Jeff Chambers and Ignacio Berroa.

Rubalcaba has the ability to make anything he attempts to play seem easy. On his early recordings his classical training seemed to hinder his abilities as a jazz pianist, and he had a tendency to overplay; by the mid-1990s, however, he was using classical music as a tool with which to create, rather than to show off, and his youthful exuberance had given way somewhat to a more mature sense of restraint. Like many Cuban musicians, Rubalcaba is not well versed in the blues, but he is a master of harmonic substitution and variation.

SELECTED RECORDINGS

Duos with J. Lovano: *Flying Colors* (1997, BN 56092-2)
As leader: of Grupo Proyecto: *Live in Havana* (1986, Messidor 15960), *Mi gran pasión* (1987, Messidor 15999), *Giraldilla* (1989, Messidor 15801-2); *Discovery: Live at Montreux* (1990, BN B21Z-95478); *The Blessing* (1991, BN B21Z-97197); *Images: Live at Mt. Fuji* (1991, BN B21Z-99492); *Rapsodia* (1992, BN B21Z-28264); *Diz* (1993, BN B21Z-30490); *Imagine: Gonzalo Rubalcaba in the USA* (1993–4, BN 30491-2); *Antiguo* (*c*1998, BN 37717-2); *Inner Voyage* (*c*1998, BN 99241-2)

BIBLIOGRAPHY

Feather–GitlerBEJ
J. Pareles: "Cuban Pianist and Band Refused Visas by US," *New York Times* (19 Aug 1989)
E. Schwartz: "US Bars Cuban Pianist," *Washington Post* (19 Aug 1989)
J. C. Coto: "Riffs: Gonzalo Rubalcaba," *DB*, lviii/8 (1991), 14
R. L. Doerschuk: "Gonzalo Rubalcaba: the Totally Amazing Jazz Pianist that the US Government Does Not Want You to Hear," *Keyboard*, xvii/8 (1991), 30 [incl. transcr.]
H. Mandel: "Gonzalo Rubalcaba: Ballads beyond Borders," *JT*, xix/6 (1991), 39
F. Gonzalez: "Gonzalo Rubalcaba: a Bud Powell for the 21st Century," *Boston Globe* (19 July 1992)
M. Hennessey: "Gonzalo: à pas de géant," *Jm*, no.417 (1992), 32
R. Guilliatt: "Politics and the Pianist," *Los Angeles Times* (20 May 1993)
H. Mandel: "Gonzalo Rubalcaba: I'll Take Manhattan," *DB*, lx/9 (1993), 16 [incl. discography]
L. Rohter: "Pop Music: Jazz and Politics Meet over the Keyboard," *New York Times* (6 May 1993)
Z. Stewart: "The Keys to Lifting an Embargo," *Los Angeles Times* (24 June 1994)
P. Elwood: "Bay Jazz Fans Get First Look at Gonzalo Rubalcaba: Cool Breeze from Cuba," *San Francisco Examiner* (30 March 1995)
M. Holston: "Gonzalo Rubalcaba," *Jazziz Presents the Key Players* (1995), winter, 54
B. Blumenthal: "Gonzalo Rubalcaba Arrives – at Last," *Boston Globe* (24 March 1996)
E. Rideout: "Man and Montuno: Gonzalo Rubalcaba Redefines Jazz Piano," *Keyboard*, xxii/8 (1996), 46 [incl. transcrs]
H. Reich: "Gonzalo Rubalcaba's Struggle to be Heard," *Chicago Tribune* (29 June 1997)
H. Mandel: "The Island of Gonzalo," *Jazziz*, xv/1 (1998), 55

GK

Rubin, Stan(ley Norman) (*b* New Rochelle, NY, 14 July 1933). Clarinetist and leader. He played clarinet in dance bands at school. In 1951, while at Princeton University, he formed a dixieland quintet, the Tigertown Five, with which he appeared at various university campuses around the Northeast. The following year the group held an engagement at Jimmy Ryan's in New York and in summer 1953 it toured Europe. It then worked at the Glen Island Casino, New Rochelle, and performed at a Carnegie Hall college band concert (1954). In 1955 it played at the Newport Jazz Festival and appeared in Stan Kenton's television special "Music '55," and in the same year Rubin modified its style to include swing and bop. After playing for Grace Kelly's wedding in Monaco in April 1956 Rubin formed a big band which was oriented towards re-creating the music of the swing era, using transcriptions; among his sidemen were Ed Polcer, Doc Cheatham, Tommy Newsom, Marty Napoleon, and other prominent musicians of that era. From 1956 to around 1959 the orchestra achieved some popularity and made approximately 50 appearances on television. During this period Rubin formed his own entertainment company, and he consequently spent most of the 1960s booking acts and performed only occasionally. When he re-formed his big band in 1973, it performed weekly in New York at the Riverboat, the Roseland, and Fat Tuesday; from 1979 the group appeared at the Red Blazer Too and from 1983 to 1986 it was resident at the Red Parrot. Rubin had to give up playing clarinet after the removal of a brain tumor in 1986, but he continued to lead his band in the 1990s. His album *Open House* (1957–8, Coral 57238) provides a good example of the sound of his big band at the height of its popularity.

BIBLIOGRAPHY

FeatherE
C. Deffaa: *Traditionalists and Revivalists in Jazz* (Metuchen, NJ, and London, 1993), 233

GK

Rubin, Vanessa (Kay) (*b* Cleveland, 14 March 1957). Singer. She received classical training, but began singing jazz early in her career. She studied journalism at Ohio State University (BA) and then returned to Cleveland, where she sang with and managed a local organ quartet and also worked in other groups. In 1982 she moved to New York, where she taught in the public school system. She studied with Barry Harris and Frank Foster at Harris's Jazz Cultural Theater, and performed variously with Stanley Cowell, Kenny Barron, George Coleman, Pharoah Sanders, Frank Foster's Loud Minority, Lionel Hampton's big band, and

Mercer Ellington's orchestra. From January 1992, following the release of her first recording as a leader, Rubin toured internationally and garnered high praise for her singing, which may be heard to good effect on her albums *Pastiche* (*c*1993, Novus 01241-63512-2) and *I'm Glad There is You* (*c*1993, Novus 01241-63170-2).

BIBLIOGRAPHY

N. Tesser: "Jazz: Ladies Be Good: Trio Brings a New Vitality to Jazz Vocal Tradition," *Chicago Tribune* (13 June 1993)
D. Kasrel: "Hearsay: Vanessa Rubin," *JT*, xxiv/7 (1994), 10
<http://www.vanessarubin.com> (1998)

SCOTT FREDRICKSON, GK

Rucker [née Cornelison]**, Ellyn (Kay)** (*b* Des Moines, IA, 29 Aug 1937). Pianist and singer. She grew up in a musical family and took up piano at the age of eight; when she was in her teens she was introduced to jazz by her brother, who played double bass. Having settled in Denver in the late 1950s she spent much of the next two decades bringing up her children, although she did perform with her husband, also a double bass player; following their divorce in 1979 she worked full-time as a musician. From the mid-1980s she toured internationally as a soloist with her own groups and with Spike Robinson, and in 1986 she made the first of several successful appearances at the North Sea Jazz Festival. In 1992 she took part in Marian McPartland's NPR show "Piano Jazz." Rucker continued to perform regularly in the Denver area through the 1990s. She may be seen with her trio in the video *Ellyn Rucker: Live in New Orleans featuring Mark Singer and Jill Frederickson* (*c*1993 [filmed 1991]); however, the double bass player is actually Mark Simon rather than Singer.

SELECTED RECORDINGS

(recorded for Capri unless otherwise indicated)

As leader: *Ellyn* (1987, 10187); *This Heart of Mine* (1988, 7409-2); with S. Robinson: *Nice Work!* (1989, 74017); *Live in New Orleans* (1991, Leisure Jazz 04900-91054)

BIBLIOGRAPHY

CarrJ; *Feather–GitlerBEJ*
D. Boyce: "Jazzkarriere: auf die altbewährte Art: Ellyn Rucker," *JP*, xxxvi/7 (1987), 14
J. Bradley: "Jazz Artist Ellyn Rucker Sheds 'Lounge Act' Label," *Denver Post* (6 Aug 1992)
D. Saunders: "Denver's Madame Jazz," *Denver Rocky Mountain News* (12 March 1995)
J. Bradley: "'Renewed' Ellyn Rucker Returns to the Weekend Scene," *Denver Post* (17 May 1998)

GK

Rudd, Roswell (Hopkins, Jr.) (*b* Sharon, CT, 17 Nov 1935). Trombonist. His father was an accomplished amateur jazz drummer. After the family moved to Clinton, New York, Rudd learned french horn from the age of 11 and taught himself to play trombone while in his teens. While studying classical music at Yale University he belonged to Eli's Chosen Six (to 1958), a dixieland band. He then went to New York and played dixieland professionally with such musicians as Pee Wee Russell, Eddie Condon, Wild Bill Davison, and Edmund Hall, and with the Saints and Sinners; he may be seen with Phil Woods and Kenny Davern in a dixieland band in the film *The Hustler* (1961). But at this same time, while working with Herbie Nichols (1960–62), whom Rudd considered his most inspiring teacher, his musical orientation shifted. He was a member of a quartet with Steve Lacy and Dennis Charles that for some time played exclusively the music of Thelonious Monk (1961–4), recorded with Cecil Taylor (1961), and joined Bill Dixon's free-jazz group (early 1962), in which Archie Shepp and Charles were also sidemen. In the summer of 1964 he recorded with Albert Ayler and with Shepp, and he was a founding member with John Tchicai and Milford Graves of the New York Art Quartet, for which he also wrote compositions and arrangements; later that year he took part in the October Revolution in Jazz. Having performed as a soloist and arranged John Coltrane's ballad *Naima* on Shepp's

Roswell Rudd at the Purcell Room, London, 1997

album *Four for Trane* (1964) he joined Shepp's group (winter 1965), with which he played in London and at the Donaueschingen Musiktage (1967). With Robin Kenyatta, Karl Berger, and Lee Konitz early in 1968 he formed the Primordial Quartet, the size and membership of which varied considerably during the next few years. In 1969 he worked with Charlie Haden's Liberation Music Orchestra, then joined a group led by Gato Barbieri that included Haden, Beaver Harris, and Lonnie Smith as sidemen; he later recorded with the group. After disbanding the Primordial Quartet in March 1970 he wrote compositions for the Jazz Composer's Orchestra (these may be heard on his album *Numatik Swing Band*, 1973).

Having studied ethnomusicology with Alan Lomax from 1964, Rudd published a brief poetic essay, "Some Quartertones around the Drone: the Universality of the Blues" (*DB*, xxxv/2 (1968), 22). Later he taught improvisation and ethnomusicology part-time at Bard College in Annandale-on-Hudson, New York (1973–6), while also driving a taxi and performing in New York City at St. James Infirmary, a club that he ran in partnership with Hod O'Brien (1974–5). He recorded and made European summer tours with Carla Bley (1976–7) and Enrico Rava (1976–8) and recorded in a duo with Giorgio Gaslini, further with Bley (1978), and as an unaccompanied soloist (1979); from 1976 he taught music ethnology and improvisation as an instructor at a community college branch campus of the University of Maine in Augusta, but lacked the academic credentials to keep this job permanently. In 1982, with Lacy, he made an album devoted to the music of Nichols and Monk. From 1986 into the 1990s he played show and dance music for older audiences at a hotel in Accord, New York, but he returned to jazz in the mid-1990s when he recorded with Allen Lowe (1993–4) and performed with Elton Dean's group Newsense in London (1996); he then took part in a few recording sessions with Dean, and as a leader made an album of trio and unaccompanied performances of Nichols's music. Early in 1999 he performed in Oakland, California, together with Tchicai and the trio led by the saxophonist Rob Scheps, and in June of that year he played in a reunion of the New York Art Quartet. Rudd brought to free jazz many of the qualities more often associated with the early jazz trombone; these include a large, warm tone, an earthy vocal sound punctuated by growls, and a deeply felt sense of rhythm.

Video oral history material in *NCH* (HCJA).

SELECTED RECORDINGS

As leader: of New York Art Quartet (with J. Tchicai): *The New York Art Quartet* (1964, ESP 1004); *Roswell Rudd* (1965, Amer. 6114); *Everywhere* (1966, Imp. 9126); *Numatik Swing Band* (1973, JCOA 1007); *Flexible Flyer* (1974, Ari. 1006); *Maine* (1976, BVHaast 011); *The Definitive* (1979, Horo 12); *Regeneration* (1982, SN 1054); with E. Dean: *Rumors of an Incident* (1996, Slam 223); *The Unheard Herbie Nichols*, i (1996, CIMP 133) [incl. unaccompanied solos]

As sideman: C. Taylor: on *The Complete Candid Recordings of Cecil Taylor* (1960–61, Mosaic 127), Jumpin' Punkins (1961); S. Lacy: *Schooldays* (1963, Emanem 3316); A. Shepp: *Four for Trane* (1964, Imp. 71); *Archie Shepp Live in San Francisco* (1966, Imp. 9118); *Archie Shepp Live at the Donaueschingen Music Festival* (1967, Saba 15148); S. Lacy: *Trickles* (1976, BS 0008); C. Bley: *Dinner Music* (1976, Watt 6); *European Tour 1977* (1977, Watt 8); E. Rava: *Enrico Rava Quartet* (1978, ECM 1122); E. Dean: *Bladik* (1996, Cuneform Rune 92); *Elton Dean's Newsense* (1997, Slam 229)

BIBLIOGRAPHY

Feather '60s; *Feather–Gitler '70s*; *GrayF*

D. Heckman: "Roswell Rudd," *DB*, xxxi/3 (1964), 14

V. Wilmer: "Trad Trombone in Outer Space," *MM* (11 Nov 1967), 8

D. Constant: "Roswell le Rude," *Jm*, no.179 (1970), 36

B. Tepperman: "Rudd, Moncur and some other Stuff," *Coda*, x/2 (1971), 8

B. McRae: "Avant Courier: Roswell Rudd: All the Way from Dixie," *JJI*, xxviii/5 (1975), 20

B. Primack: "Roswell Rudd: Transmission from the Soul," *DB*, xlv/16 (1978), 24

M. Luzzi: *Uomini e avanguardie jazz* (Milan, 1980)

P. Danson: "An Interview with Roswell Rudd," *Coda*, no.183 (1982), 4

M. Zwerin: *Close Enough for Jazz* (London, 1983)

G. Giddins: "Technicolor Repertory," *Rhythm-a-ning: Jazz Tradition and Innovation in the '80s* (New York, and Oxford, England, 1985), 168

D. DuPont: "Roswell Rudd: Interview," *Cadence*, xviii (1992), no.10, p.5; no.11, p.8

K. Whitehead: "The Return of Roswell Rudd," *Coda*, no.272 (1997), 24

<http://mindspring.com/~scala/rudd.html> (1999) [discography]

LEE JESKE/BK

Rudiments. Patterns of strokes used by percussion players. Evidence of rudimental drumming patterns dates from 15th-century Swiss military ordinances, and similar patterns were used by European drummers and taken to the USA in the 18th and 19th centuries during the numerous wars waged in North America. *Strube's Drum and Fife Instructor* of 1869 codified the most popular of these military patterns into 26 standard rudiments. In 1932 the National Association of Rudimental Drummers (NARD) adopted Strube's patterns, many of which have mnemonic names; since most sticking figures may be analyzed as belonging to one or more rudimental patterns, it is difficult to strike a drum without playing one rudiment or another. The earliest jazz drummers also invented patterns to which they applied mnemonic names (*see* Drum set, §II, 1), using them in much the same way as did their military counterparts – as a teaching device and to accompany particular melodic figures or specific dance arrangements; this practice has continued throughout the history of jazz drumming (for example, in the employment of ragtime rat-tat-tats, shuffle rhythm, and fat-back rhythm, which involves a strong backbeat).

The term rudimental drumming is often applied to the playing of Gene Krupa and several other swing and dixieland drummers of the 1930s and 1940s. At times it has been used derisively to describe the work of drummers who do not play with a jazz-like feel, but a number of well-known musicians, including Cozy Cole, Buddy Rich, Sonny Payne, Joe Morello, and Steve Gadd, have incorporated various rudiments into their playing with startling results. Rudimental patterns have also been used by other percussionists in jazz, notably the timbales player Willie Bobo and Lionel Hampton, who initially worked as a drummer and subsequently adapted his technique to the vibraphone. The patterns played on conga drum in Afro-Cuban jazz and the intricate rhythmic formulas performed on tablā in Indian music also have their basis in rudimental systems.

Jazz drummers use rudiments almost exclusively during solos, fills, and kicks, some of the most popular being the following:

(a) The roll. The roll produces a sustained sound and is achieved either by striking the sticks alternately on the drumhead in an even manner (a single-stroke roll) or by bouncing alternate sticks (a double-stroke, closed, or buzz roll). The single-stroke roll is extremely difficult to play fast, and it is commonly believed that Rich is the performer par excellence of this rudiment. The double-stroke roll and the closed or buzz roll, played at various lengths (5, 7, 9, 11, and 15 strokes) and ending with a single tap, have been used from the earliest days of jazz in patterns suited to fit the music. The most common accompaniment figure during the 1920s and 1930s is shown in ex.2; it has since been replaced

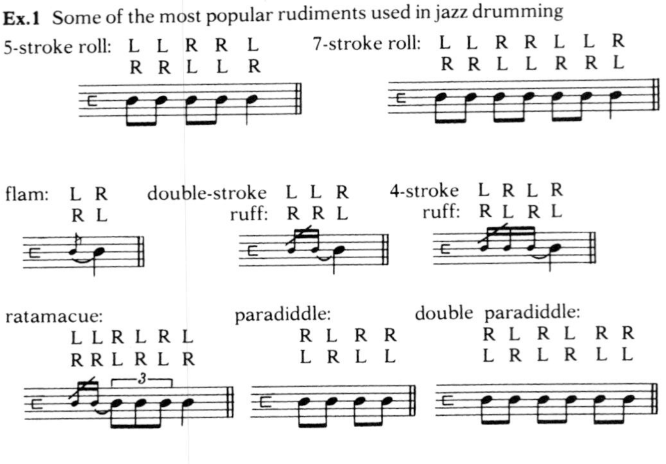

Ex.1 Some of the most popular rudiments used in jazz drumming

Ex.2 The accompanimental figure most commonly used during the 1920s and 1930s

by cymbal accompaniment patterns, although the sound still remains in the swish of the brushes. Another type of roll, the press roll, consists of a succession of double-stroke rolls of varying lengths played in march or syncopated march rhythms.

(b) The flam. The flam is a two-note pattern consisting of a principal note preceded by a grace note. Like most rudiments, flams may be played alternately or successively. Jazz drummers have executed them in a variety of ways, from the open flam (played by delaying the principal note) to the flat flam (played by striking both sticks almost simultaneously).

(c) The ruff. There are two types of ruff. The double-stroke ruff is played with one stick and consists of a principal note preceded by two grace notes, while the four-stroke ruff is played with alternate sticks and consists of a principal note preceded by three grace notes. Jazz drummers often execute a ruff before a kick.

(d) The drag. The term is used as a synonym for a double-stroke ruff and is also applied to a ruff played at a slow tempo.

(e) The ratamacue. The ratamacue is played by following a double-stroke ruff with a triplet, and may be lengthened by additional ruffs to form double ratamacues and triple ratamacues. These are well illustrated in Cozy Cole's solo *Ratamacue* (1939, Voc. 4700), recorded with Cab Calloway's band.

(f) The paradiddle. The paradiddle consists of four even notes, first starting with the right hand and then the left; double and triple paradiddles are played by adding alternate single strokes at the beginning of the figure. Permutations of the basic rudiment allow the drummer to perform a wide variety of accents and rhythmic figures, including the flam paradiddle, the paradiddle-diddle (RLRRLL, LRLLRR), and the triplet paradiddle (RLR LRR, LRL RLL). Cole's recording *Paradiddle* (1940, Voc. 5467), also with Calloway, provides a good example of this technique.

T. DENNIS BROWN

Rudolph, Steve(n Ray) (*b* Evansville, IL, 10 April 1949). Pianist. He studied trumpet from the age of eight and later attended Butler University, Indianapolis (1967–70), as a trumpet and composition major. Self-taught as a pianist, he began playing at the age of 23. He toured with the Tommy Dorsey Orchestra under the direction of Buddy Morrow (1977–8), then settled permanently in Harrisburg, Pennsylvania, where he led a quartet with John Von Ohlen and the double bass player Frank Smith (1978–80); among his weekly guest soloists were Johnny Coles, Joe Lovano, Eric Kloss, Junior Cook, and Ira Sullivan. In 1980 he founded the Central Pennsylvania Friends of Jazz, an organization that has presented concerts since its inception; Rudolph became its president in 1997. He recorded with a local group, Just Friends (1981, 1983), formed trios with the double bass player Steve Meashey and the drummer Ray Brinker (1982–4) and Hassan J. J. Wiggins and the drummer Chris Waller (1984–8), and led a big band (1983–9) with Coles and Al Grey among its sidemen. With the violinist Jorg Widmoser he co-led a band (1986–91) which included Thomas Stabenow. During this period he also worked regularly with the flutist Leslie Burrs (1986–9) and taught jazz at Elizabethtown (Pennsylvania) College (1987–90).

From 1989 Rudolph has worked primarily as an unaccompanied soloist, but he has also led a number of ad hoc jazz groups involving such distinguished musicians as Tom Harrell, Tim Warfield, Steve Turre, Grey, Matt Wilson, and Jim Snidero. In addition he worked with Mark Murphy (1993), Louie Bellson (1995–6), Kim Parker, Bill Goodwin, and Coles (in the trumpeter's last quartet, 1996–7). In 1996, with the guitarist Vinnie Valentino, he formed a quartet whose other members are Larry Gray and Bob Moses, and he in 1997 he established a trio consisting of the double bass player Paul Langosch and Goodwin. He performed at the *Jazz Times* convention in New York in October 1998 in a trio with Michael Formanek and Wilson. From 1993 Rudolph has been a partner in Rudolph & Langosch, Inc., a music consulting, telemarketing, publishing, and recording company; among the recordings issued on its label is his album *Everything I Love* (1994, R & L 41049). His album *Christmas with the Steve Rudolph Trio* (*c*1997, R & L 1054) is an excellent showcase of his playing.

GK

Rüegg, Mathias (*b* Zurich, 8 Dec 1952). Swiss pianist, composer, and arranger. He was the founder in 1977 of the Vienna art orchestra. (F. M. Coudert: "Mathias Rüegg: entre blues et Brahms," *Jm*, no.381 (1989), 38

Ruff. One of the drumstrokes collectively known as Rudiments.

Ruff, Willie (Henry, Jr.) (*b* Sheffield, AL, 1 Sept 1931). Double bass and french horn player, and teacher. He learned french horn in the army, and played in bands at the Lockbourne (Ohio) Air Force Base, where in 1947 he met Dwike Mitchell. He continued to study orchestral horn, and was also a pupil of the composer Paul Hindemith at Yale University (MA 1954). He then joined Lionel Hampton's band, with which Mitchell was already playing, and in 1955 the two musicians formed a duo. They have lectured and performed throughout the USA, and in 1959, on tour with the Yale Russian Chorus, they were the first Western jazz musicians to perform in the USSR after World War II. In 1966 they accompanied President Lyndon Johnson to Mexico, and the following year they made a film in Brazil which traced the African roots of Brazilian music. They appear with Dizzy Gillespie in the film documentary *The Legacy of the Drum* (*c*1970). As a professor of music at Yale, Ruff inaugurated the Duke Ellington Fellowship Program in 1972. In 1979, with the scientist John Rodgers, he recorded a realization of *Harmonices mundi*, a treatise by the German mathematician and music theorist Johannes Kepler. The Mitchell–Ruff duo played in China in 1981, and Ruff recorded as an unaccompanied soloist in St. Mark's basilica, Venice, in 1983. In 1994 the duo held an engagement in Chicago at the Jazz Showcase. Ruff is fluent in eight languages, and his unusual talents as both a performer and a teacher have helped to make jazz accessible to audiences throughout the world. He is the author of *A Call to Assembly: the Autobiography of a Musical Storyteller* (New York, 1991).

Oral history material in *CtY*.

SELECTED RECORDINGS

As unaccompanied soloist: *Willie Ruff at Saint Mark's* (1983, Kepler 1931)

Duos with D. Mitchell: *Mitchell–Ruff Duo* (1955, Epic 3221); *Appearing Nightly* (1957, Roul. 52002); *Jazz Mission to Moscow* (1959, Roul. 52034); *Strayhorn* (1969, Mstr. 335); *Virtuoso Elegance in Jazz* (1984, Kepler 1234)

As leader: with D. Mitchell: *Ruff–Mitchell Duo Plus Strings and Brass* (1958, Roul. 52013); with D. Mitchell and Charlie Smith: *Catbird Suite* (1961, Atl. 1374); with D. Mitchell and Elcio Melito: *Brazilian Trip* (1966, Epic 26360); with D. Mitchell and D. Gillespie: *Dizzy Gillespie and the Mitchell–Ruff Duo in Concert* (1971, Mstr. 325), *Dizzy Gillespie Live with the Mitchell–Ruff Duo* (1970, 1979–80, Book-of-the-Month 516517)

BIBLIOGRAPHY

"Willie Ruff Translates Russ Tour," *Variety*, ccxvi (7 Oct 1959), 63

"Johnson Takes Jazz on Mexico Trip," *DB*, xxxiii/11 (1966), 12

J. Blanksteen: "Computer Synthesizes 'Music of the Spheres'," *New York Times* (24 April 1979), §C, p.1

H. Schonberg: "The Planets are not Candidates for the Hit Parade," *New York Times* (24 April 1979), §C, p.1

R. Sudhalter: "Mitchell and Ruff are Well-traveled Musicians," *New York Post* (6 June 1980), 40

W. Zinsser: *Willie and Dwike: an American Profile* (New York and Toronto, 1984) [biographies]

R. Beach: "Diligence and Mentors Make a Musician's Life," *New York Times* (24 Nov 1991)

PHILIP GREENE

Ruffins, Kermit (*b* New Orleans, 1964). Trumpeter and leader. He became interested in traditional jazz at the age of 15 after following a jazz funeral and shortly afterwards took up trumpet. In 1982 he co-founded the RE-BIRTH BRASS BAND, with which he may be seen performing in the video *The JVC/ Smithsonian Folkways Video Anthology of Music and Dance of the Americas*, i (*c*1995 [filmed 1986]). He left the group in summer 1994 following the release the previous year of his album *World on a String* (1992, Justice 1101) and formed a quintet, the Barbecue Swingers; later he led a nine-piece group of the same name on the album *Swing This* (c1998, Basin Street 102). From the early 1990s he has led weekly jam sessions at New Orleans venues, notably Little People's Place, Trombone Shorty's, and Joe's Cozy Corner. Ruffins has also performed with the Olympia Brass Band, Ellis Marsalis, Lionel Hampton, and Danny Barker, among others.

BIBLIOGRAPHY

S. Aiges: "First of the Second-liners," *New Orleans Times-Picayune* (25 April 1992)

——: "Music: No Stoppin' Kermit Ruffins," *New Orleans Times-Picayune* (12 March 1993)

M. Tiserand: "Riffs: Kermit Ruffins," *DB*, lx/8 (1993), 14

P. Vacher: "Kermit Ruffins," *Jazz: the Magazine*, no.20 (1993), 11

G. Wyckoff: "Hearsay: Kermit Ruffins: Re-born Again," *JT*, xxiii/4 (1993), 10

S. Aiges: "Music: Kermit Ruffins Leaves Rebirth to Give Solo Career New Life," *New Orleans Times-Picayune* (1 July 1994)

T. Carman: "Music: Trumpeter Ready to Soar on 2nd Solo," *Houston Post* (22 Jan 1995)

"Persona: Kermit Ruffins," *New Orleans Magazine*, xxxi/7 (1997), 13

G. Wyckoff: "Jazz All-stars: Half Brass," *New Orleans Magazine*, xxxii/7 (1998), 60

<http://www.basinstreetrecords.com/kermitbio.html> (1999)

B. Taylor: "Interview with Kermit Ruffins," <http://www.wwoz.org/html/story_kermit_interview.html> (1999)

N. Ketner: "All Aboard: a Profile of Kermit Ruffins," <http://www.satchmo.com/nolavl/kermit.html> (2000)

J. Tabak and D. Bias: "Louis Armstrong's Legacy: Our Pops, Who Art in Heaven, Hallowed be thy Horn," *Offbeat* (2000), August; repr. <http://www.offbeat.com/ob2008/cover_kermit_andrews.html> (2001)

For further recordings and bibliography *see* RE-BIRTH BRASS BAND.

GK

Rugolo, Pete(r) (*b* San Piero, Sicily, 25 Dec 1915). Arranger and composer. Having moved with his family to the the USA in 1921, he grew up in Petaluma, California, and attended San Francisco State College (BA 1938). He was one of the generation of jazz composers and arrangers who studied under Darius Milhaud, who was then on the faculty of Mills College in Oakland. While still a serviceman he sold his arrangement *Opus a Dollar Three Eighty* to Stan Kenton, and he became Kenton's full-time collaborator during the band's period of greatest success (1945–9). The large number of his compositions that were recorded by Kenton includes items in all the genres associated with the band but little that was memorable outside the hothouse atmosphere of Kenton's organization. As a record producer Rugolo had the distinction of commissioning Miles Davis's famous nonet sessions of 1949–50, but the recordings with his own band in 1954 and later albums under his name showed a tendency to turn attractive ideas about orchestration into gimmickry. In the 1950s, earlier than most of his jazz-influenced colleagues, Rugolo found a niche writing background music for films and for television series such as "The Thin Man" and "Dr. Kildare."

SELECTED ARRANGEMENTS

As leader: You stepped out of a dream/Bazaar (1954, Col. 40223); *Music for Hi-fi Bugs* (1956, EmA 36082); *Out on a Limb* (1956, EmA 36115); *Reeds in Hi-fi* (1956, Mer. 20260)

Recorded by S. Kenton: Opus a Dollar Three Eighty (1944, AFRS DB87); Artistry in Percussion (1946, Cap. 289); Machito (1947, Cap. 408); Chorale for Brass, Piano and Bongo (1947, Cap. 10183); Abstraction (1947, Cap. 10184)

BIBLIOGRAPHY

"Rugged Rugolo," *Metronome*, lxiii/4 (1947), 27

W. F. Lee: *Stan Kenton: Artistry in Rhythm* (Los Angeles, 1980/*R*1994) [incl. discography; *R* without discography]

S. Woolley: "Pete Rugolo: Artistry in Arranging," *JJI*, xlii/6 (1989), 12

——: "Pete Rugolo: Interlude at Capitol," *JJI*, xliv/10 (1991), 10

——: "Pete Rugolo: Reel Jazz," *JJI*, xlviii/4 (1995), 10

BRIAN PRIESTLEY

Ruiz, Hilton (*b* New York, 29 May 1952). Pianist. He was classically trained, and performed at Carnegie Recital Hall at the age of eight. As a teenager he played in Latin bands and studied with Joe Newman, Frank Foster, and others at Newman's Jazz Interactions; his first major association as a jazz musician was with Foster (1970), and he also began working with Newman. He was a pupil of Mary Lou Williams (from 1971) and thereafter played with Clark Terry (in Syracuse, New York, *c*1971, and intermittently thereafter), Cal Massey's big band (1971–2), Freddie Hubbard and Joe

Henderson (both 1972), Jackie McLean (with whom he first performed in Europe, in 1972), Charles Mingus (briefly, 1973), Roland Kirk (intermittently, 1973–7), Betty Carter, Archie Shepp, Chico Freeman, Pharoah Sanders, Marion Brown, and Paquito D'Rivera; in addition he worked in the New York area in duos, mainly with Major Holley, but also with Ray Drummond, Jimmy Rowser, or Jamil Nasser. With Fred Hopkins and Steve McCall, Ruiz formed a rhythm section which accompanied Arthur Blythe at the Tin Palace in New York, and he led a quartet consisting of Sanders, Reggie Workman, and Idris Muhammad. In 1978 he toured with Terry from Egypt to India, and after returning to the USA he performed and recorded until the following year with George Coleman. He performed occasionally in Japan, and regularly in Europe, the latter variously with Terry's big band, Brown, Coleman (at Ronnie Scott's, London, 1979), Abbey Lincoln (with Archie Shepp in Paris, 1980), the New York All Stars (which later became the Leaders, but without Ruiz), and his own groups, including a trio (consisting of Art Davis and Walter Perkins), with which he performed and recorded in Paris in November 1981. In 1987 he recorded a tribute to Kirk with Bill Hardman, Steve Turre, Junior Cook, and others in the Vibration Society, but otherwise his groups of the 1980s and 1990s presented a Latin-jazz fusion, involving such sidemen as Sam Rivers, David Sanchez, Jerry Gonzalez, Andy Gonzalez, Daniel Ponce, Steve Berrios, Ignacio Berroa, the percussionist Giovanni Hidalgo, and Turre. In the 1990s Ruiz performed with and arranged for Tito Puente and recorded with Greg Abate (1992). He is the author, with R. Bradley, of a three-volume piano method, *Jazz and How to Play it* (*c*1987).

SELECTED RECORDINGS

As leader: *Piano Man* (1975, Ste. 1036); *Excition* (1977, Ste. 1078); *New York Hilton* (1977, Ste. 1094); *Cross Currents* (1984, Stash 248); *Something Grand* (1986, Novus 3011-1-N); *El Camino (The Road)* (1987, Novus 3024-1-N); *Strut* (1988, Novus 3053-1-N); *A Moment's Notice* (1991, Novus 3123-2-N); *Manhattan Mambo* (1992, Telarc 83322); *Live at Birdland* (1992, Can. 79532); *Heroes* (1993, Telarc 83338); *Hands on Percussion* (*c*1994, RMM 81483)

As sideman: R. Kirk: *Return of the 5000 lb Man* (1976, WB 2918); *Kirkatron* (1976, WB 2982); C. Freeman: *Beyond the Rain* (1977, Cont. 7640); G. Coleman: *Amsterdam after Dark* (1978, Tim. 129)

BIBLIOGRAPHY

Feather–Gitler '70s
C. Berg: "Hilton Ruiz: 'Making People Happy'," *JT* (1987), Dec, 13
L. Birnbaum: "Hilton Ruiz," *DB*, liv/9 (1987), 15
M. Richards: "Hilton Ruiz," *JJI*, xli/1 (1988), 6
C. Gauffre: "Hilton Ruiz: fusion et karate," *Jm*, no.380 (1989), 40
——: "Hilton Ruiz: un choix de vie," *Jm*, no.397 (1990), 27
B. Primack: "Hilton Ruz: on the Move," *JT*, xxii/1 (1992), 36

SCOTT YANOW/BK

Rully [née Urziceanu], **Aura** (*b* Bucharest, 14 Dec 1946). Romanian singer. She studied violin and voice and attended the conservatory in Bucharest (1965–7); in 1965 she toured the USSR, Poland, and Israel with Janos Kőrössi's trio. From 1966 to 1969 she performed with the Bucharest Jazz Quintet, and in 1971 she recorded as its leader. Having married the group's drummer, Ron Rully, she moved with him to Canada. She performed with Duke Ellington at the Newport Jazz Festival in 1972, then worked in Europe with Art Farmer and Slide Hampton; around 1973–4 she made further recordings as a leader. After working in Canada with Gene DiNovi (1974) and touring the USA and Japan with Quincy Jones she performed with the Thad Jones–Mel Lewis Orchestra, and in 1977, in Sweden, she recorded the album *Thad and Aura* (Four Leaf Clover 5020) with Jones. Nothing is known of her career after the late 1970s. Rully had a pure, full tone, which rose to piercing intensity when she was scat singing.

BIBLIOGRAPHY

Feather–Gitler '70s
J. Byrczek and H. Matuszewska: "Eurojazz Personalities," *JF* [intl edn], no.37 (1975), 69
R. Flohil: "Ron and Aura Rully: Powerhouse Percussion and Stunning Singing," *Canadian Composer*, no.105 (1975), 12

KIMBERLY MCCORD

Rumsey, Howard (*b* Brawley, CA, 7 Nov 1917). Double bass player. He played drums as a youth, and changed to double bass while at college. His first important engagement was with Vido Musso's band in the late 1930s. The band's pianist, Stan Kenton, formed his own ensemble in 1940, and Rumsey joined it in 1941 as the double bass player. From 1942 he worked as a freelance in southern California and in 1949 formed a group that became resident at the Lighthouse Café, Hermosa Beach, near Los Angeles. He remained associated with the club for nearly 20 years, and eventually became its manager and joint owner. The first Lighthouse All Stars was a bop group featuring Teddy Edwards, Sonny Criss, and Hampton Hawes. When in 1951 Rumsey formed a new group, still known as the Lighthouse All Stars and including Shorty Rogers, Jimmy Giuffre, and Shelly Manne, the Lighthouse became an important center for innovative jazz on the West Coast. The All Stars continued from late in 1953 with Rolf Ericson, Bob Cooper, Bud Shank, and Max Roach, who left the following year to form a hard-bop group with Clifford Brown and was replaced by Stan Levey. Thereafter Jack Sheldon (1954), Stu Williamson (1954), Conte Candoli (late 1954 – May 1955), Claude Williamson (1954–5), Frank Rosolino (1955–60), Sonny Clark, Lou Levy, and many others were members of the group, which may be seen in the film *Mad at the World* (1955) and on the television show "Lighthouse All Stars" (1962). Rumsey's excellent ensemble playing provided a discreet but solid foundation for even the most unusual textures. In the early 1960s the group was gradually replaced at the club by others, and by 1968 Rumsey had ceased playing, after having appeared in the short film *Dizzy Gillespie* (1965). In 1972 he opened a new club, Concerts by the Sea, in Redondo Beach, California. He was the nominal leader of an album celebrating the 40th anniversary of the Lighthouse All Stars in 1989, but did not play.

See also Nightclubs and other venues (Los Angeles).

SELECTED RECORDINGS

As leader: *Lighthouse*, vi (1954–5, Cont. 3504); *Music for Lighthousekeeping* (1956, Cont. 3528); *Jazz Rolls Royce* (1957, Lighthouse 5)

As sideman: S. Kenton: Concerto for Doghouse (1942, Decca 4254); C. Barnet: Skyliner (1944, Decca 18659); J. Giuffre: Big Boy (1952, Tampa 114); M. Roach: *Drummin' the Blues* (1957, Lib. 3064)

BIBLIOGRAPHY

FeatherE; *Feather '60s*; *Feather–Gitler '70s*
L. Feather: *The Passion for Jazz* (New York, 1980/*R*1990), 167
L. D. Holmes and J. W. Thomson: *Jazz Greats: Getting Better with Age* (New York, 1986)
T. Schnabel: "Rumsey: l'homme phare," *Jm*, no.348 (1986), 22
"Howard Rumsey: He Switched the Lighthouse on to Jazz," *Los Angeles Times* (11 Feb 1989)
T. Gioia: *West Coast Jazz: Modern Jazz in California, 1945–1960* (New York, and Oxford, England, 1992)

SCOTT DeVEAUX/BK

Rundqvist, Gösta (*b* Iggesund, Sweden, 8 Feb 1945). Swedish pianist. He started playing with amateur bands when he was 14 and initially pursued a non-musical profession. In 1979, when he moved to Sandviken, he became a music teacher and joined the Sandviken Big Band. Word of his talents spread via the visiting soloists he accompanied, and he eventually became recognized as one of the finest pianists in Sweden. In 1988 he began performing full-time, based in Uppsala, touring widely, and working with several groups, including the quartets of the singer Svante Thuresson and Putte Wickman, the Nogenja big band led by Bosse Broberg, and his own units, mostly trios. Influenced early on by the playing of Bill Evans (ii), Rundqvist is a versatile, adventurous, and sensitive player. His son Fredrik Rundqvist (*b* 1970) has played drums for several well-known Swedish jazz groups and occasionally works with his father.

SELECTED RECORDINGS

As leader: *Until We Have Faces* (1994, Sittel 9212); *Bernhard's Boat* (1997, Sittel 9234); *Treecircle* (1998, Opus 3 19801)

As sideman: B. Broberg and Red Mitchell: *West of the Moon* (1992, Dra. 235); S. Thuresson: *Live* (1992, Sittel 9203); Agneta Baumann: *Comes Love* (1999, Touché 011)

BIBLIOGRAPHY

G. Olson: "En trygg rorsman vid pianot" [An assured helmsman at the piano], *Orkester journalen*, lviii/3 (1990), 14

<http://www.mic.stim.se/engelsk/11/facts/rundqvist.html> (1999)

LARS WESTIN

Ruppli, Michel (*b* Coulommiers, France, 3 July 1934). French discographer. He attended the University of Paris and the Ecole Normale Supérieure des Télécommunications, and from 1960 he worked as an electronics engineer. At the same time he began to compile important discographies of jazz record labels (sometimes in collaboration with others) based on his research into the companies' ledgers and files; these discographies contain detailed information on tens of thousands of recording sessions and are far more complete and accurate than most earlier works of their kind. Ruppli also contributed discographies of individual musicians to *Jazz hot*.

WRITINGS

(selective list)

Prestige Jazz Records, 1949–1969 [*recte* 1971]*: a Discography* (n.p. [Copenhagen], 1972; rev. and enlarged 2/1980, with B. Porter, as *The Prestige Label: a Discography*)

Atlantic Records: a Discography (Westport, CT, and London, 1979)

with B. Porter: *The Savoy Label: a Discography* (Westport, CT, and London, 1980)

The Chess Labels: a Discography (Westport, CT, and London, 1983) [incl. listings for Argo and Cadet]

with B. Daniels: *The King Labels: a Discography* (Westport, CT, and London, 1985) [incl. listings for Bethlehem]

with B. Porter: *The Clef/Verve Labels: a Discography* (New York, Westport, CT, and London, 1986)

with M. Cuscuna: *The Blue Note Label: a Discography* (New York, Westport, CT, and London, 1988)

Swing (Paris, 1989)

The Aladdin/Imperial Labels: a Discography (New York, Westport, CT, and London, 1991)

with J. Lubin: *Blue Star* (Paris, 1992)

Vogue, i (Paris, 1992)

The Mercury Labels, i: *The 1945–1965 Era*; ii: *The 1956–1964 Era*; iii: *The 1964–1969 Era*; iv: *The 1969–1991 Era and Classical Recordings*; v: *Record & Artist Indexes* (Westport, CT, and London, 1993)

with J.-P. Tahmazian: *Black and Blue* (Paris, 1995)

The Decca Labels, i: *The California Sessions*; ii: *The Eastern and Southern Sessions (1934–1942)*; iii: *The Eastern Sessions (1943–1956)*; iv: *The Eastern Sessions (1956–1973)*; v: *Country Recordings, Classical Recordings, and Reissues*; vi: *Record Numerical Listings and General Artist Index* (Westport, CT, and London, 1996)

with E. Novitsky: *The MGM Labels: a Discography* (Westport, CT and London, 1998)

BIBLIOGRAPHY

Contemporary Authors, ci (1981)

BK

Rusch, Bob [Robert (D.)] (*b* New York, *c*1945). Writer. He studied clarinet and drums and played drums in workshops with Jaki Byard (1968–71) and Cedar Walton (1972). In the 1960s and 1970s he wrote for American and European periodicals, including *Down Beat*, *Jazz Journal*, and *Jazz Forum*, and in 1975 he began publishing the monthly magazine *Cadence*, which in the following years printed many wide-ranging interviews with jazz and blues musicians and reviews of recordings. Later he formed Cadence Jazz Records (1980), which by the late 1990s had issued more than 100 recordings; North Country Record Distribution (1983), which distributes the jazz and blues recordings of more than 900 small independent labels; Cadence Jazz Books (1992), which publishes reference books, histories, and discographies; and CIMP (1996), for which he had produced about 100 recordings by the turn of the century. He donated his extensive indexed collection of books and journals, covering jazz and blues literature in the English language, to the Schomburg Center for Research in Black Culture of the New York Public Library (*see* Libraries and archives, §2). Rusch is a knowledgeable, perceptive, and accurate interviewer who is adept at eliciting useful information from his subjects. Several of his interviews are incorporated in the collection *Jazz Talk: the Cadence Interviews* (Secaucus, NJ, 1984).

DANIEL ZAGER/BK

Rushen, Patrice (Louise) [Baby Fingers] (*b* Los Angeles, 30 Sept 1954). Keyboard player and singer. She studied classical piano from the age of three and turned to jazz while in her teens. After leading a group that won an award for young musicians at the Monterey Jazz Festival (1972) she played with Melba Liston, Abbey Lincoln, Gerald Wilson, Donald Byrd, and Benny Golson and recorded with Jean-Luc Ponty (1975), Stanley Turrentine (1975), and Sonny Rollins (1976); during the same period she majored in music education and piano performance at the University of Southern California. In 1977 she played piano and electronic keyboards in Lee Ritenour's group, but she left to devote more attention to singing. Rushen's first album as a leader (1974) showed the influence of bop, but she later abandoned improvisation, at which she had evinced considerable skill, in favor of a fusion of jazz and rhythm-and-blues; in the late 1970s she acquired a large following among pop audiences by performing a bland style of pop-soul. In 1982, with Ernie Watts and Ndugu Chancler, she became a member of The Meeting (for details *see* Chancler, ndugu), and in 1989 she formed a duo with Chancler, 1 + One. In 1988 she was a member of the group led by Carlos Santana and Wayne Shorter. Rushen toured Europe in 1988 and 1995 and Japan in 1989 and 1991. Through the 1990s she made only infrequent appearances in clubs in the Los Angeles area, but she remained busy in the studios, as a composer, an arranger, a performer for film and television, and a record producer. From 1999 she has served as artistic director for the Thelonious Monk Institute of Jazz Performance at the University of Southern California.

SELECTED RECORDINGS

As leader: *Prelusion* (1974, Prst. 10089); *Before the Dawn* (1975, Prst. 10098)

As leader with others: J.-L. Ponty: *Upon the Wings of Music* (1975, Atl. 18138); S. Rollins: *The Way I Feel* (1976, Mlst. 9074); L. Ritenour: *Sugarloaf Express* (1977, JVC 2)

BIBLIOGRAPHY

Feather–Gitler '70s

L. Lyons: "Profile: Patrice Rushen," *DB*, xliii/2 (1976), 30

F. Nemko: "Patrice Rushen: a New Jazz Talent Talks about her Music," *CK*, ii/6 (1976), 8

M. Zipkin: "Patrice Rushen: Rushen to the Top," *DB*, xlv/5 (1978), 16

P. Simper: "Class Act," *MM* (5 June 1982), 15

L. Pitts: "Patrice Rushen: Diminutive Drawbacks," *Musician*, no.73 (1984), 30

D. Frederick: "Patrice Rushen: a Child Prodigy Comes Home to Jazz," *Keyboard*, xii/3 (1986), 44

A. di Perna: "The Lady Plays a Vamp: Keyboard Wizard Patrice Rushen Unravels Jazz Improvisation," *Musician*, no.149 (1991), 72

F. Nemko: "Patrice Rushen's Hat Trick," *JT*, xxi/6 (1991), 28

R. L. Doerschuk: "World View Patrice Rushen: One More Sprint through the Industry Gauntlet," *Keyboard*, xx/2 (1994), 14

D. Kasrel: "Patrice Rushen: Different Routes, Similar Rewards," *JT*, xxvi/1 (1996), 38

BK

Rushing, Jimmy [James Andrew; Mr. Five by Five] (*b* Oklahoma City, OK, 26 Aug 1902 or 1903; *d* New York, 8 June 1972). Singer. His year of birth has usually been given as 1903, and thus a controversy erupted when in 1994 the US Post Office issued a commemorative stamp giving 1902. The evidence is inconclusive: Rushing's wife, Connie, gave 1902 on his death certificate and Rushing himself may have supplied information to the *ASCAP Biographical Dictionary of Composers, Authors and Publishers* (New York, 1948), which also gives 1902; however, Rushing claimed 1903 in interviews with Hentoff (1957) and Dance (1980), and he told Hague (1957, *JJ*, x/9), in preparation for a European tour: "First I have to get my mother to send me a notarized statement as to when and where I was born, that's for my passport as I never did have a birth certificate. ... I was born in Oklahoma in the year 1903."

Rushing's mother was a pianist and church singer and his father played trumpet. He reluctantly studied violin as a child and then learned piano from his uncle, a blues musician, and he sang in church choirs, glee clubs, operatic companies, and vaudeville groups; these latter activities, particularly the vaudeville performances, later manifested themselves in a mannered style of vibrato and enunciation that entered into Rushing's blues and jazz singing, especially in his early recordings. He studied music theory at Douglass High School in Oklahoma and attended Wilberforce University in the early 1920s, but as a teenager and young adult he also traveled widely as an itinerant musician; during a period in Los Angeles he performed occasionally with Jelly Roll Morton at private parties (*c*1924–5). In 1925 he toured with Walter Page briefly, then returned home to work in his father's café before singing with Page's Blue Devils (1927–9) and Bennie Moten's Kansas City Orchestra (late 1929 – April 1935). With these important bands he developed a mature singing style derived from the blues and completely idiomatic to the rhythms of jazz, an uncommon accomplishment even for experienced African-American singers in the late 1920s. He first achieved renown with Count Basie's band from 1935, his excellent intonation and robust yet sensitive manner perfectly complementing the group and helping to shape its identity. He remained with Basie regularly to October 1948 and again from June 1949 to the beginning of 1950, touring endlessly.

From 1950 to 1952 Rushing led a seven-piece group at the Savoy Ballroom in New York; his sidemen were Emmett Berry, Dicky Wells, Lucky Thompson, Rudy Powell, Al Williams, and Walter Page. While engaged in recording mainstream jazz albums for the Vanguard and Columbia labels he performed at the Newport Jazz Festival (1955–7), where he was reunited with Basie. He toured Europe as a soloist (1957–8), as a member of Benny Goodman's orchestra (1958), and again in Buck Clayton's band (1959). In New York he worked with Joe Newman and others at the Museum of Modern Art (1960–62) and with Dave Brubeck at Basin Street East (1960). While continuing to star at festivals, including those at Newport (1958, 1962) and Monterey (1960–61, 1969–70), he performed with Goodman's quartet (February 1961), worked with Harry James's orchestra in Las Vegas (December 1961), and toured Japan with Thelonious Monk (1963), Australia, New Zealand, and Japan with Eddie Condon (1964), and Europe with Basie (also 1964). As a leader he held residencies at Colonial Tavern in Toronto (1961–8), Lennie's-on-the-Turnpike in Peabody, Massachusetts (1963–9), the Jazz Workshop in San Francisco (1965–6, 1967), and the Half Note in New York (1965–72); sometimes he appeared at this last venue with the quintet of Zoot Sims and Al Cohn. Rushing's singing figures prominently in a number of films, and he portrayed a nightclub owner in *The Learning Tree* (1969).

See also Blues, §9; for illustrations *see* Blues, fig.3, and Moten, bennie.

SELECTED RECORDINGS

As leader: *Listen to the Blues* (1955, Van. 8505); *The Jazz Odyssey of Jimmy Rushing* (1956, Col. CL963); *If This Ain't the Blues* (1957, Van. 8513); *Jimmy Rushing and the Big Brass* (1958, Col. CL1152)

As sideman: W. Page: Blue Devil Blues (1929, Voc. 1463); B. Moten: Won't you be my baby? (1930, Vic. 23028); That Too, Do (1930, Vic. 22793); Liza Lee/Get Goin' (1930, Vic. 23023); New Orleans (1932, Vic. 24216); Jones–Smith, Inc. [C. Basie]: Evenin' (1936, Voc. 3441); Boogie Woogie (1936, Voc. 3459); C. Basie: Pennies from Heaven (1937, Decca 1121); Good Morning Blues (1937, Decca 1446); Georgianna (1938, Decca 1682); Sent for you yesterday and here you come today (1938, Decca 1880); The blues I like to hear (1938, Decca 2284); Do you wanna jump, children? (1938, Decca 2224); I Left my Baby (1939, Col. 35231); I want a little girl (1940, OK 5773); Goin' to Chicago Blues (1941, OK 6244); I'm gonna move to the outskirts of town (1942, Col. 36601)

SELECTED FILMS AND VIDEOS

Air Mail Special (1941); Take Me Back Baby (1941); Choo Choo Swing [Band Parade] (1943); Crazy House [Funzapoppin'] (1943); The Sound of Jazz (1957); The Subject is Jazz (no.6: Blues) (1958); Newport Jazz Festival 1962 (1962); Jazz Casual: Jimmy Rushing (1964); The Learning Tree (1969); Monterey Jazz (1973)

BIBLIOGRAPHY

ConnorBG; *McCarthyB*; *SchullerS*; *SheridanCB*

J. Armitage: "It's Blues Time, Folks, with Jimmy Rushing," *Music Mirror*, iv/8 (1957), 6

D. Hague: "Rudy Powell and Jimmy Rushing," *JJ*, x/7 (1957), 3

——: "Jimmy Rushing," *JJ*, x/9 (1957), 1

N. Hentoff: "Jimmy Rushing," *DB*, xxiv/5 (1957), 20

P. Oliver: "Jimmy Rushing: the Formative Years," *JM*, iii/10 (1957), 2

——: "Rushing in Retrospect," *Music Mirror*, iv/10 (1957), 17

P. Affeldt: "Mister 5 x 5," *Jazz Report*, vi/8 (1958), 5

R. Ellison: "Remembering Jimmy," *JJ*, xi/11 (1958), 10

"Jimmy Rushing: Link with the Past: from an Interview at the Sound Track Night Club in New Haven, Connecticut, December 1962," *Rhythm and Blues*, no.61 (1963), 8

H. McNamara: "The Odyssey of Jimmy Rushing," *DB*, xxxii/8 (1965), 22

S. Dance: "Lightly and Politely," *JJ*, xx/12 (1967), 14

G. Schuller: *Early Jazz: its Roots and Musical Development* (New York, 1968)

C. Albertson: "Jimmy Rushing: a Sturdy Branch of the Learning Tree," *DB*, xxxvi/23 (1969), 17

B. McRae: "A B Basics, no.50: Jimmy Rushing," *JJ*, xxiv/2 (1971), 32

H. Lyttelton: "Rushing," *JJ*, xxv/8 (1972), 4

D. Stewart-Baxter: "Blues and Views," *JJ*, xxv/8 (1972), 24
S. Harris: *Blues Who's Who: a Biographical Dictionary of Blues Singers* (New Rochelle, NY, 1979/*R*1994)
S. Dance: *The World of Count Basie* (New York and London, 1980), 17
M. L. Hester: *Going to Kansas City* (Sherman, TX, 1980), 123
L. Wright: *Mr. Jelly Lord* (Chigwell, England, 1980), 31
L. Gourse: *Louis' Children: American Jazz Singers* (New York, 1984), 71
J. Armitage: "Souvenirs personnels de Jimmy Rushing," *BHcF*, no.329 (1985), 20
C. Basie and A. Murray: *Good Morning Blues: the Autobiography of Count Basie* (New York, 1985/*R*1995)
T. Burke and D. Penny: "Stand up and Shout the Blues: Jimmy Rushing," *Blues & Rhythm*, no.13 (1985), 4; no.14 (1985), 4 [incl. discography]
B. Clayton and N. M. Elliott: *Buck Clayton's Jazz World* (London and New York, 1986)
"Historians Challenge Birthdate on Stamp," *San Francisco Examiner* (19 Sept 1994)

JAMES DAPOGNY/BK

Rushton, Joe [Joseph Augustine, Jr.] (*b* Evanston, IL, 1 Nov 1907; *d* San Francisco, 2 March 1964). Bass saxophonist. He took up bass saxophone in 1928, having previously played drums, clarinet, and other saxophones. In Chicago he led his own band until 1932 and performed with other bandleaders for the rest of the 1930s. During the early 1940s he worked with Jimmy McPartland and Bud Freeman and went to California as a member of Benny Goodman's group (November 1942 – September 1943), with which he performed on the soundtrack to the film *The Gang's All Here* (1943). Rushton settled in California, where he worked with the pianist and bandleader Horace Heidt (February 1944 – spring 1945) and made recordings both as a leader (1945, 1947) and as a sideman; his playing is well represented by *Carolina in the Morning* (1945, Jump 4), recorded by Floyd O'Brien's State Street Seven. From 1947 to spring 1963 he collaborated with Red Nichols, recording, touring Europe, appearing in five Snader telescriptions (1950), and playing in the film *The Five Pennies* (1958). Rushton also recorded during this period with Louis Armstrong (1947) and alongside Matty Matlock and Eddie Miller, among others, in the Rampart Street Paraders (1954).

BIBLIOGRAPHY

ChiltonW; *ConnorBG*; *FeatherE*; *Feather '60s*
A. Napoleon: "The Bass Sax in Jazz," *Sv*, no.8 (1966–7), 15; no.9 (1967), 18
R. J. Hopf: "I Wonder what's Become of Joe?," *Jazzfreund*, xxii/3 (1980), 4
P. R. Evans: "The Paul Whiteman Reunion," *MR*, xix/12 (1992), 10

Russell, Bill [William; Wagner, Russell William] (*b* Canton, MO, 26 Feb 1905; *d* New Orleans, 9 Aug 1992). Jazz historian, record producer, violinist, and composer. He played violin from the age of ten, and later studied music in Chicago (1924). After private violin tuition in New York (1927) he attended Columbia University Teachers College (1929), where he took up composition; around 1930 he dropped his surname, Wagner, to avoid comparisons with a rather more famous composer in the field. While touring with a theatrical group, the Red Gate Shadow Players, which staged classical Chinese puppet plays (1934–40), he began collecting early jazz records, reselling many through the Hot Record Exchange that he ran from 1935 with the painter Steve Smith. He contributed articles to the magazine *Jazz hot* and wrote three chapters of *Jazzmen: the Story of Hot Jazz Told in the Lives of the Men who Created it* (ed. F. Ramsey, Jr., and C. E. Smith, New York, 1939/*R*1977). Russell played an important role in rediscovering Bunk Johnson, and first recorded him in 1942. From 1944 to 1957 he undertook a historic series of recordings for his American music label, visiting Los Angeles, New Orleans, and New York to record such musicians as Baby Dodds, Bunk Johnson, Dink Johnson, George Lewis (i), Wooden Joe Nicholas, and Jim Robinson; the recordings continue to retain an influence on playing styles in Europe and Japan.

Russell was curator of the jazz archive at Tulane University, New Orleans, from 1958 to 1965, and, with Richard B. Allen, interviewed scores of veteran musicians for its oral history project. From 1967 he played in the New Orleans Ragtime Orchestra, recorded extensively, appeared at festivals, and toured Europe (1975, 1987). He may be seen in a video released as *Jazz Parades: Feet Don't Fail Me Now* (*c*1998), from Alan Lomax's documentary series "American Patchwork" of 1990. His vast knowledge and generous nature made him much sought after by jazz researchers, and he remains an inspiration to all. In his last decade he was preparing books on Jelly Roll Morton and New Orleans playing styles; *"Oh, Mister Jelly"* was published in 1999, and *New Orleans Style*, compiled and edited by Barry Martyn and Mike Hazeldine, in 1994. A concert of his compositions was given by Essential Music in New York in 1990 and again in New Orleans in 1994; his complete works were recorded in 1990 (*Made in America*, Mode 34). In 1992 his huge collection of music, recordings, publications, photographs, archival material, and memorabilia was acquired by the Historic New Orleans Collection (*see* Libraries and archives, §2).

Oral history material in *Cty* and *LNT*.

BIBLIOGRAPHY

M. Slatter: "A Portrait of Bill Russell," *JJ*, xii/9 (1959), 28
R. A. Tiug: "Shopping at Bill's," *SL*, xv/1–2 (1964), 9
T. Bethell: *George Lewis: a Jazzman from New Orleans* (Berkeley, CA, and London, 1977)
W. Carter: *Preservation Hall: Music from the Heart* (Wheatley, Oxford, England, and New York, 1991)
J. L. Anderson: "Exploring American Music," *MR*, xvii (1992), no.1, p.1; no.2, p.16
Obituaries: [various authors], *New Orleans Music*, iii/5–6 (1992)
B. Thompson: "The Extraordinary Bill Russell," *MR*, xvii/11 (1992), 10
M. Hazeldine: *Bill Russell's American Music* (New Orleans, 1993)
——: "New Orleans 1943: from the Diary of Bill Russell," *New Orleans Music*, v (1995), no.3, p.6; no.4, p.6
"Bill Russell: an American Ensemble," *Southern Quarterly*, xxxvi/2 (1998) [special issue on Russell]
P. Brady and L. Hoffman, eds.: *Jazz Scrapbook: Bill Russell and Some Highly Musical Friends* (New Orleans, 1988)
C. DeVore: "New Orleans Memories," *MR*, xxvi/2 (1998), 1; xxvi/3 (1999), 1

MIKE HAZELDINE/BK

Russell, Curly [Dillon] (*b* New York, 19 March 1917; *d* New York, 3 July 1986). Double bass player. He gained his early professional experience in the big bands of Don Redman (1941) and Benny Carter (1942–3). On returning to New York after touring he played in small groups at clubs on 52nd Street; at about this time Dizzy Gillespie and Charlie Parker were developing the musical ideas that led to the creation of bop, and in 1945 Russell joined their quintet at the Three Deuces. He was a member of Tadd Dameron's groups from 1947 to 1949, and participated in Dameron's long residencies at the Royal Roost; he also performed with Parker, Thelonious Monk (1948), and Kai Winding (at Birdland, 1949). As a freelance he worked with Bud Powell (1949, and at Birdland, September 1953), Miles Davis (1950), Stan Getz (intermittently, 1950–51), Buddy DeFranco (*c* mid- to late 1952), Coleman Hawkins (at Birdland, 1952, and Café Society, spring 1953), Art Blakey (recording while at Birdland, 1954), and Lester Young (touring, spring 1956). During a period when the responsibility for maintaining cohesion in the rhythm section rested primarily with the bass player,

Russell's consistent time-keeping and penetrating tone were greatly valued. He also recorded with Milt Buckner (1946), Serge Chaloff (1947), Allen Eager (1947), Howard McGhee and Fats Navarro (1948), Lester Young (1948), Kai Winding, Brew Moore, and McGhee (all 1949), Terry Gibbs (1949, 1951), George Wallington (1949, 1951, 1954), Powell and Sonny Stitt (both 1949–50), Herbie Steward and Zoot Sims (both 1950), Horace Silver (1952), Al Cohn (1953), Monk and Art Blakey (both 1954), Johnny Griffin (1956), Clifford Jordan and John Gilmore (1957), and Phil Woods (1957). By the late 1950s Russell was playing mainly with rhythm-and-blues groups.

Oral history material in *NjR.*

For illustration *see* Jazz (i), fig.5.

SELECTED RECORDINGS

As sideman: D. Gillespie: Salt Peanuts/Hot House (1945, Guild 1003); C. Parker: Billie's Bounce/Now's the Time (1945, Savoy 573); D. Gordon: Long Tall Dexter (1946, Savoy 603); C. Hawkins: Bean and the Boys (1946, Son. 3024); B. Powell: I'll Remember April/Off Minor (1947, Roost 513); C. Parker: Ah-leu-cha (1948, Savoy 939); S. Stitt: Sonny Side (1949, Prst. 722); B. Powell: Un poco loco (1951, BN 1577); A. Blakey: *A Night at Birdland* (1954, BN 5037–9); T. Monk: *Thelonious Monk Quintet* (1954, Prst. 180), incl. Smoke gets in your eyes

BIBLIOGRAPHY

FeatherE
"Annuaire biographique de la contrebasse," *Jm*, no.94 (1963), 28
H. Renard: "Témoinages: la chasse aux souvenirs," *Jm*, no.94 (1963), 37
J. Chambers: *Milestones*, i: *The Music and Times of Miles Davis to 1960* (Toronto, Buffalo, and London, 1983); ii: *The Music and Times of Miles Davis since 1960* (Toronto, Buffalo, and London, 1985); i and ii repr. as *Milestones: the Music and Times of Miles Davis* (1989)
A. Groves and A. Shipton: *The Glass Enclosure: the Life of Bud Powell* (Tunbridge Wells, England, 1993)

SCOTT DeVEAUX/BK

Russell, George (Allan) (*b* Cincinnati, 23 June 1923). Composer and theorist. He played drums in local clubs while a student at Wilberforce University High School. At the age of 19 he was stricken with tuberculosis, but recovered sufficiently to play in the Wilberforce college band under Ernie Wilkins. In 1944 he briefly joined Benny Carter's orchestra, but by his own account was discouraged from playing upon hearing his replacement in the band, Max Roach; the continuing effects of tuberculosis hastened his decision to abandon the drums. Around this time Russell wrote his first arrangements, for Carter and for Earl Hines. During his long illness in 1945–6 he formulated the basis of his "Lydian chromatic concept," a system of composition based on grading intervals by the distance of their pitches from a central note. After his recovery he wrote scores for Dizzy Gillespie, including *Cubana Be/Cubana Bop* (one of the earliest works to combine jazz and Latin influences), and for Buddy DeFranco (*A Bird in Igor's Yard*) and Lee Konitz (*Ezz-thetic* and *Odjenar*); meanwhile he also studied composition with Stefan Wolpe. In the late 1940s he contributed arrangements to the bands of Claude Thornhill, Artie Shaw, and Charlie Ventura and participated in the informal circle of composers and performers centered around Gil Evans in New York.

From 1950 Russell consolidated and refined his ideas on music theory, publishing them in book form as *The Lydian Chromatic Concept of Tonal Organization* (1953, 2/1959), which was immediately received as the first major contribution by a jazz musician to the field of music theory. The purported scientific and musicological basis which Russell claimed for his Lydian concept might well be met with skepticism by anyone who has had at least a modest amount

George Russell at the Queen Elizabeth Hall, London, 1995

of professional training in the history of music theory, but there is no question of its practical impact: many jazz musicians, some quite important, have taken inspiration from Russell's method. Perhaps the most concise and lucid summary is offered by Ian Carr (1995): "The basic point about this concept is that it encourages improvisers to convert chord symbols into the scales that best convey the sound of the chords. The next stage is the idea of the superimposition of one scale on another, which leads to pantonality, the presence of more than one key centre, but occurring within a dominant tonality. In other words, the music is not atonal (in no particular key), but it can accommodate some polytonality" (in *CarrJ*).

In 1956 Russell made his first recordings under his own name, as the leader of (but not a performer in) the Jazz Workshop, also known as his Small-tet, comprising Art Farmer, Hal McKusick, Bill Evans (ii), and Barry Galbraith, with Milt Hinton or Teddy Kotick on double bass, and Joe Harris, Paul Motian, or Osie Johnson on drums. Works followed on an increasingly large scale, establishing Russell, along with Gil Evans, as a leading postwar jazz composer; he combined advanced jazz idioms with an unusually rigorous concern for structure, harmony, and the balance between composition and improvisation. Perhaps the best known of these pieces, *All about Rosie*, was given its première at Brandeis University and recorded in New York in 1957, with Bill Evans as featured soloist. In 1958 Russell appeared in episode 13, "The Future of Jazz," in the television series "The Subject is Jazz." In the summers of 1958 and 1959 he taught at the Lenox (Massachusetts) School of Jazz, and about the same time he took up piano, which he played in his own jazz sextet. This was mainly a recording band (1960–62), but gave a few performances in New York and Kansas City; among the group's sidemen at various times were Don Ellis, Eric Dolphy, Chuck Israels, Steve Swallow, and Sheila Jordan (1962).

In 1963 Russell moved to Europe and taught at Lund University in Sweden and the Vaskilde Summer School in Denmark. Graced with the patronage of the director of jazz for Swedish radio, Bosse Broberg, he was able to record all of his compositions to date. Broberg also commissioned new works, including a mass, a ballet, and the *Electronic Sonata for Souls Loved by Nature*, which combined tapes with orchestral improvisation and composition. While Russell was based in Scandinavia his sextet at times included Don Cherry, who appeared with the group on tours of Europe (in the course of which he recorded in Stuttgart in 1965); Cameron Brown, Albert "Tootie" Heath, Manfred Schoof, Stanton Davis, Jan Garbarek, Terje Rypdal, Jon Christensen, and Arild Andersen were also sidemen during this period, and the last five were with Russell for a live recording in March 1970.

In 1969 Russell returned to the USA to join the faculty of the New England Conservatory, where he remained in the 1990s despite maintaining his affiliations in Europe. During the mid-1970s he ceased to compose and worked on a second volume of *The Lydian Chromatic Concept.* He made several recordings of his compositions in the late 1970s and early 1980s, among them an album as the leader of the Swedish Radiojazzgruppen (ii) (1977) and two with his own big bands in New York (1982–3); an all-star orchestra including Gary Valente, Ricky Ford, Billy Pierce, and Fred Hersch gave a retrospective performance of his most famous compositions at the Boston Globe Jazz Festival in March 1983. In 1986 Russell formed an Anglo-American group, the Living Time Orchestra, which performed in the USA, Japan, and Europe; it remained active in the late 1990s, with Andy Sheppard among its featured soloists. Russell also appeared as a guest conductor with a number of European ensembles. Among his many honors are composer awards from the magazines *Metronome* and *Down Beat*, the Oscar du Disque de Jazz, two Guggenheim fellowships, grants from the National Endowment for the Arts, the endowment's American Jazz Master Award (1990), the National Music Award, and, most significantly, a John and Catherine MacArthur Foundation Fellowship (1989).

RECORDED COMPOSITIONS

(selective list)

AS LEADER

The Jazz Workshop (1956, RCA LPM1372), incl. Ezz-thetic, Jack's Blues, Ye Hypocrite, ye Beelzebub, Round Johnny Rondo, Night Sound, Concerto for Billy the Kid, Witch Hunt, Fellow Delegates, The Ballad of Hix Blewitt, Knights of the Steamtable, The Sad Sargeant; All about Rosie, on Brandeis Jazz Festival: *Modern Jazz Concert* (1957, Col. WL127); *Jazz in the Space Age* (1960, Decca 79219), incl. Chromatic Universe, The Lydiot, Dimensions, Waltz from Outer Space; *Stratusphunk* (1960, Riv. 9341), incl. Stratusphunk, Things New; *Ezz-thetics* (1961, Riv. 9375), incl. Ezz-thetic, Lydiot, Thoughts; *The Stratus Seekers* (1961, Riv. 9412), incl. The Stratus Seekers, Pan-Daddy, Blues in Orbit, A Lonely Place; *The Outer View* (1962, Riv. 9412), incl. The Outer View, D.C. Divertimento

The George Russell Sextet at Beethoven Hall (1965, Saba 15059–60), incl. Freein' up, Takin' Lydia Home, Oh jazz, pro jazz, Volupte; *The Essence of George Russell* (1966–8, 1970, Sonet 1411–12), incl. Now and Then (1966), Othello Ballet Suite (1967), Concerto for Self-Accompanied Guitar, Electronic Organ Sonata no.1 (1968), Electronic Sonata for Souls Loved by Nature (1970); *Trip to Prillarguri* (1970, SN 1029), incl. Theme, Stratusphunk; *Listen to the Silence* (*c*1971, Concept 002); *New York Big Band* (1977–8, SN 1039), incl. Cubana Be, Cubana Bop (1977), Big City Blues, Listen to the Silence, Living Time Event V (1978); *Live in an American Time Spiral* (1982, SN 1049), incl. Time Spiral, Ezz-thetic, D.C. Divertimento; *The African Game* (1983, BN 83193); *The London Concert*, i–ii (1989, Label Bleu 6527–8), incl. Uncommon Ground, Six Aesthetic Gravities, Listen to the Silence; *It's about Time* (*c*1995, Label Bleu 6587)

RECORDED BY OTHERS

D. Gillespie: Cubana Be/Cubana Bop (1947, Vic. 20-3145); B. DeFranco: A Bird in Igor's Yard, on L. Tristano: *Crosscurrents* (1949, Cap. 11060); L. Konitz: Odjenar (1951, Prst. 753); Ezz-thetic (1951, Prst. 743); Lydian M-1, on T. Charles: *The Teddy Charles Tentet* (1956, Atl. 1229); The Day John Brown was Hanged, on H. McKusick: *Jazz Workshop* (1956, RCA LPM1366); Bill Evans (ii): *Living Time* (1972, Col. KC31490)

BIBLIOGRAPHY

CarrJ
D. Cerulli: "George Russell," *DB*, xxv/11 (1958), 15
L. Gottlieb: "Brandeis Festival Album," *Jazz: a Quarterly of American Music*, no.2 (1959), 151
J. B. Brooks: "George Russell," *JR*, iii/2 (1960), 38
M. Harrison: "George Russell: 'Jazz Workshop'," *JR*, iii/9 (1960), 28
G. Russell: "Where Do We Go from Here?," *The Jazz Word*, ed. D. Cerulli, B. Korall, and M. Nasatir (New York, 1960/*R*1987)
B. Korall: "Who is George Russell?," *DB*, xxviii/4 (1961), 14
M. Harrison: "George Russell," *Jazz on Record: a Critical Guide to the First 50 Years: 1917–1967*, ed. A. McCarthy and others (London, 1968), 251
G. Crane: *Jazz Elements and Formal Compositional Techniques in Third Stream Music* (diss., Indiana U., 1970) [incl. detailed analysis of *All about Rosie*]
P. Wilson: "George Russell's Constant Quest," *DB*, xxxix/8 (1972), 15
O. Jones: "A New Theory for Jazz," *Black Perspective in Music*, ii (1974), 63
B. Rusch: "George Russell: Interview," *Cadence*, iii/7–8 (1977), 3
D. N. Baker, L. M. Belt, and H. C. Hudson, eds.: *The Black Composer Speaks* (Metuchen, NJ, and London, 1978) [incl. list of works, discography, bibliography]
G. Giddins: "George Russell's Return," *Musician, Player & Listener*, no.13 (1978), 26
G. Buhles: "Der Jazz-Komponist George Russell und sein Lydian Concept," *JP*, xxx (1981), no.4, p.4; no.5, p.4
B. Blumenthal: "George Russell: Stratus Seeker," *DB*, l/10 (1983), 24
M. Harrison: "George Russell: Rational Anthems," *The Wire*, no.3 (1983), 30
B. Sundin: "George Russell," *Orkester journalen*, li/7–8 (1983), 8
M. Hendler: "Gedanken zum 'Lydischen Konzept' von George Russell," *Jf*, xvi (1984), 163
A. Jeanquartier: "Kritische Anmerkungen zum 'Lydian Chromatic Concept': ein Vergleich zwischen George Russells Konzept und dem Dur-Moll-System," *Jf*, xvi (1984), 9
F. Davis: *In the Moment: Jazz in the 1980s* (New York, and Oxford, England, 1986/*R*1996), 167
G. Tangerding: "George Russell," *JP*, xxxv/12 (1986), 4
S. Woolley: "George Russell," *JJI*, xxxix/10 (1986), 8 [incl. discography]
P. Benkimoun: "George Russell ou le poids des modes," *Jm*, no.398 (1990), 42
T. Blangger: "George Russell," *Coda*, no.235 (1990–91), 11
M. S. Haywood: "The Harmonic Role of Melody in Vertical and Horizontal Jazz," *ARJS*, v (1991), 109
P. Gamble: "George Russell," *JJI*, xlv/7 (1992), 15
B. Shoemaker: "Big Band Orchestral Visions," *JT*, xxii/10 (1992), 28
K. Silsbee: "George Russell: Interview," *Cadence*, xxii/6 (1996), 26
E. Nisenson: "Profile: Modes and Modalities: George Russell," *Jazziz*, xiv/4 (1997), 50
J. Fordham: "Arts: Send off the Clones: While Jazz's Young Stars are Getting all Nostalgic, 74-year-old George Russell is Motoring into the Next Century," *The Guardian* (5 March 1998)

JAMES G. ROY, JR./CARMAN MOORE/BK

Russell, Hal [Luttenbacher, Harold] (*b* Detroit, 28 Aug 1926, *d* Chicago, 5 Sept 1992). Saxophonist, trumpeter, vibraphonist, drummer, and bandleader. He began to play drums at the age of four and led a quartet while at high school; as a percussionist he received a scholarship to the University of Illinois, where he led a big band and learned trumpet. In the late 1940s he served as drummer in the big bands of Woody Herman, with whom he made his recording début, Boyd Raeburn, and Claude Thornhill. In 1950 he briefly played vibraphone with Miles Davis's quintet, and for the remainder of the decade he was based in Chicago, where he accompanied visiting musicians, notably Duke Ellington and John Coltrane. In 1959 he played an early form of free jazz as the drummer in a trio led by saxophonist Joe Daley, with whom he recorded at the 1963 Newport Jazz Festival. Russell performed with Daley and others until he moved in 1969 to Florida. The following year he returned to Chicago; there he formed his first band (1972), taught himself C-melody saxophone (1977), took up trumpet again, and learned to play tenor saxophone (1979). In 1978 he formed the five-piece NRG (i.e., "energy") Ensemble, with which he made his first recording as a leader at the age of 54. He also co-led a quartet with Joel Futterman (which recorded much later, in 1991) and recorded in a duo with the tenor saxophonist Mars Williams – later a member of the NRG Ensemble. Russell's work remained little noticed until his group toured Europe in November 1990, when it was recorded by ECM. Two further albums for ECM in 1992 – *Hal's Bells* (as an unaccompanied soloist, on which he plays 11 wind and percussion instruments and sings) and the autobiographical *The Hal Russell Story* – consolidated his reputation as one of the most idiosyncratic and individual bandleaders of his day. In his last year he also led a rock-oriented trio, the NRG 3, and was in the process of forming a new group which would use his original name: the Flying Luttenbachers. Combining rock-inflected ostinati, periods of free improvising, considerable volume, and a broadly satirical approach, Russell owed as much in his work to such rock musicians as Frank Zappa as he did to Albert Ayler, whose sound influenced his playing on tenor saxophone.

SELECTED RECORDINGS

As unaccompanied soloist: *Hal's Bells* (1992, ECM 1484)
Duos with M. Williams: *Eftsoons* (1981, Nessa 24)
As leader: *NRG Ensemble* (1981, Nessa 21); *The Finnish/Swiss Tour* (1990, ECM 1455); with J. Futterman: *Naked Colours* (1991, Silkheart 135); *The Hal Russell Story* (1992, ECM 1498)
As sideman with J. Daley: *Joe Daley Trio at Newport '63* (1963, RCA LSP2763)

BIBLIOGRAPHY

J. Litweiler: "Blowin' in from Chicago, 1986," *The Wire*, no.33 (1986), 22
J. Corbett: "Hal Russell: the Fires of Hal," *DB*, lix/4 (1992), 28 [incl. discography]
Obituary, M. Gilbert, *JJI*, xlvi/2 (1993), 23
B. Shoemaker: "To Hal & Beyond," *DB*, lxii/9 (1995), 46
D. Lewis: "Beyond Hal Russell: the Legacy of the NRG," *Coda*, no.275 (1997), 4

SIMON ADAMS

Russell, Johnny [John W.] (*b* Charlotte, NC, 4 June 1909; *d* New York, 26 July 1991). Tenor saxophonist. He grew up in New York and was taught violin from 1918; later he learned tenor saxophone, and he played both instruments in 1926 with the drummer Jimmy Campbell. He joined the band at the Strand Danceland led by the pianist Earle Howard and continued to play violin in public performance, but as far as is known he never recorded on the instrument. In the 1930s he worked with Harry White, Benny Carter (1933–4), and Willie Bryant (1935–6), among others, and recorded as a tenor saxophonist with Carter and Bryant; he toured Europe with Bobby Martin's orchestra until 1938 and played several solos with the band on the soundtrack of Erich von Stroheim's film *L'alibi* (1936). He then joined Willie Lewis (1939), with whom he worked in Switzerland and Portugal after the outbreak of war and made a number of recordings on both tenor saxophone and clarinet. After returning to the USA in September 1941 he played with Garvin Bushell (1942), various army bands (until 1945), and Cecil Scott (1945). Russell ceased full-time playing in the late 1940s, but continued to work in clubs.

SELECTED RECORDINGS

As sideman: B. Carter: Devil's Holiday (1933, Col. 2898D); M. Mezzrow: Swinging with Mezz (1933, Bruns. 6778); W. Bryant: It's over because we're through (1935, Vic. 24858); Jerry the Junker (1935, Vic. 25045); All my Life (1936, Bb 6361); I Like Bananas (1936, Bb 6436); Cross Patch (1936, Bb 6435); W. Lewis: What will I do/Happy Feet (1941, ES 4067); Lady be good (1941, ES 4072); Christopher Columbus (ES 4079); Body and Soul (1941, ES 4080); Margie (1941, ES 4081)

BIBLIOGRAPHY

ChiltonW; *McCarthyB*
J. Evensmo: *The Tenor Saxophones of Henry Bridges, Robert Carroll, Herschal* [*sic*] *Evans, Johnny Russell*, n.p. [Oslo], n.d. [?1976]) [discography]
J. Simmen: "L'imprévisible Johnny Russell," *BHcF*, no.409 (1992), 11; no.410 (1993), 36; no.411 (1993), 11
J. Evensmo: *History of Jazz Tenor Saxophone: Black Artists*, i: *1917–1934* (Oslo, 1996); ii: *1935–1939* (Oslo, 1997); iii: *1940–1944* (Oslo, 1997)

HOWARD RYE

Russell, Luis (Carl) (*b* Careening Cay, nr Bocas del Toro, Gran Colombia [now Panama], 6 Aug 1902; *d* New York, 11 Dec 1963). Bandleader, arranger, and pianist. His father, of Jamaican origins, born in what was then the Panamanian region of Colombia, was a pianist, organist, and choir director of an Anglican church. His mother, who was of Belizean and Hindustani origins, was a soloist in the choir. Russell himself is widely regarded as Panamanian, although Panama did not acquire its independence from Colombia until 1903; his widow Carline Ray reports that he took American citizenship in the early 1950s. He studied guitar, violin, organ, and piano and played in a movie theater and at the Casino Club in Colon, Panama, until he won $3000 in a lottery in 1919, which enabled him to move to New Orleans. He first played with Albert Nicholas in the band led by the drummer Arnold Du Pas at the Cadillac Club, then at Tom Anderson's in Nicholas's six-piece group, which included Barney Bigard and Paul Barbarin (1923); Russell took over leadership of the band when Nicholas left to tour with King Oliver. After touring in Louisiana, Russell returned to New Orleans, but late in 1924 went to Chicago to join Oliver; however, a disastrous fire destroyed their intended venue. He played piano and organ with Doc Cook's orchestra and worked at the Elite Club around the beginning of 1925 before gaining his first significant employment as pianist and principal arranger for Oliver's Dixie Syncopators that February; Nicholas, Bigard, and Barbarin also joined Oliver, on Russell's recommendation. They performed at the Plantation Café (to March 1927) and made recordings; Russell also recorded independently in 1926 as an accompanist to the singer Ada Brown, as a member of the Chicago Hottentots (a trio with Nicholas and Johnny St. Cyr), and as a leader. Late in April 1927 the Dixie Syncopators toured the Midwest and then traveled to New York for an engagement at the Savoy Ballroom. That summer Russell elected to leave Oliver.

Russell remained in New York, and at the Nest Club joined the band led by the drummer George Howe, which had Charlie Holmes and Teddy Hill among its sidemen. In October he took over its leadership; Bigard recalled that, when Russell sent for him, it was then a six-piece band, including Barbarin. McCarthy's (1974) account of this transitional period differs from Bigard's, but in any event Bigard soon left for Duke Ellington's orchestra and Russell brought in Louis Metcalf, J. C. Higginbotham, and Nicholas.

Gradually expanding his band to ten pieces, Russell worked at the Nest Club and then from the late 1920s into the early 1930s at the Saratoga Club, the Savoy Ballroom, Connie's Inn, and other venues, and also toured. The group broadcast and recorded with important new sidemen: J. C. Higginbothan, Henry "Red" Allen (replacing Metcalf), Pops Foster, and, strictly for sessions in September 1929, Bill Coleman; Dicky Wells replaced Higginbotham in 1931. It was during this period, especially 1929–30, that Russell's band made its most representative recordings (including several under the leadership of Oliver and Allen, and one as a small group under Higginbotham); after that, as Foster recalled in his autobiography (1971, p.141), "Luis decided to change his style. . . . When we started playing like all the other bands, finding work got tough. Why should they hire you when they've already got the same thing?"

Russell also recorded in small groups with the Jungle Town Stompers and Wilton Crawley (both 1929), Victoria Spivey (1929–30), Higginbotham (1930), and Allen (1933–5, 1937), and in an orchestra under Spike Hughes (1933). His last session as a leader was in mid-1934, when Rex Stewart was briefly a member of the band. Having accompanied Louis Armstrong for several months in 1929, the band provided the trumpeter's backing from 1935 to 1943, although by then it had lost most of its character; Russell may be seen with Armstrong in the soundie *I'll be Glad when You're Dead, You Rascal, You* (1942). He then formed another band and worked around New York, without distinction, until 1948, when he abandoned music to become a chauffeur and shopkeeper.

Although an unexceptional pianist, Russell was an important jazz bandleader of the 1920s. He attempted to adapt the New Orleans ensemble style to make his group more integrated, but the band's freshness and vigor continued to derive from its solo improvisations. Some of Allen's most characteristic early trumpet work is found in recordings with Russell, and Nicholas's clarinet improvisations around the closing ensembles of such pieces as *Panama* resemble Bigard's later work with Ellington's band; Higginbotham and Holmes also proved to be important soloists. In the mid-1990s Pedro Salazar of the Ciudad Universitaria Octavio Méndez Pereira, Universidad de Panama, and two of his colleagues established the unendowed Fundación Luis Russell, which aims to collect information on and celebrate Russell's career.

SELECTED RECORDINGS

Savoy Shout (1929, OK 8760); The New Call of the Freaks/Jersey Lightning (1929, OK 8734); Feelin' the Spirit/Doctor Blues (1929, OK 8766); Saratoga Shout/Song of the Swanee (1930, OK 8780); Louisiana Swing/On Revival Day (1930, OK 8811); Muggin' Lightly (1930, OK 8830); Panama/High Tension (1930, OK 8849); At the Darktown Strutters' Ball/Ol' Man River (1934, Ban. 33179); Ghost of the Freaks (1934, Ban. 33367); Primitive (1934, Ban. 33399)

As sideman: Chicago Hottentots: All Night Shags/Put Me in the Alley Blues (1926, Voc. 1008); K. Oliver: Doctor Jazz (1927, Voc. 1113); Call of the Freaks (1929, Vic. 38039); H. Allen: It Should Be You (1929, Vic. 38073); Dancing Dave (1930, Vic. 38121); L. Armstrong: Swing that Music (1936, Decca 866)

BIBLIOGRAPHY

ChiltonW; *McCarthyB*; *SchullerS*; *WrightK*
H. Niesen, Jr.: "Luis Russell," *Swing Music*, ii/2 (1936), 42
F. Manskleid: "Luis Russell Revisited," *JM*, iii/2 (1957), 11
A. McCarthy: "Luis Russell," *JM*, vi/6 (1960), 9
G. Hoefer: "Luis Russell," *DB*, xxix/28 (1962), 43
H. Grut: "Luis Russell," *JJ*, xvii/3 (1964), 19
P. Munnery: "Luis Russell Orchestra, 1929–1931," *Jazz Times*, iii (1966), no.6, p.7; no.7, p.7
D. Ives: "Luis Russell 1902–1963," *JJ*, xx/6 (1967), 4
E. Lambert: "Luis Russell," *JJ*, xxii/9 (1969), 6
P. Foster, T. Stoddard, and R. Russell: *Pops Foster: the Autobiography of a New Orleans Jazzman* (Berkeley, CA, Los Angeles, and London, 1971), 133
S. Dance: *The World of Swing* (New York, 1974), 253
H. Lyttelton: "Luis Russell," *The Best of Jazz*, i: *Basin Street to Harlem: Jazz Masters and Masterpieces, 1917–1930* (London, 1978), 207
R. M. Sudhalter and J. Chilton: Liner notes, *Giants of Jazz: Henry "Red" Allen* (TL 16, 1981)
F. Hoffman: *Henry "Red" Allen (Jan. 7th 1908 – Apr. 17th 1967)/J. C. Higginbotham (May 11th 1906 – May 26th 1973): Discography, 1927–1969* (Berlin, 1994)
B. Bigard: *With Louis and the Duke*, ed. B. Martyn (London, 1985)
C. E. B. Bernhardt and S. Harris: *I Remember: Eighty Years of Black Entertainment, Big Bands, and the Blues* (Philadelphia, 1986), 163
P. Carr: *Jimmy Archey: the Little Giant of the Trombone* (New Orleans, 1999)

MAX HARRISON/BK

Russell, Pee Wee [Charles Ellsworth, III] (*b* St. Louis, 27 March 1906; *d* Alexandria, VA, 15 Feb 1969). Clarinetist. He briefly studied piano, drums, and violin and took up clarinet in 1918, immediately after hearing a local performance by Alcide "Yellow" Nunez with the Louisiana Five. In the early 1920s he was already playing professionally as a clarinetist, and by the summer of 1924, when he worked alongside Jack Teagarden in Peck Kelly's Bad Boys in LaPorte, Texas, he was also doubling on bass clarinet and alto and tenor saxophones. He worked with Wingy Manone in San Antonio, Texas, on the tenor instrument from late December 1924 through the winter, then returned to St. Louis to play clarinet and alto saxophone as a colleague of Bix Beiderbecke in Frankie Trumbauer's orchestra at the Arcadia Ballroom (September 1925 – early May 1926); the three men remained together during the summer at Hudson Lake, Indiana, in a band under Jean Goldkette's nominal leadership.

Pee Wee Russell, c1939

In August 1927 Russell moved permanently to New York, where he recorded regularly with Red Nichols, under whom he also worked in the pit bands for Broadway musicals, including the Gershwins' *Strike up the Band* (late 1929 – June 1930). In the early 1930s, while playing in insignificant bands, he made outstanding recordings with the Mound City Blue Blowers, the Rhythmakers under Billy Banks and Jack Bland, and Eddie Condon. In March 1935 he joined Louis Prima's five-piece band at the Famous Door on 52nd Street in New York, and moved with the group to the Famous Door in Los Angeles in September. After making three short films with Prima in Hollywood, Russell traveled to Chicago with Prima's big band for a residency at the Blackhawk Restaurant (September 1936 – January 1937).

From mid-1937 through November 1946 Russell was resident at Nick's in New York, where he played with Condon, Bobby Hackett, Georg Brunis, Bud Freeman's Summa cum Laude Orchestra, Jimmy McPartland, Wild Bill Davison, Brad Gowans, Muggsy Spanier, Miff Mole, Sterling Bose, and other leading dixieland musicians. He continued to record and take part in numerous public jam sessions, and appeared in Condon's early evening concerts at Town Hall, the Ritz Theater, and Carnegie Hall (1942–5; these were broadcast nationally and overseas between May 1944 and April 1945). He occasionally left Nick's to work elsewhere: he was with Freeman's orchestra at Kelly's Stable in New York and the Panther Room of the Hotel Sherman in Chicago (late 1939 – spring 1940), he joined McPartland's band at the Brass Rail in Chicago (July 1940), and he later worked in New York with James P. Johnson at the Pied Piper (August 1944) and in Boston with Max Kaminsky at the Copley Terrace and the trumpeter's own short-lived venue, Maxie's (October 1945 – February 1946).

From late in 1946 Russell played at Condon's club, and in 1949 he appeared regularly on the "Eddie Condon Floor Show," an early television series. This association was less constant than the previous tenure at Nick's, where Russell returned briefly for a final time as a member of Billy Butterfield's band (early 1948). He worked in Boston again with Kaminsky (June 1948) and at the Blue Note in Chicago with Spanier and Mole (October 1948). In February 1949, with Art Hodes, he established Pee Wee and Art's Backroom in New York, and played there ostensibly in a trio, but with numerous colleagues sitting in; Willie "the Lion" Smith took Hodes's place in May. Russell traveled to Chicago and rejoined Hodes (February–April 1950), transferred to the Brass Rail to work with Brunis, and then spent the latter half of the year in California, where, suffering from the effects of longstanding and severe alcoholism, he collapsed at the end of the year.

Although he was not expected to survive, Russell recovered and in July 1951 resumed playing. He worked at the Stuyvesant Casino until 1955, while also touring with his own band, which soon included Ruby Braff, and playing elsewhere with Ray McKinley (early summer 1952), Jimmy McPartland (August 1952), George Wettling (summer 1953), and Condon (January 1954). Having played in bands with George Wein as pianist, recorded for Wein's Storyville label, and appeared at Wein's club (Mahogany Hall, in Boston), Russell participated in Wein's historic undertaking, the first Newport Jazz Festival (July 1954), as co-leader of a sextet with Hackett; he also played there in a jam session with Stan Kenton. Thereafter he was featured at Newport nearly every year through 1968. He returned to Condon's club (August 1955 – May 1956, January 1957), and worked with Hackett in New York (May–June, August–November 1956). In the late 1950s he continued to work with leading dixieland and mainstream musicians – Braff, Freeman, Buck Clayton, and Vic Dickenson – joined ad hoc all-star concert and festival bands, and twice appeared on the television show "Art Ford's Jazz Party" (1958, 1959). He was occasionally given opportunites to make modest stylistic experiments: he played the blues in a duo with Jimmy Giuffre (recorded in August 1956) and on the television show "The Sound of Jazz" (1957) and later co-led a rather unsuccessful modern jazz group with Marshall Brown (1962–3) and appeared at Newport to perform two unrehearsed numbers with Thelonious Monk (1963). In the spring of 1961 he made his first European tour, with Wein's Newport All Stars, and returned there in September 1964, after touring Australia, New Zealand, and Japan with Condon earlier that same year.

Russell's unique, complex style involved seemingly effortless variation of intentionally unorthodox timbres, growls alternating with hard attacks, and softly articulated notes held with a slow, almost sour, vibrato. He often played lines composed of greatly contrasting rhythmic values (unlike the successions of eighth-notes preferred by contemporary clarinetists) and unusual choices of pitch; by playing imperceptibly behind the beat he often gave a weighty quality to individual notes. His playing encompassed and was conditioned by the popular music of the 1930s, and is heard to best advantage on his highly individual performances of that repertory.

SELECTED RECORDINGS

As leader: Baby won't you please come home?/Dinah (1938, HRS 1000); Take me to the land of jazz (1944, Com. 596); Since my Best Gal Turned Me Down (1946, Disc 5053); *Portrait of Pee Wee Russell* (1958, Counterpoint 562); *Swingin' with Pee Wee* (1960, Swingville 2008); with C. Hawkins: *Pee Wee Russell–Coleman Hawkins All Stars* (1961, Can. 9020)

As sideman: R. Nichols: Riverboat Shuffle (1927, Bruns. 3627); Ida, Sweet as Apple Cider (1927, Bruns. 3626); Feelin' No Pain (1927, Vic. 21183); Mound City Blue Blowers: Hello, Lola/One Hour (1929, Vic. 38100); B. Banks: Oh Peter (1932, Ban. 32462); Harlem Hot Shots [B. Banks]: Baldheaded Mama (1932, Domino 123); E. Condon: Tennessee Twilight/ Madame Dynamite (1933, Bruns. 01690); Home Cooking (1933, Bruns. 6743); Love is just around the corner (1938, Com. 500); B. Freeman: Tappin' the Commodore Till (1938, Com. 508); J. P. Johnson: I've found a new baby (1938, HRS 1002); B. Hackett: A Ghost of a Chance (1938, Voc. 4565); E. Condon: Friar's Point Shuffle (1939, Decca 18040); Someday, Sweetheart (1939, Decca 18041); B. Freeman: As Long as I Live (1939, Decca 2849); Satanic Blues (1939, Decca 2781); E. Condon: It's all right here for you (1939, Com. 530); B. Freeman: Shim-me-sha-wabble (1940, Col. 35856); E. Condon: Oh, Sister! Ain't that hot?/(You're Some) Pretty Doll (1940, Com. 535); Three Deuces: Jig Walk (1941, Com. 539); The Last Time I Saw Chicago (1941, Com. 537); W. B. Davison: That's a Plenty (1943, Com. 1511); Old Folks, I would do anything for you, on G. Wettling: *George Wettling Jazz Trios* (1956, Kapp 1028); E. Condon: *Condon's Treasury of Jazz* (1956, Col. CL881)

SELECTED FILMS AND VIDEOS

Swing it (1936); Eddie Condon Floor Show (1949); Jazz Dance (1954); The Sound of Jazz (1957); Jazz USA (1960); Chicago & All that Jazz (1961); Newport Jazz Festival 1962 (1962); Jazz Alley (1968); Jimmy McPartland (*c* late 1980s); A Great Day in Harlem (1995)

BIBLIOGRAPHY

ChiltonW; *SchullerS*

E. Condon and T. Sugrue: *We Called it Music: a Generation of Jazz* (New York, 1947/*R*1988)

B. Coss: "Pee Wee Russell: the Gambling Kind," *DB*, xxx/14 (1963), 16

T. Gwaltney: "Pee Wee's Last Days," *DB*, xxxvi/12 (1969), 20

E. Condon and H. O'Neal: *The Eddie Condon Scrapbook of Jazz* (New York, 1973)

R. M. Sudhalter, P. R. Evans, and W. Dean-Myatt: *Bix: Man & Legend* (New Rochelle, NY, and London, 1974) [incl. chronology and discography], 142

W. Balliett: "Even his Feet Look Sad," *Improvising: Sixteen Jazz Musicians and their Art* (New York, 1977), 81; repr. in *BallietA (1986)*, 127; *BallietA (1996)*, 134

J. McDonough: Liner notes, *Giants of Jazz: Pee Wee Russell* (TL 17, 1981)
B. Crow: *From Birdland to Broadway: Scenes from a Jazz Life* (New York, and Oxford, England, 1992), 149
R. Hilbert with D. Niven: *Pee Wee Speaks: a Discography of Pee Wee Russell* (Metuchen, NJ, and London, 1992)
E. Anderson: "Ernie Anderson Talks about Pee Wee Russell and a New Book," *Sv*, no.153 (1993), 129
R. Hilbert: *Pee Wee Russell: the Life of a Jazzman* (New York, and Oxford, England, 1993)

JAMES DAPOGNY/BK

Russell, Ross (*b* Los Angeles, 18 March 1909; *d* Palm Springs, CA, 31 Jan 2000). Record producer and writer. He owned a record shop and in 1946 founded the record company Dial. In 1946–7 he served as Charlie Parker's personal manager, and he was also active as a lecturer on jazz. Russell contributed articles to *Down Beat*, *Jazz hot*, *Orkester journalen*, and *Jazz Review*, and his books include *Jazz Style in Kansas City and the Southwest* (Berkeley, CA, Los Angeles, and London, 1971, rev. 2/1973/*R*1997) and *Bird Lives: the High Life and Hard Times of Charlie "Yardbird" Parker* (New York, 1973/*R*1994). During the 1960s and 1970s he taught courses on Afro-American music at the University of California and Palomar College. Russell's collection was purchased in January 1981 by the University of Texas and is held at Austin (*see* Libraries and archives, §2). In 1990 he sold the Dial catalogue to Spotlite (ii).

BIBLIOGRAPHY

R. G. Reisner: "Ross Russell," *Bird: the Legend of Charlie Parker* (New York, 1962/*R*1975)
Obituaries: B. Ratliff, *New York Times* (23 March 2000); S. Voce, *The Independent* (9 Feb 2000)

Russin, Babe [Rusin, Irving] (*b* Pittsburgh, 18 June 1911; *d* Los Angeles, 4 Aug 1984). Tenor saxophonist. His name appears as Irving Rusin in his application for social security. He first performed professionally with the California Ramblers (1926). After touring Europe (1928) he traveled to New York, where he worked with Red Nichols, among others. He played with Ben Pollack in 1930 and then rejoined Nichols, with whom he remained until 1932. In the mid-1930s he was a staff musician for CBS. Having spent three months with Benny Goodman (late 1937–early 1938), and a longer period with Tommy Dorsey, he led his own band (1940–41), which undertook residencies in New York and Florida. Later he was a member of Jimmy Dorsey's group (1942–4; for illustration *see* Jazz (i), fig.3). During his military service (1944–6) he played in an AFRS band, and from the late 1940s he appeared sporadically with Goodman. He spent the latter years of his career working as a studio musician in California, although he continued to perform in reunions of Goodman's band. Russin is notable for the warm, full tone that he produced and for having kept pace with the growth and development of jazz; his early style was influenced heavily by Coleman Hawkins and Bud Freeman, but his later work reflected further stylistic innovations. He may be heard to advantage on *You Hit the Spot* (1936, Decca 689), which he recorded with Bunny Berigan's band under the leadership of the singer Bob Howard. Both his brother Jack and his sister, who was known as Sunny, were professional pianists, and Jack sometimes worked with Nichols.

SELECTED FILMS AND VIDEOS

I Dood it [By Hook and by Crook] (1943); Louis Armstrong – Bing Crosby (1951); The Glenn Miller Story (1953); The Benny Goodman Story (1955); The Swingin' Singin' Years (1960)

BIBLIOGRAPHY

ChiltonW; *FeatherE*

Russo, Bill [William Joseph, Jr.] (*b* Chicago, 25 June 1928). Composer and arranger. He attended high school with Lee Konitz and as a teenager studied with Lennie Tristano (1943–7). He played trombone in several dance bands from 1944, and from 1947 to 1950 led a rehearsal orchestra, Experiment in Jazz, while studying at De Paul University, Roosevelt College, and the Universtiy of Illinois in preparation for a legal career (later he completed a degree in English literature). However, instead he became associated from 1950 to 1954 with Stan Kenton's orchestra as a trombonist, composer, and arranger. He also studied composition privately in Chicago (1953–7); some of his arrangements were later published in *Down Beat* (intermittently, 1957–9). Russo toured Europe as the leader of a quintet in 1955. In 1958 he won a grant from the Koussevitzky Foundation and moved to New York, where he formed and conducted the Russo Orchestra, a large jazz ensemble with cellos, and taught at the Lenox (Massachusetts) School of Jazz (1957–60) and the Manhattan School of Music (1959–61). After traveling to Rome in 1961 he lived in London and conducted the London Jazz Orchestra (1962–5) and worked for the BBC. Russo returned to Chicago in 1965 and directed the Center for New Music at Columbia College (1965–75). He was composer-in-residence for the city and county of San Francisco in 1975–6, then took up work in film studios. In 1979 he resumed teaching at Columbia College, where he remained into the early 1990s, directing its Contemporary American Music program. While there he transcribed many big-band recordings, as well as some titles by small groups led by Count Basie and Duke Ellington, among others. In 1991 he founded the Chicago Jazz Ensemble, which performed both these transcriptions and new compositions, including many of his own. Russo took a tasteful and refreshingly flexible approach to this endeavor, transcribing recorded themes, accompanimental figures, and improvised solos when he felt that these were all essential to the character of the piece, but allowing his players to invent their own improvisations in contexts where the original solos were less than outstanding.

Russo composed much of Kenton's most experimental material in the 1950s and distinguished himself as a composer and arranger early in his career. His third-stream music, much of which was written in the late 1950s for the Russo Orchestra, is informed by jazz-influenced rhythms; his writing shows a sure sense of form and transition and also exploits the contrasts between disparate styles. He is the author of three texts on arranging, *Composing for the Jazz Orchestra* (Chicago and London, 1961), *Jazz Composition and Orchestration* (Chicago and London, 1968, rev. 2/1975), and *Composing Music: a New Approach* (Englewood Cliffs, NJ, 1983).

SELECTED RECORDINGS

The World of Alcina (1955, Atl. 1241); *The Seven Deadly Sins* (1960, Roul. 52063)

RECORDED COMPOSITIONS

(selective list; all recorded by S. Kenton)

Hall of Brass (1950, Cap. 28010); Bill's Blues (1952, Cap. EOX569)[EP]; on *New Concepts of Artistry in Rhythm* (1952, Cap. H383), Frank Speaking, Portrait of a Count, Twenty-three degrees north, eighty-two degrees west

SELECTED ARRANGEMENTS
(recorded by S. Kenton)

Portraits on Standards (1953–4, Cap. H462); Don't Worry 'bout Me (1955), first issued on *Some Women I've Known* (1944–63, CW 1029)

BIBLIOGRAPHY

L. Feather: "Russo: Young Man with a Mind," *MM*, xxxi (18 June 1955), 2
L. Tomkins: "In my Opinion: Bill Russo," *Crescendo*, i/3 (1962), 26
M. Sparke, ed.: *The Great Kenton Arrangers* (Whittier, CA, 1968) [incl. discography]
J. D. Dilts: "William Russo: Iconoclast in Orbit," *DB*, xxxvi/24 (1969), 15
W. F. Lee: *Stan Kenton: Artistry in Rhythm* (Los Angeles, 1980/*R*1994) [incl. discography; *R* without discography]
J. Balleras: "William Russo," *DB*, xlix/5 (1982), 26
I. Karl, ed.: *Hans Koller: the Man who Plays Jazz* (Vienna, 1993) [text in Ger. and Eng.]
C. Koch and K. Schulz: "Bill Russo oder der Versuch, Jazz und Klassik auszusöhnen," *JP*, xliii/1 (1994), 6
J. McDonough: "Tradin' Fours: at the Repertory Vanguard," *DB*, lxii/10 (1995), 36

GENEVIEVE VAUGHN/BK

Russo, Mark. Alto saxophonist, member of the YELLOWJACKETS.

Russo, Sonny [Santo J.] (*b* New York, 20 March 1929). Trombonist. He grew up in a musical family and had lessons with his father, a trumpeter and violinist, and his grandfather, who played trombone. Principally a sideman and soloist in big bands, he first worked with Buddy Morrow (1947), Lee Castle (1948), and Sam Donahue (1949), and performed and recorded with Artie Shaw (1949–50). In the 1950s he was a member of Buddy Rich's band (1951–2) and played and recorded with the clarinetist Jerry Wald (1951–2), the Sauter–Finegan Orchestra (1953–5), and Tommy Dorsey (1955–6); he also took part in sessions led by Neal Hefti (1954–5), John LaPorta (1955), and the drummer Mickey Sheen (*Have Swing Will Travel*, 1955, Herald 0105). Although he worked in Broadway shows thereafter (from 1956), he continued to record, with Sauter and Finegan (1956–*c*1961), Louie Bellson and Dinah Washington (both 1957), Toots Thielemans and Rex Stewart (both 1958), Lionel Hampton (1960), Bobby Hackett (1964), Dorothy Ashby and Benny Goodman (both 1965), and Grover Washington, Jr. (1973), and with such ensembles as Trombone Scene (1956), Urbie Green and 21 Trombones (1968), and All Star Trombone Spectacular (1977). (*FeatherE*)

Rust, Brian (Arthur Lovell) (*b* London, 19 March 1922). English discographer. He began collecting records at the age of five and from 1945 to 1960 worked in the gramophone library at the BBC, where he supervised the selection of recordings for broadcast; at the same time he wrote reviews of recordings for *The Gramophone* (1948–70). From 1960 he worked as a freelance writer of articles, liner notes, and discographies, all on early jazz, and from 1973 to 1984 he was the host of the program "Mardi Gras" for Capital Radio in London. His *Jazz Records* (1961) is the definitive discography of early jazz.

WRITINGS
(selective list)

with W. C. Allen: *King Joe Oliver* (Belleville, NJ, 1955)
with R. Harris: *Recorded Jazz: a Critical Guide* (Harmondsworth, England, 1958) [listeners' guide]
Jazz Records, i: *1897–1931* (Hatch End, nr London, 1961, 2/1962 with index by R. Grandorge); ii: *1932–1942* (Hatch End, 1965); i, ii, as *Jazz Records, A–Z, 1897–1942* (London, rev. 5/n.d. [1983]) [discography]
The Victor Master Book, ii: *1925–1936* (Stanhope, NJ, 1970) [discography; projected vol.i: 1903–25, and vol.iii: 1936–42, not pubd]
The Dance Bands (London, 1972)
with A. G. Debus: *The Complete Entertainment Discography, from the mid-1890s to 1942* (New Rochelle, NY, 1973)
The American Dance Band Discography, 1917–1942 (New Rochelle, NY, 1975)
The H.M.V. Studio House Bands, 1912–1939 (Chigwell, England, 1976)
The American Record Label Book (New Rochelle, NY, 1978)
Discography of Historical Records on Cylinders and 78s (Westport, CT, and London, 1979)
Brian Rust's Guide to Discography (Westport, CT, and London, 1980)

BIBLIOGRAPHY

M. Wyler: "Collector's Profiles, 4: Brian Rust," *JM*, ii/8 (1956), 29
J. Godbolt: "Brian Rust: King of the Zulus," *Jazz Circle News*, no.7 (1978), 18
B. Kernfeld and H. Rye: "Comprehensive Discographies of Jazz, Blues, and Gospel (Part One)," *Notes: Quarterly Journal of the Music Library Association*, li (1994), 518

ROBERT GANNON

Ruther, Wyatt (Robert) [Bull] (*b* Pittsburgh, 5 Feb 1923; *d* San Francisco, 31 Oct 1999). Double bass player. He played trombone in high school, then took up double bass, and he studied both instruments at the San Francisco Conservatory of Music (1949) and the Pittsburgh Musical Institute (1950). Based in New York in the early 1950s he performed and recorded with Dave Brubeck (1951–2) and Erroll Garner (intermittently, 1951–5; for illustration *see* GARNER, ERROLL). He toured with the singer Lena Horne (1953) and recorded as a leader (1955) and as a sideman with Toshiko Akiyoshi (1956). Ruther then went to Toronto, where he studied at the Royal Conservatory of Music (1956), played with the Canadian Jazz Quartet (1956–7) and Peter Appleyard's quartet (1957), and taught music in Ottawa, Hull (Ontario), and Toronto (1956–7). During the same period he returned to New York to record with Ray Bryant and a quintet led by Zoot Sims and Bob Brookmeyer (both 1956); he also recorded with Chico Hamilton in Los Angeles (1956). Later he performed and recorded in Hamilton's quintet, which featured Eric Dolphy (1958–9), toured and recorded with George Shearing (1959), and toured the Far East and South America as a member of Buddy Rich's sextet (1960–61). He joined Mulligan's quartet (alongside Bob Brookmeyer), with which he broadcast on radio (1962) and appeared in "Gerry Mulligan Quartet" (1963), an episode of the television series "Jazz Casual." In 1964–5 he performed and recorded with Count Basie.

Ruther appeared as a freelance in San Francisco in the late 1960s and played at the Olympic Hotel in Seattle for two years (1971–3). In 1973 he moved to Vancouver, Canada, and joined the trio led by Fraser McPherson, with which he recorded (1975), toured Canada and the Soviet Union (1978), and performed at the North Sea, Montreux, and Concord jazz festivals (1979). In the early 1980s he was a mainstay at the Ankor Hotel in Vancouver, where he accompanied, among other visiting musicians, Sammy Price and Jay McShann (both 1980–81) and Dorothy Donegan (1982). In 1984 he moved back to San Francisco, and for the next 15 years he performed regularly in Bay area clubs, often accompanying such visitors as Stan Getz or Lou Stein (both late 1980s) or playing with other locals, including John Handy and Jerome Richardson (late 1980s–1990s). He also held a regular engagement at the Bix Supper Club. Ruther's firm tone and ebullient sense of swing may be heard on *Bull in a China Shop* (1955), on which he displays a proficient technique and the influence of Jimmy Blanton on his phrasing and melodic ideas.

For further illustration *see* DOLPHY, ERIC.

SELECTED RECORDINGS

As leader with M. Hinton and W. Marshall: *Basses Loaded* (1955, RCA LPM1107), incl. Begin the Beguine, Bull in a China Shop, Crazy she calls me, I Poured my Heart into a Song

As sideman: D. Brubeck: *Modern Complex Dialogues* (1951, Alto 711); E. Garner: *Caravan* (1953, Col. CL535); *Contrasts* (1954, EmA 36001); C. Hamilton: *Gongs East* (1958, WB 1271); Bennie Green: *Catwalk* (1960, Beth. 6018); G. Mulligan: *The Quartets* (1962, Hindsight 611); F. MacPherson: *Live at the Planetarium* (1975, Conc. 92); A. O'Day: *Live at the Queen Elizabeth Theatre* (1976, Starline 9004)

BIBLIOGRAPHY

Feather '60s
J. M. Doran: *Erroll Garner: the Most Happy Piano* (Metuchen, NJ, 1985), 75
P. Elwood: "A Benefit to Help Pay Bull's Bills," *San Francisco Examiner* (9 Feb 1990)
Obituary, P. Elwood, *San Francisco Examiner* (2 Nov 1999)
P. Elwood and M. Breslow: "A Great Bay Jazz Day," *DB*, lxviii/2 (2000), 22

JOHN CURRY

Rutherford, Paul (William) (*b* London, 29 Feb 1940). English trombonist. He took up alto saxophone at the age of 14, but not long afterwards changed to trombone. After service in the RAF (1958–63), during which time he played in bands with John Stevens and Trevor Watts, he studied trombone, piano, and composition at the Guildhall School of Music and Drama, London (1964–8). During this time he played with Neil Ardley's New Jazz Orchestra (1964–6) and with Stevens and Watts ran the Little Theatre Club, presenting freely improvised music (1965–8). He was a founding member of the Spontaneous Music Ensemble in 1965, of Watts's Amalgam in 1967, and of the London Jazz Composers Orchestra in 1970. Also in 1970 he formed, with Barry Guy and Derek Bailey, the group Iskra 1903, an improvising ensemble of electric and electronic instruments; an expanded version of the group – Iskra 1912, with Maggie Nicols, Julie Tippetts, Howard Riley, and others – performed and recorded in 1972–3, and another – Oskastra, with different personnel – in the late 1980s. The original Iskra 1903 was re-formed in 1980 (but with Phil Wachsmann in place of Bailey) and performed and recorded into the 1990s. Rutherford also played with Mike Westbrook's bands (1967–78) and the Globe Unity Orchestra (1973–81, 1986), and in groups led by Tony Oxley (1969–74), Harry Miller (Isipingo, 1971), Peter Kowald (1972–6), Stevens (1982–4), Watts (1984–5), and the drummer Charlie Watts (1985–6), with whose big band he toured North America; he recorded with John Surman (1968), Manfred Schoof (1969), Bailey (in ICP, 1970), Keith Tippett's Centipede, Norma Winstone, and Don Cherry's Eternal Rhythm Orchestra (all 1971), Giorgio Gaslini (1973), Evan Parker (1979), the quartet M.L.A. Blek (1980), and Lol Coxhill (1982).

In 1983 Rutherford formed a trio with Paul Rogers and the drummer Nigel Morris, and in 1985 he performed in the USA as part of the International Trombone Workshop. He recorded in duos with Rogers (1988) and George Haslam (1989), as a member of the Free Jazz Quartet with the saxophonist Harrison Smith, the cellist Tony Moore, and Eddie Prévost (1989), in a trio with Anthony Braxton and Parker (1993), in groups led by Kenny Wheeler (1990), Mario Schiano (1991), Peter Brötzmann (1992), Fred van Hove (1996), and John Wolf Brennan and Elton Dean (both 1997), and with the Dedication Orchestra (1992, 1994). In 1995 he performed and recorded in Rome in a cooperative quintet with Schiano, Ernst Reijseger, Paul Lovens, and Kowald, and the following year he toured Japan as a member of the Berlin Contemporary Jazz Orchestra. Since 1973 Rutherford has played unaccompanied trombone. An accomplished improviser, he has worked in a wide variety of contexts, his often lyrical and mellifluous free playing sometimes aided by electronics; he has created new sonorities on the trombone by speaking into the instrument. In some of his work he has also played euphonium, notably in duos with Lovens (1976–7), on an unaccompanied solo album (1978), and with Stevens (1984).

SELECTED RECORDINGS

As unaccompanied soloist: *The Gentle Harm of the Bourgeoisie* (1974, Emanem 3305); *Old Moers Almanac* (1976, Ring 01014); *Neuph* (1978, Sweet Folk & Country 092); *1989 – and All That* (1989, Slam 301) [incl. duos with G. Haslam]

Duos: with P. Lovens: *And When I Say Slowly . . .* (1976–7, Po Torch 3); with P. Rogers: *Rogues* (1988, Emanem 4007)

As leader: *Iskra 1903* (1970–72, Incus 3–4); *Iskra/Nckpa 1903* (1992, Maya 9502); with A. Braxton and E. Parker: *Trio (London) 1993* (1993, Leo 197)

As sideman: Globe Unity Orchestra: *Live in Wuppertal* (1973, FMP 0160); Improvisors' Symposium: *Pisa 1980* (1980, Incus 37); J. Stevens: *The Life of Riley* (1984, Affinity 130); Free Jazz Quartet: *Premonitions* (1989, Matchless 18); K. Wheeler: *Music for Small and Large Ensembles* (1990, ECM 1415/6); P. Brötzmann: *The März Combo* (1992, FMP CD47)

BIBLIOGRAPHY

CarrJ; *ChiltonB*; *GrayF*
R. Williams: "Trombone Pioneer," *MM* (17 Jan 1970), 8
R. Brown: "Paul Rutherford," *JJ*, xxvi/3 (1973), 4
M. Davidson: "Blows against the Empire," *MM* (24 March 1973), 46
R. Cotterrell, ed.: *Jazz Now: the Jazz Centre Society Guide* (London, 1976)
K. Ansell: "Paul Rutherford," *Impetus*, no.6 (1977), 264
S. Lake: "Red Brassman," *MM* (30 April 1977), 40
P. Carles: "Paul Rutherford," *Jm*, no.273 (1979), 30 [incl. discography]
D. Ilic: "Paul Rutherford," *The Wire*, no.3 (1980), 6
B. Noglik: "Paul Rutherford," *Jazzwerkstatt International* (Berlin, 1981), 346 [incl. discography]
P. Renaud: *La discographie du jazz anglais* (Chaumont, France, 1985)
"Heroes," *MM* (4 Oct 1986), 28
D. Bailey: "Soundcheck: Derek Bailey Discusses the Improvising of Paul Rutherford," *Wire*, no.36 (1987), 43
E. Jost: *Europas Jazz, 1960–1980* (Frankfurt am Main, Germany, 1987), 299, 301
D. Lee: "The Gentle Harm of the Bourgeoisie: Paul Rutherford in Canada," *Coda*, no.215 (1987), 7
B. Rusch: "Paul Rutherford Interview," *Cadence*, xix/11 (1993), 9
<http://www.shef.ac.uk/misc/rec/ps/efi/musician/mrutherford.html> (1998) [incl. discography]
J. Litweiler: "Paul Rutherford: the Gentle Harm of the Bourgeoisie," *Coda*, no.279 (1998), 32

SIMON ADAMS

Rutherford, Rudy [Elman H.] (*b* Huachuca, AZ, 18 June 1924; *d* New York, 31 March 1995). Baritone and alto saxophonist and clarinetist. The details of his birth and death are taken from social security records. He played baritone saxophone in Lionel Hampton's big band for a brief period in autumn 1943 and then, from late 1943, in Count Basie's orchestra, in which he replaced Jack Washington (who was drafted); he changed to the alto instrument when Washington re-joined the orchestra in 1946. In spring of the following year Rutherford left Basie's group to join that of Teddy Buckner, and in 1951 he recorded as a member of Basie's octet; his performances on these recordings are usually attributed, mistakenly, to Serge Chaloff. Later he performed and recorded with Wilbur De Paris (1959), the rock-and-roll singer and guitarist Chuck Berry (at the Newport Jazz Festival, 1958), Buddy Tate (1960, 1964), and Earl Hines (1973–6); his appearance with Berry may be seen in the film *Jazz on a Summer's Day*. Through the late 1980s he was a member of Illinois Jacquet's big band, with which he recorded on baritone saxophone and clarinet (1987). He contributed an instructional article to *Windplayer* in 1993. Although he is best known for his work as a member of saxophone sections, Rutherford took most of his solos on clarinet.

Oral history material in *DSI* (JOHP).

SELECTED RECORDINGS

(recorded for V-disc unless otherwise indicated)

As sideman: C. Basie: Kansas City Stride (1944, 258B); Gee, baby, ain't I good to you? (1944, 289B); Playhouse no.2 Stomp (1945, 493A); High Tide (1945, 483B); W. De Paris: on *Over and Over Again* (1959–60, Atl. 1552), Would You Care (1959); E. Hines: *Swingin' Away* (1973, BL 30190)

BIBLIOGRAPHY

SheridanCB

CHRIS SHERIDAN

Růžička, Karel, Jr. (*b* Prague, 27 June 1973). Czech tenor saxophonist and leader. The son of the jazz pianist and composer Karel Růžička, he was exposed to music from an early age and for various periods of time played recorder, piano, violin, trumpet, and trombone, on which he began classical conservatory training when he was 13. While at the conservatory he also studied drums and taught himself saxophone. He played both trombone and saxophone in hard-bop bands and at summer jazz workshops in Frýdlant, in northern Bohemia. At the age of 16 he began to concentrate on tenor saxophone, though he doubles on the soprano instrument. Having begun to gain recognition for his playing in the early 1990s, he spent a brief period in New York and then returned to Prague, where he recorded with his father (*The Flight*, 1995, Melantrich 011) and deputized in Roy Hargrove's quintet (1996). From 1997 he has lived alternately in Prague and New York, where he spent two years in the house band at the Blue Note club. In addition Růžička has worked in funk, blues, and salsa bands and in other contexts. As a jazz musician he may be heard to advantage on his own album *You Know What I Mean* (1997, Arta 0080-2), which includes some of his compositions.

JAROSLAV PAŠMIK

Ryan's. Nightclub in New York, properly known as Jimmy Ryan's; *see* NIGHTCLUBS AND OTHER VENUES.

Ryerson, Ali (*b* New York, 21 Oct 1952). Flutist. Her father, the studio guitarist Art Ryerson, recorded with Frank Sinatra, Sarah Vaughan, and Erroll Garner, among others; her brothers also became musicians. She received classical training from the age of eight, and as a child she was exposed to jazz through her brothers' record collection and the jam sessions her father held at their home (Milt Hinton, Barry Galbraith, and Lou Stein were among the participants). Ryerson first performed professionally in her brothers' jazz-rock group in 1968, and she continued her classical studies at the Hartt School of Music in Hartford, Connecticut (BM classical performance 1979), and with renowned classical flutists in New York. In 1980 she spent a year playing in clubs in Montreal, then the following year she returned to New York and performed regularly at Bradley's. By the late 1980s she had moved to Brussels, where she appeared as a freelance and began what became a longstanding association with Charles Loos (with whom she recorded from 1988 to 1992). She then toured internationally with Stephane Grappelli. While performing with the violinist at Carnegie Hall around 1990 she was heard by Bob Thiele, with whom she signed a contract to record for the Red Baron label (*Blue Flute*, 1991, Red Baron AK48851); from 1994 she made recordings for Concord (including *In her own Sweet Way*, 1995, Conc. 4687). Ryerson spent a period in Carmel, California, and worked as principal flutist in the Monterey Bay Symphony Orchestra before resettling in the East in 1992. From that time she performed regularly at a restaurant in Gaylordsville, Connecticut, worked as a studio musician in New York, and toured internationally. She also recorded with Joe Beck in a duo and trio (1996) and performed with the guitarist in a duo (from 1997).

BIBLIOGRAPHY

Feather–GitlerBEJ

L. Gourse: "Ali's Odyssey," *JT*, xxii/7 (1992), 14

——: *Madame Jazz: Contemporary Women Instrumentalists* (New York, and Oxford, England, 1995), 115

<http://web.arcadis.be/beljazz/guest/ali.htm> (1999) [incl. discography]

<http://www.aent.com/concord/bios/ryerson.html> (1999)

GK

Rykodisc. Record company established in Salem, Massachussetts, in 1983. In 1994 it purchased Gramavision and reissued that label's back catalogue, as well as new recordings by Bill Frisell, Peter Apfelbaum, the trio Medeski, Martin & Wood, Ron Miles, and Myra Melford, among others. Rykodisc is a major company with a large presence in other musical genres; it has made jazz-oriented recordings for its Hannibal label, which is devoted principally to folk music.

BIBLIOGRAPHY

B. Milkowski: "Riffs: Rykodisc Acquires Gramavision Label," *DB*, lxi/11 (1994), 12

C. Morris: "Retail: Gramavision to Rejoin Indie Ranks with Ryko," *Billboard*, cvi (20 Aug 1994), 76

——: "Rykodisc Readies 1st Gramavision Catalog Releases," *Billboard*, cvi (3 Sept 1994), 12

<http://www.rykodisc.com> (2000)

GK

Rypdal, Terje (*b* Oslo, 23 Aug 1947). Norwegian electric guitarist and composer. His father played clarinet and violin and conducted a military band in Oslo. Rypdal studied classical piano and, briefly, trumpet, and taught himself to play guitar from around the age of 13. As a teenager he played in a rock-and-roll band, the Vanguards, and from 1967 to 1969 he led a blues-rock band, Dream, whose members included Jan Garbarek. He studied electrical engineering at the technical university in Trondheim, but left to pursue a career in music and instead studied the lydian chromatic concept of tonal organization with its originator, George Russell, in whose sextet and big band he also played (again with Garbarek). Rypdal first achieved recognition outside Norway at the New Jazz Meeting, Baden-Baden, Germany (1969), at which he presented some of his own compositions. He worked with Garbarek's quartet from around 1968 to 1972, and through his association with Garbarek began a permanent affiliation with the ECM label. Having taken courses in musicology at Oslo University during this same period he transferred to the city's conservatory (1970–72) and studied composition with Finn Mortensen, while also leading the pit band in the Norwegian production of the musical *Hair* (1970–71). In 1972 he appeared at the festival in West Berlin in a trio with Barre Phillips and Jon Christensen and formed the group Odyssey, with which he visited London and the USA, recorded, and performed (with Palle Mikkelborg as a guest soloist) at the Festspill in Bergen, Norway (1978). He also recorded with John Surman (1973), Mike Mantler (1975), Edward Vesala and Egil Johansen (both 1976), and Phillips (1978), in a cooperative trio with Miroslav Vitous and Jack DeJohnette (1978, 1981), and in a duo with David Darling (1983).

From 1985 to 1994 Rypdal led a trio, the Chasers, consisting of Bjørn Kjellemyr and the drummer Audun Kleive; with this group he appeared at festivals in Molde, Norway (1985), and Eastern Europe and toured the Continent and England. In 1986 he performed in a duo with Mikkelborg in Molde, and in the early 1990s he also worked with a large ensemble. After the Chasers disbanded Rypdal collaborated with the hard-rock guitarist Ronnie Le Tekro and formed a new trio, Skywards, with keyboards (rather than electric bass guitar) and drums. In 1996 Skywards recorded as a septet (with Darling and Mikkelborg among the extra members), and it appeared as a trio at major festivals in New York and Montreal; the trio returned to the New York event in 1998. In addition to his own projects, Rypdal has worked with the pianist Ketil Bjørnstad (with whom he recorded from 1993), and he has been a member of the Nordic Quartet with Karin Krog, John Surman, and Knut Riisnaes (from 1994). In 1997 he performed with Kleive and recorded with Tomasz Stańko.

Strongly influenced by Jeff Beck as well as by Jimi Hendrix, Rypdal is widely regarded as one of the most important electric guitarists in European jazz-rock; his style incorporates elements of rock and modern concert music and such novel sonorities as note clusters produced by playing the electric guitar with a violin bow. He is also one of the most important Norwegian composers of his generation; his works, which owe something to the music of Krzysztof Penderecki, include *Eternal Circulation* for symphony orchestra and jazz ensemble (1972), *Somehow it's Making Me Smile Inside* for guitar (1975), *Imagi* for dancers and big band (1984), and orchestral and chamber music.

SELECTED RECORDINGS

(all recorded for ECM)

As unaccompanied soloist: *After the Rain* (1976, 1083)

As leader: *What Comes After* (1973, 1031); *Whenever I Seem to be Far Away* (1974, 1045); *Odyssey* (1975, 1067–8); *Waves* (1977, 1110); *Descendre* (1979, 1144); with J. DeJohnette and M. Vitous: *To be Continued* (1981, 1192); *Chaser* (1985, 1303); *The Singles Collection* (1988, 1383); *If Mountains Could Sing* (1994, 1554); *Skywards* (1996, 1608)

As sideman: J. Garbarek: *Afric Pepperbird* (1970, 1007); B. Phillips: *Three Day Moon* (1978, 1123)

BIBLIOGRAPHY

R. Williams: "Song of Norway," *MM* (8 April 1972), 20

R. Hultin: "Terje Rypdal: a Great Musical Personality," *JF* [intl edn], no.27 (1974), 48

J. Sievert: "Terje Rypdal: Norwegian Composer/Guitarist," *GP*, xi/5 (1977), 30 [incl. discography]

L. Goddet: "Terje Rypdal: un son étrange venu d'ailleurs," *Jh*, no.361 (1979), 30

J. Diliberto: "Profile: Terje Rypdal," *DB*, xlvii/11 (1980), 52

B. Milkowski: "Terje Rypdal: Sculptor in Sound," *DB*, liv/10 (1987), 20

J. Nash: "Terje Rypdal," *JT* (1989), July, 20

K. M. Paulssen: "Terje Rypdal," *Jazz Nyett*, no.3 (1994), 28

I. Orvedal: "Terje Rypdal: Navigator," *Listen to Norway*, iii/1 (1995), 40

J. Woodard: "The Bridge: Guitar across the Ages: Terje Rypdal," *Jazziz*, xii/9 (1995), 72

B. Milkowski: "Terje Rypdal: Big Sky Music," *JT*, xxvii/6 (1997), 36

J. Rotondi: "Terje Rypdal: Fjord Explorer," *GP*, xxxi/9 (1997), 21

<http://www.jeffgower.com/rypdal.html> (1999) [incl. bibliography, biography, discography, list of compositions]

RANDI HULTIN

S

Saarsalu, Lembit (*b* Roosna-Alliku, nr Paide, Estonian SSR [now Estonia], 8 July 1948). Estonian saxophonist and composer. He made his début at the Tallinn International Jazz Festival in 1965 and the same year began an association with the Estonian Philharmonic Society, playing first in its dance orchestra and later in its groups Viru and Laine. After studying clarinet and brass-band conducting at the Tallinn Music School (graduating in 1975) he worked as a leader from 1978, and in 1984 he formed a duo with the Russian pianist Leonid Vintskevich. Saarsalu performed in East Africa, the Near East, Cuba, Hungary (where he appeared at festivals in Nagykanizsa, 1980, and Debrecen, 1981), Bulgaria, and Belgium. In 1986 he played in Berlin and The Hague and worked with the jazz-rock group Radar at the Bratislava Jazz Days, and in 1989 he performed in Le Mans and made the first of a succession of appearances with Vintskevich at the Lionel Hampton Jazz Festival in Moscow, Idaho (extending through the 1990s), where he also played with Hampton and with Elvin Jones. From 1995 the duo worked mainly in Germany. Several of Saarsalu's compositions incorporate elements of Estonian folk music, among them *2 x labajalg* (2 x rustic waltz) and *Ringtants* (Round dance), both on the album *Džässkvartett "Tallinn"* (1983, Mel. C60 19783007), and *Happy Childhood*, on *Land, Zemlja, Maa* (1994, Markant Music 000105); a good example of his tasteful approach to jazz standards may be heard on *I Love You* (1998, Bohème Music 809020). He is the subject of *Old Melody*, a film made for television in 1981.

WALTER OJAKÄÄR

Saba. Record label. It was owned by the company of the same name that manufactured radio receivers and tape recorders in Villingen–Schwenningen, Germany. The initial purpose of the label, established by Hans Georg Brunner-Schwer (grandson of the company's founder), was to provide recordings for use on a car tape player (the Sabamobil), first marketed in 1963. An important catalogue of jazz quickly developed; by 1967 it contained 35 albums, among them fine recordings by Oscar Peterson, Nathan Davis, the Clarke–Boland Big Band, and the group Violin Summit. During that year Saba acquired the distribution rights to 32 albums from Prestige. However, in 1968 the parent company was taken over by an American firm that did not wish to continue the recording operation. Brunner-Schwer therefore retained the rights to the catalogue (which by this time also included, among other items, an important album by the quintet led by Ben Webster and Don Byas) and founded a new record company, MPS.

BIBLIOGRAPHY

"The MPS Decade 1968–1978," *JJI*, xxxi/5 (1978), suppl.

G. Lees: *Oscar Peterson: the Will to Swing* (Toronto, 1988), 199

F. Ziegler: "Saba/MPS Discography," <http://www.fmi.unipassau.de/~schneide/music/discogr/saba.html> (1998)

K.-G. Fischer: *Jazzin' the Black Forest: Discography und Geschichte des Saba/MPS-Labels* (Berlin, 1999) [incl. discography]

BK

Saberton, Pete(r) (*b* Sheffield, England, 9 July 1950). English pianist. After attending the Northern School of Music in Manchester (1968–71) he played with the saxophonist Pete Hurt (from 1971), the National Youth Jazz Orchestra (1973), Don Rendell (1978–85), Mark Murphy (1979–85), Harry Beckett (1980–86), the saxophonists Pat Crumley (1981) and Tim Whitehead (1981–3), the BBC Radio Big Band (1981–93), John Taylor (1987), Mel Tormé (1988), Mike Westbrook (1992), the London Jazz Orchestra (early 1990s), the flutist Eddie Parker (from 1994), the drummer Pete Fairclough, Henry Lowther, the trombonist Pete Beachill, Martin Speake, and others. In 1983 he first taught at the annual Glamorgan Jazz Summer School in Wales, and the following year he recorded as a leader with James Williams's octet. In the early 1990s he led the house band which accompanied Sonny Fortune, Gary Bartz, Charles McPherson, and Jimmy Witherspoon at the Jazz Café in London. Saberton began concentrating on his own trio and sextet in 1997.

SELECTED RECORDINGS

As leader: *Year of the Buffalo* (1984, Spot. 532)

As sideman: D. Rendell: *Earth Music* (1979, Spot. 515); *Set Two* (1979, Spot. 516); P. Hurt: *Lost for Words* (1984, Spot. 525); *Umbrellas* (1994, ASC 10); P. Fairclough: *Shepherd Wheel* (1995, ASC 1); E. Parker: *Everything You Do* (1996, FMR 29); M. Speake: *Amazing Grace* (1996, Spot. 558); H. Lowther: *I.D.* (1997, Village Life 9712-2)

MARK GILBERT

Sa-Chi. Nickname of Béla Szakcsi lakatos.

Sachs, Aaron (*b* New York, 4 July 1923). Tenor saxophonist and clarinetist. He first played clarinet, which he studied privately, and alto saxophone, on which he was self-taught. In the early 1940s he worked with Babe Russin (1941), the pianist Van Alexander (1942–3), and Herbie Fields (early 1944) and performed and recorded with Red Norvo (intermittently, 1941–5) and Benny Goodman (February–June 1945). In addition he recorded, mainly on clarinet, with Eddie Heywood, Flip Phillips, and Sarah Vaughan (all 1944), Horace Henderson (1945), and Mildred Bailey (1946). From late in 1945 through April 1946 he toured and recorded as a member of Buddy Rich's big band. After leaving Rich's group in Hollywood he returned to New York, where in June 1946 he recorded on clarinet as the leader of a bop quintet that consisted of Terry Gibbs, Gene DiNovi, Clyde Lombardi, and Tiny Kahn; among the tracks from this outstanding session is an impressive rendition of *Tiny's Con*, which, like Miles Davis's better-known *Donna Lee*, has an intricate, technically challenging melody based on the chord progression of the standard popular song *Indiana*. That July Sachs worked briefly with Charlie Ventura, and by October he had rejoined Rich, with whom he remained into December 1946. The following March he played with Joe Guy in New York, and late in June he appeared in a jam session with such notable musicians as Davis, Bud Powell, and Max Roach. After a period of illness Sachs resumed his career and worked mainly as a tenor saxophonist. He toured and recorded with Earl Hines (1952–3), recorded as a leader (1954, 1956) and with Gene Krupa (1956), and was active as a freelance, performing at clubs in New York. For several years he worked sporadically with the percussionist Tito Rodriquez, and in 1959 he toured and recorded with Louie Bellson. In the early and mid-1950s he was married to Helen Merrill. Having recorded with Tom Talbert in 1956 Sachs joined several colleagues from that session for a new recording under Talbert's leadership in 1997.

SELECTED RECORDINGS

As leader: Aaron's Axe/Tiny's Con (1946, Manor 1124); Patsy's Idea/Sam Beeps and Bops (1946, Manor 1147)

As sideman: E. Heywood: How High the Moon/Sarcastic Lady (1944, Sig. 40002); T. Talbert: *This is Living!* (1997, Pipe Dream 14480)

BIBLIOGRAPHY

ConnorBG; *FeatherE*

J. Burns: "The Forgotten Boppers," *J&B*, ii/3 (1972), 4

D. Salemann, D. Hartmann, and M. Vogler: *Aaron Sachs: Discography, Solography, Bandroutes, Engagements* (Basel, Switzerland, 1989)

BK

Sachse, Helmut "Joe" (*b* Mittweida, Germany, 28 Oct 1948). German electric guitarist and flutist. While studying at the Musikhochschule in Weimar (1973–8) he performed in groups led by Manfred Schulze, including Praxis II and Schulze-Formation. In 1976 he set up his own quartet, consisting of Manfred Hering, the double bass player Christoph Winckel, and the drummer Wolfram Dix; with the addition of Hannes Zerbe, this became the quintet Osiris (1977–9), which toured with guest soloists, among them Charlie Mariano, Leo Wright, Carmell Jones, the guitarist Toto Blanke, and Rudolph Dašek. Sachse formed guitar duos with Blanke, Dašek, and Uwe Kropinski (1978–9). Having toured in a duo with Hering (1980–81), he and the saxophonist established a quartet (1982) comprising Dix and another saxophonist – either Helmut Forsthoff, Ernst-Ludwig Petrowsky, or Heiner Reinhardt. In 1981 Sachse began what became a longstanding association with the group DoppelMoppel, co-led by the brothers Conrad and Johannes Bauer (he also worked in Conrad Bauer's other small groups), and in 1983 he joined Petrowsky's trio alongside Klaus Koch (he had occasionally worked in Petrowsky's quartet from 1979).

In the mid-1980s Sachse began recording and performing as an unaccompanied soloist, and he worked sporadically in duos with George Lewis (ii) and the percussionist David Moss. He recorded with Günter Christmann (1985) and conducted workshops and performed with, among others, Tony Oxley, Howard Riley, John Stevens, Peter Brötzmann, Phil Minton, Paul Rutherford, John Tchicai, Evan Parker, Peter Kowald and Jon Rose, the double bass player Jay Oliver, Barry Altschul, Radu Malfatti, Fred van Hove, and Gerd Dudek. In the 1990s, with the tuba player Pinguin Moschner, he formed the duo If 69 Was 96 to perform the music of Jimi Hendrix, and he undertook further work with Hering, most notably in a trio with John Marshall. He also performed in a trio with Harry Beckett and Oxley, in the group Nevergreens with Moschner and Maggie Nicols, in duos with Conrad Bauer and Moss, as the leader of a quartet consisting of Forsthoff, Reinhardt, and Hering, and with the drummer Peter Hollinger in a duo which performs music by the Beatles.

SELECTED RECORDINGS

As unaccompanied soloist: *Solo* (1984, FMP 1070); *European House* (1991, FMP CD041); *Ballade für Jimi Metag* (1999, Born&Bellmann 991503)

Duos with D. Moss and G. Lewis: *Berlin Tango* (1986–7, ITM 1448)

As leader: *Helmut Sachse–Hannes Zerbe* (1981, Amiga 855858)

As sideman: H. Becker: *Pan-vielleicht Tau* (1982, FMP 1010); C. Bauer: *Round about Mittweida* (1982, FMP 0980); DoppelMoppel: *Reflections* (1986, FMP CD74); *Aventure Québécoise* (1998, Victo 065)

BIBLIOGRAPHY

M. Kunzler: *Jazz-Lexicon* (Reinbek, nr Hamburg, Germany, 1988)

R. Köhl: "Die Kunst des feinen Übergangs: Conny Bauer und Joe Sachse," *JP*, xxxix/1 (1990), 36

<http://www.helmut-joe-sachse.de/> (2000) [incl. discography]

GK

Sackville. Record company and label. The company was established in Toronto in 1968 by John Norris and Bill Smith (ii), respectively the publisher and editor of the magazine *Coda*. The label has been used to issue material in various styles, most of it newly recorded in Canada. The catalogue contains the work of Frank Rosolino, Buddy Tate, Doc Cheatham, Archie Shepp, and Humphrey Lyttelton. Sackville has been particularly active recording pianists, notably Ralph Sutton, Sir Charles Thompson, Sammy Price, Jay McShann, Abdullah Ibrahim, Don Pullen, Junior Mance, Art Hodes, Willie "the Lion" Smith, and Don Ewell. A few important reissues have also been made, among them an LP recorded in 1957 by Bill Holman's big band. Sackville expanded its activities in the 1990s: while transferring much of its catalogue to CD and offering new recordings by Sutton, McShann, the group JMOG, Don Menza, Geoff Keezer, Harold Mabern, and Keith Ingham, it became increasingly busy as a North American distributor for a number of labels, among them American Music, Chiaroscuro, Classics, Nagel-Heyer, Storyville (ii), and Timeless.

MARK GARDNER/BK

Sacramento Dixieland Jubilee [Sacramento Jazz Jubilee]. Festival held annually from 1974 in Sacramento, California. It was first organized by Bill Borcher, who continued as its executive director into the 1980s. The festival is sponsored by the Sacramento Traditional Jazz Society and has received additional funds from the city, county, and state governments. For many years it took place over four days in September, but at some point in the 1990s this was changed to four days in late May. Events are held at various indoor and outdoor venues in Sacramento. The jubilee is the largest traditional-jazz festival in the world; groups that take part are auditioned through submitted recordings. In 1985, 101 ensembles from 16 countries performed at 51 venues before a combined audience of 250,000, and in 2000 the festival presented 138 bands from throughout the world at about 40 venues before a combined audience of around 100,000. Among the groups that have performed are the Sveriges Jazz Band from Stockholm and the Jazz Band Ball Orchestra from Kraków, Poland; in 1987 the group Leningrad Dixieland made its first visit to the USA to participate. At some point in the 1990s the festival took the new name Sacramento Jazz Jubilee to reflect the expansion in style that had taken place; by that time it incorporated not only dixieland, but also Latin jazz, zydeco, blues, swing, Western swing, and gospel music.

BIBLIOGRAPHY

B. Knowles: "Jazz on the Coast: Sacto: the Chief Speaks," *MR*, xii/9 (1985), 12
<http://www.sacjazz.com> (1999)

PAUL R. LAIRD

Sadi, Fats [Lallemand, Sadi "Fats"; Lallemand, Sadi Pol] (*b* Andenne, Belgium, 23 Oct 1927). Belgian vibraphonist. He first played xylophone in a circus band, and in 1941, after hearing recordings by Lionel Hampton, he took up vibraphone. In 1945 he formed Sadi's Hot Five in Namur, then worked with the reed player Raoul Faisant and René Thomas in Brussels and with Faisant and Gus Deloof in Liège and appeared at the Cotton Club in Brussels. After performing at festivals in Nice and Paris (respectively in 1948 and 1949) and working with the Bob Shots (recording in Paris, 1949) and in Germany with the pianist Vicky Thunus, he lived from 1950 to 1961 in Paris, where he played regularly with Bobby Jaspar. He also worked with Jack Diéval (*c*1951), Henri Renaud (1952), and Aimé Barelli (touring in 1953), sang as an original member of the Blue Stars, performed and recorded with Django Reinhardt (1953), André Hodeir (from 1955), and Martial Solal (1954, 1956), and recorded with Don Byas (1955). In 1955 Sadi led a big band which included Jaspar, Jean-Louis Chautemps, Jay Cameron, and Roger Guérin, but he then served as a sideman with the bandleader Jacques Hélian (late 1955 – early 1957). After his return to Belgium he joined the orchestra of the Belgische Radio en Televisie/Radiodiffusion-Télévision Belge, led a quartet, and performed throughout Belgium and the Netherlands, often as a member of the Clarke–Boland Big Band; he made numerous recordings with Clarke and Boland, and also recorded with the European All Stars (in Berlin, 1961), Sahib Shihab (*c*1964–5, 1968), Boland's small groups (1965, 1967), and Lucky Thompson (1969). He toured the USA and South America with the singer Caterina Valente. Later he made three videos for Belgian television (*Sadi Show*, i–iii, 1972, 1973, 1975), and he continued to perform and record in the 1980s and 1990s. Sadi appeared at the Jazz Middelheim festival in 1993 and recorded again as a leader in 1994; his 70th birthday was celebrated with a tribute concert in Brussels in 1997. He is passionately devoted to the swing and bop styles.

SELECTED RECORDINGS

As leader: *Fats Sadi Como* (1953, Vogue 212); with M. Solal: *Martial Solal–Sadi Quartet* (1956, Swing 30046); *Mr. Fats Sadi, his Vibes & Friends: Ensadinado* (1966, Saba 15111); *Sadi 4tet* (1976, Rust 7611); *The Sadi Quartet* (1994, Ispahan 94101)
As sideman: S. Shihab: *Companionship* (*c*1964–5, Vogue 17243); L. Thompson: *A Lucky Songbook in Europe* (1969, MPS 15231)

BIBLIOGRAPHY

FeatherE; *Feather–Gitler '70s*; *ReclamsJ*
R. Pernet, J.-P. Schroeder, and others: *Dictionnaire du jazz à Bruxelles et en Wallonie* (Liège, Belgium, 1991)
J.-M. Hacquier: "Sadi: It Don't Mean a Thing," *Jh*, no.543 (1997), 32 [incl. discography by R. Pernet]
R. Pernet: *Belgian Jazz Discography (1897–1999)* (Brussels, 1999)

ROBERT PERNET

Sadowski, Krzysztof (*b* Warsaw, 15 Dec 1936). Polish pianist and organist. He studied piano for eleven years while at school, and after graduating from the Warsaw Institute of Technology in 1957 he took up a career in jazz, when he formed the group Modern Combo. In the early 1960s he played and recorded with Zbigniew Namysłowski's Jazz Rockers and Jan Wróblewski's Jazz Outsiders (both 1961–2) and worked with Andrzej Kurylewicz and the Swingtet, led by Jerzy Matuszkiewicz. He achieved considerable success with his own group Bossa Nova Combo (from 1963), with which he toured the USSR (1965) and Scandinavia (1967). In 1967, influenced by Jimmy Smith, he took up Hammond organ, and from 1969 to 1981 he led a hard-bop ensemble, the Organ Group. He also toured and recorded with his wife, the pop singer and flutist Liliana Urbańska. Sadowski composed many popular hits in Poland, as well as music for films, theater, radio, and television, and two suites, *Na kosmodromie* (On the cosmodrome) and *Our Common World*.

SELECTED RECORDINGS

(recorded for Muza unless otherwise indicated)

As leader: *Krzysztof Sadowski and his Hammond Organ* (1970, 0606); *Na kosmodromie* (1972, 7048); *Three Thousand Points* (1975, Polskie Nagrania 1277); *Swing and Blues* (1977, Poljazz [issue no. unknown]); *Swing Party* (*c*1979 , 1796)
As sideman: Z. Namysłowski: *Jazz Jamboree 61*, no.3: *Jazz Rockers* (1961, 0184); J. Wróblewski: *Jazz Outsiders* (1962, 0197); Z. Namysłowski: *Jazz Rockers* (1962, 0229); J. Matuszkiewicz: *Swingtet* (1963, 0262)

BIBLIOGRAPHY

J. Byrczek: "Eurojazz Personalities: Poland," *JF* [intl edn], no.18 (1972), 87
"Krzysztof Sadowski: Hammond Man," *JF* [intl edn], no.32 (1974), 19
A. Chodkowski, ed.: *Encyklopedia muzyki* (Warsaw, 1995)
K. Karpiński: "Feeling to serce jazzu" [Feeling is the heart of jazz], *JF*, no.180 (1997), 50

WOLFRAM KNAUER/ADAM CEGIELSKI, BK

Sadykhov, Vagif (Emirovich) (*b* Baku, Azerbaijan SSR [now Azerbaijan], 6 June 1946). Azerbaijani pianist. He first played jazz at the age of 12 and later completed studies in piano and composition at both the Azerbaijan Conservatory and, in 1969, the Baku Conservatory. While still a teenager he organized a student "symphojazz" group and led a trio, and in 1964 he was invited by the tenor saxophonist Vladimir Sermakashev to play in the KM Quartet at the jazz club Youth. In Moscow he worked with such musicians as Aleksey Zubov, Gennady Golstain, and Konstantin Nosov and played at the jazz clubs Sinyay Pittsa (Bluebird) and Pechora. He was a member of the band Blue Screen (1969–71), Oleg Lundstrem's orchestra (1973–7), the Azerbaijan State Variety-Symphonic Orchestra (1977–9), and Georgy Garanian's ensemble Melody (1979–85), to which he contributed compositions and arrangements; he also formed the Quintet of the Soloists of Melody (including Zubov), which recorded his first album as a leader. In 1985 Sadykhov formed a quartet with the tenor saxophonist Stanislav Grigoriev, from the following year he led a trio, and in 1990–91 he performed with Valery Ponomarev in Moscow. From 1991 he worked in the nightclub Arlekino, playing in styles other than jazz. Later, however, he was active in various ensembles with Igor Butman (from 1996) and performed in a quartet with Sergey Belichenko (1998). Sadykhov appeared at many Soviet and Russian festivals, as well as at such events in Finland, Estonia, Germany, Hungary, Poland, and the USA, and played with many other Russian musicians.

SELECTED RECORDINGS

As leader: *Tallinn Jazz Festival* (1967, Mel. 020844); *Bombay Jazz Festival* (1980, Mel. 14933); *Simple and Complex* (1983, Mel. 20281002)
As sideman with O. Lundstrem: *Sun Valley Serenade* (1976, Mel. 07077); *Music of Duke Ellington* (1977, Mel. 08473)

SERGEY BELICHENKO

Safety. In the pre-tape era, a backup recording which served as a standby should conventionally mastered takes become unusable; *see* Recording, §I, 2(ii).

Safranski, Eddie [Edward] (*b* Pittsburgh, 25 Dec ?1914; *d* Los Angeles, 10 Jan 1974). Double bass player. According to Agostinelli (1992), Safranski was born in 1912, not 1918, as given in standard reference works, but Agostinelli asserts also that Safranski died in January 1974 at the age of 59, which places his birth in 1914; this year fits best with Agostinelli's claim that Safranski graduated from high school in 1932. But to confuse matters further, Safranski's application for social security and the California death index both give 1919 as his year of birth. He learned violin as a boy and took up the double bass in high school. In 1941 he joined Hal McIntyre, with whom he played until 1945 and for whom he also wrote a number of arrangements; he then worked with Miff Mole (1945), Stan Kenton (June 1945 – December 1948), and Charlie Barnet (late 1948–1949). While he was with Kenton he became better known, and he moved to New York to seek work in radio and television; he was a staff musician at NBC and also played with Marian McPartland (in Boston, early 1950s) and Benny Goodman (1951 – March 1953). He continued to undertake studio work until the late 1960s, when he became a representative for a double bass manufacturer, running workshops and masterclasses; from that time he also played traditional and modern jazz with various groups in Los Angeles. Safranski was essentially a swing musician. As a member of a rhythm section he provided a steady, dependable beat and played with a forthright clarity and precision; his solos for Kenton were based on solid rhythms and a robust sense of the swing style.

SELECTED RECORDINGS

As leader: Spellbound/Let me Go (1946, Savoy 601); Sa-frantic/Bass Mood (1947, Atl. 851)
As sideman with S. Kenton: Painted Rhythm (1945, Cap. 250); Safranski (Artistry in Bass) (1946, Cap. 288); Concerto to End All Concertos (1946, Cap. 382); Lover (1947, Cap. 904)
As sideman with others: D. Byas: Little White Lies/You Came Along (1945, Jamboree 902); B. Goodman: East of the Sun (1952, Col. EPB1845) [EP]; Johnny Smith: Where or When (1952, Roost 558)

SELECTED FILMS AND VIDEOS

Stan Kenton and his Orchestra: Artistry in Rhythm (1945); Talk about a Lady [Duchess of Broadway] (1946); Let's Make Rhythm (1947); Charlie Barnet and his Band (1949); The Subject is Jazz [episodes 1–8, 10] (1958)

BIBLIOGRAPHY

ConnorBG; *FeatherE*
Obituary, *IM*, lxxii/11 (1974), 14
W. M. Lee: *Stan Kenton: Artistry in Rhythm* (Los Angeles, 1980/*R*1994) [incl. discography; *R* without discography]
A. Agostinelli: "Eddie Safranski: a Retrospective," *IAJE* (1992), 1 [incl. bibliography]

LEROY OSTRANSKY/BK

Sager, Jane (*b* Milwaukee, 5 June 1914). Trumpeter. She played violin and trumpet as a child, and at the age of 14 began playing the latter instrument professionally in nightclubs and ballrooms in Wisconsin. She continued earning a living as a jazz trumpeter while pursuing violin studies at Stephens College in Columbia, Missouri. After deciding to concentrate on trumpet she moved to Chicago, where she studied with Edward Lewellyn of the Chicago Symphony Orchestra and sat in with Roy Eldridge at the Three Deuces. In 1935 she joined One Armed Miller's traveling all-woman band. She played with Rita Rio's all-female band in the 1930s, then was an original member of the first all-female big band led by Ada Leonard, where she was a featured soloist on USO tours between 1940 and 1942. For the remainder of World War II she played in Johnny Richards's Orchestra, a CBS studio orchestra, the house orchestra at the Casino Gardens, and Charlie Barnet's big band. In the early 1950s she worked as the trumpet soloist with Ina Ray Hutton's all-female television band.

Oral history material at *DSI* (JOHP).

BIBLIOGRAPHY

S. Placksin: *American Women in Jazz, 1900 to the Present: their Words, Lives, and Music* (New York, 1982, London, 1985, as *Jazzwomen, 1900 to the Present: their Words, Lives, and Music*)
L. Dahl: *Stormy Weather: The Music and Lives of a Century of Jazzwomen* (London, Melbourne, Australia, and New York, 1984)
S. Tucker: *Swing Shift: "All-girl" Bands of the 1940s* (Durham, NC, 2000)

SHERRIE TUCKER

Sagmeister, Michael (*b* Frankfurt am Main, Germany, 27 July 1959). German guitarist. Self-taught, he took up guitar at the age of 13 and began playing rock and fusion. Critics, fellow musicians, and a wider public became aware of his talents in the early 1980s after he appeared as the opening act for a tour of the United Jazz and Rock Ensemble. Projects with German and international musicians such as Albert Mangelsdorff, Wolfgang Dauner, Charlie Mariano, Billy Cobham, Miroslav Vitous, and Pat Martino, membership of the Jazzensemble des Hessischen Rundfunks, a duo with Christoph Spendel (*So Near So Far*, 1987, L+R 40024), and his own trio and quartet led to Sagmeister's becoming one of the most important jazz guitarists in Germany. From the early 1980s he also taught; he was appointed professor at the Musikhochschule in Frankfurt am Main in 1999. His excellent technique may be heard to advantage on *Looking out my Window* (1987, Mood 28659) and *Soulful Questions* (1995, Bell 84065), on which he shines with virtuoso single-line phrases after the manner of Martino and blues-inflected sounds reminiscent of Pat Metheny.

BIBLIOGRAPHY

"Michael Sagmeister: ein neues deutsches Gitarren-Genie," *Fachblatt*, no.11 (1982), 49
<http://www.fantasyfactory.de/bands/sagmeister/sagmeister.html> (1999)
A. Schulz: "Michael Sagmeister: Acoustic Guitarist," *Akustik Gitarre*, vi/1 (1999), 16

WOLFRAM KNAUER

Sahara. Record company and label founded in 1971 by Errol Parker.

St. Clair, Cyrus (*b* Cambridge, MD, 1890; *d* New York, 1955). Tuba player. He began playing cornet in a local band, but later changed to tuba. Around 1925 he moved to New York, where he worked with Wilbur De Paris and Charlie Johnson (1926–30). He also recorded with Clarence Williams's orchestra (1926–30), during which period the band accompanied several singers, among them Bessie Smith (1929). In 1930 he played with Cozy Cole's Hot Cinders and in the mid-1930s he made further recordings with Williams (to 1937). Thereafter he ceased working for some time, but in 1947 he took part in Rudi Blesh's radio series "This is Jazz" (also playing double bass) and recorded with Tony Parenti's Ragtimers. St. Clair, who was capable of executing nimble bass lines on the tuba, is thought to have been the first jazz musician to play melodic solos on the instrument.

SELECTED RECORDINGS

As sideman: C. Williams: Gravier Street Blues/Candy Lips (1927, Col. 14193D); C. Johnson: Don't you leave me here (1927, Vic. 20653); C. Williams: Cushion Foot Stomp/Take your black bottom outside (1927, OK 8462); I'm goin' back to bottomland/You'll long for me (1927, Col. 14244D); Baby won't you please come home/Close Fit Blues (1927, OK 8510); Red River Blues/I need you (1928, Col. 14326D); C. Johnson: The Boy in the Boat/Walk that thing (1928, Vic. 21712); C. Williams: Close Fit Blues (1929, Grey Gull 1718); Baby, won't you please come home (1929, Grey Gull 1724); B. Smith: Nobody knows you when you're down and out (1929, Col. 14451D); C. Williams: Harlem Rhythm Dance (1933, Voc. 2602)

BIBLIOGRAPHY

ChiltonW; *McCarthyB*

B. Moon and K. L. Bright: "Last of the Tubas: Cy St. Clair – a Man all Wrapped up in his Work," *Record Changer*, vii/5 (1948), 11

T. Lord: *Clarence Williams* (Chigwell, England, 1976)

HOWARD RYE

St. Cyr, Johnny [John Alexander] (*b* New Orleans, 17 April 1890; *d* Los Angeles, 17 June 1966). Guitarist and banjoist. He taught himself to play on a homemade guitar, and from 1905 to 1908 led his own trio at lawn parties and fish fries. After playing in bands led by Manuel Gabriel and A. J. Piron (1908–9) he worked with the Superior, Olympia, and Tuxedo bands (1910–14) and Kid Ory's band (1914–17). For most of his work after this time St. Cyr played on a six-string "guitar banjo" that he had constructed himself from a banjo head and a guitar neck and fingerboard; in his later years, however, he returned to playing a regular guitar, and in the 1940s also used an electric guitar. He worked with Fate Marable's riverboat band from 1918 to 1920, and spent his last summer on the riverboats, in 1921, with Charlie Creath's band. He then concentrated on his daytime job as a plasterer. In mid-September 1923 King Oliver sent for him to travel to Chicago, strictly for the purpose of participating in two weeks of recordings with Oliver's Creole Jazz Band. St. Cyr then worked with Darnell Howard for two months at the Arcadia Ballroom before joining Doc Cook's Dreamland Orchestra, of which he was a member from 1924 to 1929. Far more significantly, he recorded with Louis Armstrong's Hot Five and Hot Seven (1925–7) and Jelly Roll Morton's Red Hot Peppers (1926), thus contributing as soloist and accompanist to the most important and historic small-group sessions in early jazz. The unusual sound St. Cyr obtained from his hybrid instrument may be heard on Armstrong's *Gut Bucket Blues*, where he plays a low single-string solo with a few accompanying chords.

While with Cook, St. Cyr began doubling in an after-hours small group led by one of Cook's sidemen, Jimmie Noone. He shared the guitar chair in this group with Bud Scott when Noone and Earl Hines went into the Apex Club in December 1927 (St. Cyr gave December 1926, but this is incorrect); however, he had lost the job to Scott by the time of Noone's Apex Club Orchestra recordings, made soon afterwards. The effects of the Depression caused Cook to reduce the size of his band in summer 1929 and St. Cyr was laid off, and after some obscure work in the region he returned to New Orleans the following year and again worked principally as a plasterer. Later he played with Paul Barbarin, Alphonse Picou, and others, and recorded as a sideman with Big Eye Louis Nelson, Raymond Burke, and Wooden Joe Nicholas (all 1949), Barbarin (1950–51, 1954), and George Lewis (i) (1954), and also as a leader (1954). He moved to Los Angeles in 1955, and he led his own band, the Young Men from New Orleans, at Disneyland from 1961 until his death. In his last years he completed all but the last of a projected five-part essay of reminiscences and autobiography, published as "Jazz as I Remember it" (*JJ*, xix (1966), no.9, p.6; no.10, p.22; no.11, p.6; xx (1967), no.1, p.14).

In ensembles St. Cyr played in the relaxed, four-beat chordal manner associated with New Orleans jazz, though he used a variety of styles in his solos, sometimes even playing high tremolos. His pioneering work on early jazz recordings, as well as his dance-hall and riverboat activities, helped set the style for America's twentieth-century dance music.

Oral history material in *LNT*.

See also Banjo; for illustrations *see* Armstrong, louis, fig.1, and Nightclubs and other venues, fig.3.

SELECTED RECORDINGS

As leader: *J. St. Cyr and his Hot Five* (1954, Slnd 212)

As sideman: L. Armstrong: Yes, I'm in the barrel/Gut Bucket Blues (1925, OK 8261); Oriental Strut/You're Next (1926, OK 8299); Chicago Hottentots: All Night Shags/Put Me in the Alley Blues (1926, Voc. 1008); D. Cook: Messin' Around (1926, OK 8390); J. R. Morton: Black Bottom Stomp/The Chant (1926, Vic. 20221); Smoke House Blues/Steamboat Stomp (1926, Vic. 20296); L. Armstrong: Jazz Lips/Skid-dat-de-dat (1926, OK 8436); Willie the Weeper/Alligator Crawl (1927, OK 8482); Wildman Blues/Gully Low Blues (1927, OK 8474); Original Creole Stompers: Some of these Days (1949, AM 535); B-flat Blues (1949, AM 532); L. Delisle: Clarinet Marmalade (1949, AM 537)

BIBLIOGRAPHY

ChiltonW

J. Lucas: "Banjo Playing and Johnny St. Cyr," *Jazz Report*, vi/2 (1959), [2]

Obituary, *SL*, xvii (1966), Sept–Oct, 107

T. Stagg and C. Crump: *New Orleans, the Revival: a Tape and Discography of Negro Traditional Jazz Recorded in New Orleans or by New Orleans Bands, 1937–1972* (n.p. [London], 1973)

B. Rust: "Johnny St. Cyr," *Sv*, no.51 (1974), 100

L. Wright and others: *Walter C. Allen & Brian A. L. Rust's "King" Oliver* (Chigwell, England, 1987)

G. Anderson: "Johnny Dodds in New Orleans," *American Music*, viii (1990), 405

B. Russell: *New Orleans Style*, comp. and ed. B. Martyn and M. Hazeldine (New Orleans, 1994), 63

BILL RUSSELL/BK

Saints and Sinners. Sextet formed in 1960 by Red Richards and Vic Dickenson. Initially a pickup band, it rapidly developed into a first-class mainstream dixieland group with polished routines and an extensive repertory unparalleled during the time for its quality and durability. The Saints and Sinners received regular bookings in Cleveland, Columbus (Ohio), Pittsburgh, and Toronto, where the band recorded its acclaimed album *Saints and Sinners* (1967, Cav-a-Bob 101). Before the group disbanded in 1970 it also made two successful tours of Europe (1968, 1969); during its first trip it recorded the album *Sugar: the Saints and Sinners in Europe* (MPS 15174). Among the group's sidemen were Herman

Autrey, Buster Bailey, Rudy Powell, Buddy Tate, Truck Parham, Barrett Deems, and the drummer George Foster. (S. Dance: "The Saints and Sinners Go Marching on," *DB*, xxxv/12 (1968), 24)

BOB WEIR

Sakata, Akira (*b* Hiroshima, Japan, 21 Feb 1945). Japanese alto saxophonist and leader. He played clarinet in a high school brass band and alto saxophone in a college band. After moving to Tokyo (1969) he performed and recorded in Japan and Europe as a member of Yosuke Yamashita's trio (1972–9). With his own group he toured Germany and France and appeared at the Newport Jazz Festival in New York (1979). From 1980 he led a trio, though he also organized various orchestras. In 1986 he recorded in a duo with Peter Kowald and in a wild improvised dialogue with Peter Brötzmann as a guest soloist with the group Last Exit (Brötzmann, Sonny Sharrock, Bill Laswell, and Ronald Shannon Jackson). Later he participated in projects with Laswell, Jackson, the Senegalese percussionist Ayib Dieng, the Gambian *kora* (plucked harp-lute) player Foday Musa Suso, and other musicians from different traditions. Sakata's performances display considerable virtuosity and an engaging sense of humor.

Sakata is also known for his writing and acting. He has created a language of his own which sounds very funny to Japanese listeners and which he uses extensively in his publications and in his appearances as an actor; his unusual comic combination of language and appearance has resulted in numerous appearances in Japan in films and on television.

SELECTED RECORDINGS

Duos with P. Kowald: on *Duos Japan* (1984, 1986, FMP 1280), Birth of Signs (1986)

As leader: *Counter Clockwise Trip* (1975, Frasco 7001); *Peking* (1977, Frasco 7023); *4 o' Clock* (1981, Better Days YF7026); *Dance* (1981, Enja 4002); *Da-da-da* (1985, VariBori BM32-2002); *Mookoe* (1988, NEC AMJ 61); *Silent Plankton* (1990, Tokuma TKCB30291)

As sideman with Last Exit: on *The Noise of Trouble: Live in Tokyo* (1986, Enemy 28JAL3080), Blind Willie

YOZO IWANAMI/KAZUNORI SUGIYAMA, BK

Salis, Antonello (*b* Villamar, nr Cagliari, Italy, 28 Feb 1950). Italian pianist and accordion player. He took up accordion at the age of seven, organ when he was 18, and then piano. From 1974 to 1978 he played in Sardinia with the trio Cadmo and then in a quintet with the alto saxophonist Sandro Satta and the trombonist Danilo Terenzi. From the late 1970s to the early 1980s he worked in groups led by Terenzi and the double bass player Marcello Melis. He first played as an unaccompanied soloist on piano in 1978; he also performed as a soloist on accordion, and he established a duo with Satta. In the 1980s he played in Mario Schiano's groups, in duos with Nana Vasconcelos (1985), the guitarist Gerard Pansanel (from 1986), and the pianist Riccardo Fassi (1986), and led a quintet with Terenzi (1982–8). In the 1990s he worked in a duo with the *'ūd* player Anouar Brahem (1990), with Evan Parker and Paolino Dalla Porta, and in Trio P.A.F., which he formed with Paolo Fresu and Furio Di Castri.

Salis is an energetic improviser, with a percussive touch and a nervous approach to the keyboard on both piano and accordion. Influenced by Cecil Taylor, he mixes clusters and single-note lines, often adding lyrical unison or octave whistling to high notes.

SELECTED RECORDINGS

(recorded for Splasc(h) unless otherwise indicated)

As unaccompanied soloist: *Orange Juice/Nice Food* (1980, HH 10); *Salis!* (1987, 136)

Duos: with M. Schiano: *Old Fashioned* (1978, Carosello 21043); with N. Vasconcelos: *Lester* (1985, SN 1157); with R. Fassi: *Joining* (1986, 113); with G. Pansanel: *Cinecittà* (1986, BLC 002); *Beatles Stories* (1990–91, 52e Rue Est 022); with S. Satta: *Live in Como* (1993, 432-2); with R. Fassi: *Live at the Vatican Radio* (1995, 634)

As leader: with P. Dalla Porta: *Canguri urbani* (1988, 174); with E. Parker and Mauro Orselli: *Improvvisazioni* (1995, Ada 02.11)

As sideman: Cadmo: *Boomerang* (1976, Vedette 8335); Trio P.A.F.: *Live in Capodistria* (1998, 625)

BIBLIOGRAPHY

D. Soutif: "Antonello Salis: du bal au free sarde," *Jm*, no.315 (1983), 41

STEFANO ZENNI

Salle Pleyel. Concert hall in Paris; *see* NIGHTCLUBS AND OTHER VENUES.

Salmi, Klaus (*b* Helsinki, 3 Dec 1908; *d* Kuopio, Finland, 10 July 1987). Finnish trombonist and bandleader. He played with Fred Pell's Novelty Buddians (1928–9), and in 1930 formed his own group, the Ramblers, which performed English and American arrangements of dance tunes; the Finnish-American alto saxophonist Wilfred "Tommy" Tuomikoski, who is regarded as having introduced jazz improvisation in Finland in 1926, played with the group in the early 1930s. The Ramblers made a large number of recordings, but only two, *Muistan sua, Elaine* (1931, Homocord 23141) and *You can't stop me from dreaming* (1938, Col. DY172), display the band's talent for jazz. After World War II Salmi worked principally as a record producer.

BIBLIOGRAPHY

O. Häme: *Rytmin voittokulku* [The triumph of rhythm] (Helsinki, 1949), 148

P. Jalkanen: *Ravintola: ja tanssiorkesterilaitoksen murros Helsingissä 1920-luvulla* [Changes in the dance orchestra in Helsinki in the 1920s] (diss., U. of Helsinki, 1975), 118; rev. as *Alaska, Bombay ja Billy Boy* (Helsinki, 1989), 94

PEKKA GRONOW

Salnave, Bertin (Depestre) (*b* Port-au-Prince, Haiti, 5 Sept 1892; *d* ? Port-au-Prince, 1970s). Haitian flutist and saxophonist. He taught himself flute as a child and in 1913 he moved to France, where he studied classical music in Paris and Montpellier. He first worked professionally with a tango band in Paris in 1918, then the following year joined Will Marion Cook's Southern Syncopated Orchestra in London. After taking up the saxophone (1920) he performed in Scandinavia with the pianist George Clapham (1921), in Belgium and Austria with Arthur Briggs, and in Spain with Crickett Smith (1925). Salnave formed his own band in the late 1920s and made recordings as a sideman and leader (1931, including *Brown Love*, Ultraphone SU5002). He played with Benny Peyton in France in 1937–8 and toured Switzerland and Romania with Leon Abbey until 1939, when he returned to Haiti and ceased full-time performing. (B. Demeusy: "The Bertin Depestre Salnave Musical Story," *Sv*, no.78 (1978), 207)

RAINER E. LOTZ

Salsa. A loosely defined term encompassing various musical styles of Cuba, Puerto Rico, and the Spanish Caribbean, and the developments of those styles as from the 1960s they incorporated elements of rhythm-and-blues, pop, and jazz and spread into a worldwide movement. While salsa emerged as a music of Puerto Ricans living in New York, its strongest musical root is the Cuban *son*. A comparable word had appeared as early as the 1930s in Cuban music (in the title of Septeto Nacional's recording *Echale salsita!*), and jazz had felt the influence of Cuban and Puerto Rican music from the 1940s (*see* AFRO-CUBAN JAZZ). However, the term salsa became common currency only in the 1960s, largely as a marketing handle for the Fania record label, which recorded many of the Afro-Caribbean musicians based in New York – notably Ray Barretto, Willie Colón, Celia Cruz, and Johnny Pacheco. The Latin soul and boogaloo dance crazes of the 1960 to 1970s, which absorbed components of rhythm-and-blues and pop, cemented the use of the expression; examples include Barretto's pop hit *El watusi*, from the album *Charanga moderna* (1962), and the title track of Cal Tjader's album *Soul Sauce* (1964, Verve 68614). By the mid-1970s it was used routinely in association with jazz contexts, though some of the musicians active in Afro-Cuban jazz objected to the term and felt that the commercialization of salsa had betrayed its authentic folk sources. Indeed, there is no clear point where Cuban music and salsa divide: cross-influence has been continuous from the 1930s. In this sense the key figures who developed and evolved Cuban musical styles throughout the twentieth century have a historical significance in the roots of salsa.

The rhythmic concept known as *clave* underpins all styles played in salsa. Sometimes the rhythm is overtly stated on the claves (as heard, for example, on *T.P.'s especial*, from Tito Puente's album *On Broadway* (1982, Conc. 207). More often it is not played but rather implied in the arrangement of every instrumental part in the ensemble; the rhythm of the tune and the accompanying figures, breaks, and solo improvisations are all phrased in order to blend with this implied rhythmic foundation. The *clave* rhythm takes a number of different forms depending on the context, all ultimately descended from various African styles. The two most common versions used in salsa are *son clave* and *rumba clave*. Both versions consist of a two-bar pattern with two accentuations in one bar and three in the other, the *rumba clave* being slightly more syncopated than the *son clave*; the rhythm may begin either with the bar with two accentuations (in which case it is referred to as "2–3" *clave*) or with the bar with three ("3–2" *clave*) (see ex.1).

Ex.1 The rhythmic patterns *son clave* and *rumba clave*

An arrangement will be based on one of these *clave* rhythms. With rare exceptions, once the *clave* pattern is set in motion it continues in the same sequence throughout the piece. However, an arranger can create the effect of shifting the direction by making a section of the form last for an odd number of bars; in this way the two-bar *clave* sequence remains undisturbed, but the next part of the piece begins with the opposite phrasing, 2–3 becoming 3–2, or vice versa. *Son clave* forms the basis of most popular dance styles (e.g., *mambo*, *son montuno*, *guaracha*), while *rumba clave* usually underpins more folkloric and religious forms, such as *rumba*, *conga de comparsa*, and *mozambique*. The melody and brass breaks in Barretto's *Tu propio dolor*, from his album *Giant Force* (1980, Fania 579), exemplify the art of arranging in *clave*, and the listener clapping along in 2–3 or 3–2 *clave* should soon feel on which direction the track is based: one version will fit almost exactly, but the other will sound out of phase.

Salsa bands make use of a great variety of instruments, evolved from the various line-ups which traditionally performed the music's Afro-Caribbean antecedents. Thus a contemporary group might include violins and flutes, which are characteristic of the *charanga* orchestra; guitar and *tres* (a guitar with three courses of strings) from the typical *son sexteto*; brass and reeds from developments in Afro-Cuban jazz of the 1940s and 1950s; and a rhythm section, typically of piano, double bass, and a veritable arsenal of percussion, with conga, bongos, and timbales usually supplemented by cowbells, maracas, *güiro*, claves, and woodblock (some of these played by singers within the group). Bands which draw more on folkloric traditions might employ *sekere*, *cajón* (a Cuban drum made from a wooden box), and *batá* drum, and the incorporation of styles from the Dominican Republic, Puerto Rico, and Colombia may call for the addition of the *tambora* (a double-headed drum) and *pandereta* (a frame drum fitted with jingles). Many of these instruments may be heard on the album *Concepts in Unity* (1975, Charly 153), by the Grupo Folklorico y Experimental Nuevayorquino.

A corresponding variety of formal structure is available to the arranger. There is evidence of the African roots of the music in the frequent use of call and response, both in the alternation of verses and choruses and in the common use of dialogues where a refrain (stated either by a chorus of vocalists or instrumentally) is interspersed with improvised statements from the lead singer (as on Cruz's *Cuando despiertes*, from the album *Fania All Stars with Celia Cruz*, SONY CDZ82352). This aspect of salsa form is referred to as the *montuno* or *coro*. Cruz's track illustrates another common element, also called a *montuno* (or, alternatively, a *guajeo*), whereby a repeated two- or four-bar phrase played by the piano functions as an accompanimental ostinato. This device has frequently been borrowed by jazz musicians, among them Chick Corea – on *Samba Song*, from his album *Friends* (1978, Pol. 6160) – and Luis Bonilla's Latin Jazz All Stars – on the title track of their album *Pasos gigantes* (1991, Can. 79507); for a portion of the tune on the latter, a modified version of John Coltrane's *Giant Steps*, a *montuno* appears within an ostinato that replaces the complex original chord progression.

Albums such as Irakere's *Irakere* (1978, Col. JC35655), *Machete* (1989–94, Xenophile 4029), by the percussionist John Santos, and *Moliendo Café (to Wisdom the Prize)* (1991, Sunnyside 1061), by Jerry Gonzalez and the Fort Apache Band, exemplify an approach which mixes traditional Cuban dance and folkloric styles with jazz to create a hybrid version of salsa. Michel Camilo, Paquito D'Rivera, and Monty Alexander are among the many others who have drawn on salsa styles in their recordings. Salsa bands may be seen playing in the video *Beats of the Heart: Salsa* (*c* mid-1980s).

BIBLIOGRAPHY

J. S. Roberts: *The Latin Tinge: the Impact of Latin American Music on the United States* (New York, and Oxford, England, 1979)

B. Sulsbrück: *Latinamerikansk percussion: rytmer og rytmeinstrumenter fra Cuba og Brasilien* (Copenhagen, 1980, 2/1985; Eng. trans., 1986, as *Latin-American Percussion: Rhythms and Rhythm Instruments from Cuba and Brazil*)

C. Gérard and M. Sheller: *Salsa! The Rhythm of Latin Music* (Crown Point, IN, 1989)

L. Goines and R. Ameen: *Funkifying the Clavé: Afro-Cuban Grooves for Bass and Drums* (New York, 1990)
F. Malabe and B. Weiner: *Afro-Cuban Rhythms for Drumset* (New York, 1990) [incl. discography, bibliography]
V. W. Boggs: *Salsiology: Afro-Cuban Music and the Evolution of Salsa in New York City* (New York, Westport, CT, and London, 1992)
R. Mauleón: *Salsa Guidebook for Piano and Ensemble* (Petaluma, CA, 1993)
C. Washburne: "Play it *Con Filin*! The Swing and Expression of Salsa," *Revista Latin de Música American/Latino Music Americana Review*, xix/2 (1998), 160
J. S. Roberts: *Latin Jazz: the First of the Fusions, 1880s to Today* (New York, 1999)
S. Steward: *Salsa: Musical Heartbeat of Latin America* (London, 1999)
B. Sulsbrück: *Congas: Tumbadoras: your Basic Conga Repertoire from Cuban Music and Salsa to Rock, Jazz & Samba* (Herning, Denmark, 1999)

RICK FINLAY

Saluzzi, Dino [Timoteo] (*b* Campo Santo, Argentina, 20 May 1935). Argentine bandoneon player. He grew up in a musical family, took up bandoneon when he was seven, and was playing professionally by the age of 14. After moving in 1952 to Buenos Aires he worked in tango orchestras. He studied composition with Jacobo Ficher, was a member again of tango orchestras and of folk groups, and from 1970 worked with such musicians as Gato Barbieri in a style of jazz that incorporated elements of Argentine folk music. In 1979 he formed a quartet, with which he toured Europe in 1983; the same year he performed with George Gruntz at the Jazzfest Berlin and made recordings as an unaccompanied soloist and with Gruntz. From 1982 through the 1990s he recorded a succession of atmospheric jazz and tango albums for ECM (among them two as an unaccompanied soloist, in 1982 and 1988); in Argentina in 1984 he recorded as a leader two albums for RCA bearing the title *Vivencias* (TLP 50162, 50361); and the following year he recorded in Europe with Palle Mikkelborg, Charlie Haden, and Pierre Favre. In 1986 he worked in a duo with Haden in Los Angeles and toured Europe with Mikkelborg, Enrico Rava, and Eddie Gomez. Saluzzi continued to work with Gruntz in the 1990s, when he also recorded as a member of Al Di Meola's World Sinfonia (1990–91) and with Maria João (*c*1995), and toured Asia and Australia (1995) as the leader of the Dino Saluzzi Family, which included Michel Benita.

BIBLIOGRAPHY

E. Janke: "Symbiose von Jazz und Tango: Dino Saluzzi," *JP*, xxxii/1 (1983), 25
M. Bourne: "Dino Saluzzi," *DB*, liii/7 (1986), 14
T. Schnabel: "Saluzzi ou la mémoire tango," *Jm*, no.354 (1986), 37
K. Brodacki: "Dino Saluzzi: Once upon a Time: Far away in the South," *JF* [intl edn], no.113 (1988), 26
L. Birnbaum: "Dino Saluzzi," *DB*, lix/11 (1992), 14
<http://www.salta.net/cultura/saluzzi.htm> (1999)

LAUREANO FERNÁNDEZ, OMAR GARCÍA BRUNELLI/BK

Salvador, Sal (*b* Monson, MA, 21 Nov 1925; *d* Stamford, CT, 22 Sept 1999). Guitarist. He grew up in Stafford Springs, Connecticut, and took violin lessons as a child. At the age of 15 he became interested in jazz when he heard recordings by Charlie Christian, and he changed to guitar after his family moved to Springfield, Massachusetts, in 1943. From 1945 he played in and around Springfield with Phil Woods, Joe Morello, Chuck Andrus, and other young musicians. Following a move in 1949 to New York, where he rehearsed with his roommates Tal Farlow, Jimmy Raney, and Woods, he secured a job in Boston as the leader of a trio including Andrus; he also toured briefly and recorded (1951) with Terry Gibbs. In summer 1952 he joined Stan Kenton's orchestra, with which he remained through 1953. From December of that year to 1960 he worked as a freelance, appeared in a two-guitar group led by Mundell Lowe (1954), and led bop groups that included Eddie Costa and Woods. During this period he twice rejoined Kenton (1955, 1970), spent a lengthy period as an accompanist to popular singers, recorded with Lennie Hambro (1956) and Don Bagley (1957), and performed with Sonny Stitt in the film *Jazz on a Summer's Day* (1958). From 1958 he also led the big band Colors in Sound, which in the early 1960s sometimes deputized for Count Basie's orchestra at Birdland. Among its members were Charlie Mariano, Joe Farrell, Nick Brignola, and Eddie Gomez, and Al Cohn and Bill Holman contributed arrangements; Brignola recalled it as one of the first rehearsal big bands in New York, anticipating that of Thad Jones and Mel Lewis. When it eventually ran into the financial difficulties that plague most big bands, Salvador disbanded in 1965 and re-formed his small group. In the 1970s he played in a guitar duo with Allen Hanlon and took a teaching position at the University of Bridgeport, Connecticut, where he became head of the guitar department; he also taught at Wesconn State University. He resumed recording as a leader in 1978 and reassembled his big band in the 1980s. In 1988 he formed a fusion group, Crystal Image. Salvador wrote more than a dozen method books, including *Sal Salvador's Complete Chord Method for Guitar* (New York, n.d. [?1956]) and *Sal Salvador's Single String Studies for Guitar* (New York, n.d. [?1961]).

Oral history material in *PEsU* (ACMJC).

SELECTED RECORDINGS

As leader: *Sal Savador Quintet* (1953, BN 5035); *Frivolous Sal* (1956, Beth. 59); *Shades of Sal Salvador* (1956, Beth. 39); *Colors in Sound* (1958, Decca 9210); *Music to Stop Smoking By* (*c*1964, Roul. 25262); *Starfingers* (1978, BH 7002); *Juicy Lucy* (1978, BH 7009); *Sal Salvador Plays Gerry Mulligan* (1984, Stash 251); of Crystal Image: *Teo Macero Presents Sal Salvador & Crystal Image* (n.d. [*c*1989], Stash 17), *Lorinda's Kitchen* (1995, Jazzmania 6017)

As sideman with S. Kenton: *New Concepts of Artistry in Rhythm* (1952, Cap. H383), incl. Invention for Guitar and Trumpet

BIBLIOGRAPHY

FeatherE
R. Alberto: "Sal Salvador: a Jazz Great for Thirty Years," *GP*, viii/7 (1974), 14
R. D. Kinkle: *The Complete Encyclopedia of Popular Music and Jazz, 1900–1950* (New Rochelle, NY, and Westport, CT, 1974)
W. F. Lee: *Stan Kenton: Artistry in Rhythm* (Los Angeles, 1980/*R*1994) [incl. discography; *R* without discography]
J. Obrecht: "Pro's Reply: Sal Salvador: Straight Talk about Guitar Lessons," *GP*, xxii/10 (1988), 16
B. Rusch: "The Questionnaire," *Cadence*, xvi/7 (1990), 75
B. Wentz: "Profile: Sal Salvador," *DB*, lvii/2 (1990), 46
M. Richards: "Nick Brignola," *JJI*, xliv/4 (1991), 6
"Interview with Sal Salvador," *The Note*, viii/3 (1996), 2
Obituary, B. Ratliff, *New York Times* (20 Oct 1999)

WILLIAM F. LEE III/BK

Samba. A dance of Brazilian and African origin. The word is also used by extension for the accompanying music, and for any music in that style, which is in duple meter, lively in tempo, and characterized by many interlocking, syncopated lines in the melody and accompaniment (ex.1). The samba first became known in the USA in the 1930s and 1940s when Vincent Youmans's *Carioca* (1933), Ary Barroso's *Brazil* (1939), and Zequinha Abreu's *Tico tico* (1943) became hits; the dance itself was introduced to the USA in 1939 at the New York World's Fair, and was popularized by the films of the singer and dancer Carmen Miranda during the next two decades. However, American jazz musicians did not adopt the idiom on a large scale until the release, in the 1950s, of such recordings as Charlie Parker's *Tico tico* (1951, Mer./Clef

Ex.1 From *Cetulio Marinho: Caboclo do matto* (1940s, Col. 36504); transcr. T. Owens

11091), Stan Kenton's *Baia* (1953, Cap. T2511), Laurindo Almeida's album *The Laurindo Almeida Quartet, Featuring Bud Shank* (1954, PJ 7, 13), Dizzy Gillespie's *Ungawa*, from his album *The Ebullient Mr. Gillespie* (1959, Verve 8328), Oscar Peterson's *Carioca*, from his LP *Warren and Youmans* (1959, Verve 62059), and Horace Silver's *Swingin' the Samba*, on *Finger Poppin' with the Horace Silver Quintet* (1959, BN 4008). In some cases a percussionist playing Brazilian instruments augmented the conventional jazz rhythm section; otherwise the guitarist, drummer, and double bass player provided the rhythmic impetus (ex.2).

Ex.2 From *Carioca Hills*, on L.A. Four: *The L.A. Four Scores!* (1975, Conc. 8); transcr. T. Owens

In the late 1950s Brazilian musicians began to play in a style known as BOSSA NOVA, which was slower and more sedate than the music customarily used to accompany the samba, employing longer themes and more elaborate, jazz-influenced harmonies. In the USA the brief craze for this style, in part instigated by the album *Jazz Samba* (1962, Verve 68432) by Stan Getz and Charlie Byrd, prompted many bop musicians to incorporate Brazilian rhythms and melodies into their music; Getz, Byrd, Peterson, Cannonball Adderley, and others recorded albums devoted entirely or mostly to sambas and bossa novas. It also encouraged many Brazilians to travel to the USA to perform and record. Although sambas and bossa novas became less faddish in the late 1960s, jazz groups regularly include them in their performances and recordings, and such pieces as Luis Bonfa's *The Gentle Rain*, *Manha de carnaval*, and *Samba de orfeu*, Antonio Carlos Jobim's *Chega de saudade*, *Samba de uma nota so*, *Triste*, and *Wave*, Michel Legrand's *Watch What Happens*, Clare Fischer's *Pensativa*, Benny Carter's *South Side Samba*, and Dizzy Gillespie's *Tanga* have become jazz standards. In addition, jazz musicians sometimes transform non-Latin pieces (such as Bronislav Kaper's ballad *Invitation* or John Coltrane's lively *Giant Steps*) into sambas and bossa novas. (*See also* LATIN JAZZ.)

BIBLIOGRAPHY

G. Duran: *Recordings of Latin American Songs and Dances: an Annotated Selected List of Popular and Folk Music* (Washington, 1942, rev. and enlarged ed. G. Chase 2/1950), 29 [incl. discography]

O. Alvarenga: *Música popular brasileña* (Buenos Aires, 1947)

C. Perry: "The Samba," *IM*, li/12 (1959), 24

J. Tynan: "The Real Story of the Bossa Nova," *DB*, xxix/28 (1962), 21

J. S. Roberts: *Black Music of Two Worlds* (New York, Washington, DC, and London, 1972/*R*[?1990])

G. Behague: "Bossa and Bossas: Recent Changes in Brazilian Urban Popular Music," *Ethnomusicology*, xvii (1973), 209

J. S. Roberts: *The Latin Tinge: the Impact of Latin American Music on the United States* (New York, and Oxford, England, 1979)

N. Goldberg: "South of the Border: the Samba," *MD*, vii/12 (1983), 106

C. McGowan and R. Pessanha: *The Brazilian Sound: Samba, Bossa Nova and the Popular Music of Brazil* (New York, 1991, 3/1998)

THOMAS OWENS

Sambeat, Perico [Pedro] (*b* Valencia, Spain, 23 July 1962). Spanish tenor saxophonist. He learned piano from the age of six but taught himself to play tenor saxophone, which he took up in 1978. In 1982 he moved to Barcelona, and while serving on the faculty of the Taller de Músics (a school dedicated to jazz and popular music) studied flute at the Barcelona conservatory; he continued his studies at the New School in 1991. In New York he played with Lee Konitz, Jimmy Cobb, Joe Chambers, and others. He has appeared throughout Spain and also toured extensively, having performed in England, Portugal, Angola, Argentina, Mexico, and France. He recorded as a leader with such sidemen as Wallace Roney, Tete Montoliu, David Kikoski, the singer Enrique Morente, and Brad Mehldau, and has also recorded as a sideman with Montoliu, Benny Golson, Paquito D'Rivera, and Curtis Fuller.

SELECTED RECORDINGS

As leader: *Perico Sambeat* (1989, EGT 531); *Punto de Partida* (1991, EGT 539); *Uptown Dance* (1992, EGT 585); *Dual Force* (1993, Ronnie Scott's Jazz House 031); *Ademuz* (1995, EGT 660)

BIBLIOGRAPHY

"Seven Spanish Jazz Musicians the World Should Know About," *Jazz Changes*, vi/2 (1999), 14

ALFREDO PAPO

Sample, Joe [Joseph Leslie] (*b* Houston, 1 Feb 1939). Pianist. His older brother played in swing and rhythm-and-blues bands, including those of Earl Bostic and Milt Larkin. Sample took up piano at around the age of seven. In his early teens he was a founding member of the group that eventually became known as the CRUSADERS, and his career remained associated with that of the band for more than 30 years. He studied at Texas Southern University and in 1958 moved to Los Angeles. Although at first he played only piano, from the 1960s he occasionally recorded on organ, then experimented with the Wurlitzer electric piano (*c*1962–1963) and often played the Fender–Rhodes electric piano, on which he developed a hard, percussive, bluesy approach. From the late 1960s Sample also worked independently of the Crusaders: he accompanied pop artists such as Diana Ross and the Jackson Five, played in the bop quintet led by Harold Land and Bobby Hutcherson (1967–8, *c*1971), and was a member of Tom Scott's quartet which, as the L.A. Express, toured and recorded with Joni Mitchell (1973–4). The last-named association led to his taking part in studio sessions with rock and folk artists, although he continued to play jazz, funk, and soul; perhaps the finest example of his use of electronic keyboards in a jazz-funk setting may be heard in his clavinet playing on *Always There*, from Ronnie Laws's album *Pressure Sensitive* (1975).

In 1987 Sample left the Crusaders. Later he became prominent in the realm of contemporary jazz. He suffered a heart attack while performing in Japan in May 1994, but he successfully underwent surgery early the following year and resumed his career in 1996. Thereafter he formed a funk octet, the Soul Committee, in which Oscar Brashear and Steve Gadd were sidemen, and toured and recorded as the leader of small groups including Jay Anderson. He also toured Europe in the group Legends, consisting of David Sanborn, Eric Gale, Marcus Miller, and Gadd, and joined Scott's re-formed L.A. Express. Apart from his filmed appearances with the Crusaders, he may be seen in the video *Al Jarreau: Tenderness* (1994).

SELECTED RECORDINGS

As leader: *Fancy Dance* (1969, Sonet 611); with R. Brown and S. Manne: *The Three* (1975, EW 10001); *Rainbow Seeker* (*c*1977, ABC 1050); *The Hunter* (*c*1982, MCA 5397)

As sideman: B. Hutcherson: *San Francisco* (*c*1971, BN 84362); T. Scott: *Tom Scott and the L.A. Express* (1973, Ode 77021); R. Laws: *Pressure Sensitive* (1975, BN LA452), incl. Always There

For further recordings and videos *see* CRUSADERS.

BIBLIOGRAPHY

E. Kriss: "Backstage with Joe Sample," *CK*, i/1 (1975), 41

B. Doerschuk: "Joe Sample: Branching out after 25 Years with the Crusaders," *CK*, v/8 (1979), 44

L. Feather: "Piano Giants of Jazz: Joe Sample," *CK*, v/5 (1979), 61

A. J. Liska: "The Lone Crusaders," *DB*, l/11 (1983), 20

G. Armbruster: "Joe Sample: Painter in Sound and Time," *Keyboard*, x/4 (1984), 44

R. L. Doerschuk: "25 Years Blending Blues, Bop, & Funk, Joe Sample Still Puts it Where He Wants it," *Keyboard*, xv/8 (1989), 60

L. Birnbaum: "Joe Sample & Bob James: Roughing up Smooth Edges," *DB*, lxiii/9 (1996), 28

B. Blumenthal: "Joe Sample's Roots Crusade," *Boston Globe* (19 April 1996)

J. Eig: "Hard Hands, Sweet Soul," *Jazziz*, xiii/7 (1996), 50

P. Myers: "Joe Sample: Soul Survivor," *JT*, xxvi/3 (1996), 34

BK

Sampler. A digital electronic device used to manipulate fragments ("samples") of recorded sound; for examples of its use in jazz contexts, *see* COMPUTERS and SYNTHESIZER.

Sampson, Deryck (*b c*1926). Pianist. He was aged 17 in 1943, when his father signed his recording contract with Joe Davis's Beacon label. Four recording sessions were held, the first in May 1943 and the last in February 1944; *Boogie In "C"* (1943, Beacon 2) and *Basin Street Boogie* (1944, Beacon 7016) sufficiently demonstrate his caliber. He also took part in several soundies as the leader of a small band accompanying the singer and dancer Mabel Lee, including *Half-past Jump Time* and *Cats Can't Dance* (both 1945). Recordings with Sampson accompanying Jackie Paris on MGM were released in 1947, but may well have been made earlier. Public appearances in New York clubs by this fine blues and boogie pianist were advertised into early 1946; however, nothing is known of his later career.

BIBLIOGRAPHY

B. Bastin: Liner notes, *Deryck Sampson: Boogie Express, 1943–1944* (Harlequin 2006, 1984)

——: *Never Sell a Copyright: Joe Davis and his Role in the New York Music Scene, 1916–1978* (Chigwell, England, 1990)

HOWARD RYE

Sampson, Edgar (Melvin) [The Lamb] (*b* New York, 31 Aug 1907; *d* Englewood, NJ, 16 Jan 1973). Saxophonist, violinist, composer, and arranger. He began playing violin as a child and took up alto saxophone as a teenager. His first engagement was with the pianist Joe Coleman (1924), after which he worked with Duke Ellington (briefly, spring 1926), Bingie Madison and the saxophonist Billy Fowler (both also in 1926), the pianist Arthur Gibbs (1927–8), Charlie Johnson (1928–30), and the bass saxophonist Alex Jackson (1930). He then played with Fletcher Henderson (June 1931 – *c* September 1932; for illustration *see* HENDERSON, FLETCHER), and recorded as solo violinist on *The House of David Blues* (1931). Sampson began composing tunes and writing arrangements while working with Rex Stewart (1933): *Stomping at the Savoy* and *Don't be that way*, which were written for Stewart's band, are among the best-known standards of the swing era; they were recorded while Sampson was a member of Chick Webb's orchestra (late 1933 – July 1936) but became better known in contemporary versions by Benny Goodman's orchestra. Sampson then became a freelance arranger, working for Webb, Goodman, Artie Shaw, Red Norvo, and Teddy Wilson. He resumed playing as music director for Ella Fitzgerald (July–November 1939) and as alto and baritone saxophonist for Al Sears (1943), and also led his own band (1949–51). During the early 1950s he performed with and wrote arrangements for the Latin bands of Marcellino Guerra, Tito Puente, and Tito Rodriguez, and in the late 1950s and early 1960s he led his own small groups; he also played in the first Henderson reunion band at the Great South Bay Jazz Festival in July 1957.

SELECTED RECORDINGS

As leader: *Swing Softly Sweet Sampson* (1956, Coral 57049)

As sideman with F. Henderson: The House of David Blues (1931, Ban. 32733)

RECORDED COMPOSITIONS

(selective list; all recorded by C. Webb with Sampson as sideman)

If dreams come true (1934, Col. CB754); Let's get together (1934, Col. CB741); Stomping at the Savoy (1934, Col. 2926D); Blue Minor (1934, OK 41572); Don't be that way (1934, Decca 483); Blue Lou (1934, Decca 1065); Facts and Figures (1935, Decca 830)

BIBLIOGRAPHY

AllenH; *ChiltonW*

[A. Barnett]: "Edgar Sampson," *Fable Bulletin: Violin Improvisation Studies*, no.11 (1999), 49 [discography]

FRANK DRIGGS

Samson, Jacky (*b* Paris, 11 April 1943). French double bass player. He first played trombone and sang with the soprano saxophonist Marc Laferrière, then studied double bass at the conservatory in Versailles. He worked with Michel Hausser (1964–5), Guy Lafitte (1965, 1968), Jean-Claude Naude's big band (1965–7), Milt Buckner, T-Bone Walker, and a sextet co-led by Maynard Ferguson and Slide Hampton (all 1968), François Guin's Swingers (1971–2), François Biensan, and the blues musician Jimmy Dawkins (1972). However, he is best known as a member of the historic Georges Arvanitas trio (1965–93), which accompanied, among others, Albert Nicholas, then Hank Mobley, Frank Foster (1968), Richard Boone (1970), Ted Curson (1971, 1978), Dexter Gordon with the trumpeter Sonny Grey (1973), Frank Wright (1978), and the violinist Françis Darizcuren (1990). Samson taught at Orly, and with Hal Singer created the soundtrack to the film *Salut l'artiste* (1974). In 1984 he led his own trio with Hervé Sellin and the guitarist André Condouant. His versatility is evident on the album *Chasin' the Blues* by Tiny Grimes (1968, BB 33017) and on *Hommage à Charles Saudrais*, recorded under his own name (1994, Paradox OO1). (F. W. Sportis: "Jacky Samson," *Jh*, no.523 (1995), 12)

MICHEL LAPLACE

Samuels, Dave [David Alan] (*b* Waukegan, IL, 9 Oct 1948). Vibraphonist and marimba player. He played drums and piano from the age of six, and during his college years he combined his interests in percussion and keyboards by taking up vibraphone and marimba. Having begun his undergraduate education in Chicago, he completed a degree in psychology at Boston University (BA 1971); while in Boston he studied with Gary Burton and David Friedman and later taught percussion and jazz improvisation at the Berklee College of Music (from autumn 1972). After moving to New York (1974) he toured internationally and recorded with Gerry Mulligan (1974–7) and performed and recorded with Carla Bley (1975) and Gerry Niewood (1975–7). In 1975 he formed a duo with Friedman in which both men played vibraphone and marimba; they toured Europe, taught in workshops and at the Manhattan School of Music, and made recordings both under Friedman's name with Harvie Swartz and Hubert Laws (1975) and as Double Image with Michael Di Pasqua and Swartz (1977–80, notably *Double Image*, 1977, Enja 2096). While continuing to work with Double Image (recording *c*1985), Samuels recorded with Spyro Gyra (from *c*1979) and played in the cooperative group Gallery (1980–82). In 1983 he began touring with Spyro Gyra, and by 1986 he had become a full-time member of the group, with which he continued to tour until 1994 and to record until 1996. He may be heard playing a marimba solo on *Morning Dance*, from the band's album of the same name (1979, Infinity 9004). During the same period he recorded with Paul McCandless (1979), Art Lande (1981), Anthony Davis (1983), and Bobby McFerrin (1984), and as an unaccompanied soloist (1981), and played with a number of European musicians (mid-1980s), among them Arild Andersen, Jukka-Pekka Uotila, John Taylor, Jon Christensen, Alex Riel, and John Surman. In the 1990s he had further reunions with Friedman, and in 1993 the two men recorded as Double Image; that same year Samuels formed the CARIBBEAN JAZZ PROJECT. He recorded twice as a sole leader in the early 1990s, as a sideman with Mulligan in 1995, and with Michael Sagmeister in 1998.

Samuels was a columnist for *Modern Drummer* and *Modern Percussionist*, and he wrote a method book, *A Musical Approach to Four Mallet Technique for Vibraphone*, i–ii (Bryn Mawr, PA, *c*1983, and New York, *c*1987), and made an instructional video, *Dave Samuels Mallet Keyboard Musicianship Steps to Excellence*, i–ii (*c*1989). Later he appeared in the video *Time Groove: the Ultimate All-star Percussion Ensemble* (*c*1991). During his career he has supplied music for television and film, and he taught at Berklee again from 1994.

BIBLIOGRAPHY

H. Nolan: "Dave Friedman and Dave Samuels: Two Man Percussion Crusade," *DB*, xliii/20 (1976), 12
J. Peterscak: "Musically Speaking," *Percussive Notes*, xiv/3 (1976), 18
S. K. Fish: "Introducing Dave Samuels," *MD*, v/2 (1981), 74
R. Mattingly: "Dave Samuels," *Modern Percussionist*, iii/1 (1986–7), 8
A. Pryor: "The Sound of Dave Samuels," *JT* (1988), June, 9
R. Mattingly: "Update: Dave Samuels," *MD*, xv/11 (1991), 8
J. Woodard: "Crossing Borders Naturally," *JT*, xxv/9 (1996), 50
<http://www.ejn.it/mus/samuels.htm> (2000)
<http://www.uoregon.edu/~splat/Dave_Samuels.html> (2000) [incl. discography]

BK

Sanborn, David (William) [Dave] (*b* Tampa, FL, 30 July 1945). Alto saxophonist. He played alto saxophone briefly at about the age of eight and again to strengthen his lungs while he was recovering from polio. Strongly influenced by Hank Crawford, he began playing rhythm-and-blues professionally at the age of 14, working in St. Louis with the singer and electric guitarist Albert King. After studying music at Northwestern University (1963–4) and the University of Iowa (1965–7) he toured and recorded with Paul Butterfield's blues band (1967–71), the soul singer Stevie Wonder (1971–3), and the rock singer David Bowie (1974); he also recorded with other soul, pop, and rock musicians. He was a soloist with Gil Evans's orchestra (at intervals from 1973 to the mid-1980s) and the Brecker Brothers (1975). From 1976 he toured and recorded as a leader, most notably during the 1980s in collaborations with Marcus Miller (who served both as his electric bass guitarist and as his producer). During this decade Sanborn's group was a forerunner in the style that came to be known as smooth jazz, but his music has much more substance than that of most groups operating in this domain. Sanborn acted as host for the television show "Sunday Night" from autumn 1988 to 1990 and of a weekly radio program, "The Jazz Show," for six years into the early 1990s. Later he toured Europe in the group Legends, consisting of Joe Sample, Eric Gale, Miller, and Steve Gadd.

Sanborn is a cautious soloist, whose immaculate playing shows complete control of the traditional formulas of gospel preaching and blues. However much the melodic content of his work may owe to the central African-American musical tradition, his remarkable tone – full-bodied, intense, and often heart wrenching – is utterly original and unprecedented, and from the 1990s has been widely copied; this raw, urgent timbre is somehow so evocative of American urban life that Sanborn has become, unusually, a celebrity as an instrumentalist in the realm of film and television, turning up time and again as a soloist on soundtracks and commercials. He has also recorded on the soprano and sopranino instruments – the latter atypically in a free-jazz context, as a sideman with Tim Berne in 1992. Collections of his recorded solos have been transcribed as *David Sanborn: Artist Transcriptions* (Milwaukee, 1989) and *The Best of David Sanborn* (transcr. T. Nystrom and R. Kerber, Milwaukee, 1994).

SELECTED RECORDINGS

(recorded for Warner Bros. unless otherwise indicated)

As leader: *Heart to Heart* (*c*1978, 3189); *Hideaway* (*c*1979, 3379); *Voyeur* (*c*1980, 3546); *As We Speak* (*c*1981, 23650); *Backstreet* (*c*1982, 23906); *Straight to the Heart* (*c*1983, 25150); with Bob James: *Double Vision* (*c*1986, 25393); *Close-up* (*c*1987, Reprise 25715-2); *Another Hand* (*c*1990, Elek. Mus. 61088-2)

As sideman: Joe Beck: *Beck* (1975, Kudu 21); H. Swartz: on *Urban Earth* (1985, Gram. 8503), Falling, Sweet Walk, Until Tomorrow; T. Berne: *Diminutive Mysteries (Mostly Hemphill)* (1992, JMT 514003-2), incl. The Unknown; M. Stern: on *Give and Take* (*c*1996, Atl. 83036-2), That's what you think

SELECTED FILMS AND VIDEOS

David Sanborn: Love and Happiness (*c*1986); Benny Carter: Symphony in Riffs (1989); Al Jarreau: Tenderness (1994)

BIBLIOGRAPHY

C. Berg: "Dave Sanborn's Alto Spectrum," *DB*, xliii/2 (1976), 11
L. Tomkins: "Dave Sanborn," *CI*, xvi/9 (1978), 23
S. Sutherland: "Crossing the R & B Bridge to Melodic Jazz," *Billboard*, xciii (2 May 1981), 35
R. Tolleson: "David Sanborn Interview: the Voice of Emotion," *DB*, l/3 (1983), 15 [incl. discography]
"David Sanborn," *SJ*, xxxviii/2 (1984), 217 [discography]
M. Gilbert: "Straight to the Heart," *JJI*, xxxviii/4 (1985), 8
G. Kalbacher: "R & B Altology: David Sanborn," *DB*, liii/8 (1986), 16 [incl. discography]
G. J. Balfany: *A Motivic Study of Twenty Selected Improvised Solos of David Sanborn and Stanley Turrentine* (diss., U. of Wisconsin, 1988)

B. Milkowski: "David Sanborn: David Sanborn's Changes of Heart," *DB*, lv/8 (1988), 16
G. Balfany: "David Sanborn," *Saxophone Journal*, xiii/4 (1989), 28
B. Wynan: "Anything Goes," *Chicago Tribune* (8 Oct 1989)
P. Freeman: "New Album: King of Sax Soloists: David Sanborn Doesn't Spend Much Time Looking Back," *San Francisco Chronicle Datebook* (3 March 1991)
C. Heim: "For David Sanborn, 'Night Music' Had a Lingering Impact," *Chicago Tribune* (9 Aug 1991)
B. Malik: "David Sanborn," *Jazz FM*, no.8 (1991), 11
T. Moon: "David Sanborn's New Direction," *JT*, xxi/7 (1991), 26
P. Smith: "David Sanborn," *Boston Globe* (23 June 1991)
J. Brown: "David Sanborn's Tenor Time," *Washington Post* (3 July 1992)
F. Goaty: "David Sanborn," *Jm*, no.421 (1992), 44
K. Goddard: *David Sanborn: the Effects of Differing Musical Idioms on Formula Usage in Improvisation* (thesis, York U., 1993)
H. Mandel: "Critical Sparring: David Sanborn Swings Back," *DB*, lx/2 (1993), 16
E. Enright: "Soul Connection: Hank Crawford & David Sanborn," *DB*, lxi/10 (1994), 17
J. Woodard: "David Sanborn: Branching out, Digging in," *JT*, xxv/5 (1995), 48
D. Holley: "David Sanborn: Made for TV," *DB*, lxv/3 (1998), 25
B. Milkowski: "David Sanborn: Inside the Music," *JT*, xxix/5 (1999), 44

BK

Sanchez, David (*b* Guaynabo, Puerto Rico, 3 Sept 1968). Puerto Rican tenor and soprano saxophonist and leader. His sister plays piano, and his brother, drums. Around the age of eight he began learning percussion, which he played in local salsa and show bands, and when he was 12 he took up saxophone. At a performing arts high school in Hato Rey, Puerto Rico, he continued his percussion studies and received classical tuition, but at the age of 15 he became interested in jazz, after hearing recordings by Miles Davis and Billie Holiday, and thereafter he concentrated on saxophone. Having moved to New York in 1988 he studied with Kenny Barron at Rutgers at Newark, New Jersey, and by 1989 he was performing in Latin-jazz groups with Hilton Ruiz, Eddie Palmieri, Paquito D'Rivera, and Charlie Sepulveda; shortly afterwards he began playing more bop-oriented material with John Hicks, Larry Ridley, Claudio Roditi, and Kenny Burrell. In 1991, on the recommendation of Roditi and D'Rivera, he joined Dizzy Gillespie's United Nation Orchestra and small groups, with which he remained until the leader's death in early 1993. In addition he worked with Slide Hampton's Jazzmasters (recording in 1993), Ray Drummond's Excursion All Stars, Danilo Pérez's group Afro-Cuban Explosion (1992), Pérez's quartet (1993–6), and Tom Harrell (late 1990s). In December 1996 Sanchez performed alongside Roy Hargrove at Umbria Jazz Winter in Orvieto, Italy, as a member of the New York/Havana/San Juan Superband, and the following year he recorded under Hargrove's leadership and then toured with Hargrove's Afro-Cuban band Crisol. From the mid-1990s he has toured as a leader, and he appeared at Brecon Jazz in 1994 and the Havana Jazz Festival in 1997; his regular sidemen are Edsel Gomez, the double bass player John Benitez (a schoolmate and colleague from *c*1980), Adam Cruz, and the percussionist Bernell Saturnino.

David Sanchez at Jazz in Marciac, France, 1993

When he is playing conventional forms of jazz Sanchez's rhythmically charged style reflects a combination of John Coltrane's sound and Sonny Rollins's bop lines, as demonstrated by his appearance as a soloist at the Chicago Jazz Festival in 1994, broadcast on National Public Radio. He is equally in command of the exquisitely tense, speech-like melodic lines that characterize the playing of the most accomplished rhythm-and-blues saxophonists. Another facet of his talent emerges mainly when he is performing in concert with his group, when he plays at rapid tempos in odd meters such as 7/4 or with changing time signatures. With his experience as a percussionist Sanchez has been able to integrate this approach, which was earlier explored most successfully by Dave Holland, into a Latin-jazz context and make musical sense of unusual rhythmic structures.

SELECTED RECORDINGS

As leader: *The Departure* (1993, Col. CK57848); *Sketches of Dreams* (1994, Col. CK67021); *Street Scenes* (1996, Col. CK67627); *Obsesión* (1997–8, Col. CK69119)

As sideman: C. Sepulveda: *Algo nuestro (Our Thing)* (1992, Ant. 314-512768-2); H. Ruiz: *Live at Birdland* (1992, Can. 79532-2); S. Debriano: *Panamaniacs* (1993, Freelance 019); H. Ruiz: *Heroes* (1993, Telarc 83338); D. Pérez: *The Journey* (1993, Novus 63166-2); J. King: *The Meltdown* (1997, Enja 9329-2)

BIBLIOGRAPHY

E. Holley: "Riffs: Sanchez Carries Dizzy's Torch," *DB*, lxi/8 (1994), 11
B. Primack: "Hearsay: David Sanchez," *JT*, xxiv/5 (1994), 11
D. Ansell: "David Sanchez," *JJI*, xlviii/5 (1995), 12
T. Quénum: "David Sanchez: Do the Right Thing!," *Jm*, no.464 (1996), 34 [incl. discography]
E. Holley: "Danilo Perez & David Sanchez: Import Duties," *DB*, lxiii/11 (1996), 32 [incl. discography]
S. Baudot: "David Sanchez," *Jh*, no.545 (1997), 19
P. Elwood: "Sanchez Brings Joyous End to S.F. Jazz Festival," *San Francisco Examiner* (10 Nov 1998)
W. Jenkins: "David Sanchez: Old and New Vibes," *JT*, xxviii/5 (1998), 46

GK, BK

Sanchez Reinoso, Raúl (Armando) (*b* Buenos Aires, 18 Dec 1908; *d* Buenos Aires, 7 Sept 1957). Argentine guitarist, banjoist, and bandleader. He formed the SANTA PAULA SERENADERS in 1933 and led the group until it disbanded in 1948.

LAUREANO FERNÁNDEZ, OMAR GARCÍA BRUNELLI

Sanders, Joe [Joseph L.] (*b* Thayer, KS, 15 Oct 1896; *d* Kansas City, MO, 14 May 1965). Pianist, singer, and bandleader. With the drummer Carleton (Allyn) Coon(, Sr.) (*b* Rochester, MN, 5 Feb 1894; *d* Chicago, 4 May 1932) he led the Coon–Sanders Novelty Orchestra, a small band which the two men formed in Kansas City in 1920. It made its first broadcast in 1921 and from December 1922 played on late-night programs, earning the nickname the Nighthawks. With additional members it began performing and recording in Chicago in 1924 as the Coon–Sanders Original Nighthawk Orchestra or the Coon–Sanders Nighthawks; Sanders's solo playing may be heard on *Deep Henderson* (1926, Vic. 20081). The band was resident at the Blackhawk, Chicago, from 1926 and toured widely during the summer. After Coon's death Sanders continued to lead a version of the band for a few months. He worked in Hollywood studios in 1934, then in May 1935 formed a new band, the Joe Sanders Original Nighthawks, which was resident at the Blackhawk until the end of the 1930s and occasionally thereafter. In the latter part of the 1940s he again worked in Hollywood studios and led a band that returned periodically to Chicago to perform at the Blackhawk. During the 1950s Sanders sang regularly with the Kansas City Opera.

BIBLIOGRAPHY

ChiltonW

P. F. Karberg: "Commercial Swing Bands, no.1: Joe Sanders and his Nighthawks," *Swing Music*, ii/3 (1936), 57

B. Colton and L. Kunstadt: "Encore: the Story of Coon–Sanders," *Record Research*, no.13 (1957), 3

R. P. Hopkins, "Three Cheers for Coon–Sanders," *Saturday Review*, xlix (25 June 1966), 58H.

H. Schultz: "The Dancing World of Coon–Sanders," *Saturday Review*, xlix (14 May 1966), 57

A. McCarthy: *The Dance Band Era: the Dancing Decades from Ragtime to Swing, 1910–1950* (London, 1971/*R*1982)

D. A. Johnson: "The Happy-go-lucky Sounds of Coon–Sanders Nighthawks," *MR*, i/3 (1974), 7

Sanders, Pharoah [Farrell; Little Rock] (*b* Little Rock, AR, 13 Oct 1940). Tenor saxophonist. He started playing professionally while in high school, trying numerous instruments before adopting tenor saxophone; after graduating in 1959 he played rhythm-and-blues and avant-garde jazz in the San Francisco Bay area, where he acquired the nickname Little Rock. In 1962 he moved to New York and worked with Billy Higgins, Don Cherry, and, unofficially, in John Coltrane's group (1965–7; for illustration *see* COLTRANE, JOHN). Here he made his mark with harsh, shrieking improvisations that combined multiphonics and sweeping runs of indefinite pitch. Remarkable examples may be heard on Coltrane's album *Live at the Village Vanguard Again* and on *Preview*, which Sanders recorded in 1968 as a principal soloist with the Jazz Composer's Orchestra. Following Coltrane's death in 1967 Sanders remained briefly with Alice Coltrane, then from 1969 to 1970 he led a group with Leon Thomas. In such performances as *The Creator Has a Master Plan*, Sanders's intense sounds were juxtaposed with tuneful melodies, usually played over serene, hypnotic vamps. He may be seen leading a quartet in the short film *It's Nation Time* (1970).

Sanders kept his home in Oakland, California, and, having worked for a while out of New York, he was again based in Oakland from the 1970s. His groups of the mid-1970s merely imitated his first successes, and his popularity declined accordingly, but after an unsuccessful flirtation with disco music (1977–8) his career revived considerably. In the 1980s both his repertory and his playing style covered a wide range,

Pharoah Sanders at Dingwalls, London, 1993

embracing not only the energetic free jazz and calm modal jazz of his earlier periods but also swing, rhythm-and-blues, and, especially, bop – as may be heard on several acclaimed albums recorded for the Theresa label in 1980–82. At that time Sanders performed most frequently as the leader of a quartet, among whose members were John Hicks and Idris Muhammad. William Henderson replaced Hicks as the regular pianist in 1982 and continued with the group into the new century; others of his sidemen in the 1990s included the Moroccan percussionist and *'ūd* player Yassir, Charnett Moffett, Ralph Penland, Sherman Ferguson, Alex Blake, the double bass player Jeff Littleton, and Winard Harper. From 1992 he spent another period in New York. In 1990 he performed on the nationally syndicated television show "Night Music," and later he made the video *Pharoah Sanders at the Keystone Korner in Japan* (1993). Although in the 1990s he mainly toured as a leader, he recorded with Sonny Sharrock (*c*1991), Randy Weston (1991, 1998), Franklin Kiermyer and the Moroccan multi-instrumentalist Maleem Mahmoud Ghania (both 1994), Steve Turre (1995), and Wallace Roney and James "Blood" Ulmer's Music Revelation Ensemble (both 1996).

SELECTED RECORDINGS

As leader: *Tauhid* (1966, Imp. 9138); *Karma* (1969, Imp. 9181), incl. The Creator Has a Master Plan; *Jewels of Thought* (1969, Imp. 9190); *Summun bukmun umyun* (1970, Imp. 9199); *Journey to the One* (1980, The. 108–09), incl. Greetings to Idris, Kazuko (Peace Child), You've got to have freedom; *Rejoice* (1981, The. 112–13); *Heart is a Melody* (1982, The. 118); *Pharoah Sanders Live* (1982, The. 116); *Ballads with Love* (1992, Venus [Jap.] 19025); *Message from Home* (1996, Verve 314-529578-2)

As sideman: J. Coltrane: *Ascension* (1965, Imp. 95); *Live at the Village Vanguard Again* (1966, Imp. 9124); D. Cherry: *Symphony for Improvisors* (1966, BN 84247); *Where is Brooklyn?* (1966, BN 84311); Jazz Composer's Orchestra: on *The Jazz Composer's Orchestra* (1968, JCOA 1001–02), Preview; S. Sharrock: *Ask the Ages* (*c*1991, Axiom 422-848957-2); R. Weston: *The Spirits of our Ancestors* (1991, Ant. 314-511896-2), incl. African Cookbook, Blue Moses; *Khepera* (1998, Verve 314-557821-2)

BIBLIOGRAPHY

GrayF
E. Van der Mei: "Pharoah Sanders: a Philosophical Conversation," *Coda*, viii/2 (1967), 2
——: "Far out Pharoah," *Jm*, no.152 (1968), 22
——: "Les confessions de Pharoah," *Jh*, no.239 (1968), 17
M. Williams: "Pharoah's Tale," *DB*, xxxv/10 (1968), 21
E. Raben: *A Discography of Free Jazz* (Copenhagen, 1969)
B. Palmer: "Pharoah Sanders," *RS*, no.57 (30 April 1970), 44
"Pharoah Sanders," *J&P*, ix/2 (1970), 3; repr. in *Black Giants*, ed. P. Rivelli and R. Levin (New York and Cleveland, 1970/*R*1980 as *Giants of Black Music*)
S. Randolph: "A Good Look at Pharoah Sanders," *JM*, no.181 (1970), 2
B. Tepperman: "Pharoah Sanders: Some Casual Impressions," *Pieces of Jazz* (1970), 22
N. Hentoff: "Pharoah Sanders," *BMI: the Many Worlds of Music* (1971), June, 7
J. Welch: "Pharoah Sanders: 'I Play for the Creator'," *DB*, xxxviii/10 (1971), 15
L. Tanter: "The Evolution of Pharoah Sanders," *Soul* (23 July 1973), 6
B. Case: "Pharoah Sanders Has Been Here and Gone," *New Musical Express* (22 June 1974), 36
E. Jost: *Free Jazz* (Graz, Austria, 1974/*R*1994)
G. Giddins: "Pharoah Sanders Goes Secular," *VV*, xxi (11 April 1977), 53
C. May: "In the Land of the Pharoah," *Black Music and Jazz Review*, i/2 (1978), 14
B. Vuijsje: *De nieuwe jazz* (Baarn, Netherlands, 1978), 114
P. Kemper: "Pharoah Sanders: zwischen Mythos und Logos," *JP*, xxviii/12 (1979), 6
K. Dallas: "Jazz: Pharoah Sanders," *MM* (28 June 1980), 26
V. Wilmer: "Rights and Rituals," *Time Out* (27 June–3 July 1980)
G. Tate: "The Son Bobs some Brand New Funk," *VV*, xxvi (29 July 1981), 49
J. Blum: "Pharoah Sanders: a Free-jazz Flower Child Blooms in a New Age," *Musician*, no.50 (1982), 36
F. Setterberg: "Pharoah Sanders: Jazz as God, Sax as Sacrament: Two Decades in Hot Pursuit of the Musical Truth," *San Francisco Examiner Image* (5 July 1987), 24; repr. in *Coda*, no.228 (1989), 8
D. Ouellette: "Pharoah Sanders," *DB*, lviii/8 (1991), 15
——: "Chasing the Trane: Saxophonist Pharoah Sanders Celebrates Jazz Legend John Coltrane," *S.F. Weekly* [San Francisco] (21 Oct 1992)
J. Fine: "Pharoah Sanders," *San Francisco Bay Guardian* (15 Nov 1995), 45
M. Johnson: "Pharoah's Return: Pharoah Sanders," *DB*, lxii/4 (1995), 20
B. Milkowski: "Pharoah Sanders: Expanding Orbit," *JT*, xxv/2 (1995), 66
J. Hamlin: "Q and A with Pharoah Sanders," *San Francisco Chronicle Datebook* (12 May 1996), 44
G. Hines: "Sanders: from Coltrane to a Spiritual Plane," *Washington Post* (24 April 1998)
<http://cyboard.com/jchrissco/bios/PS_bio.html> (2000)
<http://www.angelfire.com/id2/laotan/pharoah.html> (2000) [discography]
<http://www.dougpayne.com/AfroARTz/pharoah/> [incl. discography]
<http://www.mindspring.com/~scala/sanders.html> (2000) [discography]

BK

Sandke, Randy [Jay Randall] (*b* Chicago, 23 May 1949). Trumpeter. Primarily self-taught, he played jazz in high school and at Indiana University (1966–9), where he also performed in a rock band with his classmate Michael Brecker (1968). In 1969 he ruptured his larynx and, despite corrective surgery, abandoned the trumpet; until around 1979 he played guitar and occasionally piano instead. He then worked again as a trumpeter in Vince Giordano's Nighthawks, Bob Wilber's Bechet Legacy, with which he toured Europe (1983–4) and recorded, Benny Goodman's last big band (1985–6), in which he appeared in the PBS television special "Benny Goodman: Let's Dance: a Musical Tribute", George Wein's Newport All Stars (from 1986), Buck Clayton's big band (1988–91), and Dick Hyman's group (from 1990), among others. Sandke has led a quintet (from 1986), the New York All Stars (from 1990), including Ken Peplowski and Dan Barrett, and the Metatonal Band (from 1992), with Ted Rosenthal and Marvin "Smitty" Smith. He has also worked as an arranger for the Carnegie Hall Jazz Orchestra (from 1994). In 1997, with George Avakian, he co-produced for the JVC New York Jazz Festival the tribute concert "The Re-discovered Music of Louis (Armstrong) & Bix (Beiderbecke)," which featured Sandke and Nicholas Payton. A highly respected swing stylist, Sandke has also recorded some very agreeable forays into the bop vernacular. He has contributed to the *Annual Review of Jazz Studies* and he is the author of *An Introduction to Metatonal Music* (New York, 1998), an instructional booklet describing his own harmonic system, which he calls "metatonal."

His brother Jordan (Lewis) Sandke (*b* Chicago, 20 Feb 1946) is also a trumpeter who studied at the New England Conservatory of Music, worked with Vince Giordano's Nighthawks (1979), Jaki Byard's Apollo Stompers (from 1979), the Widespread Depression Jazz Orchestra, and Buck Clayton's big band (1988–91), and led a small group which recorded in 1985.

Video oral history in *NCH* (HCJA)

SELECTED RECORDINGS

As leader: *Wildcats* (1992, Jlgy 222); *I Hear Music* (1993, Conc. 4566); *The Chase* (1994, Conc. 4642)

As sideman: B. Wilber: *Bechet Legacy* (1984, Challenge 70018); K. Peplowski: *Steppin' with Peps* (1993, Conc. 4569); Allen Lowe: *Woyzeck's Death* (1994, Enja 9005-2)

BIBLIOGRAPHY

CarrJ; *ConnorBG*
C. Deffaa: "Profile: Randy and Jordan Sandke," *DB*, liv/3 (1987), 50
E. Cook: "Randy Sandke," *JJI*, xlix (1996), no.7, p.6; no.8, p.8

GK

Sandoval, Arturo (*b* Artemisa, Cuba, 6 Nov 1949). Trumpeter, pianist, and composer. He was self-taught on the trumpet, and by the time he was 12 was playing in a street band with adult musicians. He was one of the founding members of the Orquesta Cubana de Música Moderna, which around 1973 grew into the group Irakere. With other members of the group he recorded with David Amram in 1977. After leaving Irakere in 1981 he toured internationally with his own group, and recorded with it in Cuba. He was a protégé of Dizzy Gillespie, with whom he played in Cuba, the USA, Puerto Rico, and England; they recorded together in Finland in 1982. During the 1980s Sandoval began to tour every summer, and appeared in Europe, South America, and Japan at festivals, concerts, and clubs.

Near the end of the decade Sandoval joined Gillespie's United Nation Orchestra, and in 1989 made a video and recorded with the group in London. While touring Europe with this ensemble in 1990 he entered the American embassy in Rome to secure his defection from Cuba to the USA. Soon afterwards he recorded with Paquito D'Rivera (August 1990) and performed with Tito Puente and Chico O'Farrill in Latin-jazz settings, though he also recorded Cuban popular music in Miami (where he settled) and played classical music in Germany and Great Britain. From the early 1990s, as a member of the GRP All-Star Big Band, he recorded, made a video, and toured Japan; he also performed and recorded as a guest soloist with James Moody at the Blue Note, New York (1995). On 7 December 1998 Sandoval took American citizenship. He continues to lead a bop and Latin-jazz band, recording regularly, and to perform trumpet concertos with symphony orchestras. From the early 1990s he has been a member of the faculty of Florida International University, Miami, and has written three books on trumpet playing. Gifted with a prodigious technique, Sandoval favors aggressive, busy, extroverted improvisations.

SELECTED RECORDINGS

As leader: with D. Gillespie: *To a Finland Station* (1982, Pablo 2310889); *No Problem* (1986, Ronnie Scott's Jazz House 001); *Tumbaito* (1986, Messidor 15974); *I Remember Clifford* (*c*1992, GRP 9668); *Dreams Come True* (*c*1993, GRP 9701); *Danzòn (Dance on)* (1993, GRP 9761); *Swingin'* (*c*1996, GRP 9846)

SELECTED FILMS AND VIDEOS

A Night in Havana: Dizzy Gillespie in Cuba (1987); Dizzy Gillespie and the United Nation Orchestra: Live at the Royal Festival Hall, London (*c*1990 [filmed 1989]); GRP All-Star Big Band: Live! (*c* early 1990s)

BIBLIOGRAPHY

J. Brody: "Version latine: trompettiste à Cuba," *Jm*, no.329 (1984), 50
S. Steward: "Cubana be, cubana bop," *The Wire*, no.21 (1985), 26
J. C. Coto: "Miami Nice," *DB*, lviii/7 (1991), 19 [incl. discography]
L. Birnbaum: "Cubano Bopper & the Mambo King," *DB*, lx/6 (1993), 16
H. Mandel: "Remembering Dizzy: All Dizzy's Children," *DB*, lx/4 (1993), 24
F. Kreiger: "'Tunisias Blues': Anmerkungen zum Trompetenspiel von Arturo Sandoval," *Jf*, xxviii (1996), 29
B. Primack: "Arturo Sandoval: Both Sides Now," *JT*, xxiv/4 (1994), 38
H. Mandel: "Arturo Sandoval Comes Out Swingin'," *DB*, lxiii/10 (1996), 18 [incl. discography]
B. Primack: "Arturo Sandoval: Latin Heat Wave," *JT*, xxviii/7 (1998), 46

CRISTÓBAL DÍAZ AYALA/BK

Sands, Bobby (*b* New York, 28 Jan 1907). Tenor saxophonist. He played in New York with the saxophonist Billy Fowler (*c*1927) and in a band led by Charlie Skeete (1929). During the 1930s he worked with Claude Hopkins, with whom he made several recordings, including *Mush Mouth* (1932, Col. 2674D), and appeared in the film shorts *Barbershop Blues* (1933) and *By Request* (1936). Sands ceased full-time performing in the 1940s. (*McCarthyB*)

based on *ChiltonW*

Sandström, Nisse [Nils] (*b* Katrineholm, Sweden, 13 March 1942). Swedish tenor saxophonist. He studied music from the mid-1950s and won an amateur contest on television in 1958. In the 1960s he led free-jazz groups, but he then adopted a bop style and recorded the album *The Painter* (1972, Odeon 062-34659); this was awarded a Gold Disc by *Orkester journalen* in 1972. He performed and recorded from 1973 with Red Mitchell's Swedish group Communication, appeared in the USA and Sweden in the late 1970s with Mitchell and Tommy Flanagan, and in the 1980s worked with Rolf Ericson, with the all-star groups Jazz Inc. and Summit Meeting, and as a leader and, sometimes, a teacher. Sandström is a versatile soloist with a wide-ranging knowledge of jazz and a strong sense of harmony. He is also highly regarded as an artist; several of his paintings are based on ideas associated with jazz. (L. Westin: "Nils Sandström," *Orkester journalen*, xli/2 (1973), 6)

ERIK KJELLBERG/LARS WESTIN

Sänger, Christof (*b* Wiesbaden, Germany, 28 July 1962). German pianist. He took piano lessons as a child and later studied classical piano at the University of Mainz (1984–9). After winning the Concours International de Piano Jazz Martial Solal (1989) he played with Bill Saxton (1990–92), Richie Cole (1994, 1997), Hermeto Pascoal (1992), and Ernie Watts (1999–2000) and worked with many European and American musicians. From 1992 he led a trio. He toured South America with his own groups (1994–5) and appeared at major festivals. Sänger's mainstream-oriented piano playing incorporates Latin and classical influences, swing idioms, and moments of improvised motivic polyphony.

SELECTED RECORDINGS

As unaccompanied soloist: *Live at Montréal Jazz Festival* (1996, Laika 3510082-2)
As leader: *Chorinho* (1992, Laika 93033); *Moliendo Café* (1998, Mons 874302)

WOLFRAM KNAUER

Sangster, John (Grant) (*b* Melbourne, Australia, 17 Nov 1928; *d* Brisbane, Australia, 26 Oct 1995). Australian drummer and composer. He first played trombone, and by 1948 was a respected trumpeter in the traditional style. In 1950, however, he took up drums for an overseas tour with Graeme Bell; after this he concentrated on percussion, and his approach became increasingly progressive. From 1961 to 1967 he led a quartet at El Rocco, Sydney, which recorded in the latter year. He also worked with Don Burrows, with whom he performed at Expo 67 in Montreal and Expo 70 in Osaka, Japan. In 1977 he recorded on vibraphone with Alan Lee, and in 1987 he joined Burrows's re-formed quartet for a series of concerts. Sangster's works, which are widely performed, often draw inspiration from the Australian environment: they contain elements of both traditional and modern jazz and display his concern for color and swing. Some of his pieces in this vein may be heard on his two-volume album *Australia and All that Jazz* (1971, 1976); others of his many albums of original compositions include a three-volume set, *Lord of the Rings* (1974, 1976–7). He published an autobiography, *Seeing the Rafters* (Sydney, 1988).

SELECTED RECORDINGS

As leader: *Conjurman* (CBS BP233450); *Australia and All that Jazz*, i–ii (1971, 1976, CPS 1008, CPF 1027); *The Hobbit Suite* (1973, Swaggie 1340); *Lord of the Rings*, i–iii (1974, 1976–7, EMI 2525-6, 2548-9, 2580-81); *Landscapes of Middle Earth* (1978, EMI 2642A/B/C/D)
As sideman with T. Gould: *Gould Plays Gould* (1978, Move 3021)

BIBLIOGRAPHY

Jazz, Catalogues of Australian Compositions (Sydney, 1978) [incl. discography, list of compositions; pubn of Australia Music Centre]
A. Bisset: *Black Roots, White Flowers: a History of Australian Jazz* (Sydney, 1979, rev. 2/1987)
M. Williams: *The Australian Jazz Explosion* (London and elsewhere, 1981), 53
E. Myers: "John Sangster," *APRA Journal*, ii/10 (1982), 16
B. Johnson: *The Oxford Companion to Australian Jazz* (Melbourne, Australia, 1987)

JEFF PRESSING (with JOHN WHITEOAK)/ROGER T. DEAN

San Jacinto Hall. Venue in New Orleans; *see* NIGHTCLUBS AND OTHER VENUES.

Santamaria, Mongo [Ramón] (*b* Havana, 7 April 1922). Cuban conga player and bandleader. He was born in a poor district of Havana which was known for its Afro-Cuban culture. After traveling to the USA via Mexico as a young man in 1950, he spent seven years with Tito Puente; he also was a member of an Afro-Cuban percussion section in a big band which recorded under Dizzy Gillespie's leadership in 1954. From 1957 to 1960 he performed and recorded with Cal Tjader. His composition *Afro-blue* became a jazz standard and was recorded by Tjader, John Coltrane, Dizzy Gillespie, and others. He then formed a group based on the classic Latin *charanga* format of flute and violin, but added to it jazz-oriented brass and saxophone players. In the 1960s Santamaria recorded and toured as the leader of a series of diverse bands that combined elements of jazz with Latin and black popular music, and at various times included such musicians as Hubert Laws, Chick Corea, Herbie Hancock, and Sonny Fortune; in the early 1970s Carter Jefferson, Steve Berrios, and Armando Peraza were among his sidemen. These bands, which played both Latin jazz and Latin soul, were enormously influential on the next generation of black-American musicians – especially percussionists – and were in a large part responsible for the gradual absorption of Latin rhythms into black music. However, Santamaria always retained contact with his musical roots in recordings that ranged from early Afro-Cuban percussion performances to classic salsa, as may be seen in the films *Our Latin Thing* (1972) and *Salsa* (1976). He remained associated with jazz musicians, and recorded with Dizzy Gillespie in 1980; he may be seen in "Wolf Trap Salutes Dizzy Gillespie: an All-Star Tribute to the Jazz Master" (1988), from the television series "Great Performances." He continued to lead salsa groups, record regularly, and make international tours in the 1980s and 1990s.

Oral history material in *DSI* (JOHP).

SELECTED RECORDINGS

As leader: *Yambu* (1958, Fan. 3267); *Mongo* (1959, Fan. 3291); *Go, Mongo!* (1962, Riv. 9423); *Watermelon Man* (1962–3, Battle 96120); *Mongo at the Village Gate* (1963, Battle 96129); *Live at Jazz Alley* (1990, Conc. Picante 4427); *Mamba Mongo* (1992, Chesky 100)

As sideman: D. Gillespie: *Afro* (1954, Norg. 1003); C. Tjader: *Cal Tjader Goes Latin* (1959, Fan. 8030); *Concert by the Sea* (1959, Fan. 8038), incl. Afro-blue; D. Gillespie: *Summertime* (1980, PL 2308229), incl. Afro-blue

BIBLIOGRAPHY

M. Santamaria: "Mongo Makes some Points," ed. L. Tomkins, *CI*, x/1 (1971), 16
A. J. Smith: "Mongo Santamaria: Cuban King of Congas," *DB*, xliv/8 (1977), 19
J. S. Roberts: *The Latin Tinge: the Impact of Latin American Music on the United States* (New York, and Oxford, England, 1979)
M. Goldberg: "An Interview with Mongo Santamaria," *Percussive Notes*, xxii/5 (1984), 55
C. Larkin, ed.: *The Guinness Encyclopedia of Popular Music* (Enfield, England, and Chester, CT, 1992, rev. and enlarged 2/1995)
M. Breton: "Mongo Santamaria: Roots and Innovation," *JT*, xxiii/9 (1993), 10

JOHN STORM ROBERTS/BK

Santa Paula Serenaders. Argentine big band. Formed in 1933 as a sextet by Raúl Sanchez Reinoso, who led the group throughout its existence, it later expanded to include four saxophones, two trumpets, a trombone, two violins, an accordion, two pianos, a guitar or banjo, a double bass, drums, and one or two singers. It played jazz standards and Argentine dances (such as the *paso doble*, a two-step generally in 6/8 rhythm, and the *guaracha*, an Afro-Cuban form based on the *habanera* rhythm) and displayed in the work of some of its soloists the influence of Coleman Hawkins and Joe Venuti. Apart from a tour of Brazil in 1936 the band performed exclusively in Argentina. It recorded about 200 tracks (among them *Tiger Rag/Santa Paula Stomp*, 1935, Parl. E1130) before disbanding in 1948.

LAUREANO FERNÁNDEZ, OMAR GARCÍA BRUNELLI

Santoro, Gene (*b* New York, 31 Oct 1950). Writer. After studying music at CUNY and at the guitar center of the New School for Social Research he worked as an editor, feature writer, and columnist for the periodical of Tower Records, *Pulse* (1983–91), and contributed numerous articles to *Down Beat* (1984–93). While serving as a music critic for *The Nation* (from 1986) he was a columnist for *7 Days* (1987–9) and *Taxi* (1988–90); he then wrote essays for *Atlantic Monthly* and taught at CCNY (both from 1991). As both a music critic and a feature writer he has contributed to the *New York Post* (1988–90), the *New York Daily News* (from 1993), and *Fi* (1996–9), and he has written for the *New Yorker*, the *New York Times*, the *Village Voice*, *Rolling Stone*, and *Musician* and contributed biographies of rock musicians to *Encyclopedia Britannica*. Santoro's jazz profiles and reviews show a deep interest in social and cultural issues, and many of them have been collected in anthologies (from 1994). In 2000 he published a biography of Charles Mingus.

WRITINGS

(selective list)

Dancing in your Head: Jazz, Blues, Rock and Beyond (New York, 1994)
Stir it Up: Musical Mixes from Roots to Jazz (New York, and Oxford, England, 1997)
Myself when I am Real: the Life and Music of Charles Mingus (New York, 2000)

GK

Sarbib, Saheb [John] (*b* ?Algeria, 1944). Double bass player, composer, and leader. His father was a jazz pianist, and his brother was also a musician. He may have grown up in North Africa, where his father toured with an Algerian group, but from 1973 he was leading small groups and recording (1974, 1976) in France; his sidemen included Daunik Lazro, François Jeanneau, Muhammad Ali, and Mino Cinélu, among others. In 1977 or 1978 he moved to New York, where he continued as the leader of small groups and also of the Multinational Big Band; notable sidemen in the latter were Roy Campbell, Jack Walrath, Art Baron, Talib Qadir (later known as Talib Kibwe), Joe Ford, Jemeel Moondoc, Mark Whitecage (who was also a regular member of Sarbib's small groups), and Dave Hofstra (on electric bass guitar). In the mid- to late 1980s Sarbib appears to have ceased to perform and record; nothing is known of his life from that time. He also played piano.

SELECTED RECORDINGS

UFO! Live on Tour (1979, Cadence Jazz 1008); of Multinational Big Band: *Live at the Public Theater* (1980, Cadence Jazz 1001), *Aisha* (1981, Cadence Jazz 1010); *Seasons* (1981, SN 1048); *Jancin' at Jazzmania* (1982, Jazzmania 50325)

BIBLIOGRAPHY

B. Rusch: "Saheb Sarbib: Interview," *Cadence*, vii/12 (1981), 8

GK

Sardaby, Michel (*b* Fort-de-France, Martinique, 4 Sept 1935). French pianist of Martinique birth. His father was a pianist, and he began to play piano at the age of five. In 1954, after leading his own 18-piece band in the Caribbean, he traveled to Paris, where he received informal lessons from Art Simmons and Bud Powell. He played with the trombonist Al Lirvat, Jacques Butler, and Benny Waters (1957), worked in Paris clubs with Guy Lafitte (1960) and J. J. Johnson and Kenny Clarke (both 1961), and toured with Bill Coleman (1962). In 1964 he led his own trio with the double bass player Michel Finet and the drummer Philippe Combelle, and in 1965 he made his first recording under his own name, *Blue Sunset* (Debs 508). He then worked with Michel Attenoux, Sonny Criss, Clark Terry (1965–6), Johnny Griffin and Dexter Gordon (both 1967), the trumpeter Sonny Grey, and Hal Singer (1970); he also accompanied such bluesmen as Sonny Boy Williamson (1963), T-Bone Walker (1968), and Mickey Baker (1971). Among further recordings under his leadership are a trio album with Percy Heath and Connie Kay, *Night Cap* (1970, Debs 522); *Mike Sardaby in New York* (1972, Debs 540), on which he was accompanied by Richard Davis, Billy Cobham, and Ray Barretto; and a session with a quartet in 1975 including Davis and Billy Hart. In 1987 he led a new trio with Jack Gregg and the drummer Steve Phillip.

BIBLIOGRAPHY

Feather–Gitler '70s
D. Constant: "Jazz informations: Sardaby story," *Jm*, no.218 (1974), 5
M. Zwerin: "Michel Sardaby: Lucid, World-class Improviser," *International Herald Tribune* (9 Jan 1987), 7
L. Chevalier: "Michel Sardaby," *Jh*, no.508 (1994), 26

MICHEL LAPLACE

Sargent, Gray (*b* Attleboro, MA, 10 June 1953). Guitarist. He grew up in a musical family and, having studied piano from the ages of seven to nine, took up guitar when he was 11. From 1975 to 1985 he worked intermittently as a member of Illinois Jacquet's small groups, and in 1990 he was a member of Jacquet's big band. In the late 1980s he began what became a longstanding association with Dave McKenna; in 1992 the two men recorded in a duo at Maybeck Recital Hall in Berkeley, California, and were both members of the Concord Jazz All-Stars (with Scott Hamilton, McKenna, the double bass player Marshall Wood, and Chuck Riggs) for a performance and recording at Cape Cod, Massachusetts. Sargent was artist-in-residence at Harvard University in 1988–9, and from the early 1990s he was active in Ruby Braff's small groups. As a freelance during these years he worked in Boston with Benny Carter, Phil Woods, Marshall, Bob Wilber, Arnett Cobb, Buddy Tate, Peanuts Hucko, Frank Wess, Vic Dickenson, and Sheila Jordan, among numerous others. He recorded with George Wein's Newport Jazz Festival All-Stars (in Berne, 1989), the trumpeter Lou Colombo (1989), the reed player Billy Novick and the singer Donna Byrne (both *c*1992), Byrne and Herb Pomeroy (1996), and Ralph Sharon (late 1990s), and he appeared on the PBS program "Big Band Ballroom Bash" as member of the Artie Shaw Orchestra under the direction of Dick Johnson. Sargent recorded as a sole leader in 1993.

SELECTED RECORDINGS

Duos with D. McKenna: *Concord Duo Series*, ii (1992, Conc. 4552)
As leader: *Shades of Gray* (1993, Conc. 4571)
As sideman: Concord All Stars: *Concord All-Stars on Cape Cod* (1992, Conc. 4530); B. Novick: on *Swing So Softly* (*c*1992, Daring 3007), Sing so softly, sing so wild, The way the wind blows; R. Braff: *Live at the Regattabar* (1993, Arbors 19131); H. Pomeroy and D. Byrne: *Walking on Air* (1996, Arbors 19176)

BIBLIOGRAPHY

Feather–GitlerBEJ
F. Bouchard: "Hearsay: Gray Sargent," *JT*, xxiv/6 (1994), 13

GK

Sarin, Michael (Towne) (*b* Stockton, CA, 20 Sept 1965). Drummer. He grew up near Seattle and began private studies in drumming in 1979; later he attended the University of Washington (1983–5) and had lessons with Jerry Granelli at the Cornish Institute for the Arts (1986–8). Sarin first played with Brad Shepik (then known as Brad Schoeppach) in Seattle in 1987 and continued to work with him after moving to New York in 1989. In the 1990s he collaborated with Thomas Chapin (1992 until the saxophonist's death in 1998) and joined Dave Douglas's string group Parallel Worlds (1992); he also played with Douglas in various other groups into the new century, notably the nonet Witness. Sarin has been associated with Ned Rothenberg, both in Double Band and in Power Lines (from 1993), and has been a member of Myra Melford's band The Same River, Twice (from 1995), and Anthony Coleman's trio Sephardic Tinge (from 1997). He has performed with John Zorn and with Ben Goldberg, and in 1996 he co-led a recording with Goldberg and the guitarist John Schott; that same year he toured Europe and recorded in the Netherlands with Mark Helias's quartet.

SELECTED RECORDINGS

As leader with B. Goldberg and J. Schott: *What Comes Before* (1996, Tzadik 7120)
As sideman: D. Douglas: *Five* (1995, SN 121276-2); T. Chapin: *Haywire* (1996, Knitting Factory Works 176); *Sky Piece* (1997, Knitting Factory Works 208); D. Douglas: *Convergence* (1998, SN 121316-2); M. Melford: *Above Blue* (1998, Arabesque 0142)

STEVE SMITH

Sarmanto, Heikki (*b* Helsinki, 22 June 1939). Finnish pianist, keyboard player, and composer, brother of Pekka Sarmanto. He studied at the Sibelius Academy, Helsinki (1962–4), and at the Berklee School of Music (1968–9, 1970–71). From 1962 he played with Esa Pethman, Christian Schwindt, and his own small jazz groups, and he appeared at the Montreux (1971) and Newport (New York; 1979) jazz festivals. He made recordings as a sideman with Pethman, Schwindt, Eero Koivistoinen, and Seppo Paakkunainen, and as a soloist (including *Flowers in the Water*, 1969, Col. 5E062-34044), and toured Europe and the USA, where he has presented two of his large works, *New Hope Jazz Mass* and *Perfect Harmony*. In addition to jazz compositions he has written vocal, orchestral, and theatrical works; one such piece, with Sonny Rollins as principal soloist, is performed in the documentary film *Saxophone Colossus* (1986).

Oral history material in *FiHJ*.

BIBLIOGRAPHY

A. Granholm: *Finnish Jazz* (Helsinki, 1974, rev. and enlarged 5/1997, by M. Huuskonen, J. Muikku, and T. Vähäsilta)

J. Muikku: "Broadening out: Finnish Jazz Breaks down Barriers," *Nordic Sounds* (1989), June, 12

PEKKA GRONOW

Sarmanto, Pekka (*b* Helsinki, 15 Feb 1945). Finnish double bass player, brother of Heikki Sarmanto. After studying violin and double bass at the Sibelius Academy in Helsinki he joined his brother's band (1965). He made recordings with Eero Koivistoinen (from 1967), Edward Vesala (1969, 1983), Ted Curson (1970), his brother (from 1971), and Charlie Mariano and Juhani Aaltonen (1974), and in a quintet led by Dizzy Gillespie and Arturo Sandoval (*To a Finland Station*, 1982, Pablo 2310889); he also appeared frequently with various jazz groups in Finland and abroad. In the 1990s he recorded further with Vesala (1991 and 1994) and with UMO (1997).

Oral history material in *FiHJ*.

BIBLIOGRAPHY

A. Granholm: *Finnish Jazz* (Helsinki, 1974, rev. and enlarged 5/1997, by M. Huuskonen, J. Muikku, and T. Vähäsilta)

A. Crohns: "Aarets finske musiker" [Finnish musician of the year], *Orkester journalen*, xlvi/12 (1978), 22

PEKKA GRONOW

Sarpila, Antti (*b* Helsinki, 11 June 1964). Finnish clarinetist and saxophonist. He was originally inspired by his father, who was an amateur saxophonist, but he met Bob Wilber at the Pori Jazz Festival in 1980 and studied and played with him in the USA on several occasions; later he recorded with Wilber in Stockholm (1993) and the UK (1994). In 1984 he founded a big band specializing in swing and traditional jazz, which by 1997 had recorded eight albums, including many of his own arrangements and compositions and featuring his solo playing. He also recorded in small groups as a leader, as a co-leader with the clarinetist Alan Vaché in Germany (1995), and as a member of the Yamaha International Allstar Band (1993), the Buck Clayton Legacy (1993–4), the European Jazz Giants (1994), and the International Allstars (1995). He also works with Lars Erstrand and Ulf Johansson in the Swedish Swing Society, a quartet modeled after Benny Goodman's classic group; the quartet recorded in 1996.

Oral history material in *FiHJ*.

SELECTED RECORDINGS

As leader: *Swinging* (1991, ASCD 4); with B. Wilber: *Moments Like These* (1993, Phon. 8811); with A. Vaché: *Summit Meeting* (1995, Nagel-Heyer 027); *Antti Sarpila Meets Markku Johansson* (1996, Jardis 8801); of Antti Sarpila Swing Band: *15th Anniversary* (1996, ASCD 9)

As sideman with Yamaha International Allstar Band: *Happy Birthday Jazzwelle Plus* (1993, Nagel-Heyer 005)

BIBLIOGRAPHY

M. Huuskonen, J. Muikku and T. Vähäsilta: *Finnish Jazz* (Helsinki, 5/1997)

PEKKA GRONOW

Sarrusophone. A brass instrument of conical bore played with a double reed. A family of such instruments, ranging from the sopranino to the contrabass, was designed in the mid-19th century to substitute for the double-reed woodwind instruments (oboes and bassoons) in military bands; they continued to be played in military, brass, and wind bands, and made isolated appearances in classical scores, but were largely obsolete by the mid-20th century. The sarrusophones resemble the saxophones in compass, keywork and fingering, and tone. They are rarely used in jazz: Sidney Bechet played one (the contrabass in E♭) on *Mandy, make up your mind* (OK 40260), recorded in 1924 by Clarence Williams's Blue Five; John R. T. Davies may be heard on the bass instrument (in B♭) on *Don't monkey with it* (1963), a one-man-band recording on which he also plays all the other instruments (issued on the anthology *Sounds of Surprise*, 1927–63, Jazz Greats CD079); and Scott Robinson played contrabass sarrusophone on his album *Thinking Big* (1996, Arbors 19179).

Sasajima, Akio (*b* Hakodate, Japan, 14 March 1952). Japanese guitarist. Having taught himself guitar he performed in Sapporo with Sadao Watanabe, who encouraged him to embark on a professional career in Tokyo; however, within a year he had returned to Hakodate. In 1977 he moved to Chicago, and two years later he performed at the first Chicago Jazz Festival. Later he recorded in duos with Harvie Swartz (1989) and Ron Carter (1991) and in a trio with Swartz and Victor Lewis (1989) and toured Japan leading a quintet that consisted of Randy Brecker, Don Friedman, Swartz, and Jimmy Cobb (1991).

SELECTED RECORDINGS

Duos with R. Carter: *Akioustically Sound* (1991, Muse 5448)

As leader: *Time Remembered* (1989, Muse 5417)

As sideman with Eden Atwood: on *Today!* (*c*1992, Southport 0015), Old Devil Moon

BIBLIOGRAPHY

G. Lees and J. Reeves: *Jazz Lives: 100 Portraits in Jazz* (Toronto, 1992), 168

GK

Sash, Leon (Robert) (*b* Chicago, 19 Oct 1922; *d* 25 Nov 1979). Accordionist and leader. Blind from the age of 11, he took up accordion in his teens and began working as a professional musician when he was 16. He studied harmony and arranging and changed to the "bassetti" accordion, which has an extra manual of buttons in three rows arranged chromatically, thus producing a wider range of notes in the left hand than the standard instrument. Later he led his own groups, usually trios or quartets that included his wife, the singer and double bass player Lee Morgan. In 1954 he made some recordings for EmArcy accompanied by a syrupy vocal group that imitated brass and reed sections; although these are disappointing in some ways, they provide a fine example of Sashs's accordion playing. He led further sessions in 1956 and 1967 and made a successful appearance at the Newport Jazz Festival in 1957; a recording of this performance was issued on *Toshiko & Leon Sash at Newport* (Verve 8236; half the album is devoted to a separate performance by Toshiko Akiyoshi at the same festival). Sash also wrote arrangements for accordion groups and worked as a staff musician at WLS radio.

BIBLIOGRAPHY

FeatherE

Obituary, *DB*, xlvii/2 (1980), 12

GK

Sassetti, Bernardo (*b* Lisbon, 24 June 1970). Portuguese pianist and composer. He studied classical piano as well as with the jazz musicians Horace Parlan, Roland Hanna, and Zé Eduardo. In 1988 he played with Carlos Martins, the Moreiras Jazztet, Al Grey, John Stubblefield, Frank Lacy, and Andy Sheppard. He appeared at concerts and festivals with Art Farmer, Kenny Wheeler, Freddie Hubbard, Paquito D'Rivera, Benny Golson, Curtis Fuller, Eddie Henderson, Charles McPherson, and Steve Nelson, and as a member of the United Nation Orchestra. In the 1990s he performed and recorded with Guy Barker (including *Into the Blue*, 1994–5, Verve 527656-2) and toured internationally with his own group and as a sideman. Sassetti composed the suites *Ecos de África*, *Sons do Brasil*, and *Mundos e Mùsica para Trio*. He recorded as a leader from 1994 (notably *Salsetti*, 1994, Groove/Movieplay 107, with Paquito D'Rivera as guest soloist, and *Mundos*, 1996, EmA 532988-2), and also recorded with Conrad Herwig, the Cuban band Sierra Maestra, Carlos Barretto, and Martins. A pop-oriented session under his leadership in 1997 involved the London Philharmonic Orchestra, with Barker and the rock star Sting as guest soloists.

JOSÉ DUARTE

Sassy. Nickname of SARAH VAUGHAN.

Satchmo [Satchelmouth]. Nickname of LOUIS ARMSTRONG.

Satellites. Record company and label founded in 1987 by RYO KAWASAKI.

Sato, Masahiko (*b* Tokyo, 6 Oct 1941). Japanese pianist, composer, arranger, and leader. He studied violin and piano from the age of five, and while still in high school was a member of George Kawaguchi's group Big Four (known during his membership as Big Four Plus One). After graduating from Keio University in Tokyo he studied at the Berklee School of Music (1966–8). He then returned to Tokyo, formed a trio, and recorded his first album, *Palladium* (1969), which was critically acclaimed. Also in Tokyo he recorded with Charles Mingus and Helen Merrill (1971), and in Germany he recorded as a leader (1971) and with Attila Zoller (1971), Karl Berger (1971), and Albert Mangelsdorff (1973). Sato's best-known compositions include *Samardhi*, *Fairy Rings*, *Fall Out* (1972), *Yamataifu* (1972, played by Toshiyuki Miyama's New Herd), *Sosho* (1973), *Yun* (1976), *Kan jizai* (1976), and *Escape Velocity* (1986, recorded by Sato, Eddie Gomez, and Steve Gadd in 1988). He has written arrangements for many recordings, notably led by Nancy Wilson, Merrill, Masami Nakagawa, and Kimiko Itoh, and for the album *Maiden Voyage* (1983, Interface 7073), recorded by Art Farmer's quartet and a string section, on which Sato plays piano. In 1983 he played a large role in establishing Masor House Music College in Tokyo, where he teaches. Sato has appeared in clubs and festivals in Europe, the USA, Africa, Australia, South America, and Russia with his trio or other groups.

SELECTED RECORDINGS

As unaccompanied soloist: *Yun* (1976, Denon YX7502)

As leader: *Palladium* (1969, Express 8004); with G. Peacock: *Samardhi: Masahiko Meets Gary Peacock* (1972, Express 9003), incl. Samardhi, Fairy Rings, Fall Out; *Kan jizai* (1976, Col. YX7501); *Brink* (1983, Contl HL5027); *Double Exposure* (1988, CBS 5051); *Randooga: Live under the Sky '90* (1990, CBS 5171); *Step to Next* (1994, Pol. 1200); *Liberissimo* (1999, BAJ 0012)

As sideman with M. Togashi: *Plays BeBop*, i–ii (1991, 1992, Pol. 1076, 1097)

BIBLIOGRAPHY

Feather–Gitler '70s

M. Gourges: "Masahiko Sato," *Jm*, no.233 (1975), 37

K. Yokoi: "Masahiko Satoh: Oral History," *Cadence*, xx/8 (1994), 5

YOZO IWANAMI/KAZUNORI SUGIYAMA

Saturn. Record company and label founded by SUN RA. It should not be confused with a French company and label of the same name which was active in the 1950s.

Saucier, Edgar (T.) (*b* Bay St. Louis, MS, 29 May 1912; *d* San Francisco, 27 Dec 1962). Alto saxophonist. One of the eight children of the double bass player, trombonist, and bandleader August Saucier, he played as a teenager in his father's band before moving to New Orleans in 1928 to join the Joyland Revelers, led by the violinist and banjoist Clarence Desdune. He worked in New Orleans until the mid-1930s, when he went to Chicago and became a member of Lee Collins's band at the Derby Club. While in Chicago, Saucier recorded accompaniments to blues singers, including Ollie Shepard, Bill Gaither, and Georgia White. In late 1938 he is known to have spent time in the San Antonio area working with Boots and his Buddies and in the band of the trumpeter L. D. Harris. Back in Chicago, he played in the house band at the All Star at 43rd Street and Indiana Avenue. He was in the army from April 1941 until 1944, then from May to July 1944 he appeared at Martin's Corner with the Chicago Play-Boys, led by the drummer Judge Riley. Saucier led his own bands at the Carver Hotel in Chicago in 1946 and 1947, and in the late 1940s he worked again with Collins at the Victory Club. After moving to San Francisco (1949) he continued to perform and to lead a band until his death from a heart attack. Contempories recalled his distinctive style and tone as an early precursor of the jump and rhythm-and-blues styles, and recorded evidence bears out this judgment.

SELECTED RECORDINGS

(all recorded for Decca)

As sideman: O. Shepard: It's low down dirty shame/If it ain't love (1937, 7384); Honey Bee/Sweetheart Land (1937, 7400); No one to call you dear (1937, 7408); G. White: Careless Love (1937, 7419); Rock me daddy (1937, 7436); I'm doing what my heart says do/T'aint nobody's fault but yours (1939, 7672)

BIBLIOGRAPHY

F. J. Gillis and J. W. Miner, eds.: *Oh, didn't he Ramble: the Life Story of Lee Collins* (Urbana, IL, Chicago, and London, 1974/*R*1989)

M. Tovey: "Edgar Saucier: New Orleans Alto Saxophone," *Fn*, xvii/1 (1985), 15; xvii/6 (1986), 15 [inc. discography]

HOWARD RYE

Saudrais, Charles (*b* Paris, 7 Sept 1938; *d* ?Paris, 28 April 1993). French drummer. He first played in dixieland bands led by the pianist Armand Gordon and Raymond Fonsèque (1954–5), then worked with Henri Renaud and Roger Guérin in Berlin and Paris (1955–6). He appeared in the short film *Bill Coleman from Boogie to Funk* (1961) and performed with, among others, Chet Baker (1956), André Persiany, Barney Wilen, the Modernisticks, led by the saxophonist Bib Monville (1957), Jean Bonal (1958), Guy Lafitte (1965, 1971), Babik Reinhardt (1967), Red Mitchell (1969), Sonny Grey's big band (1973), and the singer Jan Harrington with André Persiany (1989), but is best known as a member of the historic Georges Arvanitas trio (1965–93). The group accompanied numerous distinguished soloists, including Jimmy Heath, Frank Foster (1968), Ted Curson (1971, 1978), and Frank Wright (1978); among its recordings is the album *Parisian Concert* (1973, Futura 41), when it formed the nucleus of a quintet led by Dexter Gordon, with Grey on trumpet.

MICHEL LAPLACE

Sauer, Heinz (*b* Merseburg, Germany, 25 Dec 1932). German tenor saxophonist. Self-taught, he began playing as an amateur in Frankfurt am Main during the 1950s. From 1968 to 1978 he was a member of Albert Mangelsdorff's quintet, and his best work with the group is exemplified by *Club trois*, on the trombonist's album *Tension* (1963, CBS 62336). He also played in the Jazzensemble des Hessischen Rundfunks (from 1962) and the German All Stars (1968, 1980–81). In 1974 he founded a quartet. Later he played with Bob Degen (with whom he recorded the duo album *Ellingtonia Revisited*, 1980, L+R 40007), Manfred Schoof, Günter Lenz, Ralf Hübner, and others. Originally influenced by Sonny Rollins, Sauer developed an individual voice; always experimenting, he began in the 1990s to alter his sound through the use of electronic devices, though even in free passages he maintains a feeling of swing. In the 1990s he formed, with Degen and the double bass player Stefan Schmolck, a trio which is heard on the album *Exhange* (1995, Free Flow Music 0695). His current ensemble with vibraphonist Christopher Dell and drummer Bertram Ritter remains one of the most exciting jazz ensembles in Germany.

BIBLIOGRAPHY

G. Endress: "Heinz Sauer: ein Suchender," *JP*, xxxiv/12 (1985), 4

WOLFRAM KNAUER

Saunders, Keith (Leo) (*b* Wilkes-Barre, PA, 25 Aug 1960). Pianist and leader. In 1964 his family moved to Van Nuys, California, where from the ages of eight to 15 he learned classical piano. He then abandoned this path and received lessons from Charlie Shoemake for three years; in 1982 he studied briefly with Horace Silver. In Los Angeles he worked with Roy McCurdy and Bill Watrous (both 1980–82) and in Dick Berk's group Adoption Agency, in which he served as music director (1980–83). He then played with Richie Cole (1983–9). In 1984 he moved to New York, where he performed with Tom Harrell (1985) and Lionel Hampton (1988) and founded the N.Y. HARD BOP QUINTET (1991). From 1992 he was pianist and music director for the dance group Manhattan Tap, with which he performs in the video *Manhattan Tap with the HardBop Trio* (*c*1994); he toured England with the group in 1995. In addition Saunders is a member of the trio accompanying the singer Laverne Butler and leads his own trio, which usually includes the double bass player Bim Strasberg. (*Feather–GitlerBEJ*)

For recordings *see* N.Y. HARD BOP QUINTET.

GK

Saunders, Red [Theodore Dudley] (*b* Memphis, 2 March 1912; *d* Chicago, 5 March 1981). Drummer and bandleader. Following his mother's death he was brought up by his sister in Milwaukee. In 1923 he moved to Chicago, where he first worked in 1928 with the pianist Stomp King. He spent five years working mainly in the city as a member of the Walkathonians under the leadership of the pianist Ira Coffey; this association finished in summer 1933, when the white musicians' union in Atlantic City, New Jersey, caused all of Coffey's sidemen to be fired prematurely, shortly after they had begun an engagement there. Saunders then performed with Curtis Mosby in two touring musical revues. Having returned to Chicago, he played with Tiny Parham at the Savoy Ballroom (*c*1934) and then joined the house band led by Albert Ammons at the Club DeLisa; towards the end of 1937 he took over the leadership of the ensemble from the reed player Dalbert Bright, who had replaced Ammons as leader earlier that year. In June 1945 he transferred his group, which at the time included Sonny Cohn and Leon Washington, to the Garrick Theatre Lounge. After a brief period at the Band Box in 1947 he worked again at the Club DeLisa from May 1947 until it closed early in 1958; during this period Porter Kilbert joined the band, Joe Williams served as its singer, and Sonny Blount (later known as Sun Ra) supplied arrangements. Among Saunders's many recordings is *Mistreatin' Woman Blues/Hey Bartender* (1951, OK 7061), on which Williams may be heard singing. Saunders continued to work as the leader of house bands at Roberts' Show Lounge (July – *c* December 1958) and the Regal Theater (1959–68). In addition he led a successful campaign in 1963 to integrate the white and black musicians' unions in Chicago. He continued working into the 1970s, performing with Art Hodes (1968) and Little Brother Montgomery (1969), leading his own big band (1970), and appearing in an episode of the PBS television series "Soundstage" (1974).

Oral history material in *NjR* (JOHP), *NNC*.

BIBLIOGRAPHY

ChiltonW; *FeatherE*
A. Hodes: "Sittin' in: Looking at Red," *DB*, xxxiv/16 (1967), 18
H. Rye: "Red Saunders Columbia and Okeh Sessions," *Journal of Jazz Discography*, no.5 (1979), 9
D. J. Travis: *An Autobiography of Black Jazz* (Chicago, 1983), 123
<http://hubcap.clemson.edu/~campber/saunders.html> (2000) [incl. discography]

HOWARD RYE

Saury, Maxim (*b* Enghien-les-Bains, France, 27 Feb 1928). French clarinetist. His father, a professional violinist, did not encourage him to study music. He reluctantly took up violin at the age of 12, then changed to clarinet after hearing Hubert Rostaing play with Django Reinhardt. Having first worked with amateur groups in Paris, from 1947 to 1952, apart from a period in 1949 during which he led his own trio, he played with Claude Bolling (recording in 1948–50). Later he formed a big band, the New Orleans Sound, which he led for 15 years in Paris and at many festivals in Europe. He also toured as far as North Africa (1963), Madagascar (1965), and Tahiti (1966). In 1968 he visited the USA, where he played with Barney Bigard, and he made further visits to America in 1970 and 1976. He acted and performed in a number of films, including *Printemps à Paris* (1956, with Bill Coleman) and *Les temps d'une nuit* (1963). Saury's fluid style, which is reminiscent of that of Bigard, is well represented by his album *Rendez-vous à la Nouvelle-Orléans* (1960–61, Pathé 1133–4).

BIBLIOGRAPHY

FeatherE
L. Malson: "Maxim Saury ou le sens de l'équilibre," *Jm*, no.59 (1960), 28
P. Koechlin: "Le swing et l'Afrique," *Jh*, no.189 (1963), 15
F. Levin: "Maxim Saury: Jazzman," *IAJRC Journal*, xxv/1 (1992), 75
R. Fonsèque: "Maxim Saury en 1995," *Jazz Dixie/Swing: du Ragtime au Big Band*, no.6 (1994), 16

ANDRÉ CLERGEAT

Saussois, Patrick (*b* Paris, 24 June 1954). French guitarist. He was self-taught, and was influenced mainly by Django Reinhardt, Oscar Alemán, and Grant Green. In 1977 he was introduced to Parisian jazz circles by Gilbert Leroux, and he went on to play with the soprano saxophonist Marc Laferrière, Benny Waters, Roger Guérin, the violinist Jean Toupance, the drummer Japy Gauthier (1982), and Jean-Claude Fohrenbach (1985). He accompanied the accordionist Jo Privat (1983–9), was a member of Louis Mazetier's trio (1988–92), and led his own groups. In 1991 he co-led a recording session with Georges Arvanitas (1991). He was the editor of *Jazz Swing Journal* from 1986 to 1989, and then served as an artistic director for the Djaz label, for which he recorded *Isn't it Romantic?* (1988, Djaz 88091). (F. W. Sportis: "Alma Sinti: Patrick Saussois," *Jh*, no.540 (1997), 26)

MICHEL LAPLACE

Sauter, Eddie [Edward Ernest] (*b* New York, 2 Dec 1914; *d* Nyack, NY, 21 April 1981). Arranger and composer. He was initially a drummer. He attended Columbia University and then, as a trumpeter, performed in bands on transatlantic cruise ships. After studying at the Juilliard School he became a member of Red Norvo's trumpet section in late 1935, and shortly afterwards, by mutual consent, the full-time arranger for Norvo's band. From 1939 he worked as a freelance, writing arrangements for such bandleaders as Benny Goodman (for whom he produced his most notable work) and Artie Shaw, and established a strong reputation among musicians. Suffering from tuberculosis, he was unable to work from late 1941 through much of the decade. His only period of public recognition (in the mid-1950s) stemmed from the success of a band assembled, initially for recording purposes only, by Sauter and Bill Finegan, formerly an arranger for Tommy Dorsey and Glenn Miller; he may be seen with it in the film short *The Sauter–Finegan Orchestra* (1955). Sauter continued as a freelance writer for stage, film, and television, but also produced occasional pieces of "absolute" music, such as *Q.T.* for the New York Saxophone Quartet.

Sauter's arrangements of popular song material for Norvo displayed a wealth of invention, and his deft handling of dynamics and unstilted counterpoint suggest an acquaintance with the methods of Duke Ellington. These elements were fully developed in his original works for Goodman, such as *Benny Rides Again* (1940) and *Clarinet à la King* (1941). The lightweight character of the most popular recordings by the Sauter–Finegan Orchestra, such as *Doodletown Fifers* or *Midnight Sleigh Ride* (both on the album *The Sauter–Finegan Orchestra*, 1952, RCA LPM3115, the latter an adaptation of the "Troika" from Prokofiev's *Lieutenant Kijé*), should not obscure those orchestral and contrapuntal touches that foreshadowed the explorations of Gil Evans. If some of Sauter's work seems superficial, the best is a vindication of his versatility and sensitivity; in particular, his writing for chamber string ensemble on Stan Getz's album *Focus* (1961) represents one of the most convincing fusions of jazz and nonjazz elements. Further collaborations with Getz included the film soundtrack of Arthur Penn's *Mickey One* (1965) and the *Tanglewood Concerto* (1966). A collection of his scores is held at Yale University (*see* Libraries and archives, §2).

Oral history material in *NjR* (JOHP).

RECORDED COMPOSITIONS

(selective list)

Recorded by B. Goodman: Benny Rides Again (1940, Col. 55001); Superman (1940, Col. 55002); Clarinet à la King (1941, OK 6544)

Recorded by others: A. Shaw: The Maid with the Flaccid Air (1945, Vic. 28-0406); S. Getz: *Focus* (1961, Verve 68412); on *Stan Getz & Arthur Fiedler at Tanglewood* (1966, RCA LSC2925), Tanglewood Concerto; on New York Saxophone Quartet: *The New York Saxophone Quartet* (1980, Stash 210), Q.T.

SELECTED ARRANGEMENTS

Recorded by R. Norvo: Gramercy Square (1936, Decca 691); A Porter's Love Song to a Chambermaid/I know that you know (1936, Bruns. 7744); Smoke Dreams (1937, Bruns. 7815); Remember (1937, Bruns. 7896)

Recorded by B. Goodman: How High the Moon (1940, Col. 35391); My Old Flame (1941, Col. 36754)

Recorded by A. Shaw: Summertime (1945, Vic. 28-0406)

BIBLIOGRAPHY

ChiltonW; *ConnorBG*; *SchullerS*

L. Feather: "Men Behind the Bands: Eddie Sauter," *DB*, vii/5 (1940), 17

"Coda: Eddie Sauter," *JF* [intl edn], no.71 (1981), 59

B. Laber: "The Wizards of Doodletown: the Sauter–Finegan Legacy," *The Instrumentalist*, xliv/1 (1989), 18 [incl. discography]

I. Karl, ed.: *Hans Koller: the Man who Plays Jazz* (Vienna, 1993) [text in Ger. and Eng.]

BRIAN PRIESTLEY

Savannah Syncopators. Name used on some recordings made by King Oliver and the Dixie syncopators.

Savant. Record company and label established in New York around 1997 by Barney Fields. By 2000 it had issued approximately 25 recordings, including albums by Houston Person, Charles Earland, Winard Harper, Lonnie Plaxico, and Arthur Blythe.

BIBLIOGRAPHY

E. Holley: "Riffs: Muse Founder Sells Catalog to 32 Jazz," *DB*, lxiv/3 (1997), 13

<http://www.jazzdepot.com/about.html> (2000)

GK

Savery, Finn (*b* Gentofte, Denmark, 24 July 1933). Danish pianist and composer. From the early 1950s he was active in both jazz and classical music; he worked mainly as a composer, but he also led ensembles, played briefly in a trio led by Erik Moseholm (autumn 1960 – spring 1961), and performed with the Danish Radiojazzgruppen (i) and the Radioens Big Band. As a jazz musician he preferred to perform within the conventional piano trio (accompanied by double bass and drums), but he also appeared with larger ensembles. In addition to composing music for chamber ensembles, vocal groups, films, and musicals (such as *Teenagerlove*, 1962), Savery wrote several jazz and third-stream works, usually in the form of suites.

SELECTED RECORDINGS

As leader: *New York Series* (1976, Exlibris 20013); *Waveform* (1978, Met. 15641); *Kiming* (1981, Met. 15700); *Many Moments* (1982, Met. 15818), incl. Streams; *Interplay* (1991, Canzone 33006)

As sideman with Jørn Elniff: *Music for Mice and Men* (1961, Debut 134)

BIBLIOGRAPHY

E. Christensen: "Talløse varianter mellem det enkle og det komplicerede" [Numerous variations between the simple and the complicated], *DMT (Dansk musik tidsskrift)*, lv/1 (1980–81), 15 [incl. list of works and discography]

K. Frandsen: *Politikens jazzleksikon* (Copenhagen, 1987)

B. Krarup: "Dualisme," *DMT (Dansk musik tidsskrift)*, lxx/4 (1995–6), 122

ERIK WIEDEMANN/FRANK BÜCHMANN-MØLLER

Savolainen, Jarmo (*b* Iisalmi, Finland, 24 May 1961). Finnish pianist and composer. Originally trained as a classical pianist, he turned to jazz and studied for two years at the Berklee College of Music. He performed with Jukka-Pekka Uotila (1983–6), Pekka Pohjola (1987–92), and the Avanti Orchestra. From 1985 he made recordings as an unaccompanied pianist and with Finnish and American musicians, among them *True Image* (1994, A Records 73031, with Tim Hagans, Dave Liebman, Ron McClure, and Billy Hart among his sidemen), and *Another Story* (1997, A Records 73112). He has also composed works for big bands and the Finnish Radio Symphony Orchestra.

Oral history material in *FiHJ*.

BIBLIOGRAPHY

"Key Musician," *JF* [intl edn], no.98 (1986), 16
M. Huuskonen, J. Muikku and T. Vähäsilta: *Finnish Jazz* (Helsinki, 5/1997)

PEKKA GRONOW

Savoy (i). Record label. It was established around 1931 in Chicago by the company Melrose and Montgomery. The five issues of jazz and race material were derived from Gennett. ("Afterthoughts 468," *Sv*, no.102 (1982), 240)

HOWARD RYE

Savoy (ii). Record company and label. The company was founded late in 1942 in Newark, New Jersey, by Herman Lubinsky. Among the label's first issues were items recorded in 1939 by the Savoy Dictators: these inaugurated a substantial catalogue of jazz which made Savoy one of the most important independent labels of the 1940s. From 1945 to 1952 artists and repertory were directed by Teddy Reig, who was responsible, despite Lubinsky's initial doubts, for introducing to the label several musicians of the emerging bop school. Savoy organized sessions by Charlie Parker (1945, 1947–8), Dexter Gordon and Fats Navarro (both 1946–7), J. J. Johnson (1946–7, 1949), and Serge Chaloff and Miles Davis (both 1947), the results of which are now among the most highly prized recordings of the style. Nevertheless the most successful parts of the catalogue were recordings of swing and others of jazz with a strong beat and blues feeling that later came to be categorized as rhythm-and-blues, including a notable series by Johnny Otis (1949–51). An office was opened on the West Coast in 1948; in charge of artists and repertory was Ralph Bass, who was responsible for bringing Erroll Garner to the label.

Savoy began purchasing other enterprises in 1948. The first of these was Fred Mendelsohn's label Regent; those of particular jazz interest were National, Bop, and Discovery, all of which had extensive jazz catalogues. In addition the company leased a large amount of important jazz from small organizations, notably traditional material by Mutt Carey and Punch Miller first issued by Century and Fletcher Henderson's recordings for Crown. Savoy also reissued the catalogue of the Jewell label, best known for its recordings by Boyd Raeburn of 1945–6.

Reig's successor, Lee Magid, altered the emphasis of the company's recording policy, concentrating on more commercially oriented types of African-American music, but jazz remained important under the supervision of Ozzie Cadena, who controlled artists and repertory from 1954 to 1959. Cadena instigated reissues on LP of major recordings of the 1940s and organized important bop sessions by Kenny Clarke (1954–6), Cannonball Adderley (1955), and Yusef Lateef (1957, 1959). Lubinsky established a subsidiary label, World wide, in 1958. After working for other organizations Mendelsohn returned to the company in 1960 and was responsible for its development of the largest catalogue of black gospel music; from this time jazz and other secular music began to figure less prominently. Surprisingly, the company nevertheless recorded isolated free-jazz sessions by Sun Ra (1961) and Bill Dixon and Archie Shepp (both 1964). Lubinsky died in 1974, and the following year Savoy's entire catalogue was purchased by Arista, which began a systematic program of reissues. This was continued by the company Muse (ii), which acquired the repertory around 1985. LP reissues were also made in Europe by RCA and under the Savoy name in Japan.

In 1991 Nippon Columbia acquired Savoy from Muse and initiated another program of reissues, on compact disc. The company also made new recordings, among them albums by Marc Copland and Ralph Moore. All these releases appeared under the label name Savoy Jazz; catalogue numbers for the reissues began at 101, with an SV prefix, while new issues had a CY prefix and a numbering series associated with Nippon Columbia's label Denon. A later generation of reissues came from the Time-Warner-Atlantic conglomerate; these were produced by Orrin Keepnews and returned to the high standard of documentation for which the Arista reissue series was known.

BIBLIOGRAPHY

"Savoy Stomp Off with 28 Doubles," *Jazz Circle News*, no.11 (1978), 12
A. Shaw: "Savoy Records of Newark, New Jersey," *Honkers and Shouters: the Golden Years of Rhythm and Blues* (New York, 1978), 343
M. Ruppli: *The Savoy Label: a Discography* (Westport, CT, and London, 1980)
C. Sheridan: "Savoy Records: the Hidden Treasures," *JJI*, xxxiii (1980), no.10, p.17; no.12, p.18
J. Levenson: "Blue Notes: Nippon Columbia Buys Savoy Jazz Catalog," *Billboard*, ciii (16 March 1991), 49
J. Nash: "Denon Records Purchases the Savoy Record Label," *JT*, viii/5 (1991), 38
A. Fraga, A. Tomas, and M. Carton: "Entretien avec Lee Magid: il était une foi ..." *Soul Bag*, no.33 (1994), 18

HOWARD RYE, BK

Savoy Ballroom. The name of several ballrooms, notably ones in Chicago and New York; *see* Nightclubs and other venues.

Savoy Sultans (i). Swing band. Led by Al Cooper, it was formed from a group for which Willie Bryant and John Hammond arranged an audition at the Savoy Ballroom, New York, where it became resident as the Savoy Sultans in September 1937. It comprised two trumpets, three reed instruments, and a rhythm section that occasionally included a guitar; Grachan Moncur (double bass) was among its founding members. The principal soloists were Rudy Williams (alto saxophone), Sam Massenberg (trumpet), Cyril Haynes (piano), and, successively, Ed McNeil, Sam Simmons, Skinny Brown, and George Kelly (tenor saxophone), while Cooper sometimes performed clarinet solos. The band, which was extremely popular with dancers at the Savoy Ballroom and was also much admired by other musicians, made several recordings between 1938 and 1941 (Kelly joined in this last year) and continued performing until around 1946. It played simple, straightforward written arrangements in the powerful swing style that came to be known as jump.

SELECTED RECORDINGS

(all issued under A. Cooper's name)

The Thing/Gettin' in the Groove (1938, Decca 7525); Jumpin' at the Savoy/We'd rather jump than swing (1939, Decca 2526); Jumpin' the Blues/When I grow too old to dream (1939, Decca 2930); Wishing and crying for you/Sophisticated Jump (1940, Decca 3274); Second Balcony Jump/Jackie Boy (1941, Decca 8545)

BIBLIOGRAPHY

McCarthyB
S. Dance: Liner notes, *Jumpin' at the Savoy* (MCA 1345, 1982)
C. Deffaa: "Sultan of Sax," *MR*, xvii/6 (1990), 11; repr. in *In the Mainstream: 18 Portraits in Jazz* (Metuchen, NJ, and London, 1992), 203

JOHNNY SIMMEN

Savoy Sultans (ii). Swing band. It was formed by Panama Francis to play at a concert in New York in 1974 and began performing regularly in 1979. It consisted of two trumpets, three reed instruments, and a rhythm section (including guitar). Among the members were Irvin Stokes, Franc Williams, George Kelly (who had also worked with Al Cooper's Savoy Sultans), John Smith, Red Richards, and Bill Pemberton. The group toured under Francis's direction and recorded under various leaders in Europe, and it played regularly at the Rainbow Room, New York, between 1980 and 1987. It played exactly in the spirit of the first Savoy Sultans, emphasizing the strong relationship between jazz and dancing, and it became one of the best swing and dance bands of its time. Its repertory included compositions by Kelly and other members of the group.

SELECTED RECORDINGS

P. Francis: *Gettin' in the Groove* (1979, BB 33320–21); G. Kelly: *George Kelly in Cimiez* (1979, BB 33161); J. Witherspoon: *Jimmy Witherspoon* (1980, BB 33177); P. Francis: *Grooving* (1982, Stash 218); *Everything Swings* (1984, Stash 233)

BIBLIOGRAPHY

I. Gitler: Liner notes, *Grooving* (Stash 218, 1982)
G. Giddins: *Rhythm-a-ning: Jazz Tradition and Innovation in the '80s* (New York, and Oxford, England, 1985), 12

For further recordings and bibliography *see* Francis, Panama.

JOHNNY SIMMEN

Sawada, Shungo (*b* Tokyo, 10 Feb 1930). Japanese guitarist and leader. He took up guitar at the age of 12, spent much time listening to jazz on the radio, and then began playing at military bases, where, in 1957, he took lessons from a former member of Chico Hamilton's band. A pioneer of modern jazz guitar in Japan, he formed the group Double Beats in 1954 and from 1966 led a quintet; Shotaro Moriyasu, Norio Maeda, Akitoshi Igarashi, and Motohiko Hino were among his sidemen at various times. His recordings as a leader include the albums *Shungo Sawada vs Sadanori Nakamure* (1975, Tei. GM5003) and *Shungo* (1983, Denon YX7342). Sawada performed in Japan with Benny Goodman, Stan Getz, Helen Merrill, Oscar Peterson's trio, Dizzy Gillespie, Thad Jones, and Sonny Stitt, among others, and from 1981 he was a member of Maeda's Wind Breakers. He established a recording company and label, Elec (1972), produced jazz festivals, and became the principal of Roots College of Music, a vocational school in Tokyo. In 1996 he formed a new quintet.

KAZUNORI SUGIYAMA

Saxello. A variant of the B♭ soprano saxophone; *see* Saxophone, §6(v).

Saxhorn. A family of valved brass instruments, designed by Adolphe Sax and first manufactured between 1843 and 1855, having a tapering bore, a bell of moderate flare (usually facing upwards), a deep cup-shaped mouthpiece, and usually three piston valves. The Tuba and related instruments are sometimes referred to as members of the saxhorn family; organologically, both families of instruments are classified as valved bugle horns.

Of the entire range of saxhorns (from soprano to contrabass, pitched alternately in B♭ and E♭), those most commonly found in jazz are the B♭ baritone and the E♭ alto or tenor (known in colloquial American usage as the "peck horn"); they are normally referred to as "horns" rather than "saxhorns." The name "baritone horn" is commonly applied indifferently to the baritone saxhorn and the euphonium in the USA, where makers have minimized the structural differences between the two; indeed "baritone" has become the normal term for the valved instrument pitched in B♭, and makers simply offer a range of instruments of different bores, sometimes designating the largest "euphoniums."

Saxhorns were originally intended for use in military music and found their way thence into brass and other wind bands, and from there into early jazz parade bands. The first Onward Brass Band, formed in 1885, was typical of New Orleans brass bands in including alto and baritone horns, and Feather records Eubie Blake's recollection of the use of these instruments in early jazz. They are found as late as 1946 on recordings made by the re-created Original Zenith Brass Band, on which Harrison Barnes played euphonium or baritone horn, Isidore Barbarin alto horn and mellophone, and Joe Howard tuba. Later use of saxhorns in jazz has been rare. The alto horn has been played by Dick Cary (on Bobby Hackett's *Gotham Jazz Scene*, 1957, Cap. T857) and Kate Westbrook (on Mike Westbrook's *On Duke's Birthday*, 1984, HA 2012). Paul Rutherford has played euphonium, recording duos with Paul Lovens (1976–7) and an unaccompanied solo album *Neuph* (1978, Sweet Folk & Country 092).

BIBLIOGRAPHY

L. Feather: *The Book of Jazz: a Guide to the Entire Field* (New York, 1955, 2/1965 as *The Book of Jazz from Then till Now: a Guide to the Entire Field*)

CLIFFORD BEVAN

Saxophone [sax]. A single-reed instrument invented by Adolphe Sax around 1840. Although it has remained a peripheral instrument in the classical music tradition, the saxophone has played a leading role in jazz, and it is here that its technical and expressive potential has been most fully explored.

This article deals with the members of the saxophone family in order of their importance in jazz. Reference is made to specific recordings only to exemplify unusual or particularly important uses of the instruments or to illustrate the use of rare types of saxophone; for numerous recorded examples of saxophone playing see the lists following entries on individual saxophonists.

1. The saxophone family: (i) Structure and compass (ii) General history. 2. The tenor saxophone. 3. The alto saxophone. 4. The soprano saxophone. 5. The baritone saxophone. 6. Other saxophones: (i) The C-melody saxophone (ii) The bass saxophone (iii) The sopranino saxophone (iv) The contrabass saxophone (v) The saxello (vi) The manzello (vii) The stritch (viii) The slide saxophone.

1. The saxophone family.

(i) Structure and compass. All members of the saxophone family have a conical tube of wide bore, made of metal, and a single reed; this combination of characteristics puts them in an instrumental category of their own. They overblow at the octave to yield the second register. The body of the saxophone is made of thin metal, commonly brass, flaring slightly at the bell. It has between 18 and 21 tone-holes controlled by keys (some that open holes and some that close holes), and two small "octave" or speaker keys at the mouthpiece end, which facilitate the production of notes in the high register. The fingering is based on that of the simple-system oboe combined with the Boehm system for the right hand, but a number of modifications have been made to the basic system by different instrument builders.

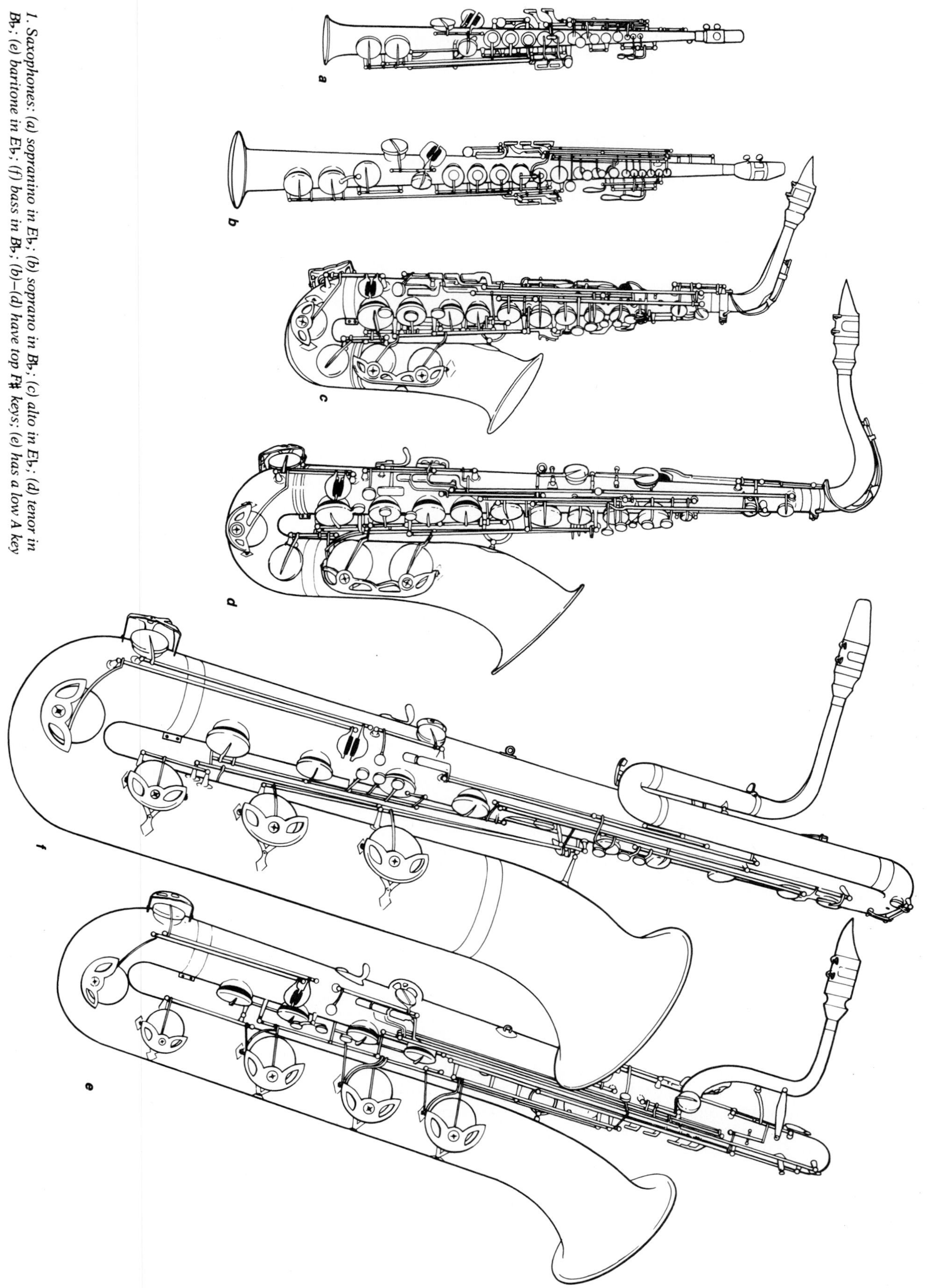

1. Saxophones: (a) sopranino in E♭; (b) soprano in B♭; (c) alto in E♭; (d) tenor in B♭; (e) baritone in E♭; (f) bass in B♭; (b)–(d) have top F♯ keys; (e) has a low A key

2. *The Weintraub Syncopators in 1933 with (left to right) bass, baritone, two tenor, two alto, and soprano saxophones*

The larger saxophones, because of the length of their tubes, have a U-bend (usually in the region of the third lowest tone-hole), a forward-tilting bell, and a detachable crook for the section above the main tone-holes. Even the soprano and sopranino instruments have sometimes been made in this configuration for the sake of uniformity, though a straight design without a crook, similar to that of the clarinet, is more characteristic.

The saxophone mouthpiece, originally made of wood but now commonly of ebonite or hard rubber (and sometimes of metal, glass, or plastic), is similar to that of the clarinet, though it has different relative proportions and interior shape. It slides over the top of the mouthpipe, which is lapped with a thin cork sheet to make an airtight joint, and the position of the mouthpiece may be minutely adjusted to allow for a certain degree of fine tuning. The variety of mouthpiece and ligature designs available, the style and hardness of the reed selected, and the relatively loose embouchure required (which gives greater flexibility of timbre, intonation, and vibrato than any other wind instrument) allow the player to shape a thoroughly individual sound; in many instances an innovative jazz saxophonist has been able to develop his own instantly recognizable style of playing, which his followers have then imitated.

The saxophone family as patented was of 14 instruments, from sopranino to contrabass, pitched alternately in F and C or E♭ and B♭; the written compass of the entire family is the same – normally *b*♭ to *f'''*, though some instruments have *a* as the lowest note and some players can extend the range to *d''''* or even *f''''* – and all but the orchestral soprano in C require transposition. The basic sounding ranges of the principal instruments discussed in this article are: sopranino in E♭, *d*♭*'–a*♭*'''*; soprano in B♭, *a*♭*–e*♭*'''*; alto in E♭, *d*♭*–a*♭*''*; tenor in C (C-melody saxophone), *B*♭*–f''*; tenor in B♭, *A*♭*–e*♭*''*; baritone in E♭, *C–a'*; bass in B♭, *A*♭*'–e*♭*'*; contrabass in E♭, *D*♭*'–a*♭.

There have been few technical developments to the saxophone in the 20th century that have affected the playing of jazz musicians. A general improvement in the mechanism has allowed smoother, faster playing, especially in the extreme low and high registers, and the addition of a high F♯ key on many models from the 1970s has extended the upper range. On the whole, however, the instrument is the same as it was in the 1920s. Plastic alto saxophones were available, particularly in the 1950s, as inexpensive student models.

From the 1960s a variety of electronic and electric attachments have been devised to modify the sound of the saxophone, but they have had short-lived success; most saxophonists content themselves with amplifying the instrument in the usual way. A few players, among them Wayne Shorter, Sonny Rollins, Tom Scott, and Michael Brecker, have explored the possibilities of synthesizer controllers in the shape of wind instruments, of which the best-known are the Lyricon (*see* SYNTHESIZER, §2(iii)) and the EWI.

(ii) General history. Of the group of saxophones pitched in F and C only the tenor in C (or C-melody) saxophone has been widely used in jazz; it is the group of instruments in E♭ and B♭ used in military music that has gained currency. In the 1920s virtually all the E♭ and B♭ members of the family (including the cumbersome bass) and the C-melody saxophone were found in jazz and dance bands, but from the 1930s jazz musicians have generally concentrated mainly on the B♭ tenor and E♭ alto and then on the soprano and baritone instruments; other saxophones have been little used but several have been taken up by free-jazz players for the timbral variety they offer (see §6 below). Early jazz woodwind players tended to specialize in the clarinet. They used the saxophone instead where its greater volume was needed or to provide a sweet, syrupy sound with a wide, fast vibrato on certain numbers.

Many techniques that came to be associated with jazz, including playing in the highest register and FALSE FINGERING, were in use among classical players by 1900, though these techniques did not become commonplace in jazz until many years later. The C-melody saxophonist and vaudeville performer Rudy Wiedoeft began recording in 1916 and took some part in bringing about the increasing popularity of the saxophone; his playing is characterized by remarkably fast tonguing, displayed in virtuoso novelty and rag pieces, many of which were his own compositions. He became well known to jazz musicians and even recorded with some (including the Cotton Pickers in 1923).

During the 1920s the saxophone came to be more widely used in jazz and commercial dance music. Such effects as Slap-tonguing, the Smear, and whinnying sounds were used in both contexts, but within a decade had come to be considered "corny," as a smoother approach gained currency. By 1930 the saxophone had become an established member of jazz ensembles, and any large group had a saxophone section consisting of alto, tenor, and baritone, with the soprano or, more often, the clarinet to give color. Such a section has remained a permanent feature of the jazz big band.

Although the saxophone's ensemble position is important, its major role in jazz is as a solo instrument (many soloists have also played in the ranks of large ensembles or big bands). The most significant soloists – Coleman Hawkins, Lester Young, and Sonny Rollins (tenor), Charlie Parker (alto), and John Coltrane (tenor and soprano) – influenced players of all saxophones and even of other instruments.

The saxophone has occasionally been used as an unaccompanied solo instrument (without rhythm section), early examples being Coleman Hawkins's *Hawk Variation* (1945, Baronet TR4) and *Picasso* (*c*1948, Clef [unnumbered].) Beginning in 1957 Sonny Rollins made the unaccompanied solo a characteristic element of his playing, and from the late 1960s members of the Association for the Advancement of Creative Musicians (notably Anthony Braxton) and other free-jazz players such as Steve Lacy began to give entire concerts and to record entire albums as unaccompanied soloists.

It is easier to attain a professional level of proficiency on more than one member of the saxophone family than it is in the case of any other family of instruments. Many players have been fluent on several saxophones, and it is not at all unusual to find a musician playing, for example, alto and tenor, and perhaps also soprano (and certainly clarinet), in early jazz, or alto, tenor, and soprano in a modern combo. Other types of doubling, involving the baritone and bass instruments, occur as well, though less commonly. For this reason, as well as because of the wide influence of important players, there has been considerable sharing of techniques and imitating of sound among saxophonists. A logical development from this trend was the formation of ensembles made up principally (though not exclusively) of saxophones, in which harmony and bass lines were usually played on saxophones rather than on the instruments that conventionally play those lines in other ensembles. A non-improvising vaudeville group, the Six Brown Brothers, made ragtime recordings between 1914 and 1920, but of greatest interest are the English trio SOS (1973–5) and especially the World Saxophone Quartet, which from its inception in 1976 stimulated the formation of many other such groups, including notably the 29th Street and ROVA saxophone quartets.

2. The tenor saxophone. In ensembles the role of the tenor saxophone, when not playing a solo, has generally been that of a supporting voice, playing, for example, a line beneath the lead alto saxophone in a big band, or doubling a trumpet melody an octave lower in rendering a bop theme. But far more important is its solo role. The tenor saxophone is the principal solo voice, not only within its own section of a big band but within the band as a whole; from the swing era onwards it has often figured equally prominently in small groups. It is perhaps rivaled only by the trumpet as the most important wind instrument in jazz.

3. John Coltrane playing tenor saxophone

Coleman Hawkins is generally regarded as the first major jazz improviser on the saxophone (though he denied this himself, mentioning Prince Robinson, Happy Caldwell, and Stump Evans). The importance of Hawkins's achievement lies in his developing an original style designed specifically for the saxophone, rather than adapting the style of the clarinet (which like many saxophonists he played early in his career). Hawkins's playing is identifiable by its powerful emotion and drive, and the huge sound he produced. His highly original technical patterns for the most part display great harmonic awareness and are not designed merely to show off speed of fingering or tonguing. His arpeggiated lines obviously owe something to clarinet styles of the day, but the tenor saxophone was always his specialty and after 1924 he was rarely heard on any other instrument. He favored a wide vibrato and large, dark tone. During the 1920s he became technically more accomplished and progressed from a heavy to a smoother articulation, abandoning the occasional use of such devices as slap-tonguing. He extended his command of the upper range, as his famous recording of *Body and Soul* (1939, Bb 10523) demonstrates (it ascends to *g‴*, sounding *f′*).

By the end of the 1920s Hawkins had become the model for most jazz tenor saxophonists. Many players developed their own styles, but the influence of Hawkins is apparent in the basic approach of Charlie Barnet, Tex Beneke, Chu Berry, Herschel Evans, Vido Musso, and Ben Webster (who was also indebted to the alto saxophonist Johnny Hodges), and a later generation, including Arnett Cobb, Illinois Jacquet (who was also influenced by Lester Young), Flip Phillips, Ike Quebec, Al Sears, Buddy Tate, and the important modern stylist Don Byas. Bud Freeman began as a disciple of Hawkins but soon went his own way and is often mistakenly referred to as an influence on Lester Young, who became the next important figure in the development of the tenor saxophone in jazz.

Young was born only five years after Hawkins, but his influence was not widely apparent until the late 1930s because, until he made his first recording in 1936, he was little known outside Minneapolis and the Midwest. His style was soon adopted by younger players as an alternative to that of Hawkins. In important matters – tone, phrasing, melody, rhythm – Young's playing differed strikingly from Hawkins's, showing the influence of the C-melody saxophonist Frankie Trumbauer and the alto saxophonist Jimmy Dorsey. The essence of Young's tenor style was a smooth, singing tone of great beauty, in strong contrast to Hawkins's aggressive sound; Young achieved this originally using a metal mouthpiece but later changed to a hard rubber one made by Brilhart, which gave a darker effect. Instead of Hawkins's constant wide vibrato, Young's vibrato was very varied and fitted each phrase: many phrases had no vibrato at all, certain notes had a light, narrow vibrato, and some passages were highlighted by a wide vibrato close to Hawkins's style. Young was relatively unconcerned with the kind of technical and harmonic exploration that interested Hawkins and concentrated instead on the shaping of the melodic line, though his melodies always express a sophisticated understanding of the harmonic substructure.

Young's concepts of melody and phrasing were so persuasive that their influence extended far beyond saxophonists to jazz performance on many instruments. From about 1940 his authority is felt in the playing of his contemporary Budd Johnson (who earlier in his career was closer to Hawkins) and in that of the next two generations of saxophonists; these included Dexter Gordon and Charlie Parker (who also admired Hawkins's technical approach), and, during the mid-1940s, Gene Ammons, Al Cohn, John Coltrane, Allan Eager, Stan Getz (at first closer to Hawkins), Wardell Gray, Lee Konitz, Jackie McLean, Warne Marsh, James Moody, Art Pepper, Sonny Rollins (who, with Coltrane, studied the playing of Hawkins, and also Parker), Zoot Sims, Sonny Stitt, and countless others. The nature of the influence Young exercised on these players is, however, far more subtle than that of Hawkins on his followers: in the work of Cohn, Eager, Getz, Gray, Konitz, Marsh, and Pepper, Young's conception of tone shows clearly, yet by the mid-1940s Parker's bop playing on alto saxophone was perhaps a more powerful influence than Young's tenor style. And while Hawkins's influence remained strong for the first 20 years during which he recorded, Young's lasted at its height no more than ten.

After World War II Sonny Rollins combined the virtuosity, rhythmic complexity, and forceful wit of the alto saxophonist Charlie Parker with a gruff Hawkins-like sound and a Youngian sense of phrasing and structure. His authoritative personality has left its mark on most tenor saxophonists since the mid-1950s, including Joe Henderson, Roland Kirk, Yusef Lateef (known for his interest in Eastern traditional music), Barney Wilen, Joe Lovano, Joshua Redman, and many others.

John Coltrane was also influenced by Parker, but he soon began to move in different directions. Coltrane's sound (usually produced using a metal mouthpiece) had a biting quality and a fierce emotional cry. He liberally employed Overblowing, the high register, and Multiphonics. There is hardly a saxophonist in the late 20th century whose playing does not reflect the influence of Coltrane's sound and an awareness, at least, of his typical melodic formulas. Such players include Bob Berg, Michael Brecker, George Coleman, Dave Liebman, Joe Farrell, Sonny Fortune, Steve Grossman, Charles Lloyd, and Branford Marsalis. The highly original work of Coltrane's younger contemporary Wayne Shorter, a brilliant improviser and composer, seems to fall somewhere between Coltrane's and Rollins's, while the younger David Sanchez replicates a combination of their styles.

Many free-jazz tenor saxophonists derive their style from Coltrane or the alto player Ornette Coleman or both, but also influential is Albert Ayler, whose extreme and unique vocalistic sounds have been taken up most strikingly by David Murray. Other important free-jazz musicians to exploit such sounds are Pharoah Sanders, Archie Shepp, Jan Garbarek (all of whom also play soprano saxophone), Gato Barbieri (only in his early work), Willem Breuker, Peter Brötzmann, and Evan Parker. Later, as free-jazz techniques became absorbed into the mainstream, James Carter explored the incorporation of these vocalistic sounds into aggressive and audacious performances of jazz standards.

3. The alto saxophone. In big bands the role of the alto saxophone has generally been to lead the saxophone section. From the early period of jazz a number of players became recognized as much for their abilities as section leaders as for their prowess as soloists; these include Johnny Hodges (with Duke Ellington), Charlie Holmes (with Luis Russell), and Earle Warren (with Count Basie).

The solo tradition for the alto saxophone was established in the mid-1920s and the two principal innovators were Jimmy Dorsey and Frankie Trumbauer. Dorsey was a showy player who utilized multiphonics and false fingerings as early as 1926 on two versions of *That's no Bargain* recorded with Red Nichols (Bruns. 3407, PAct 36576). He owed some of his approach to Rudy Wiedoeft, and occasionally developed technical display pieces in a similar way – for example, the version of *I'm just wild about Harry* recorded in 1930 (Decca F1876), the second chorus of which involves a prepared virtuoso passage of triple-tonguing, perfectly executed. Trumbauer, who specialized in alto and tenor C-melody saxophones (see §6(i) below), introduced a new lightness and poise into saxophone playing; his clear tone and delicate, cantabile phrasing were as influential on alto as on tenor players.

Johnny Hodges joined Duke Ellington in 1928 and his creamy, elegant style soon became a trademark of Ellington's music. A pupil of Sidney Bechet, Hodges brought to his alto saxophone solos a mixture of Bechet's formulaic set-piece constructions (evolved for the soprano) and a singing blues style recognizable by the way in which he held and bent the pitch of long notes. Other leading alto saxophone soloists of the 1930s included Hilton Jefferson, Willie Smith, and the brilliant and stylish Benny Carter (who was equally proficient as a trumpeter).

Charlie Parker was the leading figure in the development of bop on the saxophone. His first recordings, from 1940, suggest the strong influence of Lester Young, but also individual qualities – an unprecedented technical virtuosity, lightness, wit (including the clever interpolation of humorous quotations), long lines, and passing dissonances – all of which were to be further explored as he matured. Parker's sound had a bite to it which offended many critics, but those who called his tone thin missed its body and carrying power, as well as its unique color and personality; to achieve it Parker generally used a hard rubber mouthpiece and a hard reed. His influence extended to the saxophonists Cannonball Adderley, Ornette Coleman, Eric Dolphy, Arne Domnérus, Lou Donaldson, Jackie McLean, Charles McPherson, Charlie Mariano, Sonny Stitt, and Phil Woods, and virtually all jazz players who came to maturity during the 1950s.

An alternative to Parker's approach for the alto instrument came indirectly from the tenor playing of Young, as adapted by Lee Konitz (on alto) and Warne Marsh (on tenor). Through working with their teacher Lennie Tristano, both men found that softer reeds and a smoother melodic style gave a different method of approaching bop. Art Pepper and Paul Desmond also found similar individual new directions.

Ornette Coleman's saxophone playing has been highly controversial, but he has affected musicians of many persuasions, even Coltrane and Rollins. When he came to prominence in the late 1950s he was playing a plastic saxophone with a rubber mouthpiece; by the 1970s he had adopted an instrument made by Selmer with a metal mouthpiece and a medium-soft reed. His basic sound, which has a singing, folklike quality, and his style remain unmistakable, but these have more to do with his conception of improvised melody than with any particular characteristic of the alto saxophone.

Eric Dolphy pursued Parker's style in a different direction. His rhythms and phrasing clearly derived from Parker but his choice of pitches was highly dissonant and unpredictable. He is widely admired, even among critics with whom free jazz generally finds little favor, for his technical achievements, which included an astounding ability to leap fluently between registers. Shortly after his death his approach found a new school of practioners among members of the Association for the Advancement of Creative Musicians, including Joseph Jarman and Roscoe Mitchell, and the Black Artists Group, including Oliver Lake and Julius Hemphill; in turn the most aggressive aspects of Hemphill's style have spun off onto such players as Tim Berne and, especially, John Zorn.

Among the followers of Coleman are John Tchicai, Marion Brown, Gennady Gol'shteyn, and Vladimir Chekasin. Jimmy Lyons retained an individual approach to free jazz, based on Parker with some touches of influence from Dolphy. Gary Bartz and Sonny Fortune both found highly individual adaptations of Coltrane's style for soprano and alto saxophones.

4. The soprano saxophone. The soprano saxophone is made in two designs, one straight, the other with an outward curve at the bell; it has a clear and somewhat strident sound, though the curved instrument is noticeably less strident than the straight one. It is notoriously difficult to pitch accurately. Played without vibrato it can sound remarkably similar to the oboe, but with the right combination of reed and "lay" of the mouthpiece and with vibrato it can emulate aspects of all the other saxophones.

The first important exponent of the soprano saxophone was Sidney Bechet, who achieved a high level of virtuosity and improvisational inventiveness on the instrument by 1923 when he made his first recordings. Bechet saw the soprano saxophone as complementary to the clarinet, which at first was his main instrument, and never developed a serious interest in the other saxophones. Nevertheless he influenced Johnny Hodges and other players, such as Don Redman, Woody Herman, and Charlie Barnet, all of whom played soprano and other saxophones. In the 1930s few saxophonists specialized on soprano, with the notable exception of Emmett Mathews, and during the 1940s and 1950s it became extremely rare.

The instrument was taken up again by the iconoclastic musician Steve Lacy and by others, including the Danish player Max Bruel, but it regained its popularity only after 1960 when John Coltrane (perhaps under Lacy's influence) began to play it: virtually every musician listed above as a follower of Coltrane plays the soprano as well as the tenor saxophone. Older players who had established their reputations on alto or tenor also took up the soprano, including Dexter Gordon, Budd Johnson, Oliver Nelson, Jerome Richardson, Sam Rivers, Lucky Thompson, and even (briefly) Cannonball Adderley and Sonny Rollins. Bob Wilber, perhaps the most accomplished of Bechet's pupils, with his band Soprano Summit (led jointly with Kenny Davern), did much to popularize the instrument among traditional and mainstream jazz players; Bechet himself, through his postwar residence in France, fueled an important (though imitative) school of European soprano players, among them Jean-Pierre Bonnel and Claude Luter, and the Englishman Wally Fawkes, all of whom played the instrument regularly in the 1970s and 1980s. It has been exploited in free jazz by Lacy and, as a result of Lacy's influence, by Evan Parker; during the 1970s Wayne Shorter and Dave Liebman came to prominence as players of the soprano, and shortly afterwards Jane Ira Bloom, with an individual style that centers on a powerful tone, joined the small ranks of soprano specialists.

5. The baritone saxophone. Despite its comparatively low range, the baritone saxophone functions far more often as a melodic instrument or an inner voice within a chordal texture than as a bass instrument. Exceptions to this occur, most frequently in Latin jazz, where the stinging crispness of its tone effectively carries ostinato bass lines, as for example at the beginning of Dizzy Gillespie's *Manteca* (1947, Vic. 20-3023). The baritone saxophone has been used mainly in larger ensembles, notably in the saxophone sections of big bands. The rich color of Harry Carney's baritone playing was a staple of Duke Ellington's band sound for 50 years and Jack Washington's filled an analogous role in Count Basie's orchestra. Both men were capable, though rarely used, soloists and in their way influential. It was not until the 1950s, with the emergence of Gerry Mulligan and Lars Gullin, that a clearly defined solo school of baritone playing emerged. Other baritone players of some importance include Serge Chaloff, Leo Parker, Cecil Payne, and Ronnie Ross. Pepper Adams was admired by many musicians on account of his hard-edged sound, virtuosity, and wit. During the 1960s Coltrane's influence came through in the baritone playing of Charles Davis, John Surman, and others. Later, Hamiet Bluiett became one of the few avant-garde musicians to specialize on baritone saxophone, using such radical virtuoso techniques as overblowing in the highest register. The instrument has also found some use in dixieland and mainstream ensembles from the 1960s; a notable soloist is

John Barnes, who has played with Alex Welsh and Humphrey Lyttelton. Since the 1980s Gary Smulyan has been prominent in big bands and bop bands in the New York area.

6. Other saxophones.

(i) The C-melody saxophone. This tenor saxophone survived in jazz well into the 1920s, when Frankie Trumbauer was its principal exponent. Although he played solo pieces in the virtuoso style of Rudy Wiedoeft he was mainly an improvising jazz musician. He developed a singing tone and legato style on the instrument, making ample use of portamento and other expressive devices; his improvisations employ a natural, vocalistic articulation and a dry wit, expressed in surprising pauses and unusual phrase lengths. Many players (both African-American and white) modeled elements of their style on his: Budd Johnson, Eddie Barefield, and Lester Young have all testified to the respect Trumbauer inspired as a jazz player.

Other musicians to use the instrument in the 1920s were Stump Evans (with King Oliver), Jack Pettis, and Spencer Clark (with the California Ramblers). In the 1980s it was used infrequently by the revivalists Bob Wilber and Kenny Davern.

(ii) The bass saxophone. The instrument has occasionally been used as a substitute for the tuba or double bass. Its first, and most significant, solo exponent was Adrian Rollini, who developed a role for it as a novelty instrument, and acquired a considerable degree of facility on it; he used slap-tonguing to achieve the effect of the tuba in playing a bass line, but in his solos emerged from the ensemble and played predominantly in the upper register, effectively within the range of the baritone. Other significant players of the instrument include Charlie Jackson (with King Oliver), Billy Fowler (in Fletcher Henderson's orchestra), Spencer Clark, and, later, Joe Rushton and Vince Giordano.

After World War II the bass saxophone was still used occasionally by Boyd Raeburn, Rushton (with Red Nichols in the 1950s), and Charlie Ventura. It was also the main instrument of the bandleader Harry Gold. In free jazz Anthony Braxton has used it, as have Roscoe Mitchell and Joseph Jarman of the Art Ensemble of Chicago and Vinny Golia. In 1986 the BBC made an influential film about the use of the instrument in jazz, *The Lowest of the Low*.

(iii) The sopranino saxophone. The highest-pitched of the saxophone family, the sopranino has a range about an octave above that of the alto. It has been adopted as a doubling instrument by Joseph Jarman (from around 1969) and Anthony Braxton (from around 1973), who both use it regularly (together with many other wind instruments) to supply timbral contrast in their improvisations. Braxton plays the sopranino intermittently on his album *The Montreux–Berlin Concerts* (1975–6, Ari. 5002); on the track *29 M 36* it contrasts sharply with the sound of the contrabass. John Purcell, as a new member of the World Saxophone Quartet in the 1990s, has focused on the sopranino instrument.

(iv) The contrabass saxophone. Its range is about an octave below that of the baritone instrument and like the sopranino it has been used by Braxton (from around 1976) for purposes of timbral variety; he plays it on *73̄S Kelvin* on the anthology *Wildflowers 2: the New York Loft Jazz Sessions* (1976, Douglas 7046).

4. Roland Kirk playing the stritch

(v) The saxello. A variant of the B♭ soprano saxophone, it was manufactured by King from the 1920s, and the name was the company's trademark. It has a gentle curve in the neck, and the bell faces outwards. It is a relatively rare instrument but has been used by Bennie Maupin and Elton Dean.

(vi) The manzello. A modified version of the saxello, it was used (and named) by Roland Kirk. It has a larger bell than the saxello, which gives it a broader sound. Kirk is its sole exponent; on the track *Parisian Thoroughfare* on Jaki Byard's album *The Jaki Byard Experience* (1968, Prst. 7615) he changes between several wind instruments during the raucous introduction, plays manzello followed by tenor saxophone in the statement of the theme, and then improvises a fine bop solo on the same two saxophones.

(vii) The stritch. The stritch is Roland Kirk's modified version of the straight E♭ alto saxophone manufactured by Buescher in the late 1920s. He may be heard playing a solo on the instrument on *Skater's Waltz* from his album *Kirk's Work* (1961, Prst. 7210). Late in his career, after he suffered a stroke, his further adaptations to the original instrument involved the addition of extra keywork to allow one-handed playing.

(viii) The slide saxophone. Although examples of various types of slide saxophone were made in France during the 1920s, the only instrument to have been adopted in jazz is a

variant of the B♭ soprano, developed and played by Snub Mosley. It has a conventional saxophone mouthpiece and crook, which is attached to the head of a straight tube, held vertically, with a longitudinal opening instead of tone-holes. A slide runs inside the tube and is manipulated by the player's right hand; as the slide is pushed in, it progressively closes the longitudinal opening on the instrument's body so that the air column is restricted within the body and slide. The problem of pitching notes accurately made it a difficult instrument to master and even Mosley (who used it mostly for ballads) produced performances that were badly out of tune.

For further illustrations *see* Byas, don; Coltrane, john; Domnérus, arne; Foster, pops; Garbarek, jan; Giuffre, jimmy; Gordon, dexter; Lacy, steve; Mulligan, gerry; Pepper, art; Rollins, sonny; Shorter, wayne; Sims, zoot; Williams, mary lou; and Young, lester.

BIBLIOGRAPHY

J.-E. Berendt: *Das Jazzbuch: Entwicklung und Bedeutung der Jazzmusik* (Frankfurt am Main, Germany, 1953, rev. and enlarged 5/1981 as *Das grosse Jazzbuch: von New Orleans bis Jazz Rock*, Eng. trans., 1982, as *The Jazz Book: from New Orleans to Fusion and Beyond*)
L. Feather: *The Book of Jazz: a Guide to the Entire Field* (New York, 1957, 2/1965 as *The Book of Jazz from Then till Now: a Guide to the Entire Field*)
H. Miedema: *Jazz Styles and Analysis: Alto Sax* (Chicago, 1975) [125 transcrs. of solos by 103 players]
J. Viera: *Das Saxophon im Jazz* (Vienna, 1977)
M. Cuscuna: Liner notes, R. Kirk: *Pre-Rahsaan* (Prst. 24080, 1978)
D. Sickler: *The Artistry of John Coltrane* (New York, 1979)
P. Cohen: "The Saga of the F Alto Saxophone," *Saxophone Journal*, v/1 (1980), 10
P. Bate and J. B. Robinson: "Saxophone," *GroveI*
P. Cohen: "Vintage Saxophones Revisited," *Saxophone Journal*, x/2 (1985), 4; x/3 (1985), 4
H. R. Gee: *Saxophone Soloists and their Music, 1844–1985* (Bloomington, IN, 1986)

LEWIS PORTER

Sayama, Masahiro (*b* Amagasaki, Japan, 26 Nov 1953). Japanese pianist. He learned piano from the age of six. Inspired to play jazz at the age of 13 when he watched the film *The Glenn Miller Story*, he formed an amateur jazz band in high school, studied composition at Kunitachi College of Music in Tokyo, and embarked on a professional career in 1972. He performed with Toshiyuki Honda (1974–6), Shigeharu Mukai (1975–9), the tenor saxophonist Kazunori Takeda (1978–83), and others. In 1984 he worked with Shuichi Murakami's group Ponta Box, and in 1987 he began leading his own quartet or quintet. Sayama became a member of Masahiko Osaka's trio in 1991.

SELECTED RECORDINGS

As leader: *Hymn for Nobody* (1994, JVC VICJ210)
As sideman with S. Murakami: *Ponta Box* (1994, JVC VICJ199); *Ponta Box: the One* (1996, JVC VICJ240)

KAZUNORI SUGIYAMA

Sayles, Emanuel (René) [Manny] (*b* Donaldsonville, LA, 31 Jan 1907; *d* New Orleans, 5 Oct 1986). Banjoist and guitarist, son of George Sayles. He taught himself banjo and guitar and in 1923 toured to Pensacola, Florida. After returning to New Orleans he worked with Fate Marable and Sidney Desvigne on the SS *Capitol* and with Armand Piron on the SS *J.S.*; he also played with Desvigne at the Pythian Roof Garden in New Orleans. His banjo playing may be heard on the recordings he made in 1929 with the Jones and Collins Astoria Hot Eight. In 1933 he joined Piron's band at a country club in Metarie, Louisiana, and remained there for five years. In 1938 or 1939 he participated in another lengthy Mississippi cruise when Peter Bocage took over Piron's band on the *J.S.* He moved in 1939 to Chicago, where he worked with many leaders, including John Lindsay, and led his own small band. In 1949 he returned to New Orleans and recorded as a leader (1961–3), notably in a trio session featuring banjo duets with Narvin Kimball (accompanied by double bass).

Sayles was equally accomplished as a guitarist, and displayed a light chordal style in ensembles and a formidable single-string solo technique on the acoustic instrument; his work is especially well demonstrated on *Sayles' Broken String Blues*, made as a member of the trio led by Louis Cottrell, Jr. (1961). He worked in Cleveland with Punch Miller (1960), traveled to Japan with George Lewis (i) (1963–4), and toured with Sweet Emma Barrett (1964). From 1965 to 1968 he was again in Chicago as a house musician at Jazz Ltd. He appeared regularly at Preservation Hall, New Orleans, in 1968 and the following year performed as a soloist in Britain. During the 1970s and 1980s he continued to play, mainly in New Orleans, though he also toured with the Preservation Hall Jazz Band (1971, 1979) and others. Among the many leaders with whom he recorded were Miller (1960, 1962), Kid Howard (1961), Bocage (1961–2, 1964), Barrett (1961, 1963–4), Paul Barbarin, John Casimir, and Jim Robinson (all 1962), Lewis (1962–4), Louis Nelson (1963, 1971), Kid Thomas Valentine (1971, *c*1974, 1975, 1981, 1983), and Earl Hines (1975); he may be seen with Valentine's Preservation Hall band in the video released as *Jazz Parades: Feet Don't Fail Me Now* (*c*1998), from Alan Lomax's documentary series "American Patchwork" (1990).

Oral history material in *LNT*.

See also Banjo; for illustration *see* Humphrey.

SELECTED RECORDINGS

As leader: *Banjo on Bourbon Street* (1963, Nobility 701)
As sideman: Jones and Collins Astoria Hot Eight: Astoria Strut (1929, Vic. V38576); Damp Weather (1929, Bb 10952); P. Humphrey: *Percy Humphrey's Crescent City Joymakers* (1961, Riv. 9378); L. Cottrell, Jr.: *Bourbon Street Parade* (1961, Riv. 9385), incl. Sayles' Broken String Blues; on B. Pierce and D. Pierce/J. Robinson: *Jazz at Preservation Hall*, ii (1962, Atl. 1409), Robinson: Gettysburg March; P. Barbarin/P. Miller: *Jazz at Preservation Hall*, iii (1962, Atl. 1410), incl. Barbarin: Give it up, The Second Line; J. Casimir: on *John Casimir's Young Tuxedo Jazz Band* (1962, Icon 11), Fidgety Feet/St. Louis Blues; E. Hines: *Earl Hines in New Orleans* (1975, UP International 5057/8), incl. Bouncing for Panassié

BIBLIOGRAPHY

ChiltonW
H. Friedwald: Liner notes, L. Cottrell: *Bourbon Street Parade* (Riv. 9385, 1961)
T. Stagg and C. Crump: *New Orleans, the Revival: a Tape and Discography of Negro Traditional Jazz Recorded in New Orleans or by New Orleans Bands, 1937–1972* (n.p. [London], 1973)
B. Turnock: "Emanuel Sayles Reminiscing," *Fn*, xi/4 (1980), 4
Obituaries: L. Whittaker, *Fn*, xviii/2 (1986–7), 17; J. Simmen, *BHcF*, no.347 (1987), 22
W. Carter: *Preservation Hall: Music from the Heart* (Wheatley, Oxford, England, and New York, 1991)

HOWARD RYE

Sayles, George(, Sr.) (*b* New Orleans, *c*1880; *d* 1955 or 1956). Guitarist, father of Emanuel Sayles. He was a member of the Silver Leaf Orchestra from about 1898 until it disbanded in 1918, when he retired, though he played occasionally during the early 1920s.

MARCEL JOLY

Sbarbaro, Tony [Antonio; Spargo, Tony] (*b* New Orleans, 27 June 1897; *d* New York, 30 Oct 1969). Drummer. He began playing in New Orleans with the Frayle Brothers' Band (1911) and later with Papa Jack Laine's Reliance Band,

Merritt Brunies, and the pianist Carl Randall. In 1916 he moved to Chicago to join the Original dixieland jazz band. He was the only original member of the group to remain with the band until its final dissolution in 1956. Sbarbaro also played in New York, often appearing at Nick's, where he worked as a bandleader from at least 1939 and also as a sideman with many dixieland musicians, including Phil Napoleon, Big Chief Moore, the pianist Mike Koscalzo (with whom he recorded as a drummer and kazoo player in 1945), Muggsy Spanier, Miff Mole, and Pee Wee Russell (these last three together in 1946). In 1943 he took part in two recording sessions with Eddie Condon's band. Later he performed and recorded with Napoleon (intermittently, 1946–59) and Pee Wee Erwin (intermittently, 1954–6, 1959), recorded with Connee Boswell (1957), and made further appearances at dixieland clubs in New York with Jimmy Lytell (1957–8) and Tony Parenti. He ceased performing in the early 1960s.

Sbarbaro's early playing contrasts sharply with that of his New Orleans contemporaries Baby Dodds and Zutty Singleton. His showy technique and exuberant improvisatory style are rooted in the ragtime playing of such drummers as James Lent, Buddy Gilmore, and John Lucas. His earliest recordings, notably *Indiana*, *Dixie Jass Band One-step*, and *Tiger Rag* (all 1917), belie the idea that the equipment and playing techniques of drummers were restricted in early recording studios. His cymbal, woodblock, cowbells, snare drum, and bass drum (played by double-drumming) are clearly heard on these tracks.

Oral history material in *LNT*.

SELECTED RECORDINGS

As sideman: Original Dixieland Jazz Band: Indiana (1917, Col. A2297); Dixie Jass Band One-step (1917, Vic. 18255); Tiger Rag (1917, Aeolian Voc. 1206); Crazy Blues (1921, Vic. 18729); Fidgety Feet (1936, Vic. 25668); Original Dixieland One-step (1936, Vic. 25502); E. Condon: Mandy Make up your Mind (1943, Com. 604)

BIBLIOGRAPHY

ChiltonW; *FeatherE*
R. Goffin: *La Nouvelle-Orléans: capitale du jazz* (New York, 1946), 201
F. Manskleid: "Sixty Years of Tony Sbarbaro," *JM*, iv/9 (1958), 24
H. H. Lange: *The Fabulous Fives* (Lübbecke, Germany, 1959, rev. 2/1978, by R. Jewson, D. Hamilton-Smith, and R. Webb) [discography]
H. O. Brunn: *The Story of the Original Dixieland Jazz Band* (Baton Rouge, LA, 1960/*R*1977)
T. D. Brown: *A History and Analysis of Jazz Drumming to 1942* (diss., U. of Michigan, 1976)
W. W. Vaché, Sr.: *Pee Wee Erwin: this Horn for Hire* (Metuchen, New Jersey, 1987)
——: "Jazz Pioneer and King of the Kazoo," *MR*, xxii/5 (1995), 30

T. DENNIS BROWN/BK

Scala. Record label. It was established in England in 1911. At first the catalogue consisted of German recordings pressed in Germany, but when production resumed after World War I the repertory was expanded, drawing on American material taken from Gennett and Vocalion and including a few jazz items issued under pseudonyms. Among items recorded in London were the first made by a racially integrated jazz band, a group of British and expatriate African-American musicians who recorded under the leadership of Victor Vorzanger in mid-1922. The label was discontinued late in 1927. (B. Rust: *The American Record Label Book* (New Rochelle, NY, 1978), 275)

HOWARD RYE

Scat singing. A technique of jazz Singing in which onomatopoeic or nonsense syllables are sung to improvised melodies. Some writers have traced scat singing back to the practice, common in West African musics, of translating percussion patterns into vocal lines by assigning syllables to characteristic rhythms. However, since this allows little scope for melodic improvisation and the earliest recorded examples of jazz scat singing involved the free invention of rhythm, melody, and syllables, it is more likely that the technique began in the USA as singers imitated the sounds of jazz instrumentalists.

Scat singing was used in early New Orleans jazz, as demonstrated by Jelly Roll Morton in his *Scat Song* (1938, Library of Congress). Morton gave the credit for originating the practice to Joe Simms of Vicksburg. The most celebrated early instances are by Louis Armstrong, whose highly successful recording *Heebie Jeebies* (1926, OK 8300) established his reputation as a jazz singer; his early scat solos rival his trumpet improvisations in virtuosity, range of feeling, and variety of attacks and timbres (see ex.1, which illustrates

Ex.1 From L. Armstrong: *Hotter than that* (1927, OK 8535); transcr. J. B. Robinson

his clear imitation of a trumpet rip). Armstrong started a vogue for scat singing. It was taken up to particular effect by the Philadelphia-based Washboard Rhythm Kings, whose *Every Man for Himself* (1931, Vic. 22719) has Buck Franklin scatting as a member of the ensemble and performing in duet with the trumpet and the alto saxophone.

In the swing era, scat singing was popularized by Cab Calloway in recordings such as *The Scat Song* (1932, Bruns. 6272) and *Zaz zuh zaz* (1934, Vic. 24557); the latter title features call-and-response scatting between leader and band and also used ensemble scat singing as an arranging device, an approach later copied by commercial big bands. Scat singing was employed extensively by jump and jive bands such as the Spirits of Rhythm; their *Scattin' the Blues* (1945, Black & White 23) features Leo Watson, whose inventive and uninhibited scat singing influenced the "vout" language of Slim Gaillard, with whom he worked in the mid-1940s.

As jazz improvisation grew increasingly complex, scat singing followed suit. Ella Fitzgerald in particular made a specialty of imitating various jazz instruments and even particular soloists, thereby greatly expanding the range of timbres and attacks in scat singing (ex.2); her approach was

Ex.2 From E. Fitzgerald: *Flying Home* (1945, Decca 23956); transcr. J. B. Robinson

extremely influential and closely imitated even by such otherwise distinctive vocalists as Sarah Vaughan and Mel Tormé. Other scat singers, including Eddie Jefferson, Betty Carter, Anita O'Day, Joe "Bebop" Carroll, Carmen McRae, Jon Hendricks, Babs Gonzales, and Dizzy Gillespie, could improvise effortlessly in the complex bop idiom.

Like other jazz musicians, each scat singer adopted a

unique, immediately recognizable timbre and delivery and developed a personal stock of syllables and vocal devices; Clark Terry's distinctive "mumbling" technique and Gillespie's imitations of trumpet smears are extreme but not untypical examples. Bop scat singing was also vitiated and popularized in Charlie Ventura's groups of the late 1940s and later by Ward Swingle and the Swingle Singers, whose application of scat techniques to the classical repertory arose originally from a desire to find new solfège exercises for classically trained singers. In addition, the usefulness of bop scat singing for teaching jazz was discovered, notably by Lennie Tristano, and accounts for the relatively large number of scat-singing manuals that are in fact primers in jazz improvisation and ear training.

The 1960s saw a vast expansion of the timbres and resources available to scat singers, and the international spread of scat singing to other types of music. Leon Thomas incorporated pygmy yodeling techniques of Central Africa into his singing, while many scat singers (including Karin Krog from Norway, Urszula Dudziak from Poland, and Flora Purim from Brazil) came to jazz from other musical cultures. The extension of vocal improvisation to include sounds formerly regarded as nonmusical, such as cries, screams, sobbing, and laughter, was one of the principal innovations of this period, and at times brought jazz singing close to avant-garde art music; this is apparent, for example, in the work of Cleo Laine or, later, Lauren Newton. Dudziak in particular explored the possibilities of electronic manipulation and distortion of the voice.

Scat singing in the Louis Armstrong tradition has been an established feature of the repertory of traditional revivalist bands since the 1940s. With the bop revival in the mid-1970s there was also a revival of interest in bop scat singing, leading to comebacks for singers such as Betty Carter and Eddie Jefferson, who had previously worked in obscurity. Many young scat singers at the time regarded themselves as belonging to the classic bop tradition; among the best of these are Al Jarreau, who is particularly adept at creating vocal equivalents of complex jazz-rock rhythms, and Bobby McFerrin, whose extraordinarily wide range and mobility are evident in his unaccompanied solo performances. Contemporary scat singers have shown that this vocal art can strike out in directions of its own, independent of developments in instrumental jazz or avant-garde music.

BIBLIOGRAPHY

L. Feather: "An Explanation of Vocalese," *Jazz: a Quarterly of American Music*, no.3 (1959), 261

P. Coker and D. Baker: *Vocal Improvisation: an Instrumental Approach* (Lebanon, IN, 1981) [incl. discography]

K. Henriques: "Scatting and Bopping," *The Wire*, no.1 (1982), 14

J. BRADFORD ROBINSON

Scepter. Record company and label. The company was established in New York in 1964. It recorded several excellent albums by Art Farmer and James Moody and by the New York Jazz Sextet, which included Farmer, Moody, and Tom McIntosh; McIntosh also produced several recordings for the company. Within two years of its foundation, however, Scepter had ceased to operate. It should not be confused with a 1990s pop label of the same name.

MARK GARDNER

Schaap, Phil [Van Noorden, Philip Van Loon Guybo Schaap] (*b* New York, 8 April 1951). Disc jockey and record producer. His father, Walter Schaap, a scholar and a translator of French jazz texts, collaborated in 1937 with Hugues Panassié and Charles Delaunay in creating a bilingual jazz periodical, *Le jazz hot*. In 1970 Phil Schaap became an announcer for Columbia University's radio station WKCR; later he also worked at the radio stations WBGO and WNYC and had a syndicated program, "Jazz Session." This radio work is characterized by his encyclopedic and anecdotal knowledge of the material he plays; he is especially known for his daily WKCR program "Bird Flight," on which he discusses and plays recordings by Charlie Parker. Schaap organized jazz performances at the West End Café in 1980. He has taught at the New School for Social Research and at Princeton University, and he has written liner notes for new and reissued recordings.

As a record producer Schaap has been involved in tape vault research, the restoration of archived materials, and the production and packaging of material to be reissued. In this capacity he strives for the best possible sound and incorporates such ancillary material as alternate and incomplete takes, or assorted studio chatter, within the chronological presentation of originally released material. Though this exhaustive approach generally reflects contemporaneous trends in jazz issues, and has been much praised, it has also engendered some criticism, particularly following Schaap's reorganization of Duke Ellington's classic Columbia LP *Ellington at Newport 1956* and for his work on other Ellington reissues, notably in the decision to include a snippet of Mahalia Jackson cursing before her performance of *Come Sunday*, on the album *Black, Brown and Beige*.

BIBLIOGRAPHY

J. C. Katz: "Phil Schaap '73: One-man Jazz Radio Movement," *Columbia College Today* (1986), fall, 24

B. Ratliff: "With a Mind for Facts and a Soul for Jazz," *New York Times* (5 Oct 1996)

J. Hoffman: "Public Lives: Jazz Detective Unravels an Ellington Puzzle," *New York Times* (19 May 1999)

GK

Schaphorst, Ken(neth William) (*b* Abington, PA, 24 May 1960). Arranger, composer, leader, and educator. He attended Swarthmore (Pennsylvania) College (BA music 1982) and then studied composition at the New England Conservatory (MM 1984) and Boston University (DMA 1990). In 1985 he founded the Jazz Composers Alliance and from January 1989 he led a big band, which may be heard on the album *After Blue* (1992, Accurate 4202). Later he recorded *When the Moon Jumps* (1993, Accurate 4203) with a ten-piece ensemble and performed as a trumpet soloist on *Over the Rainbow: the Music of Harold Arlen* (1996, Accurate 4204), which involved various groups, including the trio Medeski, Martin & Wood, and the Either/Orchestra. These albums feature Schaphorst's compositions and arrangements and display an understanding of complex harmony and a sense of humor that pervades even the most serious pieces. He has taught at various schools around Boston (1984–91), and at Boston University (1986–9), the New England Conservatory (1987–8), the Phillips Academy in Andover, Massachusetts (summers 1989–93), and Lawrence University in Appleton, Wisconsin (from 1991).

BIBLIOGRAPHY

B. Rusch: "Cadence Questionnaire," *Cadence*, xvii/3 (1991), 31

G. Robinson: "Hearsay: Ken Schaphorst," *JT*, xxvii/4 (1997), 28

<http://cwis.lawrence.edu/www/dept/MUSIC/SCHAPHORST.TXT> (1998)

GK

Schärli, Peter (*b* Schötz, Switzerland, 29 May 1955). Swiss trumpeter, flugelhorn player, composer, and leader. He took up trumpet at the age of ten and first performed as a singer, pianist, and trumpeter in a blues band (1974–7). While at the Swiss Jazz School in Berne (1977–81) he performed with John Wolf Brennan (from 1977), was a member of the Uhuru-Quintet (1978–81), and toured with salsa and reggae bands. In 1982 he founded his own trio; this became a quintet in 1984, when Hans Koch was among the sidemen, and a sextet in 1988, when Glenn Ferris joined, and it performed at the Montreux International Jazz Festival in 1987 and at Jazzyatra in Bombay in 1990. It was expanded further in 1994, when Tom Varner, who had replaced Ferris temporarily for a tour of former soviet states in 1990, became a permanent member. From 1984 Schärli also led a quartet, Peter Schärli Special Choice, which initially included Urs Blöchlinger, and in 1993 he founded a third group, Don't Change your Hair for Me, which played only ballads and thus provided a forum for his sensitive playing. In addition he worked in Blöchlinger's Legfek Orchestra, co-led the Christy Doran–Peter Schärli Project (which performed at Jazz Festival Willisau in 1984), joined Doran's quartet (1990), and played in Brennan and Gabriele Hasler's group Organic Voices (recording in 1994). He has worked as a composer and trumpeter in several theaters and circuses and for films and radio plays, and in 1980 he began teaching at the jazz school in Lucerne.

SELECTED RECORDINGS

Wenn's im Sommer ins Kino schneit (1987, Plainisphare 1267-32); *Drei Seelen/Three Souls* (1988, Creative Works 1014); *Blues for the Beast* (1995, Enja 9103-2)

BIBLIOGRAPHY

J. Agrell: "West Meets East," *Brass Bulletin*, no.73 (1991), 88
<http://www.echo.ch/~schaerli_tp/index.html> (1999) [incl. discography]
L. Van Trikt: "Peter Scharli: Short Talk," *Cadence*, xxvi/4 (2000), 16

ARMIN BÜTTNER, GK

Schenkelbach, Fülöp. *See* Filu.

Scherer, Uli [Ulrich] (*b* Villach, Austria, 26 March 1953). Austrian pianist and composer. He studied music and played piano from the age of four. In 1977 he was a co-founder of the Vienna Art Orchestra, and he has remained active in nearly all of its projects, including its recordings. In the 1980s he was closely associated with Wolfgang Puschnig and performed and recorded in such projects and groups as Part of Art, Red Sun and Samul Nori (bringing together a fusion group and a group of Korean master drummers), and AM4. He played with Harry Sokal's group Timeless and performed and recorded with the Austrian writer Ernst Jandl and Lauren Newton (especially in 1988 and 1991, but also at other times). In 1995 he recorded the album *OKIPIK* in Oslo with the trumpeter Matthieu Michel (Plainisphare 1267-107). Scherer's playing draws on his varied musical experience: melodic lines in the bop style are decorated with devices often associated with free jazz.

KLAUS SCHULZ

Schertzer, Hymie. *See* Shertzer, hymie.

Schiaffini, Giancarlo (*b* Rome, 23 Oct 1942). Italian trombonist, tuba player, and leader. He studied trumpet at the age of 15 and changed to trombone when he was 17. In the early 1960s he played jazz with the trombonist Marcello Rosa and the pianist Puccio Sboto. Later he worked with the Gruppo Romano Free Jazz and led a trio with double bass and drums (both 1966–8), led a large ensemble (1967–8), and performed with Lionel Hampton (1969) and Gato Barbieri (1972). He was leader of the trio SIC, with Eugenio Colombo and the drummer Michele Iannaccone as his sidemen (1977–80), and also of another trio, with Paolo Damiani and Iannaccone (1978–80). From 1978 he performed as an unaccompanied soloist. Schiaffini worked with countless free improvisers, among them the drummer Andrea Centazzo, Bruno Tommaso, Enrico Rava, Gianluigi Trovesi, Alex Schlippenbach, Barry Guy, Kent Carter, Evan Parker, Lol Coxhill, Radu Malfatti, Tony Oxley, Kenny Wheeler, Albert Mangelsdorff, and Paul Rutherford (all late 1970s), Anthony Braxton, George Lewis (ii), Derek Bailey, and Yves Robert (all early 1980s), and Eje Thelin and Borah Bergman (both 1986). In the 1990s he led a sextet and continued to appear as an unaccompanied soloist. He is a member of the Italian Instabile Orchestra.

In 1970 Schiaffini studied classical composition in Darmstadt with Karlheinz Stockhausen, György Ligeti, and Vinko Globokar; such contemporary composers as Luigi Nono and Luciano Berio have dedicated compositions to him. One of the pioneers of free improvisation in Italy, he mixes contemporary classical compositional and improvisational techniques with free jazz. He has approached the jazz tradition – the styles of Thelonious Monk and Charlie Parker, for example – from a European point of view, decomposing and reassembling their music in fragments and going beyond standard forms. He also uses electronic devices in unaccompanied performances. He is the author of *Il trombone/The Trombone* (Milan, *c*1984).

SELECTED RECORDINGS

Duos with T. Ghiglioni: *Well Actually* (1987, Splasc(h) 117)
As leader: *Jazz a Confronto 5* (1973, Horo 5); *A tung me* (1980, L'Orchestra 70005); *Giancarlo Schiaffini* (1987, Edi-Pan 20/41); *About Monk* (1992, Pentaflowers 025); *Edula* (1994, Pentaflowers 068); with Claudio Cojaniz: *Alea* (1994, Splasc(h) 461); *As a Bird* (1994, Pentaflowers 040); *Dubs* (1997, ART PURecords 04)
As sideman: Gruppo Romano Free Jazz: *Gruppo Romano Free Jazz* (1966–7, Vedette 8342); M. Schiano: on *Original Sins* (1967–70, Splasc(h) 502), GR, Lacca a-b (1967); with L. Coxhill and A. Centazzo: *Moot* (1978, Ictus 0008); with Trio SIC: *Pezzo* (1978, Red 136); *Altri pezzi* (1978, Red 137); Italian Instabile Orchestra: *Italian Instabile Festival* (1997, Leo 262–3)

BIBLIOGRAPHY

E. Jost: *Europas Jazz, 1960–1980* (Frankfurt am Main, Germany, 1987), 99
S. A. Loewy: "Giancarlo Sciaffini: Exploring New Ground," *Coda*, no.282 (1998), 32
<http://www.shef.ac.uk/misc/rec/ps/efi/minstab.html> (1999)

STEFANO ZENNI

Schiano, Mario (*b* Naples, 22 July 1933). Italian alto saxophonist and leader. After studying piano and accordion he changed at the age of 24 to alto saxophone. He made his début in Rome in 1958, but his first important work was in the mid-1960s as a member of the Gruppo Romano Free Jazz, a trio with Marcello Melis on double bass and Franco Pecori on drums, and a quartet with Giancarlo Schiaffini, which became the leading Italian free-jazz group. He also performed with popular, folk, and theatrical ensembles, notably the folk revival group Canzoniere Italiano and Living Theatre. In the early 1970s he and Melis undertook research on Italian folk music and Schiano performed and recorded with various small groups, among them those led by Bruno Tommaso, the arranger and composer Tommaso Vittorini, Massimo Urbani, and Maurizio Giammarco. In the mid-

1970s he collaborated with the avant-garde composer Domenico Guaccero, and in 1976 he initiated what became a longstanding partnership with the trumpeter Guido Mazzon and organized the Controindicazioni festival in Penne, near Pescara. Although he was less active from the late 1970s into the mid-1980s, he returned to form the Unrepentant Ones (including Schiaffini, Tommaso, the violinist Renato Geremia, Mazzon, and others), then restarted the Controindicazioni festival in 1988 in Rome, where he discovered new talents and played with many European masters of free jazz. In 1990 he became a member of the Italian Instabile Orchestra. Gruppo Romano Free Jazz celebrated its 30th anniversary with a reunion concert in 1996.

Schiano is a pioneer of free jazz in Italy, and broke into a highly conservative musical environment when he first appeared in the 1960s. He is an instinctive player and a master of collective improvisation, able to combine Mediterranean lyricism, Neapolitan cabaret and irony, and southern Italian popular songs. He has molded many young musicians, from Massimo Urbani to Maurizio Giammarco to Sebi Tramontana.

SELECTED RECORDINGS

Duos: with G. Mazzon: *Gospel* (1977, L'Orchestra 10015); with T. Vittorini: *Swimming Pool Orchestra* (1980, Dischi della Quercia 28011)

As leader: *Original Sins* (1967–70, Splasc(h) 502); *If not Ecstatic We Refund* (1970, Cedi 8127); *Sud* (1973, Tom Orro 2001); *Partenza di Pulcinella per la luna* (1974, RCA TLP1-1117); *Concerto della Statale* (1975, Vedette 103); with G. Mazzon: *Progetto per un inno: Now's the Time* (1976, IT 70030); with D. Guaccero: *Dedé* (1977, Folkstudio 5008); with P. Rutherford, H. Bennink, and M. Mengelberg: *A European Proposal* (1978, Horo 35–36); with G. Mazzon: *Effetti Larsen* (1988, Splasc(h) P09); with S. Tramontana, V. Chekasin, and V. Tarasov: *Red and Blue* (1988; Splasc(h) 15); with D. Moye, G. Schiaffini, and M. Melis: *Uncaged* (1991, Splasc(h) 357); with Vittorino Curci: *The Friendship of Walnuts* (1996, Splasc(h) 611)

As sideman with Gruppo Romano Free Jazz: *Gruppo Romano Free Jazz* (1966–7, Vedette 8342)

For further recordings *see* ITALIAN INSTABILE ORCHESTRA.

BIBLIOGRAPHY

E. Jost: *Europas Jazz, 1960–1980* (Frankfurt am Main, Germany, 1987), 99
F. Martinelli: *Mario Schiano: discografia* (Pontedera, Italy, 1996)
<http://www.ijm.it/enartists.html> (1999)
<http://www.shef.ac.uk/misc/rec/ps/efi/minstab.html> (1999)

STEFANO ZENNI

Schifrin, Lalo [Boris] (*b* Buenos Aires, 21 June 1932). Argentine composer and pianist. He learned piano as a child and later won a scholarship to the Paris Conservatoire, where he was supervised by Charles Koechlin and studied with Olivier Messiaen. While in Paris he played with local jazz artists and in 1954 represented Argentina in the third International Jazz Festival. On his return home he established himself as a composer, arranger, conductor, and pianist who was equally at ease in popular, jazz, and art-music circles; he also formed the first Argentine big band in the Basie-Gillespie tradition. In 1958 Schifrin moved to New York, and that year worked in a trio with Eddie de Haas and Rudy Collins. He then gained recognition as the pianist in Gillespie's jazz quintet (1960-62) and recorded with other well-known jazz musicians. From 1962 he has concentrated on writing, and has become a major composer of film music; his *Jazz Suite on the Mass Texts* (1965) is highly regarded. Schifrin worked more frequently as a symphony conductor from the late 1980s and in the mid-1990s lessened his film-writing duties to concentrate on a project that he calls "Jazz Meets the Symphony."

SELECTED RECORDINGS

As leader: *Lalo Schifrin* (1962, Roul. 52088); *Ins and Outs* (*c*1983, PAlt 8055)

As sideman with D. Gillespie: *An Electrifying Evening with the Dizzy Gillespie Quintet* (1961, Verve 68401); *New Wave!* (1962, Phi. 600070)

RECORDED COMPOSITIONS

(selective list)

Recorded by others: D. Gillespie: *Gillespiana* (1960, Verve 68394); *New Continent* (1962, Lml. 86022); P. Horn: *Jazz Suite on the Mass Texts* (1965, RCA LSP3414)

SELECTED ARRANGEMENTS

Recorded by others: S. Getz: *Reflections* (1963, Verve 68554); Jimmy Smith: *The Cat* (1964, Verve 68587)

BIBLIOGRAPHY

B. Houston: "Jazz is Not an Industry!," *MM* (18 Aug 1962), 8
G. Lees: "Lalo = Brilliance," *DB*, xxix/8 (1962), 18
P. Lattes: "Les rigeurs de Lalo," *Jh*, no.210 (1965), 17
J. Tynan: "Lalo Schifrin," *BMI: the Many Worlds of Music* (1965), Nov, 11
H. Siders: "Keeping Score on Schifrin: Lalo Schifrin and the Art of Film Music," *DB*, xxxvi/5 (1969), 16
L. Tomkins: "Lalo Schifrin: my Approaches to the Film Score," *CI*, xv (1976), no.2, p.8; no.3, p.15
D. Gillespie and A. Fraser: *To be, or not ... to Bop: Memoirs* (Garden City, NY, 1979, London, 1980, as *Dizzy: the Autobiography of Dizzy Gillespie*)
T. Darter and B. Doerschuk: "Lalo Schifrin: Piano Roots of a Master Film Composer," *CK*, ix/2 (1983), 8 [incl. discography]
R. Palmer: "Reel Job," *JJI*, xxxix/2 (1986), 19 [incl. discography]
H. Lucraft: "Lalo Schifrin," *CI*, xxvi/5 (1989), 19
R. S. Brown: "Quadruple Life: an Interview with Lalo Schifrin," *Fanfare*, liv/4 (1991), 108
G. Endress: "Synthese von Jazz und sinfonischer Musik," *JP*, xlii/7 (1993), 16
H. Lucraft: "Lalo Schifrin Today," *CJM*, xxxi/5 (1994), 26
G. Endress: "Lalo Schifrin: der offene Musik-Welten-Brummler," *JP*, xlvii/11 (1998), 10

MICHAEL J. BUDDS/BK

Schildkraut, Dave(y) [David] (*b* New York, 7 Jan 1925; *d* New York, 1 Jan 1998). Alto saxophonist. He gained his first professional experience with Louis Prima (1941) and later played with Buddy Rich (intermittently from 1947) and Anita O'Day (1947). In 1953–4 he toured Europe and recorded with Stan Kenton's orchestra, and while in Berlin he appeared with the group in the film *Schlagerparade* (1953). He then performed and recorded with Pete Rugolo (1954) and George Handy (1955) and was a soloist on the album *Miles Davis Quintet* (1954, Prst. 185), from which the track *Solar* well represents his playing. In the mid-1950s he also recorded with Oscar Pettiford (1954), Ralph Burns and Eddie Bert (both 1955), Tito Puente and Chuck Wayne (both 1956), and Sam Most (1957). Following another period with Kenton (1959) he led his own quartet at clubs in New York and was active as a freelance. He then left music and worked as a civil servant in New York. Schildkraut was a fluent bop musician whose playing was occasionally mistaken for that of Charlie Parker.

BIBLIOGRAPHY

FeatherE
R. Reisner: *Bird: the Legend of Charlie Parker* (New York, 1962/*R*1975), 206
Obituary, *DB*, lxv/5 (1998), 15

Schilperoort, Peter [Bronx, Pat] (*b* The Hague, 4 Nov 1919; *d* Leiderdorp, Netherlands, 17 Nov 1990). Dutch clarinetist and saxophonist. He was self-taught as a musician. He began his career with the Bouncers (1938–9) and the Swing Papas (1939–43) and played under the bandleader Klaas van Beeck (1943). With the pianist Frans Vink he formed the Dutch Swing College, a school for jazz, in 1944 and the DUTCH SWING COLLEGE BAND the following year; he succeeded Vink as the leader in 1946. He left the Dutch Swing College in September 1955 to work in the aircraft industry and to lead a quartet and a quintet from 1956 until 1959, when he again assumed leadership of the band – a position he retained into the 1980s. He appeared with the group at the North Sea Jazz Festival in the late 1970s and early 1980s, and continued to record with it on clarinet and baritone saxophone. He also played with Jimmy Maxwell and Dicky Wells until failing health ended his career. A good example of his work is the album *Quartet and Quintet* (Dureco 51022), recorded in 1957–8.

BIBLIOGRAPHY

FeatherE
Obituaries: W. van Eyle, *JF* [intl edn], nos.125–6 (1990), 11; H. Rainey, *JJI*, xliv/3 (1991), 20

WIM VAN EYLE

Schiöpffe, William (*b* Bangkok, 6 Feb 1926; *d* Copenhagen 2 Jan 1981). Danish drummer. His father owned rubber plantations in Siam and Malaysia, and he spent his early childhood in both countries. He moved to Denmark in 1934 and played professionally with the Harlem Kiddies from 1947 to 1953. After performing in Sweden with Arne Domnérus (1953–5) he returned to Denmark to work as a freelance, and played regularly with Stan Getz during the saxophonist's stay in Scandinavia (1958–61). He then served as the house drummer at the Montmartre, Copenhagen (1962–3), and as a member of the Radiojazzgruppen (i) (1961–5) and the Radioens Big Band (1964–9). Thereafter he was inactive on account of ill-health. Schiöpffe was regarded as one of the best European drummers of his era – he was chosen to be a member of the European All Stars during the International Jazz Festival in Berlin in 1961: he played with perfect timing and a great sense of swing, and combined the best from both the swing and the bop traditions. He recorded with Harry Arnold, Svend Asmussen, Rolf Billberg, Don Byas, Domnérus, Getz, Ib Glindemann, Dexter Gordon, Lars Gullin, Bengt Hallberg, the Harlem Kiddies, Jan Johansson, Brew Moore, Erik Moseholm, Carl-Henrik Norin, Bud Powell, the Radiojazzgruppen, the Radioens Big Band, and Monica Zetterlund.

SELECTED RECORDINGS

As leader: *Drum Colours* (1957, Col. SEGK 1038)
As sideman: B. Hallberg: Whiskey Sour/Side Car (1953, Met. MEP29 [EP]); L. Gullin: Late Summer/For F. J. Fans Only (1955, Met. MEP129 [EP]); R. Billberg: Curly Curt/Opus de Funk/Ja da (1956, Sonet SXP2003 [EP]); Old Man River/I'm beginning to see the light/Yesterdays (1956, Sonet SXP2004 [EP]); S. Getz: *Imported from Europe* (1958, Verve 8331); A. Domnérus: *When Lights Are Low* (1959, Telefunken 14120); S. Getz: *Stan Getz at Large* (1960, Verve 8393-2); A. Domnérus: *Come Listen with Me* (1960, Telefunken 14179); B. Powell: *Bouncing with Bud* (1962, Sonet 31); B. Moore: *Svinget 14* (1962, Debut 137); S. Asmussen: *Two of a Kind* (1965, Met. 15177)

BIBLIOGRAPHY

E. Wiedemann: "Omkring William Schiöpffe" [About William Schiöpffe], *Jazz årbogen* (Copenhagen 1957), 37
E. Moseholm: *William Schiöpffe* (Copenhagen, 1962)
K. Frandsen: *Politikens jazzleksikon* (Copenhagen, 1987)

FRANK BÜCHMANN-MØLLER

Schlinger, Sol (*b* New York, 6 Sept 1926). Baritone saxophonist. He first played tenor saxophone in dance bands (1940–43) and then took up the baritone instrument and performed with Buddy Rich (1943). After working alternately with Tommy Dorsey (?1943–4, 1949–51) and Jimmy Dorsey (1947, 1951) he played briefly with Charlie Barnet, Jerry Gray, Herbie Fields, Louis Jordan, and the Latin dance-band leader Perez Prado. As a tenor saxophonist he toured (1952) and performed in New York (1956) with Benny Goodman; on the baritone instrument he recorded with Neal Hefti (1952), the Sauter–Finegan Orchestra (1952–3), Goodman (1954–8), Al Cohn (1954, 1956), Manny Albam (1955–7), Teddy Charles, Coleman Hawkins, Phil Woods, Don Elliott, and Bob Brookmeyer (all 1956), Urbie Green (1956, 1958, 1961), Chuck Wayne (1957), Bill Potts (1959), Benny Golson and Mundell Lowe (both 1961), and Dave Frishberg (1968). His work is well represented by Cohn's albums *Mr. Music* (1954, RCA LPM1024) and *The Sax Section* (1956, Epic LN3278). Later, as well as working as a studio musician, Schlinger performed with Goodman's big band in the television show "Swing into Spring" (1958), for recordings (1963, 1965, 1969), in concerts at Carnegie Hall (1974, 1978), and for a PBS television broadcast (1977). Although most of his work in the 1980s and 1990s involved genres other than jazz, he recorded a re-creation of music by Glenn Miller in 1983 and took part in a session led by John Pizzarelli in 1991. (*Connor BG*; *FeatherE*)

Schlippenbach, Alex(ander von) (*b* Berlin, 7 April 1938). German pianist, composer, and bandleader. He took piano lessons from the age of eight and studied composition with the composers Bernd Alois Zimmermann and Rudolf Petzold at the Staatliche Hochschule für Musik in Cologne; he also performed in the school's jazz band, which was led by Kurt Edelhagen. Schlippenbach studied jazz piano with Francis Coppieters, and in his teens he played boogie-woogie and blues before coming under the influence first of Oscar Peterson and then of Thelonious Monk and Bud Powell. From 1963 to 1965 he worked with Gunter Hampel, and from 1965 to 1968 he was a member of Manfred Schoof's quintet and sextet. His composition *Globe Unity* (1966), commissioned by RIAS radio, was performed to considerable acclaim by the Globe Unity Orchestra at the Berliner Jazztage, and his association with the orchestra continued (interrupted only in 1971–2) until 1989; in 1988 he formed a new ensemble, the Berlin Contemporary Jazz Orchestra, which he co-led from that time with his wife, Aki Takase.

From 1967 Schlippenbach led a number of small groups, most notably a trio with Evan Parker and Paul Lovens (formed in 1970, but with Michel Pilz briefly in place of Parker); this trio worked occasionally as a quartet with the addition of Peter Kowald (1973–8, recording in 1975 and 1977), Alan Silva (recording in 1981–2), or Reggie Workman. In 1976 he began what became a longstanding affiliation with Sven-Åke Johansson, with whom he had first worked in Schoof's group in the late 1960s: they appeared together most often in a duo, in which Johansson eventually performed solely as a singer; in the mid-1980s they formed a quasi-swing dance band, which included the double bass player Jay Oliver and Rüdiger Carl (recording in 1984); and in 1989 they worked on a multi-media project with Fred Frith, Wolfgang Fuchs, and Tom Cora. Schlippenbach also performed – in particular at the first Jazzyatra in Bombay (1978) – and recorded (1972, 1977) as an unaccompanied soloist. In 1973 he recorded with the Jazzensemble des Hessischen Rundfunks.

Schlippenbach formed other small groups, notably trios involving Ernst-Ludwig Petrowsky (1985, 2000), another trio with Sunny Murray and Nobuyoshi Ino (mid-1980s), a duo with Murray (recording in 1989), and a quintet consisting of

Parker, Mario Schiano, Joëlle Léandre, and Paul Lytton (for a recording in 1990). He performed and recorded (1988, 1993–4) in a duo with Takase, and recorded in duos with Lovens (1984), Sam Rivers (1997), and Tony Oxley (1998) and as a guest with the Improvisors Pool (1995) and Hampel (1997), among others. His trio appeared at the Empty Bottle Festival in Chicago in 1998 with Lytton deputizing for Lovens, and at the North Sea Jazz Festival in 2000 he and Parker amalgamated their trios to form Double Trio, a quintet consisting of Barry Guy, Lovens, and Lytton.

Schlippenbach's music combines elements of free jazz and avant-garde classical music, and his performances on such recordings as Hampel's *Heartplants* (1965) and the Manfred Schoof Quintet's *Voices* (1966) were influential in the development of free jazz in Europe. He has published some thoughts in the essays "Potenzierung musikalischer Energien: das Globe Unity Orchester" (*JP*, xxiv/3 (1975), 11); "Free Jazz" (*Neue Zeitschrift für Musik*, cxl (1979), 244); and "Orgie unerträglichsten Missklangs" (*Neue Zeitschrift für Musik*, cxli (1980), 310).

SELECTED RECORDINGS

As unaccompanied soloist: *Payan* (1972, Enja 2012); *Piano Solo* (1977, FMP 0430)

Duos with S.-Å. Johansson: *Drive* (1979, FMP 0810); *Kalfaktor A. Falke und andere Lieder* (1982, FMP 0970); Blind aber hungrig – norddeutsche Gesänge (1984, FMP S15) [EP]

Duos with others: with P. Lovens: *Stranger than Love* (1984, Po Torch 12); with A. Takase: on [various artists]: *Tutu Records Presents "Live" from Internationales Jazzfestival Münster* (1988, Tutu 888110-2), Frictitious Paragon; with S. Murray: *Smoke* (1989, FMP CD23); with A. Takase: *Piano Duets: Live in Berlin 93/94* (1993–4, FMP OWN90002); with S. Rivers: *Tangens* (1997, FMP CD99); with T. Oxley: *Digger's Harvest* (1998, FMP CD103)

As leader of small groups: *Pakistani Pomade* (1972, FMP 0110); *The Hidden Peak* (1977, FMP 0410); with S.-Å. Johansson: *Idylle und Katastrophen* (1979, Po Torch 6); *Das hohe Lied* (1981, Po Torch 16–17); *Elf Bagatellen* (1990, FMP CD27); *Physics* (1991, FMP CD50); on E. Parker: *50th Birthday Concert* (1994, Leo 212/213), Bowed Stiffly and Went Free, Hero of Nine Fingers; *Complete Combustion* (1998, FMP CD106); *Swinging the BIM* (1998, FMP CD114–15)

As sideman: G. Hampel: *Heartplants* (1965, Saba 15026); M. Schoof: *Voices* (1966, CBS 62621); *The Early Quintet* (1966–7, FMP 0540); *Wergo Jazz* (1967, Wergo 80003); M. Schiano: on *Unlike* (1990, Splasc(h) 309-2), Trend, pts 1–2; Improvisors Pool: *Backgrounds for Improvisors* (1995, FMP CD75); G. Hampel: *Legendary: the 27th of May 1997* (1997, Birth CD45)

For further recordings *see* Globe unity orchestra and Berlin contemporary jazz orchestra.

BIBLIOGRAPHY

CarrJ; *Feather–Gitler '70s*; *GrayF*

R. Williams: "Re-thinking Big Band Music," *MM* (13 June 1970), 16

S. Lake: "Center of the Globe," *MM* (2 Feb 1974), 53

"Alex Schlippenbach," *Jm*, no.234 (1975), 15

G. Rouy: "Berlin: Free Music Production," *Jm*, no.238 (1975), 12

"Swinging News: West Berlin: Schlippenbach's New Effort," *JF* [intl edn], no.48 (1977), 12

I. Storb: "Fragen an Alexander von Schlippenbach," *JP*, xxvii/10 (1978), 4

B. Ogen: "Schlippenbach–Johansson Duo," *JP*, xxviii/1 (1979), 31

L. Jeske: "Free Players from Many Lands Form Globe Unity Orchestra," *DB*, xlvii/9 (1980), 28

B. Noglik: "Alexander von Schlippenbach," *Jazzwerkstatt international* (Berlin, 1981, 2/1983) [incl. discography]

M. Thiem: "Alexander von Schlippenbach," *JF* [intl edn], no.77 (1982), 44

R. Cook: "The Indispensable Focus," *Wire*, no.30 (1986), 10

E. Jost: *Europas Jazz, 1960–1980* (Frankfurt am Main, Germany, 1987)

P. Carles, A. Clergeat, and J.-L. Comolli: *Dictionnaire du jazz* (Paris, 1988, rev. and enlarged 2/1994)

M. Kunzler: *Jazz-Lexicon* (Reinbek, nr Hamburg, Germany, 1988)

R. Kühl: "Alexander von Schlippenbach Trio," *JP*, xli/6 (1992), 32

"Albert-Mangelsdorff-Preis and Alexander von Schlippenbach," *JP*, xliii/6 (1994), 44

<http://www.shef.ac.uk/misc/rec/ps/efi/mschlipp.html> (2000) [incl. discography]

For further bibliography *see* Globe unity orchestra.

BERT NOGLIK/GK

Schlitten, Don(ald) (*b* New York, 4 March 1932). Record producer and photographer. He studied art at the High School of Music and Art and, in the late 1940s, tenor saxophone at the New York Conservatory of Modern Music. After working in the early 1950s as an artist he began his career as a record company owner and record producer for Signal, then worked for Prestige (initially serving as its art director before going on to produce sessions), Muse (ii), Onyx, Cobblestone, Xanadu, and several other companies, including MPS, Columbia, and Mercury. In the mid-1960s he co-produced, with Ira Gitler, a series of jazz concerts at the Museum of Modern Art, and he hosted the radio series "Jazz Legends" and "The Scope of Jazz" on the Pacifica network. Schlitten has maintained a parallel career as a photographer: his jazz images have appeared on album covers and posters and in numerous periodicals, books, and films; he has also given exhibitions of his work.

BIBLIOGRAPHY

Feather–Gitler '70s

L.-V. Mialy: "Don Schlitten: Xanadu Records," *Jh*, no.556 (1998–9), 25

BK

Schlott, Volker (*b* Oelsnitz, Vogtland, Germany, 20 April 1958). German saxophonist. He received lessons on clarinet as a child and later studied saxophone at the Musikhochschule Hanns Eisler in Berlin (1974–80). Having begun his professional career with the jazz-rock band Fusion (1977–80) he then played with Uwe Kropinski (1980–83), Radio Big-Band Berlin (1984–7), the Hannes Zerbe Blechband (1985–7), and Pierre Dørge's New Jungle Orchestra (from 1989). He also became a member of the wind quartet Fun Horns (1985) and Gebhard Ullmann's band Tá Lam Zehn (1992); he leads a quartet, and he has performed as an unaccompanied soloist. Schlott, who has appeared at festivals worldwide, teaches at the Musikhochschule Hanns Eisler and composes music for theater and films. His works for the Fun Horns as well as for his own bands are full of surprises, incorporating ironic hints at different musical worlds and improvisations which alternate between swinging modern jazz and a fusion of jazz, folk, and pop-rock sources. His sound has a full, singing quality.

SELECTED RECORDINGS

As unaccompanied soloist: *The 12 Seasons* (1992, Klangräume 30030), incl. Jaguar

As leader: *Why Not* (1996, Acoustic Music 319-1083-2), incl. Abschiedslied

As sideman with Fun Horns: *Der Mond ist aufgegangen* (1996, Klangräume 30300), incl. Moon Waltz

WOLFRAM KNAUER

Schlüter, Wolfgang (*b* Berlin, 12 Nov 1933). German vibraphonist. He studied piano as a child and percussion and timpani at the Hochschule für Musik in Berlin from 1950 to 1954, during which time he also played in dance bands. Later he was a member of Michael Naura's quintet (1956–63), whose band played music after that of George Shearing, the Modern Jazz Quartet, and Cannonball Adderley's group, though he also played with Rolf Kühn (1956), Horst Jankowski (1961), the German All Stars (1963), and Volker Kriegel (1978). In Hamburg in 1965 he joined the orchestra of the Norddeutscher Rundfunk, with which he remained until 1994. Schlüter recorded in duos with Naura (*Country Children*, 1977, ECM 5803) and Christoph Spendel (*Orange Town*, 1981, MRC 06664599) and, together with Naura, collaborated with the poet Peter Rühmkorff on albums of jazz and poetry that were highly acclaimed. In the 1980s and 1990s he led a swing group modeled after Benny Goodman's small bands. He has worked extensively as a composer and arranger of jazz and dance music, and he contributed the essay "Vibraphon" to *Jazzrock: Tendenzen einer modernen Musik* (edited by B. König, Reinbek, Germany, 1983). Schlüter has a virtuoso technique and has been influenced by the major American vibraphonists. (*FeatherE*; *ReclamsJ*)

WOLFRAM KNAUER

Schmidli, Peter (*b* Basel, Switzerland, 20 Sept 1937; *d* Basel, 22 Jan 2001). Swiss banjoist and guitarist. In the 1950s and 1960s he played as an amateur with local dixieland bands. Having recorded with Oscar Klein in 1968 and 1970 he joined the Tremble Kids, with whom he recorded between 1971 and 1982; at the same time he led the P. S. Corporation (to 1981), which played jazz and popular music on radio and television and made several recordings. Schmidli was a member for several years of the group Buddha's Gamblers, with which he recorded the album *Swinging with Buddha's Gamblers* (Swiss Jazz 6336) in 1982. He may be heard to good effect accompanying Danny Moss on *A Swingin' Affair* (1996, Nagel-Heyer 034).

PETER SCHWALM

Schneeze. Nickname of ART ROLLINI.

Schneider, Hawe [Hans Wolf] (*b* Leipzig, 25 April 1930). German trombonist and vibraphonist. He took up violin in 1938 and trombone in 1947, and the following year founded the Feetwarmers. He moved to West Berlin in 1951, and while studying there founded the Spree City Stompers. The group played in many film and television productions and toured in Europe and Africa; at the time Schneider was considered in most German polls to be the best traditional-jazz trombonist. From 1953 to 1968 he also ran the Eierschale, a jazz club in Berlin, and in 1957 he was a member of the first German group at the Polish jazz festival in Zopot, with guest soloist Albert Nicholas. He moved in 1968 to Nettelstedt, near Minden, where he was the curator of an automobile museum, and then in 1971 to Lenzkirch in the Black Forest. There he worked as a freelance journalist and photographer and appeared as a freelance soloist with many groups in southwest Germany and Switzerland. In 1972 he founded the group Hawe and the Hot Wave, with which he played swing, in 1973 the traditional-jazz band the Dixie Bellows, and in 1976 the Schwarzwälder Swing Gemeinschaft, a quintet in which he played vibraphone. He took part in the New Orleans Jazz & Heritage Festival in 1981 and played in various cities with Benny Waters and Preston Jackson, among others, as guest soloists. In 1992 he ceased to work as a bandleader, but he continued to play as a soloist with southwestern German bands, as well as with a Polish rhythm section in Olsztyn in 1997. He is the author of an autobiography, *... und Abends swing: ein Buch voll Jazz, nicht nur für Fans* (Hinterzarten, Germany, 1985).

SELECTED RECORDINGS

As leader: of Spree City Stompers: Who's Sorry Now?/Miss Annabelle Lee (1954, Col. DW5349); *Hot Club Melomani* (1957, Muza 0159); *Warte, warte nur ein Weilchen* (1961, Vogue 557-30)

As sideman: F. Goudie: Davenport Blues (1953, Col. DW5269); W. B. Davison: *Spree Coast Jazz* (1958, Manhattan 61162); D. Antritter: *For my Friends and Me* (1974, Haga XFOE)

GERHARD CONRAD

Schneider, Larry (*b* Long Island, NY, 1949). Tenor and soprano saxophonist. While studying biology at the University of Massachusetts he played in local jazz and rhythm-and-blues groups. In 1970 he decided to pursue a career as a musician and moved to New York, and in the mid-1970s he worked frequently with Billy Cobham, the Thad Jones–Mel Lewis Orchestra, and Horace Silver (*c*1976–9); a recording with Jim McNeely (1976) led to an association with his fellow sideman Mike Richmond. In 1978–9 he recorded with Bill Evans (ii). Schneider settled in the early 1980s in San Francisco, where he led a group with Hein van der Geyn (1981–3) and John Abercrombie among his sidemen. He toured Europe for the first time, performing as a leader at jazz festivals in Berlin and Paris. In 1986 he traveled to Paris to perform with François Jeanneau and the Orchestre National de Jazz; two years later he returned to France and recorded as the leader of a quintet consisting of Marc Ducret, David Friedman, Henri Texier, and Daniel Humair and as a sideman with Ducret. From 1988 he toured and recorded with George Gruntz's Concert Jazz Band, and in 1989 he toured and recorded in Steve Smith's Vital Information. From the late 1980s through the 1990s Schneider frequently visited France to perform in various ensembles, including a group led by Humair, a trio with François Méchali and the drummer Alain Soler, another trio with André Jaume and Éric Barret (1995), and a group performing Soler's work *J'irai valser sur vos tombes* (1995). In 1996 he performed in San Francisco in a group including Jaume, Méchali, and Soler; his own bands have often involved Andy LaVerne and Richmond. Schneider also formed a duo with the pianist Giacomo Aula and worked as a studio musician. Around 1997 he performed and recorded at the Jazz on the Coast Festival in Italy.

SELECTED RECORDINGS

Duos with A. LaVerne: *Bill Evans ... Person We Knew* (1992, Ste. 31307)

As leader: with D. Wissels: *Milanka* (1987, Tim. 254); *So Easy* (1988, Label Bleu 6516); *Just Cole Porter* (1991, Ste. 31291); *Mohawk* (1993, Ste. 31347); *Freedom Jazz Dance* (1996, Ste. 31390)

As sideman: B. Evans: *We Will Meet Again* (1979, WB 3411); S. Smith: *Vitalive!* (1989, Manhattan B21Z96692); M. Richmond: *Blue in Green* (1991, Ste. 31296)

BIBLIOGRAPHY

"Encyclopédie permanente Jazzmag," *Jm*, no.377 (1988), 39

J. Buzelin: "Larry Schneider: le franc-tireur," *Jazzman*, no.44 (1999), 29 [incl. discography]

GK

Schneider, Maria (Lynn) (*b* Windom, MN, 27 Nov 1960). Composer, arranger, and bandleader. She played piano, clarinet, and violin before studying theory and composition at the University of Minnesota (BS 1983). During the academic year 1983–4 she was at the University of Miami, but she transferred to the Eastman School to complete her graduate work in jazz and contemporary writing (MM 1985). That summer she moved to New York, where she began working as an apprentice to Gil Evans (1985–8); she was also employed occasionally as a ghost writer. From 1986 to 1991 she studied with Bob Brookmeyer. Through Brookmeyer's affiliation with Mel Lewis she wrote pieces for the Village Vanguard Orchestra and formed a rehearsal band with John Fedchock (to whom she was then married). She received the

Gil Evans Fellowship award in 1991 and the following year she formed her own big band, which performed at Visiones in New York (1993–8) and recorded the albums *Evanescence* (1992, Enja 8048-2) and *Coming About* (1995, Enja 9069-2). In 1995 she was commissioned by the Monterey Jazz Festival to present the suite *Scenes from Childhood*. Schneider and her band toured Europe and the Far East, performing and giving workshops. She has had work commissioned by and has conducted the Carnegie Hall Jazz Orchestra, the Orchestre National de Jazz (Paris), the Radioens Big Band (Denmark), and the Stockholm Jazz Orchestra, among others, and in 1998, in collaboration with the Pilobolus Dance Theater company, she presented a new work at the American Dance Festival. A volume of her scores and an interview have been published under the title *Evanescence* (Vienna, 1998).

BIBLIOGRAPHY

CarrJ
B. Marantz: "Maria Schneider: to Gil with Love," *DB*, lix/6 (1992), 24
D. Kasrel: "Hearsay: Maria Schneider," *JT*, xxiv/5 (1994), 10
T. Teachout: "Jazz: at 33, a Composer of Note," *Wall Street Journal* (7 Oct 1994)
L. Gourse: *Madame Jazz: Contemporary Women Instrumentalists* (New York, and Oxford, England, 1995), 167
M. Handler: "Riffs: Monterey Commissions New York Big Band," *DB*, lxii/12 (1995), 14
D. Heckman: "An Unexpected Candidate for Next Jazz Giant," *Los Angeles Times* (27 Feb 1995)
B. Protzman: "Maria Schneider's Composing Pains," *DB*, lxiii/11 (1996), 36
H. Reich: "A Different Beat," *Chicago Tribune* (5 July 1996)
M. Zwerin: "Little Pinky Schneider, the Leader of the Band," *International Herald Tribune* (17 Jan 1997)
B. Blumenthal: "Maria Schneider: Balancing Pen & Baton," *JT*, xxvii/7 (1998), 32
G. Thys: "Maria et les garçons," *Bleu banane*, no.3 (1998), 12

GK

Schneiderman, Rob(ert Roland) (*b* Boston, 21 June 1957). Pianist. He grew up in Palo Alto, California, where he began teaching himself piano, and from the age of 12 he lived in San Diego. He decided to pursue a career in music after coming into contact with jazz and began working professionally when he was about 16 with, among others, Peter Sprague, Eddie Harris, and Charles McPherson; he continued to play intermittently with both Harris (who died in 1996) and McPherson into the 1990s. In 1982 Schneiderman moved to New York, where he performed with such musicians as Zoot Sims, James Moody, Art Farmer, Chet Baker, Slide Hampton, and J. J. Johnson. In addition he toured regularly with the group TanaReid, of which he was a founding member in 1990, and taught at Queens College and at William Paterson College in Wayne, New Jersey. Around 1994 he returned to California to begin a doctorate in mathematics at the University of California, Berkeley.

SELECTED RECORDINGS

(all recorded for Reservoir)

New Outlook (1988, 106); *Smooth Sailing* (1990, 114); *Radio Waves* (1991, 120); *Standards* (1992, 126); *Keepin' in the Groove* (1996, 144)

BIBLIOGRAPHY

B. Primack: "Hearsay: Making Waves with Rob Schneiderman," *JT*, xxii/1 (1992), 13

GK

Schnitter, David (Bertram) (*b* Newark, NJ, 19 March 1948). Tenor saxophonist. He learned clarinet as a child but changed to tenor saxophone at the age of 15; from 1966 to 1970 he studied at Jersey City State College (BA). He began his professional career playing at weddings and as a member of various rock bands, and in 1972 he formed his own group in New York. After playing with Ted Dunbar and Wilbur Little (both 1973) and Walter Davis (at the Cellar, 1974), and during the same period leading a group at Boomer's, he began his most important association, with Art Blakey (1974–9). While with Blakey he played with Frank Foster and Ricky Ford (both 1976) and Walter Bishop, Jr. (1978), and recorded with Charles Earland, Groove Holmes, Johnny Lytle, and Red Rodney (all 1977). He worked with Freddie Hubbard from 1979, recording with him in 1980 and 1981. Schnitter then traveled to Europe, where he initially led a quintet consisting of Michael Cochrane, Dennis Irwin, Jimmy Madison, and the singer Marti Marin. Around 1983 he led a quartet with Terumasa Hino, Harold Mabern, and Billy Hart for an engagement at Sweet Basil in New York. After returning to New York in the mid-1990s he taught privately, and in 1996 he joined the faculty of the Mannes/New School (in autumn 1999 the Jazz and Contemporary Music Program there moved to the New School University). Schnitter's style is based firmly on hard bop; his sound has been compared in particular with that of Dexter Gordon, though the influences of Sonny Rollins and John Coltrane are also detectable.

SELECTED RECORDINGS

As leader (all recorded for Muse): *Invitation* (1976, 5108); *Goliath* (1977, 5153); *Thundering* (1978, 5197); *Glowing* (1979, 5222)
As sideman: S. Stitt: *In Walked Sonny* (1975, Sonet 691); A. Blakey: *Backgammon* (1976, Roul. 5003); *In my Prime* (1977–8, Tim. 114, 118); *In this Korner* (1978, Conc. 68); J. Madison: *90° with 100% Humidity* (1996, Blue Chip Jazz 878402-2)

BIBLIOGRAPHY

Feather–Gitler '70s
C. Delaunay: "Nice Plus ... Dave Schnitter," *Jh*, no.330 (1976), 20
J. Howard: "A Message from Today," *JF* [intl edn], no.70 (1981), 38

PAUL RINZLER/BK

Schnyder, Daniel (*b* Zurich, 12 March 1961). Swiss saxophonist, flutist, and composer. He learned to play cello as a child and took up saxophone at the age of 12. Later he studied saxophone, composition, and arranging at the Berklee College of Music (1980–81) and classical flute at the Conservatory of Winterthur (1982–3). After settling in New York he attended summer classes in Banff, Canada, in 1986 and 1987. Schnyder is an accomplished composer whose diverse commissions include works for the Vienna Art Orchestra, the Tonhallen Orchestra Zürich, and the NDR Big Band; his principal publishers are Edition Kunzelmann, Hal Leonard, and Universal Edition. From 1988, for Enja, he issued a series of recordings involving the techniques and instrumentation of jazz and classical music; his style tends to be vigorous but sensitive and combines the rhythmic inventions of jazz with the harmonic developments of the 20th century and earlier contrapuntal techniques. His recordings feature such players as Michael Philip Mossman (with whom he co-led a group from 1988), Mark Feldman, Michael Formanek, Dave Taylor, Kenny Drew, Jr., and Marvin "Smitty" Smith. Schnyder worked as an arranger for recordings by Franco Ambrosetti (on the album *Music for Symphony and Jazz Band*, 1990, Enja 6070-2), Lee Konitz (1997), and Abdullah Ibrahim (1997), and he performed in Australia in a trio with Drew and Taylor (1997). He is the author of *Crossing Over: Essentials for the Classical and the Jazz Flutist* (New York, 1999).

SELECTED RECORDINGS

Secret Cosmos (*c*1987, Enja 5055-2); *Daniel Schnyder* (1988, COD 31221); *The City* (1988, Enja 6002-2); *Streichquartett, Streichsextett und Jazzkomposition* (1987–8, MGB 4015 CD); *Decoding the Message* (1989, Enja 6036-2); *Winds* (1991, Koch Schwann 310121); *Mythen* (1991, Koch Schwann 310170H1); *Mythology* (1991, Enja 7003-2); *Nucleus* (1994, Enja 8068-2); *Tarantula* (1994–6, Enja 9302-2); *Words within Music* (1999, Enja 9369-2)

BIBLIOGRAPHY

P. Bürli: "Daniel Schnyder," *JP*, xlvi/1 (1997), 31
H.-J. Schaal: "Ein Wanderer zwischen den Welten," *Neue Musikzeitung*, xlvii/9 (1998), 12

MARCUS GAMMEL

Schoebel, Elmer (*b* East St. Louis, IL, 8 Sept 1896; *d* St. Petersburg, FL, 14 Dec 1970). Arranger, composer, and pianist. He first played piano for silent films and vaudeville shows, then moved to Chicago. Around 1920, at the Blatz Palm Gardens, he led a forerunner of the New Orleans Rhythm Kings, with Paul Mares or Muggsy Spanier, Georg Brunis, and Jack Pettis among his sidemen. In 1922–3 he played and wrote arrangements for the New Orleans Rhythm Kings. He then led his own band at the Midway Gardens and worked as an arranger for the Melrose Brothers Music Co. Later he became a staff arranger in New York for Warner Bros., with whom he remained until the 1940s. Thereafter he resumed playing, and he continued to perform until shortly before his death. Scarcely audible as a pianist on most of his recordings, Schoebel was most important as an arranger and composer. He arranged for publication many early jazz pieces, notably those of Jelly Roll Morton, and his work displays a development from his early, rather naive, scores to later, more sophisticated ones. Among his compositions are many popular songs and jazz standards, including *Bugle Call Rag* (his arrangement of which was later recorded as *Bugle Call Blues*), *Farewell Blues*, *Nobody's Sweetheart*, and *Prince of Wails*.

SELECTED RECORDINGS

As leader: Copenhagen/Prince of Wails (1929, Bruns. 4652)
As sideman with New Orleans Rhythm Kings: Discontented Blues/Bugle Call Blues (1922, Gen. 4967)

BIBLIOGRAPHY

ChiltonW
M. Williams: "N. O. R. K.," *Jazz Masters of New Orleans* (New York and London, 1967/*R*1978), 82

JAMES DAPOGNY

Schoenberg, Loren (Jonathan) (*b* Paterson, NJ, 23 July 1958). Tenor saxophonist, pianist, composer, arranger, bandleader, educator, and writer. He grew up in Fair Lawn, New Jersey, received piano lessons from the age of four, and took up saxophone when he was 15. Later he studied piano with Sanford Gold (1973–6) and, while attending the Manhattan School of Music (1976–80, 1986), saxophone with Lee Konitz (1976) and John Purcell (1986), among others. He worked as a sideman with Howard McGhee (1974–8), Eddie Durham (1976–85), Russell Procope (1979), Harold Ashby (1980–84), Benny Goodman (1980–85), Jo Jones (1981), Panama Francis (1982–4), Buck Clayton (1985–7), Benny Carter (from 1987), Jimmy Heath (from 1987), Gunther Schuller (from 1989), and John Lewis and the American Jazz Orchestra (1986–92); he occasionally conducted the orchestra in its final years (1990–92). Having previously conducted the WDR big band (Cologne) (1988–9), he conducted the Venezuela Jazz Symphony (1993), the Lincoln Center Jazz Orchestra (1994), and the Smithsonian Masterworks Orchestra (from 1994). From 1980 he has led his own big band, which has made numerous recordings (including *Just a-Settin' and a-Rockin'*, 1989, Musicmasters 5039-2), and various small groups, among them a quartet with Kenny Werner, John Goldsby, and Adam Nussbaum (which recorded *Sposin'*, 1990, Musicmasters 5055-2).

Aside from his work as a performer and conductor, from 1972 Schoenberg has worked as a jazz disc jockey in the New York area. From 1990 he taught in the Jazz and Contemporary Music Program at the New School for Social Research in New York (from 1996 at the Mannes/New School; from autumn 1999 at the New School University); he has also been a member of the faculties of Long Island University (1995–6) and the Manhattan School of Music (from 1996), and in 1997 he was an artistic consultant at Jazz at Lincoln Center. He is an accomplished writer whose publications have appeared in the *Annual Review of Jazz Studies*, *The Lester Young Reader*, ed. L. Porter (Washington, DC, and London, 1991), *Settin' the Tempo: 50 Years of Great Liner Notes*, ed. T. Piazza (New York and elsewhere, 1996), and the *New York Times*. In 1995 he received a Grammy Award for best album notes as co-author with Dan Morgenstern of the liner notes to *Louis Armstrong: Portrait of the Artist as a Young Man, 1923–1934* (1994, Col. Legacy CK40242).

BIBLIOGRAPHY

J. McDonough: "Swing Shift," *Chicago Tribune* (2 April 1989)
S. Nicholson: "Solid Ground," *Jazz: the Magazine*, no.13 (1992), 40

GK

Schoeppach, Brad. *See* Shepik, Brad.

Schönenberg, Detlef (*b* Berlin, 6 May 1944). German drummer. He began on accordion when he was 11 and took drum lessons from the age of 18; in the mid-1960s he became interested in free jazz. While playing with the band Rüdiger Carl Inc. (1969–72) he moved to Wuppertal (1970) and became involved in free-jazz activities there. While in Carl's trio he met Günter Christmann, with whom in 1972 he formed a duo that became known for its manner of combining free improvisation and ironic musical statements with theatrical gestures. The duo performed with the dancer Pina Bausch (1973), experimented with electronical devices (1975–6), and performed with Maggie Nicols. Schönenberg was a founding member of FMP. He belongs to the experimental school of German free jazz which endeavored to avoid traditional timekeeping roles and emphasized spontaneous improvisation, as may be heard in his duo with Christmann (*We Play*, 1973, FMP 0120) and on his unaccompanied solo album *Detlef Schönenberg spielt Schlagzeug* (1974, FMP SAJ04). In the 1980s and 1990s he abandoned idiomatic jazz improvisation and worked mainly within the field of contemporary art music.

BIBLIOGRAPHY

J. Engelhardt: "Jazzmusiker im Profil: Detlef Schönenberg, Schlagzeuger: Jazz als musikalische Sprache," *Neue Zeitschrift für Musik*, cxl/5 (1979), 553
B. Noglik: *Jazzwerkstatt international* (Berlin, 1981), 150
E. Jost: *Europas Jazz, 1960–1980* (Frankfurt am Main, Germany, 1987), 227

WOLFRAM KNAUER

Schönfeld, Friedhelm (*b* 1938). German clarinetist, saxophonist, flutist, and leader. He began playing jazz in the early 1950s but first worked professionally in a dance orchestra. In 1960 he joined the Tanzorchester des Berlin Rundfunks and began working in small groups playing jazz. While performing in Dresden in 1965 he recorded as the leader of a septet, then the following year he formed a trio consisting of Klaus Koch and Günter Sommer, which became increasingly involved in free improvisation. When the trio disbanded in 1974 Schönfeld formed another such small group with the cellist Wolfgang Weber and the drummer Dieter Keitel; it recorded in 1978 with Aladár Pege replacing Weber and in 1979 with its original members. Schönfeld also recorded with the bandleader Gunther Kretschmer (*c*1972) and the pianist Hans Rempel (1975–6) and wrote arrangements for the Tanzorchester des Berlin Rundfunks (mid-1970s). Nothing is known of his later career.

SELECTED RECORDINGS

As leader: on [no leader]: *Jazz via Dresden* (1965, Amiga 850116), Blues-Gendanken, Sparring; on *Friedhelm Schönfeld–Hubert Katzenbeier* (1972, Amiga 855307), Trio-Dimension (1972); *Friedhelm Schönfeld* (1978, Amiga 855628)

BIBLIOGRAPHY

H. D. Plümper: "Grosse Augenblicke," *JP*, xxii/3 (1973), 20
E. Jost: *Europas Jazz, 1960–1980* (Frankfurt am Main, Germany, 1987), 236

GK

Schoof, Manfred (*b* Magdeburg, Germany, 6 April 1936). German trumpeter. Having begun on piano, he did not take up trumpet until the age of 17. He attended the Musikakademie in Kassel (1955–8) and studied composition (with Bernd Alois Zimmermann), trumpet, and piano at the Hochschule in Cologne (1958–61); he wrote arrangements while he was a student for a school band and soon afterwards for orchestras led by Kurt Edelhagen and Harald Banter. From 1963 to 1965 he belonged to Gunter Hampel's quartet, then from December 1965 until 1968, with Gerd Dudek, Alex Schlippenbach, Buschi Niebergall, and the drummer Jacki Liebezeit as his sidemen, he led a quintet that was one of the first free-jazz groups in Europe. He worked with the Globe Unity Orchestra from its founding in 1966 until it disbanded in 1989, and in 1967, with Barney Wilen, Irène Schweizer, and others, he participated in a recording which brought a jazz group together with a trio of Indian classical musicians (sitar, tambura, and tablā).

In 1969 Schoof led a free-jazz orchestra on the recording *European Echoes* and, with Cees See and Peter Trunk, formed the New Jazz Trio, which incorporated into its playing elements of ethnic music; he also belonged to George Russell's orchestra (1969–71) and the Clarke–Boland Big Band (1969–72). After Trunk's death in 1973 he led a quintet and sextet with Michel Pilz (1974–9), which involved Jasper van 't Hof or Rainer Brüninghaus on keyboards, Günther Lenz on double bass, and Ralf Hübner on drums; the sextet toured Asia in 1975. Schoof also worked with Mal Waldron during this period (1974–80). Later he formed his own orchestra (1980), was a member of the European Jazz Ensemble (with which he recorded in 1987 and 1989), and wrote compositions and arrangements for big band (1983). Much in demand as a sideman with big bands – he toured and recorded with George Gruntz's Concert Jazz Band in the late 1980s and played at the concert arranged by Quincy Jones in honor of Miles Davis in 1991 – he was commissioned to write a new composition for the Berlin Contemporary Jazz Orchestra in 1995; the orchestra toured Germany giving the premières of his new compositions in 1997.

SELECTED RECORDINGS

As leader: *The Early Quintet* (1966, FMP 0540); *European Echoes* (1969, FMP 0010); of New Jazz Trio (with P. Trunk and C. See): *Page One* (1970, MPS 15276); *Horizons* (1979, Japo 60030); *Reflections* (1983, Mood 42)
As sideman: G. Russell: *Electronic Sonata for Souls Loved by Nature* (1969, SN 1034); M. Waldron: *Hard Talk* (1974, Enja 2050); European Jazz Ensemble: *At the Philharmonic Cologne* (1989, MA Music 800); Globe Unity Orchestra: *20th Anniversary* (1986, FMP CD45)

BIBLIOGRAPHY

Feather–Gitler '70s; *GrayF*; *ReclamsJ*
R. Williams: "Schoof: Apostle of the New Music," *MM* (14 March 1970), 12
H. Kumpf: "Der Komponist Manfred Schoof: Plattendokumente aus den Jahren 1965–1969," *JP*, xxii (1973), no.1, p.21; contd as "Der Komponist Manfred Schoof: Plattendokumente aus den Jahren 1970–1972," no.4, p.28
I. Storb: "Fragen an Manfred Schoof," *JP*, xxvii/7 (1978), 11
R. Reichelt: "Manfred Schoof: Beyond Free Jazz," *JF* [intl edn], no.61 (1979), 41
G. Endress: "Free Jazz, aber auch klangliches, farbiges, schönes im althergebrachten Sinn: Manfred Schoof Orchester," *JP*, xxxiii/1 (1984), 6
"On the Scene: G.D.R: Schoof on Tour," *JF* [intl edn], no.86 (1984), 16
E. Jost: *Europas Jazz, 1960–1980* (Frankfurt am Main, Germany, 1987), 60, 164

ROBERT J. IANNAPOLLO/SIMON ADAMS

Schröder, John(-Henry) (*b* Frankfurt am Main, Germany, 15 Sept 1964). German guitarist and drummer. His father, Heinrich Schröder, was a jazz drummer. He learned classical music on piano from the age of six and on guitar from the age of 11, and later he studied at the Hoch Conservatory in Frankfurt. Around the age of 16 he began working professionally and embarked on what became a long association with Christof Lauer. In 1982 he toured Asia in a quartet with Lauer and recorded with the same group as a leader. Schröder was the guitarist in Klaus Weiss's bop groups around 1982–8 and a member of Lauer's trio in 1986. In the late 1980s he joined the NDR Big Band (which recorded with Chet Baker in 1988) and the Jazzensemble des Hessischen Rundfunk, in which he performed with, among others, Heinz Sauer, Albert Mangelsdorff, and Adelhard Roidinger.

From around 1990 Schröder worked as both a guitarist and a drummer. He played guitar in a trio with Dieter Ilg and Wolfgang Haffner and in another trio with the pianist Roberto di Gioia and the double bass player Marc Abrams, and he recorded with the vibraphonist Christopher Dell and the bass player Stephan Schmolck (both 1992). As a drummer he toured with James Moody and in a trio, the Rote Bereich III, alongside the bass clarinetist Rudi Mahall and the guitarist Frank Möbius; in the same capacity he performed and recorded (1990) in the quartet Zuppa Romana (with the saxophonist Pete Weniger, di Gioia, and Abrams) and in small groups under Weniger's leadership (recording in 1998) and took part in sessions led by, among others, the pianist Markus Becker (1991) and the saxophonist Jan von Klewitz (1995). Schröder should not be confused with the drummer of same name who recorded with Eddie Condon in the early 1950s. He also plays piano.

SELECTED RECORDINGS

(recorded on guitar unless otherwise indicated)

As leader: *Deep Well* (1982, Trion 3210); with Henrik Walsdorff and Uli Jennessen: *Freedom of Speech* (1998, FMP OWN90011)
As sideman: K. Weiss: *Live at Opus 1* (1987, Jazzline 20830); H. Geller: *A Jazz Songbook* (1988, Enja 6006); Zuppa Romana: *Zuppa Romana* (1990, L+R 45030) [drums]; S. Schmolck: *Rites of Passage* (1992, L+R 45064)

BIBLIOGRAPHY

ReclamsJ

H.-J. Schaal: "John Schroeder," *JP*, xxxix/10 (1990), 12

GK

Schroeder, Gene [Eugene Charles] (*b* Madison, WI, 5 Feb 1915; *d* Madison, 16 Feb 1975). Pianist. His mother played piano and his father performed on trumpet with his own band. Schroeder learned piano (1924–7), played clarinet at high school, and studied music for a year at the University of Wisconsin (1932). He was then based in Milwaukee, where he first played with Wild Bill Davison. In 1939 he moved to New York and led his own group at the Town Topics club. He worked with Joe Marsala (from November 1940) and Marty Marsala (from late 1941), and with Davison in Chicago, Boston, and New York (from summer 1942). From October 1943 he was resident at Nick's, New York, initially in Miff Mole's group. While continuing at Nick's, he performed, recorded, and broadcast over the next two years in groups variously under the leadership of Davison, Mole, Joe Marsala, Muggsy Spanier, Pee Wee Russell, Bud Freeman, and, most often, Eddie Condon, with whose bands he also appeared in a series of concerts at Town Hall, the Ritz Theater, and Carnegie Hall in 1944–5. He was in Davison's band for the opening of Condon's club in Greenwich Village in December 1945, and he remained associated with the venue until 1960. Although he worked there mainly as a member of Davison's small group, he routinely played under Condon's leadership (in Davison's band or in other ensembles) for performances at the club (for illustration *see* NIGHTCLUBS AND OTHER VENUES, fig.5), recordings, and radio and television broadcasts; with Condon he also took part in the film short *Eddie Condon's Cavalcade of Broadway* (1951), appeared at the Newport festival (1956), and toured (notably to Britain in 1957). From 1948 to 1950 he studied with the composer Paul Creston. Schroeder was a member of the Dukes of Dixieland from 1961 to 1964, and in the late 1960s he worked with Tony Parenti.

SELECTED RECORDINGS

As leader: Liza/I ain't got nobody (1944, Black & White 33); Sweet Georgia Brown/Tea for Two (1944, Black & White 5)

As sideman: W. B. Davison: That's a Plenty/Panama (1943, Com. 1511); Riverboat Shuffle/Muskrat Ramble (1943, Com. 618); Original Dixieland One Step (1943, Com. 549); I'm Confessin' (1945, Com. 563); Wrap your Troubles in Dreams/I'm comin', Virginia (1946, Com. 628); E. Condon: Maple Leaf Rag/Jazz Me Blues (1950, Decca 27035); *Jam Session Coast-to-coast* (1953, Col. CL547); *Jammin' at Condon's* (1954, Col. CL616); *Bixieland* (1955, Col. CL719); *Condon's Treasury of Jazz* (1956, Col. CL881); *The Roaring Twenties* (1957, Col. CL1089)

BIBLIOGRAPHY

ChiltonW

E. Condon and H. O'Neal: *The Eddie Condon Scrapbook of Jazz* (New York, 1973)

O. Coyle: "Quiet Mastery," *MR*, ix/3 (1982), 1

G. Lombardi: *Eddie Condon on Record, 1927–1971* (Milan, 1987)

M. Selchow: *Profoundly Blue: a Bio-discographical Scrapbook on Edmond Hall* (Lübbecke, Germany, 1988)

M. Harrison: Liner notes, *The Complete CBS Recordings of Eddie Condon and his All Stars* (Mosaic 152, 1994)

B. Whyatt: *Muggsy Spanier: the Lonesome Road: a Biography and Discography* (New Orleans, 1995)

H. Willard: *The Wildest One: the Life of Wild Bill Davison* (Monkton, MD, 1996)

JAMES M. DORAN/BK

Schubert, Matthias (*b* Kassel, Germany, 18 April 1960). German tenor saxophonist. He took oboe lessons as a child and studied saxophone at the Swiss Jazz School (1979–81) and with Herb Geller and Walter Norris in Hamburg (1982); a fellow saxophonist, Allan Praskin, was his musical mentor (1975–90). He worked with the Euro Jazz Band (1981–5), Albert Mangelsdorff (1989–94), Gunter Hampel's Galaxy Dream Band (1984–96), and the Klaus König Orchestra (1989–96), as well as with his own bands. Schubert's playing is extremely extroverted and full of expression; even when screaming at the top range of his instrument his playing remains lyrical. He is comfortable performing modern-jazz standards as well as improvising freely; his own compositions tend to blend highly complex structures with free improvisation.

SELECTED RECORDINGS

Duos with G. Hampel: *Dialog* (1992, Birth 041)

As leader: *For Thieves and Lovers* (1992, Jazz Network 66658); *Blue and Grey Suite* (1994, Enja 9045-2)

BIBLIOGRAPHY

<http://www.jazzpages.com/MatthiasSchubert> (2001)

WOLFRAM KNAUER

Schuller. Family of musicians.

(1) Gunther (Alexander) Schuller (*b* New York, 22 Nov 1925). Composer, conductor, and writer, father of (2) Ed Schuller and (3) George Schuller. The son of a violinist with the New York Philharmonic Orchestra, he studied theory, flute, and french horn privately and played horn professionally with the American Ballet Theatre (1943), the Cincinnati Symphony Orchestra (1943–5), and the Metropolitan Opera in New York (1945–59); he began his career in jazz by recording as a french horn player with Miles Davis (1949–50).

In 1955 Schuller founded with John Lewis the Modern Jazz Society, which gave its first concert in Town Hall, New York, that same year and later became known as the Jazz and Classical Music Society. While lecturing at Brandeis University in 1957 he coined the term "third stream" to describe music that combined elements of Western art music and jazz; during the following decades he became an enthusiastic advocate of this style and wrote many works according to its principles, among them *Transformation* (1957, for jazz ensemble), Concertino (1959, for jazz quartet and orchestra; one of its movements, *Progression in Tempo*, has sometimes been performed separately), *Abstraction* (1959, for nine instruments), and Variants on a Theme of Thelonious Monk (1960, for 13 instruments), which was recorded by Ornette Coleman, Eric Dolphy, and Bill Evans (ii). His association with Lewis led to the performance and recording by the Modern Jazz Quartet of several of Schuller's works, notably *Conversation* (on *Third Stream Music*, 1957, 1959, 1960, Atl. 1345) and the Concertino. With Lewis and the conductor Harold Farberman, he led the big band ORCHESTRA U.S.A. from 1962 to 1965. In addition he oversaw the programming and performance of third-stream works at concerts and festivals (such as one at Brandeis University, 1957), and with Lewis and others he formed the Lenox School of Jazz in Massachusetts.

From 1967 to 1977 Schuller was the president of the New England Conservatory. During this period he promoted the music of Scott Joplin, Jelly Roll Morton, Duke Ellington, and Paul Whiteman by preparing editions, making transcriptions, and giving performances of their works; his recordings of music by Joplin include the opera *Treemonisha* and selections from *The Red Back Book*, a collection of orchestrated ragtime compositions. In the late 1980s, in collaboration with the jazz scholar Andrew Homzy, he reconstructed Charles Mingus's 18-movement symphony *Epitaph*; he then toured with an orchestra which gave performances of this piece, recording at the Lincoln Center and Wolf Trap in 1989 and broadcasting on NPR from the Chicago Jazz Festival in 1990, and also making a studio recording. In 1994 he contributed compositions and arrangements to Joe Lovano's album of jazz and pop standards and third-stream music, *Rush Hour* (BN 29269-2).

Schuller formed the firms Margun Music (1975) and Gunmar Music (1979), which published jazz and third-stream works by Charles Mingus, George Russell, Johnny Carisi, Ran Blake, and Jimmy Giuffre, as well as his own editions of ragtime music by Joplin, Joseph Lamb, and Eubie Blake; in 1980 he established the record company and label GM. Of his published writings the most influential have been his contributions to the *Jazz Review* (1958–60), his book *Early Jazz: its Roots and Musical Development* (1968), and the latter's sequel, *The Swing Era: the Development of Jazz, 1930–1945* (1989) [*SchullerS*].

Oral history material in *NjR*.

WORKS

(selective list)

Orch: Symphonic Tribute to Duke Ellington, 1955; Symphony for Brass and Construction, 1956; Concertino, jazz qt, orch, 1959, Passacaglia arr. jazz qt, band, Progression in Tempo pubd separately; Journey into Jazz (Schuller, N. Hentoff), nar, jazz qnt, orch, 1962; numerous arrs. and transcrs. for orch and other inst ens of works by E. Blake, J. P. Johnson, S. Joplin, J. Lamb, and others

Chamber: Jumpin' in the Future (Atonal Jazz Study), 12 insts, 1948; Twelve by Eleven, jazz nonet, 1955; Transformation, jazz ens, 1957; Abstraction, 9 insts, 1959; Conversations, jazz qt, str qt, 1959; Variants on a Theme of John Lewis, 11 insts, 1960; Variants on a Theme of Thelonious Monk, 13 insts, 1960

SELECTED RECORDINGS

As leader: *Jazz Abstractions* (1960, Atl. 1365), incl. Abstraction, Variants on a Theme of Thelonious Monk

As sideman: M. Davis: *Classics in Jazz* (1949–50, Cap. H459), incl. Deception, Moon Dreams, Rocker; Darn that Dream (1950, Cap. 1221); [no leader]: *Music for Brass* (1956, Col. CL941), incl. Symphony for Brass and Construction, Three Little Feelings; Brandeis Jazz Festival: *Modern Jazz Concert* (1957, Col. WL127), incl. Transformation; M. Davis: *Porgy and Bess* (1958, Col. CL1274); E. Dolphy: on *Vintage Dolphy* (1962–3, GMR 3005), Abstraction, Variants on a Theme of Thelonious Monk

WRITINGS

(selective list)

"Sonny Rollins and the Challenge of Thematic Improvisation," *JR*, i/1 (1958), 6; repr. in *Jazz Panorama*, ed. M. Williams (New York and London, 1962/*R*1979), 239

"Thelonious Monk," *JR*, i/1 (1958), 22; iii/6 (1960), 26; repr. in *Jazz Panorama*, ed. M. Williams (New York and London, 1962/*R*1979), 216

"Jazz and Classical Music," in L. Feather: *The Encyclopedia of Jazz* (New York, rev. and enlarged 2/1960), 497

"Third Stream Redefined," *Saturday Review*, xliv (13 May 1961), 54

Horn Technique (London, New York, and Toronto, 1962)

"The Future of Form in Jazz," *The American Composer Speaks: a Historical Anthology, 1770–1965*, ed. G. Chase (n.p. [Baton Rouge, LA], 1966), 216

Early Jazz: its Roots and Musical Development (New York, 1968)

Musings: the Musical Worlds of Gunther Schuller (New York, and Oxford, England, 1986)

The Swing Era: the Development of Jazz, 1930–1945 (New York, and Oxford, England, 1989) [*SchullerS*]

BIBLIOGRAPHY

G. Chase, ed.: *The American Composer Speaks: a Historical Anthology, 1770–1965* (n. p. [Baton Rouge, LA], 1966)

S. Mitchell: "Third Stream Visitation: a Talk with Gunther Schuller," *DB*, xxxv/4 (1968), 20

B. Persia: *Two Works for Jazz Quartet and Ensemble by Gunther Schuller* (diss., Eastman School, 1973) [on *Conversations* and *Concertino*]

R. Palmer: "Gunther Schuller: on the American Musical Melting Pot," *DB*, xliii/3 (1976), 12

D. Baker: "A Talk with Gunther Schuller," *MR*, vi/9 (1979), 5

J. Hasse: "An Interview with Gunther Schuller," *ARJS*, i (1982), 39

D. Reffkin: "The Ragtime Machine," *MR*, xi/1 (1983), 8

N. Carnovale: *Gunther Schuller: a Bio-bibliography* (New York, 1987)

R. Dyer: "At 63, Gunther Schuller Remains a Man for All Tempos," *Boston Globe* (30 April 1989)

L. Feather: "Schuller: a Man who Lives in Harmony," *Los Angeles Times* (12 March 1989)

R. Dyer: "Schuller at 65," *Boston Globe* (25 Nov 1990)

M. J. Mavrides: "The Sound of Eclectic Music," *Boston Globe* (18 March 1990)

J. Woodard: "Hail! Hail! Gunther Schuller," *Musician*, no.156 (1991), 22

J. McDonough: "'Original Intent' Comes to Jazz," *Wall Street Journal* (21 July 1992)

W. Russo: "Lifetime Achievement: Gunther Schuller: Classical to Cool to 3rd Stream," *DB*, lx/9 (1993), 24

B. Blumenthal: "Joe Lovano & Gunther Schuller: Orchestral Raps," *DB*, lxii/3 (1995), 20

R. Dyer: "Celebrating Gunther Schuller," *Boston Globe* (3 Dec 1995)

J. McLellan: "Gunther Schuller: Going for the Records," *Washington Post* (15 Nov 1998)

(2) Ed(win Gunther) Schuller (*b* New York, 11 Jan 1955). Double bass player, son of (1) Gunther Schuller. He moved to Boston in 1967 and began playing the double bass at the age of 15, performing with his fellow student Ricky Ford and studying privately and at the New England Conservatory of Music (1972–5). After a brief tour with Pat Martino he moved in 1975 to New York, where he worked with Tim Berne and Jaki Byard (both late 1970s – early 1980s) and toured and recorded with Paul Motian's quintet (*c*1982–6), Jim Pepper and Mal Waldron (both 1980s), and the orchestra that presented Charles Mingus's symphony *Epitaph*, conducted by his father (early to mid-1990s). He also worked with Gerry Hemingway, Herb Robertson, Perry Robinson, Simon Nabatov, Armen Donelian, and others, and in the mid-1980s began to lead his own group, the Eleventh Hour. Among his sidemen have been the trombonist Gary Valente, the saxophonists Joe Lovano, Craig Handy, Dewey Redman, and Mack Goldsbury, the guitarist Bill Bickford, and the drummers Victor Jones, Billy Hart, Ronnie Burrage, and Motian. From 1996 he has worked in the quartet Schulldogs with his brother George. Schuller lives in Berlin, where he teaches at the Hanns Eichler School, and New York, and around 1990 he became a resident instructor at the Schweitzer Institute, Sand Point, Idaho.

SELECTED RECORDINGS

As leader: *Inside Lookin' Out* (1988, Tutu 888004): *The Eleventh Hour* (1991, Tutu 888124); *Mu-point* (1993, Tutu 888154); *To Know Where One Is* (1994, GM 3019)

As sideman: T. Berne: *Ancestors* (1983, SN 1061); *Mutant Variations* (1983, SN 1091); P. Motian: *The Story of Maryam* (1983, SN 1074); S. Nabatov: *Circle the Line* (1986, GM 3009); P. Motian: *Misterioso* (1986, SN 1174); M. Waldron: *Quadrologue at Utopia* (1989, Tutu 888118); T. Stańko: *Caoma* (1991, Konnex 5053); J. Lovano: *Rush Hour* (1994, BN 29269-2)

BIBLIOGRAPHY

P. Wiessmueller: "Ed Schuller," *JP*, xlii/4 (1993), 12

K. Franckling: "Hearsay: Ed Schuller," *JT*, xxxvi/3 (1996), 26

H. Pekar: "Bass Notes: Acoustic's New World Order: Ed Schuller: Life Styles," *Bass Player*, ix/10 (1998), 26

(3) George (Alexander) Schuller (*b* New York, 29 Dec 1958). Drummer and leader, son of (1) Gunther Schuller. He moved to Boston in 1967, studied at the New England Conservatory of Music (BM 1982), and co-led the group Best Foreign Film (1981–4). Early in his career he worked as an assistant sound engineer at Tanglewood (1975–82) and as a jazz radio disc jockey (1976–84). In 1984 he formed the 12-piece group Orange then Blue, with which he has recorded and toured internationally. He has also worked with the singer Lisa Thorson (from 1987), the keyboard player

Eugene Maslov and his trio (1990–94), Bruce Gertz (1990–96), the vibraphonist Tom Beckham (from 1996), and Tom Varner's trio (from 1997). In 1994 he moved to New York, where he has been active as a freelance. That same year he recorded the album *Rush Hour* (BN 29269-2) with Joe Lovano and the following year he performed with his father and Lovano at Jazz at Lincoln Center and in Linz, Austria; he recorded again with Lovano, under the leadership of Bill De Arango (*c*1995). From 1996 Schuller has led the quartet Schulldogs, with the saxophonists George Garzone and Tony Malaby and his brother Ed Schuller or Mark Helias on double bass. He may be heard as a leader on *Lookin' Up from Down Below* (1986, GM 3013).

MARK TUCKER/BK (1), GK (2–3)

Schulze, Manfred (*b* Schweizerthal, Germany, 17 Aug 1934). German baritone saxophonist, clarinetist, and leader. He undertook formal studies in piano and clarinet and worked in various ensembles from 1954 to 1958. In 1962, with Ernst-Ludwig Petrowsky, he formed the hard-bop group Manfred Ludwig Sextet; it recorded in 1963 and 1964 and in 1964 accompanied and recorded with the singer Dorothy Ellison. From 1964 to 1970 he worked in groups led by Klaus Lenz (he recorded in Lenz's Modern Jazz Big Band '65 in 1965). Schulze formed the wind ensemble Bläserquintett (1969) and then led the groups Praxis II (1970–71) and Schulze Formation (1973–6). From 1973 he collaborated with the contemporary European art music pianist Hermann Keller, with whom he worked in various formations, including a duo (1974–6), the Berliner Improvisations Quartett (1976–9, recording in 1979), and the Berliner Improvisations Trio (from 1979, including a tour in autumn of that year in a quartet with the addition of Tony Oxley); these groups combined free improvisation with the recitation of written texts, as did the Jazz Werkstatt Orchester, again co-led by Schulze and Keller. Schulze was also associated with Hannes Zerbe, in whose Blechband he recorded and toured from 1980, and with whom he worked in a trio and a quintet. In the mid-1980s he re-formed his Bläserquintett, with Manfred Hering and Johannes Bauer among his sidemen; the group recorded in 1985–6 and 1994. He toured in 1986 as the leader of the ensemble Clarinet Project. By the early 1990s, suffering from Huntington's disease, Schulze was forced to retire from performance, although the Bläserquintett made a further recording under his nominal leadership in 1994 (*Konzertino*, FMP CD070). He spent much of his career working as an educator.

SELECTED RECORDINGS

As leader of Bläserquintett: *Nummer 12* (1985, FMP1090); *Viertens* (1986, FMP1230)

As sideman with Berliner Improvisations Quartett: *Berliner Improvisations Quartett* (1979, Amiga 585717)

BIBLIOGRAPHY

"Eurojazz Personalities," *JF* [intl edn], no.27 (1974), 67

E. Jost: *Europas Jazz, 1960–1980* (Frankfurt am Main, Germany, 1987), 267

M. Kunzler: *Jazz-Lexicon* (Reinbek, nr Hamburg, Germany, 1988)

A. Gerlof: "Manfred Schulze Bläser Quintett," *JP*, xliii/3 (1994), 26

B. Noglik: "An Schnittstellen von Jazz und neuer Musik," *Neue Musikzeitung*, xliii (1994), Aug–Sept, 36

D. O'Driscoll: "Johannes Bauer: Short Talk," *Cadence*, xxvii/2 (2001), 12

GK

Schutt, Arthur (R.) (*b* Reading, PA, 21 Nov 1902; *d* San Francisco, 28 Jan 1965). Pianist, arranger, and composer. He was pianist and arranger for Paul Specht's orchestra from 1918 to 1924. In New York he contributed to the emerging novelty piano idiom and recorded with many dance bands and such jazz groups as the Georgians (1922–4), led by Frank Guarente, and the Charleston Chasers (1925, 1927, 1929). During the 1920s he was closely associated with Rube Bloom and frequently alternated with him in local bands. Schutt worked with some of the most important jazz artists of the 1920s and 1930s, including Red Nichols (1926–9, 1931), the Dorsey Brothers' orchestra (1928–31), and Benny Goodman (1931, 1934); he also recorded as a soloist and leader and in the Chicago Loopers with Bix Beiderbecke and Frankie Trumbauer. In the 1940s and 1950s he was employed by film studios in Hollywood. Among his important works for piano is *Bluin' the Black Keys* (1926).

SELECTED RECORDINGS

As sideman: Georgians: I wish I could shimmy like my sister Kate (1922, Col. A3775); Charleston Chasers: Farewell Blues (1927, Col. 1539D)

RECORDED COMPOSITIONS

(selective list; all recorded by Schutt as unaccompanied soloist)

The Ghost of the Piano (1923, Regal G8032); Teasin' the Ivories (1923, Regal G8046); Rambling in Rhythm (1928, Har. 860H); Piano Puzzle (1929, OK 41243)

BIBLIOGRAPHY

ChiltonW

D. A. Jasen: *Recorded Ragtime, 1897–1958* (Hamden, CT, 1973) [incl. 78 r.p.m. recordings of jazz versions of ragtime pieces]

D. A. Jasen and T. J. Tichenor: *Rags and Ragtime: a Musical History* (New York, 1978)

DAVID THOMAS ROBERTS

Schütz, Martin (*b* Biel, Switzerland, 1954). Swiss cellist. In 1981 he performed with Werner Lüdi's group Sonnymoon at Jazz Festival Willisau. Later he and Hans Koch spent six months living in New York (1987), where they worked with leading free improvisers. In the late 1980s Schütz formed a trio with Koch and the drummer Marco Käppeli, and in 1989–90 he and Koch led various large ensembles that included the American musicians Jason Hwang, Butch Morris, Tom Cora, Andrew Cyrille, and Shelley Hirsch and the Europeans Hans Reichel and Paul Lovens; one version of this group performed and recorded at the Total Music Meeting in November 1990. From that year Schütz worked regularly in a trio with Koch and Fredy Studer, performing an amalgamation of avant-garde improvisation, rock, and electronic music which is aptly described by the title of the album *Hardcore Chambermusic* (1994); this trio recorded with the traditional Egyptian group El Nil Troop in 1995 and with a group of Cuban musicians in 1997. In addition Schütz recorded with Urs Blöchlinger (1985) and Lüdi (1987). In the 1990s he formed trios with the violinist Hans Burgener and Barre Phillips, Stephan Wittwer and Lovens, and the reed player Rüdi Hausermann and the drummer Tim Hägler; this last group recorded in 1990 and 1993. Schütz also worked regularly with the pianist Michel Wintsch (recording in a trio with Gerry Hemingway in 1994), and in 1995 he appeared with the group Switchbox at the International New Jazz Festival Moers. As well as the standard cello he plays five-string acoustic and electric instruments and various electronic devices.

SELECTED RECORDINGS

As leader: with H. Koch and M. Käppeli: *Accélération* (1987, ECM 1357), *The Art of the Staccato* (1988, Sound Aspects 033); with H. Koch: *Approximations* (1989, Intakt 018); with H. Burgener and B. Phillips:

Looking out our Window (1992, For 4 Ears 515); with S. Wittwer and P. Lovens: *Choice Chase* (1992, Intakt 032); with M. Wintsch and G. Hemingway: *Wintsch/Schütz/Hemingway* (1994, Unit 4071); with H. Koch and F. Studer: *Hardcore Chambermusic* (1994, Intakt 042), *Heavy Cairo Traffic* (1995, Intuition 3175-2), *Fidel* (1997, Intakt 056); with H. Burgener and B. Phillips: *Heat Transfer* (1998, For 4 Ears 929)
As sideman with X-Communication: *X-Communication* (1990, FMP CD33)

BIBLIOGRAPHY

B. Carnevale: "Refrain: Swiss Trio Captures Field," *Jazziz*, xvi/9 (1999), 80
<http://www.shef.ac.uk/misc/rec/ps/efi/musician/mschuetz.html> (2000) [incl. discography]

GK

Schuur, Diane (Joan) [Deedles] (*b* Tacoma, WA, 10 Dec 1953). Singer. She was blind from birth as the result of a medical accident. She began singing when she was only two and, self-taught as a pianist, was performing professionally by the time she was ten. Later she spent three years in Arizona (*c*1977–1980) before returning to the Northwest to live in Seattle. She sang primarily pop music until the mid-1970s, but in 1975 she performed with Ed Shaughnessy at the Monterey Jazz Festival. She returned to this festival in 1979 at the behest of Dizzy Gillespie and was heard there by Stan Getz, who became a mentor and helped to promote her early career; while performing with Getz on public television at the White House in December 1982 she was heard by Larry Rosen of GRP records, for which she recorded from 1984 into the 1990s. In February 1987 she recorded and broadcast on television with the Count Basie Orchestra under the direction of Frank Foster; this performance may be seen on the video *Diane Schuur & the Count Basie Orchestra* (1988). In June 1987 Schuur performed with the Mel Lewis Orchestra and Getz at the JVC Jazz Festival New York. From the late 1980s through the 1990s she continued to tour internationally, most often appearing in Japan and Europe and at major festivals; she gave concerts in South America in 1995 and 1996 and in Bangkok in 1996. In 1998 she recorded for Atlantic.

Schuur is essentially a jazz-inflected pop singer. Her early work displayed a tendency towards a brassy, overwrought sound, which may possibly have been connected with her struggles with drug addiction, which Maggin (1996) recounts. Her work from the early to mid-1990s, when it appears she overcame this problem, shows a mature and controlled presence that is much more musical and expressive.

BIBLIOGRAPHY

M. Bourne: "Diane or Deedles ... She's Schuur Dynamite," *JT* (1987), Oct, 32
J. Kaliss: "Jazz World Has Diane Schuur in Sight," *San Francisco Chronicle Datebook* (11 Sept 1988)
D. L. Maggin: *Stan Getz: a Life in Jazz* (New York, 1996)

SCOTT FREDRICKSON, GK

Schwab, Sigi [Siegfried] (*b* Ludwigshafen, Germany, 5 Aug 1940). German guitarist. Having taken up guitar at the age of 13 he played with blues, folk, and jazz groups while studying classical guitar and double bass at the Musikhochschule in Mannheim (from 1956). In 1963 he was engaged by Erwin Lehn for regular work on radio and in the studios; in 1965 he played in the RIAS Big Band in Berlin, and in 1966 he recorded his first album as an unaccompanied soloist, *Fabulous Guitar* (Phi. 843975PY). For roughly the next 15 years he was active mainly as a studio musician, recording with Wolfgang Dauner (1969–70), Peter Herbolzheimer (1971–2), Svend Asmussen (1974), George Shearing (1974), Benny Bailey (1976), and others, as well as with many pop musicians; at the same time he wrote music for films. In the 1980s he played in a duo with Chris Hinze (with whom he recorded the album *Live at the Northsea Jazz Festival*, 1980, Kt. 705), with the jazz-rock and Latin group Percussion Academia (from 1983, when it recorded the album *Rondo a tre*, Melos 703), and in a classical group, the Diabelli Trio. In the 1990s Schwab increasingly utilized ethnic elements drawn from Indian, African, and other sources in his music. He produced two series of guitar workshops for German television. (<http://www.sigi-schwab.de> (2001))

WOLFRAM KNAUER

Schwaller, Roman (*b* Frauenfeld, Switzerland, 18 Jan 1957). Swiss tenor saxophonist. He studied classical clarinet from the age of 14, changed to jazz alto saxophone when he was 17, and took up tenor saxophone while attending the Swiss Jazz School in Berne. After moving to Munich (1977) he performed and toured as a member of Klaus Weiss's quintet; in 1979 he worked in New York and made his first recording as a leader. From 1979 to 1989 he performed and recorded with the Vienna Art Orchestra, and in 1983 he formed his own quartet. He also toured, performed on radio and television, appeared at festivals in Europe, and participated in bop "battles" with Johnny Griffin and Sal Nistico (ii) in the group Three Generations of Tenor Saxophone (1983–6); the band recorded at a concert in 1985. Schwaller recorded as a sideman with Dusko Goykovich and Joe Haider (1980), Thomas Stabenow (1984), Charly Antolini (1985), Klaus Ignatzek (1986), Haider (1986, 1994), and Wolfgang Haffner (1990–91); as a co-leader with Mel Lewis (1987); and as the sole leader of small bop groups (1987, also including Lewis; 1990, 1995). In addition he made recordings as a member of the salsa group Orquestra Conexion Latina (1987), of the quintet Saxophone Connection (1991), of the saxophone quartet the Munich Saxophon Family (1990, 1993), and of the sextet the Lost Jazz Generation, which included Franco Ambrosetti and Daniel Humair (1995), and as a guest soloist with the trios Grooveyard and We Three (both 1996). In 1991 he joined the NDR big band, and in 1995 he formed another quartet of his own; in November 1996 he toured with Jimmy Cobb.

SELECTED RECORDINGS

As leader: with J. Griffin and S. Nistico: *Three Generations of Tenor Saxophone* (1985, JHM 3611); with M. Lewis: *Roman Schwaller–Mel Lewis* (1987, Bassic Sound 005)
As sideman: K. Weiss: *Density* (1980, MRC 06646195); Vienna Art Orchestra: *From No Time to Ragtime* (1982, HA 1999–2000), incl. Jelly Roll, but Mingus Rolls Better, Variations about a Liberate Proposal, Variations about N508-10 (4G); *The Minimalism of Eric Satie* (1983–4, HA 6024), incl. Vexations 1801, Vexations 1611, Vexations 2105
For further recordings *see* VIENNA ART ORCHESTRA.

BIBLIOGRAPHY

M. A. Woelfle: "Höhenflüge eines Saxophonisten: Roman Schwaller," *JP*, xlv/7–8 (1996), 32 [incl. discography]

PETER SCHWALM/BK

Schwartz, Thornal(, Jr.) [Thornel] (*b* Philadelphia, 29 May 1927; *d* Philadelphia, 30 Dec 1977). Electric guitarist. Although his first name consistently appears on recordings and in the jazz literature as Thornel, he spelled it (and that of his father) Thornal on his application for social security. He studied piano at the Landis Institute in Philadelphia. As a guitarist he held an association with the singer Freddie Cole (1952–5) and played in the organ trios of Jimmy Smith (1955–7), in whose first recordings for Blue Note he took part, Johnny Hammond (then Johnny Hammond Smith) (1958–60, 1967), and Larry Young (1960–62). In the early 1960s he worked in Philadelphia with Charles Earland, when the latter was still performing as a saxophonist, and from *c*1966 to *c*1971 he was with Jimmy McGriff. Schwartz also recorded with Jimmy Forrest (1960), the singers Sylvia Sims and Byrdie Green (both 1967), and Groove Holmes (*c*1970).

SELECTED RECORDINGS

As leader: *Soul Cookin'* (1962, Argo 704)
As sideman: L. Young: *Testifying* (1960, NewJ 8249); J. Forrest: *Forrest Fire!* (1960, NewJ 8250); L. Young: *Groove Street* (1962, Prst. 7237)

BIBLIOGRAPHY

FeatherE

GK

Schweizer, Irène (*b* Schaffhausen, Switzerland, 2 June 1941). Swiss pianist and leader. When she was eight she took up accordion, on which she initially played Swiss folk music, then at the age of 12 she began learning piano; she had stopped playing accordion by the time she was 14 or 15, at which point she took up drums. Her first work in jazz was as a drummer in dixieland bands in the mid-1950s. In 1961 she attended the Bournemouth Language School in London, and the following year, not wishing to return to Switzerland, she worked as a domestic. Through the double bass player David Willis she was introduced to the jazz spots in the city and frequented Ronnie Scott's nightly, and with the help of Scott she studied jazz piano with Eddie Thompson. Back in Switzerland by September 1962 she recorded in Zurich as a sole leader, then early in 1963 she formed a piano trio with the double bass player Uli Trepte and the drummer Mani Neumaier. This trio originally played soul jazz and was later influenced by the trio styles of Bill Evans (ii), McCoy Tyner, and Paul Bley, but during a tour of Germany in 1966 it began to explore free improvisation. It recorded with the tenor saxophonist Alex Rohr in 1964 and in its own right through 1967, when it also recorded with Manfred Schoof, Barney Wilen, and the Indian musicians Diwan Motihar (sitar and voice), Keshav Sathe (*tablā*), and Kasan Thakur (*tambūrā*). In 1968, after having disbanded her trio, Schweizer joined Pierre Favre's trio with George Mraz (replaced early on by Peter Kowald); this group performed as a quartet with the addition of Evan Parker (1968–9, recording in the latter year). In June 1969 she recorded alongside the pianists Fred van Hove and Alex Schlippenbach as a member of Schoof's large ensemble, and in March 1970 she performed in another of Favre's groups at the Deutsches Jazz Festival Frankfurt.

From 1973 to 1985 Schweizer collaborated regularly with Rüdiger Carl. They co-led a quartet (recording in 1973–4) and formed a trio with Louis Moholo (1974–7) before working extensively in a duo, and they co-led another quartet consisting of Maarten Altena and Tristan Honsinger. She may be seen in the documentary film *Rising Tones Cross* ([filmed 1984]), both in the duo with Carl and as a member of Peter Brötzmann's ensemble. She recorded in John Tchicai's quartet with Buschi Niebergall and Makaya Ntshoko at the Willisau Jazz Festival (1975), began working as an unaccompanied soloist (1976), and established, with Maggie Nicols and Lindsay Cooper, the Feminist Improvising Group (1977), which later continued as the European Women's Improvising Group (from *c*1980). In 1981 she recorded with Joe McPhee's group Po Music, and around 1984 she was a founder of the record company and label Intakt.

In 1986 Schweizer began working with Joëlle Léandre. They formed a duo (which recorded in 1986), Les Trois Dames (a trio with the singer Annick Nozati), and Les Diaboliques (a trio with Nicols which remained active in the new century), and Léandre appeared in Schweizer's small groups. At the same time Schweizer began a series of duo recordings with drummers: Moholo (1986), Günter Sommer (1987), Andrew Cyrille (1988), Neumaier and Favre (both 1990), Han Bennink (1995), and Favre again (1998). In 1987 she renewed her association with Carl by joining his quintet COWWS, which consisted initially of Phil Wachsmann, Stephan Wittwer, and the double bass player Jay Oliver.

In 1990 Schweizer and Favre set up a trio with Barre Phillips. That same year she performed and recorded with Marilyn Crispell at the Free Music Workshop, and in 1991, on the occasion of her fiftieth birthday, she recorded *Theoria*, a work commissioned for the event by the London Jazz Composers Orchestra; she also recorded in a sextet consisting of Conrad Bauer, Barry Guy, Parker, Phillips, and Paul Lytton (1991) and recorded with Mario Schiano (1992), and performed and recorded frequently as an unaccompanied soloist. In 1995 she recorded again with the London Jazz Composers Orchestra, and in late 1997 she made a rare appearance on her first jazz instrument, recording as a drummer in the small group led by the pianist Urs Voerkel. Schweizer has also worked as a producer and organizer for Canaille: International Women's Festival of Improvised Music and the Taktlos Festival.

SELECTED RECORDINGS

As unaccompanied soloist: *Wilde Señoritas* (1976, FMP 0330); *Hexensabbat* (1977, FMP 0500); *Piano Solo*, i (1990, Intakt 020), incl. The Ballad of the Sad Café, Look-In; *Many and One Direction* (1996, Intakt 044)
Duos: with R. Carl: on *Tuned Boots* (1977–8, FMP 0550), Boose, Blues, Bambus (1978); *The Very Centre of Middle Europe* (1978, HH X); with L. Moholo: *Irène Schweizer–Louis Moholo* (1986, Intakt 006); with J. Léandre: *Cordial gratin* (1986, FMP 1160); with P. Kowald: on Kowald: *Duos: Europa* (1986–9, FMP 1260), Wundenkönigin und Fühlebähr (1986); with G. Sommer: *Irène Schweizer–Günter Sommer* (1987, Intakt 007); with A. Cyrille: *Irène Schweizer–Andrew Cyrille* (1988, Intakt 008); with M. Crispell: *Overlapping Hands: Eight Segments* (1990, FMP CD30); with P. Favre: *Irène Schweizer–Pierre Favre* (1990, Intakt 009); with H. Bennink: *Irène Schweizer–Han Bennink* (1995, Intakt 010)
As leader: *Early Tapes* (1967, FMP 0590); *Messer* (1975, FMP 0290); with J. Tchicai: *Willi the Pig* (1975, Willisau 1); on *Tuned Boots* (1977–8, FMP 0550), Tuned Boots; with L. Cooper and M. Nicols: on [no leader]: *Dix improvisations, Victoriaville 1989* (1989, Victo CD009), Nicosch
As sideman: P. Favre: *Santana* (1968, Favre 1); *Pierre Favre Quartett* (1969, Wergo 80004); J. McPhee: *Topology* (1981, HA 1987/88); Paris Quartet: *Paris Quartet* (1985, Intakt 012); R. Carl: *Zwei Quintette* (1987, FMP 1210/20); London Jazz Composers Orchestra: *Theoria* (1991, Intakt 024); M. Schiano: on *Meetings* (1980, 1992–3, Splasc(h) 418-2), Three Little Songs, i–ii (1992); COWWS: *Grooves 'n' Loops* (1993, FMP CD59); Les Diaboliques: *Les Diaboliques* (1993, Intakt 033); *Splitting Image* (1994, Intakt 048); *Live at the Rhinefalls* (1997, Intakt 059)

BIBLIOGRAPHY

CarrJ; *GrayF*
J. Solothurnmann: "Irene Schweizer," *JF* [intl edn], no.17 (1972), 61
H. D. Plümper: "Wieder in Berlin – Free Music," *JP*, xxiii/6 (1974), 12
"Emil Mangelsdorff, Schweizer–Carl–Moholo im Palmegarten," *JP*, xxiv/9 (1975), 18
G. Rouy: "Irène Schweizer," *Jm*, no.235 (1975), 16 [incl. discography]
E. Caflisch: "Jobs zum Überleben: Irène Schweizer," *JP*, xv/10 (1976), 13
G. Cerutti: "Discographie: Irène Schweizer," *Jazz 360°*, no.33 (1980), 6 [discography]
H. Charlton: "Collective Impressions," *MM* (13 Sept 1980), 30
B. Noglik: "Irène Schweizer: Uncompromising Continuity," *JF* [intl edn], no.65 (1980), 34
——: "Irène Schweizer," *Jazzwerkstatt international* (Berlin, 1981, 2/1983) [incl. discography]
G. Lock: "Irene Schweizer: an Ear for Freedom," *Wire*, no.11 (1985), 12
E. Jost: *Europas Jazz, 1960–1980* (Frankfurt am Main, Germany, 1987), 156

P. Carles, A. Clergeat, and J.-L. Comolli: *Dictionnaire du jazz* (Paris, 1988, rev. and enlarged 2/1994)
M. Chenard: "Irène Schweizer," *Coda*, no.222 (1988), 11
M. Kunzler: *Jazz-Lexicon* (Reinbek, nr Hamburg, Germany, 1988)
B. Ogilvie: "Le bal d'Irène," *Jm*, no.371 (1988), 27
B. Rusch: "Irene Schweizer: Interview," *Cadence*, xvii/1 (1991), 5
I. Schaad: "Laudatio für Irène Schweizer," *JP*, xl/3 (1991), 14
B. Noglik: "Improvisationen als Symbole des Lebensstils," *Neue Zeitschrift für Musik*, cliii (1992), Oct, 32
J. Hale: "Irène Schweizer: Many and One Direction," *Coda*, no.276 (1997), 14
F. Raulin and S. Oliva: "Irène Schweizer: dialogue à six mains," *Jm*, no.469 (1997), 22
J. Solothurnman: "Wie es ist mit Irène Schweizer zu spielen: fünf Schlagzeuger und eine Pianistin," *JP*, xlvi/3 (1997), 3
<http://www.shef.ac.uk/misc/rec/ps/efi/mschweiz.html> (2000) [incl. discography]

BERT NOGLIK/GK

Schwindt, Christian [Chrisse] (*b* Helsinki, 14 March 1940; *d* Helsinki, 12 Oct 1992). Finnish drummer. He played in dance bands while he was in high school and participated regularly in jam sessions at the Old House Jazz Club in Helsinki. In the 1960s he recorded as a leader (1963–4) and as co-leader with Otto Donner of a quintet (*For Friends and Relatives*, 1965, RCA LSP10070). He was a founder and director of Love Records (1966–76), which issued many Finnish jazz albums. After the company failed, Schwindt started Kompass Records, which he operated on a part-time basis with the pianist Lasse Mårtenson. He worked mostly with entertainers but played regularly with the DDT Jazzband, a semiprofessional dixieland group. In 1972 and 1979 he recorded with Hacke Björksten. Schwindt is regarded as the most influential Finnish drummer of the 1960s.

PEKKA GRONOW

Ścierański, Krzysztof (*b* Kraków, Poland, 24 Aug 1954). Polish electric bass guitarist. Playing both jazz and rock, he was a member of the ensemble Laboratorium (1976–80), Zbigniew Namysłowski's band Air Condition (1980–82), and Krzesimir Dębski's fusion group String Connection (1982–6). He toured widely, recorded as a studio musician, and led his own trio, but above all he was acclaimed for his performances and recordings as an unaccompanied bass soloist. In the late 1980s he formed a trio with his brother, the guitarist Paweł Ścierański, and the drummer Marek Surzyn (later replaced by Jan Pluta). He made several recordings as a leader in the 1990s, including an album with Marek Bałata, Zbigniew Namysłowski, and Tomasz Stańko among his sidemen (*c*1993) and an album of solos, duos, and trios with Bernard Maseli and the drummer and percussionist José Torres (from a performance which they gave in Rotunda, Poland); he also recorded in 1998 together with Namysłowski as guest soloist with the Hungarian Bop-Art Orchestra. While remaining active as the leader of his own groups, Ścierański gives solo recitals on a regular basis.

SELECTED RECORDINGS

As unaccompanied soloist: *Krzysztof Ścierański* (1984, Savitor 013) [incl. duos with drums]; *Flying Over* (1998, Selles 0075)
Duos with Szendi Gabór: *The King is in Town* (1989, Poljazz 271)
As leader: *Bass Line* (1983, Poljazz [issue no. unknown]); *Confusion* (*c* mid-1980s, Poljazz 207); *Far Away from Home* (*c*1993, Soundpol 00736); with B. Maseli and J. Torres: *Music Painters* (1995, Gowi 27) [incl. duos and unaccompanied solos]; *Inna Bajka* (1997, Gowi [issue no. unknown])
As sideman: Laboratorium: *Laboratorium* (1980, View 0014); Z. Namysłowski: *Follow your Kite* (1980, Muza 2303); *Air Condition* (1981, IC 1130); String Connection: *Workaholic* (1982, Poljazz 107); *New Romantic Expectation* (1983, Poljazz 126); *Live* ([date unknown], Polton 008)

BIBLIOGRAPHY

H. Kumpf: "E-Bass als Kirchenorgel," *JP*, xxxiv/3 (1985), 25
"Guitar in Poland: Krzysztof Scieranski," *GP*, xxiii/12 (1989), 46
A. Chodkowski, ed.: *Encyklopedia muzyki* (Warsaw, 1995)
<http://www.alphainter.net/~skok/polskie/grupy/s/scierans/scierans.html> (2001)

ADAM CEGIELSKI, BK

Sclavis, Louis (Humbert) (*b* Lyons, France, 2 Feb 1953). French clarinetist and bass clarinetist. He took up clarinet at the age of ten and studied classical music at the conservatory in Lyons from 1968 to 1971. In the mid-1970s he turned towards free improvisation and began playing with such local groups as the Workshop de Lyons, the Marvelous Band, and a big band, La Marmite Infernale. He established associations, some enduring, with Bernard Lubat (working regularly from 1977 to 1983 and intermittently thereafter), Michel Portal (collaborating in a clarinet quartet, 1979), Henri Texier (in whose group he replaced Eric Le Lann, *c*1979), Didier Levallet, and Chris McGregor's Brotherhood of Breath (*c*1980). From the early 1980s Sclavis formed numerous groups of his own, among them the Tour de France, the personnel of which were drawn from different regions of the country (1982), a quartet that included the double bass player Bruno Chevillon (1984), and the Clarinet Trio, which mixed contemporary classical compositions with free improvisation (1988); from 1992 he was co-leader, with Dominique Pifarély, of the Acoustic Quartet (with Chevillon and Marc Ducret), and in 1994 he formed a trio with Chevillon and the drummer François Merville. In addition he worked with John Lindberg and George Lewis (ii) (*c*1984), Evan Parker, Peter Brötzmann, Tony Oxley, Lol Coxhill, Cecil Taylor (in a duo and a big band, 1988), Trilok Gurtu, and Joachim Kühn. Through the 1990s he performed in a trio with Aldo Romano and Texier; during the same period he co-led a quintet with Ray Anderson, worked in duos with Fred Frith and Ernst Reijseger, and formed a short-lived trio with Tim Berne and Noël Akchoté (1995). In striving to find new venues in which to perform and new combinations of musical and artistic style, Sclavis worked variously with folk musicians, dancers, photographers, playwrights, and film directors; he provided the score to Bertrand Tavernier's film *Ça commence aujourd'hui* (1999).

SELECTED RECORDINGS

Duos with E. Parker, H. Koch, and W. Fuchs: *Duets, Dithyrambisch* (1989, FMP CD19–20)
As leader: *Ad Augusta per angustia* (1981, Nato 14); *Clarinettes* (1984–5, Ida 004); *Rencontres* (1985, Nato 500); with Heinz Becker and J. Lindberg: *Transition* (1987, FMP 1170); *Chine* (1987, Ida 012); *Chamber Music* (1989, Ida 022); *Rouge* (1991, ECM 1458); *Ellington on the Air* (1991–2, Ida 032); with D. Pifarély: *Acoustic Quartet* (1993, ECM 1526); *Ceux qui veillent la nuit* (1994, Label Bleu 6596); *Les violences de Rameau* (1995–6, ECM 1588)

BIBLIOGRAPHY

J. Laret and G. Rouy: "Les ateliers de Douai," *Jm*, no.288 (1980), 36
C. Tarting: "Sclavis: un Louis qui parle d'or," *Jm*, no.302 (1981), 20
P. Barithel: "Sclavis: le regard de l'orrie," *Jm*, no.368 (1988), 14
P. Carles, A. Clergeat, and J.-L. Comolli: *Dictionnaire du jazz* (Paris, 1988, rev. and enlarged 2/1994)
J. D'Souza: "Startling Landscape," *JF* [intl edn], no.118 (1989), 28
P. Carles: "Louis Sclavis: 'cette émotion-là . . .'," *Jm*, no.391 (1990), 50
C. Gauffre: "Sclavis on the Air," *Jm*, no.413 (1992), 54
F. Goaty: "Quand parle le quartette dont on parle," *Jm*, no.435 (1994), 22
P. H. Ardonceau: "Les violences de Sclavis," *Jm*, no.465 (1996), 26
J. Gaudas: "Louis Sclavis, un jouglaire," *Jh*, no.534 (1996), 18
A. Jones: "Profile: Louis Sclavis," *Jazziz*, xiii/7 (1996), 46
M. Chénard: "Sonic Stories: Louis Sclavis," *Coda*, no.275 (1997), 20
<http://www.ejn.it/mus/sclavis.htm> (1999)

<http://www.netlaputa.ne.jp/~lili/> (1999) [incl. discography]

MARK GILBERT

Scobey, Bob [Robert Alexander, Jr.] (*b* Tucumcari, NM, 9 Dec 1916; *d* Montreal, 12 June 1963). Trumpeter. He spent much of his life in California, and grew up in Stockton. He took up cornet at the age of nine and changed to trumpet when he was about 14. After moving to Berkeley he played commercial music in the San Francisco Bay area and spent a period with Lu Watters's big band at Sweet's Ballroom in Oakland in 1938–9. From 1940 to 1942 and again from 1946 to 1950 he performed with Watters and the Yerba Buena Jazz Band (for illustration *see* Watters, lu). During his military service (1942–6) he was a member of an army band. In the 1950s Scobey led his own Frisco Jazz Band and in the early 1960s he lived in Chicago. With Watters and Turk Murphy, he was a key figure in the "West Coast" or San Francisco revival of traditional jazz, in which the importance of the whole band was emphasized rather than the role of individual soloists; several new compositions inspired by New Orleans jazz were added to the older repertory. Scobey recorded as a leader from 1947 to 1961; among his sidemen at various times were Clancy Hayes (1950–59), Jesse Crump (1956), Matty Matlock and Ralph Sutton (both 1956–7), Rich Matteson (1958–9), and Art Hodes (1959). He recorded as a sideman with Sidney Bechet (1953) and Bing Crosby (1957).

SELECTED RECORDINGS

As leader: All the Wrongs You've Done (1952, GTJ 74); *Bob Scobey's Frisco Band with Clancy Hayes*, i–ii (1955, GTJ 12006, 12009); *Direct from San Francisco* (1956, GTJ 12023); *The Great Bob Scobey and his Frisco Band* (1956, Jansco 6250, 6252)

As sideman: L. Watters: Working Man Blues/Big Bear Stomp (1946, West Coast 104); Chattanooga Stomp/Creole Belles (1946, West Coast 102); New Orleans Joys/Panama (1946, West Coast 115); B. Crosby: *Bing with a Beat* (1957, RCA LPM1473)

BIBLIOGRAPHY

FeatherE

B. Nicholls: "The West Coast Revival," *Music Mirror*, iii/2 (1956), 6

Obituary, *SL*, xiv/7–8 (1963), 17

J. Scobey: *He Rambled! 'Til Cancer Cut Him Down* (Northridge, CA, 1976)

J. Darensbourg: *Telling it Like it is*, ed. P. Vacher (London, 1987, Baton Rouge, LA, 1987, as *Jazz Odyssey: the Autobiography of Joe Darensbourg*)

J. Scobey: "Bob Scobey (1916–1963) and his Frisco Band: 25th Year Anniversary," *SL*, xl (1988), summer, 21

F. Levin: "I Remember Bob Scobey," *Jazzbeat*, ix/1 (1997), 15

——: "The Forgotten Ones: Bob Scobey," JJI, l/7 (1997), 17

JOHN EDWARD HASSE/BK

Scofield, John (Leavitt) (*b* Dayton, OH, 26 Dec 1951). Electric guitarist. He grew up in Wilton, Connecticut, where he took up guitar at the age of 12. As a teenager he played in rock bands and studied blues players such as Otis Rush and B. B. King and jazz musicians such as Wes Montgomery and Jim Hall. He attended the Berklee School of Music (1970–73) before making his recording début with Chet Baker and Gerry Mulligan at Carnegie Hall (November 1974). In 1975 he joined Billy Cobham's group (later the Billy Cobham–George Duke band), with which he remained until 1977. He spent a year with Gary Burton (1977) and around the same time played in the bands of Charles Mingus, Terumasa Hino, Jeremy Steig, Ron Carter, Jay McShann, and Baker. Late in 1977 he was invited to take a band to Germany, and thereafter he played frequently in Europe with a quartet (variously including Richard Beirach, Hal Galper, and Adam Nussbaum) or a trio (completed by Steve Swallow and Nussbaum). He toured worldwide with Dave Liebman in 1979–80. Late in 1982 he joined Miles Davis and remained with him until August 1985, the year in which he also played in Mino Cinélu's trio. Later he focused on his own bands in addition to recording widely as a sideman.

Scofield's 1974 début with Mulligan and Baker was largely in the jazz mainstream, but his study of post-1960 jazz and

John Scofield at Festival International du Jazz Antibes–Juan-les-Pins, France, 1986

his attraction to blues, rock, country, and other idioms led him to a new style which, along with those of Pat Metheny and Allan Holdsworth, was one of the most influential among jazz guitarists since John McLaughlin. As his album *John Scofield Live* shows, he had by the late 1970s made an extensive translation to the guitar of the polytonal approach associated with John Coltrane, McCoy Tyner, Joe Henderson, Michael Brecker, and others. He was not unique among guitar players in this respect (Pat Martino and Holdsworth had adapted similar styles with different results), but his translation was particularly idiosyncratic, and, when combined with blues and rock, it resulted in a strongly individual voice. The contrast between the earthiness of the blues and the sophistication of post-bop jazz was a major source of his distinctiveness: in straight-ahead contexts (for example, on *Softly as in a Morning Sunrise* on *John Scofield Live*) his use of light distortion and blues-rock phrasing was refreshingly unidiomatic, and in a fusion setting, as on the funk version of *Love for Sale* from Baker's album *You Can't Go Home Again*, he played with a chromaticism which was then rare among fusion guitar players. This stylistic cross-breeding was evident in almost all of his later work: he incorporated many blues and rock elements into his ostensibly lyrical trio with Swallow and Nussbaum of 1980–81, he significantly widened the idiomatic range of Davis's band (fragments of his solos were transcribed to make themes for *Decoy*), and his groundbreaking band with Gary Grainger and Dennis Chambers (1985–8) added many new dimensions to fusion.

With his album *Flat Out* (1988), which used conventional double bass and organ, Scofield moved away from highly amplified fusion towards earlier styles. In 1989 he formed a quartet with Joe Lovano which included, at various times, Charlie Haden, Marc Johnson, Dennis Irwin, Jack DeJohnette, and Bill Stewart, and which was widely acclaimed for its free-ranging embrace of rhythm-and-blues, country music, New Orleans funk, bop, and harmonically open playing reminiscent of Ornette Coleman. He also recorded in a similar style on separate albums with Bill Frisell and Metheny. From 1993 he resumed an approach, suggested by *Flat Out*, which updated the funk-blues style of the 1960s. To this end he frequently employed an organ trio and recorded with Larry Goldings, Eddie Harris, Idris Muhammad, and the trio Medeski, Martin & Wood; in keeping with the traditional character of jazz organ trios he improvised in a spare, blues-orientated manner which was largely devoid of the harmonic complexity of his earlier years. In 1996 he recorded an entire album, *Quiet*, on the acoustic guitar, an instrument he had previously played only infrequently. In the 1980s and 1990s he also recorded with numerous prominent leaders in addition to Davis, among them Henderson and Herbie Hancock.

Scofield has been a prolific composer, writing most of the material he has recorded as leader. By the late 1990s he had made highly personalized contributions to a wide variety of idioms, including bop, hard bop, modal jazz, fusion, free jazz, and rhythm-and-blues. For his quartet of the late 1970s he wrote in an updated modal and post-bop style as well as producing such rock-influenced vamp pieces as *Gray and Visceral* (on the album *John Scofield Live*). In his trio of 1980–81 he wrote chiefly in a lyrical style inspired by Jim Hall, but almost all of his writing for this group was edged with blues, and the exhilarating title track of its 1981 album *Shinola* was hard-hitting rock with jazz inflections. Scofield also wrote in a harmonically sophisticated fusion style for *Who's Who* (1979). He was a major influence on the work of Davis's 1980s band, and co-wrote three tracks on *Decoy* and provided the title track of *You're Under Arrest*. The harmonically angular style of composition which developed in that band had a significant bearing on Scofield's writing for his own fusion band of 1985–8 and was evident in such pieces as *Techno* and *Protocol* from *Still Warm*, but he also added a good measure of country and blues material. It is interesting to note that despite constant stylistic change, certain formulas recur in Scofield's writing. A prime example is the slow, menacing bass figure which defines *Gray and Visceral*: this seems to give birth to the bass riff of *Protocol* (1985), and that riff in turn was almost certainly adapted for *Stranger to the Light*, a track on the rather more abstract album *Time on my Hands* (1989).

After returning to conventional jazz instrumentation in 1989 Scofield expanded the scope of his writing to include a free harmonic style derived from Ornette Coleman (*Mr. Coleman to You*, 1990), New Orleans-style rhythm-and-blues (*Twang*, 1991), classic bop (*What They Did*, 1992), and a bluesy organ trio style (heard throughout the album *Groove Elation*, 1995). He wrote many variations on these basic models, but an enduring feature of his composition (and playing) is the habitual use of guitaristic rock and blues figures, regardless of idiom.

Scofield's performances have been transcribed by K. Chipkin and F. Amendola (*Guitar Transcriptions: John Scofield*, Winona, MN, *c*1987); Chipkin (*Time on my Hands: John Scofield*, Miami, *c*1991); and Chipkin, D. Begelman, and J. Workman (*Jazz-Funk Guitar*, i, ed. A. Buk, Miami, *c*1993), the last of which serves as a companion to a video of the same name.

SELECTED RECORDINGS

Duos with A. Mangelsdorff: on [various artists]: *Live from International Festival Munster* (1988, Tutu 888110), Alfie's Theme, The Eternal Turn-on, Gray and Visceral

As leader: *John Scofield Live* (1977, Enja 3013), incl. Gray and Visceral, Softly as in a Morning Sunrise; *Rough House* (1978, Enja 3033); *Who's Who* (1979, AN 3018); with H. Galper: *Ivory Forest* (1979, Enja 3053); *Bar Talk* (1980, AN 3022); *Shinola* (1981, Enja 4004); *Out like a Light* (1981, Enja 4038); with J. Abercrombie: *Solar* (1982–3, PA 8031); *Electric Outlet* (1984, Gram. 8405); *Still Warm* (1985, Gram. 8508), incl. Protocol, Techno; *Blue Matter* (1986, Gram. 8702); *Loud Jazz* (1987, Gram. 18-8801-1); *Pick Hits Live* (1987, Gram. R2-79405); *Flat Out* (1988, Gram. R1-79400); *Time on my Hands* (1989, BN B21S-92894), incl. Stranger to the Light; *Meant to Be* (1990, BN B21Z-95479), incl. Mr. Coleman to You; *Grace under Pressure* (1991, BN B21Z-98167), incl. Twang; *What We Do* (1992, BN B21Z-99586), incl. What They Did; with P. Metheny: *I Can See your House from Here* (1993, BN B21Z-27765); *Hand Jive* (1993, BN B21Z-27327); *Groove Elation* (1995, BN B21Z-32801); *Quiet* (1996, Verve 314-533185-2); *A Go Go* (1997, Verve 314-539979-2)

As sideman: G. Mulligan/C. Baker: *Carnegie Hall Concert* (1974, CTI 6054); B. Cobham: *A Funky Thide of Sings* (1975, Atl. 18149); C. Baker: *You Can't Go Home Again* (1977, A&M Hor. 726), include. Love for Sale; C. Mingus: *Three or Four Shades of Blue* (1977, Atl. 1700); T. Hino: *May Dance* (1977, F Disk 6002); J. McShann: *The Last of the Blue Devils* (1977, Atl. 8800); *The Big Apple Bash* (1978, Atl. 8804); L. Coryell: *Tributaries* (1978, 1979, AN 3017); D. Liebman: *Doin' it Again* (1979, Tim. 140); *If They Only Knew* (1980, Tim. 151); M. Davis: *Star People* (1982–3, Col. FC38657); *Decoy* (1983–4, Col. FC38991); *You're Under Arrest* (1984, Col. F40023); M. Johnson: *Bass Desires* (1985, ECM 1299); *Second Sight* (1987, ECM 1351); B. Wallace: *The Art of the Saxophone* (1987, Denon 33CY1648); M. Gibbs: *Big Music* (1988, Virgin Venture 27); G. Thomas: *By Any Means Necessary* (1989, JMT 834432-2); H. Hancock: *The New Standard* (1995, Verve 314-529584-2)

SELECTED FILMS AND VIDEOS

On Improvisation (1984); Jaco Pastorius: Modern Electric Bass (1985); Jazzvisions: All Strings Attached (1988); Live 3 Ways (1990); In the Pocket (*c*1992); Serious Moves (*c*1992), Jazz-Funk Guitar, i–ii (*c*1993)

BIBLIOGRAPHY

CarrJ

L. Jeske: "Profile: John Scofield," *DB*, xlvii/2 (1980), 51
D. Breskin: "John Scofield's Brilliant Career," *Musician, Player & Listener*, no.32 (1981), 24
S. Freedman: "John Scofield: Music for the Connoisseur," *DB*, xlix/9 (1982), 18 [incl. discography]
J. Ferguson: "John Scofield: Bebop Expressionist," *GP*, xvii/2 (1983), 30 [incl. discography]
M. Gilbert: "John Scofield," *JJI*, xxxvi/8 (1983), 6
J. Ferguson: "John Scofield on Recording with Miles Davis: the new 'Decoy' LP," *GP*, xviii/9 (1984), 45 [incl. discography]
C. Gauffre: "Scofield: un sideman autonome," *Jm*, no.337 (1985), 22
C. Munthe: "John Scofield med blueskänsla och fantasi" [John Scofield with blues feeling and imagination], *Orkester journalen*, liii/2 (1985), 16
J. Woodard: "John Scofield: Detours and Decoys," *Musician*, no.78 (1985), 72
P. Brodowski: "Still Warm: John Scofield Interview," *JF* [intl edn], no.104 (1987), 30
J. Ferguson: "John Scofield: Miles Beyond," *GP*, xxi/6 (1987), 78
B. Milkowski: "John Scofield: All Shades of Blue," *DB*, liv/1 (1987), 16 [incl. discography]
D. Townsend: "John Scofield," *JT* (1988), March, 11
H. Mandel: "John Scofield: Restless Guitar Player," *DB*, lvi/3 (1989), 16
D. Michel and F. Goaty: "Pièges pour Scofield," *Jm*, no.379 (1989), 40
J. Ephland: "Riffs: John Scofield," *DB*, lvii/11 (1990), 13
"John Scofield," *JP*, xl/10 (1991), 14
D. Polkow: "Beating the Odds," *Chicago Tribune* (15 March 1991)
B. Sidran: "Scofield et les notes bleues," *Jm*, no.404 (1991), 40
B. Milkowski: "John Scofield & Jack DeJohnette: Fun, Creativity, Advice, Politics & the Miles Factor," *DB*, lix/4 (1992), 16 [incl. discography]
J. Rotondi: "The Art of Improvisation," *GP*, xxvi/7 (1992), 54
J. Rotondi and J. Gore: "Displaying Grace under Pressure," *GP*, xxvi/7 (1992), 68
F. Goaty: "Scofield et Lovano, le coeur et les idées," *Jm*, no.429 (1993), 30
M. Resnicoff: "John Scofield's Standards: the Full Life of a Jazz Guitarist," *Musician*, no.178 (1993), 64
Z. Stewart: "John Scofield's New Twist on Tradition," *Los Angeles Times* (18 April 1993)
B. Blumenthal: "A Natural Jazz Pairing," *Boston Globe* (23 Sept 1994)
J. Ferguson: "John Scofield: King of the Jazz Guitar," *DB*, lxi/4 (1994), 16 [incl. discography]
"John Scofield: John Pat(ch)work," *Jh*, no.512 (1994), 28
A. Schmitz: "John Scofield," *JP*, xliii/8 (1994), 39
J. Rotondi: "Vital Organs: Abercrombie & Scofield Reanimate the Organ Combo," *GP*, xxix/2 (1995), 63
B. Primack: "John Scofield & Joe Henderson: One," *JT*, xxvi/10 (1996), 60
Z. Stewart: "John Scofield: my Unplugged Romance," *DB*, lxiii/10 (1996), 24 [incl. discography]
M. Resnicoff: "John Scofield," *GP*, xxxi/3 (1997), 29
M. Gilbert: "John Scofield," *JJI*, li/10 (1998), 6
A. Levy: "John Scofield: Rebel without a Chorus," *GP*, xxx/ii (1998), 37
J. Macnie: "Sco's Go Go," *DB*, xlv/4 (1998), 20
B. Milkowski: "Charlie Hunter, John Scofield: Conversing Guitars," *JT*, xxviii/6 (1998), 28
T. Moon: "Defender of the Groove," *Jazziz*, xv/4 (1998), 40
<http://www.serve.com/scottnew/> (1998)
<http://www.c-and-c.si/sco/index.html> (1999) [incl. discography, transcrs., and lists of 167 compositions and 42 videos]

MARK GILBERT

Scoop. On wind instruments, a Gliss rising to the beginning of a note, achieved entirely with the embouchure.

Score. Budget label established in 1957 by Aladdin and used to reissue much of the parent company's back catalogue.

Scott, Aaron (*b* Chicago, 19 June 1956). Drummer. He learned piano, accordion, trombone, and drums as a child and concentrated on drums from the age of nine. After attending the US Army Element School of Music in Norfolk, Virginia (1979–82), he studied music education and performance at the Berklee College of Music (1982–5) and conducting at the Boston Conservatory (1983–5); while in Boston he was principal timpanist and assistant conductor of the Brookline Symphony Orchestra. In 1985 he moved to Paris, where he studied conducting at L'Ecole Normale de Musique and became the drummer for and assistant conductor of the Orchestre National de Jazz; during this period he worked with various jazz groups. In 1988 Scott joined McCoy Tyner, with whom he worked in both big-band and trio settings, on tour and at festivals. He also appeared with such other well-known musicians as George Benson, Michael Brecker, Ron Carter, Chick Corea, Larry Coryell, Gil Evans, Frank Foster, Dizzy Gillespie, Joe Henderson, Freddie Hubbard, Bobby Hutcherson, Steve Lacy, Claudio Roditi, John Scofield, and Steve Swallow.

SELECTED RECORDINGS

As sideman: Orchestre Nationale de Jazz: *Orchestre Nationale de Jazz 1986* (1986, Label Bleu 6503–04); E. Watson: *Your Tonight is my Tomorrow* (1987, Owl 047); M. Tyner: *Live at Sweet Basil*, i–ii (1989, PW [Jap.] 292E6033, KICJ1); *Remembering John* (1991, Enja 6080-2); *The Turning Point* (1991, Verve 314-513573-2); *Journey* (1993, Verve 314-519941-2); *Infinity* (1995, Imp. 171)

DEBORAH GILLASPIE

Scott, Bud [Arthur, Jr.] (*b* New Orleans, 11 Jan ?1890; *d* Los Angeles, 2 July 1949). Guitarist, banjoist, and singer. He played violin and guitar from his childhood, and in the years around 1905 worked with John Robichaux and, briefly, Freddie Keppard. In 1913 he left New Orleans and performed on the southern vaudeville circuit, then in 1915 he went to New York and worked as a nightclub singer and violinist in theater orchestras. He also studied at the Institute of Musical Art and, while working in Baltimore (1917), at the Peabody Conservatory. From spring 1923 he toured the Midwest and played intermittently in Chicago with King Oliver. It is his voice heard shouting "Oh play that thing!" on Oliver's second recording (June 1923) of *Dipper Mouth Blues* (he missed the earlier session, in April 1923, at which the group's double bass player, Bill Johnson (i), played banjo and initiated this shout). Scott worked on the West Coast with Kid Ory, briefly rejoined Oliver's Creole Jazz Band in Chicago, and then returned to Ory on the West Coast before joining Curtis Mosby's Blue Blowers. He was in Chicago once again for much of 1926 with Oliver's Dixie Syncopators. Having left the band in December that year, he played banjo in and managed the orchestra at the Café de Paris, and worked in the orchestras led by Erskine Tate (1926, 1927) and Dave Peyton (playing violin, late 1926–1928). In 1927 he recorded with Johnny Dodds and participated in some of Jelly Roll Morton's finest ensemble sessions; Scott was well known for his sophisticated knowledge of harmony, and Morton referred to him as "the great guitarist" (Lomax, 1950). In the following year he became a member of Jimmie Noone's small group, the Apex Club Orchestra, and he took part in all its finest recording sessions (May–August 1928). After playing with Fess Williams (January 1929) and spending a further period with Peyton (summer 1929) Scott moved to California, where he worked with Mutt Carey's Jeffersonians in the early 1930s and led his own trio for several years. He was again a member of Ory's band (1944–8) and appeared with Louis Armstrong in the film *New Orleans* (1947). He should not be confused with the guitarist Bud Scott (c1870–c1920) who led a popular dance band throughout the Gulf Coast region.

SELECTED RECORDINGS

As sideman: K. Oliver: Dipper Mouth Blues (1923, OK 4918); J. Dodds: Oh! Lizzie/The New St. Louis Blues (1927, Bruns. 3585); J. R. Morton: Wild Man Blues/Jungle Blues (1927, Bb 10256); J. Noone: I know that you know (1928, Voc. 1184); Blues my naughty sweetie gives to me (1928, Voc. 1215); K. Ory: Muskrat Ramble/The girls go crazy (1945, Decca 25133); L. Armstrong: Where the blues were born in New Orleans/ Mahogany Hall Stomp (1946, Vic. 20-2088)

BIBLIOGRAPHY

ChiltonW
C. Chain: "Bud Scott," *Jazz Music*, iii/3 (1946); repr. in *Jazz Reprints*, i/3 (1963), 35
A. Finley: "Guitar and Vocal by Bud Scott," *Record Changer*, [vi/7] (1947), 5
A. Lomax: *Mister Jelly Roll: the Fortunes of Jelly Roll Morton, New Orleans Creole and "Inventor of Jazz"* (New York, 1950, 2/1973/*R*1993)
J. Vincent: "The Banjo in Jazz," *JJ*, xxx/3 (1977), 20
D. M. Marquis: *In Search of Buddy Bolden, First Man of Jazz* (Baton Rouge, LA, and London, 1978/*R*1993)
J. Darensbourg: *Telling it Like it is*, ed. P. Vacher (London, 1987; Baton Rouge, LA, 1987, as *Jazz Odyssey: the Autobiography of Joe Darensbourg*)
L. Wright and others: *Walter C. Allen & Brian A. L. Rust's "King" Oliver* (Chigwell, England, 1987)

DAVID FLANAGAN/BK

Scott, (C.) Calo (*b* Camaguey, Cuba, 11 March 1920; *d* Middlesex, VT, 9 Aug 1998). Cellist. He was brought up in the USA from the age of two and began playing piano when he was seven. Having taken up saxophone in his teens, he played the instrument in a US Army band in 1949. Two years later he was diagnosed with a rheumatic heart condition that forced him to give up saxophone, and he subsequently began playing cello. From the mid-1950s he worked in New York as a freelance musician and as a member of Vinnie Burke's String Jazz Quartet, with which he recorded in 1957 and, accompanying Gerry Mulligan, in 1958; he took part in other sessions with Mal Waldron (1958) and Ahmed Abdul-Malik (1961, 1962). In 1967 he recorded with Gato Barbieri, performed in John Handy's group at Carnegie Hall, and performed and recorded in Marc Levin's group Free Unit. Scott then recorded with Carla Bley (late 1960s), Archie Shepp (1971–3), and Levin (1972). Nothing is known of his later career.

SELECTED RECORDINGS

As sideman: M. Waldron: *Mal 3* (1958, NewJ 8201); A. Abdul-Malik: *The Music of Ahmed Abdul-Malik* (1961, NewJ 8266); G. Barbieri: *In Search of the Mystery* (1967, ESP 1049)

BIBLIOGRAPHY

Feather '60s

GK

Scott, Cecil (Xavier) (*b* Springfield, OH, 22 Nov 1905; *d* New York, 5 Jan 1964). Clarinetist and tenor and baritone saxophonist, brother of Lloyd Scott. He formed a trio during his teens with his brother Lloyd and Don Frye. By one account he worked regularly on riverboats as a member of Charlie Creath's band between 1921 and 1924. By another, from 1922 to 1929 he led a band with Lloyd in Ohio, Pittsburgh, and New York, where, from December 1927, it was resident at the Savoy Ballroom; it made recordings under both Lloyd's name (1927) and Cecil's (1929). Among the group's regular sidemen were Dicky Wells, Frankie Newton, and Bill Coleman; Johnny Hodges, Joe Thomas (iv), Juice Wilson, Roy and Joe Eldridge, and Chu Berry also performed with the ensemble. Cecil became sole leader in 1929 and the band toured and continued to play in clubs in New York. Clyde Bernhardt (1986) recalled Scott "doing that crazy Cab Calloway stuff in front of his band. Like he be leading and playing his sax and suddenly fall in a big split, then rise slowly as he kept blowing a hot solo." In the early 1930s these antics ended permanently and Scott's career was interrupted after a serious accident, when, according to Bernhardt, he leapt out of a fourth-story window to avoid an irate husband. Upon recovering he worked with the double bass player Ellsworth Reynolds and the pianist Earle Howard (both 1932–3), Teddy Hill (1936–7), and Alberto Socarras (until 1942) and made several recordings with Clarence Williams, Willie "the Lion" Smith, and Henry "Red" Allen. From around 1942 he led a nine-piece group that held a residency at the Ubangi Club in New York (October 1943–1944) with Henry Goodwin, Bernhardt, and Kenneth Roane among his sidemen. During the rest of the decade he led a trio and played with such musicians as Hot Lips Page and Art Hodes; he also made three soundies as a leader: *Contrast in Rhythm*, *Don't Be Late*, and *Mr. X Blues* (all 1945). From 1950 into the 1960s he worked for various leaders, including Jimmy McPartland (*c*1953) and Willie "the Lion" Smith (in Canada, 1959), and continued to lead his own small groups. Scott recorded mainly on clarinet and tenor saxophone. He played with much drive and zest and his style was characterized by quirky, idiosyncratic effects.

SELECTED RECORDINGS

As leader: Springfield Stomp (1929, Vic. 38117); *Chris Barber Presents Harlem Washboard: Cecil Scott and his Washboard Band* (1959, Col. 33SX1232)
As sideman: C. Williams: Chizzlin' Sam (1933, Col. 2829D); W. Smith: Echo of Spring (1935, Decca 7040); H. Allen: Roll along, prairie moon (1935, Voc. 2997)

BIBLIOGRAPHY

ChiltonW; *FeatherE*; *McCarthyB*
H. B. Mackey: "Everybody Loves Cecil: a Special Interview," *Jazz Record*, no.56 (1947), 8; repr. in *Selections from the Gutter: Jazz Portraits from "The Jazz Record,"* ed. A. Hodes and C. Hansen (Berkeley, CA, and London, 1977), 215
G. W. Kay: "The Springfield Story," *JJ*, v/7 (1952), 12
T. Grove and M. Grove: "Cecil Scott and his Bright Boys," *JJ*, vi/12 (1953), 29; vii/1 (1954), 3
J. Evensmo: *The Tenor Saxophones of Budd Johnson, Cecil Scott, Elmer Williams, Dick Wilson, 1927–1942* (n.p. [Oslo], n.d. [?1977]) [discography]
C. E. B. Bernhardt and S. Harris: *I Remember: Eighty Years of Black Entertainment, Big Bands, and the Blues* (Philadelphia, 1986), 159
J. Evensmo: *History of Jazz Tenor Saxophone: Black Artists*, i: *1917–1934* (Oslo, 1996); ii: *1935–1939* (Oslo, 1997)

EDDIE LAMBERT/BK

Scott, Clifford (Donley) (*b* San Antonio, TX, 21 June 1928; *d* San Antonio, 19 April 1993). Tenor saxophonist and flutist. His middle name is taken from Texas death records. He played drums in his family's band and studied piano and violin with his father (a classically trained violinist) before taking up clarinet in junior high school; by the time of his high school years he was working locally as a clarinetist and saxophonist. From 1947 into 1949 he accompanied famous blues singers as a member of the house band led by the pianist James Hopkins at the Avalon Grill; during this period Scott temporarily left San Antonio to tour west with the singer and pianist Amos Milburn, and in February 1949, while they were in Los Angeles, he made his recording début with Jay McShann. After rejoining Hopkins in 1950 he toured the USA with Lionel Hampton, then in 1952 he toured with the blues singer Roy Brown and with Roy Milton's Solid Senders, recording with both. The following year Scott rejoined Hampton for a European tour and recorded with the band in Paris. On his return to the USA he studied arranging at a music school in New York and then flute and piccolo at Florida Agricultural and Mechanical College, Tallahassee.

In 1955 Scott joined Bill Doggett's band, with which he remained until 1960. He was featured extensively on both his main instruments and contributed to the success of Doggett's 1956 hit *Honky Tonk*. During these years and afterwards he also undertook a good deal of session work, including recordings under his own name (1958–62). In 1962 he recorded with Sonny Thompson. From that same year he was based on the West Coast, where in the course of his continuing studio work for recordings, films, and television he made further albums under his own name, appeared in a band for a party scene in the film *Drums of Africa* (1963), recorded with Jimmy Witherspoon (1963), and performed with his own group on Steve Allen's television show (1964). Like many fellow studio musicians during this period, he played in the Los Angeles area in big bands led by Gerald Wilson and Onzy Matthews; around 1965 he was briefly a member of Frank Butler's sextet for an engagement at the It Club. He then toured with Ray Charles's big band (1966–8), in the course of which he was sometimes featured in tenor saxophone battles with Curtis Amy. Having returned to Los Angeles, he led the house band at the Parisian Room and around 1970 recorded with Charles. In 1973 he joined a show which toured Vietnam, entertaining servicemen. His mother's illness led in 1975 to his moving back to San Antonio, where he appeared with groups in local bars and spent 15 years as a member of the band led by the double bass player George Prado. He occasionally deputized in Jim Cullum, Jr.'s Jazz Band, and he recorded again as a leader in 1991–2.

SELECTED RECORDINGS

(recorded for King unless otherwise indicated)

As leader: Frostee Nite/Blue Lady (1960, 5472); Bushy Tail/Skitchy (1960, 5440); *Mr. Honky Tonk is Back in Town* (1991, Rose 286)

As sideman on flute: B. Doggett: Flying Home (1957, 5096); How Could You (1958, 5130); on *Dance Awhile with Doggett* (1953–8, 585), Pied Piper of Islip (1958)

As sideman on t sax: L. Hampton: [untitled LP] (1953, Vogue LD167), incl. Walkin' at the Trocadero; B. Doggett: Honky Tonk (1956, 4950); Leaps and Bounds (1956, 5101); Shindig (1957, 5070); on *Dance Awhile with Doggett* (1953–8, 585), Bone Tones (1958); J. Witherspoon: *Evenin' Blues* (1963, Prst. 7300)

BIBLIOGRAPHY

Feather '60s

H. Panassié and M. Gautier: *Dictionnaire du jazz* (Paris, rev. and enlarged 3/1987 by A. Vasset and J. Pescheux)

Obituaries: D. Penny, *Blues & Rhythm*, no.80 (1993), 20; M. Redenac, *Soul Bag*, no.131 (1993), 22

L. Brown: "The Forgotten Ones: Clifford Scott," *JJI*, xlvii/7 (1994), 12

J. Evensmo: *History of Jazz Tenor Saxophone: Black Artists*, iv: *1945–1949* (Oslo, 1999)

HOWARD RYE

Scott, Hazel (Dorothy) (*b* Port of Spain, Trinidad, 11 June 1920; *d* New York, 2 Oct 1981). Pianist and singer. She studied classical piano at the Juilliard School from the age of eight and played jazz in nightclubs and on the radio; from 1939 to 1943 she was a leading attraction at both the downtown and uptown branches of Café Society. In the 1940s she appeared in several films, and during the following decades she performed as the leader of various groups, among them a trio that consisted of Bill English and the double bass player Martin Rivera; she continued to play occasionally in nightclubs until the year of her death. Scott was best known for her jazz improvisations on familiar classical pieces, which continued a practice favored by earlier stride and ragtime pianists.

SELECTED RECORDINGS

(all recorded for Decca)

Hungarian Rhapsody no.2 (Liszt)/Valse in D Flat Major (Chopin, op.64, no.1) (1940, 18129); Hazel's Boogie Woogie (1942, 18340); Embraceable You (1942, 18341); Hallelujah (1942, 18342)

SELECTED FILMS AND VIDEOS

I Dood it [By Hook and by Crook] (1943); Something to Shout About (1943); Broadway Rhythms (1944); Rhapsody in Blue (1945); Le désordre et la nuit [Night Affair] (1958)

BIBLIOGRAPHY

"Scott, Hazel," *CBY 1943*

A. Taylor: "Hazel Scott," *Notes and Tones: Musician-to-musician Interviews* (Liège, Belgium, 1977, rev. and enlarged 2/1993)

Obituary, J. McAfee, Jr., *JSN*, ii/4 (1982), 19

D. Myter-Specner: "Hazel Scott, Jazz Pianist: Boogie-woogie and Beyond," *Jazz Research Papers*, x (1990), 75

MARK TUCKER

Scott, Little Jimmy [James Victor] (*b* Cleveland, 17 July 1925). Singer. His mother was a church pianist, and he sang in church in a vocal quartet with his siblings. In the 1940s he toured the Midwest and South in the tent show run by the contortionist Estelle "Caledonia" Young and soon became celebrated for his high-pitched, powerful voice, his small stature, and his delicate looks – the result of an unusual medical condition; while he was with Young he was given his stage name, Little Jimmy Scott, by the comedian Redd Foxx. Late in 1948 he joined Lionel Hampton, with whom he made the hit recording *Everybody's Somebody's Fool* (1950), but following an abortive solo career and business problems he retired from music. In 1955 he returned to the studios, for Savoy, and recorded some of his most moving work with such musicians as Charles Mingus, but his later efforts for the label were ruined by poor material and overdubs. In 1962 Ray Charles arranged to have Scott recorded again, but his career continued to flounder. He returned to performing in the mid-1980s, when he worked in clubs in Harlem and Newark, New Jersey. On New Year's Eve in 1988 he broadcast on NPR, and in 1989 he made two guest appearances with Illinois Jacquet's big band. Scott experienced a wave of interest in the 1990s. He abandoned his diminutive nickname and recorded once more, when his accompanists included Kenny Barron, Ron Carter, and David "Fathead" Newman.

Scott's phrasing, akin to the melodic concept of an instrumentalist, made him a favorite with jazz musicians and a powerful influence on singers from Frankie Lymon, Nancy Wilson, and Marvin Gaye to Karin Krog. He performs only standard ballads but treats them in an unconventional manner, freely singing behind or in front of the beat and drawing lyrics over from one bar to another.

SELECTED RECORDINGS

As leader: *Very Truly Yours* (1955, Savoy 12027); *Falling in Love is Wonderful* (1962, Tangerine 1501); *Lost and Found* (1969, 1972, Rhino R2-71059); *All the Way* (1992, Sire 26955-2); *Dream* (1994, Sire 45629-2)

As sideman with L. Hampton: I've been a fool (thinking you care) (1950, Decca 24864); Everybody's Somebody's Fool (1950, Decca 27176); I wish I knew (1950, Decca 28711)

BIBLIOGRAPHY

J. McDonough: "For Whatever the Reason," *Village Voice Rock & Roll Quarterly* (1988), winter, 16

——: Liner notes, *All the Way* (Sire 26955-2, 1992)

B. Loupias: "Deux voix de l'Amerique," *Jm*, no.436 (1994), 34

C. Deffaa: *Blue Rhythms: Six Lives in Rhythm and Blues* (Urbana, IL, and Chicago, 1996), 73

A. Luviano-Cordero and I. You: "Jimmy Scott: Interview," *Cadence*, xxiii/7 (1997), 5

D. Kochakian: "Great Scott: It's Jimmy!," *Blues & Rhythm*, no.137 (1999), 4 [incl. discography]

D. Richardson: "Jimmy's World," *San Francisco Examiner Magazine* (1 Oct 2000), 6

VAL WILMER

Scott, Lloyd (W.) (*b* Springfield, OH, 21 Aug 1902). Drummer, brother of Cecil Scott. He worked in a succession of bands with his brother, beginning with their first trio in 1919, and was generally billed as the leader until Cecil assumed the role in June 1929 (for further details *see* CECIL SCOTT). The pairing *Symphonic Scronch/Happy Hour Blues* (1927, Vic. 20495), recorded under Lloyd's name, is revered especially for the earliest work of Dicky Wells. Various aspects of Lloyd's drumming are prominently heard on Cecil Scott's *In a corner* (1929, Vic. 38098) and *Springfield Stomp* (1929, Vic. 38117). By 1933 he was leading his own band, but he soon abandoned music and returned to Ohio. Danny Barker recalled that he had a harelip, and that it was this deformity that ruined his career, his physical appearance causing employers to disregard his musical talent.

BIBLIOGRAPHY

McCarthyB
G. W. Kay: "The Springfield Story," *JJ*, v/7 (1952), 12
D. Barker: *A Life in Jazz*, ed. A. Shipton (London and New York, 1986), 144

HOWARD RYE

Scott, Mabel (*b* Richmond, VA, 30 April 1915; *d* Los Angeles, 19 July 2000). Singer. She started singing in church after moving to New York around 1921 and made her professional début in 1930. In the early 1930s she appeared with Cab Calloway and Charlie Johnson, and on 26 January 1934 she was on the inaugural bill at the Apollo Theatre in Harlem. The following year she sang with Jimmie Lunceford's band. Early in 1936 Scott went to Paris, where she appeared at Chez Florence; she then traveled to London for cabaret engagements and to appear in the film *Dreaming Lips*. She returned to America in December 1936 and rejoined Lunceford, but in August 1937 she went back to Europe, accompanied by Bob Mosley. Scott appeared on British television in both 1936 and 1938 and made her recording début in London in April 1938. Late that year she turned down an opportunity to star at the Folies Bergère in Paris because of language problems, and in November she was back in the USA; a further European trip was cut short by the war. From 1942 Scott toured widely from her base in Los Angeles, where during the 1940s she held a series of residencies at the Club Alabam. In 1944 she appeared with the trio led by the pianist Lorenzo Flennoy in four soundies, among them *Steak and Potatoes* and *Gee*. She resumed recording in 1946; a session with Charles Brown, to whom she was married from 1949 to 1951, included *Elevator Boogie* (1947, Exclusive 35X). Scott continued to tour and record into the mid-1950s – *No More Cryin' Blues* (1951, Coral 65057) and *Mabel Blues* (1953, Parrot 780) are good examples of her style – but after performing and recording in Australia in 1955 she became less active. She should not be confused with a pianist of the same name who held a number of residencies in Chicago clubs during the 1940s.

BIBLIOGRAPHY

"Mabel Scott Scores at Trianon," *MM*, xiv (8 Jan 1938), 9
G. Durst: Liner notes, *Fine, Fine Baby* (Jukebox Lil 606, 1983)
Obituary, B. Vera, *Blues & Rhythm*, no.152 (2000), 12

HOWARD RYE

Scott, Raymond [Warnow, Harry [Harold]] (*b* New York, 10 Sept 1908; *d* North Hills, CA, 8 Feb 1994). Bandleader and pianist. His birth year has appeared as 1909 or 1910, but both social security and California death index records give 1908; this agrees with his *New York Times* obituary, which says he was 85 years old. After studying at the Institute of Musical Art in New York he joined CBS in 1934 as a staff pianist and composer. Born Harold Warnow, he changed his legal name to Raymond Scott in late 1936. He recorded novelty pieces as the leader of a six-piece studio "quintet" (1936–8) and wrote film scores, and he also worked as an actor; his quintet appeared in a number of films, notably *Love and Hisses* (1937), and made recordings which became well known as the music accompanying such classic Warner Bros. cartoon characters as Bugs Bunny, Daffy Duck, Porky Pig, and Roadrunner. Between 1939 and 1942 he toured and recorded with his own big band, but this had neither strong soloists nor a good sense of swing. In 1942 he returned to CBS as a music director and organized a studio sextet with Emmett Berry, Jerry Jerome, and Cozy Cole among his sidemen. Over the next two years Scott expanded this ensemble to include Charlie Shavers, Ben Webster, Benny Morton, Johnny Guarnieri, George Johnson, Israel Crosby, and Specs Powell. During the 1950s and 1960s he worked in popular music as a composer, arranger, recording engineer, and conductor. He settled in California in the early 1970s and ended his career as the head of the electronic music division of Motown records. Don Byron recorded a posthumous tribute to him, performing pieces associated with the quintet on the album *Bug Music* (1996, Nonesuch 79438-2), and Michael Hashim has explored jazz-oriented elements of Scott's music. A collection of his scores and other materials is held in the Raymond Scott Archive within the Marr Sound Archives at the University of Missouri at Kansas City, and a smaller but still substantial collection is in the Rodgers and Hammerstein Archives of Recorded Sound in the Music Division of the New York Public Library (*see* LIBRARIES AND ARCHIVES, §2).

BIBLIOGRAPHY

ChiltonW; *FeatherE*
A. Ewing: "Engineer-musician Electrifies Swing World with Ideas," *DB*, iv/6 (1937), 6
G. T. Simon: *The Big Bands* (New York, 1967, rev. 4/1981)
K. E. Klein: "Going on Record again," *Los Angeles Times* (3 Sept 1993)
P. Verna: "A Committee of Fans Restores the Creations of Raymond Scott," *Billboard*, cv (18 Dec 1993), 1
B. Kragting, Jr.: "The Raymond Scott Quartet Alumni," *Sv*, no.158 (1994), 55
Obituaries: W. Grimes, *New York Times* (9 Feb 1994); M. Oliver, *Los Angeles Times* (10 Feb 1994)

BK

Scott, Ronnie [Schatt, Ronald] (*b* London, 28 Jan 1927; *d* London, 23 Dec 1996). English tenor saxophonist and bandleader. He first played soprano saxophone, and took up the tenor instrument at the age of 15; his early style reflected the influence of Coleman Hawkins. After touring with the trumpeter Johnny Claes (October 1944 – summer 1945), with whom he may be seen in the film comedy *George in Civvy Street* (*Remember the Unicorn*) (1946), Ted Heath (February 1946 – February 1947), and others, he became one of a number of British players who worked on transatlantic liners solely to travel to the USA to hear the new jazz being played by such musicians as Dizzy Gillespie, Charlie Parker, and Bud Powell (1946–8). He was a founding member of the Club Eleven late in 1948. Scott worked with Jack Parnell from spring 1951 before forming his own band late the following year; this group was notable for the quality of its music and for its talented young British players, among them Jimmy Deuchar, Derek Humble, Victor Feldman, and Phil Seamen. He enlarged the band in September 1955, but in 1956 also worked as a sideman with others, including the quintet of Tony Crombie; in 1957 he took his own sextet to the USA. From April 1957 to August 1959, with Tubby Hayes, he was the leader of the Jazz Couriers.

In December 1959 Scott established his own club in Gerrard Street, London, in partnership with the businessman and former saxophonist Peter King. (King should not be confused with the English saxophonist of the same name who played at the club's opening night.) He played at the club with his own groups, including a quintet with Deuchar (spring 1960–61) and a quartet; Stan Tracey was house pianist from 1960 to 1968, and Scott and Tracey may be seen together in a group accompanying Ben Webster on the television show "Jazz 625" in December 1964. Scott also took Deuchar and Ronnie Ross to New York to work at the Half Note with an American rhythm section.

While a member of the Clarke–Boland Big Band (1962–73), Scott recorded with the orchestras of John Dankworth (1963) and Tracey (1966), and he continued to lead his own groups – a big band which accompanied Ella Fitzgerald (1969), Nancy Wilson (1973), and other singers, an eight-piece band with Kenny Wheeler (1968–9), and a trio in which Mike Carr played Hammond organ (1971–5). From 1975 he worked with a quartet or quintet, frequently with Dick Pearce, John Critchinson, and Martin Drew. The club established its own record company and label, Ronnie Scott's Jazz House, in 1978, and initially produced an album by Scott's own quintet. It became a more prominent label in the late 1980s and 1990s, issuing historic tapes from club performances in the 1960s and new recordings by such diverse groups and artists as Irakere, the National Youth Jazz Orchestra, Al Cohn, Marian Montgomery, Roy Ayers, Peter King, and Art Themen.

After a period in which his playing tended to reflect changing fashions in American jazz, Scott settled down to improvising fluidly in a manner identifiably his own, injecting standard harmonic progressions with an individual muscularity and quirkiness. In Ronnie Scott's (which moved to larger premises in Frith Street in mid-December 1965) he specialized in presenting American jazz soloists in informal surroundings, and the establishment soon became recognized internationally as London's major center for modern jazz. He opened a second club in Birmingham in October 1991. The worldwide fame of his club did not, however, bring him self-confidence – he was always unsure of his own musical abilities – and after a period of deepening depression, exacerbated by poor health and a dental problem which had prevented him from playing from mid-1995, he took his own life in December 1996. He was the author, with M. Hennessey, of an autobiography, *Some of my Best Friends are Blues* (1979).

For illustration *see* Nightclubs and other venues, fig.1.

SELECTED RECORDINGS

As leader: Wee Dot (1949, Esquire 10036); Too marvellous for words/Have you met Miss Jones? (1951, Esquire 10131); Chasing the Bird/Little Willie Leaps (1951, Esquire 10141); Close your eyes/I didn't know what time it was (1951, Esquire 10185); *Ronnie Scott Jazz Group* (1952, Esquire 32001), incl. The Champ; Tangerine (1953, Esquire 10311); Double or Nothing (1953, Esquire 10331); *Ronnie Scott Jazz Group* (1954, Esquire 32006), incl. Fuller Bop Man; Seaman's Mission (1954, Esquire 31) [EP]; This Heart of Mine (1955, Esquire 10462); Bang (1955, Esquire 10466); with T. Hayes: *The Jazz Couriers in Concert* (1958, Tempo TAP22), incl. Some of my best friends are blues, *The Last Word* (1959, Tempo TAP26); *When I Want your Opinion, I'll Give it to You* (1963–5, Ronnie Scott's Jazz House 610); *The Night is Scott and You're so Swingable* (1965, Fon. 5332), incl. Baubles, Bangles and Beads; *Live at Ronnie's* (1968, CBS 52661), incl. Lord of the Ready River; *Serious Gold* (1978, Pye 18542); *Live at the Jazz Club*, i (1987, Esquire 328); *Never Pat a Burning Dog* (1990, Ronnie Scott's Jazz House 012)

As sideman: K. Clarke and F. Boland: *Sax No End* (1967, Saba 15138), incl. Milkshake; Pablo All Star Jam: *Montreux '77* (1977, PL 2308210)

BIBLIOGRAPHY

CarrJ; *ChiltonB*; *FeatherE*; *Feather '60s*; *Feather–Gitler '70s*; *WickesIBJ*, i

L. Tomkins: "Ronnie Scott's Opinions," *CI*, x/12 (1972), 22; xi/1 (1972), 14

C. Welch: "Ronnie Scott Trio: Band Breakdown," *MM* (21 Dec 1974), 42

R. Cotterrell, ed.: *Jazz Now: the Jazz Centre Society Guide* (London, 1976)

S. Woolley: "Ronnie Scott: Interview," *Cadence*, iv/2–3 (1978), 11

B. Case: "King of Clubs," *MM* (13 Oct 1979), 26

K. Grime: *Jazz at Ronnie Scott's* (London, 1979)

R. Scott: "The First Twenty Years," *JJI*, xxxii/10 (1979), 7

L. Tomkins: "The Club and I," *CI*, xvii (1979), no.10, p.6; no.11, p.20; no.12, p.12; contd as "The Ronnie Scott Viewpoint," xviii/1 (1979), 12

R. Ottaway: "Scott's London Roost Swings into 3d Decade as Leading Jazz Joint," *Variety* (9 Jan 1980), 195

A. Bausch: *Jazz in Europa* (Echternach, Luxembourg, 1985)

P. Renaud: *La discographie du jazz anglais* (Chaumont, France, 1985)

J. Fordham: *Let's Join Hands and Contact the Living: Ronnie Scott and his Club* (London, 1986, rev. 2/1995, as *Jazz Man: the Amazing Story of Ronnie Scott and his Club*)

M. Hennessey: *Klook: the Story of Kenny Clarke* (London, 1990)

Obituaries: G. Ramos, *Los Angeles Times* (25 Dec 1996); *New York Times* (25 Dec 1996); *The Times* (26 Dec 1996); J. Fordham, *The Guardian* (3 Jan 1997); E. Cook, *JJI*, l/4 (1997), 16; B. Priesley, *DB*, lxiv/3 (1997), 15

B. Green: "Appreciation: Ronnie Scott: the Night I Nearly Blew it with my Jazz Idol," *The Guardian* (18 Jan 1997)

M. Jackson: "Riffs: 'Have a Nice Life'," *DB*, lxiv/4 (1997), 10

T. Middleton: *Ronnie Scott Discography* (London, 1997)

CHARLES FOX/DIGBY FAIRWEATHER, SIMON ADAMS, BK

Scott, Shirley (*b* Philadelphia, 14 March 1934). Organist and pianist. She studied piano as a child and took up trumpet in high school. When, through the playing of Jimmy Smith, the Hammond organ became popular in jazz, a club owner in Philadelphia rented an instrument for her (*c*1955), and she quickly became one of the finest jazz organists. She played and recorded frequently in trios (with drums) led by Eddie "Lockjaw" Davis (*c*1955–1960) and Stanley Turrentine (1960–71), whom she married in 1961. After her marriage ended in 1971 Scott made a number of commercial recordings for the Chess label, then from 1974 she led a bop trio with Harold Vick. Later she performed and recorded with Al Grey and Jimmy Forrest (in a group co-led by both men, and under the separate leadership of each, 1977–8) and recorded with Dexter Gordon (1982).

By the late 1980s Scott was often playing piano rather than organ, and from 1989 into the 1990s she held a residency at Ortlieb's Jazzhaus in Philadelphia, where (as a pianist) she led a trio consisting of Arthur Harper on double bass and Mickey Roker on drums. She also appeared as a pianist in New York at the Village Vanguard and Birdland, and, on organ, she led a sextet on Bill Cosby's television show "You Bet your Life" (autumn 1992–1993). In 1996 Scott toured Europe, and while appearing at the Festival Jazz aux Remparts in Bayonne, France, she recorded an album as an unaccompanied piano soloist; around the same time she recorded on organ as a guest soloist with Antonio Hart. She also taught at Cheyney University, served as music director at a church in Chester, Pennsylvania, and ran a production company with Gordon's widow, Maxine Gordon. In 1997–8 she suffered health problems, but she resumed her career.

Scott is most notable as an organist. She takes advantage of the special characteristics of the Hammond organ, playing with a biting, percussive attack and using the instrument's full, fast, mechanical vibrato. A masterful improviser, she combines complex bop lines with a repertory of simple, soulful melodic formulas derived from blues and gospel music. Transcriptions of her organ work appear in *Shirley Scott in Concert* (New York, n.d.) and in the anthology *Leonard Feather's 200 Omnibus of Jazz* (Miami Beach, FL, c1975).

SELECTED RECORDINGS

(recorded for Prestige, and on organ, unless otherwise indicated)

As unaccompanied soloist: *Rencontres du cloître*, i (1996, Jazz aux Remparts 64201) [pf]

As leader: *Great Scott!* (1958, 7143); *Hip Soul* (1961, 7205); *Hip Twist* (1961, 7226); *Happy Talk* (1962, 7262); *The Soul is Willing* (1963, 7267); *Soul Shoutin'* (1963, 7312); *Blue Flames* (1964, 7338); *Everybody Loves a Lover* (1964, Imp. 73); *Queen of the Organ* (1964, Imp. 81); *One for Me* (1974, SE 7430); *Blues Everywhere* (1991, Can. 79525) [pf]; *Skylark* (1991, Can. 79705) [pf]; *A Walkin' Thing* (1992, Can. 79719)

As sideman: E. Davis: *The Eddie Lockjaw Davis Cookbook*, i–iii (1958, 7141, 7161, 7219); [no leader]: *Very Saxy* (1959, 7167); T. Curson: on *Plenty of Horn* (1961, Old Town 2003), Ahma (see ya), Flatted Fifth; S. Turrentine: *Dearly Beloved* (1961, BN 84081); *Never Let Me Go* (1963, BN 84129); *A Chip off the Old Block* (1963, BN 84150); *Hustlin'* (1963, BN 84162); *Let it Go* (1966, Imp. 9115); A. Hart: on *Here I Stand* (c1996, Imp. 208), Flamingo

BIBLIOGRAPHY

B. Gardner: "Shirley Scott: a Woman First," *DB*, xxix/27 (1962), 20

M. Jones: "Shirl's her own Girl," *MM* (23 Aug 1975), 27

S. Scott and L. Tomkins: "My Approach to the Organ, and to Music," *CI*, xiv/2 (1975), 8

D. Kasrel: "Hearsay: Shirley Scott: Piano Revisited," *JT*, xxiii/4 (1993), 10

R. Woessner: "Tube Jazz: You Bop your Life: Shirley Scott," *DB*, lx/1 (1993), 28

<http://www.dougpayne.com/shirley1.htm> (2000) [discography]

BK, JOSH FERKO (recording-list)

Scott, Stephen (*b* New York, 13 March 1969). Pianist and leader. He began learning piano with his mother at the age of five and later had classical tuition; he was introduced to jazz by Justin Robinson while they were both studying at the High School of the Performing Arts. After playing with Arnie Lawrence and Dave Burns he worked regularly with Betty Carter (March 1987–1988), and as a freelance performed with, among others, John Faddis, Terence Blanchard, Wynton and Branford Marsalis, Benny Golson, Dexter Gordon, Courtney Pine, Bobby Hutcherson, and Jimmy Cobb. He was with the Harper Brothers until 1990 and the following year he recorded with Joe Henderson. In about 1992 he was a member of Buster Williams's quintet Something More and played with Bobby Watson, both in the group Horizon and in his big band Tailor Made. Around the same time he began working with Ron Carter and leading his own groups, most of which have been trios; his sidemen have included Ray Drummond, Michael Bowie, Dwayne Burno, Ben Riley, Carl Allen, Gregory Hutchinson, and Clarence Penn. Scott performed at Bradley's in 1992 and at the Village Vanguard with Burno and Allen in 1993 and with Bowie and Hutchinson in 1996; he toured with Sonny Rollins from 1996 to 1998. As a freelance he played with Roy Hargrove (1989, 1995), Charles Fambrough (c1991), the studio group Good Fellas (1991–2), Cecil Brooks III (1993), Freddie Hubbard (1994, c1998), Mark Whitfield and Pete Yellin (both 1995), Victor Lewis (1996), and Steve Turre (1997).

Scott is one of a number of young swing and bop players who emerged in the early 1990s. He is an accomplished accompanist and soloist, and improvises in a style that is derived from Ahmad Jamal but also reflects the playing of Red Garland and Wynton Kelly. He should not be confused with the classical pianist Scott Stephens.

SELECTED RECORDINGS

As leader: *Something to Consider* (1991, Verve 849557-2); *Aminah's Dream* (1992, Verve 314-517996-2); *Renaissance* (1994, Verve 314-523863-2), incl. Poinciana, Tenderly; with R. Hargrove and C. McBride: *Parker's Mood* (1995, Verve 314-527907-2)

As sideman: Harper Brothers: *Remembrance: Live at the Village Vanguard* (1989, Verve 841723-2); J. Henderson: *Lush Life: the Music of Billy Strayhorn* (1991, Verve 314-511779-2); R. Hargrove: *Family* (1995, Verve 314-527630-2); S. Rollins: on *Sonny Rollins + 3* (1995, Mlst. 9250), Cabin in the Sky, They Say it's Wonderful; P. Yellin: *It's You or No one* (1995, Mons 874772-2); S. Rollins: *Global Warning* (1998, Mlst. 9280)

BIBLIOGRAPHY

D. Elfman: Liner notes, *The Harper Brothers* (Verve 833077-1, 1988)

J. Blum: "Hearsay: Stephen Scott: Someone to Consider," *JT*, xxii/1 (1992), 12

S. Nicholson: "Road to a Dream," *Jazz: the Magazine*, no.20 (1993), 14

E. Pooley: "Fast Track: Brief Lives: a Leader among Sidemen," *New York*, xxvi (12 July 1993), 18

M. Bourne: "All the Young Dudes," *DB*, lxi/12 (1994), 20

D. Helland: "All Together Now: Great Scott: an Emerging Jazz Leader has a Renaissance," *Piano & Keyboard*, no.173 (1995), 56

J. Macnie: "Fracturing the Mainstream: Stephen Scott & Eric Reed," *DB*, lxii/6 (1995), 22 [incl. discography]

J. Woodard: "Adventures inside the Piano," *Los Angeles Times* (8 Dec 1996)

G. Reynard: "Stephen Scott: couleur jazz," *Jh*, no.550 (1998), 24 [incl. discography]

GK

Scott, Tom [Thomas Wright] (*b* Los Angeles, 19 May 1948). Tenor saxophonist, composer, and leader. He grew up in a musical family: his father scored music for television shows, and his mother taught piano. After learning clarinet and soprano and alto saxophone he settled on the tenor instrument, and by the age of 19 he had played with the orchestras of Oliver Nelson and Don Ellis and in groups led by Howard Roberts and Roger Kellaway. On his first recording as a leader (1967) he made use of rock rhythms and electronic effects; he also included one of his best-known compositions, *Blues for Hari*. In 1970 Scott sat in with Gerry Mulligan's group at the Montreux International Jazz Festival, and in 1973 he took a quartet consisting of Joe Sample, Max Bennett, and John Guerin to an international song competition in Caracas, Venezuela. That same year he turned firmly to jazz-rock with his group the L.A. Express, a quartet (later a quintet) which toured and recorded with the singer Joni Mitchell. Its performances were hybrid, combining Mitchell's poetic folk lyrics with jazz improvisation and rock accompaniment. Bennett and Guerin provided the rhythmic underpinning alongside Sample and Larry Carlton (who were replaced respectively by Kellaway and Robben Ford in 1974). Scott was also the principal soloist on the hit recording *Jazzman* (c1974), by the songwriter Carole King. Having previously studied Indian music he toured as music director and soloist with Ravi Shankar and George Harrison in 1975; thereafter he briefly re-formed the L.A. Express with Bennett, Guerin, Ford, and the keyboard player Larry Nash.

In the late 1970s Scott's working group included Russell Ferrante, Steve Khan, and Jimmy Haslip. From that time he toured occasionally but concentrated on studio work in Los Angeles, writing and performing for many film and television soundtracks and taking part as a guest soloist in recording sessions with well-known pop artists. In the course of this work he has employed various sizes of saxophone, clarinet, flute, and recorder, as well as oboe, english horn, and lyricon, and in the early 1980s he played saxophone and lyricon in groups that blended elements of jazz and soul music. Scott toured and recorded with, and arranged music for, the GRP Big Band in the early 1990s. In 1996 he again re-formed the L.A. Express, with Sample, Ford, Steve Gadd, and Ralph MacDonald among his sidemen. He may be seen performing in the video *Jazzvisions: Echoes of Ellington*, pt 2 (1988).

SELECTED RECORDINGS

As leader: *The Honeysuckle Breeze* (1967, Imp. 9163), incl. Blues for Hari; *Rural Still Life* (1967, Imp. 9171); *Paint your Wagon* (1970, FD 114); *Great Scott* (*c*1973, A&M 4330); *Tom Scott and the L.A. Express* (1973, Ode 77021); *Apple Juice* (*c*1981, Col. FC37419); *Born Again* (*c*1991, GRP 9675)

As sideman: R. Kellaway: *Spirit Feel* (1967, PJ 20122); J. Mitchell: *Court and Spark* (*c*1974, Asy. 1001); C. King: Jazzman (*c*1974, Ode 66101); V. Feldman: *Your Smile* (*c*1974, Choice 1005)

BIBLIOGRAPHY

B. Libby: "Tom Scott: Groovy Californian," *J&P*, vi/11 (1967), 13
D. Rensin: "Tom Scott: Joni's Spark," *RS*, no.166 (1 Aug 1974), 28
L. Underwood: "Playback on Scott: Studio Brat Turned Monster," *DB*, xlii/1 (1975), 16
A. J. Liska: "Tom Scott," *DB*, xlviii/7 (1981), 28
H. Siders: "Great Scott!," *Windplayer*, iii/5 (1986), 8
L. Feather: "Tom Scott Makes the Sajak Connection," *Los Angeles Times* (8 April 1989)
J. Woodard: "Tom Scott: TV or not TV?," *DB*, lxi/3 (1994), 30

BK

Scott, Tony [Sciacca, Anthony] (*b* Morristown, NJ, 17 June 1921). Clarinetist. He began singing at the age of seven, imitating both instrumentalists and the Mills Brothers, and took up clarinet when he was about 12. At the age of 14 he formed a quartet that included Bobby Tucker and began doubling on alto saxophone. While studying at the Institute of Musical Art he took part in jam sessions at Minton's Playhouse (from 1941) and became skilled as a player in the emerging bop style – which, however, offered little work for clarinetists. From 1942 to February 1945 he served in the US Army in the New York area, playing alto saxophone in big bands, tenor saxophone in dixieland bands, and clarinet and piano in small swing groups. He performed on his preferred instrument in numerous short-lived groups, among them those of Ben Webster (1943), Sid Catlett, Trummy Young, and Earl Bostic, and led his own quartets intermittently (until 1956), the last of which numbered Bill Evans (ii) among its sidemen. Scott also appeared frequently as a saxophonist in big bands – with Buddy Rich (1946), Tommy Dorsey, Claude Thornhill (for three months in winter 1949), and, most notably, Duke Ellington (early 1953) – and he worked as an arranger (for Billie Holiday, Sarah Vaughan, and others), a pianist, and a music director (for the singer Harry Belafonte, 1955) – activities that only furthered his appetite for bop jam sessions. In the late 1950s he took part in the television shows "Omnibus" (episode v/9, 1956) and "The Subject is Jazz" (episodes 1, 3–5, 9, 11–13, all 1958).

After making a successful tour of Europe and South Africa in 1957, and in 1959 recording perhaps his finest albums (which for reasons unknown were not released for more than two decades) Scott traveled extensively from 1959 to 1965 throughout the Far East, where his performances drew on Indonesian, oriental, and Indian musics. He then returned to the USA briefly to work in nightclubs, but in the late 1960s he settled in Italy and appeared principally in Europe; in 1972 he toured as the leader of a group which included Romano Mussolini. He played and recorded in Stockholm (1972–3) and later, following an extended break from recording, made an album in England (1981) and Italy (1984). He recorded again on a regular basis for the Philology label from the late 1980s into the mid-1990s, variously as an unaccompanied soloist, in duos with Franco D'Andrea and with the pianist Renato Sellani, and as a leader.

For illustration *see* McShann, Jay.

SELECTED RECORDINGS

As unaccompanied soloist: *Like a Child's Whisper: Dialogue with Myself* (1989, 1994, Philology 78)

Duos with F. D'Andrea: *Homage to Billie Holiday: Body and Soul* (1995, Philology 119)

As leader: I cover the waterfront/Goodbye (1953, Bruns. 80242); *A Touch of Tony Scott* (1956, RCA LPM1353); *The Modern Art of Jazz* (1957, Secco 425); *South Pacific Jazz* (1958, ABC-Para. 235); *52nd Street Scene* (1958, Coral 57239); *Golden Moments* (1959, Muse 5230); *I'll Remember* (1959, Muse 5266); *Music for Zen Meditation* (1964, Verve 68634); *Music for Yoga Meditation and other Joys* (1967, Verve 68742); *Tony Scott* (*c*1969, Verve 68788); *African Bird: Come Back! Mother Africa* (1981, 1984, SN 1083); *The Clarinet Album* (1993, Philology 113)

BIBLIOGRAPHY

N. Hentoff: "Scott Free," *DB*, xxiii/21 (1956), 11
L. Feather: "A Pied Piper?," *DB*, xxiv/23 (1957), 19
G. Kopelowicz: "Tony Scott," *Jh*, no.121 (1957), 13
D. Morgenstern: "The Long-awaited Return of Tony Scott," *DB*, xxxii/25 (1965), 19
W. Balliett: "Musical Events," *New Yorker*, xliii (3 Aug 1967), 80
J. Burns: "The Forgotten Boppers," *J&B*, ii/3 (1972), 4
A. Morgan: "Ten Lessons with Tony," *J&B*, iii/1 (1973), 14
G. Endress: *Jazz Podium: Musiker über sich selbst* (Stuttgart, Germany, 1980), 160
P. Pettinger: *Bill Evans: How my Heart Sings* (New Haven, CT, and London, 1998)
<http://www.dragonfire.net/~msnyder/clarinet.scott.htm> (2000)

BK

Scott-Heron, Gil (*b* Chicago, 1 April 1949). Singer and songwriter. He grew up initially in Jackson, Tennessee, with his grandmother, who taught him to play piano. After experiencing the difficulties of being one of three young African-Americans trying to integrate into a school in Jackson (1962) he moved to New York at the age of 13; later he attended Lincoln University in Philadelphia. When he was 19 he published his first novel, *The Vulture*, and in 1970 he recorded an album of jazz and poetry. In the 1970s Scott-Heron collaborated with the pianist Brian Jackson for a number of recordings that contained spoken verse and protest songs; among these were *Pieces of a Man* (1971, including *The revolution will not be televised*), *Free Will* (1972), and *Winter in America* (1973). His album *The First Minute of a New Day* (1974) was the first recording on which he was accompanied by the Midnight Band, a proficient backup ensemble; on this album and those that followed he and his group developed a terse, concise blend of jazz and funk, over which he recited monologues or sang in a deep, mellow voice. In an era when funk and disco recordings often contained facile or meaningless lyrics and monotonously repetitive accompaniments Scott-Heron constructed songs that combined perceptive social and political comment with the exuberance of dance music and the improvisatory fluidity of jazz. Many of these carry stern reprimands to the public about such matters as the misuse of drugs or alcohol (*The Bottle*), apartheid (*Johannesburg*), and the threat of a disaster at a nuclear power plant (*We almost lost Detroit*), although he never resorts to mere preaching. *B-movie*, for example, with a long, humorous spoken introduction, is a sardonic attack on conservative politics, and *Storm Music* is a passionate, hopeful rhythm-and-blues song which predicts justice for all oppressed peoples. On *Is that jazz?* Scott-Heron traces the history of the music in terms of African-American consciousness.

In the early 1970s Scott-Heron earned a master's degree from Johns Hopkins University and taught creative writing at the University of the District of Columbia. By the middle of the decade he was working full-time as a musician and poet, and for a number of years he appeared regularly at

Blues Alley in Washington. In 1984 his long association with the label Arista ended and he moved to Britain, but in 1990 he was convicted for cocaine possession and deported. Following his return to the USA he worked in New York and toured both nationally and internationally with his small group the Amnesia Express, in which he mainly sang but also accompanied himself on an electric keyboard instrument; in 1996 and 1997 he recorded as a guest soloist with Ron Holloway. In addition to his novels he has published collections of poetry and an account of a tour with Stevie Wonder which promoted the introduction of a national holiday to celebrate Martin Luther King's birthday.

SELECTED RECORDINGS

As leader: *Pieces of a Man* (1971, FD 10143), incl. The revolution will not be televised; *Free Will* (1972, FD 10153); *Reflections* (*c*1981, Ari. 9566), incl. B-movie, Is that jazz?, Storm Music; *Moving Target* (1982, Ari. 9606)

As leader with B. Jackson: *Winter in America* (1973, SE 19742), incl. The Bottle; *The First Minute of a New Day* (1974, Ari. 4030), incl. We beg your pardon, America; *From South Africa to South Carolina* (*c*1975, Ari. 4044), incl. Johannesburg; *It's your World* (1976, Ari. 5001), incl. Bicentennial Blues; *Bridges* (c1977, Ari. 4147), incl. We almost lost Detroit; *Secrets* (1978, Ari. 4189)

As sideman with R. Holloway: on *Scorcher* (1996, Mlst. 9257), Blue Collar, Is that jazz?; on *Groove Update* (1997, Mlst. 9276), Three Miles Down, We almost lost Detroit

BIBLIOGRAPHY

R. Townley: "El Jefe's Manifesto," *DB*, xlii/8 (1975), 13
S. Loupias: "Les nouveaux poèmes de Gil Scott-Heron," *Jm*, no.275 (1979), 34
I. Pye: "Unarmed and Extremely Dangerous," *MM* (17 April 1982), 18
M. Brennan: "Target Man," *MM* (30 April 1983), 22
L. Barber: "Beam Me up (Scotty)," *MM* (24 March 1984), 25
"Shrink Rap," *MM* (29 June 1985), 21
K. Kirk: "Master of the Arts," *MM* (19 July 1986), 12
L. Goffe: "Arts: Right-on, Right out," *The Guardian* (29 May 1990)
M. Boehm: "Scott-Heron's Take on the Roots of Rap," *Los Angeles Times* (5 Dec 1992)
S. Aiges: "Changes Make Prophet of Singer," *New Orleans Times-Picayune* (7 June 1994)
P. Croom: "Gil Scott-Heron, Back from being Here All Along," *Washington Post* (8 May 1994)
W. Jenkins: "Gil Scott-Heron: Spirits Renewed," *JT*, xxiv/7 (1994), 45
M. Saunders: "30 Years on the Urban Front: Scott-Heron keeps Getting Message out," *Boston Globe* (22 Feb 1998)
J. Maycock: "Don't dis Daddy. He Sang Poetry to Conga Beats and Percussion. It was Rap, although They didn't Call it that Then," *The Guardian* (9 April 1999)
J. Sullivan: "Scott-Heron's Muse Returns to Action," *San Francisco Chronicle Datebook* (14 Feb 1999)

BK

Screwgun. Record company and label founded in 1996 by TIM BERNE.

SDR Big Band. German radio orchestra of the Süddeutscher Rundfunk, Stuttgart, led for 40 years by ERWIN LEHN.

Seamen, Phil(lip William) (*b* Burton on Trent, England, 28 Aug 1926; *d* London, 13 Oct 1972). English drummer. Having taken up drums at the age of 14, he first played in bands led by Nat Gonella (late 1945–1946), the trumpeter Ken Turner (1947), Gonella again (1948), and the violinist Joe Loss (1950–51), and performed and recorded with Jack Parnell (April 1951 – August 1954) – except for a brief period with Bert Ambrose (spring 1953). He then worked with Ronnie Scott (August 1954 – early 1957), Kenny Baker (1956–8), with whom he recorded, Dizzy Reece's quartet (1957, 1958), and Don Rendell (summer 1957 – early 1958); he also appeared as a leader in the film *The Golden Disc* (*The Inbetweeen Age*) (1958) and recorded with Stan Tracey (1958–9). Seamen was a member of the Jazz Couriers (1959), Tubby Hayes's quartet (1959–60), and Joe Harriott's pioneering European free-jazz group (late 1960 – March 1962). During the early 1960s he became involved with the blues movement in England, working with the singers Georgie Fame (from 1962) and Alexis Korner (1963). Thereafter he was employed as the resident drummer at Ronnie Scott's (1964–8), where he accompanied such soloists as Johnny Griffin, Stan Getz, Roland Kirk, and Freddie Hubbard; at the same time he worked with Dick Morrissey's quartet (1965–6), big bands led by Harry South (1965) and Burt Rhodes (1966), his own small groups (1966), Harriott's band again (occasionally in 1967, including a recording in that year), and the trio led by Tony Lee (1967–8). Later he led his own trio (from 1969) and, infrequently, a big band. In 1969–70 he played, toured, and recorded with Air Force (led by his pupil the drummer Ginger Baker), and worked as a freelance musician (1970–72), in which capacity he recorded with Tony Coe and Brian Lemon (1971), worked with John Stevens, and toured with Hubbard, though he was mainly heard performing in pubs in London.

Seamen was a technically accomplished and highly perceptive musician. Throughout his working life he maintained a brilliant, though occasionally anarchic, career, performing in theaters, working as a session musician, and frequently leading small groups in London clubs and pubs. A master of most styles from swing to rock, his catholic taste did not confine him to the bop style with which he was most closely associated.

SELECTED RECORDINGS

As leader: on *Third Festival of British Jazz* (1956, Decca LK4180), Manteca Suite; *Now! ... Live!* (1968, Vogue SVLP9220), incl. Who's afraid of the big bad wolf; *Phil on Drums!* (1971, 77 SEU53), incl. Allen's Alley

As sideman with S. Tracey: *Little Klunk* (1959, Vogue 160155)

BIBLIOGRAPHY

CarrJ; *ChiltonB*; *Feather '60s*; *Feather–Gitler '70s*
B. Blain: "I Remember Phil ...," *Jazz Now: the Jazz Centre Society Guide*, ed. R. Cotterrell (London, 1976), 25
A. Korner and others: "Phil," *The Wire*, no.2 (1983–4), 22
P. Renaud: *La discographie du jazz anglais* (Chaumont, France, 1985)
S. Goodwin: "From the Past: England's Phil Seamen," *MD*, xii/1 (1988), 44

DIGBY FAIRWEATHER/BK

Séance de boeuf (Fr.). JAM SESSION.

Sears, Al(bert Omega) (*b* Macomb, IL, 21 Feb 1910; *d* New York, 23 March 1990). Tenor saxophonist. He began his career in Buffalo and first played professionally in New York early in 1928 under James P. Johnson and Fats Waller in the pit band for the show *Keep Shufflin'*. He then worked in the big bands of Chick Webb (1928), Zack Whyte (1929), and Elmer Snowden (1931–2), with whom he appeared in the short film *Smash your Baggage* (1932). He returned to Buffalo while recovering from pneumonia and led his own groups; his singer there in *c*1933–4 and again in Cincinnati in 1937 was Helen Humes, who traveled with Sears to New York for an engagement at the Renaissance Casino in the latter year. After working with Andy Kirk (February 1941 – summer 1942) he formed a band for further work at the Renaissance Casino, made a USO tour, and spent four months with Lionel Hampton (from December 1943). In May 1944 he joined Duke Ellington's orchestra, succeeding Ben Webster as one of its principal tenor saxophonists. Sears's flamboyant and emotionally direct style is prominent on many of Ellington's recordings. He left the band in 1949 and played in a small group led by Johnny Hodges (March 1951 –

October 1952). When the recording by Hodges of Sears's composition *Castle Rock* became a commercial success he formed a music publishing company, Sylvia Music Inc. He later concentrated on rhythm-and-blues, making regular appearances at the Brooklyn Paramount theater as a soloist in the band of the pioneering rhythm-and-blues and rock-and-roll promoter and disc jockey Alan Freed. From the late 1950s he performed only infrequently, but he continued to play at reunions of Ellington's former sidemen. He became one of the first African-American executives working at ABC-Paramount. Sears claimed his personal favorite among his rhythm-and-blues solos was with Joe Turner (ii) on *Flip, Flop and Fly*, which many discographies have attributed to Grady Jackson.

SELECTED RECORDINGS

As leader: Shake Hands/Brown Baby (1949, Coral 65023); Goin' Uptown/ Tweedle Dee (1954, Herald 448); *Swing's the Thing* (1960, Swingville 2018)

As sideman with D. Ellington: I ain't got nothing but the blues (1944, Vic. 20-1623); The Blues (1944, Vic. 28-0400); Carnegie Blues (1945, Vic. 20-1644); It don't mean a thing (1945, Vic. 27-0054); Hiawatha (1946, Musi. 464); *Liberian Suite* (1947, Col. CL6073)

As sideman with others: Z. Whyte: It's tight like that/West End Blues (1929, Gen. 6798); J. Hodges: Castle Rock (1951, Clef 8944); J. Turner (ii): Flip, Flop and Fly (1955, Atl. 1053); Swingville All-Stars: *Swingville All-Stars* (1960, Swingville 2010)

BIBLIOGRAPHY

ChiltonW; *FeatherE*; *McCarthyB*; *TuckerDE*

L. Feather: *The Book of Jazz: a Guide to the Entire Field* (New York, 1957, rev. 2/1965 as *The Book of Jazz from Then till Now: a Guide to the Entire Field*)

D. Ioakimidis: "Kings of the Tenor Sax: Al Sears," *Jh*, no.126 (1957), 19 [incl. discography by K. Mohr]

K. Mohr: "Discography of Al Sears," *Jazz-Statistics*, no.12 (1959), [3]

P. Turley: "Three Forgotten Men," *JM*, iv/12 (1959), 29

V. Wilmer: "'Big' Al Sears Talks," *JM*, ix/7 (1963), 12

G. E. Lambert: "The Ellingtonians, 2: Al Sears," *JM*, xi/4 (1965), 19

B. Niquet: "Deux précurseurs: Red Prysock, Al Sears," *Soul Bag*, no.65 (1978), 7 [incl. discography by K. Mohr]

O. Peterson: "The Forgotten Ones: Al Sears," *JJI*, xl/3 (1987), 16

Obituaries: *New York Times* (26 March 1990); I. Crosbie, *JJI*, xliv/3 (1991), 18

J. Simmen: "Al Sears," *BHcF*, no.396 (1991), 1

P. Schaap: Liner notes, *Big Al Sears: Sear-iously* (Bear Family 15668, 1992)

SCOTT DeVEAUX/BK

Seaton, Lynn (Earl) (*b* Tulsa, OK, 18 July 1957). Double bass player. He played guitar from the age of seven, changed to double bass when he was nine, and began working professionally while studying at the University of Oklahoma. In September 1980 he moved to Cincinnati, where he worked with the pianist Steve Schmidt and in the Blue Wisp Big Band, with which he recorded in 1983–5; in Schmidt's group he played alongside John Von Ohlen, with whom he accompanied numerous leading musicians as a member of the house band at the Blue Wisp club. During the same period he had lessons with Rufus Reid in New York (1981) and taught at the College Conservatory of Music at the University of Cincinnati (1982–4). In the mid-1980s he was a member of Woody Herman's big band (September 1984 – June 1985, February 1986) and the Count Basie Orchestra under Thad Jones and Frank Foster (July 1985–1987; for illustration *see* Recording, fig.6), and in 1986 he moved to New York. Later he toured extensively with Tony Bennett and for six months with George Shearing and joined Howard Alden's trio (recording in 1989–90) and Buck Clayton's Swing Band. In the early 1990s Seaton performed and recorded with Ernestine Anderson and Frank Wess at the Concord Jazz Festival (1990), toured with Monty Alexander (1991–2), and played with Oliver Jones (1992). While he continued to collaborate with Wess (recording from 1993) he began working regularly in the trios of Kenny Drew, Jr., and Jeff Hamilton (both *c* mid-1990s). During an extensive career as a freelance he has performed on over one hundred albums, notably with Tim Hagans (1983), Jackie and Roy (1990), the guitarist Royce Campbell (from 1991), John Fedchock's New York Big Band (1992), Dave Stryker (1994), the DMP Big Band (1995–6), and the alto saxophonist Mark Vinci (from 1995).

While in New York Seaton taught at Long Island University, SUNY (New Paltz), and William Paterson College in Wayne, New Jersey, at Jamey Aebersold's jazz camps, and at Clark Terry's Institute of Jazz Studies; he also published the instructional book *Jazz Solos for Bass* (New York, 1996). After moving to the Dallas metropolitan area (1998) he served on the faculty at the University of North Texas and continued to work as a freelance. He has played electric bass guitar as well as the acoustic instrument.

SELECTED RECORDINGS

As leader: *Bassman's Basement* (1991, Tim. 390)

As sideman: W. Herman: *50th Anniversary Tour* (1986, Conc. 302), incl. Blues for Red, Pools; J. Colianni: *Blues-o-matic* (1988, Conc. 367), incl. Exactly like you; H. Alden: *Snowy Morning Blues* (1990, Conc. 4424), incl. Sleepy Time Gal; K. Drew: *Portraits of Mingus and Monk* (1994, Claves Jazz 50-1194), incl. Peggy's Blue Skylight; F. Wess: *Surprise! Surprise!: Live at the 1996 Floating Jazz Festival* (1996, Chi. 350); K. Drew: *Winter Flower* (1998, Mlst. 9289)

BIBLIOGRAPHY

K. Franckling: "Hearsay: Lynn Seaton: beneath the Surface," *JT*, xxiii/8 (1993), 14

W. D. Clancy and A. C. Kenton: *Woody Herman: Chronicles of the Herds* (New York and elsewhere, 1995)

<http://www.music.unt.edu/instrumental/bass/faculty/Lynn_Seaton/lynn_seaton.html> (1999) [incl. discography]

GK

Seay, Clarence (*b* Washington, DC, 7 Jan 1957). Double bass player. He attended both the Duke Ellington School of the Arts and Howard University at the same time as Wallace Roney. From the mid-1980s he worked regularly with Billy Harper, with whom he first recorded in 1989, and from 1993 he toured and recorded with Roney. Seay also accompanied Chico Freeman (1983), Lou Donaldson (1986), Helen Merrill, and Horace Silver, and recorded with Wynton Marsalis (1981), Cindy Blackman (1987, 1992), the drummer Jae Sinnett (from 1993), and as a member of the Warner All Stars (1995).

SELECTED RECORDINGS

As sideman: B. Harper: *Destiny is Ours* (1989, Ste. 1260); J. Sinnett: *House and Sinnett* (1993, Positive Music 78020); W. Roney: *Village* (1996, WB 46649)

BIBLIOGRAPHY

ReclamsJ

T. L. Stinson: "Bassnotes: Clarence Seay: Tomorrow's Tradition," *Bass Player*, viii/12 (1997), 20

GK

Sebesky, Don(ald J.) (*b* Perth Amboy, NJ, 10 Dec 1937). Composer, arranger, and trombonist. While studying at the Manhattan School of Music (1955–9) he worked with Kai Winding, Claude Thornhill, and Tommy Dorsey. He played trombone and wrote arrangements for Maynard Ferguson (1958–9) and Stan Kenton (1959–60), but then ceased playing trombone and devoted his time to composing and making arrangements, working as a leader and for Wes

Montgomery (1965, 1967–8), Buddy Rich (1968–9), Paul Desmond (1969), Freddie Hubbard (1971, 1974), and Sonny Stitt (1973). Thereafter he was rarely active in jazz contexts; however, early in 1997 he arranged for and conducted the big band of John Pizzarelli for its début at the Blue Note, New York, and in the late 1990s he arranged and recorded tributes to Bill Evans (ii) and Duke Ellington. As an arranger Sebesky is noted for paying scrupulous attention to the capabilities and limitations of the instruments for which and the players for whom he wrote; his compositions, which include scores for film and television, combine elements of jazz, classical music, and rock. He published an instructional book, *The Contemporary Arranger* (Port Washington, NY, 1975), and from 1978 to 1993 he taught a seminar on orchestration.

SELECTED RECORDINGS

As leader: *Giant Box* (1973, CTI 6031–2); *Full Cycle* (1984, Crescendo 2164); of Contemporary Arrangers Workshop: *Moving Lines* (1984, Doctor Jazz 40155)

As sideman with M. Ferguson: *A Message from Newport* (1958, Roul. 52012)

SELECTED ARRANGEMENTS

Recorded by others: W. Montgomery: *Bumpin'* (1965, Verve 68625); P. Desmond: *Bridge over Troubled Water* (1969, A&M 3032); F. Hubbard: *First Light* (1971, CTI 6013)

BIBLIOGRAPHY

FeatherE; *Feather '60s*; *Feather–Gitler '70s*

A. Smith: "Date with Sebesky," *DB*, xli/19 (1974), 16 [incl. discography]

C. Deffaa: "Out and About in New York: John Pizzarelli, Jnr, Don Sebesky, Ralph Burns, Ellington Broadway Musicals," *CJM*, xxxiv/2 (1997), 14

PATRICK T. WILL/BK

Section. A group of homogeneous instruments within a band; *see* Bands, §§2, 4.

Sedergreen, Bob [Robert Alexander] (*b* 'Akko, Palestine [now in Israel], 24 Aug 1943). Australian pianist. As a small child he lived in England, where he first studied piano. His family moved to Melbourne, Australia, in 1950 and during the 1960s he gained experience with various ensembles there. He performed and recorded with Ted Vining (from 1969), Alan Lee (1972–3), and Brian Brown (from 1974), and accompanied such visiting Americans as Dizzy Gillespie, David Baker, Phil Woods, Jimmy Witherspoon, Milt Jackson, and Lee Konitz; he toured Scandinavia with Brown in 1978. In 1984 he formed the group Blues on the Boil, which was influenced by the blues styles of Chicago and the Mississippi Delta; he also played with Onaje, a group led by Allan Browne. He is a member of the faculty of the Victorian College of the Arts in Melbourne, where he teaches in the improvisation department.

Following Australia's bicentennial celebrations, and in an attempt to capture in music the nation's cultural diversity, Sedergreen conceived a hybrid sound which falls under the banner of "world music" and established Art Attack, a group comprising flute, bagpipes, saxophones, didjeridu and clapsticks, bouzouki, drum set, electronic percussion, highland snare drums, voice, and two synthesizers; it was invited to play at the inaugural Malaysian International Jazz Festival in 1993. Also in the early 1990s he formed a duo with Tony Gould, with whom he presented at least one two-piano concert each year. In addition he continued his long association with Vining's trio through both live and recorded performances, wherein his rhythmic buoyancy, drive and musical daring are displayed in full.

SELECTED RECORDINGS

Duos with T. Gould: *Unanimity* (1993, 1995, Move 3155)

As leader of Art Attack: *Bobbing and Weaving* (1989–91, Larrikin 253)

As sideman: T. Vining and A. Lee: *Moomba Jazz '76, Live from the Dallas Brooks Hall*, i (1976, 44 Records 6357708); B. Brown: on [various artists]: *Moomba Jazz '76: Live from the Dallas Brooks Hall*, ii (1976, 44 Records 6357709), Moomba Jazzbird '76; *Upward* (1976, 44 Records 6357711); T. Vining: *The Ted Vining Trio Live at PBS-FM* (1981, Jazznote 029), incl. Impressions; *Wildflowers* (1982, Move 3051); *The Planets* (1985, Larrikin 151); Onaje: *Waltz for Stella* (1985, Larrikin 174); T. Vining: *Together* (1998, ABC 496496-2)

BIBLIOGRAPHY

A. Bisset: *Black Roots, White Flowers: a History of Jazz in Australia* (Sydney, 1979, rev. 2/1987)

A. Jackson: "Bob Sedergreen," *Jazz: the Australasian Contemporary Music Magazine*, i/6 (1981), 23

B. Johnson: *The Oxford Companion to Australian Jazz* (Melbourne, Australia, 1987)

W. Bebbington, ed: *The Oxford Companion to Australian Music* (Melbourne, Australia, 1997)

TONY GOULD

Sedric, Gene [Eugene Hall; Honey Bear] (*b* St. Louis, 17 June 1907; *d* New York, 3 April 1963). Tenor saxophonist and clarinetist. His father was the ragtime pianist Paul "Can Can" Sedric. He first worked in St. Louis with Charlie Creath and on riverboats with Fate Marable and Dewey Jackson. Late in 1922 he joined Ed Allen, and the following year he toured with Jimmy Cooper's Black and White Revue, with which he traveled to New York; there he later became a member of Sam Wooding's orchestra, with which he performed at the Nest Club in Harlem and at the Club Alabam (where the orchestra replaced that of Fletcher Henderson). From May 1925 to October 1931 he toured Europe with Wooding, except for a nine-month period in the USA. After returning to the USA he rejoined Wooding (summer 1932), worked briefly with Fletcher Henderson (1934), and performed and recorded with Alex Hill. From 1934 to 1942, except for an occasional absence, he was a sideman with Fats Waller (for illustration *see* Waller, fats); he may be seen with the group in four soundies from 1940, including *Honeysuckle Rose*, *The Joint is Jumping*, and *Your Feet's Too Big*. While Waller was working as a soloist Sedric played in Mezz Mezzrow's Disciples of Swing (November 1937) and with Don Redman (1938–9), and following Waller's death he worked as a leader in New York (from March 1943) and then in other major cities. In 1944 he joined a quartet led by the pianist Phil Moore, and late the following year he toured with Hazel Scott. He led his own groups in 1946 and 1947, and during the same period performed with a band of Waller's former sidemen under the leadership of the pianist Pat Flowers. Sedric then worked further as a leader and played with Jimmy McPartland (recording in 1950) and Bobby Hackett (1951). In 1953 he toured Europe with Mezzrow and recorded in Paris with Mezzrow and Buck Clayton; later that year he began a long association with Conrad Janis. He worked as a freelance from the late 1950s but retired on account of ill-health after playing and recording with Dick Wellstood in 1961. He published some reminiscences as "Trouping with Fats Waller" (*Jazz Record*, no.30 (1945), 10; repr. in *Selections from the Gutter: Jazz Portraits from "The Jazz Record"*, ed. A. Hodes and C. Hansen (Berkeley, CA, Los Angeles, and London, 1977), 223) and "Gene 'Honeybear' Sedric" (*BHcF*, no.26 (1953), 4).

SELECTED RECORDINGS

As leader (all recorded in 1938 for Vocalion): The Joint is Jumpin'/Off Time (4576); Choo Choo/The Wail of the Scromph (4552)

As sideman with F. Waller: Georgia May/Don't let it bother you (1934, Vic. 24714); Breakin' the Ice (1934, Vic. 24826); Something Tells Me/Don't Try to Cry your Way Back to Me (1938, Vic. 25817); You Out-smarted yourself/Hold Tight (1939, Bb 10116); The Darktown Strutters' Ball/I can't give you anything but love (1939, Bb 10573)
As sideman with others: E. Mathews: You came to my rescue (1936, Voc. 3332); The way you look tonight (1936, Voc. 3317); Cliff Jackson: Jeepers Creepers (1944, Black & White 1205)

BIBLIOGRAPHY

ChiltonW; *FeatherE*; *Feather '60s*
"Sedric Sends Shortsleeved Sophisticates," *DB*, xiii/14 (1946), 3
G. Hoefer: "The Hot Box," *DB*, xxi/5 (1954), 8
J. Bradley: "'Honeybear': Gene Sedric, 1907–1963," *Coda*, v/10 (1963), 21
L. Kunstadt: "Eugene Sedric: Gentleman Musician," *Record Research*, no.55 (1963), 3
C. Albertson: Liner notes, S. Wooding: *Sam Wooding and his Chocolate Dandies* (Biograph 12025, *c*1970)
L. Wright: *"Fats" in Fact* (Chigwell, England, 1992)
J. Evensmo: *History of Jazz Tenor Saxophone: Black Artists*, i: *1917–1934* (Oslo, 1996); ii: *1935–1939* (Oslo, 1997); iii: *1940–1944* (Oslo, 1997); iv: *1945–1949* (Oslo, 1999)

WARREN VACHÉ, SR.

See, Cees (*b* Amsterdam, 5 Jan 1934; *d* The Hague, 9 Dec 1985). Dutch drummer. A self-taught musician, he worked with the double bass player Freddy Logan (1955–6), the tenor saxophonist Jack Sels (1956–60), the Millers (1956–7, 1960), Rolf Kühn (1962), Pim Jacobs's trio (1964–6), the quartet led by the clarinetist and saxophonist Herman Schoonderwalt (1965), Teddy Wilson (1965–9), and Klaus Doldinger (1965–9). In the early to mid-1960s he was a member of a sextet for Sender Freies Berlin in Germany, which included Ack van Rooyen, Herb Geller, and Jerry van Rooyen. During the following years he worked in a group led by Dusko Goykovich and Nathan Davis (1969–72) and with Jan Hammer (1968) and Volker Kriegel (1968, 1971–3); with Manfred Schoof and Peter Trunk he belonged to the New Jazz Trio (1970–71), which made recordings (including *Page One*, 1970, MPS 15276). At around the same time he worked with Wolfgang Dauner (1971) and as a percussionist with Chris Hinze (1971–2). He also gave concerts and appeared at festivals with Schoof, Cannonball Adderley, Kenny Drew, Donald Byrd, Yusef Lateef, Dexter Gordon, Don Byas, Rita Reys, Art Farmer, Tete Montoliu, Jean-Luc Ponty, and Benny Bailey. See was proficient in many styles, notably bop, hard bop, and free jazz. (*ReclamsJ*)

WIM VAN EYLE

Seffer, Yoch'ko (*b* Miskolc, Hungary, 10 July 1939). French saxophonist and composer. He left Hungary, where he studied clarinet and saxophone, to move to France in 1956. In Paris he studied at the Conservatoire and with Nadia Boulanger, and discovered the music of the composers of the Second Viennese School – Arnold Schoenberg, Alban Berg, and Anton Webern. In 1962 he enrolled at the Ecole des Beaux-Arts, where he studied painting and sculpture. At the same time he earned his living by accompanying popular singers, and frequently played in clubs with such leading musicians as Mal Waldron, Charlie Rouse, Phil Woods, Ornette Coleman, Pharoah Sanders, Kenny Barron, and Daniel Humair. He was a member of the groups Magma (1970), Perception (1971–4), and Zao (1973–6) and led his own ensemble Speed Limit (1975–6). From 1976 he drew on the traditions of his native country with the group Neffesh Music, which played a fusion of jazz, classical, and ethnic musics; it toured the USA in 1979. Seffer took French nationality in 1981. In the 1980s he formed the Ethnic Duo (1980), a group of varied makeup which recorded *Chromophonie* (1982, 1984), a saxophone septet (1984), a quartet with Siegfried Kessler (1988), the group Mestari (1993), a big band which played Coltrane's compositions (1994), and the group Yog (1996), which presented programmatic and electronic music. His daughter Deborah Seffer (*b* 13 Aug 1969) is a jazz violinist.

SELECTED RECORDINGS

As leader: *Chromophonie*, i: *Le diable angélique* (1982, GC 2101); *Chromophonie*, ii: *Le livre de Bahir* (1984, GC 2102); *Monk Forever* (1988, Moshé Naïm 13019); *Prototype* (1989, Kid 590462); *Ghilgoul* (1995, Musea 4145); *Adama ima* (1995, Moshé Naïm 500742); *Ornette Forever* (1996, Moshé Naïm 5008242); *Magyar etno* (1997, Pannon 1028)
As sideman with Zao: *Shekina* (1975, RCA Balance 0097)

BIBLIOGRAPHY

R. Baud: "Ce que Yoch'ko sait faire," *Jh*, no.408 (1984), 43
X. Prévost: "Gros plan: Yoch'ko Seffer," *Jm*, no.351 (1986), 42
P. Carles, A. Clergeat, and J.-L. Comolli: *Dictionnaire du jazz* (Paris, 1988, rev. and enlarged 2/1994)
X. Matthyssens: "Seffer et Kessler: fous de Monk," *Jm*, no.371 (1988), 21
Fara C.: "Retrospective d'un slave," *Jazzman*, no.31 (1997), 16
A. Juliac: Liner notes, Y. Seffer: *Retrospective* (Frémeaux 70, 1997)

ANDRÉ CLERGEAT

Segal, Jerry [Gerald] (*b* Philadelphia, 16 Feb 1931; *d* Aug 1974). Drummer. He was active mainly in styles derived from bop. Having performed and recorded with Bennie Green and Pete Rugolo (both 1954) he spent a period playing at clubs in Philadelphia. He then performed and recorded with Johnny Smith and Terry Gibbs (both 1955–6), Teddy Charles (1955, 1957), and Stan Getz (1957) and collaborated with the composer Edgard Varèse. In the late 1950s he worked with Charles Mingus, Herbie Mann, and Lennie Tristano. Segal recorded with Bob Dorough (1956), Teo Macero (1957), Curtis Fuller and Hampton Hawes (1957), and Dick Cary's dixieland octet (1957), as a member of the Prestige Jazz Quartet (1957, alongside Mal Waldron, Teddy Charles, and Addison Farmer), and with Green (1958), Mose Allison (1959–60), and Dave McKenna (1960). From 1958 to 1960 he performed and recorded with Bernard Peiffer. Only the month and year of his death appear in the social security death index. (*FeatherE*)

Segure, Roger (*b* New York, 22 May 1905). Arranger. Largely self-taught, he first worked as a pianist with Midge Williams, touring the USA and the Far East; he may be heard with her on *Dinah* (1934, Col. 27884), which was recorded in Tokyo. In the late 1930s he wrote arrangements for Louis Armstrong, Andy Kirk, and John Kirby, and from 1940 to 1944 he was Jimmie Lunceford's arranger; examples of Lunceford's group performing Segure's work may be heard on *Blue Afterglow* (1940, Col. 35919) and the soundtrack to the film *Blues in the Night* (1941). After settling in Los Angeles in the late 1940s Segure worked as the music director for a television program and a dance orchestra and then as a teacher. (*FeatherE*)

Sehring, Rudi (*b* Langen, Hessen, Germany, 13 June 1930). German drummer. He began his career in the late 1940s as a member of the Joe Klimm Combo and in 1953 joined Hans Koller's group, with which he played at intervals until 1959; he also recorded as the leader of a trio (*Long John/Just You, Just Me*, 1955, Modern 06021), toured Italy and Scandinavia, and worked with Bill Russo, Lee Konitz, and Zoot Sims. From 1957 he played in the Jazzensemble des Hessischen Rundfunks in Frankfurt am Main and worked with Albert and Emil Mangelsdorff. Sehring joined the dance orchestra of Hessischer Rundfunk in 1960 and became less active in jazz. (*ReclamsJ*)

WOLFRAM KNAUER

Seifert, Zbigniew [Zbiggy] (*b* Kraków, Poland, 6 June 1946; *d* Munich, 15 Feb 1979). Polish violinist and alto saxophonist. He studied violin from the age of six and alto saxophone while in his teens. From 1965 to 1969 he led a quartet (which included Jan Jarczyk and Janusz Stefański) in which he played saxophone in a style modeled after that of John Coltrane; in its last year the quartet gave performances to some acclaim at the Polish festivals Jazz on the Odra and Jazz Jamboree, as well as at a festival in Hungary. Seifert again took up violin while playing free jazz with Tomasz Stańko's quintet (1968–73); by 1971 he had ceased playing saxophone. That year he was a guest soloist with Boško Petrovic at the festival in Ljubljana, and in 1972 he recorded with Barre Phillips and Jiří Stivín in Czechoslovakia. After moving to Germany (1973) Seifert was a member of Hans Koller's group Free Sound (1974–5) and worked as a freelance with Volker Kriegel, Joachim Kühn, Jasper van 't Hof, and others. In the USA he performed at the Monterey Jazz Festival with John Lewis (1976) and recorded with Oregon (*c*1977). On his successful album *Man of the Light* (1976) he plays with a rhythm section (consisting of Kühn, Cecil McBee, and Billy Hart) that recalls that of Coltrane; the album also includes a ballad Seifert recorded in a duo with van 't Hof. His recordings of jazz-rock and classical music were less successful, although he nonetheless fitted in perfectly as a guest soloist with Oregon during a session fusing folk-revival, classical, and jazz styles.

SELECTED RECORDINGS

As unaccompanied soloist: *Solo Violin* (1976, MRC 06645088)
As leader: *Man of the Light* (1976, MPS 15489); *Passion* (1977, Cap. ST11923)
As sideman: T. Stańko: *Purple Sun* (1973, Calig 30610); V. Kriegel: *Lift!* (1973, MPS 15390); Oregon: *Violin* (*c*1977, Van. 79397)

BIBLIOGRAPHY

"Seifert, Zbigniew," *JF* [intl edn], no.18 (1972), 89
R. Kowal: "Zbigniew Seifert: Rapid Ascent," *JF* [intl edn], no.34 (1975), 53
J.-E. Berendt: "Profile: Zbigniew Seifert," *DB*, xliv/17 (1977), 32
Obituary, *JF* [intl edn], no.58 (1979), 13
R. Kowal: "Zbigniew Seifert: a Musical Legacy," *JF* [intl edn], no.59 (1979), 42 [incl. discography]

BK

Sekere [shekere]. Gourd vessel rattle of the Yoruba people of Nigeria. It has external strikers, consisting of a network of cowrie shells. The instrument may be heard clearly on *All Blues*, from Tito Puente's album *Goza mi timbal* (1989, Conc. Picante 4399). (*GroveI*)

Selden, Fred (Laurence) (*b* Los Angeles, 22 Jan 1945). Alto saxophonist. He studied music at UCLA (BA 1966) and took private lessons in composition and arrangement with Shorty Rogers, in film music with Lalo Schifrin, and on alto saxophone with Bud Shank. After gaining a teaching credential at UCLA (1967) he led a quintet (1968–78) and performed and recorded as the lead alto saxophonist of Don Ellis's orchestra (1969–74). His playing may be heard on Ellis's album *Live at Fillmore* (1970, Col. G30243), on which *The Magic Bus Ate my Donut* provides an example of his acclaimed work as a composer and arranger. Selden worked with the big bands of Louie Bellson and Bill Holman (mid-1970s) and then led a quintet (1979–81) and a trio (1982–4) with Milcho Leviev. From 1991 he co-led with the guitarist Michael Ferenci the group Timeline, which recorded in 1994. Having resumed his education at UCLA in the latter part of the 1990s, he gained a master's degree in 1998 and began working towards a doctorate. In addition to his principal instrument Selden, who is highly regarded as a studio musician, plays flute, clarinet, and tenor and soprano saxophones. He has composed music for television programs and films and has published several books of arrangements for flute.

BIBLIOGRAPHY

Feather–Gitler '70s
J. Burger and J. Rona: "Fred Selden: a Studio Reed Player Goes Electronic," *Keyboard*, xiii/7 (1987), 54

BK

Sellin, Hervé (*b* Paris, 16 March 1957). French pianist, son of Pierre Sellin. He studied piano at the Paris Conservatoire, where he received a *premier prix*. For a time he played bop trumpet as a member of the Buds (1974). He later performed as a pianist with his father, Michel Attenoux, Geo Daly, Eddie "Lockjaw" Davis, Gérard Badini (1982), Dany Doriz (1983), Chet Baker, Jacky Samson (1984), Slide Hampton (1985), Jimmy Owens (1986), Dee Dee Bridgewater (1986–9), Jean-Loup Longnon and Brandford Marsalis (both 1990), and Ranee Lee with Harry Allen (1992). In 1989–91 his own sextet included the trumpeter Tony Russo and Jacques Bolognesi. At the French festival Jazz in Marciac he played with Guy Lafitte, François Théberge, and Denis Leloup (1997). Sellin taught at the IMFP (Institut Musical de Formation Professionnelle) in 1992 and from 1994 at the Paris Conservatoire and the Marciac summer workshops.

SELECTED RECORDINGS

As sideman: A.Villéger: *Something to Live For* (1984, Cara 012); J. Griffin: *Live at Jazz Valley* (1991, Jazz Valley 1536); Eric Aubier: *Toot Suite* (1998, Feeling Musique Paris 03)

MICHEL LAPLACE

Sellin, Pierre (*b* Le Mans, France, 8 March 1930; *d* St. Leu-la-Fôret, France, 12 Jan 1998). French trumpeter and valve trombonist, father of Hervé Sellin. He came from a family of pianists, but studied trumpet. He first played with Hubert Rostaing, the bandleader Jerry Mengo, Alix Combelle (1953–4), Buck Clayton (1953), and Lucky Thompson (1959), and in the 1960s worked with television orchestras. From 1963 he made jazzy trumpet recordings under his own name. Influenced both by Louis Armstrong and bop trumpeters, he recorded the album *Jazz Parade in New Orleans* with the Claude Gousset Big Band under the leadership of Claude Luter (1971, Vogue 804). After performing with André Persiany (1972), Claude Bolling (1973–6), François Guin (1973), and Dany Doriz (1976), he changed to trombone and played with Benny Vasseur (1981–96). Sellin taught at Paul Beuscher's school of music in Paris (1977) and later in Concarno. (Obituaries, M. Laplace, *Jh*, no.548 (1998), 11; M. Laplace, *Jazz Dixie/Swing: du Ragtime au Big Band*, no.19 (1998), 32).

MICHEL LAPLACE

Sels, Jack [Jean Jaques] (*b* Antwerp, Belgium, 29 Jan 1922; *d* Antwerp, 21 March 1970). Belgian tenor saxophonist. He studied piano in Belgium and England. In Antwerp he played saxophone with the trombonist Mickey Bunner at the

Cascade and appeared at the GI Club and the 13th Port. In 1947 he worked at the Exi Club and toured France, and the following year he played in an army big band. As the leader of Jack's All Star Bop Orchestra he performed in Antwerp and Knokke in Belgium and also in Amsterdam. After working in radio, from 1950 he again led a group. Later he played with Dizzy Gillespie in a concert of Jazz at the Philharmonic (1952) and performed at various clubs in Germany (1953). Sels made several recordings as a leader and recorded rock-and-roll (1955) and film music.

BIBLIOGRAPHY

G. Stevens: "Huldententoostelling Jazz Sels," *Jazz Middelheim Tentoostelling 1980* (Antwerp, 1980), 17

R. Pernet, J.-P. Schroeder, and others: *Dictionnaire du jazz à Bruxelles et en Wallonie* (Liège, Belgium, 1991)

R. Pernet: *Belgian Jazz Discography (1897–1999)* (Brussels, 1999)

ROBERT PERNET

Semple, Archie [Archibald Stuart Nisbet] (*b* Edinburgh, 31 March 1928; *d* London, 26 Jan 1974). Scottish clarinetist. He first worked semiprofessionally in Edinburgh, often with his brother John, a trumpeter. He led several groups before starting work as a full-time musician in spring 1952, when he joined Mick Mulligan's band in London. After touring and recording with Freddy Randall (1953 – August 1954) he worked with Alex Welsh (February 1955 – March 1963), and became an important member of the latter's band; the originality and inventiveness of his playing made a considerable impact. Semple also recorded frequently as a leader (1952, 1957–63) before illness forced him to retire. Although he was influenced by Pee Wee Russell and Edmond Hall, he found a highly personal voice that was not bound by convention. His playing made particularly effective use of the clarinet's low register and variety of timbre.

SELECTED RECORDINGS

As leader: *The Clarinet of Archie Semple* (1957–8, 77 LEU6); *It's Right Here for You* (1960, Col. 33SX1240)

As sideman with A. Welsh: *Dixieland to Duke* (1957, Nixa 507); *The Melrose Folio* (1958, Nixa 516)

BIBLIOGRAPHY

CarrJ; *ChiltonB*; *FeatherE*

R. Harris: *Jazz* (London, 1952, 5/1957), 244

S. Brown: "Semple: a Natural," *MM* (16 Feb 1974), 16

L. Taylor: "The Undiscovered Archie Semple," *IAJRC Journal*, xxiii/4 (1990), 1

N. Simpson and G. Bielderman: *Archie Semple Discography* (Zwolle, Netherlands, 1997)

L. Taylor and J. Latham: "Archie Semple," *IAJRC Journal*, xxxii/2 (1999), 56

S. Klett: "Listing of Archie Semple Recordings," *IAJRC Journal*, xxxii/2 (1999), 59

CLARRIE HENLEY

Senator. Nickname of EUGENE WRIGHT.

Senba [Takahashi], **Kiyohiko** (*b* Tokyo, 23 Dec 1954). Japanese percussionist. He grew up in a family of traditional Japanese musicians and learned *taiko* (traditional Japanese drums) from the age of three; he made his début in *kabuki* when he was ten and started on drums and percussion when he was 13. Having majored in traditional Japanese percussion, he graduated from the Tokyo University of Fine Arts and Music, though he had already begun to work professionally in other genres at the age of 19. In 1978 he joined a popular jazz-fusion group, The Square. Later he accompanied the popular singer and songwriter Akiko Yano and worked with Akira Sakata, the traditional percussion group Kodo (1981), and the Asian Fantasy Orchestra (1992). Senba recorded with Material, Jamaaladeen Tacuma, Ronald Shannon Jackson, and Kazumi Watanabe's Mobo Band, and from 1982 he led various groups of his own. While maintaining a busy studio career he has been active in traditional Japanese music, jazz, and pop. In 1994 he was appointed music director of several large productions, including *Fire Bird* and *King Lear*.

SELECTED RECORDINGS

As leader: *Haniwa* (1991, CBS–Sony SRCLK2138); *Kana shibari* (1991, CBS–Sony SRCL6038); *Buson Senba* (1998, Sony VRFL0007); *Senba* (1999, Village A 0023)

As sideman: K. Watanabe: *Mobo Club* (1984, Pol. 3113-38); Asian Fantasy Orchestra: *Asia Tour 1998* (1998, Pol. 7419)

BIBLIOGRAPHY

S. Hall: "Eastern Intrigue: Kiyohiko Senba," *Talking Drums*, iv/1 (1996), 41

KAZUNORI SUGIYAMA

Sendecki, Władysław (*b* Kraków, Poland, 1955). Polish pianist, keyboard player, and leader. After working as a classical musician early in his career he devoted himself to jazz. In 1974, with Jarosław Śmietana, he founded Extra Ball, which became Poland's leading jazz-rock group. From 1977 to 1980 Sendecki also led the group Sunship, which included Zbigniew Jaremko, Henryk Miśkiewicz, and Vitold Rek among its sidemen. Having emigrated to Sweden in 1981 he toured and recorded in an acoustic duo with Michal Urbaniak (from 1982) and toured as a member of Leszek Żądło's Polski Jazz Ensemble (1983–6). He then toured Europe and recorded in a jazz-rock group co-led by Bireli Lagrene and Jaco Pastorius; the album *Stuttgart Aria* (1986) provides excellent examples of Sendecki's work on synthesizer. From the late 1980s into the early 1990s he worked with Daniel Schnyder, though during the same period he played in Harry Sokal's group Full Circle, performed and recorded with the NDR Big Band, and recorded with Klaus Doldinger's Passport (*c*1990) and Franco Ambrosetti (1990). In 1995 he moved to Germany and recorded that year with a group co-led by Ralf Hübner and Christof Lauer. He was a founding member, with the trumpeter Ingolf Burkhardt, Detlev Beier, and Gerry Brown, of the Hamburg Jazz Quartett.

SELECTED RECORDINGS

As leader of Sunship: *Live at Aquarium* (1979, Poljazz [issue no. unknown]); *Follow Us* (1979, Muza [issue no. unknown])

As sideman: B. Lagrene and J. Pastorius: *Stuttgart Aria* (1986, Jazzpoint 1019); D. Schnyder: *The City* (1988, Enja 6002-2); *Decoding the Message* (1989, Enja 6036-2); D. Schnyder and M. Mossman: *Granulat* (1990, Red 123240); R. Hübner and C. Lauer: *Mondspinner* (1995, Free Flow Music 0796)

BIBLIOGRAPHY

L. Blomberg: "Kvintettjazz paa Polska" [Jazz quintet from Poland], *Orkester journalen*, li/10 (1983), 12

K. Mümpfer: "Mainzer Abschlusskonzert des SWF-New-Jazz-Meeting," *JP*, xxxviii/1 (1989), 42

<http://www.harrysokal.co.at/harrysokal/sendecki.html> (1999)

GK

Senensky, Bernie [Bernard Melvyn] (*b* Winnipeg, Canada, 31 Dec 1944). Canadian pianist and leader. After classical and jazz studies in Winnipeg he moved in 1968 to Toronto, where he soon emerged as the city's premier accompanist to visiting American soloists, includng Buddy DeFranco, Art Farmer, Art Pepper, and Red Rodney. He was a member of the Moe Koffman Quintet (from 1979 until the flutist's death in 2001), and he has led his own bands in a variety of configurations. Senensky has made several trio recordings since 1975, including *Rhapsody* (1993, Tim. 434). In 1991 he recorded *Re:Union* (Unity 123) with a septet and made two albums for Timeless with quartets featuring American sidemen, Gary Bartz and Bobby Watson among them. He has also recorded with Koffman, Fred Stone, and others. His playing is characterized by his obvious comfort in a wide range of styles, from swing to the assertive post-bop of his own groups. Several of Senensky's compositions have been recorded by other musicians, most notably *Lolito's Theme* by DeFranco, Rodney, and Don Thompson.

BIBLIOGRAPHY

EMC2
Mark Miller: "Bernie Senensky," *DB*, xxxxii/21 (1975), 42
L. Tomkins: "Piano Special: I'm Trying to Keep a Keyboard Balance, Says Bernie Senensky," *CI*, xix/9 (1981), 12

MARK MILLER

Senior, Milton (E.) (*b* Springfield, OH, *c*1900; *d c*1948). Saxophonist and clarinetist. He was one of the founding members in 1921 of the Synco Septet; William McKinney assumed its leadership, and the band was known as the Synco Jazz Band before it became McKinney's Cotton Pickers in 1926. Senior took part in the band's earliest recording sessions as a member of the reed section, but is not known to have taken any solos. He left McKinney in 1928 and in the early 1930s he led his own band in Toledo, Ohio, which at various times included Art Tatum and Teddy Wilson. He left music many years before his death by his own hand. (J. Chilton: *McKinney's Music: a Bio-discography of McKinney's Cotton Pickers*, London, 1978)

based on *ChiltonW*

Sepulveda, Charlie [Sepulveda (Rivera), Charles] (*b* New York, 17 July 1962). Trumpeter. At the age of eight he moved with his family to Puerto Rico. He learned trumpet at Escuela Libre de Musica (1974–9), attended the conservatory in Puerto Rico (1979–81), and performed with various groups. After returning to New York he studied at CUNY (1985–8) while serving as lead trumpeter for Eddie Palmieri (*c*1984–92), with whom he appeared on David Sanborn's television program "Night Music" (1988). He also worked in Ray Barretto's groups (1985–6) and as a freelance with, among others, Tito Puente (recording in 1990–91), the bandleader Johnny Pacheco, and the Fania All Stars. Sepulveda spent two years as lead trumpeter in Dizzy Gillespie's United Nation Orchestra (1991–3) and was a member of Danilo Pérez's group Afro-Cuban Explosion (1992). From 1989 he toured internationally and recorded with his own groups, notably a sextet, The Turnaround; his sidemen have included David Sanchez, Pérez, and Andy Gonzalez.

SELECTED RECORDINGS

Duo with H. Ruiz: on *Heroes* (1993, Telarc 83338), Con Alma
As leader: *Algo nuestro (Our Thing)* (1992, Ant. 314-512768-2)
As sideman: H. Ruiz: *Manhattan Mambo* (1992, Telarc 83322); D. Valentin: *Tropic Heat* (*c*1993, GRP 9769-2)

BIBLIOGRAPHY

Feather–GitlerBEJ
L. Mergner: "Hearsay: Charlie Sepulveda: Leading his own Way," *JT*, xxiii/2 (1993), 10

GK

Sequencer. An electronic device used to repeat, reproduce, and manipulate brief sequences of notes; for examples of its use in jazz contexts *see* Computers and Synthesizer.

SESAC. Record label. It was established in the late 1950s by the music licensing agency SESAC, Inc. (founded in 1931 as the Society of European Stage Authors and Composers). Devoted to broadcast transcriptions, the jazz catalogue included material by such musicians as Count Basie, Woody Herman, Coleman Hawkins, and Charlie Shavers. Because the recordings were made under an arrangement that forbade the use of material owned by members of ASCAP or BMI, the repertory consisted only of compositions licensed by the organization and material in the public domain. (S. Voce and B. Priestley: "SESAC: Discography of a Transcription Label," *J&B*, ii (1972), no.2, p.16; no.3, p.22)

HOWARD RYE

Session (i). A term most commonly used in jazz of a continuous period in a recording studio, but also (in the standard sense) of any period during which musicians play together, as in the expression Jam session. A player who works exclusively in recording studios, whether as a freelance or as the employee of a recording or film company, is described as a "session musician" (*see also* Bands, §3(e)) or "studio musician."

Session (ii). Record company and label. The company was established in 1943 by Phil Featheringill and D. W. Bell and was operational for about a year. It is best remembered for its recordings of unaccompanied blues and boogie-woogie piano solos by Jimmy Yancey, Alonzo Yancey, and Cripple Clarence Lofton, of traditional jazz by Punch Miller and others, and of swing by Trummy Young; 31 discs were issued. The masters were later purchased by Dante Bolletino, who issued recordings on his label Pax. Later reissues were made on Jazztone in the USA, on Vogue and Storyville in Europe, and on various private labels. ("Session: a Label Listing," *Matrix*, no.70 (1967), 10)

HOWARD RYE

Session (iii). Record label established in the early 1970s by Boris Rose.

Sessoms. Record company and label formed in 1986 by Ed Wilkerson, Jr.

Set. A group of pieces played one after the other in a public performance, and therefore a segment of a performance during which musicians are continuously on stage. A performance is normally divided into two or more "sets," each lasting from 45 minutes to an hour, between which the musicians rest; during the intermission there may be no live music, or another band or (more often) an unaccompanied soloist may play. Less commonly the term is used of shorter periods (20–30 minutes) in a continuous presentation during which the musicians never leave the stage; in this case the sets are separated by breaks of a few minutes to allow the musicians to decide on the next group of pieces to be played or to put their music in order. (*GoldJL*)

Sete, Bola [De Andrade, Djalma] (*b* Rio de Janeiro, 16 July 1923; *d* Greenbrae, nr San Rafael, CA, 14 Feb 1987). Brazilian guitarist. He grew up in a musical family, and studied at the National School of Music in Rio de Janeiro (MusM, 1949). His early work with local samba groups was followed by further study in Rio at the conservatory, and he became interested in jazz after hearing Barney Kessel. After a period as a staff guitarist with radio stations he moved in 1959 to the USA. He performed in various hotels until he was discovered by Dizzy Gillespie, with whom he played at the Monterey Jazz Festival and recorded in 1962 at the start of the craze for bossa nova. He worked with Vince Guaraldi (1963–6), led his own Brazilian group (1966–71), then performed mostly as a soloist, playing both guitar and lutar (a lute-shaped guitar of his own design). Sete may be seen performing in the film documentary *Sounds of Summer: the Concord Jazz Festival* (1970). He was a highly distinctive guitarist whose classical technique was inspired by Andrés Segovia, although his work on the electric instrument was related stylistically to that of George Van Eps, Kessel, and Tal Farlow. His playing combined harmonic ideas influenced by jazz with the rhythmic vitality of the samba.

SELECTED RECORDINGS

As unaccompanied soloist: *Ocean* (1972, Takoma 1049)
As leader: *Bossa nova* (1962–3, Fan. 3349); *Bola Sete Live at the Monterey Jazz Festival* (1966, Verve 68689)
As sideman: D. Gillespie: on *New Wave!* (1962, Phi. 600070), Chega de saudade; V. Guaraldi: *At El Matador* (1966, Fan. 8371)

BIBLIOGRAPHY

Feather '60s; *Feather–Gitler '70s*
D. McCarthy: "Bola Sete," *GP*, i/4 (1967), 8
B. Sete: "Pro's Reply," *GP*, viii/7 (1974), 6 [incl. discography]
Obituary, *San Francisco Examiner* (15 Feb 1987)

NORMAN MONGAN

Setup. A rhythmic fill played by the drummer to lead an ensemble into a break.

78 (r.p.m. disc). Generally a shellac disc of 10- or 12-inch diameter, recorded and played back at 78 r.p.m., and having a playing time of three to four minutes per side; *see* RECORDING, §I, 1(i). The last commercially issued 78 r.p.m. discs from the mid-1950s onwards were often pressed on vinyl rather than shellac.

77. Record company and label. The company was established in 1957 by Doug Dobell (*b* London, 1918; *d* Nice, France, 10 July 1987), the owner of a record store in London. The first discs to be released were 10-inch EPs, which were put out in limited quantities. Later the catalogue was expanded to include 12-inch LPs; by the mid-1970s the company had issued more than 50 albums, mostly of traditional and mainstream jazz. The catalogue included recordings made by such English musicians as Tubby Hayes, Bruce Turner, Dick Morrissey, Keith Smith, Kenny Baker, and Tony Coe and items by visiting Americans, among them Bud Freeman, Eddie Miller, Buck Clayton, Albert Nicholas, and George Lewis (i). In 1962 the company sponsored and issued the results of Jack McVea's first session as a leader in 15 years. Much of the repertory was produced by Dobell, who, as a pianist himself, was responsible for recording albums by Dick Wellstood, Dill Jones, Brian Lemon, Don Ewell, Dick Katz, Joe Turner (i), and Ralph Sutton. In addition 77 issued some albums first put out by Delmark and other small American labels.

After 1979 the company made no new recordings, although much of the repertory remained available for some years. In the early 1980s, however, Dobell began to dispose of the catalogue to other companies, selling many of the masters to Harlequin, and others (particularly of traditional jazz) to American organizations. By 1984 the company had ceased to function.

BIBLIOGRAPHY

"Record Dealer Starts New Jazz Disc Company," *Jazz News* (March 1957), 8
F. Owen: "The Sound of Dobell's," *Sv*, i/4 (1966), 20

MARK GARDNER

Severinsen, Doc [Carl Hilding] (*b* Arlington, OR, 7 July 1927). Trumpeter and bandleader. His father played violin. He took up trumpet at the age of seven and toured briefly with a big band (*c*1945) before entering the army. Later he was a member of big bands led by Charlie Barnet (intermittently, 1947–9), Tommy Dorsey (1949–*c*1951), and Benny Goodman (for a short period). After joining NBC in 1949, Severinsen worked almost continuously in television, appearing on "The Steve Allen Show" in the mid-1950s. In 1962 he became the assistant leader of Skitch Henderson's orchestra on "The Tonight Show," and in 1967 he replaced Henderson as the orchestra's leader and the program's music director; he became well known to television audiences for his virtuoso playing and quick wit. In addition to his work in television he led workshops for young brass players, conducted the Phoenix (Arizona) Pops, performed as a soloist with symphony orchestras, and led his own groups, notably Xebron, a jazz-rock quintet formed in 1981. Although his big band on "The Tonight Show" was replaced by a group under the direction of Branford Marsalis when the show's host, Johnny Carson, retired in 1992, Severinsen continued to lead his group in other settings. A good example of his work is the album *The Tonight Show Orchestra with Doc Severinsen*, i–ii (1986, Amherst 3311, 3312), on which Snooky Young, Conte Candoli, Bill Perkins, Pete Christlieb, Tommy Newsom, Ernie Watts, Ross Tompkins, and Ed Shaughnessy may be heard.

SELECTED FILMS AND VIDEOS

Charlie Barnet and his Band (1949); The Subject is Jazz, episodes 1, 4, 5, 11–13 (1958); Michael Bryan (1961)

BIBLIOGRAPHY

B. Willis: "Meet the Doc," *CI*, vi/9 (1968), 24
N. Dunlap: "Doc Severinsen: Ideal Model," *DB*, xxxvi/1 (1969), 16
G. Lees: "Tonight with Doc Severinsen," *High Fidelity/Musical America*, xx/4 (1970), 122
L. Underwood: "Doc Takes Issue," *DB*, xli/20 (1974), 12
Z. Stewart: "Doc Severinsen: Tonight's the Night," *DB*, lii/11 (1985), 16
J. Brady: "In Step with: Doc Severinsen," *Washington Post* (23 July 1989)
S. Yanow: "Doc Severinsen: the Many Facets of . . .," *DB*, lvi/2 (1989), 27
H. Phillips: "Straight Talk from Doc Severinsen," *Instrumentalist*, xlv/3 (1990), 14
G. Giddins: "Weatherbird: the Conductor's New Clothes: Doc Severinsen Swings to Black," *VV* (9 June 1992), 86
J. McDonough: "Good Night, Doc: Tonight Show Band," *DB*, lix/5 (1992), 26
B. O. Boston: "Interview: Doc Severinsen: Lessons for a Lifetime," *Teaching Music*, iv/1 (1996), 44
J. Bradley: "Trumpeter Doc Severinsen Keeps up the Pace at 71," *Denver Post* (28 Jan 1999)

MARK TUCKER/BK

Sewing, Jack (*b* Rotterdam, Netherlands, 11 Feb 1934). Dutch double bass player. He began on accordion in 1939 and took up guitar in 1948. From 1951 he played double bass in the band led by the pianist Jack Redler, and in 1956 he joined the Dixieland Pipers under the leadership of the pianist Eric Krans. In the early 1960s, with the singer and clarinetist Bob Azzam, he played for a year in Beirut and toured in Europe. Following a performance in Paris in 1965 Sewing settled in the city and spent his time repairing double basses and other stringed instruments; he also accompanied such American musicians as Johnny Griffin, Dexter Gordon, Nathan Davis, Ted Curson, Don Cherry, Jimmy Gourley, Sir Charles Thompson, and Kenny Clarke. In the late 1960s he worked in France with the Brazilian singer Silvio Sylvera, the Trinidadian trumpeter Sonny Gray, and Marc Hemmeler. During the same period he began playing with Stephane Grappelli at the Toits de Paris (1968), the restaurant within the Paris Hilton where Grappelli's career was revived, and he subsequently toured and recorded worldwide with Grappelli (to 1989). In addition he collaborated frequently with Bill Coleman, and in 1973 they recorded alongside Guy Lafitte at the Montreux International Jazz Festival. Four years later Sewing moved to Nice, where he worked for five seasons at the Grande Parade du Jazz, both performing and maintaining instruments. He also played with Lionel Hampton's big band (touring France in 1984), Teresa Brewer, and Benny Waters. In 2000 he remained on the south coast of France, repairing and manufactuing instruments and performing as a freelance.

SELECTED RECORDINGS

As sideman: B. Coleman and G. Lafitte: *Mainstream at Montreux* (1973, BL 30150); S. Grappelli: *At the Winery* (1980, Conc. 139); *Vintage 1981* (1981, Conc. 169)

MARK GILBERT

Shad, Bob [Robert Abraham] (*b* New York, 12 Feb 1920; *d* Los Angeles, 13 March 1985). Record producer and record company owner. From the early 1940s he produced rhythm-and-blues and jazz recordings for Black & White, Continental, Manor, National (iii), and Savoy, among others. In September 1948 he formed the company and label Sittin' in with, with which he continued until it was acquired by Mercury in October 1951; during the same period he worked for Castle (1948–50) and its subsidiary Jade (1949–50) and for a gospel music label, Spirituals (1949). From 1951 to 1952 he ran Jax, and in late 1952 he joined the staff at Mercury, where he initially produced blues and rhythm-and-blues recordings and later became head of artists and repertory for the popular music division. In 1954 he started the EmArcy label, and he oversaw the production of much of its jazz output before transferring to Mercury's pop label Wing. During this association Shad produced recordings for the Harlem label (1955). He formed the eponymous label Shad in 1958 and worked on pop music for the Brent label the following year. From around 1960 he was artistic director for Time (ii), for which once again he initially produced popular music before moving to jazz. In 1964 he formed Mainstream. At some earlier point in his career Shad produced gospel music for Sunrise.

BIBLIOGRAPHY

"The Shad Labels," *Blues Research*, no.16 (n.d. [?1966]), 2
M. Leadbitter: "Sittin' in with Shad," *Blues Unlimited*, no. 41 (1967), 3
T. Berkowitz: "Really Sittin' in with Shad," *Blues Unlimited*, no.53 (1968), 14
M. Kington: "Mr. Mainstream," *MM* (2 June 1973), 22
M. Leadbitter: "Sittin' in Again," *Blues Unlimited*, no.109 (1974), 9
Obituary, *Los Angeles Times* (17 March 1985)
M. Ullman: "Back to the Mainstream," *Fanfare*, xv/2 (1991), 584
N. Darwen and T. Shad: "Bob Shad – the Record Man: the Sittin' in With Story," *Blues & Rhythm*, no.100 (1995), 16 [incl. discography]

HOWARD RYE, GK

Shahid, Jaribu (Abdurahman) [Henderson, Ben] (*b* Detroit, 11 Sept 1955). Bass player. He played electric bass guitar initially and took up double bass after becoming interested in jazz. In the mid-1970s he co-founded the group Griot Galaxy with the composer and saxophonist Faruq Z. Bey; after Bey was seriously injured in a motorcycle accident in 1984 Shahid continued to lead the group, and it performed in Detroit into the 1990s. As a member of the Creative Arts Collective from the late 1970s, Shahid worked with such visiting musicians as Roscoe Mitchell, Anthony Braxton, and Muhal Richard Abrams. In 1978 he appeared with Sun Ra's Arkestra at the Ann Arbor Jazz & Blues Festival, after which he toured with the group and spent eight months with its leader in Philadelphia. Having returned to Detroit he worked with Mitchell's Sound Ensemble (from 1980) and Geri Allen's trio (late 1980s – early 1990s). From 1992 he was a member of Mitchell's Note Factory, with which he performed in Austria at the Saalfelden Jazz Festival in August 1994, and around 1993 he joined James Carter's group. In the 1990s his primary instrument was double bass, although he continued to play the electric bass guitar where appropriate.

SELECTED RECORDINGS

As sideman: Griot Galaxy: *Kins* (1981, Black & White 001); R. Mitchell: *Live at the Knitting Factory* (1987, BS 120120-1); G. Allen: *Twylight* (1989, Minor Music 801014)

BIBLIOGRAPHY

H. Boyd and L. Sinclair: *Detroit Jazz Who's Who* (Detroit, 1984)
R. L. Campbell: *The Earthly Recordings of Sun Ra* (Redwood, NY, 1994)
M. Johnston: "Jaribu Shahid," *Coda*, no.270 (1996), 22

GK

Shake. An effect produced on a brass instrument by shaking it against the lips while playing. It resembles a trill or an exaggerated vibrato, but usually covers a wider interval – often a 3rd or a 5th, but sometimes as much as an octave. It is notated by the normal symbol for the trill accompanied by the word "shake" (*see* Notation, §5 (ii), and ex.6). A succession of slow shakes occurs at the beginning of the third blues chorus of Clark Terry's solo on *Feedin' the Bean*, from Coleman Hawkins's *Back in Bean's Bag* (1962, Col. CS8791). Although the shake is essentially a brass technique it may be imitated on woodwind instruments by rapidly lipping pitches up and down (*see* Lip). On the title track of the album *Two for the Blues* (1983, Pablo 2310905) the tenor saxophonists Frank Foster and Frank Wess imitate the sound of the brass and wind sections of a big band; an element in the imitation is the execution of a shake on a held note (*see* Honk, ex.1).

BIBLIOGRAPHY

G. Schuller: *Early Jazz: its Roots and Musical Development* (New York, 1968)
A. Napoleon: "The Music Goes Down and Around: (a Case of Mistaken Identity)," *Sv*, no.37 (1971), 18
A. Blatter: *Instrumentation/Orchestration* (New York and London, 1980)
M. Laplace: "La trompette et le cornet dans le jazz et la musique populaire," pt vi, *Brass Bulletin*, no.47 (1984), 39

BK

Shakti. Fusion group. It was formed in the USA in 1973 as a trio by John McLaughlin, the South Indian violinist Lakshminarayana Shankar (brother of L. Subramaniam), and the North Indian tablā player Zakir Hussain; to suit the character of the other instruments, McLaughlin played a specially designed acoustic guitar based on the Indian *vīṇā*. After giving concerts before small audiences on the East Coast the group recorded *Shakti* (1975, Col. PC34162), in which the original members were joined by the percussionists Vikku (T. H.) Vinayakaram (whose main instrument was the *ghaṭam*, a clay pot drum) and R. Raghavan (*mṛdaṅgam*, a wooden, double-headed barrel drum). As a quartet (without Raghavan) Shakti recorded *A Handful of Beauty* (1976, Col. PC34372), then in 1977 it toured Europe and made another recording before disbanding later in the year. The name Shakti, meaning "together," refers to the union of jazz guitar improvisation with North and South Indian rhythms. The group favored fast tempos in complex meters, but its use of repetitive patterns and simple harmonies suggested links with jazz-rock. In the late 1990s Shakti re-formed to record, with the *bānsuri* player Hariprasas Chaurasia as guest soloist.

BIBLIOGRAPHY

M. Jackowski: "Lakshminarayana Shankar, the Indian Wizard of the Fiddle," *JF* [intl edn], no.48 (1977), 28
J. Szprot: "Shakti and Afterthoughts," *JF* [intl edn], no.48 (1977), 32
C. Welch: "Pot Luck," *MM* (21 May 1977), 9
C. Berg: "John McLaughlin: Evolution of a Master," *DB*, xlv/12 (1978), 12

BK

Shank, Bud [Clifford Everett, Jr.] (*b* Dayton, OH, 27 May 1926). Alto saxophonist and flutist. He studied clarinet, alto and tenor saxophones, and flute, and majored in music at the University of North Carolina (1944–6), but left when his college dance band quit the university en masse to work professionally. After a visit to New York he traveled west, and abandoned the tenor saxophone for the alto while playing with Charlie Barnet (1947–8). He played flute and alto saxophone with Stan Kenton (1950–51), and in the interim also worked for the less famous bandleaders Alvino Rey and, briefly, Art Mooney. He was drafted into the marines during the Korean War in 1952, but was discharged soon afterwards because of impaired vision. He returned to the Los Angeles area, where he became an important figure in West Coast jazz: he performed and recorded with Howard Rumsey's Lighthouse All Stars (to the end of 1955), recorded with Laurindo Almeida in a style that combined bop and Brazilian music, led his own group, including Claude Williamson, and toured with Bob Cooper and June Christy, with whom he performed in Europe and South Africa (March–June 1958). He also recorded in 1953 with Gerry Mulligan's tentet, Shelly Manne, and Chet Baker, and from 1954 as a leader or co-leader with Bill Perkins and Cooper.

In the early 1960s Shank led a local group which at times included Carmell Jones, Dennis Budimir, and Gary Peacock, and he performed at festivals and concerts in Europe and South America with such bossa nova musicians as Sergio Mendes. He also worked with the Japanese koto player Kimio Eto and the Indian sitar player Ravi Shankar. From the mid-1960s he was active principally as a studio musician, but during the bop revival of the mid-1970s he appeared occasionally with his own quintet in Los Angeles. In 1974 he formed the L.A. FOUR with Almeida, Ray Brown, and Chuck Flores (replaced by Manne, who was in turn replaced by Jeff Hamilton). Later he toured with Chet Baker, performing at Fat Tuesday's in New York in 1981, and Shorty Rogers, working from 1983 with Rogers's revived Giants, and from the late 1980s into the early 1990s with the revived Lighthouse All Stars, co-led by Rogers and Shank; he also formed a duo with Almeida. By the mid-1980s Shank had abandoned his work as a studio musician and had left the L.A. Four. After moving to Port Townsend, Washington, he established in 1984 the annual Bud Shank Jazz Workshop, which in the 1990s grew into a major event. He stopped playing flute around 1986 to concentrate on performing bop as an alto saxophonist. In 1988 he led a quartet which included Larry Grenadier and the drummer Vince Lateano, and in 1992 he appeared at Birdland in New York with a rhythm section of Kenny Barron, Lonnie Plaxico, and Victor Lewis. Shank celebrated his 70th birthday with a Canadian tour in 1996, and later that year toured the USA and performed on a Caribbean cruise ship. Throughout this new period in his career he has been consistently praised for the fire and maturity of his playing. Earlier he published a volume of transcriptions, *World's Greatest Jazz Solos: Flute* (Hollywood, 1978).

SELECTED RECORDINGS

As leader: with S. Rogers: *Shorty Rogers Compositions* (1954, Nocturne 2); *Live at the Haig* (1956, Choice 6830); *Bud Shank Quartet* (1956, PJ 1215); with L. Almeida: *Holiday in Brazil* (1958, WP 1259), *Latin Contrasts* (1958, WP 1281); of L.A. Four (with L. Almeida, R. Brown, and S. Manne): *The L.A. Four Scores!* (1975, Conc. 8); with S. Rogers: *Yesterday, Today, and Forever* (1983, Conc. 223); *This Bud's for You* (1984, Muse 5309); *That Old Feeling* (1986, Cont. 14019); with B. Perkins: *Serious Swingers* (1986, Cont. 14031); *The Doctor is In* (1991, Can. 79520); with S. Rogers: *Eight Brothers* (1992, Can. 79521); *I Told You So!* (1992, Can. 79533); with D. Lanphere and D. Goodhew: *Lopin'* (1992, Hep 2058); *New Gold!* (1993, Can. 79707); *Bud Shank Plays the Music of Bill Evans* (1996, Fresh Sound 5012); *Bud Shank Sextet Plays Harold Arlen* (*c*1996, Jimco 9502); *By Request: Bud Shank Meets the Rhythm Section* (1996, Mlst. 9273)

As sideman: S. Kenton: on [untitled EP] (1947–51, Cap. EAP1-508), Theme for Alto (1951); S. Manne: *Shelly Manne and his Men* (1953, Cont. 2503), incl. Afrodesia; L. Almeida: *Laurindo Almeida Quartet Featuring Bud Shank* (1954, PJ 7, 13); H. Rumsey: *Lighthouse*, vi (1954–5, Cont. 3504)

SELECTED FILMS AND VIDEOS

Redskin Rhumba (1948); Bud Shank–Clare Fischer Bossa Nova Show (1962); Stan Kenton and his Orchestra (1977); StudioLive with Freddie Hubbard (1981); Jazzvisions: the Many Faces of Bird (1988)

BIBLIOGRAPHY

FeatherE; *Feather–Gitler '70s*
L. Tomkins: "Bud Shank," *CI*, xviii (1979–80), no.2, p.14; no.3, p.22; no.8, p.20; no.11, p.23; xix/6 (1981), 23
C. Borg: "Bud Shank: populariserade flöten," *Orkester journalen*, xlviii/4 (1980), 8
W. F. Lee: *Stan Kenton: Artistry in Rhythm* (Los Angeles, 1980/*R*1994) [incl. discography; *R* without discography]
L. Tomkins: "Bud Shank: Enjoying a more Interesting Life," *CI*, xxii/4 (1984), 8
P. De Barros: "The Third Annual Bud Shank Workshop," *Saxophone Journal*, xi/3 (1986), 21
B. Korall: "That Old New Feeling: Bud Shank," *DB*, liii/9 (1986), 23 [incl. discography]
R. Cotterrell: "Bud Shank: a New Image," *JF* [intl edn], no.106 (1987), 23
L. Tomkins: "Back on the Road Again: Bud Shank," *CI*, xxiv/4 (1987), 8
——: "Bud Shank is Given Food for Thought," *CI*, xxiv/7 (1987), 20; contd as "Improvisation: Can it be Learned?," xxiv/8 (1987), 8
J. Blum: "Bud Shank," *JT* (1988), April, 7
L. Hildebrand: "Studio Saxophonist Bebops Back into Jazz," *San Francisco Chronicle Datebook* (14 Feb 1988)
J. Cuniff: "Riffs: Bud Shank," *DB*, lvii/12 (1990), 13
S. Woolley: "Bud Shank," *JJI*, xliv/5 (1991), 8
T. Gioia: *West Coast Jazz: Modern Jazz in California, 1945–1960* (New York, and Oxford, England, 1992), 209
G. Rouy: "Bud Shank: retour au jazz," *Jm*, no.411 (1992), 40
G. Endress: "Das neue Ich des Bud Shank," *JP*, xlii/3 (1993), 3
"Bud Shank Celebrates," *CJM*, xxxiii/4 (1996), 4
G. Jack: "Bud Shank," *JJI*, li/5 (1998), 6
T. Pérémarti: "Bud Shank, la vie quotidienne du jazzman à Hollywood," *Jazzman*, no.36 (1998), 30

WILLIAM F. LEE III/BK

Shannon, Terry [Terence] (*b* London, 5 Nov 1929). English pianist. A self-taught musician, he played piano from the age of seven. He performed and recorded with Victor Feldman and Wilton "Bogey" Gaynair (1956–9) and regularly toured and recorded with the Jazz Couriers led by Tubby Hayes and Ronnie Scott (April 1957 – April 1959). From August 1959 through the 1960s he continued to work with Hayes, as a member of both his big band and various small groups; his playing may be heard on *Blues Flues* (on the album *A Tribute to Tubbs*, 1963, Spot. SPJ902). When not with Hayes, Shannon recorded with Dizzy Reece (in London, 1956, and in Paris with Donald Byrd, 1958), Sonny Stitt (in performance at Scott's club, on the album *Sonny's Blues*, 1964, Ronnie Scott's Jazz House 603), Jimmy Deuchar, and Paul Gonsalves and Ray Nance (1965) and worked with the Jazzmakers, led by Allan Ganley and Ronnie Ross (spring 1959), Vic Lewis's orchestra (in the USA, spring 1960), his own trio, and the quintet led by Keith Christie and Deuchar (1965). In the late 1960s he joined Phil Seamen's trio, and he led a trio of his own until illness disrupted his career. Shannon resumed playing on an intermittent basis with the Pizza Express All Stars and other groups in the 1980s, and he performed in South Humberside from 1988 until returning to London in 1993. Thereafter he worked with lesser-known bands in the north of England. (*ChiltonB*; *FeatherE*)

SALLY-ANN WORSFOLD/BK

Shapiro, Artie [Arthur] (*b* Denver, 15 Jan 1916). Double bass player. He grew up in New York, played trumpet from the age of 13, and took up double bass when he was 18. After playing and recording with Wingy Manone (1934–6) he lived briefly in Washington, DC, then returned to New York, where he performed and recorded with Manone, Joe Marsala, and Tommy Dorsey (all 1937–8). From the mid-1930s he worked as a studio musician, recording with Frank Froeba and Sharkey Bonano (both 1936), Red McKenzie (1937), the Original Dixieland Jazz Band, Bud Freeman, and Chu Berry (all 1938), and Eddie Condon (1938–41). In addition he was a member of Paul Whiteman's band (late 1938–1940) and performed at Nick's in New York with Bobby Hackett (1939). Shapiro then worked briefly with Marsala (1940) and Whiteman (to spring 1941) before moving to Hollywood (1941); there he was once again active as a freelance musician, recording with Jack Teagarden (1943), Charlie LaVere (1944–5), Charlie Ventura and Joe Sullivan (both 1945), Artie Shaw (1946), and Benny Goodman (August–December 1947). From 1949 to 1959 he worked for MGM, and until 1962 he continued to record with such popular singers as Bing Crosby and Frank Sinatra. Although he is typically heard in a timekeeping role, in November 1939 Shapiro recorded one of the finest early examples of the double bass as a solo instrument in jazz on Condon's *Ballin' the Jack*.

SELECTED RECORDINGS

As sideman: C. Berry: Sittin' in/Forty-six West Fifty-two (1938, Com. 516); E. Condon: Sunday/California, Here I Come (1938, Com. 515); Ballin' the Jack (1939, Com. 531); B. Goodman: That's a Plenty/Henderson Stomp (1947, Cap. 15766); J. Stacy: *A Tribute to Benny Goodman* (1954–5, Atl. 1225)

BIBLIOGRAPHY

ChiltonW
"Metronome's Hall of Fame: Artie Shapiro," *Metronome*, lvii/7 (1941), 24

BK

Shapiro, Nat(haniel M.) (*b* New York, 27 Sept 1922; *d* New York, 15 Dec 1983). Writer and record producer. After attending Brooklyn College he worked as a national director of promotion for Mercury Records (1948–50), as a public-relations representative for BMI (1954–5), and as the director of international artists and repertory for Columbia Records (1956–66). He produced about 100 albums for Columbia, Philips, Vanguard, Epic, RCA, and other labels, including recordings by Miles Davis and Michel Legrand. With Nat Hentoff, he edited *Hear me Talkin' to ya* (1955) and *The Jazz Makers* (1957). In addition to his work in jazz he compiled (and until 1979 continued to revise) an important work entitled *Popular Music: an Annotated Index of American Popular Songs* (New York, 1964–7).

WRITINGS

(selective list)

ed. with N. Hentoff: *Hear me Talkin' to ya: the Story of Jazz by the Men who Made it* (New York and London, 1955/*R*1966)
ed. with N. Hentoff: *The Jazz Makers* (New York, 1957/*R*1979 as *The Jazz Makers: Essays on the Greats of Jazz*)

DANIEL ZAGER

Sharkey. *See* Bonano, sharkey; also the nickname of jean-pierre Morel.

Sharon, Ralph (*b* London, 17 Sept 1923). Pianist, arranger, and bandleader. In his youth he studied piano privately, and in the early 1940s he played with, among others, Carlo Krahmer (1942) and Victor Feldman (1944). After World War II he performed and recorded briefly with Ted Heath (1946) and recorded with Ronnie Scott in both the Esquire Five (1948) and the Melody Maker All Stars (1951–2). Thereafter he played and recorded in London as the leader of a sextet with Feldman among his sidemen. Sharon moved to the USA in May 1953 and became an American citizen in 1958. In New York he continued to work as a leader, recording with such distinguished swing and bop musicians as Teddy Charles, Charles Mingus, Kenny Clarke, Milt Hinton, Jo Jones, Lucky Thompson, and Oscar Pettiford. While serving as music director and pianist for Tony Bennett (1954–65, 1979 through 1990s) he wrote many arrangements for the singer, notably those for his sessions with Count Basie (1958); he also worked alongside Bennett in collaboration with Duke Ellington, Woody Herman, and Buddy Rich. In addition he recorded with Chris Connor (1955–9) and Johnny Hartman and Mel Tormé (both 1956) and worked as Rosemary Clooney's accompanist. Sharon made a number of other recordings, both with Bennett (to mid-1960s, from 1987) and as the leader of his own trio (into the early 1960s, from 1994).

SELECTED RECORDINGS

Easy Jazz (1955, London LL1488); *The Ralph Sharon Trio* (1956, Beth. 41); *Around the World in Jazz* (1957, Rama 1001); *Portrait of Harold* (1996, DRG 9147)

BIBLIOGRAPHY

ChiltonB; *FeatherE*
L. Tomkins: "Tony Bennett's Debt to British Jazz: Ralph Sharon," *CI*, xxv/5 (1988), 8; contd as "Ralph Sharon on Tony Bennett and the Art of Accompaniment," xxvi/2 (1989), 4
H. Reich: "The Right Sound," *Chicago Tribune* (20 July 1992)
R. Laber: "Of Jazz, Tony Bennett, and Hits," *Clavier*, xxxiv/6 (1995), 18
S. Woolley: "Ralph Sharon," *JJI*, xlix/12 (1996), 10

BK

Sharpe, Avery (George) (*b* Valdosta, GA, 23 Aug 1954). Bass player. His mother was a pianist and gave him piano lessons from the time he was eight. Before he was in his teens his family moved to Springfield, Massachusetts, where he played accordion. He took up electric bass guitar when he was 16 and began playing gospel music at church. While studying economics at the University of Massachusetts in Amherst (from 1972) he performed in funk bands and was inspired to buy a double bass after hearing Reggie Workman, who was a visiting teacher; he subsequently studied the instrument with Workman for about a year. He then worked as an insurance adjuster, undertook graduate work in music education at the University of Massachusetts, and played double bass in workshops led by Max Roach and Archie Shepp at the university's Andover campus. In autumn 1979 Sharpe toured Europe and recorded as a member of Shepp's big band; after the tour he left his job and joined Shepp's small group. While he was in Europe he met Art Blakey, and in 1980 he replaced Dennis Irwin in Blakey's Jazz Messengers; however, soon afterwards he transferred to McCoy Tyner's ensemble, replacing Charles Fambrough, who in turn joined Blakey. When Tyner's group disbanded (1982) Sharpe worked as a freelance (until 1984), during the course of which he appeared as a member of the Young Lions at the Kool Jazz Festival in New York (June 1982). From 1985 he worked again with Tyner in a trio and a big band, playing a six-string electric bass guitar as well as the conventional four-stringed instrument and double bass. He made his first recording as a leader in 1988, and in the mid-1990s he founded a music distribution company, Jade Enterprises, and a record company and label, JKNM, for which he recorded in 1993. Sharpe also recorded with John Blake (1985, 1997, the latter in a duo), the pianist Marc Puricelli (1991, 1995), Steve Grossman (1991), and Jeri Brown (1995).

SELECTED RECORDINGS

Duos with J. Blake: *Epic Ebony Journey* (1997, JKNM 89893)
As leader: *Unspoken Words* (1988, Sunnyside 1029)
As sideman with M. Tyner: on *Double Trios* (1986, Denon 33CY1128), Dreamer, Latino Suite, Lil' Darlin', Satin Doll; *Uptown/Downtown* (1988, Mlst. 9167); *Live at Sweet Basil*, i–ii (1989, PW [Jap.] 292E6033, KICJ1); *Remembering John* (1991, Enja 6080-2); *Infinity* (1995, Imp. 171)

BIBLIOGRAPHY

J. Howard: "Profile: Avery Sharpe," *DB*, xlviii/8 (1981), 52
J. Roberts: "Avery Sharpe: Bass Man for McCoy Tyner, Archie Shepp, Art Blakey, and other Jazz Luminaries," *GP*, xxi/5 (1987), 56
——: "Riffs: Avery Sharpe," *DB*, lvi/1 (1989), 14
L. Gourse: "Surviving as a Jazz Bassist," *Bass Player*, iv/2 (1993), 14
J. Roberts: "Bass Notes: Avery Sharpe: Takin' Care of Business," *Bass Player*, v/4 (1994), 8
M. Ervin: "Low End Theory: Avery Sharpe," *Jazziz*, xiii/7 (1996), 66

GK

Sharpe, C(larence (Hardy)) (*b* St. Louis, 5 May 1931; *d* New York, 28 Jan 1990). Alto saxophonist. Crouch (1987) gave his year of birth as 1936, and obituaries published his age as 53; however, Sharpe himself gave his year of birth as 1931 in his application for social security. His stepfather, Nathaniel Sharpe, played alto saxophone with Fletcher Henderson, and his natural father, Benjamin Hardy, was a big-band singer. He grew up in Germantown, Pennsylvania, and in his youth he played in the Philadelphia area with Cal Massey, McCoy Tyner, Lee Morgan, and Jimmy Garrison, among others. His nickname derived from his high school group, C Sharpe and the Flats. In 1956 (as Clarence Sharpe) he recorded with Lee Morgan on *Lee Morgan Indeed!* (BN 1538). In 1958 he moved to New York, where during the 1960s he worked with such musicians as Jimmy McGriff (*c*1961–2), Steve Ellington (1965–6), Kenny Dorham, Joe Henderson, and Archie Shepp. Nothing is known of his activities in the 1970s. He recorded in 1983 with the Jazz Disciples, led by the alto saxophonist Vern Fridie, and in 1985 with Freddie Redd (*Lonely City*, Upt. 27.30). In the mid- to late 1980s he led a group consisting of the pianist Frank Hewitt, the double bass player Hal Dotson, and Leroy Williams, and from around 1987 he led another group on Monday nights at the Zanzibar club, where he also worked with the trio led by the double bass player Ari Roland. Sharpe performed in Paris in 1989 with Jackie McLean, Phil Woods, Frank Morgan, and Vincent Herring in the concert Alto Summit: Tribute to Charlie Parker.

BIBLIOGRAPHY

S. Crouch: "C Sharpe: in the Shadows," *VV* (24 March 1987), 64
"En direct (Alto Summit)," *Jm*, no.384 (1989), 8
Obituaries: *New York Times* (30 Jan 1990); *DB*, lvii/4 (1990), 12; *Newsday* (2 Feb 1990)
O. Seabrook: "For sure, sa Sharpe," *Orkester journalen*, lviii/9 (1990), 37

GK

Sharpe, Jack (*b* London, 19 Aug 1930; *d* London, 4 Nov 1994). English saxophonist and bandleader. After taking up tenor saxophone in 1948 he worked with Vic Lewis, the brass player Teddy Foster, and various small groups in London. By 1953 he had left full-time music to drive a taxi. However, in 1954 he returned to work with Dizzy Reece, and from February 1955 to September 1956 he played tenor and baritone saxophone in Tubby Hayes's nine-piece band. Thereafter he performed semi-professionally, co-leading the Downbeaters with the saxophonist Mike Senn (from 1957), leading his own sextet (1958), and working with Hayes's big band; in addition he often served as an organizer and promoter for others. Having co-led a quintet with Alan Branscombe in 1985 Sharpe made a renewed impact on jazz in London the following year, when he formed a big band in tribute to Hayes. The group made three recordings, notably *Catalyst (a Tribute to Tubby Hayes)* (1987, Frog 716), which featured Al Cohn, and *Roarin'* (1989, Ronnie Scott's Jazz House 016).

BIBLIOGRAPHY

ChiltonB
Obituary, B. Davis, *JJI*, xlviii/1 (1995), 15

MARK GILBERT

Sharp Nine. Record company and label established in Westfield, New Jersey, in June 1995 by Mark Edelman. It made recordings from its inception and began to issue compact discs approximately one year later; as of the year 2000 its catalogue of 17 recordings featured such artists as Brian Lynch, David Hazeltine (including his small group, co-led with Joe Locke), Louis Hayes, Eddie Henderson, and the group One for All.

BIBLIOGRAPHY

D. Zych: "Label Watch: Sharp Nine: Exclusively Straight Ahead," *JT*, xxvii/2 (1997), 69
<http://www.sharpnine.com/> (2000)

GK

Sharps and Flats. Big band led from 1952 by NOBUO HARA.

Sharrock [née Chambers]**, Linda** [Lynda] (*b* Philadelphia, 2 April 1947). Singer. She sang in choirs at church and school, then around the age of 16 she became interested in folk music; later she changed to jazz. Having moved to New York she studied art at college, became familiar with avant-garde music, and began performing with Pharoah Sanders. In 1966 she studied music theory with Giuseppi Logan and in December of that year she married Sonny Sharrock; at this point she changed the spelling of her first name to Lynda. While touring with Herbie Mann (1969–70) and Sanders (1970–71) she continued to work with her husband (who was also a sideman in Mann's group), and the pair appeared together at a pop and jazz festival in Antibes (1971). In 1973 Sharrock performed in Istanbul, and the following year she recorded with Joe Bonner. After separating from her husband she settled in Vienna; they divorced in 1978 and she evidently reverted to the original spelling of her name, the form in which it appears in later sources. She worked with Franz Koglmann and with Eric Watson in a duo which remained active in the late 1990s, and formed what became a longstanding association with Wolfgang Puschnig: the two have performed together in various groups, notably the Pat Brothers (with Ernst Reijseger and the synthesizer player Wolfgang Mitterer, from 1984), the quartet or quintet Red Sun (with Uli Scherer, Jamaaladeen Tacuma, and, later, the guitarist Rick Iannacone, from 1986), the trio AM4 (A Monastic Quartet) (with Scherer, from 1988), the 3 Man Band (with Tacuma and the drummer Frank Samba, recording in 1991), and another trio with the pianist and guitarist Harry Pepl (1992); Red Sun has performed and recorded in collaboration with the South Korean percussion ensemble Samul Nori.

SELECTED RECORDINGS

As leader: *Linda Sharrock and the Three Man Band* (1991, Moers Music 02078-2); *Live in Vitoria-Gasteiz* (1995, Amadeo 537693-2)

As sideman with S. Sharrock: *Black Woman* (1969, Vortex 2014); *Monkey-Pockie-Boo* (1970, BYG 529337); *Paradise* (1975, Atco 36-121)

As sideman with others: J. Bonner: on *Angel Eyes* (1974, Muse 5114), Celebration; Pat Brothers: *The Pat Brothers* (1986, Moers Music 02052); Samul Nori: *Red Sun* (1989, Amadeo 841222-2); AM4: *... And She Answered* (1989, ECM 1394); W. Puschnig and the Amstettner Musikanten: *Alpine Aspects* (1991, Amadeo 511204-1); W. Puschnig: *Mixed Metaphors* (1994, Amadeo 527266-2); Red Sun and Samul Nori: *Then Comes the White Tiger* (1993, ECM 1499); W. Puschnig: *Roots & Fruits* (1996, Amadeo 537495-2)

BIBLIOGRAPHY

Feather–Gitler '70s

V. Wilmer: *As Serious as your Life: the Story of the New Jazz* (London, 1977, rev. [3]/1987)

L. Dahl: *Stormy Weather: the Music and Lives of a Century of Jazzwomen* (London, Melbourne, Australia, and New York, 1984), 181

R. Linke: "The Art of the Trio," *JP*, xxxviii/4 (1989), 32

C. Gauffre: "Linda du cri au texte," *Jm*, no.401 (1991), 36

P. Carles: "Linda au pluriel," *Jm*, no.444 (1995), 18

GK

Sharrock, Sonny [Warren Harding] (*b* Ossining, NY, 27 Aug 1940; *d* Ossining, 26 May 1994). Electric guitarist. He sang rock-and-roll with a doo-wop group, the Echoes (1954–8), and from 1959 played guitar, which he learned largely by teaching himself. As he suffered from asthma, he took up this instrument rather than his preferred one, the saxophone, and it was later often said that he endeavored to play guitar as if it were a saxophone; although this is perhaps an oversimplification, it does convey some sense of his creative approach. After attending the Berklee School of Music for one semester (from September 1961) he moved in 1965 to New York, where he played free jazz with Byard Lancaster, Pharoah Sanders, and Marzette Watts. "He developed a personal vocabulary of overdriven amplifiers, high-speed tremolos and percussive picking on muffled strings" (Pareles, 1994); passages of mandolin-like fast picking, which he termed a "buzz-saw trill," represented his effort to translate Sanders and Albert Ayler's screaming saxophone lines to the guitar. He also used a slide, applying a down-home acoustic blues guitar technique to the electric instrument. These diverse and, at the time, radical combinations of sounds later suggested comparisons with, and possibly emulations of, Jimi Hendrix, but Sharrock claimed that his style was in place by 1966, before Hendrix became famous.

Sharrock was a member of Herbie Mann's group at intervals from 1967 to 1974, and at the same time played as a sideman with Don Cherry, Wayne Shorter, and Milford Graves. From 1969 he also worked as a leader, often with his wife, Linda Sharrock (they separated in the mid-1970s and divorced in 1978), and initially formed a sextet with Ted Daniel, Dave Burrell, Sirone, and Graves. From 1975 he worked only occasionally as a sideman, but in the early 1980s he became more prominent, owing in part to the influence that his early work had exerted on avant-garde rock musicians in New York; in 1982 he recorded with the art-rock group Material, and he also toured Europe with this group. Later he performed with the group LAST EXIT (1986–94), which also involved Peter Brötzmann, Ronald Shannon Jackson, and Bill Laswell, and formed two groups, one a quartet that consisted in addition to Sharrock of an electric bass guitarist and two drummers, the other an ensemble that included Daniel and made use of synthesizers. Sharrock was among the first jazz guitarists to employ the slide and electronic distortion, and he ignored the standard jazz technique based on linear solos and chordal comping; he also used drones that were suggestive of Indian music.

SELECTED RECORDINGS

As unaccompanied soloist: *Guitar* (1986, Enemy 102)

As leader: *Black Woman* (1969, Vortex 2014); with L. Sharrock: *Paradise* (1975, Atco 36-121); *Live in New York* (1989, Enemy 108); *Highlife* (*c*1990, Enemy 119); *Ask the Ages* (*c*1991, Axiom 422-848957-2)

As sideman: P. Sanders: *Tauhid* (1966, Imp. 9138); M. Watts: *Marzette Watts* (1966, ESP 1044); H. Mann: *Memphis Underground* (1968, Atl. 1522); D. Cherry: *Eternal Rhythm* (1968, MPS 15204); W. Shorter: *Super Nova* (1969, BN 84332); Material: *Memory Serves* (1982, Elek. Mus. E1-60042); Last Exit: *Last Exit* (1986, Enemy 101); Bill Cosby: on *Where You Lay your Head* (*c*1989, Verve 314-841930-2), Why is it I can never find anything in the closet?

BIBLIOGRAPHY

GrayF

M. Walters: "A Guitarist with No Time for Chords and All that Jazz," *MM* (30 Nov 1968), 22

G. Endress: "So erregend wie Bläser: Gitarrist Sharrock," *JP*, xviii (1969), 10; Fr. trans. as "Sonny Sharrock," *Jh*, no.247 (1969), 28

J. Bisceglia and J.-L. Ginibre: "Sharrock: la dent dure et les dents longues," *Jm*, no.180 (1970), 34

M. Bourne: "Sonny Sharrock's Story," *DB*, xxxvii/12 (1970), 16

R. Williams: "Like No Other Guitarist Ever Born," *MM* (27 June 1970), 24

T. Trombert and P. Alessandrini: "La dent dur," *Jh*, no.276 (1971), 13

V. Wilmer: "The State of Sonny," *MM* (9 Oct 1971), 32

B. Vuijsje: *De nieuwe jazz* (Baarn, Netherlands, 1978), 134

S. Lake: "Sonny Sharrock," *JF* [intl edn], no.108 (1987), 30

T. Drozdowski: "Sonny Sharrock: Learning to Win Friends and Alienate People with the Father of the Free Guitar," *Musician*, no.119 (1988), 60

D. Hill: "Sonny Sharrock: Free Improvisation: an Innovator's View," *GP*, xxiii/2 (1989), 101

M. Dery: "Sonny Sharrock," *GP*, xxiv/2 (1990), 70

B. Ratliff: "Sonny Sharrock: Seize the Rainbow," *Coda*, no.234 (1990), 21

M. Sinker: "Sonny Sharrock – Melvin Gibbs: New York is Now," *Wire*, no.73 (1990), 22

D. Rubien: "Jazz Veteran Busy: Guitarist Strings Fans Along," *San Francisco Chronicle Datebook* (10 Nov 1991)

B. Milkowski: "Of Guts & Guitars: Vernon Reid & Sonny Sharrock," *DB*, lx/7 (1993), 24

Obituaries: J. Pareles, *New York Times* (31 May 1994); V. Wilmer: *The*

Guardian (4 June 1994); H. Kaiser: *San Francisco Bay Guardian* (22 June 1994); B. Milkowski, *DB*, lxi/8 (1994), 12

ROBERT J. IANNAPOLLO/BK

Shaughnessy, Ed(win Thomas) (*b* Jersey City, NJ, 29 Jan 1929). Drummer and composer. His mother played piano, and he started on that instrument at the age of nine, but changed to drums in 1943 after his father acquired a set as payment for a debt; he took lessons and soon afterwards began playing locally. He worked with bands led by the trumpeter Randy Brooks (1946) and Bobby Byrne (1946–7), then played briefly with the clarinetist Jerry Wald, Shorty Sherock, Jack Teagarden, Pete Brown, George Shearing, and others in clubs on 52nd Street in New York. From 1948 to 1950 he was a member of Charlie Ventura's band. After touring Europe with Benny Goodman's sextet and recording in Stockholm with Zoot Sims and in Paris with Roy Eldridge (1950), he played for a brief period with Lucky Millinder and with Tommy Dorsey, performed and recorded with Teddy Charles (from 1952), and became a staff drummer for CBS television. In 1953 he recorded with Chuck Wayne. As a studio musician from 1954 he recorded with Billie Holiday (1954), Mundell Lowe (1955–6), and Trigger Alpert (1956); he also appeared as a freelance with Charles Mingus and Duke Ellington (deputizing for Louie Bellson in the latter's orchestra for two months). In the late 1950s he left CBS and led the Jazz Four for two years with Charles. He recorded with Chris Connor (1957–9, 1963, this last in performance at the Village Gate, New York), Bobby Jaspar (1958, 1960), Johnny Richards (1959), Joe Newman (1961), Oliver Nelson (1961–2), Etta Jones, Sam "the Man" Taylor, Jimmy Smith, Gene Ammons, Clark Terry, Jimmy Forrest, and Teagarden (all 1962), Gary McFarland, and Johnny Hodges and Wild Bill Davis (both 1963), Shirley Scott (1966) and Count Basie (1966–7). In 1964 he joined the orchestra of the "Tonight Show," with which he moved to Los Angeles in 1972. In Los Angeles he formed a big band, Energy Force (1974), and led drumming workshops. He continued on television with Doc Severinsen's "Tonight Show" band until it was replaced by Branford Marsalis's group in 1992. Thereafter he continued to work with Severinsen's group, while also leading his own big band and quintet.

Shaughnessy's specialty is strong, driving big-band drumming. His compositions, which are in a big-band style, include *Blues detambour* and *Nigerian Walk*. Some of his earlier pieces have been recorded by Charles and Clare Fischer; his later works have been played by his own ensemble. He has contributed to *Percussive Notes*, *Crescendo International*, and *Modern Drummer*, published instructional books, notably *New Time Signatures in Jazz Drumming* (Melville, NY, n.d.) and *Stage Band Drumming* (n.d.), and made an instructional video, *Ed Shaughnessy's Drum Clinic* (*c*1983).

SELECTED RECORDINGS

As leader: *Jazz in the Pocket* (1990, Chase Music 8028)

As sideman: T. Charles: *A Word from Bird* (1956, Atl. 1274); C. Basie: *Broadway Basie's Way* (1966, Command 905); on O. Nelson: *Happenings* (1966, Imp. 9132), Jazztime USA.

BIBLIOGRAPHY

ConnorBG; *SheridanCB*

B. Coss: "Vital Statistics: Steady Eddie: and More," *Metronome*, lxx/5 (1954), 20

D. C. Hunt: "The Musician's Musician: Cases of Seven Underrated Jazzmen," *Jazz*, vi/7 (1967), 19

J. Szantor: "Eddie Shaughnessy: 'Play Like You Mean it'," *DB*, xl/7 (1973), 16

R. Cook: "Ed Shaughnessy: Swinger on Staff," *MD*, ii/3 (1978), 6

K. Ogle: "Drum Set Forum: Inside Ed Shaughnessy," *Percussive Notes*, xix/1 (1980), 38

L. Tomkins: "Ed Shaughnessy Talks Drums," *CI*, xviii/6 (1980), 6

T. Smith: "Driver's Seat: Ed Shaughnessy on the Road," *MD*, viii/3 (1984), 60

R. Flans: "Ed Shaughnessy," *MD*, x/4 (1986), 17

D. Black: "Interview: Ed Shaughnessy: an Energy Force Reflects on his Life and Music," *Jazz Educators Journal*, xix/3 (1987), 18

R. Flans: "Ed Shaughnessy: Life after the Tonight Show," *MD*, xvi/9 (1992), 22

JEFF POTTER/BK

Shavers, Charlie [Charles James] (*b* New York, 3 Aug 1917; *d* New York, 8 July 1971). Trumpeter and arranger. Encouraged by his father, an amateur banjoist and trumpeter, he took up piano, banjo, guitar, double bass, and, finally, trumpet. A fellow trumpeter, Carl Warwick, lived in their home, and he and Shavers became professional musicians together, working with lesser-known bands in New York, Washington, DC, and Philadelphia, where they were joined by Dizzy Gillespie in the trumpet section of Frankie Fairfax's band; Gillespie and Shavers practiced together, copying Roy Eldridge's recorded solos. Shavers then continued with his friend Warwick in the big bands of Tiny Bradshaw (1936) and Lucky Millinder (1937) before making a sensational impact on the New York jazz scene at the age of 19 when he joined John Kirby's sextet in November 1937 (for illustration *see* Kirby, John). He starred with the sextet in its residency at the Onyx and later in national touring and network radio broadcasts. During his time with the group he was also its principal arranger and wrote several deft compositions, including *Undecided*.

As Kirby's sextet declined in popularity Shavers worked in Raymond Scott's CBS radio orchestra in 1943 and with Benny Goodman's big band in 1944. He finally left Kirby in 1944 and in February of the following year began working in Tommy Dorsey's big band, where he was featured in spectacular arrangements that displayed his bravura approach and his talents as a jazz musician; he also sang. For the next 11 years he performed intermittently with Dorsey and in a wide variety of studio bands, but he spent the latter part of his life playing mainly in small groups, where he continued to display an astonishing versatility. In 1950 he was the leader, with Louie Bellson and Terry Gibbs, of a sextet. He toured to Europe (1952) and Japan (1953) with Jazz at the Philharmonic and joined Goodman's group (1954). From 1956, when Dorsey died, into the 1960s he frequently led his own quartet, and he was regularly at the Metropole, New York, with Coleman Hawkins, Buster Bailey, and others. He had joined the memorial Tommy Dorsey Orchestra by 1964, and toured internationally from 1965 to 1966 under the leadership of the singer Frank Sinatra, Jr. He visited Europe as a soloist (1969, 1970) and gave his final performances as a soloist with the JPJ Quartet (Budd Johnson, Dill Jones, Bill Pemberton, and Oliver Jackson) at the Half Note in New York in May 1971.

Shavers was originally influenced by Roy Eldridge, but he soon developed a bold individualism that radiated confidence and good humor. He was a well-schooled musician who displayed remarkable technical fluency, and he was able to harness this skill in agile improvisations that were particularly noteworthy for their wide dynamic range. He was one of the first jazz trumpeters to improvise long lines in the altissimo register of the instrument with complete control; however, these high-note excursions did not diminish his flexibility or the warmth of his low notes.

See also TRUMPET, §4.

SELECTED RECORDINGS

As leader: Stardust (1944, Key. 1305)

As sideman: J. Dodds: Melancholy (1938, Decca 1676); J. Kirby: Rehearsin' for a Nervous Breadown (1938, Decca 2367); Undecided (1938, Decca 2216); B. Holiday: Them There Eyes (1939, Voc. 5021); J. Kirby: Royal Garden Blues (1939, Voc. 5187); Opus 5 (1939, Voc. 5048); S. Bechet: I'm Coming, Virginia (1941, Vic. 27904); Texas Moaner (1941, Vic. 27600); Mood Indigo (1941), first issued on *The Blue Bechet* (1932, 1940–41, RCA LPV535); G. Auld, C. Hawkins, and B. Webster: Salt Peanuts (1944, Apollo 755); L. Hampton: *Just Jazz* (1947, Decca 7013), incl. Hampton: Stardust, and G. Norman [Just Jazz All Stars]: The Man I Love; N. Granz: *Norman Granz' Jam Session no.2* (1952, Clef 602), incl. Funky Blues, What is this thing called love?; S. Allen: *Jazz for Tonight* (1955, Coral 57018), incl. Limehouse Blues; All Stars: *Session at Riverside* (1956, Cap. T761), incl. Broadway; H. Singer: *Blue Stompin'* (1959, Prst. 7153), incl. Fancy Pants

SELECTED FILMS AND VIDEOS

Tommy Dorsey and his Orchestra (1951); The Steve Allen Show, no.19 (1956); Sam Donahue Fronting the Tommy Dorsey Memorial Band (1965); Jazz Scene at Ronnie Scott's (*c*1969)

BIBLIOGRAPHY

ChiltonW; *McCarthyB*; *SchullerS*
T. Hassell: "Charlie Shavers," *JM*, x/1 (1964), 6
S. Voce: "What'd I Say? Jug and Trumpet," *JJ*, xvii/3 (1964), 12
H. Panassié: "Charlie Shavers," *BHcF*, no.177 (1968), 3
L. Tomkins: "Playing Soft for the Fun of it," *CI*, viii/11 (1970), 12
S. Traill: "Charlie Shavers," *JJ*, xxiii/5 (1970), 8
Obituaries: *New York Times* (9 July 1971); *JJ*, xxiv/8 (1971), 4
A. Shaw: *The Street that Never Slept: New York's Fabled 52nd Street* (New York, 1971/*R*1977 as *52nd Street: the Street of Jazz*)
O. Bryce: "Charlie Shavers: an Appreciation," *JJI*, xxxii/11 (1979), 16
D. Gillespie and A. Fraser: *To be, or not ... to Bop: Memoirs* (Garden City, NY, 1979, London, 1980, as *Dizzy: the Autobiography of Dizzy Gillespie*)
R. Horricks: "The Man they Called Firecracker: Charlie Shavers," *CI*, xxi/6 (1983), 23
J. Chilton: *Sidney Bechet: the Wizard of Jazz* (London and New York, 1987/*R*1996), 145
S. Voce: "Buddy Childers," pt i, *JJI*, l/10 (1997), 6

JOHN CHILTON/BK

Shaw, Arnold (*b* New York, 28 June 1909; *d* Las Vegas, 26 Sept 1989). Writer. He studied English literature at the City College of New York (BS 1929) and Columbia University (MA 1931) and American literature at New York University. From 1950 to 1966 he held administrative positions with a number of popular music publishers, and in 1981 he joined the faculty of the University of Nevada, Las Vegas. In 1985 he founded the Popular Music Research Center. He was a prolific author in the areas of popular music and jazz, and in addition to his more than 150 articles, reviews, and liner notes wrote several books, among them a dictionary of American rock and pop music. He won ASCAP–Deems Taylor awards in 1968 and 1979.

WRITINGS

(selective list)

Sinatra: Twentieth-century Romantic (New York, 1965)

The Street that Never Slept: New York's Fabled 52nd Street (New York, 1971/*R*1977 as *52nd Street: the Street of Jazz*)

Honkers and Shouters: the Golden Years of Rhythm and Blues (New York, 1978)

The Jazz Age: Popular Music in the 1920s (New York, and Oxford, England, 1987)

BIBLIOGRAPHY

Obituary, A. L. Yarrow, *New York Times* (7 Oct 1989)

PAULA MORGAN

Shaw, Artie [Arshawsky, Arthur Jacob] (*b* New York, 23 May 1910). Clarinetist, bandleader, composer, and arranger. He grew up in New Haven, Connecticut, where he began playing ukulele at the age of ten and saxophone two years later. In summer 1925 he joined Johnny Cavallaro's dance band as an alto saxophonist, at which time he changed his name to Shaw. While touring with Cavallaro the following year he took up clarinet, which later became his principal instrument. From 1927 to 1929 he worked in Cleveland and established a lasting reputation as music director and arranger for an orchestra led by the violinist Austin Wylie. He then toured as a tenor saxophonist with Irving Aaronson's band, and while in Chicago in 1929 played in jam sessions with several local musicians. At the same time he discovered the music of Debussy and Stravinsky; both influences were important in his musical development.

Artie Shaw's Gramercy Five at the Strand Theatre, New York, 1945: (left to right) Dodo Marmarosa (piano), Roy Eldridge (trumpet), Shaw (clarinet), Barney Kessel (guitar), and Morris Rayman (double bass)

Later that year Shaw traveled with Aaronson to New York, where he played in Harlem jam sessions and came under the influence and tutelage of Willie "the Lion" Smith. From 1931 to 1935 he worked as a freelance studio musician and in 1936 he formed his first group, for a concert at the Imperial Theater. Shaw's unorthodox band, consisting of a string quartet, three rhythm instruments, and clarinet, created a sensation by performing his chamber composition *Interlude in B♭*. Having added two trumpets, trombone, saxophone, and a singer, he signed a recording contract with Brunswick and led a band at New York's Lexington Hotel. However, the public remained indifferent to the group's unusual style and instrumentation, and Shaw was forced to disband in March 1937.

One month later Shaw formed a conventional swing band with a new library of music by Jerry Gray, the trombonist Harry Rogers, and himself, later augmented by pieces by the best popular-song composers of the day. With this group he recorded his first big hit – Cole Porter's *Begin the Beguine* (1938). This marked his breakthrough to public fame and established him as a rival to Benny Goodman. Constitutionally and emotionally unequal to his role as a matinée idol, however, Shaw withdrew from public view in November 1939, a move which served only to provoke the publicity he sought to avoid; Georgie Auld, Shaw's tenor saxophone soloist since 1938, took over the group, but it disbanded a few months later. Through these years Shaw's band had been driven by a succession of outstanding drummers: George Wettling (1936–7), Cliff Leeman (1937–8), Wettling again (for recordings late in 1938), and Buddy Rich (1939). His singers included Leo Watson (1937–8) and Billie Holiday (March–November 1938), and Bernie Privin served as his featured trumpet soloist (1938–9).

In early 1940 Shaw worked in Hollywood on the film *Second Chorus* and recorded his next big hit, *Frenesi*, using a studio orchestra with a large string section. The success of this recording forced him on tour again with a big band augmented by nine strings; among his sidemen were Billy Butterfield, Jack Jenney, Jerry Jerome, Johnny Guarnieri, and Nick Fatool. From within this group Shaw organized the GRAMERCY FIVE, including Guarnieri (harpsichord) and Butterfield, and recorded one of his best-known compositions, *Summit Ridge Drive* (1940). Despite high critical acclaim, Shaw again dissolved his band a few months later and settled in New York to record with studio groups and to study orchestration. His last prewar band, organized in September 1941, involved Hot Lips Page, Max Kaminsky, Auld, and Guarnieri.

After enlisting in the US Navy in January 1942 Shaw was asked to form a band, which in 1943 he led throughout the Pacific war zone. Following his discharge and convalescence he organized a new group in 1944, which was by all accounts his best jazz-oriented band, including Roy Eldridge, Herbie Steward, Dodo Marmarosa, and Barney Kessel; one of its recordings, *Little Jazz* (1945), featuring Eldridge, became a classic. Shaw also continued to perform and record with a small group, drawn from the members of the big band, under the name Gramercy Five (see illustration). During the next decade he organized two more big bands, appeared at Carnegie Hall, and issued recordings on several labels. He assembled his last Gramercy Five in October 1953, and after recording with the group in February and March 1954 he went into retirement. In 1983, however, he was persuaded to reorganize his band, which he continued to conduct occasionally; it mainly performed into the 1990s under the leadership of Dick Johnson, who also plays clarinet.

Shaw was a leading musician of the swing period, and a public figure whose handsome features and eight marriages made him a darling of gossip columnists. His clarinet playing has often been compared with that of his rival Benny Goodman; though less hot than Goodman, he demonstrated superb technical facility in his recordings of fast and lively numbers and a genuine sense of jazz phrasing in ballads. The full range of his gifts is displayed in his recording *Concerto for Clarinet* (1940). Like Goodman, Shaw was an energetic spokesman for racial equality in jazz, hiring and recording such African-American musicians as Holiday, Page, and Eldridge. The Artie Shaw Collection, including music arrangements, photographs, and papers, is held in the Department of Special Collections in the main library of the University of Arizona, Tucson (*see* LIBRARIES AND ARCHIVES, §2). Shaw is the author, with A. Brilhart, of *Clarinet Method: a School of Modern Clarinet Technic* (New York, 1941/*R c*1984). A book of lead sheets to pieces composed by or associated with Shaw, individual arrangements for his big band, and transcriptions from the Gramercy Five's classic performances are published by Musicprint.

Oral history material in *DSI* (JOHP).

SELECTED RECORDINGS

As leader: Begin the Beguine (1938, Bb 7746); Any Old Time (1938, Bb 7759); Nightmare (1938, Bb 7875); *In the Blue Room/In the Cafe Rouge* (1938–9, RCA LPT6000), incl. Carioca; Deep Purple (1939, Bb 10178); Traffic Jam (1939, Bb 10385); Frenesi (1940, Vic. 26542); Summit Ridge Drive (1940, Vic. 26763); Star Dust (1940, Vic. 27230); The Blues (1940, Vic. 27411); Concerto for Clarinet (1940, Vic. 36383); Moon Glow (1941, Vic. 27405); Blues in the Night (1941, Vic. 27609); St. James Infirmary (1941, Vic. 27895); Little Jazz (1945, Vic. 20-1668)

As sideman with B. Holiday: Did I Remember?/No Regrets (1936, Voc. 3276)

SELECTED FILMS AND VIDEOS

Artie Shaw and his Orchestra (1939); Artie Shaw and his Orchestra in Symphony of Swing (1939); Artie Shaw's Class in Swing (1939); Dancing Co-ed [Every Other Inch a Lady] (1939); Second Chorus (1940); Time is All You've Got (1985)

BIBLIOGRAPHY

McCarthyB; *SchullerS*

A. Shaw: "I Finally Know what I Want to Do," *DB*, xviii/13 (1951), 1

——: *The Trouble with Cinderella: an Outline of Identity* (New York, 1952/*R*1992) [autobiography]

C. Delaunay: "Artie Shaw," *Jh*, no.118 (1957), 21

R. L. Taylor: "Middle Aged Man without a Horn," *New Yorker*, xxxviii (19 May 1962), 47

W. Smith and G. Hoefer: *Music on my Mind: the Memoirs of an American Pianist* (Garden City, NY, 1964/*R*1975)

J. Burns: "Artie Shaw," *JM*, xiii/9 (1967), 2

F. Jacobs: "Non-stop Flight: Re-appraisal of the Music of Artie Shaw," *JJ*, xx/3 (1967), 8

G. T. Simon: *The Big Bands* (New York and London, 1967, rev. 4/1981)

O. Peterson: "Artie Shaw," *JJ*, xxii (1969), no.9, p.15; no.10, p.14

"Recreating my Sound," *CI*, vii/12 (1969), 30

J. McDonough: "Artie Shaw: Nonstop Flight from 1938," *DB*, xxxvii/2 (1970), 12

G. T. Simon: *Simon Says: the Sights and Sounds of the Swing Era, 1935–1955* (New Rochelle, NY, 1971)

V. Simosko: "Artie Shaw and his Gramercy Fives," *JJS*, i/1 (1973), 34

E. L. Blandford: *Artie Shaw* (Hastings, England, 1974) [bio-discography]

B. Korst and C. Garrod: *Artie Shaw and his Orchestra* (Spotswood, NJ, and Zephyrhills, FL, 1974, rev. 2/1986) [discography]

J. McDonough: "Clarinet King Artie Shaw is Back with a New Instrument: his Band," *Chicago Tribune* (22 April 1984), 8

C. Deffaa: "Artie Shaw is Back with the Big Band at 75," *MR*, xiii/2 (1985), 1

J. McDonough: "Artie Shaw's Big Band Obsession," *DB*, liii/2 (1986), 26

R. Soar: "Artie Shaw: Update," *JJI*, xl/11 (1987), 6

G. Lees: *Meet Me at Jim and Andy's: Jazz Musicians and their World* (New York, and Oxford, England, 1988), 58

C. Deffaa: *Swing Legacy* (Metuchen, NJ, and London, 1989), 17

D. Ramsey: "On Art and Popularity: a Few Words With Artie Shaw," *JT*, xxii/4 (1992), 29
P. Vacher: "Alias Albie Snow," *Jazz CD*, i/1 (n.d. [1992]), 27
B. Blumenthal: "First Person Memories of Swing," *DB*, lxi/7 (1994), 18
J. McLeod: "Artie Shaw: Victim of Success," *JJI*, xlvii (1994), no.4, p.12; no.5, p.16
J. McDonough: "Hall of Fame: Artie Shaw," *DB*, lxiii/8 (1996), 24
W. Suppan: "Begin the Beguine: mit Artie Shaw begann es," *Jf*, xxviii (1996), 52
E. L. Blandford: "Artie Shaw and his US Navy 'Rangers' Band," *JJI*, li/3 (1998), 6
L. C. do Nascimento Silva: "Artie Shaw on Musicraft," *IAJRC Journal*, xxxi/1 (1998), 17
M. P. Zirpolo: "Artie Shaw and his Symphonic Swing – 1941," *IAJRC Journal*, xxxi (1998), no.2, p.21; no.3, p.17
"Artie Shaw's Address to the IAJRC Convention," *IAJRC Journal*, xxxii/1 (1999), 9

RICHARD WANG

Shaw, Arvell (J.) (*b* St. Louis, 15 Sept 1923). Double bass player. He was taught trombone and tuba at high school and learned double bass while playing with Fate Marable on Mississippi riverboats in 1942. After serving in navy bands he toured with Louis Armstrong's big band; his association with Armstrong's All Stars (1945–53) was interrupted in 1951, when he studied harmony and composition in Geneva. Shaw played with Armstrong intermittently until 1957, regularly from 1963 to 1965, and again intermittently until Armstrong's death. In 1958 he appeared on television and toured Europe with Benny Goodman and performed and recorded with Sidney Bechet, Teddy Buckner, Coleman Hawkins, and Sammy Price. He played in Teddy Wilson's trio from the late 1950s to the early 1960s, recording with the group in 1959 and touring Australia in 1960. From 1967 to 1969 he toured as a member of Wild Bill Davison's Jazz Giants, which included Benny Morton, Herb Hall, Claude Hopkins, and Buzzy Drootin; the rhythm section of this sextet recorded in Canada in 1969 under Hall's leadership. Between 1972 and 1974 Shaw worked with Dorothy Donegan and with Wilson again. In 1974 he performed and made recordings in France with Barney Bigard, Earl Hines, and Hopkins, and in an all-star sextet alongside Hopkins, Vic Dickenson, and Buddy Tate, and the following year he recorded with Donegan. From 1977 into the 1980s Shaw worked in pit bands on Broadway (notably for the shows *Bubbling Brown Sugar* and *Ain't Misbehavin'*) and as a freelance in the New York area; in 1985 he spent a brief period with one of Benny Goodman's last big bands. He also recorded with Lionel Hampton in 1982 and toured in "The Wonderful World of Louis Armstrong" under Keith Smith during the early 1980s. He performed at the Berne Festival in 1993, and in 1994 took part in concerts for the Louis Armstrong Archives.

SELECTED RECORDINGS

As sideman: L. Armstrong: *Louis Armstrong Plays W. C. Handy* (1954, Col. CL6334–5); A. Persiany: Concerto du blues/If it weren't for you (1956, Col. ESDF1140) [EP]; Jazz Giants: *Jazz Giants* (1968, Sack. 3002), incl. Yesterdays; D. Donegan: *The Many Faces of Dorothy Donegan* (1975, Mahogany 558101)

SELECTED FILMS AND VIDEOS

Louis Amstrong–Jack Teagarden Sextet (1948); Eddie Condon Floor Show (3 Sept 1949); Louis Armstrong and his All Stars in France (1950); Botta e risposta (1951); The Glenn Miller Story (1953); Satchmo the Great [Saga of Satchmo] (1956); Swing into Spring (1958)

BIBLIOGRAPHY

ConnorBG; *FeatherE*; *Feather '60s*; *Feather–Gitler '70s*
E. Cook: "The Wonderful World of Louis Armstrong," *JJI*, xxxiv/9 (1981), 9
P. Vacher: "Arvell Shaw," *JJI*, xxxvi/10 (1983), 12
W. W. Vaché: *Crazy Fingers: Claude Hopkins' Life in Jazz* (Washington, DC, and London, 1992)
C. Battestini and J.-P. Battestini: "Arvell Shaw," *BHcF*, no.449 (1996), 2

JOHNNY SIMMEN/BK

Shaw, Charles "Bobo" [Charles Wesley, Jr.] (*b* Pope, MS, 5 Sept 1947). Drummer and leader. He studied drums with, among others, Ben Thigpen and briefly played trombone and double bass. In the late 1960s in St. Louis he was one of the founders of the Black Artists Group; with members of that organization he went to Europe and played free jazz for a year in Paris with Anthony Braxton, Steve Lacy, Frank Wright, Alan Silva, and Michel Portal. In 1971 he recorded in St. Louis with Oliver Lake, and during the 1970s he made several albums, notably *Streets of St. Louis* (1974, Moers Music 02020), as the leader of the Human Arts Ensemble, with Lake, Lester Bowie, Joseph Bowie, and Julius Hemphill among his sidemen. In the same period he recorded with Lester Bowie (1974, 1975, 1977), Frank Lowe and Lake (both 1975), and Hamiet Bluiett (1976). After touring and recording in Europe with the Human Arts Ensemble (1977–8) Shaw returned to the USA and later recorded with Billy Bang (1984).

BIBLIOGRAPHY

P. Carles and J.-L. Comolli: *Free Jazz, Black Power* (Paris, 1971, 2/1979)
V. Wilmer: *As Serious as your Life: the Story of the New Jazz* (London, 1977, rev. [3]1987)
B. Amiard: "West B'way Blues," *Jm*, no.261 (1978), 8
D. Constant: "Human Arts Ensemble," *Jm*, no.269 (1978), 12
J. Rensen and R. van den Heijden: "Bobo Shaw and the Human Arts Ensemble/Association," *Jazz Press*, no.52 (1978), 10
A. Dutilh: "Human Arts Ensemble, à trois," *Jh*, nos.356–7 (1978–9), 54

Shaw, Clarence (Eugene) [Gene] (*b* Detroit, 16 June 1926; *d* Los Angeles, 17 Aug 1973). Trumpeter. He played piano from the age of four and trombone from the age of six, and later took classical piano lessons for two years. While convalescing from an injury during army service he heard a recording of Dizzy Gillespie playing *Hot House* and decided to take up trumpet (*c*1946). Having returned to Detroit he studied with Barry Harris and at the Detroit Institute of Music, and worked locally, with among others, Lester Young, Wardell Gray, and Lucky Thompson. In October 1956 he moved to New York, where around July 1957 he joined Charles Mingus's Jazz Workshop. Following an argument with the volatile Mingus around November of that year Shaw destroyed his trumpet, quit playing music, and moved to Chicago; ironically, he gave a party for Mingus five years later to celebrate the album *Tijuana Moods*, on which he had recorded in 1957 but which was released only in 1962. In summer of the latter year he again took up trumpet and formed his own group; thereafter he worked as Gene Shaw. After serving as music director at the Old East Inn (*c* late 1963 – April or May 1964) he again retired from music, but resumed playing in 1968. Details of his death are taken from the California death index.

SELECTED RECORDINGS

As leader: *Breakthrough* (1962, Argo 707); *Debut in Blue* (1963, Argo 726); *Carnival Sketches* (1964, Argo 743)
As sideman with C. Mingus: *Tijuana Moods* (1957, RCA LSP2533); *East Coasting* (1957, Beth. 6019); *A Modern Jazz Symposium of Music and Poetry* (1957, Beth. 6026), incl. Duke's Choice

BIBLIOGRAPHY

Feather '60s
J. Cooke: "Clarence Shaw: a Critical Study," *JM*, vii/2 (1961), 13
——: "Back on the Scene," *JM*, x/7 (1964), 11
D. DeMichael: "Shavina Philosophy," *DB*, xxxi/3 (1964), 16
J. B. Litweiler: "Caught in the Act: Gene Shaw," *DB*, xxxv/21 (1968), 32

P. Moon: "Clarence Gene Shaw: Sometime Jazz Man," *Pieces of Jazz*, no.7 (1969), 35 [incl. discography]
H. Pekar: "Gene Shaw," *Coda*, x/8 (1972), 12
B. Weir: *Clarence Gene Shaw Discography* (Cardiff, 1986, rev. 2/1986)
P. Carles, A. Clergeat, and J.-L. Comolli: *Dictionnaire du jazz* (Paris, 1988, rev. and enlarged 2/1994)
B. Rusch: "Joel Futterman: Interview," *Cadence*, xviii/3 (1992), 18

GK

Shaw, Hank [Henry; Shalofsky, Henry] (*b* London, 23 June 1926). English trumpeter. A self-taught musician, he first performed professionally with the trumpeter Teddy Foster (1943–4) and the bandleader Oscar Rabin (1945). After playing informally with Maynard Ferguson and Oscar Peterson in Canada (1947) he became a founding member of Club Eleven, London (December 1948), and worked with Vic Lewis (early 1949). He then toured Europe with Cab Kaye (December 1950 – May 1951). Shaw played in dance bands led by Roy Fox (January–March 1952) and Harry Roy (March 1952). He joined Freddy Randall's big band in Glasgow (June 1953) before working with Jack Parnell (June 1953 – July 1954), with whom he made recordings, Ronnie Scott (September 1954–1956), Tony Crombie, Don Rendell (spring 1957), and Joe Harriott (spring 1958–1960). In the 1960s he was busy as a freelance and as the leader of his own quartet. He also worked with Tony Kinsey briefly (November 1961) and recorded with Harry South (1966), Kenny Wheeler (1968), and Stan Tracey and Jon Hendricks (both 1969). Shaw was a member of Bill Le Sage's Bebop Preservation Society (1971–83), though during the same period he recorded with John Dankworth (1972–4), Kinsey (1974, 1976), and others. Examples of his playing may be heard on Le Sage's *Bebop Preservation Society* (1971, Dawn 3027) and on Red Rodney's *Red Rodney with the Bebop Preservation Society* (1975, Spot. 7). From the 1970s into the 1990s Shaw worked in John Burch's octet, and he also continued to lead his own quartet.

BIBLIOGRAPHY

ChiltonB; *FeatherE*
R. Cotterrell, ed.: *Jazz Now: the Jazz Centre Society Guide* (London, 1976)

NEVIL SKRIMSHIRE/BK

Shaw, Woody (Herman, Jr.) (*b* Laurinburg, NC, 24 Dec 1944; *d* New York, 9 May 1989). Trumpeter and leader. He grew up in Newark, New Jersey, and, having often heard his father's gospel group, the Diamond Jubilee Singers, rehearse at his home, he began to play bugle and then, at the age of 11, trumpet. When he was 14 he was placed in a YMCA big band, of which Wayne Shorter was also a member. In 1963, after many local professional jobs, he worked for Willie Bobo (with Chick Corea and Joe Farrell) and also performed and recorded as a sideman with Eric Dolphy. The following year Dolphy invited Shaw to join him in Paris; Dolphy died shortly before Shaw's departure, but he decided to make the trip nonetheless, and found steady work in Paris with Nathan Davis and such veteran expatriate American musicians as Bud Powell, Kenny Clarke, Johnny Griffin, and Art Taylor. He performed in Paris, Berlin, and London with a group that included Larry Young (recording in Germany under Davis's name), then returned to the USA to play in Horace Silver's quintet (June 1965–1966). He recorded with Young (late in 1965), Corea (1966), Jackie McLean (1967), McCoy Tyner (1968), and Andrew Hill (1969). In 1968–9 he worked intermittently with Max Roach, with whom he appeared at a festival in Iran, and in 1968–70 occasionally with Tyner. Roach fired him when he became addicted to heroin, and he worked temporarily as a studio musician and in pit orchestras for Broadway musicals. Thereafter he formed a quintet with Joe Henderson (1970) and held an important engagement with Art Blakey's Jazz Messengers (1971–2) before settling in San Francisco, where he led a group with Bobby Hutcherson; they also performed at the Montreux International Festival, Switzerland (July 1973).

Shaw was in New York in December 1974 to begin his affiliation with the Muse (ii) label and again from July 1975 as a member of the Louis Hayes-Junior Cook Quintet, which after Cook's departure became the Woody Shaw-Louis Hayes Quintet. Cook was soon replaced by Rene McLean, and then by Dexter Gordon, who adopted the band for his acclaimed homecoming performances in 1976. Shaw also became active at this time as a jazz educator, and toured holding workshops in schools and colleges into the mid-1980s. By 1977 he was working regularly as the sole leader of small groups whose style was oriented towards hard bop but also incorporated elements of modal jazz and some of the harmonic freedom associated with free jazz. Having just made his firmest statement in the free-jazz style, on portions of the album *The Iron Men* with an ad hoc group including Anthony Braxton (1977), he was contracted soon afterwards to Columbia records. Among his regular sidemen during the late 1970s were Carter Jefferson, Onaje Allen Gumbs, Stafford James, and Victor Lewis; at this time he occasionally played cornet rather than trumpet. From 1980 to 1983 his quintet included Steve Turre, Larry Willis or Mulgrew Miller, James, and Tony Reedus.

An accomplished soloist with a brilliant command of his instrument, Shaw improvised rapid, precise, subtle melodies in the tradition of Clifford Brown while maintaining a round, sweet tone, but by the early 1980s it had become clear that he would never become the stylistic innovator that critics and producers hoped for. Evidently in reaction to these pressures, his problem with narcotics intensified, and at some point he contracted AIDS from an infected needle; in addition, he had suffered since childhood from retinitis pigmentosa, a hereditary illness causing night blindness, and now his sight deteriorated significantly. Nonetheless in the mid-1980s he worked with Slide Hampton, Nathan Davis, Jimmy Woode, and others in the Paris Reunion Band, recording in Stockholm in 1985, and, after touring and recording as a leader with a group of constantly changing personnel, in 1986 he formed a short-lived new quintet with Willis, David Williams, and Teri Lynne Carrington; in the face of all his problems he somehow managed to continue to make fine new albums (1986–7). Ultimately he lost his teeth, which brought his career to an end. In 1989 he fell into the path of a subway train in Brooklyn and lost his left arm; he died of complications from this accident and AIDS.

Oral history material in *GBLnsa*.

SELECTED RECORDINGS

As leader: *Blackstone Legacy* (1970, Cont. 7627–8); *The Moontrane* (1974, Muse 5058); *The Iron Men* (1977, Muse 5160); *Rosewood* (1977, Col. JC35309); *Stepping Stones* (1978, Col. JC35560); *United* (1981, Col. FC37390); *Lotus Flower* (1982, Enja 4018); *Master of the Art* (1982, Elek. Mus. 60131); *Time is Right* (1983, Red 168); *Setting Standards* (1983, Muse 5318); *Solid* (1986, Muse 5239); *Imagination* (1987, Muse 5338); *In your own Sweet Way* (1987, In + Out 7003)

As sideman: E. Dolphy: *Iron Man* (1963, Douglas 785); H. Silver: *The Cape Verdean Blues* (1965, BN 84220); *The Jody Grind* (1966, BN 84250); L. Young: *Unity* (1965, BN 84221); C. Corea: *Tones for Joan's Bones* (1966, Vortex 2004); J. McLean: *Demon's Dance* (1967, BN 84345); A. Blakey: *Buhaina* (1973, Prst. 10067); *Anthenagin* (1973, Prst. 10076); L. Hayes and J. Cook: *Ichi-ban* (1976, Tim. 102); D. Gordon: *Homecoming* (1976, Col. PG34650)

TRANSCRIPTIONS

J. Aebersold: *A New Approach to Jazz Improvisation*, ix: *Woody Shaw: Eight Classic Jazz Originals* (New Albany, IN, 1976) [incl. solos and lead sheets to his compositions]
K. Slone: *28 Modern Jazz Trumpet Solos*, i, ed. J. Aebersold (Lebanon, IN, 1977)
D. Carley: *Woody Shaw: Jazz Trumpet Solos: Transcriptions from the Original Recordings*, comp. E. Rahn, ed. R. S. Shiff (New York, 1979/*R*1989, as *The Greatest Jazz Hits of Woody Shaw: Jazz Trumpet Solos*)
K. Slone: *28 Modern Jazz Trumpet Solos*, ii (Miami, *c*1980)

SELECTED FILMS AND VIDEOS

Jazz in Exile (1978); Jackie McLean on Mars (1979); Mal Waldron and Friends: Live at the Village Vanguard ([filmed 1986])

BIBLIOGRAPHY

A. J. Shaw: "Woody Shaw," *DB*, xlii/8 (1975), 34
E. Chadbourne: "Woody Shaw," *Coda*, no.144 (1976), 10
S. Lake: "The Intimidator," *MM*, li (2 Oct 1976), 48
L. Tomkins: "Keeping Jazz Alive ... Our Way: Louis Hayes and Woody Shaw," *CI*, xv/3 (1976), 20
W. Shaw: "My Approach to the Trumpet, and to Jazz," *CI*, xv/8 (1977), 14
C. Berg: "Woody Shaw," *DB*, xlv/14 (1978), 22
A. Baraka: Liner notes, *Woody III* (Col. JC35977, 1979); repr. in Amiri Baraka and Aminan Baraka, *The Music: Reflections on Blues and Jazz* (New York, 1987), 193
"Woody Shaw," *JF* [intl edn], no.57 (1979), 19
B. Rusch: "Woody Shaw: Interview," *Cadence*, vii/1 (1981), 12
"Woody Shaw," *SJ*, xxxvi/14 (1982), 242 [discography]
L. Reitman: "Woody Shaw: Linked to a Legacy," *DB*, l/1 (1983), 18 [incl. discography]
M. Chenard: "Shawnuff Did, Shawnuff Said," *Coda*, no.214 (1987), 4
Obituary, *New York Times* (12 May 1989)

BK

Shearer, Dick [Richard Bruce] (*b* Indianapolis, 21 Sept 1940). Trombonist. He grew up in California, took up trombone at the age of 13, and began his professional career five years later. After performing with Si Zentner (1960–61), Billy May (1961), and various groups in Los Angeles he worked briefly with Tex Beneke (1964), the pop singers the Righteous Brothers (1964–5), and Louie Bellson (1965). From 1967 to 1978 he was the lead trombonist and a soloist in Stan Kenton's band, with which he toured, recorded, and taught at workshops; in addition he sometimes stood in for Kenton as the band's director. His solo on *Chiapas*, from the album *Stan Kenton Live at Redlands University* (1970, CW 1015), is a good example of his playing. In the early 1980s, while based in Detroit, Shearer led his own band, performed in the Detroit Symphony Orchestra, and worked as a freelance. Having returned to the Los Angeles area in 1985, he recorded as the leader of a band devoted to Kenton's legacy in 1992. He has remained active as a studio musician, teacher, and music publisher.

BIBLIOGRAPHY

Feather–Gitler '70s
D. Shearer: "Growing up with the Kenton Band," *CI*, xi/10 (1973), 6
W. F. Lee: *Stan Kenton: Artistry in Rhythm* (Los Angeles, 1980/*R*1994) [incl. discography; *R* without discography], 337

BK

Shearing, George (Albert) (*b* London, 13 Aug 1919). American pianist of English birth. Blind from birth, he began playing piano at the age of three, but his only formal training in music was at the Linden Lodge School for the Blind, which he attended from the ages of 12 to 16. By 1936 he was listening to recordings of Earl Hines, Fats Waller, Teddy Wilson, Meade "Lux" Lewis, and Art Tatum. While playing piano and accordion in bands with Carlo Krahmer, Harry Parry, Bert Ambrose (1942), Stephane Grappelli, Harry Hayes (1945–7), and many others, he absorbed the musical vocabulary of jazz so quickly and convincingly that the *Melody Maker* poll voted him the top British pianist for seven consecutive years. In 1947 he emigrated to the USA (he took citizenship in 1956) and settled in New York, where he was strongly influenced by the bop style – particularly the aggressive rhythmic playing of Bud Powell. He worked as an intermission pianist at the Hickory House, and thereby was able to play with major jazz artists, most significantly joining Ella Fitzgerald's trio on Hank Jones's night off. He also held a long engagement at the Three Deuces, initially as an

George Shearing's quintet, New York, 1949: Shearing (piano), John Levy (double bass), Margie Hyams (vibraphone), Chuck Wayne (guitar), and Denzil Best (drums)

Ex.1 From *Sorry, Wrong Rhumba* (1949, Dis. 106); transcr. B. Dobbins

unaccompanied soloist and then leading a trio with Oscar Pettiford (or John Levy) and J. C. Heard; Eddie Shu sometimes joined as well, making it a quartet. Late in 1948 he co-led a quartet with Buddy De Franco including Levy and Denzil Best.

The historic "Shearing sound" originated in recordings for Discovery in 1949, made with a quintet of piano, vibraphone, guitar, double bass, and drums. Using the piano as the leading instrument, Shearing played in the block chord style known as "locked hands," which he developed from Milt Buckner's earlier model and from the chordal playing of Glenn Miller's saxophone section. In this style, each note of the melody is harmonized with a three-note chord in the right hand, the left hand doubling the melody an octave below (*see* Piano, ex.9). In Shearing's quintet the upper melody note was then doubled by the vibraphone (with the vibrato motor turned off, to strength the unison with the piano), and the lower one by the guitar (see ex.1). By popularizing this particular ensemble sound Shearing achieved commercial success on a scale rarely known in the jazz world. The quintet toured with Billy Eckstine in 1950 and again in 1951; from 1953, though still called a "quintet," it actually became a six-piece band, with the addition of the percussionist Armando Peraza. Apart from its original members (see illustration), among the many important sidemen who played in the quintet are the vibraphonists Don Elliott, Joe Roland, Cal Tjader, Emil Richards, and Gary Burton, the guitarists Toots Thielemans and Joe Pass, and the rhythm section members Ed Thigpen, Al McKibbon, Percy Brice, Israel Crosby, Vernel Fournier, Ralph Peña, Bob Whitlock, and Colin Bailey. Shearing also played accordion, notably as a bop soloist on *Cherokee/Four Bars Short* (1949).

During the late 1950s Shearing began performing classical concertos with symphony orchestras in concerts which sometimes included orchestral arrangements featuring his quintet; later in his career he would routinely intermix classical and jazz playing in the course of a performance, transforming Beethoven into bop, and vice versa. From 1968 he worked in a trio with Andy Simpkins and Stix Hooper, or with these same men in the quintet. In 1978 he finally disbanded the quintet, and formed it only for special occasions, including two weeks with Frank Sinatra at Carnegie Hall in 1981.

By this time Shearing had turned his attention elsewhere. Having earlier made unaccompanied albums for Capitol in 1956 and for the first release on his own short-lived label, Sheba, in 1969, from 1978 he performed more extensively as a soloist and in duos, which best display the full range of his abilities as a pianist and improviser. One such collaboration, with Mel Tormé, dates from 1976, when they first appeared together at Carnegie Hall. In the early 1980s they collaborated on some award-winning duo and small-group recordings, and continued to work together in the 1990s when Tormé's schedule allowed. Shearing's other steady duo partners have been the double bass players Brian Torff (1978–82), Don Thompson (1982–7), and Niel Swainson (1987–), but this duo format is by no means rigid – Shearing and Swainson, for example, worked variously with Pass, Joe Williams, and Grady Tate in the early 1990s. Shearing has also performed in duos with Jim Hall, Carmen McRae, Marian McPartland (early 1980s), and Hank Jones (at the JVC Jazz Festival, New York, 1987, and on recordings, 1988). In 1994 he re-formed the quintet for a recording, resurrecting its classic arrangements and presenting new ones; the group toured the following year. His best-known composition, *Lullaby of Birdland*, was written in 1952 as a theme for the legendary jazz club and its radio shows. Many of his own arrangements for piano have appeared in individual scores or collections of scores published variously by Big 3, Hansen, MCA, and Robbins.

Video oral history material in *NCH* (HCJA).

See also Piano, §4.

SELECTED RECORDINGS

As unaccompanied soloist: *The Shearing Piano* (1956, Cap. T909); *My Ship* (1974, MPS 15433); *Grand Piano* (1985, Conc. 281)

Duos: with B. Torff: *Blues Alley & Jazz* (1979, Conc. 110); with M. McPartland: *Alone Together* (1981, Conc. 171); with H. Jones: *The Spirit of 176* (1988, Conc. 4371)

As leader: So Rare (1947, Savoy 689); Bop's your Uncle/Sophisticated Lady (1947, Savoy 718); Cherokee/Four Bars Short (1949, Dis. 107); Sorry, Wrong Rhumba (1949, Dis. 106); Lullaby of Birdland (1952, MGM 11354); *Latin Escapade* (1956, Cap. T737); *San Francisco Scene* (1960, Cap. T1715); *Jazz Concert* (1963, Cap. T1992); with M. Tormé: *An Evening with George Shearing & Mel Tormé* (1982, Conc. 190), *An Evening at Charlie's* (1983, Conc. 248); *I Hear a Rhapsody* (1992, Telarc 83310); *Walkin'* (1992, Telarc 83333); *That Shearing Sound* (1994, Telarc 83347)

SELECTED FILMS AND VIDEOS

Stéphane Grappelli and his Quintet (1946); Conception (1951); Disc Jockey (1951); Swedish Pastry (1951); I'll Be Around (1951); Move (1951); The Magic of Music (1955); The Big Beat (1957); The Artistry of George Shearing (n.d. [?1980s]); George Shearing: Lullaby of Birdland (1992); Joe Williams: a Song is Born (1992)

BIBLIOGRAPHY

BalliettA (1996)

L. Tomkins: "George Shearing: How I Found the Sound," *Crescendo*, v/3 (1966), 15

H. Frost: "Cheers for Shearing," *DB*, xxxiv/21 (1967), 21

S. Holroyd: "Shearing: an Eight-bar Wonder," *MM* (28 Sept 1974), 65

S. Quaver: "So Now We'll be Hearing more from George Shearing," *CI*, xiii/4 (1974), 26

L. Lyons: "George Shearing: Sophisticated Jazz Piano," *CK*, ii/4 (1976), 10

L. Feather: "Piano Giants of Jazz: George Shearing," *CK*, iii/8 (1977), 39
"George Shearing," *SJ*, xxxii/3 (1978), 294 [discography]
L. Feather: *The Passion for Jazz* (New York, 1980/*R*1990), 83
L. R. Reitman: "George Shearing," *CK*, vii/3 (1981), 42
L. Lyons: *The Great Jazz Pianists, Speaking of their Lives and Music* (New York, 1983), 93
G. Shearing: "Good Times and Good Time," *CI*, xxii/2 (1984), 22
L. Feather: *The Jazz Years: Earwitness to an Era* (London and New York, 1986), 192
K. Kevorkian: "George Shearing: Tips for Jazz Apprentices from an Old Master," *Keyboard*, xiii/2 (1987), 46
W. Balliett: *American Singers: Twenty-seven Portraits in Song* (New York, and Oxford, England, 1988), 151
F. Hall: *Dialogues in Swing: Intimate Conversations with the Stars of the Big Band Era* (Ventura, CA, 1989)
F. Salamone: "George Shearing," *Cadence*, xvi/4 (1990), 5
B. Laber: "The George Shearing Legend Continues," *Clavier*, xxxi/8 (1992), 12
D. Matthews: "In Conversation with George Shearing," *CJM*, xxxi/4 (1994), 8

BILL DOBBINS/BK

Sheba. Record company and label established in 1969 by George Shearing. It ceased activity in 1973, and the following year Shearing began an association with MPS.

Sheet music. A term applied to a single item of published music, typically a piano piece or a popular song in "short score" (i.e., a version in which the accompaniment is reduced to a piano part and usually also to chord symbols or tablature so that it may be realized on plucked string instruments). For the way in which sheet music is adapted by jazz musicians for their use *see* Notation, §2.

Sheets of sound. A term coined by Ira Gitler ("Trane on the Track," *DB*, xxv/21 (1958), 16) to describe the rapid, sweeping lines, in which individual pitches are indistinguishable, played by John Coltrane from the late 1950s.

Sheik, Kid. *See* Cola, kid sheik.

Shekere. *See* Sekere.

Shelbo. Nickname of shelton Gary.

Sheldon, Jack (*b* Jacksonville, FL, 30 Nov 1931). Trumpeter and singer. He studied trumpet in Detroit from the age of 12 and first worked professionally a year later. In 1947 he moved to Los Angeles, where for two years he attended Los Angeles City College. While serving in the air force he belonged to military bands in Texas and California; following his discharge in 1952 he played West Coast jazz with his own quintet and with groups led by Howard Rumsey (briefly in 1954), Jimmy Giuffre (recording in 1955), Curtis Counce (1956–8), Art Pepper (recording in 1956, 1958, and 1960), Dave Pell (recording in 1957), Herb Geller, Wardell Gray, Stan Kenton (1958), and Benny Goodman, with whom he toured Europe (1959) and the USA (1960). In the 1960s he became well known as an actor and comedian, and in 1964–5 he portrayed a jazz trumpeter in a television series; he also recorded with Gary Burton (1963). Later he played regularly on television (on the "Merv Griffin Show"), and from around 1972 to 1973 he led a band in which he doubled on electric organ; among his sidemen were Cat Anderson, Blue Mitchell, Pepper, Dave Frishberg, and Nick Ceroli. Sheldon performed and recorded with big bands led by Bill Berry (1976–1990s) and Goodman (1978), recorded with June Christy (1977) and Woody Herman (1983), played in Herman's sextet (1986), and led small groups in the Los Angeles area; in the mid-1980s he was performing at the Smoke House in Burbank with Monty Budwig and Plas Johnson among his sidemen and in Glendale in a duo with Ross Tompkins. Sheldon's trumpet style is reminiscent of that of Miles Davis. He may be seen in a jazz context in "Stan Kenton and his Orchestra" (1962), from the television series "Jazz Scene USA," and in the video *Jack Sheldon in New Orleans* (1988).

Video oral history material in *NCH* (HCJA).

SELECTED RECORDINGS

As leader: *Jack's Groove* (1957, 1959, GNP 60); *Jazz Profile of Ray Charles* (1961, Rep. 2004); *Stand by for the Jack Sheldon Quartet* (1983, Conc. 229); *Playing for Change* (1986, Upt. 27.43); *Jack Sheldon Sings* (1992, Butterfly 7701)

As sideman: C. Counce: *The Curtis Counce Group* (1956, Cont. 3526); B. Goodman: *The Sound of Music* (1959, MGM 3810); A. Pepper: *Smack Up* (1960, Cont. 7602)

BIBLIOGRAPHY

ConnorBG; *FeatherE*; *Feather '60s*; *Feather–Gitler '70s*
S. Voce: "It Don't Mean a Thing . . . ," *JJI*, xxxiv/1 (1981), 19
H. Siders: "Live Sounds: Jack Sheldon: Ain't Misbehavin," *Windplayer*, iii/7 (1987), 27
T. Gioia: *West Coast Jazz: Modern Jazz in California, 1945–1960* (New York, and Oxford, England, 1992), 322

GARY THEROUX/BK

Shepard, Ernie [Ernest, Jr.] (*b* Beaumont, TX, 19 July 1916; *d* Hamburg, Germany, 23 Nov 1965). Double bass player and singer. He worked in Texas during the 1930s, then played in California with Gerald Wilson and the pianist Phil Moore. In 1945 he was briefly in the quintet led by Charlie Parker and Dizzy Gillespie and recorded as a singer with Lem Davis, and in 1945–6 he recorded on double bass with Eddie Heywood. In New York he performed and recorded as a singer and double bass player with Slim Gaillard (1951), Gene Ammons (1951–2, 1955), Sonny Stitt (1952), and Johnny Hodges (*c*1955). After spending some time out of work in Los Angeles, Shepard joined Duke Ellington (November 1962), with whom he toured Europe and recorded. The following year he recorded on double bass and as a scat singer with Paul Gonsalves (*Tell it the Way it is*, 1963, Imp. 55) and played double bass at a session led by Johnny Hodges (1964). Shepard left Ellington in February 1964 and settled in Germany, where he undertook a variety of session work, including engagements for radio and television.

BIBLIOGRAPHY

Feather '60s; *ReclamsJ*
D. Ellington: *Music is my Mistress* (Garden City, NY, 1973), 230

Shepherd, Dave [David Joseph] (*b* London, 7 Feb 1929). English clarinetist. He had piano lessons before teaching himself to play clarinet from the age of 16. While stationed in Hamburg, Germany, during his national service he studied with a clarinetist from the Hamburg State Opera Orchestra. After returning to England he played with the dixieland bandleader Reg Rigden (1950), the drummer Joe Daniels (1951–3), and Freddy Randall (September 1954 – January 1955); as an occasional member of the Jazz Today Unit he accompanied Billie Holiday during her visit to Britain in 1954 and performed with Gerry Mulligan. Shepherd spent a period in the New York area in 1956, and for several months he led a band that included Teddy Kotick at Casa Lou in Farmingdale. When he returned to Britain he worked again with the Jazz Today Unit (late 1956–1957) and toured with Jazz at the Philharmonic (1957). During the mid-1950s he also accompanied Mary Lou Williams on several occasions. Later he played again with Randall (1963, summer 1972–

1973) and performed with Teddy Wilson in Britain (1967, 1969, 1971), at the Montreux International Jazz Festival (1973), and in South Africa (1975). From 1980 to 1999 he was a member of the Pizza Express All Star Jazz Band, and in 1995 he joined the Great British Jazz Band. In addition Shepherd led numerous bands of his own, typically in the style of Benny Goodman, and between 1976 and 1990 he worked extensively in film and television music production.

SELECTED RECORDINGS

As leader: *Shepherd's Delight* (1969, 77 LEU12/35); with F. Randall: *Freddy Randall/Dave Shepherd All Stars* (1972, BL 12102); *Benny Goodman Classics* (1975, BL 12119); *Tribute to Benny Goodman* (1994, Avid 595)
As sideman: J. Daniels: Runnin' Wild/The Boogie Woogie March (1952, Parl. R3574); T. Wilson: on *Runnin' Wild* (1973, BL 30149), St. James Infirmary, After you've gone

BIBLIOGRAPHY

CarrJ; *ChiltonB*

MARK GILBERT

Shepherd, Shep [Berisford] (*b* Honduras, 19 Jan 1917). Drummer and arranger. He grew up in Philadelphia and was conservatory-trained. From 1932 to 1941 he worked with the bandleader Jimmy Gorham in and around Philadelphia, and in 1941–2 he played with Benny Carter. He also recorded with Artie Shaw in June 1941. After military service (1943–6) he worked extensively as an arranger, undertook a short tour with Cab Calloway (1946), played with Buck Clayton (1947), and spent three years with Earl Bostic. Shepherd was in Philadelphia from 1950 to 1952, arranging and copying for music publishers and taking part in local recording sessions. From 1952 to 1959 he was a member of Bill Doggett's group; with Doggett he composed *Honky Tonk*, which became a hit, and his driving beat contributed much to the group's popularity with dancers. Thereafter he performed and recorded prolifically as a freelance, playing for many shows on Broadway, recording with Sy Oliver, and working occasionally with Erskine Hawkins. In the mid-1960s he settled in San Francisco, where he continued to be active as a freelance.

SELECTED RECORDINGS

As sideman: B. Carter: Back Bay Boogie (1941, Bb 11341); first issued on *Benny Carter 1940–1941* (1940–41, RCA 741073), Tree of Hope (1941); B. Doggett: Tailor Made/Sweet Lorraine (1953, King 4720); *Dance awhile with Doggett* (1953–8, King 585), incl. Flying Home (1957); Honky Tonk (1956, King 4950)

BIBLIOGRAPHY

McCarthyB

based on *ChiltonW*/HOWARD RYE (recording-list)

Shepik [Schoeppach]**, Brad** (*b* Walla Walla, WA, 13 Feb 1966). Guitarist. He changed his surname to Shepik around 1998. Having played saxophone in his school band at the age of 11 he took up rock guitar when he was 13 and became interested in jazz in his late teens. He studied music at Cornish College of Arts in Seattle (BA 1988) and later played with, among others, Paul Motian's Electric Bebop Band (from 1991), Dave Douglas's Tiny Bell Trio (from 1992), the saxophonist Matt Darriau (from 1992), the saxophonist Yuri Yunakov (1995–7), Charlie Haden (1997), and Carla Bley (1997–8). In addition he led a number of his own groups, notably Babkas (from 1992) and the Commuters (from 1996), in which his sidemen included Peter Epstein, the electric bass guitarist Tony Scherr, and Kenny Wollesen; he formed the cooperative quartet Pachora in 1993 with Chris Speed, the bass player Skuli Sverrison, and Jim Black. Taking inspiration from Eastern European and Middle Eastern music, Shepik also plays a Turkish instrument, the electric *saz*, and the Bulgarian *tambura*.

SELECTED RECORDINGS

As leader: *The Loan* (1996–7, Songlines 1518)
As sideman: Babkas: *Ants to the Moon* (1995, Songlines 1505); P. Motian: *Flight of the Blue Jay* (1996, Winter & Winter 910009-2); M. Darriau: *Flying at a Slant* (1997, Knitting Factory Works 206); Pachora: *Pachora* (1997, Knitting Factory Works 207); D. Douglas: *Songs for Wandering Souls* (1998, Winter & Winter 910042-2)

BIBLIOGRAPHY

J. Marcus: "Coda: Bumpin' with Babkas," *Jazziz*, xii/8 (1995), 98
H. Pekar: "Brad Schoeppach: from Bebop to Freebop," *GP*, xxxi/7 (1997), 22
A. Levy: "Brad Shepik: Old World, Young Turk" *GP*, xxxii/7 (1998), 45

MARK GILBERT

Shepp, Archie (Vernon) (*b* Fort Lauderdale, FL, 24 May 1937). Saxophonist, playwright, and teacher. He grew up in Philadelphia, where he began on clarinet and took up saxophone at around the age of 15; he studied dramatic literature at Goddard College (BA 1959). While seeking theatrical work in New York he played alto saxophone in dance bands, but under the influence of John Coltrane he took up the tenor instrument and performed in avant-garde groups. He was a member of Cecil Taylor's quartet (1960–62) and served as co-leader of a quartet with Bill Dixon (1962–3) and with Don Cherry and John Tchicai of the New York Contemporary Five (1963–4). Thereafter he led his own groups, which involved such distinguished sidemen as Roswell Rudd (1964, 1966), Bobby Hutcherson (1965), Beaver Harris (1966–8, 1971, 1975), and Grachan Moncur III (1966–9). Shepp became an eloquent spokesman and apologist for free jazz, which he interpreted as a medium for political expression. He also wrote a play, *Junebug Graduates Tonight!*, which ran briefly in early 1967. From 1969 to 1974 he was a member of the faculty of black studies at SUNY, Buffalo, and in 1974 he transferred to the University of Massachusetts, where four years later he was named an associate professor. From the 1980s he has made regular tours of Europe, where he recorded the majority of his albums, among them a series of duos with Max Roach, Horace Parlan, Niels-Henning Ørsted Pedersen, and Jasper van 't Hof. From the 1990s his touring quartet often included the double bass player Wayne Dockery and the drummer Stephen McCraven; the group recorded in 1996 with Eric Le Lann as fifth member and co-leader, and in 2000 it performed at the North Sea Jazz Festival. Shepp also recorded in Paris in concert with Chris McGregor and the Brotherhood of Breath (1989) and in the USA as a co-leader with Kahil El'Zabar of the Ritual Trio (1999).

Shepp's early recordings abound in such elements of free jazz as collective improvisation, atonality, and harsh fragments of melody. From the mid-1960s he began to make use of powerful poems evocative of life in the black ghettos (*Malcolm, Malcolm, semper Malcolm*) and African percussion, and to play marches, slow blues, and sentimental ballads (*Prelude to a Kiss, In a Sentimental Mood*); his tone became correspondingly full-bodied, and he employed old-fashioned growls and bends and wide vibrato. Throughout this first decade of career he invented tenor saxophone melodies in an audacious, pungent, slithering manner, developing one of the most distinctive instrumental voices of the era. Shepp simplified his style radically in the early 1970s, however, as he embraced rhythm-and-blues (*Attica*

Archie Shepp at the Queen Elizabeth Hall, London, 1997

Blues), and later his academic historical pursuits prompted him to incorporate into his repertory bop (*Looking at Bird*), early blues (*Trouble in Mind*), and electronic music (*Mama Rose*).

SELECTED RECORDINGS

Duos: with M. Roach: *The Long March* (1979, HH 13); with H. Parlan: *Trouble in Mind* (1980, Ste. 1139); with N.-H. Ørsted Pedersen: *Looking at Bird* (1980, Ste. 1149); with J. van 't Hof: *Mama Rose* (1982, Ste. 1169); with H. Parlan: *Swing Low* (1991, Plainisphare 1267-73)

As leader: with B. Dixon: *Archie Shepp–Bill Dixon Quartet* (1962, Savoy 12178); with D. Cherry and J. Tchicai: *Archie Shepp and the New York Contemporary Five* (1963, Sonet 36); *Four for Trane* (1964, Imp. 71); *Fire Music* (1965, Imp. 86), incl. Malcolm, Malcolm, semper Malcolm, Prelude to a Kiss; *On this Night* (1965, Imp. 97), incl. In a Sentimental Mood; *Archie Shepp Live in San Francisco* (1966, Imp. 9118), incl. In a Sentimental Mood; *Mama Too Tight* (1966, Imp. 9134); *The Magic of Ju-Ju* (1967, Imp. 9154); *Archie Shepp Live at the Donaueschingen Music Festival* (1967, Saba 15148); *The Way Ahead* (1968, Imp. 9170); *Attica Blues* (1972, Imp. 9222); *Steam* (1976, Enja 2076); *I Know about the Life* (1981, Sack. 3026); *My Man* (1981, Impro 06); *African Moods* (1984, Cir. [Ger.] 29); *I Didn't Know about You* (1990, Tim. 370); with E. Le Lann: *Live in Paris* (1996, L'Oz 10); *True Blue* (1998, Venus 35067); with K. El'Zabar: *Conversations* (1999, Del. 514)

As sideman: C. Taylor: on *The World of Cecil Taylor* (1960, Can. 9006), Air, Lazy Afternoon; G. Evans: *Into the Hot* (1961, Imp. 9); J. Coltrane: *Ascension* (1965, Imp. 95)

WRITINGS

(selective list)

"An Artist Speaks Bluntly," *DB*, xxxii/26 (1965), 11

"On Jazz," *Jazz*, iv/4 (1965), 24

"A View from the Inside," *Down Beat Music '66* (Chicago, 1966), 39

"On Pugilism," *Jazz*, v/7 (1966), 7

"Black Power and Black Jazz," *New York Times* (26 Nov 1967)

"Fortunes Unattended: Notes on the History of Black American Music," *Lightworks*, no.10 (1978), 47

"Innovations in Jazz," *History and Tradition in Afro-American Culture*, ed. G. H. Lenz (Frankfurt am Main, Germany, and New York, 1984), 256

SELECTED FILMS AND VIDEOS

Future One (1963); Festival Pan Africain d'Alger [Pan-African Festival] (1970); Archie Shepp chez les Touaregs (1971); Imagine the Sound (1981); Archie Shepp: I am Jazz … It's my Life (*c*1990)

BIBLIOGRAPHY

GrayF

A. B. Spellman: "Introducing Archie Shepp," *Metronome* (1961), Nov, 26

"Archie méconnu," *Jm*, no.119 (1965), 50

J. Hopkins and B. Houston: "Archie Shepp: We Can't Let the Audience Escape," *MM* (7 Aug 1965), 6

L. Jones: "Voices from the Avant Garde: Archie Shepp," *DB*, xxxii/1 (1965), 18

F. Postif and G. Kopelowicz: "Archie Shepp ou la marée qui monte," *Jh* (1965), no.210, p.22; no.211, p.38

"Shepp le rebelle," *Jm*, no.125 (1965), 78

J. Cooke: "New York Nouvelle Vague, no.4: Archie Shepp," *JM*, xii/4 (1966), 2

G. Endress: "Archie Shepp Interview," *JP*, xxv/5 (1966), 122

L. Feather: "Shepp: Look Forward in Anger," *Music Maker* [London] (1966), Oct, 25

D. Heckman: "Archie Shepp," *BMI: the Many Worlds of Music* (1967), May, 22

L. Jones: *Black Music* (New York, 1967/*R*1980), 145

V. Wilmer: "The Tenorist Playwright who Speaks for Black Expressionism," *MM* (14 Oct 1967), 18

N. Hentoff: "Archie Shepp: the Way Ahead," *J&P*, vii/6 (1968), 17; repr. in *Black Giants*, ed. P. Rivelli and R. Levin (New York and Cleveland, 1970/*R*1980 as *Giants of Black Music*), 118

B. McRae: "Archie Shepp," *JJ*, xxi/1 (1968), 34

E. Raben: *A Discography of Free Jazz* (Copenhagen, 1969)

W. Roggeman: *Free en andere jazz-essays* (The Hague, 1969), 89

F. Fayenz: *Il jazz dal mito all' avanguardia* (Milan, 1970), 441

V. Wilmer: *Jazz People* (London, Indianapolis, and New York, 1970/*R*1985), 155

——: "Shepp the Teacher," *MM* (16 Oct 1971), 14

E. Jost: *Free Jazz* (Graz, Austria, 1974/*R*1994), 105

J. B. Litweiler: "Shepp: an Old Schoolmaster in Brown Suit," *DB*, xli/18 (1974), 15 [incl. discography]

B. McRae: "Avant Courier: Things Have Got to Change," *JJ*, xxvii/2 (1974), 26

L. Goddet: "Archie Shepp: le lien," *Jh*, no.320 (1975), 4

B. McRae: "Avant Courier: the Traditionalism of Archie Shepp," *JJ*, xxviii/9 (1975), 14

M. Naura: "Unsere Musik war für die Schwarzen immer relevant," *JP*, xxiv (1975), no.2, p.4; contd as "Der Schrei meines Volkes," no.3, p.4

"Discographie: Archie Shepp," *Jh*, no.325 (1976), 24

G. Pellicciotti: "Archie Shepp," *Jm*, no.243 (1976), 16

D. N. Baker, L. M. Belt, and H. C. Hudson, eds.: *The Black Composer Speaks* (Metuchen, NJ, and London, 1978)

G. Giddins: "Archie Shepp without Rhetoric," *VV*, xxiii (27 Nov 1978), 88

B. Primack: "Archie Shepp: Back to Schooldays," *DB*, xlv/21 (1978), 27
P. Kemper: "Archie Shepp: zur Sensibilität eines traditionsbewussten Avantgardisten," *JP*, xxviii (1979), no.5, p.4, no.6, p.9
B. Rusch: "Archie Shepp: Interview," *Cadence*, v/3 (1979), 3
J. Runcie: "Archie Shepp," *JJI*, xxxiii (1980), no.3, p.26; no.4, p.28
B. Stepien and N. Richmond: "Archie Shepp," *Coda*, no.171 (1980), 4
J. Reese: "Archie Shepp ou la mémoire du peuple noir," *Jh*, no.390 (1981), 10
G. Cerutti and G. Maertens: *Discographie Archie Shepp, 1960–1980* (Sierre, Switzerland, 1982)
S. Crouch: "Archie Shepp's Neoclassicist Dilemma," *VV*, xxvii (3 Feb 1982), 63
S. Freedman: "Archie Shepp: Embracing the Jazz Ritual," *DB*, xlix/4 (1982), 22 [incl. discography]
R. Sanderson: "Archie Shepp," *The Wire*, no.3 (1983), 16
G. Putschögl: "Black Music – Key Force in Afro-American Culture: Archie Shepp on Oral Tradition and Black Culture," *History and Tradition in Afro-American Culture*, ed. G. H. Lenz (Frankfurt am Main, Germany, and New York, 1984), 262
C. J. Gans: "Archie Shepp: in the Tradition," *JF* [intl edn], no.93 (1985), 36
K. Natambu: "Archie Shepp: We Must Move Toward a Critique of American Culture," *Cultures in Contention*, ed. D. Kahn and D. Neumaier (Seattle, 1985), 166
B. Smith: "Archie Shepp: Four for Trane," *Coda*, no.204 (1985), 20
G. Putschögl: "Zur Schlüsselfunktion der Musik in der Afro-Amerikanischen Kultur: Archie Shepp über die Musiktradition der schwarzen Amerikaner," *Jf*, xviii (1986), 67
C. L. Hardin: *Black Professional Musicians in Higher Education: a Study Based on In-depth Interviews* (diss., U. of Massachusetts, 1987)
B. Sidran: "Shepp: des sons pour le dire," *Jm* (1987), no.365, p.36; no.366, p.28
M. Smith: "Archie Shepp Interview," *Cadence*, xv/8 (1989), 5
N. C. Weinstein: *A Night in Tunisia: Imaginings of Africa in Jazz* (Metuchen, NJ, and London, 1992)
J. Denis: "Archie Shepp: mes années Impulse!," *Jazzman*, no.34 (1998), 10
<http://www.archieshepp.com> (2000) [incl. discography]

BK

Sheppard, Andy (*b* Warminster, England, 20 Jan 1957). English tenor and soprano saxophonist, composer, and leader. He played guitar and flute as a child and sang in his church choir until he was 11. At the age of 19 he became interested in jazz after hearing recordings by Charles Mingus and John Coltrane, and he subsequently taught himself tenor saxophone; within three weeks he had joined the ensemble Sphere led by the pianist Geoff Williams (not to be confused with the American quartet of the same name) and he later recorded with the group. He took up soprano saxophone two years later. Sheppard lived briefly in London (*c*1981) and then moved to Paris, where he joined Laurent Cugny's ensemble Big Band Lumière and worked as one of 40 saxophonists in the performance art group Urban Sax. From 1986 he lived in Bristol, and led a quintet and then a prize-winning quartet with which he gained a recording contract with Antilles. He returned briefly to Paris to tour and record in Cugny's group (late 1987–1988), for which Gil Evans was the guest conductor and arranger. In the late 1980s he joined Carla Bley's big band (1988), performed with George Russell's Living Time Orchestra, and began working regularly alongside Keith Tippett, with whom he performed in New York at the Knitting Factory (1991); he also toured and recorded in a trio with Bley and Steve Swallow.

In 1989 Sheppard formed the big band Soft on the Inside, with Gary Valente, Chris Biscoe, Ernst Reijseger, and Han Bennink among his sidemen; the following year it was the subject of a video documentary, *Soft on the Inside*. In the 1990s he led a quartet with Reijseger, Nana Vasconcelos, and Orphy Robinson (1990), and a fusion quintet, In Co-Motion, with Claude Deppa, Steve Lodder, the electric bass guitarist Sylvan Richardson, and the drummer Dave Adams (from 1991); he toured Cuba (1993) and Nigeria (1993–4) with an expanded version of the quintet, Big Co-Motion, and performed in a duo with Lodder as Small Co-Motion. He collaborated with Lodder and Vasconcelos in the trio Inclassifiable (recording in 1994) and played alongside Lodder and the saxophonist John Harle in the group 20th Century Saxophones. In 1996 Sheppard's piece *Harmattan* was given its première by the Bergen Big Band at the Cheltenham Jazz Festival; he has also composed for the BBC and for a British production of Arthur Miller's play *The Man who had all the Luck*. His company Shoddy Music, Inc., which he co-founded with Lodder, manages his film, radio, and television writing projects. As a freelance he has worked with, among others, Evan Parker, Lol Coxhill, Paul Dunmall, Harry Beckett, Elton Dean, and Stan Tracey. He may be seen leading a trio in the video *The Live Sessions* (1999). Sheppard is one of a number of tenor saxophone virtuosos who came to prominence in the mid-1980s and 1990s; his playing is more mature than that of many of them, for he improvises with melodic coherence, creativity, and a tasteful awareness of the diverse styles in which he operates.

Andy Sheppard at the Islington Festival, London, June 1988

SELECTED RECORDINGS

Duos with K. Tippett: *66 Shades of Lipstick* (1990, Editions EG 64)
As leader: *Andy Sheppard* (1987, Ant. 422-842710); *Introductions in the Dark* (1988, Ant. 422-842654); *Soft on the Inside* (1989, Ant. 422-842927-2); *Rhythm Method* (1993, BN B21Z-27798); with S. Lodder: *Moving Image* (1995–6, Verve 314-533875-2)
As sideman: G. Russell: *The London Concert* (1989, Label Bleu 6527–8); B. Dennerlein: *Hot Stuff* (1990, Enja 6050-2); C. Bley: *The Very Big Carla Bley Band* (1990, Watt 23), incl. Lo ultimo; *Songs with Legs* (1994, Watt 26); *The Carla Bley Big Band Goes to Church* (1996, Watt 27)

BIBLIOGRAPHY

CarrJ; *ChiltonB*
T. Reed: "Control Zone: Sax Appeal," *MM* (21 Nov 1987), 42

D. Baldy: "Eurosax: Andy Sheppard," *Jm*, no.382 (1989), 22
J. Fordham: "Big, Bold and Brassy," *The Guardian* (2 Nov 1989)
——: "Going to St. Ives," *The Guardian* (14 Nov 1991)
C. Parker: "Andy Sheppard," *Jazz FM*, no.6 (1991), 10
K. Whitehead: "Success (Un)formula: Persistence and the Big Break: Andy Sheppard," *DB*, lviii/9 (1991), 30 [incl. discography]
M. M. Boyd: "Andy Sheppard," *Saxophone Journal*, xvii/4 (1993), 30
A. Sheppard: "Have Horn, Will Travel," *The Guardian* (14 Jan 1994)
T. Hodgett: "A British Point of View: Andy Sheppard & John Surman," *Coda*, no.263 (1995), 18

GK

Sheppard, Bob [Robert Louis] (*b* Trenton, NJ, 5 April 1952). Saxophonist, clarinetist, and flutist. He studied music education at Glassboro State College (BS 1975), New Jersey, and jazz performance at the Eastman School (MM 1977). After teaching at Loyola University in New Orleans (1978–9) he played with Freddie Hubbard (1984–91), Billy Childs (1988–95), Scott Henderson and Tribal Tech (1985–9), the pop group Steely Dan (1992–4), Lyle Mays (1995), Mike Stern (1996–8), and Chick Corea's sextet Origin (1996–9). He also performed less frequently with Randy Brecker, Andy LaVerne (recording in 1991), Bobby Shew, and Horace Silver. In 1997 he joined Peter Erskine's trio the Lounge Art Ensemble. Sheppard may be seen in the documentary film *Toshiko Akiyoshi: Jazz is my Native Language* (1984).

SELECTED RECORDINGS

As leader: *Tell Tale Signs* (1991, Windham Hill Jazz 0129)
As sideman: Tribal Tech: *Spears* (1985, Passport 88010); *Dr. Hee* (1987, Passport J88030); S. Erquiaga: *Erkiology* (*c*1990, Windham Hill Jazz 0127); B. Childs: *His April Touch* (*c*1991, Windham Hill Jazz 0131); Jeff Beal: *Objects in the Mirror* (1990–91, Triloka 189); Terry Trotter: *A Funny Thing Happened on the Way to the Forum ... in Jazz* (*c*1995, Varese Sarabande 5707); C. Corea: *Origin: A Week at the Blue Note* (1998, Stretch 6-9020); Lounge Art Ensemble: *Lava* (1997, Fuzzy Music 04)

BIBLIOGRAPHY

H. Siders: "Live Sounds: Bob Sheppard: Saxman Plays with Electronic Elite," *Windplayer*, iii/7 (1986), 17
J. Woodard: "Riffs: Bob Sheppard," *DB*, lviii/4 (1991), 13

MARK GILBERT

Sheriff, the. Nickname of CLIFF LEEMAN.

Sherman, Herman (Edward, Sr.) (*b* New Orleans, 28 June 1923; *d* New Orleans, 10 Sept 1984). Saxophonist and bandleader. He learned clarinet at high school and later took up alto and tenor saxophone. By 1941 he had begun to work with various brass bands in New Orleans, and he soon developed into a specialist in this type of music, playing with the Eureka, Onward, and Young Tuxedo bands. In 1971 he became leader of the Young Tuxedo Brass Band, with which he toured widely in the USA and also visited Berlin (1980). Although Sherman occasionally undertook dance-band engagements, he concentrated on his work with the Young Tuxedo band, which may be heard under his leadership on the album *Jazz Continues* (1983, 504 Records 10). (M. Joly: "New Orleans, 1984," *Fn*, xv/6 (1984), 28)

ALYN SHIPTON

Sherman, Jimmy [James Benjamin] (*b* Williamsport, PA, 17 Aug 1908; *d* Philadelphia, 11 Oct 1975). Pianist and arranger. He played at local dances and worked occasionally with Jimmy Gorham's band in and around Philadelphia before his first professional engagement, with Alphonso Trent on the Great Lakes steamboats (1930); later he worked with Peanuts Holland (1931), Al Sears (1932), Stuff Smith (1933–4, 1936), and Lil Armstrong (1935, 1937). He also made recordings in 1936–7 with Putney Dandridge, Mildred Bailey, and Billie Holiday. From 1938 to 1952 Sherman served as accompanist and arranger for a vocal group, the Charioteers, with whom he toured Europe in 1948. He then returned to Pennsylvania, where he continued to play regularly into the 1970s; he held a residency from 1960 at Miss Jeanne's Crossroad Tavern which lasted for more than a decade.

SELECTED RECORDINGS

As sideman: S. Smith: It ain't right (1936, Voc. 3270); Bye Bye Baby (1936, Voc. 3300); L. Armstrong: I'm knockin' at the cabin door (1937, Decca 1272); B. Holiday: A Sailboat in the Moonlight/Born to love (1937, Voc. 3605); Without your love (1937, Voc. 3593)

based on *ChiltonW*/HOWARD RYE (recording-list)

Sherock, Shorty [Cherock, Clarence Francis] (*b* Minneapolis, 17 Nov 1915; *d* Northridge, CA, 19 Feb 1980). Trumpeter. He took up cornet as a child and played locally while he was in high school at Gary, Indiana. As a soloist he first attracted attention with Ben Pollack's band (1936), after which he served as a sideman with Jimmy Dorsey (1937–9), with whom he appeared as a soloist in the short film *Jimmy Dorsey and his Orchestra* (1938). He then worked with Bob Crosby (June 1939 – January 1940), Gene Krupa (January 1940 – March 1941), and Tommy Dorsey (April–July 1941) before forming a series of less important associations with Raymond Scott (summer 1941), Bud Freeman (late 1941), and others (to 1945); in 1944 he played several excellent solos at the first Jazz at the Philharmonic concert. Sherock led his own orchestra from March 1945 to June 1946, making the short film *Shorty Sherock and his Orchestra* (1947), and re-formed the band in 1948. He rejoined Jimmy Dorsey briefly in 1950, then during the 1950s and 1960s worked in studios in Los Angeles, playing in many different styles and contexts; he also spent a brief period with Georgie Auld in 1954. A highly respected and much sought-after musician, he continued to be active as a freelance until autumn 1979. Sherock was principally a swing trumpeter whose playing was influenced by that of Roy Eldridge, but he was also at home in the dixieland and bop styles. Although in his later years he took few solos, he continued to inject a spirit of excitement into many recordings on which he played.

SELECTED RECORDINGS

As leader: Meandering/It's the Talk of the Town (1946, Sig. 28113); Snafu/The Willies (1946, Sig. 28118)
As sideman: G. Krupa: Alreet (1941, OK 6118); Slow Down (1941, OK 6154); Jazz at the Philharmonic: Rosetta (1944, Disc 6027); I've found a new baby (1944, Clef 106); M. Matlock: *And they Called it Dixieland* (1958, WB 1262); Benny Carter: *BBB & Co.* (1962, Swingville 203)

BIBLIOGRAPHY

ChiltonW; *FeatherE*; *Feather '60s*
W. H. Miller: "Shorty Cherock," *Jazz Session* (1946), July, 24
"The Survey in Detail," *Brass Bulletin*, no.4 (1973), 39
Obituary, *DB*, xlvii/6 (1980), 12
J. Chilton: *Stomp Off, Let's Go! The Story of Bob Crosby's Bob Cats & Big Band* (London, 1983), 89

SCOTT YANOW

Sherrill (Guilmenot), Joya (*b* Bayonne, NJ, 20 Aug 1927). Singer. She worked with Duke Ellington for a short spell in 1942 and, after writing the lyrics to *Take the "A" Train*, joined his band in 1944. She married Richard Guilmenot in 1946. After four years with Ellington she became a solo singer but returned to the band to perform in the television program "A Drum is a Woman" (1956). Sherrill toured the USA in 1959, appearing in nightclubs and at army bases, then took an acting role in a Broadway play. She went to the USSR with

Benny Goodman (1962), performed and recorded with Ellington in Chicago (1963), and also recorded two albums as a leader (*c*1960, 1965). She may be seen in the television documentaries "The Duke" (1965) and "Duke Ellington: the Music Lives on" (1984), the latter from the PBS series "Great Performances." Ellington had a high regard for Sherrill, whose diction and articulation he considered excellent.

Oral history material in *CtY.*

SELECTED RECORDINGS

As leader: *Sugar and Spice* (*c*1960, Col. CS8207); *Joya Sherrill Sings Ellington* (1965, 20CF 4070)

As sideman with D. Ellington: I'm beginning to see the light (1944, Vic. 20-1618); The Blues (1944, Vic. 28-0400); on *A Drum is a Woman* (1956, Col. CL951), Carribee Joe, Zajj's Dream; on *My People* (1963, Contact 1), The Blues Ain't

BIBLIOGRAPHY

FeatherE

B. Ulanov: *Duke Ellington* (New York, 1946/*R*1975)

G. T. Simon: *The Big Bands* (New York and London, 1967, rev. 4/1981)

D. Ellington: *Music is my Mistress* (Garden City, NY, 1973, rev. 2/1982)

REG COOPER

Shertzer [Schertzer]**, Hymie** [Herman] (*b* New York, 22 April 1909; *d* New York, 22 March 1977). Alto saxophonist. His birthdate has been published in reference books as 2 April, but on his application for social security, where his name appears as Herman Shertzer, he gave 22 April. He took up violin at the age of nine and alto saxophone when he was 16. In 1934 he worked with the alto saxophonist Gene Kardos at Birdland in New York and recorded with Benny Goodman (August), and he subsequently became the lead alto saxophonist in the latter's band. After Goodman had transferred Jimmy Dorsey's former sideman Dave Matthews to this position in April 1938, Shertzer performed and recorded with Tommy Dorsey from 1938 to 1940; however, he continued to work with Goodman both during this period (January–June 1939) and in later years (June 1942 – June 1944, June–August 1945, summer 1946). In addition he recorded with Bunny Berigan (1937), Lionel Hampton (1937, 1939), and Billie Holiday (1941, 1944). In the mid-1940s he became a staff musician at NBC. As a studio player he recorded in big bands led by Ella Fitzgerald (1947, 1951, 1955), Sarah Vaughan (1949), Sy Oliver (1949, 1950), Louis Armstrong (1949–53), Artie Shaw (1950, 1953), and Goodman (1951–8). Around 1957 he recorded the album *Hymie Shertzer* (Disneyland 3017), which contained tunes that were made famous by Goodman's orchestra, and in April 1958 and April 1959 he appeared with Goodman in the television program "Swing into Spring." Shertzer maintained this affiliation, broadcasting on radio and television and recording further with Goodman intermittently from 1961 to 1969, and he continued to work as a studio musician until shortly before his death.

BIBLIOGRAPHY

ConnorBG; *FeatherE*

Obituaries: *New York Times* (24 March 1977); *DB*, xliv/10 (1977), 10

BK

Shew, Bobby [Joratz, Robert] (*b* Albuquerque, NM, 4 March 1941). Trumpeter and flugelhorn player. His given name was Joratz; Shew is his stepfather's name, which he took at the age of five. Almost entirely self-taught, he first worked professionally at the age of 13 as a trumpeter at local dances, and he decided to make music his career after performing in bands during his military service. He was briefly a member of the Tommy Dorsey Orchestra under Sam Donahue (1964–5), after which he played with Woody Herman (1965), Benny Goodman (December 1965), and Buddy Rich (1966–7, for a time as Rich's lead trumpeter). For the next nine years he lived in Las Vegas, accompanying popular singers, playing in show bands, and working in films and television. In 1973 he moved to Los Angeles, where he continued to be active as a studio musician and resumed his career in jazz. In the late 1970s Shew received critical acclaim as a sideman in the Toshiko Akiyoshi–Lew Tabackin Big Band, and he also enlivened the playing of the orchestras led by Ed Shaughnessy, Don Menza, Frank Capp and Nat Pierce, and Louie Bellson. He ceased to play in big-band settings in the early 1980s, and instead worked with many small groups, in which he performed solos on trumpet, flugelhorn, and (from the early 1980s into the early 1990s) his custom-made "Shewhorn," in which the tubing led to two separate bells (one muted, one not) that could be used in alternation.

From 1978 Shew performed and recorded as the leader of a quintet (with Bill Mays, Dick Berk, Bob Magnusson, and Gordon Brisker); later his quintets and sextets included Bill Reichenbach (ii) (from 1980), Chuck Findley, Kei Akagi, Makoto Ozone, Sherman Ferguson, Roy McCurdy, John Patitucci, Bob Sheppard, Tom Harrell, and, at various times in the 1990s, Carl Fontana, Joe LaBarbera, George Cables, Pete Christlieb, and Ralph Penland. He also played in the late 1970s with groups led by Art Pepper and Bud Shank, and in 1981 he recorded as a co-leader with Jan Allan; later he became involved occasionally in big-band work on recordings with Frank Mantooth (1987), Gerald Wilson (*c*1994) and Tito Puente (1996). From the late 1970s through the 1990s Shew performed and taught at workshops in the USA, the Far East, Europe, Australia, and New Zealand (where he hosted a jazz television series for at least five years from *c*1978), and he was a regular contributor to *Crescendo International* and *ITG Journal*. Although his tone is soft, it is easily identifiable in a big band, and he has a flawless technique. He performs exceptionally well on his album *Playing with Fire* (1986), engaging in fiery bop "battles" with his fellow trumpeter Tom Harrell on *Prelude and Blues* and other tracks.

SELECTED RECORDINGS

Duos with B. Mays: *Telepathy* (1978, Jazz Hounds 0003)

As leader: *Outstanding in his Field* (1978–9, IC 1077); *Class Reunion* (1980, Sutra 1002); *Play Song* (1981, Jazz Hounds 0002); *Shewhorn* (1982–3, Pausa 7198); *Breakfast Wine* (1983, Pausa 7171); *'Round Midnight* (1984, Mo Pro 111); *Playing with Fire* (1986, MAMA Foundation 1017), incl. Prelude and Blues; *Metropole Orchestra* (1986, 1988, Mons 6458); *Tribute to the Masters* (1995, Double-Time 101); *Heavyweights* (1995, MAMA Foundation 1013)

As sideman: T. Akiyoshi and L. Tabackin: *Kogun* (1974, RCA JPL1-0236); *Tales of a Courtesan* (1975, RCA JPL1-0723); *Insights* (1976, RCA AFL1-2678); L. Bellson: *Dynamite!* (1979, Conc. 105); *London Scene* (1980, Conc. 157)

BIBLIOGRAPHY

L. Tomkins: "Bobby Shew," *CI*, xviii/6 (1980), 16; xix (1981), no.6, p.12; no.8, p.14

"Bobby Shew: my Fantastic Life-style," *CI*, xxi/6 (1983), 22

K. Franckling: "Bobby and his Shewhorn," *JT* (1986), Sept, 15

L. Hollis: "Bobby Shew Interview," *Cadence*, xv/9 (1989), 5

B. Rusch: "The Questionnaire," *Cadence*, xvi/5 (1990), 63

D. Matthews: "Bobby Shew," *CJM*, xxviii/4 (1991), 6

J. LaBarbera: "Shew Horn," *ITG Journal*, xvii/3 (1993), 22

T. S. Jenkins: "Bobby Shew Finally Has his Cake," *Marge Hofacre's Jazz News* (1995), Nov–Dec, 20

J. Kaliss: "Hearsay: Bobby Shew: the Other Shew Drops," *JT*, xxvi/5 (1996), 24

<http://www.bobbyshew.com> (1999)

SCOTT YANOW/BK

Shibuya, Takeshi (*b* Tokyo, 3 Nov 1939). Japanese pianist and leader. He began piano lessons at the age of seven and later studied composition at Tokyo University of Fine Arts and Music. In 1963 he joined George Kawaguchi's Big Four. Later he played in Shungo Sawada's quintet and with the tenor saxophonist Takatoshi Oya, then in 1976 he formed his own trio and big band. From 1978 Shibuya was active as an accompanist to and arranger for singers, among them the jazzy pop singer Maki Asakawa.

SELECTED RECORDINGS

As unaccompanied soloist: *Shibuyan* (1982, Aketa's Disk 13)

As leader: *Dream* (1975, Trio PA7127); *Live 1989 with Takeshi Shibuya Orchestra* (1989, ACT 0001); *Essential Ellington* (1999, Crown 9152); *Shibu ryu* (1999, Titei B14F); *Home Ground Aketa Live* (1999, Aketa's Disk 79); with M. Kikuchi: *Tandem* (1999, Pol. POCJ1475)

As sideman: M. Asakawa: *Yami no naka ni okizari ni shite* (Leave me alone in the dark; 1998, Toshiba–EMI 24004); Shun Sakai: *Beyond Time* (1999, Titei B15F)

KAZUNORI SUGIYAMA

Shields. Family of musicians. The four Shields brothers rank with members of the Brunies and Laine families as among those most influential in the development of the early New Orleans style as it was played by white musicians. The oldest member of the family was the guitarist Pat Shields (*b* New Orleans, *c*1891). From 1904 to 1908 he played in a band led by the violinist Alex "King" Watzke; he also worked at various times with his younger brothers (see 1–3 below).

(1) Larry [Lawrence James] **Shields** (*b* New Orleans, 13 Sept 1893; *d* Los Angeles, 21 Nov 1953). Clarinetist. His middle name is taken from California death records. He took up clarinet at the age of 14 and less than a year later joined Nick LaRocca's first band. In mid-1915 he traveled to Chicago to replace his friend Gus Mueller in Tom Brown's Band from Dixieland, then at the peak of its historic run at Lamb's Café. After touring in vaudeville, the band picked up work in New York. January 1917 found Shields playing with LaRocca, Eddie Edwards, Henry Ragas, and Tony Sbarbaro in what shortly afterwards became the ORIGINAL DIXIELAND JAZZ BAND. Although he was unable to read music, he was widely considered to be the most accomplished member of the band and as influential as the more flamboyant LaRocca. His name shares composer credit on most of the group's instrumental specialties, including *Clarinet Marmalade*, *At the Jazz Band Ball*, and the much-disputed *Livery Stable Blues*. He toured the UK with the group in 1919–20, and remained with it until 1921. By the mid-1920s Shields was living in California, working at such venues as the 400 Club and Tent Café. In the 1930s he worked as a freelance in Los Angeles, Chicago, and New Orleans, and he toured with various reconstituted versions of the Original Dixieland Jazz Band. He finally settled in California and gradually withdrew from professional music.

SELECTED RECORDINGS

(All recorded as a sideman with the Original Dixieland Jazz Band, for Victor unless otherwise indicated)

Livery Stable Blues/Dixie Jass Band One-step (1917, 18255); Skeleton Jangle/Tiger Rag (1918, 18472); Fidgety Feet/Lazy Daddy (1918, 18564); Mournin' Blues/Clarinet Marmalade Blues (1918, 18513); Skeleton Jangle/Tiger Rag (1936, 25524); Clarinet Marmalade/Bluin' the Blues (1936, 25525); Barnyard Blues/Original Dixieland One-step (1936, 25502); Drop a Nickel in the Slot/Jezebel (1938, Bb 7454)

BIBLIOGRAPHY

ChiltonW; *FeatherE*

Obituary, *Record Changer*, xiii (1954), Feb, 4

H. O. Brunn: *The Story of the Original Dixieland Jazz Band* (Baton Rouge, LA, 1960/*R*1977)

A. Rose and E. Souchon: *New Orleans Jazz: a Family Album* (Baton Rouge, LA, 1967, rev. and enlarged 3/1984)

(2) Eddie Shields (*b* New Orleans, ?1896; *d* New Orleans, 1936). Pianist. Like his brothers, he was active in white New Orleans bands from *c*1910 and played long engagements at Toro's Cabaret, leading a band which included at various times Santo Pecora and Leon Roppolo. Afterwards he joined the band of Alcide "Yellow" Nunez, which played at Vernon's Café in Chicago. Nick LaRocca invited Shields to replace Henry Ragas in the Original Dixieland Jazz Band in New York after the latter's death in 1919, but the association did not work out and Shields returned permanently to New Orleans.

(3) Harry (P.) Shields (*b* New Orleans, 30 June 1899; *d* New Orleans, 18 Jan 1971). Clarinetist and baritone saxophonist. He spent most of his life in New Orleans, where he worked with the trumpeter Johnny Bayersdorffer and made his first recordings (*Peculiar/Dirty Rag*, OK 40337) with the pianist Norman Brownlee in 1925. Later he worked with Johnny Wiggs (1950) and the Dukes of Dixieland (1952); he was also active as a recording musician, participating in sessions with Papa Jack Laine (1951), Monk Hazel and Tom Brown (both 1954), Al Hirt (1955), and Emile Christian and Armand Hug (both 1958). The drummer and scholar John Joyce, who worked with Shields in the 1960s, was deeply impressed by his drive and intensity.

Oral history material in *LNT*.

BIBLIOGRAPHY

FeatherE

A. Rose and E. Souchon: *New Orleans Jazz: a Family Album* (Baton Rouge, LA, 1967, rev. and enlarged 3/1984)

A. Rose: "Wolf in Sheep's Clothing," *SL*, xviii (1967), Jan–Feb, 13

RICHARD M. SUDHALTER

Shihab, Sahib [Gregory, Edmund] (*b* Savannah, GA, 23 June 1925; *d* Tennessee, 24 Oct 1989). Alto and baritone saxophonist, and flutist. He studied with Elmer Snowden (1935–9), and first worked professionally in a band led by the pianist Luther Henderson (1938). After attending Boston Conservatory (1941–2) he was the lead alto saxophonist in Fletcher Henderson's band (April 1944 – spring 1946), and while in Los Angeles with Henderson recorded in small groups led by Jay McShann (August 1945). During an engagement in Chicago he left Henderson to work with Roy Eldridge, with whom he toured and recorded. In autumn 1946 he joined Ray Perry in Boston; he then became a Muslim and adopted the name Shihab, but continued to appear as Edmund Gregory on some recordings into the early 1950s.

From late 1947, when he recorded with Thelonious Monk and Art Blakey, Shihab worked with some of the most prominent modern jazz bandleaders. After a period in Buddy Johnson's orchestra (late 1947 – early 1948) he held day jobs outside of music while working occasionally with Monk (at Minton's, May 1948, and the Three Deuces, October 1948) and performing and recording regularly with Tadd Dameron (January–April 1949) and Lucky Thompson (May 1949 into 1950). He recorded with Monk again (1951), joined Illinois

Jacquet (1952), and was a member of Dizzy Gillespie's quintet (May 1953–1954). In October 1954 he rejoined Jacquet in the Jazz Parade show for a tour of Europe, in the course of which he recorded with Roy Haynes in Stockholm. Following his return to the USA he recorded with Gillespie's big band (1955–6), appeared with the quintet in the short film *Date with Dizzy* (1956), and at some point performed with Howard McGhee in Philadelphia (with whom he recorded in New York in 1955). In 1957 he recorded with John Coltrane and with Oscar Pettiford's big band, and the following year he worked in the double bass player's quintet, appeared with Dinah Washington at the Newport Jazz Festival, and recorded with Cat Anderson's big band.

In 1959 Shihab traveled to Europe with Quincy Jones in Harold Arlen's show *Free and Easy*. Apart from an extended stay in Los Angeles (1973–6) he remained in Europe into the mid-1980s, and in 1963 settled in Copenhagen. He worked with the Clarke–Boland Big Band (1961–72), Radiojazzgruppen (i), Ernie Wilkins's Almost Big Band, and other ensembles, and was also active as a soloist; in the mid-1960s he performed and recorded with Clarke and Boland's small groups and appeared with Clarke at the Blue Note in Paris. In 1965 he composed the score for a jazz ballet based on the folk tale *The Red Shoes* by Hans Christian Andersen. He may be seen with Don Cherry, George Gruntz, Henri Texier, and Daniel Humair in the German film documentary *Noon in Tunisia* (1970). In the late 1970s he was co-owner and co-producer with Kenny Drew of a publishing company and a short-lived record label, Matrix. In 1981 he recorded with Art Farmer. He returned to the USA in 1986, recorded as a soloist with Charlie Rouse in 1988, and shortly before his death visited Paris as a member of Jay McShann's Kansas City Band (June 1989).

Shihab was one of the first bop musicians to make use of the flute, but his playing on baritone saxophone, which combines a delicate tone with an inventive flow of ideas, is held by many to be his best work.

SELECTED RECORDINGS

As leader: *Jazz-Sahib* (1957, Savoy 12124); *Conversations* (1963, Debut 141), incl. Billy Boy; *Sentiments* (1971, Sto. 1008); with J. Steig, J. Moody, and C. Hinze: *Flute Summit* (1973, Atl. 50027)

As sideman: T. Monk: In walked Bud (1947, BN 548); 'Round about Midnight (1947, BN 543); Monk's Mood/Who Knows? (1947, BN 1565); Four in One/Straight no Chaser (1951, BN 1589); Ask me now (1951, BN 1591); J. Coltrane: *Coltrane* (1957, Prst. 7105); E. Wilkins: *Montreux* (1983, Ste. 1190); C. Rouse: *Soul Mates, featuring Sahib Shihab* (1988, Upt. 27.34)

BIBLIOGRAPHY

J. Lind: "Sahib Shihab's Expatriate Life," *DB*, xxx/7 (1963), 17

F. Postif: "Sahib Shihab," *Jh*, no.259 (1970), 22; repr. in *Jazz Me Blues: interviews et portraits de musiciens de jazz et de blues* (Paris, 1998), 269

R. Baggenaes: "Sahib Shihab," *Coda*, no.204 (1985), 6

D. Salemann, D. Hartmann, and M. Vogler: *Edmund Gregory, Sahib Shihab: Solography, Discography, Band Routes, Engagements, in Chronological Order* (Basel, Switzerland, 1986)

J. Chilton: *The Song of the Hawk: the Life and Recordings of Coleman Hawkins* (London and New York, 1990)

M. Hennessey: *Klook: the Story of Kenny Clarke* (London, 1990)

Obituary, M. Gardner, *JJI*, xliii/8 (1990), 21

ROLAND BAGGENAES/BK

Shih Shih Wu Ai. Record company and label founded around 1972 by MILO FINE.

Shiina, Yutaka (*b* Tokyo, 23 Sept 1964). Japanese pianist and leader. He took piano lessons from the age of three, and later, while studying composition in Tokyo at the Kunitachi College of Music (from 1982), he played jazz piano professionally. In 1989 he toured Japan as a member of Lionel Hampton's orchestra and Vincent Herring's quartet, and in 1990 he was a member, with Masahiko Osaka, of Roy Hargrove's quartet. This led to the formation the following year of the acclaimed quintet Jazz Networks (with the addition of Antonio Hart); from 1992 Shiina served as a leader of the group. He led his own trio from 1994, which consisted of Osaka and Reginald Veal for his first album as a leader and an ensuing tour of Japan. His next two recordings (1995, 1996) were with Veal and Herlin Riley as sidemen (Nicholas Payton was guest soloist on the latter), and the following album (1998) was made with Christian McBride and Clarence Penn. In 1996 Shiina toured and recorded with Dusko Goykovich (Japan) and toured with Elvin Jones's Jazz Machine (Europe). He has also worked in the quartets of Joh Yamada, Nao Takeuchi, and the saxophonist Tim Armacost, as well as in other groups, and frequently toured Europe and the USA.

SELECTED RECORDINGS

(all recorded for Novus J)

As leader: *Movin' Forces* (1994, 617); *Hittin' the Spirit* (1995, 630); *At the Moment* (1996, 639); *United* (1998, 31005)

As sideman with Jazz Networks: *Straight to the Standards* (1991, 117); *Beauty and the Beast* (1992, 601); *Blues 'n Ballads* (1993, 616); *In the Movies* (1995, 37056)

KAZUNORI SUGIYAMA

Shilkloper, Arkady (Fimovich) (*b* Moscow, 17 Oct 1956). Russian french horn player. He took up french horn while studying at the Moscow Military Music School and in 1981 graduated from the Gnesin Institute. As a student in 1978 he began to work in the Bolshoy Theater Orchestra, where he remained until 1985 as a member of the Bolshoy Brass Quintet; he then joined the Moscow Philharmonic Orchestra and played with the Moscow Horn Quintet (1985–9). In parallel with his studies at the Gnesin Institute he attended the Moscow Experimental Studio of Musical Improvisation (1976–8). His first serious jazz experience was in a duo with the double bass player Mikhail Karetnikov (1984–6), during which time he performed with the group Tri O (or Three O) (1985–9). From 1988 he played in a duo with Mikhail Alperin, and in 1991 the two men formed the Moscow Art Trio with an enthusiast of Russian traditional folklore – the singer, clarinetist, and ethnic multi-instrumentalist Sergey Starostin; this trio has toured extensively. In 1992 Shilkloper began to give concerts as an unaccompanied soloist, and in 1995 he joined the international group Pago Libre, which included John Wolf Brennan. In Russia he regularly played in a trio with Starostin and the double bass player Vladimir Volkov, in another trio led by Volkov, and with his own Acoustic Quartet, among others. He appeared at festivals in the USA, Germany, Austria, the UK, and Israel, and often in the 1990s at such events in Russia. In addition to french horn, Shilkloper plays flugelhorn, alphorn, and hunting horn.

SELECTED RECORDINGS

Duos with M. Alperin: *Wave of Sorrow* (1989, ECM 1396); *Live in Grenoble* (1993, RDM 305015)

As leader: of Acoustic Quartet: *Brass Complot* (1996, Ermatell 020); *Hornology* (1996, RDM 606144); *Live in Norway* (1998, Boheme 809007)

As sideman: Tri O: *Three O* (1989, Solyd 0031); Moscow Art Trio: *Prayer* (1991, JARO 4193); Octet Ost: *Octet Ost*, ii (1994, Amadeo 521 823); Pago

Libre: *Pago Libre* (1995, L+R 45015); M. Alperin: *North Story* (1995, ECM 1596)

SERGEY BELICHENKO

Shim, Mark (*b* Kingston, Jamaica, 21 Nov 1973). Tenor saxophonist. He lived in Canada until he was five, after which his family moved to the USA and eventually settled in Richmond, Virginia. He began playing alto saxophone around the age of 12 and took up the tenor instrument when he was about 16. Later he studied jazz at Virginia Commonwealth University (1991–3) and William Paterson College, Wayne, New Jersey (1993–4). In 1995 Shim recorded alongside Hamiet Bluiett and became a member of the Mingus Big Band. Around the same time he began working with David Murray's big band and Betty Carter, with whom he recorded (1996) and toured Europe; he also participated in Carter's Jazz Ahead education program. He made his first recording as a leader, *Mind over Matter* (BN 37628-2), in 1997. He recorded again in 1999 (*Turbulent Flow*, BN 23392-2) and from that year also toured and recorded as a member of New Directions, a band sponsored by Blue Note.

BIBLIOGRAPHY

B. Primack: Liner notes, *Mind over Matter* (BN 37628-2, 1998)
G. Robinson: "Mark Shim," *JT*, xxviii/3 (1998), 23

GK

Shimizu, Jun (*b* Kobe, Japan, 27 Feb 1928). Japanese drummer. He attended Kansei Gakuin University in Osaka until shortly after World War II. Having learned to play drums at American military bases in 1945 he began working professionally as a drummer and moved to Tokyo in 1946. There he played with the Red Hot Boys, the Gramercy Five, and the CB Nine, one of the first bop groups in Japan, and during the early 1950s he joined Toshiko Akiyoshi's Cozy Quartet and Shotaro Moriyasu's group. After a period of relative inactivity in the 1960s he led trios and quartets in the 1970s and performed with trios led by the pianist Yuzuru Sera and Norio Maeda, as well as with other groups. Shimizu is highly regarded in Japan for his sensitive, energetic, and melodic style of playing.

SELECTED RECORDINGS

As leader with Sampei Ohno: *Swing on Birdland*, ii (1977, Canyon 2005)
As sideman: S. Moriyasu: *The Historic Mocambo Session '54* (1954, Pol. 2490–91); Y. Sera: *Yuzuru Sera Live at Birdland* (1975, Vic. [Jap.] 859)

YOZO IWANAMI/KAZUNORI SUGIYAMA

Shipp, Matthew (*b* Wilmington, DE, 7 Dec 1960). Pianist and composer. He is primarily self-taught, but had some lessons from the organist at his church and received further tuition briefly as a teenager; he also played bass clarinet at high school. After a short period at the University of Delaware he attended the New England Conservatory (*c*1983–4), where he studied with Ran Blake. In 1984 he moved to New York and founded the group Convection, with William Parker, Abdul Wadud, the cellist Akua Dixon Turre, Dennis Charles, and Steve McCall among his sidemen. This marked the beginning of a long association with Parker: the pair recorded in a duo around 1994 and toured the USA in 1997, playing in a variety of venues not normally associated with jazz, and the following year they appeared at the Monterey Jazz Festival. Shipp formed a similar relationship with Rob Brown, with whom he recorded in a duo in 1987–8 and 1996. In addition he has collaborated with Roscoe Mitchell, touring the USA, touring and recording with Mitchell's group the Note Factory (1992), and recording in a duo (*c*1995). In 1990 he began working regularly in David S. Ware's quartet. From the late 1980s he has led his own trio with Parker and Whit Dickey, who was replaced in the mid-1990s by Susie Ibarra. Later he began leading a quartet with Mat Maneri, Parker, and Ibarra, and the "String" Trio, with Maneri and Parker (both mid-1990s). Shipp also recorded in groups led by Marc Edwards (1990) and Joe Morris (ii) and Ivo Perelman (both 1996), and in duos with Perelman (1996) and Morris (1997).

SELECTED RECORDINGS

As unaccompanied soloist: *Before the World* (1995, FMP CD81); *Symbol Systems* (1995, No More 01)
Duos: with R. Brown: *Sonic Explorations* (1987–8, Cadence Jazz 1037); with W. Parker: *Zo* (*c*1994, Rise 126-2); with R. Mitchell: *2-Z* (*c*1995, 2.13.61 Records 21312-2); with I. Perelman: *Bendito of Santa Cruz* (1996, Cadence Jazz 1076); with R. Brown: *Blink of an Eye* (1996, No More 3); with J. Morris: *Thesis* (1997, Hatology 506)
As leader: *Points* (1990, Silkheart 129); *Circular Temple* (1990, Quinton 1); *Prism* (1993, Brinkman 058/ROV-009-2); *Critical Mass* (1994, 2.13.61 Records 003); *By Law of Music* (1996, HA 6200); *Flow of X* (1996, 2.13.61 Records 23126-2); *The Multiplication Table* (1997, Hatology 516); *Strata* (1997, Hatology 522)
As sideman with D. S. Ware: *Great Bliss*, i–ii (1990, Silkheart 127, 128); *Flight of I* (1991, DIW 856); *Cryptology* (1994, Homestead 220-2); *Wisdom of Uncertainty* (1996, AUM Fidelity 001); *Go See the World* (1997, Col. CK69138)
As sideman with others: M. Edwards: *Black Queen* (1990, Alpha Phonics 1); R. Mitchell: *This Dance is for Steve McCall* (1992, BS 120150-2); J. Morris: *Elsewhere* (1996, Homestead 233-2); I. Perelman: *Cama de terra* (1996, Homestead 237-2)

BIBLIOGRAPHY

A. M. Griepenburg: "New Faces," *Ear*, xiv/1 (1989), 66
B. Rusch: "The Questionnaire," *Cadence*, xv/7 (1989), 33
R. Hicks: "Riffs: Matthew Shipp," *DB*, lix/10 (1992), 13
——: "Matthew Shipp," *Jazziz*, xii/5 (1995), 74
E. Brunet: "Shipp: piano, boxe et mysticisme," *Jm*, no.471 (1997), 23
S. Dollar: "The Gospel According to Matthew," *Jazziz*, xiv/10 (1997), 49 [incl. discography]
W. Jenkins: "Hearsay: Matthew Shipp," *JT*, xxvii/1 (1997), 28
S. Taylor: "The Non-verbal Act: Matthew Shipp," *Coda*, no.274 (1997), 14 [incl. discography]
T. Lépin: "Matthew Shipp: piano choc," *Jazzman*, no.42 (1998), 27
L. Nai: "Matthew Shipp: Interview," *Cadence*, xxiv/12 (1998), 14
A. Schatz: "A Jazz Pianist Stands Tall in the Rock Underground," *New York Times* (25 Jan 1998)
B. Shoemaker: "Matthew Shipp," *JT*, xxix/1 (1999), 32
R. Lopez: "The Matthew Shipp Sessionography," <http://www.velocity.net/~bb10k/SHIPP.disc.html> (2000)

GK

Shirley, Jimmy [James Arthur] (*b* Union, SC, 31 May 1913; *d* New York, 3 Dec 1989). Guitarist. His father was a musician who worked in Cleveland. Shirley first played with bands in Cincinnati (1934–6). After leading his own quartet in Cleveland he was a member of Clarence Profit's trio in New York (1937–41), then spent two years as an accompanist to Ella Fitzgerald. In 1944 he joined Herman "Ivory" Chittison's trio, with which he played intermittently for ten years. During this period he recorded for Blue Note as a sideman with Edmond Hall (1943), James P. Johnson, Art Hodes, and Sidney De Paris (all 1944), and John Hardee (1946), and for other labels with Coleman Hawkins (1943), and Sid Catlett, Billie Holiday, and Ram Ramirez (all 1946); he also led his own group for residencies at the Onyx Club (1946) and elsewhere in New York. In the 1960s he played electric bass guitar with George James (1963) and Buddy Tate (1967). Later, in 1975, he recorded in Paris as a leader and with Slam Stewart, Johnny Guarnieri, and Stephane Grappelli.

Shirley used a tremolo arm on his guitar during the 1940s which gave his playing a characteristic Hawaiian sound.

Inspired by the work of Al Casey and Teddy Bunn, he articulated his sober, blues-tinged lines with the hard, percussive attack commonly used by players who have made the transition from the acoustic to the electric instrument.

SELECTED RECORDINGS

Duo with Oscar Smith: first issued on *Blue Note 40 Years of Jazz* (1939–45, BN F667/786–9), Stardust (1945)

As leader: Jimmy's Blues (1945, BN 530); *China Boy* (1975, BB 33081)

As sideman: Wingy Carpenter: Rhythm of the Dishes and Pans/Team Up (1940, Decca 7711); Creole George Guesnon: Iberville and Franklin/Goodbye, Good Luck to You (1940, Decca 7740); C. Profit: Times Square Blues/Hot and Bothered (1940, Decca 8503); Edmond Hall: Night Shift Blues (1943, BN 29); H. Chittison: The Song is Ended/How High the Moon (1944, Musi. 315); S. De Paris: Who's Sorry Now (1944, BN 41); J. Hardee: River Edge Rock (1946, BN 521); E. Bostic: That's the groovy thing (1946, Gotham 104); S. Catlett: Organ Boogie/Shirley's Boogie (1946, Manor 8026); Organ Blues (1946, Manor 8025); W. Harris: A Love Untrue (1950, King 4445); S. Grappelli: *Steff and Slam* (1975, BB 33076)

BIBLIOGRAPHY

ChiltonW; *FeatherE*

H. Panassié and M. Gautier: *Dictionnaire du jazz* (Paris, 1954, rev. and enlarged 3/1980; Eng. trans., London, 1956, rev. A. A. Gurwitch as *Guide to Jazz*, Boston, 1956)

J. Simmen: "Jimmy Shirley," *BHcF*, no.383 (1990), 1

NORMAN MONGAN/HOWARD RYE

Shoemake, Charlie [Charles Edward] (*b* Houston, 27 July 1937). Vibraphonist and bandleader. He took up piano at the age of six and vibraphone during his last year of high school. After studying piano for a year at Southern Methodist University in Dallas he moved in summer 1956 to Los Angeles, and from 1959 to 1963 he played with, among others, Charles Lloyd, Art Pepper, and Howard Rumsey's Lighthouse All Stars; during the same period he took up a career as a studio musician and began working with his wife, the singer Sandi Shoemake, whom he had married in 1959. In the mid-1960s he recorded on vibraphone and other mallet instruments with Lalo Schifrin, Quincy Jones, Nelson Riddle, and Johnny Mandel. Shoemake was a member of George Shearing's quintet from late 1966 through 1972, and as such he recorded, toured the USA, and performed at jazz festivals. He then opened a school for jazz improvisation in Los Angeles (his best-known student is Ted Nash (ii)) and played at clubs in a ensemble co-led by Pete Christlieb (performing regularly at Donte's in the mid- to late 1970s) as well as with his own groups; among his sidemen were Tom Harrell, Hank Jones, Paul Motian, and Larance Marable. Shoemake made a number of recordings as a leader: with Christlieb he co-led a quintet session in New York with Kenny Barron, Mark Helias, and Ben Riley as the rhythm section (*Sunstroke*, 1978, Muse 5193) and with Harold Land he was co-leader of another quintet (*Stand-up Guys*, 1988, Chase Music Group 8016); he also made big-band recordings that featured arrangements by Bill Holman. In spring 1990 Shoemake closed his teaching studio and moved north to Cambria, California, and from November the following year he and his wife performed with major jazz artists at the Hamlet, a restaurant on the coast of central California. He has published transcriptions of jazz solos and contributed to *Brass Bulletin*.

BIBLIOGRAPHY

Feather–Gitler '70s

T. Stevens: "Can Jazz Performance be Taught? A Profile of Charlie Shoemake," *Brass Bulletin*, no.57 (1987), 13

Z. Stewart: "Jazz Notes: Charlie Shoemake Brings Education Home; Band Leader Bill Holman up for Grammy," *Los Angeles Times* (18 Jan 1989)

L. Feather: "A Turning Point in Careers of Charlie, Sandi Shoemake," *Los Angeles Times* (10 Jan 1990)

F. Nemko: "Charlie Shoemake: Out of the Rat Race," *California Jazz Now* (1993), Aug, 9; Sept [page number unknown]

<http://www.thegrid.net/shoemake/> (2000) [incl. discography]

BK

Shoffner, Bob [Robert Lee] (*b* Bessie, TN, 30 April 1900; *d* Chicago, 5 March 1983). Trumpeter. The first edition of this dictionary gave his birthdate as 4 April (from Erskine's published survey and interview), but Shoffner gave 30 April in his oral history interview (at *LNT*), and this date is confirmed in social security records and in Chilton's *Who's Who of Jazz*. He was brought up in St. Louis, where he began in a drum and bugle corps at the age of nine as a drummer and then took up bugle. Later he performed on trumpet in dance bands and played ragtime piano. After graduating from high school in 1916 he worked as a laborer. During his army service (1917–19) he entertained troops as a ragtime pianist and played trumpet in an army band. Shoffner first performed in a jazz band and began to improvise when he joined Charlie Creath (1919), and he worked both with Creath and with Fate Marable's band on Mississippi riverboats. Having moved to Chicago in 1921 he performed with Freddie Keppard, and in 1924 he became a member of Honore Dutrey's band. He twice worked for King Oliver as second trumpeter, on the first occasion replacing Louis Armstrong (June–August 1924) and on the second Tommy Ladnier (May 1925 – February 1927); in the interim he was a member of Dave Peyton's orchestra. He is perhaps best known as Ladnier's successor in Lovie Austin's Blues Serenaders, in which he recorded regularly for the Paramount label with Austin and Jimmy O'Bryant (1925–6). Shoffner also recorded as a soloist with a septet led by Luis Russell (1926). Thereafter he played with Charlie Elgar (1928), Erskine Tate and McKinney's Cotton Pickers (both 1931–2), and Frankie "Half Pint" Jaxon (1932–3) and was active as a freelance in New York and Chicago. In 1940 he left full-time music, but later he resumed playing and joined Franz Jackson's traditional band, with which he recorded from 1957 to 1965.

Oral history material in *LNT*.

SELECTED RECORDINGS

As sideman: J. O'Bryant: Everybody Pile/Charleston Fever (1925, Para. 12312); I. Cox: How can I miss you when I've got dead aim/I ain't got nobody (1925, Para. 12334); L. Russell: Plantation Joys/Please don't turn me down (1926, OK 8424); F. Jackson: *A Night at the Red Arrow* (1961, Pinnacle 104)

BIBLIOGRAPHY

ChiltonW

G. E. Beall: "Forgotten Giants: Bob Shoffner," *Jazz Information*, ii/11 (1940), 15

G. M. Erskine: "Ever-fresh Bob Shoffner," *DB*, xxix/2 (1962), 18

C.-U. Durr: "Bob Shoffner (in the 1920s)," *Record Research*, no.64 (1964), 3 [incl. discography]

C. Hillman: "Paramount Serenaders, 1923-1926," *Sv* (1976), no.67, p.8; no.68, p.52; (1977), no.69, p.91; no.70, p.149; no.72, p.227; no.73, p.29; no.74, p.67; (1978), no.75, p.84 [incl. discography]

L. Wright and others: *Walter C. Allen & Brian A. L. Rust's "King" Oliver* (Chigwell, England, 1987)

BK

Shook, Travis (*b* Oroville, CA, 1969). Pianist. He attended Indiana University before transferring to William Paterson College (Wayne, New Jersey), where he studied with Harold Mabern and Rufus Reid. Following graduation he moved to Seattle. In 1991 he participated in the Great American Jazz Piano Competition at the Jacksonville Jazz Festival; his victory there led to his signing a contract with Columbia records, and around 1992 he made his début, recording as the leader of a quartet consisting of Bunky Green, Ira Coleman, and Tony Williams. In 1994 he worked in a small group led by the trumpeter and saxophonist Jay Thomas, on whose recording *Rapture* (1994, Jazz Focus 013) he is heard to excellent effect. Later he toured and recorded with Sonny Simmons (1995) and performed in Europe and the USA with Betty Carter (1996).

BIBLIOGRAPHY

D. Macdonald: "Road to Stardom? – Shook Wins Piano Competition," *DB*, xlix/2 (1992), 11

B. Milkowski: "Hearsay: the Book on Travis Shook," *JT*, xxiii/7 (1993), 12

A. Pryor: Liner notes, *Travis Shook* (Col. CK53138, 1993)

P. Watrous: "Pop and Jazz in Review," *New York Times* (27 May 1993)

GK

Short, Bob [Robert Russell] (*b* Kirksville, MO, 26 Aug 1911 or 1913; *d* Shellville, CA, 4 April 1976). Tuba player. Feather gives an earlier year of birth (1911) than Short himself in his social security application (1913); the latter provides his middle name. He took up cornet at the age of eight and tuba while at high school and was playing professionally by 1928. Short worked in Los Angeles and Las Vegas and gradually began doubling on valve trombone, baritone horn, violin, piano, double bass, drums, and banjo. Following an association with Jack Teagarden (1945) he performed and recorded in Portland, Oregon, with the Rose City Stompers and with the Castle Jazz Band (1947 – early 1952), in which he initially played cornet and valve trombone and then tuba. While a member of the Castle Jazz Band he traveled to San Francisco and collaborated with Turk Murphy's dixieland ensemble (1951–4), occasionally performing on cornet; in 1953 he played that instrument and then overdubbed the tuba parts on two of Murphy's albums (among them *The Music of Jelly Roll Morton*, Col. CL559), and the following year he played tuba on Murphy's recording *Dancing Jazz* (Col. CL650). Later he worked with Bob Scobey (*c*1956–8) and the Great Pacific Jazz Band (*c* early 1960s) and led a group in San Francisco (1958). In the years 1956–61 and 1963–4 he returned to Murphy's band several times and performed mainly on tuba and double bass, although for a series of concert recordings which Murphy made at Easy Street in 1958 he performed exclusively as a cornetist. He made further recordings with the Castle Jazz Band (1957, 1959) and later took part in sessions led by Clancy Hayes (1963) and Lu Watters (1964). Short maintained a second career as a flight instructor and stunt pilot. Although he concentrated on these activities in the last decade of his life, he continued to play in dixieland bands, and in April 1970 he deputized in the Firehouse Five Plus Two. He died in a crash when an experimental plane lost its wing.

BIBLIOGRAPHY

FeatherE

J. Goggin: *Turk Murphy: Just for the Record* (San Leandro, CA, 1982), 56

H. Smith: "A Hero in Two Different Worlds," *MR*, xx/9 (1993), 1 [incl. discography]

BK

Shorter, Alan (*b* Newark, NJ, 29 May 1932; *d* Los Angeles, 5 April 1988). Flugelhorn player, brother of Wayne Shorter. His birth and death dates appear in the California death index. He initially played tenor saxophone, during which time he co-led a small group with his brother Wayne, and took up flugelhorn after lending his saxophone to someone who never returned it. On occasion he also played trumpet. At Howard University (1952–4) he was a classmate of Leroi Jones (later known as Amiri Baraka). Having moved to New York in the early 1960s he worked alongside Carla Bley and Pharoah Sanders in Charles Moffett's group, as well as with Archie Shepp (with whom he recorded in 1964), his brother Wayne (recording in 1965), and Marion Brown (recording in 1965–6). He performed in Sunny Murray's Acoustical Swing Quartet in San Francisco in August 1967 and recorded as a sole leader late in 1968. In mid-1969 or mid-1970 (sources vary) Shorter moved to Paris, where he worked regularly with Shepp, performed and recorded (*c*1970) as a leader, recorded with groups led by Alan Silva (1970) and François Tusques (recording in 1971), and published an article in *Jazz magazine* ("Vivre la new music," no.219 (1974), 10). Nothing is known of his subsequent career, although he is believed to have returned to the USA soon afterwards.

SELECTED RECORDINGS

As leader: *Orgasm* (1968, Verve 68768); *Tes-esat* (*c*1970, Amer. 6118)

As sideman: A. Shepp: *Four for Trane* (1964, Imp. 71); W. Shorter: on *The All Seeing Eye* (1965, BN 84219), Mephistopheles; M. Brown: *Marion Brown Quartet* (1965, ESP 1022); *Juba-Lee* (1966, Fon. 881012); A. Shepp: *Coral Rock* (1970, Amer. 6103)

BIBLIOGRAPHY

GrayF

D. Berger and A. Corneau: "Allan [*sic*] Shorter et le monstre magnétigue," *Jh*, no.232 (1967), 24

R. Williams: "Everybody is a Leader," *MM* (1 May 1971), 18

P. Carles, A. Clergeat, J.-L. Comolli: *Dictionnaire du jazz* (Paris, 1988, rev. and enlarged 2/1994)

H. Schreiber and T. Klatt: Liner notes, *Marion Brown Quartet* (ESP 1022-2, *c*1992)

GK

Shorter, Wayne (*b* Newark, NJ, 25 Aug 1933). Tenor and soprano saxophonist and composer. He began playing clarinet at the age of 16, then changed to tenor saxophone. From 1952 he studied music at New York University (BS 1956) and played in a local band, then in 1956 he performed briefly with Horace Silver before being drafted and serving in army bands based in New Jersey. Following his discharge in October 1958 he joined Maynard Ferguson's group, in which he first met Joe Zawinul. From 1959 to 1963 Shorter enjoyed an important association with Art Blakey's Jazz Messengers, ultimately serving as the band's music director when Lee Morgan left in 1961. After a brief period of rest and work on his own recordings he joined Miles Davis's quintet in September 1964. He remained with the group until 1970, taking up soprano saxophone in late 1968 as Davis experimented with electronic instruments and new ensembles, though during the same period he recorded regularly as a leader. Late in 1970, with Zawinul, he founded Weather Report (for illustration *see* Zawinul, Joe). Shorter also recorded a Latin-jazz album presenting Milton Nascimento (1974), which received some acclaim, and toured and recorded with Herbie Hancock's group V.S.O.P. (1976–7; *see* V.S.O.P. (i)). From the mid-1970s he devoted his time equally to playing tenor and soprano saxophones. In 1985 Shorter left Weather Report and concentrated instead on recording, making international tours with his new group and appearing in reunion concerts with many of his colleagues from the 1960s. In 1988, with Carlos Santana, he led a Latin jazz-rock group which toured internationally.

Shorter has appeared in numerous small-group reunion bands with Hancock (among them one in a tribute to Davis, early 1990s), and from 1997 the two men have toured internationally in a duo (including performances in the USA

Wayne Shorter playing at the Newport Jazz Saratoga Festival, 1987

and Argentina in 2000). In 1990 Shorter led a group consisting of Mitchel Forman, Alphonso Johnson, Terri Lyne Carrington, and Mino Cinélu, and in the mid-1990s he formed a sextet with Rachel Z, Adam Holzman, David Gilmore, the drummer Will Calhoun, and Cinélu. He was given an honorary doctorate by the Berklee College of Music in 1999, and the following year he performed with Joshua Redman and others in concert in San Francisco in a celebration of "The Music of Wayne Shorter."

In the early 1960s Shorter's tone and his ideas on tenor saxophone strongly resembled those of John Coltrane, with whom he had practiced after leaving the army. As his personal style emerged he developed varied approaches on the tenor and soprano instruments that had in common a certain terseness. Typically he plays subdued bop runs or Coltrane-like flourishes, liberally interspersed with periods of silence and sometimes with fragments of thematic material, especially as signposts in unconventional compositions. From soul music he adopted a funky style (the simplicity of which suits his sense of economy), combining a biting attack and bluesy, syncopated dance phrases with an often esoteric selection of pitches. On the soprano saxophone he produces a remarkably beautiful tone.

A few of the compositions that Shorter contributed to the Jazz Messengers are fairly straightforward tunes in the hard-bop style; the bouncy and attractive piece *One by One* (1963), for example, suggests in both title and substance that it might be heard as a creative tribute to *Blue March*, which Benny Golson had written for the Messengers a few years earlier. But, as several of his other compositions for Blakey demonstrate (notably *Joelle*, recorded in 1961, *This is for Albert*, 1962, and *On the Ginza* and *Ping-pong*, 1963), at this time Shorter was already trying out patterns of slippery harmonic relationships, although he had not quite yet found his way towards marrying these experiments with strikingly memorable and tuneful melodies. However, from 1964, when he began recording under his own name, until late in the 1960s he developed a large body of highly original and influential new compositions which are especially important for this creative union of great tunes with abstract harmony (or, by extension, with an absence of identifiable harmony).

One type of composition is represented by such pieces as *Speak No Evil* and *Witch Hunt* (both 1964). Their themes are related to conventional forms (respectively, *aaba* song form and the blues) and are firmly grounded in hard bop, involving characteristically tuneful thematic melodies, walking bass lines, swinging drum patterns, and a structure in which solos are interspersed among statements of the theme; but in these pieces Shorter's new chord progressions were pioneering in the application, to jazz, of particular aspects of extended tonality, as he constructed multiple layers of intertwining strong and weakly functional relationships. Another type of composition is illustrated by *E.S.P.* (1965) (historically significant as the title track of the album that marked Davis's turn towards a new repertory) and by *Pinocchio* (1967). Here Shorter's point of departure is again the hard-bop tradition, but his jittery melodies are set to successions of non-functional and dense harmonies that at times are grouped in asymmetrical phrases; improvisations are virtually pantonal. (For detailed analysis of Shorter's use of extended tonality and other advanced harmonic devices in pieces such as these *see* HARMONY (i), tables 2–3, ex.18 and 28, and §2.) Yet another type, which provided the inspiration for Weather Report, is represented by *Nefertiti* (1967) and *Sanctuary* (1969). Here the "accompanists" improvise while the "soloists" reiterate strange, slow-moving melodies. Later (and of less significance), much of Shorter's writing for Weather Report was based on simple dance ostinatos and lyrical melodies; the rapidly changing textures of his *Surucucú* (on the group's album *I Sing the Body Electric*, 1971–2, Col. KC31352), on the other hand, probably resulted from Weather Report's collective improvisation rather than from the composer's design.

Transcriptions of some of Shorter's solos and compositions have been published in *A New Approach to Jazz Improvisation*, xxxiii: *Jazz Classics: Wayne Shorter*, ed. J. Aebersold (New Albany, IA, 1985), and *Wayne Shorter: Saxophone Collection: Artist Transcription Saxophone* (transcr. S. Marten, Milwaukee, 1990).

SELECTED RECORDINGS

* – composed by Shorter

DUOS

With H. Hancock: *1 + 1* (*c*1996, Verve 314-527564-2)

AS LEADER

Night Dreamer (1964, BN 84173), incl. *Armageddon, *Black Nile, *Night Dreamer, *Virgo; *Juju* (1964, BN 84182), incl. *Deluge, *House of Jade, *Juju, *Mahjong, *Yes or No; *Speak No Evil* (1964, BN 84194), incl. *Fee-fi-fo-fum, *Infant Eyes, *Speak No Evil, *Wild Flower, *Witch Hunt; *The Soothsayer* (1965, BN LT988), incl. *Lady Day, *Lost, *The Soothsayer; *The All Seeing Eye* (1965, BN 84219), incl. *The All Seeing Eye, *Chaos, *Face of the Deep, *Genesis; *Adam's Apple* (1966, BN 84232), incl. *Adam's Apple, *El gaucho, *502 Blues, *Footprints

Schizophrenia (1967, BN 84297), incl. *Go, *Miyako, *Schizophrenia, *Tom Thumb; *Super Nova* (1969, BN 84332), incl. *Water Babies; *Odyssey of Iska* (1970, BN 84363), incl. *De pois do amor, o vazio; *Moto grosso feio* (*c*1971, BN LA014G); *Native Dancer* (1974, Col. PC33418), incl. *Ana Maria, *Beauty and the Beast; *Atlantis* (1985, Col. FC40055);

with D. Liebman: *Tribute to John Coltrane: Live under the Sky* (1987, Col. CK45136)

AS SIDEMAN

With A. Blakey: *The Big Beat* (1960, BN 84029), incl. *Lester left town; *Meet You at the Jazz Corner of the World* (1960, BN 84054-5); *The Witch Doctor* (1961, BN 84256), incl. *Joelle; *The Freedom Rider* (1961, BN 84156); *Caravan* (1962, Riv. 9438), incl. *This is for Albert; *Ugetsu* (1963, Riv. 9464), incl. *One by One, *On the Ginza, *Ping-pong; *Free for All* (1964, BN 84170)

With M. Davis: *E.S.P.* (1965, Col. CS9150), incl. *E.S.P., *Iris; *Live at the Plugged Nickel* (1965, CBS Sony 25AP291); *Miles Smiles* (1966, Col. CS9401), incl. *Dolores, *Footprints; *Sorcerer* (1967, Col. CS9532), incl. *Prince of Darkness; *Nefertiti* (1967, Col. CS9594), incl. *Fall, *Nefertiti, *Pinocchio; *In a Silent Way* (1969, Col. CS9875); *Bitches Brew* (1969, Col. GP26), incl. *Sanctuary

With others: G. Evans: on *The Individualism of Gil Evans* (1963–4, Verve 68555), The Barbara Song (1964); on *Previously Unreleased Recordings* (1964, Verve 68838), Barracuda; B. Timmons: *Soul Man* (1966, Prst. 7465); H. Hancock: *V.S.O.P.* (1976, Col. PG34688); Steely Dan: on *Aja* (*c*1976, ABC 10006), Aja; M. Petrucciani: on *Power of Three* (1986, BN 85133), Bimini, Limbo, Morning Blues; [no leader]: *A Tribute to Miles* (1992–3, Qwest 45059), incl. Pinocchio

For further recordings *see* WEATHER REPORT.

SELECTED FILMS AND VIDEOS

Art Blakey: the Jazz Messenger (1986); Great Performances: Miles Ahead (1986); Newport Jazz '86 (1986); Round Midnight (1986); The South Bank Show: Blue Note (1986); Art Blakey & the Jazz Messengers (1989 [filmed 1986]); Tribute to John Coltrane (*c*1987); Michel Petrucciani: Power of 3 (*c*1990 [filmed 1986]); The Manhattan Project (*c*1990 [filmed 1989]); The Music of Miles Davis (1990); The World According to John Coltrane (1991)

BIBLIOGRAPHY

L. Jones: "Introducing Wayne Shorter," *JR*, ii/10 (1959), 22
B. Page: "Shorter View," *DB*, xxvii/25 (1960), 15
R. Atkins: "Wayne Shorter," *JM*, ix/10 (1963), 14
N. Hentoff: "The Long Future of Wayne Shorter," *IM*, lxiii/9 (1965), 20
T. Logan: "Wayne Shorter: Double Take," *DB*, xli/12 (1974), 16
C. Silvert: "Wayne Shorter: Imagination Unlimited," *DB*, xliv/13 (1977), 15
M. C. Gridley: *Jazz Styles* (Englewood Cliffs, NJ, 1978, rev. 6/1997 [*recte* 1996])
A. Liska: "Wayne Shorter: Coming Home," *DB*, xlix/7 (1982), 18 [incl. discography]
R. Cook: "Wayne Shorter," *The Wire*, no.11 (1985), 31
M. Gilbert: "Wayne Shorter," *JJI*, xxxix/4 (1986), 8
S. Yanow: "The Wayne Shorter Interview," *DB*, liii/4 (1986), 17 [incl. discography]
B. Witherden: "Wayne Shorter: the Phantom Speaks," *Wire*, no.38 (1987), 14
L. Feather: "The Report: Busy Days Ahead for Shorter," *Los Angeles Times* (20 Aug 1989)
M. Gifford: "Wayne Shorter," *CI*, xxvi/3 (1989), 4
M. Martin: "Wayne Shorter," *Saxophone Journal*, xvi/4 (1992), 12
M. Rowland and T. Scherman, eds.: *The Jazz Musician* (New York, 1994), 1
J. Woodard: "The Artful Dodger's Return," *JT*, xxv/9 (1995), 30
M. Gilbert: "Wayne Shorter," *JJI*, xlix/3 (1996), 6
J. Hamlin: "For Wayne Shorter, '1 + 1' is about Three," *San Francisco Chronicle Datebook* (31 Aug 1997)
D. Heckman: "Discovery: Wayne Shorter & Herbie Hancock," *DB*, lxiv/12 (1997), 20
——: "Duet for One," *Los Angeles Times Calendar* (29 June 1997)
J. Woodard: "Shorter: Two Divided by One," *JT*, xxvii/7 (1997), 44
B. Ratliff: "With this Composer, the Work is Never Done," *New York Times* (22 April 1998)
D. Ouellette: "Ambassadors of Jazz: Wayne Shorter and Herbie Hancock Bring their Message of Celebration to the Zellerbach Stage," *San Francisco Chronicle Datebook* (30 May 1999)
<http://www.immworld.com/shorter.html> (2000)
B. Råberg: "The Music of Wayne Shorter," <http://www.orbismusic.com/wayne%20shorter/shortermainpage.html> (2000) [incl. transcrs]

BK

Shout. In jazz the word has three main applications, all having to do with a style or manner of performance.

(1) An energetic piece performed by a stride pianist. The most famous example is James P. Johnson's composition *Carolina Shout* (1921; this title probably refers to an African-American religious dance, the ring shout). By extension a shout pianist is one who plays in this style and manner. (*See* PIANO, §2.)

(2) A "blues shouter" is a rough-voiced male performer who shouts rather than sings the lyrics of the blues. The term is associated especially with singers from the Southwest, such as Jimmy Rushing and Joe Turner (ii) (*see* BLUES, §9).

(3) A "shout chorus" is a loud, spirited, climactic chorus in a performance by a big band, in which the brass section leads the whole ensemble.

SHQ. Group led by KAREL VELEBNÝ from the mid-1960s. It succeeded the S & H Quintet, which in turn succeeded the S & H Quartet (formed 1961).

Shu, Eddie [Shulman, Edward] (*b* New York, 18 Aug 1918; *d* Tampa, FL, 4 July 1986). Reed player, trumpeter, and singer. He learned violin and guitar as a child and played harmonica and tenor saxophone in vaudeville shows from the age of 17. During his military service he played trumpet and clarinet and also developed an act as a ventriloquist; after leaving the army he continued to work as an entertainer, then performed and recorded with the bands of Tadd Dameron (1947), George Shearing (1948), Buddy Rich, Lionel Hampton (1949–50), and Charlie Barnet (on the West Coast, 1950). He played with Chubby Jackson in 1952, and from 1953 to 1958 he was a member of Gene Krupa's trio, in which his versatility was fully exploited. Thereafter he worked in Cuba until the revolution, when he moved to Miami and again led his own group. In the early 1960s Shu performed as a freelance in Los Angeles before playing clarinet in Louis Armstrong's All Stars (1964–5). He rejoined Hampton briefly in 1966, but left to resume freelance work in New York. During the early 1980s he performed and taught in the Virgin Islands, and in 1985 he settled in Florida. Shu was an extremely talented performer on each of the instruments he played.

SELECTED RECORDINGS

As leader: *I only Have Eyes for Shu* (1954, Beth. 1013)

As sideman: K. Winding: *Dixieland vs Birdland* (1953, MGM 231); G. Krupa: *The Rocking Mr. Krupa: Sing, Sing, Sing* (1953, Clef 627), incl. Harmonica Shu Boogie; *Drummer Man* (1956, Verve 2008); *Hey! Here's Gene Krupa* (1957, Verve 8300); L. Armstrong: *The Best Live Concert* (1965, Festival 200)

BIBLIOGRAPHY

ChiltonW; *FeatherE*; *Feather '60s*

BRIAN PEERLESS

Shuffle. (1) A dance step of indefinite southern African-American origin, perhaps dating from the 18th century, in which the feet are moved rhythmically across the floor without being lifted.

(2) A rhythm derived from the dance step. The term is onomatopoeic, "sh" describing its characteristic smoothness (and especially its sound when played on the snare drum). The alternation of long and short syllables (shuf-fle, shuf-fle, . . .) evokes its distinguishing rhythm (ex.1), a subdivision of

Ex.1 A typical shuffle rhythm

the beat into uneven triplets which is more specific than the fundamental swing or boogie-woogie rhythm only in that it is usually played legato and at a relaxed tempo. The shuffle rhythm is generally confined to earlier styles of jazz, up to and including swing; however, it is not unknown in later styles, and may be heard, for example, on a version of *Birdland* recorded in concert by Weather Report and included on the album *8:30* (*c*1979, Col. PC2-36030). Although the rhythm is most often executed on the snare drum using brushes, some drummers, notably Paul Barbarin, were adept at producing it with sticks on the cymbal.

(3) A term used in the titles of jazz pieces, principally in the late 1920s and the 1930s; although the shuffle rhythm was widely used during this period, such pieces are not necessarily associated with the dance step or the rhythm. The term was introduced after the success of the revue *Shuffle Along* (1921) by Noble Sissle and Eubie Blake, a work which included, but was by no means restricted to, the shuffle dance step. Later titles confuse the rhythmic meaning of the term: no clear rhythmic thread ties together such a diverse body of pieces as King Oliver's *Showboat Shuffle* (1927, Voc. 1114), Frankie Trumbauer's *Riverboat Shuffle* (1927, OK 40822), Duke Ellington's *Syncopated Shuffle* (1929, OK 8746) and *Showboat Shuffle* (1935, Bruns. 7461), and Jan Savitt's *Futuristic Shuffle* (1938, Bb 7733). A late and unusual example, in the hard-bop style, is Charles Mingus's *Boogie Stop Shuffle* (on his album *Mingus Ah Um*, 1959, Col. CL1370), which calls attention to the relationship of shuffle to boogie-woogie; Mingus presents the shuffle rhythm most clearly in the tune's opening melody rather than as an underlying motif, and the tempo is far too fast for a characteristic shuffle.

Shull, Tad [Thomas Barclay, Jr.] (*b* Norwalk, CT, 15 Oct 1955). Tenor saxophonist. He first played alto saxophone and later changed to the tenor instrument and studied with John Mehegan and Dave Liebman; in his early teens he played in a youth swing band in Westport, Connecticut. After attending the New England Conservatory (1974–6) he gained bachelors and masters degrees in political science from Columbia University. Shull led his own small groups and from 1981 was a member of the Widespread Jazz Orchestra, as it was then known; also in 1981 he worked with Bob Wilber and with the Smithsonian Jazz Masterworks Orchestra. In 1985 he recorded as a sideman with the trumpeter Jordan Sandke and Jaki Byard. Having recorded as a sole leader in 1990–91, from 1993 he recorded with Eric Alexander and Ralph Lalama in the group Tenor Triangle, in which they were accompanied by Mel Rhyne's trio. Shull plays with a thick, robust tone, and his style recalls that of such transitional swing to bop tenor saxophonists as Lucky Thompson and Don Byas.

SELECTED RECORDINGS

(recorded for Criss Cross unless otherwise indicated)

As leader: *In the Land of Tenor* (1991, 1071)

As sideman: Widespread Jazz Orchestra: *Swing is the Thing* (1982, Adelphi 5015); *Paris Blues* (1984, Col. FC40034); Tenor Triangle and M. Rhyne: *Tell it Like it Is* (1993, 1089); *Aztec Blues* (1994, 1143)

BIBLIOGRAPHY

Feather–GitlerBEJ

GK

Shulman, Joe [Joseph] (*b* New York, 12 Sept 1923; *d* New York, 2 Aug 1957). Double bass player. He worked briefly with Les Brown (1942), then toured the USA and Europe with Glenn Miller's Army Air Force Band (1943–4); while in Paris he recorded with Django Reinhardt (1944) and Mel Powell (1945). After returning to New York he performed and recorded with Buddy Rich (late 1945 – *c* March 1946) and Claude Thornhill (1947) and toured with Dave Barbour and Peggy Lee (1948, 1950). In 1949 he worked again with Thornhill, participated in Miles Davis's famous "Birth of the Cool" recording sessions (for illustration *see* JAZZ (i), fig.6), joined Barbara Carroll's trio, and played with Lennie Tristano at Carnegie Hall. The following year he recorded in a trio with Duke Ellington and Billy Strayhorn and toured and recorded with Lester Young's quartet. Shulman married Carroll in 1954 and continued to work with her trio until his death.

SELECTED RECORDINGS

As sideman: C. Thornhill: Anthropology (1947, Col. 38224); *The Uncollected Claude Thornhill and his Orchestra* (1947, Hep 108); M. Davis: Move/Budo (1949, Cap. 15404); Jeru/Godchild (1949, Cap. 60005)

BIBLIOGRAPHY

FeatherE

F. Büchmann-Møller: *You Just Fight for your Life: the Story of Lester Young* (New York, Westport, CT, and London, 1990), 149

BK

Shy, Robert (Marshall) (*b* Lexington, KY, 20 May 1939) Drummer. He began playing drums when he was seven and worked professionally from the age of 16. In 1963 he moved to Chicago as a member of the Three Souls organ trio (with Sonny Cox, alto, and Kenneth Prince, organ). From 1972 to 1974 he toured and recorded extensively with Roland Kirk, with whom he may be seen in the video *The One-man Twins* (1996), filmed at the Montreux Jazz Festival in 1972; he also worked with Sonny Stitt and intermittently with Eddie Harris, notably at the Red Sea Jazz Festival in 1991. Much in demand in Chicago, Shy performed at major clubs, performed annually at the Chicago Jazz Festival, and recorded for local labels. As the drummer for the house rhythm section at the Jazz Showcase (Willie Pickens's trio) he accompanied such artists as Ari Brown, Ron Carter, Jodie Christian, Charles Davis, Von Freeman, Frank Lacy, Frank Morgan, Nicholas Payton, Claudio Roditi, Ira Sullivan, Malachi Thompson, and Cedar Walton.

SELECTED RECORDINGS

As sideman: Three Souls: *Dangerous Dan Express* (1964 Argo 4036); R. Kirk: *Bright Moments* (1973, Atl. 2-907); W. Pickens: *It's About Time* (1981, 1986–7, Southport 8); Jackie Allen: *Never Let Me Go* (1994, Lake Shore Jazz 005); Joannie Pallatto: *Passing Tones* (1994–5, Southport 0032); V. Freeman and E. Petersen: *Von & Ed* (1998, Del. 508); W. Pickens: *A Jazz Christmas* (1998, Southport 0056)

DEBORAH GILLASPIE

Sickler, Don (*b* Spokane, WA, 6 Jan 1944). Trumpeter, arranger, conductor, and record producer. He began playing piano at the age of four and took up trumpet when he was ten; in his early teens he organized a dixieland ensemble and later he formed a dance band. He studied music at Gonzaga University, Spokane (BA 1967), and trumpet performance at the Manhattan School of Music (MM 1970). After graduation he worked in show bands and with Gene Roland's rehearsal big band, and from the late 1970s he was a member of Philly Joe Jones's septet. In the 1980s he played with Jones's Dameronia, for which he also wrote arrangements and served as music director. Following the drummer's death in 1985 Sickler led the group, which recorded under his leadership in 1989. For a while each year between 1987 and 1991 he led a quartet for nightclub appearances in Paris. During the same period he toured Japan as a member of Art

Blakey's big band (1987–9) and led the group Superblue (1988–9), with which he performed internationally. In 1989 he led an octet for a tribute concert to Charlie Parker in Paris with Johnny Griffin, Jackie McLean, Cecil Payne, Duke Jordan, Ron Carter, and Roy Haynes among his sidemen. He was a member of Clifford Jordan's big band from 1990 until the tenor saxophonist's death in 1993, and in 1991 he began working regularly with T. S. Monk's groups. Sickler plays flugelhorn as well as trumpet and has worked as a conductor: he directed a Gil Evans retrospective at the Kool Jazz Festival (1983), the Thelonious Monk Reunion Orchestra at the Chicago Jazz Festival (1986) and the Festival du Théâtre de Boulogne-Billancourt (1987), and other ensembles assembled for special events at Lincoln Center, Carnegie Hall, and elsewhere; he may be seen conducting in the video *Carnegie Hall Salutes the Jazz Masters*, from a concert sponsored by Verve, which was recorded and released in 1994.

In the 1970s Sickler began working as a managing editor for E. B. Marks and as a production manager for Big 3 Music Corporation, for which he published transcriptions of compositions and solos by Joe Henderson and John Coltrane. In 1980 he formed his own publishing companies, Second Floor Music and Twenty-Eighth Street Music; by the 1990s Second Floor Music, distributed by Hal Leonard, was responsible for publishing the transcribed music of more than 200 artists. Many of Sickler's performances as both a leader and a sideman include "classic" arrangements he has written from his own transcriptions. From 1987 he worked regularly as a record producer for Blue Note, Muse (ii), and Verve.

SELECTED RECORDINGS

As leader: *The Music of Kenny Dorham* (1983, Upt. 27.17); *Superblue*, i–ii (1988, 1989, BN B1-91731, B21-92997); *Nightwatch* (1990, Upt. 27.39)

As sideman: Dameronia: *To Tadd with Love* (1982, Upt. 27.11); *Look, Stop, Listen* (1983, Upt. 27.15); [various artists]: *Birdology*, i–ii (1989, Verve 841132-2, 841133-2); T. S. Monk: *Changing of the Guard* (1993, BN B21Z-89050)

BIBLIOGRAPHY

B. Pulliam: "Riffs: Don Sickler," *DB*, lvii/10 (1990), 12

T. Pérémarti: "Focus: Don Sickler: l'homme-orchestra," *Jazzman*, no.34 (1998), 12

GK

Siddik, Rasul (*b* ?St. Louis, *c*1950s). Trumpeter. Nothing is known of his early life. He appears to have first recorded in 1979 with the St. Louis Creative Ensemble, which included Joseph Bowie and Charles "Bobo" Shaw, and he recorded again in San Francisco in 1982 as a member of the Contemporary Art Movement, a large ensemble led by the flutist Karlton Hester. By the mid-1980s he was performing regularly in Michele Rosewoman's large ensemble New Yoruba (1984), in Henry Threadgill's Sextett (*c*1984–*c*1989; on all but one of the group's recordings his surname is misspelled as Sadik), and in Lester Bowie's Brass Fantasy, with which he recorded (1986–7) and toured internationally; during the same period he recorded with Oliver Lake (1986) and in Julius Hemphill's Big Band (1988). In the late 1980s he began what became a longstanding association with David Murray, first in the latter's octet (with which he recorded in 1987, 1992, and *c*1999) and then from the early 1990s in the saxophonist's big band (recording in 1991–2). Siddik is a member of the Association for the Advancement of Creative Musicians, and at its twenty-fifth anniversary concert in 1990 he appeared in a quartet alongside the pianist Adegoke Steve Colson, Lake, and Joseph Jarman.

By the late 1990s Siddik was living in Paris, where he recorded with the double bass player Christian Blazer (1995), performed in a trio led by Bobby Few (January 2000), and appeared at Sunny Murray's nightclub Studio des Islett. He has continued his affiliation with David Murray, appearing in the octet at the Chicago Jazz Festival in 2000. In December 2000 he was co-leading a small group with the Italian saxophonist Romano Partesi; he is also a member of the large ensemble Nova Ghost Sect*tet, led by the saxophonist Ghasem Batamuntu.

SELECTED RECORDINGS

As sideman with H. Threadgill: *Subject to Change* (1984, About Time 1007); *You Know the Number* (1986, Novus 3013-1-N); *Easily Slip into Another World* (1987, Novus 3025-1-N); *Rag, Bush and All* (1988, Novus 3052-2-N)

As sideman with others: O. Lake: on *Gallery* (1986, Gram. 8609), Le Sport Suite; D. Murray: *Hope Scope* (1987, BS 120139-2); Rod Williams: on *Destiny Express* (1990, Muse 5412), Mama Laura

GK

Side. In recording parlance, one face of a disc. During the 78 r.p.m. era the word was used, by extension, to mean the musical number recorded on one side of a disc, and hence, in the most general way, the recording itself. The use of "side" to mean a musical number became inappropriate with the introduction of long-playing discs (each side of which usually contains several numbers) and in this sense the word was superseded by "track."

Sideman. Any member of a band other than the leader.

Sides, Doug(las Joseph) (*b* Los Angeles, 10 Oct 1942). Drummer. He studied at the University of Southern California, New York University, and the Berklee School of Music. While in Boston he also took lessons from Alan Dawson, and in 1961 he performed with Illinois Jacquet. In Los Angeles he worked with Teddy Edwards (with whom he appeared in 1962 in "Teddy Edwards Sextet," an episode in the television series "Jazz Scene USA"), Lionel Hampton, Johnny Griffin (recording in July 1962), Howard Rumsey (1962–3), Curtis Amy's group with Dupree Bolton (recording in March 1963), Harold Land, Sonny Stitt (recording in 1963), Charles Kynard, and Buddy Collette (recording in 1964). Following military service (1964–6) he was in San Francisco with the organist Merle Saunders (1967) and John Handy (1967–8); with Handy he went to New York in June 1967 for a performance recorded at the Village Gate. After returning to Los Angeles Sides was a member of the quintet led by Bobby Hutcherson and Harold Land (1969–70) and played with Phineas Newborn (1970), the singer O. C. Smith (1970–72), Blue Mitchell (with whom he recorded in New York in 1971), and Land again. In 1974 he performed and recorded with Kai Winding in Phoenix, Arizona, and the following year he traveled to Johannesburg, South Africa, where he recorded with Abdullah Ibrahim's group. Later he toured Europe with Abbey Lincoln (1980) and the USA and Canada with Jon Hendricks (1982–3). While on a tour of Europe with the show *Sophisticated Ladies* in 1988 he recorded in the Netherlands with the tenor saxophonist Joe van Enkhuisen.

In 1989 Sides moved to Amsterdam, where he led his own groups (recording in *c*1990 and 1997) and worked locally with Benny Bailey. He toured with Griffin, Tete Montoliu, Steve Grossman, Tom Harrell, Walter Bishop, Jr. (recording in Milan in 1991), Ralph Sutton, Ranee Lee, Hank Jones, Oliver Jones (with whom he appeared on Dutch television), and others, and recorded with the pianist Don Bennett (1994, 1997) and the double bass player Fritz Kisse (mid-1990s).

SELECTED RECORDINGS

As leader: *Sumbio* (1997, Laika 35100882)

As sideman: C. Amy: *Katanga* (1963, PJ 70); J. Handy: *New View!* (1967, Col. CS9497); B. Mitchell: *Blue Mitchell* (1971, Mstr. 315); W. Bishop: *Midnight Blue* (1991, Red 123251-2); D. Bennett: *Solar* (1994, Can. 79723)

BIBLIOGRAPHY

Feather–GitlerBEJ

GK

Sidran, Ben (*b* Chicago, 14 Aug 1943). Radio and television presenter, pianist, singer, writer, and producer. He grew up in Racine, Wisconsin, took up piano at the age of seven, and as a teenager played in a local dance band and led a bop trio. While attending the University of Wisconsin he played in a rock-and-roll and blues-rock band with Steve Miller and Boz Scaggs, both of whom later became successful pop musicians. From 1967 to 1970 Sidran worked towards a PhD in American studies at the University of Sussex, during which time he performed and recorded in London with Miller and various British rock groups; he later recorded with the Rolling Stones, Peter Frampton, and Eric Clapton. In 1970 he became a producer for Capitol records in Los Angeles. He then taught communication arts at the University of Wisconsin, and in 1973 he resumed producing and performing. Later he produced a jazz series for the television show "Sound Stage" (*c*1977) and the program "Jazz Alive!" for National Public Radio (NPR) (from *c*1980); he replaced the latter's original host, Billy Taylor (ii), in 1981. When "Jazz Alive!" was discontinued in 1984 owing to cuts in funding, Sidran began presenting a new interview and music radio program, "Sidran on Record"; in addition he worked as a jazz critic for the NPR news program "All Things Considered" and made an instructional video, *Jazz Class*, with Richard Davis (1985). In June 1988 he took over as the presenter of the cable television program "New Visions," which incorporated live interviews and performances, and music videos, and covered various kinds of music.

Sidran began performing and recording regularly in the early 1970s, and from the late 1980s his sidemen were Bob Malach, the keyboard player Ricky Peterson, the bass player Billy Peterson, and the drummer Gordon Knudtson; he appears with this group, along with the guest soloists Phil Woods and Miller, in the video *Ben Sidran: on the Live Side* (*c*1988 [filmed 1986]). Around 1990 he formed the record label Go Jazz, which was licensed and marketed by the Mesa Bluemoon record company; the label's first four releases were by Sidran, Malach, the singer Georgie Fame, and Ricky Peterson, all of whom toured together late in 1991. In 1997 in Chicago he presented a program called "A Jazzy Chanukah," in which he led a band with Eddie Daniels, Gil Goldstein, and Steve Khan among his sidemen.

Sidran's most obvious point of reference as a performer is Mose Allison, but unlike Allison's his voice possesses an affected sense of cool. His piano playing reflects his early experience with bop, although most of his recordings place him within lighter fusion-oriented settings. Sidran is the author of *Black Talk* (New York, 1971/*R*1981), which is derived from his dissertation, and *Talking Jazz: an Illustrated Oral History* (San Francisco, 1992, rev. and enlarged 2/1995), a collection of transcriptions of radio interviews; he has also contributed to a number of periodicals, notably *Jazz Magazine*.

SELECTED RECORDINGS

As leader: *Bop City* (1983, Ant. 1012); *Have You Met . . . Barcelona* (1987, Orange Blue 002); *Cool Paradise* (*c*1990, Go Jazz R21S-79350)

BIBLIOGRAPHY

CarrJ

B. Holland: "Sidran Replacing Taylor as Host of 'Jazz Alive!'," *Billboard* (9 Oct 1982), 36

S. Sutherland: "Ben Sidran Turns himself On: New Album Targets Fusion Audience," *Billboard*, xcvii (7 Dec 1985), 53

P. Elwood: "Ben Sidran: it Ain't Art, but People Like it," *San Francisco Examiner* (7 March 1986)

T. Schnabel and C. Gauffre: "Ben Sidran: paroles et musique," *Jm*, no.354 (1986), 32

P. Carles, A. Clergeat, and J.-L. Comolli: *Dictionnaire du jazz* (Paris, 1988, rev. and enlarged 2/1994)

M. Baillie: "Ben Sidran: Professin' the Blues," *JJI*, xlii/9 (1989), 8

K. Lynch: "Riffs: Ben Sidran," *DB*, lvi/8 (1989), 15

S. Morse: "'New Visions' Gives Jazz a Cable Showcase," *Boston Globe* (14 Jan 1989)

K. Franckling: "Hearsay: Go Jazz . . . Goes Sidran . . .," *JT*, xxii/1 (1992), 13

J. Bessman: "Self-made Set Teaches Sidran Life Lessons: DNA Picks Up his '93 Album of Jewish-oriented Jazz," *Billboard* (10 Dec 1994), 73

G. Endress: "Jazz – ein Lifestyle: Ben Sidran," *JP*, xlv/7–8 (1996), 22

H. Reich: "'Jazzy Chanukah' Fails to Light a Fire," *Chicago Tribune* (23 Dec 1997)

GK

Signal. Record company and label. The company was established in New York in 1955 by Jules Colomby, Harold Goldberg, and Don Schlitten. It developed a reputation for well prepared, perfectly engineered recordings which were issued in attractive liners. The catalogue included albums by Duke Jordan, Cecil Payne, Red Rodney, and Gigi Gryce, as well as an LP by an all-star sextet recorded at the Five Spot, New York, as a tribute to Charlie Parker. Signal also introduced the Jazz Laboratory series, in which each album contained music by a quartet (saxophone and rhythm section) on one side, and the identical performance, but with the sound from the saxophone microphone omitted, on the other. These proved extremely useful as an aid to practicing improvisation and anticipated, together with contemporaneous recordings on the Music Minus One label, the "jazz play-along" series of Jamey Aebersold that became enormously popular among students of jazz from the mid-1970s onwards. Part of Signal's catalogue was sold to Savoy, which later reissued various items, among them the albums by Payne and Gryce and the tribute to Parker.

MARK GARDNER/BK

Signature. Record company and label. It was established in New York in the early 1940s by Bob Thiele. Before ceasing operations in the late 1940s it issued recordings by Coleman Hawkins (including his famous verson of *The Man I Love*), James P. Johnson, Flip Phillips, Earl Hines, Eddie Heywood, Barney Bigard, Dicky Wells, Bill De Arango, Art Hodes, and Anita O'Day (her first ten sides as a leader), among others. Signature was revived briefly in the late 1950s as the label of Thiele and Steve Allen's company Hanover Signature, and new recordings by Ray Bryant, Toots Thielemans, Jimmie Rowles, Terry Gibbs, and Tony Scott appeared on it. Most of the early catalogue was reissued by Thiele on his labels Flying Dutchman and Doctor Jazz. In 1993 the Signature logo was revived briefly for a series of reissues on compact disc.

BIBLIOGRAPHY

"Thiele Launches Hanover Signature Diskery Operation with Steve Allen," *Variety*, ccxiv (20 May 1959), 7
J. Levenson: "Jazz: Blue Notes," *Billboard*, cv (28 Aug 1993)
B. Thiele and B. Golden: *What a Wonderful World: a Lifetime of Recordings* (New York, and Oxford, England, 1995)
<http://www.cjnetworks.com/~roryb/1996/thiele.html> (2000)

GK

Signorelli, Frank (*b* New York, 24 May 1901; *d* New York, 9 Dec 1975). Pianist and composer. After studying piano with a cousin, Pasquale Signorelli, he played with the ORIGINAL MEMPHIS FIVE (1917), the Original Dixieland Jazz Band (1921), and again with the Original Memphis Five (until 1926, recording to 1931). He then worked with Joe Venuti (September 1926) and Adrian Rollini's New Yorker Band (September–October 1927), and recorded with Venuti (1927–31), in a duo with Eddie Lang (1927–8), and with Frankie Trumbauer and Bix Beiderbecke (1927). Over the course of the 1920s he also recorded prolifically in many pseudonymous studio groups, the majority of which involved a fellow member of the Original Memphis Five, Phil Napoleon. Later he accompanied Bunny Berigan at sessions led by Red McKenzie (1936) and performed after its re-formation with the Original Dixieland Jazz Band (1936–8) and with Paul Whiteman (1938). In the 1940s he joined Bobby Hackett (1943), recorded as a leader and as a sideman with Napoleon (1946), and appeared at Nick's in New York with Hackett (1947) and Napoleon (briefly, 1949). Signorelli re-formed the Original Memphis Five in the mid-1950s, including its clarinetist of the early to mid-1920s, Jimmy Lytell; the group recorded as accompanists to Connee Boswell (1956) and under Miff Mole's leadership (1958) and performed on radio and television. At the same time Signorelli performed as an unaccompanied soloist in Greenwich Village. Among his compositions are *I'll Never be the Same* (recorded by Billie Holiday and Teddy Wilson, 1937), *Stairway to the Stars* (recorded by Ella Fitzgerald, 1939), and *A Blues Serenade* (recorded by Johnny Hodges, 1938).

SELECTED RECORDINGS

As leader: St. Louis Hop/A Blues Serenade (1926, PAct 36535); Margie/Jingling the Bells (1946, Davis 9001)
As sideman (all recorded for OKeh): B. Beiderbecke: Royal Garden Blues/Goose Pimples (1927, 8544); T. Dorsey: Daddy, Change your Mind/You can't Cheat a Cheater (1929, 41422); J. Venuti: Little Buttercup (I'll Never be the Same) (1931, 41506)

BIBLIOGRAPHY

ChiltonW; *FeatherE*
R. M. Sudhalter, P. R. Evans, and W. Dean-Myatt: *Bix: Man and Legend* (New Rochelle, NY, and London, 1974)

JAMES M. DORAN/BK

Sikała, Maciej (*b* Gdańsk, Poland, 7 Sept 1961). Polish tenor saxophonist. While studying jazz and pop music at the academy of music in Katowice (from which he graduated in 1987) he played in a big band and in Kazimierz Jonkisz's small group (with which he recorded in 1984). In 1993 he joined the groups Quintessence and Miłość; the latter, which includes Leszek Możdżer, recorded with Lester Bowie in 1995. In the mid-1990s Sikała had an opportunity to play with Kenny Wheeler, and he made a number of recordings as a sideman, notably with Krzysztof Herdzin, Piotr Wojtasik, and Piotr Rodowicz. In 1996 he became a member of Wojtasik's quintet. Sikała recorded as the leader of a trio in 1998 and made another album under his own name in 2001.

SELECTED RECORDINGS

As leader: *Blue Destinations* (1998, Power Bros. 00153)
As sideman: K. Jonkisz: *XYZ* (1984, Poljazz 198); Quintessence: *Infinity* (1993, E. Kulm Productions 002); Miłość: *Taniec smoka* (Dragon's dance) (1994, Gowi 15); P. Rodowicz: *Mingus Mingus* (1994, Gowi 23); Leszek Kułakowski: *Black and Blue* (1994, Polonia 031); L. Bowie and Miłość: *Not Two* (1995, Gowi 25); Miłość: *Asthmatic* (1995, Gowi 34); Quintessence: *Live* (1995, E. Kulm Productions 003); K. Herdzin: *Chopin* (1995, Polonia 056); P. Wojtasik: *Lonely Town* (1995, Power Bros. 00137); L. Możdżer: *Talk to Jesus* (1996, Gowi 35); P. Wojtasik: *Escape* (1998, Power Bros. 00177)

BIBLIOGRAPHY

M. Bogdanowicz: "Maciej Sikała: Interview," *JF*, no.169 (1996), 28

ADAM CEGIELSKI, BK

Silkheart. Record company and label. It was formed in Stockholm around 1985 by Lars Olof Gustavsson and Keith Knox and began to issue albums around 1987, initially offering recordings by Dennis Gonzalez, Steve Lacy, Ahmed Abdullah, and Charles Brackeen. Later items included the début recording of Charles Gayle. By late 1999 Silkheart had issued approximately 49 albums, with Joel Futterman, David S. Ware, and Ernest Dawkins among the other performers well presented by its output. The first 25 releases were on both LP and CD, but from the early 1990s Silkheart limited itself to compact discs. Its production policies, which recall those of ESP-disk, allow the performer complete artistic control of the recording and its packaging.
(<http://www.silkheart.se/cgi-bin/cgiwrap/silk/silk.cgi?aboul> 2000)

GK

Silva, Alan (Treadwell) (*b* Bermuda, 22 Jan 1939). Double bass player and leader. He grew up in Brooklyn, New York, where he studied piano and violin from the age of ten and trumpet for three years with Donald Byrd; he later attended the New York College of Music and around 1962 took up double bass. Having taken an interest in free jazz he worked in the Free Form Improvisation Ensemble with Burton Greene and in 1964 took part in the October Revolution in Jazz. He played with Sun Ra during the latter half of 1964, doubling as a cellist, and then worked with Cecil Taylor (1965–9, with whom he performed in Europe in 1966), and Albert Ayler (1966–8); he also recorded with Sunny Murray (1966). In 1969 Silva settled in France, where he performed and recorded with Murray and Archie Shepp, formed the Celestrial [*sic*] Communication Orchestra, a free-jazz group of varying membership, and the Celestrial Strings, and recorded with Grachan Moncur III, Dave Burrell, and Jimmy Lyons. In 1970 he appeared as a string player in Sun Ra's large orchestra. During the early 1970s he was a member of trios and quartets with Frank Wright, Bobby Few, and Muhammad Ali, and in 1972 the four men founded the cooperative publishing and production company Center of the World Productions (for details *see* ALI, MUHAMMAD). Silva also recorded with François Tusques (1971), Franz Koglmann and Bill Dixon (1976), and the ICP Tetterettet (1977). From the mid-1970s he lived and taught in both New York and Paris, where he established the Institute for Artistic and Cultural Perception (IACP); he recorded again with Murray and Greene (both 1979), Taylor and Dixon (both 1980), and

Few (1983), as well as with Andrew Hill (1980), Alex Schlippenbach's quartet (1981–2), and the Globe Unity Orchestra (1982, 1986). In the 1990s he settled in Germany.

SELECTED RECORDINGS

As leader: *Luna Surface* (1969, BYG 529312); *Seasons* (1970, BYG 529342–4)

As sideman: C. Taylor: *Unit Structures* (1966, BN 84237); *Conquistador!* (1966, BN 84260); *Great Paris Concert* (1966, Fre. 147309–10); A. Ayler: *Albert Ayler in Greenwich Village* (1966–7, Imp. 9155); Jazz Composer's Orchestra: on *The Jazz Composer's Orchestra* (1968, JCOA 1001–2), Communications no.11; S. Murray: *Big Chief* (1969, Pathé-Marconi 10096); *Hommage to Africa* (1969, BYG 529303)

BIBLIOGRAPHY

D. Caux: "Alan Silva à Paris," *Jh*, no.249 (1969), 9; contd as "Un Rayonnant Silva," no.250 (1969), 6
D. Caux and M. Chiari: "Alan Silva: de la contrebasse au violon," *Jh*, no.247 (1969), 21 [incl. discography]
J. Bisceglia: "Alan Silva: un sideman et ses leaders," *Jm*, no.182 (1970), 32
J. M. Damian: "Silva viole Royan," *Jm*, no.189 (1971), 18
P. Griffiths: "The Silva Lining," *MM* (15 May 1971), 32
P. Gros-Claude and P. Carles: "Communication Celestrielle," *Jm*, no.186 (1971), 9
V. Wilmer: "Silva: Making History," *MM* (5 April 1975), 41
——: *As Serious as your Life: the Story of the New Jazz* (London, 1977, rev. [3]/1987)
P. Carles: "Alan Silva ou le triangle des Bermudes," *Jm*, no.280 (1979), 38 [incl. discography]
P. Carles and S. Loupien: "Les écoles d'Alan Silva," *Jm*, no.278 (1979), 50
G. Arnaud: "L'IACP: entretien avec Alan Silva," *Jh*, no.397 (1983), 35
<http://www.mindspring.com/~scala/silva.html> (1999) [discography]
L. Nai: "Alan Silva Interview," *Cadence*, xxv/7 (1999), 5

ANDRÉ CLERGEAT/BK

Silva, Michael (*b* New York, 12 Nov 1925; *d* France, 1990). Drummer. After military service (1943–5) he worked for the Norman Diller Dancers, Hot Lips Page, Cyril Haynes, and the entertainer Sammy Davis, Jr. (1958–68). In 1971 he settled in France, where he performed and recorded with many visiting and expatriate African-American musicians, including the blues singer and guitarist Clarence "Gatemouth" Brown (1972) and Arnett Cobb, Milt Buckner, Candy Johnson, Al Casey, Helen Humes, Sy Oliver, and Sonny Thompson (all 1973); he also worked with Claude Bolling's big band. His group accompanied the tap-dancer Jimmy Slyde on the album *Special Tap Dance* (1974, BB 33066). Silva toured France and continued to perform in Paris, where he led a quartet (1979), played in duos with the pianists Bob Vatel (1981) and Red Richards (1983), and again accompanied Slyde (1985). (J.-P. Battestini: "Michael Silva," *BHcF*, no.218 (1972), 10)

HOWARD RYE

Silvano, Judi [née Silverman, Judith; Lovano, Judith Silverman] (*b* Philadelphia, 8 May 1951). Singer. Her professional name is a combination of her maiden name and her married name. She studied education at Temple University, Philadelphia (BS 1974), and toured the USA and Europe in various modern dance groups (1972–6); from 1973 to 1975 she was an adjunct faculty member at Temple and at Antioch College, Ohio. She later studied arranging with Bob Brookmeyer and Manny Albam (both 1992–4) and performance with Barry Harris (1992–5). In 1976 Silvano moved to New York, where she continued to work as a dancer. In 1981 she began performing with Joe Lovano, whom she married, and Kenny Werner, and from 1982 to 1987 she and Lovano led the Windance Ensemble, which combined jazz and modern dance. From the late 1980s she recorded and toured with a number of Lovano's groups, notably World Ensemble (from 1989), with which she visited Europe, Universal Language (from 1992), his third-stream ensemble Symbiosis (from 1993), and Celebrating Sinatra (from 1996). She toured Scandinavia in 1994 as a singer with Werner's big band. Between 1990 and 1995 Silvano led her own ensemble, Voices of Jupiter, which generally consisted of four voices, two brass or reed players, and a rhythm section, and in 1996 she formed the group Vocalise, which included Vic Juris, Drew Gress, and Victor Lewis. In addition she has worked as a choral director and professional church singer from 1990, and has taught at the Newark campus of Rutgers from 1997. Silvano has a beautiful soprano singing voice and excels in abstract vocalizing. She can accurately span large intervals and is most effective providing improvised counterpoint to other melody instruments.

SELECTED RECORDINGS

As leader: *Dancing Voices* (1991, JSL 0002); *Vocalise* (1996, BN 52390-2)

As sideman with J. Lovano: *Universal Language* (1992, BN B21Z-99830); *Rush Hour* (1994, BN 29269-2)

GK

Silver [Silva], **Horace (Ward Martin Tavares)** (*b* Norwalk, CT, 2 Sept 1928). Pianist, bandleader, and composer. As a child he was exposed to Cape Verdean folk music performed by his father, who was of Portuguese descent. He began studying piano at the age of 12 and took up tenor saxophone while in high school, when his influences were blues singers such as Memphis Slim, and boogie-woogie and bop pianists, especially Bud Powell and Thelonious Monk. In 1950 Stan Getz made a guest appearance in Hartford, Connecticut,

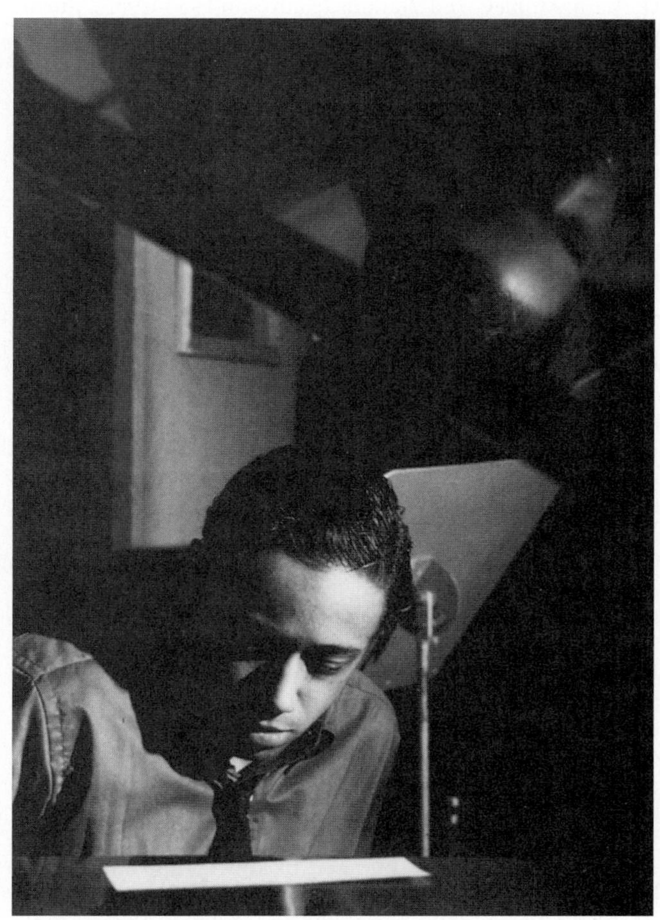

Horace Silver, 1956

with Silver's piano trio, and subsequently engaged the group to tour regularly with him. Silver remained with Getz for a year, during which time three of his compositions, *Penny*, *Potter's Luck* (written for Tommy Potter), and *Split Kick*, were recorded.

By 1951 Silver had developed sufficient confidence to move to New York, where he performed as a freelance with such established professionals as Coleman Hawkins, Lester Young (with whom he toured for about five months), Terry Gibbs, Oscar Pettiford, and Art Blakey. He was virtually the house pianist at Birdland, accompanying Slim Gaillard, Bill Harris (i), Serge Chaloff, and others, and also played in jam sessions at the Paradise Club with many other leading bop and swing musicians, including Charlie Parker, Sonny Rollins, and Hot Lips Page. In 1952 he was engaged by Lou Donaldson for a recording session with Blue Note; this led to his own first recordings as a leader, in which capacity he maintained an exclusive relationship with Blue Note for the next 28 years, although he made landmark recordings as a sideman with Miles Davis in 1954. From 1953 he played in groups with Blakey. When their quintet was recorded at Birdland in October 1953 their sidemen were Kenny Dorham, Donaldson, and Gene Ramey, and in February 1954, again at Birdland, Clifford Brown, Donaldson, and Curley Russell; both of these sessions were issued under Blakey's nominal leadership. He then led a quartet including Hank Mobley, Doug Watkins, and Arthur Edghill at Minton's Playhouse, where Dorham and Blakey sat in. From this experience came Silver and Blakey's lasting quintet with Dorham, Mobley, and Watkins (*c* autumn 1954–1955), during which time the group took the name the Jazz Messengers and recorded under both Silver's and Blakey's name; Donald Byrd replaced Dorham at the end of 1955. Silver left the group in the spring of 1956, for reasons undisclosed, and by the middle of the year he was performing and recording solely as the leader of his own quintet. Blakey continued as leader of the Jazz Messengers.

Silver's music was a major force in modern jazz on at least four counts. He was the first important pioneer of the style known as Hard bop, which combined elements of rhythm-and-blues and gospel music with jazz, influencing pianists such as Bobby Timmons, Les McCann, and Ramsey Lewis. Second, the instrumentation of his quintet (trumpet, tenor saxophone, piano, double bass, and drums) served as a model for small jazz groups from the mid-1950s until the late 1960s. Further, Silver's ensembles provided an important training ground for young players, many of whom (such as the trumpeters Dorham, Brown, Byrd, Art Farmer, Blue Mitchell, and Woody Shaw, tenor saxophonists Mobley, Clifford Jordan, Junior Cook, and Joe Henderson, and drummers Roy Brooks and Louis Hayes) later led similar groups of their own; other notable members of his groups were Gene Taylor, Carmell Jones, Roger Humphries, and Randy Brecker. Finally, Silver refined the art of composing and arranging for his chosen instrumentation to a level of craftsmanship as yet unsurpassed in jazz. He is a prolific composer, and one of very few jazz musicians to record almost exclusively original material; his work consistently combines simplicity and profundity in a rhythmically infectious style which, despite its sophistication, sounds completely natural. A number of his compositions have become jazz standards, notably *The Preacher*, *Doodlin'*, *Opus de Funk*, *Señor Blues*, *Sister Sadie*, *Peace*, *Nica's Dream*, *Filthy McNasty*, and *Song for my Father*.

At the end of 1970 Silver married, disbanded the quintet, and focused on writing lyrics and music for a series of three albums, *The United States of Mind.* He resumed touring in 1973. Tom Harrell, Bob Berg, and Michael Brecker were members of the reconstituted quintet during this period, when Silver recorded a number of albums featuring the quintet with ensembles of brass, woodwind, percussion, voices, and strings, but his music had little impact on developments in jazz, and by the end of the decade he was in semi-retirement.

After finally leaving Blue Note, in 1981 Silver founded his own record company, Silveto, devoted to his explicitly spiritually minded compositions; a subsidiary label, Emerald, focused on his straightforward hard-bop performances. He toured with new quintets including Harrell, Bob Maize (1983–4), and Carl Burnett, and many younger sidemen, as he – like Blakey, Miles Davis, Woody Herman, and other "living legends" – continued to serve as a mentor to emerging musicians: Ralph Moore (1981–5), Brian Lynch (1983–5), and the double bass player Luther Hughes (1985); Dave Douglas, Vincent Herring, and the double bass player Brian Bromberg, with Burnett (1987); and Michael Philip Mossman, Ralph Bowen, Clarence Seay, and Yoron Israel (1990). From about 1987, when the singer Andy Bey began performing regularly with the quintet, to about 1992, Silver confined his touring to the summer months in order to be at home during the school year to take sole care of his teenage son; these brief tours were ambitious, embracing the USA, Europe, Japan, and Brazil, as he presented a wide range of material from his impressive and influential library of original works. From 1994, after recovering from serious physical ailments suffered the previous year, he toured and recorded with the Silver Brass Ensemble, comprising six brass players, Rickey Woodard, and a rhythm section of himself, Maize, and Burnett.

Silver is the author of *The Art of Small Combo Jazz Playing, Composing, and Arranging* (Milwaukee, 1995),which includes scores for some of his best-known pieces. Lead sheets to his compositions are by J. Aebersold: *A New Approach to Jazz Improvisation*, xvii: *Eight Jazz Classics by Horace Silver* (New Albany, IN, 1978); *A New Approach to Jazz Improvisation*, xviii: *Eight Jazz Classics by Horace Silver* (New Albany IN, 1979). A volume of piano transcriptions has been published by A. Smith: *The Horace Silver Collection* (Milwaukee, n.d. [*c*1996]).

Oral history material in *GBLnsa*.

Principal publishers: Hansen, Silhouette.

See also Piano, §5.

SELECTED RECORDINGS

(recorded for Blue Note unless otherwise indicated)

As leader: Opus de Funk (1953, 1625); *Horace Silver and the Jazz Messengers* (1954, 5058), incl. Doodlin'; *Horace Silver and the Jazz Messengers* (1955, 5062), incl. The Preacher; *Six Pieces of Silver* (1956, 1539), incl. Señor Blues; *Blowin' the Blues Away* (1959, 4017), incl. Sister Sadie, Peace; *Horace-scope* (1960, 84042), incl. Nica's Dream; *Doin' the Thing* (1961, 84076), incl. Filthy McNasty; *Song for my Father* (1964, 84185), incl. Song for my Father; *The Cape Verdean Blues* (1965, 84220); *That Healin' Feelin' (The United States of Mind, Phase I)* (1970, 84352); *Total Response (Phase II)* (*c*1971, 84368); *All (Phase III)* (*c*1973, 84420); *Silver 'n' Brass* (1975, LA406); *Silver 'n' Wood* (1976, LA581); *Silver 'n' Voices* (1977, LA708); *Silver 'n' Percussion* (1977, LA853); *Silver 'n' Strings Play the Music of the Spheres* (1978–9, LWB 1033); *The Hardbop Grandpop* (1996, Imp. 192)

As sideman: S. Getz: Penny (1950, Roost 556); Potter's Luck (1950, Roost 538); Split Kick (1950, Roost 526); A. Blakey: *A Night at Birdland* (1954, 5037–9); M. Davis: Four (1954, Prst. 898); *Miles Davis Quintet* (1954, Prst. 185), incl. Solar; *Miles Davis* (1954, Prst. 182), incl. Walkin'; *Miles Davis Quintet* (1954, Prst. 187), incl. Airegin, Oleo, Doxy; A. Blakey: *The*

Jazz Messengers at the Café Bohemia (1955, 1507–8); S. Rollins: *Sonny Rollins*, ii (1957, 1558)

SELECTED FILMS AND VIDEOS

Jazz USA, no.7 (1960); Jazz Goes to College (1966–7); Jazz at the Maltings (1969); Jazz in Piazza (1974); A Great Day in Harlem (1995)

BIBLIOGRAPHY

N. Hentoff: "Even Mynheers Turn to Silver," *DB*, xxiii/22 (1956), 17
"Horace Silver: the Rumors and the Facts," *DB*, xxvii/14 (1960), 18
B. Gardner: "Inside the Horace Silver Quintet," *DB*, xxx/14 (1963), 20
M. Kazan: *Horace Silver* (Brussels, 1964)
D. Morgenstern: "That Durable Horace Silver," *DB*, xxxii/26 (1965), 18
B. McRae: "Horace Silver," *JB*, iii/10 (1966), 14
M. Williams: *The Jazz Tradition* (New York, 1970, rev. 2/1983), 178
J. H. Klee: "Horace Silver's United States of Mind," *DB*, xxxviii/7 (1971), 16
V. Wilmer: "Horace Silver," *J&B*, i/11 (1972), 14
H. Nolan: "In Pursuit: Horace Silver," *DB*, xl/15 (1973), 16
L. Lyons: "Horace Silver: Father of Funk," *CK*, ii/1 (1976), 18
J. R. Taylor: "Horace Silver Discography," *Radio Free Jazz*, xviii (1977), March, 21
L. Feather: "Piano Giants of Jazz: Horace Silver," *CK*, v/9 (1979), 68
M. Cuscuna: "Horace Silver's Blue Note Swan Song," *DB*, xlvii/11 (1980), 16
F. Foster: "On Horace Silver: Take a Deeper Look," *JSN*, ii/1 (1980), 8
M. Ullman: *Jazz Lives: Portraits in Words and Pictures* (Washington, DC, 1980), 79
L. Lyons: *The Great Jazz Pianists, Speaking of their Lives and Music* (New York, 1983), 120
E. S. Meadows: "Prolegomenon to the Music of Horace Silver," *Jf*, xviii (1986), 123
J. Rozzi: "Horace, Hard Bop, and the Healing Process: Horace Silver," *Coda*, no. 239 (1991), 34
J. Goldberg: "The Finest Pieces of Silver," *Musician*, no. 168 (1992), 34
B. Milkowski: "It's Got to Be ... Horace Silver," *JT*, xxiii/7 (1993), 34
——: "Got That Healin' Feelin': Horace Silver," *DB*, lxi/9 (1994), 24 [incl. discography]
T. Owens: *Bebop: the Music and its Players* (New York, and Oxford, England, 1995), 153
Z. Stewart: "Down Beat's 61st Annual Readers Poll Hall of Fame: Horace Silver," *DB*, lxiii/12 (1996), 28
D. Ouellette: "Horace Silver: Treasure Chest of Tunes," *DB*, lxiv/12 (1997), 53
J. Woodard: "Horace Silver: Feeling the Healing," *JT*, xxviii/1 (1998), 32

BILL DOBBINS/BK

Silvertone. Record label. It was the main label of the mail-order organization Sears–Roebuck and was established shortly before World War I. During the 1920s it was used to issue material from many companies. Most of the material of jazz interest was derived from Gennett and Paramount, often from their race series. Issues from these labels were invariably made under pseudonyms and often with alternative tune titles, which has created many problems for discographers. Pseudonyms were also often used for items from other companies. The label appears to have been discontinued at the end of 1930, but it was briefly revived in 1940 for the release of recordings from Columbia and OKeh, including items by Benny Goodman.

BIBLIOGRAPHY

J. Godrich and J. McKenzie: "Silvertone 3500 Series," *Matrix*, no.56 (1964), 3
R. M. W. Dixon and J. Godrich: *Recording the Blues* (London, 1970), 54
B. Rust: *The American Record Label Book* (New Rochelle, NY, 1978), 277
A. Sutton: *Directory of American Disc Record Brands and Manufacturers, 1891–1943* (Westport, CT, and London, 1994), 139

HOWARD RYE

SIMA [Sydney Improvised Music Association Inc.]. Australian non-profit association founded in Sydney in 1984, at a time when performance opportunities for contemporary jazz and improvised music in the city were poor. With modest public funding, the intention of the organization was to demonstrate the existence of an audience for contemporary jazz which was being ignored. Activities in the first two years involved staging short concert series and mini-festivals, and the success of these encouraged SIMA to seek funding for weekly performances – a strategy initiated in 1987. From 1989 to 1997 the association was based at the Strawberry Hills Hotel, where more than 100 performances by local artists took place annually; occasionally overseas artists were presented as well. In March 1999 SIMA moved to the Side on Café. Its activities figure in the video *Dr. Jazz* (1998).

BIBLIOGRAPHY

B. Johnson: *The Oxford Companion to Australian Jazz* (Melbourne, Australia, 1987)
J. Clare [G. Brennan, pseud]: *Bodgie Dada and the Cult of Cool* (Sydney, 1995)

PETER RECHNIEWSKI

Šima, Jan (*b* Prague, 17 Oct 1911). Czech bandleader. In 1934 he joined the Harry Harden Orchestra, for which he wrote arrangements and in which he may have played piano. From 1935 to 1937 he led the Gramoklub Orchestra, which gave the first jazz concert in Prague and afforded to such young soloists as Kamil Behounek the opportunity to perform. Joe Turner (i) recorded two tracks with the orchestra in 1936 (*Joe Turner Stomp/Joe Turner Blues*, Ultraphon A11400).

GERHARD CONRAD

Simeon, Omer (Victor) (*b* New Orleans, 21 July 1902; *d* New York, 17 Sept 1959). Clarinetist and saxophonist. He took up clarinet after he moved with his family to Chicago in 1914, and received lessons from Lorenzo Tio, Jr. (1918–20). He worked in the band led by his brother Al Simeon, a violinist, and then with Charlie Elgar's Creole Orchestra, in which he played clarinet, alto saxophone, and eventually soprano saxophone as well, in Chicago and Milwaukee (1923–7). In 1926 he recorded with Jelly Roll Morton, and immediately became one of Morton's favorite clarinetists. His playing on *Black Bottom Stomp* is typical of his fluent and imaginative style; passages in which he displays the warm beauty of the instrument's low register are contrasted with others of biting intensity. He also contributed a solo on bass clarinet to Morton's *Someday Sweetheart*, providing an early (though not terribly significant) instance of the use of this instrument in jazz.

In April 1927 Simeon joined King Oliver in Milwaukee and toured with him to St. Louis and New York. Stranded in Baltimore a month later with what was left of Oliver's Dixie Syncopators, he rejoined Elgar in Milwaukee and Chicago and then went back to New York, where he played with Luis Russell (summer 1928) and recorded again with Morton and Oliver (both 1928). After returning to Chicago he worked with Erskine Tate (autumn 1928–1930), while also playing occasionally with Elgar's band and making an important series of recordings with Jabbo Smith's small group; these offer numerous extended examples of his playing of sweet melodies and freewheeling improvisations on clarinet and alto and tenor saxophone (1929). Following a stint with Dave Peyton's orchestra at the Regal Theater, Simeon became lead alto saxophonist in Earl Hines's big band, based at the Grand Terrace (March 1931 – July 1937; for illustration *see* Hines, Earl). He deputized for Buster Bailey in Fletcher Henderson's orchestra for two weeks in 1936, left Hines in a dispute over money and became a member of Horace Henderson's band (August 1937 – September 1938), but returned to Hines's group (until 1940). In 1940 he joined Walter Fuller's big band, also at the Grand Terrace, and in 1941 that of Coleman Hawkins, then worked with Fuller again, but mainly in Minneapolis (late 1941 – summer 1942). He was a member of Jimmie Lunceford's orchestra from 1942. While with the band Simeon also recorded with Kid Ory in Hollywood (1944–5). Following Lunceford's death in 1947 he remained with the group until 1950 under the leadership of Eddie Wilcox. He spent the rest of his life working in New York, where he performed and recorded regularly with Wilbur De Paris (1951–9); he toured Africa with De Paris in 1957, and he may be seen with him in the early jazz episode of the television series "The Subject is Jazz" (1958).

Oral history material in *LNT*.

SELECTED RECORDINGS

As leader: Smoke House Blues/Beaukoo Jack (1929, Bruns. 7109)

As sideman with J. R. Morton (all for Victor): Black Bottom Stomp/The Chant (1926, 20221); Sidewalk Blues/Dead Man Blues (1926, 20252); Steamboat Stomp (1926, 20296); Someday Sweetheart (1926, 20405) [bass cl]; Doctor Jazz (1926, 20415); Shoe Shiner's Drag/Shreveport [Stomp] (1928, 21658); Georgia Swing/Mournful Serenade (1928, 38024)

As sideman with K. Oliver: Doctor Jazz (1927, Voc. 1113); Showboat Shuffle/Every Tub (1927, Voc. 1114); Willie the Weeper/Black Snake Blues (1927, Voc. 1112); Aunt Hagar's Blues (1928, Voc. 1225); I'm watching the clock (1928, Bruns. 4469)

As sideman with Jabbo Smith (all 1929, for Brunswick): Jazz Battle (4244); Little Willie Blues/Sleepy Time Blues (7058); Take your Time/Sweet and Low Blues (7061); Take Me to the River/Ace of Rhythms (7071); Let's get together/Sau Sha Stomp (7065); Michigander Blues (7069); Decatur Street Tutti/Till Times Get Better (7078)

As sideman with E. Hines (all 1934, for Decca): That's a Plenty (182); Maple Leaf Rag (218); Rosetta (337); Angry (183); Wolverine Blues/Rock and Rye (577)

As sideman with others: J. Lunceford: *Back Door Stuff* (1944, Decca 18594); K. Ory: Blues for Jimmie Noone/Get out of here (1944, Crescent 2); W. De Paris: *Rampart St. Ramblers* (1952, Atl. 141, 143)

BIBLIOGRAPHY

ChiltonW

H. Rosenberg and E. Williams: "Omer Simeon," *Jazz Information*, ii/1 (1940), 7

E. Keartland: "Discography of Omer Simeon," *Hot Notes*, ii/5 (1947), 14

A. Lomax: *Mister Jelly Roll: the Fortunes of Jelly Roll Morton, New Orleans Creole and "Inventor of Jazz"* (New York, 1950, London, 1952, 2/1973/*R*1993)

H. Panassié: "Omer Simeon," *BHcF*, no.92 (1959), 3

J. R. T. Davies: "The Curious Case of the Forgotten Years," *Sv*, i/1 (1965), 8

G. Schuller: *Early Jazz: its Roots and Musical Development* (New York, 1968), 211

H. Openeer, Jr.: "Omer Simeon," *Doctor jazz*, no.42 (1970), 6; no.43 (1970), 4 [incl. discography]

S. Dance: *The World of Earl Hines* (New York, 1977/*R*1983)

O. Simeon: "Mostly about Morton," *Selections from the Gutter: Jazz Portraits from "The Jazz Record,"* ed. A. Hodes and C. Hansen (Berkeley, CA, Los Angeles, and London, 1977), 92

L. Wright: *Mr. Jelly Lord* (Chigwell, England, 1980)

W. J. Schafer: "Clarinet Kings," *MR*, x/11 (1983), 1

L. Wright and others: *Walter C. Allen & Brian A. L. Rust's "King" Oliver* (Chigwell, England, 1987)

"The Walter C. Allen Interviews," *Sv*, no.147 (1991), 87

K.-U. Dürr: *The Recordings of Omer Simeon* (Hamburg, Germany, 1996)

BILL RUSSELL/BK

Simmen, Johnny [Hans Georg] (*b* Brugg, Switzerland, 7 April 1918). Swiss writer. His numerous articles have appeared in magazines published in Belgium, France, Germany, Switzerland, the UK, and Canada, and he has given lectures on jazz in several countries. One of the most knowledgeable jazz writers, he specializes in musicians of the pre-bop era and writes with a deep understanding of the improviser's craft; his biographical features clearly indicate the trust and confidence that his subjects, who are usually veteran musicians, place in him. Although Simmen studied piano for seven years he never played professionally, but his knowledge of keyboard technique makes his articles on jazz pianists particularly incisive. His extraordinarily acute musical ear allows him to recognize jazz soloists with ease, and his lectures on individual musicians are models of learned enthusiasm.

WRITINGS

(selective list)

"Carnet de notes, xvii: Mrs. Emily Kraft-Banga and Mr. Kaiser Marshall," *BHcF*, no.208 (1971), 4; no.209 (1971), 7; rev. Eng. trans. in *Sv*, no.41 (1972), 176

"Kenneth J. Hollon: Portrait of an Unsung Musician," *Coda*, xi/9 (1974), 2

"Crystal Clear," *Coda*, xii/3 (1975), 25 [on Bill Coleman]

"Sandy Williams," *BHcF* (1984), no.315; p.3; no.316, p.2; no.317, p.4; no.318, p.7; no.319, p.1; Eng. trans., abbreviated, in *Sv*, no.116 (1984–5), 48 [incl. discography]

"Joe Turner," *Sv*, no.123 (1986), 97

JOHN CHILTON

Simmonds, Mark (Bentley) (*b* Christchurch, New Zealand, 21 July 1959). New Zealand saxophonist and leader. He was a founding member of Keys Music Association in Sydney, which brought him into contact with a number of different experimental musicians; among those with whom he worked were the rock band Ol' 55 and the rhythm-and-blues group Dynamic Hepnotics. In the 1970s he performed with Chris Abrahams, Serge Ermoll, Phil Treloar, and others, and in the 1980s he founded the Freeboppers; the group's recordings reveal the intensity of his style. Simmonds also worked with the Australian Art Orchestra and spent periods of time based in several other capital cities in Australia besides Sydney.

SELECTED RECORDINGS

As leader: on Jamie Fielding: *Notes from the Underground* (1981–92, AIJA 006-008), Duality of Opposites Suite (1983); on *Beyond El Rocco* (1988, Vox Australis 017-2) [film soundtrack], Kings Cross Drag

As sideman: Keys Music Association: *The March of the Five Limbs* (1981–2, KMA 8301-2); S. Ermoll: *Dedication to Horst Liepolt* (1980, Janda Jazz 1002); *Jungle Juice* (1986, Larrikin 193); Umbrellas: *Age of Elegance* (1986–9, The Sound of Music 1002); on *Beyond El Rocco* (1988, Vox Australis 017-2) [film soundtrack], P. Treloar: Shades of Bhairau

BIBLIOGRAPHY

J. Shand: "No Slaves: Mark Simmonds," *Australasian Jazz 'n' Blues*, i/5 (1994), 7

J. Clare [G. Brennan, pseud.]: *Bodgie Dada and the Cult of Cool* (Sydney, 1995)

W. Bebbington, ed: *The Oxford Companion to Australian Music* (Melbourne, Australia, 1997)

ROGER T. DEAN

Simmons, Art(hur Eugene) (*b* Glen White, WV, 5 Feb 1926). Pianist. In April 1946 he went to Europe with a combat engineer unit and was transferred to the 17th Special Services Band. Following World War II he stayed in Germany, where he studied music for three years, and in 1949 he settled in Paris. While continuing his studies at the Paris Conservatoire and the Ecole Normale de Musique he played in a jam session with Charlie Parker and Kenny Clarke during the Paris Jazz Festival (1949), shared a residency with Aaron Bridgers at Chez Inez, and then worked with Don Byas, Robert Mavounzy, and Nelson Williams. By 1951 he was leading a group at the Ringside Club. He generally worked with his own trio at venues such as L'Intrigue, but he also played with Dizzy Gillespie, collaborated with Quincy Jones on arrangements for the Double Six, and toured to London with American singers, among them Bertice Reading. Simmons became the resident pianist at the Mars Club, where he played in a trio with Michel Gaudry, Pierre Cullaz, and Elek Bacsik among his sidemen at various times; in this capacity he accompanied Carmen McRae and, in 1958, Billie Holiday. In 1963 he moved with the manager of the Mars, the singer Nancy Holloway, when she opened her own nightclub; there he worked in a duo with Art Taylor, but by 1963 he had become part-owner of the Living Room, where he alternated sets with Bridgers. An impeccable accompanist in the style of Hank Jones, Simmons also wrote arrangements for Barclay and other labels. He worked in Majorca, Spain, in 1971, then returned to the USA and retired from music.

SELECTED RECORDINGS

As leader: on [album title unknown] (1959, Ducretet-Thomson 450V254), Don't ever leave me, Et tu me regarde, No Problem

As sideman: D. Byas: A pretty girl is like a melody (1950, BStar 208); Somebody Loves Me (1952, BStar 268); Riviera Blues (1952, BStar 267); That Old Feeling (1952, BStar 270); R. Mavounzy: Pick Yourself Up/Perdido/Sonny's Boy/Sid's Bounce (1954, Pathé 45EA14) [EP]; Eddie Barclay: Ne m'laissez pas comme ça/Place blanche (1957, Barclay 72133); Double Six and Q. Jones: *Les Double Six Meet Quincy Jones* (1960, Ducretet-Thomson 450V255); L. Bennett: *Echoes and Rhythms of my Church* (1963, Bel Air 411052)

BIBLIOGRAPHY

V. Wilmer: "Art Simmons," *JJ*, xiv/8 (1961), 11
M. Hennessey: *Klook: the Story of Kenny Clarke* (London, 1990)
S. Chambon: "Art Simmons in Paris," *Jm*, no.512 (2001), 8

VAL WILMER

Simmons, John (Jacob) (*b* Haskell, OK, 14 June 1918; *d* Los Angeles, 19 Sept 1979). Double bass player. He first played trumpet, then took up double bass. He worked with Nat "King" Cole and recorded in Los Angeles with Teddy Wilson's quintet (1937), then moved to Chicago, where he played in the bands of Johnny Letman (late 1940), Roy Eldridge (December 1940–1941), Benny Goodman (July–September 1941), and Cootie Williams and Louis Armstrong (both 1942). He worked in CBS radio orchestras, performed briefly with Duke Ellington (*c* October 1943), appeared in the acclaimed film *Jammin' the Blues* (1944), then played with Eddie Heywood in Los Angeles and Illinois Jacquet in New York (both 1945). Between 1944 and 1946 he also recorded with James P. Johnson, Hot Lips Page, Sid Catlett, Ben Webster, Billie Holiday, the Kansas City Six, Heywood, Sidney De Paris, Erroll Garner, Al Casey, Coleman Hawkins, Bud Freeman, André Previn, Emmett Berry, John Hardee, Don Byas, Benny Carter, Bill De Arango, Billy Kyle, and Russell Procope. Later he recorded with Ella Fitzgerald (1947), Sir Charles Thompson (1947–8), Thelonious Monk (1948), Lee Young, Cecil Payne, and Billy Taylor (ii) (all 1949). From 1949 to 1952 he played in Garner's trio in New York, and as a member of Bill Doggett's trio he recorded with Eddie "Lockjaw" Davis (1949) and Tyree Glenn (1951). After further studio work, including dates with Sonny Stitt and Wilson (both 1952), Davis (*c*1952), Louie Bellson and a Norman Granz jam session group (both 1953), Buddy Rich (1953, 1955), and Art Tatum (1955), he performed with Harry Edison and in Scandinavia with the quintet led by Rolf Ericson and Duke Jordan (1955); in 1956 he recorded in New York with Maynard Ferguson's Birdland All Stars and Tadd Dameron, in Stockholm with Ernestine Anderson, and in New York with Matthew Gee. Illness prevented Simmons from working steadily thereafter, but he recorded with Edison in 1958 and played with Phineas Newborn in 1959–60. He was equally at home as a member of mainstream and bop groups, and his round tone and sensitive, solid playing is heard to advantage on the recordings he made with Catlett.

Oral history material in *NjR* (JOHP).

SELECTED RECORDINGS

As sideman: T. Wilson: Ain't Misbehavin' (1937, Bruns. 7964); Just a Mood (1937, Bruns. 7973); H. L. Page: My gal's gone/The blues jumped a rabbit (1944, Com. 593); S. Catlett: Sleep/Linger awhile (1944, Com. 546); Memories of You/Just a Riff (1944, Com. 1515); I never knew/Love for Sale (1945, Cap. 10032); R. Ericson: Flight to Jordan (1956, Met. 192) [EP]; This time the dream's on me (1956, Met. 193) [EP]; P. Newborn: *Piano Portraits* (1959, Roul. 52031), incl. Star Eyes; *I Love a Piano* (1959, Roul. 52043), incl. Real Gone Guy

SELECTED FILMS AND VIDEOS

Jammin' the Blues (1944); Jam Session (1944); Boy! What a Girl (1947)

BIBLIOGRAPHY

ChiltonW; *FeatherE*; *Feather–Gitler '70s*
Obituary, *DB*, xlvi/18 (1979), 13
J. Doran: *Erroll Garner: the Most Happy Piano* (Metuchen, NJ, and London, 1985) [incl. discography]

JOHNNY SIMMEN/BK

Simmons, Norman [Sarney] (*b* Chicago, 6 Oct 1929). Pianist, arranger, and teacher. Simmons reported to the Lewises (2000) that he was given the forename Sarney but was originally called Billy; he registered for school as Norman. He studied piano at the Chicago School of Music (1945–9) and first performed with Clifford Jordan (1946). Around 1950 he deputized for Lou Levy for two weeks in the group led by Bill Harris (i) at the Blue Note in Chicago. After taking time off to practice in Minneapolis he returned to Chicago, where in July 1952 he began an engagement at the Capitol Lounge as a member of Coleman Hawkins's small group. He then joined Paul Bascomb's group (1953). Soon afterwards he worked as the house pianist at the Bee Hive (1953–6), where once again he accompanied Hawkins before forming a trio with Vernel Fournier and Victor Sproles. This trio supported such distinguished soloists as Gene Ammons, Sonny Stitt, Lester Young, Dexter Gordon, Sonny Rollins, J. J. Johnson and Kai Winding, Charlie Parker, Wardell Gray (with whose sextet it recorded in 1955), and Ira Sullivan and Red Rodney (with whom Simmons, Sproles, and Roy Haynes recorded that same year). When the Bee Hive closed in 1956 the trio continued on its own, performing and recording with Simmons as its leader. Simmons also led a band at the C & C Lounge in Chicago (1957–9), with such sidemen as Booker Little, Frank Strozier, Bobby Bryant, and Bill Lee, and accompanied Dakota Station (1958) and Ernestine Anderson (1959).

After moving to New York (1959) Simmons wrote arrangements for recordings issued by Riverside (including Johnny Griffin's *The Big Soul Band*, 1960, 1179), performed and recorded in a quintet with Griffin and Eddie "Lockjaw" Davis, undertook further work with Staton (in particular a recording at Storyville in Boston in 1961), and, most significantly, accompanied Carmen McRae (1960–69), with whom he appeared in "Carmen McRae" (1963), an episode of the television series "Jazz Casual." He then accompanied Betty Carter, with whom he made several recordings in concert (1969–71). Having deputized for, and then replaced, Roland Hanna in Roy Eldridge's band and Hank Jones in Tyree Glenn's band (late 1960s/early 1970s), he later recorded with Eldridge (1976) and in a group led by Scott Hamilton and Warren Vaché (1978, 1979), during which time he temporarily alternated with their regular pianist, John Bunch. He recorded while on tour with Anita O'Day in Japan in 1976, and in 1979 accompanied O'Day, Helen Humes, and Joe Williams; that same year he founded Milljac Record Productions, for which he recorded three albums as a leader. Simmons led a trio and continued to write arrangements into the 1980s. In addition to his work with singers (he made further tours with Anderson in the 1980s and with Williams from the 1970s into the 1990s) he performed as an unaccompanied soloist (notably for a series of engagements at the Café des Copains, Toronto) and in duos and trios. He recorded with Philip Harper's sextet in 1994.

Simmons is the composer of the well-known tune *Jan* (1953). He taught on the Jazzmobile from 1974 into the mid-1990s and on the faculties of William Paterson College, Wayne, New Jersey (1982–97), and the New School for Social Research, New York (for about three years).

Video oral history material in *NCH* (HCJA).

SELECTED RECORDINGS

As leader: *Norman Simmons Trio* (1956, Argo 607); *Ramira the Dancer* (1976, Spot. 13); *13th Moon* (1986, Milljac 1003)

As sideman: R. Rodney: *Modern Music from Chicago* (1955, Fan. 3208); E. Davis: *Battle Stations* (1960, Prst. 7282); B. Carter: *Finally Betty Carter* (1969, Roul. 5000); J. Williams: *Every Night: Live at Vine Street* (1987, Verve 833236-1); *Ballad and Blues Master* (1987, Verve 314-511354-2)

BIBLIOGRAPHY

Feather '60s
M. Gardner: "Norman Simmons," *JM*, no.188 (1970), 4; no.189 (1970), 2; no.190 (1970), 14; no.191 (1971), 6
J. Olsson: "Norman Simmons," *Orkester journalen*, xlvii/12 (1979), 9 [discography]
L. Gourse: *Louis' Children: American Jazz Singers* (New York, 1984), 262, 278
S. Troup: "His Excellence Keeps Him Scarce," *Newsday* (29 Nov 1985), 7
L. Gourse: "Norman Simmons: I am the Blues," *JT* (1987), March, 7
B. Rusch: "The Questionnaire," *Cadence*, xv/11 (1989), 65
D. Palmer: "Riffs: Norman Simmons," *DB*, lix/9 (1992), 13
A. Lewis and L. Lewis: "Norman Sarney Simmons," *Cadence*, xxvi/3 (2000), 5

JAMES M. DORAN/BK

Simmons, Sonny [Huey] (*b* Sicily Island, LA, 4 Aug 1933). Alto saxophonist. He moved with his family in the early 1940s to Oakland, California, where in 1950 he began teaching himself to play saxophone, starting on the tenor instrument and changing about a year later to the alto. During the 1950s he worked in rhythm-and-blues groups while playing bop at jam sessions in San Francisco; in 1961 he played with Charles Mingus at the Jazz Workshop. He had met Prince Lasha in 1954, and in the early 1960s the two performed and recorded together. Later Simmons appeared on the East and West coasts in groups that included his wife, Barbara Donald, and in the late 1960s he moved to Woodstock, New York. After returning to the West Coast in 1970 he performed in the San Francisco area with Lasha and Bobby Hutcherson. In the early 1970s, together with Donald, he retired from music to look after their small children. They both resumed playing four years later, and in the late 1970s they ran a jazz club in the Hotel DeAnza; they also played with Elvin Jones in San Jose in 1978. The family moved to Seattle around 1980, but soon afterwards the couple split up (they never divorced) and Simmons returned to San Francisco. As a consequence of the debilitating effects of alcoholism he became homeless; he spent many years in San Francisco, working mainly as a street musician and only occasionally securing jobs in clubs. In 1982 he recorded with Michael Marcus; the results were released a decade later, and late in 1992 Simmons recorded a trio album, *Ancient Ritual*, with his son Zarak Simmons (*b* 25 Dec 1965) on drums and Charnett Moffett on double bass, which received some critical acclaim. Thereafter he enjoyed several periods of international touring, though he still struggled for steady work. In addition to his principal instrument he played tenor saxophone, heckelphone, oboe, and english horn.

SELECTED RECORDINGS

As leader: *Staying on the Watch* (1966, ESP 1030); with P. Lasha: *Firebirds* (1967, Cont. 7617); *Music from the Spheres* (1967–8, ESP 1043); *Manhattan Egos* (1969, Arhoolie 8003); *Rumasuma* (1970, Cont. 7623); *Burning Spirits* (1971, Cont. 7625–6); *Ancient Ritual* (1992, Qwest 45623-2); *American Jungle* (1995, Qwest 46543-2); *Transcendence* (1996, CIMP 113)

As sideman: P. Lasha: *The Cry!* (1962, Cont. 7610); Elvin Jones and J. Garrison: *Illumination* (1963, Imp. 49); E. Dolphy: *Conversations* (1963, FM 308)

BIBLIOGRAPHY

J. Tynan: "Take Five," *DB*, xxx/9 (1963), 40
L. Feather: "Blindfold Test: Sonny Simmons," *DB*, xxxv/10 (1968), 33
R. Russell: "Sonny Simmons," *Jh*, no.267 (1970), 16
D. C. Hunt: "Sonny Simmons," *J&P*, x/5 (1971), 20
P. Soberanis: "Sonny's Side of the Street," *San Francisco Chronicle Datebook* (13 June 1989)
J. Fine: "Sonny Soars," *San Francisco Bay Guardian* (2 Nov 1994)
R. Grosman and P. Richard: "Out of Nowhere," *Jh*, no.524 (1995), 30
H. Mandel: "Tradin' Fours: Back from Hell," *DB*, lxii/66 (1995), 36
M. Oricchio: "Burning Spirit: Sonny Simmons Rises to Reclaim the Career that Held So Much Promise then Slipped through his Fingers," *San Jose Mercury News* (16 June 1995)

DAVID WILD/BK

Simon, Edward [Morillo, Eduardo Simon] (*b* Punta Cardón, Venezuela, 27 July 1969). Venzuelan pianist. His father played guitar, and one of his brothers played trumpet; another brother, Marlo Simon, is a drummer and recorded as a sideman with Charles Fambrough in 1994 and as a sole leader in the late 1990s. Simon took up electric organ before beginning classical piano studies; from the age of ten he performed in the family's band, and in his early teens he also played trombone in school. In 1984 he moved to Philadelphia to attend the Performing Arts High School. He then studied at the University of the Arts (Philadelphia) (1986–9) and the Manhattan School of Music (1989) and took private lessons in jazz piano with Harold Danko. After graduation he worked with Greg Osby (1989), Kevin Eubanks (1989–93), Horizon (the quintet led by Bobby Watson and Victor Lewis, 1989–94), Herbie Mann (1990–94), Paquito D'Rivera's Havana–NY Ensemble (intermittently, 1990–94), and Lewis's own small groups (1992–3). From 1993, when he was placed third in the Thelonious Monk International Jazz Piano Competition, he was a member of the United Nation Orchestra under D'Rivera, and from 1994 he performed with Terence Blanchard. As a freelance during these years Simon recorded with the alto saxophonist Dave Binney (1989), Claudio Roditi (1990), Craig Handy (1991), Charlie Sepulveda (1992), Carl Allen (1992–3), Conrad Herwig (1993), Fambrough (1994), Terrell Stafford (1995), Mark Turner (1995), the guitarist Freddie Bryant (1997), and Jon Gordon (1998), among others. From the late 1990s he directed the Latin Jazz Ensemble at the University of the Arts.

SELECTED RECORDINGS

As leader: *Beauty Within* (1993, Audioquest 1025); *Edward Simon* (1995, Kokopelli 1305); *La bikina* (1998, Mythology 10982)

As sideman: B. Watson: *Post-Motown Bop* (1990, BN B21Z-95148); *Present Tense* (1991, Col. CK52400); C. Handy: *Split Second Timing* (1991, Arabesque 101); V. Lewis: *Family Portrait* (1992, Audioquest 1010); B. Watson: *Midwest Shuffle* (1993, Col. CK57697); T. Blanchard: *Romantic Defiance* (1994, Col. CK67042); T. Stafford: *Time to Let Go* (1995, Can. 79702); J. Gordon: *Currents* (1998, Double-Time 136)

BIBLIOGRAPHY

Feather–GitlerBEJ
F. Bouchard: "Hearsay: Edward Simon," *JT*, xxiv/7 (1994), 13

<http://www.mythologyrecords.com/edbio.html> (1999) [incl. discography]

GK

Simon, George T(homas) (*b* New York, 9 May 1912; *d* New York, 13 Feb 2001). Writer and record producer. He played drums in his own band while attending Harvard University (BA 1934) and later for a brief period in Glenn Miller's orchestra (1937), which he had helped to organize. After working as an associate editor of *Metronome* (1935–9) he served as its editor-in-chief (1939–55); during his period there he changed the magazine's orientation away from articles on instrument making and publishing towards items on recording and the work of such big-band leaders as Bunny Berigan, Benny Goodman, and the Dorsey brothers. He wrote much of the material in *Metronome* himself (under pseudonyms) before engaging Barry Ulanov and others as staff writers. Later he supervised artists and repertory for the record company Jazztone and served as the program director of the Jazztone Society (1956–7), a mail-order scheme. He was also a writer, producer, and consultant for several television programs (including the "Timex All Time Jazz" series) and the president of Bouree Productions (1958–60), a record production company. From 1961 to 1972 he was the executive director of the National Academy of Recording Arts & Sciences. Simon produced jazz recordings for Capitol, Columbia, Victor, and Warner Bros. and wrote about jazz in the *New York Herald Tribune* (1961–4) and the *New York Post* (1980–81). He won the ASCAP–Deems Taylor Award in 1968 for his book *The Big Bands* (1967) and a Grammy Award in 1978 for his liner notes to the album *Bing Crosby: a Legendary Performer* (RCA CPL1-2086(e), 1977).

WRITINGS

(selective list)

The Feeling of Jazz (New York, 1961)
The Big Bands (New York, 1967, rev. and enlarged 2/1971, rev. 3/1974, 4/1981)
Simon Says: the Sights and Sounds of the Swing Era, 1935–1955 (New Rochelle, NY, 1971)
Glenn Miller and his Orchestra (New York, 1974/*R*1980)
with others: *The Best of the Music Makers* (Garden City, NY, 1979)

BIBLIOGRAPHY

Obituary, B. Ratliff, *New York Times* (16 Feb 2001)

DANIEL ZAGER

Simon, Maurice (James) (*b* Houston, 26 March 1929). Saxophonist. Having worked in Texas with Russell Jacquet (1943–4) he moved to Los Angeles (*c*1945), where he played and recorded on tenor saxophone with Jacquet and Gerald Wilson; he recorded on the baritone instrument with Wilson's big band accompanying Dinah Washington (1946) and with Maxwell Davis (1949). In 1949–50 he performed and recorded with Illinois Jacquet, and from 1950 to 1953 he led a group with his brother Freddie, a trumpeter. After playing briefly with Count Basie (*c* May–June 1953) he worked in New York with Cootie Williams and performed and recorded with Cab Calloway and Wild Bill Davis (both 1958). During the 1960s he led groups that accompanied singers in Las Vegas and Los Angeles, recorded with Jimmy Witherspoon (1961), and worked with Ray Charles (1967). Later he played tenor, alto, and baritone saxophones with the Duke Ellington Orchestra under Mercer Ellington (1974–5). A robust and earthy player in swing and rhythm-and-blues styles, Simon may be heard to advantage playing tenor saxophone on his recording *The Saint/Frenchie* (1949, Down Beat 207) and the baritone instrument on Helen Humes's *You Played on my Piano* (1952, Decca 48282).

BIBLIOGRAPHY

FeatherE; *Feather–Gitler '70s*; *SheridanCB*
J. Evensmo: *History of Jazz Tenor Saxophone: Black Artists*, iv: *1945–1949* (Oslo, 1999)

Simon, Stafford [Pazuza] (*b c*1908; *d* New York, 1960). Tenor saxophonist. He first came to general notice as a member of Willie Bryant's orchestra, with which he made his recording début in April 1938. That same year he appeared in the film *Swing*, directed by Oscar Micheaux, as a member of the band led by the alto saxophonist Leon Gross. From 1939 into 1940 he worked as a freelance and recorded with Louis Jordan, the blues singer Ollie Shepard, and the dance-band leader Fred Rich. By May 1940 he had joined Benny Carter, with whom he recorded and made a tour of the Midwest. Simon recorded with Jordan again in 1941 before becoming a member of Lucky Millinder's orchestra; he may be seen in the soundies which Millinder made in 1941, and in one of these, *Four or Five Times*, he takes a solo. After leaving Millinder (late in 1943) he formed his own band, then worked with George James (1944). In 1946 he was briefly with Rex Stewart and also recorded with the Brooklyn Buddies, led by the pianist Kenny Watts. Simon joined Clyde Bernhardt's Blue Blazers in 1947, staying until mid-1948, and thereafter led his own small band in the New York area. He died on the bandstand at the Savannah Club, New York.

SELECTED RECORDINGS

As sideman: W. Bryant: On the Alamo (1938, Decca 1772); O. Shepard: Jitterbugs broke it down (1940, Decca 7761); L. Jordan: June Teenth Jamboree (1940, Decca 7723); L. Millinder: Rock, Daniel (1941, Decca 3956); Big Fat Mama (1941, Decca 4041); Apollo Jump (1941, Decca 18529); Mason Flyer/Little John Special (1942, Bruns. 03406); R. Stewart: That's Rhythm (1946, Mer. 8008); C. Bernhardt: Good Woman Blues/If it's any news to you (1947, Son. 109)

BIBLIOGRAPHY

ChiltonW
C. E. B. Bernhardt and S. Harris: *I Remember: Eighty Years of Black Entertainment, Big Bands, and the Blues* (Philadelphia, 1986)
N. Hazlewood: "The Jump Bands: Louis Jordan, 1938–42" *Sv* (1989), no.137, p.164; no.138, p.218
J. Chilton: *Let the Good Times Roll: the Story of Louis Jordan and his Music* (London and New York, 1992), 68
J. Evensmo: *History of Jazz Tenor Saxophone: Black Artists*, ii: *1935–1939* (Oslo, 1997); iii: *1940–1944* (Oslo, 1997); iv: *1945–1949* (Oslo, 1999)

HOWARD RYE

Simpkins, Andy [Andrew] (*b* Richmond, IN, 29 April 1932; *d* Los Angeles, 2 June 1999). Double bass player. His first instruments were clarinet and piano, which he took up respectively at the ages of ten and 14 and played though two years of study at Wilberforce University in Ohio; he began to play double bass while in the army (1953). In 1956 he was a founding member of the Four Sounds, which the following year became the Three sounds, and he remained with the group until 1968; it played swing and bop tinged with the blues, and was highly successful. Simpkins also recorded film soundtracks during this period: one of his notable performances is an eerie duet with Ray Brown for *In Cold Blood* (1967). From 1968 to 1974 he toured and recorded with George Shearing; he also performed with Carmen McRae and Joe Williams, and recorded with Clare Fischer (1971). Later he took part as a sideman in sessions with Stephane Grappelli and Shearing (1976), Dave Mackay (*c*1977), Lorez Alexandria (1977, 1980, 1984, 1992), the drummer John Dentz, Ernie Watts and Chick Corea (both 1980), and Don Menza and Buddy DeFranco (both 1981); from around 1977 into the 1990s he made several albums as a leader. In the late 1970s he toured with Monty Alexander, recording in Germany (1977) and Japan (1979), as well as participating in a session locally, in Hollywood (1978). From 1979 through the 1980s he was a member of the trio that accompanied Sarah Vaughan. He worked in Mike Wofford's small groups, recording in the 1980s and 1990s under the pianist's name and together as sidemen with others (including Alexandria and the guitarist Dan Papaila), and he was a member of Gerry Wiggins's trio for many years. Fine examples of his playing may be heard on an album recorded with Wiggins in 1995, including *Alexander's Ragtime Band*, on which he scat sings in a two-octave unison above the nimble solo bass line. He appeared regularly in the Los Angeles area in clubs and studios, and in the latter capacity recorded as a sideman with Terry Gibbs (1982, 1990), Charles McPherson (1983), Joe Pass, Charlie Shoemake and Harold Land (both 1988), Jimmy Smith (1989, 1993), Sue Raney, Mackay (1990), Scott Hamilton (1991), Teddy Edwards (1992), and Ron Affif (1992–3).

SELECTED RECORDINGS

As leader: of the Three Sounds (with B. Dowdy and G. Harris): *Bottoms Up* (1959, BN 4014), *Moods* (1960, BN 84044); with D. Mackay: *Happying* (*c*1977, Studio 7403); *Love Will Win* (*c*1982, Dis. 883); *Summer Strut* (*c*1983, Dis. 892); *Comin' at Ya* (*c*1990, MAMA 1002)

As sideman: G. Shearing: *The George Shearing Trio* (1971, Sheba 103); M. Alexander: *Jamento* (1978, Pablo 2310826); *Monty Alexander in Tokyo* (1979, Pablo 2310836); S. Vaughan: *Crazy and Mixed Up* (1982, PT 2312137); J. Pass: *One for my Baby* (1988, Pablo 2310936); R. Affif: *Ron Affif* (1992, Pablo 2310949); G. Wiggins: *Soulidarity* (1995, Conc. 4706), incl. You're mine, you, Strip City, Alexander's Ragtime Band

BIBLIOGRAPHY

FeatherE; *Feather '60s*; *Feather–Gitler '70s*

J.-L. Ginibre and P. Carles: "Dictionnaire de la contrebasse," *Jm*, no.166 (1969), 56

Obituaries: K. Mathieson, *The Scotsman* (26 Aug 1999); A. Morgan, *JJI*, lii/8 (1999), 14

K. Silsbee: "Andy Simpkins Interview," *Cadence*, xxvi/8 (2000), 11

DIANNA RHYAN/BK

Simple Acoustic Trio. Polish group formed in 1990 by MARCIN WASILEWSKI.

Simpson, Cassino (Wendell) (*b* Chicago, 22 July 1909; *d* Elgin, IL, 27 March 1952). Pianist. He reportedly once claimed to have been born in Venice, Italy, but there seems no substantial evidence for this. Early in his career he was given lessons by Zinky Cohn. In Chicago he recorded with the trumpeter Bernie Young (1923) and worked with Arthur Sims's orchestra; from around 1926 this group was led by Young, with whom he remained until spring 1930. During the same period he performed and made several recordings with Jabbo Smith, among them *Little Willie Blues* (1929, Bruns. 7058), on which he plays a particularly fine solo, *Take your Time* (1929, Bruns. 7061), and *Ace of Rhythms* (1929, Bruns. 7071). He also worked with Erskine Tate and recorded as a freelance, and from around 1931 to 1933 he led his own bands, which included Smith and Milt Hinton. He then accompanied Frankie "Half Pint" Jaxon, but the association ended abruptly when Simpson was charged with attempting to kill Jaxon. Shortly afterwards, on 29 March 1935, he was admitted to a mental hospital, where he continued performing and in 1942 recorded piano solos which were issued on LP after his death (*Cass Simpson: Traditional Piano Stylist*, Para. 109). The few recordings of his work confirm the view of his contemporaries that Simpson was an exceptional pianist whose playing became increasingly impressive towards the end of his short career.

BIBLIOGRAPHY

ChiltonW; *McCarthyB*

J. S. Shipman: "Cassino Simpson," *JJ*, viii/11 (1955), 1

J. Simmen: "Cassino Simpson," *Sv*, no.28 (1970), 123, rev. and enlarged in *BHcF*, no.206 (1971), 6

A. Vollmer: "Rhythm Aces," *Sv*, no.86 (1979–80), 70

HOWARD RYE

Sims, Ray (C.) (*b* Wichita, KS, 18 Jan 1921). Trombonist, brother of Zoot Sims. After gaining experience in dance bands he recorded with Anita O'Day and worked briefly with Benny Goodman (both 1947); as a member of Goodman's septet he recorded *How High the Moon* (Cap. 20127). From 1947 to 1957 he played trombone and sang ballads with Les Brown; during this period he played alongside other members of Brown's band in Dave Pell's octet (1953–7). While working and recording with Harry James (1957–69) he made occasional recordings with such leaders as Bill Holman (1957–8), Red Norvo (1958), and Charlie Barnet (1959). Later he recorded again with James (1973), as a singer with Corky Corcoran (1973), and as a trombonist and singer in his brother's quintet (*The Swinger*, 1979–80, Pablo 2310861).

SELECTED FILMS AND VIDEOS

Les Brown (1948); Les Brown and his Band of Renown (1949); Connee Boswell and Les Brown's Orchestra (1950); Harry James and his New Swinging Band (1965)

BIBLIOGRAPHY

FeatherE; *Feather '60s*

R. D. Kinkle: *The Complete Encyclopedia of Popular Music and Jazz, 1900–1950* (New Rochelle, NY, and Westport, CT, 1974) [incl. discography]

Sims, Zoot [John Haley] (*b* Inglewood, CA, 29 Oct 1925; *d* New York, 23 March 1985). Tenor saxophonist and leader, brother of Ray Sims. He grew up in a family of vaudeville artists and played drums and clarinet as a child; he took up tenor saxophone when he was 13. He worked as a professional musician from the age of 15, touring in dance bands, and while with the obscure dance band of Kenny Baker (not the English jazzman of that same name) he acquired his nickname, Zoot, taken from the then-current nonsense language popularized by Slim Gaillard (other fellow Baker bandsmen were called Scoot and Voot). Engagements in February 1943 and from October 1943 to January 1944 marked the start of a long affiliation with Benny Goodman. In 1944 Sims played in New York at Café Society (Uptown) with Bill Harris (i) and recorded with this group under the nominal leadership of Joe Bushkin, then performed in California with Sid Catlett. After serving in army bands he worked again with Goodman (1946–7) and also with Gene Roland. From 1947 to 1949 he was a member of Woody Herman's big band, where Roland's writing for four tenor saxophones led to the establishment of the famous saxophone section known as the Four Brothers (for illustration *see* HERMAN, WOODY, fig.1*b*); Sims is the second soloist (following Stan Getz) to be heard on Herman's recording of *Keen and Peachy* and the first on *Four Brothers* (both 1947). At this time Sims was one of Herman's eight sidemen plagued by heroin addiction. After leaving Herman he played briefly with Buddy Rich, replaced Wardell Gray in Good-

Zoot Sims (right) and Al Cohn in Toronto, 1960

man's bop group (October 1949), toured Europe with Goodman's reconstituted swing sextet (including Roy Eldridge), and worked with Chubby Jackson (1950) and Elliot Lawrence (1951), but performed and recorded principally as a freelance; his recordings included a session with Al Cohn (1952). Following a brief period in Stan Kenton's band (1953) he toured Europe and recorded as a sideman with Gerry Mulligan's groups (1954–6).

Having recorded further sessions with Cohn (1956, 1957), for about four months in 1957 the two men toured as coleaders of a swing and bop quintet (see illustration). Later performances and recordings by Cohn and Sims's quintet included engagements at the Half Note in New York three or four times annually from 1959 through the 1960s, residencies in London (1962, 1967), and tours of Europe (1965), Scandinavia (1974), and Japan (1978). On occasion the group became a sextet with the addition of a third tenor saxophonist, Richie Kamuca, and from time to time it served as Jimmy Rushing's band. Throughout these years Sims also worked apart from Cohn. Having visited Europe with Goodman in May 1958, he remained for several months and toured with a Jazz at Carnegie Hall show before returning to the USA in October. He played as a soloist in Mulligan's Concert Jazz Band (1960), joined Red Norvo's nonet (January 1961), toured South America with Curtis Fuller (July 1961), worked as a soloist at Ronnie Scott's in London (autumn 1961), and toured the USSR with Goodman (1962). With Jazz at the Philharmonic he performed at the Newport Jazz Festival (1963) and later toured England (1967) and Europe (1975). He worked in Clark Terry's big band (1967), participated in reunions with Herman (1972, 1976), toured Europe (1972) and Australia (1973) with Goodman once again, and performed at the Grande Parade du Jazz in Nice with ensembles that played in styles ranging from dixieland to bop. In August 1979 he gave his last concert with Goodman. Sims also led informally organized rhythm sections of piano, bass, and drums from the late 1960s to the end of his life. In October 1979 he played at Fat Tuesday in New York with one such group, including Jimmy Rowles, Major Holley, and Mousey Alexander; the bass players Michael Moore (i), Bob Cranshaw or George Mraz and the drummer Mickey Roker also worked in quartets with Sims and Rowles during these years.

Sims was one of several leading white tenor saxophonists whose playing was closely modeled on that of Lester Young, but had a good dose of bop melodic formulas thrown into the mix. Like Stan Getz, he produced a beautifully rounded and breathy tone. He was a tireless, exuberant performer who had a seemingly perfect sense of swing. In his last decade he doubled as a soprano saxophonist.

Oral history material in *GBLnsa*.

SELECTED RECORDINGS

As leader: Don't worry about me (1950, Vogue 5054); Tangerine/Zootcase (1952, Prst. 1348) [EP]; with A. Cohn: *From A to Z* (1956, RCA LPM1282), *Al and Zoot* (1957, Coral 57171), *You 'n' Me* (1960, Mer. 60606), *Body and Soul* (1973, Muse 5016); *Zoot at Ease* (1973, FaD 2000); with J. Venuti: *Joe and Zoot* (1974, Chi. 128); *Nirvana* (1974, GM 533); *Zoot Sims and Friend* (1975, CJ 21); with J. Venuti: *Joe Venuti/Zoot Sims* (1975, Chi. 142)

As sideman: W. Herman: Keen and Peachy (1947, Col. 38213); Four Brothers (1947, Col. 38304); G. Mulligan: *Concert Jazz Band* (1960, Verve 68388); P. Adams: *Encounter* (1968, Prst. 7677); C. Basie: *Basie and Zoot* (1975, Pablo 2310745)

SELECTED FILMS AND VIDEOS

Woody Herman and his Orchestra (1948); Flash (1962); The Shelly Manne All Stars (1970); Jazz on Stage: The Zoot Sims Quartet (1970); All Star Swing Reunion (1986); Norman Granz présente improvisation: documents exceptionnels et inédits des plus grands noms de jazz (n.d.)

BIBLIOGRAPHY

BalliettA (1986); *BalliettA (1996)*
B. Hodgkins: "Zoot," *Metronome*, lxvi/12 (1950), 16
I. Gitler: "The Colorful World of Zoot Sims," *DB*, xxviii/8 (1961), 20
A. Entwhistle: "Zoot Sims: Fratricidal Enigma," *JM*, no.164 (1968), 10
M. Bourne: "Zoot Sims: Elemental Elegance," *DB*, xliii/20 (1976), 13
C. Carrière and A. Tercinet: "Zoot Sims," *Jh*, nos.339–40 (1977), 24
A. Astrup: *The John Haley Sims Discography* (Lyngby, Denmark, 1980; suppl. 1983; suppl. 1990)
G. Endress: *Jazz Podium: Musiker über sich selbst* (Stuttgart, Germany, 1980), 122
D. Long: "Zoot Sims: Interview," *Cadence*, ix/5 (1983), 5
B. Rusch: "Zoot Sims: Interview," *Cadence*, x/11 (1984), 5; xi/1 (1985), 5
Obituary, J. S. Wilson, *New York Times* (24 March 1985)
M. Jones: *Talking Jazz* (London, 1987), 66
D. K. Ramsey: *Jazz Matters: Reflections on the Music and Some of its Makers* (Fayetteville, AR, 1989), 215
R. A. Luckey, ed.: *West Coast Jazz Saxophone Solos: Fifteen Recorded Solos from 1952–1961* (Lafayette, LA, c1996) [incl. transcrs.]

BK

Simtaine, Félix (*b* Verviers, Belgium, 1938). Belgian drummer and bandleader. From the mid-1950s he played in dixieland and hard-bop groups. He appeared with Philip Catherine at the Montreux Jazz Festival (1969), accompanied the organist Rhoda Scott (1969–73), then played in jazz-rock groups, though he also accompanied such visiting soloists as Joe Henderson, Chet Baker, J. R. Monterose, Dave Pike, Lou Bennett, Jimmy Gourley, Dusko Goykovich, Slide Hampton, Pepper Adams, and Tete Montoliu. From 1978 through the 1990s he led the Act Big Band, consisting of many leading Belgian players; Michel Herr served as its music director. Simtaine recorded with Eric Legnini's group, with Joe Lovano as guest soloist (1994), and as a member of Lew Tabackin's trio (1996); in 1996 he toured variously with Gary Smulyan, with Dave Turner, and to Shanghai in a trio with Charles Loos and Philippe Aerts. He also played in Phil Abraham's quartet and in Paris in Jean-Loup Longnon's sextet. In 1998 he celebrated the twentieth anniversary of the Act Big Band with a concert, and in 2000 he formed the group Ten-Tamarre.

SELECTED RECORDINGS

(recorded for Igloo unless otherwise indicated)

As leader: of Act Big Band: *Act Big Band* (1981, Les Lundis d'Hortense 1002); *Extremes* (1986, 044); of Act Big Band and other ensembles: *Intensive Act* (1995–6, 125)

As sideman: M. Herr: *Ouverture éclair* (1977, Oryx 001); E. Legnini: *Rhythm Sphere* (1994, 117); L. Tabackin: *L'archiduc: Round about Five* (1996, 127)

BIBLIOGRAPHY

R. Pernet, J.-P. Schroeder, and others: *Dictionnaire du jazz à Bruxelles et en Wallonie* (Liège, Belgium, 1991)

R. Pernet: *Belgian Jazz Discography (1897–1999)* (Brussels, 1999)

<http://www.jazzinbelgium.org/mus/felix.htm> (2000) [incl. discography]

BK

Sinatra, Frank [Francis Albert] (*b* Hoboken, NJ, 12 Dec 1915; *d* Los Angeles, 14 May 1998). Singer. His parents were Italian immigrants from whom he inherited a predilection for the bel canto style of singing. He first attracted widespread attention while singing for radio programs in New York, and was engaged as a big-band vocalist with Harry James in 1939. This was followed by a three-year period with Tommy Dorsey (1940–42; for illustration *see* Dorsey, Tommy), during which he became a celebrity among young people on a scale matched only by Benny Goodman before him and later by Elvis Presley and the Beatles. After leaving Dorsey he was constantly in demand as a soloist, singing as many as 100 songs daily on a tight touring and recording schedule. Inevitably this overexposure began to tell on Sinatra's voice and popularity, and from 1947 his career entered a noticeable decline. He continued to make recordings for Columbia, generally of ballads, but failed to match his former success, and by 1952 he was without a recording contract.

The following year, however, Sinatra re-established himself in the public eye through a non-singing role in the film *From Here to Eternity*, and signed a new recording contract with Capitol which placed him in a more congenial, jazz-oriented context. There followed a long series of best-selling recordings using arrangements by Billy May, Gordon Jenkins, and, most notably, Nelson Riddle, whose expert handling of big band and strings drew out the many facets of Sinatra's musical personality to excellent advantage. From this point Sinatra projected an image as a "swinger" rather than a balladeer, though he continued to excel in ballad performances as well. Once again he began to dominate the popularity polls for male vocalists. Other important film roles followed, both in musicals such as *Guys and Dolls* (1955), *High Society* (1956), and *Can-can* (1960) and in non-singing roles, particularly in *The Man with the Golden Arm* (1955; *see* Films, §I, 4(iv)). The years around 1960 probably represented the crest of his popularity. He ceased to record for Capitol, and founded his own record company and label, Reprise, in 1961. For this organization he recorded with Count Basie (1962–6) and Duke Ellington (1967). He announced his retirement in 1971, but this proved impossible for a man so quintessentially a public performer, and from 1973 he resumed his career with national and international tours, television spectaculars, and recordings. He received the Presidential Medal of Freedom in 1985.

Sinatra is best known as a popular singer, but he is nevertheless highly respected in jazz circles, above all for his relaxed and subtle sense of swing. Although improvisation is not one of the main characteristics of his style, whenever he departed radically from the given material he always did so with excellent taste and to expressive purpose. From Dorsey he adopted certain key aspects of jazz phrasing, particularly regarding breathing; later he expressed a debt to Billie Holiday. But the crucial innovations in Sinatra's approach were based (unwittingly) on the Italian bel canto tradition, particularly his legato attack (known to his detractors as "mooing"), his handling of portamento and rubato, and his sensitive modulation of vowel sounds. Like Crosby, he made full use of the microphone, but with a new awareness of its potential as an "instrument" for achieving a wide range of dynamics and for magnifying the expressive effects of singing at medium volume. His lightness of breath and "forward" vocal production permitted an extraordinarily clear enunciation and allowed him to concentrate on shading and nuance. Though Sinatra spawned countless imitators – few popular singers outside the rock tradition entirely escaped his influence – none was able to match the note of almost autobiographical sincerity in his singing, the result of a unique fusion of a turbulent and controversial public career and an intuitive penetration and projection of the meaning of a song and its lyric.

SELECTED RECORDINGS

As leader with C. Basie: *An Historical Music First* (1962, Rep. 1008); *It Might as Well be Spring* (1964, Rep. 1012); *Frank Sinatra/Count Basie at the Sands* (1966, Rep. 1019)

As sideman with T. Dorsey: Without a Song (1941, Vic. 36396); Everything happens to me (1941, Vic. 27359)

BIBLIOGRAPHY

E. J. Kahn: *The Voice* (New York, 1947)

M. Romano: "Swingin' Frankie," *Jh*, no.115 (1956), 12

A. Shaw: *Sinatra: Twentieth-century Romantic* (New York, 1965)

A. I. Lonstein and V. R. Marino: *The Compleat Sinatra: Discography, Filmography, Television Appearances, Motion Picture Appearances, Radio Appearances, Concert Appearances, Stage Appearances* (Ellenville, NY, 1970, 2/1979 as *The Revised Compleat Sinatra: Discography, Filmography, Television Appearances, Motion Picture Appearances, Radio Appearances, Concert Appearances, Stage Appearances*, suppl. 1991)

H. Pleasants: "Frank Sinatra – a Great Vocalist Retires," *Stereo Review*, xxvii/5 (1971), 59 [incl. discography]

K. Barnes: *Sinatra and the Great Song Stylists* (London, 1972)

H. Pleasants: *The Great American Popular Singers* (New York, 1974)

E. Wilson: *Sinatra: an Unauthorized Biography* (New York, 1976)

J. Ridgway: *The Sinatra File* (Birmingham, England, 1977-80)

J. Rockwell: *Sinatra: an American Classic* (New York, 1984)

G. L. Doctor: *The Sinatra Scrapbook* (New York, 1991)

R. W. Ackelson: *Frank Sinatra: a Complete Recording History of Techniques, Songs, Composers, Lyrics, Arrangers, Sessions and First-issue Albums, 1939–1984* (Jefferson, NC, 1992)

J. Howlett: *Frank Sinatra* (New York, 1994)

S. Britt: *Frank Sinatra: a Celebration* (New York, 1995)

W. Friedwald: *Sinatra!: the Song is You: a Singer's Art* (New York, 1995)

D. Holder: *Completely Frank: Life of Frank Sinatra* (London, 1995)

S. Petkov and L. Mustazza, eds.: *The Frank Sinatra Reader* (New York, and Oxford, England, 1995)

E. A. Vare, ed.: *Legend: Frank Sinatra and the American Dream* (New York, 1995)

D. Clarke: *All or Nothing at all: a Life of Frank Sinatra* (London, 1997)

J. Lahr: *Sinatra: the Music and the Man* (New York, 1997)

J. Collis: *The Complete Guide to the Music of Frank Sinatra* (London, 1998)

Obituaries: S. Holden, *New York Times* (16 May 1998); B. A. Folkart and A. Martinez, *Los Angeles Times* (16 May 1998); B. Crowther, *JJI*, li/8 (1998), 18

L. Mustazza: *Ol' Blue Eyes: a Frank Sinatra Encyclopedia* (Westport, CT, and London, 1998)

HENRY PLEASANTS/BK

Singer, Hal [Harold; Cornbread; Oklahoma] (*b* Tulsa, OK, 8 Oct 1919). Tenor saxophonist and bandleader. He first learned violin, then from 1933 played clarinet and alto saxophone. After changing to tenor saxophone he worked from time to time with Ernie Fields (1938–42), Nat Towles and Tommy Douglas (both 1939–42), and the trumpeter Lloyd Hunter (1941–2). He then moved to New York with Jay McShann and performed there with Hot Lips Page (1943),

Roy Eldridge (1944), Don Byas (1945), Henry "Red" Allen and Sid Catlett (both 1946–7), and Lucky Millinder and Duke Ellington (both 1948). As a member of Page's band he recorded with various blues singers, notably Wynonie Harris, in 1947; on Harris's *Blow your Brains Out* he takes the first and third solos in a succession of tenor saxophone "chase" choruses with Tom Archia, and on *Blowin' to California* his is the second tenor saxophone solo, following that of Archia.

In 1948 Singer, who had been known to his fellow musicians as Oklahoma, gained the nickname Cornbread, after the title of one of his first recordings as a leader. Over the next ten years (1949–58) he toured with his own band, and during the same period he recorded as an accompanist to many rhythm-and-blues performers. He then worked as a house musician at the Metropole in New York (1958–61). In the early 1960s he toured with a trio and led a band in New York while studying at the Juilliard School. Following a tour of Scandinavia he settled in Paris (1965), where he led a succession of bands, including a group with Jimmy Woode (1971–2) and a quartet with Georges Arvanitas (1972–8). In addition he performed and recorded extensively with various visiting Americans, among them T-Bone Walker, Johnny Letman, Eddie "Cleanhead" Vinson, and Jimmy Witherspoon. In 1986–7 he was a member of the cast of the Paris show *Black and Blue*, and in 1989 he toured Germany with Joe Newman and traveled to Russia to appear in the film *Taxi Blues* (1990), a Franco-Russian co-production. His autobiography, *Hal Singer: Jazz Roads* (Paris, 1990), which he wrote together with his wife, Arlette Singer, was published in French. In the 1990s Singer visited Africa (1995), was associated with Michel Legrand, and recorded in a duo with the pianist Bernard Maury (1997).

SELECTED RECORDINGS

Duos with B. Maury: *Prints in the Sand* (1997, BB 648-2)

As leader: A Plug for Cliff/Cornbread (1948, Savoy 671); on [various artists]: *Honkers and Shouters: Roots of Rock 'n' Roll*, vi (1948–61, Savoy 2234), Loose Riff (1949); *Blue Stompin'* (1959, Prst. 7153); with M. Buckner: *Milt and Hal* (1968, BB 33016)

As sideman: W. Harris: Blow your Brains Out/Lollipop Mama (1947, King 4226); Blowin' to California (1947, King 4252); Good Rockin' Tonight (1947, King 4210); Arbee Stidham: Stidham Jumps (1949, Vic. 22-0000); J. Letman: *A Funky Day in Paris* (1968, BB 33015); T-Bone Walker: on *Feeling the Blues* (1968, BB 33019), Feeling the Blues, Gee, baby, ain't I good to you, I hate to see you go, Late Blues, Leavin' You Behind

BIBLIOGRAPHY

ChiltonW; *FeatherE*; *Feather–Gitler '70s*

A. McCarthy: "The Hal Singer Story," *JM*, iv/11 (1959), 11

C. Roby: "Blue Stomping at the Trois Mailletz," *JB*, ii/11 (1965), 4

J. Elliott: "All Tenor Players Owe Something to Hawkins," *CI*, iv/12 (1966), 10

J. Pescheux: "Hal Singer," *BHcF*, no.155 (1966), 7

C. Scheneider: "Le prêcheur à la pêche," *Jh*, no.437 (1987), 27

K. Mohr: "Conversations avec Hal Singer," *Soul Bag*, no.119 (1990), 8; "Hal Singer Discography," 12

J. Pescheux: "Avec Hal Singer sur les routes de jazz," *BHcF*, no.389 (1991), 1

F. W. Sportis: "Hal Singer: les anches ... de Duke Ellington," *Jh*, no.514 (1995), 38

J. Evensmo: *History of Jazz Tenor Saxophone: Black Artists*, iii: *1940–1944* (Oslo, 1997); iv: *1945–1949* (Oslo, 1999)

HOWARD RYE

Singing.

1. General: (i) The place of singing and singers in jazz (ii) Jazz vocal techniques and styles. 2. The precursors of jazz singing. 3. The influence of the blues. 4. Early jazz singers. 5. The swing era. 6. Singers and styles of the 1940s and 1950s. 7. New directions after 1960.

1. General.

(i) The place of singing and singers in jazz. Jazz has developed its own tradition of singing and has evolved a number of distinctive techniques and styles. Both historically and stylistically it is closely allied to other forms of popular music and its connection with classical music is remote. Few jazz singers (or vocalists, as they are normally called in jazz) have a classical training or bring to their performance classical techniques of breathing, voice production, and vibrato (a notable exception is Sarah Vaughan). Similarly the traditional naming of the voices according to range, though it is sometimes found in writing on jazz, is not altogether appropriate: singers whose voices fall into the alto (or contralto), tenor, and baritone ranges are far more often found than are sopranos and basses, but many singers anyway employ techniques (such as falsetto and scat yodeling, see below) that carry the voice out of the basic range.

Jazz singing arises from and overlaps with two other traditions – the blues and popular song. The definition of a singer as a blues, jazz, or popular singer is often controversial, especially as there is no clear distinction in terms of repertory. Particularly in the earlier periods of jazz, the numbers a singer was called upon to perform consisted almost entirely of items from the blues and popular repertories; the distinction in these periods lies rather in the character of the accompaniment, the way in which the singer interacts with the instruments in the group, and the style of delivery and expression. The first of these considerations is often the most important: for example, a blues singer whose personal style differs in no significant way from that of other singers in the genre might be regarded as a jazz singer because he or she was singing with a jazz band.

The importance of the singer in jazz has varied according to style and period. In early jazz, performances of the blues and vaudeville numbers often involved singers (usually women), but performances of marches and ragtime pieces were always instrumental. Once popular songs began to enter and indeed dominate the repertory (from the 1920s) the singer found a regular place in jazz performance. The singing of popular songs reached its zenith during the swing era, when jazz and popular music effectively merged and every big band had at least one singer. It continued through the bop era (alongside new styles of jazz singing) and into Latin jazz, especially that in bossa nova style. Nevertheless, the prominence of the popular song did not eclipse the blues, which has continued to form part of the jazz repertory.

At periods when instrumentalists were almost always male, singing was an important route by which women entered jazz. While a large proportion of leading male singers have been first and foremost instrumentalists (Louis Armstrong, Jack Teagarden, and Clark Terry, for example), most female singers have tended to concentrate on singing alone. All of the greatest jazz singers have been American: although there are fine European and Latin American singers, including Alice Babs, Annie Ross, and Urszula Dudziak, none has been nearly so influential as such non-American instrumentalists as Django Reinhardt, Stephane Grappelli, Jean-Luc Ponty, Albert Mangelsdorff, Toots Thielemans, and Airto Moreira. The reasons for this are not altogether clear, though they may have to do with the importance of the English language in the jazz singing repertory and the centrality of the African-American musical heritage, with its characteristic timbres and modes of expression and delivery.

The place of the singer in jazz is different from that of any other member of the jazz ensemble for several reasons. In a band the singer almost always performs as a soloist even when he or she is technically a sideman. In those rare instances where the singer's line is integrated into an instrumental ensemble passage (as with the wordless vocalizing of Kay Davis in some of Duke Ellington's numbers) the voice still does not blend thoroughly with the instrumental sound. Singers have often been bandleaders (among them Bessie Smith, Cab Calloway, and Billy Eckstine) but neither this role nor that of a sideman in another leader's band signifies the same degree of success for a singer as it does for an instrumentalist. The most important landmark in the careers of some jazz singers is not the joining or leading of a band but the graduation from affiliation with an ensemble to work as a solo artist, touring and recording in varied settings, as did, for example, Ella Fitzgerald; in jazz and popular music such a singer is said to be working as a "single." The finest singers sometimes collaborate with one another, though less often than is the case with leading instrumentalists. Important examples include Louis Armstrong with Jack Teagarden and a number of vocal ensembles, notably the duo of Jackie Cain and Roy Kral, the trios Lambert, Hendricks, and Ross and the Boswell Sisters, and the quartets the Mills Brothers, the Novi Singers, and Manhattan Transfer. The Swingle Singers, whose scat versions of classical music are of questionable taste and peripheral importance to jazz, the Double Six, and the Vienna Art Choir are among the few large vocal ensembles.

(ii) Jazz vocal techniques and styles. Despite its derivation from and connection with blues and popular song, jazz has developed its own vocal techniques and practices, not all of which fall into the category of conventional singing.

Scat singing, in which the voice is used as a surrogate instrument and the singer employs nonsense syllables rather than words, was a regular element in early jazz and swing; it gained greater importance in bop, and was later also adapted to fusions of jazz and soul music. Scat singing and some other styles of jazz singing often involve the use by male singers of the falsetto range and by low-voiced female singers of an equivalent high range. Many kinds of wordless vocalizing are exploited by jazz singers, from expressive growls and screeches to gentle humming, from vocal sounds that are close to speech (notably Clark Terry's mumbling) to convincing imitations of the timbres of particular instruments. One technique that is unrivaled is Leon Thomas's scat yodeling. A form of vocal practice that is, in a way, the converse of scat singing is Vocalese, an instrumental melody reproduced vocally with added text.

Besides these exceptional practices, jazz singers have adopted a great variety of approaches to the delivery of lyrics, ranging from careful interpretation to distortion in the interests of other aspects of the performance (line, vocal inflection, timbre, etc.). A controversial figure is Sarah Vaughan, who has been criticized for concentrating on instrumental sound rather than on meaning, and consequently destroying the sense of the words she sings. It should be said in her defense that the lyrics of popular songs of the 1920s to the 1940s are often trite and sentimental, if not sometimes nonsensical, and a lack of clarity is therefore small loss compared with the gain in the quality of the vocal sound. Among those who have evolved alternative approaches to such lyrics are Fats Waller, whose treatments ranged from serious to satirical (see Berger, 1973), and Billie Holiday, who developed an ability to infuse them with depth and meaning.

The use of vocal sounds in jazz is by no means confined to singers: many instrumentalists vocalize while playing. A number of performers provide a vocal accompaniment to their improvised instrumental lines, most often in unison or at the octave above or below, but sometimes at other intervals; exponents include Ray Perry (violin), Slam Stewart and Major Holley (double bass), George Benson (electric guitar), Tania Maria (piano), and Roland Kirk (flute). The important technique of humming or singing through the instrument is used in the production of Multiphonics and the Growl and is intrinsic to playing the Kazoo; performers sometimes incorporate the same practice in their improvisations – Dewey Redman, for example, has developed a unique manner of humming through the tenor saxophone. Vocal sounds and effects, often of a less "musical" kind, are employed in some free jazz, notably by the members of the Art Ensemble of Chicago, and many of the instrumental gestures associated with the style have an inherently vocal character. (It is interesting, given these aspects of the music, that there have been only a few singers of significance in free jazz.)

An unusual form of vocal production used occasionally in jazz is whistling. The notable exponents are Toots Thielemans, the bop whistler Ron McCroby, and Joel Brandon. Although the rather smooth and saccharine sound of whistling does not generally meld well with the characteristic timbres of jazz, Brandon takes a different approach, producing a raspy sound that is well suited to the genre; a fine example may be heard in his duo with Chico Freeman, *The Ditty*, on Freeman's album *You'll Know When You Get There* (1988, BS 120128-2).

In the mid-1920s the introduction of the microphone revolutionized the practice of popular singing, allowing singers to explore a much broader range of dynamic variation than had previously been possible, and leading to a new, intimate style of delivery, which in some cases involved whispering, speaking, or half-speaking the lyrics of songs. Singers used the microphone not only to amplify volume but also to project notes in extreme registers and of subtle timbres. With the widespread availability from the 1970s of electronic sound-modifying devices of a more varied and complex kind, the range of sound effects available to performers increased enormously. The singers to have exploited the possibilities offered by electronics most creatively are Urszula Dudziak and Jay Clayton.

2. The precursors of jazz singing. The roots of jazz singing are to some extent more clearly traceable than those of instrumental jazz and in many respects predate them. During the late 19th century such forms as the work song and the spiritual presaged the birth of vocal jazz, and by the turn of the century the Blues was becoming established as a song form. All these styles were cultivated exclusively by African-Americans. The work song, sung to pace the execution of manual labor, often followed a pattern of Call and response, while the spiritual, a kind of sacred folksong performed in church or less formally in the fields, had a more song-like structure. The opinions of musicians and scholars differ as

to whether the blues grew out of the work song or the spiritual. Early groups, such as the Jubilee Singers of Fisk University, who from the 1870s transferred the spiritual to the concert hall, employed the bent notes and other inflections that characterize the blues, though these nuances were often eliminated in performances for white (particularly European) audiences.

3. The influence of the blues. The way in which the blues developed into a vocal form can only be guessed, since the transition took place before the era of the phonograph and in a stratum of society about which written documentation is scarce. The nature of early blues is perhaps best represented by the recordings of primitive country blues made in the 1920s by Blind Lemon Jefferson and in the 1920s and 1930s by Leadbelly (Huddie Ledbetter). These songs were based on the 12-bar Blues progression. They often followed what became the traditional lyric pattern, one similar to that of classical English verse and familiar through the works of Shakespeare, which made use of the iambic pentameter:

> I love to hear my baby call my name
> She calls so sweet and calls so doggone plain.

Both men accompanied themselves on guitar and made extensive use of Blue notes (usually the flatted third and seventh). Jefferson developed a plaintive, moaning vocal style, suited to the melancholy cast of his lyrics, while Leadbelly had a more varied, robust approach, with a full, rough tone and a harsh vibrato. Leadbelly moved, late in his career, to New York, where he became popular in nightclubs and the concert hall.

A separate tradition of blues singing was established by a group of women, who were the first to record the blues, in the early 1920s. Several of them grew up in vaudeville and were thus accustomed to a performing tradition much closer to jazz than were street musicians such as Jefferson and Leadbelly. They sang with powerful emotion, full voices, and a wide range of expression, and are regarded as contributing important elements to the development of jazz singing style. They were usually accompanied by pianists or small groups: Fletcher Henderson's orchestra, Clarence Williams's small ensembles, and Lovie Austin's Blues Serenaders were among the bands that supplied accompanists. Some female blues singers had their own groups – Mamie Smith's Jazz Hounds was the group in which Coleman Hawkins began his career – and they sometimes worked with soloists of the first rank, most notably Louis Armstrong.

Ma Rainey, the first of the classic female blues singers, recorded some 90 songs in the 1920s, but the blues became known to an African-American audience mainly through the work of Mamie Smith (fig.1), whose *Crazy Blues* (1920, OK 4160), the first highly successful Race record, set a vital precedent. It was the passionate, rasping sound and strong personality of Bessie Smith that did most to create the legendary status of the female blues singers and their songs alike. She recorded predominantly for race record series, toured the Theater Owners' Booking Association circuit, and starred in the all-black film *St. Louis Blues* (1929). The success of her first recording, *Down-hearted Blues* (1923, Col. A3844), written by another early blues artist, Alberta Hunter, and her many other recordings through the rest of the decade established her as an imperiously individual stylist. However, by the time Smith made her last recording in 1933 the blues as a pure vocal form had lost much of its popularity, and jazz singing was no longer confined to the blues.

1. Mamie Smith, 1922

4. Early jazz singers. In contrast to the blues, born out of slavery in the American South, other vocal traditions developed in other parts of the USA. Midwestern ragtime had scarce significance for jazz singing, its manifestation in jazz being exclusively instrumental, but in New York the emergence from similar roots of popular songwriting under the broad banner of Tin Pan Alley was of great importance. The origins of Tin Pan Alley go back to the 1880s and the publication of various forms of vaudeville music, including so-called ragtime songs. This tradition entered jazz after World War I, when individual popular songs and songs written for the musical theater were taken up by jazz musicians. (For numerous examples *see* Forms, §1(i)(a)).

Ethel Waters was the first singer to move away from a strong association with the blues into a broader-based style that encompassed popular songs of the day. By comparison with the blues singers her voice had more of the characteristics generally considered typical of popular singing: her timbre was cleaner, her phrasing more relaxed, and her personality both more conventional and more positive. These qualities may be heard on her many recordings, such as the highly successful *Dinah* (1925, Col. 487D).

Louis Armstrong, whose early performances included blues which he both sang and played, was also able to break away into new stylistic areas. He was the first important exponent of the technique of scat singing; a good example (and one of the earliest) is provided by *Heebie Jeebies* (1926, OK 8300), recorded with the Hot Five. In due course scat singing became an important element in jazz singing, particularly in the bop period, though some of the great singers, including Billie Holiday, never employed it. Armstrong's contribution transcended such novelties. He

Ex.1 Louis Armstrong's reworking of the melody of *I can't give you anything but love* (1929, OK 8669; original song by Dorothy Fields and Jimmy McHugh): transcr. B. Kernfeld

brought to jazz the ability to imbue even the most trivial popular song with a gruff emotional integrity, which established him in vocal jazz as firmly as his playing had in instrumental jazz. On recordings of popular songs such as *I can't give you anything but love* (1929, OK 8669) he drastically alters the melodic line to suit his own concept of the song. While saxophones offer in the background a staid, literal rendering of the melody, Armstrong centers large parts of his new melody on repeated pitches, introduces fragments of scat singing to fill spaces between phrases, and delivers brief excerpts from the original line, almost always placing all these elements well ahead of or behind the beat, rarely on it (ex.1). Although he remained a masterful blues singer, he gradually enlarged his scope until he could successfully interpret anything from a nonsense song to a ballad in a beguiling vocal performance.

Armstrong's rejection of the orthodox approach to singing inspired numerous imitators. Some of these were, like him, trumpeters – Henry "Red" Allen, Roy Eldridge, Wingy Manone, and Louis Prima, for instance, not only imitated

Armstrong's trumpet playing but also translated his melodic style of wind improvisation into vocal terms. However, it has rightly been said that every singer, male or female, whether an instrumentalist or not, has come under the influence of the unique impact of Armstrong's work in the 1920s and 1930s. Even Waters copied Armstrong in her own rendition of *I can't give you anything but love* (1932, Bruns. 6517).

5. The swing era. The big band, which developed from the mid-1920s, came to great prominence in the 1930s, when for the first time jazz merged with popular music, producing the style known as swing. Every big band included a singer, if indeed it was not led by one, and many featured two (a man and a woman) to present the hit songs of the day. Some singers were integrated into ensembles in a memorable fashion, as was the case with Kay Davis, Adelaide Hall, Ivie Anderson, Betty Roche, Joya Sherrill, and Alice Babs in Duke Ellington's orchestra; they performed not only popular songs (many newly composed by Ellington), but also blues, and works by Ellington that involved a semiclassical style of singing. Of great importance, too, was the work of forceful blues singers in Count Basie's orchestra (see below). In other settings singers were merely accessories to a more important instrumental ensemble; strikingly there is no vocal part in almost any of the greatest hits made by Benny Goodman's orchestra (one of the most popular bands of the time), even though the ensemble gave countless performances with singers.

The most creative and influential singers of the swing era did a considerable amount of work outside the big bands. Despite the attempts of Sophie Tucker and other white singers to imitate African-American styles, no important white jazz singers emerged until 1929–30, when Mildred Bailey and Jack Teagarden, both of whom moved with ease between small groups and big bands, made their first recordings. Bailey brought an effortless vocal production, a light timbre, and swinging vitality to her performances of popular songs, some of them influenced by the blues and spirituals but most quite conventional products of Tin Pan Alley. Hoagy Carmichael's *Rockin' Chair* became the theme song of her numerous radio broadcasts in the 1930s; among her several recordings of this song is a representative version made in 1937 (Voc. 3553).

Jack Teagarden was exposed as a youth to the sound of African-American spirituals sung at revivalist meetings. He became a master of the trombone and a singer who brought his rich, warm tone to songs in many different styles from genuine blues to such popular numbers as *I've got a right to sing the blues*, which became the theme song of his big band in the 1940s. Teagarden later entered into a close association with Armstrong, and (under Armstrong's leadership) they recorded vocal duets together, including the pairing *Back o' Town Blues/St. James Infirmary* (1947, Vic. 40-4006); they occasionally sang in harmony but for the most part alternated phrases or choruses, responding to and building upon each other's improvised paraphrasing of a familiar melody or lyric. Teagarden's lazy, relaxed sound established him as the only white male jazz singer of consequence of the time.

Lee Wiley, who sang with Paul Whiteman, Eddie Condon, Willard Robison, and other prominent bandleaders in the 1930s and 1940s, was another white jazz singer to develop a distinctive style. Her huskily erotic interpretations of songs by Gershwin and Cole Porter were marked by a wide vibrato and a sensitive understanding of lyrics. Many of her best-known recordings were made with dixieland bands.

In the mid-1930s two singers came to prominence, Billie Holiday and Ella Fitzgerald, whose influence on the development of jazz singing was to be decisive. Holiday made two attempts at affiliations with big bands, but she was at her most effective in small and medium-sized groups, perhaps because her inventive, irrepressible gift for improvisation was confined by big-band arrangements. Her sound, rugged and rasping, owed something to the influence of both Armstrong and Bessie Smith, though most of her best work involved standard popular songs rather than the blues; she also contributed to the composition of several songs that she performed superlatively, including *God bless the child* (1941, OK 6720) and a poignant piece about a lynching, *Strange Fruit* (1939, Com. 526). Like many jazz singers, Holiday mostly had to work with inferior material; a number of songs are remembered only because she gave them immortality (on recordings made in the 1930s and 1940s) by improvising memorably on their melodies and investing their trite lyrics with a profound depth. Although her voice deteriorated in later years, the emotional impact of her performances was without parallel. Her influence has been felt by every other singer from Frank Sinatra onwards.

Ella Fitzgerald, by contrast, moved freely during this period between Chick Webb's orchestra and her own recording octet. Her voice, with its clear, bell-like tone, was the antithesis of Holiday's. Delightful recordings with Webb, including *Sing Me a Swing Song* (1936, Decca 830), established her as a leading vocalist of the swing era. In the 1940s, unlike Holiday, she ventured into the bop style and became one of the first successful modern scat singers, as for example on her version of *How High the Moon* (1947, Decca 24387). But her most significant work was a series of albums of the compositions of Duke Ellington (often with Ellington's orchestra), Irving Berlin, Cole Porter, and others, recorded in the 1950s for Norman Granz's labels. Her rhythmic versatility, wide compass, and full, appealing tone proved adaptable to many different styles in the course of her long career, during which she continued to broaden her range.

Alongside the synthesis of popular music and jazz that is the chief characteristic of big-band style, the blues continued to be cultivated by male singers, who came to be known as "blues shouters." Working initially in the Southwest, they sang the blues in a raw, raucous style. First and foremost in this line of modern blues singers was Jimmy Rushing, a member of Walter Page's Blue Devils, Bennie Moten's orchestra, and, most importantly, Count Basie's orchestra. Later notable exponents were Joe Turner (ii), who worked as a soloist or in a duo with the boogie-woogie pianist Pete Johnson, Jimmy Witherspoon with Jay McShann's orchestra, and Joe Williams with Count Basie. Rushing, whose talent for blues singing may be heard on Basie's *Boogie Woogie* (1936, Voc. 3459), also performed popular songs, and some of his early recordings with Moten (1930) were in a heavy-handed vaudeville style. Williams eventually became accepted not only as a pre-eminent blues performer but also as a consummate interpreter of rhythmic popular songs and ballads.

Among leading male singers of the swing era, Cab Calloway and Billy Eckstine offered a contrast to the gruff approaches established separately by Armstrong and the blues shouters. It is not coincidence that both were from the northern states. They favored clarity of sound, and they enunciated in a manner closer to conventional American English than to African-American speech. Calloway's piercing timbre and humorous, mock-Hebrew scat singing may be heard on his *Minnie the Moocher* (1931, Bruns. 6074), Eckstine's creamy baritone on Earl Hines's *Jelly Jelly* (1940, Bb 11065).

While most singers during the swing era were associated with current popular songs, standards, or the blues, one young musician broke out of the mold in 1937. Maxine Sullivan, with her recording of the Scottish folksong *Loch Lomond* (Voc. 3654), established the possibility of bringing together traditional music and jazz, adapting the original song by making subtle variations to the melody and setting it against a jazz-oriented accompaniment. This famous performance, however, had no immediate successors. The idea emerged again, independently and much later, with the explosion of non-American jazz from the 1960s onwards (see below, §7).

6. Singers and styles of the 1940s and 1950s. With the emergence of bop in the 1940s and of succeeding styles such as cool jazz, progressive jazz, and third stream, the fortunes of the singer in jazz underwent a dramatic change. From a situation in which there was at least one singer in almost every big band and the leading ensembles were almost all big bands, there developed one in which the most important and innovative ensembles were small groups, concentrating overwhelmingly on instrumental music and having no place for a singer as a permanent member. While there were many prominent singers, such as Sarah Vaughan, who maintained groups of their own or worked successfully as soloists, and while singers continued to occupy their old position in bands that pursued existing styles of jazz, the major groups at the forefront of change – those, for example, of Charlie Parker, Charles Mingus, Thelonious Monk, Miles Davis, John Coltrane, Art Blakey, Horace Silver, Tadd Dameron, Fats Navarro, and many others – though they might from time to time work and record with singers, did not regularly include a singer among their personnel. (A notable exception is Dizzy Gillespie's bop big band, of which the singer Joe "Bebop" Carroll was a member from 1949.)

Despite a certain curtailment of opportunities for singers, the bop era saw a blossoming of jazz vocal techniques, notably scat singing. The impetus for this came from the new style itself: singers wishing to explore bop improvisation, to imitate with the voice the playing of soloists such as Parker and Gillespie, found scat an appropriate vehicle. The technique developed and broadened (as did other aspects of vocal production such as range, timbre, and special effects) into a well-established virtuoso practice, as convincing in its way as the parallel instrumental one. The 1940s also saw the development by Eddie Jefferson of vocalese, though the technique was not widely used until the 1950s, when it was taken up by King Pleasure and Lambert, Hendricks, and Ross.

Among the singers who maintained the tradition of the big-band vocalist in the bop era was Anita O'Day, who came to prominence as a member of Gene Krupa's and Stan Kenton's orchestras. She became a symbol of the so-called hip singer of the 1940s, with a loose, casual style involving musicianly extemporizing. Her highly individual, husky voice gained her popularity and inspired others, notably June Christy and Chris Connor, both of whom later followed her into Kenton's orchestra.

A high level of musicianship marked out several influential singers whose careers were launched in the 1940s and 1950s. Dinah Washington, Sarah Vaughan, and Carmen McRae, for example, were all not only superb singers but also competent pianists. Washington, who toured with Lionel Hampton's orchestra, had a tart, vinegary sound, which was superbly suited to the blues; but after making a series of blues hits (among them *Evil Gal Blues*, 1943, Key. 605) she achieved even greater acceptance as a singer of popular songs, often with fine jazz accompanists. Vaughan made her recording début as a leader with a group that included Dizzy Gillespie, an association that indicates her close allegiance to the bop movement; her acute ear for chord changes enabled her to bring new and vivid life to such old songs as *East of the Sun* (1944, Contl 6031). But her involvement with bop was more important for the affiliations she established – with bands led by Gillespie and Parker – than for her singing style. Over the years her range and repertory expanded continuously. Many observers felt that she could have been a successful opera singer and she went some way in that direction in numerous semiclassical performances in the 1970s and 1980s.

Carmen McRae, though four years older than Vaughan and Washington, was all but unknown until the early 1950s; at the start of her career she spent some years as an intermission pianist at a Harlem club, but her talents as a singer gradually emerged and the influence of Billie Holiday (who was a close friend) became apparent. Later she developed a more personal, occasionally sardonic, style, and her work became greatly respected among her fellow singers.

An even more accomplished musician than these three was Mel Tormé, who was still in his teens when he formed a highly acclaimed vocal group, the Mel-Tones; the group's recordings with Artie Shaw's orchestra have continued to be available. Tormé was an extraordinarily versatile and authoritative performer, one of the few jazz singers to seem equally at home in a pop song and a wordless bop number. Like Joe Williams and McRae he is widely esteemed by other singers.

Eddie Jefferson is believed to have been the first singer and lyricist to devise texted versions of instrumental improvisations. Although solos such as Coleman Hawkins's famous *Body and Soul* made intricate and demanding vocal vehicles, vocalese was taken up by other singers in the 1950s, notably King Pleasure, Jon Hendricks, and Annie Ross (who recorded her own words to solos by Wardell Gray and Art Farmer). Towards the end of the decade Hendricks and Ross joined Dave Lambert (already established as a bop singer) to form the trio Lambert, Hendricks, and Ross (fig.2). They recorded two albums of vocalese on orchestral numbers by Count Basie's band, mostly with lyrics by Hendricks; the first, *Sing a Song of Basie* (1957, ABC-Para. 223), promptly established them as the most innovative new vocal group. Hendricks continued to perform vocalese, leading a group with his wife and two daughters into the 1990s.

Betty Carter, though she had worked with Lionel Hampton's orchestra between 1948 and 1951, came to the attention of most jazz fans and critics somewhat belatedly. Her style, always jazz-oriented, and marked by great melodic freedom and a gift for making a blue note work anywhere, brought her acclaim and popularity during the 1960s and 1970s, and even more success thereafter. Also a late beginner was Sheila Jordan, who made her recording début in 1962 but failed to

2. *Lambert, Hendricks, and Ross at the Newport Jazz Festival, 1960*

gain more than a minimal following until much later; her buoyant, sensitive singing and sometimes poignant way with ballads took many years to win over audiences and critics alike. In the 1980s she was heard most often in an unusual setting, accompanied solely by the double bass player Harvie Swartz, and within this limited context creating provocative routines; she continued in this vein with Cameron Brown as her accompanist in the late 1990s.

7. New directions after 1960. The styles of jazz that evolved after 1960 have in general called less often for singers than those of the preceding period. Free jazz only rarely finds a regular place for singing, and one of the principal characteristics that distinguishes jazz-rock from rock music, and fusion from pop music, is the absence of vocal parts. However, other hybrids, those of jazz with bossa nova, soul music, rap music, and numerous non-Western musical traditions, have provided more scope for singers, a number of whom have explored various individual and eclectic styles that combine the extended techniques of avant-garde art music with different elements of jazz.

In the mid-1960s Astrud and João Gilberto introduced authentic bossa nova singing into jazz, sometimes performing songs with Portuguese lyrics. A decade later the Brazilian pop-music singer Milton Nascimento collaborated with Wayne Shorter, and in the late 1980s Nascimento's soaring style of wordless vocalizing was adopted by the Pat Metheny Group. In the early 1970s Urszula Dudziak created jazz-rock versions of Polish folksongs in her work with Michal Urbaniak's group Fusion. From the 1980s various other singers have brought sounds as diverse as Russian folk music, Dogan (Senegalese) tribal songs, native-American chant, and the Italian bel canto tradition into postmodern cross-genre hybrids with jazz.

The most original new jazz singer to emerge in the 1970s was Bobby McFerrin, who developed a unique manner of equipping his mostly wordless and usually unaccompanied performances with a variety of sound effects. Among his formidable arsenal of vocal techniques are rapid leaps of register (giving the impression of his singing both melody line and accompaniment), bitonality, chest thumping for percussive effects, and an enormous range of "nonmusical" sounds such as shrieks and grunts. By the mid-1980s, however, McFerrin had drifted away from jazz into other genres.

More popular than McFerrin with general audiences were Al Jarreau (fig.3) and the electric guitarist George Benson. Jarreau is a virtuoso scat singer who also performed in a more pop-oriented style with groups of that character, but proved in performances such as *Take Five* (on his album *Look to the Rainbow*, 1977, WB 3052) that he was one of the most creative jazz scat singers ever. Benson, like Nat "King" Cole in the 1940s, sacrificed what might have been a triumphant career as a jazz musician to pursue commercial success in popular music.

As the merging of elements of avant-garde jazz and contemporary European improvised music came into vogue, free-jazz singers began to garner recognition; the most notable exponents are Karin Krog, Shelley Hirsch, Jeanne Lee, Lauren Newton (on, for example, *Variations about N508-10 (4G)* and *Variations about Silence*, on the Vienna Art Orchestra's album *From No Time to Ragtime*, 1982, HA 1999–2000), and Norma Winstone. A very different hybrid has involved the integration of jazz with rap, as heard, for example, in the improvised rap on *I'm burnin' up*, by Black Indian, Sub-Zero, and Kokayi, on Steve Coleman and the Five Elements' album *Curves of Life* (1995, Novus 31693-2), and Avenda "Khadijah" Ali and Moishe Naim's rap on *Search for Live*, on Ornette Coleman's album *Tone Dialing* (*c*1995, Harmolodic 314-527483-2).

However, it is by no means the case that, because singers are not always at the spearhead of the newest styles in jazz, their art has declined. Alongside the innovatory developments, former styles continue to flourish, maintained both

3. Al Jarreau, New York, 1977

by the performers who created them and by new adherents. Thus opportunities for singers are plentiful in types of jazz that have now entered the mainstream, from blues (as sung, for example, by Cassandra Wilson on her album *Blue Light 'til Dawn*, c1993, BN B21Z-81357), to ballads (Shirley Horn's album *The Main Ingredient*, 1995, Verve 314-529555-2), to scat singing (as heard on Dee Dee Bridgewater's version of *On a Clear Day*, from her album *Live in Paris*, 1986, Affinity 172), to bop vocalese and a revival of the union of jazz singing and beat poetry (both of which are central to Kurt Elling's repertory (*Close your Eyes*, 1994, BN B21Z-30645).

BIBLIOGRAPHY

J. Rowe, ed.: *Vocal Jazz* (London, n.d. [1945])
J.-E. Berendt: *Das Jazzbuch: Entwicklung und Bedeutung der Jazzmusik* (Frankfurt am Main, Germany, 1953, rev. 2/1959 as *Das neue Jazzbuch*, Eng. trans., New York, 1962; rev. and enlarged 5/1981 as *Das grosse Jazzbuch: von New Orleans biz Jazz Rock*, Eng. trans., Westport, CT, 1982, as *The Jazz Book: from New Orleans to Fusion and Beyond*)
L. Feather: *The Book of Jazz: a Guide to the Entire Field* (New York, 1957, 2/1965 as *The Book of Jazz from Then till Now: a Guide to the Entire Field*)
——: "An Explanation of Vocalese," *Jazz: a Quarterly of American Music*, no.3 (1959), 261
M. Berger: "Fats Waller: the Inside Outsider," *JJS*, i/1 (1973), 3
H. Pleasants: "Bel Canto in Jazz and Pop Singing," *Music Educators Journal*, lix/9 (1973), 54
——: *The Great American Popular Singers* (New York, 1974)
W. Balliett: *American Singers* (New York, 1979, rev. and enlarged 2/1988, as *American Singers: Twenty-seven Portraits in Song*)
D. Bogle: *Brown Sugar: Eighty Years of America's Black Female Superstars* (New York, 1980/*R*1990)
S. Placksin: *American Women in Jazz, 1900 to the Present: their Words, Lives, and Music* (New York, 1982, London, 1985, as *Jazzwomen, 1900 to the Present: their Words, Lives, and Music*)
K. Grime: *Jazz Voices* (London, 1983)
L. Dahl: *Stormy Weather: the Music and Lives of a Century of Jazzwomen* (London, Melbourne, Australia, and New York, 1984)
L. Gourse: *Louis' Children: American Jazz Singers* (New York, 1984)
B. Crowther and M. Pinfold: *The Jazz Singers: from Ragtime to the New Wave* (Poole, England, 1986)
L. Federighi: *Cantare il jazz: l'universale vocale afroamericano* (Rome, 1986)
V. Lupo: *Vocal Groups in Modern Jazz, Vocalese: storia, discografia, biografie* (Ferrara, Italy, 1986)
G. Lees: *Singers and the Song* (New York, and Oxford, England, 1987, rev. and enlarged 2/1998, as *Singers and the Song II*)
F. Billard: *Les chanteuses de jazz* (Paris, 1990)
U. Buechter-Roemer: *New Vocal Jazz: Untersuchungen zur zeitgenössischen improvisierten Musik mit der Stimme anhand ausgewählter Beispiele* (Frankfurt am Main, Germany, 1991)
W. Friedwald: *Jazz Singing: America's Great Voices from Bessie Smith to Bebop and Beyond* (New York, 1992)
B. Crowther and M. Pinfold: *Singing Jazz: the Singers and their Styles* (London, 1997)
R. S. Schiff, ed.: *The Jazz Vocalists: a Tribute to the Singers and the Songs of the Jazz and Swing Eras* (New York, 1997)
P. Roland, ed.: *Jazz Singers* (London, 1999)

BK (1), LEONARD FEATHER (2–6), BK, GK (7)

Single (i). In jazz parlance a performer who pursues a career as a soloist; the word is often applied to singers who are accompanied by a pianist or a small group, or pianists who play as unaccompanied soloists.

Single (ii). In popular-music usage, a disc having a single musical number on each side (or occasionally a complete piece covering both sides). The term is mostly applied to the 7-inch 45 r.p.m. disc that has a playing time normally of $3\frac{1}{2}$ to 4 minutes per side. From the late 1970s it also referred to the 12-inch single that can run for up to about 12 minutes per side, and in the digital era it refers to a compact disc holding only one track (of any length). (It is not customarily used to refer to the 78 r.p.m. disc.) *See* Recording, §I, 3(ii).

Singleton, Zutty [Arthur James] (*b* Bunkie, LA, 14 May 1898; *d* New York, 14 July 1975). Drummer and leader. He played drums in several important New Orleans bands, such as those of Papa Celestin and Luis Russell, and from 1921 to 1923 worked in Fate Marable's riverboat groups, with which he made his first recordings in 1924. The following year he recorded with Charlie Creath in St. Louis, and by 1927 had moved to Chicago, where after playing with Doc Cook and Jimmie Noone he joined the band led by the pianist Clarence Jones. His recordings with Louis Armstrong in 1928 and in a trio with Jelly Roll Morton and Barney Bigard in 1929 made Singleton well known in the jazz world. He played on the majority of the delightful tracks recorded in an amalgamated New Orleans and swing style by a racially mixed band, the Rhythmakers, under the leadership of Billy Banks and the nominal leadership of Jack Bland.

Singleton's style was sufficiently flexible and progressive to keep him active during the height of the swing era. He led his own group at the Three Deuces (1935, 1936), Nick's (he was the first African-American musician to be regularly employed at this venue), the Village Vanguard, Kelly's Stable (1939–40), and Jimmy Ryan's (1941–3), and at other times accompanied performers such as Roy Eldridge (September 1936–1937) and, also at Nick's, Sidney Bechet (1938). During these years he participated in important recording sessions under Pee Wee Russell (1938, including trio tracks by "Pee Wee, Zutty, and James P." [Johnson]), Lionel Hampton (1939), Morton (1939–40), Henry "Red" Allen (1940), Wingy Manone (1941), the Three Deuces (with Russell and Joe Sullivan, 1941), and Art Hodes and Joe Marsala (both 1942).

Zutty Singleton at Jimmy Ryan's in New York, 1941

After traveling to Los Angeles in 1943, Singleton worked with Fats Waller's group in the film *Stormy Weather*. While he intermittently led his own bands, he also joined the bands of Paul Howard and T-Bone Walker, recorded with the Capitol Jazzmen, played in Kid Ory's New Orleans revival group on Orson Welles's radio show (1944), and was a member of Slim Gaillard's trio (1945). In later years he worked mainly as a freelance in New York, either leading his own dixieland bands or working with such traditional and mainstream musicians as Gaillard, Wingy Manone, Eddie Condon, Joe Marsala, Nappy Lamare, and – after a residency with Art Hodes in Chicago (1950) – Bobby Hackett. He toured Europe in 1951–3, and worked variously with Mezz Mezzrow, Hot Lips Page, and Bill Coleman. Following his return to New York he appeared for a number of years at the Stuyvesant Casino, the Central Plaza, and the Metropole. Late in 1954 he joined Wilbur de Paris. He held a long residency at Ryan's with Tony Parenti from 1963 and with Max Kaminsky from 1969 until he was incapacitated in 1970 by a stroke.

Singleton's career and musical development closely resemble those of Baby Dodds, with whom he is often, and sometimes unfavorably, compared. Unlike Dodds, however, he incorporated the innovations of 1920s Chicago drummers into his playing, thereby forming a link from the New Orleans style to later swing drummers, notably Sid Catlett. He was among the first drummers to use the sock cymbals (a forerunner of the hi-hat) and wire brushes, both of which appear on his recordings with Armstrong (1928); and he was particularly innovative on his recordings with Morton and Victoria Spivey (1929), where he may be heard playing rim shots, ride patterns on the top cymbal, unchoked cymbal crashes, and offbeat accents on the bass drum, all of which later became familiar features of jazz drumming. Although Singleton played solo choruses at least from the mid-1920s, and was famous for his imaginative breaks and fills (transcriptions by G. Wettling in *DB*, vii/19, 1940), he is known primarily as an expert and highly musical accompanist, as is attested by the many important musicians of several generations who sought him out for recording sessions.

Oral history material in *LNT*, *NjR* (JOHP), *NjR*.

SELECTED RECORDINGS

As leader: King Porter Stomp/Shim-me-sha-wabble (1940, Decca 18093); *Zutty and the Clarinet Kings* (1967, Fat Cat's Jazz 100-101)

As sideman: F. Marable: Frankie and Johnny (1924, OK 40113); L. Armstrong: A Monday Date/Sugar Foot Strut (1928, OK 8609); West End Blues (1928, OK 8597); Muggles (1928, OK 8703); V. Spivey: Funny Feathers (1929, OK 8713); J. R. Morton: My Little Dixie Home/That's like it ought to be (1929, Vic. 38601); B. Banks: Yellow Dog Blues (Ban. 32502); J. Bland: Who Stole the Lock (1932, Ban. 32605); P. W. Russell: Dinah (1938, HRS 1000); Pee Wee, Zutty, and James P.: I've Found a New Baby/Everybody Loves my Baby (1938, HRS 1002); J. R. Morton: Climax Rag (1939, Bb 10442); Three Deuces: Jig Walk/About Face (1941, Com. 539); Deuces Wild (1941, Com. 537); F. Waller: Moppin' and Boppin' (1943, Vic. 40-4003); S. Gaillard: Dizzy Boogie (1945, Beltone 753); Flat Foot Floogie (1945, Beltone 758)

SELECTED FILMS AND VIDEOS

Stormy Weather (1943); New Orleans (1947); Love that Brute (1950); L'aventure du jazz (1970)

BIBLIOGRAPHY

ChiltonW; *SchullerS*
P. Tanner: "'Zutty': The Story of Zutty Singleton," *Jazz Music*, nos.1–3 (1943)
H. Panassié: "Zutty Singleton, le plus grand drummer du monde, est arrivé en France," *BHcF*, no.12 (1951), 3
M. Williams: "Zutty Singleton, the Pioneer Jazz Forgot," *DB*, xxx/30 (1963), 18
W. Balliett: "Zutty," *Such Sweet Thunder* (Indianapolis, 1966), 282
M. Williams: "Zutty," *Jazz Masters of New Orleans* (New York and London, 1967/*R*1978), 178
M. Jones: "Satchmo's Master Drummer," *MM*, 1 (26 July 1975), 29
T. D. Brown: *A History and Analysis of Jazz Drumming to 1942* (diss., U. of Michigan, 1976), 245
S. Dance: *The World of Earl Hines* (New York, 1977), 53
J. Chilton: *Sidney Bechet: the Wizard of Jazz* (London and New York, 1987/*R*1996)
L. Wright: *"Fats" in Fact* (Chigwell, England, 1992)

J. BRADFORD ROBINSON/BK

Siobud, André (*b* Guadeloupe, *c*1915). Guadeloupe tenor saxophonist and clarinetist. In the 1940s he recorded with many bands and musicians in Paris, among them Freddie Jumbo, the guitarist Jean Ferret, the Ensemble Swing du Hot Club Colonial (*c*1943), and Harry Cooper (1943). He performed in the antillean style, and on his recordings as a clarinetist (including Ferret's *Swing Guitars*, 1943, Pathé 2187) he uses the vibrato characteristic of Creole music in his jazz improvisations. His name is given as Sylvio Siobud in some sources. (A. Boulanger: Liner notes, *Jazz and Hot Dance in Martinique*, Harl. 2018, 1985)

RAINER E. LOTZ

Sirone [Jones, Norris] (*b* Atlanta, 28 Sept 1940). Double bass player. He first played trombone and took up double bass at the age of 17. Between 1957 and 1961 he played in Atlanta with The Group, a cooperative ensemble in which George Adams was a sideman. After moving to New York (1965) he helped to form the free-jazz group Untraditional Jazz Improvisational Team with Dave Burrell and performed and made recordings with Marion Brown (1966), Gato Barbieri (1967), and Pharoah Sanders, Noah Howard, and Sonny Sharrock (all 1969). During the latter half of the 1960s he also worked with Sunny Murray, Albert Ayler, Archie

Shepp, Sun Ra, Bill Dixon, Rashied Ali, Don Cherry, and Jackie McLean. From 1971 to 1977 Sirone was a member of the Revolutionary ensemble, which he formed with Leroy Jenkins and the drummer Frank Clayton (who was soon replaced by Jerome Cooper). In addition he made recordings with Clifford Thornton (1972), Roswell Rudd (1973), Dewey Redman (1973–4), Cecil Taylor (1973, 1978), and Walt Dickerson (1982).

Sirone played in a group with Jason Hwang at some point in the early 1980s, appeared in the documentary film *Rising Tones Cross* (1984), and was a member of Phalanx from its formation in April 1984 until it disbanded around 1988. In the latter year he recorded three albums in small groups led by Charles Gayle. He also worked with bands based in Berlin, notably the Unity Ensemble, led by Conrad Bauer and Ulrich Gumpert. In Vienna in April 1990 he performed in *Streetlife*, a drama about a jazz musician in New York, which he wrote and composed in collaboration with his wife, Veronika Nowag-Jones, and the following summer he appeared at European festivals in a reunion of the Revolutionary Ensemble. During the same period he played alongside Ahmed Abdullah, Brown, Billy Bang, Fred Hopkins, and Andrew Cyrille in another band known as The Group. He recorded with Taylor again in Berlin in 1993.

For further recordings *see* Phalanx and Revolutionary ensemble.

SELECTED RECORDINGS

As sideman: D. Redman: *The Ear of the Behearer* (1973, Imp. 9250); C. Taylor: *3 Phasis* (1978, New World 303); *One Too Many, Salty Swift, and Not Goodbye* (1978, HH 2); C. Gayle: *Spirits Before* (1988, Silkheart 117); C. Taylor: *Always a Pleasure* (1993, FMP CD69)

BIBLIOGRAPHY

Feather–Gitler '70s
P. Carles and J.-L. Comolli: *Free Jazz, Black Power* (Paris, 1971, 2/1979)
V. Wilmer: "Sirone is One Hell of a Dirty Bass Player," *MM* (15 July 1972), 44
R. Riggins: "The Revolutionary Ensemble," *DB*, xl/19 (1973), 15
V. Wilmer: *As Serious as your Life: the Story of the New Jazz* (London, 1977, rev. [3]/1987)
H. J. Schaal: "Sirone," *JP*, xxxix/11 (1990), 20
"Sirone: 'Amerika braucht eine Revolte!'," *Jazzthetik*, iv/11 (1990), 18

BK

Sissle, Noble (Lee) (*b* Indianapolis, 10 July 1889; *d* Tampa, FL, 17 Dec 1975). Singer, songwriter, and bandleader. He sang professionally from 1908, and worked as a singer and dancer through his years at De Pauw University, Greencastle, Indiana (1913), and Butler University, Indianapolis (1914 – May 1915). He formed his first orchestra in 1915 and then left university to form a duo with Eubie Blake in Baltimore. After working in society dance bands led by Bob Young and James Reese Europe he resumed his songwriting and performing partnership with Blake, then in September 1916 rejoined Europe in New York. He became a drum major in Europe's 369th US Infantry band, with which he toured overseas in 1918; he remained in the band until its leader was murdered in May 1919. In the 1920s Sissle achieved much success as a singer and songwriter in vaudeville and on Broadway with Blake (for illustration *see* Blake, eubie), with whom he produced the shows *Shuffle Along* (1921) and *In Bamville* (soon renamed *The Chocolate Dandies*) (1924) and performed in Europe, mainly in London (1925–6), but also in Dublin and Paris. In summer 1927 he returned alone to Europe to perform in France, and in July 1928 he was persuaded by Cole Porter to form a 12-piece band for a residency at Les Ambassadeurs in Paris. The band performed in France, Belgium, and Britain; among Sissle's sidemen were Otto Hardwick, Sidney Bechet, Johnny Dunn, Bubber Miley, Demas Dean, Buster Bailey, Juice Wilson, Arthur Briggs, Tommy Ladnier, and Russell Smith. Sissle also continued working in vaudeville duos in 1928–9, during periods when his orchestra was idle. He led orchestras in Paris (summer 1931), New York (1933, 1934, 1935), and Chicago (1934). In 1935 he organized a new band called the International Orchestra, with Lena Horne as the singer, which performed throughout the USA and was resident at Billy Rose's Diamond Horseshoe in New York from 1938 to 1942 and again from 1945 until the mid-1950s; during World War II Sissle toured for the USO. From the 1960s he managed his own publishing company and worked occasionally as a leader.

Although he is best known as a composer and lyricist, with Blake and others, Sissle's importance in jazz was chiefly as a bandleader and singer. He made recordings throughout his career as a singer under other leaders, including several with James Reese Europe and various studio orchestras before 1920 and with studio bands in Britain in the 1920s; he also recorded many sides with Blake as his accompanist. Two pairings made in London in 1929 are perhaps the most important recordings ever made by an African-American showband: *Kansas City Kitty/On the Lazy Amazon* (HMV B5731) and *Camp Meeting Day/Miranda* (HMV B5709). The best jazz recordings that carry his name are those made in 1937–8 with a small group, the Swingsters, drawn mainly from his band, though Sissle himself took little part in them; his activities as a leader are perhaps more accurately represented by *Basement Blues* (1931, Bruns. 6129). He can be seen on film in the DeForest Phonofilm *Snappy Songs* (1923), accompanied by Eubie Blake, and with his band in *That's the Spirit* (1933).

Oral history material in *NN-Sc* (HBc).

BIBLIOGRAPHY

ChiltonW; *McCarthyB*
B. Howard: "Noble Sissle International Star," *DB*, ix/19 (1942), 21
J. R. T. Davies: "Eubie Blake: his Life and Times, pt ii: Blake and Noble Sissle," *Sv*, ii/7 (1966), 7
G. Fernett: *Swing Out: Great Negro Jazz Bands* (Midland, MI, 1970/*R*1993)
R. Kimball and W. Bolcom: *Reminiscing with Sissle and Blake* (New York, 1973)
Obituary, *New York Times* (18 Dec 1975)
P. Carr: "Travellin' Man: the Story of Demas Dean," *Sv*, no.72 (1977), 207
C. Goddard: *Jazz away from Home* (London and New York, 1979)
H. Rye: "Visiting Firemen, 7: Eubie Blake and Noble Sissle," *Sv*, no.105 (1983), 88
J. Chilton: *Sidney Bechet: the Wizard of Jazz* (London and New York, 1987/*R*1996), 79
R. Badger: *A Life in Ragtime: a Biography of James Reese Europe* (New York, and Oxford, England, 1995)

JOHN GRAZIANO/BK

Sitar. A large, plucked, fretted string instrument used chiefly in the classical repertory of the South Asian subcontinent. It became familiar to Western audiences in the late 1960s when it was used by several rock musicians, and was introduced to jazz soon after; Miles Davis recorded in 1969 with a group that included a sitar. In the same year Collin Walcott played sitar on the title track of Tony Scott's album *Homage to Lord Krishna* (Verve 68788), and he later came to be regarded as the most important sitarist in jazz; he played the instrument regularly in the groups Oregon and Codona. A fine example of jazz sitar playing is Walcott's solo on the track *Witchi-tai-to* from Oregon's album *Out of the Woods* (1978, Elek. 154). John Scofield recorded on electric sitar with Herbie Hancock in 1995, but this is not a significant performance, and since

Walcott's death in 1984 the sitar has remained a rather peripheral instrument in jazz contexts.

BK

Sit in. To play with a band of which one is not a member, either by advance invitation or on the spur of the moment; an outsider is said to sit in when, for example, he plays for one engagement or set or participates in a jam session.

Sittin' in With. Record label. It was operated by Bob Shad for about three years from 1948. Its catalogue contained notable recordings by John Hardee, Julian Dash, Wardell Gray, and other musicians of the late swing period. The label was also used to put out a small number of bop recordings, though the latter style was better represented on Shad's label Jax (1951–2). Shad later became the owner of Mainstream, which also had a considerable jazz catalogue. On some issues and pressings the label name appears as Sittin' In rather than Sittin' in With.

BIBLIOGRAPHY

"The Shad Labels," *Blues Research*, no.16 (n.d. [?1966]), 2

A. Shaw: *Honkers and Shouters: the Golden Years of Rhythm and Blues* (New York, 1978), 140

N. Darwen and T. Shad: "Bob Shad the Record Man: the Sittin' in With Story," *Blues & Rhythm*, no.100 (1995), 16 [incl. discography]

HOWARD RYE

Six, Jack (*b* Danville, IL, 26 July 1930). Double bass player. He studied trumpet from 1945 to 1947 and then worked in Chicago, Los Angeles, and New York, where he studied composition for a year at the Juilliard School (1955–6). He played double bass as a freelance with Tommy Dorsey's ghost band under Warren Covington and then with the big bands of Claude Thornhill (1958) and Woody Herman (1959–60), while also studying with Wendell Marshall. He worked with Don Elliott (1960–64), Jimmy Raney (1961), and Kenny Davern (at Nick's, *c*1961), and was a member of the Dukes of Dixieland (recording in 1963) and a small group led by Herbie Mann (recording in 1964). From 1966 to 1968 he played with Kenny Davern and Dick Wellstood at the Ferryboat in Brielle, New Jersey. In 1968 he joined Dave Brubeck's quartet, with Gerry Mulligan, and he remained with the group for two years after Mulligan's departure in 1972; he also recorded with Tal Farlow (1969), Illinois Jacquet (1974), Jay McShann (1978), Susannah McCorkle (1980), and the pianist Jack Reilly (1981), and worked as a freelance in New York (1970s). From 1981 to 1985 Six was music director at the Claridge Hotel and Casino in Atlantic City, New Jersey. He resumed playing with Brubeck in the 1980s, and by 1990 was again working full-time in the pianist's group. His playing is well represented by his recordings with Brubeck, including the album *All the Things We Are* (1973–4), on which he plays a well-constructed solo on *Here's that Rainy Day*. In addition to his work in jazz he has written several classical compositions.

SELECTED RECORDINGS

As sideman with D. Brubeck: *Compadres* (1968, Col. CS9704), incl Amapola; *All the Things We Are* (1973–4, Atl. 1684), incl. Here's that Rainy Day; *Late Night Brubeck* (1993, Telarc 83345); *Young Lions and Old Tigers* (1994–5, Telarc 83349)

BIBLIOGRAPHY

Feather–Gitler '70s

F. M. Hall: *It's About Time: the Dave Brubeck Story* (Fayetteville, AR, 1996)

LAWRENCE KOCH/BK

Six Winds. Danish group founded in 1979 by Jørgen Emborg and UFFE MARKUSSEN. It should not be confused with the Dutch group DE ZES WINDEN, which has also been known by its equivalent English name, Six Winds.

Sizzle cymbal. A cymbal with holes drilled around its edge in which rivets are loosely fastened; these sustain its sound and alter its timbre (*see* DRUM SET, §I, 5). A similar effect is achieved by suspending a light chain on the surface of a cymbal.

SJIN. *See* STICHTING JAZZ EN GEÏMPROVISEERDE MUZIEK IN NEDERLAND.

Sjösten, Lars (*b* Oskarshamn, Sweden, 7 May 1941). Swedish pianist, composer, arranger, and leader. Initially inspired by the leading bop and hard-bop musicians, he performed and toured Europe in Eje Thelin's quintet (1962–6), then played at the Gyllene Cirkeln club and later at other venues in Stockholm and on domestic tours with Swedish and visiting American soloists, including Dexter Gordon, Ben Webster, Brew Moore, Art Farmer, Sonny Stitt, and Steve Lacy. From 1964 to 1976 he played and recorded with Lars Gullin, who became a chief influence on his work as a composer; like those of Gullin, many of Sjösten's pieces combine the language of American jazz with the melodious tradition of Nordic romanticism. Sjösten also recorded with Idrees Sulieman (1964), Bernt Rosengren (1965), George Russell (1967), Putte Wickman (1970), Rolf Ericson, Gordon, and Moore (all 1971), and Gunnar Nilson (1971, 1972). During the late 1960s he undertook radio and studio work and toured Sweden with Ericson and Czechoslovakia with Rosengren. From the early 1970s Sjösten has led several ensembles, toured widely, and made recordings, principally under his own name; his group recorded with Lee Konitz in 1983 and toured Sweden with Konitz in the early 1990s.

Oral history material in *SSsv*.

SELECTED RECORDINGS

As leader: *Gutår!* (1972, Phi. 6316016); *Select Notes* (1980, Caprice 1216); *Bells, Blues and Brotherhood* (1980–81, Dra. 46); with L. Konitz: *Dedicated to Lee: Lars Sjösten Plays the Music of Lars Gullin* (1983, Dra. 66); *Roots and Relations* (1988, Dra. 164); *In Confidence* (1990, Dra. 197)

As sideman: L. Gullin: *Portrait of my Pals* (1964, Col. SSX1010); B. Moore: *Brew's Stockholm Dew* (1971, Sonet 624); D. Gordon: *The Shadow of your Smile* (1971, Ste. 1206)

BIBLIOGRAPHY

Feather–Gitler '70s

B Möller: "Vår lysande Sjösten" [Our shining Sjösten], *Orkester journalen*, xxxiv/11 (1966), 9

A. von Konow: "Swing är en gudagåva" [The ability to swing is a gift of God], *Orkester journalen*, xlix/4 (1981), 10

L. Westin: "Spelar på allvar och lek" [Serous-minded yet playful], *Orkester journalen*, lxiiii/6 (1997), 2

<http://www.mic.stim.se/engelsk/11/facts/sjoesten.html> (2000)

LARS WESTIN, BK

Ska. A musical style resulting from the coalescence in Jamaica in the late 1950s of local *mento* and *burron* rhythms with New Orleans rhythm-and-blues. Its chief influence on jazz has been through its derivative form REGGAE. (R. Steffens, "Ska," *Grove7*).

MARK GILBERT

Skatalites [Ska-talites]. Jamaican popular band. It was formed in 1964 by the island's leading jazz musicians: Johnny "Dizzy" Moore (trumpet), Don Drummond (trombone), Lester "Ska" Sterling (alto saxophone), Roland Alphonso and Tommy McCook (tenor saxophones), Donat Roy "Jackie" Mittoo (piano), Jerome "Jah Jerry" Hines (or Haines) (guitar), Lloyd Brevett (double bass), and Lloyd Knibbs (drums). Schooled in swing and bop, the group played ska. The Skatalites were influenced by Art Blakey's Jazz Messengers, Dexter Gordon, and Earl Bostic, and rhythmically by the 1952 recordings of the blues singer Rosco Gordon, but the producer Clement "Coxsone" Dodd was the catalyst who recorded and promoted them; his sessions frequently involved other musicians, notably Ernest Ranglin. In less than two years among the group's prolific output were dozens of popular singles, among them *Addis Ababa*, *Confucious*, *Fidel Castro*, *Christine Keeler*, and *Guns of Navarone*. (Discographical information on the original issues is lacking; *Foundation Ska*, issued in 1997, offers a definitive collection of reissues of singles recorded in the years 1964–6.) These repeated a successful format: the theme, followed by improvised jazz solos played over ska rhythms that increasingly foreshadowed the reggae style, and then a reprise of the theme. Highly influential both in and outside the Caribbean (on the group Jazz Jamaica, for example), the Skatalites re-formed in New York in 1984 with Sterling, Alphonso, Brevett, and Kibbs. They were joined at that time by younger musicians, including the trumpeter Nathan Breedlove and the trombonist Will Clark, and featured guest appearances by McCook.

SELECTED RECORDINGS

Foundation Ska (1964–6, Heartbeat 185–6); *Return of the Big Guns* (1984, Island 9775); *Hip-bop Ska* (1994, Shanachie 45019); *Ska-mania* (1996, Dojo 266); *Ball of Fire* (1997, Island Jamaica Jazz 4005)

BIBLIOGRAPHY

S. Clarke: *Jah Music: the Evolution of the Popular Jamaican Song* (London, 1980), 64
L. O'Neill: "Skatalites: a Conversation with Original Skatalites' Tommy McCook," *Reggae Report*, xii/9 (1994), 16
G. Robinson: "Skatalites," *Windplayer*, no.51 (1995), 14
K. Bennett: "The Skatalites: Jazzin' up Themselves," *Rhythm Music*, v (1996), Dec, 14
S. Barrow and P. Dalton: *The Rough Guide to Reggae* (London, 1997), 9
B. Keyo: Liner notes: Skatalites: *Foundation Ska* (Heartbeat 185–6, 1997)
J. Preston: Liner notes, Skatalites: *Ball of Fire* (Island Jamaica Jazz 4005, 1997)
R. Finnis: Liner notes, R. Gordon: *Bootin': the Best of the RPM Years* (Ace 694, 1998)
Obituary [T. McCook], S. Barrow, *The Guardian* (16 June 1998)

VAL WILMER

Skeat, Bill [William Frederick James] (*b* London, 25 July 1928; *d* nr Gerrards Cross, England, 4 July 1999). English alto and tenor saxophonist, brother of Len Skeat. When he was 16 he began teaching himself clarinet, which he later played for two years in an army band. He worked with Carl Barriteau briefly in 1948 and spent much of the next three decades playing jazz and popular music in various bands. After a number of engagements with Joe Newman and Yank Lawson at the Pizza Express in London he became more involved with prominent jazz musicians. He deputized for Bob Wilber at the 1978 Newport Jazz Festival and was later a member of Wilber's big band. During the late 1980s he worked with Digby Fairweather, toured Belgium and Germany with the Chas-tet (1988), and played with Bill Berry in Spain (1988) and at the Monterey Jazz Festival (1989). He also performed as a guest soloist with Bruce Forman in San Francisco, with Eiji Kitamura and others in Japan, in Australia, in New Zealand, and in Russia; his playing may be heard to advantage on his album with the Bolshoi Theater Orchestra, *For Adults Only* (*c*1997, Jazzmuse 9903). Skeat worked as a lead alto saxophonist and as a soloist on the tenor instrument.

BIBLIOGRAPHY

ChiltonB
Obituary, P. Vacher, *JJI*, lii/9 (1999), 19

GK

Skeat, Len [Leonard] (*b* London, 25 Feb 1937). English double bass player, brother of Bill Skeat. He learned clarinet with his brother and took up double bass in his late teens. In the early 1960s he worked with Tommy Whittle and in Eddie Thompson's trio, then played briefly in Ted Heath's group, with which he appeared on German television, before joining a BBC radio big band. He was a member of Stephane Grappelli's ensemble between 1973 and 1977, during which time he toured the USA and Australia. He then worked in the group Velvet (1977–1980s), with Digby Fairweather, Ike Isaacs (ii), and the guitarist Denny Wright, and played in the Pizza Express All Stars (1980–1990s). Skeat was a member of the quartets led by Danny Moss and Whittle, and worked in Thompson's trio, with which he recorded (1978–83) and accompanied Roy Williams (1981) and Spike Robinson (1984). During the same period he was active as a freelance accompanying various visiting musicians, including Bill Watrous (recording in 1982), Ruby Braff, Joe Newman, Scott Hamilton, Harry Edison, Billy Eckstine, and Lionel Hampton. He performed with Bob Rosengarden in New York and in 1980 he recorded with a quintet led by Williams and John Barnes named the Gruesome Twosome. The following year he appeared at the Grande Parade du Jazz in Nice as a member of the Jazz Journal All Stars. From 1989 he recorded regularly alongside Brian Lemon in a group led by Charly Antolini, and he continued his freelance work with Bob Wilber, Kenny Baker's re-formed Dozen, Digby Fairweather's Half Dozen, the Great British Jazz Band (recording in 1994 and 1996), and in quintets led by Dave Shepherd, and Alan Barnes and the trumpeter Bruce Adams; he also performed with the singer Val Wiseman in the show *Lady Sings the Blues* and made recordings with George Masso (1992, 1994), Harry Allen and Randy Sandke's Buck Clayton Legacy (both 1993), Danny Moss (1994), and the clarinetists Alan Vaché and Antti Sarpila (1995); a number of these were made while he was house bass player for the German label Nagel-Heyer.

SELECTED RECORDINGS

As sideman: S. Grappelli: *I Got Rhythm* (1973, BL 30158); E. Thompson: *When Lights are Low* (1980, Hep 2007); G. Masso: *The Wonderful World of Gershwin* (1992, Nagel-Heyer 001); D. Moss: *Weaver of Dreams* (1994, Nagel-Heyer 017)

BIBLIOGRAPHY

CarrJ; *ChiltonB*
D. H. Matthews: "Len Skeat," *CI*, xxvii/2 (1980), 20

GK

Skidmore, Alan (Richard James) (*b* London, 21 April 1942). English tenor saxophonist, son of Jimmy Skidmore. In the early 1960s he worked with Alexis Korner and the drummer Eric Delaney, and in 1965 he played with Ronnie Scott. From that year until 1969 he participated in jazz workshops for German radio and television in Hamburg with, among others, Dave Holland, Chick Corea, Albert Mangelsdorff, and John Surman, and in 1966 he recorded film music with Herbie Hancock. His performance with

Kenny Wheeler, John Taylor, Harry Miller, and Tony Oxley at the Montreux International Jazz Festival in 1969 earned him a scholarship to the Berklee School of Music, which he declined. In 1970 he began an association with the organist and singer Georgie Fame that continued through the 1990s. Skidmore led a quintet with Malcolm Griffiths, Taylor, Chris Laurence, and Tony Levin as his sidemen (1970) and performed at concerts with Mike Gibbs, Mike Westbrook, Chris McGregor, and Ian Carr's Nucleus (1971). In 1973 he formed the trio SOS with Mike Osborne and Surman; after this disbanded (1975) he toured with the George Gruntz Concert Jazz Band (1976–82). Though principally a saxophonist, Skidmore has doubled on drums, and he may be heard to advantage as a drummer on *Wherever I am,* recorded by SOS in 1975.

While with Gruntz, Skidmore played with Ali Haurand in a number of groups, notably Third Eye, various manifestations of the European Jazz Quartet and the European Jazz Quintet, and the trio SOH (from 1978, with Oxley). Later he was a guest soloist with West German Radio and Television (1981–4) and toured India and Southeast Asia with the WDR Radio Band (1984). In 1985 he formed the quartet Tenor Tonic, with Levin, Paul Dunmall, and Paul Rogers, and thereafter he toured extensively with this group. Among his major activities in the mid- to late 1980s were guest appearances with Elvin Jones's Jazz Machine at Ronnie Scott's (1986), tours of the USA (1986–7) and Italy (1987) with a big band led by the drummer Charlie Watts, and work in Britain, the USA, Spain, and Germany with Stan Tracey's groups (1988–90). During the 1990s he played under the composer and bandleader Colin Towns in the Mask Orchestra (from 1991), with the Dedication Orchestra (1992–4, celebrating South African jazz in Britain), and with Delaney (at the Guinness Cork Jazz Festival, 1994). Skidmore led his own bands and recording sessions throughout the 1980s and 1990s, often in tribute to his major influence, John Coltrane. In 1999 he visited Cape Town and recorded with the drumming group Amampondo.

SELECTED RECORDINGS

As leader: *Once upon a Time* (1969, Deram 11); *TCB* (1970, Phi. 6308041); of SOS (with M. Osborne and J. Surman): *SOS* (1975, Ogun 400), incl. Wherever I am; of SOH (with T. Oxley and A. Haurand): *SOH* (1979, Ego 4011), *SOH Live!* (1981, View 0018); *East to West* (1984, 1992, Miles Music 081); *Tribute to Trane* (1988, Miles Music 075); *After the Rain* (1988, 1998, Miles Music 084); with Amampondo: *The Call* (1999, Provocateur 1018)

As sideman: E. Delaney and L. Bellson: *Repercussion* (1963, EMI 169); G. Fame: *Walking Wounded* (1995, Go Jazz 60362); C. Towns: *Dreaming Man with Blue Suede Shoes* (1997–8, Provocateur 1017)

BIBLIOGRAPHY

CarrJ; *ChiltonB*; *WickesIBJ*, i

L. Evans: "Reed Clinic," *Crescendo*, iv/10 (1966), 24

L. Henshaw: "Alan Follows in Dad's Footsteps," *MM* (15 March 1969), 11

I. Carr: "Notes on Some Virtuosi," *Music Outside: Contemporary Jazz in Britain* (London, 1973), 12

B. Case: "In the Tradition," *Jazz Now: the Jazz Centre Society Guide*, ed. R. Cotterrell (London, 1976), 73

C. J. Gans: "Alan Skidmore: All in the Family," *JF* [intl edn], no.76 (1982), 35

M. Hennessey: "Europajazz," *JT* (1987), Nov, 18

S. Graham: "Keeper of the Flame," *Jazzwise*, no.26 (1999), 34

MARK GILBERT

Skidmore, Jimmy [James Richard] (*b* London, 8 Feb 1916; *d* Welwyn, England, 23 April 1998). English tenor saxophonist, father of Alan Skidmore. A self-taught musician, he took up guitar at the age of 18 and first performed on this instrument and as a singer before taking up tenor saxophone when he was 20. Having joined Harry Parry's group in summer 1942 he appeared in the short film *Harry Parry and his Radio Rhythm Club Sextet* (1942); he may also be seen with Ted Heath, George Shearing, and others in the short film *Theatre Royal* (1943). He transferred from Parry's band to Harry Roy's sextet (summer 1942), played regularly at the No.1 Swing Club in London (from its opening in October 1942), joined Carlo Krahmer (1943), and performed and recorded with the Spirits of Rhythm, led by Frank Deniz (1944). In the late 1940s he played with the Vic Lewis–Jack Parnell Jazzmen (1945) and other groups under Lewis's sole leadership (1946, December 1947), performed with an all-star British group led by the reed player Derek Neville at the Nice Jazz Festival (1948), spent a brief period with Victor Feldman (1948), and toured Germany with Dill Jones (1949). Skidmore was then a member of Ralph Sharon's sextet (?July 1950 – December 1951) and Kenny Baker's sextet (March–September 1952); he rejoined Baker in the mid-1950s, played in the Jazz Today Unit, and worked in a band led by the drummer Eric Delaney (summer 1954 – October 1956). Thoughout this first portion of his career he also played with many lesser-known musicians, and he recorded with George Chisholm (1944), Lewis (1945, 1947), Sharon (1950–52), and Baker (1951, 1955, 1956). From October 1956 to September 1960 (except for a period of illness late in 1957) he was a member of Humphrey Lyttelton's band, with which he toured the USA; he is heard to advantage on *Humphrey Lyttelton Plays Standards* (1960, Col. 33SX1305). During the 1970s and 1980s Skidmore often appeared as the leader of small groups with sidemen such as Kathy Stobart and Tommy Whittle; in the latter decade he was also a member of a quartet led by the pianist Colin Peters. He continued to lead his own group in the 1990s, and in 1996 celebrated his 80th birthday in performance with his son, Alan, who had sometimes played in Jimmy's earlier groups.

BIBLIOGRAPHY

CarrJ; *ChiltonB*; *FeatherE*

R. Cotterrell, ed.: *Jazz Now: the Jazz Centre Society Guide* (London, 1976)

Obituaries: [A. Shipton], *The Times* (10 April 1998); T. Middleton, *JJI*, li/6 (1998), 16

NEVIL SKRIMSHIRE/BK

Skiffle. A hybrid style of popular music that has affinities with jazz and country blues. The term "skiffle" appears originally to have been applied in the USA during the 1930s to entertainment provided at rent parties, which encompassed blues, barrelhouse, boogie-woogie, and other styles of African-American popular music. This music was revived in the 1950s, mostly by white players, who learned the repertory from touring African-American performers and from recordings. Skiffle bands played in a style loosely based on that of the spasm bands from New Orleans and such groups as the Mound City Blue Blowers, led by Red McKenzie. They often included acoustic guitar, harmonica, kazoo, jug, washtub bass, and washboard or drums, and the chordal and melodic instruments provided a simple three- or four-chord accompaniment to a vocal part.

While the skiffle revival of the 1950s embraced the USA and Germany, it gained most ground in Great Britain. The earliest recordings by Chris Barber (1951) and Ken Colyer (1954), made with skiffle groups drawn from their jazz bands, exemplified the style of such ensembles, but the best-known recording of the period was *Rock Island Line* (1954,

Decca F10647), by Lonnie Donegan with Barber's group. Donegan's work was modeled on that of the blues singer and guitarist Leadbelly (Huddie Ledbetter). Donegan and his imitators enjoyed considerable popularity until about 1959, when skiffle gave way, both in the USA and Europe, to "beat" music and rock-and-roll.

See also Jug band, Spasm band, and Washboard band.

BIBLIOGRAPHY

D. Boulton: *Jazz in Britain* (London, 1958), 126
G. Melly: *Revolt into Style: the Pop Arts in Britain* (London, 1970), 28
C. McDevitt: *Skiffle: the Definitive Inside Story* (London, 1997)
M. Dewe: *The Skiffle Craze* (Aberystwyth, Wales, 1998) [incl. discography]

ALYN SHIPTON

Skins. Slang term for drums; *see* Drum set.

Skipper, the. Nickname of Henry Franklin.

Skjoldborg, Anker (*b* Copenhagen, 11 Dec 1903; *d* Los Angeles, 3 April 1986). Danish tenor saxophonist and bandleader. He began his career as the first Danish jazz drummer, then took up saxophone and played both instruments with Valdemar Eiberg (1923–5) and Kai Ewans (1927) and in the group We Three, with Otto Lington and Leo Mathisen (1927–8). Thereafter he worked exclusively as a saxophonist, with Lington (1928–9), with Bernard Etté and others in Germany (1929–31), with the dance-band leader Kai Julian in Denmark (1932–3), and with bands in Italy (1933–4). From 1935 to 1939 he led a fine band in Denmark which made several recordings, including *Rug Cutters Swing* (1936, Odeon D759). Skjoldborg emigrated to the USA in 1939 and later worked as a draftsman in the Los Angeles area. (E. Wiedemann: *Jazz i Danmark i tyverne, trediverne og fyrrerne: en musikkulturel undersøgelse* [Jazz in Denmark in the twenties, thirties, and forties: a study of musical culture] (Copenhagen, 1982) [incl. discography])

ERIK WIEDEMANN

Skowron, Janusz (*b* Warsaw, 23 May 1957). Polish pianist and keyboard player. Skowron, who is blind, made his professional début in 1980 with Kazimierz Jonkisz's quartet. From 1981 to 1984 he was a member of Krzesimir Dębski's popular small fusion group String Connection, and during the same period he recorded both with this band and with the double bass player Zbigniew Wegehaupt. From 1985 he was most frequently with Tomasz Stańko, with whose group Freelectronic he recorded while on tour in 1987; he also performed with the group Bassspace and with Krzysztof Popek's ensemble Young Power and led his own small group, Carte Blanche. Later he recorded with the drummer Zbigniew Lewandowski (1989, 1993). From 1990 to 1993 he was a member of Zbigniew Namysłowski's quartet, and in 1997 he joined the fusion group Walk Away.

SELECTED RECORDINGS

As sideman: K. Jonkisz: *Tiritaka* (1980, Muza 2301); String Connection: *Workaholic* (1982, Poljazz 107); *New Romantic Expectation* (1983, Poljazz 126); Z. Wegehaupt: *Sake* (1983–4, Poljazz 129); String Connection: *Live* (1984, Polton 008); T. Stańko: *Witkacy-Peyotl* (1984–6, Poljazz 154–5); *The Montreux Performance* (1987, ITM 0023); *Chameleon* (1989, Utopia [issue no. unknown]); *Tales for a Girl* (1991, Polonia 046); Z. Namysłowski: *Without a Talk* (1991, P&J 002-1); *The Last Concert* (1991, Polonia 002)

BIBLIOGRAPHY

A. Chodkowski, ed.: *Encyklopedia muzyki* (Warsaw, 1995)
M. Brzywczy: "Janusz Skowron," *JF*, no.205 (2000), 55
A. Kosowska-Czubaj: "That Fascinating Rhythm," *Warsaw Voice* (26 March 2000); repr. <http://www.warsawvoice.pl/v596/Cult02.html> (2001)

ADAM CEGIELSKI, BK

Sky. Nickname of George Tyndale.

Slack, Freddie [Frederic Charles] (*b* nr Westby, WI, 7 Aug 1910; *d* Hollywood, CA, 10 Aug 1965). Pianist and leader. After playing piano in Johnny Tobin's band in Chicago, in 1931 he moved to Los Angeles. He toured and recorded with Ben Pollack (1934–6), then worked with Jimmy Dorsey (*c* September 1936 – August 1939). Between August 1939 and 1941 he was a soloist in the band led by Will Bradley and Ray McKinley, and he became well known for his boogie-woogie playing on such recordings as *Beat me daddy, eight to the bar* (1940, Col. 35530). In 1941–2 he recorded with Joe Turner (ii), whose versions of *Rocks in my Bed* and *Goin' to Chicago* (1941, Decca 4093) demonstrate his ability to perform in a blues idiom far removed from the boogie-woogie style. Slack formed his own band in 1942 and had a hit with his recording of *Cow Cow Boogie* (1942, Cap. 102). In the remainder of the 1940s he continued to record as a leader and appeared in the film *Follow the Boys* (1944), and during the 1950s he played at clubs in California.

BIBLIOGRAPHY

ChiltonW; *FeatherE*; *Feather '60s*
G. T. Simon: *The Big Bands* (New York, 1967, rev. 4/1981), 93
C. Garrod and B. Korst: *Will Bradley and his Orchestra; Freddie Slack and his Orchestra* (Zephyrhills, FL, 1986, rev. 2/1997) [discography]

Slagle, Steve(n Bryce) (*b* Los Angeles, 18 Sept 1951). Alto saxophonist and flutist. He moved to the East Coast with his family in the early 1960s and to Boston in 1970; there he studied at the Berklee College of Music and worked with John Scofield, Harvie Swartz, Joey Baron, and Stevie Wonder. Having settled in New York (1977) he played lead alto saxophone in Machito's Afro-Cuban Orchestra (1977–8) and was a member of Steve Kuhn's band (1977–9). Between 1979 and 1981 he worked with Eddie Palmieri and Lionel Hampton, and during the same period he played tenor saxophone with Woody Herman. In the 1980s he performed with Brother Jack McDuff (1981), Carla Bley (1981–5), and Charlie Haden's Liberation Music Orchestra (1982), and toured Brazil with Milton Nascimento (1986). He was a member of Ray Barretto's group (1988–91), and then joined the Mingus Big Band (1991), in which he has served as music director.

From the mid-1980s Slagle has toured internationally and recorded as the leader of his own groups; his sidemen have included Tim Hagans, Ryan Kisor, Kenny Drew, Jr., Mike Stern, Adam Nussbaum, and Jeff Hirshfield. In 1999 he co-led a small group with Dave Stryker which toured the USA and recorded. He worked for the Jazz and Contemporary Music Program (at the New School for Social Research, then from 1996 at the Mannes/New School) until it transferred to the New School University in 1999, and has also taught at the Manhattan School of Music, where he has led a saxophone quartet. Besides his principal instruments he plays soprano saxophone and alto clarinet.

SELECTED RECORDINGS

As leader: *Rio Highball* (1985, Atl. 81657); *Smoke Signals* (*c*1991, Panorama 1); *The Steve Slagle Quartet* (1992, Ste. 31323); *Spread the Word* (1994, Ste. 31354); *Reincarnation* (1994, Ste. 31367); *Alto Blue* (1997, Ste. 31416); *Steve Slagle Plays Monk* (1997, Ste. 31446)

As sideman: S. Kuhn: *Motility* (1977, ECM 1094); *Non-fiction* (1978, ECM

1124); C. Haden: *The Ballad of the Fallen* (1982, ECM 1248); D. Stryker: *Strike Zone* (1990, Ste. 31277); *Passage* (1991, Ste. 31330); Mingus Big Band: *Nostalgia in Times Square* (1993, Dreyfus 36559); D. Stryker: *Full Moon* (1993, Ste. 31345); Mingus Big Band: *Live in Time* (*c*1995, Dreyfus 36583)

GK

Slap-bass [slap]. An effect produced on the double bass by means of an exaggerated pizzicato technique: the string is drawn away from, or across, the fingerboard at high tension and then released suddenly so that the resulting note is accompanied by a percussive click or slapping sound as the string hits the fingerboard. Slap-bass was first used in New Orleans jazz; an early recorded example occurs in John Lindsay's accompaniment to the clarinet and banjo solos in Jelly Roll Morton's *Black Bottom Stomp* (1926, Vic. 20221). It was taken up by double bass players in the big bands of the 1930s, notably Pops Foster, who interchanged it with bowing and conventional pizzicato on many of his recordings with Luis Russell and with Louis Armstrong, for example, on *Swing that Music* (1936, Decca 866). During the swing era the technique ceased to be widely used, but it re-emerged during the New Orleans revival in the 1940s, through the playing of Alcide "Slow Drag" Pavageau (with Bunk Johnson and George Lewis (i)) and Ed "Montudi" Garland (with Kid Ory). Traditional and revival bands continue to use the effect occasionally.

In other styles of jazz slap-bass is normally employed for comic purposes or as a conscious archaism, as on Charles Mingus's recording *Cocktails for Two*, on *My Favorite Quintet* (1965, Charles Mingus 009). However, as part of the reawakening of interest in early jazz styles during the 1990s, some contemporary mainstream players incorporated slap-bass into their solo playing with the idea of further exploring its potential as a percussive and tonal effect; notable among these are Rodney Whitaker (in the Lincoln Center Jazz Orchestra and various of the small groups led by Wynton Marsalis) and Roland Guerin, both in his own groups and with Marcus Roberts's trio. Slap-bass has also been incorporated into the vocabulary of avant-garde and free-jazz players. Barry Guy employed it in several of his pieces for unaccompanied double bass, and Steve Berry in his work with the Mike Westbrook Brass Band. A similar effect, often known simply as slapping, is used on the ELECTRIC BASS GUITAR. (A. Shipton: "Styles of New Orleans Bass Playing," *Fn*, vii/1 (1976), 18)

ALYN SHIPTON

Slap-tonguing. A technique used in playing single-reed wind instruments. Using the length of the tongue, slightly arched, the player presses hard against the reed, at the same time sucking so as to create a vacuum between reed and tongue; he then draws the tongue sharply away so that the vacuum is broken and the reed is released, producing a dull slapping sound. The technique may be used alone, in which case the pitch of the note being fingered is only faintly heard (this is particularly effective in a low register), or to give a loud percussive attack to notes blown in the usual way.

Slap-tonguing was used extensively by such early reed players as Bob Fuller, Sticky Elliott, and Stump Evans and formed a major element in the styles of musicians who strove for novelty effects as a primary aim, such as Ted Lewis, Boyd Senter, and Fess Williams – though Williams combined it with an intense blues sensibility in a manner that is sometimes surprisingly effective; his employment of this and other novelty devices may be heard on *Nobody but my baby is getting my love* (1926, first issued on the album *Fess Williams and his Royal Flush*, 1925–7, Fountain 116). A later practitioner, on clarinet, was Joe Darensbourg, whose use of the technique may be heard on Kid Ory's *Yaaka hula hickey dula* (1950, Col. CL845). Although it has been adopted on most saxophones it is especially successful on the bass instrument, and is heard to advantage in traditional and swing ensembles in which players such as Adrian Rollini used bass saxophone in place of tuba or double bass. Because its execution is physically awkward, slap-tonguing may lead to a disjointed style of playing which is the antithesis of swing; Coleman Hawkins employed it as a melodic device in early improvisations, but he quickly discarded it in favor of a smoother approach to articulation.

ALYN SHIPTON

Slickaphonics. Group founded in 1980 by Ray Anderson, Mark Helias, and Steve Elson; its other members were the guitarist Allan Jaffe (ii) and the drummer Jim Payne. It made two recordings, in 1982 and 1983, before disbanding in 1987, and performed a repertory that was oriented predominantly towards funk but also drew from avant-garde jazz.

BIBLIOGRAPHY

D. Soutif: "Le free funk de Slickaphonics," *Jm*, no.314 (1983), 36
M. Wangler: "Slickaphonics," *JP*, xxxiv/1 (1985), 18

GK

Slide (i). In such instruments as the TROMBONE, a telescopic joint used to extend or reduce the sounding length of the instrument's tubing and thus to alter the fundamental.

Slide (ii). In jazz parlance a synonym for GLISS.

Slide cornet [slide trumpet]. Name used colloquially to refer to the soprano trombone; *see* TROMBONE, §1.

Slide saxophone. A saxophone fitted with a slide instead of tone-holes; the only instruments of the type used in jazz were one designed and played by Snub Mosley and one played by Roland Kirk. *See* SAXOPHONE, §6(viii).

Slim and Slam. Duo formed in the late 1930s by SLIM GAILLARD and SLAM STEWART.

Slinger, Cees [Cornelis Ernst] (*b* Alkmaar, Netherlands, 19 May 1929). Dutch pianist. He played with dance bands from the age of 12 and appeared with Rita Reys at the Sheherazade club in Amsterdam for six months in 1954. Over the next three years he worked as a pianist (and with one group as a double bass player) before forming the Diamond Five, which performed six nights a week at the Sheherazade from 1958 to 1962, often accompanying visiting Americans. Although he then worked in the steel industry, first as a purchaser and later as a personnel manager (1962–74), he continued to play jazz, appearing with the bandleader Boy Edgar (1965–73), René Thomas (1966), Ben Webster (during his stay in Amsterdam, 1966–9), Johnny Griffin and Art Taylor (both 1967–8), Dexter Gordon (1970), and the Diamond Five (1972–3). Slinger returned to full-time music in 1974 and performed on a radio program with his group and American guests in 1974–5. Thereafter, as well as playing with local musicians, he worked with numerous

Americans, notably Philly Joe Jones, with whom he toured and gave isolated concerts in Europe (1976–7, 1985). He led a sextet, Just in Case (1978), octets (1982–3, 1995), and his 70th Birthday Dreamband (1999, at the North Sea Jazz Festival), and worked more briefly with Dizzy Gillespie and Griffin (1977), Slide Hampton (1984, 1985), Clifford Jordan (1985), Lou Donaldson (1986), Archie Shepp and James Moody (both 1988), Freddie Hubbard (1988, 1991), Benny Waters and Jimmy Knepper (both 1989), Scott Hamilton (1991), Jon Faddis (1993), and Buddy DeFranco and Terry Gibbs (1994). Between 1979 and 1989 Slinger taught at the conservatory in Rotterdam, and from 1986 to 1989 he organized performances at the Jazz Inn Party in Noordwijk, in the Netherlands.

SELECTED RECORDINGS

As leader: *Brilliant* (1964, Fon. 680520TL); *Back Together* (1973, BASF 16-25301-5); *Live at the North Sea Jazz Festival* (1982, Limetree 198224); *Slingshot* (1985, Tim. 225)

As sideman: D. Gordon: *Live at the Amsterdam Paradiso* (1969, Catfish 5C188-24336–7); B. Webster: *For the Guv'nor* (1969, Imperial 5C054-24049); *Ben at his Best* (1970, RCA 741060); A. Queen and D. Goykovich: *A Day in Holland* (1983, Nilva 3407)

MARK GILBERT

Sloane [née Morvan], **Carol (Spurr)** [Vann, Carol] (*b* Providence, RI, 5 March 1937). Singer. She first performed professionally at the age of 14. After settling in New York she worked in the Les and Larry Elgart Orchestra (1958–60). Early in her career she had appeared as Carol Vann, but Larry Elgart changed her stage surname to Sloane. In 1960 she occasionally deputized for Lambert, Hendricks, and Ross. In autumn 1961 she performed at the Village Vanguard and appeared at the pop festival that replaced the Newport jazz event that year in a performance that was highly praised. She recorded twice for Columbia in the early 1960s and spent the rest of the decade working steadily as a freelance. In 1969 she moved to North Carolina, where she wrote reviews for *Down Beat*, worked as a legal secretary, and occasionally sang in local clubs; she recorded again in 1975. In 1977 she returned to New York and began working with the New York Jazz Quartet, which toured and recorded in Japan. She was again in North Carolina in 1981, booking for local clubs and giving infrequent local performances, but continued touring and recording in Japan. In 1985 she moved to Boston and remained active as a singer, recording and touring regularly. Her work included an affiliation with the Concord All Stars in 1992 and a two-week stand at the Rainbow and Stars in New York in 1998.

SELECTED RECORDINGS

As leader: *Out of the Blue* (1961, Col. CL1766); *Sophisticated Lady* (1977, Trio 25039); *As Time Goes By* (1982, Eastwind 706); *Love You Madly* (1988, Cont. 14049); *The Songs Carmen Sang* (1995, Conc. 4663)

BIBLIOGRAPHY

H. Cutler: "Carol Sloane," *Cadence*, xiii/4 (1987), 5

W. Balliett: *American Singers: Twenty-Seven Portraits in Song* (New York, and Oxford, England, 1988), 223

E. Santosuosso: "Carol Sloane's Warm Vocals," *Boston Globe* (22 Aug 1989)

F. Bouchard: "Credit Where Credit's Due," *DB*, lxv/11 (1998), 53

GK

Slocum, Melissa (*b* New York, 26 July 1961). Double bass player. She grew up in Ohio, where her father played French horn with the Cleveland Orchestra and her mother, a professor of medieval history, played viola. She took up piano at the age of three and was encouraged by her parents to study classical music. When she was 12 she began playing electric bass guitar, and a year later she started working professionally. Slocum was gifted in her academic studies as well as in music, and she finished high school at the age of 15. She completed a degree in classical piano performance at Youngstown State University when she was 18, then spent an additional year at Youngstown studying for a second degree in art history, in which she specialized in Egyptian art. In 1981 she moved to New York to pursue graduate work in art, and shortly afterwards she took up double bass, which she studied with Lisle Atkinson on the Jazzmobile and later privately. After playing regularly at Augies (1983) she became the bass player for Ted Curson's late-night sessions at the Blue Note (1984) and was a member of the house band at Arthur's Tavern (1985–6).

In 1986 Slocum received a grant to study with Rufus Reid and gave up her academic work in the field of art. From that year until 1989 she worked with Dakota Staton, Lionel Hampton, Art Blakey, Bobby Enriquez, Walter Davis, and Ralph Peterson, Jr.; among her recordings from this period are Charli Persip's *No Dummies Allowed* (1987, SN 1179) and *Ralph Peterson Presents the Fo'tet* (1989, BN B21Z-95475). In 1992 she was a founding member of Diva, and she played with the band in its first year and from 1994 to 1997. Slocum continued her studies at the Manhattan School of Music (gaining master's degrees in jazz bass, 1994, and classical bass, 1996) and the Mannes College of Music (1997–8) and then took part in the DMA program for double bass performance at SUNY, Stonybrook, concentrating on the early Italian Baroque period. While working for this degree she appeared as a freelance with Kevin Mahogany, the Ellington Big Band, and the trumpeter Roy Merriweather, and worked as the house bass player for the Broadway show *Phantom of the Opera*. (S. Stein: "Hearsay: Melissa Slocum," *JT*, xxi/6 (1991), 11)

LARA PELLEGRINELLI

Slow drag [drag]. *See* Dance.

Slyde, Jimmy [Godbolt, Jimmy] (*b* Atlanta, 2 Oct 1927). Tap-dancer. His family moved to Boston while he was still a baby. He received dance tuition from 1939 and later studied violin at the New England Conservatory. In 1949 he made his professional début with the tap-dancer Jimmy Mitchell, known as Sir Slyde; they called themselves the Slyde Brothers, and it was at this point that he adopted the stage name Jimmy Slyde. In the 1950s he toured seaside resorts along the East Coast with various shows and worked in California with Teddy Edwards and Hampton Hawes. He visited Europe in 1966 and toured South America with the Legends of Jazz in the show *1000 Years of Jazz* in the early 1970s. In 1972 he returned to Europe with Milt Buckner and Jo Jones and settled in France, where he recorded *Just You, Just Me* (1974, BB 33066) as co-leader with Michael Silva. In 1985 he was featured in the Paris show *Black and Blue*, and he went back to the USA for its run on Broadway. In the 1990s he gave weekly tap-dancing shows in New York clubs, presented Jimmy Slyde and Friends (including Gregory Hines) at the Jacob's Pillow Summer Dance Festival (1996), appeared at the White House with Claude Williams and Savion Glover (1998), performed in Rio de Janeiro at the third Tap Encontro (May 1998), worked with the Lincoln

Center Jazz Orchestra, and made appearances at other festivals. From 1999–2000 Slyde was featured in Savion Glover's touring show *Foot Notes*.

SELECTED FILMS AND VIDEOS

L'aventure du jazz (1972); The Cotton Club (1984); About Tap (1985); 'Round Midnight (1986); Tap (1989); Dance in America: Tap (1989)

BIBLIOGRAPHY

J.-P. Battestini: "Jimmy Slyde parle ...," *BHcF*, no.288 (1973), 6
R. E. Frank: *Tap! The Greatest Tap Dance Stars and their Stories, 1900–1955* (New York, 1990, rev. and enlarged 2/1994), 257
S. Harper: "Une interview avec Jimmy Slyde," <http://www.domain.com.br/clientes/steven/french/others.html> (1998)
<http://arts.endow.gov/explore/Heritage00/SlydeBio.html> (1999)
J. Ott: "Interview with Jimmy 'Slyde' Godbolt," <http://arts.endow.gov/explore/Heritage00/Slyde.html> (1999)

HOWARD RYE

Smack. Nickname of Fletcher Henderson.

Smalls, Cliff [Clifton Arnold] (*b* Charleston, SC, 3 March 1918). Pianist. He first toured with the Carolina Cotton Pickers (1935–42) and then worked with Earl Hines, playing trombone and second piano (autumn 1942–1946). Following periods with Billy Eckstine (1948–50) and Earl Bostic's popular small group (1950–51) he was forced into temporary retirement by injuries sustained in a road accident; when he returned to work he collaborated with Al Sears (1953) and Bennie Green (1953–6). Smalls then played alto and baritone saxophone in rhythm-and-blues groups and backed such singers as Clyde McPhatter, Brook Benton (for seven years), and Smokey Robinson. Later he resumed playing jazz and worked with Sy Oliver (from 1968). He recorded both as a leader and as a sideman, with Eddie Barefield (1973), a quintet led by Paul Gonsalves and Roy Eldridge (1973), Buddy Tate (1975), Milt Hinton (1976), and Oliver Jackson (1977, 1982). In the 1990s his poor health limited him to occasional appearances with his own group in New York; he no longer recorded with any frequency, though he still provided arrangements for other leaders. Smalls played in a personal style that combined harmonic subtlety with a flexibility and drive reminiscent of Hines.

SELECTED RECORDINGS

As leader: *Swing and Things* (1976, MJR 8131); *Cliff Smalls* (1978, BB 33134)
As sideman: C. Hastings: first issued on *Count Red Hastings* (1948–50, Krazy Kat 823), Baboo (1949); B. Green: *Bennie Green Blows his Horn* (1955, Prst. 210); *Bennie Green and Art Farmer* (1956, Prst. 7041); P. Gonsalves: *Mexican Bandit Meets Pittsburgh Pirate* (1973, Fan. 9646); S. Oliver: *Yes, Indeed* (1973, BB 33048); B. Tate: *The Texas Twister* (1975, MJR 8128); O. Jackson and H. Henry: *Real Jazz Express* (1977, BB 33126); O. Jackson: *Le quartet* (1982, BB 33180)

BIBLIOGRAPHY

ChiltonW; *Feather–Gitler '70s*
S. Dance: *The World of Earl Hines* (New York, 1977), 261
A. Balalas: "Cliff Smalls," *BHcF*, no.271 (1979), 5

PETER VACHER

Smalls' Paradise. Nightclub in New York; *see* Nightclubs and other venues.

SME. *See* Spontaneous music ensemble.

Smear. An exaggerated Bend of a semitone or a tone down and then up again, executed with a harsh or "dirty" tone; it is most often associated with brass instruments in jazz. An example may be heard in bar 23 of Louis Armstrong's solo on *Wolverine Blues* (1940, Decca 3105). (M. Laplace: "La trompette et le cornet dans le jazz et la musique populaire," pt vi, *Brass Bulletin*, no.47 (1984), 39)

Smetaček, Pavel (*b* Prague, 4 Jan 1940). Czech clarinetist, saxophonist, and bandleader. He studied clarinet at the Prague Conservatory from 1957 and the same year founded the Traditional Jazz Studio, with which he recorded regularly from 1959. Through his association with the studio he worked with such musicians as Albert Nicholas, Benny Waters (with whom he recorded in 1976), and Tony Scott, and toured internationally. In 1977 he took part in the New Orleans Jazz & Heritage Festival. Smetaček's work is well represented on the recording *Traditional Jazz Studio, 1959–1979* (1959–79, Sup. 11152606H). In 1991 he ended his musical career and became a member in Italy of the diplomatic service of the Czech Republic. (G. Conrad: "Pavel Smetaček und das Traditional Jazz Studio," *Der Jazzfreund*, no.94 (1979), 4)

GERHARD CONRAD

Śmietana, Jarosław [Jarek] (*b* Kraków, Poland, 29 March 1951). Polish guitarist, composer, and leader. While still a student in the jazz department of the academy of music at Katowice (from which he graduated in 1974) he made his professional début with Klaus Lenz's big band at the International Jazz Jamboree, Warsaw (1972). In 1974, with Władysław Sendecki, he founded Extra Ball, which became Poland's leading jazz-rock group and won many prizes; that year Śmietana himself won the award for the best soloist at the festival Jazz on the Odra at Wrocław. During international tours he performed at major European events such as the North Sea Jazz Festival (The Hague) and Jazz Ost-West (Nuremberg); he also appeared with Extra Ball and the Katowice Big Band at American festivals in Reno, Nevada, and Berkeley, California (1978), and later he made a coast-to-coast tour of the USA with Extra Ball (1980). He disbanded this group in 1984 and two years later formed another ensemble, Sounds, which played contemporary jazz in a straight-ahead manner with Latin and rock elements; Piotr Baron was among its members. In the early 1980s Śmietana also led a successful big band, the Symphonic Sounds Orchestra. A virtuoso player and a prolific composer, he recorded numerous albums as a leader and worked with many of Poland's foremost jazz musicians, including Zbigniew Namysłowski, Janusz Muniak, Zbigniew Seifert, and Jan Wróblewski. He continued to lead small groups through the 1990s, notably a hard-bop quintet consisting of Eddie Henderson, Baron, Andrzej Cudzich, and the drummer Greg Bandy, which performed at Jazz Jamboree in Warsaw in 1994, and a quartet co-led by John Abercrombie for a recording session in New York in 1999. In 2000 he toured as co-leader with Gary Bartz of the African Lake Band, as co-leader with Tomasz Szukalski of a quartet, and as the leader of a band in which John Purcell was a sideman.

SELECTED RECORDINGS

As leader: *Birthday* (1976, Muza 1414); *Go Ahead* (1979, Muza 1795); *Mosquito* (1981, Poljazz 104); *Talking Guitar* (1983, Muza 2197); *From One to Four* (1987, Poljazz 191); *Sound Colors* (1987, Muza 2537); *Cooperation* (1992, Gowi 03); *Ballads and other Songs* (1993, Starling 0004); *Live at the Jazz Jamboree* (1993–4, Gowi 33); *Flowers in Mind* (1994, Koch Jazz 3850); with W. Karolak: *Phone Consultations* (1996, Gowi 36); with J. Abercrombie: *Speak Easy* (1999, PAO 10610)
As sideman with Z. Seifert: *Kilimanjaro* (1978, Poljazz 101–2)

BIBLIOGRAPHY

K. Czyż: "Jarosław Śmietana: Rolling Straight Ahead," *JF* [intl edn], no.73 (1981), 44

A. Chodkowski, ed.: *Encyklopedia muzyki* (Warsaw, 1995)

<http://muzyka.onet.pl/jazz/jsmietana/> (2000) [incl. discography]

PAWEŁ BRODOWSKI/BK

Smith, Ben(jamin J.) (*b* Memphis, 1 March 1905). Alto saxophonist and clarinetist. After playing with lesser-known ensembles in Tennessee and Texas he led his own band, the Blue Syncopators (1927–9). He worked briefly in Omaha, Nebraska, and led a group in Kansas City, then played with the bandleaders Jesse Stone (1929), George E. Lee (1930), Grant Moore, and Eli Rice. In 1932 he led the White Hut Band in Pittsburgh and Philadelphia. Later he worked with Blanche Calloway and Charlie Gaines, and directed and took part in recording sessions by the Washboard Rhythm Kings. Around 1934 he moved to New York, where he played with Fess Williams, Claude Hopkins (*c* March 1937 – January 1938), and Jabbo Smith (1938). He then performed and made recordings with Hot Lips Page, with whose band his warm-toned clarinet playing may be heard to advantage. During the 1940s Smith worked with Lucky Millinder, Andy Kirk (*c* April 1942–1944), and Snub Mosley (1945–*c*1947), but he was mainly active as the leader of his own groups. As well as continuing to lead bands in the 1950s he organized his own business as an arranger and copyist and owned a record company. Around 1953 he took up tenor saxophone to play with rhythm-and-blues groups.

SELECTED RECORDINGS

As sideman: Washboard Rhythm Kings: Underneath the Harlem Moon (1932, Vic. 23373); Ikey and Mikey (1932, Vic. 23380); Georgia Washboard Stompers: Lulu's back in town (1935, Decca 7095); H. L. Page: He's Pulling his Whiskers (1938, Decca 7451); Down on the levee (1938, Decca 7433)

BIBLIOGRAPHY

ChiltonW; McCarthyB

F. Driggs: "Ben Smith," *Record Research*, no.29 (1960)

O. Flückiger: "Biography and Discography of Ben Smith," *Jazz Statistics*, no.21 (1961), 9; no.23 (1961), 9; no.24 (1961), 8

T. Zwicky: "I'm Gonna Beat Me Some Washboard: the Washboard Rhythm Kings and Affiliated Groups (1930–35)," *Sv*, no.19 (1968), 3; no.20 (1968–9), 47; no.22 (1969), 148 [incl. discography]

HOWARD RYE

Smith, Bessie (*b* Chattanooga, TN, 15 April 1894; *d* Clarksdale, MS, 26 Sept 1937). Singer. She had begun her professional career by 1909 and briefly joined Ma and Pa Rainey's company in Atlanta the following year. During the 1910s she performed in various touring minstrel shows and cabarets, and by the 1920s she was a leading artist in African-American shows and cabarets, on the Theater Owners' Booking Association circuit, and at the 81 Theatre in Atlanta. After further tours she was sought out by Clarence Williams to record in New York. Her first recording, *Downhearted Blues*, established her as the most successful African-American performing artist of her time; she recorded regularly until 1928 with important early jazz instrumentalists such as Williams, James P. Johnson, and various members of Fletcher Henderson's band, including Louis Armstrong, Charlie Green, Joe Smith, and Tommy Ladnier. Though based in New York, during this period she also toured throughout the South and North, performing to large audiences. In 1929 she appeared in the film *St. Louis Blues* (*see* FILMS, §I, 1, and fig.1). By then, however, alcoholism had severely damaged her career, as did the Depression, which affected the recording and entertainment industries. A recording session, her last, was arranged in 1933 by John Hammond for the increasing European jazz audience; it featured among others Jack Teagarden and Benny Goodman. By 1936 Smith was again performing in shows and clubs, but she died, following an automobile accident, before her next recording session had been arranged.

Bessie Smith, c1923

Smith was unquestionably the greatest of the vaudeville blues singers, and brought the emotional intensity, personal involvement, and expression of blues singing into the jazz repertory with unexcelled artistry. *Baby Doll* and *After you've gone*, both made with Joe Smith, and *Nobody knows you when you're down and out*, with Ed Allen on cornet, illustrate her capacity for sensitive interpretation of popular songs. Her broad phrasing, fine intonation, blue-note inflections, and wide, expressive range made hers the measure of jazz-blues singing in the 1920s (for further discussion of her vocal technique *see* GROWL). She made almost 200 recordings, of which her remarkable collaborations with Armstrong are among her best. Although she excelled in the performance of slow blues, she also recorded vigorous versions of jazz standards. Joe Smith was her preferred accompanist, but possibly her finest recording (and certainly the best-known in her day) was *Back Water Blues*, with James P. Johnson. Her voice had coarsened by the time of her last session, but few jazz artists have been as consistently outstanding.

See also BLUES, §3.

SELECTED RECORDINGS

(recorded for Columbia unless otherwise indicated)

Duos: with C. Williams: Down Hearted Blues/Gulf Coast Blues (1923, A3844); with F. Henderson: Bleeding Hearted Blues (1923, A3936); with Irving Johns: Jail House Blues (1923, A4001); Sam Jones Blues (1923,

13005D); with F. Henderson: Any Woman's Blues (1923, 13001D); Squeeze Me (1926, 14143D)

As leader: Pinchbacks – Take 'em Away (1924, 14025D); Weeping Willow Blues (1924, 14042D); The St. Louis Blues/Cold in Hand Blues (1925, 14064D); Cake Walkin' Babies (from Home) (1925, 35673); Careless Love Blues (1925, 14083D); J. C. Holmes Blues (1925, 14095D); Baby Doll (1926, 14147D); Back Water Blues (1927, 14195D); After you've gone (1927, 14197D); Alexander's Ragtime Band (1927, 14219D); Trombone Cholly (1927, 14232D); Mean Old Bed Bug Blues/A good man is hard to find (1927, 14250D); Dyin' by the Hour/Foolish Man Blues (1927, 14273D); Empty Bed Blues (1928, 14312D); Nobody knows you when you're down and out (1929, 14451D); Long Old Road/Shipwreck Blues (1931, 14663D); Gimme a pigfoot (1933, OK 8949)

BIBLIOGRAPHY

C. Van Vechten: "Negro 'Blues' Singers: an Appreciation of Three Coloured Artists who Excel in an Unusual and Native Medium," *Vanity Fair*, xxvi/1 (1926), 67

B. Rust: "On Bessie Smith," *Hot Notes*, ii/2 (1947), 6

P. Oliver: *Bessie Smith* (London, 1959); repr. in *Kings of Jazz*, ed. S. Green (South Brunswick, NJ, and New York, 1978)

J. Gee: "Big Hearted Bessie Smith: my Wife," *Blues Unlimited* (1964), no.15, p.3; no.16, p.5

G. Schuller: *Early Jazz: its Roots and Musical Development* (New York, 1968), 226

C. Albertson: *Bessie: Empress of the Blues* (New York, 1972/*R*1982)

S. Harris: *Blues Who's Who: a Biographical Dictionary of Blues Singers* (New Rochelle, NY, 1979/*R*1994)

E. Brooks: *The Bessie Smith Companion: a Critical and Detailed Appreciation of the Recordings* (Wheathampstead, nr St. Albans, England, and New York, 1982/*R*1989)

L. Abbott and D. Seroff: "Bessie Smith: the Early Years," *Blues & Rhythm*, no.70 (1992), 8

F. Martin: *Bessie Smith* (Paris, 1994)

PAUL OLIVER

Smith, Betty (*b* Sileby, nr Leicester, England, 6 July 1929). English tenor saxophonist. She learned piano from the age of six and saxophone from the age of nine and began to play jazz while a teenager. After touring the Middle East with the pianist Billy Penrose (1948) she performed and toured (together with her husband, the double bass player Jack Peberdy) in Freddy Randall's band (June–November 1950, 1953 – February 1957; recording in 1953–5). She then led her own quintet (1957–64), played and sang in Ted Heath's orchestra, and worked as a guest soloist on radio and television programs; she had her own program on Radio Luxembourg. From the mid-1970s she was a member of the Best of British Jazz, with Kenny Baker, Don Lusher, and Jack Parnell, and her playing is well represented on the group's recording *Exactly Like You* (1981, ASV ALM4001). Smith also sang with the group led by the soprano and alto saxophonist Eggy Ley in the 1980s, but illness late in the decade forced her gradually to withdraw from performance. (*CarrJ*; *ChiltonB*)

NEVIL SKRIMSHIRE

Smith, Bill [William O(verton)] **(i)** (*b* Sacramento, CA, 22 Sept 1926). Clarinetist and composer. He took up clarinet as a child and was playing with the Oakland Symphony Orchestra by the age of 15. Later he studied at the Juilliard School and with the composer Darius Milhaud at Mills College (MA 1951); with his fellow student Dave Brubeck he founded an octet which performed and recorded between 1947 and 1951. While teaching at the University of Southern California he recorded in Los Angeles with Red Norvo (1957) and Shelly Manne (1957, 1958) and on three occasions with Brubeck's quartet (1959–61) as a replacement for Paul Desmond; he also composed for Brubeck. In 1960 Smith won a Guggenheim Fellowship for composition, and he spent the next six years based in Italy; during this period he organized a bop quartet, the American Jazz Ensemble, with which he toured and recorded in Europe and the USA. From 1966 he directed the Contemporary Music Group at the University of Washington, Seattle. He visited Italy again in the years 1977–80 and recorded in Rome with Enrico Pieranunzi's trio. Thereafter he toured internationally and made recordings with Brubeck, in whose group he alternated in or shared the reed position with Jerry Bergonzi (1980s) and Bobby Militello (1990s); while playing with Brubeck he sometimes used an electronic processor to modify the sound of his clarinet. Under the name William O. Smith he has composed and performed many classical works, some of which contain elements of jazz.

SELECTED RECORDINGS

As leader: *Sonorities* (1977, Edi-Pan 801); *Colours* (1978, 1980, Jazz Music 807)

As sideman with D. Brubeck: *Concord on a Summer Night* (1982, Conc. 198), incl. Take Five; *Blue Rondo* (1986, Conc. 317); *Moscow Night* (1987, Conc. 4353); *Late Night Brubeck* (1993, Telarc 83345); on *Night Shift* (1993, Telarc 83351), Blues for Newport

BIBLIOGRAPHY

Feather '60s

P. Rehfeldt: "William O. Smith," *The Clarinet*, vii/3 (1980), 42 [incl. discography]

G. Endress: "Intuitives Verständnis mit Dave Brubeck," *JP*, xxxii/6 (1983), 4

L. Tomkins: "Bill Smith," *CI*, xxi (1983), no.5, p.6; no.6, p.16

L. L. Pierce: "William O. Smith: I. C. S. Commission," *The Clarinet*, xiv/4 (1987), 26 [incl. discography]

"The Clarinet Can be King Again, Says Bill Smith," *CI*, xxv/10 (1988), 24

F. M. Hall: *It's About Time: the Dave Brubeck Story* (Fayetteville, AR, 1996)

BK

Smith, Bill [William Ernest] **(ii)** (*b* Bristol, England, 12 May 1938). Canadian writer, editor, saxophonist, and clarinetist of English birth. He studied aeronautical design and played drums and trumpet in England before moving to Toronto in 1963. He immediately became art director of *Coda* magazine, and rose to the position of co-publisher with John Norris in 1967; he succeeded Norris as editor in 1976. He was also co-founder with Norris of Sackville in 1968. Having taken up saxophone and clarinet in Toronto, he developed a modest, conversational style and began performing in freely improvised settings in the mid-1970s, first with the pianist Stuart Broomer, then with the Bill Smith Ensemble (1980–89) and as the sopranino saxophonist in Zes Winden (1986–8). He moved the editorial offices of *Coda* to Hornby Island, northwest of Vancouver, in 1989 and thereafter played saxophone and drums locally. (The magazine's business office remains in Toronto, under Norris.) The Smith Ensemble (David Prentice, violin; David Lee, double bass) recorded both as a trio and with guests Leo Smith (*Rastafari*, 1983, Sack. 3030) and Joe McPhee (*Visitation*, 1983, Sack. 3036). Smith was co-producer (with Ron Mann) of a feature-length documentary about the October Revolution in jazz, *Imagine the Sound* (1981), and published a collection of his jazz photography and reminiscences, *Imagine the Sound*, no.5: *The Book* (Toronto, 1985).

BIBLIOGRAPHY

EMC2

M. Miller: "A New King of Jazz Moves in," *Canadian Composer*, no.114 (1979), 16

——: "Bill Smith," *Boogie, Pete & the Senator: Canadian Musicians in Jazz, the Eighties* (Toronto 1987), 232

MARK MILLER

Smith, Brian (*b* Wellington, New Zealand, 3 Jan 1939). New Zealand saxophonist and flutist. Although he studied piano for four years, he was largely self-taught as a reed player. After playing in local rock, jazz, and dance bands he moved to England in 1964, and the following year he joined Alexis Korner's Blues Incorporated. He then played at Ronnie Scott's (1966–7) and worked as a member of big bands led by Maynard Ferguson and Tubby Hayes (both 1969). Smith later recorded with Ferguson (1970–74) and played for his tours of Japan and the USA (1972, 1974). In 1969 he joined Ian Carr's group Nucleus, with which he worked extensively until 1982; his playing is well represented on the album *Roots* (1973, Vertigo 6360100). He also performed with Gordon Beck's group Gyroscope (*c*1968), Annie Ross, and Graham Collier (early 1970s), and played or recorded with Mike Westbrook (1969), Neil Ardley (1969, 1976), Mike Gibbs (1970), the Spontaneous Music Ensemble (1970, 1971), and Keith Tippett's group Centipede (1971). Smith was a member of the groups Pacific Eardrum (1975–6) and Paz (recording *c*1976), and with Nucleus in 1978 he appeared at the first Jazzyatra in India. In 1982 he returned to New Zealand, where he formed his own quartet; in 1984 its album *Southern Excursions*, recorded on the New Zealand label Ode, was voted Australian Jazz Record of the Year. Based in Auckland, he has been a member of Space Case, led by the drummer Frank Gibson, with whom he recorded the album *Rendevous* (1988, Ode [issue number unknown]).

Smith should not be confused with the American free-jazz double bass player Brian Smith, who recorded with Barry Altschul and Fred Anderson (both 1978), Muhal Richard Abrams (1980), Henry Threadgill (1982), and the World Bass Violin Ensemble (1982–3), or with the English tenor saxophonist Brian Smith (*b* Lancaster).

BIBLIOGRAPHY

CarrJ
R. Cotterrell, ed.: *Jazz Now: the Jazz Centre Society Guide* (London, 1976), 167
P. Renaud: *La discographie du jazz anglais* (Chaumont, France, 1985)

DIGBY FAIRWEATHER/BK

Smith, Buster [Henry] (*b* Alfdorf, nr Ennis, TX, 24 Aug 1904; *d* Dallas, 10 Aug 1991). Alto saxophonist, clarinetist, and arranger. He grew up on a farm, then moved with his family to Celina (just north of Dallas) and, in 1920, into Dallas. Having taught himself to play clarinet, he worked with local groups in Dallas from around 1923, but by 1925, when he joined Walter Page's Blue Devils, a territory band based in Oklahoma that performed in Kansas City and the Southwest, he had taken up alto saxophone. Among others in the band by 1928 were Hot Lips Page, Jimmy Rushing, Count Basie, and Eddie Durham, all of whom later left to play with Bennie Moten. In 1931 Smith assumed leadership of the band, which now included Lester Young and which later became known as the 13 Original Blue Devils. After the group disbanded late in 1933 he settled in Kansas City, where he too joined Moten's group; this disbanded after the death in 1935 of its leader. Smith became a member of a band led by Basie, which involved other musicians who had worked with Moten, and which performed in Kansas City at the Reno Club; when Basie moved to New York he remained in Kansas City, played with Claude Hopkins, Julia Lee, and Andy Kirk, and wrote arrangements for Nat Towles. In 1937 he formed his own group, with Jay McShann, Fred Beckett, and Charlie Parker, who was then 17 years old, among his sidemen; a year later he moved with the band to New York, where, unable to secure engagements as a leader, he worked instead as an arranger for Basie, Benny Carter, and Snub Mosley and as a sideman with Don Redman. He moved late in 1942 to Dallas and led small groups at clubs and hotels; David "Fathead" Newman was a member of his group in the late 1940s. Although Smith ceased playing saxophone in 1959, he continued to work on piano and electric bass guitar until his retirement around 1980 and intermittently thereafter until the last years of his life; in the mid- to late 1980s he was the electric bass guitarist in a local ensemble of veteran players, the Legendary Revelations.

Smith's importance lies in his work as an arranger and above all in his having been a mentor of Parker. His few recordings (including *Cherry Red*, 1939; *I ain't got nobody*, 1940; and *Moten's Swing*, 1940) reveal an approach close to that of Parker's early style and sometimes that of his mature work. It is not to diminish Parker's importance as the originator, with Dizzy Gillespie, of a completely new language of jazz to note that several elements of his style – his tone and attack, certain turns of phrase, and his basically linear conception – may be traced to Smith's buoyant, fluent playing and warm sound.

Oral history material in *NjR* (JOHP).

SELECTED RECORDINGS

As leader: *The Legendary Buster Smith* (1959, Atl. 1323)
As sideman: W. Page: Blue Devil Blues/Squabblin' (1929, Voc. 1463); D. Redman: Chew, Chew, Chew (1939, Vic. 26258); Ain't I good to you? (1939, Vic. 26266); Pete Johnson: Cherry Red/Baby, Look at you (1939, Voc. 4997); H. L. Page: I ain't got nobody/Gone with the Gin (1940, Decca 7714); E. Durham: I Want a Little Girl/Moten's Swing (1940, Decca 18126)

SELECTED ARRANGEMENTS

Recorded by C. Basie: Smarty (1937, Decca 1379); One o'Clock Jump (1937, Decca 1363); The Blues I Like to Hear (1938, Decca 2284)
Recorded by H. L. Page: Gone with the Gin (1940, Decca 7714)

BIBLIOGRAPHY

D. Gazzaway: "Conversations with Buster Smith," *JR*, ii/11 (1959), 18; iii/1 (1960), 11; contd as "Buster and Bird: Conversations with Buster Smith," iii/2 (1960), 12 [incl. discography]
——: "Before Bird: Buster," *JM*, vii/11 (1962), 4
B. Rusch: "Buster Smith: Interview," *Cadence*, iv/4 (1978), 14
M. L. Hester: *Going to Kansas City* (Sherman, TX, 1980), 15
T. Schuller: "The Buster Smith Story," *Coda*, no.217 (1987), 4
A. Govenar: *Meeting the Blues* (Dallas, 1988), 39
N. W. Pearson, Jr.: *Goin' to Kansas City* (Urbana, IL, and London, 1988)
Obituaries: P. Watrous, *New York Times* (15 Aug 1991); T. Burke, *Blues & Rhythm*, no.64 (1991), 16; M. Redenac, *Soul Bag*, no.125 (1992), 19
A. Vasset: "Buster Smith," *BHcF*, no.399 (1992), 35

GUNTHER SCHULLER

Smith, Cal [Carl Lee] (*b* Cave City, KY, 7 March 1903; *d* Louisville, KY, summer 1937). Banjoist and guitarist. He was one of six brothers who formed the Smith Brothers String Band in their hometown in 1916–17; the group was led by Smith's elder brother the violinist, trumpeter, and banjoist Clarence Smith (*c*1897–1940s). When Clarence joined the army in 1917, the family and band moved to Jeffersonville, Ohio, and in 1919 Cal became a member of Henry Smith's Jug Band in Louisville (Henry Smith, a jug blower, was unrelated but sometimes claimed to be Cal Smith's brother to capitalize on the latter's reputation). In the 1920s and early 1930s Smith worked regularly with the bands of Earl McDonald and Clifford Hayes and played banjo on most of the recordings by the Louisville jug-band musicians. In July 1926 he worked with W. C. Handy in Memphis. He is one of the three banjoists on the Dixieland Jug Blowers' *Banjoreno*

(1926, Vic. 21473). In 1926 he took up guitar and quickly developed into a major creative artist with whom few well-known visiting musicians cared to duel. His recordings on this instrument amply justify the awe in which his playing was held by Louisville musicians; however, major success eluded him, and he succumbed to tuberculosis at the age of 34.

SELECTED RECORDINGS

(all recorded for Victor)

As sideman. C. Hayes: Blue Guitar Stomp (1927, 20955); Tenor Guitar Stomp (1928, 23346); Blue Harmony (1928, 21583); The Petter's Stomp (1928, 21584); Clef Club Stomp (1928, 38011); Bare-foot Stomp (1928, 21489); Dance Hall Shuffle (1929, 38557); Everybody Wants my Tootelum (1929, 38529); Shady Lane Blues (1929, 23407); Kentucky Jazz Babies [C. Hayes]: Old Folks Shake (1929, 38616); S. Thomas [S. Wallace]: You gonna need my help (1929, 38502); B. Ferguson: Please don't holler, mama/Try and treat her right (1931, 23297)

BIBLIOGRAPHY

L. Wright, comp. [from material supplied by F. Cox, J. Randolph, and J. Harris]: *The Jug Bands of Louisville* (Chigwell, England, 1993 [*recte* 1994])

F. Cox, J. Randolph, and J. Harris: "The Jug Bands of Louisville," *Sv* (1993), no.155, p.164; no.156, p.204; (1994), no.157, p.4; no.158, p.43; no.159, p.83; no.160, p.145; (1995), no.161, p.188; no.162, p.203

B. Bogert: Liner notes, *Clifford Hayes & the Louisville Jug Bands*, i–iv (RST 1501-2, 1502-2, 1503-2, 1504-2, 1994)

HOWARD RYE

Smith, Carl [Tatti] (*b* Marshall, TX, *c*1908). Trumpeter. He first worked with Terrence Holder's band in Kansas City, Missouri (1931), and then played mainly on the West Coast with the bandleader Gene Coy (1931–4). Having returned to Kansas City, he worked with Count Basie. In Chicago he made recordings as the nominal co-leader of Jones–Smith, Inc., a sextet actually led by Basie. Smith left Basie in March 1937 and until 1940 worked principally with Skeets Tolbert and his Gentlemen of Swing; he also performed with Hot Lips Page in 1939. Later he played occasionally with Leon Abbey and Benny Carter, and in 1944 he was a member of Chris Columbus's band. After World War II Smith moved to South America, where he continued to play into the 1950s.

SELECTED RECORDINGS

As leader of Jones–Smith, Inc.: Shoe Shine Boy (1936, Voc. 3441); Boogie Woogie/Lady be good (1936, Voc. 3459)

As sideman with S. Tolbert: I can't go for you (1940, Decca 7722)

BIBLIOGRAPHY

McCarthyB; *SheridanCB*

based on *ChiltonW*

Smith, Carrie (Louise) (*b* Fort Gaines, GA, 25 Aug 1941). Singer. She was brought up in Newark, New Jersey, and sang in a local church choir, with which she made recordings at the Newport Jazz Festival in 1957. However, she performed only occasionally until 1970, when she toured with the band led by the pianist and singer Big Tiny Little (1970–72). After working with Tyree Glenn (1973) she joined the New York Jazz Repertory Company, with which she visited the USSR in 1975. In the course of her first tours of Europe she recorded the albums *Do your Duty* (1976, BB 33103), accompanied by a group which included Vic Dickenson and Panama Francis, and *When You're Down and Out* (1977, BB 33119), with George Kelly and Ram Ramirez among her sidemen, and sang at the Grande Parade du Jazz, Nice (1979). She continued to perform in the USA and frequently returned to Europe, touring there with Yank Lawson's band in 1987 and appearing that same year at the Guinness Cork Jazz Festival in Ireland. From January 1989 to around 1991 she was one of the stars of the Broadway musical *Black and Blues*. Smith remained active into the new century, mainly with small groups, though she also sang with a big band at Carnegie Hall in 1994. She frequently worked with Bross Townsend, with whom she recorded in 1992 (in Paris) and in 1995, in which year they appeared at the Oslo Jazzfestival; she has made many other festival appearances. She may be seen in the television show "TV Gospel Time #7" (1962).

BIBLIOGRAPHY

Feather–GitlerBEJ

E. Townley: "The Carrie Smith Story," *JJ*, xxix/11 (1976), 4

J. C. Arnaudon: "Un talent nouveau: Carrie Smith," *Pj*, no.13 (1977), 93

M. Cullaz: "A Touch of Gospel," *Jh*, nos.351–2 (1978), 50

G. Endress: "Stimme aus Gospel und Blues: Carrie Smith," *JP*, xxvii/10 (1978), 8

S. Harris: *Blues Who's Who: a Biographical Dictionary of Blues Singers* (New Rochelle, NY, 1979/*R*1994)

"Überzeugend mit Gospel, Blues and Jazz: Carrie Smith," *JP*, xxxiii (1984), 6

C. Deffaa: "Carrie Smith," *MR*, xviii/2 (1990), 19

——: "Carrie Smith: Singing the Blues on Broadway," *JT*, xxi/1 (1991), 49

HOWARD RYE

Smith, Carson (Raymond) (*b* San Francisco, 9 Jan 1931; *d* Las Vegas, 2 Nov 1997). Double bass player. He first played and recorded West Coast jazz in Los Angeles with Gerry Mulligan (1952–3), Chet Baker (1953–5), Russ Freeman (1955–6), and Chico Hamilton (1955–7), with whom he appeared in the short film *Cool and Groovy* (1956); he also recorded with Clifford Brown and Dick Twardzik (both 1954) and with Billie Holiday in a concert at Carnegie Hall (1956). Later he worked as a freelance in Los Angeles (late 1950s), toured and recorded with Stan Kenton (1959), and recorded with Hamilton (1959) and Charlie Barnet (1960). After moving to Las Vegas, Smith performed and recorded with Charlie Teagarden (1962) and recorded in a sextet led by Teagarden and Lionel Hampton (1963). In 1964 he toured Japan with Georgie Auld and appeared with Mulligan at the Hollywood Bowl, and two years later he recorded with Buddy Rich. In Las Vegas he played with Arno Marsh and Carl Fontana and worked for ten years at the 4 Queens Hotel, where on Monday nights he accompanied such visiting players as Art Farmer, Lew Tabackin, Zoot Sims, and Baker (*c* January 1985). In addition he traveled to Denver to appear regularly at Dick Gibson's annual Colorado Jazz Party and took a prominent role as a soloist in a reunion concert with Hamilton's quintet in Milan in 1989.

SELECTED RECORDINGS

As sideman with G. Mulligan (all recorded in 1953): The lady is a tramp/Turnstile (Fan. 528); Lover Man/Lady be good (PJ 609); Carson City Stage (PJ 611); Makin' Whoopee (PJ 604); *Gerry Mulligan Quartet* (PJ 5), incl. Jeru, Love me or leave me, Swing House

As sideman with C. Hamilton: *Reunion* (1989, SN 121191-2)

BIBLIOGRAPHY

FeatherE; *Feather '60s*

R. Gordon: *Jazz West Coast: the Los Angeles Jazz Scene of the 1950s* (London and New York, 1986)

Obituaries: J. Fordham, *The Guardian* (8 Dec 1997); G. Jack, *JJI*, li/2 (1998), 30

BK

Smith, Charles Edward (*b* Thomaston, CT, 8 June 1904; *d* New York, 16 Dec 1970). Writer. In the mid-1930s he provided scripts for "Saturday Night Swing Session," the first series of jazz programs to be broadcast live on network radio. With Fred Ramsey, he collaborated on the writing of scripts for "Jazz in America" (1942–3), a series of radio programs produced by the Office of War Information, and on the compilation of *Jazzmen* (1939), an important early anthology, for which he also contributed essays; he wrote *The Jazz Record Book* (1942) with Ramsey and others, as well as many reviews, articles, and liner notes. In 1959 he received the "Silver Medal" award from *Down Beat*. Smith was a founder of the Institute of Jazz Studies, where his personal papers are now held.

WRITINGS
(selective list)

ed. with F. Ramsey, Jr.: *Jazzmen: the Story of Hot Jazz Told in the Lives of the Men who Created it* (New York, 1939/*R*1977)
with F. Ramsey and others: *The Jazz Record Book* (New York, 1942/*R*1978) [listeners' guide with discography]
"Jack Teagarden," "Pee Wee Russell," "Billie Holiday," *The Jazz Makers*, ed. N. Shapiro and N. Hentoff (New York, 1957/*R*1979, as *The Jazz Makers: Essays on the Greats of Jazz*), 59, 103, 276

DANIEL ZAGER

Smith, Charlie [Charles] (*b* New York, 15 April 1927; *d* New Haven, CT, 15 Jan 1966). Drummer. He first played professionally with various groups in New York in 1947, and the following year he joined Ella Fitzgerald. Later he performed and recorded with such artists as Hot Lips Page, Erroll Garner, Benny Goodman, Slim Gaillard, Oscar Peterson, Artie Shaw, Joe Bushkin, and Slam Stewart. In addition he was a member of Duke Ellington's orchestra, although this was only for a brief period (to March 1951), reportedly because Juan Tizol and Willie Smith agreed to join Ellington from Harry James's band on the condition that the leader also engaged James's drummer, Louie Bellson. In 1952 Smith appeared in a television show with Charlie Parker and Dizzy Gillespie. Thereafter he worked with Billy Taylor (ii) (1952–4), Aaron Bell (1954–6, 1958), and Wild Bill Davison (1959) and performed as a freelance. He then moved to New Haven, where he played in a trio with Dwike Mitchell and Willie Ruff (recording in 1961). Towards the end of his life he was active as a composer and teacher. A proficient drummer in both bop and swing styles, he was known especially for his brush work.

SELECTED RECORDINGS

As leader: on *Jazzville*, iii (1956, Dawn 1114), Blues for Sale, Flying Home
As sideman: E. Garner: *Piano Selections* (1949, Atl. 109); S. Gaillard: Yip roc Heresy/The Hip Cowboy (1951, Clef 8956); B. Taylor: *Billy Taylor Trio* (1954, Prst. 184); H. Renaud: *Henri Renaud All Stars* (1954, Swing 33320–21); H. Mann: *Sultry Serenade* (1957, Riv. 234)

BIBLIOGRAPHY

FeatherE
B. Korall: "A Blast from the Past: the Great Drummers of Duke Ellington," *MD*, xxi/12 (1997), 82

RICK MATTINGLY

Smith, Clara (*b* Spartanburg, SC, 1894; *d* Detroit, 2 Feb 1935). Singer. She began working in vaudeville around 1910, and by 1918 was a principal performer on the Theater Owners' Booking Association circuit. For the next five years she toured, mainly in the South, before traveling in 1923 to New York, where she sang at clubs in Harlem and made her first recordings. Thereafter, until her last sessions in 1932, she worked in studios with such distinguished musicians as Fletcher Henderson, Don Redman, Coleman Hawkins, Louis Armstrong, Charlie Green, and Joe Smith. In 1924 she opened a theatrical club in New York, but continued to tour extensively, working as far afield as the West Coast (1924-5). She appeared frequently in revues in Harlem from 1928 to 1931; in the early 1930s she worked with Paul Barbarin in New York, and also performed in Detroit and Cleveland.

Smith recorded exclusively for Columbia, whose catalogue also included the work of Bessie Smith, and the fame of the latter has undoubtedly distracted audiences from Clara Smith's work. She was often known as the "Queen of the Moaners" – this facet of her style may be heard on *Awful Moanin' Blues* – but actually had a lighter tone than her contemporary. During the early part of her career she displayed a penchant for very slow tempos, but from about 1925 she developed a richer sound and a greater emotional range that mark her as one of the most important vaudeville blues singers.

SELECTED RECORDINGS
(all recorded for Columbia)

Duos: with F. Henderson: I never miss the sunshine/Awful Moanin' Blues (1923, A4000); with Lem Fowler: Whip it to a Jelly (1926, 14150D)
As leader: Death Letter Blues/Prescription for the Blues (1924, 14045D); Shipwrecked Blues/My John Blues (1925, 14077D); with B. Smith: My Man Blues (1925, 14098D); It's tight like that (1929, 14398D); Papa I don't need you now (1929, 14398D)

BIBLIOGRAPHY

ChiltonW
C. Van Vechten: "Negro 'Blues' Singers: an Appreciation of Three Coloured Artists who Excel in an Unusual and Native Medium," *Vanity Fair*, xxvi/1 (1926), 67
L. M. G. Arntzenius: *Amerikaansche kunstindrukken* (Amsterdam, 1927) [colln of previously pubd articles]; Eng. trans., pp.169ff, as "Clara Smith, Eyewitness Account 1926," *Juke Blues*, no.46 (2000), 52
H. Panassié and M. Gautier: *Dictionnaire du jazz* (Paris, 1954; Eng. trans., London, 1956, rev. A. A. Gurwitch as *Guide to Jazz*, Boston, 1956), 285
P. Oliver: "Clara Voce: a Study in Neglect," *JM*, iv/2 (1958), 8
S. Harris: *Blues Who's Who: a Biographical Dictionary of Blues Singers* (New Rochelle, NY, 1979/*R*1994), 466
E. Brooks: *The Bessie Smith Companion: a Critical and Detailed Appreciation of the Recordings* (Wheathampstead, nr St. Albans, England, and New York, 1982/*R*1989), 31, 93
D. Seroff: "Blues Itineraries: Clara Smith on the Road," *Whiskey, Women, and . . .*, nos.12-13 (1983), 58
E. Townley: "The Forgotten Ones: Clara Smith," *JJI*, xxxviii/7 (1985), 16

HOWARD RYE

Smith, Colin (Ranger) (*b* London, 20 Nov 1934). English trumpeter. He learned piano briefly at around the age of seven, played clarinet and banjo in his mid-teens, and took up trumpet at the age of 19. After performing and recording with Terry Lightfoot (1956 – early 1957) he formed his own group, but then played again with Lightfoot (late 1957–1958); he also performed and recorded with Archie Semple (May 1958). While working with Cy Laurie (1958–60) he deputized in Acker Bilk's group (1959). He was a member of Bilk's band from May 1960 to June 1966, after which he performed as a freelance. Smith gave up music to pursue sailing, but rejoined Bilk in 1968. From 1971 he was active as a freelance, working with the band of Tony Coe and John Picard, and others; he recorded with the blues singers Willie Mabon (1973) and Cousin Joe Pleasant (1974). From 1974 he led the Dixieland All Stars, from the mid-1970s he was a member of Stan Greig's London Jazz Big Band, and in 1978 he recorded with Rocket 88, led by the trombonist Ian Stewart. In 1983 Smith became a member of the Pizza Express All Stars, and throughout the decade he also worked in the Midnite Follies, Greig's Boogie Band, and the big bands of Bob Wilber and the drummer Charlie Watts. In 1992 he again joined Bilk, with whom he recorded in 1993 (*Chalumeau – That's my Home*, Apricot 1) and toured

Germany in 1996, though he maintained his associations with the Pizza Express All Stars, Wilber, Tommy Whittle, and others.

BIBLIOGRAPHY

CarrJ; *ChiltonB*
M. Jones: "Star Sidemen: 10 Years as a Bilk Man," *MM* (7 Nov 1970), 12

GK

Smith, Crickett [William Cricket] (*b* Nashville, 15 Aug 1883; *d* ?New York, ? late 1947). Cornetist and trumpeter. After touring in vaudeville shows as a youth he played and recorded in New York with James Reese Europe's Clef Club Society Orchestra (1913–14) and Ford Dabney (1917–19) and in Europe with Louis Mitchell's Jazz Kings (1919–24); *Montmartre Rag/Wabash Blues* (1922, Pathé 6566) is a good example of his work with the last-named group. In 1923 he took over the leadership of Mitchell's band and renamed it the Real Jazz Kings. He led his own group in Spain (1925, 1931–3), worked in Paris (1928–31), then was associated with Herb Flemming (1933–4), Leon Abbey (1936–7), Teddy Weatherford (1937–8), and others, playing in Ceylon, Java, and India, where he recorded again as leader of his own group, the Symphonians; he may be heard playing a solo on *Taj Mahal* (1936, Rex 7994). He returned to the USA probably in 1943.

For illustration *see* NIGHTCLUBS AND OTHER VENUES, fig.1.

BIBLIOGRAPHY

R. Gulliver: "Crickett Smith," *IAJRC Journal*, xii/3 (1979), 3
P. Darke: "The Mystery of Crickett Smith," *Sv*, no.111 (1984), 90

RAINER E. LOTZ

Smith, Derek (Geoffrey) (*b* London, 17 August 1931). English pianist. He took up piano at the age of seven and worked professionally from his teenage years as both a bandleader and a sideman. Having played with Kenny Graham (early 1950s) he performed and recorded with John Dankworth's big band (spring 1954 – September 1955), alongside Allan Ganley in the New Jazz Quintet (from September 1955), and with his own groups (1954–7); he also recorded with Vic Ash (1954, 1956) and Kenny Baker, Jimmy Skidmore, and Bertie King (all 1956) and worked in Baker's Dozen and as a studio musician for the BBC. After emigrating to the USA (April 1957) he was the leader of a trio (1957) consisting of Connie Kay and Percy Heath. Around 1960 he led a trio that included John Drew and which recorded in 1961 as the British Jazz Trio; in the latter year he appeared alongside Georgie Auld in a jazz group in the television program "Michael Bryan," and that November he toured South America with Benny Goodman. From 1967 to 1972 Smith was the pianist in the big band that played on "The Tonight Show"; when the show moved to Los Angeles in 1972 he remained in New York and performed on other television programs, notably that of the comedian Dick Cavett.

Smith worked in Goodman's group again several times (1969, 1971, 1972, 1973), on the last occasion touring Australia. In the 1970s and 1980s he made several albums under his own name, as well as recording with such leaders as Goodman (1971), the singer Marlena Shaw (1972, 1973), Bill Watrous (1975), Buddy DeFranco and Nick Brignola (both 1977), Sal Salvador and Dick Meldonian (both 1978), and Arnett Cobb (1978, 1980). In 1983 he toured Japan with Benny Carter. Through the 1980s and 1990s he worked in a trio with Milt Hinton and Bob Rosengarden and performed as a freelance, in which capacity he recorded in a duo with Dick Hyman (1983, 1998) and as a sideman with Svend Asmussen (1983), Louie Bellson (intermittently from 1986), Flip Phillips (1993), Hinton (1994–*c*1995), and Watrous (2000). He also appeared at international festivals and parties, often in swing-oriented settings with such musicians as Phillips, Ken Peplowski, Johnny Frigo, Bucky Pizzarelli, Hyman, and Roger Kellaway.

Video oral history material in *NCH* (HCJA).

SELECTED RECORDINGS

As leader: *The Man I Love* (1978, Prog. 7035); *The Derek Smith Trio Plays Jerome Kern* (1980, Prog. 7055)

As sideman: S. Asmussen: *June Night* (1983, Doctor Jazz FW39150); M. Hinton: *The Trio 1994* (1994, Chi. 322); B. Watrous: *Live at the Half Note* (2000, HighNote 4908)

BIBLIOGRAPHY

ConnorBG; *FeatherE*
E. Cook: "Derek Smith," *JJI*, xliv/2 (1991), 8
E. Berger: *Bassically Speaking: an Oral History of George Duvivier* (Metuchen, NJ, and London, 1993), 183, 197

BK

Smith, Floyd [Wonderful] (*b* St. Louis, 25 Jan 1917; *d* Indianapolis, 29 March 1982). Guitarist. From 1932 he played ukulele, working locally with Dewey Jackson and Charlie Creath, and from July 1934 to 1936 he performed on acoustic guitar in the Crackerjacks under the pianist Eddie Johnson. He first recorded on electric guitar as a member of the Jeter–Pillars Orchestra (1937–8). Smith then played with Andy Kirk (1939–42), with whom he recorded one of the first notable blues solos on electric guitar on his showpiece *Floyd's Guitar Blues* (1939); the track features his outrageously original conception of applying a downhome bottleneck guitar technique to an electric instrument. During military service (May 1942–1945) Smith had an opportunity to take part in a jam session in Paris with Django Reinhardt. Following another period with Kirk (late 1945 – September 1946) he led his own trio in Chicago and worked with Wild Bill Davis (*c*1952–1957) and Horace Henderson. Later he played with various ensembles in St. Louis and with Bill Doggett in New York (1959–64). In 1964 he formed another group, with which he moved to Indianapolis, and towards the end of the 1960s he played in Atlantic City, New Jersey, in a duo with the organist Hank Marr. While visiting Europe with Davis in 1972, he recorded in France as a leader and with Davis, Buddy Tate, and Al Grey.

SELECTED RECORDINGS

As leader: *Floyd's Guitar Blues* (1972, BB 30046)

As sideman. A. Kirk: Floyd's Guitar Blues (1939, Decca 2483); Six Men and a Girl: Mary Lou Williams Blues/Tea for Two (1940, Vars. 8193); E. Hines: The Day Will Come/Bop Omlette [*sic*] (1948, MGM 266); W. B. Davis: I ain't feeling so good (1953, OK 7021); Things ain't what they used to be (1953, Epic 7047); on *At Birdland* (1951–5, Epic LN3118), Night Train (1954); April in Paris/Lullaby of Birdland (1954, OK 9137); B. Tate and W. B. Davis: *Buddy Tate & Wild Bill Davis* (1972, BB 33054)

BIBLIOGRAPHY

ChiltonW; *FeatherE*
J. Obrecht: "Pro's Reply: Floyd Smith," *GP*, xiii/11 (1979), 8
Obituary, J. McAfee, Jr., *JSN*, ii/4 (1982), 20

HOWARD RYE, BK

Smith, Frank [Francis Percival] (*b* Sydney, 30 July 1927; *d* Melbourne, Australia, 18 Feb 1974). Australian reed player and teacher. After first performing in a group led by his father he played extensively during the 1940s and 1950s with dance bands in Sydney, among them those led by Frank Coughlan and the trombonist Ralph Mallen. He studied at the New South Wales Conservatorium of Music and became an important and influential teacher; many of his pupils later became prominent jazz musicians. In the late 1950s he moved to Melbourne, where he worked as a studio musician and composed for radio and television. He also acted as the music director for many visiting musicians, including the singers Billy Eckstine and Andy Williams. In 1959–60 he led his own group at the Embers in Melbourne. His playing is well represented on *Ockeration* from the album *Music Maker 1957 All Stars* (*c*1957, Parl. AuPMD07511).

BIBLIOGRAPHY

A. Bisset: *Black Roots, White Flowers: a History of Jazz in Australia* (Sydney, 1979, rev. 2/1987)

B. Johnson: *The Oxford Companion to Australian Jazz* (Melbourne, Australia, 1987)

TONY GOULD

Smith, Howard (Stanley) (*b* Ardmore, OK, 19 Oct 1910; *d* 12 July 1988). Pianist. Chilton, in *Who's Who of Jazz*, gives his forename as Harold and his nickname as Howard, but in his application for social security Smith gave his forenames as Howard Stanley. From 1919 he lived with his family in Montreal, and in 1933 he moved to New York, where the following year he played briefly with Benny Goodman at Billy Rose's Music Hall and recorded with Adrian Rollini. After working with Ray Noble (1935) he performed and recorded alongside Woody Herman in Isham Jones's Juniors (1935 – early 1936) and recorded with Red Norvo (1936) and Glenn Miller (1937). From spring 1937 to January 1940 he toured and recorded with Tommy Dorsey, and he may be heard playing a solo on Dorsey's *Boogie Woogie* (1938, Vic. 26054). Smith appears as a member of the Saturday Evening Post All-American Jazz Band in the film *Syncopation* (1942). Later he worked as a studio musician. The social security death index gives his last-known residence as New York. (*FeatherE*; *ChiltonW*)

Smith, Jabbo [Cladys] (*b* Pembroke, GA, 24 Dec 1908; *d* New York, 16 Jan 1991). Trumpeter and singer. After spending his early childhood in Savannah, Georgia, at the age of six he entered the Jenkins Orphanage at Charleston, South Carolina. He began playing trombone, but progressed to cornet, and traveled with the orphanage band to New York and Florida. In addition to receiving brass tuition in the Jenkins band, he was introduced to jazz technique by Gus Aiken. His first professional job was on trumpet with the bandleader Harry Marsh in Philadelphia (1924–5), after which he joined Aiken in Atlantic City; he then transferred to Charlie Johnson's Paradise Ten, in which he stayed from 1925 to 1928. Smith recorded with Johnson, whose band played regularly in New York at Smalls' Paradise, and took part as a freelance in other recording sessions, notably with Duke Ellington in November 1927, when he produced a masterly solo on *Black and Tan Fantasy* that demonstrated his originality in a strikingly different approach to the piece from that of Ellington's regular trumpeter Bubber Miley. In February 1928 he joined James P. Johnson's pit orchestra for the revue *Keep Shufflin'*, in which he was a prominent soloist along with Fats Waller and the drummer Carl "Battle Axe" Kenny. A contingent from this band, under the name the Louisiana Sugar Babes, recorded music from the show in March 1928, and subsequently Smith traveled with the production to Chicago, where it closed. He remained there, working as a freelance for several leaders, among them Carroll Dickerson, Earl Hines, Erskine Tate, Charlie Elgar, Tiny Parham, and Fess Williams. In 1929 he recorded 19 titles for Brunswick with his Rhythm Aces; these confirm his reputation as one of the most outstanding and innovative trumpeters of the late 1920s, second only to Louis Armstrong. The majority of the Rhythm Aces sides were composed by Smith, and pieces such as *Jazz Battle* and *Decatur Street Tutti* demonstrate his extraordinary speed and range, in playing which he foreshadowed the attack of Roy Eldridge and the high register agility of Dizzy Gillespie.

Despite his ability as a soloist and composer, Smith's temperament and a casual attitude to copyright meant that he failed to capitalize on his talent, and he drifted through the early 1930s playing as a sideman and occasional leader in Chicago and Milwaukee. He also worked in Toledo and Detroit (with Sammy Price) before spending a period with Claude Hopkins (1936–8). In 1938, with an eight-piece band, he recorded four of his compositions for Decca which constitute the high point of his achievement as a composer, quirky singer, and flamboyant, controlled, yet imaginative trumpeter.

In the early 1940s Smith worked in Newark, New Jersey, with Don Lambert and then returned to Milwaukee, where in 1958 he temporarily abandoned playing. He took up performing and recording again in 1961 at the instigation of Marty Grosz, but despite a consistently creative flow of ideas his technical brilliance had already faded, and this was to be true of the majority of his later recordings, which only hinted at his former talents as a brass player. Nevertheless, as a singer and composer he continued to show his customary ability to surprise. He played sporadically in Milwaukee in the late 1960s and appeared as a trombonist at the Oude Stijl Jazz Festival Breda in 1971, heralding the start of a lengthy period of rediscovery and lionization as a living legend. In 1977, once more playing trumpet, he recorded in the Netherlands, toured there and in Britain with Sammy Rimington, and worked in Chicago, New Orleans, and Milwaukee. From 1979 to 1982 he played and sang in the off-Broadway show *One Mo' Time* and traveled with the production, despite the first in a series of debilitating strokes, to many parts of the USA, including Philadelphia and Los Angeles. He toured Europe again in 1982 with the Hot Antic Jazz Band from Nîmes, France. With this group he made a systematic effort to document and record his original compositions. His last appearance as a trumpeter was at the Breda event in 1983, but he continued to work occasionally in New York and on tour as a singer, notably with Don Cherry's band Collaboration, which appeared at the Village Vanguard and Jazzfest Berlin in 1986.

Smith's long periods of obscurity and final return to fame well after the peak of his powers should not occlude his originality and influence as one of the most forward-thinking and technically brilliant trumpeters of the 1920s and 1930s. His attack, speed, and range influenced many later players, among them Dizzy Gillespie.

Oral history material in *CtY*, *LNT*, *NjR* (JOHP), and *NjR*.

See also Trumpet, §4.

SELECTED RECORDINGS

As leader: Jazz Battle (1929, Bruns. 4244); Sweet and Low Blues (1929, Bruns. 7061); Decatur Street Tutti/Till times get better (1929, Bruns. 7078); Rhythm in Spain/More Rain, More Rest (1938, Decca 1980); Absolutely/How can Cupid be so stupid (1939, Decca 1712); *Hidden Treasure*, i–ii (1961, Jazz Art 520699, 520700); *Jabbo Smith and the Hot Antic Jazz Band* (1982, Memories 05)

As sideman: D. Ellington: Black and Tan Fantasy (1927, OK 40955); C. Johnson: Charleston is the best dance after all (1928, Vic. 21491)

BIBLIOGRAPHY

D. DeMicheal: "Focus on Jabbo Smith," *DB*, xxviii/17 (1961), 22
H. Pekar: "Jabbo Smith," *JJ*, xviii/7 (1965), 8
G. Schuller: *Early Jazz: its Roots and Musical Development* (New York, 1968), 207
L. Terjanian: "The Legendary Cladys 'Jabbo' Smith," *Pj*, no.7 (1972), 32
O. Coyle: "Jabbo Smith: his Horn is Hot again," *MR*, iii/9 (1976), 1
M. Hinton: "Milt on Jabbo," *MM* (6 Aug 1977), 32
"Jabbo: Legend who Came Back from the Dead," *MM* (3 Sept 1977), 34
A. Vollmer: "Rhythm Aces," *Sv*, no.86 (1979–80), 70
J. Chilton: *A Jazz Nursery: the Story of the Jenkins' Orphanage Bands of Charleston, South Carolina* (London, 1980), 27
W. Balliett: "Starting at the Top," *Jelly Roll, Jabbo and Fats* (New York, and Oxford, England, 1983), 63; repr. in *BallietA (1986)*; *BallietA (1996)*
E. Cook: "Jabbo Smith," *JJI*, xxxvii/4 (1984), 6
J. Reldy: "Gabbin' with Jabbo," *BHcF*, no.319 (1984), 7
M. Laplace: "Jabbo Smith: le méconnu," *Brass Bulletin*, no.49 (1985), 47
A. Shipton: "Jabbo Smith: Hidden Treasure," *Fn*, xviii/3 (1987), 15
M. Laplace: *Jabbo Smith: the Misunderstood and the "Modernistic"* (Menden, Germany, 1988)
A. Shipton: *Fats Waller: his Life & Times* (Tunbridge Wells, England, and New York, 1988)
C. Deffaa: *Voices of the Jazz Age* (Wheatley, Oxford, England, Urbana, IL, and Chicago, 1990), 188
Obituaries: P. Watrous, *New York Times* (18 Jan 1991); E. Cook, *JJI*, xliv/5 (1991) 17
J. Simmen: "Cinq enregistrements presque toujours passés sous silence, et qui montrent Jabbo Smith en pleine possession de ses moyens," *BHcF*, no.397 (1991), 6
L. Terjanien: "The Legendary Cladys Jabbo Smith," *BHcF*, no.464 (1997), 4; no.465 (1997), 7; no.466 (1998), 3

ALYN SHIPTON

Smith, Jimmie [James Howard] (*b* Newark, NJ, 27 Jan 1938). Drummer and arranger. After studying at the Al Germansky School for Drummers in Newark (1951–4) and the Juilliard School (1959–60) he recorded in the New York area with Jimmy Forrest (1960), Larry Young (1960, 1962), Pony Poindexter, Jimmy Witherspoon, and Gildo Mahones (all 1963), Jimmy McGriff (*c*1963–5), and Groove Holmes (1965). He performed and recorded with Lambert, Hendricks, and Ross (1962–3, appearing at the Newport Jazz Festival in 1963) and toured and recorded with Erroll Garner (autumn 1967–1974). Having settled in California (mid-1970s) he played with Benny Carter (1975, 1978) and performed and recorded with Bill Henderson (1975, 1979), Hank Jones (1976), Harry Edison (1976–8, recording in groups led by Edison and Eddie "Lockjaw" Davis and Edison and Zoot Sims), and Terry Gibbs (1978). At the Montreux International Jazz Festival in 1977 he recorded in performance with Carter, Davis, Milt Jackson, Dizzy Gillespie, and Count Basie. On account of his clear, crisp sound and his reliable sense of swing Smith has been much sought after as a sideman. He took part in sessions with Sonny Criss (1975), Ernestine Anderson, Plas Johnson, and Phineas Newborn (all 1976), Lorez Alexandria (1977–8), Tommy Flanagan (1978), Bob Cooper (1979), Marshall Royal and Great Guitars (both 1980), Barney Kessel, Herb Ellis, and Gibbs and Buddy DeFranco (all 1981), Al Cohn (1983), Carter (1985), Anderson (1986), Red Holloway (1987), and Dave McKenna (1988). In 1993 he recorded in concert in Japan with Jimmy Smith and Kenny Burrell.

SELECTED RECORDINGS

As sideman: J. Forrest: *Forrest Fire* (1960, NewJ 8250); G. Holmes: *Soul Message* (1965, Prst. 7435); S. Criss: *Crisscraft* (1975, Muse 5068); *Out of Nowhere* (1975, Muse 5089); H. Roberts: *The Real Howard Roberts* (1977, Conc. 53); J. Smith: *The Master* (1993, BN B21Z-30451)

BIBLIOGRAPHY

Feather–Gitler '70s
J. M. Doran: *Erroll Garner: the Most Happy Piano* (Metuchen, NJ, 1985), 106

CHRIS SHERIDAN

Smith, Jimmy [James Oscar, Jr.] (*b* Norristown, PA, 8 Dec 1925). Organist and leader. He first learned piano, largely from his parents and through self-instruction, and at the age of nine won a talent contest, playing boogie-woogie on the "Major Bowes Amateur Hour" radio program in Philadelphia. Later, in 1942, before joining the navy, he formed a song-and-dance act with his father at local nightclubs. Following his discharge in 1947 he returned to Philadelphia and studied harmony and theory at the Halsey Music School, double bass at the Hamilton School of Music (1948), and piano at the Ornstein School of Music (1949–50) – though, by his own testimony, without ever learning to read music, so extraordinary was his ability to play by ear. From 1949 he worked in obscure local rhythm-and-blues bands. In 1953, in the midst of a long period with Don Gardner and his Sonotones, Smith took up the Hammond organ, after hearing Wild Bill Davis. He acquired a formidable reputation in the Philadelphia area before making his extremely successful début in New York at the Café Bohemia in 1956, when he began a long association with the drummer Donald Bailey (to 1963). An appearance at Birdland and a highly acclaimed performance at the Newport Jazz Festival in 1957 launched his international career as the first important jazz player on his instrument. Although the organ had been played previously in jazz (for example, by Fats Waller and Count Basie), it was usually treated as a novelty instrument. Smith spent the next 20 years touring, visiting Israel in 1974 and Europe in 1975. He then settled in Los Angeles, where, with his wife Lola, he opened his own club, Jimmy Smith's Jazz Supper Club. He resumed touring in the early 1980s,

Jimmy Smith playing a Hammond organ

recording an outstanding album with Eddie Harris at the Keystone Korner in San Francisco (1981) and performing in New York (1982, 1983).

After a disastrously unproductive five-year association with Quincy Jones's Quest label, during a portion of which time he lived in Nashville and found little opportunity to perform, Smith settled in Sacramento, California, in 1989. He recorded immediately (with the double bass player Andy Simpkins covering the bass lines as Smith recovered from a broken left arm) and later that year appeared at the Chicago Jazz Festival with some of his favorite soloists from years past – Stanley Turrentine, Lou Donaldson, and Kenny Burrell; the following year he performed with Turrentine, Burrell, and Grady Tate in New York. With Hammond organ trios having come back into fashion, Smith resumed touring widely in the 1990s with Herman Riley as his tenor saxophonist. He may be heard in performance with Burrell and the unrelated drummer Jimmie Smith in Japan on a recording from December 1993. He performed in Britain and Ireland in 1994, and toured Europe in 1995.

Smith recognized that the organ could be suitable for jazz only if its articulation and timbre were altered from the manner in which Waller and Basie practiced. Proceeding from the approach of his mentor Wild Bill Davis (the first important soloist on the Hammond instrument), Smith emphasized the lower-pitched draw bars, to produce a fundamental timbre that was mellow and full-bodied by comparison with that of earlier jazz organists; he used this in combination with the high-pitched percussion stop on the instrument's upper keyboard, which effectively placed a fleeting grace note at the front of each fundamental note and thus gave a biting edge to his melodies. He also discarded the instrument's cheesy, built-in electronic vibrato in favor of the two-speed mechanical vibrato produced by the spinning of the external Leslie speaker. He was the first to make the organ effectively serve as a group (minus drums), providing walking bass lines with his feet, chordal accompaniment in his left hand, and a solo line in his right, and he set the standard instrumentation for a hard-bop group: organ, electric guitar, and drums, perhaps with saxophone (usually tenor saxophone) as well. These innovations and his powerful style, which combined rhythm-and-blues elements with the more sophisticated bop vocabulary, have influenced virtually every later jazz organist, including Don Patterson, Brother Jack McDuff, Jimmy McGriff, Groove Holmes, Larry Young, Joey DeFrancesco, and Larry Goldings.

See also Organ, §2.

SELECTED RECORDINGS

A New Star – a New Sound: Jimmy Smith at the Organ, i–iii (1956, BN 1512, 1514, 1525), incl. The Champ; *A Date with Jimmy Smith*, i–ii (1957, BN 1547–8); *The Sermon* (1957–8, BN 4001); *Crazy Baby* (1960, BN 4030); *Midnight Special* (1960, BN 84078); *Back at the Chicken Shack* (1960, BN 84117); *The Unpredictable Jimmy Smith: Bashin'* (1962, Verve 68474), incl. Walk on the Wild Side; *The Cat* (1964, Verve 68587); *Organ Grinder Swing* (1965, Verve 68628); with W. Montgomery: *The Dynamic Duo* (1966, Verve 68678); with E. Harris: *Keystone Korner: All the Way Live* (1981, Mlst. 9251–2), incl. Eight Counts for Rita; *Off the Top* (1982, Elek. 52418); *Prime Time* (1989, Mlst. 9176); *The Master* (1993, BN B21Z-30451)

SELECTED FILMS AND VIDEOS

Jazz Scene USA: Jimmy Smith Trio (1962); Get Yourself a College Girl (1964); Smith, James O. Organist USA (1965); Jazz 625 (1966); Midnight Special (1992); Carnegie Hall Salutes the Jazz Masters (1994)

BIBLIOGRAPHY

L. Feather: "Jimmy Smith," *Jm*, no.26 (1957), 17
F. Postif: "New Stars on the Horizon: Jimmy Smith," *Jh*, no.120 (1957), 13
P. Adler: "Jimmy Smith: objectif lune," *Jh*, no.181 (1962), 28
J. Cooke: "The Electric Organ in Jazz: Jimmy Smith and some Others," *JM*, vii/11 (1962), 11
B. Gardner: "Jimmy Smith: Reaching the People," *DB*, xxix/14 (1962), 17
D. Ioakimidis: "Inédit en France, voici, présenté le premier organiste moderne: Jimmy Smith," *Jh*, no.178 (1962), 19
"Jazz Spectacular: Jimmy Smith," *Rhythm & Blues*, no. 63 (1964), 20
H. Siders: "Jimmy Smith: a New Deal for the Boss," *DB*, xxxvii/20 (1970), 14
L. Birnbaum: "Jimmy Smith: Sermonizing in the '70s," *DB*, xliv/21 (1977), 22
B. Doerschuk: "Jimmy Smith," *CK*, iv/8 (1978), 26
G. Giddins: "Return of the Organ Grinder," *Rhythm-a-ning: Jazz Tradition and Innovation in the '80s* (New York, and Oxford, England, 1985), 166
S. Nicholson: "The Incredible Jimmy Smith," *Jazz Express*, nos.143–4 (1992), 6
M. Jackson: "Cat Napped!," *Jazz on CD*, no.11 (1994), 12
R. L. Doerschuk: "12 Who Count: Jimmy Smith," *Keyboard*, xxi/4 (1995), 58
D. Ouellette: "Jimmy Smith: the B-3 Messiah," *DB*, lxii/1 (1995), 30 [discography]
R. Palmer: "Jimmy Smith on Record," *JJI*, l/11 (1997), 6

BILL DOBBINS/BK

Smith, Joe [Joseph C.; Joseph E.] (*b* Ripley, OH, 28 June 1902; *d* New York, 2 Dec 1937). Trumpeter, brother of Russell Smith. Allen (1974), who gives Smith's middle initial as "E." rather than "C.," notes that he should not be confused with the white violinist Joseph C. Smith, the bandleader Joe Smith of the Martha Lee Club Orchestra, or a West Indian called Joe Smith who worked with Benny Peyton in France. Smith's father led a brass band in Cincinnati, and all six of his brothers were also trumpeters. As a child he played an instrument belonging to one of his elder brothers before acquiring his own. Around 1919 he left home to perform professionally and about a year later first went to New York, where he worked with Kaiser Marshall. In Chicago he joined Fletcher Henderson's Black Swan Jazz Masters accompanying Ethel Waters, with whom he toured (January–July 1922); he recorded with her under the name Joe Smith's Jazz Masters in May in Long Island City, New York. He then toured as far as California and recorded in a similar capacity with Mamie Smith (October 1922 – June 1923). On his return to New York he worked as a freelance, and his recordings over the next half decade included many sessions with singers, among them Alberta Hunter (1923), Rosa Henderson (1924), Waters (1924, 1925, 1927), Trixie Smith (1925), Ma Rainey (1926), and, most notably, Bessie Smith (in several dates with Henderson's men, 1924–7).

From March to November 1924 Smith directed the band for a revue by Noble Sissle and Eubie Blake which received its première in Rochester as *In Bamville* and took a new title, *The Chocolate Dandies*, when it opened in New York City that September. He was a member of Henderson's orchestra from April 1925 to October 1928. After working in the band for Lew Leslie's *Blackbirds* show he served as a member of McKinney's Cotton Pickers (summer 1929 – November 1930 and August–December 1931) until his drinking became excessive and he began consistently to miss performances. He settled in Kansas City, Missouri, but ill-health prevented him from performing regularly; he attempted to play with Henderson's band in Detroit, but shortly afterwards entered a sanatorium in New York.

For a brief period in the 1920s Smith was considered to be the chief rival of Louis Armstrong, who, like Smith, had also played as a soloist with Henderson. However, the styles of the two men were entirely different, Smith relying mainly on a mellow tone, subtle inflections, and lyrical playing in the middle register of the instrument. His very personal style and gentle lyricism attracted few followers in his own generation, and this, combined with his early retirement, has sometimes obscured his merits. He was particularly adept with the plunger mute, producing a touching, vocal sound which enhanced several of the recordings he made with Bessie Smith, whose favorite accompanist he was, though some of his finest work was done in accompaniment to Waters. His ability to accompany so effectively two singers with such disparate approaches evidences an unusual sensibility.

SELECTED RECORDINGS

As sideman: E. Waters: Tell 'em bout me (when you reach Tennessee)/ You'll need me when I'm long gone (1924, Para. 12214); Maggie Jones: Mamma (1925, Col. 14074D); B. Smith: Cake Walking Babies (1925, Col. 35673); F. Henderson: What-cha-call-'em Blues (1925, Col. 395D); M. Rainey: Chain Gang Blues (*c*1925, Para. 12338); Bessemer Bound Blues (*c*1925, Para. 12374); E. Waters: Tell 'em about me/I've found a new baby (1925–6, Col. 561D); B. Smith: Money Blues (1926, Col. 14137D); Baby Doll (1926, Col. 14147D); Lost You Head Blues (1926, Col. 14158D); F. Henderson: The Stampede (1926, Col. 654D); B. Smith: Young Woman's Blues (1926, Col. 14179D); Clara Smith: You don't know who's shakin' your tree (1926, Col. 14192D); F. Henderson: Rocky Mountain Blues (1927, Col. 970D); Stockholm Stomp/Have it Ready (1927, Bruns. 3460); B. Smith: There'll be a hot time in the old town to-night (1927, Col. 14219D); Trombone Cholly (1927, Col. 14232D); F. Henderson; Fidgety Feet (1927, Bruns. 3521); McKinney's Cotton Pickers: Gee, ain't I good to you? (1929, Vic. 38097)

BIBLIOGRAPHY

AllenH
W. G. Woods: "Joe Smith," *Australian Jazz Quarterly*, no.13 (1951), 12
B. Houghton: "Joe Smith: a Biography and Appreciation," *JJ*, xviii/12 (1965), 18
W. C. Allen: "Addenda: Joe Smith," *JJ*, xx/8 (1967), 6
H. Panassié: "Il y a 30 ans, le 1er décembre 1937 [*sic*], mourait Joe Smith," *BHcF*, no.173 (1967), 4
G. Schuller: *Early Jazz: its Roots and Musical Development* (New York, 1968), 234
J. Chilton: *McKinney's Music: a Bio-discography of McKinney's Cotton Pickers* (London, 1978), 27
C. Sheridan: "The Forgotten Ones: Joe Smith," *JJI*, xxxiv/12 (1981), 12
J. Chilton: *The Song of the Hawk: the Life and Recordings of Coleman Hawkins* (London, 1990)

JOHN CHILTON/BK

Smith, John (William) (*b* Atlanta, 27 Nov 1908). Guitarist. In Atlanta he played banjo with the pianist J. Neal Montgomery in the late 1920s; in New York he studied guitar with Edwin Colts in the early 1930s while playing in Otto Hardwick's band and working as a freelance. As a member of Teddy Hill's band (1932–9) he toured Europe in 1937. He played in both the big band and the small group of Fats Waller (June 1939 – summer 1940), then toured with the Mills Brothers until late in 1942, when he joined Benny Carter's orchestra. After working briefly in Dizzy Gillespie's big band he played with Cab Calloway (1946–8, and at intervals to 1951), performed as a solo singer and guitarist for a number of years, and played banjo and guitar with Wilbur De Paris (1958–66). He retired from music before resuming his career as a guitarist with Panama Francis and his Savoy Sultans (ii) from the late 1970s into the 1980s.

SELECTED RECORDINGS

As sideman: first issued on F. Waller: *Hitherto Unpublished Piano, Vocals and Conversation, no.1* (1935, 1939, HMV CLP1042), Honeysuckle Rose [no.2] (1939); P. Francis: *Grooving* (1982, Stash 218)

BIBLIOGRAPHY

ChiltonW
Battestini: "John Smith," *BHcF*, no.279 (1980), 10
E. Townley: "From Down in Atlanta, GA: an Interview with John Smith," *Sv*, no.99 (1982), 91
D. Barker: *A Life in Jazz*, ed. A. Shipton (London and New York, 1986), 176
L. Wright: *"Fats" in Fact* (Chigwell, England, 1992)

EDDIE LAMBERT/BK

Smith, Johnny [John Henry, Jr.] (*b* Birmingham, AL, 25 June 1922). Guitarist and leader. He taught himself trumpet, violin, and viola before specializing on electric guitar. From 1947 to 1953 he worked as a studio musician for NBC in New York, playing trumpet and guitar. In 1952 he organized his own group and recorded *Moonlight in Vermont* (Roost 542), which *Down Beat* named "jazz record of the year." Under the pseudonym Sir Jonathan Gasser he played on the album *Jazz Studio* (1953, Decca 8058) with an all-star group that included Bennie Green, Hank Jones, and Kenny Clarke. During the 1950s Smith recorded prolifically as a leader and led groups at Birdland in New York. After moving to Colorado Springs in February 1958, he opened a music shop in 1961 and performed and taught; however, he continued to record in New York until 1968. In 1976 he made unaccompanied recordings in Colorado Springs, and in the late 1970s he toured England with Bing Crosby. Smith received an honorary doctorate from the University of Colorado in 1986. The following year he sold his music shop, and thereafter he performed only occasionally. He published a method book, *The Complete Johnny Smith Approach to Guitar* (Pacific, MO, *c*1980).

BIBLIOGRAPHY

FeatherE; *Feather '60s*
L. Henshaw: "Smith to a D," *MM* (18 Feb 1979), 47
R. Yellin: "Johnny Smith," *GP*, xvi/1 (1982), 36 [incl. discography]
T. Reig and E. Berger: *Reminiscing in Tempo: the Life and Times of a Jazz Hustler* (Metuchen, NJ, and London, 1990), 105

BK

Smith, Johnny Hammond. *See* HAMMOND, JOHNNY.

Smith, Keith (John) (*b* London, England, 19 March 1940). English trumpeter. He began playing locally, and worked with the San Jacinto Jazz Band (1957) and the double bass player Mickey Ashman before forming his own Climax Jazz Band. While touring the USA he recorded with George Lewis (i) in New Orleans (1965). In 1966 he performed in Europe as a member of the New Orleans All Stars, which included Jimmy Archey, Darnell Howard, Alton Purnell, Pops Foster, and Cié Frazier; he then moved to the USA, where he made a recording with Capt. John Handy (1966), performed at Eddie Condon's, and worked with Tony Parenti and Zutty Singleton. He led his own band and performed and recorded in Denmark with Papa Bue's Viking Jazz Band (1972–4). After returning to England in 1975 Smith formed the band Hefty Jazz (with Ian Wheeler as co-leader from 1976 to 1979) and promoted a record label of the same name; among his recordings as the group's leader are *Up Jumped the Blues* (1978, Hefty Jazz 105). In 1981 he began performing on tour with such presentations as "The Wonderful World of Louis Armstrong" (including five former members of Armstrong's All Stars) and "100 Years of Dixieland Jazz"; these shows continued in the 1990s with tributes to Cole Porter and George Gershwin. A further tribute to Armstrong in 1994 featured Joe Muranyi.

BIBLIOGRAPHY

CarrJ; *ChiltonB*
K. Smith: "In my Opinion," *JJ*, xxii/8 (1969), 13
R. Laing: "I'm only Interested in Music which Works!," *JJI*, xxxii/5 (1979), 7
E. Cook: "The Wonderful World of Louis Armstrong," *JJI*, xxxiv/9 (1981), 6
T. Dash: "Profile on Keith Smith," *Fn*, xvi/6 (1985), 4
"Keith Smith's Hefty Jazz," *Jazz Express*, no. 92 (1988), 8

DEREK COLLER/BK

Smith, Leo. *See* SMITH, WADADA LEO.

Smith, (Dr.) Lonnie (*b* Buffalo, 3 July 1942). Organist. By his own account the nickname "Dr." derives from other musicians saying, "You doctor up the music." He grew up in a musical family in which his grandmother, mother, and aunt sang in a gospel quartet, and he first played trumpet and tuba in school; later he sang professionally in rhythm-and-blues vocal groups. After taking up organ in the early 1960s he toured with the singer Miss Sammy Bryant and worked in Buffalo accompanying visiting Motown artists. Around 1965, while sitting in with Brother Jack McDuff, he met George Benson; shortly afterwards he joined Benson's group in Pittsburgh, and in 1967 he traveled with it to New York. Smith then performed with Lou Donaldson (from *c*1967) and Ronnie Cuber (1969–70); he also toured with, among others, Dizzy Gillespie, Grover Washington, Jr., Ron Carter, Frank Foster, Leon Thomas, and Willis "Gator" Jackson, and worked with such pop and soul singers and groups as Gladys Knight, Dionne Warwick, Etta James, Esther Phillips, the Impressions, and the Coasters. From around 1985 he again toured and recorded with Donaldson. Smith first recorded as a sole leader in 1966, and in 1992–3 he led a trio with John Abercrombie and Marvin "Smitty" Smith. From the late 1980s he recorded as a freelance with, among others, the guitarist Richie Hart (1988–9), Jimmy Ponder (1988–90), Ron Holloway (1993), the Essence All Stars (*c*1995), the saxophonist Terry Myers (1995), Turk Mauro (with whom he doubled on piano; 1995–6), the saxophonist Jesse Jones, Jr. (1996), the saxophonist Eric Allison (1996–7), and Javon Jackson (1996, 1998). Through much of his career he has been mistaken for Lonnie Liston Smith.

SELECTED RECORDINGS

As leader: *Finger Lickin' Good* (1966, Col. CS9496); *Think!* (1968, BN 84290); *Live at the Club Mozambique* (1970, BN 31880-2); *Afro Blue* (1993, Musicmasters 65167)

As sideman: G. Benson: *The Most Exciting New Guitarist on the Jazz Scene Today: it's Uptown with the George Benson Quartet* (1966, Col. CS9325); *The George Benson Cookbook* (1966, Col. CS9413); L. Donaldson: *Alligator Boogaloo* (1967, BN 84263); J. Ponder: *Come on Down* (1990, Muse 5375); L. Donaldson: *Play the Right Thing* (1990, Mlst. 9190); T. Mauro: *Hittin' the Jug: the Music of Gene Ammons* (1995, Mlst. 9246); Chartbusters: *Mating Call* (1995, Prst. 11002); J. Jackson: on *A Look Within* (1996, BN 36490-2), Peggy's Blue Skylight/Duke Ellington's Sound of Love, Zoot Allures; T. Mauro: on *The Truth* (1996, Mlst. 9267), A Joyful Feeling, What a difference a day made [both p]

BIBLIOGRAPHY

Feather–GitlerBEJ

A. Cohen: "Rockin' the House," *DB*, lxiv/10 (1997), 34 [incl. discography]

<http://www.fantasyjazz.com/chartbustersbio.html> (1999)

<http://www.theatreorgans.com/grounds/doodlin/smithl.html> (1999) [incl. discography]

GK

Smith, Lonnie Liston(, Jr.) (*b* Richmond, VA, 28 Dec 1940). Keyboard player. His father sang and played with a gospel group, the Harmonizing Four. After graduating in music education from Morgan State University (BS 1961) Smith went to New York, where he worked with Betty Carter (1963–4), Roland Kirk (1964–5), Art Blakey (1966–7), Joe Williams (1967–8), Pharoah Sanders (1969–71), Gato Barbieri (1971–3), and Miles Davis (1972–*c*1973). In the last three groups he tended to supply harmonic drones by reiterating shimmering or rhythmic chordal patterns. In 1974, with one of his brothers, the singer Donald Smith, he formed the Cosmic Echoes. Although this group was soundly criticized in jazz record reviews for its use of predictable improvisations, bland funk vamps, and sugary lyrics, its album *Expansions* (1975) reached high positions on the jazz, pop, and soul charts. During the late 1970s the Cosmic Echoes achieved considerable popularity through its performances on the club circuit, and Smith continued to lead the group through the 1990s. In 1997 he formed his own record company and label, Loveland. He may be seen in the video *Teruo Nakamura and Lonnie Liston Smith in Concert at Godspell* (1983).

SELECTED RECORDINGS

As leader: *Expansions* (*c*1975, FD 10934); *Renaissance* (*c*1977, RCA APL1-1822)

As sideman: P. Sanders: *Karma* (1969, Imp. 9181); S. Turrentine: on *Sugar* (1970, CTI 6005), Sugar; G. Barbieri: *Fenix* (1971, FD 10144); M. Davis: *Big Fun* (1972, Col. PG32866)

BIBLIOGRAPHY

M. Cullaz: "Lonnie Liston Smith J° a beaucoup de choses à raconter," *Jh*, no.282 (1972), 14

E. Chadbourne: "Astral Travelling," *Coda*, xi/4 (1973), 2

A. J. Smith: "Lonnie Liston Smith: Cosmic Head on Electronic Neck," *DB*, xliii/1 (1976), 12 [incl. discography]

R. Palmer: "Lonnie Liston Smith's Power for the People," *RS*, no.279 (30 Nov 1978), 35

"Lonnie Liston Smith: the Messenger," *Afro-American* (13 May 1989)

M. White: "Lonnie Liston Smith," *Jazz Express*, no.138 (1992), 9

BK

Smith, (Edward) Louis (*b* Memphis, 20 May 1931). Trumpeter and leader. He took up trumpet at the age of 13 and studied music at Tennessee State University (BM); while touring with the Tennessee State Collegians he performed in New York at Carnegie Hall. After pursuing graduate work in music at the University of Michigan he played with an army band (1954–5) and then taught at a high school in Atlanta. Smith traveled to the New York area and recorded two fine albums (1957, 1958) as the leader of hard-bop quintets with such distinguished sidemen as Tommy Flanagan, Duke Jordan, Cannonball Adderley (who used the pseudonym Buckshot la Funke), Charlie Rouse, Paul Chambers, and Art Taylor. In 1958 he recorded with Kenny Burrell and toured briefly with Horace Silver. However, as he was uninterested in the rigor and low pay of life as a touring jazz musician, he returned to teaching, though in 1960 he recorded in New York with the Young Men from Memphis, a group consisting of Booker Little, Phineas Newborn, Calvin Newborn, Frank Strozier, Charles Crosby, and George Coleman. Later he led a quartet in Louisville, Kentucky (1967), and played in local groups while teaching at the University of Michigan (from *c*1969). In 1978–9 he recorded as a leader in New York; Coleman and Harold Mabern (another colleague from Memphis) are among his sidemen on the outstanding album *Just Friends* (1978). Smith made further recordings in the early 1990s.

SELECTED RECORDINGS

As leader: *Here Comes Louis Smith* (1957, BN 1584); *Smithville* (1958, BN 1594); *Just Friends* (1978, Ste. 1096)

As sideman: K. Burrell: *Blue Lights*, i–ii (1958, BN 1596–7); Young Men from Memphis: *Down Home Reunion* (1960, UA 4029)

BIBLIOGRAPHY

FeatherE

M. Gardner: "Wilber Harden and Louis Smith: Forgotten Faces of the Fifties," *JJ*, xxi/5 (1968), 19 [incl. discography]

——: Liner notes, *Just Friends* (Ste. 1096, 1978)

BK

Smith [née Robinson], **Mamie** (*b* Cincinnati, 26 May 1883; *d* New York, ?30 Oct 1946). Singer and entertainer. She toured as a dancer with Tutt-Whitney's Smart Set Company when in her early teens, and gained a reputation as a singer in Harlem clubs and theaters before World War I. In 1918, at the Lincoln Theater in Harlem, she took a prominent role in Perry Bradford's musical revue *Made in Harlem*, in which she sang *Harlem Blues*. In 1920 she became the first African-American jazz-blues singer to record when she took part in a session in place of Sophie Tucker. Shortly afterwards she had a huge success with *Crazy Blues* (a retitled version of *Harlem Blues*), which made a fortune both for the singer and her promoter Bradford; it was also important in that it opened the way for the subsequent recording of other African-American singers. Following this, Smith had many engagements, touring nationally with her Jazz Hounds, which at times between 1920 and 1923 included Johnny Dunn (replaced by Bubber Miley), Garvin Bushell, and Coleman Hawkins. Later she appeared as the featured singer in her own shows. She also made several films, both short subjects and full-length features, notably with Lucky Millinder's band in *Paradise in Harlem* (1940). She possessed a lively stage personality, was extremely attractive, and had a strong voice. Many of her best recordings were made with her Jazz Hounds. *Jenny's Ball* gives a good indication of her appeal as a singer. Smith was a vaudeville performer rather than a blues singer and, unlike Bessie Smith, seldom used the blues form or blues inflections.

For illustration *see* SINGING, fig.1.

SELECTED RECORDINGS

That thing called love (1920, OK 4113); Crazy Blues (1920, OK 4169); I ain't gonna give nobody none o' this jelly-roll (1922, OK 4752); The Darktown Flappers' Ball (1922, OK 4767); Goin' Crazy with the Blues (1926, Vic 20210); Jenny's Ball (1931, OK 8915)

BIBLIOGRAPHY

ChiltonW
D. Burley: "'Crazy Blues' and the Woman who Sold 'em," *Amsterdam News* (17 Feb 1940); contd as "The 'Crazy Blues'," (24 Feb 1940, 2 March 1940, 9 March 1940, 16 March 1940)
L. Kunstadt and B. Colton: "Mamie Smith: First Lady of the Blues," *Record Research*, no.31 (1960), 7
S. B. Charters and L. Kunstadt: *Jazz: a History of the New York Scene* (Garden City, NY, 1962/*R*1981)
P. Bradford: *Born with the Blues: ... the True Story of the Pioneering Blues Singers and Musicians in the Early Days of Jazz* (New York, 1963)
W. Smith and G. Hoefer: *Music on my Mind: the Memoirs of an American Pianist* (Garden City, NY, 1964/*R*1975), 102
R. C. Foreman, Jr.: *Jazz and Race Records, 1920–32: their Origins and their Significance for the Record Industry and Society* (diss., U. of Illinois, 1968)
R. M. W. Dixon and J. Godrich: *Recording the Blues* (London, 1970)
D. Stewart-Baxter: *Ma Rainey and the Classic Blues Singers* (New York and London, 1970)
S. Harris: *Blues Who's Who: a Biographical Dictionary of Blues Singers* (New Rochelle, NY, 1979/*R*1994)
S. Placksin: *American Women in Jazz, 1900 to the Present: their Words, Lives, and Music* (New York, 1982, London, 1985, as *Jazzwomen, 1900 to the Present: their Words, Lives, and Music*), 21
J. Chilton: *Sidney Bechet: the Wizard of Jazz* (London and New York, 1987/*R*1996), 57
G. Bushell and M. Tucker: *Jazz from the Beginning* (Wheatley, Oxford, England, 1988, Ann Arbor, MI, 1990), 21
D. D. Harrison: *Black Pearls: Blues Queens of the 1920s* (New Brunswick, NJ, 1988)
L. Wright: *"Fats" in Fact* (Chigwell, England, 1992)

PAUL OLIVER

Smith, Marvin "Smitty" [Smith, Marvin (O., II); Smitty] (*b* Waukegan, IL, 24 June 1961). Drummer. After studying at the Berklee College of Music he played in New York for two years with Jon Hendricks's group (from December 1980) and with John Hicks, Bobby Watson, and Slide Hampton. In the early to mid-1980s he worked as a freelance musician, recording with Archie Shepp (1982, 1984), Terence Blanchard and Branford Marsalis (both 1983), and Hamiet Bluiett and David Murray (both 1984) and recording (1983–4) and performing in a quintet led by Frank Foster and Frank Wess; during the same period he played with Ray Brown, Ron Carter, and Hank Jones. Smith performed and recorded frequently with Peter Leitch (1984–95) and with Steve Coleman and Five Elements and Dave Holland's small groups (both 1985–92). Among his studio engagements were sessions with Kevin Eubanks, Mulgrew Miller, and Cassandra Wilson (all 1985), The Jazztet, Art Farmer, Sonny Rollins, Buddy Montgomery, and Watson (all 1986), and Donald Byrd, Benny Golson, and George Shearing (1987).

Smith made his first album as a leader in 1987 and later that year played in the touring band of the rock musician Sting. He continued to maintain a busy career as a freelance, in which context he recorded with, among others, Diane Reeves, Emily Remler, Monty Alexander, and Grover Washington, Jr. (all 1988), David "Fathead" Newman and Ray Drummond (both 1989), Eubanks (1989, 1991, 1993), Kip Hanrahan and the singer Michelle Hendricks (both 1990), the M-Base collective and Harvie Swartz (both 1991), Miller and JoAnne Brackeen (both 1992), Steve Marcus, Bheki Mseleku, the pianist Stefan Karlsson, and Billy Taylor (ii) (all 1993), and Michel Camilo, Robin Eubanks, and McCoy Tyner (all 1994). In 1995 he moved to Los Angeles to join the house band of the NBC television program "The Tonight Show," led by Kevin Eubanks, but he remained in demand for recordings, performing at sessions led by Joe Locke and Lonnie Smith (both 1995), Jay Hoggard and Don Byron (both 1996), Larry Coryell, Kenny Drew, Jr., and Farmer (all 1998), and Michel Sardaby (1999).

Smith is a versatile drummer whose jazz playing shows the strong influence of Max Roach. He has proved himself to be a master of jazz-funk drumming and irregular time signatures, notably in his recordings with Coleman and Five Elements; he also incorporates elements of rock into his playing.

SELECTED RECORDINGS

As leader: *Keeper of the Drums* (1987, Conc. 325); *The Road Less Traveled* (1989, Conc. 4379)

As sideman: J. Hendricks: *Love* (1981, Muse 5258); D. Holland: *Seeds of Time* (1984, ECM 1292); S. Coleman: *Motherland Pulse* (1985, JMT 850001); Jazztet: *Back to the City* (1986, Cont. 14020); B. Montgomery: *Ties of Love* (1986, Landmark 1512); E. Remler: *East to Wes* (1988, Conc. 4356); D. Holland: *Extensions* (1989, ECM 1410); S. Coleman: *Black Science* (1990, Novus 3119-2-N); M. Tyner: *Prelude and Sonata* (1994, Mlst. 9244); P. Leitch: *Colours and Dimensions* (1995, Reservoir 140); D. Byron: *No-vibe Zone: Live at the Knitting Factory* (1996, Knitting Factory Works 191); K. Drew, Jr.: *Secrets* (1998, TCB 98502)

SELECTED FILMS AND VIDEOS

M-BASE Jams at BAM (*c*1989 [filmed 1988]); Stanley Jordan: Cornucopia (c1990, [filmed 1989]); Dave Holland Quintet: Vortex (*c*1994)

BIBLIOGRAPHY

J. Levenson: "Profile: Marvin Smitty Smith," *DB*, lii/11 (1985), 52
C. Stern: "Marvin 'Smitty' Smith: Drum History in Transition," *MD*, x/3 (1986), 22
H. Mandel: "Marvin 'Smitty' Smith: Drummer with a Heartbeat," *DB*, lv/5 (1988), 22 [incl. discography]
R. Mattingly: "Marvin 'Smitty' Smith: Down for the Long Count," *Musician*, no.155 (1991), Sept, 72
B. Shoemaker: "Marvin 'Smitty' Smith: Jazz, not Pizza," *JT*, xxii/9 (1992), 38
R. Mattingly: "Marvin 'Smitty' Smith: the Art of Self-discovery," *MD*, xvii/4 (1993), 20

M. Seidel: "Ray Drummond & Marvin 'Smitty' Smith: Rhythm Leaders," *DB*, lx/3 (1993), 24 [incl. discography]

RICK MATTINGLY

Smith, Michael (Joseph) (*b* Tiline, KY, 13 Aug 1938). Keyboard player, composer, and leader. From around the age of six he played piano in a white Baptist church, and he was initially influenced entirely by the music that was performed there; however, when he was 14 his home was supplied with electricity, and he began to listen to other kinds of music on the radio. While in the navy he had informal lessons with David Baker and served as a recruiter in Chicago, where he played regularly in jazz clubs; later he studied privately with Ran Blake, at the New England Conservatory, and at the Juilliard School. He traveled in the USA and Europe with the Paul Bley Synthesizer Show and recorded as a leader in Copenhagen and as a member of Anthony Braxton's quartet in Paris (both 1972). After moving to Paris (1973) he performed and recorded as an unaccompanied soloist and with Steve Lacy and Noah Howard (all 1974). In 1975 he settled in Sweden, and the following year he recorded in a duo with Lacy in Oslo and as a leader (*Austin Stream*, FMP SAJ09). He continued to work with Lacy until around 1978. Smith's compositions, which include *Symphony for Geomusic* (*c*1973), gained several Swedish awards in the late 1970s and early 1980s. In 1984 he recorded as an unaccompanied pianist and synthesizer player, but by this point in his career his music had little relation to jazz.

BIBLIOGRAPHY

Feather–Gitler '70s
S. Traill: "Meet Michael Smith," *JJ*, xxiv/4 (1971), 10
M. Fine: "Michael Smith: Interview," *Cadence*, xi/9 (1985), 11

BK

Smith, Paul (Thatcher) (*b* San Diego, 17 April 1922). Pianist and arranger. His mother, the singer Constance Farmer, and his father, the trumpeter Lon Smith, were vaudeville performers. He began piano lessons at the age of eight, played in a dance band at school, and first worked professionally when he was 16. Three years later, in 1941, he toured with Johnny Richards. During most of his army service (1943–5) he was in a band led by Ziggy Elman, and following his discharge he worked with Les Paul (1946–7), the singing group the Andrews Sisters (1947), and Tommy Dorsey (1947–9). During the 1950s, because of his technical proficiency, improvising skill, and reading ability, he became a staff pianist for NBC in Los Angeles and a busy studio musician. Smith is highly regarded as an accompanist, and worked with the singers Steve Lawrence, Eydie Gormé, Dinah Shore, Jo Stafford, Bing Crosby, Sammy Davis, Jr., and many others in jazz and popular music; his skill is illustrated beautifully by a duo album made in 1960 with Ella Fitzgerald. During the late 1950s and early 1960s he alternated with Lou Levy in Fitzgerald's instrumental trio, and from 1978 he was her regular accompanist for most of her remaining career. During that time he gradually disengaged from constant studio work, and from 1977 to 1991, when not performing with Fitzgerald, he played on weekends at the Velvet Turtle in Redondo Beach. He also became active as a private teacher, and he published ten books of instructional materials, including *The Pianist's Handbook* (1981), *How to Play Ballads* (1982), and two collections of Charlie Parker's solos arranged for unaccompanied piano (1987, 1988). In the 1990s he continued to perform occasionally at clubs and concerts.

Video oral history material in *NCH* (HCJA).

SELECTED RECORDINGS

Duos with E. Fitzgerald: *Let No Man Write my Epitaph* (1960, Verve 4043)
As leader: *Paul Smith Quartet* (1953, Skylark 13); *Jazz Spotlight on Cole Porter and George Gershwin* (1979, Outstanding 023); *Jazz Spotlight on Duke Ellington and Richard Rodgers* (1979, Outstanding 024); *At Home* (1983, Outstanding 022); *Jazz on Broadway* (2000, Vertical Jazz 5504–2)
As sideman with E. Fitzgerald: *Ella Fitzgerald Sings the Cole Porter Song Book* (1956, Verve 4001); *Ella Fitzgerald Sings the Rodgers and Hart Song Book* (1956, Verve 4002); *Ella in Berlin: Mack the Knife* (1960, Verve 4041); *A Perfect Match: Basie and Ella* (1979, Pablo 2312110)
As sideman with others: A O'Day: *Pick Yourself up with Anita O'Day* (1956, Verve 2043); Stuff Smith: *Cat on a Hot Fiddle* (1959, Verve 8339)

BIBLIOGRAPHY

H. Lucraft: "This Pianist Needs a Ten-gallon Hat," *MM* (17 July 1954), 9
G. F. Wrisch: "Meister der Präzision: Paul Smith," *vierViertel*, viii/12 (1954), iv
B. Doerschuk: "Backstage with Paul Smith," *CK*, iv/1 (1978), 6
J. S. Wilson: "Paul Smith: Keyboard Giant," *JT* (1981), Oct, 7
S. Nicholson: *Ella Fitzgerald: a Biography of the First Lady of Jazz* (London, 1993, New York, 1994; addns, 1996, as *Ella Fitzgerald, 1917–1996: a Biography of the First Lady of Jazz*)
P. D. Atteberry: "Paul Smith Interview," *Cadence*, xx/6 (1994), 5

THOMAS OWENS

Smith, Pine Top [Clarence] (*b* Troy, AL, 11 June 1904; *d* Chicago, 15 March 1929). Singer and pianist. His nickname reportedly derived from a childhood game of stretching a wire across pine trees and speaking into tin cans attached at each end, as if the cans were telephones. He taught himself piano while living in Birmingham (1918–20). After moving to Pittsburgh in 1920 he toured as a pianist and tap-dancer in various revues, including that of Ma Rainey, before being discovered by the pianist Charles "Cow Cow" Davenport. In 1928–9 he made a number of recordings in Chicago, of which eight were released. Among these was the remarkably successful *Pine Top's Boogie Woogie*, probably the most influential and widely imitated of all blues recordings; a re-creation of a rent-party dance or "boogie," it at once established and popularized the blues piano style known as Boogie-woogie. Most of Smith's recordings were novelty pieces or comic monologues; only *Pine Top's Blues*, which he sang in a high, even petulant and childlike, voice, was in the traditional blues vein. He greatly influenced Albert Ammons, who used the "powerhouse" rhythm of left-hand walking bass figures, but his own playing had a light, rolling quality also evident in the playing of his contemporaries Cripple Clarence Lofton, Charles Avery, and Romeo Nelson. He was accidently shot during a brawl in the masonic lodge where he was performing.

SELECTED RECORDINGS

Pine Top's Boogie Woogie/Pine Top's Blues (1928, Voc. 1245); I'm sober now (1929, Voc. 1266); Now I ain't got nothin' at all (1929, Voc. 1298)

BIBLIOGRAPHY

W. Russell: "Boogie Woogie," *Jazzmen: the Story of Hot Jazz Told in the Lives of the Men who Created it*, ed. F. Ramsey, Jr., and C. E. Smith (New York, 1939/*R*1977), 187
J. Bentley: "Pine Top Smith," *Jazz Report*, ii/7 (1962), 11
B. Hall and R. Noblett: "The Birth of the Boogie," *Blues Unlimited*, no.133 (1979), 10
F. Wilford-Smith: "I Saw Pine Top Spit Blood, or How Pine Top Smith Didn't Die," *Blues Unlimited*, no.139 (1980), 34

PAUL OLIVER

Smith, Russell (Taylor) [Pops] (*b* Ripley, OH, 5 Feb 1890; *d* Los Angeles, 27 March 1966). Trumpeter, brother of Joe Smith. His full name and date of birth are taken from his application in 1937 for social security, on which he gives his current employment as with Fletcher Henderson at the Grand Terrace. He played alto horn before changing to trumpet at the age of 14. Having begun playing professionally in 1906 or 1907, around 1910 he settled in New York, and in 1915 he was a member of the pianist (Joe) Jordan's Syncopated Orchestra in London. He served in army bands for many years and then performed in revues. In November 1925 he joined Henderson, with whom he played first trumpet until 1941 (for illustration *see* Henderson, fletcher); during this period he left Henderson from time to time, to play in the show *Blackbirds* (from October 1928), to work with lesser-known bands (until April 1929), and to perform with the orchestras of Horace Henderson (1933), Benny Carter (December 1934), Claude Hopkins (1935 – September 1936), and Carter again (mid-1939–1940). He was a member of Cab Calloway's band from late 1941 to early 1946, and appeared with the group in the soundies *Blues in the Night* and *Minnie the Moocher* (both 1942), then until around 1950 performed with Noble Sissle. In the 1950s he settled in California, where he played occasionally and worked as a teacher. Smith's assured technique and flawless reading of lead trumpet parts was much admired by other musicians, but writers often criticized his stiff staccato playing on the recordings he made with Fletcher Henderson up to about 1932. He had been performing for many years before Louis Armstrong's influence began to transform jazz in the mid-1920s, and he took some time to adapt to the flexible, legato phrasing of the new style. His impeccable and exemplary work as a lead trumpeter in the 1940s and 1950s did not always receive due recognition.

SELECTED RECORDINGS

As sideman: H. Henderson: Happy Feet (1933, Parl. R1792); Rhythm Crazy (1933, Parl. R1743); F. Henderson: Big John's Special (1934, Decca 214); Down South Camp Meetin' (1934, Decca 213); B. Carter: Everybody Shuffle (1934, Voc. 2870); Pom Pom (1940, Decca 3262); Cuddle up, huddle up (1941, Bb 11197)

BIBLIOGRAPHY

AllenH
A. Judd: "A Portrait of Russell Smith," *JJ*, xx/4 (1967), 5
W. Smith and G. Hoefer: *Music on my Mind: the Memoirs of an American Pianist* (Garden City, NY, 1964/*R*1975), 75
H. Rye: "Visiting Firemen 14: Joe Jordan 1915," *Sv*, no.134 (1988), 55

JOHNNY SIMMEN/BK

Smith, Ruthie [Ruth Elaine Foster] (*b* Manchester, England, 24 Nov 1950). English saxophonist and singer. She first trained as a concert singer and cellist, then taught herself to play saxophone and eventually mastered the alto, tenor, and soprano instruments. After working with rock bands, including the Stepney Sisters, she joined Soulyard and the South African group District Six, with which she recorded the album *Akuzwakale* (1984, D6 001). A founding member of the Guest stars, she taught improvisation and was one of the organizers of the women's workshop band Sisterhood of Spit and the first women's jazz festival held in London, Early Evening Jazz (1982); she played in the Lydia D'Ustebyn Swing Orchestra and with Gale Force 17, led by the french horn player Sharon Freeman. With the a cappella group the Hipscats, comprising the singers Jim Dvorak, Josefina Cupido, Laka Daisical, Jan Ponsford or Caroline Gillfillan, and Smith (and later the pianist Alastair Gavin as well) she created memorable vocal harmonies. A resilient, swinging improviser, Smith has also played free music with Mervyn Afrika, the double bass player Julia Doyle, and John Stevens, and, with Dvorak, in Toot Sweet. Her compositions include big-band pieces for the combined Guest Stars and District Six groups and an extended piece, *The Toot Suite*.

Oral history material in *GBLnsa*.

For further recordings *see* Guest stars.

BIBLIOGRAPHY

CarrJ
V. Wilmer: "Swinging Sisters," *Observer Magazine* (17 May 1981), 30
——: "Back in the Soulyard," *City Limits* (16–22 July 1982), 37
D. Ilic: "Conversations," *City Limits* (25 Nov – 1 Dec 1983), 49

VAL WILMER

Smith, Sonelius (Larel) (*b* Hillhouse, MS, 17 Dec 1942). Pianist and composer. He grew up in a musical family which in 1948 moved to Memphis; at the age of nine he began classical piano studies and in 1958 he started playing jazz. While studying at Arkansas Agricultural, Mechanical and Normal College (BS MusEd 1969), from 1965 to 1968 he performed six nights per week in a quintet; he also formed a group with John Stubblefield, which appeared at the Intercollegiate Jazz Festival in St. Louis several times during the late 1960s. In autumn 1969 Smith moved to New York, where he performed briefly with Kenny Dorham and Roy Brooks, and in November of that year he joined Roland Kirk, with whom he toured and recorded into summer 1971. In addition he worked with Robin Kenyatta and Rashied Ali, was a member of a sextet co-led by Stubblefield and Warren Smith (ii) (1971–2), and performed as a freelance with, among others, Frank Foster, Harold Vick, Donald Byrd, Elvin Jones, Archie Shepp (with whom he appeared on television in Italy), Freddie Hubbard, Art Blakey, and Lionel Hampton.

In the mid-1970s Sonelius Smith played in Stanley Cowell's Piano Choir (with which he recorded *c*1973–4) and with the alto saxophonist Shamek Farrah (1974–8). As a member of the group Flight to Sanity, alongside Olu Dara, Byard Lancaster, and Don Moye, he performed and recorded at the Wildflower loft sessions in New York in 1976, and later in the decade he worked in small groups led by J. R. Mitchell (recording in 1978) and in a quartet consisting of Kalaparusha Maurice McIntyre, Warren Smith, and Wilber Morris. Later he played with Andrew Cyrille (recording in 1982), and from the mid-1980s he maintained an affiliation with David Murray, both in a duo and as a member of Murray's quartet and big band (recording with these latter ensembles in the early 1990s). He worked again in Cowell's Piano Choir in the mid-1990s (recording in 1994) and recorded in a big band led by the trombonist Jack Jeffers (1995). From 1973 to 1986 Smith taught in a community arts program established at the New Muse Community Museum in Brooklyn, and in the late 1990s he taught at the Harlem School of the Arts. He has composed music for the theater.

SELECTED RECORDINGS

As sideman: on [various artists]: *Wildflowers*, ii: *The New York City Loft Sessions* (1976, Douglas 7046), Flight to Sanity: The Need to Smile; A. Cyrille: *The Navigator* (1982, SN 1062); D. Murray: *Body and Soul* (1993, BS 120155-2)

BIBLIOGRAPHY

Feather–Gitler '70s

GK

Smith, Steve(n Bruce) (*b* Brockton, MA, 21 Aug 1954). Drummer and leader. While attending the Berklee College of Music (1972–6) he studied with Peter Erskine and Alan Dawson and played with a big band led by the trumpeter Lin Biviano (1973–4) and with Buddy DeFranco. Between 1976 and 1978 he toured and recorded with Jean-Luc Ponty, and in 1977 he recorded with Gil Goldstein. He then joined the rock group Journey, with which he performed and recorded from 1978 to 1985 and again in 1996–7. In 1981 he formed a jazz-fusion ensemble, Vital Information, with David Wilczewski, Tim Landers, and Dean Brown among his sidemen; in later years Tom Coster, Larry Grenadier, Frank Gambale, and Jeff Andrews were members. Smith also recorded with Coster (1983–4), Jeff Berlin (1984), the keyboard player Kit Walker (1987–9), and the synthesizer player Michael Manring (1994). He toured and recorded with Steps Ahead (1986–94), recorded and appeared with the Buddy Rich ghost band (1991–9), and worked with Ahmad Jamal (1987), Stanley Clarke, Randy Brecker, and Allan Holdsworth (all 1988), and Eliane Elias, Victor Bailey, and Brecker again (all 1990). In 1998 he recorded with Scott Henderson and the electric bass guitarist Victor Wooten, Frank Gambale and the electric bass guitarist Stuart Hamm, and Larry Coryell and Coster, and the following year he recorded with Jerry Goodman, the keyboard and harmonica player Howard Levy, and the electric bass guitarist Oteil Burbridge. Smith is a versatile drummer who has the ability to blend the power of rock with the finesse and intricacy of bop.

SELECTED RECORDINGS

As leader of Vital Information: *Vital Information* (1983, Col. FC38955); *Global Beat* (1986, Col. FC40506); *Vitalive!* (1989, Manhattan B21Z96692); *Where We Come From* (1997, Intuition 3218-2)

As leader with others: with S. Henderson and V. Wooten: *Vital Tech Tones* (1998, Tone Center 40002); with L. Coryell and T. Coster: *Cause and Effect* (1998, Tone Center 40022)

As sideman: J.-L. Ponty: *Enigmatic Ocean* (1977, Atl. 19110); T. Coster: *Ivory Expedition* (*c*1982, Fan. 9623); K. Walker: *Fire in the Lake* (1989, Windham Hill 0117); Steps Ahead: *N. Y. C.* (*c*1991, Intuition 3007-2)

SELECTED FILMS AND VIDEOS

Steps Ahead: Live in Tokyo 1986 (*c*1986); Steve Smith, i–ii (*c*1987, *c*1988); Buddy Rich Memorial Scholarship Concert, tape 3 (1991)

BIBLIOGRAPHY

R. Flans: "Steve Smith: Journeyman," *MD*, v/4 (1981), 14

C. Stern: "Drums," *Musician, Player & Listener*, no.40 (1982), 59

R. Tolleson: "Journeying to Jazz: Steve Smith," *DB*, l/10 (1983), 17

R. Flans: "Steve Smith," *MD*, x/8 (Aug 1986), 16

J. Woodard: "Steve Smith: Long Day's Journey into Jazz," *Musician*, no.104 (1987), 86

R. Flans: "Steve Smith," *MD*, xvii/2 (1993), 22 [incl. discography]

——: "Steve Smith, Journey Revisited," *MD*, xxi/4 (1997), 49 [incl. discography]

L. Hildebrand: "Journey beyond the Rock World," *San Francisco Chronicle Datebook* (20 Sept 1998)

C. Levin: "Forget Radio," *DB*, lxv/11 (1998), 50

J. Woodard: "Blast Off: Steve Smith and Vital Information," *JT*, xxviii/9 (1998), 34

<http://www.journey.simplenet.com/journey/members/smith/index.html> (1999)

RICK MATTINGLY

Smith, Stuff [Le Roy Gordon; Hez(ekiah)] (*b* Portsmouth, OH, 13 Aug 1909; *d* Munich, 25 Sept 1967). Violinist, singer, and composer. According to his birth certificate he was born on 13 August, but for some reason he celebrated his birthday on the 14th – hence the latter date in many sources. The same certificate spells his forename as Leroy, but later, whenever he signed in full, his preferred form was Le Roy. He was sometimes called Hezekiah or Hez, but this was not a given name. Following early studies with his father and performances with his family's band he won a scholarship to Johnson C. Smith University (Charlotte, North Carolina), but around October 1926 he began touring with Aunt Jemima's Revue. During this period (extending into 1927) he acquired his nickname, Stuff – reportedly after having applied it to others whenever he failed to remember their name.

Smith joined Alphonso Trent in Lexington, Kentucky, late in 1927. He had been drawn into jazz through the work of Joe Venuti with Eddie Lang, but around this time, like many others, he was deeply influenced by Louis Armstrong's recordings with his Hot Five and Hot Seven. In the course of Trent's tours of the South- and Midwest he became the orchestra's compère and conductor, as well as its principal soloist. In 1928 he left Trent in Iowa to perform with Jelly Roll Morton in New York, but quit two weeks later because he felt that his playing could not be heard. He rejoined Trent in Arkansas and remained with the band until 1930, touring to Canada and the Northeast and making a few recordings, among them his first as a featured singer, *After You've Gone* (1930). He then spent several years in Buffalo leading a group that included Peanuts Holland, Joe Thomas (iii), and, later, Jonah Jones.

Early in 1936 Smith moved to New York, where he led a sextet at the Onyx Club with Jones and Cozy Cole among his sidemen; here he began using an amplified violin. He may be seen in action at the Onyx (with a contemporary dubbed-in soundtrack) in a fragment of a film documentary short, *The March of Time*, iii/7: *The Birth of Swing* (1937). Clyde Hart joined the group shortly before its residency at the Famous Door in Hollywood (summer 1937 – early 1938). Around March 1938 Smith was obliged to declare bankrupcy and disband, but by May he had formed a new group that worked mainly in New York and Chicago; his sidemen again included Cole (to November 1938) and Jones (to May 1940), until each joined Cab Calloway. In spring 1942 he took over a group with a number of Fats Waller's former sidemen, but in the autumn, while working in Los Angeles, they collectively fired their leader – reportedly owing to Smith's eccentric behavior (which was expressed in, and in some ways essential to, his musical style).

From spring 1943 Smith performed and broadcast in Chicago as the leader of a trio that consisted of Jimmy Jones and John Levy. In August 1944 they moved to New York, where they recorded and held an engagement at the Onyx (to spring 1945). Jones left the trio and was replaced briefly first by Erroll Garner and then by Billy Taylor (ii). Over the next decade, while based in Chicago once again, Smith toured nationally with lesser-known musicians; he recorded with Sun Ra (then unknown; 1948 or 1949) and with Dizzy Gillespie (1951). This lull in his career was followed by a series of excellent recordings for Norman Granz in 1956–7 and 1959, as well as a session with Nat "King" Cole for Capitol in 1956. He traveled to Europe in spring 1957 with Granz's Jazz at the Philharmonic, but left the tour owing to illness. During the latter half of 1958 he appeared in several episodes of the television series "Art Ford's Jazz Party" (for illustration *see* Films, fig.5). He worked in the Los Angeles area, performed twice at the Monterey Jazz Festival (1961 and 1962), and held a residency at the Royal Tahitian Room in Ontario, California (1963–4), then joined Joe Bushkin's group at the Embers in New York; however, again illness ended the engagement. Early in 1965 Smith settled in Copenhagen. During this final phase of his career he performed frequently throughout Europe, apart from a period of recovery after a major operation in Paris (1965), and remained quite popular with audiences. His late recordings include the renowned *Violin Summit* with Svend Asmussen, Stephane Grappelli, and Jean-Luc Ponty, made in Basel, Switzerland, in September 1966. Other violinists with whom Smith broadcast or recorded in Europe were Ray Nance and two of his long-standing Danish admirers, Poul Olsen and Søren Christensen. His residencies with Kenny Drew and Niels Henning Ørsted-Pedersen at the Montmartre in Copenhagen are well documented on several albums, notably *Swingin' Stuff*.

Smith's famous performances at the Onyx brought together the straightforward swing trumpet playing and drumming of Jones and Cole with their leader's performance style, involving risqué, off-the-wall monologues, humorous lyrics, and audacious improvisations. Smith was an innovative musician: he played violin in a raucous style and with a sense of swing that was of unequaled intensity. Harmonically his work was extremely adventurous and in its context often dissonant, and he evolved radical techniques to accommodate his wildly inventive ideas. Wide vibrato, hoarse tone, expressive intonation, and rhythmic creativity are all hallmarks of his style. Dizzy Gillespie has cited Smith as a profound influence upon his playing.

SELECTED RECORDINGS

As leader: I'se a Muggin' (1936, Voc. 3169); After You've Gone/You'se a Viper (1936, Voc. 3201); Old Joe's Hittin' the Jug (1936, Voc. 3270); Knock, Knock, Who's There? (1936, Voc. 3300); Upstairs (1937, Decca 1287); Stop-look (1944, Asch 353-2); Desert Sands (1944, Asch 353-3); Perdido (1945, Selmer Y7140); Is, is (1944, Savoy 528); Up Jumped the Devil (*c*1949, Town & Country 505); *Have Violin, Will Swing* (1957, Verve 8282); *Stuff Smith* (1957, Verve 8206); with D. Gillespie: *Dizzy Gillespie and Stuff Smith* (1957, Verve 8214); with S. Grappelli: *Violins No End* (1957, Pablo 2310907); *Cat on a Hot Fiddle* (1959, Verve 8339); with H. Ellis: *Alone Together* (1963, Epic 16039); *Swingin' Stuff* (1965, Met. 15188); *Black Violin* (1965, Saba 15147); with S. Grappelli: *Stuff and Steff* (1965, Barclay 84110); with S. Asmussen, S. Grappelli, and J.-L. Ponty: *Violin Summit* (1966, Saba 15099)

As sideman with A. Trent: Black and Blue Rhapsody/Nightmare (1928, Gen. 6710); After You've Gone (1930, Gen. 7161); D. Gillespie: Caravan (1951, Dee Gee 3601); E. Fitzgerald: *Ella Fitzgerald Sings the Duke Ellington Song Book* (1956, Verve 4008–9); N. Cole: *After Midnight* (1956, Cap. W782)

BIBLIOGRAPHY

ChiltonW

G. Hennesey-Richards: "The Swing Sensation from Buffalo," *Rhythm* (1936), Nov, 37

Y. Bruynoghe: "Stuff Smith, Mad Genius of the Violin," *Jazz 57*, no.6 (1957), 3

F. Tenor: "Les dompters de violins ou du swing sur quatre cordes," *Jm*, no.27 (1957), 28

J. Pescheux: "Stuff Smith," *BHcF*, no.150 (1965), 3

V. Wilmer: "Stuff Smith: the Genius of Jazz Violin," *JB*, ii/6 (1965), 16

Obituary, *DB*, xxiv/23 (1967), 13

D. Morgenstern: "Jazz Fiddle," *DB*, xxxiv/3 (1967), 16

R. Balagri: "Stuff Smith: le violent du violon," *Jm*, no.175 (1970), 34

A. Shaw: *The Street that Never Slept: New York's Fabled 52nd Street* (New York, 1971/*R*1977 as *52nd Street: the Street of Jazz*)

S. Dance: *The World of Swing* (New York, 1974), 176

M. Glaser and S. Grappelli: *Jazz Violin* (New York and elsewhere, 1981) [incl. transcrs.]

M. L. Hester: "Hot Stuff!," *MR*, xi/6 (1984), 8

A. Barnett and E. Løgager: *Stuff Smith: Pure at Heart* (Lewes, England, 1991)

H. Grässer: *Jazz Violin* (Bonn, 1991)

A. Barnett: *Desert Sands: the Recordings and Performances of Stuff Smith: an Annotated Discography and Biographical Source Book* (Lewes, England, 1995; suppl., 1998, as *Up Jumped the Devil*)

MATT GLASER/BK

Smith, Tab [Talmadge] (*b* Kinston, NC, 11 Jan 1909; *d* St. Louis, 17 Aug 1971). Alto, soprano, and tenor saxophonist, arranger, and bandleader. He began his musical studies on piano, and played C-melody saxophone before taking up the alto and soprano instruments. From 1927 to 1929 he led the Carolina Stompers, after which he spent a brief period with Ike Dixon in Baltimore. He then played with Eddie Johnson's Crackerjacks (1931–3), Fate Marable (1934), Lucky Millinder and the Mills Blue Rhythm Band (1936–7), and Frankie Newton (1938–9); he also recorded with Henry "Red" Allen (1936–7) and with several small swing groups accompanying Billie Holiday (March 1938, March–July 1939). In 1940 he worked briefly with Teddy Wilson, Count Basie, Millinder, and Eddie Durham, and at the end of the year he rejoined Basie, with whom he remained until spring 1942; he may be seen with the band in the soundies *Air Mail Special* and *Take Me Back, Baby* (both 1941). Smith was with Millinder's band again from 1942 to 1944, but thereafter he directed his own groups, and enjoyed great success at the Savoy Ballroom in New York in the late 1940s. In 1951 he moved to St. Louis, where his band was resident at the 20th Century Club; after 1952 the popularity of their recordings for the Chicago-based United label (1951–7) brought him back to prominence. He retired again to St. Louis in 1960.

Smith was highly regarded as a soloist on both alto and soprano saxophone and in his own groups in the 1940s and 1950s also provided effective solos on tenor saxophone. The recordings of his own groups for the rhythm-and-blues market include a proportion of saccharine ballads but are otherwise among the finest examples of the later development of the jump style. Among his best-known arrangements are *Barrel House* and *Tab's Blues*.

SELECTED RECORDINGS

* – composed by Smith; † – arranged by Smith

As leader: Tab Steps Out (1944, Regis 7000); Granny Dodging at the Savoy (1945, 20C 20-45) Jumpin' at the Track/Morning Blues (1945, Southern 125); Fat Mouth Blues (1945, Hub 3009); Because of You/Dee Jay Special (1951, United 104) [t sax]; Red, Hot and Blue/These Foolish Things (1952, United 140); Jump Time (1952, United 171) [t sax]; A Bit of Blues (1952, United 124); Top 'n' Bottom (1952, United 190)

As sideman: Mills Blue Rhythm Band: Red Rhythm/St. Louis Wiggle Rhythm (1936, Col. 3135D); H. Allen: Algiers Stomp (1936, Voc. 3302); Mills Blue Rhythm Band: In a Sentimental Mood (1936, Col. 3148D); †Barrel House (1936, Col. 3156D); Mr. Ghost Goes to Town (1936, Col. 3158D); F. Newton: Tab's Blues (1939, Voc. 4821); C. Basie: *†Blow Top (1940, OK 5629); †You can't run around (1940, OK 5673); Rockin' the Blues (1940, OK 6010); †The Jitters (1941, OK 6095); †Take Me Back, Baby (1941, OK 6440); *†Platterbrains (1941, OK 6508); *†Harvard Blues (1941, OK 6564); L. Millinder: *†Mason Flyer (1942, Bruns. 03406); *†Shipyard Social Function (1943, Decca 18674); C. Bernhardt: The Lady in Debt (1945, Musi. 345); Scandal-monger Mama (1945, Musi. 348)

BIBLIOGRAPHY

ChiltonW; *McCarthyB*; *SheridanCB*

S. Dance: "Lightly and Politely: 199: Alto Attitudes," *JJ*, vi/11 (1953), 17

R. Horricks: *Count Basie and his Orchestra: its Music and its Musicians* (London and New York, 1957), 175

M. Pinfold: "The Forgotten Ones: Tab Smith," *JJI*, xxxv/10 (1982), 8

J. Bernholm: Liner notes, *I Don't Want to Play in the Kitchen* (Saxophonograph 503, 1985)

P. Carr: Liner notes, *Joy! At the Savoy* (Saxophonograph 509, 1986)

D. Périchon: "Tab Smith: le mal entendu," *BHcF* (1997), no.456, p.1; no.457, p.4; no.458, p.8

FRANK DRIGGS/HOWARD RYE, BK

Smith, Teddy [Theodore] (*b* Washington, DC, 22 Jan 1932; *d* Washington, late Aug 1979). Double bass player. He played with Betty Carter (1960), then performed and recorded with Clifford Jordan and Kenny Dorham (both 1961–2); he may be heard on Dorham's album *El matador* (1962, UA 15007). After working with Jackie McLean and Slide Hampton (1962–3) he joined Horace Silver's hard-bop quintet, with which he recorded *Song for my Father* (1964, BN 84185) and performed at jazz festivals in Paris, Antibes, and Montreux (all 1964). He also recorded with Sonny Rollins (1964–5) and Sonny Simmons's free-jazz group (1966).

BIBLIOGRAPHY

Feather '60s
Obituary, *Coda*, no.169 (1979), 38

Smith, Tommy [Thomas William] (*b* Luton, England, 27 April 1967). Scottish saxophonist. He grew up in Edinburgh, where he began to play tenor saxophone at the age of 12. In 1982 he studied classical flute, clarinet, piano, and saxophone at Broughton High School and played with the European Youth Jazz Orchestra. The following year he appeared with Niels-Henning Ørsted Pedersen, Gordon Beck, Philip Catherine, and Jon Christensen on Oscar Peterson's television show "Jazz at the Gateway," led a trio at the Leverkusen Jazz Festival, toured Britain with the New York Jazz Quintet, and recorded his first two albums as leader. He began studying at the Berklee College of Music in Boston in January 1984, and in the summer of that year he led a group of fellow students on a tour of Britain and Scandinavia. Later he recorded with another Berklee-based group, Forward Motion, co-led by Terje Gewelt (1984–5) and began a two-year stint with Gary Burton (1985–7). In 1988 he made the first of four albums for Blue Note, featuring John Scofield and Jack DeJohnette, and in 1989 he presented six programs on BBC television in which he played with Chick Corea, Tommy Flanagan, and others. Beginning in the late 1980s he wrote and performed a number of classically orientated pieces for saxophone and orchestra. He was appointed director of music at the National Jazz Institute of Scotland and established the Scottish National Jazz Orchestra in 1995. In 1997 he recorded in New York with Kenny Barron. Smith first came to prominence as a virtuoso exponent of a style based on the playing of John Coltrane and Michael Brecker, among others, but he later added to this a more reflective, folk-flavored approach redolent of Jan Garbarek. In the 1990s he made a number of powerfully conceived and executed recordings inspired by poetry and art.

SELECTED RECORDINGS

As leader: *Paris* (1992, BN International 80612); *Misty Morning and No Time* (1994, Linn 040); *Beasts of Scotland* (1996, Linn 054); *The Sound of Love* (1997, Linn 084)

As sideman: Forward Motion: *The Berklee Tapes* (1984, Hep 2026); *Progressions* (1985, Hep 2033); G. Burton: *Whiz Kids* (1986, ECM 1329)

BIBLIOGRAPHY

C. Wright: "Tommy Smith's Giant Steps," *JJI*, xxxviii/2 (1985), 23
K. Mathieson: "Tommy Smith: Back to Forward," *Wire*, no.41 (1987), 7
C. Wright: "Profile: Tommy Smith," *DB*, liv/10 (1987), 44
K. Mathieson: "Melody in Motion," *Wire*, no.50 (1988), 35
D. H. Matthews: "Tommy Smith," *CI*, xxvi/5 (1989), 16
N. Hadsley: "Tommy Smith," *Jazz FM*, no.6 (1991), 8
N. A. Lee: "Beasts of Scotland," *Jazz Times* (1996), Dec
A. Simpson: "Cool Cat among the Cream," *Glasgow Herald* (18 March 1996)
K. Mathieson: "Music for your Spheres," *Jazzwise*, no.2 (1997), 4
——: "Tommy Smith," *Saxophone Journal*, xxii/1 (1997), 28
B. Donaldson: "Interview with Tommy Smith," *Marge Hofacre's Jazz News* (2000), spring, 36

MARK GILBERT

Smith, Trixie [Lee, Bessie] (*b* Atlanta, 1895; *d* New York, 21 Sept 1943). Singer. After studying at Selma University she moved to New York (*c*1915). From around 1918 she worked on the Theater Owner's Booking Association circuit, and in the early 1920s she began to record regularly. Between 1920 and 1933 she performed frequently in New York's black theaters, both as a singer and an actor, and in January 1922 she won a blues contest. Under the pseudonym Bessie Lee she performed on Broadway and recorded for Silvertone. Later she appeared in the films *The Black King* (1931) and *Birthright* (1938).

Smith recorded prolifically as a leader (1921–5), as a sideman with Jimmy Blythe (1926), and as the leader of various all-star groups (1938–9); among the bands that accompanied her in recording sessions were groups led by James P. Johnson (1921), Fletcher Henderson (1922, 1924–5, whose ensemble featured Louis Armstrong in 1925), and Sidney Bechet (1938). By the late 1930s her formerly girlish, bright, penetrating voice had taken on a full-bodied quality, and there was a more direct sexual nature to her performances that departed from the typically coy double entendres of classic blues and vaudeville and which pointed towards styles of singing later used in rhythm-and-blues and soul.

SELECTED RECORDINGS

Trixies Blues [*sic*] (1922, Black Swan 2039); Ride, Jockey, Ride/Choo Choo Blues (1924, Para. 12245); You've got to beat me to keep me/Mining Camp Blues (1925, Para. 12256); The world's jazz crazy and so am I/ Railroad Blues (1925, Para. 12262); Love me like you used to do (1925, Para. 12330); Freight Train Blues (1938, Decca 7489); Trixie Blues/My Daddy Rocks Me (1938, Decca 7469); He may be your man (but he comes to see me sometime) (1938, Decca 7528); My Daddy Rocks Me, pt ii/No Good Man (1938, 1939, Decca 7617)

BIBLIOGRAPHY

CarrJ
P. Tanner: "Veteran Blues Singer Trixie Smith is Dead," *MM* (27 Nov 1943), 4
R. C. Foreman, Jr.: *Jazz and Race Records, 1920–32: their Origins and their Significance for the Record Industry and Society* (diss., U. of Illinois, 1968)
D. Stewart-Baxter: *Ma Rainey and the Classic Blues Singers* (New York and London, 1970), 81
S. Harris: *Blues Who's Who: a Biographical Dictionary of Blues Singers* (New Rochelle, NY, 1979/*R*1994)
D. D. Harrison: *Black Pearls: Blues Queens of the 1920s* (New Brunswick, NJ, 1988), 244

BK

Smith, Viola (*b* Mt. Calvary, WI, 29 Nov 1912). Drummer. She started out in a family band, the Schmitz Sisters (later the Smith Sisters) Orchestra (1925–38), which was featured in "Jack Fine's Band Box Revue" (1934–6) and on the "Major Bowes Show" on NBC Radio (1936–7). In 1938 she and her sister, the saxophonist Mildred Smith, organized the Coquettes All Girl Orchestra, a hot swing band renowned for Viola's drum technique (she was compared with Chick Webb and Gene Krupa) and for arrangements by Gene Gifford, Eddie Durham, and Louise Sorenson. Smith appeared on the cover of *Billboard* on 24 February 1940. In 1942 she joined Phil Spitalny's orchestra, and she made guest appearances with Bob Crosby and Woody Herman; the latter offered her a job. While working with Spitalny in New York she studied with Cozy Cole. She later developed a solo act, "Viola and her 17 Drums." Her last job as a drummer was with an all-girl band in the Kit Kat Club in the Broadway version of *Cabaret* (1966–70). (S. Tucker: *Swing Shift: "All-girl" Bands of the 1940s*, Durham, NC, 2000)

SHERRIE TUCKER

Smith, (Ishmael) Wadada Leo (*b* Leland, MS, 18 Dec 1941). Trumpeter and flugelhorn player. His father was the blues musician Little Bill (Alex) Wallace, and B. B. King and others regularly played in the family home. Leo Smith (as he was known until the mid-1980s) played mellophone and french horn before taking up trumpet. After high school he worked in rhythm-and-blues and army bands, then in 1967 he became a member of the ASSOCIATION FOR THE ADVANCEMENT OF CREATIVE MUSICIANS (AACM). With Leroy Jenkins and Anthony Braxton, he was leader of the CREATIVE CONSTRUCTION COMPANY (late 1967–1970), which performed in Europe (1969–70) and, with other AACM members, recorded in New York (1970). In 1970 Smith made the documentary film *See the Music* with Marion Brown. Later that year, in New Haven, Connecticut, he formed New Dalta Ahkri, a two- to five-piece group whose members included Henry Threadgill, Anthony Davis, the double bass player Wes Brown, Bobby Naughton, Oliver Lake, and the reed player Dwight Andrews. In 1971 Smith established his own record label, Kabell. Shortly after publishing a pamphlet explaining his musical philosophy (*Notes (8 Pieces) Source a New World, Music: Creative Music*, 1973) he studied ethnomusicology at Wesleyan University (1974–5). He then worked with Braxton again (1976) and with Derek Bailey's group Company in London (1977), and led a trio with Peter Kowald and Günter Sommer (into the early 1980s).

In the 1980s Smith became involved in Rastafarianism and reggae music and took the Rastafari forename Wadada; in the late 1990s he added yet another forename, Ishmael. From 1987 to 1993 he taught at Bard College (Annandale-on-Hudson, New York), and during the late 1980s he led the group NDA, which included Brandon Ross. In collaboration with the choreographer Barbara Chang he made *Irrational Fullness* (1990), a video of music and dance. In 1991 he formed the group Wadada and the Electric Warriors, and in 1993 he spent a season in Japan under a grant to write a piece based on a classic story of the Heike and Genji people. Smith then took the Dizzy Gillespie chair as a member of the faculty of the California Institute for the Arts (autumn 1993), where he continues to develop a personalized notion of music theory and musical notation which he calls Ankhrasmation. He has performed in a number of settings in the Los Angeles area and participates regularly in the series New Music Monday, which began at the Alligator Lounge (to 1997) and continues at Luna Park (from 1998). Smith became leader of a music and poetry group, N'Da Kulture, which originally consisted of the *bānsuri* (bamboo flute) player David Philipson, Glenn Horiuchi (until his death in 2000), the tuba player William Roper, Sonship Theus, and his wife, the poet Harumi Makino Smith, and in 1998 he formed two avant-garde fusion groups – NOK, and, with Henry Kaiser as co-leader, the 12-piece Yo Miles!, in which the electric bass guitarist Michael Manring, Steve Smith, and the members of ROVA have served as sidemen.

Smith's preference for music that displays lyricism, pleasing timbres, and sustained calmness sets him apart from many of his colleagues in free jazz. He also plays flute, percussion, and non-Western instruments, and he has composed in many genres, including large-scale works for the theater and music for chamber groups.

For illustrations *see* JAZZ (i), fig.9, and LACY, STEVE.

SELECTED RECORDINGS

As unaccompanied soloist: *Creative Music* (1971, Kabell 1); *Solo Music Ahkreanvention* (*c*1981, Kabell 4)

As leader: *Reflectativity* (1974, Kabell 2); *The Mass on the World* (1978, Moers 01060); *Divine Love* (1978, ECM 1143); *Spirit Catcher* (1979, Nessa 19); *Rastafari* (1983, Sack. 3030); with V. Golia and Bertram Turetzky: *Prataksis* (1997, Nine Winds 199)

As sideman: A. Braxton: *Three Compositions of New Jazz* (1968, Del. 415); *Silence* (1969, Fre. 40123); Creative Construction Company: *Creative Construction Company* (1970, Muse 5071, 5097); A. Davis: *Hemispheres* (1983, Gram. 8303)

WRITINGS

(selective list)

Notes (8 Pieces) Source a New World, Music: Creative Music (1973)

"Thoughts of an Improvisor," *JF* [intl edn], no.23 (1973), 43

"M1 (American Music)," *Black Perspective in Music*, ii/2 (1974), 111

"Lecture/Workshop May 27th 1978," *Musica* [London], no.18 (1978), suppl., ii

BIBLIOGRAPHY

GrayF

V. Wilmer: "Leo Smith: Aware of the Hazards," *MM* (11 Sept 1971), 32

B. Smith: "Leo Smith," *Coda*, no.143 (1975), 2 [incl. discography]

G. Giddins: "Theory and Practice in Leo Smith," *VV* (17 May 1976), 98

B. Ness: "Profile: Leo Smith," *DB*, xliii/16 (1976), 36

K. Ansell: "Leo Smith," *Impetus*, no.6 (1977), 259

S. Arcangelli: "Parla Leo Smith," *Musica jazz*, xxxiii/8–9 (1977), 26

S. Lake: "Bound for Glory: Muhal Richard Abrams, Leo Smith, Roscoe Mitchell," *MM* (1 Jan 1977), 22

V. Wilmer: *As Serious as your Life: the Story of the New Jazz* (London, 1977, rev. [3]/1987)

——: "Leo, Lion of the Trumpet," *MM* (11 June 1977), 28

B. Rusch: "Leo Smith: Interview," *Cadence*, iii/10 (1978), 29

G. Rouy: "L'esthétique noire selon Leo Smith," *Jm*, no.277 (1979), 30

——: "Leo Smith pour la musique créative," *Jm*, no.278 (1979), 80 [incl. discography]

G. Cerutti: "Discographie de Leo Smith," *Jazz 360°*, no.24 (1980), 7

B. Ogan: "Free Jazz – Multilateral: Smith–Kowald–Sommer," *JP*, xxix/10 (1980), 24

R. Palmer: "Jazz: Leo Smith's Avant-garde Delta Blues," *RS* (10 July 1980), 26

B. Smith: "Leo Smith: Rastafari," *Coda*, no.192 (1983), 4

E. Lieb: "Leo Smith's World Music: Jazz Meets Jah," *Option* (1986), Jan–Feb, 42

N. Weinstein: "Reggae or Not: Jazz Goes Dread?," *DB*, liv/3 (1987), 63

L. Birnbaum: "Meet the Composer: Wadada Leo Smith," *Ear: New Music News*, xiii/5 (1988), 22

G. Lock: "Wadada Leo Smith," *Jazz: the Magazine*, no.22 (1993), 8

J. Woodard: "A Virtuoso of Variation," *Los Angeles Times Calendar* (29 Nov 1998), 55

<http://shoko.calarts.edu/~wls/> (2000)

D. Rubien: "Channeling Davis' Wondrous Spirit: Eclectic Yo Miles! Regroups for a CD and Encore Performance," *San Francisco Chronicle Datebook* (27 Feb 2000), 38

BK

Smith, Warren (Doyle) [Smitty] **(i)** (*b* Middlebourne, WV, 17 May 1908; *d* Santa Barbara, CA, 28 Aug 1975). Trombonist. He grew up in a musical family and played piano from the age of seven. In 1920 he moved with his family to Dallas, where he learned to play cornet and saxophone, and later, trombone; in 1924 he worked professionally for the first time as a trombonist, and over the next few years he doubled on saxophone. After he had begun to concentrate exclusively on trombone he played in Chicago with the drummer Abe Lyman (1928–35) and toured and recorded with Bob Crosby (*c* February 1937 – May 1940; for illustration *see* CROSBY, BOB); he may be heard to advantage on Crosby's *Till We Meet Again* (1939, Decca 2825). Between 1940 and 1945 he appeared in and around Chicago with Wingy Manone, among others. He then moved to California, where he performed and recorded with Crosby (1945), Pete Dailey (1947–9), and Lu Watters (1949–50) and played with Jess Stacy (1950) and Nappy Lamare (1951). Although Smith was associated mainly with dixieland bands, he played briefly in New York with Duke Ellington in summer 1955. Later he recorded with Bob Scobey (1956, 1957), played and recorded with Joe Darensbourg (1957–60), and worked with Wild Bill Davison and Ben Pollack. In the early 1960s he joined Red Nichols, with whom he toured Japan in summer 1964. He continued to play in California until 1975.

BIBLIOGRAPHY

ChiltonW; *FeatherE*; *Feather–Gitler '70s*

J. Chilton: *Stomp Off, Let's Go! The Story of Bob Crosby's Bob Cats & Big Band* (London, 1983)

Smith, Warren (Ingle, Jr.) [Wis] **(ii)** (*b* Chicago, 4 May 1932). Percussionist. He grew up in a musical family, learned saxophone and clarinet with his father (a reed player and music publisher) from the age of three, and took up drumming when he was six. After attending the University of Illinois (BS in music education, 1957) and the Manhattan School of Music (MM in percussion, 1958) he performed and recorded with Johnny Richards's big band (1959–64), and formed the Composer's Workshop Ensemble (1961), which continued to rehearse, perform, and record occasionally into the late 1990s; among his sidemen were Jimmy Owens, Johnny Coles, the saxophonist George Barrow, Kalaparusha Maurice McIntyre, Garnett Brown, Herb Bushler, Bross Townsend, Howard Johnson (ii), and the trombonist Jack Jeffers. He also toured with Nat "King" Cole (1964), performed and recorded with Sam Rivers (1964–76), and recorded with Aretha Franklin (1960s).

In 1968 Smith took part in a jazz-influenced recording session led by the rock singer Van Morrison. That same year he established Studio WIS, a percussion studio at which M' BOOM RE: PERCUSSION, of which he was a founding member, rehearsed from 1970; at the same time he played in Gil Evans's orchestra (1968–76), for which he also wrote compositions, was a member of the New York Jazz Repertory Company (1968–70) and Collective Black Artists, and recorded with Gene Ammons and Sonny Stitt (1973). In 1976 he recorded with Anthony Braxton and, with Andrew White, led a tribute to John Coltrane; later he made recordings as a leader (1977, 1982) and as a sideman with George Russell (1978), Julius Hemphill (1980), Muhal Richard Abrams (1983, 1990), Buddy Montgomery and Herb Robertson (both 1986), the bandleader James Jabbo Ware and Braxton (both 1993), and Jeffers's NY Classic Big Band (1995). In 1995 he recorded an album of duos with Kent Jordan, Stanley Cowell, Steve Novosel, the drummer Chief Bey, and the poet and rap singer Amirou Willingham which was very well received. Smith worked with Hemphill from 1975 until the leader's death in 1995, and he remained a member of M' Boom Re: Percussion until 1998; he continued to work with Abrams, Ware, and Jeffers in the late 1990s, and in May 1999 he performed in a drum choir with Rashied Ali, Andrew Cyrille, and Sunny Murray at the Vision Festival, New York.

Smith served as a member of Broadway pit orchestras from 1958 (*West Side Story*) into the late 1990s (notably for the jazz-oriented show *Jelly's Last Jam*, 1991–2). He also remained busy in the 1990s as a studio musician and in various concert settings, and in 1992 he performed in Anthony Davis's opera *X: the Life and Times of Malcolm X*. He taught in public schools (1958–*c*1969) and at Adelphi University (*c*1969–71) and was a founder, with Makanda Ken McIntyre and others, of the Afro-American program at SUNY, Old Westbury (1971), where he remained until his retirement from teaching in 1996.

SELECTED RECORDINGS

Duos: with Hidefumi Toki: Warren Smith and Toki (1977, RCA [Japan] RVL8501) [EP]; with K. Jordan, S. Cowell, S. Novosel, C. Bey, and A. Willingham: *Cats are Stealing my Shit* (1995, Mapleshade 05332)

As leader of Composer's Workshop Ensemble: *Cricket Poem Song* (1982, Miff 1006)

As sideman: G. Evans: *Montreux Festival '74* (1974, Phi. 6043); S. Rivers: *Essence* (1976, Cir. [Ger.] 1); M. Roach: *M' Boom Re: Percussion* (1979, Col. IC36247); J. Hemphill: *Flat Out Jump Suite* (1980, BS 0040); M. R. Abrams: *Rejoicing with the Light* (1983, BS 0071); *View from Within* (1984, BS 0081); *Blu Blu Blu* (1990, BS 0117); M. Roach: on *To the Max!* (1990–91, Enja 7021–22), M' Boom Re: Percussion: A Quiet Place, Dance, pt.3, Street Dance (1991)

BIBLIOGRAPHY

Feather–Gitler '70s

A. J. Smith: "Profile: Warren Smith," *DB*, xlii/11 (1975), 30

R. Mattingly and S. K. Fish: "M'Boom," *MD*, vii/9 (1983), 8

E. Hazell: "Warren Smith," *Coda*, no.211 (1986), 18

B. Rusch: "Warren Smith," *Cadence*, xiv/3 (1988), 5

ED HAZELL/BK

Smith, William O(verton). *See* BILL SMITH (i).

Smith, Willie [William McLeish] (*b* Charleston, SC, 25 Nov 1910; *d* Los Angeles, 7 March 1967). Alto saxophonist. He attended Fisk University in Nashville, where he came to the attention of Jimmie Lunceford, and from 1929 to 1942 he played in Lunceford's well-known swing band (for illustration *see* LUNCEFORD, JIMMIE), establishing a reputation as a highly competent section leader and superior soloist; he also wrote some characteristic early arrangements for the group (*Sophisticated Lady*, *Mood Indigo*, *Rose Room*) and occasionally sang. After leaving Lunceford to become a member of Charlie Spivak's orchestra (summer 1942 – April 1943) and to work alongside Clark Terry and Gerald Wilson in a US Navy band, Smith played mainly in Harry James's band (late 1944 – March 1951, 1954-64), with interruptions to replace Johnny Hodges briefly in the Duke Ellington Orchestra (March 1951 – spring 1952), to play with Billy May's orchestra (1952), to tour with Jazz at the Philharmonic (1953), and to lead his own small jazz and rhythm-and-blues groups in Los Angeles. Along with Hodges and Benny Carter, Smith was the oustanding soloist on his instrument during the swing period. He played in a driving, broken-chord style and had a distinctive manner of slipping momentarily out of the background harmonies to create bitonal effects. Smith's papers are held in the Archive Center of the National Museum of American History, Smithsonian Institution, Washington, DC (*see* LIBRARIES AND ARCHIVES, §2).

SELECTED RECORDINGS

As sideman: J. Lunceford: Sophisticated Lady (1934, Decca 129); Mood Indigo/Rose Room (1934, Decca 131); Blue Blazes (1939, Voc. 4667); Uptown Blues (1939, Voc. 5362); H. James: Who's sorry now? (1945, Col. 36973); Moten's Swing (1946, Col. 37351); D. Ellington: Caravan/Indian Summer (1951, Mercer 1968)

SELECTED FILMS AND VIDEOS

Jimmie Lunceford and his Dance Orchestra (1936); Caravan (1952); Sophisticated Lady (1952)

BIBLIOGRAPHY

ChiltonW; *McCarthyB*; *SchullerS*

"Willie Smith," *Ebony* (1949), June, 41

S. Dance: *The World of Swing* (New York, 1974), 93

J. BRADFORD ROBINSON

Smith, Willie "the Lion" [Bertholoff, William Henry Joseph Bonaparte] (*b* Goshen, NY, 25 Nov 1897; *d* New York, 18 April 1973). Pianist and composer. Born Bertholoff, he took the surname Smith from his stepfather. He grew up in Newark, New Jersey, where his mother's keyboard playing in the African-American Baptist church sparked his early interest in music; independently, and for non-musical reasons, he adopted Judaism in his youth and later served as a cantor in Harlem. He started playing piano at the age of

Willie "the Lion" Smith at the RCA Victor recording studios, New York, 1960s

six. After a largely informal music education he began to work professionally in Atlantic City and New York while still in his teens, and soon became one of the most illustrious and influential proponents of the stride or Harlem ragtime style. By one of his several accounts, he earned his nickname "the Lion" during World War I through his heroism at the front. On his discharge from the army in 1919 he established himself in the forefront of New York's stride pianists. The friendship and mutual admiration he enjoyed with Duke Ellington during these early years were musically documented in Ellington's *Portrait of the Lion* (1939) and Smith's *Portrait of the Duke* (1957).

Smith performed at Leroy's in Harlem in 1919–20 and in the latter year recorded Mamie Smith's pioneering *Crazy Blues*. After touring in obscure shows he returned to Harlem, where he played with Bubber Miley and Jimmy Harrison (*c*1923) and worked with Sidney Bechet at the Rhythm Club; when Bechet left in the spring of 1925 he took over the band and brought in Johnny Hodges. He continued at this venue, renamed the Hoofers Club, with the jam-session format giving way to a quartet including Benny Carter. He played in another little-known show, performed at countless Harlem rent parties with his friends Fats Waller and James P. Johnson, and in the early 1930s held a long engagement at Pods' and Jerry's (which had taken over the Hoofers Club premises), where Bechet and the young Artie Shaw sat in. Smith then transferred to the emerging scene on 52nd Street, working at the Onyx and the Famous Door (1934–5), at which time he recorded and broadcast with Clarence Williams and Eva Taylor. But he remained virtually unknown to the general public until 1935, when Decca issued a series of his recordings with groups. His solo recordings for Commodore in 1939, however, best illustrate the full maturity of his style. The eight original pieces recorded during this session clearly reveal his acknowledged interest in classical music and stand as masterpieces of stride piano literature, comparable with earlier works by Johnson and Waller. Of particular interest are the counterpoint in *Passionette* and the impressionistic qualities in *Echoes of Spring*, inspired by images of clouds, trees, and morning in a New York park.

Smith played in Bechet's trio and then recorded twice (1939, 1941). In between he accompanied Joe Turner (ii) in an awkward duo blues session (1940), Smith's refinement and Turner's rawness being fundamentally incompatible. During the 1940s his popularity grew as Artie Shaw and Tommy Dorsey performed arrangements of his compositions. He worked regularly in New York – most notably in 1944 at the Pied Piper as a member of Max Kaminsky's band and in individual stride "battles" with Johnson – and in Toronto. The success of a tour of Europe and North Africa from December 1949 to February 1950 was representative of the increased recognition and respect that he enjoyed in his final years. In the 1950s he played regularly at the Central Plaza. He continued to perform at festivals during the 1960s and the early 1970s, and also made two further tours of Europe (1965, 1966). Smith's flamboyant behavior as an entertainer, and his dashing appearance, with derby hat and fat cigar, became almost legendary. His blending of ragtime, impressionism, and counterpoint, coupled with his ability to contrast delicate and subtle melodic lines with passages of intense swing, constituted a unique contribution to the jazz tradition. Some of his recorded solos, transcribed and annotated by R. Scivales, appear in *Harlem Stride Piano Solos* (Katonah, NY, *c*1990).

Oral history material in *NjR*.

SELECTED RECORDINGS

As unaccompanied soloist: Echoes of Spring/Fading Star (1939, Com. 521); Rippling Waters/Finger Buster (1939, Com. 522); Morning Air/Passionette (1939, Com. 523); Concentrating/Sneakaway (1939, Com. 524); *Willie "The Lion" Smith* (1949, Collection Hugues Panassié 004/005); *Reminiscing the Piano Greats* (1950, Vogue LD008) [oral history]; *Memoirs* (1967, RCA LSP6016) [oral history]

As leader: *The Lion Roars* (1957, Dot 3094), incl. Portrait of the Duke

As sideman: M. Smith (1920, OK/Phonola 4169); Alabama Jug Band [Clarence Williams]: Somebody Stole my Gal (1934, Decca 7041)

SELECTED FILMS AND VIDEOS

Jazz Dance (1954); The Subject is Jazz: Ragtime (1958); Jazz 625 (1965); L'aventure du jazz (1970)

BIBLIOGRAPHY

A. Shaw: *The Trouble with Cinderella: an Outline of Identity* (New York, 1952/*R*1992), 223

W. Smith and G. Hoefer: *Music on my Mind: the Memoirs of an American Pianist* (Garden City, NY, 1964/*R*1975)

H. Panassié: "Willie Smith 'le Lion'," *BHcF*, no.152 (1965), 3

J. Simmen: "Some Piano Compositions of Willie 'the Lion' Smith Played by other Musicians," *Sv*, no.44 (1972-3), 44; no.45 (1973), 98

Obituary, *New York Times* (19 April 1973)

L. Feather: "Piano Giants of Jazz: Willie 'the Lion' Smith," *CK*, iii/10 (1977), 55

M. G[autier] P[anassié]: "Une visite au Lion," *BHcF*, no.289 (1981), 3

J. Chilton: *Sidney Bechet: the Wizard of Jazz* (London and New York, 1987/*R*1996)

J. Collinson: "Willie 'the Lion' Smith," *Sv*, no.132 (1987), 211; no.133 (1988), 27; no.134 (1988), 63; no.135 (1988), 94; no.136 (1988), 147; no.137 (1989), 192; no.138, (1989), 205 [discography]

BILL DOBBINS/BK

Smithsonian Institution. United States government historical complex, agency, and cultural institution established in August 1846 by an act of the US Congress. Its main building, completed and opened in 1855, was originally designed to house an art gallery, a library, a chemical laboratory, lecture halls, and museum galleries. By the year 2000 its facilities consisted of 16 museums and galleries, the National Zoo, and numerous research facilities, both in the USA and abroad; all but three of the museums are located in Washington, DC. The institution's first secretary, Joseph Henry, a scientist, strove to develop the Smithsonian as the country's first major research institute for science; its second secretary, Spencer Baird, developed the institution as a national museum.

In 1970 Martin Williams was named director of the Jazz and American Cultural Studies Program in the Division of Performing Arts of the Smithsonian Institution. From 1972 to 1984, under a grant from the NEA, the Smithsonian conducted a Jazz Oral History Project; from 1980 the tapes and transcripts of its 122 interviews have been housed at the Institute of Jazz Studies at Rutgers in Newark, New Jersey (*Njr* (JOHP)). From the early 1970s to 1998 the institution operated its own record company and label, the Smithsonian Collection, offering, within the realm of jazz, important anthologies of reissues of items by Dizzy Gillespie, John Kirby, Teddy Wilson, King Oliver, Louis Armstrong and Earl Hines, Fletcher Henderson, and Duke Ellington, as well as the compilations *Big Band Jazz*, *Singers and Soloists of the Big Bands*, and, most notably, Williams's *Smithsonian Collection of Classic Jazz*, which has served as a basis for jazz education courses worldwide.

In 1987, in collaboration with the Thelonious Monk Institute, the Smithsonian sponsored the first Thelonious Monk International Jazz Piano Competition. In 1988 it acquired the Duke Ellington collection (*see* LIBRARIES AND ARCHIVES, §2), and early the following year, in conjunction with the Oberlin Conservatory of Music, it initiated Jazz Masterworks Editions, with the aim of publishing transcriptions and analyses of classic jazz recordings; unfortunately the project failed after only three volumes devoted to individual pieces recorded by Ellington (among them Billy Strayhorn's *Take the "A" Train*). Around this time the institution received a $5 million permanent endowment honoring John Hammond and allowing free concerts to be given at the National Museum of American History.

In 1990, following the US Congress's passing of a bill which declared jazz a "rare and valuable national American treasure," the institution established the Smithsonian Jazz Masterworks Orchestra, again at the history museum. The bill authorized funding for various projects, including this ensemble, which was then founded by the museum's curator of American music, John Edward Hasse, together with Gunther Schuller and David Baker; in autumn 1999 Baker became its sole music and artistic director. The orchestra gave its first performances in June 1991 and from that time has presented an annual concert series; it also toured the USA and recorded the album *Big Band Treasures Live* (1993–6, Smithsonian Collection RJ44).

In 1992, in partnership with the Lila Wallace–Readers Digest Fund (which gave a $7 million grant), the Smithsonian began a cultural program, America's Jazz Heritage – a ten-year initiative to research and present the history of jazz through exhibitions, performances, recordings, radio broadcasts, publications, and educational programs, both at the institution and across the USA. Headquartered at the Smithsonian Institution Traveling Exhibition Service (SITES), it coordinates the Smithsonian Jazz Alliance, a consortium of individuals who research or work to preserve the history of jazz. The America's Jazz Heritage program has included the symposium and concert series "Sung & Unsung: Jazzwomen," held in conjunction with 651, a theater and arts center in Brooklyn; the Jazz Oral History Program (*DSI* (JOHP)), under which more than 100 new interviews had been conducted by 1999, when the reactivated oral history program became moribund; the activities of the Smithsonian Jazz Masterworks Orchestra; and a "Jazz Smithsonian" radio series.

In 1997, as a bequest from Ella Fitzgerald, the Archives Center of the National Museum of American History received Fitzgerald's memorabilia (her sheet music and music scores went to the Library of Congress). The museum also acquired Rex Stewart's papers, material from the Schiffmans, who ran the Apollo Theatre, Ernie Smith's film collection, and the Jimmie Lunceford band library (*see* LIBRARIES AND ARCHIVES, §2).

BIBLIOGRAPHY

R. Harrington: "On the Beat: All that Jazz, at Smithsonian," *Washington Post* (10 Oct 1990)
J. Litweiler: "The Feast of Jazz: Transcription Program Rates High on List of '89 Milestones," *Chicago Tribune* (4 Jan 1990)
"IAJE News: Smithsonian Announces Jazz Expansion," *Jazz Educators Journal*, xxiii/4 (1991), 13
I. Molotsky: "Smithsonian Expands Jazz Program," *New York Times* (24 April 1991)
M. Schramm: "The Smithsonian Jazz Masterworks Orchestra," *JT*, xxi/7 (1991), 23
W. K. Self: "News: Swingin' at the Smithsonian," *DB*, lviii/7 (1991), 11
R. Harrington: "Smithsonian Jazz Program Gets $7 Million," *Washington Post* (22 May 1992)
J. McDonough: "'Original Intent' Comes to Jazz," *Wall Street Journal* (21 July 1992)
J. Bradley: "Roots of Jazz Remembered at Smithsonian Masterworks Show," *Denver Post* (7 April 1996)
C. Santiago: "When this Jazz Band Plays, it's Not Just Music – it's History," *Smithsonian*, xxvii/6 (1996), 74
R. Harrington: "Ella Fitzgerald's Bequest to America," *Washington Post* (25 April 1997)
D. Helland: "Repertory Big Bands: Jazz's Future-Past," *DB*, lxiv/1 (1997), 34
A. Pollard: "Jammin': Jazz – an American Treasure: Celebrating the 10th Anniversary of HCR 57," *International Musician*, xcvi/7 (1997), 8
P. Applebome: "Smithsonian Shuts Down Book and Record Units," *New York Times* (8 April 1998)
<http://www.americanhistory.si.edu/music/bandmbrs.htm> (2000)
<http://www.si.edu/> (2000)

GK

Smitty. Nickname of MARVIN "SMITTY" SMITH and of WARREN SMITH (i).

Smock (Shipp), Ginger [née Smock, Emma; Colbert, Emma S(mock); Shipp, Emma] (*b* Chicago, 3 June 1920; *d* Las Vegas, 13 June 1995). Violinist. She grew up in Los Angeles from the age of six and attended Jefferson High School, Los Angeles City College, and the Zoellner Conservatory of Music under Otto Klemperer; she studied violin with Edith Smith. As a child she was a soloist at the Hollywood Bowl and on radio. After playing light concert music, she was first engaged as a jazz violinist in 1943 at Randini's in Los Angeles, where she deputized for Stuff Smith; Smith encouraged her, and his horn-like approach influenced her staccato style. During the mid-1940s she worked with the organist Nina Russell and the pianist Mata Roy in a trio known as the Sepia Tones. She recorded only sporadically, initially in a bop vein with the double bass player Vivien Garry in 1946. Smock was one of the first African-American women to host her own television show: she led the all-women group the Chicks and the Fiddle on the CBS network's KTSL in Los Angeles (1951) and, on KTLA, hosted "Dixie Showboat," on which she appeared with house orchestras under Jack Teagarden, Rosy McHargue, and others (1952–3). From 1953 to 1955 she toured with the Red Caps, led by the guitarist and singer Steve Gibson. For a decade from the mid-1970s she worked with orchestras in Las Vegas, and later she was active as a solo violinist in the church. She always worked professionally as Ginger Smock. Colbert, her surname from a brief marriage in the 1940s, appears in some discographies and liner notes without any indication that the person referred to is, in fact, Smock; the surname Shipp is from her marriage in 1970.

SELECTED RECORDINGS

As leader: *On the S. S. Catalina with the Shipmates and Ginger* (1961, Venise 7015)

As sideman: V. Garry: Body and Soul/A woman's place is in the groove (1946, Vic. 40-0144); Operation Mop (1946, Vic. 20-2352); Cecil Count Carter: Strange Blues (1953, Federal 12130); Gingerbread (1953, Federal 12135); the Greats: Fiddler's Rock (1958, Ebb 145)

BIBLIOGRAPHY

J. Reeves with A. Barnett, ed.: "Ginger Smock: Issued and Unissued Recordings on Disc and Tape," *Fable Bulletin: Violin Improvisations Studies*, i/3 (1994); addns and corrections in iii/10 (1998)

B. Y. Cox: *Central Avenue: its Rise and Fall, 1890–c.1955* (Los Angeles, 1997), 309

ANTHONY BARNETT

Smoker, Paul (Alva) (*b* Muncie, IN, 8 May 1941). Trumpeter and leader. He grew up in Davenport, Iowa, and had piano lessons from the age of six; when he was ten, after hearing Harry James on the radio, he took up trumpet and studied both classical and jazz playing. He later attended the University of Iowa (BM 1964, MA 1965, MFA 1967, DMA 1974). From 1960 to 1961 he worked with Dodo Marmarosa for a series of engagements in Rock Island, Illinois, and in the mid-1960s he had lessons for a short time with Doc Severinsen and played briefly in Bill Chase's band. Between 1968 and 1971 Smoker taught at the University of Wisconsin in Oshkosh and recorded and performed in Chicago; given his later inclination towards the avant garde, it is interesting to note that at this time he played mainly in bop and swing groups and was unaware of the Association for the Advancement of Creative Musicians. Having finished his doctorate he taught at the University of Northern Iowa (1975–6) and at Coe College in Cedar Rapids, Iowa (from 1976), where he ran a jazz program. In addition he worked with Art Pepper (1976–7) and Frank Rosolino (1978).

In 1981 Smoker formed a trio with the double bass player Ron Rohovit and Phil Haynes, his student at the time; Drew Gress replaced Rohovit in 1990. In 1983 he met Anthony Braxton, who, after hearing his demonstration tape, invited the trumpeter to perform with him in Germany later that year. Smoker appeared with Braxton's large ensemble at the Victoriaville Jazz Festival in 1988, and between 1993 and 1996 he performed and recorded in Europe with various other groups led by Braxton, including the Charlie Parker Project. In 1987 he was a founding member of the cooperative group Joint venture, in which he played alongside Gress, Haynes, and Ellery Eskelin (who was replaced by Don Byron in 1996). During this time he played with Dave Liebman (1987), the percussionist Damon Short (from 1988), and in Haynes's group Four Horns and What?. He left Coe College in 1990 and moved to upstate New York. In the 1990s he continued to work with his trio and performed with the drummers Gregg Bendian (from 1994), Lou Grassi (from 1998), and Gerry Hemingway (from 1999), and recorded with Short (1990), the saxophonist Randy McKean (1991), Dave Taylor (1993), and Bendian (1996). In 1996 Smoker and Vinnie Golia co-founded a quartet with Ken Filiano and Haynes as their sidemen.

SELECTED RECORDINGS

As leader: *QB* (1984, Alvas 101); *Mississippi River Rat* (1984, Sound Aspects 006); *Alone* (1986, Sound Aspects 018); *Come Rain or Come Shine* (1986, Sound Aspects 024); *Genuine Fables* (1988, HA 6126); with V. Golia: *Halloween '96* (1996, CIMP 129), *Halloween, the Sequel* (1997, Nine Winds 0207)

As sideman: P. Haynes: *4 Horns & What?* (1989, Open Minds 2402); D. Short: *All of the Above* (1990, Southport 0028); R. McKean: *So Dig this Big Crux* (1991, Rastacan 012); G. Bendian: *Counterparts* (1996, CIMP 105)

For further recordings *see* Joint venture.

BIBLIOGRAPHY

CarrJ

K. Whitehead: "Profile: Paul Smoker," *DB*, lv/11 (1988), 48

B. Rusch: "The Questionnaire," *Cadence*, xv/8 (1989), 30

C. MacMillan: "Paul Smoker: Music from the Heart," *Coda*, no.228 (1989), 26

L. Van Trikt: "Paul Smoker: Interview," *Cadence*, xx/12 (1994), 18

<http://ourworld.compuserve.com/homepages/damonshort/smoker.htm> (1998)

L. M. Svirchev: "Paul Smoker: a Product of my Musical Experience," *Coda*, no.279 (1998), 28

GK

Smooth jazz. A largely instrumental style that emerged in the early 1990s and which is derived from the romantic side of soul music. It is essentially a continuation of the sweet soul style of players such as Grover Washington, Jr., as exemplified on his album *Winelight* (1980, Elek. 6E-305) – a style that in the 1970s and 1980s had been called "crossover" or "jazz lite." The term "smooth jazz" and the growth of the music it describes came about as a response to the demand for light, undemanding music from ratings-conscious radio stations with a brief to play jazz. The soft, easily assimilated character of smooth jazz made it palatable to a wide audience with little interest in unprefixed jazz, and musicians, broadcasters, and record companies formed a symbiotic, profit-driven triangle which perpetuated the style. It was a particularly welcome development for stations such as Jazz FM in London, which, before the advent of a popular subgenre containing the word "jazz," had had to defend a playlist dominated by soul, blues, and blues-rock.

Because of his huge success in the 1990s with albums such as *One Breath* (*c*1992, Ari. 07822-18646-2), the saxophonist Kenny G is often seen as the inventor of smooth jazz, but the template had been drawn by Washington and others. The style has developed various shadings, but most typically it features a three- or four-chord soul vamp over which a saxophone generates synthetic, carefully calculated passion from a limited palette of diatonic, pentatonic, and blues phrases. Frequently it creates a sense that it is ballad-oriented soul music in which saxophone, guitar, or piano takes the place of the voice. The illusion of singing, allowing a point of entry for non-jazz listeners, is often made real, in an understated manner, by the presence of subtle vocal choirs or vocal "hooks" low in the recording mix, or of sung choruses without a sung verse. Aside from Kenny G, other prominent smooth jazz players in the 1990s included the pianists Bob James and David Benoit, the saxophonists Boney James, Warren Hill, Richard Elliott, Najee, George Howard, Eric Marienthal, and Nelson Rangell, and the guitarists Marc Antoine, Peter White, Chuck Loeb, and Norman Brown. The apparently easy success of leading performers resulted in a proliferation of formulaic, musically stagnant imitations, but ambitious and imaginative musicians added extra content within the constraints of the style. Among these were Art Porter on saxophone (notably on his album *Straight to the Point*, 1993, Verve Forecast 314-517997-2), Loeb and Jeff Golub on guitar, Jeff Lorber on keyboards, and the groups the Yellowjackets (featuring Bob Mintzer), Fourplay, and Metro. As heard on his album *Close-up* (*c*1987, Reprise 25715-2), the saxophonist David Sanborn is perhaps the epitome of the player whose music seems to contain the key components of smooth jazz yet rarely sounds smooth, synthetic, or formulaic.

BIBLIOGRAPHY

E. Tiegel: "Riffs: Smooth Moves on the Air," *DB*, lxiii/12 (1996), 10
P. Watrous: "The Jazz is 'Lite,' but the Radio Profits are Heavy," *New York Times* (6 June 1997)

MARK GILBERT

Smulyan, Gary (H.) (*b* Long Island, NY, 4 April 1956). Baritone saxophonist. He took up alto saxophone while he was at school and had lessons with Joe Dixon; later he studied composition with Bob Brookmeyer. As a teenager he played in house bands at local jazz clubs, sitting in with Lee Konitz, Chet Baker, Jimmy Knepper, and George Coleman, among others. He changed to baritone saxophone to work with Woody Herman's Young Thundering Herd (May 1978 – May 1980). Having moved to New York he deputized for Gary Prebeck in the Mel Lewis Orchestra. He eventually replaced Prebeck in 1981 and took part in a tour of Australia in 1983, during which he performed and taught at the Sydney Conservatorium; he may be seen in the video *Jazz at the Smithsonian: Mel Lewis and the Jazz Orchestra* (1982). Smulyan continued to work with the group after Lewis's death in 1990, when it became known as the Vanguard Jazz Orchestra. In addition he has performed with Lee Konitz's nonet, Mike LeDonne's quintet (1988–90), Gene Harris and the Phillip Morris Superband (from 1989), the Carnegie Hall Jazz Band, Joe Henderson's big band (1992), the Mingus Big Band, and Charli Persip's Superband. In the early 1990s he was a member of the orchestra which performed Charles Mingus's posthumously reconstructed symphony *Epitaph* under the direction of Gunther Schuller, and around 1993 he toured and recorded with Diana Ross. Following Gerry Mulligan's death he formed the Three Baritone Saxophone Band (1996) with Ronnie Cuber and Nick Brignola, who has sometimes been replaced by Charles Davis on tour. As a freelance he has recorded with Rob Schneiderman (1991, 1997), Bill Evans (iii) (1993), Benny Green and Kevin Mahogany (both 1994), Michel Camilo and Freddie Hubbard (both 1994–5), Conrad Herwig (1996), Tom Harrell (1996–7), and Roseanna Vitro (1997). Smulyan has performed as a soloist in France, Italy, and Scandanavia, usually accompanied by local rhythm sections, and has taught occasionally at William Paterson College in Wayne, New Jersey. He also plays bass clarinet.

SELECTED RECORDINGS

As leader: *The Lure of Beauty* (1990, Criss Cross 1049); *Saxophone Mosaic* (1993, Criss Cross 1092); *Gary Smulyan with Strings* (1996, Criss Cross 1129)
As sideman: M. LeDonne: *'Bout Time* (1988, Criss Cross 1033); M. Lewis: *Soft Lights and Hot Music* (1988, MusicMasters 20172); *The Lost Art* (1989, MusicMasters 60222); M. LeDonne: *The Feeling of Jazz* (1990, Criss Cross 1041); R. Schneiderman: *Radio Waves* (1991, Reservoir 120); C. Herwig: *The Latin Side of John Coltrane* (1996, Astor Place 4003); Three Baritone Saxophone Band: *The Three Baritone Saxophone Band Plays Mulligan* (1997, Dreyfus 36588)

BIBLIOGRAPHY

M. Bourne: "Riffs: Gary Smulyan," *DB*, lix/10 (1992), 14
A. Lewis and L. Lewis: "Gary Smulyan: a Short Talk," *Cadence*, xviii/12 (1992), 13
G. Boudry: "Gary Smulyan: Pepper Spirit," *Jh*, no.525 (1995), 14 [incl. discography]
J. Woodard: "Mulligan View: the Baritone Saxophone Band," *JT*, xxviii/5 (1998), 50

GK

Smythe, Pat(rick) (*b* Edinburgh, 2 May 1923; *d* London, 6 May 1983). Scottish pianist. While studying to become a lawyer he spent a period in London in the late 1950s and played in clubs with musicians such as Dizzy Reece (early 1958). Not long afterwards he put aside his career in law to become a professional musician. He performed and recorded in Joe Harriott's quintet (alongside Shake Keane, Coleridge Goode, and Phil Seamen) from 1960 to 1964, during which period he played on occasion with Tubby Hayes's quartet, led his own group (1961–2), and worked with Bobby Wellins and Annie Ross; he recorded with Keane (1961) and Paul Gonsalves (1963), as well as under his own name (1962). Smythe stayed with Harriott from 1965 to 1967 as a member of the free-jazz group Indo-jazz Fusions (led by Harriott and the violinist John Mayer), and his playing may be heard to advantage on *Abstract Doodle*, on the group's album *Personal Portrait* (1967, Col. SCX6249). While continuing this intermittent affiliation with Harriott he worked with his own trio (1965–6) and led other bands for radio broadcasts; at some point his groups included the emerging musicians Dave Holland, John McLaughlin, and Allan Holdsworth. In 1968 he joined Peter King's quartet. He directed the London Jazz Ensemble, contributed arrangements to the BBC Radio Big Band and the Radioens Big Band in Denmark, and accompanied such leading jazz instrumentalists as Stan Getz, Ben Webster, Sonny Stitt, Gonsalves, and Zoot Sims, and such singers as Anita O'Day, Blossom Dearie, Tony Bennett, and Mark Murphy. During the 1970s Smythe played in the group Coe, Wheeler and Co. (led by Tony Coe and Kenny Wheeler, from April 1970), Wheeler's big band, and other groups led by Wheeler, and worked with Ronnie Ross, Ronnie Scott, John Stevens, Tony Kinsey, John Dankworth, and the quintet led by Holdsworth and Ray Warleigh. He also accompanied the singers Elaine Delmar (1970s – early 1980s) and Sandra King (early 1980s). From 1986 to 1996 a fund in support of young musicians operated as a memorial to the pianist.

BIBLIOGRAPHY

CarrJ; *ChiltonB*; *Feather '60s*
R. Cotterrell, ed.: *Jazz Now: the Jazz Centre Society Guide* (London, 1976)
B. Priestley: "Pat Smythe: a Sad Loss," *The Wire*, no.4 (1983), 17

NEVIL SKRIMSHIRE

Snader telescription. Three-minute film musicals of a single performance by a singer or group intended for replay on independent American television stations. Snader telescriptions were made from 1950 to around 1952 (*see* Films, §II, 3).

Snaer, Albert (Joseph) (*b* New Orleans, 29 Jan 1902; *d* Napa County, California, 26 June 1962). Trumpeter. After playing locally with the Excelsior Brass Band he worked for several years on riverboats. In 1925–6 he performed and made recordings with Dewey Jackson, including *She's crying for me* (1926, Voc. 1040), on which he is the soloist playing without a mute. He then worked with his own band, co-led with the banjoist George Augustin, and with Fate Marable (1928), and moved to New York (*c*1930), where he played briefly with Andy Kirk and others. From 1932 to 1941 he was intermittently with Claude Hopkins, and he may be seen with the band in the short films *Barbershop Blues* (1933) and *By Request* (1936). He was also a member of Leroy Smith's orchestra (1936). Later he ceased to work as a full-time musician but continued to play occasionally, with Sidney Bechet (1949), Frank "Big Boy" Goudie (early 1960s), and others. In the late 1950s Snaer moved to the West Coast. His death was erroneously reported in summer 1960; his place and date of death appear in the California death index.

BIBLIOGRAPHY

McCarthyB
J. De Donder: "Reminiscing with Mary Sayles: Some Notes on Albert Snaer," *Fn*, xii/4 (1981), 25

based on *ChiltonW*

Snare drum. The principal drum in the jazz drum set. *See* DRUM SET, esp. §§I, 3; II, 1–4; *see also* BRASS BAND.

Snidero, Jim [James J.] (*b* Redwood City, CA, 29 May 1958). Alto saxophonist. After attending the University of North Texas (1977–81) he worked with Brother Jack McDuff (1981–2), then joined Toshiko Akiyoshi's big band (1983). He has played with Frank Wess (1985), Frank Sinatra (1991–5), Eddie Palmieri (from 1994), Walt Weiskopf (1994–5), and the Mingus Big Band (from 1996). In 1984 he formed his own quintet and recorded and performed with many distinguished sidemen, among them the trumpeters Brian Lynch (with whom Snidero in turn has worked as a sideman from 1986; 1984–9), Tom Harrell (1989–92), and Tim Hagans (1992–5); the pianists Benny Green (1987–91) and Mulgrew Miller (1991); the double bass players Peter Washington and Dennis Irwin; and the drummers Billy Hart (1984–6, 1989), Louis Hayes (1990), Gene Jackson (1993), and Adam Nussbaum (from 1996). Based in New York, Snidero teaches in the Jazz and Contemporary Music Program at the New School University, and he has published an 11-volume series of jazz etude books keyed to play-along CDs. He performs often in Europe, and in 1998 toured Japan and Australia. He is a highly energetic player whose concept as an improviser started to show a stronger maturity in the mid-1990s.

SELECTED RECORDINGS

As leader: *Live* (1989, Red 123228-2); *While Your* [*sic*] *Here* (1991, Red 123241-2); *Vertigo* (1994, Criss Cross 1112); *Standards + Plus* (1997, Double-Time 130)
As sideman: T. Varner: *Jazz French Horn* (1985, New Note 1004); T. Akiyoshi: *Wishing Peace* (1986, Ken 001); B. Lynch: *Peer Pressure* (1986, Criss Cross 1029); T. Akiyoshi: *Desert Lady* (1993, Col. CK57856)

BIBLIOGRAPHY

K. Franckling: "Hearsay: Jim Snidero: Consistency and Commitment," *JT*, xxiii/4 (1993), 11
Z. Stewart: "Honesty of Expression," *DB*, lxv/6 (1998), 43
V. Lo Conte: "Jim Snidero," *Cadence*, xxvi/7 (2000), 5

GK

Snow, Valaida [Valada; Little Louis] (*b* Chattanooga, TN, 2 June 1904; *d* New York, 30 May 1956). Trumpeter, singer, and dancer. Her mother taught her to play several instruments and her sisters Alvada (Alvaida), Hattie, and Lavada (Lavaida) (*b* 1914) also became professional entertainers. She was known as Valada and her sister as Lavada until 1931. Her year of birth is in doubt; the earliest known source gives 1905, but by the time of her death, at the age of "47," she had lost four years by stages. However, City of Chattanooga records show the birth of an unnamed female child to J. V. and Etta E. Snow on 2 June 1904 and it seems almost certain that this is Valaida. Her first major engagement was at Barron Wilkins's cabaret in Harlem in 1922. In the early 1920s she toured the USA in various revues, including Noble Sissle and Eubie Blake's *Chocolate Dandies* (1924–5), and in August 1926 she went to China with Jack Carter's band for a one-year residency at the Plaza Hotel, Shanghai, after which she toured extensively in Asia. Snow joined *Blackbirds of 1929* in Paris and returned to the USA to work in *Keep Shuffling*, but in June 1930 traveled again to Paris and embarked on an extensive tour of northern and eastern Europe with Louis Douglas. Back in the USA in 1931, she toured with *Rhapsody in Black*, in which she fronted Pike Davis's Orchestra. In 1933 she joined Earl Hines's band in Chicago, but recorded only as a singer, though she played trumpet with the band in public performance. After leaving Hines in June 1933 she led an all-female band in an act with the dancers the Berry Brothers (she had married Ananias Berry in 1929).

From August 1934 to May 1935 Snow was in London in *Blackbirds of 1934*, and in January 1935 she began a series of band recordings for Parlophone through which she became the only female horn player of the vintage or swing eras to be extensively documented on record. After returning to the USA she worked at the Los Angeles Cotton Club, and again with Hines (March to June 1936). In August 1936 she was back in Britain, where she resumed recording and toured with Ken Johnson's Emperors of Jazz. She then appeared in Paris, Dublin, and Cannes, France, before touring Europe with a band led by Johnny Pillitz. She recorded in London with this band, then undertook further extensive European touring, which took her to Sweden in mid-1939. That September she moved to Denmark, where she remained after the country was occupied by the Nazis in April 1940. Her work permit was withdrawn in February 1941, but she was able to work in Sweden later in the year. She was then returned to Denmark. After Germany declared war on the USA she was interned from March 1942 until the Danish authorities could arrange her repatriation, via Sweden, in May of that year.

Snow resumed her career in April 1943, leading the Sunset Royal Orchestra, and in autumn 1943 was resident at the Rhumboogie in Chicago. In 1945 she settled in California, but from mid-1946 she was again touring, and continued to do so for the rest of her life, most often as a singer. She made two soundies with the Ali Baba Trio in 1946. In late 1953 she held a residency at the Crown Propeller Lounge, Chicago, with Sax Mallard's band.

Sometimes billed as 'Little Louis' in the 1930s, Snow was heavily influenced by Louis Armstrong as both a trumpeter and singer. She nonetheless developed an individual style, heard to best advantage on her European recordings; her rhythmic poise, growled notes, and effervescent scat singing place her in a high rank among jazz singers. However, her later work emphasizes more commercial aspects of her singing style and rarely recaptured the *joie de vivre* which is so conspicuous in her work up to 1940.

SELECTED RECORDINGS

As leader: on *Valaida*, ii: *1935–1940* (Harlequin 18), Poor Butterfly (1935); I Wish I Were Twins/I Can't Dance (I Got Ants in my Pants) (1935, Parl. F118); Imagination (1935, Parl. F230); Swing is the Thing (1937, Parl. F891); I got rhythm (1937, Parl. F1048); I can't believe that you're in love with me (1937, Parl. F923); My Heart Belongs to Daddy (1939, Sonora 3557); I can't give you anything but love/St. Louis Blues (1940, Tono 21166); Some of these Days/Carry Me Back to Old Virginny (1940, Tono 21194); St. Louis Blues (1945, AFRS Jubilee 145)

SELECTED FILMS AND VIDEOS

Pièges (1939); Patience and Fortitude (1946); If You Only Knew (1946)

BIBLIOGRAPHY

ChiltonW
R. Atwood: "Bride of a Month, Pretty 'In Bamville' Star tells of Hopes and Ambitions," *Pittsburgh Courier* (29 March 1924)
J. J. Adams: "Valaida, Back Home, Vows Love for USA and 'Nias'," *New York Amsterdam Star-News* (12 June 1942)
R. Kimball and W. Bolcom: *Reminiscing with Sissle and Blake* (New York, 1973)
H. Stonor: "Can't We Talk it Over," *Sv*, no.66 (1976), 213
H. T. Sampson: *Blacks in Blackface: a Source Book on Early Black Musical Shows* (Metuchen, NJ, 1980)
S. Placksin: *American Women in Jazz, 1900 to the Present: their Words, Lives, and Music* (New York, 1982; London, 1985, as *Jazzwomen, 1900 to the Present: their Words, Lives, and Music*)
R. Reitz: Liner notes, *Hot Snow: Valaida Snow, Queen of the Trumpet, Sings and Swings* (Rosetta RR1305, 1982)
L. Dahl: *Stormy Weather: the Music and Lives of a Century of Jazzwomen* (London, Melbourne, Australia, and New York, 1984)
H. Rye: "Visiting Firemen 9: The Blackbirds and their Orchestras," *Sv* (1984), no.112, p.133; no.114, p.216
G. Huygens: "Valaida Snow: reine noire de la trompette," *PJ*, no.20 (1986), 14
M. Clausen: Liner notes, *Valaida*, ii: *1935–1940* (Harlequin 18, 1992)
H. Rye: Liner notes, *Valaida*, i: *1935–1937* (Harlequin 12, 1992)
J. Canérot and A. Carbuccia: "Les Jazzmen américains dans les longs métrages français de fiction (1933–1958)," *BHcF*, no.458 (1997), 1
H. Rye: "Visiting Fireman 17: Valaida Snow," in *Storyville 1998/9*, ed. L. Wright (Chigwell, England, 1999), 116 [incl. discography]

HOWARD RYE

Snowden, Elmer (Chester) [Pops] (*b* Baltimore, 9 Oct 1900; *d* Philadelphia, 14 May 1973). Bandleader, banjoist, and guitarist. Having begun on guitar as a child, he went on to play mandolin, banjo-mandolin (with eight strings), tenor banjo, and the modern banjo. He worked in Baltimore with Eubie Blake (1915) and in Washington as a member of Duke Ellington's trio (1919–20) before leading his own bands. His first groups, in Washington and Atlantic City, New Jersey, included Otto Hardwick and Artie Whetsol (1921–3). These two traveled with Snowden to New York and were joined by Sonny Greer and Ellington (1923); with Bubber Miley (replacing Whetsol) and Charlie Irvis, this group became known as the Washingtonians (and later, without Snowden, as the Duke Ellington Orchestra). By this time Snowden was also doubling on soprano, C-melody, and baritone saxophones. Published remembrances of his groups and their venues are somewhat inconsistent, but details are firm enough to make clear his importance as a jazz bandleader. Among the members of his bands in New York were Miley, Jimmie Lunceford, Count Basie (replaced by Claude Hopkins), Tricky Sam Nanton, Harry White, Ernest Hill, and Tommy Benford at the Bamville Club and Henry Goodwin, Nanton (replaced by Charlie Irvis), Happy Caldwell, Cliff Jackson, Cyrus St. Clair, and Manzie Johnson at the Nest Club (concurrently, *c*1926). Caldwell's roommate at the time, Rex Stewart, recalled that they played together in Snowden's band, and he mentioned his participation in jobs at both of these venues. Further complicating these recollections are accounts of Stewart, Jimmy Harrison, Prince Robinson, Joe Garland, Freddy Johnson, Bob Ysaguirre, and Manzie Johnson having toured and performed at the Nest Club between mid-1927 and October 1928; individual surveys of these sidemen's careers suggest a different sequence, placing their association with Snowden earlier, in 1925–6 or 1926 alone.

In any event, the parade of young jazz notables continued: Frankie Newton, Al Sears, Hardwick, and Fats Waller were with Snowden at the Hot Feet Club (summer 1927), and Newton, Garvin Bushell, Rudy Powell, Bingie Madison, Hardwick, and Fats Pichon at the Furnace Club. While playing in the show *Blackbirds of 1930*, he began to lead the Smalls' Paradise Orchestra, including Gus Aiken, Sears, Hardwick, Waymon Carver, Don Kirkpatrick, Dick Fulbright, and Sid Catlett; Eldridge, Dicky Wells, Bushell, and Howard Johnson later joined this band and participated in the short film *Smash your Baggage* (1932). After settling in Philadelphia (1933) Snowden taught banjo, mandolin, and saxophone. He worked in Luckey Roberts's society orchestra (1935–9), led small groups in the Northeast and in Canada (1941–63), and then moved to Berkeley, California. He was well received in 1963 at the Monterey Jazz Festival, where he led an unusual quartet with Darnell Howard, Pops Foster, and the young drummer Tony Williams. He also taught and played with Turk Murphy, and in 1967 made a tour of Europe. In 1994 there appeared a previously unissued collection of tracks from Snowden's 1960 session with Lonnie Johnson; Snowden's outstanding jazz solos, delivered in a style firmly rooted in Piedmont blues, suggest the need for a reconsideration of his stature among jazz guitarists.

For illustration *see* Washingtonians.

SELECTED RECORDINGS

As leader: *Harlem Banjo* (1960, Riv. 9348)
As sideman: Viola McCoy: West Indies Blues (1924, Voc. 14801); Bessie Smith: I ain't got nobody (1925, Col. 14095D); Te Roy Williams: Oh Malinda/Lindbergh Hop (1927, Har. 439); Lonnie Johnson: *Blues and Ballads* (1960, Bluesville 1011); *Blues, Ballads, and Jumpin' Jazz*, ii (1960, Original Blues Classics 570-2)

BIBLIOGRAPHY

McCarthyB
H. P. [H. Panassié]: "Elmer Snowden," *BHcF*, no.34 (1954), 6
B. Demeusy: "Elmer Snowden Discography," *JJ*, xvi/4 (1963), 15
D. Ives: "Elmer Snowdon [sic]," *JJ*, xvi/1 (1963), 26
"Elmer Snowden: the Bandleader who Fired Basie!," *CI*, vi/5 (1967), 16
L. Muscutt: "Discovering Elmer," *Sv* (1968), no.16, p.3; no.17, p.4; no.18, p.4
S. Dance: *The World of Swing* (New York, 1974), 45
F. Dutton: "Birth of a Band," *Sv*, no.80 (1978–9), 44; no.91 (1980), 7; no.98 (1981–2), 45
G. Bushell and M. Tucker: *Jazz from the Beginning* (Wheatley, Oxford, England, and Ann Arbor, MI, 1990), 77
R. Stewart and C. P. Gordon: *Boy Meets Horn* (Wheatley, Oxford, England, and Ann Arbor, MI, 1991), 73
M. Tucker: *Ellington: the Early Years* (Oxford, England, Urbana, IL, and Chicago, 1991)

HOWARD RYE, BK

Socarras (Estacio), Alberto (*b* Manzanillo, Cuba, 19 Sept 1901; *d* New York, 26 Aug 1987). Reed player, flutist, and bandleader. His year of birth has been published as 1908, but in his application for social security he gave 1901 as well as his full name, Alberto Socarras Estacio. After working with local orchestras he moved to the USA, where in the late 1920s he recorded with Clarence Williams and others. He was the first important jazz flutist, and he may be heard to advantage on the instrument on Lizzie Miles's *You're such a cruel papa to me* (1928, Col. 14335D); he plays alto saxophone on the paired track on this issue, *My difrent kind of man*. From 1928 to 1933 he worked in orchestras for revues, during which time he made a tour of Europe. He continued to record occasionally, and his clarinet and alto saxophone playing on *Big Ben* (1930, Col. 14557D), by Bennett's Swamplanders, is an example of his more emotive work. From the 1930s Socarras led his own bands with such sidemen as Prince Robinson, Cecil Scott, Edgar Sampson, Cab Calloway, and Mongo Santamaria, though he also worked with Benny Carter (1933) and Sam Wooding (1935). His band played for three years at the Cotton Club around 1937. For many years he played classical music, and in 1945 he performed as a soloist at Carnegie Hall. He continued to be active as a teacher into the 1970s.

Oral history material in *NjR* (JOHP).

BIBLIOGRAPHY

H. Friedwald: "The Alberto Socarras Story," *Sv*, no.90 (1980), 220

based on *ChiltonW*

Society band. A type of dance band active in the early years of the 20th century; *see* Bands, §4(i). More generally, the term might be applied to any sort of group working in a setting involving an extremely affluent or "high-class" audience and employer; Whitey Mitchell satirized the experience in his essay "My First 50 Years with Society Bands" (*DB*, xxviii/3 (1961), 20).

Sock. A hard blow, hence in jazz argot a strong accent, or to play with heavy accentuation, loudly and propulsively. "Sock rhythm" or "sock style" is used of a style of playing characterized by heavy off-beat accents. A "sock chorus" is the final chorus of a lively piece, played in a hardhitting, emphatic manner (*see* Forms, §2); the term is used chiefly of early jazz.

Sock cymbal. Name originally applied to the Charleston cymbal and used to describe a pair of pedal-operated cymbals on a low stand; later it was also applied to the hi-hat (*see* Drum set, §I, 5).

Socolow, Frank (*b* New York, 18 Sept 1923; *d* New York, 30 April 1981). Tenor saxophonist. In the early 1940s he played in big bands, including that led by Georgie Auld (1942). He then toured and recorded with Boyd Raeburn's orchestra (1944–5), Chubby Jackson (1947–9, visiting Scandinavia in the winter of 1947–8), and Artie Shaw (1949–50); in some recordings, notably Jackson's *Tiny's Blues* (1949, Col. 38623), he played alto saxophone. Socolow continued to be associated intermittently with Raeburn (for illustration *see* Raeburn, boyd), performing in his band in 1947 and recording with him again in 1948 and 1956–7. During the 1940s he also recorded with Sid Catlett (1944) and Johnny Bothwell (1945), as the leader of a bop quintet with Freddie Webster and Bud Powell among its members (1945), and with Buddy DeFranco and Charlie Ventura (1949). From 1950 he worked as a freelance in New York, in which capacity he recorded with Charlie Parker (1950), Sal Salvador (1953), Terry Gibbs (1955, 1956), Cecil Payne (*Patterns of Jazz*, 1957, Signal 1204), Manny Albam (1957–62), Gene Krupa (1958), Teddy Charles (1959), and Joe Morello (1961). In addition Socolow recorded as a leader (*Sounds by Socolow*, 1956, Beth. 70) and played and recorded with Johnny Richards (1957–9).

Oral history material in *NjR*.

BIBLIOGRAPHY

FeatherE
Obituary, *DB*, xlviii/10 (1981), 13

Soft jazz. *See* Smooth jazz.

Soft Machine. English jazz-rock group. It was formed in Canterbury in 1966 by the keyboard player Mike Ratledge, the drummer Robert Wyatt, the electric bass guitarist Kevin Ayers, and the electric guitarist Daevid Allen. In 1967 the group was involved in the psychedelic movement in London and worked in avant-garde theatre in St. Tropez. The following year it toured the USA as a support act to Jimi Hendrix and recorded its eponymous first album in New York. Its next recording was more jazz oriented, and its third album, *Third* (1970), on which Elton Dean, Marc Charig, and the trombonist Nick Evans performed, confirmed this new direction; by this time Ayers and Allen had left, and Hugh Hopper was the group's electric bass guitarist. *Third* was the last album by Soft Machine to feature Wyatt's singing, which at times showed the influence of pop music; thereafter the group's performances were entirely instrumental, and following Wyatt's departure in autumn 1971 Ratledge remained as the only founding member. Other notable British jazz players passed through Soft Machine, among them Allan Holdsworth, the soprano saxophonist Alan Wakeman, the reed player Jimmy Hastings, Alan Skidmore, John Etheridge, Roy Babbington, and John Marshall.

Frequent changes of personnel often radically altered the character of the group's music, but Soft Machine was one of the most adventurous, influential, and enduring of English fusion bands. Although the albums *Third*, *Fourth* (1970), and *5* (1971–2) are generally thought to have the greatest jazz content, in some listeners' minds the rock and funk vamps of later recordings by Soft Machine may overshadow the presence of substantial and accomplished jazz solos by Holdsworth (on *Hazard Profile Part 1*, from *Bundles*, 1974) and Wakeman (on *Ban Ban Caliban*, from *Softs*, 1976). In 1978 two groups derived from Soft Machine – Soft Heap and Soft Head – were started by former members. Soft Machine itself effectively disbanded in December of that year, though it recorded a final album in 1980 to fulfil a contractual obligation. In 1999 Dean, Keith Tippett, Marshall, and Hopper gave a concert in Germany; their group was retrospectively named SoftWare.

SELECTED RECORDINGS

Third (1970, Col. CG30339); *Fourth* (1970, Col. C30754); *5* (1971–2, Col. KC31604); *Bundles* (1974, Harvest 4044); *Softs* (1976, Harvest 4056)

BIBLIOGRAPHY

WickesIBJ, i
M. Watts: "The Softs Blow Hot and Cold in Holland," *MM* (31 Oct 1970), 24
"The Soft Machine File," *MM* (9 Dec 1972), 51 [incl. individual biographies]
K. Dallas: "Soft Machine," *MM* (5 April 1975), 18 [incl. individual biographies]
R. Williams: "The Softs Parade," *MM* (30 July 1977), 35
P. Renaud: *La discographie du jazz anglais* (Chaumont, France, 1985)

MARK GILBERT

SOH. Trio formed in 1978 by the tenor saxophonist Alan Skidmore, the drummer Tony Oxley, and the double bass player Ali Haurand.

Sokal, Harry (*b* Vienna, 18 March 1954). Austrian soprano and tenor saxophonist, leader, and composer. He began to play jazz together with the keyboard player Peter Wolf when he was ten. In 1976 he joined a funk band which included the Austrian pianist Peter Ponger and the Swiss drummer Joris Dudli, and later that year he worked professionally in his own band, Timeless, with Dudli, the Swiss double bass player Heiri Känzig, and Uli Scherer. In 1977 he was a co-founder of the Vienna Art Orchestra, and one year later he became a member of Art Farmer's European quintet; with Farmer he performed at the Viennese club Jazzland, recorded, and toured the USA, appearing at Sweet Basil in New York. He was also the Austrian member of Palle Mikkelborg's EBU big band. In 1985 he performed in France with Michel Portal, Jean-François Jenny-Clark, Aldo Romano, Joachim Kühn, Dave Holland, Mino Cinélu, Daniel Humair, and the Austrian guitarist Harry Pepl. He led his own trio (with Känzig and the Swiss drummer Jo Jo Mayer), with which he performed at festivals in Moers and Cologne, Germany; Helsinki; Montpellier, France; and Skopje, Yugoslavia. He also toured twice with Carla Bley's big band. He joined Friedrich Gulda's Paradise Band in 1990, and two years later formed his own band, Depart. After leaving the Vienna Art Orchestra in the early 1990s he worked in New York with Lonnie Plaxico and Ronnie Burrage, and he taught at the Bruckner conservatory in Linz, Austria. Sokal is one of the most important post-Coltrane saxophonists in Europe. He has recorded with the Vienna Art Orchestra, the pianist and guitarist Stephen Ferguson, Jean-Paul Bourelly, Plaxico, Farmer, and his own groups (including the album *Rave the Jazz: Live*, 1996, PAO 450314).

BIBLIOGRAPHY

R. Urmann: "Harry Sokal," *JP*, xli/6 (1992), 36
<http://www.harrysokal.co.at> (2000)

KLAUS SCHULZ

Martial Solal at the Cheltenham International Jazz Festival, England, 1999

Solal, Martial (*b* Algiers, 23 Aug 1927). French pianist, composer, arranger, and leader. He studied piano with his mother, an opera singer, from the age of seven. After working locally in Algiers from 1942, he settled in 1950 in Paris, where he played with Django Reinhardt and Don Byas (recording with both in 1953), Lucky Thompson (recording in 1956, 1959, and 1961), and Kenny Clarke (playing in the house band at the Club Saint-Germain from 1956 and recording in 1956 and 1957). He was the leader of a trio which first recorded in 1953 and during the 1950s included such musicians as Pierre Michelot (who was also with Clarke in the band at the Club Saint-Germain), Jean-Louis Viale, and Christian Garros. In 1956 he made his first recordings as an unaccompanied pianist, and in 1959 he established a quartet, with Roger Guérin and Daniel Humair, and appeared at the Newport Jazz Festival with Teddy Kotick and Paul Motian. Principally he worked as the leader of trios with Guy Pedersen and Humair (1960–65) and Gilbert Rovère and Charles Bellonzi (1965–8), though among other members of his small groups were Michelot (to 1968) and Jean-François Jenny-Clark (from 1967). In 1968 Solal recorded in Italy with Lee Konitz. From 1974 into the 1980s the two men played and recorded as a duo and in small groups, and broadcast throughout Europe; they also appeared together at the Antibes–Juan-les-Pins Jazz Festival (1974), the Berliner Jazztage (1980), and the Grande Parade du Jazz (1980–81). Solal later gave concerts in a duo with Phil Woods (1994) and performed and recorded as the leader of trios with Marc Johnson and Peter Erskine (1995) and Gary Peacock and Motian (1997).

Solal has the ability to accommodate his playing to widely varying styles: he was a member of a trio with two double basses (Rovère and Jenny-Clark, 1969–71), and has occasionally worked as leader of a big band, making several recordings (1956, 1957, 1962, 1981), broadcasting in Paris (1980), and performing at the Montreux International Jazz Festival (1984). He has composed and performed extensively in contemporary art music and in a third-stream style bringing together jazz and classical music, and he has published didactic jazz piano pieces after the model of Béla Bartók's *Mikrokosmos*. He has also written music for more than 20 films (he may be seen in the short films *Hi-fi à gogo* (1958) and *Les temps d'une nuit* (1963)). In 1990 the diversity of his musical activities was celebrated in a series of concerts in Paris. His best music, however, has been made in a conventional trio of piano, double bass, and drums, and shows a grasp of form uncommon among improvisers; *Jordu* (from *Jazz à Gaveau*), for example, develops entirely from seemingly unimportant melodic, harmonic, and rhythmic alterations to the theme, and *Gavotte à Gaveau* (from the same LP) gradually integrates dissimilar fragments into a tight structure.

SELECTED RECORDINGS

As unaccompanied soloist: *Nothing but Piano* (1975, MPS 15447); *Bluesine* (1983, SN 1060); *Improvisations* (1991, Erato 45795); *Martial Solal improvise pour France Musique* (1994, JMS 071)

Duos: with L. Konitz: *Duplicity* (1977, Horo 17–18); with T. Thielemans: *Martial Solal and Toots Thielemans* (1992, Erato 45795): with M. Portal: *Martial Solal and Michel Portal* (1992, Erato 45799); with D. Lockwood: *Martial Solal and Didier Lockwood* (1993, JMS 067); with M. Portal: *Fast Mood* (1999, BMG 743216931); with J. Griffin: *Martial Solal and Johnny Griffin* (1999, Dreyfus 36610)

As leader: *Modern Sounds* (1953–4, Vogue 200); *Martial Solal Live* (1959–85, Stefanotis Flat and Sharp 1963); *Jazz à Gaveau* (1963, Col. FPX221), incl. Jordu, Gavotte à Gaveau; *Martial Solal at Newport* (1963, RCA LSP2777); *Suite for Trio* (1978, MPS 15497); *Martial Solal Big Band*

(1981, Gaumont Musique 753804); *Triangle* (1995, JMS 18674-2); *Just Friends* (1997, Dreyfus 36592)
As sideman with L. Konitz: *Impressive Rome* (1968, Campi 12003); *Jazz à Juan* (1974, Ste. 1072)

BIBLIOGRAPHY

FeatherE; *Feather '60s*; *Feather–Gitler '70s*
A. Clergeat: "Martial Solal," *Jh*, no.56 (1951), 29
J.-L. Ginibre: "Autopsie dans un miroir," *Jm*, no.83 (1962), 20
P. Koechlin and J. Tronchot: "Humair et Pedersen, que pensez-vous du trio Solal?" *Jh*, no.177 (1962), 14
C. Lenissois and J. Gilson: "Solal," *Jh*, no.188 (1963), 26
M. Harrison: "Two from Solal," *JM*, no.152 (1967), 7
B. Priestley: "Postwar Pianists," in A. McCarthy and others: *Jazz on Record: a Critical Guide to the First 50 Years: 1917–1967* (London, 1968), 351
M. Williams: *Jazz Masters in Transition, 1957–69* (New York and London, 1970/*R*1980), 119
J.-C. Levinson: "Quelques réflexions sur Martial Solal," *Jh*, no.287 (1972), 18
A. Dutilh: "Martial Solal," *Jh*, no.306 (1974), 16
J. Laret: "Martial Solal," *Jm*, no.289 (1980), 18
J. Laurents: "Martial Solal," *Jm*, no.290 (1980), 18
D. Soutif: "Martial Solal," *Jm*, no.283 (1980), 15
G. Endress: "Martial Solal," *JP*, xxxi/3 (1982), 12
X. Prévost: "Martial Solal: la tentation contemporaine," *Jm*, no.320 (1983), 26
R. Palmer: "Pianos in the Background," *JJI*, xxxvii/11 (1984), 16
J. Bens and X. Prévost: "Soleil Solal," *Jm*, no.346 (1986), 26
J. Reese: "Martial Solal: France's Virtuoso Pianist Likes to be Difficult," *Musician*, no.125 (1989), 26
L. Giraudo: "Martial Solal," *Jm*, no.408 (1991), 14
F. Bergerot: "Solal–Lockwood: pas de deux," *Jazzman*, no.170 (1993), 11
P. Anquetil: "Martial Solal ... colossal," *Jazzman*, no.177 (1994), 1
P. Benkimoun: "Le défi Solal," *Jm*, no.452 (1995), 22
P. Carles: "Martial Solal," *Jm*, no.450 (1995), 7
F. Cruz: "Solal–Johnson–Erskine: le triangle isocèle," *Jazzman*, no.6 (1995), 20
P. Anquetil: "Solal–Peacock–Motian: la belle équippe," *Jazzman*, no.28 (1997), 16
F. Raulin and S. Oliva: "Martial Solal en face des touches," *Jm*, no.466 (1997), 34

MAX HARRISON/ANDRÉ CLERGEAT, BK

Solid State. Record label, founded around 1966 as a subsidiary of UNITED ARTISTS.

Solo Art. Record company and label. The company was established by Dan Qualey, and in 1939–40 the label was used to issue recordings of piano solos. Apart from one disc by Art Hodes these were all of boogie-woogie, including material by Meade "Lux" Lewis, Albert Ammons, Pete Johnson, Jimmy Yancey, and Cripple Clarence Lofton; 15 78 r.p.m. records were issued before the label ceased to operate. Recordings by Yancey and Lofton not issued by Solo Art were made available by Riverside in the 1950s. (B. Rust: *The American Record Label Book* (New Rochelle, NY, 1978), 279)

HOWARD RYE

Soloff, Lew(is Michael) (*b* New York, 20 Feb 1944). Trumpeter. He played piano and ukulele from the age of five and took up trumpet when he was ten; the activities of his father, who was a dancer and managed a nightclub, allowed him to hear live music regularly from his early childhood. One summer, when he was around 19, he led a quartet which consisted of Patti Bown, Steve Davis (i), and Curtis Boyd. He studied at the Juilliard and Eastman schools of music and gained degrees in trumpet performance and music education from the latter institution in 1965. Later he played in New York with Tony Scott, Machito, Gil Evans (from spring 1966), and Tito Puente and in a rehearsal band led by Joe Henderson and Kenny Dorham (1965–7). In May 1968 he joined Blood, Sweat and Tears as a replacement for Randy Brecker, and he took part in international tours and recording sessions with the group until September 1973. In addition he performed with Clark Terry (at Carnegie Hall, 1970), recorded with Mongo Santamaria (1970, 1972), and played and recorded in the Thad Jones–Mel Lewis Orchestra (intermittently, 1968–76). Soloff toured and recorded with Evans from 1973 until the leader's death in 1988, after which he sometimes worked with Evans's son, the trumpeter Miles Evans.

Soloff was busy as a studio musician. In 1974 he recorded with both Robin Kenyatta and Stanley Clarke, and the following year he organized a quintet with Jon Faddis. He recorded with Sonny Stitt (1976), Stanley Turrentine (1976–7), George Russell (1978, 1980), Spyro Gyra and Teo Macero (both 1983), and Franco Ambrosetti and Bill Evans (iii) (both 1985). In 1987, in a concert entitled "Ornette Coleman Celebration" at Weill Recital Hall, Carnegie Hall, he performed as the soloist in *The Sacred Mind of Johnny Dolphin*. Under the leadership of the keyboard player David Matthews he played in the MANHATTAN JAZZ QUINTET and the Manhattan Jazz Orchestra, and from 1984 through the 1990s he recorded more than 25 albums with these ensembles and took part in various tours, especially to Japan. From 1988 he toured and recorded as a soloist with Carla Bley's big band. Soloff played lead trumpet for the Lincoln Center Jazz Orchestra and the Carnegie Hall Jazz Band (both from *c*1992) and the Mingus Big Band (by 1993). In the early to mid-1990s he led his own septet or sextet, in which Ray Anderson, Bill Evans (iii), Pete Levin, Gil Goldstein, Joe Beck, Mark Egan, Danny Gottlieb, Kenwood Dennard, Mino Cinélu, Don Alias, and Manolo Badrena were among his sidemen at various times; in 1996 the band became a quintet, Food Group, in which Beck, Egan, and Gottlieb were regular members, and Evans (iii) (1996) and Arthur Blythe (1998) appeared as guest soloists. As a sideman Soloff recorded with Peter Erskine (1988), Daniel Schnyder (1988–9), Charles Earland (1989), Ricky Ford (1991), John Clark (1992), Anderson (from 1994) and Paquito D'Rivera (1996). As well as maintaining a long association with the faculty of the Manhattan School of Music, he taught at SUNY, Purchase, and the Mannes/New School (both 1997).

Video oral history material in *NCH* (HCJA).

SELECTED RECORDINGS

As leader: *But Beautiful* (1987, PW K28P6468); *With a Song in my Heart* (1999, Mlst. 9290)
As sideman: S. Stitt: *Stomp Off, Let's Go* (1976, FD 1538); Mike Gibbs: *Big Music* (1988, Venture 27), incl. Pride Aside; D. Schnyder: *The City: Eight Compositions* (1988, Enja 6002); Manhattan Jazz Quintet: *Manhattan Blues* (1990, Sweet Basil 001); C. Bley: *The Very Big Carla Bley Band* (1990, Watt 23), incl. Strange Arrangement; *Big Band Theory* (1993, Watt 25), incl. Birds of Paradise; R. Anderson: *Don't Mow your Lawn* (1994, Enja 8070-2); C. Bley: *The Carla Bley Big Band Goes to Church* (1996, Watt 27)

BIBLIOGRAPHY

J. H. Klee: "The Uses of Adversity: Lew Soloff," *DB*, xl/3 (1973), 18
M. Jones: "Solo Soloff Minus Tears," *MM*, l (11 Oct 1975), 48
A. J. Smith: "Lew Soloff: Seeking the Right Sound," *DB*, xliv/3 (1977), 14
M. Bourne: "Lew Soloff: Big Band Brass Man," *DB*, liv/9 (1987), 24 [incl. discography]
D. Gross: "Lew Soloff," *Windplayer*, iv/5 (1987), 28
H. Mandel: "Remembering Dizzy: All Dizzy's Children," *DB*, lx/4 (1993), 24
G. Reynard: "Lew Soloff: musique actuelle," *Jh*, no.526 (1995–6), 16

BK

Solography. A type of DISCOGRAPHY listing solos recorded by an individual performer.

Soloist. Any musician who plays or sings a solo. *See* Bands, §3(c); *see also* Improvisation, §2.

Solomon, Clifford (T.) [Cliff "King"] (*b* Los Angeles, 17 Jan 1931). Tenor, alto, and soprano saxophonist. He began as a clarinetist, but changed to saxophone in 1944. In 1948–9 he was a member of Roy Porter's big band, then worked in Phoenix, where he joined Lionel Hampton. He was briefly with Floyd Ray in 1950, after which he played with Charles Brown until 1952. He rejoined Hampton in 1952–3 and toured Europe in late 1953. In August 1953 he made recordings under the name Cliff "King" Solomon. In 1954–5 he was again with Brown. He worked in Alaska in 1955–6, and played in Roy Milton's band in 1956–7. From 1962 to 1964 Solomon was a member of Onzy Matthews's Big Band, after which he toured with Ike and Tina Turner in a band which became known as The Goodtimers and later worked with Johnny Otis (from 1969); they can be seen at the 1970 Monterey Jazz Festival in the film *Play Misty for Me* (1971). Solomon was music director for Ray Charles from 1974 to 1987, then for Otis in 1988–90. In 1990 he joined the band which the guitarist Danny Caron had formed for Brown; he recorded several albums with Brown.

SELECTED RECORDINGS

As leader: But Officer (1953, OK 7010)

As sideman: J. Otis: *The Spirit of the Black Territory Bands* (1990, Arhoolie 384), incl. Harlem Nocturne, Rock-a-Bye Basie; C. Brown: *Honey Dripper* (1994, Verve 314-529848-2)

BIBLIOGRAPHY

R. Porter: *There and Back*, ed. D. Keller (Wheatley, Oxford, England, and Baton Rouge, LA, 1993) [incl. discography]

R. Weinstock: "Clifford Solomon," *Living Blues*, no.118 (1994), 25

HOWARD RYE

Solomon, Reuben (*b* Rangoon, Burma, 1918). British clarinetist. While at college in Burma in the late 1930s he organized a cooperative group, the Jive Boys. After the Japanese invaded Burma in 1942 he was evacuated to India and played as a freelance before joining Teddy Weatherford at the Grand Hotel, Calcutta; among the recordings he made with a small group from the band is *One Dozen Roses* (1942, Col. FB40231). Solomon left Weatherford at the end of 1944 and formed a new Jive Boys group, which recorded extensively, then after Weatherford's death (1945) he took some of the former's members and augmented his own group to 14 pieces. He also wrote arrangements for this new band. He emigrated to Australia after World War II and worked initially as a musician in Sydney.

BIBLIOGRAPHY

K. P. Darke: "Teddy Weatherford's Indian Recording Sessions 1941–45," *Matrix*, nos.107–8 (1975), 3

P. Darke and R. Gulliver: "Teddy Weatherford," *Sv*, no.65 (1976), 175

——: "Roy Butler's Story," *Sv*, no.71 (1977), 178

PETER DARKE

Solo-tone mute. A name under which the double mute has been manufactured; *see* Mute, §2(b).

Sommer, Günter ("Baby") (*b* Dresden, Germany, 25 Aug 1943). German drummer. He first played trumpet, studying in school and privately and also playing in local dance bands; at the age of 15 or 16 he took up drums. While attending the Musikhochschule in Dresden (1962–6) he worked professionally in the band led by Klaus Lenz, with which he recorded in 1965. In 1966 he joined Friedhelm Schönfeld's trio, in which he began to perform free jazz; he remained with Schönfeld until 1974, though at the same time he was a member of the Manfred Ludwig Sextet, co-led by Ernst-Ludwig Petrowsky and Manfred Schulze (1968–9), Ulrich Gumpert's jazz-rock group SOK (1971–3), and Gumpert's Jazz-Werkstatt Orchester (1972). Later he played in Petrowsky's trio alongside Klaus Koch (1972–9), in the group Synopsis, consisting of Conrad Bauer, Petrowsky, and Gumpert (1973–9), and in a duo with Gumpert (from 1973), which also recorded as a trio with the addition of Manfred Hering (1973 and 1979). In the mid-1970s he formed duos with the contemporary European art-music composer and multi-instrumentalist Hans-Karsten Räcke and with the church organist Hans-Günther Wauer; he recorded with Wauer in 1981 and again in the mid-1980s, and the two men occasionally played in a trio with John Tchicai.

In 1977 Sommer began performing and recording as an unaccompanied soloist; his works in this vein have been presented under the appellation Hornmüsik. In the late 1970s he worked in Gumpert's Workshop Band (recording in 1978–9), co-founded, with Peter Kowald and Wadada Leo Smith, a trio in which he recorded (1979 and 1981) and toured internationally, and recorded in the large ensemble Interjazz IV and with Clarinet Summit (both 1979). In 1980 he joined Fred van Hove's ensemble ML DD4, with which in 1982 he recorded and toured Europe and Japan, and in 1984 he formed the group Zentral-Quartett, which consists of the former members of Synopsis. During the 1980s Sommer worked in trios with Albert Mangelsdorff and Peter Brötzmann (recording in 1982) and Brötzmann and Barre Phillips (recording in 1988), and collaborated with Irène Schweizer, both in her small groups and in a duo (the latter in 1987). In the 1990s he was active in Ekkehard Jost's ensembles, recorded with Mario Schiano (1991), and took part in Herbert Joos's Südpool Jazz Projects (1992 and 1994).

Sommer was influenced early on by Art Blakey, most notably in regard to rhythmic pulse and swing; later he came under the sway of Han Bennink, whose performances he credits with answering all of the questions he had regarding free playing. In addition to the standard drum kit he uses found objects, many made of sheet metal, and he is particularly concerned with the combined timbres of his various instruments.

SELECTED RECORDINGS

(recorded for FMP unless otherwise indicated)

As unaccompanied soloist: *Hörnmusik* (1979, 0790); *Hörnmusik III: Sächsische Schatulle* (1988, 1992, Intakt 027)

Duos: with U. Gumpert: *Versaumnisse* (1979, 0740); on [various artists]: *Snapshot* (1979, R5), Jazz now-und später, Machschlag-aufgewärmt; with I. Schweizer: *Irène Schweizer–Günter Sommer* (1987, Intakt 007); with Cecil Taylor: *Riobec* (1988, CD2); on C. Taylor: *In East Berlin* (1988, CD13/14), Puuc

As leader: with U. Gumpert: *The Old Song* (1973, 0170); on [various artists]: *Snapshot* (1979, R5), Anophelismücke; with P. Brötzmann and B. Phillips: *Reserve* (1988, CD17)

As sideman: F. Schönfeld: on *Friedhelm Schönfeld–Hubert Katzenbeier* (1972, Amiga 855307), Trio-Dimensionen (1972); Synopsis: *Gruppe Synopsis* (1974, Amiga 855395); U. Gumpert: *Echos von Karolinenhof* (1979, 0710); E.-L. Petrowsky: on [various artists]: *Snapshot Jazz Now: Jazz aud der DDR* (1979, LP SP1), Enfant, Talar; *Selb-Viert* (1979, 0760); Clarinet Summit: *Clarinet Summit Live: You Better Fly Away* (1979, MPS 15557); W. L. Smith: *Touch the Earth* (1979, 0730); ML DD 4: *Was macht ihr denn?* (1982, SAJ42); M. Schiano: *And So On* (1991, Splasc(h) 368-2); Zentral-Quartett: *Plie* (1994, Intakt 037)

BIBLIOGRAPHY

GrayF; *ReclamsJ*

H. D. Plümper: "Grosse Augenblicke," *JP*, xxii/3 (1973), 20

"Eurojazz Personalities," *JF* [intl edn], no.27 (1974), 67
"On the Bandstand," *JF* [intl edn], no.43 (1976), 19
"Keeping Time with Drummers," *JF* [intl edn], no.47 (1977), 36
M. Laages: "Jazz aktuell: etwas gänzlich eigenes: Gumpert–Hering–Sommer," *JP*, xxix/5 (1980), 15
B. Ogan: "Free Jazz – Multilateral: Smith–Kowald–Sommer," *JP*, xxix/10 (1980), 24
R. Reichelt: "Günter Sommer: Baby Comes of Age," *JF* [intl edn], no.67 (1980), 47
H. Charlton: "Jazz: Snapshots of East Germany," *MM* (19 Sept 1981), 21
"Dico Disco & Co.," *Jm*, no.298 (1981), 64
B. Noglik: "Ernst-Ludwig Petrowsky, Günter Sommer," *Jazzwerkstatt international* (Berlin, 1981, 2/1983) [incl. discography]
G. F. Margull: "Hans-Günther Wauer – Günter 'Baby' Sommer," *JP*, xxxi/11 (1982), 12
W. Eschner: "Günter 'Baby' Sommer & Dynamo Big Band," *JP*, xxxv/2 (1986), 20
N. Ionescu: "On the scene – Romania: Sommer tour," *JF* [intl edn], no.108 (1987), 17
E. Jost: *Europas Jazz, 1960–1980* (Frankfurt am Main, Germany, 1987)
M. Kunzler: *Jazz-Lexicon* (Reinbek, nr Hamburg, Germany, 1988)
D. Martin: "Günter Sommer: la liberté venue de l'est," *Jm*, no.376 (1988), 18
"Encyclopédie permanente Jazzmag," *Jm*, no.393 (1990), 45
"Hors les murs: Günter Sommer," *Jm*, no.404 (1991), 56
J. Solothurnmann: "Wie es ist mit Irène Schweizer zu spielen: fünf Schlagzeuger und eine Pianistin," *JP*, xlvi/3 (1997), 3
<http://www.jazzinbelgium.org/mus/vanhove.htm> (2000)

BERT NOGLIK/GK

Sonet. Record company. It was founded in 1956 by Sven Lindholm and Gunnar Bergström, who remained its managers into the late 1980s. Another executive, Dag Häggqvist, joined the organization in 1960. At this point Sonet acquired Gazell (i), the label which John Engelbrekt had founded in spring 1949 and which Häggqvist had re-established in 1957. The company quickly expanded, setting up a subsidiary of the same name in Denmark; this in turn acquired the Danish firm Storyville, which had been active from the early 1950s in recording traditional jazz in Copenhagen. The organization later established branches in England, Finland, and France, as well as publishing houses in England and Scandinavia, a film and video production company, and a fine-art division.

Sonet's catalogue offers a wide variety of music, including folk music (much of which was produced by Sam Charters) and most styles of jazz. The company has issued albums by many notable musicians, among them (on Gazell) Zoot Sims and Toots Thielemans (both 1950), Svend Asmussen (1969), Arne Domnérus (1969–70), and Rolf Ericson (1971); (on Storyville) Chris Barber (1953–4), Papa Bue (1956–77), Sahib Shihab (1971), and the quintet led by Lee Konitz and Warne Marsh (1975); (on Danish Sonet) Archie Shepp and the New York Contemporary Five (1963) and Asmussen (1978); (on Norwegian Sonet) Karin Krog (1970); and (on Swedish Sonet) Lars Gullin (1953, 1958), Bengt Hallberg (1968), Thielemans (1972), Domnérus (1972–9), and Al Cohn and Zoot Sims (both 1974). In addition the repertory contains material reissued from many sources, in particular recordings made in Finland by Jukka Tolonen and items from the catalogues of Chiaroscuro and Roulette. In the 1980s Sonet issued particularly important recordings by Zoot Sims (1984) and Chet Baker and Benny Carter (both 1985), all of which were produced by Charters and released in the USA on Charters's label Gazell (ii). In the late 1980s Polygram acquired Sonet, and in the mid-1990s it was absorbed, together with other Polygram subsidiaries, into the Universal Music Group. Häggqvist had left Polygram by 1993 when he started Gazell Music AB, which has released a few compact discs on the revived Gazell label.

ERIK KJELLBERG/LARS WESTIN, GK

Song form. A term applied to the forms common in the refrains of popular songs and therefore in the jazz pieces based on them; *see* Forms, esp. §1(i)(a).

Songlines. Record company and label formed in Vancouver, Canada, in 1992 by Tony Reif. Its catalogue offered around 30 recordings by mid-2000 and featured such jazz and avant-garde performers as Dave Douglas, Ellery Eskelin, Jerry Granelli, François Houle, Andy Laster, Ben Monder, Paul Plimley, Brad Shepik, Chris Speed, and the saxophonist Patrick Zimmerli.

BIBLIOGRAPHY

F. Bouchard: "Label Watch: Songlines: Brave New Worlds," *JT*, xvii/7 (1997), 62
<http://www.songlines.com/> (2000)

GK

Sonora. Record company and label. The label was established in Sweden in 1932. There were two swing series in its catalogue: the first was issued from January 1937 to December 1941 and consisted of items put out as part of the company's main series but given a distinctive label and number; the second, inaugurated in August 1940, was a separately numbered series which ran until 1948. While both were devoted mainly to the work of local musicians, there were a number of items recorded during visits to Sweden by Valaida Snow and Peanuts Holland. Sonora also released recordings made in Sweden by Benny Carter in 1936.

BIBLIOGRAPHY

B. Englund: *Sonora II: Swing-series* (Stockholm, 1974)
——: Liner notes, *Jubileumsskivan Sonora 50 år* (Son. 6363062, 1982)

HOWARD RYE

Sønstevold, Gunnar (*b* Elverum, Norway, 26 Nov 1912; *d* Oslo, 18 Oct 1991). Norwegian pianist. From 1932, with Kalle Engstrøm, Øivind Bergh (later replaced by the guitarist and saxophonist Finn Westbye), and the saxophonist and drummer Svein Øvergaard, he was a member of the Funny Boys; the quartet toured Europe and made one recording in 1938 before disbanding the following year. Sønstevold then led small groups in Norway. During World War II he moved to Sweden, where he recorded with Gösta Törner and Thore Jederby. After 1945, however, he was largely inactive in jazz; he studied music in Vienna from 1960 to 1967 and later became well known in Norway as a composer of symphonic works and of music for films and the theater. Sønstevold's playing is exemplified by his recording *You got me woodooed/It Happened in Kaloha* (1940, Col. DS1219).

Oral history material in *NOnj*.

BIBLIOGRAPHY

O. Angell, J. E. Vold, and E. Økland: *Jazz i Norge* (Oslo, 1975)
K. Michelsen, ed.: *Cappelens musikkleksikon* (Oslo, 1978)
B. Stendahl: *Jazz, Hot & Swing: jazz i Norge, 1920–1940* (n.p. [Oslo], 1987) [incl. discography]
J. Bergh: *Norwegian Jazz Discography, 1905–1998* (Oslo, 1999)

VIDAR VANBERG

Sony. Record corporation and electronics manufacturer. It was founded in 1946 in Tokyo by Akio Morita and Masaru Ibuka as the electronics manufacturer Tokyo Tsushin Kogyo.

In 1958 it changed its name to Sony Corporation, and from that time it established itself as one of the world's largest manufacturers of consumer electronics. It became involved in the recording industry in 1968 when, with CBS Records, Inc., it formed CBS/Sony Group, Inc., in order to market Columbia and Japanese recordings in Japan, Macao, and Hong Kong; over time this became the largest record company in Japan, selling both Japanese popular music and international pop, jazz, and classical recordings. In the 1970s CBS/Sony first issued the important jazz albums *Miles Davis Quintet in Tokyo* (1964, SONX60064R) and *Miles Davis at the Plugged Nickel* (1965, 25AP291, 25AP1).

In November 1987 Sony purchased the CBS records group, though the deal was not finalized until the following year. Sony continued to use the label names Columbia, CBS, and Epic for its recordings of popular music and jazz and until January 1991 maintained the company name Columbia Records, Inc., for its recording activities in the USA. Thereafter it became Sony Music Entertainment, Inc. (SME), a division of the Sony Corporation of America; Sony Music, which is in turn a division of SME, handles the corporation's labels, including Columbia, Epic, and Legacy (for its activities in jazz since this period of acquisition and renaming *see* Columbia and Legacy). In Japan recording operations are with Sony Music Entertainment Japan (SMEJ), a division of Sony.

BIBLIOGRAPHY

P. J. Boyer: "Sony and CBS Records: What a Romance!" *New York Times* (18 Sept 1988)
F. Goodman: "CBS Records Sold to Sony," *RS*, no.517 (14 Jan 1988), 17
J. Lippman: "CBS and Sony Wrangle over Records Unit Sale," *Variety* (24 Feb 1988), 480
"CBS Records Changes Name," *New York Times* (16 Oct 1990)
P. Verna: "CBS Records to Become Sony Music Entertainment," *Billboard*, cii (27 Oct 1990), 6
A. White: "CBS Records Buys Columbia Trademark from EMI Music," *Billboard*, cii (2 June 1990), 4
D. Jeffrey: "Sony Music Creates Two Record Groups, Promotes Execs," *Billboard*, cvi (22 Jan 1994), 11
"Sony Dividing Labels in Europe," *Billboard*, cviii (13 Jan 1996), 43
L.-V. Mialy: "Didier Deutsch: Columbia, Legacy, Sony," *Jh*, no.556 (1998–9), 25

GK

Soph, Ed(ward Bingham) (*b* Coronado, CA, 21 March 1945). Drummer. He studied drumming in Houston, where he played informally with Arnett Cobb. While studying English at North Texas State University (1963–8, BA) he was a member of the university's renowned big band and worked for summer seasons with Ray McKinley and Stan Kenton (1965). He then toured and recorded with Woody Herman (1968–*c*1971) before returning to university to undertake a brief period of graduate study. Having moved to New York (1971) he worked as a freelance, touring (1973) and recording (the album *Giant Steps*, 1973, Fan. 9432) with Herman and recording with Bill Watrous (1974) and Clark Terry (1974–5). Later he recorded with Joe Henderson (1977), toured from Egypt to India with Terry (1978), and recorded in Australia with Dave Liebman and at the Monterey Jazz Festival with Herman (both 1979); he rejoined Herman's band in 1979. From the late 1970s he taught both privately and at colleges and workshops, and in 1987 he became a permanent member of staff at the University of North Texas; he contributed articles about drumming to *The Instrumentalist*, *Modern Drummer*, and *Percussive Notes*, wrote three method books, and released an instructional video, *The Drum Set: a Musical Approach* (*c*1987). In the 1990s he played with Marvin Stamm's quartet and recorded in small groups based in Texas led by the saxophonists Howie Smith (1991, 1993), Marchel Ivory (1994), and Tony Campise (1995), as well as in an ensemble led by Stamm's pianist Joe LoCascio (*c*1996).

BIBLIOGRAPHY

Feather–Gitler '70s
M. Rozek: "Profile: Ed Soph," *DB*, xliii/11 (1976), 3
S. K. Fish: "Ed Soph: Idealist," *MD*, ix/11 (1985), 18
R. Mitchell: "Three Generations of Jazz: Drummers Keep the Beat in Houston," *Houston Chronicle* (12 Sept 1993)
W. D. Clancy with A. C. Kenton: *Woody Herman: Chronicles of the Herds* (New York and elsewhere, 1995)

BK

Sopranino clarinet. The highest member of the clarinet family in common use, normally pitched in E♭; *see* Clarinet, §§1 and 2.

Sopranino saxophone. The highest instrument of the saxophone family, normally pitched in E♭; *see* Saxophone, §6(iii).

Soprano. In general musical terminology the highest vocal part or range; the word is also used as a qualifying adjective to distinguish those members of certain families of instruments (especially wind) that are pitched in that range (e.g., "soprano clarinet" is the full name of the principal member of the Clarinet family, though the qualifying adjective is not normally used in this case). In jazz argot "soprano" is used alone to mean the soprano saxophone (*see* Saxophone).

Soprano clarinet. The principal member of the clarinet family, pitched in B♭, A, or C; *see* Clarinet, §§1 and 3.

Soprano saxophone. The soprano instrument of the saxophone family, normally pitched in B♭; *see* Saxophone, §4.

Soprano Summit. Group led by Bob Wilber and Kenny Davern. The two musicians first played together at the Colorado Jazz Party of 1972, and worked together at intervals before forming a full-time partnership in 1974. Soprano Summit was established shortly thereafter with the addition of a rhythm section, which included the guitarist Marty Grosz. The original concept of the front-line musicians was to re-create the soprano saxophone and clarinet duos of Sidney Bechet and Mezz Mezzrow, but they drew on a wider instrumentation when later Wilber played alto saxophone and Davern took up the C-melody instrument. The group made a number of recordings and toured the USA and Europe; it was also the first jazz ensemble to play in South Africa to nonsegregated audiences. It disbanded in 1979, and then resumed performing as Soprano Reunion in the late 1980s, by which time Davern was concentrating strictly on the clarinet. The group remained active intermittently through the 1990s.

SELECTED RECORDINGS

Soprano Summit (1973, World Jazz 5); *Chalumeau Blue* (1976, Chi. 148); *In Concert* (1976, Conc. 29); *Soprano Reunion* (1990, Chi. 311); *Yellow Dog Blues* (1995, Chi. 339); *Reunion at Arbors* (1998, Arbors 19183)

BIBLIOGRAPHY

"Soprano Summit," *Full Swing*, i/3 (1976), 3
D. Coller and B. Whyatt: "Soprano Summit Discography," *JJI*, xxxv (1982), no.4, p.22; no.5, p.43

DEREK WEBSTER/BK

SOS. Trio formed in 1973 by the saxophonists Alan Skidmore, Mike Osborne, and John Surman. Its playing on the eponymous album *SOS*, recorded in 1975 (Ogun 400), foreshadows that of the World Saxophone Quartet and raises questions about the trio's possible influence on that much more famous group, particularly in its manner of combining dance-based ostinatos with free and funk-oriented improvisation.

BK, GK

Soskin, Mark (Samuel) (*b* New York, 12 July 1953). Pianist. He studied classical piano from the age of seven, became involved in jazz while studying at the University of Colorado in 1972, and the following year transferred to the Berklee School of Music, Boston. After moving to San Francisco he played in local salsa bands and worked as a freelance, then toured and recorded with Billy Cobham and the CBS All Stars (both 1977) and extensively with Sonny Rollins (1978–93). Having settled in New York around 1980, he worked with George Russell (1981), Herbie Mann's Jasil Brazz (from 1983), Claudio Roditi (from the 1980s), Stanley Turrentine (1988, 1994–5), and Bobby Watson (1995–6), while remaining active as a freelance with Latin-jazz bands. Soskin led a trio with Harvie Swartz and Adam Nussbaum (1990–93) which became a quartet with the addition of Joe Locke (1993–4), and he formed ongoing duos with Swartz and with Cameron Brown. With Swartz and Joe LaBarbera he co-led the group Spirits (1994–5) and with Chip Jackson and Danny Gottlieb he formed the cooperative Contempo Trio; this last group recorded with Ravi Coltrane as a fourth member (1991) and played again later as a trio (1996–7). Soskin has also worked as an instructor at the Manhattan School of Music.

SELECTED RECORDINGS:

As leader: *Overjoyed* (1987, Jazz City 660.53.020)

As sideman: S. Rollins: *Sunny Days, Starry Nights* (1984, Mlst. 9122); *Sonny Rollins Plays G-Man* (1986–7, Mlst. 9150); *Falling in Love with Jazz* (1989, Mlst. 9179); H. Mann: *Caminho de casa* (1990, Chesky 40); Contempo Trio: *No JAMF's Allowed* (1991, Jazzline 11137-2); H. Meurkens: *A View from Manhattan* (1993, Conc. 4585); C. Roditi: *Free Wheelin'* (1994, Reservoir 136)

BIBLIOGRAPHY

B. Milkowski: "Profile: Mark Soskin," *DB*, lvi/1 (1989), 48

GK

Souchon, Edmond(, Jr.) [Doc; Tuig, R. A.] (*b* New Orleans, 25 Oct 1897; *d* New Orleans, 24 Aug 1968). Guitarist and writer. He trained as a physician in Chicago and was largely self-taught as a guitarist. Souchon was a founding member of the Six and Seven Eighths Band, a string nonet which enjoyed considerable popularity between about 1911 and the early 1920s. In 1945 he helped to revive this group as a quartet, and in 1949 and 1959 he made some recordings of the early string band repertory, among them *High Society* (1949, New Orleans 1000); the ensemble continued to perform until the 1960s. As well as recording as a leader (1955, 1958, 1959) he often played and recorded with such New Orleans musicians as Johnny Wiggs (1950, 1954–7, 1958), the double bass and tuba player Sherwood Mangiapane, Papa Jack Laine (1951), Raymond Burke (1952), and Paul Barbarin (1956).

Although he was not a founder of the New Orleans Jazz Club, Souchon was an early president of the organization. He produced its weekly radio program on WWL for several years and was the editor of its journal, *Second Line*, from 1951 until his death, contributing to it frequently under the pseudonym R. A. Tuig. In addition he wrote articles for such periodicals as *Jazz* and *Jazz Report*, and with Al Rose he compiled *New Orleans Jazz: a Family Album* (Baton Rouge, LA, 1967, rev. and enlarged 3/1984). Souchon assisted in the establishment of the National Jazz Foundation in 1942 and of the New Orleans Jazz Museum in the 1950s. He owned around 2000 recordings of early New Orleans jazz, which he donated to the New Orleans Public Library; his collection of materials relating to folk music and jazz is held in the William Ransom Hogan Jazz Archive at Tulane University in New Orleans (*see* Libraries and archives, §2). ("Biographical Data on Dr. Edmond Souchon, II," *SL*, xx (1968), 97)

Soul jazz [funk, funky jazz]. A type of Hard bop dating from the mid-1950s. Played most often in small groups led by a tenor or alto saxophonist, a pianist, or a Hammond organist, it is characterized by simple, tuneful themes and improvisations, modeled on the speech inflections of African-American preachers in the sanctified churches. Themes are sometimes 16 (rather than 12 or 32) bars long and are occasionally in 6/8 meter. Harmonic progressions and riffs often emphasize the subdominant and the plagal cadence (IV–I) long associated in church music with the singing of the word "amen." In most respects, however, the definable differences between soul jazz and hard bop – the instrumentation, structures of tunes, melody, harmony, rhythm, and techniques of improvisation – are negligible, and the stylistic labels connote feeling and atmosphere rather than distinctive musical characteristics.

The words "soul" and "funk" describe the essential qualities of the style, which were perceived as distinguishing it from the cold, intellectualized West Coast jazz of the period. "Funk" (an African-American dialect word referring to body odor) is the older term, implying earthiness; an early occurrence of the word in this sense is found in the title of a piece recorded by Horace Silver in 1953 – *Opus de Funk*. "Soul" evokes the emotional and spiritual depth of African-American culture and in particular suggests links with the gospel church; "soul" was also used in titles during the 1950s, but the term "soul jazz" achieved widespread currency only from 1960, when Cannonball Adderley's quintet began to be promoted as a soul-jazz group on the Riverside label.

Other exponents of the style, which has persisted virtually unchanged, include Gene Ammons (late in his career), Charles Earland, Groove Holmes, Willis "Gator" Jackson, Les McCann, Brother Jack McDuff, Jimmy McGriff, Charles Mingus (in those of his performances influenced by gospel music), Harold Ousley, Don Patterson, Houston Person, Shirley Scott, Johnny Hammond, Bobby Timmons, Stanley Turrentine, and Harold Vick. Among a new generation of devotees are Paul Bollenback, Joey DeFrancesco, Larry Goldings (his organ trio with Peter Bernstein and Bill Stewart), Ron Holloway, and the tenor saxophonist Robert Stewart.

The terms "funk" and "soul" later became more widely known in connection with styles of popular music; the former was used for the hard, percussive dance rhythm originated by the singer and bandleader James Brown, and the latter for the style that blended elements of gospel and rhythm-and-blues. Once established these genres were in turn combined with jazz when fusions of jazz with other styles became fashionable. Hybrids of jazz and soul music, and of jazz and the popular style funk, however, have little in common with soul jazz.

BIBLIOGRAPHY

D. Heckman: "Soul jazz and the Need for Roots," *JM*, viii/1 (1962), 5
P. Tamony: "Funk," *Americanisms: Content and Continuum* (San Francisco, *c*1969)
R. F. Thompson: *Flash of the Spirit* (New York, 1983)

BK

Soul Note. Record label. It was founded in 1979 in Milan by Giovanni Bonandrini as a companion to his label Black Saint. By the mid-1980s it had become extremely important; on it are issued recordings by such renowned hard-bop and free-jazz musicians as Billy Harper, George Adams, Dannie Richmond, Giorgio Gaslini, Billy Bang, Bill Dixon, Art Farmer, George Russell, and Paul Motian. From the 1990s it has reissued much of its existing catalogue on CD and recorded such new American talents as Tom Varner, Craig Harris, Mark Dresser, and Ellery Eskelin, as well as major Italian players, including Enrico Pieranunzi, Maurizio Giammarco, and Gianluigi Trovesi. It has also initiated the complete reissue of Gaslini's recordings. Management of the label has transferred to Bonandrini's son Flavio. Although not dedicated to free jazz in the same way as its companion Black Saint, Soul Note does embrace numerous examples of the style.

BIBLIOGRAPHY

F. Davis: *In the Moment: Jazz in the 1980s* (New York, and Oxford, England, 1986/*R*1996), 206
J. Levenson: "Jazz: Blue Notes," *Billboard*, cii (7 July 1990), 62
F. Fini: *Soul Note: a Label Discography* (Imola, Italy, 1997)
<http://www.blacksaint.com> (2000)

STEFANO ZENNI, BK

Soundie. A three-minute film of a single performance intended for replay on a kind of jukebox in bars and clubs, each play costing 14 cents. Soundies were produced between 1940 and 1946 (*see* Films, §II, 2, and Recording, §II, 3).

Sound recording. *See* Recording.

Sousaphone. A type of bass Tuba named for the American bandmaster John Philip Sousa and built in the circular shape of the helicon.

South, Eddie [Edward Otha] (*b* Louisiana, MO, 27 Nov 1904; *d* Chicago, 25 April 1962). Violinist. His extensive music education began at the age of ten with a German violinist and with Charles Elgar; later he studied at Chicago's College of Music. In 1918–19 he and Juice Wilson were featured as the Gold Dust Twins with Freddie Keppard's band. From 1923 to 1927 he recorded with and was the music director of Jimmy Wade's Moulin Rouge Orchestra, after which he joined Erskine Tate's orchestra as first violinist and recorded as a leader. He traveled in 1928 to Europe, where he toured, and studied both at the Paris Conservatoire and in Budapest. In 1931 he returned to Chicago and organized and recorded with a band which included Everett Barksdale; Milt Hinton joined in 1932, and in December of that year the group went to Hollywood for an engagement at the Ballyhoo. In 1934 South broadcast regularly from Chicago over CBS radio station WBBM with an eight-piece band in which Ed Burke was a sideman; he then led 10- and 12-piece orchestras. He was again in Paris in 1937, and the historic recordings he made with Django Reinhardt and Stephane Grappelli during this visit represent the peak of his output. In the Netherlands the following year he recorded his composition *Black Gypsy*, which he had written in 1934. Over the next two decades he continued to lead his own groups, held residencies in New York, Chicago, Milwaukee, and the Los Angeles area, and made recordings, notably a remarkable series of transcriptions with a trio and quartet involving Billy Taylor (ii) in 1944. South directed the string section at Lionel Hampton's Carnegie Hall concert in 1945, performed almost daily on radio in New York during the mid-1940s, and in 1946 was employed in a recording band accompanying country singers. He performs two titles in his sole film appearance, in the African-American film *Stars on Parade* (1946). In 1947 he recorded in a modernistic blues vein, under the pseudonym Bill Dougherty, in a band led by Earl Hines. Following a long recuperation from tuberculosis in 1950 he remained in Chicago, where he appeared on television and recorded two albums. He played his last engagement in April 1962.

South was one of the finest classically trained violinists ever to play jazz. He had a dark tone, a powerful bowing attack, and an immaculate left-hand technique. At fast tempos he achieved a considerable sense of swing, whereas in slower pieces he employed a more rhapsodic style inspired by Hungarian and gypsy music – as exemplified by *Hejre Kati*, which he chose as his theme. Fourteen transcriptions of his own compositions, including *Black Gypsy*, and of compositions by others were published as *Eddie South: Violin Solos with Piano Accompaniment* over the course of the years 1936 to 1943.

SELECTED RECORDINGS

Hejre Kati (1931, Vic. 22847); Nagasaki (1933, Vic. 24383); Eddie's Blues (1937, Swing 8); Dinah (1937, Swing 12); Improvisation sur le premier mouvement du Concerto en ré mineur de Jean-Sébastien Bach/ Interprétation Swing du premier mouvement du Concerto en ré mineur de Jean-Sébastien Bach (1937, Swing 18); Black Gypsy (1938, Bruns 81504); first issued on *The Dark Angel of the Fiddle: the Complete Standard Transcriptions* (1944, Soundies 4120), Kol Nidre; Swinging the Blues (1947, Contl 6045); *The Distinguished Violin of Eddie South* (1958, Mer. 20401)

BIBLIOGRAPHY

E. South: "Are We Dissatisfied?" *Rhythm* (1930), Nov, 23
E. South with F. Avendorph: "My Foreign Travels and Experiences," *Chicago Defender* (12, 19, and 26 Dec 1931; 2 and 16 Jan 1932)
H. Panassié: *Douze années de jazz (1927–1938): souvenirs* (Paris, 1946), 233
L. Lawrence: "Eddie South Saw a Sign, Faith Saved Life," *Milwaukee Journal* (19 March 1951), 1
The Torchbearer: "Look Forward Angel," *Flash* (1951), Aug, 16
L. Feather: "Back Comes Eddie South: and He's Still a Virtuoso," *MM*, xxviii (15 Nov 1952), 3
D. Morgenstern: "Jazz Fiddle," *DB*, xxxiv/3 (1967), 16
R. Gulliver: "The Recordings of Jimmy Wade," *IAJRC Journal*, vii/3 (1974), 3
——: "Jimmy Wade," *Sv*, no.56 (1974–5), 55
J. Brown: Liner notes, *The Dark Angel of the Fiddle* (Trip 5803, late 1970s)
B. Niquet: "Edward Otha South, 1904–1962," *Pj*, no.14 (1978), 17
M. Glaser and S. Grappelli: *Jazz Violin* (New York and elsewhere, 1981) [incl. transcrs.]
B. Crowther: "The Forgotten Ones: Eddie South," *JJI*, xxxvi/8 (1983), 12 [incl. discography]
H. Rye: "Visiting Firemen, 8: Eddie South," *Sv*, no.108 (1983), 207
S. Glaess: *Die Rolle der Geige im Jazz* (Berne, 1991 [*recte* 1992]), 65 [incl. transcrs.]
H. Crowder with H. Speck: *As Wonderful as All That: Henry Crowder's Memoir of his Affair with Nancy Cunard, 1928–1935* (Navarro, CA, 1987), 49
A. Barnett: "Eddie South: Film, Airchecks, Transcriptions, Issued and Unissued Sessions," *Fable Bulletin: Violin Improvisations Studies*, i/4 (1994); addns and corrections in i/8 (1996); ii/9 (1997)
H. Openneer: "Het debuut van Eddie South in Nederland," *NJA Bulletin*, no.15 (1995), 38

A. Barnett: *Black Gypsy: the Recordings of Eddie South: an Annotated Discography and Itinerary* (Lewes, England, 1999)
——: Liner notes, *Black Gypsy: The Complete Victor, Gramophone, and ARC Recordings, 1927–1934* (Frog DGF36, 2000)

MATT GLASER/ANTHONY BARNETT

South, Harry [Henry Percy] (*b* London, 7 Sept 1929; *d* London, 12 March 1990). English pianist, arranger, and composer. He started on drums in 1943, but gave up the instrument on being stricken with tuberculosis in 1945; during a year-long period of hospitalization he studied arranging and composition. Having taken up piano, from late 1948 to 1950 he performed at Club Eleven, London's foremost bop venue. He continued his career as a performer with several lesser-known groups from 1952, but more significantly wrote material for Ronnie Scott's band (1954–5) and performed with Tony Crombie, Tubby Hayes (April 1955 – September 1956), and Joe Harriott (1958–60), with whom he also worked in Germany. In 1959 he formed an all-star big band which broadcast on the BBC. After working with John Dankworth (late 1959 – early 1960s) and the Jazztet led by Ronnie Ross and the trumpeter Bert Courtley (April 1960 – February 1961), he was with Dick Morrissey in India (from September 1961); on their return to England in October 1962 the two men formed a quartet. From 1966 South led (and that year recorded with) his own big band. In the late 1960s he worked occasionally with Harriott again and was associated for some time with the British rhythm-and-blues influenced pop singer Georgie Fame, with whom he recorded and toured as pianist and music director, notably for two weeks with Count Basie's band (April 1968). Later he worked as a music director for Annie Ross and wrote arrangements for Sarah Vaughan, Buddy Rich, and Jimmy Witherspoon. Thereafter South concentrated on writing music for films and television, and in the 1970s and 1980s achieved considerable success in this field. He composed a number of scores for the National Youth Jazz Orchestra, which in 1990 recorded *Portraits*, his suite of 15 pieces (Hot House 1007).

SELECTED RECORDINGS

As leader: *Presenting the Harry South Big Band* (1966, Mer. 20081)
As sideman: D. Morrissey: *Storm Warning* (1965, Mer. 20077MCL); G. Fame: *Sound Venture* (1966, EMI SX6076)

BIBLIOGRAPHY

ChiltonB; *FeatherE*; *SheridanCB*
P. Gammond, ed.: *The Decca Book of Jazz* (London, 1958), 238
R. Cotterrell, ed.: *Jazz Now: the Jazz Centre Society Guide* (London, 1976)

DIGBY FAIRWEATHER/SIMON ADAMS, KEN RATTENBURY, BK

Southall, Henry (Branch) (*b* Richmond, VA, 25 Aug 1931). Trombonist. After playing informally while a student he worked with Stan Kenton in 1958. From October 1962 to 1966 he toured and recorded with Woody Herman, whom he rejoined in 1968; among the recordings he made with Herman is the album *My Kind of Broadway* (1965, Col. CS9157). Nothing else is known of his career.

BIBLIOGRAPHY

Feather '60s
W. D. Clancy with A. C. Kenton: *Woody Herman: Chronicles of the Herds* (New York and elsewhere, 1995)

Southpaw, the. Nickname of JOHN LEITHAM.

Southport. Record company and label formed by BRADLEY PARKER-SPARROW.

Southwest jazz. *See* KANSAS CITY JAZZ.

Space Jazz Trio. Italian trio formed in 1984 by the pianist Enrico Pieranunzi, with the double bass player Enzo Pietropaoli and a succession of drummers: Fabrizio Sferra, Roberto Gatto, Alfred Kramer, and John Arnold. As well as working in its own right, the group accompanied numerous visiting musicians, recording with Chet Baker, Lee Konitz, and Phil Woods (all 1988). The Space Jazz Trio is influenced by the classic piano trio of Bill Evans (ii) and Chick Corea's work in trio settings and is notable for the virtually telepathic interaction of its members.

SELECTED RECORDINGS

Autumn Song (1984, Enja 4094); *Space Jazz Trio*, i–ii (1986, 1988, yvp 3007, 3015); with C. Baker: *Little Girl Blue* (1988, Philology 21); with L. Konitz: *Blew* (1988, Philology 26); with P. Woods: *Phil's Mood* (1988, Philology 27), *Live at the Corridonia Jazz Festival 1991* (1991, Philology 211-2)

GK

Spanier, Muggsy [Francis Joseph] (*b* Chicago, 9 Nov 1901; *d* Sausalito, CA, 12 Feb 1967). Cornetist and leader. Whyatt (1995) discovered that Spanier was born in 1901, not 1906, as widely given; the social security death index confirms 1901. From around 1910, after his parents separated, he grew up in an orphanage, which proved to be a hateful experience, although he was afforded an opportunity to play drums and then cornet; when he was 13 his father, a semiprofessional classical pianist, bought Spanier his own cornet, which he later studied with players from the Chicago Opera and Chicago Symphony orchestras. He was also an aspiring baseball player, and his friends gave him the nickname of the renowned manager of the New York Giants, John McGraw: "Muggsy."

Spanier began his professional career in 1920 with Elmer Schoebel's band. He then played with a lesser-known dixieland band while absorbing the sounds of King Oliver's Creole Jazz Band in local performances. He was first recorded as a member of the Bucktown Five (1924) and Stomp Six (1925), both of which included Volly De Faut and Mel Stitzel. After a brief period with Husk O'Hare's Wolverines he played with Frank Teschemacher and Jess Stacy in the band led by the tenor saxophonist Floyd Town (*c*1926–8), with which he made regional broadcasts. He then joined Charlie Pierce and participated in several classic Chicago-jazz recording sessions under Pierce's name and those of the Chicago Rhythm Kings and the Jungle Kings (1928). In 1929 he became an important member of Ted Lewis's orchestra, with which he performed in two films (1929, 1935). In December 1936 he joined Ben Pollack's group, but serious illness, partly the effect of alcoholism, forced him to leave early in 1938. On his recovery the following year he organized his Ragtime Band (see illustration), an eight-piece dixieland group that included Georg Brunis, Rod Cless, Nick Caiazza, and Joe Bushkin, with which he made a series of 16 recordings that contributed substantially to the New Orleans revival of the 1940s. From April 1939 the group performed at the Panther Room and Off Beat Room in Chicago and Nick's in New York, but it was forced to disband at the end of the year through lack of commercial success.

Spanier briefly rejoined Lewis, led a recording group with Sidney Bechet called the BIG FOUR (1940), and played in Bob Crosby's dixieland big band (mid-1940 – February 1941). For a short time he led his own big band, modeled on Crosby's (1941 – September 1943), with Vernon Brown, Irving Fazola, and Caiazza among his sidemen, but thereafter he played and recorded almost exclusively in small dixieland groups. In New York from March 1944 he worked with Art Hodes at Jimmy Ryan's and then with Miff Mole and Pee Wee Russell in the band at Nick's. He played once again with Lewis (May–August 1944) and then returned for a lengthy engagement at Nick's, where eventually first Russell and then Mole left; Spanier took over leadership of the band in April 1947, just after having participated in a number of broadcasts of Rudi Blesh's weekly radio show "This is Jazz." In November 1947, with Mole once more as one of his sidemen, Spanier took his band to the new Blue Note club in Chicago. He then worked in New York at Nick's, on Eddie Condon's television show (March 1949), with Bechet (February 1950), and in Chicago at the Blue Note and Jazz Ltd. (the latter from early 1949 to 1950), and appeared in a concert in Hollywood (October 1950). In the 1950s he toured nationally with a six-piece group that initially included Darnell Howard, Floyd Bean, and Truck Parham; having made a number of appearances at the Club Hangover in San Francisco with this ensemble, Spanier settled in the bay area in 1957 and joined Earl Hines for further engagements at the Hangover. From October 1959 he resumed touring widely with his own group, and in 1960 he toured Europe as a soloist. He retired in 1964 after appearing in a self-titled episode of the television series "Jazz Casual" and performing at the Newport Jazz Festival.

Spanier played in a clipped middle-register style that was closer to King Oliver's than Louis Armstrong's and unusual for his generation. He was not a virtuoso soloist, but his strong, simple lead parts in the New Orleans style ideally suited the music he favored from 1939, and his recordings in that year with his Ragtime Band remain models for reinterpretive traditional jazz.

Oral history material in *DLC* (American Life Histories: Manuscripts from the Federal Writers' Project, 1936–1940) and *LNT*.

See also Blues, §8.

SELECTED RECORDINGS

As leader: of Bucktown Five: Mobile Blues/Someday, Sweetheart (1924, Gen. 5405); Big Butter and Egg Man (1939, Bb 10417); At the Jazz Band Ball/Livery Stable Blues (1939, Bb 10518); Relaxin' at the Touro (1939, Bb 10532); At Sundown (1939, Bb 10719); (What did I do to be so) Black and Blue (1939, Bb 10682); *Spanier in Chicago* (1958, VJM LC2)

As sideman: C. Pierce: Bull Frog Blues/China Boy (Para. 12619); Jazz Me Blues/Sister Kate (1928, Para. 12640); Chicago Rhythm Kings: There'll be some changes made/I've found a new baby (1928, Bruns. 4001); Mound City Blue Blowers: The Darktown Strutters' Ball/You Rascal, You (1931, OK 41526)

BIBLIOGRAPHY

ChiltonW; *McCarthyB*

H. Panassié: *Douze années de jazz (1927–1938): souvenirs* (Paris, 1946), 55

G. Hoefer: "Muggsy Still a Driving, Communicative Jazzman," *DB*, xviii/9 (1951), 2

N. Shapiro and N. Hentoff, eds.: *Hear me Talkin' to ya: the Story of Jazz by the Men who Made it* (New York and London, 1955/*R*1966), 115

L. Gushee: "Muggsy Spanier," *JR*, i/2 (1958), 40

M. Jones: "Muggsy Flies in for 30 Minutes after 30 Years," *MM* (2 April 1960), 14

C. H. Garrigues: "Jazzman without a Home," *San Francisco Chronicle* (13 Feb 1961)

M. Harrison: "Backlog, 15: Muggsy Spannier [*sic*]," *JM*, x/2 (1964), 6

R. Hadlock: *Jazz Masters of the Twenties* (New York, 1965/*R*1985)

E. Ward: "Muggsy Spanier Discography," *Jazz Register*, i–ii (1965–6)

W. Esposito: "The Spanier Big Band," *JJ*, xx/10 (1967), 10

Obituary, *San Francisco Chronicle* (13 Feb 1967)

I. Crosbie: "The Big Band Muggsy Spanier," *Coda*, xii/2 (1974), 8

D. Curran: "Hear that Ragtime Band," *Selections from the Gutter: Jazz Portraits from "The Jazz Record,"* ed. A. Hodes and C. Hansen (Berkeley, CA, Los Angeles, and London, 1977), 182

A. Hubner: "Muggsy Spanier," *Selections from the Gutter: Jazz Portraits from "The Jazz Record,"* ed. A. Hodes and C. Hansen (Berkeley, CA, Los Angeles, and London, 1977), 174

J. Chilton: *Stomp Off, Let's Go! The Story of Bob Crosby's Bob Cats & Big Band* (London, 1983)

D. Fairweather, "Muggsy Spanier," *The Blackwell Guide to Recorded Jazz*, ed. B. Kernfeld (Oxford, England, and Cambridge, MA, 1991, 2/1995), 162

B. Whyatt, *Muggsy Spanier: the Lonesome Road: a Biography and Discography* (New Orleans, 1995)

Members of Muggsy Spanier's Ragtime Band at the Panther Room, Hotel Sherman, Chicago, 1939: (left to right) Bob Casey (double bass), Marty Greenberg (drums), Spanier (cornet), Georg Brunis (trombone), and Rod Cless (clarinet)

D. Coller: "Floyd Town," *Storyville 1996/7*, ed. L. Wright (Chigwell, England, 1997), 156

J. R. TAYLOR/BK

Spann, Les(lie L., Jr.) (*b* Pine Bluff, AR, 23 May 1932; *d* 24 Jan 1989). Electric guitarist and flutist. While studying music education and flute at Tennessee State University (1950–57) he performed with local bands. Although he was principally a guitarist, he frequently played flute. Following graduation he performed and recorded with Phineas Newborn (1957) and worked briefly with Ronnell Bright and then with Dizzy Gillespie (August 1958 – August 1959); in 1959 he took part in a recording session with Gillespie that resulted in two albums, *The Ebullient Mr. Gillespie* (Verve 6068) and *Have Trumpet, Will Excite* (Verve 6047). From 1959 to 1961 he toured Europe and recorded with Quincy Jones, and during the same period he recorded with Abbey Lincoln, Ben Webster, Duke Ellington, and Johnny Hodges. Spann recorded on flute as the leader of a hard-bop quintet (1960) that included Julius Watkins and Tommy Flanagan; he also made recordings as a guitarist with Nat Adderley and as a flutist and guitarist with both Benny Bailey and Randy Weston. Later he took part in sessions led by Curtis Fuller and Charlie Shavers (both 1961), Red Garland, Jerome Richardson, Wild Bill Davis, and Charles Mingus (all 1962), Duke Pearson (1965), Sonny Stitt and Eddie "Lockjaw" Davis (both 1966), and Hodges (1967).

BIBLIOGRAPHY

FeatherE
M. C. J.: "Les Spann," *Jm*, no.61 (1960), 29 [incl. discography]

Spargo, Tony. *See* SBARBARO, TONY.

Sparks, Ernie. Pseudonym of DAVID BEE.

Sparks, Melvin (Herman) [Sparks Hassan, Melvin] (*b* Houston, 22 March 1946). Electric guitarist. His middle name is taken from Texas birth records. His mother was a gospel singer in their church and his brother was a drummer. He began playing drums at the age of nine, took up guitar about two years later, and was introduced to the music of Billy Harper and Michael Carvin at a jazz night for teenagers that was held at his mother's café; he learned to play jazz and blues by accompanying recordings on the café's jukebox. While at high school he wrote arrangements for the school's jazz band and began performing with such visiting singers as Hank Ballard and Joe Turner (ii). From the age of 16 he toured with various soul singers, including Jackie Wilson and Sam Cooke, as a member of the Upsetters, which was formerly Little Richard's band.

Sparks lived briefly in Los Angeles before moving to New York in the mid-1960s. Between 1966 and 1969 he played in Brother Jack McDuff's group, in which he replaced Grant Green after a recommendation by George Benson, and from 1969 to 1972 he worked with Lou Donaldson. During the same period he took part in a number of soul-jazz recording sessions for Blue Note, with Lonnie Smith (1968–9) and the organist Reuben Wilson (1969), and for Prestige, with Charles Earland (1969), Charles Kynard, Sonny Phillips, Rusty Bryant, and Idris Muhammad (all 1970), the organist Leon Spencer (1970–2), and Sonny Stitt (1971); he made his first recording as a leader in 1970. In 1975 he converted to Islam and changed his name to Melvin Sparks Hassan, although he has continued to appear professionally under his original name. After working with Earland (1978–82) he joined Big Nick Nicholas and Hank Crawford (both 1983), and then led a group at the club Gates in New Canaan, Connecticut (mid-1980s). Sparks has recorded with, among others, Houston Person (1977, 1980), Johnny Lytle (1981), Jimmy McGriff (1983, 1988), and the organist Ron Levy (*c*1995). In the late 1990s he continued to lead own groups and to work with Crawford.

SELECTED RECORDINGS

As leader: *Spark Plug* (1971, Prst. 10016); *Akilah!* (1971, Prst. 10039); *Texas Twister* (*c*1975, Eastbound)

As sideman: L. Smith: *Think!* (1968, BN 84290); R. Wilson: *Blue Mode* (1969, BN 84343); C. Earland: *Black Talk* (1969, Prst. 7758); L. Donaldson: *Everything I Play is Funky* (1969–70, BN 84337); L. Spencer: *Sneak Preview* (1970, Prst. 10011); S. Stitt: *Turn it On!* (1971, Prst., 10012)

BIBLIOGRAPHY

K. Whitehead: "Profile: Melvin Sparks," *DB*, liii/5 (1986), 46
<http://209.249.8.78/sparks2.htm> (1999)

JOSH FERKO, GK

Sparrow. *See* PARKER-SPARROW, BRADLEY.

Spasm band. An ensemble consisting largely of homemade instruments. Spasm bands were active in New Orleans during the first three decades of the 20th century and performed a repertory of blues, ragtime, and the popular songs of the day. They were generally made up of a chord-playing instrument, such as a ukulele or guitar, a kazoo or comb-and-paper, and various percussion instruments – for example, washboard or tambourine. Some instruments associated with the "second line" of marching bands (the popular following that accompanied street parades) were also used, notably the boom-bam, a broom handle on which metal bottle-tops are nailed to give an effect similar to that of the metal discs in the shell of a tambourine.

BIBLIOGRAPHY

D. Barker: *A Life in Jazz*, ed. A. Shipton (London and New York, 1986)
F. Ramsey, Jr., and C. E. Smith, eds.: *Jazzmen: the Story of Hot Jazz Told in the Lives of the Men who Created it* (New York, 1939/*R*1977), 52

Spaulding, James (Ralph, Jr.) [Jimmy] (*b* Indianapolis, 30 July 1937). Alto saxophonist and flutist. His father, the guitarist Jimmy Spaulding, worked regionally in the 1930s and 1940s and was a member of Indiana's first interracial band, the Bobcats Orchestra (not to be confused with Bob Crosby's white band of the same name); Teddy Wilson often visited the Spauldings' home for informal playing. After beginning on a toy bugle, Spaulding took up C-melody saxophone and then alto saxophone in high school, where he doubled on clarinet and flute and developed a preference for the latter instrument. He worked locally in rhythm-and-blues bands, then enlisted in the army (1954 – August 1957) and served at an Indiana base as a musician in repertory and jazz bands; he also visited Indianapolis for performances with Freddie Hubbard and Larry Ridley in their quintet, the Jazz Contemporaries.

Spaulding studied music from autumn 1957 in Chicago, where he performed and recorded with Sun Ra. After working as a freelance in the Midwest from 1960 to 1961, he went to New York in 1962 and worked with his own group and performed and recorded with Hubbard (1962–9). He also played with Roy Haynes and Randy Weston (both *c*1965) and Max Roach (touring Europe, 1966) and recorded with Art Blakey (1963) and, for the Blue Note label, with

Grant Green (1964), Duke Pearson (1964, 1966–7), Wayne Shorter (1965, 1967), Bobby Hutcherson (1965, 1968), Stanley Turrentine, Larry Young, Horace Silver, and Hank Mobley (all 1966), and McCoy Tyner (1967). Later he recorded with Archie Shepp (1969, 1971).

While resuming his university studies Spaulding played with a variety of musicians, among them Silver, Hutcherson, Budd Johnson, Milt Jackson, and Bob Wilber, and he performed occasionally as the leader of his own small ensembles. He spent the summer of 1974 in the Duke Ellington Orchestra under Mercer Ellington, but was obliged to quit so that he could complete his degree at Livingston College, Rutgers (MusEd 1975). From 1976 through the mid-1980s he recorded only occasionally, notably with Ricky Ford (1977, 1984, 1986–7), but the album *Ashanti* (1981) by Alvin Queen includes some particularly good examples of his playing. He toured Europe with Weston at some point in the 1980s, was a member of David Murray's octet (recording in 1987 and 1992) and big band (recording in 1992), and in the early 1990s spent a period with Murray as a provisional member of the World Saxophone Quartet. During the same time he recorded again with Hutcherson and Sun Ra (both 1989) and made a succession of acclaimed albums as a leader. Spaulding is a highly creative hard-bop soloist and has a fiery, driving style on alto saxophone; his flute playing is light and lyrical.

SELECTED RECORDINGS

As leader: *James Spaulding Plays the Legacy of Duke Ellington* (1976, Sto. 1019); *Brilliant Corners* (1988, Muse 5369); *Gotstabe a Better Way!* (1988, Muse 5413); *Songs of Courage* (1991, Muse 5382); *Blues Nexus* (1993, Muse 5467); *The Smile of the Snake* (1996, HighNote 7006)

As sideman: F. Hubbard: *Breaking Point* (1964, BN 84172); W. Shorter: *The Soothsayer* (1965, BN LT988); F. Hubbard: *Backlash* (1966, Atl. 1477); D. Pearson: *Sweet Honey Bee* (1966, BN 84252); H. Mobley: *A Slice of the Top* (1966, BN LT995); W. Shaw: *Woody III* (1978, Col. JC35977); A. Queen: *Ashanti* (1981, Nilva 3402)

BIBLIOGRAPHY

Feather '60s; *Feather–Gitler '70s*

D. C. Hunt: "James Spaulding: for Spee's Sake," *J&P*, no.12 (1968), 23

D. Wallace: "James Spaulding," *JJ*, xxiii/4 (1970), 6

B. Rusch: "James Spaulding," *Cadence*, xiv/12 (1988), 5; xv/2 (1989), 12

H. Geerken and B. Hefele: *Omniverse Sun Ra* (Wartaweil, Germany, 1994)

C. Wolff: "Profile: James Spaulding: Hooking this Thing up," *Jazziz*, xvi/2 (1999), 62

ROLAND BAGGENAES/BK

Speake, Martin (John) (*b* Barnet, England, 3 April 1958). English alto saxophonist. He began playing saxophone at the age of 16 after hearing the album *The Ornette Coleman Trio at the Golden Circle* and then studied music at Southgate Technical College (1975–7) and classical saxophone at Trinity College of Music (LTCL and FTCL, 1977–81). In the 1980s he worked with the octet led by John Williams (iii) (mid-1980s), Itchy Fingers (1984–8), John Warren (1985), Simon Purcell's group Jazz Train (1986), and Julian Argüelles and Jim Mullen (both 1986–7) and as a member of a trio with the double bass player Ronan Guilfoyle and Steve Argüelles (1989). From 1988 he led his own groups, in some of which he collaborated with Paul Motian; later he toured with Motian, Bobo Stenson, and Mick Hutton in the UK and Ireland (May 2000). In the 1990s Speake worked as a sideman with, among others, Billy Jenkins (1994, recording in 1990–91), Phil Lee (1995), Stan Tracey's octet (1997), and Don Weller's big band (1998). He began teaching at the Royal Academy of Music in 1989 and at Middlesex University in 1990.

SELECTED RECORDINGS

As leader: *Amazing Grace* (1996, Spot. 558); *Trust* (1996, 33 Jazz 035); with Nikki Iles: *The Tan T'ien* (1996–7, FMR CD51-V0898)

As sideman: Itchy Fingers: *Quark* (1987, Virgin 2438); B. Jenkins: *Entertainment USA* (1990–91, Babel 9401)

BIBLIOGRAPHY

CarrJ; *ChiltonB*

J. Fordham: "The East End Triangle," *The Guardian* (5 Sept 1998)

M. Kelly: "Martin Speake," *Avant*, no.12 (1999), 52

MARK GILBERT

Spearman, Glenn (*b* New York, 14 Feb 1947; *d* Berkeley, CA, 8 Oct 1998). Tenor saxophonist. His father was an opera singer. He moved to Concord, California, with his mother when he was 11 and had his first music lessons with his stepfather, who played classical violin, clarinet, and jazz piano; he began playing jazz at the age of 19, while attending Colorado State University on an athletic scholarship. Around 1967 he transferred to San Jose State College, but shortly afterwards he left and moved to Berkeley, where he performed and studied with Charles Tyler and worked with Donald Garrett, Sonny Simmons, Prince Lasha, Frank Lowe, Bert Wilson, and the East Bay Jazz Ensemble; he also played in a group co-led by Tyler and Butch Morris, with which he appeared in Los Angeles. During the 1970s Spearman lived in Paris (from 1972), where he led the band Emergency (until 1973), and then in Rotterdam, where he joined the Dutch Jazz Society and worked in the Sunshine Creative Orchestra and with Han Bennink. In 1976 he toured Germany, France, and the Netherlands in the Sea Ensemble. Having moved to New York (1978) he worked and studied with Raphé Malik. In the early 1980s he performed with Cecil Taylor's big band at Lush Life and then played briefly in his group Unit and in his Dance Orchestra.

From 1984 Spearman lived in Oakland and in 1986 he recorded with William Parker and the drummer Paul Murphy as Trio Hurricane. In addition he led another trio, with the double bass player Ben Lindgren and the drummer Donald Robinson as his sidemen, and formed Double Trio, in which he worked with Lindgren, Robinson and the trio Room – Larry Ochs, the pianist Chris Brown, and the percussionist William Winant. He also played in a duo with Lindgren. Spearman performed in New York as a member of the New York Free Jazz Quintet alongside Malik, Parker, and Karen Borca, and in 1992 he appeared with Lisle Ellis's quartet at the DuMaurier International Jazz Festival in Vancouver, Canada. He performed in a trio with Paul Plimley and Ellis in 1994 and that same year formed the group G-Force, with Ellis, Robinson, and the guitarist James Reuthier as his sidemen. In December 1995 he directed a performance and recording of John Coltrane's *Ascension* at San Francisco's Great American Music Hall, which involved ROVA, Dave Douglas, Malik, Brown, Ellis, the double bass player George Cremaschi, and Robinson. The following year he recorded with Malik's quartet at the Fire in the Valley Festival in Amherst, Massachusetts. He taught at Mills College in Oakland from 1993. With his ferocious free-jazz style and warm timbre, Spearman created a slightly mellow version of Albert Ayler's approach of the mid-1960s. As well as tenor saxophone, he played wooden flute.

SELECTED RECORDINGS

Duos with D. Robinson: *Night after Night* (1981, Musa-Physics 0001)

As leader: of Double Trio: *Mystery Project* (1992, BS 120147-2); of G-Force: *Let it Go* (1994, Red Toucan 9308); of Double Trio: *The Fields* (1994, BS 120197-2)

As sideman: Trio Hurricane: *Suite of Winds* (1986, BS 120102-2); R. Malik: *21st Century Texts* (1991, FMP CD43); L. Ellis: *Elevations* (1993, Victo 027); on *What We Live Fo(u)r* (1994, BS 120156-2), Addressing the Ancestors; R. Malik: *Short Form* (1996, Eremite 05)

BIBLIOGRAPHY

D. Rubien: "Free-jazz Sax Man has it Down Code Perfect," *San Francisco Chronicle Datebook* (15 Dec 1991)
B. Rusch: "Glenn Spearman: Interview," *Cadence*, xx/5 (1994), 5
G. Awad: "Coda: Glenn Spearman," *Jazziz*, xii/3 (1995), 98
D. Ouellette: "Riffs: San Francisco's New Brew," *DB*, lxii/7 (1995), 10
<http://www.blacksaint.com/V2/bios/gspearman.html> (1999)
K. Waxman and R. Lopez: "The Glenn Spearman Discography," <http://www.velocity.net/~bb10k/SPEARMAN.disc.html> (2000)

GK

Speed, Chris(topher Patrick) (*b* Seattle, 12 Feb 1967). Tenor saxophonist and clarinetist. He studied classical clarinet and piano until 1986 and took up tenor saxophone in his teens; while at high school he performed locally with his classmates Andrew D'Angelo and Jim Black. Later he attended the New England Conservatory (BM 1990) in Boston, where he worked in the group Human feel with D'Angelo and Black (from 1987) and performed and recorded with Orange then Blue. After moving to New York (1992) Speed continued to play with Human Feel and formed the group Pachora (1992) with Brad Shepik, the double bass player Skuli Sverrison, and Black. In addition he joined Tim Berne's Bloodcount (1992), Dave Douglas's sextet and his octet Sanctuary (both 1993), and Myra Melford's group The Same River, Twice and Erik Friedlander's Chimera (both 1994); later he was a member of John Zorn's Bar Kokhba (1996) and worked with Mark Dresser, Ben Perowsky's trio, and the quintet Claudia, led by the drummer John Hollenbeck (all from 1996). At the Knitting Factory in February 1995 he performed his *Un-Big Band Suite* , a tribute to Albert Ayler, with an 11-piece ensemble that included the trumpeter Cuong Vu, Curtis Hasselbring, Andy Laster, D'Angelo, Ellery Eskelin, Friedlander, Dresser, and Black. Speed has also worked in Black's quartet alongside Anthony Coleman and the double bass player Tony Scherr and in Vu's Vu-tet, with which he appeared at the Tampere Jazz Happening in Finland (1998). From 1997 he has led the quartet Yeah, No, with Vu, Sverisson, and Black as his sidemen.

SELECTED RECORDINGS

As leader: *Yeah, No* (*c*1997, Songlines 1524); *Deviantics* (*c*1998, Songlines 1517)

As sideman: Orange then Blue: *While You Were Out …* (1992, GM 3028), incl. Truth is Marching In; Human Feel: *Welcome to Malpesta* (1994, New World 80450-2); T. Berne: *Lowlife: the Paris Concert* (1994, JMT 514019-2); *Poisoned Minds: the Paris Concert* (1994, JMT 514020-2); D. Douglas: *In our Lifetime* (1994, New World 80471-2); E. Friedlander: *Chimera* (1995, Avant 057); M. Melford: *The Same River, Twice* (1996, Gram. 79513); T. Berne: *Saturation Point* (1997, Screwgun 70004); J. Emery: *Spectral Domains* (1997, Enja 9344-2); Pachora: *Pachora* (*c*1997, Knitting Factory 207); J. Granelli: *Enter, a Dragon* (*c*1998, Songlines 1521); M. Dresser: *Eye'll be Seeing You* (*c*1998, Knitting Factory 211)

BIBLIOGRAPHY

T. Conrad: "Tradin' Fours: Feeling their Way," *DB*, lxiii/5 (1996), 42
<http://www.screwgunrecords.com/speed.htm> (1999) [incl. discography]

GK

Speers, Stewie [Speer, Stewart] (*b* Melbourne, Australia, 26 June 1928; *d* Sydney, 16 Sept 1986). Australian drummer. In the late 1950s he became known for his skill in several styles; he played traditional jazz with Roger Bell, Bob Barnard, Frank Traynor, and others as well as performing in a more modern idiom with Brian Brown at Jazz Center 44 in Melbourne. Later, in Sydney, he worked at El Rocco with groups led by John Sangster, Judy Bailey, the pianist Col Nolan, and Don Burrows. In 1967 he joined a rock group, Max Merritt and the Meteors, and toured the UK, where he later performed with Alexis Korner. Having returned in 1980 to Sydney, he remained active, playing with several important musicians.

SELECTED RECORDINGS

As leader with Barry Duggan: *A Tribute to Stewart* (1981, BDLP 001)

As sideman: B. Brown: *The Brian Brown Quintet* (1956, Score 006); C. Nolan: *Col Nolan and the Soul Syndicate* (1966, CBS BP233319); first issued on Tom Baker: *Jazz Live at Soup Plus* (1985, 2MBS Jazz-4), Memories of You, Someday my prince will come

BIBLIOGRAPHY

A. Bisset: *Black Roots, White Flowers: a History of Australian Jazz* (Sydney, 1979, rev. 2/1987)
B. Johnson: *The Oxford Companion to Australian Jazz* (Melbourne, Australia, 1987)
J. Clare [G. Brennan, pseud.]: *Bodgie Dada and the Cult of Cool* (Sydney, 1995)
W. Bebbington, ed: *The Oxford Companion to Australian Music* (Melbourne, Australia, 1997)

JEFF PRESSING (with JOHN WHITEOAK)/ROGER T. DEAN (recording-list)

Spencer, O'Neill [William] (*b* Cedarville, OH, 25 Nov 1909; *d* New York, 24 July 1944). Drummer. He first performed with Al Sears in Buffalo (1930) and then worked with several well-known jazz bands and leaders, among them the Mills Blue Rhythm Band (1931–6, including an appearance in the short film *Mills Blue Rhythm Band*, 1933), Henry "Red" Allen (recording in 1935 and 1936), John Kirby's sextet (July 1937–1941), and Mildred Bailey (recording from 1938 to 1942). In 1938 he played washboard and drums on several recordings with Johnny Dodds and his Chicago Boys and recorded with his own trio, which consisted of Buster Bailey (clarinet) and Billy Kyle (piano). During the same period he also worked as a singer, making recordings with Kirby, Dodds, Jimmie Noone (1937), the organist Milt Herth (1937–9), and Andy Kirk and Noble Sissle (both 1938), as well as with his own trio. Towards the end of his career he played briefly with Louis Armstrong's big band (*c* September 1941) and then rejoined Kirby (1942); suffering from tuberculosis, he collapsed while performing with Kirby in June 1943 and was obliged to retire. Spencer's drumming style was accurate and disciplined, especially in his work with large groups, where his fills were subtle and imaginative.

For illustrations *see* Kirby, john, and Mills blue rhythm band.

SELECTED RECORDINGS

(recorded for Decca unless otherwise indicated)

As leader: Afternoon in Africa (1938, 1873); Baby, won't you please come home (1938, 1941)

As sideman: Mills Blue Rhythm Band: Ridin' in Rhythm (1933, Col. CB734); M. Herth: The Dippsy Doodle/That's a Plenty (1937, 1553); J. Dodds: Wild Man Blues (1938, 2111); Peetie Wheatstraw: Little Low Mellow Mama (1939, 7578); B. L. Barker: You ain't had no blues/Marked Woman (1939, 7648); Helen Proctor: Cheatin' on Me/Blues at Midnight (1939, 7666); J. Kirby: Close Shave (1941, Vic. 27568); Mabel Robinson: Me and my Chauffeur/I've got too many blues (1942, 8601)

BIBLIOGRAPHY

ChiltonW; *FeatherE*
A. von Konow: "Nyyansernas Maestare O'Neill Spencer" [O'Neill Spencer, the Master of Subtle Variation], *Orkester journalen*, lviii/9 (1990), 25
B. Korall: *Drummin' Men: the Heartbeat of Jazz: the Swing Years* (New York and Toronto, 1990), 322

T. DENNIS BROWN/BK

Spendel, Christoph (Josef) (*b* Bytom, Poland, 19 July 1955). German pianist. He received piano lessons from the age of five. Having moved to Germany in 1963, he later studied the instrument at the Robert Schumann Institut in Düsseldorf and the Folkwang Hochschule in Essen. He started his professional career with the band Jazztrack (1975–9) and then worked with the guitarist Toto Blanke (1978–9) and in a celebrated duo with Wolfgang Schlüter (1978–90). From 1983 he was active principally with his own bands. He appeared at major European and international festivals, gave concerts as an unaccompanied soloist (from 1978), and performed with such musicians as Albert Mangelsdorff, Christof Lauer, and Wolfgang Dauner. On his own recordings he collaborated with many American colleagues, including Bill Evans (iii), Jeremy Steig, Steve Gadd, Bob Mintzer, Lonnie Plaxico, and Jim Pepper, as well as with Michal Urbaniak. In the late 1980s Spendel was a member of the popular band Special EFX, based in New York. From the late 1990s he was involved in appearances as a soloist, with his acoustic band and his Electric Band (formed in 1997), and in a duo with Michael Sagmeister. Spendel is equally comfortable with the standard jazz repertory and with percussion-dominated funk-, hip-hop-, and Latin-influenced fusion music; his jazz playing may be heard to advantage on *Paula* (on the album *Back to Basics*, 1987, Blue Flame 4007-2), his use of hip-hop elements on *Flight 408* (1997, BMG 3985019-2, 1997), and his incorporation of world music on *Warrior for Peace: in Memory of Mr. Yitzhak Rabin* (on *The Three Worlds*, 1999, Konnex 5088). He is also a noted teacher, and in 1999 he was appointed professor at the Musikhochschule in Frankfurt am Main.

BIBLIOGRAPHY

G. Endress: "Jazztrack: mit Jazz lässt sich leben," *JP*, xxiv/8 (1975), 3
H. Bruns: "Christoph Spendel: Piano-Crossover von Klassik, Jazz und HipHop," *Keyboards*, (1998), Dec, 80
U. Goeman: "Christoph Spendel: the Best of Two Worlds," *JP*, xlviii/1 (1999), 3
<http://www.spendel.com/english/index.html> (1999)

WOLFRAM KNAUER

Sperling, Jack [John, Jr.] (*b* Trenton, NJ, 17 Aug 1922). Drummer. He started on violin at about the age of four, but after a short time changed to drums. Largely self-taught, he began playing in local professional bands when he was 15. His first major engagement, from July 1941 to the following spring, was with Bunny Berigan's big band. He then went to New York, where he studied drumming for several months. During his military service (1942–6) he played in navy bands, including one led by Tex Beneke (1943–5), and following his discharge he was a member of the Glenn Miller ghost band, led by Beneke (March 1946 – autumn 1949), whose pianist was Henry Mancini. From 1949 to 1954 he played with Les Brown's big band, and from 1954 to 1957 he appeared on Bob Crosby's daily television show. He also recorded with Eddie Miller (*c*1957) and with Dave Pell's octet (1953, 1955, 1957). In the late 1950s Mancini used Sperling on soundtracks for the television shows "Peter Gunn" and "Mr. Lucky," and soon he became one of the busiest studio drummers in Los Angeles; from 1959 to 1972 he was a staff musician for NBC. As time permitted he played in local clubs, and he recorded with Pete Fountain (1959–63), Crosby and Benny Goodman (both 1960), Charlie Barnet (1962, 1966), Brown (1963), Bob Florence (*c*1968), and others; in 1961 and 1962 he joined Fountain for a few weeks at Fountain's new French Quarter Inn in New Orleans. After leaving NBC in 1972 he often performed with Brown (through the 1990s), and otherwise worked as a freelance; he appeared regularly at festivals, notably in a concert at the Aurex Jazz Festival in Tokyo in 1983.

An early imitator of Gene Krupa's flamboyant solo style, Sperling soon concentrated on timekeeping and taking a supportive role within the rhythm section. His skill as a mainstream drummer endeared him to many famous bandleaders and entertainers during his career and earned him a place in many hundreds of recording sessions.

SELECTED RECORDINGS

As sideman: D. Pell: *I Had the Craziest Dream* (1955–7, Cap. T925); B. Crosby: *The Bob Cats in Hi Fi* (1957, Coral 57170); H. Mancini: *The Music from Peter Gunn* (1958, RCA LPM1956), P. Fountain: *Pete Fountain Presents Jack Sperling and his Fascinating Rhythm* (1961, Coral 57341); C. Barnet: *Big Band 1967* (1966, Vault 9004); B. Florence: *Pet Project* (*c*1968, WP 1860); P. Hucko: *Peanuts Hucko with his Pied Piper Quintet* (1979, World Jazz 15); L. Brown: *Digital Swing* (1986, Fan. 9650)

SELECTED FILMS AND VIDEOS

Les Brown and the Band of Renown (1949); Connee Boswell and Les Brown's Orchestra (1950); Stars of Jazz (1957); The Swingin' Singin' Years (1960); Jazz Scene USA: Pete Fountain Sextet (1962)

BIBLIOGRAPHY

FeatherE
"A Man Can Stand it Only So Long," *DB*, xxix/1 (1962), 11
T. Borst: "Portraits: Jack Sperling," *MD*, vii/3 (1983), 68
B. Korall: "Jack Sperling: a Lifetime of Swing," *MD*, xx/2 (1996), 90

THOMAS OWENS

Sphere. Bop quartet. It was organized in the early 1980s by the tenor saxophonist Charlie Rouse, the pianist Kenny Barron, the double bass player Buster Williams, and the drummer Ben Riley. Its first album, *Four in One* (1982, Elek. Mus. 60166), was devoted entirely to the music of Thelonious (Sphere) Monk, though Barron explained later that he did not realize at the time that Sphere was Monk's middle name, and had selected the name independently. Thereafter the group performed a repertory of standards and the members' own compositions. Sphere recorded again in 1983, 1985, and 1987 (for further details *see* WILLIAMS, BUSTER); the 1985 album is a recording of a concert the group gave in Italy. Rouse died in 1988; with Gary Bartz on saxophone, the group re-formed for a recording in 1997 and tour in 1998.

BIBLIOGRAPHY

J. Levenson: "Sphere: Monk and Beyond," *DB*, li/1 (1984), 22
K. Franckling: "'A Universal Circle': Sphere," *JT* (1987), Dec, 9

Spider. Nickname of CYRIL HAYNES.

Spikes brothers. The brothers Benjamin "Reb" Spikes (*b* Dallas, 31 Oct 1888; *d* Los Angeles, 24 Feb 1982), a pianist, and Johnny (John Curry) Spikes (*b* Dallas, 22 July 1881; *d* Los Angeles, 28 June 1955), a drummer, started their careers playing duets in 1906. Details regarding both Reb Spikes (his date of death) and Johnny Spikes (his full name and birth and death dates) are taken from the California death index. They operated the Pastime Theater in Muskogee, Oklahoma, booking traveling jazz bands and blues singers, engaged Jelly Roll Morton in 1911, and toured with Morton in McCabe's minstrel show. In 1915 Reb played saxophone on San Francisco's Barbary Coast in Sid Le Protti's So Different Orchestra. The brothers settled in Los Angeles in 1919, opened their music store at 12th Street and Central Avenue, and became a major force in the local music scene. Reb soon formed the Majors and Minors Orchestra. The Spikes brothers composed and published music (for example, *Someday Sweetheart*, 1920); they published Jelly Roll Morton's *Froggie Moore* in 1923 and wrote the lyrics to Morton's *Wolverine Blues*. They also formed the Sunshine Record Company and in 1921 or 1922 produced the first African-American New Orleans jazz recordings, by Kid Ory's Creole Jazz Band (*see* Spikes' seven pods of pepper). In the same year they opened the Dreamland Café, a nightclub at 4th and Central. Ory's Creole Jazz Band was featured at their after-hours venue, Wayside Park Café, at Leak's Lake, in the Watts district of Los Angeles; Morton booked the bands, and King Oliver's group played there in 1922. The Spikes brothers' music store closed during the Depression, and Reb Spikes spent his later years in the real estate business.

BIBLIOGRAPHY

F. Levin: "The Spikes Brothers: a Los Angeles Saga," *JJ*, iv/12 (1951), 12
R. Macnic: "Reb Spikes: Music Maker," *Sv*, no.21 (1969), 100
T. Stoddard: *Jazz on the Barbary Coast* (Chigwell, England, 1982, rev. 2/1998)

FLOYD LEVIN

Spikes' Seven Pods of Pepper. Recording group. In 1921 or spring 1922 (sources disagree), under the direction of the Spikes Brothers agency and using the name Spikes' Seven Pods of Pepper, Kid Ory's Original Creole Jazz Band became the first African-American jazz band involving musicians from New Orleans to record commercially (earlier jazz tracks were recorded by Wilbur Sweatman, W. C. Handy's Memphis Blues Band, Eubie Blake's Jazzola Orchestra, and Mamie Smith's Jazz Hounds). Ory's group had been active on the West Coast (first as Kid Ory's Brownskinned Babies) from 1919. The personnel for the recording band consisted of Ory (trombone), Mutt Carey (cornet), Freddie Washington (piano), Ed "Montudi" Garland (whose double bass, however, is inaudible), Ben Borders (drums), and Dink Johnson, a pianist and drummer who had recently taken up clarinet and replaced Ory's usual clarinetist, Wade Whaley. The sextet recorded two titles, *Ory's Creole Trombone* and *Society Blues* (1921/1922, Nordskog 3009), but during the same session, as Ory's Sunshine Orchestra, it made a further four as the accompanying band for the singers Roberta Dudley and Ruth Lee.

BIBLIOGRAPHY

R. MacNic: "Reb Spikes: Music Maker," *Sv*, no.21 (1969), 100
P. Vacher: Liner notes, D. Johnson: *Dink's Good Time Music* (Nola 12, 1977)
H. Rye, Liner notes, *Kid Ory and his Creole Jazz Band, 1922–1947* (Document 1002, 1996)
For further bibliography *see* Nordskog.

MIKE HAZELDINE

Spill. A Gliss falling from the end of a note.

Spirits of Rhythm. String band. It grew out of a group known variously as the Sepia Nephews, Ben Bernie's Nephews, and the Five Cousins, which included the tiple players Wilbur and Douglas Daniels and (from 1929) the singer and tiple player Leo Watson. After the ensemble was augmented in 1932 by the addition of the guitarist Teddy Bunn it changed its name to the Spirits of Rhythm, and it first recorded under this title the following year; a fifth member, Virgil Scoggins, played various homemade percussion instruments. The band worked successfully in New York on 52nd Street, in Hollywood, and on tour, becoming one of the most influential string bands of the decade (*see* String band) and acquiring a special significance for its role in establishing the Onyx as a successful jazz club in 1934; it was noted for its driving rhythmic style and good-humored songs (often with comic or nonsensical lyrics). It may be heard to advantage on such recordings as *I got rhythm/Rhythm* (1933, Bruns. 01715) and may be seen on the soundies *Yes, Indeed* and *Alabamy Bound* (both 1941). The Spirits of Rhythm remained active until 1946 and at various times included Wellman Braud, Marlowe Morris, and Zutty Singleton. In 1934 it made recordings accompanying Red McKenzie.
See also Tiple.

BIBLIOGRAPHY

A. Shaw: *The Street that Never Slept: New York's Fabled 52nd Street* (New York, 1971/*R*1977 as *52nd Street: the Street of Jazz*)
M. Jones: Liner notes, *The Spirits of Rhythm, 1933–34* (JSP 1088, 1985)

FRANK DRIGGS

Spivak, Charlie [Charles] (*b* Kiev, Ukraine, 17 Feb 1907; *d* Greenville, SC, 1 March 1982). Trumpeter and bandleader. He arrived in the USA as a small child and grew up in New Haven, Connecticut, where he began to learn trumpet at the age of ten. Between 1924 and 1931 he worked mostly with an orchestra led by the violinist Paul Specht. Although he was not a jazz musician, Spivak was in great demand among jazz bandleaders during the 1930s for his sweet tone and wide range, and his playing enlivened the trumpet sections of Ben Pollack (1931–4), the Dorsey Brothers (late 1934 – spring 1935), Ray Noble (1935), Bob Crosby (November 1937 – August 1938), Tommy Dorsey (August 1938 – *c* June 1939), and Jack Teagarden (1939); in 1936–7 he was said to be the highest-paid studio musician in New York. In November 1939 Glenn Miller financed Spivak's first orchestra; this soon disbanded, but his second group, which included such sidemen as Dave Tough (1941–2) and Willie Smith (1943), prospered until 1959, when it also broke up. Spivak, who was billed as "the sweetest horn in the world," enjoyed great popularity as the result of his band's success. After working in Florida, Las Vegas, and South Carolina he led a new orchestra in the late 1970s on a tour of the South. In 1983, the year after his death, his collection of music was donated to Furman University (Greenville, South Carolina).

SELECTED RECORDINGS

As leader: Let's Go Home (1941, OK 6366); Autumn Nocturne (1941, OK 6476); Star Dreams (1941, OK 6546); *The Uncollected Charlie Spivak* (1943–6, Hindsight 105)
As sideman: G. Miller: Time on my Hands (1937, Bruns. 7915); B. Crosby: South Rampart Street Parade (1937, Decca 15038)

SELECTED FILMS AND VIDEOS

Hoagy Carmichael (1939); Hop, Skip and Jump (1942); Pin-up Girl (1943); Follow the Boys (1944); Charlie Spivak and his Orchestra (1949)

BIBLIOGRAPHY

ChiltonW
G. T. Simon: *The Big Bands* (New York, 1967, rev. 4/1981), 426
C. Garrod: *Charlie Spivak and his Orchestra* (Spotswood, NJ, and Zephyrhills, FL, 1974, rev. 3/1996) [discography]
Z. Knauss: *Conversations with Jazz Musicians* (Detroit, 1977), 178
G. Buck: "Charlie Spivak," *Jazzology Newsletter*, viii/3 (1982), 2
J. Chilton: *Stomp Off, Let's Go! The Story of Bob Crosby's Bob Cats & Big Band* (London, 1983), 74

SCOTT YANOW

Spivey, Victoria (Regina) (*b* Houston, 15 Oct 1906; *d* New York, 3 Oct 1976). Singer and pianist. The daughter of the leader of a string band, she learned piano as a child and by the age of 12 was performing at the Lincoln Theatre in Dallas. After working with local artists, including the blues singer and guitarist Blind Lemon Jefferson, she commenced her recording career in St. Louis; *Black Snake Blues*, to her own piano accompaniment, was an instant success. Her voice was lean and nasal and she made much use of moaned syllables. A partnership in the late 1920s with Lonnie Johnson produced many notable titles. In 1929 Spivey appeared in *Hallelujah!*, an all-African-American film directed by King Vidor, and also recorded several titles with Henry "Red" Allen's New York Orchestra. She toured with her husband, the dancer Billy Adams, in the 1930s; she also worked with Louis Armstrong, and occasionally made recordings – often of a mildly risqué nature – such as *Good Cabbage*. In the late 1940s she settled in New York, where she continued to perform in jazz clubs. In 1962 she formed her own Spivey record company and recorded a number of well-known singers as well as her own works, reviving an old partnership with Johnson on *Somebody's got to go*. Her voice remained strong and her vivacious stage personality undiminished even in her last years. She performed in Europe in 1963 and toured the USA up to the time of her death.

Oral history material in *NN-Sc* (HBc).

SELECTED RECORDINGS

As unaccompanied soloist: Black Snake Blues (1926, OK 8338)
As leader: T. B. Blues (1927, OK 8494); Murder in the First Degree (1927, OK 8581); Moaning the Blues (1929, Vic. 38546); Good Cabbage (1937, Voc. 03639); *The Queen and her Knights* (1965, Spivey 1006), incl. Somebody's got to go
As sideman with H. Allen: Funny Feathers Blues (1929, Vic. 38088)

BIBLIOGRAPHY

J. Failows: "Victoria Spivey: Queen Vee," *Coda*, v/7 (1963), 2
D. Stewart-Baxter: "Blues & Views," *JJ*, xxii/7 (1964), 22
"Blues Elpees on the Spivey Label," *JM*, xi/7 (1965), 25
V. Wilmer: "Victoria: the Black Queen with Class," *MM* (13 Sept 1975), 38
P. Garon and A. O'Neal: "Victoria Spivey, 1906–1976," *Living Blues*, no.29 (1976), 5
S. Harris: *Blues Who's Who: a Biographical Dictionary of Blues Singers* (New Rochelle, NY, 1979/*R*1994)
S. Placksin: *American Women in Jazz, 1900 to the Present: their Words, Lives, and Music* (New York, 1982, London, 1985, as *Jazzwomen, 1900 to the Present: their Words, Lives, and Music*), 33
D. D. Harrison: *Black Pearls: Blues Queens of the 1920s* (New Brunswick, NJ, 1988), 146

PAUL OLIVER

Splasc(h). Italian record company and label. It was founded in 1982 as a cooperative (from a financial point of view), with its president, Peppo Spagnoli, managing its operations. Until 1999 the company recorded only Italian jazz. It offered a fresh outlet to young musicians emerging in the 1980s and later issued recordings by both new players and such established masters as Gianluigi Trovesi, Paolo Fresu, Paolo Damiani, Luca Flores, Stefano Battaglia, and Pino Minafra; Splasc(h) became the principal label documenting the recent history of Italian jazz. In 1990 it initiated a 500 series, reissuing historical albums of Italian avant-garde jazz, and in 1999 it started a new series with such American musicians as Sheila Jordan, Anthony Braxton, and Butch Morris. (F. Fini, *Splasc(h): a Label Discography*, Imola, Italy, 1997)

STEFANO ZENNI

Splash cymbal. A small cymbal used for special and novelty effects; *see* DRUM SET, §I, 5.

Spoerri, Bruno (*b* Zurich, 16 Aug 1935). Swiss saxophonist, composer, and electronic sound designer. After studying psychology, he took up a career in film music composing and sound recording, specializing from 1965 in electronic music; in 1968 he began to give unaccompanied concerts in this medium. He also played in and led modern jazz groups and jazz-rock groups (including Jazz Rock Experience, which he co-led with Hans Kennel from 1969 to 1971), and from 1971 to 1977 he served as music director for the Zurich Jazz Festival. Spoerri taught computer music at the conservatory in Zurich and elsewhere and in 1985 became a director of the Swiss Center for Computer Music; he formed a duo with Reto Weber and played jazz with the Mulligan Project and in the quartet Movin' On, consisting of Albert Mangelsdorff, Christy Doran, and Weber.

SELECTED RECORDINGS

Duos with R. Weber: *Controlled Risk* (1988, Konnex 5017)
As sideman: on *Switzerjazz* (1995, TCB 96452), The Survivors: In a Sentimental Mood, It's you or no one; A. Mangelsdorff: *Shake, Shuttle and Blow* (1999, Enja 9374-2)

BIBLIOGRAPHY

<http://www.computerjazz.ch> (2000) [incl. discography by O. Flückiger]

OTTO FLÜCKIGER

Spontaneous Music Ensemble [SME, Spontaneous Music Orchestra, SMO]. British free-jazz group. It was founded as a cooperative band by the drummer John Stevens and the saxophonist Trevor Watts late in 1965, and in January 1966 began an important engagement at the Little Theatre Club, London. Stevens worked consistently with the group until his death in 1994, providing a connecting thread through its many changes in personnel. Watts left temporarily in 1967. Singers were first included in 1969, but the group was pared down to a duo (Stevens and Watts) in 1973, and later worked for a time as the 20-piece Spontaneous Music Orchestra (from 1975). From the 1980s the group has functioned mainly as a trio. Among its members have been the guitarists Derek Bailey and Roger Smith, the violinist Nigel Coombes, the trumpeters Ian Carr and Kenny Wheeler, the double bass players Barry Guy and Dave Holland, the saxophonists John Butcher and Evan Parker, the trombonist Paul Rutherford, and the singers Maggie Nicols, Julie Tippetts, and Norma Winstone. One of the finest free-jazz bands, the Spontaneous Music Ensemble performed its collective improvisations in a nonhierarchical, nonlinear, often abstract style, frequently involving dialogues between the musicians with no preconceived structures of any sort.

SELECTED RECORDINGS

Withdrawal (1966, Emanem 4020); *Summer 1967* (1967, Emanem 4005); *Karyobin* (1968, Isl. 9079); *Face to Face* (1973, Emanem 303); *Eight-five Minutes*, pts i–ii (1974, Emanem 3401–02); *Hot and Cold Heroes* (1980, 1991, Emanem 4008); *A New Distance* (1994, Acta 8)

BIBLIOGRAPHY

GrayF; *WickesIBJ*, i
V. Schonfield: "Caught in the Act: Spontaneous Music Ensemble/Derek Bailey, Little Theatre Club," *DB*, xxxv/1 (1968), 41
R. Williams: "SME on Record," *MM* (7 March 1970), 8
M. Harrison: "The Spontaneous Music Ensemble," *J&B*, ii/12 (1973), 8
M. Patton: "SME," *MM* (11 June 1977), 39
P. Renaud: *La discographie du jazz anglais* (Chaumont, France, 1985)
E. Jost: *Europas Jazz, 1960–1980* (Frankfurt am Main, Germany, 1987), 280
R. Parry: "Spontaneous Music Ensemble," *Coda*, no.218 (1988), 22
For further bibliography *see* STEVENS, JOHN.

SIMON ADAMS

Spoon. Nickname of JIMMY WITHERSPOON.

Spörri, Bruno. *See* SPOERRI, BRUNO.

Spotlite (i). The name of several nightclubs, notably one in New York; *see* Nightclubs and other venues.

Spotlite (ii). Record company and label. The company was established by Tony Williams (who should not be confused with the drummer of the same name) in 1968. Though originally based in London, in 1974 it moved to Sawbridgeworth, Hertfordshire. Its first release (in a limited pressing of 99 copies) was of broadcasts by Billy Eckstine's orchestra; this was followed by the comprehensive reissue (on six LPs) of all the available material recorded by Charlie Parker for Dial. Eventually the company rereleased Dial's entire catalogue, and made further contributions to the collecting and organizing of Parker's material when it compiled sets of his recordings made in Sweden, France, and the USA. A great deal of broadcast material from the 1940s and 1950s was issued in a well-received series, Jazz off the Air. In 1973 Spotlite began making new recordings, the first of which was an album made in London by Pepper Adams. During the 1970s the company was largely responsible for rekindling interest in such bop musicians as Joe Albany, Al Haig, and Red Rodney, and in the 1980s it began to provide an important outlet for the work of such English musicians as Peter King and Don Rendell. By 1987 Spotlite had issued more than a hundred LPs, and with the advent of compact discs it began to concentrate on making new recordings by such underrepresented British artists as Jim Richardson, John Williams (iii), Martin Speake, Brian Dee, Harry Beckett, Dave Cliff, John Horler, and Elaine Delmar. In 1990 Spotlite purchased the Dial catalogue from Ross Russell. It should not be confused with Spot Lite, a pop and country-and-western label founded in 1989.

MARK GARDNER/MARK GILBERT

Sprague, Peter (Tripp) (*b* Cleveland, 11 Oct 1955). Electric guitarist. He was brought up in Colorado until he was eight, when his family moved to Del Mar, California. At the age of 12 he began playing guitar and later he studied with Pat Metheny in Boston (1976) and with Yoshiaki Masuo in New York. Sprague formed the Dance of the Universe Orchestra in San Diego and worked with Bob Mover in Montreal and New York (recording in 1977), then returned to San Diego, where he continued to work in the 1990s. He played with Charles McPherson and occasionally with Chick Corea, and recorded as a freelance with the GRP All Star Big Band (1992), David Benoit (1992, 1994), and Billy Childs (1994). In 1988 he began teaching at the Musicians Institute in Los Angeles.

SELECTED RECORDINGS

As leader: *Dance of the Universe* (1979, Xan. 176); *The Message Sent on the Wind* (1982, Xan. 193)

As sideman: C. McPherson: *Free Bop!* (1978, Xan. 170); D. Benoit: on *Letter for Evan* (1992, GRP 9687-2), Take 6, Waiting for Love

BIBLIOGRAPHY

J. Ferguson: "Peter Sprague: Bebopper Meets Synth," *GP*, xx/7 (1986), 66

GK

Spring, Bryan (*b* London, 24 Aug 1945). English drummer. He took up drums at the age of six and was largely self-taught, though he later studied with Philly Joe Jones. In the early 1960s he worked as a freelance musician in London, then joined Stan Tracey, with whom he performed and recorded between 1965 and 1977; he may be heard to advantage on Tracey's album *Bracknell Connection* (1976, Steam 103). During the same period he played and recorded with Frank Ricotti (1967–9), the octet of John Williams (iii), Joe Harriott (1969), Tubby Hayes, the Bebop Preservation Society, led by Bill Le Sage (1971 – autumn 1972), Klaus Doldinger's Passport (1972), and Ian Carr's Nucleus (1974); he also joined Keith Tippett's Centipede, a group co-led by Dick Morrissey and the guitarist Terry Smith (1975), and the quartet of Dick Heckstall-Smith (1976). In 1979 he became joint leader with Don Weller of the Weller–Spring Quartet, with which he recorded the same year (*Commit No Nuisance*, Affinity 44); the group toured with Hannibal Peterson in 1981 and remained active into the early 1990s. In 1992 Spring joined Alan Skidmore's quartet, with which he can be heard on *East to West* (1992, Miles Music 08). From the mid-1990s he led his own quartet and trio.

BIBLIOGRAPHY

CarrJ; *ChiltonB*; *FeatherE*
R. Cotterrell, ed.: *Jazz Now: the Jazz Centre Society Guide* (London, 1976)
P. Renaud: *La discographie du jazz anglais* (Chaumont, France, 1985)

DIGBY FAIRWEATHER/SIMON ADAMS, BK

Springer, Joe [Joseph] (*b* New York, 22 May 1916; *d* Florida, Dec 1985). Pianist. He first played professionally in 1931 in Coney Island, New York. In 1935 he worked with Wingy Manone, and in 1940 he played at the Hickory House with Louis Prima, with whom he made his recording début. He then joined Buddy Rich and performed and made recordings (including *That Drummer's Band*, 1942, Col. 36819) with Gene Krupa (1942–3). Thereafter he worked with Oscar Pettiford, Tiny Grimes, with whom he recorded *Groovin' with Grimes* (first issued on *The Changing Face of Harlem: the Savoy Sessions*, 1944, Savoy 2208), Ben Webster, Charlie Barnet, Jimmy McPartland, and others; in the mid-1940s he was a regular accompanist for Billie Holiday. In 1952 Springer played briefly with Rich, and during the 1960s he worked as a freelance in New York before moving to Florida. The social security death index, from which his date of death is taken, gives his last known residence there as Cocoa and states that he died in Florida.

based on *ChiltonW*/HOWARD RYE

Sproles, Victor (*b* Chicago, 18 Nov 1927). Double bass player. After private musical study, followed by army service, he worked as house double bass player at the French Poodle, Chicago. He then took up a residency at the Bee Hive, where as a member of Norman Simmons's trio (with Vernel Fournier) he played with such visiting performers as Charlie Parker and Wardell Gray (both 1955), Sonny Stitt, Lester Young, and Dexter Gordon. During this period he also worked with Sun Ra, with whom he recorded regularly in 1956–7. After the Bee Hive closed in 1956 Sproles recorded with Stan Getz (1958), performed and recorded in Chicago with Ira Sullivan (1958–9), and toured and recorded with Johnny Griffin and Eddie "Lockjaw" Davis (both 1960). He then toured Europe and Japan with Carmen McRae (recording in 1963–4 and appearing in "Carmen McRae," an episode of the television series "Jazz Casual," 1963); Simmons was also one of McRae's sidemen during this time. For two periods between 1964 and 1968 Sproles worked with Art Blakey's Jazz Messengers, again touring Europe and Japan; he may be seen in the episode "Art Blakey and the Jazz Messengers" from the BBC television series "Jazz 625" (1965). In addition he recorded with Lee Morgan (1965, 1967), Lee Konitz (1966), and Andrew Hill (1968). Between

1969 and 1972 he often worked at the Half Note, New York, with Al Cohn and Zoot Sims, Anita O'Day, Jimmy Rushing, and James Moody. In 1969 he began a long association with Clark Terry, with whom he performed at the Montreal Expo and toured Europe in 1975. Sproles played with Simmons again in 1981 at the Chicago Kool Jazz Festival, and, with other musicians who had formerly worked at the Bee Hive (including Clifford Jordan), the two men recorded the album *Hyde Park after Dark* in celebration of the club's heyday.

SELECTED RECORDINGS

As sideman: R. Rodney: *Modern Music from Chicago* (1955, Fan. 3208); I. Sullivan: *Nicky's Tune* (1958, Del. 422); L. Morgan: *The Rumproller* (1965, BN 84199); C. Terry: *Ain't Misbehavin'* (1979, PT 2312105); Hyde Park after Dark: *Hyde Park after Dark* (1981, BH 7014)

BIBLIOGRAPHY

Feather–Gitler '70s

J.-L. Ginibre and P. Carles: "Dictionnaire de la contrebasse," *Jm*, no.166 (1969), 56

J. Litweiler: Liner notes, *Hyde Park after Dark* (BH 7014, 1983)

WILLIAM S. BROCKMAN/BK

Spyro Gyra. Jazz-rock group, founded in 1974 in Buffalo by the alto saxophonist Jay Beckenstein and the pianist Jeremy Wall. From around 1975 or 1976 the group's members included the electric guitarist Chet Catallo (to 1984), the electric bass guitarist David Wolford (to 1981), the drummer Eli Konikoff (to 1983), and the percussionist Rubens Bassini (to 1980); Wall was replaced by the keyboard player Tom Schuman in 1978, but he continued to work with the band as a producer, composer, arranger, and studio pianist. This long-lived ensemble kept its members for reasonably lengthy periods of time, and this stability added to the cohesive nature of its sound; among later sidemen were the electric guitarist Julio Fernandez (from 1984), the electric bass guitarists Kim Stone (*c*1981–6), Roberto Vally (1987), Oscar Cartaya (1988–92), and Scott Ambush (from 1992), the drummers Richie Morales (1983–91) and Joel Rosenblatt (from 1991), and the percussionists Gerardo Velez (*c*1980–85), and Manolo Badrena (*c*1985–7). In its first decade the group's albums also involved numerous studio musicians, most notably the vibraphonist Dave Samuels, who by 1983 had become a regular member; Samuels toured with the band through 1993 and recorded with it into the late 1990s.

Spyro Gyra acquired a loyal following in Buffalo soon after it was formed; its name is a misspelling of spirogyra, a biological term Beckenstein jokingly gave a club owner as the group's name. Its first recording, issued on an independent label, achieved considerable commercial success, and its second album, *Morning Dance* (1979), became popular with rock audiences, but the group's emphasis on instrumental music rather than songs prevented it from achieving widespread exposure on radio. Much of the ensemble's popularity, therefore, was generated by means of performances. During the 1970s Spyro Gyra undertook several long, demanding tours of small clubs across the USA; by the end of the decade it had gained enough of an audience to fill the major concert halls. From the 1980s it toured the world, performed at the Kool and JVC festivals in New York, among others, and continued to record with substantial success; in 1997 it released its twentieth recording in 20 years (*20/20*). Beckenstein's mellifluous playing and Wall's production have consistently helped to define the group's sound, which is characterized by funk and Latin rhythms and structures derived from those of popular songs. Transcriptions of some of the group's compositions appear in *Catching the Sun: plus Highlights from Morning Dance and Spyro Gyra* (Buffalo, NY, 1980) and *The Best of Spyro Gyra: Original Scores for Saxophone, Keyboards, Guitar, Bass, Drums & Percussion* (Milwaukee, *c*1989).

SELECTED RECORDINGS

(recorded for MCA unless otherwise indicated)

Spyro Gyra (1976, Amherst 1014); *Morning Dance* (1979, Infinity 9004); *Catching the Sun* (1980, 5108); *Carnaval* (1980, 5149); *Freetime* (1981, 5238); *Incognito* (1982, 5368); *City Kids* (1983, 5431); *Access All Areas* (1983, 6893); *Alternating Currents* (1986, 5606); *Breakout* (1986, 5753); *20/20* (1997, GRP 9867)

BIBLIOGRAPHY

J. H. Hunt: "Spyro Gyra," *DB*, xlvi/8 (1979), 33

J. Aikin: "Tom Schuman and Jeremy Wall: Synthesizers and Smokebombs with Spyro Gyra," *Keyboard*, vii/8 (1981), 16

P. Rothbart: "Spyro Gyra: Relaxin' at 30,000 Volts," *DB*, xlviii/10 (1981), 14 [incl. discography]

G. Santoro: "The Spyro Gyra Interview," *DB*, liii/9 (1986), 20 [incl. discography]

H. Grey: "Spyro Gyra: Perfect Quest," *JT*, xxv/4 (1995), 42

J. Widran: "Tradin' Fours: Unsuspecting Legends," *DB*, lxiv/9 (1997), 37

<http://www.spyrogyra.com> (1998)

PATRICK T. WILL/GK

Squadronaires. British dance band. It was formed in 1940 as the principal dance orchestra of the RAF and comprised musicians from leading British dance bands. Among its original personnel were George Chisholm, Tommy McQuater, the saxophonist Andy McDevitt, the pianist Ronnie Aldrich, and the drummer Jock Cummings. It broadcast regularly on radio and made recordings for Decca (e.g., *That's a Plenty*, 1941, F8127); its repertory included a number of big-band versions of well-known dixieland numbers. By 1947 the Squadronaires had become a civilian orchestra; it continued performing and recording under the leadership of Aldrich until it disbanded in 1964.

Oral history material in *GBLnsa* ("Miller, Jimmy").

BIBLIOGRAPHY

"There's Something in the Air," *Fanfare*, iv/6 (1946), 4

A. McCarthy: *The Dance Band Era: the Dancing Decades from Ragtime to Swing, 1910–1950* (London, 1971), 142

T. Middleton: *The Squadronaires R. A. F. Dance Orchestra: an Exploratory Discography, 1940–1945* (London, 1976)

——: *The Squadronaires*, i: *1940–1946* (London, 1996) [discography]

NEVIL SKRIMSHIRE

Squires, Bruce (Willmarth) (*b* Berkeley, CA, 21 Jan 1910; *d* North Hollywood, CA, 8 May 1981). Trombonist. His middle name is taken from California death records. He first played in the early 1930s with lesser-known bands. From May 1935 to February 1937 he was with Ben Pollack, and among the recordings he made with the group are *Spreadin' knowledge around/Zoom zoom zoom* (1936, Voc. 3342), issued under the name the Dean and his Kids. Thereafter Squires played with Jimmy Dorsey (February 1937 – January 1938), Gene Krupa (January 1938 – March 1939), Benny Goodman (May–August 1939), Harry James (1939–40), Freddie Slack (1940–41), and Bob Crosby (summer 1942). After World War II he worked mainly as a studio musician, and he continued to perform into the 1970s.

BIBLIOGRAPHY

ConnorBG

J. Chilton: *Stomp Off, Let's Go! The Story of Bob Crosby's Bob Cats & Big Band* (London, 1983)

based on *ChiltonW*

Stabenow, Thomas (*b* Kirchberg, Germany, 11 Sept 1952). German double bass player. While studying double bass at the Musikhochschule in Stuttgart (1975–80) he joined the Ulmer Jazz Quintet (December 1976). Later he recorded with Emil Mangelsdorff, the clarinetist Heinz Schönberger, and Klaus Doldinger's trio (all 1978), Frederic Rabold (1979), the saxophonist Bernd Konrad (1980), and Lauren Newton and the Human Music Association (both 1982). From the early 1980s Stabenow led his own groups, among them a quartet whose members were Johannes Faber, the pianist Jörg Reiter, and the drummer Michael Kersting; it recorded in 1982 and again in 1984. Another of his quartets, Straight Four, consisted of Benny Bailey, the tenor and soprano saxophonist Wolfgang Engstfeld, and Christof Lauer. At some point in the 1980s he formed the record company and label Bassic-Sound. He worked in Peter Herbolzheimer's Rhythm Combination & Brass (from 1986), with Roman Schwaller (from *c*1987), and in Klaus Weiss's various groups (from *c*1987), including a trio with Rob van Bavel (from 1991) and Saxophone Connection, and in the late 1980s he formed the cooperative group Trio Concepts, with the pianist Klaus Wagenleiter and the drummer Harald Rüschenbaum. In the early 1990s Stabenow played with Wolfgang Haffner. As a freelance he performed with, among numerous others, Johnny Griffin (recording in 1987), Ack van Rooyen, Toots Thielemans, Albert Mangelsdorff, Charly Antolini's Jazz Power, Stan Getz, Charlie Mariano, David Friedman, Diane Reeves, Al Porcino's big band, Joe Haider's Jazz Orchestra, the WDR big band, and the SDR big band. In the 1990s he also recorded with the pianist Joe Keineman (1991), the Südpool Jazz Project (1991), the saxophonists Harvey Wainapel and Jurgen Seefelder (both 1992), the singer Rachel Gould (1993), the trumpeter Franz Weyerer, the pianist Larry Porter, the vibraphonist Florian Poser, and the violinists Hajo Hoffman and Jörg Widmoser (all 1994), the drummer Joe Baudisch (from 1995), and Frank Foster, the saxophonist Johannes Enders, the saxophonist Till Martin, and the quintet led by the trumpeter Ingolf Burkhardt and the trombonist Ludwig Nuss (all 1996). Stabenow taught from 1984 at the Musikhochschule in Stuttgart and from 1996 at the Musikhochschule in Mannheim.

SELECTED RECORDINGS

Duos with Lothar Schmitz: *Sweet Peanuts* (1991, Bassic-Sound 007); with J. Seefelder: *Visitation* (1992, Bassic-Sound 008)

As leader: *Human Spirit* (1992, Bassic-Sound 009); *What's New* (1995, Bassic-Sound 014)

As sideman: L. Newton: *Timbre* (1982, hat Music 3511); K. Weiss: *Live at Opus 1* (1987, Jazzline 20830); Trio Concepts: *More* (1989, YVP 3019); K. Weiss: *L.A. Calling* (1991, L+R 45033); H. Wainapel: *At Home/On the Road* (1992, Jazzmission 101); R. Gould: *More of Me* (1993, Bassic-Sound 010); R. Schwaller: *Welcome Back from Outer Space* (1995, Jazz Haus Musik 3605); J. Baudisch: *The Meeting of the Two Tenors* (1996, Acoustic Music 319.1135.2)

BIBLIOGRAPHY

ReclamsJ

"Ausgezeichnet: Thomas Stabenow," *JP*, xxxv/7 (1986), 4

<http://www.jazzrecords.com/bassic/thomas.htm> (1999) [incl. discography]

GK

Stabulas, Nick [Nicholas] (*b* New York, 18 Dec 1929; *d* nr Great Neck, NY, 6 Feb 1973). Drummer. After working initially as a commercial musician he performed and recorded in New York with Phil Woods (1954–7); good examples of his solo playing may be heard on the tracks *Be my love*, *Woodlore*, *Get Happy*, and *On a slow boat to China*, on Woods's album *Woodlore* (1955, Prst. 7018). Stabulas also took part in sessions with such musicians as Jon Eardley (1955–6), Jimmy Raney (1955, 1957), Eddie Costa and Friedrich Gulda (both 1956), George Wallington (1956–7), Al Cohn (1956–7, 1960), Zoot Sims and Gil Evans (both 1957), Mose Allison (1957–8), and Carmen McRae and Don Elliott (both 1958). Later he worked with Chet Baker, Kenny Drew, and Bill Evans (ii), and in 1964 he appeared at the Half Note as a member of Lennie Tristano's group in a concert that was recorded and broadcast on television as "Jazz at the Half Note," an episode of the television series "Look up and Live." Stabulas continued to work until he was killed in an automobile accident in 1973. (*FeatherE*; *Feather–Gitler '70s*)

Stacy, Jess (Alexandria) (*b* Bird's Point, MO, 11 Aug 1904; *d* Los Angeles, 1 July 1995). Pianist. He was largely self-taught, and gained his first professional experience on riverboats during the early 1920s. He moved in the mid-1920s to Chicago, where he worked alongside Muggsy Spanier and Frank Teschemacher in the band led by the tenor saxophonist Floyd Town (*c*1926–8) and took part in regional broadcasts. He was most influential during his tenure with Benny Goodman's orchestra (July 1935 – July 1939), though, apart from his lengthy contribution to *Sing, sing, sing* from the acclaimed Carnegie Hall concert in 1938 (released only two decades later), he was given scarcely any opportunity with Goodman to play solos. His highly personal style was technically precise and rhythmically incisive, containing elements derived from the playing of both Earl Hines and Teddy Wilson. His first solo recordings, made in 1935, include the earliest recorded versions of Bix Beiderbecke's *Flashes* and *In the Dark*, and while with Goodman he also made important recordings with Lionel Hampton, Harry James, Eddie Condon, and Bud Freeman. Stacy continued working and recording with popular big bands throughout the 1940s, including those led by Bob Crosby (September 1939–1942), Goodman (December 1942 – March 1944), and Tommy Dorsey (December 1944 – June 1945). He then formed his own big band (July 1945 – May 1946), featuring Lee Wiley, his wife at the time. After one last period with Goodman (November 1946 – mid-March 1947) he moved to California, made a second unsuccessful effort to establish a big band (until about April 1948), and then played mostly as an unaccompanied soloist in bars, where the work was unrewarding. Not long after a brief reunion with Goodman (December 1959 – January 1960) he ceased to be a professional musician. However, he reappeared at the 1974 Newport Jazz Festival New York, performed at the Dixieland Jubilee in Sacramento, California, and gave a last concert in 1979 for the New Jersey Swing Club. A volume of transcriptions of his work, *Piano Solos*, was published in 1944.

Oral history material in *LNT*, *NjR*.

SELECTED RECORDINGS

As unaccompanied soloist: In the Dark/Flashes (1935, Para. 2233); Candlelights/Ain't goin' nowhere (1939, Com. 517); *Stacy Still Swings* (1974, Chi. 133)

As sideman: L. Hampton: Stomp (1937, Vic. 25535); On the Sunny Side of the Street (1937, Vic. 25592); H. James: Life Goes to a Party (1937, Bruns. 8035); B. Goodman: *Carnegie Hall Concert* (1938, Col. SL160), incl. Sing, sing, sing; E. Condon: Beat to the Socks (1938, Com. 502); Carnegie Jump/Carnegie Drag (1938, Com. 1500); B. Goodman: One O'Clock Jump (1938, Vic. 25792); Topsy (1938, Vic. 26107); B. Crosby: Spain (1940, Decca 3248); That Da Da Strain (1942, Decca 25293)

SELECTED FILMS AND VIDEOS

Sweet and Lowdown (1944); Sarge Goes to College (1947); March of the

Bobcats (1951); Muskrat Ramble (1951); Panama (1951); Who's Sorry Now? (1951)

BIBLIOGRAPHY

ConnorBG
"Is Jess Stacy the Greatest White Pianist?," *Music and Rhythm*, ii/6 (1941), 84
R. Hadlock: "The Chicagoans," *Jazz Masters of the Twenties* (New York, 1965/*R*1985), 106
E. Condon and H. O'Neal: *The Eddie Condon Scrapbook of Jazz* (New York, 1973)
W. Balliett: "Back from Valhalla," *Improvising: Sixteen Jazz Musicians and their Art* (New York, 1977), 97; repr. in *BallïettA (1986)*, 151; *BallïettA (1996)*, 165
L. Feather: "Piano Giants of Jazz: Jess Stacy," *CK*, v/3 (1979), 68
M. Grosz: Liner notes, *Giants of Jazz: Frank Teschemacher* (TL 23, 1982)
J. Chilton: *Stomp Off, Let's Go! The Story of Bob Crosby's Bob Cats & Big Band* (London, 1983)
D. Coller: "Jess Stacy: the Recent Past," *MR*, xi/9 (1984), 16
B. Rusch: "Jess Stacy: Interview," *Cadence*, xii/5 (1986), 8
L. D. Holmes and J. W. Thomson: *Jazz Greats: Getting Better with Age* (New York, 1986)
K. Keller: *Oh, Jess!: a Jazz Life: the Jess Stacy Story* (New York, 1989)
F. Levin: "Jess Stacy: a Retrospection," *IAJRCJ*, xxvi/3 (1993), 56
Obituary, *New York Times* (4 Jan 1995)
D. Coller: "Floyd Town," *Storyville 1996/7*, ed. L. Wright (Chigwell, England, 1997), 156

BILL DOBBINS/BK

Stadler, Heiner (*b* Lessen, Poland, 4 Sept 1942). German composer and pianist. He grew up in Hamburg, Germany, where he studied piano and composition (1960–64). Having moved to New York (*c*1965) he led rehearsal groups with Thad Jones, Tom McIntosh, John Gilmore, Roger Kellaway, and Reggie Johnson among his sidemen. In 1966 he recorded his composition *Fugue 2*, conducting a sextet that comprised Jimmy Owens, Garnett Brown, Joe Farrell, Don Friedman, Barre Phillips, and Joe Chambers, and the following year the New York Jazz Sextet performed his piece *No Exercise*. During another period in Hamburg Stadler studied harmony (1968–70) and wrote arrangements for James Moody (1969). After returning to New York he formed a record company, Labor (1974), on which he issued his own recordings as well as those of such jazz musicians as the saxophonist Tyrone Washington. His first two albums, *Brains on Fire*, i–ii, are compilations of pieces that he recorded between 1966 and 1973, notably a duo recording of his composition *Love in the Middle of the Air* by Dee Dee Bridgewater and Reggie Workman. In 1978 he recorded his own arrangements of works by Charlie Parker and Thelonious Monk. Later Marilyn Crispell and Workman recorded two versions of his piece *Three Problems* (1988), which were included on a reissue of Stadler's album *Jazz Alchemy*.

Stadler has been active mainly as a composer and arranger, and the majority of recordings under his leadership involve musicians interpreting his work. At his best he succeeds in blending the harmonic sensibilities of contemporary art music with the expressiveness of jazz (especially free jazz), creating a type of chamber jazz that is reminiscent of the finest compositions of George Russell and Jimmy Giuffre.

SELECTED RECORDINGS

* – composed by Stadler

As leader: *Brains on Fire*, i–ii (1966, 1971, 1973, Labor 7001–02), incl. *Fugue 2 (1966), *Love in the Middle of the Air (1973); *Jazz Alchemy: Six Pieces for Trumpet, Bass and Drums* (1975, Labor 7006); *A Tribute to Monk and Bird* (1978, Tomato 2-9002); first issued on *Jazz Alchemy* (1975, 1988, Tomato 2696702), *Three Problems (1988)

BIBLIOGRAPHY

Feather–Gitler '70s
P. Carles, A. Clergeat, and J.-L. Comolli: *Dictionnaire du jazz* (Paris, 1988, rev. and enlarged 2/1994)
M. Kunzler: *Jazz-Lexicon* (Reinbek, nr Hamburg, Germany, 1988)

GK

Stafford, George (*b c*1898; *d* New York, spring 1936). Drummer. After performing with Sam Wooding in Atlantic City, New Jersey, he moved to New York, where he accompanied his sister, the singer Mary Stafford; however, he did not take part in any of her recording sessions, probably because of the difficulties many companies had in recording a drum kit at this early date. Around 1920, back in Atlantic City, he joined Charlie Johnson's band, with which he played and recorded regularly until shortly before he died. He also recorded with Eddie Condon (1929), Henry "Red" Allen (1935), and Mezz Mezzrow (1936), among others.

SELECTED RECORDINGS

As sideman: C. Johnson: Don't forget you'll regret (1925, Emerson 10856); Birmingham Black Bottom (1927, Vic. 20551); You ain't the one (1928, Vic. 21247); Charleston is the best dance after all (1928, Vic 21491); The Boy in the Boat/Walk that Thing (1928, Vic. 21712); H. Allen: Rosetta/Body and Soul (1935, Voc. 2965); I'll never say "never again" again (1935, Voc. 2956)

BIBLIOGRAPHY

E. Condon and T. Sugrue: *We Called it Music: a Generation of Jazz* (New York, 1947/*R*1985), 186

based on *ChiltonW*/HOWARD RYE

Stafford, Gregg [Gregory Vaughan] (*b* New Orleans, 6 July 1953). Cornetist, trumpeter, and leader. He began playing music professionally in 1974. In 1976 he gained a degree in elementary education from Southern University in New Orleans, and from 1985 he has taught in the New Orleans school system. He took over the leadership of the Young Tuxedo Brass Band in 1984 and then in 1992 assumed a leadership role both in the Heritage Hall Jazz Band and (replacing Kid Sheik Cola) in one of the Preservation Hall jazz bands, with which he has appeared on Tuesday nights into the new century. In the early 1990s Stafford toured with Wynton Marsalis in an ensemble that paid tribute to Louis Armstrong. Having spent more than a decade in Danny Barker's group the Jazz Hounds, he took over as its leader in March 1994, following Barker's death. He recorded an album as a leader in 1998 and another as co-leader with the English clarinetist Brian Carrick in 1999; he has also worked regularly with Michael White (ii), with whom he recorded in 1987. Stafford may be seen in the video *New Orleans Jazz is Alive in 2000* (2001).

SELECTED RECORDINGS

As leader: *That Man from New Orleans* (1998, Jazz Crusade 3033–4); with B. Carrick: *Streets of the City* (1999, Jazz Crusade 3053)
As sideman with M. White: on *Jazz in New Orleans – the Eighties: Shake it and Break it* (1981, 1987, 504 S6), Careless Love, Hindustan, Royal Garden Blues, Sing on, Streets of the City (1987)

BIBLIOGRAPHY

M. Joly: "Gregg Stafford: New Orleans, the New Generation," *SL*, xxxvi (1984), spring, 28
"Won't Walk Away from the Music," *New Orleans Times-Picayune* (15 Oct 1993)
G. Chapman: "Welcome Touch of New Orleans," *Toronto Star* (30 Jan 1995)
L. E. Elie: "Traditions Resurrected," *New Orleans Times-Picayune* (29 Aug 1997)
<http://www.dertien.be/tweeentwintig/orleans.htm> (2001)

GK

Stafford, Terrell (Lamark) (*b* Miami, 25 Nov 1966). Trumpeter. He was classically trained and studied trumpet performance at the University of Maryland (BS 1988) and Rutgers (MM 1991). After beginning his career in the pit orchestras of various Broadway musicals he worked with Bobby Watson's Horizon (1989–93), Kenny Barron (1990), Shirley Scott (1994), Stephen Scott and Don Braden (both 1995), Bruce Barth (1996), Cedar Walton (1997), and McCoy Tyner, the Carnegie Hall Jazz Band, and the Lincoln Center Jazz Orchestra (all from 1997). From 1989 he co-led a quintet with Tim Warfield and the following year he formed his own group. Stafford has taught at Cheyney (Pennsylvania) University (1993–6) and Temple University (from 1996).

SELECTED RECORDINGS

As leader: *Time to Let Go* (1995, Can. 79702); *Centripetal Force* (1997, Can. 79718)

As sideman: B. Watson: *Present Tense* (1991, Col. CK52400); *Midwest Shuffle* (1993, Col. CK57697); T. Warfield: *A Cool Blue* (1994, Criss Cross 1102); *A Whisper in the Midnight* (1995, Criss Cross 1122)

BIBLIOGRAPHY

L. Blumenfeld: "Tradin' Fours: Cut Straight to the Jazz," *DB*, lxii/12 (1995), 52

D. Zych: "Hearsay: Terrell Stafford: Rising up," *JT*, xxv/10 (1995), 28

GK

Stage band. A term used in American schools as a synonym for "big band"; *see* Bands, esp. §§4(ii) and (iii).

Stahl, Dave [David] (*b* Reading, PA, 23 Jan 1949). Trumpeter. After studying music education at the Pennsylvania State University (BS 1970) he played in an army band in Washington, DC. Between 1973 and 1975 he toured and recorded as lead trumpeter with Woody Herman, and he may be heard to advantage on the tracks *Superstar* and *Montevideo*, on Herman's *The Herd at Montreux* (1974, Fan. 9470). Stahl spent two periods with Count Basie (April–October 1975, January–June 1980) and in the interim led his own group (from April 1977), which was based in Reading. In addition he played in bands accompanying pop artists, and he spent most of the 1980s and 1990s working as the lead trumpeter for the entertainer and actress Liza Minnelli. He recorded occasionally in studio big bands, notably that of Bill Evans (iii) (1993) and the memorial Buddy Rich Orchestra (1994); early in 1999 he played lead trumpet in the Vanguard Jazz Orchestra. Among his recordings as a leader are *Anaconda* (1987, Abee Cake 1001) and *Live at Knight's* (*c*1990, Abee Cake 3005). On *Scream Machine*, from the former album, he plays in a full-bodied, high-pitched melodic style after the manner of Maynard Ferguson. However, Stahl performed in a more restrained setting as the leader of a bop quintet which took its members from his big band; in 1979 these ensembles featured Sal Nistico (ii).

BIBLIOGRAPHY

Feather–Gitler '70s; *SheridanCB*

R. J. Robbins: "Reviewed Recently: Dave Stahl Big Band," *CI*, xvii/11 (1979), 8

<http://www.davestahl.com> (2000)

BK

Stamm, Marvin (Louis) (*b* Memphis, 23 May 1939). Trumpeter and flugelhorn player. He began to learn trumpet formally at the age of 12 and later studied at North Texas State University (BMus 1961); in his final year at college he worked briefly with Buddy Morrow and Stan Kenton. In spring 1961 he joined Kenton's Mellophonium Orchestra, and his concise, tightly muted trumpet tone may be heard to great effect on many of the band's finest recordings from the early 1960s. He remained with Kenton for two years, after which he worked with Woody Herman (1965–6). Stamm then embarked on a career as a studio musician in New York, but he retained an enthusiasm for jazz performance, playing as a member of the Thad Jones–Mel Lewis Orchestra (1966–72) and with Duke Pearson (1967–70). He recorded mainly with studio big bands, but in 1968 he made several recordings with smaller groups, notably a sextet led by Frank Foster; he also played in a sextet called Jazz for a Sunday Afternoon which included Chick Corea, Richard Davis, and Elvin Jones. Stamm led his own quartet intermittently during the 1970s, and from autumn 1974 to mid-1975 he worked with Benny Goodman; he made three tours with Frank Sinatra.

Stamm appeared with Dizzy Gillespie's big band in the video *Jazz in America: Lincoln Center, New York* (1982). Not long afterwards he set aside his lucrative studio career and renewed his connection with jazz, not only as a performer but also as a touring jazz educator. He was a founding member of Bob Mintzer's big band (recording with it from 1983) and of the American Jazz Orchestra in 1986, he toured and recorded as a soloist with George Gruntz's Concert Jazz Band from 1987 into the 1990s, and he played regularly in Louie Bellson's big band (recording from 1990) and intermittently in those of Maria Schneider and the pianist Rich Shemaria (recording with the latter in 1990). As a soloist he toured in a duo with Bill Mays (from 1995) and in a quartet with Mays or Joe LoCascio on piano and Ed Soph on drums; while on tour he and Mays also appeared with numerous student and professional ensembles.

SELECTED RECORDINGS

As leader: *Machinations* (1968, Verve 68759); *Stammpede* (1982, PAlt 8022); *Bop Boy* (1990, Musicmasters 65065); *Mystery Man* (1992, Musicmasters 65085)

As sideman: S. Kenton: *Sophisticated Approach* (1961, Cap. ST1674); *Adventures in Blues* (1961, Cap. ST1985); *Adventures in Time* (1962, Cap. ST1844); W. Herman: *Jazz Hoot* (1966, Col. CS9352); B. Mays: *Mays in Manhattan* (1996, Conc. 4738)

BIBLIOGRAPHY

Feather '60s; *Feather–Gitler '70s*

B. Houston: "Marvin Stamm: Not Just an Up-tempo Specialist," *MM* (19 March 1966), 8

M. Rozek: "Marvin Stamm: Technical Magic/Subtle Persuasion," *DB*, xliii/8 (1976), 19

G. Kalbacher: "Trumpetman Marvin Stamm: Business before Pleasure," *DB*, li/2 (1984), 29 [incl. discography]

P. Dorian: "Marvin Stamm: the Educator's Musician," *Jazz Educators Journal*, xx/4 (1988), 32

D. Matthews: "Marvin Stamm," *CI*, xxvii/7 (1990), 9

S. Woolley: "Marvin Stamm," *JJI*, xliv/3 (1991), 14

"Marvin Stamm," *The Note*, iv/3 (1992), 10

J. M. Rohner: "A Clinician's View of Music Programs," *Instrumentalist*, xlvi/11 (1992), 10

G. Lees: *Leader of the Band: the Life of Woody Herman* (New York, and Oxford, England, 1995)

B. Primack: "Jazz Clinicians Stamm & Liebman: Two for the Road," *JT*, xxvii/8 (1997), 158

<http://marvinstamm.com/> (1999) [incl. discography]

STAN WOOLLEY/BK

Standard. A composition, usually a popular song, that becomes an established item in the repertory; by extension, therefore, a song that a professional musician may be expected to know. Standards in jazz include popular songs from the late 19th century (e.g., *When the saints go marching in*), songs from Broadway musicals and Hollywood films by composers such as George Gershwin, Jerome Kern, Harold

Arlen, Irving Berlin, Cole Porter, and Richard Rogers, and tunes newly composed by jazz musicians (e.g., Thelonious Monk's *Round Midnight*, Dizzy Gillespie's *A Night in Tunisia*, and John Coltrane's *Giant Steps*). Jazz musicians themselves, however, distinguish further between these categories, referring to the first as comprising dixieland standards, the second as unqualified or mainstream standards, and the last as jazz standards; it is the consensus that the essential repertory of standards is comprehended within the mainstream category. Many jazz performances are based on standards, taking not only the melody but also the harmonies of the entire piece, or more often the refrain only, as the theme (*see* Forms, esp. §1); part of the impact of a performance based on a standard derives from its being familiar to the listeners, who are better able to appreciate skillful arrangement and inventive improvisation because they know the original work.

ROBERT WITMER

Stankiewicz, (Jakub) Kuba (*b* Wrocław, Poland, 7 Dec 1963). Polish pianist and educator. From 1985 to 1987 he was a member of Zbigniew Namysłowski's group, and around the same time he worked in Jan Wróblewski's band. After gaining a degree in piano performance at the Berklee College of Music (1990) he joined the Artie Shaw Orchestra under Dick Johnson (1990). Back in Poland he taught at an annual jazz workshop in Pulawy from 1991 to 1997, and in 1993 he joined the faculty of the Hochschule für Musik und Darstellende Kunst in Graz, Austria. He led his own quartet (1993–6), with Henryk Miśkiewicz, the double bass player Adam Cegielski, and the drummer Cezary Konrad as his sidemen, which recorded the album *Northern Song* (1993, Gowi 09), and joined the Traveling Birds Quintet (1994), alongside Piotr Baron, Piotr Wojtasik, Darek Oleszkiewicz, and Konrad, whose albums include *Return to the Nest* (1995, Polonia 041). In 1995 he established a trio and in 1998 another quartet. While continuing at the Hochschule into the new century, Stankiewicz worked with Scott Hamilton (1996–7), Art Farmer (1996–9), and Sheila Jordan (1997–8).

ADAM CEGIELSKI, BK

Stańko, Tomasz (*b* Rzeszów, Poland, 11 July 1942). Polish trumpeter, leader and composer. His father was an attorney and a professional violinist. Stańko received classical tuition on violin and piano, then in 1959 took up trumpet, which he studied at a music school in Kraków. In 1962, with Adam Makowicz, he co-founded the group Jazz Darings; it first played hard bop, and then, when Janusz Muniak replaced Makowicz, took up free jazz; it was one of the first European groups to be influenced by Ornette Coleman. Stańko worked with Krzysztof Komeda (1963–7) and Andrzej Trzaskowski (1965–9) and was the leader of a quintet (1968–73) which included Muniak and Zbigniew Seifert (initially performing as a saxophonist) and with which he appeared at numerous European jazz festivals. He also performed in the Globe Unity Orchestra and recorded with the orchestra of the Studio Jazzowe Polskiego Radia (Polish Radio Jazz Studio) under Jan Wróblewski (1969). In the early 1970s he performed and recorded with Don Cherry's Eternal Rhythm Orchestra and in a group led by Michal Urbaniak. He led a quartet that involved Edward Vesala and Tomasz Szukalski (1974–8) and worked in Vesala's ensembles, with which he recorded in 1976 and 1979. Stańko played with Makowicz again as a member of Urbaniak's group in 1974, and the following year they formed the Tomasz Stańko–Adam Makowicz Unit, consisting of Szukalski and Czesław Bartkowski, and made a successful tour of Germany; in the mid-1970s this group recorded twice under Bartkowski's leadership.

Stańko took occasional solo engagements from 1978, and in 1980 he recorded as an unaccompanied soloist at the Taj Mahal and the Karla Caves temple in India. He played in Vesala's group Heavy Life with, among others, Howard Johnson (ii), Chico Freeman, James Spaulding, and Reggie Workman (recording in 1980), and he was a member of Sławomir Kulpowicz's group In/formation. In the 1980s he recorded with Gary Peacock (1981), in Vesala's trio (1983), and as a guest soloist with the NDR big band (1984), performed in a trio with Jack DeJohnette and Rufus Reid (1983), and was a member of Cecil Taylor's Orchestra of Two Continents (recording in 1984). He also formed his own groups: a small ensemble including Kulpowicz (early to mid-1980s) and Freelectronic (1985), in which Janusz Skowron was a sideman; Freelectronic performed in Graham Collier's *Hoarded Dreams* at the Camden Jazz Festival that year and recorded at the Montreux International Jazz Festival in 1987. In 1988 Stańko worked with Taylor again in the European Orchestra.

In 1991 Stańko recorded as co-leader, with the reed player Vlatko Kucan, of a quintet that involved the double bass player Jay Oliver and Billy Elgart. From that same year he worked in groups led by the reed player Nicolas Simion (recording in 1991, 1994, and 1995), performed and recorded in a cooperative quartet with the saxophonist and flutist Sigi Finkel, Ed Schuller, and Elgart, and led a trio consisting of Arild Andersen and Jon Christensen. In 1993 he established a quartet with Bobo Stenson, Anders Jormin, and Tony Oxley, and in Poland that same year he formed another quartet, in which the Simple Acoustic Trio (comprising Marcin Wasilewski, the double bass player Sławek Kurkiewicz, and the drummer Michał Miśkiewicz) served as his rhythm section. In the late 1990s Stańko formed two other ensembles: one, ranging in size from quartet to septet, performs the music of Komeda; the other, established in 1998, is a sextet consisting of John Surman, Dino Saluzzi, the violinist Michelle Makarski, Jormin, and Christensen. Stańko also composes music for film and theater.

SELECTED RECORDINGS

As unaccompanied soloist: *Music from Taj Mahal and Karla Caves* (1980, Leo 011)

As leader: *Music for K* (1970, Muza 0607); *Purple Sun* (1973, Calig 30610); *Balladyna* (1975, ECM 1071); *Almost Green* (1978, Leo 008); *Witkacy-Peyotl* (1984–6, Poljazz 154–5); *Bluish* (1991, Power Bros. 00113); with S. Finkel, E. Schuller, and B. Elgart: *Caoma* (1991, Konnex 5053); *Bosonossa and Other Ballads* (1993, Gowi 08); *Matka Joanna* (1994, ECM 1544); *Leosia* (1996, ECM 1603); *Litania* (1997, ECM 1636); *From the Green Hill* (1998, ECM 1680)

As sideman: K. Komeda: *Astigmatic* (1965, Muza 0298); E. Vesala: *Satu* (1976, ECM 1088); G. Peacock: *Voice from the Past–Paradigm* (1981, ECM 1210); N. Simion: *Transylvanian Dance* (1994, Tutu 888164-2)

BIBLIOGRAPHY

CarrJ; *Feather–Gitler '70s*; *Feather–GitlerBEJ*; *GrayF*; *ReclamsJ*

J. Byrczek and B. Czajkowska: "On Free Jazz Stańko, Trzaskowski, Wróblewski," *JF* [intl edn], nos.13–14 (1971), 70

R. Kowal: "Tomasz Stańko: Jazz is the Message," *JF* [intl edn], no.18 (1972), 51

"Stańko Quintet Disbanded," *JF* [intl edn], no.27 (1974), 25

K. Czyż: "Tomasz Stańko: Hat-trick," *JF* [intl edn], no.33 (1975), 41 [incl. discography]

"Poland: Stańko Solo," *JF* [intl edn], no.59 (1979), 15

E. Jost: *Europas Jazz, 1960–1980* (Frankfurt am Main, Germany, 1987)

M. Kunzler: *Jazz-Lexicon* (Reinbek, nr Hamburg, Germany, 1988)
H. Kumpf: "Tomasz Stanko: 'Man muss sich selbst helfen': der prominente Jazzmusiker über die ökonomische Krise in Polen," *JP*, xl/6 (1991), 20
S. Graham: "Tomasz Stańko: Still Daring at Fifty," *JF* [intl edition], no.133 (1992), 33
G. Kleinert: "Bründl–Stanko–Riessler," *JP*, xliii/3 (1994), 22
K. Mümpfer: "Tomasz Stanko–Vitold Rek," *JP*, xlv/12 (1996), 32
M. Piechnat: "Dramatiker med integritet" [Dramatist with integrity], *Orkester journalen*, lxiv/11 (1996), 24
M. Zwerin: "The Soul of Polish Jazz and the Free Market," *International Herald Tribune* (3 Oct 1997)
J. Denis: "Le cinéma de Tomasz Stanko," *Jazzman*, no.34 (1998), 14
S. Hopkins and D. Hill: "Tomasz Stanko: Anger, Lyricism and Power," <http://motion.state51.co.uk/features/stanko/> (2000)
<http://www.mediapolis.com/ecm-cgi-bin/background?1603> (2000)
D. Wayne: "A Conversation with Tomasz Stanko," <http://www.jazzweekly.com/interviews/stanko.htm> (2000)

BERT NOGLIK/GK

Stapleton, Bill [William John] (*b* Blue Island, IL, 4 May 1945; *d* 14 July 1984). Trumpeter and arranger. While studying music at North Texas State University (1963–7, 1971) he was a member of the renowned student big band. From 1972 to 1974 he worked with Woody Herman, playing trumpet and flugelhorn, and his style is well represented on *The Raven Speaks* (1972, Bellaphon 19132); during this period he arranged five pieces, including the title track, for Herman's album *Giant Steps* (1973, Fan. 9432). Stapleton then worked with Neal Hefti (1974) and Bill Holman (1974–5), and later he recorded with Alan Broadbent (*c*1979) and performed with Herman at the Concord Jazz Festival (1981). The social security death index gives only his date of death.

BIBLIOGRAPHY

Feather–Gitler '70s
W. D. Clancy with A. C. Kenton: *Woody Herman: Chronicles of the Herds* (New York and elsewhere, 1995)

Stark, Bobby [Bobbie; Robert Victor] (*b* New York, 6 Jan 1906; *d* New York, 29 Dec 1945). Trumpeter. He studied alto horn, piano, and reed instruments before taking up trumpet. He played with Chick Webb intermittently (1926–7), then worked with Fletcher Henderson (November 1927 – early 1934; for illustration *see* HENDERSON, FLETCHER), though in 1932 he spent a brief period with Elmer Snowden; he was Henderson's principal trumpet soloist for about a year until Rex Stewart joined the band. After a brief period with Charlie Turner's Arcadians he returned to Webb (July 1934; for illustration *see* WEBB, CHICK), and remained with the band under Ella Fitzgerald (1939–40). He served in the army, then worked with Garvin Bushell and, in September 1944, joined Benny Morton's sextet.

Stark's early playing was craggy and full of bravura, marked by a staccato attack and daring melismas, which, though they were often unsuccessful musically, were somewhat redeemed by deft turns of phrase. The spectacular work he produced in 1928 was very similar to that of Jabbo Smith during the same period. From the early 1930s his solos had a lissome smoothness that was sometimes reminiscent of Bill Coleman's playing; there was more intensity in his work which, along with his phrasing and figuration (of, for example, *King Porter's Stomp*, 1933), influenced Roy Eldridge, especially in his early work with Henderson. Long lines spun from a motif were characteristic of Stark's playing and his invention became more artfully dazzling as time went on; a good example of his improvisation is provided by *Squeeze me* (1937). In the late 1930s he used smears and heightened rubato and his low register gained an attractive sibilant resonance. His late work resembled Harry Edison's in style.

SELECTED RECORDINGS

As sideman: Chocolate Dandies: Bugle Call Rag/Dee Blues (1930, Col. 2543D); F. Henderson: My sweet tooth says I wanna (1931, Vic. 22786); Honeysuckle Rose (1932, Col. 2732D); King Porter's Stomp (1933, Voc. 2527); H. Henderson: Rhythm Crazy (1933, Parl. R1743); C. Webb: Clap hands! Here comes Charley (1937, Decca 1220); Squeeze me (1937, Decca 1716); Spinnin' the Webb (1938, Decca 2021); Liza (1938, Decca 1840)

BIBLIOGRAPHY

AllenH; *ChiltonW*; *McCarthyB*; *SchullerS*
R. Stewart and C. P. Gordon: *Boy Meets Horn* (Wheatley, Oxford, England, and Ann Arbor, MI, 1991), 109

BOB ZIEFF

Starr. Record label. It was established by the Starr Piano Company of Richmond, Indiana, which was the parent company of the label GENNETT. The company's first records were issued using the Starr label in 1915. The name was maintained by the Starr Company of Canada, originally a record distributing business, which in mid-1919 began issue on its own label Starr; these records were pressed in Canada by Compo. A considerable quantity of jazz from Gennett's catalogue was issued on Canadian Starr, with a heavy emphasis on more popular styles. Issues were also made of material from other American labels, but the link with Gennett ended late in 1925 when Canadian Starr was purchased by Compo, which transferred the operation from London, Ontario, to Toronto.

BIBLIOGRAPHY

J. Kidd: "Canadiana: the Starr–Gennett Story," *Matrix*, no.59 (1965), 13; no.61 (1965), 9
B. Rust: *The American Record Label Book* (New Rochelle, NY, 1978), 282
A. Robertson: "Canadian Gennett and Starr–Gennett 9000 Numerical," *Record Research*, nos.195–6 (1983), 1; nos.197–8 (1983), 7; nos.199–200 (1983), 10; nos.201–2 (1983), 10; nos.203–4 (1983), 8
A. Sutton: *Directory of American Disc Record Brands and Manufacturers, 1891–1943* (Westport, CT, and London, 1994), 144

HOWARD RYE

Starr, Henry (*b* Washington, DC, 22 Aug 1901; *d* Alameda, CA, 12 Sept 1962). Pianist and singer. His birth date and place of death appear in the California death index. When he was a child his family moved to California, and he later attended the University of California at Berkeley. In the late 1910s he met Jelly Roll Morton, for whom he substituted at the Rex Café in Oakland. From 1924 to 1929 he was the pianist with Curtis Mosby's Dixieland Blue-Blowers, and his early style can be heard on a private recording of *All Night Blues* made by Mosby's band in 1924, issued on *Curtis Mosby/Henry Starr: Recorded on the West Coast and in London, 1924–1939* (Jazz Oracle 8003). He later worked as an unaccompanied soloist, emphasizing his non-jazz singing, and became known as a radio artist. In 1928 he made his only unaccompanied recordings: *Mr. Froggie/Willow Tree* (Flexo 148). He moved to New York in 1934 and teamed up with the singer Ivan Harold Browning to form a cabaret act which performed at the Cotton Club and toured throughout Europe up to 1939. Starr later resumed his solo career in San Francisco.

BIBLIOGRAPHY

J. Wilby and C. J. Bray: Liner notes, *Curtis Mosby/Henry Starr: Recorded on the West Coast and in London, 1924–1939* (Jazz Oracle 8003, 1996)

HOWARD RYE

Starr, Kay [Starks, Kathryn La Verne] (*b* Dougherty, nr Sulphur, OK, 21 July 1922). Singer. She grew up in Dallas. At the age of 13 she joined Joe Venuti, with whose band she remained until 1939, when she sang briefly with Glenn Miller and Bob Crosby. She was known initially for her deep-voiced white blues style. Between 1943 and 1945 she performed and recorded with Charlie Barnet, though during the same period she sang at a session led by Wingy Manone (1944) and recorded the track *If I could be with you* (1945, Cap. 10031) with the Capitol Jazzmen, an all-star group with Bill Coleman, Buster Bailey, Benny Carter, Max Roach, Coleman Hawkins, and Nat "King" Cole among its members. Starr received widespread acclaim from the mid-1940s, singing in a popular style oriented towards country music; she performed on her own television show and recorded as a leader accompanied by Venuti and Barney Bigard (both 1946), Red Norvo (1947), Red Nichols (1947, 1949), Ben Webster (1961), and Count Basie (1968). After working only occasionally for several years she performed with small swing groups in London (1983) and New York (1985) and recorded *Live at Freddy's* (1986, Baldwin Street Music 202), accompanied by a trio that consisted of John Basile (guitar), John Goldsby (double bass), and Ronnie Zito (drums). In the 1990s she appeared in nostalgic hit-song revues.

BIBLIOGRAPHY

FeatherE
G. Giddins: "A Starr is Reborn," *VV*, xxx (12 Nov 1985), 48

Stateside. Record label, operated from 1962 to 1974 by Emi, used specifically to issue in the UK material first put out in the USA by American independent companies. It was revived in 1986.

Statesmen of Jazz. All-star swing group, founded in 1994. Organized by the American Federation of Jazz Societies, it has usually appeared as a sextet drawn from a pool of 30 distinguished members, among them Clark Terry, Irvin Stokes, Joe Wilder, Al Grey, Benny Powell, the trombonist Spiegel Wilcox, Buddy Tate, Benny Waters, Jane Jarvis, Milt Hinton, Claude Williams, Panama Francis, and Eddie Locke. It made a video late in 1994, performed at the Sacramento Jazz Jubilee in 1995, and recorded (including the album *Statesmen of Jazz*, 1994, Arbors 201) and toured internationally, notably in Japan in September 1997. (G. Gibson: "Statesmen of Jazz: Living Legends Keeping Jazz Alive for All Ages," *AARP Bulletin*, xxxviii/6 (1998), 24)

State Street Ramblers. Name used by several informally organized bands that recorded for the Gennett label. Their repertory reflected the music played at rent parties on Chicago's South Side. The bands were formed by the pianist Jimmy Blythe, who took part in all their recording sessions: one in August 1927 with the drummer Baby Dodds, the clarinetist Johnny Dodds, and the cornetist Natty Dominique, during which three tracks were recorded; two in February and April of 1928 with the alto saxophonist Joe Walker and the washboard player W. E. "Buddy" Burton; two in July 1928 with the clarinetist Angelo "Alvin" Fernandez, the alto saxophonist Baldy McDonald, the double bass player Bill Johnson, and the drummer Clifford "Snags" Johnson, during which 16 tracks were recorded (these were probably influenced by the recordings that Doc Poston made with Jimmie Noone); and two on 17 and 20 March 1931 with the trombonist Roy Palmer, the drummer Jasper Taylor, the kazoo player Alfred Bell, the clarinetist Darnell Howard, and the banjoist Ed Hudson, during which 17 tracks were recorded. Blythe frequently used the same groups, or much the same ones, to record for rival companies: thus sessions by the Dixieland Thumpers (for Paramount, 1927), the Chicago footwarmers (for OKeh, 1927), and J. C. Cobb's Grains of Corn (for Vocalion, 1928) often took place within weeks of those of the State Street Ramblers; sometimes these groups even recorded the same material. Little Brother Montgomery also led a band called the State Street Ramblers in the mid-1970s.

SELECTED RECORDINGS

The Weary Way Blues/Cootie Stomp (1927, Gen. 6232); My Baby/Pleasure Mad (1928, Gen. 6454); Barrel House Stomp/Kentucky Blues (1931, Champion 16320)

BIBLIOGRAPHY

C. Hillman and M. Tovey: "Chicago South Side, 1927–1932," *Sv*, no.124 (1986), 14; no.130 (1987), 124
C. Hillman: Liner notes, *The State Street Ramblers*, i (Gannet 1003, n.d. [*c*1996])

MIKE HAZELDINE

Staton, Dakota (*b* Pittsburgh, 3 June 1931). Singer. Her year of birth has been published widely, and incorrectly, as 1932. She sang from early childhood and was an accomplished dancer by the age of five. As a teenager she took classical singing lessons, but after hearing Dinah Washington she chose to concentrate on a blues style and joined the cast of *Bogey Fowler's Fantastic Rhythm*, an African-American revue based in Pittsburgh. From the age of 18 until she moved to Detroit in 1950 Staton sang with the orchestra of the bandleader Joe Westray. After performing in clubs in the USA and Canada she began recording in 1954, and she achieved critical success and popular acclaim for her album *The Late, Late Show* (1957), on which she performed standards and scat solos accompanied by a swing sextet that included Jonah Jones and Hank Jones. In addition she recorded with George Shearing (1957), performed at Town Hall in New York (1959), toured with Benny Goodman (*c*1960), and recorded at the Newport Jazz Festival (1963). In 1965 she moved to England, and three years later she sang with Kurt Edelhagen's big band at the Deutsches Jazz Festival in Frankfurt am Main. Having returned to the USA (early 1970s) she recorded two albums oriented towards soul jazz and gospel (*c*1972, 1973). Staton remained active through the 1980s and 1990s, appearing at clubs and festivals and making several new recordings which were well received.

SELECTED RECORDINGS

The Late, Late Show (1957, Cap. T876); *Dynamic!* (1958, Cap. T1054); *Dakota at Storyville* (1961, Cap. ST1649); *Dakota Staton* (1990, Muse 5401); *Darling Please Save your Love for Me* (1991, Muse 5462); *Isn't this a Lovely Day* (1992, Muse 5502); *A Packet of Love Letters* (1999, HighNote 7008)

BIBLIOGRAPHY

FeatherE; *Feather–Gitler'70s*
J. Olsson: "Man måste vara trogen sin publik: Dakota Staton" [One must truly love one's public: Dakota Staton], *Orkester journalen*, xlv/11 (1977), 6
L. Dahl: *Stormy Weather: the Music and Lives of a Century of Jazzwomen* (London, Melbourne, Australia, and New York, 1984), 155
C. Narita: "An Interview with Dakota Staton on February 9, 1986," *Artist and Influence 1986* (New York, 1986), 115
P. Smith: "Dakota Staton: Still Singin' the Blues, Thank You," *Boston Globe* (18 Jan 1991)

B. Donaldson: "Interview with Dakota Staton," *Marge Hofacre's Jazz News* (2000), spring, 5

BK

Stauffer, Teddy [Stauffifere, Ernest Henry] (*b* Morat am Murtensee, Switzerland, 2 May 1909; *d* Acapulco, Mexico, 27 Aug 1991). Swiss bandleader. He played saxophone and violin in and around Berne in 1927, and in 1929 he began performing in Germany with his own band under the name Teddy and his Band; the group was first billed as the Original Teddies in June 1929. In the early 1930s Stauffer led the band on transatlantic steamships, and he rose to prominence in 1936 through its performances in Berlin and its highly successful recording *Goody Goody* (1936, Tel. 478). The group toured Germany and Switzerland and recorded prolifically until the outbreak of World War II, when Stauffer settled in Zurich. In 1939 he formed a new group under the name the Original Teddies (also known as the Teddies and the International Teddies), which he led in performances and on a large number of recordings (including *Stop, It's Wonderful*, 1940, ES 4007) until 1941. He then moved to Acapulco de Juárez, Mexico, where he became a nightclub owner; although he ceased full-time performing he recorded in Mexico (1944, 1950), Los Angeles (1946), and Zurich (1947). In the 1960s and 1970s he worked in radio and television studios in London and Berlin.

BIBLIOGRAPHY

T. Stauffer: *Es war und ist ein herrliches Leben* (Berlin, Frankfurt am Main, Germany, and Vienna, 1968)

O. Flückiger: "Zur Geschichte der Schweizer Jazz- und Hot-Dancebands," *Jazz + Classic* [Muttenz, Switzerland], v/6 (1978), 14; vi/4 (1979), 13

J. Schütte and A. Stöcklin: *Teddy Stauffer: Discographie der Original Teddies (Teddy Stauffer und Eddie Brunner) und der kleinen Formationen mit Musikern der Teddies* (Menden, Germany, 1983)

W. J. Stock: "Teddy Stauffer: Swing ist ein guter Rhythmus," *JP*, xxxii/2 (1983), 16

RAINER E. LOTZ

Steam. Record label established in 1965 by STAN TRACEY.

Stearns, Marshall W(inslow) (*b* Cambridge, MA, 18 Oct 1908; *d* Key West, FL, 18 Dec 1966). Writer. He learned to play drums before attending Harvard University as an undergraduate (BS 1931) and law student (1932–4), then studied medieval English literature at Yale University (PhD 1942); at graduate school he was a founder of the United Hot Clubs of America, a jazz appreciation society. While pursuing a career as a professor in English literature at several universities he served as a columnist on jazz for *Variety* and *Saturday Review*, contributed to *Down Beat*, *Record Changer*, *Esquire*, *Harper's*, and *Life*, and edited articles on jazz for *Musical America*. In 1950 he received a Guggenheim Fellowship to begin work on *The Story of Jazz* (1956), a historical survey that became widely used. He developed a course on jazz at New York University in 1950 and another at Hunter College, where he settled the following year. Stearns founded the INSTITUTE OF JAZZ STUDIES in 1952 and later became its first executive director; he also taught music at the New School for Social Research (1954–66) and was a consultant in the 1950s to the US State Department and the Voice of America. In 1956 he accompanied Dizzy Gillespie's band on a tour of the Middle East sponsored by the State Department. He was an advisor for the television series "The Subject is Jazz" (1958), and around the same time he taught at the School of Jazz in Lenox, Massachusetts. Later, with his second wife, Jean Stearns (née Barnett), he wrote a pioneering survey of jazz dance (1968).

See also LIBRARIES AND ARCHIVES, §2.

WRITINGS

(selective list)

The Story of Jazz (New York, 1956, London, 1957, rev. and enlarged 2/1958, enlarged 1970)

with J. Stearns: *Jazz Dance: the Story of American Vernacular Dance* (New York and London, 1968/*R*1979)

BIBLIOGRAPHY

E. Condon and R. Gehman, eds.: *Eddie Condon's Treasury of Jazz* (New York, 1956/*R*1975), 205

Obituaries: *New York Times* (19 Dec 1966); *Publishers Weekly* (2 Jan 1967); J. F. Szwed, *Journal of American Folklore*, 80 (1967), 300; J. R. Taylor, *JJS*, i/1 (1973), 82

R. Reisner, "Reminiscences of Marshall Stearns," *JJS*, i/1 (1973), 84

DANIEL ZAGER/BK

Steckar, Marc (*b* Cherbourg, France, 1 June 1935). French trombonist, bass trombonist, and tuba player. He studied cello and trumpet, then trombone (1957–9), and first played with the drummer Benny Bennett (1958), Aimé Barelli (1959–60), and Nat "King" Cole (1960). Later he worked with Raymond Fonsèque's group T4 (1960–62), the pianist Jacques Denjean (1962), the trumpeter Sonny Grey (1967, 1970), Slide Hampton, Dexter Gordon (1970), and Ivan Jullien (1970–71). From 1970 he specialized on tuba, and in 1978 recorded an album on this instrument as an unaccompanied soloist. He worked regularly with the singer Claude Nougaro (1973–83), but he was also a member of big bands led by the arranger Claude Cagnasso (1978), Martial Solal (1980), the double bass player Bob Quibel (1981-5), Gérard Badini (1986–94), and Jay McShann (1989), and improvised in freer styles with the Caratini–Fosset Onztet (1981–3) and Michel Portal (1983). From the 1980s he has written for brass ensembles and led tuba ensembles such as Tubapack (from 1980), Elephant Tuba Horde (1987), and Steckar Trinity (1989). He enjoys great success in popular brass music circles and as a teacher. His playing is well represented on the album *En concert: turbanisation* (*c*1984, Ida 001).

BIBLIOGRAPHY

F. Billard: "Les voix graves de Marc Steckar," *Jm*, no.305 (1982), 36

R. Fonsèque: "Les créations de Marc Steckar," *Gazette des cuivres*, no.5 (1990), 5

Y. Rémy: "Marc Steckar compositeur renouvelle le répertoire des batteries-fanfares," *Gazette des cuivres*, no.27 (1997), 20

MICHEL LAPLACE

Steel drum. A tuned percussion instrument, usually made from an oil drum, that developed in Trinidad during the 1930s and 1940s. The head of a steel drum contains several depressions, each of which produces a different pitch; the instrument is played with rubber-headed sticks. The instrument came to be used occasionally in jazz in the late 1970s; its best-known exponent has been Andy Narell, who usually plays steel drum solos over Latin jazz and jazz-rock ostinatos, and who sometimes also uses it in highly chromatic bop passages, such as those that occur in Victor Feldman's *Seven Steps to Heaven*, recorded by Narell on his first album, *Hidden Treasure* (1979, IC 1053).

BK

Steele, Joe [Joseph Alexander Ellis] (*b* Savannah, GA, 17 Dec 1899; *d* New York, 5 Feb 1964). Pianist. The details of his birth and his full name appear in his application for social security. After studying at the New England Conservatory he performed and made recordings with the Savoy Bearcats (1926), notably *Bearcat Stomp* (Vic. 20307). He worked with the banjoist Henri Saparo at the Bamboo Inn, New York (1927), and in the late 1920s led his own band there; among his sidemen were Ward Pinkett, Langston Curl, Jimmy Archey, Charlie Holmes, and Joe Garland. In 1929 he made two recordings as a leader, *Coal-yard Shuffle/Top and Bottom* (Vic. 38066), on the second of which he takes a solo. As a member of the orchestra led by the trumpeter Pike Davis he toured with the show *Rhapsody in Black* (1931–2). Later he performed mainly with Chick Webb (1932–6), with whom he also recorded (1933–4); he may be heard playing a solo on *When dreams come true* (1934, Col. CB754). (*McCarthyB*)

based on *ChiltonW*

Steepee [Steepy]. Nickname of BRANFORD MARSALIS.

Steeplechase. Record company and label. The company was established by Nils Winther in Copenhagen in 1972, and that year issued its first LP, recorded by Jackie McLean at the Montmartre Jazzhus. From that time Winther developed one of the leading European bop-oriented catalogues. Its main series contains material recorded in both Copenhagen and New York; especially well represented are Dexter Gordon, Walt Dickerson, Tete Montoliu, Clifford Jordan, Duke Jordan, Kenny Drew, and Niels-Henning Ørsted Pedersen. The catalogue embraces several other brief series, which consist of reissues or first issues of material recorded (chiefly by Gordon and Bud Powell) between 1959 and 1965; an isolated session recorded in 1946 under Don Redman's leadership; three albums recorded direct-to-disc; and several blues recordings. From the late 1980s through the 1990s the company reissued much of its catalogue on CD and made well over 200 additional new recordings, by Paul Bley, Stanley Cowell, Harold Danko, Billy Harper, Andy LaVerne, Ron McClure, Doug Raney, Dave Stryker, Larry Willis, and many others. To facilitate sales in the USA, Winther established the company Steeplechase Productions in Chicago in 1978. Within Denmark, Steeplechase also served as a distributor for other important European labels, including ECM, Enja, Circle (iii), and Black Saint.

BIBLIOGRAPHY

A. Penchansky: "Danish Label into U.S. Market," *Billboard*, xci (15 Dec 1979), 71
C. Sheridan: "In the Tradition: the Story behind SteepleChase Records," *Radio Free Jazz*, xx (1979), 9
G. Buhles: "Drei Unabhängige – ein Spektrum der Stile: FMP, Enja, SteepleChase," *HiFi-Stereophonie*, xix (1980), March, 308
G. Rouy: "Nils Winther: Steeplechase ou sept ans de production," *Jm*, no.286 (1980), 28
P. H. Larsen: "SteepleChase," *Musical Denmark*, no.36 (1985), 21
F. Morey: *Jazz indépendant: cinq labels d'aujourd-hui: Chabada, ECM, Hat-Hut, Nato, Steeplechase* (Paris, 1988)
<http://www.steeplechase.dk/> (2000)

BK

Stefański, Janusz (Maria) (*b* Kraków, Poland, 14 June 1946). Polish drummer. He studied percussion at the Fryderyk Chopin School of Music and at the high school of music in Kraków (graduating from the latter in 1972). In the 1960s he performed with Zbigniew Seifert (1965–9), with a fellow sideman from Seifert's quartet, Jan Jarczyk (during the same period), and with Tomasz Stańko (1967). In 1969 he joined the orchestra of the Studio Jazzowe Polskiego Radia (Polish Radio Jazz Studio) under Jan Wróblewski (recording that year); he also performed and recorded with Stańko (1968–73), Hans Koller's Free Sound (1973–6), Seifert's Various Spheres (1975–6), and Zbigniew Namysłowski (1976–8). In 1978, with Tomasz Szukalski (tenor and soprano saxophone) and Namysłowski's former sidemen Sławomir Kulpowicz (piano) and Paweł Jarzębski (double bass), Stefański formed the cooperative group The Quartet; he is heard to advantage on its album *Loaded* (1979, Leo 010). During the late 1970s and early 1980s he worked in Austria, playing and recording with Koller (1979–80) and the Vienna Art Orchestra (1981), and occasionally touring with Leszek Żądło's Polski Jazz Ensemble (1983, 1985). From 1993 he has taught at Johannes-Gutenberg-Universität in Mainz, Germany.

BIBLIOGRAPHY

J. Byrczek: "Eurojazz Personalities: Poland," *JF* [intl edn], no.18 (1972), 87
K. Brodacki: "Janusz Stefański: 'I Envy Horn Players'," *JF* [intl edn], no.66 (1980), 42 [incl. discography]
I. Bodnar: "Wywiad nieautoryzowany: Janusz Maria Stefański," *Jazzi mazagine* [Poland], no.23 (1998), 58

WOLFRAM KNAUER

Stegmeyer, Bill [William John] (*b* Detroit, 8 Oct 1916; *d* Long Island, NY, 19 Aug 1968). Clarinetist. After studying at Transylvania College in Lexington, Kentucky, he performed with and worked as a staff arranger for the dance-band leader Austin Wylie (1937). He then played alto saxophone and clarinet with Glenn Miller (1938), undertook radio work in Detroit, and performed and recorded with Bob Crosby (June 1939 – May 1940). Having moved to New York (1942) he worked as an arranger and played and recorded with Billy Butterfield (1944–7) and Yank Lawson (1944–5). In the mid-1940s he made recordings with Bobby Hackett (1943, 1946), with Una Mae Carlisle (1944), as a leader (*Sentimental Journey/Frantic Rhapsody*, 1945, Sig. 15014), and with Pearl Bailey and Billie Holiday (both 1945–7). Between 1948 and 1950 he was a staff arranger for a radio station in Detroit, and from 1950 to 1958 he arranged popular music for the television program "Hit Parade" in New York. In addition he played clarinet in a band led by Lawson and Bob Haggart (1951–4, 1959–60, 1965), and he may be heard performing a duet feature with Peanuts Hucko in *Lover*, on the group's album *All Star Jazz Concert* (1954, Decca 8151–2). Stegmeyer also recorded with Jimmy McPartland (1953, 1955–7), Will Bradley (1953), and Ruby Braff (1956). During the 1960s he worked as a staff conductor at CBS.

BIBLIOGRAPHY

ChiltonW; *FeatherE*
J. Chilton: *Stomp Off, let's Go! The Story of Bob Crosby's Bob Cats & Big Band* (London, 1983)

Steig, Jeremy (*b* New York, 23 Sept 1943). Flutist. He began playing recorder at the age of six, studied flute from the age of 11, and started performing professionally when he was 15. In 1961 he worked with Paul Bley and Gary Peacock. His career was interrupted in 1962 by a motorcycle accident, but he made his recording début (as a leader) the following year, and in 1966 played with the popular singer Tim Hardin. In 1967 he formed Jeremy and the Satyrs, one of the first bands consistently to play jazz-rock. It initially included Eddie Gomez and Warren Bernhardt; Gomez had earlier joined Bill Evans (ii), and Steig in turn spent a period as a guest soloist with Evans's trio (autumn 1968 – early 1969), broadcasting on television, sitting in at the Village Vanguard and the rock venue Fillmore East, and recording. He collaborated frequently with Gomez until around 1980 and continued to lead his own groups. Later, while active mainly recording soundtracks to accompany cartoons and working as a painter, he recorded with Gomez (1987, 1992), Christoph Spendel (1989), and the keyboard player and singer Tom Lellis (*c*1993); more significantly, he made a jazz recording as a leader in 1991 which received some critical acclaim.

In his jazz-oriented activities Steig turned gradually from playing harmonically sophisticated standards, such as *Willow weep for me*, to a style of melodic improvisation that is modally oriented. His desire to encompass a variety of sounds led him to play all the instruments in the flute family, to exploit a wide range of performance techniques, and to make use of such electronic devices as the ring modulator and the wa-wa pedal.

SELECTED RECORDINGS

Duos with E. Gomez: *Outlaws* (1976, Enja 2098)

As leader: *Flute Fever* (1963, Col. CS8964), incl. Willow weep for me; *Jeremy and the Satyrs* (1967, Rep. 6282); *Monium* (1974, Col. KC32579); *Firefly* (1977, CTI 7075); with E. Gomez: *Rain Forest* (1980, CMP 12); *Jig Saw* (1991, Triloka 7190-2)

BIBLIOGRAPHY

W. Balliett: *Such Sweet Thunder* (Indianapolis, 1966), 182

A. Heineman: "Jeremy and the Satyrs: Potential Unlimited," *DB*, xxxv/12 (1968), 17

W. Diehans: "Jeremy Steig," *JP*, xxviii/5 (1979), 14

H. Boehm: "Aspekte zur Entwicklung des Floetenspiels im Jazz zwischen 1950 und 1980," *Jf*, xx (1988), 10

P. Pettinger: *Bill Evans: How my Heart Sings* (New Haven, CT, and London, 1998)

DAVID FLANAGAN/BK

Stein, Johnny [John (Hountha); Hountha, ?Philip John, Jr.] (*b* New Orleans, 15 June 1891 or 1895; *d* New Orleans, 30 Sept 1962). Drummer. His mother's surname had been Stein from an earlier marriage, and his elder half-brother was Emile Stein; although his real name was Philip John or John Philip Hountha, Jr. (accounts are contradictory), he took their surname. In 1915 he formed a band in New Orleans, the other members of which were Alcide "Yellow" Nunez, Eddie Edwards, Henry Ragas, and Nick LaRocca, and in March 1916 took it to Chicago to play a long engagement at the Schiller Café. In May that year Edwards, Ragas, and LaRocca left him to form the Original Dixieland Jazz Band; Stein afterwards claimed that the credit for their success belonged to him because he had brought the nucleus of the group together. After their departure he organized a new band to fulfill his contract at the Schiller Café. He then moved to New York to join the Original New Orleans Jazz Band led by the pianist Jimmy Durante, with which he played during 1918–19; he returned to the band (by now known as Jimmy Durante's Jazz Band) in 1920, and took part in its recording *Why Cry Blues* (1920, Gen. 9045). Stein continued to perform as a leader and with other bands in New York and Chicago before returning to New Orleans in 1961.

BIBLIOGRAPHY

H. O. Brunn: *The Story of the Original Dixieland Jazz Band* (Baton Rouge, LA, 1960/*R*1977)

Obituaries: *New Orleans States-Item* (30 Sept 1962) [as Hountha]; *SL*, xiv/3–4 (1963), 9 [as Stein]

KARL KOENIG

Stein, Lou(is) (*b* Philadelphia, 22 April 1922). Pianist. He learned to play saxophone and piano as a child and worked informally with Buddy DeFranco, Charlie Ventura, and Bill Harris (i) before joining Ray McKinley's band in 1942. In the mid-1940s he was a member of Glenn Miller's Army Air Force Band, although he worked with the group only in the USA and did not tour abroad. After performing again and recording (1946–7) with McKinley he worked in Ventura's group, with which he recorded his composition *East of Suez* (1947). During the 1950s Stein played a variety of styles, notably dixieland, bop, and popular music; he performed and recorded with Yank Lawson and Bob Haggart (1951–60) and Billy Butterfield (1954) and made recordings with Kai Winding (1951–2), Benny Goodman and Sarah Vaughan (both 1952), the Sauter–Finegan Orchestra (1952–3, 1958), Neal Hefti (1952–4), Joe Newman (1954), Louie Bellson (1955–6), Edgar Sampson (1956), Peanuts Hucko (1956–7), Henry "Red" Allen and Coleman Hawkins (both 1957), and Lester Young (1958). Between 1954 and 1956 he also recorded several times as a leader.

Although Stein played little jazz during much of the 1960s, he recorded and toured Europe with Joe Venuti in 1969 and 1971–2 and recorded as a leader from 1971 and as an unaccompanied soloist from 1976. In the 1970s and 1980s he performed at and served as the music director of several annual jazz parties in the USA, notably the Odessa Jazz Party in Texas. He appeared at the Internationales Jazzfestival Bern (1981, 1982, 1984, 1986), the North Sea Jazz Festival (1986), and the JVC Grande Parade du Jazz Nice (with Ruby Braff, 1987) and toured throughout Europe alongside Butterfield, Trummy Young, Hucko, Marty Napoleon, and Gus Johnson in the band Tribute to Louis Armstrong. In 1987 he toured briefly in the USA with Lawson and Haggart and in northern Europe as a member of a group that consisted of Lawson, George Masso, Jim Galloway, Jake Hanna, and three pianists – himself, Ralph Sutton, and Dick Wellstood (October–November). Stein continued to record under his own name, as well as in a duo with McKinley (1981) and as a sideman with Flip Phillips (1981), Nick Fatool (1987), Lawson and Haggart (1987), and Lawson (1988). In the 1980s he contributed regularly to *Sheet Music Magazine* and *Keyboard Workshop*.

SELECTED RECORDINGS

As unaccompanied soloist: *Tribute to Tatum* (*c*1976, Chi. 149); *Live at the Dome* (1981, Dreamstreet 106); *Solo* (1984, Audiophile 198)

As leader: *Go Daddy* (n.d., Pullen Music 2140)

As sideman: C. Ventura: *East of Suez* (1947, Nat. 9048); All Stars: *Session at Riverside* (1956, Cap. T761); Y. Lawson: *Something Old, Something New, Something Borrowed, Something Blue* (1988, Audiophile 240)

BIBLIOGRAPHY

FeatherE

BK

Stenfalt, Norman (Vivian) (*b* Ilford, England, 20 Feb 1922; *d* Clacton-on-Sea, England, 24 Nov 1991). English pianist and arranger. He began playing piano at the age of five and became a professional musician when he was 16. In 1940–41 he worked with, among others, Nat Gonella and Johnny Claes, and in 1942 he joined the RAF band at Northolt. While serving in the RAF (to 1945) he performed as a civilian with Harry Hayes and Ted Heath and arranged music for the bandleader Geraldo. Following his discharge he co-led a group with Hayes (1945–6) and worked as a pianist and arranger with Heath (spring 1946 – November 1948) and

Bert Ambrose (late 1948 – summer 1951). With Kenny Baker he played in a duo for the London stage production of *A Streetcar Named Desire* (1949–50) and took part in broadcasts of the BBC radio program "Baker's Dozen" (mid-1950s). In addition he worked with Ronnie Scott (1952–4, recording in 1957), Jack Parnell's orchestra (1954–5), and Scott's big band (summer 1955–1956). From 1957 until the late 1980s he was again a member of Parnell's group, which during this period became the house orchestra for the television company ATV. In the last decade of his life Stenfalt played with the memorial Ted Heath Orchestra led by Don Lusher.

SELECTED RECORDINGS

As sideman: R. Scott: *Presenting the Ronnie Scott Sextet* (1957, Phi. BBL7153); K. Baker: *Date with the Dozen* (1957, Nixa 19020); D. Lusher: *The Don Lusher Big Band Pays Tribute to the Great Bands*, i (1985, Horatio Nelson 110)

BIBLIOGRAPHY

ChiltonB
Obituary, T. Middleton, *JJI*, xlv/2 (1992), 24

MARK GILBERT

Stenson, Bobo [Bo Gustav] (*b* Västerås, Sweden, 4 Aug 1944). Swedish pianist and composer. After beginning his career in jazz with the Swedish tenor saxophonist Börje Fredriksson (recording in 1966–7) he played with Red Mitchell (1968–71, recording in 1969) and Jan Garbarek, with whom he co-led a quartet (1973–6). He toured Africa and performed at the Festival Mondial du Jazz Antibes–Juan-les-Pins with Stan Getz (1970) and recorded with George Russell's orchestra and Terje Rypdal (both 1971) and Putte Wickman and Bernt Rosengren (both 1973). With Palle Danielsson he formed Rena rama in 1971; this was among the first jazz groups in Europe to incorporate into its playing elements of folk music, in particular that of Bulgaria and India. In the 1970s, with Okay Temiz, Stenson formed the group Oriental Wind, which performed at the Jazzyatra festival in Bombay in 1980. Later he recorded an album with the Karnataka College of Percussion that combined jazz with the classical music of south India. From 1988 he has toured and recorded with Charles Lloyd, in whose group he forms a rhythm section with Anders Jormin and Billy Hart; he also made two acclaimed albums as the leader of a trio consisting of Jormin and Jon Christensen (1993, 1998) and recorded as a sideman with Lars Danielsson (1985, 1991), Don Cherry (1993), and Tomasz Stańko (1994–7), and in a cooperative quartet with Danielsson, Dave Liebman, and Christensen (1994, 1997, the latter date from a performance in New York).

SELECTED RECORDINGS

(recorded for ECM unless otherwise indicated)

As leader: with J. Garbarek: *Witchi-tai-to* (1973, 1041), *Dansere* (1975, 1075); *Reflections* (1993, 1516); *War Orphans* (1998, 1604)
As sideman: L. Danielsson: *New Hands* (1985, Dra. 125); *Poems* (1991, Dra. 209); T. Stańko: *Matka Joanna* (1994, 1544); C. Lloyd: *All my Relations* (1994, 1557); T. Stańko: *Litania: the Music of Krzysztof Komeda* (1997, 1636)

BIBLIOGRAPHY

A. Westin: "Bobo Stenson," *Orkester journalen*, xliv/1 (1976), 10
J. Scherwin: "Bobo Stenson," *Dagens nyheter* (8 March 1984), 9
E. Kjellberg: *Svensk jazzhistoria: en översikt* [Swedish jazz history: an overview] (Stockholm, 1985), 249
C. Lundberg: "Skimrande Stenson" [Brilliant Stenson], *Orkester journalen*, lv/5 (1987), 17
J. Scherwin: "Profile," *Musik* [Sweden], no.4 (1996), 7
L. Westin: "Känslan är Kärnan" [Feeling is the essence], *Orkester journalen*, lxiv/12 (1996), 2
——: "'Inte det lättaste att få spelningar med pianotrio'" [Not easy to get gigs with a piano trio], *Orkester journalen*, lxiv/2 (1997), 5
J. Woodard: "Hearsay: Bobo Stenson," *JT*, xxvii/1 (1997), 24
<http://www.mic.stim.se/engelsk/11/facts/stenson.html> (1998)

PEKKA GRONOW

Stephenson, Louis (George Alexander) (*b* Cashew Ground, St. Ann's, Jamaica, 2 June 1907; *d* London, 3 Feb 1994). Jamaican alto saxophonist, singer, and double bass player. As a bandboy and clarinetist with Jamaica's West India Regiment he traveled to England in 1924 for the British Empire Exhibition. In Kingston, Jamaica, he played for silent films and became a soloist particularly noted for his tone quality. He worked as a steward on luxury liners cruising to Canada before returning to England in 1935 to join the drummer Happy Blake. A founding member of Leslie Thompson's all-black band fronted by Ken "Snake Hips" Johnson, he accompanied Valaida Snow, then in 1937 he joined Benny Carter in the Netherlands. Stephenson broadcast with Carter and his guest soloist Coleman Hawkins, recorded with Carter, and went with the latter to Paris. He also played in Holland with Eddie South and the singer Mabel Mercer. Predominantly a section player, he worked in nightclubs with Latin and commercial bands, but he influenced a new generation of saxophonists at after-hours sessions. He changed to double bass after the war and played and sang on tour with Jiver Hutchinson and the saxophonist Freddie Grant, but he reverted to reed instruments for a visit to Berlin with Rex Stewart in 1948. Stephenson worked in a vocal trio with Lauderic Caton before retiring from music in 1952.

Oral history material in *GBLnsa*.

SELECTED RECORDINGS

As sideman: B. Carter: Skip it/Lazy Afternoon (1937, Decca F42136); I ain't got nobody (1937, Decca F42125); Blues in my Heart (1937, Decca F42128); R. Stewart: Bei dir war es immer so schön (1948, Amiga 1164) 1165)

BIBLIOGRAPHY

R. Harris: "Swing Show-case Disclosures, no.4: Alto Saxophone," *Discography* (15 Sept 1943), 6
F. Dennis: "In those Days," *City Limits* (27 May – 2 June 1983), 10
J. Chilton: *The Song of the Hawk: the Life and Recordings of Coleman Hawkins* (London and New York, 1990), 136
V. Wilmer: "How We Met: Lauderic Caton and Louis Stephenson," *Independent on Sunday Review* (7 Feb 1993)
Obituaries: V. Wilmer, *The Guardian* (5 Feb 1994); V. Wilmer, *JJI*, xlvii/7 (1994), 20

VAL WILMER

Stephenson, Ronnie [Ronald] (*b* Sunderland, England, 26 Jan 1937). English drummer. In his early teens he joined a band led by his elder brother, the pianist Bobby Stephenson. He performed locally and toured with a singer, and during his national service he played in the Royal Signals Band (1955–7). After leaving the army he worked with the trumpeter Don Smith, intially in Luton and then in Newcastle upon Tyne (1958–60), where he became a founding member of the EmCee Five (with Mike Carr, Ian Carr, the saxophonist Gary Cox, and Spike Heatley). In London he played with John Dankworth (1960–63) and then with Stan Tracey at Ronnie Scott's (1963–9), where he accompanied many leading American visitors. During the same period he worked with Jack Parnell, Scott, and Tubby Hayes, and was active as a studio musician. In 1969, following a tour of Germany with the singer Tom Jones, he joined Kurt Edelhagen's orchestra in Cologne. He then moved to Berlin and played with, among others, the SFB Big Band under the pianist Paul Kuhn (1972–80) and the orchestra at the Theater des Westens (1981–95); he also taught at the University of Berlin (1990–93). In 1995 he gave up drums on medical advice and moved to Scotland.

SELECTED RECORDINGS

As leader with K. Clare: *Drum Spectacular* (1966, Col. TWO146)

As sideman: W. Montgomery: *Live in Europe* (1965, Philology W97.2); S. Tracey: *Alice in Jazzland* (1966, Col. SX6051); T. Hayes: *100% Proof* (1966, Fon. STL5410); B. Goodman: *King of Swing's London Date* (1969, Phi. 6308023); R. Kühn: *Big Band Connection* (1993, Blue Flame Jazz 39840622)

BIBLIOGRAPHY

ChiltonB

MARK GILBERT

Steps Ahead. Group formed under the name Steps in 1979 by the vibraphonist Mike Mainieri. It grew from informal associations among studio musicians in New York who had toured together and played in jam sessions; the other original members were the tenor saxophonist Mike Brecker, the keyboard player Don Grolnick, the double bass player Eddie Gomez, and the drummer Peter Erskine. The group toured Japan, where it recorded three albums. In 1983 Grolnick was replaced by the pianist Eliane Elias, who performed with the band, now known as Steps Ahead, on its album of the same name (the first it made in the USA). Elias was in turn succeeded in 1984 by the keyboard player Warren Bernhardt, whose expert synthesizer playing defined to a large degree the sound of the group's successful album *Modern Times* (1984). Gomez and Bernhardt left later the next year and were replaced by various studio musicians, who performed on the album *Magnetic* (1986), a commercially oriented recording. By late 1986 Brecker was co-leader of the quintet, which included Mike Stern (electric guitar), Darryl Jones (electric bass guitar), and Steve Smith (drums); it disbanded after a tour of Japan that year. The original group's repertory was characterized by a spare texture that showed to advantage the virtuoso playing of its members.

Mainieri had revived Steps Ahead, under his sole leadership, by 1989, when its members were Bendik Hofseth, Rachel Z, Jimi Tunnell, Victor Bailey, and Smith; later editions of the group involved Jeff Andrews in place of Tunnell and Bailey (1992) and a quintet consisting of the saxophonist Donny McCaslin, Rachel Z, James Genus or Bailey, and Clarence Penn (1995).

SELECTED RECORDINGS

Smokin' in the Pit (1979, Better Days YB7010–11); *Step by Step* (1980, Better Days YF7020); *Steps Ahead* (1983, Elek. Mus. 60168); *Modern Times* (1984, Elek. Mus. 60351); *Magnetic* (1986, Elek. 960441-1); *NYC* (1989, Intuition 3007); *Yin-Yang* (1992, NYC 6001-2)

BIBLIOGRAPHY

H. Mandel: "Steps Ahead," *DB*, l/8 (1983), 18 [incl. discography]
M. Gilbert: "Mike Mainieri," *JJI*, xxxvii/12 (1984), 10
E. Rose and L. Fradkin: "Stepping Out," *Music Technology* (1987), Jan, 76
M. Bourne: "Mike Mainieri & Steps Ahead: Hitting it Heavy," *DB*, lvi/7 (1989), 20
D. Kasrel: "Hearsay: New Steps: Mike Mainieri," *JT*, xxiii/2 (1993), 9
G. Robinson: "Mike Mainieri: Staying Steps Ahead," *JT*, xxv/5 (1995), 54
R. Mattingly: "Mike Mainieri: the Paths Less Traveled," *Percussive Notes*, xxxv/4 (1997), 8

PATRICK T. WILL/BK

Stereo(phonic) recording. A term applied to techniques of sound recording (and playback) that produce the effect of sound coming from different directions in three-dimensional space; *see* RECORDING, esp. §I, 3(iii).

Stern, Leni [née Thora, Magdalena; Thora-Stern, Magdalena] (*b* Munich, 28 April 1952). German electric guitarist. After pursuing an acting career in Germany and France she went in 1978 to the Berklee College of Music in Boston, where she studied film scoring until 1980; around 1979 she married Mike Stern. The couple moved to New York in 1981, and in 1983 Leni Stern formed a group with Paul Motian and her former guitar teacher Bill Frisell. From 1985 she led several recording sessions featuring such prominent players as Frisell, Motian, Harvie Swartz, Bob Berg, Hiram Bullock, Dennis Chambers, Lincoln Goines, Wayne Krantz, David Sanborn, Bob Malach, Gil Goldstein, Michael Formanek, Russell Ferrante, and Didier Lockwood. She also took part in collaborative projects with the slide guitar specialist David Tronzo (from 1988), Krantz (from 1991), Mike Mainieri (1994), and the singer and guitarist Larry John McNally (1997). In 1997 she formed a record label, Leni Stern, the first issue of which focused on her singing. Her music is characterized by a lyrical blend of jazz, funk, blues, and country. She has contributed an instructional article to *Guitar Player* and she is the author of *Composing and Compositions* (Miami, 1994).

SELECTED RECORDINGS

Duos with W. Krantz: *Separate Cages* (1996, Alchemy 1007)

As leader: *Clairvoyant* (1985, Passport 88015); *The Next Day* (1987, Passport 88035); *Secrets* (1988, Enja 5093-2); *Closer to the Light* (1989, Enja 6034-2); *Ten Songs* (1992, Lipstick 890092); *Black Guitar* (1997, Leni Stern 910220419-2)

BIBLIOGRAPHY

B. Milkowski: "Riffs: Leni Stern," *DB*, liv/2 (1987), 14
D. Patrick: "Leni!," *JT* (1988), March, 9
G. Endress: "Ein neuer Stern am Jazzhimmel," *JP*, xxxviii/8 (1989), 39
M. Bourne: "Frets 'R' Us: Leni Stern," *DB*, lvii/5 (1990), 24
G. Santoro: "Leni Stern's Egalitarian Jazz," *Musician*, no.143 (1990), 94
J. Gress: "Leni Stern: Improvisation Meets Composition," *GP*, xxvii/3 (1993), 105
B. Milkowski: "Not your Standard Arrangement: the Ballad of Mike & Leni Stern," *GP*, xxvii/3 (1993), 92
K. Micallef: "Hearsay: Leni Stern," *JT*, xxiv/4 (1994), 12
A. Ellis: "Jazz Tripping," *GP*, xxxii/8 (1998), 78
G. Endress: "Leni Stern: 'I Wish I Had Played a Better Solo'," *JP*, xlviii/2 (1999), 15

MARK GILBERT

Stern, Mike [Michael Philips] (*b* Boston, 10 Jan 1953). Electric guitarist. His mother, a classical pianist, gave him his first music lessons and he took up guitar at the age of 12. He listened to rock and blues as a youth and was influenced by the guitarists B. B. King, Jimi Hendrix, and Eric Clapton. While attending the Berklee College of Music, where he was a pupil of Pat Metheny and Mick Goodrick, he became interested in jazz. In 1976 Metheny recommended him for a vacancy with Blood, Sweat and Tears, and Stern remained with this group for two years. Later he worked with Billy Cobham (1980–81, recording in London in the latter year) and joined Miles Davis's new band (1981); during the same period he took part in jam sessions in rhythm sections with Jaco Pastorius, Jeff Andrews, Harvie Swartz, Adam Nussbaum, Victor Lewis, Joey Baron, Ronnie Burrage, and others at the 55 Grand club in the Soho district of New York. After leaving Davis in 1983 he played with Pastorius's group Word of Mouth. Around this time he made his first recordings as a leader, and in 1985 he toured again with Davis. He toured with David Sanborn (summer 1986) and worked with Steps Ahead and in bands led by Swartz and Michael Brecker (1987–9).

From around 1987 into the 1990s Stern worked frequently

Mike Stern at the Royal Festival Hall, London, 1992

with Bob Berg, and from 1989 to 1992 they co-led a quartet with Lincoln Goines and Dennis Chambers which toured Europe and Japan in 1990. He was a regular at the 55 Bar in Greenwich Village, where his trio played jazz standards; from 1992 the other members of the trio were Goines or Andrews on bass and Ben Perowsky or Dave Weckl on drums. He also toured with the reconstituted Brecker Brothers band (1992, 1994), Bireli Lagrene (1992), and Joe Henderson (1993) and as a leader with Andrews and Weckl (1994) in a trio which performed and recorded as a quartet with the addition of Bob Malach. In 1998 Stern's group once again included Chambers. His many recordings as a sideman during the late 1980s and the 1990s include albums with Shunzo Ohno and Lew Soloff (both 1986), Berg (from 1987), Jukka-Pekka Uotila (1987, 1989), Eric Le Lann (1989), Pete Levin and the group Chroma (both 1990), Jerry Bergonzi (*c* early 1990s), Dieter Ilg (1991), Motohiko Hino (1991, 1993), Tiger Okoshi (from 1993), Carola Grey (1994), Jim Hall (1995), and Alex Riel (1997). He has been married to Leni Stern from around 1979, but these two formidable guitarists have not worked together, in the belief that a professional collaboration would upset their relationship. Stern's style draws from both hard rock and bop. Volumes of his improvisations have been published as *Mike Stern Guitar Transcriptions* (Milwaukee, 1992) and *Jazz Guitar Solos: Mike Stern* (transcr. D. Kynaston and ed. T. Kynaston, Kalamazoo, MI, *c*1992).

See also Blues, §13.

SELECTED RECORDINGS

As leader: *Upside Downside* (1986, Atl. 81656); *Jigsaw* (1989, Atl. 82027-2); *Odds or Evens* (*c*1991, Atl. 82297-2); *Standards (and other Songs)* (1992, Atl. 82419-2); *Is What it Is* (*c*1993, Atl. 82571-2); *Give and Take* (1997, Atl. 83036-2)

As sideman: M. Davis: *The Man with the Horn* (1980–81, Col. FC36790); *We Want Miles* (1981, Col. C2-38005); *Star People* (1982–3, Col. FC38657); H. Swartz: *Urban Earth* (1985, Gram. 8503); *Smart Moves* (1986, Gram. 8607); L. Soloff: *Yesterdays* (1986, PW K28P6448); J.-P. Uotila: *Jukkis Uotila Band Live* (1989, Stunt 18909); H. Swartz: on *In a Different Light* (1990, Blue Moon 79153), Alone Together, Softly as in a Morning Sunrise, Sonny Moon for Two; M. Hino: *Sailing Stone* (1991, Gram. R2-79473); C. Grey: on *The Age of Illusions* (1994, Jazzline 11139), The Age of Illusions; T. Okoshi: *Two Sides to Every Story* (1994, JVC 2039)

SELECTED VIDEOS

Steps Ahead: Live in Tokyo 1986 (n.d.); Newport Jazz '87 (1987); Brecker Brothers: Live in Barcelona (1992); Return of the Brecker Brothers (*c*1993); Chroma: Music on the Edge (n.d.)

BIBLIOGRAPHY

H. Mandel: "Profile: Bill Evans, Mike Stern, and Mino Cinelu," *DB*, xlviii/11 (1981), 52
B. Milkowski: "Mike Stern: Bebop Rocker with Miles Davis," *GP*, xvi/11 (1982), 113
J. Chambers: *Milestones*, ii: *The Music of Miles Davis since 1960* (Toronto, Buffalo, and London, 1985)
J. Ferguson: "Mike Stern: the Jazz Voice of the Late '80s?," *GP*, xxi/3 (1987), 56 [incl. discography]
B. Milkowski: "Mike Stern's New Lease on Life," *DB*, liv/8 (1987), 28 [incl. discography]
J. Woodard: "Mike Stern's Either/or Fusion Philosophy," *Musician*, no.107 (1987), 40
F. Goaty: "Mike Stern: après Miles," *Jm*, no.371 (1988), 38
J. Woodard: "Playing from the Heart," *Los Angeles Times* (26 Nov 1989)
M. Joyce: "Stern, Yearning for More: a Fusion Guitarist Gets to Play Lead," *Washington Post* (15 May 1991)
K. Micallef: "Mike Stern's (Not So) Standard Issue," *JT*, xxii/10 (1992), 58
B. Blumenthal: "Mike Stern's Straight-ahead Side," *Boston Globe* (10 Jan 1993)
B. Milkowski: "Not your Standard Arrangement: the Ballad of Mike & Leni Stern," *GP*, xxvii/3 (1993), 95
——: "Jim Hall & Mike Stern: Six String Rapport," *JT*, xxiv/6 (1994), 36
Y. Le Goff and R. Grosman: "Rencontre," *Jh*, no.530 (1996), 10
M. Point: "Tradin' Fours: a Fretboard Heretic Returns," *DB*, lxiii/4 (1996), 40
<http://rugmd0.chem.rug.nl/~lensink/stern/> (1998)
B. Milkowski: "Mike Stern's Party Mix," *JT*, xxix/10 (1999), 58

BILL MILKOWSKI/BK

Stern, Peggy [Margaret] (*b* Philadelphia, 22 Sept 1946). Pianist. She studied classical piano at the Eastman School (BM 1968) and the New England Conservatory (MM 1970), and began improvising only when she was in her late twenties, by way of fleshing out figured bass parts in a Renaissance ensemble. In 1981 she led an octet, which included Julian Priester and Richie Cole, after which she began a series of associations with rhythm-and-blues and Latin bands. She worked regularly with Lee Konitz from 1992 to 1995 and sporadically thereafter, and led her own trios from the early 1990s. Stern taught at the Cornish Institute (Seattle) between 1981 and 1989, and from 1991 at SUNY-Purchase. She also plays synthesizer.

SELECTED RECORDINGS

Duos with L. Konitz: *The Jobim Collection* (1993, Philology 68.2)

As leader: with L. Konitz: *Lunasea* (1992, SN 121249-2); *Pleiades* (1993, Philology 82.2); *The Fuchsia* (*c*1996, Koch 7837); *Room Enough* (*c*1997, Koch 7851)

As sideman with L. Konitz: *Rhapsody*, i, ii (1993, PW 174, 210)

BIBLIOGRAPHY

D. Kasrel: "Hearsay: Peggy Stern," *JT*, xxvii/4 (1997), 27

GK

Stevens, John (William) (*b* Brentford, England, 10 June 1940; *d* London, 13 Sept 1994). English drummer, cornetist, and pocket trumpet player. He played drums from the age of 17, and while in the RAF belonged to an orchestra with Trevor Watts and Paul Rutherford (1958–63). From 1963 he worked in London in groups led by Tubby Hayes, Ronnie Scott, and Stan Tracey and in a quartet with John McLaughlin, Jeff Clyne, and Ian Carr. In 1965 he formed two groups: one a septet involving Kenny Wheeler and Alan Skidmore, in which he played contemporary modern jazz, and the other, formed late that year with Watts, the Spontaneous music ensemble (SME), in which he pursued his interest in free improvisation. From January 1966 the SME performed regularly for several years at the Little Theatre Club in London and underwent many changes in size and membership; among those who worked with the ensemble were Rutherford, Derek Bailey, Evan Parker, Wheeler, Julie Tippetts, and the double bass players John Ryan, Clyne, Barry Guy, Dave Holland, and Barre Phillips. Stevens also belonged to Watts's group Amalgam and worked with Stan Tracey, Dudu Pukwana, John Tchicai, and such rock musicians as John Lennon and Yoko Ono. From 1978 he performed less often with the SME; from 1992 until his death the group was a trio (with the saxophonist John Butcher and the guitarist Roger Smith).

In 1971 Stevens co-led, with his fellow drummer Phil Seaman, the sextet Splinters, with Hayes, Tracey, Wheeler, and Clyne as sidemen. He formed the John Stevens Dance Orchestra in 1974 and the jazz-rock band Away in 1975. From 1977 to 1981 he worked in a trio with Guy and Howard Riley which was sometimes, with the addition of Watts, expanded to a quartet. From 1981 Stevens worked regularly with the Norwegian saxophonist Frode Gjerstad, and the two men formed a trio, Detail, with the pianist Eivin One Pederson. When Pederson left in 1982 Stevens and Gjerstad formed another trio in which double bass – Johnny Dyani (to 1986), Paul Rogers, and then Kent Carter – replaced the piano; Bobby Bradford also appeared as a guest soloist on cornet. In 1989 the quartet of Stevens, Gjerstad, Carter, and Bradford toured Norway and recorded with Billy Bang. From 1982 Stevens also led the ten-piece band Folkus, which included Rutherford, and the 12-piece group Freebop, with Bradford, Parker, Courtney Pine, and Peter King among its ranks at various times. He continued to work with Detail (as a trio with Gjerstad and Carter), to lead other bands, and to perform as a sideman in a wide variety of settings right up to his untimely death in 1994. He may be seen in a duo with Bailey in the video *Gig*, taped at a pub in 1992.

From 1968 Stevens became increasingly involved in jazz education and community projects. He ran frequent workshops and in 1985 published *Search and Reflect*, a manual of workshop pieces. From 1983 he was music director of the Jazz Centre Society's Outreach Community Music Project, and he later became the main force in Community Music Ltd, an independent charity, working in community and summer projects with schizophrenics and children and devising an improvisation course for teachers. Shortly before his death he completed *Celebration With Voices*, for 60-piece choir, string quartet, and jazz octet. One of the most vital and imaginative musicians in Britain, Stevens contributed enormously to the growth and appreciation of free and improvised jazz in the country, as well as inspiring and informing many younger musicians and people outside jazz through his numerous educational and community projects.

SELECTED RECORDINGS

Duos: with T. Watts [as Spontaneous Music Ensemble]: *Face to Face* (1973, Emanem 4003); with F. Gjerstad: *Sunshine* (1984, Impetus 18428); with D. Bailey: *Playing* (1992, Incus CD14); with E. Parker: *Corner to Corner* (1993, Ogun 005)

As leader of Spontaneous Music Ensemble (with others): *Challenge* (1966, Eyemark 1002); *Karyöbin* (1968, Isl. 9079); *So, What Do You Think?* (1971, Tangent 118); *A New Distance* (1994, Acta 8)

As leader of trios: with B. Guy and H. Riley: *No Fear* (1977, Spot. 556), *Facets* (1979, Impetus 38002); Detail: *Backwards and Forwards/Forwards and Backwards* (1983, Impetus 18203), *Ness* (1987, Impetus 28509), *Less/More* (1989–90, Circulasione Totale 909089)

As leader of other bands: Amalgam: *Amalgam Plays Blackwell and Higgins* (1972, A Records 002); John Stevens Dance Orchestra: *A luta continua* (1977, 1979, 1981, Konnex 5056); Away: *Integration* (1978, Red 009); Folkus: *The Life of Riley* (1984, Affinity 130); [quartet]: *New Cool* (1992, Jazz Label 006); John Stevens Ensemble: *Blue* (1993, That's Jazz 2008)

BIBLIOGRAPHY

CarrJ; *GrayF*; *WickesIBJ*, i

"Stevens: Ring in the New Wave (British)," *MM* (8 Jan 1966), 6

C. Welch: "Stevens: a Sadder but Wiser Avant Gardist," *MM* (18 Feb 1967), 8

V. Schonfield: "Rule Brittania?," *DB*, xxxv/14 (1968), 24

R. Williams: "John Finds a Place for Amateurs," *MM* (16 May 1970), 8

——: "Total Honesty is John's Motivation," *MM* (27 March 1971), 12

——: "Stevens: Getting in a Jam," *MM* (22 July 1972), 14

I. Carr: *Music Outside: Contemporary Jazz in Britain* (London, 1973), 39

K. Hyder: "Stevens: Searching for Space to Play," *MM* (17 March 1973), 52

B. Case: "Digestible Wig Bubbles Explained," *New Musical Express* (23 Aug 1975), 24

S. Lake: "Stevens: up, up, and Away," *MM* (30 Oct 1976), 33

M. Paton: "Away Day," *MM* (18 June 1977), 32

K. Hyder: "Best of British, no.3: John Stevens," *JJI*, xxxi/4 (1978), 35

D. Blake: "4 to the Bar," *MM* (24 March 1979), 52; (23 June 1979), 52

V. Wilmer: "Freedom Sweet," *MM* (10 Feb 1979), 32

J. Shand: "John Stevens: Free Jazz Pioneer," *Jazz* [Sydney], no.11 (1982), 24

A. Turner: "John Stevens: Spontaneous Music," *The Wire*, no.1 (1982), 30; no.2 (1982), 30

P. Renaud: *La discographie du jazz anglais* (Chaumont, France, 1985)

E. Jost: *Europas Jazz, 1960–1980* (Frankfurt am Main, Germany, 1987), 52, 280

Obituaries: *The Guardian* (16 Sept 1994); *The Times* (27 Sept 1994)

<http://www.shef.ac.uk/misc/rec/ps/efi/mstevens.html> (1998) [incl. biography by M. Davidson, discography]

ED HAZELL/SIMON ADAMS

Stevenson, George (Edward) (*b* Baltimore, 20 June 1906; *d* New York, 21 Sept 1970). Trombonist. He studied saxophone and trombone and first performed locally with his Baltimore Melody Boys. After moving to New York (1928) he played trombone with, among others, Charlie Johnson (1932–3), Rex Stewart (1934), Fletcher Henderson (mid-1935–1936), Claude Hopkins (1936), Ovie Alston (1937), Baron Lee (1938), and Lucky Millinder (1939 – early 1944). In the mid-1940s he worked with Cootie Williams and Roy Eldridge (both 1944) and Cat Anderson (1947), and as a freelance (from 1948) he performed with such musicans as Tony Parenti, Chris Columbus, Don Redman, and Sy Oliver. His playing is represented particularly well by *Trombone Blues* (1956), which he recorded while on tour in Europe with Sammy Price's Blusicians (1955–6). After returning to the USA Stevenson made recordings with Willie "the Lion" Smith (1957) and Stewart (1958) and led his own band in Wantagh, New York (late 1950s). In the 1960s he performed with Joe Thomas (iv), Lem Johnson, and Max Kaminsky, among others.

SELECTED RECORDINGS

As sideman: R. Stewart: Stingaree/Baby, ain't you satisfied? (1934, Voc. 2880); S. Price: *The Price is Right* (1956, Jzt. 1260), incl. Trombone Blues; R. Stewart: on *Rendezvous with Rex* (1958, Felsted 7001), My kind of gal, Tillie's Twist

BIBLIOGRAPHY

AllenH; *ChiltonW*; *FeatherE*

HOWARD RYE

Stevenson, Tommy [Steve; Henry J., Henry Thomas] (*b* *c*1914; *d* New York, Oct 1944). Trumpeter. In 1933 he joined Jimmie Lunceford, with whom he made a number of recordings (1933–4). After leaving Lunceford in about May 1935 he performed and recorded with Blanche Calloway (with whom he appears consistently from June 1935 through 1936 in band listings in the *International Musician* as Henry J. Stevenson) and Don Redman (May 1938 – January 1940, including one listing as H. Thomas Stevenson). He then worked with Slim Gaillard's small group and Coleman Hawkins's big band (the latter from July 1940) and later with Lucky Millinder and Cootie Williams. Stevenson died of pneumonia while with Williams. His solo playing may be heard on Lunceford's *Stomp it Off* (1934, Decca 712), on which he is the unmuted player. (*ChiltonW*; *McCarthyB*)

HOWARD RYE

Steward, Herbie [Herbert Bickford] (*b* Los Angeles, 7 May 1926). Tenor and alto saxophonist. His middle name is taken from California birth records. He took up clarinet at the age of nine and about four years later changed to tenor saxophone, which he began playing professionally in his early teens. He performed with the tenor saxophonist Bob Chester (*c* mid-1942 – autumn 1943), Freddie Slack, and Barney Bigard, recorded with Barney Kessel (1945), and recorded in the big bands of Artie Shaw (1944–6) and Alvino Rey (1946). With Stan Getz, Zoot Sims, and Jimmy Giuffre, he worked in the saxophone section of Gene Roland's band in Los Angeles; through that association he became an original member of Woody Herman's Second Herd (formed in September 1947) and played one of the solos on the first recording of *Four Brothers* (1947). He left Herman on 31 December 1947 (or by another account, two weeks later), before *Four Brothers* became an unexpected hit record, and thus it was his replacement, Al Cohn, who came to be better known to the general public as one of the Four Brothers (with Getz, Sims, and Serge Chaloff). Steward then worked as a freelance, spending a brief period with Red Norvo, and played with the orchestras of Shaw (1949), Tommy Dorsey, Elliot Lawrence (1950–51), Claude Thornhill, and Harry James. He joined James's big band in summer 1951 as a tenor saxophonist, but soon transferred to the lead alto chair, which had recently been vacated by Willie Smith; Smith returned to the band in 1954, in turn replacing Steward. In the mid-1950s Steward moved to Las Vegas, where he worked in orchestras accompanying shows; he later played film music in Hollywood. From that period he performed and recorded jazz only occasionally: he played on the album *Four Brothers Together Again* (1957) with three other former sidemen of Herman's. Around 1970 he moved to San Francisco to work as a studio musician, and later he recorded with Kessel (1975) and as a leader (1981). In 1985 he performed at the Chicago Jazz Festival in a tribute to Sims, and in 1987 he appeared at the North Sea Jazz Festival. He remained active in the San Francisco area in the 1990s. Steward is renowned for his versatility and exceptional sight-reading; his playing is cool and restrained and his phrasing is notable for its clarity and simplicity.

SELECTED RECORDINGS

As leader: *Passport to Pimlico* (1950, Roost 515); with S. Chaloff, A. Cohn, and Z. Sims: *Four Brothers Together Again* (1957, Vik 1096); *The Three Horns of Herb Steward* (1981, FaD 139)

As sideman: W. Herman: Four Brothers (1947, Col. 38304); B. Kessel: *Barney Plays Kessel* (1975, Conc. 9)

BIBLIOGRAPHY

FeatherE; *Feather '60s*

A. Morgan: "Woody's Tenors," *JM*, vi (1960–61), no.7, p.4; no.8, p.13; no.12, p.9

J. A. Treichel: *Woody Herman and the Second Herd, 1947–1949* (n. p., 1978), 13 [discography]

S. Woolley: "Herbie Steward: a Steward's Inquiry," *JJI*, xlii/3 (1989), 12

J. Anderson: "The Forgotten Ones: Herbie Steward," *JJI*, xlviii/5 (1995), 16

DAVE GELLY/BK

Stewart, Bill [William Harris] (*b* Des Moines, IA, 18 Oct 1966). Drummer. His father played trombone and his mother conducted choirs. He taught himself drums from the age of seven, when he received his first set, and learned to read music through piano lessons; while at high school he played in a local pop band. Having studied classical percussion briefly at the University of Northern Iowa in Cedar Falls (1984–5) he transferred to William Paterson College in Wayne, New Jersey, where he was taught by Eliot Zigmund, Dave Samuels, Harold Mabern, Rufus Reid, and Horacee Arnold. From 1986 to 1991 he toured and recorded with Armen Donelian, and in 1987 he recorded with the tenor saxophonist Scott Kreitzer. In spring 1988 he graduated with a degree in jazz studies and performance, and the following year he moved to New York. There Stewart played in local

Bill Stewart at the JVC Grande Parade du Jazz Nice, France, 1989

jam sessions and worked as a freelance, and in 1989 he began what became a lengthy association with Larry Goldings, in whose trio he toured internationally and recorded. He then toured the USA and Europe with Maceo Parker, performed with Joe Lovano, and played in Lee Konitz's quartet alongside Kenny Werner and Ron McClure (all 1990–91). From November 1990 to May 1995 he was a member of John Scofield's quartet, after which he led his own groups, which have included Seamus Blake and the pianist Bill Carrothers, and worked again as a freelance. In 1993 he performed in James Moody's quartet at the first Newark Jazz Festival. Around this time he formed a cooperative trio with Scott Colley and Chris Potter and toured with Jim Hall and with Charlie Haden's Liberation Music Orchestra. Having played with the Blue Note All Stars between December 1995 and January 1996, he rejoined Scofield in April 1996 and toured Europe in a trio alongside Steve Swallow that spring. Stewart has recorded with Marc Copland (from 1990), Kevin Hays and Ron McClure (both 1990), Parker, Konitz, Lovano, and Fred Wesley (all 1990–91), Don Grolnick and Jon Gordon (both 1992), Potter, Tim Hagans, Blake, and Walt Weiskopf (all 1993), Bob Belden and the pianist Peter Delano (both 1993–4), Andy LaVerne and Marty Ehrlich (both 1995), and George Garzone, Ingrid Jensen, and Bill Charlap (all 1996).

Stewart's playing is influenced by the approach to the cymbal of Billy Higgins and Jack DeJohnette and Higgins and Roy Haynes's playing of the snare drum. His tom-tom work, his rock drumming, and the free-jazz aspects of his style reflect the work of DeJohnette, while his tight swing feeling recalls that of Higgins. He is an unobtrusive drummer, although he has the ability to create a dialogue with those he is accompanying.

SELECTED RECORDINGS

As leader: *Think Before You Think* (1989, Jazz City 660.53.024); *Snide Remarks* (1995, BN B21Z-32489); *Telepathy* (1996, BN 53210-2)

As sideman: L. Konitz: *Zounds* (1990, SN 121219-2); J. Lovano: *Landmarks* (1990, BN B21Z-96108); R. McClure: *Never Forget* (1990, Ste. 31279); J. Scofield: *Meant to Be* (1990, BN B21Z-95479); L. Goldings: *Intimacy of the Blues* (c1991, Minor Music 801017); D. Grolnick: *Nighttown* (1992, BN B21Z-98689); J. Scofield: *Hand Jive* (1993, BN B21Z-27327); S. Blake: *The Call* (1993, Criss Cross 1088); M. Ehrlich: *New York Child* (1995, Enja 9025-2); L. Goldings: *Big Stuff* (1996, WB 46271-2); B. Charlap: *Distant Star* (1996, Criss Cross 1131); P. Metheny: *Trio 99→00* (1999, WB 9-47632-2)

BIBLIOGRAPHY

B. Milkowski: "Up & Coming: Bill Stewart," *MD*, xv/9 (1991), 54
L. Birnbaum: "Up and Drumming: the Next Generation of Percussion," *DB*, lx/11 (1993), 27
T. Quénum: "Gros plan: Bill Stewart," *Jm*, no.440 (1994), 24
L. Birnbaum: "Bill Stewart: Nobody's Clone," *DB*, lxii/10 (1995), 30 [incl. discography]
B. Milkowski: "Hearsay: Surprise Kit: Bill Stewart," *JT*, xxv/9 (1995), 27
K. Micallef: "Bill Stewart: in Full Swing," *MD*, xx/3 (1996), 42
——: "Profile: Bill Stewart: Elements of Surprise," *Jazziz*, xiv/6 (1997), 62 [incl. discography]

GK

Stewart, Bob [Robert Alvin] (*b* Sioux Falls, SD, 3 Feb 1945). Tuba player. He appears erroneously in the *Music Index* as Bob (Robert Album) Stewart; his questionnaire for this dictionary gives Robert Alvin. He grew up in Ohio, New York City, and, from 1953, Newport, Rhode Island, played trumpet from the age of ten, and studied trumpet and tuba at the Philadelphia College of the Performing Arts (1962–6, BME). After teaching in public schools he played traditional jazz at Your Father's Moustache in Philadelphia and in 1968 moved to New York; the same year he was an original member of the tuba ensemble Gravity, led by Howard Johnson (ii). He worked in Sam Rivers's big band (1968–75), Frank Foster's Loud Minority (from 1975), the orchestras of Gil Evans (1976–82, making his first tour of Europe in 1976) and Carla Bley (1976–88), with Charles Mingus (1971), in small groups led by Arthur Blythe (from 1973), and with McCoy Tyner (1973, 1980), the Globe Unity Orchestra (from 1978), David Murray's big band (from 1983), Lester Bowie's Brass Fantasy (from 1984), Charlie Haden's Liberation Music Orchestra (1984–7), and Henry Threadgill's orchestra (1986).

In 1987 Stewart formed his First Line Band and made his first album and first tour (of Europe) as a leader. He made further tours of Europe in 1988 and 1989, and led the band (usually as a quintet) into the late 1990s; Stanton Davis, Steve Turre, Carlos Ward, Jerome Harris, Idris Muhammad, Art Baron, and Riley Mullins were among his sidemen at various times. He also continued his associations with Johnson, Foster, Blythe, Bowie, and Murray through the 1990s. From 1987 to 1995 he was a member of Don Cherry's quintet, and in 1992 he recorded in a cooperative quartet with Christof Lauer, Wolfgang Puschnig, and Thomas Alkier. In 1995 he formed a duo with Dave Burrell and began playing with Max Roach's brass quintet (to 1997), Don Byron's Silent Film Project, Ray Anderson's quartet Pocket Brass, and again with Threadgill's orchestra. Late in the decade he toured with a trio consisting of Blythe and Arto Tunçboyaciyan and in a quartet led by Blythe, and he appeared at the Willisau festival in Switzerland in a duo (Heavy Metal) with Anderson. Having taken a ten-year break to concentrate on touring as a performer, Stewart resumed teaching in 1993 as director of the jazz program at LaGuardia High School for the Performing Arts in New York; he had studied at Columbia Teachers College from 1979 to 1981 and later completed graduate work at Lehman College, CUNY (MME 1996).

Stewart has an unusual command of the tuba throughout the instrument's range and he constructs bass lines of great rhythmic and melodic complexity. He should not be confused with the white crooning singer Bob Stewart, who recorded as a leader in the 1980s and 1990s.

SELECTED RECORDINGS

As leader: *First Line* (1987, JMT 880014); with C. Lauer, W. Puschnig, and T. Alkier: *Bluebells* (1992, CMP 56); *Then and Now* (1996, Postcards 1014)

As sideman: Jazz Composer's Orchestra: *The Jazz Composer's Orchestra* (1968, JCOA 1001–2); A. Blythe: *The Grip* (1977, IndN 1029); C. Bley: *European Tour 1977* (1977, Watt 8); A. Blythe: *Bush Baby* (1977, Adelphi 5008); G. Evans: *Gil Evans Live at the Royal Festival Hall* (1978, RCA PL25209); Globe Unity Orchestra: *Intergalactic Blow* (1982, Japo 60039); H. Johnson and Gravity: *Right Now!* (1996, Verve 314-537801-2)

BIBLIOGRAPHY

L. Jeske: "Profile: Bob Stewart," *DB*, xlvii/12 (1980), 48
B. Case: "Jazz: Tuba or Not Tuba," *MM*, lvii (9 Jan 1982), 23
R. Hepola: "The Jazz Niche," *T.U.B.A. Journal*, xvii/2 (1989), 10 [incl. discography]
S. H. Thompson: "Bob Stewart: Tenacious Tuba," *JT* (1989), Sept, 15
K. Whitehead: "Bob Stewart: Interview," *Cadence*, xvi/10 (1990), 9
M. Goldenberg: "Bob Stewart," *Windplayer*, viii/6 (1991), 26
B. Milkowski: "Hearsay: Bob Stewart," *JT*, xxvi/8 (1996), 23
"6th Annual Down Beat Achievement Awards for Jazz Education: Achievement Awards: Bob Stewart," *DB*, lxiv/5 (1997), 50
B. Bennett: "Bass Notes: Jazz Bass on Tuba: Bob Stewart: Bottom Brass," *Bass Player*, ix/2 (1998), 3
R. Hicks: "Bob Stewart," *Coda*, no.283 (1999), 22

ED HAZELL/BK

Stewart, Buddy (*b* Derry, NH, 1922; *d* New Mexico, 1 Feb 1950). Singer. As a child he had a successful career in vaudeville. He later worked in a vocal trio and, after moving to New York, in a duo with Martha Wayne, whom he married; in the early 1940s they both sang in the vocal groups associated with the bands of Glenn Miller and Claude Thornhill. With Dave Lambert and Gene Krupa's band Stewart made the first vocal recording in the bop style – *What's This?* (1945). He continued to be associated with Lambert and two other fellow sidemen in Krupa's group, Charlie Ventura and Red Rodney: in 1946, under Rodney's leadership, Stewart and Lambert recorded *Wahoo*, a wordless variant on the tune *Perdido*, and in 1947 Stewart was a principal soloist with Ventura's ensemble (he was also voted "leading band vocalist" by *Down Beat*). The following year Kai Winding left Ventura to form his own group and Stewart went with him; in 1949 he sang with Charlie Barnet's band and performed again with Lambert and Winding. He was killed in an automobile accident. Although Stewart was known for his warm interpretation of ballads, his major contribution to jazz lies in his pioneering efforts in bop vocalese, both alone and with Lambert.

SELECTED RECORDINGS

As leader: If Love is Trouble/Hee haw (1948, SiW 515); Laughing Boy/Shawn (1948, SiW 512)

As sideman: G. Krupa: What's this? (1945, Col. 36819); A tender word will mend it (1945, Col. 36846); D. Lambert: Perdido (Wahoo) (1946, Key. 657); C. Ventura: Synthesis (1947, Nat. 9036); Pennies from Heaven (1947, Nat. 9077); first issued on C. Parker: *What's This?* (1949, SCAM 3), Deedle, What's This?; C. Barnet: Bebop Spoken Here (1949, Cap. 640)

BIBLIOGRAPHY

FeatherE

LAWRENCE KOCH

Stewart, Louis (*b* Waterford, Ireland, 5 Jan 1944). Irish electric guitarist. A visit to New York in 1961 with a showband led by the clarinetist Jim Doherty stimulated his passion for jazz, and following his return to Ireland he studied intensively and then played with a trio led by the pianist Noel Kelehan. After winning an award as the outstanding European soloist at the Montreux International Jazz Festival (1968), where he performed with Doherty's quartet, he played with Tubby Hayes (1968), toured three times with Benny Goodman (1969–71), and worked in radio and television in Ireland (1971–5). Stewart was then a member of Ronnie Scott's quartet (July 1975–1979), performed with George Shearing (1977–80), and toured Australia with Blossom Dearie (1979). In the 1980s he was based in Dublin and worked as a freelance, playing with, among others, Stephane Grappelli and Spike Robinson, and developing particularly fruitful associations with Scandinavian musicians. As well as maintaining these Nordic connections in the 1990s he toured Britain with Mundell Lowe and Doug Raney (1993), played with Shearing (touring Europe and the USA in 1995), and performed extensively in Germany and Ireland with the German guitarist Heiner Franz. He appeared less frequently with Art Farmer, Stephen Keogh, Michael Moore (i), J. J. Johnson, the London Big Band, Mark Murphy, Kenny Davern, Warren Vaché, and Joe Williams. In 1998 he was awarded an honorary doctorate by Trinity College, Dublin.

SELECTED RECORDINGS

Duos with H. Franz: *I Wished on the Moon* (1999, Jardis 20027)

As leader: with 4 Sure: *Good News* (1986, Villa 001); *Overdrive* (1993, Hep 2057)

As sideman with G. Shearing: *Paper Moon* (1995, Telarc 83375)

BIBLIOGRAPHY

CarrJ; *ChiltonB*

L. Henshaw: "The Source of Stewart," *MM* (15 April 1978), 59

S. Britt: "Louis Stewart," *The Jazz Guitarists* (Poole, England, 1984), 116

R. Comiskey: "Louis the First," *Jazz News*, iii/5 (1989), 23

M. J. Summerfield: *The Jazz Guitar: its Evolution, its Players and Personalities since 1900* (Blaydon on Tyne, England, 4/1998)

MARK GILBERT

Stewart, Michael "Patches" [Michael Kenneth] (*b* New Orleans, 31 July 1955). Trumpeter. He played french horn briefly before taking up trumpet at the age of 11; later he studied theory at Xavier University. After moving to Los Angeles he played extensively with the Brothers Johnson (1979–80), Quincy Jones (1981–2), Al Jarreau (1983–91), and Marcus Miller (from 1989). More occasionally he worked with George Duke, Stanley Turrentine, the keyboard player Bobby Lyle, Lenny White, Patrice Rushen, the alto saxophonist Everette Harp, the soprano saxophonist George Howard, David Benoit, and David Sanborn.

SELECTED RECORDINGS

As leader: *Blue Patches* (1997, Hip Bop 8016); *Penetration* (1998, Hip Bop 8018)

As sideman: B. Lyle: on *Rhythm Stories* (1993, Atl. 82590), Funk Street; D. Sanborn: *Hearsay* (1994, Elek. 61620-2); M. Miller: *Tales* (*c*1994, PRA 60501); *Live and More* (1996, Dreyfus 36585)

BIBLIOGRAPHY

T. Terrell: "Michael 'Patches' Stewart," *JT*, xxvii/7 (1997), 22

MARK GILBERT

Stewart, Rex (William, Jr.) (*b* Philadelphia, 22 Feb 1907; *d* Los Angeles, 7 Sept 1967). Cornetist and bandleader. His father sang and played several instruments, his mother was a pianist, and several of his uncles and an aunt were musicians. Brought up in Washington, DC, from the age of seven, Stewart studied piano, violin, and alto horn before taking up cornet. Having later learned trombone and saxophones as well, he worked as a multi-instrumentalist in minor New York groups from 1921. After playing cornet with Elmer Snowden at the Bamville and Nest clubs (1925–6) he joined Fletcher Henderson's band as a cornetist around May 1926. Feeling unequal to this position, which Louis Armstrong had previously filled, and by his own account having been harrassed relentlessly by Charlie Green, he left in late October to join Horace Henderson's Wilberforce College group, but in November 1928 he returned to Fletcher Henderson, with whom he remained (with interruptions) until early 1933, contributing many solos in a forceful, good-humored style, indebted equally to Armstrong, Bubber Miley, and Bix Beiderbecke. During this period he was also a member of McKinney's Cotton Pickers (summer 1931 and November 1931 – February 1932), and occasionally when circumstances allowed he played concurrently with both bands. In spring 1933 he worked with Fess Williams, and then led a big band at the Empire Ballroom in New York and on tour (*c* June 1933 – autumn 1934). His saxophonist Edgar Sampson wrote *Blue Lou*, *Stomping at the Savoy*, and *Don't Be That Way* for this big band; Ward Pinkett, Rudy Powell, Ram Ramirez, and Sid Catlett were also in the group.

Late in 1934, after working as a freelance and then spending a little over one week in Luis Russell's orchestra, Stewart joined the Duke Ellington Orchestra, beginning his most creative period. During his 11 years with the band he created a distinctive element in Ellington's ensemble sound, particularly with his mock-conversational "talking" style and the novel HALF-VALVE effects which he explored from 1937. He was the co-composer of several of Ellington's pieces (including *Boy Meets Horn* and *Morning Glory*), and also led excellent small-group recording sessions using other members of Ellington's band. In July 1943 he played with Benny Carter in Southern California, then led his own band and spent another period with Ellington (October 1943 – December 1945). Stewart formed his own group early in 1946 and made a long tour of Europe (1947–9), during which he lectured on jazz at the Paris Conservatoire (1948). He spent the latter part of 1949 as a freelance in Australia. In the early 1950s he entered semiretirement, but led the Fletcher Henderson reunion band in 1957 and 1958 and during this same period led bands at Eddie Condon's club. In his later years he became well known as a writer of urbane, anecdotal pieces on jazz, several of which were reprinted posthumously as *Jazz Masters of the Thirties* (New York and London, n.d. [1972]); an autobiographical collection (with C. P. Gordon) appeared later as *Boy Meets Horn* (Wheatley, Oxford, England, and Ann Arbor, MI, 1991); Stewart's papers are held in the Archive Center of the National Museum of American History, Smithsonian Institution, Washington, DC (*see* LIBRARIES AND ARCHIVES, §2).

Oral history material in *NjR*.

For illustrations *see* BANDS, fig.3, and HENDERSON, FLETCHER.

SELECTED RECORDINGS

As leader: Rexatious/Lazy Man's Shuffle (1936, Var. 517); Fat Stuff Serenade (1939, Voc. 5448); Low Cotton (1939, Swing 203); Finesse (1939, Swing 70); Linger Awhile (1940, Bb B11057); Mobile Bay (1947, BStar 74); with D. Wells: *Chatter Jazz* (1959, RCA LSP2024)

As sideman: F. Henderson: The Stampede (1926, Col. 654D); Singin' the Blues (1931, Col. 2565D); D. Ellington: Trumpet in Spades (Rex's Concerto) (1936, Bruns. 7752); Braggin' in Brass (1938, Bruns. 8099); Boy Meets Horn (1938, Bruns. 8306); Subtle Lament (1939, Bruns. 8344); Morning Glory (1940, Vic. 26536); Dusk (1940, Vic. 26677); Take the "A" Train (1941, Vic. 27380); Perdido (1941, Vic. 27880); Main Stem (1942, Vic. 20-1556)

SELECTED FILMS AND VIDEOS

Hellzapoppin' (1941); Hot Chocolate [Cottontail] (1941); Jam Session (1942); Duke Ellington and his Orchestra (1943); Rendez-vous de Juillet (1949); The Sound of Jazz (1957); Jazz on a Summer's Day (1960)

BIBLIOGRAPHY

AllenH; *ChiltonW*; *McCarthyB*; *SchullerS*; *TuckerDE*

H. Oakley: "Rex Stewart," *Jh*, 1st ser., no.14 (1936), 6

B. Fleagle: "Rex," *HRS Society Rag* ([1940]), Aug, 10

C. Wilford: "Rex Stewart as I Knew Him," *Jazz Music*, viii/43 (1943), 7; repr. in *Record Changer*, vi/5 (1947), 11

G. E. Lambert: "Rex Stewart," *JM*, iii/11 (1958), 2

B. Houghton: "Rex in Perspective," *JJ*, xix/5 (1966), 18

J. Postgate: "Rex Stewart," *JM*, xii/3 (1966), 3

S. Voce and A. Judd: "Rexatious," *JJ*, xxi (1968), no.2, p.14; no.3, p.12; no.4, p.12

G. Conrad: "Rex Stewart in Berlin," *JJ*, xxiv/3 (1971), 13

F. Thorne: "Rex William Stewart, Jr.," *Jazz Masters of the Thirties*, ed. R. Stewart (New York and London, n.d. [1972]), 209

G. M. Colombé: "Rex Stewart in Europe, 1966," *JJ*, xxvi/8 (1973), 22

J. Simmen: "Crystal Clear," *Coda*, xii/1 (1974), 25

B. Bastin, ed.: "Trumpet (At)tributes: More Johnny Simmen Snippets," *Sv*, no. 125 (1986), 163

J. Sutherland: "Rex Stewart: Man with a Horn," *Coda*, no.l211 (1986), 4

M. Jones: *Talking Jazz* (London, 1987), 78

G. Bushell and M. Tucker: *Jazz from the Beginning* (Wheatley, Oxford, England, 1988, Ann Arbor, MI, 1990), 121

V. Wilmer: "Fatstuff Afterhours: an Interview with Rex Stewart," *Coda*, no.238 (1991), 24

J. BRADFORD ROBINSON/BK

Stewart, Slam [Leroy Elliott] (*b* Englewood, NJ, 21 Sept 1914; *d* Binghamton, NY, 10 Dec 1987). Double bass player and leader. His birth name is unknown; in the oral history held at *NjR* (JOHP), he mentions that he was adopted, but declines to give details. He took up violin at around the age of six and double bass while in high school. Befriended by his adopted father's employer, he was able to afford to study for one year at the Boston Conservatory, where he heard the violinist Ray Perry humming and playing in unison and decided to adapt that gimmick to the double bass by humming an octave above the bowed instrument; this became Stewart's excessively overused musical signature, heard in his bass melodies through more than four decades of recordings.

After playing locally during his studies in Boston, Stewart worked with Peanuts Holland in Buffalo (1936) and then began to perform in the New York area. He first attracted attention in 1937 in a novelty duo called "Slim and Slam" with Slim Gaillard, when they performed on Martin Block's radio show "The Make Believe Ballroom"; their riff tune *The Flat Foot Floogie* became extremely popular. Stewart toured with Gaillard, making further recordings and appearing in the film *Hellzapoppin'* (1941), until the guitarist was inducted in 1942. He also performed with the Spirits of Rhythm (spring 1939), played in Van Alexander's dance orchestra (1940), and led a trio at Kelly's Stable, New York (late 1940).

Early in 1943 Stewart went to Hollywood to perform as a member of Fats Waller's group in the film *Stormy Weather*. While he was there, Tiny Grimes took Gaillard's place in the duo, and soon afterwards the two men played at a jam session with Art Tatum, as a result of which Tatum's trio was formed (for illustration *see* TATUM, ART). Stewart, gifted with perfect pitch and a great facility with American popular songs, was perhaps the only one of Tatum's various accompanists to remain unperturbed by the pianist's harmonic impetuosity. The trio played mainly at the Three Deuces in New York, during which time Stewart also recorded with Lester Young (December 1943), joined Johnny Guarnieri's trio at the same venue, and played in Grimes's quartet (both 1944). Late in 1944 Tatum returned to the Los Angeles area and Stewart took over leadership of the trio, with Erroll Garner serving as pianist at the Three Deuces and on tour to early 1946. Stewart also was the double bass player in Benny Goodman's quintet and sextet from late January to November 1945. He performed with Don Byas, Red Norvo, and Teddy Wilson in an acclaimed concert recorded at Town Hall, New York, on 9 June 1945, and during the course of that year made important studio recordings with Dizzy Gillespie, Norvo, and Byas. In 1946 Billy Taylor (ii) replaced Garner in the trio, which also worked as a quartet with the addition of Doc West. After being reunited with Tatum in spring 1946, Stewart resumed leading the trio, now with Taylor and John Collins; Mary Lou Williams was a member in 1947.

In May 1948 Stewart performed with Garner at the Festival International de Jazz in Paris. He then moved to Los Angeles and resumed working with Tatum; Everett Barksdale was their companion in the trio into the early 1950s. Stewart played with Roy Eldridge's quartet (1953), Beryl Booker (1953–5), and the singer and pianist Rose Murphy (1956–1960s), and appeared with Gaillard at the Great South Bay Jazz Festival in Great River, New York (July 1958). In the mid-1960s he moved to Binghamton, New York, where he worked in television studios and from 1971 taught music at schools and SUNY, Binghamton, and produced concerts. He continued to perform, leading a trio in New York City (late 1968), making a final appearance with Gailliard at the Monterey Jazz Festival (1970), and touring Europe with Milt Buckner and Jo Jones (April 1970). After appearing with Goodman at the Newport Jazz Festival New

York (1973) he toured widely with the clarinetist (1973 – March 1976), returning to Europe in 1974. Although he suffered a heart attack and a stroke, he performed at the Grand Parade du Jazz in Nice, France, in July 1977. That same year he worked in New York with Bucky Pizzarelli; in 1978 their duo appeared frequently on the "Today Show" on NBC television. Stewart rejoined Goodman in 1979 and in June 1985, and he toured with Illinois Jacquet from around 1980 to 1981. In May 1984 he received an honorary doctorate in music from SUNY, Binghamton, and in 1986 he was prominently featured in the public television special "Benny Goodman: Let's Dance." Although best known for his unique solo style, Stewart was also a fleet accompanist, as is evident from his early bop recordings with Gillespie, and especially his remarkable saxophone and bass duos with Byas at Town Hall.

Oral history material in *CtY, NjR* (JOHP).

SELECTED RECORDINGS

Duos with D. Byas: Indiana (1945, Jazz Star 47101); I got rhythm (1945, Jazz Star 47102)

As leader: *Slam Stewart* (1972, BB 33027); *Slamboree* (1972, BB 33049)

As sideman: S. Gaillard: The Flat Foot Floogie (1938, Voc. 4021); L. Young: Afternoon of a Basieite/Sometimes I'm Happy (1943, Key. 604); J. Guarnieri: Bowing Singing Slam (1944, Savoy 530); A. Tatum: Topsy (1944, Asch 4522); D. Gillespie: Groovin' High (1945, Guild 1001); All the Things You Are (1945, Musi. 488); R. Norvo: Slam Slam Blues (1945, Dial 1045); D. Byas: Three o'Clock in the Morning (1945, Super Disc 1006); A. Tatum: *Art Tatum Trio* (1952, Cap. H408)

SELECTED FILMS AND VIDEOS

Hellzapoppin' (1941); Stormy Weather (1943); Boy! What a Girl (1947); Harlem Follies (1950)

BIBLIOGRAPHY

J. Burns: "Slim & Slam," *JJ*, xxi/9 (1968), 4

F. Borromeo: "Slam Stewart Discography," *DF*, no.21 (1970) – no.31 (1972); contd in no.36 (1976), 1

L. Tomkins: "How my Bass Started Singing," *CI*, xiii/4 (1974), 17

D. Long: "Slam Stewart," *Cadence*, viii (1982), no.9, p.8; no.11, p.8

J. M. Doran: *Erroll Garner: the Most Happy Piano* (Metuchen, NJ, and London, 1985), 59

——: "Slam Stewart Interview," *ARJS*, iii (1985), 131

J. Simmen: "Ceux qui s'en vont: Slam Stewart," *BHcF*, no.366 (1989), 19

BK

Stichting Jazz en Geïmproviseerde Muziek in Nederland. Organization formed in August 1965 as Stichting Jazz in Nederland (SJIN) to foster an interest in jazz in the Netherlands and to administer the annual award of the Wessel Ilcken Prize (later known as the Boy Edgar Prize, then as the Dutch National Jazz Prize). The organization first included musicians on its managing board in November 1970 and worked with the BIM (Beroepsvereniging van Improviserende Musici [Professional association of improvising musicians]) from its formation in November 1971. The organization also advised the Dutch government on the granting of subsidies for performance to jazz musicians. Its headquarters were in Amsterdam. At the beginning of 1997 it was absorbed into the MUZIEK EN THEATER NETWERK.

WIM VAN EYLE

Stichting National Jazz Archief. Dutch foundation formed in 1980 to run the National Jazz Archief in Amsterdam (*see* LIBRARIES AND ARCHIVES, §2). It later took the name Nederlands Jazz Archief.

Stick. The standard beater used by the jazz drummer; *see* DRUM SET, §I, 8.

Stief, Bo (*b* Copenhagen, 15 Oct 1946). Danish bass player. He began his career as a freelance, in 1963, playing at the Montmartre Jazzhus. In the following years he toured Europe with Dollar Brand (1964), Don Cherry (1966), Palle Mikkelborg, and Krysztof Komeda. From 1966 to 1968 he was a member of a quintet led by Alex Riel and Mikkelborg, after which he was with Eje Thelin and joined the Danish Radiojazzgruppen (i). Later he worked in Riel and Mikkelborg's octet V8 (1970–75) and Mikkelborg's group Entrance (1975–85), and with the pianist Niels Thybo (1990s). He began leading his own groups in 1980, first a trio, which in 1982 became a quintet, and from the 1990s the bands Chasing Dreams and Dream Machine. Much in demand as an accompanist in Europe, Stief performed and recorded with, among others, Dexter Gordon, Bobby Jones, Arne Domnérus, Terje Rypdal, Jan Garbarek, Francy Boland, Peter Herbolzheimer, Joachim Kühn, Carla Bley, Ben Webster, Jackie McLean, Philip Catherine, Niels Lan Doky, Toots Thielemans, Zoot Sims, Al Cohn, Stan Getz, Didier Lockwood, Allan Botschinsky, Eddie Harris, Frank Rosolino, Frans Bak, Jasper van 't Hof, Dizzy Gillespie, Manfred Schoof, the EBU Big Band, Miles Davis, Eddie "Lockjaw" Davis, and the Tolvan Big Band.

SELECTED RECORDINGS

As leader: *Hidden Frontiers* (1986–7, Replay 3505); *Chasing Dreams* (1993, Col. 475548-2); *Heart & Destiny* (1997–8, Dream Song Music/Kilofon 9904); with N. Thybo and Lennart Gruvstedt: *Trio Music* (1998, Stunt 19810)

As sideman: Entrance: *Entrance* (1977, Met. 15612), incl. Cream; F. Rosolino: *In Denmark* (1978, Vantage 507); A. Botschinsky: *Allan Botschinsky Quintet* (1982, Stunt 8301); M. Davis: *Aura* (1985, Col. CK45332); N. L. Doky: *The Truth* (1987, Sto. 4144); A. Domnérus: *When Lights Are Low* (1988, Salut 8434); P. Mikkelborg: *Anything but Grey* (1992, Col. 471614-2)

BIBLIOGRAPHY

K. Frandsen: *Politikens jazzleksikon* (Copenhagen, 1987)

I. Rod: "To play betyder at lege" [To play means to play], *Jazz Special*, no.42 (1998), 22

ERIK WIEDEMANN/FRANK BÜCHMANN-MØLLER

Stinson, Albert (Forrest, Jr.) (*b* Cleveland, 2 Aug 1944; *d* Boston, 2 June 1969). Double bass player. He played piano, trombone, and tuba as a child and double bass from the age of 14. During his short career he performed with Terry Gibbs (from 1961), Chico Hamilton (1962–5), and Charles Lloyd's quartet (briefly from late 1965), then worked as a freelance in California (from 1966); he also toured with John Handy (1967) and Larry Coryell (1969). Stinson had reliable intonation, a virtuoso technique, and a clear, sharp attack that recalled the playing of Charles Mingus; his solos were notable for the elegance of their structure.

SELECTED RECORDINGS

As sideman: C. Hamilton: *Passin' Thru* (1962, Imp. 29); *A Different Journey* (1963, Rep. 96078); *Man from Two Worlds* (1963, Imp. 59); D. Budimir: *The Session with Albert* (1964, Rev. 14); C. Hamilton: *El Chico* (1965, Imp. 9102)

BIBLIOGRAPHY

J. W. Hardy: "Caught in the Act," *DB*, xxxiii/5 (1966), 34

M. Hennessey: "Albert and the New Breed of Bass Players," *MM* (2 Sept 1967), 6

D. C. Hunt: "Al Stinson: Exciting New Bass Face," *J&P*, vii/8 (1968), 40

Obituary, *DB*, xxxvi/15 (1969), 7

JOHN VOIGT

Stitt, Sonny [Edward] (*b* Boston, 2 Feb 1924; *d* Washington, DC, 22 July 1982). Saxophonist. The son of musicians, he studied piano before taking up clarinet and alto saxophone.

Sonny Stitt

In Saginaw, Michigan, where he grew up, he received lessons informally from the local saxophonist Big Nick Nicholas and from Wardell Gray, who, in the absence of an African-American hotel in the town, often stayed in Stitt's room. Before graduating from high school he toured widely during summer vacations in bands which included Nicholas and Thad Jones. He then joined Sabby Lewis in Boston (*c*1942) and became a member of the 'Bama State Collegians (1942–3), with whom he traveled from Detroit to New York. There he began to participate in bop jam sessions. He played alto saxophone in Tiny Bradshaw's big band (July 1943–1944), then joined Billy Eckstine's big band (late April – autumn 1944), which included such young bop players as Fats Navarro, Dexter Gordon, Gene Ammons, and Art Blakey. His association with the leaders of the new bop movement continued in Dizzy Gillespie's sextet and big band (March–June 1946). Having become addicted to heroin, Stitt had his New York City police cabaret card taken away, and late in 1946 or early in 1947 he traveled to Chicago, where he played with Ammons and Miles Davis in jam sessions, joined Johnny Griffin's group at Saturday night dances at the Pershing Ballroom, and led his own bands. In the summer of 1947 he moved to Detroit and worked with Gillespie, Davis, and Charlie Parker.

After returning to New York Stitt began playing tenor and baritone saxophones as well as alto, often in a quintet that he founded with Ammons in autumn 1949. In December he made outstanding recordings as a leader with Bud Powell, Curley Russell, and Max Roach; this quartet was joined by Davis, Benny Green, and Serge Chaloff for a concert at Carnegie Hall later that same month. During 1950 and 1951 Ammons and Stitt often worked at Birdland, and thereafter they played together occasionally (until 1955). In 1954 Stitt had spent a brief period in Los Angeles as a member of the new Max Roach–Clifford Brown Quintet, but he left before they recorded. He rejoined Gillespie early in 1958 for three months. He twice toured Britain with Jazz at the Philharmonic (1958, 1959), and, after appearing in the film *Jazz on a Summer's Day* (1960), returned to Europe as a replacement for John Coltrane in Davis's quintet (September 1960). He left Davis early in 1961, and was reunited with Ammons for performances in Chicago (late 1961 – February 1962) and recordings. Later he visited Japan in a sextet with Johnson and Clark Terry (1964), toured widely with the Giants of Jazz (1971–2, with Gillespie, Kai Winding, Thelonious Monk, Al McKibbon, and Blakey), and performed at the Newport Jazz Festival New York and in Europe in *The Musical Life of Charlie Parker* (1974). But his principal activity was as a freelance leader and soloist, in which capacity he recorded more than 100 albums. He toured Europe in 1964, performed at the Gyllene Cirkeln in Stockholm in 1966, returned to Scandinavia in 1967, and thereafter visited Europe routinely; a performance at the Umbria Jazz Festival is preserved in the film *Jazz in piazza* (1974). He also went again to Japan, where he recorded several times, as well as to Israel and Brazil. Fond of competitive jam sessions, he often sought out saxophone "battles"; among his colleagues in this activity, after Ammons, were Art Pepper, Eddie "Lockjaw" Davis, Sonny Rollins, Paul Gonsalves, Zoot Sims, Ricky Ford, and finally Red Holloway, with whom he toured England in 1980. His last performance took place in Japan just a few days before his death.

Stitt's early recorded solos show clearly that he was a disciple of Charlie Parker; he used Parker's favorite melodic formulas and imitated his tone quality and vibrato. Only small details of phrasing and articulation – an occasional slight hesitation in connecting notes in a Parkeresque phrase, or a subtly different way of tonguing – betray the imitator. Over the years he gradually added a number of individual melodic formulas to his vocabulary, but Parker's influence always dominated his solos on the alto saxophone, even when he used the Varitone, an electronic sound-modifying attachment which he adopted soon after its appearance on the market in 1966. He probably turned initially to the tenor and baritone saxophones in an effort to escape his image as Parker's follower; the baritone instrument proved to be but a temporary diversion, but the tenor opened up new lines of musical thought for him. He made his most distinctive statements on this instrument, which he played frequently from 1950.

SELECTED RECORDINGS

As leader: All God's Chillun Got Rhythm/Sunset (1949, Prst. 705); Sonny Side (1949, Prst. 722); Bud's Blues (1949, Prst. 706); Imagination (1950, Prst. 733); with G. Ammons: Chabootie (1950, Prst. 741); *Sonny Stitt Plays Arrangements from the Pen of Quincy Jones* (1955, Roost 2204); *Personal Appearance* (1957, Verve 8324); with D. Gillespie and S. Rollins: *Duets with Sonny Rollins and Sonny Stitt* (1957, Verve 8260), *Sonny Side Up* (1957, Verve 8262); *Burnin'* (1958, Argo 661); *Sonny Stitt Sits in with the Oscar Peterson Trio* (1959, Verve 8344); *A Little Bit of Stitt* (1959, Roost 2235); *Sonny Side Up* (1960, Roost 2245); with G. Ammons: *Boss Tenors* (1961, Verve 68426); *Sonny Stitt Plays Bird* (1963, Atl. 1418); with P. Gonsalves: *Salt and Pepper* (1963, Imp. 52); *What's New!!! Sonny Stitt Plays the Varitone* (1966, Roul. 25343); *Tune-Up!* (1972, Cob. 9013); *Constellation* (1972, Cob. 9021); *So Doggone Good* (1972, Prst. 10074); *12!* (1972, Muse 5006); *In Walked Sonny* (1975, Sonet 691); *Good Life* (1980, Trio 25015)

As sideman: D. Gillespie: Oop bop sh-bam/That's Earl, Brother (1946, Musi. 383); Bebop Boys: Boppin' a Riff (1946, Savoy 588); Fat Boy (1946, Savoy 587); G. Ammons: Blues up and down/You Can Depend on Me (1950, Birdland 6005); Seven Eleven (1950, Prst. 725); Modern Jazz Sextet: *The Modern Jazz Sextet* (1956, Norg. 1076); Giants of Jazz: *The Giants of Jazz* (1971, Atl. 2-905)

BIBLIOGRAPHY

D. B. Bittan: "Don't Call me Bird," *DB*, xxvi/10 (1959), 19
L. Tomkins: "Sonny Stitt Says There's No Successor to Bird," *MM* (16 May 1959), 6
M. Jones: "Stitt, Parker, and the Question of Influence," *JM*, v/11 (1960), 9
M. Williams: "Sonny Stitt in the Studio," *JJ*, xvi/8 (1963), 12
M. Delorme and P. Koechlin: "Stitt le laconique," *Jh*, no.200 (1964), 27
R. Scott: "But This Time, my Prince Has Come," *MM* (9 May 1964), 10
B. McRae: *The Jazz Cataclysm* (London, South Brunswick, NJ, and New York, 1967/*R*1985), 20
J. Burns: "Early Stitt," *JJ*, xxii/10 (1969), 6
J. A. Mitchell: "Gallery: Sonny Stitt," *JM*, ii/4 (1978), 25
A. Pepper and L. Pepper: *Straight Life: the Story of Art Pepper* (New York and London, 1979, rev. 2/1994) [incl. discography by T. Selbert]
B. Case: "How Stitt Lost his Bottle," *MM* (15 Aug 1981), 20
A. Levitt: "Le nouveau style de Stitt," *Jm*, no.304 (1982), 16
Obituaries: *Los Angeles Times* (23 July 1982); *New York Times* (24 July 1982); G. Giddins, *VV* (10 Aug 1982), repr. in *Rhythm-a-ning: Jazz Tradition and Innovation in the '80s* (New York, and Oxford, England, 1985), 108
"Sonny Stitt," *SJ*, xxxvi/3 (1982), 240 [discography]
J. Chambers: *Milestones*, ii: *The Music and Times of Miles Davis since 1960* (Toronto, Buffalo, and London, 1985), 25
D. Salemann, D. Hartmann, and M. Vogler: *Sonny Stitt: Solography, Discography, Band Routes, Engagements, in Chronological Order* (Basel, Switzerland, 1986)
W. Enstice and P. Rubin: *Jazz Spoken Here: Conversations with Twenty-two Musicians* (Baton Rouge, LA, and London, 1992), 240

THOMAS OWENS/BK

Stitzel, Mel(ville J.) (*b* Germany, 9 Jan 1902; *d* Chicago, 31 Dec 1952). Pianist and arranger. He was brought up in Chicago. In 1923 he made several recordings as a member of the New Orleans Rhythm Kings (for illustration *see* NEW ORLEANS RHYTHM KINGS), among them *Maple Leaf Rag* (Gen. 5104) and – credited in some sources as his own composition – *Tin Roof Blues* (Gen. 5105). He also recorded with Muggsy Spanier in the Bucktown Five (1924) and Stomp Six (1925) and in a trio with Benny Goodman (1928). From 1925 he played and wrote arrangements for a large number of bands in Chicago, and he continued performing regularly in the 1930s. Stitzel later led his own band (1940s) and worked with Danny Alvin (early 1950s).

based on *ChiltonW*

Stivín, Jiří (*b* Prague, 23 Nov 1942). Czech flutist, alto and tenor saxophonist, and composer. His mother was an actress. Although he learned violin in his youth, he initially studied cinematography at the Prague Film Academy (FAMU; 1961–5). Following graduation he began to play flute, on which he took classical lessons through much of the 1960s; he was self-taught on saxophone, which he learned while playing in rock bands early in that decade. He then worked with the keyboard player Martin Kratochvíl in the band Jazz Q (1964–7) and in Karel Velebný's group SHQ (1967–9) and recorded in Pavel Smetáček's group Traditional Jazz Studio (1966 or 1967) and with Velebný's nonet (1968). In 1969 he studied with John Dankworth at the Royal Academy of Music in London and played in the Scratch Orchestra, an experimental ensemble led by the avant-garde composer Cornelius Cardew.

After returning to Prague Stivín worked in the new music group Quax, and in 1970 he re-formed Jazz Q (recording in March of that year); he also joined the Czechoslav radio big band and a band led by Milan Svoboda. By late that year he had formed the free-jazz group Stivín and Co. Jazz Systém, which in 1972 recorded as a sextet including Rudolf Dašek, Barre Phillips, and Zbigniew Seifert. From 1971 to 1975 he worked frequently and recorded with Dašek in the duo Systém Tandem. He recorded with Gustav Brom (1974), in a trio with Dašek and Tony Scott (1978), in a duo with Pierre Favre (1979), and with the ensemble Interjazz IV (1979); as a leader he recorded an album of his own compositions (*Zodiak*, 1976) and with a large ensemble involving such leading European improvisors as Albert Mangelsdorff, Radu Malfatti, Willem Breuker, Trevor Watts, Alan Skidmore, Rüdiger Carl, Tony Oxley, Louis Moholo, and Günter Sommer.

In the 1980s, while continuing to lead Stivín and Co. Jazz Systém, Stivín began performing as an unaccompanied soloist (often supported by taped accompaniment) and with the percussionist Alan Vitouš, as well as recording with Velebný (1980) and the singer Mirka Křivánková (1984). Reunited with Dašek, he performed in the duo Systém Tandem again from 1985. In the early 1990s he began an association with Ali Haurand: they performed regularly in a duo, as members of the group Pantomime & Jazz with the mime Milan Sládek, and as fellow sidemen in the European Jazz Ensemble. At some point he formed a duo with Wolfgang Lackerschmid, and around 1998 he recorded again in a duo with Favre.

In addition to his work in jazz, from 1975 Stivín has performed and recorded concertos for recorder by Georg Philipp Telemann and Antonio Vivaldi, as well as works by other pre-classical composers. He has written a large corpus of film, theater, and concert music, he teaches at the conservatory in Prague and at annual jazz workshops in Frýdlant, Bohemia, and he gives educational concerts for children. He was the subject of the documentary *Jří Stivín, méně známý český kameraman* [Jiří Stivín, a lesser-known Czech cameraman], directed for Czech television by Jan Malíř Radim Smetana.

His son Jiří Stivín, Jr., is a drummer and his daughter Zuzana Stivínová is a singer; in the early 1990s they recorded in Stivín and Co. Jazz Systém, and father and son have recorded an album of duos.

SELECTED RECORDINGS

Duos with R. Dašek: *Systém Tandem* (1974, Japo 60008); *Reunion* (1989, Sup. 111224-2)
As leader: *Five Hits in a Row* (1972, Sup. 1151229); *Zodiak* (1976, Sup. 1152015); *Inspiration with Folklor* (*c*1992, Arta 10004); with R. van den Broek and A. Haurand: *Bordertalk* (1994, Konnex 5068)
As sideman with K. Velebný: *SHQ* (1967, ESP 1080)

BIBLIOGRAPHY

Feather–Gitler '70s
H. Rothová: "O jednotě v ruznosti" [On unity in diversity], *Hudební rozhledy*, xxxvi/5 (1983), 222
J. Veverková: "Dva večery se Stivínem" [Two evenings with Stivín], *Hudební rozhledy*, xxxvii/2 (1984), 62
——: "Stivínovy besidky v městské knihovně" [Stivín's get-togethers in the municipal library], *Hudební rozhledy*, xxxvii/6 (1984), 262
F. Schulz: "Jiří Stivín/Rudolf Dašek," *JP*, xxxv/3 (1986), 29
M. Kunzler: *Jazz-Lexicon* (Reinbek, nr Hamburg, Germany, 1988)
I. Poledňák: *Mne všechno dvakrát, aneb, O Jiřím Stivinovi* [Twice as much for me, or, On Jiří Stivín] (Prague, 1989)
A. Matzner, I. Poledňák, and I. Wasserberger, eds.: *Encyklopedie jazzu a moderní populární hudby* (Prague, 1990) [incl. transcriptions]
S. Barancicova: "Pocta svate Cecilii a Stivínovi" [Homage to St. Cecilia and Stivín], *Hudební rozhledy*, xlvi/1 (1993), 21
<http://music.taxoft.cz/ascii/jiri_stivin/> (2000) [incl. discography]
<http://www.hudba.cx/jmena/stivin_e.htm> (2001)
<http://www.jazzbox.com/eje/playerslist.html> (2001)

BERT NOGLIK/GK

Stobart, Kathy [Florence Kathleen] (*b* South Shields, England, 1 April 1925). English tenor saxophonist. She grew up in a musical family and studied piano and then saxophone. At the age of 14 she joined a band in Newcastle, and late in 1942 she moved to London, where she played with various informal groups and with such visiting players as Peanuts Hucko and Art Pepper. From the latter part of World War II to 1948 she worked in bands led by the Canadian pianist Art Thompson, who was at that time her husband; they played briefly in Palm Springs, California, before returning to the UK in May 1948. During this period Stobart also worked with Vic Lewis (spring 1947). She appeared as a soloist in Sweden (September 1948), toured and recorded with Lewis (from spring 1949, including an appearance at the Festival International de Jazz, Paris), and performed in the Netherlands. Later she formed her own ensemble, which included Derek Humble, Dill Jones, and the trumpeter Bert Courtley; it recorded in 1951 but disbanded soon afterwards, when Stobart renewed her association with Lewis. Having divorced Thompson and married Courtley she went into semiretirement while she brought up her family. During this period she worked as a session musician and deputized briefly for Jimmy Skidmore in Humphrey Lyttelton's band (late 1957 into 1958). She played with Tony Kinsey (1959), Eddie Thompson's quintet (1960), and Courtley's sextet (April 1961–*c*1962), formed her own group, and worked with Courtley's band in the last years of his life (he died in 1969).

While teaching for nearly two decades at the City Literary Institute, Stobart studied clarinet at the Guildhall School of Music, led a quintet, worked with John Picard (late 1960s – early 1970s), and, most notably, was a member of Lyttelton's band (late 1969–1978). In the mid-1970s her own groups included Harry Beckett and John Burch, and from 1979 into the early 1980s she co-led a band with the vibraphonist Lennie Best; among her recordings as a leader is the album *Arbeia* (1978, Spot. 509). Thereafter she led her own quintet and sextet, played on cruise ships, and appeared as a guest soloist with Lyttelton, with whom she recorded the album *Movin' and Groovin'*, 1983, BL 760504). She also played in New York with Marian McPartland and with Zoot Sims, at the first British women's jazz festival (1982), and with Gail Thompson's band Gail Force (1986). From the late 1980s into the early 1990s she co-led another quintet with the saxophonist Joan Cunningham, then in spring 1991 she rejoined Lyttelton. She continues to be active as a teacher, and she also plays alto, soprano, and baritone saxophones.

BIBLIOGRAPHY

CarrJ; *ChiltonB*; *Feather '60s*
P. Pitt: "Kathy's Crown," *MM* (16 Sept 1972), 30
H. Witt: "Queen of the Tenor," *MM* (17 Feb 1973), 50
L. Tomkins: "The Kathy Stobart Story," *CI*, xii/8 (1974), 14
R. Cotterell, ed.: *Jazz Now: the Jazz Centre Society Guide* (London, 1976)
D. Eberhard: "Eine ungewöhnliche Karriere Kathy Stobart," *JP*, xxxi/6 (1982), 11
V. Wilmer: "Kathy Stobart: Music in my Blood," *JF* [intl edn], no.76 (1982), 43
S. Worsfold: "Kathy Stobart: Interview," *Turntable* (1986), July

SALLY-ANN WORSFOLD/BK

Stock arrangement. A simplified, strictly practical arrangement in a conventional style, usually commercially available in published form; *see* ARRANGEMENT, §1.

Stockhausen, Markus (Pirol) (*b* Cologne, Germany, 2 May 1957). German trumpeter and composer. His father is the composer Karlheinz Stockhausen. He took up piano at the age of six and trumpet when he was 12, then from 1974 to 1982 he studied piano and both classical and jazz trumpet in Cologne at the Musikhochschule – this last with Manfred Schoof. Stockhausen appeared frequently in performances of his father's works from 1974 into the 1990s and worked as an independent classical composer and soloist. At the same time he sustained a career in jazz: he played in and led various ensembles, among them the quintet Key (1974–9), the Rainer Brüninghaus Group (1980–84), Kairos (1984–90), Aparis (1989–96), and Possible Worlds (1993–5), and performed in duos with Jasper van 't Hof (1980), Gary Peacock (1988–9), the pianist Fabrizio Ottaviucci (1987), and his sister, the pianist Majella Stockhausen. In addition he worked with the double bass player Enrique Diaz (1990–99), Michel Portal (1997), Antoine Hervé (1997–8), and Arild Andersen (1999), and toured worldwide for the Goethe Institut. He has also collaborated regularly with his brother Simon (Tobias Jonas Martin) Stockhausen (*b* Bensberg, Germany, 5 June 1967), both on recordings (notably the first album by Aparis) and on various film and theater scores. From 1996 he has taught at the Musikhochschule in Cologne.

SELECTED RECORDINGS

Duos with J. van 't Hof: *Aqua sansa* (1980, Fran 01012)
As leader: *Cosi lontano* (1988, ECM 1371); *Sol mestizo* (1995, ACT 9222-2); with WDR Big Band: *Jubilee* (1996, EMI Classics 7243-5-56265-2-3)
As sideman: R. Towner: *City of Eyes* (1988, ECM 1388); Aparis: *Aparis* (1989, ECM 1404); M. Portal: *Dockings* (1997, Label Bleu 6604); M. Riessler: *Honig und Asche* (1997, Enja 9303-2)

BIBLIOGRAPHY

M. Stockhausen: "Der Dämpfergürtel," *Brass Bulletin*, no.54 (1986), 38
J. Beckman: "Om at klinge igennem" [How to project sound], *DMT: Dansk musik tidsskrift*, lxii/3 (1987–8), 131
A. Beyer: "At forstaa livets dybder: et interview med Markus Stockhausen" [Understanding the depths of life: an interview with Markus Stockhausen], *DMT: Dansk musik tidsskrift*, lxiii/6 (1988–9), 203
"Markus Stockhausen," *JP*, xxxix/9 (1990), 10
R. Bratfisch: "Markus und Simon Stockhausen," *JP*, xlv/5 (1996), 19
<http://www.jazzpages.com/MarkusStockhausen/index_e.htm> (1999)

MARK GILBERT

Stokes, Irvin (*b* Greensboro, NC, 11 Nov 1926). Trumpeter. In 1947 he moved to New York, where in 1949 he recorded in a sextet led by the alto saxophonist Charlie Singleton. During the 1950s he toured with Mercer Ellington and worked mainly in big bands, including those of Tiny Bradshaw, Andy Kirk, Jimmie Lunceford, Erskine Hawkins, Duke Ellington, and Buddy Johnson (1956–8). He then played with the sextet led by the guitarist Austin Powell (1959–60) and recorded with Bobby Donaldson (1960) and Lou Donaldson (1963). In the 1970s Stokes was active mainly in bands for Broadway musicals, including *Hair*, and in 1978 he toured Europe with the Thad Jones–Mel Lewis Orchestra. From the following year he performed regularly with Panama Francis's Savoy Sultans (ii), and his playing is well represented on the group's recordings; he also worked with George Kelly's bands into the late 1990s, recording with them in Nice, France, in 1979 and in New York in 1982. He toured Europe in 1982 with Illinois Jacquet and in 1984 with Oliver Jackson, with whom he recorded as co-leader. Later he made further tours with Jackson (until 1989) and with Jacquet's big band (1988–9) and toured with the Count Basie Orchestra under Frank Foster (1990). In the 1990s Stokes played regularly at Sunday brunches at Sweet Basil in New York, initially deputizing for Doc Cheatham; following Cheatham's death in 1997 he continued under Chuck Folds, alternating with Spanky Davis as the group's trumpeter. In 1999–2000 he worked with the Statesmen of Jazz and Jacquet's Jazz Legends.

SELECTED RECORDINGS

As leader with O. Jackson: *Broadway* (1984, BB 33151)
As sideman: L. Donaldson: on *A Man with a Horn* (1961–3, BN 21436-2), Hipty Hop, Soul Meetin' (1963); P. Francis: *Gettin' in the Groove* (1979, BB 33320–21); G. Kelly: *Live! At the West End Cafe* (1982, Vanacore 440)

BIBLIOGRAPHY

J. Simmen: "Irvin Stokes: une voix importante sur la scène d'aujourd'hui," *BHcF*, no.327 (1985), 3
E. Enright: "Trad-brunch Tradition," *DB*, lxvi/1 (1999), 50

HOWARD RYE

Stoller, Alvin (Aaron) (*b* New York, 7 Oct 1925; *d* Los Angeles, 19 Oct 1992). Drummer. His middle name is taken from the California death index. His first professional engagement, with the pianist Van Alexander, was quickly followed by work with the bandleaders Raymond Scott and Teddy Powell. Later he played with many of the foremost bands of the time, including those of Benny Goodman (1942), Charlie Spivak (1943–5), Tommy Dorsey (1945–7), Georgie Auld (1949), Harry James (1950, 1951), Jerry Gray (1950–52), Billy May (1951–7), Charlie Barnet (1954, 1956), Maynard Ferguson (1955–6), Claude Thornhill, and Bob Crosby. By the 1950s Stoller was active as a studio musician, but he also took part in many sessions with small groups, most of which were produced by Norman Granz: among those with whom he recorded were Erroll Garner (1949), Billie Holiday (1952, 1956–7), Roy Eldridge (1953), Harry Edison (1953, 1956–7), Ben Webster (1953, 1957), Art Tatum (1955), Herb Ellis (1955–6), Ella Fitzgerald (1956, 1957), Buddy DeFranco (1957), Coleman Hawkins (1957), and Benny Carter (1966). In 1986 he toured Australia with May.

SELECTED RECORDINGS

As sideman: E. Garner: I Surrender, Dear/Love Walked In (1949, Savoy 701); H. Edison: *Sweets at the Haig* (1953, PJ 4); A. Tatum: *The Art Tatum–Roy Eldridge–Alvin Stoller–John Simmons Quartet* (1955, Clef 679); M. Ferguson: *Around the Horn with Maynard Ferguson* (1955–6, EmA 36076); H. Ellis: *Ellis in Wonderland* (1955–6, Norg. 1081); C. Hawkins: *The Genius of Coleman Hawkins* (1957, Verve 8261); B. Carter: *Additions to Further Definitions* (1966, Imp. 9116)

SELECTED FILMS AND VIDEOS

Pin-up Girl (1943); The Fabulous Dorseys (1947); The Secret Fury [Blind Spot] (1950); Summer Love (1958); Bob Crosby Golden Anniversary Tribute (1986)

BIBLIOGRAPHY

FeatherE
Obituary, P. Robinson, *JJI*, xlvi/3 (1993), 10

SCOTT YANOW

Stomp. A term variously applied in early jazz to rhythmic swing or, as in blues, to a heavy, strongly marked beat. It is undoubtedly derived from "stamp," and its use in jazz arises from the dances associated with ragtime and early blues forms, which were characterized by stamping steps. The word was frequently used in titles such as Jelly Roll Morton's *King Porter Stomp* (1906) and *Black Bottom Stomp* (1925) and Edgar Sampson's *Stompin' at the Savoy* (1934).

A "stomp chorus" is the final chorus of a lively piece, played in a loud, spirited manner (*see* FORMS, §2); the term is used mostly of early jazz. A bandleader "stomps (or kicks) off" by striking the beat of a piece with his heel on the floor; this marks the tempo and gives a signal to the musicians so that they begin playing in time and together.

GUNTHER SCHULLER

Stomp Off. Record company and label. It was established in York, Pennsylvania, around 1979 by Bob Erdos, and its first album was recorded in October 1979 and issued in November 1980. From that time it has produced more than 350 albums of traditional and Chicago jazz and has made new ragtime recordings both by unaccompanied solo pianists and by ensembles. Performers and groups who have recorded regularly for Stomp Off include Marty Grosz, Keith Ingham, Humphrey Lyttelton, Bent Persson, the Black Eagle Jazz Band, the Jim Cullum Jazz Band, James Dapogny's Chicagoans, the South Frisco Jazz Band, Paris Washboard, the Swedish Jazz Kings, and the Swiss group Kustbandet.

BIBLIOGRAPHY

T. des Plantes: "Stomp Off: No Small Feat," *MR*, xiii/11 (1986), 7
R. Byler: "Stomp Off!," *JJI*, xl/5 (1987), 12
<http://www.stompoffrecords.com/> (2000)
<http://www.trombone-usa.com/jazz-labels_s.htm> (2000)

GK

Stone, Fred(die) (*b* Toronto, 9 Sept 1935; *d* Toronto, 10 Dec 1986). Canadian flugelhorn player, composer, and conductor. He studied music from the age of 12 and began playing trumpet in Toronto dance bands when he was 16. Later he studied composition with Gordon Delamont (1955–60). From the mid-1950s through the 1960s he worked in Toronto studio ensembles, and he was a soloist with several symphony orchestras in performances of third-stream pieces, notably Norman Symonds's *The Nameless Hour* and *Democratic Concerto*. He led his own jazz big band in the 1960s, and was also associated with Ron Collier (1960–73), Phil Nimmons (1965–70), and Rob McConnell and the Boss Brass (1968–70). From 24 March to 6 September 1970 he toured with Duke Ellington's orchestra, which recorded his composition *Maiera* (first issued on the CD *Duke Ellington and his Orchestra, 1965–72*, Musicmasters 5041-2); his flugelhorn playing is featured on *Aristocracy à la Jean Lafitte* (on the album *New Orleans Suite*, 1970, Atl. 1580). Thereafter Stone taught in Toronto and led several groups. He was a strong influence on the city's younger and most venturesome musicians, many of whom passed through Freddie's Band, an improvising ensemble that he founded in 1984 and directed through a form of "conduction."

BIBLIOGRAPHY

EMC2; *Feather–Gitler '70s*
B. Smith: "The Fred Stone Interview," *Coda*, no.209 (1986), 4
M. Miller: "Fred Stone," *Boogie, Pete & the Senator: Canadian Musicians in Jazz: the Eighties* (Toronto, 1987), 241

EDDIE LAMBERT/MARK MILLER

Stone, Jesse [Calhoun, Charles E. [Chuck]] (*b* Atchison, KS, 16 Nov 1901; *d* Altamonte Springs, FL, 1 April 1999). Bandleader, singer, pianist, arranger, and record producer. He was brought up in St. Joseph and Kansas City, Missouri, and began his professional career at the age of five as a singer and dancer in a traveling variety act with his parents, who gave him a formal musical education. Having played piano in a trio with the saxophonist Theodore Thyus, he formed his first band, the Blues Serenaders, in 1918, initially a quartet of piano, drums, violin and cello, though it later developed into a larger ensemble with woodwind and brass; Coleman Hawkins played cello and later C-melody saxophone with the band. Stone directed, played piano, and arranged music for the group, which performed a variety act in the St. Joseph area that involved dancing and conjuring tricks; with the help of the agent Frank Rock, he established an early network of venues for touring appearances, and in the early 1920s he pioneered jazz radio broadcasting in St. Joseph. He continued to lead the Blues Serenaders until 1928. Its recording of *Starvation Blues* (1927) is an exceptional example of the development of Southwestern big-band jazz, successfully combining blues feeling with arranged ensemble passages to create space for the band's main soloist, the trumpeter Albert Hinton. A transcription by Schuller (1968) suggests that Stone, while artfully creating the impression of collective improvisation, had arranged the interwoven brass parts of the final ensemble, and Stone later confirmed in interviews that he wrote out the majority of the band's ensemble passages as part of the process of teaching his key soloists to improvise.

After leading the Blue Moon Chasers in and around Dallas, Stone joined George E. Lee and helped Terrence Holder form a new band (1929). He then worked as Lee's music director and arranger (1930–31) and directed the Kansas City Rockets with Thamon Hayes (1932–4). From 1935 he led the Cyclones (with such sidemen as Jabbo Smith and Budd Johnson) in Chicago and wrote arrangements for Earl Hines, among others; he also worked briefly as second pianist in Hines's orchestra. In 1937 he moved to New York as a staff writer for Mills Music and made two recordings with another orchestra. He later became staff arranger at the Apollo Theatre, writing for the bands that played there as well as for portions of revues, such as *Strivers' Row* (March 1941), co-written with James P. Johnson, Dan Burley, and Abram Hill. From 1942 to 1944 he wrote arrangements for and coached the International Sweethearts of Rhythm. Stone continued working as a leader in the 1940s, often featuring himself as a light-voiced blues shouter with a conversational style; he performed overseas on a tour sponsored by the US State Department, when he led a band that included Franz Jackson. The outstanding composition from this stage of his career was the song *Idaho*, which became a standard after being recorded in 1942 by Les Hite and Benny Goodman (the latter in an arrangement by Deane Kincaide rather than Stone himself).

From the late 1940s Stone began working as an artists and repertory manager for the rhythm-and-blues catalogues of several companies (but principally Atlantic), though at the same time he wrote numerous compositions for both instrumentalists and vocalists. Among these were *Cole Slaw* for Frank Culley, *Shake, Rattle & Roll* for Joe Turner (ii), and *It should have been me* for Ray Charles. His songs were also performed by groups such as the Clovers and the Drifters. Much of his later work was produced under the pseudonym Charles E. (or Chuck) Calhoun, and he led recording bands under this name in 1955–6. He retired briefly to California in the late 1950s, but soon returned to the business, and in the early 1960s he embarked on a professional and personal partnership with Evelyn McGee (who worked under the name Evelyn McGee Stone), a former singer with the International Sweethearts of Rhythm. The couple toured widely as the Jesse Stone Duo, with Evelyn playing drums as well as singing, until they retired from full-time performing in 1978. Even then Stone remained active as a composer and arranger, playing and arranging music for his wife's recordings, and appearing in occasional concerts and regularly at a Sunday brunch close to his home near Orlando, Florida, until 1995. His last professional engagement was at Disney World in Orlando, four weeks before his death.

Stone was one of the first territory bandleaders in the Midwest and a significant composer and music director in the territories, Chicago, and New York. As a songwriter and composer he generally favored simple repetitive melodies with catchy, punning lyrics. He was credited by Ahmet Ertegun as being largely responsible, through the instrumentation and recording balance of the groups whose sessions he produced for Atlantic, for the basic sound of rhythm-and-blues as it emerged from jazz.

Oral history material in *NjR* (JOHP).

SELECTED RECORDINGS

* – arranged by Stone

† – with Stone as singer

As leader. *Starvation Blues/*Boot to Boot (1927, OK 8471); *Wind Storm/*Snaky Feeling (1937, Var. 521); †Sneaky Pete/†I came home unexpectedly (1947, Vic. 20-2670); first issued on *Jesse Stone, alias Charles 'Chuck' Calhoun* (1947–58, Bear Family 15695), *Easy Walkin' (1949)

As sideman with E. M. Stone: **It's my Time* (1988, Bee Cee 17441)

SELECTED ARRANGEMENTS

Recorded by J. Lunceford: Sassin' the Bass (1939, Voc. 5016)
Recorded by H. Leonard: Snaky Feeling (1940, Bb 11083)
Recorded by C. Calloway: Papa's in bed with his britches on (1940, OK 5731)
Recorded by L. Hite: Idaho (1942, Hit 7002)

BIBLIOGRAPHY

ChiltonW; *McCarthy B*
F. S. Driggs: "Kansas City and the Southwest," *Jazz: New Perspectives on the History of Jazz*, ed. N. Hentoff and A. J. McCarthy (New York, 1959/R1974), 189
G. Schuller: *Early Jazz: its Roots and Musical Development* (New York, 1968), 288
R. Russell: *Jazz Style in Kansas City and the Southwest* (Berkeley, CA, Los Angeles, and London, 1971, rev. 2/1973/R1997), 117
C. Gillett: *Making Tracks: Atlantic Records and the Growth of a Multi-billion-dollar Industry* (London, 1975)
D. A. Handy: *The International Sweethearts of Rhythm* (Metuchen, NJ, and London, 1983, rev. 2/1996)
N. W. Pearson, Jr.: *Goin' to Kansas City* (Urbana, IL, and London, 1988)
J. Chilton: *The Song of the Hawk: the Life and Recordings of Coleman Hawkins* (London and New York, 1990), 5
P. Gettelman: "Forefather of Rock 'n' Roll Aging as Gracefully as Music," *Orlando Sentinel* (16 Nov 1993)
J. Wexler and D. Ritz: *Rhythm and Blues: a Life in American Music* (New York, 1993, London, 1994)
C. Battestini and J.-P. Battestini: "Jesse Stone," *BHcF*, no.440 (1995), 3; no.441 (1995), 5; no.442 (1995), 6; no.444 (1996), 11
P. A. Grendysa: Liner notes, *Jesse Stone, alias Charles 'Chuck' Calhoun* (Bear Family 15695, 1995)
Obituaries: T. Burke, *Blues & Rhythm*, no.139 (1999), 21; J. Périn, *Soul Bag*, no.155 (1999), 47; B. Dahl, *Living Blues*, no.146 (1999), 49

HOWARD RYE, ALYN SHIPTON

Stop-time. A technique used to focus attention on a singer or an instrumental soloist. An ensemble or pianist repeats in rhythmic unison a simple one- or two-bar pattern consisting of sharp accents and rests, while the soloist takes command. Meter and tempo remain intact; only the texture of the accompaniment changes. An unusual instance in ragtime may be found in Scott Joplin's *Ragtime Dance* (1906). The technique is common in jazz: famous examples occur during Johnny Dodds's clarinet solos on King Oliver's two recorded versions of *Dipper Mouth Blues* (1923, Gen. 5132; OK 4918) and Louis Armstrong's trumpet solo on *Potato Head Blues* (1927, OK 8503).

A more recent type of stop-time occurs in urban blues and related popular genres where, in the four opening tonic bars of the 12-bar blues progression, the group places a heavy accent on the downbeat of each bar and then gives way to the singer.

BIBLIOGRAPHY

G. Schuller: *Early Jazz: its Roots and Musical Development* (New York, 1968)

E. A. Berlin: *Ragtime: a Musical and Cultural History* (Berkeley, CA, Los Angeles, and London, 1980/*R*1984 with addns)
B. Kernfeld: *The Blackwell Guide to Recorded Jazz* (Oxford, England, and Cambridge, MA, 1991, rev. 2/1995)

BK

Storaas, Vigleik (*b* Bergen, Norway, 9 Feb 1963). Norwegian pianist and composer. After studying jazz at the music conservatory in Trøndelag (1982–4) he settled in Trondheim. He was a member of the groups Kråboel (1981–3), Soeyr (1983–5), and Fair Play (1985–8), and then led his own group Lines (1987–92). He toured periodically with Karin Krog and John Surman (1992–5), his own trio (from 1992), and the Nordic Quartet, comprising Krog, Surman, and Terje Rypdal (from 1994).

SELECTED RECORDINGS

As leader: *Lines* (1988, Odin 4026); *Bilder* (1994, Curling Legs 18); *Andre bilder* (1996, Curling Legs 35)
As sideman with Nordic Quartet: *Nordic Quartet* (1994, ECM 1553)

JOHS BERGH

Story, Nat(haniel Edward) (*b* Oak Station, nr East Paducah, KY, 8 Aug 1904; *d* Evansville, IN, 21 Nov 1968). Trombonist. In the 1920s he worked on the Mississippi riverboats with Fate Marable and Floyd Campbell, and in the early 1930s he moved to New York, where he played with Luis Russell (with whom he recorded) and Sam Wooding (both 1934), among others. He joined Chick Webb around August 1936 (for illustration *see* Webb, chick) and stayed after Webb died in 1939 to work under Ella Fitzgerald's leadership. Story made a number of recordings with both leaders, mainly as leader of the section, but he may be heard as a soloist on Webb's *Pack up your sins and go to the devil* (1938, Decca 1894). He left the band in 1940, and after playing with Andy Kirk and Lucky Millinder he ceased to work as a full-time musician, though he continued to perform into the 1960s.

BIBLIOGRAPHY

McCarthyB
J. Simmen: "Carnet de notes, 15: Nat Story 'Mr Pinch-Penny'," *BHcF*, no.189 (1969), 10
F. Driggs: "Story's Story," *Sv*, no.79 (1978), 24

based on *ChiltonW*

Storyville (i). The name of the brothel district of New Orleans around the turn of the century. It has been adopted for various purposes in jazz: as the name of a number of nightclubs (*see* Nightclubs and other venues), at least two record labels (see Storyville (ii) and Storyville (iii)), and a notable journal (see Appendix 1: Bibliography (Periodicals)).

Storyville (ii). Record company and label. The company was formed by George Wein in Boston in 1951 and evolved from the club of the same name that he had opened the previous year. The catalogue contained recordings made both at the club and in studios; it included albums by Lee Konitz, Serge Chaloff, Toshiko Akiyoshi, Ruby Braff, Vic Dickenson, Ellis Larkins, Sidney Bechet, Johnny Windhurst, Joe Newman, Zoot Sims, and Jo Jones. Several singers also made recordings for the label, among them Lee Wiley, Jackie Cain, and Roy Kral.

Storyville leased some material from other companies, notably the results of a session recorded by Buck Clayton in Paris. It was at its most active in 1953–5, but thereafter Wein's increasing involvement with the Newport Jazz Festival and associated activities began to demand most of his time. The label had virtually been discontinued by the late 1950s. Parts of the catalogue were issued contemporaneously on Vogue in the UK and France, and a few albums have been rereleased in Japan, but there has been no comprehensive reissue program.

MARK GARDNER

Storyville (iii). Record company and label; the company began recording traditional jazz in Copenhagen in the early 1950s and shortly thereafter was taken over by Sonet.

Stovall, Don(ald) [Donnie] (*b* St. Louis, 12 Dec 1913; *d* New York, 20 Nov 1970). Alto saxophonist. He first played with Dewey Jackson (1930–31) and Fate Marable (1932–3), then worked with Lil Armstrong (1936) and Peanuts Holland (1936–8). After moving to New York he recorded with Armstrong, Pete Johnson (*627 Stomp*, 1940, Decca 18121), the trumpeter Joe Brown and Sammy Price (both 1940–41), and Snub Mosley (1941). He also played with Eddie Durham, Mercer Ellington, and Cootie Williams. From 1942 to 1949 he was a member of Henry "Red" Allen's sextet, with which he made a number of recordings, including his own composition *Count Me Out* (1946, Vic. 20-1956); he may be seen playing this number and four others in soundies made with Allen in 1946. Stovall ceased to play in 1951, when he took a job with a telephone company.

BIBLIOGRAPHY

ChiltonW
J. Simmen: "Don Stovall: an Appreciation," *Coda*, x/2 (1971), 31
——: "Un des grands swingmen du saxophone: Don Stovall," *BHcF*, no.207 (1971), 11
F. Hoffman: *Henry "Red" Allen (Jan. 7th 1908 – Apr. 17th 1967)/J. C. Higginbotham (May 11th 1906 – May 26th 1973): Discography, 1927–1969* (MS, Berlin, rev 2/1994) [unpubd typescript]
J. Chilton: *Ride, Red, Ride: the Life of Henry "Red" Allen* (London, 1999)

FRANK DRIGGS

Stowell, John (*b* New York, 30 July 1950). Electric guitarist. He grew up in Connecticut and began playing guitar in his early teens; later he studied with John Mehegan. Around 1976 he began an association with David Friesen, with whom he worked in small groups and in a duo until 1981. During the same period he recorded as a leader (1977) and performed with Milt Jackson (1977), Pete Christlieb, Bill Watrous, and Conte Candoli (all 1980). At some point he settled in Portland, Oregon. Stowell toured and recorded with Paul Horn from 1983, when they performed in the USSR, and in 1985 he worked with Art Farmer. Although he is often compared with Jim Hall, his playing style owes a debt to that of Mick Goodrick, as may be heard on his duo recording with Friesen (1978). He recorded again as a leader in 1992 and contributed articles to *Guitar Player* in 1996 and 1999.

SELECTED RECORDINGS

Duos with D. Friesen: *Through the Listening Glass* (1978, IC 1061)
As sideman with D. Friesen: *Star Dance* (1976, IC 1019); on *Waterfall Rainbow* (1977, IC 1027), Dancing Spirits before the Lord, Waterfall Rainbow

BIBLIOGRAPHY

Feather–GitlerBEJ
T. Schnabel: "Profile: John Stowell," *DB*, xlvi/6 (1979), 30
L. Coryell: "John Stowell's Beautiful Bebop," *GP*, xxiii/3 (1989), 42
J. Ferguson: "Intro: John Stowell's Jazz: Delicate & Determined," *GP*, xviii/4 (1994), 22

<http://www.cyboard.com/JohnStowell/> (1999) [incl. discography]

GK

Straight. A colloquial term used both verbally and in notation to indicate musical elements which are to be played with strictly even subdivisions of the beat ("straight eighths" referring, for example, to eighth-notes of equal duration) rather than in the irregular lilt of swing; *see* Beat, §3).

RICK FINLAY

Straight ahead. A term describing a conventional, simple, or straightforward approach to playing in the bop style and its derivatives; in some contexts it also carries connotations of a positive, forceful manner. It may be applied to the playing of a soloist or a group, or to the style of a piece.

Straight mute. *See* Mute, §2(a).

Strange, Pete(r Charles) (*b* London, 19 Dec 1938). English trombonist and arranger. He played violin before taking up trombone, and as a teenager he performed and recorded with the Southern Jazz Band, led by the banjoist Eric Silk (1956), and the trumpeter Teddy Layton (1957–8). After military service (1958–60) he resumed working with lesser-known groups in London and was a sideman in Bruce Turner's Jump Band (August 1961–1964); he also worked with the drummer Johnny Armatage, with Mick Mulligan, and with visiting American musicians. Strange quit working as a full-time musician but continued to play regularly with numerous groups, including that of Freddy Randall, with whom he recorded in 1971; during the 1970s he worked in Turner's Reunion Band, co-led the Swingtet with the trumpeter Clive Peerless, and performed with Lennie Hastings, Digby Fairweather, and the double bass player Ron Russell, with whom he toured Czechoslovakia. From the mid-1970s Strange again worked full-time, with Alan Elsdon, among others; he was a founding member in January 1978 of the Midnite Follies Orchestra and in September 1980 of Five-a-Slide, with which he recorded in 1981. In March 1983 he began what became a longstanding association with Humphrey Lyttelton, for whose groups he also supplied arrangements. When not with Lyttelton he appeared as a freelance, occasionally co-led groups with Peerless, and played in the group Slide-by-Slide. In 1994, with Fairweather, he formed the Great British Jazz Band.

SELECTED RECORDINGS

As sideman: B. Turner: *Accent on Swing* (1962, Sonet 2025); *Going Places* (1963, Phi. BL7590); H. Lyttelton: *Beano Band* (1989, Calligraph 021); Great British Jazz Band: *Jubilee* (1994, Can. 79720); *A British Jazz Odyssey* (1996, Can. 79740)

BIBLIOGRAPHY

CarrJ; *ChiltonB*

GK

Strata-East. Record company and label founded in 1971 by Charles Tolliver and Stanley Cowell.

Strata Institute. Group formed by Steve Coleman and Greg Osby consisting of musicians associated with M-Base. It made two recordings (1988 and 1991). The second, *Transmigration* (DIW 860), featured Von Freeman, whose playing influenced both Coleman and Osby; this album is a fine example of the group's style, which melds bop-oriented jazz with the funkier M-Base sound. Among the others who performed with the Strata Institute were David Gilmore (guitar), Kenny Davis (double bass), and Marvin "Smitty" Smith (drums).

GK

Strayhorn, Billy [William; Swee' Pea] (*b* Dayton, OH, 29 Nov 1915; *d* New York, 31 May 1967). Composer, arranger, and pianist. Hadju's biography disclosed Strayhorn's true date of birth (not 19 November, as in all previous sources). As a youth in Hillsborough, North Carolina, and Pittsburgh he received an extensive training in music. In December 1938 he submitted a composition to Duke Ellington, who was so impressed by the young man's talent that three months later he recorded Strayhorn's *Something to live for* with the composer as pianist. Four more of Strayhorn's pieces were recorded during 1939 – *I'm checkin' out, goo'm bye* and *Grievin'* by Ellington, and *Barney goin' easy* and *Lost in Two Flats* by Barney Bigard – as well as a work by Ellington written as a tribute, *Weely (a Portrait of Billy Strayhorn)*. After

Billy Strayhorn at Civic Hall, Los Angeles, 1945

serving briefly as a pianist in Mercer Ellington's orchestra, Strayhorn joined Duke Ellington's band as associate arranger and second pianist, and for nearly three decades, while based mainly in New York but also in Paris, he worked in close collaboration with the leader. The two men were so attuned to one another musically, and Strayhorn's work was such a perfect complement to Ellington's, that it is now impossible to establish the exact extent of the former's contribution to Ellington's oeuvre. Their relationship was described in flattering terms by Ellington in his autobiography (1973). Strayhorn collaborated on more than 200 items in Ellington's repertory, notably such standards as *Take the "A" Train* (one of the band's theme tunes) and *Satin Doll*. His ballads, including *Lush Life*, *Something to live for*, *Day Dream*, *After all*, *Passion Flower*, *Chelsea Bridge*, *Lotus Blossom*, and *Blood Count*, are harmonically and structurally among the most sophisticated in jazz. Strayhorn was a technically fluent pianist, and made a notable contribution to several small-group recordings by various of Ellington's sidemen, among them Cootie Williams (1939), Bigard (1939–40), Johnny Hodges (1939, 1947, 1956–8), the Ellingtonians (1950), the Coronets (1950–51), Louie Bellson (1952), Ben Webster (1954), and Clark Terry (1957); he also recorded a number of titles in a trio with Ellington and either Wendell Marshall or Joe Shulman, which were issued on an album under his own name (*Billy Strayhorn Trio*, 1950, Mercer 1001). Published versions of his works issued by Billy Strayhorn Manuscript Editions are "drawn directly from his original handwritten scores."

RECORDED COMPOSITIONS

(selective list)

* – with Strayhorn as sideman

Recorded by D. Ellington: *(I want) Something to live for (1939, Bruns. 8365); I'm checkin' out, goo'm bye (1939, Col. 35208); Grievin' (1939, Col. 35310); Take the "A" Train (1941, Vic. 27380); *After all (1941, Vic. 27434); *Chelsea Bridge (1941, Vic. 27740); Raincheck (1941, Vic. 27880); *Johnny come lately (1942, Vic. 20-1556); Midriff (1946, Swing 230); Satin Doll (1953, Cap. 2458); Upper Manhattan Medical Center, on *Historically Speaking: the Duke* (1956, Beth. 60); Such Sweet Thunder (1957), on *Such Sweet Thunder* (1956–7, Col. CL1033); *Far East Suite* (1966, RCA LSP3782); Blood Count, on *"... and his Mother Called him Bill"* (1967, RCA LSP3906)

Recorded by others: B. Bigard: Barney goin' easy (1939, Voc. 5378); *Lost in Two Flats (1939, Voc. 5422); J. Hodges: Day Dream (1940, Bb 11021); Passion Flower (1941, Bb 30-0817); Charlotte russe (Lotus Blossom), on *Johnny Hodges* (1947, Mercer 1000); Lush Life, on J. Coltrane: *Lush Life* (1957–8, Prst. 7188); A. Farmer: *Something to Live for: the Music of Billy Strayhorn* (1987, Cont. 14029); J. Henderson: *Lush Life: the Music of Billy Strayhorn* (1991, Verve 314-511-779-2); Dutch Jazz Orchestra: *Portrait of a Silk Thread: Newly Discovered Works of Billy Strayhorn* (1995, Dutch Jazz 95001)

BIBLIOGRAPHY

SchullerS; *TuckerDE*

B. Coss: "Ellington & Strayhorn, Inc.," *DB*, xxix/12 (1962), 22

S. Dance: *The World of Duke Ellington* (London and New York, 1970/*R*1981)

D. Ellington: *Music is my Mistress* (Garden City, NY, 1973; index by H. F. Huon separately pubd, Melbourne, Australia, n.d. [?1977], rev. 2/1982), 109

D. Jewell: *Duke: a Portrait of Duke Ellington* (London and New York, 1977, 2/1978)

J. L. Collier: *Duke Ellington* (New York and London, 1987)

L. Feather: "Billy Strayhorn: the Man Beside the Duke," *San Francisco Chronicle Datebook* (27 Oct 1991)

G. Schuller, ed., and B. Wallarab, transcr.: *Take the "A" Train: 1941* (Washington, DC, *c*1993)

J. Gill: *Queer Noises: Male and Female Homosexuality in Twentieth-century Music* (London, 1995)

D. Hajdu: *Lush Life: a Biography of Billy Strayhorn* (New York, 1996)

E. Holley: "Riffs: Billy Strayhorn Revisited," *DB*, lxiii/9 (1996), 10

JOSÉ HOSIASSON

Strazzeri, Frank (John) (*b* Rochester, NY, 24 April 1930). Pianist. He began playing alto saxophone and clarinet in 1942, then changed to piano, which he studied at the Eastman School. In 1952 he accompanied visiting jazz musicians (among them Roy Eldridge, J. J. Johnson, and Billie Holiday) as the house pianist at a club in Rochester. Two years later he moved to New Orleans, where he performed with Sharkey Bonano and Al Hirt. After playing with Charlie Ventura (1957–8) he performed in Las Vegas, then joined Woody Herman's band (1959). In 1960 he settled in Los Angeles and took Vince Guaraldi's place in Howard Rumsey's Lighthouse All Stars; he played at the Lighthouse with Conte Candoli, Frank Rosolino, Art Pepper, Bud Shank, and Bob Cooper, worked as a studio musician for Pacific Jazz, Verve, and Atlantic (recording with Herb Ellis, Terry Gibbs, Curtis Amy, Carmell Jones, and Red Mitchell), and toured with Joe Williams, Maynard Ferguson, and the Lighthouse group. From time to time he worked with Pepper, with whom he appeared in an episode of the television show "Jazz Casual" in 1964 and recorded in 1964 and 1968. He was a member of Kenny Dorham's quintet for about two months (*c*1965), and he recorded with Oliver Nelson's orchestra (1967). In the late 1960s he formed a house rhythm section at Donte's club with Chuck Berghofer and Nick Ceroli, and he had intermittent affiliations with many other prominent jazz musicians, notably Shelly Manne, Joe Pass, Sal Nistico (ii), Dexter Gordon, and Billy Higgins.

After touring with Elvis Presley and spending three years with Les Brown's band in the early 1970s, Strazzeri joined Cal Tjader's quintet in 1974, and he accompanied Kai Winding late in the trombonist's career, recording in 1974 and 1977. From 1973 he has led his own groups, including a sextet that initially consisted of Candoli, Rosolino, Don Menza, Gene Cherico, and Dick Berk. Having accompanied Chet Baker briefly around 1960 and again in the late 1970s, he served as the pianist and music coordinator for Bruce Webber's documentary film on Baker, *Let's Get Lost*, released in 1989. He made recordings with Louie Bellson (in London, 1980, 1982), Menza (1981), and Tal Farlow and Bill Perkins (both 1984), and in the mid-1980s took part in further sessions in a duo with Perkins and as a leader, in the course of which he returned exclusively to the piano, following a decade of unsatisfying albums where he recorded on electronic keyboards. Strazzeri leads the sextet Woodwinds West, including Bob Cooper, Perkins, and Jack Nimitz, which recorded (1992, 1994) and made a video (1992). He also recorded in the 1990s in a duo with Perkins and as a sideman with Perkins (1993) and Louie Bellson (1995). His generally conservative playing reflects the relaxed approach and technical competence of the finest keyboard players in Los Angeles.

Video oral history material in *NCH* (HCJA).

SELECTED RECORDINGS

As unaccompanied soloist: *Relaxin'* (1982, Seabreeze 1007)

Duos with B. Perkins: *Two as One* (1990, Interplay 8611); *Warm Moods* (1991, Fresh Sounds 191)

As leader: *After the Rain* (1976, Cat. 7607); *Straz* (1977, Cat. 7623); *Kat Dancin'* (1985, Dis. 933); *Litle Giant* (1989, Fresh Sound 184); of Woodwinds West: *Woodwinds West* (1992, Jazz Mark 111); *Somebody Loves Me* (1994, Fresh Sound 5003)

As sideman: C. Jones: *The Remarkable Carmell Jones* (1961, PJ 29); C. Tjader: *Last Night when We Were Young* (1975, Fan. 9482); D. Menza: *First Flight* (1976, Cat. 7617); *Hip Pocket* (1981, PAlt 8010); B. Perkins: *Journey to the East* (1984, Cont. 14011)

BIBLIOGRAPHY

H. Wong: "Profile: Frank Strazzeri," *DB*, xliii/1 (1976), 32

B. Rusch: "Frank Strazzeri: Interview," *Cadence*, xxi/9 (1995), 5

ROBERT L. DOERSCHUK/BK

Stretch. Record company and label formed in 1992 by Chick Corea and his business manager Ron Moss. Besides releasing albums by Corea (including material the pianist had recorded for Warner Brothers, *c*1977–80), it recorded and issued albums by Bob Berg, Billy Childs, Robben Ford, John Patitucci, and Eddie Gomez. Initially affiliated with GRP, Stretch entered into an agreement with Concord late in 1996; it then reissued much of its back catalogue (approximately 15 albums) and continued to produce new material, notably recordings by Avishai Cohen, Dave Weckl, and Steve Wilson, as well as further items by Corea and Berg. As of the year 2000 its catalogue numbered about 35 albums.

(<http://www.concordrecords.com/mainpage/stretch.html> (2000))

GK

Stretch out. To improvise for an extended period, sufficiently long to allow a thorough working out of the possibilities offered by a theme. The term implies an unexpectedly lengthy, inventive, even self-indulgent solo in a context in which a short improvisation would be normal, and presumably derives from the consequent "stretching out" or extension of the piece as a whole. A renowned example of such a solo is Paul Gonsalves's 27-chorus improvisation on Duke Ellington's *Diminuendo and Crescendo in Blue* at the Newport Jazz Festival in 1956 (the recording of which was issued on the album *Ellington at Newport*, Col. CL934).

Stride. A style of solo jazz piano; *see* Piano, §2.

String band. Any ensemble consisting largely or wholly of string instruments. The string-band tradition is an independent one that has developed in parallel with jazz, and the characteristic types of ensemble have their roots in blues, ragtime, and society music from the turn of the century. Later influences have been elements of gypsy and Eastern European music.

In his interviews with Alan Lomax for the Library of Congress, Jelly Roll Morton recalled the repertory of waltzes, schottisches, and quadrilles played by the string groups of New Orleans in the early 1900s. No recordings from this period exist, but Edmond Souchon recorded with a typical ensemble, the Six and Seven Eighths Band, in 1949. Its instrumentation consisted of mandolin, steel guitar, guitar, and double bass, and it performed in a style that was to some extent a precursor of skiffle, as may be heard on *High Society* (1949, New Orleans 1000).

Similar string ensembles (the members of which possessed a considerable degree of virtuosity) performed ragtime music. The principal instrument used in these ragtime bands was the banjo, and the recordings of Fred Van Eps, Sr. (for example, *Florida Rag*, 1912, Vic. 17308), made with a trio of two banjos and piano, illustrate the early style. Among the earliest African-American string bands to record was an assembly of musicians from the Clef Club in New York, who traveled to Britain in 1915 under the leadership of Dan Kildare and recorded as Ciro's Club Coon Orchestra with an instrumentation of two banjos (one sometimes replaced by a banjolin, a hybrid of the banjo and mandolin), cello, piano, double bass, and drums. On recordings such as *Yaaka hula hickey dula* (1916, Col. E638), while remaining within the overall feel of ragtime timing and beat, the group gets close to a form of proto-jazz, in which the melodic lead (on the banjolin) is underpinned by improvised banjo countermelodies and accented cross-rhythms from the drums. Ragtime later came to be performed on guitar (notably by the Rev. Gary Davis and his protégé Stefan Grossman) and flourished predominantly as a solo tradition; banjo-based ensembles were therefore less common until the ragtime revival of the 1970s.

A more enduring style was that of the blues-based ensembles, such as those led by Lonnie Johnson. Johnson made many blues recordings with his brother James "Steady Roll" Johnson in string bands consisting of guitar, banjo, and violin; the brothers were each adept at playing all three instruments. Johnson commanded a formidable guitar technique, and his solo work (best demonstrated on his remarkable tour de force *To do this you gotta know how*, 1926, OK 40695), together with a series of guitar duets recorded with Eddie Lang (including *Bull Frog Moan/A Handful of Riffs*, 1929, OK 8695), set the pattern for string-band jazz of the late 1920s. With Joe Venuti, Lang had previously recorded duets which combined the rhythmic, chordal work of the guitar with a swinging and melodic violin line; *Stringing the Blues* (1926, Col. 914D) is one of the earliest recorded duets for violin and guitar and was as influential as Lang's work with Johnson.

Lang's recordings (under his own name and under the pseudonym Blind Willie Dunn) coupled the musical language of blues and early jazz with a string technique as dextrous as that of the best ragtime players. His style reached its high point in his duets with Carl Kress, notably *Pickin' my Way* (*Guitar Mania*, pt i) (1932, Bruns. 6254). As early as 1927 Lang was involved in another series of string-band recordings that influenced many string and vocal groups of the 1930s. These were with Red McKenzie, whose skiffle or spasm-band style involved the use of homemade and string instruments as accompaniment to popular or simple blues singing.

McKenzie recorded in the mid-1930s with the most influential American string band of the decade, the Spirits of Rhythm. This ensemble was renowned for its driving rhythmic pulse, obtained by chordal work on tiples (played by Leo Watson and the brothers Wilbur and Douglas Daniels) and guitar (Teddy Bunn); other instruments were double bass and homemade percussion. The group's repertory of songs with nonsense or scat lyrics, often incorporating Harlem slang or "jive" talk (for example, *My Old Man*, 1933, Bruns. 6728), became particularly associated with American string bands; it also formed the basis for the work of Slim and Slam (Slim Gaillard and Slam Stewart), whose most important recording, *The Flat Foot Floogie* (1938, Voc. 4021), was made with guitar, bowed double bass, piano, and drums.

During the mid-1930s there were parallel developments in Europe in the work of the Quintette du Hot Club de France, an instrumental band consisting of three guitars, double bass, and violin. The principal members of the quintet, Stephane Grappelli and Django Reinhardt, emulated the approach of Venuti and Lang, allowing the melodic lines to pass from the violin to the guitar; Reinhardt played a combination of single-string, chordal, and tremolo solos (the last accomplished by rapid strumming with the right hand) against a solid 4/4 pulse in the rhythm guitars and bass. But the quintet also made use of the harmonic vocabulary of Romany music and the Central European guitar tradition. Reinhardt employed the conventional guitar keys of E, A, and B in many of his compositions and made free use of augmented chords and whole-tone scales. The temperament of these sharp keys proved a strong contrast to those more usual in jazz (such keys as F, B♭, and E♭ allowing brass and woodwind instruments to play together with ease) and gave a characteristic edge to the group's performances. (Johnson and Lang, however, had already demonstrated the flexibility of string ensembles in respect of keys in *Have to change keys to play these blues*, 1928, OK 8637.)

After World War II the universal adoption of the electric guitar led to the virtual discontinuation of the string-band tradition. From 1939 Reinhardt added clarinet or saxophone and drums to the instrumentation of the quintet, and he began to meld his own style with the bop approach of Charlie Christian. Even groups which had started out in emulation of the Quintette du Hot Club de France followed a similar path, though the German violinist Helmut Zacharias used a harpsichord on some of his 1949 quintet recordings to retain the string-band timbre, and possibly to offset the plummy amplified guitar sound of Coco Schumann. Grappelli continued to work sporadically with string-band accompaniment, and in the 1970s and 1980s he returned to a formula similar to that of the quintet when he played with a trio of two guitars and double bass, led initially by the English guitarist Diz Disley and later by Martin Taylor or John Etheridge. In his last years Grappelli scaled down his accompaniment further, to just Marc Fosset on guitar and Jean-Phillippe Viret on double bass, yet his performances retained the essential freedom and lightness characteristic of a string band.

Other Romany players, including Reinhardt's brother Joseph and son Babik, Christian Escoudé, Rafael Fays, Paul Ferret, and Bireli Lagrene, kept alive the style of the Quintette du Hot Club de France, though Lagrene later largely abandoned the acoustic guitar and played in various fusion styles. In the Netherlands, both Fapy Lafertin and Stochelo Rosenberg maintained the Hot Club style through the 1990s, whereas the Limberger family band from Belgium (Les Manouches de Piotto's) played a brand of gypsy jazz that owed more to the folk traditions of Hungary and Romania than to Reinhardt's direct influence. In Britain, following Disley's example, several groups played string-band jazz in a style broadly reminiscent of the Hot Club de France. These include Johnny Van Derrick's Hot Club d'Angleterre, Le Jazz, Gary Potter and Gipsy Jazz, and, most importantly, Martin Taylor's Spirit of Django, which added accordion and saxophone to an instrumentation of three guitars, acoustic bass guitar, and percussion. This band worked with Grappelli on some of his final recordings.

Generally speaking, the string-band tradition was not continued by bop ensembles – even players from within the string tradition such as Lagrene or Philip Catherine choosing a different type of accompaniment when they ventured into this stylistic territory. Other such ensembles involving guitarists (such as Great Guitars, or the various duos and trios led by Kenny Burrell, John McLaughlin, Larry Coryell, and Al Di Meola) have not looked to the string-band tradition in terms of either ensemble or improvisatory style, and the most successful attempt to meld the string-band style with bop remains the body of work by two French brothers, the guitarists Boulou and Elios Ferré.

BIBLIOGRAPHY

C. Delaunay: "The Founding of the String Quintet," *Django Reinhardt: souvenirs* (Paris, 1954; Eng. trans., London, 1961, rev. 2/1981/*R*1993)
I. Cruickshank: *The Guitar Style of Django Reinhardt and the Gypsies* (Woodcote, nr Reading, England, 1982, rev. and enlarged 2/1985)
M. Jones: "Teddy Bunn, the Spirit of Rhythm," *The Spirits of Rhythm, 1933–34* (JSP 1088, 1985) [liner notes]
F. Billard and A. Antonietto: *Django Reinhardt: un géant sur son nuage* (Paris, 1993)
H. Rye and T. Brooks: "Visiting Firemen 16: Dan Kildare," *Storyville 1996/7*, ed. L. Wright (Chigwell, England, 1997), 30
R. E. Lotz: Liner notes, *The Earliest Black String Bands*, i: *Dan Kildare* (Document 5622, 1998)

ALYN SHIPTON

String bass. *See* Double bass.

Stringle, Julian (Marc) (*b* Marlow, England, 13 June 1967). English clarinetist and saxophonist. He formed a dixieland band when he was 12 and appeared on television with Acker Bilk at the age of 14. After attending Latymer Music School and the London College of Music, where he studied clarinet and composition, he toured Europe as the leader of a quintet. As a freelance he recorded with pop musicians, performed with visiting American players, and worked as a composer for television, film, and advertising. In 1995 he recorded the album *Pathfinder* (Mabley Street 9501) and around the same time he joined Digby Fairweather's band, with which he may be heard on *Twelve Feet off the Ground* (1998, Flat Five 03). Stringle has toured in a Latin jazz quintet and has continued to lead his own group. He also plays flute and piano. (*ChiltonB*)

GK

String Trio of New York. Trio formed in 1977 by Billy Bang (violin), James Emery (guitar), and John Lindberg (double bass). Bang's position as violinist later transferred successively to Leroy Jenkins (temporarily, *c*1985), Charles Burnham (1986–91), Regina Carter (1991–7), and Diane Monroe (from 1997). The trio, which has toured internationally and recorded, draws equally from contemporary art music and jazz, especially free jazz, but with elements of popular music also worked into the mix (e.g., a delightfully perverted reggae tune or a harmonically complex evocation of bluegrass).

SELECTED RECORDINGS

Rebirth of a Feeling (1983, BS 0068); *Natural Balance* (1986, BS 0098); *Ascendant* (1990, Stash 532); *Time Never Lies* (1991, Stash 544); *Intermobility* (1992, Arabesque 0108); *Octagon* (1992, BS 120131-2); *Blues ...?* (1993, BS 120148-2); *String Trio of New York with Anthony Davis* (1996, Music & Arts 994); *Faze Phour: a Twenty Year Retrospective* (1997, BS 120168-2)

BIBLIOGRAPHY

K. Whitehead: "String Trio of New York: a Decade of Perseverance," *DB*, liv/11 (1987), 26 [incl. discography]
<http://www.johnlindberg.com/stringtrio/index.htm> (2000) [incl. discography]

BK

Stripling, (Lloyd) Byron (*b* Atlanta, 20 April 1961). Trumpeter and singer. He grew up in a musical family in Kentucky and Boulder, Colorado, and sang and played trumpet in church after his family settled in St. Paul, Minnesota. He studied music at the Interlochen Academy (1978–9) and the Eastman School of Music (1979–82), and while at Eastman toured with Clark Terry's big band (1981). He joined Lionel Hampton's big band in 1984 and played lead trumpet in the big bands of Woody Herman (September 1983 – 1984) and Count Basie (1984–8), the latter just after

Basie's death and under the leadership of Eric Dixon, Thad Jones, and Frank Foster; in 1987 he recorded with the band under the leadership of Diane Schuur. He also played in Dizzy Gillespie's big band at some point before joining Basie. For three months in 1988 he portrayed Louis Armstrong in the touring production of *Satchmo.* He then rejoined Basie's group, under Foster. Stripling made a number of recordings during his two tenures with this band. He left it in 1989 to lead his own quintet, which performed at the Newport Jazz Festival that summer. In the 1990s he played in pit orchestras for Broadway shows and also worked with the American Jazz Orchestra, the Lincoln Center Jazz Orchestra, the Carnegie Hall Jazz Band, the GRP All-Star Big Band (recording in 1993), the pianist David Matthews's Manhattan Jazz Orchestra, and Mitchell's All-Star Orchestra, with several of which he recorded in the early 1990s; in 1999 he recorded his first session as a leader (*Stripling Now! Byron Stripling*, Nagel-Heyer 2002). He is sought after as a soloist by pops orchestras across the USA and frequently appears at colleges and high schools as a performer, teacher, and motivational speaker. Stripling can capture the spirit and style of Louis Armstrong with his voice and instrument, but has also developed his own style, bridging early jazz and bop with a soaring tone and infectious musical personality.

Video oral history material in *NCH* (HCJA).

BIBLIOGRAPHY

C. Hall: "Byron Stripling," *DB*, lvii/12 (1990), 13

W. D. Clancy with A. C. Kenton: *Woody Herman: Chronicles of the Herds* (New York and elsewhere, 1995), 337

J. LaBarbera: "An Interview with Byron Stripling," *ITG Journal* [Journal of the International Trumpet Guild], xx/2 (1995), 34

MONK ROWE

Stritch. A modified version of the straight E♭ alto saxophone, used and named by Roland Kirk; *see* Saxophone, §6(vii).

Strittmatter, Mac [Max] (*b* Basel, Switzerland, 2 March 1914; *d* Colombo, Sri Lanka, 12 March 1980). Swiss clarinetist and saxophonist. Educated in architecture, he played harmonium, violin, and guitar before taking up clarinet and saxophone. Having first performed locally in amateur bands, he left Basel to take a professional engagement in Surabay, Java, but he returned in 1938 and the following year worked with Fred Böhler. He was drafted into the Swiss Army at the outbreak of the war and established a musical cabaret for soldiers. Following his discharge he formed a group which gradually grew into a big band (from 1944), with his wife, Molly McCormick, as its singer; from 1947 he reduced this to a smaller group which toured Switzerland, the Netherlands, and elsewhere. Later, in Berne, Strittmatter opened a music shop and manufactured amplifiers. In the late 1970s he moved to Colombo, Sri Lanka, where he performed in clubs. He specialized in playing "dirty" (i.e., with a gruff, vocalized timbre), and he may be heard to advantage on two tracks as a leader, *Wham* (1944, first issued on the anthology *Jazz in Switzerland*, Elite Special 9544002/1) and *Yesterdays* (1954, Tell 30151). (A. Schwaninger and A. Gurwitsch: *Swing discographie*, Geneva, 1945)

OTTO FLÜCKIGER

Stroll. *See* Lay out.

Strong, Jimmy (*b* 29 Aug 1906; *d* South Carolina, April 1977). Clarinetist and tenor saxophonist. In the early 1920s he performed in Chicago with the Nighthawks, led by the pianist Lottie E. Hightower, and after touring with a show in 1925 played with several bands in California. He then returned to Chicago and worked with Carroll Dickerson (1927, 1929) and the big band led by the clarinetist Clifford King (1928). Strong is best known for the recordings he made as a member of Louis Armstrong's Hot Five and Savoy Ballroom Five in 1928 and 1929. He worked with Cassino Simpson (1931), led his own group, and joined Zinky Cohn (1937) and Jimmie Noone's big band (1939); he then moved to Jersey City, New Jersey, where he again worked as a leader, at the Blue Room Club (from October 1940). Thereafter he appears to have retired from music. Although his clarinet playing was rather harsh and brittle, and less attractive than his tone on tenor saxophone, Strong was known and recorded mainly as a clarinetist. The date of his death is taken from the social security death index, which gives his last known residence as Andrews, South Carolina.

SELECTED RECORDINGS

(all 1928; on clarinet unless otherwise indicated)

As sideman: C. Dickerson: Missouri Squabble (Bruns. 3990) [t sax]; L. Armstrong: Fireworks (OK 8597); Don't jive me (Col. 36376); Knee Drops (OK 8631) [t sax]; No (OK 8690); Muggles (OK 8703)

BIBLIOGRAPHY

McCarthyB

J. Evensmo: *History of Jazz Tenor Saxophone: Black Artists*, i: *1917–1934* (Oslo, 1996)

based on *ChiltonW*/HOWARD RYE

Strozier, Frank (R.) (*b* Memphis, 13 June 1937). Alto saxophonist, flutist, clarinetist, and pianist. He began learning piano while at school in Memphis; after moving to Chicago (1954) he worked with other Memphis musicians, such as Harold Mabern, George Coleman, and Booker Little, and also played with Walter Perkins's group MJT + 3 (recording in 1959–60). In 1959 he settled in New York, where he appeared with Miles Davis for a brief period (1963, alongside Mabern and Coleman) and with Roy Haynes's quartet. He recorded with Johnny Griffin's Big Soul Band (1960) and with his own small groups (1960–62), as well as with those led by Sam Jones (1962), Booker Ervin (1963), and McCoy Tyner (1964). After six years in Los Angeles, during which he performed with Chet Baker (recording in 1965) and groups led by Shelly Manne (1965–*c*1967) and Don Ellis (1968), he returned to New York (1971); he joined the Jazz Contemporaries, led by the drummer Keno Duke (recording in 1974), and the New York Jazz Repertory Company, recorded as a leader (1976–7), and played with Horace Parlan (1977). He performed in Europe in 1978 and at Town Hall in New York in 1980. After recording as an alto saxophonist with the double bass player Stephen Roane in 1983 he abandoned jazz for seven years. On 31 March 1990 he returned to the genre as a pianist, giving a concert at Carnegie Hall in a trio with Roane and Curtis Boyd. Strozier was a dynamic and committed performer on saxophone with a blues-based style that enlivened any context in which he appeared; his tone and phrasing had a biting edge reminiscent of Jackie McLean's playing.

SELECTED RECORDINGS

As leader: *Waltz of the Demons* (1960, VJ 1007); *Cool, Calm and Collected* (1960, VJ 2-911); *Remember Me* (1976, Ste. 1066); *What's Goin' On* (1977, Ste. 17001)

As sideman with R. Haynes: *Cymbalism* (1963, NewJ 8287)

BIBLIOGRAPHY

Feather '60s; *Feather–Gitler '70s*
P. B. Matthews: "Observations," *Cadence*, xv/5 (1990), 33

BRIAN PRIESTLEY

Stryker, Dave [David Michael] (*b* Omaha, NE, 30 March 1957). Electric guitarist. After teaching himself to play guitar from records he moved in 1978 to Los Angeles, where he studied with the former Crusaders guitarist Billy Rogers. In 1980 he received a jazz study grant from the National Endowment for the Arts and moved to New York. He toured the USA and Canada with Brother Jack McDuff (1984–5) and worldwide with Stanley Turrentine (1986–95) and Kevin Mahogany (from 1996). In 1988 he began a series of recordings as leader in which he worked with Joey Calderazzo, Adam Nussbaum, Joey DeFrancesco, Mulgrew Miller, and others, and played in a style which often showed the influence of Grant Green, Wes Montgomery, Pat Martino, and John Scofield. Stryker produced a compilation album of Rogers's work in 1993 in which he himself was featured as rhythm guitarist. He also worked widely as a teacher in small-group and big-band settings. A selection of scores of his compositions has been published as *The Music of Dave Stryker* (1995, Klampenborg, Denmark).

SELECTED RECORDINGS

As leader: *First Strike* (1989, Someday 1011); *Guitar on Top* (1991, Ken Music 019); *Blue Degrees* (1992, Ste. 31315); *Full Moon* (1993, Ste. 31345); *Nomad* (1994, Ste. 31371); *Blue to the Bone* (1996, Ste. 31400); *All the Way* (1997, Ste. 31455)
As sideman: S. Turrentine: *Live at Blues Alley* (1991, Blues Alley Music 110004); T. Reedus: *Minor Thang* (1995, Criss Cross 1117); S. Turrentine: *T Time* (1995, MusicMasters 65124-2); L. Schneider: *Ali Girl* (1997, Ste. 31429); Danny Walsh: *D's Mood* (1997, Ste. 31428); S. Slagle: *Steve Slagle Plays Monk* (1997, Ste. 31446); K. Mahogany: *Another Time, Another Place* (1997, WB 9-46699-2)

BIBLIOGRAPHY

M. J. Summerfield: *The Jazz Guitar: its Evolution and its Players* (Gateshead, England, 1978, 4/1998, as *The Jazz Guitar: its Evolution, Players and Personalities since 1900*)
B. Rusch: "The Questionnaire," *Cadence*, xvii/10 (1991), 29
S. Gribetz: "Dave Stryker: on Top of Strings," *JT*, xxii/6 (1992), 11
B. Milkowski: "5 Young Kings of Swing," *GP*, xxvii/2 (1993), 87
——: "Hearsay: Dave Stryker: Big Time," *JT*, xxvi/3 (1996), 22

MARK GILBERT

Strzelczyk, Maciej (*b* Łódź, Poland, 17 Aug 1959). Polish violinist. He came to prominence during the years 1983 to 1986, when he won several prizes for his performances at jazz festivals in Poland and Belgium. Among the many Polish musicians with whom has worked are Kazimierz Jonkisz, Zbigniew Namysłowski, Tomasz Stańko, and Włodzimierz Nahorny, and he made a tour of Poland with Philip Catherine. From 1997, together with Piotr Rodowicz and the guitarist Krzysztof Woliński, he has performed and recorded tributes to Stephane Grappelli and Django Reinhardt as a member of the World Strings Trio.

SELECTED RECORDINGS

As leader: *Music for M* (1995, Polonia 045); *Jobim* (1995, Polonia 055)
As sideman: K. Jonkisz: *XYZ* (1984, Poljazz 198); *Outsider* (1986, Muza 2453); Z. Namysłowski: *The Last Concert* (1991, Polonia 002); T. Stańko: *A Farewell to Maria* (1994, Gowi 12); W. Nahorny: *Piosenki Lwowskie* (Lvov songs) (1995, Polonia 066); *Myths* (1997, Polskie Radio 200); *Fantazja Polska* (Polish fantasy) (2000, Polskie Radio 228)

BIBLIOGRAPHY

P. Smolinski: "Dobry jazz mozna grać nawet na grzebieniu" [Good jazz can even be played on a comb], *Jazzi magazine* [Poland], no.9 (1995), 44
<http://www.a1artists.net/artists/worldstrings/members.html> (2001)

ADAM CEGIELSKI, BK

Stuart, Kirk [Kincheloe, Charles] (*b* Charleston, WV, 13 April 1934; *d* 17 Dec 1982). Pianist. Following a conservatory training he worked as an accompanist to Billie Holiday (1956) and then toured and recorded as a pianist, arranger, and conductor for the singers Della Reese (1957–9) and Sarah Vaughan (1961–3); he may be heard to advantage on Vaughan's album *Sassy Swings the Tivoli* (1963, Mer. 60831), which was recorded in Copenhagen. Stuart later led his own group in Los Angeles and recorded with Al Grey (1965) and again with Reese (1967). Thereafter he taught at Howard University for several years, led his own group at clubs in Las Vegas, and accompanied Joe Williams in Los Angeles and Washington, DC; he appears in the video *Jazz at the Smithsonian: Joe Williams* (1982). He died after undergoing surgery on his spleen.

BIBLIOGRAPHY

Feather '60s
Obituary, *JT* (1983), March, 8

Stuart, Rory (John) (*b* New York, 9 Jan 1956). Guitarist. He played drums as a child and took up acoustic guitar at the age of 13. He is primarily self-taught, although he studied classical guitar from 1971 to 1973; he also played electric bass guitar at school and took a course in music which was taught by Jaki Byard. Stuart studied biology for a short time at Stanford University in Palo Alto, California, where he met Tuck Andress, but in 1975 he decided to pursue a career in music and moved to Boulder; there he attended the University of Colorado and played in Jerry Granelli's band Visions (1977). He then lived in San Francisco briefly, studying with the guitarist Dave Creamer and playing with Andress, and spent periods in Paris and New York before returning to Boulder. While touring with Brother Jack McDuff (1978) he was injured in an automobile accident, and after he had recovered he performed locally in Colorado.

In 1981 Stuart toured again with McDuff, and around the same time he moved to New York, where he formed a quartet that included Alex Foster and Kim Richmond. He played with Errol Parker's tentet (1981–90, 1992), Charlie Rouse (1982), Larry Coryell, Vic Juris, and Chuck Loeb in the Modern Guitar Masters Summit II (1983), Steve Nelson (1984), Jeanie Bryson (1984–90, 1996, 1998), Steve Coleman (1984–6), Bill Doggett (1985–6, 1989), Charles Earland (1986), Makanda Ken McIntyre (1986–8), the Cadence All Stars (1988), the trombonist Michael Vlatkovich (1987, 1992, 1994), Ernie Krivda (1989, 1995), Michael Cochrane (1990–91), Keith Copeland's Coalition (1991–2), and Ivo Perelman (1996). In 1982 he began leading his own quartet, in which he has worked regularly with Armen Donelian (piano), Calvin Hill or Anthony Cox (double bass), and Keith Copeland (drums), although Marc Copland, Chip Jackson, Stafford James, the double bass player Leon "Boots" Maleson, Ronnie Burrage, John Riley, and Newman Taylor Baker have also performed with the group. In 1986 he established a duo with the saxophonist Glenn Wilson, and in 1992 he led a septet consisting of John Stubblefield, Dannie Moore, Wilson, Donelian, Hill, and Copeland. Stuart contributed an instructional article to *Guitar Player* in 1988, and from 1992 he has taught at the New School for Social Research (from 1996 the Mannes/New School; from autumn 1999 the Jazz and Contemporary Music Program at the New School University).

SELECTED RECORDINGS

Duos with G. Wilson: *Bittersweet* (1990, 1992, Sunnyside 1057)
As leader: *Nightwork* (1983, Cadence 1016); *Hurricane* (1986, Sunnyside 1021)
As sideman: E. Parker: *Live at the Woolman Auditorium* (1985, Sahara 1014); Cadence All Stars: *Lee's Keys Please* (1987, Tim. 284); G. Wilson: *Blue Porpoise Avenue* (1990, Sunnyside 1074); I. Perelman: *Revelation* (1996, CIMP 134)

BIBLIOGRAPHY

B. Rusch: "Rory Stuart: Interview," *Cadence*, x/1 (1984), 11
J. Ferguson: "Rory Stuart: Jazz Hurricane," *GP*, xxii/3 (1988), 76 [incl. transcr.]

GK

Stubblefield, John(, IV) (*b* Little Rock, AR, 4 Feb 1945). Tenor and soprano saxophonist. He worked initially with rhythm-and-blues bands (1961–7) and took a degree in music education at the Agricultural, Mechanical and Normal College in Pine Bluff, Arkansas (BS 1967). After moving to Chicago he joined the Association for the Advancement of Creative Musicians, studied with Muhal Richard Abrams and George Coleman, and recorded with Joseph Jarman (1968). He continued his formal music education at Vandercook College (1968–70) and the University of Indiana (1969). During the late 1960s he led his Hot Five, which consisted of Leo Smith, Frank Gordon, Amina Claudine Myers, Malachi Favors, and Thurman Barker, and performed with Jarman and Lester Bowie. In 1971 he moved to New York, where he worked with a big band organized by the Collective Black Artists and with Mary Lou Williams, in whose group he initially played flute; during his first year in the city he and Warren Smith (ii) co-led a sextet with Sonelius Smith and Wayne Dockery among their sidemen. Stubblefield also played with Frank Foster's big band, Charles Mingus, the Thad Jones–Mel Lewis Orchestra, and Tito Puente, and in 1972 he performed and recorded at Town Hall with Anthony Braxton. The following year he recorded in Europe with Abdullah Ibrahim and worked with Miles Davis, and in 1974 he recorded with McCoy Tyner (playing oboe and flute), Gil Evans (at the Montreux International Jazz Festival), and Bowie. In 1975 he appeared further with Evans, as well as with sextets led by Cecil McBee and by Billy Taylor (ii). From 1976 to 1977 he played alongside Onaje Allen Gumbs and Buddy Williams in a quartet, the Basic Black Band, and performed as a sideman in groups led by Nat Adderley and Roy Haynes; he also recorded as a sideman with Adderley (1976) and Sonny Phillips (1977) and as a leader (from 1976). Around the late 1970s or early 1980s he was a member of Reggie Workman's group.

Later Stubblefield led Giant Steps (1982–3), which included Anthony Jackson and either Buddy Williams, Billy Hart, or Victor Lewis on drums. Through the 1980s and 1990s he led a quartet in which, at various times, Al Dailey, Mulgrew Miller, George Cables, Mike Nock, Mickey Tucker, McBee, Lewis, Marvin "Smitty" Smith, and Keith Copeland served as his sidemen. Having recorded with Kenny Barron (1980) and Teo Macero (1983) he worked with Roy Brooks (*c* early 1980s), Freddie Hubbard's quintet (1985), Tyner's big band (from 1985), Teruo Nakamura's Rising Sun Band and Barron's quintet (both from 1986), George Russell's sextet (1987), Jerry Gonzalez's Fort Apache Band (from 1988), and Louis Hayes's quintet (1989–90); from 1986 he deputized for David Murray in the World Saxophone Quartet. Around 1992 he joined the Mingus Big Band and Hart's group. As well as recording with many of these ensembles, he took part in sessions led by Julius Hemphill (1988), Ibrahim (1989), and Craig Harris and Larry Willis (both 1993). He has been active as a teacher, working on the Jazzmobile (1974–94) and lecturing, leading seminars, and organizing workshops at numerous universities and colleges.

Stubblefield has been much in demand in settings that range from bop to free jazz. His improvisatory signature is a continuous and relentlessly aggressive exploration of his instrument's altissimo register, which seems to reflect in a jazz context the ostentatious rhythm-and-blues tenor saxophone style that he experienced early in his career.

SELECTED RECORDINGS

As leader: *Confessin'* (1984, SN 1095); *Bushman Song* (1986, Enja 5015)
As sideman: A. Braxton: *Town Hall 1972* (1972, Trio 3008-9); L. Hayes: *The Crawl* (1989, Can. 79045); L. Willis: *A Tribute to Someone* (1993, Audioquest 1022)

BIBLIOGRAPHY

G. Urban: "Jazzmobile Introduced Fine New Musicians to Area," *Times Record* [Albany, NY] (5 Aug 1975), 24
A. J. Smith: "Profile: John Stubblefield," *DB*, xliii/2 (1976), 30
V. Wilmer: *As Serious as your Life: the Story of the New Jazz* (London, 1977, rev. [3]/1987)
I. Leymarie: "John Stubblefield: 'l'AACM m'a sauvé la vie'," *Jm*, no.346 (1986), 34
G. Endress: "Bushman," *JP*, xxxvi/11 (1987), 6
S. Schwartz: "John Stubblefield: Interview," *Cadence*, xix/2 (1993), 5
R. Grosman: "Working: John Stubblefield," *Jh*, no.525 (1995), 26

BK

Stubø, Thorgeir (*b* Narvik, Norway, 12 Nov 1943; *d* Narvik, 22 Oct 1986). Norwegian electric guitarist. He played in northern Norway with the pianist Terje Bjorklund, the tenor saxophonist Henning Gravrok, and others. His recording of his own compositions, *Notice* (1981, Odin 1), was the first made on the Norwegian Jazz Federation's own label. He made further bop recordings with Doug Raney (1983), in a quintet with Bernt Rosengren, Egil Kapstad, Egil Johansen, and the double bass player Terje Venaas (1984), in a group with Alex Riel (1985), and with Raney and Art Farmer (1986). He named Tal Farlow as the principal influence on his style.

RANDI HULTIN

Studer, Fredy (*b* Lucerne, Switzerland, 16 June 1948). Swiss drummer and percussionist. A self-taught musician, he took up drums at the age of 16 and first played rock music in groups with Christy Doran. In 1970 he moved to Rome, where he worked with Doran, Urs Leimgruber, and the double bass player Bobbi Burri in the electric free-jazz quartet Om (1972–82) and in a trio with Rainer Brüninghaus and Markus Stockhausen (1981–4); another trio, in which he performed with Doran and Stefan Wittwer, was known as Red Twist & Tuned Arrow, an anagram of its members' surnames. Studer played with Joe Henderson, Joachim Kühn, Albert Mangelsdorff, Enrico Rava, Tomasz Stańko, Miroslav Vitous, Eberhard Weber, and Kenny Wheeler, and he recorded with John Tchicai (1971), in a rhythm section alongside Wolfgang Dauner and Pierre Favre in the group String Summit (1980), and with Paul Motian and Nana Vasconcelos in Favre's percussion quartet Singing Drums (1984). In the late 1980s he was a member of a band led by Charlie Mariano and Jasper van 't Hof, and in 1990 he joined Doran's quartet. Later he played with Doran, Phil Minton, Django Bates, and Amin Ali in an ensemble that was initially called Doran, Studer, Minton, Bates, & Ali Play the Music of Jimi Hendrix (from 1993); Tom Cora replaced Bates in 1994, and the group toured as a quartet (without Cora) in 1995–6.

With Hans Koch and Martin Schütz, Studer formed in 1990 a trio which played a mixture of avant-garde improvisation, classical chamber music, and heavy metal; it toured Europe, and in 1995 it recorded in Egypt. In addition Studer recorded with André Jaume (1989) and performed contemporary art music with the Japanese percussionist Izawa Nakamura. In the course of his career he has made tours of the USA, Central and South America, the Caribbean, North Africa, and Japan.

SELECTED RECORDINGS

As leader: with C. Doran and S. Wittwer: *Red Twist & Tuned Arrow* (1986, ECM 1342); with B. Burri and Oliver Magnenat: *Musik für zwei Kontrabasse, elektrische Gitarre und Schlagzeug* (1990, ECM 1436); with C. Doran, P. Minton, D. Bates, and A. Ali: *Doran, Studer, Minton, Bates & Ali Play the Music of Jimi Hendrix* (1993, VMG 8098); with J. Tacuma: *Race the Time* (1997, MGB 973)
As sideman with P. Favre: *Singing Drums* (1984, ECM 1274)

BIBLIOGRAPHY

CarrJ
M. Bettine: "Fredy Studer: Swiss Timekeeper," *MD*, xvii/5 (1993), 30
M. Buholzer: "Christy Doran und Fredy Studer: Half a Lifetime zusammen," *JP*, xliv/4 (1995), 37
M. Bettine: "Fredy Studer: Are You Cross-culturally Experienced?," *MD*, xx/8 (1996), 12

BK

Studio musician. A musician who works mainly in recording studios, whether as a freelance or as the employee of a recording or film company or of a television or radio station; *see also* SESSION (i).

Sturgis, Ted [Columbus] (*b* Cape Charles, VA, 25 April 1913; *d* 18 Oct 1995). Double bass player. The name Fred Sturgis, which had been thought to be an error made by early discographers, does appear in some contemporary sources; the explanation for this is not known. Sturgis began playing piano at the age of five. In 1934 he moved to New York and worked with Roy Eldridge and Jacques Butler (both 1935), Blanche Calloway (1936), Tommy Stevenson (1936–7), and the trumpeter Eddie Mallory (1937–8), in whose band he doubled on alto saxophone. Late in 1939 he rejoined Eldridge at the Arcadia Ballroom and made his first recordings. In the early 1940s he was with the bandleader Bardu Ali (1940), Benny Carter (1940–41), Fletcher Henderson (1941), and Louis Armstrong (1942–3), with whom he may be seen in the film *Jam Session* (1943), then joined Paul Bascomb (1944) and recorded again with Eldridge (1943, 1945). Sturgis went to Europe with Don Redman in autumn 1946. Following his return he worked with Ben Webster (1947–8), Buster Harding (1948), Milt Buckner (1949), and Joe Thomas (iii) (1950). In the 1950s and 1960s he was active as a freelance. He was involved in several USO tours, during which he often played piano, and he occasionally made further recordings, notably with Cozy Cole in 1954. In 1970 he appeared as a member of Buddy Tate's band in the film *Jazz Odyssey*, playing electric bass guitar, and in the 1970s he was again a member of Eldridge's band for a long residency at Jimmy Ryan's in New York. He remained active and in 1988 toured Europe with the Harlem Blues and Jazz Band. His date of death is taken from the social security death index, which gives his last known residence as New York.

SELECTED RECORDINGS

As sideman: R. Eldridge: *Arcadia Shuffle* (1939, Jazz Archives 14); Pluckin' the Bass (1939, Vars. 8107); High Society/Muskrat Ramble (1939, Vars. 8154); D. Redman: *For Europeans Only* (1946, Ste. 6020–21), incl. I got rhythm; M. Buckner: Oo-be-doop/M. B. Blues (1949, MGM 10504); J. Thomas: Sittin' Around (1950, King 4434); Sooey, sooey baby (1950, King 4401); B. Tate, P. Quinichette, and J. McShann: *Kansas City Joys* (1976, Sonet 716)

BIBLIOGRAPHY

AllenH; *ChiltonW*

HOWARD RYE

Stuyvesant Casino. Ballroom in New York; *See* NIGHTCLUBS AND OTHER VENUES.

Sublett, John. *See* BUBBLES, JOHN.

Subramaniam, L(akshminarayana) (*b* Madras, India, 23 July 1947). Indian violinist and leader. In his youth he learned violin and performed in classical concerts. After a period reading medicine he traveled to the USA to study Western music as a graduate at the California Institute for the Arts (MFA). In 1973–4 he toured the USA and Europe with the rock guitarist George Harrison and the sitar player Ravi Shankar, performing a fusion of Indian music and rock, and in 1978 he composed for and recorded with Stu Goldberg and made a series of duo recordings with Larry Coryell and his first album as a leader. Later he recorded as a member of the group Rainbow with John Handy and the sarod player Ali Akbar Khan (the album *Fantasy without Limit*, 1979, Trend 524), as the leader of a quartet consisting of Coryell, George Duke, and Tom Scott (*c*1982), and as a leader with Stephane Grappelli (the album *Conversations*, 1984, Mlst. 9130); he also appeared in the television program "L. A. Jazz, no.2" (1981). Thereafter he remained a leading violinist in various expressions of and fusions with south Indian classical music, notably a tour with Grappelli and Yehudi Menuhin in 1993, and generally had little further connection to the jazz tradition. His brother Lakshminarayana Shankar, another violinist, was a member of John McLaughlin's group Shakti.

BIBLIOGRAPHY

L. Underwood: "L. Subramaniam," *DB*, xlvii/11 (1980), 53
J. De Souza: "Laxminarayana Subramaniam: the Emperor of Violinists," *JF* [intl. edn], no.102 (1986), 30

Substitute [sub]. A musician employed on an occasional or short-term basis; *see* BANDS, §3.

Substitute chord. A chord used to replace one in a given harmonic progression; *see* HARMONY (i), §1(v)(b).

Substitute fingering. *See* FALSE FINGERING.

Subtone. A soft, caressing, breathy tone, produced in the lowest range of the saxophone or clarinet by carefully controlled suppression of the higher partials of a note. Subtone is produced by means of a small, slow, but steady stream of air, projected through a tight embouchure; the player must blow firmly to prevent the sound from breaking or fading altogether, but gently so that the upper partials of the note are not produced. On the saxophone, especially the tenor, the effect contrasts with the Honk, a loud low-pitched sound in which the high partials are prominent.

Subtone occurs most often in ballads. Ben Webster used it freely, as for example on Sid Catlett's *Memories of You* (1944, Com. 1515), notably in bar 7 of his opening statement of the theme. Another characteristic use is in bossa nova melodies, following the example of Stan Getz in the theme of

Desafinado, on his album *Jazz Samba* (1962, Verve 68432). John Coltrane's recording of *Alabama*, on *Live at Birdland* (1963, Imp. 50), offers a clear example of the contrast between subtone, heard on the lowest pitches of the descending phrase of the theme at every statement throughout the performance, and Coltrane's normal penetrating tone.

BK

Suchanek, Bronisław (*b* Bielsko-Biała, Poland, 30 Aug 1948). Polish double bass player. He studied double bass at the high school of music in Katowice (1967–72) and while still a student played with the Silesian Jazz Quartet (late 1960s), Jan Wróblewski (1970), the pianist Mieczysław Kosz (1971), and Tomasz Stańko (1969–72). From 1969 he worked regularly with the orchestra of the Studio Jazzowe Polskiego Radia (Polish Radio Jazz Studio) under Wróblewski, then in the mid-1970s he moved to Sweden, where he performed and recorded both with the tenor saxophonist Urban Hansson (1976) and with Radiojazzgruppen (ii) under the leadership of George Russell (1977), and played with Roland Hanna and Don Cherry; he took Swedish citizenship in 1983. In that same year, 1983, he played in the group G.A.P. (based in Austria and including Benny Bailey), and in 1983 and 1985 he toured with Leszek Żądło's Polski Jazz Ensemble. In 1989 he toured and recorded with Okay Temiz. Suchanek moved in 1991 to the USA and settled in New England, although he retains his Swedish citizenship. In 1994 he became a member of the Artie Shaw Orchestra under Dick Johnson and began teaching at the University of Southern Maine, in Gorham, Maine. He recorded two albums with the trombonist Rick Stepton, and he may be heard as a soloist on *Old Folks*, recorded as a fellow sideman with Stepton in a big band led by the trumpeter and arranger John Allmark.

SELECTED RECORDINGS

As sideman: T. Stańko: *Jazz Message from Poland* (1972, JG 030); R. Stepton: *Blue Collar Trombone* (1996–7, Brownstone 9804); *Stiff Upper Lip* (1998, Brownstone 9904); John Wilkins: *Strollin'* (1998, Brownstone 2-0004); J. Allmark: *The John Allmark Jazz Orchestra featuring Clay Osborne* (*c*2000, Whaling City Sound 007), incl. Old Folks

BIBLIOGRAPHY

J. Byrczek: "Eurojazz Personalities: Poland," *JF* [intl edn], no.18 (1972), 87
<http://www.usm.maine.edu/~mus/faculty/suchanek.htm> (2001)

WOLFRAM KNAUER/ADAM CEGIELSKI, BK

Sudhalter, Dick [Richard M(errill); Napoleon, Art] (*b* Boston, 28 Dec 1938). Trumpeter, cornetist, leader, and writer. He began on cornet at the age of 12, played in his high-school bands, and formed a dixieland band with his fellow students, who included Roger Kellaway and Steve Kuhn. Following studies at Oberlin College, Ohio (BA 1960), he moved to Austria, where he worked as an English teacher; while there he routinely crossed the border with Germany to play in jazz bands in Munich. He returned to the United States (1962) and served in a US Army band, then went back to Munich and played cornet in the jazz ensemble of Bavarian state radio (1963–4). From 1964 to 1972 he lived primarily in London and worked as a staff reporter for United Press International (UPI); during this time he led the group Anglo-American Alliance (1967–8) and became active as a jazz writer under the pseudonym Art Napoleon (in particular he wrote a notable article on brass mutes; *see* Mute, bibliography). After leaving UPI he remained in London, where he worked as a sideman in Sandy Brown's quintet (1972–4) and led various groups, among them the New Paul Whiteman Orchestra (1974–5). In 1975 he returned to the USA to produce and perform in the New York Jazz Repertory Company's concert tribute to Bix Beiderbecke; by the end of the year he had moved to New York and had become an administrator for that organization (to 1978). He was a jazz critic for the *New York Post* (1978–83) and also produced concerts and wrote liner notes. Sudhalter led the New California Ramblers (1976–8), the recording band Friends with Pleasure (1980–81), and the Puck Dance Orchestra (1983–5), played in Loren Schoenberg's big band (1980–96), and was a member of a cooperative group, the Classic Jazz Quartet, with Joe Muranyi, Marty Grosz, and Dick Wellstood (1984–7). He continued to perform with Grosz in the 1990s, made a reunion recording in Britain (1994), and also recorded as a leader, with Kellaway (1998).

Sudhalter is highly regarded for his work as an instrumentalist and arranger in repertory groups which focus primarily on white jazz of the mid- to late 1920s. He has published a controversial history, *Lost Chords: the Contributions of White Musicians to Jazz, 1915–45* (New York, and Oxford, England, 1998), and he is a co-author, with P. R. Evans and W. Dean-Myatt, of *Bix: Man and Legend* (New Rochelle, NY, and London, 1974).

SELECTED RECORDINGS

As leader: *The New Paul Whiteman Orchestra* (1974, Argo 167); *After Awhile: Dick Sudhalter and his London Friends* (1994, Challenge 70014); *Melodies Heard, Melodies Sweet* (1998, Challenge 70055)
As sideman with Classic Jazz Quartet: *The Classic Jazz Quartet* (1984, Jlgy 138)

BIBLIOGRAPHY

Feather–Gitler '70s
D. Fairweather: "Anglo-American: a Portrait of Dick Sudhalter," *JJ*, xxv/6 (1972), 4
J. H. Klee: "Richard Sudhalter: Bix is the Start of Something Big," *MR*, iii/8 (1976), 9
L. Feather: "Jazz: Dick Sudhalter Leads Double Life," *Los Angeles Times* (1 Feb 1981)
C. Deffaa: "Ad Lib: for Love of Bix," *DB*, lii/10 (1985), 61
W. R. Stokes: "The Classic Jazz Quartet," *JT* (1986), Aug, 8
C. Deffaa: "An Interview with Richard Sudhalter," *MR*, xviii/5 (1991), 1
——: *Traditionalists and Revivalists in Jazz* (Metuchen, NJ, and London, 1993), 170
D. Zych: "Label Watch: Challenge Records: Vineyard Harvest," *JT*, xxvii/3 (1997), 61

GK

Sudler, Monnette (Leigh) (*b* Philadelphia, 5 June 1952). Guitarist and singer. Her mother was a pianist and singer who taught her to play piano. She took up guitar when she was eight and began formal lessons at the age of 14; initially she performed the type of finger-style guitar music associated with the folk revival, but after two years she began playing jazz. In 1970–71 she studied theory, harmony, and piano at the Berklee School of Music, where she developed a technique that blended plectrum and finger styles. She also attended Combs College in Philadelphia and later received tuition in composition and drumming from the drummer Dwight James. After returning to Philadelphia in 1971 Sudler worked with Khan Jamal and Byard Lancaster in the group Sounds of Liberation, with which she appeared at the Newport Jazz Festival New York the following year, and in 1974 she toured Germany as the conductor of an orchestra for the show *Miss Black America*. Around 1974–5 she spent a year in Sam Rivers's big band, during which time she performed at the Newport festival, and in 1976 she played there again alongside Dave Holland and Jack DeJohnette as a member of Rivers's quartet.

Sudler first recorded for Steeplechase in 1976, and her third album for that company was recorded in performance at the Café Montmartre in Copenhagen during a tour of Europe, when she led a quartet with the pianist Oliver Collins, the double bass player Kenneth Kellum, and the drummer Newman Taylor Baker; she worked with this group into the early 1980s. In the late 1970s she played in the Philadelphia Change of the Century Orchestra and in Sunny Murray's ensemble Untouchable Factor (recording *c*1978). Sudler toured with Hugh Masekela in 1980 and in spring of that year she led a trio with Fred Hopkins and Baker at the Women's Jazz Festival in New York. Little is known of her later musical activities, although she recorded again with Jamal in 1989 and released a fusion album in spring 1991, on which she sang as well as played. Following a drunk-driving accident in 1993 she was incarcerated for vehicular manslaughter and thereafter performed infrequently.

SELECTED RECORDINGS

As leader: *Time for a Change* (1976, Ste. 1062); *Brighter Days for You* (1977, Ste. 1087); *Live in Europe* (1978, Ste. 1102)

As sideman: S. Murray: *Apple Cores* (*c*1978, Philly Jazz 1004); K. Jamal: *Don't Take No* (1983, 1989, Stash 20)

BIBLIOGRAPHY

GrayF
"Monette Sudler," *Jm*, no.235 (1975), 17
J. Shapiro: "Monnette Sudler: Contemporary Jazz Stylist," *GP*, xiii/2 (1980), 92 [incl. discography and transcr.]
R. F. Grass: "Profile: Monnette Sudler," *DB*, xlviii/1 (1981), 50
P. Carles, A. Clergeat, and J.-L. Comolli: *Dictionnaire du jazz* (Paris, 1988, rev. and enlarged 2/1994)
D. Kasrel: "Hearsay: Monnette Sudler," *JT*, xxi/6 (1991), 10
J. Lloyd: "Jazz: from Phila. and back for Guitarist," *Philadelphia Inquirer* (26 June 1992)
K. Stark: "Monnette Sudler: Dreaming Modest Dreams," *Philadelphia Inquirer* (18 March 1997)

GK

Sulieman, Idrees (Dawud ibn) (*b* St. Petersburg, FL, 7 Aug 1923). Trumpeter. After playing for four years with the Carolina Cotton Pickers he joined Earl Hines's orchestra (1943) and then spent about two years in New York and Boston with Sabby Lewis's big band (late 1943 – *c*1945). He worked in Benny Carter's big band in 1945–6, recorded with Thelonious Monk in 1947, and became a member of Cab Calloway's band the following year. Later he worked with many other big bands, including those of Mercer Ellington, Erskine Hawkins (1950), and Count Basie and Lionel Hampton (both briefly in 1951). He recorded with both Tadd Dameron and Max Roach in 1953 and between 1956 and 1958 with Dizzy Gillespie's big band, Mal Waldron, Coleman Hawkins, Bobby Jaspar and George Wallington, Gene Ammons, and several all-star groups organized by Prestige. In 1956 he played in Friedrich Gulda's ensemble of American musicians, and in 1958–9 he worked with Randy Weston. Sulieman toured Europe in the late 1950s with a group led by the pianist Oscar Dennard, and in 1961 he settled in Stockholm, where he recorded with Eric Dolphy (1961) and began playing alto saxophone, although trumpet remained his principal instrument. From 1963 to 1973 he was a member of the Clarke–Boland Big Band. In 1964 he moved to Copenhagen, and from that time has played mainly in Denmark; he worked with the Radioens Big Band from the early 1970s. In 1991 he recorded in New York with Weston's big band. Sulieman's playing is rooted in the bop tradition; indeed, it has been said that he was one of the first musicians to adopt the bop style.

SELECTED RECORDINGS

As leader: *Now is the Time* (1976, Ste. 1052); *Bird's Grass* (1976, Ste. 1202)

As sideman: T. Monk: Humph (1947, BN 560); Evonce (1947, BN 547); Suburban Eyes/Thelonious (1947, BN 542); M. Waldron: *Mal 1* (1956, Prst. 7090); on *Mal 2* (1957, Prst. 7111), From this moment on, One by one, The way you look tonight; H. Parlan: *Arrival* (1973, Ste. 1012); Radioens Big Band: *By Jones, I Think We've Got it* (1978, Met. 15629), incl. New York City, Tip Toe

BIBLIOGRAPHY

SheridanCB
J. G. Jepsen: "Idrees Sulieman diskografi," *Orkester journalen*, xxxii/12 (1964), 46; xxxiii (1965), no.1, p.30; no.2, p.27
M. Gardner: Liner notes, *Now is the Time* (Ste. 1052, 1976)
G. Henderson: "Idrees Sulieman: Interview," *Cadence*, v/9 (1979), 3
M. Hennessey: *Klook: the Story of Kenny Clarke* (London, 1990)

ROLAND BAGGENAES/BK

Sulieman, Jamil. *See* NASSER, JAMIL.

Sullivan, Charles (Henry) [Adilifu, Kamau (Muata)] (*b* New York, 8 Nov 1944). Trumpeter, flugelhorn player, and bandleader. He took up trumpet when he was ten and had lessons for two years with his uncle, but then gave up. After graduating from high school he became interested in music once again, and he later studied at the Manhattan School of Music (BA 1967) and performed intermittently for off-Broadway theater productions (from 1965). He then played with Lionel Hampton (1968) and Roy Haynes's Hip Ensemble (1969), toured briefly as lead trumpeter with Count Basie (1970), and worked with Lonnie Liston Smith (1971), Sy Oliver (1972), and Norman Connors (1973). In 1973 he toured Europe and recorded with Abdullah Ibrahim, after which he worked intermittently with Sonny Fortune, recording in 1974–5 and touring the USA in 1978. Sullivan also recorded as a leader (1974) and with Carlos Garnett and Bennie Maupin (both 1974), Kenny Barron and Charles Greenlee (both 1975), Ricky Ford, Eddie Jefferson, and Walter Davis (all 1977), and Woody Shaw (1978–9). From 1978 he led his own small group, with Kenny Kirkland, Cecil McBee, and Keith Copeland as his sidemen, and a big band, Black Legacy. Two years later he changed his name to Kamau (Muata) Adilifu. Apart from occasional appearances with the big bands led by Frank Foster (early 1980s) and Mercer Ellington and McCoy Tyner (both late 1980s) and with the Carnegie Hall Jazz Band (early 1990s), he worked mainly in Broadway pit orchestras and had little further recognition in jazz until a new recording in 1995 won popular acclaim; he released this album with his new forename, *Kamau*, as its title, but under his former name, Charles Sullivan, because that was more familiar to the jazz audience.

SELECTED RECORDINGS

As leader: *Kamau* (1995, Arabesque 0121)

As sideman: B. Maupin: on *The Jewel in the Lotus* (1974, ECM 1043), Excursion, Mappo; R. Ford: *Loxodonta Africana* (1977, New World 204); M. Tyner: *Uptown/Downtown* (1988, Mlst. 9167), incl. Blues for Basie, Uptown

BIBLIOGRAPHY

Feather–Gitler '70s
L. A. Emenari III: "Profile: Charles Sullivan," *DB*, xlvii/10 (1980), 50
S. Gribetz: "Hearsay: Kamau Adilifu," *JT*, xxvi/8 (1996), 25

BK

Sullivan, Ira (Brevard, Jr.) (*b* Washington, DC, 1 May 1931). Trumpeter, saxophonist, and flugelhorn player. He grew up in a musical family and at the age of four began to learn trumpet and saxophone with his parents. Although he concentrated on trumpet, when he began to play engagements during his high-school years it was more often as a tenor saxophonist. During the 1950s he was based in Chicago, except for a brief period with Art Blakey in New York (1956), at which time he also recorded as a soloist on J. R. Monterose's first album. His skill on both his instruments (and soon on alto and baritone saxophones as well) and his mastery of the bop style became widely known, and he played with many prominent musicians. Always reluctant to travel, having settled in Florida in the early 1960s Sullivan had fewer opportunities to play with major jazzmen, though he appeared regularly in Miami and Fort Lauderdale. He was seldom heard outside Florida until 1980, except for taking part occasionally in recording sessions: in Berkeley, California, in 1977, for example, he was paired with Harold Land as a tenor saxophonist in Red Garland's group.

During the 1960s Sullivan tired of bop and evolved a freer style, and at the same time he took up soprano saxophone and flutes. Through contact with younger players at the University of Miami (among them Pat Metheny, Jaco Pastorius, Danny Gottlieb, and Mark Egan) he began to teach. In 1980 he formed a quintet with his friend Red Rodney. On Sullivan's insistence it played new compositions rather than bop standards, and as a consequence its music was among the most creative and stimulating of the 1980s. It also formed a favorable setting for Sullivan's playing and enabled him to demonstrate his remarkable ability to create an individual and original style on each of his instruments. He continued touring as a freelance in the 1990s and returned regularly to Chicago, where he appeared at clubs and recorded with the vibraphonist Jim Cooper (1991), Lin Halliday (1991–3), and the saxophonist Frank Catalano (1997); he also recorded a quiet duo album with Joe Diorio in Pennsylvania (1993) and as a member of big bands led by the reed player Barry Ross in Miami (1996) and by Melton Mustafa in Fort Lauderdale (1997). In the latter part of his career Sullivan has played flugelhorn as well as trumpet, while continuing to double on flute and soprano saxophone.

SELECTED RECORDINGS

As leader: *Nicky's Tune* (1958, Del. 422); *Bird Lives!* (1962, VJ 3033); *Horizons* (1967, Atl. 1476); *Ira Sullivan* (1975–6, A&M Hor. 706); *Peace* (1978, Gal. 5114); *Multimedia* (1978, Gal. 5137); with R. Rodney: *Live at the Village Vanguard* (1980, Muse 5209); *Ira Sullivan Does it All* (1981, Muse 5242); with R. Rodney: *Night and Day* (1981, Muse 5274), *Sprint* (1982, Elek. Mus. 60261)

As sideman: R. Rodney: *Red Rodney: 1957* (1957, Signal 1206); R. Kirk: *Introducing Roland Kirk* (1960, Argo 669); R. Garland: *Red Alert* (1977, Gal. 5109), incl. The Whiffenpoof Song; L. Halliday: *Delayed Exposure* (1991, Del. 449); *East of the Sun* (1992, Del. 458), incl. Will you still be mine; *Where or When* (1993, Del. 468)

BIBLIOGRAPHY

FeatherE; *Feather–Gitler '70s*

D. DeMicheal: "Ira Sullivan: Legend in the Making," *DB*, xxvii/19 (1960), 18

D. D. Spitzer: "Ira Sullivan: Living Legend," *DB*, xxxix/3 (1972), 14 [incl. discography]

G. Rouy: "Ira Sullivan," *Jm*, no.290 (1980), 38; no.291 (1980), 36; no.292 (1980), 44 [incl. discography]

N. Tesser: "Ira Sullivan: Multi Mystique," *DB*, xlviii/2 (1981), 21 [incl. discography]

K. Brodacki: "Ira Sullivan: a Gift of Music," *JF* [intl edn], no.93 (1985), 30

SCOTT YANOW

Sullivan, Joe [O'Sullivan, Joseph Michael] (*b* Chicago, 4 Nov 1906; *d* San Francisco, 13 Oct 1971). Pianist and composer. He was gifted with perfect pitch and, like his eight older siblings, took classical piano lessons as a child. Later he continued his classical studies at the Chicago Conservatory (1922–3), but from his youth he concentrated mostly on popular styles. During the early 1920s he became friends with members of the Austin High School Gang and began working professionally. On securing a musicians' union card he found his surname printed as Sullivan, as he was known thereafter. He played with fellow sideman George Wettling in an obscure band on the vaudeville circuit before obtaining regular work in Chicago, where he appeared with many bandleaders and performed on radio; he also furthered his informal jazz education by sitting in with Jimmie Noone's band at the Nest Club and the Dodds brothers at Kelly's Stables. His memorable recording début was made in December 1927 with Red McKenzie and Eddie Condon's Chicagoans, when he played a powerful, driving solo on *China Boy*.

In 1928, together with other men associated with Chicago jazz, Sullivan went to New York. He held engagements with Red Nichols (1929–30), Roger Wolfe Kahn (1930), and Red McKenzie's Mound City Blue Blowers (to 1932), and then worked as an unaccompanied pianist at the Onyx Club (1932). With the help of John Hammond he participated in a succession of broadcasts and recordings in 1932–3, including sessions with Benny Goodman, Ethel Waters, and Billy Banks, and as a soloist. After rejoining Kahn (spring 1933) he traveled to Los Angeles (October 1933) and the following year became Bing Crosby's accompanist. In 1935 he made further recordings as an unaccompanied soloist. During an engagement with Bob Crosby's orchestra from September to

Joe Sullivan at Café Society, New York, 1941

December 1936 he became ill with tuberculosis, but after a lengthy recovery he resumed working in mid-1938 as a soloist and with ensembles; from June to September 1939 he was again with Crosby's band.

Having commenced an engagement in mid-October 1939 at Café Society as the leader of a white band of six to seven pieces, in the following month Sullivan formed one of the earliest racially integrated ensembles in New York. His sidemen were the trumpeter Murray Steinberg (soon replaced by Ed Anderson), Benny Morton, Edmond Hall, Danny Polo, the double bass player Henry Turner, and the drummer Johnny Wells. These last two men were replaced in early spring 1940 by Billy Taylor (i) and Yank Porter, at which time Sullivan led the group in a jazz sequence in the documentary film *The Fight for Life* (1940). Following a summertime stint at Nick's, Sullivan re-formed his group for a return to the downtown location of Café Society (October–November 1940), probably with Joe Thomas (iv), Claude Jones, Hall, Taylor, and Eddie Dougherty. He then transferred for the remainder of the year to the Famous Door, with Joe Thomas (iv), Jones (replaced by the tenor saxophonist Ernie Powell), Chauncey Haughton (replaced by Albert Nicholas), Hayes Alvis, and Dougherty (replaced by Manzie Johnson).

For some years thereafter Sullivan traveled frequently between the East and West coasts, fulfilling short-lived engagements and recording sporadically. He participated in the NBC radio show "Chamber Music Society of Lower Basin Street" (early 1941), gave concerts in New York, toured, and recorded with Eddie Condon's groups (1941–2). During a period in Los Angeles, from late 1943 to May 1945, he appeared with Jack Teagarden in two films; their performance in *Stars and Violins* (1944) was included in two later film anthologies. After returning to New York Sullivan recorded with Wild Bill Davison in September and served as the intermission pianist at Condon's new club from its opening in December 1945 until August 1948. Between March and July 1947 he took part in seven episodes of Rudi Blesh's radio show "This is Jazz" as a soloist and band pianist.

Among Sullivan's notable later achievements were his solo on *After you've gone* (1951) and his recording of eight unpublished compositions by Fats Waller (1952). He led a house band including Lee Collins at the Club Hangover in San Francisco in the summer of 1953, served as the club's intermission pianist in September of that year, and returned there as intermission pianist from June 1955 through 1960 (with occasional breaks). In 1963 he appeared at the Monterey Jazz Festival, improvised music for a film about blind children, *Who's Enchanted?*, and began playing at the Trident in San Francisco, but he was taken ill at the Newport Jazz Festival the following year and thereafter performed only infrequently.

Sullivan was strongly influenced by the blues and the stride piano style of Waller; he also drew inspiration from Earl Hines, Jimmie Noone, and Louis Armstrong. He typically exploited the resources of his instrument with the bravura of a concert pianist, improvising with tremendous animation and ferocity of attack. A strong rhythmic pulse of four beats to the bar was usually present in his playing, and at times broke through even the poignant lyricism with which he interpreted slow or medium-tempo ballads such as *I cover the waterfront*. Among his best-known compositions are *Gin Mill Blues*, *Little Rock Getaway*, and *Farewell to Riverside*.

SELECTED RECORDINGS

As unaccompanied soloist: Honeysuckle Rose/Gin Mill Blues (1933, Parl. R1686); Little Rock Getaway/Onyx Bringdown (1933, Parl. R2006); My Little Pride and Joy (1935, Bruns. 02136); Little Rock Getaway/Just Strolling (1935, Decca 600); Forevermore (1941, Com. 538); *Fats Waller First Editions* (1952, Epic 1003); *New Solos by an Old Master* (1953, Riv. 202), incl. I cover the waterfront, Farewell to Riverside; *Mr. Piano Man* (1955, Down Home 2), incl. In the middle of a kiss; *Joe Sullivan* (1963, Pumpkin 112)

As leader: Oh, Lady Be Good (1940, Voc. 5496)

As sideman: McKenzie and Condon's Chicagoans: China Boy (1927, OK 41011); Chicago Rhythm Kings: I've found a new baby (1928, Bruns. 4001); E. Condon: Indiana (1928, Parl. R2932); R. Nichols: Shim-me-sha-wabble (1930, Bruns. 80005); B. Banks: Oh Peter (1932, Col. 35841); Spider Crawl (1932, Ban. 32459); J. Venuti: In de Ruff (1933, Col. CB686); E. Condon: Home Cooking (1933, Bruns. 6743); There'll be some changes made (1939, Decca 18041); B. Crosby: Till we meet again (1939, Decca 2825); E. Condon: Mammy O'Mine (1942, Com. 1509); G. Wettling: *George Wettling's Jazz Band* (1951, Col. CL6189), incl. After you've gone, Collier's Clambake; E. Condon: *Chicago and all that Jazz* (1961, Verve 68441), incl. China Boy

SELECTED FILMS AND VIDEOS

The Fight for Life (1940); Stars and Violins (1944); Hi, Good Lookin'! (1944); Rhythm Masters: a Decade of Band Hits (1948); Chicago & All that Jazz (1961); Who's Enchanted? (1963); Jazz Casual (1963)

BIBLIOGRAPHY

D. Biggar: "Gin Mill Joe," *Piano Jazz*, no.1 (1945), 22
O. Keepnews: "On Piano: Joe Sullivan," *Record Changer*, viii/5 (1949), 9
R. Hadlock: *Jazz Masters of the Twenties* (New York, 1965/*R*1985)
K. Gallacher: "Joe Sullivan: a Study in Neglect," *JJ*, xx/4 (1967), 2
R. Hadlock: "Joe Sullivan: the Last Days," *J&B*, iii/3 (1973), 6
N. P. Gentieu: "Notes for a Bio-discography of Joe Sullivan," *JJS*, iv/2 (1977), 33; *ARJS*, i (1982), 128; ii (1983), 81; iii (1985), 11
R. Hadlock: Liner notes, *Joe Sullivan* (TL 27, 1982)
J. Chilton: *Stomp Off, Let's Go! The Story of Bob Crosby's Bob Cats & Big Band* (London, 1983)
M. Selchow: *Profoundly Blue: a Bio-Discographical Scrapbook on Edmond Hall* (Lübbecke, Germany, 1988), 87

NORMAN P. GENTIEU/BK

Sullivan, Maxine [Williams, Marietta] (*b* Homestead, PA, 13 May 1911; *d* New York, 7 April 1987). Singer. She sang as a child, and first attracted attention in New York in 1937 in Claude Thornhill's band, particularly with her successful recording *Loch Lomond*; she took the stage name Maxine Sullivan for this recording, which typecast her as a singer of folk and light-classical material for the rest of her career. Having already begun to sing at the Onyx, she starred there from autumn 1937 with a sextet led by John Kirby, where her gentle delivery, pristine enunciation, and light sense of swing perfectly complemented the group's concept of chamber jazz. She appeared in two Hollywood film musicals, *Going Places* (opposite Louis Armstrong, 1938) and *St. Louis Blues* (1939), again with Armstrong in the failed Broadway show *Swingin' the Dream* (November 1939), and yet again with him in the last revue at the Cotton Club (until June 1940). Sullivan and Kirby married in 1938. She joined Kirby's group on a sponsored network radio show, "Flow Gently, Sweet Rhythm," and shared engagements with the sextet at prestigious venues until 1942, when the couple divorced and Sullivan married Cliff Jackson. She toured the South for six weeks with Benny Carter's big band and then embarked upon a solo career, occasionally performing on valve trombone and flugelhorn. Wishing to spend more time with her teenage daughter, and having grown exceedingly weary of *Loch Lomond*, she retired in 1957 and devoted herself to community work, but she appeared on an episode of "Art

Ford's Jazz Party" in 1958. After Jackson's death in 1970 she founded the House that Jazz Built, a cultural center in the Bronx.

Sullivan resumed singing in the late 1960s. She worked with Bobby Hackett and recorded with Bob Wilber in 1969 before joining the World's Greatest Jazz Band of Bob Haggart and Yank Lawson, with which she performed regularly during the 1970s. During this second phase of her musical career Sullivan's voice retained its soft tone but her approach was much more energetic, emotional, and swinging than before. She appeared in two Broadway shows, receiving a Tony nomination in 1979 for her work in *My Old Friends*. She performed at clubs, on cruises, and at festivals, toured Japan with Scott Hamilton (1984), and sang with Doc Cheatham's group (1985). Her album *The Great Songs from the Cotton Club* was nominated for a Grammy Award in 1986.

Oral history material in *NjR* (JOHP), *NjR*, *NN-HBc*.

For illustration *see* Films, fig.5.

SELECTED RECORDINGS

Loch Lomond (1937, Voc. 3654); Nice work if you can get it (1937, Voc. 3848); St. Louis Blues (1938, Vic. 25895); When your lover has gone/My Ideal (1942, Decca 18555); *The Complete Charlie Shavers with Maxine Sullivan* (1956, Period 1113); *The Queen* (1981–5, Kenneth 2052-5); *The Great Songs from the Cotton Club by Harold Arlen and Ted Koehler* (1984, Stash 244); *Uptown* (1985, Conc. 288)

BIBLIOGRAPHY

L. Feather: "58 Inches of Swing," *Rhythm*, no.128 (1938), 13
D. Burley: "Maxine Sullivan 'Proving Self' as Worthy of Fame She Achieved with Loch Lomond," *New York Amsterdam News* (10 June 1939), 16
A. Gray: "Sepia Cinderella: New Light on the Story of Maxine Sullivan's Scottish Swing," *Rhythm*, no.140 (1939), 58
A. Shaw: *The Street that Never Slept: New York's Fabled 52nd Street* (New York, 1971/*R*1977 as *52nd Street: the Street of Jazz*)
R. Johnson: "Maxine Sullivan," *Coda*, xi/6 (1974), 26
S. Traill: "Maxine Sullivan," *JJ*, xxviii/11 (1975), 6
B. Rusch: "A Talk with Maxine Sullivan," *Cadence*, i/10 (1976), 4
R. D. Johnson: "Sullivan Swing," *MR*, v/12 (1978), 10
M. Berger, E. Berger, and J. Patrick: *Benny Carter: a Life in American Music* (Metuchen, NJ, and London, 1982)
D. J. Travis: *An Autobiography of Black Jazz* (Chicago, 1983), 451
C. Deffaa: "Still Gently Swinging," *MR*, xii/10 (1985), 10
J. S. Wilson: "Maxine Sullivan: 50 years a Singer and Still Growing," *New York Times* (15 Dec 1985), §II, 29
Obituary, L. Feather, *Jazz Express*, no.84 (1987), 7
J. Simmen: "Ceux qui s'en vont: Maxine Sullivan," *BHcF*, no. 356 (1988), 31
C. Deffaa: *Swing Legacy* (Metuchen, NJ, and London, 1989), 83

J. BRADFORD ROBINSON/BK

Sulzmann, Stan(ley Ernest) (*b* London, 30 Nov 1948). English saxophonist. He took private lessons on saxophone and clarinet from the age of 13 and two years later joined Bill Ashton's London Youth Jazz Orchestra (which became the National Youth Jazz Orchestra). From 1969 to 1972 he attended the Royal Academy of Music. He first played with the Clarke–Boland Big Band (1971), Mike Gibbs (from 1971), John Taylor and Kenny Wheeler (both from the early 1970s), Volker Kriegel, Eberhard Weber, and Zbigniew Seifert (all 1973), Phil Woods and Clark Terry (both 1978), and Gordon Beck (from the mid 1970s). Later he worked with Gil Evans's British orchestra (1983), the European Jazz Ensemble (from 1983), the Hilversum Radio Orchestra (early 1980s), the NDR Big Band in Hamburg (1980s), the London Jazz Orchestra, Allan Botschinsky's quintet (in Denmark in the mid-1990s), the New York Composers Orchestra (mid-1990s), David Murray's big band (1997), Paul Clarvis and Bruno Castellucci (both 1998), and others. He has led his own small groups and has taught regularly in London at the Guildhall School of Music, the Royal Academy of Music, and Trinity College of Music.

SELECTED RECORDINGS

Duos: with J. Taylor: *Everybody's Song but my Own* (1986, Loose Tubes 004); with M. Copland: *Never at All* (1992, FMR 0528193); with Nikki Iles: *Treasure Trove* (1995, ASC 7)
As leader: *Feudal Rabbits* (1990, Ah Um 011)
As sideman: K. Clarke and F. Boland: *Change of Scenes* (1971, Verve 2304034); G. Evans: *The British Orchestra* (1983, Mole 8); K. Wheeler: *Flutter by, Butterfly* (1987, SN 1146); *Music for Large & Small Ensembles* (1990, ECM 1415–16); P. Clarvis: *For all the Saints* (1996, Village Life 97123); B. Castellucci: *Lost and Found* (1997, Quetzal 107)

BIBLIOGRAPHY

CarrJ; *ChiltonB*
M. Pearson: "Stan Sulzmann," *JJI*, l/4 (1997), 12

MARK GILBERT

Summa cum Laude Orchestra. Octet formed in 1939 by Bud Freeman.

Sun (i). Record label. It was established in Canada in the very early 1920s and drew its repertory from OKeh's catalogue. The issues include some of Mamie Smith's earliest recordings. (B. Rust: *The American Record Label Book* (New Rochelle, NY, 1978), 284)

HOWARD RYE

Sun (ii). Record company and label. The company was established in 1973 in Paris by Sébastien Bernard and flourished during the mid-1970s. It concentrated on recording American free-jazz musicians who were resident in France, among them Frank Wright and Noah Howard. (S. Loupien: "Deux stratégies phonographiques en France: Sun par Sébastien Bernard," *Jm*, nos.266–7 (1978), 26)

BK

Sunnyside. Record company and label. It was established in New York in 1982 by François Zalacain and Christine Berthe. At first it recorded mostly unaccompanied pianists and ensembles without drums, but later it expanded its repertory to include the work of more standard groups. Among its most important musicians are Kirk Lightsey, Lee Konitz, Rufus Reid, James Williams, Billy Pierce, Harold Danko, Jerry Gonzalez, Kenny Werner, Geoff Keezer, Eddie Higgins, Armen Donelian, and Meredith D'Ambrosio.

BIBLIOGRAPHY

D. Zych: "Label Watch: Sunnyside's Zalacain: No Excuse for a Bad Recording," *JT*, xxi/7 (1991), 36
<http://www.sunnysidezone.com/> (2000)

BK

Sun Ra [Blount, Herman (Poole); Blount, Sonny; Le Sony'r Ra] (*b* Birmingham, AL, 22 May 1914; *d* Birmingham, 30 May 1993). Composer, bandleader, and keyboard player. He was gifted with a remarkable ear for music and evidently absorbed everything from his older sister's piano studies; he secretly taught himself to read music, so that when his great-aunt gave him a piano at the age of 10 or 11 he astonished his friends and family by immediately playing it with skill. While at Industrial High School he studied with the renowned African-American music educator Fess Whatley and he began working in bands. Around 1932 (accounts are conflicting) he toured to Chicago with a collegiate swing band; in December 1934, while touring north again in a band nominally led by Whatley, he joined the Chicago musicians' union, as Sonny Blount. He studied liberal arts (including music) at Alabama State Agricultural and Mechanical Institute in 1935–6, then resumed his playing career. In the South and Midwest over the next decade he worked with lesser-known groups and as the leader of a band that performed only occasionally. After being drafted in the autumn of 1942 he suffered bitter experiences, particularly a two-month period of imprisonment, in his effort to be recognized as a true conscientious objector; he was finally reclassified and discharged in March 1943.

Blount left Birmingham permanently in 1946. He went to Chicago, but then returned to the South temporarily as a member of Wynonie Harris's band, with which he first recorded. He played piano in Fletcher Henderson's orchestra at the Club DeLisa in Chicago from summer 1946 to May 1947, and first attracted attention as an arranger; he continued to be associated with the DeLisa for the next five years, acting as rehearsal pianist and musical copyist for Red Saunders's band and performing at the club when Saunders was elswhere. He also worked at an after-hours venue, the Congo Club, from late 1947, accompanying Gene Ammons, Billie Holiday, and other notable soloists as a member of a rhythm section that came to be led by Gene Wright. He was a member of Wright's ten-piece big band Dukes of Swing at the Pershing Hotel from 1947 until late December 1948, when Wright disbanded and joined Count Basie; in October of the latter year Blount accompanied Coleman Hawkins. He played at striptease clubs and sporadically led a big band whose members by 1950 included Harold Ousley, John Jenkins, Von Freeman, Wilber Ware, and Vernel Fournier, and a small group with Ousley, Ware, and Fournier.

In the late 1940s Blount became immersed in Egyptian studies, and in 1951 he joined a secret society in Chicago "whose members studied the occult, advocated a form of Black Nationalism, and frequently preached about outer space." He formed a trio with Pat Patrick in 1950, and "in 1952, he proclaimed his vocation: that he was not human, but rather of an angel race; that he was to serve as the Cosmic Communicator, bringing the Creator's message to benighted Planet Earth. Accordingly, he changed his name to Le Sony'r Ra – Ra after the Egyptian sun god, Le from his last name, Sony for reasons both heliocentric and mundane, and an extra r to bring the total up to a lucky 9 letters. This is the name that appears on his passport. ... Sun Ra is technically his stage name. Upon changing his name, he began calling his band an Arkestra (a respelling that just happens to include 'Ra' both forwards and backwards)" (Campbell, in Geerken and Hefele, 1994). Hand in hand with his otherworldliness came a desire to keep his names fluid; variant spellings of Blount and Le Sony'r Ra abound, and the word Arkestra appears in dozens of combinations: Myth-Science Arkestra, Solar Arkestra, Intergalactic Arkestra, and so forth.

From the mid-1950s the Arkestra became significant in Chicago's emerging avant-garde jazz movement and began to issue recordings, although for some years the substantial avant-garde elements were more programmatic than musical. John Gilmore, Sun Ra's most important and permanent sideman (except for his few months with Art Blakey in 1965) and Julian Priester joined in 1954, and Charles Davis became a member in 1956, the year in which Sun Ra established Saturn, his longstanding record company and label; issue numbers on Saturn share the same quality of changeability that characterized the leader's approach to names. Ronnie Boykins and Marshall Allen came into the Arkestra at Priester's departure in late 1957 or early 1958, and Hobart Dotson and James Spaulding joined in the latter year. At the end of the decade the group began to appear in futuristic costume, and its musical orientation had moved from rhythm-and-blues and a delightfully twisted take on cool jazz to a somewhat stultifying preoccupation with deliberate melody and static harmony. Perhaps Sun Ra's most satisfyingly adventuresome piece from the 1950s is *A Call for All Demons* (1956), which presents a wonderfully humorous combination of atonal improvising and Latin dance rhythms: it might best be described as a free-jazz mambo.

Sun Ra moved to New York in 1961. In 1963, when Clifford Jarvis, the alto saxophonist Danny Davis, the bass clarinetist Robert Cummings, and the wind player and percussionist James Jacson joined him, he recorded a startlingly original and eccentric album, *Cosmic Tones for Mental Therapy*, i; through its mix of rumbling drums, blaring horns, and weird keyboard effects, this serves as a signpost marking his emergence as a unique avant-garde musician. A two-volume set, *The Heliocentric Worlds of Sun Ra*, and an intervening album, *The Magic City* (all 1965), mark the full blossoming of his free-jazz period, in which the Arkestra explores timbre with scarce regard for beat or meter. Works such as *Cosmic Chaos* show a radical, complex, often frenetic idiom and an obsession with percussion instruments; during this period the leader contributed as a soloist on piano, electric celeste, clavioline, "astral space organ" (the Hammond B-3), bass marimba, harp, timpani, bongos, "cosmic" side drums, and other keyboard and percussion instruments.

Although over the years he often had little work, Sun Ra kept his band together; inspired by their leader's intense devotion to his music, the players rehearsed constantly. From 1966 to 1972 the group's most regular job was at Slug's Saloon on Monday nights. The singer June Tyson joined in 1968, and later that year Sun Ra moved the band's home to Philadelphia. Its performance style changed yet again from 1970, when Sun Ra reintroduced conventional jazz and blues styles into his repertory, while adding extra-musical elements – dancers, acrobats, jugglers, fire eaters, and a light show – as well as more singers and instrumentalists. Over the previous two decades he had been a pioneer in the use of unconventional keyboards: he was a capable pianist, but made notable recordings on electric piano (from 1956), clavioline (from 1963), and Moog synthesizer (from 1969); he also performed on other conventional and unusual keyboard instruments, including celesta, organ, and rocksichord – an electric keyboard that combines the sharp attack of a harpsichord with the glossy, sustained sound of an electric piano. Complementing this experimental spirit in keyboard use was his unusual expertise in matters of recording technology; Campbell notes that in the 1970s he carried this fascination too far, adopting the rock music practice of amplifying every instrument, regardless of need, and ignoring the qualities of space and silence that heretofore were crucial elements in his revolutionary personal style.

The Arkestra gave concerts at the Fondation Maeght in Saint Paul de Vence, France, in August 1970, then toured Europe (October–November 1970; October–December 1971, including a trip to Cairo). In 1971 the bass clarinetist Elmo Omoe replaced Cummings; Patrick left in 1973, and Boykins after a performance in Paris later that same year. For its fourth European tour, in 1976, the Arkestra comprised

Sun Ra with members of his Arkestra, Central Park, New York, 1987

Tyson, three dancers, and 19 instrumentalists, among them Ahmed Abdullah, Craig Harris, Gilmore, Allen, Danny Davis, Omoe, Jacson, Jarvis, and, again, Patrick. It toured West Africa in February 1977 and later that year gave its first Halloween concert in New York; later it appeared annually in the Halloween parade in Greenwich Village. It played on the television show "Saturday Night Live" in May 1978. During this period Sun Ra attempted to adapt his band's style to the markets for soul and disco, but its looseness was incompatible with the demands of these genres. He rediscovered his youthful interests, bringing Henderson's music into the group, as well as pieces associated with Duke Ellington, and he began to appear as an unaccompanied soloist, revealing that he had retained considerable skill as a stride, swing, and blues pianist. A documentary film, *Sun Ra: a Joyful Noise*, was made in 1980, directed by Robert Mugge; it wonderfully captures Sun Ra's stature as a poet, philosopher, and radical African-American politician as well as the musical virtuosity of the band and its leader. Still employing freely improvised solos in busy combinations with microtonal melodies and electronic effects, he was now often juxtaposing standard jazz tunes or personalized dance ostinatos with aleatory solo work on such instruments as piccolo, violin, and synthesizer in addition to saxophones and trumpets. (For observations on the complexity of collective improvisation in so large a group *see* BANDS, §1.)

The Arkestra toured Europe annually in the 1980s and into the early 1990s, until the leader's health failed; it returned to Egypt in 1983 and gave its first concerts in Japan in 1988. Gilmore, Allen, Omoe, and Jacson remained central to its performances, and Patrick was a member yet again from 1985 to 1988, during which time Sun Ra added two new thematic areas to his repertory: songs associated with Billie Holiday and tributes to Walt Disney characters. He also may be heard as a hauntingly weird singer on the jazz standard *Beautiful Love* (1986). In 1989 he made further television appearances, on "VH1-Jazz" with Don Cherry and also on the show "Night Music."

In the mid-1960s Sun Ra's activities merged somewhat uncomfortably with the free-jazz movement, and he may be regarded as one of its leading exponents. From any broader perspective he is unclassifiable: a wildly creative, one-off musician and poet. While he is underrated by those who perceive mainly the clowning elements of his art, he is held in awe by many listeners who have come to understand that an outlandish, pseudo-galactic world was from his perspective less absurd than racist America, and that the "signifying" elements of his theatricality and repertory were underpinned by a deeply serious philosophy and by music-making of the highest order.

See also ALLEN, MARSHALL, BLUES, §12, and JAZZ (i), §VI, 3.

SELECTED RECORDINGS

Angels and Demons at Play (1956, 1960, Saturn 9956-2-O/P), incl. A Call for All Demons (1956); *Jazz by Sun Ra* (1956, Tran. 10); *Sound of Joy* (1957, Del. 414), incl. Reflections in Blue; *Sun Ra Visits Planet Earth* (1958, Saturn 9956-11-A/B); *Jazz in Silhouette* (1958, Saturn K70P3590-91); *The Lady with the Golden Stockings* (*The Nubians of Plutonia*) (1958–9, Saturn 9956-11-E/F); *We Travel the Spaceways* (1959–60, Saturn 5445); *Rocket Number Nine Take off for the Planet Venus* (*Interstellar Low Ways*) (1959–60, Saturn 9956-2-M/N); *The Futuristic Sounds of Sun Ra* (1961, Savoy 12169)

When the Sun Comes Out (1962–3, Saturn 2066); *Cosmic Tones for Mental Therapy* (1963, Saturn 408); *The Heliocentric Worlds of Sun Ra*, i (1965, ESP 1014); *The Magic City* (1965, Saturn 711); *The Heliocentric Worlds of Sun Ra*, ii (1965, ESP 1017), incl. Cosmic Chaos; *Nothing Is* (1966, ESP 1045); *The Solar Myth Approach*, i–ii (*c*1967–70, BYG 529340–41); *Live at Montreux* (1976, Saturn 87976); *Visions* (1978, Ste. 1126); *The Other Side of the Sun* (1978–9, Sweet Earth 1003); *Reflections in Blue* (1986, BS 0101); *Hours After* (1986, BS 120111-2), incl. Beautiful Love

SELECTED FILMS AND VIDEOS

The Cry of Jazz (1959); Space is the Place (1974); A Joyful Noise (1980); Mystery, Mr. Ra (1984)

BIBLIOGRAPHY

GrayF
B. McRae: "Sun Ra," *JJ*, xix/8 (1966), 15
L. Jones: *Black Music* (New York, 1967/*R*1980)

T. Fiofari: "The Music of Sun Ra: Space Age Music," *Negro Digest*, xix/3 (1970), 23
R. Townley: "Sun Ra," *DB*, xl/21 (1973), 18
E. Jost: *Free Jazz* (Graz, Austria, 1974/*R*1994)
B. McRae: "Avant Courier: Another Look at Sun Ra," *JJ*, xxviii/12 (1975), 14
H. Pekar: "Sun Ra," *Coda*, no.139 (1975), 2
J.-E. Berendt: "Sun Ra und sein schwarzer Kosmos," *Ein Fenster aus Jazz: Essays, Portraits, Reflexionen* (Frankfurt am Main, Germany, 1977), 109
V. Wilmer: *As Serious as your Life: the Story of the New Jazz* (London, 1977, rev. [3]/1987)
B. Primack: "Captain Angelic: Sun Ra," *DB*, xlv/9 (1978), 14
J. Buzelin and A. R. Hardy: "Disco Sun Ra," *Jh*, no.361 (1979), 15; no.362 (1979), 23
H. Geerken: *Chronological Discography of the Acoustic Works of Sun Ra, 1956–1981* (Athens, 1982)
L. Lyons: *The Great Jazz Pianists, Speaking of their Lives and Music* (New York, 1983), 83
T. Stahl: *Sun Ra Materialen/Sun Ra Materials* (Freudenberg, nr Siegen, Germany, 1983, rev. and enlarged 2/1987) [Ger. and Eng. texts; incl. discography]
J. Litweiler: *The Freedom Principle: Jazz after 1958* (New York, 1984/*R*1990), 129
F. Davis: *Outcats: Jazz Composers, Instrumentalists, and Singers* (New York, and Oxford, England, 1990), 24
A. S. Chase: *Sun Ra: Musical Change and Musical Meaning in the Life and Work of a Jazz Composer* (thesis, Tufts U., 1992)
Obituaries: *New York Times* (31 May 1993); K. Karim: "Sun Set in Alabama," *Jazz on CD*, i/4 (1993), 72
R. L. Campbell: *The Earthly Recordings of Sun Ra* (Redwood, NY, 1994)
H. Geerken and B. Hefele: *Omniverse Sun Ra* (Wartaweil, Germany, 1994) [incl. discography, comprehensive bibliography]
J. Gill: *Queer Noises: Male and Female Homosexuality in Twentieth-century Music* (London, 1995)
B. Kernfeld: *What to Listen for in Jazz* (New Haven, CT, and London, 1995)
J. F. Szwed: *Space is the Place: the Lives and Times of Sun Ra* (New York, 1997)

BK

Sunrise. Record label. A subsidiary of RCA, it was operational for about a year from August 1933, and its catalogue included a fair proportion of jazz recordings. All items issued on Sunrise were also put out on Bluebird.

BIBLIOGRAPHY

B. Rust: "A Glimpse of the Past: Sunrise and Timely Tunes," *Sv*, no.16 (1968), 17
A. Sutton: *Directory of American Disc Record Brands and Manufacturers, 1891–1943* (Westport, CT, and London, 1994), 146

HOWARD RYE

Sunset (i). Record label. It existed in California from 1922 to 1926. On it were issued some of the earliest recordings made on the West Coast of African-American jazz, notably important items by the California Poppies (1923) and the Stompin' Six (1925), both groups associated with the pianist Sonny Clay.

BIBLIOGRAPHY

B. Rust: *The American Record Label Book* (New Rochelle, NY, 1978), 286
H. Rye: "West Coast Recordings 1922–1935," *Collectors Items*, no.40 (1987), 14
A. Sutton: *Directory of American Disc Record Brands and Manufacturers, 1891–1943* (Westport, CT, and London, 1994), 146

HOWARD RYE

Sunset (ii). Record label. It was operated in Hollywood from 1944 to 1946 by Eddie Laguna, who recorded several prominent jazz musicians, including Howard McGhee, Willie Smith, and Charlie Ventura. (A. Morgan: "Sunset Records: a Listing," *Discographical Forum*, no. 2 (1960), 2)

HOWARD RYE

Sunset Cafe. Nightclub in Chicago; *see* NIGHTCLUBS AND OTHER VENUES.

Sunset Crystal Palace. Nightclub in Kansas City; *see* NIGHTCLUBS AND OTHER VENUES.

Sunshine. Record label. It was established by John C. Spikes and Benjamin "Reb" Spikes in Los Angeles in 1921 or 1922. Its catalogue contained only three items, but these are notable in that they were the first recordings made by an African-American jazz band from New Orleans, Ory's Sunshine Orchestra. These were recorded by NORDSKOG, and were also issued on that company's label.

BIBLIOGRAPHY

F. Owen: "A Glimpse of the Past, 12: Sunshine & Nordskog," *Sv*, no.21 (1969), 94
A. Sutton: *Directory of American Disc Record Brands and Manufacturers, 1891–1943* (Westport, CT, and London, 1994), 146

HOWARD RYE

Sunshine, Monty (*b* London, 8 April 1928). English clarinetist. His father was a violinist. Self-taught, he first played flute and later, while serving in the RAF, took up clarinet. He was a founding member of the Crane River Jazz Band, with which he performed and recorded from 1949 to 1952. From late 1952 to early 1953 he worked with Chris Barber, then in spring 1953 joined Ken Colyer's Jazzmen. The following year the personnel of Colyer's group formed a new band, which was led by Barber (for illustration *see* BARBER, CHRIS). After leaving Barber in December 1960 Sunshine began to work as a leader; among his sidemen were Johnny Parker, Rod Mason, and the trombonist Geoff Sowden. Later he recorded again with the Crane River Jazz Band, which held reunions from 1972 to 1978, and from 1975 with Barber, including a series of fortieth anniversary concerts in 1994. At some point he played with Graeme Bell's band in Australia. Sunshine worked in a touring show with Lonnie Donegan in the 1980s while continuing to perform and record with his own band; Donegan in turn recorded with Sunshine's band around 1987.

SELECTED RECORDINGS

As leader: *Gotta Travel On* (1991, Tim. 570)
As sideman with C. Barber: Wild Cat Blues (1953, Sto. KB206); *Forty Years Jubilee (1954–1956)* (1954–6, Tim. 586); Hushabye (1956, Nixa 2011)

SELECTED FILMS AND VIDEOS

Momma Don't Allow (1955); Chris Barber's Jazz Band (1956); Holiday (1957)

BIBLIOGRAPHY

CarrJ; *ChiltonB*
R. Harris: *Jazz* (London, 1952, 5/1957)
D. Boulton: *Jazz in Britain* (London, 1958)
M. Sunshine and T. Brown: "My Seven Years with Barber," *MM* (14 Jan 1961), 3
G. Bielderman: *Monty Sunshine Discography* (Zwolle, Netherlands, 1994, rev. 2/1995)

NEVIL SKRIMSHIRE/BK

Suomen Jazzliitto [Finnish Jazz Federation, FJF]. Organization formed in 1966 by Pekka Gronow and others to promote jazz in Finland. It organizes and sponsors jazz performances, lectures, tours, and workshops, as well as the Finnish National Jazz Days, held each November in various cities. The federation issued the periodical *Rytmi* from 1967 to 1981 and also published several books on jazz in Finland, including Åke Granholm's *Finnish Jazz* (Helsinki, 1974, rev. and enlarged by M. Huuskonen, J. Muikku, and T. Vähäsilta 5/1997) and Hans Westerberg's *Suomalaiset jazzlevytykset, 1932–1976/a Finnish Jazz Discography, 1932–1976* (Helsinki, 1977). Its Yrjö (Georgie) award has been given annually from

1967 to the Finnish jazz musician of the year. Suomen Jazzliitto has 41 affiliates in Finland and belongs in turn to the International Jazz Federation and Nordjazz. In 2000 the federation's president was Klaus Järvinen and its executive director was Timo Vähäsilta.

PEKKA GRONOW

Suonsaari, Klaus (Henrikki) (*b* Iitti, Finland, 7 Nov 1959). Finnish drummer. His mother and sister both played piano, and his great-uncle Harry Bergström is a well-known Finnish film music composer. He learned piano from the age of six, changed to drums when he was 14, and attended the Oulunkyla pop-jazz conservatory and the Lahti conservatory (1973–9). During the same period he was a member of the Heinola Big Band and led a quintet, Blue Train (both 1974–9); he also studied at the Eastman School of Music (1976–7) and the Berklee College of Music (1979–84). While in Boston he performed in Herb Pomeroy's big band (1981–4). He worked from 1980 with Scott Robinson and Niels Lan Doky and from 1985 with the singer Laverne Butler. In 1988 he performed with Muhal Richard Abrams and with UMO, and the following year he toured with Diana Krall and accompanied the cabaret singer Bobby Short, for whom he also provided arrangements. He played with the Vanguard Jazz Orchestra in 1991. Suonsaari again led his own small group from 1984 and first recorded as a sole leader in 1987; for a tour of the USA in 1994 his bandmembers were Lew Tabackin, Renee Rosnes, and Niels-Henning Ørsted Pedersen.

SELECTED RECORDINGS

As leader: *Reflecting Times* (1987, Sto. 4125); *True Colours* (1992, L+R 45080); with N.-H. Ørsted Pedersen and N. L. Doky: *Klaus Suonsaari, Niels-Henning Ørsted Pedersen, Niels Lan Doky Play Harrell* (*c*1992, Jazz Alliance 10010); *Inside Out* (1994, SN 121274-2)

As sideman with S. Robinson: *Multiple Instruments* (1984, Multijazz 101); *Thinking Big* (1996, Arbors 19179)

BIBLIOGRAPHY

Feather–GitlerBEJ

P. B. King: "Musicians Bring Hot Jazz to the US from Finland," *Star Tribune* [Minneapolis] (20 Jan 1994)

GK

Superbone. A hybrid trombone with both slide and valves, designed and used by Maynard Ferguson; *see* TROMBONE.

Super Disc. Record label. It existed from 1945 to 1947; the proprietors were Irvin Feld, Israel Feld, and Viola Marsham. The catalogue was devoted to race records and included important material by Don Byas, Sid Catlett, and others. ("Super Disc," *Blues Research*, no.16 (n. d. [?1966]), 12)

HOWARD RYE

Superior. Record label. It was established by the Starr Piano Company after that organization discontinued Gennett; the discs were apparently sold in chain stores. Between December 1930 and June 1932 339 issues were made, including many race and jazz items.

BIBLIOGRAPHY

G. W. Kay: "The Superior Catalog," *Record Research*, no.37 (1961), 1; no.38 (1961), 10; no.39 (1961), 19; no.41 (1962), 11; no.42 (1962), 11; no.43 (1962), 19; no.47 (1962), 19; no.48 (1963), 10

R. M. W. Dixon and J. Godrich: *Recording the Blues* (London, 1970)

B. Rust: *The American Record Label Book* (New Rochelle, NY, 1978), 287

A. Sutton: *Directory of American Disc Record Brands and Manufacturers, 1891–1943* (Westport, CT, and London, 1994), 147

HOWARD RYE

Supersax. Ensemble of studio musicians. Based in the Los Angeles area, it made its début late in 1972 at Donte's in North Hollywood, performing arrangements of the improvised solos of Charlie Parker. At first it was led by Buddy Clark and Med Flory, and consisted of Flory and Bill Perkins (alto saxophones), Warne Marsh and Jay Migliori (tenor saxophones), Jack Nimitz (baritone saxophone), Conte Candoli (trumpet), Ronnell Bright (piano), Clark (double bass), and Jake Hanna (drums). Clark left the group in 1975 and Flory became its leader and chief arranger. Over the years other Los Angeles-based musicians have played in this part-time group, including the trumpeter Blue Mitchell, the trombonists Carl Fontana and Frank Rosolino, the alto saxophonists Joe Lopes and Lanny Morgan (from 1978), the tenor saxophonists Don Menza and Ray Reed (from 1982), the pianists Walter Bishop, Jr., and Lou Levy (from 1974), the double bass players Fred Atwood, Monty Budwig, Dave Carpenter and Trey Henry, and the drummers John Dentz, Larry Marable, Ralph Penland, and Frank Capp. In the mid-1980s the group recorded three albums with L. A. Voices, a vocal quintet in which Flory sang, and in the 1990s Flory added a full brass section for some performances. Occasionally Supersax has appeared in American cities outside the Los Angeles area, and in 1975 and 1990 the group performed in Japan. In 1981 it made a video recording released only in Japan, *Let the Bird Fly*; another video, of its first Japanese tour, has also been made.

A typical arrangement by Supersax begins with the theme played in a block-chord harmonization, with the melody doubled at the lower octave by the baritone saxophonist. Parker's solo, played in the same manner, follows. After solos by one or more players, the piece ends with the block-chord harmonization of the theme. In the late 1970s Flory began adding arrangements of solos by Bud Powell and John Coltrane, as well as of his own solos in the style of Charlie Parker. However, the foundation of the group's repertory remains such classic Parker solos as *Koko*, *Just Friends*, *Parker's Mood*, and *Star Eyes*, which were on the Grammy-award winning inaugural album *Supersax Plays Bird*. Materials relating to Supersax are at the Library of Congress in Washington, DC (*see* LIBRARIES AND ARCHIVES, §2).

SELECTED RECORDINGS

Supersax Plays Bird (1972, Cap. ST11177), incl. Koko, Just Friends, Parker's Mood, Star Eyes; *Supersax Plays Bird*, ii: *Salt Peanuts* (*c*1973, Cap. ST11271); *Supersax Plays Bird with Strings* (1974, Cap. ST11371); *Live in 75: the Japanese Tour*, i–ii (1975, Hindsight 618, 622); *Chasin' the Bird* (1977, MPS 15491); *Dynamite!* (1978, MPS 15492); *Supersax & L. A. Voices*, iii: *Straighten up & Fly Right* (1986, Col. FC40547); *Stone Bird* (1988, Col. FC44436); *Bird Lives!* (1992, CEMA 57081)

BIBLIOGRAPHY

H. Siders: "Caught in the Act: Supersax Plays Bird," *DB*, xl/3 (1973), 30

R. Townley and T. Hogan: "Supersax: the Genius of Bird x Five," *DB*, xli/19 (1974), 13

M. Morgan: "Caught in the Act: Supersax," *DB*, xlv/5 (1978), 39

A. Scott: "Med Flory," *JT* (1987), Dec, 21

M. Daniels: "Med Flory & Supersax & L. A. Voices," *L. A. Jazz Scene*, no.62 (1992), 23

THOMAS OWENS

Supertone (i). Record label. It was used in 1924 by the mail-order company Sears-Roebuck to release material drawn from Olympic and Paramount. The company later revived the name for the issue in 1928–30 of repertory first put out on Gennett; this included a considerable number of race records. In 1930–31 recordings made by Brunswick of such musicians as Benny Goodman and Red Nichols were issued on Supertone under pseudonyms; this S2000 series also involved a sequence of race recordings. (A. Sutton: *Directory of American Disc Record Brands and Manufacturers, 1891–1943* (Westport, CT, and London, 1994), 147)

HOWARD RYE

Supertone (ii). Record label. It was established in the 1920s by Straus and Schram, a company that owned a store in Chicago. The catalogue was drawn from Grey Gull, Columbia, Paramount, and Pathé. (A. Sutton: *Directory of American Disc Record Brands and Manufacturers, 1891–1943* (Westport, CT, and London, 1994), 148)

HOWARD RYE

Supreme. Record label. It was established on the West Coast late in 1947 by Al Patrick and was devoted to race records. Jimmy Witherspoon was the most important musician in the catalogue, which also included Buddy Tate and Jay McShann. The label was used to issue Fletcher Henderson's last commercial recording. Trading ceased in December 1950, after a ruinous lawsuit against Decca over an alleged cover version of a rhythm-and-blues recording, and the masters were acquired by Swing Time. Supreme should not be confused with the earlier label of the same name, a subsidiary of Grey Gull from 1926 to 1929. (G. A. Moonoogian: "Supreme," *Whiskey, Women, and . . .* , no.16 (1987), 24)

HOWARD RYE

John Surman at the Queen Elizabeth Hall, London, 1997

Surman, John (Douglas) (*b* Tavistock, England, 30 Aug 1944). English baritone and soprano saxophonist. He learned clarinet from the age of 14 and later took up baritone saxophone. While still at school he played in jazz workshops organized by Mike Westbrook (1958–62), then studied at the London College of Music (1962–5) and London University Institute of Education (1965–6); in 1966 he worked with Pete Lemer. He continued to play with Westbrook until 1968 and to record with him until 1975, and while performing in his group at the 1968 Montreux International Jazz Festival won an award as best soloist: his work with Westbrook may be heard to best effect in his baritone solo on *Outgoing Song* on *Citadel/Room 315* (1975). During the late 1960s he also played with Humphrey Lyttelton's small group and big band, Ronnie Scott's octet (1968), Chris McGregor (recording in 1968), Maynard Ferguson (early 1969), Graham Collier, Mike Gibbs, Dave Holland, and John McLaughlin. In 1970 he toured Europe with Francy Boland's big band; he recorded in that same year with the European Jazz All Stars, in groups led by Harry Beckett, Eddy Louiss, and Alan Skidmore, and as co-leader with Michel Portal.

Surman formed the first of his own groups in 1968 and recorded as a leader the same year. From 1969 to 1972 he toured internationally with Barre Phillips and Stu Martin as The Trio, which also recorded in 1971 incorporated in a big band and again that same year in Prague within the big band of Slide Hampton and the arranger Vaclav Zahradnik; the group re-formed in 1977 as Mumps with the addition of Albert Mangelsdorff. From October 1973 to 1975 Surman played with Mike Osborne and Skidmore in the saxophone trio SOS. Thereafter he collaborated with the Carolyn Carlson dance company at the Paris Opéra (1974–9), recorded in duos with Karin Krog (1977), Stan Tracey (1978), and Jack DeJohnette (1981) and in groups led by Friedrich Gulda (1976), Phillips (1976–9), Mick Goodrick (1978), and Miroslav Vitous (1979–82), worked with Azimuth, and performed and recorded in Barry Altschul's quartet (1983). He worked regularly with Vitous and for many years with Krog, touring Australia with each respectively in 1983 and 1985, and gave numerous concerts with DeJohnette through the 1980s.

Surman has been active from 1981 with an ensemble of 11 brass and rhythm players known as the Brass Project. He worked with Collier's big band Hoarded Dreams and Gil Evans's British Orchestra (both 1983), toured in a group with Kenny Wheeler, Phillips, and John Taylor (1985), in a duo with Mangelsdorff (1986), and again with Evans (1986 and 1987), and recorded with Krog (1982, 1986), as a member of Paul Bley's quartet (1986, 1991), and with John Abercrombie (1992). In 1993 and 1994 he recorded two contrasting quartet albums, the first with three British musicians – Taylor (on piano), Chris Laurence (bass), and John Marshall (drums), who had collaborated twenty years previously on *Morning Glory* – and the second with the Nordic Quartet, consisting of the pianist Vigleik Storaas, the guitarist Terje Rypdal, and the singer Krog.

Surman's prodigious talent was first noticed during his time as a soloist with Westbrook. He is remarkable for having transferred John Coltrane's characteristic phrasing to the baritone saxophone, a feat requiring considerable technical powers. He has also utilized for the first time the extreme upper register of the baritone by his mastery of its harmonics, thus expanding its versatility as a solo instrument. As a member of The Trio, his incredible range and wide tonal coloration brought him international acclaim, establishing him as one of the world's finest baritone saxophonists since Harry Carney, whom Surman acknowledges as a major influence. With SOS he employed synthesizers and electronic techniques, pre-programming synthesizer parts over which the three saxophones improvised in performance; he further developed this aspect of his work throughout the 1970s. Surman's personal style is one of stunning dexterity, technical mastery, and emotional depth, his playing mixing a harsh, forceful delivery with softer lyricism. The fluency and range he achieved early in his career on both baritone and soprano saxophones may be heard on the innovative jazz-rock album *Extrapolation* (1969), recorded with McLaughlin. Soon after making this recording he turned to more personal methods of expression, and his solos on *Westering Home* (1972), using bass clarinet and a variety of other instruments in addition to the two saxophones, explore folk-related themes, at the same time making effective use of multiple recording techniques. Between 1979 and 1994 he recorded five further solo albums, each one consisting of improvised solo lines over his own synthesizer accompaniments. His intensely personal music is often evocative and atmospheric, and draws heavily on his knowledge and experience of English and European folk, brass-band, classical, and church music. In recent years his interests have widened to include non-European folk music, as may be heard in his collaboration with the Tunisian *'ūd* player Anouar Brahem on *Thimar* (1997). He has won jazz polls for both his performing and his recording work, and as a composer has received commissions for ballet scores and church music: *Proverbs and Songs* – eight Biblical texts set to music, with Surman accompanied by Taylor (on organ) and the Salisbury Festival Choir – was commissioned by the Salisbury Festival and premièred in Salisbury Cathedral in July 1996. His work with the Brass Project in association with John Warren demonstrates his often neglected strengths as a composer and arranger.

SELECTED RECORDINGS

(recorded for ECM unless otherwise indicated)

As unaccompanied soloist: *Westering Home* (1972, Isl. 10); *Upon Reflection* (1979, 1148); *Withholding Pattern* (1984, 1295); *Private City* (1987, 1366); *Road to St. Ives* (1990, 1418); *A Biography of the Rev. Absalom Dawes* (1994, 1528)

Duos: with S. Tracey: *Sonatinas* (1978, Steam 106); with J. DeJohnette: *The Amazing Adventures of Simon Simon* (1981, 1193)

As leader: *John Surman* (1968, Deram 1030); *How Many Clouds Can You See?* (1969, Deram 1045); *Morning Glory* (1973, Isl. 9237); of SOS (with M. Osborne and A. Skidmore): *SOS* (1975, Ogun 400); *Such Winters of Memory* (1982, 1254); *Adventure Playground* (1991, 1463); *The Brass Project* (1992, 1478); *Stranger than Fiction* (1993, 1534); *Nordic Quartet* (1994, 1553); *Proverbs and Songs* (1996, 1639); with A. Brahem and D. Holland: *Thimar* (1997, 1641)

As sideman: J. McLaughlin: *Extrapolation* (1969, Marmalade 608007); M. Westbrook: *Marching Song* (1969, Deram 1047–8); The Trio: *The Trio* (1970, Dawn 3006); J. McLaughlin: *Where Fortune Smiles* (1970, Dawn 3018); The Trio: *Conflagration* (1971, Dawn 3022); M. Westbrook: *Citadel/Room 315* (1975, RCA SF8433), incl. Outgoing Song; B. Phillips: *Mountainscapes* (1976, 1076); K. Krog: *Cloud Line Blue* (1977, Pol. 2382093); M. Vitous: *Journey's End* (1982, 1242); G. Evans: *The British Orchestra* (1983, Mole 8); P. Bley: *The Paul Bley Quartet* (1987, 1365), incl. After Dark; *In the Evenings Out There* (1991, 1488); J. Abercrombie: *November* (1992, 1502); M. Alperin: *First Impression* (1997, ECM 1664)

BIBLIOGRAPHY

CarrJ; *ChiltonW*; *GrayF*; *WickesIBJ*, i

C. Bird: "John Surman," *MM* (9 Dec 1967), 4

V. Schonfield: "World Class Baritone from West Country," *MM* (12 Aug 1967), 6

L. Henshaw: "Now Surman Joins the British Jazz Brain Drain," *MM* (14 June 1969), 10

M. Cullaz: "John Surman, Barre Phillips, Stu Martin: Interview," *Jh*, no.259 (1970), 16

R. Williams: "Surman: the Happy Wanderer," *MM* (14 March 1970), 8

J. Byrczek and R. Kowal: "The Trio: Surman Phillips Martin," *JF* [intl edn], nos.13–14 (1971), 62

R. Williams: "Surman for Today," *MM* (28 April 1973), 25

M. Paton: "Surman on the Mount," *MM* (22 April 1978), 52

L. Tomkins: "A Meeting with Mumps: John Surman and Albert Mangelsdorff," *CI*, xvi (1978), no.6, p.23; no.7, p.14

G. Rouy: "Ici Londres: John Surman," *Jm*, no.273 (1979), 3

R. Cotterrell: "John Surman: Perpetual Motion," *JF* [intl edn], no.76 (1982), 25

P. Danson: "John Surman," *Coda*, no.189 (1983), 12

L. Gourse: "John Surman," *DB*, lii/12 (1985), 25

G. Lock: "Save the Wail," *The Wire*, no.14 (1985), 35

P. Renaud: *La discographie du jazz anglais* (Chaumont, France, 1985)

E. Jost: *Europas Jazz, 1960–1980* (Frankfurt am Main, Germany, 1987), 335

J. Fordham: "A Tradition with a Vision," *The Guardian* (20 Jan 1989)

B. McRae: "Upon Reflection: John Surman," *JJI*, xlii/7 (1989), 14

B. Witherden: "John Surman: No Profit in his own Country," *Wire*, no.76 (1990), 20

D. O'Driscoll: "A Different Kind of Music," *JF* [intl edn], no.132 (1992), 30

T. Hodgett: "Saxophonists Andy Sheppard and John Surman: a British Point of View," *Coda*, no.263 (1995), 20

G. Endress: "John Surman," *JP*, xlvii/12 (1998), 3

<http://www.rojac.co.at/rojac/surman> (1999) [discography]

SIMON ADAMS

Suter, Robert (*b* St. Gallen, Switzerland, 30 Jan 1919). Swiss pianist. In 1937 he left St. Gallen to study piano, theory, and composition at the conservatory in Basel; at the same time he discovered jazz, which he began to play in local clubs. He worked with the clarinetist Peter Wyss in a traditional jazz band, the Barrelhouse Boys, and in 1948, together with Wyss, formed the Darktown Strutters; the group's recordings include *Morning Mood* (1950, Chant du Monde 29138) and the album *Queer Dance* (1956, HMV 113). While maintaining a distinguished career as a composer of contemporary classical music and teaching at the academy of music in Basel, Suter played with such artists as Edmond Hall, Jimmy Archey, Wild Bill Davison, and Tommy Benford.

Video oral history material in *CHW* (JdA).

OTTO FLÜCKIGER

Sutton, Mynie [Myron Pierman] (*b* Niagara Falls, Canada, 9 Oct 1903; *d* Niagara Falls, 17 June 1982). Canadian alto saxophonist and bandleader. He traveled with dance bands based in Buffalo and Cleveland from 1924 to 1931, then introduced the Canadian Ambassadors in Aylmer, Quebec, late in 1931. One of Canada's few black jazz bands during the 1930s, the Ambassadors were based in Montreal from 1933 and held extended engagements at Connie's Inn, the Hollywood Club, and the Café Montmartre; the group also traveled in Quebec and Ontario. At one time or another Sutton's musicians included the pianists Buster Harding and Lou Hooper. With the demise of the Ambassadors, Sutton returned in 1941 to Niagara Falls, where he again led a dance band and then played in smaller groups for many years. He did not record commercially; an amateur recording of an arrangement of a tune based on *Honeysuckle Rose* (recorded *c*1947) was issued on the anthology *Jazz and Hot Dance in Canada, 1916–1949* (Harl. 2023, 1986). His collection of photographs and other materials is now in the archives of Concordia University, Montreal; *see* Libraries and archives, §2.

Oral history material in *CaQMG*.

BIBLIOGRAPHY

J. Gilmore: *Swinging in Paradise: the Story of Jazz in Montreal* (Montreal, 1988)

——: *Who's Who of Jazz in Montreal: Ragtime to 1970* (Montreal, 1989)

M. Miller: *Such Melodious Racket: the Lost History of Jazz in Canada, 1914–1949* (Toronto, 1997)

JACK LITCHFIELD/MARK MILLER

Sutton, Ralph (Earl) (*b* Hamburg, nr St. Louis, 4 Nov 1922). Pianist. He began classical piano lessons at the age of nine and two years later was working in a country dance band led by his father, a violinist; he became the group's leader when he was in high school. He learned to play jazz from radio broadcasts and recordings and developed a special devotion to Fats Waller. His musical studies continued at Northeast Missouri State University, but he left in his second year to join Jack Teagarden's band in New York in December 1942. Soon afterwards he was drafted into the army, and served from February 1943 to April 1945. As a sideman with the guitarist Joe Schirmer he played in and around St. Louis, though he also performed at the Village Vanguard, New York, for a month in 1945. In 1947 he returned to New York with Teagarden, and appeared for about six weeks at the Famous Door until Teagarden left to join Louis Armstrong's All Stars. That same year he took part in the weekly radio show "This is Jazz."

In 1948 Sutton worked with Albert Nicholas and Art Trappier, first in a trio at Jimmy Ryan's, then under Max Kaminsky's leadership at the Village Vanguard, and once again in a trio, in St. Louis. From July of that year he was the intermission pianist at Eddie Condon's club in New York; at the same time he played in distinguished all-star bands at Condon's Tuesday night jam sessions, participated in Condon's radio and television shows, and occasionally deputized for Gene Schroeder in a band led by Wild Bill Davison at Condon's club. He also gave concerts in England and Switzerland as an unaccompanied soloist (June 1952), led a quartet with Edmond Hall, Walter Page, and drummer Charlie Lodice at the Club Hangover in San Francisco (summer 1954), and performed at the London House in Chicago (January 1956). In July 1956 he finally left Condon's to settle in San Francisco.

Sutton toured with Bob Scobey into 1957 and then played at the Club Hangover as an intermission pianist and as a temporary replacement in Earl Hines's band while Hines was in Europe. He continued in the role of intermission pianist at Easy Street and also returned to the London House (January 1958) and performed in St. Louis (June 1959). In 1960 he accompanied Jimmy Rushing and appeared on the NBC television show "Those Ragtime Years," and he returned twice to Condon's, in 1961 and 1962. From 1963 he participated in Dick Gibson's annual Colorado Jazz Parties, as a result of which he was invited to initiate a similar event in Odessa, Texas. He worked with Bob Crosby's Bob Cats in New York in the autumn of 1966, but his major performances from 1965 to 1969 were in Aspen, Colorado, at the Rendezvous, a restaurant run by Sunnie Anderson, who became his second wife; there he performed as a soloist and in ad hoc small groups involving such players as Davison, Ruby Braff, Peanuts Hucko, Lou McGarity, Edmond Hall, Clancy Hayes, Morey Feld, Jack Lesberg, Al Hall, Milt Hinton, Jake Hanna, Cliff Leeman, and Mousie Alexander. Again as a result of Gibson's Jazz Parties, where he was heard annually as a member of the Eight, Nine, and finally (in 1968) Ten Greats of Jazz, in November 1968 Sutton became a founding member of the World's Greatest Jazz Band, and played regularly with the group until September 1974.

After working with Hucko's quartet in Denver from October 1974 through March 1975, Sutton once again became a freelance. He remained a fixture at the Colorado and Odessa parties into the 1990s, and occasionally returned to the World's Greatest Jazz Band before it disbanded; in October 1975, at the end of one of several European tours with that ensemble, he remained overseas to tour as a soloist. For many years thereafter he gave concerts and participated in European festivals, both as an unaccompanied soloist and in small groups, often with Gus Johnson on drums and sometimes with Pee Wee Erwin (1980) or Hucko (1980, 1981) featured as soloist. Sutton made his first visit to Australia in 1979, and returned there in 1981 with Braff and in 1988 with Kenny Davern; from 1985 he toured annually in Japan. He played in Denver through the latter part of the 1970s, performed in a duo and small groups with Johnson in Billings, Montana, from 1979 to 1983, and was a soloist at Hanratty's in New York briefly in 1980 and 1982 and then for long periods at the Café des Copains in Toronto from 1983 to 1991, when this venue closed. From 1979 into the 1990s he also performed and recorded internationally with Jay McShann in a duo and a quartet (with Hinton and Johnson), billed as "the last of the whorehouse piano players." In these last decades Sutton's accompanied performances routinely involved a rhythm section of Lesberg or Hinton with Johnson (until the latter's retirement in 1990) or Jake Hanna. In 1992 he suffered a stroke which affected his left hand, but he soon recovered and resumed his career. He may be seen in the video *Flip Phillips' 80th Birthday Party Featuring the All-Stars* (*c*1996 [filmed 1995]).

Ralph Sutton at the Brecon Jazz Festival, Wales, 1994

Sutton's playing is in the Harlem stride tradition of Fats Waller, James P. Johnson, and Willie "the Lion" Smith; it is characterized by a robust but tastefully controlled technique, an impeccably precise sense of rhythm, and an ebullient dancing quality. He performs works such as Bix Beiderbecke's *In a Mist* and Meade "Lux" Lewis's *Honky Tonk Train* in their original form; jazz standards, popular songs, and rags, however, are metamorphosed and enriched with melodic innovations of remarkably expressive power and vitality, including arabesque-like figures and riffs ingeniously adapted from traditional jazz motifs. In the 1980s and 1990s he was playing with undiminished drive, verve, and virtuosity, his repertory broader than before, and his basic style enhanced by a sparkling, melodious treble and subtle polyrhythms.

Video oral history material in *NHC* (HCJA).

SELECTED RECORDINGS

As unaccompanied soloist: Dill Pickles/St. Louis Blues (1949, Cir. [USA] 1053); Whitewash Man/Carolina in the Morning (1949, Cir. [USA] 1052); In a Mist (1950, Com. 1525); *Ragtime* (*c*1962–3, Roul. 25232), incl. Honky Tonk Train; *The Other Side of Ralph Sutton* (1980, Chaz Jazz 107); *Ralph Sutton at Café des Copains* (1983–7, Sack. 2-2019); *Ralph Sutton at Maybeck: Maybeck Recital Hall Series*, xxx (1993, Conc. 4586)

Duos: with A. Trappier: In the Dark/Flashes (1950, Com. 639); When You're Smiling/Squeeze Me (1950, Com. 641); with G. Wettling: *Ralph Sutton at the Piano* (1952, Cir. [USA] 413), incl. Fascination, Drop me off in Harlem, Bee's Knees; with R. Braff: *Ralph Sutton & Ruby Braff* (1980, Chaz Jazz 101-2); with J. McShann: *Ralph Sutton & Jay McShann: the Last of the Whorehouse Piano Players* (1980, Chaz Jazz 103-4); with K. Davern: *Ralph Sutton & Kenny Davern* (1980, Chaz Jazz 105-6); with E. Miller: *We've Got Rhythm* (1982, Chaz Jazz 110); with J. Lesberg: *Live at Hanratty's* (1982, Chaz Jazz 111); with P. Hucko: *Big Noise from Wayzata* (1982, Chaz Jazz 112); with V. Dickenson: *Blowin' Bubbles* (1982, Chaz Jazz 114); with D. Hyman: *Dick Hyman/Ralph Sutton* (1993, Conc. 4603)

As leader: *Suttonly* (1966, Solo 103); with W. B. Davison: *Together Again!* (1977, Sto. 4027); *The Jazzband* (1982, Chaz Jazz 113); with B. Barnard: *Partners in Crime* (1983, Avan-Guard 505); *Easy Street* (1991, Sack. 2040)

As sideman with G. Wettling: *George Wettling's Jazz Band* (1951, Col. CL6189)

BIBLIOGRAPHY

R. Johnson: "Ralph Sutton," *Coda*, xii/5 (1975), 9

J. D. Shacter: *Piano Man: the Story of Ralph Sutton* (Chicago, 1975; rev. and enlarged [2]/1994, as *Loose Shoes: the Story of Ralph Sutton*) [incl. discography]

"Caught in the Act," *MM* (23 June 1979), 61; (21 June 1980), 24

G. Endress: "Ralph Sutton," *JP*, xxix/11 (1980), 6

J. De Muth: "Ralph Sutton: on the Road with a Jazz Piano Veteran," *Keyboard*, vii/12 (1981), 30

D. Coller: "Ralph Sutton recalls . . .," *New Orleans Music*, ii/3 (1991), 13

L. Lewis and A. Lewis: "Ralph Sutton Interview," *Cadence*, xvii/9 (1991), 5

P. D. Atteberry: "Short Talk with Ralph Sutton," *Cadence*, xxi/8 (1995), 19

NORMAN P. GENTIEU/BK

Suzuki, Chin. Name by which YOSHIO SUZUKI is also known.

Suzuki, Hiromasa [Colgen] (*b* Tokyo, 26 May 1940). Japanese pianist, arranger, and leader. He took piano lessons from the age of 11, began to play jazz while attending Keio University, Tokyo, and made his début with George Kawaguchi's Big Four. After playing with the Bluecoats, led by Shigenori Obara, and the quartet led by the drummer Akira Ishikawa he joined Terumasa Hino's quintet in 1968, following the departure of Masabumi Kikuchi; thereafter he contributed greatly to the group's success. From 1979 to 1986 he led a quintet, The Players, though he also led a trio and was active as a studio musician. Suzuki taught piano and arranging in Tokyo at Ann School of Music.

SELECTED RECORDINGS

As leader: *Colgen World* (1976, Toshiba LF91019); of The Players: *Galaxy* (1979, Village A 0013), *Wonderful Guy* (1979, Village A 0014); *With my Whole Heart* (1996, Crown 9135)

As sideman: T. Hino: *Hi-nology* (1969, Col.–Tact 7691); Salena Jones: *Melodies of Love* (1980, JVC VIJ28007)

KAZUNORI SUGIYAMA

Suzuki, Isao [Hisao; Oma] (*b* Tokyo, 2 Jan 1946). Japanese double bass player and leader. He first played double bass at American military bases. Later he recorded with the pianist Shotaro Mariyasu (1954), played with Hidehiko Matsumoto (1961–4) and Sadao Watanabe (1964–5), and led a bop group in Tokyo (1965–9); he also recorded with Hampton Hawes (1968). In New York he worked with Art Blakey (1969–70) and performed with Thelonious Monk, Ella Fitzgerald, Wynton Kelly, Ron Carter, Charles Mingus, Paul Desmond, Bobby Timmons, and Jim Hall, usually in duos. In 1971 he returned to Japan, where he appeared as a sideman with Kenny Burrell's quartet and Mal Waldron's trio, among others, and worked again as the leader of various groups, including Soul Family, which in 1975 included Kazumasa Akiyama. He doubled on cello on a number of his albums recorded between 1973 and 1976 and played piccolo bass on others from 1978 into the 1980s. From 1984 he co-led, with Hideto Kanai, an organization for bass players, the Japan Bass Players Club. In 1987 Suzuki opened his own venue in Osaka to help further the careers of younger musicians.

SELECTED RECORDINGS

(recorded for Three Blind Mice unless otherwise indicated)

Blow Up (1973, 15); *Blue City* (1974, 24); *Black Orpheus* (1976, 63); *Hip Dancin'* (1976, EW 8044); *Ako's Dream* (1976, 76); *Yo ko* (1984, King K35Y6003); *My Spare Time* (1978, JVC VIJ6011)

BIBLIOGRAPHY

Feather–Gitler '70s

KAZUNORI SUGIYAMA, BK

Suzuki, Shoji (*b* Yokohama, Japan, 16 Aug 1932; *d* Tokyo, 10 Sept 1995). Japanese clarinetist and leader. His father played violin in orchestras accompanying silent films, and all three of his brothers became professional musicians. He grew up in Zushi from 1945 (after Yokohama was bombed) and began practicing on his elder brother's clarinet; he turned professional at the age of 16. After playing successively with four bands, including Fumio Nanri's Hot Peppers, in 1952 he formed a quintet, the Rhythm Aces, modeled after Benny Goodman's classic small groups; in tribute to Goodman's forthcoming appearance in Japan in January 1957 he made several recordings in this style. Later in 1957 he had considerable success with a Hawaiian-style pop recording, *Suzukake no michi* (Sycamore road), on which Peanuts Hucko played. His swing quintet recorded in New York with Hucko as guest soloist in 1962, and in spring 1966 Suzuki spent a month deputizing for Hucko at Eddie Condon's club. He continued to lead the Rhythm Aces in Japan into the mid-1990s, making further recordings with this group, and also performed with Hucko, Helen Merrill, and others in a concert tour of Japan in 1983.

SELECTED RECORDINGS

Shoji Suzuki Quintet (1956, Rockwell 502); *Shoji Suzuki Best Selection* (1957, Vic. [Jap.] BVCJ2609), incl. Suzukake no michi (Sycamore road); *Shoji Suzuki Recital at Sankei Hall: Kojyo no tsuki* (1959, Vic. [Jap.] JV5009); *Swing on my Mind: Tribute to Benny Goodman* (1988, Alfa Jazz 32R2-13); *Swing is my Life* (1992, Alfa Jazz ALCR231)

BIBLIOGRAPHY

T. Hirai: "News from Japan," *The Clarinet*, xxiii/4 (1996), 44

KAZUNORI SUGIYAMA, BK

Suzuki, Yoshio [Chin] (*b* Nagano, Japan, 21 March 1946). Japanese double bass player and pianist. He learned piano and violin from an early age, took up guitar in his teens, and played piano in a band at Waseda University in Tokyo. At the suggestion of Sadao Watanabe he changed to double bass, then performed with Watanabe's quartet from 1969 and with Masabumi Kikuchi's sextet from 1971. After moving to New York (1973) he worked with Stan Getz (1974), Art Blakey and the Jazz Messengers (1974–6), and the quintet of Bill Hardman and Junior Cook (1977–82); he also played with Dave Liebman, Sonny Rollins, Chet Baker, Lee Konitz, and Sonny Stitt, among others, and studied at the Juilliard School. Suzuki returned to Tokyo in 1984 and led the groups Matsuri (1984–92) and East Bounce (from 1992).

SELECTED RECORDINGS

Duos with K. Fujiwara (as the group Vino Rosso): *Bass & Bass* (1999, King KICJ368)

As leader: *Friends* (1973, CBS–Sony SOPL192); *Matsuri* (1979, CBS–Sony 25AP1611); *Wings* (1981, Trio PAP25013); *Morning Picture* (1984, JVC JMI28005); *Fairy Tale* (1987, JVC VDJ1078); *Alone in the Pacific* (1989, King KICP118); *The Moment* (1992, Video Arts 1002); *The East Bounce Collection* (1997, Video Arts 1015)

As sideman with A. Blakey: *Backgammon* (1976, Roul. 5003)

YOZO IWANAMI/KAZUNORI SUGIYAMA

Svenska Hotkvintetten. Swedish recording quintet, formed in 1939. Its instrumentation was modeled after that of the Quintette du Hot Club de France, which had visited Sweden in the spring of 1939; the group's original members were the violinist Emil Iwring, the guitarists Sven Stiberg (also its arranger), Kalle Löhr, and Folke Eriksberg, and the double bass player Roland Bengtsson. The Svenska Hotkvintetten may be heard to advantage on two recordings made for Columbia in 1940, *Opus 5* (1210) and *Honest and Truly/ Wham* (1199); the group disbanded in 1942. (L. Westin: Liner notes, *Swedish Hot 1939–41*, Dra. 223, 1992)

ERIK KJELLBERG/LARS WESTIN

Svensson, Esbjörn (*b* Västerås, Sweden, 16 April 1964). Swedish pianist and composer. While attending the Kungliga Musikhögskolan (Royal College of Music) in Stockholm he worked in the bop-based band led by the drummer Fredrik Norén (1985–8). After concentrating for a couple of years on pop music and studio work he became involved in jazz again. In the early 1990s, with the double bass player Dan Berglund and his childhood friend the drummer Magnus Öström, he formed the Esbjörn Svensson Trio (EST). While remaining within the traditional concept of a jazz piano trio, albeit sometimes with an energetic approach more often associated with rock, EST has managed, as have few jazz groups, to reach a wide and youthful audience. It has toured extensively throughout Europe and has collaborated with a variety of jazz and pop artists, including the singers Viktoria Tolstoy and Louise Hoffsten. Svensson's piano style is basically influenced by that of Keith Jarrett and Chick Corea. He is also a member of Nils Landgren's Funk Unit, in which he makes use of a range of keyboard instruments.

SELECTED RECORDINGS

Duos with N. Landgren: *Swedish Folk Modern* (1997, ACT 9257-2)

As leader: *When Everyone Has Gone* (1993, Dra. 248); *Mr. & Mrs. Handkerchief* (1995, Prophone 028); *Esbjörn Svensson Plays Monk* (1996, Superstudio Gul C-1-7432-1-3768-02); *Winter in Venice* (1997, Superstudio Gul C-2-74321-9612); *From Gagarin's Point of View* (1999, Superstudio Gul C-3-7432-16481-02); *Good Morning Susie Soho* (2000, Superstudio Gul C-4 73204-7000-773)

As sideman: Peter Danemo: *Baraban* (1991, Dra. 206); Jazz Furniture: *Jazz Furniture* (1994, Caprice 21449); K. Andersson and EST: *Intromotion* (1996, LCM C130); V. Tolstoy: *White Russian* (1996–7, BN 7243-8-21220-2-9); N. Landgren: *Live in Montreux* (1998, 9265-2)

BIBLIOGRAPHY

B. Borgström: "Jag vill visa mig" [I want to show who I am], *Orkester journalen*, lxii/4 (1994), 2

L. Westin: "Spränger gränserna" [Blasts through the borders], *Orkester journalen*, lxvi/4 (1998), 2

H. Gregory: "Good Morning, Piano Lovers," *JR*, no.14 (2000), 8

LARS WESTIN

Svensson, Reinhold (*b* Husum, nr Örnsköldsvik, Sweden, 20 Dec 1919; *d* Stockholm, 23 Nov 1968). Swedish pianist, composer, and arranger. Almost blind from an early age, he made his professional début recording some solo piano works (1941–2). From 1942 to 1948 he played in a quintet led by the violinist Hasse Kahn; the group was then taken over by Putte Wickman, who expanded it into a sextet, and Svensson remained as a member until 1960. Svensson quickly made his name as a swing pianist, though he made use of bop idioms; in 1949 he performed successfully at the Paris Jazz Fair. He took part in many recording sessions, and his quintet recordings in the style of George Shearing (for example, *Tasty Pastry*, 1952, Met. 245) brought him fame in the USA and elsewhere; he also recorded as the leader of a trio and, as Hammond Olson, on the Hammond organ. Svensson made many well-worked arrangements for Wickman's group and contributed compositions of his own, including *Lobster's Delight* (1955, Odeon SD5851) and *Impressions* (1957, Odeon GEOS64) [EP].

BIBLIOGRAPHY

"Svenskt stjärnalbum" [Swedish star album], *Orkester journalen*, xii/6 (1944), 5

"På omslaget" [On the cover], *Orkester journalen*, xxiv/5 (1956), 4

R. Dahlgren: "Reinhold Svensson," *Orkester journalen*, xxxvii/1 (1969), 8

ERIK KJELLBERG

Svoboda, Milan (*b* Prague, 10 Dec 1951). Czech pianist, bandleader, and composer. His mother was a pianist and musicologist, and he grew up in a musical family; he learned classical piano from around the age of five and later studied organ at the Prague Conservatory, musicology at Charles University, and composition at the Academy of Music in Prague. In the 1960s he began to listen to jazz, and in 1974 he founded a jazz-rock group, the Prague Big Band. This group was especially significant politically: rock was forbidden at that time (because of its potentially subversive lyrics), but instrumental jazz-rock offered a means of presenting a similar musical aesthetic. The band remained active into the mid-1980s. In 1979 Svoboda founded a small ensemble to play a mixture of jazz-rock and jazz standards; this group has remained active into the new century (although it was inoperative during the academic year 1984–5, which the leader spent at the Berklee College of Music in Boston). In 1987, at the summer jazz workshop in Frýdlant, northern Bohemia, he formed a new large ensemble, Contraband. Svoboda has written music for film and theater.

SELECTED RECORDINGS

(recorded for P&J Music unless otherwise indicated)

Duos with Michal Gera: *Duo* (1991, 003-1)

As leader: *Dedication* (1990, 001-2); of Contraband: *Live at Viersen* (1991, 004-1); with T. Lakatos: *Milan Svoboda & Tony Lakatos* (1997, 014-2); of Contraband: *Family* (1998, Lotos 0068-2)

JAROSLAV PAŠMIK

Swaggie. Record company and label. The company was established in Australia in 1949 by Graeme Bell. During its first decade it was devoted mainly to the documentation of

Australian jazz, especially of the traditional revival in that country, and it retained this role into the 1980s. However, the label became more widely known internationally in the early 1960s, when it was used for an extensive series of reissues, on 7-inch LPs, of vintage jazz; the material was drawn from all the major American companies, obtained by leasing agreements with their Australian branches and agents. This series was succeeded in the 1970s by a similar sequence of 12-inch LPs which drew mainly on American Decca and (through Australian EMI) on OKeh and the French label Swing. In the 1980s an additional series, Vintage Jazz Archives, was devoted to the definitively programmed chronological reissue (using dubbings of the highest quality) of early jazz. Swaggie was managed by Nevill Sherburn. Some further reissues were made on compact disc in the 1990s.

BIBLIOGRAPHY

N. Sherburn and G. Hulme: "The Swaggie Label," *Matrix*, no.23 (1959), 3; no.24 (1959), 11; no.27 (1960), 3; nos.29–30 (1960), 37; nos.35–6 (1961), 29

"Reissue Listing: Swaggie," *JM*, no.169 (1969), 26

N. Sherburn: "Swaggie Jazz Collector Series," *Matrix*, nos.81–8 (1969–70) [series of suppls.]

HOWARD RYE

Swainson, Neil (James Sinclair) (*b* Victoria, Canada, 15 Nov 1955). Canadian double bass player. He toured with Paul Horn (1975–7) and then moved to Toronto, where he worked with Moe Koffman (1978–82) and accompanied many visiting American musicians in local clubs. He traveled occasionally outside Canada with Woody Shaw (1983–7) and George Shearing (from 1985), and in 1988 became Shearing's regular touring partner. With Don Thompson, Pat LaBarbera, and Joe LaBarbera, he formed the Toronto-based quartet JMOG (Jazz Men on the Go) in 1992. He toured in Canada and recorded in 1994 as a member of the quintet Free Trade, consisting of Ralph Bowen, Renee Rosnes, Peter Leitch, and Terry Clarke. In addition to his own hard-bop album *49th Parallel* (1987, Conc. 396) and JMOG's *JMOG* (1992, Sack. 2031), he recorded with Shaw, Shearing, Jay McShann, Sam Noto, Doc Cheatham (1983–5), Ed Bickert (from 1985), Leitch (1981, 1986, 1991), Walter Norris (1990), Geoff Keezer (1993), and many others; the range of his recordings reflects his versatility as an accompanist and soloist of great warmth, melodic assurance, and technical dexterity. (G. Sutherland: "Best of Both Worlds," *Jazz Report*, viii/2 (1995), 16)

MARK MILLER

Swallow, Steve [Stephen W.] (*b* New York, 4 Oct 1940). Bass player and composer. He grew up in in Fair Lawn, New Jersey, and studied classical piano from the age of six. Having become acquainted with jazz through his father's interest he took up trumpet in junior high school, although he soon began to play double bass as well and discovered that he had a far greater talent on this instrument. While a student at Yale he played professionally with visiting dixieland and swing musicians, including Bud Freeman, Jimmy McPartland, Buddy Tate, Buck Clayton, Rex Stewart, and Dickie Wells. In autumn 1959 he began an apprenticeship with Paul Bley, and that winter he went to New York to join Bley while continuing to work with mainstream jazz bands. In summer 1960 he toured Germany with a colleague from prep school and Yale, the wind player Ian Underwood, performing pieces by Thelonious Monk and Ornette Coleman.

Back in New York, Swallow worked with Freeman and resumed his association with Bley as a member of the Jimmy Giuffre Three, in which setting he recorded several albums (1961–2) and toured Europe. After a brief period with George Russell and Benny Goodman (the latter in autumn 1962 and early 1963) he mastered an advanced bop style while a member concurrently in 1963 of the Art Farmer–Jim Hall Quartet (with Walter Perkins), Giuffre's Three, and Marian McPartland's trio (with Pete LaRoca); he also worked as a freelance with Freeman, João Gilberto, Sheila Jordan, Chico Hamilton, the quintet of Al Cohn and Zoot Sims, that of Clark Terry and Bob Brookmeyer, and Chick Corea. He continued in Farmer's quartet, for which he persuaded Farmer to engage LaRoca (replacing Perkins) and Steve Kuhn (replacing Hall), both of whom had earlier worked in a trio with Swallow. In 1964 he appeared in "Art Farmer Quartet Featuring Jim Hall" (1964), from the television series

Steve Swallow at the Bracknell Jazz Festival, England, 1984

"Jazz Casual," and in the middle of that year he joined Stan Getz's group, in which he began his long and productive association with Gary Burton. While with Getz he made a brief appearance with Dave Burns, Charles McPherson, Corea, and Al Dreares in a nightclub scene in the film *Sweet Love, Bitter* (*It Won't Rub Off, Baby*) (1966). He became a member of Burton's quartet in 1967, and shortly afterwards he took up electric bass guitar.

In 1970 Swallow moved to Bolinas, California, where he played in a small group with Art Lande and Mike Nock, led his own trio (including Bill Connors), and focused on mastering the electric instrument. He returned east in 1973, rejoined Burton, and became a key figure in working out a jazz vocabulary for the electric bass. Unlike rock bass players, he uses no distorting devices, concentrating instead on facility and precision of attack and on new melodic patterns suitable to a jazz context. In the mid-1970s he taught at the Berklee College of Music in Boston, but left teaching to return to performing and to direct his attention increasingly to composing – most notably in *Home* (1979), a setting of poems by Robert Creeley. In 1978 he joined Carla Bley's orchestra, and in the early to mid-1980s he toured widely with Burton, Carla Bley, John Scofield, and Mike Gibbs; later he appeared only occasionally with Burton's small groups. He recorded and toured in reunions with Giuffre and Paul Bley (from December 1989 into the 1990s) and in a quartet with Scofield, Pat Metheny, and Bill Stewart (1994), and also recorded with Henri Texier (1988), Joe Lovano (1992–3), Rabih Abou-Khalil (1992, 1994), and Motohiko Hino (1993). In 1994 he gave a concert at the London Jazz Festival and performed with Paul Motian's Electric Bebop Band. He recorded with Kuhn, John Taylor, and others in 1995, and toured Europe with Scofield and Stewart (spring 1996) and as the leader of a quintet including Chris Potter, Mick Goodrick, and Adam Nussbaum (November 1996). In 1997 he formed Trio 2000 with Potter and Motian, and a quintet consisting of Ryan Kisor, Potter, Mick Goodrick, and Adam Nussbaum; he continued working with Scofield and recording widely as a freelance. Most significantly he has spent many years with Carla Bley, performing in, writing for, and producing recordings for her ensembles. From 1988 he has appeared with her in a duo (it may be seen in the videos *Very, Very Simple*, 1987, and *Duets*, 1988), and from 1991 in her trio with Andy Sheppard.

SELECTED RECORDINGS

Duos with C. Bley: *Duets* (1988, Watt 20); *Go Together* (1992, Watt 24)
As leader: with G. Burton: *Hotel Hello* (1974, ECM 1055); *Home* (1979, ECM 1160); *Carla* (1986–7, XtraWatt 2); *Swallow* (1991, XtraWatt 6); *Real Book* (1993, XtraWatt 7); *Deconstructed* (1996, XtraWatt 9)
As sideman: J. Giuffre: *Fusion* (1961, Verve 68397); G. Russell: *Ezz-thetics* (1961, Riv. 9375); J. Giuffre: *Thesis* (1961, Verve 68402); P. Bley: *Footloose* (1962–3, Savoy 12182); P. LaRoca: *Basra* (1965, BN 84093); G. Burton: *Duster* (1967, RCA LSP3835); *A Genuine Tong Funeral* (1967, RCA LSP3988); C. Bley: *Social Studies* (1980, Watt 11); J. Scofield: *Shinola* (1981, Enja 4004); *Out Like a Light* (1981, Enja 4038); C. Bley: *Night-glo* (1985, Watt 16); *Sextet* (1986–7, Watt 17); *Songs with Legs* (1995, Watt 26)

BIBLIOGRAPHY

CarrJ
M. Williams: "Steve Swallow," *DB*, xxx/27 (1963), 22
J. Rosenbaum: "Steve Swallow: Renegade Jazz Bassist," *GP*, xv/12 (1981), 60
H. Mandel: "Steve Swallow: Bass in Progress," *DB*, xlix/11 (1982), 21
W. P. Hinely: "The Strings of Change," *JF* [intl edn], no.80 (1983), 36; no.81 (1983), 34
P. Carles: "Swallow, le bassiste de Carla," *Jm*, no.352 (1986), 46
J. Roberts: "Steve Swallow," *GP*, xxi/11 (1987), 58 [incl. discography]
P. Carles: "Carla & Steve: Passion Flower," *Jm*, no.397 (1990), 56
M. Bourne: "Carla Bley & Steve Swallow: Making Sweet Music," *DB*, lviii/4 (1991), 19 [incl. discography]
K. Franckling: "Carla Bley's 'Normal' Big Band," *JT*, xxii/1 (1992), 26 [incl. interview with Swallow]
J. Roberts: "Dancing in the Dark: an Interview and Private Lesson with Steve Swallow," *Bass Player*, iii/4 (1992), 50
M. Jarrett: "Big Bangs Theory," *Jazziz*, xii/8 (1995), 50
P. Kober: "Jazz: Steve Swallow," *Jh*, no.529 (1996), 26 [incl. discography by G. Reynard and Y. Sportis]
C. Jisi: "Meet the Advisory Board: Steve Swallow," *Bass Player*, viii/3 (1997), 26
<http://www2.pcom.net/rminer/SteveSwallow.html> (1999) [discography]

J. BRADFORD ROBINSON/BK

Swan. Nickname of HOWARD JOHNSON (i).

Swana, John (*b* Norristown, PA, 26 April 1962). Trumpeter. He took up trumpet at the age of 11 and later attended Temple University (BMus 1987). From the mid-1980s he performed in Philadelphia with, among others, Philly Joe Jones, Hank Mobley, Don Patterson, Shirley Scott, Mickey Roker, and Cecil Payne. Swana worked mainly as a freelance, but from the early 1990s he also led various small groups, notably one with Johnny Coles as co-leader (1996–7) and another with Joe Magnarelli (1998); he made his first recording under his own name in 1990. From 1996 to 1998 he toured with the drummer Gerry Gibbs (son of Terry Gibbs), and in 1996 he performed in Eric Alexander's group at the Molde International Jazz Festival in Norway. As a sideman he recorded with Peter Leitch (1991), Chris Potter (1992), Alexander (1992, 1994), Charles Fambrough (1994, *c*1997), the pianist Orrin Evans and Clarence Penn (both 1996), and Benny Golson (1997). Swana is an underrated hard-bop trumpeter who plays with a full, round, and, when needed, brash sound that combines the lyricism of Clifford Brown's style with the emotional intensity of Lee Morgan's.

SELECTED RECORDINGS

(recorded for Criss Cross unless otherwise indicated)

As leader: *The Feeling's Mutual* (1993, 1090); *In the Moment* (1995, 1119); with J. Magnarelli: *Philly–New York Junction* (1998, 1150)
As sideman: C. Potter: *Presenting Chris Potter* (1992, 1067); E. Alexander: *Full Range* (1994, 1098); O. Evans: *Justin Time* (1996, 1125); C. Penn: *Penn's Landing* (1996, 1134); B. Golson: *Remembering Clifford* (1997, Mlst. 9278)

BIBLIOGRAPHY

Feather–GitlerBEJ
B. Primack: "Hearsay: John Swana," *JT*, xxix/1 (1999), 21

GK

Swanerud, Thore (*b* Stockholm, 18 June 1919; *d* Stockholm, 8 Dec 1988). Swedish pianist, vibraphonist, and composer. He became a professional musician at the age of 18 and in the 1940s performed and recorded with several of the leading Swedish bands, including those of Miff Görling, Simon Brehm, and Stan Hasselgård. From 1949 to 1951 he led a sextet, and thereafter he ran his own trios for many years, though he also worked as an arranger and orchestra leader in studios and theaters. He recorded with James Moody (1949) and Ernestine Anderson (1956) and made recordings as a leader into the 1980s (including *Star Dust*, 1984, Dra. 100); among his best-known compositions is the lyrical *Södermalm*. While he commenced his career playing in the swing tradition, Swanerud was later influenced by modern trends and won a reputation as a fine soloist and accompanist.

Oral history material in *SSsv*.

BIBLIOGRAPHY

"Svenkst stjärnalbum" [Swedish star-album], *Orkester journalen*, ix/3 (1941), 5

L. Westin: "Swanis: en av våra stora" [Swanis: one of our greats], *Orkester journalen*, lvii/33 (1989), 33

ERIK KJELLBERG/LARS WESTIN

Swanton, Lloyd (*b* Sydney, 14 Aug 1960). Australian bass player and composer. He studied jazz at the New South Wales Conservatorium of Music (1979–80) and composition at the Guildhall School of Music in London (1986). In 1980 in Sydney he joined The Benders, and in 1985 he took part in the group's international tour, which included an appearance at the Montreux International Festival. From the mid-1980s Swanton was highly sought after as an accompanist on double bass for overseas jazz artists visiting Australia, and he made a large number of jazz and popular recordings. His versatility and command of various jazz idioms involved him with such important Australian ensembles as The Necks, Clarion Fracture Zone, the bands of Vince Jones and Mike Nock, and Bernie McGann's trio. In 1991 Swanton's interest in merging jazz with ethnic and popular music led to the formation of his group The Catholics, which ultimately became his primary focus. The band recorded three albums in the 1990s.

SELECTED RECORDINGS

As leader of The Catholics: *The Catholics* (1992, Spiral Scratch 0011); *Simple* (1993, Rufus 009); *Life on Earth* (1996, Rufus 022)

As sideman with The Necks: on *Beyond El Rocco* (1988, Vox Australis 017-2) [film soundtrack], The Royal Family; *Next* (1988–90, Spiral Scratch 0004); *Sex* (1989, Spiral Scratch 0002); *Aquatic* (1994, Fish of Milk 0002); *Silent Night* (1995, Fish of Milk 0004); *Piano Bass Drums* (1996–7, Fish of Milk 0005)

As sideman with B. McGann: *At Long Last* (1983, Emanem 3601); *Ugly Beauty* (1991, Spiral Scratch 0010); *McGann McGann* (1994, Rufus 011); *Playground* (1996, Rufus 023)

As sideman with others: The Benders: *E* (1982, Hot 1002); *False Laughter* (1983, Hot 1006); D. McRae: *Southern Roots* (1987, Emanem 3603); Wizards of Oz: *Soundtrack* (1988, EmA 834531-1); D. Barlow: *Horn* (1989, Spiral Scratch 0003); V. Jones: *Come in Spinner* (1989, ABC 838984-2); Clarion Fracture Zone: *What this Love Can Do* (1993, Rufus 010); *Less Stable Elements* (1995, Rufus 020)

BIBLIOGRAPHY

B. Johnson: *The Oxford Companion to Australian Jazz* (Melbourne, Australia, 1987)

J. Clare [G. Brennan, pseud.]: *Bodgie Dada and the Cult of Cool* (Sydney, 1995)

ANDREW HARRISON

Swartz, Harvie (*b* Chelsea, MA, 6 Dec 1948). Double bass player. Having played piano from childhood, he took up double bass in 1967 during his second year at the Berklee School of Music and played both instruments locally in jazz bands. After graduating in 1970 he spent four months in Europe, and while in Denmark worked with Dexter Gordon, Johnny Griffin, Brew Moore, Jimmy Heath, Kenny Drew, and Art Taylor. He played electric bass guitar in a pop band and then reverted to the acoustic instrument, which he played in Boston with Mose Allison, Chris Connor, and Al Cohn and Zoot Sims. In 1972 he moved to New York, where, with Mike Abene, he accompanied such singers as Connor, Jackie Cain and Roy Kral (recording in 1973), and Jackie Paris; he later worked with Thad Jones and Mel Lewis and with Gil Evans. He also performed as a studio electric bass guitarist in soul, pop, and country music. Swartz worked regularly in the mid-1970s at Richard's Lounge in Lakewood, New Jersey, accompanying (among others) Lee Konitz, Jan Hammer, and John Abercrombie, and from 1974 to at least 1976 was a member of Barry Miles's Silverlight, in which he doubled as an electric bass guitarist. He played with several of David Friedman's groups (recording between 1975 and 1981), notably a trio with Eddie Daniels (1976) and Double Image (a cooperative quartet with Dave Samuels and Michael Di Pasqua); Swartz and Friedman also recorded as sidemen in Daniel Humair's trio (1979). He then performed in the big band led by the pianist David Matthews (1976), recorded in a duo with Bob Degen (1977), toured and recorded with Steve Kuhn (1977–81) – whose quartet included Sheila Jordan – and toured widely and recorded in a duo with Jordan (1978–95).

In the 1980s Swartz experimented with unusual instrumental combinations: his album *Underneath it All*, for instance, features an ensemble of double bass, piano, flugelhorn, cello, percussion, and drums. In 1982–3 he led the Harvie Swartz String Ensemble, which included Terry King (violin) and Erik Friedlander (cello), and in 1986 he formed his own pop-flavored fusion band, Urban Earth. Intermittently from 1982 he worked in New York with Mike Stern (often in a trio with Victor Lewis), and performed with Kenny Barron (in a duo from the mid-1980s), Bill Mays, Jim Hall, John Scofield, Al Di Meola, and Louie Bellson (recording in 1993). He joined an ensemble of five basses, piano, and drums organized by Rufus Reid, and recorded with Leni Stern (1985, 1988), Toots Thielemans (1988), Akio Sasajima, the saxophonist John Mastroianni and Sherrie Maricle, and Mays (all 1989), Mick Goodrick (1990), Paquito D'Rivera and Bernie Senensky (both 1991), and Hendrik Meurkens (1993–4); he may be seen with Thielemans in the video *Toots! In New Orleans* (1988), and he also appeared in videos with Pat Martino, Jordan, Jay Clayton, and Jane Ira Bloom. He taught at the Manhattan School of Music (1983 through the 1990s) and at the Eastman School (summer 1990). After spending periods studying and performing in Cuba, in the latter half of the 1990s Swartz led the band Eye Contact, with which he explored his interest in Afro-Cuban and other Latin music traditions; the group appeared at the JVC festival in New York in 1998 and recorded in 1999. From the 1980s Swartz ceased to play electric bass guitar. In addition to the double bass, he has utilized a four-string (and later, five-string) "vertical bass," combining the acoustic instrument's conventional neck with a solid body and electronic pickups.

SELECTED RECORDINGS

Duos with S. Jordan: *Old Time Feeling* (1982, PAlt 8038); *Songs from Within* (1989, MA 014)

As leader: *Underneath it All* (1980, Gram. 8202); *Urban Earth* (1985, Gram. 8503); *Smart Moves* (1986, Gram. 8607); *In a Different Light* (1990, Blue Moon 79153); *Arrival* (1991, Novus 63174-2); of Eye Contact: *Havana Mañana* (1999, Bembe 2024-2)

As sideman: B. Miles: *Barry Miles and Silverlight* (1974, Lon. 651); D. Friedman: *Futures Passed* (1976, Enja 2068); D. Humair: *Trip Hip Trip* (1979, Owl 014); S. Kuhn: *Last Year's Waltz* (1981, ECM 1213); S. Jordan: *Lost and Found* (1989, Muse 5390); A. Sasajima: *Time Remembered* (1989, Muse 5417)

BIBLIOGRAPHY

Feather–Gitler '70s

A. J. Smith: "Profile: Harvie Swartz," *DB*, xliii/5 (1976), 32

B. Reidinger: "Jazz Catalyst: Harvie Swartz," *JT* (1988), Sept, 7

R. Gaspar: "Old Guys in Suits and Ties Blowing Saxophones: the Harvie Swartz Interview," *Coda*, no.227 (1989), 10

P. Booth: "Profile: Harvie Swartz," *DB*, lvii/1 (1990), 44

J. Rosenbaum: "Harvie Swartz: Versatility and Eclecticism," *Strings*, iv/5 (1990), 17

F. Salamone: "Harvie Swartz Interview," *Cadence*, xix/8 (1993), 5

C. Jisi: "Harvie Swartz: Mastering the Bass at his own Pace," *Bass Player*, vii/7 (1997), 52

WILLIAM S. BROCKMAN/BK

Swayze, Edwin [King] (*b* Marshall, TX, 13 June 1906; *d* New York, 31 Jan 1935). Trumpeter. He played with Alex Hill and in 1924 joined Alphonso Trent, with whom he performed intermittently until 1928. In 1925–6 he toured and made several recordings with the singer Sammy Lewis (including *Hateful Papa Blues*, on which he plays an excellent muted solo); he also toured with Jelly Roll Morton and in 1928 made two recordings with him in New York. The following year he worked with Chick Webb and traveled to Europe, where in 1930 he joined Herb Flemming's International Rhythm Aces and led the Plantation Band for a residency in Amsterdam. After returning to New York, Swayze recorded regularly with Cab Calloway (from July 1931), performed with Webb and Sam Wooding, and played and provided arrangements for the bandleader Eugene Kennedy (1932); he then rejoined Calloway's band, with which he remained until his death. Because of its pronunciation, Swayze's name has consistently been misspelled Swayzee.

SELECTED RECORDINGS

As sideman: S. Lewis: Just too late/Somebody I can call my own (1926, OK 8285); Hateful Papa Blues (1926, Voc. 1029); Levee Serenaders (J. R. Morton): Midnight Mama/Mr. Jelly Lord (1928, Voc. 1154); C. Calloway: 'Long about Midnight (1934, Vic. 24592)

BIBLIOGRAPHY

McCarthyB

D. Raichelson: Liner notes, *Jazz in Harlem, 1926–1931* (Arcadia 2008, 1976)

A. Barnett and E. Løgager: *Stuff Smith: Pure at Heart* (Lewes, England, 1991), 12

A. Barnett: *Desert Sands: the Recordings and Performances of Stuff Smith: an Annotated Discography and Biographical Source Book* (Lewes, England, 1995; suppl., 1998, as *Up Jumped the Devil*)

based on *ChiltonW*/HOWARD RYE

Sweatman, Wilbur (C.) (*b* Brunswick, MO, 7 Feb 1882; *d* New York, 9 March 1961). Clarinetist, bandleader, and composer. After beginning on piano with lessons from his sister Eva, he taught himself to play clarinet and violin. His first professional work was in vaudeville with a "pickaninny" band led by Nathaniel Clark Smith (*c*1897–8). In 1902 he was assistant leader of P. G. Lowery's concert band with Forepaugh and Sells Circus, and later that year he joined Mahara's Minstrels band under the leadership of W. C. Handy. In 1903 he formed his own band in Minneapolis and recorded cylinders for a local music store. Sweatman moved to Chicago in 1908 and led trios at the Grand and Monogram theatres, accompanying acts and writing music for tabloid shows. He returned to vaudeville in 1911 as a soloist and met with great acclaim. Having moved to New York in 1912 he led the Lafayette Theatre orchestra in Harlem for a short while in 1914, then went back to vaudeville with a band which included Crickett Smith. During World War I he appeared in many benefits, and at Brighton Beach in the summer of 1919 led a band which included Freddie Keppard. He continued to work through the 1920s in vaudeville, and in March 1923 employed Duke Ellington, Sonny Greer, and Otto Hardwick with his act. He provided music for the opening of Connie's Inn in 1923 with a band that included Coleman Hawkins. In the 1920s and 1930s he ran his own booking agency, handling both African-American and white musicians. Sweatman retired from performance in the early 1930s to concentrate on booking acts, publishing music, and managing musicians' estates, most notably Scott Joplin's. He made a few appearances in the 1940s, including a residency at Paddell's Club in New York and some high school gala concerts with Handy, and made his last (private) recordings in 1951.

Although Sweatman is best remembered for his ability to play three clarinets simultaneously, as the composer of *Down Home Rag*, and for giving employment to a youthful Duke Ellington, his role in the development and popularization of jazz demands reappraisal. His long career in vaudeville took ragtime and jazz across the USA to African-American and white audiences alike, and his Columbia recordings of 1918–20 sold extremely well and are the first African-American jazz recordings consistently to feature collective improvisation and embellishment. Sweatman's accompanying bands were a nursery for young jazz musicians, including most notably (besides those already mentioned) Sidney Bechet, Wellman Braud, Cozy Cole, Jimmie Lunceford, Count Basie, Claude Hopkins, and Teddy Bunn. It may be argued that the 1917 recordings by the Original Dixieland Jazz Band were not the first jazz recordings in the conventional sense, but that this honor really belongs to Sweatman's improvised solo recordings of *Down Home Rag*, made in December 1916 (Emerson 7161 and 5163), despite the non-jazz accompaniment. More interesting musically is a jazz session of April 1917, in which Sweatman's clarinet playing is accompanied by five African-American saxophonists: *Joe Turner Blues* (Pathé 20167) is arguably the earliest African-American recording for which no historical apologia is necessary.

BIBLIOGRAPHY

ChiltonW; *McCarthyB*

M. Berresford: "Wilbur Sweatman: Everybody's Crazy 'bout the doggone Blues but I'm Happy," *The Gunn Report*, no. 61 (1975), 16

L. Kunstadt and B. Cotton: "Daddy of the Clarinet: Wilbur Sweatman," *Record Research*, no.24 (1959), 3; repr. in *Black Perspective in Music*, xvi/2 (1988), 227

M. Tucker: *Ellington: the Early Years* (Oxford, England, Urbana, IL, and Chicago, 1991)

M. Berresford: "Ragtime to Jazz 1" (Tim. CBC1-035, 1997) [liner notes]

EDDIE LAMBERT/HOWARD RYE, MARK BERRESFORD

Swedish Radio Big Band. Group led from 1956 to 1965 by HARRY ARNOLD.

Swedish Radio Jazz Group. *See* RADIOJAZZGRUPPEN (ii).

Swee' Pea. Nickname of BILLY STRAYHORN.

Sweethearts of Rhythm. Name given to various bands led in the 1950s by the singer Anna Mae Winburn after the INTERNATIONAL SWEETHEARTS OF RHYTHM disbanded.

Sweets. Nickname of HARRY EDISON.

Swell, Steve (*b* Newark, NJ, 6 Dec 1954). Trombonist. His father played saxophone and clarinet and his sister is a church organist and choir conductor. He learned clarinet briefly with his father when he was nine but changed to trombone a year later, after an injury to his hand temporarily limited the movement of his fingers; while at school he played in a big band with Danny Gottlieb. At the age of 15 he heard Roswell Rudd's free-jazz style on the album *Archie Shepp Live in San Francisco* and as a result changed his perspective on how to play. From 1973 to 1975 he attended

Jersey City College, during which time he frequented free-jazz performances in lofts in New York and began playing with the drummer Lou Grassi. Having moved to the city (1975) he worked in salsa groups, deputized in Broadway pit bands, and studied with Rudd and Grachan Moncur III in the Jazz Interactions program (1975–7). In the early 1980s he was a member of the house band at the revived Roseland Ballroom and in 1983 he performed with Lionel Hampton's orchestra. The following year he joined Buddy Rich's ensemble, but he left after a short time because his style of improvisation conflicted with the leader's conception. He performed and recorded (1984, 1988) with Jaki Byard's big band and appeared at Carnegie Hall in Makanda Ken McIntyre's group (1985). Swell made his first tour of Europe with Herb Robertson's Bud Powell band in 1988 and returned later that year with Hank Roberts's Black Pastels. In the 1990s he toured internationally and recorded with Tim Berne's Caos Totale (*c*1990–93) and Joey Baron's Barondown (1991–5) and worked with John Zorn's Cobra, Joe Gallant's Illuminati, William Parker's Little Huey Creative Music Orchestra, Grassi's Pogressions, and Phillip Johnston's Big Trouble (recording in 1994–5); in New York he was a featured soloist in a performance of Anthony Braxton's opera *Shala Fears for the Poor.* In 1994 he established a duo with the saxophonist Chris Kelsey and began leading the group Space, Time, Swing with Perry Robinson; he has also led two quartets, one of which includes Rudd. Swell has recorded with, among others, Tom Varner (1990, 1992), the drummer Tom Schmidt (1995), and the alto saxophonist Christopher Cauley and Michael Formanek (both 1996).

SELECTED RECORDINGS

Duos with C. Kelsey: *Observations* (1996, CIMP 108)
As leader: *Out and About* (1996, CIMP 116); *Moons of Jupiter* (*c*1997, CIMP 149)
As sideman: T. Berne: *Pace Yourself* (1990, JMT 834442-2); J. Baron: *Raisedpleasuredot* (1993, New World 80449-2); T. Berne: *Nice View* (1993, JMT 314-514013-2); T. Schmidt: *Rabble* (1995, Koch 7918-2); L. Grassi: *PoGressions* (1995, Cadence Jazz 1062); J. Baron: *Crackshot* (1995, Avant 059); M. Formanek: *Nature of the Beast* (1996, Enja 9308-2); C. Cauley: *Finland* (1996, Eremite 06)

BIBLIOGRAPHY

V. Tarrière: "Plus haut perché, le nouveau Baron," *Jm*, no.446 (1995), 84
B. Rusch: "Steve Swell: Interview," *Cadence*, xxiv/2 (1998), 5
<http://home.earthlink.net/~sdswell/> (1998)

GK

Swift, Duncan (*b* Rotherham, England, 21 Feb 1943; *d* Bewdley, England, 8 Aug 1997). English pianist and trombonist. He played piano in local bands from the age of 14 and then took up trombone. After moving to the Midlands with his family (1960) he performed as a trombonist (1961–2) and as a pianist with lesser-known groups. Swift took a degree at the Birmingham School of Music and gained diplomas from the Royal Academy of Music, and from 1968 to 1978 he taught music in schools. During this period he led the New Delta Jazzmen (1974–7) and began playing piano with Kenny Ball; he worked with Ball occasionally at first (1977–8) and later full-time (1979–83), and may be heard on the album *Greensleeves* (1982, Tim. 505). Between 1983 and 1987 Swift ran a public house in Bewdley, after which he returned to music; in 1988–9 he worked with the reed player Pete Allen. In the 1990s he concentrated on performances as an unaccompanied soloist and recorded *The Broadwood Concert* (1990, Big Bear 543), although he continued to play in bands from time to time.

BIBLIOGRAPHY

CarrJ; *ChiltonB*
Obituaries: A. Shipton, *The Guardian* (18 Sept 1997); P. Hawes, *JJI*, l/10 (1997), 17

MARK GILBERT

Swing (i). (1) A quality attributed to jazz performance. Although basic to the perception and performance of jazz, swing has resisted concise definition or description. Most attempts at such refer to it as primarily a rhythmic phenomenon, resulting from the conflict between a fixed pulse and the wide variety of actual durations and accents that a jazz performer plays against that pulse (*see* Beat, esp. §3). However, such a conflict alone does not necessarily produce swing, and a rhythm section may even play a simple fixed pulse with varied amounts or types of swing. Clearly other properties are also involved, of which one is probably the forward propulsion imparted to each note by a jazz player through manipulation of timbre, attack, vibrato, intonation, or other means; this combines with the proper rhythmic placement of each note to produce swing in a great variety of ways.

(2) The name given to a jazz style and to a related phase of popular music which originated around 1930 when New Orleans jazz was in decline; it is characterized by a greater emphasis on solo improvisation, larger ensembles, a repertory based largely on Tin Pan Alley songs, and above all the more equal weight given to the four beats of the bar (hence the term "four-beat jazz" occasionally applied to this style). This important change in jazz rhythm took place gradually between 1930 and 1935 as the tuba was superseded by the double bass (played in the walking bass style) and the banjo by the rhythm guitar, and the basic pulse was transferred from the snare drum to the hi-hat or ride cymbal. The harmonic rhythm in swing was generally much faster than in New Orleans jazz, sometimes changing as often as twice a bar, and soloists were expected to improvise melodies freely over these "changes." There was a notable increase in instrumental virtuosity among soloists in this period; some of the most prominent were Henry "Red" Allen, Roy Eldridge, Coleman Hawkins, Chu Berry, Benny Goodman, Johnny Hodges, and Lester Young. At the same time instruments not previously regarded as suitable for solo work began to be given solo roles, including the drums (Gene Krupa and Chick Webb), double bass (Jimmy Blanton), vibraphone (Lionel Hampton and Red Norvo), and guitar (Django Reinhardt and Charlie Christian). The development of swing coincided with the emergence by 1932 of the 13-piece dance band (consisting of 3 trumpets, 2 trombones, 4 reed instruments, piano, guitar, double bass, and drum set); the music was thus most often played in "big bands" such as those led by Duke Ellington, Fletcher Henderson, Count Basie, Jimmie Lunceford, Benny Goodman, Artie Shaw, and Earl Hines (*see* Bands, §4 (iii); *see also* Battle of bands). However, the musicians often preferred to work in smaller groups, which allowed more scope for solo improvisation and extended their repertory beyond the confines of dance music. Important small ensembles working in this style included Goodman's groups, the Brunswick recording bands led by Teddy Wilson, the John Kirby Sextet, Fats Waller and his Rhythm, and various ad hoc recording groups drawn from the Ellington and Basie bands (*see also* Bands, §4 (iv)). The swing rhythm section became an important element in rhythm-and-blues and hence in early rock-and-roll, and was

also used by some traditional jazz groups from the early 1940s. A simple relaxed style of swing, played chiefly by small groups, developed in the late 1930s and became known as Jump (early rhythm-and-blues). Although in the late 1940s the swing style ceased to be the dominant movement in jazz, it continued to attract excellent players such as Ruby Braff, Rolf Kühn, Claude Bolling, and Scott Hamilton, and remained commercially viable.

Around 1989 a so-called swing revival got underway in San Francisco and gradually spread nationally. It has been flourishing since 1996, when the film *Swingers* was released, and is becoming an international phenomenon. The nature of the revival has more to do with swing-era fashion (such as zoot suits and wide ties) and swing-era dances (*see* DANCE) than with the classic big-band music of that time. The focus of its sounds is jump and rock-and-roll, though it also draws from many disparate styles, both earlier and later, and the electric guitar has an anachronistic centrality in a typical band – "it's swing as imagined by rockers" (Harrington, 1998).

See also FORMS, §3; JAZZ (i), §IV, 1, 2; and WESTERN SWING.

BIBLIOGRAPHY

McCarthyB; *SchullerS*
A. Hodeir: *Hommes et problèmes du jazz, suivi de La religion du jazz* (Paris, 1954; Eng. trans., rev. Hodeir, as *Jazz: its Evolution and Essence*, New York, 1956/*R*1975)
G. T. Simon: *The Big Bands* (New York, 1967, rev. 4/1981)
G. Schuller: *Early Jazz: its Roots and Musical Development* (New York, 1968), 6ff
M. C. Gridley: *Jazz Styles* (Englewood Cliffs, NJ, 1978, rev. 6/1997 [*recte* 1996])
C. Bohländer: *Die Anatomie des Swing* (Frankfurt am Main, Germany, 1986)
I. Gitler: *Swing to Bop: an Oral History of the Transition in Jazz in the 1940s* (New York, and Oxford, England, 1987)
W. Barlow and C. Finley: *From Swing to Soul: an Illustrated History of African American Popular Music from 1930 to 1960* (Washington, DC, 1994)
T. J. Hennessey: *From Jazz to Swing: Afro-American Jazz Musicians and their Music, 1890–1935* (Detroit, 1994)
D. W. Stowe: *Swing Changes: Big Band Jazz in New Deal America* (Cambridge, MA, and London, 1994)
B. Kernfeld: *What to Listen for in Jazz* (New Haven, CT, and London, 1995)
T. Scanlan: *The Joy of Jazz: Swing Era, 1935–1947* (Golden, CO, 1996)
E. Wood: *Born to Swing* (London, 1996)
R. Harrington: "Back in the Swing," *Washington Post* (26 Oct 1998)
V. Vale and M. Wallace, eds.: *Swing! The New Retro Renaissance* (San Francisco, 1998)

J. BRADFORD ROBINSON/BK

Swing (ii). Record label. It was established in Paris in 1937; artists and repertory were directed by Charles Delaunay and Hugues Panassié, and the recordings were made and marketed by the French branch of EMI. As well as the recordings of the Quintette du Hot Club de France, the catalogue contained extensive documentation of the work of such American visitors to France as Benny Carter, Coleman Hawkins, Dicky Wells, and Garland Wilson. From 1940 to 1944, though jazz was frowned upon in France by the occupying Nazi regime, demand for the music increased and the label's operations flourished. Items were issued during this period by local and Antillean musicians and also by Americans who had escaped internment, such as Harry Cooper. In 1946 Delaunay went to the USA and organized several recordings specifically for issue in France. In 1948 control of the label passed to Vogue, which Delaunay joined as manager of artists and repertory. Swing's back catalogue remained the property of EMI. Vogue continued to issue discs, some of them LPs, on Swing throughout the 1950s; among these were items leased from such small American enterprises as Dial, Pacific Jazz, and Fantasy, as well as recordings made in France. The name was used in the 1980s by the American company DRG for an important series of reissues of early jazz and swing, including material originally issued in France on Swing before 1948.

BIBLIOGRAPHY

C. Delaunay: "Swing a 20 ans," *Jh*, no.125 (1957), 13
I. Frésart: "Swing: a Numerical Listing of the 78 r.p.m. Issues," *Matrix*, nos.62–79 (1965–8) [series of suppls.]
C. Delaunay: *Delaunay's Dilemma: de la peinture au jazz* (Mâcon, France, 1985)
M. Ruppli: *Swing* (Paris, 1989)

HOWARD RYE

Swingle, Ward (Lamar) (*b* Mobile, AL, 21 Sept 1927). Singer and leader. He is gifted with perfect pitch and as a child took up clarinet, oboe, and piano; together with his siblings he sang in an imitation of a popular vocal group of that era, the Andrews Sisters. From 1943 to 1945 he played alto saxophone and sang with the big band of the songwriter Ted Fio Rito. After receiving a master's degree from the Cincinnati Conservatory he studied piano on a Fulbright scholarship in Paris (1951), where he later settled (1956) and worked with the Blue Stars (1957–61) and performed and recorded with the Double Six (1959–61). In 1962, with Christiane Legrand, he formed the Swingle Singers, a vocal ensemble that became well known for performing scat jazz versions of pieces from the classical repertory, in particular those of J. S. Bach; it toured the USA and Europe and recorded with the Modern Jazz Quartet (1966), Stan Getz (1971), and André Hodeir (1972). After it disbanded in 1973, Swingle formed another group, Swingle II, which also performed conventionally and which established a large repertory that included madrigals, ragtime, popular songs, and rock. Under the name the Swingle Singers it recorded in 1979 and performed into the late 1980s. Swingle later published a reminiscence, *Swingle Singing* (Delaware Water Gap, PA, 1999).

BIBLIOGRAPHY

Feather '60s
M. Kerner: "Ward Swingle has New Four-four Ensemble," *Christian Science Monitor* (2 June 1978), 23
E. Wilcox: "Spotlight on Ward Swingle," *Music Educators Journal*, lxxvi (1989), Nov, 47
M. Becker: "Ward Swingle," *JP*, xli/4 (1992), 16
M. Zwerin: "Making Bach Swing: Saga of Ward Swingle," *International Herald Tribune* (28 April 1999)

Swingle Singers. French vocal group. The eight academically trained singers were brought together in Paris in 1962 by Ward Swingle and Christiane Legrand to improve their sight-singing and musicianship. They developed a distinctive style, performing scat arrangements of Baroque and classical instrumental music, in which they added a jazz bass and percussion as accompaniment, embellished rhythmic sections, and improvised solos. They toured Europe and the USA, and made several successful recordings. In summer 1973 the group disbanded and Swingle formed a new, British, group, Swingle II. Making less use of scat singing, it performed a wider repertory, including madrigals, early jazz, and pop songs, and introduced new music by such composers as Luciano Berio.

BIBLIOGRAPHY

M. Zwerin: "Making Bach Swing: Saga of Ward Swingle," *International Herald Tribune* (28 April 1999)

RAYMONDE S. KRAMLICH

Swingsters. Name used in the early 1950s by the CRUSADERS.

Swingville. Record label founded in 1960 as a subsidiary of PRESTIGE.

Swope, Earl (Bowman) (*b* Hagerstown, MD, 4 Aug 1922; *d* Washington, DC, 3 Jan 1968). Trombonist, brother of Rob Swope. His parents, a sister, and two other brothers were also musicians. He began his professional career at the age of 20 with Sonny Dunham's orchestra, before playing with Boyd Raeburn (1943–4), Georgie Auld (1945), Don Lamond (in Washington, 1945) and Buddy Rich (1945–7); when he joined Woody Herman's Second Herd he was replaced in Rich's band by his brother Rob. He was one of the few trombonists in the 1940s to develop a style that was not influenced by J. J. Johnson; he played in a modern barrelhouse style, which is clearly heard on the recordings he made with small groups led by Serge Chaloff and Stan Getz during the period he was with Herman (September 1947–1949); he also performed in the film shorts *Woody Herman and his Orchestra* (1948) and *Herman's Herd* (1949). In the 1950s he played with Elliot Lawrence (1950–51) and was a freelance player for some time in New York and Washington; then he again worked regularly in bands, playing in Jimmy Dorsey's last orchestra (1957) and with Louie Bellson (1959), with whom he recorded in Los Angeles. He spent the 1960s as a freelance in Washington, playing jazz of a commercialized type.

SELECTED RECORDINGS

As sideman: B. Rich: Dateless Brown/It Couldn't be True (*c*1945, Mer. 3001); S. Chaloff: Gabardine and Serge (1947, Savoy 978); A Bar a Second (1947, Savoy 906); W. Herman: That's Right (1948, Cap. 15427); Lemon Drop (1948, Cap. 15365); *Classics in Jazz* (1948–50, Cap. T324), incl. Lollypop (1949); S. Getz: Stan Gets Along (1949, Savoy 966); Fast (1949, Savoy 947); Not Really the Blues (1949, Cap. 57-837)

BIBLIOGRAPHY

FeatherE; *Feather–Gitler '70s*

I. Gitler: *Jazz Masters of the Forties* (New York, n.d. [?1966]/*R*1983 with discography)

J. Burns: "Bopping Bones," *J&B*, ii/7 (1972), 16

J. A. Treichel: *Keeper of the Flame: Woody Herman and the Second Herd, 1947–1949* (n.p. [Zephyrhills, FL], 1978)

W. D. Clancy with A. C. Kenton: *Woody Herman: Chronicles of the Herds* (New York and elsewhere, 1995)

LAWRENCE KOCH

Swope, (George) Rob(ert) [Bob] (*b* Washington, DC, 2 Dec 1926; *d* Washington, 9 Jan 1967). Trombonist, brother of Earl Swope. He recorded with the clarinetist Jerry Wald (1947) and performed and recorded with Buddy Rich (1947), Chubby Jackson (1948 – early 1949), Gene Krupa (1949–50), and Elliot Lawrence (1950–51). During the 1950s he led a trio in Washington, where he also belonged to The Orchestra, a big band that accompanied Charlie Parker (1953) and Dizzy Gillespie (1955). In New York he performed and recorded with the trumpeter Larry Sonn (1957) and worked briefly with Boyd Raeburn, Claude Thornhill, Jimmy Dorsey, and Louie Bellson. Later he returned to Washington and worked again as a leader. As a soloist Swope may be heard to advantage on *Godchild* (1949, Col. 38451), which he recorded with Jackson. (*FeatherE*)

Syeed, Luqman Abdul. *See* STEVE DAVIS (i).

Symonds, Nelson (*b* Halifax, or Hammonds Plains, near Halifax, Canada, 24 Sept 1933). Canadian guitarist. He toured in Canada and the USA with a carnival (1955–8), then settled in Montreal, where in the mid-1960s he came to notice accompanying visiting Americans (including Art Farmer, Benny Golson, Jimmy Heath, and Booker Ervin). With his own groups he took extended engagements in local clubs (including the Black Bottom and Rockhead's Paradise) and from the 1980s through the mid-1990s was a mainstay of the Festival International de Jazz de Montréal, where he received the Prix Oscar-Peterson in 1996. Despite the high regard in which he has been held, Symonds effectively went unrecorded until the 1990s; his intense and roughly virtuoso hard-bop style is documented by his own album *Getting Personal* (1991, Justin Time 44), as well as recordings with Dave Turner, including *Thanks for the Hospitality* (1993, DSM 3001).

Oral history material in *CaQMG*.

BIBLIOGRAPHY

EMC2

M. Miller: "My Head Will Never Get Big," *Jazz in Canada: Fourteen Lives* (Toronto, Buffalo, and London, 1982), 146

——: "Nelson Symonds," *Boogie, Pete & the Senator: Canadian Musicians in Jazz: the Eighties* (Toronto, 1987), 250

MARK MILLER

Symphonic jazz. A term coined in the 1920s partly in connection with attempts, some of them sponsored by Paul Whiteman, to fuse jazz with classical forms, and therefore a predecessor of the term THIRD STREAM. The tendency emerged before jazz was identified as such, and there are a number of works such as Frederick Delius's *Appalachia* (1896, rev. 1903), subtitled "Variations on an old Slave Song," which reveal a keen perception of specifically American song and dance idioms.

Perhaps symphonic jazz may be said to have begun with George Gershwin's one-act opera *Blue Monday* (1922), although a variety of comparable works appeared during the same period from both the classical and jazz camps, among them two ballets – Darius Milhaud's *La création du monde* (1923) and Cole Porter's *Within the Quota* (1923, revived as *Times Past*, 1970). It was *Blue Monday*, however, that led Whiteman to commission *Rhapsody in Blue* (1924), undoubtedly the most famous piece of symphonic jazz. Other pieces by Gershwin followed, such as the Piano Concerto (1925) and the folk opera *Porgy and Bess* (1935), which may be considered the movement's peak.

Whiteman meanwhile obtained a considerable number of other pieces from both classical and jazz composers, such as George Antheil's Jazz Symphony (1925, rev. 1955) and Ferde Grofé's *Metropolis* (*c*1928). These in turn were a stimulus for a variety of other works, notably in England. Indeed, though associated primarily with the 1920s, the tendencies embodied in symphonic jazz remained until the arrival in the late 1950s of third stream music. Later commissions by Whiteman included *The Blue Belles of Harlem* from Duke Ellington (1942) and *Scherzo à la russe* from Igor Stravinsky (1944).

Although the label "symphonic jazz" is in the strictest sense confined to Whiteman's circle, the principles implied therein clearly embrace a larger repertory. Ellington had always been aware of the endeavors of his predecessors, and began to step outside the normal time limits and functional purposes of much early jazz with such multisectional works as *Creole Rhapsody* (1931, two versions, *see* FORMS, §3), *Reminiscing in Tempo* (1935), and a number of other pieces. Classical music continues to be affected by jazz, notable instances being Stefan Wolpe's Quartet for trumpet, tenor saxophone, piano and percussion (1950) and Michael Tippett's Symphony no.3 (1970–72). Jazz likewise remains influenced by the large forms of classical music, examples including Carla Bley's opera *Escalator over the Hill* (1968–71), a latter-day *Porgy and Bess*, and Charlie Haden's *Ballad of the Fallen* (1982). None of this later music should be described as symphonic jazz, yet it would have been considerably different without that movement's earlier examples of cross-fertilization.

For further discussion *see* BANDS, §4, esp. (ii), and JAZZ (i), §III,4.

BIBLIOGRAPHY

P. Whiteman and M. M. McBride: *Jazz* (New York, 1926)
J. Sypniewski: *Ein Problem der Gegenwartsmusik: Jazz, unter besonderer Berücksichtigung des symphonisches Jazz (George Gershwin)* (diss., U. of Zurich, 1949)
M. Harrison: *A Jazz Retrospect* (Newton Abbot, England, 1976, rev. 2/1977/ *R*1991)

MAX HARRISON

Symphonola. Record label. It was owned by the Larkin Company of Buffalo and was used to issue items produced by Emerson in 1918 and 1919. The catalogue included some of Emerson's recordings of the Louisiana Five.

BIBLIOGRAPHY

B. Rust: *The American Record Label Book* (New Rochelle, NY, 1978), 291
A. Sutton: *Directory of American Disc Record Brands and Manufacturers, 1891–1943* (Westport, CT, and London, 1994), 149

HOWARD RYE

Synco Jazz band. Big band formed from the Synco Septet by William McKinney; in 1926 it became known as MCKINNEY'S COTTON PICKERS.

Syncopation. In measured music an effect of rhythmic displacement created by articulating weaker beats or metrical positions that do not fall on any of the main beats of the bar, while stronger beats are not articulated; *see* BEAT, §4(iii).

Synthesizer. An electronic instrument capable of generating and processing a wide variety of sounds. Synthesizers were first used as tools for composition in electronic music studios, but in the 1960s they began to play an increasingly important role in performance and to be used extensively by jazz musicians. However, in the 1990s this usage greatly diminished.

1. Technological development. 2. Use: (i) Introduction (ii) Keyboard synthesizers (iii) Other control devices (iv) Role of the synthesizer.

1. TECHNOLOGICAL DEVELOPMENT. The earliest instruments that employed the principles of synthesis were constructed in the mid-1950s, but it was not until 1964 that synthesizers were manufactured on a commercial basis. These instruments employed analogue synthesis, in which continuously varying voltages are used to control the operation of sound sources (oscillators) and sound processors (filters, modulators, envelope shapers, and mixers); this was the basis for synthesizers until the establishment of the digital instrument in the early 1980s. As technology advanced, various refinements and capabilities were added; for example, the first analogue synthesizers were monophonic (playing only one note at a time), but varying degrees of polyphony were added during the 1970s.

The analogue process can be imitated by a digital synthesizer, which combines discrete units of information in rapid succession. By the late 1980s the combination of the digital synthesizer and microprocessors led to the production of keyboard units which offered not only sound synthesis but also data storage (enabling immediate recall of previously programmed settings), sampling (the digital recording of external sounds, usually with the object of playing them back via the keyboard), and sequencing (programming the keyboard to play a series of notes); because they fulfilled so many functions, such multi-purpose units became known as workstations. Most digital synthesizers can also be linked to computers and other electronic devices, usually by means of MIDI (Musical Instrument Digital Interface), a system of standard code signals that was introduced in 1983 and updated in 1992. As digital synthesis developed there was a marked increase in the capability of instruments to produce polyphonic sounds and to play different timbres simultaneously.

In the late 1980s many manufacturers relinquished pure digital synthesis in favour of sample-and-synthesis, in which samples of "real" instruments are combined with synthesized sound. At the same time, reflecting a renewed interest in old analogue synthesizers, several companies began producing machines which contained digital samples of analogue synthesizer sounds. By 1999 some units featured physical modeling, in which computer software was used to alter the sounds of both conventional instruments and analogue synthesizers.

Some early synthesizers were controlled by touch-plates and ribbons, but the most common controller has been the standard chromatic keyboard. By the mid-1980s other systems had been considerably improved, and controllers resembling wind instruments, electric guitar, and (especially) drums had become quite common. However, by the mid-1990s changing fashions had reduced the demand for such controllers. Synthesizer technology also led to the development of the drum machine, a combined synthesizer and sequencer designed to play drum sounds; some units also included other instruments such as keyboards and bass.

2. USE.

(i) Introduction. During the late 1960s the modular synthesizer was in regular use in both rock and avant-garde art music, and its currency in these styles undoubtedly contributed to its adoption by jazz musicians. By 1970 many pianists had taken up electric piano in addition to or sometimes instead of the acoustic instrument, and several also doubled on electronic organ; for these players the synthesizer represented a logical extension of the means at their disposal. Small monophonic keyboard synthesizers such as the Minimoog, unlike any other keyboard instruments used in jazz, allowed the musician to play a melody line in any of a multitude of timbres, to inflect it with pitch bends and portamento (which are extremely idiomatic to jazz), and to vary the sustaining properties of notes; in general it provided a versatility of expression otherwise unavailable. Polyphonic synthesizers further expanded this facility and gave the player the opportunity to voice chords in

previously unobtainable colorations. The centrality of timbral manipulation to the concept of synthesis led to the instrument's adoption in styles such as free jazz and jazz-rock, in which the exploration of new sounds was prevalent. Accordingly, most musicians in older styles with long-established conventions, such as swing and mainstream jazz, avoided the synthesizer.

(ii) Keyboard synthesizers. Experiments combining jazz and taped electronic music took place as early as 1951, and the use of home-made electronic instruments and the investigation of the potential of signal processors was begun in the mid-1960s, notably by Gil Melle. However, the synthesizer itself was not adopted in jazz on a widespread basis until after 1968, when the manufacture of Robert Moog's modular system began on a larger scale. Early users of the modular Moog included Sun Ra (who played the instrument on his album *My Brother, the Wind*, i, 1969, Saturn 521), Emil Richards, Oliver Nelson, Dick Hyman, Richard Teitelbaum of Musica Elettronica Viva, and Paul Bley (collaborating with Annette Peacock in the Bley-Peacock Synthesizer Show); although it was designed for use in the studio, it was employed in concerts by some of these musicians, as well as by other players. Bley also used the ARP 2500 modular system for about four years before abandoning electronic instruments; it may be heard to advantage on his album *Revenge: the Bigger the Love the Greater the Hate* (1969, Pol. 244046). Of the two other synthesizers to be produced on a commercial basis before 1970, the Buchla and the Synket, only the latter found favor with improvising artists, among them Bill Smith (i) and the Gruppo di Improvvisazione Nuova Consonanza, and then only on a limited scale.

The first portable keyboard synthesizer, Moog's Minimoog, appeared in 1970; it remained a firm favorite with musicians for many years. Indeed, many continued to play it into the late 1990s, despite the vast technological superiority of later models, because its particularly rich timbre was not matched by other instruments; however, in the 1990s sampling and physical modeling closely imitated the sounds of such analogue machines without the instability and unreliability associated with the originals. The original Minimoog may be heard on Sun Ra's album *It's After the End of the World* (1970, MPS 15289). This instrument and two similar synthesizers, the Odyssey and the 2600, which were introduced in 1971 by ARP, were only monophonic, but they offered a wide range of sounds and resources in a single small unit, and they also introduced a pitch-bend controller. This is operated by the left hand and normally takes the form of a wheel – as on the Minimoog, which provides an average compass of pitch variation of a minor 3rd (though in some machines it is as much as an octave) upwards or downwards.

The development of jazz-rock by Miles Davis's group from the late 1960s, and by several of his former colleagues from 1971 (in such ensembles as Weather Report, Return to Forever, and the Mahavishnu Orchestra), was closely linked with the proliferation of electronic instruments within the realm of jazz. From playing electric piano with Davis, Herbie Hancock, Chick Corea, and Joe Zawinul soon turned to synthesizers, although another of Davis's sidemen, Keith Jarrett, did not. For example, Hancock used the ARP Odyssey for the bass line at the beginning of *Chameleon* (from the album *Headhunters*, 1973, Col. KC32731), Corea played particularly interesting Minimoog solos on the tracks *Nite Sprite* and *Lenore* (from the album *The Leprechaun*, 1975, Pol. 6062), and Zawinul made use of the ARP 2600 to simulate a trombone on *River People* (from Weather Report's album *Mr. Gone*, c1978, Col. JC35358). (In addition musicians that had worked with Davis who were not keyboard players, notably Wayne Shorter, John McLaughlin, and Billy Cobham, explored synthesizer controllers in other forms (see (iii) below).) Others who adopted the Minimoog at an early stage were Sun Ra, George Duke, and Jan Hammer, who used it as a solo instrument on such recordings as the Mahavishnu Orchestra's *Birds of Fire* (1972, Col. KC31996).

From the late 1960s other companies began to manufacture synthesizers in Europe, Japan, and the USA. In 1974 the American company Oberheim produced the first commercially available polyphonic instruments, the Four-, Six-, and Eight-voice models. Among the first jazz musicians to use these were Corea, Zawinul (who played an Oberheim on the title track of Weather Report's album *Black Market*, c1976, Col. PC34099), Lyle Mays, and Hammer. Hammer controlled the synthesizer by means of the Probe, a four-octave portable keyboard which is suspended from the shoulder like a guitar; this and other similar keyboard controllers such as the Clavitar (played by Hancock and Duke) permitted the musician to move around on stage while performing and to step forward to take solos.

Gil Evans introduced parts for the synthesizer into his scores in 1971 and Quincy Jones frequently employed the instrument from the mid-1970s. Free-jazz musicians such as Michael Waisvisz (working with Steve Lacy and Willem Breuker) and Wolfgang Dauner also began to explore its possibilities. In the second half of the decade it became more widely accepted, particularly (but by no means exclusively) by jazz-rock musicians, many of whom assembled substantial arrays of keyboards that surrounded them in performance on three sides. But the increasing use of electronic instruments did not mean that the piano was abandoned. Indeed several keyboard players avoided the synthesizer for long periods of their careers, notably Hancock and Corea, who took up the instrument again after many years in 1985. Outside jazz-rock a number of musicians, particularly in Europe, made periodic use of the synthesizer; these included Neil Ardley, Alvin Curran, Gordon Beck, George Gruntz, Jasper van 't Hof, members of the group Nucleus, Stan Tracey, John Taylor, Vyacheslav Ganelin, Graham Collier, Muhal Richard Abrams, and Chris Barber.

In 1976 the first fully polyphonic instruments appeared, beginning with the Polymoog, which was for some time Teitelbaum's main instrument; this was followed by Sequential Circuits's Prophet 5 and several models each from Korg, Oberheim, Roland, and Yamaha. All of these enabled the user to create a huge variety of sounds. Most of them also offered some form of programmability, a storage facility which memorizes timbres that can then be recalled instantly as required (on non-programmable synthesizers sounds are lost as soon as the setting is changed). Around this time new companies began manufacturing larger, computer-based instruments, including the PPG Wave Computer, the Fairlight CMI, and the Synclavier. Largely because of their cost these highly sophisticated digital systems were employed in jazz relatively rarely, although van't Hof and Oscar Peterson used the PPG and Hancock and Hammer the Fairlight. Among those who performed on the Synclavier were Corea, Duke, Peterson, Jean-Luc Ponty, and Mays, who played the instrument on the title track of Pat Metheny's album *Offramp* (1980, ECM 1190). Cheaper digital synthesizers began to appear in the early 1980s; Yamaha's DX7, which was first manufactured in 1983, rapidly became the best-selling synthesizer ever produced. An extremely versatile, fully programmable machine, it could imitate many other instruments with remarkable fidelity and found favor with such established jazz musicians as Sun Ra, Davis, and John Surman. In the 1990s an interest in reviving earlier forms of jazz led some performers to begin playing original analogue synthesizers again.

Unlike most other commodities, digital equipment becomes cheaper as the technology develops. Thus, whereas analogue synthesizers were available in the 1970s only to the more successful musicians, digital instruments can be afforded by those less affluent. An important consequence of this in the 1980s was the widespread adoption of the instruments by the professional and amateur alike. However, in the 1990s the interest in swing, bop, and other earlier jazz forms considerably lessened that effect.

(iii) Other control devices. Several control systems have been developed that make the synthesizer available to musicians other than keyboard players. Special drums or drum pads may be used to trigger percussion sounds, which are either synthesized or, on later equipment, sampled. These included the Moog drum, which controlled a Minimoog and was first manufactured in the early 1970s; it was used by Billy Cobham from 1973 and played by Joe Gallivan in Gil Evans's orchestra in 1975. One of the most popular drum synthesizer systems among jazz musicians was the Simmons set, which was played by Cobham, Jon Hiseman, Bill Bruford, Steve Smith (in Steps Ahead), and Tony Williams. Cobham was also one of the first jazz musicians to explore the potential of the electronic drum machine. Although the rhythmic rigidity of the device discouraged its widespread adoption in jazz, it was employed to good effect by certain jazz-rock musicians, notably Hancock and Bill Evans (iii). A controller for pitched percussion, Simmons's Silicon Mallet, resembles a vibraphone; it was introduced in 1987 and played by such musicians as Orphy Robinson in Courtney Pine's Jazz Warriors.

Two controllers in the form of wind instruments were developed in the mid-1970s. The Lyricon was played for a time by Wayne Shorter (on *Black Market*, among other recordings), Sonny Rollins (on such pieces as *Tai-chi*, on his album *Don't Ask*, 1979, Mlst. 9090), Tom Scott, Michal Urbaniak, Bennie Maupin, and Klaus Doldinger. The Electronic Valve Instrument (EVI), invented by Nyle Steiner and sometimes known as the Steinerphone, was employed by several members of Sun Ra's Arkestra. In 1987 the Japanese company Akai began production of an updated EVI and a related controller, the Electronic Wind Instrument (EWI); the latter was used by such musicians as Michael Brecker (on his album *Michael Brecker*, 1987, MCA/Imp. 5980) and Phil Todd of Nucleus. The introduction in the same year of a new model by Yamaha, the WX7, indicated substantial interest in wind controllers, but by the late 1990s the use of such instruments, along with the guitar synthesizer discussed below, had declined. In the early 1990s perhaps half of a performance by Brecker featured the EWI, but by 1997 he was playing his first instrument, tenor saxophone, almost exclusively.

Controllers in the form of guitars, known as guitar synthesizers, were introduced by Roland in 1977 and by ARP (the Avatar) the following year; these were played by John Abercrombie, Bill Frisell, Terje Rypdal, David Torn, Mike Stern (in Steps Ahead), and John McLaughlin. Pat Metheny used such an instrument to trigger a Synclavier on the title track of *Offramp* (1981, ECM 1216) and also played the Roland GR300; Lee Ritenour and Allan Holdsworth employed the computerized SynthAxe. However, by the late 1990s only Metheny made persistent use of the guitar synthesizer. Holdsworth, a progressive musician who had embraced the SynthAxe with enthusiasm in the 1980s, abandoned it a few years later in the face of adverse reaction from his audiences.

(iv) Role of the synthesizer. During the late 1960s the use of the synthesizer was restricted largely to the recording studio because the equipment was bulky and difficult to transport. More portable instruments were developed by the early 1970s which became popular in live performance. In the 1980s the synthesizer was often a studio instrument of choice; several jazz recordings of this period depended heavily on synthesizers, drum machines, and sophisticated digital effects. The best-known of these is Miles Davis's album *Tutu* (1986, WB 254904), on which the majority of the instrumental sounds, other than the trumpet, are synthetic; recordings by Don Cherry, Eddie Harris, Bill Evans (iii), and Jamaaladeen Tacuma also made considerable use of such equipment. At first it was difficult to reproduce complex synthesized sounds in concerts, but digitization, and in particular MIDI, largely eliminated such problems. Some pianists who did not use the synthesizer in performance employed it in the studio, often as a tool for composition; these included Oscar Peterson and Ray Charles.

Other musicians who were not principally keyboard players occasionally played synthesizers both in the studio and on stage; among these were Davis, Ralph Towner, Jean-Luc Ponty, and John Surman. Particularly interesting is Surman's technique of setting the instrument to play repetitive patterns and slowly changing textures, over which he then performed saxophone solos; this may be heard to advantage on the track *Sunday Morning*, from the album *Such Winters of Memory* (1982, ECM 1254). George Lewis (ii) developed a program that enabled a computer to respond to a soloist's playing by instantly composing an appropriate accompaniment in a free-jazz style, which was then sent to a synthesizer via MIDI. In the 1980s many ensembles used at least one instrument and several groups comprehended two or more synthesizer players.

In the 1990s the growing popularity of earlier, non-electric forms of jazz generally reduced the role of the synthesizer; among those who continued to use it were Adam Holzman, Jim Beard, and Tom Coster. Coster was at the forefront of synthesizer-based fusion in the mid-1990s, but his readoption of his first keyboard, the accordion, in 1998 shows how pervasive was the retrospective mood of the period.

BIBLIOGRAPHY

C. Harman: "Music Moves into the Future," *BMI: the Many Worlds of Music* (1970), summer, 10

D. Rubinstein: Liner notes, H. Hancock: *Treasure Chest* (WB 2807, 1974)

R. Townley: "Hancock Plugs In," *DB*, xli/17 (1974), 13

T. Darter: "Chick Corea: Multi-keyboardist Giant," *CK*, i/1 (1975), 20

H. Nolan: "Jan Hammer: Saved by the Synthesizer," *DB*, xliii/5 (1976), 17

L. Underwood: "Chick Corea: Soldering the Elements, Determining the Future," *DB*, xliii/17 (1976), 13

D. Milano and others: "Herbie Hancock," *CK*, iii/11 (1977), 26

D. Milano: "An Introduction to Polyphonic Synthesizers," *CK*, iv/4 (1978), 10

——: "Jan Hammer," *CK*, iv/10 (1978), 20

C. Silvert: "Joe Zawinul: Wayfaring Genius," *DB*, xlv (1978), no.11, p.13; no.12, p.21
M. Davis: "Lyle Mays," *CK*, vi/10 (1980), 12
J.-E. Berendt: *Das Grosse Jazzbuch: von New Orleans bis Jazz Rock* (Frankfurt am Main, Germany, 1981; Eng. trans. as *The Jazz Book: from New Orleans to Fusion and Beyond*, Westport, CT, 1982)
D. Forte: "Pat Metheny," *GP*, xv/12 (1981), 90
G. Armbruster: "Oscar Peterson: a Jazz Piano Giant Talks about his Synthesizer Debut," *Keyboard*, ix/10 (1983), 56
J. Diliberto and K. Haas: "Lyle Mays: Straight Talk on Synths," *DB*, 1/7 (1983), 25
L. Lyons: "Chick Corea," "Herbie Hancock," "Joe Zawinul," *The Great Jazz Pianists, Speaking of their Lives and Music* (New York, 1983)
H. Davies: "Electronic Instruments," *GroveI*
H. Mandel: "Jean-Luc Ponty's Electronic Muse," *DB*, li/1 (1984), 18
D. Roberts and H. Davies: "Synthesizer," *GroveI*
B. Milkowski: "Allan Holdsworth's New Horizons," *DB*, lii/11 (1985), 19
T. Mulhern: "Allan Holdsworth, Lee Ritenour: SynthAxe," *GP*, xx/6 (1986), 109
R. Valentino: "Le altre elettroniche," *Nuova Atlantide: il continente della musica elettronica 1900–1986* (Venice, Italy, 1986) [exhibition catalogue; incl. discography]
B. Doerschuk and others: "Miles Davis: the Picasso of Invisible Art," *Keyboard*, xiii/10 (1987), 64
J. Aikin: "Plug in Here: the ABC's of Techno-music Literacy," *Keyboard*, xiv/6 (1988), 34
D. Milano and others: "American Synthesizer Builders," *Keyboard*, xiv/5 (1988), 42
J. Rothstein: *MIDI: a Comprehensive Introduction* (Madison, WI, 1992)
P. Trynka, ed.: *Rock Hardware* (London, 1996)

HUGH DAVIES/MARK GILBERT

Szabados, György (*b* Budapest, 13 July 1939). Hungarian pianist, composer, and arranger. He formed a band in 1955, and in 1963 presented a program of his compositions at the Dália youth jazz club in Budapest. He performed mostly as a soloist and with small groups, and from the late 1960s was regarded as Hungary's leading exponent of avant-garde jazz; in 1972 he led a quintet in a performance of his *Psalm of the Axe* at the festival in Donostia, Spain, and won first prize in the free-jazz category. He has written works for chamber orchestra and ballets, and has recorded several of his own compositions, including the title tracks of his albums *B–A–C–H Impressions* (1964), *The Wedding* (1974), and *Adyton* (1982). From 1982 he performed occasionally with Anthony Braxton, with whom he recorded an album of duos in 1984, and in the mid-1980s he formed the Makuz Orchestra. Szabados developed his style of free jazz evidently without knowing of parallel trends in the USA. He has been influenced by folk music and by the works of such composers as Béla Bartók. He is the author, with T. Váczi, of *A zene kettős természetű fénye* (Double natured light of the music) (Budapest, 1990).

SELECTED RECORDINGS

As unaccompanied soloist: *A szent főnixmadár dürrögései* [Ruttings of the sacred phoenix bird] (1991, Szabados 001)
Duos with A. Braxton: *Szabraxtondos* (1984, Krém 17909)
As leader: *B–A–C–H Impressions* (1964, Qual. 7279–80); *The Wedding* (1974, Hungaroton 17475); *Adyton* (1982, Krém 17724); *A szarvassá vált fiák* [Sons turned into stags] (1985, Krém 37215); *Homoki zene* [Sands music] (1991, Adyton 05); *Elfelejtett énekek* [Forgotten songs] (1996, Fonó/Adyton 012); with Roscoe Mitchell: *Jelenés* [Revelation] (1997, Fonó 038-2)

BIBLIOGRAPHY

G. Turi: *Azt mondom: jazz* [I say that: jazz] (Budapest, 1983), 79
B. Noglik: "György Szabados Forgotten Songs," *Jazz* [Basel, Switzerland], no.6 (1985)
G. Turi: *Jazz from Hungary* (Budapest, 1987), 22
G. G. Simon: *The Book of Hungarian Jazz* (Budapest, 1992)
——: *Magyar jazzdiszkografia, 1905–1994* (Budapest, 1994)

GÉZA GÁBOR SIMON, RAINER E. LOTZ (with BERT NOGLIK)

Szabo, Frank (J.) (*b* Budapest, 16 Sept 1952). Trumpeter. He left Hungary following the failed revolution in 1956. After studying in Los Angeles with Tom Scott (1962–9) he played in Las Vegas and toured with Harry James (1970–71); he also performed, recorded, and toured in Europe, Japan, and the USA with Ray Charles (1971). From 1971 into the 1990s he was a freelance musician in the Los Angeles area, working in television and films as well as recording studios and in concert; his jazz recordings include more than 30 albums as a sideman, mainly with big bands, notably with Louie Bellson, Count Basie, Chuck Mangione, the Capp–Pierce Juggernaut, Grover Mitchell, Don Menza, Gene Harris, Bill Holman, Charlie Shoemake, Teddy Edwards, the saxophonist Roger Neumann, and Gerald Wilson. He also toured with Basie (December 1974 – October 1975, January–September 1983) and Bellson (performing in England in 1980), and worked on occasion with Buddy Rich, Harry Edison, and Woody Herman.

BIBLIOGRAPHY

Feather–Gitler '70s; *SheridanCB*
G. G. Simon: *Magyar jazzdiszkografia, 1905–1994* (Budapest, 1994)

BK, GÉZA GÁBOR SIMON

Szabó, Gábor (*b* Budapest, 8 March 1936; *d* Budapest, 26 Feb 1982). Guitarist, composer, arranger, and bandleader. He played in modern jazz groups in Hungary from 1952 and made his first recording for a film soundtrack in 1955 as a member of Lajos Martiny's band. The following year he began his studio recording career in jazz and also recorded for a Voice of America broadcast in Budapest, but he left Hungary after the failed revolution. While attending the Berklee School of Music he was a member of Marshall Brown's International Youth Band, which performed at the Newport Jazz Festival in 1958. In 1959 a Berklee big band under the direction of Herb Pomeroy recorded Szabó's composition and arrangement *Dilemma*. From 1962 to 1965 he played West Coast jazz as a member of Chico Hamilton's quintet and in 1964 he was named "best new jazz guitarist" by *Down Beat*. He made his first recording as a leader in 1965 and that same year arranged Hamilton's score to Roman Polanski's film *Repulsion*; he also toured with Charles Lloyd, Gary McFarland, Bob Thiele's New Happy-Times Orchestra, the singer Lena Horne, the percussionist Coke Escovedo, and Charles Earland. From 1969 his playing became strongly influenced by blues and rock, and his composition *Gypsy Queen* was recorded in various stylistic settings, the best known version being by the Latin rock guitarist Carlos Santana. After settling in Los Angeles he worked in television. In his last years Szabó moved freely between the USA and Hungary, where he broadcast on Hungarian television (1971, 1978, 1981) and played in jazz clubs with, among others, the Interbrass Band, Csaba Deseő and Aladár Pege (1974), the drummer Imre Kőszegi (1974, 1978), and the pianist Attila Garay (1981). In 1979 Szabó's band recorded with Chick Corea as guest soloist.

SELECTED RECORDINGS

As leader: *Gypsy '66* (1965, Imp. 9105); *Jazz Raga* (1966, Imp. 9128); *The Sorcerer* (1967, Imp. 9146); *More Sorcery* (1967, Imp. 9167); *Femme fatale* (1979, Pepita 707)
As sideman: [no leader]: *Jazz in the Classroom* (1959, Berklee 4), incl. Dilemma; C. Hamilton: *Drumfusion* (1962, Col. CS8607); *Passin' Thru* (1962, Imp. 29); *Man from Two Worlds* (1963, Imp. 59); P. Desmond: *Skylark* (1973, CTI 6039)

BIBLIOGRAPHY

FeatherE; *Feather–Gitler '70s*
P. Rivelli: "Gabor Szabo," *Jazz*, v/8 (New York, 1966), 8
D. DeMicheal: "Gabor Szabo: Jazz and the Changing Times," *DB*, xxxiv/20 (1967), 17
P. Senoff: "Gabor Szabo Interview," *J&P*, ix/9 (1970), 37
M. Summerfield: "Gabor Szabo," *The Jazz Guitar: its Evolution and its Players* (Gateshead, England, 1978, 4/1998, as *The Jazz Guitar: its Evolution, Players and Personalities since 1900*)
L. Tomkins: "Gabor Szabo," *CI*, xviii/4 (1979), 20
H. Wong: Obituary, *DB*, xlix/6 (1982), 14
K. Libisch: *Feketére festve. Szabó Gábor gitárművész bio-diszkográfiája* [Painted black: bio-discography of the guitar artist Gabor Szabo] (Budapest, 1993, 4/1998)

FRANK A. DIBUSSOLO/GÉZA GÁBOR SIMON

Szabó, Sándor (*b* Törökszentmiklós, Hungary, 21 March 1956). Hungarian guitarist and composer. After private classical guitar studies he began to investigate the music of a great variety of cultures and became increasingly involved with improvisation; the influences of Arabia, India, the Far East, and his homeland may be clearly heard in his playing. Szabó has regularly toured Europe and the USA, appearing at numerous festivals. He has given performances on a 16-string guitar, and he has composed and played contemporary experimental music, introducing a new electronic sound which he calls AmbiMorph. He has recorded as an unaccompanied soloist and has also made a number of recordings with the drummer and percussionist Balázs Major, among them a trio album with the guitarist Gilbert Isbin.

SELECTED RECORDINGS

As unaccompanied soloist: *Alexandria* (1997, Acoustic Music 319-1118.2); *Gaia and Aries* (1998, Acoustic Music 319-1156-2)
Duos with B. Major: *Ritual of a Spiritual Communion* (1986, Leo 157)
As leader: with B. Major and G. Isbin: *The Clear Perception of Provenance Within* (1987, Hwyl 2); SzaMaBa Trio: *Hypnos* (1988–92, Tandem-Ferdinandus–Hungarian Society for Jazz Research 2002)

BIBLIOGRAPHY

G. G. Simon: *The Book of Hungarian Jazz* (Budapest, 1992)
——: *Magyar jazzdiszkografia, 1905–1994* (Budapest, 1994)
——: *Magyar jazztörtéret* [Hungarian jazz history] (Budapest, 1999)

GÉZA GÁBOR SIMON

Szafran, Lora (*b* Krosno, Poland, 24 July 1960). Polish singer. After graduating from the jazz department at the academy of music in Katowice she sang in the groups Walk Away (1986–8) and New Presentation (1988–94). She gave successful performances at festivals in Sopot (1990) and at Bregenz, Austria, and Cesme, Turkey (both 1991), and worked with such leading musicians as Jan Wróblewski, Włodzimierz Nahorny, Andrzej Jagodziński, Henryk Miśkiewicz, and Bernard Maseli, with whom she recorded an album in which themes by Chopin have been set to original lyrics (1994).

SELECTED RECORDINGS

As leader: *W górę głowa* (Heads up) (1991, Polskie Nagrania 108)
As sideman: New Presentation: *Lonesome Dancer* (1989, Polskie Nagrania 2840); *You've Changed* (1992, Power Bros. 00117); B. Maseli: *Tylko Chopin* (Only Chopin) (1994, Polskie Nagrania 056)

BIBLIOGRAPHY

A. Chodkowski, ed.: *Encyklopedia muzyki* (Warsaw, 1995)

ADAM CEGIELSKI, BK

Szakcsi Lakatos, Béla [Szakcsi; Sa-Chi] (*b* Budapest, 8 July 1943). Hungarian keyboard player, composer, arranger, and leader. In 1970 he gave a performance to great acclaim in Aladár Pege's quartet at the Montreux International Festival, and thereafter he played both in his own and in Pege's groups. From 1987 he recorded for GRP simply as Szakcsi or Sa-Chi. In the 1990s he spent periods in Switzerland and France and performed and recorded with the Hungarian reed player Victor Burghardt and with Yoch'ko Seffer; late in the decade he gave concerts with the Hungarian drummer Imre Kőszegi.

SELECTED RECORDINGS

Duos with I. Kőszegi: *Journey in Time* (1997, Hsart 1)
As leader: *Sa-Chi* (1988, GRP 1045), *Straight Ahead* (1993, GRP 97582); with V. Burghardt: *La magia dell' improvviso: Live* (1994–6, Matagot 0301)
As sideman: A. Pege: *Montreux Inventions* (1970, Hungaroton 17418); Special EFX: *Mystique* (1987, GRP 1033); *Double Feature* (1987, GRP 1048)

BIBLIOGRAPHY

G. Turi: *Azt mondom: jazz* [I say that: jazz] (Budapest, 1983), 137
——: *Jazz from Hungary* (Budapest, 1987), 23
G. G. Simon: *The Book of Hungarian Jazz* (Budapest, 1992)
——: *Magyar jazzdiszkografia, 1905–1994* (Budapest, 1994)

GÉZA GÁBOR SIMON

Szukalski, Tomasz [Szakal] (*b* Warsaw, 8 Jan 1948). Polish tenor and soprano saxophonist and bass clarinetist. He played piano from the age of five and later studied clarinet at school and at the high school of music in Warsaw (from 1968). In 1964 he began to play tenor saxophone in amateur dixieland bands. By 1970 he had established a national reputation, and thereafter he performed and recorded with Zbigniew Namysłowski (1971–5) and Tomasz Stańko (intermittently from 1973). He played regularly with the orchestra of the Studio Jazzowe Polskiego Radia (Polish Radio Jazz Studio), which Jan Wróblewski led until 1977, and in 1978 he joined the cooperative group The Quartet. This group, consisting of Sławomir Kulpowicz, Paweł Jarzębski, and Janusz Stefański, started a trend in Poland for a return to acoustic jazz, following a period during the 1970s when electric instruments had been popular. Later Szukalski recorded in a cooperative fusion trio with Wojciech Karolak and Czesław Bartkowski (1984) and as the leader of a quartet including Bartkowski (1986). He performed with his trio into the 1990s, and in 2000 he worked as the co-leader of a quartet with Jarosław Śmietana. Szukalski is experienced in many different styles but acknowledges in particular the influence of Jan Garbarek's quartet of the 1970s.

SELECTED RECORDINGS

As leader: with W. Karolak and C. Bartkowski: *Time Killers* (1984, Poljazz 62); *Tina Kamila* (1986, Muza 2250); *Tina Blues* (1986, Wipe 7084); *Body and Soul* (1988, Muza 2807)
As sideman: T. Stańko: *Twet* (1974, Muza 1138); *Balladyna* (1975, ECM 1071); E. Vesala: *Rodina* (1976, Love 189); *Satu* (1976, ECM 1088); T. Stańko: *Almost Green* (1978, Leo 008); The Quartet: *Loaded* (1979, Leo 010); E. Vesala: *Neitsytmatka* (Maiden voyage) (1979, Polarvox 11014)

BIBLIOGRAPHY

J. Byrczek: "Eurojazz Personalities: Poland," *JF* [intl edn], no.18 (1972), 87
R. Kowal: "Tomasz Szukalski: 'Music Must Pack a Punch'," *JF* [intl edn], no.41 (1976), 51 [incl. discography]
J. Hawryluk: "Tomasz Szukalski," *Ruch muzyczny*, xxxvii/13 (1993), 3

WOLFRAM KNAUER/ADAM CEGIELSKI, BK

T

Tabackin, Lew(is Barry) (*b* Philadelphia, 26 March 1940). Saxophonist and flutist. He first learned flute, took up tenor saxophone in high school, and attended the Philadelphia Conservatory of Music (BM 1962) – though his studies outside this institution, notably with the composer Vincent Persichetti, had more impact on his development. Towards the end of a period of army service (1962–5) he played in New Jersey with Tal Farlow and Don Friedman, among others. He then moved to New York, where he worked with big bands led by Les and Larry Elgart, Cab Calloway (briefly in 1965), Buddy Morrow, Maynard Ferguson (recording *c*1966), Thad Jones and Mel Lewis, Clark Terry, Duke Pearson (recording in 1967–8), Chuck Israels, and Joe Henderson. In 1967 he first played with Toshiko Akiyoshi, at a concert which she gave in Town Hall, New York. Tabackin led a trio at La Bohème, Philadelphia, in 1968–9, and played in other small groups with Elvin Jones, Donald Byrd, Attila Zoller, and Roland Hanna. In 1969 he worked on television with Doc Severinsen in "The Tonight Show" and then with Bob Rosengarden in "The Dick Cavett Show"; that same year he appeared as a soloist in Europe with the Hamburg Jazz Workshop and the Radiojazzgruppen (i) and in the International Jazz Quartet (with Daniel Humair, George Gruntz, and Israels).

Toshiko Akiyoshi and Lew Tabackin, June 1979

In 1970, with Akiyoshi (whom he had married the previous year), Tabackin formed a quartet which toured Japan and appeared at the Expo '70 jazz festival. The couple moved to North Hollywood in mid-1972 and jointly led a big band from March 1973, which continued to perform, with Tabackin as a principal soloist, until around 1984 (for details *see* Akiyoshi, toshiko); in 1983 they returned to New York. Tabackin also played in a variety of other contexts, notably in recording sessions with the big bands of Louie Bellson (1977) and Bill Berry (1978), in a small group led by Shelly Manne, and in his own small groups – often a trio, which in its first years frequently included Billy Higgins. After leaving Akiyoshi's band he toured internationally as a soloist. He formed small groups with Dannie Richmond in the years before the drummer's death in 1988, and that year he toured with Dave Holland and then as a replacement for Buddy Tate (who was ill) in Buck Clayton's big band. From 1989 into the 1990s he made a succession of small-group albums as a leader which received some cricial acclaim (these were mainly for the Concord label, for which he also recorded as a guest soloist with Harold Alden in 1996). In 1992, in the course of the making of a video documentary (released in 1993), he was heard again with Akiyoshi's big band and interviewed.

Tabackin's flute playing combines a classical approach with an oriental flavor that is often enhanced by the style of Akiyoshi's distinctive arrangements. His work on tenor saxophone, by contrast, is based firmly in the jazz tradition; its idiom and timbre display an individual blend of influences from many of the performers active before John Coltrane.

Video oral history material in *NCH* (HCJA).

SELECTED RECORDINGS

As leader: with T. Akiyoshi: *Kogun* (1974, RCA JPL1-0236); *Tabackin* (1974, RCA RVP6271); *Black and Tan Fantasy* (1979, JAM 5005); with T. Akiyoshi: *Farewell to Mingus* (1980, JAM 003); *Lew Tabackin Quartet*

(1983, Ewd 90025); *Desert Lady* (1989, Conc. 4411); *I'll Be Seeing You* (1992, Conc. 4528); *What a Little Moonlight Can Do* (1994, Conc. 4617); *Live at Vartan Jazz* (1994, Vartan Jazz 003); *Tenority* (1996, Conc. 4733)
As sideman: D. Byrd: *Electric Byrd* (1970, BN 84349); S. Manne: *Essence* (1977, Gal. 5101); F. Hubbard: *Sweet Return* (1983, Atl. 80108); H. Alden: on *Take your Pick* (1996, Conc. 4743), The Gig, How Deep is the Ocean

SELECTED FILMS AND VIDEOS

Southern Crossing (1980); Toshiko Akiyoshi: Jazz is my Native Language (1984); Toshiko Akiyoshi's Jazz Orchestra Featuring Lew Tabackin: Strive for Jive (1993)

BIBLIOGRAPHY

Feather–Gitler '70s
Z. Stewart: "Toshiko Akiyoshi/Lew Tabackin," *Musician, Player & Listener*, i/9 (1977), 24
L. Feather: "Lew Tabackin: Tabackin Road," *DB*, xlv/2 (1978), 14
Liner notes, *Tabackin* (IC 1038, 1978)
"Lew Tabackin," *Jazz Echo*, no.39 (1979), 6
C. Sheridan: "The Manchurian Candidate," *JJI*, xxxii/1 (1979), 6
G. Endress: *Jazz Podium: Musiker über sich selbst* (Stuttgart, Germany, 1980), 174
L. Feather: *The Passion for Jazz* (New York, 1980/*R*1990), 109
C. Kuhl: "Akiyoshi & Tabackin: Interview," *Cadence*, viii/7 (1982), 8
H. Hill: "Lew Tabackin: Tenor Gladness," *Coda*, no.197 (1984), 4
M. Richards: "Lew Tabackin," *JJI*, xlii (1989), no.1, p.6; no.2, p.20
For further recordings and bibliography *see* Akiyoshi, toshiko.

DAVID WILD/BK

Tabane, Philip (Nchipi) (*b* Pretoria, *c*1940). South African guitarist, singer, flutist, and percussionist. He took up electric guitar in 1954 and started performing four years later. From 1961 he led groups known usually as Malombo (but also as Malombo Jazzmen, Venda-Malombo, and Malombo Jazz Band). The first such group was a cooperative formed with Julian Bahula and the flutist Abbey Cindi which appeared to great acclaim as the Malombo Jazzmen at the Castle Lager Jazz Festival in 1963 and 1964. It disbanded when Bahula left for Britain, but Tabane later re-formed it as a duo with his nephew Gabriel Mabi Thobejane on percussion (1970); the two men toured South Africa, appeared at the Newport New York, Montreux, and North Sea festivals, and performed with the addition of Bheki Mseleku for a tour in 1977. During this period Pharoah Sanders, Miles Davis, Max Roach, Clark Terry, and Herbie Mann made guest appearances with Malombo. Thobejane left to join Sipho Gumede and Khaya Mahlangu in the group Sakhile in 1982, and thereafter Malombo continued as a trio comprising Tabane and the percussionists Oupa Mahapi Monareng and Raymond "Fish" Mphunye Motau. They may be seen in the documentary video *The Malombo Men* (1999); another video of a performance by Malombo is held in the collection of the Caribbean Cultural Center in New York.

Tabane comes close to being *sui generis* – almost unthinkable in jazz. Malombo means "spirit" in Sotho, and Tabane's mother was a *sedupe* (a type of traditional healer) who taught him songs and the mysticism of sound. While it is unlikely that he has heard recordings by Jimi Hendrix, he uses guitar amplifiers and effects as an intergral part of his own sound in a similar way. He appreciated Wes Montgomery and others, but the influence of American jazz seems minimal in his personal language. Performances often incorporate his playing up to six flutes simultaneously (including two nose flutes), "Malombo drums" (wooden and cowhide instruments made by Tabane and his percussionists), singing, and dancing. His music, almost all of which he composes, is a personal reinvention of Venda music inspired by free-jazz improvisation. He has been awarded an honorary doctorate from the University of Venda.

SELECTED RECORDINGS

As leader of Malombo: *Pele pele* (Atl. ATC8003, 1976); *Sangoma* (Atl. ATH4024, 1978); *Malombo* (Kaya 300, 1984); on [various artists]: *The Indestructible Beat of Soweto*, iii (Earthworks 17, 1990), Machaba

BIBLIOGRAPHY

O. Musi: "Malombo Jazz Trio," *Drum* [Johannesburg] (1964), Nov, 35
J. Goodwin: "The Sound of Music: African," *Christian Science Monitor* (31 March 1977)
J. Pareles: "Malombo," *New York Times* (10 May 1988)
——: "Jazz Festival: from African Roots, New Rhythms," *New York Times* (24 June 1989)
<http://www.music.org.za/artists/malombo/> (2000)

DARIUS BRUBECK

Tabányi, Mihály (*b* Pilis, Hungary, 1 Feb 1921). Hungarian accordionist, composer, arranger, and bandleader. He became well known when he won first prize in an accordion competition and made a film in Budapest in 1940. He first recorded as a swing soloist in 1942 and from 1942 to 1949 led several jazz and dance-music recording bands; he also toured Europe, Lebanon, and the USA as a leader. Among his sidemen were Elek Bacsik, Attila Zoller, and the tenor saxophonist Rudolf Wirth. He made further recordings as a leader from the early 1950s to 1963, with Aladár Pege, Andor Kovács, Gyula Kovács, and Lajos Dudás among his sidemen. In the 1990s he gave concerts and made new recordings as a featured soloist with the Palermo Boogie Gang. His playing may be heard to advantage on *Suzy* (1949), one of his own arrangements.

SELECTED RECORDINGS

As leader: Suzy (1949, Tonalit C307); *Tabányi együttes* [Tabányi ensemble] (1962, Qual. 7170-71); *The Pinocchio Ensemble*, i–ii (1963, Qual. 7231, 7234)
As sideman with Palermo Boogie Gang: *Red Hot Blues* (1993, Mafioso 1001)

GÉZA GÁBOR SIMON, RAINER E. LOTZ

Tabbal, Tani (Abdul-Batin) (*b* Chicago, 16 Jan 1954). Drummer. He worked with Phil Cohran in Chicago, then in 1976 moved to Detroit, where he joined Griot Galaxy, an ensemble led by the saxophonist Faruq Z. Bey and Jaribu Shahid; after Bey was injured in a motorcycle accident in 1984 Tabbal helped to organize the group into the 1990s. In the early 1980s he joined Roscoe Mitchell's Sound Ensemble (1980) and worked alongside Hugh Ragin in Mitchell's trio (recording in 1981). Around this time he formed a cooperative trio with Spencer Barefield and the saxophonist Anthony Holland which performed and recorded at Nickelsdorf Konfrontationen (1984). Later he was a member of Geri Allen's trio (late 1980s – early 1990s). Tabbal continued his association with Mitchell in the group Note Factory from 1992, and from around 1993 he toured and recorded with James Carter. He also performed with Oscar Brown, Jr., and Jackie McLean, and recorded as part of the collective M-Base in the group Strata Institute (1988), and with Rod Williams (1989–90) and Cassandra Wilson (1990); he may be seen in the video *M-BASE Jams at BAM* (*c*1989 [filmed 1988]). In addition to the drum set he plays various other percussion instruments, including *tablā* and *djembe*.

SELECTED RECORDINGS

As leader with S. Barefield and A. Holland: *Trans-dimensional Space Window* (1981, Trans-African 001); *Live at Nickelsdorf Konfrontationen* (1984, Sound Aspects 007)
As sideman: R. Mitchell: *More Cutouts* (1981, Cecma 1003); Griot Galaxy: *Kins* (1981, Black & White 001); *Opus krampus* (1984, Sound Aspects 004); R. Mitchell: *Live at the Knitting Factory* (1987, BS 120120-2); Strata Institute: *Ciphersyntax* (1988, JMT 834425-1); S. Barefield: *Xenogenesis*

(1990, CAC 002); G. Allen: *Maroons* (1992, BN B21Y-99493); C. Taborn: *Craig Taborn Trio* (1994, DIW 618); J. Carter: on *The Real Quietstorm* (1994, Atl. 82742-2), The Stevedore's Serenade; R. Mitchell: *Nine to Get Ready* (1997, ECM 1651)

BIBLIOGRAPHY

H. Boyd and L. Sinclair: *Detroit Jazz Who's Who* (Detroit, 1984), 60

GK

Tablā. A pair of small drums played with the hands and used chiefly in the classical repertory of the South Asian subcontinent; one drum is a metal kettle, the other cylindrical and wooden. The instrument became well known to audiences in the West in the late 1960s when several rock musicians incorporated into their work South Asian musical elements and instruments, and in the following years it came to be used in jazz as well. The tablā player Zakir Hussain undertook a collaboration with John Handy that resulted in a surprisingly effective fusion of bop, modal jazz, and Indian classical music; this may be heard to advantage on Handy's album *Karuna Supreme* (1975, MPS 15455). Hussain later worked in the group Shakti with John McLaughlin. A number of tablā players have been members of jazz-rock groups; the best known of these is Badal Roy, who played with McLaughlin, Dave Liebman (on, for example, Liebman's album *Lookout Farm*, 1973, ECM 1039), and Miles Davis. The tablā has also been used in groups that draw on diverse styles of jazz (including free jazz and jazz-rock), classical music, and folk music of various cultures. Collin Walcott played tablā in several groups of this kind, notably Oregon (as a member of which he recorded an unaccompanied tablā solo on the track *Story Telling*, from the album *Out of the Woods*, 1978, Elek. 154) and Codona; Trilok Gurtu joined Oregon following Walcott's death in 1984 and emerged as another important practitioner of the instrument.

In the hands of musicians schooled in the traditional techniques of playing the instrument, the tablā has enriched jazz: it has brought to the music many complex rhythms that are entirely independent of the African sources from which most jazz rhythms are drawn. However, it has also been used by jazz musicians who have sought to exploit its timbre while replacing the rhythms that are indigenous to the instrument with conventional jazz rhythms, or with new ones; in these cases the results have been consistently disappointing.

BK

Taborn, Craig (Marvin) (*b* Minneapolis, 20 Feb 1970). Pianist. He began playing at the age of 12 and studied classical music for three years, but he also gained interest in other types of music from his father, who was himself a pianist. In his teens he took up jazz, and he worked professionally from the age of 16. While studying at the University of Michigan in Ann Arbor he performed in Detroit and joined James Carter's quartet (*c*1993), with which he toured internationally and recorded. Following graduation he moved to New York, where he continued his affiliation with Carter and worked with Marcus Belgrave, Roscoe Mitchell, Craig Harris, Graham Haynes, Reggie Workman, and Mat Maneri, among others. In 2000 he joined Tim Berne's groups Quicksand (a trio with Tom Rainey) and Composure (a quartet with Rainey and Marc Ducret). Taborn recorded as the leader of a trio in 1994, and from that time has led his own small groups. He recorded on electric piano for one of Bill Laswell's dub projects and as a member of the Innerzone Orchestra, led by the producer Carl Craig, which blends jazz improvisation with techno.

SELECTED RECORDINGS

As leader: *Craig Taborn Trio* (1994, DIW 618)

As sideman: J. Carter: *JC on the Set* (1993, DIW 875), incl. Blues for a Nomadic Princess, Lunatic; *Jurassic Classics* (1994, DIW 886), incl. Equinox, Oleo; H. Ragin: *An Afternoon in Harlem* (1998, Justin Time 127)

BIBLIOGRAPHY

J. Woodford: "Craig Taborn '95: Non-piano Man," *Michigan Today*, xxvii/2 (1995), 13; repr. <http://www.umich.edu/~newsinfo/MT/95/Jun95/mt22j95.html> (2000)

G. Boudry: "Craig Taborn: L'avant-garde? Une tradition . . . ," *Jh*, no.534 (1996), 32 [incl. discography]

GK

Tacuma, Jamaaladeen [McDaniel, Rudy] (*b* Hempstead, NY, 11 June 1956). Electric bass guitarist. He grew up in Philadelphia and as a teenager sang in a doo-wop group. At the age of 13 he took up double bass and began playing in local bands. His first major engagement was with Charles Earland (1973–4), after which he played with the soul singer Edwin Birdsong. In 1975 he joined Ornette Coleman's electric band Prime Time, with which he recorded in Paris; during his stay there he converted to Islam and took a Muslim name. After leaving Prime Time Tacuma began recording as a leader for Gramavision. His first album, *Show Stopper*, combined the HARMOLODIC THEORY of Coleman with a funky dance style derived from rhythm-and-blues. *Music World* was recorded with musicians from all over the world at studios in the USA, Europe, and Asia. Tacuma also worked as a sideman with Jeff Beck, James "Blood" Ulmer, and Kip Hanrahan. He formed Double Exchange, a duo with Cornell Rochester, played in a trio with Max Roach and the Latin-rock guitarist Carlos Santana, joined the Firespitters, accompanying Jayne Cortez, worked with Bill Laswell in the Golden Palominos, was a member of the group New York Art/Noise, and performed and recorded again with Prime Time (mid-1980s). In 1983 his own harmolodic group, Jamaal, toured Japan, where he made use of traditional Japanese instruments and added Kazumi Watanabe to the group; during this same period he led Cosmetic, a group based in Philadelphia that played dance music. In 1985 he founded his own company, Jam-All Productions, and in 1987–8 he spent another period with Prime Time. His principal association from the late 1980s through the 1990s was with Wolfgang Puschnig, variously in groups (including Alpine Aspects) under the saxophonist's leadership, as a co-leader, in a duo, as a sidemen with Linda Sharrock, and as a member of the band Red Sun, which recorded in collaboration with Samul Nori, a group of Korean master drummers (1989, 1993, 1996). In the 1990s Tacuma also made further albums in a dance vein as a leader and recorded with Pink, Inc. (a trio with George Garzone and the drummer Alex Deutsch, 1991), in a duo with the drummer Dennis Alston (1992), with his group Basso Nouveau (four bass players and a drummer) (at the Moers Festival in Germany, 1993), and in David Murray's Fo Deuk Revue, which presented a fusion of rap and jazz (1996).

Tacuma is a highly innovative musician; he achieves the melodic agility of a soloist without neglecting his instrument's rhythmic role. Among electric bass guitarists in jazz, he is one of the most extreme in the use of a bright, piercing, metallic timbre, which lends itself to the precise definition of pitch that characterizes his approach. *Caravan*, recorded in a duo with Puschnig (1991), shows off his technical mastery; more importantly, it offers one of most convincing demonstrations of how funky dance rhythms can be absorbed into the jazz tradition.

SELECTED RECORDINGS

Duos with W. Puschnig: *Gemini-Gemini* (1991, ITM Pacific 970063), incl. Caravan
As leader: *Show Stopper* (1982–3, Gram. 8301); *Renaissance Man* (1983–4, Gram. 8308); *Music World* (1985, Gram. 8613)
As sideman: O. Coleman: *Dancing in your Head* (1975, A&M Hor. 722); *Body Meta* (1975, AH 1); J. Ulmer: *Tales of Captain Black* (1978, AH 7); O. Coleman: *Of Human Feelings* (1979, Ant. 2001); *Ornette and Prime Time: Opening the Caravan of Dreams* (1985, Caravan of Dreams 85001); *In All Languages* (1987, Caravan of Dreams 85008); W. Puschnig: *Pieces of the Dream* (1988, Amadeo 837322-2); L. Sharrock: *Linda Sharrock and the Three Man Band* (1991, Moers Music 02078)

BIBLIOGRAPHY

C. Tinder: "Jamaaladeen Tacuma: Electric Bass in the Harmolodic Pocket," *DB*, xlix/4 (1982), 19 [incl. discography]
C. J. Gans: "Jamaaladeen Tacuma: 21st Century Electrical Bass Guitarist," *JF* [intl edn], no.80 (1983), 51
B. Milkowski and C. Stern: "Jamaaladeen Tacuma: Breaking Bass Barriers," *GP*, xvii/5 (1983), 76 [incl. discography]
S. Lake: "A Renaissance Man for All Seasons," *The Wire*, no.21 (1985), 18
J. Nash: "Jamaaladeen Tacuma," *JT* (1989), June, 34
P. Carles, A. Clergeat, and J.-L. Comolli: *Dictionnaire du jazz* (Paris, rev. and enlarged 2/1994)
<http://ernie.bgsu.edu/~jeffs/tacuma.html> (1998) [discography]

BILL MILKOWSKI/BK

Tada, Seiji (*b* Takamatsu, Japan, 10 May 1960). Japanese alto saxophonist and leader. He took piano lessons from the age of seven and played flute and conducted brass bands through his years in high school. At Okayama University, when he was 20, he taught himself to play alto saxophone. He worked as a banker after graduation and performed as an amateur for five years in Takamatsu, then moved in 1988 to Tokyo to start a professional career. There he performed with the Bop Band, led by the trumpeter Hiroshi Murata (1990–93), Tomonao Hara, Masahiko Osaka, Junko Onishi's Jazz Workshop (1996–7), Motohiko Hino's group Art Directions (1997–9), and the big bands of the trombonist Kenichi Tsunoda and Yoshihiko Katori. While serving, with his fellow alto saxophonist Joh Yamada, as co-leader of the group Alto Nakayoshi Koyoshi (from 1993), he established his own quartet (1996) and the group Slash! (1998). Tada doubles on soprano saxophone and flute.

SELECTED RECORDINGS

As leader: *The Gig* (1997, Somethin' Else 5587); *Slash!* (1999, East Works 0012)
As sideman: T. Hara and M. Osaka: *def* (1994, King KICJ203); J. Onishi: *The Sextet* (1997, Somethin' Else 5586); M. Hino: *Club Toko*, i (1998, East Works 0007)

KAZUNORI SUGIYAMA

Tafenau, Raivo (*b* Mustla, Estonian SSR [now Estonia], 20 Nov 1963). Estonian reed player, composer, and leader. He studied accordion at the Pärnu Children's Music School (graduating in 1979) and saxophone at both the Tallinn Georg Ots Music School (graduating in 1988) and the Tallinn State Conservatory (to 1989). In 1991 he joined the quintet led by the pianist Urmas Lattikas, and in 1992 he was a soloist on an international television broadcast, "Europe Jazz Night." He also recorded with the European Broadcasting Union Big Band (1992), with which he appeared as a soloist in Barcelona (1993) and Budapest (1994), by which time he had become a member of the jazz orchestra of Estonian Radio. Between 1994 and 1996 Tafenau performed at several festivals in Finland, Germany, and Denmark. Thereafter he led his own groups and, most notably, formed a duo with the bass clarinet player Meelis Vind. As a studio musician he contributed to innumerable jazz and pop projects, and he was the principal soloist in the Estonian Dream Big Band, formed in 1998 (its first concert was conducted by Frank Foster). Tafenau may be heard to advantage as an accordionist on *Accordéon Bohémian: polkast sambani* (1995, Forte 0032-2) and as a virile reed player on his first album with his quintet, *Alone Together* (1999, Eesti Raadio 01/99).

WALTER OJAKÄÄR

Tag. A phrase (usually of a few bars, sometimes no more than a motif) added to the end of a theme, a chorus, or (most often) an entire piece. It may or may not be related thematically to the rest of the piece; a frequent practice is to repeat (once, twice, or a few times) the last two or four bars of the final chorus. Sometimes jazz musicians playfully stretch out the tag, utilizing solo breaks and a succession of false endings; one such example may be heard at the end of Charles Mingus's *Jelly Roll*, on the album *Mingus Ah Um* (1959, Col. CL1370). *See* Forms.

Tailgate. The style of trombone playing used in New Orleans jazz. In about 1900 the slide trombone replaced the valve trombone in popularity because of its ability to play portamentos, or "slurs." The portamento (*see* Gliss) became modish just as jazz was developing, and as a consequence became part of the New Orleans style. Early bands frequently played on advertising wagons, and it was supposed that the trombonist must stand on the wagon's "tailgate" so that he would have room to play. The tailgate style was derived mainly from trombone patterns in marches. The trombone, usually carrying an inner voice, supplies connecting links between the main phrases of the song in the middle or low register, frequently moving between harmony notes of successive chords by scalar or chromatic movement, or portamentos. The trombone may also undergird the melody with a pedal point, usually on the tonic or fifth.

JAMES LINCOLN COLLIER

Takahashi, Tatsuya (*b* Yamagata, Japan, 24 Dec 1931). Japanese bandleader and tenor saxophonist. He played professionally from 1951 and worked at American military bases near Sendai before moving to Tokyo in the late 1950s; his early style was influenced by that of Hidehiko Matsumoto. In 1961 he joined the alto saxophonist Keiichiro Ebihara and his Lobsters, and from 1966 he led Tokyo Union, a big band that made an acclaimed recording, *Scandinavian Suite*, in 1977; he also appeared at the festivals in Monterey (California) and Montreux (Switzerland). Tokyo Union disbanded in 1989. From 1992 Takahashi directed student and amateur big bands, and in 1996 he formed the group Jazz Groovys. His saxophone playing owes much to the work of Sonny Rollins, and the style of his band is strongly rhythmic. He has commissioned arrangements by, among others, Slide Hampton, Chikara Ueda, and Toshiyuki Honda.

SELECTED RECORDINGS

As leader: *Maiden Voyage* (1976, Three Blind Mice 3001); *Scandinavian Suite* (1977, Three Blind Mice 1005); *Funpico* (1978, WB 8004); *Black Pearl* (1980, Vic.–Zen 5001); *Chasin' the Duke* (1983, Carnival RJL8063); *Beauties* (1984, TDK T28P1007); *Keeping Count* (1986, King K32Y6129); *Tatsuya Takahashi Plays Miles & Gil* (1988, King K32Y6268); *TT & TU*

Best Selections (1989, JVC 28005); *Secret Love* (1992, Aeolus 001); *Señor Blues* (1995, Aeolus 004)
As sideman: Naoki Nishi: *Straight No Chaser* (1981, Full House PAP25001); Shuji Atsuda: *Blues on my Mind* (1999, Atsuda 261204)

BIBLIOGRAPHY

J. McDonough: "Tokyo Union," *Billboard*, xcii (8 Nov 1980), 52
"Tokyo Union Big Band Splits with Leader," *Billboard*, cii (10 Feb 1990), 72

YOZO IWANAMI/KAZUNORI SUGIYAMA

Takase, Aki (*b* Osaka, 26 Jan 1948). Japanese pianist and leader. Her mother, a piano teacher, began to give her lessons at the age of three, and she studied classical piano through her years at Tohogakuen Music University, from which she graduated in 1972; she also played double bass while in high school. She began her professional career in 1971 in the group led by the alto saxophonist Yoshio Otomo and then performed in bands led by Yoshio Ikeda, Motohiko Hino, the alto and soprano saxophonist Hidefumi Toki, and Joe Henderson. Her first recording was made in 1978, and her second, in December 1980, was as the leader of a quartet including Dave Liebman. In 1982 she performed in New York with Cecil McBee, Bob Moses, and Sheila Jordan. Having visited Europe regularly from 1981 (she appeared with her trio at the Berlin Jazz Festival that year, performed as an unaccompanied soloist in Nuremberg in June 1982, and toured with her quartet in 1983), she moved to Germany in 1986. She formed duos with Maria João (touring worldwide, 1987–93), her husband, Alex Schlippenbach (1990), David Murray (1991), and the bass clarinetist Rudi Mahall (1997, when they recorded together), and co-led the Berlin Contemporary Jazz Orchestra with Schlippenbach. From 1993 Takase led her own trio, which toured in 1994 (with Reggie Workman and Rashied Ali), and in autumn 1994 her septet of Japanese musicians (in which Issei Igarashi and Nobuyoshi Ino were sidemen) toured and recorded in Europe. She wrote for and toured with a string quartet involving Tristan Honsinger in autumn 1995, and continued to appear both unaccompanied and in duos. Takase teaches piano at the Hanns-Eisler Music College in Berlin.

SELECTED RECORDINGS

As unaccompanied soloist: *Perdido* (1982, Enja 4034); *Shima shoka* (1990, Enja 6062)
Duos: with A. Schlippenbach: on *Internationales Jazzfestival Münster* (1988, Tutu 888110), Frictitious Passages; with D. Murray: *Blue Monk* (1991, Enja 7039); with A. Schlippenbach: *Piano Duets: Live in Berlin 93/94* (1993–4, FMP OWN90002); with R. Mahall: *Duet for Eric Dolphy* (1997, Enja 9109-2)
As leader: *Minerva's Owl* (1980, Contl HL5010); *ABC* (1982, Tei.–Union ULP5505) *Close-up of Japan* (1992, Enja 7075-2); *Clapping Music* (1993, Enja 8090-2)
As leader of Berlin Contemporary Jazz Orchestra (with A. Schlippenbach): *Berlin Contemporary Jazz Orchestra* (1989, ECM 1409); *The Morlocks and Other Places* (1993, FMP CD61); *Live in Japan 1996* (1996, DIW 922)

BIBLIOGRAPHY

CarrJ
D. Kasrel: "Hearsay: Aki Takase," *JT*, xxiv/7 (1994), 12
<http://www.ejn.it/mus/takase.htm> (2000)

KAZUNORI SUGIYAMA, GK

Takayanagi, Masayuki [JoJo] (*b* Tokyo, 22 Dec 1932; *d* Tokyo, 23 June 1991). Japanese guitarist. He taught himself to play guitar during his high school years and made his professional début in 1951. In 1954, while performing with Toshiko Akiyoshi, Sadao Watanabe, and Hampton Hawes, he formed his own quartet, New Direction. From 1959 through 1965 he took a leading role in various experimental activities under the banner of Shinseiki Ongaku Kenkyusyo (New Century Music Laboratory, a forum for avant-garde musicians), and in 1961 he formed the cooperative quartet Jazz Academy with Masahiko Togashi, Masabumi Kikuchi, and another of the laboratory's central figures, Hideto Kanai. Takayanagi formed a bossa nova band in 1967. Later in his career he founded a tango group (1989) – he performed fluently in more traditional jazz styles as well – but he mainly led bands oriented towards free jazz, including the groups Jazz Contemporary and Tee & Company. In 1980 he performed at the International New Jazz Festival Moers. Once dubbed as "the Sonny Sharrock, Derek Bailey, James Blood Ulmer, and Fred Frith of Japan," Takayanagi was one of the most avant-garde Japanese musicians of his time. From the late 1980s he appeared mainly as an unaccompanied soloist, performing free improvisations.

SELECTED RECORDINGS

(recorded for Three Blind Mice unless otherwise indicated)

As unaccompanied soloist: *Lonely Woman* (1982, PAP25030); *Action Direct* (1985, ALM UR6); *Inanimate Nature* (1990, Jinya Disc B01)
Duos with K. Abe: *Kaitaiteki kokan* (Exchanging feelings in a divisive manner; 1970, DIW 414); with M. Togashi: *Pulsation* (1983, PW K28P6244); with J. Zorn: *Experimental Performance* (1986, Mobys 1750)
As leader: with H. Kanai: *Ginparis Session* (1963, 9); *Independence* (1970, Tei.–Union JUP3); *Free Form Suite* (1973, 10); *Axis: Another Revolvable Thing* (1975, Offbeat 1005, 1009); *Cool JoJo* (1979, 5018); *Moers New Jazz Festival '80* (1980, 5023)
As leader of Tee & Company: *Sonnet* (1977, 5004); *Dragon Garden* (1977, 5006); *Spanish Flower* (1977, 5008)

BIBLIOGRAPHY

B. McRae: "Tomorrow is Now," *JJI*, xlix/5 (1996), 14

KAZUNORI SUGIYAMA

Take. In recording (both sound recording and film) the recorded result of a single uninterrupted performance, whether complete or partial. The word is usually applied in sound recording to each of the attempts made at a single session to record any one piece, and these different versions are designated "first take," "second take," etc. In sound recording during the 78 r.p.m. era, each take was assigned a "take number," generally a numeral or a letter, which is a component of the MATRIX NUMBER, usually its last element. The takes might be numbered in chronological order of successful attempts; this was the usual practice in the 1920s. However, by the 1930s many companies evaluated all takes, then assigned take numbers in order of preferred performance, the best version being called the "first take"; for example, most original issues on Decca 78s are take "A." Procedures were by no means standardized. A third practice may be found, for example, in sessions recorded by Dial, which numbered takes chronologically, including incomplete takes (some less than 30 seconds in duration) interspersed among complete ones.

The concept of a take lost some of its meaning with the advent of mastering on magnetic tape, because of the possibilities inherent in editing on tape. Nonetheless, a considerable amount of jazz, especially improvised jazz, continues to be recorded without significant alteration of tapes through editing. Moreover, a spoiled or abridged take might include within it, for example, a fine unissued improvisation, and, if interest in an artist proves sufficient, a record company may decide to issue this material, just as companies have released different takes from the 78 r.p.m. era. Examples abound in late (and sometimes posthumous) issues of material recorded by John Coltrane and Charles Mingus: such issues may consist of alternative takes of titles previously issued, rejected takes (i.e., previously unissued titles), or full takes (i.e., titles previously issued only in edited or abridged versions).

Correspondingly, although the take number has lost much of its significance in the modern era of recording, some companies have continued to assign such numbers to sections of a master tape; as before, the take number forms a component of a number that identifies the attempts at a single title. In this case the take number has no relationship to the various types of numbers (for example, issue numbers or pressing numbers) that may appear on an album, except in those instances where an entire album comprises a single take: apart from listening, one may distinguish between the two takes of Coltrane's album-long performance of *Ascension* (both released under the same cover as Imp. 95) only by finding which of the two numbers is etched onto the space between the centermost groove and the label.

HOWARD RYE, BK

Takeuchi, Nao (*b* Tokyo, 18 April 1955). Japanese tenor saxophonist and leader. He started piano lessons at the age of three but taught himself to play tenor saxophone when he was 17; later he doubled on flute and bass clarinet. After joining Elvin Jones's Japanese Jazz Machine (1990) he became a member of Issei Igarashi's group (1991), Shota Koyama's group Ichigo Ichie (1996), the band led by the Hammond organ player Toshihiko Kankawa (1998), and the saxophone quartet Saxophobia (1998). His own quartet consisted of Yutaka Shiina, Shigeo Aramaki, and Dairiki Hara from 1995, but in 1998–9 he toured and recorded with an American rhythm section of Rod Williams, Jaribu Shahid, and the drummer Eli Fountain. Takeuchi is a powerful free-jazz tenor saxophonist.

SELECTED RECORDINGS

As leader: *Live at Bash* (1997, CAB 0009); *More than You Know* (1998, Off Note 27); *Talking to the Spirits* (1999, Off Note 31)

As sideman: S. Koyama: *Ichigo Ichie* (1996, Off Note 15), T. Kankawa: *Uganda* (1998, P-Vine 9410)

KAZUNORI SUGIYAMA

Talbert, Thomas (Robert) [Tom(my)] (*b* Crystal Bay, MN, 4 Aug 1924). Composer and arranger. He was primarily self-taught as a pianist and became interested in arranging at the age of 15, having heard big-band performances on the radio. After serving in the military during World War II he moved to the West Coast. He led his own group from 1946 to 1949 and toured with Anita O'Day. In the 1950s he wrote arrangements for Claude Thornhill, Tony Pastor, Kai Winding, Oscar Pettiford, and Don Elliot, among others. Talbert returned in the mid-1960s to Minnesota, where he led a 12-piece band, and from 1975 he lived in southern California; there he worked as a studio arranger (into the mid-1980s) and led a big band and a septet (through the 1990s).

SELECTED RECORDINGS

As leader: Stop your Knockin'/I've Got You under my Skin (1947, Para. 112); *Bix, Duke, Fats* (1956, Atl. 1250); *Louisiana Suite and Other Instrumentals* (1977, Sea Breeze 107); *This is Living!* (1997, Pipe Dream 14480)

BIBLIOGRAPHY

FeatherE

Z. Stewart: "A Mixture of Moods: from Foot-tapping Swing to Ethereal Sounds, Arranger-composer Tom Talbert's Works Spring from his Devotion to Two Schools of Music," *Los Angeles Times* (19 Aug 1994)

<http://www.pipedreampromotions.com/tombio.html> (1999)

GK

Talbot, Jamie [James Robert] (*b* London, 23 April 1960). English alto saxophonist. While in school he played with the London Schools Symphony Orchestra and with the National Youth Jazz Orchestra (1976–82). After studying at the Royal College of Music (1978–9) he toured and recorded in the 1980s and 1990s with, among others, Clark Tracey, Stan Tracey, Jack Sharpe, John Dankworth, the composer Colin Towns, Guy Barker, the arranger and big-band leader Richard Niles, Shorty Rogers, and Bud Shank. In addition he played occasionally with Ella Fitzgerald, Frank Sinatra, Nelson Riddle, Gil Evans, Mel Tormé, and Quincy Jones and worked widely in commercial recording studios. Although his principal work has been on alto saxophone in the bop style, Talbot has latterly been inspired by the example of Eddie Daniels to play clarinet in both jazz and classical contexts.

SELECTED RECORDINGS

As leader: *Altitude* (1985, Move 21)

As sideman: C. Tracey: *Suddenly Last Tuesday* (1986, Cadillac 1013); S. Tracey: *Live at Ronnie Scott's* (1986, Steam 113); *Genesis* (1987, Steam 114); J. Sharpe: *Catalyst* (1987, Frog 716); G. Barker: *Isn't It* (1991, Spot. 545); C. Tracey: *We've Been Expecting You* (1992, 33JAZZ 007); C. Towns: *Nowhere & Heaven* (1996, PVC 1013); G. Barker: *What Love Is* (1998, EmA 558331-2)

BIBLIOGRAPHY

ChiltonB

MARK GILBERT

Tana, Akira (*b* San Jose, CA, 14 March 1952). Drummer and leader. He played piano, trumpet, and drums as a child and began drumming in rock bands in the San Francisco Bay area as a teenager. While living in Boston he gained degrees in sociology and East Asian studies from Harvard University (1974) and in percussion from the New England Conservatory (1979). During the same period he worked with the Paul Winter Consort (1977), Helen Humes (1977–8), Jaki Byard, Sonny Stitt, Hubert Laws, and Sonny Rollins (all 1978), and Milt Jackson (1979) and began an association with Art Farmer that lasted until 1986. Having moved to New York (1979) he worked with Johnny Hartman (1979), the Heath Brothers (1979–82), Stanley Cowell (1980), the singer Sylvia Sims (1980–84), Zoot Sims (1980–85), Al Cohn (1982–5), Jimmie Rowles and Slide Hampton (1983), Cedar Walton (1984), Jim Hall (1985–6), Farmer and Benny Golson (in the Jazztet, 1985–7), George Coleman (1986–7), the singer Lena Horne (1986, 1993–4), and Paquito D'Rivera (1988–9).

In 1990 Tana and Rufus Reid formed the quintet TanaReid, which originally consisted of Jesse Davis, Ralph Moore, and Rob Schneiderman, and which was active through the 1990s. Among its later members were Dan Faulk (who replaced Moore in 1991), Craig Bailey (who replaced Davis in 1992), and John Stetch (who replaced Schneiderman on piano *c*1994); Mark Turner succeeded Faulk around 1994. Tana also worked with James Moody (1989–92), J. J. Johnson and Ray Bryant (1991), the Asian American Jazz Trio (1992, alongside Kei Akagi and Reid), Manhattan Transfer (1993), Sonny Fortune (1995–6), and the rhythm-and-blues singer Ruth Brown (1997–9); in March 1997 he led Akira Tana and the Japanese All Stars for a performance and recording at the Kennedy Center in Washington, DC. Tana is a versatile drummer whose playing ranges from driving hard-bop timekeeping to delicate, impressionistic coloring, enhanced by a wide dynamic spectrum that allows him to build effectively the intensity of the music when accompanying soloists and to create powerful climaxes. As an adjunct faculty member at Queens College (from 1989), Jersey City State College (from 1994), and Rutgers (from 1995), he has been active as a teacher and made a number of recordings.

SELECTED RECORDINGS

As leader of TanaReid (with R. Reid): *Blue Motion* (1993, Evidence 22075); *Looking Forward* (1994, Evidence 22114); *Back to Front* (1998, Evidence 22206)

As sideman: Heath Brothers: *Live at the Public Theatre* (1978, Col. FC36374); A. Farmer: *Warm Valley* (1982, Conc. 212); Z. Sims: *Suddenly it's Spring* (1983, Pablo 2310898); J. Hall: *Jim Hall's Three* (1986, Conc. 298); J. Heath: *Peer Pleasure* (1987, Landmark 1514); J. Moody: *Sweet and Lovely* (1989, Novus 3063-2-N); Project G7: *Tribute to Wes Montgomery*, i–ii (1992, Evidence 22049, 22051); Asian American Jazz Trio: *Sound Circle* (1992, Evidence 22108); L. Horne: *We'll be Together Again* (1993, BN B21X-28974); R. Brown: *A Good Day for the Blues* (1999, Bull's Eye 1166196132A)

BIBLIOGRAPHY

W. Friedwald: "Jazz Cymbalism: Give the Drummer Some (Jazz Drummers Name their Own and other Drummers' Best Recordings)," *VV* (30 Aug 1988), 26

J. Potter: "Akira Tana: from Sideman to Leader," *MD*, xv/11 (1991), 30

L. Gourse: "TanaReid," *Jazziz*, vii/3 (1994), 71

"Interview with Akira Tana," *The Note*, vi/2 (1994), 2

A. Lewis and L. Lewis: "Akira Tana Interview," *Cadence*, xxii/2 (1996), 5

E. Holley: "Riffs: TanaReid/Hal Galper Double Tour Takes Educational Slant," *DB*, lxiv/2 (1997), 12

<http://www.jazzcorner.com/tana/tanahome.html> (1999)

<http://www.tanareid.com/tanareidhome.html> (1999)

RICK MATTINGLY

Tangerding, Götz (*b* Donauwörth, Germany, 25 June 1961; *d* Munich, 29 July 1991). German pianist. He was classically trained and studied at the conservatory in Augsburg, at the Swiss Jazz School in Berne, and with Jaki Byard at the New England Conservatory; he also received tuition in composition from George Russell and worked with Russell's New York big band (recording in 1978). After playing in the group Bhakti (*c*1980–81) he led his own trio, which consisted of Christian Stock on double bass and Rudi Roth or Heim Weidferhofer on drums; the group toured with Karlheinz Miklin (recording in 1987) and Ray Pizzi and performed with such guest soloists as Wolfgang Lackerschmid, Sheila Jordan, and Monty Waters. Tangerding died of an AIDS-related illness.

SELECTED RECORDINGS

(all recorded for Bhakti Jazz)

First Step (1980, 20); *Crystallizations* (1982, 21); *A la ala: a Voice in Jazz* (1982, 22); *Porque no* (1987, 25); *Jazztracks* (1989–90, 26)

BIBLIOGRAPHY

T. Fitterling: "Jazz aktuell: engagierte Spielfreude: Götz Tangerding Trio," *JP*, xxxi/2 (1982), 22

M. Wangler: "Jazz aktuell: Pianist Kunstgriffe: Götz Tangerding," *JP*, xxxv/5 (1986), 28

Obituary, T. Fitterling, *JP*, xl/9 (1991), 56

GK

Tanggaard, Aage (*b* Hasseris, Denmark, 25 Feb 1957). Danish drummer. Following lessons with Ed Thigpen and Michael Carvin he played from the late 1970s with Jørgen Emborg's quartet and Thomas Clausen's trio. From 1980 he has been active mainly as a freelance, but he has also played in the Radiojazzgruppen (i), Ernie Wilkins's Almost Big Band, the NDR Big Band (Hamburg), the NDR Symphony Orchestra (Hannover), Finn Savery's trio, the quintet led by Arne Domnérus and Rune Gustafsson, and Duke Jordan's trio (with which he toured Japan). He is a permanent member of Svend Asmussen's quartet. Tanggaard recorded with Frank Foster (1982), John McNeil and Bernt Rosengren (both 1983), Red Holloway, Horace Parlan, and Doug Raney (all 1984), Paul Bley (1985), Chet Baker (1985, 1988), Roland Hanna (1987), Red Rodney (1988), and Ben Besiakov and Bob Rockwell (both 1990), and he accompanied such visiting musicians as Joe Bonner, Stan Getz, Johnny Griffin, John Lewis, Lee Konitz, Toots Thielemans, and Putte Wickman. He teaches at Det Rytmiske Musikkonservatorium in Copenhagen.

SELECTED RECORDINGS

As sideman: T. Clausen: *Rain* (1980, Matrix 29202); F. Foster: *The House that Love Built* (1982, Ste. 1170); J. McNeil: *I've Got the World on a String* (1983, Ste. 1183); E. Wilkins: *Montreux* (1983, Ste. 1190); A. Domnérus: *Happy Together!* (1995, Lady Bird 0019); S. Asmussen: *Fit as a Fiddle* (1996, Dacapo 9429)

BIBLIOGRAPHY

K. Frandsen: *Politikens jazzleksikon* (Copenhagen, 1987)

FRANK BÜCHMANN-MØLLER

Tanksley, Francesca [Chessie] (*b* Vicenza, Italy, 21 Nov 1957). Italian pianist. She grew up in Munich, where she began studying piano at the age of seven. Having attended the Berklee College of Music from 1974 to 1976 she returned to Germany, and in 1977 began playing professionally with various European jazz groups while studying liberal arts at a Munich campus affiliated to the University of Maryland (AA 1978). She then moved to New York (1980) and worked with Melba Liston & Co. (to 1982), with which she appeared in the PBS television series "Women in Jazz: a Matter of Taste" and performed at Carnegie Hall, accompanying Dizzy Gillespie (1981). As well as recording and touring internationally with the quintets of Erica Lindsay (from 1982) and Billy Harper (from 1983), Tanksley has worked with Cecil Payne, David "Fathead" Newman, Clifford Jordan, Nick Brignola, and Charles Davis. In 1990 she formed her own trio, with which she has performed in New York and at various American festivals. After studying music at a SUNY campus (BA 1993) and at Queens College, New York (MA 1995), she joined the faculty of the Jazz and Contemporary Music Program at the New School for Social Research (from 1996 at the Mannes/New School; from autumn 1999 at the New School University). Tanksley is one of the most imaginative piano soloists playing in the style pioneered by McCoy Tyner.

SELECTED RECORDINGS

As sideman: E. Lindsay: *Dreamer* (1989, Can. 79040); B. Harper: *Destiny is Yours* (1989, Ste. 31260); *Live on Tour in the Far East*, i–iii (1991, Ste. 31311, 31321, 31366); *Somalia* (1993, Omagatoki 7107); *If our Hearts could only See* (*c*1997, DIW 931)

BIBLIOGRAPHY

M. Unterbrink: *Jazz Women at the Keyboard* (Jefferson, NC, and London, 1983), 164

GK

Tanner, Paul (Ora Warren)(*b* Skunk Hollow, nr Newport, KY, 15 Oct 1917). Trombonist and educator. He grew up in Wilmington, Delaware, from the age of six and learned piano before starting on trombone when he was 13. In the summer of 1938 he found work in a club in Atlantic City, where Glenn Miller heard him and engaged him as a sideman. Tanner remained with Miller's band until its breakup in September 1942 (for illustrations *see* Miller, glenn, and Mute, fig.3), at which time he joined Charlie Spivak's band. In 1943 he entered the army; following his discharge in 1945 he joined Les Brown's band, after which he was a member of the memorial Miller band, led by Tex Beneke (1946–51). In 1951 he settled in Los Angeles to enroll at the University of

California and soon became first-chair trombonist at ABC, a position he held until 1968. During that time he played for Neal Hefti, Henry Mancini, Billy May, Nelson Riddle, Pete Rugolo, and many other leaders. From 1958 to 1981 he taught at UCLA, and thereafter he lectured on a freelance basis; in 1984 he donated his collection of 78 r.p.m. and LP recordings to the Music Library Special Collections at UCLA (*see* LIBRARIES AND ARCHIVES, §2).

Although he was not noted as an improvising soloist, Tanner's warm tone quality and skill in the upper register made him a valuable lead player in big bands and orchestras. He wrote compositions and arrangements for trombone and piano, arrangements for big band, and trombone methods, and he published, with B. Cox, the memoir *Every Night was New Year's Eve: ... on the Road with Glenn Miller* (Tokyo, 1992); with M. Gerow, one of the best-known textbooks in the USA, *A Study of Jazz* (Dubuque, IA, 1964, rev. 8/1997); and, with D. W. Megill, *Jazz Issues: a Critical History* (Madison, 1995).

SELECTED FILMS AND VIDEOS

Sun Valley Serenade (1941); Orchestra Wives (1942); Discovering Jazz (1969)

BIBLIOGRAPHY

Feather '60s; *Feather–Gitler '70s*
L. Feather: "A History Class with a Beat," *Los Angeles Times* (15 July 1979)
C. Miller: "Musician Travels Far from Skunk Hollow," *San Diego Union* (15 May 1986)
J. Tumpak: "Paul Tanner: from Skunk Hollow to Glenn Miller to UCLA," *L.A. Jazz Scene*, no.148 (1999), 23

THOMAS OWENS

Tap-dance. *See* DANCE.

Tapscott, Horace (Elva) (*b* Houston, 6 April 1934; *d* Los Angeles, 27 Feb 1999). Pianist, composer, and leader. He began piano studies at the age of six with his mother, the pianist Mary Lou Malone, and took up trombone two years later. His family moved to Los Angeles in 1943 and he studied trombone in school, playing with Frank Morgan in a high-school band; other young associates from this period included Don Cherry and Billy Higgins. Tapscott worked with Gerald Wilson's orchestra before graduating from Jefferson High School in 1952. After studying briefly at Los Angeles City College he enlisted in the air force, and served in a band in Wyoming (1953–7). He then returned to Los Angeles and worked with various local bands before touring as a trombonist with Lionel Hampton (1959 – early 1961), for whom he also wrote a number of arrangements and at times sat in on piano. By the early 1960s he was playing piano exclusively, in part because of persistent dental problems resulting from an automobile accident during his high-school years.

By the end of 1961 Tapscott had formed the Pan Afrikan Peoples Arkestra, which at various times included Arthur Blythe, Stanley Crouch, Azar Lawrence, Marcus McLaurine, Roberto Miranda, the brothers Butch and Wilber Morris, David Murray, the saxophonist Michael Session, Sonship Theus, and Jimmy Woods. The purpose of the Arkestra was to preserve, develop, and perform African-American music within the community. Its rapid growth and branching off into related social and artistic activities led to the formation in 1963 of a larger organization, the Underground Musicians Association (UGMA), of which the Pan Afrikan Peoples Arkestra was a component. By the late 1960s the organization's continued evolution led to broader community involvement, symbolized by a change of name to the Union of God's Musicians and Artists Ascension (UGMAA). Although activities had tapered off by the mid-1980s, both the Arkestra and UGMAA continued to play a role in their community in the 1990s.

Between the late 1950s and early 1970s Tapscott recorded with Lou Blackburn (1963) and Onzy Matthews (1963, accompanying Lou Rawls), arranged and conducted the music for two albums for the singer (and, later, Black Panther Party leader) Elaine Brown, and composed and conducted the material for Sonny Criss's album *Sonny's Dream (Birth of the New Cool)* (1968, Prst. 7576); his first album as a leader was made one year later. From 1978 through the mid-1980s he recorded for Interplay and Nimbus, two labels formed by enthusiasts for Tapscott's music. He recorded with the Arkestra, as an unaccompanied soloist, in a duo with the drummer Everett Brown, with his trio (notably a session in performance at the Lobero Theater in Santa Barbara, California), and as the leader of a sextet. In the 1990s he became increasingly busy with writing and international touring. His commissioned composition *Two Shades of Soul* was the centerpiece of the 17th annual Asian-American Jazz Festival in San Francisco in 1998. With S. Isoardi, he wrote his autobiography, *Songs of the Unsung: the Musical and Social Journey of Horace Tapscott* (forthcoming). His date of death appeared in some obituaries as 28 February 1999; he actually died on the 27th, at ten minutes before midnight.

SELECTED RECORDINGS

As leader: *The Giant is Awakened* (1969, FD 107); *The Call* (1979, Nimbus 246); *Live at Lobero*, i–ii (1981, Nimbus 1369, 1258); *The Dark Tree*, i–ii (1989, HA 6053, 6083); *Aiee! The Phantom* (1995, Arabesque 0119); *Thoughts of Dar es Salaam* (1996, Arabesque 0128)

BIBLIOGRAPHY

Feather–Gitler '70s
D. Keller: "Horace Tapscott," *JT* (1982), Oct, 8
J. Weiss and C. Gauffre: "Horace Tapscott: l'autre West Coast," *Jm*, no.321 (1983), 28 [incl. discography]
E. Cohen: "Horace Tapscott Talking: 'A Legacy to Pass on'," *Cadence*, x (1984), no.7, p.8; no.8, p.12 [incl. discography]
R. Mitchell: "Horace Tapscott," *DB*, lv/1 (1988), 13
D. Rubien: "Black Pianist's Key to Preserve a Jazz Heritage," *San Francisco Chronicle Datebook* (10 April 1988)
B. Hershon: "Horace Tapscott," *California Jazz Now*, i/4 (1991), 7; rev. as "Horace Tapscott," *JJI*, xlv/7 (1992), 10
B. Ratliff: "Horace Tapscott: Staring No in the Face," *Coda*, no.242 (1992), 7
D. Richardson: "Quiet Giant," *San Francisco Bay Guardian* (3 Aug 1994)
M. Smith: "Horace Tapscott," *Cadence*, xxi/8 (1995), 5
C. Bryant and others, eds.: *Central Avenue Sounds: Jazz in Los Angeles* (Berkeley, CA, Los Angeles, and London, 1998), 282
A. Cohen: "Horace Tapscott: Papa's Optimism: the Final Interview," *DB*, lxvi/5 (1999), 28
Obituary, D. Heckman, *Los Angeles Times* (2 March 1999)
K. Silsbee: "Dollar Short," *New Times Los Angeles* (25–31 March 1999), 70

STEVEN L. ISOARDI

Tarasov, Vladimir (Petrovich) (*b* Arkhangel'sk, Russian SFSR [now Russia], 29 June 1947). Russian drummer, composer, and educator. Although he was largely self-taught as a musician, he brought his skill to perfection and came to be regarded as the best all-round drummer and percussionist in the USSR. He played drums from 1961 and worked with the saxophonist Vladimir Rezitski in 1967–8; harrassed by the government for attempting to open a jazz club, he then moved to Vilnius, where in 1969 he formed a duo with Vyacheslav Ganelin; this became the Ganelin Trio (later known as the G–T–Ch Trio) when they were joined by Vladimir Chekasin in 1971. Tarasov made recordings with the trio (which disbanded in 1987), in a duo with Ganelin, and as a soloist (*Atto*, 1984, Mel. C60 23565004). Later he formed an unusual duo of two drummers with Andrew Cyrille, with whom he toured the Soviet Union (1987), North America (1990), and Europe (1990), and recorded the album *Galaxies* (1990, Music & Arts 672). In addition to his work in jazz Tarasov played percussion in the Lithuanian State Symphony Orchestra. A member of the Lithuanian Composers' Union from 1990, he formed the Lithuanian Art Orchestra (LAO) at the Lithuanian Music Academy in 1991. He wrote and performed music for films and concerts and organized multi-media projects in museums and galleries in several countries. In the 1990s he taught improvising in Berlin (1991) and Bremen (1994) and appeared at many concerts and festivals in Europe, Japan, and the USA, sometimes when on tour with ROVA. He is the author of *Trio* (Vilnius, 1998).

BIBLIOGRAPHY

B. Noglik: "Wjatscheslaw Ganelin, Wladimir Tschekassin, Wladimir Tarassow," *Jazzwerkstatt international* (Berlin, 1981), 29 [incl. discography]
F. Maino: "Ganelin, Tarasov, and Chekasin: Interview," *Cadence*, ix/1 (1983), 19
A. Duncan: "Soviet Trio Takes Daring Liberties with Familiar Jazz Styles," *Christian Science Monitor* (30 June 1986), 29
D. Richardson: "A Different Drummer," *San Francisco Bay Guardian* (4 July 1990)
H. Kumpf: "Vladimir Tarasov," *JP*, xlii/6 (1993), 13
For a video appearance, further recordings, and bibliography *see* Ganelin, vyacheslav.

WALTER OJAKÄÄR

Tardy, Greg(ory John) (*b* New Orleans, 3 Feb 1966). Tenor saxophonist and clarinetist. He grew up in a musical family: his father and mother were both opera singers, his sister played flute, and his brother played trumpet; his mother also recorded as a jazz singer. Tardy trained as a classical clarinetist and performed as such while attending Carroll College in Waukesha, Wisconsin (1984–6), and the University of Wisconsin in Milwaukee (1986–8). When he was 21 he took up tenor saxophone, which he played in a local funk and fusion band in order to fund his clarinet studies. In 1988 he majored in jazz harmony at the Wisconsin Conservatory of Music, and in 1991 he attended the University of New Orleans. From 1985 to 1991 he performed various genres of popular music in Milwaukee, St. Louis, and New Orleans; in this last city he worked with funk bands led by the Neville Brothers and Allen Toussaint.

In the 1990s Tardy became more involved with jazz and performed occasionally with Ellis Marsalis, the Olympia Brass Band (1992–3), and Elvin Jones's Jazz Machine (1993–5); in the middle of the decade, by which time he was based in New York, he began touring with Nicholas Payton's quintet. As a freelance he worked with, among others, John Hicks, Jay McShann, Roy Hargrove, the group TanaReid, Rashied Ali, Brian Lynch, Russell Gunn (recording in 1996), and Steve Coleman (recording in 1997 with the big band Council of Balance). From 1996 to 1998 he was a member of a big band led by the pianist Jason Lindner and a sextet led by the double bass player Omar Avital, and he appeared regularly with both groups at Smalls. During the same period he collaborated with Tom Harrell and led his own small ensembles (both 1997). Later he joined Andrew Hill's sextet (recording in 1999) and performed with Dave Douglas at the Bell Atlantic Jazz Festival in New York (1999). Tardy also plays flute.

SELECTED RECORDINGS

As leader: *Serendipidity* (1997, Imp. 256)
As sideman: R. Gunn: *Gunn fu* (1996, HighNote 7003); T. Harrell: *The Art of Rhythm* (1997, RCA 68924-2), incl. Petals Dance [cl]

BIBLIOGRAPHY

Feather–GitlerBEJ

GK

Tarto, Joe [Tortoriello, Vincent Joseph] (*b* Newark, NJ, 22 Feb 1902; *d* Morristown, NJ, 24 Aug 1986). Tuba and double bass player and arranger. He performed with several lesser-known bandleaders in the early 1920s, then from 1925 played with Red Nichols, Miff Mole, the Dorsey Brothers, Eddie Lang, Phil Napoleon, Bix Beiderbecke, and others. As an arranger Tarto worked with a number of bandleaders, including Fletcher Henderson and Chick Webb; he composed and arranged *Black Horse Stomp*, which Henderson recorded in 1926 (Har. 153). *I must have that man*, recorded by Joe Venuti, is an excellent example of his skill as an arranger, and includes one of his better solos. Tarto recorded with such singers as Ethel Waters, Sophie Tucker, Bing Crosby, and the Boswell Sisters. After 1930 he played jazz only occasionally, and worked mostly with radio, theater, pit, and symphony orchestras. He also played with Nichols (1935–6), and was associated intermittently for some 25 years with Paul Whiteman. During the late 1940s he performed at Nick's, New York. Thereafter he led a band, the New Jersey Dixieland Brass Quintet, periodically into the 1980s, and also worked with other traditional jazz musicians. In 1984 he was a guest soloist at the Oude Stijl Jazz Festival at Breda in the Netherlands.

SELECTED RECORDINGS

As sideman: R. Nichols and M. Mole: Black Bottom Stomp (1926, Edison 51878); M. Mole: The Darktown Strutters' Ball (1927, OK 40784); J. Venuti: I must have that man (1928, OK 41133); E. Waters: Am I Blue? (1929, Col. 1837D); E. Lang: Freeze and Melt (1929, OK 8696)

BIBLIOGRAPHY

AllenH
W. Miller: "Joe Tarto," *Australian Jazz Quarterly*, no.7 (1948), 3
J. Tarto and H. Openeer: "A Joe Tarto Story," *Doctor jazz*, no.33 (1968), 5
W. Vaché, Sr.: "Joe Tarto: a Tribute," *Jersey Jazz*, v/3 (1977), 4; repr. in *Jersey Jazz*, x/3 (1982), 9
——: "Tuba King: Joe Tarto," *JJI*, xxxiii/8 (1980), 14
S. Hester: Liner notes, *Joe Tarto, Titan of the Tuba* (Broadway Intermission 108, 1981)
C. Deffaa: "Joe Tarto: Last of the Five Pennies," *MR*, xii/4 (1985), 1; repr. in *Voices of the Jazz Age: Portraits of Eight Vintage Jazzmen* (Wheatley, Oxford, England, Urbana, IL, and Chicago, 1990), 106

CHIP DEFFAA

Tate, Buddy [George Holmes] (*b* Sherman, TX, 22 Feb 1912; *d* Chandler, AZ, 10 Feb 2001). Tenor saxophonist and leader. His year of birth appears in many sources variously as 1913, 1914, or 1915, but 1912 (from his passport and in the social security death index) accords better with accounts of his career, because he started on alto saxophone at about the age of 12 (i.e., 1924) and had already begun his professional career by 1927, if not earlier. He worked with Terrence Holder (1930–33), Count Basie (replacing Lester Young in March 1934), and Andy Kirk (again following Young, late 1934 to summer 1935), and played with Nat Towles. In 1939 he replaced Herschel Evans in Basie's band, with which he remained for ten years, to summer 1948 (for illustration *see* Films, fig.3). He then performed with Hot Lips Page, Lucky Millinder, and Jimmy Rushing (1950–52), and formed his own band, which was resident at the Celebrity Club in

Harlem from 1953 to 1971; the band also appeared at the Savoy Ballroom until it closed in 1957. Among Tate's sidemen during this period were Pat Jenkins, Eli Robinson, Skip Hall (replaced by Sadik Hakim), and Everett Barksdale (playing electric bass guitar). He also played with other leaders and occasionally again with Basie. He toured Europe (1959, 1961) and recorded (1960–61) with Buck Clayton.

Tate returned to Europe as a leader and with the Saints and Sinners; he made particularly fine recordings in France in a trio with Milt Buckner (organ) and Wallace Bishop (drums) (1967–8). In 1975 he led a band with Paul Quinichette at the West End Café, New York, and later performed and recorded with Jay McShann and Jim Galloway in Canada. He was co-leader of a band with Bob Rosengarden at New York's Rainbow Room, and in the late 1970s and early 1980s performed and recorded with Scott Hamilton. Concurrently in the 1980s he toured with the Texas Tenors, led by Illinois Jacquet, and he replaced Jimmy Forrest in Al Grey's group (*c*1980–1987). He appeared at jazz festivals in Newport (1980) and Cork (1983, 1985) and regularly at the Grande Parade du Jazz, Nice, and in 1991 was a featured soloist at the Chicago and JVC (New York) festivals. In the 1990s he performed and recorded with Lionel Hampton's Golden Men of Jazz, and in the latter half of the decade he was also a member of the Statesmen of Jazz. Tate had a big tone and an exceptional command of the harmonics in the upper register, which he used as an extension of the tenor saxophone's normal range.

Oral history material in *MoKmh, NjR* (JOHP); video oral history material in *NCH* (HCJA).

SELECTED RECORDINGS

As leader: *Jumpin' on the West Coast* (1947, Fre. 30128); *Celebrity Club Orchestra*, i (1954, BB 33006); *Buddy Tate and his Orchestra* (*c*1955, Halo 50322), incl. Skip it; with B. Clayton: *Buck & Buddy* (1960, Swingville 2017); *Buddy Tate Featuring Milt Buckner* (1967, BB 33014), incl. When I'm Blue; *Celebrity Club Orchestra*, ii (1968, BB 33020); with E. Warren: *The Count's Men* (1973, RCA LPL1-5034); *The Texas Twister* (1975, MJR 8128); *Hard Blowin': Live at Sandy's* (1978, Muse 5249); with S. Hamilton: *Scott's Buddy* (1980, Conc. 148); *The Great Buddy Tate* (1981, Conc. 163); *The Ballad Artistry of Buddy Tate* (1981, Sack. 3034); with A. Cohn and S. Hamilton: *Tour de force* (1981, Conc. 172); with A. Grey: *Just Jazz* (1984–5, Reservoir 110); with H. Person and N. Simkins: *Just Friends* (1990, Muse 5418)

As sideman: C. Basie: Rock-a-bye Basie (1939, Voc. 4747); Taxi War Dance (1939, Voc. 4748); Let Me See (1940, OK 6330); Super Chief (1940, OK 5673); It's Sand, Man! (1942, Col. 36647)

SELECTED FILMS AND VIDEOS

Choo Choo Swing [Band Parade] (1943); Hit Parade of 1943 [Change of Heart] (1943); Reveille with Beverly (1943); Buck Clayton and his All Stars (1961); L'aventure du jazz (1970); Born to Swing (1972); The Great Rocky Mountain Jazz Party (1977); To the Count of Basie (1979); Mary Lou Williams: Music on my Mind (1990); The Texas Tenors (n.d.)

BIBLIOGRAPHY

ChiltonW; *McCarthyB*; *SheridanCB*
H. Panassié: "Buddy Tate," *BHcF*, no.61 (1956), 3
B. Tate and F. Driggs: "My Story," *JR*, i/2 (1958), 18
F. Driggs: "The Buddy Tate Story," *JM*, v/2 (1959), 2
L. Jones: "Showtime at the Old Corral: Buddy Tate at the Celebrity Club," *JR*, ii/3 (1959), 11
J. Mansion: "Dig . . . Dingue . . . Dong . . ., iii: The Swinging Gentleman," *BHcF*, no.116 (1962), 6
J. R. Haddon: "Buddy Tate," *JM*, xii/6 (1966), 9
J. Poinsot, L. Verdeaux, and P. Walter: "Quelques propos de Buddy Tate," *BHcF*, no.181 (1968), 10
B. Esposito: "Tate the Tenor," *JJ*, xxv/2 (1972), 14
L. Verdeaux: "Buddy Tate vous parle," *BHcF*, no.240 (1974), 10
J. Simmen: "Crystal Clear," *Coda*, no.144 (1976), 29
S. Woolley: "Tate à tête," *JJ*, xxx/2 (1977), 6
B. Case: "Buddy & the 'President'," *MM* (1 Dec 1979), 37
J. Pescheux and J.-P. Battestini: "Buddy Tate en Europe," *BHcF*, no.271 (1979), 3
S. Dance: *The World of Count Basie* (New York and London, 1980), 111
M. L. Hester: *Going to Kansas City* (Sherman, TX, 1980), 115
S. Klett: "Buddy Tate: Interview," *Cadence*, vi/5 (1980), 15
J. Norris and B. Smith: "Buddy Tate: the Texas Tenor," *Coda*, no.195 (1984), 4
M. L. Hester: "Tate on Tenor," *MR*, xiv/8 (1987), 14
D. Kochakian: "Buddy Tate," *Whisky, Women, and . . .*, no.16 (1987), 32 [incl. discography by D. Penny]
N. W. Pearson, Jr.: *Goin' to Kansas City* (Urbana, IL, and London, 1988/*R*1994)
K. Brodacki: "The Big Sound of Buddy Tate," *JF* [intl edn], no.119 (1989), 30
J. Evensmo: *History of Jazz Tenor Saxophone: Black Artists*, ii: *1935–1939* (Oslo, 1997); iii: *1940–1944* (Oslo, 1997)
H. O'Neal: *Les fantômes de Harlem: l'histoire du quartier mythique de jazz* (Levallois-Perret, France, 1997)
Obituary, B. Ratliff, *New York Times* (13 Feb 2001)

EDDIE COOK/BK

Tate, Erskine (*b* Memphis, 19 Dec 1895; *d* Chicago, 17 Dec 1978). Bandleader. He grew up in a musical family and moved as a teenager to Chicago, where he studied at the American Conservatory of Music; in 1912 he began playing violin professionally. From 1919 to 1928 he led an orchestra that was resident at the Vendome Theater and made the recordings *Cutie Blues/Chinaman Blues* (1923, OK 4907) and *Static Strut/Stomp off, let's go* (1926, Voc. 1027). This ensemble played at various theaters before working regularly at the Savoy Ballroom (1931–8) and the Cotton Club. As the leader of the most prominent theater orchestra in Chicago, Tate provided invaluable training for young musicians, among them Louis Armstrong, Boyd Atkins, Buster Bailey, Jimmy Bertrand, Earl Hines, Milt Hinton, Darnell Howard, Guy Kelly, Freddie Keppard, Omer Simeon, Jabbo Smith, and Teddy Weatherford. Around 1945 he retired from performing to concentrate on teaching, in which capacity he continued to work into the mid-1970s. Although mainly a violinist, he played and taught most orchestral instruments.

BIBLIOGRAPHY

ChiltonW; *McCarthyB*
"From our Files . . . the Incomplete Story of Erskine Tate's Orchestra," *Jazz-Statistics*, no.9 (1959), 6
T. J. Hennessey: "The Black Chicago Establishment, 1919–1930," *JJS*, ii/1 (1974), 15
S. Dance: *The World of Earl Hines* (New York, 1977)
P. Van Vorst: "Erskine Tate," *MR*, vi/6 (1979), 6

MICHAEL TOVEY

Tate, Frank (Eastman) (*b* Washington, DC, 18 July 1943). Double bass player. He grew up in Arlington, Virginia, and was originally a trumpeter, but changed to double bass at the age of 23. He led the house band at Blues Alley (1972–5), then left to work with Bobby Hackett in Cape Cod and shortly afterwards with Dave McKenna. He continued to perform with McKenna occasionally until around 1979, but in 1975 moved to New York, where he worked as a freelance, deputized for Red Balaban at Eddie Condon's club, and accompanied Marian McPartland (1975–9). After touring and recording with Zoot Sims (1980–83) he took a group that included Spanky Davis, Al Cohn, John Bunch, and Billy Hart to the Queen's University Festival in Ireland in 1983; he returned there in 1985 with Scott Hamilton, McKenna, Davis, and others. Tate worked with Pearl Bailey from 1984 through the late 1980s, the Alden–Barrett Quintet from 1985 into the 1990s, and Ruby Braff's bands, among them a trio with Howard Alden. He has played at various jazz parties and festivals worldwide. His bass utilizes an added fifth string, tuned to *B'*.

Oral history material in *PES* (ACMJC).

SELECTED RECORDINGS

(all recorded for Concord)

As sideman: H. Alden and D. Barrett: *Swing Street* (1986, 4349); *The A.B.Q. Salutes Buck Clayton* (1989, 4395); K. Peplowski: *Mr. Gentle and Mr. Cool* (1990, 4419); R. Braff: *Cornet Chop Suey* (1991, 4606); *Ruby Braff and his New England Songhounds*, i–ii (1991, 4478, 4504); H. Alden: *Misterioso* (1991, 4487)

BIBLIOGRAPHY

"Interview with Frank Tate," *The Note*, iii/1 (1991), 2

M. Richards: "Frank Tate," *JJI*, xlv (1992), no.2, p.18; no.3, p.10

GK

Tate, Grady (B.) (*b* Durham, NC, 14 Jan 1932). Drummer and singer. He began singing as a small child, played drums from the age of five, and was at first self-taught; he learned jazz drumming while serving in the air force (1951–5). On his discharge he returned to Durham, where he studied theater, literature, and psychology at North Carolina College and worked part-time as a musician. He then moved to Washington, DC (1959), played with Wild Bill Davis until early in 1962, and in 1963 moved to New York to work with Jerome Richardson and in Quincy Jones's big band. Later he played with Duke Ellington, Count Basie, Jimmy Smith, Wes Montgomery, Roland Kirk, Stan Getz, Kenny Burrell, Bill Evans (ii), Oscar Peterson, Lalo Schifrin, Oliver Nelson, J. J. Johnson, Kai Winding, Billy Taylor (ii) (1966), Clark Terry (in his big band, 1967), and Zoot Sims. Much of this work was as a house drummer for Verve in orchestral and big-band settings from 1964 to 1969, though he occasionally worked for other labels, in similar instrumental contexts or in small-group sessions, with Nelson (1964), Nat Adderley (1965), Eric Kloss and Shirley Scott (both 1966), Eddie "Lockjaw" Davis, Getz, Duke Pearson (all 1967), Johnny Hammond (1968), and Taylor (1969); perhaps the finest moment among these is to be heard on Getz's album *Sweet Rain*, where Tate invents a magnificently disorienting drum introduction to Dizzy Gillespie's composition *Con Alma*. He also accompanied several jazz and popular singers, including Peggy Lee, Ella Fitzgerald, Astrud Gilberto, Chris Connor, Ray Charles, Blossom Dearie, Lena Horne, and Sarah Vaughan, recorded albums as a singer in a quasi-popular idiom, worked as an actor, and played in the big band for "The Tonight Show" on NBC television (1968–74). Tate deputized for Ben Riley in the New York Jazz Quartet (recording with the group in 1978), played intermittently in Ray Bryant's trio (with which he recorded in 1976 and 1978), and recorded as a sideman with Zoot Sims (1975), Benny Carter and Jiggs Whigham (both 1976), Earl Hines, Howard McGhee, and Taylor (all 1977), Clifford Jordan (1978), and Peterson (1979).

Tate remained active as a freelance, playing with Sonny Stitt in Tokyo in 1980, appearing at the Lincoln Center in the video *Jazz in America* (1983) and at Town Hall in the celebration of the reactivated Blue Note label (1985), and recording with Milt Jackson (1981), Joe Beck (1983), Ray Brown, Jane Jarvis, and Monty Alexander (all 1985), Gerry Mulligan and Scott Hamilton (1986), Smith (1986), Dado Moroni (in Rome), Eric Gale, Brother Jack McDuff, and Houston Person (all 1987), Lionel Hampton and Peggy Lee (both 1988), and Claude Williams (1989). As a singer he held an engagement at the Hotel Méridian in Paris in 1988 and recorded in 1991–2. Again on drums, he was a member of Lionel Hampton's Golden Men of Jazz (from 1991), performed and recorded with George Shearing in New York (1992), toured with Smith and Burrell (1993), and recorded with Bill Easley, Person and Buddy Tate, and Carol Sloane (all 1990), John Hicks and Abbey Lincoln (both 1992), the saxophonist Lisa Pollard (1993), Jarvis (1995), and Dee Dee Bridgewater and Bob Dorough (both 1997).

As a drummer Tate is highly regarded for his forceful, driving playing and for his ability to adapt to a wide range of musical styles; his singing is curiously overrated in many circles, perhaps because its mannered eccentricity appeals to some listeners, or perhaps simply because of the novelty of his maintaining these two discrete musical roles.

Video oral history in *NN-Sc* (LAJOHP).

SELECTED RECORDINGS

As leader (all as singer): *Feeling Life* (1969, Skye 7); *After the Long Ride Home* (1969, Skye 17); *Master Grady Tate* (*c*1977, Imp. 9930); *TNT* (1991, Mlst. 9193); *Body and Soul* (1992, Mlst. 9208)

As sideman (all as drummer): O. Nelson: *More Blues and the Abstract Truth* (1964, Imp. 75); J. Smith and W. Montgomery: *The Dynamic Duo* (1966, Verve 68678); S. Getz: *Sweet Rain* (1967, Verve 68693), incl. Con Alma; R. Kirk: *Now Please don't you Cry Beautiful Edith* (1967, Verve 68709); Q. Jones: *Walking in Space* (1969, A&M Hor. 3023); Z. Sims: *Zoot Sims and the Gershwin Brothers* (1975, Pablo 2310744); B. Taylor: *Live at Storyville* (1977, West 54 8008); New York Jazz Quartet: *Blues for Sarka* (1978, Enja 3025); O. Peterson: *Silent Partner* (1979, Pablo 2312103); R. Rodney: *The 3 R's* (1979, Muse 5290); R. Brown: *Don't Forget the Blues* (1985, Conc. 293); G. Shearing: *I Hear a Rhapsody: Live at the Blue Note*, i (1992, Telarc 83310); J. Jarvis: *Jane Jarvis Jams* (1995, Arbors 19152)

BIBLIOGRAPHY

R. Palmer: "Grady Tate," *JJ*, xxiii/11 (1970), 18

E. Meadow: "Grady Tate: He'd Rather Sing," *DB*, xxxviii/10 (1971), 18

C. Iero: "Grady Tate," *MD*, iii/3 (1979), 22

B. Korall: "Exploring the Versatility of Grady Tate," *IM*, lxxxiii/1 (1984), 6

K. Franckling: "Riffs: Grady Tate," *DB*, lix/2 (1992), 15

J. KENT WILLIAMS/BK

Tatum, Art(hur, Jr.) (*b* Toledo, OH, 13 Oct 1909; *d* Los Angeles, 5 Nov 1956). Pianist.

1. Life. 2. Musical style.

1. Life. As he had seriously impaired vision (he was blind in one eye and had only partial sight in the other), Tatum attended special classes at the Jefferson School (a local elementary school), the School for the Blind in Columbus, Ohio (1924), and the Toledo School of Music. He studied piano in Toledo with Overton G. Rainey, and learned to read music with the aid of glasses as well as by the Braille method. Violin, guitar, and accordion are variously mentioned as additional instruments in his early musical development. He was gifted with superb rentential powers and an infallible sense of pitch, and learned from piano rolls, phonograph recordings, radio broadcasts, local musicians, and the touring ensembles he encountered in the area around Toledo and Cleveland. Playing for drinks, tips, and free meals, Tatum and his friends spent weekends frequenting local night spots during the Prohibition years. His ability to go without sleep was remarkable even to the stalwarts who accompanied him then, and this ceaseless energy would remain characteristic throughout his life: professional engagements were followed by excursions to after-hours spots for the challenges of cutting competitions and all-night sessions. He was playing professionally in Toledo by 1926 and in 1929 had his own 15-minute live radio program at WSPD, broadcast on the NBC Blue radio network.

Tatum named Fats Waller as his primary inspiration, with the popular radio pianist Lee Sims, whose interpretations were rich in harmony and filigree, as an important secondary influence. In 1932 he traveled to New York as part of a two-piano team, with Francis Carter, accompanying

Adelaide Hall, and recorded with her in August. In March 1933 he made his first unaccompanied solo recordings, for Brunswick, and these were major successes. After leaving Hall he worked in Cleveland (1934–5), performed at the Three Deuces, Chicago (1935), and spent a considerable time in Hollywood (1936–7) working in various clubs and playing for private parties. He made his only overseas tour, to England, in March 1938, and in the late 1930s and early 1940s appeared regularly in New York and Los Angeles. With Nat "King" Cole's successful jazz trio as a model, Tatum founded his own influential trio with Slam Stewart (double bass) and Tiny Grimes (electric guitar) at the Streets of Paris in Hollywood in 1943 (see illustration). Grimes left the following year, but Tatum continually returned to this format, using Everett Barksdale regularly in the 1950s.

In the early 1940s Tatum performed in a variety of settings with many of the great musicians of his era, and in 1947 he made a cameo appearance in the film *The Fabulous Dorseys*. He held extended engagements in New York at the Three Deuces (1944, 1945) and the Downbeat Club (1945, 1946, 1947), in Los Angeles at Billy Berg's (1946), again in New York at the Famous Door (1947) and the downtown location of Café Society (1949–50), and at the Surf, Los Angeles (1950), and the Embers, New York (1951). In 1953 he gave an unaccompanied solo concert at Brandeis University. That year he began an association with the record producer Norman Granz that led to a number of outstanding small-group recordings with such prominent musicians as Benny Carter, Roy Eldridge, Lionel Hampton, Ben Webster, and Jo Jones. Also, from 1953 to 1956 Granz recorded Tatum in a long series of more than 120 unaccompanied performances which reveal the state of his musical maturity and his extraordinary imagination. Tatum remained active, touring just weeks before his death from kidney failure.

2. Musical style. Tatum transported the art of jazz piano improvisation beyond the real and imagined confines of his day. His first professional solo recordings in 1933 were seen as a challenge to his own and future generations of jazz and popular pianists. His technical abilities, lightness of touch, and control of the full range of the instrument were unprecedented among popular pianists. He had an unerring sense of rhythm and swing, a seemingly unlimited capacity to expand and enrich a melody, and a profound and continually evolving grasp of substitute harmonies. The thematic element was as strategic as the harmonic structure to the architecture of Tatum's recorded improvisations; extended departures from audible melodic references points, as heard in his solo on *Exactly like You* (1944), are rare. Ex.1 shows several variations of the opening melodic notes of *After You've Gone* (1934), including (1*c*) rhythmic and harmonic intensification, and (1*a*) extension and variation of the melody; (1*d*) new melodic material involving harmonic variety and a different manner of syncopation; (1*e*) a slashing scalar figure in each hand (bar 55) and then a return to the melody (bar 56); and (1*f*) double-time stride in the left hand.

Most often Tatum chose models from the standard popular repertory, though he also interpreted the blues and sometimes performed parodies on light classical pieces. Only occasionally did he play original works. He was often described as having two distinct musical personalities: in his professional appearances he was thoroughly business-like, obliging audiences with almost literal repetitions of his recorded performances, seldom taking encores, and, in a studio, rarely recording more than one take of a performance. Among friends he was inclined to play (and sing) the blues, to improvise for hours on a given chord sequence, and to depart radically and dramatically from the original tune.

Art Tatum (piano) with Slam Stewart (double bass) and Tiny Grimes (guitar) at the Three Deuces, New York, 1944

Ex.1

(a) The first two bars of the melody of *After You've Gone*, by H. Creamer and T. Layton (1918)

(b)–(f) From *After You've Gone* (1934, Bruns. 01862); transcr. B. Edstrom

(b)

(c)

(d)

(e)

(f)

His performances are preserved on more than 600 recordings (as unaccompanied soloist, with his trios, and with other ensembles), which provide ample evidence of his uncommonly creative genius as an improviser.

Tatum integrated the practices and characteristic gestures of the stride and swing keyboard traditions, at the same time transforming them through his virtuosity. His early impact on his contemporaries was enormous, memorable, and the stuff of legends: people did not believe their ears, and, when they saw him perform, they did not believe their eyes. With hands that seemed to glide horizontally across the keyboard, he played the piano with an uncommon ease and grace, shielding in simplicity his tremendous strength, technical agility, and control of nuance even in the finest details. Simple decorative techniques became complex harmonic sweeps of color; traditional repetitive patterns were expanded and intensified; rhythmic-melodic ideas were introduced with unpredictable and ever-changing combinations of notes per beat even in the most rapid passages. In ex.2, a six-bar excerpt from *Aunt Hagar's Blues* (1949), melodic rhythms are so subtly controlled that the melodic line seems to be propelled by its own internal dynamic: tossed upwards from a turning figure, the line loses speed as it climbs to its highest point; the two-bar descent seems to contain the most delicate application of brakes as it returns to its starting-point.

Later generations of jazz musicians were impressed by Tatum's elaboration of the original harmonies of a tune, particularly his use of complex passing harmonies and voicings, and by the textural variety of his work, which frequently led to contrapuntal relationships among lines in different registers. He could apply different variation techniques simultaneously, and used subtle rhythmic intensification and relaxation to give clear identity and shape to his phrases. Tatum's creativity and flexibility stood on a foundation characterized by his intimate understanding of the traditions of jazz piano performance, superb technical skills, rhythmic solidity and security, an orchestral embrace of the full range of the keyboard, impeccable delivery, affection for his material, and joy in performance. He remains a gigantic musical presence both for the gifts he shared during his lifetime and for those he bequeathed to the future.

See also PIANO, §2, and fig.1.

SELECTED RECORDINGS

As unaccompanied soloist: Tea for Two (1933, Bruns. 6553); Tiger Rag (1933, Bruns. 6543); After You've Gone (1934, Bruns. 01862); Liza [take A] (1934, Decca 1373); Liza [take D] (1934, also Decca 1373); Gone with the Wind/Stormy Weather (1937, Decca 1603); Elegie (1940, Decca 18049); Sweet Lorraine/Get Happy (1940, Decca 18050); St. Louis Blues (1940, Decca 8550); Begin the Beguine/Rosetta (1940, Decca 8502); *California Melodies* (1940, Memphis Archives 7007), incl. Get Happy, The Shout, I got rhythm; Hallelujah/Memories of You (1945, American Recording Artists 4501); Yesterdays (1949, Just Jazz 69); Willow Weep for Me/Aunt Hagar's Blues (1949, Cap. 15520); Nice work if you can get it/Dancing in the Dark (1949, Cap. 15519); Sweet Lorraine (1949, Cap. 15713)

Piano Music (1949, Cap. H216), incl. Blue Skies; *Art Tatum Piano Discoveries* (1950, 1955, 20CF 3033), incl. Mr. Freddie Blues (1950), I cover the waterfront (1955); *The Genius of Art Tatum*, ii (1953, Clef 613), incl. Makin' Whoopee, Memories of You; *The Genius of Art Tatum*, iii (1953, Clef 614), incl. Embraceable You, Come Rain or Come Shine; *The Genius of Art Tatum*, vi (1953, Clef 657), incl. Jitterbug Waltz, Night and Day; *The Genius of Art Tatum*, v (1953, Clef 618), incl. Stompin' at the Savoy; *The Genius of Art Tatum*, viii (1953, Clef 659), incl. Ain't misbehavin', All the Things you are; *The Genius of Art Tatum*, x (1953, Clef 661), incl. Too marvelous for words

As leader: With Plenty of Money and You (1937, Decca 1198); *Pieces of Eight* (1939–55, Smithsonian 029), incl. Exactly like You; Stompin' at the Savoy/Last Goodbye Blues (1941, Decca 8536); Corinne, Corinna/Lonesome Graveyard Blues (1941, Decca 8563); I got rhythm/I ain't got nobody (1944, World Jam Session 32); Dark Eyes (1944, Comet 1); Body and Soul (1944, Comet 2); Flying Home (1944, Comet 3); Boogie (1944, Asch 4521); with B. Carter and L. Bellson: *The Art Tatum–Benny Carter–Louis Bellson Trio* (1954, Clef 643), incl. Idaho, Blues in B Flat

with L. Hampton and B. Rich: *The Lionel Hampton–Art Tatum–Buddy Rich Trio* (1955, Clef 709), incl. More than you know; *The Art Tatum Trio* (1956, Verve 8118), incl. Trio Blues; with B. Webster: *The Art Tatum–Ben Webster Quartet* (1956, Verve 8220), incl. All the things you are, Night and Day, Where or When; with E. Barksdale and S. Stewart: *The Art*

Ex.2 Bars 31–6, the melody only, from *Aunt Hagar's Blues* (1949, Cap. 15520); transcr. B. Edstrom

Tatum Trio (1955–6, Jazz Anthology 5138), incl. I Cover the Waterfront, Soft Winds

As sideman: A. Hall: This Time It's Love (1932, Bruns. 6362); L. Feather: Esquire Bounce/Esquire Blues (1943, Com. 547); My Ideal (1943, Com. 548); B. Bigard: Please don't talk about me when I'm gone (1945, Black & White 14); Blues for Art's Sake (1945, Black & White 13); L. Hampton: *Lionel Hampton and his Giants* (1955, Norg. 1080), incl. Verve Blues

TRANSCRIPTIONS

The Famous Style Piano Solo Album (London, 1939); selections repr. in C. Bolton, ed.: *Art Tatum – Piano Solos* (London, 1980)

M. Feldman, ed. and transcr.: *Art Tatum Improvisations*, i–ii (New York, 1939, 1946); selections repr. in C. Bolton, ed.: *Art Tatum – Piano Solos* (London, 1980), and in *The Genius of Art Tatum – Piano Solos* (New York, 1981)

F. Paparelli, ed. and transcr.: *5 Jazz Piano Solos by Art Tatum* (New York, 1944)

J. Distler: *Art Tatum* (New York, 1981)

B. Edstrom, transcr., and R. Schiff: *The Art Tatum Collection* (Milwaukee, 1996)

Art Tatum Solo Book (Milwaukee, 1998)

BIBLIOGRAPHY

SchullerS

A. Duckett: "Art Tatum: What a Blind Man," *New York Age Defender* (5 May 1954)

W. Balliett: "Art and Tatum," *Saturday Review*, xxxvii (24 Oct 1955), 44; repr. in *BallietA (1986), BallietA (1996)*

A. Hodeir: "Art Tatum: a French Critic Evaluates the Music of a Great Pianist," *DB*, xxii/17 (1955), 9

B. Taylor: "Billy Taylor Replies to Art Tatum Critic," *DB*, xxii/19 (1955), 17

O. Keepnews: "Art Tatum," *The Jazz Makers*, ed. N. Shapiro and N. Hentoff (New York, 1957/*R*1979 as *The Jazz Makers: Essays on the Greats of Jazz*), 156; repr. in *The View from Within: Jazz Writings, 1948–1987* (New York, and Oxford, England, 1988), 74

M. Gibson: "The Paradox of Art Tatum," *JJ*, xiii/10 (1960), 3

M. Williams: "The Real Art Tatum," JR, iii/6 (1960), 28; repr. in *Jazz Masters in Transition, 1957–69* (New York and London, 1970/*R*1980)

D. Katz: "Art Tatum," *Jazz Panorama*, ed. M. Williams (New York and London, 1962/*R*1979)

J. Mehegan: *Jazz Improvisation*, ii: *Jazz Rhythm and the Improvised Line* (New York, 1962)

T. Rosenkranz: "Reflections on Art," *DB*, xxix/14 (1962), 15

J. Mehegan: *Jazz Improvisation*, iii: *Swing and Early Progressive Piano Styles* (New York, 1964)

R. Spencer: "Art Tatum Discography," *JJ*, xix/10 (1966), 13

——: "The Tatum Story," *JJ*, xix/8 (1966), 6

——: "The Tatum Style," *JJ*, xix/9 (1966), 11

A. Bridgers: "Tatum the Master by Aaron, the Pupil," *Music Maker* (1967), July, 14

W. Balliett: "One Man Band," *New Yorker*, xliv (7 Sept 1968); repr. in *Ecstasy at the Onion* (New York and Indianapolis, 1971), 111

S. Rothman: "The Art of Tatum," *Blade Sunday Magazine* [Toledo, OH] (14 June 1970), 4

D. Morgenstern: Liner notes, Art Tatum: *God is in the House* (Onyx 205, 1972)

R. Stewart: *Jazz Masters of the Thirties* (New York and London, n.d. [1972]), 181

V. Genova: *Melodic and Harmonic Irregularities Found in the Improvisations of Art Tatum* (thesis, U. of Pittsburgh, 1978)

J. A. Howard: *The Improvisational Techniques of Art Tatum* (diss., Case Western Reserve U., 1978)

D. C. Brigaud: *Art Tatum: essai pour une discographie des enregistrements hors commerce* (Paris, 1980) [incl. listings of radio broadcasts, film music, and V-discs]

Keyboard, vii/10 (1981) [special issue]

H. Lyttelton: *The Best of Jazz*, ii: *Enter the Giants, 1931–1944* (London, 1981), 113

B. Taylor: "An Art Tatum Recollection and Analysis," *Keyboard*, vii/10 (1981), 36

A. Laubich and R. Spencer: *Art Tatum: a Guide to his Recorded Music* (Metuchen, NJ, 1982) [bio-discography]

A. B. Spellman: Liner notes, *Giants of Jazz: Art Tatum* (TL 24, 1982)

A. Balalas: "Art Tatum," *BHcF* (1983), no.304, p.3; no.305, p.6 [incl. Fr. trans. of interview by W. Conover]

F. A. Howlett: *An Introduction to Art Tatum's Performance Approaches: Composition, Improvisation, and Melodic Variation* (diss., Cornell U., 1983)

H. Rye: "Visiting Firemen, 8(f): Art Tatum," *Sv*, no.108 (1983), 216

M. Williams: "Art Tatum: not for the Left Hand Alone," *American Music*, i/1 (1983), 36

R. Callender and E. Cohen: *Unfinished Dream: the Musical World of Red Callender* (London, 1985)

S. Rothman: "Art Tatum's Toledo Years," *Toledo Blade* (30 June 1985)

D. Asher: "Keys of the Kingdom," *Jazzletter*, ix/3 (1990), 1

S. Mayer: "Tatum & Liszt at the Keyboard," *Keyboard Classics*, x/2 (1990) 12

J. L. Anderson: "He Played Like the Wind," *MR*, xviii/6 (1991), 1

D. Hyman, *Piano Pro* (Katonah, NY, 1992)

J. Lester: *Too Marvelous for Words: the Life and Genius of Art Tatum* (New York, and Oxford, England, 1994)

S. Mayer: "The Tatum–Horowitz Connection," *Keyboard Classics*, xiv/6 (1994), 34

T. Piazza, ed.: *Setting the Tempo: 50 Years of Great Jazz Liner Notes* (New York and elsewhere, 1996)

R. Scivales: *The Right Hand According to Tatum* (Bedford Hills, NY, 1998) [incl. transcrs.]

A. Tercinet: "Piano intempérant: Art Tatum, le 'Chopin fou'," *Jazzman*, no.34 (1998), 22

FELICITY HOWLETT

Tavaglione, Steve(n Alan) [Tav] (*b* Riverside, CA, 1 Dec 1950). Saxophonist and EWI player. After teaching himself to play saxophone he worked with Sly and the Family Stone (1974) and was co-leader of the group Caldera (1976–9). In the 1980s and 1990s he played with George Benson (1980–87), Diana Ross (1990), and John Patitucci (1991–5) and performed occasionally with such musicians as Dave Weckl, the trumpeter Jeff Beal, Gary Willis, Frank Gambale, the Brazilian bandleader Sergio Mendes, Vinnie Colaiuta, Mark Isham, Allan Holdsworth, the popular singer Holly Cole, and Lee Ritenour. Tavaglione has worked extensively in commercial recording studios in California and brought a harmonically oblique yet highly melodic flavor to many fusion and straight-ahead recordings in the 1990s.

SELECTED RECORDINGS

As leader: *Blue Tav* (1990, Creatchy 1006); *Silent Singing* (1998, Unitone 4701-2)

As sideman: Caldera: *Dreamer* (1979, Cap. 6385); F. Gambale: *Live* (1988, Legato 1003); MVP: *Truth in Shredding* (1990, Heading West 652507); *Centrifugal Funk* (1991, Heading West 652508); S. Mendes: *Brasileiro* (1991, Elek. 61315-2); J. Patitucci: *Another World* (1993, GRP 9725-2); D. Weckl: *Hard-wired* (1993, GRP 9760-2); V. Colaiuta: *Vinnie Colaiuta* (1994, Stretch 00132); M. Isham: *Blue Sun* (1995, Col. CK67227); G. Willis: *No Sweat* (1996, Alchemy 1009)

BIBLIOGRAPHY

H. Siders: "Live Sounds: Steve Tavaglione," *Windplayer*, v/ii (1988), 29

MARK GILBERT

Taylor, Art(hur S., Jr.) (*b* New York, 6 April 1929; *d* New York, 6 Feb 1995). Drummer. He began on drums at a fairly late age (*c*1948). Having played in a church in Harlem with Sonny Rollins and Jackie McLean and worked with Howard McGhee, he performed and recorded with Oscar Pettiford (1950–51), Coleman Hawkins (late 1950–1952, 1955), Buddy DeFranco (1952), Bud Powell (1953–5, intermittently to the mid-1960s), Art Farmer (1954–5, recording in 1955), George Wallington (1954–6), and Miles Davis (in the studio with Davis's quintet, 1955 and 1956; in performance with it, 1957; and in the studio with Gil Evans's orchestra and Davis, 1957). In New York he led the group Taylor's Wailers at The Pad, a club in Greenwich Village, until 1956; he also made several trips to Europe, the first of which was with Donald Byrd and Bobby Jaspar (1958), and played with Thelonious Monk (1959). While living in France (from 1963) and Belgium (from 1970) Taylor played frequently with Johnny Griffin and Dexter Gordon and toured the USA. A collection of his interviews with other jazz musicians was published as *Notes and Tones: Musician-to-musician Interviews* (Liège, Belgium, 1977, rev. and enlarged 2/New York, 1993). After moving back and forth between Europe and the USA through the early 1980s, he settled in New York in 1984 and became the host of an interview program on radio station WKCR. He reorganized Taylor's Wailers in the late 1980s and recorded in 1991–2; among his sidemen were the double bass player Tyler Mitchell (with whom he worked from the mid-1980s), Abraham Burton, Willie Williams, Jacky Terrasson, and Marc Cary (replacing Terrasson). Taylor recorded prolifically (especially in the late 1950s, when he was house drummer for Prestige) and may be heard on nearly 300 recordings, including John Coltrane's *Giant Steps* (1959), the title track of which well illustrates Taylor's bop style.

SELECTED RECORDINGS

(recorded for Prestige unless otherwise indicated)

As leader: *Taylor's Wailers* (1957, 7117); *A. T.'s Delight* (1960, BN 4047); *Mr. A. T.* (1991, Enja 7017-2); *Taylor's Wailers* (1992, Verve 314-519677-2)

As sideman with J. Coltrane: *Dakar* (1957, 7280); *Soultrane* (1958, 7142); *Black Pearls* (1958, 7316); *Giant Steps* (1959, Atl. 1311)

As sideman with others: B. Powell: The Glass Enclosure (1953, BN 1628); M. Davis: *Milt and Miles* (1955, 7034); E. Hope and F. Foster: *Wail, Frank, Wail* (1955, 7021); J. McLean: *4, 5 and 6* (1956, 7048); M. Waldron: *Mal 2* (1957, 7111); M. Davis: *Miles Ahead* (1957, Col. CL1041); R. Garland: *Soul Junction* (1957, 7181); *Dig it* (1957–8, 7229); T. Thielemans: *Man Bites Harmonica* (1957–8, Riv. 257); G. Ammons: *Groove Blues* (1958, 7201); *Blue Gene* (1958, 7146); D. Gordon: *A Day in Copenhagen* (1969, MPS 15230); J. Griffin: *Live in Tokyo* (1976, Phi. [Jap.] RJ7160); T. Flanagan: *Thelonica* (1984, Enja 4052); S. Grossman: *Do it* (1991, Dreyfus 36550)

BIBLIOGRAPHY

I. Gitler: "Art Taylor," *DB*, xxvii/21 (1960), 23
M. Gibson: "Art Taylor," *JJ*, xv/3 (1962), 17
N. Hentoff: "Soundings: Art Taylor," *J&P*, ix/8 (1970), 9
V. Wilmer: "Taylor's New Tricks," *MM* (18 April 1970), 8
S. Crouch: "Drumming up a Book," *VV*, xxvii (19 Oct 1982), 36
J. Chambers: *Milestones*, i: *The Music and Times of Miles Davis to 1960* (Toronto, Buffalo, and London, 1983)
J. Chilton: *The Song of the Hawk: the Life and Recordings of Coleman Hawkins* (London and New York, 1990)
P. Watrous: "Pop/Jazz: Art Taylor: Improviser, Instructor, Inspiration," *New York Times* (6 March 1992)
M. Bourne: "Jazz Artists, Jazz Chroniclers: Arthur Taylor & Milt Hinton," *DB*, lx/12 (1993), 32 [incl. discography]
A. Groves and A. Shipton: *The Glass Enclosure: the Life of Bud Powell* (Tunbridge Wells, England, 1993)
B. L. Johnson: "Words and Music by Art Taylor," *ARJS*, vi (1993), 253 [incl. transcrs.]
B. Primack: "Art Taylor: Still Wailin' after all these Years," *JT*, xxiii/9 (1993), 40
R. McIlroy: "The Art of Noise, Noise of Art: *Mr. A. T.*," *Coda*, no.254 (1994), 21
R. Mattingly: "Arthur Taylor: Jazz Elder Statesman Lives On," *MD*, xviii/5 (1994), 20
Obituaries: P. Watrous, *New York Times* (7 Feb 1995); R. Van Horn, *MD*, xix/6 (1995), 126; M. Gardner, *JJI*, xlviii/6 (1995), 20
F. W. Sportis: "Art Taylor: les tambours se sont tous," *Jh*, no.519 (1995), 20
F. Postif: *Jazz Me Blues: interviews et portraits de musiciens de jazz et de blues* (Paris, 1998), 32

JEFF POTTER/BK

Taylor, Billy [William, Sr.] **(i)** (*b* Washington, DC, 3 April 1906; *d* Fairfax, VA, 2 Sept 1986). Double bass and tuba player. He began playing tuba in his teens. After moving to New York (1924) he worked with Elmer Snowden (1925) and Charlie Johnson (1927–9) and, as a member of Duke Ellington's orchestra, recorded with the singer Ozie Ware (1928). He recorded with McKinney's Cotton Pickers in 1929, and toured with the group from 1931 until it disbanded the following year, when he returned to New York and again worked with Johnson (1932–3). In 1934 he recorded with Benny Morton (including his composition *Taylor Made*, which he also arranged), performed and recorded with an important new group, Fats Waller and his Rhythm (April–November), and briefly joined Louis Metcalf, whose band at the Renaissance Casino was taken over by Fletcher Henderson (*c* November–December). Taylor came to prominence as a double bass player with Ellington (1935–40), when he shared bass duties first with Hayes Alvis and later with Jimmy Blanton; he may be seen with Ellington in the short film *Symphony in Black* (Alvis on the left, Taylor on the right; 1935). He also recorded with other members of Ellington's band, including Barney Bigard (1936–9), Cootie Williams (1937–9), and Johnny Hodges (1938–9). After leaving Ellington he was with Joe Sullivan at Café Society from March 1939 to early 1940 and again in the autumn of that year, after briefly deputizing in Coleman Hawkins's band at the Savoy Ballroom (August 1940). He then spent a period with Henry "Red" Allen (November 1940 – July 1941), remaining with the group when it moved from Café Society to Kelly's Stable; he also recorded with Art Tatum during this period.

From 1942 Taylor worked as a studio musician. He rejoined Williams (1944) before playing with Bigard (1944–5) and Morton (1945), and he also recorded with many other leaders, including Edmond Hall (1943–4), the De Paris brothers, Hawkins, and Johnny Guarnieri (all 1944), Don Byas, J. C. Higginbotham (1945), and Teddy Wilson (1945–7). From 1945 he worked as a freelance in New York (with such musicians as Cozy Cole, 1945, 1949), and in Washington, where during the 1960s he occasionally appeared at Blues Alley.

His son Billy, Jr. (*d* Washington, 15 Nov 1977), was also a double bass player. Another jazz and popular musician of this name was the black English drummer and singer Billy [William] Taylor (*b* Manchester, England, 31 Jan 1898), who played in Britain with Thompson's Negro Band (1923–9) and on the continent with Freddy Johnson's orchestra (1933–4) and Coleman Hawkins (1935). Nothing is known of the saxophonist Billy Taylor and the singer Billy Taylor, both mentioned fleetingly in McCarthy's *Big Band Jazz* (1974).

Oral history material in *CtY*.

SELECTED RECORDINGS

As leader: Carney-val in Rhythm/Night Wind (1944, Key. 615); Taylor Made/Flight of the Be-bop (1947, HRS 1045)

As sideman: O. Ware: Santa Claus, bring my man back to me/I Done Caught You Blues (1928, Vic. 21777); Bessie Smith: Gimme a pigfoot (1933, OK 8949); B. Morton: Taylor Made (1934, Col. 2924D); D. Ellington: Tough Truckin'/Indigo Echoes (1935, Col. 37297); It was a sad night in Harlem (1936, Bruns. 7710); Steppin' into Swing Society (1938, Bruns. 8063); Subtle Lament (1939, Bruns. 8344); R. Stewart: Montmartre/Solid Old Man (1939, Swing 56); Finesse/I know that you know (1939, Swing 70); J. Guarnieri: These Foolish Things/Salute to Fats (1944, Savoy 511)

BIBLIOGRAPHY

AllenH; *ChiltonW*; *FeatherE*; *McCarthyB*; *SchullerS*

C. Carrière: "Pitter Panther Patter: les bassistes de Duke Ellington," *Jh*, no.316 (1975), 10

J. Chilton: *McKinney's Music: a Bio-discography of McKinney's Cotton Pickers* (London, 1978)

J. Simmen: "Les Billy Taylor," *BHcF*, no.351 (1987), 1

M. Selchow: *Profoundly Blue: a Bio-discographical Scrapbook on Edmond Hall* (Lübbecke, Germany, 1988)

R. Stewart and C. P. Gordon: *Boy Meets Horn* (Wheatley, Oxford, England, and Ann Arbor, MI, 1991), 156

L. Wright: *"Fats" in Fact* (Chigwell, England, 1992)

F. Hoffman: *Henry "Red" Allen (Jan. 7th 1908 – Apr. 17th 1967)/J. C. Higginbotham (May 11th 1906 – May 26th 1973): Discography, 1927–1969* (MS, Berlin, 2/1994) [unpubd typescript]

LAWRENCE KOCH/BK

Taylor, Billy [William (Edward), Jr.] **(ii)** (*b* Greenville, NC, 24 July 1921). Pianist, educator, and leader. His birthdate appeared incorrectly as 21 July in "interviews" published in 1980 and 1995; he confirmed that the correct date is 24 July, as many sources give it. He was brought up in Washington, DC, and took piano lessons from the age of seven. His family favored classical music, but an uncle introduced him to the music of the great jazz pianists, and he copied recordings by Fats Waller, Teddy Wilson, and others. In high school he doubled as a tenor saxophonist, but, feeling overwhelmed by the abilities of schoolmate Frank Wess, soon abandoned that pursuit. While studying music at Virginia State College (BMEd 1942) he performed professionally; he sat in one evening with the Count Basie Orchestra and met Jo Jones, who became in effect his jazz mentor and a faithful supporter of his career. In 1944 Taylor moved to New York and immediately secured two brief but extraordinary engagements, playing with Ben Webster's four-piece swing group at the Three Deuces and, while Webster was on break, with Dizzy Gillespie and Oscar Pettiford's bop quintet across the street at the Onyx (their intended pianist, Bud Powell, being highly unreliable). He worked as a freelance with John Kirby, Noble Sissle, Ethel Waters, and others, performed with Eddie South in both New York and Chicago (1944), and played in New York with Foots Thomas. In 1945 he joined Cozy Cole's group – including the bass player Billy Taylor (i) (no relation) – in the show *The Seven Lively Arts* and performed and recorded with Stuff Smith. Early in 1946 he toured as a member of Slam Stewart's trio as a replacement for Erroll Garner. He was in Europe from autumn 1946 to spring 1947 with Don Redman and with small groups generated from this band (without Redman).

On his return to New York, Taylor and Budd Johnson co-led a group with Kenny Dorham, John Collins, Lloyd Trotman, and Charlie Smith, and performed in Haiti at the National Exposition. Subsequently Taylor played with Machito and explored Latin jazz in his own groups. During the winter of 1950–51 Artie Shaw took over Taylor's quartet; this edition of Shaw's Gramercy Five played at the New York restaurant Iceland. In 1951 Taylor became house pianist at Birdland, where he supported Lester Young, Dizzy Gillespie, Roy Eldridge, Stan Getz, Lee Konitz, Gerry Mulligan, Charlie Parker, and other soloists in all-star bop groups that usually incorporated a rhythm section of Taylor with Charles Mingus and Art Blakey, Oscar Pettiford and Jo Jones, or Pettiford and Blakey. From 1952 he performed principally as the leader of his own trio with the bass player Earl May (1951–9) and the drummers Charlie Smith (1952–4) and Ed Thigpen (1956–8).

Billy Taylor (ii), New York, 1946

Taylor's interest in jazz education was first manifested during the 1950s in four brief primers on jazz piano styles. In these years he also wrote magazine articles, lectured at music schools, held jazz workshops, and served as music director for the television series "The Subject is Jazz" (1958). Through these activities, and later, through his involvement in Jazzmobile, which he helped to establish in 1965, he became an articulate and respected spokesman for the arts in general and jazz in particular. In the early 1960s his trio (with sidemen Joe Benjamin and drummer Ray Moscow) performed only intermittently, while Taylor focused on work as a disc jockey in New York and continued his educational activities. He wrote one of the most influential political songs of the civil rights decade, *I wish I knew how it would feel to be free.* From 1969 to 1972 he led an 11-piece band for the "David Frost Show" on television while working concurrently in jazz clubs in a trio with Bob Cranshaw (double bass) and Bobby (Robert) Thomas (Jr.) (drums).

By the 1970s Taylor had written six further booklets on piano styles, combo arranging, and harmony. At the University of Massachusetts he earned a DME in 1975 for his dissertation *The History and Development of Jazz Piano: a New Perspective for Educators*; he published a further work, *Jazz Piano: History and Development*, in 1982. He appeared in the film *Shepherd of the Night Flock* (1977), contributed regularly to *Contemporary Keyboard* magazine (May 1977 – September 1980), and was the founder and director of the radio program "Jazz Alive!" From 1981 through the 1990s he presented interviews and reports and played on CBS television, making regular appearances on Charles Kuralt's show "Sunday Morning." His trio continued with the bass player Victor Gaskin and the drummers Thomas, Freddie Waits (*c*1980), Keith Copeland (1980s), and Thomas again (*c*1988 to the early 1990s).

Taylor served as an American cultural representative in the Soviet Union (summers 1987–8). He joined the faculty of the Brooklyn campus of Long Island University, while keeping up a wide lecturing and performing schedule and remaining devoted to the Jazzmobile. In 1988 he founded his own record label, Taylor Made, and received a Jazz Masters fellowship from the National Endowment for the Arts. By the 1990s he held the Wilber D. Barrett chair at the University of Massachusetts, and in 1994 his career was celebrated at Carnegie Hall in "Billy Taylor: My First 50 Years in Jazz" during the JVC Jazz Festival. Around this time Chip Jackson replaced Gaskin in his trio; his drummers were Carl Allen and then Steve Johns. He continued to host new series for National Public Radio, including "Billy Taylor's Jazz from the Kennedy Center" (from October 1994); an appearance at Jazz Plaza in Havana, Cuba, in December 1997 was among his ongoing festival tours. In the 1990s Taylor also devoted considerable attention to ambitious compositions; his works include the Suite for Jazz Piano and Orchestra (1973), *Homage*, *Siesta: Tucson* (both *c*1990), *Conversations* (*c*1991), and *Step into my Dream* (*c*1994). Materials relating to his career are at the Library of Congress in Washington, DC (*see* Libraries and archives, §2).

Oral history material in *DSI* (JOHP) and *NjR*; video oral history material in NCH (HCJA).

SELECTED RECORDINGS

As unaccompanied soloist: The Very Thought of You (1946, Swing 234); *Solo* (1988, Taylor Made 1002)

As leader: *Piano Panorama* (1951, Atl. 113); *Jazz at Storyville* (1952, Roost 406); *A Touch of Taylor* (1955, Prst. 7001); *One for Fun* (1959, Atl. 1329); *Sleeping Bee* (1969, MPS 15234); *Where've You Been?* (1980, Conc. 145); *You Tempt Me* (1985, Taylor Made 1004); *Billy Taylor and the Jazzmobile All Stars* (1989, Taylor Made 1003); *Dr. T* (*c*1992, GRP 9692); *It's a Matter of Pride* (*c*1993, GRP 9753)

BIBLIOGRAPHY

S. A. Pease: "Taylor: One of the Creators among the Progressives," *DB*, xvii/16 (1950), 12
A. Hodeir: "Critic's Reply to Billy Taylor," *DB*, xxii/22 (1955), 34
B. Nicholls: "Billy Taylor," *Music Mirror*, iii/10 (1956), 12
B. Taylor: "Progressive Jazz," *DB*, xxiii/5 (1956), 11
D. Gold: "Billy Taylor," *DB*, xxv/1 (1958), 16
F. H. Mitchell: "A Matter of Ego," *DB*, xxviii/22 (1961), 22
D. Morgenstern: "Taylor-made Frostings," *DB*, xxxviii/5 (1971), 18
A. Shaw: *The Street that Never Slept: New York's Fabled 52nd Street* (New York, 1971/*R*1977 as *52nd Street: the Street of Jazz*)
W. Fowler: "How to Complete the Spectrum of your Music Education," *DB*, xli/7 (1974), 36
L. Lyons: "Billy Taylor: Jazz Pianist, PhD," *CK*, ii/6 (1976), 18
Z. Knauss: *Conversations with Jazz Musicians* (Detroit, 1977), 202
A. J. Smith: "Jazzmobile: Billy Taylor and Dave Bailey, Magnetizing the Arts," *DB*, xliv/20 (1977), 14
W. A. Brower: "Jazz Alive!: Ad-free Radio Taylored for you," *DB*, xlvi/9 (1979), 18
B. Parker-Sparrow: "Billy Taylor Presents America's Classical Music," *DB*, xlvii/5 (1980), 24
L. P. Bass: "Marathon Man of Jazz Education," *Music Educators Journal*, lxviii/5 (1982), 31
L. Lyons: *The Great Jazz Pianists, Speaking of their Lives and Music* (New York, 1983), 176
J. Roberts: "Billy Taylor: Primarily Piano," *DB*, lii/3 (1985), 26
J. Simmen: "Les Billy Taylor," *BHcF*, no.351 (1987), 1
K. Kevorkian: "Billy Taylor: New Frontiers for the Ambassador of Jazz," *Keyboard*, xv/2 (1989), 32
P. Elwood: "Billy Taylor Keyed in on a Grand Scale," *San Francisco Examiner* (26 May 1991)
J. McDonough: "Billy Taylor: the Player's Advocate," *DB*, lviii/2 (1991), 28 [incl. discography]
K. Franckling: "Billy Taylor's 50 Years in Jazz," *JT*, xxiii/2 (1993), 32
Z. Stewart: "Riffs: Pianist Taylor Notches 50 Years of Jazz Mobility," *DB*, lxi/3 (1994), 11
Z. Anglesey: "Riffs: Taylor Tapes Radio Shows at Kennedy Center," *DB*, lxii/12 (1995), 12
P. Matthews: "Billy Taylor: Interview," *Cadence*, xxi (1995), no.10, p.19; no.11, p.21; no.12, p.5; xxii (1996), no.1, p.19; no.2, p.11; no.3, p.10
E. Rideout: "Billy Taylor: 75 Years of Art and Advocacy," *Keyboard*, xxiii/4 (1997), 56

BILL BENNETT/BK

Taylor, Cecil (Percival) (*b* New York, 15 March 1929). Pianist, composer, and leader. For many years he avoided divulging his year of birth, which was thought to be 1933; it is actually 1929, as Taylor told Whitney Balliett and as confirmed privately by Gary Giddins, who examined Taylor's passport. He grew up on Long Island, where his mother, a highly cultured woman who played the piano, encouraged him to begin piano lessons at the age of five. Later he also studied percussion with a timpanist, which probably influenced his percussive approach to the keyboard. In 1952 he entered the New England Conservatory, where he studied piano and theory; however, he soon detected a lack of appreciation in the academic world for the aesthetic values of African-American culture. After exploring the music of Dave Brubeck, Lennie Tristano, and Igor Stravinsky, he came under the decisive influence of Duke Ellington, Thelonious Monk, and Horace Silver. He worked very briefly with Hot Lips Page and Johnny Hodges (*c*1953). In 1956 he made his first important recording, *Jazz Advance*, in a quartet with Steve Lacy, Buell Neidlinger, and Dennis Charles. In the same year he held a six-week engagement at the Five Spot in New York, which virtually established that club as a major forum for new jazz; he also made appearances at the Newport Jazz Festival in 1957 and the Great South Bay Jazz Festival in 1958 which won him considerable prestige. With Archie Shepp in place of Lacy, Taylor's free-jazz quartet performed briefly as a controversial replacement for the hard-bop band in the play *The Connection* (autumn 1960). In the summer of 1961 Taylor worked on weekends with Shepp and Charles in Greenwich Village at Raphael's, where Jimmy Lyons (ii) began sitting in with the group; Lyons then worked with the quartet at the Five Spot. Despite critical recognition, none of these sporadic events captured a large audience for Taylor's music or secured him further work, and by 1962, when he was given the *Down Beat* "new star" award for pianists, he was, ironically, unemployed, and the quartet had broken up.

The previous autumn, in October 1961, Taylor contributed three tracks to *Into the Hot*, an album issued under the name and sponsorship of the arranger Gil Evans (but without the latter's musical participation) in a failed attempt by Evans to gain greater public acceptance for Taylor's music. But the recording session was nonetheless significant in helping to assemble one of Taylor's most important groups; in addition to Shepp, his principal sidemen on these tracks were Lyons, the saxophonist who would remain Taylor's favorite colleague in groups spanning roughly a quarter of a century (to Lyons's death in 1986), Sunny Murray, who became under Taylor's direction the leading exponent of free-jazz drumming, and Henry Grimes, who served as a bass player with Taylor intermittently to 1966.

In the autumn of 1962 the pianist held what was, for him, a stand of unparalleled length, 13 weeks at the Take Three club in Greenwich Village in a trio with Lyons and Murray; Grimes also sat in from time to time. Then, for seven weeks from the end of 1962 into 1963, the trio made a fairly successful tour of Denmark, where Albert Ayler joined and returned home with them. But in the USA they failed to secure further public performances: throughout the following decade Taylor faced a baffling combination of high critical acclaim and little or no work. The personal satisfaction of his experiences at the Take Three and in Scandinavia confirmed his full-time commitment to music, but by his own account he was nevertheless obliged to live on welfare for half a decade, until finally, from 1967, music provided him an income for subsistence. He made perhaps one major concert appearance each year, but otherwise worked sporadically in nightclubs for modest to low pay. These difficulties undoubtedly stemmed from the unrelenting demands posed by his music on the listener. Taylor himself said of his piano style that he tries "to imitate on the piano the leaps in space a dancer makes." Although in the 1950s and early 1960s he frequently incorporated single-note melodies and conventional rhythms in his playing, by the late 1960s he was concentrating on clusters and glissandos produced with open palms, fists, elbows, and forearms, and making use of dense, aperiodic rhythms that seemed to bear little resemblance to those traditionally associated with jazz. Indeed, Taylor's later work is more akin to the European avant garde than the jazz of his predecessors.

Taylor participated in the October Revolution in Jazz (1964) and was a member of the related Jazz Composers Guild (1964–5), by which time Andrew Cyrille was his drummer and Alan Silva provided a second double bass. Taylor worked at the Village Vanguard for five weeks in 1965, and in 1968 he recorded as a soloist with the Jazz Composer's Orchestra. Sam Rivers was with Taylor from about 1968 to 1970, most notably when both joined Lyons and Cyrille in residency at the Fondation Maeght in Paris in 1969. After a brief and unsatisfying venture into college teaching at the University of Wisconsin (1970–71), and with Lyons and Cyrille as artists-in-residence at Antioch College (1971–3), Taylor found his professional career began to gather momentum, and from 1973 he worked fairly regularly, either as a solo pianist or as the leader of his own group; in that same year his group toured Japan, Europe, and America. Among exceptions to a schedule dominated by European concerts and recordings were a three-week stand at the Five Spot with Lyons and Cyrille in 1975 (Cyrille's last year with Taylor); a controversial duo concert with Mary Lou Williams, who rather foolishly criticized Taylor's style and attempted to influence his performance (1977); duo concerts with Max Roach (December 1979); a few days at Fat Tuesday's, New York (1980), with Murray joining a quintet that had toured Europe late the previous year (Lyons, the violinist Ramsey Ameen, Silva, and Jerome Cooper); and, during the mid-1980s, very occasional work in New York with his then-current working group, including Lyons, William Parker, and Rashid Bakr.

Taylor renewed his duo with Roach at the Ravenna Jazz festival in Italy in 1984. Following Lyons's death, Taylor engaged Carlos Ward for a European tour in 1987, but later that year his group included Leroy Jenkins, Thurman Barker, and Freddie Waits. Most notably, in 1988 Taylor's music was celebrated in a month-long festival in Berlin involving an array of distinguished European avant-garde musicians; many of the consistently excellent solo, duo, and group performances were recorded by FMP and issued both separately and in a boxed set, the latter including extensive notes on Taylor's music. During the early 1990s Taylor organized the Feel Trio with William Parker and Tony Oxley; they are featured in the video *Burning Poles*.

In 1991 Taylor was awarded a McArthur Foundation "genius" grant-in-aid and for the first time had some financial security. Not having been invited to participate in the Jazz at Lincoln Center concert series, owing to assertions that his music did not fit the jazz department's definition of jazz, he rented Alice Tully Hall in 1994 and gave a concert as an unaccompanied soloist that was highly acclaimed. Other activities of the mid-1990s included small-group performances involving Mark Helias, Bakr, Barker, and Lisle Ellis, and, in October 1994, an orchestral performance in San Francisco. Taylor remains completely uncompromising as an artist, and, after nearly 50 years in jazz, is still a controversial figure.

Oral history material in *NjR*.

See also Improvisation, §3; Jazz (i), §VI, 1; and Piano, §5, and fig.3.

SELECTED RECORDINGS

As unaccompanied soloist: *Silent Tongues* (1974, Ari. 1005); *Air Above Mountains (Buildings Within)* (1976, Enja 3005); *Fly! Fly! Fly! Fly! Fly!* (1980, MPS 15575); *For Olim* (1986, SN 1150); *Erzulie Maketh Scent* (1988, FMP CD18)

Duos: with M. Roach: *Historic Concerts at McMillin Theatre, Columbia University, New York* (1979, SN 1100–01); with G. Sommer: *Riobec* (1988, FMP CD2); with P. Lovens: *Regalia* (1988, FMP CD3); with L. Moholo: *Remembrance* (1988, FMP CD4); with H. Bennink: *Spots, Circles and Fantasy* (1988, FMP CD5); with T Oxley: *Leaf Palm Hand* (1988, FMP CD6); with D. Bailey: *Pleistozaen mit Wasser* (1988, FMP CD16)

As leader: *Jazz Advance* (1956, Tran. 19); *Looking Ahead!* (1958, Cont. 3562); *Hard Driving Jazz* (1958, UA 4014); *The World of Cecil Taylor* (1960, Can. 9006); *The Complete Candid Recordings of Cecil Taylor* (1960–61, Mosaic 127), incl. O.P.; with B. Neidlinger: *New York R&B* (1961, Barnaby 31035); *Cecil Taylor Live at the Cafe Montmartre* (1962, Debut [Den.] 138); *Unit Structures* (1966, BN 84237); *Conquistador!* (1966, BN 84260); *Nuits de la Fondation Maeght* (1969, Shandar 83507/83508/83509); *Dark to Themselves* (1976, Enja 2084); *Three Phasis* (1978, New World 303); *One too Many, Salty Swift, and Not Goodbye* (1978, HH 2); *The Eighth* (1981, HA 6036); *Winged Serpent (Sliding Quadrants)* (1984, SN 1089); *Olu Iwa* (1986, SN 121139); *Live in Bologna* (1987, Leo 404–05); *Alms/Tiergarden (Spree)* (1988, FMP CD8–9); *The Hearth* (1988, FMP CD11); *In Florescence* (1989, A&M 5286); of Feel Trio: *Celebrated Blazons* (1990, FMP CD58)

As sideman: G. Evans: on *Into the Hot* (1961, Imp. 9), Pots, Bulbs, Mixed; Jazz Composer's Orchestra: on *The Jazz Composer's Orchestra* (1968, JCOA 1001–2), Communications no.11

SELECTED FILMS AND VIDEOS

Ambitus (1967); De l'autre côté du chemin de fer (1967); L'invention (1967); Imagine the Sound (1981); Cecil Taylor: Münchner Klaviersommer (1984); Burning Poles (*c*1992)

BIBLIOGRAPHY

BallietA (1986); *BallietA (1996)*; *GrayF*

G. Schuller: "Reviews: Recordings," *JR*, ii/1 (1959), 28

B. Coss: "Cecil Taylor's Struggle for Existence: Portrait of an Artist as a coiled Spring," *DB*, xxviii/22 (1961), 19

P. Binchet: "Portrait: Cecil Taylor," *Jm*, no.100 (1963), 45

J. Goldberg: *Jazz Masters of the Fifties* (New York and London, 1965/*R*1980)

N. Hentoff: "The Persistent Challenge of Cecil Taylor," *DB*, xxxii/5 (1965), 17

F. Paudras: "Cecil Taylor," *Jh*, no. 206 (1965), 24

A. B. Spellman: "Cecil Taylor," *Four Lives in the Bebop Business* (New York, 1966/*R*1970 as *Black Music: Four Lives*), 1–76
D. Berger: "Cecil Taylor à la Trace," *Jh*, no.227 (1967), 15
L. Jones: *Black Music* (New York, 1967/*R*1980), 104
M. Le Bris: "Interview," *Jh*, no.248 (1969), 20
F. Pinguet: "Cecil Taylor le Solitaire," *Jh*, no.248 (1969), 14
F. Pinguet and M. Cullaz: "Cecil Taylor: deux nuits à la Fondation Maeght," *Jh*, no.253 (1969), 11
E. Raben: *A Discography of Free Jazz* (Copenhagen, 1969)
V. Wilmer: *Jazz People* (London, Indianapolis, and New York, 1970/*R*1985), 23
P. Griffith: "Taylor raconte octobre et la suite," *Jm*, no.188 (1971), 26
E. Jost: *Free Jazz* (Graz, Austria, 1974/*R*1994)
P. Carles and F. Marmande: "Cecil Taylor," *Jm*, no.234 (1975), 26
J. B. Figi: "Cecil Taylor: African Code, Black Methodology," *DB*, xlii/7 (1975), 12
M. Jones: "Is Taylor a Genius?," *MM* (30 Aug 1975), 35
B. Smith: "Unit Structures," *Coda*, xii/4 (1975), 2
N. Hentoff: *Jazz Is* (New York, 1976/*R*1991), 225
V. Wilmer: *As Serious as your Life: the Story of the New Jazz* (London, 1977, rev. [3]/1987)
B. Rusch: "Cecil Taylor: Interview," *Cadence*, iv/1 (1978), 3
B. Vuijsje: *De nieuwe jazz* (Baarn, Netherlands, 1978), 178
Jazz 360°, no.22 (1979) [incl. discography by G. Cerutti; special Cecil Taylor issue]
P. Rothbart: "Orchestrating the Collective Consciousness," *DB*, xlvii/4 (1980), 17
T. Darter: "Piano Giants of Jazz: Cecil Taylor," *CK*, vii/5 (1981), 56
G. Giddins: *Riding on a Blue Note: Jazz and American Pop* (New York, and Oxford, England, 1981), 274
M. Hames: *Albert Ayler, Sunny Murray, Cecil Taylor, Byard Lancaster & Kenneth Terroade on Disc and Tape* (Ferndown, England, 1983)
L. Lyons: *The Great Jazz Pianists, Speaking of their Lives and Music* (New York, 1983), 301
M. Buholzer and U. Breger: "Cecil Taylor: Interview," *Cadence*, x/12 (1984), 5
J. Litweiler: *The Freedom Principle: Jazz after 1958* (New York, 1984), 200
D. Soutif: "My Taylor is Roach," *Jm*, no.332 (1984), 36
B. Doerschuk: "Cecil Taylor: in the Eye of the Hurricane," *Keyboard*, xi/1 (1985), 38 [incl. discography]
G. Giddins: "Pick a Card, any Card," *Rhythm-a-ning: Jazz Tradition and Innovation in the '80s* (New York, and Oxford, England, 1985), 7
K. Lynch: "Cecil Taylor and the Poetics of Living," *DB*, liii/11 (1986), 22 [incl. discography]
S. Lake, B. Noglik, E. Jost, D. Werts, and others: Liner notes, *Cecil Taylor in Berlin '88* (FMP CD0–CD18, *c*1989)
M. Buholzer, A. Schmitt-Rosenthal, and V. Wilmer: *Auf der Suche nach Cecil Taylor* (Hofheim, Germany, 1990)
F. Davis: *Outcats: Jazz Composers, Instrumentalists, and Singers* (New York, and Oxford, England, 1990), 42
G. Giddins, ed.: "Cecil Taylor: the Space of 61 Years Danced Through," *VV: Voice Jazz Special* (26 June 1990)
G. Santoro: "Cecil Taylor: An American Romantic," *DB*, lvii/6 (1990), 16
T. Meissgang, ed.: *Semantics: neue Musik im Gesprach* (Hofheim, Germany, 1991)
P. Landolt and R. Wyss, eds.: *Die lachenden Aussenseiter: Musikerinnen und Musiker zwischen Jazz, Rock und Neuer Musik: die 80er und 90er Jahre* (Zurich, 1993)
J. M. Reynolds: *Improvisation Analysis of Selected Works of Albert Ayler, Roscoe Mitchell and Cecil Taylor* (diss., Univ. of Wisconsin, 1993)
C. Laban and K. L. Williams: "Riffs: Taylor Holds Recital on Lincoln Center Turf," *DB*, lxi/6 (1994), 11
<http://www.shef.ac.uk/misc/rec/ps/efi/musician/mtaylor.html> (1998)

BILL DOBBINS/BK

Taylor, Creed (*b* Lynchburg, VA, 13 May 1929). Record producer. He played trumpet in school bands and read psychology at Duke University. In 1954 he became head of artists and repertory for Bethlehem; in 1956 he left to join ABC-Paramount, where in 1960 he founded the label Impulse! and produced albums by, among others, Gil Evans, Oliver Nelson, and Ray Charles. Late in 1961 Taylor joined Verve as its chief executive and principal producer; he initially suspended all its releases for a period of six months and dropped numerous older musicians who were associated with Norman Granz's Jazz at the Philharmonic, retaining only Ella Fitzgerald, Dizzy Gillespie, Stan Getz (whose bossa-nova albums he produced), Oscar Peterson, and Johnny Hodges. Later he engaged Jimmy Smith, Cal Tjader, Wes Montgomery, and Bill Evans (ii) to record for the label; with such artists he issued a large number of albums that became best sellers and often blended jazz instrumentation with string sections and other light-orchestral accompaniments more commonly associated with popular music. In 1967 Taylor moved to A&M and soon thereafter he formed Creed Taylor, Inc. (CTI). Its recordings were initially distributed by A&M, but it became independent two years later when Taylor began managing the distribution; Freddie Hubbard and Stanley Turrentine were CTI's most successful artists. The company went bankrupt in the late 1970s, but Taylor re-formed it around 1991.

Taylor will be remembered for his attempts to blur artistic and commercial boundaries in an effort to sell jazz to a wide audience. Apart from those issued for CTI, his most famous recordings (and those most often critically maligned) are several orchestral albums he produced for Wes Montgomery in the mid- to late 1960s which became immensely popular.

BIBLIOGRAPHY

Feather–Gitler'70s
M. Hennessey: "Crossover Crusader," *JJI*, xxxii/11 (1979), 19
A. Ingram: *Wes Montgomery* (Gateshead, England, 1985/*R*1993), 34
R. Horricks: "Clef/Verve: Creed Taylor and After," *CI*, xv/6 (1988), 24

GK

Taylor, Dave [David Michael] (*b* New York, 6 June 1944). Bass trombonist. He played trumpet and then tuba, and settled on trombone when he was at high school; while studying at the Juilliard School from 1962 (BS *c*1965, MS 1968) he changed to bass trombone. From 1967 he played in the American Symphony Orchestra under Leopold Stokowski, and in the late 1960s he spent a year teaching in a school before pursuing a full-time career as a musician; by this time he had became involved in studio work, and he eventually performed as a section player on hundreds of recordings. Shortly thereafter he began playing in jazz bands led by Thad Jones and Mel Lewis, George Russell, Chuck Israels, and Larry Elgart, although he did not become a soloist until around 1981, when he was again working in Russell's big band. He later joined George Gruntz's concert band (*c*1983), Bob Mintzer's big band (*c*1985), and Gil Evans's orchestra, and taught at the Manhattan School of Music (from 1989).

In 1979 Taylor began commissioning pieces for bass trombone, and he gave his first solo recital at Carnegie Hall in 1984; in later performances he incorporated jazz into his repertory. In 1984 he formed an ensemble with Jim Pugh, and in 1989 he performed in Europe as a member of Ray Anderson's "Small" World Trombone Quartet, which was actually a trio with Annie Whitehead, as illness had forced Albert Mangelsdorff to withdraw from the group. In the early 1990s he joined the New York Trombone Quartet and a trio led by Frank Lacy, and from 1993 he worked with Paul Smoker's Brass Group and from 1996 with John Clark. He also formed a cooperative classical and chamber-jazz trio with Daniel Schnyder on tenor saxophone and Kenny Drew, Jr., on piano, which appeared at the Barossa Music Festival in Australia (1997). Taylor has continued to perform as a classical trombonist, in which context he has collaborated with the Lincoln Center Chamber Society and the New York Chamber Orchestra.

SELECTED RECORDINGS

As leader: with J. Pugh: *The Pugh–Taylor Project* (1984, DMP 448); *Past Tells* (*c*1993, New World 80436)

As sideman: G. Evans: *Bud & Bird* (1986, EB K19P6455–6), incl. Groove from the Louvre; G. Gruntz: on *Blues 'n Dues Et cetera* (1991, Enja 6072-2), General Cluster

BIBLIOGRAPHY

M. Bourne: "Profile: Dave Taylor," *DB*, lv/8 (1988), 52

D. Yeo: "David Taylor, Bass Trombone: an Appreciation and Interview," *International Trombone Association Journal*, xix/4 (1991), 30; xx/1 (1992), 14

GK

Taylor, Eva [Gibbons, Irene] (*b* St. Louis, 22 Jan 1895; *d* Mineola, NY, 31 Oct 1977). Singer. As a child she worked in traveling shows and toured Australia and New Zealand (*c*1904–6), Europe (1906), and Australia again (1914–15). In 1921 she moved to New York and married Clarence Williams. From 1922 (when she assumed the stage name Eva Taylor) she worked on radio and in stage shows and revues and recorded both as a soloist and as a sideman. She made a large number of recordings with Williams's group (1924–41), one of the finest of which is *Cake-walking Babies from Home* (1925, OK 40321). Although it is aimed at the vaudeville blues and jazz audience, much of her recorded output consists of contemporary pop songs appropriately performed and is of enduring value primarily for its often excellent accompaniments. Taylor ceased full-time performing in the 1940s and sang only occasionally in the 1950s and early 1960s, but from the mid-1960s she made visits to England, New York, Copenhagen, and Sweden. In England in 1967 she recorded *Eva Taylor and her Anglo-American Boyfriends* (Audubon AAN), which reveals an emotional depth often lacking in her earlier work.

BIBLIOGRAPHY

W. Smith and G. Hoefer: *Music on my Mind: the Memoirs of an American Pianist* (Garden City, NY, 1964/*R*1975), 208

"Looking Back with Eva," *Sv*, no.14 (1967–8), 17; no.15 (1968), 18; no.16 (1968), 19

R. C. Foreman, Jr.: *Jazz and Race Records, 1920–32: their Origins and their Significance for the Record Industry and Society* (diss., U. of Illinois, 1968)

A. Napoleon: "The Return of Eva Taylor," *JJ*, xxi/1 (1968), 30

T. Lord: *Clarence Williams* (Chigwell, England, 1976)

S. Harris: *Blues Who's Who: a Biographical Dictionary of Blues Singers* (New Rochelle, NY, 1979/*R*1994)

based on *ChiltonW*

Taylor, Gene [Calvin Eugene] (*b* Toledo, OH, 19 March 1929). Double bass player. He lived in Detroit from 1936 and played sousaphone and, for a brief period, piano before taking up double bass. Having achieved prominence as a member of Horace Silver's quintet (1958–64), he performed and recorded with another member of the group, Blue Mitchell; he also played in Duke Pearson's trio, which recorded in 1959, and recorded with Roland Alexander in 1961 and with Silver's drummer Roy Brooks in 1963. In 1966 Taylor was the house bass player at the Newport Jazz Festival. He was a sideman in big bands led by Howard McGhee and by Pearson, and he recorded with Pearson's octet in 1967 and with Eddie Jefferson in 1969. From 1966 to 1968 he worked with Nina Simone, for whom he wrote the song *Why? (The King of Love is Dead)*, a tribute to Martin Luther King, Jr., and in the late 1960s he was a member of Teddy Wilson's trio; he also accompanied the folksinger Judy Collins (1968–76). In the 1970s he played in New York in Frank Foster's big band the Loud Minority. Taylor was a member of duos and trios led by Duke Jordan, Barry Harris (recording in 1975), and Cedar Walton, and he toured Japan with Buddy Rich, Philly Joe Jones, Louie Bellson, Charli Persip, and Junior Mance (this last in 1977) and the western US with Billy Taylor (ii) (1978); he recorded with Eric Kloss (1972) and Walter Bolden (1977). In 1980 he appeared at Carnegie Hall, and in the late 1980s he accompanied Jimmy Witherspoon for nightclub appearances in New York. Taylor taught music in the New York public schools from 1985 to 1987, and informally from 1991, and he hosted jam sessions at his home. He has a relaxed, confident manner, and a style marked by short, percussive notes played with a swinging intensity.

SELECTED RECORDINGS

As sideman: H. Silver: *Finger Poppin'* (1959, BN 4008); *Blowin' the Blues Away* (1959, BN 4017); *Horace-scope* (1960, BN 84042); B. Mitchell: *The Cup Bearers* (1963, Riv. 9439); D. Pearson: *The Right Touch* (1967, BN 94267); E. Jefferson: *Come Along with Me* (1969, Prst. 7698); B. Harris: *Barry Harris Plays Tadd Dameron* (1975, Xan. 113)

BIBLIOGRAPHY

FeatherE; *Feather '60s*; *Feather–Gitler '70s*

B. Sidran: *Talking Jazz: an Illustrated Oral History* (Petaluma, CA, 1992, rev. and enlarged 2/1995)

JOHN VOIGT/BK

Taylor, Jasper (*b* Texarkana, TX, 1 Jan 1894; *d* Chicago, 7 Nov 1964). Drummer, washboard player, and percussionist. He first worked as a drummer in Texas before touring with Young Buffalo Bill's Wild West Show (1912) and with the Dandy Dixie Minstrels (to Mexico). In 1913 he was in Memphis, where he worked in theaters and performed with Jelly Roll Morton. During an association with W. C. Handy that began that same year Taylor first experimented with playing rhythms on a washboard. In 1917 he moved to Chicago, though he also recorded with Handy in New York; he may be heard playing xylophone on Handy's *That Jazz Dance* and woodblocks on *The Old Town Pump* – recordings which show that he was in the forefront of the development of jazz percussion. During World War I he served with a military band in France. He then played with Will Marion Cook and Handy in New York, and from summer 1920 (or possibly earlier) to spring 1923 he worked in Canada (mainly in Quebec City and Montreal) as a member of Millard Thomas's Famous Chicago Jazz Band and Novelty Orchestra. Playing variously drums, washboard, and percussion, he made many recordings, notably with Morton (1923), Jimmy O'Bryant's Washboard Band (1924–5), Clarence Williams (in the pianist's Blue Grass Foot Warmers and Dixie Washboard Band), Jimmy Blythe, and Freddie Keppard (all 1926), and Fess Williams (1927–8); by the time of the sessions with Blythe, Keppard, and Fess Williams he had settled in Chicago. Taylor also recorded on washboard as a leader (1927, 1928) and, as a drummer, took part in a classic series of recordings by Reuben Reeves (1929). He left music for some years in the 1930s, but later worked with such musicians as Punch Miller (1945), Natty Dominique (1952), and Lil Armstrong (1959–60), and led his own band (1962). Although he is remembered mainly for having introduced the washboard as a musical instrument, he was also a versatile percussionist. The rhythmic accuracy and sophisticated accentuation of his work with Reeves fully support his reputation as one of the finest drummers of his generation.

Oral history material in *LNT*.

SELECTED RECORDINGS

As leader: Stomp Time Blues/It must be the blues (1927, Para. 12409); Jasper Taylor Blues/Geechie River Blues (1928, Voc. 1196)

As sideman: W. C. Handy: That Jazz Dance (1917, Col. A2419); The Old Town Pump (1917, Col. A2417); J. O'Bryant: Red Hot Mama/Drunk

Man's Strut (1924, Para. 12246); Washboard/Brand New Charleston (1925, Para. 12265); Skoodlum Blues (1925, Para. 12260); Clarinet Get Away (1925, Para. 12287); Dixie Washboard Band: Boodle am/I've found a new baby (1926, Ban. 1781); F. Keppard: Stock Yards Strut/Salty Dog (1926, Para. 12399); R. Reeves: Papa Skag Stomp/Bugle Call Blues (1929, Voc. 1297); Blue Sweets/Texas Special Blues (1929, Voc. 1411)

BIBLIOGRAPHY

ChiltonW
C. Hillman: "Paramount Serenaders, 1923–1926," *Sv*, no.67 (1976), 8; no.70 (1977), 149; no.72 (1977), 226 [incl. discography]
D. Griffiths: *Hot Jazz from Harlem to Storyville* (Lanham, MD, New Brunswick, NJ, and London, 1998), 60

MICHAEL TOVEY

Taylor, John (*b* Manchester, England, 25 Sept 1942). English pianist. He had no formal musical education but drew instinctively on the influences of Oscar Peterson, Bill Evans (ii), and, later, Herbie Hancock. After early professional experience in dance bands he moved in 1964 to London, where he worked frequently in a trio accompanying singers; his first important engagement was with Tommy Whittle at the Hopvine. Later he was associated with Alan Skidmore (recording in 1969 and 1971), John Surman (recording in 1969–73), John Dankworth and Cleo Laine (1970–73), and especially Norma Winstone, whom he married (1972). He also took part in sessions led by Graham Collier (1970), Harry Beckett (1970–71), Mike Gibbs (1970, 1972), and Volker Kriegel (1971–3). For six years in the 1970s he led a sextet with Kenny Wheeler among his sidemen; he played in Ronnie Scott's band for six months (1977) and accompanied leading American bop musicians at Scott's club.

From 1977 Taylor was best known for his work as a performer in and a composer for the trio Azimuth, in which he collaborated with Winstone and Wheeler; his dynamic, romantic style combined with Winstone's singing and Wheeler's plangent flugelhorn playing to produce strikingly individual results. He toured and recorded with Jan Garbarek (1977–8) and recorded as a sideman with Martin Drew, Jon Eardley, and Stan Sulzmann (all 1977), Louis Stewart (1979), Arild Andersen (1981), Miroslav Vitous (1982), Wheeler (1983), and Enrico Rava (1986). In 1983 he performed with Surman in Australia and worked in Gil Evans's British orchestra. He formed duos with Sulzmann, Tony Coe, and Steve Argüelles, and performed with Charlie Mariano; later he played with Tommy Smith (1988) and Ian Carr's Orchestra UK (1989). In the 1990s Taylor led his own groups (notably Foil, which toured on the Contemporary Music Network) and continued to play in Azimuth and to perform as a sideman with Wheeler. He formed duos with Michael Garrick and Wheeler, and from 1992, with Palle Danielsson, he was a member of Peter Erskine's European trio. During the same period he recorded with Uli Beckerhoff (1992), Surman (1993 and 1996, the latter as an organist in a concert at Salisbury Cathedral), and Eric Vloeimans (1998). In 1996 he appeared as a guest soloist with Karsten Houmark, and in February 1999 he performed alongside Winstone under David Murray's leadership in London. He has taught at the Musikakademie in Cologne.

SELECTED RECORDINGS

As unaccompanied soloist: *Solo* (*c*1992, Sentemo 30592)
As leader: *Decipher* (1971, MPS 15316); of Azimuth (with K. Wheeler and N. Winstone): *Azimuth* (1977, ECM 1099), *Azimuth '85* (1985, ECM 1298)
As sideman: J. Surman: *How Many Clouds Can You See?* (1969, Deram 1045); J. Dankworth: *Full Circle* (1972, Phi. 6308122); J. Surman: *Morning Glory* (1973, Isl. 9237); R. Scott: *Serious Gold* (1977, Pye 18542); J. Eardley: *Namely Me* (1977, Spot. 17); K. Wheeler: *Double, Double You* (1983, ECM 1262); *Music for Large & Small Ensembles* (1990, ECM 1415–16); *The Widow in the Window* (1990, ECM 1417); P. Erskine: *You Never Know* (1992, ECM 1497); *Time Being* (1993, ECM 1532); K. Houmark: *Dawn* (1996, Sto. 4211)

BIBLIOGRAPHY

CarrJ; *ChiltonB*; *WickesIBJ*, i
R. Cotterrell, ed.: *Jazz Now: the Jazz Centre Society Guide* (London, 1976)
A. Macintosh: "John Taylor & Norma Winstone: a Jazz Partnership," *JF* [intl edn], no.59 (1979), 38
P. Renaud: *La discographie du jazz anglais* (Chaumont, France, 1985)
F. Raulin and S. Oliva: "John Taylor: une expérience d'abord physique," *Jm*, no.467 (1997), 78
<http://www.ejn.it/mus/taylor.htm> (1999)

CHRIS SHERIDAN/BK

Taylor, Mark (Thomas) (i) (*b* Chatanooga, TN, 22 May 1961). French horn player. He had classical lessons from an early age and was introduced to the jazz playing of Julius Watkins by Jerry Coker while studying at the University of Tennessee (Bmus 1986). From 1988 to 1990 he attended the New England Conservatory, and while in Boston he studied with George Russell and Dave Holland and worked with Jimmy Giuffre; during the same period he performed and recorded with Orange then blue, as a member of which he took part in a tour sponsored by the US State Department of Turkey, Cyprus, and Syria. From 1989 he worked with Max Roach's Chorus and Orchestra and in his group So What Brass 5, with which he toured the USA in 1998. In addition he performed with the large ensembles of Oliver Lake (recording in 1988) and Sam Rivers, toured with Abdullah Ibrahim's Ekaya (1990), and joined Muhal Richard Abrams's big band and octet (both 1990). While he was a member of Henry Threadgill's Very Very Circus (1990–95) he deputized in Lester Bowie's Brass Fantasy (1991–5) and worked in Grover Mitchell's big band (1992–5). In 1997 Taylor formed the group Quiet Land Project with Myra Melford and Fred Hopkins, who was replaced by Brad Jones the following year. He then worked alongside Ken Filiano and Matt Wilson as the leader of Tré-O and formed Circle Squared, a quartet with Melford, Jones, and Wilson, and another such group that included the pianist Lafayette Harris. In December 1998 he led a large brass ensemble at Blues Alley in Washington, DC. From the late 1990s Taylor wrote music for film, dance, and theater, and in 1998 he composed scores for the short films *Confessions of a Curbed Dog* and *Role Reversal.* He should not be confused with the saxophonist Mark Taylor.

SELECTED RECORDINGS

As leader: *Quiet Land* (1995, Mapleshade 05232)
As sideman: H. Threadgill: *Too much Sugar for a Dime* (*c*1992, Axiom 314-514258-2); Michael Shea: *Last Night while You Slept* (1993, Accurate 5007); H. Threadgill: *Makin' a Move* (*c*1995, Col. CK67214)

BIBLIOGRAPHY

"Auditions: Mark Taylor," *DB*, lvii/2 (1990), 62
P. Elwood: "Memorable Jazz: So What," *San Francisco Examiner* (5 March 1998)
M. Joyce: "Top Brass," *Washington Post* (15 Dec 1998)
<http://home.earthlink.net/~taymons/biopage.htm> (1999)

GK

Taylor, Mark (Anthony) (ii) (*b* London, 7 Nov 1962). English drummer. He began teaching himself drums when he was five and became a professional musician at the age of 16, when he performed briefly with Eddie Thompson's trio. A year later he toured with Al Cohn, after which he worked on cruise ships and in dixieland bands, and then played more modern styles with such visiting Americans as Johnny

Griffin, Pharoah Sanders, Kenny Barron, Bobby Watson, and George Coleman; he may be heard alongside Julian Joseph and Dave Green in the rhythm section accompanying Coleman and Peter King on Coleman's album *Blues Inside Out* (1995, Ronnie Scott's Jazz House 046). In the late 1980s and 1990s Taylor worked in Britain with the pianist Geoff Castle, John Dankworth, John Taylor, Gordon Beck, Dick Morrissey, Alan Barnes, Alec Dankworth, Mike Carr, and the Pizza Express Modern Jazz Sextet; in addition he played with Kenny Drew and Niels-Henning Ørsted Pedersen in Herb Geller's quartet, with which he recorded the album *Birdland Stomp* (1990, Fresh Sound 0174) in Barcelona. He also spent periods in the USA, where he recorded in New York with Lew Tabackin's group and with Chris Flory's trio (both 1996) and appeared in Coleman's quartet at the JVC Jazz Festival New York (1998). He should not be confused with the saxophonist Mark Taylor. (*ChiltonB*)

BK

Taylor, Martin (*b* Harlow, England, 20 Oct 1956). English guitarist. He was introduced to guitar at the age of four by his father, the double bass player and guitarist Buck Taylor; although he was completely self-taught, Ike Isaacs (ii) was later an important mentor. Turner turned professional at the age of 15 and worked with a variety of British players through the 1970s, among them Lennie Hastings (from late 1972), Alex Welsh, Alan Elsdon (September 1975 into 1976), Dave Shepherd, and Roy Williams and John Barnes (1978). In 1979 he joined Stephane Grappelli, with whom he toured internationally into the 1990s; he appears in the video *Stephane Grappelli in New Orleans* (1989). During the 1980s he toured with, among others, Buddy DeFranco, Emily Remler, Louis Stewart, and the Great Guitars, and towards the end of the decade he began concentrating on performances as an unaccompanied soloist, basing his guitar style particularly on the piano playing of Art Tatum and Bud Powell. In 1994 Taylor formed a group, the Spirit of Django, to perform a wide range of music inspired by Django Reinhardt, and the following year it toured Asia. Later he was awarded an honorary doctorate by the University of Paisley in Scotland in recognition of his outstanding career in music. He has also worked with Peter Ind, the mandolin player David Grisman, Teresa Brewer, Claire Martin, the singer Carol Kidd, and the guitarist Chet Atkins. Taylor is one of the featured performers in the video *World of Fingerstyle Jazz Guitar* (*c*1998) and the subject of another, *Martin Taylor in Concert* (*c*1999 [filmed 1996]). He published an instructional book, *Jazz Guitar Artistry of Martin Taylor* (Newcastle upon Tyne, England) in 1990.

SELECTED RECORDINGS

As unaccompanied soloist: *A Tribute to Tatum* (1983, Hep 2032)

Duos: with P. Ind: *Triple Libra* (1979, Wave 24); with S. Grappelli: *We've Got the World on a String* (1981, Angel DS37886); *Reunion* (1993, Linn 022)

As leader: *Sarabanda* (1987, Gala 13-9018-1); *Don't Fret* (1990, Linn 014); *Change of Heart* (1991, Linn 016); *Spirit of Django* (1994, Linn 030); *Gypsy* (1996, Linn 090)

As sideman: B. DeFranco: *On Tour: UK* (1983, Hep 2023); S. Grappelli and T. Thielemans: *Bringing it Together* (1984, Cymekob 801-2); B. DeFranco: *Groovin'* (1984, Hep 2030); S. Grappelli and Vasar Clements: *Together at Last* (1985, Flying Fish 421); D. Grisman: *Tone Poems II* (1995, Dawg 18)

BIBLIOGRAPHY

CarrJ; *ChiltonB*

L. Tomkins: "The Guitar and the Musician: Martin Taylor," *CI*, xxi/8 (1983), 20; contd as "I'm Contemporary, but of an Older School, Says Martin Taylor," xxi/9 (1983), 12; contd as "Jazz Must be *Presented* Right, Stresses Martin Taylor," xxi/12 (1983), 16

D. Forte: "Martin Taylor: Leading British Jazz Stylist at Grappelli's Side," *GP*, xviii/1 (1984), 38

C. Deffaa: "Martin Taylor: from England with Chops," *JT* (1989), May, 16

D. Matthews: "Martin Taylor: a Unique Guitar Talent," *CI*, xxvi/8 (1989), 8

——: "Around the World with Martin Taylor," *CJM*, xxix/1 (1992), 13; contd as "Martin Taylor," xxix/2 (1992), 16

P. Hilborne: "Style File: Martin Taylor," *Guitarist*, x/4 (1993), 138

P. Tingen: "Intro: Martin Taylor: British Jazz Giant," *GP*, xxvii/12 (1993), 16

B. Milkowski: "Hearsay: Martin Taylor: Beyond Django," *JT*, xxvi/2 (1996), 29

——: "Intro: Martin Taylor: Possessed by the Spirit of Django," *GP*, xxx/5 (1996), 20

J. Ohlschmidt: "Martin Taylor: Dazzling Fingerstyle Jazz," *Acoustic Guitar*, viii (1997), July, 66

C. Lockhart: "String Thing," *Jazzwise*, no.13 (1998), 20

M. Summerfield: *The Jazz Guitar: its Evolution, Players and Personalities since 1900* (Blaydon on Tyne, England, 4/1998)

MARK GILBERT

Taylor, Mike [Michael] (*b* London, 1938; *d* 1969). English pianist, composer, and arranger. He learned piano as a child and played clarinet briefly. After military service he led various groups, ranging from quartets to octets, which included such musicians as Jack Bruce, Jon Hiseman, the drummer Ginger Baker, the trumpeter Frank Powell, the trombonist John Mumford, and the tenor saxophonist Dave Gelly. In 1966 he recorded the album *The Mike Taylor Trio* (1966, Col. SX6137); this includes the track *Abena*, which offers a particularly fine example of his work. As well as composing for his own ensembles (his style is well represented by the tracks *Half Blue* and *Black and White Raga* from the album *Pendulum*, 1965, Col. SX6042) Taylor wrote arrangements and pieces for the New Jazz Orchestra, Norma Winstone, and the rock group Cream. He is believed to have committed suicide; his body was found on the beach near Leigh-on-Sea, Essex.

SALLY-ANN WORSFOLD

Taylor, Sam "the Man" [Samuel Leroy, Jr.] (*b* Lexington, TN, 12 July 1916; *d* 5 Oct 1990). Tenor and baritone saxophonist and clarinetist. His full name appears in his application for social security. After working with the singer Scat Man Crothers (1937–8) and the Sunset Royal Orchestra (1939–41, with which he made his recording début under the leadership of the bandleader Doc Wheeler in 1941) he performed and recorded with Cootie Williams (1941–3, 1944–6) and Lucky Millinder (1943–4, 1946). During an association with Cab Calloway (1946–52) he toured South America and the Caribbean (1951–2) and made notable recordings with Milt Hinton (1947) and Clyde Bernhardt (1949). As a session musician (from 1952) Taylor made a large number of recordings, many of them in a style oriented towards rhythm-and-blues; he recorded under his own name (from *c*1954) and with the singer Big Maybelle (1952–4), Ella Fitzgerald and Ray Charles (both 1953), the singer Ella Johnson (1954–5, accompanied by the orchestra led by her brother, Buddy Johnson), Jesse Stone (1955), Louis Jordan (1956), Joe Turner (ii) (1957), and Sy Oliver (1958), among others. He led his own bands into the 1960s and toured Japan, where he enjoyed considerable success, in 1963. Only his date of death appears in the social security death index. Taylor's characteristic driving swing and intense blues feeling enabled him to function successfully in both swing and rhythm-and-blues contexts and often to merge the two approaches, as may be heard on recordings that he made alongside Taft Jordan, Hinton, and Panama Francis in a quintet called the Blues Chasers.

SELECTED RECORDINGS

As leader: Deliver Me (1961, Savoy 1597)

As sideman: L. Millinder: Shipyard Social Function (1943, Decca 18674); C. Williams: Blue Garden Blues (1944, Hit 7108); first issued on *Capitol Jazz Classics*, ii (1943–6, Cap. M11057), That's the Lick (1946); L. Millinder: Fare thee well, Deacon Jones (1946, Decca 24495); M. Hinton: Oo-la-fee/And Say it Again (1947, Staff 604); C. Calloway: Rooming House Boogie/I beeped when I shoulda bopped (1949, Bb 30-0012); Blues Chasers: Birmingham Special/Old Fashioned Blues (1952, MGM 11409); Big Maybelle: first issued on *Big Maybelle: the OKeh Sessions* (1952–5, Epic 38456), Hair Dressin' Woman (1954); H. L. Page: Ain't nothin' wrong with that, baby (1953, King 1404); E. Johnson: It used to hurt me/Well do it (1954, Mer. 70459)

SELECTED FILMS AND VIDEOS

Film Vodvil Series 2, no.2 (1944); Big Fat Mamas (1946); Hello Bill (1946); I Want a Man (1946)

BIBLIOGRAPHY

FeatherE

H. Panassié and M. Gautier: *Dictionnaire du jazz* (Paris, 1954; Eng. trans., London, 1956, rev. A. A. Gurwitch as *Guide to Jazz*, Boston, 1956), 310

P. Roth: "Leroy Sam 'The Man' Taylor," *Jazz Podium*, iv/12 (1955), 13 [discography]

J. Evensmo: *History of Jazz Tenor Saxophone: Black Artists*, iii: *1940–1944* (Oslo, 1997); iv: *1945–1949* (Oslo, 1999)

HOWARD RYE

TCB [Taking Care of Business]. Record company and label. It was formed in the mid-1980s in Basel, Switzerland, by the drummer Peter Schmidlin, who initially operated it as a part-time venture. Its first issues were made on LP around 1987 and consisted of compilations derived from Swiss radio broadcasts; these involved a rhythm section, including Schmidlin, accompanying such soloists as Benny Bailey, Johnny Griffin, Slide Hampton, and Woody Shaw. Later the company released new material on CD by, among others, Bailey and Thomas Moeckel; however, its catalogue failed to make commercial inroads, and it appears to have ceased operations briefly in the early 1990s.

Schmidlin began to operate TCB as a full-time venture late in 1992, and the following year it relocated to Lausanne; by the mid-1990s its headquarters were in Montreux. From 1993 new recordings and releases have been predominantly of bop-oriented material, but the company has also issued previously unreleased material by Benny Goodman, further recordings of the Swiss radio performances (under the rubric Swiss Radio Days) by, among others, Art Blakey (1960), Buck Clayton (1961), and Cannonball Adderley (1963), fusion or jazz-rock material, and world music. Its main series of bop-related recordings, which as of 2000 numbered more than 75 albums, features such performers and groups as Lynne Arriale, Bailey, Kenny Drew, Jr., George Gruntz, the N.Y. Hardbop Quintet, George Robert, James Weidman, Buster Williams, and Phil Woods, as well as numerous lesser-known American and European musicians. (<http://www.tcb.ch/the_company.html> (2000))

GK

Tchicai, John (Martin) (*b* Copenhagen, 28 April 1936). Danish saxophonist and bandleader. His father was Congolese, his mother Danish. He grew up in Århus, where he played violin from the age of ten and clarinet and alto saxophone from the age of 16; he studied alto saxophone for three years at the Royal Danish Music Conservatory in Copenhagen. In 1962 he appeared at festivals in Helsinki, where he met Archie Shepp, and Warsaw, where he made his first recording (as the leader of a quintet). After moving to New York he played with Shepp and Don Cherry in the New York Contemporary Five (1963) and with Roswell Rudd and Milford Graves in the New York Art Quartet (1964–5); with both groups he toured Europe and made recordings. He also recorded as a member of the Jazz Composers Guild and with Shepp, John Coltrane, and Albert Ayler. In 1966 he returned to Denmark, where he led the workshop ensemble Cadentia Nova Danica (1967–71), with which he performed in London in 1968. For several years from 1972 he performed less frequently and worked principally as a teacher.

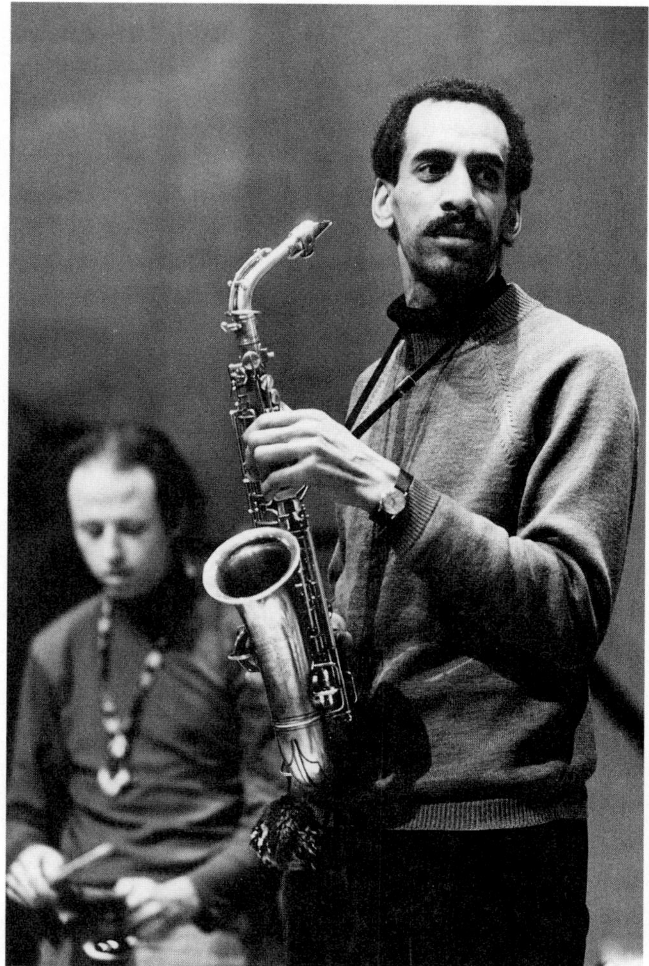

John Tchicai during a free-jazz concert called Natural Music, Lady Margaret Hall, Cambridge, England, 1969; Barre Phillips plays percussion in the background

Tchicai resumed playing full-time in 1977, when he joined Strange Brothers, led by the saxophonist Simon Spang-Hanssen, and Johnny Dyani's group; the following year he appeared with the Danish All Stars at the Jazzyatra in India. In the 1980s he played with the Dutch saxophone sextet De Zes Winden and Cecil Taylor's Two Continents Ensemble and joined Pierre Dørge's New Jungle Orchestra, with which he appeared at the Chicago Jazz Festival (1986); he rejoined Dyani's group for a tour of America. In 1989 he formed a duo with Vitold Rek, which recorded in 1991. In 1990 Tchicai was honored with a lifetime achievement grant from the Danish Ministry of Culture, and in 1991 he moved to Davis,

California, to be near his daughters. Thereafter he played with Charles Gayle and led his own group, the Coyote Ensemble (later renamed the Archetypes). He also recorded as co-leader with Irène Schweizer (1975) and the singer Yusef Komunyakaa (1997), in duos with the saxophonist André Goudbeek (1977–8) and the pianist and percussionist Hartmut Geerken (1980), and with ICP (from 1968), the Berlin Jazz Workshop Orchestra (1978), Chris McGregor (1981), the guitarist Giancarlo Nicolai, the pianist Kristian Blak, Curtis Clark, and the opera librettist Paul Haines. In autumn 1996 he was appointed to lead improvisational groups at the University of California in Davis, and in June 1999 he traveled to New York for a performance and recording in a reunion of the New York Art Quartet.

Early in his career Tchicai favored a staccato attack and a dry tone that recalled the work of Lee Konitz and Ornette Coleman, but in 1982 he changed to the tenor instrument and began to employ a fuller sound in a style influenced by Sonny Rollins and Archie Shepp. In addition to saxophone he plays bass clarinet proficiently. He was instrumental in creating a Danish style of world music, and he has composed for both small and large ensembles. He published a method book, *Advice to Improvisers: Compositions and Exercises for All Instruments* (Copenhagen, 1987).

SELECTED RECORDINGS

As unaccompanied soloist: *Solo* (1977, FMP SAJ12); *Live in Athens* (1980, Praxis 101)

Duos: with A. Goudbeek: *Duets* (1977, SVM 2); *Barefoot Dance* (1978, Marge 07); with H. Geerken: *Continent* (1980, Praxis 102); with P. Dørge: *Ball at Louisiana Museum of Art* (1981, Ste. 1174)

As leader: with D. Cherry and A. Shepp: *Archie Shepp and the New York Contemporary Five* (1963, Sonet 36); of New York Art Quartet (with R. Rudd): *The New York Art Quartet* (1964, ESP 1004); of Cadentia Nova Danica: *Afrodisiaca* (1969, MPS 15249); *Real Tchicai* (1977, Ste. 1075); *John Tchicai & the Strange Brothers* (1977, FMP SAJ15); *Timo's Message* (1984, BS 0094); *Grandpa's Spells* (1992, Sto. 4182); of Archetypes: *Love is Touching* (1995, B&W/X-Talk 055); with Y. Komunyakaa: *Love Notes from the Madhouse* (1997, 8th Harmonic Breakdown 8001)

As sideman: A. Ayler: *New York Eye and Ear Control* (1964, ESP 1016); A. Shepp: *Four for Trane* (1964, Imp. 71); Jazz Composers Guild Orchestra: on *Communication* (1964, Fon. 881011), Roast; J. Coltrane: *Ascension* (1965, Imp. 95); J. Dyani: *Witchdoctor's Son* (1978, Ste. 1098); P. Dørge: *Ballad Round the Left Corner* (1979, Ste. 1132); *Pierre Dørge and the New Jungle Orchestra* (1982, Ste. 1162); *Brikama* (1984, Ste. 1188); C. Taylor: *Winged Serpent* (1984, SN 1089); J. Dyani: *Angolian Cry* (1985, Ste. 1209); P. Dørge: *Very Hot: Even the Moon is Dancing* (1985, Ste. 1208); Zes Winden: *Elephants Can Dance* (1988, Sack. 3041); Ok Nok Kongo + 3 Jokers: *Plays Thomas Agergaard & John Tchicai* (1997, Sto. 4220); P. Dørge: *Giraf* (1998, Dacapo 9440)

BIBLIOGRAPHY

GrayF

J.-L. Comolli: "Tchicai sans chique," *Jm*, no.137 (1966), 28

D. Morgenstern: "John Tchicai: a Calm Member of the Avant-garde," *DB*, xxxiii/3 (1966), 20

A. Barnett: "John Tchicai: of Three Continents," *JM*, no.164 (1968), 2

V. Wilmer: "Tchicai in Full Control," *MM* (12 Oct 1968), 8

R. Williams: "It Must be Good – it's Danish!," *MM* (22 Nov 1969), 8

M. Caloum: "John Tchicai: jours tranquilles à Copenhague," *Jm*, no.189 (1971), 26

C. Flicker and G. Noël: "Je m'appelle John Tchicai," *Jh*, no.272 (1971), 9 [incl. discography]

E. Jost: *Free Jazz* (Graz, Austria, 1974/*R*1994), 109

M. Hames: *John Tchicai on Disc and Tape* (Ferndown, England, 1979) [discography]

G. Cerutti: *Discographie de John Tchicai* (Sierre, Switzerland, n.d. [?1980]; rev. and enlarged 2/n.d. [?1982] as *Guidebook John Tchicai*, rev. and enlarged 3/n.d. [?1986] as *John Tchicai Discography (on Records), 1962–1985*)

G. Rouy: "John Tchicai: jours tranquilles à Copenhague," *Jm*, no.286 (1980), 26

B. Noglik: "John Tchicai," *Jazzwerkstatt international* (Berlin, 1981), 399 [incl. discography]

K. Yianoulopoulos: "'Die eigene spirituelle Erfahrung spüren lassen': John Tchicai," *JP*, xxxi/4 (1982), 4 [incl. discography]

C. Irgens-Møller: "Tchicai: et begreb" [Tchicai: a notion], *Dansk musik tidsskrift*, lxi/3 (1986–7), 111

P. N. Wilson: "In Marrakech: Jazzworkshop mit John Tchicai," *JP*, xxxvi/2 (1987), 22

R. Baggenæs: "John Tchicai," *Coda*, no.221 (1988), 16

H. Geerken: "Motte motte motte," *JP*, xxxix/9 (1990), 14

P. Pullman: "Jazz Obsessions: the Danish Connection," *VV* (28 Aug 1990), 71

A. Kirkegaard: "John Tchicai," *Copyright* [Copenhagen], no.6 (1991), 45

D. Richardson: "Hail and Farewell: Saxophonist John Tchicai Featured in Final Show at Koncepts," *San Francisco Bay Guardian* (4 March 1992)

D. Rubien: "John Tchicai: Danish Delight," *San Francisco Chronicle Datebook* (24 Oct 1993), 23

N. van Bergen Garner: "John Tchicai," *Jazz Special*, no.28 (1996), 13

M. Trouchon: "John Tchicai," *Opprobrium*, no.3 (1996), 82 [incl. discography]

<http://dcn.org/go/jomnamo/> (2000) [incl. discography]

<http://www.info.net.nz/opprobrium/3/tchicai.html> (2000) [incl. discography]

OLE MATTHIESSEN/ERIK WIEDEMANN/
FRANK BÜCHMANN-MØLLER

Teagarden. Family of musicians.

(1) Helen Teagarden [née Giengar] (*b* Oklahoma City, 3 Jan 1890; *d* Oct 1982). Pianist. She taught piano in Chappel, Nebraska, and later (around 1920) in Oklahoma City, and was largely responsible for the musical education of her children. While she was not particularly a jazz-oriented player, she did appear at the Monterey Jazz Festival in 1963 in a band that was led by (2) Jack Teagarden and included (3) Norma and (4) Charlie Teagarden. The correct spelling of her maiden name and details of her birth appear in her application for social security, and the social security death index gives her last-known residence as Las Vegas. (J. D. Smith and L. Guttridge: *Jack Teagarden: the Story of a Jazz Maverick*, London, 1960/*R*1988)

(2) Jack [Weldon Leo] **Teagarden** [Big T] (*b* Vernon, TX, 29 Aug 1905; *d* New Orleans, 15 Jan 1964). Trombonist and singer. He started learning piano with his mother (1) Helen Teagarden when he was five, then turned to baritone horn, and took up trombone at the age of ten. He began playing professionally as a teenager, working mainly in the Southwest with local bands, including Peck Kelley's Bad Boys (1921–3, 1924), the Original Southern Trumpeters (1924), and Doc Ross's Jazz Bandits (1924–7). He then went to New York, where he played briefly with Wingy Manone. After working as a freelance for a while he joined Ben Pollack's band in June 1928, though he continued to play and record with other musicians such as Red Nichols, Louis Armstrong, Benny Goodman, and Eddie Condon, including sessions under the nominal leadership of Irving Mills, with the pseudonymous group Johnny Walker and his Orchestra (directed by Goodman), with the Mound City Blue Blowers, and in an ad hoc studio group led by Joe Venuti and Eddie Lang. He left Pollack while in Chicago in May 1933, and after brief associations with Manone and lesser-known leaders he became a member of Paul Whiteman's band in December 1933. For one month in 1936 he played after hours at the Hickory House on 52nd Street in New York with his fellow Whiteman sidemen Frankie Trumbauer and his brother (4) Charlie Teagarden in a group known as the Three T's. Teagarden remained as a star soloist and singer with Whiteman until December 1938. He then set up his own big band, a venture which was successful musically but financially unrewarding, as it ended with his being declared bankrupt in 1946. He led a sextet from late 1946 until he joined the first Louis Armstrong All Stars in July 1947 (see

Jack Teagarden (trombone) with Louis Armstrong (trumpet) and Bobby Hackett during a rehearsal for a concert by Armstrong's All Stars at Town Hall, New York, May 1947

illustration), then formed his own dixieland group, also known as the All Stars, in August 1951. Except for a reunion with Pollack in 1956, he continued to lead small groups, which included such musicians as Don Ewell, Max Kaminsky, Dick Wellstood, his brother Charlie, and his sister (3) Norma Teagarden, until his death. One such group, co-led by Earl Hines, toured Europe (autumn 1957) and another visited the Far East (September 1958 – January 1959).

Teagarden is considered by many critics to be the finest of all jazz trombonists, but his style was so personal that he had few followers and founded no school. Significantly, he grew up in rough southwestern towns containing large African-American populations, and was far more familiar than most early white jazz players with African-American spirituals, work songs, and the blues, having experienced them first-hand from earliest childhood. As a consequence he was one of the first white jazz musicians to master the blues, and probably the first to make use of blue notes. He usually detached his solo line markedly from the ground beat, weaving lazy arabesques of melody. He tended to play in the upper register of the instrument, and his cloudy tone, at first relatively rough, grew smoother in his later years. Because of his deceptively simple style, few listeners realized how technically adroit he was; he was particularly skilled in playing lip trills, which became a prominent feature of his style. Teagarden is also considered one of the finest jazz singers. His vocal style was much simpler than that of his highly decorative playing, but characterized by a similar lazy quality, and his husky voice was particularly suitable for the blues (*see* Blues, §4). Teagarden's recorded output is very consistent, but especially fine are his performances on *Knockin' a Jug* (1929), *Jack hits the road* (1940), and *Makin' Friends* (1928), the last named including an eccentric solo played with the bell of the trombone removed.

Oral history material in *LNT*.

SELECTED RECORDINGS

As leader: A Hundred Years from Today (1933, Bruns. 6716); Stars Fell on Alabama (1934, Bruns 6993); What did I do to be so black and blue? (1941, Decca 3844); Blues after Hours (1947, Vic. 20-2458); A Jam Session at Victor (1947, Vic. 40-0138); with B. Hackett: *Jazz Ultimate* (1957, Cap. T933); *The Swingin' Gate* (1960, 1963, Giants of Jazz 1026); *Jack Teagarden Sextet in Person* (1963, Fanfare LP32-132)

As sideman: Roger Wolfe Kahn: She's a great great girl (1928, Vic. 21326); E. Condon: Makin' Friends (1928, OK 41142); R. Nichols: After You've Gone (1930, Bruns. 4839); I. Mills: Diga diga doo (1928, PAct 36902); Bugle Call Rag (1928, PAct 36945); E. Condon: I'm gonna stomp, Mr. Henry Lee/That's a Serious Thing (1929, Vic. 38046); B. Pollack: My Kinda Love (1929, Vic. 21944); L. Armstrong: Knockin' a Jug (1929, OK 8703); I. Mills: Strut, Miss Lizzie (1930, Bruns. 4983); B. Pollack: If I could be with you (one hour tonight) (1930, Ban. 0747); R. Nichols: The Sheik of Araby (1930, Bruns. 4885); J. Walker: Basin Street Blues (1931, Col. 2404D); J. Venuti and E. Lang: Beale Street Blues (1931, Voc. 15864); B. Goodman: I gotta right to sing the blues (1933, Col. 2835D); Moon Glow (1934, Col. 2927D); F. Trumbauer: I hope Gabriel likes my music (1936, Bruns. 7613); E. Condon: Serenade to a Shylock (1938, Com. 1501); B. Freeman: Jack hits the road (1940, Col. 35854); L. Armstrong: Rockin' Chair (1947, Vic. 40-4004); St. James Infirmary (1947, Vic. 40-4006); Jack-Armstrong Blues/Rockin' Chair (1947, Vic. 20-2348); C. LaVere: Lover (1950, Jump 32); B. Hackett: *Coast Concert* (1955, Cap. T692); *Gotham Jazz Scene* (1957, Cap. T857)

SELECTED FILMS AND VIDEOS

Ben Pollack and his Park Central Orchestra (1929); Me and the Boys (1929); The Happiness Remedy (1931); Hoagy Carmichael (1939); Birth of the Blues (1941); Louis Armstrong–Jack Teagarden Sextet (1948); Eddie Condon Floor Show (3 different films, all 1949); Botta e risposta (1951); Basin Street Blues (1952); Stars Fell on Alabama (1952); The Glass Wall (1953); Ban Nhac Teagarden (1958); Jack Teagarden in Thailand (1958); The Jack Teagarden Show (1958); Jazz on a Summer's Day (1960); Chicago & All that Jazz (1961); The Jack Teagarden Sextet: Far East Tour: 1958–1959 (1989)

BIBLIOGRAPHY

McCarthyB; *SchullerS*

W. Scholl: "The New Vocal Sensation: Jack Teagarden," *MM*, x (26 May 1934)

C. Wilford: "An Anatomy of Teagarden," *Jazz Music*, no.6 (1943); repr. in *Jazz Reprints*, i/1 (1962), 12

L. Feather: *The Book of Jazz: a Guide to the Entire Field* (New York, 1957, 2/1965 as *The Book of Jazz from Then till Now: a Guide to the Entire Field*)

C. E. Smith: "Big Gate," *JM*, iii/8 (1957), 2

J. Tynan: "Teagarden Talks," *DB*, xxiv/5 (1957), 19

G. Hoefer: "The Change in Big T," *DB*, xxvi/24 (1959), 18

J. D. Smith and L. Guttridge: *Jack Teagarden: the Story of a Jazz Maverick* (London, 1960/*R*1988)

H. J. Waters, Jr.: *Jack Teagarden's Music: his Career and Recordings* (Stanhope, NJ, 1960)

W. Balliett: "Slow Sleeper," *Dinosaurs in the Morning* (Philadelphia, 1962), 207

M. Kaminsky and V. E. Hughes: *My Life in Jazz* (New York, 1963/*R*1981)

B. James: "Blues for Jack Teagarden," *JJ*, xvii/3 (1964), 2

R. Hadlock: *Jazz Masters of the Twenties* (New York, 1965/*R*1985), 172

H. Woodfin: "Say it Simple: the Art of Jack Teagarden," *JM*, xii/9 (1966), 10

M. Williams: "In Praise of Jack Teagarden," *JJ*, xxi/6 (1968), 4

——: *Jazz Masters in Transition, 1957–69* (New York and London, 1970/*R*1980)

R. Blesh: "Big T," *Combo, USA: Eight Lives in Jazz* (Philadelphia and London, 1971), 58

R. Russell: "Jack Teagarden and the Texas School," *Jazz Style in Kansas City and the Southwest* (Berkeley, CA, Los Angeles, and London, 1971, rev. 2/1973/*R*1997), 120

G. Sloan: "Something Old, Something New," *Newsletter of the ITA*, vii/1 (1979), 3 [incl. transcr.]

H. Lyttelton: *The Best of Jazz*, ii: *Enter the Giants, 1931–1944* (London, 1981), 92

D. Chamberlain and R. Wilson, eds.: *The Otis Ferguson Reader* (Highland Park, IL, 1982), 104

W. Balliett: "Profiles: Jack Teagarden," *New Yorker*, lx (2 April 1984), 47; repr. in *BalliettA (1986)*; *BalliettA (1996)*

G. Sloan: "The Body and Soul of Jazz Trombone," *The Instrumentalist*, xl/4 (1985), 14 [incl. transcr.]

H. Mückenberger: *Meet Me Where they Play the Blues: Jack Teagarden und seine Musik* (Gauting, Germany, 1986)

G. Sloan: "You're in Teagarden Country," *ITA Journal*, xiv/2 (1986), 26

C. Garrod: *Jack Teagarden and his Orchestra* (Zephyrhills, FL, 1993) [discography]

(3) Norma (Louise) Teagarden [Friedlander, Norma (Louise)] (*b* Vernon, TX, 29 April 1911; *d* San Francisco, 5 June 1996). Pianist. She was taught by her mother, (1) Helen Teagarden, and began playing as a solo pianist in dance halls and clubs in 1926 to supplement her income as a telephone switchboard operator. After working in Oklahoma City and New Mexico she moved in 1941 to California, where she led her own groups in San Pedro and Long Beach. The following year she joined the big band led by her brother (2) Jack Teagarden, with whom she stayed until 1946. She made her first recordings in a small group drawn from his band, among them *Big "T" Blues* (1944, Com. 592), in which he compliments her on her playing, and during the same period she was informally recorded playing her specialty, *Little Rock Getaway* (first issued on the album *Big T and the Condon Gang*, 1944, Pumpkin 33155). From 1946 to 1949 she was the leader of her own band, following which she took up teaching. Teagarden then performed with a variety of bands, notably those of Ben Pollack and Ada Leonard, and in 1953–4 she was a member of Jack's small group. On leaving her brother's band she married and withdrew from public performance, although she continued to teach. She emerged occasionally into the limelight, and in 1963 she made recordings with Jack and (4) Charlie Teagarden at the Monterey Jazz Festival, notably *Basin St. Blues* (first issued on J. Teagarden: *The Swingin' Gate*, Giants of Jazz 1026). In 1975 she played on a jazz cruise and resumed an active performing career; later that year she took up a permanent residency at the Washington Street Bar and Grill in San Francisco. In 1983, at the Sacramento Dixieland Jubilee, she was elected "Empress of Jazz," and she continued to work on the West Coast well into the 1990s, often with her Marin County Band, with which she toured Britain in 1986. She also played and recorded in the Netherlands during the 1980s.

BIBLIOGRAPHY

FeatherE
S. Placksin: *American Women in Jazz, 1900 to the Present: their Words, Lives, and Music* (New York, 1982)
B. Doerschuk: "Norma Teagarden: Queen of Stride Piano," *Keyboard*, x/5 (1984), 28
C. McFadden: "Miss Norma," *San Francisco Examiner* (14 Nov 1985)
A. C. Williams: "The Enduring Grace of Norma Teagarden," *MR*, xiv/3 (1987), 1
J. Kaliss: "The Greening of Teagarden," *San Francisco Chronicle Datebook* (27 Aug 1989)
P. Elwood: "Tribute: Norma Teagarden," *San Francisco Examiner Image* (31 March 1991), 23
Obituaries: *San Francisco Chronicle* (8 June 1996); P. Elwood, *San Francisco Examiner* (14 June 1996); [A. Shipton,] *The Times* (27 June 1996)

(4) Charlie [Charles] **Teagarden** [Little T] (*b* Vernon, TX, 19 July 1913; *d* Las Vegas, NV, 10 Dec 1984). Trumpeter. After first working with bands in Oklahoma he joined Ben Pollack in New York in 1929. He recorded there with various bands, notably those of Joe Venuti and Eddie Lang (1931), Red Nichols (1931), and Roger Wolfe Kahn (1932), before following his brother (2) Jack Teagarden into Paul Whiteman's orchestra (1933). While he was with Whiteman (1933–40) he made club appearances with Jack and Frankie Trumbauer in the Three T's and also recorded with a larger group of the same name (*I'se a muggin'*, 1936, Vic. 25273). In September 1940 he joined Jack's big band, with which he performed intermittently throughout the decade, although he also led his own band briefly in 1942. Thereafter he spent a number of periods with his brother's small groups, while also playing with Jimmy Dorsey (1948–50), Pollack (1950–51), and Bob Crosby (1954–8). In 1959 Teagarden moved to Las Vegas and gradually withdrew from performing in favor of a career in the musicians' union, for which he worked throughout the 1970s. He also led his own quartet, however, which recorded the album *Big Horn* in 1962 (Coral 757410). (*ChiltonW*; *FeatherE*; *Feather '60s*)

(5) Cub [Clois Lee] **Teagarden** (*b* Vernon, TX, 16 Dec 1915; *d* ?Riverton, NY, June 1969). Drummer. In 1929 he joined Frank Williams's Oklahomans as drummer and singer, and during the 1930s he played with various groups. While he was a member of the band led by his brother (2) Jack Teagarden from 1939 to 1940, his tenure was relatively unsuccessful, and he was soon replaced by Dave Tough. He then performed with the Oklahoma Symphony Orchestra and briefly led his own band before moving to California, where he worked as a freelance. He virtually ceased to play in 1948. (*FeatherE*)

ALYN SHIPTON (1, 3–5), JAMES LINCOLN COLLIER/BK (2)

Teague, Thurman (*b* Illinois, 1910). Double bass player. He first performed on banjo and guitar in Chicago, then in the early 1930s played regularly with the guitarist Jack Goss. After changing to double bass he worked with Ben Pollack and later with the pianist and bandleader Vincent Lopez and others. His solid, rhythmic playing may be heard to advantage on *I never knew what a gal could do* (1937, Col. 36159), by Santo Pecora and his Back Room Boys. From 1939 to 1944 Teague played with Harry James. Thereafter he worked with Red Nichols (1945–6) and was active as a studio musician on the West Coast.

based on *ChiltonW*

Tebar, Ximo (*b* Valencia, Spain, 30 March 1963). Spanish guitarist. He studied guitar at the age of seven, beginning in the flamenco style, but when he was 15 took up Brazilian music and jazz. From the age of 17 he has led the Ximo Tebar Jazz Group. He has accompanied such important soloists as Johnny Griffin, Tete Montoliu, Lou Bennett, Pedro Iturralde, Lonnie Smith, and Jorge Pardo. In 1989 he perfomed in Italy with the European Big Band, in 1990 he toured Russia and Central America, and in 1992 he participated in an international guitar festival in France. From 1994 he has appeared at many European festivals. Tebar has recorded as a leader with Bennett (1992, 1995), Idris Muhammad (1992, 1997–), and Joey DeFrancesco (1998–), and in 1998 he performed in Madrid as a member of the Champs, a trio with Muhammad and DeFrancesco.

SELECTED RECORDINGS

As leader: *Aranzazu* (1988, Difusio Mediterranea 39); *Ania del gnomo* (1990, Eligeme Discos 0007); *Live in Russia* (1991, Difusio Mediterranea 43); with L. Bennett and I. Muhammad: *Hello Mr. Bennett* (1992, WEA 0630-18789-2); *Son Mediterraneo* (1995, WEA 0630-10993-2); *So What* (1997, WEA 0630-18790-2)

ALFREDO PAPO

Teddies. *See* ORIGINAL TEDDIES.

Teddy Wilson School for Pianists. Record label. Its material was recorded in 1938–9 by the American Record Corporation and made available for sale by the school, which was based in New York. Five 78 r.p.m. discs were released, all unaccompanied solos by Wilson; the discs were issued with scores and analytical texts. (J. Callanan: Liner notes, *Teddy Wilson: the Complete 'School for Pianists' Recordings, 1938–1939*, Meritt 23, 1984)

HOWARD RYE

Tee [Ten Ryk]**, Richard (Edward)** (*b* New York, 24 Nov 1943; *d* New York, 11 July 1993). Keyboard player. He studied in New York at the High School of Music and Art and the Manhattan School of Music, and at some point he simplified his surname, changing it from Ten Ryk to Tee. He first became active as a sideman during the soul-jazz era, when the dance rhythms of African-American popular music were being reintegrated into the mainstream of jazz: he recorded with Shirley Scott and Les McCann (both 1969), Gary Burton (1969–70), Hank Crawford (1969–75), Herbie Mann, King Curtis, and Snooky Young (all 1971), Stanley Turrentine (1971, 1973), Grover Washington, Jr. (1971–3), Roland Kirk (1971, 1975), David "Fathead" Newman (1972), Ron Carter (1973, 1975), Hubert Laws (1974, 1980), Jimmy Witherspoon (1975), and Carla Bley (1976). With Young, Tee may be heard to advantage as an organist on *Lil' Darlin'* and as a pianist on *The Checkered Hat*, both on *The Boys from Dayton* (1971, 1975 MJR 8130); the other tracks on this album were taken from an unrelated session which was recorded in 1975 under Norris Turney's leadership and in which Tee did not take part. From 1974 to 1984 Tee led his own funk group, Stuff, with the guitarists Eric Gale and Cornell Dupree, the electric bass guitarist Gordon Edwards, and either Steve Gadd or Chris Parker on drums. During the same period he played in Gadd's group the Gadd Gang, worked with many popular entertainers and commercial groups, and recorded film soundtracks. Tee later recorded with Gadd and Sadao Watanabe (both 1984) and Ronnie Cuber (1985) and made the album *The Bottom Line* (1985, EB 6364) under his own name. Thereafter he led a funk band, RTC (Richard Tee Commission), which consisted of the saxophonist Lennie Pickett, John Tropea, Will Lee, and Gadd; the group toured on its own and accompanying the singer Paul Simon, and it appeared on the popular television program "Saturday Night Live."

SELECTED FILMS AND VIDEOS

Grover Washington, Jr., in Concert (1981); On Studio Piano [Contemporary Piano] (*c* early 1980s); Steve Gadd, ii: In Session (1985)

BIBLIOGRAPHY

J. Stix: "Richard Tee: from New York Session Work to 'Stuff'," *CK*, iii/11 (1977), 16 [incl. discography]

J. Coryell and L. Friedman: *Jazz-rock Fusion* (New York and London, 1978)

D. Townsend: "Keyboardist to the Stars, on his Own," *Washington Times* (1 Oct 1990)

Obituary, *New York Times* (26 July 1993)

BK

Teepe, Joris (*b* Rijswijk, Netherlands, 27 Nov 1962). Dutch bass player. He studied electric bass guitar (BA 1990) and double bass (MA 1991) at the Hilversum Conservatory/Amsterdam Conservatory, where he played in a big band which accompanied such visiting musicians as Slide Hampton and the singer Deborah Brown. In 1992 he moved to New York and received tuition from Ron Carter and Peter Washington. The following year he began collaborating with Don Braden, both in a quartet and as the co-leader of a quintet; their sidemen have included Tom Harrell, Cyrus Chestnut, Kevin Hays, Renee Rosnes, David Hazeltine, Carl Allen, Cecil Brooks III, Tony Reedus, and Billy Drummond. Between 1995 and 1997 Teepe performed and recorded with the tenor saxophonist Barend Middelhoff, and in 1996 he began working with the alto saxophonist Brad Leali and with the Intercontinental Jazz Trio, in which he plays alongside the American saxophonist Tim Armacost and the Japanese drummer Shingo Okudaira. He has recorded with the saxophonist Maximilian Geller (1996), and with Brooks and Grant (both *c*1997), and has led his own groups.

SELECTED RECORDINGS

As leader: *Bottom Line* (1995, Mons 874770)

As sideman: D. Braden: *Landing Zone* (1994, Landmark 1539-2); B. Middelhoff: *Soil* (1995, A-Records 73026); Intercontinental Jazz Trio: *Live at the Bimhuis* (*c*1996, Via Jazz 992040-2)

BIBLIOGRAPHY

"Joris Teepe – Don Braden," *JP*, xliv/10 (1995), 20

<http://www.jazzrecords.com/musicians/joris_teepe.htm> (1998)

GK

Teitelbaum, Richard (Lowe) (*b* New York, 19 May 1939). Composer and synthesizer player. He studied music at Yale University (MM 1964), then traveled to Italy on a Fulbright scholarship. While there, with other composers based in Rome, he formed Musica Elettronica Viva for the performance of live electronic music; the group continued to perform and record collaborative improvisations, mainly in Europe, until 1970, during which time it was joined by Steve Lacy and the trombonist Garrett List. Teitelbaum then returned to the USA for further study, and at Wesleyan University formed the World Band with musicians from the Middle and Far East who shared his interest in collective improvisation. He later taught at the California Institute of the Arts, the Art Institute in Chicago, and York University in Toronto. From 1974 he performed with Anthony Braxton, with whom he made such recordings as the duo albums *Time Zones* (1976, Fre. 41037) and *Open Aspects* (1982, HA 1995–6), and later, *Duet: Live at Merkin Hall* (New York) (1994, Music & Arts 949). He also recorded in a quartet with George Lewis (ii) (*Homage to Charles Parker*, 1979, BS 0029), and presented his multi-tiered amalgamation of synthesized and "natural" instruments, of avant-garde European art music and jazz, variously composed and improvised, in his *Concerto Grosso* (1985, HA 6004), recorded in a trio with Braxton and Lewis.

BIBLIOGRAPHY

M. Dery: "The Arcane Experiments of Richard Teitelbaum," *Keyboard*, xv/7 (1989), 74

R. M. Radano: *New Musical Figurations: Anthony Braxton's Cultural Critique* (Chicago and London, 1993)

JOAN LA BARBARA/BK

Telarc. Record label. Its parent company, Telarc International, was founded in Cleveland in 1977 by Jack Renner and Robert Woods. Telarc built its reputation as a classical music label (it was the first such American label to record digitally), then in 1989 it formed a jazz division and began issuing jazz recordings on CD. It had recorded and issued an LP by Mel Lewis in 1979, and this was its first "new" jazz issue in 1989; its second, released in October 1990, was from material recorded by André Previn the previous year. Thereafter Telarc's jazz division has documented the work of predominantly veteran musicians, notably Oscar Peterson (from 1990), George Shearing (from 1992), and Ray Brown, Dave Brubeck, and Jim Hall (all from 1993); other sessions have involved the Count Basie Orchestra, Frank Morgan, George Coleman, Harry Edison, Dizzy Gillespie, Al Grey, Lionel

Hampton, Slide Hampton, Ahmad Jamal, Gerry Mulligan, and Joe Williams. Its catalogue also features some performers of the younger generation, including Jeanie Bryson, the trumpeter Jeremy Davenport, Cody Moffett, Vanessa Rubin, and Hilton Ruiz. In May 1992 Telarc initiated a reissue series devoted to Lionel Hampton, Paul Desmond, and, especially, Erroll Garner (in particular recordings made from the mid-1960s to the early 1970s for the MGM and London labels), and in 1996 it began to issue fusion and world music on the imprint Telarc Jazz Zone. By late 2000 its jazz catalogue exceeded 160 albums.

BIBLIOGRAPHY

D. Lander: "The Audio Interview: Telarc's Jack Renner: Recording without a Net," *Audio*, lxviii/7 (1984), 30
"Telarc Reveals New Directions," *Billboard*, c (22 Oct 1988), 89
I. Lichtman: "Telarc Jazzes up its Image with DMP Label Distrib Deal," *Billboard*, ci (22 July 1989), 90
H. Reich: "Digital Duo," *Chicago Tribune* (1 Feb 1989)
D. Zych: "Label Watch: Telarc's Distinguished Profile," *JT*, xxii/5 (1992), 24
E. Holley: "Telarc Enters Contemporary Zone," *DB*, lxiii/4 (1996), 15
B. Milkowski: "Label Watch: Telarc: on the Sonic Forefront," *JT*, xxvii/4 (1997), 77
<http://www.telarc.com/about/history6.asp> (2000)

GK

Temiz, Okay (*b* Ankara, 11 Feb 1939). Turkish drummer, percussionist, and leader. Through his mother, who played *'ūd* and *jumbush* and performed Turkish classical music, he was introduced to traditional folk musics from Turkey, Macedonia, and the Middle East. He took up trumpet, trombone, and double bass before studying percussion at the conservatory in Ankara in the mid-1950s, and in 1955 he was inspired to play jazz after hearing Charli Persip perform with Dizzy Gillespie's band. Around this time he began working professionally as a drummer in dance bands, with which he toured Germany, Denmark, and Sweden, and met and played with, among others, Maffy Falay, Don Cherry, Johnny Dyani, and Dollar Brand. In Sweden he worked alongside Dyani in Cherry's trio (from 1969, recording in 1969, 1971) and was a member of Falay's group Sevda (through summer 1972); he then joined Dyani and Mongezi Feza in Music for Xaba and toured with the group Rena Rama. From around 1977 he led Oriental Wind, which included Bobo Stenson and Lennart Åberg, the Okay Temiz Ensemble, and the Magnetic Band. After living in Sweden for a number of years he moved to Finland in 1993 and formed the group the Romans, with which he continued to tour internationally and record in the late 1990s. In much of his work Temiz has combined the folk music of Turkey and other Eastern European countries with jazz. He plays percussion instruments from various parts of the world, including *cuíca* and *berimbau* from Brazil and talking drums and *kalimba* from Africa, and he often uses drum sets in which he has replaced the standard drums with comparitively spongey-sounding Turkish *darabukkas*.

SELECTED RECORDINGS

As leader: with J. Dyani and M. Feza: *Music for Xaba* (1972, Sonet 642); *Live in Bremen* (1981, Jaro 007); of Oriental Wind: *Bazaar* (1981, Sonet 864); *Magnetic Band in Finland 1995* (1995, Ano Kato 2004)
As sideman: D. Cherry: *Live in Ankara* (1969, Sonet 669); *Don Cherry* (1971, BYG [Jap.] 4012–13); *Blue Lake* (1971, BYG [Jap.] 4022–23); M. Falay: *Sevda* (1972, Caprice 31); J. Dyani: *Rejoice* (1972, Cadillac 1017); D. Cherry: *Dona nostra* (1993, ECM 1448)

BIBLIOGRAPHY

T. B. Lyrhed: "Okay faar musiken att svaeva ... " [Okay makes the music soar ...], *Orkester journalen*, li/4 (1983), 10
M. Scheiner: "Zwischen Orient und Okzident: Okay Temiz," *JP*, xxxii/11 (1983), 16
L. Blomberg: "Nya vindar i Oriental Wind" [New direction of Oriental Wind], *Orkester journalen*, liv/4 (1986), 20
D.-C. Martin: "Orient Express," *Jm*, no.393 (1990), 22
<http://www.goldenhorn.com/okaytemiz.html> (1999) [incl. discography]
<http://yunus.cmpe.boun.edu.tr/~hocaoglu/famous.htm> (1999) [incl. discography]

GK

Temperance Seven. English traditional jazz band. It was formed in late December 1955 to perform dance music of the 1920s. Its original members were the cornetist Douglas Gray, the trombonist and singer Paul McDowell, the clarinetist Joe Clarke, the banjoist and saxophonist Philip Harrison, the double bass player Brian Wright, and the drummer Brian Innes. Innes remained a longstanding member while gradual changes in personnel brought into the band the trumpeter and euphonium player Cephas Howard, the reed player Alan Cooper, the pianist Colin Bowles, the tuba player Clifford Bevan (replaced by Martin Fry in 1958), and, in 1959, the banjoist John Gieves-Watson. Clarke died in 1959 and was replaced by John R. T. Davies, who supplied arrangements and played trombone, trumpet, and alto saxophone. In 1961 the reed player Ray Whittam succeeded Harrison and Bevan replaced Bowles; Bevan also served as the group's music director. In the course of further changes in personnel the trumpeter and sousaphone player Bobby Mickleburgh joined in 1962. The musicians' adoption of fanciful nicknames was characteristic of their humorous approach. The band made several recordings, including *The Temperance Seven, 1961* (1961, Parl. PMC1152); the most successful were *You're driving me crazy* and *Pasadena*, which reached the top of the popular music charts in the UK in 1961. The band also appeared in *It's Trad Dad, Toto da notte* (both 1962), and other films. After a period of relative inactivity, in the early 1970s it performed as the New Temperance Seven. With many further changes in membership, but Howard, Gieves-Watson, Davies, and Innes remaining as its directors, the Temperance Seven continued to work in the 1980s and 1990s.

BIBLIOGRAPHY

ChiltonB
R. Coleman: "One Over the Eight, that's the Temperance Seven," *MM* (1 April 1961), 6
——: "The Temperance Seven: a Sober Survey," *MM* (9 Dec 1961), 2
"The Temperance Seven: Personal Appearance," *Jazz News*, v/28 (1961), 16
I. Berg, I. Yeomans, and N. Brittan: *Trad: an A to Z Who's Who of the British Traditional Jazz Scene* (London and elsewhere, 1962), 70
B. Matthew: *Trad Mad* (London, 1962)
G. Martin and J. Hornsby: *All you Need is Ears* (London, 1979)
D. Clarke, ed.: *The Penguin Encyclopedia of Popular Music* (London and elsewhere, 1989)

BRIAN INNES

Temperley, Joe [Joseph] (*b* Cowdenbeath, Scotland, 20 Sept 1929). Scottish baritone saxophonist. He first learned cornet and then alto saxophone, but after taking up the tenor instrument (around 1945) he joined Harry Parry (1949), with whom he recorded and toured the Middle East. Later he performed and recorded with Jack Parnell (autumn 1952 – March 1954) and Tony Crombie (October 1954 – March 1955) and worked with Dizzy Reece (1954) and lesser-known groups, including his own. After playing with Carl Barriteau (spring 1955) he took up baritone saxophone to join Tommy Whittle (autumn 1955). He recorded with Jazz Unit Today and George Chisholm (both 1956) and worked with the saxophonist Oscar Rabin (1956) and Phil Seamen's quintet

(1957), but first achieved national prominence as a member of Humphrey Lyttelton's band (1958–65), with which he played tenor and then baritone saxophone; he made several important recordings with the group and toured the USA (1959). He may be seen in the film *The Small World of Sammy Lee* (1962).

In 1965 Temperley settled in New York, where he worked with Woody Herman (1966–7), Buddy Rich, Joe Henderson, Duke Pearson, and the Jazz Composer's Orchestra, and recorded with the Thad Jones–Mel Lewis Orchestra (1969), Clark Terry (1970), and Eumir Deodato (1973). In October 1974, as Harry Carney's replacement, he toured and recorded with Duke Ellington's orchestra (at that time led by Mercer Ellington). He then resumed his freelance activities, which included regular tours as a soloist in Britain, an activity which continued through the 1990s; he recorded with Benny Waters in Edinburgh in 1980. In the 1980s he played in the Broadway show *Sophisticated Ladies*, performed on numerous film soundtracks, and, late in the decade, worked in Buck Clayton's big band and recorded in a group with Benny Carter, Jimmy Heath, Frank Wess, and Hal Geller. For the BBC he organized, performed in, and hosted the documentary "Temperley's Town" ("Jazz Apple") featuring Clayton's group, a duo of Temperley and Milt Hinton, an interview with Mulgrew Miller, a quintet comprising Temperley, Eddie Barefield, and a rhythm section of Sammy Price, Arvell Shaw, and the drummer Ronnie Cole, and other prominent musicians; it was broadcast early in 1990.

Temperley was a founding member of the Lincoln Center Jazz Orchestra, with which he remained active in the late 1990s. He continues to work as a freelance, in which capacity he played in Joe Henderson's big band and appeared at Zinno's in New York with Mike LeDonne's trio (1991) and with Junior Mance and Calvin Hill (1996). In 1996 he was also a member of Benny Carter's big band for a concert at the Library of Congress in Washington. He is a mentor and co-founder of the Fife Youth Jazz Orchestra program in Scotland, and he has taught at the Manhattan School of Music.

Temperley regularly doubles on bass clarinet and soprano saxophone and plays other saxophones and flute as well, but the baritone remains his principal instrument. The broad base of his style has won him praise from such diverse players as Charles Mingus and Warren Vaché; that he took the place of a musician of Carney's caliber in Ellington's orchestra was a colossal achievement and shows him to be a player of high standing.

Video oral history material in *NCH* (HCJA).

SELECTED RECORDINGS

Duos with D. McKenna: *Sunbeam and Thundercloud* (1995, Conc. 4703)
As leader with J. Knepper: *Just Friends* (1978, Hep 2003); *Nightingale* (1991, Hep 2052); *Concerto for Joe* (1993–4, Hep 2062)
As sideman: H. Lyttelton: *Humph Plays Standards* (1960, Beth. 6063), incl. Prelude to a Kiss; B. Clayton: *Le vrai Buck Clayton* (1964, 77 LEU11); M. Ellington: *Continuum* (1974–5, Fan. 9481)

BIBLIOGRAPHY

CarrJ; *ChiltonB*; *FeatherE*; *Feather–Gitler '70s*
M. Gardner: "Speaking my Mind, the Musician's Viewpoint: Baritone Saxophonist Joe Temperley," *Coda*, viii/2 (1967), 8
V. Wilmer: "Versatile Joe," *MM* (26 Jan 1974), 47
M. Jones: "Joe's Happy Road to the Isles," *MM* (6 March 1976), 42
D. H. Matthews: "Joe Temperley," *CI*, xxvi/7 (1989), 12
M. Richards: "Joe Temperley," *JJI*, xlii (1989), no.4, p.6, no.5, p.10
"Interview with Joe Temperley," *The Note*, v/2 (1993), 5
B. Bernotas: "Joe Temperley," *Saxophone Journal*, xxi/6 (1997), 19

DIGBY FAIRWEATHER/BK

Temple block. A spherical wooden slit-drum used in jazz from the 1920s to produce novelty effects; *see* Drum set, §I, 7(ii).

Templin, Lutz [Ludwig] (*b* Düsseldorf, Germany, 18 June 1901; *d* nr Stuttgart, Germany, 7 March 1973). German bandleader. He studied violin and composition, and during the 1930s he worked as a tenor saxophonist and arranger for various dance bands. In 1941 he formed his own big band, which worked in radio and recording studios (1941–9); its swing recordings include *Immer wieder tanzen/Rhythmus in Dosen* (1942, Grammophon 47705). Under the name Charlie and his Orchestra the band made recordings of arrangements by American jazz musicians; these were broadcast on radio by the German authorities with added texts that purveyed propaganda against the Allies. Because of the bombardment of Berlin, Templin's orchestra was evacuated in 1943 to Stuttgart, where it performed until 1944. Templin continued to work in and around Stuttgart, and for a short time he was music director of the dance orchestra of Süddeutscher Rundfunk.

BIBLIOGRAPHY

R. E. Lotz: Liner notes, *Charlie and his Orchestra: Propaganda Swing* (Discophilia 13UTC1–2, 1975)
H. H. Lange: Liner notes, *Die grossen Tanzorchester, 1930–1950: Lutz Templin* (Pol. 2437629–30, ?1978)
H. J. P. Bergmeier and R. E. Lotz: *Hitler's Airwaves: the Inside Story of Nazi Radio Broadcasting and Propaganda Swing* (New Haven, CT, and London, 1997)

RAINER E. LOTZ

Tempo (i) (It.). The "time" of a piece of music, hence the speed at which the performance proceeds; for a discussion of tempos in jazz *see* Beat, esp. §2.

Tempo (ii). Record label. It was established by the Tempo Record Society of London, and issue began in September 1946. The catalogue contained two series. The A- sequence was used to issue new recordings by British bands, mostly of traditional jazz; the R- series contained reissues of early jazz from American labels no longer in operation. The last issues were made in October 1952; early the following year the operation was taken over by British Vogue, which immediately discontinued the reissue series. No further issues in the A- series were made until 1955, when British Decca, which had absorbed Vogue, used the label to release new material by such bop artists as Ronnie Scott, Tubby Hayes, Don Rendell, Victor Feldman, Dizzy Reece, and Jimmy Deuchar. (G. Hulme and B. Holland: "Tempo," *Matrix*, no.44 (1962), 3; no.45 (1963), 11; no.46 (1963), 15; no.47 (1963), 21)

HOWARD RYE

Tenor. In general musical terminology the vocal part or range lying below the alto and above the baritone; the word is also used as a qualifying adjective to distinguish those members of certain families of instruments (especially wind) that play in that range (e.g., tenor horn; *see* Saxhorn). In jazz argot "tenor" is used alone to mean the tenor saxophone (*see* Saxophone); "tenor man" (also sometimes "tenor") is used of the player of that instrument.

Tenor cor. *See* Mellophone.

Tenor [alto] **horn.** The alto instrument of the SAXHORN family, pitched in E♭; it normally plays the alto part, occasionally the tenor.

Tenor saxophone. The tenor instrument of the saxophone family, normally pitched in B♭; it was formerly found also in C (the C-melody saxophone). *See* SAXOPHONE, §2.

Terai, Naoko (*b* Fujisawa, Japan, 1 May 1967). Japanese violinist and leader. She took violin lessons from the age of four and was inspired to become a jazz musician after hearing a recording by Bill Evans (ii), *Waltz for Debby*. In 1986 she began working professionally, performing and recording with Shigeharu Mukai, Mal Waldron, and others. In 1995 she made a notable album as a sideman with Kenny Barron (*Things Unseen*, Verve 314-537315-2), and in 1998 she formed her own quartet. Her recordings as a leader include *Thinking of You* (1998, Video Arts 1031) and *Pure Moment* (1999, Video Arts 1033).

KAZUNORI SUGIYAMA

Terminal vibrato. A vibrato of increasing breadth introduced in the course of a note; a sustained note begins without vibrato, then gradually develops towards the end of the note a pitch oscillation which becomes broader or quicker, or both. The effect often occurs at the end of a phrase. Hodeir coined the term to describe a characteristic of Dicky Wells's playing and referred to Louis Armstrong's use of the effect; he gave two instances of it in Wells's playing, including the latter's solo on Count Basie's *Panassié Stomp* (1938; ex.1). Schuller discussed many examples in

Ex.1 Opening phrase of D. Wells's solo on C. Basie: *Panassié Stomp* (1938, Decca 2224); transcr. B. Kernfeld

Armstrong's music, noting that Armstrong sometimes ended a terminal vibrato with a Shake. The effect is notated by a representational symbol (see ex.1).

BIBLIOGRAPHY

A. Hodeir: *Hommes et problèmes du jazz, suivi de La religion du jazz* (Paris, 1954; Eng. trans., rev. Hodeir, as *Jazz: its Evolution and Essence*, New York, 1956/*R*1975)

G. Schuller: *Early Jazz: its Roots and Musical Development* (New York, 1968)

BK

Termos, Paul (*b* Hilversum, Netherlands, 15 Jan 1952). Dutch alto saxophonist and composer. His birthdate appears incorrectly in Whitehead (1998). He played guitar from the age of ten and attended the Amsterdam Conservatory from 1970 to 1980. There he took up clarinet, studied composition, and began collaborating with Guus Janssen and the drummer Wim Janssen, as well as with the English guitarist Peter Cusack. He took up alto saxophone on his own, in 1977. Soon he became recognized as a composer of concert music, often with a jazz flavor: one piece has a skewed boogie-woogie bass, and *Groundwork* (1993; recorded on *Paul Termos*, 1990–97, Composers Voice 60) consists of brass-quintet variations on *Cherokee*. A saxophone concerto (1983) reflects his own playing, which is indebted to the styles of Steve Lacy and Lee Konitz for its conceptual clarity. In the 1980s Termos worked with Misha Mengelberg, Guus Janssen, and Maarten Altena, and played in trios with Janssen alongside Wim Janssen (1984–9) or Han Bennink (1990–97). He combined his various influences in the Termos Tentet (1988–92), which included Peter van Bergen, Wolter Wierbos, Ernst Glerum, and Wim Janssen, and in which simple elegant game pieces formed a part of the group's repertory. In 1995 he founded Dubbel Expres, a sextet with van Bergen and Wim Janssen, sometimes supplemented by two classical soprano singers and a harpist. In the late 1990s he also played Ornette Coleman's music in groups led by Eric Boeren, and in 1998 he spent a month in India with his trio. As a composer his pieces (for improvisers or reading musicians) are notable for the transparent simplicity of the materials and for a riff-based melodicism that seems to be indebted equally to jazz and minimalism. Termos is also inspired by pop music of the early 1960s, as heard on *For Sandy Nelson* (on the album *POK*), a tribute to the rock-and-roll drummer who had several instrumental hits during that decade, and *Sam the Sham was a Pharao* [*sic*] (on the album *Shakes and Sounds*), based on *Wooly Bully* (1965), by the rock group Sam the Sham and the Pharaohs.

SELECTED RECORDINGS

As unaccompanied soloist: *Solo 84–85* (1984–5, Claxon 86.17)

As leader: with G. Janssen, P. Cusack, and P. Lytton: *Groups in Front of People 2* (1978, Bead 15); with G. Janssen and W. Janssen: *POK* (1988-9, Geestgronden 3), incl. For Sandy Nelson; *Shakes & Sounds* (1990, Geestgronden 5), incl. Sam the Sham was a Pharao; *Death Dance of Principles* (1992, 1995, Geestgronden 16)

As sideman: M. Altena: *Tel* (1982, Claxon 83.12); *Rondedans* (1984, Claxon 85.15); E. Boeren: *Cross Breeding* (1995, BIMhuis 005)

BIBLIOGRAPHY

K. Stevens: "Over het compeneren of het schrijven voor improvisatoren" [About composing or writing for improvisers], *Jazz freak*, xvi/3 (1989), 20

H. te Loo: "Wij leven in muzikaal heel vruchtbare periode" [We live in a musically very fertile period], *Jazz nu*, no.129 (1989), 436

B. Andriessen: *Tetterettet: interviews met Nederlandse improviserende musici* (Ubbergen, Netherlands, 1996), 176

P.-U. Hiu: *Het hondered componisten boek* (Hilversum and Haarlem, Netherlands, 1997)

——: "Why would I start doing sums as a composer," *Key Notes*, xxxi/2 (1997), 10

K. Whitehead: *New Dutch Swing* (New York, 1998), 257, 271

KEVIN WHITEHEAD

Terrasson, Jacky [Jacques-Laurent] (*b* Berlin, 27 Nov 1966). French pianist and leader. His father was French and his mother was African-American, and he was brought up in Paris. He took up classical piano when he was five and had additional lessons in jazz from the age of 13; two years later he enrolled at the Lycée Lamartine, a performing arts school, where he met Stephane Paudras (the son of Bud Powell's patron, Francis Paudras), who introduced him to the Paris jazz milieu. Encouraged by Francis Paudras, Terrasson moved to Boston around 1985 and studied arranging for two semesters at the Berklee College of Music; during this period he spent four months playing Hammond B-3 organ at Wally's. He then moved to Chicago and worked regularly at Blondie's in a trio with the double bass player Dennis Carroll and the drummer Marshall Thompson. In 1986 he returned to France to serve in the French Army, after which he worked regularly with Dee Dee Bridgewater and Barney Wilen and as a freelance throughout Europe.

From 1990 Terrasson lived in New York, where he participated in jam sessions at Augie's, with the double bass player Tyler Mitchell and Antoine Roney, as a member of Jesse Davis's house band; he later recorded with Davis (1992). In summer 1991 he toured Europe and recorded in Ray Brown's trio Two Bass Hits, and in France during the same period he appeared at jazz festivals and recorded in a duo with Tom Harrell. After returning to the USA he joined Art Taylor's Wailers and worked in bands led by Wallace Roney (recording in 1991) and Tony Williams. In 1993 Terrasson joined Betty Carter, with whom he toured Europe, and towards the end of the year he won the Thelonious Monk International Piano Competition; he subsequently signed a contract with Blue Note. His first album was recorded with his working trio, in which Ugonna Okegwo and Leon Parker were his sidemen, and was released in January 1995; Parker left the group in the same year, although he returned to play briefly in 1997. Between July 1996 and September 1997 Ali Jackson was his replacement. From summer 1996 Terrasson spent a period based in San Francisco, and later that year he performed with Carter at Yoshi's in Oakland. He recorded as co-leader with Cassandra Wilson in 1997. Having returned to New York he appeared in a duo with Danilo Pérez in Houston in 1998, and early in 1999 he added a saxophonist and a harmonica player to his trio to tour in support of his album *What it is*. As a freelance he recorded with Guy Lafitte (1991), Antoine Roney and Sebastian Whittaker (both 1992), Cindy Blackman (1992, 1997), Javon Jackson (1993, 1995), and Diane Reeves (*c*1994). Apart from his skill on the acoustic instrument Terrasson is, after Chick Corea, one of the few musicians to play the Fender-Rhodes electric piano convincingly in a jazz context, as is evident on the title track of Blackman's recording *In the Now* (1997); although the liner notes claim the contrary, he plays electric piano on the other tracks as well.

SELECTED RECORDINGS

Duos with T. Harrell: *Moon and Sand* (1991, Jazz aux Remparts 64007)

As leader: *What's New* (1992, Jazz aux Remparts 64003); *Lover Man* (1993, Venus 79033); *Jacky Terrasson* (1994, BN B21Z-29351-2); *Reach* (*c*1995, BN B21Z-35739-2); with C. Wilson: *Rendezvous* (1997, BN 55484-2); *Alive* (1997, BN 59651-2)

As sideman: R. Brown: *Ray Brown's New Two Bass Hits* (1991, Capri 74034-2); J. Davis: *As We Speak* (1992, Conc. 4512); S. Whittaker: *One for Bu!!* (1992, Justice 0203); C. Blackman: *Telepathy* (1992, Muse 5437); Grand Central: *Sax Storm* (1993, Alfa Jazz 9528); J. Jackson: *When the Time is Right* (1993, BN B2NA-89678); C. Blackman: *In the Now* (1997, HighNote 7024)

BIBLIOGRAPHY

CarrJ

P. Carles, A. Clergeat, and J.-L. Comolli: *Dictionnaire du jazz* (Paris, 1988, rev. and enlarged 2/1994)

M. Laverdure: "Gros plan: Jacky Terrasson," *Jm*, no.421 (1992), 24

K. Bennett: "Trading Fours: Herbie Hancock and Jacky Terrasson," *Musician*, no.189 (1994), 56

L. Birnbaum: "Don't Wanna be no Young Lion: Jacky Terrason & Cyrus Chestnut," *DB*, lxi/6 (1994), 22

E. Holly: "Riffs: Terrasson Takes Top Prize at Monk Competition," *DB*, lxi/2 (1994), 10

M. D. Carnegie: "The World at his Fingertips: Eclectic Influences help Make Terrasson Jazz's Hottest Pianist," *Washington Post* (26 March 1995)

C. Gauffre: "Terrasson en trois sets," *Jm*, no.445 (1995), 40

R. Grosman: "Recontre: Jacky Terrasson, Paris–New York," *Jh*, no.519 (1995), 13 [incl. discography]

D. Helland: "All Together Now: Jacky Terrasson: Blue Note Special," *Piano & Keyboard*, no.175 (1995), 55

D. Zych: "Hearsay: Jacky Terrasson," *JT*, xxv/3 (1995), 12

G. Endress: "Jacky Terrasson," *JP*, xlv/6 (1996), 22

M. Laverdue: "Le double passeport de Jacky Terrasson," *Jm*, no.456 (1996), 17

D. Richardson: "Kind of Blue (Note)," *San Francisco Bay Guardian* (25 Dec 1996)

D. Zych: "Jacky Terrasson: a Fresh Voice, a New Language," *JT*, xxvi/4 (1996), 34

P. Watrous: "A Reunion of Improvisers," *New York Times* (13 June 1997)

R. Mitchell: "Jazz Duo Combines Talent during Cullen Presentation," *Houston Chronicle* (7 Dec 1998)

B. Blumenthal: "With Quint, Terrasson Discovers New Textures," *Boston Globe* (9 June 1999)

GK

Terrell, Pha (Elmer) (*b* Kansas City, MO, 25 May 1910; *d* Los Angeles, 14 Oct 1945). Singer. In the early 1930s he sang, danced, and worked as a compère at the 18th Street Club, Kansas City. He was recruited in 1933 by Andy Kirk, with whom he performed and made recordings (including *Blue Illusion*, 1936, Decca 772, and *I don't stand a ghost of a chance*, 1939, Decca 2915) until 1941. Thereafter he worked in Indianapolis with the bandleader Clarence Love and toured and performed on the West Coast as a soloist.

BIBLIOGRAPHY

McCarthyB

L. Gourse: *Louis' Children: American Jazz Singers* (New York, 1984), 77

A. Kirk, as told to A. Lee: *Twenty Years on Wheels* (Wheatley, Oxford, England, and Ann Arbor, MI, 1989)

based on *ChiltonW*

Territory band. A term applied to dance bands of the 1920s and early 1930s that worked in the South and West of the USA. It is normally used of bands that were based in small regional capitals and made extended tours of the outlying area, playing in local dance halls. Because of the lack of recording opportunities the work of territory bands is poorly documented, and the contribution of individual bands to the formation of KANSAS CITY JAZZ is difficult to trace. From the mid-1920s there were more than 100 active territory bands, among the most important being those of Alphonso Trent (Dallas), Doc Ross (El Paso and Oklahoma City), Troy Floyd (San Antonio), Walter Page (Oklahoma City), and Jesse Stone (Missouri and Kansas).

See also BLUES, §6.

BIBLIOGRAPHY

McCarthyB; *SchullerS*

G. Schuller: *Early Jazz: its Roots and Musical Development* (New York, 1968)

R. Russell: *Jazz Style in Kansas City and the Southwest* (Berkeley, CA, Los Angeles, and London, 1971/*R*1983, rev. 2/1973/*R*1997)

M. L. Hester: *Going to Kansas City* (Sherman, TX, 1980)

N. W. Pearson, Jr.: *Goin' to Kansas City* (Urbana, IL, and London, 1988)

J. BRADFORD ROBINSON

Terroade, Kenneth (*b* Galina, St. Mary, Jamaica, 1944). Jamaican tenor saxophonist and flutist. He started on flute, took up tenor saxophone in 1961, and moved to London the following year to live with his mother. While continuing his schooling he worked in rock bands, then began to play jazz with John Surman, Mike Osborne, Dave Holland, Mike Westbrook, the South African saxophonist Ronnie Beer, and Chris McGregor. In 1968 he was a member of the Hot Shot Delivery Service, led by the saxophonist Roy Voce, and traveled to Paris at the invitation of Sunny Murray. There he became part of the city's radical free-jazz ferment, his stamina and abrasive sound providing an excellent foil for Murray's desperate, free-wheeling percussion. Terroade played with the French drummer Claude Delcloo and many Americans in exile, among them Lester Bowie, Dave Burrell, Archie Shepp, and Alan Silva. He also went to New York, where he played with Murray and Clifford Jarvis. In 1970 he returned to Britain and worked with McGregor's Brotherhood of Breath and the South African drummer Selwyn

Lissack, co-led a group with Ray Draper, and toured with the popular musician Dr. John. He moved between Jamaica and New York in the 1970s and 1980s, playing music of a spiritual nature with Count Ossie's Mystic Revelation of Rastafari and working as a farmer; at some point he performed with the reggae musician Bob Marley. Later he returned to New York, where he confined his musical activities to the church.

SELECTED RECORDINGS

(recorded for BYG and in 1969 unless otherwise indicated)

As leader: *Love Rejoice* (529322)

As sideman: S. Murray: *Sunshine* (529348); A. Silva: *Luna Surface* (529312); C. Delcloo and Arthur Jones: *Africanasia* (529306); S. Lissack: *Friendship Next of Kin/Facets of the Universe* (Goody 30006); S. Murray: *Never Give a Sucker an Even Break* (529332); D. Burrell: *La vie de bohème* (529330)

BIBLIOGRAPHY

D. Constant: "L'homme de la Jamaique," *Jm*, nos.169–70 (1969), 14
R. Williams: "Ken Terroade: a Name to Watch," *MM* (11 Oct 1969), 8
V. Wilmer: "Growing Day by Day," *MM* (13 June 1970), 16
——: "Ray Draper: Just Call Me a Musician," *MM* (27 June 1970), 24
P. Carles and J.-L. Comolli: *Free Jazz, Black Power* (Paris, 1971)
M. Hames: *Albert Ayler, Sunny Murray, Cecil Taylor, Byard Lancaster, and Kenneth Terroade on Disc and Tape* (Ferndown, England, 1983)

VAL WILMER

Terry, Clark(, Jr.) [Mumbles; Cee Tee] (*b* St. Louis, 14 Dec 1920). Trumpeter, flugelhorn player, scat singer, and bandleader. As a child he made a trumpet from a hose, using a kerosene funnel as a mouthpiece. In high school he finally gained access to a real instrument, a valve trombone, before changing to trumpet. He began his professional career with Fate Marable in St. Louis and then embarked on tours in the Reuben and Cherry Carnival Show and with Ida Cox. He played jazz in a navy band which included Willie Smith and Gerald Wilson (1942–5). After a brief stint in Lionel Hampton's big band he spent 18 months directing George Hudson's big band for residencies at the Club Plantation in St. Louis and in 1946 at the Apollo Theatre in Harlem. He then performed with Charlie Barnet (1947–8), rejoined Hudson briefly, and spent short periods with Charlie Ventura and Eddie "Cleanhead" Vinson before becoming a member of Count Basie's big band and small groups (September 1948 – mid-1951). Terry maintained an important affiliation with Duke Ellington from 1951 to 1959, during which time he began doubling on flugelhorn. During this period he took part in many of Ellington's suites and acquired a lasting reputation for his wide range of styles (from swing to hard bop), technical proficiency, and infectious good humor; in the questionnaire for this dictionary he gave his "institution(s) attended" as "University of Ellingtonia." After leaving Ellington he traveled to Europe with Quincy Jones in Harold Arlen's blues opera *Free and Easy*.

After his return to New York in March 1960, Terry became a frequent performer in studios and the first African-American staff musician at NBC, in which capacity he appeared regularly on the "Tonight Show." Having introduced his unique "mumbling" scat singing on a recording with Oscar Peterson's trio in 1964, he made this technique famous on the "Tonight Show," with which he remained until 1972, when the show was transferred to California and he elected to stay in New York. Despite his commitment to studio work he found time for many significant activities in jazz. He was a principal soloist in Gerry Mulligan's Concert Jazz Band (1960–64), and he co-led with Bob Brookmeyer a

Clark Terry at the JVC Grande Parade du Jazz Nice, France, 1987

quintet whose members included at various times Tommy Flanagan, Roger Kellaway or Hank Jones, Bill Crow or Bob Cranshaw, and Dave Bailey (1961–7). In 1967, in between television shows, he toured with Jazz at the Philharmonic and also founded a big band. This long-lived ensemble was drawn from a pool of sidemen including the trumpeters Ernie Royal, Marvin Stamm, Jimmy Owens, Randy Brecker, Virgil Jones, Lew Soloff, and Jimmy Nottingham; the trombonists Melba Liston, Jimmy Cleveland, Julian Priester, Janice Robinson, and Eddie Bert; the saxophonists Phil Woods, Zoot Sims, Frank Wess, George Coleman, Joe Temperley, Charles Davis, and, much later, Branford Marsalis; the rhythm section players Don Friedman, Duke Jordan, Ron Carter, Joe Benjamin, Victor Sproles, Grady Tate, Mousie Alexander, and Ed Soph; and the arranger Ernie Wilkins. By 1970 the group was known as Clark Terry's Big B-A-D Band. In the 1970s Terry began to concentrate increasingly on the flugelhorn, from which he obtains a remarkably full, ringing tone. Through this and the following decades he also toured regularly with small groups, including Peterson's.

Early in 1978, with Hilton Ruiz as his pianist, Terry embarked on a state department-sponsored tour from Egypt to India, where he led an international big band at the Jazz Yatra in Bombay. In 1987 he disbanded the Big Bad Band and formed a nonet, Clark Terry's Spacemen, including Virgil Jones, Jimmy Hamilton, Norris Turney, Heywood

Henry, Aaron Bell (on piano rather than bass), Victor Gaskin, and Butch Ballard. He starred in and acted as host for a concert at the 1989 New York Jazz Festival. Terry has been involved in jazz education since the 1960s, and in autumn 1994 he launched a four-year jazz degree program at the Clark Terry International Institute of Jazz Studies at Teikyo Westmar University in LeMars, Iowa. On 14 December 1994 he commenced a year-long touring celebration culminating in his 75th birthday. In the late 1990s he was a member of the Statesmen of Jazz. His humor and command of jazz styles are nowhere more apparent than in his mumbling (which may be heard to fine effect on *The Orator (C. T.'s Sermon)*, recorded with James Williams in 1993) and in his instrumental "dialogues" with himself, in which he plays brief contrasting passages, alternating between trumpet and flugelhorn or playing one instrument, muted and unmuted (as heard, for example, on his album with Oscar Peterson's trio in 1964).

Oral history material in *CtY*, *NjR*, and *TNF*; video oral history material in *NCH* (HCJA) and *NN-Sc* (LAJOHP).

SELECTED RECORDINGS

Duos with R. Mitchell: *Clark Terry–Red Mitchell* (1986, Enja 5011)
As leader: *Introducing Clark Terry* (1955, EmA 36007), incl. Kitten, Swahili; *Serenade to a Bus Seat* (1957, Riv. 237); *The Happy Horns of Clark Terry* (1964, Imp. 64); *Big B-A-D Band* (1970, Etoile IA); *Memories of Duke* (1980, PT 2312118); *The Clark Terry Spacemen: Squeeze Me* (1989, Chi. 309); *What a Wonderful World* (1993, Red Baron 53750); *Shades of Blues* (1994, Challenge 70007)
As leader with B. Brookmeyer: *Tonight* (1964, Mstr. 6043); *The Power of Positive Swinging* (1964, Mstr. 6054); *Mumbles* (1965, Mstr. 6066); *Gingerbread Man* (1966, Mstr. 6086)
As sideman: D. Ellington: *A Drum is a Woman* (1956, Col. CL951); J. Hodges: *The Big Sound* (1957, Verve 8271); C. Hawkins: *Back in Bean's Bag* (1962, Col. CS8791); O. Peterson: *The Oscar Peterson Trio Plus One: Clark Terry* (1964, Mer. 60975); James Williams: *Talkin' Trash* (1993, DIW 887), incl. The Orator (C. T.'s Sermon)

SELECTED FILMS AND VIDEOS

Sugar Chile Robinson – Billie Holiday – Count Basie and his Sextet (1950); Duke Ellington in Europe (1959); Jazz 625: Clark Terry Quintet (1965); Jazz from Newport (1966); The Great Rocky Mountain Jazz Party (1977); Clark Terry Big Bad Band (n.d.); Gibson Jazz Concert (*c*1982); J. J. Johnson All Star Jam (n.d. [filmed 1982]); Clark Terry Quartet (1985); All-Star Swing Reunion (1986); Duke Ellington in Amsterdam and Zurich (1991); Flip Phillips' 80th Birthday Party featuring the All-Stars (1995); Statesmen of Jazz (*c*1995 [filmed 1994]); Norman Granz présente improvisation: documents exceptionnels et inédits des plus grands noms de jazz (n.d.)

BIBLIOGRAPHY

SheridanCB
M. Walker: "Clark Terry Discography (1947–1960)," *JM*, vii/10 (1961), 18; vii/11 (1962), 18
D. Morgenstern: "Why is this Man so Happy?" *DB*, xxxiv/11 (1967), 16
V. Wilmer: "Happiness is Clark Terry," *JJI*, xx/11 (1967), 6; rev. as "The Sweet Smell of Success," *Jazz People* (London, Indianapolis, and New York, 1970/*R*1985), 103
S. Dance: *The World of Duke Ellington* (London and New York, 1970/*R*1981), 182
A. Van Starrex and T. O'Reilly: "Clark Terry: View and Interview," *Coda*, ix/5 (1970), 2
E. Wilkins: "My Friend Clark Terry," *DB*, xl/2 (1973), 17
A. J. Smith: "Clark Terry: Jazz Ed, Mumbles Style," *DB*, xliii/19 (1976), 12
B. Rusch: "Clark Terry: Interview," *Cadence*, iii/6 (1977), 3
A. Morgan: "Clark Terry: Jazz Ambassador," *JJI*, xxxi/5 (1978), 6
L. Birnbaum: "Clark Terry: Big B-A-D Brassman," *DB*, xlviii/9 (1981), 22
C. Terry: "Clark Terry and his Jolly Giants: the African Safari, 1979," *JSN*, ii/4 (1982), 137
S. Floyd: "An Oral History: the Great Lakes Experience," *Black Perspective in Music*, xi/1 (1983), 41
D. J. Travis: *An Autobiography of Black Jazz* (Chicago, 1983), 457
S. Voce: "Clark Terry," *JJI*, xxxix/12 (1986), 10; xl/1 (1987), 16
K. Franckling: "A Conversation with Clark Terry," *JT* (1987), Dec, 16
A. Stevens: "Clark Terry," *CI*, xxiv/4 (1987), 16
D. Ramsey: *Jazz Matters: Reflections on the Music and Some of its Makers* (Fayetteville, AR, 1989), 232
L. Fisher: "Clark Terry Discusses his Experiences with the Bands of Duke Ellington and Count Basie," *Jazz Research Papers*, x (1990), 32
W. Enstice and P. Rubin: *Jazz Spoken Here: Conversations with Twenty-two Musicians* (Baton Rouge, LA, and London, 1992), 269
P. B. King: "Mellow with Age," *Pittsburgh Post-Gazette* (4 Nov 1994), 16
M. Seidel: "Clark Terry: Reminiscin' with a Legend," *DB*, lxi/10 (1994), 22 [incl. discography]
B. Blumenthal: "Clark Terry: Reflections on a Brilliant Career," *JT*, xxv/8 (1995), 30
J. McDonough: "Clark Terry: Jazz Ambassador," *DB*, lxiii/6 (1996), 16 [incl. discography]

J. BRADFORD ROBINSON/BK

Teschemacher, Frank [Tesch] (*b* Kansas City, MO, 13 March 1906; *d* Chicago, 1 March 1932). Clarinetist, alto saxophonist, and violinist. He spent his childhood in Chicago, where he studied violin, mandolin, banjo, and alto saxophone. Around 1922 he was one of the so-called Austin High School Gang of young Chicago jazz musicians (see illustration); he played with Jimmy McPartland, Bud Freeman, and other members of this group in the Blue Friars, the Red Dragons, and Husk O'Hare's Wolverines (this last engagement from spring 1925 to 1926), and also joined Freeman and Eddie Condon in Wingy Manone's group at the Merry Gardens ballroom (autumn 1924). From 1926 he occasionally performed in commercial dance orchestras, but his principal employment brought him together with Muggsy Spanier and Jess Stacy in the group led by the tenor saxophonist Floyd Town, which, Stacy recalled, was routinely mistaken for an African-American band by those who listened to its radio broadcasts (Whyatt, 1995, p.21).

Four members of the Austin High School Gang, Chicago, c1927: (left to right) Frank Teschemacher, Jimmy McPartland, Dick McPartland, and Bud Freeman, with Freeman's brother Arnie Freeman

Teschemacher also played with Spanier, Stacy, and George Wetting at the Cottage Grove (*c*1927) and made definitive Chicago-jazz recordings with McKenzie and Condon's Chicagoans (1927), the Chicago Rhythm Kings, Charles Pierce and his Orchestra, the Louisiana Rhythm Kings, and the Jungle Kings (all April–May 1928). In June 1928 he went to New York, and the following month temporarily took Gil Rodin's place in Ben Pollack's orchestra and recorded with Red Nichols (under Miff Mole's name) and Condon. After working with Nichols in Sam Lanin's orchestra in Atlantic City he returned to Chicago to join Ted Lewis and numerous lesser-known bandleaders, who used him mainly as an alto saxophonist and violinist. Around 1930, on clarinet and doubling on drums, he joined Stacy's Aces, a small group playing for dance marathons at the Merry Gardens.

Teschemacher's importance rests primarily on his performing style as a clarinetist, though he played that instrument regularly only from 1925 to about 1930. His dirty tone resembles (and may have influenced) that of Pee Wee Russell and the young Benny Goodman. His low-register solo on *Darktown Strutters Ball*, including ragtime figurations after the manner of Jimmie Noone (but lacking Noone's precise execution), was frequently copied; this type of sound is uncharacteristic of Teschemacher, who typically played in the instrument's mid- to high range. Poor intonation and insecure technique mar many of his recordings, of which he made about three dozen before his early death in an automobile accident. Many listeners may have difficulty comprehending the consistent high praise which he received from his talented colleagues, but Stacy offers a simple explanation that rings true: "He had always drunk too much when he reached the recording studio, so the world will never hear just how great he really was" (Keller, 1989, p.85).

SELECTED RECORDINGS

As sideman: McKenzie-Condon Chicagoans: Sugar/China Boy (1927, OK 41011); Nobody's Sweetheart/Liza (1927, OK 40971); Jungle Kings: Friars Point Shuffle/Darktown Strutters Ball (1928, Para. 12654); M. Mole: Shim-me-sha-wabble (1928, OK 41445); E. Condon: Oh! Baby/Indiana (1928, Para. R2932)

BIBLIOGRAPHY

J. Van Praag: "Frank Teschmaker [*sic*]," *Jh*, 1st ser., no.8 (1936), 8
T. Tolley: "Frank Teschmacher [*sic*]: a Biographical and Critical Study," *Pickup*, ii/4 (1947), 2
N. Shapiro and N. Hentoff, eds.: *Hear me Talkin' to ya: the Story of Jazz by the Men who Made it* (New York and London, 1955/*R*1966), 118
R. Hadlock: *Jazz Masters of the Twenties* (New York, 1965/*R*1985), 106
B. Esposito: "Jazz Juxtaposition: Bix . . . Tesch," *JJ*, xxv/10 (1972), 4
V. Simosko: "Frank Teschemacher: a Reappraisal," *JJS*, iii/1 (1975), 28
M. Grosz: Liner notes, *Giants of Jazz: Frank Teschemacher* (TL 23, 1982)
T. Tolley: "Teschemacher and the Chicagoans in New York: an Investigation," *Sv*, no.111 (1984), 84
B. Whyatt: "Tesch and the Chicagoans: More Ideas and Thoughts," *Sv*, no.114 (1984), 204
K. Keller: *Oh, Jess!: a Jazz Life: the Jess Stacy Story* (New York, 1989)
R. Hilbert: *Pee Wee Russell: the Life of a Jazzman* (New York, and Oxford, England, 1993)
W. H. Kenney: *Chicago Jazz: a Cultural History, 1904–1930* (New York, and Oxford, England, 1993)
B. Whyatt: *Muggsy Spanier: the Lonesome Road: a Biography and Discography* (New Orleans, 1995)
D. Coller: "Floyd Town," *Storyville 1996/7*, ed. L. Wright (Chigwell, England, 1997), 156

J. R. TAYLOR/BK

Tevelian, Meg(uerditsch) (*b* ?Turkey, 1902; *d* Vienna, 23 Oct 1976). Armenian guitarist. He fled Turkey in 1921 on account of the persecution of the Armenian people and settled in Berlin, where by the 1930s he was highly sought after for concert, dance, and studio work. Among the bandleaders with whom he played and recorded were Michael Jary (1939–40), Willy Berking (1939–42), Kutte Widmann (1940–41), Horst Winter and Helmuth Zacharias (both 1941–2), Benny de Weille (1941–3), and Primo Angeli and Willy Stech (both 1942–3). His most significant recordings were made as a leader in 1941 with personnel from the bands of Ernst van 't Hoff and Jean Omer, and include his own arrangement of *Lieselott* (Pallas 1205). Tevelian moved to Vienna in 1943 and later left music to work for an oil company. (K. Schulz: "Sehen Sie, ich lebe weiter: die Meg Tevelian-Story," *Der Jazzfreund: Mitteilungsblatt für Jazzfreunde in Ost und West*, xii/4 (1970), 4)

RAINER E. LOTZ

Tex. Nickname of JESSE POWELL.

Texier, Henri (*b* Paris, 27 Jan 1945). French double bass player and leader. He studied piano from the age of nine and performed with an amateur dixieland group when he was 14. In 1960 he developed an interest in modern jazz, and the following year he began teaching himself double bass. He led his own small group, worked in Jef Gilson's big band (*c*1962–5), and performed at Le Chat qui Pêche and the Blue Note accompanying such musicians as Chet Baker, Kenny Drew, Bud Powell, Donald Byrd, and Bill Coleman. In 1965 he appeared as the leader of a quintet at jazz festivals in Boulogne and Comblain-la-Tour and formed another quintet that included Enrico Rava, Michel Portal, and Aldo Romano. As a sideman he performed with Don Cherry, Mal Waldron, Steve Lacy, and Barney Wilen (1965) and accompanied Lee Konitz, René Thomas, and Dexter Gordon, among others (1966). After a brief period in the military in 1967 Texier played later that year at the first free-jazz festival to be held in Paris, and in 1968 he worked with Hampton Hawes, Dave Pike, and Art Farmer. From 1968 to 1972 he was a member of Phil Woods's European Rhythm Machine alongside Gordon Beck and Daniel Humair, after which he formed the group Total Issue, which performed folk and folk-rock music; during the same period he worked as a freelance, joined Jean-Luc Ponty's trio, and played electric bass guitar in George Gruntz's Piano Conclave. He also recorded with Larry Schneider (1968), Flavio Ambrosetti (1976), Jimmy Gourley (*c*1977), and Claude Barthélémy (1979).

From 1976 Texier performed and recorded as an unaccompanied soloist, augmenting his performances on double bass with flute, cello, piano, *'ūd*, electric bass guitar, percussion, his own voice, and bombarde. With Didier Lockwood and Jean-Charles Capon he worked in a string trio which recorded in 1979, and from 1978 to 1981 he was a member of a trio with Humair and François Jeanneau. In the early 1980s he began participating in reunions of Portal's ensemble Unit, of which he was not an original member. Around this time he formed a quartet, in which his sidemen were, first, from 1981 to 1982, Philippe Deschepper, Eric Le Lann, and Bernard Lubat, and then, from 1982, Deschepper, Louis Sclavis, and the drummer Jacques Mahieux. The group performed with Joe Lovano as a guest soloist at a jazz festival, Le Temps du Jazz, in Amiens in 1986, and the following year at the Europa Jazz Festival in Le Mans it was augmented by Dewey Redman, Kenny Wheeler, and Bagdad de Quimperlé – a group of bell-ringers, bagpipers, and bombarders. Pietro Tonolo joined Texier in 1988. Texier also led the Transatlantik Quartet, which consisted of Lovano, Steve Swallow, and Romano, and in 1988 he worked in a quartet alongside Lovano, Redman and Romano, and in a cooperative trio with Eric Barret and Romano which recorded that year. Later he performed and recorded with Lovano in his Wind Ensemble (1989) and with his quartet in New York (1993).

From 1990 Texier worked in a trio with Romano and Sclavis; it toured Africa in 1991 and 1993 and performed throughout Europe into the late 1990s. At the British International Jazz Awards in Cannes, France, in 1991 he appeared in a trio with Jeanneau and Humair, and the following year he formed the group Azur with Glenn Ferris, Bojan Zulfikarpasic and the drummer Tony Rabeson; from the early 1990s he was also a member of the collective group Zhivaro. In 1994 he recorded with Claudio Fasoli, and in 1995 he established the Sonjal Sextet, in which he worked at various times with the alto saxophonist Sébastien Texier, Julien Lourau, the baritone saxophonist François Corneloup, Zulfikarpasic, Noël Akchoté, and Mahieux; in the late 1990s Zulfikarpasic joined his small group. Texier may be seen in the documentary film *Noon in Tunisia* (1970).

SELECTED RECORDINGS

(recorded for Label Bleu unless otherwise indicated)

As unaccompanied soloist: *Amir* (1975–6, Eurodisc 913082); *Varech* (1977, Eurodisc 913087)

As leader: with F. Jeanneau and D. Humair: *Humair, Jeanneau, Texier* (1979, Owl 016), *Akagera* (1980, JMS 012); with J. Lovano: *Paris–Batignolles* (1986, 6506); with E. Barret and A. Romano: *Barret/Romano/Texier* (1988, Carlyne 13); *Izlaz* (1988, 6515); *Colonel Skopje* (1988, 6523); with F. Jeanneau and D. Humair: *Up Date 3.3* (1990, 6530); *An Indian's Week* (1993, 6558); with L. Sclavis and A. Romano: *Carnet de routes* (1994–5, 6569); *Mad Nomad(s)* (1995, 6568); *Mosaic Man* (1998, 6608)

As sideman: F. Jeanneau: on *Ephémère* (1977, Owl 07), Complicité; J. Lovano: *Worlds* (1989, 6524); P. Tonolo: *Tresse* (1992, Splasc(h) 386); C. Fasoli: *Ten Tributes* (1994, RAM 4517)

BIBLIOGRAPHY

C. Tarting: "Actualité: Henri Texier Quartet," *Diapason–Harmonie*, no.322 (1986), 18

P. Carles, A. Clergeat, and J.-L. Comolli: *Dictionnaire du jazz* (Paris, 1988, rev. and enlarged 2/1994)

F. M. Coudert: "Sur la piste des Zhivaro," *Jm*, no.369 (1988), 39

——: "Texier de haut en bass," *Jm*, no.379 (1989), 22

G. Le Querrec: "Le tropique des concerts par le griot du trio," *Jm*, no.394 (1990), 20

P. Benkimoun: "Zhivaro, les séducteurs de têtes," *Jm*, no.421 (1992), 36

C. Gauffre: "Le trio du griot bis d'Afrique," *Jm*, no.429 (1993), 20

O. Gasnier: "Henri Texier et sept hérauts et caetera," *Jm*, no.455 (1996), 18

GK

Tharpe, Sister Rosetta [Thorp [née Nubin], Rosetta] (*b* Cotton Plant, AR, 20 March 1915; *d* Philadelphia, 9 Oct 1973). Singer and guitarist. She was brought up in Chicago, where she was influenced by her mother's singing of spirituals and was attracted to blues guitar techniques and to the ecstatic religion of the Sanctified Church. She gained a reputation as a singer-evangelist in Chicago. From 1934 to 1938 she worked in a trio with her mother and her husband, Pastor Thorp (she modified his name for her stage name). According to Panama Francis, she was heard by Cotton Club talent scouts in a Miami church, and sometime before mid-October 1938 she had moved to New York and was appearing in the *Cotton Club Parade of 1939*. She became known for her compositions and her electrifying performances. Just before Christmas that year she took part in the first "From Spirituals to Swing" concert at Carnegie Hall and sang with Cab Calloway; she also performed at Café Society downtown, and with Benny Goodman, and returned to Carnegie Hall for the second such concert late in 1939. Her first recording was a lively and rhythmical version of *Hide me in thy bosom* with the secularized title *Rock me*, which she performed both in theaters and churches, altering the lyrics to suit the location. Later she sang in Lucky Millinder's big band, making a number of recordings. Tharpe had a hit with *Strange things happening every day*, recorded with Sammy Price's trio, and she recorded several outstanding vocal duets with her mother, Katie Bell Nubin (1880–1969), and with Sister Marie Knight, playing guitar in a vivid style recalling that of Big Bill Broonzy. On later, religious, recordings, she used choirs and accompanying groups that tended to cloud the bright sound of her voice and the brilliance of her guitar playing, which she offset by using an electric instrument. She toured Europe from November 1957 to April 1958, performing in Great Britain with Chris Barber's Jazz Band and Mick Mulligan, returned to Europe with the American Folk Blues Gospel Caravan in April–May 1964, and again as a freelance soloist visited France (October 1964) and toured the continent (November–December 1966, 1970). She appeared in several episodes of the television show "Gospel Time" (n.d.).

SELECTED RECORDINGS

As leader: Rock me (1938, Decca 2243); Strange things happening every day (1944, Decca 18669)

As sideman with L. Millinder: Rock Daniel (1941, Decca 3956); I want a tall skinny papa (1942, Decca 18386)

SELECTED FILMS AND VIDEOS

Four or Five Times (1941); Shout, Sister, Shout (1941); The Lonesome Road (1941); Blues & Gospel Train (1964); L'aventure du jazz (1970)

BIBLIOGRAPHY

G. Boatfield: "Sister Rosetta Tharpe and the Gospel Singers," *JJ*, x/11 (1957), 3

W. Hamilton, Jr.: "Sister Rosetta Tharpe," *Jazz News* (1957), Nov, 6

J. Demêtre: "Sister Rosetta Tharpe est à Paris," *Jh*, no. 129 (1958), 16

T. Heilbut: *The Gospel Sound: Good News and Bad Times* (New York, 1971, rev. 2/1985)

C. Hayes: *A Discography of Gospel Records, 1937–1971* (n.p. [Copenhagen], 1973)

H. Panassié: "Rosetta Tharpe," *BHcF*, no.232 (1973), 3

Obituary, *Black Perspective in Music*, ii (1974), 227

R. Reitz: Liner notes, *Sister Rosetta Tharpe: Gospel-Blues-Jazz* (Rosetta 1317, [n.d.])

PAUL OLIVER/HOWARD RYE

Theater Owners' Booking Association [TOBA]. An organization formed in January 1921 by two white theater owners based in Tennessee – Milton B. Starr of Nashville and Sam Revin of Chattanooga – in order to manage vaudeville bookings for African-American performers efficiently. The association has erroneously been dated earlier, having been confused with an organization which Sherman H. Dudley had formed in 1913 and extended in 1919, when he joined with a white entrepreneur based in Pensacola, Florida, to form the Southern Consolidated Circuit. Dudley brought his competing circuit into TOBA in mid-1921 and at that point became co-director with Starr and Revin. By 1923 the association extended to 85 houses in most of the major cities and several smaller towns in the South, Southwest, and Midwest. The acts booked into the theaters were primarily abbreviated versions of musical comedies (tabloid shows), though solo singers, comedy teams, song-and-dance duos, and specialty acts (jugglers, acrobats, etc.) also appeared. While it was notorious for its demanding schedules and low pay, the organization enabled many African-Americans to appear before black audiences and created steady employment for such performers as Ma Rainey, Bessie Smith, and

Ethel Waters. A number of early jazz musicians, including Bennie Moten and Count Basie, also started their careers on the circuit. By 1932, however, the Depression, competition from the film industry, and personal conflicts among theater owners led to the demise of the organization, and nearly all its houses were converted to motion picture theaters.

BIBLIOGRAPHY

J. A. Jackson: "A Survey of the Negro in American Life and in the Amusement World," *Billboard* (6 Aug 1921), 60
L. Hughes and M. Meltzer: *Black Magic: a Pictorial History of the Negro in American Entertainment* (Englewood Cliffs, NJ, 1967/*R*1990), 66
M. Stearns and J. Stearns: *Jazz Dance: the Story of American Vernacular Dance* (New York, 1968)
H. T. Sampson: *Blacks in Blackface: a Source Book on Early Black Musical Shows* (Metuchen, NJ, 1980)
T. Riis: *Black Musical Theatre in New York, 1890–1915* (diss., U. of Michigan, 1981)
T. Vincent: *Keep Cool: the Black Activists who Built the Jazz Age* (London and East Haven, CT, 1995)

THOMAS RIIS/HOWARD RYE

Théberge, François (*b* Montreal, 18 May 1963). Canadian saxophonist, composer, and arranger. He was active in jazz in Montreal from 1982 to 1985, then studied arrangement at the University of Rochester (MM 1989), where he was an assistant to Bill Dobbins; during the same period he toured the world for 14 months as an arranger and saxophonist with the memorial Glenn Miller Orchestra (1986–7). In 1990, on Dobbins's recommendation, he became the leader of and played saxophone with the French regional orchestra Rhône-Alpes. He moved in 1991 to Paris, where he formed a quintet, made several recordings, and with Lionel Belmondo formed the Big Band Belmondo. In 1993–4 Théberge played with Dave Liebman, Johnny Griffin, and Hervé Sellin, gave a series of concerts in Portugal with his own group, and appeared at a number of festivals in France and elsewhere. The following year, again with Belmondo, he formed the group Sax Generation. He toured Japan with Kenny Werner (1996) and went to the USA with the Fensters, a group with which he made several recordings. In 1997 he founded the Composer's Workshop (again including Belmondo), with which he recorded his first album as a leader. In 1995 he was appointed a professor at the Conservatoire National Supérior in Paris.

SELECTED RECORDINGS

As leader: of Composer's Workshop: *Asteur* (1997, Lazer Production 591532); *François Théberge and the Medium Band* (1999, Round 2468)
As sideman: J.-M. Pilc: *Big One* (1992, EMP 890); Fensters: *Jazz Music*, i (1992, Arta 10035); C. Barretto: *Impressoes* (*c*1993, Groove-Movieplay 101); M. Zwerin: *Zip* (1996, Verve 529466-2)

BIBLIOGRAPHY

"François Théberge: le sax et la plume," *Jazzman*, no.17 (1996), 21
"Guide des nouveaux talents," *Jazzman*, no.24 (1997), 13

JACQUES ABOUCAYA

Thelin, Eje (Eilert) (*b* Jönköping, Sweden, 9 June 1938; *d* Stockholm, 18 May 1990). Swedish trombonist. He worked with dixieland groups while in his early teens, then played bop in Sweden with the drummer Joe Harris (1958–9) and Putte Wickman (1959–60), and led a quintet that won acclaim in Europe (1961–5). In the mid-1960s he played with George Russell and led a quartet with Barney Wilen, and in 1967 he joined the faculty of the Musikakademie in Graz, Austria; at the same time he performed and recorded with many European free-jazz musicians, notably Joachim Kühn, with whom he led groups. In 1970 he was named "new star" on the trombone by *Down Beat*. After returning to Sweden in 1972 Thelin continued to work as a leader until 1980, after which he was mainly active as a composer and occasional guest soloist with various ensembles. He appeared with George Gruntz's Concert Jazz Band, worked in the European Jazz Ensemble, and formed the group E.T. Project (1986). Early in his career Thelin developed a fluent style that owed something to the work of J. J. Johnson. He turned to free jazz in the mid-1960s, and later became known for his ensemble leadership and for his compositions for large groups, often inspired by the work of Gil Evans; his playing and writing showed an ability to contrast sensitively melodies of different shapes, rhythmic statements, and lush textures.

SELECTED RECORDINGS

So Far (1963, Col. SSX1005); *At the German Jazz Festival* (1964, Met. 15158); *Acoustic Space* (1970, Odeon E062-34180); *Eje Thelin Group* (1974, Caprice 1091); *Live – 76* (1976, Caprice 2007); *Bits & Pieces* (1980, Phono Suecia 9); *Polyglot* (1981, Caprice 1291); *E.T. Project Live at Nefertiti* (1986, Dra. 128); *Raggrupamento* (1989, Phono Suecia 56)

BIBLIOGRAPHY

B. Sundin: "Unga jazzmusiker: Eje Thelin" [Young jazz musician: Eje Thelin], *Orkester journalen*, xxviii/11 (1960), 14
L. Hansson: "Eje Thelin diskografi," *Orkester journalen*, xxxv/12 (1967), 48
L. Westin: "Eje Thelin," *Orkester journalen*, xli/1 (1973), 9 [incl. discography]
——: "Trials and Tribulations of a Swedish Trombonist," *DB*, xliii/16 (1976), 18
——: "Vill ha debatt och solidaritet: Eje Thelin" [Wants to have debate and solidarity: Eje Thelin], *Orkester journalen*, xliv/3 (1976), 10
M. Kunzler: *Jazz-Lexicon* (Reinbek, nr Hamburg, Germany, 1988)
L. Westin: "Eje Thelin: virtuos och visionär" [Eje Thelin: virtuoso visionary], *Orkester journalen*, lviii/7–8 (1990), 33

ERIK KJELLBERG/GK

Thelonious Monk Institute. Non-profit educational organization. It was founded in 1986 by the family of Thelonious Monk (headed by T. S. Monk), together with Maria Fisher, a longtime supporter of the arts who founded the Beethoven Society of America and the American Opera School. In 1986 Fisher underwrote a concert that raised funds for a Monk foundation, with the aim of building a monument and perhaps a small conservatory in Monk's hometown in North Carolina, and the institute produced a television documentary, "Celebrating a Jazz Master: Thelonious Sphere Monk," broadcast on PBS that same year. From 1987 an office was established in Washington, DC, and the Monk Institute held annual jazz competitions, initially with assistance from the Smithsonian Institution. At first these events focused only on piano performance (1987–9), but afterwards they involved not only piano (again in 1993 and 1999), but also trumpet (1990, 1997), saxophone (1991, 1996), drums (1992), composition (from 1993), singing (1994, 1998), guitar and bass (1995), and Latin and African hand drumming (2001).

Educational programs began around 1989 with the Thelonious Monk Institute's Jazz in the Classroom program, which funded workshops for elementary-school children. When Fisher died in 1992 she left a bequest of $1.1 million directed towards further cultural and educational programs. These have included, from 1995, Jazz Sports (in both Los Angeles and Washington), and, from 1996, a summertime educational program, the Thelonious Monk Institute Jazz Colony at Jazz Aspen Snowmass. In the mid-1990s the institute produced two television specials for ABC. From 1995 to 1999 it maintained the Thelonious Monk Institute of Jazz Performance at the New England Conservatory, offering free tuition to select groups of students; Ron Carter served as artistic director, with Clark Terry, Herbie Hancock, Jimmy

Heath, Wynton Marsalis, Wayne Shorter, Grover Washington, Jr., and Slide Hampton among those who held brief appointments as artist-in-residence. In 1999 this program transferred from Boston to the University of Southern California in Los Angeles and Patrice Rushen became its artistic director. The following year the Monk Institute began offering public schools access to a web-based jazz curriculum, Jazz in America: the National Jazz Curriculum.

BIBLIOGRAPHY

P. Keepnews: "Jazz: Blue Notes," *Billboard*, xcix (21 Feb 1987), 29
T. Wilborn: "Monk Conservatory Announced," *DB*, lv/10 (1988), 13
J. Probber: "Thelonious Monk Memorial Will Help Jazz Live," *New York Times* (22 Jan 1989)
P. Stewart: "Aspiring Jazz Musicians May Soon Have an Alternative to Smoky Cabarets," *New York Times* (2 Sept 1990)
P. Watrous: "Monk Jazz Contest Moving to New York," *New York Times* (5 March 1992)
J. Levenson: "Jazz: Blue Notes," *Billboard*, cv (18 Dec 1993), 35
P. Watrous: "With New Backing, Jazz Competition Plans New Riffs," *New York Times* (22 Nov 1995)
R. Harrington: "The Monk Institute: a Major Player in Jazz," *Washington Post* (24 Nov 1996)
B. Korall: "Pop & Jazz Scene: Monk Institute Moves Ahead," *IM*, xciv/1 (1996), 16
J. Potter: "Contemporary Grooves: Theme and Variations Park (Thelonious Monk Institute, Down Beat Magazine and Universal to Establish Jazz Center at E Zone Entertainment Center in Orlando, Fla.)," *IM*, xcv/9 (1996), 17
P. Watrous: "Jazz's New Gig: Go Along and Get Along," *New York Times* (28 Nov 1996)
K. Franckling: "Tradin' Fours: First Monk Institute Class Graduates with the Goods," *DB*, lxiv/9 (1997), 64
S. Fromartz: "Mr. Monk Goes to Washington," *Jazziz*, xiv/4 (1997), 38
P. Gallo: "Music: LA County Jazzed by Monk Deal," *Variety* (2 June 1997), 20
D. Heckman: "Music Center Gives Jazz a Major Gig. Partnership: the Thelonious Monk Institute Becomes an Affiliate. Herbie Hancock Will be Artistic Director of the $1.2-million Program," *Los Angeles Times* (28 May 1997)
——: "Riffs: Cross-country Jazz Alliance," *DB*, lxiv/8 (1997), 12
P. Watrous: "A Los Angeles Project Aims to Nourish the Jazz City's Roots," *New York Times* (28 May 1997)
B. Blumenthal: "Monk Institute Program to Leave NEC for USC," *Boston Globe* (28 Sept 1998)
——: "Monk Sextet: Up the Learning Curve," *Boston Globe* (10 Dec 1998)
S. Fromartz: "Circa 1983: the Route to the Monk Institute," *Jazziz*, xvi/2 (1999), 72
B. Ratliff: "A Contest Befitting Monk Competition Shows Where Jazz Piano is Today," *New York Times* (19 Oct 1999)
<http://www.monkinstitute.com> (2000)
J. Murph: "Prelude: Ingenuity Sparks Monk Piano Competition," *Jazziz*, xvii/2 (2000), 12
B. Ratliff: "Critic's Notebook: Monk Contest Puts Focus on Latin Rhythms," *New York Times* (12 Sept 2000)

GK

Theme. In jazz a harmonized melody, often 16 or 32 bars long, or in some cases (notably the blues progression) simply a series of harmonies, used as the basis for a piece or section of a piece; *see* Forms.

Themen, Art(hur Edward George) (*b* Manchester, England, 26 Nov 1939). English tenor saxophonist. He was self-taught as a musician. While studying medicine at Cambridge he played with the university's jazz group (1959–62). After moving to London to continue his medical training he worked with the blues-rock musicians Jack Bruce (from 1962) and Alexis Korner (1963). In 1965 he was a member of the international Peter Stuyvesant Jazz Orchestra at the jazz festival in Zurich. He then performed with the rock singers Rod Stewart and Joe Cocker, the drummer Charlie Watts (1965–7), Michael Garrick (*c*1968–1971), and Graham Collier (recording, 1975–8), and in the late 1960s also co-led quintets with Dick Heckstall-Smith, the saxophonist Dave Gelly, and Barbara Thompson. In 1974 Themen began an association with Stan Tracey, working as a member of various of his groups, ranging from duo to octet; his playing may be heard to advantage on *Stan Tracey's Hexad Live at Ronnie Scott's* (1985, Steam 113). He toured extensively with Tracey, visiting India, South America, and Indonesia, as well as performing throughout the UK (to 1995). He also toured and recorded with American musicians, including Al Haig and Sal Nistico (ii), and performed with Nat Adderley, George Coleman, and Billy Mitchell. In the 1990s he worked further with Garrick and in a quintet with Don Weller (including, in 1994, a club date with Bobby Wellins), as well as with Henry Lowther's group Quarternity, with Kincade, the group led by the drummer Alan Jackson, and with Alan Cohen's big band. In 1996 he set up his own quartet with the pianist John Chitchinson, the double bass player Dave Green, and the drummer Dave Barry, and the same year recorded *First Moves* (Ronnie Scott's Jazz House 052). Also in 1996 he recorded a collection of standards in a duo with Howard Riley, *Classics (Live)* (Slam 222). Themen is a rarity in jazz in that he pursues a successful career as a consultant orthopedic surgeon; as a saxophonist his playing has an almost quirky originality.

BIBLIOGRAPHY

CarrJ; *ChiltonB*
R. Cotterrell, ed.: *Jazz Now: the Jazz Centre Society Guide* (London, 1976)
D. Gelly: "The Best of British, no.1: Art Themen," *JJI*, xxxi/1–2 (1978), 6
M. Pearson: "Doing it for Art: the Art Themen Story," *JJI*, lii/1 (1999), 6

DIGBY FAIRWEATHER/SIMON ADAMS, BK

Theresa. Record company and label. The company was founded by Allen Pittman and B. Kazuko Ishida in 1975 in El Cerrito, California. During the years 1980 to 1987 it established an important catalogue, including, most notably, material by Pharoah Sanders, John Hicks, and George Coleman, but by 1986, when it moved to Albany, California, the company was suffering financial difficulties. From the late 1980s it was largely inactive. Around 1992 Evidence (ii) purchased much of Theresa's back catalogue and reissued it on compact disc. (H. Gray: *Producing Jazz: the Experience of an Independent Record Company*, Philadelphia, 1988)

BK

Theselius, Gösta (*b* Stockholm, 9 June 1922; *d* Stockholm, 24 Jan 1976). Swedish tenor saxophonist, pianist, composer, and arranger. He first worked as a tenor saxophonist in recording sessions with Thore Jederby (1940, 1941) and thereafter played with big bands led by Håkan von Eichwald (1940–41), Sam Samson (1941–3), Lulle Ellboj (1943–6), and Thore Ehrling (recording in 1944, 1951, and 1953), as well as in a bop-oriented group led by Simon Brehm (1947–8). While initially he gained a reputation as a fine soloist in a style derived from that of Chu Berry, he later modernized his playing somewhat; by the late 1940s he sounded more like Vido Musso or Charlie Ventura, and by the time of his last recordings as a tenor saxophonist, in 1954, he had been impressed by the school of players who followed Lester Young (Brew Moore, Zoot Sims, and others). Theselius was also well known as a fluent and versatile arranger (he was the principal arranger for Ellboj during his tenure with that band). His arrangements and compositions represent some of the best-integrated Swedish jazz writing of the 1940s and 1950s, and they show the influence of the leading American swing orchestras and the more modern big bands, such as those led by Stan Kenton, Dizzy Gillespie, and Boyd Raeburn. In addition to his arrangements of a number of his own compositions (detailed below) he arranged *Sunday* for Harry Arnold (on the album *This is Harry*, 1957) and a number of tracks heard on Arnold's album *Studio Sessions* (1956–68, Dra. 296), notably *Moonlight in Vermont*. As a pianist he played and recorded with such musicians as James Moody (1949), Arne Domnérus (1949–50), Charlie Parker (1950), and Benny Bailey (1959).

RECORDED COMPOSITIONS

(selective list)

As leader: Siesta (1949, Met. 101); Three Without a Key (1956, RCA S52) [EP]

Recorded by others: S. Samson: Express (1942, Bruns. A83007); L. Ellboj: Hot Gravy (1945, Col. DS1600); Ulf Linde: Three Without a Key, pts 1–3 (1951, Cavalcade 502, 503); Jazzkritikerorkestern: *Cream of the Crop* (1951, Cupol 9007); H. Arnold: on *This is Harry* (1957, Met. 15006), Six-Ten

BIBLIOGRAPHY

"Svenskt stjärnalbum" [Swedish star-album], *Orkester journalen*, x/1 (1942), 5

"Våra arrangörer" [Our arrangers], *Estrad*, iv/2 (1942), 7

"Årets musiker" [Musician of the year], *Estrad*, xiv/1 (1952), 5

"På omslaget" [On the cover], *Orkester journalen*, xxi/5 (1953), 4

R. Dahlgren: "Gösta Theselius in memoriam," *Orkester journalen*, xliv/3 (1976), 6

ERIK KJELLBERG/LARS WESTIN

Theus, Sonship [Woodrow, Jr.; Woody] (*b* Los Angeles, 21 June 1952). Drummer and percussionist. He began piano lessons when he was seven and changed to drums and percussion at the age of 13. From 1966 to 1968 he was in the band led by the pianist Larry Nash, Jazz Symphonics, which became the house band at the Club Tropicana, known as "the Birdland of the West." While there he met and was befriended by Elvin Jones and Tony Williams, who became his two most important teachers. While still in his teens he played with John Klemmer, Charles Lloyd, Joe Henderson, and Freddie Hubbard, and recorded with Bobby Hutcherson (1971), and Hadley Caliman and Woody Shaw (both 1972). In the late 1970s he toured with the soul singer Marvin Gaye, played in McCoy Tyner's band, and then joined John McLaughlin. In the early 1980s Theus started performing with Horace Tapscott's Pan Afrikan Peoples Arkestra in Los Angeles; he remained with the Arkestra until Tapscott's death in 1999, and in 1995 performed with it at the Moers Festival in Germany. He recorded with Tapscott as part of his trio and octet, and with other members of the Arkestra, including the saxophonist and flute player Dadisi Komolafe (1983), Curtis Clark (1984), and the saxophonist Michael Session (1990). In 1982, with Michel Petrucciani and Palle Danielsson, he toured Europe with Charles Lloyd's quartet in the saxophonist's return to jazz after a long retirement; their performance at the Montreux Jazz Festival was recorded on LP and their appearance at the Antibes–Juan-les-Pins Jazz Festival was released on video. During that European tour Theus also performed and recorded with Bobby McFerrin in Copenhagen. He returned to Europe in 1989 with James Newton, and later recorded under the flutist's leadership (1994). During the 1990s he was active in gospel music, performing regularly at his church. He also recorded as a sideman with Wadada Leo Smith and the group N'da Kulture (1997), and he performed and recorded with the quartet led by the pianist Nate Morgan (1998).

SELECTED RECORDINGS

As sideman: B. Hutcherson: *Head On* (1971, BN 84376); H. Caliman: *Iapetus* (1972, Mstr. 342); W. Shaw: *Song of Songs* (1972, Cont. 7632); M. Tyner: *The Greeting* (1978, Mlst. 9085); H. Tapscott: *Live at Lobero*, i–ii (1981, Nimbus 1369, 1258); C. Lloyd: *Montreux 82* (Elek. Mus. 60220); *A Night in Copenhagen* (1983, BN BT85104); D. Komolafe: *Hassan's Walk* (1983, Nimbus 3035); C. Clark: *Phantasmagoria* (1984, Nimbus 3368); H. Tapscott: *Octet Live* (1987, Americana 3002); M. Session: *'n Session* (1990, ITM Pacific 970074); J. Newton: *Suite for Frida Kahlo* (1994, AudioQuest 1023); L. Smith: *Golden Hearts Remembrance* (1997, Chap Chap 002)

STEVEN L. ISOARDI

Thiam, Mor (Dogo) (*b* Dakar, Senegal, *c*1942). Senegalese percussionist and singer. He began drumming at the age of eight and first performed in public when he was 12. In 1968, at the behest of the dancer and choreographer Katherine Dunham, he traveled to St. Louis, where he became involved in the Black Artists Group and began working as an instructor at Southern Illinois University. In the early 1970s he played with Freddie Hubbard and recorded with Nancy Wilson and B. B. King, the latter two affiliations in an effort to benefit African drought victims. Thiam's involvement with jazz dates mainly from 1990, when he toured and recorded as one of a trio of African drummers with the World Saxophone Quartet and became a member of Don Pullen's Afro-Brazilian Connection, with which he remained until Pullen's death in April 1995. In the early 1990s he joined Ray Drummond's Excursion All Stars (with which he recorded in 1992 and 1994) and began working with Hamiet Bluiett, notably in a cooperative trio with D. D. Jackson (from 1997). He also performed in groups led by Craig Handy and Carlos Ward, and in 1991 he recorded at a session led by the reed player Joseph Celli and the *kayagŭm* player Jin Hi Kim.

Thiam's main professional activities have fallen outside of jazz. He has led the African drum ensembles Drums of Fire and United Ballet Africa, worked extensively as an artistic consultant (notably at the Epcot Center at Disney World in Orlando, Florida), and taught at Southern Illinois University, the University of Dakar in Senegal, the University of Miami, and Boston University. In the late 1990s he was serving as executive director of the Institute for the Study of African Culture in Atlanta and as artistic director for both the annual World Drum and Dance Summit and the National Black Arts Festival's World Drummers March for Peace, and he recorded in Dakar as the leader of an ensemble of African drummers and singers. He has also published an instructional book (1980).

SELECTED RECORDINGS

Duos with A. Cyrille: on Cyrille: *Ode to the Living Tree* (1994, Venus 79098), Coast to Coast, Water, Water, Water

As sideman: World Saxophone Quartet: *Metamorphosis* (1990, Elektra Nonesuch 9-79258-2); J. Celli and J. H. Kim: *No World (Trio) Improvisations* (1991, O.O. Discs 4); D. Pullen: *Kele mou bana* (1991, BN B21S-98166); *Ode to Life* (1993, BN B21Z-89233); *Live ... Again* (1993, BN B21Z-30271)

BIBLIOGRAPHY

S. Dollar: "Rhythm of the Drums Beats in Player's Soul," *Atlanta Constitution* (17 March 1993)

A. Mundundu and K. Nketia: "Conversations with Mor Thiam," *Voice of African Music*, v/4 (1998), repr. at <http://www.africanchorus.org/Voam/Voam541.htm> (1999)

<http://www.africanchorus.org/Voam/Voam51.htm> (1999)

<http://www.justin-time.com/hiband/bio/thiam_m.html> (1999)

A. Mundundu and K. Nketia: "Conversations with Mor Thiam," *Voice of African Music*, vi/1 (1999), repr. at <http://www.africanchorus.org/Voam/Voam611.htm> (1999)

GK

Thiele, Bob [Robert] (*b* New York, 27 July 1922; *d* New York, 30 Jan 1996). Record producer. He learned clarinet as a teenager, played in a local dance band, and worked as a disc jockey. Between 1942 and January 1945 he and a friend produced the magazine *Jazz;* they also ran jam sessions at Kelly's Stable. Thiele formed the Signature record label, which recorded in the 1940s, and from around 1953 he produced pop hits for Coral. After leaving Coral in the late 1950s he worked for Dot (1959–60), Hanover-Signature (1960–63), and Roulette (1963–4). From 1962 to 1971 he was a producer at Impulse! records, and in 1969 he formed the Flying dutchman label, distributed by RCA. In the 1980s he set up Doctor jazz, distributed by Columbia, but he changed the label's name to Red baron in the early 1990s after Sony purchased Columbia.

Thiele will best be remembered for his championing and recording of John Coltrane and other free-jazz musicians, including Pharoah Sanders, Archie Shepp, and Albert Ayler, during the mid- to late 1960s. His other projects for Impulse! involved mostly aging swing musicians but also took in some fine late period hard-bop recordings. His later labels focused more on attempts at popularization: for example, he recorded his wife, Teresa Brewer (they married in 1972), in various settings, notably with Count Basie and Duke Ellington, and assembled all-star studio groups.

BIBLIOGRAPHY

Feather–Gitler '70s
B. Primack: "Bob Thiele: the Red Baron Flies Again," *JT*, xxi/8 (1991), 34
B. Thiele and B. Golden: *What a Wonderful World: a Lifetime of Recordings* (New York, and Oxford, England, 1995)
Obituaries: P. Watrous, *New York Times* (1 Feb 1996); *DB*, lxiii/4 (1996), 15

GK

Thielemans, Toots [Jean Baptiste] (*b* Brussels, 29 April 1922). Harmonica player, guitarist, and whistler. He played the accordion from the age of three and took up chromatic harmonica when he was 17. In the early 1940s, under the influence of Django Reinhardt, he taught himself to play guitar. He toured Europe from mid-April to early June 1950 with an all-star group under the leadership of Benny Goodman, and the following year he emigrated to the USA; he took American citizenship in 1958. From 1953 to 1959 he was a member of George Shearing's quintet. He then worked as a freelance, traveling between the USA and Sweden; he first recorded his best-known composition, *Bluesette*, on which he both played guitar and whistled, in Stockholm in 1961. From the 1960s Thielemans obtained regular work as an instrumentalist and whistler in American recording studios, and he was often featured as a soloist with Quincy Jones's orchestra. From the early 1970s he made annual trips to Brussels and began to appear more frequently in public as the leader of swing and bop quartets. He also recorded at the Montreux International Jazz Festival as a sideman with Oscar Peterson (1975) and Dizzy Gillespie (1980), as well as with Paquito D'Rivera (1984). In 1981 he toured Japan as a guest soloist with Jaco Pastorius's big band Word of Mouth, and in the mid-1980s he led a European quartet that included Michel Herr and Bruno Castellucci and an American quartet consisting of Fred Hersch, Marc Johnson, and Joey Baron. Later in the decade he made the video *Toots Thielemans in New Orleans* (1988), where he was accompanied by Hersch, Harvie Swartz, and Adam Nussbaum. In the 1990s he continued to tour in jazz settings and recorded an album of jazz standards in a duo with Martial Solal (1991), two albums of Brazilian jazz (1992), and another album of jazz standards as the leader of various ad hoc all-star groups (1994). From 1995 he has performed with Kenny Werner.

Thielemans's whistling is excessively sweet and cute. His guitar playing, although completely professional, is not exceptional. But his work on harmonica is rivaled only by that of Larry Adler and Stevie Wonder in popular genres, and is unequaled in jazz. His lush timbre is revealed in such pretty songs as *Brown Ballad*, and he improvises on the harmonica with the dexterity expected of an accomplished bop saxophonist.

SELECTED RECORDINGS

Duos with M. Solal: *Martial Solal, Toots Thielemans* (1991, Erato 292-45795-2)
As leader: *Man Bites Harmonica* (1957–8, Riv. 257); *Time Out* (1958, Decca 9204); *Toots Thielemans* (1961–2, ABC-Para. 482), incl. Bluesette; *Toots Thielemans Captured Alive* (1974, Choice 1007); *Live in the Netherlands* (1980, PL 2308233); *Only Trust your Heart* (1988, Conc. 355); *The Brasil Project*, i–ii (1992, Private Music 82101-2, 82110-2); *East Coast West Coast* (1994, Private Music 82120-2)
As sideman: G. Shearing: Body and Soul (1953, MGM 11493); *On Stage!* (1958, Cap. T1187); Q. Jones: on *Smackwater Jack* (1971, A&M 3037), Brown Ballad; O. Peterson: *The Oscar Peterson Big Six at Montreux* (1975, Pablo 2310747); D. Gillespie: *Dizzy Gillespie at Montreux, 1980* (1980, PL 2308226)

BIBLIOGRAPHY

ConnorBG
D. Morgenstern: "Triple Threat Toots Thielemans," *DB*, xxxviii/20 (1971), 11
L. Henshaw: "Harmonica King," *MM* (20 Dec 1975), 10
R. Cotterrell: "Toots Thielemans: a Traveling Man," *JF* [intl edn], no.55 (1978), 33
B. Primack: "Toots Thielemans: Miracle Harmonica Man," *DB*, xlv/14 (1978), 25
L. Tomkins: "Toots Thielemans," *CI*, xvi (1978), no.8, p.20; no.9, p.8
A. Berle: "Toots Thielemans," *GP*, xiii/1 (1979), 34
D. Francfort and G. Rouy: "Tout tout Toots sur Thielemans," *Jm*, no.309 (1982), 54
J. Levenson: "Riffs: Toots Thielemans," *DB*, lv/12 (1988), 14
R. Pernet, J.-P. Schroeder, and others: *Dictionnaire du jazz à Bruxelles et en Wallonie* (Liège, Belgium, 1991)
L. Gourse: "Toots Thielemans: Samba Rhapsody," *JT*, xxii/7 (1992), 52
M. Bourne: "The Harmonicat: Toots Thielemans," *DB*, lx/8 (1993), 22
D. Heckman: "There's More to Music than Saxes and Pianos," *Los Angeles Times Calendar* (11 May 1997)
J. Lowe: "Toots Thielemans: Home is Where the Harp is," *JT*, xxviiii/6 (1998), 42
S. Woolley: "Toots Thielemans: Jazz with a Smile and a Tear," *JJI*, li/6 (1998), 12
B. Blumenthal: "Jazz Original Toots Thielemans is Still Searching for Something New," *Boston Globe* (31 Jan 1999)
R. Pernet: *Belgian Jazz Discography (1897–1999)* (Brussels, 1999)
<http://www.tootsthielemans.com> (2000)

BK

Thigpen, Ben(jamin F.) (*b* Laurel, MS, 16 Nov 1908; *d* St. Louis, 5 Oct 1971). Drummer, father of Ed Thigpen. At the age of 15 he joined Bobby Boswell's band in South Bend, Indiana. Having accompanied a dance team, he settled in Chicago and studied with Jimmy Bertrand. He played throughout the Midwest with Al Wynn (1925), Doc Cheatham (1926), Charlie Elgar (1927–8), the singer and dancer Eli Rice, and the trombonist J. Frank Terry (late 1928–1930). For 17 years from 1930 he was a member of Andy Kirk's Clouds of Joy (for illustration *see* Williams, mary lou), during which time he earned the respect of his colleagues for his steady, swinging beat; occasionally he sang with the band. After leaving the Clouds of Joy in 1947 he settled in St. Louis, where he led groups and performed with the Singleton Palmer Orchestra through the 1960s.

SELECTED RECORDINGS
(all recorded for Decca)

As sideman with A. Kirk: Walkin' and Swingin' (1936, 809); Lotta Sax Appeal/Bearcat Shuffle (1936, 1046); Git (1936, 931); Jump Jack Jump/ Ghost of Love (1938, 2226); Honey/Mary's Idea (1938, 2326)
As sideman with M. L. Williams: Corny Rhythm/Isabelle (1936, 1021); Baby Dear/Harmony Blues (1940, 18122)

BIBLIOGRAPHY

ChiltonW; *McCarthyB*
Obituary, *DB*, xxxviii/20 (1971), 9

J. KENT WILLIAMS

Thigpen, Ed(mund Leonard) (*b* Chicago, 28 Sept 1930). Drummer and jazz educator, son of Ben Thigpen. His birthdate has been published in reference sources as 28 December, but Lees (1991), in his essay on Thigpen, gives 28 September. He spent his infancy in St. Louis, and after his parents separated he grew up with his mother in Los Angeles, where he remained with another family after she died. His first professional engagement was with Buddy Collette in 1948. He played in rhythm-and-blues bands, joined Cootie Williams at the Savoy Ballroom, New York (September 1951 – February 1952), and then served as a drummer in the army (until November 1954). After returning to New York he worked with Dinah Washington (whose trio he joined just after his discharge), Gil Melle (late 1954–1957), Johnny Hodges, Lennie Tristano (for a few weeks only), Bud Powell (for a few months in 1956), Jutta Hipp (for about six months, also in 1956), and Billy Taylor (ii) (1956–8), and recorded with Toshiko Akiyoshi (1954, 1956), Dorothy Ashby, Bernard Pfeiffer, and Ira Sullivan (all 1956), Paul Quinichette and John Coltrane, Mal Waldron, Mundell Lowe, and Eddie "Cleanhead" Vinson (all 1957), Teddy Charles, Shorty Baker, and Aaron Bell (all 1958), and Blossom Dearie (1958–9).

From 1959 to June 1965 Thigpen worked with Ray Brown in a trio led by Oscar Peterson, who had earlier used a guitarist in place of a drummer; the group, which was highly acclaimed, toured widely and made many recordings. His occasional work as a freelance during the same period included sessions with Teddy Edwards and Howard McGhee (1961) and Gene Ammons (1962). In December 1965 he joined Ella Fitzgerald's accompanying group and the following year toured with her. He moved to Los Angeles in 1967 to work again as a freelance, but was with Fitzgerald again from 1968 to July 1972. After moving to Copenhagen that September he taught at the Malmö Conservatory in Sweden and performed with his group Action-re-action. His wife, who was Danish, died in childbirth, and Thigpen remained in Copenhagen to look after their two children; only after they had grown up did he resume making regular visits to the USA. He performed with leading jazz musicians resident in and visiting Copenhagen, and recorded as a sideman with Toots Thielemans (1972), Johnny Griffin, Horace Parlan, and Tony Scott (all 1973), Duke Jordan (1973, 1975), Rune Gustafsson (1973–7), Helen Humes, Gerry Wiggins, Major Holley, and Sir Charles Thompson (all 1974), Arne Domnérus and Red Rodney (both 1976), Svend Asmussen (1978, 1984), Clark Terry (1978, 1986), Kai Winding (1979), Thad Jones (1979, 1984), Benny Carter and Teddy Wilson (both 1980), Kenny Drew (1980–83), Ernie Wilkins (1980–81, 1986), Art Farmer (1981), Kim Parker (1981–2, 1985), Monty Alexander and Guido Manusardi (both 1985), Boulou Ferré (1985–6), the Berlin Contemporary Jazz Orchestra (1989), Oliver Jones (1991), Eric Watson (1994), and John Lindberg (1997). Thigpen toured the USA with his own trio (*c*1992), played in a quartet with Watson, Lindberg, and Albert Mangelsdorff (recording in 1994–5 under Lindberg's name), and performed and recorded with the all-star group Roots (1995).

Thigpen is respected for his energetic, swinging style, his sensitivity to timbre and dynamics, and his facility with sticks and brushes. He frequently uses his hands and timpani mallets on the drum set, and has explored diverse percussion instruments and styles, both Western and non-Western, in his performances. He is the author of *Talking Drums* (Toronto, 1965), *Rhythm Analysis and Basic Coordination* (Copenhagen, 1977), and *The Sound of Brushes* (Copenhagen, 1981), and has led workshops in Europe and North America.

SELECTED RECORDINGS

As leader: *Out of the Storm* (1966, Verve 68663); *Action-re-action* (1974, GNP 2098); *Young Men & Old* (1989, Tim. 330); *Mr. Taste* (1991, Justin Time 43-2)
As sideman with O. Peterson: *Fiorello!* (1959, Verve 8366); *The Trio: Live from Chicago* (1961, Verve 68420); *West Side Story* (1962, Verve 68454)
As sideman with others: D. Ashby: *The Jazz Harpist* (1956, Reg. 6039); J. Coltrane and P. Quinichette: *Cattin'* (1957, Prst. 7158); J. Griffin: *Blues for Harvey* (1973, Ste. 1004); A. Farmer: *Manhattan* (1981, SN 1026); K. Parker: *Havin' myself a Time* (1981, SN 1033); J. Lindberg: *Quartet Afterstorm* (1994, BS 120162-2); *Resurrection of a Dormant Soul* (1995, BS 120172-2)

SELECTED FILMS AND VIDEOS

Oscar Peterson Trio (1958); The Subject is Jazz, nos.6–7, 10–12 (1958); Jazz USA, no.5 (1960); Newport Jazz Festival 1962 (1962); Ella (1964); Jazz 625: Oscar Peterson Trio (1964); Eddie "Lockjaw" Davis, i–ii ([filmed 1985]); Eddie "Lockjaw" Davis & Johnny Griffin ([filmed 1985]); Svend Asmussen Quartet ([filmed 1986]); The Essence of Brushes (*c*1991)

BIBLIOGRAPHY

D. DeMicheal: "Edmund Thigpen: Gentleman and Jazzman," *DB*, xxviii/18 (1961), 17
L. Tomkins: "The Ed Thigpen Story," *Crescendo*, iv/1 (1965), 14
H. McNamara: "Ed Thigpen: on the Move," *DB*, xxxiv/6 (1967), 18
L. Tomkins: "There's Action, Reaction, and Interaction in Europe Says Ed Thigpen," *CI*, xiv/5 (1975), 6
M. Hurley: "Ed Thigpen: Intercontinental Swinger," *MD*, vi/7 (1982), 16
E. Soph: "Drum Set Forum: Ed Thigpen," *Percussive Notes*, xxiii/2 (1985), 22
G. Lees: *Oscar Peterson: the Will to Swing* (Toronto, 1988), 141
A. Scott: "Ed Thigpen: No Name Tag Required," *JT* (1988), Nov, 12
G. Lees: *Waiting for Dizzy* (New York, and Oxford, England, 1991), 181
B. Milkowski: "Ed Thigpen: Living the Art," *MD*, xvii/2 (1993), 28
"Ed Thigpen: Swing Feeling," *Jh*, no.549 (1998), 20 [incl. discography by G. Reynaud]

J. KENT WILLIAMS/BK

Thilo, Jesper (*b* Copenhagen, 28 Nov 1941). Danish alto and tenor saxophonist and clarinetist. He completed studies on clarinet at the Royal Danish Music Conservatory in Copenhagen, and first worked with the bandleader Arnvid Meyer and in a quintet with Bent Jædig. Following military service (1965–6) he became a member of the Radioens Big Band, with which he remained intermittently for 25 years. He was again with Meyer until 1973, and from 1968 until the mid-1970s he played with Beatkapel, led by the pianist, arranger, and composer Niels Jørgen Steen. In 1978 he established his own successful quartet, though from 1980 he was also a member of Ernie Wilkins's Almost Big Band and later of Steen's groups Saxmaniacs and A-Team. Thilo is versatile and much in demand as a soloist; his early playing was modeled after that of Ben Webster and Coleman Hawkins, but he developed a style reminiscent of Dexter Gordon and Eddie "Lockjaw" Davis. His imaginative and impressive solos may be heard on recordings with Meyer, Steen, Gugge

Hedrenius, the Radioens Big Band, Finn Savery, Wilkins, Wild Bill Davison, Børge Roger Henrichsen, Al Grey, Roland Hanna, Clark Terry, Harry Edison, Hank Jones, and the big band led by the conductor Jens Klüver.

SELECTED RECORDINGS

As leader: *Jesper Thilo Quartet* (1980, Music Mecca 128); *Swingin' Friends* (1980, Sto. 4065); *Jesper Thilo Quintet Featuring Harry Edison* (1986, Sto. 4120); *We Love Him Madly* (1992, Music Mecca 1025-2); *Don't Count Him Out* (1993, Music Mecca 1035-2); *Movin' Out* (1994, Music Mecca 1045-2); *Thank You Mr. Hat* (1997, Music Mecca 2045-2)

As sideman: Radioens Big Band: *By Jones, I Think We've Got it* (1978, Met. 15629); *A Good Time was Had by All* (1978, Met. 15644); E. Wilkins: *Ernie Wilkins' Almost Big Band Live* (1981, Matrix 29203); *Montreux* (1983, Ste. 1190); T. Flanagan: on *Flanagan's Shenanigans* (1993, Sto. 4191), For Lena and Lennie; Radioens Big Band: *A Little Bit of Duke* (1994, Dacapo 9420); H. Chaix: *Jesper Thilo Strikes up the Band* (1998, Sack. 2050)

BIBLIOGRAPHY

A. von Konow: "Jesper Thilo: mångsidig mästermusikant" [Jesper Thilo: a versatile master musician], *Orkester journalen*, li/10 (1983), 17
J. J. Gjedsted: "Joy in Playing," *Musical Denmark*, no.35 (1983–4), 10
K. Frandsen: *Politikens jazzleksikon* (Copenhagen, 1987)
A. Astrup: "Jesper Thilo," *JJI*, xliii/8 (1990), 6
G. Giddins: "WeatherBird: Jazz Danish," *VV* (2 April 1991), 68
L. Tømming: "Jesper Thilo," *Musikeren*, no.10 (1995) 20

FRANK BÜCHMANN-MØLLER

Thin Man. Nickname of NOBLE WATTS.

Third stream. A term coined by Gunther Schuller, in a lecture at Brandeis University in 1957, for a type of music which, through improvisation or written composition or both, synthesizes the essential characteristics and techniques of contemporary Western art music and various ethnic or vernacular musics. At the heart of this concept is the notion that any music stands to profit from a confrontation with another; thus composers of Western art music can learn a great deal from the rhythmic vitality and swing of jazz, while jazz musicians can find new avenues of development in the large-scale forms and complex tonal systems of classical music.

The term was originally applied to a style in which attempts were made to fuse basic elements of jazz and Western art music – the two mainstreams joining to form a "third stream." This style had been in existence for some years, and is exemplified by such pieces as Red Norvo's *Dance of the Octopus* (1933, Bruns. 6906), Ralph Burns's *Summer Sequence* (recorded by Woody Herman's band, 1946, Col. 38365-7), George Handy's *The Bloos* (1946, Jazz Scene [unnumbered]), Robert Graetinger's *City of Glass* (recorded by Stan Kenton's orchestra, 1951, Cap. 28062-3), Alec Wilder's *Jazz Suite* (1951, Col. 39727), and Rolf Liebermann's *Concerto for Jazz Band and Orchestra* (recorded by the Sauter–Finegan Orchestra, ?1956, Vic. LPM1888). Since the late 1950s the application of the term has broadened, notably through the work of Ran Blake, to encompass fusions of classical music with elements drawn not only from African-American sources but also from other ethnic musics, such as Greek folk and popular music, and Sephardic, Armenian, Japanese, and Hindu traditional music.

The third-stream movement attracted much controversy and has often erroneously been allied with the SYMPHONIC JAZZ movement of the 1920s; symphonic jazz, however, lacked the essential element of improvisation. Other critics have seen the movement as an inevitable outcome of postwar eclecticism and stylistic and technical synthesis. Third stream, like all musical syntheses, courts the danger of exploiting a superficial overlay of stylistic exotica on an established musical idiom, but genuine cross-fertilization has occurred in the work of musicians deeply rooted in dual traditions.

Composers and performers associated with the third-stream movement include J. J. Johnson (*Poem for Brass*, on the album *Music for Brass*, 1956, Col. CL941); André Hodeir (*On a Blues*, on the album *American Jazzmen Play André Hodeir's Essais*, 1957, Savoy 12104); Milton Babbitt (*All Set*, on the Brandeis Jazz Festival album *Modern Jazz Concert*, 1957, Col. WL127); Bill Russo (*An Image of Man*, on the album *An Image: Lee Konitz with Strings*, 1958, Verve 8286); Gunther Schuller (*Concertino for Jazz Quartet and Orchestra*, on the Modern Jazz Quartet's album *Modern Jazz Quartet and Orchestra*, 1960, Atl. 1359); Don Ellis (*Improvisational Suite no.1*, on the album *How Time Passes*, 1960, Can. 9004); Bill Smith (i) (*Concerto for Jazz Soloist and Orchestra*, 1962, CRI 320); Jimmy Giuffre (*Three We*, on the album *Free Fall*, 1962, Col. CS8764); Larry Austin (*Improvisations for Orchestra and Jazz Soloists*, 1967, Col. MS6733); Mike Mantler (*13*, on the album *13-3/4* (recorded with Carla Bley), 1975, Watt 3); Ran Blake (*Jim Crow* and *Silver Fox*, both on the album *Wende*, 1976, Owl 05; *Portfolio of Dr. Mabuse*, 1977, Owl 29); Anthony Braxton (*Composition 82*, on the album *For Four Orchestras*, 1978, Ari. 8900); Wadada Leo Smith (*The Burning of Stones*, on the album *Spirit Catcher*, 1979, Nessa 19); and Steve Lacy (*Worms*, on the Globe Unity Orchestra's album *Compositions*, 1979, Japo 60027). A large number of third-stream works have been published by Margun Music; others have been issued by such publishers as MJQ Music, C. F. Peters, and Cireco Music.

See also FORMS, §4.

BIBLIOGRAPHY

G. Schuller: "Jazz and Classical Music," *FeatherE*
——: "'Third Stream' Redefined," *Saturday Review*, xliv (13 May 1961), 54
——: "The Future of Form in Jazz," *The American Composer Speaks: a Historical Anthology, 1770–1965*, ed. G. Chase (n.p. [Baton Rouge, LA], 1966), 216
G. Crane: *Jazz Elements and Formal Compositional Techniques in Third Stream Music* (thesis, Indiana U., 1970)
C. J. Stuessy, Jr.: *The Confluence of Jazz and Classical Music from 1950 to 1970* (diss., Eastman School, 1970)
R. Blake: "Teaching Third Stream," *Music Educators Journal*, lxiii/4 (1976), 30
M. Harrison: *A Jazz Retrospect* (Newton Abbot, England, 1976, rev. 2/1977/*R*1991)
L. Lyons: "Ran Blake: Pianist and Teacher from the Third Stream," *CK*, iv/10 (1978), 16
A. Lange: "Ran Blake's Third Stream Visions," *DB*, xlvii/2 (1980), 24
E. Santosuosso: "Third Stream: a Label for an 'Anti-label' Music," *Boston Globe* (19 July 1980), §A, p.9
G. Schuller: "The Avant-garde and Third Stream," *Mirage* (New World 216, 1985) [liner notes]
M. Williams: "Third Stream Problems," *Jazz Heritage* (New York, and Oxford, England, 1985)
G. Schuller: "Third Stream Revisited," *Musings: the Musical Worlds of Gunther Schuller* (New York, and Oxford, England, 1986)

GUNTHER SCHULLER

Thollot, Jacques (*b* Vaucresson, France, 9 Oct 1946). French drummer, keyboard player, and composer. A student of Kenny Clarke, he also studied composition, and he made his professional début in the 1960s accompanying Bud Powell, Walt Dickerson, Joachim Kühn, Barney Wilen, Don Cherry, and, most notably, Eric Dolphy. He joined Jef Gilson's big band (1960) and then Cherry's New York Total Music Company, and played free jazz with Steve Lacy in France and Italy. After a period of inactivity he recorded an album on which he played drums, piano, and organ (1971). Between 1975 and 1978 he made two further albums as a leader, with, most notably, François Jeanneau among his sidemen, and in 1978 he recorded the album *Cinq hops*, on which his compositions extended beyond the strict confines of jazz. He then appeared in Paris with his own group (1980) and performed and recorded with Siegfried Kessler, Jean-François Jenny-Clark, and Bernard Vitet. He gave a concert as the leader of an 18-piece orchestra in 1981 and then reduced his activities once more. Thollot began playing regularly again in 1990 in various groups, including those of the brass player Jac Berrocal and the keyboard player Tony Hymas, where he was able to give priority to his work as a composer whose style is not limited by existing jazz conventions.

SELECTED RECORDINGS

As leader: *Quand le son devient aigu, jeter la girafe à la mer* (1971, Futura 24); *Cinq hops* (1978, Free Bird 03); with J.-F. Jenny-Clark and T. Hymas: *A Winter's Tale* (1992, Nato 777725); *Tenga Nina* (1995, Nato 777701)

As sideman: D. Cherry: *Eternal Rhythm* (1968, MPS 15204); M. Portal: *Our Meanings and our Feelings* (1969, Pathé C054-10525); S. Rivers: *Configuration* (1995, Nato 777711)

BIBLIOGRAPHY

N. Akchoté: "Entretien avec Jacques Thollot," *Jm*, no.455 (1996), 70

JACQUES ABOUCAYA

Thomas, Fathead [George] (*b* Charleston, WV, *c*1903; *d* New Haven, CT, Nov 1930). Singer. From 1925 until his death he was the featured singer with McKinney's Cotton Pickers (for illustration *see* McKinney's cotton pickers), and his remarkable tenor voice was a significant element in the band's style and popularity. He also played saxophone with the group, but was not prominent as a soloist. In addition Thomas recorded with Duke Ellington (1926). He was killed in an automobile accident.

SELECTED RECORDINGS

As sideman with McKinney's Cotton Pickers: Baby, won't you please come home? (1930, Vic. 22511); Okay baby/I want a little girl (1930, Vic. 23000); Cotton Picker's Scat (1930, Vic. 23012)

BIBLIOGRAPHY

J. Chilton: *McKinney's Music: a Bio-discography of McKinney's Cotton Pickers* (London, 1978)

based on *ChiltonW*

Thomas, Foots [Walter Purl] (*b* Muskogee, OK, 10 Feb 1907; *d* Englewood, NJ, 26 Aug 1981). Reed player and arranger, brother of Joe Thomas (ii). He grew up in Topeka, Kansas, and began his career as a musician while attending college. After moving to New York in 1927 he worked with Jelly Roll Morton, Luis Russell, and the pianist Joe Steele (1928), and in 1929 joined the Missourians. He remained a member of this band after Cab Calloway assumed its leadership (for illustration *see* Calloway, cab), and he contributed many arrangements to its repertory, including *Minnie the Moocher*, recorded in 1931 (Bruns. 6074); he may be seen with the band in the short films *Hi-de-ho* (1937), *Blues in the Night* (1942), and *Minnie the Moocher* (1942). According to Benny Payne (in Calloway's autobiography), Thomas acquired his nickname because of his extremely large feet. He left the band in 1943, played for a brief period with Don Redman, and in 1944 worked as a leader. In 1948 he ceased playing to pursue a successful career as an agent, manager, and music publisher. Thomas played alto, tenor, and baritone saxophones, clarinet, and flute; he may be heard as a soloist on early recordings by the Missourians and Calloway, but in his later years he worked chiefly as a section player and arranger.

Oral history material in *NjR* (JOHP).

SELECTED RECORDINGS

As leader: Every Man for himself (1944, Joe Davis 8128); Bird Brain (1945), first issued on *The Walter "Foots" Thomas All Stars* (1944–5, Prst. 7584)

As sideman: J. R. Morton: Crazy Chords (1930, Vic. 23307); C. Calloway: Bugle Call Rag (1931, Bruns. 6196)

BIBLIOGRAPHY

ChiltonW; *FeatherE*; *McCarthyB*; *SchullerS*

C. Calloway and B. Rollins: *Of Minnie the Moocher and Me* (New York, 1976), 154

L. D. Holmes and J. W. Thomson: *Jazz Greats: Getting Better with Age* (New York, 1986)

EDDIE LAMBERT/BK

Thomas, (Daniel) Gary (*b* Baltimore, 10 June 1961). Saxophonist and flutist. He played a variety of wind instruments during his teenage years, including saxophone during his last year in high school, and studied classical music at the Peabody Conservatory in Baltimore (1974–6) before discovering jazz. In 1978–9 he attended Howard University in Washington, DC. He then played with Jack DeJohnette's Special Edition (1985–93), Miles Davis (December 1986 – June 1987 and sporadically until the end of 1988), and Michele Rosewoman (from 1986). He also recorded as a sideman with Wallace Roney, Steve Coleman, Greg Osby, Cassandra Wilson, Cecil Brooks III, and others, appeared in the video *M-Base Jams at BAM* (*c*1989 [filmed 1988]), and worked with Cindy Blackman. In April 1994 he performed at a concert sponsored by Verve which was recorded on video as *Carnegie Hall Salutes the Jazz Masters*. In 1996 he was appointed director of jazz studies at Johns Hopkins University in Baltimore, and in June 1997 he began touring and recording with John McLaughlin. Thomas has led his own groups, including Seventh Quadrant, from the late 1980s, most often for recording purposes; among his sidemen have been Paul Bollenback, Tim Murphy, Renee Rosnes, Anthony Cox, Terri Lyne Carrington, and the guitarist Marvin Sewell. Although he took part in a number of straight-ahead sessions as a sideman, his most original work is as a leader in fusion settings: these recordings typically blended funk rhythms with dense textures and dark, polytonal harmony to create a forbidding, Gothic atmosphere; Thomas frequently used an electronic device which thickened the timbre of the saxophone by adding frequencies below the note sounded on the instrument. Unusually, he often played flute in this context, its light, lyrical quality standing in contrast to the turbid backgrounds and the electronically enhanced muscularity of his sound on tenor saxophone. Later he produced recordings in which jazz improvisation took second place to rap vocals. By his own account, Thomas was influenced by Billy Harper, Eddie Harris, and Woody Shaw and not, as is often assumed, John Coltrane (though the work of Harper and Shaw was shaped strongly by Coltrane). Contrary to common opinion, he was not associated with M-Base, although he played frequently with its leading members.

SELECTED RECORDINGS

As leader: *Seventh Quadrant* (1987, Enja 5047); *Code Violations* (1988, Enja 5085); *By Any Means Necessary* (1989, JMT 834432-2); *While the Gate is Open* (1990, JMT 834439-2); *The Kold Kage* (1991, JMT 849151-2); *Till We Have Faces* (1992, JMT 514000-2); *Exile's Gate* (1993, JMT 514009-2); *Overkill* (1994-5, JMT 514024-2)

As sideman: J. DeJohnette: *Irresistible Forces* (1987, MCA/Imp. 5992); W. Roney: *Verses* (1987, Muse 5335); S. Coleman: *Sine die* (1987–8, Pangaea 42150); J. DeJohnette: *Audio-visualscapes* (1988, MCA/Imp. 8029); W. Roney: *Intuition* (1988, Muse 5346); M. Rosewoman: *Contrast High* (1988, Enja 5091); *The Standard Bearer* (1989, Muse 5372); C. Brooks III:

The Collective (1989, Muse 5377); C. Wilson: *Jumpworld* (1989, JMT 834434-2); W. Roney: *Obsession* (1990, Muse 5423); J. DeJohnette: *Earthwalk* (1991, BN B21Z-95590); U. Caine: *Sphere Music* (1992, JMT 514007-2); M. Rosewoman: *Harvest* (1992, Enja 7069-2); U. Caine: *Toys* (1995, JMT 514012-2); J. McLaughlin: *The Heart of Things* (1997, Verve 314-539153-2)

BIBLIOGRAPHY

G. Rouy: "Trois saxes de Miles," *Jm*, no.367 (1987–8), 37
M. Gilbert: "Gary Thomas," *JJI*, xliv/3 (1991), 6
B. Shoemaker: "Gary Thomas: Pure Propulsion," *DB*, lvii/7 (1991), 26
B. Malik: "Gary Thomas," *Jazz: the Magazine*, no.16 (1992), 11
B. Primack: "Gary Thomas: Pushing the Envelope," *JT*, xxiii/5 (1993), 34
L. Jurgeit: "Gary Thomas," *JP*, xliv/10 (1995), 18
R. Grosman: "Gary Thomas," *Jh*, no.527 (1996), 11

MARK GILBERT

Thomas, Joe [Joseph William; Brother Cornbread] **(i)** (*b* New Orleans, 3 Dec 1902; *d* New Orleans, 18 Feb 1981). Clarinetist. In 1923, having bought an Albert system clarinet for $5.00, he began his career playing with the trombonist Joe Harris. Later he worked with the trombonist Jack Carey, Kid Rena, and Chris Kelly. In 1940 he recorded privately with the trumpeter Charles "Duke" Derbigny, and in 1941 as a leader; these tracks, rediscovered and issued in the 1960s, are in the small-band swing idiom. From the early 1940s Thomas led a band at the H & J Tavern for several years. He joined Papa Celestin's band in 1951, and continued to play and record with the group under the leadership both of the trombonist Eddie Pierson and the banjoist Albert French. He also recorded with Freddie Kohlman (1955) and Punch Miller (1961), worked with Harold Dejan's Olympia Brass Band (1963), and appeared with Sweet Emma Barrett in a show filmed for Swedish television in 1968. In 1975 he took Joe Darensbourg's place in the Legends of Jazz, with which he toured until 1978. Thomas was well known for his singing and his sense of humor. His solo on Pierson's *In Gloryland* alone places him in the front rank of New Orleans clarinetists.

Oral history material in *LNT*.

SELECTED RECORDINGS

As leader: first issued on [no leader:] *New Orleans Style, 1937–41* (1937–41, MONO 12), Eh la bas #1, Eh la bas #2 (1941)
As sideman: first issued on [no leader:] *New Orleans Style, 1937–41* (1937–41, MONO 12), D. Derbigny: I can do most anything for you, Sweet Georgia Brown (1940); on [no leader:] *Recorded in New Orleans*, ii (1956, GTJ 12020), E. Pierson: Gettysburg March, In Gloryland, Bill Bailey; A French: *A Night at Dixieland Hall* (1963, Nobility 702)

BIBLIOGRAPHY

T. Stagg and C. Crump: *New Orleans, the Revival: a Tape and Discography of Negro Traditional Jazz Recorded in New Orleans or by New Orleans Bands, 1937–1972* (n.p. [London], 1973)
M. MacMurray: "Joseph 'Brother Cornbread' Thomas," *SL*, xxxi (1979), spring, 16
Obituary, M. Tovey, *Fn*, xii/6 (1981), 28

BILL RUSSELL/HOWARD RYE

Thomas, Joe [Joseph, Jr.] **(ii)** (*b* Muskogee, OK, 23 Dec 1908). Tenor and alto saxophonist, brother of Foots Thomas. After performing with the Virginia Ravens (1927) he toured Pennsylvania and Ohio with Jelly Roll Morton's band and recorded with the group in New York (1929–30). He then played with Cozy Cole (1930), Blanche Calloway, the bandleader Vernon Andrade (1934), and the pianist Dave Martin (early 1940s). Having retired from full-time performing (1949) he worked as a singing coach and in the artists and repertory departments of Decca (1949–50) and Victor (1950–51). No discography distinguishes him adequately from Joe Thomas (iii), and besides the sessions with Morton (on which he and Foots Thomas may not always be identified securely) the only recordings on which he is reasonably certain to have played are those of 1951 with Big John Greer (for Victor) and the orchestra of the pianist Howard Biggs led by the singer Titus Turner (for OKeh); he may have recorded with Barney Bigard in 1945 and Billie Holiday in 1947 and 1949, but since he performed rarely after 1950 it is unlikely that he is the Joe Thomas who took part in many sessions from 1956 into the 1970s.

BIBLIOGRAPHY

FeatherE
L. Wright: *Mr Jelly Lord* (Chigwell, England, 1980), 62

HOWARD RYE

Thomas, Joe [Joseph Vankert] **(iii)** (*b* Uniontown, PA, 19 June 1909; *d* Kansas City, 3 Aug 1986). Tenor saxophonist. He began playing on alto saxophone with Earl Hood and Horace Henderson (1930–31), then changed to the tenor instrument and worked with Stuff Smith (1932) and the drummer Guy Jackson (1933). From 1933 to 1947 he was with Jimmie Lunceford, and his ebullient personality as both singer and saxophone soloist played a major role in establishing the band's success (for illustration *see* LUNCEFORD, JIMMIE); he may be see with it in the film short *Jimmie Lunceford and his Orchestra* (1936). After Lunceford's death Thomas became leader of the band with Eddie Wilcox, but he left to form his own group, a seven-piece swing and rhythm-and-blues ensemble consisting of other former members of the Lunceford–Wilcox–Thomas Band – the trumpeter Johnny Grimes, the trombonist Dicky Harris, the double bass player George Duvivier, and the drummer Joe Marshall – together with the baritone saxophonist Ben Kynard and the pianist George Rhodes; it recorded from 1949 to 1951. He then joined his family's undertaking firm, but continued to play occasionally: he appeared at the Newport Jazz Festival in 1970, recorded as the leader of a quartet with Jimmie Rowles in 1979, and made a fine album as co-leader with Jay McShann in a re-creation of his seven-piece group (and reunion with Grimes, Harris, and Duvivier) in 1982. Thomas was inspired by Coleman Hawkins and Chu Berry, and when playing solos tended to remain close to the melody and concentrate on the tune's rhythmical aspects. His huge and occasionally grainy tone influenced an entire generation of saxophonists in the 1940s; he may be heard to advantage as a singer on his own titles *You're buggin' me* and *You're just my kind*. Materials relating to his career are held as the Joseph V. Thomas Collection in the Miller Nichols Library at the Kansas City campus of the University of Missouri; *see* LIBRARIES AND ARCHIVES, §2.

SELECTED RECORDINGS

As leader: Don't blame me/For Boobs Only (1945, Melodisc 113); You're buggin' me (1945, Melodisc 114); Harlem Hop (1949, King 4401); Blue Shadows/Raw Meat (1950, King 4385); Big Foot (1950, King 4421); You're just my kind/Buttons (1951, King 4474); *Raw Meat* (1979, Upt. 27.01); with J. McShann: *Blowin' in from K.C.* (1982, Upt. 27.12)
As sideman with J. Lunceford: Black and Tan Fantasy (1934, Decca 453); Posin' (1937, Decca 1355); Le jazz hot (1939, Voc. 4595); Baby won't you please come home? (1939, Voc. 4667); I'm alone with you (1939, Col. 35484); *Jimmy* [sic] *Lunceford* (1940, Alamac QSR2422), incl. Stardust; *Jimmie Lunceford and his Orchestra 1940* (1940, Cir. [USA] 11), incl. Annie Laurie; What's your story, morning glory? (1940, Col. 35510); Moonbeams (1948, Manor 1111)

BIBLIOGRAPHY

ChiltonW; *FeatherE*
"Le saxo ténor Joe Thomas," *BHcF*, no.76 (1958), 3
B. Niquet: "Les Joe Thomas," *Pj*, no.8 (1973), 76 [incl. discography]

R. Sunenblick: Liner notes, *Blowin' in from K.C.* (Upt. 2712, 1983)
Obituary, *New York Times* (8 Aug 1986)
J. Simmen: "Ceux qui s'en vont: Joe V. Thomas (19 juin 1909 – 3 août 1986)," *BHcF*, no.345 (1987), 14
E. Berger: *Bassically Speaking: an Oral History of George Duvivier* (Metuchen, NJ, and London, 1993), 82
J. Evensmo: *History of Jazz Tenor Saxophone: Black Artists*, i: *1917–1934* (Oslo, 1996); ii: *1935–1939* (Oslo, 1997) ; iii: *1940–1944* (Oslo, 1997)

FRANK DRIGGS/HOWARD RYE, BK

Thomas, Joe [Joseph Lewis] **(iv)** (*b* Webster Groves, MO, 24 July 1909; *d* New York, 6 Aug 1984). Trumpeter. He first played in the lesser-known bands of Cecil Scott (1928), the pianist Darrel Harris (1929), the saxophonist Eli Rice (1930–32), Shuffle Abernathy (1932–3), the drummer Harold Flood (1933), and Ira Coffey (1933–4). After a brief period with Fletcher Henderson (*c* March–May 1934) he joined the little-known Ferman Tapp at Smalls' Paradise in Harlem (September 1934) and then Charlie Turner's Arcadians. In mid-1935, around the time that Fats Waller took over Turner's band, Thomas rejoined Henderson (to September 1936). He continued in big bands with Willie Bryant (1937), Claude Hopkins (1938–9), and Benny Carter (1939–40); some sources also place him in James P. Johnson's band from December 1939 to November 1940, but the pianist suffered a stroke in August 1940, and thus the chronology of Thomas affiliations during this period awaits further research. After briefly leading his own band he played with Joe Sullivan (also briefly, 1941), toured and recorded with Waller's big band (1942), and was in Teddy Wilson's sextet at Café Society (August 1942 – October 1943). He was with Barney Bigard at the Onyx Club from the latter part of 1944 into 1945. From the late 1940s he worked extensively as a freelance, participating in concerts by Eddie Condon's band at Town Hall and Carnegie Hall (*c*1947) and working with Cozy Cole (1948), Bud Freeman (in Chicago, 1949), Eddie Barefield and Sid Catlett (also in Chicago, *c*1950), Willie "the Lion" Smith (at the Central Plaza, New York, 1952), the Fletcher Henderson reunion bands under Rex Stewart's direction (1957–8), and Hopkins again (recording in 1961, performing in 1966), though he occasionally led his own groups. Ill-health curtailed his activities during the 1970s. Thomas was a great admirer of Louis Armstrong. He was noted for his superb, big tone and his understated style of playing staccato, which was heard to best advantage at slow and medium tempos.

Oral history material in *NjR* (JOHP).

SELECTED RECORDINGS

As leader: on [no leader:] *Trumpet Interlude* (1943–6, 1955, EmA 36017), Pocatello (1946); Black Butterfly (1946, Key. 642)

As sideman: Lil Armstrong: Bluer than Blue (1937, Decca 1299); on [no leader:] *Jazz Odyssey*, iii: *The Sounds of Harlem* (1920s–1940s, Col. C3L33), B. Carter: When lights are low; B. Carter: Sleep (1940, Voc. 5399); A. Tatum: Lucille (1941, Decca 8577); Rock Me Mama/Lonesome Graveyard Blues (1941, Decca 8563); R. Eldridge: Don't Be that Way/St. Louis Blues (1944, Key. 607); C. Cole: Thru' for the Night (1944, Key. 1301); on [no leader:] *Alto Altitude* (1944–6, ?1953, EmA 36018), P. Brown: That's my Weakness Now, It's the Talk of the Town (1944); R. Norvo: Russian Lullaby (1944, Key. 1310)

BIBLIOGRAPHY

ChiltonW; *McCarthyB*; *SchullerS*
W. Balliett: *Dinosaurs in the Morning* (Philadelphia, 1962/*R*1978), 62
A. J. McCarthy: "Joe Thomas," *JM*, ix/6 (1963), 12
J. Postgate: "The St. Louis Sound," *JM*, no.158 (1968), 2
B. Niquet: "Les Joe Thomas," *Pj*, no.8 (1973), 76 [incl. discography]
F. H. Trolle and W. H. Coverdale, "Joseph Lewis Thomas [Joe Thomas–trumpet]: a Discography and Short Biography," *IAJRC Journal*, xii/3 (1979), 12
M. Berger, E. Berger, and J. Patrick: *Benny Carter: a Life in American Music* (Metuchen, NJ, and London, 1982)
J. Evensmo: *The Trumpets of Dizzy Gillespie, 1937–1943, Irving Randolph, Joe Thomas* (n.p. [Oslo], n.d. [?1982]) [discography]
J. Simmen: "Joseph Lewis 'Joe' Thomas," *BHcF* (1985), no.324, p.21; no.325, p.16
L. Wright: *"Fats" in Fact* (Chigwell, England, 1992)

FRANK DRIGGS/BK

Thomas, Joe (v) (*b* Newark, NJ, 16 June 1933). Flutist and tenor saxophonist. He studied music before moving in 1949 to Canada, where he worked with the singer Dee Dee Ford. After returning to Newark he led with the drummer Bill Elliott a quintet that recorded in 1963. In the following years he made several recordings as a leader, on which his sidemen included Jimmy Ponder (1969, 1972) and Ernie Royal, Garnett Brown, and Seldon Powell (all 1972); he may be heard to advantage on *Joy of Cookin'* (*c*1972, GrM 504). Thomas also recorded an album of his own compositions with a big band led by Chico O'Farrill (1971). (B. Niquet: "Les Joe Thomas," *Pj*, no.8 (1973), 76 [incl. discography])

Thomas, John (L.) (*b* Louisville, KY, 18 Sept 1902; *d* Chicago, 7 Nov 1971). Trombonist. He was brought up in Chicago, where his first professional work was with the orchestra led by the saxophonist Clarence Miller (1923). Later he played with Erskine Tate (1927–8), Dave Peyton, Fess Williams, and Jerome Pasquall (all 1928) and toured with Freddie Keppard. While in California he worked with Speed Webb and others; he then returned to Chicago (*c*1930), where he performed with Tate, Cassino Simpson (1931), and Reuben Reeves (1933). After playing briefly with McKinney's Cotton Pickers in Detroit and Buffalo (late 1934) he worked with Zack Whyte. In spring 1937 Thomas toured with Nat "King" Cole's band in the revue *Shuffle Along*. He performed again with Tate (*c*1940) and spent a short period with the guitarist Walter Dysett (1944), then abandoned performing for ten years. In late 1960 he joined Franz Jackson's band the Original Jass All-Stars, with which he performed regularly until summer 1965. References to Thomas's presence at recording sessions early in his career are open to doubt, but it is generally accepted that he is the trombonist on Louis Armstrong's *Melancholy Blues* (1927, OK 8496); his playing may be heard to advantage on Jackson's album *Franz Jackson and the Original Jass All-Stars* (1961, Riv. 9406). (B. Demeusey: "The Musical Career of John Thomas," *JJ*, xx/1 (1967), 23)

based on *ChiltonW*

Thomas, Kid. *See* VALENTINE, KID THOMAS.

Thomas, (Amos) Leon(, Jr.) [Leone] (*b* East St. Louis, IL, 4 Oct 1937; *d* New York, 8 May 1999). Singer. While studying music at Tennessee State University he was a member of a local group with Hank Crawford. After moving in 1958 to New York he performed at the Apollo Theatre, where he took part in a show that later toured on the African-American theater circuit, in which setting he was accompanied by Art Blakey's quintet. He joined Count Basie briefly in 1961 and again, after army service and further work as a freelance, from February 1964 to spring 1965, in the course of which he sang with Basie's orchestra on the television shows "The Big Bands" (New York, September 1964) and "Jazz from WGN-TV" (Chicago, March 1965). He then worked with Randy Weston, Roland Kirk, Benny Powell, Joe Newman, Tony Scott, and Mary Lou Williams (with whom he later recorded, c1970) in the New York area, and with Horace Tapscott in Los Angeles (1967). While performing and recording from 1969 to 1972 with Pharoah Sanders he gained considerable attention for his virtuosity. Later he performed and recorded as a leader. According to Feather and Gitler he changed his forename from Leon to Leone in 1976, but he evidently did not stick with this decision and soon afterwards was billed once again as Leon Thomas. From the late 1970s his career was disrupted by personal problems. He toured with Freddie Hubbard in 1979 and recorded as a leader in Milan with Hubbard among his sidemen, but shortly thereafter was fired from the band. In the late 1980s he toured with Joe Henderson's quintet (1985) and made two recordings, one with Gary Bartz's group at a club in Maryland (1987). In autumn 1995 he took a trio to London. Thomas's work was characterized by a unique, glottal approach to scat singing and a style of yodeling that is strongly suggestive of African pygmy music; a spectacular example of his dexterity as a bop scat singer may be heard on *One*, from his first album as a leader (1969).

Video oral history material in *NN-Sc* (LAJOHP).

SELECTED RECORDINGS

As leader: *Spirits Known and Unknown* (1969, FD 10115), incl. One; *The Leon Thomas Album* (1970, FD 10132); *Blues and the Soulful Truth* (c1972, FD 10155); *Full Circle* (1973, FD 10167); with G. Bartz: *Precious Energy* (1987, Mapleshade 512694); *The Leon Thomas Blues Band* (1988, CBS/Portrait RK44161)

As sideman: P. Sanders: *Karma* (1969, Imp. 9181); J. Hodges: on *Three Shades of Blue* (1970, FD 10120), Disillusion Blues; P. Sanders: on *Shukuru* (1985, The. 121), Mas in Brooklyn, Sun Song

BIBLIOGRAPHY

Feather–Gitler '70s; *SheridanCB*

N. Hentoff: "Spirits Known and Unknown," *Black Giants*, ed. P. Rivelli and R. Levin (New York and Cleveland, 1970/*R*1980 as *Giants of Black Music*), 113

J. H. Klee: "Leon Thomas: Avant-garde with Roots," *DB*, xxxvii/25 (1970), 18

D. Stewart-Baxter: "Blues & Views," *JJ*, xxiii/12 (1970), 25; xxiv/1 (1971), 29

A. Taylor: *Notes and Tones: Musician-to-musician Interviews* (Liège, Belgium, 1977, rev. and enlarged 2/1993)

"Gab den Jazzgesang neue Dimensionen Leon Thomas," *JP*, xliii/2 (1994), 20

M. Fordham: "Leon Thomas," *Jazz on CD*, no.18 (1995), 58

Obituaries: B. Ratliff, *New York Times* (14 May 1999); L. Prangell, *JJI*, lii/7 (1999), 16

LEE JESKE/BK

Thomas, Millard G(alwston) (*b* Collinsville, IL, ?1880s; *d* New York, May 1955). Pianist, composer, and bandleader. He studied music at the University of Nebraska and in 1917 led the Caddo Orchestra in Shreveport, Louisiana, and Chicago. By 1920 he had moved to Canada. His Chicago Novelty Orchestra (CNO) was based in Quebec City (1920–22) and Montreal (1922–7); usually a quintet, it included Jasper Taylor (1920–23) and the multi-instrumentalist Charles Harris. It appeared in theaters, hotels, and dance halls and, in 1923, on Montreal radio station CKAC. Thomas recorded eight items in Montreal with the CNO (1924–5), two as an unaccompanied soloist (*Blue Ivories/Reckless Blues*, 1924, Ajax 17974), and four in which he is thought to have accompanied the clarinetist Theodore West (1925). After moving about 1928 to New York he wrote lyrics for a Broadway musical, *Brown Buddies* (1930).

BIBLIOGRAPHY

J. Litchfield: *The Canadian Jazz Discography, 1916–1980* (Toronto, Buffalo, and London, 1982)

J. Gilmore: *Who's Who of Jazz in Montreal: Ragtime to 1970* (Montreal, 1989)

M. Miller: *Such Melodious Racket: the Lost History of Jazz in Canada, 1914–1949* (Toronto, 1997)

JACK LITCHFIELD/MARK MILLER

Thomas, René (François August Nicholas) (*b* Liège, Belgium, 25 Feb 1927; *d* Santander, Spain, 3 Jan 1975). Belgian guitarist. He was essentially self-taught, but was early influenced by Django Reinhardt. He first worked as a freelance with various Belgian and French musicians, most notably Bobby Jaspar, Jacques Pelzer, and Fats Sadi. Having been introduced to Jimmy Raney's style by Jimmy Gourley in Paris in 1952, he became one of Raney's most ardent disciples in Europe, and his first important engagements were with visiting Americans in Paris, among them Chet Baker (1955). In 1956 he moved to Montreal. He played with Jackie McLean and Cecil Payne, then visited New York, where he performed and recorded with Sonny Rollins and with Toshiko Akiyoshi (both 1958); he also worked with Rollins in Philadelphia in 1958, and he returned to New York in 1960 to record as a leader, with J. R. Monterose among his sidemen.

In 1961 Thomas returned to Europe, and he performed in August of that year at the third Festival de Comblain-la-Tour in Belgium. He was co-leader of a quintet with Jaspar (to 1962) and toured with Chet Baker (1962). From 1962 to 1966 he played intermittently, alternating with Gourley, with Kenny Clarke at the Blue Note in Paris. He made further recordings as a leader with Jaspar (1961), as a leader with Baker (1962), and as sole leader (1963–4, with Pelzer among his sidemen in 1963); he also participated in sessions led by Baker (1962, 1964), Lou Bennett (1962–4, 1966), the pianist and organist Ingfried Hoffman and Sonny Criss (both 1963), and Jack Sels (1965). After a period of practice in Liège, he resumed performing with, among others, the tenor saxophonist Robert Jeanne, Monterose, and a quartet involving players with whom he had worked in Paris in the mid-1960s – René Urtreger, Gilbert Rovère, and Charles Bellonzi. In March 1969 he recorded under Lucky Thompson's leadership. He then toured throughout Europe with Eddy Louiss and with Stan Getz (1969–72), with whom he also played in Mexico. He appeared in the film documentary *Three Days in April* (*Jazz in Belgium*) (1972), undertook further work with Bennett and Pelzer, appeared in a duo with Christian Escoudé and in a trio with Art Taylor, and in the mid-1970s again shared membership with Gourley in Clarke's group. He suffered a fatal heart attack the day after a performance with Bennett and Al Jones early in 1975. Thomas's playing combined the precise approach of Raney with the adventurous spirit of Reinhardt to form an innovative style, and his influence among guitarists in Europe was widespread.

SELECTED RECORDINGS

As leader: *Guitar Groove* (1960, Jlnd 27); *Meeting Mr. Thomas* (1963, Barclay 84091); with K. Clarke and E. Louiss: *Eddy Louiss–Kenny Clarke–René Thomas* (1972, RCA CY3004); *Hommage à ... René Thomas* (1974, Tim. 398)

As sideman: S. Rollins: *Brass/Trio* (1958, Metro. 1002); B. Jaspar: *The Bobby Jaspar Quartet at Ronnie Scott's 1962* (1962, Mole 11); C. Baker: *Chet is Back* (1962, RCA LPM10307); S. Getz: *Dynasty* (1971, Verve 68802)

BIBLIOGRAPHY

FeatherE; *Feather–Gitler '70s*

J.-L. Ginibre: "L'homme aux lunettes d'écaille," *Jm*, no.86 (1962), 33

M. Hennessey: "Great Guitar Belgian Style," *MM* (13 Feb 1965), 6

J. Gilmore: *Who's Who of Jazz in Montreal: Ragtime to 1970* (Montreal, 1989)

M. Hennessey: *Klook: the Story of Kenny Clarke* (London, 1990)
R. Pernet, J.-P. Schroeder, and others: *Dictionnaire du jazz à Bruxelles et en Wallonie* (Liège, Belgium, 1991)
J. M. Hacquier and J.-P. Schroeder: "René Thomas: la legende du Roi René," *Jh*, no.530 (1996), 19 [incl. discography]
J.-P. Schroeder: "Les chemins de Thomasiana," *Jh*, no.530 (1996), 24

NORMAN MONGAN/BK

Thomas, Walter. *See* THOMAS, FOOTS.

Thompkins, Eddie [Edward A.] (*b* Kansas City, MO, 1908; *d* Tennessee, 17 April 1943). Trumpeter and singer. Many sources spell his name "Tompkins." He played with Terrence Holder, the bandleader Eli Rice, Jesse Stone, and the clarinetist Grant Moore before entering the University of Iowa in 1926. While a student he worked with George E. Lee and others. Thereafter he rejoined Moore, then played with Holder, Benny Moten, Tommy Douglas, and Rice (1931). In late 1933 he joined Jimmie Lunceford, with whom he performed and made recordings until 1939; he may be seen in the short film *Jimmy Lunceford and his Dance Orchestra* (1937). He died in a shooting accident during military service.

SELECTED RECORDINGS

As sideman with J. Lunceford (all recorded for Decca): Mood Indigo (1934, 131) [first tpt solo]; Black and Tan Fantasy [second tpt solo]/Since my best gal turned me down (1934, 453); Honest and truly (1937, 1219); Ragging the scale (1937, 1364)

BIBLIOGRAPHY

McCarthyB
H. Panassié: "Jimmy Lunceford and his Orchestra," *Jh*, no.21 (1937), 3
G. Minish: "The Forgotten Ones: Eddie Tompkins," *JJI*, xlv/12 (1992), 14

based on *ChiltonW*

Thompson, Barbara (Gracey) (*b* Oxford, England, 27 July 1944). English saxophonist and flutist. She began classical music lessons on clarinet at the age of ten and took no interest in jazz until she was 18. She studied flute, clarinet, piano, and composition at the Royal College of Music in London for three years, and also learned saxophone privately. In 1965 she joined Neil Ardley's New Jazz Orchestra, with which she made recordings intermittently until 1978; while a member of this ensemble she met Jon Hiseman, whom she later married. During the same period she played with other jazz and rock musicians, including an all-woman group, the She Trinity (which toured West Germany and Britain), Art Themen (as co-leader of a quintet, 1969), John Dankworth, Cleo Laine, Mike Gibbs, Don Weller, Don Rendell (recording in 1974), Wolfgang Dauner, and Charles Loos (April 1975). Around 1972 she formed the jazz-rock group Paraphernalia, which established an identity about three years later when the keyboard player Colin Dudman joined it; among her other sidemen have been Pete Lemer, Roy Babbington, and, from 1979, Hiseman. She has continued to tour and make recordings with the group, with which she may be seen in the video *Barbara Thompson's Paraphernalia: Live in Concert* (filmed 1990). From 1973 to 1980 she also led a Latin-jazz nonet, Jubiaba, and from the late 1980s a big band, Moving Parts. She performed and recorded with the United Jazz and Rock Ensemble (from 1975), toured Europe as a soloist (1980s and 1990s), and worked in the band Sans Frontières (1990s). In 2001 the effects of Parkinson's disease forced her to retire from playing. Thompson has composed music for films and television and big bands (from the 1970s), a saxophone concerto (1989), and suites of songs. She is a partner with Hiseman in their recording studio and related activities.

SELECTED RECORDINGS

As unaccompanied soloist: *Songs from the Centre of the Earth* (1990, Black Sun [issue number unknown])
As leader: *Barbara Thompson's Paraphernalia* (1978, MCA 2852); *Live in Concert* (1980, MCA 309); *Mother Earth* (1982, VeraBra 5); *Shadow Show* (1983, VeraBra 10); *Pure Fantasy* (1984, VeraBra 8); *Barbara Thompson's Special Edition* (1985, VeraBra 2017-2); *Heavenly Bodies* (1986, VeraBra 15); *A Cry from the Heart* (1987, VeraBra 21–22); *Breathless* (1990–91, VeraBra 2057-2); *Everlasting Flame* (1993, VeraBra 2058-2); *Lady Saxophone* (1995, VeraBra 2166-2)
As sideman: D. Rendell: *Just Music* (1974, Spot. 502); N. Ardley: *Kaleidoscope of Rainbows* (1976, Gull 1018); United Jazz and Rock Ensemble: *The Break Even Point* (1979, Mood 23600); *United Live Opus Sechs* (1984, Mood 28642)

BIBLIOGRAPHY

CarrJ; *ChiltonB*; *WickesIBJ*, i
B. van Rooyen: "Barbara Thompson: Woman in Jazz," *JF* [intl edn], no.48 (1977), 39
V. Geibel: "Gespräch mit Barbara Thompson," *JP*, xxvii/12 (1978), 22
M. Hennessey: "Barbara Thompson," *JJI*, xxxiii/3 (1980), 27

STAN BRITT/BK

Thompson, Butch [Richard Enos] (*b* Marine, MN, 28 Nov 1943). Pianist and clarinetist. After playing with local bands he moved to Minneapolis and St. Paul, where he joined the Hall brothers' New Orleans Jazz Band in 1962; the group worked for more than 20 years at the Mendota Emporium, playing frequently with well-known guest artists such as George Lewis (i), Kid Thomas Valentine, Pops Foster, Manuel Manetta, Ray Burke, Art Hodes, and Eubie Blake. Thompson also led his own trio, which in 1974 began a 12-year engagement with Garrison Keillor's radio show "A Prairie Home Companion"; this became the USA's most popular radio program, and Thompson was heard (on both piano and clarinet) by millions of listeners each week. He toured extensively both as a soloist and with the trio, appearing in Europe, the Far East, and South America as well as in the USA, and also toured with the Black Eagle Jazz Band of Boston (recording in 1975–6), the New Orleans Ragtime Orchestra (1977), his own King Oliver Centennial Band (in Europe and the USA from 1985 to *c*1989), and Geoff Bull's Olympia Jazz Band (*c*1991); in 1979 he participated in a performance captured on the video *Jam Session*, nos.i–ii, from the television series "After Hours with Art Hodes." His duo projects have included recordings with the drummer Hal Smith, James Dapogny, and, in 1994, Doc Cheatham. He has been a regular contributor to *Mississippi Rag*.

SELECTED RECORDINGS

As unaccompanied soloist: *Minnesota Public Radio* (*c*1978, Prairie Home Companion 34817); *A'Solas* (1981, Stomp Off 1037), incl. Creepy Feeling; *New Orleans Joys* (1989, Daring 3001)
Duos: with H. Smith: *If You Don't Shake: Echoes from Storyville*, i (1984, Stomp Off 1075); with J. Dapogny: *How Could We Be Blue?* (1988, Stomp Off 1183) [incl. 2 tracks on cl]
As leader with Charlie DeVore and H. Smith: *Echoes from Storyville*, ii (1984, Stomp Off 1116)
As sideman with K. T. Valentine [cl]: *Kid Thomas at San Jacinto Hall* (1965, San Jacinto 4), incl. Merry Christmas Blues

BIBLIOGRAPHY

H. Gilltrap: "Talking Ragtime," *Fn*, xvi/4 (1985), 15
D. Reffkin: "The Ragtime Machine," *MR*, xxi/1 (1993), sec.2, p.1

BILL RUSSELL

Thompson, Chuck [Charles Edmund] (*b* New York, 4 June 1926). Drummer. Following piano studies in New York he learned drums for five years in Hollywood. He worked in Los

Angeles with the trumpeter Charlie Echols (1943) and played and recorded briefly in New York with Charlie Parker's bop quintet (1946), the other members of which included Joe Albany and Miles Davis. In 1947 he worked with Howard McGhee and Benny Carter, recorded with Gerald Wilson, and performed and recorded with the quintet of Dexter Gordon and Wardell Gray; two years later he made recordings as a member of the Kenton All Stars (alongside Art Pepper and Hampton Hawes, among others), in concert with Erroll Garner, and with Sonny Criss. After recording again with Gray (1950) and Gordon (1952, 1955) he was associated with Hawes (1955–6); the two recorded as sidemen with Barney Kessel and Red Mitchell (both 1955) and in a trio with Mitchell (1955–6). Thompson recorded further with Criss in Los Angeles (1956) and worked as a freelance in San Francisco, where he played in a quartet at the Cellar (1959). Nothing is known of his later activities.

SELECTED RECORDINGS

As sideman: W. Gray: The Great Lie (1947, Jazz Selection 805); D. Gordon: Bikini (1947, Dial 1022); H. Hawes: *Hampton Hawes Trio*, i (1955, Cont. 3505); R. Mitchell *Jam for your Bread* (1955, Beth. 38); H. Hawes: *This is Hampton Hawes*, ii: *The Trio* (1955–6, Cont. 3515), incl. Section Blues

BIBLIOGRAPHY

FeatherE
R. Gordon: *Jazz West Coast: the Los Angeles Jazz Scene of the 1950s* (London and New York, 1986)
T. Gioia: *West Coast Jazz: Modern Jazz in California, 1945–1960* (New York and Oxford, England, 1992)

Thompson, Danny [Daniel Henry Edward] (*b* Teignmouth, England, 4 April 1939). Double bass player. After teaching himself to play double bass he became involved during the 1960s with jazz in London, working with Tubby Hayes's student orchestra, John Burch, Ronnie Scott, Stan Tracey, and John McLaughlin, among others, and accompanying visiting Americans. From 1964 to 1966 he played with Alexis Korner's Blues Incorporated, in which he developed a special musical relationship with the drummer Terry Cox, and in 1968 he and Cox formed the rhythm section in the commercially successful folk-jazz group Pentangle. Around this time he was a member of a trio with McLaughlin and the saxophonist and flutist Tony Roberts that gave a concert in 1967, a recording of which was not released until the late 1990s. Thompson remained with Pentangle until it disbanded in 1973. In the meantime he developed a career as a session player which led to work with such pop and folk artists as John Martyn and Richard Thompson. In 1987 he formed the group Whatever, with Roberts and the guitarist Bernie Holland among his sidemen; as its name suggests, the ensemble drew on a wide range of musical styles, including jazz, folk, and world music, after the manner of the trio with McLaughlin and Roberts. In 1992 Thompson founded the Jazz Label, which has recorded various musicians, notably John Etheridge.

SELECTED RECORDINGS

Danny Thompson Trio: Live 1967 (1967, What Disc 3); *Whatever* (1987, Hannibal 1326); *Whatever Next* (1989, Ant. 8743); *Elemental* (1990, Ant. 8753)

BIBLIOGRAPHY

CarrJ; *ChiltonB*; *WickesIBJ*, i
<http://www.dirtynelson.com/linen/feature/56thompson.html> (1999)

MARK GILBERT

Thompson, Don(ald Winston) (*b* Powell River, Canada, 18 Jan 1940). Canadian double bass player and pianist. He worked in Vancouver with the pianist Chris Gage and others (1960–65), and toured in the USA with John Handy's quintet (1965–7), with which he appears in the Canadian short film *John Handy at the Blue Horn* (1965). In 1969 he settled in Toronto, but continued to tour on occasion, playing double bass with Paul Desmond (1975–6), double bass and piano with Jim Hall (1975–82), and double bass and occasionally two-piano duets with George Shearing (1982–7). In Toronto, Thompson was a member of Rob McConnell's Boss Brass on double bass (1969–82) and piano (1988–93) and also worked with Ed Bickert, Lenny Breau, Jane Bunnett, the singer Trudy Desmond, Sonny Greenwich, the Dave McMurdo Jazz Orchestra, Kenny Wheeler, and many visiting American musicians. He has led his own bands as a vibraphonist or pianist in mainstream and contemporary jazz styles; his vibraphone playing is in the tradition of Milt Jackson, while his piano playing has latterly revealed the influence of Keith Jarrett.

SELECTED RECORDINGS

Duos with G. Shearing: *Live at the Cafe Carlyle* (1984, Conc. 246)
As leader: *Country Place* (1976, PM 008); with E. Bickert: *Dance to the Lady* (1980, Sack. 4010); *A Beautiful Friendship* (1984, Conc. 243); *Winter Mist* (1990, Jazz Alliance 1004)
As sideman: J. Handy: *Live at the Monterey Jazz Festival* (1965, Col. CS9262); S. Greenwich: *The Old Man and the Child* (1970, Sack. 2002); J. Hall: *Live!* (1975, A&M Hor. 705); P. Desmond: *The Paul Desmond Quartet Live!* (1975, A&M Hor. 850); F. Rosolino: *Thinking about You* (1976, Sack. 2014); J. McShann: *Tuxedo Junction* (1980, Sack. 3035); E. Remler: *Take Two* (1982, Conc. 195); D. McMurdo: *Different Paths* (1993, Sack. 2-2034)

BIBLIOGRAPHY

EMC2
M. Miller: "Don Thompson: Sideman in the Spotlight," *JF* [intl edn], no.58 (1979), 34 [incl. discography]
B. Smith and D. Lee: "Don Thompson," *Coda*, no.190 (1983), 4 [incl. discography]
L. Tomkins: "Don Thompson," *CI*, xxii/3 (1984), 20
M. Miller: "Don Thompson," *Boogie, Pete & the Senator: Canadian Musicians in Jazz: the Eighties* (Toronto, 1987), 262
B. King: "Don Thompson: the Abstract Truth," *Jazz Report*, ii/5 (1989), 1
——: "A Musical Genius," *Jazz Report*, viii/4 (1995), 12
P. Murray: "Don Thompson," *Bass Player*, vi/3 (1995), 50

MARK MILLER

Thompson, Eddie [Edgar Charles] (*b* London, 31 May 1925; *d* London, 6 Nov 1986). English pianist. He was born blind and learned piano as a child. In 1947 he joined Freddy Randall, and in 1949 he went to Paris with Carlo Krahmer before joining Victor Feldman's sextet in England. In the early 1950s he led a quintet and a trio and also played with Tony Crombie and Ronnie Scott. He worked with dance bands and in radio studios and made recordings as a leader of small groups (1954–9), while also performing and recording with Vic Ash (1954) and Randall (December 1955 – July 1956), the latter after brief affiliations with the brass player Bobby Mickleburgh and the Jazz Today Unit (both 1955). In 1957–8 Thompson was a member of Tommy Whittle's quartet, with which he went to the USA. He then re-established his own quintet and trio, which held a residency at Scott's club, and appeared as an unaccompanied soloist at the Downbeat club (1960). During the ten years he spent in the USA (1962–72) he was resident for some time at the Hickory House, New York, where around 1963 his trio included Mickey Roker; he performed at various other clubs and recorded as a leader (1963, 1970) and as a soloist (1970). After returning to Britain Thompson toured as a soloist, in a duo with Roger Kellaway, and with his trio, visiting the USA, Australia, New Zealand, and Europe, and he performed on television and radio. His recordings from 1978 include *When Lights are Low* (1980, Hep 2007) and *Memories of You* (1983, Hep 2021), with his trio, and albums in which the trio accompanied Roy Williams (1981) and Spike Robinson (1984). He played frequently at clubs in London, and in 1985 worked with Kellaway in New York. A brilliant pianist, Thompson was also well known for the dry wit and occasionally anarchic sense of humor he brought to his performances.

Oral history material in *GBLnsa*.

BIBLIOGRAPHY

CarrJ; *ChiltonB*
P. Brand: "The Scene is Different in the States, Says Eddie Thompson," *Crescendo*, iii/3 (1964), 24
"If You're Blind, Piano is the Most Natural Instrument, Says Eddie Thompson," *CI*, ix/7 (1971), 8
"Welcome Home, Eddie," *CI*, xiii/5 (1974), 18
R. Cotterrell, ed.: *Jazz Now: the Jazz Centre Society Guide* (London, 1976)
Obituary, *JJI*, xxxix/12 (1986), 4
A. Stevens: "Eddie in the States," *MM* (1 Nov 1995), 51

DIGBY FAIRWEATHER/BK

Thompson, Gail (Alison) (*b* London, 15 June 1958). English saxophonist, composer, and conductor. She began playing clarinet at the age of 14 and changed to tenor saxophone a year later. In 1977 she played saxophone in the musical *Bubbling Brown Sugar* and taught music at South East London Technical College, and in 1980 she managed Macari's music shop in London and appeared at Camden Jazz Week with her band, the Gail Thompson Approach. Thompson founded the school Music Works in the Brixton area of London in 1986, and that same year she formed the group Gail Force and, with Courtney Pine and Gary Crosby, the Jazz warriors. In the mid-1980s she performed and recorded with a big band led by the drummer Charlie Watts and worked with Art Blakey during his visits to Britain. After she developed multiple sclerosis in 1986 her playing career was curtailed and she concentrated instead on composing and conducting; she has written music for her own ensembles as well as for Stan Tracey and the Midland Big Band, among others. In the early 1990s, having traveled widely in Africa, she formed the group Jazz Africa. Thompson has also worked in television and as a concert promoter.

SELECTED RECORDINGS

As leader: *Gail Force* (1994, EFZ 1005); *Jazz Africa* (1995, Enja 9053-2)

BIBLIOGRAPHY

ChiltonB
"Sidelines: Gail Force," *MM* (14 March 1987)

MARK GILBERT

Thompson, Leslie (Anthony Joseph) (*b* Kingston, Jamaica, 17 Oct 1901; *d* London, 26 Dec 1987). Jamaican trumpeter. He trained with the band of the West India Regiment and played in cinemas and performed in recitals before moving to London in 1929. The following year he joined Spike Hughes's group, with which he played trumpet and trombone until 1932; he may also be heard on double bass on the band's recording of *Sirocco* (1932, Decca F2844). After touring France, Italy, and Switzerland with Louis Armstrong (1934–5) Thompson formed a band with the encouragement of Ken "Snake Hips" Johnson; the latter danced with the group in 1936 and assumed its leadership the following year. Thompson recorded with Armstrong in Paris (1934) and with Benny Carter in London (1936–7), then played in a band led by Edmundo Ros. Following military service in World War II he performed at clubs and dance halls in London, but he ceased to work as a professional musician in 1954.

Oral history material in *GBLnsa*.

BIBLIOGRAPHY

O. Wright and K. Wright: "My Face is my Fortune," *Sv*, no.83 (1979), 196; no.84 (1979), 215
J. Green: "Leslie Thompson," *Black Perspective in Music*, xii (1984), 98
L. Thompson and J. P. Green: *An Autobiography* (Crawley, England, 1985)
V. Wilmer: "Leslie Thompson: a Pioneer Remembers," *Wire*, no.25 (1986), 16
Obituary, V. Wilmer, *Wire*, no.49 (1988), 12

JEFFREY P. GREEN

Thompson, Lucky [Eli] (*b* Columbia, SC, 16 June 1924). Tenor and soprano saxophonist. He first toured with the 'Bama State Collegians, and in 1943 he moved to New York. After six months with Lionel Hampton he became a member of Billy Eckstine's bop orchestra (1944) and spent a year with Count Basie (November 1944 – October 1945). He then went to Los Angeles, where he was in great demand as a studio musician. He took part in more than 100 recordings in two years, both as a leader (he later cited as a personal favorite the magnificent version of *Just One More Chance* recorded in 1947) and as a sideman, with Boyd Raeburn, Slim Gaillard, Jimmy Mundy, and Dodo Marmarosa; in 1946 he participated in sessions with Charlie Parker and Dizzy Gillespie.

After returning to New York (1948) Thompson led his own band at the Savoy (1951–3), recorded with Thelonious Monk (1952), and made a major contribution to the session in which Miles Davis recorded *Walkin'* (1954). In 1955 he played with Jo Jones for one of the studio jam sessions organized by the Vanguard label, and the following year he made a number of recordings as a sideman with Milt Jackson in New York (January) and as a leader in Paris (February–April). He then joined Stan Kenton, whose band was touring France, and returned with Kenton to the USA. According to one account, his opportunities for a career in America declined thereafter because he was blacklisted by Joe Glaser, Louis Armstrong's manager, after an argument during an airplane flight on which he refused to allow Glaser's star to leave the aircraft first; in any event, following another session with Jackson in January 1957, Thompson lived in France until 1962. During this period he mastered the soprano saxophone and worked steadily throughout Europe.

Thompson spent a period of comparative inactivity in the mid-1960s, then from 1968 to 1971 he lived again in France. He toured widely and recorded as a leader in Switzerland (in concert in 1968 with Buddy Tate, Milt Buckner, and Wallace Bishop as his sidemen, and in 1969 with lesser-known players), in Germany (1969), in Poland (1969, with Adam Makowicz in his quartet), and in Spain (1970, with Tete Montoliu). In 1973–4 he taught at Dartmouth College and at Yale University, after which, disillusioned with the music business, he retired. He was briefly in Canada before moving to an island off the coast of Savannah, Georgia; in exchange for dental work, he sold his instruments to a dentist in Savannah (these were later purchased by Pat LaBarbera). While living in Atlanta he was badly beaten, and he later moved to Denver, to Oregon, and, in the late 1980s, to Seattle; there he became a hermit and then a homeless person before entering the Columbia City Assisted Living facility in August 1994.

Thompson was an important player whose style drew on the work of Coleman Hawkins and Don Byas, tempered by the lighter tone of Lester Young and his own creative approach. In his contributions to Parker's historic Dial session of March 1946, he does not sound entirely comfortable playing in a bop context, but he contributes a sense of weird melodic adventurousness which distinguishes his work from that of the classic swing tenor saxophonists; by the time of Monk's similarly important Blue Note session of 1952 and Davis's landmark date for Prestige in 1954, he had refined this aspect of his hybrid swing and bop style. He was one of the first of the modern group of soprano saxophonists.

SELECTED RECORDINGS

As leader: Just One More Chance/Boppin' the Blues (1947, Vic. 20-2504); From Dixieland to Bop (1947, Vic. 20-3142); *Lucky Thompson Featuring Oscar Pettiford* (1956, ABC–Para. 111, 171); *Lucky Strikes* (1964, Prst. 7365); *Body and Soul* (1970, Ensayo 35); *I Offer You* (1973, GrM 517)

As sideman: C. Basie: Taps Miller (1944, Col. 36831); I didn't know about you (1944, Col. 36766); D. Washington: My Lovin' Papa (1945, Apollo 371); My voot is really vout/Blues for a Day (1945, Apollo 388); D. Marmarosa: How High the Moon (1946, Atomic 225); D. Gillespie: Diggin' Diz (1946, Dial 1004); C. Parker: Moose the Mooche/Yardbird Suite (1946, Dial 1003); Ornithology/Night in Tunisia (1946, Dial 1002); T. Monk: Skippy/Let's Cool One (1952, BN 1952); Hornin' In/Carolina Moon (1952, BN 1603); Sixteen (1952), first issued on *More Genius of Thelonious Monk* (1947, 1952, BN [Jap.] BNJ61011); M. Davis: *Miles Davis* (1954, Prst. 182), incl. Blue and Boogie, Walkin'; M. Jackson: Flamingo (1956), on *Meet Milt Jackson* (1949, 1954, 1956, Savoy 12061); *The Jazz Skyline* (1956, Savoy 12070); *Jackson'sville* (1956, Savoy 12080); *Plenty, Plenty Soul* (1957, Atl. 1269)

BIBLIOGRAPHY

SheridanCB
L. Feather: *Inside Be-bop* (New York, 1949/*R*1977 as *Inside Jazz*), 98
Y. Bruynoghe: "Lucky Thompson," *Swing Time*, no.17 (1952), [3]
N. Hentoff: "Lucky Thompson," *DB*, xxiii/7 (1956), 9; contd as "Call him Lucky(?)," xxiii/9 (1956), 14
R. Horricks: "Lucky Thompson: a Jazz Musician without a School," *JM*, i/11 (1956), 6
——: *Count Basie and his Orchestra: its Music and its Musicians* (London, 1957), 180
V. Wilmer: "Lucky Thompson," *JM*, viii/7 (1962), 12
T. Williams: *Lucky Thompson Discography and Biography*, i: *1944–51* (London, *c*1967)
M. Gardner: "Lucky Thompson in the Sixties," *Coda*, ix/1 (1969), 3
C. Kuhl: "Lucky Thompson: Interview," *Cadence*, viii (1982), no.1, p.10; no.2, p.8
H. A. Mims: "E. L. 'Lucky' Thompson: in Search of what the Creator Intended for Him," *JSN*, ii/4 (1982), 102
M. Jones: *Talking Jazz* (London, 1987), 72
B. Wilber: *Music was not Enough*, ed. D. Webster (London and New York, 1987), 36
D. Norwood: Liner notes, *Lucky Thompson, the Beginning Years* (IAJRC 1001, 1991)
M. D. Watson: "Lucky Thompson: a Survey of his Work," *JJI*, xliv (1991), no.4, p.20; no.5, p.14
A. von Konow: "Lucky," *Orchester journalen*, lxii/6 (1994), 19
M. Hennessey: "Lucky Thompson: a Giant Forgotten," *CJM*, xxxiv/5 (1997), 19; contd as "Lucky Thompson: the Vultures are Still out There," xxxiv/6 (1997–8), 18
B. Donaldson: "Lola Pedrini: the 'Jazz Angel' of Seattle," *Marge Hofacre's Jazz News* (1998), Jan–Feb, 12

SCOTT YANOW/BK

Thompson, Malachi (Richard) (*b* Princeton, KY, 21 Aug 1949). Trumpeter and leader. He grew up in Chicago, learned piano briefly at an early age, and took up trumpet when he was 11 after hearing a performance by Count Basie's orchestra. Having worked in local rhythm-and-blues bands, in 1969 he joined the Association for the Advancement of Creative Musicians (AACM); through 1973 he was a member of the AACM Experimental Big Band. He also played in the Southern Christian Leadership Council's Operation Breadbasket Big Band, which performed at political rallies and protest marches. While attending Malcolm X College in Chicago, Thompson led a small ensemble that won an award for the best group at the Amherst Jazz Festival, and he subsequently received a scholarship to attend Governor's State University, where he studied composition (BA 1974).

After moving to New York (1974) Thompson worked regularly in small groups led by Kalaparusha Maurice McIntyre (*c*1974–81) and Roland Alexander (1976–80); he also performed with Jackie McLean, Joe Henderson, and the big bands of Sam Rivers (1975–80) and Sam Wooding (1976–9) and toured on the Jazzmobile. From 1975 to 1980, with the trumpeter Norman Spiller, he co-led a brass ensemble, Brass Proud, which usually consisted of seven or eight trumpets and a rhythm section; among its sidemen were Olu Dara, Lester Bowie, Ahmed Abdullah, and Tommy Turrentine. In 1979 he toured and recorded in Europe as a member of Archie Shepp's 30-piece big band; he worked in Shepp's smaller groups until 1980 and maintained an association with the saxophonist into 1988. In 1980 he was a founding member of Bowie's Hot Trumpet Repertory Company – a trumpet choir without rhythm section – which later became Brass Fantasy (1982–7).

In 1978 Thompson founded a small group, the Freebop Band, and after leaving Shepp in 1980 he reduced his freelance work to concentrate on this ensemble; his principal saxophonist was Carter Jefferson (until his death in 1993), although James Spaulding, Joe Ford, Gary Bartz, Oliver Lake, Roland Alexander, Ron Bridgewater, David Murray, Billy Harper, George Adams, and Paul Quinichette also played saxophone with the group; Al Dailey and Victor Lewis were among its other members. From around 1983 Thompson lived alternately in Washington, DC, and New York, before moving around the mid-1980s to Vienna; there he performed with his own ensembles, notably the Freebop Band and an all-star big band. However, in 1989, having been diagnosed with t-cell lymphoma, he returned to Chicago. With his cancer in remission he re-formed the Freebop Band, and in 1991 he began leading the big band Africa Brass. Two years later he organized the Hyde Park/Kenwood Jazz Festival and founded the Sutherland Community Arts Initiative, a non-profit organization involved in preserving the Sutherland Theater (in which Thompson lives) and developing an awareness of the history of music in Chicago's South Side; by 1997 he had received state and federal funding to develop the theater into a venue for the arts and to create music projects to promote the aims of his organization.

SELECTED RECORDINGS

(recorded for Delmark unless otherwise indicated)

As leader: *The Seventh Son* (1972, RA 102); *Spirit* (1984, 1987, 442); *The Jaz Life* (1991, 453); *Lift Every Voice* (1992, 463); *New Standards* (1993, 473); *Buddy Bolden's Rag* (*c*1995, 481); *Freebop Now!* (1998, 506)

As sideman: K. M. McIntyre: *Kwanza* (1977, Bayside 6015); *Ram's Run* (1981, Cadence Jazz 1009)

BIBLIOGRAPHY

T. Nuccio: "Profile: Malachi Thompson," *DB*, l/10 (1983), 50
P. Carles, A. Clergeat, and J.-L. Comolli: *Dictionnaire du jazz* (Paris, 1988, rev. and enlarged 2/1994)
N. A. Lee: "Malachi Thompson: New Odds, New Standards," *JT*, xxiv/8 (1994), 45
J. Corbett: "Malachi Thompson's Flesh against Steel," *DB*, lxii/7 (1995), 32 [incl. discography]
H. Reich: "Riffs: Venue Revivalist," *DB*, lxiv/7 (1997), 10
L. Blumenfeld: "Traditions," *Jazziz*, xv/6 (1998), 19

GK

Thompson, Rudolph [Jazz-Lips] (*b* Louisville, KY, 13 Dec 1913; *d* Louisville, 20 Sept 1956). Jug blower. He began playing on the streets with the Mud Gutters Jug Band at the age of 12. The following year he was engaged by Whistler for a trip to St. Louis, during which the 13-year-old made recordings with the band, including *The Vamps of "28"* (1927, OK 8469). He played frequently with Whistler's band up to 1932, recording again in 1931 (*Folding Bed/Hold that Tiger*, Vic. 23305). Thompson continued working with various leaders, including Clifford Hayes, until 1949, when he joined the Henry Miles Jug Band; he remained with Miles until his death, which was caused by lesions on his lungs resulting from the force of his playing.

BIBLIOGRAPHY

L. Wright, comp. [from material supplied by F. Cox, J. Randolph, and J. Harris]: *The Jug Bands of Louisville* (Chigwell, England, 1993 [*recte* 1994])
F. Cox, J. Randolph, and J. Harris: "The Jug Bands of Louisville," *Sv* (1993), no.155, p.164; no.156, p.204; (1994), no.157, p.4; no.158, p.43; no.159, p.83; no.160, p.145; (1995), no.161, p.188; no.162, p.203
B. Bogert: Liner notes, *Clifford Hayes & the Louisville Jug Bands*, i–iv (RST 1501-2, 1502-2, 1503-2, 1504-2, 1994)

HOWARD RYE

Thompson, Sir Charles [Charles Phillip] (*b* Springfield, OH, 21 March 1918). Pianist, organist, and composer. His family was musical, and his stepmother was a pianist. He first studied violin and briefly played tenor saxophone, but took up piano as a teenager. He became involved in jazz after his father, a minister, was transferred to Parsons, Kansas, and Thompson entered high school in Kansas City. He began his professional career playing with midwestern territory bands, including those of the trumpeter Lloyd Hunter (1937) and Nat Towles (1937–9); later Horace Henderson, after taking over Towles's band (with Thompson no longer a member), recorded Thompson's composition and arrangement *Smooth Sailing* (1940, OK 5900). By this time Thompson had worked with the bandleader Floyd Ray in the Los Angeles area (*c*1939) and toured with Lionel Hampton's band (1940). He joined George Clarke in Buffalo, and then went to New York to play with the Harlem Dictators and with Lee and Lester Young at the downtown location of Café Society (autumn 1942 – January 1943); it was Lester who dubbed him Sir Charles. Around this time he also contributed arrangements to the big bands of Count Basie (including *My, What a Fry*, 1942), Jimmy Dorsey, Hampton, and Fletcher Henderson.

Through a number of engagements on 52nd Street in the mid-1940s Thompson became familiar with the emerging bop style. In 1945 he worked with Howard McGhee in the band that Coleman Hawkins took to California; his solo on Hawkins's *Stuffy* is a characteristically witty and concise single line that makes effective use of silences. He may be seen with the band in the film *The Crimson Canary* (1945), but his part on the soundtrack is ghosted by a lesser player. On his return to New York later the same year Thompson performed and recorded with Charlie Parker. In 1946 he joined Lucky Millinder's big band and from 1947 to 1948 he played in the group led by Illinois Jacquet, who recorded his most popular composition, *Robbins' Nest*; he rejoined Jacquet in 1952. During the 1950s he worked as a freelance, performing mostly as an organist, but he played piano with Parker in Boston in 1953 and, more significantly, figured prominently as a piano soloist in the first mainstream jazz sessions recorded by Vic Dickenson and Buck Clayton in 1953–4.

In the late 1950s Thompson worked with Earl Bostic and then led a quartet at Count Basie's nightclub (1959). He joined Clayton for a European tour (a moment of which is captured in the Belgian film *Buck Clayton and his All Stars*, 1961), worked with Clayton in Toronto in 1963, and returned to Europe with Jazz at the Philharmonic in 1964 (in which setting he participated in the "Coleman Hawkins Sextet" episode of the British television series "Jazz 625") and again with the show *Jazz from a Swinging Era* in 1967. Living variously on the West Coast, where he often worked with Vernon Alley, and in Toronto, Paris, and Zurich, he continued to lead small groups through the 1970s and 1980s. In 1990 he appeared as an unaccompanied soloist and in a three-piano trio with Dick Hyman and Roger Kellaway at the JVC Jazz Festival in New York. He recorded an album as a leader in 1993–4 in New York and Tokyo.

Oral history material in *NjR* (JOHP).

SELECTED RECORDINGS

As unaccompanied soloist: *Portrait of a Piano* (1984, Sack. 3027)
As leader: If I Had You (1945, Apollo 757); 20th Century Blues (1945, Apollo 759); Mad Lad (1947, Apollo 773); *Bop This* (1953, Van. 8003); *Sir Charles Thompson with Coleman Hawkins* (1954, Van. 8009); *Rockin' Rhythm* (1961, Col. CS8463); *Hey, There!* (1974, BB 33071); *Stardust* (1993–4, PW 225)
As sideman: C. Hawkins: Ladies Lullaby (1945, Asch 3552); Stuffy (1945, Cap. 15254); I. Jacquet: Robbins' Nest (1947, Apollo 769); V. Dickenson: *The Vic Dickenson Septet*, i–ii (1953, Van. 8001–2); B. Clayton: *The Huckle-buck and Robbins' Nest* (1953, Col. CL548); V. Dickenson: *The Vic Dickenson Septet*, iii–iv (1954, Van. 8012–13)

BIBLIOGRAPHY

ChiltonW; *McCarthyB*
K. Gallacher and B. Fairweather: "Sir Charles Thompson," *JJ*, xv/3 (1962), 11
S. Dance: *The World of Count Basie* (New York and London, 1980), 333
J. Chadwick: "Sir Charles Thompson," *JJI*, xli/4 (1988), 8 [incl. discography]
F. Büchmann-Møller: *Just Fight for your Life: the Story of Lester Young* (New York, Westport, CT, and London, 1990)
J. Chilton: *The Song of the Hawk: the Life and Recordings of Coleman Hawkins* (London and New York, 1990)
M. Richards: "Sir Charles Thompson," *JJI*, xliii (1990), no.1, p.8; no.2, p.26
L. Bukowski: Liner notes, C. Thompson: *Takin' Off* (Del. 450, 1992)

SCOTT DeVEAUX/BK

Thompson, Sonny [Alphonso] (*b* Memphis, 22 Aug 1916; *d* Chicago, 11 Aug 1989). Pianist and leader. His place of birth was thought to be Centreville, Mississippi, but in his application for social security he gave Memphis. After moving as a child to Chicago he studied at the Chicago Conservatory of Music. He led a band accompanying Rosetta Howard in New York in 1940 and appeared at Café Society Uptown in 1941. In the mid-1940s he returned to Chicago, where he first recorded as an unaccompanied soloist in 1946. The following year he formed a small group in the jump style and began recording with it. Between two tours with the blues singer and pianist Memphis Slim in 1948 he was intermission bandleader at the Savoy Ballroom in New York. In the ensuing years his band toured widely, especially after an association with the King label brought commercial success in the rhythm-and-blues market. Thompson also recorded with other King artists, including Lucky Millinder, Bullmoose Jackson, Wynonie Harris, and the singer Lula Reed, who became his wife. From 1953 Thompson and Reed toured together in package shows which by 1957 were billed as rock-and-roll shows. In 1959 he became the director of artists and repertory for King in Chicago, and from 1960 to 1964 he was the pianist on the recordings by the blues singer and guitarist Freddie King. He visited several European countries with a touring Chicago Blues Festival in 1972. A superlative blues, boogie, and jump-band pianist, Thompson was influenced in his youth by Earl Hines and Art Tatum; however, it was only during this tour, in France, that he had an opportunity to display, in a recording session, his creative understanding of their virtuoso swing and stride styles, as well as an awareness of Thelonious Monk's more eccentric approach to these traditions of jazz piano playing.

SELECTED RECORDINGS

As unaccompanied soloist: Southside Boogie (1946, Sultan 2502); Sonny's Boogie (1946, Sultan 2503)

As leader: Long Gone (1947, Miracle 126); Sugar Cane (1950, King 4345); Frog Legs (1950, King 4364); Blues for the Night Owls (1950, King 4399); Mellow Blues (1951, King 4488); Real Real Fine (1952, King 4554); Cat on the Keys (1954, King 4746); *Moody Blues* (1956, King 568); *Mellow Blues for Late Hours* (1959, King 655); *Sonny Thompson Swings in Paris* (1972, BB 33051)

As sideman with B. Jackson: Nosey Joe (1952, King 4524); Bearcat Blues (1952, King 4551)

BIBLIOGRAPHY

T. Burke and D. Penny: "Screaming Boogie," *Blues & Rhythm*, no.37 (1988), 9

Obituaries: D. Penny, *Blues & Rhythm*, no.48 (1989), 23; D. Nelson, *Living Blues*, no.89 (1989), 39; R. Pruter, *Juke Blues*, no.18 (1989), 17; M. Radenac, *Soul Bag*, no.119 (1990), 22

A. Vasset: "Sonny Thompson," *BHcF*, no.387 (1991), 27

HOWARD RYE

Thornhill, Claude (*b* Terre Haute, IN, 10 Aug 1909; *d* New York, 1 July 1965). Bandleader, composer, arranger, and pianist. He started piano lessons at the age of ten and two years later was working in dance bands. After studying piano and composition at the Cincinnati Conservatory and the Curtis Institute he recorded with Bud Freeman (1935), Chick Bullock (1935–7), and Billie Holiday (1938) and performed and recorded with Benny Goodman (1934–5), Ray Noble (1935), and Maxine Sullivan (1937–8). For Sullivan he arranged a lightly swinging version of *Loch Lomond*, which became a hit (1937, Voc. 3654); he also wrote arrangements for radio orchestras and for jazz bands, including those of Goodman and Skinnay Ennis. In 1937 he recorded as a leader and from spring 1940 led his own big band. With Conrad Gozzo, Irving Fazola (replaced in 1942 by Danny Polo), Barry Galbraith, and (briefly) Dave Tough among his sidemen, and with Bill Borden, Thornhill himself, and, from November 1941, Gil Evans as principal arrangers, he developed a strikingly original big-band sound that emphasized static textures, without vibrato, in the lower registers and depended for coloristic effect on several instruments usually associated with classical music, including the french horn and bass clarinet.

In late October 1942 Thornhill was inducted into the navy, where he served for a period in Artie Shaw's band and toured the Pacific as a bandleader. In April 1946 he re-formed his group, continuing along the same stylistic lines, but with bop melodies as a new and prominent element explored by his arrangers Evans and Gerry Mulligan and such leading members of his ensemble as Red Rodney, Lee Konitz, Polo, Mulligan, Galbraith, Joe Shulman, and Bill Barber, whose tuba served as a member of the soft-toned brass section rather than interfering with Shulman's bass lines. Their creative and immaculately clean and delicate interpretation of Evans's arrangement of Dizzy Gillespie's fast bop theme *Anthropology* (1947) provides a particularly noteworthy example of Thornhill's style, which influenced Miles Davis's recordings in 1949 for Capitol and many musicians who followed. Additionally this band offered a curiosity in the little-known singer Gene Williams, who sounds so identical to Harry Connick, Jr., that one wonders if the young Connick took Williams as a model. Thereafter, apart from a two-month period as music director for Tony Bennett in 1957, Thornhill led a number of less successful bands which served as training grounds for such players as Bob Brookmeyer, Gene Quill, and Bill Crow in the early 1950s (at which time Mulligan continued to supply arrangements), and Jimmy Knepper, Willie Dennis, and J. R. Monterose in the mid-1950s; some of these bands may be seen in two short films and a television show, each entitled *Claude Thornhill and his Orchestra* (1947, 1950, 1965).

SELECTED RECORDINGS

As leader: Gone with the Wind (1937, Voc. 3595); Snowfall/Where or when (1941, Col. 36268); Autumn Nocturne (1941, Col. 36435); There's a Small Hotel (1942, Col. 36725); A Sunday Kind of Love (1946, Col. 37219); Anthropology (1947, Col. 38224); *The Uncollected Claude Thornhill and his Orchestra* (1947, Hep 108), incl. Snowfall, Robbins' Nest, Deed I Do, Donna Lee, Polka Dots and Moonbeams, Anthropology; Polkadots and Moonbeams (1947, Col. 38437); *Claude on a Cloud* (1958, Decca 8722)

As sideman with B. Freeman: What is there to say?/Keep Smilin' at Trouble (1935, Para. 2285)

BIBLIOGRAPHY

BallietA (1996); *SchullerS*

M. W. Stearns: *The Story of Jazz* (New York, 1956, London 1957, enlarged 1970)

N. Hentoff: "The Birth of the Cool," *DB*, xxiv (1957), no.9, p.15; no.10, p.16

E. Edwards, Jr.: "A Claude Thornhill Discography," *JM*, viii/11 (1963), 13; ix/1 (1963), 16

A. Morgan: "Claude Thornhill," *JM*, viii/11 (1963), 11

G. T. Simon: *The Big Bands* (New York and London, 1967, rev. 4/1981)

I. Crosbie: "Prophet without Honor," *JJ*, xxiv (1971), no.3, p.6; no.4, p.28

C. Garrod: *Claude Thornhill and his Orchestra* (Spotswood, NJ, and Zephyrhills, FL, 1971, rev. 4/1996) [discography]

I. Crosbie: "Claude Thornhill," *Coda*, no.142 (1975), 2

P. D. Castle: *Aspects of Style in the Repertory of the Claude Thornhill Orchestra, 1940–1948* (diss., U. of Illinois, 1981)

J. Chambers: *Milestones*, i: *The Music and Times of Miles Davis to 1960* (Toronto, Buffalo, and London, 1983)

M. Zwerin: *Close Enough for Jazz* (London, 1983) [autobiography], 23

B. Crow: *From Birdland to Broadway: Scenes from a Jazz Life* (New York, and Oxford, England, 1992), 99

RONALD M. RADANO/BK

Thornton, Argonne. *See* HAKIM, SADIK.

Thornton, Clifford (Edward, III) (*b* Philadelphia, 6 Sept 1936; *d* Geneva, *c*1983). Cornetist and trumpeter. He played piano before taking up trumpet. After attending Temple University (1954–6) he worked with Ray Draper (1956–7), studied with Donald Byrd (1957), and toured Korea and Japan with an army band (1958–61). In New York he performed and recorded with Sun Ra (1962), worked with Pharoah Sanders (1963–7), and played with John Tchicai (1966); in December 1966 he recorded there on trombone and cornet with Marzette Watts (the album *Marzette Watts*, ESP 1044). Thornton formed the New Arts Ensemble, a free-jazz group, with which he recorded as a leader in 1967. Over the following years he appeared at a festival in Amougies, Belgium (1969), and performed and recorded in Paris with Dave Burrell and Sunny Murray (1969) and with Archie Shepp and his own band (1969–70); in 1970 he recorded an album with Shepp at the Antibes–Juan-les-Pins Jazz Festival (*Archie Shepp Live in Antibes*, BYG 529338–9). While a member of the faculty at Wesleyan University (1969–75) Thornton recorded again with Shepp (1972), wrote compositions, and led groups for both performances and recordings (1971, 1972, 1974). In 1976 he became an educational counselor at the African American Institute, an organization supported by UNESCO.

BIBLIOGRAPHY

Feather–Gitler '70s
V. Wilmer: "Clifford Thornton," *J&B*, ii/2 (1972), 12
P. Carles: "Clifford Thornton: pour l'exemple," *Jm*, no.208 (1973), 14 [incl. discography]
V. Wilmer: *As Serious as your Life: the Story of the New Jazz* (London, 1977, rev. [3]/1987)
D. Constant: "Clifford Thornton," *Jm* (1978), no.262, p.40; no.263, p.34 [incl. discography]

Thornton, (Hanson Lee) Steve (*b* New York, 1 Aug 1954). Percussionist. He was inspired to play conga and bongo drums after hearing recordings of Mongo Santamaria, with whom he toured and recorded from 1974 to 1976. From 1968 he worked regularly with New York salsa bands and also led his own group, the Young Explosives. In 1972 he toured the USA with the singer Jon Lucien and later joined Harry Belafonte's band, with which he toured and recorded as conga drummer for four years. Thornton has recorded with artists as diverse as the pop singers Anita Baker and Tracey Chapman, Carter Jefferson (1978), Dizzy Gillespie, Miles Davis (*You're Under Arrest*, 1984–5, Col. FC40023), Ronnie Cuber (1985), Michel Petrucciani (1987), and Greg Osby (1989); he may be seen performing with Davis at the New Orleans Jazz and Heritage Festival in the documentary video *Miles Ahead*, from the television series "Great Performances." He also worked regularly with Lonnie Liston Smith (1979–85), Tania Maria (1982–96), and McCoy Tyner (1985–8, including *Double Trios*, 1985, Denon CC33CY1128). Thornton's music incorporates a broad variety of ethnic styles, and he easily adapts to others, as is well evidenced in his work with the Malaysian group Raihan. (F. M. Coudert: "Les bleus de Miles," *Jm*, no.330 (1984), 40)

RUSS GIRSBERGER

Thornton, Teri [Avery, Shirley Enid] (*b* Detroit, 1 Sept 1934; *d* Englewood, NJ, 2 May 2000). Singer. She began playing piano and singing as a youngster, but did not perform professionally until she was 19. By the late 1950s she was working in Chicago. She moved to New York in 1960, and at the behest of Cannonball Adderley and Johnny Griffin she was recorded by Orrin Keepnews for Riverside. Her début album, *Devil may Care* (1960–61, Riv. 9352), was followed by a rendition of *Somewhere in the Night* (on the album of the same name, 1963, Dauntless 4306), which became a hit and served as the theme to the television program "Naked City." However, by the late 1960s Thornton's career was in decline, and around the mid-1970s she settled in southern California, where she worked outside of music. In 1979 she began performing again, and by the early 1980s she had returned to New York; later she appeared regularly at the restaurant clubs Zinno's and Cleopatra's Needle. Thornton was diagnosed with bladder cancer after collapsing during a performance at the Internationales Jazzfestival Bern in summer 1998. She made a temporary recovery and took first prize at the Thelonious Monk International Jazz Vocal Competition later that year; on the strength of this award she signed a contract with Verve, which released a recording that she had made independently in June 1997, *I'll be Easy to Find* (Verve 314-547755-2).

BIBLIOGRAPHY

J. Koransky: "Voice of Experience Wins Monk Competition," *DB*, lxv/12 (1998), 18
J. Wadler: "A Jazz Triumph after Decades of Bad Breaks," *New York Times* (6 Oct 1998)
P. Watrous: "Tearing Down the House at a Jazz Competition," *New York Times* (28 Sept 1998)
B. Holland: "Jazz Singer Teri Thornton Back in Business with New Verve Set," *Billboard*, cxi (25 Sept 1999), 18
<http://www.vervemusicgroup.com/afeatures/teri_thornton/main.html> (2000)
F. Jung: "My Conversation with Teri Thornton," <http://www.allaboutjazz.com/iviews/TThornton.htm> (2000)
Obituary, B. Ratliff, *New York Times* (7 May 2000)
A. Starita: "A Jazz Singer's Story," <http://salon.com/ent/music/feature/2000/02/01/thornton/index.html> (2000)

GK

Threadgill, Henry (Luther) (*b* Chicago, 15 Feb 1944). Alto saxophonist, composer, and leader. As a child he played percussion in street marching bands and taught himself to play piano; later he took up baritone saxophone, and he began clarinet in high school. In the early 1960s he played hard bop and free jazz in a sextet with Joseph Jarman and Roscoe Mitchell and performed with Muhal Richard Abrams's Experimental Band and Phil Cohran's Heritage Ensemble. Later in the decade he became a member of the Association for the Advancement of Creative Musicians and toured with the gospel singer Jo Jo Morris (1965–7). Following a period of military service (during which he played in an army rock band) he worked in the house band at a blues club in Chicago and recorded with Abrams. Threadgill then studied flute, piano, and composition at the American Conservatory of Music (gaining the BM) and at Governors State University. In 1971 he formed the coopera-

Henry Threadgill at the Royal Festival Hall, London, 1996

tive trio Reflection with Steve McCall and Fred Hopkins; after the group reassembled as Air in 1975 he toured and recorded regularly with it and also composed most of its repertory. In the mid-1970s he moved to New York, where he became the leader of the Windstring Ensemble and the Society Situation Orchestra. He worked as a sideman with Mitchell, Olu Dara, and David Murray (recording in 1980–82) and then founded a sextet (which in fact had seven members – Threadgill regarded the two drummers as one element of the ensemble – and which he indicated by calling the group the Henry Threadgill Sextett); its longstanding members were Hopkins, Diedre Murray, and Pheeroan akLaff, with Rasul Siddik, Craig Harris, Ray Anderson, Frank Lacy, John Betsch, and Reggie Nicholson among others who spent periods in the group. Around the late 1980s Threadgill contributed compositions to ROVA and to the American Jazz Orchestra.

In the 1990s Threadgill, who traveled widely, began to spend substantial periods each year in India; he established legal residence in Goa in 1994, though he continued to base his musical activities in the USA. From 1990 to 1995 he led his Very Very Circus, initially comprising french horn (played by Mark Taylor (i)), the leader's alto saxophone and flute, two electric guitars (Brandon Ross and Masujaa), two tubas (Edwin Rodriguez, Marcus Rojas), and drums; later he added two percussionists to the group. He then founded the Make a Move quintet, again including Ross. His three-movement work *Mix for Orchestra* was given its début by the Brooklyn Philharmonic Orchestra in 1993.

Threadgill constructs his solos around fragmentary motifs; although his improvisations are well thought out, his playing, with its dry but urgent tone, remains exciting. His compositions, which incorporate improvised elements, became increasingly complex in the 1980s. Those recorded by his Sextett (1982–9) reflect a concern with death and employ unpredictable voicings and rhythms that are determinedly askew.

SELECTED RECORDINGS

(most tracks recorded as leader composed by Threadgill)

As leader of Air (with S. McCall and F. Hopkins): *Air Song* (1975, Why Not 7123); *Air Time* (1977, Nessa 12); *Air Lore* (1979, AN 3014), incl. Buddy Bolden's Blues, King Porter Stomp, The Ragtime Dance, Weeping Willow Rag; *Air Mail* (1980, BS 0049); *80° Below '82* (1982, Ant. 1007); of New Air (with P. akLaff and F. Hopkins): *Air Show no.1* (1986, BS 0099)

As leader: *X-75 Volume 1* (1979, AN 3013); *When Was That?* (1982, About Time 1004); of Sextett: *Just the Facts and Pass the Bucket* (*c*1983, About Time 1005), *Subject to Change* (1984, About Time 1007), *You Know the Number* (1986, RCA Novus 3013-1-N); *Easily Slip into Another World* (1987, RCA Novus 3025-1-N); *Rag, Bush and All* (1988, Novus 3052-2-N); of Very Very Circus: *Spirit of Nuff . . . Nuff* (1990, BS 120134-2), *Live at Koncepts* (*c*1991, Taylor Made 10292), *Too Much Sugar for a Dime* (*c*1992, Axiom 314-514258-2), *Song out of my Trees* (1993, BS 120154-2); *Carry the Day* (*c*1994, Col. CK66995); of Very Very Circus and other groups: *Makin' a Move* (*c*1995, Col. CK67214); of Make a Move: *Where's your Cup?* (1996, Col. CK67617)

As sideman: M. R. Abrams: on *Young at Heart, Wise in Time* (1969, Del. 423), Wise in Time; R. Mitchell: on *Nonaah* (1976–7, Nessa 9–10), Nonaah (1977); M. R. Abrams: *1-0QA+19* (1977, BS 017); R. Mitchell: on *L-R-G, The Maze, S II Examples* (1978, Nessa 14-15), The Maze

BIBLIOGRAPHY

GrayF
J. Blum: "Henry Threadgill: Beyond Air," *JT* (1983), Sept, 10
G. Giddins: *Rhythm-a-ning: Jazz Tradition and Innovation in the '80s* (New York, and Oxford, England, 1985), 185
H. Mandel: "Henry Threadgill: Music to Make the Sun Come Up," *DB*, lii/7 (1985), 26 [incl. discography]
L. Van Trikt: "Henry Threadgill: Interview," *Cadence*, xi/9 (1985), 5
S. Buchanan: "Henry Threadgill," *Be-bop and Beyond*, iv/2 (1986), 21
F. Davis: *In the Moment: Jazz in the 1980s* (New York, and Oxford, England, 1986/*R*1996), 217
M. Smith: "Henry Threadgill," *Cadence*, xiv/10 (1988), 25
K. Lynch: "Henry Threadgill: Composer, Bandleader, and Alchemist," *DB*, lvi/2 (1989), 20 [incl. discography]
F. Davis: *Outcats: Jazz Composers, Instrumentalists, and Singers* (New York, and Oxford, England, 1990), 59
D. Rubien: "Threadgill's Circus Comes to Town," *San Francisco Chronicle* (2 May 1991)
W. Enstice and P. Rubin: *Jazz Spoken Here: Conversations with Twenty-two Musicians* (Baton Rouge, LA, and London, 1992), 282
L. Birnbaum: "Outside Moves In: Henry Threadgill Inks a Major-label Deal," *DB*, xlii/3 (1995), 16 [incl. discography]
L. Blumenfeld: "The Sideways: Henry Threadgill," *Jazziz*, xii/3 (1995), 22
J. Macnie: "Henry Threadgill: 'Global Jelly Roll' with the Bismarck of Jazz," *Musician*, no.197 (1995), 40
V. Tarrière: "Henry Threadgill: je ne suis un citoyen du monde," *Jm*, no.452 (1995), 33
D. Richardson: "Movin' Out," *San Francisco Bay Guardian* (26 June 1996), 61
T. Scherman: "Music Like Nobody Else's, Not for Everyone," *New York Times* (7 Jan 1996)

HOWARD MANDEL/BK

Three Blind Mice. Record label. Its parent company, TBM, was established in Japan in June 1970 by Takeshi ("Tee") Fuji, and by 1999 its headquarters were in Yokohama. Its more than 130 albums include recordings by such musicians as Hiroshi Fukumura, Nobuo Hara, Motohiko Hino, Terumasa Hino, Masaru Imada, Hideto Kanai, Fumio Karashima, George Kawaguchi, Hidehiko Matsumoto, Kosuke Mine, Toshiyuki Miyama, Kenji Mori, Teruo Nakamura, Toshio Oida, Shunzo Ono, George Otsuka, Isao Suzuki, Tatsuya Takahashi, Masayuki Takayanagi, Takao Uematsu, and Tsuyoshi Yamamoto.

GK

Three Deuces. The name of several nightclubs, notably ones in Chicago and New York; *see* NIGHTCLUBS AND OTHER VENUES.

Three Eddies. Tap-dancing trio. The leader of the act was Tiny (Earle) Ray (*b* New Jersey, 1887), who began his professional career as a child dancer in the act of Gussie Francis. The other two original members were Chick (Layburn) Horsey (*b* Chester, ?PA., 1903) and Shakey (Clarence) Beasley (*b* Orange, ?NJ, 1898). The group appeared in New York at Club Alabam (1924) and the Plantation (1925) before traveling to Europe with Sam Wooding and the show *Chocolate Kiddies*, which opened in Berlin on 20 May 1925. Beasley had been replaced by Charles Woody by the time they appeared in *Blackbirds of 1926* in Paris in May 1926. The Three Eddies remained with the show through its British run from September 1926 into 1927 and returned to Britain in 1930; they may be seen in the film *Elstree Calling* (1930) performing *Dance around in your bones* and *Doin' the new low-down*.

BIBLIOGRAPHY

B. H. Behncke: "Sam Wooding and the Chocolate Kiddies at the Thalia-Theater in Hamburg, 28th July, 1925 to 24th August, 1925," *Sv*, no.60 (1975), 214
H. Rye: "Visiting Firemen 9: the Blackbirds and their Orchestras," *Sv*, no.112 (1984), 133
S. Bourne: *Black in the British Frame: Black People in British Film and Television, 1896–1996* (London and Washington, DC, 1998), 69

HOWARD RYE

360 Degree Music Experience. Cooperative group formed in 1968 by BEAVER HARRIS with Grachan Moncur III and Dave Burrell.

Three Motions. Band formed from within the REFORM ART UNIT.

Three of a Kind. Cooperative trio formed in 1993 by the pianist Peter Madsen, the double bass player Dwayne Dolphin, and the drummer Bruce Cox, who had first worked together as the rhythm section of a group led by Fred Wesley (recording in 1992); they also toured and recorded with Wesley in 1994. Three of a Kind recorded an eponymous début album in 1993 (Minor Music 801039) and in 1996 made a second album, *Drip Some Grease* (Minor Music 801056); it also recorded in support of Stanley Turrentine (*c*1994) and the singer Annette Lowman (1995).

GK

Three Sounds. Instrumental trio. In 1956 the drummer Bill Dowdy formed a quartet, the Four Sounds. The following year this group became a trio, the Three Sounds; the other members were the pianist GENE HARRIS and the double bass player Andy Simpkins. In 1958 the ensemble traveled to New York, where it began making recordings and achieved considerable popularity, particularly among patrons of supper clubs. It specialized in playing standards, employing a swing style enlivened with occasional bop figures and hints of the blues. Among its best recordings are *Willow, weep for me* (which may be heard on the album *Introducing the Three Sounds*, 1958, BN 1600), and *Summertime* and *Poinciana* (from *Here we Come*, 1960, BN 84088), as well as the album *Blue Hour* (1960, BN 84057) made with Stanley Turrentine. It also recorded with the guest leaders Nat Adderley (1958), Lou Donaldson (1959), and Anita O'Day (1962). Dowdy left the group in 1966, as did Simpkins two years later; Harris led larger ensembles called the Three Sounds, which played jazz-rock, until 1974. (*Feather '60s*)

LEROY OSTRANSKY

Three T's. Group formed in 1936 by Jack and Charlie Teagarden and Frankie Trumbauer; *see* TEAGARDEN family, (2) JACK.

Thumb piano. *See* LAMELLAPHONE.

Tibbetts, Steve [Stephen Horton] (*b* Madison, WI, 3 Oct 1954). Guitarist, percussionist, and leader. Influenced by his father, who played folk guitar, he first learned ukulele and baritone ukulele. Self-taught as a guitarist, he took up that instrument at the age of 13, and in his teens he performed in local rock groups. He studied art at Macalester College in St. Paul, Minnesota, and while there produced his first recording (1975–6) and founded a record company, Frammis. After graduating in 1976 he remained in St. Paul, produced his second recording, and then from 1981 recorded for ECM. His long-time collaborator was the percussionist Marc Anderson. Tibbetts was a traveling faculty member of the Naropa Institute (based in Boulder, Colorado), and in this capacity he studied drumming in Indonesia (1988) and studied in Nepal and Bali (early 1990s); while in Nepal he recorded with a group of Tibetan Buddhist singers led by Choying Drolma (1994–6), and later he toured the USA with Drolma and two of her fellow nuns (1999).

Tibbetts's muse is strongly influenced by ethnic musics. His principal creative tool is really the recording studio; he is a master at using sound loops and other technological devices to manipulate and produce new sounds, and his recordings offer densely layered musical tapestries. His music is perhaps best understood as a combination of the early 1970s acoustic guitar work of John McLaughlin and the hard-rock playing of Jimi Hendrix, filtered through his own pan-cultural musical vision.

SELECTED RECORDINGS

Duos with M. Anderson: *Northern Song* (1981, ECM 1218)

As leader: *Steve Tibbetts* (1975–6, Frammis BZZ-77); *Yr* (1980, Frammis 1522-25); *Safe Journey* (1983, ECM 1270); *Exploded View* (1985–6, ECM 1335); *Big Map Idea* (1987–8, ECM 1380); *The Fall of Us All* (*c*1993, ECM 1527); with C. Drolma: *Chö* (1994–6, Hannibal 1404)

BIBLIOGRAPHY

J. Diliberto: "Profile: Steve Tibbetts," *DB*, xlvi/10 (1982), 53
D. Forte: "New Directions in Acoustic Steel-string: Steve Tibbetts," *GP*, xix/2 (1985), 82
J. Woodard: "Acoustic Rebirth: the Wooding of America," *Musician*, no.107 (1987), 52
A. Jones: "Steve Tibbetts: the New Faces," *Coda*, no.223 (1988–9), 30 [incl. discography]
D. Emerson: "Frets 'R' Us: Steve Tibbetts," *DB*, lvii/5 (1990), 24
J. Nash: "Steve Tibbetts: Musical Mapmaker," *JT* (1990), March, 9
J. Rotondi: "Eastern Aura Meets Midwestern Crunch: Steve Tibbetts," *GP*, xxxi/10 (1994), 77
D. Ouellette: "Tradin' Fours: Beaten, Squeezed & Stroked," *DB*, lxiv/3 (1997), 39
<http://members.aol.com/Cuneiform4/tibbetts.html> (1999)
<http://www.steppinin.com/> (1999)

GK

Tiberi, Frank (*b* Camden, NJ, 4 Dec 1928). Tenor saxophonist. He took lessons on clarinet from the age of eight and later studied bassoon with a member of the Philadelphia Orchestra, but he was self-taught on saxophone and flute; when he was 12 his father died, and he subsequently began working professionally to help support the family. After graduating from high school he played with the bandleader Bob Chester (1948–9), Benny Goodman's small group (1954–5), Urbie Green (who had then taken over Goodman's group, with Rolf Kühn as clarinetist), and Dizzy Gillespie (late 1950s, in Philadelphia). During the 1960s Tiberi worked as a freelance musician on the East Coast and in film and television studios, and in October 1969 he joined Woody Herman's band as lead tenor saxophonist, though he also played bassoon and flute. In the 1970s and 1980s he toured Europe with Herman and recorded and performed at jazz festivals in Monterey (1970, 1979) and Japan (1982); he is heard to advantage on Herman's album *Thundering Herd* (1974, Fan. 9452). One of Herman's longest-serving sidemen, Tiberi led the band during Herman's absences (1977, 1986, 1987) and after his death, and he has written a number of arrangements for it. While continuing to lead the group, which in 1996 gave a performance at the JVC Jazz Festival in New York to some acclaim, Tiberi made his first album as a leader around 1999 (*Tiberian Mode*, NY Jam [unnumbered]), with Joe Lovano and George Garzone as fellow tenor saxophone soloists and a rhythm section that consisted of either Andy LaVerne or James Williams, Ray Drummond, and Adam Nussbaum. He teaches at the Berklee College of Music.

See also BASSOON.

BIBLIOGRAPHY

Feather–Gitler '70s
S. Woolley: "The Reign of Tiberi," *MM* (5 Nov 1977), 48
G. Endress: "Frank Tiberi," *JP*, xxvi/10 (1987), 3
"Heard from the Herd," *CI*, xxiv/12 (1987), 24
W. D. Clancy with A. C. Kenton: *Woody Herman: Chronicles of the Herds* (New York and elsewhere, 1995), 279
S. Woolley: "Frank Tiberi," *JJI*, liii/2 (2000), 20

BK

Timbales. A pair of cylindrical, single-headed drums used in Latin American dance music, and in fusions of this music with rock and soul. The instrument has also been employed in Afro-Cuban jazz: Machito included timbales among the many percussion instruments in his orchestras from the 1940s to the 1980s, and the percussionist Willie Bobo often played the instrument (on, for example, his album *Bobo's Beat*, 1963, Roul. 52097).

Time (i). A word loosely used for meter and sometimes also applied in other contexts to do with rhythm and tempo (*see* BEAT); a member of the rhythm section who plays with rhythmic accuracy, consistency, and fluency is often said to have "good time." Also, in notated jazz, an instruction indicating that the drummer should maintain a conventional accompanimental pattern (e.g., swing rhythm), rather than supplying a particular accentuation reinforcing a motif played by the ensemble; used in this sense, "time" stands in opposition to the term "figure" (*see* NOTATION, §5(iv)).

RICK FINLAY

Time (ii). Record company and label. The company was established in New York in 1960; until operations ceased around 1966 it produced a series of excellent albums under the artistic direction of Bob Shad. The catalogue included material by Max Roach, Kenny Dorham, Booker Little, Sonny Clark, Tommy Turrentine, Stanley Turrentine, Terry Gibbs, Marian McPartland, and Bennie Green. A few of the discs were also released by Oriole in the UK. Time's masters were comprehensively reissued (in replicas of the original liners) in Japan in the 1980s.

MARK GARDNER

Timeless. Record company and label. The company was founded in 1975 in Wageningen, the Netherlands, by Wim Wigt. Although it has recorded the work of ensembles as diverse as Lionel Hampton's swing orchestra and Machito's salsa band, the company's principal series of issues is devoted to bop, especially hard bop, and in its first decade it offered important recordings by such artists as Cedar Walton, Art Blakey, and George Adams; Tommy Flanagan, Pharoah Sanders, and Archie Shepp are among those who recorded for the label in later years. A second, smaller series consists of traditional-jazz and swing recordings led by such musicians as Chris Barber (who prepared a historical anthology for the label), Papa Bue, and Peanuts Hucko. In the 1990s Timeless established the subsidiary labels World Wide Jazz and, for both jazz and classical music, Limetree. By the turn of the new century it had issued more than 600 albums.

The company also sponsored the Timeless All Stars, a sextet formed by Wigt around 1981. Its original members were Harold Land, Curtis Fuller, Bobby Hutcherson, Walton, Buster Williams, and Billy Higgins. The group recorded two albums (1982–3) and toured Europe regularly in the 1980s, but seldom performed in the USA. In 1989 it involved George Bohanan rather than Fuller and David Williams rather than Buster Williams, but it seems to have been inactive after 1992, when it appeared at a festival in South Carolina.

BIBLIOGRAPHY

P. Carles: "Deux faces du disque: Timeless, Hat Hut," *Jm*, no.338 (1985), 42
J. Hamlin: "The Timeless All Stars: Famed Jazzmen Set for a Rare Gig," *San Francisco Chronicle Datebook* (13 April 1986), 20
D. Zych: "Label Watch: Timeless Swing," *JT*, xxiii/1 (1993), 26
<http://www.timeless-records.com> (2000)

BK

Timely Tunes. Record label. It was a subsidiary of RCA Victor and was operational between April and July 1931. Among its 41 issues were recordings by Dave Nelson and Blanche Calloway that were made specifically for Timely Tunes and not put out on any other labels in the Victor group. (B. Rust: "A Glimpse of the Past: Sunrise and Timely Tunes," *Sv*, no.16 (1968), 17)

HOWARD RYE

Timmons, Bobby [Robert Henry] (*b* Philadelphia, 19 Dec 1935; *d* New York, 1 March 1974). Pianist and composer. The son of a minister, he learned piano from the age of six and later served as a church organist, an experience which clearly helped to shape his future jazz playing. After moving to New York (1954) he played bop with Kenny Dorham's Jazz Prophets (February–April 1956), Chet Baker (April 1956 – January 1957), Sonny Stitt (February–August 1957), and Maynard Ferguson (August 1957 – March 1958). While a member of Art Blakey's Jazz Messengers (July 1958 – September 1959), with whom he toured Europe, he became well known for his composition *Moanin'*, a funky, gospel-oriented tune; at this same time the piece was further popularized by Lambert, Hendricks, and Ross, with Jon Hendricks setting lyrics to Timmons's melody. From October 1959 to February 1960 Timmons worked with Cannonball Adderley and recorded two further soul-jazz compositions that became hits, *This here* (also called *Dis here*) and *Dat dere*. He was with Blakey again from March 1960 through June 1961, and began to work and to record as a leader, but thereafter his career declined rapidly, because of alcoholism and artistic frustration: Timmons was a sophisticated and versatile pianist, but he became stereotyped and inhibited by the success of his simple compositions.

SELECTED RECORDINGS

As leader: *This Here is Bobby Timmons* (1960, Riv. 317); *Easy Does It* (1961, Riv. 9363)

As sideman: K. Dorham: *'Round about Midnight at the Cafe Bohemia* (1956, BN 1524); C. Baker: *Chet Baker and Crew* (1956, PJ 1224); Lee Morgan: *The Cooker* (1957, BN 1578); P. Adams: *10 to 4 at the Five Spot* (1958, Riv. 265); A. Blakey: *With the Jazz Messengers* (1958, BN 4003), incl. Moanin'; *At the Jazz Corner of the World* (1959, BN 4015–6); C. Adderley: *The Cannonball Adderley Quintet in San Francisco* (1959, Riv. 311), incl. This here, Hi-fly; *Them Dirty Blues* (1960, Riv. 1170), incl. Dat dere; Lee Morgan: *Leeway* (1960, BN 4034); A. Blakey: *The Freedom Rider* (1961, BN 84156); *Jazz Messengers* (1961, Imp. 7), incl. I hear a rhapsody, You don't know what love is; K. Dorham: *Matador* (1962, UA 15007), incl. Melanie

BIBLIOGRAPHY

B. Gardner: "Timmons in a Tempest," *DB*, xxvii/24 (1960), 14
M. Gardner: "Timmons: Soul and Honesty," *MM* (30 March 1974), 20
Obituaries: *DB*, xli/7 (1974), 10; *New York Times* (2 March 1974)
P. Keepnews: "Remember Bobby," *Moanin'* (Mlst. 47031, 1975) [liner notes]
M. Hennessey: "The Enduring Message of Abdullah Ibn Buhaina," *JJI*, xxx/9 (1977), 8
L. Feather: "Bobby Timmons," *CK*, vi/8 (1980), 48

BK

Timpani. Kettledrums which are capable of producing notes of definite pitch; these may be altered by tightening or slackening the drumhead by means of screws or other mechanisms. Timpani have occasionally been used in jazz; *see* DRUM SET, §I, 9.

Tinkler, Scott (Cameron) (*b* Melbourne, Australia, 2 Oct 1965). Australian trumpeter and composer. He began performing professionally in 1983, working in small groups with Mark Simmonds, Dale Barlow, and Paul Grabowsky, as well as with Billy Harper, Steve Lacy, and others. In 1993 in Melbourne he formed his own quartet, which recorded two successful albums; he then recorded with his trio in Sydney. Tinkler toured Europe and the USA in 1997, when he recorded at the Knitting Factory in New York, and then spent 18 months teaching and performing in Europe. After returning to Australia he settled in Byron Bay. He has also performed in Africa and Asia.

SELECTED RECORDINGS

As leader: *Back of my Head* (1994, Origin 05), *Hop to the Cow* (1994, Origin 013); *Dance of Delulian* (1996, Origin 028); *Tabas* (1997, ABC 823055-2); *Sofa King* (1997, Origin 046); with Ian Chaplin: *The Future in Today* (1997, Jazzhead Mush 33082)

As sideman: Australian Art Orchestra: *Ringing the Bell Backwards* (1994, Origin 008); M. Simmonds: *Fire* (1994, Birdland 002)

ROGER T. DEAN

Tinney, Al(len) (*b* Ansonia, CT, 28 May 1921). Pianist. As a child performer he appeared in the original production of Gershwin's *Porgy and Bess* in 1935. In the forefront of the movement that crystallized into the bop idiom, he led the house band from 1939 to 1943 at Monroe's Uptown House in New York; at various times it included Charlie Parker, Max Roach, Little Benny Harris, George Treadwell, and the trumpeter Victor Coulsen. Although Tinney's professional studio work is limited to a single session with the singer Clarence Palmer and the Jive Bombers in 1957, his harmonically advanced, flowing, and lightly percussive style mark him as an important forerunner of such early modern pianists as Bud Powell, George Wallington, Al Haig, and Duke Jordan. Repelled by the influence of drugs in jazz, from 1946 he turned increasingly to commercial music. In 1968 he settled in Buffalo, New York, where he has remained active, performing regularly with local and visiting jazz musicians. He has also held positions as co-director of an instrumental music program at a New York state prison detention center and as lecturer at SUNY Buffalo; he received an honorary doctorate from Buffalo State College in May 1999. In January 2000 Tinney and the singer Peggy Farrell made a new album at Fanny's, a restaurant where he works on Saturdays (*Peg & Al: the Al Tinney Trio with Peggy Farrell*, Border City 1000).

BIBLIOGRAPHY

L. Feather: *Inside Be-bop* (New York, 1949/R1977 as *Inside Jazz*), 15

D. Gillespie and A. Frazer: *To be, or not . . . to Bop: Memoirs* (Garden City, NY, 1979, London, 1980, as *Dizzy: the Autobiography of Dizzy Gillespie*), 205

J. Patrick: "Al Tinney, Monroe's Uptown House, and the Emergence of Modern Jazz in Harlem," *ARJS*, ii (1983), 150

I. Gitler: *Swing to Bop: an Oral History of the Transition in Jazz in the 1940s* (New York, and Oxford, England, 1985), 77

S. DeVeaux: *The Birth of Bebop: a Social and Musical History* (Berkeley, Los Angeles, and London, 1997)

B. Donaldson: "Allen Tinney Interview," *Cadence*, xxvi/5 (2000), 17

JAMES PATRICK

Tio. Family of musicians active in New Orleans.

(1) Papa [Antoine Louis] **Tio** (*b* Eureka Colony, Mexico, 4 Feb 1862; *d* New Orleans, 10 July 1922). Clarinetist, brother of (2) Lorenzo Tio, Sr. Kinzer (1993) reports that Tio signed his name Louis and believes that jazz writers have assumed that he spelt it Luis on account of his Mexican birth; his parents were born in Louisiana, and as "free persons of color" they were able to emigrate to Mexico in 1859. Tio received tuition in classical music before the family returned to New Orleans around 1878. Later he made a national tour with the Georgia Minstrels (1887) and was a member of the Excelsior Brass Band (mid-1880s–1890s) and the Lyre Club Symphony Orchestra (1890s). He may have played in a dance band led by Manuel Manetta as early as 1910 and certainly performed alongside Peter Bocage in Manetta's band at the Tuxedo Dance Hall from 1912 to 1913, after which he retired from dance-band work. It is possible that he worked with John Robichaux late in his career. By 1910 Tio had adapted his playing to the emerging jazz idiom and was working successfully as a teacher of the "split-time" style; among his pupils were Achille and George Baquet, Barney Bigard, and Albert Nicholas.

Oral history material in *LNT*.

BIBLIOGRAPHY

ChartersJ

[J. De Donder:] "The Second Hundred Years, no.4: the Tio Family," *Fn*, xix/6 (1988), 27; contd in *New Orleans Music*, iv/3 (1993), 14

C. E. Kinzer: *The Tio Family: Four Generations of New Orleans Musicians, 1814–1922* (diss., Louisiana State U., 1993)

——: "The Tios of New Orleans and their Pedagogical Influence on the Early New Orleans Clarinet Style," *Black Music Research Journal*, xvi/2 (1996), 279

R. H. Knowles: *Fallen Heroes: a History of New Orleans Brass Bands* (New Orleans, 1996)

(2) (Augustin) Lorenzo Tio, Sr. (*b* Tampico, Mexico, 28 Aug 1867; *d* New Orleans, 10 June 1908). Clarinetist, brother of (1) Papa Tio. He had formal music lessons before his family returned to New Orleans around 1878 and received additional tuition from his brother. From the mid-1880s into the 1890s he played E♭ clarinet with the Excelsior Brass Band, and in 1889 he was a founding member of the Lyre Club Symphony Orchestra. He worked intermittently with John Robichaux from 1898 and toured with a minstrel company around 1900. Tio was noted in the Creole music community for the purity of his tone, the excellence of his musicianship, and his influence as a teacher.

Oral history material in *LNT*.

BIBLIOGRAPHY

ChartersJ

[J. De Donder:] "The Second Hundred Years, no.4: the Tio Family," *Fn*, xix/6 (1988), 27; contd in *New Orleans Music*, iv/3 (1993), 14

C. E. Kinzer: *The Tio Family: Four Generations of New Orleans Musicians, 1814–1922* (diss., Louisiana State U., 1993)

——: "The Tios of New Orleans and their Pedagogical Influence on the Early New Orleans Clarinet Style," *Black Music Research Journal*, xvi/2 (1996), 279

R. H. Knowles: *Fallen Heroes: a History of New Orleans Brass Bands* (New Orleans, 1996)

(3) Lorenzo (Anselmo) Tio, Jr. (*b* New Orleans, 21 April 1893; *d* New York, 24 Dec 1933). Clarinetist, son of (2) Lorenzo Tio, Sr. He was brought up in Bay St. Louis, Mississippi, but returned to his birthplace in New Orleans during late childhood. By the time he was nine he was playing in parade bands. From about 1910 he performed occasionally with Freddie Keppard's Olympia Orchestra and regularly in the Onward Brass Band, which he joined after a brief period with Papa Celestin and Bebe Ridgley's Tuxedo Brass Band. He worked at a dance hall, the 102 Ranch, first with Keppard (*c* November 1912–1913) and then with Celestin and Ridgley's dance band (1914–15), which continued from autumn 1915 under Ridgley alone. After spending about two years in Chicago (1916 – summer 1918) working with Charlie Elgar and Manuel Perez he returned to New Orleans and resumed playing with Celestin and Ridgley. He worked in the Maple Leaf Orchestra in 1919, then became a member of A. J. Piron's orchestra, with which he also played in New York; his recordings with this group reveal his instrumental brilliance. When Piron finally left the group in 1928 it continued in New Orleans as the Creole Serenaders. In 1930 Tio decided to settle in New York, where in 1932–3 he held a residency at the Nest Club. His most lasting influence came through the success of his many pupils, who included Paul Barnes, Barney Bigard, Louis Cottrell, Jr, Jimmie Noone, Omar Simeon, Albert Nicholas, Darnell Howard, Harold Dejan, and Don Albert. It is also said that he supplied Duke Ellington, via Bigard, with ideas for several compositions, most notably a sketch for the second theme of *Mood Indigo*.

Oral history material in *LNT*.

For illustrations *see* Bands, fig.1, and Brass band, fig.1.

SELECTED RECORDINGS

(all as sideman with A. J. Piron)

Bouncing Around (1923, OK 40021); New Orleans Wiggle (1923, Vic. 19233); Bright Star Blues (1924, Col. 99D); Lou'siana Swing (1924, OK 40189); Red Man Blues (1925, Vic. 19646)

BIBLIOGRAPHY

ChartersJ
B. Bigard: *With Louis and the Duke*, ed. B. Martyn (London, 1985)
[J. De Donder:] "The Second Hundred Years, 4: the Tio Family," *Fn*, xix/6 (1988), 27; contd in *New Orleans Music*, iv/3 (1993), 14
C. E. Kinzer: *The Tio Family: Four Generations of New Orleans Musicians, 1814–1922* (diss., Louisiana State U., 1993)
——: "The Tios of New Orleans and their Pedagogical Influence on the Early Jazz Clarinet Style," *Black Music Research Journal*, xvi/2 (1996), 279

ALDEN ASHFORTH/BK (1, 2), JOHN CHILTON/BK (3)

Tiple [tipple]. A small guitar of Spain, Colombia, Guatemala, Puerto Rico, and Venezuela. Although the tiple's size and tuning are not standard, the instrument usually has four metal strings (or four courses, each consisting of two or three strings), which are tuned to the same pitches as the four upper strings of the guitar. The most important tiple players in jazz were three members of the Spirits of Rhythm, Leo Watson and the brothers Wilbur Daniels and Douglas Daniels, who played tiples with courses of multiple strings; like the group's guitarist, Teddy Bunn, they generally did not use a plectrum, even when one string alone was used to play a solo. The tiples provided the group with a chordal backing that was lighter than that afforded by guitars in other string bands; the instrument was also well suited to the playing of incisive solos, which tonally were reminiscent of those played on the mandolin, but which had a somewhat deeper timbre. The Spirits' recording of *I'll be ready when the great day comes* (1933, Bruns. 6728), on which solos are taken alternately on tiple and guitar, demonstrates clearly the contrasting sound of the two instruments. The tiple was seldom used in jazz after the late 1930s, though it was revived briefly in the early 1970s by the English blues singer and guitarist Alexis Korner.

BIBLIOGRAPHY

R. Brown: "Jazz at the Docks," *JJ*, xxv/4 (1972), 28
M. Jones: Liner notes, *The Spirits of Rhythm, 1933–34* (JSP 1088, 1985)

ALYN SHIPTON

Tippett, Keith (Grahame) (*b* Bristol, England, 25 Aug 1947). English pianist, composer, and leader. He learned classical piano between the ages of four and 18 and joined the choir at St Thomas the Martyr Beckett in Bristol when he was five; he also played tenor horn between the ages of 13 and 18 and studied classical organ for three years from the age of 16. After playing traditional jazz and bop in Bristol he moved to London in 1967. The following year he met Marc Charig, the trombonist Nick Evans, and Elton Dean at a jazz summer school in Barry in south Wales, and he subsequently formed a sextet with these three musicians, plus the double bass player Jill Lyons and the drummer Alan Jackson; among the group's later personnel were the double bass players Jeff Clyne, Roy Babbington, and Harry Miller and the drummers Bryan Spring and John Marshall. In November 1970 Tippett assembled a 50-piece orchestra, Centipede, which featured jazz, rock, and classical musicians and remained active until 1976. From 1971 to the late 1970s he led the trio Ovary Lodge, initially with Babbington and the percussionist Frank Perry; later he was joined by his wife, Julie Tippetts, and Babbington was replaced by Miller. During this decade Tippett was virtually the house pianist for the London-based label Ogun, and his 22-piece orchestra Ark (from 1978) featured almost all of its artists. In the same period he played in duos with, among others, Stan Tracey (as T'n'T, recording in 1974), Howard Riley, and Hans Reichel and in ensembles led by Trevor Watts, Dean, Dudu Pukwana, Miller, Peter Brötzmann, Evans, Louis Moholo, and Riley; he recorded with all of these group leaders (except Brötzmann) between 1974 and 1981.

In the 1980s Tippett worked increasingly in trios and duos and as an unaccompanied soloist. He made a three-volume series of albums as a soloist, *Mujician* (named after his young daughter's description of his profession), and recorded in a duo with Moholo and in trios with Moholo and the saxophonist Larry Stabbins, Julie Tippetts and Maggie Nicols, and Tippetts and the German percussionist Willi Kellers. At the end of the decade he formed an improvising quartet with Paul Dunmall, Tony Levin, and Paul Rogers to which he transferred the name Mujician. In 1991 this group, joined by Tippetts, visited Tbilisi in Georgia to play with 12 local musicians and then returned with them to perform in London and at the Bath International Music Festival. Tippett also recorded (1990) and performed at the Knitting Factory, New York (1991) in a duo with Andy Sheppard.

As well as performing with Mujician in the 1990s Tippett played with and arranged for the Dedication Orchestra (alongside Moholo, among others, celebrating South African jazz in Britain), appeared worldwide as an unaccompanied soloist, worked in Dunmall's octet, and was a member of a quartet with Evan Parker. In 1995 the Kreutzer String Quartet commissioned Tippett to write a piano quintet; the performance of the work, *Linückia*, at the Bath International Music Festival in 1996 was later broadcast on BBC Radio 3. In April 1996 Mujician toured South Africa and performed with the South African group Ingoma, and the following year it toured with Ingoma in Britain. In 1997 Tippett formed the 21-piece orchestra Tapestry to perform his composition *First Weaving*. In September 1999 he appeared at a Soft Machine tribute concert in Germany in a quartet (with Dean, the electric bass guitarist Hugh Hopper, and Marshall) which was retrospectively named SoftWare. He was the artistic director of the Rare Music Club in Bristol in the late 1990s and taught at the Dartington International Summer School and the Welsh College of Music and Drama.

SELECTED RECORDINGS

As unaccompanied soloist: *Mujician* (1981, FMP SAJ37); *Mujician III (August Air)* (1987, FMP CD12); *The Dartington Concert* (1990, Editions EG 2106); *Friday the Thirteenth* (1997, Nippon Rediffusion Ltd 10001)

Duos: with Peter Fairclough: *Wild Silk* (1995, ASC 8); with J. Tippetts: *Couple in Spirit II* (1996, ASC 12)

As leader: *Dedicated to You but You Weren't Listening* (1971, Vertigo 6360 024); of Centipede: *Septober Energy* (1971, RCA Neon 9); of Ark: *Frames (Music for an Imaginary Film)* (1978, Ogun 003/004); with W. Kellers and J. Tippetts: *Twilight Etchings* (1993, FMP CD65); of Mujician: *Colours Fulfilled* (1997, Cuneiform Rune 102)

BIBLIOGRAPHY

CarrJ; *ChiltonB*; *WickesIBJ*, i
R. Cotterell, ed.: *Jazz Now: the Jazz Centre Society Guide* (London, 1976), 174
K. Ansell: "No Gossip from the Mujician," *The Wire*, no.2 (1982), 10
P. Renaud: *La discographie du jazz anglais* (Chaumont, France, 1985)
E. Jost: *Europas Jazz, 1960–1980* (Frankfurt am Main, Germany, 1987), 331
B. Morton: "A Partnership of Note," *Sunday Times* (19 July 1992)
M. Chenard: "Now & Then: Keith Tippett," *Coda*, no.258 (1994), 12
D. Albert: "Jazz: Jazz Brotherhood Play Jo'burg," *The Star* [Johannesburg] (24 April 1996)
<http://www.alpes-net.fr/%7Ebigbang/musicians/keithtippett.html> (2000) [incl. discography]
<http://www.shef.ac.uk/misc/rec/ps/efi/mtippett.html> (2000) [incl. discography]

MARK GILBERT

Tippetts [née, Driscoll], **Julie (Dawn)** (*b* London, 8 June 1947). English singer. Encouraged by her father, the trumpeter Reg Driscoll, she sang in London coffee bars from 1959, and she performed with his band in 1963. After singing with Brian Auger in the rhythm-and-blues band Steampacket from 1964 to 1966 she became a member of the Brian Auger Trinity, when the singers Rod Stewart and Long John Baldry left in the latter year; she enjoyed international success with the group's version of Bob Dylan's *This Wheel's on Fire* (1968). She left the group after an American tour in 1968 and returned to England, where the following year she released her first solo album. In 1970 she married the pianist Keith Tippett; she collaborated with him in Centipede (1970–75), Ovary Lodge (from 1973), and Ark (1975–8), and also performed with him in a duo, occasionally contributing lyrics. In 1975–6 she sang with her own group, Butterfly, and in 1976 she formed the vocal quartet Voice with Maggie Nicols, Brian Ely, and Phil Minton; she also worked with the Spontaneous Music Ensemble (1971), Carla Bley (recording in 1973–4), Harry Miller (recording in 1978), Derek Bailey and Company (1982), and Working Week (1984–5). From the mid-1980s she has performed and recorded with her husband in a duo and in a trio, the third member of which is at different times Nicols, the drummer Willi Kellers, or Louis Moholo; she also performs unaccompanied and in a duo with Nicols, and has recorded an album of poetry as part of John Wolf Brennan's Hextet. From the 1970s Tippetts moved away from the blues and rock style of her early work and began to favor wordless, free improvisation, creating contrapuntal interplay with other members of the ensemble; her performances are remarkable for their total improvisation, stark contrasts of range, technique, timbre, and volume, and intense delivery.

SELECTED RECORDINGS

As unaccompanied soloist: *Shadow Puppeteer* (1999, La Cooka Ratcha 101)
Duos: with M. Nicols: *Sweet and S'ours* (1978, FMP SAJ38); with K. Tippett: *Couple in Spirit* (1987, Editions EG 52)
As leader: *1969* (1969, Pol. 2383077); *Sunset Glow* (1975, Utopia 601); with K. Tippett and M. Nicols: *Mr Invisible and the Drunken Sheilas* (1987, FMP SAJ61)
As sideman with J. W. Brennan: *Through the Ear of a Raindrop* (1997, Leo 254)

BIBLIOGRAPHY

P. Renaud: *La discographie du jazz anglais* (Chaumont, France, 1985)

SIMON ADAMS

Tiptoe. A subsidiary record label of Enja.

Tissendier, Claude (*b* Toulouse, France, 1 Oct 1952). French clarinetist, saxophonist, arranger, and leader. From 1969 to 1975, while playing in local jazz groups, he pursued classical studies at the conservatory in Toulouse. On his arrival in Paris in 1977 he joined Claude Bolling's big band and then played with other big bands: Ornicar, Gérard Badini's Swing Machine, those of Jean-Loup Longnon and François Laudet, and others. In 1983 he formed a group in homage to John Kirby, and the album it made in 1985 received considerable critical acclaim. Three years later Tissendier founded the group Saxomania (comprising four saxophones and rhythm section) to perform the repertory of swing and bop in original arrangements. Its recordings provided him with the opportunity to collaborate with several important soloists, notably Benny Carter, Spike Robinson, Phil Woods, Guy Lafitte, and Clark Terry. With its leader playing in a style which drew both from the classic elegance of Carter and from the dexterity of Charlie Parker, Saxomania interpreted the music of Benny Goodman's quartet (1993) as well as that of Duke Ellington, Billy Strayhorn, and Johnny Hodges (1996). In 1997 the group toured the UK and Scandinavia.

SELECTED RECORDINGS

As leader: *Tribute to John Kirby* (1985, Ida 006); *Saxomania featuring Benny Carter* (1988, Ida 017); *Saxomania featuring Spike Robinson* (1989, Sacem 1522); *Saxomania featuring Phil Woods* (1991, Ida 031); *Saxomania featuring Guy Lafitte* (1993, Ida 038); *Saxomania featuring Clark Terry* (1995, Ida 040); *Swingtime* (1998, Djazz 710); *Carrots for Hodges* (1999, Djazz 716); *Ellington Moods* (1999, Frémeaux 433)
As sideman: C. Bolling: *Black, Brown and Beige* (1989, Adès 671); *Cinemadreams* (1995, Milan 35501); *A Drum is a Woman* (1996, Milan 40906)

BIBLIOGRAPHY

D. Waterhouse: "French Polish," *JJI*, xxxviii/11 (1985), 16
M. Richard: "A propos de John Kirby," *Jazz Swing Journal*, no.3 (1987), 26
"Encyclopédie permanente *Jazzmag*," *Jm*, no.390 (1990), 51
A. Legrand: "Claude Tissendier: gardien de la flamme," *Jazzman*, no.20 (1996), 16
"Swingtime-Interview," *Jh*, no.564 (1999), 29

ANDRÉ CLERGEAT

Tite, B. D. (*b* Louisville, KY, *c*1870; *d* Louisville, *c*1935). Jug blower, banjoist, and guitarist. He began playing banjo with string bands around 1888. In the mid-1890s he rambled through the South and took up the jug after hearing it played as an instrument in southwest Virginia while working with the fiddler Cy Anderson. Anderson's group reached Louisville in 1900, after which it resumed touring along the Ohio and Mississippi rivers. Tite took over the band when Anderson retired in 1909. In 1917 he disbanded and joined Whistler's Jug Band, with which he made recordings in 1924, including *Jerry o'Mine* (Gen. 5554) and *I'm a Jazz Baby* (Gen. 5614). He gave up jug blowing in 1925 and thereafter played only occasionally on banjo or guitar. He is thought to have been the first professional jug blower in Louisville and the originator there of the jug-band tradition.

BIBLIOGRAPHY

L. Wright, comp. [from material supplied by F. Cox, J. Randolph, and J. Harris]: *The Jug Bands of Louisville* (Chigwell, England, 1993 [*recte* 1994])
F. Cox, J. Randolph, and J. Harris: "The Jug Bands of Louisville," *Sv* (1993), no.155, p.164; no.156, p.204; (1994), no.157, p.4; no.158, p.43; no.159, p.83; no.160, p.145; (1995), no.161, p.188; no.162, p.203
B. Bogert: Liner notes, *Clifford Hayes & the Louisville Jug Bands*, i–iv (RST 1501-2, 1502-2, 1503-2, 1504-2, 1994)

HOWARD RYE

Tizol, Juan [Vincente Martinez] (*b* San Juan, 22 Jan 1900; *d* Inglewood, CA, 23 April 1984). Valve trombonist and composer. After working in a municipal concert orchestra in San Juan he moved to the USA in 1920 and worked for a long period at the Howard Theatre in Washington, where he met Duke Ellington. He played briefly with Bobby Lee's Cotton Pickers and the White Brothers Band, then joined Ellington in September 1929. He left to join Harry James in April 1944 and thereafter spent most of his time alternating between the two bands, interspersed among periods working with other leading artists, such as Louie Bellson and Pearl Bailey, and as a studio musician. He was with Ellington from March 1951 to late 1953 and again in 1960 and 1961. He retired to California and later lived in Las Vegas.

In February 1953 Tizol and the band's new double bass player Charles Mingus started a dangerous fight (Tizol with a machete, Mingus with a fire axe); Ellington, showing no hesitation about whom he felt was more valuable to the band, immediately fired Mingus. Tizol was rarely heard playing solos with Ellington's orchestra, but his large, yet unassertive, tone and great mobility made him a key voice in the ensemble. He contributed a number of compositions to the band, such as *Moonlight Fiesta*, *Pyramid*, *Caravan*, and *Perdido*; the latter two have become standards. These works, with their Latin-American melodies and rhythms, reflect Tizol's Puerto Rican background, and his thematic statements on such numbers as *Caravan* and *Moonlight Fiesta* delineate their exotic mood perfectly. Tizol's film appearance on *Caravan* is revealing not merely because of the opportunity to see the composer and player in action, but because Ellington's approach to the structure of the piece diverges significantly and engagingly from the regularized 64-bar *aaba* popular-song form that *Caravan* normally takes in its countless manifestations as a jazz standard.

Oral history material in *CtY*, *NjR* (JOHP).

For illustrations *see* Bands, fig.3; Trombone; and Trumpet.

SELECTED RECORDINGS

As sideman: D. Ellington: Twelfth Street Rag (1931, Bruns. 6038); Caravan (1937, Master 131); Lost in Meditation (1938, Bruns. 8083); Pyramid (1938, Bruns. 8168); Battle of Swing (1938, Bruns. 8923); Raincheck (1941, Vic. 27880); *Duke Ellington and his Orchestra* (1941, Temple 550), incl. Perdido; The Coronets: Moonlight Fiesta (1951, Mercer 1967)

SELECTED FILMS AND VIDEOS

Check and Double Check (1930); Bundle of Blues (1933); Belle of the Nineties [It Ain't No Sin] (1934); Murder at the Vanities (1934); Symphony in Black (1934); Duke Ellington and his Orchestra (1943); Reveille with Beverly (1943); Caravan (1952); The Hawk Talks (1952); The Mooche (1952); Mood Indigo (1952); Solitude (1952); Sophisticated Lady (1952); V.I.P.'s Boogie (1952)

BIBLIOGRAPHY

McCarthyB; *SchullerS*; *TuckerDE*

S. Dance: *The World of Duke Ellington* (London and New York, 1970/*R*1981)

D. Ellington: *Music is my Mistress* (Garden City, NY, 1973, rev. 2/1982)

K. R. Dietrich: *Joe "Tricky Sam" Nanton, Juan Tizol and Lawrence Brown: Duke Ellington's Great Trombonists, 1926–1951* (diss., U. of Wisconsin, 1989)

K. Dietrich: *Duke's Bones: Ellington's Great Trombonists* (Rottenburg, Germany, 1995)

EDDIE LAMBERT/BK

Tjader, Cal(len Radcliffe, Jr.) (*b* St. Louis, 16 July 1925; *d* Manila, 5 May 1982). Vibraphonist and leader. His parents performed in vaudeville shows (his father was a dancer and his mother had been an aspiring concert pianist), and at the age of four Tjader worked with them as a tap-dancer. He later expressed regret for playing little attention to the piano lessons he received from his mother after they moved to the West Coast to open a dance studio. He began to play drums while in high school and found work with a dixieland band before serving in the navy (1943–6). While studying at San Jose State College (1946–7) and then at San Francisco State College, and playing drums with Dave Brubeck's octet (1948) and trio (1949–51), he began to double as a vibraphonist. Following graduation (BA 1950) he toured with Brubeck's trio, led a group including Jerome Richardson and Vernon Alley, worked with Alvino Rey, and again led his own group.

In 1953 Tjader joined George Shearing's highly successful quintet, playing both vibraphone and percussion. During this period he became interested in Latin music, and his bongo playing may be heard to advantage on Shearing's *Wrap your Troubles in Drums* (1953). After leaving Shearing in April 1954 he joined the house band at the Blackhawk in San Francisco, but soon afterwards formed his own quintet, which played a blend of Latin and Afro-Cuban music and jazz. In 1957, to Tjader's delight, the percussionists Willie Bobo and Mongo Santamaria abruptly left Tito Puente's band and joined him after Puente disapproved of their having recorded with him; his group also included Gene Wright (1955 – autumn 1957) and Al McKibbon (autumn 1957–1959) on bass. By the end of the decade Tjader had achieved great popularity. Although he remained based on the West Coast, and held numerous residencies at the Blackhawk during the 1960s, he made a tour of the eastern USA late in 1959 and during the 1960s and 1970s appeared frequently in New York; Steve Berrios was a longstanding member of the group from around 1968 into the 1980s. Tjader's recordings range from almost pure salsa (with Puente and Eddie Palmieri) to jam sessions (with such musicians as Luis Gasca and the saxophonist José "Chombo" Silva). Ironically, the album *La onda va bien* (1979), which won a Grammy Award, was recorded with musicians who at that time were relatively unknown, including Mark Levine and Poncho Sanchez.

SELECTED RECORDINGS

As leader: *Cal Tjader: Vibist* (1953, Savoy 9036); *Cal Tjader Plays Afro-Cuban* (1954, Fan. 3-17); *Cal Tjader Plays Tjazz* (1955, Fan. 3211); *Mas ritmo caliente* (1957, Fan. 3262); with S. Getz: *Cal Tjader–Stan Getz Sextet* (1958, Fan. 3266); *Concert by the Sea* (1959, Fan. 8038); *West Side Story* (1960, Fan. 8054); *Warm Wave* (1964, Verve 68585); *Soul Sauce* (1964, Verve 68614); *Breathe Easy* (1977, Gal. 5107); *La onda va bien* (1979, Conc. 113); *The Shining Sea* (1981, Conc. 159); *A fuego vivo* (1981, Conc. 176)

As sideman: D. Brubeck: *Dave Brubeck Trio* (1950, Fan. 3-1, 3-2, 3-4); G. Shearing: Mood for Milt (1953, MGM 11677); Wrap your Troubles in Drums/Easy to Love (1953, MGM 11600)

SELECTED FILMS AND VIDEOS

Salute to Song (1957); The Big Beat (1957); Jazz Scene USA: the Cal Tjader Quintet (1962); For Singles Only (1967); Sounds of Summer: the Concord Jazz Festival (1970)

BIBLIOGRAPHY

J. Tynan: "Cal Tjader: not that he's Tjaded with Concerts, but he Prefers his Tjazz in Saloons," *DB*, xxiv/17 (1957), 17

D. A. Ramsey: "Cal Tjader," *JM*, viii/9 (1962), 7

R. Carr: "Bossa Nova? It's Beautiful," *Crescendo*, ii/7 (1964), 18

H. Siders: "The Latinization of Cal Tjader," *DB*, xxxiii/18 (1966), 21

J. S. Roberts: *The Latin Tinge: the Impact of Latin American Music on the United States* (New York, and Oxford, England, 1979)

Obituary, *New York Times* (6 May 1982)

F. M. Hall: *It's About Time: the Dave Brubeck Story* (Fayetteville, AR, 1996)

JOHN STORM ROBERTS/BK

T. J. Kirk. Cooperative quartet of the mid-1990s comprising the electric guitarists Charlie Hunter, John Schott, and Will Bernard and the drummer Scott Amendola. Originally known as James T. Kirk (after the main character in the television program "Star Trek"), the group was forced to change its name by Paramount studios, which owns the series; both the original name and its revision as T. J. Kirk refer to the players' principal influences: T(helonious Monk), J(ames Brown, and Roland) Kirk. Although it made several tours and recordings, and despite its increasing popularity, the group disbanded in 1997. Its quirky blend of funk, rock, and jazz may be heard on *T. J. Kirk* (*c*1994, WB 45885) and *If Four Was One* (*c*1996, WB 46262). (J. Rotondi: "Profile: T. J. Kirk: Three Wise Jazz Guys," *GP*, xxix/8 (1995), 25)

GK

TOBA. *See* THEATER OWNERS' BOOKING ASSOCIATION.

Togashi, Masahiko (*b* Tokyo, 22 March 1940). Japanese drummer, percussionist, composer, and leader. His father played double bass. He learned violin from the age of six, took up drums and made his début as a drummer with his father's swing band when he was 14, and then moved into other jazz styles. After playing bop with Sadao Watanabe and his Cozy Quartet (1956) and working with Toshiko Akiyoshi and Tony Scott (1950s) he formed the group Jazz Academy (1961), with Hideto Kanai, Masabumi Kikuchi, and Masayuki Takayanagi. He was active as a leader from 1965, when Yosuke Yamashita appeared as his sideman in what is considered to be the first Japanese free-jazz group, and he accompanied such visitors to Japan as Sonny Rollins, Ornette Coleman, Lee Morgan, and Blue Mitchell. An accident in 1969 left him unable to play drums, and the following year he played percussion exclusively; he also wrote compositions that show a strong oriental influence. Togashi resumed performing as a drummer in the mid-1970s and toured and recorded with Don Cherry and Charlie Haden in Europe in 1979. He then performed with Yamashita, Masahiko Sato, the contemporary art music composer and pianist Yuji Takahashi, Steve Lacy, Gary Peacock, and others. In 1988 he recorded as the leader of a trio consisting of Lacy and Jack DeJohnette. Togashi led the group J. J. Spirits in the 1990s and recorded with Paul Bley in 1999.

SELECTED RECORDINGS

Duos: with M. Kikuchi: *Poesy* (1971, Phi. FX8518); with I. Suzuki: *A Day of the Sun* (1979, PW GP3187); with Y. Yamashita: *Kizashi* (An omen; 1980, Phonogram 4132); with S. Lacy: *Eternal Duo* (1981, PW K28P-6219); *Eternal Duo '95* (1995, Take One 1)

As leader: *We Now Create* (1969, Vic. [Jap.] SMJX10065); *Speed and Space* (1970, Union JUP1); *Song for Myself* (1974, EW 7006); *Rings* (1975, EW 9001–02); *Spiritual Nature* (1975, EW 8013); *Essence* (1976, Denon YX7513); *Sketch* (1977, Denon YX7516); *Song of Soil* (1979, PW GP3206); *Al-alarf: Improvisation Jazz Orchestra* (1980, PW K22P-6021–22); *Flame Up* (1981, PW K28P-6205); *Spiritual Moments* (1981, PW K28P-6138); *Follow the Dream* (1984, PW K25P-6328–29); *Scene* (1987, Cornelius CCD701); *Voices* (1988, NEC Avenue A29C-1018); of J. J. Spirits: *Plays BeBop*, i–ii (1991, 1992, Pol. 1076, 1097); with T. Hino and M. Kikuchi: *Triple Helix* (1993, Enja 8056-2); *Inter-action* (1995, Take One 2); *Echo* (1999, Sony 2168)

As sideman with M. Sato: *Palladium* (1969, Express 8004)

BIBLIOGRAPHY

Togashi Masahiko Discography (n.p. [Japan], 1995)

<http://www2s.biglobe.ne.jp/~emac/togashi/index.html> (2000) [incl. discography]

YOZO IWANAMI/KAZUNORI SUGIYAMA

TOK. Trio formed in 1976 by the pianist TAKASHI KAKO, the drummer Oliver Johnson, and the double bass player Kent Carter.

Toko. Nickname of MOTOHIKO HINO.

Tokyo Union. Big band led from 1966 by TATSUYA TAKAHASHI.

Tolbert, Skeets [Campbell Arelius] (*b* Calhoun Falls, SC, 14 Feb 1909; *d* Houston, 30 Nov 2000). Bandleader, clarinetist, and alto saxophonist. His family moved to Lincolntown, North Carolina, when he was very young, and he later attended Johnson C. Smith University in Charlotte. Acquaintance with the violinist Dave Taylor and the pianist Jimmy Gunn led in 1929 to his joining Taylor's Dixie Serenaders, with which he made his recording début in May 1931. He left in March 1934 to move to New York and worked for a summer season with Charlie Alexander at Glens Fall, New York; he then joined the relief band at the Savoy Ballroom. Tolbert performed with Fats Waller in 1936 before becoming a member of a band fronted by the athlete Jesse Owens early in 1937. Having joined Snub Mosley at the Black Cat, he took over the leadership of the band there when Mosley left. This group moved to the Café Creole (April–June 1938) and then to the Plantation Club (until February 1939); at various times it included Freddie Green (who was lured away from the Black Cat by Count Basie) and Kenny Clarke. By the time it first recorded as Tolbert's Gentlemen of Swing in March 1939 Carl Smith and Lem Johnson were among its sidemen.

Over the next three years Tolbert's group recorded some of the definitive examples of the then-current jump style and featured a range of singers of varying talent. The Gentlemen of Swing returned to the Plantation for a residency from July 1939 to February 1940. Later Johnson was replaced by the tenor saxophonist Otis Hicks (early in 1940) and Red Richards took over the piano chair. The band was featured at the Queens Terrace Club in Woodside, New York, from May 1940 to April 1941 and was then at the Famous Door before playing for a summer season at Asbury Park, New Jersey. While at The Place in Greenwich Village the group made its final recordings, in July 1942, but in 1944 four soundies were filmed (*No, No Baby*, *'Tis You Babe*, *Blitzkreig Bombardier*, and *Corn Pone*) which show it to good effect. The band toured eastern cities until Tolbert, who had gained a master's degree at Columbia University, disbanded around 1946 to return to Charlotte as supervisor of high school instrumental music. In 1948 he joined the music faculty at Southern University in Houston, and he was active for many decades thereafter in the American Federation of Musicians; he also ran a music store.

SELECTED RECORDINGS

(all recorded for Decca)

As leader [cl]: Bouncing Rhythm (1939, 7630)

As leader [a sax]: Get Up (1939, 7570); Swing Out (1939, 7669); Papa's in bed with his britches on (1940, 7751); I can't go for you (1940, 7722); Jumpin' Jack (1940, 7791); Fill Up (1942, 8617)

BIBLIOGRAPHY

ChiltonW, McCarthyB

J. Hammond and I. Townsend: *John Hammond on Record: an Autobiography* (New York, 1977), 177

W. O. Smith: *Sideman: the Long Gig of W. O. Smith: a Memoir* (Nashville, 1991)

N. Haslewood: "The Jump Bands – no.3: Skeets Tolbert and his Gentlemen of Swing," *Sv*, no.156 (1993), 220; no.157 (1994), 16

Obituary, D. Penny, *Blues & Rhythm*, no.157 (2001), 25

HOWARD RYE

Tolkachev, Vladimir (Nikolayevich) (*b* Serov, Russian SFSR [now Russia], 17 June 1951). Russian alto, tenor, and soprano saxophonist, leader, arranger, and educator. In

1970 he began to work in various ensembles in Sverdlovsk, Ukraine, and the following year he completed his studies at Sverdlovsk Music College. He first played jazz in the group led by the pianist Vladimir Lukachev (1972) and then worked in the dance orchestra at Ural, a "house of culture" (1973–5). In 1975 he moved to Novosibirsk and studied saxophone at the Novosibirsk State Philharmony. He formed the Musical Improvising Trio with Sergey Panasenko (double bass) and Sergey Belichenko (drums), joined the Novosibirsk State Circus orchestra, and from 1977 played with Igor Dmitriev and others in the group Zolotoye Gody Dhaza (Jazz Golden Years). The trio continued until 1979 and appeared at many jazz festivals; in 1981 it was reconstituted as a quartet, Homo Liber, and then, with the addition of the pianist and composer Yuri Yukachev, as a quintet. Also in 1981 Tolkachev began teaching saxophone at the conservatory; from 1985 he organized and led its student big band, which took the name EuroSib International Orchestra in 1991 and became the orchestra of the Novosibirsk State Philharmony in 1995.

SELECTED RECORDINGS

Duos with Y. Yukachev (as Homo Liber): *Homo Liber* (1983, Leo 129)
As leader: *School Copybook* (1991, Ermatell 010); *Jazz at the Old Fortress* (1992, Shark Taronasi 011479); Siberian Jazz: *Anthologue*, i (1993, Ermatell 008)
As sideman with Homo Liber: *Siberian Four* (1982, Leo 114); *Document* (1986, Leo 806)

SERGEY BELICHENKO

Tolley, David (*b* Melbourne, Australia, 12 Oct 1936). Australian double bass player, composer, and performance artist. In his late adolescence and early twenties, when he was devoted to American jazz and its culture, he played with such hard-bop stalwarts as Stewie Speers and with Keith Hounslow. In the late 1950s and early 1960s he pursued parallel careers as an artist (particularly as a sculptor) and a jazz double bass player, working mainly in Melbourne. Having stopped making sculpture in 1969, he was active in the 1970s in free jazz, particularly with Brian Brown, exploring signal processing of the double bass, as well as extended acoustic techniques on the instrument. With his partner, Dur-é Dara, he formed Connections in 1975. Soon afterwards he ceased playing and focused instead on analogue electronics and his "art" ensemble False Start, which merged and saw no division among music, theatre, art, and performance. The ensemble produced a series of "events" until 1981, involving many other performers; two albums recorded in a duo with Dara are representative of this period. After a diversion into "bent-pop" in EX (a duo with the composer, guitarist, and poet Daevid Allen) Tolley withdrew from public appearances between 1981 and 1993. When he re-emerged it was with digital technology, computer-generated sound, and a renewed involvement with the double bass. His new ensemble, That, presented "spontaneously composed interactive performance," and began recording and releasing substantial amounts of material on limited edition CD-ROM. Tolley also engaged with Pipeline, renewing an earlier association with Phil Treloar, and he collaborated extensively with the guitarist and composer Ren Walters, in a trio format of That with Dara, and in the production of *Moments of Alchemy*, a 50-minute work performed with the Australian Art Orchestra and elsewhere. From 1996 he also worked in a trio, This, with the clarinetist Brigid Burke and the double bass player Gary Costello. Tolley's activities in the late 1990s involved interaction with other musicians not only in real-time in performance, but also in computer time in remixing and reprocessing shared materials.

SELECTED RECORDINGS

Duos: with D. Dara: *Cutheart* (1980, Cleopatra 30); *You Know You Know* (1981, Cleopatra 209); with D. Allen (EX): *Don't Stop* (1983, Shanghai 220); with K. Hounslow: first issued on *Keith Hounslow, My Jazz Life, 50 Years of Playing Jazz in Australia: an Autobiography* (1947–*c*1997, Keith Hounslow Label [unnumbered]), That's a Surprise (*c*1970s)
As sideman: on [various artists:] *Moomba Jazz '76: Live from the Dallas Brooks Hall*, ii (1976, 44 Records 6357709), B. Brown: Moomba Jazzbird '76; That: *That's BASSic* (1995, Muscle Music 001); *That*, i (1998, Origin 023)

BIBLIOGRAPHY

D. Cahill: "David Tolley: Iconoclast," *Sounds Australian*, xvii (1998), autumn, 16
J. Clare [G. Brennan, pseud.]: *Bodgie Dada and the Cult of Cool* (Sydney, 1995)
J. Whiteoak: *Playing ad lib: Improvisatory Music in Australia, 1836–1970* (Sydney, 1999)

ROGER T. DEAN

Tolliver, Charles (*b* Jacksonville, FL, 6 March 1942). Trumpeter. He grew up in New York and took up cornet at the age of eight. After spending three years at Howard University in Washington, DC, he returned to New York, where he performed and recorded with Jackie McLean (1964). This was the first of several brief associations that Tolliver formed with leading bop musicians, among them Art Blakey and Sonny Rollins. Later he played in Gerald Wilson's big band in California (1966–7) and in Max Roach's quintet (1967–9). Late in 1968 he went to Copenhagen to conduct the Radioens Big Band. The following year he formed Music, Inc., a bop quartet that occasionally expanded to become a big band, and in July he took the quartet to Copenhagen to perform at the Montmartre. During the next few years, as the group made frequent trips to Europe, the members of its rhythm section included the pianists Stanley Cowell and John Hicks, the double bass players Cecil McBee, Steve Novosel, Reggie Workman, and Clint Houston, and the drummers Jimmy Hopps and Clifford Barbaro; Ron Mathewson also joined for one European tour.

In 1971 Tolliver and Cowell founded Strata-East Records, an innovative company that allowed participating jazz musicians to control the rights to their own recordings. Music, Inc. performed and recorded until the late 1970s, and in the early 1980s Tolliver led a quartet in Europe. As a sideman he toured with Workman in 1972 and worked in Hicks's quintets and sextets from 1982. From around 1988 to 1990 he toured and recorded with Louis Hayes's group, which also worked under the trumpeter's leadership, with John Stubblefield, George Cables, Houston, and Hayes as sidemen. His only recordings from this period were as the leader of a quartet involving Alain Jean-Marie at a performance in Berlin in 1988 (for Strata-East) and three albums with Hayes in 1989. In the 1990s he joined the faculty of the Jazz and Contemporary Music Program at the New School for Social Research (from 1996 at the Mannes/New School; from autumn 1999 at the New School University).Tolliver is a sensitive, swinging, consistently inventive hard-bop trumpeter who plays with a bright, but rounded, timbre. He has recorded a number of his own compositions, notably the fine bop waltz *Peace with Myself*.

Oral history material in *NN-Sc* (LAJOHP).

SELECTED RECORDINGS

As leader: *Paper Man* (1968, Arista 1002), incl. Peace with Myself; *The Ringer* (1969, Pol. 583750); *Live at Slugs* (1970, SE 1972, 19720); *Music Inc. Big Band* (1971, Pol. 2383138); *Live in Tokyo* (1973, SE 19745); *Impact* (1975, SE 19757)

As sideman: J. McLean: *It's Time* (1964, BN 84179); R. Ayers: *Virgo Vibes* (1967, Atl. 1488); H. Silver: *Serenade to a Soul Sister* (1968, BN 84277); M. Roach: *Members Don't Git Weary* (1968, Atl. 1510); L. Hayes: *Light and Lively* (1989, Ste. 31245); *The Crawl* (1989, Can. 79045); *Una Max* (1989, Ste. 31263)

BIBLIOGRAPHY

V. Wilmer: "What Charles Tolliver Can Use," *DB*, xxxvi/4 (1969), 16

——: "Making it Alone," *MM* (10 Oct 1970), 18

R. Williams: "Tolliver's Travels," *MM* (2 Sept 1972), 18

E. Chadbourne: "Strata East," *Coda*, xii/3 (1975), 7

V. Wilmer: "Tolliver's Five-year Plan," *MM* (24 May 1975), 44

A. Taylor: *Notes and Tones: Musician-to-Musician Interviews* (Liège, Belgium, 1977/*R*1982), 76

<http://www.powerup.com.au/~msafier/tolliver/tolliver.html> (1999) [discography]

<http://www.serecs.com/CharlesTolliver.html> (2000)

BK

Tolonen, Jukka (*b* Helsinki, 16 April 1952). Finnish guitarist. With Pekka Pöyry and others he founded the jazz-rock group Tasavallan Presidentti, which was active from 1969 to 1974. He later pursued a career as a soloist with his own groups, among them the Jukka Tolonen Band (1976–86, with the Swedish guitarist Costa Apetrea), Oreo Moon, and Bill's Boogie Band. A brilliant solo player on both acoustic and electric instruments in jazz and rock styles, he made many recordings as a leader (1971–8, including *The Hook*, 1974, Love 113) and with others, such as Charlie Mariano (1974) and Eero Koivistoinen (1970, 1973, 1976).

BIBLIOGRAPHY

A. Granholm: *Finnish Jazz* (Helsinki, 1974, rev. and enlarged 5/1997, by M. Huuskonen, J. Muikku, and T. Vähäsilta)

P. Gronow: "Three Heroes (the Electric Guitar in Finland)," *Finnish Music Quarterly* no.1 (1991), 59

S. Bruun and J. Lindfors: *Jee jee jee: suomalaisen rockin historia* [Yeah, yeah, yeah: a history of Finnish rock] (Helsinki, 1998)

PEKKA GRONOW

Tom Anderson's. Nightclub in New Orleans; *see* NIGHTCLUBS AND OTHER VENUES.

Tomkins, Les(lie Charles) (*b* London, 31 Oct 1930). English writer. In 1950 he ran a jazz club near London in which a number of well-known British bop musicians performed, and from 1957 to 1960 he was the secretary of an informal group known as the Contemporary Jazz Society. To broaden the society's activities he began to interview musicians, including Americans who were visiting England; some of these interviews were later published in *Melody Maker* (1959–60). In 1961–2 Tomkins was a freelance contributor to *Jazz News*, and in 1962 he began an association with *Crescendo* which continued into the 1980s; he was its editor and art editor from 1966 to 1967 and served as a freelance editor, contributor, and art director from 1970. Throughout this association he published each month three or four interviews with jazz musicians, which now represent a major archive of source material for the study of jazz. Later he was a reviewer for and contributor to the *Jazz Rag* (from 1991) and produced and presented a radio series, "Jazz Greats," for the BBC. He has also written liner notes and program notes. In the late 1990s the label Ronnie Scott's Jazz House began to issue music which Tomkins had recorded at Scott's club in the 1960s.

BK

Tomkins, Trevor (Ramsey) (*b* London, 12 May 1941). English drummer and educator. His surname was misspelled Tompkins in the first edition of this dictionary. He began listening to jazz at the age of 13 on Voice of America broadcasts. After playing trombone he took up drums and at first played mostly commercially oriented music, working with jazz groups only informally. He was initially self-taught, but later studied harmony, theory, and orchestral percussion at the Blackheath Conservatory of Music and the Guildhall School of Music. Late in 1962 he became a full-time jazz musician when he joined Don Rendell; he was then a member of the quintet led by Rendell and Ian Carr (1963–9), and he may be heard to advantage with this ensemble on *Tan san fu*, from the album *Dusk Fire* (1966, Col. ESX6064). During the same period he played on the transatlantic liner *Queen Elizabeth* and worked with Neil Ardley's New Jazz Orchestra and with lesser-known bands. He performed and recorded with Michael Garrick from 1969 to the mid-1970s, worked with the vibraphonist Frank Ricotti late in 1969, and rejoined Rendell in 1970. In the 1970s and 1980s he was with Barbara Thompson (recording with her group Jubiata in 1978), as well as with Keith Tippett, John Taylor, Carr's group Nucleus, Mike Westbrook, Dick Morrissey, Henry Lowther, John Picard, Kenny Wheeler, Tony Coe, the London Jazz Big Band, and others. Tomkins was also associated with such visiting American musicians as Ben Webster, Tal Farlow, Joe Newman, Spike Robinson, Art Farmer, Sonny Stitt, Pepper Adams, and Phil Woods, and in 1986 he toured the UK as a member of Lee Konitz's European quartet, with which he played regularly. He appeared many times at Ronnie Scott's club and participated in several broadcasts and recording sessions. From the late 1980s he played with Brian Priestley, and he worked with Marian Montgomery (recording at Scott's club in 1989), the double bass player Phil Bates, and his own groups. He has also maintained a long, distinguished, and pathbreaking career as a percussion teacher, bringing jazz drumming into England's most prestigious institutions: he is on the faculty of the Guildhall School and was a visiting professor at the Royal Academy of Music.

BIBLIOGRAPHY

CarrJ; *ChiltonB*

R. Cotterell, ed.: *Jazz Now: the Jazz Centre Society Guide* (London, 1976), 175

P. Renaud: *La discographie du jazz anglais* (Chaumont, France, 1985)

S. Goodwin: "Trevor Tomkins: a Teacher's Perspective," *MD*, xiii/6 (1989), 26

SALLY-ANN WORSFOLD/BK

Tommaso, Bruno (*b* Rome, 20 Nov 1946). Italian double bass player, leader, educator, and composer. A cousin of Giovanni Tommaso, he began to play free jazz in 1967 with Mario Schiano. In 1972 he studied jazz at the Conservatorio di S. Cecilia in Rome, from which he graduated in double bass in 1973 and where he later studied composition. In addition to his affiliation with Schiano, which continued until 1974, he worked as a sideman with Franco D'Andrea's Modern Art Trio (1969–72), the quintet led by the trumpeter and flugelhorn player Cicci Santucci and the tenor saxophonist Enzo Scoppa (1970–72), Nunzio Rotondo's group (1970–73), the pianist Martin Joseph (1973–4), Enrico Pieranunzi (1974–9), the quintet led by Dino Piana and Oscar Valdambrini (1978–9), and, most significantly, Giorgio Gaslini (1973–6). In the mid-1970s he began to conduct big bands, first at the Scuola Popolare di Musica del Testaccio in Rome (1976–9), and then in Florence (1980 – early 1990s), the Marche region (the Marche Jazz Orchestra, from 1981), Siena, Barga, Matera, Segni, and elsewhere. He also taught jazz arranging, composition, and conducting and helped to spread jazz orchestras for young musicians throughout Italy. In the 1990s, when he emerged as a composer for jazz orchestra, he performed and recorded his own music, collaborated with Enrico Rava on opera and jazz projects (works by Puccini in 1993, *Carmen* in 1995), composed for many institutions and festivals (contributing, for example, to Pino Minafra's Banda project for jazz group and folk brass band), and conducted orchestras throughout Europe. From 1990 to 1995 he led Meditango, a group playing a mixture of jazz and tango, and in late 1990s he worked with Eugenio Colombo. In 1990 he became the double bass player with and a composer for the Italian Instabile Orchestra; he left it in 1999. He also plays with Renaissance, folk, and tango groups.

Tommaso is one of the most important jazz educators in Italy. He played a major role in the growth of big-band writing and performing there in the 1970s and 1980s, opening up possibilities at a time when there was no official support for teaching jazz in the country.

SELECTED RECORDINGS

Duos with G. Gaslini: *Canti di popolo in jazz* (1975, PDU 6043)

As leader: *12 variazioni su un tema di Jerome Kern* (1981, Splasc(h) 18); of Meditango: *Meditango* (1993, Onyx Jazz Club 001); with Vittorino Curci: *Nux erat* (1993, CMC 9934-2); *6x30: anche i numeri danno poesia* (1995, Onyx Jazz Club 004); *Oltre Napoli, la notte* (1997, Dischi della Quercia 128026-2)

As sideman: Modern Art Trio: *Modern Art Trio* (1970, Vedette 8434); M. Schiano: *If not Ecstatic We Refund* (1970, Cedi 8127); G. Gaslini: *Colloquio con Malcolm X* (1974, PDU 6004); Domenico Guaccero and M. Schiano: *Dedé* (1977, Folkstudio 5008); Italian Instabile Orchestra: *Live in Noci and Rive de Gier* (1991–2, Leo 182); E. Rava: *Rava l'opéra va* (1993, Label Bleu 6559); Italian Instabile Orchestra: *Skies of Europe* (1994, ECM 1543); Italian String Trio: *From Gronigen to Mulhouse* (1994, Splasc(h) 416); E. Rava: *Carmen* (1995, Label Bleu 6579); [various artists]: *Il diritto e il rovescio* (1996, Siena Jazz 1-04-96); La Banda: *La Banda* (1996, Enja 9326-2); G. Trovesi: *Around Small Fairy Tales* (1998, SN 121341-2)

BIBLIOGRAPHY

S. Zenni: "Il giardino dei sentieri che si biforcano, ovvero le *Dodici variazioni su un tema di Jerome Kern* di Bruno Tommaso, ovvero il jazz europeo ai bivi della Storia," *Proceedings of the Meetings La musica di ricerca alle soglie degli anni Novanta/New Music from Russia* (Noci, Italy, 1992)

"Ten Italian Musicians the World Should Know about . . .," *Jazz Changes*, iv/2 (1997), 16

<http://www.ejn.it/mig/tommaso.htm> (1999)

<http://www.shef.ac.uk/misc/rec/ps/efi/minstab.html> (1999)

STEFANO ZENNI

Tommaso, Giovanni (*b* Lucca, Italy, 20 Jan 1941). Italian double bass player, composer, and leader. A cousin of Bruno Tommaso, he took up piano at the age of 12, but changed to double bass when he was 15. In 1956 he played jazz with the Quintetto di Lucca, consisting of Antonello Vannuchi (vibraphone), Gaetano Mariani (guitar), his brother Vito Tommaso (piano), and Giampiero Giusti (drums); from 1960 to 1966 the group continued as a quartet, without Mariani. During the same period Tommaso worked with the pianist Amedeo Tommasi (1960–64) and Gato Barbieri (1963–5). From the late 1960s he played on and composed for television, and as a freelance he accompanied leading American players in Italian clubs. After spending a further period with Barbieri (1971) he co-led, with Franco D'Andrea and Claudio Fasoli, the jazz-rock group Perigeo (1972–7), which performed in Europe and the USA, and worked again with D'Andrea (1977–8) and with Enrico Rava (1978–80). In 1978 he formed a quartet with Maurizio Giammarco and Enrico Pieranunzi, and in the 1980s and 1990s he led his own hard-bop quintets, which launched the careers of such young talents as Massimo Urbani, Paolo Fresu, the trumpeter Flavio Boltro, the pianist Danilo Rea, and Roberto Gatto. He directed workshops at the Umbria Jazz Festival from 1986 and taught jazz at the Conservatorio di F. Morlacchi in Perugia from 1993 to 1995. In 1999 he rejoined Rava, with whom he continues to play into the new century.

Influenced by the classic sound of Blue Note recordings of the 1950s and 1960s, Tommaso's quintets have always followed the conventions of hard bop while playing haunting melodies and chorus forms loosened to allow the soloists free space.

SELECTED RECORDINGS

As leader: *The Healthy Food Band* (1970, RCA KOLS1015); *Via G.T.* (1986, Red 196); *To Chet* (1988, Red 220); with F. D'Andrea and R. Gatto: *Kick Off* (1988, Red 123225-2), *Airegin* (1991, Red 123252-2); *Over the Ocean* (1993, Red 123526-2); *Third Step* (1998, Ricordi 74321-582552)

As sideman: Quintetto di Lucca: *Quintetto di Lucca* (1959, RCA EPA30-338); Quartetto di Lucca: *Quartetto di Lucca* (1962, RCA PLM10361); Perigeo: *Abbiamo tutti un blues da piangere* (1973, RCA DPSL10609); *Genealogia* (1974, RCA TPL1-1080); *La valle dei templi* (1975, RCA TPL1-1175); E. Rava: *Ah* (1979, ECM 1166)

BIBLIOGRAPHY

CarrJ

S. G. Biamonte: "Giovanni Tommaso: da quintetto a quintetto," *Musica jazz*, liv/8–9 (1998), 14

C. Pecoraro, ed.: *Giovanni Tommaso: querent'anni di jazz* (Salerno, Italy, 1998)

<http://www.ijm.it/enartists.html> (1999)

STEFANO ZENNI

Tompkins, Eddie. *See* THOMPKINS, EDDIE.

Tompkins, Ross (*b* Detroit, 13 May 1938). Pianist. He studied at the New England Conservatory. In New York he performed and recorded at intervals with Kai Winding (1960–67) and with Joe Newman (mid-1960s); he also played briefly with Eric Dolphy (1964), Wes Montgomery (1966), Bob Brookmeyer and Clark Terry's quintet (1966), Roy Eldridge, and Benny Goodman (1968) and recorded with Eddie "Lockjaw" Davis. He performed frequently with Bobby Hackett (1965–70) and the quintet led by Al Cohn and Zoot Sims (1968–72). In 1971 he moved to Los Angeles, where he played in Louie Bellson's big band and, until 1992, the orchestra of "The Tonight Show" under Doc Severinsen. Tompkins recorded in duos with Herb Ellis (1975) and Jack Sheldon (1991), as a leader (from 1977), and as co-leader with Joe Venuti (1977) and Red Norvo (1979); in addition he took part in sessions as a sideman with Bellson (1974–82), Ellis (in studio quartets, 1978, 1983; and in a quartet at the Montreux International Jazz Festival, 1979), Venuti and George Barnes (at the Concord Jazz Festival, 1976), Zoot Sims (1976), Howard Roberts (1977), Snooky Young and Marshal Royal (1978–9), Harry Edison and Sheldon (both 1983), Young and Bob Cooper (1985), Spike Robinson (1988), and Dick Hafer (1994), as well as in small groups led by a fellow member of Severinsen's band, Tommy Newsom (from 1990). From around 1988 he worked with Bill Berry and from the mid-1980s with Sheldon.

Video oral history material in *NCH* (HCJA).

SELECTED RECORDINGS

As unaccompanied soloist: *Scrimshaw* (1976, Conc. 28); *Aka "the Phantom"* (*c*1992, Prog. 7090)

Duos with H. Ellis: *A Pair to Draw to* (1975, Conc. 17)
As leader: with J. Venuti: *Live at Concord '77* (1977, Conc. 51); with R. Norvo: *Red and Ross* (1979, Conc. 90); *Symphony* (*c*1984, FaD 146)
As sideman: E. Davis: *Lock, the Fox* (1966, RCA LSP3652); H. Roberts: *The Real Howard Roberts* (1977, Conc. 53); L. Bellson: *Prime Time* (1977, Conc. 64); Concord All Stars: *Festival Time* (1979, Conc. 117); J. Sheldon: *Stand by for the Jack Sheldon Quartet* (1983, Conc. 229); D. MacDonald: *The Doug MacDonald Trio* (1990, Cexton 5678); T. Newsom: *Tommy Newsom and his T.V. Jazz Stars* (1990, Laserlight 15331); D. Hafer: *Pres Impressions: Dedicated to the Memory of Lester Young* (1994, Fresh Sound 5002); T. Newsom: *Tommy Newsom and L.A. Big Band All Stars* (1996, Planet Earth 2410); J. Hanna: *The Joint is Jumpin'* (1998, Arbors 19148)

BIBLIOGRAPHY

Feather–Gitler '70s
S. Traill: "Ross Tompkins," *JJI*, xxxiii/10 (1980), 41

PAUL RINZLER/BK

Tom Terrific. Nickname of ALAN TURNBULL.

Tom-tom. Single or double-headed rod-tensioned drum. Mounted on the bass drum, or free-standing, two or more of them have generally been used in the drum set from the 1940s onwards; *see* DRUM SET, esp. §§I, 4; II, 4, 5.

Ton-Art. Small group formed in Austria in the mid-1980s by the trumpeter Klaus Peham, the alto saxophonist Bernhard Spahn, the bass clarinetist Johann Carl Steiner, the electric guitarist Burkhard Stangl, the double bass player Werner Dafeldecker, and the drummer Paul Skrepek. It appears to have disbanded by the mid-1990s. Its recordings *Ant Ort* (*c*1987, Extraplatte 63) and *Zu* (1989, HA 6034) exemplify its blend of contemporary art music and free improvisation. Franz Koglmann and Tom Varner recorded as guest soloists with the group, respectively in 1989 and 1991.

GK

Toneff, Radka (*b* Oslo, 25 June 1952; *d* Oslo, 21 Oct 1982). Norwegian singer and composer. She studied at the conservatory in Oslo from 1971 to 1975, while at the same time working with various jazz-rock groups. From around 1975 she became established as one of the country's best new jazz singers, performing in a soft but intense style, and from 1975 to 1982 she led her own quintet, which included such musicians as Jon Balke on piano, Jon Eberson on guitar, and Arild Andersen on bass; much of its repertory was based on modern poetry, with music composed by Toneff. In the last year of her life she often worked in a duo with the Swedish-American pianist Steve Dobrogosz. From the mid-1980s many young Scandinavian jazz singers have been inspired by, and have copied, her style.

SELECTED RECORDINGS

Duos with S. Dobrogosz: *Fairytales* (1982, Odin 03)
As leader: *Winter Poem* (1977, Zarepta 1439); *It Don't Come Easy* (1979, Zarepta 34015); *Live in Hamburg* (1981, Odin 4044)

JOHS BERGH

Tonolo, Pietro (*b* Mirano, Italy, 30 May 1959). Italian tenor and soprano saxophonist. After studying violin he began to play saxophone professionally in Milan in 1979 with Franco D'Andrea, the pianist Luigi Bonafede, the drummer Gianni Cazzola, the tenor saxophonist Larry Nocella, and Massimo Urbani. He often worked with Enrico Rava between 1981 and 1986, and he was a member of Gil Evans's orchestra in 1982, again in 1984–5 in New York, and in 1987 at the Umbria Jazz Festival. From 1983 he led his own groups and appeared in clubs, theaters, and concert halls throughout Italy, in Europe, and in the USA, with Kenny Clarke, Roswell Rudd, Sal Nistico (ii), Chet Baker (in New York, 1985), Lee Konitz, John Surman, George Lewis (ii), Barry Altschul, Joe Chambers, Aldo Romano, Kenny Wheeler, Dave Holland, Tony Oxley, Steve Swallow, and Paul Motian. In 1986 Tonolo formed a duo and a quartet with Rita Marcotulli, and in 1988 he first played with Henri Texier and Enrico Pieranunzi and wrote arrangements for the Italian big band Keptorchestra. From the mid-1990s he was a member of Mario Raja's saxophone quartet Arundo Donax. Influenced by Sonny Rollins and Warne Marsh, Tonolo improvises in a swinging hard-bop style.

SELECTED RECORDINGS

(recorded for Splasc(h) unless otherwise indicated)

As unaccompanied soloist: *Monologues* (1996–7, 645)
As leader: *Quartet, Quintet, Sextet* (1985, 105); *Slowly* (1990, 324); *Alliance* (1990, Pentaflowers 023); *Tresse* (1992, 386); *Simbiosi* (1994, 431); *Disguise* (1996, 492); with Danilo Rea: *Sotto la luna* (1999, Egea 069)
As sideman: G. Manusardi: *A Bridge into the New Generation* (1981, 102); E. Rava: *Andanada* (1986, SN 1064); M. Raja: *Ellington* (1994, 427); G. Tommaso: *Over the Ocean* (1993, Red 123256-2); Keptorchestra: *Sweet Sixteen* (1993, Caligola 2001-2); Marcello Tonolo: *Seed Journey* (1997, Caligola 2023-2); Arundo Donax: *Arundo Donax* (1999, BMG 74321-68585-2)

BIBLIOGRAPHY

<http://www.ijm.it/enartists.html> (1999)

STEFANO ZENNI

Tononi, Tiziano (*b* Milan, 18 Nov 1956). Italian drummer, composer, and leader. A self-taught rock drummer, he began to play jazz in the mid-1970s; he then studied with Andrew Cyrille and Bob Moses and with a classical percussion teacher. In 1981 he played with the Democratic Orchestra Milano and, with the tenor saxophonist Daniele Cavallanti, a close colleague, founded Nexus, one of the longest-lived Italian jazz groups. Nexus played throughout Europe and featured such guests as Glenn Ferris, Mark Dresser, and Herb Robertson; it should not be confused with contemporary Swedish and Canadian groups of the same name. In the mid-1980s Tononi also began to work with Tiziana Ghiglioni, Giancarlo Schiaffini, Gianluigi Trovesi, Pierre Favre, Maggie Nicols, Cyrille, Barre Phillips, Dresser, and Dewey Redman. In 1985 he founded the percussion group Moon on the Water. Tononi played with the Jazz Chromatic Ensemble from 1989 and the Italian Instabile Orchestra from 1990, and later joined the trio led by the trombonist and tuba player Beppe Caruso. In 1995 he composed music for the film *Ketchup*, and in 1997 he formed the Multiphonics Tuba Trio with the multi-instrumentalist Renato Geremia and Michel Godard. He has composed successful homages to Don Cherry (*Awake Nu*, recorded in 1996) and Roland Kirk (*We Did it, We Did it!*, recorded in 1999).

A powerful drummer, Tononi bases his style on the sounds and techniques of traditional percussion music, especially those of native Americans and from the Orient. He has the driving swing of a conventional jazz drummer and utilizes a wide variety of cymbals, gongs, bells, and other percussion instruments. His compositions are after the manner of Charles Mingus in a free-jazz context; they consist of suites in several movements, with effective changes of tempo, meter, and atmosphere.

SELECTED RECORDINGS

(recorded for Splasc(h) unless otherwise indicated)

Duos with D. Cavallanti: *Udu Calls* (1996, 496)
As leader of Nexus (with D. Cavallanti): *Open Mouth Blues* (1983, Red 169); *Night Riding* (1985, Red 190); *Urban Shout* (1988, 170); *The Preacher and*

the Ghost (1991, 349); *Free Spirits* (1994, 421); *We Still Have Visions* (1997–8, 657–8)
As leader of Moon on the Water: *Moon on the Water* (1985, Buscemi 2); *Mr. Doubles* (1989, Innowo 814); *Think with your Ears* (1996, Sensible 008)
As leader of other groups: *Going for the Magic* (1987, 13); *Ketchup* (1995, Sensible 010); *Awake Nu* (1996, 487–8); of Multiphonics Tuba Trio (with R. Geremia and M. Godard): *Tre cose* (1997, 635); of The Society of Freely Syncopated Organic Pulses: *We Did it, We Did it!* (1999, 811–13)
As sideman: Democratic Orchestra Milano: *Invenzioni* (1983, Bull 004); D. Cavallanti: *The Leo* (1987, Red 216); T. Ghiglioni: *Yet Time* (1988, 150); G. Trovesi: *Les boîtes à musique* (1988, 152); U. Petrin and Guido Mazzon: *Other Line* (1990, 317); G. Schiaffini: *About Monk* (1992, Pentaflowers 025); T. Ghiglioni: *S.O.N.B.* (1992, 370); Jazz Chromatic Ensemble: *Skydreams* (1995, 473); B. Caruso: *Mr. C* (1997, 647)
For further recordings *see* ITALIAN INSTABILE ORCHESTRA.

BIBLIOGRAPHY

<http://www.ijm.it/enartists.html> (1999)
<http://www.shef.ac.uk/misc/rec/ps/efi/minstab.html> (1999)

STEFANO ZENNI

Tonooka [Morris]**, Sumi** (*b* Philadelphia, 3 Oct 1956). Pianist. Her father was African American and her mother Japanese American, and she later took her mother's maiden name as a stage name. She left high school at the age of 15 and moved to Boston, where she had lessons with Margaret Chaloff and Charlie Banacos. In 1973 she lived in Connecticut and then Detroit, where she studied and performed with Marcus Belgrave. Having returned to Philadelphia (1974) she studied at the Philadelphia College of Performing Arts and received private tuition from Bernard Peiffer, Mary Lou Williams, Stanley Cowell, and Dennis Sandole; she performed in local clubs and worked with various musicians, including Odean Pope and Philly Joe Jones. In 1983 she moved to New York and attended the New School for Social Research and performed as an unaccompanied soloist at a SoHo supper club in Green Street. She made her first recording as a leader in 1984. The following year Tonooka was awarded a grant by the Japanese American Cultural Organization and composed a three-part suite, *Out from the Silence*, which was inspired by her family history – in particular her mother's experience in Manzinar, a World War II internment camp for Japanese Americans; the piece combined traditional Japanese instruments, in particular the *shakuhachi* (notched flute) and *koto*, with a jazz ensemble, and was used for the soundtrack to *Susumu* (1991), a film which told the same story. She recorded with John Blake in 1988 and the saxophonist Bobby Zankel in 1991 and led a trio with Lewis Nash and Rufus Reid at the Monterey Jazz Festival in 1994.

SELECTED RECORDINGS

As leader: *With an Open Heart* (1984, Radiant 5601); *Taking Time* (1990, Can. 79502); *Here Comes Kai* (1991, Can. 79516)
As sideman: J. Blake: *A New Beginning* (1988, Gram. 18-8808-1); B. Zankel: on *Seeking Spirit* (1991–2, Cadence Jazz 1050), Block Party, Cause and Effect, Heritage, Rush Hour, Spherical Motion (1991)

BIBLIOGRAPHY

F. Davis: *In the Moment: Jazz in the 1980s* (New York, and Oxford, England, 1986/R1996), 90
L. Gourse: "Sumi Tonooka: Secret Piano Places," *JT* (1990), Aug, 7
W. Minor: "Pianist & Composer Sumi Tonooka," *Coda*, no.258 (1994), 26
L. Gourse: *Madame Jazz: Contemporary Women Instrumentalists* (New York, and Oxford, England, 1995), 36

GK

Tony the Tiger. Nickname of TONY PURRONE.

Toot. Nickname of T. S. MONK.

Top cymbal. Name by which the ride cymbal is also known; *see* DRUM SET, §§I, 5; II, 5, 6.

Top of the beat, on. Expression used to describe the performance of a player or singer who (deliberately or unintentionally) places notes slightly before or too precisely on the beat as it is articulated by the rhythm section or implied by the playing of the rest of the ensemble; *see* BEAT, §2.

Torff, Brian (Quade) (*b* Hinsdale, IL, 16 March 1954). Double bass player. He took up double bass at the age of 11 and electric bass guitar when he was 13; in his mid-teens he played mainly the electric instrument, but while studying at the Berklee College of Music and the Manhattan School of Music he concentrated on jazz and double bass. Following graduation he toured with Cleo Laine (1974) and briefly with Erroll Garner (for the last ten days of the pianist's career, in February 1975). In New York he played with David Amram and Laine and performed and recorded at the Cookery in a duo with Mary Lou Williams (1975). Later he toured and recorded (at Carnegie Hall, 1978) with Stephane Grappelli and performed and recorded with Marian McPartland (1978, 1979). For three and a half years he played in a duo with George Shearing (1979–83), with whom he recorded the album *Blues Alley & Jazz* (1979, Conc. 110), and during the same period he took part in sessions led by Jackie Cain and Roy Kral (1979, 1980), Eiji Kitamura (1980), and Shearing and Mel Tormé (1982). In 1985 he made an album of his own programmatic compositions and improvisations, *Hitchhiker of Karoo* (Quade 2601). Between 1989 and 1991 Torff accompanied Clark Terry, James Moody, Jimmy Cobb, and Red Rodney, and later in the 1990s he worked with Larry Coryell and Milt Hinton. In 1997 he formed a jazz fusion trio, Thunderstick, which recorded that same year under his leadership and which included Joe Beck. He also played with Laurence Hobgood and Paul Wertico in the trio Union, which recorded albums of jazz standards and original compositions (notably *State of the Union*, 1998, Naim 038), formed a duo with the French pianist Florence Melnotte (*c*1999), and recorded with Eddie Higgins (2000). Torff has taught in Connecticut at the University of Bridgeport (1989–93) and at Fairfield University (from 1993).

BIBLIOGRAPHY

A. J. Smith: "Profile: Brian Torff," *DB*, xliii/12 (1976), 34
J. M. Doran: *Erroll Garner: the Most Happy Piano* (Metuchen, NJ, 1985), 114
B. Milkowski: "Brian Torff," *JT*, xxviii/3 (1998), 25
<http://www.faculty.fairfield.edu/faculty/Btorff/> (2000) [incl. discography]

BK

Tormé [Torme], **Mel(vin Howard)** (*b* Chicago, 13 Sept 1925; *d* Los Angeles, 5 June 1999). Singer and songwriter. A professional performer from the age of four, he studied piano and drums, and while still in his teens toured as singer, arranger, and drummer with a band led by the comedian Chico Marx (1942-3), appeared in the film *Higher and Higher* (1943), led a vocal swing group, the Mel-Tones, and made his first recordings. After his discharge from the army in 1946 he focused on working in films and, from the early 1950s, television, and became known as a first-rate arranger. Although the sophistication and jazz orientation of his best singing precluded widespread appeal, Tormé achieved periodic success in nightclubs, on television, and through recordings, and was widely admired by fellow musicians. In the 1950s and early 1960s he made numerous jazz albums with small groups, with Marty Paich's Dek-tette, and with other ensembles, and from the 1960s he produced television shows and developed his career as an actor and writer. His activities as a jazz musician came to the fore through an association with George Shearing in the 1980s and 1990s, when the two men performed and recorded together in a quartet and as a duo. Tormé also recorded and toured with Paich's revived Dek-tette (1988), toured the USA with a quintet that included Ken Peplowski (1995), and made the jazz-oriented video *Live from the Ambassador Hotel* (*c*1990s) and several more acclaimed recordings. He suffered a stroke in August 1996.

Tormé was one of the finest pop and jazz singers of his generation. Early in his career his high, husky voice caused him to be nicknamed "the Velvet Fog," but in time it deepened into a well-controlled baritone. His wide-ranging repertory included sentimental ballads, swing numbers with big bands, and popular songs in jazz arrangements that involved scat singing; like Ella Fitzgerald, to whom his scat-singing technique was deeply indebted, Tormé was equally comfortable improvising or taking a more straightforward approach to American popular song in settings involving large studio orchestras. He composed around 300 popular songs, notably *The Christmas Song* (1946). Apart from his diverse work in entertainment, he pursued a successful career as a writer, and published autobiographical material, a biography of Buddy Rich, remembrances of fellow musicians, and two novels.

SELECTED RECORDINGS

As leader: *Lulu's Back in Town* (1956, Beth. 52); *Live at the Crescendo* (1957, Beth. 6020); *Mel Tormé Swings Shubert Alley with the Marty Paich Dek-tette* (1960, Verve 6146); *I Dig the Count, I Dig the Duke* (1960–61, Verve 68491); *Live at the Maisonette* (1974, Atl. 18129); with G. Shearing: *An Evening with George Shearing & Mel Tormé* (1982, Conc. 190), *An Evening at Charlie's* (1983, Conc. 248); with R. McConnell: *Mel Tormé, Rob McConnell and the Boss Brass* (1986, Conc. 306); with G. Shearing: *Mel and George "Do" World War II* (1990, Conc. 4471); *Fujitsu–Concord Jazz Festival in Japan '90* (1990, Conc. 4481); *The Great American Songbook* (1994, Telarc 83328); *An Evening with ...* (1996, Conc. 4736)

As sideman with Artie Shaw: What is this thing called love? (1946, Musi. 390); Get out of town (1946, Musi. 389)

WRITINGS

(selective list)

It Wasn't All Velvet: an Autobiography (New York, 1990)

Traps, the Drum Wonder: the Life of Buddy Rich (New York, and Oxford, England, 1991)

My Singing Teachers: Reflections on Singing Popular Music (New York, 1994)

BIBLIOGRAPHY

"Tormé, Mel," *CBY 1983*

J. McDonough: "The Velvet Fog in Mellow Pose: Mel Torme," *DB*, xliii/9 (1976), 16

M. R. Pitts and L. H. Harrison: *Hollywood on Record: the Film Stars' Discography* (Metuchen, NJ, 1978)

W. Balliett: "Profiles: a Vast Minority," *New Yorker*, lvii (16 March 1981), 49; repr. in *American Singers: Twenty-seven Portraits in Song* (New York, and Oxford, England, rev. 2/1988), 143

K. Franckling: "Mel Torme: at the Top of his Game," *JT* (1986), Feb, 12

C. Deffaa: *Swing Legacy* (Metuchen, NJ, and London, 1989), 210

E. Santosuosso: "Mel Torme: He's Still Doing it his Way," *Boston Globe* (28 Aug 1992)

P. Elwood: "Tormé is Back on the Bus for Concert Tour," *San Francisco Examiner* (24 March 1995)

Obituary, S. Holden, *New York Times* (6 June 1999)

MICHAEL J. BUDDS/BK

Torn, David (Mitchell) (*b* Amityville, NY, 26 May 1953). Electric guitarist. He began playing piano at the age of seven and attended classes at Leonard Bernstein's Music for Young Composers when he was 12. In his teens he studied flamenco and jazz guitar, and in 1973 he attended the Berklee College of Music for one semester; thereafter he had private jazz guitar lessons with John Abercrombie and Pat Martino. Torn developed a textural rather than linear approach to playing his instrument and worked largely in this manner with Jan Garbarek and Eberhard Weber (1983–7), Don Cherry (1979–80), Mark Isham (1987–90), and the keyboard players David Sylvian (1988–90) and Ryuichi Sakamoto (1997–9). He also performed as a soloist or "texturalist" for film soundtracks by Carter Burwell, Isham, Michael Shrieve, and Michael Whalen, and played on an occasional basis with Joachim Kühn, Trilok Gurtu, Bill Bruford, Jack Bruce, Cassandra Wilson, and Pharoah Sanders. Torn led various recording groups, and in 1998 he worked with his fellow guitarists Vernon Reid and Elliott Sharp in the group Gtr Obliq. He is the subject of a two-part video, *Painting with Guitar* (*c*1994), and the author of an instructional article, "Loop Guru: Dave Torn Decodes the Art of Electronic Looping," which was published in *Guitar Player* (xxx/9 (1996), 57). In 1992 he suffered a brain tumor which caused the loss of hearing in his left ear.

SELECTED RECORDINGS

As leader: *Best Laid Plans* (1984, ECM 1284); *Cloud about Mercury* (1986, ECM 1322); *Polytown* (1993, CMP 1008); *What Means 'Solid,' Traveller?* (1995, CMP 1012); with V. Reid and E. Sharp: *Gtr Obliq* (1998, Knitting Factory Works 233)

As sideman: Everyman Band: *Everyman Band* (1981, ECM 1234); J. Garbarek: *It's OK to Listen to the Gray Voice* (1984, ECM 1294); M. Shrieve: *Stiletto* (1988, Novus 3050-2-N)

BIBLIOGRAPHY

B. Milkowski: "Profile: David Torn," *DB*, liv/2 (1987), 48

J. Woodard: "Soundpage," *GP*, xxi/11 (1987), 32

J. Diliberto: "David Torn: Arrogant Ambient Music from a Guitarist who's Not that Sure He's a Guitarist," *Musician*, no.119 (1988), 38

B. Milkowski: "David Torn: Neo-psychedelic Renegade," *GP*, xxv/5 (1991), 64

J. Diliberto: "Riffs: Torn Recovers from Brain Trauma, Reclaims Career," *DB*, lxi/4 (1994), 12

J. Woodard: "Jazz Guitar Mutants," *Musician*, no.189 (1994), 62

B. Milkowski: "Hearsay: David Torn," *JT*, xxv/6 (1995), 18

J. Gress: "Torn Curtain: Behind David's Psychoactive Sheets of Sound," *GP*, xxx/9 (1996), 57 [incl. transcrs.]

B. Rorick: "Home Studio: David Torn," *Musician*, no.220 (1997), 82

J. Rotondi: "David Torn: What Means Stoopit, Traveller?," *GP*, xxxi/1 (1997), 65

MARK GILBERT

Törner, Gösta (*b* Stockholm, 27 Oct 1912; *d* Stockholm, 11 Nov 1982). Swedish trumpeter and bandleader. Active as a professional musician from the late 1920s, he became one of Sweden's earliest and most consistent hot jazz improvisers and one of its finest trumpeters. Between 1936 and 1938 he made several recordings in small-band jam sessions with the Sonora Swing Swingers under the leadership of Thore Jederby, among them *Louisiana* and *Easy Swing*. These were the first of their kind in Sweden, and Törner's playing shows the influence of Louis Armstrong (whom he had heard and met in Stockholm in 1933) and Bix Beiderbecke; later on he also drew inspiration from the playing of Bobby Hackett and Roy Eldridge. Törner worked with a large number of Swedish bands of the 1930s and 1940s – notably those led by the double bass player Sune Lundwall (1933–5), Arne Hülphers (1937–40), the drummer Sven Fors (1940–42), and Thore Ehrling (1941–50). From 1940 to 1949 he was elected into most of the annual Swedish all-star bands, and in this last year he was a member of the Swedish group that played at the Paris Jazz Fair. In the 1940s he also led jam session broadcasts over the sole national radio channel in Sweden.

Törner was much in demand for studio work, played in theaters for revue, and led numerous groups of his own from 1943 until his retirement from music in the mid-1960s. The Svenskt Visarkiv, Stockholm, holds scores used by his orchestras, as well as his many comic strips and portrait drawings of jazz stars, which he published in *Orkester journalen* (1936–52); *see* Libraries and archives, §2.

Oral history material in *SSsv*.

SELECTED RECORDINGS

As leader: I found a new baby (1943, Tel. A5369); Queen Street Blues (1944, Tel. A5388); with B. Laine: Blues Cupol/Ain't Misbehavin' (1947, Cupol 4011); At the Jazz Band Ball (1949, Artist B3008); *Living Legend* (1964, Phon. NOST7607), incl. Lazy River

As sideman: Swing Swingers: Louisiana (1936, Son. 3217); Easy Swing (1936, Son. 3218); T. Jederby: Bix idé (1941, Scala 395); Rhythm is our Business (1941, Odeon D5013); Parisorkestern 1949: Body and soul/ Idaho (1949, Cupol 4224)

BIBLIOGRAPHY

"Svenskt stjärnalbum" [Swedish star-album], *Orkester journalen*, iv/11 (1936), 3

"Mannen bakom orkestern" [The man behind the orchestra], *Estrad*, vi/6 (1944), 11

B. Nyquist: "Gösta: vår första stora jazzartist" [Gösta: our first great jazz artist], *Orkester journalen*, l/11 (1982), 33

B. Westin: *Gösta Törner: musikanare, tecknare* [Gösta Törner: musician, sketch-artist] (Stockholm, 1993)

ERIK KJELLBERG/LARS WESTIN

Toshiko. *See* Akiyoshi, toshiko.

Totah, Nobby [Nabil (Marshall)] (*b* Ramallah, Transjordan [now Jordan], 5 April 1930). Double bass player. His nickname is often misspelled Knobby. He emigrated to the USA in 1944 to attend school in Providence, Rhode Island, studied political science at Haverford College (graduated 1952), and took up double bass in 1953. While serving in the US Army he was a member of a military band and played in Japan with Hampton Hawes and Toshiko Akiyoshi (1953–4). In 1954 he worked briefly with Charlie Parker, and the following year he undertook his first engagements with Gene Krupa and Johnny Smith, with both of whom his association continued for many years; he also performed with Les Elgart (1955) and Cy Coleman (1955–7), performed and recorded with Zoot Sims (at intervals, 1956–9), and worked with Eddie Costa (1957), Herbie Mann (1958–61), Bobby Hackett (with whom he appeared in the television show "Bobby Hackett," 1961), Sol Yaged (1961), and Teddy Wilson (1960–64). In the 1970s he played with Max Kaminsky and Benny Goodman (both 1976) and Hazel Scott (1978–80) and recorded with Lee Konitz (1977). Totah was a member of Peter Duchin's band in New York in the 1980s, and from 1972 into the 1990s he led small groups of his own (recording in 1987 and 1997); among his sidemen were Horace Parlan, Mike Longo, Attila Zoller, and Pepper Adams. He also recorded in New York with the singer Stephanie Nakasian (1988, 1990). Totah's style is that of an accompanist: he plays simple bass lines behind the beat, which support the soloist rather than display his own virtuosity.

SELECTED RECORDINGS

As leader: *More Double Bass* (1987, 1997, Consolidated Artists 928)

As sideman: Z. Sims: *Zoot* (1956, Argo 608); B. Jaspar: *Bobby Jaspar Quartet* (1956, Col. FPX123); G. Wallington: *Jazz at Hotchkiss* (1957, Savoy 12122); T. Farlow: *This is Tal Farlow* (1958, Verve 8289); H. Mann: *Family of Mann* (1961, Atl. 1371)

BIBLIOGRAPHY

FeatherE; *Feather '60s*

J. Bany: "Double Double-bass," *International Society of Bassists*, xiii/1 (1986), 25

JOHN VOIGT

Touff, Cy(ril James) (*b* Chicago, 4 March 1927). Bass trumpeter. He received piano lessons from the age of six, then learned C-melody saxophone, xylophone, and trumpet. After playing trombone in an army band with Conte Candoli and Red Mitchell (1944–6) he returned to Chicago, where he studied with Lennie Tristano and worked with Bill Russo, Charlie Ventura, Ray McKinley, and Boyd Raeburn. Touff took up bass trumpet in the late 1940s and performed, recorded, and toured the USA and Europe with Woody Herman from late 1953 to mid-1956. In 1954 he recorded in Paris as a member of the Herdsmen (a group of Herman's sidemen) and as a soloist on several tracks of the album *The Woody Herman Band!* (Cap. T560); in addition he recorded with Nat Pierce's and Dick Collins's nonet (1954) and as the leader of various West Coast jazz groups (1955). He then worked as a freelance in Chicago, played in dance bands, and recorded as the leader of a dixieland sextet (*c*1956) and a hard-bop quintet (1958) and as a sideman with Chubby Jackson and Lorez Alexandria (both 1957). Later he made recordings in Chicago with the drummer Fred Wacker (1965) and alongside Clifford Jordan and Von Freeman, among others, in the sextet Hyde Park after Dark (1981). In the early 1980s Touff worked in studios and with local groups.

BIBLIOGRAPHY

FeatherE

J. Tracy: "Meet Cy Touff; the Man who Brought Bass Trumpet to Prominence," *DB*, xxii/25 (1955), 14

E. Jost: *Jazzmusiker: Materialen zur Soziologie der afro-amerikanischen Musik* (Frankfurt am Main, Germany, Berlin, and Vienna, 1981), 223

R. Gordon: *Jazz West Coast: the Los Angeles Jazz Scene of the 1950s* (London and New York, 1986)

W. D. Clancy with A. C. Kenton: *Woody Herman: Chronicles of the Herds* (New York and elsewhere, 1995), 217

Tough, Dave [Dav(e)y; David Jaffray] (*b* Oak Park, IL, 26 April 1907; *d* Newark, NJ, 9 Dec 1948). Drummer. Balliett (1985) gives his middle name Jaffray and his year of birth as 1907 from his birth certificate, procured by the researcher Harold Kaye; these details have appeared incorrectly in many sources. As the leading intellectual and free spirit in the Austin High School Gang in the mid-1920s, Tough had a formative influence on the Chicago style of white jazz. He played with these teenage friends as the Blue Friars (1923–4), but then ceded his position to Gene Krupa in order to join Husk O'Hare's Wolverines. In 1927 he played in jam sessions at the Three Deuces and worked alongside Eddie Condon, accompanying silent movies, before leaving Chicago to embark with his wife and Danny Polo for Europe; he thus missed the seminal McKenzie and Condon recording sessions, for which Krupa was the drummer. Tough and Polo joined George Carhart's New Yorkers Tanzorchestra for performances in Belgium and Germany, where, in Berlin in September 1927, Tough made his first recordings. He worked as a freelance in Europe, was a member of Mezz Mezzrow's trio in Paris (March 1929), and rejoined the New Yorkers. After returning to the USA in May 1929, he worked briefly with Benny Goodman and toured and recorded with Red Nichols.

Tough was largely incapacitated for the next six years, suffering from alcoholism. He played for a brief period with Ray Noble's dance orchestra in New York (1935), then worked with Tommy Dorsey's big band (February 1936 –

1 January 1938), during which time he wrote an advice-to-drummers column for *Metronome* magazine. He spent short periods with Red Norvo and Bunny Berigan before replacing Krupa in the Benny Goodman Orchestra and Quartet (mid-March–October 1938), and played again with Dorsey (December 1938 – June 1939). Tough was a leading drummer of the swing period: two prominent features of his playing with Dorsey – his ride patterns on Chinese cymbal (and later on large Turkish cymbal) and his irregular bass drum figures – were far in advance of their time, becoming widespread only in the bop style of the 1940s.

Tough deputized for Ray McKinley in Jimmy Dorsey's orchestra (July 1939) and toured with Jack Teagarden's big band (August–September) while also playing and recording with Bud Freeman's Summa Cum Laude Orchestra (intermittently, August 1939 – January 1940), after which his health failed once again. In May 1940 he rejoined Mezzrow, and the following July made further recordings with Freeman; September found him playing in Joe Marsala's small group on 52nd Street in New York, and occasionally from October 1940, and regularly from January to April 1941, he worked again with Goodman. In March 1941 he participated in one of Charlie Christian's informal recording sessions, the results of which were released under Goodman's name. After rejoining Marsala, Tough toured with the big bands of Artie Shaw (August–December 1941), Woody Herman, Charlie Spivak (to April 1942), and Claude Thornhill. He enlisted that summer to join Shaw's Navy Band and toured the South Pacific until receiving a medical discharge in February 1944. He then adapted to the progressive big-band style as a member of Woody Herman's First Herd (April 1944 – September 1945; for illustration *see* HERMAN, WOODY, fig.1*a*.), with which he made several classic recordings and appeared in the film *Earl Carroll Vanities* (1945). Because he was now drinking excessively once again, Tough began to miss performances. He left Herman's band after suffering a seizure while touring the South. His final years, when not interrupted by ill-health or the effects of alcoholism, were spent in settings as varied as the group led by Charlie Ventura and Bill Harris (i) at the Three Deuces in New York (March–May 1947) and the traditional band of Muggsy Spanier in Chicago (November 1947 – January 1948). According to Kaye's research, Tough fell and fractured his skull on 8 December 1948 and died the next morning. However, death notices appeared only two days later, on 11 December, and obituaries the following day; hence an incorrect date of death has appeared in some sources.

Among white musicians of the 1920s and 1930s, Tough was probably the first to acquire a thorough understanding of African-American jazz drumming, which he admired deeply. Unusually versatile, he was comfortable in any group. Chubby Jackson, in published reminiscences of the period with Herman, marveled at Tough's ability to manipulate time, discreetly altering accents (before, on, or behind the beat) or even changing the tempo slightly to energize a given piece or to accord with a particular soloist.

SELECTED RECORDINGS

As sideman: New Yorkers: Hoosier Sweetheart (1927, Homokord 42420); Louisiana Rhythm Kings (1929, Voc. 15828); T. Dorsey: Royal Garden Blues/Ja-da (1936, Vic. 25326); Marie/Song of India (1937, Vic. 25523); B. Goodman: The Blues in your Flat/The Blues in my Flat (1938, Vic. 26044); Dizzy Spells (1938, Vic. 25822); Big John Special (1938, Vic. 25871); B. Freeman: Tappin' the Commodore Till (1938, Com. 508); B. Goodman: Opus 1/2 (1938, Vic. 26091); Bumble Bee Stomp (1938, Vic. 26087); E. Condon (1939, Decca 18040); J. Teagarden: Wolverine Blues (1939, Col. 35297); Beale Street Blues/Swingin' on the Teagarden Gate (1939, Col. 35323); B. Freeman: 47th and State (1940, Col. 35854); Shim-me-sha-wabble (1940, Col. 35856); Prince of Wails (1940, Col. 35853); B. Goodman: A Sm-o-o-oth One/Good Enought to Keep (Air Mail Special) (1941, Col. 36099); W. Herman: Apple Honey (1945, Col. 36803); Caldonia (1945, Col. 36789); Goosey Gander (1945, Col. 36815); Northwest Passage (1945, Col. 36835)

BIBLIOGRAPHY

E. Condon and T. Sugrue: *We Called it Music: a Generation of Jazz* (New York, 1947/*R*1988)
L. Feather: "Dave," *Eddie Condon's Treasury of Jazz*, ed. E. Condon and R. Gehman (New York, 1956/*R*1975), 162
J. Lucas: "Tough Stuff," *JJ*, xii/6 (1959), 5
R. Hadlock: "The Chicagoans," *Jazz Masters of the Twenties* (New York, 1965/*R*1985), 106–44
W. Balliett: "Jazz: Little Davy Tough," *New Yorker*, lxi (18 Nov 1985), 160; repr. in *BalliettA (1986)*, 121; *BalliettA (1996)*, 128
S. Voce: *Woody Herman* (London, 1986)
B. Korall: "Remembering Dave Tough," *MD*, xii/9 (1988), 32
R. Stewart and C. P. Gordon: *Boy Meets Horn* (Wheatley, Oxford, England, and Ann Arbor, MI, 1991), 137
H. S. Kaye: "Dave Tough with the New Yorkers in Europe," in *Storyville 1998/9*, ed. L. Wright (Chigwell, England, 1999), 5

BK

Toussaint, Jean (*b* Aruba, Lesser Antilles, 27 July 1957). Antillean tenor saxophonist. He grew up in St. Thomas in the US Virgin Islands and was initially a singer, performing in the high-pitched manner of the young Michael Jackson, but in his mid-teens, after his voice had broken, he took up alto saxophone; while at high school he had piano lessons. Having changed to tenor saxophone, he spent four semesters at the Berklee College of Music (*c*1978–80) and then worked in Boston (until 1982). From August 1982 to November 1986 he was a member of Art Blakey's Jazz Messengers, with which he toured internationally and made several albums; he also recorded with Kirk Lightsey. Late in 1986 he moved to London to perform and to teach at the Guildhall School of Music and Drama. He led a quartet that included either Jason Rebello or Julian Joseph on piano and either Alec Dankworth or Dave Green on double bass and a jazz-rock group, Nazaire, in which Rebello, Joseph, and the guitarist Tony Rémy all performed. As a sideman he appeared with Rebello, Joseph, Bheki Mseleku, Andy Hamilton, and Claire Martin, among others, and recorded with Nathan Davis (1987), Mseleku (*c*1991), and Hamilton (1994). Toussaint continued to lead groups in the late 1990s, one of which was co-led by Hugh Fraser (from 1996) and another of which involved Rebello (1997).

SELECTED RECORDINGS

As leader: of Nazaire: *Who's Blues* (1991, Ronnie Scott's Jazz House JHCD 019); *What Goes Around* (*c*1991, World Circuit 029); *Life I Want* (*c*1995, New Note 1001); with H. Fraser: *Back to Back* (1996, Jazz Focus 025)
As sideman: A. Blakey: *Blue Night* (1985, Tim. 217); K. Lightsey: *Kirk 'n Marcus* (1986, Criss Cross 1030)

BIBLIOGRAPHY

I. Gitler: Liner notes, A. Blakey: *Art Blakey Live at Sweet Basil* (1985, PW 6357)
M. Hennessey: "Europajazz," *JT* (1988), Nov, 21
"Gros plan," *Jm*, no.418 (1992), 10
A. Titmuss: "Shooting the Messenger," *Jazz: the Magazine*, no.14 (1992), 20
J. Fordham: "Bringing the Message Home," *Jazz UK*, no.6 (1995), 8
——: "Rebel Rebello: the Comeback," *The Guardian* (13 Sept 1997)

BK

Towles, Nat (C.) (*b* New Orleans, 10 Oct 1905; *d* Berkeley, CA, 29 Nov 1962). Bandleader and double bass player. His birth month has appeared in jazz literature as August, but October is given in both the social security and California death indexes; the latter also provides his death information, which has also been mis-reported. The son of the double bass player Phil (Charlie) Towles, he first learned guitar and violin; after changing to double bass he worked with the Melody Jazz Band (1922) and Buddy Petit and Henry "Red" Allen (both 1923). In 1923 he formed the Creole Harmony Kings, which played in New Orleans and toured Oklahoma, Texas, and New Mexico (1923–7). During this period he also worked briefly with Fate Marable (*c*1925). He left New Orleans in 1929 as a member of the Seven Black Aces, led by the banjoist Thomas Benton. Thereafter he led his own band in Jackson, Mississippi (1930–33). He assumed leadership in 1935 of a student band at Wiley College, Austin, Texas, with which he performed in Dallas. It held a very successful engagement in Omaha, Nebraska (1936–7), and toured the Southwest; among its members were Money Johnson, Fred Beckett, Henry Coker, Sir Charles Thompson, and Buddy Tate. Although most of his sidemen joined Horace Henderson in 1940, Towles continued to work as a leader; his few recordings include *There you are/Strictly Swing* (1943, Tower 1257). He ceased performing after moving to California in 1959.

BIBLIOGRAPHY

ChiltonW; McCarthyB
J. Lucas: "Nat Towles Recalls Crescent City Jazz," *DB*, xi/12 (1944), 3
K. Mohr: "Nat Towles," *Jh*, no.119 (1957), 15
F. S. Driggs: "Kansas City and the Southwest," *Jazz: New Perspectives on the History of Jazz*, ed. N. Hentoff and A. J. McCarthy (New York, 1959/*R*1974), 189
"The (Incomplete) Story of Nat Towles Orchestra," *Jazz Statistics*, no.10 (1959), 8
A. McCarthy: "The Nat Towles Story," *JM*, no.168 (1969), 2
R. Russell: *Jazz Style in Kansas City and the Southwest* (Berkeley, CA, Los Angeles, and London, 1971, rev. 2/1973/*R*1997), 69
P. Vacher: "The Forgotten Ones: Nat Towles. Buddy Tate Talks about the Thirties Dance Band Leader," *JJI*, xli/9 (1988), 10
P. Love: *A Thousand Honey Creeks Later: my Life in Music from Basie to Motown – and Beyond* (Hanover, NH, and London, 1997)

HOWARD RYE

Towner, Ralph (N.) (*b* Chehalis, WA, 1 March 1940). Acoustic guitarist. Born into a musical family, he studied trumpet, taught himself piano, and later received a BA in composition from the University of Oregon (1963). He then took up guitar, studying classical technique with Karl Scheit in Vienna in 1963 and again in 1967. After his return to the USA he worked in small jazz groups with Jimmy Garrison (1969–70) and Jeremy Steig (1969–71), mainly as a pianist. He rose to prominence with a notable solo for 12-string guitar issued on Weather Report's *I Sing the Body Electric* (1971). In 1970 Towner had joined the Paul Winter Consort, and late that year he and his fellow sidemen left Winter to found the group Oregon, with which Towner explored a highly individual mixture of classical, rock, jazz, and Indian musics. He also played with Gary Burton (1974–5) and toured in a duo with John Abercrombie (mid-1970s–1980s). He is one of the few postwar jazz guitarists to specialize in the acoustic guitar, which he plays in a "pianistic" manner, drawing on the instrument's full range and often carrying on several processes simultaneously in different registers. Although his work is only tenuously connected with jazz, he performs well in duos with jazz musicians. His solo performances, almost always based on his own compositions, unite a wide range of material, from impressionism to folk music, with unusual coherence. His best-known composition is *Icarus*, popularized by the Winter Consort.

SELECTED RECORDINGS

As unaccompanied soloist: *Diary* (1973, ECM 1032), incl. Icarus; *Solo Concert* (1979, ECM 1173); *Blue Sun* (1982, ECM 1250)
Duos: with G. Burton: *Matchbook* (1974, ECM 1056), incl. Icarus; with J. Abercrombie: *Sargasso Sea* (1976, ECM 1080); *Five Years Later* (1981, ECM 1207); with G. Burton: *Slide Show* (1985, ECM 1306); with G. Peacock: *Oracle* (1993, ECM 1490)
As leader: of Oregon (with P. McCandless, G. Moore, and C. Walcott): *Music of Another Present Era* (1972, Van. 79326); *Solstice* (1974, ECM 1060); of Oregon: *Roots in the Sky* (1979, Elek. 6E224); *Old Friends, New Friends* (1979, ECM 1153); *City of Eyes* (1988, ECM 1388)
As sideman with Weather Report: on *I Sing the Body Electric* (1971–2, Col. KC31352), The Moors

BIBLIOGRAPHY

CarrJ
L. Lyons: "Ralph Towner: Oregon's Classical/Jazz Master," *GP*, ix/12 (1975), 10
C. Mitchell: "Ralph Towner: a Chorus of Inner Voices," *DB*, xlii/12 (1975), 16
J. Reese: "La guitare pianistique de Ralph Towner," *Jh*, no.378 (1980), 10
L. Nowakowski: "Ralph Towner: Acoustic Eclectic," *DB*, l/5 (1983), 14
J. Woodard: "Ralph Towner: Chamber-made Jazz," *JT*, xxvi/4 (1996), 42

J. BRADFORD ROBINSON/BK

Town Hall. Concert hall in New York, which was used frequently for performances of jazz; *see* Nightclubs and other venues.

Townsend, Bross (Elvie, Jr.) (*b* Princeton, KY, 18 Oct 1933). Pianist. He was introduced to music by his father, a pianist who played in the tradition of Earl Hines, and took up formal piano studies at the age of seven. In 1951 the family moved to Cleveland, and Townsend accompanied such local singers as Little Jimmy Scott and Wynonie Harris while studying arranging and composition at the Cleveland Institute of Music. From 1953 he toured and worked as freelance with Gene Ammons, John Coltrane, and such blues musicians as Memphis Slim and Jimmy Reed. He settled in New York in 1959 and remained active there in the late 1990s. An open-minded musician, he is comfortable not only in rhythm-and-blues, soul music, and conventional jazz groups, but also in avant-garde settings (including the Composer's Workshop Ensemble of Warren Smith (ii)); among the musicians with whom he has collaborated are Carrie Smith, Woody Herman, Diana Ross, and Kalaparusha Maurice McIntyre. He formed a duo with Bob Cunningham and the trio the Dynamic 3B's with Cunningham and Bernard Purdie, and he also appeared as an unaccompanied soloist. Townsend lost his sight in the mid-1990s, but continued to perform, and toured Europe several times.

SELECTED RECORDINGS

As leader: *I Love Jump* (1995, Claves Jazz 50-1095)
As sideman: W. Smith: *Composer's Workshop Ensemble* (1972, SE 1972/3); Dynamic 3B's: *After Hours with the 3B's* (*c*1992, 3B's 001); Arvell Shaw: *A Tribute to Satchmo* (*c*1991, Victoria 92022); B. Brooks: *The Big Sound of Bubba Brooks* (1995, Claves Jazz 50-1359)

OTTO FLÜCKIGER

Township jazz. A synthesis of American swing and South African traditional or urban popular music. In the 1940s Zacks Nkosi was a forerunner of this style, which flourished in South Africa in the 1950s. Barney Rachabane's composition *Kwela Mama* is also representative of the genre, and its practitioners Kippie Moeketsi and Ntemi Piliso later became members of the African Jazz Pioneers, a group which revived township jazz in the 1980s.

Toyama, Yoshio (*b* Tokyo, 5 March 1944). Japanese trumpeter, singer, and leader. At the age of 13 he taught himself to play trumpet, mainly influenced by Hollywood films featuring jazz. A specialist in New Orleans jazz and the playing and singing style of Louis Armstrong, he graduated in 1966 from Waseda University in Tokyo, where he was very active in the New Orleans Jazz Club. He lived in New Orleans from 1968 to 1969 with his wife, Keiko, who plays banjo and piano, and studied under and performed with many legendary players, including George Lewis (i), Jim Robinson, and Danny Barker. In summer 1970 he led a band in Osaka, then in 1971 and 1972 he toured Europe and the USA as a member of Barry Martyn's New Orleans Jazz Band. After returning briefly to New Orleans and then in spring 1973 to Japan, Toyama led his Dixieland Saints from 1975; the group first performed at the Sacramento Dixieland Jubilee in 1978, and it appeared annually in the Los Angeles area at the Classic Jazz Festival (and its successor from 1996, the Sweet and Hot Music Festival). From 1981 into the 1990s it held a residency at the Japanese location of Disneyland. Toyama appeared in Denver in 1994 as a member of Ralph Sutton's All Stars. He also heads, with Keiko, the Louis Armstrong Fans' Association of Japan, which regularly donates musical instruments to children of New Orleans.

SELECTED RECORDINGS

Duos with D. Ewell: *Duet* (1975, Overseas 76)

As leader: with D. Ewell: *Do You Know What it Means to Miss New Orleans* (1975, Offbeat 1007); *The Saints* (1976, RCA RVL8503); *Dixieland Saints* (1978, Toyama 01); *Satchmo Forever* (1978, Far East 85002); *Tribute to Louis Armstrong* (1981, Far East 85018); *What a Wonderful World* (1996, Denon COCC13558)

As sideman: B. Martyn: *Boston Concert* (1971, Dixie 8); A. Purnell: *Alton Purnell with Barry Martyn's Band at the 100 Club* (1972, 77 SEU12/44)

BIBLIOGRAPHY

R. Fehring and R. Fehring: "Toyamas Spread New Orleans Sounds," *SL*, xxxvii (1985), summer, 28

J. Bradley: "Tokyo Trumpeter Does Satchmo Proud," *Denver Post* (20 Sept 1994)

KAZUNORI SUGIYAMA

Tracey, Clark (*b* London, 5 Feb 1961). English drummer, son of Stan Tracey. He played piano and vibraphone initially and took up drums at the age of 13; later he studied with Bryan Spring. From 1978 he has played in a number of bands with his father, including a long-lasting quartet and another quartet, Fathers and Sons (1990s), alongside John and Alec Dankworth. In addition he has accompanied numerous visiting Americans on a occasional basis, among them Scott Hamilton, Johnny Griffin, and Pharoah Sanders. He has had associations with an ensemble co-led by Buddy DeFranco and Martin Taylor (1984–6), and with Charlie Rouse (1988), Alan Skidmore (performing in Hong Kong in 1989), Tommy Smith (late 1980s), and Guy Barker (touring in 1992). In the early 1980s Tracey began leading and recording with his own small groups, which at various times have involved Django Bates, Iain Ballamy, Guy Barker, Jamie Talbot, Mark Nightingale, Dave O'Higgins, Nigel Hitchcock, Gerard Presencer, Mornington Lockett, Jean Toussaint, and Alan Barnes. From 1990 he has worked with his wife, Tina May, and with Claire Martin. As well as performing Tracey has composed and arranged for small groups, string quartets, and big bands, both for his own projects and under commission.

SELECTED RECORDINGS

As leader: *Suddenly Last Tuesday* (1986, Cadillac 1013); *Stiperstones* (1987, Steam 115); *We've Been Expecting You* (1992, 33 Jazz 007); *Full Speed Sideways* (1994, 33 Jazz 018); with D. Newton: *Bootleg Eric* (1998, ASC 23)

As sideman: S. Tracey: *The Poet's Suite* (1984, Steam 111); B. DeFranco and M. Taylor: *Garden of Dreams* (1986, Projazz 661); T. May: *Never Let Me Go* (1991, 33 Jazz 005); G. Barker: *Isn't it?* (1991, Spot. 545); S. Tracey: *Portraits Plus* (1992, BN International 80696); *Live at the Queen Elizabeth Hall* (1994, BN International 31139); B. Wellins: *Satin Album* (1996, Jazzizit 9607)

BIBLIOGRAPHY

CarrJ; *ChiltonB*

B. Rusch: "The Questionnaire," *Cadence*, xxii/4 (1996), 35

M. Pearson: "Living the Tradition," *Jazz UK*, no.20 (1998), 11

MARK GILBERT

Tracey, Stan(ley William) (*b* London, 30 Dec 1926). English pianist and composer, father of Clark Tracey. He began on accordion before taking up the piano at the age of 13, and was largely self-taught; he first worked as a professional musician at the age of 16. In the course of his service in the RAF he led a group, including Vic Ash, on a USO tour of Germany. During the 1950s he played in various bands, among them Eddie Thompson's quintet, in which he played accordion (1950–51). After working with the drummer Laurie Morgan and, in August 1951, Cab Calloway, Tracey was a member of Kenny Baker's octet (October 1951 – March 1952, September–December 1952) and quartet (August 1953 – November 1954), and played with Ash's quartet, Tony Crombie, Ronnie Scott (early 1956), Carl Barriteau, Kenny Graham, and the drummers Ivor Kirchins and Basil Kirchins. He went to the USA with Scott in February 1957, but from April resumed working in London briefly with Dizzy Reece, with the Kirchins together, and with Basil Kirchin before joining Ted Heath's orchestra as pianist, vibraphonist, and arranger the following September.

Stan Tracey (right) and Gil Evans in London during an interview at Radio London's studios, February 1978

Tracey rejoined Crombie late in 1959, then early in 1960 became a member of Ronnie Scott's quintet, which, following a brief retirement, he returned to in December 1960, under the co-leadership of Scott and Jimmy Deuchar. He led his own trio at Scott's club from that time to 1968, and as house pianist worked with a large number of visiting American soloists, notably Zoot Sims, Sonny Rollins, and Ben Webster, in whose quintet he appeared, together with Scott, on the television show "Jazz 625" in December 1964. Up to the mid-1960s Tracey had performed as a pianist (and occasionally as a vibraphonist), apparently influenced by the work of Thelonious Monk and Duke Ellington, but at this point it became apparent that he was not only a remarkable soloist, his style pungent, percussive, and harmonically daring, but also an exceptionally original composer. In 1964 he established a quartet which included Bobby Wellins, and the following year, with this ensemble, he recorded his suite based on Dylan Thomas's *Under Milk Wood*, a work generally considered a masterpiece of British jazz. Thereafter he wrote a number of suites for big band, notably *Alice in Jazzland* (1966), *Seven Ages of Man* (1969), and *Genesis* (1987), several of which he recorded on his own label, Steam (established in 1965); material from Steam was reissued on Blue Note in the 1990s.

With Sonny Rollins,Tracey recorded the soundtrack to the film *Alfie* (1966); except for the title tune (by Burt Bacharach) he composed all of the music (which has been mistakenly attributed to Rollins). He recorded as a sideman with Joe Harriott (1967) and Neil Ardley (1971) and made arrangements of some of Ellington's compositions (recorded on the album *We Love You Madly*, 1968, Col. SX6320). For much of the early 1970s he composed for and played in small groups, and during a short period improvised in the free-jazz manner, although his work retained its highly individual harmonic character. From 1976 to 1985 Tracey led an octet, and in 1979 he formed a sextet, later known as Hexad; he worked regularly in duos with such musicians as Tony Coe, Alan Skidmore, Mike Osborne (recording in 1972 and 1976), Keith Tippett (recording in 1974), and John Surman, with whom he recorded on piano synthesizer in 1978. He also led a quartet (which from 1978 comprised Art Themen, Roy Babbington, and his son Clark Tracey), a quintet which toured the UK in 1988 (with the addition of Skidmore), and an orchestra. He played in the big band led by the drummer Charlie Watts (1985–6) and in Fathers and Sons, alongside his son Clark and John and Alec Dankworth (late 1980s). He toured Hong Kong with Skidmore (1989) and recorded with Guy Barker (1991), among others. In December 1996 his 70th birthday was celebrated with a concert at the Queen Elizabeth Hall, London, featuring Tracey in a number of settings, from unaccompanied soloist to full orchestra. He has taught at Goldsmiths' College and the Guildhall School of Music.

Oral history material in *GBLnsa*.

SELECTED RECORDINGS

* – composed by Tracey

As unaccompanied soloist: *Stan Tracey . . . in Person* (1966, Col. SX6124), incl. *Let them crevulate

Duos: with K. Tippett: *TNT* (1974, Steam 104); with J. Surman: *Sonatinas* (1978, Steam 106)

As leader: *Little Klunk* (1959, Vogue 160155), incl. *Little Klunk; *Under Milk Wood* (1965, Col. 33SX1774), incl. *Cockle Row, *No good boyo, *Under Milk Wood; *Alice in Jazzland* (1966, Col. SX6051), incl. *Afro-Charlie meets the white rabbit; **Seven Ages of Man* (1969, Col. SCX6413); **Salisbury Suite* (1977, Steam 105); **Crompton Suite* (1981, Steam 109); **The Poets' Suite* (1984, Steam 111); **Genesis* (1987, Steam 114); *Portraits Plus* (1992, BN International 80696)

BIBLIOGRAPHY

CarrJ; *ChiltonB*; *Feather '60s*; *Feather–Gitler '70s*; *WickesIBJ*, i
M. Jones: "Tracey: So Busy Doing Nothing," *MM* (15 Oct 1966), 8
S. Lake: "Freedom and Stan Tracey," *MM* (3 May 1975), 58
S. Tracey: "Freedom is Nothing without Self-discipline," *CI*, xiv/1 (1975), 24
R. Cotterrell, ed.: *Jazz Now: the Jazz Centre Society Guide* (London, 1976)
J. Solothurnmann: "Stan Tracey," *JF* [intl edn], no.46 (1977), 44 [incl. discography]
P. Renaud: *La discographie du jazz anglais* (Chaumont, France, 1985)
"Stan Tracey: a British Legend," *CI*, xxv/3 (1988), 5
M. Davidson: "Call and Response: Letters," *Cadence*, xvi/1 (1990), 66
A. Hamilton: "Tracey in Blue," *Wire*, no.111 (1993), 18
J. Fordham: "Half-century Stan," *Boz Incorporating Jazz Express*, no.7 (1994), 7
M. Pearson: "Stan Tracey," *JJI*, xlvii/3 (1994), 6

CHARLES FOX/DIGBY FAIRWEATHER, SIMON ADAMS, BK

Track. (1) The groove in a phonograph disc; *see* Recording, §1.

(2) One of two or more discrete musical items on a single side of a disc, hence by extension such items on an EP (*see* Recording, §I, 3(ii)) or any form of Album. On microgroove discs the items are normally but not always marked off by narrow bands that carry an unmodulated spiral groove.

(3) One of two or more paths on magnetic recording tape receiving information from a single input channel; hence by extension the single voice or line recorded, whether on tape or by digital means. *See* Recording, §I, 3.

Trad. A style of traditional jazz current in Britain between the mid-1950s and the early 1960s. The term was applied to a particularly commercial and simplified form of revivalist jazz which was modeled on the serious attempts of Ken Colyer and Chris Barber to re-create New Orleans styles. Trad bands followed the instrumentation of New Orleans groups (trumpet, trombone, clarinet, banjo, double bass, drums, and occasionally piano); the principal and most influential were those of Barber, Acker Bilk, and Kenny Ball. Their repertory was bland, ranging from jazz interpretations of popular songs and nursery rhymes (such as Barber's *Bobby Shaftoe*, 1954, Decca F10492) to cloying, sentimental clarinet solos, notably those of Monty Sunshine (with Barber) and Bilk, whose greatest hit was his theme music for the television series "Stranger on the Shore." The brief vogue for trad resulted in part from shrewd marketing techniques, which featured such anachronistic touches as the association of Bilk's band with bowler hats and Victorian waistcoats.

A number of bands were formed to exploit the commercial potential of trad, but they proved short-lived, and after riots at the Beaulieu Festival in 1961 and the rift between supporters of traditional and modern styles of jazz, the repertory lost popularity. Some elements of the style have remained in use in continental Europe (notably in Germany and the Netherlands), but trad in its strict sense was a spent force by 1965. Among the other most important bands in the trad movement were Beryl Bryden's Back Room Boys, Forrie Cairns and the Clansmen, Dick Charlesworth and his City Gents, the Clyde Valley Stompers, the Mike Cotton Jazzmen, Mike Daniels and his Delta Jazzmen, Alan Elsdon and his Jazz Band, the Fairweather–Brown All Stars, Terry Lightfoot and his New Orleans Jazzmen, the London City Stompers, Jim McHarg's Scottsville Jazz Band, the Sonny Morris Jazz Band, Mike Peters's Florida Jazz Band, Alex Revell's Jazz Band, and Bob Wallis and his Storyville Jazzmen.

BIBLIOGRAPHY

R. Harris: *Jazz* (London, 1952, 5/1957)
——: *Enjoying Jazz* (London, 1961)
I. Berg, I. Yeomans, and N. Brittan: *Trad: an A to Z Who's Who of the British Traditional Jazz Scene* (London and elsewhere, 1962)
B. Matthew: *Trad Mad* (London, 1962)
G. Melly: *Revolt into Style: the Pop Arts in Britain* (London, 1970)
J. Godbolt: *A History of Jazz in Britain, 1950–1970* (London, 1989)

ALYN SHIPTON

Trade. In jazz to divide a chorus between or among solo players, so that each takes a phrase in turn. The length of phrases traded is usually four bars, but eight-bar and two-bar phrases and even single bars are also treated in this way; the players are said to "trade fours" ("eights," "twos," "ones"). *See* FORMS, §1(ii); *see also* CHASE.

Traditional jazz. A term that arose in polemical writings of the late 1930s to distinguish NEW ORLEANS JAZZ of the 1920s from the swing style of the 1930s; it was later applied to the music of New Orleans revival groups and is now used almost exclusively in that sense. Beginning in 1938, four forces led to a revival of a supposedly authentic New Orleans style: first, several nationally prominent black jazz musicians (Sidney Bechet, Jelly Roll Morton, and Jimmie Noone) were recorded playing a purportedly traditional repertory using traditional instrumentation; second, a significant number of white musicians, both in the USA (Turk Murphy and Lu Watters in San Francisco) and elsewhere, turned to recordings of New Orleans jazz of the 1920s for models (during the 1980s, in an attempt to re-create earlier performance practice, some groups using instruments of the period played exact transcriptions of recordings); third, a number of older black New Orleans musicians who had never or rarely played outside Louisiana were recorded by white aficionados; finally, older dixieland musicians, many of whom had retired to New Orleans, were recorded from the mid-1950s, often under the auspices of the New Orleans Jazz Club. The music of the third group (beginning with the recordings made under Kid Rena's leadership in 1940 and continuing with those of Bunk Johnson and George Lewis (i)) has come to be regarded as the authentic bearer of the New Orleans tradition of jazz, which is thought to continue in the music still played in New Orleans at Preservation Hall. However, this revival style, often excellent in its own right, was a locally evolved idiom that responded to market forces (an appetite for folklore, nostalgia, and primitivism) rather than a resurrection of a type of music that was originally more cosmopolitan and technically demanding. Whatever the case, the traditional-jazz movement has a very large and devoted audience and many active performers, especially outside the USA, with an eclectic repertory and performing style. In this most generalized usage, the term traditional jazz is sometimes used interchangeably with the term DIXIELAND.

See also JAZZ (i), §§IV, 7, V, 10.

BIBLIOGRAPHY

Second Line (1950–)
W. L. Grossman and J. W. Farrell: *The Heart of Jazz* (New York, 1956/*R*1976)
A. J. McCarthy: "The Re-emergence of Traditional Jazz," *Jazz: New Perspectives on the History of Jazz*, ed. N. Hentoff and A. J. McCarthy (New York, 1959/*R*1974), 303
Footnote (1969–89)
Mississippi Rag (1973–)
T. Stagg and C. Crump: *New Orleans, the Revival: a Tape and Discography of Negro Traditional Jazz Recorded in New Orleans or by New Orleans Bands, 1937–1972* (n.p. [London], 1973)
T. Ikegami: *New Orleans Renaissance on Record* (Tokyo, 1980) [discography]
New Orleans Music (1989–)
B. Bissonette: *The Jazz Crusade: the Inside Story of the Great New Orleans Jazz Revival of the 1960s* (Bridgeport, CT, 1992) [incl. discography]

LAWRENCE GUSHEE

Traill, (Eric) Sinclair [Sinc] (*b* Camborne, England, Dec 1904; *d* Brighton, England, 10 Jan 1981). English writer and editor. After a brief career in banking he began to write about jazz, and with Bill Elliott he developed the feature "Collector's Corner" for *Melody Maker*. During World War II he served with the RAF in India, where he produced a program for the radio network of the armed forces, reviewed records for the Forces magazine *Victory*, and, most significantly, arranged and supervised a series of unaccompanied piano recordings by Teddy Weatherford. He then moved to London, where from 1946 to 1947 he published the magazine *Pick Up*. He is best known for having edited *Jazz Journal* (from 1977 known as *Jazz Journal International*) from May 1948 until his death. As an editor Traill won respect for his taste, tact, fairness, humor, and considerable flamboyance.

WRITINGS

(selective list)

ed.: *Play that Music: a Guide to Playing Jazz* (London, 1956)
ed.: *Concerning Jazz* (London, 1957)
ed. with G. Lascelles: *Just Jazz* (London, 1957–60) [four annual vols.: incl. D. Coller and E. Townley: *Jazz Discography, 1956* [–*1957*]; F. Dutton and E. Townley: *Jazz Discography, 1958*; G. Cherrington: *Jazz Discography, 1959/60*]
with E. Kirkeby and D. P. Schiedt: *Ain't Misbehavin': the Story of Fats Waller* (London and New York, 1966)

BIBLIOGRAPHY

Obituary, R. Laing and others, *JJI*, xxxiv/3 (1981), 4

ROBERT GANNON

Tram. Nickname of FRANKIE TRUMBAUER.

Tramontana, Sebi [Sebastiano] (*b* Rosolini, nr Siracusa, Italy, 12 Dec 1960). Italian trombonist. As a teenager he purchased a soprano saxophone, taught himself to play it, and performed with Stefano Maltese's groups; he also played baritone saxophone at that time. In 1982 he changed to trombone and studied at the conservatory in L'Aquila while working in Rome with the pianist Martin Joseph, Eugenio Colombo, and Mario Schiano. In 1986 he joined the New Talents Orchestra and the following year he formed a trio with the double bass player Daniel Studer and the drummer Roberto Altamura. Later he performed with Paul Rutherford, Barry Guy, Colombo, the reed player Co Streiff, and the french horn player Martin Mayes. In 1990 he joined the Italian Instabile Orchestra. Tramontana first appeared as an unaccompanied soloist in Rome in 1992. From 1994 he worked with Georg Gräwe, touring in Europe and recording in a duo. In 1996 he played with Gruppo Romano Free Jazz for that band's 30th anniversary reunion and appeared at the festival at Roccella Jonica with Barre Phillips, Michel Doneda, and two dancers and at the Victoriaville festival with Schiano, Evan Parker, Paul Lovens, and Guy. He formed a duo with Joëlle Léandre in 1997 and in 1999 he played in Chicago with Léandre, Giancarlo Schiaffini, the trombonist Jeb Bishop, and other musicians. Tramontana lives in Munich, where he works as a music therapist.

A master of unaccompanied perfomance, Tramontana uses electronic devices to widen and change the sound of his instrument and adds elements of theater through careful use of body movements and sounds. His playing has harsh overtones reminiscent of the style of early New Orleans trombonists.

SELECTED RECORDINGS

Duos: with J. Léandre: *E' vero* (1997, Leo 275); with G. Gräwe: *Schz!* (1998, Splasc(h) 670)
As leader: with M. Schiano, V. Chekasin, and V. Tarasov: *Red and Blue* (1988; Splasc(h) 15); *Il giorno del santo* (1992, Wind 12)
As sideman: Antonio Moncada: *The True Story of Twelve Colours* (1992, Splasc(h) 394); M. Schiano: *Social Security* (1996, Victo 043); G. Gräwe: *Concert in Berlin* (1996, Wobbly Rail 007); Italian Instabile Orchestra:

Italian Instabile Festival (1997, Leo 262–3); Südpool Project: *Marcia funebre: the Italian Suite* (1998, Leo 45106); S. Maltese: *Open Letter to Mingus* (1998, Musica Jazz 1122)

BIBLIOGRAPHY

R. Valentino: "Sebi Tramontana: grazie all'elettronica mi sento meno solo," *Musica jazz*, lii/12 (1996), 34
<http://www.ijm.it/enartists.html> (1999)
<http://www.shef.ac.uk/misc/rec/ps/efi/minstab.html> (1999)

STEFANO ZENNI

Transcription (i). In jazz the act of fixing in notated form music that is entirely or partly improvised, or for which no written score exists; also the resulting notated version itself. The term is also applied to the traditional practice of memorizing and reproducing a recorded improvisation without necessarily notating it. It should not be confused with Transcription (ii), the process of copying sound from one source to another, or Transcription (iii), a type of sound recording. This article deals with the principles, purposes, techniques, and history of transcription and discusses its value as a means of disseminating jazz and as a tool for studying it. For a discussion of the ways in which transcribers have adapted the symbols of standard Western notation to jazz *see* Notation, §4.

1. Introduction. 2. Techniques and applications. 3. History.

1. Introduction. As with other forms of music transmitted by oral tradition, there was little need initially for jazz to be notated. Much of it was improvised or relied on certain musical conventions – melodic patterns, chord progressions, rhythmic devices – known to and shared by players and learned through imitation. Although musicians might glean similar principles of melodic, harmonic, and rhythmic transformation from published compositions (e.g., theme and variations, arrangements of popular songs), they could absorb the distinctive sounds of jazz and the specific techniques of jazz improvisation only through listening to the music.

The first musicians who wished to learn jazz had to find ways to translate the music they heard into something they could play. Most commonly they achieved this by developing their aural memory – by learning something in one context and attempting to re-create it later in another; by imitating phrases played by teachers or colleagues; and by copying parts directly from recordings or piano rolls, often by slowing down the speed at which these were being played and repeating passages many times. Many musicians who engaged in such activities had no need of notation, but some found it a useful bridge between the acts of listening and performing; by notating a solo, a player might come to understand the basic principles of improvisation and thereby generate fresh, original statements. Thus transcriptions facilitated analysis as well as performance.

2. Techniques and applications. Transcription as practiced by jazz musicians is usually a self-taught skill. There are no fixed rules for transcribing jazz, nor is there a standard set of symbols used to indicate pitch inflection, articulation, rhythmic deviation, and other expressive devices. Transcription is merely an extension of the technique, learned by every music student, of taking aural dictation, in which it is necessary to listen accurately, to construe analytically, and to notate. Repetition is an integral part of the process; accordingly, tape recorders are generally easier to work with than record players, and reel-to-reel machines offer more flexibility than do cassette players. With digital technology, difficult passages may sometimes be unraveled with the help of a function which allows the listener to create a loop that repeats between any two selected points; however, even this operation is no match for the flexibility of manipulating a reel-to-reel tape by hand to hear a particular moment of sound, or for the simplicity of playing such a recording at half-speed, whereby complex chords, sounding an octave lower than normal, and rhythms may be revealed. A graphic equalizer may further assist the transcriber to perceive cloudy textures.

Transcription becomes considerably more complicated for those wishing to study jazz. Unlike performing musicians, who may adopt an attitude of practical efficiency towards transcription, scholars have been concerned to bring a high level of detail and scientific rigor to the task. These different approaches roughly follow Charles Seeger's categories of "prescriptive" and "descriptive" notation (described in his article in *Musical Quarterly*, 1958), and also reflect the different philosophies behind performing and study editions. Whereas the player might intuitively know how to interpret or adjust notated rhythms to make them sound like the rhythms in a recorded performance, the scholar is interested in describing them as precisely as possible; in an effort to give a faithful graphic representation of an aural document, scholarly transcriptions therefore tend to exhibit a plethora of signs and symbols. Yet ironically, the more the transcriber travels in the direction of accuracy and precision, the more he or she departs from a score that may actually have been used in performance or one that may easily be read and interpreted in the future.

Western notation is weak in its ability to represent the rhythms and timbres of jazz. Thomas Owens (1974) made a preliminary attempt to analyze a slow-paced solo by Charlie Parker using the melograph model C (an electronic instrument that produced graphic representation of pitch and amplitude over time). Owens found that the machine (which was designed by Seeger) revealed many complex details of pitch, duration, and vibrato; for example, some scale steps received a variety of intonations in different contexts, and many notes were of lengths for which we have no symbols (e.g., fifteenth notes or nineteenth notes). However, on account of the "extreme rhythmic complexity of Parker's improvised melody," it revealed a high margin of error in reading pitches.

Milton Stewart and Richmond Browne, building on the hand graph method described by Bruno Nettl in *Theory and Method in Ethnomusicology* (New York, 1964), proposed a "grid" notation to help show more clearly the rhythmic displacement in an improvised solo. This makes use of vertical lines of different lengths within bars to indicate subdivisions of the beat, and then positions the pitches of a solo in relation to the lines. Stewart also added superscript symbols designed to give "a clear visual representation of articulation patterns and the resultant structures" (1982). But the resulting transcriptions, while in theory more accurate, are difficult to use. Neither the melograph nor the grid notation system has been widely adopted by transcribers of jazz. It was hoped that computer-aided transcription might yield a greater degree of precision in measuring the parameters of the music, but there is no strong evidence of any meaningful developments in this direction, and it may be that computers are essentially too rigid to reflect the subtleties of jazz; moreover, even if a computerized analysis were set up to capture the minutiae of the music, the resulting transcription would inevitably be unreadable in any kind of practical musical way.

No matter how much transcribers aim for accuracy, consistent notational practice, and expressive detail in their scores, the goal of capturing the essential element of jazz on paper may ultimately remain elusive; somehow it is a process at odds with the aesthetic values of the music and the creative spirit of its practitioners. Lee Castle acknowledged this problem and spoke for all transcribers in his preface to *Louis Armstrong's Immortal Trumpet Solos* (New York, 1947) when he wrote, "I have tried to compile what I think to be typical Louis. It wasn't easy, for black dots on white paper just can't express what's in his soul." And in many instances players have found it impossible to reproduce their own solos: James Moody, for example, on examining a transcription of his recording of *Cherokee*, exclaimed good-humoredly, "I don't even know how to play all those things" (1973).

3. History. While many professional jazz musicians regard transcription as an integral part of their own education, few have discussed the transcribing process in any detail (though Andrew White presents an account of his approach to the subject in *A Treatise on Transcription*, 1978); writers on jazz have also largely passed over the subject. As a result the history of jazz transcription still awaits fuller documentation and can be suggested only in broad outline. The informal process of transcribing jazz – copying solos or individual parts from recordings – probably began as soon as the latter became available, in the late 1910s. Even earlier, players had engaged in the same activity as they strove to emulate what they heard others perform in clubs, cabarets, and dance halls, at parades, and on riverboats. Recordings, however, made it easier for musicians to absorb other ideas and techniques, and at least one major figure, Freddie Keppard, supposedly resisted making them for fear that rivals would steal his tricks.

From the 1920s professional jazz musicians have used the transcribing process to learn from other professionals. When Charlie Parker, at the age of 16, worked in the band led by George E. Lee, he reportedly played solos taken from recordings made by Lester Young. (David Baker, at Indiana University, and other contemporary jazz educators have maintained the tradition, requiring students to memorize improvisations by Young, Parker, Armstrong, and other outstanding soloists.)

Another application of the technique, in which musicians have been obliged to re-create solos they or others have played in earlier performances, has been common in big bands: Tommy Dorsey, for example, required Buddy De-Franco constantly to reproduce the first solo he had improvised on *Opus no.1*, and Thad Jones cited the onus of repeating his original solo on *April in Paris* (with its interpolation of *Pop Goes the Weasel*) as a reason for his leaving Count Basie's orchestra. New members of bands with a long history of recording – such as that led by Duke Ellington – were often expected to know important solos played by their predecessors and to reproduce them as an act of homage; this was also an acknowledgment that such solos helped define the identity of the piece in question as well as the ensemble itself. Several trumpeters in bands led by Fletcher Henderson and Benny Goodman, among others, paid lip service to King Oliver's solo on *Dippermouth Blues* when they performed *Sugar Foot Stomp*. The same respect for instrumentalists has been shown by singers, among them Eddie Jefferson, King Pleasure, and Jon Hendricks, who have set lyrics to notable recorded solos, and by groups such as Supersax, which has specialized in performing arrangements of Charlie Parker's improvisations.

It is not possible to define precisely the moment when transcriptions were first notated. A signal event, however, was the appearance in 1927 of two collections of Louis Armstrong's improvisations, *50 Hot Choruses for Cornet* and *125 Jazz Breaks for Cornet*, published by Melrose Brothers of Chicago. The former publication claimed in its foreword that it differed from others of its type: "The solos in this book depart in principle of production from any solos on the market. They are genuine improvisations obtained, not by the old method of the artist writing down his solos one note at a time, but from actual recordings." Armstrong supposedly recorded his improvisations in the Melrose offices, where presumably a staff member notated them. Although no copy of these recordings has been traced, the "hot choruses" in the collection do bear a resemblance to the work of Armstrong in the late 1920s, so perhaps the publisher's claim may be believed. In addition the foreword made clear the practical application of the solos: "All that is necessary is to place this book on the music stand next to the orchestration – then when the orchestration reaches the cornet strain read your book instead of the orchestration." In the same way, *125 Jazz Breaks for Cornet* offered the jazz soloist solutions that Armstrong himself had employed, or might employ, in the relevant context.

In 1927 Melrose also advertised collections of solo breaks by Benny Goodman and Glenn Miller and arrangements of solos by Frankie Trumbauer, Ted Lewis, Jelly Roll Morton, Goodman, Miller, and Armstrong. Some of these publications may have involved the use of transcription, but it is difficult to determine how much; the arrangers employed by Melrose, and other publishers, may have been working from lead sheets, orchestrations, actual recordings, their own imagination, or any combination of these. Indeed, when staff arrangers produced sheet music or orchestrated versions of jazz pieces that had already been recorded, they sometimes incorporated solos taken from the recording. Examples of this may be found in sheet-music versions of Duke Ellington's *The Creeper* and *Birmingham Breakdown* published by Gotham Music Service in 1927.

In the 1930s transcriptions began to appear in periodicals aimed at jazz musicians, such as *Metronome* and *Down Beat*; Armstrong's *West End Blues* was the first transcribed solo to be published in the latter, in 1936. As writers turned their attention to jazz subjects they sometimes used transcriptions to illustrate their points. An early instance of this may be found in Roger Pryor Dodge's article "Jazz Trumpets and Harpsichords" (*Hound and Horn*, 1934), in which the author transcribed several versions of Bubber Miley's trumpet solo on different recordings of Ellington's *Black and Tan Fantasy*. Many transcribed music examples appeared in Winthrop Sargeant's *Jazz, Hot & Hybrid* (1938), and the composer Lou Harrison helped with notation in Rudi Blesh's history of jazz *Shining Trumpets* (1946).

The early 1940s saw the publication of a number of folios of transcriptions (or what were advertised as transcriptions). Like the volumes published in the 1920s, these were intended for players who wished to imitate their musical idol, or at least to perform in a style that was strongly identified with a particular soloist. The Robbins Music Corporation issued a series devoted to pianists, among them Teddy Wilson, Earl

Hines, Bob Zurke, Fats Waller, Mary Lou Williams, Willie "the Lion" Smith, and Art Tatum. Some of these folios included the word "transcription" in their titles, while others used "arrangement" or a similar euphemism (for example, *Teddy Wilson Piano Patterns*, *Rube Bloom Piano Impressions*). Again, the question of whether these publications contained actual transcriptions or merely arrangements in the style of major figures has yet to be answered fully. The uniform length of most of the solos raises doubts about authenticity; whereas the average recorded or live performance would be fairly extended, the published versions often end tidily after one or two choruses.

Other publishing firms that issued folios of transcriptions were M. M. Cole in Chicago and Harms and Leeds in New York. Leeds published a major series of solos by boogie-woogie and blues pianists and also collections of "warm-up exercises" by such artists as Rex Stewart and J. C. Higginbotham; the volume by the last named was said to contain "exact transcriptions from original recordings made by J. C. Higginbotham." The practice of identifying the soloist as the transcriber was unusual, and frequently the identity of the transcriber (or arranger) was not revealed; when in 1947 Leeds issued *Louis Armstrong's Immortal Trumpet Solos*, however, the transcriber was a well-known trumpeter and admirer of Armstrong, Lee Castle, who also wrote a preface to the collection.

As jazz education burgeoned in the 1960s and 1970s, there was a corresponding growth in the publication of transcriptions. The second of John Mehegan's four volumes on jazz improvisation, *Jazz Rhythm and the Improvised Line* (1962), consists largely of transcribed solos by artists ranging from Bessie Smith to Oscar Peterson. Some enterprising transcribers, such as Jamey Aebersold and Andrew White, started their own mail-order distribution services, while others, among them Don Sickler, Dave Berger, and Alan Campbell, have had their transcriptions issued by major publishing firms; Sickler later formed his own company. Many more transcribers, however, work in isolation and do not circulate their scores beyond a limited geographical area.

From the 1980s, while transcriptions continued to serve a practical pedagogical function, their use broadened through the jazz repertory movement and the increasing interest in jazz shown by musicologists and music theorists. Transcriptions are essential for musicians active in jazz repertory groups, which aim to re-create past styles and recorded performances, since in many cases the original scores (or any other kind of written parts the players may have used) are unavailable or have been lost. The accuracy of such transcriptions, as well as their faithfulness to the original recordings and flexibility of interpretation, varies considerably, depending on the musicians involved and the context in which they are performing. Among the major figures who have been involved in jazz repertory are Gunther Schuller (who has transcribed and performed compositions by Morton, Ellington, and others), Chuck Israels (leader of the National Jazz Ensemble), Martin Williams (who organized the Smithsonian Jazz Repertory Ensemble), Gary Giddins and John Lewis (who formed the American Jazz Orchestra), and Doug Richards and Andrew Homzy (both of whom have established successful repertory ensembles in colleges).

Transcriptions intended for the purpose of study rather than performance may be found in musicological and theoretical dissertations on jazz; among these are works by Thomas Owens on Charlie Parker, Charles Blancq on Sonny Rollins, Lewis Porter on John Coltrane, Franz Kerschbaumer on Miles Davis, Barry Kernfeld on Cannonball Adderley, Coltrane, and Davis, Scott DeVeaux on Coleman Hawkins and Howard McGhee, Ron Radano on Anthony Braxton, Mark Tucker on Duke Ellington, Felicity Howlett on Art Tatum, Steve Larsen on versions of Thelonious Monk's *'Round Midnight*, and Greg Smith on Bill Evans (ii). Some published works are also notable for their inclusion of transcriptions – for example, Schuller's *Early Jazz* (1968), Brian Priestley's *Mingus: a Critical Biography* (1982), and *Benny Carter: a Life in American Music* (1982), by M. Berger, E. Berger, and J. Patrick – as are such periodicals as the *Annual Review of Jazz Studies*, the *Journal of Jazz Studies*, and *Jazzforschung*.

By the mid-1980s only one major scholarly edition of transcriptions had appeared – James Dapogny's *Ferdinand "Jelly Roll" Morton: the Collected Piano Music* (1982). This volume represented a landmark in the history of jazz transcription and is exemplary in its thoroughness, attention to detail, and high editorial standards; it is a source intended for both study and performance, and thus accommodates the aims of scholars as well as those involved with repertory. In 1989 the Smithsonian Institution, in conjunction with the Oberlin Conservatory of Music, initiated the Jazz Masterworks Editions with the aim of publishing transcriptions and analyses of classic jazz recordings; unfortunately the project failed after only three volumes, which were devoted to individual pieces recorded by Ellington (among them Billy Strayhorn's *Take the "A" Train*).

Far more influential is Jamey Aebersold's series *A New Approach to Jazz Improvisation*, which he began in 1967 and which by 2000 numbered 87 volumes. These method books combine aspects of a lead sheet with those of transcription, whereby the melody and chord progression to a given popular standard or jazz tune is transcribed from a particular "definitive" (i.e., first, or most popular) recording, and that transcription of the theme is followed by the transcription of a solo from the same recording. Although they offer little of substance from a theoretical standpoint, Aebersold's volumes exhibit meticulous care in the transcription of melodies and chord progressons of famous jazz recordings and are enormously popular with those involved in jazz education. The demand for such "accurate" transcriptions has fostered the democratization of the music, enabling a great many more people to play jazz in a reasonably idiomatic manner. However, with too much emphasis placed upon notation and the notion of a definitive recorded version, this approach engenders the fossilization of jazz, and it is debatable whether it is entirely beneficial for the future of the music.

BIBLIOGRAPHY

C. Seeger: "Prescriptive and Descriptive Music Writing," *Musical Quarterly*, xliv/2 (1958), 184

"James Moody's solo 'Cherokee'," *DB*, xl/15 (1973), 38

T. Owens: "Applying the Melograph to 'Parker's Mood'," *Selected Reports in Ethnomusicology*, ii/1 (1974), 167

A. N. White III: *A Treatise on Transcription* (Washington, DC, 1978)

M. L. Stewart: "Grid Notation: a Notation System for Jazz Transcription," *ARJS*, i (1982), 3

T. S. Koger: "Fifty Years of *Downbeat* Solo Jazz Transcriptions: a Register," *Black Music Research Journal* (1985), 43

D. Morgenstern: "Comments on Fifty Years of *Downbeat* Solo Jazz Transcriptions," *Black Music Research Journal* (1986), 23

M. S. Haywood: "Melodic Notation in Jazz Transcription," *ARJS*, vi (1993), 271

B. Kernfeld: *What to Listen for in Jazz* (New Haven, CT, and London, 1995)

MARK TUCKER/BK

Transcription (ii). The process of copying sound from one source to another; also the result of such a process; in some cases the term is synonymous with "dubbing" (and "dub"). It is applied to a number of types of recording: for example, to one made from the radio (*see* Air check); to one made from a performance that is broadcast – in which case the recording is made simultaneously with the broadcast but not from the radio (and may or may not be used as a transcription in the sense described in Transcription (iii)); and to the converting of a recording made by analogue means (e.g., a multitrack magnetic tape recording) into a digital recording.

HOWARD RYE

Transcription [broadcast transcription] **(iii).** A recording (on disc or tape) produced for sale or distribution to radio stations for broadcasting. The term is commonly applied only to discs. Almost all such "transcriptions" are recorded specially in the studio (as, for example, in the case of sessions by Fats Waller and Clarence Williams for Lang–Worth and by Roy Eldridge and Louis Jordan for World), but some derive from performances broadcast live and simultaneously recorded, and a few (chiefly those made by AFRS) from commercially available recordings. In the 1930s and 1940s broadcast transcriptions were recorded on 16-inch discs that played at $33\frac{1}{3}$ r.p.m., allowing up to 15 minutes of playing time; some were recorded from the center outwards (a technique known as "center start"), rather than from the rim inwards (the conventional "rim-start" technique); and many were cut vertically at a time when commercial discs were cut laterally. As well as securing longer-playing time, these characteristics ensured that any change in audio quality perceived by listeners was an improvement, since the sound quality of disc recordings deteriorates towards the center. Taken together they had the incidental advantage that the recordings could not be played except on equipment available in radio stations. However, the advantages of exclusivity were quickly sacrificed by transcription companies once microgroove recordings, which offered superior reproduction, became available.

For a short period in the early years of sound films, before the development of optical methods of recording sound on film, transcription technology (i.e., the 16-inch disc recorded at $33\frac{1}{3}$ r.p.m.) was used to provide synchronized soundtracks. Thus in a few cases soundtracks are preserved independently of the films to which they belong; an example is Duke Ellington's *Black and Tan Fantasy* (1929), the soundtrack of which is preserved on an RKO transcription disc.

The term "transcription turntable" is sometimes applied to a turntable used for playing microgroove recordings, which shares certain technical characteristics with the turntables used by radio stations to play broadcast transcriptions in the 1930s and 1940s.

See also Recording, esp. §II, 3.

HOWARD RYE

Transition. Record company and label. The company was established by Tom Wilson in Cambridge, Massachusetts, in 1955. Although it remained in existence only for about two years it established an important reputation by enabling Donald Byrd, Cecil Taylor, Herb Pomeroy, Jay Migliori, Doug Watkins, and Sun Ra to make their first recordings as leaders. Around 20 albums were issued, among them three by Byrd, one by Johnny Windhurst, and Curtis Fuller's studio début. The company also sponsored sessions by Fuller that included John Coltrane, but issued only one of the four tracks that resulted; the remaining material was later released by Blue Note under Coltrane's name. Rather than liner notes, the albums were accompanied by booklets that contained information about the music. Transition's catalogue was acquired around 1958 by United Artists, for whom Wilson was by that time working as a producer. Some of the repertory was issued in different formats by Esquire in England; other items were put out by Delmark. From 1979 several of Transition's albums were released in Japan in replicas of the original packages. Later, Delmark and Blue Note reissued Transition material on CD.

MARK GARDNER

Trappier, Art(hur Benjamin) [Traps] (*b* Georgetown, SC, 28 May 1910; *d* New York, 17 May 1975). Drummer. He first played professionally in New York in 1928 with the pianist Charlie Skeete, and worked there in the 1930s with Tiny Bradshaw, Blanche Calloway, and Buddy Johnson. After performing with Sidney Bechet in summer 1941 he worked extensively with Fats Waller from mid-autumn 1941 until the pianist disbanded in mid-January 1943 (for illustration *see* Waller, fats). He performed and recorded with a number of other traditional and swing musicians, among them Wilbur De Paris (1944), James P. Johnson (recording for Blue Note in 1944), and Edmond Hall, with whom he was resident at the downtown location of Café Society (June 1944 – November 1945). In the late 1940s Trappier worked with Louis Armstrong (1945), Sy Oliver (on tour), Albert Nicholas, and Punch Miller (recording) (all 1947), Ralph Sutton (1948, in a trio with Nicholas in New York and St. Louis, and in Max Kaminsky's band in New York), and Tony Parenti and Wingy Manone (both 1949). He then appeared at Jimmy Ryan's and the Central Plaza with Bechet (February 1950), Hot Lips Page (1950–51), and others; during the same period he recorded in a duo with Sutton (1950), rejoined Bechet for a tour of Chicago, Toronto, and the northeast (September–November 1951), and performed with Sammy Benskin (1951). In the 1950s and 1960s he played with various dixieland bands, including his own, and he toured Canada with Willie "the Lion" Smith (1957) and recorded with Rex Stewart (January 1958); he continued as a freelance player in the New York area until his death. Trappier's recordings demonstrate his unobtrusive, subtle style.

SELECTED RECORDINGS

Duos with R. Sutton: In the Dark/Flashes (1950, Com. 639); Sweet Lorraine/Three Little Words (1950, Com. 640)

As sideman with: F. Waller: We Need a Little Love/The Jitterbug Waltz (1942, Bb 11518); Swing Out to Victory (1942, Bb 11569)

BIBLIOGRAPHY

ChiltonW; *FeatherE*

J. D. Shacter: *Piano Man: the Story of Ralph Sutton* (Chicago, 1975, rev. and enlarged [2]/1994, as *Loose Shoes: the Story of Ralph Sutton*)

J. Chilton: *Sidney Bechet: the Wizard of Jazz* (London and New York, 1987/*R*1996)

M. Selchow: *Profoundly Blue: a Bio-discographical Scrapbook on Edmond Hall* (Lübbecke, Germany, 1988)

L. Wright: *"Fats" in Fact* (Chigwell, England, 1992)

T. DENNIS BROWN/BK

Trap set [traps]. *See* Drum set.

Travis, Nick [Travascio, Nicholas Anthony] (*b* Philadelphia, 16 Nov 1925; *d* New York, 7 Oct 1964). Trumpeter. After playing with Vido Musso (1942) and Woody Herman (intermittently, 1942–4) he performed in Paris during his military service. He then worked with Ray McKinley (intermittently, 1946–50), Benny Goodman (1948–9), Gene Krupa and Ina Ray Hutton (both late 1940s), Tommy Dorsey and Tex Beneke (both 1950), Herman (1950–51), Jerry Gray, Bob Chester, and Elliot Lawrence (all 1951), and Jimmy Dorsey (1952–3). He was a principal soloist in the Sauter–Finegan Orchestra from 1953 to 1956; the following year he became a member of the NBC staff in New York, and he was active into the 1960s as a studio musician. From 1960 to 1962 he toured and recorded with Gerry Mulligan's Concert Jazz Orchestra, and in 1963 he played with a ten-piece band led by Thelonious Monk at Lincoln Center and Carnegie Hall. Travis was considered an excellent and versatile trumpeter with a strong, clear tone; he spent most of his career playing in big bands, but may be heard as a bop soloist on recordings with the quintets led by Al Cohn and Zoot Sims and also as the leader of his own quintet.

SELECTED RECORDINGS

As leader: *The Panic is On* (1954, RCA LPM1010)

As sideman: A. Cohn: *Al Cohn with Nick Travis, Horace Silver, Curley Russell, and Max Roach* (1953, Prog. 3004); E. Sauter and B. Finegan: *Inside Sauter–Finegan* (1953, RCA LPM1003); E. Lawrence: *Swinging at the Steel Pier* (1956, Fan. 3236); Z. Sims: *Zoot!* (1956, Riv. 228); M. Albam: *The Jazz Giants of our Time* (1957, Coral 57173); W. Herman: *The Herd Rides Again* (1958, Ev. 5003)

BIBLIOGRAPHY

FeatherE

Obituary, *DB*, xxxi/30 (1964), 10

W. D. Clancy with A. C. Kenton: *Woody Herman: Chronicles of the Herds* (New York and elsewhere, 1995)

FREDERICK A. BECK

Travo, Manuel. Pseudonym of DAVID BEE.

Traxler, Gene [Eugene Frederick] (*b* Chambersburg, PA, 28 June 1913; *d* 18 July 1991). Double bass player. His full name appears on his application for social security. He was taught by his father to play a number of instruments, including piano, which he studied for two years, violin, which he learned for eight years, and double bass, which he took up as a teenager. After leading his own seven-piece band in high school he worked with local groups in the early 1930s and played in Baltimore and Buffalo. He recorded with Joe Venuti (1934), worked with Joe Haymes, and played and sang with Tommy Dorsey's band (1935–40). Thereafter he performed in New York at the Hickory House as a member of Joe Marsala's group, with which he made several recordings (among them *Three o'Clock Jump/Reunion in Harlem*, 1940, General 3001), worked as a studio musician for NBC (*c*1942–5), and recorded with Benny Goodman (1944). From 1945 to 1972 Traxler played in the band for the "Arthur Godfrey Show" on CBS television, and from 1972 to 1978 he performed with a show band in Florida; he then retired. He recorded with Connee Boswell in 1956. The social security death index gives only his date of death. (H. Sanford: *Tommy and Jimmy: the Dorsey Years*, New Rochelle, NY, 1972)

BK

Traynor, Frank [Thomas Francis] (*b* Melbourne, Australia, 8 Aug 1927; *d* Melbourne, 22 Feb 1985). Australian trombonist. After making his début as a jazz musician on piano (1944) he changed to trombone and performed and recorded with Len Barnard (1949–55). In 1956 he formed the Jazz Preachers, which he led until his death. The band toured regularly and made many recordings of traditional jazz, some of which were issued in Europe and North America as well as in Australia; the most commercially successful of these was the single *Sweet Patootie* (1962, W&G 1524), which was a hit in Australia. In 1961 he opened Frank Traynor's, a folk and jazz club in Melbourne, which became known internationally. He was an important figure in the revival of traditional jazz in Australia in the 1950s and 1960s, organizing concerts and festivals and teaching, as well as performing and recording. A representative example of Traynor's later work, recorded by his Jazz Preachers in 1979 and first issued on an album of unknown title on the unnumbered Roseleaf label, was reissued on the CD compilation *Keith Hounslow, My Jazz Life, 50 Years of Playing Jazz in Australia: an Autobiography* (1947–*c*1997, Keith Hounslow Label [unnumbered]).

BIBLIOGRAPHY

A. Bisset: *Black Roots, White Flowers: a History of Jazz in Australia* (Sydney, 1979, rev. 2/1987)

B. Johnson: *The Oxford Companion to Australian Jazz* (Melbourne, Australia, 1987)

TONY GOULD

Treadwell, George (McKinley) (*b* New Rochelle, NY, 21/23 Dec 1918/1919; *d* New York, 14 May 1967). Trumpeter. His birthdate has been published as 21 December 1919, but in his rather scrawled application for social security the day given is almost certainly 23 December, and the year may be 1918. After performing in New York in the house band at Monroe's Uptown House (1941–2) he worked with Benny Carter's orchestra on the West Coast (late 1942). He then played with Ace Harris's Sunset Royals and Tiny Bradshaw and performed and recorded with Cootie Williams (late 1943 – early 1946). As a member of J. C. Heard's group (1946–7) he made several recordings, notably *The Walk/Heard but not Seen* (1946, Contl 6022), and he gave perhaps his finest recorded performance when Heard's group accompanied Etta Jones on *Mean to Me/Osculate me, daddy* (1946, Vic. 20-2941). While with Heard he met Sarah Vaughan, whom he subsequently married (1947); during the same period he recorded with Vaughan (1946, 1947) and with Dicky Wells and Ethel Waters (both 1946). Treadwell ceased playing trumpet to become Vaughan's manager, a role which he retained after their divorce. In the 1950s he managed such rhythm-and-blues musicians as the Drifters and Ruth Brown, worked as an artists and repertory agent, and wrote songs (from 1959). (*ChiltonW*; *FeatherE*; *Feather–GitlerBEJ*)

HOWARD RYE

Treloar, Phil(lip Maurice) (*b* Sydney, 7 Dec 1946). Australian drummer and composer. He learned drums privately and studied timpani at the New South Wales Conservatorium of Music. In 1968 he joined Alan Lee's quartet, and from 1972 to 1975 he played in the seminal Jazz Co-op, with Roger Frampton on piano, Jack Thorncraft on double bass, and Howie Smith on saxophone. In 1976 he performed with Frampton and Barry Guy, and he continued in several other projects with the former, including Intersection, which toured central Asia in 1984, after which Treloar studied in India. As a sideman he worked with, among others, Errol Buddle and Judy Bailey (1970s), Bernie McGann (1976–82), and Bruce Cale, Mark Simmonds, Dale Barlow, and Mike Nock (1980s). Around 1981 he created *Double Drummer*, a work for slides, tape, and improvising drummer. He then led Expansions (1981–2) and the innovative group Feeling to Thought (1987–9). In 1989 he moved to Melbourne and taught at La Trobe University, and in 1992 he moved again, to Kanazawa, Japan, where he practiced and composed in relative isolation. Treloar is a fluent improvising drummer of subtlety who has a strong melodic conception. As a composer he has written for settings ranging from unaccompanied percussion instruments to chamber orchestra, mostly seeking fresh ways to combine improvisation and composition. His piece *(. . . And then) Sunrise* was recorded by the percussionist Tom O'Kelly on an album of the same title (1991, Vic. [Jap.] VICC80).

SELECTED RECORDINGS

As leader of Feeling to Thought: on *Beyond El Rocco* (1988, Vox Australis 017-2) [film soundtrack], Shades of Bhairau

As sideman: Jazz Co-op: *Jazz Co-op* (1974, Phi. 6641225); Pipeline: *In the Pipeline* (1993, Tall Poppies 095)

BIBLIOGRAPHY

J. Shand: "No Big Deal," *Jazz* [Sydney], ii/7 (1982), 6

J. Clare [G. Brennan, pseud.]: *Bodgie Dada and the Cult of Cool* (Sydney, 1995)

N. Saintilian, A. Schultz, and P. Stanhope: *Biographical Directory of Australian Composers* (Sydney, 1996)

JOHN SHAND

Tremble Kids. Swiss dixieland group formed in the mid-1950s by the clarinetist Werner Keller. At various times Charly Antolini, Peter Giger, Henri Chaix, Oscar Klein, Raymond Droz, Peter Schmidli, Isla Eckinger, and Klaus Weiss were among its members. The group recorded prolifically until 1963, with Bill Coleman and Wild Bill Davison appearing as guest soloists in 1957 and 1958 respectively, and it continued to record on a regular basis until 1980; the albums *The Tremble Kids are Back* (1971, MPS 15327) and *Jumpin' the Blues* (1978, Intercord 145016) are representative of its style. In 1994 a septet that included Klein, Keller, Chaix, Schmidli, and Antolini recorded as the Tremble Kids All Stars.

BIBLIOGRAPHY

F. Ewald: "A Swingin' Reunion: the Tremble Kids are Back," *JP*, xxiii/4 (1974), 18

E. Elvers and G. Bielderman: *Werner Keller – Tremble Kids Discography* (Zwolle, Netherlands, 1997)

GK

Trenner, Donn [Donald R.] (*b* New Haven, CT, 10 March 1927). Pianist. He studied classical piano, played in the big band of the songwriter Ted Fiorito (1943–5), and led a military band (1946). With his wife, the singer Helen Carr, he worked in Buddy Morrow's orchestra (1947), led a trio in San Francisco (1948), and performed and recorded with Charlie Barnet (1950–51). From 1952 to 1953 he played with Jerry Gray, Stan Getz, Georgie Auld, and Charlie Parker; his excellent solo playing may be heard in a recording of a performance he made with Parker (*On the Coast*, 1952, Jazz Showcase 5007); he also recorded with Auld (1952). Trenner performed and made recordings with Les Brown at intervals from 1953 to 1960; during the same period he took part in sessions led by Dave Pell (1954, 1955), his wife (1955), Howard McGhee (1956), Betty Roche (her album *Take the "A" Train*, 1956, Beth. 64), and Frank Capp (1960), and worked briefly in New York with Oscar Pettiford and Anita O'Day (1957). After recording with Ben Webster (1961) he served as music director and pianist for Steve Allen's television program (1962–4) and as producer and conductor for Allen's recordings; among his sidemen were Conte Candoli, Herb Ellis, and Frank Rosolino. Trenner's composition *Leave it to me*, which was used by Allen as his commercial-break theme in the 1960s, may be heard on the album *Anita O'Day and the Three Sounds* (1962, Verve 68514). Trenner recorded as a pianist with Ellis in 1963 and as the leader of his own band accompanying Nancy Wilson in 1968. In the 1970s he was active as a bandleader and music director, and in 1983 he played with Gerry Mulligan at a jazz festival in Stockholm. In 1998 he recorded with the Big Band All Stars. (*FeatherE*; *Feather '60s*)

Trent, Alphonso [Alphonse] **(E.)** (*b* Fort Smith, AR, 24 Aug 1905; *d* Fort Smith, 14 Oct 1959). Bandleader and pianist. He performed in Arkansas and Oklahoma before taking over a small territory band, Eugene Crook's Synco Six, in 1924. The band, which included Snub Mosley, Terrence Holder, and A. G. Godley, continued touring in these states before expanding to ten pieces the following year to begin a long tenure at the Adolphus Hotel, Dallas, where Trent presented light classics, jazz, and dance music for white audiences only. The group's performances and radio broadcasts made it the most successful and respected of the early southwestern jazz bands. It toured Texas late in 1926, returned to the Adolphus, and then in 1927 began a period of extensive touring; Stuff Smith joined in Kentucky late that year. The band's recordings of 1928 show a polished ensemble style as advanced as that of Duke Ellington or Fletcher Henderson at that time, and include excellent improvised solos by Smith, Mosley, and a trumpeter thought to be Peanuts Holland. In 1930 the group recorded again and played for one week at the Savoy Ballroom in New York with notable success, but Trent refused further offers to work on the East Coast because he was afraid of losing his best soloists to other bandleaders; he instead took an engagement at the Plantation Club in Cleveland, where ironically the band lost all of its arrangements in a fire. Trent returned to the Southwest and in 1932 went home to support his parents. Other musicians had taken over the leadership of the orchestra by the time of its final recording session, which included Holland, Harry Edison, Mosley, Hayes Pillars, and Teddy Wilson's brother, the trombonist Gus Wilson. These recordings, from March 1933, show a remarkable ensemble precision and swing, which influenced Jimmie Lunceford later in the decade. The group then disbanded, and from 1934 Trent led various lesser ensembles in the Southwest, including one in 1938 that featured Charlie Christian; he later worked in real estate, although he was still leading a quintet locally in 1958.

Oral history material in *NjR* (JOHP) [Snub Mosley]

SELECTED RECORDINGS

Louder and Funnier/Gilded Kisses (1928, Gen. 6664); Black and Blue Rhapsody/Nightmare (1928, Gen. 6710); After you've gone/St. James Infirmary (1930, Gen. 7161); Clementine/I've found a new baby (1933, Champion 16587)

BIBLIOGRAPHY

McCarthyB

"Alphonso Trent's Band to Rank with Greatest in Country Soon," *Pittsburgh Courier* (6 Sept 1930)

F. Driggs: "Kansas City and the South West," *Jazz: New Perspectives on the History of Jazz*, ed. N. Hentoff and A. J. McCarthy (New York, 1959/*R*1974), 189

G. Schuller: *Early Jazz: its Roots and Musical Development* (New York, 1968), 299

G. Fernett: *Swing Out: Great Negro Jazz Bands* (Midland, MI, 1970/*R*1993), 41

Advertisement for an appearance of Alphonso Trent and his orchestra at the Showboat, New Lebanon, NY, September 1931

R. Russell: *Jazz Style in Kansas City and the Southwest* (Berkeley, CA, Los Angeles, and London, 1971/*R*1983, rev. 2/1973/*R*1997)
S. Dance: *The World of Swing* (New York, 1974), 176
L. Wright: "(Very) Young Man with a Horn," *Sv*, no.97 (1981), 26; no.98 (1981–2), 52
N. W. Pearson, Jr.: *Goin' to Kansas City* (Urbana, IL, and London, 1988)
M. L. Hester, "Tops in the Territory," *MR*, xviii/3 (1991), 16
A. Barnett: *Desert Sands: the Recordings and Performances of Stuff Smith: an Annotated Discography and Bibliographical Source Book* (Lewes, England, 1995; suppl., 1998, as *Up Jumped the Devil*)

J. BRADFORD ROBINSON/BK

Triangle. Record label. The catalogue was issued between 1922 and 1925 by the Bridgeport Die & Machine Company. The repertory was derived mostly from the New York Recording Laboratories and included items by Jelly Roll Morton, Fletcher Henderson, and the Original Memphis Five that had previously been put out on Paramount. Some recordings from Emerson's catalogue and one of Duke Ellington's first recordings as a leader (originally made for Blu-disc) were also released on Triangle.

BIBLIOGRAPHY

C. Kendziora: "Behind the Cobwebs: Triangle," *Record Research*, no.93 (1968), 93
B. Rust: *The American Record Label Book* (New Rochelle, NY, 1978), 295
A. Sutton: *Directory of American Disc Record Brands and Manufacturers, 1891–1943* (Westport, CT, and London, 1994), 152

HOWARD RYE

Tribal Tech. Jazz-rock group. It was formed in 1984 by the guitarist Scott Henderson and the electric bass guitarist Gary Willis, who have been its principal members throughout; they have worked alongside various others, notably the saxophonist Bob Sheppard, the keyboard players Pat Coil, David Goldblatt, and Scott Kinsey, the drummers Steve Houghton and Kirk Covington, and the percussionist Brad Dutz. The group recorded the first of many albums in 1985 and was still recording and touring internationally in the late 1990s. Weather Report was a primary and abiding influence on Henderson and Willis, who wrote most of the group's highly virtuoso material. However, Henderson also introduced elements of heavy rock and blues, and the group frequently tempered its generally serious intent with gentle musical irony.

SELECTED RECORDINGS

Spears (1985, Passport 88010); *Dr. Hee* (1987, Passport 88030); *Nomad* (1988, Relativity 88561-1028-2); *Tribal Tech* (1990, Relativity 88561-1049-2); *Illicit* (1992, Blue Moon R27-9180-2); *Face First* (1993, Blue Moon R2-79190); *Reality Check* (1994, Blue Moon 2-92549)

BIBLIOGRAPHY

K. Micallef: "Tribal Tech: a Graphic Tour," *JT*, xxii/6 (1992), 41

MARK GILBERT

Tribe. Collective organization and record label formed in Detroit in 1972 by Marcus Belgrave, the trombonist Phil Ranelin, and Wendell Harrison; later they were joined by Harold McKinney. Tribe was organized during one of the city's more violent periods to provide an outlet for channeling energies into positive and creative actions through music. Its recordings, which combine jazz with some rock and pop elements and also incorporate aspects of free-jazz improvisation, were issued under each of the founding member's names. In 1974 it began to publish a quarterly magazine. All of its activities ceased in 1977.

BIBLIOGRAPHY

M. Fine: "A Look at Tribe," *Cadence*, ii/1 (1976), 11

Message from the Tribe: an Anthology of Tribe (Universal Sound 5, 1996) [liner notes]

GK

Trío Argentina Argentine trio. It was formed in 1984 by the pianist Jorge Navarro, the double bass player Alfredo Remus, and the drummer Pocho Lapouble. The group recorded the albums *Pasando* (1984, EMP 3003) and *Carlitos* (1985, Amadeo 829447-1) with Karlheinz Miklin, performed regularly in Buenos Aires, and toured Austria and Germany.

LAUREANO FERNÁNDEZ, OMAR GARCÍA BRUNELLI

Trio da Paz. Cooperative trio formed in 1991 by the guitarist Romero Lubambo, the double bass player Nilson Matta, and the drummer Duduka da Fonseca. The three men had played together from 1986 in Fonseca's studio as the rhythm section for his group the New York Samba Band and toured with Herbie Mann in the late 1980s; they first recorded as Trio da Paz for an instructional video that Fonseca made in 1990, but did not actually begin working under the name until the following year. The trio continued to record through the decade.

SELECTED RECORDINGS

Brazil from the Inside (1992, Conc. 4524); *Black Orpheus* (1994, Kokopelli 1299); *Partido Out* (*c*1997, Malandro 71005)

BIBLIOGRAPHY

B. Primack: Liner notes, Trio da Paz: *Partido Out* (Malandro 71005, 1998) [repr. in <http://www.worldbop.com/malandro/partidoout/liner.html> (1999)]

GK

Trio Midnight. Hungarian trio formed in 1990 by the pianist Kálmán Oláh (*b* 1970), the double bass player János Egri (*b* 1966), and the drummer Elemér Balázs (*b* 1967). After performances in France and Italy the trio won first prize at an international jazz contest in Belgium in September 1995. Its style draws on the modern mainstream of jazz and on twentieth-century art music, as may be heard on the albums *Trio Midnight with Strings* (1995, Fonó 026-2) and *Live in Budapest* (1996, Pannon Jazz 1035). (G. G. Simon: Liner notes, *Live in Budapest*, Pannon Jazz 1035, 1997).

GÉZA GÁBOR SIMON

Trio 3. Trio formed in 1989 by OLIVER LAKE, Reggie Workman, and Andrew Cyrille.

Trio Transition. Cooperative trio formed in 1987 by the pianist Mulgrew Miller, the double bass player Reggie Workman, and the drummer Freddie Waits; it was active until 1989 and recorded two albums: *Trio Transition* (1987, DIW 808) and *Trio Transition with Special Guest Oliver Lake* (1988, DIW 829).

GK

Trip. Record company and label. The company was established by the producer Fred Norsworthy in 1974 in Rahway, New Jersey. It developed mainly from a licensing agreement with Polydor whereby it reissued material that had originally been put out on EmArcy, Limelight, and Mercury. It also ran a subsidiary label, Up Front. Operations ceased in 1979.

BK

Trippel, Fritz [Little Fritz] (*b* Chur, Switzerland, 10 Dec 1937). Swiss pianist. He studied with Joe Turner (i) in 1954–6 and from 1957 toured Austria, France, Switzerland, the Netherlands, and Germany with such musicians as Albert Nicholas (who gave him the nickname Little Fritz) and Don Byas. After working with the Swiss dixieland group the Tremble Kids (1960–61) he joined Kurt Weil's orchestra (1962), then led a band that included Oscar Klein and Wallace Bishop (1963–4). Later he played in the Far East and Southeast Asia (at intervals from 1969 to 1977). In Chur he worked until 1998 not only as a pianist but also as a concert promoter, record producer, and journalist; he also played intermittently in New Orleans, and in 1999 he appeared as an unaccompanied soloist in Bangkok and at hotels in Switzerland. His albums as a leader of small groups include *Whisky Time* (1964, Phi. 625101), *Coffee Time at the Atlantis* (1964, Phi. 843801), and *Blues for Eddie Jones* (1997, Jazz Time 001).

PETER SCHWALM

Tristano, Lennie [Leonard Joseph] (*b* Chicago, 19 March 1919; *d* New York, 18 Nov 1978). Pianist, teacher, and leader. He first studied with his mother, an amateur pianist and opera singer, and later at a school for the blind, where from 1928 to 1938 he learned piano and several wind instruments and received a thorough grounding in music theory. He then entered the American Conservatory in Chicago, and graduated with a BMus in 1943. During these years he played piano and wind instruments semiprofessionally in a wide variety of jazz settings and began teaching jazz privately. By 1945 he had attracted his first important pupils – Billy Bauer, Lee Konitz, and Bill Russo – and was drawing critical attention with his performances in Chicago clubs. His earliest solo and trio recordings, though not issued until 1977, were made at this time.

In 1946 Tristano moved to New York, where he immediately attracted a cult following and made his first studio recordings. He performed with Charlie Parker and Dizzy Gillespie in concerts and broadcasts and was named *Metronome* magazine's "musician of the year" for 1947. (He contributed two articles on bop to the magazine during that year.) In 1948 he acquired an important new pupil in Warne Marsh, and when Konitz and Bauer rejoined him shortly thereafter he had the basis of his now famous sextet. The recordings of this group in 1949 are representative of Tristano's powers as an improviser and group leader at the highest level, but they caused controversy among musicians and sold poorly.

Having by then attracted a large number of private students, including Bud Freeman, Sal Mosca, and Peter Ind, in 1951 Tristano founded a school of jazz in New York, the first significant institution of its kind. For his teaching staff he used his most important pupils, including Konitz, Marsh, Bauer, and Mosca. From this point he increasingly withdrew from public life, appearing rarely and issuing only a few experimental recordings as an adjunct to his teaching. He gradually lost his staff as his pupil-disciples embarked on their own careers, and in 1956 he dissolved his school to live in semiseclusion as a private teacher on Long Island. He performed occasionally at the Half Note (1958–9 and 1964–5), and in the course of the engagement in 1964 his quintet was videotaped for the television show "Look up and Live: Jazz at the Half Note." He also performed at the Berliner

Lennie Tristano (piano) with Lee Konitz (alto saxophone) and Warne Marsh (tenor saxophone) at the Isis Theater, Indianapolis, September 1959

Jazztage and on European television shows (1965), and in Harrogate, England (1968); he made his last public appearance in the USA in 1968. In 1973 French television broadcast an hour-long documentary interview on his life and work. After his death many of his recordings were reissued and a number of private tapes made by his students became commercially available; later, under his daughter's direction, these were distributed on CD on the Jazz Records label.

Tristano's music stands apart from the main tradition of modern jazz, representing an alternative to bop which poses severe demands of ensemble precision, intellectual rigor, and instrumental virtuosity. Rather than the irregular cross-accents of bop, Tristano preferred an even rhythmic background against which he concentrated on linear melody and focused his complex changes of time signature. Typically, his solos consisted of extraordinarily long, angular strings of almost even eighth-notes provided with subtle rhythmic deviations and abrasive polytonal effects. He was particularly adept in his use of different levels of double time and was a master of the block-chord style of George Shearing, Dave Brubeck, and others, carefully gauging the accumulation of dissonance. His experiments in multitrack recording and overdubbing, beginning in 1951 with *Ju-Ju* (not issued until 1971), inspired similar performances by Bill Evans (ii) and others in the 1960s. With his groups he also explored free collective improvisation, most notably in *Intuition* and *Digression* (1949). Although he was accused at the time of being willfully experimental, "free" performances of this sort were in fact part of Tristano's teaching practice (many were taped privately by Bauer) and pointed the way to similar experiments by Charles Mingus and Ornette Coleman in the late 1950s.

Tristano excelled as a teacher, demanding and receiving firm loyalty from his pupils, many of whom sacrificed more lucrative careers to continue their work with him. His method stressed advanced ear training and a close analysis of the work of several seminal jazz improvisers, including Louis Armstrong, Earl Hines, Roy Eldridge, Charlie Parker, and Bud Powell. Because of his knowledge of several instruments and broadminded approach Tristano attracted players of different instruments and schools, among them such established musicians as Freeman, Art Pepper, and Mary Lou Williams. Perhaps more than in his own scant recordings, Tristano's influence is felt most strongly in the work of his best pupils – many of whom also became outstanding teachers – and in his example of high-mindedness and perfectionism, characteristics which presupposed for jazz the highest standards of music as art. Bauer published several of Tristano's compositions, including a collection as *Jazz Lines, no.1* (Albertson, NY, 1958).

See also Piano, §§4 and 5.

SELECTED RECORDINGS

Yesterdays (1946, Jazz Guild 1008); Out on a Limb (1946, Key. 647); I surrender dear/Coolin' off with Ulanov (1947, Key. 680); A Ghost of a Chance (1947, Vic. 27-0145); Abstraction (1947, Cupol 9003); Dissonance (1947, Selmer Y7154); Progression/Retrospection (1949, NewJ 832); Subconscious-Lee/Judy (1949, NewJ 80001); Wow/Crosscurrent (1949, Cap. 60003); Marionette/Sax of a Kind (1949, Cap. 60013); Yesterdays/Intuition (1949, Cap. 1224); Digression (1949, Cap. EAP1-491); Ju-Ju/Passtime (1951, Jazz 101); *Lennie Tristano* (1955, Atl. 1224); *New York Improvisations* (1955–6, Elek. 96-0264-1); *The New Tristano* (1960–62, Atl. 1357)

BIBLIOGRAPHY

B. Ulanov: "Master in the Making," *Metronome*, lxv/8 (1949), 14

J. S. Wilson: "Lennie Tristano: Watered Down Bop Destroying Jazz," *DB*, xvii/20 (1950), 1

H. Pekar: "Lennie Tristano," *JR*, ii/6 (1960), 13

B. Coss: "Lennie Tristano Speaks Out," *DB*, xxix/24 (1962), 19

H. Pekar: "Lennie Tristano," *JM*, viii/4 (1962), 6

G. Endress: "Lennie Tristano," *JM*, xi/12 (1966), 21

I. Gitler: *Jazz Masters of the Forties* (New York, 1966/*R*1983 with discography), 226-61

A. Suprin: "Lennie Tristano: Feeling is Basic," *DB*, xxxvi/21 (1969), 14

J. Delmas: "Tristano et ses fils," *Jh*, no.325 (1976), 6; no.326 (1976), 6

J. F. McKinney: *The Pedagogy of Lennie Tristano* (diss., Fairleigh Dickinson U., 1978)

C. Sheridan: "Lennie Tristano," *JP*, xxviii/2 (1979), 12
L. Feather: "Piano Giants of Jazz: Lennie Tristano," *CK*, vi/1 (1980), 60
H. Hollenstein: *Lennie Tristano on LPs [sic] Records* (Sierre, Switzerland, 1984) [discography]
R. Beirach: "Lennie Tristano's 'Line Up': the Essence of Bebop from a Neglected Pioneer of Jazz Piano Overdubbing," *Keyboard*, xi/7 (1985), 44
H. Hellhund: *Cool Jazz: Grundzüge seiner Entstehung und Entwicklung* (Mainz, Germany, 1985), 36-148
J. W. Susat: *Discography of the "Uncompromising Lennie Tristano"* (Menden, Germany, 1986)
F. Billard: *Lennie Tristano* (Montpellier, France, 1988)
F. Bellard: "Lenny Popkin: ma Tristano Story," *Jm*, no.313 (1992), 32; no.314 (1993), 40
G. Jack: "Peter Ind," *JJI*, xlix/6 (1996), 6
B. Bauer with T. Luba: *Sideman: the Autobiography of Billy Bauer* (New York, 1997)
<http://www2.pcom.net/rminer/LennieTristano.html> (1999) [discography]

J. BRADFORD ROBINSON/BK

Trombar, Frank. Pseudonym of FRANKIE TRUMBAUER.

Trombone. A brass instrument of mainly cylindrical bore, with a cup-shaped mouthpiece. It is usually considered the tenor–baritone counterpart of the trumpet.

1. The trombone family. 2. Use.

1. THE TROMBONE FAMILY. In its most familiar form the trombone has a U-shaped telescopic tube known as a slide, by means of which the player alters the sounding length of the instrument's tubing, hence changing the pitch; this form of the instrument is known as the slide trombone. By the 17th century there existed a complete family of soprano, alto, tenor, and bass trombones. The upper and lower limits of the trombone's range are dependent on the player's ability to control his embouchure. The tenor in B♭ became, and has remained (especially in jazz), the most widely used; it has a complete chromatic compass from *E* to around *f′* and, in addition, seven pedal notes – E′ to *B♭′*. Some players prefer the B♭/F tenor–bass trombone, which has a thumb-operated valve (also known as a "trigger" or "plug") that lowers the pitch of the instrument by a perfect 4th and adds the chromatic pitches between *C* and *E♭* to the compass. The B♭/F/E and B♭/F/D bass trombones have a second valve that allows a *B♮′* to be played; this second valve also facilitates the playing of fast passages in the lower register. The B♭/F, B♭/F/E, and B♭/F/D instruments, built with a wide bore, may all be considered bass trombones. Their larger bore enables the player to produce a more robust, sonorous tone. Composers and arrangers show an increasing tendency to assume the presence of a two-valved instrument, regularly writing parts including notes as low as *C′*, though pitches below *F′* are mainly used only as held notes. A soprano trombone (often described as a slide cornet) has also been used in jazz very occasionally, principally as a novelty doubling instrument, though more often for photographic poses (for example by Freddie Keppard, *c*1911, for illustration *see* NELSON, BIG EYE LOUIS; and Louis Armstrong, 1923, for illustration *see* OLIVER, KING) than in performance. It is limited by having a slide that moves through only six positions (as opposed to seven on the other members of the trombone family), and its tone compares unfavorably with that of the cornet and trumpet.

The valve trombone (generally a tenor instrument in B♭) was invented in the early 19th century and has a system of valves instead of a slide. The advantages of compactness, and for some purposes a greater technical facility, must be set against the disadvantages of a constant need to correct intonation by changes in embouchure and the greater difficulty of producing a sensitive legato. These intonation problems are compounded on some instruments by the addition of a fourth valve that lowers the compass by a 4th.

Some attempts have been made to produce hybrid instruments with both a slide and valves (as in the trombone duplex made by G. A. Besson, Paris, in the 1840s). These combine the versatility and expressive capabilities of the slide trombone with the technical facility of the valve instrument. On the valide, adopted by Brad Gowans, the slide, though generally locked, can be brought into operation when needed for glissandos and other effects. The superbone, invented by Maynard Ferguson in the 1970s, is a tenor trombone with a large bore that has valves played with the right hand and a slide controlled by the left.

2. USE. While the slide trombone may appear clumsy and the manipulation of the slide cumbersome, the inherent freedom from the fixed pitches of a tonal scale which this allows adapts the instrument well for use in any and all styles of jazz. The ease with which bends, blue notes, and glisses (*see* BEND, BLUE NOTE (i), and GLISS) may be produced on the slide trombone, simply by exploiting its basic technique, contrasts with the difficulty of executing those effects on many other instruments used in jazz. These factors go some way towards explaining the pre-eminence in jazz of the slide trombone over the valve trombone, which, though more agile, is perhaps less well suited to most styles of jazz. The valve instrument was often used in parade bands, which influenced early jazz, but it had declined in popularity by around 1900 and was not used again widely until the 1940s, when players were faced with the technical demands of bop. An important aspect of jazz trombone playing is the use of different types of mute to produce not only a quieter sound but also a variety of special effects (*see* MUTE, §3).

The trombone, like most instruments in jazz, has both an ensemble and a solo function. In the earliest jazz groups it played a bass line in the polyphonic texture collectively improvised by the melody instruments. In later styles a single trombone in an ensemble usually plays an inner line or doubles the melody played by another instrument (perhaps at the lower octave); a trombone section forms the foundation for the brass grouping.

In the 1920s brass sections usually consisted of two trumpets and one trombone until Henderson (1927) and Ellington (1929) added a second trombone, thus introducing the potential for four-part brass harmony. In the 1930s Ellington's band expanded to include a six-piece brass section (three trumpets and three trombones). Kenton's use of four trombones (with five trumpets) in the 1940s yielded a practical and long-lasting pattern for the big band. This section of four instruments (usually three tenors and one bass) may be used to play a riff in unison; to play as a four-voice unit in combination with the rhythm section, in which case the first or lead tenor trombone would normally play the melody; or to carry inner voices within passages for all the brass and reeds. Even the bass trombone, despite its name, rarely plays bass lines; in a big band the double bass (or electric bass guitar) usually provides the bass line while the bass trombone plays a low-pitched inner voice, often in unison or at the octave with the baritone saxophone when a full, rich sound is required.

In early jazz and swing styles the trombone was often used as a solo instrument. In later contexts it has sometimes been overshadowed by other instruments, but nonetheless has found a place as a distinctive solo voice in bop and free jazz, and also (though less prominently) in jazz-rock.

The various playing styles of jazz trombonists, whose technical capabilities have possibly improved more markedly over the course of jazz history than those of any other instrumentalists, are connected by clear lines of descent. Blesh (1946) observed that the trombone inherited the functions of the baritone and alto horns (*see* Saxhorn) in the early jazz band. As its deeper notes could serve both contrapuntal and rhythmic purposes, the trombone forged an important link between the melody instruments (trumpet and clarinet) and the rhythm section. Syncopated impetus could be achieved with considerable economy of means: Ike Rodgers, who recorded in Chicago (1929–34), is described by Keepnews and Grauer (1956) as "a crude trombonist (said to be able to play 'only two notes')." Jim Robinson, who recorded with Sam Morgan in 1927 and later played with the bands of Bunk Johnson and George Lewis (i), demonstrated on *Tishomingo Blues* (1945, Decca 25131), recorded with Johnson, that only a very few more notes were necessary to fulfill the instrument's function in the ensemble – an occasional staccato accent in the appropriate part of the bar was sufficient. Other trombonists, however, gave more prominence to the type of contrapuntal tenor part heard in American military bands of the Civil War period; these more proficient players included Georg Brunis and, in particular, Kid Ory, who exploited the portamento and vibrato effects that form an intrinsic part of the trombone's Tailgate style. Ory's use of such effects may be heard on his showpiece *Ory's Creole Trombone* (1927, Col. 35838), recorded with Louis Armstrong's Hot Seven, as well as on later recordings such as *Snag it* (1947, Cir. [USA] 12001), recorded with his own band.

Miff Mole is usually considered the first jazz trombonist fully to have mastered the instrument. During his association with Red Nichols (1925–8) he demonstrated both a trumpet-like clarity of attack and an ability to produce a sweet, legato, controlled sound; he is heard to advantage on *Nothing does-does like it used to do-do-do* (1927, PAct 36707), recorded with Nichols's Red Heads. Mole is an acknowledged influence on the trombonists and bandleaders Jack Teagarden, Tommy Dorsey, and Glenn Miller; classical orchestral musicians were also influenced by his technique. Trummy Young, however, felt that Mole displayed a virtuoso command of the instrument at the expense of the jazz content of his playing. Jimmy Harrison, a member of Fletcher Henderson's band from 1926 to 1931, also made a lasting effect on other players; his sonorous tone, bold ideas, and flexible technique led to his being called "the father of swing trombone."

Tricky Sam Nanton, who worked with Ellington from 1926, developed the "growl and plunger" technique to contribute to the "jungle" sound of Ellington's early recordings (*see* Jungle music). When Ellington added a second trombone to his orchestra in 1929 he chose the valve trombonist Juan Tizol, whose tone blended equally well with trumpets and reeds. The duet by Nanton and Tizol on the 1931 version of Ellington's *Creole Rhapsody* (Bruns. 6093) is one of the first recorded trombone duets. Ellington's orchestra demonstrated the range of approaches to the trombone current in jazz when Nanton and Tizol were joined in 1932 by a third distinctive soloist, Lawrence Brown (see illustration), whose playing explored the lyrical and legato possibilities of the slide trombone. Tizol was one of few players to employ the valve trombone before the bop era. Others were the trumpeter Jabbo Smith, who played the valve instrument on his recording of *Lina Blues* (1929, Bruns. 7087), and the cornetist Wild Bill Davison, who between 1933 and 1941 also performed on valve trombone.

Throughout the swing era a variety of styles of trombone playing flourished. Tommy Dorsey was known for his sumptuous interpretations of sentimental ballads; Vic Dickenson was a noted blues player, with a husky tone; J. C.

Duke Ellington's trombone section, 1933: (left to right) Tricky Sam Nanton, Juan Tizol, and Lawrence Brown; Tizol is playing a valve trombone

Higginbotham had a rich, powerful, raucous sound, reminiscent of the earlier Gutbucket style; and Benny Morton was noted for his controlled vibrato and imaginative improvisations. Louis Armstrong's favorite trombonist was Jack Teagarden, who had an outstanding technique and a strongly personal blues style; his recordings with Armstrong include *Some Day* (1947, Vic. 202530). An element of humor is associated with the styles of many trombonists, including Trummy Young and Dicky Wells; the latter was also known for his legato playing.

While the revival of traditional jazz during the late 1930s and early 1940s embraced a renewed interest in the tailgate style and related approaches to playing, concurrently the bop style evolved from swing, and trombonists took on the new challenge of executing fast-moving bop melodies. Between 1944 and 1950 Bill Harris (i) demonstrated a wide expressive range with a precisely controlled vibrato and almost veiled tone in slow numbers, as well as a new rhythmic vigor in faster ones. The most important trombonist of the period was J. J. Johnson, who showed that fast-moving bop melodies could be played on the slide trombone at a time when the technical demands of the style had resulted in the valve trombone coming back into popular use. He developed a fluid technical facility similar to that of bop saxophonists and comparable with Dizzy Gillespie's mastery of the trumpet. From 1954 to 1956 Johnson performed in a duo with Kai Winding that influenced a whole generation of players; a good example of their playing is *This could be the start of something* from the album *The Great Kai and JJ* (1960, Imp. 1). While players such as Frank Rosolino, Carl Fontana, and Bill Watrous followed their example, the influence of Morton and Teagarden could still be heard in the playing of Bennie Green and Lou McGarity respectively. A notable exponent of the bass trombone in this period was George Roberts, who performed and recorded with the big bands of Gene Krupa (1950) and Stan Kenton (1951–7).

Harris and Johnson, and a number of lesser players, occasionally played the valve trombone as well as the slide trombone. Some trombonists, though, concentrated on the valve instrument to the exclusion of the slide trombone. The most notable of these was the West Coast musician Bob Brookmeyer, whose playing is well represented on the album *Stan Getz at the Shrine Auditorium* (1954, Norg. 2000). From the 1970s there has been a revival in many American and European orchestras of the nineteenth-century Italian valved contrabass trombone, usually termed *cimbasso*. Primarily intended for use in operas by Verdi and others, its unique timbre is increasingly attracting film composers. The German tuba player Heiko Triebener plays cimbasso with the Bamberger Symphoniker Big Band.

The playing of Slide Hampton, who has used the technique of circular breathing, and of the brilliant Jimmy Knepper, who is best known for his work with Charles Mingus, provided a link between bop and the free-jazz styles of the 1960s. During that decade several European free-jazz musicians, notably Eje Thelin, Paul Rutherford, and Albert Mangelsdorff, came to prominence alongside the American Roswell Rudd. These players, among others, have explored the expressive potential of the trombone by the use of Multiphonics, achieved through adjustments of the embouchure in combination with humming into the instrument. Mangelsdorff has recorded both as an unaccompanied soloist and as a leader; his playing in this manner is well represented by *Mahusale* from the album *Albert Mangelsdorff Live in Tokyo* (1971, Enja 2006). Thelin also experimented with electronic effects, attaching a pickup to his instrument. Rutherford (an admirer of Robinson), Mangelsdorff, and Rudd, together with such younger players as Ray Anderson and George Lewis (ii), have adopted and exaggerated techniques and sounds from early jazz playing, which are well suited to the expressiveness of free jazz – a raw, brassy tone, distorted pitches, "splatting," and exuberant portamentos. Lewis has also explored a new context for trombone playing by improvising together with a computer-programmed synthesizer.

The trombone is of little importance in jazz-rock and other fusions. Such medium-sized groups as Chicago, Tower of Power, and Blood, Sweat and Tears (all closer to rock music than to jazz) have included a trombone within a three- to five-piece wind section, playing both boppish lines and simple riffs in the style of rock or soul music. Many modern big bands, such as those of Gil Evans, Thad Jones and Mel Lewis, Toshiko Akiyoshi and Lew Tabackin, and Maynard Ferguson, have regularly performed tunes based on rock rhythms and harmonies. Trombonists have taken solos in this context but no innovatory players of great significance have emerged; solos usually consist of lines in the bop style superimposed on a rock accompaniment, or distorted gesturing in a manner reminiscent of some electric guitarists. Among the few players to make notable original contributions in fusion styles are Barry Rogers, in the group Dreams, Wayne Henderson, heard in the 1970s as one of the principal melodic voices of the Crusaders, and Watrous, who for a time was the leader of a jazz-rock group. Ferguson has performed and recorded regularly on his superbone; a fine example of his playing style is the improvised exchange with the baritone saxophonist Bruce Johnstone on the track *Superbone Meets the Bad Man*, from Ferguson's album *Chameleon* (1974, Col. KC33007).

For further illustrations *see* Johnson, j. j.; Mangelsdorff, albert; Miller, glenn; and Teagarden.

BIBLIOGRAPHY

R. Blesh: *Shining Trumpets: a History of Jazz* (New York, 1946, London, 1949, rev. and enlarged 2/1958/R1975)
J.-E. Berendt: *Das Jazzbuch: Entwicklung und Bedeutung der Jazzmusik* (Frankfurt am Main, Germany, 1953, rev. 2/1959, Eng. trans., New York, 1962; rev. and enlarged 5/1981, Eng. trans., Westport, CT, 1982, as *The Jazz Book: from New Orleans to Fusion and Beyond*)
O. Keepnews and B. Grauer, Jr.: *A Pictorial History of Jazz: People and Places from New Orleans to Modern Jazz* (New York and London, 1956, rev. 2/1968/R1981)
D. Heckman: "Jazz Trombone: Five Views," *DB*, xxxii/2 (1965), 17 [incl. transcrs.]
G. Schuller: *Early Jazz: its Roots and Musical Development* (New York, 1968)
D. Baker: *Jazz Styles & Analysis: Trombone: a History of the Jazz Trombone via Recorded Solos, Transcribed and Annotated* (Chicago, 1973)
A. C. Baines: "Trombone," *GroveI*
M. Laplace: "Le trombone dans le jazz et la musique populaire," *Brass Bulletin* (1985), no.50, p.36; no.51, p.40; no.52, p.20

CLIFFORD BEVAN

Tropea, John (*b* New York, 7 Jan 1946). Electric guitarist. He studied privately with Sal Salvador (1962–4) and attended the Berklee School of Music (1964–7). Among the musicians with whom he played are Billy Cobham (early 1970s), Eumir Deodato (1972–9), Spyro Gyra (1979–80), Terumasa Hino (1980), Ron Carter (1981), Richard Tee, Tom Scott, the pop musician Dr. John, David Sanborn, Jon Faddis (all early 1980s), and Ralph McDonald and Will Lee (both 1980s–1990s). In addition he has worked extensively as a studio arranger and guitarist (from 1970) and collaborated with such pop artists as Roberta Flack, Alice Cooper, James Brown, and Paul Simon. In 1975 Tropea formed a group with the guitarist David Spinozza.

SELECTED RECORDINGS

As leader: *Short Trip to Space* (1976, Marlin 2204); *NY Cats Direct* (1986, DMP 453)

As sideman: E. Deodato: *Deodato 2* (1973, CTI 6029), incl. Super Strut; T. Hino: *Daydream* (1980, Flying Disk VIJ28003)

SELECTED FILMS AND VIDEOS

John Tropea (n.d. [filmed 1975]); Short Trip to Space (n.d. [filmed 1977]); To Touch You Again (n.d. [filmed 1979])

MARK GILBERT

Trotman, Lloyd (Nelson) (*b* Boston, 25 May 1923). Double bass player. After studying at the New England Conservatory he began performing in Boston and toured with Blanche Calloway as a member of a band led by the reed player Joe Nevils (1941). In 1945 he moved to New York, where that year he played with Stuff Smith's trio (alongside Erroll Garner), Eddie Heywood, Hazel Scott, Duke Ellington (for two weeks in November), and Pete Brown. Later he worked with Edmond Hall and Billy Taylor (ii) (both 1948, the latter for a six-week tour of Haiti), Boyd Raeburn (1948–9), Wilbur De Paris (1949–51), and Johnny Hodges (1951–2). From the late 1940s he was active mainly as a studio musician, notably for King, Atlantic, and Groove, and in this role he took part in sessions led by, among others, Lucky Millinder (1952), Ray Charles (1953), and Joe Turner (ii) (1956–8). In addition he recorded with Oscar Pettiford (1950), in a trio with Bud Powell and Art Blakey (1955), and with Henry "Red" Allen (1957); he later performed with Allen at the Shakespearian Festival in Stratford, Ontario (1958), accompanying the poet Langston Hughes, and at the Newport Jazz Festival (1959). Trotman spent the last eight years of his career as a musician playing in a duo with the pianist Billy Rowland, after which he retired from music (1978) to work in a bank.

SELECTED RECORDINGS

As sideman: D. Ellington: Light (1945, AFRS Date with the Duke 41); J. Hodges: Castle Rock (1951, Clef 8944); Globe Trotter (1951, Clef 8954); Sideways/A Pound of Blues (1952, Clef 8961); Who's Excited/Sweeping the Blues Away (1952, Clef 8977); Standing Room Only (1952, Norg. 64 [EP]); L. Millinder: Please be Careful (1952, King 4545); R. Charles: Mess Around (1953, Atl. 999)

BIBLIOGRAPHY

FeatherE

D. Kochakian: "Bey Perry," *Whiskey, Women, and . . .*, no.15 (1985), 48

——: "Charlie Cox," *Whiskey, Women, and . . .*, no.15 (1985), 44

——: "Lloyd Trotman: the Big Beat!," *Whiskey, Women, and . . .*, nos.18–19 (1989), 4

HOWARD RYE

Troup, Bobby [Robert William] (*b* Harrisburg, PA, 18 Oct 1918; *d* Sherman Oaks, CA, 7 Feb 1999). Singer and songwriter. His father was a pianist and owned a retail music store, a business which Troup planned to enter after studying business at the Wharton School of the University of Pennsylvania; while in college he wrote the chart-topping popular song *Daddy* (1941). After graduation he enlisted in the US Marines, but worked as a staff writer for Tommy Dorsey before entering military service. In 1946, following his discharge, he moved to Los Angeles to pursue a career as a songwriter; en route he began writing what became a major hit, *Route 66*, as a commemoration of his journey. During the 1940s and 1950s he worked as a pianist and led local groups, performing with such musicians as Howard Roberts and Bob Enevoldsen (1954–5). In 1954 he met Julie London and helped to launch her singing career; they married in 1959. In the 1950s he also began acting and contributed songs to the films *The Girl Can't Help It* (1956) and *Man of the West* (1958), among others; from 1956 to 1958 he hosted the television program "Stars of Jazz." From the 1960s his acting career flourished and he also appeared on various television programs. His sophisticated singing style may be heard on the recordings *Bobby Troup Sings Johnny Mercer* (1955, Beth. 19) and *The Distinctive Style of Bobby Troup* (1955, Beth. 35).

BIBLIOGRAPHY

FeatherE

Obituaries, *New York Times* (10 Feb 1999); H. Lucraft, *CJM*, xxxvi/2 (1999), 10

SCOTT FREDRICKSON, GK

Trovajoli, Armando (*b* Rome, 2 Sept 1917). Italian pianist and composer. He formed a group modeled after the Benny Goodman Sextet in 1944 and studied piano at the conservatory in Rome, from which he graduated in 1949; the same year he performed at the Paris Jazz Fair in a trio with Kramer Gorni and Gil Cuppini. In 1950 he recorded as the leader of trios with Franco Cerri and the drummer Paolo Tagliaferri, and with Cuppini and Roberto Nicolosi; he also recorded with Django Reinhardt, Stephane Grappelli, Toots Thielemans, and Flavio Ambrosetti. From 1956 to 1958 he led an orchestra for RAI that played arrangements by, among others, Bill Russo and Bill Holman; among his sidemen were Cuppini and Oscar Valdambrini. Trovajoli recorded as the leader of a quartet, a sextet, and a big band (1956–8), and his playing may be heard to advantage on *Pick Yourself up* (1959, RCA LPM10019). He wrote film scores from 1952 and musical comedies from the 1960s. His importance lies in his work as a pianist, and in his having formed one of the first big bands in Italy and introduced jazz to a large audience through his film and television scores.

ADRIANO MAZZOLETTI

Trovesi, Gianluigi (*b* Nembro, nr Bergamo, Italy, 10 Jan 1944). Italian alto saxophonist, clarinetist, composer, and leader. At the age of 15 he took up clarinet and joined the local brass band. He attended the Instituto Musicale in Bergamo and the Liceo Musicale in Piacenza, graduating from the latter institution in 1965, and then studied composition from 1967 to 1972. He played with the Sestetto Jazz di Bergamo (1969–72), Gigi Chichellero's big band (1973–4), Franco Cerri (1974–6), Giorgio Gaslini (1977–82), and the Mitteleuropa Orchestra, led by the arranger and composer Andrea Centazzo (1980–81). In 1978 he began to play with the RAI Orchestra in Milan and formed a trio with Paolo Damiani and the drummer Gianni Cazzola. He also appeared as an unaccompanied soloist, in which setting he utilizes electronic devices. Trovesi was a member of Tiziano Tononi's group Nexus (1989–91) and Paolo Fresu's sextet (1991–5), and in 1992 he formed an octet which toured throughout Europe to some acclaim. In the mid-1990s he performed and recorded in a duo with Gianni Coscia and in 1998 he became the leader of a nonet. He is a member of the Italian Instabile Orchestra.

Trovesi has brought together popular medieval dances, Renaissance Venetian brass music, Mediterranean and north Italian folk music, popular Italian brass-band music, free jazz, and (for a period in the late 1970s to mid-1980s) electronic music, all organized in deeply expressive, complex, often multi-layered structures. In the 1990s he explored unusual instrumentation: his octet consisted of three reed and brass players, cello, two double basses, drums, and percussion, and the nonet comprises three trios – popular, classical, and jazz. As a soloist he was influenced first by Eric Dolphy and later, on alto saxophone, by David Sanborn's distinctive timbre; his phrasing on clarinet has been affected by Italian folk traditions.

SELECTED RECORDINGS

Duos with G. Coscia: *Radici* (1995, Egea 050)
As leader: *Baghèt* (1978, Dischi della Quercia 28008); *Cinque piccole storie* (1980, Dischi della Quercia 28010); with P. Damiani: *Roccellanea* (1983, Ismez Polis 26001); *Dances* (1985, Red 181); *Les boîtes à musique* (1988, Splasc(h) 152); *From G to G* (1992, SN 121231-2); *Les hommes armés* (1996, SN 121311-2); *Around Small Fairy Tales* (1998, SN 121341-2); *Round About a Midsummer's Dream* (1999, Enja 9384-2)
As sideman: G. Gaslini: *Live at the Public Theatre in New York* (1980, Dischi della Querchia 2Q28009); P. Fresu: *Ossi di seppia* (1991, Splasc(h) 350), G. Coscia: *Il bandino* (1993, DDD 74321-16354-2); P. Fresu: *Ensalada mistica* (1994, Splasc(h) 415); E. Rava: *Carmen* (1995, Label Bleu 6579); T. Ghiglioni: *Spellbound* (1996, Yvp 3058)

BIBLIOGRAPHY

D. Soutif: "Gianluigi Trovesi: entre avant-garde et moyen-age," *Jm*, no.315 (1983), 34
A. Bazzurro: "Gianluigi Trovesi," *Musica jazz*, l/2 (1994), 37
"Ten Italian Musicians the World Should Know about . . .," *Jazz Changes*, iv/2 (1997), 16
D. Ouellette: "Musician at Play," *DB*, lxv/6 (1998), 44
<http://www.ijm.it/enartists.html> (1999)
<http://www.shef.ac.uk/misc/rec/ps/efi/minstab.html> (1999)

STEFANO ZENNI

Trowers, Robert (*b* New York, 3 March 1957). Trombonist. He grew up in a musical family, and played piano and viola before taking up trombone at the age of 15; later he studied at CCNY (1975–80). His first work was with, among others, Ray Draper's big band (1978), Jaki Byard's Apollo Stompers (1978–9), Abdullah Ibrahim (1979, 1981), and Cecil Payne (1980). In the 1980s he was a member of Lionel Hampton's orchestra (1982–5) and the big bands of Sam Wooding (1984) and Illinois Jacquet (1986–7). In 1987 he joined the Count Basie Orchestra under Frank Foster, and he remained with the band when Grover Mitchell took over in 1995; in the 1990s he also toured with the Lincoln Center Jazz Orchestra. As the leader of a small bop group Trowers made a number of recordings from 1992, notably *Point of View* (1994, Conc. 4656); in addition he recorded as a sideman in small ensembles led by Jesse Davis (*As We Speak*, 1992, Conc. 4512, and *High Standards*, 1994, 4624) and Randy Sandke (1993) and as a soloist in groups accompanying Susannah McCorkle (1993–4). He worked as a science teacher at public schools in New York from 1984 to 1987 and later taught at the Brooklyn Conservatory of Music.

BIBLIOGRAPHY

Feather–GitlerBEJ
J. Ferguson: "Hearsay: Robert Trowers: Point–Counterpoint," *JT*, xxv/8 (1995), 26

GK

Trueheart, John (*b* Baltimore, *c*1900; *d* New York, 1949). Guitarist and banjoist. From the early 1930s he worked with his close friend Chick Webb in Baltimore and then in New York, performing and making recordings (including *Blue Minor*, 1934, Decca 172, and *Don't be that way*, 1934, Decca 483). In 1937 his career was interrupted by illness, but two years later he rejoined Webb. After the latter's death Trueheart remained with the band under Ella Fitzgerald's leadership until mid-1940. Thereafter he played with Art Hodes (1943) and others before he was forced to retire through ill-health.

based on *ChiltonW*

Trujillo, Bill [William Lee] (*b* Los Angeles, 7 July 1930). Tenor saxophonist. He started playing clarinet at the age of four and was reading music before he learned to read words; some time later he studied at Westlake Music College in Los Angeles. While in his teens he performed in local dance bands, and in 1950–51 he played with the guitarist Alvino Rey. From mid-1953 to March 1954 he performed and recorded with Woody Herman's New Third Herd, and he may be heard playing a brief solo on the band's recording *The Moon is Blue* (1953, Mars 1002). After leading his own quartet at the Key Club in Chicago (1955) Trujillo toured Europe with Bill Russo (summer 1955) and worked with Charlie Barnet (1956–7) and Jerry Gray (1958); he made recordings with all three leaders. He then toured and recorded with Stan Kenton from around August 1958 to 1959 before moving to Las Vegas in 1960; there he performed with numerous visiting jazz musicians and continued to work through the 1990s, leading small groups and teaching privately. In August 1997 he led a quartet at Chadney's Club in Burbank, California, with Lou Levy among his sidemen, and in 1999 he recorded his first album as a leader, *It's Tru* (Sea Breeze 3033). Besides his principal instrument Trujillo plays other saxophones, clarinets, and flute.

BIBLIOGRAPHY

FeatherE
A. Morgan: "Woody's Tenors," *JM*, vi (1960–61), no.7, p.4; no.8, p.13; no.12, p.9
W. D. Clancy with A. C. Kenton: *Woody Herman: Chronicles of the Herds* (New York and elsewhere, 1995)

BK

Trumbauer, Frankie [Orie Frank; Trombar, Frank; Tram] (*b* Carbondale, IL, 30 May 1901; *d* Kansas City, MO, 11 June 1956). Alto and C-melody saxophonist and bandleader. Having briefly played violin, trombone, and piano without developing any special interest in these instruments he acquired a C-melody saxophone in 1912 and immediately became deeply devoted to it; by his early teens he was already leading bands at local parties. After serving in US Navy bands during the last year of World War I he resumed playing professionally, working mainly in Missouri and Illinois. He joined the Benson Orchestra in Chicago early in 1923 and that year recorded with the group in Camden, New Jersey. From March 1924 to July 1925 he was a member of the Ray Miller Orchestra and from September 1925 to May 1926 he led a band in St. Louis with Bix Beiderbecke, who became his close associate. The two men later worked together in an orchestra contracted by Jean Goldkette (May 1926 – September 1927, when Trumbauer served frequently as leader) and then in orchestras led by Adrian Rollini (September–October 1927) and Paul Whiteman (from October 1927). By this time Trumbauer's originality was easily discernible, and in 1927 he gained his own recording contract with OKeh, leading to the creation of some of the most important recordings of the era by white jazz musicians. These performances reveal Trumbauer and Beiderbecke, together with Eddie Lang, at the peak of their inspiration. In 1934, while still with Whiteman, Trumbauer led his own recording band, which included several young "swing" stars, such as Bunny Berigan. He appeared with Whiteman's band in the short film *King of Jazz* (1929) and the film *Thanks a Million* (1935). After a brief spell (late 1936 – early 1937) as a member of the Three T's with Jack and Charlie Teagarden he left Whiteman in July 1937 and moved to California. As Frank Trombar he led his own big band for local residencies and touring (late 1937 – February 1940). He was a test pilot during World War II, after which he played briefly in studio groups (1945–7), but he then left music altogether to work in aeronautics.

Although Trumbauer played most members of the saxophone family he specialized on alto and C-melody saxophones; he was the only successful jazz specialist on the C-melody instrument. His graceful, light-toned improvisations were extremely individual, and they were acknowledged to have influenced the tenor saxophone style of Lester Young, who was greatly impressed by the recording of *Singin' the Blues* (1927) which Trumbauer made in the company of Beiderbecke. Trumbauer introduced delicacy into the art of jazz saxophone playing: he was a model of musical poise when improvising, and his long, singing phrases were beautifully constructed and delivered in a restrained but attractive tone. His individuality was effectively displayed on many of his recordings with Paul Whiteman's orchestra, where his pithy sense of understatement and dry, delicate tone stood out against the lush backgrounds. Later he had difficulty adjusting to the new swing style, and in his recordings from the mid-1930s his timing often appeared stiff and uneasy and his phrasing anachronistic.

SELECTED RECORDINGS

As leader: Trumbology (1927, OK 40871); Clarinet Marmalade/Singin' the Blues (1927, OK 40772); Ostrich Walk/Riverboat Shuffle (1927, OK 40822); I'm coming, Virginia/'Way down yonder in New Orleans (1927, OK 40843)

As sideman with P. Whiteman: You took advantage of me (1928, Vic. 21398)

BIBLIOGRAPHY

M. Brian: "America's Public Swing Star Number One," *MM*, xiv (10 Sept 1938), 10

D. Dexter: "Giants of Jazz," *DB*, vii/21 (1940), 10

"Frank Trumbauer Quits Jazz," *DB*, vii/13 (1940), 13

F. Trumbauer: "The Good Old Days," *DB*, ix/8 (1942), 6

R. M. Sudhalter, P. R. Evans, and W. Dean-Myatt: *Bix: Man & Legend* (New Rochelle, NY, and London, 1974)

P. R. Evans and L. F. Kiner with W. Trumbauer: *Tram: the Frank Trumbauer Story* (Metuchen, NJ, and London, 1994)

JOHN CHILTON/BK

Trumpet. A brass instrument made in a range of pitches from sopranino to bass.

1. Technical aspects. 2. The importance of jazz trumpet playing. 3. The trumpet in early jazz. 4. The swing era. 5. Bop and traditional jazz. 6. Free jazz, fusion, and the continuation of established styles.

1. Technical aspects. The trumpet generally has three valves and tubing of a mainly cylindrical profile; the tubing is "folded" through several reversals, so that it lies parallel in a horizontal plane, with the bell pointing forwards. The mouthpiece of the modern trumpet is cup-shaped and relatively shallow. The written compass of the trumpet in B♭ (the principal member of the modern trumpet family) is *f♯–c‴* (sounding *e–b♭″*), though many players add a further octave to the upper limit of the range, and some another octave still.

Jazz musicians almost all play the standard trumpet in B♭. Dizzy Gillespie adopted an instrument (first patented in 1866 by the Schreiber Cornet Manufacturing Company of New York) in which the familiar outline of the trumpet is modified so that the bell points upwards at an angle of 45°. A few players have used other members of the trumpet family: those who have taken up the bass trumpet in B♭ include Cy Touff (as a soloist within Woody Herman's trombone section), Johnny Mandel (in several bands during the 1950s), and Ray Premru (in the 1960s in Kenny Baker's group); Don Cherry specialized in a pocket instrument, also in B♭ (for illustration *see* Cherry, Don); and Don Ellis, under the influence of the Czech player Jaromír Hnilička, has played the four-valve "quarter-tone" trumpet. In the early 1970s Maynard Ferguson invented a combination valve and slide trumpet known as the Firebird; the slide mechanism, operated by the left hand, allows the player effortlessly to produce such effects as blue notes and glisses. Ellis and Al Hirt occasionally used the instrument, and Ferguson may be heard playing it on his album *Hollywood* (1982, Col. FC37713).

2. The importance of jazz trumpet playing. The general approach to trumpet playing in the 20th century has been influenced significantly by jazz musicians. In Western art music, while the trumpet was prominent as a concertante instrument in the Baroque era, for the following two centuries it held at best a secondary position within the orchestra. In the military tradition, although the trumpet was always considered the principal melodic instrument, the demands made by the music on players were not extreme. From the late 19th century, however, with the ad hoc experimentation within brass bands in the southern USA (particularly those in New Orleans) and, later, with the evolution of jazz (and notably the innovations of Louis Armstrong), the concept of how the trumpet might be played was brought to a level far higher than had previously been imagined.

Among the developments brought about by these musicians, all later carried over into other genres, were an extension of the upper range (to *e♭‴*); a potpourri of personal approaches to the use of vibrato (including Terminal vibrato) of varying amplitude and speed, produced by the chin, the diaphragm, or the motion of the right hand; the ability to execute smoothly various kinds of Gliss (including the rip, the doit, and the fall off); a number of manipulations of the embouchure and fingers to achieve such effects as the Growl, the Half-valve, and the Smear; the production of an airy tone by tightening the lips more than usual and blowing with force so that part of the lip tissue does not vibrate; the playing of Multiphonics by tightening or relaxing the lips unduly and blowing between the partials or by the act of simultaneously playing and singing, which results in various tones and beats being created (best workable in the low register); the invention of new mutes to achieve an array of new timbres (*see* Mute); and the achievement of a technical facility previously unknown, not merely in scale passages, but also in the negotiation of difficult chromatic intervallic leaps which are not idiomatic to the instrument.

3. The trumpet in early jazz. For historical and sociological reasons the soprano brass instrument in early jazz bands was the Cornet. However, the word "cornet" was used in the USA in the 19th century to refer to any soprano brass instrument that played the melodic part, a usage that implied a somewhat interchangeable nature between trumpet and cornet; since many players who began on cornet later took up trumpet as well as or instead of the former, the

history of the two instruments in jazz is best considered as a single continuous tradition.

In New Orleans the leader of brass and jazz bands, and of related groups, was most frequently a cornetist, who would take the most prominent role by playing the melody; as well as being the player with the most volume, he was generally the finest musician in the ensemble. There are numerous accounts among jazz brass players of musicians beginning in their youth as drummers and gradually working their way from the lower brass instruments to the higher, with the position of cornetist being the coveted goal. Universally credited as being the first accomplished cornetist was the legendary Buddy Bolden, who was renowned for his authoritative style. Among those influenced by Bolden were Manuel Perez, Buddy Petit, and, notably, Freddie Keppard; Keppard used his powerful tone over a much wider compass than hitherto, as may be heard on *Stock Yards Strut* (1926, Para. 12399), and exhibited a new delight in exploiting the instrument's technical possibilities.

The typically brusque melodic style and four-square rhythmic approach of New Orleans cornetists was characteristic of King Oliver's playing when he moved from that city to Chicago in 1918, yet his performance of blues numbers was distinctively vocal. Oliver was a good leader and his bands were notable for their integrated teamwork. He was also a considerable influence on other musicians – particularly Mutt Carey, a reliable lead player renowned (like Oliver) for his muted effects, and Tommy Ladnier, a fluent improviser whose relaxed yet controlled phrasing had implicit swing without explicit syncopation. Oliver's Creole Jazz Band was augmented after only a month in Chicago by the arrival of Louis Armstrong, which brought into existence a team of two cornets. This was the first of many such pairings: among Oliver's later partners were Bob Shoffner, Louis Metcalf, and Dave Nelson, while George Mitchell and Natty Dominique appeared together in recording bands led by Johnny Dodds, contributing to the distinctive sound heard, for example, on *Come on and stomp, stomp, stomp* (1927, Bruns. 3568).

Armstrong first recorded on trumpet on 28 May 1926, and soon jettisoned many earlier attitudes, contributing a new approach not only to trumpet playing but also to the wider field of jazz. Using a technique that was basically conventional, his tone was remarkable for its clarity and often sheer beauty, particularly in the control of sustained notes and apposite use of vibrato. He developed a range of three octaves and was one of the first to include chords of the minor and diminished seventh in his improvisations. Most importantly, he created the idea of the featured soloist within the integrated New Orleans sound. His overall gift was that of communication, which he achieved through the exquisite simplicity of his ideas, his subtle use of syncopation and rubato, and the undisputed authority of his playing; a good example of a performance displaying these characteristics is *Sweethearts on Parade* (1930, Col. 2688D).

In the late 1920s most cornet players found it advisable to take up trumpet. A notable exception was Bix Beiderbecke, who nevertheless had a considerable influence over the course of jazz trumpet development. His restrained, elegant, and sensitive playing, improvising close to the melody, indicated the possibilities of the "cool" approach 20 years before its time. Unlike Armstrong, who modified his tone as the situation seemed to demand, Beiderbecke rarely altered his, which was for the most part straight, with only a slight vibrato at the end of certain notes and phrases.

The matter of tone assumed increasing importance during the 1920s. Bubber Miley, the foremost soloist in Duke Ellington's orchestra from 1923 to 1929, had a great melodic gift, but is remembered more for establishing the band's "jungle" sound, typified on *East St. Louis Toodle-oo* (1927, Vic. 21703). Miley was influenced by Oliver's use of mutes, and his growl and wa-wa techniques were subsequently

Part of Duke Ellington's brass section at a recording session for BBC Radio, London, 1933: (left to right) Freddie Jenkins (trumpet), Lawrence Brown (trombone), Cootie Williams (trumpet), and Juan Tizol (valve trombone)

adopted by other sidemen in Ellington's band – Cootie Williams, Rex Stewart, Ray Nance, and Clark Terry.

Big bands began to emerge from the mid-1920s, and consequently trumpeters began to work in trumpet sections or, more generally, with trombonists in brass sections. The size of trumpet sections gradually increased, from Oliver's two instruments in 1922 to Fletcher Henderson's three in 1924. Paul Whiteman foreshadowed a development of the 1930s by including a section of four players in his band in 1928, and by 1951 the trumpets in Stan Kenton's orchestra numbered five; four, however, remained the norm.

4. The swing era. By the late 1920s the primacy of the soprano brass instrument – now generally the trumpet rather than the cornet – was being challenged by the saxophone, and aspects of saxophone performance began to affect the way in which trumpeters played. Armstrong's influence, which extended far beyond other trumpeters, was felt especially in the playing of such leading figures as Jabbo Smith and Henry "Red" Allen, but his emphasis on relaxed melody was beginning to give way to an exploration of dexterity. Smith, who in 1928 succeeded Armstrong in Carroll Dickerson's band, introduced the fast fingering techniques and frequent use of the high register that later became characteristic of bop trumpeters. He also suffered the major drawback of such a style: a thin tone, resulting from the speed of the air through the instrument not allowing full resonance. This may be clearly heard on *Jazz Battle* (1929, Bruns. 4244). There was an even closer approach to bop in Allen's inclination to obscure the joins between phrases. He too included fast-moving passages as an integral part of his style, but unlike Smith, who showed considerable skill in obtaining high notes, Allen tended to use force, often introducing smears and rips into his playing. His vibrato, however, was generally more restricted than was usual for the time.

Of those influenced by Allen, Roy Eldridge was arguably the most important, yet his playing in the high register perhaps owed more to Smith's control than Allen's force. His rhythmic drive has been compared with that of Armstrong, and his virtuoso technique allowed him to use saxophone-like phrasing, as may be heard on Chu Berry's *Forty-six West Fifty-two* (1938, Com. 516).

A smoother and more gentle trumpeter than Eldridge, Buck Clayton employed a wider vibrato, often resorting to the use of a cup mute and showing a preference for traditional harmonies. Charlie Shavers also owed a debt to Allen. He had a strong technique and a remarkable range that allowed him to obtain extreme high and low notes in close proximity; while his style was often very syncopated, his playing at slower tempos is sometimes considered sentimental.

A wider use of the trumpet's high register, possibly stemming from Armstrong's inclination to build up to a climax literally through increasingly higher notes, became noticeable during the 1930s and 1940s. Cat Anderson was the most celebrated high-note specialist in Ellington's orchestra, but Maynard Ferguson, in Kenton's bands of the 1940s and later in his own groups, was most consistently impressive in the high tessitura up to and including *e*♭''''; a good example of his playing may be heard on *MacArthur Park* on the album *M. F. Horn* (1970, Col. C30466).

5. Bop and traditional jazz. By the 1940s the saxophone was the most important instrument in jazz, and as a result the most significant development in brass playing (first for the trumpet and later for the trombone, french horn, and tuba) was the acquisition of a non-idiomatic technical facility that would enable players to rival the facility of bop saxophonists. This was achieved first by Dizzy Gillespie, the most innovative trumpeter after Armstrong. Gillespie's contribution, like Armstrong's, marked a stylistic turning point. Through a remarkable technique he was able to give full vent to his fluent skill for improvisation, utilizing a harmonic rather than a melodic basis. He had scant use for vibrato, but for the most part the notes came so fast that tone was of little importance. In 1947, with *Cubana Be/Cubana Bop* (Vic. 20-3145) and *Manteca* (Vic. 20-3023), he introduced a new element: Afro-Cuban jazz.

Fats Navarro and Clifford Brown were virtuoso players and remarkable improvisers, playing difficult and sophisticated bop solos, yet maintaining a warm, beautiful, velvety tone. They were the precursors of the hard-bop trumpeters that emerged during the 1950s, such as Donald Byrd, Lee Morgan, Freddie Hubbard, and, later, Woody Shaw.

Unable and unwilling to play so high, so fast, or with such precision as Gillespie, Navarro, and Brown, Miles Davis became a strong influence on trumpet players of the 1950s. His introverted, cool style involved even less vibrato than Gillespie's, and at times his notes seemed to be implied rather than stated. While over three decades he led his groups through several landmarks in the evolution of jazz styles, Davis's own playing changed little, though he took up the stemless harmon mute in 1954 to produce a brooding sound so striking that subsequent users of the effect may be said to be only imitating Davis.

Concurrent with developments in bop and related styles was a renewed interest in early cornet and trumpet playing, beginning with the rediscovery in New Orleans of Bunk Johnson and leading to the widespread popularity of traditional jazz and trad bands. While this movement had no great consequences for the development of trumpet styles, it did allow the instrument, among a wide circle of musicians, to re-establish its principal role within the jazz ensemble.

6. Free jazz, fusion, and the continuation of established styles. There have been only a small number of important trumpeters in free jazz – notably Don Cherry (playing a pocket instrument), Bill Dixon, Don Ellis, Lester Bowie, Mike Mantler, and Wadada Leo Smith – and fewer in jazz-rock, the most important being Davis, Ferguson, and Chuck Mangione (who later took up flugelhorn). Significant developments in the 1960s and 1970s in the role and capabilities of the trumpet were rare, contrasting sharply with the changes affecting, for example, the saxophone and the instruments of the rhythm section. Dixon and Bowie differentiated themselves from others not by developing new effects, but by bringing heavy emphasis to the special effects that had been developed in early jazz and swing. Ellis's work with the quarter-tone trumpet has had little influence. Ferguson adapted his playing to jazz-rock with no change whatsoever in his high-pitched melodic style. Ellis and Davis both explored electronic devices, Ellis working, for example, with a ring modulator, Davis with a fuzz box and a wa-wa pedal (as may be heard on his album *Live-Evil*, 1970, Col. G30954), but their experiments had more to do with synthesized sound than with trumpet playing; in Davis's case

it served only to make the instrument sound more like a cheap electric guitar than a trumpet.

Thus, after the unprecedented early achievements of jazz trumpeters in mainstream and bop styles, the trumpet seems to have reached a halt in its development. Perhaps the emergence of musicians such as Wynton Marsalis, classically trained and equally at home performing a trumpet concerto with a symphony orchestra or working with Art Blakey and Herbie Hancock, may give some clue as to the part to be played by a straight, clear tone, faultless technique, and lively imagination.

For further illustrations *see* ALLEN, HENRY "RED"; BOWIE, LESTER; DAVIS, MILES, fig.2; ELDRIDGE, ROY; ELLIS, DON; HUBBARD, FREDDIE; MARSALIS, WYNTON; MEZZROW, MEZZ; NAPOLEON, fig.1a; and TEAGARDEN.

BIBLIOGRAPHY

A. McCarthy: *The Trumpet in Jazz* (London, 1945)
R. Blesh: *Shining Trumpets: a History of Jazz* (New York, 1946, London, 1949, rev. and enlarged 2/1958/*R*1975)
I. Lang: *Jazz in Perspective: the Background of the Blues* (London and elsewhere, 1947/*R*1976)
R. Harris: *Jazz* (London, 1952, 5/1957)
J.-E. Berendt: *Das Jazzbuch: Entwicklung und Bedeutung der Jazzmusik* (Frankfurt am Main, Germany, 1953, rev. 2/1959, Eng. trans., New York, 1962; rev. and enlarged 5/1981, Eng. trans., Westport, CT, 1982, as *The Jazz Book: from New Orleans to Fusion and Beyond*)
O. Keepnews and B. Grauer, Jr.: *A Pictorial History of Jazz: People and Places from New Orleans to Modern Jazz* (New York and London, 1956, rev. 2/1968/*R*1981)
L. Feather: *The Book of Jazz: a Guide to the Entire Field* (New York, 1957, 2/1965 as *The Book of Jazz from Then till Now: a Guide to the Entire Field*)
B. Ulanov: *A Handbook of Jazz* (New York, n.d. [?1957]/*R*1975)
N. Hentoff and A. J. McCarthy, eds.: *Jazz: New Perspectives on the History of Jazz by Twelve of the World's Foremost Jazz Critics and Scholars* (New York and Toronto, 1959/*R*1974)
J. Goldberg: *Jazz Masters of the Fifties* (New York and London, 1965/*R*1980)
G. Schuller: *Early Jazz: its Roots and Musical Development* (New York, 1968)
M. Williams: *The Jazz Tradition* (New York, 1970, rev. 2/1983)
G. Collier: *Inside Jazz* (London, 1973)
A. J. Smith: "Maynard Ferguson: Conquistador of Double High C," *DB*, xliv/16 (1977), 14
M. Laplace: "La trompette et le cornet dans le jazz et la musique populaire," *Brass Bulletin*, no.42 (1983), 16; no.43 (1983), 44; no.44 (1983), 54; no.45 (1984), 38; no.46 (1984), 23; no.47 (1984), 39

CLIFFORD BEVAN

Trunk, Peter (*b* Frankfurt am Main, Germany, 17 May 1936; *d* New York, 31 Dec 1973). German double bass player. After participating in concerts and broadcasts in Germany with Kenny Clarke and Zoot Sims (both 1957) and Stan Getz (1958) he performed and recorded with Albert Mangelsdorff (1958–61). He also recorded with Sims and the dixieland group the Two Beat Stompers (both 1958) and Hans Koller (1958–9). Thereafter he performed and made recordings with Klaus Doldinger (1963–7) and Dusko Goykovich (1965, 1966) and took part in sessions with Tete Montoliu (1962, 1968), Benny Bailey (1964), Don Byas and Ben Webster (1968), Volker Kriegel (1968, 1971), and Kurt Edelhagen (1972); he is heard to advantage on *Ben Webster Meets Don Byas* (1968, Saba 15159). Having worked with Manfred Schoof in 1969, Trunk recorded with him as a member of the New Jazz Trio in 1970–71. He died in an automobile accident.

BIBLIOGRAPHY

FeatherE; *ReclamsJ*
J.-E. Berendt: "In memoriam Peter Trunk," *Ein Fenster aus Jazz: Essays, Portraits, Reflexionen* (Frankfurt am Main, Germany, 1977), 159

Trzaskowski, Andrzej (*b* Kraków, Poland, 23 March 1933; *d* Warsaw, 16 Sept 1998). Polish pianist and composer. He played piano as a child and later studied musicology at the university in Kraków (1952–7); he also took private lessons in composition and contemporary music theory and was active at the Studio Elektroniczne Muzyki Współczesnej (Electronic Studio of Contemporary Music). In 1951 he helped to form Melomani, one of the first Polish swing and bop groups. In 1958 he played and recorded with the Jazz Believers, a quintet that included Wojciech Karolak and Jan Wróblewski, and worked with another quintet, led by Jerzy Matuszkiewicz. The following year he formed his own hard-bop group, the Wreckers, which toured the USA for a month in 1962 as the Andrzej Trzaskowski Quintet and appeared at jazz festivals in Washington, DC, and Newport, Rhode Island. As the leader of small groups Trzaskowski performed and recorded with American musicians visiting Poland, such as Stan Getz (1960) and Ted Curson (1965–6). Many leading Polish musicians, among them Zbigniew Namysłowski, Tomasz Stańko, and Michal Urbaniak, played with his groups early in their careers. Trzaskowski began to incorporate avant-garde techniques in his work from 1964. In the late 1960s he worked regularly for Norddeutscher Rundfunk in Hamburg, West Germany, writing more than 20 compositions and participating in workshops, then from 1975 to 1991 he led the Orkiestra Polskiego Radia i Telewizji Studio S1 (Orchestra of Polish Radio and Television Studio S1). Although he was an excellent pianist, from the early 1970s he concentrated more on composition. He wrote music for films and theater, two jazz ballets, and *Nihil novi*, a third-stream work performed by Don Ellis at the International Jazz Jamboree in Warsaw in 1962. From 1992 until his death in 1998 Trzaskowski taught at the Fryderyk Chopin School of Music in Warsaw.

SELECTED RECORDINGS

As leader: *The Wreckers* (1960, Muza 0133); *The Andrzej Trzaskowski Quintet* (1965, Muza 0258), incl. Synopsis; *Andrzej Trzaskowski Sextet Featuring Ted Curson* (1966, Muza 0378)
As sideman: *Stan Getz w Polsce* (Stan Getz in Poland) (1960, Muza 0329); Jazz Workshop Ost-West: *Jazz Workshop Ost-West* (1965, Col. SMC83875)

BIBLIOGRAPHY

Feather–Gitler '70s
J. Byrczek: "Eurojazz Personalities: Poland," *JF* [intl edn], no.18 (1972), 87
"Andrzej Trzaskowski," *JF* [intl edn], no.42 (1976), 8
E. Jost: *Europas Jazz, 1960–1980* (Frankfurt am Main, Germany, 1987), 44
"Andrzej Trzaskowski: Życiorys" [Andrzej Trzaskowski: biography], *JF*, no.189 (1998), 2

WOLFRAM KNAUER/ADAM CEGIELSKI

Tsfasman, Aleksandr (Naumovich) (*b* Zaporozh'ye, Ukraine, 14 Dec 1906; *d* Moscow, 20 Feb 1971). Russian bandleader, pianist, and composer. In 1926 he formed the orchestra AMA-Jazz (the jazz ensemble of the Assotsiyatsia Moskovskikh Avtorov [Association of Moscow Authors]), which became the first jazz band in the USSR to broadcast on radio (1928) and the first to make a recording (*Hallelujah*, 1929). While leading the band he studied piano at the Moscow P. I. Tchaikovsky State Conservatory, from which he graduated in 1930; that same year AMA-Jazz disbanded. He led other bands from the mid-1930s, then the jazz orchestra of Vsesoyuznoe Radio (All-union radio) from 1939 to 1946, and made many recordings. Tsfasman was the first improvising virtuoso in soviet jazz. Among his compositions are jazz pieces, two piano concertos, film scores, music for the stage, and popular songs. The album *Aleksandr Tsfasman: kompozitor, pianist, dirizher* (Mel. 33M60 3658992) includes several previously unissued tracks recorded in the 1930s and 1940s.

BIBILIOGRAPHY

S. F. Starr: *Red and Hot: the Fate of Jazz in the Soviet Union, 1917–1980* (New York, and Oxford, England, 1983, rev. 2/1994, as *Red and Hot: the Fate of Jazz in the Soviet Union, 1917–1990*)

"Aleksandr Tsfasman," *Sovetskaya muzyka*, no.3 (1986), 79

WALTER OJAKÄÄR

Tsilis, Gust William (*b* Chicago, 14 April 1956). Vibraphonist and marimba player. He initially played piano and drums and took up vibraphone only when he enrolled at the Berklee College of Music in 1974; it was later again that he began playing marimba. In 1981 he moved to New York, and he led his own groups from the mid-1980s. In addition he toured and recorded with Herb Robertson (1987) and Arthur Blythe (from 1989), recorded with Lindsey Horner (1989) and the saxophonist Karl Denson (1994), and performed and recorded with the Enja Band, alongside Willie Williams, Uri Caine, Michael Formanek, and Cecil Brooks III (December 1992). Tsilis has worked as a record producer for Enja and Ken and as the manager of the jazz club Visiones.

SELECTED RECORDINGS

As leader: *Pale Fire* (1986–7, Enja 5061); *Heritage* (1991, Ken 018); *Sequestered Days* (1991, Enja 6094-2); *Wood Music* (1993, Enja 7093-2)

As sideman: A. Blythe: *Hipmotism* (1991, Enja 6088-2); K. Denson: on *Chunky Pecan Pie* (1994, Minor Music 801041), Banana Boy

BIBLIOGRAPHY

Feather–GitlerBEJ

B. Milkowski: "Caught: Enja All-Stars," *DB*, lx/3 (1993), 52

——: "Hearsay: Gust Tsilis: Knockin' on Wood," *JT*, xxiii/8 (1993), 12

GK

Tuba. A valved brass instrument of wide conical bore. The tubing is usually coiled into an elliptical shape and terminates in a wide bell (usually pointing upwards) and a deep, cup-shaped mouthpiece. The instrument has an open fundamental of 8′ *C* (or lower) and is equipped with three to six (usually four, rarely seven) valves to alter the length of the tubing and hence the pitch. It is generally used in jazz as the bass or contrabass member of the band.

A group of related instruments, in various shapes and sizes, may be said to constitute a tuba family; its members are known generically as brass bass. The most important are the euphonium (sometimes referred to, especially in the USA, as the baritone horn, *see* Saxhorn), which is essentially a tenor tuba in B♭; and the helicon and sousaphone, which are both types of bass tuba distinguished from the rest of the family by their circular shape. The lower members of the saxhorn group are also sometimes regarded as forming part of the tuba group. The sousaphone, named after the composer and bandmaster John Philip Sousa, is used mainly in marching bands. Like the helicon (now almost obsolete, but used by Rich Matteson on recordings by Bob Scobey's Frisco Jazz Band in the 1950s and 1960s), it encircles the player, resting on the left shoulder and passing under the right arm, with the bell pointing forwards above the player's head; this form was devised to facilitate carrying the instruments while marching. Some upright tubas have been made with the bell facing forwards; this "recording" bell was introduced during the 1920s, when the tuba often substituted for the double bass in recording studios.

As an important military instrument the tuba was commonly found in early marching bands, though by the early 1900s the double bass was normally preferred in jazz bands. (This might not have been the case had more tuba players of the caliber of Cyrus St. Clair been available.) During the 1920s the sousaphone was used to provide the crisp attack necessary to the fulfilling of the primarily rhythmic function of the bass instruments; Paul Whiteman's orchestra, for example, included two. Driven from the dance band by the double bass when swing became the predominant style in jazz, the tuba reappeared during the dixieland revival of the 1940s; in dixieland it is often found in conjunction with the banjo (just as the double bass is usually paired with the guitar).

In the later 1940s the tuba began to be used in a different role in such bands as those of Claude Thornhill and Miles Davis, where it was valued because it offered a deep brass sound combined with considerable agility. It left the rhythm section to join the brass section, in which, since its timbre was similar, it was frequently linked with the orchestral horn. Gil Evans used the instrument in a consistently imaginative way; among the first to play tuba in his arrangements was Bill Barber, who as a member of Miles Davis's nonet took part in the recordings (1949–50) that were later issued collectively as *The Birth of the Cool*. Don Butterfield, playing in groups led by Sonny Rollins, Cannonball Adderley, Charles Mingus, and others in the 1950s and 1960s, became known for the exceptional agility and virtuosity of his solos. Howard Johnson (ii), who played tuba in the bands of Archie Shepp and Evans (he may be heard as a soloist on *Thoroughbred* from Evans's *Svengali*, 1973, Atl. 1643), formed the first jazz tuba ensemble in 1968, and remains, with Bob Stewart, the leading jazz tuba player; his group Gravity includes Stewart, Joe Daly, and Earl McIntyre.

The euphonium also enjoyed a revival in postwar jazz: the orchestra assembled in London in 1964 for Benny Golson incorporated a euphonium alongside its four orchestral horns, and the instrument was played by Kiane Zawadi and occasionally by Maynard Ferguson. In 1976 Rich Matteson co-founded the Matteson–Phillips Tuba-Jazz Consort, an ensemble of three euphoniums, three tubas, and rhythm section. Michel Godard has been influenced by both Johnson and Stewart. In addition to his duo with Marc Ducret, Godard uniquely plays jazz on one of the tuba's French ancestors, the serpent. His recordings (on both instruments) include *Le chant du serpent* (1989, Label la Lichère 37).

For illustration *see* Jazz (i), figs.2 and 6.

BIBLIOGRAPHY

O. Keepnews and B. Grauer, Jr.: *A Pictorial History of Jazz: People and Places from New Orleans to Modern Jazz* (New York and London, 1956, rev. 2/1968/*R*1981)

C. J. Bevan: *The Tuba Family* (London and New York, 1978)

M. Laplace: "Les tubas dans le jazz et les musiques populaires," *Brass Bulletin*, no.56 (1986), 18; no.57 (1987), 84

CLIFFORD BEVAN

Tubs. Slang term for drums; *see* Drum set.

Tuck & Patti. Duo formed around 1979 by the guitarist Tuck Andress and the singer Patti Cathcart (*b* San Francisco, 4 Oct 1960); the couple were married in 1981. They performed in the San Francisco Bay area and made their first recording around 1987. Andress and Cathcart have been highly acclaimed and have gained a reputation around the world for their blend of jazz, rhythm-and-blues, and pop. Both are virtuosos and may be heard to fine effect on *Tears of Joy* (*c*1987, Windham Hill 0111), *Love Warriors* (1988, Windham Hill 0116), and *Learning How to Fly* (*c*1994, Epic 64439).

For bibliography *see* ANDRESS, TUCK.

GK

Tucker, Ben(jamin Mayer) (*b* Nashville, 13 Dec 1930). Double bass player. He began playing trumpet at the age of 12 and tuba in his last year of high school (1948–9). While studying music at Tennessee State University he took up double bass and appeared at clubs in Nashville. Following military service he performed and recorded in Los Angeles in the West Coast jazz groups of Warne Marsh and Bill Perkins (both 1956), Art Pepper (1956–7, 1958), and Chico Hamilton (1958). He then moved to New York, where in 1959 he made recordings and appeared with Kenny Burrell and Roland Hanna; in the same year he toured with Chris Connor. In 1961 he performed and recorded in Rio de Janeiro as a member of an all-star bop group that included Kenny Dorham, Al Cohn, and Zoot Sims. In the early 1960s Tucker was associated with Herbie Mann and Billy Taylor (ii). He also worked extensively as a studio musician, performing at sessions with, among others, Yusef Lateef (1960), Lou Donaldson (1960, 1961), Marian McPartland (1960, 1963), Dave Bailey, Connor, and Grant Green (all 1961), Gerry Mulligan and Vi Redd (both 1962), Illinois Jacquet (1963, 1968), Mose Allison and Dave Burrell (both 1964), Eddie "Lockjaw" Davis and Teddy Edwards (both 1967), Pat Martino (1967–8), Taylor (1967, 1969), and Harold Vick (1975). In the early 1970s he settled permanently in Savannah, Georgia, where he has been active as a musician and businessman and has taken a prominent role in cultural and business activities affecting the city's African-American community.

Oral history material in *TNF*.

SELECTED RECORDINGS

As sideman: A. Pepper: *The Omega Man* (1957, Omega Tape 7020); G. Green: *Sunday Morning* (1961, BN 84099), incl. Exodus, So What; H. Mann: *Standing Ovation at Newport* (1965, Atl. 1445), incl. Comin' Home Baby

BIBLIOGRAPHY

FeatherE; *Feather '60s*

R. Gordon: *Jazz West Coast: the Los Angeles Jazz Scene of the 1950s* (London and New York, 1986)

<http://www.coastaljazz.com/fame/tucker/> (2000)

BK

Tucker, Bobby [Robert Nathaniel, Jr.] (*b* Morristown, NJ, 8 Jan 1923). Pianist. Having taken piano lessons from the age of four, he began performing when he was 14 and later studied in New York at the Institute of Musical Art. While serving in the army in Cheyenne, Wyoming (from 1943), he played trombone in a military band and piano in a dance band alongside George Duvivier. In 1946, following his discharge, he became accompanist first to Mildred Bailey and then, in the autumn, to Billie Holiday, with whom he remained until summer 1949; during the same period he played in clubs on 52nd Street with Lucky Thompson and Stuff Smith. He continued to make recordings with Holiday in the 1950s (1951, 1954, 1955; notably *I thought about you*, 1954, Clef 89150) and also took part in a session led by Marshal Royal (1953). In 1949 Tucker joined Billy Eckstine, with whom he toured the USA, Europe, Australia, and Japan; he began writing arrangements for the singer in the 1960s and remained his accompanist until the latter's death in 1993. That year he recorded with Joe Wilder (*No Greater Love*, Evening Star 103), and in 1994 he directed a big band accompanying Nancy Wilson at Carnegie Hall, New York, and toured for three months with Tony Bennett.

BIBLIOGRAPHY

ChiltonW; *FeatherE*

J. Chilton: *Billie's Blues: a Survey of Billie Holiday's Career, 1933–1959* (London, 1975)

E. Southern: "'Mr. B' of Ballad and Bop," *Black Perspective in Music*, viii (1980), 64 [incl. biography of Tucker]

E. Berger: *Bassically Speaking: an Oral History of George Duvivier* (Metuchen, NJ, and London, 1993)

D. Clarke: *Wishing on the Moon: the Life and Times of Billie Holiday* (London and New York, 1994)

L. Gourse: "Bobby Tucker: Light and Shade," *Jh*, no.519 (1995), 28

HOWARD RYE, BK

Tucker, George (Andrew) (*b* Palatka, FL, 10 Dec 1927; *d* New York, 10 Oct 1965). Double bass player. He studied double bass at the New York Conservatory of Modern Music (1948), and his early performing experience included engagements with Earl Bostic, John Coltrane, and Jackie McLean. In the 1950s Tucker was a member of the house bands at the Continental Lounge, Minton's Playhouse, and The Playhouse, where he also appeared with Horace Parlan and Booker Ervin. After playing with Jerome Richardson and Junior Mance he toured with Lambert, Hendricks, and Bavan (1962–3). He recorded with Freddie Redd and Clifford Jordan (both 1957), Curtis Fuller (1957–8), Bennie Green (1958–60), Richardson (1959), Johnny Hammond (1959–60), Oliver Nelson, Eric Dolphy, Arnett Cobb, Buddy Tate, and Lou Donaldson (all 1960), frequently with Ervin, Parlan, Stanley Turrentine, and Shirley Scott (all 1960–61), and with Dexter Gordon and Howard McGhee (both 1961), Sonny Red (1961–2), Walt Dickerson and Ted Curson (both 1962), Pony Poindexter and Jimmy Witherspoon (both 1963), Gildo Mahones (1963–4), Willis "Gator" Jackson (1964), and Carmell Jones, Charles McPherson, and Lucky Thompson (all 1965). In 1965 Tucker appeared in Boston with Jaki Byard's group. Although he was associated mainly with hard-bop groups and swing musicians strongly oriented toward the blues, he accompanied Jack Teagarden at the Monterey Jazz Festival in 1963, and in 1965 performed and recorded with Earl Hines's trio, accompanying Coleman Hawkins.

SELECTED RECORDINGS

As sideman: C. Jordan: *Cliff Craft* (1957, BN 1582); E. Dolphy: *Outward Bound* (1960, NewJ 8236); H. Parlan: *Us Three* (1960, BN 4037); D. Gordon: *Doin' Allright* (1961, BN 84077); Lambert, Hendricks, and Bavan: *At Newport '63* (1963, RCA LSP2747); C. Hawkins: *Coleman Hawkins with the Earl Hines Trio* (1965, Pumpkin 105); J. Byard: *Live at Lennie's* (1965, Prst. 7419, 7477)

BIBLIOGRAPHY

Obituary, *DB*, xxxii/24 (1965), 12

D. C. Hunt: "Unforgettable," *JM*, no.162 (1968), 14

P. S. Friedman: "Discography: George Tucker," *JM*, no.163 (1968), 24; no.166 (1968), 30; no.167 (1969), 30

BRENDA PENNELL/BK

Tucker, Mickey [Michael B.] (*b* Durham, NC, 28 April 1941). Pianist. He grew up in Rankin, Pennsylvania, and learned piano from the age of six. The family returned to the South when he was 12 years old, and Tucker continued his studies in North Carolina and then in Atlanta, where he entered Morehouse College at the age of 15. He taught and performed in Mississippi from 1961 to 1964 and then moved to New York; there he joined the singer Damita Jo (1965), with whom he made his first visit to London. He was a sideman for the comedian Timmie Rogers (1966–7) and the pop group Little Anthony and the Imperials (1967–8), and then joined James Moody, with whom he worked strictly as an organist (1969–72). Having deputized briefly in the Thad Jones–Mel Lewis Orchestra (1973) he worked with Roy Brooks (1973–5) and the group Final Edition (1975); he also recorded on organ with Roland Kirk (1971), on electric piano and organ with Willis "Gator" Jackson (1973–4), and on piano with Eric Kloss (1973, 1976), Eddie Jefferson (1974, 1976), and David Schnitter (1976). His preference was for piano, which he used for his own albums, though the first of his LPs (from 1975) includes a track on which he played Hammond organ.

Tucker toured Europe and North Africa with Art Blakey (1976), toured Europe and recorded with Frank Foster (1977–9), and toured Japan and recorded in Tokyo with Archie Shepp (1978–9). In New York he recorded with Junior Cook, Philly Joe Jones, Billy Harper, and Charles McPherson (all 1977), Bill Hardman (1978), Johnny Lytle (1980), and Jimmy Ponder (1983), made further albums under his own name (1977–9), and played in the New York Giants (alongside Ted Dunbar, *c*1980–1981). In the mid-1980s he performed and recorded (1983, 1986) with the reconstituted Jazztet of Art Farmer and Benny Golson. Later he worked with Junior Cook (recording in 1988–9), made a recording in concert with Louis Hayes (1989), and recorded again with Hardman (in Copenhagen, 1989) before settling in Melbourne, Australia (late 1989), where he performs regularly. Tucker has returned to New York or traveled to Denmark from time to time to fulfill recording commitments (including sessions with Cook, 1991, Dunbar 1991, and Foster, 1998, and his first album as an unaccompanied soloist, in 1994), and he also has recorded several sessions in Australia. He frequently travels within the country as an invited guest soloist or to accompany visiting American jazz musicians, and he has appeared at major Australian festivals.

SELECTED RECORDINGS

As unaccompanied soloist: *Gettin' There* (1994, Ste. 31365)
As leader: *Triplicity* (1975, Xan. 128); *Sweet Lotus Lips* (1978, Denon YX7535); *Mister Mysterious* (1978, Muse 5174); *The Crawl* (1979, Muse 5223); *Blues in Five Dimensions* (1989, Ste. 31258); *Hang in There* (1991, Ste. 31302)
As sideman: J. Moody: *Never Again* (1972, Muse 5001); E. Kloss: *Essence* (1973, Muse 5038); E. Jefferson: *Things are Getting Better* (1974, Muse 5043); A. Farmer and B. Golson: *Back to the City* (1986, Cont. 14020); B. Hardman: *What's Up* (1989, Ste. 31254); L. Hayes: *The Crawl* (1989, Can. 79045); J. Cook: *You Leave Me Breathless* (1991, Ste. 31304);

BIBLIOGRAPHY

Feather–Gitler '70s
A. Lewis and L. Lewis: "Mickey Tucker: Interview," *Cadence*, xix/5 (1993), 13

PAUL RINZLER/BK

Tuig, R. A. Pseudonym under which EDMOND SOUCHON contributed to the journal *Second Line*.

Tuncboyaçiyan [Tuncboyaçi], **Arto** (*b* Galataria, nr Istanbul, 4 Aug 1957). Armenian percussionist. He has worked under both spellings of his surname. At the age of 11 he began performing professionally in bands with his older brother, and from around 1972 he worked in Europe. Later he moved to New York (*c*1981), and he eventually settled in New Jersey. In the mid-1980s he became a member of Ed Schuller's ensembles, and he played in Gust William Tsilis's group Alithea (recording in 1986) and in Armen Donelian's quintet (1986–91). In addition he performed with Al Di Meola's band World Sinfonia (from 1990), Marc Johnson's Right Brain Patrol (from 1991 into mid-1990s), Arthur Blythe (from *c*1991), and Hank Roberts's trio Little Motor People (recording in 1992); he took part in recording sessions with Jim Pepper (1988), Mitch Watkins (1989), Dino Saluzzi and Ellery Eskelin (both 1991), Bob Berg (1992–4), Jay Anderson (1994), Linda Sharrock (1995), Oregon (1996), Bill Evans (iii) (1997), and Mike Mainieri's American Diary project (*c*1998). In 1986 Tuncboyaçiyan was a founding member of Night Ark, with which he performed in October 1998 at an international jazz festival in Yerevan, Armenia, alongside Donelian, Johnson, and its other remaining original member, the *'ūd* player Ara Dinkjian. With Dave Samuels and others he took part in a percussion concert under Tom Rainey's leadership, and in the late 1990s he worked in a trio with Joe Zawinul and Fareed Haque and in a quintet with Zawinul, Haque, Matthew Garrison, and Gene Lake. Shortly thereafter Tuncboyaçiyan, Garrison, Lake, and Jim Beard formed the group Walking Fish, and in 1999 Tuncboyaçiyan performed and recorded with Maria Pia De Vito and Rita Marcotulli in the trio Triboh. He makes his own instruments as well as playing traditional ethnic percussion instruments such as *djembe*. He may be seen playing in the video *An Evening of Dance by Zonnie J. Bauer* (n.d. [filmed 1988]), for which he also wrote the music.

SELECTED RECORDINGS

Duo with G. Moore: on Oregon: *Northwest Passage* (1996, Intuition 3191-2), Don't Knock on my Door
As leader with M. P. De Vito and R. Marcotulli: *Triboh* (1999, Polo Sud 026)
As sideman: G. W. Tsilis: *Pale Fire* (1986, Enja 5061); S. Nabatov: *Inside Lookin' Out* (1988, Tutu 888004); A. Donelian: *The Wayfarer* (1990, Sunnyside 1049); M. Johnson: *Right Brain Patrol* (1991, JMT 849153); H. Roberts: *Little Motor People* (1992, JMT 514005); M. Johnson: *Magical Labyrinth* (1994, JMT 514018)

BIBLIOGRAPHY

<http://www.forthnet.gr/libra-music/arto.html> (1999)

GK

Tunnell, Jimi [James Gilliland] (*b* Denton, TX, 8 July 1958). Electric guitarist. He took up classical and jazz trumpet at the age of ten, and while following the jazz program at North Texas State University (1977–9) he settled on electric guitar as his primary instrument. After college he formed the group 360 with the keyboard player Robbie Kilgore and began working with jazz musicians in New York. In 1988 he joined Mike Mainieri's Steps Ahead, and during a three-year association with the group he introduced singing into its live performances. In addition he played with Bob Belden (1991, 1993), Dennis Chambers (1991–2), and Adam Holzman (1992) and led and recorded with Trilateral Commission (1991–2), a group which reflected his admiration for Weather Report. Tunnell has also been active as a freelance guitarist, singer, and producer with the multi-media artist Laurie Anderson, Omar Hakim, Teo Macero, and Tom Coster. In 1990 he became partner, artist, and producer at Damfino Productions in New York, working on commercials and film scores.

SELECTED RECORDINGS

As leader: *Trilateral Commission* (1991–2, 101 South 877083)
As sideman: B. Belden: *Straight to my Heart* (1989–91, BN B21Z-95137); D. Chambers: *Getting Even* (1991, 101 South 877079); A. Holzman: *Overdrive* (1991–2, Lipstick 89025); Steps Ahead: *Yin-yang* (1992, NYC 6001-2)

BIBLIOGRAPHY

B. Milkowski: "Redefining the F-word: Five New Faces in Fusion", *GP*, xxv/6 (1991), 68

MARK GILBERT

Turbinton, Earl(, Jr.) [Naim Akban Ben-Tur; the African Cowboy] (*b* New Orleans, 23 Sept 1941). Saxophonist. He took up saxophone at the age of 12. In the early 1960s he was a founding member of the Jazz Workshop, an organization that offered free music lessons to local inner-city children and ran a club promoting modern jazz; it was Turbinton's hope that it would become the modern-jazz equivalent of Preservation Hall, but the venture failed. Turbinton had begun working professionally as a studio musician in the late 1950s, and he toured with the soul singer Jerry Butler, in groups accompanying numerous Motown acts, notably Diana Ross and the Supremes, the Temptations, and the Four Tops (from the mid-1960s), and with B. B. King (late 1960s – early 1970s). In addition he recorded with Joe Zawinul (*Zawinul*, 1970, Atl. 1579), with King in Los Angeles (1971), and with Buster Williams in New York (1975), after which he returned to New Orleans, where he continued to perform into the late 1990s. In the 1980s Turbinton took the nickname the African Cowboy as part of a protest against the policies of President Reagan, who had played cowboys in films and was in the process of reducing US government funding for the arts. He recorded as a leader in 1987 (*Brothers for Life*, Rounder 2064) and around 1998 (*Dominion and Sustenance*, Prog. 7067-2), and in 1993 he led a pianoless trio. His brother Willie Tee (Wilson Turbinton) is a pianist and keyboard player.

BIBLIOGRAPHY

J. A. Simon: "Profile: Earl Turbinton Jr.," *DB*, xlv/15 (1978), 26
"High Flying Jazz," *New Orleans Times-Picayune* (24 Dec 1993)
L. E. Elie: "Rare Cowboy Rides his Sax," *New Orleans Times-Picayune* (1 May 1998)

GK

Turnaround [turnback]. A chord pattern at the end of the final phrase of a chorus which leads back to the beginning of the theme; *see* Harmony (i), §1(v)(b).

Turnbull, Alan (Lawrence) [Tom Terrific] (*b* Melbourne, Australia, 23 Nov 1943). Australian drummer. He began playing professionally at the age of 14 and was influenced by Stewie Speers and Graham Morgan. In 1961 he was with Frank Smith at the Embers in Melbourne, and in 1965 he moved to Sydney, where he worked regularly with John Sangster, Don Burrows, and others. In 1972 he appeared with Burrows's quartet at the Montreux and Newport jazz festivals; he may be heard to advantage on the album *Live at Montreux* (CPRS 1010). The following year he performed in Don Banks's *Nexus* with the Sydney Symphony Orchestra. Turnbull maintained his association with Burrows into the 1980s, but only intermittently thereafter, and continued to play and record as a sideman; he worked with Gary Burton, Milt Jackson, Sonny Stitt, Phil Woods and Joe Henderson (both 1981), and George Cables (1985). Perhaps his most notable later work was with Dale Barlow and the pianist Cathy Harley, but he remained busy in many other settings in the 1980s and 1990s.

SELECTED RECORDINGS

As sideman: D. Burrows: *Just the Beginning* (1970, Cherry Pie 1009); Jazz Co-op: *Jazz Co-op* (1976, 44 Records 6357706); E. Buddle: *Buddles Doubles* (1977, M7 216); B. Bertles: *Moontrane* (1979, Batjazz 2070); D. MacRae: *Southern Roots* (1986–7, Emanem 3603); D. Barlow: *Horn* (1989, Spiral Scratch 0003); C. Harley: *Tuesday's Tune* (1995, Rufus 028)

BIBLIOGRAPHY

A. Bisset: *Black Roots, White Flowers: a History of Jazz in Australia* (Sydney, 1979, rev. 2/1987)
J. Shand: "Alan Turnbull," *Jazz: the Australasian Contemporary Music Magazine*, ii/[9] (1982), 22
B. Johnson: *The Oxford Companion to Australian Jazz* (Melbourne, Australia, 1987)
J. Clare [G. Brennan, pseud.]: *Bodgie Dada and the Cult of Cool* (Sydney, 1995)
W. Bebbington, ed: *The Oxford Companion to Australian Music* (Melbourne, Australia, 1997)

JEFF PRESSING (with JOHN WHITEOAK)/ROGER T. DEAN (recording-list)

Turner, (Malcolm) Bruce (*b* Saltburn, England, 5 July 1922; *d* Newport Pagnell, England, 28 Nov 1993). English alto and soprano saxophonist, clarinetist, and leader. He taught himself clarinet at school and took up alto saxophone while in the RAF (1943). After a short spell with a bop group in 1947 he played dixieland with Freddy Randall from 1948 to 1950, apart from two periods as a sideman in a band on the *Queen Mary*. He then led a quartet on the ship with Dill Jones and Peter Ind, and, while visiting New York, studied with Lee Konitz. Turner worked again with Randall (November 1950 – January 1953), then with Humphrey Lyttelton (January 1953 – March 1957), and from 1957 to 1965 led the Jump Band; this group was featured in Jack Gold's film *Living Jazz* (1961), for which Turner arranged the music. From May 1964 to February 1966 Turner worked once more with Randall and occasionally re-formed the Jump Band to accompany American jazzmen, including Don Byas, with whom the group appeared on the television show "Jazz 625" (1966). He was a member of Acker Bilk's band from May 1966 to June 1970. In the early 1970s he worked variously with the Jump Band, Wally Fawkes and John Chilton's Feetwarmers, Ind, and Lyttelton; he was with Lyttelton regularly from 1974 to 1988, while also working with Stan Greig (1975–6), Ind, Alex Welsh (late 1970s), and Dave Green. In the early 1990s he led small groups.

Turner's style on alto saxophone was highly individual, reflecting the early influence of Pete Brown as well as that of Charlie Parker and Konitz, whereas his playing on soprano saxophone was similar to that of Bob Wilber. His performances on clarinet were flexible and varied in style. He was extremely self-critical and continually analyzed his own performances.

SELECTED RECORDINGS

As leader: with W. Fawkes: The Sheik of Araby/Fishmouth/Exactly like you/Oh Baby (1954, Decca 6193) [EP]; *Accent on Swing* (1959, International Jazz Club 4)
As sideman: F. Randall: Tight Lines/Baby won't you please come home? (1951, Parl. 3494); H. Lyttelton: *Live at the Royal Festival Hall* (1954, Parl. 1032); *Midnight at Nixa* (1956, Nixa 3); K. Smith: *Up Jumped the Blues* (1978, Hefty Jazz 105); D. Green: *Fingers Remembers Mingus* (1979, Spot. 521)

BIBLIOGRAPHY

ChiltonB; *FeatherE*
H. Lyttelton: *I Play as I Please: the Memoirs of an Old Etonian Trumpeter* (London, 1954)
——: *Second Chorus* (London, 1958)
M. Jones: "Turner Turns the Corner," *MM* (14 Oct 1961), 7
D. Oliver: *B. Turner Jump Bands* (Summerhill, Suffolk, England, 1968)
S.-A. Worsfold: "Bruce Turner: Confessions of a Jazz Maverick," *JJI*, xxx (1977), no.5, p.6; no.6, p.22
B. Turner: *Hot Air, Cool Music* (London, 1984) [incl. discography]
Obituary, *The Times* (1 Dec 1993)

REG COOPER/BK

Turner, Charlie [Fat Man] (*b* early 20th century; *d* 27 Oct 1964). Tuba and double bass player and bandleader. He played with Doc Cheatham (1926), then recorded with Richard M. Jones's Jazz Wizards (1927), and his imaginative tuba playing may be heard to advantage on *Boar Hog Blues* (1927, Vic. 21203). After touring with Jelly Roll Morton he moved to New York as a member of Marion Hardy's Alabamians (1929). By 1933 he was leading his own band, which, under the name Turner's Arcadians, was resident at the Arcadia Ballroom in 1934. Between November 1934 and around May 1935 this group was used by Fletcher Henderson for various engagements, and from 1935 to 1938 some of its members, including Turner himself, formed the nucleus of Fats Waller's touring band. Turner also recorded with Waller's Rhythm and with Emmett Mathews; *You came to my rescue* (1936, Voc. 3332), recorded with the latter, provides a good example of his double bass playing. Thereafter he worked in a backup group for Ethel Waters (1938–9). He was previously thought to have rejoined Waller in 1941–2, but the bass player on these sessions is actually Cedric Wallace.

BIBLIOGRAPHY

AllenH
H. Dial: *All that Jazz about Jazz: the Autobiography of Harry Dial* (Chigwell, England, 1984)
L. Wright: *"Fats" in Fact* (Chigwell, England, 1992)

HOWARD RYE

Turner, Danny [James Daniel] (*b* Farrell, PA, 8 March 1920; *d* New York, 14 April 1995). Alto saxophonist. Having first learned piano for two years and played clarinet, he took up alto saxophone while at high school in Niagara Falls, New York, and formed a gospel vocal quartet with his brothers. He played his first engagements at the age of 18 in the Buffalo area. After moving to Philadelphia (1948), where he worked with Red Garland, he recorded with Sabby Lewis (1949) and then toured briefly with the vocal group Four Kings and a Queen and with Gerald Wilson's band accompanying Billie Holiday (early 1950s). From 1954 he spent about four years in Milt Buckner's trio, and he is heard to advantage on *Rockin' with Milt* (1955, Cap. T642). In the 1960s Turner played intermittently with Machito and recorded with Dakota Staton (1963), Brother Jack McDuff (1963, 1966–7), Ray Charles (1964), Jimmy Witherspoon and Pat Martino (both 1967), and Jimmy McGriff (1968–9). He worked as a substitute in Count Basie's band early in 1969 and again from 1971; later he became a full-time member, initially playing tenor saxophone (from May 1975) and then serving as lead alto saxophonist (from 1983). In addition he recorded as the leader of a quartet (*First Time Out*, *c*1983, Hemisphere 0001). Following Basie's death in 1984, Turner continued to work with the memorial Basie orchestra into the 1990s, successively under Thad Jones, Frank Foster, and Grover Mitchell; in the 1980s, at times when the group was not busy, he also played in Mitchell's big band. He doubled on clarinet and flute.

BIBLIOGRAPHY

SheridanCB
P. Vacher: "Counting the Score," *MM*, li (3 Jan 1976), 27
D. J. Gibson: "Count Basie Saxophone Section Celebrates 50th Anniversary," *Saxophone Journal*, xi/3 (1986), 40; xi/4 (1987), 39
Obituary, P. Vacher, *The Guardian* (20 May 1995)
J. Evensmo: *History of Jazz Tenor Saxophone: Black Artists*, iv: *1945–1949* (Oslo, 1999)

BK

Turner, Dave [David Bruce] (*b* Montreal, 8 May 1949). Canadian alto saxophonist and leader. He played keyboards with rhythm-and-blues bands in Montreal (1968–74) and began studying saxophone in 1970. He was a member of Andrew Homzy's Sax No End in 1975 and worked locally with salsa groups before joining Vic Vogel's big band in 1979. His own groups have included a sextet co-led by the trumpeter Ron DiLauro (1983–90), a quartet featuring Nelson Symonds (1992–6), and a Latin ensemble (from 1997). From 1984 he has made several trips to Europe, working with local rhythm sections in Belgium and Holland. Turner, a stirring player influenced by Johnny Hodges, Earl Bostic, and Cannonball Adderley, has recorded as lead alto saxophonist and featured soloist with Vogel and has made several albums with his own groups, notably *For the Kindness of Strangers* (1988, Justin Time 29).

MARK MILLER

Turner, Henry (Benton) (*b* Quincy, FL, 28 June 1903 or 1904; *d* New York, 26 July 1980). Double bass player. In his application for social security Turner supplies his middle name and his year of birth as 1903, one year earlier than the date in standard reference sources. He studied at the Tuskegee Institute, Alabama, after which he worked in Hartford, Connecticut (1925), playing tuba and trombone. In 1929 he was a member of Don Albert's Ten Happy Pals. In New York he was with the bandleader Charlie Skeete before joining Claude Hopkins at the Venetian Gardens, and he remained with Hopkins until his career was interrupted by illness in 1936. Following his recovery he joined Snub Mosley (1937), then played with Sidney Bechet (1938) and Joe Sullivan (1939–40). His dependable, swinging rhythm work was later heard with Louis Jordan (1940–41), George James (1942–3), Garvin Bushell (1944), Lem Johnson (1945, *c*1947), Herman "Ivory" Chittison (1946), Bobby Sands (1947–8), Harry Dial (1949–52), and Wilbur De Paris (1957). Turner then worked as a freelance, performing and recording regularly, and played for radio and television.

SELECTED RECORDINGS

As sideman: J. Sullivan: Low Down Dirty Shame (1940, Voc. 5531); I can't give you anything but love (1940, Voc. 5496); L. Jordan: Saint Vitus Dance (1941, Decca 8581); Brotherly Love (1941, Decca 8560); L. Johnson: Walkin' the boogie/Oo wee baby (1945, Queen 4125)

BIBLIOGRAPHY

McCarthyB

based on *ChiltonW*/HOWARD RYE (recording-list)

Turner, Joe [Joseph H.] **(i)** (*b* Baltimore, 3 Nov 1907; *d* Montreuil, France, 21 July 1990). Pianist. He was first taught piano by his mother when he was five. Around 1925 he moved to New York and enjoyed much popularity among musicians in Harlem, working with June Clark (1927–8), Benny Carter (1929), and Louis Armstrong (1930). He accompanied the singer Adelaide Hall in a piano duo with Alex Hill and then with Francis Carter; he and Carter toured Europe with Hall in 1931. Turner performed as a soloist throughout Europe until 1939, and then in the USA. After working as a member of an army band led by Sy Oliver (1944–5) and with Rex Stewart (1946) he returned to Europe and played in Hungary (1948) and Switzerland (1949–62). He then settled in Paris, where from 1962 he held a residency at La Calvados; he also performed in Britain, Switzerland, and the USA, where he held annual residencies at the Cookery from 1976 to 1978. Turner was influenced mainly by James P. Johnson, Fats Waller, Art Tatum, and Erroll

Garner. A true stride pianist, he performed test pieces of the genre with faultless phrasing, a brilliant technique, and a strong sense of swing.

SELECTED RECORDINGS

As unaccompanied soloist: *Stridin' in Paris* (1952, Vogue 047); *Joe Turner* (1955, Tell 542); *Joe's Back in Town* (1974, BB 33064), incl. Harlem Strut; *Another Epoch: Stride Piano* (1975–6, Pablo 2310763)

Duos: with T. Benford: The Ladder/Loncy (1939, Swing 71); with P. Francis: *Effervescent* (1976, BB 33102)

As leader: with A. Nicholas: *Joe & Nick + Two* (1958, Col. SEGZ2019) [EP]; *Joe Turner Trio* (1971, BB 33031)

As sideman with J. Šima: Joe Turner Stomp/Joe Turner Blues (1936, Ultraphon A11400)

BIBLIOGRAPHY

J. Simmen: "Joe Turner and the Pianists in my Life," *Coda*, vii/4 (1965), 2

M. Jones: "Joe Turner Strides out," *MM* (17 June 1972), 26

B. Rusch: "A Talk with Joe 'Stride' Turner," *Cadence*, ii/2 (1976), 7

R. Zabor: "Nights at the Cookery," *Musician, Player & Listener*, no.14 (1978), 50

J. R. Burden: "Conversation with . . . Joe Turner: 'Last of the Stride Pianists'," *Black Perspective in Music*, ix/2 (1981), 183

H. Rye: "Visiting Firemen, 10(a): Adelaide Hall, Joe Turner, and Francis J. Carter," *Sv*, no.114 (1984), 211

J. Simmen: "Joe Turner," *Sv*, no.123 (1986), 97

——: "A Personal Survey of the Recordings of Joe Turner," *Sv*, no.124 (1986), 140

——: ": Joe Turner," *BHcF* (1991), no.387, p.4; no.388, p.1; no.389, p.4; no.390, p.1

R. Juon-Turner and D. Koran: Liner notes, *Joe Turner 1907–1990: the Giant of Stride Piano in Switzerland* (Jazz Connoisseur 9106-2, n.d. [1993])

JOHNNY SIMMEN/HOWARD RYE

Turner, (Big) Joe [Joseph Vernon] **(ii)** (*b* Kansas City, MO, 18 May 1911; *d* Inglewood, CA, 24 Nov 1985). Singer. He began working as a barman and cook at the age of 14 in various clubs in Kansas City. There he became known as "the singing bartender" and attracted the attention of such bandleaders as Bennie Moten, Andy Kirk, and Count Basie, with whom he subsequently toured. From the mid-1930s he was frequently accompanied by Pete Johnson, with whom he appeared at the "From Spirituals to Swing" concert at Carnegie Hall in 1938 shortly before recording his first titles. *Roll 'em, Pete*, with spectacular piano playing by Johnson, is an example of Turner's forceful, half-shouted vocal style; tension is built up towards the close of the piece by his use of repeated phrases.

In April 1939 Turner began an association with the boogie-woogie piano trio of Johnson, Albert Ammons, and Meade "Lux" Lewis, first at Café Society in New York and then at the Hotel Sherman in Chicago, and at the end of the year he starred in a second "From Spirituals to Swing" concert. He had numerous engagements at both the downtown and the new uptown location of Café Society (to 1942), performed with Duke Ellington in Hollywood in the show *Jump for Joy* (summer 1941), and toured the USA with Lewis. He then sang at the Swanee Inn in Hollywood in duos with Lewis (1943) and Joe Sullivan (1944), and toured with Johnson and Ammons (1944) and Luis Russell (1945) before going into a venture as co-owner with Johnson of the Blue Room, a club in Los Angeles.

Over the next three decades Turner continued to tour extensively. Although he was best known as a "blues shouter" and began to be marketed quite successfully in the emerging rhythm-and-blues field, he was a musical and sensitive singer on slow blues (*see* BLUES, §9). With his relaxed singing style and the hot tone, strength, and subtle inflections of his voice, he soon became recognized as a model for other jazz-blues singers. His recording of *Shake Rattle and Roll* precipitated a revolution in popular music, though it was Bill Haley and his Comets who made a reputation out of the rock-and-roll theme. In spite of his many popular hits, Turner remained at his best in jazz-blues performances, a setting to which he returned intermittently from 1956. He was reunited with Johnson for a European tour with Jazz at the Philharmonic in 1958 and for performances at the Newport and Great South Bay jazz festivals. Later, in spring 1965, he traveled to Europe with Buck Clayton to work with Humphrey Lyttelton's band. From the late 1960s Turner was based in southern California. He remained in demand for concerts, sang in several television shows (including "Oscar Peterson Presents" for the CBS network in 1974), and made further European tours with Milt Buckner (1971) and Basie (1972, 1974). He also performed at the Cookery in New York (1976–7), went to Kansas City to star in the documentary

Joe Turner (ii) (far right) with (from left) Harold Blacksheer, Lionel Hampton, Jack McVea, and Pete Johnson, Los Angeles, c1947

film *The Last of the Blue Devils* (1979), and gave concerts with Basie's orchestra at the Great American Music Hall in San Francisco (April 1980).

Oral history material in *NjR* (JOHP), *NjR*.

SELECTED RECORDINGS

Duo with P. Johnson: Roll 'em, Pete (1938, Voc. 4607)

As leader: Piney Brown Blues (1940, Decca 18121); Old Piney Brown is gone (1948, Swingtime 154); Shake Rattle and Roll (1954, Atl. 1026); *Joe Turner Sings Kansas City Jazz* (1956, Atl. 1234), incl. You're driving me crazy; *Big Joe Rides Again* (1959, Atl. 1332); with C. Basie: *The Bosses* (1973, Pablo 2310709)

As sideman: P. Johnson: Cherry Red/Baby, Look at You (1939, Voc. 4997); A. Tatum: Wee Baby Blues (1941, Decca 8526); Last Goodbye Blues (1941, Decca 8536); Corrine, Corrina (1941, Decca 8563); Lucille (1941, Decca 8577)

SELECTED FILMS AND VIDEOS

Showtime at the Apollo (1955); Rhythm & Blues Revue (1955); Rock 'n' Roll Revue [Harlem Rock 'n' Roll] (1955); Shake, Rattle and Rock! (1956); Monterey Jazz (1970); The Last of the Blue Devils (1979); Fiddler's Dream (1985)

BIBLIOGRAPHY

SchullerS
J. Demêtre: "Joe Turner," *Jh*, no. 114 (1956), 16
P. H. Oliver: "Boss of the Blues," *Jazz Music Mirror*, v/5 (1958), 4
H. J. Mauerer: *The Pete Johnson Story* (New York, and Frankfurt am Main, Germany, 1965) [incl. discography]
V. Wilmer: "Blues for Mr. Turner," *JB*, ii/7 (1965), 4; rev. as "The Boss of the Blues: Joe Turner," *DB*, xxxii/24 (1965), 16; rev. version repr. in *Jazz People* (London, Indianapolis, and New York, 1970/*R*1985), 144
P. Clinco: "Joe Turner," *Living Blues*, no.10 (1972), 20
G. Von Tersch, "Big Joe Turner," *Living Blues*, no.8 (1972), 32
H. Lyttelton: *Take it from the Top: an Autobiographical Scrapbook* (London, 1975), 110
A. Shaw: *Honkers and Shouters: the Golden Years of Rhythm and Blues* (New York, 1978), 45
W. Balliett: *American Singers* (New York, 1979, rev. and enlarged 2/1988 as *American Singers: Twenty-Seven Portraits in Song*), 42
S. Harris: *Blues Who's Who: a Biographical Dictionary of Blues Singers* (New Rochelle, NY, 1979/*R*1994)
D. Pomus: "Joe Turner," *Whiskey, Women, and . . .*, no.11 (1983), 3
T. Burke and D. Penny: "Big Joe Turner," *Blues & Rhythm*, no.11 (1985), 4; no.12 (1985), 4
Obituaries: *New York Times* (24 Nov 1985); *JJI*, xlix/2 (1986), 21; R. Werinstock and D. Pomus, *Living Blues*, no.69 (1986), 11
M. K. Aldin: "'Hey Cousin, How You Doin'?': an Appreciation of Big Joe Turner," *Blues & Rhythm*, no.16 (1986), 25
B. Clayton and N. M. Elliott: *Buck Clayton's Jazz World* (London and New York, 1986), 175
D. Garçon: "Bad Luck Blues," *Soul Bag*, no.105 (1986), 34
N. W. Pearson, Jr.: *Goin' to Kansas City* (Urbana, IL, and London, 1988/*R*1994), 107
E. Komara: "From the Archive," *Living Blues*, no.114 (1994), 76

PAUL OLIVER/BK

Turner, Mark [Nat] (*b* Fairborn, OH, 10 Nov 1965). Tenor saxophonist. He grew up in southern California from the age of four, took up clarinet when he was about nine and alto saxophone in his early teens, and changed to the tenor instrument around the age of 16. Having first studied visual arts at Long Beach College from 1987, he attended the Berklee College of Music toward the year's end (BM performance 1990). In 1991 he toured with the memorial Glenn Miller Orchestra and joined Delfeayo Marsalis's quintet, with which he recorded, toured, and appeared the following year at Kimball's in San Francisco. He then moved to New York, where he worked in a record shop and performed as a street musician, before spending a year in New Orleans studying with Ellis Marsalis. After returning to the Northeast he settled in New Haven, Connecticut, and worked frequently in New York. As well as playing in Kurt Rosenwinkel's small ensembles, Turner joined the group TanaReid around 1994 and toured and recorded with Jimmy Smith the following year, and in April 1998 he led a group at Sweet Basil. As a freelance he recorded with Ryan Kisor (*c*1993), the trumpeter Derrick Shezbie (1993), Carl Allen's Manhattan Projects (1993–4), Jonny King and Seamus Blake (both 1994), Jon Gordon and Edward Simon (both from 1995), James Moody, and the pianist George Colligan (both 1997). Turner's playing, with his adventurous use of harmony, suggests an unusual blend of the styles of John Coltrane and Warne Marsh, recalling that of Marsh in particular in the manner of his phrasing. He tends to avoid the extreme registers of his instrument and instead produces a flat-edged, rather pungent timbre in the middle range. He also plays soprano saxophone.

SELECTED RECORDINGS

As leader: *Mark Turner* (1995, WB 46701); with J. Moody: *Warner Jams*, ii: *The Two Tenors* (1997, WB 46212); *In this World* (1998, WB 47074)

As sideman: D. Marsalis: *Pontius Pilate's Decision* (1991–2, Novus 63134-2); Manhattan Projects: *Echoes of our Heroes* (1993, Evidence 22154); J. King: *In from the Cold* (1994, Criss Cross 1093); J. Smith: on *Damn!* (1995, Verve 314-527631-2), The One Before This, Scrapple from the Apple, This Here; J. Gordon; *Witness* (1995, Criss Cross 1121); G. Colligan: *The Newcomer* (1997, Ste. 31414); E. Simon: *La bikina* (1998, Mythology 10982)

BIBLIOGRAPHY

G. Giddins: "Turner Classic Moves," *VV* (14 April 1998), 118
G. M. Stern: "Airtime: Mark Turner: You Don't Have to be Twenty Years Old to Succeed," *Windplayer*, no.58 (1998), 10
<http://www.allaboutjazz.com/iviews/mturner.htm> (1999)
<http://www.wbjazz.com> (1999)

GK

Turner, Matt(hew Lee) (*b* Platteville, WI, 30 Dec 1966). Cellist. His father played jazz saxophone and directed his high school orchestra, and his mother was a classical violinist and pianist. He learned classical piano and cello and began improvising at an early stage, and from around the age of 13 he had jazz lessons on both instruments. Later he studied cello at Lawrence University in Appleton, Wisconsin (BM 1989), and third-stream music at the New England Conservatory (MM 1991), where he was taught by Joe Maneri. In 1993 he returned to Appleton, and from that year until 1996 he lectured in jazz at Lawrence. From 1989 through the 1990s he performed and recorded on both his instruments in a duo with Jeff Song, who played electric bass guitar and *kayagŭm* (a Korean 12-string zither) and sang. In addition he toured and recorded with an ensemble led by the guitarist Scott Fields and collaborated with Ken Schaphorst (from 1994); around 1996 he worked in a trio with Curtis Hasselbring and Dane Richeson which performed Schaphorst's arrangements of Harold Arlen's music. From 1997 Turner performed an avant-garde blend of rock and funk as the leader of the group Chum, with Song and the drummer John Mettam among his sidemen.

SELECTED RECORDINGS

Duos with J. Song: *In vivo* (*c*1993, Asian Improv 0016)

As sideman: J. Song: *The Other Pocket* (1995, Music & Arts 975); S. Fields: *Disaster at Sea* (1996, Music & Arts 961); K. Schaphorst: on *Over the Rainbow (The Music of Harold Arlen)* (*c*1996, Accurate 4204), I've Got the World on a String

BIBLIOGRAPHY

"Auditions: Matt Turner," *DB*, xxii/10 (1985), 62
B. Rusch: "The Questionnaire," *Cadence*, xxiv/11 (1998), 36
<http://www.cello.org/freepage/mturner.htm> (1999) [incl. discography]

GK

Turney, Norris (William) (*b* Wilmington, OH, 8 Sept 1921; *d* Kettering, OH, 17 Jan 2001). Alto saxophonist. He took piano lessons for about a year from the age of 11 before changing to saxophone. While still in high school he deputized in Fate Marable's band for a week. After working in Ohio with the tenor saxophonist A. B. Townsend he toured with the Jeter–Pillars Orchestra and in 1945 played with Tiny Bradshaw in Chicago. He performed and recorded with Billy Eckstine in New York (1945–6), returned to Ohio, then worked in Philadelphia with Elmer Snowden (1951); in 1967 he toured Australasia with Ray Charles. Turney substituted for Johnny Hodges in Duke Ellington's band in 1969, then served as a regular member of the band until 1973. During the following decade he worked in pit orchestras in New York, and in the 1980s he resumed his career in jazz as a member of Panama Francis's Savoy Sultans (ii) and of George Wein's Newport All Stars, with which he toured internationally. In the late 1980s he joined Clark Terry's Spacemen. In 1990 he settled in Dayton, Ohio, but he continued to be involved in bands on the East Coast, playing in the American Jazz Orchestra, the Lincoln Center Jazz Orchestra, and the Duke's Men, and recording as a sideman with Jodie Christian's small group (1996). A versatile musician, Turney was among the most lyrical of alto saxophonists as well as an adept player of flute and clarinet.

Oral history material in *CtY*; video oral history material in *NCH* (HCJA).

SELECTED RECORDINGS

As leader: N. Turney and S. Young: *The Boys from Dayton* (1971, 1975, MJR 8130); *I Let a Song* (1979, BB 33140); *Big Sweet 'n Blue* (1993, Mapleshade 02632)

As sideman: D. Ellington: *The Seventieth Birthday Concert* (1969, SolS 19000); *Toga brava Suite* (1971, UA 92); R. Eldridge: *What it's All About* (1976, Pablo 2310766); C. Anderson: *Cat Anderson Plays W. C. Handy* (1978, BB 33163); P. Francis: *Gettin' in the Groove* (1979, BB 33320–21); J. Christian: *Front Line* (1996, Del. 490)

BIBLIOGRAPHY

Feather–Gitler '70s

B. Rusch: "Norris Turney: Interview," *Cadence*, v/2 (1979), 18

M. Richards: "Norris Turney," *JJI*, xxxix/6 (1986), 12

R. Orgill: "Young and Old in Jazz Collaboration," *Wall Street Journal* (14 Oct 1992)

C. Melville: "Fame at Last for Norris Turney?," *CJM*, xxxiii/1 (1996), 8

Obituary, B. Ratliff, *New York Times* (22 Jan 2001)

MARTIN RICHARDS

Turnham, Floyd (Payne, Jr.) (*b* Spokane, WA, 23 Jan 1909; *d* Los Angeles, 5 May 1991). Saxophonist. His mother, Edythe Turnham, was a pianist and bandleader, and his father played drums. In 1924 he joined his mother's group, Knights of Syncopation, and in 1928 he moved with the band to Los Angeles when it was invited to tour on the Orpheum Circuit. He formed his own group in 1939, and it was later incorporated into Les Hite's orchestra, with which Turnham toured and recorded from 1940 to 1942. At that point he became a member of Bardu Ali's Lincoln Theater orchestra, and during the war he also worked with the big bands of the guitarist Ceelle Burke and Gerald Wilson. When rhythm-and-blues became popular Turnham concentrated on tenor and baritone saxophones and joined groups led by Joe Liggins and Roy Milton; he recorded on the baritone instrument with Milton in October 1955, and it is reported that he toured with Liggins in May 1950. During the 1950s he took part in many rhythm-and-blues recordings in Los Angeles and was invited to lead the house band for Jake Porter's new label, Combo (1953); playing the baritone instrument he provided a fine accompaniment on *Beer Drinkin' Woman*, by the blues shouter Cledus Harrison (1953, Combo 26), and performed an extended solo on his own recording *Rocket Ride* (1953, Combo 27). He performed with such local rhythm-and-blues artists as T-Bone Walker and the singer and pianist Nellie Lutcher, and in 1951 he worked briefly in Duke Ellington's orchestra (replacing Johnny Hodges). Later he played at burlesque houses and undertook a series of club residencies in Orange County with his own organ trio (1964–75). Thereafter he was semi-retired – he continued to play at weekends – until he joined the Legends of Jazz in 1979; he may be heard to advantage with this group as a clarinetist on *Sheik of Araby* and as a tenor saxophonist on *When you're smiling* and *Red River Blues* (all 1979, from the album *The Legends of Jazz*, 1979–80, Blue Boy 1001). In 1984 Turnham visited Europe, where he impressed listeners with his powerful, full-toned style on tenor saxophone.

BIBLIOGRAPHY

P. De Barros and E. Calderon: *Jackson Street After Hours: the Roots of Jazz in Seattle* (Seattle, 1993)

C. Bryant and others, eds.: *Central Avenue Sounds: Jazz in Los Angeles* (Berkeley, CA, Los Angeles, and London, 1998)

PETER VACHER

Turn the rhythm [beat, time] **around.** Accidentally or deliberately to redefine meter over a long period by the displacement of normal accents or the disturbance of phrase structures; *see* Beat, §4(iii).

Turre, Steve (*b* Omaha, NE, 12 Sept 1948). Trombonist, shell player, and leader. He grew up in Lafayette, California (in the San Francisco Bay area), and took up trombone at the age of ten; in his early teens he played in a band with his elder brother, a saxophonist. Although he entered Sacramento State College on a football scholarship, he read music theory there for two years before transferring to North Texas State University, where he studied in 1968–9 and played in a band led by Hannibal Peterson. Having returned to San Francisco he recorded with the Latin rock group Santana (1970) and played sporadically with Roland Kirk. After touring with Ray Charles (1972) he worked briefly with Woody Shaw, then traveled to New York with Art Blakey's Jazz Messengers and toured Europe with the Thad Jones–Mel Lewis Orchestra (both 1973). Between 1974 and 1976 Turre performed and recorded on trombone and electric bass guitar with Chico Hamilton. During this period he played trombone with Shaw (1974–5), on whose album *Moontrane* his solos are particularly prominent. Following another association with Kirk (from mid-1976 until the saxophonist's death in late 1977) Turre was a member of and wrote arrangements for Slide Hampton's World of Trombones; he also worked as a composer and arranger for Max Roach, led his own quartet, toured with Cedar Walton, and played in various Afro-Cuban groups, notably Conjunto Libre. In spring 1980 he returned to Shaw's band, with which he made a number of recordings and remained until 1986. While with Shaw he performed and recorded with Jerry Gonzalez's Fort Apache Band (early 1980s) and joined Lester Bowie's Brass Fantasy (by 1985, when he first recorded with the group).

At some point Turre completed his undergraduate studies at the University of Massachusetts, Amherst, and in 1986 he gained a master's degree in trombone studies at the Manhattan School of Music. That same year he joined the house band of the television program "Saturday Night Live" (with which he remained through the 1990s), led a quartet and a quintet for a short period, and formed the group

Explorations, which comprised six shell and brass players, congas, timbales, and double bass. In 1988 he toured and recorded (December) with Bob Stewart's group the First Line Band, toured Europe with Brass Fantasy, and joined and recorded with McCoy Tyner's big band; in addition he performed in Dizzy Gillespie's Latin Jazz All Stars (with which he may be seen in "Wolf Trap Salutes Dizzy Gillespie: an All-Star Tribute to the Jazz Master" (1988), from the PBS television series "Great Performances"). He subsequently became a founding member of Gillespie's United Nation Orchestra, and he appears in the video *Dizzy Gillespie and the United Nation Orchestra: Live at the Royal Festival Hall, London* (*c*1990 [filmed 1989]).

By 1992 Turre was leading a sextet that included a cello (played by his wife, Akua Dixon Turre) and a violin (played by John Blake and Regina Carter, among others); its rhythm section consisted of Danilo Pérez, Cecil McBee, and Marvin "Smitty" Smith in 1992, and Mulgrew Miller, Buster Williams, and Lewis Nash in 1997. Also in the 1990s Turre co-led a quintet with Harold Land (1993), played with the Leaders (*c*1993–4), joined McCoy Tyner's Afro-Cuban All Stars (1995), and toured as the leader of a quartet with Stephen Scott, Williams, and Louis Hayes as his sidemen (1997); he was a member of the Carnegie Hall Jazz Band and recorded with Larry Gales (1990), Don Braden (1991), Christian McBride (1994), and the Mingus Big Band (1997), among others. He has taught at William Paterson College in Wayne, New Jersey, and at the Manhattan School of Music.

Turre is principally a trombonist and plays in a brash, extroverted, and emotive manner that draws from both jazz and popular styles; he doubles on didjeridu and, more significantly, sea shells (specifically conches and tridents), and he is probably best known for the skill with which he plays these objects. He began experimenting with shells shortly after meeting Kirk, and from the time of his affiliations with Blakey and Hamilton he has used them increasingly in performance, blowing into informal sets of four or five shells of different size, thus yielding different ranges of pitch which he modifies by cupping his hand within the shell (akin to the technique used by french horn players); he was also inspired by Kirk to adopt circular breathing and to play two shells at once.

SELECTED RECORDINGS

As leader: *Viewpoint* (1987, Stash 270); *Fire and Ice* (1988, Stash 275); with R. Eubanks: *Dedication* (1989, JMT 834433-1); *Right There* (1991, Ant. 314-510040-2); *Sanctified Shells* (1992, Ant. 314-514186-2); *Rhythm Within* (*c*1994, Ant. 314-527159-2)

As sideman: W. Shaw: *Moontrane* (1974, Muse 5058); on *For Sure!* (1979, Col. FC36383), Opec; *United* (1981, Col. FC37390), incl. Blues for Wood; *Master of the Art* (1982, Elek. Mus. 60131); M. Tyner: *Uptown/Downtown* (1988, Mlst. 9167), incl. Lotus Flower; D. Gillespie: *Dizzy Gillespie and the United Nation Orchestra: Live at the Royal Festival Hall* (1989, Enja 6044-2), incl. Dizzy Shells, Tin tin deo

BIBLIOGRAPHY

Feather–Gitler '70s
T. Nuccio: "Steve Turre," *DB*, xlix/9 (1982), 53
D. Pagani: "Steve Turre: Interview," *Cadence*, xi/4 (1985), 5
M. Bourne: "Steve Turre: Trombone Straight from the Hip," *DB*, liv/12 (1987), 24 [incl. discography]
H. Frühauf: "Steve Turre," *JP*, xxxvi/3 (1987), 10
"Steve Turre," *JT* (1988), June, 15
M. M. Margetts: "Steve Turre," *Windplayer*, vi/4 (1989), 10
T. Pérémarti: "Steve Turre: coquilles Saint-Jazz," *Jh*, no.461 (1989), 30
C. Deffaa: "The State of the Trombone: Talking with Slide Hampton & Steve Turre," *JT*, xxi/9 (1991), 32
J. Kaliss: "Live from NY: Steve Turre," *San Francisco Chronicle Datebook* (27 Oct 1991)
B. Blumenthal: "Steve Turre Sounds the Trumpet: Ah, Make that Trombone and Conch," *Boston Globe* (29 Jan 1993)
P. Cole: "Sanctified Sound: Steve Turre," *DB*, lx/3 (1993), 21 [incl. discography]
P. Benkimoun: "Steve Turre," *Jm*, no.463 (1996), 7
J. Eig: "Tradin' Fours: Exotic Resonance," *DB*, lxiv/12 (1997), 64
R. Grosman: "Steve Turre: l'homme à la conque," *Jh*, no.538 (1997), 21
W. Jenkins: "Steve Turre," *JT*, xxvii/8 (1997), 46
J. D'Souza: "Steve Turre," *Coda*, no.277 (1998), 12
<http://www.cybercomm.net/~dmackey/snlband/steveturre.html> (1999) [discography]

BK

Turrentine, Stanley (William) (*b* Pittsburgh, 5 April 1934; *d* New York, 12 Sept 2000). Tenor saxophonist, brother of Tommy Turrentine. As a child he played piano by ear. When he was about ten years old his father, a tenor saxophonist who had played with the Savoy Sultans (i), provided introductory lessons, demanding that Turrentine produce a handsome sound on each note of the instrument from bottom to top; he was otherwise self-taught. After touring in rhythm-and-blues groups, including Lowell Fulson's band (featuring Ray Charles), and working with Tadd Dameron, he replaced John Coltrane in Earl Bostic's group (1953), playing alongside his brother. He served in the army for three years and then rejoined his brother in Max Roach's group (1959–60).

Turrentine achieved his reputation in the 1960s, when he made a number of recordings for Blue Note, both as a leader and as a sideman, notably with Jimmy Smith and Shirley Scott (who was at that time Turrentine's wife); he also recorded with Dizzy Reece, Duke Jordan, Art Taylor (1960), Horace Parlan (1960–61), Ike Quebec (1962), Kenny Burrell (1963–4), Duke Pearson (1967), and Horace Silver (1968), all for Blue Note. Influenced by Don Byas, Coleman Hawkins, and Sonny Rollins, he played in an earthy blues style characterized by brief moans and wails; an individualized whooping sound on the note *e*♭″ was his particular musical signature. Turrentine continued working in small groups with Scott until 1971, but from 1965 he also began to record with larger ensembles, producing work that appealed to a large popular market; *Sugar*, for which he composed the title track, was the first of a number of albums that appeared on the charts throughout the 1970s, when he maintained a popularity unusual by jazz standards. He met little success producing his own pop albums in the early 1980s, and in 1984, when the Blue Note label was revived, returned to soul jazz. He toured through the 1990s in reunions with Smith and Burrell, as a freelance, and as the leader of a small group whose longstanding members were Kei Akagi, Dave Stryker, and Mark Johnson; Charles Fambrough and Dwayne Dolphin are among others who also worked in the band, which may be seen in a performance at the Village Gate broadcast on the television special "Stanley Turrentine: Jazz USA" (1990). Turrentine made recordings reviving the style of his early 1970s orchestral successes with the CTI label, including one for MusicMasters in 1993. A volume of transcriptions was published by H. Butler: *The Stanley Turrentine Collection* (Milwaukee, n.d. [1990s]).

SELECTED RECORDINGS

As leader: *Stan "the Man" Turrentine* (*c*1959–60, Time 52086); with Three Sounds: *Blue Hour* (1960, BN 84057); *Up at Mintons*, i–ii (1961, BN 84069–70); *Z. T.'s Blues* (1961, BN 84424); *Jubilee Shout* (1962, BN 84122); *Never Let Me Go* (1963, BN 84129); *A Chip off the Old Block* (1963, BN 84150); *Let it Go* (1966, Imp. 9155); *Common Touch* (1968, BN 84135); *Sugar* (1970, CTI 6005); *Pieces of Dreams* (1974, Fan. 9465); *Betcha* (1979, Elek. 217); *Tender Togetherness* (1981, Elek. 534); *Straight Ahead* (1984, BN 85105); *Wonderland* (1986, BN 85140); *More than a*

Mood (1992, MusicMasters 01612-65079-2); *If I Could* (1993, MusicMasters 01612-65103-2)
As sideman: M. Roach: *Quiet as it's Kept* (1960, Mer. 20491); J. Smith: *Midnight Special* (1960, BN 84078); *Back at the Chicken Shack* (1960, BN 84117); K. Burrell: *Midnight Blue* (1963, BN 84123); S. Scott: *Everybody Loves a Lover* (1964, Imp. 73)

BIBLIOGRAPHY

M. James: "Introducing Stanley Turrentine," *JM*, vii/5 (1961), 7
H. Nolan: "Dues on Top of Dues: Stanley Turrentine," *DB*, xlii/18 (1975), 12
B. Primack: "Stanley Turrentine: We're in the Marketplace Now!," *DB*, xlv/17 (1978), 13
L. Tomkins: "Tenor Integrity for the People: Stanley Turrentine," *CI*, xix (1981), no.9, p.6; no.10, p.12
G. Kalbacher: "The Blue Notes of Mr. T.," *DB*, lii/5 (1985), 16 [incl. discography]
E. Holley, Jr.: "Stanley Turrentine: the Timeless Tenor," *JT*, xxii/8 (1992), 61
J. Jones IV: "Stanley Turrentine: Mr. T's Mood Swings," *DB*, lix/10 (1992), 27 [incl. discography]
Obituaries: B. Ratliff, *New York Times* (14 Sept 2000); [A. Shipton], *The Times* (14 Sept 2000)

BK

Turrentine, Tommy [Thomas Walter, Jr.] (*b* Pittsburgh, 22 April 1928; *d* New York, 13 May 1997). Trumpeter, brother of Stanley Turrentine. His father played tenor saxophone with Al Cooper's Savoy Sultans, and Tommy began learning trumpet in his early teens. He played with Benny Carter (1946), Earl Bostic (1952–5), Charles Mingus (1956), and Max Roach (1959–60) and performed in the big bands of Billy Eckstine, Dizzy Gillespie, and Count Basie (October 1950). In the early 1960s he worked as a freelance in New York, and his best recordings, made with such leaders as his brother, Horace Parlan, Jackie McLean, Sonny Clark, and Lou Donaldson, date from this period. He also recorded with Paul Chambers and Booker Ervin (both 1960), Ahmed Abdul-Malik (1961), Dexter Gordon (1962), Big John Patton (1963), and Archie Shepp (1966). He was briefly a member of Mingus's group again early in 1964, but thereafter was largely inactive, though he took part in a recording session with Philly Joe Jones in 1977 and with Sun Ra's orchestra in December 1988. Turrentine's lyrical, full-toned playing was stylistically related to that of Gillespie and Fats Navarro, and his crisp, long-breathed solos invariably displayed a fine sense of balance and structure. He unfortunately recorded only one album as a leader.
Video oral history material in *NN-Sc* (LAJOHP).

SELECTED RECORDINGS

(recorded for Blue Note unless otherwise indicated)

As leader: *T. Turrentine* (1960, Time 70008)
As sideman: H. Parlan: *Speakin' my Piece* (1960, 4043); *On the Spur of the Moment* (1961, 4074); J. McLean: *A Fickle Sonance* (1961, 84089); S. Clark: *Leapin' and Lopin'* (1961, 84091); S. Turrentine: *Jubilee Shouts* (1961–2, LA883J2); L. Donaldson: *The Natural Soul* (1962, 84108)

BIBLIOGRAPHY

FeatherE
N. Hentoff: Liner notes, *T. Turrentine* (Time 70008, 1960)
——: Liner notes, H. Parlan: *Speakin' my Piece* (BN 4043, 1961)
Obituary, M. Gardner, *JJI*, l/7 (1997), 17

MARK GARDNER/BK

Tusa, Frank (*b* New York, 1 April 1947). Double bass player. He grew up in a musical family and played guitar for about two years before taking up double bass at the age of ten. After working in the orchestra for a Broadway show he served as a musician in the army. He then performed and recorded with Paul Bley (1970–71), worked with Horacee Arnold (1971) and in the trio Open Sky with Dave Liebman and Bob Moses (1972–4), played with Dave Holland and Collin Walcott, and taught at workshops. From 1973 to 1976 Tusa performed, recorded, and toured Europe alongside Richard Beirach, Jeff Williams, and Badal Roy as a member of Liebman's group Lookout Farm; around the same period he worked as a freelance with Barry Miles, Booker Ervin, Don Cherry, Freddie Hubbard, Lee Konitz, and Harold Mabern. In addition he recorded on electric bass guitar with Dom Um Romão (1973) and made albums with Beirach (*Eon*, 1974, ECM 1054) and as a leader (*Father Time*, 1975, Enja 2056). Later he joined Beirach (1976) in the trio Eon (which took its name from the aforementioned album of 1974) and played a fusion of Indian ragas and jazz-rock with Roy and worked as a freelance with Art Blakey (both 1977). From 1983 to around 1989 he worked in the San Francisco Bay area with the group Bebop and Beyond, with which he recorded in 1984.

BIBLIOGRAPHY

C. Berg: "Frank Tusa: Triple Threat Bassman," *DB*, xliv/15 (1977), 20
D. Liebman and others: *Lookout Farm: a Case Study of Improvisation for Small Jazz Group* (n.p., 1978)

Tusques, François (*b* Paris, 27 Jan 1938). French pianist, leader, and composer. He was initially self-taught on piano but later studied at a conservatory. Having led his own trio, in 1965, with Bernard Vitet, he co-founded the first free-jazz group in France. He then played with Barney Wilen (recording in 1968), Sunny Murray (recording in 1968–9), Clifford Thornton (recording in 1970), Beb Guérin, Michel Portal, and François Jeanneau, among others. In 1969 he formed the Intercommunal Free Dance Orchestra, which included the Guinean saxophonist Jo Maka, the Algerian percussionist Guem, the trombonist Ramadolf Adolf Winkler, and the trumpeter Michel Marre; in the late 1970s the ensemble performed folk music together with the Spanish singer Carlos Andreù and a group of Breton musicians. In the early 1970s Tusques also began to work as an unaccompanied soloist. From around 1980 he composed for the theater, television, and film (*Les yeux des oiseaux*, 1984) and collaborated with the poet Violetta Ferrer, and in the early 1990s he began to perform music set to the poetry of Jean de la Croix and Guillaume de Machaut, among others; during this period he abandoned many of the free-jazz elements of his style in favor of a lusher, more romantic approach.

SELECTED RECORDINGS

As unaccompanied soloist: *Piano dazibao*, i–ii (1970, Futura 14, 32); *Génération* (*c*1988, Paysages 001), incl. Variations sur l'appel du Komintern
As leader: *Free Jazz* (1966, Mouloudji 13507); *Intercommunal Music* (1971, Shandar 10010); *Le jardin des délices* (1991–2, In Situ 139)
As sideman: S. Murray: *Big Chief* (1968, Shandar 10008); B. Vitet: *La guêpe* (1971, Futura 05)

BIBLIOGRAPHY

GrayF
M. Le Bris: "François Tusques," *Jh*, no.247 (1969), 32
P. Carles: "Tusques: d'où viennent lessons justes?," *Jm*, no.202 (1972), 22
S. Loupien: "François Tusques: pour une nouvelle musique bretonne," *Jm*, no.280 (1979), 30
E. Jost: *Europas Jazz, 1960–1980* (Frankfurt am Main, Germany, 1987), 378
P. Carles, A. Clergeat, and J.-L. Comolli: *Dictionnaire du jazz* (Paris, 1988, rev. and enlarged 2/1994)
Fara C.: "François Tusques: sarcasmes et jubilation," *Jm*, no.424 (1993), 44
R. Latxague: "Entrevues: Francois Tusques," *Jm*, no.469 (1997), 8

GK

Tutu. Record company and label founded in Starnberg, Germany, in 1988 by Horst Weber (one of the founders of

Enja) and Peter Weismuller. Its first release was a recording by Mal Waldron dating from 1987, and by 2000 it had issued approximately 50 new albums. Marty Cook, the saxophonist Gunther Klatt, Jim Pepper, Ed Schuller, the saxophonist Nicolas Simion, Waldron, and Monty Waters figure prominently in its catalogue. (<http://www.jazzrecords.com/tutu/about.htm> (2000))

GK

Tuxedo Big Band. French big band of sixteen instrumentalists and a singer, founded in 1983 by Paul Chéron. The Tuxedo Big Band may be considered as a French territory band, insofar as its region of activity since 1990 has been restricted to the south of France, although it has appeared in Paris at summer festivals. A repertory band, it aims to revive the music of the big bands of the 1930s, notably those of Jimmie Lunceford and Chick Webb. While preserving the spirit and appearance of its models, it benefits from the interactions of such excellent soloists as Michel Pastre and the singer Mariannick Saint-Céran, as well as an astonishingly supple rhythm section.

SELECTED RECORDINGS

Rhythm is our Business (1994, TBB 101); *Siesta at the Fiesta* (1996, TBB 102); *To Ella and Chick* (1998, TBB 103); with B. Wilber: *Fletcher Henderson Unrecorded Arrangements for Benny Goodman* (1999, Arbors 19229)

BIBLIOGRAPHY

"Les Bananes épluchées," *Jazz Dixie/Swing: du Ragtime au Big Band*, no.6 (1995), 6
A. Doutard: "L'imprévue résurrection de l'orchestre Jimmie Lunceford," *BHcF*, no.451 (1996), 9
S. Dance: "Laying on Mellow," *BHcF*, no.455 (1997), 3
A. Clergeat: Liner notes, *To Ella and Chick* (TBB 1073, 1998)

ANDRÉ CLERGEAT

Tuxedo Brass Band. *See* ORIGINAL TUXEDO ORCHESTRA.

Tuxen, Erik (*b* Mannheim, Germany, 4 July 1902; *d* Copenhagen, 28 Aug 1957). Danish bandleader. He was trained as a classical musician and conducted theater orchestras for several years. From 1932 to 1936 he led an important big band, which included Kai Ewans, Leo Mathisen, and Peter Rasmussen among its members and made several outstanding recordings, among them two for Polyphon in 1933, *New York* (XS50204) and *Københavnerrhapsodie* (XS50201). From 1936 until his death Tuxen was the conductor of the Danish Radio Orchestra. (E. Wiedemann: *Jazz i Danmark i tyverne, trediverne og fyrrerne: en musikkulturel undersøgelse* [Jazz in Denmark in the twenties, thirties, and forties: a study of musical culture] (Copenhagen, 1982) [incl. discography])

ERIK WIEDEMANN

Twardzik, Dick [Richard] (*b* Danvers, MA, 30 April 1931; *d* Paris, 21 Oct 1955). Pianist. From late 1950 into 1951 he played bop in Boston with Serge Chaloff, and in the latter year he participated in a broadcast with Charlie Parker. He then worked with Charlie Mariano (1951–2) and toured with Lionel Hampton. In 1954 he recorded with Chaloff and supplied a moody, difficult, but strangely attractive three-part composition as the title track of the saxophonist's album *The Fabel of Mabel* (Sto. 317); Twardzik takes brief, quirky piano solos on several tracks. After recording as a leader that year he joined Chet Baker for a European tour in 1955. His playing may be heard to advantage on Baker's acclaimed album *Rondette* (1955, Barclay 84009), which was recorded shortly before Twardzik died of a drug overdose.

BIBLIOGRAPHY

FeatherE
A. Morgan: "Dick Twardzik," *JM*, ix/9 (1963), 27 [discography]
R. Williams: "Chet Baker," *MM* (7 Aug 1976), 13
T. Gioia: *West Coast Jazz: Modern Jazz in California, 1945–1960* (New York and Oxford, England, 1992), 184
V. Simosko: Liner notes, *The Complete Serge Chaloff Sessions* (Mosaic 147, 1993)

BK

Twelve Clouds of Joy. Name sometimes used by the Kansas City jazz band led from 1929 to 1948 by ANDY KIRK.

29th Street Saxophone Quartet. Group formed in 1982 by the saxophonists Ed Jackson, Rich Rothenberg, and Jim Hartog; Marty Ehrlich, Kenny Garrett, and Steve Wilson joined briefly before Bobby Watson became a permanent member later that year. It toured Europe in late 1982 and internationally thereafter, and achieved considerable success, although it was never well known in the USA. Along with the World Saxophone Quartet and ROVA, the group was the leading American quartet of its kind, and of the three it provided the most irresistible dance rhythms; its members combined crisp swinging ostinatos, based on bop, blues, and funk, with diverse approaches to improvisation. Unlike the World Saxophone Quartet, which made a number of disappointing recordings, particularly in its first ten years, the 29th Street Saxophone Quartet was consistently able to transfer the energy of its concert performances to its albums, at times adding lighthearted scat singing, rap, and poetry. It disbanded in 1996.

SELECTED RECORDINGS

Pointillistic Groove (1983, Osmosis 6002); *Watch your Step* (1985, New Note 1002); *The Real Deal* (1987, New Note 1006); *Live* (1988, Red 123233-1); *Underground* (1990, Ant. 848415-2); *Your Move* (*c*1992, Ant. 314-512524-2); *Milano New York Bridge* (1992–3, Red 123262-2)

BIBLIOGRAPHY

G. Giddins: "Weatherbird: Saxophone Colossi," *VV* (20 Nov 1984)
L. Jänichen: "29th Street Saxophone Quartet," *JP*, xxxiv/3 (1985), 24
P. Bloom: "29th Street Saxophone Quartet: Sax Rap," *DB*, liv/2 (1987), 26
D. H. Matthews: "The 29th Street Saxophone Quartet," *CI*, xxvi/5 (1989), 18
J. Fordham: "Arts: You Can't Beat the Lessons of the Street," *The Guardian* (21 Aug 1990)
R. Urmann: "29th Street Saxophone Quartet," *JP*, xxxix/1 (1990), 38
J. Woodard: "Four-sided Swing," *DB*, lviii/7 (1991), 18

GK, BK

Two-beat. A term applied to music in which the first and third beats of a bar in 4/4 meter are accented. It is pertinent to the marches and rags on which early jazz drew, and therefore to some pieces from the jazz repertory; slow ballads may also be performed with two-beat accentuation. *See* BEAT, §4(ii).

Twofer. In popular parlance a double ALBUM (albums containing three discs are also usually categorized for convenience as twofers). The term derives from the phrase "two for the price of one"; originally some record companies did indeed market two discs at the price of one, though often the playing time of the two together might scarcely exceed that of a single disc. Latterly the double album came to cost nearly as much as two separate LPs. The term has not been applied to compact discs.

Twos. Two-bar phrases, as in the expression "to trade twos"; *see* Forms, §1(ii).

Two-step. *See* Dance.

Tyler, Alvin "Red" (*b* New Orleans, 5 Dec 1925; *d* New Orleans, 3 April 1998). Tenor and baritone saxophonist. Having been drafted at the end of World War II, he played saxophone in a navy band, and following his discharge in 1946 he enrolled at the Grunewald School of Music in New Orleans. He joined Dave Bartholomew's band and in December 1949 took part in the first recording sessions by the singer and pianist Fats Domino. Tyler remained prominent throughout the 1950s among the city's rhythm-and-blues personnel and busy as a studio musician, accompanying a great variety of blues, rhythm-and-blues, and popular artists, including Little Richard, as well as Joe Turner (ii), Charles Brown, and Amos Milburn on their visits to New Orleans. In the studio he normally played baritone saxophone, whereas for club work he preferred the tenor instrument. In the late 1950s he served as artists and repertory man and house musician for Johnny Vincent's Ace label, and in 1961 he was a founder of the organization and record label A.F.O. After this enterprise failed, in 1966 Tyler formed his own Parlo Records, but this too soon collapsed and that same year he took a job as a sales representative. Thereafter he was involved in studio work only occasionally, though he continued to play in clubs and led the house band at Mason's, South Claiborne, for many years in the 1960s and 1970s; Edward Frank and Chuck Badie were among his sidemen. His studio work in the 1960s had been largely chart-oriented, and his recordings for Rounder accompanying Clarence "Gatemouth" Brown (1981) and James Booker (1982) on tenor saxophone brought him back to prominence; he made two albums as a leader, *Heritage* (1985, Rounder 2047) and *Graciously* (1986, Rounder 2061), mainly featuring his own compositions in a swing and hard-bop style. Tyler retired from his day job in 1990 and joined the touring band of the rock performer Dr. John, with which he visited Europe; he also worked with Lillian Boutté. In 1995 he was leading a band at Snug Harbor, New Orleans, and in 1997 he performed at a cross-generational summit with Nicholas Payton.

BIBLIOGRAPHY

J. Broven: *Walking to New Orleans: the Story of New Orleans Rhythm and Blues* (Bexhill-on-Sea, England, 1974, Gretna, LA, 1983, as *Rhythm & Blues in New Orleans*)

J. Hannusch: *I Hear you Knockin': the Sound of New Orleans Rhythm and Blues* (Ville Platte, LA, 1985), 239

J. Berry, J. Foose, and T. Jones: *Up from the Cradle of Jazz: New Orleans Music since World War II* (Athens, GA, and London, 1986)

L. Benicewicz: "Alvin Tyler: a Man and his Horn," *Blues Gazette*, no.3 (1996), 32

Obituaries: *New Orleans Music*, vii/4 (1998), 24 [repr. of obituary in *New Orleans Times-Picayune*]; E. LeBlanc, *Blues & Rhythm*, no.130 (1998), 19; J. Hannusch, *Blues Access*, no.34 (1998), 61; J. Hannusch, *Living Blues*, no.141 (1998), 50; M. Redenac, *Soul Bag*, no.151 (1998), 40

HOWARD RYE

Tyler, Charles (Lacy) (*b* Cadiz, KY, 20 July 1941; *d* Toulon, France, 27 June 1992). Baritone and alto saxophonist and teacher. He studied piano, clarinet, and alto saxophone as a youth, and after entering military service in 1958 played baritone saxophone in an army band. He moved in 1960 to Cleveland, where he performed with Albert Ayler, then to New York, where he became involved in free jazz and performed and recorded with Ayler; he was the most constant member of the tenor saxophonist's groups from 1963 to 1966. In 1967–8 he studied with David Baker at Indiana University. He spent the latter half of 1969 touring in a rock group, while based in Denver, and then moved to California and worked in the Los Angeles area. Having moved north to secure a teaching certificate at the University of California, Berkeley, he taught music in Oakland at North Peralta Community College and Mills College (1971–3). He returned to New York in 1974, toured Sweden in 1975, and then settled in New York to lead his own groups, including a quartet with Ronnie Boykins on double bass and Steve Reid on drums, a trio without bass, and a big band, the New Music Orchestra, with Arthur Blythe, David Murry, Julius Hemphill, Dewey Redman, Ahmed Abdullah, Boykins, John Ore, Abdul Wadud, Reid, and others.

In the mid-1970s Tyler performed with John Fischer's group Interface and in 1978 he operated a free-jazz club, the Brook, in an 8th floor loft at 40 West 17th Street. Later he played with Frank Lowe and Cecil Taylor. He recorded as a member of Billy Bang's quintet (1981–2) and as a guest soloist with Hal Russell's NRG Ensemble (1982). In summer 1984 he toured Europe and played in Chicago as a member of Sun Ra's Arkestra, then immediately returned to Europe to perform with Khan Jamal – mainly in Denmark, but also in Germany and elsewhere in Scandinavia – from autumn 1984 into 1985, when he settled in France. While based in Europe he recorded with Steve Lacy's trio (1986) and worked with Johnny Dyani, Wilbur Little, Willem Breuker, Didier Levallet and Dennis Charles, Bobby Few, Oliver Johnson, Alan Silva's Celestrial Communication Orchestra, and many others. Illness prevented him from playing the demanding baritone instrument after 1989, and his final sessions as a leader were recorded on the tenor and alto saxophones, which require somewhat less exertion to blow. Tyler may be seen in a documentary of the New York avant-garde scene, *Rising Tones Cross* (1984).

SELECTED RECORDINGS

As leader: *Charles Tyler Ensemble* (1966, ESP 1029); *Eastern Man Alone* (1967, ESP 1058); *Live in Europe* (1975, Akba 1010); *Saga of the Outlaws* (1976, Nessa 16); *Sixty Minute Man* (1979, Adelphi 5011); *Folk and Mystery Stories* (1980, Sonet 849); *Definite* (1981, Sto. 4098–9); *Folly Fun Music Magic* (1990, 1992, Blue Regard 1941); *Mid Western Drifter* (1991, Bleu Regard 1942)

As sideman: A. Ayler: *Spirits Rejoice* (1965, ESP 1020); B. Bang: *Rainbow Gladiator* (1981, SN 1016); K. Jamal: *Dark Warrior* (1984, Ste. 1196)

BIBLIOGRAPHY

GrayF

C. Flicker: "Charles Tyler," *Jm*, no.255 (1977), 18

M. Cuscuna: Liner notes, *Saga of the Outlaws* (Nessa 16, 1978)

T. Johnson: "New Outlets for New Music," *VV* (10 Feb 1978)

C. J. Safane: "Charles Tyler: the Saga of a Saxophonist," *Music Journal*, xxxvii/6 (1979), 18

E. Jost: *Jazzmusiker: Materialen zur Soziologie der afro-amerikanischen Musik* (Frankfurt am Main, Germany, Berlin, and Vienna, 1981), 123

J. Litweiler: "Charles Tyler," *DB*, li/5 (1984), 56

C. Gauffre and J. Sorano: "Gros plan: Charles Tyler," *Jm*, no.344 (1985), 26

N. Weinstein: "Charles Tyler's Saga of the Outlaws: Jazz at the Threshold of a Shootout," *Noh Quarter*, ii/3 (1987), 40

Obituary, V. Wilmer, *The Guardian* (1 Oct 1992)

C. Gauffre: "Charles Tyler: la saga d'un outlaw," *Jm*, no.453 (1995), 42

J. Schwartz: *Albert Ayler: his Life and Music* (<http://ernie.bgsu.edu/~jeffs/ayler.html>, 1997) [incl. bibliography]

DAVID G. SUCH/BK

Tyndale, George (Sybornia) [Sky] (*b* Manchester, Jamaica, 15 June 1913; *d* Dorking, England, 4 Dec 1991). Jamaican tenor saxophonist and clarinetist. He started on clarinet and worked in Bermuda and on Canadian cruise ships before taking up saxophone. As a key soloist in the society band of the pianist Milton McPherson he became the leading tenor saxophonist of his generation in Jamaica. In 1945 he moved to England to join Jiver Hutchinson, with whom he remained for five years and made tours of India and Europe. He then worked in Cambridge with the trumpeter Ken Turner. With Cab Kaye he toured Belgium and Holland (1950–51), after which he rejoined Hutchinson to tour Sweden and worked with Joe Harriott. A generous, expansive soloist in the style of Ben Webster, Tyndale developed a reputation for reliability as a section player and worked with Ted Heath, Harry Gold, and the Squadronaires. He recorded with Caribbean singers and appeared extensively in nightclubs, in particular with Joe Appleton's band and for a period as a leader at the Sunset, a rendezvous popular with London's black population. Tyndale attained national prominence when he changed to baritone saxophone on joining John Dankworth's orchestra in 1960; he then spent several years with semi-professional groups.

SELECTED RECORDINGS

As sideman: J. Hutchinson: Cherokee/She's Funny that Way (1947, Sup. C18166); Annie Laurie/I Can't Get Started (1947, Sup. C18167); Exactly like You/Rosetta (1947, Sup. C18168); C. Kaye: Saturday Night Fish Fry/School-bop (1951, Astraschall 4005); Mood Indigo/Solitude (1951, Astraschall 4001); P. Pitterson: Mango Time (1951, Esquire 5-053) [cl]; Ivan Browne: Little Fly (1954, London CAY108); Rupert Nurse: Lord Kitchener "Birth of Ghana" (1956, Melodisc 1390); on [no leader:] *African Waltz* (1960, Col. SEG8137), J. Dankworth: African Waltz, Moanin'; J. Dankworth: *The Criminal* (1960, Col. SEG8037)

BIBLIOGRAPHY

Obituary, V. Wilmer, *The Independent* (23 Jan 1992)
J. Dankworth: *Jazz in Revolution* (London, 1998)

VAL WILMER

McCoy Tyner at the Royal Festival Hall, London, 1997

Tyner, (Alfred) McCoy [Saud, Sulaimon] (*b* Philadelphia, 11 Dec 1938). Pianist, composer, and leader. He began to study piano formally at the age of 13 and later took theory lessons at the Granoff School of Music. He had his own jazz group while in high school and played locally with Lee Morgan. His early influences included Richie and Bud Powell (who at that time, as neighbors without a piano, would come to Tyner's house to practice), as well as Art Tatum and Thelonious Monk. In Philadelphia he worked with Cal Massey, Jimmy Garrison, and Albert "Tootie" Heath; in 1957 this group had a week-long engagement with John Coltrane, with whom Tyner regularly rehearsed. He also worked locally with Benny Golson, who took Tyner to San Francisco for a three-week stand at the Jazz Workshop with Curtis Fuller, Leroy Vinnegar, and Lennie McBrowne. This in turn led to his first important engagment, in 1959, when he joined the Benny Golson-Art Farmer Jazztet.

Tyner achieved international acclaim as the pianist in Coltrane's quartet from July 1960 to December 1965; he recorded prolifically and in the process made pathbreaking contributions to the development of jazz style. During the same period he also made a comparatively conservative and somewhat unambitious series of albums under his own name for the Impulse label, his performances focusing on conventional renditions of jazz standards (1962–4). He toured Japan (1966) and the US (1967) with Art Blakey's Jazz Messengers. While associated with the Blue Note label (1967–70) Tyner drew more heavily upon his own compositions and the style associated with Coltrane – an approach which would later bring him great success – but these were difficult years: his trumpeter Woody Shaw recalled that, for lack of work, they jokingly called Tyner's group "the Starvation Band." In this decade his various ad hoc all-star recording groups incorporated, for the Impulse label, Garrison and Elvin Jones (who had been his fellow sidemen with Coltrane), as well as Art Davis, Henry Grimes, Roy Haynes, Heath, Thad Jones, and John Gilmore; for the Blue Note label, band members included Shaw, Gary Bartz, Bobby Hutcherson, Herbie Lewis, Freddie Waits, Joe Henderson, Ron Carter, Lee Morgan, and Wayne Shorter.

Tyner began to record with Milestone in 1972, and despite a somewhat less famous cast of sidemen (featuring Sonny Fortune and then Azar Lawrence on saxophone) his later albums gained him a large popular following. He toured and recorded with the Milestone Jazzstars in 1978, and in the early 1980s led small groups which included Bartz, John Blake, and Avery Sharpe (replaced by John Lee in 1982). From 1984 Tyner worked in a trio with Sharpe and Louis Hayes; later in the decade he also toured in all-star groups with Freddie Hubbard and Frank Morgan. On 31 December 1987 his trio appeared with Stephane Grappelli on the PBS new year's special "Jazz at Ethel's Place." From 1989 through the 1990s he continued to lead small groups, with Sharpe and Aaron Scott filling out his rhythm section, either on their own as a trio or supporting such soloists as Howard Johnson (ii) (who had also appeared with Tyner in the 1980s),

Hutcherson (1992), Eddie Henderson, Billy Harper, and Fortune (together in 1994), Michael Brecker (1996), and Henderson, Harper, and Bartz (together in 1997). Concurrently, from 1995 Tyner led his Afro-Cuban All Stars, featuring the trombonist Steve Turre, the tenor saxophonist David Sanchez, and the trumpeter Claudio Roditi with Sharpe and several Cuban and Puerto Rican percussionists, among them Mongo Santamaria. In 1998 he led a quartet that included Joshua Redman, Christian McBride, and Brian Blade.

Tyner also performed as an unaccompanied soloist, in duos with George Adams, John Scofield (both 1989), Grappelli (1990–91), and Hutcherson (1993), and as the leader of an outstanding big band. In this orchestral setting he brought a freshness to the often stultifying conventions of big-band arranging by overlaying the expected combination of riffs and solos onto the type of open-ended chordal ostinato which he developed as a member of Coltrane's combo. Formed in Philadelphia in 1984, the big band was soon performing in New York nightclubs, including the Village Vanguard, Fat Tuesday's, and the Blue Note, where it made the first of its Grammy-award winning albums. The group featured Henderson, Kamau Adilifu, Turre, Harper, Johnson, Ricky Ford, Joe Ford, Junior Cook, John Stubblefield, and of course Tyner himself. Tyner's music has been a major influence in the adoption in jazz of quartal and quintal harmonies, modes and pentatonic scales, and African rhythmic elements. Two volumes of transcriptions of his solos have been published: *Inception to Now* (New York and Hialeah, FL, 1983) and B. Leso: *McCoy Tyner: Artist Transcriptions: Piano* (Milwaukee, 1992).

Video oral history material in *NN-Sc* (LAJOHP).

See also PIANO, §5.

SELECTED RECORDINGS

As unaccompanied soloist: *Echoes of a Friend* (1972, Mlst. 9055); *Revelations* (1988, BN B21S-91651); *Things Ain't What They Used to Be* (1989, BN B21S-93598) [incl. duos with G. Adams and with J. Scofield]; *Soliloquy* (1991, BN B21Z-96429); *Live at Warsaw Jazz Festival 1991* (1991, Jazzmen 660.50.008)

Duos with S. Grappelli: *One on One* (1990, Mlst. 9181–2); *Live in Warsaw* (1991, Who's Who in Jazz 21047)

As leader: *Inception* (1962, Imp. 18); *Reaching Fourth* (1962, Imp. 33); *Nights of Ballads and Blues* (1963, Imp. 39); *Today and Tomorrow* (1963–4, Imp. 63); *The Real McCoy* (1967, BN 84264); *Expansions* (1970, BN 84388); *Sahara* (1972, Mlst. 9039); *Song for my Lady* (1972, Mlst. 9044); *Enlightenment* (1973, Mlst. 55001); *Supertrios* (1977, Mlst. 55003); *Four Times Four* (1980, Mlst. 55007); *Just Feelin'* (1985, PAlt 8083); with J. McLean: *It's About Time* (1985, BN 85102); *Double Trios* (1986, Denon 33CY1128); with F. Morgan: *Major Changes* (1987, Cont. 14039); *Uptown/Downtown* (1988, Mlst. 9167); *Live at Sweet Basil*, i–ii (1989, PW 292E6033, KICJ1); *Remembering John* (1991, Enja 6080-2); *The Turning Point* (1991, Verve 314-513573-2); *Infinity* (1995, Imp. 171)

As sideman with J. Coltrane: *My Favorite Things* (1960, Atl. 1361); *Impressions* (1961, 1963, Imp. 42); *Coltrane* (1962, Imp. 21); with J. Hartman: *John Coltrane and Johnny Hartman* (1963, Imp. 40); *Selflessness* (1963–5, Imp. 9161); *Live at Birdland* (1963, Imp. 50); *A Love Supreme* (1964, Imp. 77); *Ascension* (1965, Imp. 95); *Kulu se Mama* (1965, Imp. 9106); *First Meditations* (1965, Imp. 9332); *Om* (1965, Imp. 9140); *Meditations* (1965, Imp. 9110)

As sideman with others: A. Farmer and B. Golson: *Meet the Jazztet* (1960, Argo 664); J. Henderson: *Page One* (1963, BN 84140); A. Blakey: *A Jazz Message* (1963, Imp. 45); W. Shorter: *Night Dreamer* (1964, BN 84173); *Juju* (1964, BN 84182); J. Henderson: *Inner Urge* (1964, BN 84189); D. Murray: *David Murray Special Quartet* (1990, DIW 843)

SELECTED FILMS AND VIDEOS

Jazz Casual: the John Coltrane Quartet (1963); Soundstage: Down Beat Jazz Awards (1975); Harvest Jazz (1982); The Coltrane Legacy (1987); Jazzvisions: Implosions (1988); The World According to Coltrane (1991)

BIBLIOGRAPHY

S. Dance, "Tyner Talk," *DB*, xxx/28 (1963), 18
A. Bashier: "McCoy Tyner," *JJ*, xix/12 (1966), 29
D. Ioakimidis: "À l'ombre de Coltrane: McCoy Tyner," *Jh*, no.217 (1966), 20
A. Gerber: "Tyner: l'ombre après la lumière," *Jm*, no.177 (1970), 20
F. J. Kofsky: *Black Nationalism and the Revolution in Music* (New York, 1970, rev. and enlarged as *Black Nationalism and the Revolution in Music: Social Change and Stylistic Development in the Art of John Coltrane and Others, 1954–1967*, diss., U. of Pittsburgh, 1973/*R*1991), 207
M. Bourne: "McCoy Tyner," *DB*, xl/20 (1973), 14
V. Wilmer: "Tyner – Keeping it Clean," *MM* (8 Sept 1973), 16
P. Brodowski: "McCoy Tyner: Outburst of Energy," *JF* [intl edn], no.33 (1975), 38
M. Gourgues: "McCoy Tyner," *Jm*, no.234 (1975), 18
M. Luzzi: "Discographia McCoy Tyner," *Musica jazz*, xxxi/12 (1975), 45; xxxii (1976), no.1, p.47; no.2, p.47; no.3, p.46; xxxiii/3 (1977), 48
L. Underwood: "McCoy Tyner: Savant of the Astral Latitudes," *DB*, xlii/15 (1975), 12
J.-E. Berendt: "McCoy Tyner: Echoes of a Friend," *Ein Fenster aus Jazz: Essays, Portraits, Reflexionen* (Frankfurt am Main, Germany, 1977), 75
Z. Stewart: "Tyner," *Musician, Player and Listener*, no.10 (1977–8), 26
D. Clark: "Milestone Jazzstars on Tour," *DB*, xlv/19 (1978), 16
L. Feather: "Piano Giants of Jazz: McCoy Tyner," *CK*, iv/8 (1978), 54
B. Vuijsje: *De nieuwe jazz* (Baarn, Netherlands, 1978), 120
D. Wild: "McCoy Tyner: the Jubilant Experience of the Classic Quartet," *DB*, xlvi/13 (1979), 18
——: *The Recordings of John Coltrane* (Ann Arbor, MI, 1979)
P. Danson: "McCoy Tyner: USA," *Coda*, no.180 (1981), 4
B. Doerschuk: "McCoy Tyner," *CK*, vii/8 (1981), 28
H. Rock: "Profiling McCoy Tyner," *JSN*, ii/3 (1981), 10
L. Lyons: *The Great Jazz Pianists, Speaking of their Lives and Music* (New York, 1983), 235
P. Rinzler: "McCoy Tyner: Style and Syntax," *ARJS*, ii (1983), 109-49
J. Diliberto: "McCoy Tyner: Piano Visionary," *DB*, li/2 (1984), 20 [incl. discography]
B. Rusch: "McCoy Tyner: Interview," *Cadence*, x/1 (1984), 5
O. Keepnews: *The View from Within: Jazz Writings, 1948–1987* (New York, and Oxford, England, 1988), 180
K. Franckling: "McCoy Tyner," *JT* (1989), Nov, 24
F. Postif: *Les grandes interviews de Jazz hot* (Paris, 1989)
Z. Stewart: "Tyner," *Musician, Player and Listener*, i/10 (1990–91), 26
P. Brodowski: "McCoy Tyner Solo," *JF* [intl edn], no.128 (1991), 24
Y. Fujioka with L. Porter and Y. Hamada: *John Coltrane: a Discography and Musical Biography* (Metuchen, NJ, and London, 1995)
B. Primack: "The Real McCoy," *JT*, xxvi/1 (1996), 28
J. Corbett: "Trane-crossing," *DB*, lxv/3 (1998), 16

BILL DOBBINS/BK

Tzigane. Nickname of ELEK BACSIK, using the word widely used to describe gypsies and their music.

Tzizit, Rav. Pseudonym under which JOHN ZORN has recorded.

'Ūd. Short-necked plucked lute of the Arab world. Until the mid-1980s the only significant exponent of the instrument in jazz was Ahmed Abdul-Malik (not coincidentally a man of Egyptian descent), who plays the *'ūd* on his own albums (the first of which was *Jazz Sahara*, 1958, Riv. 287), as well as on a version of *India* captured on John Coltrane's album *The Other Village Vanguard Tapes* (1961, Imp. 9325); here Coltrane was striving for a non-Western musical "otherness," and the fact that an instrument of the Arab world was utilized on a piece called *India* perhaps reveals something about an American audience's uncritical sense of this "other." Later, with a fusion of jazz and "world music" having come into vogue, the *'ūd* player Rabih Abou-Khalil recorded numerous albums in jazz and jazz-related contexts, beginning with *Between Dusk and Dawn* (1986, MMP 170886). The instrument also figures in Sam Newsome's group of the mid- to late 1990s, Global Unity. (*GroveI*)

BK

UDJ. *See* UNION DEUTSCHER JAZZMUSIKER.

Uematsu, Takao (*b* Tokyo, 16 April 1947). Japanese tenor saxophonist. Self-taught, he played clarinet and alto saxophone from the age of 13 and later specialized on the tenor instrument. From 1965 he performed in the groups led by the drummer Akira Ishikawa, the guitarist Kiyoshi Sugimoto, George Otsuka, Terumasa Hino (at the Berlin Jazz Festival, 1971, and the Newport Jazz Festival New York, 1972), Motohiko Hino, and Takeo Moriyama, among others. He also played with Mal Waldron, Reggie Workman, Steve Gadd, and Eddie Gomez.

SELECTED RECORDINGS

As leader: *Debut* (1970, Three Blind Mice 3); *Straight Ahead* (1977, Trio PAP9100); *Come From With* (1992, East Works 6632)

As sideman: T. Hino: *At Berlin Jazz Festival '71* (1971, JVC SMJX10128); *Fuji* (1972, JVC SMJX10135); M. Hino: *Wild Talk* (1989, Meldac 30002); T. Honda: *Ease* (1992, Fun House 2072)

KAZUNORI SUGIYAMA

UGMA. Acronym of the Underground Musicians Association, an organization formed in 1963 by HORACE TAPSCOTT.

UGMAA. Acronym of the Union of God's Musicians and Artists Ascension, an organization formed in the late 1960s by HORACE TAPSCOTT; it was an outgrowth of his earlier Underground Musicians Association (UGMA).

UHCA [United Hot Clubs of America]. Record label. It was established in 1936 by Milt Gabler, who ran the enterprise from his Commodore Music Shop in New York. Its catalogue included items leased from many of the most important companies of the 1920s and 1930s; in many cases UHCA's recordings were pressed directly from original masters. At first the records were sold only by means of a subscription scheme, though later they became more widely available.

BIBLIOGRAPHY

G. Millstein: "For Kicks," *New Yorker*, xxii (9 March 1946), 40; xxii (16 March 1946), 34; repr. as "The Commodore Shop and Milt Gabler," *Eddie Condon's Treasury of Jazz*, ed. E. Condon and R. Gehman (New York, 1956/*R*1975), 98

B. Rust: *The American Record Label Book* (New Rochelle, NY, 1978), 297

G. Wheeler: *Jazz by Mail: Record Clubs and Record Labels 1936 to 1958, including Complete Discographies for Jazztone and Dial Records* (Manassas, VA, 1999), 291

A. Sutton and K. Nauck: *American Record Labels and Companies: an Encyclopedia (1891–1943)* (Denver, 2000), 210

HOWARD RYE

Ukulele [ukelele]. A small instrument resembling a guitar, usually associated with the music of Hawaii. It has four plucked strings that are generally tuned *a'–d'–f♯'–b'* or *g'–c'–e'–a'*. The instrument's best-known exponent in jazz is Ike Edwards (also known as Ukulele Ike), who recorded in a duo with Adrian Rollini (*That's all there is*, 1925, PAct 025132) and later made recordings as a leader with such sidemen as Red Nichols, Miff Mole, and Jimmy Dorsey (until 1935); he used the instrument both to play solo melodies and to provide rhythmic, chordal accompaniment. The ukulele playing of Roy Smeck, which relied to a greater extent than that of Edwards on pyrotechnics and perhaps as a result gained a larger following, was seldom as musically rewarding. Other jazz ukulele players, such as Frank Crumit and the singer Annette Hanshaw, used the instrument only to provide chordal accompaniment.

In African-American jazz, the ukulele was employed effectively by the Pebbles (Baxter White and Alphonsus Agee) on their *Hot Pebble Blues/Deep Henderson* (1927, Vic. 20774). The pianist Louis Hooper occasionally used it for accompaniments, as on Monette Moore's *Memphis Blues*

(1925, Ajax 17124), while in the 1960s Victoria Spivey recorded numerous ukulele accompaniments to her own singing. The instrument was also played in a jazz context by the Hawaiian guitarist King Benny [Benjamin Keakahiawa] Nawahi Nawahi (*b* 3 July 1899; *d* 29 Jan 1985), most notably with the African-American group which he led in the early 1930s at the Chinaland Restaurant, New York, and which recorded as the Georgia Jumpers (*Ukulele Benny/The Big Feet Rag* (1931, Col. 14620D).

JULIAN F. V. VINCENT, DAVID C. PHILLIPS/HOWARD RYE

Ukulele banjo. *See* BANJULELE.

Ulanov, Barry (*b* New York, 10 April 1918; *d* New York, 30 April 2000). Writer. His father was concert master for the conductor Arturo Toscanini. He was interested in jazz from a young age and attended Columbia University (AB 1939) to be closer to the jazz movement in Harlem; while a student he published articles on jazz in *The Spectator.* Following graduation he edited *Swing: the Guide to Modern Music* (*c*1939–40), *Listen* (1940–42), and the *Review of Recorded Music* (1945–6). As the editor of *Metronome: Modern Music and its Makers* (1943–55) he changed the focus of the journal from classical music and white swing groups to other aspects of jazz, notably bop and its African-American components; in 1950 he designed the *Metronome Yearbook.* In addition Ulanov organized all-star bop groups which broadcast on WOR (1947) and published biographies of Duke Ellington (1946) and Bing Crosby (1948). He taught music at the Juilliard School (1946) and English at Princeton University (1950–51) and Barnard College (from 1951); after gaining a PhD from Columbia he continued to teach English at Barnard from 1956 until his retirement in 1988. In the 1950s he was a columnist for *Down Beat* (1955–8) and published two overviews of jazz history. Towards the end of the 1960s he edited a work that explored modern culture and the arts, but thereafter he concentrated on a combined exploration of religion and psychology.

Ulanov was one of the early champions of bop and its substyles (especially the work of Lennie Tristano and his cool-jazz disciples), and he strove to bring a wider exposure to the idiom through both his writings and his editorial position at *Metronome.* His overviews of jazz were among the first works of this nature to be published by an American author.

WRITINGS
(selective list)

Duke Ellington (New York, 1946)
The Incredible Crosby (New York, 1949)
A History of Jazz in America (New York, 1952/*R*1972)
A Handbook of Jazz (New York, n.d. [?1957]/*R*1975)

BIBLIOGRAPHY

"Ulanov Joins 'Down Beat'," *DB*, xxii/7 (1955), 1
Obituary, B. Ratliff, *New York Times* (7 May 2000)

GK

Ullmann, Gebhard (*b* Bonn, 2 Nov 1957). German saxophonist and bass clarinetist. He took lessons on classical flute from the age of six and later studied flute and saxophone at the Musikhochschule in Hamburg (1983–4). From 1983 he performed and recorded with the guitarist Andreas Willers, both in a duo and as co-leader of small groups which included the drummer Nikolaus Schäuble. He was a member of Die Elefanten (1984–94), Minimal Kidds (1987–8), Günter Lenz's Springtime (from 1992), and the Hannes Zerbe Blechband, while also leading his own groups, among them the quartet Basement Research (based in New York), a ten-piece woodwind and accordion ensemble, Tá Lam Zehn (based in Berlin), the trio Trad Corrosion, and a clarinet trio (heard on *Clarinet Trio: Oct. 1, '98*, 1998, Leo Lab 058). Ullmann collaborated with such musicians as Paul Bley, Ellery Eskelin, the double bass player Joe Fonda, Bobby Previte, Alex Schlippenbach, Enrico Rava, and many others. He has appeared at concerts and festivals worldwide, and his active touring schedule and the experience of foreign cultures have contributed to the openness of his music, which makes use of Turkish, African, and Asian traditions (such as gamelan) as well as European influences. He is a brilliant orchestrator of complex, unpredictable compositions and an instrumentalist who understands how to merge compositional structure and improvisational freedom. The varied bands with which he works on a regular basis continually offer new challenges and the opportunity to see how the same composition might work in different settings. He may be heard to advantage on *Tá Lam* (1991, 1994, Songlines 1520-2), or by comparing versions of his *D. Nee No* on the albums *Faust* (with Die Elefanten, 1992, Klangräume 30150), *Basement Research* (by his quartet, 1993, SN 121271-2), and *Trad Corrosion* (in a trio with Willers and Phil Haynes, 1995, Nabel 4673).

BIBLIOGRAPHY

K. Noffke: "Gebhard Ullmann: Power und Pläne," *JP*, xl/3 (1991), 16
W. Kampmann: "Gebhard Ullmann Interview," *Jazzthetik*, vi/12 (1992), 40
<http://gebhard-ullmann.com/> (1999) [incl. discography]
R. Wissmann: "Gebhard Ullmann: Berliner 'Weltmusik'," *JP*, xlviii/9 (1999), 8

WOLFRAM KNAUER

Ulmer, James "Blood" [Musawwir, Damu Mustafa Abdul] (*b* St. Matthews, SC, 2 Feb 1942). Electric guitarist, singer, leader, and composer. At home he learned guitar, and from the ages of seven to 13 he played and sang baritone voice parts with his father's gospel group, the Southern Sons. He began his professional career playing with soul-jazz and rhythm-and-blues groups in Pittsburgh (1959–64) and around Columbus, Ohio (1964–7), including those of Jimmy Smith, Groove Holmes, and the organist Hank Marr; he made his first recordings in 1964 and toured Europe in 1966–7 in Marr's group, in which George Adams was also a member. While mainly rehearsing for four years in Detroit, Ulmer played with Big John Patton's soul-jazz group and traveled east with the organist to record for Blue Note in 1969 and again in 1970. He took his own band to New York early in May 1971 and performed for nine months at Minton's Playhouse, where he was able to introduce many of his new dance tunes. During his first years in New York he worked with Rashied Ali, Larry Young, and Paul Bley. He joined Art Blakey briefly, then in 1973 began to study and perform with Ornette Coleman, which brought about a dramatic change in his career. He embraced Coleman's HARMOLODIC THEORY, according to which all the instruments in an ensemble are regarded as equally important and engage in harmonically free improvisation. In the late 1970s Ulmer led groups (notably the MUSIC REVELATION ENSEMBLE) that presented daring new blends of funk, avant-garde jazz, and hard rock, but his originality gradually diminished as he sought greater precision. His tendency to abandon jazz elements and rely on increasingly rigid structures culminated in an album appropriately entitled *Black Rock* (1982), but thereafter he returned to more complex stylistic blends.

Ulmer often toured Europe and Japan in the 1980s. From around 1983 he led Odyssey, a trio consisting of violin, electric guitar, and drums, and in 1984 he became a member, with Adams, Ali, and others, of the group PHALANX. The Music Revelation Ensemble had continued without him for a period in the early 1980s, and then disbanded, but the group reunited, with Ulmer, for a reunion recording in 1988, and the musicians resumed performing and recording together on a regular basis from 1990. From the late 1980s Ulmer also led a rhythm-and-blues group; it toured Europe in the early 1990s as a quartet (comprising the electric guitarist Ronnie Drayton, Ali's son Amin Ali on electric bass guitar, and Randy Weston's son Grant Calvin Weston on drums) and then continued as a trio (with Amin Ali and the drummer Aubrey Dayle). He recorded in a trio with Bill Laswell and Ronald Shannon Jackson in Zurich in 1990 and in a duo with Karl Berger in Germany in 1994. In 1996 or 1997 he founded yet another eclectic band, Third Rail, consisting of Laswell, Amina Claudine Myers, the keyboard player Bernie Worrell, and the drummer Joseph "Zigaboo" Modeliste, which performed an amalgam of jazz, blues, rock, soul, and rap. In 1999 he led the New Jazz Art Quartet, whose members were John Hicks, Reggie Workman, and Rashied Ali.

The melody of Ulmer's composition *Black Sheep* (which he recorded in 1986) was published in *Guitar Player* (xxiv/5 (1990), 94).

SELECTED RECORDINGS

As leader of Music Revelation Ensemble: *No Wave* (1980, Moers 01072); *Music Revelation Ensemble* (1988, DIW 825)

As leader of Odyssey: *Odyssey* (1983, Col. BFC38900); *Live at the Caravan of Dreams* (1986, Caravan of Dreams 85004)

As leader of other groups: *Tales of Captain Black* (1978, AH 7); *Are You Glad to Be in America?* (1980, Rough Trade 16); *Freelancing* (1981, Col. ARC37493); *Black Rock* (1982, Col. ARC38285); *America, Do You Remember the Love?* (1986, BN 85136), incl. Black Sheep; *Blues Allnight* (1989, In + Out 7005-2); *Music Speaks Louder than Words* (1996, DIW 910)

As sideman: R. Ali: *Rashied Ali Quintet* (*c*1973, Survival 102); A. Blythe: *Lenox Avenue Breakdown* (1978, Col. JC35638); D. Murray: *Children* (1984, BS 0089); *David Murray* (1986, DIW 8009)

BIBLIOGRAPHY

G. Giddins: "Jazz-funk," *VV*, xxiv (25 June 1979), 53

R. Palmer: "The Futuristic Jazz-funk of James Ulmer," *RS*, no.319 (12 June 1980), 23

C. J. Safane: "The Harmolodic Diatonic Funk of James 'Blood' Ulmer," *DB*, xlvii/10 (1980), 22

B. Caux: "James Blood Ulmer: les contes du capitaine Blood," *Jh*, no.381 (1981), 34

B. Loupias: "James Blood Ulmer: un sang nouveau pour nos sillons?," *Jm*, no.294 (1981), 34 [incl. discography]

N. Tesser: "Ulmer and Jackson's New Fusion," *Musician*, no.33 (1981), 82

C. May: "Blood Change," *Black Music and Jazz Review*, v/8 (1982), 19

G. Giddins: "Harmolodic Hoedown," *VV*, xxix (27 March 1984), 38

S. Lake: "Blood: off the Tracks," *The Wire*, no.22 (1985), 24

D. Reinert: "James 'Blood' Ulmer: Ich spiele nur Gitarre . . .," *JP*, xxxv/4 (1986), 16

R. M. Jackson: "Blood: Red, White & Blue Note," *Jazziz*, iv/3 (1987), 53

D. Rubien: "Two Guitar Masters Give Instrument Unheard-of-range," *San Francisco Chronicle Datebook* (10 Dec 1989), 51

W. Hetfield: "Rare Blood: the Guitar According to James Blood Ulmer," *GP*, xxiv/5 (1990), 90

J. Litweiler: "Free Spirit, Free Jazz," *Chicago Tribune* (21 March 1990)

S. Adams: "James 'Blood' Ulmer," *JJI*, xlv/9 (1992), 10

F. Bruckert: "James Blood Ulmer et l'harmolodic diatonic funk: une musique futuriste entre jazz, punk et soul," *Jazz Notes*, no.22 (1993), 15

B. Ratliff: "James Blood Ulmer," *Coda*, no.249 (1993), 18

A. Robinson: "James 'Blood' Ulmer," *Jazz Express*, no.152 (1993), 13

K. A. Kunze: "Der Gitarrist auf der Kanzel: James Blood Ulmer und die Sprache des Blues," *Jazzthetik*, vii/12–viii/1 (1993–4), 44

R. Hicks: "James 'Blood' Ulmer," *Jazziz*, xi/5 (1994), 55

H. Mandel: "Tales of Captain Blood: James Blood Ulmer," *DB*, lxi/4 (1994), 22

B. Primack: "Hearsay: James Blood Ulmer," *JT*, xxiv/4 (1994), 11

C. Tabarini: "James Blood Ulmer: Tales of Captain Black," *Viva la musica*, no.162 (1994), 27

D. Ouellette: "He's Been Working on the Third Rail: Jazz Guitarist Ulmer Gets Big-name Band Ready to Roll," *San Francisco Chronicle Datebook* (20 July 1997), 43

<http://www.geocities.com/BourbonStreet/Quarter/7055/Ulmer/index.htm> (2000) [incl. discography by R. Stubenrauch and bibliography]

For further recordings and bibliography *see* PHALANX.

BK

Umbria Jazz. Festival held in the Umbria region of Italy, principally in the city of Perugia. It was founded by Carlo Pagnotta, who continued as its producer into the late 1990s. Umbria Jazz began as a free annual outdoor event in the years 1973 to 1976, but was then discontinued because of crowd disturbances; it was resumed in 1982. The festival takes place for ten to 12 days in July at indoor and outdoor venues in Perugia, which in 1999 included the Teatro Morlacchi, Teatro del Pavone, Piazza del Bacio, Piazza IV Novembre, Giardini del Frontone, Ristorante la Taverna, and Contrappunto Jazz; audiences at the outdoor events have reached 30,000. Umbria Jazz has often staged events in other towns in the region, notably Terni, Foligno, Orvieto, and Città di Castello, and in 1995 there were performances for two days in Cortona, Tuscany. From 1985 it has hosted the Berklee Summer School as part of the Umbria Jazz Clinics. Events are held at other times of year as well, notably Umbria Jazz Winter in Orvieto (from 1993, December to January) and the Jazz & Soul Easter Festival (from 1997, spring).

BIBLIOGRAPHY

Un mare di facce: dieci anni di Umbria Jazz (Rome, 1984)

Vent'anni di Umbria Jazz (Perugia, Italy, 1993)

Umbria & Jazz: 25 anni di musica (Cinisello Balsamo, Italy, 1998)

<http://www.umbriajazz.com> (1999)

PAUL R. LAIRD

Umezu, Kazutoki [Dr. Umezu; Kappo] (*b* Sendai, Japan, 17 Oct 1949). Japanese alto saxophone and reed player. He took up clarinet at the age of 12 and later majored in the instrument at Kunitachi College of Music, Tokyo, graduating in 1972; while still a student he played with Toshinori Kondo's trio. From 1974 to 1976 he lived in New York, where he performed with Oliver Lake, Arthur Blythe, Ahmed Abdullah, and Ted Daniel, among many others. Upon returning to Japan he formed, with the pianist Yoriyuki Harada, the Seikatsu Kojo Iinkai Orchestra, a group which enjoyed great popular success until it disbanded in 1981; his next group, DUB (Dr. Umezu Band), also achieved wide popularity. In the 1980s he joined R. C. Succession, a popular Japanese rock band. From 1988, when DUB disbanded, Umezu led various ensembles, including the seven-piece group Shakushain (formed in 1989), an 18-piece klezmer orchestra, Betsuni Nanmo Klezmer (from 1992), and Nazo, which blended elements of middle-Eastern music, pop, and jazz (from the mid-1990s); in addition he appeared as one of the guest performers with Third Person, the duo of Tom Cora and the percussionist Samm Bennett (1990–94). With these groups he toured and recorded in Japan, Europe, and the USA. In the 1990s Umezu worked with Yosuke Yamashita, Masahiko Togashi, Fumio Itabashi (playing in Indonesia and Hong Kong in 1994 and in Thailand in 1995), and the drummer Yoshisaburo Toyozumi, and with a number of musicians associated with improvised music in New York, among them John Zorn, George Lewis (ii), Fred Frith, Marc Ribot, Ned Rothenberg, and Wayne Horvitz. He composed music for several Japanese films, produced concerts for a number of Japanese musicians, and performed, mainly with Asian artists, in many other genres, including blues, the folk revival, the traditional musics of Japan and Korea, and music for dance.

SELECTED RECORDINGS

Duos: with Y. Harada: *Danke* (1980, Next Wave 25PJ1007); with T. Cora: *Abandon all Improvisation* (1987, Umisushi 1001)

As leader: *This is Music is This?* (1978, Tei. 18911); *Dance, Dance, Dance* (1979, Tei. 18912); *Dynamite* (1983, Barca L28N1011); *Danger* (1987, Toshiba–EMI 8326); *Diva* (1988, Avenue 1008); *Cinema* (1989, Avenue 1001); *'94 Live* (1995, Axel 002); *Ahiru & Waltz* (1996, Nani 101–02); *Asian Fantasy Orchestra* (1998, Polydor 7419)

BIBLIOGRAPHY

<http://www.j-music.com/umezu/profile.html> (2000) [incl. discography]

KAZUNORI SUGIYAMA, BK

UMO [Uuden Musiikin Orkesteri; New Music Orchestra]. Finnish big band. Founded in 1975 as a co-operative band by the country's leading jazz musicians, UMO became a full-time professional orchestra in 1984 with the support of the ministry of culture, the city of Helsinki, and the Finnish Broadcasting Company. Its first conductor was Heikki Sarmanto, but his duties were soon taken over by Esko Linnavalli, who held the post for fifteen years (1975–90). He was followed by Markku Johansson (1992–3), Rick Shemaria (1994–6), Eero Koivistoinen (1996–8) and Sarmanto again (from 1998). UMO has regularly presented both Finnish and foreign guest soloists and conductors, both in concert and on recordings. One of the first guests was Thad Jones, who conducted the band on several occasions and helped to mold its style. Since then it has featured more than 200 guests, including Dizzy Gillespie, Mercer Ellington, Clark Terry, and Muhal Richard Abrams, and recorded 16 albums. UMO has made several tours in the USA and Europe: in the 1990s it toured with the singer Natalie Cole and Manhattan Transfer.

SELECTED RECORDINGS:

Thad Jones, Mel Lewis & UMO (1978, RCA PL40096); *UMO Jazz Orchestra* (1998, Naxos Jazz 86010-2); *Day Dreamin': the Music of Billy Strayhorn* (1998, FSR 02)

BIBLIOGRAPHY

T. Sandberg: "UMO Jazz Orchestra," *Finnish Music Quarterly* no.3 (1998), 40

PEKKA GRONOW

Underground Musicians Association [UGMA]. Organization formed in 1963 by HORACE TAPSCOTT.

Union Deutscher Jazzmusiker [UDJ]. German professional organization. It was established in Marburg in 1973 to promote the interests of jazz musicians in the Federal Republic of Germany. Aiming to enhance the reputation of jazz, and to gain wider recognition for it, the UDJ has made many efforts to represent the case for the music to state bodies and other organizations. It has also encouraged the teaching of jazz in German schools and sponsored the Deutsches Jazz Forum, a program of concerts, seminars, and discussions held for two days each November and presented in various jazz centers throughout Germany. From 1985 the organization supported the German–French Jazz Ensemble, led by Albert Mangelsdorff and Jean-François Jenny-Clark. The UDJ is a member of the Deutscher Musikrat (German Music Council) and of the International Jazz Federation. In 1987 it had about 500 members and was led by Mangelsdorff and Peter Ortmann; a decade later its executive committee included Joe Viera, Manfred Schoof, Sigi Busch, Dieter Ilg, and Ortmann, while Rainer Brüninghaus, Wolfgang Dauner, Klaus Doldinger, Gunter Hampel, Ekkehard Jost, and Eberhard Weber were serving as advisors. In 2000 it was based in Bonn. (<http://www.udj.de/> (2000))

BERT NOGLIK

Union of God's Musicians and Artists Ascension [UGMAA]. Organization formed in the late 1960s by HORACE TAPSCOTT as an outgrowth of his earlier Underground Musicians Association (UGMA).

Unit. Record company and label. It was founded in Switzerland in 1983 by four improvising musicians – Urs Blöchlinger, the trombonist Paul Haag, Hans Kennel, and the tenor saxophonist Jürg Solothurnmann – who had been unable to get their own music released on existing labels. Having initially been advised by a five-person selection committee on new releases, the label nearly failed in 1991. However, it was revived with a more business-oriented approach, and in 1998 it was taken over by René Aeberhard. Unit documents improvised music in Switzerland and releases many début recordings. The company requires that Swiss musicians participate in each recording in some capacity (not necessarily musical), although this policy does not exclude performances by foreigners. Unit has released more than 30 LPs and 80 CDs, including albums by John Wolf Brennan, Pierre Favre, Hans Koch, Urs Leimgruber, and Irène Schweizer. All its recording artists become members of the Verein Improvisierender Musiker der Schweiz (VIMS; Association of Improvising Musicians of Switzerland), which aims to improve conditions for improvised music in the country. Unit also organizes an annual festival of Swiss improvised music.

SIMON ADAMS

United. Record company and label. The company was established in Chicago in 1951 by Lew Simpkins (who had formerly been responsible for artists and repertory with Miracle and Premium) and Leonard Allen. The label and its subsidiary, States (launched in 1952), were used to issue a wide range of African-American music. The best-remembered jazz recordings were by Tab Smith, Paul Bascomb, and Jimmy Forrest, whose *Night Train* (1951, United 110) became a hit throughout the USA. Simpkins died in May 1953, but Allen continued the company until 1957. United's masters were purchased in 1975 by Delmark, which embarked on a program of important reissues and also put out some items from the repertory that had not previously been released.

BIBLIOGRAPHY

B. Koester: "The United/States Masters," *Blues Unlimited*, no.123 (1977), 14; no.124 (1977), 11

R. Pruter: "Obituary: Leonard Allen," *Living Blues*, no.67 (1986), 39

R. Pruter and J. O'Neal: "Leonard Allen and the United/States Story," *Living Blues* (1990), no.92, p.37; no.93, p.34; (1991), no.95, p.41

HOWARD RYE

United Artists. Record company and label. The company was established in New York in 1958 as a subsidiary of the film company of the same name. It quickly assembled a remarkably comprehensive catalogue that contained a wide variety of mainstream and modern jazz. Among its most notable recordings were the excellent album *Money Jungle* by

Duke Ellington, Charles Mingus, and Max Roach, and the only recording made jointly by John Coltrane and Cecil Taylor. In addition the company released albums by Art Blakey, Roy Ayers, Count Basie, Billie Holiday, Bill Potts, Art Farmer, Curtis Fuller, Thad Jones, Mose Allison, Ruby Braff, Gerry Mulligan, the Modern Jazz Quartet, Betty Carter, Dave Lambert, Rex Stewart, Oliver Nelson, Benny Golson, Herb Pomeroy, Booker Little, Milt Jackson, Howard McGhee, Bud Freeman, Teddy Charles, Kenny Dorham, Zoot Sims, and Billy Strayhorn. This extensive repertory was produced by Tom Wilson, Jack Lewis, Alan Douglas, and George Wein. Around 1966 United Artists established an offshoot, Solid State, which achieved considerable artistic and commercial success and is best known for a long series of albums by the Thad Jones–Mel Lewis Orchestra. In 1979 United Artists was purchased by EMI, at which point control of the company's material passed to Manhattan, a subsidiary of Capitol within the EMI conglomerate. After Manhattan revived the Blue Note label in 1985 it reissued much of the United Artists catalogue under the Blue Note name; later Manhattan was discontinued and Blue Note itself controlled the United Artists material. When *Money Jungle* was reissued in 1987 it included four previously unreleased tracks; this suggests that there may be a considerable amount of unissued material in the United Artists archive.

MARK GARDNER

United Hot Clubs of America. *See* Uhca.

United Jazz and Rock Ensemble. International group based in Germany. Originally called the Elf-1/2-Ensemble, it was organized by Wolfgang Dauner in 1975 for a television series in Stuttgart. The popularity of this show convinced the participating musicians to continue their work, and in 1977 the group took the name United Jazz and Rock Ensemble. It brought together some of the most innovative musicians from jazz and rock in Europe: Ack van Rooyen and Ian Carr (trumpets), Albert Mangelsdorff (trombone), Charlie Mariano and Barbara Thompson (saxophones), Volker Kriegel (guitar), Dauner (keyboards), Eberhard Weber (double bass and electric bass guitar), and Jon Hiseman (drums). The membership of the ensemble remained reasonably constant from its formation: Kenny Wheeler joined in 1978, Weber was replaced by Dave King in the mid-1980s, and the trumpeter Johannes Faber was added to the group occasionally in the 1980s; Mariano left in 1994, to be replaced by Christof Lauer, and Thorsten Benkenstein (trumpet) and Peter O'Mara (guitar) appeared with the band in the late 1990s.

After the group's first public appearance, in July 1976, the musicians met about once a year to tour and record, and the band soon became one of the most popular European jazz-rock ensembles. It recorded for Mood, which was originally founded to produce recordings by the United Jazz and Rock Ensemble only, but soon thereafter also released albums by others. The band's own albums were highly successful, and its *Live im Schützenhaus* (1977) became the best-selling jazz LP produced in Germany.

SELECTED RECORDINGS

(all recorded for Mood)

Live im Schützenhaus (1977, 28600); *Teamwork* (1978, 22999); *The Break-even Point* (1979, 23600); *Live in Berlin* (1981, 28628); *United Live Opus Sechs* (1984, 33621); *Round Seven* (1987, 33606); *Na endlich!* (1991, 6382); *Die Neunte von United* (1996, 6472); *United Jazz and Rock Ensemble Plays Albert Mangelsdorff* (1998, 6552); *X* (1999, 6582)

BIBLIOGRAPHY

"On the Bandstand: the United Jazz + Rock Ensemble," *JF*, no.55 (1978), 20

V. Kriegel: "Jazz & Rock," *Jazzrock: Tendenzen einer modernen Musik*, ed. B. König (Reinbek, Germany, 1983), 35-77

A. Höll: "The United Jazz & Rock Ensemble," *JP*, xxxiv/12 (1985), 32

H. Kumpf: "10 Jahre United Jazz & Rock Ensemble," *JP*, xxxiv/5 (1985), 27

G. Endress: "20 Jahre United Jazz + Rock Ensemble," *JP*, xliii/10 (1994), 3

WOLFRAM KNAUER

United Nation Orchestra. Big band founded in 1988 by Dizzy Gillespie and led after his death by Paquito D'Rivera.

United Phonographs Corporation [UPC]. Record company. It was established by the Wisconsin Chair Company at Sheboygan, Wisconsin, and in the early 1920s issued recordings on Puritan and Paramount. (A. Sutton and K. Nauck: *American Record Labels and Companies: an Encyclopedia (1891–1943)* (Denver, 2000), 300)

Unity. Record company and label. It was established around 1987 in Toronto by the saxophonist Alex Dean, the double bass player Kieran Overs, and the trumpeter John MacLeod to issue their recordings; later Barry Elmes was involved in its operations. By the mid-1990s Unity had released more than 150 albums featuring, among others, Dean, Overs, MacLeod, Elmes, Hugh Fraser, Jacek Kochan, Mike Murley, P. J. Perry, and Bernie Senensky; the groups Chelsea Bridge Quartet and Fourth Inversion are also well represented in its catalogue. Around 1996 Unity was acquired by Page Music, which after changing the label name to UP (for Unity Page) continued to produce new recordings and to maintain the back catalogue. Unity should not be confused with other labels of the same name, most of which have issued hip-hop and other dance musics. (<http://www.pagemusic.com> (2001))

GK

Universal Music Group. The name given to the record company Mca in 1996, one year after it was purchased by the Canadian spirits manufacturer Seagrams. In 1998 the Universal Music Group absorbed Polygram when it too was purchased by Seagrams, and thereafter its jazz division operated as the Verve Music Group (see Verve).

Unt, Toivo (*b* Tallinn, Estonian SSR [now Estonia], 6 March 1951). Estonian double bass player. He took up electric bass guitar while at school and in 1967–8 performed in the rock group Kristallid. From 1969 he played double bass in the National Opera Estonia. He graduated from the Tallinn Georg Ots Music School (1971) and then enrolled at the Tallinn State Conservatory, but this period of study was ended by service in the Soviet Navy (1972–5). Having resumed his permanent position in the opera orchestra, he spent some years in a television ensemble and played in the rock group Hõim (1980) and the jazz-rock group Radar (1980–82). In the 1980s and 1990s he was a member of three bands involving Baltic and Scandinavian musicians: the Scan Trio, the Baltic Quartet, and the Gimer Trio. He played with innumerable compatriots and also accompanied such visiting musicians as Ted Curson, Leroy Jones, and Judy Niemack; in 1987 he engaged in a memorable jam session with Dave Brubeck's quartet in Tallinn. Unt has appeared at festivals in ten European countries and participated in radio jazz workshops in Hungary, Finland, and Estonia. In 2000 he founded the Nômme Jazz Festival in a suburb of Tallinn, with Ted Curson and Ryo Kawasaki as featured performers.

SELECTED RECORDINGS

It's Four of Them (1995, Sittle 9222); *Relaxin' at the Viru* (1998, Viru Entertainment 001); *Take it or Leave it* (1998, Green May Oy 001)

WALTER OJAKÄÄR

Uotila, Jukka-Pekka [Jukkis] (*b* Helsinki, 23 Aug 1960). Finnish drummer. He moved to New York in 1980, studied with Louis Hayes and Bob Moses, and soon found employment with various jazz groups in the city, including those of Randy Brecker, Bob Berg, Mike Stern, Gil Evans, and McCoy Tyner. After returning to Finland he taught jazz at the Sibelius Academy in Helsinki from 1986 and was appointed associate professor there in 1992; from 1986 to 1993 he was assistant conductor of UMO. His work may be heard to advantage on the album *Jukkis Uotila Band Live*, recorded in Copenhagen by a quintet consisting of Berg, Stern, Lars Jansson, and Lars Danielsson (1989, Stunt 18909). Uotila also recorded with Chet Baker and Bob Rockwell (both 1986), Joe Bonner (1987), Doug Raney and Jørgen Emborg (both 1988), and Lennart Ginman and Kirk Lightsey (1990).

Oral history material in *FiHJ*.

BIBLIOGRAPHY

P. Silas: "I Want to Teach the World to Jazz," *Finnish Music Quarterly* no.2 (1989), 97

M. Huuskonen, J. Muikku and T. Vähäsilta: *Finnish Jazz* (Helsinki, 5/1997)

PEKKA GRONOW

UP [Unity Page]. The name which the Unity record company took after it was acquired by Page Music around 1996.

Upbeat. The beat or subdivision of the beat that immediately precedes the first beat of the bar or downbeat; *see* Beat, §4(i).

Upchurch, Phil (*b* Chicago, 19 July 1941). Electric guitarist. He began playing ukulele at the age of 12 and guitar when he was 13. Largely self-taught, he first worked professionally with rhythm-and-blues groups (1957–62) and as a session musician in Chicago, recording with such popular artists as Muddy Waters, Jimmy Reed, and Chuck Berry; in 1961 his own group had a Top 40 hit, *You Can't Sit Down* (recorded late the previous year). From 1965 to 1967 he served in the US Army in Germany, where he often played jazz in clubs. After returning to the USA he toured with the Staple Singers, co-led a group with the soul singer Donny Hathaway, and resumed his studio work in Chicago; he recorded as a leader (1967, 1969) and with Jimmy Smith (1968), Woody Herman, Brother Jack McDuff, and John Klemmer (all 1968–9), and Dizzy Gillespie (1969). From 1969 to 1970 Upchurch was a member of Ramsey Lewis's quartet, after which he worked with Quincy Jones in California and on a tour of Japan (1972). He again returned to Chicago, and in the mid-1970s he joined George Benson's group, with which he toured until 1981; during this period he made several recordings as a leader, including *Phil Upchurch* (*c*1978, Marlin 798), and recorded with Jones, Cannonball Adderley, and Grover Washington, Jr. (all 1974), the Crusaders (1980), and Mose Allison (1982). In the 1980s he settled in the Los Angeles area. He toured with Smith, and he continued to record as a freelance and to lead his own small groups through the 1990s; in 1998 he formed a 20-piece band, the Phil-Harmonic Orchestra.

Although Upchurch is known primarily as an electric guitarist, he also worked throughout his career on electric bass guitar and often played both instruments at the same recording session. He is much admired both for his tasteful, articulate accompaniments and as a soloist. A volume of transcriptions of his solos was published as *12 x 12* (Pacific, MO, 1995). In the mid-1990s the Vestax Corporation created and marketed a high-quality guitar called the Phil Upchurch model.

SELECTED RECORDINGS

As leader: You Can't Sit Down, pts i–ii (1961, Boyd 1026); *Feeling Blue* (1967, Mlst. 9010); *Phil Upchurch/Tennyson Stephens* (1974–5, Kudu 22); *Free and Easy* (1982, Jam 007); *Revelation* (1983, Jam 001); *Phil Upchurch Presents the L.A. Jazz Quintette* (1986, Pro Arte 631); *Phil Upchurch Trio* (1987, King 6459); *Whatever Happened to the Blues* (1996, GoJazz 5019/Bean Bag 55566)

As sideman: C. Adderley: *Pyramid* (1974, Fan. 9455); G. Benson: *Breezin'* (1976, WB 2919); Joe Williams: *Nothin' but the Blues* (1983, Delos 4001); C. McRae: *Fine and Mellow: Live at Birdland West* (1987, Conc. 4342); R. Holloway: *Locksmith Blues* (1989, Conc. 4390); J. Smith: *Prime Time* (1989, Mlst. 9176); *Sum Serious Blues* (1993, Mlst. 9207); Joe Williams, *Feel the Spirit* (1994, Telarc 83362); J. Pisano: on *Conversation Pieces* (1994–5, Pablo 2310963), Ribbit

BIBLIOGRAPHY

Feather–Gitler '70s

D. Morgenstern: "Phil Upchurch: Studio Soul," *DB*, xxxvi/13 (1969), 13

A. Shay: What it's Like to Be a Musician (Chicago, 1972)

C. Mitchell: "Jammin' with Phil," DB, xli/11 (1974), 13

M. J. Summerfield: *The Jazz Guitar: its Evolution and its Players* (Gateshead, England, 1978, 4/1998, as *The Jazz Guitar: its Evolution, Players and Personalities since 1900*)

J. Sievert: "Sharing Leads with George," *GP*, xiii/7 (1979), 87 [incl. discography]

J. Ferguson: "Phil Upchurch: from '50s R & B to '80s Pop: Fusing Blues, Funk, and Jazz," *GP*, xix/2 (1985), 56 [incl. discography]

R. Pruter: *Chicago Soul* (Chicago, and Oxford, England, 1991)

J. Ferguson: "Phil Upchurch: the Guitar's Greatest Challenges," *JT*, xxiii/6 (1993), 34

R. Grosman: "Phil Upchurch," *Jh*, no.503 (1993), 13

<http://www.nutbutton.com/upchurch.html> (1997)

M. Lewis: "Phil Upchurch Likes his Jazz Funky," *San Diego Union-Tribune* (30 Jan 1997)

G. Robinson: "Phil Upchurch," *JT*, xxvii/6 (1997), 22

<http://www.philupchurch.com> (2001)

THOMAS OWENS

Upper Austrian Jazz Orchestra. Austrian big band. It was formed in 1991 by Upper Austrian jazz musicians as a leaderless cooperative. In 1993 its principal soloists were the Canadian trumpeter Ingrid Jensen and the Austrian saxophonists Klaus Dickbauer and Christian Maurer. In the mid-1990s the band rehearsed and performed monthly in the most important Viennese jazz club, Porgy & Bess. Its arrangements were written by Frank Foster, Bill Holman, Don Menza, Frank Mantooth, Bob Florence, and its own gifted pianist, Helmar Hill. In 1995 the band gave several concerts with Kenny Wheeler, who wrote and rehearsed a complete program which was recorded as *Upper Austrian Jazz Orchestra Plays the Music of Kenny Wheeler* (West Wind 2097). In 1997 the orchestra played some of the larger-scale works of Charles Mingus and of the Austrian trumpeter and composer Franz Hautzinger. It toured Britain and Canada in 1998.

KLAUS SCHULZ

Up tempo. Fast.

Uptown. Record company and label established in Montreal in the late 1970s by Bob Sunenblick. It began recording in 1979, and among its first issues were albums by Joe Thomas (iii) and J. R. Monterose. Around 1981 the producer Mark Feldman joined the company, and from that time its operations were based mainly in New York. Uptown released approximately 40 of its own recordings, including further items by Monterose (in a duo with Tommy Flanagan) and Thomas (as co-leader with Jay McShann), as well as albums by Dicky Wells, Hod O'Brien, Allen Eager, Pepper Adams, Philly Joe Jones's group Dameronia, Johnny Coles and Frank Wess, Kenny Barron, Barry Harris, Al Grey and Buddy Tate, Al Cohn, Claudio Roditi, and Flanagan (all made between 1981 and 1986). Other releases were broadcast recordings by Serge Chaloff, Charlie Parker, Chet Baker, and Sonny Clark, dating variously from the years 1946–55, and a collection of concert recordings by Dodo Marmarosa made between 1956 and 1962. In 1987 Feldman left the company to form Reservoir music, which subsequently issued some recordings he had made for Uptown and reissued some of Uptown's own albums; thereafter Sunenblick continued to operate Uptown in Montreal. The company appears to have ceased making new recordings around 1990, but it continued through the late 1990s to issue material sporadically, notably new collections of broadcast material from the 1950s by Lee Wiley, Parker, and Coleman Hawkins.

GK

Urbani, Massimo (*b* Rome, 8 May 1957; *d* Rome, 24 June 1993). Italian alto saxophonist. He took up clarinet at the age of 11 but soon changed to alto saxophone. In 1972 he studied jazz with Giorgio Gaslini at the conservatory in Rome. Having been discovered by Mario Schiano, with whom he worked from 1972 to 1974, he played with the jazz-rock group Area (1974), Enrico Rava (1974–8), and Enrico Pieranunzi (1980–81). In 1979 he formed his first quartet, which from 1980 included Danilo Rea on piano and Furio Di Castri on double bass. On account of personal problems he was unable to lead his group on a steady basis, and instead worked and played in jam sessions with various rhythm sections, often below his talent. He died of a drug overdose.

Urbani was one of the greatest and wildest of Italian jazz musicians. His idol was Charlie Parker, but he was attracted by John Coltrane and Ornette Coleman too. All his music had an overwhelming energy: his sound was bright and forceful but also had a singing quality. Within the conventional setting of chorus forms his imagination was without boundaries; at his best in informal sessions, he was a virtuoso player with a great control of long, complex lines and an irresistible sense of swing.

SELECTED RECORDINGS

Duos with M. Melillo: *Duet Improvsations for Yardbird* (1987, Philology 214)

As leader: *Jazz a confronto 13* (1974, Horo 13); *Invitation* (1977, 1983–4, Philology 58); *360° Aeutopia* (1979, Red 146); *Dedication to A.A. & J.C./ Max's Mood* (1980, Red 160, 165); *Easy to Love* (1987, Red 208); *Round about . . . Max with Strings* (1991, Sentemo 30392); *The Blessing* (1993, Red 123257-2)

As sideman: M. Schiano: *Sud* (1973, Tom Orro 2001); E. Rava: *Jazz a confronto 14* (1974, Horo 14); E. Pieranunzi: *Isis* (1980, SN 1021)

BIBLIOGRAPHY

M. Piras: "Massimo Urbani," *Musica jazz*, li/10 (1995), 37

L. Viotto: "Urbani: discografia completa," *Musica jazz*, li/10 (1995), 46

C. De Scipio: *Vita, morte, musica di Massimo Urbani* (Rome, 1999)

<http://www.ijm.it/enartists.html> (1999) [discography]

STEFANO ZENNI

Urbaniak, Michal [Michał] (*b* Warsaw, 22 Jan 1943). Polish violinist, tenor saxophonist, and bandleader. He studied classical violin from the age of six, and when he was 15 he won – but declined – a scholarship to study with David Oistrakh in Moscow, choosing instead to concentrate on his new love, jazz; he took up soprano saxophone, then tenor saxophone, and briefly played dixieland and swing before settling into the hard-bop style. However, he worked as a classical violinist while playing tenor saxophone with Zbigniew Namysłowski (1961), Andrzej Trzaskowski's Wreckers (1962–4, including a tour of the USA in 1962), and Krzysztof Komeda (1962–5). From 1965 he led a group in Scandinavia with Urszula Dudziak, whom he married in 1967, and after returning to Poland in 1969 he formed the eclectic group Constellation, with Dudziak, Adam Makowicz, Czesław Bartkowski, and Paweł Jarzębski (replaced in 1972–3 by Roman Dyląg). In the course of this affiliation he was named the best soloist at the 1971 Montreux International Jazz Festival and thus won a scholarship to the Berklee School of Music, but again he declined the opportunity.

By 1974 Urbaniak had moved to New York and formed the jazz-rock group Fusion, which he led until 1977; the group's playing exploited the unusual scat singing of Dudziak, and some of the pieces in its repertory, such as *New York Batsa* (1974), used the melodies and irregular meters of Polish folk music. Later Urbaniak performed and recorded with Dudziak and as a leader; he also worked as a sideman with Archie Shepp and recorded as a soloist with Don Pullen (the latter in 1976). In the 1980s he continued to lead Constellation and formed acoustic duos with Larry Coryell, with whom he toured and recorded from around 1982–4, and Władysław Sendecki, for tours and recordings from 1982. He wrote extensively for films from the late 1980s, recorded as a leader of small groups playing in bop and modal-jazz styles in the early 1990s, and in the mid-1990s formed the group Urbanator to play a fusion of jazz and hip-hop.

Like Jean-Luc Ponty, Urbaniak played the electric violin and the violectra (an electronic bowed string instrument that sounds an octave lower than the violin) before taking up a five-string hybrid instrument (the lowest string on which was tuned to *c*) and later a six-string instrument (with the addition of a string tuned to *F*); he uses electronic pedals to alter his instrument's timbre. Although he is best known as a violinist, he prefers saxophone, which he resumed playing in his work with Urbanator.

SELECTED RECORDINGS

Duos with L. Coryell: *The Larry Coryell–Michal Urbaniak Duo* (1982, Key. 716)

As leader: *Super Constellation* (*c*1973, CBS 65744); *Constellation in Concert* (1973, Muza 1010); *Atma* (1974, Col. KC33184), incl. New York Batsa; *Fusion III* (*c*1975, Col. PC33542); *Urbaniak* (1977, IC 1036); *Music for Violin and Jazz Quartet* (1980, JAM 001); *Take Good Care of my Heart* (1984, Ste. 1195)

As sideman: R. Kühn: *Solarius* (1964, Amiga 850046); [no leader:] *Jazz Workshop East–West* (1965, Col. SMC83875); *New Violin Summit* (1971, MPS 15335); M. Davis: on *Tutu* (1986, WB 25490), Don't lose your mind

BIBLIOGRAPHY

B. Lojkowna: "Jazz and Nostalgia in the Urbaniak Style," *JF* [intl edn], no.8 (1970), 75

J. Byrczek: "Eurojazz Personalities: Poland," *JF* [intl edn], no.18 (1972), 93

R. Urbach: "Michal Urbaniak," *Blues Notes*, iv/4 (1972), 20

D. Zimmerle: "Michal Urbaniak Group," *JP*, xxi/3 (1972), 66

S. Czajkowski: "Michal Urbaniak," *JF* [intl edn], no.21 (1973), 45

J.-R. Masson and G. Rouy: "Onze européens parlent de leur musique: Michal Urbaniak," *Jm*, no.220 (1974), 32

R. Townley: "Profile: Michal Urbaniak," *DB*, xli/17 (1974), 38

R. Waschko: "Any Good Music Can Sell . . . Michal Urbaniak Talks," *JF* [intl edn], no.30 (1974), 41

"Michal Urbaniak: kein Stitz zwischen zwei Stilen," *JP*, xxv/11 (1976), 15
C. J. Gans: "Michal Urbaniak: New York Serenade," *JF* [intl edn], no.73 (1981), 34
L. Jeske: "Michal Urbaniak: Stranger in a Strange Land," *DB*, xlix/5 (1982), 22 [incl. discography]
"Michal Urbaniak: Let's Go Back to the Future," *Jazz World*, no.61 (1984), 3
A. Bausch: *Jazz in Europa* (Echternach, Luxembourg, 1985), 115
M. Bourne: "Riffs: Rhythm and Blu," *DB*, liv/2 (1987), 15
B. Milkowski: "Michal Urbaniak: Michal's Musical Mysteries," *DB*, lv/12 (1988), 24
R. Hultin: *Jazzens tegn* (Oslo, 1991; Eng. trans., London, 1998, as *Born under the Sign of Jazz*)
T. Green: "Funk is the Preacher," *Jazziz*, xi/7 (1994), 31
S. Graham: "Michal Urbaniak," *Jazz on CD*, no.16 (1995), 46
K. Thomas: "Michal Urbaniak: Urban-influenced Jazz Creates a New Genre: Acid Jazz," *Windplayer*, no.57 (1997), 24
<http://www.urbaniak.com> (2000)
C. Szabó: "Michal Urbaniak's Unofficial Discography," <http://members.aol.com/szabocsaba/private/urbaniak.html> (2001)

BK

Urban Sax. French saxophone group formed in 1973 by the multi-instrumentalist Gilbert Artman. Its basic eight pieces is enlarged for performances to about fifty personnel, incorporating female choristers and dancers, all rendered anonymous by wearing masks and a strange white, black, or metal body suit. Each of the group's concerts is unique, because each is a function of the topography of the place where it is held (most often in an open-air setting). Their music, which is repetitive, develops in waves of sound, its spiraling motifs resulting in a strange magic of which recordings can give only a vague idea; a better understanding of its impact may be gained from the video *Live in Tokyo: mirage de son* (1991). Since the inauguration of the Forum des Halles in Paris in 1979, Urban Sax has appeared throughout the world, notably at the carnival of Venice (1981), the world summit of heads of state in Versailles (1982), the inauguration of the museum of contemporary art in Vienna (1993), and the Baalbeck festival in Lebanon (1998).

SELECTED RECORDINGS

Urban Sax 2 (1978, Cobra 37017); *Fraction sur le temps* (1982, Celluloid 66789); *Spiral* (1991, EPM1125); *Live in Tokyo* (1991, Teichiku 48045); *Live in Jakarta* (1995, Awa 95002)

BIBLIOGRAPHY

M. Calonne: "Les manifs d'Urban Sax," *Jm*, no.280 (1979), 36
D. Elliott: "Saxophones of the Apocalypse," *JF* [intl edn], no.89 (1984), 24
W. Panke: "Guerilleros der Kulturpolitik: Urban Sax," *JP*, xxxiv/7 (1985), 10
P. Carles, A. Clergeat, and J.-L. Comolli: *Dictionnaire du jazz* (Paris, 1988, rev. and enlarged 2/1994)

ANDRÉ CLERGEAT

Urso, Phil(ip) (*b* Jersey City, NJ, 2 Oct 1925). Tenor saxophonist. He was brought up in Denver from the age of ten, took up clarinet when he was 13, and studied tenor saxophone at high school; at the age of 16 he joined the navy. Having moved to New York (1947) he played and recorded with Elliot Lawrence (1948–50) and Woody Herman (late 1950 – May 1951). He then performed with Jimmy Dorsey (1951) and Miles Davis (1952) and recorded as a sideman with Don Elliott and Terry Gibbs (both 1952) and Oscar Pettiford (1953) and as the leader of small groups (1953, 1954, 1956, 1958); at one of these sessions (1954) he and Bob Brookmeyer led a quintet in which the sidemen were Horace Silver, Kenny Clarke, and Percy Heath. After working as a freelance musician Urso was with Chet Baker from late 1954 into 1955 and spent about a year playing clarinet and tenor saxophone in a band in Las Vegas. In mid-1956 he rejoined Baker, with whom he toured the USA and then worked in Los Angeles, performing in the trumpeter's small group and recording with both the small group and a big band.

Urso played in the Birdland All Stars in 1957 and worked briefly with Herman that same year before touring in Claude Thornhill's band; the latter group disbanded in 1959 and Urso moved back to Denver. Thereafter he played intermittently with Baker, recording in New York (January 1965) and performing at a restaurant in Pueblo, Colorado (summer 1966), at the Half Note in New York (1972), at a hotel in Denver (March 1985), and in Europe. During a visit to Miami in 1986 he recorded in a sextet which he co-led with Eddie Higgins, the trumpeter Pete Minger, and Allen Eager. However, from the 1960s into the 2000s his principal activity was working as the leader of small groups in Denver, where he also taught music. In the mid-1990s he made a video, *A Night with Phil Urso*, at a party in Boulder, Colorado. Urso is one of the many tenor saxophonists of the 1950s to be influenced strongly by Lester Young.

For illustration *see* JACKSON, MILT.

SELECTED RECORDINGS

As leader: *New Trends of Music*, xii (1953, Savoy 8059) [EP], incl. Little Pres, Three Little Words; with E. Higgins, P. Minger, and A. Eager: *Taking Sides* (1986, Spinster 0008)
As sideman: W. Herman: By George (1951, MGM 10975); C. Baker: *Chet Baker and Crew* (1956, PJ 1224); A. Pepper and C. Baker: *Playboys* (1956, WP 1234)

BIBLIOGRAPHY

FeatherE
A. Morgan: "Woody's Tenors," *JM*, vi (1960–61), no.7, p.4; no.8, p.13; no.12, p.9
I. Gitler: Liner notes, B. Moore and others: *Brothers and Other Mothers*, ii (Savoy 2236, 1979)
A. Katz: "Denver Jazzman has Legendary Past," *Denver Post* (4 March 1990)
S. Woolley: "Phil Urso," *JJI*, xliv/8 (1991), 10
W. D. Clancy with A. C. Kenton: *Woody Herman: Chronicles of the Herds* (New York and elsewhere, 1995), 166
N. Provizer: "Tip of the Horn to Sax Man Phil Urso," *Rocky Mountain News* (19 Dec 1996)

BK

Urtreger, René (*b* Paris, 6 July 1934). French pianist. From the age of four he studied classical piano with such well-known teachers as Marguerite Long. He began playing jazz when he was 17, belonged to a student band, and after winning an amateur contest in 1953 worked professionally with Buck Clayton and Don Byas. Following army service (to 1957) he worked regularly at the Club Saint-Germain in Paris, where he often played in Kenny Clarke's group and accompanied many American soloists, including Miles Davis (with whom he recorded the soundtrack to the film *Ascenseur pour l'échafaud*, 1957), Lester Young, Lionel Hampton, Stan Getz, Chet Baker (with whom he had recorded earlier, in October 1955), Johnny Griffin, Milt Jackson, Dexter Gordon, and Stuff Smith and Stephane Grappelli (recording in 1965); he also joined Clarke at the Blue Note early in 1959. From 1960 to 1961 he was a member of the trio HUM with Daniel Humair and Pierre Michelot, and for much of 1963 he was again with Clarke at the Club Saint-Germain and on tour in Europe and North Africa.

Urtreger interrupted his career in jazz for several years, during which he worked principally as an accompanist for French popular singers, though he was again with Clarke at the Blue Note in 1965–6; he also performed in 1968 with Ben Webster and Johnny Griffin and in 1969 with Jimmy

Gourley, with whom he later recorded (1972). After 1977 he worked regularly again as a jazz musician, both as an unaccompanied soloist and as a leader of small groups, one of which toured France with Sonny Stitt in 1982, and others of which involved Christian Escoudé, Eric Le Lann, Niels-Henning Ørsted Pedersen, Jean-François Jenny-Clark, and Michelot. From 1985 he often appeared at the club Le Montana in Paris. In 1999 HUM made new recordings which were issued together with a reissue of the trio's albums of 1960 and 1979. Although Urtreger's playing is frequently likened to that of Bud Powell, he apparently developed his style before becoming familiar with Powell's music.

SELECTED RECORDINGS

As leader: *Trio* (1955, Barclay 84003); with D. Humair and P. Michelot: *HUM* (1960, Vega 837), *HUM* (1960, 1979, 1999, Sketch 33306–08); *Jazzman* (1985, Carlyne 010); *Serena* (1990, Carlyne 017); *Move* (1995, BB 647)

As sideman: M. Davis: *Ascenseur pour l'échafaud* (1957, Fon. 460603); L. Young: *Lester Young in Paris* (1959, Verve 8378)

BIBLIOGRAPHY

H. Olier: "René Urtreger," *Jh*, no.93 (1954), 14
R. Mouly: "René ou le blues pour Marianne," *Jm*, no.63 (1960), 20
J. Chesnel: "Le roi René," *Jh*, no.358 (1979), 32
F. Marmande: "René Urtreger," *Jm*, no.283 (1980), 8
B. Franceschi: "René Urtreger," *Jm*, no.288 (1980), 19
Y. Lucas: "Urtreger renaît," *Jm*, no.293 (1981), 22
J. M. Bernard: "Pur et tendre Urtreger," *Jh*, no.429 (1986), 16
M. Hennessey: *Klook: the Story of Kenny Clarke* (London, 1990)
P. Anquetil: "René Urtreger: piano forte tête," *Jazzman*, no.175 (1994), 5

ANDRÉ CLERGEAT/BK

Urziceanu, Aura. *See* RULLY, AURA.

Usselton, Billy [William Hugh] (*b* New Castle, PA, 2 July 1926; *d* Tempe, AZ, 5 Sept 1994). Tenor saxophonist. He performed and recorded in swing bands led by Sonny Dunham (1946–8), Ray Anthony (1948–50, 1951–3), and Tommy Dorsey (1950), and during his second period with Anthony he led a group with Bill Harris (i). From 1954 to 1960 he was the principal tenor saxophonist with Les Brown's band, in which capacity he performed, recorded, and toured Europe, North Africa, and the Far East. In 1956 Usselton made his first recording as a leader, *His First Album* (Kapp 1051), and in 1960 he recorded with Frank Capp.

BIBLIOGRAPHY

FeatherE
Obituary, *Washington Post* (9 Sept 1994)

Utyosov, Leonid (Osipovich) (*b* Odessa, Ukraine, 21 March 1895; *d* Moscow, 10 March 1982). Russian singer and bandleader. He studied violin as a child, worked in theaters from 1911, and sang roles in operettas. Later he staged shows in which he sang, danced, played violin, and conducted an orchestra and a choir, and in 1929 he formed a jazz theater orchestra, which he led until 1975. Among the members of the orchestra were several capable jazz musicians; the band acquired a large following, gave thousands of concerts, recorded many tracks (of which seven, dating from 1932 to 1934, are included on *Perviïe shagi* (Mel. M60 45827006), the first album in the series Anthology of Soviet Jazz), and appeared in a film comedy, *Veselïe rebyata* (Merry fellows; 1934). Utyosov was named People's Artist of the USSR in 1965. (S. F. Starr: *Red and Hot: the Fate of Jazz in the Soviet Union, 1917–1980*, New York, and Oxford, England, 1983, rev. 2/1994, as *Red and Hot: the Fate of Jazz in the Soviet Union, 1917–1990*)

WALTER OJAKÄÄR

Vaché, Warren(, Jr.) (*b* Rahway, NJ, 21 Feb 1951). Cornetist. He studied piano from around the age of six and trumpet from when he was about 11, and later changed to cornet and flugelhorn. He began his career playing traditional jazz with his father, a double bass player, bandleader, jazz writer, and impresario, and studied trumpet with Pee Wee Erwin (1970–80). He first earned critical acclaim for a performance with the New York Jazz Repertory Company at Carnegie Hall in 1975, at which he re-created solos by Bix Beiderbecke. He worked with Benny Goodman (intermittently, 1975–85) and was a member of the house band at Eddie Condon's club (1976–9). In 1976 he began playing with Scott Hamilton, forming an association which continued fruitfully into the mid-1980s. They recorded more than 15 albums, and played together under the leadership of Goodman and Woody Herman, in the Concord Super Band (1979–82), and with the Newport Jazz Festival All-Stars (from 1984). Vaché also played with Hamilton's quintet, and in 1985 he appeared in a film, *The Gig*. Later he recorded as a sideman with Dan Barrett (1987) and Howard Alden (1989), and as a leader (1993, 1996). In the 1990s he worked as a freelance (touring Europe) and with a trio.

Vaché became a leading exponent of swing in the 1980s. He was the first major player since Ruby Braff to be inspired by the work of Louis Armstrong (whose influence can clearly be heard on *Cadillac Taxi*, for example), but he also took elements from the playing of other musicians (notably Clifford Brown) and formed them into a style that is immediately recognizable as his own. In 1993, as the leader of a recording session that included Houston Person, Richard Wyands, Joe Puma, Michael Moore (i), and Billy Hart, he dipped into the repertory of bop. Both Vaché and Hamilton have expanded upon the swing tradition, and together they tend to establish the character of any group with which they play.

Vaché's brother, the clarinetist Alan Vaché (*b c*1953), has been a member of Jim Cullum's Jazz Band for over two decades. He made several recordings as a leader from 1982 into the 1990s.

Video oral history material in *NCH* (HCJA).

SELECTED RECORDINGS

(recorded for Concord unless otherwise indicated)

As leader: *First Time Out* (1976, MonE 7081); *Jersey Jazz at Midnight* (1978, Jersey Jazz 1002); *Polished Brass* (1979, 98); *Iridescence* (1981, 153), incl. Sweet and Slow; *Midtown Jazz* (1982, 203); *Horn of Plenty* (1993, Muse 5524)

As leader with S. Hamilton: *In New York City* (1978, 70); *Skyscrapers* (1979, 111), incl. Cadillac Taxi

As sideman: B. Goodman: *Fortieth Anniversary Concert* (1978, Lon. 2PS918-9); D. Hyman: *Music of Jelly Roll Morton* (1978, Smithsonian 006); Concord Super Band: *In Tokyo* (1979, 80); *Concord Super Band II* (1979, 120); W. Herman: *A Concord Jam* (1980, 142); Newport Jazz Festival All-Stars: *The Newport Jazz Festival All-Stars* (1984, 260)

BIBLIOGRAPHY

ConnorBG
M. Jones: "Trumpet out of Time," *MM* (14 June 1980), 19
S. Klett: "Warren Vaché Jr.: Interview," *Cadence*, vi/1 (1980), 11
B. Korall: "Warren Vaché," *IM*, lxx (1980), Jan, 10
J. Wilson: "Cornet Player who Turned Away from Dixieland," *New York Times* (19 Nov 1982), §C, p.6
D. Morgenstern: "Warren Vaché: Classic Cornet," *DB*, l/2 (1983), 24 [incl. discography]
C. Deffaa: "A Profile of Warren," *MR*, xii/5 (1985), 7; repr. in *Swing Legacy* (Metuchen, NJ, and London, 1989), 319
F. Davis: *In the Moment: Jazz in the 1980s* (New York, and Oxford, England, 1986/*R*1996), 82
A. R. Vaché: "Family Ties," *MR*, xvi/5 (1989), 16
G. Endress: "Warren Vaché," *JP*, xxxix/2 (1990), 11
"Interview with Warren Vache [*sic*]," *The Note*, iii/3 (1991), 8
F. Levin: "Warren Vaché, Jr.," *JF* [intl edn], no.133 (1992), 30
J. McLeod: *Jazztrack* (Sydney, 1994), 231
T. Hodgett: "An Interview with Cornetist Warren Vache [*sic*]," *Coda*, no.271 (1998), 8

CHIP DEFFAA/BK

Valdambrini, Oscar (*b* Turin, Italy, 11 May 1924; *d* Rome, 26 Dec 1996). Italian trumpeter and composer. He studied violin and trumpet as a child and in 1948 took part in a jam session with Rex Stewart. With Gianni Basso he led a quintet that recorded in 1952, and performed and recorded with the Sestetto Italiano (1955–7). In 1955 the two men formed the Basso–Valdambrini Quintet, for many years the best-known group in modern Italian jazz, which from 1962, with the addition of the valve trombonist Dino Piana, operated frequently as a sextet. Valdambrini worked with Armando Trovajoli as a trumpeter and arranger (1957–8) and played in orchestras led by Gil Cuppini (1964–71), Giorgio Gaslini (1968–9), Duke Ellington (1968–9), and Maynard Ferguson (1970–71). In 1972 he formed another sextet with Basso, and on the latter's departure in 1974 he led the group as a quintet, then as a sextet that remained active into the 1980s and performed with Dusko Goykovich and Kai Winding. From 1972 he also worked with the Television Orchestra of Rome, in which capacity he played with Frank Rosolino,

Conte Candoli, Freddie Hubbard, Franco Ambrosetti, Ernie Wilkins, and Mel Lewis. He rarely gave concerts in the 1980s and 1990s on account of health problems. Valdambrini had a central role in the emergence of a modern jazz movement in Italy. Playing in a style close to that of Art Farmer, with a brilliant and warm timbre, he mixed dynamic and complex bop lines with a sensibility for lyrical melody. His best-known original works include *Gin Blues* (1952), *Lo struzzo Oscar*, and *Lotar* (1959).

SELECTED RECORDINGS

As leader with G. Basso: Gin Blues (1952, Col. CJ1002); *Basso–Valdambrini Quintet* (1959, Music 2079), incl. Lotar, Lo struzzo Oscar; *The Best Modern Jazz in Italy* (1962, RCA PML10326)
As leader with D. Piana: *Afrodite* (1976, Vedette 8337)

BIBLIOGRAPHY

FeatherE; *Feather–Gitler '70s*

ADRIANO MAZZOLETTI/STEFANO ZENNI

Valdés, Chucho [Jesús, Sr.] (*b* Quivicán, nr San Antonio de los Baños, Cuba, 9 Oct 1941). Cuban keyboard player, composer, and bandleader. As a teenager he directed a band led by his father, Bebo Valdés (who defected to Sweden in 1963). In 1967, with Arturo Sandoval and Paquito D'Rivera, he formed the Orquesta Cubana de Música Moderna, then around 1973 he and other members of this group established Irakere. He became its music director the following year, and in 1981, after D'Rivera and Sandoval left the group, he became its leader. He may be seen in the video *Irakere: Live at Ronnie Scott's* (*c* early 1990s), filmed in 1987 in the course of the band's annual month-long residencies at this London club (1986–96). He has made numerous recordings with the group, and has also recorded occasionally as an unaccompanied soloist and a leader. Valdés teaches at the Beny Moré School of Improvised Music, the Escuela Nacional de Arte, and El Instituto Superior de Arte, and serves as president of Jazz Plaza (the annual Havana jazz festival). He worked at the Banff Centre for the Arts in Alberta, Canada, in 1995, and the following year obtained an educational visa enabling him to lecture and perform in the USA with two other members of Irakere. At the Umbria Winterfest in Italy (late 1996) he performed with the New York/Havana/San Juan Superband, which then recorded under Roy Hargrove's leadership (January 1997) and took the name Crisol; Valdés returned to America to tour as a sideman with Crisol in 1997. At some point during these last two years (accounts are unclear) he also held a week-long residency at Bradley's in New York, gave three concerts with the Lincoln Center Jazz Orchestra, and appeared at the Village Vanguard with Hargrove. His activities in Cuba from 1997 have involved unaccompanied performance and the formation of a new quintet of trumpet, piano, double bass, drums, and percussion. He continues to perform in the USA, and in 1998 at the Chicago Jazz Festival gave his last performance with Irakere; he then handed its leadership over to his son, Luis, and toured with his own quartet. His compositions include *100 años de juventud* (1979).

SELECTED RECORDINGS

As unaccompanied soloist: *Lucumi* (1986, Messidor 15976)
As leader: *Solo Piano* (1991, BN CDP7-80597-2)
For further recordings *see* Irakere.

BIBLIOGRAPHY

J. Brody: "Chucho, le piano d'Irakere," *Jm*, no.334 (1984), 10
S. Steward: "Cubana be, cubana bop," *The Wire*, no.21 (1985), 26
F. Bouchard: "Hands Across the Gulf: Chucho Valdes," *JT*, xxvi/8 (1996), 50
——: "Riffs: Chucho Valdés Lights up a Havana in Boston," *DB*, lxiii/5 (1996), 12
M. Holston: "Cuba!: a Chat with Chucho," *Jazziz*, xv/1 (1998), 58
J. Koransky: "Chucho Valdés: 'The Piano Plays Me'," *DB*, lxvi/3 (1999), 29

CRISTÓBAL DÍAZ AYALA/BK

Valdez, Carlos "Patato" (*b* Havana, 4 Nov 1926). Cuban conga player and percussionist. His nickname has often been misspelled as "Potato." He moved in 1953 to the USA, where he played with the Latin bands of Machito and Tito Puente. From 1959 to 1972 he played with Herbie Mann, with whom he toured Africa in 1960 and made several recordings (including *Live at Newport*, 1963, Atl. 1413). He also recorded with Kenny Dorham (1955), Art Blakey (1957), Dizzy Gillespie (1959, 1971), Art Taylor (1960), Max Roach (1961), Duke Pearson (1968), Dave Liebman (1974), and the pianist Jorge Dalto (1985), made recordings demonstrating Latin percussion techniques, and recorded as a leader (*Masterpiece*, 1984–5, EFA 15827-2). From the mid-1980s until the leader's death in 1993 he performed and recorded as a member of Mario Bauzá's big band. He also recorded with the trombonist Papo Vazquez (1991), Hilton Ruiz (1993), and the pianist Bebo Valdés (1994), and as a co-leader with José Luis "Changuito" Quintana and Orestes Vilató (*Ritmo & Candela: Rhythm at the Crossroads*, *c*1994, Mlst. 9503-2).
Oral history material in *DSI* (JOHP).

BIBLIOGRAPHY

FeatherE; *Feather '60s*
J. Brody: "Carlos Patato Valdes," *Jm*, no.340 (1985), 28

CATHERINE COLLINS

Valente, Gary (L.) (*b* Worcester, MA, 26 June 1953). Trombonist. He began playing trombone at the age of eight, taking initial instruction from his father, Frank Valente, who was also a trombonist. At the New England Conservatory (1971–4) he studied composition with Jaki Byard and recorded with the New England Conservatory Jazz Repertory Orchestra (1974). In 1973 he joined Tony Dagradi's group Inner Visions. After moving to New York (1977) he became a member of George Russell's Living Time Orchestra (with which he recorded in 1978) and performed in Byard's big band the Apollo Stompers (1978–80), which held a weekly residency at Ali's Alley and also toured. In 1978 he recorded with the double bass player Marcello Melis, and in 1979 he joined Carla Bley, with whose small and large ensembles he appeared as a featured soloist into the new century. He worked in the large group led by the pianist Larry Harlow (1980–81), toured the USA with Maynard Ferguson (1981), and toured and recorded (1982) in Charlie Haden's Liberation Music Orchestra. From 1982 to 1986 Valente taught at the New England Conservatory, and from the mid-1980s he worked in Ed Schuller's group Eleventh Hour. He held extended associations with Cab Calloway (1985–94), Joe Lovano's World Ensemble (1989–96, recording in Amiens, France, in 1989 at the festival Le Temps du Jazz), and Andy Sheppard's large ensembles Soft on the Inside and Big Co-Motion (to 1995); he is featured on Sheppard's recording *Soft on the Inside* (1989) and appears in the video documentary of the same name (1990). From 1987 to 1990 he co-led a quintet with the tenor saxophonist Bob Hanlon.

While continuing with Bley, Valente toured Europe with Don Byron in 1994, and that year he was a founding member, with Craig Harris, Ray Anderson, and George Lewis (ii), of the cooperative trombone quartet Slideride, which performed at the International New Jazz Festival Moers in 1996. He worked in George Gruntz's Concert Jazz Band and the Louis Armstrong Legacy Band (under the leadership of Arvell Shaw) (both from 1994), David Murray's big band (from 1995), Lester Bowie's Brass Fantasy (1995–9, recording in 1997), and Chico O'Farrill's Afro-Cuban Big Band (1996–7). In the late 1990s Slideride participated in a tribute to Duke Ellington co-led by James Newton and Murray, and during the same period Valente formed a new quintet consisting of Lew Soloff, the pianist Arturo O'Farrill, Jr., the double bass player Tim Engles, and the drummer Vinnie Johnson. In 1999 he performed in Bley's group 4+4 at the Lugano Estival Jazz.

SELECTED RECORDINGS

As leader with R. Anderson, C. Harris, and G. Lewis: *Slideride* (1994, HA 6165)

As sideman with C. Bley: *Social Studies* (1980, Watt 11); *Live!* (1981, Watt 12), incl. The lord is listening to ya, hallelujah!; *Fleur Carnivore* (1988, Watt 21); *The Very Big Carla Bley Band* (1990, Watt 23); *Big Band Theory* (1993, Watt 25); *The Carla Bley Big Band Goes to Church* (1996, Watt 27)

As sideman with others: T. Dagradi: *Oasis* (1980, Gram. 8001); C. Haden: *The Ballad of the Fallen* (1982, ECM 1248); G. Schuller: *Looking Up from Down Below* (1986–8, GM 3013), incl. Pasta Episodes (n.d.); J. Lovano: *Worlds* (1989, Label Bleu 6524); A. Sheppard: *Soft on the Inside* (1989, Ant. 422-842927-2), incl. Adventures in the Rave Trade (Smoking), Rebecca's Silk Stockings; on *Rhythm Method* (1993, BN B21Z-27798), Sofa Safari; E. Schuller: *The Force* (1994, Tutu 888166-2), incl. The Force, Playing for Keeps; Joe Mulholland: *Second Sight* (1995, Jazzheads 9497); M. Maneri: *Acceptance* (1996, Hatology 512)

GK

Valentin, Dave (*b* New York, 29 April 1952). Flutist. His year of birth has appeared in reference sources as 1952, 1953, and 1954, but he gives 1952 in his video oral history. He learned percussion as a child and was playing conga and timbales professionally by the age of 13. When he was 17 he began teaching himself flute, and he later studied with Hubert Laws. From the late 1970s Valentin played a fusion of Latin music, funk, and jazz as the leader of various groups, with the pianist and electronic keyboard player Bill O'Connell, Lincoln Goines, either Richie Morales or Robby Ameen on drums, and either Sammy Figueroa or Giovanni Hidalgo on percussion. In addition he recorded with the violinist Noel Pointer and the singer Patti Austin (both 1977), Lee Ritenour (1977–8), Dave Grusin (1978, *c*1997), Chris Connor (1987), David Benoit (*c*1987), Eliane Elias (*c*1997), and Dave Samuels and Nnenna Freelon (both *c*1998). Valentin plays conventional Western flutes as well as ethnic instruments collected on his travels around the world. He may be seen in the video *Wolf Trap Salutes Dizzy Gillespie: a Tribute to the Jazz Master* (1988), which was taken from an episode of the television series "Great Performances."

Video oral history material in *NCH* (HCJA).

SELECTED RECORDINGS

As leader: *Kalahari* (*c*1984, GRP 1009); *Live at the Blue Note* (1988, GRP 9568); with H. Mann: *Two Amigos* (1990, GRP 9606); *Tropic Heat* (*c*1993, GRP 9769)

As sideman with E. Elias: on *The Three Americas* (*c*1997, BN 53328-2), Caipora, Crystal and Lace, The Time is Now, An Up Dawn

BIBLIOGRAPHY

T. Sabournin: "Dave Valentin Escapes Pop-jazz," *VV* (8 Oct 1980), 76

P. Carles, A. Clergeat, and J.-L. Comolli: *Dictionnaire du jazz* (Paris, 1988, rev. and enlarged 2/1994)

J. M. Davis: "Dave Valentin: '... Not Too Spicy, but Just Right ...'," *Windplayer*, v/5 (1988), 10

D. Townsend: "Dave Valentin," *JT* (1988), Jan, 13

W. R. Pinckney, Jr.: "Puerto Rican Jazz and the Incorporation of Folk Music: an Analysis of New Musical Directions," *Latin American Music Review/Revista de musica Latino Americana*, x/2 (1989), 236

M. Holston: "A Magic Flute with Crossover Tones," *Américas*, xliv/2 (1992), 56

L. Kohanov: "Dave Valentin's Family Portrait," *JT*, xxii/4 (1992), 31

<http://fantasma.com/artist_rep/artist-dave_valentin.html> (1999)

GK

Valentine, Jerry [Gerald Graham] (*b* Chicago, 13 Sept 1914; *d* New York, Oct 1983). Arranger and trombonist. His date of birth has been published as 14 September, but he gave 13 September, as well as his full name, in his application for social security. Although he received tuition in piano, composition, and harmony as a youth, he taught himself to play trombone. He worked initially with Earl Hines as a composer and arranger and then performed and recorded with and composed and arranged for Billy Eckstine (1944–7). Later he worked as an artists and repertory adviser for National (iii) (1950–52) and wrote arrangements for sessions by the Prestige Blues Swingers (1958, 1959), an all-star group that included Art Farmer, Pepper Adams, and Coleman Hawkins. Details of his death are taken from the social security death index.

SELECTED ARRANGEMENTS

Recorded by E. Hines: The Jitney Man (1941, Bb 11535); Second Balcony Jump (1942, Bb 11567)

Recorded by B. Eckstine: Blowin' the Blues Away (1944, DeLuxe 2001); I'll wait and pray (1944, DeLuxe 2002); on *Billy Eckstine Orchestra 1945* (1945, Alamac 2415), Love me or leave me

BIBLIOGRAPHY

FeatherE; *McCarthyB*

I. Gitler: *Jazz Masters of the Forties* (New York, 1966/*R*1983 with discography), 277

Valentine, Kid Thomas [Thomas, Kid; Valentine, Thomas] (*b* Reserve, LA, 3 Feb 1896; *d* New Orleans, 16 June 1987). Trumpeter and bandleader. He began playing at the age of ten. When he was 14 he joined the Pickwick Brass Band, of which his father was a member, and four years later he formed a band with Edmond Hall and other members of Hall's family. In 1922 he moved to New Orleans, where from the early 1930s he led his own band. He became associated with the dance-hall proprietor Specks Rodriguez in the late 1930s, playing for him at various venues in Louisiana – notably at the Moulin Rouge in Marrero (from World War II into the 1950s). Valentine made his first recordings in 1951. He began working at Preservation Hall when it opened in 1961 and in the mid-1980s continued to lead his band the Algiers Stompers, sometimes under the name of the PRESERVATION HALL JAZZ BAND; he also toured overseas with the group on numerous occasions. Its regular members included Emanuel Paul, Louis Nelson, Joe Butler, and the drummer Sammy Penn; Alcide "Slow Drag" Pavageau and Albert Burbank are among others who spent a substantial period with the group. Valentine may be seen in the film documentary *'Til the Butcher Cuts Him Down* (1971) and the television documentary "American Patchwork: Songs and Stories of America, no.101: Jazz Parades: Feet Don't Fail Me Now" (1990).

Valentine developed an individual style that was allusive, elliptical, impressionistic, and, above all, rhythmic. A superb lead trumpeter, he would state the melody sparsely but in a forthright manner, before exploding into a progression of little rhythmic clusters of white-hot notes, jabbing through the ensemble with his wide vibrato and searing tone. His use of various mutes was a strong characteristic of his playing; on *Panama*, for example, he generally employed a plunger mute in a performance that was both electrifying and highly comical, then changed to a metal derby to build to the climax of the piece. Occasionally, on slower numbers such as *Just a closer walk with thee*, he could be heard taking a solo; using a harmon mute he played softly and with great poignancy.

Oral history material in *LNT*.

SELECTED RECORDINGS

As leader: *Kid Thomas' Algiers Stompers* (1951, AM 642); *Kid Thomas at Moulin Rouge* (1956, Center 14); *Kid Thomas Valentine's Creole Jazz Band* (1959, 77 LA9), incl. Panama; *Kid Thomas and his Algiers Stompers* (1965, Jazz Crusade 2006); *Kid Thomas at Kohlman's Tavern* (1968, La Croix 4–5); on *Original Jass Band and Kid Thomas' Jazz Band in Scandinavia* (1964, 1971, Rarities 16), Just a closer walk with thee (1971); *Kid Thomas 1981* (1981, Lulu White's Black Label 033)

As sideman with J. Robinson: *Jim Robinson and his New Orleans Band* (1964, Center 8)

BIBLIOGRAPHY

H. Souchon: "Speck's Moulin Rouge," *SL*, vii/2 (1956), 7

T. Bethell: "Kid Thomas: his Recordings," *Jazz Times*, iv (1967), no.6, p.7; no.7, p.9; no.8, p.27; no.9, p.9

R. B. Allen: Liner notes, *Thomas Valentine at Kohlman's Tavern* (New Orleans 7201, 1972)

T. Stagg and C. Crump: *New Orleans, the Revival: a Tape and Discography of Negro Traditional Jazz Recorded in New Orleans or by New Orleans Bands, 1937–1972* (n.p. [London], 1973)

C. De Vore: "The True New Orleans Sound of Kid Thomas Valentine," *MR*, i/4 (1974), 1

D. M. Marquis: "The King of Old-time Jazz," *Passages: the Magazine of Northwest Orient Airlines*, ix/2 (1978), 10

B. Martyn: "The People Pleaser from Algiers," *Fn*, xi/1 (1979), 14

M. Tovey: "Kid Thomas Valentine: his Musical Background and Early Years," *Fn*, xi/1 (1979), 4

Almost Slim [J. Hannusch]: "Kid Thomas," *Wavelength*, i/6 (1981), 12

B. Martyn: "Rattle of a Simple Man," *Fn*, xviii/6 (1987), 21

P. Van Vorst: "A New Orleans Original: Kid Thomas Valentine (1896–1987)," *MR*, xiv/10 (1987), 1 [incl. discography]

W. Carter: *Preservation Hall: Music from the Heart* (Wheatley, Oxford, England, and New York, 1991)

R. H. Knowles: *Fallen Heroes: a History of New Orleans Brass Bands* (New Orleans, 1996)

J. De Donder: "Sweet Memories: Kid Thomas Valentine and his Dixieland Band," *New Orleans Music*, vi/5 (1997), 6

D. Griffiths: *Hot Jazz from Harlem to Storyville* (Lanham, MD, New Brunswick, NJ, and London, 1998), 42

MICHAEL TOVEY/BK

Valide. A hybrid trombone with both slide and valves used in jazz by Brad Gowans; *see* TROMBONE, §1.

Vamp. A short passage, which is simple in rhythm and harmony, played in preparation for the entry of a soloist; it is usually repeated ad libitum until the soloist is ready, hence the rubric "vamp till ready." The term is applied to the technique of playing ostinatos before or between solos, and, by extension, during or after solos. For example, on Miles Davis's recording of *Someday my prince will come* (on the album of the same title, 1961, Col. CS8456), Wynton Kelly improvises a delicate piano ostinato until Davis enters with the melody, and the band repeats the vamp at the end of the piece. Although the term "vamp" may be almost synonymous with "ostinato," it carries the additional idea that duration is at the discretion of a soloist. In jazz-rock, Latin jazz, and other fusions of jazz and popular music, and especially in modal jazz, an entire piece may be based on a succession of open-ended vamps. Vamps have also made their way into jazz through borrowings from various types of ethnic music, as heard, for example, in Abdullah Ibrahim's use of a typical Xhosa harmonic pattern (the alternation of two major chords separated by a whole tone) on *Namhanje (Today)* from his album of duos with Johnny Dyani, *Echoes from Africa* (1979, Enja 3047). (B. D. Kernfeld: *Adderley, Coltrane, and Davis at the Twilight of Bebop: the Search for Melodic Coherence (1958–59)* (diss., Cornell U., 1981), 158)

DEANE L. ROOT/BK

Van Bavel, Rob (*b* Breda, Netherlands, 16 Jan 1965). Dutch pianist. His father was a classical pianist, and he studied classical piano and accordion. He heard jazz at the Old Style Jazz Festival in his home town and began playing jazz piano after listening to recordings by Oscar Peterson, Bill Evans (ii), and Chick Corea. From 1982 he studied piano at the conservatory in Rotterdam. After gaining his degree in 1987, and that same year placing second in the Thelonious Monk Jazz Piano Competition in Washington, DC, he studied composition and arranging. From 1990 van Bavel has been a member of the quintet led by Jarmo Hoogendijk and Ben van den Dungen; he also played with the Dutch Jazz Orchestra and in the quartets of the tenor and soprano saxophonist Ad Colen and the singer Ronald Douglas, and worked with such Americans as Woody Shaw, Slide Hampton, Johnny Griffin, and Bob Mintzer. He has led his own octet, trio, and quintet (with the tenor saxophonist John Ruocco among his sidemen), and has recorded with the quintet (*Daydreams*, 1989, RVB 9101/89) and in a duo with the double bass player Marc van Rooij (*Duo*, 1994, RVB 9103/94). He teaches at the Royal Conservatory in The Hague and at Amsterdam's high school for fine arts.

WIM VAN EYLE

Van Bergen, Peter (*b* Tubbergen, Netherlands, 13 March 1957). Dutch tenor saxophonist and E♭ and contrabass clarinetist. He started on flute at the age of nine and changed to alto (1980) and then tenor saxophone (1981) while at the Royal Conservatory in The Hague (1977–84). From 1980 to 1982 he led a trio (with Martin van Duynhoven, and sometimes Wilbur Little) which played Thelonious Monk's compositions. Soon afterwards he assembled the first edition of LOOS, his major creative outlet, whose membership stabilized in 1990 with the pianist Gerard Bouwhuis, the electric guitarist Huib Emmer, and the drummer Paul Koek (replaced in 1997 by Johan Faber), sometimes augmented by the electric guitarist Patricio Wang and the singer and actor Dennis Rudge. Its sound – often characterized by long silences followed by a cued dissonant chord – was influenced both by Monk and by van Bergen's period in Hoketus (1983–5), an orchestra organized by the composer Louis Andriessen, which played music of similar conceptual rigor.

LOOS places complex restrictions on the role of the improvising soloist, van Bergen included. As a saxophonist his work is better displayed in various improvised meetings with European and North American musicians. He is attracted to the extreme sounds of Evan Parker (with whom he studied in 1990–92) and John Gilmore; he manipulates split-tones and overtones with precision on all his instruments, sometimes modified through electronic devices.

Van Bergen played in Cecil Taylor's Berlin orchestra in 1988 and in 1992 became a member of the reed trio Holz für Europa (with Wolfgang Fuchs and Hans Koch). His taste for gaming strategies and strong clear ideas made him a natural ally of Maarten Altena (1985–95) and Guus Janssen (from the early 1990s), as in the opera *Noach*, where van Bergen's elephantine howls were given prominence. When drafted into a more traditional setting, however, he is a thoughtful melodic improviser with a sumptuous tone and a gentle touch on old ballads.

SELECTED RECORDINGS

As leader of LOOS: *Fundamental* (1992, Geestgronden 10); *De tragische handeling [Actus tragicus]* (1995, Composers' Voice 58); *Armstrong* (1999, Okkadisk 12034)

As sideman: M. Altena: *Quick Step* (1985, Claxon 86.16); C. Taylor: *Alms/ Tiergarten (Spree)* (1988, FMP CD8–9); King Übü Örchestrü: *Binaurality* (1992, FMP CD49); G. Janssen: *Noach: an opera off Genesis* (1994, Composers' Voice 42–43 and Geestgronden 13); Holz für Europa: *Comité imaginaire* (1995, FMP CD84)

BIBLIOGRAPHY

F. van Leeuwen: "Ik heb een hekel aan gezellig getoeter" [I dislike happy tooting], *Jazzjaarboek*, vi (1987), 60

H. van Westen: "In Loos is meer aan de hand dan in de bebop revival" [Loos is about more than the bebop revival], *Jazz nu*, no.115 (1988), 316

J. Corbett: "Quick Reeds from Europe: 3 Saxophone Trailblazers," *Option*, no.55 (1994), 44

J. Oskamp: "You Can Hear the Players Thinking During the Silence," *Key Notes*, xxix/2 (1995), 7

B. Andriessen: *Tetterettet: interviews met Nederlandse improviserende musici* (Ubbergen, Netherlands, 1996), 229

K. Whitehead: *New Dutch Swing* (New York, 1998), 296

KEVIN WHITEHEAD

Van Breedam, Camiel (*b* Boom, Belgium, 29 June 1936). Belgian trombonist. He studied piano from 1948 to 1954, in 1966 took up tuba, which he played in a local brass band, and in 1969 changed to trombone and traditional jazz. With his brother Johnny, a trumpeter and the leader of the Red Roses Brass Band, he opened the Jazzclub het Veerhuis in Willebroek in 1970 (*see* Nightclubs and other venues); the following year they formed the Fondy Riverside Bullet Band, with which Camiel later recorded (*Red Roses for a Blue Lady*, 1982, Fondy 7775). He made frequent visits to New Orleans, performed at festivals in Europe, and recorded several albums with such musicians as Alvin Alcorn and the pianist Jeannette Kimball. He continued to perform and record with the Fondy Riverside Bullet Band in the 1990s. Van Breedam plays a style of traditional jazz influenced by the work of Jim Robinson. (P. Chielens and J. Gerber: "Het dubbeltalent van Camiel Van Breedam," *'t pebbeltje*, no.17 (1986), 8)

MARCEL JOLY

Vance, Dick [Richard Thomas] (*b* Mayfield, KY, 28 Nov 1914 or 1915; *d* New York, July or August 1985). Trumpeter and arranger. His essential dates have appeared in reference sources as 28 November 1915 and July or August 1985; the social security death index reports his death as having taken place in July 1985 but gives a birthdate of 28 November 1914. He grew up in Cleveland, where he studied violin before taking up trumpet. After touring with the trombonist and bandleader Frank Terry (1932–4) and working for brief periods with Lil Armstrong (1934–5), Kaiser Marshall (at the Ubangi Club and Harlem Uproar House, 1935), and Willie Bryant, he served as the lead trumpeter in Fletcher Henderson's band (1936 – summer 1938), in which he also occasionally sang; he remained lead trumpeter even after Russell Smith (formerly in that role) rejoined the band in October 1936. Vance then transferred to Chick Webb's group as a trumpeter and arranger (?summer 1938–1939), and following the leader's death he remained in the band under Ella Fitzgerald's leadership (1939–41). During the 1940s he wrote arrangements for several bands, including those of Glen Gray, Cab Calloway, Don Redman, Billy Eckstine, and Harry James; he also performed with Redman, Barnet, Eddie Heywood (1944-5), Henderson again (briefly in March 1944, and for several months in 1950), and many others. Vance was a member of the trumpet section in Duke Ellington's band in 1951–2 and arranged most of the items on the album *Ellington '55* (1953–4, Cap. W521). He then worked as a freelance into the 1980s. In 1969 he toured abroad with his own band, which appeared in the film *L'aventure du jazz* (1970). He played with Eddie Barefield (recording an album as a soloist with the latter's small group, *c*1970), gave a performance in Paris in a group accompanying Carrie Smith (1977), and took part in the shows *One Mo' Time* and *Bubbling Brown Sugar*; he also taught a jazz course at CUNY. Vance's playing is not well represented on recordings, but he may be heard at his best with Henderson's group on *Sextet* (1950); his warm tone and lyrical swing style on this album suggest the reasons for his popularity during his prime.

SELECTED RECORDINGS

As leader: on [no leader]: *L'aventure du jazz II* (1969, Jazz Odyssey 002), Tin Roof Blues

As sideman: M. L. Williams: Stardust (1944, Asch 5521); F. Henderson: *Sextet* (1950, Alamac 2444); R. Stewart: on *The Big Reunion* (1957, Jzt. 1285), Honeysuckle Rose; on [no leader:] *A Basket of Blues* (1962, Spivey 1001), L. Hegamin: Number 12

BIBLIOGRAPHY

AllenH; *ChiltonW*; *FeatherE*; *Feather–Gitler '70s*; *McCarthyB*

C. Battestini and J.-P. Battestini: "Dick Vance," *BHcF*, no.296 (1982), 8

SCOTT YANOW

Van de Geyn, Hein (Petrus Johannes) (*b* Schijndel, Netherlands, 18 July 1956). Dutch double bass player. He learned classical violin for 15 years, began playing electric bass guitar in his teens, and later studied classical music at a conservatory in Tilburg (1974–9). His success as the leader of a bop band at the Laren Jazz Festival (1977) persuaded him to take up double bass seriously, and he subsequently studied jazz double bass at a conservatory in Rotterdam (1979–80); he was greatly influenced by Scott LaFaro's recordings. In 1979 Van de Geyn recorded with the alto saxophonist Mark Lewis, and the following year he traveled to the USA to tour with his group. He lived in Seattle before moving in 1981 to San Francisco, where he played with John Abercrombie and Larry Schneider. After returning to Europe (1983) he worked with, among others, Philip Catherine (from 1985), Chet Baker (1985–8, touring Japan in 1987), Dee Dee Bridgewater (1988–96), and Tete Montoliu (1992). In addition he played in a duo with Lee Konitz (1990–2) and gave recitals as an unaccompanied soloist (from 1995). From 1994 he led the group Baseline, which was initially a trio with Abercrombie and Joe LaBarbera and became a quartet when the dancer Annabelle Lopez Ochoa joined in 1998. Van de Geyn co-founded the record company and label Challenge with Anne de Jong and Joost Leijen in 1994 and was appointed head of the bass section of the jazz department at the Royal Conservatory in The Hague in 1996.

SELECTED RECORDINGS

As leader of Baseline (all recorded for Challenge): *Why Really* (1994, 70002); *Standards* (1994, 70023); *Returns* (1996, 70047)

Duos: with L. Konitz: *Hein Van de Geyn Meets Lee Konitz* (1990, September 5110); with Leonardo Ameudo: *Dolphin Dance* (1994, Challenge 70008)

As sideman: H. Verbeke: *Mo de bo* (1985, Tim. 246); J. Lovano: *Solid Steps* (1986, Jazz Club 6011); L. Schneider: *Milanka* (1987, Tim. 254); C. Baker: *Four: Chet Baker in Tokyo* (1987, PW [Jap.] K28P6495); P. Catherine: *September Sky* (1988, September 5106); *I Remember You* (1990, Criss Cross 1048); K. Wheeler: *California Daydream* (1991, Musicdisc 500292); P. Catherine: *Moods*, i–ii (1992, Criss Cross 1060–61); T. Montoliu: *Music for Anna* (1992, Mas 002); D. D. Bridgewater: *Keeping Tradition* (1992, Verve 314-519607-2); *Love and Peace: a Tribute to Horace Silver* (*c*1994, Verve 314-527470-2); E. Pieranunzi: *Seaward* (1995, SN 121272-2); T. Thielemans: *Chez Toots* (1996, Private Music 01005-82160); Soesja Citroen: *Songs for Lovers and Losers* (1996, Challenge 70034); L. Konitz: *Dialogues* (1997, Challenge 70053)

BIBLIOGRAPHY
F. Marmande: "La vie du jazz," *Jm*, no.403 (1991), 28
M. Bedin: "Hein Van de Geyn," *Jh*, no.557 (1999), 16

MARK GILBERT

Van den Broeck, Rob(bert) (*b* Hilversum, Netherlands, 1 Dec 1940). Dutch pianist. After studying graphic design at the Rietveld Academy in Amsterdam and music in Hilversum he played with a jazz-rock ensemble, the Chris Hinze Combination (1972–4), and worked with such visiting Americans as Ben Webster. In 1974 he formed the ensemble Free Fair, which comprised the saxophonist Dick Vennik, the double bass player Harry Emmery, and Eric Ineke; the group expanded in 1979 to include four trumpets and four trombones and broadcast from Hilversum with the Metropole Orchestra in 1999. Van den Broeck also joined the jazz-rock group Third Eye in 1974, which had been founded earlier by Ali Haurand and the Dutch pianist Jan Huydts (whom van den Broeck replaced). Between 1975 and 1977 he played piano alongside the guitarist Eef Albers for the Dutch Ballet Theatre, and from 1977 he toured and recorded with Haurand and various others, notably Gerd Dudek, in a trio and in the European Jazz Quartet, the European Jazz Quintet, and the European Jazz Ensemble; the European Jazz groups remained active into the 2000s. In the late 1990s van den Broeck worked in an ensemble with the singer Masha Bijlsma, Benny Bailey, Tony Lakatos, and the double bass player Gulli Gudmanson, formed a duo with the double bass player Wiro Mahieu, and led a quartet which consisted of Dudek, Mahieu, and Tony Levin.

SELECTED RECORDINGS

Duos with W. Mahieu: *Departures* (1997, Greenhouse 1004)
As leader: *Heavy Duty* (1986, Tim. 220); with G. Dudek and A. Haurand: *Pulque* (1993, Konnex 5055); with A. Haurand and J. Stivín: *Bordertalk* (1994, Konnex 5068); *Halloween Time* (1999, VIA 9920842)
As sideman: E. Albers: *Skyrider* (1981, Vara Jazz 206); J. Farrell and L. Hayes: *Vim 'n' Vigor* (1983, Tim. 197); M. Bijlsma: *Profile* (1998, Jazzline 11157)

MARK GILBERT

Van den Dungen, Ben [Bernardus Bartholomeus] (*b* The Hague, 29 Oct 1960). Dutch tenor and soprano saxophonist. After graduating from the Royal Conservatory in The Hague, in 1983 he formed a successful and long-lived quintet with Jarmo Hoogendijk (for recordings *see* HOOGENDIJK, JARMO). He also played with Nueva Manteca (from 1984), the guitarist Paul Hock (from 1987), Fra Fra Sound (1987–9), Loek Dikker (1988–91), Eveline and the Groove Movement (1992–7), Brand New Orleans (1994–6), and Louis van Dijk's Super Band and the Cubop City Big Band (both from 1996). In addition to performing with such American jazz musicians as Mal Waldron, Art Taylor, Woody Shaw, Jimmy Knepper, Kirk Lightsey, Lester Bowie, and Cindy Blackman, van den Dungen has worked with many leading musicians in Latin music. He teaches at the Rotterdam Conservatory and leads workshops.

WIM VAN EYLE

Vander(schueren), Maurice (*b* Paris, 11 June 1929). French organist and pianist. He performed and recorded with Don Byas (1951, 1955), Django Reinhardt (1952–3), Bobby Jaspar (1952, 1954, 1955), Jimmy Raney (1954), Stephane Grappelli (1955–6), Chet Baker (1956, 1977), and Kenny Clarke (1957, 1959, 1980), and undertook extensive studio work with Roger Guérin's group Les Baroques (1964) and Pierre Gossez and Boulou Ferré (both 1964–5). From 1965 he accompanied the singer Claude Nougaro, though at the same time he worked as a leader (recording occasionally from 1955). He appeared in the film short *Max Roach (Ciné jazz)* (1967), took part with several pianists in the recording of *Piano Puzzle* (1970, Saravah 10011, 10015), and performed as a sideman with Ivan Jullien (1968), Johnny Griffin (1975), Richie Cole (1980), Benny Powell (1981), Art Farmer (1989), and Stephane Grappelli (with the accordionist Marcel Azzola, 1994). He is highly regarded for his inspired bop style, which bears some resemblance to that of Bud Powell; his blues playing may be heard on a recording with Joe Newman, *Blues on the Champs-Elysées* (1956, Véga V35S758).

BIBLIOGRAPHY
A. Clergeat: *Dictionnaire du jazz* (Paris, 1966)
J. P. André: *Dictionnaire du jazz* (Paris, 1988)
F. W. Sportis: "Le jazz ... et la java," *Jh*, no.561 (1999), 34 [incl. discography]

MICHEL LAPLACE

Vandermark, Ken (*b* Warwick, RI, 11 Sept 1964). Tenor saxophonist, clarinetist, bass clarinetist, and leader. He grew up in Boston and studied film at McGill University in Montreal, where he took up saxophone and joined a trio, Fourth Stream (which recorded around 1984). Having returned to Boston in 1986 he worked in the trio Lombard Street with the double bass player Peter Warren and the drummer Curt Newton. In 1989 he settled in Chicago. He deputized for the saxophonist Mars Williams in Hal Russell's NRG Ensemble, though after Russell's death he became a permanent member of the group. From 1991 he worked alongside the electric guitarist Todd Colburn and the drummer Michael Zerang in a quartet led by the double bass player Kent Kessler. The following year he took over the group's leadership, and around 1994 Colburn was replaced by Daniel Scanlan, who played violin, cornet, and electric guitar; the quartet performed weekly at the Hothouse club until it disbanded around 1996.

Vandermark performed with the pianist Jim Baker and the drummer Steve Hunt in the cooperative trio Caffeine (recording *c*1994) and played in the "no-wave" group the Flying Luttenbachers (1992–4). In 1994 he joined Hamid Drake and Kessler in the DKV trio. He was a member of the group Steam (with Baker, Kessler, and the drummer Tim Mulvena) from 1995, and in the same year he formed Cinghiale, a free-jazz reed duo with Williams. In addition he worked in Williams's Witches & Devils, which payed tribute to Albert Ayler, the Boston-based trio Tripleplay, with the double bass player Nate McBride and Newton, and FJF (originally Free Jazz Four), with Mats Gustafsson, Kessler, and Hunt. As well as these and more transitory groups, often involving the same musicians, he led the Barrage Double Trio (until 1995, involving Williams, Kessler, McBride, Drake, and Newton), the Steelwood Trio (until 1997, with Kessler and Newton), the Vandermark 5 (from *c*1996), and an instrumental rhythm-and-blues group, the Crown Royals. In 1996 he appeared as the leader of a sextet at the International New Jazz Festival Moers and performed and recorded in Chicago in a trio with Joe McPhee and Kessler. In Sweden that same year he recorded with the AALY Trio, led by Gustafsson, which plays after the manner of Ayler's free-jazz trio, and with this group he toured the USA in 1998, recording in Chicago. From 1997 Vandermark concentrated on Steam, the Vandermark 5, and the DKV trio, while maintaining associations with the NRG Ensemble, Caffeine, the Barrage Double Trio, and Cinghiale. He also performed with various visiting free-jazz musicians such as Peter Brötzmann and Joëlle Léandre and worked occasionally with Fred Anderson and with the drummer Robert Barry (a former sideman of Sun Ra). In June 1999 he was awarded a prestigious "genius" grant by the MacArthur Foundation, but on the strength of his recordings it is unclear why.

Vandermark is a creative and energetic musician whose work reflects the eclectic approach of his generation; his saxophone playing and compositional style are situated in free-jazz, funk, and rock, and he routinely combines elements of these and various other genres into a musical pastiche. The same approach has been pursued by Matt Wilson and many others from Boston and New York.

SELECTED RECORDINGS

As leader: *Solid Action* (1994, Platypus 002); with J. McPhee and K. Kessler: *A Meeting in Chicago* (1996, Eighth Day 80008); with AALY Trio: *Hidden in the Stomach* (1996, Silkheart 149); of Vandermark 5: *Target or Flag* (1997, Atavistic 106)

As sideman: Lombard Street: *All that Falls* (1989, [self-produced cassette]); NRG Ensemble: *Calling all Mothers* (1993, Quinnah 05); Caffeine: *Caffeine* (*c*1994, Okka Disk 12002); Steelwood Trio: *International Front* (1995, Okka Disk 12005); Steam: *Real Time* (1996, Eighth Day 80010); F. Anderson: *Fred Anderson/DKV Trio* (1996, Okka Disk 12014)

BIBLIOGRAPHY

P. Margasak: "Sax at Large," *Chicago Tribune* (22 July 1993)
A. Cohen: "Riffs: Vandermark Debut Explores Internal Grooves," *DB*, lxi/4 (1994), 14
D. Lewis: "Beyond Hal Russell: the Legacy of NRG," *Coda*, no.275 (1997), 4
P. Margasak: "Post no Bills," *Chicago Reader* (4 April 1997); repr. <http://www.chireader.com/hitsville/970404.html>
<http://pages.ripco.com:8080/~nailhead/history2.html> (1998)
<http://www.portaudio.com/bios/vandermark_bio.html> (1998)
J. Corbett: "Freedom Fighters: Ken Vandermark & Joe McPhee Compare Notes on Creative Music Renaissances," *DB*, lxvi/1 (1999), 38 [incl. discography]
B. Meyer: "Arts & Etc.: Quick, Name a Jazz Band that Ken Vandermark *isn't* in," *Chicago Tribune* (11 April 1999)

BK, GK

Van Dijk, Louis (*b* Amsterdam, 27 Nov 1941). Dutch pianist. He studied piano and organ at the Sweelinck Conservatory in Amsterdam and from 1960 to 1964 led a quartet with the vibraphonist Carl Schulze; he also appeared at the jazz festival in Loosdrecht, near Hilversum, in 1961. With John Engels and the double bass player Jacques Schols he formed a trio in 1964 that remained in existence until the late 1970s and made several recordings, including *Triology* (1975, CBS 80527). He recorded often as an unaccompanied soloist and performed or recorded with the arranger and conductor Rogier van Otterloo, Ann Burton, Rita Reys, the classical pianist Daniel Wayenberg, Pim Jacobs, Niels-Henning Ørsted Pedersen, Toots Thielemans, the Dutch Swing College, and the singer Soesja Citroen (1996). He works with his group Louis and Friends (with his daughter, the singer Selma van Dijk, Frits Landesbergen, and the double bass player Edwin Corzilius), and his Superband, which includes, among others, Jarmo Hoogendijk and Ben van den Dungen. Van Dijk is also a classical pianist who specializes in the works of J. S. Bach; he has played with a number of symphony orchestras.

WIM VAN EYLE

Van Duynhoven, Martin (*b* Boxmeer, Netherlands, 13 June 1942). Dutch drummer. He took up snare drum as a child and later studied at the conservatory in Tilburg (1959–60). In 1963 he moved to Amsterdam and became involved in performances associated with the art movement Fluxus. (He has been interested in visual arts as long as in music, and sees his second career as a designer – where his work has a clean and stylishly orderly look – as influencing his clean and orderly drumming.) As one of the busiest drummers in the Netherlands, van Duynhoven toured and performed in the 1960s and 1970s with Don Byas, Ben Webster, Dexter Gordon, Mal Waldron, and Roswell Rudd, among others, as well as with such Dutch leaders as the trumpeter Boy Edgar, the trumpeter and pianist Nedly Elstak, and Theo Loevendie. In 1976 he studied with Andrew Cyrille in New York, and on his return he recorded an album of music scored for four drummers, two tenor saxophones, and banjo. He led his own groups in the 1980s and 1990s, and made a second, typically precise, album under his own name. In the latter decade, however, he was heard mostly with Ab Baars's trio.

Van Duynhoven tunes his drums carefully and produces a wealth of timbres from his hi-hat and other cymbals; a careful listener, he often visits clubs and jam sessions to hear other drummers. His meticulous style can be especially effective when juxtaposed with more overtly expressive players, as in Baars's trio.

SELECTED RECORDINGS

As leader: *In A.M.* (1976, [no label]); *Uitkrant* (1987–92, MVD 9602)

As sideman: N. Elstak: *The Machine* (1968, ESP 1076); B. Edgar: *Live in Shaffy* (1973, White Elephant 888.017); R. Rudd: *Maine* (1976, BVHaast 011); T. Loevendie: *Orlando* (1977, Waterland 003); A. Baars: *Sprok* (1994, Geestgronden 14); *A Free Step* (1997, Geestgronden 20)

BIBLIOGRAPHY

E. Determeyer: "De heldere hectische wereld van Martin van Duynhoven" [The hectic, transparent world of Martin van Duynhoven], *Jazz nu*, no.75 (1985), 120
K. Stevens: "In Gesprek met ... Martin van Duynhoven" [In conversation with Martin van Duynhoven], *Jazz freak*, xii/3 (1985), 95
T. Beetz: "Het ergste is niet gekleed" [The worst is not being dressed for the occasion], *Jazz nu*, no.115 (1988), 302
K. Whitehead: *New Dutch Swing* (New York, 1998), 115

KEVIN WHITEHEAD

Van Eps, George (Abel) (*b* Plainfield, NJ, 7 Aug 1913; *d* Newport Beach, CA, 29 Nov 1998). Guitarist. He was brought up in a musical family; his mother played piano and his father, Fred (F.) Van Eps, Sr. (*b* 30 Dec 1878; *d* Los Angeles, Co., 22 Nov 1960), was an internationally known ragtime banjoist (*see* Banjo). George taught himself banjo and by the age of 11 was playing professionally; two years later, influenced by Eddie Lang, he took up guitar, and by the time he was 15 he was active as a teacher. He played with Smith Ballew (1929–31, working for a six-month period alongside Lang) and with Freddy Martin (1931–3), Benny Goodman (1934–5), and Ray Noble (1935–6). From 1936 to 1940 he worked as a freelance studio musician in Hollywood, where he wrote a definitive text on guitar playing and designed a seven-string guitar (adding a bass string tuned to *A'*) which enabled him to play his own bass lines. After a further period with Noble (1940–41) he worked in his father's sound recording laboratory (1941–3), then returned to the West Coast to continue as a freelance; he took part in the film *Pete Kelly's Blues* (1955) and the subsequent television series of the same name (1959). Despite illness Van Eps continued to play at festivals in the 1960s and 1970s, and in 1986 he performed in Europe with Peanuts Hucko. He participated in Dick Cathcart's Pete Kelly reunions in the late 1980s. Later he recorded with Howard Alden in a small group and in a duo, in the process inspiring the younger guitarist to take to the seven-string instrument – hence the clever CD titles *13 Strings* (Van Eps's seven plus Alden's six, recorded in a quartet in 1991), followed by *Seven and Seven* (their duo of 1992). By this time Van Eps had taken his move toward playing in the bass range literally one step further, and was tuning all seven strings down one whole step (thus *G'-D-G-c-f-a-d'*). In 1993 he performed with Alden and toured in Ed Polcer's Salute to Eddie Condon. His unique sound and innovative harmonic mastery are well represented by *Lover* and *The Blue Room*, on the album *Soliloquy*.

Van Eps was the author of instructional books, including a *Guitar Method* (Ft. Lauderdale, FL, n.d.) and a celebrated series, *Harmonic Mechanisms*, i–iii (Pacific, MO, 1980–82). Transcribed collections of his compositions and solos have appeared as *Van Eps Collection* (Boston, *c*1970s), *Original Guitar Solos* (Ft. Lauderdale, FL, *c*1980s), and *Guitar Solos* (Pacific, MO, *c*1993).

Van Eps had three brothers, all of whom were professional musicians: John(ny) (18 Feb 1906 – 29 Jan 1997), a saxophonist and clarinetist, also worked with Ballew when George and Bobby were in the band; later he recorded with Tommy Dorsey and Joe Haymes (both 1935), Ray Noble (1936), Larry Clinton (1938–9), Jack Teagarden (1939), and Will Bradley (1941). Freddy (Fred, Jr.) (2 July 1907 – April 1980), a trumpeter, played with the California Ramblers (1928–31) and worked as an arranger for Jack Teagarden's orchestra (1939). Bobby (Robert) (*b* New Jersey, 10 March 1909; *d* Los Angeles Co., 23 April 1986), a pianist, worked with Red Nichols (1928, 1958), Smith Ballew (1929–30), Freddy Martin (1933), the Dorsey brothers (1934–5), Jimmy Dorsey (1935–7), and Kid Ory (1961).

SELECTED RECORDINGS

As unaccompanied soloist: *Soliloquy* (1968 or 1969, Cap. ST267), incl. The Blue Room, Lover

Duos: with Frank Flynn: *My Guitar* (1966, Cap. ST2533); with H. Alden: *Seven and Seven* (1992, Conc. 4584)

As leader: I wrote it for Jo/Kay's Fantasy (1949, Jump JA1); *Mellow Guitar* (1956, Col. CL929); *George Van Eps' Seven-string Guitar* (1967, Cap. ST2783); with H. Alden: *13 Strings* (1991, Conc. 4464)

As sideman: A. Rollini: Somebody Loves Me (1934, Decca 359); R. Norvo: Bughouse (1935, Col. 3079D); R. Noble: Dinah (1935, Vic. 25223); E. Miller: Back Home/It's easy to remember (1946, Jump 16); J. Stacy: Indiana (1951, Bruns. 80172); M. Matlock: *Pete Kelly's Blues* (1955, Col. CL690); W. B. Davison: *Wild Bill Davison Plays the Greatest of the Greats* (1958, Dixieland Jubilee 508)

BIBLIOGRAPHY

ChiltonW; *FeatherE*; *Feather '60s*; *Feather–Gitler '70s*

J. Tynan: "George Van Eps: a Master Guitarist's Reflections and Comments," *DB*, xxxi/21 (1964), 16

M. J. Summerfield: *The Jazz Guitar: its Evolution and its Players* (Gateshead, England, 1978, 4/1998, as *The Jazz Guitar: its Evolution, Players and Personalities since 1900*)

M. Grosz and L. Cohn: Liner notes, *Giants of Jazz: the Guitarists* (TL 12, 1980), 23

T. Greene: "George Van Eps: Harmonically Speaking, the Greatest Ever," *GP*, xv/8 (1981), 78 [incl. discography]

J. Ferguson: "George Van Eps on Eddie Lang," *GP*, xvii/8 (1983), 85

I. Mairants: "George Van Eps: Living Legend and Guitarist Extraordinary," *Classical Guitar*, v/11 (1987), 18

M. Falcon: "Between Two Worlds: George Van Eps: the Gentle Jazz Giant of New Jersey, Master of the Seven-string Guitar," *Soundboard*, xix/4 (1993), 73

J. Ferguson: "Harmonic Major," *GP*, xxviii/1 (1994), 77

Obituaries: P. Watrous, *New York Times* (7 Dec 1998); A. Shipton, *The Times* (28 Dec 1998); A. Levy, *GP*, xxxiii/4 (1999), 39

BRIAN PEERLESS

Van Gelder, Rudy (*b* Jersey City, NJ, *c*1925). Recording engineer. In the late 1940s he created a recording studio in the living room of his parents' home in Hackensack, New Jersey, and began recording as a hobby. An optometrist by profession, he became the principal recording engineer for Blue Note in 1953, and the following year he began working for Prestige (to 1969) and Savoy as well. After abandoning optometry, in July 1959 he moved into a newly built home and studio in Englewood Cliffs, New Jersey. He also made numerous recordings for Cadet, CTI, Elektra Musician, Enja, GRP, Impulse!, Kudu, Milestone, Muse (ii), Reservoir, Riverside, and Verve.

Van Gelder's skill at getting a proper mix of instruments directly onto the master tape (long before multiple-channel recording existed) was exemplary, and his clean, crisp, well-balanced drum-kit sounds were especially noteworthy. Perhaps his most distinctive aural signature was the tight, boxy sound of his small Steinway grand piano. Although his output slowed from the frenetic pace he set during the 1950s and 1960s, he continued to work, and in the late 1980s he changed to digital technology.

BIBLIOGRAPHY

B. Korall: "Rudy van Gelder: the Well-tempered Engineer," *Metronome*, lxxii/1 (1956), 24

P. Nahman: "Monsieur van Gelder," *Jm*, no.83 (1962), 30

M. Cuscuna: "The Blue Note Story" (New York, 1984) [liner notes enclosed with many Blue Note reissues]

M. Seidel: "Rudy Van Gelder," *DB*, lvii/9 (1990), 22

"The Rudy Van Gelder Interview," *Mosaic Records Catalogue*, no.9 (*c*1991), 22

T. Pérémarti: "Chasin' the Trane: Coltrane's Sound," *Jh*, no.491 (1992), 44

T. Owens: *Bebop: the Music and its Players* (New York, and Oxford, England, 1995), 255

B. Cardvilland: "All that Jazz," <http://njmonthly.com/issues/aug97/articles/jazz.html> (1997)

C. Hovan: "Rudy Van Gelder Interview," <http://www.allaboutjazz.com/iviews/vangelder.htm> (1999)

<http://npr.org/ramfiles/weed/19990130.weed.05.ram> (1999) [radio interview]

THOMAS OWENS

Vanguard. Record company and label. The company was established in New York in 1950 by Maynard Solomon and Seymour Solomon. Although devoted mainly to classical music, it also made important contributions to the jazz repertory. The label Vanguard Jazz Showcase was used between 1953 and 1959 to issue recordings produced by John Hammond. These were put out under the sponsorship of the magazine *Down Beat* (the logo of which also appeared on the record labels) and included, most importantly, the first issues of recordings made in 1938–9 at concerts in Hammond's series "From Spirituals to Swing." Among other items, newly recorded for the label between 1953 and 1957, were albums by Vic Dickenson, Sir Charles Thompson, Buck Clayton, Urbie Green, Mel Powell, Jimmy Rushing, Ruby Braff, Don Elliott, Count Basie (in the first recordings made for commercial purposes of performances at the Apollo Theatre, New York), and Rolf Kühn.

While its jazz activities decreased in the 1960s, during the following decade Vanguard made recordings of jazz-rock and other types of fusion, most importantly by Larry Coryell and Oregon. The company was purchased by the Welk Music Group of Santa Monica, California, in 1986, but in 1990 Seymour Solomon reacquired the classical catalogue. The Welk Music Group's reissues on compact disc were then organized into three areas: the Vanguard Sessions Series, drawn from in-house recording sessions and including some previously unreleased material; the Generations Series, offering a varied collection of folk, blues, and bluegrass; and a revival of the Vanguard Jazz Showcase, but involving compilations from various sessions rather than corresponding in a logical way to the original issues. In 2000 the collection "From Spirituals to Swing" was reissued with 14 previously unreleased tracks (12 from these concerts and two from one of Hammond's sessions misleadingly woven into the original LPs).

BIBLIOGRAPHY

<http://www.vanguardrecords.com/history-m.html> (2000)
H. Rye: "From Spirituals to Swing," *Names & Numbers*, no.16 (2001), 7

BK

Vanguard Jazz Orchestra. Big band which sustained and continued the traditions of the Thad Jones–Mel Lewis Orchestra and its successor, the Mel Lewis Jazz Orchestra; it was formalized as the Vanguard Jazz Orchestra following Lewis's death in 1990 and took its name from the Village Vanguard, the group having played at the New York club on Monday nights from the era of the Jones–Lewis orchestra. By the mid-1990s its ad hoc leaders were John Mosca and Dick Oatts. It continued to perform much of the repertory associated with its predecessors (notably the arrangements of Jones and Bob Brookmeyer), but it also commissioned new works from Jim McNeely, a former orchestra member; in 1997 it recorded *Lickety Split: the Music of Jim McNeely* (New World 80534).

BIBLIOGRAPHY

B. Korall: "Riffs: 30 Years of Monday Nighters," *DB*, lxiii/2 (1996), 10
M. Holston: "Big Bands: Still in the Vanguard," *Jazziz*, xv/2 (1998), 35
<http://www.nyjam.com/content/artists/vanguard.html> (2000)

GK

Van Ha Trio. Belgian rhythm section. Formed in 1965, its original members were the double bass player Roger Van Haverbeke (*b* Ostend, Belgium, 1930), the drummer Freddy Rottier, and the pianist Tony Bauwens (later replaced by Johan Clément). It accompanied many leading American soloists, including Clark Terry, Johnny Griffin, Art Farmer, Joe Newman, and Jerome Richardson.

ROBERT PERNET

Van Hove, Fred (*b* Antwerp, Belgium, 19 Feb 1937). Belgian pianist. He studied classical piano from the age of ten, became interested in bop in the early 1950s, and by 1962 had developed a modal style of playing that showed the influence of John Coltrane. After meeting Peter Brötzmann at a festival in Comblain-la-Tour, Belgium, he joined the latter's quartet; later he played in a trio with Brötzmann and Han Bennink (1969–75). He also worked as an unaccompanied soloist (from 1970) and in a duo with the saxophonist Cel Overberghe (1972–4) and recorded with Manfred Schoof's orchestra (1969), Don Cherry and the New Eternal Rhythm Orchestra (1971), and Lol Coxhill (1979, 1983), among many others. Following a dispute with the organizers of the 1972 Middelheim Jazz Festival over higher rates paid to visiting American musicians, van Hove formed the musicians collective WIM (Werkgröp Improviserende Musici), of which he has remained chairman.

From 1978 van Hove led groups whose names utilized the initials ML. The first of these, MLA (Musica Libera Antwerpen), was a septet of three stringed instruments, three brass instruments, and piano. In 1979 he formed MLA Blek, comprising Marc Charig, Radu Malfatti, and Paul Rutherford. From 1980 to 1982 he led MLDD 4 with Charig, Phil Wachsmann, and Günter Sommer. When he was artist-in-residence at the Deutscher Akademischer Austauschdienst in Berlin in 1983, all three groups played concerts and performed with local musicians in a series of MLBB (Berliner Begegnungen [Berlin encounters]). In 1984 he formed the trio MLB III (Musica Libera Belgicae) with the saxophonist André Goudbeek and the percussionist Ivo vander Borght; a new trio with the singer Annick Nozati and Johannes Bauer recorded and toured in 1988. In the 1990s his main group was t'Nonet, formed in 1991 and involving musicians from all his previous groups.

In 1984 van Hove formed the Belgisch Pianokwartet, with four pianists at two grand pianos. It originally consisted of Christian Leroy, Eddy Loozen, and Walter Hus; Marilyn Crispell later replaced Hus, and the group took a new name, t'Pianokwartet. From the mid-1980s onwards van Hove toured Japan several times, playing unaccompanied solos and duos with a wide variety of musicians, including Peter Kowald, Evan Parker, and Barry Guy. He also continued to perform alone and in duos throughout Europe, working with, among others, Steve Lacy, Albert Mangelsdorff, Wachsmann, and Brötzmann again (in Antwerp in 1995).

Besides his work in jazz, van Hove has, from 1976, provided solo accompaniment to silent films, to comedies, and to animations, written music for films and the theater, and collaborated with poets and painters. As an organist he has recorded (1979), performed at festivals in Sinzig, Germany (1980, 1982), and Lille, France (1982), and toured Germany (1985). He has regularly held improvisation seminars and workshops in Belgium, the Netherlands, Germany, Britain, and, from 1990, at the Département d'Etudes Musicales of the University of Lille.

SELECTED RECORDINGS

(recorded for FMP unless otherwise indicated)

As unaccompanied soloist: *Live at the University* (1974, Vogel 004); *Verloren maandag* (1977, SAJ11); *Church Organ* (1979, SAJ25); *Prosper* (1981, SAJ39); *Letzte* (1986, SAJ58); *Passing Waves* (1997, Nuscope 1001)

Duos: with C. Leroy: *Au pavillon de la garde* (1981, Igloo 010); with B. Guy: *Assist* (1985, Jazz & Now 4); with S. Lacy: on *Five Facings* (1996, CD85), Twenty-one

As leader: with P. Brötzmann, H. Bennink, and A. Mangelsdorff: *The End* (1971, 0050), *Live in Berlin '71* (1971, CD34–5); with P. Brötzmann and H. Bennink: *Brötzmann, van Hove, Bennink* (1973, 0130), *Outspan nr.2* (1974, 0200); of MLA Blek: *MLA Blek* (1980, SAJ32); of MLDD 4: *Was macht ihr denn?* (1982, SAJ42); of MLBB: *Berliner Begegnung* (1983, SAJ47); of MLB III: *MLB III* (1988, BVHaast 073); with J. Bauer and A. Nozati: *Johannes Bauer/Annick Nozati/Fred van Hove* (1988, Amiga 8 56411); of t'Nonet: *Suite for B... City* (1996, CD88)

As sideman: P. Brötzmann: *Machine Gun* (1968, 0090); M. Schoof: *European Echoes* (1969, 0010); D. Cherry: *Actions* (1971, Wergo 1010); L. Coxhill: *Couscous* (1982–3, Nato 157); R. Malfatti: *Ohrkiste* (1992, ITM Classics 950013); J. Bauer: *Organo pleno* (1992, CD56)

BIBLIOGRAPHY

GrayF
G. Rouy: "Belgique: Fred Van Hove," *Jm*, no.220 (1974), 24 [incl. discography]
——: "Fred van Hove: une force c'est manifestée parmi nous," *Jm*, no.262 (1978), 35
G. Märtens: "Fred van Hove," *Jazz 360°*, no.18 (1979), 2
B. Noglik: "Fred van Hove," *Jazzwerkstatt international* (Berlin, 1981), 47 [incl. discography]
B. Shoemaker: "Fred van Hove: Belgium," *Coda*, no.180 (1981), 12 [incl. discography]
J.-L. Leroy: "Propos de et sur Fred van Hove," *Jazz 360°*, no.56 (1983), 4
G. Cerutti: *Fred van Hove Discography, 1968–1983 (on Records)* (Sierre, Switzerland, 1984)
E. Jost: *Europas Jazz, 1960–1980* (Frankfurt am Main, Germany, 1987), 121
<http://www.shef.ac.uk/misc/rec/ps/efi/mvanhove.html> (1998) [incl. discography]

M. Chénard: "Tearing Down Walls: Fred van Hove," *Coda*, no.284 (1999), 18 [incl. discography]

ROBERT J. IANNAPOLLO/SIMON ADAMS

Van Kemenade, Paul (*b* Rotterdam, Netherlands, 17 May 1957). Dutch alto saxophonist. He took up alto saxophone at the age of 13, studied at the Brabants Conservatory in Tilburg, and became a professional musician in 1976. He led his own groups (including a quintet, heard on *Live*, 1996, HLPm 73083) and worked with the double bass players Ed de Vos and Niko Langenhuijsen, the group Brevis, Willem van Manen's Contraband, the octet led by the double bass player Eric van der Westen, and the guitarist Maurice Leenaars. As a member, with Wolter Wierbos (trombone) and Jan Kuiper (guitar), of the cooperative Podium Trio, van Kemenade toured internationally and recorded the albums *Take One* (1992, CD Diskus 04) and *Podium Trio with Jamaaladeen Tacuma and Cornell Rochester* (1996, RN Disc 006). He also appeared as a freelance with a large number of musicians, among them Han Bennink, Ernst Glerum, Misha Mengelberg, Wierbos, Sean Bergin, the Berlin Contemporary Jazz Orchestra, the Surinam Music Ensemble, Alex Schlippenbach, Aki Takase, Kenny Wheeler, Louis Moholo, Jasper van 't Hof, and Cecil McBee. He has taught jazz workshops from 1979, and he organizes programs for various jazz concert series and festivals.

WIM VAN EYLE

Van Lake, Turk [Hovsepian, Vanig] (*b* Boston, 15 June 1918). Guitarist and composer. He was first associated with big bands and wrote arrangements for Chick Webb (1937) and performed and recorded with Charlie Spivak and Teddy Powell (both 1941). After working with Georgie Auld (1941–2) he played with Sam Donahue (1942) and performed and recorded with Charlie Barnet (1943–4); a second period with Auld (1944–5) was followed by work as an arranger for Count Basie, Lionel Hampton, Buddy Rich, and Benny Goodman (1945–8). Later Van Lake recorded with Terry Gibbs (1953, 1955, 1956), Sarah Vaughan (1955), and Eddie "Cleanhead" Vinson (1957), led his own quartet, performed and recorded with the trumpeter Les Elgart (1954–8), and toured and recorded with Goodman (November 1958 – April 1959); he is heard to advantage on *Cheerful Little Earful/Lollypop* (1953, Bruns. 80219), which he recorded with Gibbs. During the 1960s he accompanied various singers, among them Nancy Wilson. In addition he toured the USSR with Goodman (1962) and recorded with Herbie Mann (1965). (*ConnorBG*; *FeatherE*; *Feather '60s*)

van Manen, Willem (Christiaan) (*b* Amsterdam, 3 Sept 1940). Dutch trombonist, composer, and leader. In the late 1950s he played dixieland. When he later became interested in modern jazz he took private lessons from a classical trombonist to improve his technique, and by 1968 he was an esteemed improviser in ensembles led by the arranger and bandleader Boy Edgar, Theo Loevendie, and Hans Dulfer. He also performed with Willem Breuker and the ICP, and in 1974 became a mainstay of Breuker's Kollektief, with which he recorded and toured extensively for a decade. In 1972 van Manen was a founder of the modern wind ensemble de Volharding, of which he remained a principal member until 1998, and together with the saxophonist Herman de Wit he founded a big band for amateur musicians, de Boventoon. In 1979 his interest in exploring new possibilities for the big-band repertory led to his own "alternative" 13-piece group, the Springband, which was succeeded in 1985 by the 14-piece Contraband. In 1979 he recorded his first album as a leader, the eponymous *Willem van Manen*, on which he demonstrated his ample technique and his witty, sophisticated approach to improvisation. From the 1980s he has been recognized as a composer who fuses contemporary classical traditions and jazz elements in a variety of settings, from symphonic pieces to chamber opera; his composition *Trajekten*, written in 1981, was recorded by Orkest de Volharding on *Trajekten 1972–1992* (1991–2, NM Classics 92021).

SELECTED RECORDINGS

As unaccompanied soloist and in duos with M. Mengelberg: *Willem van Manen* (1979, BVHaast 027) [also incl. trio tracks]

As leader of Contraband: *Hittit* (1997, BVHaast 9802)

As sideman: W. Breuker: *Muziek in Amsterdam* (1980, BVHaast 502); L. Cuypers: *Zeeland Suite and Johnny Rep Suite* (1974, 1977, BVHaast 9307)

BIBLIOGRAPHY

R. Koopmans: "Willem van Manen over trombonisten" [Willem van Manen about trombone players], *Jazz nu*, iv/5 (1982), 168

B. Vuijsje and S. Korteweg: "Ik verbeeld me dat ik de trombone in Nederland heb geëmancipeerd" [I'd like to think that I have emancipated the trombone in the Netherlands], *Jazzjaarboek*, v (1986), 24

B. Andriessen: *Tetterettet* (Ubbergen, Netherlands, 1996), 78

K. Whitehead: *New Dutch Swing* (New York, 1998), 73

ERIK VAN DEN BERG

Vann [Vanslembrouck], **Erwin** (*b* Anvers, Belgium, 17 Dec 1963). Belgian tenor and soprano saxophonist. Self-taught on flute from the age of seven, he later studied classical flute and saxophone (1975–83), and then jazz (from 1983), taking courses or masterclasses with Richard Beirach, Roger Kellaway, Joe Lovano, and Dave Liebman (1987–9). In 1985 he joined the BRT (Belgische Radio & Televisie) Big Band, and in 1986 he became a member of Richard Rousselet's quintet and of Felix Simtaine's Act Big Band, with which he recorded that same year (the album *Extremes*, Igloo 044) and again in 1996. Vann led his own quintet from 1988, and in 1989 he formed a trio including Dré Pallemaerts, with which he recorded the album *Some Sounds* (1990, Jazz Club de Belgique 6012). The trio continued through the 1990s, sometimes expanded to a quartet with the addition of various guest soloists, among them Marc Ducret. In 1997 Vann recorded with Paolo Fresu. He has taught at the academy of music in Amay and at the conservatories in Ghent, Brussels, and Luxembourg.

BIBLIOGRAPHY

R. Pernet, J.-P. Schroeder, and others: *Dictionnaire du jazz à Bruxelles et en Wallonie* (Liège, Belgium, 1991)

J. M. Hacquier: "Erwin Vann," *Jh*, no.535 (1996), 14

R. Pernet: *Belgian Jazz Discography (1897–1999)* (Brussels, 1999)

<http://www.jazzinbelgium.org/mus/vann.htm> (2000) [incl. discography]

BK

Van Roon, Marc (*b* The Hague, 2 Nov 1967). Dutch pianist and composer. He studied in New York and at the Royal Conservatory in The Hague (1985–91), during which time he worked with Clark Terry and Dave Liebman. As the leader of a trio he toured Europe and the USA and appeared at festivals, including the North Sea event; the group has recorded from 1988 (notably *Relaxin'*, 1991, Mirasound 399047). Van Roon also recorded as the leader of a group including Liebman (*Falling Stones*, 1994, Mons 874730), with the saxophonist Dick de Graaf (1995), and in the cooperative European Jazz Trio, consisting of the double bass player

Frans van der Hoeven and the drummer Roy Dackus (from 1995; in particular *Immortal Beloved*, 1996, Meldac 30019, and with Art Farmer as guest soloist, 1997–8). While continuing to work with his trio, van Roon plays with the Ebony band, in the trio for the singer Peggy Larson, and with Ack van Rooyen and Tony Overwater. He composed ballet music for Djazzex and the Nederlands Danstheater. (<http://ourworld.compuserve.com/homepages/air/Marc2.htm> (1999))

WIM VAN EYLE

Van Rooyen, Ack (*b* The Hague, 1 Jan 1930). Dutch trumpeter and flugelhorn player. He first toured with a big band at the age of 16, performing for troops in Indonesia. He attended the Royal Conservatory in The Hague (1947–50) and played with Ernst van 't Hoff (1951) while working in the Arnhem Symphony Orchestra. In 1954 he joined a sextet led by his brother, the trumpeter Jerry van Rooyen, and then was a member of the Ramblers (1955–7). He worked in France with Aimé Barelli (1957–60), Kenny Clarke, Lucky Thompson, Barney Wilen, and others, and in Germany for Sender Freies Berlin as a member of a sextet which included Herb Geller, Jerry van Rooyen, and Cees See (1960–67); he also played with Hans Koller and Åke Persson. From 1967 to 1978 he lived in Stuttgart, where he joined Erwin Lehn's orchestra and Wolfgang Dauner's Radio Jazz Group; he was a founding member of Peter Herbolzheimer's Rhythm Combination and Brass (1969) and of the United Jazz and Rock Ensemble (1975), and remains with both. Van Rooyen made recordings with big bands led by Klaus Weiss (in performance at the Domicile in Munich, 1971), Friedrich Gulda (1972), Charlie Antolini (1972–80), Slide Hampton (1974), Gustav Brom (1976), and Koller (1977, 1980), and with Eberhard Weber (1973) and the quartet of the guitarist Stephan Dietz (1978); at the same time he worked as an arranger for radio orchestras. As a member of the German All Stars he toured South America in 1968 and Asia in 1972, and recorded in 1969. In 1977, with Dauner, Albert Mangelsdorff, Werner Schretzmeier, and Volker Kriegel, he founded the record company and label Mood.

In 1979 Van Rooyen toured with Clark Terry, Gil Evans, and Lee Konitz, and he taught in Germany. In the following year he returned to settle in the Netherlands, where he was active as a freelance; he appeared on television with Evans and Louie Bellson and performed at the North Sea Jazz Festival with Shelly Manne, Dizzy Gillespie, and his own ensembles. He joined the Skymasters (broadcasting with Konitz in 1980 and 1982), and he recorded with Jerry van Rooyen and the Metropole Orchestra (1981), with Barbara Dennerlein and Herbolzheimer's big band (1986), and as a soloist in small groups led by the singer Sylvia Droste (1983), the Dutch guitarist Eef Albers (also 1986), the German tenor saxophonist Paul Heller (1994), and the singer Soesja Citroen (1996). In the 1990s he often worked with the Dutch Jazz Orchestra (recording in 1993) and Netherlands Concert Jazzband and in a duo with the pianist Jörg Reiter (recording in 1991), as well as performing and recording with Herbolzheimer, and touring and recording annually with the United Jazz and Rock Ensemble. He teaches at the Royal Conservatory of The Hague and holds workshops and coaches bands throughout Europe.

SELECTED RECORDINGS

As leader: *Didn't We?* (1970, RCA LSP10299); *Homeward* (1982, Mood 28633); with Metropole Orchestra: *Colores* (*c*1989, Koala 21)

As sideman: E. Weber: *The Colors of Chloe* (1973, ECM 1042); B. Dennerlein: *Tribute to Charlie* (1986, Koala 14)

BIBLIOGRAPHY

CarrJ

G. Endress: "Ack van Rooyen," *JP*, xxxv/8 (1986), 4

WIM VAN EYLE

Van Ruller, Jesse (*b* Amsterdam, 21 Jan 1972). Dutch guitarist. He took up guitar at the age of seven and later attended the conservatory in Hilversum (1990–95). He continued his studies at Miami University, Ohio (MM 1995), and in 1995 won the Thelonious Monk International Jazz Guitar Competition in Washington, DC. While teaching at the conservatory in Amsterdam, van Ruller has played with Pim Jacobs, Rita Reys, the group Fleurine Plus Five, Christian McBride, Ralph Moore, Tom Harrell, George Duke, Mike Stern, Kenny Washington, the band SfeQ, the Metropole Orchestra, Harry Connick, Jr., Joe Lovano, and the Dutch Jazz Orchestra. He may be heard with his own quintet on the albums *European Quintet* (1996, Bluemusic 1002) and *Herbs, Fruits, Balms and Spices* (1998, Bluemusic 1003). (A. Ballhorn: "Jesse van Ruller," *JP*, xlv/3 (1996), 24)

WIM VAN EYLE

Van 't Hof, Jasper (*b* Enschede, Netherlands, 30 June 1947). Dutch keyboard player. His father was a professional trumpet player and his mother a classical singer. He began piano lessons at the age of five. By the age of 19 he was performing at jazz festivals with Pierre Courbois and the guitarist Toto Blanke, among others; with Blanke he formed a quartet that appeared at the jazz festival in Loosdrecht, near Hilversum, in 1970. He played in Association PC (1970–72), led by Courbois, and with Chris Hinze (1973, recording in 1974), George Gruntz's group Piano Conclave (1974), and Archie Shepp (1974). From 1973 he led the group Pork Pie with Charlie Mariano and Philip Catherine; other members of this group were Jean-François Jenny-Clark and Aldo Romano (who were replaced by Bo Stief and John Marshall for its last recording in 1975).

By 1976 the members of Pork Pie had become too busy with other projects to maintain a commitment to the group, and in January of that year van 't Hof resumed playing with Blanke in a cooperative free jazz trio with Edward Vesala, though he continued to work with Mariano into the 1980s, often as a duo, and he formed small groups involving Jenny-Clark, Romano, Stief, and Marshall. He also worked with Jean-Luc Ponty (1975–7), Mouzon (intermittently into the late 1980s), and Manfred Schoof (recording in 1976–7, performing in 1977). From 1974 he recorded many albums as a leader, with such sidemen as Zbigniew Seifert, John Lee, and Gerry Brown (1974) and Bob Malach (1977–1990s); his group Eyeball, which recorded in 1980, consisted of Malach, Didier Lockwood, Steif, and Romano. He also recorded in duos with Shepp (1982, 1987) and Malach (from *c*1990) and in the trio Total Music with Hinze and Sigi Schwab (both 1982), and he performed and recorded as an unaccompanied soloist. In 1981 he led a quartet which included Christof Lauer. In 1985, during a concert tour of Africa with Trilok Gurtu, he founded his successful group Pili Pili, featuring a fusion rhythm section together with African percussion and such soloists as Schoof and Tony Lakatos; it recorded regularly into the 1990s. Van 't Hof also recorded with Uli Beckerhoff (1987), Mariano (1991), David Friedman (1992), and Greetje Bijma (1996). In 1993 he toured Britain with Barbara Thompson's band Sans Frontières, and 1994 he formed a trio, Freezing Screens, with Pierre Favre and Bijma, which recorded in concert in Germany in that year.

SELECTED RECORDINGS

As unaccompanied soloist: *Solo Piano* (1987, Tim. 286)
As leader: *My World of Music* (1981, Kt. 3-100); with P. Catherine and C. Mariano: *Sleep my Love* (1978–9, CMP 5); with J. Kühn: *Balloons* (1982, MPS 15590); *Pili pili* (*c*1985, Kt. 731); with E. Watts: *Face to Face* (1994, VeraBra 2063-2); *Tomorrowland* (1996, Challenge 70040)

BIBLIOGRAPHY

P. Carles: "Pays-bas: Jasper van 't Hof," *Jm*, no.220 (1974), 31 [incl. discography]
R. Reichelt: "Jasper van 't Hof: 'I Just Want to Play with Everyone who is Able to Communicate'," *JF* [intl edn], no.43 (1976), 27
K. Mümpfer: "Jasper van 't Hof: Just Friends," *JP*, xlii/6 (1993), 39
"Jasper van 't Hof," *JP*, xliii/3 (1994), 16

WIM VAN EYLE/BK

Van 't Hoff, Ernst (*b* Zandvoort, Netherlands, 13 July 1908; *d* Brussels, 17 May 1955). Dutch bandleader and pianist. He played piano on the radio (1937–40) and in his own band. In 1940 he formed a big band under orders from the Germans during their occupation of the Netherlands. This group performed principally in Germany and to a lesser degree in the Netherlands and Belgium; although in theory forbidden to do so, it nonetheless played jazz, as evidenced by the recording of *Pennsylvania 6-5000*, *Johnson Rag* (both Grammophon 47521), and *In the Mood* (Grammophon 47522) in Berlin in 1941. In 1944 van 't Hoff led the band, which now had 36 members, in performances for the American troops in Europe; it disbanded around 1946, then was re-formed for a brief period in 1951.

WIM VAN EYLE

Van Vliet, Toon (*b* Rotterdam, Netherlands, 20 June 1922; *d* Zandvoort, Netherlands, 5 Nov 1975). Dutch tenor saxophonist. He studied clarinet, and after changing to tenor saxophone in 1945 he entertained the American troops in Europe. He worked with the Pacific Boptet and Ernst van 't Hoff (1951), a group led by Wessel Ilcken and Rita Reys (1952–3), the pianist Boy Edgar (1960–64), and the VARA Dance Orchestra (1960–70); among those with whom he recorded were Ilcken (1955–7), the Rhythme All Stars (1958–60), Reys (1962), and Edgar (1965–75). Van Vliet modeled his playing after Sonny Rollins and Al Cohn; his style is well represented by his recording *Toon Van Vliet* (1959, BVHaast 059).

WIM VAN EYLE

VAO. *See* VIENNA ART ORCHESTRA.

Vapirov, Anatoly (Petrovich) (*b* Berdyansk, Ukrainian SSR [now Ukraine], 24 Nov 1947). Russian saxophonist, clarinetist, and composer. He played in the Leningrad Jazz Club from 1965 and in 1966–7 was a member of the student quintet at the Leningrad N. A. Rimsky-Korsakov State Conservatory, from which he graduated as a clarinetist in 1971. From 1967 to 1976 he played tenor saxophone (occasionally as a soloist) in the orchestra of the Leningradsky Myuzik-Kholl. He returned to the Leningrad Conservatory to teach saxophone (1976–82), gained a graduate degree in saxophone (1979), and led the student jazz band (1981–2). He also recorded in Sofia and made the first of five annual appearances at the jazz festival in Slanchev Bryag (near Burgas, Bulgaria, 1978). In 1983 he formed the ensemble Zolotïe Godï Dzhaza (which consisted of Latvian, Ukrainian, and Russian musicians) and the Trio Sovremennovo Kamernovo Dzhaza, and, having been sent to Siberia by the authorities, conducted the dance ensemble of the Buryat (then Russian SFSR) Philharmonic Society in Ulan-Ude (1983–4). Between 1974 and 1998 Vapirov performed in ten European countries and the USA. In 1992, having settled in Bulgaria, he became artistic director of the jazz festival Varna Summer. Vapirov's work may be heard to advantage on *Misteriya* (1980, Mel. C60 135756), a recording of his own composition for jazz soloist and symphony orchestra. He has also written a concerto for clarinet and strings, a suite, a symphony for strings, an oratorio, a rock-ballet, and the ballet *Macbeth*, a set of ten jazz scenes. (H. J. Schaal: "Perestroyka Blues: Who is Who im sowjetischen Jazz der 80er Jahre," *JP*, xxxix/4 (1990), 28)

WALTER OJAKÄÄR

Variety (i). Record label. It was established in 1926 and was used to issue, under pseudonyms, items from Cameo's catalogue. It is not known who owned the label, or for how long it existed, but it had apparently ceased to operate before the formation of the American Record Corporation.

BIBLIOGRAPHY

B. Rust: *The American Record Label Book* (New Rochelle, NY, 1978), 299
A. Sutton and K. Nauck: *American Record Labels and Companies: an Encyclopedia (1891–1943)* (Denver, 2000), 213

HOWARD RYE

Variety (ii). Record label. It was established in February 1937 by Irving Mills as a low-price counterpart to his label MASTER. Artists and repertory were supervised by Helen Oakley (later Helen Oakley Dance). Among the 171 discs issued between 1 April and 15 October 1937 were recordings by Cab Calloway and by small groups made up of members of Duke Ellington's orchestra, as well as much other important jazz. Recording and manufacture were undertaken by the American Record Corporation, and by the end of 1937 the musicians' contracts and Variety's catalogue had been transferred to ARC's label Vocalion.

BIBLIOGRAPHY

H. Dance: Liner notes, J. Hodges: *Hodge Podge* (CBS 52587, 1969)
B. Whyatt: "Discography: Master and Variety," *Vintage Jazz Monthly* (1970), April, 2
B. Rust: *The American Record Label Book* (New Rochelle, NY, 1978), 299
S. Placksin: *American Women in Jazz, 1900 to the Present: their Words, Lives, and Music* (New York, 1982, London, 1985, as *Jazzwomen, 1900 to the Present: their Words, Lives, and Music*), 122
J. Prohaska: "Irving Mills – Record Producer: the Master and Variety Record Labels," *IAJRC Journal*, xxx/2 (1997), 1
A. Sutton and K. Nauck: *American Record Labels and Companies: an Encyclopedia (1891–1943)* (Denver, 2000), 213

HOWARD RYE

Varner, Tom [Thomas Lindsay] (*b* Morristown, NJ, 17 June 1957). French horn player and leader. He grew up in Millburn, New Jersey, and took up french horn while at elementary school. He later attended Oberlin College, Ohio (1975–7), and briefly took private lessons from Julius Watkins (1976) before transferring to the jazz program at the New England Conservatory (BM 1979), where he studied with Jaki Byard; he later had lessons with Dave Liebman (1981). In 1979 he moved to New York and led a quartet with

Ed Jackson, Fred Hopkins or Ed Schuller, and Billy Hart until 1985, when he formed a quintet with Jim Snidero, Kenny Barron, Mike Richmond, and Victor Lewis. Between 1986 and 1990 he led a trio with Richmond and Bobby Previte, and in 1989 he formed another quintet, in which he worked alongside Jackson, the tenor saxophonist Rich Rothenberg or Ellery Eskelin, Richmond or Drew Gress, and Tom Rainey or Phil Haynes. While with this group Varner led the chamber quartet Hemoglobin (1992–4), with Mark Feldman, Lee Konitz, and Lindsey Horner, and the trio American Songs, with the guitarist Pete McCann and George Schuller (from 1996). In addition to leading his own ensembles he worked in Liebman's sextet (1982), and with Previte (1982–8), George Gruntz's Concert Jazz Band (1983–91), John Zorn (1984–8), and Urs Blochlinger (1985–92). In the 1990s he played with Peter Schärli, with whom he toured the USSR (1990), the Ton-Art ensemble (1990–94), Franz Koglmann (1991–4), Steve Lacy's octet (1993–6), and the East Down septet and Schärli's Special Sextet (both from 1994).

SELECTED RECORDINGS

As leader: *The Tom Varner Quartet* (1980, SN 1017); *Covert Action* (1987, New Note 1009); *Long Night, Big Day* (1990, New World 80410-2); *The Mystery of Compassion* (1992, SN 121217-2); *Martian Heartache* (1996, SN 121286-2); *Swimming* (1999, Omnitone 11903)

As sideman: B. Previte: *Pushing the Envelope* (1987, Gram. 18-8711-1); Ton-Art: *Mal vu, mal dit* (1991, HA 6088); S. Lacy: *Vespers* (1993, SN 121260-2); E. Jackson: *Wake up Call* (1994, New World 80451-2)

BIBLIOGRAPHY

J. Agrell: "Jazz and the Horn: Tom Varner," *Brass Bulletin*, no.47 (1984), 55
K. Whitehead: "Riffs: Tom Varner," *DB*, lvii/11 (1990), 13
M. Chénard: "Tom Varner: Love of the Single Line," *Coda*, no.260 (1995), 22
T. Panken: "Misfits no More," *DB*, lxvi/4 (1999), 52
L. Van Trikt: "Tom Varner Interview," *Cadence*, xxv/3 (1999), 16
<http://www.tomvarnermusic.com> (2000)

GK

Varro, Johnny [John Robert] (*b* New York, 11 Jan 1930). Pianist and leader. He studied piano from the age of ten, and as a teenager sat in at Jack Crystal's Commodore jam sessions, where he was encouraged by Joe Sullivan and Willie "the Lion" Smith. From 1947 into the early 1950s he worked as a freelance at the Central Plaza and Stuyvesant Casino, New York. In 1953, after being discharged from the military, he toured the Midwest with Bobby Hackett and Nappy Lamare. Following his return to New York he worked at Nick's with Phil Napoleon (1954–6) and Pee Wee Erwin and as a member of the cooperative band Empire City Six, with which he recorded in 1957. That same year he became an intermission pianist at Condon's. He appeared with Napoleon at the Newport Jazz Festival in 1959, and in 1960 replaced Gene Schroeder in Condon's house band, which also performed at the London House in Chicago in September. Through the early 1960s he performed with Yank Lawson, Wild Bill Davison (recording *c*1961), and Hackett, and played at the Metropole, the Roundtable, the Embers, Condon's, and other New York venues. He was a member of Edmond Hall's quartet regularly in 1963 and intermittently in 1964 and 1965, when he moved to Miami. There he led a local jazz trio and worked with Napoleon, Billy Butterfield, and Flip Phillips; he also toured with the Dukes of Dixieland from 1967 to 1968. In 1979 Varro moved to Los Angeles, where he led his own group, J. R. and the Heavyweights, and performed with Eddie Miller, Dick Cathcart, and Bob Havens. He toured Europe in 1986 with Davison (recording in Germany), and thereafter returned annually, touring variously with Kenny Davern, Bob Wilber, Phillips, Lawson, Peanuts Hucko (*c*1993), and others; he has also toured the Far East. In September 1993 he moved to the Tampa Bay area of Florida, where he formed a new group, Johnny Varro and the Swing 7; it has performed at jazz festivals and jazz parties throughout the USA. Although not well known, Varro is a fine swing pianist whose influences include Jess Stacy, Teddy Wilson, and Mel Powell.

SELECTED RECORDINGS

As leader: *Everything I Love* (1992, Arbors 19114); *Swing 7* (1994, Arbors 19138)

As sideman: Empire City Six: *Empire City Six* (1957, ABC-Para. 210); E. Condon: *Eddie Condon's All Stars with Wild Bill Davison* (1961, Sto. 242)

BIBLIOGRAPHY

W. W. Vaché, Sr.: *Pee Wee Erwin: this Horn for Hire* (Metuchen, NJ, 1987)
M. Selchow: *Profoundly Blue: a Bio-discographical Scrapbook on Edmond Hall* (Lübbecke, Germany, 1988)
C. Deffaa and S. Dance: Liner notes, *Everything I Love* (Arbors 19114, 1994)
W. Vaché, Sr.: "A Visit with Johnny Varro," *MR*, xxi/11 (1994), 1

GK

Varsity. Record label. The principal label of the United States Record Corporation, it was founded in 1939 by Eli Oberstein, formerly an executive of Victor, to issue records more cheaply than major companies. The popular 8000 series included some of the more commercially oriented jazz of the period, while the 6000 race series was used mainly to reissue older material from Paramount, Crown, and Gennett. The parent company ceased to operate late in 1940, but its masters were purchased by Musicraft and were later made available on several labels, many associated with Oberstein.

BIBLIOGRAPHY

R. Wile: "The United States Record Corporation and its Successors: Some Afterthoughts," *Record Research*, i/4 (1955), 8
F. Dutton, J. Godrich, M. Wyler, and J. McKenzie: "The Varsity 6000 Race Series," *Matrix*, no.32 (1961), 3 [corrections in no.40 (1962), 17]
J. Godrich and R. M. W. Dixon: *Blues & Gospel Records, 1902–1942* (Hatch End, nr London, 1964, rev. and enlarged 3/1982 as R. M. W. Dixon and J. Godrich: *Blues & Gospel Records, 1902–1943*), 25
R. M. W. Dixon and J. Godrich: *Recording the Blues* (London, 1970), 100
B. Rust: *The American Record Label Book* (New Rochelle, NY, 1978), 300
A. Sutton and K. Nauck: *American Record Labels and Companies: an Encyclopedia (1891–1943)* (Denver, 2000), 213

HOWARD RYE

Vasconcelos, Nana (Juvenal de Hollanda) (*b* Recife, Brazil, 2 Aug 1945). Brazilian percussionist. At the age of 12 he played bongos and maracas in a band led by his father, a professional guitarist. In the mid-1960s he worked as a drummer in Rio de Janeiro, and while performing with Milton Nascimento he learned to play several indigenous instruments, including the *berimbau*. Later he was taken by Gato Barbieri to Argentina, the USA (1971), and Europe. In July 1972 he recorded with Rolf Kühn in Cologne. He lived for two years in Paris, where he worked with handicapped children and recorded with Baikida Carroll (June 1974). During this period he played occasionally in Sweden with Don Cherry, and in 1975 he recorded with Joachim Kühn in Ludwigsburg, Germany. From 1976 to 1977 he toured and recorded with Egberto Gismonti, then in 1978, with Cherry and Collin Walcott, he founded the trio Codona, which performed a style of jazz that incorporated characteristics of African, Asian, and South American music; when Codona disbanded in 1984 after Walcott's death, Vasconcelos joined Cherry's group Nu. He was also a member of Pat Metheny's

Nana Vasconcelos at the Bracknell Jazz Festival, England, 1986

group (March 1981–1983), and with Metheny he was co-composer of *Barcarole* and *Eighteen* (both recorded in 1981). During the early 1980s he also toured Europe in a duo with Trilok Gurtu, and in a cooperative quartet with Gurtu, Jan Garbarek, and the violinist Lakshminarayana Shankar.

In 1983 Vasconcelos began to use drum machines, and not long thereafter he toured Europe with a group of break dancers from New York, playing the drum machine "live" (i.e., typing out polyrhythmic patterns, rather than pre-programming them). He toured Brazil as a soloist (1986), toured and recorded with Jack DeJohnette's group Special Edition (1987–8), joined Gurtu's trio (1988), and worked with Arild Andersen (*c* late 1980s – mid-1990s) and with Jean-Marie Machado's Septuor Vibracordes (1990). In 1990 he became a member of Andy Sheppard's quartet, alongside Ernst Reijseger and Orphy Robinson, and together with Sheppard and Steve Lodder he formed the trio Inclassifiable (recording in 1994). His own group, Bushdance, toured extensively in Europe.

Vasconcelos recorded often as a freelance from the 1970s, notably with Zbigniew Seifert (1978), Jon Hassell (1978–80), the reed player Dwight Andrews, Jay Hoggard, and Woody Shaw (all 1979), Terumasa Hino (1979–80), Pierre Favre, Jim Pepper, and Enrico Rava (all 1984), Mark Helias (1987), Gary Thomas (1989), Eliane Elias (1989, 1992–3), the singer Ingrid Sertso (1993), and Ivo Perelman (1994), as well as with numerous artists working in the areas of pop, avant-garde rock, and Brazilian music.

Like Airto Moreira, Vasconcelos is a master of unconventional percussion: the subtle melodies and rhythms he creates on *berimbau* and *cuíca* transform these instruments into strikingly original solo voices.

SELECTED RECORDINGS

Duos with J. DeJohnette: on *Irresistible Forces* (1987, MCA/Imp. 5992), Conclusion, Introduction

As leader: *Saudades* (1979, ECM 1147); of Codona (with D. Cherry and C. Walcott): *Codona*, ii (1980, ECM 1177); *Codona*, iii (1982, ECM 1243)

As sideman: R. Kühn: *The Day After* (1972, MPS 15378); B. Carroll: *Orange Fish Tears* (1974, Palm 13); E. Gismonti: *Danca des cabecas* (1976, ECM 1089); C. Walcott: *Codona* (1978, ECM 1132); P. Metheny: *Offramp* (1981, ECM 1216), incl. Barcarole, Eighteen; *Travels* (1982, ECM 1252–3); P. Favre: *Singing Drums* (1984, ECM 1274); M. Helias: on *The Current Set* (1987, Enja 5041), Greetings from L.C.; E. Elias: *Eliane Elias Plays Jobim* (1989, BN B21S-93089)

SELECTED FILMS AND VIDEOS

Batouka: 1st International Festival of Percussion (1986); Jack DeJohnette's Special Edition: Live at the Montreal Jazz Festival 1988 (1988); The Soul of Samba (1990); Bossa Nova (1993)

BIBLIOGRAPHY

L. Jeske: "Profile: Nana Vasconcelos," *DB*, xlix/2 (1982), 52

<http://www.rojac.co.at/rojac/vasconcelos> (1999) [incl. discography and list of videos by J. Haidenbauer]

<http://www.ejn.it/mus/vasconce.htm> (2000)

BK

Vasseur, Benny [Bernard] (*b* Cambrai, France, 7 March 1926). French trombonist. He studied solfège and classical piano at the conservatory in Cambrai and played trombone in the college orchestra; he continued to study the latter instrument at the Paris Conservatoire from 1946. After having appeared in the amateur band of the Hot Club de Versailles he made his professional début with Claude Bolling, then in 1948 replaced Sandy Williams in Rex Stewart's band for a tour of Scandinavia. That same year he played at the opening of the Club Saint-Germain and began appearing at other principal Parisian clubs with such musicians as Bill Coleman, Roy Eldridge, Django Reinhardt, Hot Lips Page, Benny Carter, Albert Nicholas, Big Chief Moore, and Buck Clayton; he may be seen with Eldridge in the documentary film short *Autour d'une trompette* (1952). From 1951 Vasseur spent two years in Aimé Barelli's big band, performing in Paris and on the Côte d'Azur, after which he joined Michel Attenoux. As a member of Claude Luter's band (1953–7) he played with Sidney Bechet, with whom he had first worked in 1949. In 1957 André Paquinet and Vasseur formed a two-trombone group in imitation of the bop quintet Jay and Kai (led by J. J. Johnson and Kai Winding), though its repertory reached back further, as is evident from their album *Dixie Trombone*. In 1960 Vasseur began collaborating with the singer Annie Cordy, and he appeared frequently in studio orchestras accompanying such popular singers as Liza Minnelli, Frank Sinatra, Tony Bennett, and Sammy Davis, Jr. In 1965 he served as one of the trombonists in François Guin's group Four Bones. He then joined Claude Bolling's Show Biz Band, with which he remained into the new century.

SELECTED RECORDINGS

As leader with A. Paquinet: *Dixie Trombone* (1958, Festival 128)
As sideman: S. Bechet: On the Sunny Side of the Street (1949, BStar 129); R. Eldridge: Tu disais que tu m'aimais (1950, Vogue 5072); S. Bechet: *En concert* (1954, Vogue 30001); G. Lafitte: *Guy Lafitte: son saxo-tenor et son orchestre* (1954, Pathé 1057), incl. You can depend on me; C. Bolling: *Black, Brown and Beige* (1989, Adès 14168); *Warm up the Band* (1991, Col. 468699)

BIBLIOGRAPHY

M. Servoles: "Silhouette du Hot Club," *Jh*, no.35 (1949), 26
P. Gaskell and A. Fell: "French Trombone Maestro Logs a Half Century of Jazz," *MR*, xxiv/3 (1997), 25
F. W. Sportis: "Benny Vasseur," *Jh*, no.538 (1997), 13
J. Vastra: "Un Jubilee Rag pour Benny Vasseur," *Jazz Dixie/Swing: du Ragtime au Big Band*, no.15 (1997), 45

ANDRÉ CLERGEAT

Vatcher, Michael (Gordon) (*b* Modesto, CA, 12 Nov 1954). Drummer. His full name is taken from California birth records. From the age of ten he lived with his family in Humboldt county, California, where he played in rock bands and studied with Jerry Moore, the father of Michael Moore (ii); as a teenager he played with Michael Moore in the fusion band Joint Session. In 1977 he moved to New York, and the following year he traveled to Amsterdam with the mime group Available Jelly and, with Moore and Ernst Reijseger, formed the cooperative trio Nomofo. In the early 1980s he lived alternately in New York and Amsterdam, but by 1984 he had settled in Amsterdam. Vatcher was a member of Tristan Honsinger's This, That, and the Other from the early to the mid-1980s (recording in 1985). In addition he worked in Available Jelly under Moore's leadership (from *c*1984), in Maarten Altena's octet (*c*1985–94), and in cooperative groups with Moore and Ernst Glerum – one with the guitarist Franky Douglas and another with the slide guitarist Dave Tronzo. In the late 1980s he performed and recorded (1987) in the USA with John Zorn's Ornette Coleman tribute band Spy vs. Spy, and in 1990 he became a member of the trio Braamdejoodevatcher with Michiel Braam and Wilbert de Joode. At the October Meeting in Amsterdam the following year he performed and recorded in a trio with George Lewis (ii) and Steve Beresford. Later he played in two of Tom Cora's last groups (1996–8) and appeared at the festival Les Trois Jours in a quartet with Paul Dunmall, Tobias Delius, and Paul Rogers (May 1999). He also worked in other groups led by Braam and in Eric Boeren's small ensembles, and with the alto saxophonist and composer Paul Termos, Peter van Bergen's LOOS, Evan Parker (briefly in 1995), the group Diftong, a Roland Kirk tribute group led by the Dutch saxophonist Frans Vermeerssen, and the viola player Ig Henneman; in addition he collaborated with the Dutch anarchist rock group Ex, the new-music composer Gene Carl, the viola player Maurice Hortshuis in Amsterdam Drama, and Douglas.

SELECTED RECORDINGS

As sideman: Available Jelly: *In Full Flail* (1988, Ear-Rational 1013); M. Altena: *Cities & Streets* (1989, HA 6082); M. Moore: *Négligé* (1989, 1992, Ramboy 04); on [no leader]: *October Meeting 1991: Anatomy of a Meeting* (1991, BIMhuis 004), Saturday, Another Sunday

BIBLIOGRAPHY

K. Whitehead: *New Dutch Swing* (New York, 1998)

GK

Vauchant(-Arnaud), Léo [Arnaud, Noël Léon Marius] (*b* Cauzan, France, 24 July 1904; *d* Hamptonville, NC, 25 April 1991). French trombonist and arranger. He studied cello but later changed to trombone (his father was a trombonist). In 1917 he moved to Paris, where he led a group of his own (1924) and studied orchestration with the composer Maurice Ravel (1924–7), in consideration of which he gave advice on the notation of trombone solos in two of Ravel's works. He played with the Chicago Hot Spots (1924), Paul Gason's band (1925), the bandleader and percussionist Fred Mélé, Irving Aaronson (1927), Lud Gluskin (1927–8), Jack Hylton (in England and Germany, 1928–30), and Gregor (1930), with whom he made a film short at the Olympia Theatre. Having appeared as a guest with Ray Ventura and the Collegians from 1929, he made recordings with them in 1931, including *The girl friend of a boy friend of mine* (Virginia 221D), on which he played solos on both cornet and trombone. He also worked in the USA with Fred Waring's band (1931–6), the Casa Loma Orchestra, the singer Russ Columbo (1932), Roger Wolfe Kahn's band, and the drummer Abe Lyman. Later he arranged film music in Hollywood. Vauchant-Arnaud's playing showed control and flexibility over a wide range of the instrument; he was the first French jazz trombonist to become well known.

BIBLIOGRAPHY

L.-V. Maily: "Le légendaire Léo Vauchant," *Jh*, no.256 (1969), 26
——: "Léo Vauchant vous parle," *Jh*, no.257 (1970), 23
C. Goddard: *Jazz away from Home* (London and New York, 1979), 261
M. Laplace: "Ravel et le nouveau trombone (Vauchant, Dorsey, Mole, Paquinet)," *Brass Bulletin*, no.47 (1984), 34
——: *Portraits of French Jazz Musicians* (Menden, Germany, 1985), 13
Obituary, *Jh*, no.484 (1991), 15
M. Laplace: "Trombone: style archaïque & style moderne," *Jh*, no.537 (1997), 20

MICHEL LAPLACE

Vaughan, Sarah (Lois) [Sassy; the Divine One] (*b* Newark, NJ, 27 March 1924; *d* Los Angeles 3 April 1990). Singer and leader. Her mother played piano and her father, guitar. As a child she learned piano and sang in the choir of the First Mount Zion Baptist Church, Newark, where at the age of 12 she became organist. In October 1942 she won an amateur contest at the Apollo Theatre; shortly afterwards, in April 1943, she joined Earl Hines's big band as second pianist and singer to Hines and Billy Eckstine. Eckstine formed his own bop-oriented big band early in 1944, and Vaughan joined him a few months later, making her first recording with his orchestra on 31 December. She left Eckstine after about a year, and thereafter, except for a brief stay in John Kirby's group in winter 1945–6, she worked only as a soloist. After George Treadwell (her manager and first husband) refashioned her stage appearance and repertory she achieved considerable success on television, in recordings from the late 1940s, and in international performances from the early 1950s. Although she began to perform predominantly slow, popular ballads with heavy vibrato to the accompaniment of "easy listening" orchestras, her early associations with bop musicians (especially Dizzy Gillespie and Charlie Parker, with whom she recorded *Lover Man* in 1945) established her lasting reputation as a jazz singer. This reputation endured in part because of her tendency to treat her voice more as a

Sarah Vaughan singing with Joe Benjamin (double bass) and Roy Haynes (drums) at Birdland, New York, c1954

jazz instrument than as a vehicle for lyrics: she negotiated wide leaps within her full-bodied contralto range, improvised subtle melodic and rhythmic embellishments, and made fluid alterations of timbre – from a bell-like clarity to a bluesy growl.

During the five-year contract with Columbia that marked her rise to stardom (1949–54), Vaughan recorded often with studio orchestras and only once in a jazz context (with Miles Davis in 1950). A new contract with Mercury (1954–9) allowed her to pursue a dual career: for Mercury she made commercial discs, including her hit *Broken-hearted Melody* (1958), while for EmArcy, Mercury's jazz subsidiary, she recorded with Clifford Brown, Cannonball Adderley, the sidemen of Count Basie's orchestra, and other jazz musicians. She combined these activities under later contracts with Roulette, Mercury, and Columbia (1960–67). In 1971, after a five-year absence from recording, she began once again to make popular albums, occasionally employing a jazz-flavored accompaniment, as on her album with Oscar Peterson, Joe Pass, Ray Brown, and Louie Bellson in 1978. In public performances Vaughan was accompanied by a trio of piano, double bass, and drums, either alone or as the nucleus of a big band or symphony orchestra. Among the members of her group were Jimmy Jones (1947–52; 1954–7), John Malachi (1952–4), Joe Benjamin (1953–5), Roy Haynes (1953–8), Richard Davis (1957–63), Ronnell Bright (1958–60, 1963), Percy Brice (1959–61), Roland Hanna (1960), Kirk Stuart (1961–3), Buster Williams (1963), Bob James (1965–8), Chick Corea (1968), Jan Hammer (1970–71), Jimmy Cobb (1970–78), Bob Magnusson (1971–2, 1975–6), Bill Mays (1971–2), the pianist Carl Schroeder (1972–8), Ron McClure (1972–3), Ray Brown (1974), Frank De la Rosa (1974–5), Walter Booker (1976–8), Mike Wofford (1979, from 1983), Andy Simpkins (from 1979), Roy McCurdy (1979), Grady Tate (1980), and Harold Jones (from 1980); from 1978 to 1980 the trio became a quartet under the leadership of Vaughan's then manager, conductor, and husband, Waymon Reed.

Vaughan recorded prolifically, sometimes scat singing (in a manner deeply indebted to Ella Fitzgerald), occasionally offering bouncy swing tunes, but predominantly singing slow ballads, in which context her tone and technique routinely awed listeners and fellow musicians. Whether as a consequence of her experimental jazz spirit, or simply from a lack of good judgement, her performances could be extremely mannered, and they evidenced a curiously inconsistent relationship to the African-American tradition, as heard, for example, in the contrast between *One Mint Julep* (1962), on which her phrasing is embarrassingly lame, sounding almost like a parody of the rhythm-and-blues style, and her famous rendition of *Ain't No Use* (1961), one of the greatest and most profound recordings of blues-based jazz singing.

SELECTED RECORDINGS

As leader: Body and Soul (1946, Musi. 494); I Cover the Waterfront (1947, Musi. 503); It's Magic (1947, Musi. 557); Mean to Me (1950, Col. 38899); Lullaby of Birdland (1954, EmA 6099); *In the Land of Hi-fi* (1955, EmA 36058); *Sassy* (1956, EmA 36089); Broken-hearted Melody (1958, Mer. 71477); *No Count Sarah* (1958, Mer. 20441); *The Divine One* (1961, Roul. 52060), incl. Ain't No Use; *After Hours* (1961, Roul. 52070); *You're Mine You* (1962, Roul. 52082), incl. One Mint Julep; *Sarah + 2* (1964, Roul. 52118); *Sassy Swings Again* (1967, Mer. 21116); *Sarah Vaughan–Michel Legrand* (1972, Mstr. 361); *Live in Japan* (1973, Mstr. 401); *How Long Has This Been Going On?* (1978, Pablo 2310821); *Crazy and Mixed Up* (1982, PT 2312137); *Brazilian Romance* (1987, Col. FM42519)

As sideman: B. Eckstine: I'll wait and pray (1944, DeLuxe 2002); on *Billy Eckstine* (1945, Alamac 2415), Mean to Me; D. Gillespie: Lover Man (1945, Guild 1002); J. Kirby: It might as well be spring (1946, Crown 108)

SELECTED FILMS AND VIDEOS

Sarah Vaughan and Herb Jeffries (1950); Disc Jockey (1951); The Nearness of You (*c*1952); Perdido (*c*1952); Listen to the Sun (1978); Sarah Vaughan: Live from Monterey (1984); Jazz Class (1985); Sass and Brass: a Jazz Session (1986); American Masters: Sarah Vaughan: the Divine One (1991)

BIBLIOGRAPHY

P. Leslie: "They Call her the Musical Miracle," *MM*, xxix (24 Jan 1953), 3

B. Eckstine: "Crazy People Like Me: When Sarah Vaughan Began to Sing," *MM*, xxx (21 Aug 1954), 5

D. Gold: "Soulful Sarah," *DB*, xxiv/11 (1957), 13

B. Gardner: "Sarah," *DB*, xxviii/5 (1961), 18

R. Leydi: *Sarah Vaughan* (Milan, 1961)

G. Kopelowicz: "Tendre et divine Sarah," *Jm*, no.96 (1963), 25

G. Hoefer: "The First Big Bop Band," *DB*, xxxii/16 (1965), 23

B. Quinn: "Sassy '67," *DB*, xxxiv/15 (1967), 20

M. Williams: "Sarah Vaughan: Some Notes on a Singer before it's Too Late," *JJ*, xxi/7 (1968), 36

——: *The Jazz Tradition* (New York, 1970, rev. 2/1983), 214

L. Robinson: "The Divine Sarah," *Ebony*, xxx/6 (1975), 94

M. Jones: "Symphonies for Sarah," *MM* (14 Aug 1976), 47

W. Balliett: "New York Notes," *New Yorker*, liii (18 July 1977), 80

S. Dance: *The World of Earl Hines* (New York, 1977/*R*1983)

A. J. Smith: "Sarah Vaughan: Never Ending Melody," *DB*, xliv/9 (1977), 16 [incl. discography]

E. Southern: "'Mr. B' of Ballad and Bop," *Black Perspective in Music*, vii (1979), 182; viii (1980), 54

"Sarah Vaughan," *SJ*, xxxiv/4 (1980), 178 [discography]

J. Liska: "Sarah Vaughan: I'm Not a Jazz Singer," *DB*, xlix/5 (1982), 19 [incl. discography]

M. L. Stewart: "Stylistic Environment and the Scat Singing Styles of Ella Fitzgerald and Sarah Vaughan," *Jf*, xix (1987), 61

D. Brown: *Sarah Vaughan: a Discography* (New York, 1991)

G. Giddins: *Faces in the Crowd: Players and Writers* (New York, and Oxford, England, 1992), 73

L. Gourse: *Sassy: the Life of Sarah Vaughan* (New York and Toronto, 1993)

BK

Vault. Record company and label. The company was established by Jack Lewerke in Los Angeles in 1965 and remained in operation into the 1970s. Its first release was an album by Jack Wilson, who later recorded a second LP for the label. The catalogue included two albums by Hampton Hawes, a collection of material by Charlie Barnet, and a splendid LP recorded by Larry Bunker's quartet with Gary Burton at Shelly's Manne-Hole.

MARK GARDNER

V-disc. Record label. It was established in October 1943 for the issue of records to the US Armed Services; the term is also used, by extension, for the discs themselves.

The operation was run by the Music Section of the Special Services Division, under the management of Captain Robert Vincent. Artists and repertory were supervised by Steve Scholes and Walt Heebner (both previously employees of RCA Victor), Morty Palitz (previously with Decca), and Tony Janak (previously with Columbia); Palitz was replaced by George T. Simon in 1944. At first the records were intended only for the army, but from July 1944 until September 1945 there was also a V-disc program for the navy, in which material was issued under different catalogue numbers. In addition there was a brief series of discs issued for the Marine Corps. The records were distributed to military personnel around the world and to posts in the USA for use on public address systems, and they were used on short-wave broadcasts by the Office of War Information and the Office of Inter-American Affairs.

The V-disc catalogue contained recordings made for commercial purposes (including both reissues and items or versions not previously issued); broadcasts; and the results of sessions specially organized by the management. The repertory forms a treasury of jazz and includes notable work by many of the most important musicians of the day, in all styles then current. The program was established in the middle of a long recording ban by the American Federation of Musicians (July 1942 to November 1944) and was, to some extent, a result of it, in that V-disc's administration developed the scheme partly because no new material was being recorded at the time. The AFM agreed that its members could participate in the project provided that the records were not sold and that the masters were ultimately destroyed. The nonprofit basis of the scheme enabled the management to organize sessions by groups of musicians who under other circumstances might never have recorded together because they were each under contract to different record companies; among the most notable examples of this are the recordings of concerts given (under the sponsorship of the magazine *Esquire*) by an ensemble led by Louis Armstrong, Coleman Hawkins, and Art Tatum.

The operation was maintained after World War II under Janak's direction, but it ceased in 1949. The circumstances under which the discs were produced has meant that an official program of reissues has been impossible. However, because the material put out on V-discs is historically so important, and often of such high quality, demand for it has been great, and extensive unofficial reissue schemes have been undertaken by several companies, chiefly in Europe and Japan. In 1997 E. P. "Digi" DiGiannantonio, who had been responsible for the separate navy, marine corps, and coast guard V-disc programs, formed the V-disc Corporation in Reston, Virginia, and began a cassette issue and custom-taping service.

See also Recording, §II, 5.

BIBLIOGRAPHY

S. Wante and W. DeBlock: *V-disc Catalogue*, i (Antwerp, Belgium, 1954)
K. Teubig: *V-disc Catalogue*, ii (Berlin, 1976)
R. S. Sears: *V-discs: a History and Discography* (Westport, CT, and London, 1980; suppl., 1986)
S. F. Bedwell: "V-disc Clarifications," *IAJRC Journal*, xxx/2 (1997), 26
——: "Unknown V-discs: Identifying Undocumented Masters," *IAJRC Journal*, xxxii/4 (1999), 36
——: "Corrections to Unknown V-discs," *IAJRC Journal*, xxxii/3 (2000), 43

HOWARD RYE

Veal, Reginald (*b* Chicago, 5 Nov 1963). Double bass player. He grew up in New Orleans, learned piano from the age of eight, and later played electric bass guitar in his father's gospel group. After high school he took up double bass on the advice of Branford and Wynton Marsalis, had lessons with Ellis Marsalis at the New Orleans Center for the Cultural Arts, and attended Southern University, where he studied bass trombone with Alvin Batiste and played trombone in the marching band. He worked initially with Ellis Marsalis (1986–9), with whom he toured Southeast Asia, and then joined the quintet led by Donald Harrison and Terence Blanchard (July 1986, recording in 1987–8). Between December 1987 and late 1993 he was a member of Wynton Marsalis's group, and from the early 1990s he toured with the Lincoln Center Jazz Orchestra. Although he settled in Atlanta in 1994 he continued an intermittent association with both Wynton Marsalis and the Lincoln Center orchestra; he appears with Marsalis in the videos *Accent on the Offbeat* (*c*1994) and *Garth Fagan's Griot New York* (*c*1995). In the mid-1990s Veal toured and recorded with Branford Marsalis, both in the hip-hop ensemble Buckshot LeFonque and in his trio (recording in 1996). He also worked in Wycliffe Gordon's and Ron Westray's group Bone Structure, toured and recorded with Harry Connick, Jr. (from late 1980s) and Marcus Roberts (late 1980s), and toured with Dianne Reeves (1999); he recorded with Mark Whitfield (*c*1990), Nicholas Payton (1994), Leroy Jones (1995–6), Courtney Pine (*c*1996), and Eric Reed and the tenor saxophonist Greg Tardy (both 1997). In 1994, as a freelance, he took part in a remarkable recording of a concert performance alongside Herlin Riley as a member of Junko Onishi's trio at the Village Vanguard.

Veal is an under-appreciated musician whose large, woody tone and rhythmically adept, elastic sense of swing fit comfortably into the diverse settings in which he works. His contribution to Wynton Marsalis's septet, and particularly his interaction with Riley therein, was essential to its early success in re-creating small-group swing performances.

SELECTED RECORDINGS

As sideman: W. Marsalis: *Levee Low Moan: Soul Gestures in Southern Blue*, iii (*c*1987–8, Col. CK47975); D. Harrison and T. Blanchard: *Black Pearl* (1988, Col. CK44216), incl. Dizzy Gillespie's Hands; M. Whitfield: *The Marksman* (*c*1990, WB 26321); W. Marsalis: *Citi Movement (Griot New York)* (1992, Col. C2K53324); M. Roberts: *Gershwin for Lovers* (*c*1994, Col. CK66437); J. Onishi: *Live at the Village Vanguard*, i–ii (1994, BN B21Z-31886, 33418-2); B. Marsalis: *The Dark Keys* (1996, Col. CK67876); E. Reed: *Pure Imagination* (1997, Imp. 244)

BIBLIOGRAPHY

<http://jazzradio.org/reginald.htm> (1999)

GK

Veasley, Gerald (*b* Philadelphia, 28 July 1955). Electric bass guitarist. He was introduced to gospel music at an early age by his uncle, who was a member of the Dixie Hummingbirds, and he also listened to rhythm-and-blues. When he was 12 he took up electric bass guitar, on which he was influenced by the funk and pop bass guitarists James Jamerson, Larry Graham, and Willie Weeks. After school he studied law at the University of Pennsylvania, but at the age of 21, following the death of his father, he decided to pursue a career as a musician. At this time he began to listen to jazz double bass players in an effort to improve his understanding of improvisation; later he studied classical and flamenco guitar to refine his technique. From the late 1970s into the 1990s Veasley worked in the group Reverie. In 1980 he joined the rhythm section of Odean Pope's Saxophone Choir, and during an appearance at the North Sea Jazz Festival later that year Pope, Veasley, and the drummer Cornell Rochester played as a trio after the larger group's repertory had been exhausted; they continued to perform and record together thereafter.

In 1984 Veasley and Rochester formed another band, with which they recorded the following year. Veasley also worked with the Japanese avant-pop singer Mari Okubu, and while continuing his association with Pope he joined a small group led by Grover Washington, Jr., with which he toured and recorded into the 1990s. At the same time he deputized for John Lee and Avery Sharpe in McCoy Tyner's trio and worked with John Blake and in Joe Zawinul's Syndicate (from summer 1988 to 1995), with which he appears in the video *Newport Jazz '90* (1990). Having tried various five-string electric bass guitars (from 1985) he began using a six-string model while with Zawinul, and by the end of his time with the group he was playing this instrument exclusively; the additional strings were tuned a fourth below and a fourth above the normal range of the bass guitar. In addition Veasley toured and recorded with the fusion group Special EFX, Harry Sokal's Full Circle, the percussionist George Jinda in the ensemble World News, and the Head's Up Superband (late 1990s), and he recorded in pop-jazz settings with Bobby Lyle, among others. He made his first recording as a sole leader around 1992 and from the mid-1990s concentrated mostly on his own groups. He may be seen in the instructional video *Gerald Veasley: Solo Bass Techniques*.

SELECTED RECORDINGS

As leader: with C. Rochester: *One Minute of Love* (1985, Gram. 8505); *Look Ahead* (*c*1992, Heads Up 3016)

As sideman with O. Pope: *Almost Like Me* (1982, Moers Music 01092); *Out for a Walk* (1990, Moers Music 02072)

BIBLIOGRAPHY

C. Jisi: "Gerald Veasley: the Zawinul Syndicate's Bass Hit Man," *GP*, xxiii/11 (1989), 35 [incl. discography and transcr.]

D. Kasrel: "The Very Versatile Gerald Veasley," *JT*, xxi/2 (1991), 25

D. Heckman: "Sideman/Frontman: Gerald Veasley," *JT*, xxii/8 (1992), 57

B. Milkowski: "Riffs: Gerald Veasley," *DB*, lix/11 (1992), 13

C. Jisi: "Gerald Veasley Looks Ahead," *Bass Player*, iv/1 (1993), 53 [incl. discography and transcr.]

B. Milkowski: "Brotherly Love & Bass: a Roundtable: Philly Style!," *Bass Player*, vii/11 (1996), 52

GK

Vee-Jay. Record company and label. The company was established in Gary, Indiana, in late 1952 or early 1953 by Vivian Carter and James C. Bracken; its name is derived from the initials of their first names. Later it had its headquarters in Chicago. It immediately established itself as a prominent label for rhythm-and-blues, though it also issued some blues and gospel material; artists and repertory were handled by Calvin Carter, and the house band included Red Holloway and Vernel Fournier. Vee-Jay issued LPs from 1957, and the following year it instituted a jazz division which was overseen by Sid McCoy; albums followed by Bennie Green and Gene Ammons (1958), Walter Perkins and MJT + 3 (1959), Paul Chambers (1959), Wynton Kelly (1959), Bill Henderson (1959, 1960, 1961), and Frank Strozier (1960). These jazz recordings appeared in Vee-Jay's main numerical series, but from 1960 jazz appeared in a separate 3000 series. Among the earliest were a reissue of Kelly's album and new recordings by Wayne Shorter (his first as a leader, from 1959, and another dating from 1962), Lee Morgan, MJT + 3, Louis Hayes, Chambers, and Eddie Higgins (all 1960), Kelly (1960–61), Eddie Harris (1961–3), and Ira Sullivan (1962); Harris's album *Exodus to Jazz* (1961, 3016) was a substantial hit. Vee-Jay seems to have ceased to record jazz at some point in 1963, and despite success in other areas it began to experience financial and managerial troubles around the same time. In 1964 a new jazz series numbered from 2500 was used for reissues; jazz reissues also appeared on the subsidiary label Exodus early in 1966.

In late 1962 or early 1963 the company established a second office in Los Angeles, and by 1964 its operations were headquartered there. In early 1965 Bracken bought out the Los Angeles contingent, and by October that year the headquarters were again in Chicago. Early in 1966 Vee-Jay filed for bankruptcy, and by May that year it ceased operations. From 1967 to 1990 the company was owned by Betty Chiapetta; she and Randy Wood (a former employee and one-time label president) bought the company out of bankruptcy in 1967, though Wood sold off his stake the following year; at the time of purchase they set up the holding company Vee-Jay International, which from around 1967 into the early 1970s leased out Vee-Jay's masters to such companies and labels as Springboard (which issued material first on its label Upfront and later on Trip), Charly, and Buddah.

Around 1972 Vee-Jay began to record and issue new material and to reissue some of its jazz albums, in part on a revived and extended 3000 series; these endeavors were overseen by the saxophonist Pat Britt. In the mid-1970s the company also reissued its own material in the "Epitaph Historical Jazz" series, and it licensed recordings by Django Reinhardt, Art Tatum, John Kirby, and others. In the mid- to late 1980s portions of its catalogue were leased to the Chicago label Chameleon, which unfortunately reissued some of the material on compact discs of poor quality. Around this time the Suite Beat label also reissued some of Vee-Jay's back catalogue.

In 1990 Chiapetta sold the company to Rockwood Music Group, which established the limited partnership Vee-Jay, Inc., to operate autonomously within the Rockwood organization; around 1992 it initiated a comprehensive reissue program, but this effort had failed by the mid-1990s. In 1993 Vee-Jay's CD recordings and other memorabilia were donated to the Schomburg Center for Research in Black Culture in Harlem. The company was reactivated in 1999 as Vee-Jay Limited Partnership, run by Michelle Taylor Management; from that time it has functioned essentially as a holding company, licensing masters out to other companies and labels. Reissues of jazz appear on CD variously on Koch Jazz (in an expanded form including alternate takes) and Collectables (straight reissues of the original LPs). In 2000

Mosaic (ii), in conjunction with Rhino, reissued a boxed set of material relating to recordings under the leadership of Morgan and Shorter, as well as another set devoted to Kelly and Chambers. Throughout its history Vee-Jay's jazz material has appeared on a Japanese label of the same name, as well as on Charly, Trip, Joy, Fresh Sound, and GNP. The company has been the subject of a radio documentary on WKRS, New York (1994), and a television documentary series, "Record Row: Cradle of Rhythm & Blues" (early 1997).

BIBLIOGRAPHY

Obituary, C. Baker, *Living Blues*, viii (1972), 11 [James Bracken]
A. Shaw: *Honkers and Shouters: the Golden Years of Rhythm and Blues* (New York, 1978), 315
B. Turner: "Vee-Jay Records," *Blues Unlimited*, nos.135–6 (1979), 21
N. George: "The Rhythm & the Blues: Suite Beat Buys Vee Jay's Catalog, Releases 52 Titles," *Billboard*, xcviii (9 Aug 1986), 26
Z. Stewart: "Music's the Staff of Life for Sax Player Pat Britt," *Los Angeles Times* (13 Sept 1986)
E. Calloway: "Former Vee Jay Records Owner Vivian Carter Made History," *Chicago Defender* (20 June 1989), 16
Obituary, N. Darwen, *Blues & Rhythm*, no.47 (1989), 11 [Vivian Carter]
D. Hoekstra: "Vee Jay Records Back in Business," *Chicago Sun-Times* (28 Oct 1992)
D. Russell: "Vee-Jay Catalog Reactivated Via Rockwood Music," *Billboard*, civ (11 July 1992), 57
J. Bessman: "Vee-Jay Records Revisits Catalog for Boxed Set," *Billboard*, cv (30 Oct 1993), 8
"Blues News," *Living Blues*, no.107 (1993), 7
A. Vigoda: "Down Memory Lane," *USA Today* (20 Oct 1993)
D. Whiteis: "Rocky Road to Reissue," *DB*, lx/2 (1993), 10
M. Joyce: "Label Watch: Vee-Jay Revived," *JT*, xxiv/2 (1994), 28
D. Hinckley: "Award-winning," *Daily News* [New York] (31 March 1995)
R. Cromelin: "TV Review: Vee-Jay, Seminal R & B Label, Lives on in 'Record Row'," *Los Angeles Times* (21 Feb 1997)
M. Callahan and D. Edwards: "The Vee-Jay Story," <http://www.bsnpubs.com/veejay.html> (2000) [incl.discography]
<http://www.jazzinstituteofchicago.org/index.asp?target=/jazzgram/bronzeville/sutherland.asp> (2000)
<http://www.mabry.argentinacity.com/vincent.html> (2000)
<http://www.oldies.com/merchandising/vee-jay.cfm> (2000)

GK

Velebný, Karel (*b* Prague, 17 March 1931; *d* Prague, 7 March 1989). Czech vibraphonist, bass clarinetist, tenor saxophonist, pianist, arranger, and composer. He studied at the Prague Conservatory and played under V. Bradač and J. Šubert. He performed and from 1959 to 1961 recorded with Karel Krautgartner and Kamil Hála; at the same time he was a member of Studio 5 with Ludek Hulan. In 1961 he formed the S & H Quartet (later the S & H Quintet, then SHQ), which played cool jazz and hard bop; with the group he played at festivals in Landskrona, Sweden (1963), Bled, Yugoslavia (1964), and Berlin (1964), toured many European countries, and made recordings in 1962-6 and 1971 (including *SHQ a přátele* (SHQ and friends), 1965, Sup. SV9004). He led the band until his death. From 1967 to 1969 he taught at the conservatory in Frýdlant, Ostrava, Bohemia, where in 1984 he founded the annual summer jazz workshop. He was awarded the Jaroslav Ježek prize in 1974. In 1984, in Frýdlant, he founded the Letni jazzová dílna (Summer jazz workshop), which took place annually. Velebný's best-known compositions include *Family Chronicle*, *Atila*, *Vernisáž* (Varnishing-day), and *Vycházka s neurotickým psem* (Walk with a neurotic dog). (*ReclamsJ*)

GERHARD CONRAD

Velvetone [velvet-tone]. An alternative name for the bucket mute; *see* MUTE, §2(g).

Velvet Tone. Record label. It was established by Columbia in 1926. At first the catalogue was the same as that of another subsidiary, Harmony (*see* HARMONY (ii)), but in 1930 the label was used to issue a separate race series, the 7000V sequence. It was discontinued in June 1932. (A. Sutton and K. Nauck: *American Record Labels and Companies: an Encyclopedia (1891–1943)* (Denver, 2000), 215)

Venable, Lucius. Name under which LUCKY MILLINDER was known early in his career.

Vendome Theater. Movie theater in Chicago; *see* NIGHTCLUBS AND OTHER VENUES.

Ventura, Charlie [Venturo, Charles] (*b* Philadelphia, 2 Dec 1916; *d* Pleasantville, NJ, 17 Jan 1992). Tenor saxophonist and bandleader. Around 1934 he learned to play C-melody saxophone, and took up the alto instrument before finally settling on tenor saxophone, which he was soon playing after the manner of Chu Berry and Coleman Hawkins in jam sessions with Roy Eldridge, Dizzy Gillespie, Bill Harris (i), Vido Musso, and Buddy DeFranco. He played with Gene Krupa (1942–3) and Teddy Powell (autumn 1943 – June 1944), then worked as principal soloist in Krupa's new trio and big band (1944–6), with which he appeared in the film *George White's Scandals* (1945); while still with Krupa he also performed with Jazz at the Philharmonic early in 1945 and again in 1946. Two decades later Stan Getz recorded a sentimental parody of Ventura's most famous solo with Krupa, *Dark Eyes*; it was issued and subsequently deleted from reissues when Getz protested angrily that it was meant to be a private joke only, not a public insult.

In June 1946 Ventura launched his own big band, including Tony Scott and Neal Hefti, but found more regular work from 1947 as the leader of a sextet, which initially included Harris, Ralph Burns, Bill De Arango, Curley Russell, and Dave Tough; Buddy Stewart soon joined as its singer, establishing the band's trademark, which involved melodies performed by instruments and voice in unison. Later that year Kai Winding replaced Harris and Shelly Manne took over from Tough. In 1948 Ventura formed a new big band, which included his younger brothers the baritone saxophonist Ben (Benjamin), the tenor saxophonist Ernie (Ernest), and the trumpeter Pete (Peter), but soon reduced it to an octet, retaining Ben Ventura, Roy Kral, Jackie Cain, and Bennie Green. In autumn 1948 the group took up the slogan "Bop for the People," and presented numerous clever arrangements of their characteristic unison melodies, now with a bop flavor. Ventura, who often played baritone saxophone during this period, was the principal soloist, although his driving improvisations were more firmly rooted in the swing era than the intricate bop style. During 1949 the octet's personnel changed frequently, with Conte Candoli, Boots Mussulli, Dave McKenna, Red Mitchell, Ed Shaughnessy, and Betty Bennett among his sidemen, and by the end of the year Ventura realized that his efforts to popularize bop had failed. He led another big band (December 1949–1951) and then formed the Big Four (a quartet with Marty Napoleon, Chubby Jackson, and Buddy Rich, 1951). While running his own club, Ventura's Open House, in Lindenwald, New Jersey (near Philadelphia), he performed again with Krupa (1952–3), Cain and Kral (1953), and McKenna (1954,

1956), worked as a disc jockey in Camden, New Jersey (1953), and appeared as a soloist with Stan Kenton (1954). Despite long bouts of illness he continued to work with Krupa intermittently until the end of the 1960s, and also led his own small groups in Las Vegas (1958–61), Minneapolis, and Denver (early 1960s). He returned to Las Vegas to work as a disc jockey (1970–72), and then played in Windsor, Connecticut (1972–5) and Fort Lauderdale, Florida (from 1975), until dental problems forced his retirement.

Four transcriptions of Ventura's solos were published as *Charlie Ventura Saxophone Solos with Piano Accompaniment* (New York, *c*1950).

SELECTED RECORDINGS

As leader: C. V. Jump (1946, Sunset 10054); How High the Moon (1946, Nat. 7015); East of Suez (1947, Nat. 9048); Baby, baby all the time/I'm forever blowing bubbles (1947–8, Nat. 9057); Euphoria (1948, Nat. 9055); Pina Colada (1948, Nat. 9066); Boptura (1949, Vic. 203552); If I had you (1949, Decca 11074); High on an Open Mike, first issued on *Charlie Ventura in Concert* (1949, Gene Norman 1); Ha! (1949, Vic. 20-3594); *Chazz 1977* (1977, FaD 115)

As sideman with G. Krupa: Leave up Leap (1945, Col. 36802); Dark Eyes (1945, Col. 36802); Stompin' at the Savoy/Body and Soul (1945, Col. 38214)

BIBLIOGRAPHY

J. Egan: "How Ventura Unit Got, Stays that Way," *DB*, xvi/5 (1949), 13
A. Morgan: "Retrospection," *JJ*, v/11 (1952), 14
G. Hoefer: "Charlie Ventura," *IM*, lxiii (1964), July, 12
J. Burns: "Swing Tenors," *JJ*, xix/12 (1966), 13
R. Cotterell: "A Personal View of Charlie Ventura," *JM*, no.147 (1967), 4
J. Burns: "Lesser Known Bands of the Forties, no.5: Charlie Ventura and Chubby Jackson," *JM*, no.163 (1968), 14
V. Schonfeld: "Charlie Ventura Reconsidered," *J&B*, i/1 (1971), 37
W. F. Lee: *Stan Kenton: Artistry in Rhythm* (Los Angeles, 1980/*R* 1994) [incl. discography; *R* without discography]
J. Liska: "Ventura Hits the Comeback Boulevard," *Philadelphia Daily News* (1 March 1981)
R. Palmer: "Stan Getz: Part Two of an Appraisal," *JJI*, xxxvii/1 (1984), 14
I. Gitler: *Swing to Bop: an Oral History of the Transition in Jazz in the 1940s* (New York, and Oxford, England, 1985)
S. Woolley: "Charlie Ventura," *JJI*, xxxix/3 (1986), 14
M. Vitez: "A Gift of Teeth for a Gifted Man," *Philadelphia Inquirer* (26 Feb. 1991)
Obituaries: *Los Angeles Times* (19 Jan 1992); *New York Times* (19 Jan 1992); *Philadelphia Daily News* (20 Jan 1992)

BK

Ventura, Ray(mond) (*b* Paris, 16 April 1908; *d* Palma de Mallorca, Spain, 30 March 1979). French bandleader. From 1924 he played piano in an amateur band that became known as the Collegiate Five in 1925 and recorded for Columbia as the Collegians from late 1928. In January 1929 he became the leader of the group, which two years later evolved into a professional show band (a versatile type of dance orchestra, the instrumentation of which was modeled on that of a big band); it made several recordings, including *St. Louis Blues/St. James Infirmary* (1932, Decca F2851). Ventura remained popular in France until 1939 (among those who performed with him as sidemen were Philippe Brun, Alix Combelle, and Guy Paquinet). He then led big bands in South America (1942–4) and again in France (1945–9); he also made a number of films. Ventura played an important role in introducing jazz to a large audience in France.

BIBLIOGRAPHY

M. Laplace: "Ray Ventura Discography," *Jazz Press*, no.49 (1978), 10
——: "Ray Ventura & His Collegians," *Memory Lane*, no. 62 (1984), 16

MICHEL LAPLACE

Venuti, Joe [Giuseppe] (*b* Philadelphia, 16 Sept 1903; *d* Seattle, 14 Aug 1978). Violinist. An irrepressible practical joker, he delighted in giving out incorrect information about his life, including false statements about his place and date of birth, which John Chilton finally identified conclusively. Other facts of Venuti's career are necessarily somewhat shaky owing to this impishness. He grew up in Philadelphia, where he learned solfeggio from his grandfather and studied classical violin, but devoted himself to popular music. He also formed a longstanding musical partnership there with Eddie Lang (see illustration). They separated temporarily in 1924 when Lang joined the Mound City Blue Blowers and Venuti traveled to Detroit to play with Jean Goldkette; he recorded with Goldkette and directed the Book-Cadillac Hotel Orchestra, one of several of the leader's dance bands. After playing in Atlantic City, New Jersey (summer 1925), Venuti moved to New York, where he and Lang worked with

Joe Venuti (right) with Eddie Lang, New York, c1929

Roger Wolfe Kahn's dance orchestra (October 1925 – June 1926) and in Broadway theater orchestras. Usually in Lang's company, Venuti played with most of the leading white jazz musicians of the period, including Goldkette (in performances and recordings in the New York area, January 1926 – September 1927, but not in the latter's touring band, based in Detroit), Red Nichols (March 1927; May–June 1928), Bix Beiderbecke (in the Broadway Bellhops, a recording band of September 1927), and Adrian Rollini and Frankie Trumbauer (both September–October 1927 and both with Beiderbecke). Venuti and Lang's recordings, especially an outstanding set of violin and guitar duos (1926–8), were highly influential in Europe, serving as a model for the quintet led by Django Reinhardt and Stephane Grappelli in Paris. The two men led bands in Atlantic City and New York before working with the Paul Whiteman Orchestra (May 1929 – May 1931), apart from a period of absence in 1929 after Venuti broke his arm. He recorded with Hoagy Carmichael and made further recordings with Trumbauer, Beiderbecke, and Lang, including an acclaimed session of 22 October 1931 by "Joe Venuti–Eddie Lang and their All Star Orchestra," including Benny Goodman and Jack Teagarden. Venuti and Lang rejoined Kahn in spring 1932 and last recorded together in February 1933, shortly before the guitarist's death.

After touring Europe in 1934, Venuti led a moderately successful big band from 1935 to 1943, served as a studio musician for MGM in California in 1944 and then returned to a small-group format. In this setting he toured frequently, visiting Europe in 1953, from his base in the Los Angeles area and, from 1963, in Seattle. An acclaimed performance at the Newport Jazz Festival in 1968, Dick Gibson's Colorado Jazz Parties from 1968 onwards, and the London Jazz Expo in 1969 marked the beginning of his return from several decades of relative obscurity, and during the 1970s he toured internationally on a regular basis. His many recordings during this last decade with such important musicians as Zoot Sims, Marian McPartland, and Earl Hines demonstrate that he had retained his prowess even at an advanced age. Venuti is considered the most important violinist in early jazz, with a full tone, a jocular style, and a strong sense of rhythm.

See also Violin.

SELECTED RECORDINGS

Duos: with E. Lang: Black and Blue Bottom/Stringing the Blues (1926, Col. 914D); Wild Cat/Sunshine (1927, OK 40762); Doin' Things/Goin' Places (1927, OK 40825); with M. McPartland: *The Maestro and Friend* (1974, Hal. 112); with B. Pizzarelli: *Nightwings* (*c*1974, FD BDL1-1120); with E. Hines: *Hot Sonatas* (1975, Chi. 145); with D. McKenna: *Alone at the Palace* (1977, Chi. 160)

As leader: Cheese and Crackers (1927, OK 40897); Penn Beach Blues (1927, OK 40947); Dinah (1928, OK 41025); Doin' Things/Wild Cat (1928, Vic. 21561); My Honey's Lovin' Arms (1928, OK 41251); Runnin' Ragged/ Apple Blossoms (1929, OK 41361); Raggin' the Scale (1930, OK 41432); I've found a new baby (1930, OK 41469); Little Buttercup (I'll never be the same) (1930, OK 41506); Beale Street Blues/After you've gone (1931, Voc. 15864); Farewell Blues/Someday Sweetheart (1931, Voc. 15858); The Jazz Me Blues/In de Ruff (1933, Col. 686); with Z. Sims: *Joe and Zoot* (1974, Chi. 128); with J. Albany: *Joe Venuti and Joe Albany* (1974, Horo 41–42); *Blue Fours* (1974, Chi. 134); with Z. Sims: *Joe Venuti/Zoot Sims* (1975, Chi. 142); with G. Barnes: *Live at the Concord Summer Festival* (1976, Conc. 30); with R. Tompkins: *Ross Tompkins and Joe Venuti Live at Concord '77* (1977, Conc. 51)

As sideman: J. Goldkette: It's the Blues (Blues no.14) (1924, Vic. 19600); R. W. Kahn: I'm sitting on top of the world (1925, Vic. 19845); J. Goldkette: Dinah (1926, Vic. 19947)

SELECTED FILMS AND VIDEOS

King of Jazz (1930); Garden of the Moon (1938); Syncopation (1942); Disc Jockey (1951); The Wizard of Waukesha (1979); Jazz at the Top! Remembering Bix Beiderbecke? (1998 [filmed 1976])

BIBLIOGRAPHY

ChiltonW

C. Emge: "Venuti Part of 'Golden Era' of Jazz," *DB*, xvii/ 24 (1950), 3

B. Crosby and P. Martin: *Call Me Lucky* (New York, 1953/*R*1993)

L. Feather and J. Tracy: *Laughter from the Hip* (New York, 1963/*R*1979 as *Laughter from the Hip: the Lighter Side of Jazz*)

R. Hadlock: *Jazz Masters of the Twenties* (New York, 1965/*R*1985), 239

D. Morgenstern: "Jazz Fiddle," *DB*, xxxiv/3 (1967), 16

G. T. Simon: *The Big Bands* (New York, 1967, rev. 4/1981), 486

D. M. Bakker: "Venuti-Lang and Friends," *Micrography*, no.5 (1969), 3

J. McCaffrey: "Hot Violin," *Coda*, ix/2 (1969), 2

R. M. Sudhalter, P. R. Evans, and W. Dean-Myatt: *Bix: Man & Legend* (New Rochelle, NY, and London, 1974)

B. Englund: "Joe Venuti in Scandinavia in 1934," *Sv*, no.58 (1975), 138

J. H. Klee: "Hear the One about Joe Venuti?" *MR*, ii/10 (1975), 4

L. Feather: *The Pleasures of Jazz: Leading Performers on their Lives, their Music, their Contemporaries* (New York, 1976), 68

L. Tomkins: "Octogenarian Giant of Jazz: Joe Venuti," *CI*, xvi/2 (1977), 14

A. Polillo: Liner notes, *I Grandi del Jazz: Joe Venuti* (I Grandi del Jazz 04, 1979)

M. Ullman: *Jazz Lives: Portraits in Words and Pictures* (Washington, DC, 1980)

G. Giddins: "A Penchant for Mayhem," *Riding on a Blue Note: Jazz and American Pop* (New York, and Oxford, England, 1981), 79

M. Glaser and S. Grappelli: *Jazz Violin* (New York and elsewhere, 1981) [incl. transcrs.]

Jazz String Newsletter, ii/1 (1983) [complete issue]

D. Hyman: "Bix Beiderbecke and Joe Venuti," *Keyboard*, xi/6 (1985), 76 [incl. transcr.]

G. Lees: *Waiting for Dizzy* (New York, and Oxford, England, 1991), 22

C. Garrod: *Joe Venuti and his Orchestra* (Zephyrhills, FL, 1993) [discography]

BK

Venuto, Joe [Joseph] (*b* New York, 20 June 1929). Vibraphonist and leader. He received a master's degree from the Manhattan School of Music, and after playing in clubs and dance bands in New York (late 1940s) he led his own quartet (1950–52). Venuto was a percussionist with the Sauter–Finegan Orchestra from 1953 to 1956 and continued to record with the band into the 1960s. After a brief association with Benny Goodman (1956) he worked as a percussionist in the orchestra at Radio City Music Hall (1956–8), performed and recorded with Johnny Richards (1958–9), and was active as a studio musician. He recorded on vibraphone with Jack Teagarden (1958), on marimba with Rex Stewart (1959), and on both instruments as a leader (1959). He is heard to advantage on *Redhead* (1959, Design 1047), which he recorded with Stewart, and on his own album *Sounds Different* (1959, Ev. 5053). Later he took part in sessions led by Budd Johnson and Shirley Scott (both 1963), Joe Mooney (1964), and Oliver Nelson, Gunther Schuller, and Johnny Hodges (all 1966). (*FeatherE*)

Verploegen, Angelo (*b* Oss, Netherlands, 22 Dec 1961). Dutch trumpeter and flugelhorn player. He played flugelhorn in a wind band from the age of 11 and took up trumpet when he joined a local big band when he was about 16. After moving to Amsterdam in 1980 he spent two years following a course in musicology at the university and a further two years at the Sweelinck Conservatory, where he studied trumpet and piccolo trumpet. From his arrival he played in a wide variety of settings, from small improvising groups to big bands. In 1987 Verploegen was a founder of the Houdini's. The group recorded regularly in its first 11 years and made many appearances in New York and at the Festival International de Jazz de Montréal, a tribute to its ensemble blend and mastery of the hard-bop style; on *Cooee* (1996), Verploegen's personal statement, it leaned towards a more airy and open style. In 1980 Verploegen began to work with the Dutch sound poet Jaap Blonk, and in the 1990s he played with the fusion guitarist Corrie van Binsbergen and in the cooperative band Zut Alors!, which included Michael Moore (ii). From 1997 to 1999 he was a member of the New Concert Big Band (later renamed the Jazz Orchestra of the Concertgebouw), conducted by Henk Meutgeer; he has continued to deputize in this group. Late in the decade he formed a trio, TOÏS, with the double bass player Tjitze Vogel and the drummer Bram Wijland. He has handled artists and repertory for the labels A (ii) and Buzz (both 1998–2000) and Jazz Impuls Nederland (from 2001), and he has taught trumpet at the Hogeschool voor de Kunsten in Utrecht (from 2001). Verploegen is an excellent section player and a soloist with decisive timing, a tart and piercing upper-register sound, and a full tone and accurate sense of pitch in the lower register.

SELECTED RECORDINGS

As leader of TOÏS: *An Angel's Work is Never Done* (1997, Via 992031-2)
As sideman: C. van Binsbergen: *Alles beweegt* (1989, BVHaast 9005); J. Blonk: *Splinks* (1992, Kontrans 739); Zut Alors!: *Pie Dough* (1992, J.B. 26); Houdini's: *Hybrid* (1994, Challenge 70004); *Cooee* (1996, Challenge 70045); C. van Binsbergen: *Corrie en de grote brokken* (1997, Via 992031-2); New Concert Big Band: *Festival* (1998, Via 992050-2)

BIBLIOGRAPHY

J. de Valk: "Met swingende tred door de instellingen" [Swinging through the institutions], *Jazz nu*, no.160 (1992), 323
M. Koster: "Het aapje is gezien" [We've seen the monkey], *Jazz nu*, no.225 (1998), 22

KEVIN WHITEHEAD

Verse. In popular music, that section of a song in which the tune remains constant but the text changes with each repetition; for the use of the melodies of song verses in jazz pieces *see* FORMS, esp. §1(i)(a).

Vertical cut recording. A term applied to a sound-recording technique that utilizes variations in the depth of the spiral groove on a cylinder or disc; *see* RECORDING, esp. §I, 1(i).

Verve. Record company and label. The company was established in Los Angeles in 1956 by NORMAN GRANZ around the time he became Ella Fitzgerald's manager, and at first issued new recordings that Granz had supervised in December of the previous year. In addition to offering Fitzgerald's now-classic "songbooks" (collections of American popular song, sung to the accompaniment of studio orchestras or jazz groups), Verve became one of the major companies recording swing and bop musicians of the era, issuing material from hundreds of important new sessions. Granz's earlier labels, CLEF and Norgran, were absorbed into the new company, and Verve reissued many items from the catalogues of both. Late in 1960 MGM bought the company from Granz, but it continued to issue new recordings, most notably those directed by Creed Taylor between 1961 and 1967. Much material from Verve's catalogue appeared in Europe and Japan under the same name, but the company also entered into agreements whereby numerous albums were issued on the labels Columbia and HMV in England and on Barclay and Blue Star in France. In 1967 Polydor purchased Verve, and the following year the company ceased to operate. However, its catalogue continued to be rereleased in the 1970s and 1980s by affiliated companies in the USA, England, France, Germany, and Japan; the most ambitious reissue project was undertaken by Polygram, using the Verve label, on which it also put out new albums. Granz retained the rights to Verve's extensive collection of recordings by Art Tatum and later released them on his new label, PABLO.

From the late 1980s important new recordings have continued to appear on Verve, especially through its French branch, which recorded Kenny Barron, Dee Dee Bridgewater, Charlie Haden, and Randy Weston, among many others, and its American operations. While the artists involved in the latter are too numerous to be detailed, mention must be made of the effect which new Verve albums had in reviving the careers of Shirley Horn and Joe Henderson. In the early 1990s Polygram formed the Verve Music Group, incorporating Antilles (which in 1992 transferred from another arm of Polygram and in 1995 became Verve/Antilles), the French label Bird-ology, the German label JMT, and its own labels Verve, Verve Forecast (focusing on acid jazz, fusion, and smooth-jazz styles), and Verve World. In 1994 it celebrated its "50th" (actually 48th) anniversary with a concert given at Carnegie Hall by leading musicians for Verve, past and present. In 1995 Verve signed a contract with Ornette Coleman to issue recordings on the saxophonist's label Harmolodics. In 1998 Seagrams purchased Polygram, which was then absorbed into the Universal Music Group. Its jazz division continued to operate as the Verve Music Group, which at that time controlled jazz material from A&M, Argo, Blue Thumb, Decca, GRP, Impulse!, MCA, Mercury, Sonet, Verve, and other labels.

BIBLIOGRAPHY

A. Morgan: "The Verve History of Jazz," *JJI*, xxxi/4 (1978), 18
M. Ruppli and B. Porter: *The Clef/Verve Labels: a Discography* (New York, Westport, CT, and London, 1986)
R. Palmer: "The Verve Story," *JJI*, xl/11 (1987), 13
B. Milkowski: "In Search of the New Fusion: Electric Jazz," Billboard, civ (4 July 1992), suppl., J2
B. Primack: "Label Watch: Verve: Living up to the Legend," *JT*, xxiii/9 (1993), 24
F. Alkyer: "Verve: Fine Time at 50," *DB*, lxi/8 (1994), 10
L. Blumenfeld: "Verve to Imprint Harmolodics," *DB*, li/10 (1994), 11
B. Kohlhaase: "A Stellar Birthday Celebration for 50 Years of Verve," *Los Angeles Times* (4 April 1994)
S. McElfresh: "Verve Concert, Reissues to Celebrate Recording Roots," *DB*, lxi/3 (1994), 10
P. Watrous: "A Label. A Vision. A Golden Anniversary," *New York Times* (3 April 1994)
D. Richardson: "The Nerve of Verve," *Piano & Keyboard*, no.172 (1995), 30
T. Tolley "Verve Records," *Coda*, no.268 (1996), 12
B. Bambarger: "Polygram Restructures its Philips, Verve Groups," *Billboard*, cix (5 April 1997), 3
L.-V. Mialy: "Chuck Mitchell," *Jh*, no.556 (1998–9), 29
D. Heckman: "All that Jazz: Verve Music Group is Ready to Get Down to Business," *Los Angeles Times* (19 Feb 1999)
<http://www.seagram.com/company_info/history/universal.html> (2000)
<http://www.vervemusicgroup.com/aboutus/> (2000)

BK

Very Very Circus. Group led from 1990 to 1995 by HENRY THREADGILL.

Vesala, Edward [Martti] (*b* Mäntyharju, Finland, 15 Feb 1945; *d* Yläne, Finland, 4 Dec 1999). Finnish drummer, percussionist, composer, leader, and record producer. He studied percussion at the Sibelius Academy, Helsinki (1965–7), and in the late 1960s played with Seppo Paakkunainen and others; he made the first of a number of recordings as a leader in 1969. In the early 1970s he performed with Jan Garbarek and toured Central Europe, and in 1974 he began working with Tomasz Stańko; later he recorded in a cooperative free-jazz trio with Gerd Dudek and Buschi

Niebergall (1977) and as a sideman with Kenny Wheeler (1979). During the late 1970s Vesala founded his own record label, Leo (*see* Leo (ii)), on which he recorded as a leader and as a sideman with Stańko (1978), Juhani Aaltonen (1978, 1981), and Charlie Mariano (1980). From 1984 he led Sound and Fury, a workshop ensemble for young Finnish musicians. He continued to record as a leader, and as a sideman with the electric guitarist Jimi Sumen (1991–2). Vesala's playing, at first influenced chiefly by the free jazz of the 1970s, became increasingly colored by ethnic music as a result of his travels in India, Indonesia, and China. His compositions, which include jazz and vocal works, combine elements of free jazz, ethnic music, and avant-garde concert music. His philosophy, which stressed the importance of personal emotional expression, is reflected in his recording *Ode to the Death of Jazz* (1990). In the late 1990s he became increasingly reclusive and lived mainly in his country house.

SELECTED RECORDINGS

(recorded for ECM unless otherwise indicated)

As leader: *Nan Madol* (1974, 1077); *Satu* (1976, 1088); *Heavy Life* (1980, Leo 009); *Mau-Mau* (1982, Johanna 2071); *Lumi* (1986, 1339); *Ode to the Death of Jazz* (1990, 1413); *Nordic Gallery* (1994, 1541)

As sideman: J. Garbarek: *Triptykon* (1972, 1029); T. Stańko: *Balladyna* (1975, 1071)

BIBLIOGRAPHY

A. Granholm: *Finnish Jazz* (Helsinki, 1974, rev. and enlarged 5/1997, by M. Huuskonen, J. Muikku, and T. Vähäsilta)

J. Sermila: "Edward's Thoughts: Interview with Edward Vesala," *JF* [intl edn], no.28 (1974), 46

T. Vähäsilta: "Edward Vesala: a Drummer from the North," *JF* [intl edn], no.92 (1985), 30

J. Muikku: "Edward Vesala: the Sound and the Fury," *Finnish Music Quarterly* no.4 (1991), 44

F. Reutemann: "Edward Vesala: Sound and Fury," *JP*, xl/2 (1991), 49

PEKKA GRONOW

Via. Record company. It was established as a record distribution company in Hilversum, Netherlands, in 1990 by Ben Gieskes. In 1995 it initiated a number of subsidiary labels, including Via Jazz, on which it has released more than 15 albums, mainly of small groups led by Michiel Borstlap, Yuri Honing, Han Bennink, and Joris Teepe, among others. In June 1998 it acquired the rights to ESP-disk, and shortly afterwards it began a reissue program using reproductions of artwork from the original albums and offering a vastly improved sound by comparison with that on earlier reissues from ESP-disk. Via opened additional offices in Wetteren, Belgium, in early 1998 and in London in October 1999.

BIBLIOGRAPHY

<http://www.rattaymusic.de/Labels/VIA%20Jazz%20Info.html> (2000)

<http://www.viarecords.com> (2000)

GK

Viale, Jean-Louis (*b* Neuilly-sur-Seine, France, 22 Jan 1933; *d* Paris, 10 May 1984). French drummer. He played as an amateur with Sacha Distel and René Urtreger (1951) and as a professional at Le Tabou in Paris with Henri Renaud, Bobby Jaspar (with whom he recorded in 1953–5), and Jimmy Gourley. In Paris he belonged to a band formed by Gigi Gryce that recorded with Clifford Brown (1953), and he also played regularly at the Club Saint-Germain. During the 1950s he performed with George Wallington, Django Reinhardt, René Thomas, Jimmy Raney, Thelonious Monk, Stephane Grappelli, Frank Foster, Barney Wilen, and Urtreger; many of these affiliations date from a period when he was mainly accompanying Distel, who was by that time working as a popular singer. From around 1956 Viale again concentrated on his work in jazz, performing at the Blue Note with Lester Young, Stan Getz, Martial Solal, and Zoot Sims (with whom he appears in the short film *Flash*, 1962). He led a group for a brief period at the Club Saint-Germain and worked frequently as a studio musician. In the mid-1960s he was associated with Johnny Griffin, Roger Guérin, Ivan Jullien, Raymond Fol, the Double Six, and Eddy Louiss. Injuries from an automobile accident interrupted his career in 1968, but he soon resumed playing with Thomas, Barney Kessel, Jim Hall, and Grappelli (all 1969), Johnny Hammond, Slide Hampton, Jack Diéval, and Guérin (all 1970), Urtreger (1970, 1975), and Benny Bailey (1978). From the mid-1970s, however, he became progressively less active. Viale was highly regarded by soloists for his vitality as a drummer and his steady beat.

SELECTED RECORDINGS

As sideman: D. Reinhardt: [untitled EP] (1953, BStar 6830); G. Wallington: *A Day in Paris* (1953, Vogue 171); G. Gryce and C. Brown: *Gigi Gryce–Clifford Brown Sextet* (1953, Vogue 175); H. Renaud: *Henri Renaud Plays Gigi Gryce* (1953, Vogue 174); Z. Sims: *Zoot Sims Sextet* (1953, Vogue 170); F. Foster: *Frank Foster Quartet* (1954, Vogue 209); R. Urtreger: *Trio* (1955, Barclay 84003); B. Kessel: *Limehouse Blues* (1969, BL 173)

BIBLIOGRAPHY

J.-L. Ginibre: "Test: pièges pour Jean-Louis," *Jm*, no.114 (1965), 30

ANDRÉ CLERGEAT/BK

Vian, Boris (*b* Paris, 10 March 1920; *d* Paris, 22 June 1959). French cornetist, songwriter, and jazz critic. In 1934 he began to play trumpet in a group with his brother, the drummer Alain Vian. Influenced by Bix Beiderbecke, he then played cornet with Claude Abadie (1943–7, 1949–50), with whom he recorded *Tin Roof Blues* (1946, Swing 212), and he led his own group at Le Tabou in Paris (1949). He may be seen along with his brother in the film *Le désordre à vingt ans* (1967); by 1950, however, he had ceased to play trumpet. He recorded as a singer with the Fol brothers (1947), and later recorded some of his own songs with the pianist Jimmy Walter and Claude Bolling (1955). Together with Michel Legrand, he wrote the first French rock-and-roll tunes (1956), and his hit song *Le blues du dentiste* was recorded by Henri Salvador with Quincy Jones (1958). In his writing Vian's general approach to the interpretation of jazz style and aesthetics followed that of André Hodeir, and he promoted African-American bop artists. He contributed to *Jazz hot* (1946–58) and *Combat* (1946–50), edited *Jazz News* (1948–50), and translated Dorothy Baker's jazz novel *Young Man with a Horn*. Vian's work as a novelist includes *J'irai cracher sur vos tombes* (Paris, 1946), under the "African-American" pseudonym Vernon Sullivan, which he pretended to have translated; the book was important in the French intellectural movement later dubbed "Le Désordre" and the bohemian culture in St. Germain-des-Prés with which the jazz of the era was associated. Some of his writings have been edited in a bilingual volume by G. Pestureau as *Jazz in Paris: Chroniques de jazz pour la station de radio WNEW, New York (1948–1949)* (n.p., 1997).Vian was also a jazz producer for Philips (1955–9) and briefly for Barclay.

BIBLIOGRAPHY

P. Boggio: *Boris Vian* (Paris, 1993)

M. Laplace: "La classic hot music," *Jazz Dixie/Swing: du Ragtime au Big Band*, no.1 (1993), 21

F. Ténot: *Boris Vian, le jazz et Saint-Germain* (Paris, 1993)

J. Campbell: *Paris Interzone: Richard Wright, Lolita, Boris Vian and others on the Left Bank, 1946–1960* (London, 1994)
M. Laplace: "Quelques immortels du cornet," *Jazz Dixie/Swing: du Ragtime au Big Band*, no.8 (1995), 40
J. Gilson: "Enregistrements Jef Gilson & Boris Vian," *Jazz Dixie/Swing: du Ragtime au Big Band*, no.11 (1996), 33
J. Thys: "Latitude de l'attitude: de Vian à Gainsbourg via Goraguer," *Bleu Banane*, no.1 (1997), 22
N. Bertolt: "Cité Véron," *Jh Spécial 2000* (1999), 36
C. Delaunay: "Geil-de-Launay," *Jh Spécial 2000* (1999), 38
H. Sportis and Y. Sportis: "Boris Vian," *Jh Spécial 2000* (1999), 34
F. Ténot: *Boris Vian, le jazz à Saint-Germain* (Paris, 1999)

MICHEL LAPLACE

Vibraphone [vibraharp, vibes]. A tuned percussion instrument consisting of a set of metal bars arranged like a piano keyboard; in contrast with the two ranks of a xylophone, all the bars are mounted on one level, facilitating the use of three or four mallets and the playing of chords. Each bar is suspended over a tube resonator containing a revolving vane or metal disc; the rotation of the vane causes a repeated opening and closing of the resonator, producing a vibrato. The speed of rotation, and thus of the vibrato, is controlled by an electric motor. When no vibrato is desired, the motor is switched off and the vanes rest in a vertical position, leaving the resonators fully open. The vibraphone has a compass of three octaves ascending from *f* and is usually played with rubber-tipped or yarn-wound rubber mallets. It has a foot-controlled sustaining device that operates in a similar way to the sustaining pedal of a piano.

The vibraphone was introduced in the USA in 1916 as a "steel marimba" and became popular as a jazz instrument in the early 1930s. Adrian Rollini used the vibraphone as a doubling instrument, and Lionel Hampton, who began his career as a drummer, played vibraphone in a short, improvised introduction to Louis Armstrong's *Confessin'* (OK 41448), which he recorded in July 1930 with Les Hite's band; Hampton later became the first outstanding vibraphone soloist, first as a sideman with Benny Goodman in the mid-1930s, then as the leader of his own band from 1940. His use of a fast vibrato and the crisp, brilliant articulation which reveals his background as a drummer may be heard to advantage on his album *Hamp in Harlem* (1979, Tim. 133). Red Norvo took up the vibraphone in 1944 and played it like the xylophone (which had earlier been his principal instrument), in that he did not use vibrato; his playing is well represented by his recording *Hallelujah/Slam Slam Blues* (1945, Dial 1045). Milt Jackson, who played with Dizzy Gillespie from 1945 and with the Modern Jazz Quartet from 1951 into the 1980s, did much to make the vibraphone popular as a jazz instrument; his use of a slow vibrato and of soft mallets of his own invention helped to define his distinctive, flowing style, which is exemplified by his recording *Plenty, Plenty Soul* (1957, Atl. 1269). Other important players have included Margie Hyams, a member of George Shearing's quartet, Teddy Charles, who in the 1950s prefigured some aspects of avant-garde jazz, Bill Le Sage, Bobby Hutcherson, and Terry Gibbs, whose playing in the 1950s displayed great virtuosity. In the 1960s the vibraphone was used as a doubling instrument by Victor Feldman and Tubby Hayes.

Gary Burton has been routinely credited with having independently brought vibraphone technique to a new level of virtuosity by playing with two mallets in each hand, a practice which he had taken up in the early 1960s. The facts are actually rather more complicated. Rollini and Norvo in earlier decades, and Hutcherson contemporaneously with Burton, had each spent periods using four mallets, but had abandoned the idea. However, Mike Mainieri (who is five years older than Burton) had been using a four-mallet technique from childhood, not by discovering it on his own, but by taking lessons in classical performance; and Burton himself had come to see the older vibraphonist play and to discuss techniques (their manner of holding the mallets was not the same). In any event, whatever the original source of four-mallet technique, it was unquestionably Burton's widely admired playing which popularized the approach, to the extent that it has come to be considered a part of the basic vocabulary of a jazz vibraphonist. Burton also devised a method of "bending," or slightly lowering, pitches by holding a hard-headed beater against a bar at its nodal point (the point at which the bar is suspended by a cord) and then striking the bar with a soft-headed beater and pulling away the other beater instantly. A good example of his innovative

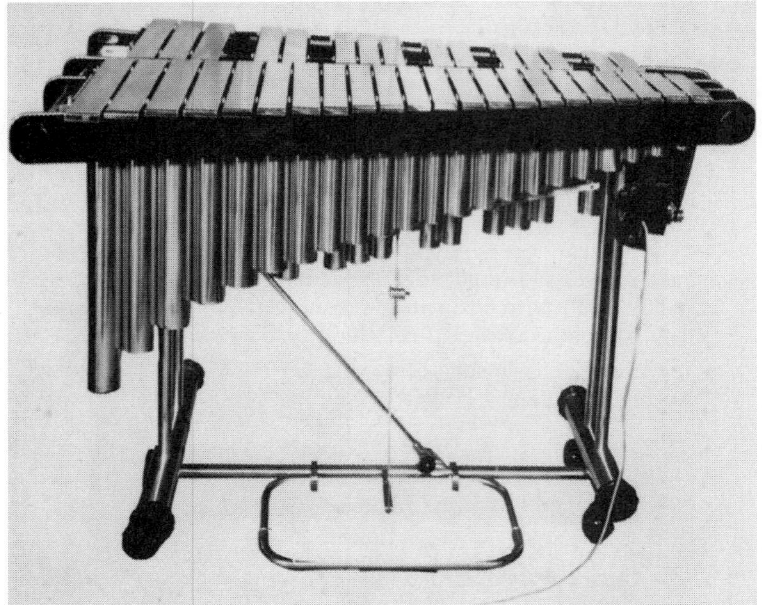

(a)

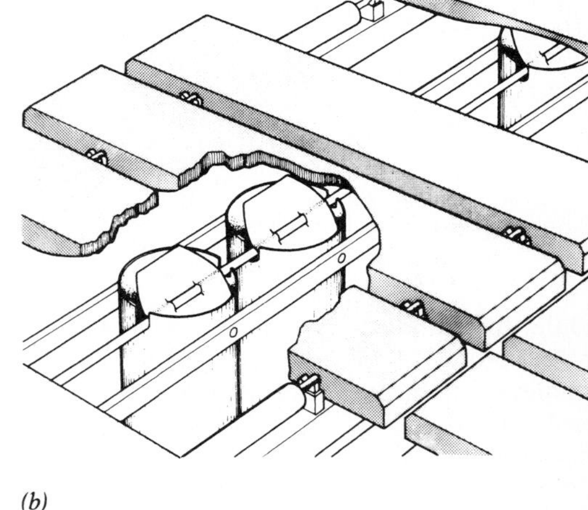

(b)

1. (a) Vibraphone; (b) diagram to show position of vanes in vibraphone resonators

playing is provided by his album *In the Public Interest* (1973, Pol. 6503), and in particular by its track *Dance*.

The vibraphone has been used as a free-jazz instrument by Walt Dickerson, Gunter Hampel, Karl Berger, and Jay Hoggard. In the 1970s Mainieri invented an electronic vibraphone, the Synthivibe.

For further illustrations *see* Hampton, lionel; Jackson, milt; and Mingus, charles.

BIBLIOGRAPHY

J.-E. Berendt: *Das Jazzbuch: Entwicklung und Bedeutung der Jazzmusik* (Frankfurt am Main, Germany, 1953, rev. 2/1959, Eng. trans., New York, 1962; rev. and enlarged 5/1981, Eng. trans., Westport, CT, 1982, as *The Jazz Book: from New Orleans to Fusion and Beyond*)
L. Feather: *The Book of Jazz: a Guide to the Entire Field* (New York, 1957, 2/1965 as *The Book of Jazz from Then till Now: a Guide to the Entire Field*)
J. Blades: *Percussion Instruments and their History* (London, 1970, rev. [3]/1984)
G. Collier: *Inside Jazz* (London, 1973)
R. Schietroma: "Mike Mainieri," *Percussive Notes*, xxii/1 (1983), 56
T. S. Gunderson: *A Pedagogical Approach to Solo Jazz Vibraphone Developed through an Analysis of Common Performance Practice* (diss., U. of Northern Colorado, 1992)
S. Rehbein: "The Contemporary Jazz Vibraphonist: the Electronic Expansion of the Acoustic Sound Spectrum," *Jazz Research Papers*, xiv (1994), 120

CLIFFORD BEVAN/BK

Vick, Harold (Edward) (*b* Rocky Mount, NC, 3 April 1936; *d* New York, 13 Nov 1987). Tenor saxophonist. His uncle Prince Robinson gave him a clarinet when he was 13, and three years later he began playing tenor saxophone. He performed while a student of psychology at Howard University, playing mainly with rhythm-and-blues bands. From 1960 to 1964 he played in Jack McDuff's soul-jazz group and also worked with other organists such as Jimmy McGriff, Big John Patton, Wild Bill Davis, Groove Holmes, and Larry Young. He then played with Walter Bishop, Jr., intermittently from 1964 until around 1969 and secured a contract for a few albums as a leader after giving a fine performance in Donald Byrd's group at Carnegie Hall around 1965; his first album, *Steppin' Out* (1963), displayed his penchant for the blues. During this period he also worked with Philly Joe Jones, Howard McGhee, and Ray Charles, played in the house band at the Apollo Theatre, New York, led a quintet including Woody Shaw and Bishop (*c*1967), performed in two plays, and appeared in Dizzy Gillespie's big band at the Newport Jazz Festival (1968). Comfortable on various types of saxophone, flute, and clarinet, in 1969 Vick joined the Negro Ensemble Company as a multi-woodwind player and toured Europe with it. Over the next five years he played in soul bands accompanying King Curtis (1969–70) and Aretha Franklin (1970–74), and while with the latter's group was also a member of Jack DeJohnette's jazz-rock band Compost, which played a blend of jazz, rock, and highly chromatic or atonal music (1971–3); with this ensemble Vick's blues style was a galvanizing force, as appropriate in this context as it was on soul-jazz recordings.

After recovering from a heart attack Vick renewed his involvement with soul jazz, performing and recording with Shirley Scott (1974–*c*1976), and again with McGriff (1980–81), while working for many years as studio musician (in which capacity he performed in three films) and as a freelance jazz player.

SELECTED RECORDINGS

As leader: *Steppin' Out* (1963, BN 84138); *Caribbean Suite* (1966, RCA LSP3677); *Straight Up* (1966, RCA LSP3761); *Don't Look Back* (1974, SE 7431); *Commitment* (1975, Muse 5054)
As sideman: J. McDuff: *Goodnight, It's Time to Go* (1961, Prst. 7220); J. Patton: *Along Came John* (1963, BN 84130); *Oh Baby!* (1965, BN 84192); J. DeJohnette: *Compost* (1972, Col. 31176); S. Scott: *One for Me* (1974, SE 7430)

SELECTED FILMS AND VIDEOS

Stardust Memories (1980); The Cotton Club (1984); School Daze (1988)

BIBLIOGRAPHY

Feather–Gitler '70s
Liner notes, *Steppin' Out* (BN 84138, 1964)
M. Gardner: "Harold Vick," *JM*, no.171 (1969), 4 [incl. discography]
L. Tomkins: "Harold Vick," *CI*, xiv/3 (1975), 14
J. De Muth: "Shirley Scott Trio Interview," *Cadence*, i/9 (1976), 11
M. Gardner: "Harold Vick," *Coda*, no.148 (1976), 8
Obituary, *New York Times* (17 Nov 1987)

ANDREW WAGGONER

Victo. Record company and label. The company was established in the late 1980s in Victoriaville, Quebec, Canada, to issue recordings made at the Festival International Musique Actuelle Victoriaville; later it issued studio recordings as well. As of 2000 Victo had released more than 70 albums, which feature music ranging from freely improvised unaccompanied piano solos to experimental rock; the first seven recordings were on both LP and CD, though all later issues were restricted to CD only. The Victo catalogue maintains a strong focus on artists from Europe and Quebec, including Derek Bailey, Conrad Bauer, Jean Derome, Barre Phillips, Paul Plimley, and Carlos Zingaro, but it also offers items by such noteworthy musicians from the USA as Anthony Braxton, Marilyn Crispell, Fred Frith, Charles Gayle, Roscoe Mitchell, and David Murray.

BIBLIOGRAPHY

<http://victo.qc.ca> (2000)
<http://www.netculture.net/~ork/HTML/Victo.htm> (2001)

GK

Victor. Record company and label. The company was established (as the Victor Talking Machine Company) in 1901 in Camden, New Jersey, by Eldridge R. Johnson. From its inception it was closely associated with Emile Berliner's Gramophone Company, with which it shared the rights to use equipment patented by Berliner; it also used the "dog and gramophone" logo that later became the trademark of His Master's Voice (HMV). The company issued some of the earliest recordings connected with jazz – those made in 1913–14 by James Reese Europe's Society Orchestra; Reese's discs were issued in territories other than the USA on HMV, and this marked the beginning of an arrangement that lasted until 1957 whereby much of Victor's material was put out on various HMV labels throughout the world.

In 1917 Victor issued the first discs by the Original Dixieland Jazz Band. This early involvement was not sustained, however, and the label was not noted for jazz in the early 1920s, when artists and repertory were directed by Edward T. King. The company was slow to record for the growing race market; it abandoned auditions for a race series in 1921, and discontinued a further attempt (though it included discs by Lizzie Miles and Rosa Henderson) after only a few issues. Most jazz recorded during this period was of the more polite type, notably the work of Paul Whiteman (with Victor from 1920 to 1928) and A. J. Piron's New Orleans Orchestra (1923–5).

After King was succeeded in November 1926 by Nat Shilkret, however, Victor quickly established a reputation for its jazz catalogue with long series by Jelly Roll Morton (1926–30), Bennie Moten (1926–32), Duke Ellington (1927–

30), McKinney's Cotton Pickers (1928–31), and King Oliver and the Missourians (both 1929–30). The company also made many field recordings, undertaking an extensive documentation of the work of jug bands in Memphis from 1927 to 1930. At first race records were issued as part of the general series, but a separate sequence, the V38000s, was started in January 1929. After a few dozen issues this was dedicated solely to recordings of instrumental music; a new series, the V38500s, was established for vocal music some three months later.

The making of these significant recordings and the establishment of the new series coincided with a corporate change: on 4 January 1929 Victor was sold and took a new name, the Radio–Victor Company of America. From 1930 it was known as RCA Victor, but its principal label continued into 1946 as Victor. Following this takeover, in 1931–2 the activities of the Victor label were drastically reduced. Nevertheless, noteworthy recordings appeared during this period by the Washboard Rhythm Kings. Both race series were discontinued in 1930 but were replaced the following year with two new sequences: the 23000s for instrumental and the 23250s for vocal recordings.

From the 1930s Victor's catalogue contained important recordings by Fats Waller (1934–42), Lionel Hampton (1937–40), and Benny Goodman's big band and small groups (1935–9), and many of the company's recordings of the 1940s, especially those of Sidney Bechet (1940–41) and Ellington (1940–46), have come to be regarded as classics. In September 1931 Victor launched a series of experimental long-playing discs; these Program Transcriptions (so called, it is thought, because they looked like broadcast transcriptions and needed to be played on similar equipment) included material recorded specifically for the series by Louis Armstrong and Duke Ellington. It was discovered in the early 1980s that at many of Victor's sessions of this period (among them those that produced Ellington's Program Transcriptions) two recordings of the same performance were taken, one each from two spatially separated microphones. Although only one from each pair of recordings was issued, in several cases a test pressing of the other has survived; when played simultaneously the two versions produce a perfect stereophonic sound (*see* Recording, §II, 3).

When referring to Victor's output up to the end of the 78 r.p.m. era (i.e., into the early 1950s), jazz enthusiasts and discographers have customarily referred to the label name (Victor) rather than the company name (RCA Victor); however, the company actually ceased to use the sole name Victor somewhat earlier, from February 1946, when records began to appear with the full name RCA Victor. For a history of the company and label from this point onwards *see* Rca victor.

For illustration *see* Films, fig.4.

BIBLIOGRAPHY

H. Panassié: *144 Hot Jazz Bluebird and Victor Records* (Camden, NJ, 1939)
R. M. W. Dixon and J. Godrich: *Blues & Gospel Records, 1902–1942* (Hatch End, nr London, 1964, rev. and enlarged 4/Oxford, England, 1997, as R. M. W. Dixon, J. Godrich, and H. Rye: *Blues & Gospel Records, 1890–1943*), xxiv
J. Godrich: "The Victor Race Series," *Blues Unlimited* (1964), no.10, p.8; no.11, p.8; no.12, p.10; no.13, p.12; no.14, p.14; no.15, p.12; no.16, p.13; no.17, p.12
D. Mahony: "Notes on Victor Master Numbers," *Matrix*, no.68 (1966), 3
R. M. W. Dixon and J. Godrich: *Recording the Blues* (London, 1970)
R. D. Kinkle: "Victor Numerical List," *The Complete Encyclopedia of Popular Music and Jazz, 1900–1950* (New Rochelle, NY, and Westport, CT, 1974), iv, 2044
B. Rust: *The American Record Label Book* (New Rochelle, NY, 1978), 303
B. Kay: Liner notes, D. Ellington: *Reflections in Ellington: the 1932 Band in True Stereo* (Everybody's 3005, 1985)
D. Spottswood: "When the Wolf Knocked on Victor's Door ...," *78 Quarterly*, no.5 (1990), 63
A. Sutton and K. Nauck: *American Record Labels and Companies: an Encyclopedia (1891–1943)* (Denver, 2000), 216, 335

HOWARD RYE

Vidacovich, John (Joseph, Jr.) [Johnny V.] (*b* New Orleans, 27 June 1949). Drummer. He took up drums at school around the age of 11 and began formal lessons a year later, after acquiring his first drum set; by the time he was 16 he was performing professionally. Later he studied (BME 1972) and then taught (from 1982) at Loyola University. From the late 1970s he has maintained long-lasting associations with Alvin "Red" Tyler (to 1998) and Tony Dagradi's group Astral Project; in addition he toured and recorded with Dave Liebman, John Scofield, Bobby McFerrin, Mose Allison, and Ray Anderson. Vidacovich may be seen in the video *New Orleans Jazz and Second Line Drumming* (*c*1995), which he made with Herlin Riley, and he has recorded twice as a sole leader.

SELECTED RECORDINGS

As sideman: A. Tyler: *Graciously* (1986, Rounder 2061); J. Scofield: *Flat Out* (1988, Gram. R1-79400); M. Allison: *My Backyard* (1989, BN B21S-93840); S. Masakowski: *What it Was* (1993, BN B21Z-80591); T. Dagradi: *Live at the Columns* (1993, Turnipseed 07); R. Margitza: *Game of Chance* (1996, Challenge 70044)

BIBLIOGRAPHY

B. Grady: "Drummer is Beat from Global Gigs," *New Orleans Times–Picayune* (25 Jan 1990)
R. Santelli: "The Drummers of New Orleans: Johnny Vidacovich," *MD*, xiv/10 (1990), 37
S. Aiges: "Music: Mastering the Mysterious Rhythms of the Street," *New Orleans Times–Picayune* (21 April 1995)
E. Enright: "The Funk inside the Van," *DB*, lxvi/11 (1999), 32

GK

Vienna Art Orchestra [VAO]. Austrian big band formed in Vienna in 1977 by the Swiss pianist, composer, and arranger Mathias Rüegg. He modified the normal instrumentation of a big band by using fewer trumpets, trombones, and saxophones and adding tuba and vibraphone. All of the Austrian members of the first VAO later became leading jazz musicians in the country: the trumpeter Karl "Bumi" Fian, the trombonist Christian Radovan, the saxophonists Wolfgang Puschnig and Harry Sokal, the vibraphonist Fritz "Woody" Schabata, the pianist Uli Scherer, and the drummer Wolfgang Reisinger. In 1983 Rüegg formed the Vienna Art Choir, which consisted of about 12 singers, and recorded with members of the orchestra that same year. In 1984 the VAO toured the USA for 16 concerts and received recognition in the *Down Beat* critics poll, and thereafter it toured Europe, India, and Africa and appeared at festivals in Montreux, East Berlin, Molde (Norway), Bombay, Willisau (Switzerland), Vienna, Palermo (Sicily), Paris, Barcelona, Cologne (Germany), Rome, Mozambique, and San Sebastian (Spain), among others (1985–90). In 1989–90 Puschnig, Sokal, and the singer Lauren Newton left the band, and the trombonist Joseph Bowie, the Austrian saxophone players Klaus Dickbauer and Florian Bramböck, the drummer Thomas Alkier, and the singer Alexandra Naumann joined. Among the soloists with whom the band has played are John Surman, George Lewis (ii), Karin Krog, and Art Farmer.

The orchestra's wide-ranging repertory has included the music of Scott Joplin, Lennie Tristano, Anthony Braxton,

Hans Koller, and the French composer Erik Satie. In the early 1990s new works were contributed by Puschnig, Werner Pirchner, Bramböck, and the Swiss composer and arranger Daniel Schnyder. During this period the VAO made further extensive tours, and appeared in Seville (Spain), Helsinki, and Utrecht (Netherlands). In 1993 it performed with the singers Betty Carter, Gabrielle Goodman, and Helen Merrill at the Festival International de Jazz de Montréal, and recorded music by Duke Ellington and Charles Mingus at the Five Spot in New York; in Vienna that same year, Rüegg founded, with financial help from the Viennese community, the jazz club Porgy & Bess, which became the most important venue for contemporary jazz musicians in Austria. In the mid-1990s the trombonist Christian Muthspiel, the tenor saxophonist Herwig Gradischnig, the pianist Reinhard Micko, the double bass player Robert Riegler, and the singers Ali Gaggl and Cornelia Giese (all Austrians) joined the orchestra; during this period Herbert Joos remained one of its principal soloists. The VAO took part in the Gunther Schuller festival in Linz, Austria, in 1996, and it celebrated its twentieth anniversary in 1997 with the release of a set of three CDs consisting of ballads sung by Sheila Jordan, Carter, Merrill, and Urszula Dudziak, together with *Nine Immortal Nonevergreens for Eric Dolphy* and a concerto for "voice and silence." Between 1979 and 1997 the band recorded nearly 30 albums presenting various annual projects.

SELECTED RECORDINGS

From No Time to Rag Time (1982, HA 1999–2000); *The Minimalism of Erik Satie* (1984, HA 2005); *Perpetuum Mobile* (1985, HA 2024); *Nightride of a Lonely Saxophone Player* (1985, Moers Music 02054–5); *Two Little Animals* (1987, Moers Music 02066); *Blues for Brahms* (1988, Amadeo 839105-2); *Innocence of Clichés* (1989, Amadeo 841646-2); *The Original Charts of Duke Ellington and Charles Mingus* (1993, Verve 521998-2); *Vienna Art Orchestra Plays for Jean Cocteau* (1994, Verve 529290-2); *20th Anniversary* (1997, Verve 537095-2) [consists of *Powerful Ways: Nine Immortal Nonevergreens for Eric Dolphy*; *Quiet Ways: Ballads*; *Unexpected Ways: a Concerto for Voice & Silence*]

BIBLIOGRAPHY

GrayF
G. Kühn: "Das Wiener Art Orchester," *JP*, xxix/12 (1980), 18
H. Hollenstein: "Le Weiner Art Orchester," *Jazz 360°*, no.35 (1981), 3
K. Schulz: "Austria: Vienna Art Orchestra," *JF* [intl edn], no.71 (1981), 11
J. Solothurnmann: "Mathias Rüegg & Vienna Art Orchestra," *JF* [intl edn], no.79 (1982), 30
J. Solothurnmann and G. Endress: "Vienna Art Orchestra," *JP*, xxxi/10 (1982), 4
M. Buholzer: "Jazz et Satie: Vienna Art," *Jm*, no.335 (1985), 27
F. Davis: "Vienna Art Orchestra: Variations on a Big Band Theme," *DB*, lii/2 (1985), 26; repr. in *In the Moment: Jazz in the 1980s* (New York, and Oxford, England, 1986/*R*1996), 75
K. Ansell: "Vienna Art Orchestra," *Wire*, no.24 (1986), 24
P. J. Butler: "Is 20 Years Enough?" *DB*, lxiv/9 (1997), 10
M. Rüegg: *Vienna Art Orchestra, 1977–1997* (Vienna, 1997)

KLAUS SCHULZ

Viera, Joe [Josef] (*b* Munich, 4 Sept 1932). German tenor saxophonist. He studied piano and saxophone privately from 1948 to 1956. From the mid-1950s he was active in a variety of settings, playing dixieland with the Riverboat Seven (1957–65), modern jazz with Albert Mangelsdorff and in a duo with the pianist Erich Ferstl (1962–5), and free jazz with his own trio (1966–8). Later he co-led a quartet with the trombonist Ed Kröger (1968–73) and led a sextet (1976–94). A prominent jazz educator in Germany, he became a professor at the University of Duisburg in 1981 and published several method books on jazz and improvisation. He was a founding member of the International Jazz Federation (1969) and the Union Deutscher Jazzmusiker (1973). In 1970 he founded the festival Internationale Jazzwoche Burghausen, for which he serves as music director, and from 1972 he organized regular workshops at the Studienzentrum für zeitgenössische Musik Burghausen; in the late 1990s he offered workshops throughout Europe. He has remained active in various duos and as the leader of a quartet and a big band. Viera's playing, which draws from both free and conventional styles, may be heard to advantage on *Sections*, from a quartet album with Kröger, *Essay in Jazz* (1971, Universal Edition 20052), and on *Boogie Stop Shuffle*, from his sextet's album *Kontraste* (1978, Calig 30619).

SELECTED WRITINGS

Grundlagen der Jazzharmonik (Vienna, 1970)
Grundlagen der Jazzrhythmik (Vienna, 1970)
Arrangement und Improvisation (Vienna, 1971)
Neue Formen – freies Spiel (Vienna, 1971)
Der Free Jazz: Formen und Modelle (Vienna, 1974)
Das Saxophon im Jazz (Vienna, 1977)
Jazz: Musik unserer Zeit (Schäftlach, Germany, 1992)

BIBLIOGRAPHY

D. Zimmerle: "Es bleibt noch viel zu tun ...: Gespräch mit Joe Viera und Ed Kröger," *JP*, xx/11 (1971), 392
G. Endress: "Joe Viera: unermüdlicher Einsatz für den Jazz," *JP*, xl/2 (1991), 24

WOLFRAM KNAUER

Vignola, Frank (J.) (*b* Islip, NY, 30 Dec 1965). Guitarist and banjoist. His father played accordion and banjo, and his brother is a trumpeter. He took up guitar at the age of five, learning initially with his father and from recordings by Django Reinhardt, Joe Pass, and Bucky Pizzarelli; over the next decade he concentrated on the styles of Reinhardt and Pass. When he was 12 he began playing banjo, and two years later he won the Grand National Banjo Championship in Canada; around this time he recorded on the instrument. From the age of 14 he was active as a professional musician, and as a teenager he spent a period playing in rock bands. In the mid-1980s he worked with the ragtime pianist Max Morath, Ken Peplowski, and the violinist Andy Stein, among others; he was also a member of Vince Giordano's Nighthawks, with which he appeared in the film *Bloodhounds on Broadway* (1989).

Late in 1987 Vignola formed a quintet, Hot Club (after the Quintette du Hot Club de France), which held a successful engagement at Michael's Pub early the following year. By 1990 he was also performing in New York in duos and trios involving, among others, Herman Foster, Frank Tate, John Goldsby, and Joe Ascione. That same year he joined Ed Polcer's quartet, and with the tuba player Sam Pilafian he established the quartet Travelin' Light; he may be seen in the video *Tuba Clinic: featuring Sam Pilafian, Tuba, with Frank Vignola on Guitar* (*c*1993). Later he worked with Peplowski again (recording in 1992), performed in Claude Williams's quartet (1994), and, with Howard Alden and Jimmy Bruno, formed the Concord Jazz Guitar Collective. His group Unit Four recorded a fusion album in 1995. Around 1997 he and Ascione formed the record and publishing company Venture Music, which released recordings, videos, and instructional materials. He has taught at Boston University and Arizona State University.

Vignola has worked principally as an acoustic guitarist for much of his career, playing in a swing style modeled after that of Reinhardt. However, under the influence of Concord's record producers, his recorded output in the latter half of the 1990s explored a fusion style.

SELECTED RECORDINGS

(recorded for Concord unless otherwise indicated)

As leader: *Appel Direct* (1993, 4576); *Let it Happen* (1994, 4625); with H. Alden and J. Bruno: *Concord Jazz Guitar Collective* (1995, 4672); of Unit Four: *Look Right, Jog Left* (1995, 4718)

As sideman: K. Peplowski: *The Natural Touch* (1992, 4517); J.-E. Kellso: *Chapter 1* (1993, Arbors 19125); Travelin' Light: *Cookin' with Frank and Sam* (1995, 4647)

BIBLIOGRAPHY

Feather–GitlerBEJ

S. Holden: "Reinhardt's Hot Club Back in Style," *New York Times* (22 Jan 1988)

B. Delatiner: "Guitarists's Passion for Gypsy Jazz," *New York Times* (29 Jan 1989)

B. Eichenberger: "Satisfied with 'Happy Music': Feel-good Jazz Suits Travelin' Light Guitarist Just Fine," *Columbus Dispatch* (22 July 1993)

J. Ferguson: "Frank Vignola: Ripping Jazzman Takes Control," *GP*, xviii/3 (1994), 16

J. Lloyd: "Jazz: a Guitarist who Cooks – with a Wok and a Steamer," *Philadelphia Inquirer* (24 March 1995)

S. R. B. Iyer: "Jazz Group Keeps Guitar Master's Spirit Alive," *Columbus Dispatch* (9 Jan 1997)

——: "Guitarist Stays True to Lifelong Love of Jazz," *Columbus Dispatch* (4 Oct 1999)

<http://visionx.com/jazz/iviews/Vignola.htm> (2000)

<http://www.aent.com/concord/biogs/vignola.html> (2000)

GK

Viking Jazz Band. Name by which a septet led by Papa Bue was known from 1958.

Village Gate. Nightclub in New York; *see* Nightclubs and other venues.

Village Vanguard. Nightclub in New York; *see* Nightclubs and other venues.

Villegas, Enrique [Mono] (*b* Buenos Aires, 3 Aug 1913; *d* Buenos Aires, 10 July 1986). Argentine pianist. He studied with Alberto Williams at the Conservatorio Nacional (graduated 1932) and began his career as a classical pianist, giving the first performances in Argentina of Ravel's Concerto in G and in 1934 of Gershwin's *Rhapsody in Blue*. After working from 1943 to 1944 as a leader of jazz groups he settled in New York (1955), where he recorded with Milt Hinton and Cozy Cole (1955–7). In 1964 he returned to Buenos Aires and recorded two albums in a trio (*Cuerpo y alma*, 1965, Trova 1, and *Tributo a Monk*, 1967, Trova 12), and also as an unaccompanied soloist (1967, 1968), in a duo with Jorge López Ruiz (1968), and with Paul Gonsalves (1968). Villegas moved again to New York in 1970 and remained there for a year. Later he recorded in a trio (1973) and a free-jazz quartet (1975) and performed at the Teatro Colón (1975); he made his last recording in 1977.

LAUREANO FERNÁNDEZ, OMAR GARCÍA BRUNELLI

Villéger, André (*b* Rosny-sous-Bois, France, 12 Aug 1945). French saxophonist. He took up clarinet at the age of 18 and made a modest début in a traditional-jazz group in 1965. After studying soprano saxophone he served as a member of Raymond Fonsèque's group (1968–70). He then took up the alto, tenor, and baritone instruments and played with Les Lutéciens, the Cocoro Steel Band (1972–5), and the house group at the Hôtel Méridien in Paris, where he had occasion to accompany such American musicians as Milt Buckner, Sir Charles Thompson, Joe Newman, Lionel Hampton, Harry Edison, Sam Woodyard, and Illinois Jacquet. Villéger joined Claude Bolling's Show Biz Band in 1975, though he also worked with the Mélanie Jazz Sextet, the Jazz Five, Polygruel, Chute Libre (which included Mino Cinélu), the Anachronic Jazz Band, and the Caratini Jazz Ensemble. In all these groups he displayed his considerable talent as an improviser, as elegant as he is fiery.

SELECTED RECORDINGS

Duos with P. Milanta: *Duke Ellington and Billy Strayhorn's Sound of Love* (1999, Jazz aux Remparts 64011)

As leader: *Something to Live For* (1984, Cara 012); *Connection* (1990, Jazz aux Remparts 59641)

As sideman: Mélanie Jazz Sextet: *It Feels so Good* (1975, Open 01); Anachronic Jazz Band: *Anachronic Jazz Band*, i–ii (1976, 1978, Open 02, 09), incl. Daahoud; F. Biensan: *Jumpin' with Sam* (1980, BB 33149); C. Bolling: *Live at the Méridien* (1984, CBS FM39245); F. Biensan: *Almost Cried* (1994, Jazz aux Remparts 64006); P. Caratini: *Darling Nellie Gray* (1999, Label Bleu 6625)

BIBLIOGRAPHY

J.-M. Bramy: "André Villéger, ou la solitude d'un ténor de fond," *Le jazzophone*, no.17 (1984), 28

——: "André Villeger," *Jh*, no.432 (1986), 50

B. Joyeux: "Gros plan: André Villéger," *Jm*, no.356 (1986), 40

ANDRÉ CLERGEAT

Vincent, Ron(ald David) (*b* Warwick, RI, 18 Oct 1951). Drummer. He studied at the Berklee School of Music (BA Mus Ed 1973) and later worked with Carmell Jones (1980–82) and John McNeil's quartet (1984–8). In 1989 his own quartet, which included Dave Douglas, toured France, where it performed at the Grenoble Jazz Festival. The following year Vincent began working with Gerry Mulligan. He was a member of Mulligan's Re-Birth of the Cool tentet in the early 1990s and recorded and toured internationally with his last quartet until the saxophonist's death in 1996. During the same period he joined Bill Charlap (1990), with whom he recorded in a trio with Michael Moore (i) (1997), and worked with Helen Merrill (1990–92), Art Lande (1991–3), Maurizio Giammarco (from 1992), Carol Sloane (from 1993), the pianist Steve Million (recording in 1995), and the Gerry Mulligan All Star Tribute Band, led by Ted Rosenthal (from 1996). In January 1997 he gave a concert as the leader of a quintet, with Randy Brecker, Chris Potter, Charlap, and Moore as his sidemen. Vincent has also been active in jazz workshops.

SELECTED RECORDINGS

As leader with B. Charlap, T. Rosenthal, and Dean Johnson: *The Gerry Mulligan Songbook* (1996, Chi. 349)

As sideman: G. Mulligan: *Dream a Little Dream* (1994, Telarc 83364); S. Million: *Million to One* (1995, Palmetto 2014-2); G. Mulligan: *Dragonfly* (1995, Telarc 83377)

GK

Vinding, Mads (*b* Copenhagen, 7 Dec 1948). Danish double bass player. A self-taught musician, he began playing professionally at the age of 16. In the 1970s he worked with Finn Savery's trio, Thomas Clausen, and the Crème Fraîche Big Band, and from 1978 with the Radioens Big Band and Svend Asmussen. In the 1980s he was a member of Ernie Wilkins's Almost Big Band, formed a duo with Kenny Drew, and played with many Swedish jazz groups, including those led by the pianist and organist Kjell Öhman and by Nils Lindberg. Vinding, whose playing both technically and in its melodic refinement is reminiscent of that of Niels-Henning Ørsted Pedersen, has accompanied countless visiting musicians, and from the 1990s was often teamed with Alex Riel in rhythm sections. One of the most prolifically recorded Danish jazz musicians, he may be heard with Drew, Jesper Thilo, Kim Parker, Johnny Griffin, Duke Jordan, Doug

Raney, Wilkins, Dexter Gordon, Howard McGhee, Art Farmer, Lindberg, Bob Brookmeyer, Roland Hanna, Clausen, Dorothy Donegan, Savery, Kai Winding, the singer Sylvia Vrethammar, the pianist Rune Öfwerman, Hank Jones, Asmussen, Idrees Sulieman, the singer Magni Wentzel, the Radioens Big Band, Rune Gustafsson, Putte Wickman, and the trombonist Torolf Mølgaard.

SELECTED RECORDINGS

As leader: *Danish Design* (1974, Sonet 2560); *The Kingdom (Where Nobody Dies)* (1997, Stunt 19703); *Daddio Don* (1998, Stunt 19813); *Six Hands, Three Minds, One Heart* (1999, Stunt 0052)

As sideman: F. Savery: *New York Series* (1976, Exlibris 20013); A. Farmer: *Manhattan* (1981, SN 1026); K. Drew: *Playtime: Children's Songs* (1982, Met. 15695); E. Wilkins: *Montreux* (1983, Ste. 1190); D. Raney: *Guitar, Guitar, Guitar* (1985, Ste. 1212); S. Asmussen: *Fiddler Supreme* (1989, Intim Music 006); T. Clausen: *Café noir* (1991, M.A. Music 004); B. Brookmeyer: *Old Friends* (1994, Sto. 8292); Marc Bernstein: *Blue Walls* (1998, Sto. 4223)

BIBLIOGRAPHY

J. Arntzen: "Jesper Lundgaard; Mads Vinding," *MM: tidskrift for rytmisk music m.m.*, xiv/4 (1982), 8

K. Frandsen: *Politikens jazzleksikon* (Copenhagen, 1987)

L. Tømming: "Mads Vinding og kongeriget" [Mads Vinding and the kingdom], *Musikeren*, nos.7–8 (1997), 10

FRANK BÜCHMANN-MØLLER

Vining, Ted [Edward Norman] (*b* Melbourne, Australia, 22 Aug 1937). Australian drummer and leader. He began playing jazz in the Melbourne area around 1958, and early in his career worked in bands led by Alan Lee, Keith Hounslow, and Brian Brown; he was a key member of Brown's bands between 1965 and 1979. In 1970 he formed a trio consisting of Bob Sedergreen and the double bass player Barry Buckley; fuelled by Vining's assertive style, this remains arguably the tightest-knit, hardest-swinging band in Australian jazz. From 1965 Vining's work in advertising took him to other cities for several lengthy periods, and his time in Brisbane (1981–6) was especially significant. He formed Musiikki-oy with several emerging talented young musicians, all of whom followed Vining when he returned to Melbourne; Musiikki-oy is a high-energy band whose performances juxtapose open improvisations and a strong rhythmic pulse. Vining was the artistic director of the Melbourne Moomba Jazz Festival from 1976 to 1979 and executive director of the Montsalvat Jazz Festival in 1995–6.

SELECTED RECORDINGS

As leader: *Moomba Jazz '76, Live from the Dallas Brooks Hall*, i (1976, 44 Records 6357708); *Number One* (1977, 44 Records 6357712); on *Beyond El Rocco* (1988, Vox Australis 017-2) [film soundtrack], Trio; of Musiikki-oy: *The Cone Centre* (1990, Spiral Scratch 0006), *Without Warning* (1992, The Deconditioned [unnumbered]); *Together* (1998, ABC 496496-2)

As sideman: Jamie Fielding: on *Notes from the Underground* (1981–92, AIJA 006–008), One-upmanship (1983); B. Brown: *The Planets* (1985, Larrikin 151); K. Hounslow: first issued on *Keith Hounslow, my Jazz Life, 50 Years of Playing Jazz in Australia: an Autobiography* (1947–*c*1997, Keith Hounslow Label [unnumbered]), Milestones, Our love is here to stay (1989)

BIBLIOGRAPHY

N. Meyers: "Ted Vining: in the Jazz Wilderness," *Jazz: the Australasian Contemporary Music Magazine*, iii/5 (1983), 10

B. Johnson: *The Oxford Companion to Australian Jazz* (Melbourne, Australia, 1987)

J. Clare [G. Brennan, pseud.]: *Bodgie Dada and the Cult of Cool* (Sydney, 1995)

W. Bebbington, ed: *The Oxford Companion to Australian Music* (Melbourne, Australia, 1997)

ADRIAN JACKSON

Vinnegar, Leroy (*b* Indianapolis, 13 July 1928; *d* Portland, OR, 3 Aug 1999). Double bass player. Vinnegar's day of birth has sometimes been given as 3 July, but he confirmed in *Cadence* (1989) that 13 July is correct. A self-taught musician, he first worked in his home town, where, with Wes Montgomery, he was a member of the quintet led by the trumpeter Roger Jones. He then played in Chicago (1952–4), principally as house double bass player at the Beehive, where he worked in rhythm sections with Junior Mance and Norman Simmons, accompanying such musicians as Charlie Parker, Lester Young, Howard McGhee, Sonny Stitt, and Johnny Griffin; he also played in a trio at the Blue Note. After moving to Los Angeles in August 1954, initially to serve as Art Tatum's deputy bass player (when Red Callendar was unavailable) Vinnegar achieved a considerable reputation, and from 1955 to 1958 he recorded with, among others, Stan Getz, Frank Morgan, Shorty Rogers, Herb Geller, Chet Baker, Dexter Gordon, Cy Touff, Stan Levey, Conte Candoli, Serge Chaloff, Buddy Collette, Quincy Jones, Art Pepper, Richie Kamuca, Elmo Hope, Buddy DeFranco, Pepper Adams, Terry Gibbs, Harold Land, and Sonny Rollins. He worked with Getz at Zardi's in Los Angeles (summer 1955) and on a West Coast tour (1956), toured with Shelly Manne for 18 months, and was a member, with Manne and André Previn, of the trio that recorded the best-selling jazz album *My Fair Lady* (1956). In 1957 he began an affiliation with Ben Webster, with whom he recorded in groups led by Benny Carter and Barney Kessel; that same year he made his first recordings as a leader, on which he made a feature of his virile walking bass lines and played only pieces with titles that pertained to the act of walking.

During the mid-1950s Vinnegar also played locally with Geller, Kessel, Pete Candoli, and Chico Hamilton, and with Carl Perkins he formed a trio and rhythm sections within various small groups; this affiliation ended in 1958, when Perkins died and Vinnegar was involved in an automobile accident which nearly killed him and permanently damaged his left lung. He continued playing with Webster into the early 1960s, made further recordings with the tenor saxophonist in groups variously involving Carter, Gerry Mulligan, Jimmy Witherspoon, Helen Humes, and Barney Bigard, and appeared in 1959 on television with Webster and Mulligan's group. Also from 1959 Vinnegar collaborated frequently with Joe Castro and Teddy Edwards, sharing leadership duties with them on several occasions; their group made a tour of Europe. As a freelance he recorded sessions with Paul Smith and Sonny Stitt (both 1959), Conte Candoli again (1960), Herb Ellis, Kenny Dorham and Jackie McLean, and McGhee (all 1961), and Victor Feldman (1962); his second album as a leader (1962–3) included his compositions *For Carl* and *Hard to Find*.

Thereafter Vinnegar spent a period as a member of the Jazz Crusaders (recording at the Lighthouse in Hermosa Beach, California, 1966) and worked as a freelance with both jazz and semicommercial ensembles. He toured Japan with an all-star group in 1964 and recorded with Gerald Wilson and Georgie Auld (both 1963), Cedar Walton (1967), Les McCann and Eddie Harris (1969), Collette (1973), Sonny Criss (1975), and the quintet led by McGhee and Edwards (1979). He also performed in the episode by the Hampton Hawes Trio for the television series "Jazz on Stage" (1970) and in the film *Some Call it Loving* (1973). In 1980 he toured West Africa with a group sponsored by Xanadu Records. He made several further appearances on television in the early

1980s as a member of the Panama Hats, a group that accompanied the actor and banjoist George Segal. Heart and lung problems stemming from his earlier accident led to his needing to spend extended periods on an oxygen tank; he also had to avoid work in clubs, because of the cigarette smoke, and to leave Los Angeles, because of the smog. From 1986 through the 1990s he was based in Portland, Oregon. He also toured Europe with Edwards, and New York and Alaska with his own trio. Vinnegar is best known for his walking bass lines, but occasionally played melodic solos, employing short, riff-like phrases and strong rhythmic punctuation; he had a keen sense of swing.

SELECTED RECORDINGS

As leader: *Leroy Walks* (1957, Cont. 3542); *Leroy Walks Again* (1962–3, Cont. 3608), incl. For Carl, Hard to Find; *Walkin' the Basses* (1992, Cont. 14068-2)

As sideman: S. Getz: *West Coast Jazz* (1955, Norg. 1032), incl. Shine; *For Musicians Only* (1956, Verve 8198); S. Chaloff: *Blue Serge* (1956, Cap. T742), incl. All the things you are, The Goof and I, A Handful of Stars, I've got the world on a string, Susie's Blues; S. Getz: *The Steamer* (1956, Verve 8294); S. Manne: *My Fair Lady* (1956, Cont. 3527), incl. Wouldn't it be loverly?; E. Hope: *Meditations* (1957, PJ 33); H. Land: *Harold in the Land of Jazz* (1958, Cont. 3550); T. Edwards: *Sonny Rollins at Music Inn/ Teddy Edwards at Falcon's Lair* (1959, Metro. 1011), incl. Billie's Bounce; L. McCann: *Les McCann Plays the Truth* (1960, PJ 2); P. Newborn: *The Great Jazz Piano of Phineas Newborn* (1961–2, Cont. 7611); *The Newborn Touch* (1964, Cont. 7615); L. McCann and E. Harris: *Swiss Movement* (1969, Atl. 1537)

BIBLIOGRAPHY

FeatherE; *Feather '60s*; *Feather–Gitler '70s*
L. Koenig: Liner notes, *My Fair Lady* (Cont. 3527, 1956)
B. Rusch: "Leroy Vinegar Interview," *Cadence*, xv/3 (1989), 5
T. Gioia: *West Coast Jazz: Modern Jazz in California, 1945–1960* (New York, and Oxford, England, 1992)
D. Bogle: "Leroy Vinnegar: Still Walkin' on Long-awaited Release," *DB*, lxi/3 (1994), 11
B. Goodwin: "Leroy: the Long and Long of it: Short Version," *The Note*, vi/2 (1994), 9
J. Kaliss: "Hearsay: Leroy Vinnegar," *JT*, xxiv/3 (1994), 11
Obituaries, *The Oregonian* (Portland) (4 Aug 1999); *San Francisco Chronicle* (6 Sept 1999); S. Woolley, *JJI*, lii/10 (1999), 18

LAWRENCE KOCH/BK

Vinson, Eddie "Cleanhead" [Eddie L.] (*b* Houston, 18 Dec 1917; *d* Los Angeles, 2 July 1988). Alto saxophonist and singer. His grandfather played violin and his parents were pianists. He took up alto saxophone in 1934 and by the following year had joined Arnett Cobb and Illinois Jacquet in Chester Boone's big band, in which he played saxophone and sang the blues; he remained in the band under the leadership of Milt Larkin (1936–40) and Floyd Ray (1940–41). Vinson then toured the South with the blues musicians Big Bill Broonzy and Lil Green (*c*1941) before working in New York with Cootie Williams (1942–5). The hit recording of *Cherry Red Blues* that he made with Williams in 1944 marked his emergence as a popular singer. He then led a big band (1946–7) and a septet which included John Coltrane, Red Garland, and Johnny Coles (*c*1948). Thereafter his popularity waned, but he continued to work steadily, if in obscurity, and to lead occasional recording sessions, with Eddie "Lockjaw" Davis, Wynton Kelly, Larkin, Joe Wilder, Tyree Glenn, Buddy Tate, Milt Buckner, Gene Ramey, Slide Hampton, and Charlie Rouse among his sidemen in the years 1949 to 1952. In 1969 his career received new impetus after he made a tour of Europe with Jay McShann, during which he recorded *Wee Baby Blues*, an album that received much critical acclaim. From the early 1970s he performed and recorded regularly in ensembles led by swing and rhythm-and-blues musicians, including Count Basie (to Europe, April–May 1972; albums 1980, 1981) and Johnny Otis. As a leader he held a long engagement at the Rubaiyat Lounge in Los Angeles, performed at other major clubs such as the Village Vanguard, Keystone Korner, Sweet Basil, and Jazz Showcase, and toured internationally, giving performances in Berlin (1974) and England (1980) and participating in numerous European festivals. He also appeared in an episode of the television show "Oscar Peterson and Friends" in 1980.

Vinson was a sophisticated, forceful bop saxophonist who played with searing intensity. His blues singing was characterized by an intentionally broken falsetto with which he punctuated line endings, and he performed his earthy, humorous lyrics in a deliberately understated manner. He was also the composer of the bop standards *Tune-up* and *Four*, both of which were popularized by Miles Davis.

SELECTED RECORDINGS

As leader: Cleanhead Blues (1946, Mer. 8023); Kidney Stew Blues (1946, Mer. 8028); Alimony Blues (1947, Mer. 8076); Person to Person (1952, King 4582); *Back Door Blues* (1961, Riv. 3502); *Wee Baby Blues* (1969, BB 33021); *Eddie Vinson and the Muse All-Stars Live at Sandy's* (1978, Muse 5208); *Mr. Cleanhead's Back in Town* (1980, JSP 1046)

As sideman: C. Williams: Cherry Red Blues (1944, Hit 7084); Juice Head Baby (1944, Cap. 237); C. Terry: *Yes, the Blues* (1981, Pablo 2312127); C. Basie: *Kansas City Six* (1981, Pablo 2310871)

SELECTED FILMS AND VIDEOS

Cootie Williams and his Orchestra (1944); Monterey Jazz (1973); America's Music: the Blues (1986)

BIBLIOGRAPHY

S. Dance: "Eddie Vinson of Houston," *Jazz*, vi/7 (1967), 13
C. Gillett: "Eddie 'Cleanhead' Vinson," *J&B*, i/11 (1972), 4
V. Wilmer: "Cleanhead Opens up Berlin," *MM* (18 May 1974), 36
N. Hess: "They Call Me Mr. Cleanhead," *Blues Unlimited*, no.114 (1975), 4
H. Nolan: "Just Call Me Cleanhead," *DB*, xlii/9 (1975), 16 [incl. discography]
L. Tomkins: "Eddie Vinson," *CI*, xx/5 (1981), 21
L. Birnbaum: "Eddie Cleanhead Vinson," *DB*, xlix/10 (1982), 28 [incl. discography]
D. Penny and T. Burke: "Eddie 'Cleanhead' Vinson," *Blues & Rhythm*, no.20 (1986), 4
M. K. Aldin: "Eddie 'Cleanhead' Vinson," *Living Blues*, no. 82 (1988), 39
T. Burke: "'Goodbye Mr. Cleanhead: Things ain't what they used to be': a Tribute to Eddie Vinson," *Blues & Rhythm*, no.38 (1988), 7
J. Simmen: "Ceux qui s'en vont: Eddie 'Mr. Cleanhead' Vinson," *BHcF*, no.368 (1989), 22
A. Tomas: "Eddie Vinson: Monsieur 'Cleanhead'," *Jh*, no.461 (1989), 65

BK

Vintskevich, Leonid (Vladislavovich) (*b* Kursk, Russian SFSR [now Russia], 1 April 1949). Russian pianist. He started to play jazz in 1964, performing in groups in Kazan and Sochi, and attended Kursk Music College from 1968 and Kazan State Conservatory from 1973. After leading a trio (1978–9) he began to perform as an unaccompanied soloist, and in 1983 he established a duo with Lembit Saarsalu which appeared at festivals in Russia, as well as in Prague (1984), Leipzig and Berlin (both 1985), Riga (Latvia), Tbilisi (Georgia), and The Hague (all 1986), and the USA (1989, 1993). He is a director of the annual Russian cultural fund festival Jazz Province.

SELECTED RECORDINGS

Duos with L. Saarsalu: *Two Play Jazz* (1984, Mel. 7659505); *Night Blues* (1986, Mel. 8779009); *No So Bad* (n.d., Mat Records 97794)

As sideman: Trinity: *Unity* (n.d., SCB-Music [issue number unknown); Targa Novoje Mond Trio: *Land zemlja maa* (n.d., Markant Music 000105); Talliner Jazz Quintet: [title unknown] (n.d., ASP 31195)

SERGEY BELICHENKO

Vinyl. Record company and label. It was founded in West Berlin by Gerd Peeckel and Manfred Schiek in 1976, and over the next few years it produced albums by Trevor Watts's group Amalgam, Ken Hyder's Talisker, Howard Riley, Alan Skidmore, John Stevens, Keith Tippett, and others. It appears to have ceased operations in the late 1970s.

BIBLIOGRAPHY

N. Skrimshire: "UK Distribution for Independent Labels," *JJI*, xxxii/1 (1979), 28

R. D. Laing and C. Sheridan: *Jazz Records: the Specialist Labels* (Copenhagen, 1981), 603

M. Fine: "Globe Trotting: West Germany: Vinyl/View," *Cadence*, xi/5 (1985), 22

GK

Viola, Al(fred) (*b* New York, 16 June 1919). Electric guitarist. He took up guitar around the age of ten and was largely self-taught. After playing in Virginia in an army band with Jimmie Rowles, Gil Evans, and Joe Mondragon (1942–5) he moved to California (1946), where he recorded with André Previn (1947) and toured with a trio led by the pianist Page Cavanaugh (1946–9). This group performed and recorded with Frank Sinatra in 1946–7; Viola's association with Sinatra continued intermittently until 1980 and included a world tour in 1962. From 1949 Viola was active as a studio musician, playing with Bobby Troup (1950–54), Ray Anthony (1955–6), Harry James (1957, 1962) and Marty Paich (late 1950s); he also worked occasionally with Buddy Collette and Les Brown, and he may be heard to advantage with Collette on *Buddy's Best* (1957, Dooto 245). Thereafter he took part in sessions led by Jimmy Witherspoon (1959, 1961), Helen Humes (1961), and June Christy (1963) and worked with Anthony, Stan Kenton, Nelson Riddle, Pete Rugolo, and Gerald Wilson.

During the 1960s Viola was a staff musician for television. Towards the end of that decade and in the 1970s he recorded several times, as an unaccompanied soloist (on acoustic guitar), as a leader, and as a sideman with, among others, Lionel Hampton, and he played mandolin on the soundtrack of the film *The Godfather* (1972). Later he worked with Collette and Terry Gibbs (both 1980s and 1990s) and resumed performing with Cavanaugh (1987), with whom he recorded two new albums (notably *The Digital Page*, i, 1989, Star Line 9001). From 1989 into the 1990s he held a residency at the Money Tree in Hollywood.

SELECTED FILMS AND VIDEOS

Romance on the High Seas [It's Magic] (1948); A Song is Born (1948); Some Came Running (1959)

BIBLIOGRAPHY

Feather–Gitler '70s

F. Nemko: "Al Viola," *GP*, xi/4 (1977), 24 [incl. discography]

L. Tomkins: "Al Viola," *CI*, xv (1977), no.10, p.20; no.12, p.8

L. Underwood: "Profile: Al Viola," *DB*, xlvi/7 (1979), 36

D. Forte: "Profile: Al Viola: Sinatra's Rejuvenated Sideman," *GP*, xxviii/10 (1994), 19

BK

Violin. The soprano member of the family of string instruments that includes the viola and cello. It was in existence in a three-stringed form by the 1520s, and by the early 17th century had become the backbone of the Western orchestra. The modern orchestral violin is of wooden construction and has four strings, tuned *g–d′–a′–e″*. Amplified violins have been in use in jazz since the 1930s, some players making use of an external microphone, "bug," or pickup, and others employing an internal pickup or transducer similar to that of an electric guitar. This has allowed the advent (from the 1960s) of solid-bodied instruments, "outline" shaped violins, and alterations in the number of strings; some jazz violinists play five- or six-string variants.

In jazz the violin has traditionally been played with the bow (arco) rather than plucked with the fingers (pizzicato). Following established practice in Western art music, the instrument is most frequently held under the player's chin; however, other less orthodox playing positions are also used, for example, where the instrument is held on the player's chest with the neck pointing floorwards, in the manner of old-time country fiddlers. As in classical playing, the strings are stopped with the left hand and are bowed or plucked with the right hand. The employment of effects units has materially altered some aspects of playing, and, just as with the guitar, modern amplification has made different stopping and plucking techniques both audible and useable.

Among African-American musicians the violin was a significant component of music on plantations, both in accompanying dance and as part of string bands which played for white slave-owners and African-American communities alike. A high level of virtuosity was achieved by such concert artists as John Thomas Douglass (1847–1886) and Walter Craig (1854–192?), and it is reasonable to assume that comparable skills were developed by those who played in the string bands that pioneered jazz forms shortly after the beginning of the 20th century. The degree to which such bands employed syncopation is not recorded, but it is known that New Orleans ensembles, among them the Big Four String Band, the Excelsior String Band, the Tio and Doublet String Band, and the Union String Band, played a repertory based on cakewalks and rags, and that for the most part they were led by violinists. The most significant violinists in the city in this pre-jazz period were Henry Nickerson and John Robichaux. Robichaux later ran a society dance orchestra, but as early as 1913 he augmented this with a full string section, including six violinists.

The earliest notated examples of the use of the violin in a jazz-related context are in the ragtime orchestras of the early 20th century. Most orchestral arrangements of ragtime – for example, those that appear in *The Red Back Book of Rags* (*c*1915) – included parts for violin (sometimes, indeed, parts for two violins), which were of equal melodic and structural importance to that of the clarinet or trumpet. The nature of the instrument's role may be heard in the recordings of the New Orleans Ragtime Orchestra (notably *The New Orleans Ragtime Orchestra*, 1971, Arhoolie 1058), a group that endeavored to re-create the sound of an early ragtime ensemble.

In the society orchestras of New Orleans the violin gradually became subservient to brass and woodwind instruments. A recording such as A. J. Piron's *Lou'siana Swing* (1924, OK 40189) provides a late example of the violin being employed as a full and equal member of the front line. Ironically, Piron's trumpeter, Peter Bocage, was an accomplished violinist (he played the instrument in Bunk Johnson's Superior Band), but he largely forsook the violin in favor of the trumpet on account of the latter's greater potential for jazz.

Territory bands, such as those led by Andy Kirk and Alphonso Trent, often included a violin in their instrumentation; while he was with Trent in the late 1920s Stuff Smith developed an innovative horn-like approach and experimented with acoustic and electric amplification. A more elemental, country-style soloist who played with both groups was Claude Williams, who later took up guitar and worked briefly on both instruments in Count Basie's orchestra; he was still playing violin into the 21st century. Eddie South first rose to prominence in the 1920s in Chicago as music director of Jimmy Wade's orchestra. The multi-instrumentalist Juice Wilson, by all accounts an accomplished violinist, worked with South in Freddie Keppard's band and later recorded with Noble Sissle in London (*Kansas City Kitty*, 1929, HMV B5731) before drifting into obscurity in Europe and North Africa. Edgar Sampson, another multi-instrumentalist who concentrated on violin in the late 1920s, recorded with Charlie Johnson and in the 1930s with Fletcher Henderson and Ethel Waters. The only woman to be identified as having recorded early hot improvisations on violin was the classically trained black – probably Puerto-Rican – American Angelina Rivera (with Spencer Williams and Josephine Baker in Paris in 1926). Some big bands of the mid-1920s incorporated violin sections, the principal example being that of Paul Whiteman, where the section was led by Matty Malneck. By and large these sections were used to play chordal or simply arranged melodic accompaniments, and did not involve any element of improvisation or solo playing. The same holds for the string sections added to big bands by Artie Shaw in the 1930s and by Earl Hines and Tommy Dorsey in the 1940s. Leaders of other ensembles, notably Erskine Tate, Clarence Black, Leon Abbey, and Carroll Dickerson (whose orchestras were resident at such Chicago theaters as the Vendome and the Savoy), and Leroy (not Stuff) Smith (in New York), played violin in addition to directing their bands. Another highly regarded violinist of the 1920s was Attwell Rose in Los Angeles.

Gradually the violin reasserted its position as a solo instrument. This was particularly owing to the work of four musicians – Joe Venuti, Stephane Grappelli, Stuff Smith, and South. Venuti established his reputation through his duet recordings with the guitarist Eddie Lang (beginning with *Stringing the Blues*, 1926, Col. 914D), and the two men developed one of the most significant partnerships of the early swing era. Similarly, Grappelli formed an association with the guitarist Django Reinhardt; in the Quintette du Hot Club de France they produced some of the most enduring, sophisticated, and swinging jazz ever recorded, with the metallic sound of Reinhardt's guitar perfectly complementing the mellow, sustained line of Grappelli's violin. Smith played an important role as a leader and soloist in small swing groups; his solos, which were full of risk-taking and fiery ideas, were pitted against those of the trumpeter Jonah Jones, who was also a combative melodic improviser. South, a classically trained musician with a virtuoso technique, was influenced by Hungarian and gypsy music (he recorded with Reinhardt and Grappelli), but he was also adept at highly organized and controlled swing.

The multi-instrumentalist Darnell Howard recorded as a member of a three-violin section in W. C. Handy's orchestra in 1917 and later as a soloist with Earl Hines, notably on three versions of *Cavernism* (among them 1933, Bruns. 6541; 1934, Decca 183). Other significant violinists of the swing era were Svend Asmussen, Ray Nance, and Ray Perry. Asmussen was one of several Scandinavian violinists (others were Frank Ottersen and Hasse Kahn) influenced by Venuti and Smith. Nance, a protégé of South, recorded his best work, such as his extended rhapsodic opening solo on the nocturne *Moon Mist* (1942, Vic. 27856), as a member of Duke Ellington's orchestra; however, his solo ventures, including a collaboration with the tenor saxophonist Paul Gonsalves (*Just-a-Sittin' and a-Rockin'*, 1970, BL 191), were also notable.

During the 1940s Perry, best known for swing recordings with a small-group offshoot of Lionel Hampton's orchestra (notably *Altitude*, 1940, Vic. 27316), emerged as a transitional figure between the harmonic invention of Smith and the emergent bop style. Despite his efforts, and those of Smith's protégée Ginger Smock (with the double bass player Vivien Garry in 1946), bop lacked solid representation on violin until the 1950s. Dick Wetmore produced a studied, understated, eponymous album in 1953 (Beth. 1035) and later recorded with Vinnie Burke and Gerry Mulligan. Odd Wentzel-Larsen in Norway and the Dane Søren Christensen (with Al Killian in Sweden) recorded bop improvisations in 1949–50. Harry Lookofsky, who had played in the NBC Symphony Orchestra under Arturo Toscanini, recorded brilliant bop (*Miracle in Strings*, 1954, Epic 7081; *Stringsville*, 1959, Atl. 1319) in which his solos, as well as his multitrack section work, bear all the hallmarks of convincing improvisation but are in fact conceived almost entirely as, and executed from, arrangements. Jean-Luc Ponty's early explorations in the 1960s, before he turned to free jazz and fusion, were in a bop vein, but it was not until Elek Bacsik made two albums in the 1970s that uncompromising, fully accomplished bop improvisations could be heard on record; the best example is *Bird and Dizzy: a Musical Tribute* (1975, FD 11082). In the 1980s Max Roach developed convincing bop arrangements for strings in his double quartet.

Different approaches to violin technique have led to a wide range of styles among jazz players: some have drawn on the techniques of classical and folk players, while others have invented original methods. Grappelli, retaining the tonal aesthetic of the classical violin tradition, explored the potential for flowing melodic lines, as may be heard on *Sweet Sue* (on the album *Homage à Django Reinhardt*, 1972, Festival 120). Venuti and Asmussen made more use of the instrument's harmonic resources and employed the bow in a percussive manner; Asmussen's technique is well represented by *Some of these Days* (1940, Odeon D408). Smith revolutionized the vocabulary of jazz violinists with his wild, biting attack, wide vibrato, unorthodox fingerings, and expressive intonation; a good example of his attack is recorded on *After you've gone* (1936, Voc. 3201). A particularly novel bowing technique was devised by Venuti to allow the player to sustain chords of three or four notes: this involved removing the pin from the frog of the bow, wrapping the bow hair around all four strings, and holding the stick of the bow underneath the body of the violin. The results may be heard on *Almost like being in love*, on the album *Joe Venuti and his Violin* (*c*1955, Jazz Man 336). Perry is reputed to have introduced the idea of singing in unison with the violin (a device also adopted by Asmussen and the double bass players Slam Stewart and Major Holley), but his own ventures in that area appear never to have been recorded.

The acoustical and musical demands of many types of modern jazz and rock have led to modifications in the way in which the violin is played. Jazz musicians have always found that the relatively quiet sound of the instrument has placed them at a disadvantage. Augustus Stroh attempted to overcome this problem at the beginning of the 20th century when he invented a type of violin that incorporated elements of the gramophone. In the late 1930s Smith was among the earliest players to amplify his instrument electronically. From the 1980s the majority of jazz violinists have relied on amplification, making use of a microphone, a transducer, or an electric violin (in which the transducer is built into the body of the instrument). Following on from amplification, violinists have adopted electronic devices to enhance the instrument's timbre. These include time-delay, echo, and reverberation units, equalizers, and wa-wa pedal.

Creative players have shown that the violin is an instrument of great flexibility in jazz. Zbigniew Seifert, for example, executed fast trills as a substitute for vibrato, while Ponty has chosen to abandon vibrato altogether. Others, such as Michael White (i) and John Blake, have experimented with non-Western tonal systems or have made extensive use of sliding pitch. Blake studied Carnatic (south Indian) music for a number of years and incorporates elements of that vocabulary into his playing; in the 1980s he recorded in various styles, both as a leader and as a soloist with Cecil McBee, Wynton Marsalis, James Newton, McCoy Tyner, and Steve Turre.

Early free-jazz violinists, often classically trained, such as Michel Sampson with Albert Ayler, and Ramsey Ameen with Cecil Taylor, took their cue mainly from the explorations of Ornette Coleman, who was self-taught on the instrument. He performs in an intense, percussive manner, using unorthodox fingerings and bowing positions (a good example of his playing may be heard on *Falling Stars*, on the album *The Ornette Coleman Trio at the Golden Circle*, 1965, BN 84224-5). Coleman's playing on alto saxophone incorporates elements drawn from other forms of music, including the blues of his native Texas, and his violin playing is similarly eclectic. Without stemming his innate gifts as a melodist, he draws on such source material as the country hoedown. Two notable free-jazz violinists who came to the fore in the immediate wake of Coleman are Leroy Jenkins and Billy Bang, both of whom consistently play outside the equal-tempered system. Jenkins, like his 1960s associate Anthony Braxton (who takes a similar approach to reed instruments), brings to the idiom a virtuoso classical technique: on his recording *For Players Only* (1975, JCOA 1010) he incorporates at different points effects associated with 20th-century art music (for example, playing sul ponticello, with and without a mute) and produces singing sustained tones in the high register of the instrument; the album also offers an example of a solo played through a wa-wa pedal. However, like another of his associates from this period, the trumpeter Leo Smith, and unlike Braxton, Jenkins often finds his points of reference in the blues. His playing in the late 1990s in the trio Equal Interest exploited the acoustic properties of the instrument (and of the viola, on which he doubles) to explore unusual timbres along with the flute of Joseph Jarman and harmonium of Myra Melford.

A resurgence of interest in the improvisational possiblities of the violin during the 1990s spawned a number of exceptionally gifted violinists who successfully combined free playing and organized structures in individualistic ways. Among these are India Cooke, Mat Maneri, and Jim Nolet. Cooke displays lyrical sensitivity and imaginative strength in interpreting a repertory of jazz standards and original pieces, but most significantly explores the improvisational possibilities of music drawn from other genres – in particular pieces for the folk fiddle, as exemplified by *Logan's Reel*, on her début album *Redhanded* (1996, Music and Arts 951). Maneri has used a variety of acoustic and electric instruments, but his highly unorthodox approach is colored by the influence of his father, the clarinetist and saxophonist Joe Maneri. Together they explore extremely slow tempi, mictrotonal variations in pitch, and timbres that range from rasps to smooth, vibratoless clear notes. Maneri is principally an ensemble player, and much of the strength of his work comes from his ability to blend with other musicians to create moving tonal effects. Nolet is an equally strong ensemble player, having been a member of bands led by Butch Morris and David Murray, and of the Jazz Passengers. By incorporating harmonics, pizzicato, double-stopping, and rapidly executed fragmented motifs, Nolet captures some of the ecstatic qualities of Murray's bass clarinet work; the two can be directly compared on *My Three Corners*, on Nolet's album *With You* (1993, Knitting Factory Works 150).

Examples of more conventional approaches to improvisation may be heard in the playing of Mark Feldman and Regina Carter. Feldman's contributions to Dave Douglas's string ensemble are among his most notable work. Carter brings a classical technique to an exceptional stylistic range. She has recorded funk under her own name and free jazz with Oliver Lake, but her forte is to combine these elements into a retrospective swing style; this is demonstrated in her own recordings and in her work with Kenny Barron, Wynton Marsalis (on an international tour in performances of his oratorio *Blood on the Fields*, 1997), and Cassandra Wilson (*Seven Steps*, on the latter's album *Traveling Miles*, 1999, BN 54123-2). A similarly retrospective approach is taken by the French violinist Didier Lockwood, who employs harmonics on both electric and acoustic instruments to add an ethereal texture to his ballad playing, as on *I remember Alby*, from his album *Round about Silence* (1998, Dreyfus 36595). His fellow countryman Dominique Pifarély has explored the interstices between jazz and contemporary classical composition in his duo with the pianist François Couturier.

Some musicians have sought ways of expanding the range of the violin downwards. Ponty and Michal Urbaniak played the violectra, an electric instrument sounding an octave below the conventional violin; both men later took up a five-string electric violin (the lowest string on which was tuned to *c*) and Urbaniak performs on a six-string model (with the addition of a string tuned to *F*). The six-string instrument is used by Wolfgang Muthspiel; his chordal approach to the violin, drawing on of his experience as a guitarist, opens up new possibilities for combining pizzicato effects with electronics. He also used electronic repeat loops and effects to play duets with himself on guitar and six-string violin. The tenor violin, which has a range between that of the viola and the cello, has been used in jazz by Lookofsky and Asmussen. Lakshminarayana Shankar plays a ten-string violin with two necks, an instrument that he designed himself.

For illustrations *see* Asmussen, svend; Films, fig.5; Grappelli, stephane; and Ponty, jean-luc.

BIBLIOGRAPHY

ChartersJ

J.-E. Berendt: *Das Jazzbuch: Entwicklung und Bedeutung der Jazzmusik* (Frankfurt am Main, Germany, 1953, rev. and enlarged 5/1981 as *Das grosse Jazzbuch: von New Orleans bis Jazz Rock*, Eng. trans. as *The Jazz Book: from New Orleans to Fusion and Beyond*, Westport, CT, 1982), 288

D. Morgenstern: "Jazz Fiddle," *DB*, xxxiv/3 (1967), 16

E. Jost: *Free Jazz* (Graz, Austria, 1974/*R*1994)

M. Glaser and S. Grappelli: *Jazz Violin* (New York and elsewhere, 1981) [incl. transcrs.]

G. Lowinger: *Jazz Violin: Roots and Branches* (New York and London, 1981) [incl. transcrs.]

Jazz String Newsletter (Milwaukee, 1982–3)
J. L. Lieberman: *Blues Fiddle* (New York and elsewhere, 1986) [incl. transcrs.]
S. Glaess: *Die Rolle der Geige im Jazz* (Berne, 1991 [*recte* 1992]) [incl. transcrs.]
A. Barnett, ed.: *Fable Bulletin: Violin Improvisation Studies* (1993–2000 [first series]) [incl. transcrs.]
J. L. Liebermann: *Improvising Violin* (New York, 1995) [incl. transcrs.]
H. Grässer with A. Holliman: *Electric Violins: Design und Technik der elektrischen Streichinstrumente/Design and Technique of Electric Bowed String Instruments* (Frankfurt am Main, 1998) [text in Ger. and Eng.]
D. Lockwood with F. Darizcuren: *Cordes & Ame: Méthode d'improvisation et de violon jazz* (Paris, 1998)

MATT GLASER, ALYN SHIPTON/ANTHONY BARNETT, ALYN SHIPTON

Violoncello. *See* Cello.

Viseur, Gus(tave Joseph) (*b* Lessines, Belgium, 17 May 1915; *d* Le Havre, France, 25 Aug 1974). Belgian accordionist. He met Django Reinhardt in Paris in 1934 and was a member of the orchestra led by the pianist Boris Sarbek, then worked in France and Belgium with Philippe Brun, Joseph Reinhardt, and his own quintet. After touring the USA in 1963 he interrupted his career as a performer to open a record shop in Le Havre, but he resumed playing around 1970. Viseur made several recordings as a leader, using such sidemen as Eddie Brunner, Oscar Alemán, Brun, Reinhardt, and Roger Guérin. (R. Pernet: *Belgian Jazz Discography (1897–1999)*, Brussels, 1999)

ROBERT PERNET

Vitet, Bernard [Babar] (*b* Paris, 26 May 1934). French trumpeter, multi-instrumentalist, and composer. He studied cinematography until 1952, when he took up trumpet after hearing a performance by Miles Davis. Having made his professional début with Jean-Claude Fohrenbach's big band he performed and recorded with Georges Arvanitas (1960–61). In the early 1960s he appeared regularly in groups at American military bases in France and at the Club Saint-Germain, where he played with such important musicians as Don Byas, Chet Baker, Johnny Griffin, André Hodeir, Martial Solal, Barney Wilen, and Michel Portal. In 1965 Vitet formed a free-jazz group with François Tusques, the first of its kind in France; their sidemen were Beb Guérin, Jean-François Jenny-Clark, and Aldo Romano. The following year, with Jean-Louis Chautemps, he composed the score for the film *Les cœurs verts* and began writing music for the theater. Later he co-founded the ensemble Jazzex (late 1960s) and worked with a number of other free-jazz musicians and groups, notably Anthony Braxton, Steve Lacy, Sunny Murray's Swing Unit (recording 1968–9), Archie Shepp, Alan Silva's Celestrial Communication Orchestra (recording 1969–70, 1978, 1982), Tusque's Intercommunal Free Dance Music Orchestra (recording *c*1982), the Globe Unity Orchestra, and the Groupe de Recherche Musicale. In addition he recorded as an unaccompanied soloist, as a leader, and with the multi-instrumentalists Jean Guérin (1971) and Jac Berrocal (1976). In 1972 Vitet performed and recorded as a member of Portal's group Unit, and around the same time he began making musical instruments which he used for specific performances; these included a reeded trumpet, a double flute, a variable tension double bass, and the dragoon – a giant *balafon* with a keyboard made of frying pans and flower pots.

With the guitarist Francis Gorgé and the synthesizer player and singer Jean-Jacques Birgé, Vitet formed Un Drame Musical Instantané in 1976, which provided accompaniment for silent films, literature readings, and radio and stage performances; it performed both as a trio and as a 15-piece orchestra. After Gorgé had left the group Vitet and Birgé continued working as a duo in collaboration with various guests, among them the Balanescu String Quartet, Raymond Boni, Dee Dee Bridgewater, and Kent Carter. Vitet also plays violin, and in the 1990s he began singing in the group Carton.

SELECTED RECORDINGS

Duos with Helène Sage: *Supposons le problème résolu* (*c*1984, GRRR 1008)
As leader: *La guêpe* (1971, Futura 05)
As sideman: G. Arvanitas: *Soul Jazz* (1960, Col. FPX193); J. Gilson: on *Enfin* (1962–3, Club de l'Echiquier 1002), Fable of Gutenberg, Le grand bidou, Three for One (1963); F. Tusques: *Free Jazz* (1966, Mouloudji 13507); A. Silva: *Luna Surface* (1969, BYG 529312); *Seasons* (1970, BYG 529342–4); M. Portal: *Michel Portal Unit à Châteauvallon* (1972, Chant du Monde 74526); Un Drame Musical Instantané: *Les bons contes fonts les bons amis* (1982, GRRR 1006)

BIBLIOGRAPHY

P. L. Rossi: "Un homme libre," *Jm*, no.114 (1965), 40
H. Lecomte: "Le souffle continu," *Jh*, no.394 (1982), 27
E. Jost: *Europas Jazz, 1960–1980* (Frankfurt am Main, Germany, 1987), 415
P. Carles, A. Clergeat, and J.-L. Comolli: *Dictionnaire du jazz* (Paris, 1988, rev. and enlarged 2/1994)
F. Marmande: "Un Drame Musical Instantané en trois actes et trois personnages," *Jm*, no.389 (1990), 24
<http://www.hyptique.com/ONLINE/drame/> (1999)

GK

Vitous [Vitouš], **Miroslav (Ladislav)** (*b* Prague, 6 Dec 1947). Czech double bass player. He learned violin and piano before taking up double bass and, while studying at the Prague Conservatory, won a scholarship to the Berklee School of Music (1966). In 1967 he moved to New York, where he played with Art Farmer, Freddie Hubbard, the quintet led by Bob Brookmeyer and Clark Terry, and Miles Davis, then worked with Herbie Mann (1968–70); he also recorded with Donald Byrd (1967), Chick Corea and Jack DeJohnette (both 1968), Wayne Shorter (1969), and Larry Coryell (1970). In 1970 he toured with Stan Getz, rejoined Mann, and, with Shorter and Joe Zawinul, was a founding member of Weather Report. Vitous left the group in 1973 and spent several years experimenting with electric bass guitars. After he resumed playing double bass he joined the faculty of the New England Conservatory (1979); later he became head of the jazz department there (1983). He remained active as a performer: between 1979 and 1982 he led a quartet consisting of John Surman, Kenny Kirkland or John Taylor, and Jon Christensen, and in 1981 he joined Chick Corea's Trio Music, alongside Roy Haynes. In 1988 Vitous left the conservatory and moved to Germany, and the following year he began giving concerts as an unaccompanied soloist. With Enrico Rava, Franco D'Andrea, and Daniel Humair, he formed the cooperative Quatre; this group recorded in 1989 and 1991 and performed at the Chicago Jazz Festival shortly before disbanding in 1991. In the early 1990s Vitous recorded and then toured with Jan Garbarek, both in a duo and in a trio with Peter Erskine, then in 1993 he formed another trio, with the pianist Aydin Esen and Trilok Gurtu. He also recorded with Laszlo Gardony (1986), Vic Juris and John Etheridge (1988), Fredy Studer (1988), Steve Kuhn (1989), Humair (1991), and Franco Ambrosetti (1997).

Vitous is best known for his work with Weather Report, in which he applied to jazz-rock the approach developed by Scott La Faro of treating the double bass as a lyrical, melodic instrument rather than as a timekeeper; his virtuoso use of the bow was also unusual. With his quartet and other musicians (notably Corea) he moved to bop and other styles of playing, which were better suited to these innovations. His arco playing may be heard to advantage on *Silver Lake*, from his album *First Meeting* (1979). From around 1992 he began using a MIDI (Musical Instrument Digital Interface) link between his double bass and a computer to generate sampled orchestral sounds as he played.

SELECTED RECORDINGS

(recorded for ECM unless otherwise indicated)

As unaccompanied soloist: *Emergence* (1985, 1312)
Duos with J. Garbarek: *Atmos* (1992, 1475)
As leader: *Infinite Search* (1969, Embryo 524); *Terje Rypdal–Miroslav Vitous–Jack DeJohnette* (1978, 1125); *First Meeting* (1979, 1145), incl. Silver Lake; *Miroslav Vitous Group* (1980, 1185); with T. Rypdal and J. DeJohnette: *To Be Continued* (1981, 1192); *Journey's End* (1982, 1242); with J. Garbarek and P. Erskine: *Star* (1991, 1444)
As sideman: C. Corea: *Now He Sings, Now He Sobs* (1968, SolS 18039); *Trio Music* (1981, 1232/33); *Trio Music: Live in Europe* (1984, 1310); S. Kuhn: *Oceans in the Sky* (1989, Owl 056); Quatre: *Earthcake* (1991, Label Bleu 6539); D. Humair: *Edges* (1991, Lable Bleu 6545)

BIBLIOGRAPHY

M. Bateson: "Avant Courier: Miroslav Vitous," *JJI*, xxxvi/3 (1983), 16
F. Bouchard: "Miroslav Vitous: Both Sides of the Bass," *DB*, li/9 (1984), 18
A. Matzner, I. Poledňák, and I. Wasserberger, eds.: *Encyklopedie jazzu a moderní populární hudby* (Prague, 1990)
B. Glasser: "Miroslav Vitous," *Jazz FM*, no.20 (1993), 10
J. Roberts: "Miroslav Vitous: Beyond Bass," *Bass Player*, iv/5 (1993), 9
B. Shoemaker: "Miroslav Vitous: Slavic Soul," *JT*, xxiii/3 (1993), 30
<http://www.ejn.it/mus/vitous.htm> (2000)

BK

Vitro [née Wickliffe]**, Roseanna (Elizabeth)** (*b* Hot Springs, AR, 28 Feb 1951). Singer. As a teenager she sang country and pop music with her sister on local radio stations. From the early 1970s she was working in Houston, where by the late 1970s she sang blues and rock and met Arnett Cobb, who became her mentor and with whom she later appeared at the Village Vanguard in New York. She then spent two years at Houston's Green Room, where she hosted a local radio broadcast featuring her own group, Roseanna with Strings and Things, as well as such visiting musicians such as Bill Evans (ii), Tommy Flanagan, and Joe Williams – all of whom encouraged her to go to New York. After moving there in 1980 she studied at the Manhattan School of Music and with Kenny Werner and Fred Hersch, and soon afterwards she toured with Lionel Hampton. Vitro performed throughout the United States and was broadcast on WBGO-FM (Newark, New Jersey) and on National Public Radio; she was also a guest on Marian McPartland's radio show "Piano Jazz." In the late 1990s she hosted a jam session for singers at Cleopatra's Needle in New York. She has taught at Jersey City College.

SELECTED RECORDINGS

As leader: *Listen Here* (1982, Texas Rose Music 1001); *Softly* (*c*1993, Conc. 4587-2); *Passion Dance* (1994–5, Telarc 83385)

BIBLIOGRAPHY

D. Zych: "Hearsay: Truth and Dare: Roseanna Vitro," *JT*, xxvi/3 (1996), 23
M. G. Nastos: "Riffs: Vitro Makes Major Label Debut," *DB*, lxi/2 (1994), 16

SCOTT FREDRICKSON, GK

Vlach, Karel (*b* Prague, 8 Oct 1911; *d* Prague, 26 Feb 1986). Czech bandleader. He worked with an amateur orchestra in Prague in 1938 and became a professional musician in 1941, leading a big band which from 1945 included such musicians as Karel Krautgartner and the tenor saxophonist Milan Ulrich. From 1947 he worked in the theater, television, radio, and films, while continuing to lead his own swing band, which until the mid-1950s was the foremost group of its kind in Czechoslovakia. Vlach gave many concerts at home and abroad, and between 1939 and the 1970s made more than 2000 recordings.

SELECTED RECORDINGS

Vlach Stomp (1943, Ultraphon B12957); Relaxin' (1945, Ultraphon 14309); Greeting the Orchestra (1953, Sup. C24530); *Let us Dance* (1953-8, Sup. 13169)

BIBLIOGRAPHY

G. Conrad: Vlach Stomp – Die Geschichte von Karel Vlach und seinem Orchester (Fox auf 78, Frühjahr 99)

GERHARD CONRAD

Vloeimans, Eric (*b* Huizen, Netherlands, 24 March 1963). Dutch trumpeter, flugelhorn player, and composer. He graduated from the College of Music in Rotterdam in 1989, and that same year he studied with Donald Byrd in New York, toured the USA with the Duke Ellington Orchestra under Mercer Ellington, and played a concert as a member of Frank Foster's big band, again in New York. He joined Riccardo Del Fra for a tribute to Chet Baker in France (1992) and Lalo Schifrin for a tribute to Dizzy Gillespie at the North Sea Jazz Festival (1993) and worked as a freelance with the group Vaalbleek, Michiel Borstlap, Pierre Courbois, Jasper van 't Hof, Paul van Kemenade, the singer Masha Bijlsma, Tony Overwater, the pianist Marcus Schinkel, the singer Carmen Gomes, Hein van de Geyn, the European Jazz Ensemble, the guitarist and *'ud* player Ergan Ogur, Jarmo Savolainen, the group Bik Bent Braam, Chris Hinze, and the New Concert Big Band. Vloeimans excels at composing and playing ballads.

SELECTED RECORDINGS

As leader: *No Realistics* (1992, Art in Jazz 991004); *First Floor* (1994, Challenge 70011); *Bestiarium* (1996, Challenge 70038); *Bitches and Fairy Tales* (1998, Challenge 70061)

WIM VAN EYLE

Vocalese. A term for the practice of jazz Singing in which texts (newly invented) are set to recorded jazz improvisations. The word is a pun on the term "vocalise," combining the ideas of a jazz "vocal" and a private language (indicated by the suffix "-ese"). Eddie Jefferson performed vocalese from the 1940s, but the best-known early recordings were made by King Pleasure, including his version of Jefferson's *Moody's Mood for Love* (1952, Prst. 924), based on a saxophone solo by James Moody, and his own setting of *Parker's Mood* (1953, Prst. 880), using Charlie Parker's blues improvisation of that title. Other important practitioners of vocalese were Dave Lambert, Annie Ross, and above all Jon Hendricks, who was extremely inventive in creating texts to capture the feeling of the original solos. In 1957 Lambert, Hendricks, and Ross (later Yolande Bavan) formed a vocal trio which attained some commercial success with their vocalese; it disbanded in 1964, but Hendricks continued to create and perform such pieces into the 1980s with a group comprising members of his family. Although the singing of vocalese is most closely associated with the bop style, it was also practiced later by such popular singers as the Pointer Sisters, the vocal quartet Manhattan Transfer (*Vocalese*, 1985, Atl. 81266), and New York Voices.

BIBLIOGRAPHY

L. Feather: "An Explanation of Vocalese," *Jazz: a Quarterly of American Music*, no.3 (1959), 261

B. K. Grant: "Purple Passages or Fiestas in Blue? Notes Toward an Aesthetic of Vocalese," *Representing Jazz*, ed. K. Gabbard (Durham, NC, and London, 1995), 285

J. BRADFORD ROBINSON/BK

Vocalion. Record company and label. The company was a division of the Aeolian Company, a firm of piano manufacturers based in New York. In 1916 it began issuing vertical-cut records – including a now famous series by the Original Dixieland Jazz Band (1917) – and in January 1920 it issued its first lateral-cut discs. At first the records bore the name Aeolian Vocalion; the first word was dropped shortly before the company was sold around 1924 to Brunswick–Balke–Callender, which owned the label BRUNSWICK. Thereafter the new administration operated the two enterprises separately, but there was considerable interchange of artists and repertory and the histories of the labels are interconnected. Although Vocalion had made race records before its purchase by Brunswick, only in 1926 was a race series formally established. The Vocalion 1000 series, recorded under the supervision of Jack Kapp, and later of J. Mayo Williams, is well remembered for its issue of material by King Oliver, Jimmie Noone, and Duke Ellington.

In December 1920 a British subsidiary was established which recorded its own repertory and also provided material for several other labels, among them Coliseum and Guardsman; some of these were employed to issue American recordings, often under pseudonyms, that had been leased to British Vocalion. Rights to the label's name in the UK were later acquired for use by an autonomous English organization, the Vocalion Record Company, of Hayes, which drew its American repertory from Gennett. British Vocalion remained in existence (but no longer used the label name) and issued material on such labels as Broadcast. Its affiliate in Australia continued to use the label name Vocalion for issue of material from Gennett and American Brunswick. In addition for a few months in 1927 records were issued on a Vocalion label by the British branch of Brunswick, drawing on material from Gennett and American Brunswick.

In the USA Vocalion was taken over in 1930 (with the rest of Brunswick–Balke–Collender) by Warner Brothers and then sold in December 1931 to Consolidated Film Industries, which already owned the AMERICAN RECORD CORPORATION. The new management discontinued the 1000 series in July 1933 but recommenced race issues the following September in a 25000 series; the catalogue numbers were later changed to an 02500 series. Numbers in this sequence ran parallel with the general series, with the prefix zero being used to denote race records. In several instances, however, the same issue number was employed (once with, and once without, the prefix) for two different items – a practice which has caused discographers much confusion. Among the important jazz issued on Vocalion in the 1930s were recordings by Billie Holiday (see illustration) and by Duke Ellington's small groups. Although ARC and Brunswick were taken over by CBS in 1938, issue continued on Vocalion until 1940, when the name was phased out in favor of the name OKeh; concurrently, in 1938 the pre-1932 catalogues of Vocalion and Brunswick were taken over by the American branch of Decca. The numerical series, however, was maintained, and many early Vocalion recordings were reissued on OKeh with their original numbers.

Label for "Trav'lin' All Alone," recorded by Billie Holiday for Vocalion (New York, 13 September 1937)

In England the Vocalion Record Company was purchased in 1932 by Crystalate; the label name was revived in 1936, most notably for issue of a swing series drawn from ARC and Brunswick. Decca purchased Crystalate in March 1937 and continued the Swing Series until 1940; this eventually ran to 247 issues and is now considered a particularly important catalogue. The label was used again by British Decca in October 1951 for the issue of its series Origins of Jazz. This ceased in 1954 after 41 items. Vocalion then remained dormant until 1962, when British Decca adopted the name for its subsidiary label Vogue after rights to the latter trademark reverted to the French parent company. The name Vocalion was dropped in 1968 but used again in 1976 for a short series (also put out in France) of reissues of early jazz and popular music taken from Brunswick's pre-1932 catalogue.

BIBLIOGRAPHY

E. Jackson and L. Hibbs: *Decca, Brunswick, Vocalion Encyclopedia of Swing* (London, 1941)

W. H. Parry: "The English Vocalion Continental Series C0001," *Discophile*, no.18 (1951), 6

S. Wante: "Decca 'J' and Vocalion 'C,' 'S,' and '500' Series," *Jazz Music*, iv/7 (1951), 21; iv/8 (1952), 18; v/7 (1954), 14

R. M. W. Dixon and J. Godrich: *Blues & Gospel Records, 1902–1942* (Hatch End, nr London, 1964, rev. and enlarged 4/Oxford, England, 1997, as R. M. W. Dixon, J. Godrich, and H. Rye: *Blues & Gospel Records, 1890–1943*)

A. G. Cox: "Discography of the Vocalion Swing Series, 1936–1940," *JJ*, xix (1966), no.3, p.22; no.4, p.17; no.5, p.25; no.6, p.38; no.8, p.38

P. Burgis: "Discs from Down Under," *Sv*, no.11 (1967), 4

R. M. W. Dixon and J. Godrich: *Recording the Blues* (London, 1970)

R. D. Kinkle: "Vocalion Numerical List," "Vocalion–Okeh Numerical List," *The Complete Encyclopedia of Popular Music and Jazz, 1900–1950* (New Rochelle, NY, and Westport, CT, 1974), iv, 2245, 2255

F. Dutton: "Numbers Runners Blues," *Sv*, no.79 (1978), 8

B. Rust: *The American Record Label Book* (New Rochelle, NY, 1978), 318

F. Dutton: "Numbers Runners Blues, 2," *Sv*, no.106 (1983), 125

P. Pelletier: "The Vogue–Vocalion Label," *Record Information*, no.1 (1983), 24

A. Sutton and K. Nauck: *American Record Labels and Companies: an Encyclopedia (1891–1943)* (Denver, 2000), 223

HOWARD RYE

Vogel, Vic(tor Stéfan) (*b* Montreal, 3 Aug 1935). Canadian pianist, bandleader, composer and arranger. He began his career during the late 1950s in Montreal dance and show bands, then for the next 30 years divided his time between jazz and studio work. In the early 1960s he was the pianist, trombonist, and arranger for the tentet led by the saxophonist Lee Gagnon, and in 1968 he formed his own big band. Vogel's orchestra, which clearly reflects its leader's avowed admiration for Duke Ellington, toured France in 1982 but has otherwise worked close to home; it has appeared annually at the Festival International de Jazz de Montréal, where Vogel received the Prix Oscar-Peterson in 1992. Its recordings include *Le Big Band* (1984, Grudge 4524) with Zoot Sims as soloist. Vogel has also recorded as an unaccompanied soloist: *Piano Solo* (1993, BYC 202). He arranged the music heard at the opening and closing ceremonies of the 1976 Olympic Games in Montreal and has prepared programs for jazz soloists (Woody Shaw, Oliver Jones, Nelson Symonds) with string or symphony orchestras.

Oral history material in *CaQMG*.

BIBLIOGRAPHY

EMC2

M. Miller: "Vic Vogel Gives 'em Hell," *Globe and Mail* (Toronto, 29 Jan 1982), 11

——: "Vic Vogel," *Boogie, Pete & the Senator: Canadian Musicians in Jazz: the Eighties* (Toronto, 1987), 276

MARK MILLER

Vogue. Record company and label. The company was established in France in 1948; artists and repertory were directed by Charles Delaunay. The extensive jazz catalogue included recordings by such native musicians as Henri Renaud, American expatriates – most notably Sidney Bechet – and visitors from the USA, including Clifford Brown, Bobby Jaspar, Jimmy Raney, and Art Farmer, as well as reissues of American material. The company also held licenses to distribute in France recordings made by small American companies; among those with important jazz catalogues were King, Coral, Contemporary, Good Time Jazz, Hot Record Society, Blue Note, and Fantasy (some of this material was issued on the label Jazz Selection, which Vogue administered).

A subsidiary was established in1951 in England. While this was taken over by British Decca five years later it retained its autonomy until 1962, when the Vogue trademark reverted to the parent company. After using the name Vocalion for this catalogue for a brief period, Decca absorbed the label into its general operations. Vogue set up a new British subsidiary within the group of companies controlled by Pye. The French company remained important for jazz into the 1980s, when its catalogue included the noteworthy reissue series Jazz Legacy as well as new recordings by Gérard Badini and Claude Luter. Reissue programs have continued into the new century.

BIBLIOGRAPHY

P. Pelletier: "The Vogue–Vocalion Label," *Record Information*, no.1 (1983), 24

C. Delaunay: *Delaunay's Dilemma: de la peinture au jazz* (Mâcon, France, 1985)

M. Ruppli: *Vogue*, i (Paris, 1992)

HOWARD RYE

Voicing. A term applied in jazz to the particular sonority of a chord, which depends on the vertical ordering, spacing, and instrumental distribution of its component notes; *see* HARMONY (i), §1(iv).

Voigt, Andrew (*b* Kentucky, *c*1956). Alto saxophonist, member of ROVA.

Volonté, Eraldo (*b* Milan, 5 Feb 1918). Italian tenor saxophonist and composer. He played violin in dance bands, then in 1936 took up tenor saxophone. In the 1940s he played in orchestras led by Enzo Ceragioli, Bruno Martelli, Kramer Gorni, and Aldo Rossi. He performed and recorded bop with big bands and small groups, both as a leader (1947–76) and as a sideman with Gil Cuppini (1948–74); he also worked with Glauco Masetti's Sestetto Jazz Moderno (1956–8). Later he recorded with an octet led by the pianist Piero Umiliani (1958), with big bands led by Umiliani (1963, 1966), Giorgio Gaslini (1968), and the double bass player Giorgio Azzolini (1971–2), and in a small group led by the double bass player Giorgio Buratti (1970). Volonté's playing may be heard to advantage on his recording *Zoot* on the album *IIIrd Festival del Jazz del San Remo* (1958, Carish 15301); among his compositions are *Eclypso* (1966) and *Dedicated to Duke Ellington* (1975).

ADRIANO MAZZOLETTI

Von Eichwald, Håkan (*b* Turku, Finland, 2 April 1908; *d* Stockholm, 1 April 1964). Swedish bandleader of Finnish birth. A child prodigy who made his début as a pianist at the age of six, von Eichwald studied piano and conducting and started working as a leader of theater orchestras in Stockholm in 1926, when he was only 18. At the dance restaurant Kaos from 1930 to 1932 he led a big band which made a number of recordings (notably *Rhythm*, 1932, Tel. A1228) and which was eventually taken over by Arne Hülphers. In 1936 he formed a new dance orchestra which toured Europe and made recordings in both Sweden and Germany. Although von Eichwald was not himself a jazz musician, his bands of the 1930s included many of the best Swedish jazz soloists (among them Thore Ehrling, who in 1938 formed his own band mainly with fellow sidemen from von Eichwald's ensemble). After disbanding in 1940 von Eichwald was active mainly as a conductor of symphony orchestras and operettas. (B. Englund: "Håkan von Eichwald: han hade flera vitt skilda karriärer" [Håkan von Eichwald: he had several widely differing careers], *Orkester journalen*, xliii/12 (1975), 12 [incl. discography]; xliv/1 (1976), 12)

ERIK KJELLBERG/LARS WESTIN

Von Essen, Eric (*b* Chicago, 30 June 1954; *d* Sweden, 14 Aug 1997). Double bass player. His father was Swedish and his mother, who was from India, performed classical Indian dance. During the 1960s he lived with his family in New Haven, Connecticut, where he studied piano and double bass and also learned to play guitar, tablā, and chromatic harmonica. In the mid-1970s he moved west to study composition at the University of California, Los Angeles; although he left the university after a year to work as a performer, he later completed his BA. In summer 1978 he studied tablā in India. While working in the Los Angeles area von Essen developed associations with many musicians, most importantly Alex Cline, Nels Cline (with whom he recorded in a duo in 1980), Vinny Golia, the violinist Jeff Gauthier, and the pianist Wayne Peet; in 1979 he formed the group Quartet Music with the Cline brothers and Gauthier. From the early 1980s he appeared regularly at Linda's, a bar in Los Angeles, performing with such pianists as Alan Broadbent, Lou Levy, Gerry Wiggins, and Jimmie Rowles; he continued to work with Levy and Rowles into the 1990s, recording under Levy's leadership (1992–3), under Rowles (1988, *c*1994), and with Rowles in a trio accompanying Jeri Brown (1994). Von Essen was one of two double bass players in Golia's large ensemble, and he performed and recorded, apart from Quartet Music, with Nels Cline (1987), Alex Cline (1987, 1992), and Gauthier (1993). As a freelance he performed and recorded in the quintet led by Art Farmer and Frank Morgan (1989) and recorded with the tenor saxophonist Greg Marvin (1989), the pianist Dave Ferris (1991), the pianist Jeff Colella (*c*1995), and Yusef Lateef (1995), among others. He also played cello. Von Essen died of a heart attack shortly after moving to Sweden, where he had accepted a teaching position in Haparanda.

SELECTED RECORDINGS

(recorded for Nine Winds unless otherwise indicated)

Duos with N. Cline: *Elegies* (1980, 0105)
As sideman with Quartet Music: *Quartet Music* (1980, 0106); *Ocean Park* (1984, 0113); *Windows on the Lake* (1986, 0122)
As sideman with others: V. Golia: *Compositions for Large Ensemble* (1982, 0110), incl. Iki; G. Marvin: *Taking Off!* (1989, Tim. 348); L. Levy: *Lunarcy* (1992, Verve 314-514317-2); A. Cline: *Montsalvat* (1992, 0174); J. Brown: *A Timeless Place* (1994, Justin Time 70)

BIBLIOGRAPHY

<http://www.cogent.net/~legoat/eric.htm> (1999)
K. Silsbee: "Against the Grain: the Genius of Jazz Bassist Eric von Essen," <http://www.newtimesla.com/archives/1997/12251997/music1.html> (1999)

GK

Von Essen, Reimer. *See* Essen, reimer von.

Von Ohlen, John [Baron] (*b* Indianapolis, 13 May 1941). Drummer and bandleader. He played accordion and piano as a child and had lessons on the latter instrument for ten years from the age of five; when he was ten he took up trombone, and around the age of 17, when the drummer of the big band of which he was a member failed to appear for a rehearsal, he began playing drums. Von Ohlen enrolled at North Texas State College but was uninterested in his courses and soon left to tour as a musician. He worked initially as a trombonist, but once again changed to the drum set out of necessity; this time he stayed with the instrument, and from 1963 he played it exclusively in professional settings. In 1967 he recorded with Woody Herman at the Monterey Jazz Festival, and in 1967–8 he toured with Billy Maxted's Manhattan Jazz Band; later he worked with Herman for a year (1969). After touring the USA and recording with Stan Kenton (1970–72) he organized and led a 17-piece band in Indiana and recorded as the leader of a quartet (1973). From around 1979 to the mid-1980s he led the Blue Wisp Big Band in Cincinnati, where the group made several successful albums; it recorded another album in 1984 during a performance at Carmelo's Jazz Club in Sherman Oaks, California. In the 1980s and 1990s Von Ohlen was a member of a big band led by the pianist Steve Allee.

SELECTED RECORDINGS

As leader: *The Baron* (1973, CW 3001); of Blue Wisp Big Band: *Butterfly* (1982, Mopro 101), *The Smooth One* (1983, Mopro 103), *Live at Carmelo's Jazz Club* (1984, Mopro 109), *Rollin' with Von Ohlen* (1985, Mopro 112)
As sideman with S. Allee: *Downtown Blues* (1999, Sea Breeze 2095)

BIBLIOGRAPHY

Feather–Gitler '70s
"These Great Leaders May Not be Replaced, Says Drummer John Von Ohlen," *CI*, x/8 (1972), 24
S. Fish: "John Von Ohlen: Natural Style," *MD*, ix/3 (1985), 16

BK

Von Schlippenbach, Alexander. *See* Schlippenbach, alex.

Voynow, Dick [Richard Fabian] (*b* Illinois, 21 Oct 1899; *d* Los Angeles, 15 Sept 1944). Pianist. His full name and details of his birth are taken from the California death index. He replaced the pianist Dud Mecum in the Wolverines during the band's first residency at the Stockton Club, Hamilton, Ohio. Later he became its business manager and nominal leader, and he continued in this role after most of the original members had left. The band toured regularly until 1926 and sporadically thereafter, and performed on one occasion with Smith Ballew. Voynow may be heard to advantage on *Riverboat Shuffle* (1924, Gen. 5454) and *Royal Garden Blues* (1924, Gen. 20062), both recorded with the Wolverines. From the late 1920s he worked as an executive for recording companies. (R. M. Sudhalter, P. R. Evans, and W. Dean-Myatt: *Bix: Man & Legend*, New Rochelle, NY, and London, 1974)

For illustrations *see* Recording, fig.3, and Wolverines.

based on *ChiltonW*

V.S.O.P. (i). Group led by Herbie Hancock. Its name derived from the title of the album (Col. PG34688) documenting a retrospective concert of Hancock's music given at the Newport Jazz Festival in New York in 1976, where three groups performed: a quintet consisting of Hancock, the trumpeter Freddie Hubbard, the saxophonist Wayne Shorter, the double bass player Ron Carter, and the drummer Tony Williams; Hancock's sextet as it had been in 1971–3; and a jazz-rock group. Hancock viewed the appearance of these diverse ensembles in the same program as a "Very Special One-time-only Performance." In 1977 he used the initials of this phrase to name the quintet (all the members of which, with the exception of Hubbard, had been members of Miles Davis's famous quintet of the mid-1960s) when it toured the USA and performed in Tokyo and London; during the same year the ensemble, also known simply as the Quintet, recorded the album *V.S.O.P.: the Quintet* (Col. C2-34976). The group was reunited in 1979 and gave a concert in Japan, and a second version of the quintet, V.S.O.P. II (consisting of Hancock, Carter, Williams, and Wynton and Branford Marsalis), toured in 1983 (for illustration *see* Hancock, herbie).

BIBLIOGRAPHY

P. Keepnews: "Notes: Hancock," *Jazz Magazine*, ii/1 (1977), 24
L. Lyons: "Herbie Hancock: V.S.O.P., New Musical Directions," *CK*, iii/11 (1977), 28
R. Palmer: "Hancock's All-star Reunion," *RS*, no.249 (6 Oct 1977), 28
H. Saal and A. Kuflik: "Jazz Comes Back!," *Newsweek*, xc (8 Aug 1977), 51
I. Gitler: "Jazz Fests Italian Style," *JT* (1983), August, 5
H. Mandel: "Herbie Hancock: Keeping his Ears and Options Open," *JT* (1983), August, 10
K. Silsbee: "The Playboy Jazz Fest," *JT* (1983), August, 5

THOMAS OWENS

V.S.O.P. (ii). Record label. It was established in the early 1980s by CBS to issue several collections of recordings by Louis Armstrong. The initials stand for "Very Special Old Phonography."

V.S.O.P. (iii). Record company and label. It was established in the early 1980s by Jeff Barr to reissue, first, albums by J. R. Monterose and Elmo Hope, and then a succession of albums originally recorded in the 1950s for the Mode and Tampa labels. From the mid-1980s it also released new recordings by, among others, Danny D'Imperio, Pete Jolly, Herb Geller, and a quintet led by Bob Cooper and Conte Candoli.

GK

Vuckovich, Larry [Lazar Milutin; El Vucko] (*b* Kotor, Montenegro, 8 Dec 1936). Pianist. His father lived in the USA from 1910 to 1921, during which period he obtained American citizenship; thus Vuckovich was born a US citizen. At the age of six he took up piano, and a year later at the conservatory in Kotor he began taking classical lessons and studying Balkan folk music and theater. In 1951 he moved with his family to San Francisco, where as a teenager he sat in at local clubs and had lessons with Vince Guaraldi; later he studied music at San Francisco State College and with Richard Wyands. He became a full-time musician in 1960. In 1965 he joined Jon Hendricks, with whom he toured North America and Europe, and at the Monterey Jazz Festival the following year he and Hendricks performed with the quartet of Elvin Jones and Booker Ervin. Vuckovich then went to Europe, where he toured with Philly Joe Jones (recording in a quintet alongside Dizzy Reece, Isla Eckinger, and Bent Jaedig at a festival in Pescara, Italy, in 1969), recorded with Mark Murphy (1969, in Bremen, as a member of a rhythm section with Jimmy Woode and Kenny Clare), worked as house pianist at the Domicile Club in Munich (1969–70), and performed with such visiting musicians as Dexter Gordon, Clifford Jordan, Slide Hampton, and Dave Holland. After returning to San Francisco (1970) he worked in Guaraldi's two-piano group and with Hendricks in the singer's show *Evolution of the Blues* (*c*1974–6). From 1979 to 1983 he appeared regularly at the Keystone Korner, accompanying numerous visiting musicians, often with Larry Grenadier on double bass. In addition he broadcast on NPR's programs "Downtown Jazz" and "Jazz Alive."

Having settled in New York in 1985, Vuckovich led a quintet that included Charles McPherson and Tom Harrell and worked with various musicians, notably in duos with Michael Moore (i), Walter Booker, and Harvie Swartz. While based in New York he performed in San Francisco (1987) as the leader of a trio with Booker and Jimmy Cobb as his sidemen and Frank Morgan as guest soloist. In 1990 he returned once more to San Francisco. There he held a long engagement at Club 36 in the Grand Hyatt Hotel (1990–98) and then led a trio at another club, Shanghai 1930; around 1991 he was filmed in performance for PBS's series "Club Date." In the late 1990s he formed the record company and label Tetrachord Music.

Vuckovich has been acclaimed for his merger of the rhythms of bop with Eastern European scales and harmonies, but he is equally impressive as an interpreter of the standard jazz repertory.

SELECTED RECORDINGS

As unaccompanied soloist: *Deja Vuk* (1999, Musette 9402)
As leader: *Blue Balkan* (1980, IC 1096); *City Sounds, Village Voices* (1981, PA 8012); *Blues for Red* (1984, Hot House 1001)
As sideman: D. Goykovich: *As Simple as it is* (1970, Session 851); C. Collins: *Blues on my Mind* (1979, Conc. 95)

BIBLIOGRAPHY

R. Tolleson: "Profile: Larry Vuckovich," *DB*, li/11 (1984), 48
P. Elwood: "Music: Ex-local Boy Back from New York with a Hot Band," *San Francisco Examiner* (12 Sept 1986)
——: "Prodigal Son Vuckovich Back in Town with his own Brand of Jazz," *San Francisco Examiner* (8 Feb 1987)
D. Sutro: "The 'Balkan Bopper' Mixes Jazz with Yugoslav Folk," *Los Angeles Times* (11 June 1991)
M. Breslow and D. Guaraldi: *Jazzography: Profiles of Regional Jazz Musicians who Perform in San Francisco* (Glenview, IL, 2000), 34

GK

Vukán, George [György] (*b* Budapest, 21 Aug 1941). Hungarian pianist, composer, arranger, and bandleader. Following a successful performance with Clark Terry at the Montreux International Festival in 1969 he played in his own groups and with leading Hungarian musicians. In 1981 he founded the Super Trio, and in 1986 the Creative Art Ensemble (CAE), combining the 22-piece Budapest Brass Ensemble with the Super Trio. In 1990 he formed the CAE Trio with Balázs Berkes on double bass and Elemér Balázs on drums. He made his first recording as an unaccompanied pianist in 1992, playing ragtime pieces from the era of the Austro-Hungarian monarchy.

SELECTED RECORDINGS

As unaccompanied soloist: *Dunapalota Ragtime* (1992, Hotelinfo-Ferdinandus 2001); *Live in Tata* (1993, Pannon Jazz 1994)
As leader: *Clarification* (1980, EMI-Col. 14C062-71168); of Super Trio: *Together Alone* (1981, Krém 17691), *Birthday Party* (1986, Krém 37047); of CAE Trio: *Chopin–Vukán: 12 Preludes op.28* (1994, CAE 004), *Debussy–Vukán: Children's Corner* (1994, CAE 005)
As sideman: C. Terry: *At the Montreux Jazz Festival* (1969, Pol. 2391011); E. Balázs: *Fly Bird* (1995, Pannon Jazz 1008); B. Berkes: *Forever* (1996, Pannon Jazz 1016)

BIBLIOGRAPHY

G. Turi: *Azt mondom: jazz* [I say that: jazz] (Budapest, 1983), 123
——: *Jazz from Hungary* (Budapest, 1987), 29
G. G. Simon: *The Book of Hungarian Jazz* (Budapest, 1992)
——: *Magyar jazzdiszkografia, 1905–1994* (Budapest, 1994)
——: *Magyar jazztőrtéret* [Hungarian jazz history] (Budapest, 1999)

GÉZA GÁBOR SIMON

Vyšniauskas, Petras (*b* Plungė, USSR [now Lithuania], 11 June 1957). Lithuanian saxophonist and clarinetist. He played accordion from the age of four, began lessons on clarinet and accordion in 1964, and continued his clarinet studies at the conservatory in Klaipėdas and at the Lithuanian music academy; in 1968 he took up saxophone, which he studied later with Vladimir Chekasin at the academy. From 1982 until 1988 his quartet (with the saxophonist Vytautas Labutis, the double bass player Leonid Shinkarenko, and the drummer Gediminas Laurinavičius) performed throughout the USSR, and during the 1980s Vyšniauskas began to develop international affiliations, playing with Steve Lacy, Theo Jörgensmann, and Tomasz Stańko, among others. His music began to incorporate elements of Lithuanian folk music, particularly in his quartet. He recorded in 1984 as a member of Vyacheslav Ganelin's trio, and in 1989 in concert in Vienna, both as an unaccompanied soloist and with Ganelin and others. In 1991 he formed a duo with the Lithuanian folk singer Veronika Povilionienė. Vyšniasukas also recorded in a duo with the Lithuanian drummer Arkadij Gotesman (1990) and in a trio with the pianist Christoph Baumann and the double bass player Jacques Siron (1991). In the 1990s he formed a trio with Ganelin and Gotesman, which performed in Israel (where Ganelin and Gotesman were both living) and in Lithuania, where it recorded in 1995.

SELECTED RECORDINGS

Duos with V. Povilionenė: *L[e˙]k,sakale* (1993, Lituanus 034)
As leader: with J. Siron and C. Baumann: *Nuit balte* (1991, Unit 4063); Octet Ost II (1994, Amadeo 521823-2)
As sideman with V. Ganelin: Inverso (1984, Leo 140)

BIBLIOGRAPHY

"Petras Vyšniauskas Quartet: Vilnius, Lithuania," *Coda*, no.214 (1987), 26

B. Noglik: "Petras Vyšniauskas: New Jazz from Lithuania," *Day In Day Out*, no.6 (1990), 86

J. Gaudas: "Petras Vyšniauskas," *Jh*, no.507 (1994), 10

B. Jahnke: "Jazz in Lithuania," <http://visionx.com/jazz/articles/a0399_04.htm> (1999)

O. Molokoyedov: "Jazz in Lithuania (Notes of an Observer)," <http://www.vilniusjazz.it/press/396llch.htm> (1999)

AUŠRA LISTAVIČIŪTĖ

Wachsmann, Phil(ipp John Paul) (*b* Kampala, Uganda, 5 Aug 1944). British violinist. His father was a German ethnomusicologist who went to Uganda to escape Hitler's persecution. He took up violin at the age of nine, then the following year left Uganda and later studied music in England (gaining a BA at Durham University), the USA (1965–6), and Paris (with Nadia Boulanger, 1968–9) and taught at Durham University (1969–70). In 1971 he formed the group Chamberpot, which drew on many sources, including the music of Anton Webern, and from that time concentrated on free improvisation, developing the use of electronics as an integrated extension of the technical capabilities of the violin. Among the jazz musicians and groups with whom he has worked are Derek Bailey (1973–) and Bailey's group Company (1982–6), a trio with Paul Lytton and Radu Malfatti (1974–5), another with Howard Riley and Barry Guy (recording *c*1976), Tony Oxley (1977–), the London Jazz Composers Orchestra (1979–), Fred van Hove (1979–84, including van Hove's group ML DD 4), Guy and Paul Rutherford (in the re-formed Iskra 1903, 1980–), the Electric String Trio (1981–), the King Übü Orchestrü (1984–), Rüdiger Carl (recording in 1987), Georg Gräwe (1988–), Trio Raphiphi (with Malfatti and Phil Minton, recording in 1990), Mario Schiano (1992), and Evan Parker's Electro-Acoustic Ensemble (recording in 1996). During the 1990s he worked with the Swedish improvisation trio Gush – the saxophonist Mats Gustafsson, the pianist and keyboard player Stan Sandell, and the percussionist Raymond Strid – in the quartet Gushwachs. Among his compositions are *Colour Energy Reaction* (1981), for film and orchestra, and other mixed-media works that have been written in collaboration with dancers and artists. Wachsmann was one of the founders in 1975 of the record label Bead.

SELECTED RECORDINGS

As unaccompanied soloist: *Writing on Water* (1984–5, Bead 23); *Chathuna* (1997, Bead CD003)

As leader: with P. Lytton: *Some other Season* (1997, ECM 1662); with Gush (of Gushwachs): *Gushwachs* (1997, Bead CD002)

BIBLIOGRAPHY

CarrJ

R. Cotterrell, ed.: *Jazz Now: the Jazz Centre Society Guide* (London, 1976)

P. Renaud: *La discographie du jazz anglais* (Chaumont, France, 1985)

B. Rusch: "Philipp Wachsmann Interview," *Cadence*, xxiii/5 (1997), 5

SIMON ADAMS

Wackerman, Chad [Charles August] (*b* Long Beach, CA, 25 March 1960). Drummer. He grew up in a musical family (his father is a drummer and junior high school music director) and played drums from the age of six; although he was reluctant to do so, he also learned violin and viola at his parents' request. While studying with Chuck Flores (1973–7) and at California State University, Long Beach (1978–80), he played in a pop and rock band at Disneyland and then transferred with that group's rhythm section into Bill Watrous's ensemble (1978). After touring with the pop singer Leslie Uggams (1979) he worked for seven years with Frank Zappa (from 1981); during this association he made several tours and recordings and appeared in a number of the leader's promotional videos, notably *The Frank Zappa Halloween Special*, which was recorded in concert at the New York Palladium in 1982. From that year he maintained a long affiliation with Allan Holdsworth, with whom he toured and recorded on a number of occasions. In 1985–6 Wackerman toured with the Australian rock group Men at Work, and in 1987 he appeared on Barbra Streisand's television special "One Voice" and performed on her album of the same name. Later he toured with John Patitucci (1994), Joe Sample (1996), and alongside Bill Bruford, Luis Conte, and Doudou Ndiaye Rose in the World Drummers Ensemble (1996); he also toured and recorded with the guitarist Andy Summers (1989–92) and Banned from Utopia (1995), a group devoted to Zappa's music. He may be seen with Buddy Rich's big band on the video *Buddy Rich Memorial Concert*, v (1994). In 1994 Wackerman moved to Australia, where he recorded with a variety of Australian pop artists and formed the Chad Wackerman Group.

SELECTED RECORDINGS

As leader: *Forty Reasons* (1991, CMP 48); *The View* (1993, CMP 64); *Scream* (1999, Metalimbo 06466-2)

As sideman with F. Zappa: *Thing-fish* (1984, Barking Pumpkin 74201); *Make a Jazz Noise Here* (*c*1990, Barking Pumpkin D2AS74234); *The Best Band You Never Heard in your Life* (*c*1990, Barking Pumpkin D2AS74233)

As sideman with others: B. Watrous: *I'll Play for You* (1980, FaD 134); A. Holdsworth: *Metal Fatigue* (1984, Enigma 74002); Ed Mann: *Perfect World* (1990, CMP 45); Tom Grant: *The View from Here* (*c*1992, Verve Forecast 314-517657-2)

BIBLIOGRAPHY

D. Levine: "Chad Wackerman: Enjoying All Challenges," *MD*, vii/5 (1983), 14

Freff: "Frank Zappa's Scott Thunes and Chad Wackerman," *Musician*, no.70 (1984), 70
R. Flans: "Chad Wackerman," *MD*, xii/12 (1988), 20 [incl. discography]
K. Micallef: "Hearsay: Chad Wackerman: Forty Reasons to Buy his Record," *JT*, xxi/8 (1991), 8
<http://home.earthlink.net/~unclemeat/wackerman.html> (1999)

RICK MATTINGLY

Wade, Jimmy [James F.] (*b* Jacksonville, IL, *c*1895; *d* Chicago, 12 Oct 1933). Trumpeter, pianist, and bandleader. After leading his own band at Queen's Hall, Chicago (*c*1916), he spent several years as the music director of the band that accompanied Lucille Hegamin, working in Seattle and New York. He left in the early 1920s and returned to Chicago, where he played with Doc Cook. Later he formed his own band, which included Eddie South and Teddy Weatherford. The group held many residencies in Chicago and also performed in New York at the Savoy Ballroom (1926) and the Club Alabam (1927). Among its recordings are *Someday Sweetheart/Mobile Blues* (1923, Para. 20295), the latter of which offers a particularly good example of Wade's solo trumpet playing. South acted as director of the band during the mid-1920s. Later in the decade Wade worked occasionally as a sideman with other leaders. After 1930 he was active mainly with his own ensembles, touring the Midwest. His date of death was given by his widow.

BIBLIOGRAPHY

McCarthyB
T. J. Hennessey: "The Black Chicago Establishment, 1919–1930," *JJS*, ii/1 (1974), 15
R. Gulliver: "Jimmy Wade," *Sv*, no.56 (1974–5), 55 [incl. discography]

based on *ChiltonW*

Wadud, Abdul (Khabir) [DeVaughn, Ronald] (*b* Cleveland, 30 April 1947). Cellist. He learned cello from the age of nine and later studied at Youngstown State University (1966–7) and Oberlin College Conservatory (1968–70), where he played in the Black Unity Trio as well as with Stanley Cowell and Cecil Bridgewater; while there he met Julius Hemphill, with whom he worked fruitfully thereafter, and took his Muslim name. With Harold Danko and the drummer Mike Smith he formed a trio in which he played double bass as well as cello. From 1970 to 1977 he was a member of the New Jersey Symphony Orchestra, and in 1972 he gained a master's degree in performance at SUNY, Stony Brook. He first worked with Arthur Blythe, another long-time associate, in 1976, and in the 1970s he played and recorded with Frank Lowe (1975), Hemphill (recording in a duo, 1976), George Lewis (ii) (1977), Oliver Lake (1978), Leroy Jenkins (in a duo, 1979), Sam Rivers, Cecil Taylor, David Murray, Chico Freeman, and others. From 1980 he worked with Anthony Davis in various settings, including a trio with James Newton (1982–4), the octet Episteme, and, later, the orchestra for Davis's opera *X: the Life and Times of Malcolm X*; he also worked with John Purcell. In 1985 he was a founding member of the Black Swan Quartet, consisting of Akbar Ali on violin, another cellist, Eileen Folson, and Reggie Workman on double bass; the group improvises on European classical structures. Wadud was a member of Marty Erhlich's Dark Woods Ensemble in the early 1990s. He continued to play with Hemphill until the saxophonist's death in 1995; the two men recorded together in a trio in 1991 and again in a duo in 1992. Through his sophisticated use of bowing and plucking techniques Wadud expanded the cello's role in jazz as both an accompanying and a solo instrument; an especially fine example may be heard on Hemphill's lengthy track *The Hard Blues* (1972), where Wadud's cello playing ranges from the avant garde to an evocation of a country blues guitarist.

SELECTED RECORDINGS

As unaccompanied soloist: *By Myself* (1977, Bishara Music BR101)
As leader with A. Davis and J. Newton: *I've Known Rivers* (1982, Gram. 8201)
As sideman: J. Hemphill: *Dogon, A. D.* (1972, Mbari 5001); *'Coon Bid'ness* (1972, 1975, Ari. 1012), incl. The Hard Blues (1972); A. Blythe: *The Grip* (1977, IndN 1029); J. Hemphill: *Raw Materials and Residuals* (1977, BS 0015); A. Blythe: *Illusions* (1980, Col. JC36583); M. Ehrlich: *Emergency Peace* (1990, New World 80409-2)

BIBLIOGRAPHY

D. Lee: "Abdul Wadud," *Coda*, no.176 (1980), 8
L. Jeske: "Abdul Wadud: Profile," *DB*, xlix/11 (1982), 52
H. Smith: "Black Swan Quartet: in the Tradition of Originality and Artistic Achievement," *Strings*, iii/3 (1989), 46

ED HAZELL/BK

Wah-wah. *See* Wa-wa.

Waits, Freddie [Frederick Douglas; Dahoud] (*b* Jackson, MS, 27 April 1943; *d* New York, 18 Nov 1989). Drummer. He first played drums for blues and rhythm-and-blues singers such as Memphis Slim, John Lee Hooker, Percy Mayfield, and Sam Cooke. In the early 1960s he toured and recorded with soul singers associated with the Motown label, but while in Detroit also played jazz with Cecil McBee, Kirk Lightsey, and Bennie Maupin. He then twice toured Brazil as a member of the Paul Winter Consort before settling around 1965 in New York, where he performed in styles ranging from swing to free jazz; his early affiliations there were with Kenny Dorham, Cedar Walton, Gerald Wilson's big band, and Sonny Rollins's trio, and he also began a long association with the Jazzmobile in Harlem. In 1967 he joined Sir Roland Hanna in the New York Jazz Sextet; although not the regular drummer in this ensemble and its continuation, the New York Jazz Quartet, he evidently deputized on occasion for a number of years. From 1968 to 1970 he also performed and recorded with McCoy Tyner and toured with Ella Fitzgerald; these activities in turn overlapped with intermittent membership for three years in Freddie Hubbard's band, brief affiliations with Walter Bishop, Jr., Joe Williams, Gary Bartz, Hubert Laws, Jimmie Heath, and several distinguished jazz and pop singers, and membership in Lee Morgan's band, which recorded in 1971. By this time Waits was sometimes known as Dahoud rather than Freddie.

Although Waits normally played the conventional drum set, his work with Max Roach's ensemble M' Boom re: percussion (from 1971) demonstrated his command of a wide array of percussion instruments. He made several European tours with this ensemble, while also accompanying Billy Taylor (ii) (1971–5) and rejoining Fitzgerald at the Newport Jazz Festival (1973). Among the many other jazz musicians with whom he recorded through the 1960s and 1970s were Ray Bryant (1966), Johnny Hodges (1968), Andrew Hill (1968–9), Richard Davis (1972), James Moody (1973), and Maupin and Bobby Jones (both 1974).

In 1973 Waits once again became active in popular music, notably on PBS on the television series "Soul." The following year he toured Europe and Africa with the memorial Duke Ellington Orchestra under Mercer Ellington's direction; he also performed and recorded with the group in 1975, and he served as an accompanist to Jimmy Heath, Stan Getz, and the drummer Grady Tate (who at the time was presenting himself as a singer). In 1976 he joined the faculty in the Livingston College Music Department at Rutgers, the State University of New Jersey. With Horacee Arnold and Billy Hart, he formed Colloquium III, a percussion group that first performed in early 1979. During this period he also recorded with Teddy Edwards (1976), Curtis Fuller (1978), Bill Dixon (1980), and Hill again (1980). He continued to work with M' Boom Re:Percussion and with Hanna through the 1980s, and in 1987 recorded with Hanna's trio; that same year he also played in a quintet led by Cecil Taylor. From 1987 to 1989 he was in We Three with Stanley Cowell and Buster Williams and in Trio Transition with Mulgrew Miller and Reggie Workman, each trio touring Japan and making recordings. His final European tours were with M' Boom Re: Percussion and Jay Hoggard. Waits may well have been the most versatile drummer of the century. Among those capable of playing perfectly within the rigid restraints of Motown drumming, no other player flourished equally well in the most outrageously creative of free-jazz ensembles or in a dozen other styles falling between these two extremes.

SELECTED RECORDINGS

As leader with S. Cowell and B. Williams: *We Three* (1987, DIW 807)
As sideman: A. Hill: *Grass Roots* (1968, BN 84303); M. Tyner: *Expansions* (1968, BN 84338); R. Davis: *Epistrophy and Now's the Time* (1972, Muse 5002); J. Moody: *Feelin' it Together* (1973, Muse 5020); B. Maupin: *The Jewel in the Lotus* (1974, ECM 1043); B. Jones: *Hill Country Suite* (1974, Enja 2046); M. Roach: *M' Boom Re: Percussion* (1979, Col. IC36247); B. Dixon: *Bill Dixon in Italy* (1980, SN 1008, 1011); M' Boom Re: Percussion: *Collage* (1984, SN 1059); J. DeJohnette: *The Jack DeJohnette Piano Album* (1985, Landmark 1504); R. Hanna: *Persia my Dear* (1987, DIW 805); Trio Transition: *Trio Transition with Special Guest Oliver Lake* (1988, DIW 829)

BIBLIOGRAPHY

Feather-Gitler '70s
B. Primack: "Drummers Colloquium III: Multiple Percussionists Horacee Arnold, Billy Hart, Freddie Waits," *DB*, xlvi/17 (1979), 25
C. Iero: "Colloquium III: Freddie Waits, Horacee Arnold, Billy Hart," *MD*, iv/1 (1980), 12
R. Mattingly and S. K. Fish: "M' Boom," *MD*, vii/9 (1983), 8
Obituary, *New York Times* (22 Nov 1989)
J. Potter: "Life Experience: Frederick Waits," *MD*, xiv/2 (1990), 24
J. Simmen: "Freddie Waits," *BHcF*, no.385 (1990), 31

BK

Waits, Nasheet (*b* New York, *c*1971). Drummer, son of Freddie Waits. He took up drums in his youth, when he was friends with Abraham Burton and Eric McPherson, both of whom were instrumental in his later playing jazz. Waits attended Morehouse College in Atlanta but returned to New York after his father's death in November 1989. By the following year he had entered the music program at Long Island University (BA 1996) and begun private studies with Michael Carvin; later he studied with Max Roach. From 1993 to around 1998 he performed extensively in Antonio Hart's ensembles, though during the same period he played with Joe Lovano, Geri Allen, Jaki Byard, and Mario Bauzá, and recorded with Philip Harper (1993) and Antoine Roney (1995). Thereafter he became much in demand as a sideman, working with Hamiet Bluiett, Marc Cary, Stanley Cowell, Stefon Harris, Andrew Hill, Jason Moran, the pianist and keyboard player James Hurt, the pianist Orrin Evans, and Greg Osby, as well as in New Directions, a group sponsored by Blue Note and consisting of Osby, Mark Shim, Moran, Harris, and Tarus Mateen. Waits has also performed in the New York All Stars (alongside Jesse Davis and Jacky Terrasson), recorded and performed with the singer Lenora Zenzalai Helm (1998) and Michael Marcus (1999), and recorded with, among others, Anthony Wonsey (1998). In the year 2000 he began associations with both Jackie McLean and Fred Hersch.

SELECTED RECORDINGS

As sideman: P. Harper: *Soulful Sin* (1993, Muse 5505); A. Roney: *Whirling* (1995, Muse 5546); A. Hart: *Here I Stand* (1997, Imp. 208); A. Wonsey: *Open the Gates* (1998, Criss Cross 1162); M. Marcus: *In the Center of it All* (1999, Justin Time 130); M. Cary: *Trillium* (c1999, Jazzateria 20304-2); J. Moran: *Facing Left* (2000, BN 23884-2)

BIBLIOGRAPHY

B. Ratliff: "Propelled by Different Drummers," *New York Times* (15 Oct 1999)
<http://www.writerscenter.org/pojazzbios.html> (2000)
T. Terrell: "Burning Hot Son: Nasheet Waits," *JT*, xxx/9 (2000), 44 [incl. discography]

GK

Waits, Tom [Thomas Alan] (*b* Pomona, CA, 7 Dec 1949). Songwriter and composer. His family moved to San Diego when he was 12 years old, but after graduating from high school he returned regularly to the Los Angeles area to try to find work there as a musician. From 1972 he was active as a storyteller-pianist and guitarist, accompanied, whenever finances allowed, by his group the Nocturnal Emissions (tenor saxophone, double bass, and drums). His subjects were crude and vulgar, concerning life in greasy diners, striptease clubs, urban bus stations, and smoky bars, and his language was a slang of the 1940s and 1950s; his humor, however, was intellectually perceptive. His tales, funny at first, became increasingly morbid during the 1970s, and his already gravelly voice began to be affected by an excess of cigarettes and alcohol. He made a number of recordings for Asylum records, the finest of which was probably *Nighthawks at the Diner* (1975), a concert performance which demonstrated his witty, improvisatory style. During the early 1980s Waits labored over the music for Francis Ford Coppola's film *One from the Heart* (1982). With the recording *Swordfishtrombones* (1983) he ceased to focus on lyrics and began to explore a broad spectrum of instrumental sounds, making use of synthesizers, bagpipes, and exotic percussion in addition to conventional jazz instruments. In 1983 he moved from Los Angeles to New York, where he concentrated on a new career as an actor; later he settled in Santa Rosa, in northern California. He made a tour of Europe with a sextet in 1985, and in 1988 he recorded an album in concert with his group. From the late 1980s into the 1990s Waits concentrated on acting in films (including *Big Time*, 1988) and on writing for both films and musical theater, and he performed only occasionally. In 1998 he recorded an album of new songs, and the following year he toured in support of that album.

SELECTED RECORDINGS

Closing Time (1972, Asy. 5061); *The Heart of Saturday Night* (1974, Asy. 7E-1015); *Nighthawks at the Diner* (1975, Asy. 7E-2008); *Small Change* (1976, Asy. 7E-1078); *Foreign Affairs* (1977, Asy. 7E-1117); *Blue Valentine* (1978, Asy. 6E-162); *Heartattack and Vine* (1980, Asy. 6E-295); *Swordfishtrombones* (1983, Isl. 90095-1); *Rain Dogs* (1985, Isl. 90299); *Bone Machine* (1992, Isl. 512580)

BIBLIOGRAPHY

S. Lake: "Waits: the Great White Hope," *MM* (4 Oct 1975), 16
M. Hohman: "Bitin' the Green Shiboda with Tom Waits," *DB*, xliii/12 (1976), 14
D. McGee: "Tom Waits," *RS*, no.231 (27 Jan 1977), 11
J. A. Scott: "On the Way to Burma Shave: Tom Waits and Ballad Form," *Popular Music and Society*, vii/2 (1980), 103 [analysis of lyrics]

P. Keepnews: "Singer Shuns 'Popularity Contest': Waits not Waiting for a Hit," *Billboard*, xcix (16 Nov 1985), 49
E. Murphy: "Tom Waits: the Drifter Finds a Home," *RS*, no.466 (30 Jan 1986), 20
D. Infusino: "Tom Waits Takes a Walk on the Dark Side," *Christian Science Monitor* (17 Dec 1992), 13
R. Rense: "Waits in Wonderland," *San Francisco Chronicle* (13 Dec 1992)
A. Sweeting: "A Mellower Prince of Melancholy," *The Guardian* (15 Sept 1992)
R. Palmer: "Tom Waits: All-purpose Troubadour," *New York Times* (14 Nov 1993)
R. Hilburn: "Tracking an Elusive Character," *Los Angeles Times Calendar* (6 June 1999), 6
G. Kot: "Reepers and Weepers: Tom Waits Brings his Avant-cabaret Music Back to Chicago," *Chicago Tribune* (29 Aug 1999)
J. Sullivan: "The Long Waits: Return of an Ageless Artist," *Boston Globe* (19 Sept 1999)
——: "Variations on a Twisted Persona," *San Francisco Chronicle Datebook* (18 April 1999), 34

BK

Wakenius, Ulf (Karl Erik) (*b* Halmstad, Sweden, 16 April 1958). Swedish guitarist. He taught himself to play guitar from the age of 11 and later attended the music high school in Gothenburg (1984–5). He first came to international notice through Guitars Unlimited (not to be confused with the French band of the mid- to late 1960s), a duo with the guitarist Peter Almqvist, which toured and recorded extensively from 1980. From 1987 Wakenius led his own quintet with Lars Jansson, Lars Danielsson, and others. He was a member of a trio led by Niels-Henning Ørsted Pedersen (from 1988), worked as a guest soloist with Ray Brown's trio (from 1994), and played in Oscar Peterson's group (from 1997). He also performed on an occasional basis with Svend Asmussen, Herbie Hancock, Joe Henderson, Jim Hall, Bob Berg, Randy Brecker, Bill Evans (iii), Toots Thielemans, Flora Purim, Larry Coryell, the fusion band Grafitti (touring the USA in 1993), Jonas Hellborg, Steve Swallow, Johnny Griffin, and others. His first inspirations – Django Reinhardt, Wes Montgomery, and Joe Pass – are discernible in his work with Brown and Peterson, but in a fusion context (with Grafitti, for example) his playing is often reminiscent of that of John Scofield.

SELECTED RECORDINGS

Duos with P. Almqvist: *Introducing Guitars Unlimited* (1980, Sonet 923); *Extraordinaire* (1993, Music/Music 18)
As leader: *Urban Experience* (1983, Dragon 60); *Venture* (1991, L+R 45052); *First Step* (1992, Imogena 034); *New York Meeting* (1994, Bellaphon 45082); *Dig In* (1995, Sittel 9230); *Enchanted Moments* (1995, Dra. 278)
As sideman: N. L. Doky: *Friendship* (1990, Mlst. 9183); Grafitti: *Good Groove* (1993, Lipstick 89020-2); N.-H. Ørsted Pedersen: *Those Who Were* (1996, Verve 314-533232-2); *This Is All I Ask* (1997, Verve 314-539695-2); R. Brown: *Summertime* (1997, Telarc 83430)

BIBLIOGRAPHY

M. J. Summerfield: *The Jazz Guitar: its Evolution and its Players* (Gateshead, England, 1978, 4/1998, as *The Jazz Guitar: its Evolution, Players and Personalities since 1900*)
K. Jonsson: "Tre unga svenska gitarrister" [Three young Swedish guitarists], *Musikrevy*, xli/7–8 (1986), 248
C. Burden: "From Stockholm to New York," *String Jazz News*, i/6 (1995), 12
"Gitarrsnille med flera sidor" [Guitar master with several sides to his artistry], *Orkester journalen*, lxiv/4 (1996), 2
G. Olson: "Ulf Wakenius i narbild" [A close-up of Ulf Wakenius], *Jazzstage* (1996), April, 6
<http://www.mic.stim.se/engelsk/11/facts/wakenius.html> (1999)

MARK GILBERT

Walcott, Collin (*b* New York, 24 April 1945; *d* Magdeburg, Germany, 8 Nov 1984). Sitar and tablā player and percussionist. His mother was a classical pianist. He learned to play violin, snare drum, and timpani, and during his teens was resident percussionist at the Yale Summer School of Music in Norfolk, Connecticut, where he became familiar with both the European and Indian classical traditions. In 1966 he graduated from Indiana University, where his major subject was percussion, then went to the University of California, Los Angeles, and studied sitar with Ravi Shankar and tablā with Alla Rakha. After moving to New York he performed and recorded a blend of bop and oriental music with Tony Scott (1967–9). Walcott recorded on sitar with Miles Davis's fusion group (1972), and he performed with John Abercrombie's trio at the Village Vanguard (1975); this same band recorded Walcott's first album as a leader later that year. But he was principally involved in three groups devoted to combining jazz improvisation and instrumentation with elements of a wide range of classical and ethnic music: the Paul Winter Consort (1970–72), with which he appeared in the films *Such Good Friends* and *Raga*; Oregon (with Ralph Towner, Paul McCandless, and Glen Moore, all former members of the Winter Consort, 1970–84); and – as an outgrowth of his tenure at the Naropa Institute in Boulder, Colorado, where he and Don Cherry were teachers – Codona, a cooperative trio with Cherry and Nana Vasconcelos (1978–84). He died in a bus crash.

SELECTED RECORDINGS

As leader: *Cloud Dance* (1975, ECM 1062); *Grazing Dreams* (1977, ECM 1096); *Codona* (1978, ECM 1132)
As sideman: T. Scott: *Music for Yoga Meditation and other Joys* (*c*1967, Verve 68742); P. Winter: *Icarus* (*c*1972, Epic 31643); M. Davis: *On the Corner* (1972, Col. KC31906); E. Gismonti: *Sol do meio dia* (1977, ECM 1116)

BIBLIOGRAPHY

M. Bourne: "The Natural Timbre of Oregon," *DB*, xli/16 (1974), 14
M. Zipkin: "Oregon: out of the Woods, into the World," *DB*, xlvi/5 (1979), 13
H. Howland: "Master Percussionist: Oregon's Collin Walcott," *MD*, v/4 (1981), 24
Freff: "Book-ends: Oregon's Collin Walcott and Glen Moore," *Musician*, no.70 (1984), 68
S. L. Larsen: *Some Aspects of the Album "Out of the Woods" by the Chamber Ensemble "Oregon"* (thesis, U. of Oregon, 1981)
Obituary, *New York Times* (10 Nov 1984)

BK

Waldron, Mal(colm Earl) (*b* New York, 16 Aug 1925). Pianist, composer, and leader. Published sources have almost universally given his year of birth as 1926; Waldron asserts in his second interview for *Cadence* (1988) that this was a fiction he had invented in 1943 (effectively to "regain" one of the two years he was then giving the army), and that the correct year is 1925. He first aspired to become a classical pianist, and played jazz on alto saxophone, changing to piano only when he was a student at Queens College, CUNY (where he gained a BA in composition). After graduating he worked with various bands around New York, making his professional début at Café Society with Ike Quebec in 1950, and his first recording with Quebec that same year. He joined Charles Mingus (1954) and played at the Newport Jazz Festival with his Jazz Composer's Workshop (1955) and Jazz Workshop (1956). Late in 1956 Waldron formed his own quintet, which included Gigi Gryce and Idrees Sulieman, and from 1956 to 1958 he recorded frequently as a leader and as a sideman for the Prestige label, notably with Gene Ammons, Jackie McLean, Ray Draper, Teo Macero, John Coltrane, Paul Quinichette, Frank Wess, Herbie Mann, Steve Lacy, and various ad hoc studio groups involving Donald Byrd, Art Farmer, Thad Jones, Kenny

Mal Waldron

Burrell, and others; he also recorded on other labels with Teddy Charles (1956–7, 1960). He was Billie Holiday's accompanist from April 1957 until her death in 1959, after which he worked with Abbey Lincoln and Max Roach and continued his activities as a studio musician. During the early 1960s he played in New York with a quintet led by Eric Dolphy and Booker Little.

After suffering a nervous breakdown in 1963 Waldron had to relearn the fundamentals of playing, which he did partly by studying his own recordings. Having scored the music for and performed in the film *The Cool World* (1963) he went to Europe, and during a period in Paris was invited to write for another film, *Trois chambres à Manhattan* (1964). He played with Kenny Clarke, Ben Webster, Jimmy Gourley, and others at such venues as the Blue Note and Le Chat qui Pêche, spent a further period working in Rome (on radio), Bologna, and Cologne, then in 1967 settled in Munich. (By his own account, he was in Paris in June 1965, but sources on films and Clarke suggest a somewhat earlier visit.) He performed frequently with expatriate and visiting musicians, among them Steve Lacy and Archie Shepp, and also became popular in Japan, where he first appeared in 1970; he renewed his association with McLean in concert in Japan in 1976. In 1975 he began making return visits to the USA, where in the late 1970s to early 1980s he performed mainly as an unaccompanied soloist, though he also led a trio with Calvin Hill and Horacee Arnold (and then a quartet with the addition of Charlie Rouse), a duo with Cameron Brown, and another quartet with Joe Henderson, Herbie Lewis, and Freddie Waits. His European affiliations of this same period included various groups involving Manfred Schoof, Steve Lacy, Jimmy Woode, and Makaya Ntshoko, as well as duos with Lacy and with Johnny Dyani.

In September 1986 Waldron's quintet with Woody Shaw, Rouse, Reggie Workman, and Ed Blackwell recorded two albums and made a video at the Village Vanguard; the following month at Sweet Basil he made a recording of the Dolphy–Little repertory, with Donald Harrison and Terence Blanchard in place of the original leaders and Dolphy and Little's former sidemen Richard Davis and Blackwell filling out the rhythm section. He worked further with Lacy, recording in a quintet at Sweet Basil in 1987 and continuing their duo, which toured and recorded periodically through the 1990s; he also appeared at the Festival International de Jazz de Montréal in a duo with Andrew Hill in 1988, led a quintet including Ricky Ford and Sonny Fortune in New York in 1989, and performed in a duo with Chico Freeman in 1990. In the 1990s Waldron moved to Brussels. He recorded in duos with George Haslam in England and Jeanne Lee in Paris in 1994, and in 1995 celebrated his 70th birthday with a concert in Japan, for which he composed and performed a piece commemorating the 50th anniversary of the bombing of Hiroshima. He maintained a busy touring schedule in the late 1990s.

As a player and composer Waldron draws heavily upon Thelonious Monk's spare, angular style; his improvisations are based on motivic repetition with a minimum of development, or on strict mathematical structures. His composition *Soul Eyes* was first recorded in 1957 and became a jazz standard. As well as jazz pieces he has written several film and ballet scores.

SELECTED RECORDINGS

As unaccompanied soloist: *Blues for Lady Day* (1972, BL 30142); *Mingus Lives* (1979, Enja 3075); *Update* (1986, SN 1130)

Duos: with S. Lacy: *Herbe de l'oubli* (1981, Hat Music 3515); *Sempre amore* (1986, SN 1170); *Hot House* (1990, Novus 3098-2); *Let's Call This … Esteem* (1993, Slam 501); with G. Haslam: *Mal Waldron/George Haslam* (1994, Slam 305); with J. Lee: *After Hours* (1994, Owl 077); with S. Lacy: *Communique* (*c*1996, SN 121298)

As leader: *Mal 1* (1957, Prst. 7090); *Mal 2* (1957, Prst. 7111); *Impressions* (1959, NewJ 8242); *The Quest* (1961, NewJ 8269); *Free at Last* (1969, ECM 1001); with G. Peacock: *First Encounter* (1971, Cat. 7906); *Mal Waldron with the Steve Lacy Quintet* (1972, Amer. 6124); *Up Popped the Devil* (1973, Enja 2034); *Hard Talk* (1974, Enja 2050); *One-upsmanship* (1977, Enja 2092); *One Entrance, Many Exits* (1982, PAlt 8014); *Encounters* (1984, Muse 5305); *The Git Go* (1986, SN 1118); *The Seagulls of Kristiansund* (1986, SN 1148-1); *No More Tears (for Lady Day)* (1988, Tim. 328); *Quadrologue at Utopia*, i (1989, Tutu 888118)

As sideman: C. Mingus: *Moods of Mingus* (1955, Savoy 15050); *Pithecanthropus erectus* (1956, Atl. 1237); [no leader]: *Interplay for Two Trumpets & Two Tenors* (1957, Prst. 7112), incl. Soul Eyes; B. Holiday: *Lady in Satin* (1958, Col. CL1157); E. Dolphy: *Eric Dolphy at the Five Spot* (1961, NewJ 8260); M. Roach: *Percussion Bitter Sweet* (1961, Imp. 8); D. Harrison and T. Blanchard: *Eric Dolphy & Booker Little Remembered Live at Sweet Basil* (1986, PW K28P-6450); *Fire Waltz* (1986, PW K28P-6476)

SELECTED FILMS AND VIDEOS

The Sound of Jazz (1957); The Cool World (1963); Trois chambres à Manhattan (1965); Appunti per un film sul jazz (1965); Mal Waldron (*c*1971); Mal Waldron and Friends: Live at the Village Vanguard ([filmed 1986])

BIBLIOGRAPHY

GrayF
M. Cullaz: "Mal Waldron," *Jh*, no.251 (1969), 20
I. Gitler: "Mal Content on the Continent," *Radio Free Jazz*, xvii/10 (1976), 5
R. Baggenaes: "Mal Waldron," *Coda*, no.153 (1977), 2
"Mal Waldron," *SJ*, xxxii/11 (1978), 286 [discography]
K. Whitehead: "Mal Waldron: Interview," *Cadence*, vi/10 (1980), 5
N. Mackey and H. Gray: "Notes from an Expatriate: a Conversation with Pianist/Composer Mal Waldron," *JSN*, ii/2 (1980–81), 18
B. Blumenthal: "Mal Waldron," *DB*, xlviii/4 (1981), 28 [incl. discography]

B. Priestley: *Mingus: a Critical Biography* (London, Melbourne, Australia, and New York, 1982)
E. Cohen: "Mal Waldron: a Profile," *Coda*, no.192 (1983), 26
B. Doerschuk: "Mal Waldron: Life on the Borderline," *Keyboard*, x/7 (1984), 42 [incl. discography]
L. Darroch: "Mal Waldron," *JT* (1985), April, 12
D. Palmer: "Jazz Pianist as Prince of Darkness and Earl of Emotion," *Musician*, no.76 (1985), 25
H. Cutler: "Mal Waldron," *Cadence*, xiv/5 (1988), 5
M. Glassman: "Mal Waldron," *Coda*, no.223 (1988–9), 10
A. Mathiesen: *Mal Waldron: a Black Artist: a Discography* (Copenhagen, 1989)
G. Rouy and T. Bruneau: "Waldron et Bruneau: Two for Eric," *Jm*, no.391 (1990), 18
F. Postif: *Jazz Me Blues: interviews et portraits de musiciens de jazz et de blues* (Paris, 1998), 39
M. Zwerin: "Mal Waldron: Looking for Musical Surprises," *International Herald Tribune* (22 Jan 1998)

ROBERT L. DOERSCHUK/BK

Walk Away. Polish quintet. It was first formed in 1983 as a student hard-bop quintet led by the drummer Krzysztof Zawadzki, then re-formed in 1985, with the saxophonist Adam Wendt, the keyboard player and composer Zbigniew Jakubek, the vibraphonist Bernard Maseli, and the double bass player Jacek Niedziela as Zawadzki's sidemen. The group had turned towards a fusion style by the late 1980s, when Niedziela joined Zbigniew Namysłowski's quartet; his place was taken by a succession of electric bass guitarists. Maseli left the group in 1995 but returned in the new century, at which time the other members were Zawadzki, Wendt, the electric bass guitarist Tomasz Grabowy, and Janusz Skowron (who had joined in 1997). Walk Away has performed or recorded in collaboration with Lora Szafran (1986–8), Urszula Dudziak (from the 1990s), Michal Urbaniak, Ewa Bem, and many visiting American fusion players, notably Mike Stern, Eric Marienthal, Bill Evans (iii), Dean Brown, Randy Brecker, David Fiuczynski, Frank Gambale, Victor Bailey, and Joey Calderazzo. Among its dozen albums (the majority made for its own label, W.A.) is *Live at the Warsaw Jazz Festival 1991* (Jazzman 660.50.003).

BIBLIOGRAPHY

"M. Kydrynski: "Walk Away," *JF* [intl edn], no.119 (1989), 34
<http://www.walkaway.home.pl> (2001)

ADAM CEGIELSKI, BK

Walker, Mike [Michael Joseph Sebastian] (*b* Salford, England, 12 July 1962). English electric guitarist. He taught himself to play guitar from records. From the early 1990s he worked with Roy Powell, Tommy Smith (1992–3), Mike Gibbs, Kenny Wheeler, and Steve Swallow (all from 1993), Julian Argüelles (from 1994), Anthony Braxton (1994), George Russell's Living Time Orchestra (1996), Bill Frisell and the pianist Steve Plews (1996), and the drummer Pete Fairclough (1997). He also led his own free improvising quartet and in 1998 toured Scotland with a sextet which played his own compositions; in the same year he toured Norway with Powell's quartet and played in Portugal with Mário Laginha. He taught from 1990 at Salford College of Music and from 1995 at Leeds College of Music, and in 1998 was appointed professor of guitar and theory at the Hochschule für Musik Franz Liszt in Weimar, Germany. Walker has effected a particularly outstanding synthesis of the styles of John Scofield, Frisell, and Allan Holdsworth.

SELECTED RECORDINGS

As sideman: M. Gibbs: *By the Way* (1993, Ah Um 016); R. Powell: *A Big Sky* (1994, Totem 101); J. Argüelles: *Home Truths* (1995, Babel 9503); G. Russell: *It's About Time* (1996, Label Bleu 6587); S. Plews: *Anywhere* (1996, ASC 15); P. Fairclough: *Permission* (1997, ASC 18)

BIBLIOGRAPHY

ChiltonB
P. Martin: "Long-distance Walker," *Jazz UK*, no.4 (1995), 8

MARK GILBERT

Walker, Sammy [Samuel Osmond; Jumping Sam; Little Sammy] (*b* Kingston, Jamaica, 16 March 1923; *d* Hamburg, Germany, 2 Feb 1986). Jamaican tenor saxophonist. As Little Sammy Walker he played with "Jamaica's Count Basie," the drummer Redver Cooke, and formed a group with Roy Burrowes before traveling around 1946 to the USA. In 1948 he moved to England and worked briefly in Birmingham with Dizzy Reece, though he also played with Pete Pitterson and Andy Hamilton. In London he joined forces with emerging bop musicians in the radical big band led by the drummer Leon Roy, which involved both black and white musicians (1949–50), and worked with Reece, Pitterson, Tony Crombie, Phil Seamen, and others. He toured Europe with Cab Kaye (1950–51), when he shared the front line with Dave Wilkins and George Tyndale, and played calypso with the clarinetist and saxophonist Freddy Grant (1951). When he returned to Britain he recorded with Reece and Bruce Turner, and with the Guyanese pianist Mike McKenzie as accompanist to American and Caribbean singers. In 1953 Walker was in Germany with Wallace Bishop. Late in 1955 he settled in continental Europe, where he worked with George Maycock (with whom he is featured in the film *Jazz: Rhythmus der Zeit*, 1957), the American trumpeter Claude Dunson, the Jamaican trombonist Herman Wilson, and others. He played again in Britain in 1961, appearing with Wilson and Jimmy Skidmore and in Birmingham with Andy Hamilton. Although he lived in Germany from 1966, he toured Sweden regularly and also worked in Italy, France, Finland, and Lebanon. His bands included African and Caribbean musicians. A driving player who could switch from a booting rhythm-and-blues style to poised and elegant improvisation, he was working in show bands on Hamburg's Reeperbahn at the time of his death from kidney failure.

SELECTED RECORDINGS

As leader: Makin' Whoopee/Girl of my Dreams (1953, Lyragon 715); *Sammy's Hat* (1981, Sam Walker Six 66.22568-01)

As sideman C. Kaye: Saturday Night Fish Fry/School-bop (1951, Astraschall 4005); Mood Indigo/Solitude (1951, Astraschall 4001); B. Turner: I Cried for You/The Piccolino (1953, Lyragon 714); George Browne (Young Tiger): Calypso Be (1953, Parl. MP119); Marie Bryant and M. McKenzie: Little Boy (1953, Lyragon 709); R. Mavounzy: Pick yourself up/Perdido/Sonny's Boy/Sid's Bounce (1954, Pathé 45EA14) [EP]; T. Crombie: *Modern Jazz at the Royal Festival Hall, London* (1954, Decca LK4087); D. Reece: *The Dizzy Reece Quintet* (1955, Tempo LAP3); G. Maycock: Lonely Man Blues/Maycock's Hop (1956, Phi. 47001H); That's right, what's wrong?/Walkin' Sam (1956, Phi. 47002H); D. Reece: A Variation on Monk (1957, Tempo EXA84) [EP]

BIBLIOGRAPHY

C. van Poorten: "Cab Kaye and his All Coloured Band in Rotterdam," *Rhythme* [Netherlands], no.6 (1950), 21
P. Leslie: "Jazz is Where You Find it ... no.2: the Sugar Hill Club," *MM* (20 June 1953), 3
J. Cowley: Liner notes, *Caribbean Connections: Black Music in Britain in the Early 1950s*, ii (New Cross 006, 1986)
V. Wilmer: "Skanking Ahoy," *Mojo* [London], no.56 (1998), 54

VAL WILMER

Walker, T-Bone [Aaron Thibeault; T-Bow] (*b* Dallas, 28 May 1910; *d* Los Angeles, 16 March 1975). Guitarist, singer, and leader. Dance (1987) gives his birthplace as Dallas, though most earlier sources, including Walker himelf in an interview (Greenough, 1947), state that he was born in Linden, Texas. At the age of eight he led the blues singer Blind Lemon Jefferson around the streets of Dallas. He developed quickly as a banjoist, guitarist, and dancer and as a teenager played with a medicine show, after which he ran away from home to tour with Ida Cox; he also appeared with Ma Rainey at the Houston Coliseum and played one-nighters and held a residency at the Tip Top as a member of a high-school band led by the saxophonist Lawson Brooks. Around 1929 he won a talent contest in which the prize was a week's touring to Houston with Cab Calloway. That year he recorded two blues numbers under the name Oak Cliff T-Bone. From 1933 to 1935 he worked as dancer with a white dance band led by Count Bulaski, with which he visited Oklahoma City in 1935; while there he jammed with Charlie Christian and took lessons from Christian's teacher. Walker moved to Los Angeles in 1936 and found employment as a dancer with Big Jim Wynn's band at Little Harlem. In the late 1930s he worked at the Club Alabam, the Trocadero, and Billy Berg's before going on a nationwide tour with Les Hite's band. By this time he was experimenting with amplifying his guitar. Back in Los Angeles he played at Little Harlem and other clubs. In 1942 he traveled to Chicago to begin a two-year residency at the Rhumboogie, accompanied initially by Milt Larkin's band and later by the band of the pianist Marl Young, with which he recorded. He also went on USO tours accompanied by Wynn's band.

Having returned Los Angeles in 1946, Walker began a long series of recordings accompanied by a variety of swing and jump musicians. He soon formed his own accompanying group, using Wynn as its leader, which worked one-nighters across the country. These road tours continued into the 1960s, interspersed with residencies at such venues as the Flame Show Bar and the Frolic Bar in Detroit and the New Slipper Club in San Francisco. In 1962 he toured Europe with a Blues Festival package, and he made further European tours, visiting Britain and France in 1965 and working with Jazz at the Philharmonic in 1966; he may be seen the documentary film *Jazz at the Philharmonic* (1967). Another Blues Festival tour in 1968–9 spawned several recording dates in France. In the 1960s Walker became a regular on festival circuits – he performed in another documentary film, *Monterey Jazz* (1968) – and after 1970 he appeared frequently with the Johnny Otis Show; he was at the Grande Paradu du Jazz, Nice, in 1971, and at the Montreux Jazz Festival in 1972. He played at Carnegie Hall in New York in 1970 and 1973 and at such venues as the Parisian Room, Los Angeles (1972–3), as well as in Canada. His career was ended in 1974 by a stroke from which he never fully recovered.

Walker is widely regarded as the founding father of post-1945 blues guitar. His style, closely related to that of Christian, had a critical influence on such blues guitarists as B. B. King and Albert King, and through them on all subsequent developments in blues. While he both performed and recorded with Chicago blues players in the 1960s and after, Walker's own work remained firmly rooted in the Californian jump-band tradition of the 1940s. Musicians who were involved in his recordings in the period 1946 to 1954 include Al Killian, Teddy Buckner, George Orendorff, Bumps Myers, Jack McVea, Maxwell Davis, Lloyd Glenn, and Billy Hadnott.

SELECTED RECORDINGS

Duos with Douglas Fernell [as Oak Cliff T-Bone]: Trinity River Blues/Wichita Falls Blues (1929, Col. 14506D)

As leader: You Don't Love Me Blues/Mean Old World Blues (1945, Rhumboogie 4003); T-Bone Boogie/Evenin' (1945, Rhumboogie 4002); She is going to ruin me (1945, Old Swing-Master 11); No Worry Blues/Don't Leave Me Baby (1946, Black & White 111); Call it Stormy Monday (1947, Black & White 122); first issued on *The Blues of T-Bone Walker* (1947, Music for Pleasure 1043), The Natural Blues; First Love Blues/T-Bone Shuffle (1947, Comet T53); Vacation Blues (1947, Cap. 57-70012); Inspiration Blues (1947, Comet T51); Stollin' with Bone (1950, Imperial 5071); You Don't Love Me (1950, Imperial 5086); The hustle is on/Baby broke my heart (1950, Imperial 5081); Alimony Blues/Life is Too Short (1951, Imperial 5153); *T-Bone Blues* (1955–7, Atl. 8020)

As sideman with L. Hite (v): T-Bone Blues (1940, Vars. 8391)

As sideman with others (all on guitar): J. Witherspoon: *Evenin' Blues* (1963, Prst. 7300); E. Vinson: *Wee Baby Blues* (1969, BB 33021); J. McShann: on *Confessin' the Blues* (1969, BB 33022), Confessin' the Blues, Four Days Rider, Hootie's Ignorant Oil, Keep your hand off her, Roll 'em

BIBLIOGRAPHY

FeatherE; *Feather60s*; *Feather–Gitler70s*

J. Greenough: "T-Bone Blues: T-Bone Walker's Story in his own Words," *Record Changer*, vi/8 (1947), 5; repr. in *Rhythm & News*, no.1 (1980), 27

J. Morgantini: "Avec T-Bone Walker," *BHcF*, no.153 (1965), 7

F. Kofsky: "T-Bone Walker & B. B. King Interview," *Jazz & Pop*, viii/10 (1969), 15

J. O'Neal and A. O'Neal: "Living Blues Interview: T-Bone Walker," *Living Blues*, no.11 (1972), 20; no.12 (1973), 24

Obituary, *Living Blues*, no.21 (1975), 6

S. Harris: *Blues Who's Who: a Biographical Dictionary of Blues Singers* (New Rochelle, NY, 1979/*R*1994)

P. Notini: Liner notes, *T-Bone Walker: the Inventor of Electric Blues Guitar* (Blues Boy 304 , 1983)

F. Le Mouhaër: "T-Bone Walker," *Soul Bag*, no.100 (1984), 9 [incl. discography by D. Groslier and others]

H. O. Dance: *Stormy Monday: the T-Bone Walker Story* (Baton Rouge, LA, and London, 1987) [incl. discography by D. Groslier and others]

H. O. Dance and B. Vera: Liner notes, *The Complete Recordings of T-Bone Walker, 1940–1954* (Mosaic 130, 1990)

Y. Le Goff: "T-Bone Blues," *Jh*, no.511 (1994), 38

T. Russell: *The Blues Collection 16: T-Bone Walker* (London, 1994)

J. Sallis: *The Guitar Players: One Instrument and its Masters in American Music* (New York, 1982, rev. 2/1994), 155

HOWARD RYE

Walking bass. (1) In jazz, a line played pizzicato on a double bass in regular crotchets in 4/4 meter, the notes usually moving stepwise or in intervallic patterns not necessarily restricted to the main pitches of the harmony. The style arose as the use of stride piano patterns declined, and its first master was Walter Page in the late 1920s and early 1930s; it has since become *lingua franca* for jazz bass players, allowing them to contribute pulse, harmony, and counter-melody simultaneously.

(2) In boogie-woogie piano style, a repeating left-hand pattern of broken octaves. *See* BOOGIE-WOOGIE, ex.2.

GUNTHER SCHULLER

Wall, Dan(iel Lee, Jr.) (*b* Atlanta, 7 Sept 1953). Pianist and organist. In his last year at high school he led a piano trio at the Carousel in Atlanta. Following studies at the Berklee College of Music and private lessons with the pianist Ray Santisi (1972–3) he played with Karl Ratzer (1974–7). While working with Jeremy Steig (1977–82) he recorded as a member of a quartet led by Ike Isaacs (i), accompanying Maxine Sullivan (1978). In addition he collaborated with Steve Grossman and Jimmy Madison (both 1980–82), the popular composer Henry Mancini (1984–5), and Eddie Gomez (1989–92). In 1992 he joined a trio with John Abercrombie and Adam Nussbaum, and from 1996 he worked with, among others, Jerry Bergonzi and the trombonist Christoph Schweitzer. Wall has also led a number of his own groups: New Ice Age (with Ratzer and Jeff Berlin as co-leaders, 1974–7), a trio with Isaacs and Steve Ellington (1978–80), and the Dan Wall Group (1985–8), in which he performed alongside his wife, the singer Carol Veto; in 1994 he formed another trio with Veto among his sidemen. He has been active as a teacher and, from 1979, as a studio musician, on soundtracks, commercials, and pop recordings. His chief influence as an organist is Larry Young.

SELECTED RECORDINGS

Duos with E. Krivda: *Golden Moments* (1995, Koch Jazz 3-7310-2)
As leader: *The Trio* (1979, Audiophile 143); *Song for the Night* (1980, Landslide 378); *Off the Wall* (1996, Enja 9310)
As sideman: J. Abercrombie: *While We're Young* (1994, ECM 1489); *Tactics* (1996, ECM 1623); K. Ratzer: *Saturn Returning* (1996, Enja 9351-2); J. Bergonzi: *Just Within* (1996, Double-Time 127); *Lost in the Shuffle* (1998, Double-Time 142)

BIBLIOGRAPHY

F.-J. Hadley: "Riffs: Dan Wall," *DB*, lx/9 (1993), 15

MARK GILBERT

Wall, Murray (James) (*b* Melbourne, Australia, 28 Sept 1945). Australian double bass player. His elder brother played clarinet and saxophone in Australian dixieland groups. Initially a trumpeter, Wall taught himself to play double bass by listening to recordings by Oscar Pettiford. From 1962 he performed regularly and accompanied many visiting soloists, including Clark Terry, Mel Tormé, and Billy Eckstine. In 1979 he moved to the USA. From 1981 to 1985 he played with Jon Hendricks, with whom he toured Europe and Israel and appeared on a PBS television tribute to Thelonious Monk. Wall worked with Benny Goodman's last bands (December 1985 – June 1986) and thereafter appeared frequently in swing groups under the leadership of Ken Peplowski, Marty Grosz, Keith Ingham, Frank Vignola, Chuck Wilson, and Spanky Davis; he may be seen with Peplowski in the video *Ken Peplowski Quintet: Live at Ambassador Auditorium* (*c*1995 [filmed 1994]). He also performed with the big bands of Buck Clayton and Grover Mitchell, Jimmy Ryan's All Stars, Annie Ross, Richard Wyands, Kenny Davern, and Claude Williams.

SELECTED RECORDINGS

As sideman: K. Peplowski: *The Natural Touch* (1992, Conc. 4517): M. Grosz: *Just for Fun!* (1996, Nagel-Heyer 039); B. Aronov: *The Best Thing for Me* (1997, Arbors 19200)

BIBLIOGRAPHY

ConnorBG; *Feather–GitlerBEJ*

GK

Wallace, Bennie (Lee, Jr.) (*b* Chattanooga, TN, 18 Nov 1946). Tenor saxophonist and clarinetist. He played clarinet from the age of 12 and later changed to tenor saxophone. After studying music at the University of Tennessee (BM 1968) he played in small groups at various local after-hours clubs, and while working in Denver, Colorado, he met Gary Burton, who encouraged him to move to New York. In 1971 he made his professional début with Monty Alexander. Thereafter he became involved with the loft-jazz movement and worked with many significant avant-garde musicians, among them Sheila Jordan (1976). Wallace then formed his own trio, which consisted initially of Eddie Gomez and Eddie Moore (1977–9); Moore was replaced by either Dannie Richmond or Alvin Queen (1979–82). The trio was joined occasionally by such guests as Tommy Flanagan, Chick Corea, and Jimmy Knepper.

During the 1980s Wallace was a member of a quartet that worked in the USA, Europe, and Japan; this group sometimes included Ray Anderson, with whom Wallace had played intermittently from 1976. Throughout the decade he appeared frequently at festivals in Europe and in Japan. A contract with Blue Note led to two special recordings (1985, 1987) that drew heavily upon his Southern musical influences and featured such artists as the blues-rock guitarist Stevie Ray Vaughan and the singer and pianist Dr. John; during this time Wallace also recorded in a more traditional setting for Denon and as a guest soloist with Mose Allison (1987). Later he moved to Los Angeles to work in films, and he composed the scores to *Blaze* (1990) and *White Men Can't Jump* (1992). While in California he continued to perform and record with small bands that involved variously Queen, Jimmy Rowles, Jerry Hahn, and Gerald Wilson's son, the guitarist Anthony Wilson. Wallace returned to the New York area in 1997 to resume a full-time career in jazz and recorded three times the following year – with Gerald Wilson, with Mulgrew Miller, and, once again, with Flanagan; he appeared with Wilson's group at the Jazz Standard in April 1998.

Although Sonny Rollins was a major initial inspiration, Wallace's highly personal, emotionally charged improvisatory style also shows the influence of such disparate musicians as Eric Dolphy, Ben Webster, and the rhythm-and-blues tenor saxophonists, most notably Red Prysock.

SELECTED RECORDINGS

The Fourteen Bar Blues (1978, Enja 3029); *The Free Will* (1980, Enja 3063); *Bennie Wallace plays Monk* (1981, Enja 3091); *The Bennie Wallace Trio and Chick Corea* (1982, Enja 4028); *Big Jim's Tango* (1982, Enja 4046); *Twilight Time* (1985, BN 85107); *The Art of the Saxophone* (1987, Denon CY1648); *The Old Songs* (1993, Audioquest 1017); *Bennie Wallace* (1998, Audioquest 1051); *Someone to Watch over Me* (1999, Enja 9356-2)

BIBLIOGRAPHY

A. D. Franklin: "Benny Wallace Inside and Out," *JT* (1982), Nov, 5
——: "The Development of a Contemporary Jazz Artist: Excerpts from an Interview with Bennie Wallace," *Jazz Research Papers*, ii (1982), 89
——: "Bennie Wallace: Interview," *Cadence*, ix/4 (1983), 5
C. Kuhn: "Bennie Wallace: Interview," *Cadence*, ix/5 (1983), 8
R. Latxague: "Le chouchou de Chattanooga," *Jm*, no.348 (1986), 31
J. Dulzo: "Saxophonist Blow in – Southern Style," *Detroit News* (7 April 1989)
R. Urmann: "Unbändig hot, melodiebesessen: Bennie Wallace," *JP*, xl/2 (1991), 48
Z. Stewart: "Riffs: Bennie Wallace," *DB*, lx/9 (1993), 14
B. Milkowski: "The Ballad of Bennie Wallace," *JT*, xxix/5 (1999), 56

STAN WOOLLEY/DAVID FRANKLIN

Wallace, Cedric (*b* Miami, 3 Aug 1904 or 1909; *d* ?New York, 19 Aug 1985). Double bass player. His year of birth has been published as 1909, but in his application for social security he gave 1904. After moving to New York he worked at the Saratoga Club (1932) and played with Jimmie Lunceford. From 1938 to 1942 he performed and made recordings with Fats Waller (for illustration *see* Waller, Fats), and he may be seen with Waller's group in four soundies from 1941, including *Your Feet's Too Big* and *Ain't Misbehavin'*. He was also a member of the group formed after Waller's death by the singer Pat Flowers from the leader's former sidemen. Later Wallace worked with Gene Sedric, Garland Wilson, and others before forming his own band, which held residencies at several clubs in New York during the 1940s, notably at Le Ruban Bleu. He continued to work into the 1970s.

SELECTED RECORDINGS

As sideman: F. Waller: *Fats Waller "Live"*, ii (1938–40, Giants of Jazz 1035); Pantin' in the Panther Room (1941, Bb 11175); P. Flowers: Googie woogie (1946, Vic. 20-2698); Texas and Pacific (1946, Vic. 20-2125)

BIBLIOGRAPHY

ChiltonW
L. Wright: *"Fats" in Fact* (Chigwell, England, 1992)

HOWARD RYE

Wallace, Sippie [née Thomas, Beulah Belle] (*b* Houston, 1 Nov 1898; *d* Detroit, 1 Nov 1986). Singer, songwriter, and pianist. Several members of her family were musicians, and she began performing at an early age. In 1923 she made her first recordings, singing in a blues style; later she was accompanied by King Oliver, Louis Armstrong, Sidney Bechet, and other important musicians. In her earliest work she attempted to project a vocal weightiness similar to that of Ma Rainey, though later she sang in a manner better suited to the lighter, prettier qualities of her voice, which may be heard to advantage on *I'm a mighty tight woman*. From the mid-1930s her repertory was mainly gospel music, but in 1965 she began singing jazz and blues once more. From that date she performed throughout the USA and Europe, and in 1979 she began an association with James Dapogny which continued into the mid-1980s. She performed *Women be Wise* with the singer Bonnie Raitt on the David Letterman television show in April 1982 and in that same year was the subject of a documentary short film, *Sippie*. In the following year her album *Sippie* was nominated for a Grammy Award. Wallace composed most of her own songs, which are notable for the shapeliness and dignity of their melodies. *Special Delivery Blues* is a fine example of her work.

Oral history material in *NjR* (JOHP).

SELECTED RECORDINGS

Duos: with C. Williams: Caldonia Blues (1924, OK 8144); with L. B. Montgomery and R. Sykes: *Sippie Wallace Sings the Blues* (1966, Sto. 198)

As leader: Special Delivery Blues (1926, OK 8328); The Flood Blues (1927, OK 8470); I'm a mighty tight woman (1929, Vic. 38502); Bedroom Blues (1945, Mer. 2010); *Sippie* (1982, Atl. 19350)

BIBLIOGRAPHY

R. P. Harwood: "'Mighty Tight Woman': the Thomas Family and Classic Blues," *Sv*, no.17 (1968), 16
B. Rusch: "Sippie Wallace: Interview," *Cadence*, iv/10 (1978), 14
E. Townley: "The Texas Nightingale," *Sv*, no.108 (1983), 227
P. Oliver: "Mighty Tight Woman," *Blues off the Record: Thirty Years of Blues Commentary* (Tunbridge Wells, England, and New York, 1984), 143
Obituary, J. Simmen, *BHcF*, no.348 (1987), 26

JAMES DAPOGNY

Wallen, Byron (*b* London, 17 July 1969). English trumpeter, electronic keyboard player, and leader. He first played piano and euphonium and later took up trumpet, which instrument he continued to study at Sussex University, where he read psychology. Wallen performed in Britain and other parts of Europe with the singer Cleveland Watkiss (1991), John Stevens's quartet, Gary Crosby, and others, and later joined Crosby's Nu Troop and worked with the saxophonist Ed Jones (1995–6). In 1995 he formed his own group, Sound Advice, which combines African music, contemporary classical music, bop, and rap, and may be heard on the album *Sound Advice* (1995, B&W 63).

BIBLIOGRAPHY

ChiltonB
S. S. Lwin: "Something in the City: Byron Wallen," *Jazz Express*, nos.143–4 (1992), 14

GK

Waller, Fats [Thomas Wright] (*b* New York, 21 May 1904; *d* Kansas City, MO, 15 Dec 1943). Pianist, organist, singer, bandleader, and composer.

1. Life. 2. Works and style.

1. Life. His father, Edward Waller, a baptist lay preacher, conducted open-air religious services in Harlem, at which as a child Fats Waller played reed organ. He played piano at his public school and at the age of 15 became organist at the Lincoln Theatre on 135th Street. His father hoped that Waller would follow a religious calling rather than a career in jazz, but after the death of his mother, Adeline Waller, in 1920 he moved in with the family of the pianist Russell Brooks. Through Brooks, Waller met James P. Johnson, under whose tutelage he developed as a pianist, and through whose influence he came to make piano rolls, starting in 1922 with *Got to cool my doggies now*. There is scant evidence to support Waller's claims that during his formative years as a pianist he studied with Leopold Godowsky or that he studied composition with Carl Bohm at the Institute for Musical Art.

In October 1922 Waller made his recording début as a soloist for Okeh with *Muscle Shoals Blues* and *Birmingham Blues*. He began a series of recordings the same year as accompanist for several blues singers, including Sara Martin, Alberta Hunter, and Maude Mills. In 1923 a collaboration with Clarence Williams led to the publication of Waller's *Wild Cat Blues*, which Williams recorded with his Blue Five, including Sidney Bechet (July 1923). Another composition, *Squeeze Me*, was published the same year, and these began to establish Waller's reputation as a composer of material performed and recorded by other artists. 1923 also saw his broadcasting début for a local Newark station, followed by regular engagements on WHN, New York. Waller went on to broadcast as a singer and soloist to the end of his life. During the early 1920s he continued as organist at the Lincoln and Lafayette theaters, New York.

In 1927 Waller recorded his own composition *Whiteman Stomp* with Fletcher Henderson's orchestra; Henderson also made use of other works by Waller, including *Crazy 'bout my baby* and *Stealin' Apples*. Waller's other work as a composer with the lyricists Edgar Dowell, J. C. Johnson, Andy Razaf, and Spencer Williams produced such songs as *Honeysuckle Rose* and *Black and Blue*. With Razaf he worked on much of the music for the African-American Broadway musical *Keep Shufflin'* (1928). Their later collaborations for the stage included the shows *Load of Coal* and *Hot Chocolates* (which opened in May 1929 and transferred on to Broadway on 20 June; it incorporated the song *Ain't Misbehavin'* as a vehicle first for Cab Calloway and later Louis Armstrong). Waller's Carnegie Hall début was on 27 April 1928, when he was piano soloist in a version of Johnson's fantasy *Yamekraw* for piano and orchestra.

In 1926 Waller began his recording association with Victor, his principal record company for the rest of his life, with the organ solos *St. Louis Blues* and his own *Lenox Avenue Blues*. Although he recorded with various groups, including Morris's Hot Babes (1927), Fats Waller's Buddies (1929) (one of the earliest interracial groups to record), and McKinney's Cotton Pickers (1929), his most important contribution to the Harlem stride piano tradition was a series of solo recordings of his own compositions: *Handful of Keys*, *Smashing Thirds*, *Numb Fumblin'*, and *Valentine Stomp* (1929). After sessions with Ted Lewis (1930), Jack Teagarden (1931), and Billy Banks's Rhythmakers (1932), performances

Fats Waller and his Rhythm with the Deep River Boys at a recording session for Victor, New York, July 1942: (left to right) Gene Sedric (tenor saxophone), Cedric Wallace (double bass), Al Casey (guitar), John "Bugs" Hamilton (trumpet), the Deep River Boys (vocal quartet), Art Trappier (drums), and Waller (piano)

in Otto Hardwick's big band at the Hot Feet Club in Greenwich Village (1931) and with Les Hite's band on the West Coast at Frank Sebastian's New Cotton Club, and broadcasts in Cincinnati from 1932 on his long-running show "Fats Waller's Rhythm Club" and "Moon River" (on which he played organ), he began in May 1934 the voluminous series of recordings with a small band known as Fats Waller and his Rhythm. This six-piece group usually included Herman Autrey (sometimes replaced by Bill Coleman or John "Bugs" Hamilton), Gene Sedric or Rudy Powell, and Al Casey.

Waller appeared in two films while in Hollywood in 1935: *Hooray for Love!* and *King of Burlesque* (*see* Films, §II, 1). For tours and recordings he often led his own big band. This began as an expanded version of the band led by his bass player (Charlie Turner's Arcadians), and in 1935, with most members of the Rhythm (as well as Don Redman, among others), it made its first recording.

In 1938 Waller undertook a European tour, recording in London with his Continental Rhythm as well as making solo pipe-organ recordings for HMV. His second European tour in 1939 was terminated by the outbreak of war, but while in Britain he recorded his *London Suite*, an extended series of six related pieces for solo piano: "Piccadilly," "Chelsea," "Soho," "Bond Street," "Limehouse," and "Whitechapel." It is Waller's longest composition and represents something of his aspirations to be a serious composer rather than just the author of a string of hit songs.

The last few years of Waller's life involved frequent recordings and extensive tours of the USA. In early 1943 he returned to Hollywood to make the film *Stormy Weather* with Lena Horne and Bill Robinson, in which he led an all-star band which included Benny Carter and Zutty Singleton. He undertook an exceptionally heavy touring load in that year, as well as collaborating with the lyricist George Marion, Jr., on the score for the stage show *Early to Bed* (which opened in Boston on 24 May 1943). The touring, constant abuse of his system through overeating and overdrinking, and the nervous strain of many years of legal trouble over alimony payments all took their toll, and his health began to break down. He was taken ill during a return visit to the West Coast as solo pianist at the Zanzibar Room, Hollywood, and died of pneumonia while traveling back to New York by train with his manager Ed Kirkeby.

2. Works and style. Waller's greatest importance lies in his several contributions to jazz piano. His original stride pieces in the Johnson tradition (*Handful of Keys*, *Smashing Thirds*, *Numb Fumblin'*, *Valentine Stomp*, *Viper's Drag*, *Alligator Crawl*, and *Clothes Line Ballet*), composed and recorded between 1929 and 1934, clearly illustrate his imaginative and broadly expressive style. The fullness and variety of his tone are still unsurpassed, and he used a wide dynamic range to great expressive and dramatic effect. Harmonically, he sometimes added inner pitches to the customary octaves or 10ths in the left hand, producing richly voiced three-note chords; his chromatic alterations and passing tones undoubtedly influenced Art Tatum. His melodies were perhaps even more tuneful than those of his mentor Johnson. Initially, Waller's use of rhythm as an unaccompanied soloist is in the classic stride tradition, its characteristics including occasional three-beat cross-rhythms in the left hand. All of these features were present in his playing by 1929, as is made clear by *My feelin's are hurt* (ex.1), which was recorded in that year, but by 1934 he began to incorporate left-hand ostinatos (*Viper's Drag*) and boogie-woogie patterns (*Alligator Crawl*) into his style, despite a contractual stipulation that he would not play boogie-woogie on his concert or club appearances. His late solos (all 1941) draw on a much wider stylistic vocabulary, which he applied both to his own compositions and pieces by others, from classical pastiche (*Honeysuckle Rose*) to variations in tempo (*Georgia on my Mind*) to explorations of dynamic range and pedal effects (*Ring Dem Bells*).

With his group Fats Waller and his Rhythm, Waller produced many musically rewarding sessions for Victor during the 1930s. These were characterized by a bustling, energetic style of small-group swing, exemplified by *Dinah*

Ex.1 *My feelin's are hurt* (1929, Vic. 38613); transcr. B. Dobbins

(1935), *I've got my fingers crossed* (1935), *S'posin'* (1936), and *'Tain't Good* (1936). Occasionally Waller's exuberant vocals threatened to blow apart his band's cohesion and swing (*12th Street Rag*, 1935) and, as he became famous for his comic as well as his musical talents, he was frequently called upon to lampoon otherwise unsaleable songs (*Us on a Bus*, 1936, or *I love to whistle*, 1938). Nevertheless he was not without a tender, lyrical side, and his recordings with Bill Coleman from 1934–5 include some of his most sensitive band work, notably his atmospheric organ playing behind Coleman's trumpet on *Night Wind*. His most popular recordings, in particular the song *My very good friend the milkman*, were not his jazziest, and his most effective ensemble jazz recordings were his two 12-inch 78 rpm sides of instrumental versions of *Blue, turning grey over you* and *Honeysuckle Rose* (1937), where the extra playing time coaxed more relaxed and interestingly structured performances from his band.

In a big-band context, Waller's solo and rhythmic gifts were less obvious, although his recording of *I got rhythm* (1935) preserves his stage "cutting contest" with his fellow pianist Hank Duncan. His later big bands were unexceptional save for his use of his "Rhythm" as an integral part of every performance, rather than following the usual "band-within-a-band" format of the swing era. There are signs that he was genuinely exploring new ground towards the end of his career with the big-band arrangement of *The Jitterbug Waltz* (1942).

Waller was the first significant jazz organist (for a discussion of his style *see* ORGAN). During the mid-1930s he was one of the first musicians to employ the CELESTA in jazz and frequently played the instrument in combination with the piano.

Waller's successful popular songs *Ain't Misbehavin'* (1928) and *Honeysuckle Rose* (1929) are among the best known of a voluminous catalogue of compositions; on account of his vicarious life style he may also have written dozens more that are not definitely attributed to him. Some, but by no means all, of his songs were in a comic vein. However, his own comic and satirical talents as a performer brought him a following as an entertainer rivaling that of Louis Armstrong. Because of this, the serious side of his musical personality was little appreciated during his lifetime and remained largely underdeveloped. As a singer he could give creditable jazz renditions of songs which he considered to have real musical merit. His vocal style, clearly in the tradition established by Armstrong, showed a tasteful and highly personal use of vibrato. On his own novelty songs, such as *Your feet's too big*, his use of comic effects and spoken or shouted asides showed at times a genuine sense of comedy; more often, however, he used his wit to draw subtle but unmistakable attention to the vapidity of the material he was expected to record. Unfortunately, Waller's public often demanded more of his exaggerated stage personality than of his unique creative gifts. Some of his recorded solos, transcribed and annotated by R. Scivales, appear in *Harlem Stride Piano Solos* (Katonah, NY, *c*1990). About 630 discs (variously 78 r.p.m. commercial recordings, transcriptions, test pressings, and acetates) are held as the Fats Waller Collection at the World Music Archives of Wesleyan University, Middletown, Connecticut (see LIBRARIES AND ARCHIVES, §2). Oral history material in *LNT*.

WORKS

Selective list; complete listing in L. Wright, *"Fats" in Fact* (Chigwell, England, 1992), 422. Dates of stage shows are those of first performance; other dates are those of copyright as recorded in the Library of Congress.

STAGE

Keep Shufflin' (A. Razaf), 27 Feb 1928; Connie's Hot Chocolates (H. Brooks, Razaf), May 1929; Fireworks of 1930 (with J. P. Johnson), 28 June 1930; Hello 1931! (with A. Hill), 29 Dec 1930; Early to Bed (G. Marion, Jr.), 17 June 1943

INSTRUMENTAL

Organ: Soothin' Syrup Stomp, 1927; Sloppy Water Blues, 1927; Messin' Around with the Blues, 1927; Lenox Avenue Blues, 1927; Fats Waller Stomp, 1927

Pf: Hog Maw Stomp, 1924; Alligator Crawl, 1925 (as House Party Stomp, renamed 1927); Old Folks Shuffle (with C. Williams), 1926; The Digah's Stomp, 1928; Gladyse, 1929; Valentine Stomp, 1929; Viper's Drag, 1930; Handful of Keys, 1930; Numb Fumblin', 1930; Smashing Thirds, 1931; African Ripples, 1931; Clothes Line Ballet, 1934; Functionizin', 1935; Paswonky, 1936; Black Raspberry Jam, 1936; Bach up to Me, 1936; Fractious Fingering, 1936; Lounging at the Waldorf, 1936; London Suite, 1939; Jitterbug Waltz, 1942

Orch: Whiteman Stomp (with J. Trent), 1927

SONGS

Wild Cat Blues (with C. Williams), 1923; In Harlem's Araby (J. Trent), 1924; Anybody here want to try my cabbage (A. Razaf), 1924; Squeeze Me (Razaf), 1925; Georgia Bo-Bo (J. Trent), 1926; I'm goin' huntin' (with J. C. Johnson), 1927; Come on and stomp, stomp, stomp (C. Smith, I. Mills), 1927; Ain't Misbehavin' (Razaf), 1929; Sweet Savannah Sue (H. Brooks, Razaf), 1929; What did I do to be so black and blue (with Brooks) (Razaf), 1929; Zonky (Razaf), 1929; Honeysuckle Rose (Razaf), 1929; My fate is in your hands (Razaf), 1929; Blue, turning grey over you (Razaf), 1929; I'm crazy 'bout my baby and my baby's crazy 'bout me (A. Hill), 1931; My feelin's are hurt (Razaf), 1931; How can you face me (Razaf), 1932; Keepin' out of mischief now (Razaf), 1932; Strange as it seems (Razaf), 1932; You're breakin' my heart (S. Williams), 1933; Ain't cha glad (Razaf), 1933; Stealin' Apples (Razaf), 1936; Joint is jumpin' (Razaf), 1938; Hold my Hand (Johnson), 1938; Yacht Club Swing (with H. Autrey and Johnson), 1938; Spider and the Fly (Razaf, Johnson), 1938; You can't have your cake and eat it (S. Williams), 1939; Old Grand Dad, 1940; All that meat and no potatoes (E. Kirkeby), 1941; Slightly Less than Wonderful (G. Marion, Jr.), 1943

Principal Publishers: Joe Davis, Mills, Southern Music, Williams.

SELECTED RECORDINGS

(recorded for Victor unless otherwise indicated)

AS UNACCOMPANIED SOLOIST

Piano: Got to cool my doggies now (1922, QRS 2149) [piano roll]; Muscle Shoals Blues/Birmingham Blues (1922, OK 4757); Handful of Keys/Numb Fumblin' (1929, 38508); Ain't Misbehavin' (1929, 22092); Sweet Savannah Sue (1929, 22108); Valentine Stomp (1929, 38554); My feelin's are hurt/Smashing Thirds (1929, 38613); African Ripples/Alligator Crawl (1934, 24830); Clothes Line Ballet/Viper's Drag (1934, 25015); I ain't got nobody (1937, 25631); Piccadilly/Chelsea (1939, HMV B10059); Soho/Bond Street (1939, HMV B10060); Limehouse/Whitechapel (1939, HMV B10061); Georgia on my Mind (1941, 27765); Carolina Shout/Ring Dem Bells (1941, 27563); Honeysuckle Rose (1941, 20-1580)

Organ: St. Louis Blues/Lenox Avenue Blues (1926, 20357); Messin' Around with the Blues/Stompin' the Bug (1927, 20655); Rusty Pail (1927, 20492); Swing low, sweet chariot (1938, HMV B8818); Go down, Moses/Deep River (1938, HMV B8816); Lonesome Road (1938, HMV B8845); That

Old Feeling (1938, HMV B8849) [duo with Adelaide Hall]; *Fats Waller at the Organ* (1939, Riv. 1021), incl. Go down, Moses, Hallelujah! I'm a bum, Hand me down my walkin' cane, Swing low, sweet chariot [Hammond organ]

AS LEADER

Small group: The Minor Drag (1929, 38050); Honeysuckle Rose (1934, 24826); Night Wind (1935, 24853); Dinah (1935, 25471); My very good friend the milkman (1935, 25075); 12th Street Rag (1935, 25087); I've got my fingers crossed (1935, 25211); Us on a Bus (1936, 25295); It's a sin to tell a lie (1936, 25342); Fractious Fingering (1936, 25652); S'posin' (1936, 25415); 'Tain't Good (1936, 25478); Swingin' them jingle bells (1936, 25483); Honeysuckle Rose/Blue, turning grey over you (1937, 36206); I love to whistle (1938, 25806); Yacht Club Swing (1938, Bb 10035); *Fats Waller "Live at the Yacht Club"* (1938, Giants of Jazz 1029); Squeeze Me (1939, Bb 10405); Your feet's too big (1939, Bb 10500)

Big band: I got rhythm (1935, HMV HE2902); In the gloaming (1938, 25847); Let's break the good news (1938, 25830); Chant of the Groove (1941, Bb 11262); The Jitterbug Waltz (1942, Bb 11518)

AS SIDEMAN

F. Henderson: The Chant (1926, Col. 817D) [organ]; Whiteman Stomp (1927, Col. 1059D); McKinney's Cotton Pickers: Plain Dirt/Gee, ain't I good to you (1929, 38097); T. Lewis: Dallas Blues/Royal Garden Blues (1931, Col. 2527D); J. Teagarden: You rascal, you (1931, Col. 2558D); B. Banks: Mean Old Bed Bug Blues (1932, Ban. 32502)

SELECTED FILMS

Hooray for Love (1935); King of Burlesque (1935); Honeysuckle Rose (1941); Your Feet's Too Big (1941); The Joint is Jumping (1941); Ain't Misbehavin' (1941); Stormy Weather (1943)

BIBLIOGRAPHY

L. G. Feather: "... And his Rhythm: a Discological Survey of 'Fats' Waller," *Swing Music*, i/8 [*recte* 9] (1936), 244
D. E. Dexter: "Immortals of Jazz," *DB*, viii/2 (1941), 10
——: "Thomas Waller of Concert Stage isn't the Mellow Fats of Backroom Jazz," *DB*, ix/3 (1942), 3
K. Bright and I. Cavanaugh: "That Harmful Little Armful: Fats Waller in his Formative Years," *The Crisis*, li (1944), 109
H. Panassié: *Douze anneés de jazz (1927–1938): souvenirs* (Paris, 1946), 79
M. Gautier: "A Night with Fats Waller," *JJ*, ii/6 (1949), 11
R. Cooke: "The Genius of Thomas 'Fats' Waller," *JJ*, v/5 (1952), 13
M. Mezzrow: "Fats Waller," *BHcF*, no.18 (1952), 3; Eng. orig. pubd *JJ*, vi/5 (1953), 21, as "Memories of 'Fats'"
J. R. T. Davies: *The Music of Thomas "Fats" Waller* (London, 1953); rev. in *Sv*, nos.2–12 (1965–7) [discography]
G. Sedric: "Sedric vous parle de Fats Waller," *BHcF*, no.28 (1953), 3; Eng. orig. pubd *JJ*, vii/5 (1954), as "Talking about 'Fats' Waller"
H. Smith: "Walleresque," *Record Research*, i/5 (1955), 8
N. Shapiro and N. Hentoff, eds.: *The Jazz Makers* (New York, 1957/*R*1979 as *The Jazz Makers: Essays on the Greats of Jazz*)
C. Fox: *Fats Waller* (London, 1960); repr. in *Kings of Jazz*, ed. S. Green (South Brunswick, NJ, and New York, 1978)
S. B. Charters and L. Kunstadt: *Jazz: a History of the New York Scene* (Garden City, NY, 1962/*R*1981)
Coda, v/10 (1963) [special issue devoted to Waller]
R. Hadlock: *Jazz Masters of the Twenties* (New York, 1965/*R*1985)
M. Harrison: "Fats Waller," *JM*, xi/10 (1965), 21
B. Kumm: "Reflections on Fats," *Sv*, i/2 (1965), 2; i/6 (1966), 4
E. Kirkeby, D. P. Schiedt, and S. Traill: *Ain't Misbehavin': the Story of Fats Waller* (London and New York, 1966/*R*1978) [incl. rev. version of discography in *Sv*]
H. Panassié: "Destruction of a Theme: an Analysis of some Fats Waller Piano Solos," *JJ*, xix/7 (1966), 27
M. Williams: "The Comic Mask of Fats Waller," *JJ*, xix/6 (1966), 5
B. Kumm: "Further Facets of Fats," *Sv*, no.23 (1969), 179
H. Panassié: "Fats Waller in Paris," *Sv*, no.40 (1972), 140
M. Berger: "Fats Waller: the Outside Insider," *JJS*, i/1 (1973), 3
T. Magnusson: "Fats Waller with Gene Austin on the Record," *JJS*, iv/1 (1976), 75
L. Feather: "Piano Giants of Jazz: Fats Waller," *CK*, iii/2 (1977), 41
J. Vance: *Fats Waller: his Life and Times* (Chicago, 1977/*R*1992)
M. Waller and A. Calabrese: *Fats Waller* (New York and London, 1977/*R*1997) [incl. discography and list of compositions]
W. Balliett: "Jazz: Fats," *New Yorker*, liv (10 April 1978), 110
H. Rye: "Fats Waller in Britain: Some Native Reactions," *Sv*, no.81 (1979), 83
H. Rye and J. Beaton: "Fats Waller's British Diary," *Sv*, no.81 (1979), 85
M. Gautier-Panassié: "Fats Waller," *BHcF*, no.286 (1981), 3; no.287 (1981), 3
H. Lyttelton: *The Best of Jazz*, ii: *Enter the Giants, 1931–1944* (London, 1981), 30
W. Balliett: "Fats," *Jelly Roll, Jabbo and Fats* (New York, and Oxford, England, 1983), 85
H. Dial: *All this Jazz about Jazz* (Chigwell, England, 1984), 55
P. S. Machlin: *Stride: the Music of Fats Waller* (Boston and London, 1985)
P. Malham: "Fats Waller: the Broadcasts," *Collectors Items*, no.33 (1985), 12
J. Simmen: "Herman Autrey [suite] une parenthèse: les autres trompettes de Fats," *BHcF*, no.336 (1986), 8
A. Shipton: *Fats Waller* (Tunbridge Wells, England, and New York, 1988)
B. Singer: *Black and Blue: the Life and Lyrics of Andy Razaf* (New York and Toronto, 1992)
L. Wright: *"Fats" in Fact* (Chigwell, England, 1992)
H. Rye: *"Fats" in Fact: the Reissues* (Chigwell, England, 1993)
L. Wright, comp.: "Corrections and Additions to 'Fats' in Fact," *Sv*, no.153 (1993), 104; no.162 (1995), 215
P. S. Machlin: "Fats Waller Composes: the Sketches, Drafts, and Lead Sheets in the Institute of Jazz Studies Collection," ARJS, vii (1994–5), 1
L. Wright, comp.: "'Fats' in Fact: a Further Up-date," *Storyville 1996/7* (Chigwell, England, 1997) [colln of essays], 168
S. Budiansky: "Resurrecting Fats," *Atlantic Monthly*, cclxxxv (2000), March, 100

ALYN SHIPTON (1), BILL DOBBINS/ALYN SHIPTON (2)

Wallgren, Jan (Edvard) (*b* Baerum, Norway, 21 Feb 1935; *d* Ystad, Sweden, 2 June 1996). Swedish pianist and composer. He grew up in Stockholm, started playing piano at an early age, and soon became interested in both classical music and jazz. Influenced in the latter realm mainly by the great bop pianists, he was recognized as one of the most talented young players in Sweden when he left music in 1956 to work in his family's machine-tool business. When he resumed playing in the early 1960s his encounter with the music of the American composer Alan Hovhaness was an overwhelming experience that changed his focus and inspired him to study Indian and oriental music and to investigate the possibilities of modality and uneven metric patterns. In the mid-1960s he played a raga-influenced type of jazz in the quartet led by the trumpeter Bengt Ernryd. From the late 1960s he toured widely, leading groups ranging in size from trio to tentet, performing as an unaccompanied soloist, and composing for the radio jazz groups in Sweden and Poland. In 1975, with Lars Westin, he was co-founder of the record company and label Dragon.

Wallgren wrote music for the theatre and eventually for string quartet and other chamber ensembles; his opera *Balagantjyk* received its première in Stockholm in 1985, and his requiem, *För levande och döda* (For the living and the dead), based on poetry by Tomas Tranströmer, was performed in several Swedish cathedrals in the 1990s. He was much in demand as a teacher in colleges in Stockholm, Malmö, and elsewhere; his mission, as he put it, was "to re-establish the musical climate from the era of Bach and before, when all professional musicians were improvisers and composers as well as interpreters of music written by others." This aim was significant also in his work as an organizer and artistic director of a number of festivals, in a radio series on musical history and theory, in his own performances, and in his compositions – including the requiem, which incorporates elements of improvisation.

SELECTED RECORDINGS

(all recorded for Dragon)

As unaccompanied soloist: *Standards and Blueprints* (1989, 1993, 246)
As leader: *Lavoro in corso* (1984, 89); *Raga, Bebop and Anything* (1995, 303)
As sideman with B. Ernryd: *Bengt Ernryd Quartet* (1964–5, 1)

BIBLIOGRAPHY

L. Westin: "Säljer tubkrökar och jazz" [Trades in steel bends and jazz], *Orkester journalen*, xlii/3 (1974), 6
G. Litterst: "Jazzpianist und Komponist aus Schweden: Jan Edvard Wallgren," *JP*, xxxii/11 (1983), 12
J. Solothurnmann: "Der Preis der Offenheit: der Schwedische Pianist und Komponist Jan Wallgren in der Schweiz," *Dissonanz/Dissonance*, no.39 (1994), 24
Obituary, L. Westin, *Orkester journalen*, lxiii/7–8 (1996), 45

LARS WESTIN

Wallin, Bengt-Arne (*b* Linköping, Sweden, 13 July 1926). Swedish trumpeter, flugelhorn player, arranger, and composer. After playing in Linköping and with Malte Johnson's big band in Gothenburg (1948–50) he went to Stockholm, where he made his reputation as an excellent trumpeter in the swing and modern mainstream styles. He was a member of Seymour Österwall's band (1951–2), then played and recorded with Arne Domnérus's orchestra (1953–65) and in Harry Arnold's Radiobandet (1955–65). Wallin also became well known as a composer and arranger, notably with Domnérus's orchestra; his album *Old Folklore in Swedish Modern* (1962, Dux 1700), which he recorded as the leader of a studio band, represents the earliest large-scale attempt to fuse jazz with Swedish folk melodies. He has composed several scores for films and the theater, and his writing for orchestra shows great skill and invention. Other recordings which he has made as a leader include *Varmluft* (1970, Sonet 2528), on which Clark Terry is the featured soloist, and *Miles from Duke* (1986, Phono Suecia 28). From the 1970s into the 1990s Wallin taught at the Kungliga Musikgskolan (Royal College of Music) in Stockholm.

BIBLIOGRAPHY

FeatherE; *Feather–Gitler '70s*
"På omslaget" [On the cover], *Orkester journalen*, xxii/11 (1954), 4
L. Westin: "Inspirerande inspirerad" [Inspiringly inspired], *Orkester journalen*, lxiii/7–8 (1995), 2
"Pionier des Folk-Jazz: Bengt-Arne Wallin," *JP*, xlvi/6 (1997), 10
<http://www.mic.stim.se/engelsk/11/facts/wallin.html> (2000)

ERIK KJELLBERG

Wallin, Per Henrik (*b* Karlsborg, Sweden, 17 July 1946). Swedish pianist and composer. Having studied piano from an early age, he decided around 1970 to become a professional musician. While he initially gave performances as an unaccompanied soloist and worked in duos with his childhood friend Sven-Åke Johansson (touring in Germany), and occasionally with Eje Thelin, he eventually formed his own trio, with the saxophonist Lars-Göran Ulander and the drummer Peter Olsen. In 1978 he established another trio, consisting of Torbjörn Hultcrantz and Erik Dahlbäck on drums (replaced in 1986 by Leif Wennerström). Wallin also continued to perform as a soloist, and he formed a duo with his wife, the actor and writer Saara Salminen, to create a spontaneous interplay of theater, poetry, and music. He worked occasionally with the American drummer Steve Reid, Johnny Dyani, and others, and sometimes enlarged his trio (to as many as 12 pieces) to play his adventuresome compositions and arrangements. A crippling accident in 1988 left him partly paralyzed and wheelchair bound, but except for periods of convalescence he has maintained his musical activities. From 1998 he has performed and recorded with a new trio, consisting of Wennerström and the double bass player Peter Janson. He published an essay, "Om improvisation" [On improvisation] in *Jazz Special* (no.54 (2000), 54).

With its rich flow of seemingly free improvisations, Wallin's trio of 1978–88 was one of the most acclaimed and influential Swedish jazz groups of its time. Many of the pieces played by the trio were in the form of sketches or fragments that functioned, together with melodic quotations from a variety of musical sources (opera, jazz standards, marches, and more), as starting points for improvised development. The group's performances had a wide emotional range, from hilariously funny to affectingly dramatic. Wallin himself is a virtuoso and melodically inventive instrumentalist, influenced primarily by Art Tatum, Bud Powell, and Thelonious Monk.

SELECTED RECORDINGS

(recorded for Dragon unless otherwise indicated)

As unaccompanied soloist: *One Knife is Enough* (1982, Caprice 1273); *Deep in a Dream* (1985, 290); *Moon over Calcutta* (1987, 143)
Duos with S.-Å. Johansson: *Magnetische Hunde* (1986, FMP S19)
As leader: *The New Figaro* (1975, 5); *River High Running* (1979, 22); *Per Henrik Wallin Trio* (1979, Caprice 1185); *Raw Material* (1981, 48); *Blues Work* (1982, 35); *Fourth Balcony Jump* (1983, Rev. 43); *Knalledonia* (1984, 77); *Where is Spring?* (1986–7, 175); *Coyote* (1986–7, 320); *Dolphins Dolphins Dolphins* (1991, 215); *Blues for Allan* (1998, Flash 8); *9.9.99* (1999, Stunt 202)

BIBLIOGRAPHY

L. Westin: "Per Henrik Wallin," *Orkester journalen*, xlvii/12 (1979), 10; xlviii (1980), no.1, p.8; no.2, p.10
J. Strand: "Utan kompromisser" [Without compromise], *Orkester journalen*, lxvi/7–8 (1998), 2

LARS WESTIN

Wallington, George [Figlia, Giacinto] (*b* Palermo, Sicily, 27 Oct 1924; *d* New York, 15 Feb 1993). Pianist, composer, and leader. His family emigrated to the USA in 1925. His father, an opera singer, taught Wallington solfeggio. He studied classical piano at the Vincent School of Music and left high school early to perform jazz professionally. He was a member of a pioneering bop group led by Dizzy Gillespie and Oscar Pettiford at the Onyx club on 52nd Street (winter 1943–4), and he played in New York in jam sessions with Charlie Parker at the Three Deuces (?1945). Around this time he acquired the stage name George Wallington, when Stan Getz began to call him, jokingly, "Lord Wallington," owing to his elegant manner of dressing. After playing swing in Joe Marsala's quartet for a year he performed and recorded bop with groups led by Parker (1946), Serge Chaloff and Allan Eager (both 1947), Kai Winding (at the Royal Roost and Bop City, 1949–*c*1951), Terry Gibbs and Brew Moore (both 1949), Al Cohn (1950), Gerry Mulligan (1951), and Zoot Sims and Red Rodney (both 1952). In summer 1953 he made a brief tour of Europe with Lionel Hampton – his only appearance in a big band. Following an engagement as the leader of a trio at the Composer Room in the Park Chambers Hotel (1954–5), he took a quintet including Donald Byrd, Jackie McLean, Paul Chambers, and Art Taylor into the Café Bohemia in July 1955, recording there in September and taking over Oscar Pettiford's role as music director that autumn. Phil Woods replaced McLean and Teddy Kotick succeeded Chambers. In May 1956 Wallington began another long engagement at the Composer Room; Nick Stabulas took Taylor's place around this time. After further club work, mainly as the leader of a trio, in 1960 he left music to work in his family's air-conditioning business; however, he resumed playing professionally in the early 1980s, and recorded an album as a soloist in 1984.

Wallington improvised clean, rapid, single-note lines in the manner of Bud Powell (though he met Powell only after having joined Gillespie's quintet in 1943). Despite his talent as a performer, however, his reputation rests more on his compositions: *Lemon Drop* was recorded by Woody Herman (1948), Gene Krupa (1949), and Woods (1957), and *Godchild* by Winding and Miles Davis (1949); both were performed frequently.

SELECTED RECORDINGS

As unaccompanied soloist: on Metronome All Stars: *Metronome All Stars, 1956* (1956, Verve 8030), Lady Fair; *Virtuoso* (1984, Interface 7092)

As leader: *George Wallington Trio* (1951, Prog. 3001); *George Wallington Trio* (1952, Prst. 136), incl. Tenderly [unaccompanied solo]; *The Workshop of the George Wallington Trio* (1954, Norg. 24); *Live! at Cafe Bohemia* (1955, Prog. 7001); *Jazz for the Carriage Trade* (1956, Prst. 7032); *Knight Music* (1956, Atl. 1275), incl. Godchild

As sideman: S. Chaloff: Gabardine and Serge (1947, Savoy 978); K. Winding: Wallington's Godchild (1949, Roost 500); B. Jaspar: *Bobby Jaspar with George Wallington* (1957, Riv. 240); P. Woods: *Phil Woods Sextet* (1957, Mode 127), incl. Lemon Drop

BIBLIOGRAPHY

L. Feather: "Pen Portrait: George Wallington," *MM*, xxviii (8 March 1952), 4

J. Burns: "George Wallington," *JJ*, xviii/1 (1965), 24

J. Goodwin: "George Wallington: a Discography of Known Recordings," *JJ*, xxvii/2 (1974), 56 [incl. listing of compositions]

M. Gardner: "Piano Peer: the Legendary 'Lord' George Wallington," *JJI*, xxxviii/5 (1985), 10

Obituary, *New York Times* (16 Feb 1993)

BK

Walrath, Jack (Arthur, Jr.) (*b* Stuart, FL, 5 May 1946). Trumpeter, composer, arranger, and leader. He was brought up in Montana and began playing trumpet in 1955. From 1964 to 1968 he studied at the Berklee School of Music, and while in Boston he performed with other students and in backup groups for rhythm-and-blues singers. After moving to the West Coast in 1969 he worked as joint leader of the groups Change (with Gary Peacock) and Revival (with Glenn Ferris) and toured for a year with Ray Charles's band. In September 1973 he went to New York, where he played with Latin bands; he then worked with Charles Mingus (1974–8), to whose last recordings he contributed orchestrations. He then spent a year with Joe Morello and in 1978 also began a long affiliation with Charli Persip's band (to 1990, recording three albums in the 1980s). He worked with Sam Rivers from around 1979 to 1986, recording with him in Berlin in 1982, and in the 1980s he toured Europe with Dannie Richmond and with the British band Spirit Level and played in the orchestra and small groups of Muhal Richard Abrams (with which he recorded from 1989). He was a member of Mingus dynasty, of which he served as music director from autumn 1989 until the group disbanded around 1994; in the early 1990s he toured with the orchestra which gave performances of Mingus's posthumously reconstructed symphony *Epitaph*, and from 1991 he was one of a number of members who served as leader of the Mingus Big Band for its weekly sessions at the Time Café in New York. Throughout the 1990s he was a member of George Gruntz's band, and in 1997 he worked with Ray Anderson; he recorded with the New York Composers Orchestra (1992), Cecil Brooks, III (1993), the orchestras of Joe Lovano and Richie Cole (both 1994), and Hamiet Bluiett (1995).

Walrath also formed his own groups, and until 1985 was leader principally of a quintet; for a performance and recording at the Umbria Jazz Festival in 1983 the group included Glenn Ferris, whose sense of musical humor fits well with Walrath's own. In 1986 he began leading a quintet or sextet known as the Masters of Suspense, which remained active in the late 1990s, though he also recorded as the leader of the group Hard Corps in 1995 and in other formats under his own name. His playing is fluent and exciting and reflects the impact of bop (*Blue 'n Boogie* with Bluiett, 1995) and later styles; a wide-ranging eclecticism is immediately evident on such recordings as the album *Serious Hang* (1992). In addition to his work with clearly jazz-oriented ensembles he gave concerts and made a recording where his band Masters of Suspense was expanded into an orchestra which included strings; these performances incorporated aspects of gospel music, calypso, European art music, and Japanese and North African forms. Walrath is also active as an arranger and has composed prolifically for his own groups, often inventing impishly clever and descriptive titles (e.g., *Ray Charles on Mars*, *Revenge of the Fat People*, *Monk on the Moon*, *Killer Bunnies*, *Wake up and wash it off* [after J. S. Bach's cantata *Wachet auf*], and the like); this wordplay often translates musically into delightful and irreverent send-ups of established styles.

SELECTED RECORDINGS

Duos with L. Willis: *Portraits in Ivory & Brass* (1992, Mapleshade 02032)

As leader: *Demons in Pursuit* (1979, Gatemouth 1002), incl. Ray Charles on Mars; *Revenge of the Fat People* (1981, Stash 221); *A Plea for Sanity* (1982, Stash 223); *Wholly Trinity* (1986, Muse 5362); *Killer Bunnies* (1986, Spot. 25); of Masters of Suspense: *Master of Suspense* (1986–7, BN 46095), incl. Monk on the Moon; *Neohippus* (1988, BN B11E-46905); *Out of the Tradition* (1990, Muse 5403), incl. Wake up and wash it off; of Masters of Suspense: *Serious Hang* (1992, Muse 5475), of Hard Corps: *Journey, Man!* (1995, Evidence 22150)

As sideman: C. Mingus: *Changes One*, *Changes Two* (1974, Atl. 1677–8); C. Persip: *In Case You Missed it* (1984, SN 1079), incl. Marching out and dancing in; *No Dummies Allowed* (1987, SN 1179), incl. Thruway Traffic; M. R. Abrams: *Blu Blu Blu* (1990, BS 120117-2), incl. Bloodline; *Familytalk* (1993, BS 120132-2); Mingus Big Band: *Nostalgia in Times Square* (1993, Dreyfus 36559); H. Bluiett: *Young Warrior, Old Warrior* (1995, Mapleshade 02932), incl. Blue 'n Boogie

BIBLIOGRAPHY

Feather–Gitler '70s

A. J. Smith: "Profile: Jack Walrath," *DB*, xlv/6 (1978), 32

"Chords and Discords: Jack Walrath on me, myself an Eye," *DB*, xlvi/12 (1979), 11

B. Priestley: *Mingus: a Critical Biography* (London, Melbourne, Australia, and New York, 1982), 202

A. Galuszka: "Gut Feelings: Jack Walrath," *JF* [intl edn], no.133 (1992), 24

L. Leventhal: "Jack Walrath," *Windplayer*, ix/1 (1992), 10

B. Rusch: "The Questionnaire," *Cadence*, x/3 (1992), 34

K. L. Williams: "Jack of All Trades: Jack Walrath," *DB*, lxi/6 (1994), 30 [incl. discography]

M. Gammel: "Jazz Walrath and the Masters of Suspense," *JP*, xliv/6 (1996), 38

BRIAN PRIESTLEY/BK

Walton, Cedar (Anthony, Jr.) (*b* Dallas, 17 Jan 1934). Pianist. He was taught piano by his mother and studied music at the University of Denver (1951–4). In 1955 he went to New York to play jazz but was drafted into the army, and in Germany he played with Leo Wright, Don Ellis, and Eddie Harris. After returning to New York he recorded with Kenny Dorham (1958–9), John Coltrane and Abbey Lincoln (both 1959), Jimmy Heath and Clifford Jordan (both 1960–62), and Sonny Red (1961), and played in J. J. Johnson's group (1958–60) and the Jazztet (1960–61). From 1961 to 1964, with Wayne Shorter and Freddie Hubbard, he was a member of Art Blakey's Jazz Messengers; in addition to recording with Blakey, he took part in a few sessions under the leadership of Hubbard. He toured Japan as a member of Jackie McLean's quintet (1965) and spent some months as Lincoln's accompanist (1965–6). As an occasional house pianist for Prestige (1967–9) Walton played on recordings by Teddy Edwards, Houston Person, Eric Kloss, Sonny Criss, Pat Martino, and Charles McPherson, and led his own groups. During the same period he recorded with Blue Mitchell (1962, 1966), Eddie Harris (1964–6), Jordan (1965), Joe Henderson (1966), Lee Morgan (1966–8), Hank Mobley (1967), and Stanley Turrentine (1969), and performed and recorded with Art Farmer (1965, 1967). In the early 1970s he co-led a group with Mobley (mid-1970 – 1972) and rejoined Blakey for a tour of Japan (1973).

From the mid-1960s Walton performed frequently as the

leader of a quartet; in the 1970s to early 1980s its members were Jordan, George Coleman, or Bob Berg, and Sam Jones and Billy Higgins. The quartet took the name Eastern Rebellion in 1975. When working under Jordan's leadership it appeared as the Magic Triangle, and in 1977 it recorded as a sextet under Jones. Its rhythm section of Walton, Jones, and Higgins appeared independently of the group's saxophonists, in quartets under Farmer (1975) and Idrees Suliemann (1976), and in a quintet under Farmer and McLean (1977); later, with Tony Dumas rather than Jones on double bass, Berg and Walton worked under Higgins's leadership (recording in 1979–80). In the 1970s Walton recorded as a freelance with Johnny Coles (1971), Dexter Gordon (1972), Lucky Thompson (1972–3), Joe Chambers (1973), Mitchell (1975, 1977), James Spaulding (1976), Ray Brown (1977), Berg (1977–8), and Philly Joe Jones (1978). By 1976, when he recorded as a sideman with Milt Jackson in Tokyo, he had begun a long association in the latter's group which continued into the 1990s.

In 1981, when Sam Jones died, David Williams took his place in Eastern Rebellion. Thereafter Walton began to make regular tours of the USA, Europe, and Japan as the leader of a trio, which often included Higgins and usually involved David Williams or Ron Carter, though Buster Williams and Dumas also appeared as the group's double bass player; the trio accompanied Frank Morgan in performance and in a recording session (mid- to late 1980s), recorded with Jordan and Slide Hampton (1985), Dale Barlow (1985), Steve Grossman (1985, 1993), Dave Pike (1986), and James Clay (1989), and performed and recorded with Charles Lloyd (1993–4). From around 1981 into the early 1990s Walton and Higgins were also members of the Timeless All Stars (*see* TIMELESS), and in 1990 a reactivated version of Eastern Rebellion toured and recorded with Ralph Moore playing alongside David Williams and Higgins. From 1995, when Moore joined the band for "The Tonight Show" on television, Vincent Herring at times took his place in Eastern Rebellion, which continued to tour on a regular basis.

In the mid-1970s Walton experimented with funk rhythms and the electric piano as the leader of Soundscapes, and in the early 1980s he formed the Modern Jazz Masters, consisting of Bill Hardman, Berg, Buster Williams, and Louis Hayes. Later he led a sextet including both Moore and Herring (1996) and another sextet consisting of James Moody, Curtis Fuller, Stefon Harris, and his two long-standing compatriots David Williams and Higgins (2000). Walton has performed occasionally as an unaccompanied soloist and in duos with various double bass players. Among his later recordings as a freelance are albums with David "Fathead" Newman (1980), Junior Cook and Gordon (both 1981), Bobby Hutcherson (1982), Woody Shaw and Don Sickler (both 1983), Brown (in Tokyo), Benny Carter, and Hank Crawford (all 1984), James Morrison (at the Montreux Jazz Festival, 1986), Red Holloway (1987), Judy Niemack (1988), Christopher Hollyday (1988–9), Kenny Burrell and Madeline Eastman (both 1991), Carmen Bradford and Terumasa Hino (both 1993), Carmen Lundy (1994), Rickey Woodard (1994–5), Morgan (1995), Eric Alexander (1997), Joe Farnsworth (1998), and Phil Woods and Johnny Griffin (1998). His better-known compositions are *Bolivia*, *Mosaic*, and *Ugetsu*; transcriptions of some of his compositions, including *Bolivia*, have been published in *A New Approach to Jazz Improvisation*, xxxv: *Nine Jazz Originals: Cedar Walton*, ed. J. Aebersold (New Albany, IA, 1985).

SELECTED RECORDINGS

As unaccompanied soloist: *Piano Solos* (*c*1981, Clean Cuts 704); *Cedar Walton at Maybeck: Maybeck Recital Hall Series*, xxv (1992, Conc. 4546)
Duos with D. Williams: *Off Minor* (1990, Red 123242)
As leader: *Spectrum* (1968, Prst. 7591); with H. Mobley: *Breakthrough* (1972, Cob. 9011); *A Night at Boomer's* (1973, Muse 5010, 5022); *Eastern Rebellion* (1975, Tim. 101), incl. Bolivia; *Animation* (*c*1978, Col. JC35572); *Cedar Walton* (1985, Tim. 223); *Manhattan Afternoon* (1992, Criss Cross 1082); *Ironclad* (1989, Monarch 1005); with R. Carter and B. Higgins: *My Funny Valentine* (1991, Sweet Basil 660.55.010); *St. Thomas* (1991, Evidence 22161); *Bambino* (1993, Evidence 22213)
As sideman: K. Dorham: *This is the Moment* (1958, Riv. 275); A. Farmer and B. Golson: *Big City Sounds* (1960, Argo 672); A. Blakey: *Mosaic* (1961, BN 84090), incl. Mosaic; *Caravan* (1962, Riv. 9438); *Ugetsu* (1963, Riv. 9464), incl. Ugetsu; H. Mobley: *Far Away Lands* (1967, BN 84425); L. Morgan: *Caramba* (1968, BN 84289); C. Jordan: *On Stage* (1975, Ste. 1071); Timeless All Stars: *It's Timeless* (1982, Tim. 178); B. Higgins: *Billy Higgins Quintet* (1993, Sweet Basil 8003)

SELECTED FILMS AND VIDEOS

Freddie Hubbard: Live at the Village Vanguard (1984); Ron Carter and Art Farmer: Live at Sweet Basil with Billy Higgins and Cedar Walton (1990); Don Menza Quintet: Live in New Orleans (1991)

BIBLIOGRAPHY

G. Giddins: Liner notes, *A Night at Boomer's* (Muse 5010, 1973)
L. Tomkins: "Cedar Walton," *CI*, xiv (1976), no.7, p.20; no.8, p.6
L. Lyons: "Cedar Walton," *CK*, iii/2 (1977), 12
B. Case: "Cedar Walton: Earning the Steinway," *MM* (3 Feb 1979), 25
A. Moorhead: "Cedar Walton's Major League Play," *DB*, xlviii/1 (1981), 26 [incl. discography]
D. Lund: "Cedar Walton," *CI*, xxii/1 (1982), 22
L. Hildebrand: "The Cedar Walton Trio: Jazz Pianist Runs Free in his 'Briar Patch'," *San Francisco Chronicle Datebook* (11 Jan 1987), 40
W. Minor: "Frank Morgan and Cedar Walton: the Inaccessibility of Art(ists)," *Coda*, no.225 (1989), 13
B. Blumenthal: "Walton Brings his Sound to Boston," *Boston Globe* (19 April 1992)
B. Primack: "Eastern Rebellion: Artful Endurance," *JT*, xxv/4 (1995), 45
J. Hamlin: "Cedar Walton Makes it All up: Author of Myriad Jazz Classics Presents 'Autumn Sketches' at Monterey Jazz Festival," *San Francisco Chronicle Datebook* (15 Sept 1996), 46
D. Heckman: "Stepping up with Cedar," *Los Angeles Times Calendar* (2 June 1996), 7
F. Postif: *Jazz Me Blues: interviews et portraits de musiciens de jazz et de blues* (Paris, 1998), 417
G. Buium: "Cedar Walton Interview," *Cadence*, xxvii/4 (2001), 5

BK

Walton, Greely (Frank) (*b* Mobile, AL, 4 Oct 1904; *d* New York, 9 Oct 1993). Tenor and baritone saxophonist. He first played violin, and studied music at the University of Pittsburgh. After taking up tenor saxophone he worked with Elmer Snowden (1926), Benny Carter (1929), and others, then joined Luis Russell's band (1930). He performed and made recordings with this ensemble until 1937, remaining with it under Louis Armstrong's leadership. Thereafter he worked with the bandleader Vernon Andrade (from 1938), Horace Henderson (from September 1941), Cootie Williams (on baritone saxophone, 1942–3), and Cab Calloway (1943–5). He then became music director of Eddie "Cleanhead" Vinson's band, in which he played baritone saxophone (1945–7), and during this period he served as music director for the popular vocal group the Ink Spots. Walton was briefly with Claude Hopkins at the Zanzibar Club, New York, before playing in Afro-Cuban bands; he also performed with Noble Sissle. From 1948 he worked mostly with Sy Oliver, playing for radio and television shows. He taught flute in the early 1950s and ceased playing in 1955.

SELECTED RECORDINGS

As sideman: H. Allen: Singing Pretty Songs (1930, Vic. 23338); L. Russell: Panama (1930, OK 8849); Ease on Down (1930, Voc. 1579); You Rascal You (1931, Vic. 22793); L. Armstrong: Mahogany Hall Stomp (1936, Decca 824)

BIBLIOGRAPHY

ChiltonW; *McCarthyB*
D. Griffiths: "Greely Walton's Life Story," *Sv*, no.107 (1983), 165
J. Simmen: "Greely Frank Walton," *BHcF*, no.424 (1994), 4
J. Evensmo: *History of Jazz Tenor Saxophone: Black Artists*, i: *1917–1934* (Oslo, 1996); ii: *1935–1939* (Oslo, 1997)
D. Griffiths: *Hot Jazz from Harlem to Storyville* (Lanham, MD, London, and Rutgers, 1998), 172

based on *ChiltonW*

Waltz. In jazz parlance (and quite independent of its connotations for dance) a term which might be applied to any piece in 3/4 time (*see* BEAT, §I).

Wanzo, Mel(vin) [Muhammad, Melvin Wahid] (*b* Cleveland, 22 Nov 1930). Trombonist. He studied music at Youngstown University (1948–52) and then, while stationed in Kentucky, played in an army band directed by Cannonball Adderley. After performing in the 1950s with Joe Turner (ii), the singer Ruth Brown, and other rhythm-and-blues musicians he worked principally in big bands; from 1958 to 1961 he continued his studies at the Cleveland Institute of Music. Later he toured and recorded with the Glenn Miller Orchestra (under Ray McKinley's direction, 1965–8) and Woody Herman (1966–8) and was a member of Count Basie's orchestra (1969–80), with which he appeared in the film *The Last of the Blue Devils* (1979); he also recorded with the Capp–Pierce Juggernaut (1981). Following Basie's death in 1984 he rejoined Basie's orchestra, then led by Thad Jones, and remained with it into the early 1990s, under Frank Foster. Although principally a section player, Wanzo may be heard as a soloist on the track *The Left-hand Corner*, on the album *Count Basie Live in Japan '78* (1978, Pablo 28MJ3473).

BIBLIOGRAPHY

Feather–Gitler '70s
D. Hameed and A. K. Mustafaa: "Melvin Wahid Muhammad (Melvin Wanzo): Muslim Musician with Heart, Soul and Experience," *American Muslim Journal* (9 Feb 1990), 24

DANIEL ZAGER/BK

Ward, Carlos (Nathaniel) (*b* Ancon, Panama Canal Zone, 1 May 1940). Saxophonist. After moving to the Seattle area in 1953 he took up clarinet, then in 1955 changed to saxophone and played in local rock-and-roll groups. While in the US Army he joined a military band (1961) and was sent to Germany; following his discharge he remained in Europe and performed with Albert Mangelsdorff, Dollar Brand (who later took the name Abdullah Ibrahim), Don Cherry, and Karl Berger. In April 1965 he returned to Seattle, where in October he worked with John Coltrane at The Penthouse. He then moved to New York, where he played with Coltrane, Sunny Murray, and Sam Rivers. In 1967 he went west with Murray and settled in San Francisco; for some time he played only on weekends. He returned to New York in 1969, played and recorded with the funk group B. T. Express, performed with Murray (at the Newport Jazz Festival) and Rashied Ali's quartet, and joined the Jazz Composer's Orchestra Association; he was also a member of a group led by David Izenzon that included Berger, Gato Barbieri, and Barry Altschul, and at some point he played with Alice Coltrane.

From 1972 Ward toured and recorded with Ibrahim's groups, with which he may be seen in the videos *A Brother with Perfect Timing* (1986) and *The Cry of Reason: Beyers Naudé: an Afrikaaner Speaks Out* (1987); he recorded with the Jazz Composer's Orchestra (under Grachan Moncur III), Paul Motian, and Clifford Thornton (all 1974), and Kip Hanrahan (1980–82). He worked into the 1980s with groups led by Carla Bley, and in 1985 he was a member of the cooperative quintet Nu, with Cherry, Nana Vasconcelos, Mark Helias, and Ed Blackwell. Ward then joined Cherry's quintet for performances in New York (1986) and a tour of Central America (1987) and replaced Jimmy Lyons (ii) in Cecil Taylor's group (1986). In 1987 he formed his own quartet, consisting of Charles Sullivan, Alex Blake, and Ronnie Burrage; the following year, as a leader at the North Sea Jazz Festival, he recorded with a different group, including Woody Shaw. Ward was a featured soloist in Don Pullen's group African-Brazilian Connection from 1990 until the pianist's death early in 1995; during this same period he played in Frank Lowe's group Saxemble (also known as Saxemple), and in 1992 he performed and recorded at Yoshi's in Oakland, California, as a member of Blackwell's group. He was reunited with Berger for duo recordings in 1994, and in 1995–6 he recorded with a big band led by Bob Stewart.

SELECTED RECORDINGS

Duos with A. Ibrahim: *Live at Sweet Basil*, i (1983, Ekapa 004)
As sideman: K. Berger: *Karl Berger Quartet* (1966, ESP 1041); D. Brand: *Underground* (1972, Trio PAP9018); D. Cherry: *Relativity Suite* (1973, JCOA 1006); R. Rudd: *Numatik Swing Band* (1973, JCOA 1007); R. Ali: *New Directions in Modern Music* (1973, Survival 103); C. Bley: *Dinner Music* (1976, Watt 6); A. Ibrahim: *Ekaya* (1983, Ekapa 005); *Water from an Ancient Well* (1985, Black Hawk 50207); D. Pullen: *Kele mou bana* (1991, BN B21S-98166); F. Lowe: *Inappropriate Choices* (1991, ITM Pacific 970062); D. Pullen: *Live ... Again: Live at Montreux* (1993, BN B21Z-30271)

BIBLIOGRAPHY

CarrJ
L. Gabel: "Carlos Ward: Expressway to Creative Truth," *DB*, xlii/13 (1975), 17 [incl. discography]
I. Vroedindewey: "De stille gebeden van Carlos Ward" [The silent prayers of Carlos Ward], *Jazz nu*, no.77 (1985), 236; repr. as "Carlos Ward: a Love Supreme," *Coda*, no.202 (1985), 24 [incl. discography]
A. Lewis and L. Lewis: "Interview: Carlos Ward," *Cadence*, xxiv/9 (1998), 5
L. Rasmussen: *Abdullah Ibrahim: a Discography* (Copenhagen, 1999)

DAVID WILD/BK

Ward, Helen (*b* New York, 19 Sept 1916; *d* Arlington, VA, 21 April 1998). Singer. The feature article in *Swing* (1939) gives her year of birth as 1913; elsewhere it appears as 1916. She was taught piano as a child and began singing in her teens. After performing on radio station WOR in New York (1933) she became a staff musician at NBC and sang with Benny Goodman on the radio show "Let's Dance" (December 1934 to May 1935). Through 1936 she toured and made several recordings with Goodman (including *Goody-goody* (1936, Vic. 25245), which displays her exuberant, swinging style). During the period 1937–42, while being a wife and mother, she sang only on recordings; she was accompanied by various musicians, among them Gene Krupa (1936–8), Teddy Wilson (1936–7, 1940, 1942), Bob Crosby, with whom she also sang on radio broadcasts (1939), Joe Sullivan (1940), and Harry James (1941). After 1942 she performed with Hal McIntyre, recorded with Red Norvo (1943), James (*c*1944), Wild Bill Davison (1952), and Peanuts Hucko (1956–7), and toured and recorded (1953, 1957, 1958) with Goodman. After a long period of inactivity, she resumed performing and recording in 1979; in 1981 she made the album *The Helen Ward Song Book* (Lyricon 1001).

BIBLIOGRAPHY

ConnorBG

"Vocalist of the Month: Helen Ward," *Swing*, ii/7 (1939), 31
R. D. Kinkle: *The Complete Encyclopedia of Popular Music and Jazz, 1900–1950* (New Rochelle, NY, and Westport, CT, 1974) [incl. discography]
L. Dahl: *Stormy Weather: the Music and Lives of a Century of Jazzwomen* (London, Melbourne, Australia, and New York, 1984), 132
M. L. Hester: "Queen of Swing," *MR*, xxiii/8 (1996), 14
Obituary, B. Crowther, *JJI*, li/7 (1998), 18

SCOTT FREDRICKSON

Ware, Bill(, III) (*b* East Orange, NJ, 28 Jan 1959). Vibraphonist. He studied theory and composition at Montclair State University (BA 1982) and received tuition on the Jazzmobile and performed in its big band. In 1982 he began teaching Latin percussion at William Paterson College in Wayne, New Jersey, and in the same year, together with other musicians at the college, he formed a Latin-jazz band, AM Sleep, which recorded and toured in the Northeast. Ware was a founding member of the Jazz Passengers in 1987, with which he has toured internationally and recorded, and in 1990 he performed in Japan with a group that was later known as Bill Ware and the Club Bird All Stars. In New York, while continuing to lead his own groups and playing with the Jazz Passengers, he joined the acid-jazz group Groove Collective; he worked with each of these bands through the 1990s, and in the middle of the decade he toured the USA and recorded with the pop group Steely Dan. Ware has also served as a bass player and a pianist in Latin groups, recorded with a number of pop musicians, including David Byrne, and collaborated with such jazz musicians as John Lurie and Marc Ribot.

SELECTED RECORDINGS

As leader: *Long and Skinny* (*c*1993, Knitting Factory Works 131); *Vibes* (1997, Knitting Factory Works 210)
As sideman: M. Pavone: *Song for (Septet)* (1993, New World 80452-2); Jerome Harris: *Hidden in Plain View* (1995, New World 80472-2); Vibes: *With Drawn* (*c*1999, Knitting Factory Works 242)

BIBLIOGRAPHY

<http://www.groovecollective.com/billw.htm> (1999)

GK

Ware, David S(pencer) (*b* Plainfield, NJ, 7 Nov 1949). Tenor saxophonist and leader. From the age of ten he played successively alto, baritone, and tenor saxophones, and from 1967 to around 1969 he attended the Berklee School of Music. With Marc Edwards among his sidemen, around 1970 he formed the group Apogee, which performed in Boston until its members moved together to New York in 1973; the following year he played in Cecil Taylor's orchestra at Carnegie Hall. In the mid-1970s Ware performed and recorded with Andrew Cyrille (1974–6), worked in a trio with Raphé Malik, and toured Europe and recorded with Taylor (1976–7). In 1977 he made the first two of his many albums as a leader and became a member of a group led by Barry Harris, with whom he also recorded in a duo that year. Around this time he resumed his association with Cyrille, with whom he recorded in Milan in 1978 and 1980.

Ware drove a taxi in New York from 1981 to 1995, a lean period for anyone attempting to survive as a free-jazz musician. Nonetheless he toured Europe twice in 1981 as the leader of a quartet and around 1981–2 worked occasionally in a duo with Milford Graves; in 1985 he returned to Europe for another tour, leading a trio that consisted of Peter Kowald on double bass and various drummers, among them Thurman Barker and Louis Moholo. Two years later he recorded as a sideman with Ahmed Abdullah, and in 1988 he performed and recorded as the leader of a quartet that included William Parker (with whom he first played in Taylor's orchestra); Matthew Shipp became the group's pianist in 1990, with, successively, Edwards, Whit Dickey, and Susie Ibarra on drums.

Ware's style is a raucous, dissonant brand of free jazz that relies heavily on overblowing and multiphonics; it is exemplified by his playing on Cyrille's album *Metamusicians' Stomp* (1978) and on his quartet's radical transformation of the pop standard *The Way We Were*, from his album *Go See the World* (1997).

SELECTED RECORDINGS

As leader: *Passage to Music* (1988, Silkheart 113); *Great Bliss*, i–ii (1990, Silkheart 127–8); *Flight of I* (1991, DIW 856); *Third Ear Recitation* (1992, DIW 870); *Earthquation* (1994, DIW 892); *Cryptology* (1994, Homestead 220-2); *Dao* (1995, Homestead 230-2); *Wisdom of Uncertainty* (1996, AUM Fidelity 001); *Go See the World* (1997, Col. CK69138), incl. The Way We Were
As sideman: C. Taylor: *Dark to Themselves* (1976, Enja 2084); A. Cyrille: *Metamusicians' Stomp* (1978, BS 0025); A. Abdullah: *Ahmed Abdullah and the Solomonic Quintet* (1987, Silkheart 109)

BIBLIOGRAPHY

B. Case: "Aw, Come on! Doncha Feel Just a Tiny Bit Scared of Cecil?," *New Musical Express* (21 Aug 1976), 33
V. T. Gbezo: "David S. Ware: du silence à la musique," *L'Independant du jazz*, no.17 (1979)
B. Rusch: "David Ware: Interview," *Cadence*, vi/1 (1980), 5
J. Quist: "David S. Ware at 12," *Jazz nu* (1982), May, 342
P. Margasak: "Riffs: David S. Ware Sharpens Edge, Deepens Vision," *DB*, lxi/2 (1994), 12
M. Bäumel: "David S. Ware: diese Stille ist Balance," *JP*, xliv/6 (1995), 26
A. Cohen: "David S. Ware: Third Ear Recitation," *Coda*, no.260 (1995), 28
T. Jousse: "David S. Ware: entre le cristal et la fumée," *Jm*, no.447 (1995), 26
G. Reynard: "Davis S. Ware," *Jh*, no.525 (1995), 15
K. L. Williams: "Tenor Madness: David S. Ware – Charles Gayle," *DB*, lxii/1 (1995), 35
F. Médioni and A. Pierrepont: "David S. Ware," *Jm*, no.467 (1997), 20
S. Dollar: "Explosive Saxophonist Takes Jazz Improv to New Heights," *Atlanta Journal Constitution* (27 Sept 1998)
—— "Objects May be Closer than They Appear," *Jazziz*, xv/10 (1998), 49
B. Ratliff: "Taking a Monkish Delight in the Serious and Spare," *New York Times* (15 Oct 1998)
B. Shoemaker: "David S. Ware: Rapturous Sounds," *JT*, xxviii/8 (1998), 52
T. Lépin: "David S. Ware et la chanson de Roland," *Jazzman*, no.45 (1999), 24
"David S. Ware," <http://lejazz.simplenet.com/09/us/inter/view2.htm> (2000)
G. Good: "WNUR Interview: David S. Ware," <http://www.nwu.edu/jazz/artists/ware.david/interview.html> (2000)
R. Lopez: "The David S. Ware Discography," <http://www.velocity.net/bb10k/WARE.disc.html> (2000)
W. Sacks: "In Conversation with David S. Ware: Improvisation, Meditation and the Crystalline Idea," <http://www.furious.com/perfect/davidsware.html> (2000)

BK

Ware, Leonard [L. W.] (*b* Richmond, VA, 28 Dec 1909; *d* New York state, March 1974). Guitarist and composer. He studied at Tuskegee Institute, where he played oboe in the band. In the early 1930s he changed to guitar and formed a trio that held various engagements in New York until the late 1940s, when he ceased full-time performing. In 1938 he recorded *Hold Tight* (*Want some sea food, mama*)/*Jungle Drums* (Voc. 4537) with Sidney Bechet, the first of which was his own composition, and in the same year he took part in the first "From Spirituals to Swing" concert, for which he replaced Eddie Durham at a late stage as the electric guitar soloist with the Kansas City Six; he may be heard with the group on *After You've Gone* (first issued under Count Basie's name on the album *Lester–Amadeus*, 1937–8, Phontastic 7639). Ware also made recordings as a sideman with Buddy Johnson (who featured him on *Southern Exposure*, 1941, Decca 8562), Joe Turner (ii) (1941, 1945), and the blues singer Albinia Jones (1944, 1945), and as a leader (1947). The social security death index gives his last known residence as New York City.

BIBLIOGRAPHY

ChiltonW; *FeatherE*

H. Panassié and M. Gautier: *Dictionnaire du jazz* (Paris, 1954; Eng. trans., London, 1956, rev. A. A. Gurwitch as *Guide to Jazz*, Boston, 1956), 331

HOWARD RYE

Ware, Munn [Winfred Nettleton] (*b* Quincy, MA, 12 Feb 1909; *d* Daytona Beach, FL, 9 Aug 1970). Trombonist. His birthdate appears on his application for social security. He took up piano at the age of 11, but in his early teens, after his parents died, he went to live with relatives in Montclair, New Jersey, and there took up banjo. While at Bowdoin College in Brunswick, Maine, he learned cornet, and afterwards began playing professionally on that instrument in Massachusetts; he began doubling on trombone around 1940, and from 1942 to 1946 he served as a trombonist in an army band. Following his discharge he played from autumn 1946 in New York clubs and restaurants in bands led by Tony Parenti, Wild Bill Davison, and Danny Alvin, and from June 1947 he worked regularly at Jazz Ltd. in Chicago with the band led by the clarinetist Bill Reinhardt. At this time he also recorded with Sidney Bechet, Muggsy Spanier, and Doc Evans; his playing may be heard to advantage on Bechet's *Maryland my Maryland/Careless Love* (1949, Jazz Limited 201). After stints with Max Kaminsky, Henry "Red" Allen, and others he moved in 1952 to Florida, where he organized bands for performances on the Daytona Beach pier and worked variously as an arranger, freelance performer, and bandleader; he recorded with Evans again in Tampa in December 1965.

BIBLIOGRAPHY

ChiltonW

"Munn Ware," *SL*, xvii (1966), 59

K. L. Kramer: "Munn Ware: a Personal Memoir," *SL*, xxiii (1969–70), 429

J. Chilton: *Sidney Bechet: the Wizard of Jazz* (London and New York, 1987/*R*1996)

BK

Ware, Wilbur (Bernard) (*b* Chicago, 8 Sept 1923; *d* Philadelphia, 9 Sept 1979). Double bass player. He played drums in church before taking up double bass, but was also a tap-dancer in his youth. As a teenager he studied with Truck Parham. After serving in an army air force band that toured the Pacific arena (September 1943 – January 1946) he was associated with Stuff Smith, Roy Eldridge, and Sonny Stitt in Milwaukee (1946). His career was impeded by problems with drugs and alcohol, but later he worked with Johnny Griffin and Joe Williams (both 1953), Junior Mance and Sonny Rollins (both 1954), and Eddie "Cleanhead" Vinson (1954–5) and recorded with Griffin (1954). On the strength of his performance of *Cherokee* while sitting in with the Clifford Brown–Max Roach Quintet at the Beehive, he was engaged to lead the house rhythm section, in which capacity he accompanied Thelonious Monk and Griffin and then Art Farmer. The consequences of further problems with narcotics ended this brief affiliation.

Early in 1956 Ware worked with Ira Sullivan, and in June he joined Art Blakey's Jazz Messengers and moved to New York, where he became a house double bass player for Riverside. He also worked for Blue Note, recording with such important musicians as Lee Morgan and Zoot Sims (both 1956), Monk, Sonny Clark, Gerry Mulligan, and Kenny Drew (all 1957), Toots Thielemans (1957–8), and Griffin and Blue Mitchell (both 1958), and leading his own groups. Having worked briefly with Stan Getz (1956) and Ray Bryant and Herbie Nichols (both 1957), he led a band that involved the Adderley brothers, Wynton Kelly or Duke Jordan, and Philly Joe Jones; more significantly, he played with John Coltrane in Monk's quartet at the Five Spot during the latter half of 1957 and in Sonny Rollins's trio for a recording in concert at the Village Vanguard in November of that year. He appeared with Griffin, Clark, and Jones at the Café Bohemia (*c*1959) and with J. R. Monterose in Albany (summer 1959), participated in the Cliff Walk Festival in Newport, Rhode Island (July 1960), and recorded with Tina Brooks, Clifford Jordan, and Grant Green (1961). Illness forced Ware to return to Chicago in 1963, and he played infrequently until 1968, when he joined Archie Shepp's group; the previous summer he had appeared with Blue Mitchell and Elvin Jones in New York. He performed and recorded sporadically with Shepp into the early 1970s, and he also worked with Jordan (intermittently to 1976), Rollins and Monk (both at the Village Vanguard in 1969), Red Garland and Jones (*c*1972), and Sun Ra (1973). Ware's heavy tone, percussive yet buoyant attack, and short notes were reminiscent of the styles of Wellman Braud and Walter Page, but his harmonic inventiveness, apparent for example on *Blues for Tomorrow*, was wholly modern. Unlike many of his contemporaries, who played legato solos, he developed his solos (such as that on *Softly, as in a Morning Sunrise*) rhythmically and motivically. In this way his was a foretaste of the free-jazz style.

Oral history material in *NjR* (JOHP).

SELECTED RECORDINGS

As leader: *The Chicago Sound* (1957, Riv. 252)

As sideman: J. Griffin: *The Johnny Griffin Quartet* (1954, Argo 624); Z. Sims: *Zoot!* (1956, Riv. 228); K. Drew: *This is New* (1957, Riv. 236); on *Blues for Tomorrow* (1957, Riv. 243), [no leader:] Blues for Tomorrow; T. Monk: *Monk's Music* (1957, Riv. 242); *Thelonious Monk with John Coltrane* (1957, Jlnd 946); S. Clark: *Dial S for Sonny* (1957, BN 1570); *Mulligan Meets Monk* (1957, Riv. 247); E. Henry: *Seven Standards and a Blues* (1957, Riv. 248); S. Rollins: *A Night at the Village Vanguard* (1957, BN 1581), incl. Softly, as in a Morning Sunrise; T. Thielemans: *Man Bites Harmonica* (1957–8, Riv. 257); B. Mitchell: *Big Six* (1958, Riv. 273); C. Jordan: *Starting Time* (1961, Jlnd 952); G. Green: *Standards* (1961, BN 21284); A. Shepp: *For Losers* (1969, Imp. 9188)

BIBLIOGRAPHY

B. Crow: "Introducing Wilbur Ware," *JR*, ii/11 (1959), 14

G. Kopel: "Au tableau d'honneur des pinceurs de cordes: Wilbur Ware et Scott La Faro," *Jm*, no.54 (1959), 16

H. Pekar: "The Development of the Modern Bass," *DB*, xxix/26 (1962), 20

V. Wilmer: "Ware on the Bass," *MM* (12 June 1971), 14

J. Litweiler: "Remembering Wilbur Ware," *DB*, xlvi/18 (1979), 27 [incl. discography]

Obituary, *New York Times* (13 Sept 1979)

JOHN CURRY/BK

Warfield, Tim(othy Reginald, Jr.) (*b* York, PA, 2 July 1965). Tenor saxophonist. Primarily self-taught, he began playing alto saxophone at the age of nine and changed to the tenor instrument while at high school. He attended Howard University in the early 1980s, but left to concentrate on jazz performance. In 1990 he began working with Marlon Jordan, the recording group Tough Young Tenors, and the Jazz Futures, with which he recorded and appeared at the JVC Newport Jazz Festival in 1991. In the same year he placed third in the Thelonious Monk International Jazz Saxophone Competition, behind Joshua Redman and Eric Alexander.

Warfield worked with Shirley Scott in a number of contexts and appeared with her as a member of the house band in Bill Cosby's television show "You Bet your Life" (*c*1991–2). He later recorded and toured Europe with Jimmy Smith (1995) and worked with Christian McBride's quartet (1995–7) and Nicholas Payton (from 1995). Around 1993 he formed a quintet with Terrell Stafford, Cyrus Chestnut, Tarus Mateen, and Clarence Penn. Warfield is one of a number of tenor saxophone virtuosos to have emerged in the 1980s and 1990s. Influenced by Wayne Shorter's mid-1960s style and that of John Coltrane in the early 1960s, his improvisations convey motivic work, terse, fleet, varied lines, and soulful, screaming passages in the instrument's altissimo register, while maintaining a sense of clarity and form.

SELECTED RECORDINGS

As leader: *A Cool Blue* (1994, Criss Cross 1102); *A Whisper in the Midnight* (1995, Criss Cross 1122); *Gentle Warrior* (1997, Criss Cross 1149)

As sideman: Tough Young Tenors: *Alone Together* (1991, Ant. 422-848767-2); J. Smith: *Damn!* (1995, Verve 314-527631-2); T. Stafford: *Time to Let Go* (1995, Can. 79702); N. Payton: *Gumbo nouveau* (1995, Verve 314-531199-2); Orin Evans: *Justin Time* (1996, Criss Cross 1125)

BIBLIOGRAPHY

D. Michel: "Quatre futurs antérieurs: Tim Warfield," *Jm*, no.410 (1991), 32

GK

Warland [Vandennheuvel]**, Jean** (*b* Brussels, 23 Oct 1926). Belgian double bass player. He played accordion from the age of four and took up double bass only in 1945. In 1949 he joined a Belgian bop group, and that May he appeared in Toots Thielemans's quartet at the Festival International de Jazz in Paris. In the 1950s he recorded with Thielemans in Brussels (1951), performed in orchestras led by Jean Omer, Fud Candrix (recording in 1953), Francis Bay, Jean Robert, Gus Deloof, Bobby Naret, and Stan Brenders, and worked as a studio musician with Jos Aerts, Al Goyens, Jack Sels, and others; while touring France with the bandleader Jacques Hélian (1956–7) he recorded in Paris in Henri Renaud's trio and octet, both of which included Kenny Clarke (1957). He played with Aimé Barelli in Monte Carlo for two years, then returned to Paris, where he recorded with Barelli (*c*1959) and accompanied such soloists as J. J. Johnson, Lee Morgan, Martial Solal, Lucky Thompson, Allen Eager, Barney Wilen, and Michel Legrand. In the early 1960s he recorded in Brussels with Fats Sadi (*c*1960) and in Cologne with Karl Drewo and Dusko Goykovich (both 1961) and Heinz Kretzschmar (1962). After touring worldwide with the singer Catherina Valente he was based in Cologne, where he at times replaced Jimmy Woode as the double bass player in the Clarke–Boland Big Band (*c*1967–71), served as a member of the WDR Big Band (1967–92), and recorded with Sahib Shihab (1968), Francis Coppieters (1968–9), Charly Antolini (1968–72), and Benny Bailey (1971). He also played with Dizzy Gillespie, Horace Parlan, Tony Scott, Tony Coe, Ronnie Scott, and others. In 1976 he recorded again with Sadi.

While continuing to work in Cologne, where he recorded with the WDR Big Band (1984) and Barbara Dennerlein (1986), Warland appeared in Belgium with such musicians as Goyens, Phil Abraham, and Richard Rousselet, and recorded with the Belgian All Stars Big Band (1980–81), again with Coppieters and Thielemans (both 1986), and later with Guitars Big Band (1996). From 1993 he led the group Sax No End in tributes to the music of Francy Boland, and in 1997 he fronted the Brussels Jazz Orchestra in another tribute to Boland at the Jazz Middelheim Festival (Antwerp). In 1999 he formed a sextet devoted to Duke Ellington's legacy and another group, Sax Port, consisting of Belgian and German musicians. Arrangements by Warland were recorded by the BRT (Belgische Radio & Televisie) Big Band (1984) and by Félix Simtaine's Act Big Band (1986).

SELECTED RECORDINGS

As sideman: T. Thielmans: Fhes [*sic*: She's] funny that way/It had to be "Bird" (1949, Pacific 2324); Boppin' at the Doge/Crazy Bop (1949, Pacific 2327); H. Renaud: *Henri Renaud et son orchestre (trio et octette)* (1957, Ducretet-Thomson 300V027); K. Drewo: *Clap Hands, Here Comes Charlie* (1961, Met. 15141); T. Thielemans: *Just Friends* (1986, Jazzline 20812)

BIBLIOGRAPHY

R. Pernet, J.-P. Schroeder, and others: *Dictionnaire du jazz à Bruxelles et en Wallonie* (Liège, Belgium, 1991)

R. Pernet: *Belgian Jazz Discography (1897–1999)* (Brussels, 1999)

<http://www.jazzinbelgium.org/mus/warland.htm> (2000)

<http://www.musikkultur.de/kuenstler/jeanward.htm> (2000)

BK

Warleigh, Ray(mond Kenneth) (*b* Sydney, 28 Sept 1938). Australian alto saxophonist and flutist. He started on flute and then clarinet as a youth, and was inspired to take up saxophone in his late teens after hearing Paul Desmond. In 1959 he began performing professionally. The following year he moved to England, where he worked at first with Alexis Korner, and later performed and recorded with such diverse musicians as John Stevens (early 1966), Tubby Hayes (recording in his big band in 1966), Chris Pyne (also 1966), Humphrey Lyttelton (1968), Ronnie Scott (summer 1968 – early 1970), and John Warren's big band (1970). In 1968 he made his first recording as a leader (*Ray Warleigh's First Album*, Phi. 7881), which involved both a jazz band and an orchestra. He was associated in the late 1960s and early 1970s with various groups led by Stevens, including the Spontaneous Music Ensemble, and he played with Mike Gibbs (recording in 1969, 1972, and 1975), Mike Westbrook (recording in 1971), Mick Pyne, and Kenny Wheeler. Thereafter he worked with Paz, Allan Holdsworth, and the drummer Tommy Chase; he recorded two new albums under his own name (1977, 1978), the latter as a leader with Chase. In the early 1980s Warleigh was a member of the radio band at Westdeutscher Rundfunk in Cologne, Germany, with which he accompanied such visiting Americans as Freddie Hubbard, Dizzy Gillespie, and Max Roach, and he played in the big bands led by Peter Herbolzheimer (recording in 1984), the drummer Charlie Watts, and Wheeler, with whom he may be heard on *Music for Small and Large Ensembles* (1990, ECM 1415–16). He worked during the 1980s with the group Blind Alley led by the trombonist Derek Wadsworth and into the 1990s with the London Jazz Orchestra; he also led his own groups and recorded with the Dedication Orchestra in 1992. He continues to pursue an extensive freelance career. Warleigh is a versatile musician, comfortable in many different styles; in addition to alto saxophone he also plays the soprano, tenor, and baritone instruments, and clarinet.

BIBLIOGRAPHY

ChiltonB

"How Some of Today's Top Men Started," *MM* (29 Oct 1966), 17

R. Cotterrell, ed.: *Jazz Now: the Jazz Centre Society Guide* (London, 1976), 178

P. Renaud: *La discographie du jazz anglais* (Chaumont, France, 1985)

B. Sivyer: "Ray Warleigh: Sydney Sax Player Blows his Trumpet," *TNT Magazine*, no.178 (1987), 17

SIMON ADAMS

Warlop, Michel (*b* Douai, France, 23 Jan 1911; *d* Bagnères-de-Bigorre, France, 20 March 1947). French violinist. He studied music for some years. After first playing with Gregor (1932–4) he led a big band that backed such popular singers as Maurice Chevalier and Germaine Sablon (1934–5). In 1934, under the pseudonym Waclaw Niemczyk, he recorded classical violin and piano duos with Leon Kartun. He also worked with the group Jazz du Poste Parisien and in 1935 with the accordionist Louis Richardet. Warlop recorded as a leader and sideman with Stephane Grappelli and Django Reinhardt (1934–7), in a violin trio with Grappelli and Eddie South (accompanied by a rhythm section, 1937), and in a duo with Garland Wilson (1938). In the 1940s he was a member of an orchestra led by Raymond Legrand (1940–43), led a string septet (1941–3), and conducted the Orchestre Symphonique de Paris in a performance of his composition *Noël du prisonnier* (1942). Warlop's playing is exemplified by his recording *Tempête sur les cordes* (1941, Swing 115).

BIBLIOGRAPHY

A. Hodeir: "Panorama du jazz français," *BHcF*, 1st ser., no.1 (1945), 9
D. Nevers: Liner notes, *Special Michel Warlop* (Jazz Time 251272-2, 1989) [in Fr. and Eng.]

MICHEL LAPLACE

Warmdaddy. Nickname of WESSELL ANDERSON.

Warner Bros. Record company and label. Warner Bros. was founded as a film company in California in 1923 by Jack Warner and his three brothers, and in 1927 it was a pioneer of sound films. It first entered the recording industry in April 1930 when it purchased Brunswick–Balke–Collender (*see* BRUNSWICK). In November of that year it established MELOTONE as a subsidiary of Brunswick, and in December it revived the British label Brunswick. In 1931 it formed the subsidiary label PANACHORD as a British counterpart to American Brunswick's subsidiary Melotone, and that December it sold Brunswick to Consolidated Film Industries, which owned the American Record Company. That same year the rights to use the trademark name Brunswick in Britain, and to issue there material recorded by American Brunswick, were purchased by British Decca.

In 1958 Warner Bros. formed its own record company and label, and shortly afterwards it made and issued jazz albums by Chico Hamilton (1958–9), Matty Matlock (1958–60), and Paul Desmond (1959); it began issuing recordings in Britain in 1960. In 1963 it acquired from Frank Sinatra the label REPRISE, which it subsequently used to release pop and rock music. Later it acquired ATLANTIC (1967). Around 1969 Warner Bros. was purchased by Kinney National Services Corporation; in 1970 Kinney purchased Elektra to form the conglomerate WEA, but each record division (Warner Bros., Elektra, Atlantic) continued to operate independently. From the early 1960s into the mid-1970s the only significant foray into jazz by Warner Bros. was to produce Herbie Hancock's recordings of October 1969 to December 1971. In the mid-1970s it again ventured into the jazz marketplace, manufacturing and distributing ECM recordings in the USA and producing recordings on its own label; the latter were mainly by fusion artists such as David Sanborn, Al Jarreau, Michael Franks, Larry Carlton, and George Benson, but there was also material by Chick Corea, Bill Evans (ii), Roland Kirk, and a group co-led by Warne Marsh and Pete Christlieb. By the early 1980s Warner Bros. had again minimized its jazz activities but maintained some focus on fusion and pop-oriented material; in the mid-1980s it contracted Bob James and Miles Davis.

In 1989 WEA was acquired by Time, Inc., and the resulting merger formed the corporation Time-Warner. In 1990 Warner Bros. again turned towards jazz when it signed Mark Whitfield. The following year Matt Pierson was engaged to head its artists and repertory department and to serve as a staff producer, and in 1995 he became head of the jazz division. Pierson's involvement marked the start of Warner Bros.' first major commitment to developing a jazz catalogue; from 1991 it recorded, among others, Kenny Garrett, Larry Goldings, Brad Mehldau, Joshua Redman, Wallace Roney, and Mark Turner. By the year 2000 it featured roughly 15 performers, several operating within the bop revival, and the remainder associated with the soft-jazz and contemporary-jazz arenas.

Around 1995 Warner Bros. moved its headquarters to New York and changed the name of its music division to Warner Music Group, within which Warner Bros. and other associated labels are subsidiary companies. From 1996 reissues have appeared under the name Warner Archives or Reprise Archives, depending upon the original source; another Warner Music Group company, Rhino, has managed the back catalogue.

BIBLIOGRAPHY

B. Rust: *The American Record Label Book* (New Rochelle, NY, 1978)
J. Williams: "WB's Lourie Turns a New Page: Will Launch own Policy and Sign 'a Few More' Acts," *Billboard*, xcii (15 Nov 1980), 56
F. Goodman: "Warner Bros. Reactivates Reprise," *RS*, no.509 (24 Sept 1987), 33
J. Levenson: "Jazz Artist Bob James Joins Warner Bros. as A & R Exec," *Billboard*, ciii (13 July 1991), 8
——: "Warner Reshapes Jazz Agenda," *Billboard*, cv (31 July 1993), 1
S. Yanow: "Label Watch: Warner Brothers: Getting in Gear," *JT*, xxiii/5 (1993), 60
M. A. Gillen: "Warner Goes Online with Jazz Promotion," *Billboard*, cvi (19 Nov 1994), 58
——: "Warner Bros. Reorganizes Jazz Division: But its Mission Won't Change, Says Senior VP," *Billboard*, cvii (18 March 1995), 6
"Question of the Week," *MM* (11 Feb 1995), 43
"WB, Postal Service to Promote Jazz Stamp Series," *Billboard*, cvii (19 Aug 1995), 6
M. Newman: "Warner, Reprise Bring Back Classics," *Billboard*, cviii (27 July 1996), 7
J. Woodard: "Label Watch: Warner Brothers Records: Gaining Land-speed," *JT*, xxvi/5 (1996), 69
<http://www.timewarner.com/corp/about/music/wmg/about.html> (2000)
<http://www.wbjazz.com/catalog.cfm> (2000)

GK

Warren, Butch [Edward Rudolph] (*b* Washington, DC, 8 Sept 1939). Double bass player. He started his career at the age of 14 in a band led by his father, then played in and around Washington with Gene Ammons and Stuff Smith (*c*1956–7). After moving to New York to work with Kenny Dorham (1958–60) he became a house musician at Blue Note and recorded with Sonny Clark (1961), Donald Byrd (1961, 1963), Jackie McLean (1961–3), Herbie Hancock, Dexter Gordon, Grant Green, and Stanley Turrentine (all 1962), and Kenny Dorham, Joe Henderson, Hank Mobley, and Horace Parlan (all 1963). He also recorded with Elmo Hope (1961) and played in New York clubs with Clark (1961–2) and Gordon (1962). In 1963–4 he was the regular double bass player in Thelonious Monk's quartet, touring Europe and Japan and making several recordings, including the tracks that made up the LP side devoted to Monk's appearance at the Newport Jazz Festival in 1963 (the other side of this album was of Miles Davis's group at the same event in 1958); he may be seen in the video *Thelonious Monk: '63 in Japan* (*c*1987). Warren then returned to the Washington area and performed with jazz groups on a local television show (1966–7) and accompanied touring pop groups such as the Platters (1966); at this time he also played regularly with Walter Bishop, Jr., at the Bohemian Taverns, a Washington club. Owing to illness he ceased to be active during the late 1960s and early 1970s, but he resumed his career in 1975, when he played with both Howard McGhee and Richie Cole. Thereafter he continued to perform in the Washington area with his own groups or as a sideman. He performed with the trumpeter Webster Young in 1996 and with Cecil Payne in 1997.

Warren's playing is notable for his buoyant, well-articulated beat and supportive walking lines. His solos, though somewhat limited in range, are tasteful and effective, as may be heard on *Rainy Blues* (1962) with McLean and *Stuffy Turkey* (1964) with Monk.

SELECTED RECORDINGS

As sideman with T. Monk: *Monk in Tokyo* (1963, CBS–Sony 69–70); *Miles and Monk at Newport* (1958, 1963, Col. CS8978); *Big Band and Quartet in Concert* (1963, Col. CS8964); *It's Monk's Time* (1964, Col. CS8984), incl. Stuffy Turkey

As sideman with others: E. Hope: on *High Hope* (1961, Beacon 401), Crazy, Maybe so, Mo is on; D. Byrd: *Royal Flush* (1961, BN 84101); J. McLean: *A Fickle Romance* (1961, BN 84089); S. Clark: *Leapin' and Lopin'* (1961, BN 84091); D. Byrd: *Free Form* (1961, BN 84118); H. Hancock: *Takin' Off* (1962, BN 84109); D. Gordon: *Go!* (1962, BN 84112); *A Swingin' Affair* (1962, BN 84133); J. Mclean: *Tippin' the Scales* (1962, BN 84427), incl. Rainy Blues; S. Turrentine: *Jubilee Shout* (1962, BN LA883J2); G. Green: *Feelin' the Spirit* (1962, BN 84132); H. Parlan: *Happy Frame of Mind* (1963, BN 84134); J. Henderson: *Page One* (1963, BN 84140)

BIBLIOGRAPHY

Feather '60s

P. Lattes: "Ornette et les autres je sais qu'ils savent ce qu'ils font," *Jh*, no.197 (1964), 26

JOHN CURRY

Warren, Earle [Earl Ronald] (*b* Springfield, OH, 1 July 1914; *d* Springfield, 4 June 1994). Alto saxophonist. He played piano, banjo, and ukulele in a family band before taking up C-melody, tenor, and finally alto saxophone. From 1930, when he began working professionally, he added an "e" to his name to distinguish himself from Hines and other jazz musicians named Earl. He led his own groups and toured around the Midwest with various bands, both African-American and white, before joining the Count Basie Orchestra in April 1937 (for illustrations *see* Basie, count, and Films, fig.3). At first he shared baritone and lead alto saxophone duties with Jack Washington, then from 1938 to May 1945 he assumed the lead alto position; he also played clarinet and sang ballads. In the late 1940s he led his own bands and worked intermittently with Basie, and during the 1950s he became a manager of rhythm-and-blues and pop groups. From 1957 Warren made a number of tours and recordings with Buck Clayton, and in 1967 he toured Europe as a soloist. He performed in *Born to Swing* (1972), a film about former sidemen of Basie's band. In 1973 he formed the Countsmen, a group that played regularly at the West End club in New York throughout the 1970s. He settled in Geneva in the early 1980s and continued to play at international festivals until he retired from music in 1992. Although he rarely played as a soloist with Basie, Warren provided the melodic lead for many of the band's greatest recordings. Later in his career, however, he proved himself an able, energetic, and extrovert swing soloist.

Oral history material in *NjR* (JOHP), *NjR*.

SELECTED RECORDINGS

As leader: Circus in Rhythm (1944, Savoy 508); *The Countsmen* (1973, RCA LFL1-5034); *Earle Warren* (1974, RCA LFL1-5066), incl. Blues in my Heart

As sideman: C. Basie: Out the Window (1937, Decca 1581); Jumpin' at the Woodside (1938, Decca 2212); B. Clayton: *One for Buck* (1961, Col. 33SX1390); *Jazz from a Swinging Era* (1967, Fon. 200); *Buck Clayton Jam Session* (1974–6, Chi. 132, 143, 152)

SELECTED FILMS AND VIDEOS

Choo Choo Swing [Band Parade] (1943); Crazy House [Funzapoppin'] (1943); Hit Parade of 1943 [Change of Heart] (1943); Reveille with Beverly (1943); The Sound of Jazz (1957); Buck Clayton and his All Stars (1961); Born to Swing (1972)

BIBLIOGRAPHY

McCarthyB; *SheridanCB*

V. Wilmer: "Earl Warren's Story," *JJ*, xiii/8 (1960), 11

P. J. Sullivan: "Earle Warren," *JJ*, xx/11 (1967), 10

E. Warren: "Before Basie: Reminiscences of a Veteran Jazz Musician," *Coda*, viii/1 (1967), 12

A. J. McCarthy: Liner notes, *Earle Warren* (RCA LFL1-5066, 1974)

J. McDonough: "Helen Humes: Still the Talk of the Town," *DB*, xliii/10 (1976), 17

S. Dance: *The World of Count Basie* (New York and London, 1980), 71

B. Rusch: "Earle Warren: Interview," *Cadence*, vi (1980), no.7, p.15; no.9, p.9

E. Warren: "Meine Liebe: das Altsaxophon und Basie," *JP*, xxix/4 (1980), 4

J. Simmen: "Earle Warren, 1982," *BHcF*, no.303 (1983), 7

Obituaries: P. Watrous: *New York Times* (7 June 1994); J. Fordham, *The Guardian* (1 July 1994)

BK

Warren, John (*b* Montreal, 23 Sept 1938). Canadian baritone saxophonist and composer. He taught himself music before studying at McGill University Conservatory in 1959–61. From 1968 he led his own band in England, which at times included John Surman, Kenny Wheeler, John Taylor, Henry Lowther, Malcolm Griffiths, Alan Skidmore, and Ray Warleigh. In addition he played and recorded with Mike Westbrook's bands (1967–76), Bob Downes (1969), and Alan Cohen, and toured with the London Jazz Composers Orchestra (1972). He recorded his composition *Tales of the Algonquin* with John Surman in 1971 (Deram 1094), and later composed for and directed Surman's Brass Project (1981, 1992), touring with the group in 1984 and 1990. Among his other principal works are *Solent Suite* (1979), *Six Tributes for 13 Players* (1985), and *Plus Four and Four More* (1986). He teaches regularly at summer schools, including those at Dartington, Devon, and Barry, Wales. (R. Cotterrell, ed.: *Jazz Now: the Jazz Centre Society Guide*, London, 1976)

DIGBY FAIRWEATHER

Warren, Peter (*b* Hempstead, NY, 21 Nov 1935). Double bass player. He first played cello, and made his début at Carnegie Recital Hall, New York, at the age of 17; he then attended the Juilliard School and performed with the Atlanta Symphony Orchestra. He took up double bass in Las Vegas and studied with Chuck Israels in New York. From 1965 to 1967 he toured with the pop singer Dionne Warwick. He then settled in New York and became a member (with David Izenzon) of the New York Bass Revolution, which featured ten double bass players. During a period in Europe (from 1970) he collaborated in Belgium with three other double bass players on the album *Bass Is*, recorded for the new label Enja, worked with Chick Corea and John Surman, and recorded with Rolf Kühn (1970), Jean-Luc Ponty, Don Cherry, Terumasa Hino, Masahiko Sato, and Albert Mangelsdorff (all 1971), Anthony Braxton (1972), and Tomasz Stańko (1974), among others. After his return to the USA (1974) Warren joined Jack DeJohnette (to 1975) and recorded with Carla Bley (1975). In 1976 he was awarded a grant by the NEA to compose and perform cello music. Later he worked again with DeJohnette in Special Edition (1979–80) and played in a group with John Scofield and Mike Stern in New York (1982).

SELECTED RECORDINGS

As leader: with D. Holland, Jamie Faunt, and Glen Moore: *Bass Is* (1970, Enja 2018); *Solidarity* (1981, Japo 60034)

As sideman: M. Sato: *Trinity* (1971, Enja 2008); A. Mangelsdorff: *Spontaneous* (1971, Enja 2064); J. DeJohnette: *Cosmic Chicken* (1975, Prst. 10094); *Tin Can Alley* (1980, ECM 1189)

BIBLIOGRAPHY

Feather–Gitler '70s

L. Jeske: "Profile: Peter Warren," *DB*, xlix/9 (1982), 52

WILLIAM S. BROCKMAN/BK

Warwick. Record company and label. The company was founded by Morty Craft in New York in 1960. For a brief period it made jazz recordings, including four important LPs produced by Teddy Charles: one of a concert given by his quartet at the Museum of Modern Art, New York; one by Curtis Fuller; an album by Pepper Adams and Donald Byrd on which Herbie Hancock made his studio début; and *The Soul of Jazz Percussion*, which contained the work of such musicians as Booker Little, Curtis Fuller, Bill Evans (ii), Mal Waldron, Byrd, and Adams. Warwick also released an album by Ralph Burns; thereafter, however, the company ceased to be involved with jazz.

MARK GARDNER

Warwick, (William) Carl [Bama] (*b* Birmingham, AL, 27 Oct 1917). Trumpeter. He moved north from Brookside, Alabama, in 1930, and thereafter he grew up in Charlie Shavers's home; early in 1936 Warwick and Shavers (who had come to regard themselves as brothers) traveled to Philadelphia to join the bandleader Frank Fairfax, in whose big band they formed a trumpet section with Dizzy Gillespie. Later they transferred to Tiny Bradshaw's orchestra (mid-1936) and the Mills Blue Rhythm Band, which Gillespie also joined and in which they recorded (1937). The two then separated: Shavers became a member of John Kirby's sextet, and Warwick continued to work in big bands under the leadership of Teddy Hill and Edgar Hayes (both 1937), Don Redman (1938), and Bunny Berigan (1939).

Having served as the music director of an army band, Warwick worked with Woody Herman (September 1944 – August 1945), Buddy Rich (1946, 1947), and various commercial bands; he may be seen with Herman's First Herd in the film *Earl Carroll Vanities* (1946). Later he led his own ensemble in California (early 1950s), played briefly with Lucky Millinder (1953), and led a group with Brew Moore in San Francisco (1954–5). After touring and recording with Gillespie in 1956–7, he worked as a freelance and as a leader; he made another recording with Gillespie in 1961. From 1966 he was the music director of the New York City Correctional Institute, and in 1972 he played with Benny Carter at the Newport Jazz Festival New York. Warwick worked mainly as a section player in big bands and rarely took solos.

BIBLIOGRAPHY

ChiltonW; *FeatherE*; *Feather–Gitler '70s*; *McCarthyB*

W. Balliett: "Super Drummer," *Improvising: Sixteen Jazz Musicians and their Art* (New York, 1977), 151; repr. in *BallietttA (1986)*; *BallietttA (1996)*

D. Gillespie and A. Fraser: *To be, or not … to Bop: Memoirs* (Garden City, NY, 1979, London, 1980, as *Dizzy: the Autobiography of Dizzy Gillespie*)

A. Shipton: *Groovin' High: the Life of Dizzy Gillespie* (New York, and Oxford, England, 1999)

BK

Washboard band. An instrumental group that employs the washboard as a rhythm instrument. The board is played by drawing a nail, fork, or thimbles over the corrugations to produce a loud, staccato rhythm. Cowbells, woodblocks, and improvised metallophones were often attached to add tonal variety. Early washboard bands also included string instruments and were frequently augmented by other improvised instruments such as a washtub bass or kazoo, as well as a harmonica. They are closely related to the children's "spasm bands" of New Orleans. The group of white musicians led by Stalebread Lacoume in 1897 is the best documented but it may not have included a washboard player. Washboards were frequently used to accompany blues singers, at least one of whom, Washboard Sam (Robert Brown), played a washboard while taking vocal parts. Almost alone among folk instruments the washboard was sometimes used by jazz bands, examples being Floyd Casey's crisp and forceful rhythms on numerous recordings by Clarence Williams, including *Beer Garden Blues* (1933, Voc. 2541), and Jimmy Bertrand's driving accompaniments to Louis Armstrong with Erskine Tate's Vendome Orchestra on *Stomp off, let's go* (1926, Voc. 1027) (*see also* Drum set, §I, 10). In the early 1930s the related groups of the Washboard Rhythm Kings and Washboard Serenaders recorded extensively; on the former's version of *Shoot 'em* (1931, Vic. 22814) the washboard is played by the drummer Jimmy Spencer, who also provides the vocal part. Sometimes a band included two trumpets and three reed instruments, but as the novelty appeal of the instrument declined the washboard returned to the folk idiom of blues. In the postwar years zydeco bands (francophone African-American groups in Louisiana and Texas) frequently used washboards, and washboards have occasionally been employed from the 1940s by traditional revivalist bands; in 1959 the British trombonist Chris Barber organized a reunion session of members of Clarence Williams's Washboard Band under the leadership of Cecil Scott (*Harlem Washboard*, Col. 33SX1232). A later development in zydeco bands, blending urban blues with Louisiana Creole music, was the wearing of a corrugated metal vest, played with thimbles; this variant instrument was introduced by Cleveland Chenier, the brother of the leading zydeco accordionist Clifton Chenier.

BIBLIOGRAPHY

B. Rust: Liner notes, *Clarence Williams Jug and Washboard Band* (Phi. 13653 A-JL, 1962)

P. Oliver: "Jug and Washboard Bands," *Jazz on Record: a Critical Guide to the First 50 Years: 1917–1967*, ed. A. McCarthy and others (London, 1968), 332

T. Zwicky: "I'm Gonna Beat me some Washboard: the Washboard Rhythm Kings and Affiliated Groups, 1930–35," *Sv*, no.19 (1968), 3; no.20 (1968–9), 47; no.22 (1969), 148

J. Broven: *South to Louisiana: The Music of the Cajun Bayous* (Gretna, LA, 1983/*R*1987) [incl. discography]

C. Pou: "Le washboard entre dans le XXIème siècle," *Jazz Dixie/Swing du ragtime au big band*, no.15 (1997), 14

F. Quétier: "Le washboard," *Jazzomaniac*, no.27 [details unknown]; repr. in *Jazz Dixie/Swing du ragtime au big band*, no.17 (1997), 37

J. Vastra: "Art Fell et Peter Gaskel roulent pour la planche: le washboard en France," *Jazz Dixie/Swing du ragtime au big band*, no.17 (1997), 35

PAUL OLIVER

Washboard Rhythm Kings. Recording group. It had no fixed personnel and usually consisted of local musicians from the areas around Camden, New Jersey, and Philadelphia. Regular members were Ben Smith and Cal Wade (saxophones), Eddie Miller or Clarence Profit (piano), Taft Jordan (trumpet), and Teddy Bunn (guitar). As musicians often played several instruments during a session, exact identification is impossible to determine. Jake Fenderson and Leo Watson were among the many singers who recorded with the group. After recording 12 titles for Vocalion as the Alabama Washboard Stompers in 1930–31, the group recorded 20 titles for Victor in 1931 as the Washboard Rhythm Kings. During 1932 an enlarged band recorded 24 titles for Victor and 21 for Vocalion; the following year it recorded for Columbia, Bluebird, and Vocalion, and in 1934–5 it recorded as the Georgia Washboard Stompers for Decca. The large number of the band's recordings made in the years of the Depression reflect changing tastes in music. These were issued under a variety of names, including the Rhythm Kings, the Washboard Rhythm Band, and the Washboard Rhythm Boys. The Washboard Rhythm Kings that recorded for Bluebird in Chicago in November 1935 had no connection with the group.

SELECTED RECORDINGS

Pepper Steak (1932, Vic. 22958); Tiger Rag (1932, Vic. 24059); I Would Do Anything for You/Spider Crawl (1932, Voc. 1734); Sloppy Drunk Blues (1932, Vic. 23380); Dog and Cat/Old Man Blues (1933, Ban. 32978)

BIBLIOGRAPHY

T. Zwicky: "I'm Gonna Beat Me Some Washboard: the Washboard Rhythm Kings and Affiliated Groups, 1930–35," *Sv*, no.19 (1968), 3; no.20 (1968–9), 47; no.22 (1969), 148

J. Evensmo: *History of Jazz Tenor Saxophone: Black Artists*, i: *1917–1934* (Oslo, 1996), 117

MIKE HAZELDINE

Washington, Buck [Ford Lee] (*b* Louisville, KY, 16 Oct 1903; *d* New York, 31 Jan 1955). Pianist, singer, and trumpeter. From around 1912 he worked with John W. Sublett (who took the name John Bubbles) in the comedy and dance act Buck and Bubbles. They performed in shows on Broadway, visited England (1930), toured Europe (1936), and appeared in several films, among them *Calling All Stars* (1937) and *Cabin in the Sky* (1942). Washington also recorded with Louis Armstrong (the duet *Dear Old Southland*, 1930, OK 41454) and Coleman Hawkins (1934), led the band that accompanied Bessie Smith in her last recording session (1933), and recorded as a piano soloist (*Old-fashioned Love*, 1934, Col. 2925D). His only recordings as a trumpeter are those he made privately in 1944 (first issued on untitled album, Ristic SAG). Washington ceased to perform with Bubbles in 1953 and worked with the singer Timmie Rogers in a group led by Jonah Jones (1953-4).

BIBLIOGRAPHY

ChiltonW; *FeatherE*

L. Feather: "Mr. Washington of Buck & Bubbles," *MM*, xii (14 Oct 1936), 2

M. Mezzrow: "Ford Lee 'Buck' Washington," *BHcF*, no.48 (1955), 3

M. Stearns and J. Stearns: *Jazz Dance: the Story of American Vernacular Dance* (New York and London, 1968), 212

J. Simmen: "'Buck & Bubbles': Jazz Dance, Song, Entertainers," *Coda*, x/2 (1971), 6; Fr. trans. as "Un grand chanteur de jazz: Bubbles," *BHcF*, no.216 (1972), 3

H. Rye: "Visiting Firemen, 10: Buck Washington (Buck & Bubbles)," *Sv*, no.114 (1984), 213

HOWARD RYE

Washington, Dinah [Jones, Ruth(a Lee)] (*b* Tuscaloosa, AL, 29 Aug 1924; *d* Detroit, 14 Dec 1963). Singer. According to Ono (2000), her given name was Rutha, not Ruth, as it is commonly published. She grew up in Chicago, where she played piano for and directed her church choir. From the age of 15 she performed alternately in nightclubs as a singer and pianist and in Sallie Martin's gospel choir. She was given the name Dinah Washington by the manager of the Garrick Stage Bar, where she was heard by Lionel Hampton, and subsequently she worked as a member of Hampton's band (1943–6). Having recorded several blues hits in 1943, she enjoyed a successful solo career from 1946. Washington's singing was characterized by high-pitched, penetrating sounds, precise enunciation, contrasts between tender understatement and gospel-inspired intensity, and an entrancing languor. Like Ray Charles, she could rework any type of material. From 1949 to 1955 her rhythm-and-blues, classic blues, pop, and country recordings consistently reached the top ten on the rhythm-and-blues chart in the USA. *What a difference a day makes* (1959) marked her breakthrough into the general pop market, where she obtained several other gold records, some in duet with the singer Brook Benton, before her early death from an accidental overdose of sleeping pills. The Portrait Collection at the New York Public Library holds a number of photographs of Washington.

SELECTED RECORDINGS

As leader: Evil Gal Blues (1943, Key. 605); Trouble in Mind (1951, Mer. 8269); *After Hours with Miss "D"* (1953–4, EmA 36028); *Dinah Washington Sings for Those in Love* (1955, EmA 36011); *The Swingin' Miss "D"* (1956, EmA 36104); *Dinah Washington Sings Fats Waller* (1957, EmA 36119); *Dinah Washington Sings Bessie Smith* (1957–8, EmA 36130); with T. Gibbs: *Newport '58* (1958, EmA 36141); What a difference a day makes (1959, Mer. 71435); with B. Benton: Baby (you got what it takes) (1959, Mer. 71565); *Dinah '62* (1962, Roul. 25170)

As sideman with L. Hampton: Blowtop Blues (1945, Decca 23792)

SELECTED FILMS AND VIDEOS

Basin Street Review (1955); Harlem Jazz Festival (1955); Jazz on a Summer's Day (1960); The Swingin' Singin' Years (1960)

BIBLIOGRAPHY

L. Feather: "Feather's Nest," *DB*, xix/10 (1952), 16

Obituary, S. Tonneay, *Rhythm & Blues Panorama*, no.28 (1964), 5

B. Niquet: "Queen Dinah," *Jh*, no.266 (1970), 20 [discography]

A. Shaw: *Honkers and Shouters: the Golden Years of Rhythm and Blues* (New York, 1978)

S. Harris: *Blues Who's Who: a Biographical Dictionary of Blues Singers* (New Rochelle, NY, 1979/*R*1994)

G. Endress: *Jazz Podium: Musiker über sich selbst* (Stuttgart, Germany, 1980)

L. Feather: *The Jazz Years: Earwitness to an Era* (London and New York, 1986), 183

J. Haskins: *Queen of the Blues: a Biography of Dinah Washington* (New York, 1987) [incl. discography]

M. Jones: *Talking Jazz* (London, 1987/*R*2000), 265

R. Reitz: "Long Live the Queen!: Dinah Washington," *Hot Wire*, vi/3 (1990), 34

G. Giddins: *Faces in the Crowd: Players and Writers* (New York, and Oxford, England, 1992), 87

T. T. Ono: Liner notes: *Queen of the Juke Box "Live" 1948–1955* (Baldwin Street Music 310, 2000)

BK

Washington, Freddie (*b* Houston, *c*1900). Pianist. After moving to California around 1918 he joined Kid Ory in Oakland in 1921, and he took part in the band's pioneering recordings. During the 1920s and 1930s he led his own band and also played with Ed "Montudi" Garland and Paul Howard. In 1944 he made recordings (including *Barney's Bounce/Lulu's Mood*, Cap. 10022) with Zutty Singleton. He remained active into the 1960s. (F. Krieger: "*Society Blues*: zur Geschichte und Analyse der ersten schwarzen Jazz-Schallplattenaufnahmen," *Jf*, xxiv (1992), 99 [incl. transcrs.])

based on *ChiltonW*

Washington, George (*b* Brunswick, GA, 18 Oct 1907). Trombonist and arranger. He grew up in Jacksonville, Florida. After studying at Edward Waters College (in Jacksonville) (1922) he worked locally and in Philadelphia. His first important engagements were with Luckey Roberts, the pianist Arthur Gibbs, and Charlie Johnson in New York during the mid- and late 1920s. He worked with Don Redman in 1931 and the following year became associated with Benny Carter; he recorded with Carter's band under the leadership of Spike Hughes. Thereafter he played with and wrote arrangements for the Mills Blue Rhythm Band (intermittently to 1936; for illustration *see* MILLS BLUE RHYTHM BAND), worked as a staff arranger for Irving Mills, and made recordings with Henry "Red" Allen. Later he played with Fletcher Henderson (*c* December 1936 – May 1937) and Louis Armstrong (mid-1937–1943). Washington then moved to the West Coast, where he worked in 1945 with Horace Henderson and Carter, with whom he recorded. From 1946 he was a member of Johnny Otis's recording bands, and he played with the latter's groups until 1958. After recording in 1947 with Count Basie he led his own band for many years in California and Las Vegas. In 1953 he joined Carter's band for a West Coast tour. Washington was with Joe Darensbourg in 1960, after which he worked as a freelance studio musician and arranger.

SELECTED RECORDINGS

As sideman: Mills Blue Rhythm Band: Jazz Cocktail (1932, Ban. 32608); African Lullaby (1934, Col. 3038D); H. Allen: We're gonna have smooth sailing/Whose honey are you? (1935, Ban. 33355)

BIBLIOGRAPHY

AllenH; *ChiltonW*

HOWARD RYE

Washington, Grover, Jr. (*b* Buffalo, 12 Dec 1943; *d* New York, 17 Dec 1999). Saxophonist. His father played saxophone in a big band in the Buffalo area, and one of his uncles was an alto saxophonist. He began on piano, took up saxophone at the age of ten, and before his teens was already performing in local clubs; when he was 16 he toured with a rhythm-and-blues group. Having played tenor saxophone and electric bass guitar in organ trios (1963 – April 1965) he performed in army bands (May 1965–1967) and then moved to Philadelphia, where he worked mostly with organists, notably Charles Earland and Johnny Hammond. His fine playing on tenor saxophone for Earland led to a series of soul-jazz recordings for several leaders on the Prestige label (1970–71). Washington was engaged to record as a tenor saxophonist with Hank Crawford in 1971, but after the latter failed to arrive for the session he was given the opportunity to make his first recording as a leader; *Inner City Blues*, on which he played alto saxophone, was a huge success. Shortly afterwards he formed a touring band, the personnel of which changed frequently over the years; during the mid-1970s he was also obliged by his recording company to use studio sidemen. *Mister Magic*, which reached no.1 on several charts (1975), was the first of his many albums to win gold or platinum records. Though he worked mainly as a leader for the remainder of his life, he occasionally took part as a guest soloist in recording sessions by others, among them Billy Cobham (1987), Charles Fambrough (*c*1991), and Vanessa Rubin (*c*1993), and in the mid-1990s he recorded and then toured in the quartet Urban Knights with Ramsey Lewis, Victor Bailey, and Omar Hakim.

Washington's repertory included jazz standards of the 1920s to the 1960s, but his strength lay in a blend of jazz and soul music, where he improvised clipped, bluesy melodies over precise, highly syncopated ostinato accompaniments. From the late 1970s he also played flute, and he may be seen, unusually, performing on baritone saxophone in the film *Blues Brothers 2000* (1998).

SELECTED RECORDINGS

As leader: *Inner City Blues* (1971, Kudu 03); *Mister Magic* (1974, Kudu 20); *Live at the Bijou* (*c*1977, Kudu 36–7); *Winelight* (1980, Elek. 6E-305); *Skylarkin'* (*c*1980, Motown 7-933R1); with K. Burrell: *Togethering* (1984, BN 85106); *Then and Now* (*c*1987, Col. OC44296); *All my Tomorrows* (*c*1993, Col. CK64319)

As sideman: C. Earland: *Living Black!* (1970, Prst. 10009); J. Hammond: *What's Goin' On?* (1971, Prst. 10015)

SELECTED FILMS AND VIDEOS

Grover Washington, Jr., in Concert (1981); Newport Jazz '88 (1988); Blues Brothers 2000 (1998)

BIBLIOGRAPHY

H. Mandel: "Grover Washington, Jr.: No Tricks to Mister Magic's Music," *DB*, xlii/13 (1975), 14

S. Bloom: "Grover Washington, Jr.: Class Act of Commercial Jazz," *DB*, xlvi/8 (1979), 12 [incl. discography]

"Grover Washington, Jr.: Evolution of an Artist," *Radio Free Jazz*, xx (1979), July, 10

A. J. Liska: "Grover Washington, Jr.: the Midas Touch," *DB*, l/4 (1983), 14 [incl. discography]

H. Boulware: "Sax Man Grover," *Chicago Tribune* (21 Feb 1990)

F. A. Salamone: "Grover Washington: a Short Talk," *Cadence*, xvi/5 (1990), 5

S. Aiges: "Grover Washington: Getting Respect from Critics at Last," *New Orleans Times-Picayune* (24 Sept 1994)

K. L. Williams: "Prove it: Grover Washington Jr. Flexes Straightahead Chops," *DB*, lxi/9 (1994), 16

Obituaries: T. Kelley, *New York Times* (19 Dec 1999); [A. Shipton,] *The Times* (20 Dec 1999)

<http://www.gwjrmusic.com> (2000)

BK

Washington, Jack [Ronald] (*b* Kansas City, KS, 17 July 1907 or 1910; *d* Oklahoma City, OK, 28 Nov 1964). Baritone and alto saxophonist. His year of birth appears in the jazz literature as 1910, but social security records give 1907. He began his professional career with the pianist Paul Banks in 1926 and made his first recordings the following year with Jesse Stone. He then worked with Bennie Moten (1927–35), Buster Moten (1935), the pianist and tuba player Leslie Sheffield (1935–6), and Count Basie (1936 – November 1943). Following army service Washington rejoined Basie in July 1946, and remained until the pianist disbanded at the beginning of 1950. Thereafter he took various day jobs, but during the 1950s he continued to play regularly with Bobby Knott's band in Oklahoma City.

Although Washington's opportunities as a soloist were limited, particularly in Basie's orchestra (with its emphasis – both in arrangements and recordings – on two tenor saxophonists), he was an exceptionally gifted player. He progressed from emulating Harry Carney to a more fluid and highly expressive style of his own; this is especially noticeable in his recordings with smaller groups, such as Basie's sextet accompanying Jimmy Rushing on *Somebody Stole my Gal*.

For illustrations *see* BASIE, COUNT, FILMS, fig.3, and MOTEN, BENNIE.

SELECTED RECORDINGS

As sideman: B. Moten: New Vine Street Blues (1929, Vic. 23007); C. Basie: Topsy (1937, Decca 1770); *Count Basie at the Famous Door* (1938–9, Jazz Archives 41), incl. Doggin' Around, Indiana; Jive at Five (1939, Decca 2922); Somebody Stole my Gal (1940, Col. 35500); *Count Basie* (1947–50, RCA LPM1112), incl. Lopin'

SELECTED FILMS AND VIDEOS

Air Mail Special (1941); Take Me Back, Baby (1941); Choo Choo Swing [Band Parade] (1943)

BIBLIOGRAPHY

ChiltonW; *FeatherE*; *McCarthyB*; *SheridanCB*

R. Horricks: *Count Basie and his Orchestra: its Music and its Musicians* (London and New York, 1957), 183

FRANK DRIGGS

Washington, Kenny (*b* New York, 29 May 1958). Drummer, brother of Reggie Washington. Devoted to jazz from childhood, he later studied drums with Rudy Collins and percussion at the High School for Music and Arts in New York; while a student he played classical violin for many years. He performed and recorded in various groups led by Lee Konitz (1977–8), played for a brief time with Walter Davis and with various musicians on the Jazzmobile, then worked with Betty Carter (1978–9) and Johnny Griffin (1980); he continued to perform in the 1980s and 1990s with Griffin, with whom he may be seen in the videos *Johnny Griffin at the Village Vanguard* (1981) and *Eddie "Lockjaw" Davis & Johnny Griffin* (filmed *c*1985). In the late 1970s he began working extensively as a freelance musician in New York, playing and recording with Kenny Burrell, Ron Carter, Frank Wess, Milt Jackson, George Coleman, and Cedar Walton. He twice replaced Dannie Richmond in Mingus Dynasty (recording in 1982 and 1987) and he toured and recorded with Dameronia under Don Sickler's leadership (1989). He worked with Tommy Flanagan's trio (*c*1988–9), Hank Jones, Benny Golson, Benny Carter's small groups and big band (1989 into the 1990s), Clark Terry (1990), Greg Abate (1991–2), Dizzy Gillespie (1992), and the Carnegie Hall Jazz Band – with most of whom he recorded.

Although he is reported to have toured with Nnenna Freelon in 1992, Washington prefers to stay in the New York area, where from the mid-1980s into the late 1990s he was a house drummer for Criss Cross; he took part in sessions with Hod O'Brien, Richard Wyands, Michael Weiss, Ralph Lalama, Gary Smulyan, Mike LeDonne, Brian Lynch, Eric Alexander, Mel Rhyne, and many others. He also made a number of recordings for Muse before its demise, notably with James Spaulding, Buck Hill, Wallace Roney, and Teddy Edwards and Houston Person. During this same period he recorded as a freelance for other labels, with Jean Toussaint (1987), Walter Davis, Bobby Watson, and Phil Woods (all 1988), Ralph Moore (1988, 1990), Jim McNeely and Larry Willis (both in Copenhagen, 1989), Joshua Breakstone (1989, 1990), Mulgrew Miller, Christian Escoudé, Michal Urbaniak, and Milt Jackson (all 1990), George Cables (1991), Konitz (1992), Ronnie Mathews and Benny Green (both 1994), Craig Bailey (1995), Louis Smith (*c*1996), and Person (*c*1997). In April 1994 he performed in the concert celebrating the Verve label's fiftieth anniversary, and he may be seen on the resulting video released later that same year, *Carnegie Hall Salutes the Jazz Masters*. In 1998 he worked with Lou Donaldson's group, and in 1999 he toured with Flora Purim. A hard-bop revivalist who is also comfortable in delicate trios or a big-band swing setting, Washington has distilled and combined the best elements from the work of earlier drummers and innovators to form his own style, which is characterized by the taste and clarity of his execution. Having inherited his father's passion for record collecting and jazz history, he has developed a second career as a disc jockey at the jazz station WBGO in Newark, New Jersey.

SELECTED RECORDINGS

As sideman: B. Carter: *The Audience with Betty Carter* (1979, Bet-Car 1003); J. Griffin: *Call it Whachawana* (1983, Gal. 5146); M. LeDonne: *'Bout Time* (1988, Criss Cross 1033); R. Moore: *Images* (1988, Landmark 1520-2); T. Flanagan: *Jazz Poet* (1989, Tim. 301); J. Breakstone: *Self-portrait in Swing* (1989, Cont. 14050); J. Spaulding: *Brilliant Corners* (1989, Muse 5369); M. LeDonne: *The Feeling of Jazz* (1990, Criss Cross 1041); J. Griffin: *Dance of Passion* (1992, Ant. 512604-2); L. Konitz: *Jazz Nocturne* (1992, Evidence 22085); T. Edwards and H. Person: *Horn to Horn* (1994, Muse 5540)

BIBLIOGRAPHY

B. Korall: "Up and Coming," *MD*, ix/4 (1985), 30

K. Micallef: "Kenny Washington: Manhattan's Underground Jazz Master," *MD*, xv/6 (1991), 30

L. Birnbaum: "First Inspirations," *DB*, lix/11 (1992), 26

H. Mandel: "Remembering Dizzy: All Dizzy's Children," *DB*, lx/4 (1993), 24

M. Bourne: "All the Young Dudes," *DB*, lxi/12 (1994), 20

K. Micallef: "Kenny Washington: his Big Band Stand," *JT*, xxiv/11 (1994), 61

A. Lewis and L. Lewis: "Kenny Washington: Interview," *Cadence*, xxi/4 (1995), 5

CHUCK BRAMAN/BK

Washington, Leon [Diamond] (*b* Jackson, MS, 27 June 1909; *d* ?Chicago, Feb 1973). Tenor saxophonist and clarinetist. His family moved in 1912 to Chicago, where he took up clarinet and then tenor saxophone. He worked with Zinky Cohn in Habor Springs, Michigan (1926), and performed in Chicago before touring with the trumpeter Bernie Young and his Creolians (1931–3). Later he played with Carroll Dickerson (1934–5) and toured with the big bands of Louis Armstrong (June–October 1935) and Fats Waller. After returning to Chicago (1936) he performed in a group with the trumpeter Jimmy Cobb at the Annex Café and served as a sideman in Earl Hines's band (February 1937 – late 1938). From 1938 to either 1963 or 1968 (sources disagree as to the correct date) Washington was a member of Red Saunders's band; he performed with the group throughout its 18-year residency at the Club De Lisa (1940–58) and at the Regal Theater, and he took part in dozens of jazz and rhythm-and-blues sessions with Saunders and with others; he may be heard with Saunders on *Hallelujah/Red's Boogie Woogie* (1945, Savoy 596). The social security death index provides the month and year of his death. (*ChiltonW*)

ARMIN BÜTTNER

Washington, Mack [William; McWashington, Willie] (*b* Kansas City, MO, 1908; *d* Kansas City, 1 Oct 1938). From 1926 he performed and made recordings with Bennie Moten (for illustration *see* MOTEN, BENNIE), and in 1936 he joined Count Basie at the Reno Club, Kansas City. After being replaced by Jo Jones he worked with Buster Smith.

SELECTED RECORDINGS

(all recorded for Victor)

As sideman with B. Moten: Missouri Wobble (1926, 20422); Moten Stomp (1927, 20955) South (1928, 38021); Terrific Stomp (1929, 38081); Loose like a Goose (1929, 38123); Toby (1932, 23384)

BIBLIOGRAPHY

ChiltonB; *McCarthyB*; *SheridanCB*

HOWARD RYE

Washington, Peter (Mark) (*b* Los Angeles, 28 Aug 1964). Double bass player. He took up classical double bass in his early teens but also played electric bass guitar and guitar in local rock groups. While studying English at the University of California (1982–6) he developed an interest in jazz. He then worked as a freelance in the San Francisco Bay area, performing with John Handy, Bobby Hutcherson, Harold

Land, Frank Morgan, Ernestine Anderson, Ernie Andrews, Chris Connor, and others. In 1986 he moved to New York, where he played with Art Blakey's Jazz Messengers (April 1986 – September 1988), Jim Snidero (*c*1987–91), Ralph Moore (*c*1988–93), the trios of Michael Weiss (1989–94) and Tommy Flanagan (from 1991), Lew Tabackin (*c*1992–6), Javon Jackson and Billy Drummond (both from 1993), and David Hazeltine's trio (from 1995). In 1995 he was a founding member of the cooperative group One for All, and in 1997 he first toured and recorded in the ghost band The Jazz Messengers: the Legacy of Art Blakey, under the direction of Benny Golson. He also worked in the Carnegie Hall Jazz Band. In 1998 he toured in the quartet New York Jazz Group with David Sanchez, Renee Rosnes, and Drummond. From the late 1980s Washington appeared extensively as a freelance with, among others, Golson (recording in 1989 and 1995), Milt Jackson, Mingus Dynasty, Teddy Edwards, Hank Jones, Randy Brecker, Geoff Keezer (recording in 1990), Toshiko Akiyoshi's orchestra (at Carnegie Hall), Hutcherson and Mulgrew Miller (recording with these last three in 1991), Tom Harrell (recording in 1991 and 1993), Dizzy Gillespie (touring and recording in the trumpeter's group Diamond Jubilee in 1992), and Kenny Burrell (recording at the Village Vanguard in 1993).

Washington is seemingly able to do everything expected of the best double bass players in modern jazz styles, a task he carries out with such aplomb that time and again reviewers call attention to his contribution (bass players are frequently accorded no mention by critics). As of the late 1990s he had taken part in more than 140 recording sessions (approximately one-quarter of which were for Criss Cross), notably with Steve Turre (1987), Benny Green and Robin Eubanks (both 1988), Donald Byrd (1989), Brian Lynch (1989, 1995), Lewis Nash, Cecil Brooks III, Charles Davis, and Barry Harris (all 1990), Ralph Lalama and John Swana (both 1990, 1995), Stephen Scott, Charlie Sepulveda, and George Cables (all 1991), Tom Williams (1991, 1993), Jimmy Ponder (1991, 1994), Ricky Ford (1992), Rob Bargad (1992–3), Eric Alexander (1992, 1994), Walt Weiskopf (1992, 1995), Stanley Cowell, Valery Ponomarev, and Sanchez (all 1993), Ronald Muldrow (1993–4), Mike LeDonne (1993, 1998), David "Fathead" Newman, Jesse Davis, Rob Schneiderman, Charles McPherson, Russell Gunn, Greg Gisbert, and Dado Moroni (all 1994), Rosnes, Bobby Broom, and Jonny King (all 1995), Richard Wyands (1995, 1996), Andy LaVerne, Mark Elf, and Claire Martin (all 1996), Tim Hagans and Marcus Printup, Red Holloway, Kenny Drew, Jr., Rich Perry, Conrad Herwig, and Bill Charlap (all 1997), Phil Woods (1998), Swana and Magnarelli (1998), and Andy Bey, Byron Stripling, and the alto saxophonist Andy Fusco (all *c*1998). He may be seen performing in David Berger's group in the video *The Harlem Nutcracker* (*c*1996).

SELECTED RECORDINGS

As sideman: R. Moore: *Furthermore* (1990, Landmark 1526-2); G. Keezer: *Here and Now* (1990, BN B21Z-99691); Walter Bishop, Jr.: *What's New* (1990, DIW 605); M. Miller: *Time and Again* (1991, Landmark 1532-2); L. Tabackin: *I'll Be Seeing You* (1992, Conc. 4528); Grant Stewart: *Downtown Sounds* (1992, Criss Cross 1085); M. LeDonne: *Soulmates* (1993, Criss Cross 1074); T. Flanagan: *Lady Be Good ... for Ella* (1993, Verve 314-521617-2); E. Alexander: *Full Range* (1994, Criss Cross 1098); J. Ponder: *Something to Ponder* (1994, Muse 5541); D. Hazeltine: *4 Flights Up* (1995, Sharp Nine 1002); B. Drummond: *Dubai* (1995, Criss Cross 1120); A. LaVerne: *Bud's Beautiful* (1996, Ste. 31399); T. Flanagan: *Sea Changes* (1996, Evidence 22191); D. Hazeltine: *The Classic Trio* (1996, Sharp Nine 1005); Jazz Messengers: the Legacy of Art Blakey: *Live at the Iridium* (1997, Telarc 83407); M. LeDonne: *To Each his Own* (1998, Double-Time 135)

BIBLIOGRAPHY

Feather–GitlerBEJ

GK

Washington, Reggie [Reginald Reuben] (*b* New York, 28 July 1962). Electric bass guitarist, brother of Kenny Washington. At the age of seven he performed on congas in the Washington Brothers, a group with his brother Kenny. He began to learn cello when he was eight and later took up bass, beginning on electric bass guitar at the age of ten and double bass when he was 13; his style was heavily influenced by both Melvin Gibbs on the electric instrument and Sam Jones on the acoustic bass. Washington's first important job was with Chico Hamilton, whom he joined in 1982; in 1987 he was a founding member of Hamilton's group Euphoria, with which he toured Europe and recorded in 1990. In the mid-1980s he worked regularly in Ronald Shannon Jackson's Decoding Society (recording in 1986 at the Caravan of Dreams in Fort Worth), then performed with Carlos Ward before joining Jean-Paul Bourelly (1987), with whom he has continued to play into the new century. He also worked with the electric keyboard player and pianist Clyde Criner (*c* late 1980s).

Around 1990 Washington began working with Steve Coleman, initially in the latter's ensemble Five Elements, and later in the Mystic Rhythm Society, Metrics, and the Council of Balance big band, as well as in Reflex, a trio comprising Coleman, Washington, and Gene Lake; he stopped performing with Coleman late in 1996, but continued to record with the saxophonist into the late 1990s. In the mid-1990s he played both double bass and electric bass guitar in Branford Marsalis's hip-hop-oriented band Buckshot LeFonque. On the electric instrument he also played with Marvin "Smitty" Smith (1991–2), Steps Ahead (*c*1993), Andy Milne (recording in 1997), Don Byron's group Existential Dread (from 1997), Oliver Lake's Steel Quartet (alongside the steel drum player Lyndon Achee; from 1999), the saxophonist Rob Miller, and the singer Marc Ledford. He toured with Joseph Bowie in the ensemble Defunkt Stripped (1998–9), and recorded with Cassandra Wilson (1990), Ronnie Cuber (1993), Greg Osby (mid-1990s), and Uri Caine (*c*1999). In addition Washington has appeared as a leader, notably of Reuben's Bass Choir, comprising three or four bass players and a drummer, and of a small group including Gene Lake and David Gilmore. In 2001 he was working regularly with Bourelly, Oliver Lake, the saxophonist Jay Rodriguez, and the contemporary rhythm-and-blues singer and electric bass guitarist Me'Shell Ndegéocello.

SELECTED RECORDINGS

As sideman: C. Wilson: *She who Weeps* (1990, JMT 834443-2); C. Hamilton: *Arroyo* (1990, SN 121241-2); M-Base Collective: *Anatomy of a Groove* (1991–2, DIW 864); S. Coleman: *The Tao of Mad Phat (Fringe Zones)* (1993, Novus 63160-2); *Curves of Life* (1995, Novus 31693-2); A. Milne: *Forward to Get Back* (1997, d'Note 2005); S. Coleman: *Genesis & the Opening of the Way* (1997, RCA 2152934-2); O. Lake: *Kinda' Up* (1999, Justin Time 136)

BIBLIOGRAPHY

R. Grosman: "Five Elements: Coleman Dynasty," *Jh*, no.525 (1995), 10
<http://www.gitarrebass.de/magazine/9910/reggie.htm> (2001)

GK

Washington, Steve (*b* Philadelphia, *c*1900; *d* Boston, *c* Jan 1936). Banjoist and singer. From 1931 he worked with several bands in Pennsylvania, and in the early 1930s he recorded as a banjoist, singer, guitarist, mandolin player, and occasional clarinetist with the Washboard Rhythm Kings (1931-3). After working as a soloist in cabarets he recorded as a leader (1933), accompanied by Benny Goodman, Joe Venuti, and others, and with the Georgia Washboard Stompers (1934, 1935). From 1934 until his death from pneumonia he was a principal soloist with the Sunset Royal Orchestra, led by the pianist Ace Harris.

SELECTED RECORDINGS

As sideman: Chicago Hot Five: Star Dust/You can't stop me from loving you (1931, Vic. 23285); Washboard Rhythm Kings: Pepper Steak (1932, Vic. 22958); Sentimental Gentleman from Georgia/It don't mean a thing if it ain't got that swing (1932, Voc. 1724); The Scat Song (1932, Voc. 1725); Ash Man Crawl (1932, Vic. 23367) [cl]; Say it isn't so (1932, Vic. 23364)

BIBLIOGRAPHY

ChiltonW

T. Zwicky: "I'm Gonna Beat Me Some Washboard: the Washboard Rhythm Kings and Affiliated Groups (1930–35)," *Sv*, no.19 (1968), 3; no.20 (1968–9), 47; no.22 (1969), 148 [incl. discography])

HOWARD RYE

Washingtonians. Group formed in 1923 by Elmer Snowden. Led by Duke Ellington from the winter of the following year, its other members were the trumpeter Bubber Miley, the trombonist Charlie Irvis (later replaced by Tricky Sam Nanton), the saxophonist Otto Hardwick, the banjoist Fred Guy (who replaced Snowden in spring 1925), and the drummer Sonny Greer. Between 1923 and 1927 the group was based at the Hollywood Club (renamed the Kentucky Club in 1924), and on 4 December 1927, when Ellington enlarged the band to begin appearing at the Cotton Club, the name Washingtonians was abandoned, although it continued to appear until 1929 on recordings the orchestra made for Brunswick, Cameo, and Harmony. (M. Tucker: *Ellington: the Early Years*, Oxford, England, Urbana, IL, and Chicago, 1991)

For recordings *see* Ellington, Duke.

MARK TUCKER

Wasilewski, Marcin (*b* Sławno, Poland, 11 Nov 1975). Polish pianist. He graduated in piano from the high school of music in Koszalin (1994) and in jazz piano from the academy of music in Katowice (1999). In 1990, while at the former institution, he formed the Simple Acoustic Trio with his fellow students Sławek Kurkiewicz on double bass and Michał Miśkiewicz on drums. The group performed at a festival in France in 1993 and later that same year became the rhythm section accompanying Tomasz Stańko, with whom it has toured internationally and recorded into the new century. The trio has also accompanied Tomasz Szukalski, Michal Urbaniak, Janusz Muniak, and Henryk Miśkiewicz, and it has served as a house band at the Jazz Jamboree and at the Warsaw Summer Jazz Days, where it has worked with numerous other leading soloists.

SELECTED RECORDINGS

As leader of Simple Acoustic Trio: *Komeda* (1995, Gowi 22); *Simple Acoustic Trio* (1996, Hilargy 091)

As sideman with T. Stańko: *Balladyna-Theatre Play Compositions* (1994, Gowi 16)

ADAM CEGIELSKI, BK

Waso. Belgian gypsy string band. It was formed in the early 1970s from a larger gypsy ensemble led by the multi-instrumentalist Piotto (Limberger), whose son Vivi Limberger became the group's rhythm guitarist; the other members were the double bass player Michel Verstraeten and the virtuoso guitarist Fapy Lafertin. In the late 1970s the leadership was taken over by Koen de Cauter, who played clarinet, saxophone, and solo acoustic guitar; he began to concentrate on guitar in 1981, and Lafertin's place was taken by the British saxophonist Bill Greenow. Though it continued to record until at least 1995, the group ceased to perform regularly during the early 1990s, and by the end of the decade both Limberger and De Cauter were focusing on their respective family bands. The group's playing is an engaging blend of string-band music in the style of the

Duke Ellington's Washingtonians, New York, 1925: (left to right) Sonny Greer (drums), Charlie Irvis (trombone), Bubber Miley (trumpet), Elmer Snowden (banjo), Otto Hardwick (saxophone), and Ellington (piano)

Quintette du Hot Club de France and Hungarian and Romany folk idioms. A typical recording is *Waso Live in Laren* (1980, Pol. 2925111).

BIBLIOGRAPHY

I. Cruickshank: *The Guitar Style of Django Reinhardt and the Gypsies* (Woodcote, nr Reading, England, 1982, rev. and enlarged 2/1985)

R. Pernet: *Belgian Jazz Discography (1897–1999)* (Brussels, 1999)

ALYN SHIPTON

Watanabe, Fumio (*b* Tochigi, Japan, 29 Dec 1938). Japanese drummer, brother of Sadao Watanabe. He started singing at clubs in 1955, then changed to drums and made his professional début with Shungo Sawada's group in 1957. Later he joined, among others, Masao Yagi's trio and the quartet led by the tenor saxophonist Kazunori Takeda, worked with his brother's group (1968–9, 1973) and the trios led by Takehiro Honda (1970) and Yosuke Yamashita (1972), and played with David Izenzon in Ornette Coleman's trio (1967, in Tokyo). Watanabe led his own quintet and the trio Big Bird (consisting of Tsuyoshi Yamamoto and the double bass player Tsutomu Okada) from 1976. In 1995 he performed with Junior Mance and Barry Harris.

SELECTED RECORDINGS

As leader: *Fumio* (1979, Better Days YX7592ND); *Groovin' High* (1982, Union VLP5506)

As sideman: S. Watanabe and C. Mariano: *Iberian Waltz* (1968, Col.–Tact XMS10012); S. Watanabe: *Dedicated to Charlie Parker* (1969, Col.–Tact XMS10018); T. Honda: *This is Honda* (1972, Trio PA7005); Tomoki Takahashi: *Make Someone Happy* (1997, Aketa's Disc 67)

KAZUNORI SUGIYAMA

Watanabe, Kazumi (*b* Tokyo, 14 Oct 1953). Japanese guitarist and leader. He took piano lessons at the age of eight, studied guitar with Sadanori Nakamure at the Yamaha Music School in Tokyo when he was 12, and performed and recorded professionally while still in his teens. After working in groups led by Isao Suzuki, Masaru Imada, the alto saxophonist Yoshio Otomo, the alto and soprano saxophonist Hidefumi Toki, and, most importantly, Sadao Watanabe, he played jazz-rock from the mid-1970s and formed the successful group Kylyn in 1979. That same year he toured the world as a guest soloist with the Japanese pop group Yellow Magic Orchestra, and in the early 1980s he took a similar role with Steps (1982), the Brecker Brothers, and Jaco Pastorius's band Word of Mouth (1983). In 1983 he formed the Mobo Band, with the saxophonist Mitsuru Sawamura, the pianist Ichiko Hashimoto, the electric bass guitarist Gregg Lee, the drummer Shuichi Murakami, and Kiyohiko Senba; with the band he played with several American musicians and performed frequently in New York. Thereafter he continued to tour in the USA and Europe and formed a trio in which he played both electric guitar and guitar synthesizer. Watanabe toured Asia in 1988, performed at the Montreux Jazz Festival in 1989, and in 1990 presented a musical, *Django 1953* (devoted to Django Reinhardt's legacy), and toured with Yosuke Yamashita. He has composed and arranged jazz and classical pieces for unaccompanied guitar.

SELECTED RECORDINGS

(recorded for Polydor–Domo unless otherwise indicated)

Infinite (1971, Express ETJ60001); *Endless Way* (1975, Col. YQ7511); *Milky Shade* (1976, Tei.–Union GU5003); *Olives Step* (1977, Col.–Better Days YX7580); *Kylyn* (1979, Col.–Better Days YX7595); *Tochika* (1980, Col. YX7265); *Dogatana* (1981, Col.–Better Days YF7037); *Mobo* (1983, Trio–Domo AW 20008-7); *Mobo Splashes* (1985, H33P20050); *Spice of Life* (1987, H33P+20145); *Kilo Watt* (1989, 20348); *Romanesque* (1990, 2433); *Resonance Vox* (1994, 1389); *Es prit* (1996, 1346); *One for All* (1999, 1451)

BIBLIOGRAPHY

Feather–Gitler '70s

J. Ferguson: "Fusion Virtuoso: Kazumi Watanabe," *GP*, xx/4 (1986), 12 [incl. discography]

B. Riedinger: "Kazumi Watanabe," *JT* (1988), Nov, 10

D. Heckman: "Watanabe: Point Man for Japan's Fusion Foray in US," *Los Angeles Times* (21 Oct 1989)

B. Milkowski: "Profile: Kazumi Watanabe," *DB*, lvii/5 (1990), 54

<http://www.isa.utl/pt/HCP/outrosmusicos.html> (2000)

YOZO IWANAMI/KAZUNORI SUGIYAMA, BK

Watanabe, Sadao (*b* Utsunomiya, Japan, 1 Feb 1933). Japanese alto and soprano saxophonist, flutist, leader, and educator, brother of Fumio Watanabe. His father was a professional musician who played *biwa* and sang. Watanabe was attracted to jazz at an early age and learned to play clarinet in high school. In 1951 he moved to Tokyo, where he changed to alto saoxphone and in 1953 began flute studies with Ririko Hayashi of the Tokyo Philharmonic Orchestra. He also joined Toshiko Akiyoshi's Cozy Quartet, and in 1956, when Akiyoshi went to the USA, took over leadership of the group. From 1962 to 1965 he attended the Berklee School of Music and played and wrote arrangements for the school's Jazz in the Classroom series. While in the USA he worked with Gary McFarland, Chico Hamilton, and Gábor Szabó (1965). After returning to Tokyo, Watanabe was appointed director of the new Yamaha Institute of Popular Music, whose curriculum and teaching methods were modeled after those of Berklee. From 1966 he presented concerts in Tokyo and toured internationally with his own quartet, which performed a repertory of bop, Brazilian music, jazz-rock, soul, and pop music. He recorded in New York with Chick Corea (1970) and in Tokyo with the Galaxy All Stars (1978); he also made more than 70 albums as a leader. In 1976 he became the first jazz musician to receive the annual Grand Prix Award from his government's cultural agency, and in 1995 he received an honorary doctorate from Berklee. Having made numerous visits to Africa from the 1970s, and having incorporated African music and instruments into his performances, Watanabe is believed to be the first major Japanese jazz musician to have performed in South Africa (early in 1992, after the country's political revolution). He remained busy touring and recording into the new century, and also maintained a separate career publishing several books of photographs. Watanabe plays with a round, polished timbre and adds growls for expressive effect.

SELECTED RECORDINGS

As leader: with C. Corea: *Round Trip* (1970, Van. 79344); *I'm Old Fashioned* (1976, EW 8037); *My Dear Life* (1977, FDisk VIJ6001); *Bird of Paradise* (1977, FDisk 6017); *California Shower* (1978, FDisk VIJ6023); *Fill up the Night* (1983, WEA 32XD341); *Rendezvous* (1984, WEA 4323); *Parker's Mood* (1985, WEA 32XD355); *Birds of Passage* (1987, WEA 32XD810); *Elis* (1988, WEA 25P2-2143); *Sweet Deal* (1992, WEA 4400); *In Tempo* (1994, Fun House 2177); *Go Straight ahead 'n' Make a Left* (1997, Verve 1373); *Remembrance* (1999, Verve 1446)

As sideman: C. Hamilton: on *El Chico* (1965, Imp. 9201), Strange; Galaxy All Stars: on *Live Under the Sky* (1978, Gal. 95001), Confirmation, I'll remember April

BIBLIOGRAPHY

M. E. Lash: "Japan's First Jazz School," *DB*, xxxvi/10 (1969), 40

L. Feather: "Profile: Sadao Watanabe," *DB*, xliv/10 (1977), 39

——: "Sadao Watanabe: Back on the Track," *JT* (1984), Jan, 7

B. Joyeux: "Gros plan: Sadao Watanabe," *Jm*, no.356 (1986), 41

G. Kalbacher: "Sadao Watanabe's Bop/Pop Chops," *DB*, liv/1 (1987), 19 [incl. discography]

E. Forrester: "Sadao Watanabe," *Windplayer*, v/4 (1988), 10

J. D'Souza: "Sadao Watanabe: Moving with the Times," *JF* [intl edn], no.124 (1990), 24
E. Tiegel: "Profile: Sadao Watanabe," *Jazziz*, xii/10 (1995), 46 [incl. discography]

KAZUNORI SUGIYAMA, BK

Waterland. Record company and label founded in 1975 by LOEK DIKKER.

Waters, Benny [Benjamin] (*b* Brighton, MD, 23 Jan 1902; *d* Columbia, MD, 11 Aug 1998). Tenor, soprano, and alto saxophonist, clarinetist, and arranger. He played piano and reed instruments as a child and first worked with Charlie Miller (1918–21). He studied at the New England Conservatory and subsequently became a teacher; among his pupils was Harry Carney. While playing and writing arrangements for Charlie Johnson (1926–31) he recorded with King Oliver and Clarence Williams. Despite his claim to have worked for three years with Fletcher Henderson, he left the group in 1935 after about six months and rejoined Johnson (1936–7). He then performed and recorded with Hot Lips Page (1938, 1941), Claude Hopkins (1940–41), and Jimmie Lunceford (1942). After leading his own band for four years he joined Roy Milton's rhythm-and-blues group. He played New Orleans jazz with Jimmy Archey from 1949, and when the group toured Europe he decided to stay; he settled eventually in Paris, where, until the end of the 1960s, he worked at the club La Cigale. He may be seen in the film documentary *Premier festival européen de jazz* (1954). He toured extensively in Europe in the 1970s and 1980s, playing at many festivals as well as recording, and also worked in New York during several brief visits early in the 1980s. In October 1991 he left Paris to live in New York, but he continued to tour internationally in the late 1990s, becoming quite literally the elder statesman of jazz. In New York he celebrated his 95th birthday with a three-night stand at Birdland and his 96th with a series of concerts at the Jazz Standard. From 1994 he was a member of the Statesmen of Jazz, and late that year he appeared in the group's eponymous video. He toured France and Germany in 1997, and, with the Statesmen of Jazz, made his first visit to Japan in September of that year.

Waters was principally a tenor saxophonist and had a big tone reminiscent of that of Coleman Hawkins. He was also a fine blues clarinetist and an excellent singer. After having moved freely among his various instruments for decades, in the 1990s he concentrated on playing alto saxophone.

Oral history material in *NjR* (JOHP), *NjR*; video oral history material in *NCH* (HCJA).

SELECTED RECORDINGS

As leader: *Benny Waters and Traditional Jazz Studio, Prague* (1976, I giganti del jazz 9); *When You're Smiling* (1980, Hep 2010); *On the Sunny Side of the Street* (1981, JSP 1027); *From Paradise (Small's) to Shangri-La* (1987, Muse 1987); *Swingin' Again* (1993, Jazz Point 1037)

As sideman: H. L. Page: If I were you/Small Fry (1938, Bb 7684); R. Milton: Sympathetic Blues/The Hucklebuck (1949, Specialty 328); on *Roy Milton*, iii: *Blowin' with Roy* (1947–53, Specialty 7060), Blowin' with Roy (1950); Great Traditionalists in Europe: *The Great Traditionalists in Europe* (1969, MPS 15228)

BIBLIOGRAPHY

AllenH; *McCarthyB*
P. Vacher: "La Cigale 1963," *JM*, ix/11 (1964), 10
C. Roby: "Benny Waters avec jazz hot," *Pieces of Jazz*, no.4 (1968), 29
P. Vacher: "Benny Waters," *JM*, no.169 (1969), 5
A. Stevens: "Waters: 73 and Still Swinging," *MM* (26 April 1975), 60
R. Baggenaes: "Benny Waters," *Coda*, no.151 (1976), 8
D. Tarrant and R. Cooper: "Benny Waters Discography," *Journal of Jazz Discography*, no.2 (1977), 11; no.3 (1978), 2
M. Jones: "Cool Blues Drive," *MM* (18 Nov 1978), 62
P. Vacher: "The Peripatetic Benny Waters," *JJI*, xxxiii/7 (1980), 11
B. Osgood: "Benny Waters: the First 80 Years," *MR*, x/2 (1982), 6
B. Waters: *The Key to a Jazzy Life* (n.p. [Toulouse], n.d. [1985])
C. Deffaa: "No Still Waters Here," *MR*, xv/10 (1988), 13; rev. and expanded in *Voices of the Jazz Age: Portraits of Eight Vintage Jazzmen* (Wheatley, Oxford, England, Urbana, IL, and Chicago, 1990), 28
M. Joyce: "Benny Waters, Jazz Birthday Boy," *Washington Post* (10 Jan 1992)
"Benny Waters Still Swingin'," *JP*, xliii/4 (1994), 15
M. Bourne: "Riffs: Waters Plays on at 95," *DB*, lxiv/5 (1997), 12
H. O'Neal: *Les fantômes de Harlem: l'histoire du quartier mythique de jazz* (Levallois-Perret, France, 1997)
B. Bernotas: "Benny Waters," *Saxophone Journal*, xxii/5 (1998), 24
Obituaries: B. Ratliff, *New York Times* (13 Aug 1998); B. Barnes, *Washington Post* (14 Aug 1998); A.V[asset], *BHcF*, no.475 (1998), 26
A. Zimmerman: "A Legend Passes on," *IAJRC Journal*, xxxi/4 (1998), 29

REG COOPER/BK

Waters, [née Howard], **Ethel** (*b* Chester, PA, 31 Oct 1896; *d* Chatsworth, CA, 1 Sept 1977). Singer. She grew up in the Philadelphia area, where she came more strongly under the influence of white vaudeville singers, such as Nora Bayes and Fanny Brice, than did her southern contemporaries. Early in her career she sang "coon" songs, and became an outstanding example of the group of black singers known as "cake-walking babies" to distinguish them from southern classic blues singers such as Ma Rainey and Bessie Smith. Some of her performances from the mid-1920s (she began recording in 1921) foreshadow the scat-singing devices later developed by Louis Armstrong and Ella Fitzgerald, and the film *On with the Show* (1929) shows her unambiguously as a jazz singer. Later, in the 1930s, Waters found the mainstream of popular music, including jazz, congenial, and brought to it a combination of tragedy (in Harold Arlen's *Stormy Weather*, 1933) and comedy (in H. I. Marshall's *You can't stop me from loving you*, 1931) which, in its range, was unsurpassed by any other popular singer. Among the fine jazz instrumentalists who accompanied her in recording sessions were Fletcher Henderson (1921–6), Joe Smith (1922, 1924–7), Coleman Hawkins (1925), James P. Johnson and Clarence Williams (both 1928), Duke Ellington (1932), and Benny Carter (1939). From the late 1930s she began appearing on the stage, and her acting career eventually eclipsed her accomplishments as a singer in the public eye (for illustration *see* FILMS, fig.3), but she may be seen as a jazz singer in the films *Bubbling Over* (1934) and *Stage Door Canteen* (1943), the latter with Count Basie and his Orchestra.

Waters was the first black entertainer to move successfully from the vaudeville and nightclub circuits to what Blacks called "the white time" (the West Indian Bert Williams had done this earlier in the *Ziegfield Follies*, but in blackface). Her vocal resources were adequate though unexceptional, but this shortcoming was mitigated by an innate theatrical flair that enabled her to project the character and situation of every song she performed. The early recordings of Mildred Bailey, Lee Wiley, and Connee Boswell clearly reflect a debt to Waters, and most other popular singers of the time came under her influence to some degree. From 1960 to 1975 Waters toured with the evangelist Billy Graham, singing with less vocal prowess than before but with an undiminished ability to characterize her material.

SELECTED RECORDINGS

Kind Lovin' Blues (1922, Black Swan 14117); Go back where you stayed last night (1925, Col. 14093D); Tell 'em 'bout me/I've found a new baby (1925–6, Col. 561D); I can't give you anything but love (1932, Bruns. 6517); Stormy Weather (1933, Bruns. 6564); Dinah (1934, Decca 234); Stop myself from worryin' over you (1939, Bb 11284)

BIBLIOGRAPHY

C. Van Vetchen: "Negro 'Blues' Singers: an Appreciation of Three Coloured Artists who Excel in an Unusual and Native Medium," *Vanity Fair*, xxvi/1 (1926), 67
E. Waters and C. Samuels: *His Eye is on the Sparrow* (New York and London, 1951/*R*1992) [autobiography]
"Ethel Waters – Her Radio Bow – 1922," *Record Research*, i/2 (1955), 10
C. Ellis: "Ethel Waters: Jazz Singer," *Sv*, no.22 (1969), 128
J. Nelson: "Ethel Waters on Record," *Coda*, x/1 (1971), 2
H. Panassié: "Ethel Waters," *BHcF*, no.207 (1971), 3
E. Waters [and C. Samuels]: *To me it's Wonderful* (New York and elsewhere, 1972) [autobiography]
H. Pleasants: *The Great American Popular Singers* (New York 1974)
——: "Happy Birthday, Ethel Waters," *Stereo Review*, xxxvii/4 (1976), 119
S. Harris: *Blues Who's Who: a Biographical Dictionary of Blues Singers* (New Rochelle, NY, 1979/*R*1994)

HENRY PLEASANTS/BK

Waters, Monty [Monville Charles] (*b* Modesto, CA, 14 April 1938). Alto saxophonist. He received his first lessons on piano from his mother and an aunt before studying the same instrument and saxophone with a private teacher. In San Francisco he co-led a big band with Dewey Redman and Art "Shaki" Lewis and then worked with Jon Hendricks (1965–8); he also played with King Pleasure and Miles Davis. After moving in 1968 to New York with Hendricks he performed with, among others, Elvin Jones, Joe Lee Wilson, Philly Joe Jones, George Coleman, and Woody Shaw; he recorded with Wilson (1975), Errol Parker (1976–80), Billy Higgins (1979), and Charli Persip (1980, 1984), and a good example of his playing may be heard on Higgins's album *The Soldier* (1979, Tim. 145). Later Waters was based in Europe, where he performed as a guest soloist with Götz Tangerding's trio (*c*1990) and recorded as a sideman with Marty Cook (1990) and as the leader of several hard-bop ensembles (1991, 1996, 1997). In 1995 he began performing jazz and blues as a singer and an alto saxophonist in a duo with the German guitarist Titus Waldenfels; in 1999 in Slovakia they recorded both in their duo and with a group led by the violinist L'ubo Šamo. (*Feather–Gitler '70s*)

BK

Watkins, Derek (Roy) (*b* Reading, England, 2 March 1945). English trumpeter, flugelhorn player, and cornetist. His father, the brass player and dance-band leader George Watkins, taught him to play cornet. From the age of six he performed with the Spring Gardens Brass Band, and as a teenager he appeared with his father's band at the Majestic Ballroom in Reading. From 1963 to 1965 he worked with the bandleader Jack Dorsey at the Astoria Ballroom in London, and during the remainder of the 1960s he played with, among others, Ted Heath, John Dankworth, Harry South's big band, Tubby Hayes, Kenny Wheeler, Maynard Ferguson, Stan Tracey, Mike Gibbs, a band led by Bobby Lamb and the trombonist Ray Premru, the Clarke–Boland Big Band, and Neil Ardley. In the 1970s he toured Europe and recorded in Stockholm with Benny Goodman (1970–71) and recorded with various studio groups in the USA. Watkins has been active in studio and freelance work from the 1980s, playing in orchestras accompanying popular singers and in big bands led by Wheeler, Julian Joseph, Stan Sulzmann, and Mark Nightingale.

SELECTED RECORDINGS

As leader: *First Brass* (1984, MA Music NU158-3); *Increased Demand* (1988, MA Music A705-2); *Over the Rainbow* (1995, Zephyr 2); with W. Vaché: *Stardust* (1996, Zephyr 9)
As sideman: K. Clarke and F. Boland: *At Her Majesty's Pleasure* (1969, BL 28416); B. Goodman: *Live in Stockholm* (1970, London SPB21); K. Wheeler: *Music for Large & Small Ensembles* (1990, ECM 1415–16)

BIBLIOGRAPHY

ChiltonB
S. Wick: "My Name is Watkins: Derek Watkins," *Brass Bulletin*, no.108 (1999), 28

MARK GILBERT

Watkins, Doug(las) (*b* Detroit, 2 March 1934; *d* nr Holbrook, AZ, 5 Feb 1962). Double bass player. He first left Detroit to tour with James Moody (1953), then returned to play with Barry Harris's trio (1954); this association enabled him to accompany such visiting musicians as Stan Getz, Charlie Parker, and Coleman Hawkins. In 1954 he performed in New York with Kenny Dorham and Hank Mobley, worked at Minton's Playhouse, and joined the Jazz Messengers; he left the group in 1956 to play with Horace Silver's quintet. His prolific work as a freelance, mainly for Prestige and Blue Note, included recordings with Mobley (1955–7), Gene Ammons (1956–61), Phil Woods and Art Farmer (both 1956), Sonny Rollins (1956, 1958), Donald Byrd (1955–6, 1959–61), Jackie McLean (1956, 1961), Kenny Burrell, Bobby Jaspar, John Coltrane, Curtis Fuller, and Lee Morgan (all 1957), Tina Brooks (1958), Coleman Hawkins with Red Garland, the blues singer Big Joe Turner, and Benny Golson (all 1959), Dizzy Reece (1960), and Billy Taylor (ii) (1961). Watkins took part in performances and recordings by Charles Mingus's Jazz Workshop when Mingus was playing piano in 1960. He died in an automobile accident.

SELECTED RECORDINGS

As leader: *Watkins at Large* (1956, Tran. 20); *Soulnik* (1960, NewJ 8238)
As sideman: H. Silver: *Horace Silver and the Jazz Messengers* (1954, BN 5058); A. Blakey: *The Jazz Messengers at the Cafe Bohemia* (1955, BN 1507–8); S. Rollins: *Saxophone Colossus* (1956, Prst. 7079), incl. Blue Seven; H. Silver: *Six Pieces of Silver* (1956, BN 1539); S. Rollins: *Newk's Time* (1957, BN 4001); L. Morgan: *Candy* (1957–8, BN 1590); G. Ammons: *Blue Gene* (1958, Prst. 7146); J. Turner: *Big Joe Rides Again* (1959, Atl. 1332), incl. Rebecca; G. Ammons: *Boss Tenor* (1960, Prst. 7180); J. McLean: *Bluesnik* (1961, BN 84067)

BIBLIOGRAPHY

FeatherE; *Feather '60s*
Obituaries: *IM*, lx/10 (1962), 33; *DB*, xxix/6 (1962), 15
J.-L. Ginibre and P. Carles: "Dictionnaire de la contrebasse," *Jm*, no.166 (1969), 59
D. Ansell: "The Forgotten Ones: Doug Watkins," *JJI*, xl/5 (1987), 21
F. Postif: *Jazz Me Blues: interviews et portraits de musiciens de jazz et de blues* (Paris, 1998), 27

DIANNA RHYAN/BK

Watkins, Earl (Thomas, Jr.) (*b* San Francisco, 29 Jan 1920). Drummer. After playing with a navy band (1942–5) he led his own groups in the San Francisco Bay area and made recordings with Wilbert Baranco (1946), among them *Night and Day/Weeping Willie* (Black & White 41). Later he worked as a sideman in various ensembles, notably with Flip Phillips (1952) and the bands of Muggsy Spanier (mid-1950s) and Bob Scobey (1954–5, 1956). From 1955 to 1961 he was a member of Earl Hines's group, which was resident at a number of venues in San Francisco, notably Club Hangover. While in Chicago in 1961 this ensemble recorded for Riverside, and Watkins's varied playing may be heard to advantage on the album *A Monday Date* (Riv. 9398). Watkins also made recordings as a freelance and with Kid Ory (1957, 1959, ?1960). (*FeatherE*)

HOWARD RYE

Watkins, Joe [Watson, Mitchell] (*b* New Orleans, 24 Oct 1900; *d* New Orleans, 13 Sept 1969). Drummer. He first studied piano, though his chief interest was always drums, and about 1918 he taught himself to play. He worked with Kid Howard, Isaiah Morgan, Herb Morand, and Punch Miller, but is best known for his long tenure with George Lewis (i), which began in 1946. Later he toured Europe and Japan with the band, and his playing and singing may be heard to advantage on *George Lewis in Japan* (1963, GHB 16). In addition to his many sessions with Lewis, he also recorded with Howard and Emanuel Sayles in 1962. On account of ill-health he played irregularly after 1966.

Oral history material in *LNT*.

BIBLIOGRAPHY

T. Dash: "An Afternoon with Joe Watkins," *Fn*, i (1970), no.4, p.6; no.5, p.4

T. Stagg and C. Crump: *New Orleans, the Revival: a Tape and Discography of Negro Traditional Jazz Recorded in New Orleans or by New Orleans Bands, 1937–1972* (n.p. [London], 1973)

BILL RUSSELL

Watkins, Julius (*b* Detroit, 10 Oct 1921; *d* Short Hills, NJ, 4 April 1977). French horn player. He took up french horn at the age of nine, but in order to earn his living played trumpet with the big bands of Ernie Fields (1943–6) and Milt Buckner (1949–50), although he did have an opportunity to record on french horn as a soloist with Kenny Clarke early in 1949. Thereafter he performed exclusively on french horn, on which he was the first to improvise fluently in the bop style. He studied at the Manhattan School of Music for three years, then recorded with Thelonious Monk and Sonny Rollins (1953), toured with Pete Rugolo (1954), and, with Charlie Rouse, joined Oscar Pettiford's sextet. In 1956 he and Rouse, with Gildo Mahones, Pettiford, and Ron Jefferson, formed Les Modes (later the Jazz Modes), a bop quintet; at times the group was enlarged to include the singer Eileen Gilbert and additional instrumentalists, such as Sahib Shihab and Chino Pozo. When it disbanded for lack of work, Watkins played briefly with George Shearing (1959) and Quincy Jones (1961). Thereafter he worked as a freelance orchestral player in Broadway shows and as a session musician, recording with Phil Woods (1960), John Coltrane (1961), Jimmie Heath (1961–2), Tadd Dameron (1962), Milt Jackson (1963), Freddie Hubbard (1963) and, most frequently, Gil Evans (1958–64). In mid-1965 he joined Charles Mingus's octet. Later, after recording with the Jazz Composer's Orchestra and Evans once again (both 1969), he briefly joined Mingus's sextet (late 1971). At the end of his career he taught, played in the Symphony of the New World, and continued to perform in theater orchestras.

SELECTED RECORDINGS

As leader of Jazz Modes (with C. Rouse): *Jazzville* (1956, Dawn 1101); *The Jazz Modes* (1958, Atl. 1306)

As sideman: M. Buckner: Yesterdays (1949, MGM 10632); K. Clarke: Don't Blame Me (1949, Cen. 1502); [Clarke:] French Licks (1949), first issued on M. Jackson: Roll 'em Bags (1949, 1956, Savoy 12042); T. Monk: Let's call this/Think of one (1953, Prst. 1352); O. Pettiford: *Bass by Oscar Pettiford* (c1956, Beth. 6); J. Heath: *The Quota* (1961, Riv. 9372); P. Sanders: *Karma* (1969, Imp. 9181)

BIBLIOGRAPHY

J. S. Wilson: "The Horn that Nobody Wants," *DB*, xxvi/19 (1959), 15

J. Agrell: "Jazz and the Horn: Julius Watkins," *Brass Bulletin*, no.41 (1983), 20

Obituaries: *DB*, xliv/12 (1977), 12; *New York Times* (8 April 1977)

BK

Watkins, Mitch(ell Allan) (*b* McAllen, TX, 1 Aug 1952). Guitarist. He studied choral music at Texas Christian University (1970–71) and composition at the University of Texas (1972–7). His work has encompassed popular music, country, classical music, and jazz. From 1976 to 1981 he was a member of a jazz group, Passenger, in Austin, and during the late 1970s and early 1980s he toured with such popular artists as Leonard Cohen and Joe Ely. Later he performed and recorded internationally with Bennie Wallace (1987), Jack Walrath (1990), and Barbara Dennerlein (from 1989). Between 1991 and 1994 he toured in Europe and Japan with Friedrich Gulda, with whom he appeared in symphonic settings. Watkins has also performed and recorded with his own group from 1983.

SELECTED RECORDINGS

As leader: *Underneath it All* (1989, Enja 5099-2); *Curves* (1990, Enja 6054-2); *Strings with Wings* (1992, TipToe 888814-2); *Humhead* (1995, Dos 7501)

As sideman: B. Wallace: *Border Town* (1987, BN B21Y-48014); B. Dennerlein: *Straight Ahead* (1988, Enja 5077); *Hot Stuff* (1990, Enja 6050-2); *That's Me* (1992, Enja 7043-2); *Junkanoo* (1996, Verve 314-537122-2)

BIBLIOGRAPHY

T. Carman: "Jazz Guitarist Watkins is Still a Travelin' Man," *Houston Post* (31 Oct 1990)

B. Milkowski: "Redefining the F-word," *GP*, xxv/6 (1991), 65

J. Nash: "Mitch Watkins: a Man for all Musical Seasons," *JT*, xxi/3 (1991), 24

B. Milkowski: "Pro Shop: a Tool for Every Task: Mitch Watkins' Guitar Setups," *DB*, lx/10 (1993), 54

D. Forte: "Intro: Mitch Watkins: Austin City, No Limits," *GP*, xxix/5 (1995), 20

M. J. Summerfield: *The Jazz Guitar: its Evolution and its Players* (Gateshead, England, 1978, 4/1998 as *The Jazz Guitar: its Evolution, Players and Personalities since 1900*)

MARK GILBERT

Watrous, Bill [William Russell, II] (*b* Middletown, CT, 8 June 1939). Trombonist. He was introduced to music by his father, the trombonist Ralph Watrous, and took up trombone at the age of five. Although he had music lessons in high school he was largely self-taught, and he gained early experience by playing in local dixieland bands and big bands. During his military service he was transferred from San Diego to the Brooklyn Navy Yard and thus found opportunities to study in New York with Ed Wilcox and Herbie Nichols. He first played professionally with Billy Butterfield, and from 1962 to 1967 he was a member of Kai Winding's various groups, which included from two to five trombones. At the same time he worked as a freelance musician with many studio groups and big bands, among them those led by Quincy Jones and Maynard Ferguson (recording with both in 1964), Johnny Richards, Woody Herman (recording in 1967), and Thad Jones and Mel Lewis (intermittently, and not on recordings). From 1965 to 1968 he played in the orchestra for Merv Griffin's television show, and from 1967 to 1969 he was a staff musician at CBS. In 1971 Watrous became a member of the jazz-rock group Ten Wheel Drive, and in 1973 he recorded with Mike Gibb's big band. He came to prominence as the leader of the big band Manhattan Wildlife Refuge, which was active from 1973 to 1977; among his sidemen were Joe Beck, Dick Hyman, Ed Soph, Ed Xiques, and the trumpeter Danny Stiles. In the late 1970s he moved to Los Angeles, where he continued to record frequently (often with Stiles), to lead a big band occasionally (from 1978, recording in 1987 and 1996), and to work in studios, notably with Bill Berry's septet (1978) and Nick Brignola's quintet (1979). In 1980 he gave a series of concerts in Germany with Winding and Albert Mangelsdorff in Trombone Summit, a group formed especially for the purpose, and back in the USA he formed a quartet; in 1982 he performed and recorded in London. He occasionally co-led groups with Carl Fontana, and he appeared in St. Louis several times in the 1990s, one of which, in 1999, was with Fontana. Watrous has been active for many years giving workshops in schools and colleges. His effortless virtuosity and fluid solo style have had a significant influence on other trombonists.

Video oral history material in *NCH* (HCJA).

SELECTED RECORDINGS

As leader: *'Bone Straight Ahead* (1972–3, FaD 101); *Manhattan Wildlife Refuge* (1974, Col. KG33090); *The Tiger of San Pedro* (1975, Col. PC33701); *I'll Play for You* (1980, FaD 134); *Coronary Trombossa* (1982, FaD 136); *Roarin' Back into New York, New York* (1982, FaD 144); *Someplace Else* (1986, Soundwings 2100); *Reflections* (1987, Soundwings 2104); *Bone-ified* (*c*1991, GNP 2211); *Space/Available* (1996, Double-Time 124)

As sideman: J. Witherspoon: *Blues for Easy Livers* (1965–6, Prst. 7475); W. Herman: *Woody Live: East and West* (1965, 1967, Col. CS9493); D. Stiles: *In Tandem* (1974, FaD 103); B. Berry: on *Shortcake* (1978, Conc. 75), Royal Garden Blues; N. Brignola: *L.A. Bound* (1979, Sea Breeze 2003)

SELECTED FILMS AND VIDEOS

Soundstage: Down Beat Jazz Awards (1975); The Great Rocky Mountain Jazz Party (1977); Bill Watrous (1982)

BIBLIOGRAPHY

Feather–Gitler '70s

S. Marks: "Bill Watrous: Swinging Refuge in the Wilds of Manhattan," *DB*, xlii/11 (1975), 14

S. Britt: "Bill Watrous," *JJI*, xxxv/11 (1982), 10

L. Tomkins: "The Most Musical Trombone of Bill Watrous," *CI*, xx/10 (1982), 20; contd as "Me and my Big Bands: Bill Watrous," xx/11 (1982), 6; contd as "Button up your Overtones, Advises Bill Watrous," xx/12 (1982), 16

"'Wild' Bill Watrous on Jazz Trombone," *The Instrumentalist*, xxxvi/11 (1982), 20

R. Hepola: "The Complete Bill Watrous Jazz and Solo Discography," *ITA* [International Trombone Association] *Journal*, xiv/4 (1986), 42

B. Baker: "Bill Watrous: Hitting his Stride," *The Instrumentalist*, xlii/4 (1987), 17

S. Yanow: "Bill Watrous: Horn o' Melody," *DB*, lv/5 (1988), 19 [incl. discography]

W. Enstice and P. Rubin: *Jazz Spoken Here: Conversations with Twenty-two Musicians* (Baton Rouge, LA, and London, 1992), 294

G. Robinson: "Bill Watrous," *Windplayer*, ix/5 (1992), 10

N. A. Lee: "Hearsay: Bill Watrous," *JT*, xxvii/8 (1997), 26

Z. Stewart: "Tradin' Fours: the Fastest Slide in the West," *DB*, lxiv/5 (1997), 54

SCOTT YANOW/BK

Watson, Bobby [Robert Michael, Jr.] (*b* Lawrence, KS, 23 Aug 1953). Alto saxophonist, composer, arranger, and leader. His mother played gospel music on piano, and his father was a saxophonist; the family lived in Lawrence (to *c*1962), Bonner Springs, Kansas (*c*1963–5), and Minneapolis (*c*1965–70) before settling permanently in Kansas City, Kansas (*c*1971). Watson took up drums as a child, began lessons on piano around the age of ten, changed to clarinet a year later, and doubled on tenor saxophone from around 1968; having played his reed instruments in a family band and at his maternal grandfather's church, he transferred from tenor saxophone to the alto instrument in 1970, while at high school in Minneapolis. After attending Kansas City (Kansas) Community College he continued his education at the University of Miami, where he gained a degree in theory and composition (*c*1974); with a fellow student, Curtis Lundy, he formed a sextet which accompanied Carmen Lundy in the Miami area. Late in August 1976 Watson traveled to New York, and from 1977 to 1981 he performed, recorded, and toured with Art Blakey's Jazz Messengers; during this period he served as Blakey's music director for two years and composed and arranged several pieces for the band. Thereafter he played with George Coleman (1981), Louis Hayes (1982), and John Hicks (from 1982), recorded with Ricky Ford and Sam Rivers (both 1982), and performed (*c*1982–4) and recorded (1983) with Panama Francis and the Savoy Sultans (ii).

After Curtis Lundy had recorded under Watson's leadership (1977), the two men led a small group (intermittently from 1979) which later took the name Horizon (1981). In 1983, with Lundy and another business partner, Watson formed the record company New Note, for which he recorded as a leader. In addition he performed and recorded with and wrote arrangements for the 29TH STREET SAXOPHONE QUARTET from 1982 until it disbanded in 1996. He toured Europe and made recordings as the leader of hard-bop groups (1983–5) and recorded as a sideman with Charli Persip (1984) and Frank Gordon, Curtis Lundy, and Carmen Lundy (all 1985). In 1985–6 he worked with Klaus Ignatzek, recording with the pianist's ensemble at performances in Switzerland and Germany, and in 1987 he played at the Bass Clef in London.

Watson and Lundy ended their partnership in 1988, and from that year until 1993 Horizon toured internationally and recorded as a quintet co-led by Watson and Victor Lewis. During this period either Melton Mustafa or Terrell Stafford played trumpet, Benny Green, Edward Simon, Stephen Scott, or Geoff Keezer took the piano chair, and Carroll (V.) Dashiell(, Jr.) (who recorded with the group in 1989 and 1990), Christian McBride, or Essiet Essiet played double bass; at New Year 1992 the group broadcast on PBS. Watson also performed alongside Irvin Stokes and Art Baron, among others, in the High Court of Swing, with Baron's group the Duke's Men, and with an all-star group, the Jazz Giants, which was organized by George Wein. He recorded with Hicks (1988), Peter Leitch (1988–9), and Louis Hayes (1989), led a big band, Tailor Made (recording in December 1992), and took part in performances of Charles Mingus's posthumously reconstructed symphony *Epitaph* (early 1992). Later he toured as the leader of a quartet, Urban Renewal (1997), and was a member of T. S. Monk's band (1997–8). In autumn 2000 he began teaching at the University of Missouri–Kansas City Conservatory of Music.

Video oral history material in *NCH* (HCJA).

SELECTED RECORDINGS

* – composed by Watson

As leader: with Curtis Lundy: *Beatitudes* (1983, New Note 11867), incl. *To See her Face; *Gumbo* (1983, Amigo 851); *Appointment in Milano* (1985, Red 184), incl. *Appointment in Milano; *Round Trip* (1985, Red 187); *The Year of the Rabbit* (1987, New Note 1008); *The Inventor* (1989, BN B21Y-91915); *Post-Motown Bop* (1990, BN B21Z-95148); *Present Tense* (1991, Col. CK52400); *Midwest Shuffle* (1993, Col. CK57697), incl. *Mable is Able

As sideman: A. Blakey: *In my Prime* (1977–8, Tim. 114, 118), incl. *Time will Tell (1978); *Album of the Year* (1981, Tim. 155), incl. *In Case You Missed it; C. Persip: *In Case You Missed it* (1984, SN 1079); K. Ignatzek: *Live in Switzerland* (1985, Nabel 8627)

For further recordings *see* 29TH STREET SAXOPHONE QUARTET.

BIBLIOGRAPHY

R. Watson: "Pro Session: Arranging and Composing for the Jazz Messengers," *DB*, xlvi/17 (1979), 90

B. Rusch: "Bob Watson: Interview," *Cadence*, vii/12 (1981), 5

C. Wagner: "Bobby Watson: Originalität ist ungeheuer wichtig," *JP*, xxxiv/1 (1985), 12

J. Giscard and D. Piatkowski: "Bobby Watson," *Coda*, no.210 (1986), 10 [incl. discography]

P. Bloom: "29th Street Saxophone Quartet," *DB*, liv/2 (1987), 26 [incl. discography]

C. Berg: "Bobby Watson: Horizons Unlimited," *JT* (1990), April, 7

G. Reynard: "Bobby Watson: le jazz c'est la vie," *Jh*, no.472 (1990), 3

K. Whitehead: "Bobby Watson: Son of the Inventor," *DB*, lvii/5 (1990), 19
B. Bernotas: "Bobby Watson," *Windplayer*, viii/2 (1991), 10
P. A. Harris: "Not Elementary for Watson: Jazz is 'Music You Have to Think About,' the Saxophonist Says," *St. Louis Post-Dispatch* (29 Dec 1991)
J. Woodard: "Bop Beyond Motown: Bobby Watson & Horizon," *DB*, lviii/7 (1991), 17
B. Blumenthal: "Stardom on Horizon for Bobby Watson," *Boston Globe* (10 May 1992)
C. Deffaa: "Bobby Watson: Now's the Time," *JT*, xxii/5 (1992), 27
H. Reich: "Jazz: in the Groove: Bobby Watson Finally Finds the Audience He Deserves," *Chicago Tribune* (2 Aug 1992)
F. Gonzales: "Watson Makes it Elementary," *Boston Globe* (13 June 1993)
M. Richards: "Bobby Watson," *JJI*, xlvi/3 (1993), 6
J. Macnie: "Between Legends & Lions," *DB*, lxii/7 (1995), 26
J. Mair: "Bobby Watson," *Saxophone Journal*, xix/4 (1995), 54 [incl. discography]
<http://www.jazzcorner.com/watson/index2.html> (2000)
V. Lo Conte: "Bobby Watson: Interview," *Cadence*, xxvi/9 (2000), 16

BK

Watson, Eric (*b* Wellesley, MA, 5 July 1955). Pianist. Le Bec (1988) reports that he was born in Pennsylvania, but Watson himself confirms it was Wellesley. He took up piano at the age of nine, but only began to take it seriously when he was 15. As a teenager he played in a local rock group, and in 1972 he formed a quartet which performed in the Boston area. He studied classical piano at the conservatory at Oberlin College in Ohio (1974–8) and after graduating he moved to France, where he worked with dance companies and as an unaccompanied soloist. In May 1981 he performed in a trio with Jean-François Jenny-Clark and Daniel Humair, and six weeks later he played in Central America in a trio that included Cesarius Alvim. Having spent three months in the USA he returned to France in October 1981, and the following year he formed a duo with John Lindberg, thus beginning a long association.

Watson went back to the United States in 1983 and spent much of the next two years composing and practicing, although he played with Ray Anderson and Barry Altschul and performed and recorded in a trio with Lindberg and John Carter in July 1983. Later he gave a concert as an unaccompanied soloist at Carnegie Hall and played with a dance company at Radio City Music Hall in New York. In the mid-1980s he traveled again to France, where he continued to work unaccompanied and with guest soloists. He formed a trio with Jean-Paul Céléa and Aaron Scott and duos with both Lindberg and Linda Sharrock; the duo with Lindberg was dormant for a period, but Watson resumed performing with him in 1988, after Scott had left the trio to join McCoy Tyner. Albert Mangelsdorff recorded with Watson and Lindberg in 1992, and two years later these three formed a quartet with Ed Thigpen; the group made a number of recordings with Lindberg as the leader which have been widely acclaimed. In addition Watson recorded in a duo with Joëlle Léandre (1991) and as a member of Steve Lacy's groups (1992) and collaborated with the singer Nicholas Isherwood (from *c* early 1990s).

Watson is uncompromising in his musical vision and has not received the recognition that he is due. He is as comfortable with the works of Charles Ives as he is with avant-garde jazz, his principal idiom, and although there are definite classical elements to his style he is nevertheless a jazz pianist of the highest order.

SELECTED RECORDINGS

As unaccompanied soloist: *Child in the Sky* (1985, Owl 040)
Duos: with J. Lindberg: *Shoot First* (1989, Ear Rational 1010); *The Memory of Water* (1990, Label Bleu 6535); *Soundpost: Works for Piano and Double Bass* (1990, 1992, 1995, Music & Arts 920); with J. Léandre: *Palimseste* (1991, HA 6103)
As leader: *Conspiracy* (1982, Owl 027); *Your Tonight is my Tomorrow* (1987, Owl 047); with J. Lindberg and A. Mangelsdorff: *Dodging Bullets* (1992, BS 120108-2); *Punk Circus* (1994, Freelance 023)
As sideman with J. Lindberg: *The East Side Suite* (1983, Sound Aspects 001); *Quartet Afterstorm* (1994, BS 120162-2); *Resurrection of a Dormant Soul* (1995, BS 120172-2)

BIBLIOGRAPHY

C. Béthune: "Elementaire mon cher Eric," *Jm*, no.309 (1982), 56
J.-Y. Le Bec: "Les demains de Watson," *Jm*, no.369 (1988), 19
P. Carles, A. Clergeat, and J.-L. Comolli: *Dictionnaire du jazz* (Paris, 1988, rev. and enlarged 2/1994)
B. Aimé: "Comment Watson sans watts sonne," *Jm*, no.408 (1991), 64
B. Rusch: "John Lindberg: Interview," *Cadence*, xviii/4 (1992), 5
M. Zwerin: "Eric Watson: a 'Recovering Classical Pianist'," *International Herald Tribune* (1 Feb 1996)

GK

Watson, Gilbert (*b* Glasgow, 31 Oct 1896; *d* Peterborough, Canada, 12 Aug 1959). Canadian pianist and bandleader. He was taken to Canada as a child and studied piano in Toronto, where he formed a dance orchestra (*c*1923). Under the influence of his trumpeter, the American Curtis Little, he soon moved towards a "hot dance" style. The band played locally in the mid-1920s on radio and appeared at Sunnyside and Ginn's pavilions and the Prince George Hotel. The ten numbers it recorded in 1925–6 (including *St. Louis Blues*, Domino 21563) are among the earliest jazz recordings made by a Canadian band. Watson later turned away from jazz, and retired in 1942 after several years as a society bandleader at Toronto's Old Mill.

BIBLIOGRAPHY

J. Litchfield: *The Canadian Jazz Discography, 1916–1980* (Toronto, Buffalo, and London, 1982)
M. Miller: *Such Melodious Racket: the Lost History of Jazz in Canada, 1914–1949* (Toronto, 1997)

JACK LITCHFIELD/MARK MILLER

Watson, Leo (*b* Kansas City, MO, 27 Feb 1898; *d* Los Angeles, 2 May 1950). Singer. He began his career as a soloist, but from 1929 he performed as a singer and tiple player in a novelty act called Ben Bernie's Nephews. After changing its name to the SPIRITS OF RHYTHM (1932) the five-man group recorded (1933), held several successful engagements, and toured. Watson also recorded as a double bass player, singer, and washboard player with the Washboard Rhythm Kings in 1932, and he worked at Kelly's Stable with Teddy Bunn in the Harlem Highlanders. In 1937 he joined John Kirby at the Onyx Club, New York; as well as singing, he occasionally played drums and trombone. He then worked with Artie Shaw (1937–8) and Gene Krupa (April–December 1938) before rejoining the Spirits of Rhythm in 1939; in that year he also played briefly with Jimmy Mundy and made four recordings as a leader. After appearing at the New York World's Fair (1940) the group moved to California, where it appeared in the film *Panama Hattie* (1942) and continued to play intermittently until about 1945. In spite of ill-health Watson then again worked on his own as a drummer and singer, and made further recordings. His highly individual "stream-of-consciousness" style of scat singing was so original for his time that it is surprising Watson is not better known. His recordings are both entertaining and impressive.

SELECTED RECORDINGS

As leader: The Man with the Mandolin/Utt da zay (1939, Decca 2750); Ja da/It's the tune that counts (1939, Decca 2959); Sunny Boy/Tight and Gay (1946, Sig. 1007); Snake Pit/Jingle Bells (1946, Sig. 1004)

As sideman: Spirits of Rhythm: I got rhythm/Rhythm (1933, Bruns. 01715); A. Shaw: Fee fi fo fum (1937, Bruns. 7952); L. Feather: For he's a jolly good fellow (1938, Com. 528); G. Krupa: Nagasaki (1938, Bruns. 8188); Tutti Frutti (1938, Bruns. 8211)

BIBLIOGRAPHY

ChiltonW; FeatherE

A. Shaw: *The Street that Never Slept: New York's Fabled 52nd Street* (New York, 1971/*R*1977 as *52nd Street: the Street of Jazz*)

M. Davidson: "Leo Watson: a Giant Lost in Time," *J&B*, iii/2 (1973), 14

——: "Leo Watson Discography," *DF*, no.33 (1974), 17; no.34 (1976), 15; no.36 (1976), 1 [addns and corrections]

D. Chamberlain and R. Wilson, eds.: *The Otis Ferguson Reader* (Highland Park, IL, 1982), 117

L. Gourse: *Louis' Children: American Jazz Singers* (New York, 1984), 149

L. Feather: *The Jazz Years: Earwitness to an Era* (London and New York, 1986), 95

LAWRENCE KOCH

Watt. Record label. Its parent company, Watt Works, Inc., was established near Woodstock, New York, in 1973 or 1974 by Mike Mantler and Carla Bley; its general managers have been Mantler (to 1990), the couple's daughter Karen Mantler (1990–93), and Ilene Mark (from 1993). The Watt catalogue comprises material recorded under the leadership of either Bley (around 20 albums, including three in a duo with Steve Swallow, one in a cooperative trio with Andy Sheppard and Swallow, and the majority with her own small and large ensembles) or Mike Mantler (nine albums). In the mid-1980s Watt Works formed the subsidiary label XtraWatt to issue recordings by Karen Mantler, Swallow, the electric keyboard player Steve Weisberg, and Orchestra Jazz Siciliana, and in the mid- to late 1990s Karen Mantler started another subsidiary label, Say Watt, to release further recordings made by her or by Weisberg.

BIBLIOGRAPHY

R. D. Laing and C. Sheridan: *Jazz Records: the Specialist Labels* (Copenhagen, 1981)

The Watt Family Scrapbook (Munich, 1994)

<http://www.fmi.uni-passau.de/~schneide/discogr/watt.html> (2000)

GK

Watters, Lu(cius Carl) (*b* Santa Cruz, CA, 19 Dec 1911; *d* Santa Rosa, CA, 5 Nov 1989). Bandleader, trumpeter, composer, and arranger. His full name is taken from the California death index. He was brought up in Rio Vista, northern California, and became a member of the drum and bugle corps at St. Joseph's Military academy. However, he also greatly enjoyed jazz, and after the family moved to San Francisco in 1925 he formed his own band; at the age of 17 he became a self-taught arranger and a professional trumpeter, touring on cruise ships. He received a scholarship to study music at the University of San Francisco but concurrently worked as a musician at the Palace Hotel, and soon left college to concentrate on his chosen profession. Through the mid-1930s he toured the USA with the little-known big band of Carol Lofner, and at one point accompanied Bing Crosby. After Lofner's group held a two-month-long engagement in New Orleans Watters became devoted to earlier styles and began to tire of the swing-era repertory. A few years later he organized a series of traditional-style jam sessions at the Big Bear, a tavern in a canyon east of Berkeley and Oakland, California; Turk Murphy, Bob Helm, Wally Rose, Clancy Hayes, Dick Lammi, and the drummer Bill Dart were among those who played at these sessions.

To satisfy contemporary audiences, in 1938 Watters founded a 12- to 14-piece swing orchestra, including Bob Scobey, Helm, the banjoist Russ Bennett or Hayes, and Squire Gersh, for a long engagement at Sweet's Ballroom in Oakland. The band inserted traditional jazz pieces into its performances as circumstances allowed, until finally in the autumn of 1939 Watters was fired for personal and musical insubordination. Early the following year he began rehearsing a small group to revive the New Orleans style of King Oliver, Kid Ory, and others. He reorganized this in the summer, when a new pianist, Forrest Browne, taught the band some of Jelly Roll Morton's compositions, and again in December of that year, when it opened at the Dawn Club in San Francisco as the Yerba Buena Jazz Band, comprising a front line of Watters and Scobey (trumpets), Murphy (trombone), and Helm (clarinet), and a rhythm section of Browne, Hayes (banjo), Lammi (tuba), and Dart. By the time of Watters's first recordings, late in 1941, Rose had replaced

Lu Watters's Yerba Buena Jazz Band at the Dawn Club, San Francisco, 1946: (left to right) Harry Mordecai (banjo), Turk Murphy (trombone), Watters (trumpet), Bill Dart (drums), Bob Scobey (trumpet), Bob Helm (clarinet), Wally Rose (piano), and Dick Lammi (tuba)

Brown, the clarinetist Ellis Horne had replaced Helm, and Bennett and Hayes were together as banjoists (Hayes doubling on guitar); by the time of a further session in March 1942 Gersh had succeeded Lammi. On its own the rhythm section also interpreted ragtime compositions at a separate session held that same month; these jazzy ragtime recordings were released under Watters's name, a practice which the band continued throughout the decade.

The Yerba Buena Jazz Band remained at the Dawn Club until the autumn of 1942, after which time Murphy and Watters enlisted in the navy. While stationed in Hawaii, the trumpeter led a 24-piece concert band and a jazz band. Following his discharge in September 1945 he re-formed the Yerba Buena band and from March to November 1946 was back at the Dawn Club with Scobey, Murphy, Helm, Rose, the banjoist Harry Mordecai, Lammi, and Dart (see illustration). This venue failed at the end of the year, and in mid-June 1947, with a few changes in personnel, the Yerba Buena band opened its own cooperative club, Hambone Kelly's, in El Cerrito, California, with Watters serving as both cook and bandleader. Mutt Carey, Kid Ory, and James P. Johnson appeared there as guest soloists in 1949. The club failed the following year. Murphy (who quit the band in 1949) and Scobey went on to form long-lived revivalist bands of their own, but, apart from a brief period of bandleading during the mid-1950s, Watters left music permanently to work as a carpenter and then as a cook, while devoting much attention to his hobbies, geology and ornithology. He briefly organized a reduced version of the Yerba Buena band to publicize a successful effort to prevent a nuclear power plant from being built at Bodega Bay, California, in 1963. Apart from this event, he remained a recluse, deflecting all efforts to get him involved in the ever-growing traditional jazz scene. Shortly before his death, and after repeated refusals in earlier years, he attended the tenth Santa Rosa (California) DixieJazz Festival to accept their Jazz Man of the Year award.

Watters was an enormously influential bandleader. In the late 1930s, a few years before his rise to fame, other small bands were recorded playing in a hybrid dixieland-swing style (notably those led by Bob Crosby and Muggsy Spanier, and a number of ensembles involving such pioneering African-American players as Sidney Bechet and Morton). But the element of alleged historical authenticity projected by Watters's group set it apart and stimulated a large-scale revival of New Orleans jazz throughout the world (though with some stultifying results, particularly in a consequent overemphasis on the use of banjo and tuba rather than guitar and double bass). Watters also provided his band with a number of arrangements and original compositions, such as *Big Bear Stomp* and *Emperor Norton's Hunch*.

See also Rose, wally.

SELECTED RECORDINGS

* – composed by Watters

Muskrat Ramble (1941, Jazz Man 3); Maple Leaf Rag (1941, Jazz Man 1); London Blues/Sunset Cafe Stomp (1942, Jazz Man 14); Milenberg Joys (1942, Jazz Man 13); Riverside Blues/Cake Walkin' Babies (1942, Jazz Man 5); Working Man Blues/*Big Bear Stomp (1946, West Coast 104); *Antigua Blues (1946, West Coast 101); *Sage Hen Strut (1946, West Coast 116); *Emperor Norton's Hunch (1946, West Coast 107); *Annie Street Rock (1946, West Coast 105)

BIBLIOGRAPHY

E. Williams: "Lu Watters' Yerba Buena Jazz Band," *Jazz Information*, ii/16 (1941), 37

B. Colburn and G. Williams: "That Frisco Jazz Band," *Jazz*, i/3 (1942), 10

E. Bayley, Jr., and B. Kinnell: "Reincarnation: the First of Two Articles on the Yerba Buena Band," *American Jazz* (n.d. [1945]), 11

R. A. Oxtot: "The Story of the Yerba Buena Band," in M. Jones and A. McCarthy, *Jazz Review* (London, 1945), 10

H. E. Avery: "Still Watters . . . ," *Pickup*, i/2 (1946), 19

N. Ertegun: "The Lu Watters Band," *Record Changer*, v/3 (1946), 15; repr. in *Jazzbeat*, iii/2–3 (1991–2), 5

"Music: Second Generation," *Time*, xlvii (26 June 1946), 77

C. Shain: "Lu Watters Yerba Buena Jazz Band," *Jazz Session* (1946), July, 24

P. F. Elwood: "The Rise and Fall of the Dawn Club," *Pickup*, ii/4 (1947), 6

R. J. Gleason: "Lu Watters Drops Nitery; Plans Big Nationwide Tour," *DB*, xviii/3 (1951), 3

——: "Yerba Buena Band Scattered to the Winds," *DB*, xviii/22 (1951), 13

B. Nicholls: "The West Coast Revival," *Music Mirror*, ii/11 (1955), 10

M. W. Stearns: *The Story of Jazz* (New York, 1956, London, 1957, rev. and enlarged 1970/*R*1974)

G. Hulme: "Lu Watters: a Discography," *Matrix*, no.24 (1959), suppl. pp.i–xiii; nos.35–6 (1961), 35

D. Dexter, Jr.: *The Jazz Story: from the 90's to the 60's* (Englewood Cliffs, NJ, 1964)

P. Martin: "Lu Watters: the Legend, the Man," *MR*, xii/7 (1985), 1

Obituaries: *San Francisco Chronicle* (7 Nov 1989); *JJI*, xliii/1 (1990), 25; Jack Retter, *New Orleans Music*, i/3 (1990), 26

F. Levin: "The Lu Watters Influence on Today's Traditional Jazz Scene," *IAJRC*, xxiii/2 (1990), 36

B. Dexter: "Lu Watters: the Man, the Band, and the Legend," *Jazzbeat*, iii/2–3 (1991–2), 8

H. Smith: "Lu Watters: an Appreciation," *Jazzbeat*, iii/2–3 (1991–2), 3

L. Wright: "Visits with Lu," *MR*, xix/7 (1992), 10

N. Ertegun, L. Koenig, P. Elwood, and others: Liner notes: *Lu Watters' Yerba Buena Jazz Band: the Complete Good Time Jazz Recordings* (Good Time Jazz 4409-2, 1993)

J. Buchanan: *Emperor Norton's Hunch: the Story of Lu Watters' Yerba Buena Jazz Band* (Sausalito, CA, 1996)

WILLIAM H. TALLMADGE/BK

Watts, Ernie [James Ernest] (*b* Norfolk, VA, 23 Oct 1945). Saxophonist and leader. He grew up in Detroit and then in Wilmington, Delaware, and took up baritone saxophone at school when he was 13; in his mid-teens he changed to the tenor instrument after discovering John Coltrane's work with Miles Davis. Following studies in classical music in Wilmington and music education at the State Teachers College in West Chester, Pennsylvania, he enrolled at the Berklee School of Music. As an alto saxophonist and flutist he toured and recorded with Buddy Rich from October 1966 to March 1968, when he moved to Los Angeles. He then worked as a studio musician and as a staff musician for NBC, playing tenor saxophone in Doc Severinsen's orchestra for the "Tonight Show" from 1972 until the orchestra was retired from the program in 1992. In addition he played with Gerald Wilson, performed and recorded with Bobby Bryant (1969), toured various French-speaking countries in West Africa for two months with Oliver Nelson, and recorded with Jean-Luc Ponty (1969), Cannonball Adderley (1972), and Leonard Feather (*c*1975). In the mid- to late 1970s he was a member of the group Karma, in which he played alongside Oscar Brashear and George Bohanon, and then of Lee Ritenour's jazz-rock band Friendship.

Watts recorded with Sadao Watanabe (1977, 1978), Anita O'Day (1978), J. J. Johnson (1980), and Wilson (1981), toured as a saxophonist with the Rolling Stones (1981), and received a Grammy Award (1982) for his performance on the soundtrack to the film *Chariots of Fire*. Thereafter he recorded with Tom Scott and Stanley Clarke (both 1983) and Ritenour (from 1983) and continued to work in studios; he was a soloist with Charlie Haden's Liberation Music Orchestra, led his own fusion quartet, and appeared in the video *Rit Special: Lee Ritenour Live* (1984). In 1982, alongside Patrice Rushen and Ndugu Chancler, he became a member of The Meeting (*see* Chancler, ndugu), and in 1986 he began touring and recording in Haden's Quartet West.

In 1987 Watts moved to a home near Boulder, Colorado. Although he undertook further studio work for recordings, films, and television (notably an appearance in "Implosions," an episode of the series "Jazzvisions," 1988), he reduced this kind of occupation considerably and became more active in jazz settings, touring internationally as a leader or a freelance soloist, often in the context of jazz workshops. He led two quartets, one in America and another in Europe (from 1993), which consisted of Jasper van 't Hof, Bo Stief, and Aldo Romano, and formed a trio (2000) with Mitchel Forman and Ed Shaughnessy as his sidemen. In addition he performed and made recordings with Dave Grusin and continued to work with Ritenour and Severinsen; around 1998 he recorded a tenor saxophone "battle" with Pete Christlieb and Rickey Woodard. Transcriptions of his solos have been published by J. Roberts as *Ernie Watts: Saxophone Collection: Artist Transcription Series* (Milwaukee, 1995).

SELECTED RECORDINGS

As leader: *Ernie Watts Quartet* (1987, JVC 3309); *Reaching up* (1993, JVC 2031); *Unity* (1994, JVC 2046)

As sideman: L. Feather: *The Night Blooming Jazzmen* (*c*1975, Mstr. 348); C. Haden: *Haunted Heart* (1991, Verve 314-513078-2); *Always Say Goodbye* (1993, Verve 314-521501-2)

BIBLIOGRAPHY

Feather–Gitler '70s
S. Y. Bradley: "Ernie Watts," *DB*, xlvi/9 (1979), 35
Z. Stewart: "Ernie Watts: Watts Happening," *DB*, li/11 (1984), 26 [incl. discography]
L. Feather: "Haden and Watts: They Lead 4 Lives," *Los Angeles Times* (15 Oct 1989)
F. Gonzalez: "Saxophonist Ernie Watts is Very Busy *Not* Being a Star," *Boston Globe* (24 Feb 1989)
R. Latxague: "Watts New," *Jm*, no.382 (1989), 40
T. Price: "Ernie Watts," *Saxophone Journal*, xiv/1 (1989), 28 [incl. discography]
D. Heckman: "The Good Life: Ernie Watts," *JT*, xxiv/2 (1994), 50
C. Levitan: "Ernie Watts," *Windplayer*, no.53 (1995), 14
J. Widran: "Recharging the Dream," *DB*, lxiii/12 (1996), 52
D. Meriwether: *Mister, I am the Band!: Buddy Rich, his Life and Travels* (North Bellmore, NY, 1998)
Z. Stewart: "Tenors West: Pete Christlieb & Ernie Watts," *DB*, lxv/2 (1998), 29
<http://cjd.com/ernie/> (2000)
<http://darkwing.uoregon.edu/~splat/Ernie_Watts.html> (2000)

BK

Watts, Grady (*b* Texarkana, TX, 30 June 1908; *d* Florida, Jan 1986). Trumpeter. He studied at the University of Oklahoma and began his professional career in Louisiana. After working with several bandleaders (1929–30) he was a soloist in the Casa Loma Orchestra (1931–42; for illustration *see* CASA LOMA ORCHESTRA); his solo playing may be heard on *No Name Jive* (1940, Decca 3089), one of many recordings he made with the band. Watts ceased full-time performing in 1945. The social security death index shows his last-known residence as Vero Beach, Florida.

based on *ChiltonW*

Watts, Jeff "Tain" (*b* Pittsburgh, 20 Jan 1960). Drummer. He began lessons on snare drum around the age of nine, acquired his first drum set when he was about 14, and played timpani in the Pittsburgh Youth Symphony Orchestra. Having studied classical music at Duquesne University he transferred to the Berklee College of Music, where he initially studied vibraphone rather than drums and was a classmate of Marvin "Smitty" Smith, Branford Marsalis, Kevin Eubanks, Victor Bailey, and Wallace Roney; during this period he deputized for Smith in the college's jazz-rock ensemble and worked in a quartet with Donald Harrison. In summer 1981 he recorded with Wynton Marsalis, and after his final semester he toured and recorded regularly from early 1982 to February 1988 in the trumpeter's quintet. In the mid-1980s he recorded with Branford Marsalis (1983, 1986), Big Nick Nicholas (*c*1983–5), Sadao Watanabe (in a bop quartet alongside James Williams and Charnett Moffett, July 1985), McCoy Tyner (1986), and Donald Brown (1987), and performed and recorded with Stanley Jordan at the Village Vanguard (1985).

Thereafter Watts was a member of Branford Marsalis's small groups, which often included Kenny Kirkland and Robert Hurst, and in 1992 he moved to Los Angeles to work with Branford in the house band for "The Tonight Show"; they left the show late in 1993 but continued their association. In 1991 Watts recorded as a co-leader with Charles Fambrough and Kirkland under the name Jazz from Keystone, and around this time he performed as a sideman on recordings by both musicians. Later he worked regularly with Ron Affif (from *c*1995), Danilo Pérez, Kenny Garrett, and Michael Brecker (all from *c*1996), and Ravi Coltrane (from 1997), and recorded as a sole leader (1998). As a freelance Watts has recorded with the pianist Harry Miller, Marlon Jordan, and James Williams (all 1988), Harry Connick, Jr., and Victor Bailey (both *c*1989), Sonny Rollins, Ricky Ford, and Larry Willis (all 1989), Geri Allen (1990), Ellis Marsalis (1990, 1993), Courtney Pine (1990, *c*1997), Stephen Scott (1991), Betty Carter and the trumpeter Sal Marquez (both *c*1992), Hurst (1992), Joe Ford (*c*1993), the trumpeter Derrick Shezbie (1993), Mark Whitfield (1994), Joey Calderazzo (1994–5), Greg Osby (*c*1996), Billy Childs and Sonny Fortune (both 1996), the Doky brothers (1996–7), and Paul Bollenback (1997).

Watts's facility rivals that of Elvin Jones and Tony Williams, and he plays in a non-derivative blend of both their styles. Like Jones, Watts is a thunderous drummer whose hard-driving style is a potent and significant contribution to the settings in which he works; he is also a remarkably sensitive accompanist on ballads.

SELECTED RECORDINGS

(recorded for Columbia unless otherwise indicated)

As leader: *Citizen Tain* (1998, CK69551)

As sideman with W. Marsalis: *Think of One* (1982, FC38641); *Black Codes from the Underground* (1985, FC40009); *J Mood* (1985, FC40308); *Live at Blues Alley* (1986, G2K40675)

As sideman with B. Marsalis: *Crazy People Music* (1990, CK46072); *The Beautyful Ones are Not Yet Born* (1991, CK46990); *Bloomington* (1991, CK52461); *The Dark Keys* (1996, CK67876); *Requiem* (1998, CK69655)

As sideman with others: J. Williams: *Meet the Magical Trio* (1988, EmA 838653-2); R. Ford: *Hard Groovin'* (1989, Muse 5373); G. Allen: *Maroons* (1990, BN B21Z-95139); C. Pine: *Within the Realms of our Dreams* (1990, Ant. 422-848244-2); E. Marsalis: *Whistle Stop* (1993, CK53177); R. Affif: *52nd Street* (1995, Pablo 2310958); D. Pérez: *Panamonk* (1996, Imp. 190); M. Brecker: *Two Blocks from the Edge* (*c*1997, Imp. 260); R. Coltrane: *Moving Pictures* (1997, RCA 2155887-2)

SELECTED FILMS AND VIDEOS

Branford Marsalis: Steep (1987); Jacksonville Jazz Festival VII (1987); Wynton Marsalis: Blues & Swing (*c*1987); Stanley Jordan: Cornucopia (*c*1990 [filmed 1989]); Branford Marsalis: The Music Tells You (1992)

BIBLIOGRAPHY

CarrJ
C. Stern: "Jeff Watts," *MD*, ix/9 (1985), 8
M. Bourne: "Jeff Watts," *DB*, liv/2 (1987), 46
T. Quénum: "Jeff Watts," *Jm*, no.396 (1990), 39
K. Micallef: "Jeff 'Tain' Watts: Bigtains' Drum Adventure," *MD*, xxiii/11 (1999), 52
B. Milkowski: "Rein of 'Tain'," *JT*, xxix/9 (1999), 28
T. Pauken: "Time with Tain," *Jazziz*, xvi/9 (1999), 56

GK

Watts, Marzette (*b* Montgomery, AL, 9 March 1938; *d* Nashville, March 1998). Alto saxophonist. He played piano in his youth. While attending Alabama State College he became a founding member of a civil rights organization, the Student Non-Violent Coordinating Committee, and on account of his association with this group he was obliged by the governor of Alabama to leave the state. In New York he attended college and shared a loft with Leroi Jones, where he had a painting studio; he and Jones were active in the Organization of Young Men and eventually began holding functions in their loft. After graduating from college in 1962 Watts studied painting at the Sorbonne in Paris and took up saxophone in order to support himself. The following year he returned to New York, where he had lessons with Don Cherry and began playing in his loft with, among others, Jiunie Booth, Henry Grimes, J. C. Moses, and Cherry; in addition he performed in Thompson Square Park and elsewhere around the city. In 1965 he decided he was serious about music and moved to Denmark to study, and in December 1966 in New York he recorded *Marzette Watts* (ESP 1044), an outstanding free-jazz album on which his reputation is based. Having recorded for Savoy in 1968 Watts began writing film scores, and he eventually produced some of his own underground films; around the late 1960s or early 1970s he gave up performing and worked as a record producer, and he opened a recording studio opposite his loft, at 27 Cooper Square. He then lived alternately in Europe and New York, and at some point he taught at Wesleyan University; later he settled in California, and in May 1997 he was living in Santa Cruz, California. He died from heart failure. (L. Nai: "Marzette Watts: Interview," *Cadence*, xxiv/8 (1998), 11)

GK

Watts, Noble [Thin Man] (*b* Deland, FL, 17 Feb 1926). Tenor saxophonist. He attended Florida Agricultural and Mechanical College, Tallahassee (from 1942), and came to notice first as a member of the Griffin Brothers Orchestra (1951–2) and then with Paul Williams (until 1956). His playing was heavily featured in both groups, which exemplify the simplified overtly emotional style (of which Watts was one of the most effective practitioners) through which swing and jump transmuted first to rhythm-and-blues and then to rock-and-roll. Williams's group was the house band for the television series "Showtime at the Apollo" (1955), and Watts may be seen in compilation films and videos derived from it, including *Rock 'n Roll Revue* (1955) and *Rhythm and Blues Revue* (1956). During the same period he appeared in accompaniment to many blues and rhythm-and-blues singers. Between 1957 and 1959 he recorded a series of forceful instrumentals alongside the guitarist Wild Jimmy Spruill; *Hard Times*, also known as *The Slop*, achieved some commercial success, and Watts recorded similar material for various labels through the 1960s. He then returned to Florida, where he played with local groups. Around 1986 he teamed up with a blues-rock band, the Midnight Creepers; three resulting albums (1987, 1990, 1993) largely reflect the aesthetic of that band's music despite the presence of Nat Adderley on the second and a reunion with Spruill on the third. Watts continued to work as a session musician in the 1990s.

SELECTED RECORDINGS

As leader: Mashing Potatoes/Pig Ears and Rice (1954, De Luxe 6066); Hard Times (1957, Baton 249); The Slide/Shakin' (1958, Baton 254)

As sideman: Griffin Brothers Orchestra: Shuffle Bug (1951, Dot 1071); The Teaser (1951, Dot 1095); Comin' Home (1952, Dot 1105); Amos Milburn: Let's have a party (1953, Ala. 3218); Margie Day: Take out your false teeth baby (1954, Decca 48317); P. Williams: Give it up (1956, VJ 234); South Shore Drive (1956, VJ 268)

BIBLIOGRAPHY

K. Mohr and B. Niquet: "Noble Watts Discography," *Soul Bag*, no.84 (1981), 18; repr. in *Pj*, no.18 (1982), 115

J. Sasfy: "Blues from a Honker," *Washington Post* (7 Feb 1986); repr. in *Blues & Rhythm*, no.19 (1986), 14

HOWARD RYE

Watts, Trevor (Charles) (*b* London, 26 Feb 1939). English alto and soprano saxophonist. Having first started on cornet, in his mid-teens he took up saxophone, which he played during his service in the RAF (1959–63). He became a founding member of the New Jazz Orchestra in 1963, and also played with various blues and rock musicians, including Long John Baldry, the singer Rod Stewart, and the singer and harmonica player Sonny Boy Williamson (1963–4). In 1965, after setting up the Little Theatre Club in London with Paul Rutherford and John Stevens to promote improvised music, he formed with Stevens the Spontaneous music ensemble, a seminal free-improvisation group. He left the ensemble in 1967 (though he worked with it again in the 1970s) and with Barry Guy and Rutherford formed Amalgam, whose style mixes elements of jazz, improvised music, folk, and rock; members included Stevens, Bobby Bradford, Harry Miller, the electric bass guitarist Colin McKenzie, the electric guitarist Keith Rowe, Keith Tippett, and Stan Tracey, and in the mid-1980s the rock drummer Liam Genocky and the folk violinist Peter Knight. Watts also formed the String Ensemble (1976), the Universal Music Group (1978), the Drum Orchestra (1982), and Moiré Music (1982), which worked in groups ranging from six to 14 musicians. In 1990 these last two groups merged to form the Moiré Music Drum Orchestra, built around four or five African drummers and an electric bass guitarist. The orchestra toured North and South America in 1990, and may be heard on *Live in Latin America*, i. During the 1990s the core of the orchestra performed as the Moiré Music Trio, with Colin McKenzie on bass and Paapa J. Mensah or Marc Parnell on percussion.

Besides leading these groups, Watts joined the London Jazz Composers Orchestra (1970), with which he remained associated (recording into the 1990s), and played in Open Circle (with Danny Thompson and John Stevens, 1973–4). He also worked with Don Cherry (1966), Steve Lacy (1966–74), Rashied Ali (with Amalgam, 1967), Miller's quintet, Louis Moholo, Pierre Favre, Bob Downes, Bobby Bradford (recording in 1973), Tracey (1973–4), Stevens's Dance Orchestra (1979–82), Tippett (1976, 1978–80), Archie Shepp (1981), and Elton Dean (recording in 1989–90). He formed his own record label, Arc, in 1983.

One of the few musicians in Britain to have mastered the innovations of Ornette Coleman, Watts has consistently broken new ground in his music, and he has contributed significantly to the establishment of an indigenous jazz-related music in Britain. His distinctive style combines rugged intensity with lyricism and a strong melodic line. In Moiré Music the rhythmic drive and layering of themes that he first explored with the String Ensemble come together successfully; the group's style echoes African and other musics and shows parallels with the structures and momentum of minimalist music. The Moiré Music Drum Orchestra draws on African rhythms much more explicitly.

SELECTED RECORDINGS

As leader: of Amalgam: *Wipe Out* (1979, Impetus 47901), *Over the Rainbow* (1983, Arc 01); of Moiré Music: *Trevor Watts' Moiré Music* (1986, Arc 02), *With One Voice* (1988, Arc 03); of Moiré Music Drum Orchestra: *Live in Latin America*, i (1990, Arc 06), *A Wider Embrace* (1993, ECM 1449); of Moiré Music Trio: *Trevor Watts' Moiré Music Trio* (1995, Intakt 039)

As sideman: Spontaneous Music Ensemble: *Birds of a Feather* (1971, BYG 529023); B. Bradford: *Love's Dream* (1973, Emanem 302); S. Lacy: *Saxophone Special* (1974, Emanem 3310)

BIBLIOGRAPHY

CarrJ; *ChiltonB*; *Feather-Gitler '70s*; *WickesIBJ*, i

V. Schonfield: "Out of SME and on the Right Road Now," *MM* (16 Dec 1967), 6

T. Yason: "Watts: Finding our Lost Rhythm," *MM* (24 April 1971), 12

I. Carr: *Music Outside: Contemporary Jazz in Britain* (London, 1973), 39

M. Davidson: "Watts: Rhythm is the Essence," *MM* (27 Jan 1973), 43

R. Cotterrell, ed.: *Jazz Now: the Jazz Centre Society Guide* (London, 1976)

K. Ansell: "Beyond the Mainstream: Closer to the Music of Trevor Watts," *JJI*, xxxiii/7 (1980), 30

M. Stamm: "Trevor Watts," *JP*, xxx/2 (1981), 30

M. Johnston: "Trevor Watts," *Coda*, no.185 (1982), 12

K. Ansell: "In Phase with Trevor Watts' Moiré Music," *The Wire*, no.9 (1984), 36

P. Renaud: *La discographie du jazz anglais* (Chaumont, France, 1985)

B. Rusch: "The Questionnaire," *Cadence*, xvi/1 (1990) 33

——: "Trevor Watts Interview," *Cadence*, xvii/12 (1991), 5

M. Johnston: "Moire Music: Trevor Watts," *Coda*, no.257 (1994), 30

<http://www.shef.ac.uk/misc/rec/s/efi/mbailey.html> (1998) [incl. discography]

SIMON ADAMS

Wave. Record company and label. Established in New York in 1961, the company developed from the activities of two recording studios (one in Queens, one in Manhattan) owned by PETER IND, at which he recorded the work of many of his colleagues and friends (among them Lee Konitz, Warne Marsh, Ronnie Ball, Joe Puma, Sheila Jordan, and Al Levitt). In addition, at the establishment in Manhattan Ind engineered sessions for Bethlehem. The first album on the label (released in England by Esquire) was issued under Ind's name, and included items he had recorded with Ball, Sal Mosca, Jordan, and others. Thereafter the company's activities declined until Ind, English by birth, returned in the late 1960s to London, where he revived Wave and issued from his archives material by Mosca, Marsh, and Konitz. He also recorded a series of new albums with his quartet and sextet, as well as two LPs of double bass solos and various other discs. Among items by others released on Wave at this time were a reunion recording made in London by Konitz and Marsh, a collection by the New Paul Whiteman Orchestra of re-creations of the sound of Whiteman's original band, and albums by Buddy DeFranco and Martial Solal. After a further period during which operations were suspended, Ind reactivated the company in the late 1980s, releasing much of the back catalogue and planning new projects. At this time Wave's studios were located in the same building that housed Ind's nightclubs, the Bass Clef and the Tenor Clef; these closed in 1994, and he sold the building, but Wave has continued to operate, issuing compact discs into the new century.

MARK GARDNER

Wa-wa [wah-wah]. The ululating sound achieved by regularly bringing into play and cutting out treble frequencies in the course of a note; the term is onomatopoeic. On brass instruments the wa-wa is created by means of muting (*see* MUTE), notably with the harmon or plunger mute, on woodwind instruments (saxophones, clarinets, and flutes) by FALSE FINGERING. A signal-processing device, generally operated by a pedal, can apply the wa-wa effect to notes played on any electrified instrument; it is associated especially with the electric guitar but has also been widely used with electric piano (for example, by Herbie Hancock and Joe Zawinul), violin (by Jean-Luc Ponty and Michal Urbaniak), and trumpet (by Miles Davis). A good example of the electronic wa-wa may be heard on Ponty's *Imaginary Voyage*, on the album of the same name (1976, Atl. 19136), beginning shortly after the introduction to the second part of the piece.

BK

Wax (i). The material in which sound recordings were cut until the early 1940s (*see* RECORDING, §I, 1 and 2), hence figuratively the shellac-based material of which most 78 r.p.m. discs are made; also, in jazz argot, to record.

Wax (ii). Record label established in 1946 by AL HALL.

Wayland, Hank [Frederic Gregson] (*b* Fall River, MA, 21 Jan 1906; *d* Los Angeles Co., 27 March 1983). Double bass player. He was taught to read music by his father and played in a band at high school. After moving to New York in 1926 he worked in several theater and studio orchestras, and in mid-1934 he performed and recorded with Benny Goodman. He made recordings as a studio musician with such leaders as Red Norvo (1934), Artie Shaw (1936), Bunny Berigan (1937–9, including *Jazz Me Blues*, 1939, Vic. 26244), and Larry Clinton (1939–41). In 1941–2 he was a member of Bob Chester's band, and in 1943 he then settled on the West Coast, where he played briefly with Eddie Miller's big band, again worked in studios, and performed with various leaders, among them Wingy Manone. The social security death index gives his last-known residence as La Crescenta, California. Details of his death are given in the California death index.

based on *ChiltonW*

Wayne, Chuck [Jagelka, Charles] (*b* New York, 27 Feb 1923; *d* Jackson, NJ, 29 July 1997). Guitarist. He first played mandolin, then changed to guitar and played with Clarence Profit (1941). After military service (1942–4) he worked on 52nd Street with Joe Marsala (1944–6), with whom he may be heard on several recordings from this period. At the same time he became involved with the bop movement and took part in several important early recording sessions with Little Benny Harris (under Clyde Hart's leadership) and Dizzy Gillespie; he also recorded with Barney Bigard, Helen Humes (1944), Slam Stewart, Willie Bryant (1945), Phil Napoleon, Bill Harris (i) (1946), Coleman Hawkins, and Lester Young (1947). He performed and recorded with Woody Herman's First Herd (May–December 1946), and while with Herman composed *Sonny*, which Miles Davis later appropriated and claimed as his own composition, under a new title, *Solar*. Wayne worked with the pianist Phil Moore (1947), and Barbara Carroll, Harris, and Stan Hasselgård (all 1948). From 1949 to 1952 he was a regular member of George Shearing's quintet (for illustration *see* SHEARING, GEORGE), with which he made several soundies in 1951, including *Conception*, *Move*, and *Swedish Pastry*. For most of the 1950s he worked as a freelance in New York, where he recorded with Billy Taylor (ii) (1952), Sam Most (1953), John Mehegan (1954), Dick Katz (1958), and Gil Evans (1958–9), and from 1954 to 1957 he toured with Tony

Bennett. He also wrote and performed the music for a production on Broadway of the play *Orpheus Descending* by Tennessee Williams (1957). Thereafter he was a member of staff at CBS (1959–71), and from that time he appeared frequently on television and continued to play occasionally at clubs. From 1972 to 1976 he performed and recorded with Joe Puma, and in 1975 he recorded with Duke Jordan. In the mid-1980s he was active as a teacher at Westchester Conservatory of Music, White Plains, New York, and he continued to teach in the 1990s; he wrote four books on rudiments of theory for jazz guitarists, including, with R. Patt: *Guitar Arpeggio Dictionary: a Library of over 2000 Arpeggios* (New York, *c*1965). Wayne's playing had a mellow tone and he displayed unusual technical facility; his style of improvising remained firmly rooted in bop.

SELECTED RECORDINGS

Duos with J. Puma: *Interactions* (1973, Choice 1004)
As leader: *The Guitar of Chuck Wayne* (1953, Savoy 15035); *Tapestry* (1963, Focus 333); *Morning Mist* (1964, Prst. 7367); *Traveling* (1976, Prog. 7008)
As sideman: C. Hart: Dee Dee's Dance/Little Benny (1944, Savoy 598); D. Gillespie: Groovin' High/Blue 'n' Boogie (1945, Guild 1001); C. Hawkins: Half Step Down Please/Jumpin' for Jane (1947, Vic. 20-3143); G. Shearing: Sorry, Wrong Rhumba/Cottontop (1949, Dis. 106)

BIBLIOGRAPHY

FeatherE; *Feather '60s*; *Feather–Gitler '70s*
B. Hodgins: "Chuck," *Metronome*, lxvii/4 (1951), 15
L. Feather: *The Book of Jazz: a Guide to the Entire Field* (New York, 1957, 2/1965 as *The Book of Jazz from Then till Now: a Guide to the Entire Field*)
D. Cerulli: "Chuck Wayne," *DB*, xxv/7 (1958), 19
R. Cole: "Interview: Chuck Wayne," *Cadence*, xxii/8 (1996), 5
Obituaries: B. Ratliffe, *New York Times* (1 Aug 1997); *The Guardian* (14 Aug 1997); *JJI*, l/9 (1997), 14

SCOTT DeVEAUX/BK

Wayne, Frances (Claire) [Bertucci, Chiarina Francesca] (*b* Boston, 26 Aug 1924; *d* Boston, 6 Feb 1978). Singer and leader. After traveling to New York with a group led by her brother, the tenor saxophonist Nick Jerret, she worked with Charlie Barnet, with whom she recorded *That Old Black Magic* (1942, Decca 18541). During a period with Woody Herman (late summer 1943 – February 1946) she married Neal Hefti and made her first recording as a leader (1945). Later she moved to California, where she sang in the short film *Shorty Sherock and his Orchestra* (1947), recorded under her own name accompanied by Hefti's orchestra (1947), and appeared as a soloist in clubs. Following a period of semi-retirement, during the early 1950s she rejoined Hefti and recorded with him several times in New York. In addition she made a number of recordings as a leader, among them the album *The Warm Sound* (1957, Atl. 1263), which was made up from several small-group sessions with such swing and bop musicians as Jerome Richardson, Milt Hinton, Al Cohn, and Hank Jones. In the mid-1970s Wayne performed occasionally as a soloist, accompanied by such sidemen as Richie Kamuca and Frank Capp, and in 1975 she sang again with Hefti's orchestra.

BIBLIOGRAPHY

FeatherE; *Feather–Gitler '70s*
H. Webman: "Hefti's Band Full of Surprises: May be Eastern Crew of '52," *DB*, xix/12 (1952), 8
L. Feather: "Frances Wayne," *MM* (30 Nov 1974), 26
Obituary, *DB*, xlv/7 (1978), 10
W. D. Clancy with A. C. Kenton: *Woody Herman: Chronicles of the Herds* (New York and elsewhere, 1995)

BK

WDR Big Band (Cologne). German radio big band. In 1947 the regional radio station Nordwestdeutscher Rundfunk (NWDR; later the radio and television station Westdeutscher Rundfunk (WDR)), based in Cologne, established the Kölner Tanz- und Unterhaltungsorchester (Cologne Dance and Entertainment Orchestra), a large ensemble combining the instrumentation of a big band with a string section. It became the Tanzorchester in 1967, at which time the string section was reassigned to another WDR radio orchestra; in the meantime Kurt Edelhagen had established a successful big band for WDR, which he led on radio, on tour, and in recording sessions from 1957 to 1973. By the late 1970s the WDR Tanzorchester had lost much of its popularity, and the decision was made to transform it into a jazz big band modeled after that of Edelhagen. In 1980 it became the WDR Big Band, and in 1985 Jerry van Rooyen was engaged to organize and direct the ensemble; 50 per cent of its repertory was to be commissioned from guest conductors and arrangers. Bill Dobbins replaced van Rooyen as principal director in 1994. The WDR Big Band has recorded in its own right, as well as in support of such guest soloists, composers, and arrangers as Bob Brookmeyer, Eddie Harris, Joachim Kühn, and Jim McNeely.

BIBLIOGRAPHY

H.-J. von Osterhausen: "Die WDR Big Band: zwischen Kontinuität und Veränderung," *JP*, xlvii/2 (1998), 8
<http://www.jazzeitung.de/ausgabe9805/wdr.htm> (1999)
<http://www.dacapo-records.dk/kunstnere/wdrbigband.html> (2000)
<http://www.wdr.de/radio/orchester/big_band/en/history/> (2000)

GK

Weatherford, Teddy (*b* Pocahontas, VA, 11 Oct 1903; *d* Calcutta, 25 April 1945). Pianist. He moved to New Orleans at the age of 12 and began learning piano two years later. From 1922 he was in Chicago, where he became Earl Hines's chief rival; he played at the Moulin Rouge Café with Jimmy Wade (1923–5), at the Vendome Theater with Erskine Tate (1925–6), and briefly as an unaccompanied soloist at the Dreamland. In 1926 he sailed to the Far East with an orchestra led by the drummer Jack Carter. Weatherford led his own band in Singapore, Manila, and Shanghai, and in 1934 returned to the USA, where he recruited Buck Clayton's big band for a residency at the Candidrome Ballroom in Shanghai. From 1936 to 1940 he played at the Taj Mahal Hotel in Bombay, though during the same period he recorded in Paris (1937) and played in Colombo, Ceylon, at the Galle Face Hotel (1939). After his contract in Bombay expired Weatherford took up an engagement at the Galle Face for a year (1940–41), then returned to India, where his band played at the Grand Hotel in Calcutta.

SELECTED RECORDINGS

As unaccompanied soloist: Tea for Two/Weather Beaten Blues (1937, Swing 5); Weather Blues/Maple Leaf Rag (1937, Swing 315)
As sideman: J. Wade: Someday Sweetheart/Mobile Blues (1923, Para. 20295); E. Tate: Static Strut/Stomp Off, Let's Go (1926, Voc. 1027)

BIBLIOGRAPHY

ChiltonW
R. Harris and M. Jones: "Collectors' Corner: the Late Teddy Weatherford," *MM*, xxi (19 May 1945), 4
J. H. Wareing: "Some Reminiscences of Teddy Weatherford," *Jazz Forum*, no.4 (Fordingbridge, England, 1947), 10
K. P. Darke: "Teddy Weatherford's Indian Recording Sessions, 1941–45," *Matrix*, nos.107–8 (1975), 3
P. Darke and R. Gulliver: "Teddy Weatherford," *Sv*, no.65 (1976), 175
B. Clayton and N. M. Elliott: *Buck Clayton's Jazz World* (London and New York, 1986)

JAMES M. DORAN

Weather Report. Jazz-rock group. It was founded in December 1970, the original members being Joe Zawinul (keyboards), Wayne Shorter (soprano and tenor saxophone), Miroslav Vitous (double bass), Alphonse Mouzon (drums), and Airto Moreira (additional percussion). Over the years the group underwent many personnel changes, with Zawinul and, until 1985, Shorter serving as the only constant members. Important later players in the group included Dom Um Romao (1971–4), Alex Acuña (1975–7), Alphonso Johnson (1974–6), Peter Erskine (1978–82), and particularly Jaco Pastorius (1976–81). From 1982 Weather Report comprised Shorter, Zawinul, Victor Bailey, Omar Hakim, and the percussionist José Rossy. Its membership continued to change, however. Mino Cinélu replaced Rossy in 1984, and Erskine left Steps Ahead to rejoin the group around 1985, replacing Hakim. After fulfilling several outstanding commitments in 1985, Shorter took extended leave; with Zawinul as sole leader and Steve Khan as Shorter's replacement, the quintet performed from 1986 under a new name, Weather Update, but it disbanded soon thereafter. Other instrumentalists and singers contributed to individual recordings throughout the life of the group. A reunion recording and tour, announced in 1996, never materialized.

Weather Report's first albums provided several remarkable instances of unconventional collective playing, though their music remained accessible to a large audience. Discarding the traditional jazz roles of soloist and accompanist, the players took the lead by turn and created textures that were continuously changing; they elided tonal ostinato themes with improvisations and alternated unmetered passages with others underpinned by rock or Latin rhythms. Excellent examples of this novel approach to ensemble improvisation are *Seventh Arrow* and *Umbrellas* (1971) or *Crystal* and *Surucucú* (1971–2). By 1972 Zawinul dominated the group, which had moved towards rock. He had a preference for dance rhythms and fixed arrangements featuring complex electronic effects. His striving for commercial success precipitated the many personnel changes in the group but also led to its resounding hit *Birdland* (1976). *Havona* (also 1976) demonstrated Pastorius's unusual command of the electric bass guitar as well as the group's continuing ties to jazz improvisation. Transcriptions from the quintet's recordings appear in *Best of Weather Report* (Milwaukee, 1988).

See also Harmony (i), §2, and exx.27 and 28; for illustration *see* Zawinul, Joe.

SELECTED RECORDINGS

(all recorded for Columbia)

Weather Report (1971, KC30661), incl. Seventh Arrow, Umbrellas; *I Sing the Body Electric* (1971–2, KC31352), incl. Crystal, Surucucú; *Sweetnighter* (*c*1973, KC32210); *Mysterious Traveller* (*c*1974, KC32494); *Tale Spinnin'* (*c*1975, PC33417); *Black Market* (*c*1976, PC34099); *Heavy Weather* (1976, PC34418), incl. Birdland, Havona; *Mr. Gone* (*c*1978, JC35358); *8:30* (*c*1979, PC2-36030); *Night Passage* (*c*1980, JC36793); *Weather Report* (*c*1981, FC37616); *Domino Theory* (1983, FC39147); *Sportin' Life* (1984, FC39908)

SELECTED FILMS AND VIDEOS

Soundstage: Downbeat Jazz Awards (1975); Rio Monterey Jam (1981); Weather Report: in Concert (*c* mid-1980s)

BIBLIOGRAPHY

D. Morgenstern: "Weather Report: Outlook Bright and Sunny," *DB*, xxxviii/11 (1971), 14
L. Goddet: "Weather Report," *Jh*, no.317 (1975), 20
B. McRae: "Weather Report," *JJ*, xxix/6 (1976), 10
K. Dallas: "Weather Report," *MM* (29 Oct 1977), 56
M. C. Gridley: *Jazz Styles* (Englewood Cliffs, NJ, 1978, rev. 6/1997 [*recte* 1996])
L. Lyons: "This Year's Weather Report," *High Fidelity/Musical America*, xxviii/9 (1978), 115
C. Silvert: "Joe Zawinul: Wayfaring Genius," *DB*, xlv (1978), no.11, p.13; no.12, p.21
L. Birnbaum: "Weather Report Answers its Critics," *DB*, xlvi/3 (1979), 14
L. Blumenthal: "Weather Report," *DB*, xlviii/2 (1981), 14
A. Liska: "On the Road with Weather Report," *DB*, xlix/10 (1982), 21
C. Murray: "Weather Report," *The Wire*, no.3 (1983), 4
P. Davis: "Weather Report: Fine and Warm," *CI*, xxii/4 (1984), 12
J. Zawinul and G. Armbruster: "The Evolution of Weather Report," *Keyboard*, x/3 (1984), 49
Z. Stewart: "Riffs: Weather Report to Re-form," *DB*, lxiii/4 (1996), 14
<http://www.members.harborcom.net/~jmayer/jordu/weather.htm> (2000)

BK

Webb, Chick [William Henry] (*b* Baltimore, 10 Feb 1909; *d* Baltimore, 16 June 1939). Drummer and bandleader. His nickname referred to his small stature. Though it continues to circulate, the story that Webb was dropped and severely injured in infancy is almost certainly untrue; an alternative and likely account explains that he became a diminutive hunchback after suffering tuberculosis, then a common inner-city disease. He played homemade drums from a very young age and acquired a proper set at the age of 12. Around 1925 he moved to New York, and during the following year he established his first band, which included Bobby Stark, Johnny Hodges, Don Kirkpatrick, and Webb's boyhood friend John Trueheart; Elmer Williams joined soon afterwards. The group performed at the Savoy Ballroom in January 1927 and transferred to Rose Danceland in December. While struggling for steady work, Webb managed to make his first recordings in June 1928 under a pseudonym, the Jungle Band, to perform in the short film *After Seben* (1929), and to work at Roseland, the Cotton Club (July 1929), the Savoy, and Roseland again (March 1931), at which point he traded Benny Morton and Russell Procope to Fletcher Henderson in exchange for Benny Carter and Jimmy Harrison. However, the exchange proved less attractive than it initially seemed, as Carter soon left, after supplying a few recorded arrangements, and Harrison was suffering from terminal cancer.

In 1932 Webb's big band toured as accompaniment to Louis Armstrong. The first of numerous lengthy residencies at the Savoy Ballroom from 1933 marked its emergence as one of the outstanding bands of the swing period. Although the group had only a few prominent soloists, including Taft Jordan and Sandy Williams, during its years of prolific recording activity it developed a distinctive style thanks in part to the compositions and arrangements provided by Edgar Sampson (e.g., *Let's get together*, *Stomping at the Savoy*, *Don't be that way*, and *Blue Lou*) and especially to Webb's forceful drumming. In April 1935 Ella Fitzgerald was engaged as the band's singer, and it achieved popular success with performances of such tunes as *A-tisket, A-tasket* (1938). Webb's band remained at the Savoy (see illustration), regularly defeating rival bands in the ballroom's famous cutting contests. After Webb's early death, Fitzgerald led the group until 1942, when it disbanded.

Webb was universally admired by drummers for his forceful sense of swing, accurate technique, control of dynamics, and imaginative breaks and fills. Although he was unable to read music, he committed to memory the arrangements played by the band and directed performances from a raised platform in the center of the ensemble, giving cues with his drumming. Using specially constructed bass-drum pedals and cymbal holders, he could range effortlessly over a large drum set that offered a wide selection of colors. Unlike drummers of the 1920s, he used the woodblocks and

Chick Webb and his band at the Apollo Theatre, New York, in the late 1930s: (left to right) Mario Bauzá (trumpet), Beverly Peer (double bass), Bobby Stark (trumpet), Nat Story and Sandy Williams (trombones), Bardu Ali (conductor), Webb (drums), Ella Fitzgerald (voice), George Matthews (trombone), Tommy Fulford (piano), Teddy McRae and Wayman Carver (tenor saxophones), Hilton Jefferson (alto saxophone), Taft Jordan (trumpet), Garvin Bushell (alto saxophone, clarinet, flute), and ? Bobby Johnson (guitar)

cowbell only for momentary effects, and varied his playing with rim shots, temple-block work, and cymbal crashes. In his celebrated two- to four-bar fills, he abandoned earlier jazz drumming formulae for varied mixtures of duple- and triple-meter patterns. Webb was seldom given to long solos, but his style is well represented on *Liza* (1938), a superior response to Gene Krupa's solo performance with Benny Goodman's band on *Sing, sing, sing*.

SELECTED RECORDINGS

As leader: Let's get together (1934, Col. CB741); Stomping at the Savoy (1934, Col. 2926D); Blue Minor (1934, OK 41572); Don't Be that Way (1934, Decca 483); What a Shuffle (1934, Decca 1087); Blue Lou (1934, Decca 1065); Go Harlem (1936, Decca 995); Clap Hands! Here comes Charley (1937, Decca 1220); I got rhythm (1937, Decca 1759); Squeeze Me (1937, Decca 1716); Harlem Congo (1937, Decca 1681); Midnite in a Madhouse (1937, Decca 1587); A-tisket, A-tasket/Liza (1938, Decca 1840)

BIBLIOGRAPHY

AllenH; *McCarthyB*; *SchullerS*
H. Oakley: "The Rise of a Crippled Genius," *DB*, iv/12 (1937), 4; v (1938), no.1, p.9; no.2, p.9
J. P. Noonan: "The Secrets of Chick Webb's Drumming Technique," *DB*, v/9 (1938); repr. in *DB*, xxxix/13 (1972), 26
N. Dodson, "10,000 Bid Farewell to Chick Webb," *Philadelphia Afro American* (24 June 1939)
S. B. Charters and L. Kunstadt: *Jazz: a History of the New York Scene* (Garden City, NY, 1962/*R*1981)
S. Dance: Liner notes, *Chick Webb: A Legend*, i: *(1929–1936)* (Decca 79222, 1967); *Chick Webb: King of the Savoy*, ii: *(1937–1939)* (Decca 79223, 1967)
G. T. Simon: *The Big Bands* (New York, 1967, rev. 4/1981), 440
D. M. Bakker: "Chick Webb, 1928–1939," *Micrography*, no.31 (1974), 4
T. D. Brown: *A History and Analysis of Jazz Drumming to 1942* (diss., U. of Michigan, 1976), 424
M. Berger, E. Berger, and J. Patrick: *Benny Carter: a Life in American Music* (Metuchen, NJ, and London, 1982)
J. L. Collier: *Louis Armstrong: an American Genius* (New York, 1983, London, 1984, as *Louis Armstrong: a Biography*), 256
G. Murphy: "Chick Webb: the Mighty Atom Remembered by Greg Murphy," *JJI*, xxxix/4 (1986), 10
B. Korall: "Chick Webb: the Total Experience on Drums," *MD*, xii/1 (1988), 26
B. Crowther: "Chick Webb and the Home of Happy Feet," *JJI*, xlii/3 (1989), 14
B. Korall: *Drummin' Men: the Heartbeat of Jazz: the Swing Years* (New York and Toronto, 1990), 7
G. Giddins: *Faces in the Crowd: Players and Writers* (New York, and Oxford, England, 1992), 111

J. BRADFORD ROBINSON/BK

Webb, George (Horace) (*b* London, 8 Oct 1917). English pianist and bandleader. In 1942 he formed a band which shortly afterwards became known as George Webb's Dixielanders; its members included Wally Fawkes and Eddie Harvey. It began by performing once a week at the Red Barn in Barnehurst, Kent (*see* NIGHTCLUBS AND OTHER VENUES), then, through its recordings (including *South*, 1946, Decca F8735) and performances on radio and in clubs, the group stimulated the jazz-band movement that came to be known as "trad." After the Dixielanders disbanded in 1948 Webb joined his former sideman Humphrey Lyttelton, with whom he performed until 1951, when he ceased full-time playing. He ran several jazz clubs and worked in jazz promotion and as a booking agent. He again led his own band in 1972–4, and he continued to perform in the 1980s and 1990s at his own pubs and in reunions with Lyttelton's group.

Oral history material in *GBLnsa*.

BIBLIOGRAPHY

CarrJ; *ChiltonB*
R. Harris and M. Jones: "Collectors' Corner: Rave for Webb," *MM* (21 July 1945), 4
O. Bryce: "The George Webb Dixielanders," in C. Jones, ed.: *Eye Witness Jazz*, ii (London, 1946), 8
C. Wilford: "The English Revivalists," *Jazz Music*, iii/5 (1947), 24
H. Lyttelton: *I Play as I Please: the Memoirs of an Old Etonian Trumpeter* (London, 1954), 116
D. Boulton: *Jazz in Britain* (London, 1958)
J. Godbolt: *A History of Jazz in Britain, 1919-50* (London, Melbourne, Australia, and New York, 1984), 200

DEREK COLLER

Webb, Speed [Lawrence Arthur] (*b* Peru, IN, 18 July 1906; *d* South Bend, IN, 4 Nov 1994). Bandleader and drummer. His nickname refers to his ability in high school as a baseball pitcher. He began by learning violin and mellophone, but changed to drums. After performing locally in 1923, he helped to form a cooperative band, the Hoosier Melody Lads, in 1925; he later assumed leadership of the band and in 1926 led it in a recording session for Gennett (though the results were not issued). It moved to California (1926), where it was resident at various clubs and appeared in several films (1928–9), the soundtracks of which, however, may have been recorded by studio orchestras (*see* FILMS, §I, 2). From 1929 Webb led a number of bands, mostly conducting them but occasionally playing drums and singing; among his sidemen were Roy Eldridge, Teddy Buckner, Vic Dickenson, Teddy Wilson, and Art Tatum. Webb ceased full-time performing in 1938. In 1942 he took a degree in sanitary science, anatomy, and embalming and became a successful professional. Later he became active in local politics in South Bend, Indiana.

BIBLIOGRAPHY

ChiltonW; *McCarthyB*
D. Schiedt: "Speed Webb," *JM*, no.165 (1968), 2
G. Fernett: *Swing Out: Great Negro Dance Bands* (Midland, MI, 1970/*R*1993), 57
D. Schiedt: *The Jazz State of Indiana* (Pittsboro, IN, 1977), 94
K. Stratemann: *Negro Bands on Film*, i: *Big Bands, 1928–1950: an Exploratory Filmo-discography* (Lübbecke, Germany, 1981)
Obituary, P. Vacher, *JJI*, xlviii/4 (1995), 20

EDDIE LAMBERT

Webber, John (Robert) (*b* St. Louis, 5 Aug 1965). Double bass player. His mother was a pianist. He played electric bass guitar from the age of 11 and changed to double bass when he was 15. Later he studied at Northern Illinois University (1983–4) and Roosevelt University (1984–5) and performed in Chicago with, among others, Von Freeman and Brad Goode. In 1987 he moved to New York, where he initally worked in the the quintet of Bill Hardman and Junior Cook and in group Bopera House, co-led by Tardo Hammer and the trumpeter John Marshall; in 1991 he recorded with Cook. Webber joined Michael Weiss's group in 1989. The following year he toured and recorded with Christopher Hollyday, and from the mid-1990s he toured with Johnny Griffin's quartet (which also included Weiss). He is also a member of Jimmy Cobb's small group Cobb's Mob, with which he recorded in 1998. As a freelance Webber played with Lou Donaldson, David Hazeltine, Diana Krall, Annie Ross, and Mike LeDonne, and recorded with Peter Bernstein (1992), Eric Alexander (1992, 1996–7), Chris Flory (1993), Doug Lawrence (*c*1996), Etta Jones and Jim Rotondi (both 1997), Ryan Kisor (1998), and Horace Silver (1999).

SELECTED RECORDINGS

As sideman: J. Cook: *You Leave Me Breathless* (1991, Ste. 31304); C. Flory: *City Life* (1993, Conc. 4589); M. Weiss: *Power Station* (1996, DIW 924); E. Alexander: *Modes for Mabes* (1997, Del. 500); R. Kisor: *The Usual Suspects* (1998, Lightyear 54267)

BIBLIOGRAPHY

Feather–GitlerBEJ

GK

Weber, Eberhard (*b* Stuttgart, Germany, 22 Jan 1940). German double bass player, leader, and composer. He was taught by his father to play cello from the age of six, but took up double bass as his main instrument in 1956 and played in school orchestras, dance bands, and local jazz groups. As a participant in the Düsseldorf Amateur Jazz Festival (1961–3) he met Wolfgang Dauner, with whom he played over the next eight years, first in a duo (or trio, with Fred Braceful) and later in the group Et Cetera. He recorded with Baden Powell

Eberhard Weber playing at the Roundhouse Arts Centre, London, during the Camden Jazz Week, 1980

in 1967 and Stephane Grappelli in 1971. From 1972 Weber used an electric double bass with an extra string at the top, and in 1976 he added another string above that; this greatly increased the potential of the double bass as a solo instrument by extending its range and making its sound more penetrating, and thereafter Weber ceased to perform on cello. After working with Dave Pike's group, which included Volker Kriegel (1972–3), he led the group Spectrum with Kriegel (1973–4).

Weber won international renown with the recording *The Colours of Chloe* (1973), which well represents his playing: he has rejected African-American influences in favor of an inspirational aesthetic that emphasizes the importance of melody, and compositional techniques, borrowed from the composer Steve Reich, that use contrasting ostinato patterns in different voices. Impressed by this album, Gary Burton later engaged Weber for an American tour and two recordings (1974, 1976), featuring him explicitly as a melodic voice rather than in the usual role of a bass player. In 1974 Weber formed the group Colours, which became highly successful; initially consisting of Charlie Mariano, Rainer Brüninghaus, and Jon Christensen (who was replaced by John Marshall around 1977), it toured the USA in 1976, 1978, and 1979, and continued performing until 1981. He also recorded with Monty Alexander (1974), Ralph Towner (1974, 1977), Benny Bailey (1976), and Pat Metheny (1977). From 1975 to 1987 he played with the United Jazz and Rock Ensemble and from 1981 into the 1990s he was a sideman with Jan Garbarek. In the early 1980s he also wrote film music and gave solo concerts; he made an acclaimed recording as an unaccompanied soloist in 1993 and then toured as such.

SELECTED RECORDINGS

As unaccompanied soloist: *Pendulum* (1993, ECM 1518)
As leader: *The Colours of Chloe* (1973, ECM 1042); *Silent Feet* (1977, ECM 1107); *Fluid Rustle* (1979, ECM 1137); *Later that Evening* (1983, ECM 1231); *Chorus* (1984, ECM 1288)
As sideman: Baden Powell: *Poema on Guitar* (1967, Saba 15150); S. Grappelli: *Afternoon in Paris* (1971, MPS 15303); V. Kriegel: *Mild Maniac* (1974, MPS 15403); G. Burton: *Ring* (1974, ECM 1051); R. Towner: *Solstice* (1974, ECM 1060); G. Burton: *Passengers* (1976, ECM 1092); United Jazz and Rock Ensemble: *Live im Schützenhaus* (1977, Mood 28-600); Kate Bush: *The Dreaming* (1982, Elec. 64589)

BIBLIOGRAPHY

Feather–Gitler '70s
M. Henkels: "An Interview with Eberhard Weber," *JF* [intl edn], no.40 (1976), 54
T. Schnabel: "Eberhard Weber: Interview," *Cadence*, iii/1–2 (1977), 6
L. Tomkins: "Eberhard Weber," *CI*, xvi (1977–8), no.7, p.6; no.8, p.14
K. Ansell: "Eberhard Weber," *Impetus*, no.7 (1978), 296
K. Brodacki: "Eberhard Weber: 'Honest Music'," *JF* [intl edn], no.59 (1979), 34
M. Naura: "Eberhard Weber: der Mann mit dem Reisebass," *JP*, xxxi/12 (1982), 8
U. J. Messerschmidt: "Einige Anmerkungen zum Werdegang des Jazzbassisten Eberhard Weber," *Jf*, no.19 (1987), 9–39 [incl. transcrs. and discography]
M. Tucker: "Eberhard Weber," *JJI*, xl/1 (1987), 12 [incl. discography]
S. Graham: "Naked Bass," *Jazz on CD*, no.15 (1995), 62
M. Jansson: "Eberhard Weber: the Bass as Orchestra," *Bass Player*, vi/8 (1995), 21

GÜNTHER HUESMANN/BK

Weber, Reto (*b* Solothurn, Switzerland, 20 Aug 1953). Swiss drummer. He took up drums at the age of 14, played with local amateur blues and jazz groups, and studied percussion in Basel. In 1973 he gave concerts as an unaccompanied soloist with his voluminous drum set, touring Europe, Asia, Africa, and the Americas. In 1978 he was a founder of an international percussion orchestra. He formed a duo with Bruno Spoerri, with whom he also worked in a quartet with Albert Mangelsdorff and in the quartet MSRW, alongside Mangelsdorff and Ernst Reijseger. In addition to teaching at the Swiss Jazz School in Berne, Weber has played for films, theatrical productions, and dance.

SELECTED RECORDINGS

As unaccompanied soloist: *Love Percussion Song* (1978, Gold 11067)
Duos with B. Spoerri: *Controlled Risk* (1988, Konnex 5017)
As sideman with MSRW: *Movin' On* (1990, Elite 76357)

OTTO FLÜCKIGER

Webster, Ben(jamin Francis) (*b* Kansas City, MO, 27 March 1909; *d* Amsterdam, 20 Sept 1973). Tenor saxophonist. He studied violin in elementary school and taught himself piano. After a brief period at Wilberforce University he worked as a pianist in Amarillo, Texas. There he met Budd Johnson, who gave Webster a chance to try to play alto saxophone. He practiced this instrument for a few months while living with Lester Young's family in Albuquerque, New Mexico, and returned to Amarillo early in 1930 as an alto and then a tenor saxophonist in Gene Coy's Happy Black Aces. Despite this relatively late start, Webster was a leading figure on the instrument. He played with the bands of Jap Allen (summer 1930 – early 1931) and Blanche Calloway (from March 1931) before becoming a member of the important southwestern bands of Bennie Moten (late 1931 – early 1933) – he contributed solos to Moten's famous recording session for Victor in 1932 – and Andy Kirk (1933 – July 1934). In 1934 he moved to New York, where in July he was retained for Fletcher Henderson's band. He then joined the big bands of Benny Carter (late 1934) and Willie Bryant (*c*February 1935), but also spent two brief spells as a substitute in Duke Ellington's orchestra (1935, 1936) and recorded in small studio bands accompanying Billie Holiday at a number of the early sessions under her own name and that of Teddy Wilson (1935–7). He then played in Cab Calloway's orchestra (1936 – July 1937), rejoined Henderson in Chicago (autumn 1937), and worked with Stuff Smith and Roy Eldridge (1938). Webster recalled his attempts during this decade to play like Coleman Hawkins. "One day ... Clyde Hart heard me playing. He was a pretty subtle cat and he said: 'Well you did it, you finally did it. You sound just like Hawk.' I got the message. I packed all the Hawk records up and set about trying to find something for myself. That would be around 1938" (Shaw, 1973, p.3).

From April 1939 Webster was the pricipal soloist in Teddy Wilson's big band, but left when he was offered a permanent engagement in 1940 with Ellington's orchestra, which until that time had lacked an important soloist on tenor saxophone. Under Ellington's influence Webster's style matured remarkably: his striking, slightly unfocused tone, great rhythmic momentum, and distinctive rasping timbre at moments of tension played a key role in many of Ellington's masterpieces of the period, and he soon became established, with Chu Berry and Herschel Evans, as a leading exponent of the style fashioned by Hawkins. After leaving Ellington in August 1943 he worked in small bands and in these settings excelled in warm renditions of popular ballads. He was a sideman in Sid Catlett's quartet, which recorded in March 1944. After playing with John Kirby, later that year he joined Henry "Red" Allen's band at the Garrick Stage Bar in Chicago. Early in 1945 he was with Stuff Smith's Mad Threesome at the Onyx Club in New York, but from October 1944 he mainly led his own small groups in New York and Chicago. He worked with Ellington again from November 1948 to September 1949.

When sober Webster was much loved as a gentle man. However, for many years he was a heavy and sometimes uncontrollable drinker (his nickname was "The Brute"), and he experienced personal problems leading to his semiretirement from 1950 to 1952, during which time he began to live in Los Angeles with his mother. He then resumed an active career. He toured and recorded with Jazz at the Philharmonic in the 1950s and made numerous recordings as a studio musician, particularly as an accompanist to such singers as Holiday, Ella Fitzgerald, and Carmen McRae, and including a remarkable collection of instrumental ballads with Art Tatum (1956). He led small groups, with, at the end of the 1950s, Jimmie Rowles, Jim Hall, Leroy Vinnegar or Red Mitchell, and Frank Butler, among others. In 1962, shortly after his mother died, Webster returned to New York. In December 1964 he moved permanently to Europe and lived in Amsterdam before settling in Copenhagen. He played frequently in clubs and at festivals with European and expatriate or visiting American musicians, among them Bill Coleman, Buck Clayton, Don Byas, Kenny Drew, Stan Tracey, Tete Montoliu, Wilson, Niels-Henning Ørsted Pedersen, and Alex Riel.

Webster is the subject of John Jeremy's documentary *The Brute and the Beautiful* (1989). While he was renowned for his aggressive swing style, even more significant is that he may be credited with defining a distinct and lasting approach to ballad playing, in which the jazz improviser, rather than launching into the sort of double-time arabesques heard in Hawkins's famous version of *Body and Soul* (1939), maintains the feeling of an exceptionally slow tempo while inventing a complex melody that is both heady and tender. A volume of transcriptions of Webster's solos has been published by J. Alexander: *Ben Webster's Greatest Transcribed Solos* (Lebanon, IN, 1995). The Ben Webster Collection, including his photos, films, and personal papers, is held in the Syddansk Universitetsbibliotek–Odense Universitetsbibliotek in Odense, Denmark (*see* LIBRARIES AND ARCHIVES, §2).

For illustrations *see* BANDS, fig.3, and CARTER, BENNY.

SELECTED RECORDINGS

As unaccompanied soloist: first issued on *Soulville* (1957, Verve 833551-2), Boogie-woogie, Roses of Picardy, Who [pf]

As leader: Honeysuckle Rose/Blue Skies (1944, Savoy 553); *The Consummate Artistry of Ben Webster* (1953, Norg. 1001); *Music for Loving* (1953–4, Norg. 1018), incl. My Funny Valentine, Sophisticated Lady; *Ben Webster Plays Music with Feeling* (1954–5, Norg. 1039), incl. Blue Moon, Chelsea Bridge; with A. Tatum: *Art Tatum–Ben Webster Quartet* (1956, Verve 8220); *Soulville* (1957, Verve 8274); *Coleman Hawkins Encounters Ben Webster* (1957, Verve 8327); with G. Mulligan: *Gerry Mulligan Meets Ben Webster* (1959, Verve 8343); *Ben Webster Meets Oscar Peterson and his Trio* (1959, Verve 8349); with H. Edison: *Ben Webster and Sweets Edison* (1962, Col. CS8691); *See You at the Fair* (1964, Imp. 65); *Duke's in Bed* (1965, BL 190); with D. Byas: *Ben Webster Meets Don Byas* (1968, Saba 15159)

As sideman with B. Moten: Toby (1932, Vic. 23384); The Blue Room/Milenberg Joys (1932, Vic. 24381); New Orleans (1932, Vic. 24216)

As sideman with D. Ellington: Conga brava (1940, Vic. 26577); Cotton Tail (1940, Vic. 26610); All too Soon (1940, Vic. 27247); Blue Serge (1941, Vic. 27356); Main Stem (1942, Vic. 20-1556)

As sideman with others: F. Henderson: Limehouse Blues (1934, Decca 157); B. Carter: Dream Lullaby (1934, Voc. 2898); T. Wilson: I'll see you in my dreams (1936, Bruns. 7816); F. Henderson: Sing you sinners (1937, Voc. 4125); J. Teagarden: St. James Infirmary/Shine (1940, HRS 2006); The world is waiting for the sunrise/Big Eight Blues (1940, HRS 2007); S. Gaillard: Ra-da-da-da (1942), first issued on B. Webster: *Giants of Jazz: Ben Webster* (1932–62, TL 21); S. Catlett: Sleep (1944, Com. 546); Memories of You (1944, Com. 1515); B. Morton: Conversing in Blue (1945, BN 46); B. Carter: Time out for the blues (1949, Modern 858); J. Witherspoon: *Roots* (1962, Rep. 96057)

SELECTED FILMS AND VIDEOS

Jam Session (1942); Cottontail (1942); The Sound of Jazz (1957); The Brute and the Beautiful (1989)

BIBLIOGRAPHY

AllenH; *McCarthyB*; *SchullerS*; *SheridanCB*
"Ben Webster Plays that Big Tenor," *DB*, xxii/20 (1955), 12
D. Cerulli: "Ben Webster," *DB*, xxv/13 (1958), 16
B. Houghton: "Ben Webster: a Biography and Appreciation," *JJ*, xv/12 (1962), 10
L. Tomkins: "Ben Webster Speaking," *Crescendo*, iii/7 (1965), 22
V. Wilmer: "Warm and Websterish," *JB*, ii/2 (1965), 19
E. Lambert: "Quality Jazz no.9: Ben Webster," *JJ*, xxi/3 (1968), 24
S. Dance: *The World of Duke Ellington* (London and New York, 1970/*R*1981), 125
R. Stewart: *Jazz Masters of the Thirties* (New York and London, n.d. [1972]), 120
J. Shaw: "Ben Webster," *JJ*, xxvi/11 (1973), 2
J. Evensmo: *The Tenor Saxophone of Ben Webster, 1931–1943* (n.p. [Oslo], n.d. [?1978]) [discography]
G. Matzorkis and J. Chilton: "Ben Webster," *Giants of Jazz: Ben Webster* (TL 21, 1981) [liner notes]
Y. Delmarche and I. Fresart: *A Discography of Ben Webster, 1931–1973* (n.p. [Surhout, Belgium], n.d. [1983])
J. S. Wilson: "Ben Webster: a Jazz Great is Still Being Discovered," *New York Times* (9 Feb 1986), II, 30
M. Jones: *Talking Jazz* (London, 1987), 78
M. Hinton and D. G. Berger: *Bass Line: the Stories and Photographs of Milt Hinton* (Philadelphia, 1988)
R. Stewart and C. P. Gordon: *Boy Meets Horn* (Wheatley, Oxford, England, and Ann Arbor, MI, 1991), 197
P. Langhorn and T. Sjøgren: *Ben: the Music of Ben Webster: a Discography* (Copenhagen, 1996)
J. Evensmo: *History of Jazz Tenor Saxophone: Black Artists*, i: *1917–1934* (Oslo, 1996); ii: *1935–1939* (Oslo, 1997)

BK

Webster, Freddie (*b* Cleveland, 1916; *d* Chicago, 1 April 1947). Trumpeter. After leading his own band as a teenager (when Tadd Dameron and Earl Bostic were among his sidemen) and playing with Earl Hines (February–August 1938) and Erskine Tate (also 1938) he moved to New York, where he spent short periods with various orchestras. He then worked with Benny Carter (?1939–1940, 1943), Eddie Durham (1940), Lucky Millinder (1940 – mid-1941, late 1941–1942, 1944), Hines again (*c* July–October 1941), Jimmie Lunceford (*c* October 1942 – January 1943), Cab Calloway (spring 1945), John Kirby's sextet (late 1945), Dizzy Gillespie's big band (1946), and Sonny Stitt (1947). Very few of his solos were recorded; he may be heard at his best on *I fell for you* (1945), by "Miss Rhapsody" (Viola Wells), and he also plays outstandingly on Sarah Vaughan's *You're not the kind* (1946). (It is unaccountable that he is best known for his playing on Vaughan's *If you could see me now* (1946), for he can be heard on only eight bars of the song.) Webster was a harmonically adventurous trumpeter and an early influence on Miles Davis. He has become something of a legendary figure. Gillespie said of him: "Freddie Webster probably had the best sound on a trumpet since it was invented."

SELECTED RECORDINGS

As sideman with L. Millinder: on *Lucky Millinder, 1941–3* (1941–3, Alamac 2425), Sweet Georgia Brown (1941); Savoy (1942, Decca 18353); Hurry Hurry (1944, Decca 18609)

As sideman with others: Sonny Boy Williams: Savoy is jumpin'/Honey it must be love (1942, Decca 8643); Reverse the Charges/Rubber Bounce (1942, Decca 8651); F. Socolow: The Man I Love/Reverse the Changes (1945, Duke 112); Miss Rhapsody: He may be your man/I fell for you (1945, Savoy 5532); S. Vaughan: If you could see me now/You're not the kind (1946, Musi. 380)

BIBLIOGRAPHY

ChiltonW
G. Hoefer: "The Hot Box: Freddy Webster," *DB*, xxviii/25 (1961), 48; xxix/1 (1962), 42 [incl. discography]
H. Pekar: "Freddie Webster," *JM*, viii/8 (1962), 12
I. Gitler: *Jazz Masters of the Forties* (New York, 1966/*R*1983 with discography), 89
D. Gillespie and A. Fraser: *To be, or not ... to Bop: Memoirs* (Garden City, NY, 1979, London, 1980, as *Dizzy: the Autobiography of Dizzy Gillespie*), 227
J. Chambers: *Milestones*, i: *The Music and Times of Miles Davis to 1960* (Toronto, Buffalo, and London, 1983), 32

SCOTT YANOW

Webster, Paul (Francis) (*b* Kansas City, MO, 24 Aug 1909; *d* New York, 6 May 1966). Trumpeter. He played on a part-time basis before becoming a professional musician around 1927. He worked with George E. Lee, Bennie Moten (summer 1927 – summer 1928, and intermittently thereafter into the early 1930s), the pianist Paul Banks's Rhythm Aces (in Kansas City, mid-1930), the tuba and double bass player Jap Allen (*c*1930), Jimmie Lunceford (1931), Tommy Douglas (*c*1931), and the singer Eli Rice (1933–4). After he rejoined Lunceford (spring 1935; for illustration *see* LUNCEFORD, JIMMIE) he began to specialize in playing in the high register. Some of his best work was done with Lunceford, and his playing is well represented on *For Dancers Only* (1937, Decca 1340); he appears in the short film *Jimmie Lunceford and his Dance Orchestra* (1936). In 1944 he left Lunceford for Cab Calloway, with whom he played at intervals into the 1950s. Webster also worked under other bandleaders, including Charlie

Barnet (1946–7, 1952–3), Sy Oliver (1947), Eddie Wilcox, and Count Basie (in New York, spring 1950). He ceased full-time playing in 1953, but continued to perform into the 1960s.

BIBLIOGRAPHY

ChiltonW; *McCarthyB*

J. Simmen: "Carnet de notes, 2: un LP où l'on entend beaucoup Paul Webster," *BHcF*, no.159 (1966), 3

EDDIE LAMBERT

Weckl, Dave [David Joseph] (*b* St. Louis, 8 Jan 1960). Drummer. He began playing drums at the age of eight and was introduced to big-band and dixieland styles by his father, an amateur pianist. When he was 16 he began working professionally with pop and jazz groups, and from 1979 to 1981 he studied jazz at the University of Bridgeport in Connecticut. As a member of the group French Toast, which later became Michel Camilo's band, Weckl met Anthony Jackson, through whom he gained studio work in New York. He subsequently played with Chick Corea in both his Elektric Band and his Akoustic Band (1985–92) and was active as a sideman with, among others, Camilo, Steve Khan, the Brecker Brothers, Mike Stern, John Patitucci, Eddie Daniels, Chuck Loeb, the MANHATTAN JAZZ QUINTET, and Dave Grusin. In 1990 he made the first of several recordings as a leader.

SELECTED RECORDINGS

As leader: *Master Plan* (1990, GRP 9619); *Heads Up* (1992, GRP 9673)

As sideman: M. Stern: *Upside Downside* (1986, Atl. 81656); C. Corea: *Light Years* (1987, GRP 1036); GRP Super Band: *GRP Super Live in Concert* (1987, GRP 2-91650); M. Camilo: *Michel Camilo* (1988, Portrait RK44482); J. Patitucci: *On the Corner* (1989, GRP 9583); S. Khan: *Public Access* (1989, GRP 9599); F. Gambale: *Thinking Out Loud* (1995, JVC 2045-2)

SELECTED FILMS AND VIDEOS

The Chick Corea Elektric Band: Live in Madrid (1986); Chick Corea Elektric Band: Inside Out; The Buddy Rich Memorial Scholarship Concert, no.1 (*c*1990)

BIBLIOGRAPHY

S. K. Fish: "Up and Coming: Dave Weckl," *MD*, viii/4 (1984), 82

G. Santoro: "Profile: Dave Weckl," *DB*, lii/9 (1985), 49

J. Potter: "Dave Weckl," *MD*, x/10 (1986), 16

B. Beuttler: "Dave Weckl: New Drumslinger in Town," *DB*, liv/12 (1987), 16

R. Mattingly: "Dave Weckl," *MD*, xiv/9 (1990), 18

R. Tolleson: "Dave Weckl: Turning the Beat Around," *DB*, lvii/11 (1990), 19 [incl. discography]

O. Gasnier and F. Goaty: "Dave Weckl: my Drummer is Rich," *Jm*, no.402 (1991), 40

K. Micallef: "In the Eye of the Hurricane," *JT*, xxii/7 (1992), 39

J. Woodard: "Elektric/Akoustic Afterlife," *DB*, lxi/4 (1994), 32

R. Mattingly: "Dave Weckl," *MD*, xxii/4 (1998), 48

<http://www.daveweckl.com> (1999)

MARK GILBERT

Weersma, Melle (*b* Harlingen, Netherlands, 22 Jan 1908; *d* Putten, Netherlands, 14 Sept 1988). Dutch bandleader and arranger. He studied piano and played with the Electorians (1926–8), under the bandleader Juan Llossas (in Germany, 1931–2), and with the drummer Bobby 't Sas (1933). In 1934 he formed a big band, the Red, White and Blue Aces, that played in a musically adventurous style and achieved little success; the following year he moved to London in February to write arrangements for Jack Hylton and to Chicago in October to write arrangements for Benny Goodman and the conductor André Kostelanetz. He went to Argentina in 1938, then returned to the Netherlands after ending his career as a musician. He is the composer of the well-known song *Penny Serenade*, recorded by, among others, Nat Gonella (1938). Weersma may be heard leading his big band on the pairing *Honolulu Blues/Red Indian Chase* (1934, Decca F42022).

WIM VAN EYLE

Wehner, Heinz (*b* Menden, Germany, *c*1910; *d c*1944). German bandleader, violinist, trumpeter, and singer. He studied at the Hanover Conservatory at the age of 12; after moving to Berlin around 1930, he formed a trio and then led a sextet. At the beginning of 1935 he formed a dance band which played in a style similar to that of the Casa Loma Orchestra; the players varied in number from 10 to 15 and included Willy Berking. The band, which earned a reputation for the refinement of its playing, made numerous recordings for Telefunken from 1935 to 1942; *White Jazz* (1935, M6118) and *Bugle Call Rag* (1936, A2007) are particularly fine recorded examples of German swing. Wehner was killed in action during World War II. (G. Conrad: *Heinz Wehner: eine Bio-Discographie*, Menden, Germany, 1989)

GÜNTHER HUESMANN

Weidman, James (Edward, Jr.) (*b* Youngstown, OH, 23 July 1953). Pianist. His father, a saxophonist, led a local soul group in which he later played organ. Weidman took up piano around the age of eight and became acquainted with jazz through recordings in his father's collection. When he was 14 his father returned to playing saxophone, and he joined the latter's group as an organist and learned to improvise. He had classical lessons from the age of 18 into his third year at Youngstown State University, where he studied performance and music education; during his final semesters he concentrated on classical music and jazz, and he graduated in 1976. Two years later he moved to New York, where he worked as a freelance with Pepper Adams, Cecil Payne, and Sonny Stitt, among others, before playing with Bobby Watson (1981). While accompanying Abbey Lincoln (1982–91) he performed with her in France (1983) and toured and recorded with Steve Coleman's Five Elements (1987–91), playing both piano and electronic keyboards. He was a member of Jay Hoggard's group from around 1987 into the 1990s, and between 1991 and 1993 he worked with Cassandra Wilson, again doubling on electronic keyboards. Weidman worked primarily as a pianist from 1991: he co-led the group Taja with Talib Kibwe, which recorded around 1995, and led his own trio, with Belden Bullock and Marvin "Smitty" Smith as his regular sidemen. In 1993 he became music director for Kevin Mahogany's group, with which he played organ while touring in 1996.

SELECTED RECORDINGS

As leader: with T. Kibwe: *Taja: a Night at Birdland* (*c*1995, Rise Up 1000-5); *People Music* (1996, TCB 96302)

As sideman: J. Hoggard: *The Fountain* (1991, Muse 5450); A. Queen: *I'm Back* (1992, Nilva 3421)

BIBLIOGRAPHY

G. Reynard and J. Szlamowicz: "Recontre: James Weidman," *Jh*, no.550 (1998), 12 [incl. discography]

<http://www.jazzcorner.com/weidman/index.html> (1999) [incl. discography]

GK

Weil, Kurt (*b* Zurich, 2 Jan 1932). Swiss vibraphonist. He studied trombone and piano before taking up vibraphone and in 1952 joined Rio de Gregori's dance band. From 1955 he was based in Stockholm as a member of Hacke

Björksten's groups, which toured with Stan Getz and Tony Scott. Weil started his own band in 1957. It toured Sweden and performed initially in a popular vein, but in 1958 altered its style more towards jazz; George Gruntz, Daniel Humair, and visiting American soloists appeared with the group during this time. Later, while touring mainly in Scandinavia (into the 1970s), it returned to popular styles. Weil finally disbanded the group and returned to Switzerland to work in the recording industry as an artists-and-repertory man. He hosted a jazz radio show, worked for nine years in a marketing position for the GRP label, and then in 1995 resumed playing vibraphone and formed a new band. This new group, with Joe Beck, Mark Egan, and Danny Gottlieb among its sidemen, toured internationally and recorded the albums *Late but Not too Late* (1997, Col. 487866) and *Movin' Forward – Reachin' Back* (2000, TCB 20302).

OTTO FLÜCKIGER

Wein, George (Theodore) (*b* Boston, 3 Oct 1925). Pianist, singer, and impresario. He studied classical piano from the age of seven with Margaret Chaloff (the mother of Serge Chaloff) and took lessons from Sam Saxe (1935–45) and Teddy Wilson. As a youth he formed a 13-piece dance band, with which he played until 1941, and while still in his teens he appeared at nightclubs in Boston. Later he played with Max Kaminsky (1946), Edmond Hall (1949), and Wild Bill Davison (1949). In 1950 he graduated from Boston University, organized groups for the Savoy in Boston, and opened his own club, Storyville, for which he engaged well-known dixieland and swing players; the following year he established a record company of the same name (*see* Storyville (ii)). By 1952 Wein had opened a second club presenting these types of musicians, Mahogany Hall, and at the end of that year he became a member of its house band, the Mahogany Hall All Stars, led by Vic Dickenson. (For the complex history of the Storyville club and Mahogany Hall *see* Nightclubs and other venues). Wein also played with Bobby Hackett (1950–54), and performed and recorded at his clubs and elsewhere with Davison (1951), Sidney Bechet (1951, 1953), Ruby Braff (1951, 1954–79), Jo Jones (*c*1953), Pee Wee Russell (1953), Dickenson (*c*1953 and *c*1956), and Jimmy McPartland. He taught jazz history at Boston University from 1954.

Wein is best known as the founder of the Newport jazz festival, which he first organized in February 1954 with financial support from Louis and Elaine Lorillard. At the same time he continued to work as a performer: he put together, and was a member of, Bechet's group at the World's Fair in Belgium in 1958, and from the late 1950s he toured internationally as the leader of the Newport Festival All-Stars, alongside Buck Clayton, Braff, Dickenson, Russell, Bud Freeman, Barney Kessel, and Red Norvo In 1969 he recorded in Paris with Stephane Grappelli and Joe Venuti. Wein founded the Boston Globe Jazz & Heritage Festival in 1966, and by the 1970s he was involved in the organization of several international festivals, such as the Grande Parade du Jazz in Nice (from 1974), and had formed a company, Festival Productions Inc. in New York, to manage this area of his activities; he also formed the New York Jazz Repertory Company (1974). In 1982 he revived the Newport Jazz Festival All-Stars (its other members were Warren Vaché, Norris Turney, Harold Ashby, Scott Hamilton, Slam Stewart, and Oliver Jackson), with which he performed widely in the USA and in 1986 appeared at the Madarao festival in Japan and toured Europe. The group continued to tour and record in the late 1980s and the 1990s with Vaché, Clark Terry, Nicholas Payton, Al Grey, Ricky Ford, Illinois Jacquet, Flip Phillips, Red Holloway, Gray Sargent, Howard Alden, Eddie Jones, and Kenny Washington among its sidemen. Wein also issued a small number of recordings on the George Wein label in the mid-1980s; these albums were quickly absorbed into the Concord label, which reissued the material on both LP and CD.

Throughout these years Wein's activities as a promoter continued to grow, and by the 1990s Festival Productions was running several dozen festivals worldwide. But during this decade the pre-eminence of Wein's JVC Jazz Festival, New York, was increasingly challenged by the concurrent What is Jazz? Festival, whose organizer, Michael Dorf (of the Knitting Factory), was widely praised for offering a much less conservative program than Wein. With the acquisition of a corporate sponsorship in 1997, the Knitting Factory event, retitled the Texaco New York Jazz Festival, rivaled Wein's own. Perhaps not coincidentally, in March 1998 Wein reached an agreement to sell 80 per cent of Festival Productions to BET (Black Entertainment Television), though he remained centrally involved and that year organized a JVC festival that was larger and lasted longer than ever before.

"Wein … has spent most of his career working for the good of the music. One may agree or disagree with his notion of what constitutes jazz and his occasional wily attempts to co-opt critics. But through his presence in New York and the world, he has consistently kept jazz in view as an important, culturally significant form of entertainment" (Watrous, 1995).

See also Festivals.

SELECTED RECORDINGS

As leader: *George Wein and the Newport All-Stars* (1962, Imp. 31); *The Newport Jazz Festival All-Stars* (1984, Conc. 260); *Bern Concert '89* (1989, Conc. 4401); *Swing that Music* (1993, Col. CK53317)

As sideman with S. Grappelli and J. Venuti: *Venupelli Blues* (1969, BYG 529122)

BIBLIOGRAPHY

FeatherE; *Feather '60s*; *Feather–Gitler '70s*

N. Hentoff: "Self Promotion: it Pays," *DB*, xxiv/11 (1957), 15

J. H. Klee: "Jazz from J to Z," *MR*, iii/9 (1976), 5

S. Traill: "From Newport to Nice to New Orleans," *JJI*, xxxi/7 (1978), 22

L. Tomkins: "George Wein," *CI*, xvii (1979), no.11, p.6; no.12, p.16

L. Tomkins: "Festivals, Musicians and Me, by George Wein," *CI*, xx/ii (1981), 6

K. Franckling: "George Wein's Long Run," *JT* (1985), Oct, 12

M. Brown: "The Man who Keeps Jazz in our Blood," *Sunday Times* (6 July 1986), 44

J. Chilton: *Sidney Bechet: the Wizard of Jazz* (London and New York, 1987/*R*1996)

G. Endress: "Wein-Lese: Gesprach mit dem Festivalmacher und Pianisten George Wein," *JP*, xxxvii/5 (1988), 8

M. Selchow: *Profoundly Blue: a Bio-discographical Scrapbook on Edmond Hall* (Lübbecke, Germany, 1988)

F. M. Coudert and B. R. Rocha: "Wein ou le double jeu," *Jm*, no.383 (1989), 48

"Interview with George Wein," *The Note*, iii/2 (1991), 10

E. Cook: "George Wein," *JJI*, xlvi/12 (1993), 6

R. Hilbert: *Pee Wee Russell: the Life of a Jazzman* (New York, and Oxford, England, 1993)

G. A Borgman: "Drummer for the Giants of Jazz," *MR*, xxi/8 (1994), 48, 25ff

J. McLeod: *Jazztrack* (Sydney, 1994), 208

P. Watrous: "Grand Potentate of Jazz," *New York Times* (11 June 1995)

——: "Two Festivals Compete for What's Hot in Jazz," *New York Times* (19 June 1997)

P. Elwood: "Jazz Festivals Play to a New Audience," *San Francisco Examiner* (27 March 1998)

P Watrous: "Jazz Festival Company Being Sold to BET Network," *New York Times* (18 March 1998)
B. Ratliff: "Once Rivals, Two Jazz Impresarios Agree to Disagree," *New York Times* (30 May 1999)

JAMES M. DORAN/BK

Weinert, Susan (*b* Neuenkirchen, Germany, 24 June 1965). German electric guitarist. After attending a number of Jamey Aebersold's summer camps in Europe in the 1980s she embarked on a career as a leader, working usually in a trio with the bass player Martin Weinert and the drummer Hardy Fischötter. Although she was inspired at first by such players as Wes Montgomery and Jim Hall, most of her work from the 1990s is characterized by a fluent command of the styles of a later generation of guitarists, among them Allan Holdsworth, Scott Henderson, and John Scofield. In addition to leading her own group Weinert has worked in Europe with Mike Mainieri's Steps Ahead (1993) and with the American electric bass guitarist Jimmy Earl.

SELECTED RECORDINGS

(all recorded for VeraBra)

Mysterious Stories (1992, 2111-2); *Crunch Time* (1994, 2144-2); *The Bottom Line* (1996, 2177-2)

BIBLIOGRAPHY

L. Trampert: "Susan Weinert: das Trio als Herausforderung," *Gitarre & Bass* (1993), Feb, 38
G. Endress: "Susan unheimlich gebucht: Susan Weinert Band," *JP*, xliii/11 (1994), 26
F. Sichmann: "Susan Weinert Band: Family Affair," *Fachblatt* (1994), Dec, 34
M. Fluck: "Susan Weinert," *Feedback* (1996), Oct–Nov, 16
J. Urbanek: "The Bottom Line: das dritte Album der Susan Weinert Band," *Gitarre & Bass*, (1996), June, 66
<http://www.jazzpages.com/SusanWeinert/index.htm> (1999)

MARK GILBERT

Weintraub Syncopators. German band. It was founded as an amateur group in Berlin in 1924 by the pianist Stefan Weintraub (*b* Breslau, Germany (now Wrocław, Poland), 14 Aug 1897; *d* Sydney, 10 Sept 1981) and the clarinetist and alto saxophonist Horst Graff. The pianist and arranger Friedrich Holländer (*b* London, 18 Oct 1896; *d* Munich, Jan 1976) assumed the leadership in 1927 when Weintraub began to play drums. By 1928 the band was playing a more extreme style of hot jazz than any band in Germany and was highly successful. In that year it made the first of many recordings of hot dance music (*Up and at 'em/Jackass Blues*, Odeon O2353), and in 1930 appeared in the film *Der blaue Engel* with Marlene Dietrich and recorded with her. The band made concert tours and worked in radio and theater in Germany until 1933, then toured Italy (1934), Scandinavia, the USSR (1935), Japan (1936–7), China (1937), and Australia (1937), where it disbanded around 1938. (H. J. P. Bergmeier: *The Weintraub Story Incorporating the Ady Rosner Story* (Menden, Germany, 1982) [incl. discography])

For illustration *see* SAXOPHONE, fig. 2.

GÜNTHER HUESMANN

Weiskopf, Walt(er David) (*b* Fort Gordon, GA, 30 July 1959). Tenor saxophonist. He grew up in Syracuse, New York, and attended the Eastman School of Music (BM 1980). Later he toured with the big bands of Buddy Rich (1981–2) and Toshiko Akiyoshi (1983–96) and, while continuing his studies at Queens College, CUNY (MM 1989), worked with the drummer Roland Vasquez (from 1987). He also led a quartet (1985–90), which consisted of his brother Joel on piano, Jay Anderson, and Jeff Hirshfield, and then a sextet (from 1990), with his brother, Conrad Herwig, the saxophonist Andy Fusco, Peter Washington, and Billy Drummond. Weiskopf is the author of *Intervallic Improvisation* (New Albany, IN, 1995) and, with R. Ricker, *Coltrane: a Player's Guide to his Harmony* (New Albany, 1990) and *The Augmented Scale in Jazz* (New Albany, 1993).

SELECTED RECORDINGS

As leader: *Mindwalking* (1990, Iris 1003); *Simplicity* (1992, Criss Cross 1075); *Night Lights* (1995, Double Time 106)
As sideman: J. Snidero: *Vertigo* (1994, Criss Cross 1112); B. Drummond: *Dubai* (1995, Criss Cross 1120)

GK

Weiss, Doug(las John) [Doogala] (*b* Chicago, 30 Nov 1965). Double bass player. He played piano from the age of five and took up double bass when he was ten. While in high school he performed with local symphony orchestras and chamber ensembles, and late in his teens he began to play jazz; in summer 1982 he toured Scandinavia with the Blue Lake Fine Arts Camp International Jazz Band. The following year he enrolled at William Paterson College (Wayne, New Jersey) (BFA), where he studied privately with Todd Coolman; later he also had private lessons with Rufus Reid and Gary Peacock. In 1987 he began what became a longstanding association with Chris Potter, and from 1988 to 1989 he worked with Joe Williams. He was also a member of Jeff Williams's small groups, notably Coalescence (1991–6, in which he played alongside Kevin Hays), and of Joe Roccisano's nonet (recording in 1994 and 1997). From 1994 to 1998 Weiss was a sideman in Toshiko Akiyoshi's orchestra, and from the mid-1990s he worked with Hays (recording in 1994–5), the saxophonist Ilhan Ersahin (in whose trio, with Kenny Wollesen, he recorded in 1995–6 and performed at numerous Turkish jazz festivals into the new century), Al Foster (with whom he recorded around 1996 and appeared at the Graz Jazz Meeting in 1997), the guitarist Dawn Thomson (recording in 1997), and the tenor saxophonist John Nugent (recording from *c*1997).

Late in 1995 Weiss performed with the Blue Note All Stars, consisting of Tim Hagans, Greg Osby, Hays, and Bill Stewart, but he was replaced by Essiet Essiet for the group's recording, made early the following year. Later he worked with Mark Turner (1997–9), the pianist George Colligan (from 1997), Eddie Henderson (from 1999), and the pianist Bill Carrothers and Randy Brecker (both 2000). He also played with Dominique Eade, and the saxophonists David Bixler and Anton Schwartz, and recorded with the trombonist Nils Wogram (1994) and the saxophonists Joel Frahm, John McKenna, and Adam Kolker (all 1998). Weiss is a member of the cooperative ensemble Subterranean Sextet, alongside Myron Walden (alto saxophone and bass clarinet), John Cowherd (piano), John Hart, Monte Croft, and Brian Blade; in 2000 it was performing regularly at Smalls in New York, and that same year it appeared at the JVC Jazz Festival New York. In 1991 Weiss began teaching in the Jazz and Contemporary Music Program at the New School for Social Research (from 1996, at the Mannes/New School, and from 1999, at the New School University).

SELECTED RECORDINGS

As sideman: C. Potter: *Sundiata* (1993, Criss Cross 1107); K. Hays: *Go Round* (1995, BN B21Z-32491-2); D. Thomson: *Happenstance* (1997, NY Jam 1198); J. McKenna: *Apparition* (1998, Igmod 49902-2)

BIBLIOGRAPHY

"Auditions: Doug Weiss," *DB*, lii/11 (1985), 62
"Mus. Ed. Report," *DB*, liii/12 (1986), 13
<http://www.fundementiacom/musicians2.htm#doug> (2000)

GK

Weiss, Klaus (*b* Gevelsberg, Germany, 17 Feb 1942). German drummer. He studied drumming from the age of ten; although largely self-taught, he took lessons briefly from Stuff Combe at the Musikhochschule in Cologne (1959–60). As a member of the Jazzopaters (from 1958) he accompanied Nelson Williams and the singer Inez Cavanaugh; later he worked with the Tremble Kids (1960) and Klaus Doldinger (1962–5). In Paris he accompanied Johnny Griffin, Kenny Drew, and Bud Powell (1963), recorded with the German All Stars (1963), and formed a trio with which he accompanied such visiting soloists as Leo Wright, Don Byas, and Wilton "Bogey" Gaynair (1965). In 1965 he toured in a group that included Sal Nistico (ii) and Dusko Goykovich and played with Don Menza, and the following year his trio toured as accompanists to Booker Ervin. Weiss was a member of Erwin Lehn's big band (1967–8), after which he took up residence near Munich and played with the jazz ensemble of Bayerischer Rundfunk, led by Joe Haider, and worked with Friedrich Gulda (1969–70). He appeared frequently at the Domicile club and performed and recorded as the leader of various ensembles, notably a quartet, which recorded the album *Mythologie* (1971, BASF 2021111), and a group consisting of members of the Thad Jones–Mel Lewis Orchestra, which recorded the album *The Git Go* (1974, BASF 20224066). During the first half of the 1970s Weiss also played in Horst Jankowski's sextet and in the trios of Bobby Jones and Eugen Cicero. He toured with Mal Waldron and with Goykovich's big band (1975–7), led a quintet which accompanied such soloists as Nistico, Roman Schwaller, and Clifford Jordan (1978–83), and played with Tete Montoliu, Eddie "Lockjaw" Davis, and the WDR and NDR big bands. In the 1980s he toured with Jordan and Horace Parlan, worked with Jerome Richardson, and established a new quintet. In 1991 Weiss formed a trio consisting of Rob van Bavel and Thomas Stabenow, which that same year recorded *L.A. Calling* (L+R 45033).
(<http://www.jazzrecords.com/klausweiss/index.htm> (2000) [incl. M. Hennessey: "Klaus Weiss: a Profile"; also incl. discography])

WOLFRAM KNAUER/BK

Weiss, Michael (David) (*b* Dallas, 10 Feb 1958). Pianist. He attended Indiana University (BM 1981) and following his graduation moved to New York. There he worked with Jon Hendricks (1982), Junior Cook's quartet (1983–4), in Cook's quintet with Bill Hardman (1983–7, touring Europe in 1986), and semi-regularly with Lou Donaldson (1984–8) and Art Farmer (1986). In 1987 he began a lasting association with Johnny Griffin, serving as the latter's music director and touring internationally. In 1989, when he was placed second in the Thelonious Monk International Piano Competition, he performed in the quintet led by Farmer and Clifford Jordan, and that same year he formed a trio, using the bass players Peter Washington, Dennis Irwin, or John Webber and the drummers Lewis Nash, Ben Riley, Al Harewood, Kenny Washington, or Leroy Williams; the trio, which remained in existence until 1994, appeared on the CBS television show "Night Watch" in 1990. In 1991 he performed in a duo with Cook at Scullers in Cambridge, Massachusetts, a performance which was broadcast early in 1992 on the National Public Radio show "Jazzset." Weiss played in the orchestra presenting Charles Mingus's symphonic piece *Epitaph* (1991), the Smithsonian Jazz Masterworks Orchestra (1991–4), and the Vanguard Jazz Orchestra (from 1991), with Charles McPherson (recording in 1994), and again with Farmer (1996–7). From 1995 he has led small groups with such sidemen as Eric Alexander, Steve Davis (iii), Webber, and Joe Farnsworth. During much of his career he has been active as a freelance, working with, among many others, George Coleman, Slide Hampton, Frank Wess, and Cecil Payne, and in a duo with Barry Harris; in collaboration with Harris he wrote the liner notes to *The Complete Bud Powell on Verve* (1994, Verve 5-314-521669-2). He also served on the faculties of Long Island University (1986) and Queens College, CUNY (1996–7). In summer 2000 Weiss's composition *El Camino* earned him the grand prize in the Thelonious Monk International Jazz Composers Competition.

SELECTED RECORDINGS

As leader: *Presenting Michael Weiss* (1986, Criss Cross 1022); *Power Station* (1996, DIW 924)
As sideman: J. Griffin: *The Cat* (1990, Ant. 422-848421-2); C. McPherson: *First Flight Out* (1994, Arabesque 0113); D. Raney: *Back in New York* (1996, Ste. 31409)

BIBLIOGRAPHY

B. Blumenthal; "Cook, Weiss Exemplify a Jazz Tradition," *Boston Globe* (20 Oct 1991)
T. Panken: "Digging the Foundation," *DB*, lxv/12 (1998), 71
P. B. Matthews: "Michael Weiss Interview," *Cadence*, xxv (1999), no.7, p.21; no.8, p.5

GK

Weiss, René (*b* Geneva, 1900; *d* Geneva, 28 Aug 1984). Swiss trombonist. After studying music, he played with the Illarez Orchestra (1922) and the bandleader and pianist Jean Yatov (1924). He then moved to Berlin, where he worked with the violinist Marek Weber, Béla Dajos's band, Ben Berlin (1928), the double bass player Teddy Sinclair (1929), and Lud Gluskin (1930), to whom he returned in 1932 to make recordings. In France he performed with Ray Ventura (1931–6), Guy Paquinet (1934–5), the orchestra of the Paramount theater (1937–8), and Fred Adison's band (1938). In 1939 Weiss left France for Switzerland, where he played with Teddy Stauffer and led a group that made recordings in 1942–3 (among them *Boogie woogie* (1943, Col. ZZ1086), which well represents his style of playing).

MICHEL LAPLACE

Weiss, Sammy [Samuel M.] (*b* New York, 1 Sept 1910; *d* Encino, CA, 18 Dec 1977). Drummer and bandleader. From 1931 he performed and recorded in New York with the alto saxophonist and singer Gene Kardos (1931–8), Benny Goodman (1934), Tommy Dorsey (1935–6), Louis Prima (1935, 1937), and Artie Shaw (1936). He also worked with Paul Whiteman and made numerous recordings as a freelance with such musicians as Adrian Rollini (1935), Wingy Manone (1935, 1936), Miff Mole (1937), Louis Armstrong and Lil Armstrong (both 1938), and the pianist and singer Erskine Butterfield (1940, 1942) and also in a trio with Johnny Guarnieri (1944). After moving to California (May 1945) he formed his own orchestra, which became very successful; he continued to work as a leader through the

1960s, though he briefly rejoined Goodman from December 1946 to January 1947. Weiss's playing may be heard on Lil Armstrong's *Let's get happy together* (1938, Decca 1904) and Butterfield's *Tuxedo Junction* (1940, Decca 3042). While he was principally a drummer he also played vibraphone. (*ConnorBG*)

based on *ChiltonW*

Weiss, Sid (*b* Schenectady, NY, 30 April 1914; *d* San Bernadino Co., CA, 29 March 1994). Double bass player. He played violin, clarinet, and tuba before changing to double bass in his teens. Having begun to perform in New York in 1931 he worked with Louis Prima (1934), Wingy Manone (1935–6), Charlie Barnet (1936), Artie Shaw (1936, September 1937–1939), Joe Marsala (from November 1939), and Tommy Dorsey (March 1940 – November 1941; for illustration *see* DORSEY, TOMMY). He then spent several periods with Benny Goodman's band (October 1941 – June 1942, late 1942 – early 1943, June 1943 – January 1945). Following an overseas tour with Hal McIntyre (1945) he played mainly in studios, recording with such musicians as Muggsy Spanier, Pee Wee Russell, and Cozy Cole (all 1944), Duke Ellington and Bud Freeman (both 1945), and Wild Bill Davison (1947); he also played with Eddie Condon and Joe Bushkin. In August 1954 he moved to Los Angeles, where he ceased full-time performing, though he continued to work occasionally as a freelance. Weiss's playing may be heard to advantage with Adrian Rollini and his Tap Room Gang on *Nagasaki* (1935, Vic. 25085) and with Cole on *Jump Awhile* (1944, Savoy 518). The social security death index gives his date of death and his last-known residence, Lake Elsinore, California; state death records place his death in San Bernadino County. (*ConnorBG*)

based on *ChiltonW*

Weldon, Jerry [Gerard Joseph, Jr.] (*b* New York, 27 Sept 1952). Tenor saxophonist. He attended Rutgers University, at the campus at Newark, New Jersey (BA music 1981), and studied privately with Paul Jeffrey, George Coleman, Kenny Barron, and David Baker. Between 1982 and 1988 he was a featured soloist in Lionel Hampton's big band, with which he appears in the video *Newport Jazz '88.* He joined Brother Jack McDuff's Heating System in 1988 and continued to work with the group in the 1990s. From 1990 to 1993 he toured with the big band of Harry Connick, Jr., and he performed in the videos *Swingin' out When* (*c*1991 [filmed 1990]) and *You Didn't Know Me When.* In 1991 Weldon was a founding member of the N.Y. Hardbop Quintet. He also worked with Jimmy McGriff (1993–7) and Al Grey (from 1995), and co-led a number of small groups with the organist Bobby Forrester and Joe Magnarelli.

SELECTED RECORDINGS

As leader with B. Forrester: *Five by Five* (1993, Cats Paw 2101); *The Second Time Around* (*c*1995, Cats Paw 2501)
As sideman: N.Y. Hardbop Quintet: *The Clincher* (1994, TCB 95202); J. McDuff and J. DeFrancesco: *It's about Time* (1995, Conc. 4705); A. Grey: *Me 'n Jack* (1995, Pullen Music 2350); N.Y. Hardbop Quintet: *Rokermotion* (1996, TCB 96352)

GK

Weller, Don(ald Arthur Albert) (*b* Croydon, England, 19 Dec 1940). English tenor saxophonist. His year of birth is given as 1947 in Carr, Fairweather, and Priestley's *Jazz: the Rough Guide*, but according to Weller himself he was born in 1940. Although he played classical clarinet and jazz tenor saxophone in his teenage years he did not turn professional until he was 30. He then led the jazz-rock group Major Surgery (1970–79), performed and recorded with Stan Tracey (from 1976), and co-led a quartet with Bryan Spring for several years (from 1978); the Weller–Spring quartet toured and recorded in Britain in 1981 with Hannibal Peterson as guest soloist. In the 1970s Weller also worked with Harry Beckett's Powerhouse Section and in various groups with Art Themen, and in the 1980s he performed and recorded with Gil Evans in Britain and co-led a quintet with Bobby Wellins. Later he performed and recorded frequently with Tina May (1990s) and began leading his own big band (1995), for which he wrote compositions and arrangements; it toured Britain in autumn 1998.

SELECTED RECORDINGS

As leader: of Major Surgery: *First Cut* (1977, Next 1); with B. Spring: *Commit No Nuisance* (1979, Affinity AFF 44); with S. Tracey: *Play Duke, Monk and Bird* (1988, Emanem 3604); *Live* (1996, 33 Jazz 032)
As sideman: S. Tracey: *The Bracknell Connection* (1976, Steam 103); H. Peterson: *Poem Song* (1981, Mole 6); T. May: *Never Let Me Go* (1991, 33 Jazz 005); S. Tracey: *Portraits Plus* (1992, BN International 80696); D. Newton and C. Tracey: *Bootleg Eric* (1998, ASC 23)

BIBLIOGRAPHY

CarrJ; *ChiltonB*
B. Case: "Anything for the Easy Life," *MM* (22 Dec 1979), 18
P. Kelly: "Don's Four by Three," *Jazz UK*, no.15 (1997), 15

MARK GILBERT

Wellins, Bobby [Robert Coull] (*b* Glasgow, 24 Jan 1936). Scottish tenor saxophonist. Both his parents were professional musicians. Having started on piano, he was taught alto saxophone and harmony by his father and later studied keyboard harmony. In 1953 he moved to London, where he worked as a tenor saxophonist with Buddy Featherstonhaugh (autumn 1956 – summer 1957, recording in 1956). He visited America while with Vic Lewis (1958) and France with John Burch and Jeff Clyne (spring 1959). Once again in London, he played with Tony Crombie (1959; recording in 1960–61), Tony Kinsey (1960), Tommy Whittle (1960–61), and others. In 1961 he gave a memorable concert performance of his composition *Culloden Moor.* His most important affiliation was with Stan Tracey, in the New Departures Quartet and in a quartet and big band under Tracey's name, from the early 1960s into the early 1970s; he took a prominent role on Tracey's successful recording *Under Milk Wood* (1965). Wellins was inactive for some years owing to his heroin addiction, but in 1975 he overcame this problem and gradually resumed playing. From 1977 through the 1990s he performed and recorded as the leader of small groups, particularly a quartet with the pianist Peter Jacobson, the bass players Adrian Kendon or Kenny Baldock, and the drummer Spike Wells. He also toured and then recorded (1980) with Jimmy Knepper, and he was a soloist in Charlie Watts's big band (1985–6). In the 1990s he was a member of orchestras led by Kenny Wheeler and Bob Wilber and worked with John Barnes and Spike Robinson in Tenor Madness (1996), as well as appearing as a freelance with other small groups. From the late 1970s onwards he has worked as a teacher, principally in the jazz department at the West Sussex Institute of Higher Education in Chichester.

Wellins's playing is notable for its combination of passion and intelligence, which distinguishes, in particular, the albums *Jubilation* (1978) and *Dreams are Free* (1979); both these recordings demonstrate the reconciliation of keen spontaneity with a structured approach to collective improvisation, in the finest tradition of such music.

SELECTED RECORDINGS

As leader: *Jubilation* (1978, Vortex 1); *Dreams are Free* (1979, Vortex 2); *Birds of Brazil* (1989, Sungai 11); *Nomad* (1992, Hot House 1008)
As sideman with S. Tracey: *Under Milk Wood* (1965, Col. 33SX1774)

BIBLIOGRAPHY

ChiltonB; *Feather '60s*; *WickesIBJ*, i
L. Tomkins: "Bobby Wellins Looks Forward," *CI*, xvii/1 (1978), 12
S. Wells: "Best of British, no.6: Bobby Wellins," *JJI*, xxxi/8 (1978), 10
M. James: Review of *Jubilation* (1978) and *Dreams are Free* (1979), *JF* [intl edn], no.76 (1982), 54
M. Pearson: "Bobby Wellins," *JJI*, xliii/12 (1990), 10
——: "Head and Heart," *Jazz: the Magazine*, no.21 (1993), 19

MICHAEL JAMES/BK

Wells, Dicky [Dickie; William] (*b* Centerville, TN, 10 June 1907; *d* New York, 12 Nov 1985). Trombonist. He grew up in Louisville, Kentucky, where, after taking up baritone horn when he was ten and changing to trombone at the age of 16, he played in local bands as a teenager and encountered the playing of Jimmy Harrison. Having moved to New York in 1926 as a member of Lloyd Scott's band, which was then taken over by Scott's brother Cecil Scott (1930), he worked with Elmer Snowden (1930–31). He then began playing in better-known African-American bands, including those led by Benny Carter (autumn 1932–1933, December 1933 – early 1934), Fletcher Henderson (*c* May–December 1933), where he first made a name for himself, and Teddy Hill (1934–7); in the course of a European tour with Hill he recorded as a leader in Paris (July 1937). He was also a sideman in important recording sessions with Spike Hughes (with Carter's band, 1933), Henry "Red" Allen (1934, 1935), and Pee Wee Russell and Billie Holiday (both 1938).

Dicky Wells, 1935

In July 1938 (just before the last two sessions) Wells joined Count Basie's highly influential big band, where he formed a famous trombone team with Benny Morton. He remained in Basie's band until late 1945 (for illustration *see* FILMS, fig.3), when illness forced his departure; he also recorded as a leader for the Signature label in 1943 and as a member of the Kansas City Six and Kansas City Seven in 1944. He played with J. C. Heard at Café Society in New York from January 1946, with Willie Bryant from June of that same year, and then with Sy Oliver (1946–7), and recorded again in 1946 as a leader and as a sideman with Buck Clayton. In October 1947 he rejoined Basie in California, and once again was a mainstay of the group, until it disbanded in January 1950; he stayed on to play in Basie's octet the following month.

Wells began the 1950s in Jimmy Rushing's group. He recorded with Paul Quinichette in 1952, and went to France that October and toured Europe with Bill Coleman. He returned to the USA in February 1953, joined Lucky Millinder (autumn 1953) and Earl Hines (at the Crescendo in Hollywood, July 1954), and then settled in New York as a freelance musician. He was reunited with Basie for the television show "The Sound of Jazz" (1957) and participated in the Henderson reunion bands of 1957–8. He twice revisited Europe as a member of Buck Clayton's All Stars (autumn 1959, spring 1961) and toured with Ray Charles (November 1961 – spring 1963) before joining the house band led by Reuben Phillips at the Apollo Theatre in Harlem. Wells traveled to Europe as a freelance soloist in 1965. In 1967 he took a day job, but he continued to play, touring Europe with Buddy Tate late in 1968 and appearing at the New Orleans Jazz Festival in 1969. In 1972 he was a member of Carter's big band at the Newport Jazz Festival. From mid-1977 he worked with the group of veteran musicians known as the Countsmen, and he made further tours of Europe with Earle Warren and Claude Hopkins in 1978. In the early 1980s he performed in a big band.

Wells was one of a group of trombonists in the 1930s who developed further the legato style of Jimmy Harrison. He played in a rich, flamboyant style filled with portamentos, smears, and growls. He has many excellent brief solos on Basie's recordings, but his best-known performances are as the leader of a group recorded in Paris in 1937, some of which include Django Reinhardt. He should not be confused with Dickie Wells, the owner of both the Ebony and Dickie Wells's Shim Sham Club, New York.

SELECTED RECORDINGS

As leader: Bugle Call Rag/Between the Devil and the Deep Blues Sea (1937, Swing 6); I got rhythm/Japanese Sandman (1937, Swing 27); Sweet Sue/Hangin' around Boudon (1937, Swing 16); I've found a new baby/Hot Club Blues (1937, Swing 3); Dinah/Nobody's Blues but my Own (1937, Swing 39); Lady Be Good/Dicky Wells Blues (1937, Swing 10); I got rhythm/I'm fer it too (1943, Sig. 90002); Linger Awhile/Hello Babe (1943, Sig. 28115); Drag Nasty Walk (1946, HRS 1018)
As sideman: F. Henderson: King Porter's Stomp (1933, Voc. 2527); C. Basie: Texas Shuffle (1938, Decca 2030); Panassié Stomp (1938, Decca 2224); Jive at Five (1939, Decca 2922); Dickie's Dream (1939, Voc. 5118); Take me back, baby (1941, OK 6440) E. Berry: *Beauty and the Blues* (1959, Col. 33SX1246)

SELECTED FILMS AND VIDEOS

Smash yo' Baggage (1933); Choo Choo Swing [Band Parade] (1943); Hit Parade of 1943 [Change of Heart] (1943); Reveille with Beverly (1943);

The Sound of Jazz (1957); Buck Clayton and his All Stars (1961); Born to Swing (1973)

BIBLIOGRAPHY

McCarthyB; *SchullerS*
H. Panassié: *Douze années de jazz (1927–1938): souvenirs* (Paris, 1946), 217
A. Hodeir: *Hommes et problèmes du jazz, suivi de La religion du jazz* (Paris, 1954; Eng. trans., rev. Hodeir, as *Jazz: its Evolution and Essence*, New York, 1956/*R*1975)
R. Horricks: *Count Basie and his Orchestra: its Music and its Musicians* (London and New York, 1957), 89
M. Jones: "Wells: Fond Memories of an Old Boss," *MM* (20 Oct 1965), 6
D. Wells and S. Dance: *The Night People: Reminiscences of a Jazzman* (Boston and London, 1971, rev. 2/1992)
G. Colombe: "How do they Age so Well? Lawrence, Dicky and Vic," *JJ*, xxix/8 (1976), 4
L. Jeske: "The Return of Dicky Wells," *JJI*, xxxi/8 (1978), 6
H. Lyttelton: *The Best of Jazz*, i: *Basin Street to Harlem: Jazz Masters and Masterpieces, 1917–1930* (London, 1978), 157
S. Dance: *The World of Count Basie* (New York and London, 1980), 88
J. Evensmo: *The Flute of Wayman Carver, the Trombone of Dickie Wells, 1927–1942, the Tenor Saxophone of Illinois Jacquet* (n.p. [Oslo], n.d. [?1983]) [discography]

JAMES LINCOLN COLLIER/BK

Wells, Henry (James) (*b* Dallas, 1906). Trombonist and singer. Having studied music at Fisk University and Cincinnati Conservatory he began playing professionally in 1926. He worked with Jimmie Lunceford (1929 – early 1935), with whom he made several recordings (1933–4, including *Jazznocracy*, 1934, Vic. 24522), Claude Hopkins (1932), and Cab Calloway. His association with Andy Kirk (1936–9, 1940–41, 1946) was interrupted by a period in which he led his own big band and worked with Gene Krupa and Teddy Hill, and another when he served in the army. Wells recorded frequently with Kirk and from 1940 served as his principal vocalist. After leaving Kirk he worked with Rex Stewart (1946) and Sy Oliver (1946–8), and in the 1960s he performed in California. (*McCarthyB*)

based on *ChiltonW*

Wells, Johnny (*b* Kentucky, *c*1905; *d* New York, 25 Nov 1965). Drummer. After performing as a singer, comedian, and dancer at the Apex Club in Chicago he joined Jimmie Noone's band, which was resident there from around late 1926. He rejoined the band later in the 1920s and recorded with it extensively between 1928 and 1931. Wells then moved to New York, where he performed and recorded with Joe Sullivan (1940).

SELECTED RECORDINGS

As sideman: J. Noone: I know that you know (1928, Voc. 1184); Every Evening (1928, Voc. 1185); Apex Blues (1928, Voc. 1207); J. Sullivan: Oh, Lady be good/I can't give you anything but love (1940, Voc. 5496)

based on *ChiltonW*/HOWARD RYE (recording-list)

Wells, Spike [Michael John] (*b* Tunbridge Wells, England, 16 Jan 1946). English drummer. As a child he studied classical piano, organ, cello, and singing; he was the head chorister at Canterbury Cathedral in 1959 and took part as a treble soloist in a recording of Vaughan Williams's Mass in G minor. His interest in jazz began to develop at the age of 11. As a drummer he is largely self-taught, although he had lessons in London with Philly Joe Jones (1966–7) and Kenny Clarke (1969). Wells played with Tubby Hayes (1968–73) and with Ronnie Scott and Humphrey Lyttelton (both 1969–70), and led a trio and a quartet with Marc Charig and Jeff Clyne among his sidemen (1969–70). From 1968 to 1970 he accompanied numerous visiting Americans as the house drummer at Ronnie Scott's, and around the same time he toured Britain with Roland Kirk (1969) and performed in Scandinavia with Stan Getz (1970). In addition he appeared at European festivals with Kenny Wheeler, Sandy Brown, Scott, and Arild Andersen. In 1974 Wells began working as a solicitor, and in 1995 he became a parish priest in Brighton. At the same time he continued his musical activites: he held longstanding affiliations with Bobby Wellins (1977–95) and Peter King (1980–89), and led a quintet with Norwegian sidemen for a tour of Norway (early 1980s), a quartet consisting of the saxophonist Geoff Simkins, Colin Purbrook, and Dave Green (mid-1980s), and a trio with the pianist Liam Noble and Chris Laurence (from 1996).

SELECTED RECORDINGS

As sideman: T. Hayes: *Live 1969* (1969, Harlequin 3006); P. King: *East 34th Street* (1983, Spot. 424); Spike Robinson: *London Reprise* (1984, Capri 44360); B. Nerem: *More than You Know* (1987, Gemini 56); M. Pyne: *My Romance* (1990, Spot. 66023); B. Wellins: *Nomad* (1992, Hot House 1008)

BIBLIOGRAPHY

ChiltonB
B. Priestley: "The Musical Obituary of Spike Wells," *MM* (24 Oct 1970), 32

MARK GILBERT

Wellstood, Dick [Richard McQueen] (*b* Greenwich, CT, 25 Nov 1927; *d* Palo Alto, CA, 24 July 1987). Pianist. His mother, a professionally trained church organist, was a graduate of the Institute of Musical Art (later the Juilliard School). He took some lessons before reaching the age of 10, but was largely self-taught and learned to play boogie-woogie and stride during the mid-1940s. From 1945 to 1950 he performed in amateur and professional dixieland groups, nearly all involving Bob Wilber. These bands accompanied Sidney Bechet in New York, Chicago, and Philadelphia clubs from 1947 to 1949 and recorded with the clarinetist, though Wellstood was later somewhat embarrassed by the results, as his playing was not yet near Bechet's standard. When Jimmy Archey left Wilber, Wellstood joined the former's group (1950), which later toured Europe (1952). After a brief further engagement with Bechet (mid-August 1953) he studied law, while playing intermittently with Roy Eldridge and regularly in Conrad Janis's Tailgate Five (1953–60); a brilliant scholar, fluent in Latin, he qualified as a lawyer, but did not practice until 1985.

From the late 1950s Wellstood played in New York as a soloist, holding a long engagement at Condon's, or as an accompanist to a large number of swing and dixieland musicians, including (besides Eldridge) Henry "Red" Allen, Ben Webster, Coleman Hawkins, Wild Bill Davison, Vic Dickenson, and Buster Bailey, mainly at the Metropole club. In 1960 he appeared on the television show "Those Ragtime Years." He also worked in the folk revival, recording with Bob Dylan and directing recordings for Odetta (1962). He played at Nick's, mainly with Davison (1962–3), joined Janis in the play *Marathon'33*, starring Julie Harris (1963), and then played for jam sessions at an obscure New York venue, Bourbon Street. After touring army bases in Greenland with Carl Warwick's band, he joined Gene Krupa's quartet, with which he toured South America (1965) and Israel (1966). From 1966 to 1968 he performed with Kenny Davern in Brielle, New Jersey, but opportunities for band work diminished as rock became increasingly popular. Apart from touring New England in a band with Punch Miller and Capt. John Handy (1970) and deputizing for six weeks in 1975 for Ralph Sutton in the World's Greatest Jazz Band of Yank

Lawson and Bob Haggart, in the 1970s he played with Paul Hoffman's society orchestra, but concentrated principally on developing a career as a solo pianist. In this capacity he appeared for many years at the Newport Jazz Festival, regularly toured Europe, worked intermittently in a duo with Davern from 1978 and in the Blue Three with Davern and Bob Rosengarden (early 1980s), and was resident at Hanratty's in New York from 1979 to 1985. Except for a period from 1985 when he temporarily abandoned music to work as a lawyer, from 1984 to 1987 he was a member of the cooperative Classic Jazz Quartet, with Dick Sudhalter, Joe Muranyi, and Marty Grosz; he continued as an unaccompanied player at Bemelman's lounge in the Carlyle Hotel, New York (1986–7), resumed his duo with Davern, and also played in a two-piano duo with Dick Hyman.

Wellstood was a witty, anti-intellectual intellectual who playfully challenged the conventions of jazz literature in his occasional writings and interviews. Although he also recorded ragtime during the craze for that genre in the early 1970s and made rare nods towards a modern repertory (*Giant Steps*, *Lush Life*), his strength was as a stride pianist, where he carried on the styles of James P. Johnson, Willie "the Lion" Smith, Fats Waller, and Art Tatum. Some of his recorded solos, transcribed and annotated by R. Scivales, appear in *Harlem Stride Piano Solos* (Katonah, NY, *c*1990).

SELECTED RECORDINGS

As unaccompanied soloist: *Alone* (1970–71, Jlgy JCE73); *From Ragtime On* (1971, Chi. 109); *At the Cookery* (1975, Chi. 139); *Swingin' on a Baby Grand* (1976, 88 Upright 005); on *Piano Giants* (1980, Swingtime 8202), Giant Steps; *Marion McPartland's Piano Jazz with guest Dick Wellstood* (1981, The Jazz Alliance 12007); *Diane* (1985, Swingtime 8207); *Swinging at the Sticky Wicket* (1986, Arbors 19188); *After You've Gone* (1987, Unisson 1008)

Duos: with D. Hyman: *I Wish I Were Twins* (1983, Swingtime 8204); with K. Davern: *Never in a Million Years* (1984, Challenge 70019); with D. Hyman: *Stride Monsters* (1986, Unisson 1006)

As leader: *From Dixie to Swing* (*c*1972, Classic Editions 10); with P. Ind: *Some Hefty Cats!* (1977, Hefty Jazz 100); with M. Grosz: *Take Me to the Land of Jazz* (1978, Aviva 6001)

As sideman: R. Eldridge: *Swing Goes Dixie* (1956, Verve 1010); J. Venuti and Z. Sims: *Joe and Zoot* (1974, Chi. 128); Classic Jazz Quartet: *The Classic Jazz Quartet* (1984, Jlgy 138)

BIBLIOGRAPHY

D. Wellstood: "Waller to Wellstood to Williams to Chaos," *JR*, iii/7 (1960), 10

D. Morgenstern: "The Life-flight of a Surrealistic Bent Eagle," *DB*, xxxiv/7 (1967), 22

D. Wellstood: "Walking with a King: a Memory of Sidney Bechet," *Down Beat Music '71* (1970), 29

M. Jones: "Wellstood: Barroom Blues," *MM* (2 Feb 1974), 51

"Richard McQueen Wellstood," *PJ*, no.11 (1975), 72

M. Kington: "Jazz in Britain: Dick Wellstood," *JJ*, xxix (1976), 16

J. Simmen: "Crystal Clear," *Coda*, no.146 (1976), 25

M. Jones: "Wellstood in his Stride," *MM* (12 March 1977), 40

R. D. Johnson: "Many Faces of Wellstood," *MR*, vi/2 (1978), 10

L. Tomkins: "Dick Wellstood," *CI*, xvi (1978), no.6, p.10; no.8, p.6

F. Kappler, D. Wellstood, and W. Rouder: Liner notes, *Giants of Jazz: James P. Johnson* (TL 18, 1981)

W. Balliett: "Easier than Working," *Jelly Roll, Jabbo and Fats* (New York, and Oxford, England, 1983), 97; repr. in *BallietA (1986)*, 311; *BallietA (1996)*, 381

J. Chilton: *Sidney Bechet: the Wizard of Jazz* (London and New York, 1987/*R*1996)

Obituaries: *New York Times* (27 July 1987); E. Cook, *JJI*, xl/9 (1987), 22

B. Wilber with D. Webster: *Music was not Enough* (London and New York, 1987)

J. Norris: "Dick Wellstood: Mister Stride," *Coda*, no.220 (1988), 30

J. D. Shacter: *Loose Shoes: the Story of Ralph Sutton* (Chicago, rev. and enlarged [2]/1994), 273

N. Hentoff: "Review: Recording: Swinging at the Sticky Wicket," *New York Times* (5 June 1998)

E. N. Meyer: *Giant Strides: the Legacy of Dick Wellstood* (Lanham, MD, and London, 1999) [bio-discography]

BK

Welsh, Alex (*b* Edinburgh, 9 July 1929; *d* London, 25 June 1982). Scottish trumpeter, singer, and bandleader. He first played cornet, and worked with Archie Semple (1951) and Sandy Brown (1953). After moving to London in 1954 he formed his own group, which within a year had played several times at the Royal Festival Hall, made its first broadcasts and recordings, and established a reputation for its dedication to the dixieland style and the excellence of its playing. From 1955 it made several tours overseas, and in 1968 it played to great acclaim at the Newport Jazz Festival. The band accompanied many American soloists, including Bud Freeman, Wild Bill Davison, Earl Hines, and Ruby Braff. In 1957 Welsh was invited to join Jack Teagarden, but did not accept. Fred Hunt and Lennie Hastings were among his longstanding sidemen; although his ensemble was noted for its few personnel changes, by 1966 the trombonist Roy Crimmins had been replaced by Roy Williams and the clarinetist Archie Semple by John Barnes and Al Gay, who between them played seven different reed instruments. This gave the band a greater tonal variety and, although it retained its early ideals, it began to approach other forms of jazz and became highly regarded for its versatility. During this period the group appeared on television in the show "Alex Welsh" (*c*1963), the series "All that Jazz" (1964) and "Jazz 625" (three episodes from 1966, with Dicky Wells, Freeman, and Henry "Red" Allen), and, later in the decade, other jazz series evidently not preserved on film and video. Welsh continued to work as a leader until shortly before his death, and in 1978 he toured Australia in the show "Salute to Satchmo."

SELECTED RECORDINGS

Dixieland to Duke (1957, Nixa 507); *The Melrose Folio* (1958, Nixa 516); *Music of the Mauve Decade* (1959, Col. 33SX1219); *Echoes of Chicago* (1962, Col. 33SX1429); *Strike One* (1966, Strike One 102); *Vintage '69* (1969, Col. SCX6333); *The Melody Maker Tribute to Louis Armstrong*, i–iii (1970, Pol. 2460123-5); *Alex Welsh in Concert* (1971, BL 12115-6); *Band Showcase*, i–ii (1973, BL 12120-21)

BIBLIOGRAPHY

CarrJ; *ChiltonB*; *Feather '60s*; *Feather–Gitler '70s*

G. A. L. Smith: "Out of the Wilderness: the Alex Welsh Band," *JM*, vii/11 (1962), 14

M. Jones: "The Welsh Wizard," *MM* (19 Feb 1972), 14

R. Cotterrell, ed.: *Jazz Now: the Jazz Centre Society Guide* (London, 1976), 179

G. Smith: "Salute to Alex," *MM* (17 June 1978), 46

Obituary, R. Crimmins, D. Fairweather, H. Gold, and M. Jones, *JJI*, xxxv/8 (1982), 24

G. Bielderman: *Alex Welsh Discography* (Zwolle, Netherlands, 1990, rev. 2/1993)

CLARRIE HENLEY/BK

Wendholt, Scott (*b* Patuxant River, MD, 21 July 1965). Trumpeter. He grew up in Denver and played trumpet from around the age of eight; his local contemporaries included Javon Jackson, Greg Gisbert, and John Gunther. After attending Indiana University (BMus 1987) he moved to Cincinnati, where he played in John Von Ohlen's Blue Wisp Big Band. Around 1990 he settled in New York. There he studied with Dave Liebman and worked initially in Latin bands; from 1991 to 1994 he led a jazz band at Augie's, and in 1992 he joined Vincent Herring. Wendholt also worked with Bruce Barth (1993–5), Carl Allen (from *c*1993), and Don Braden and joined numerous big bands: the Carnegie Hall Jazz Band, the Vanguard Jazz Orchestra, the Mingus Big Band, and the orchestras of Maria Schneider, Toshiko Akiyoshi, Louie Bellson, Bob Mintzer, Woody Herman, and

Joe Roccisano. He recorded with, among others, Klaus Suonsaari and Darrell Grant (both 1994) and the pianist Roberta Piket (1996).

SELECTED RECORDINGS

As leader: *The Scheme of Things* (1993, Criss Cross 1078); *From Now On* (1995, Criss Cross 1123)

As sideman: K. Suonsaari: *Inside Out* (1994, SN 121274-2); B. Barth: *Morning Call* (1994, Enja 8084-2); D. Grant: *The New Bop* (1994, Criss Cross 1106); R. Piket: *Unbroken Line* (1996, Criss Cross 1140)

BIBLIOGRAPHY

Feather–GitlerBEJ

<http://www.doubletimejazz.com/dtr128.htm> (1999)

GK

WenHa. Record company and label founded by WENDELL HARRISON.

Werner, Kenny [Kenneth] (*b* New York, 19 Nov 1951). Pianist. Carles, Clergeat, and Comolli (2/1994) give the year of his birth as 1952 and Stewart (1998) has his date of birth as 11 November, but in a questionnaire for this dictionary Werner gave 19 November 1951. He was classically trained from the age of seven and studied at the Manhattan School of Music (1969–70). While attending the jazz studies course at the Berklee School of Music (1971–3) he befriended Joe Lovano, and the two men have worked together periodically since that time. He toured and recorded with Archie Shepp (1980–84) and led his own trio, with Ratzo Harris and Tom Rainey (1981–95), which toured Europe several times. In New York he gave concerts of his works at Symphony Space in 1985 and 1987 and worked as a sideman with Ron Carter, Dizzy Gillespie, Al Cohn, Joe Henderson, and Gunther Schuller. Werner has had a longstanding working relationship with Bob Brookmeyer, who has been both a mentor and collaborator; he also played with the Mel Lewis Orchestra (after Lewis's death the Vanguard Jazz Orchestra; 1985–95), Eddie Gomez (1989–90), Lee Konitz (1993–6), Tom Harrell (1995–7), and Toots Thielemans (from 1995). In the 1990s he arranged the music for Christopher Hollyday's album *And I'll Sing Once More* (1992, Novus 01241-63133-2), served as music director for the singer Roseanna Vitro (from the mid-1990s), and accompanied other singers in the course of extensive freelance work. He taught at the New School for Social Research, New York (1987–93), and later published the method book *Effortless Mastery: Liberating the Master Musician Within* (New Albany, IN, 1997).

Werner, an iconoclast, is an extremely adaptive stylist whose empathy for a given musical situation makes him highly valued as a sideman, especially with singers. His playing draws from the styles of Bill Evans (ii) and Keith Jarrett, as well as from his experience in classical music. He is also, among jazz musicians, one of the few to use synthesizers in interesting ways, as heard, for example, on *Body and Soul*, recorded with Konitz.

SELECTED RECORDINGS

As unaccompanied soloist: *Beyond the Forest of Mirkwood* (1980, Enja 3061); *Meditations* (1992, Ste. 31327); *Copenhagen Calypso* (1993, Ste. 31346)

Duos with C. Potter: *Concord Duo Series*, x (1994, Conc. 4695)

As leader: *298 Bridge Street* (1981, AMF 1015); *Introducing the Trio* (1989, Sunnyside 1038); *Press Enter* (1991, Sunnyside 1056); *Live at Visiones* (1995, Conc. 4675)

As sideman: A. Shepp: *Soul Song* (1982, Enja 4050); *Down Home New York* (1984, SN 1102); P. Erskine: *Transition* (1986, Denon 33CY-1484); J. Lovano: *Village Rhythm* (1988, SN 1182); M. Lewis: *The Lost Art* (1989, Limelight 820815-2); L. Konitz: *Zounds* (1990, SN 1219); J. Lovano: *Landmarks* (1990, BN B21Z-96108); L. Schoenberg: *Sposin'* (1990, Musicmasters 5055-2); P. Erskine: *Sweet Soul* (1991, Novus 02141-63140-2); J. Lovano: *Universal Language* (1992, BN B21Z-99830); L. Konitz: on *Rhapsody*, ii (1993, PW 210), Body and Soul; R. Vitro: *Passion Dance* (1994–5, Telarc 83385)

BIBLIOGRAPHY

P. Carles, A. Clergeat, and J.-L. Comolli: *Dictionnaire du jazz* (Paris, rev. and enlarged 2/1994)

D. Heckman: "Werner Finds the Keys to the 'Master Musician Within'," *Los Angeles Times* (13 March 1998)

A. Merlin: "Qui fait couac?: Kenny Werner: esprit es-tu là?," *Jazzman*, no.33 (1998), 14

Z. Stewart: "Kenny Werner: I'd Better Write a Book," *DB*, lxv/11 (1998), 42 [incl. discography]

M. Zwerin: "A Master of Bebop Buddhism in No-man's Land," *International Herald Tribune* (13 March 1998)

GK

Werner, Lasse [Lars (Olof)] (*b* Stockholm, 22 May 1934; *d* Stockholm, 3 Feb 1992). Swedish pianist, composer, leader, and writer. He started out in the late 1940s as a tenor saxophonist but soon changed to piano, on which he was influenced mainly by Bud Powell and Thelonious Monk. In the 1950s he led his own groups and played for long periods in Germany, where he accompanied Lester Young in 1956; this recording was later issued on Onyx, on whose typically outrageous liner notes Werner is misidentified as Horst Ornimert. He recorded with a trio in 1959, and in 1960 he made an album as co-leader of a quartet with Bernt Rosengren. Werner also wrote jazz criticism for *Orkester journalen* (1957–67). He took part in the Swedish productions in Stockholm of Jack Gelber's play *The Connection* (1963, 1965), and he accompanied Don Ellis in much-debated musical "happenings" and free improvisations at the club Gyllene Cirkeln (1963). From the mid-1960s he worked regularly with the alto saxophonist Christer Boustedt and others in the group Lasse Werner och hans Vänner (Lasse Werner and his Friends), with which Dave Liebman made his first recording while in Stockholm in 1967. Into the 1970s Werner's group gave performances that combined bop, free jazz, and improvised, burlesque theatrical episodes. After suffering a stroke related to diabetes in 1978 Werner made only a few further appearances.

Oral history material in *SSsv*.

SELECTED RECORDINGS

As leader: with B. Rosengren: *Bombastica* (1960, Jlnd 26); *Lasse Werner och hans Vänner* (1967, Love 2); *Kropp & själ* (Body and soul) (1971–4, Dra. 2); *Därför dricker jag* (That's why I'm drinking) (1967, 1978, Dra. 20); *Saxofonsymfonin* (The saxophone symphony) (1972–5, Dra. 6)

As sideman with L. Young: *Lester Young in Europe* (1956, Onyx 218)

BIBLIOGRAPHY

L. Kleberg: "Man saltar i pianot bara en gång" [You must salt the piano only once], *Orkester journalen*, xxxii/7–8 (1964), 18

L. Westin: "Lars Werner," *Orkester journalen*, xlii/6 (1974), 6

Obituary, L. Westin, *Orkester journalen*, lx/3 (1992), 56

ERIK KJELLBERG/LARS WESTIN

Wertico, Paul (*b* Chicago, 5 Jan 1953). Dummer. Self-taught, he started on drums when he was 12, and by the age of 15 he was working professionally in many styles; he cites Roy Haynes as his primary jazz influence. In 1978 he declined an offer to join Pat Metheny and chose instead to remain a member of the band led by the saxophonist Joe Daley at the Jazz Showcase in Chicago. During the early 1980s he played in a group with Steve Rodby (Metheny's bass player) and the guitarist Ross Traut. In 1983 he finally joined Metheny, with whom he has toured internationally and recorded extensively. Independent of Metheny's regular group, Wertico toured Argentina in a quartet with Metheny,

Charlie Haden, and Ernie Watts in February 1986; in 1988 they toured California, Japan, and Hong Kong, and in 1993 Wertico and his wife, the keyboard player Barbara Unger-Wertico, toured as members of Metheny's band Secret Story. Wertico also performed and recorded in a duo with the drummer and percussionist Gregg Bendian and toured Poland with his own trio (1994). In 1996, with Bendian, Metheny, and Derek Bailey, he gave a series of concerts at the Knitting Factory, New York. He has worked extensively as a freelance, accompanying pop groups, folk singers, blues musicians, and other jazz musicians; his jazz recordings include albums with Kurt Elling, Paul Horn, and Ken Nordine, and he has performed with Von Freeman, Evan Parker, and Roscoe Mitchell. From around 1973 he has been a leader or co-leader of various groups in the Chicago area. In 1992 he became an instructor at Northwestern University, and he has written columns for several drumming magazines and made two instructional videos.

Wertico is a highly melodic and versatile drummer whose rhythmic flexibility has allowed Metheny's group to explore different polyrhythmic foundations. Although he is most often associated with the jazz mainstream, his tastes are wide-ranging and he is noted for his forays into the avant garde, both through his drumming and through his involvement in producing the group's recordings and live performances.

SELECTED RECORDINGS

Duos: with G. Bendian: *Bang* (1993–4, Truemedia 96731)
As leader: *The Yin & Yout* (1992, Intuition 2150-2); *Live in Warsaw!* (1994, Igmod 49802); with D. Bailey, P. Metheny, and G. Bendian: *The Sign of Four* (1996, Knitting Factory Works 197)
As sideman with P. Metheny: *First Circle* (1984, ECM 1278); *Still Life (Talking)* (1987, Geffen 24145); *Letter from Home* (1989, Geffen 24245); *We Live Here* (1994, Geffen 24729); *Quartet* (1996, Geffen 24978); *Imaginary Day* (1997, WB 9-46791-2)
As sideman with K. Elling: *Close your Eyes* (1994, BN B21Z-30645)

SELECTED FILMS AND VIDEOS

Fine Tuning your Performance (1987); The Babe (1992); Pat Metheny Group: More Travels (1992); Pat Metheny: Secret Story: Live (1993 [filmed 1992]); Sound Work of Drumming (*c*1994); Pat Metheny Group: We Live Here: Live in Japan 1995 (1995)

BIBLIOGRAPHY

CarrJ
R. Flans: "Paul Wertico: a Musical Conversation," *MD*, ix/12 (1985), 14
B. Milkowski: "Paul Wertico's Drum Obsession," *DB*, lii/5 (1985), 26
——: "Paul Wertico's Secret Story," *MD*, xix/1 (1995), 36
H. Reich: "Stardom is Beating a Path to Drummer Paul Wertico," *Chicago Tribune* (14 March 1996)
<http://pubweb.acns.nwu.edu/~pwe574/paul.htm> (1997)
A. Budofsky: "Paul Wertico: 'Give the Drummer's Sum/8x12'," *Hot Trax* [suppl. to *MD*] (1998), 35

GK

Wesley, Fred(, Jr.) (*b* Mobile, AL, 4 July 1943). Trombonist. His father led a local rhythm-and-blues big band and was head of the music department at Mobile Central High School. From the age of three he learned piano with his grandmother, and after playing trumpet briefly he changed to trombone when he was about 12; one of his earliest influences was the trombonist in his father's band. Later he played drums in a small group with his father. He attended Alabama State University (AA music) and toured for a short time in Ike and Tina Turner's band (*c*1962) and with Hank Ballard and the Midnighters. During his military service he played in an army band in Huntsville, Alabama, following which he spent two periods with James Brown (1967–70, 1971–5); in the interim he worked in studios and wrote film scores in Los Angeles. After leaving Brown, Wesley worked in various groups led by the funk singer George Clinton, for which he often provided arrangements, and between January and November 1978 he played in Count Basie's orchestra, replacing Henry Coker. From the mid-1970s he performed and toured with Maceo Parker and the tenor saxophonist Pee Wee Ellis (his bandmates from his time with Brown) under various group names, including the J.B.s, the Horny Horns, and Pee Wee Ellis's All Stars, and he later recorded under Parker's leadership. Around 1995 he toured and recorded as the leader of a group with Hugh Ragin, the saxophonist Carl Benjamin, Peter Madsen, Dwayne Dolphin, and Bruce Cox as his sidemen. Wesley is one of the best soul and funk trombonists of his generation; an example of his jazz playing may be heard on his album *New Friends* (*c*1991, Minor Music 1016).

BIBLIOGRAPHY

SheridanCB
H. Bordowitz: "The Three Funkateers," *American Visions*, viii/6 (1993), 44
B. Milkowski: "Hearsay: at the Junction: Fred Wesley," *JT*, xxv/8 (1995), 24
<http://ourworld.compuserve.com/homepages/PJebsen/FW-91.htm> (1998)
<http://www.funky-stuff.com/wesley/> (1999) [incl. transcr.]

GK

Wess, Frank (Wellington) (*b* Kansas City, MO, 4 Jan 1922). Flutist and tenor and alto saxophonist. He grew up in Sapulpa, Oklahoma, and in Washington, DC. Having first learned to play alto saxophone, under the strong influence of Lester Young he changed to the tenor instrument. He worked with Blanche Calloway and during World War II served in army bands, then played briefly with Billy Eckstine (for illustration *see* Eckstine, Billy), Eddie Heywood, Lucky Millinder, and Bullmoose Jackson before returning to Washington. In 1949 he took up flute. From June 1953 to August 1964 he was a member of Count Basie's big band, in which, at first, he played tenor saxophone; his smooth, light tone provided a contrast to the rougher and larger sound produced by Frank Foster. Later, at Basie's request, he performed on alto saxophone (1957–64). Most importantly, Wess established the flute as an appropriate instrument for jazz; his swinging improvisations were played with a pleasing classical timbre, and he avoided many of the special effects that later became frequent in jazz flute playing. During his years with Basie he recorded with Thad Jones (1954, 1957, 1960), Kenny Clarke and Milt Jackson (both 1955), Joe Newman (1955–60), Foster (1956), Kenny Burrell (1956–7), Dorothy Ashby (1956, 1958), the Prestige All Stars (1957), J. C. Heard (1958), and Etta Jones and Lem Winchester (both 1960).

From 1964 Wess recorded advertising jingles, performed in pit bands for Broadway shows, and worked in studio bands for television. While concentrating on these activities, from 1967 into the 1970s he was a member of Clark Terry's big band, and, in a departure from his normal stylistic realm, in 1968 he recorded free jazz with the Jazz Composer's Orchestra. He played in Basie's reunion bands of July 1973 and July 1976, became a member of the New York Jazz Quartet in 1974, and performed and recorded in Howard McGhee's group in 1978. With Foster he performed and recorded in the 1980s and 1990s as the leader of a quintet called Two Franks; their rhythm section consisted of Kenny Barron and Marvin "Smitty" Smith, with either Rufus Reid or Ray Drummond on double bass. From around 1981 Wess was a member of

Dameronia, and in January 1985 he appeared in Woody Herman's sextet at the St. Regis Hotel in New York. He played in Buck Clayton's big band (late 1980s), worked in the Philip Morris Superband under Gene Harris (1988 – early 1990s), recorded in Benny Carter's octet (1988), performed with Carter at the Chicago Jazz Festival (1989), and recorded with Billy Taylor (ii) and the Jazzmobile All Stars in New York (1989). From 1989 to 1990 Wess toured and recorded several times in Japan and California in a big band, variously under his sole leadership, with Harry Edison as his co-leader, or accompanying Mel Tormé.

Wess has continued to tour and record as the leader of small groups, as well as giving jazz workshops. In the 1990s his freelance recording activities included sessions with Ernestine Anderson (1990, in performance at the Concord Jazz Festival), Edison's sextet (1990, at a club in New York), Grover Mitchell (1990), Toshiko Akiyoshi, Jeannie and Jimmy Cheatham, and Susannah McCorkle (all 1991), Louie Bellson, Carter, and John Pizzarelli (all 1992), Carol Sloane (1993, 1996), Howard Alden (1994, when he made one track in a duo with Michael Moore (i)), Dick Hyman (1994, 1996), Ernie Andrews, Harris's quartet, and Mike Longo (all 1995), Jimmy McGriff and Byron Stripling (both 1998), and Jane Jarvis and Frank Vignola (both 1999).

Video oral history material in *NCH* (HCJA).

SELECTED RECORDINGS

As leader: *Frank Wess Quintet* (1954, Com. 20031); *North, South, East ... Wess* (1956, Savoy 12072); *Frank Wess Quartet* (1960, Mdsv. 8); *Yo Ho!* (1963, Prst. 7231); with F. Foster: *Two for the Blues* (1983, Pablo 2310905), *Frankly Speaking* (1984, Conc. 276); with H. Edison: *Dear Mr. Basie* (1989, Conc. 4420); *Tryin' to Make my Blues Turn Green* (1993, Conc. 4592); *Going Wess* (1993, Town Crier 518); *Surprise! Surprise!* (1996, Gemini 84); *Surprise, Surprise!* (1996, Chi. 350)

As sideman: C. Basie: Basie Goes Wess (1953, Clef 89112); T. Jones: *The Fabulous Thad Jones* (1954, Debut 12), incl. Elusive; C. Basie: *April in Paris* (1955–6, Verve 8012), incl. The Midgets; [no leader:] *After Hours* (1957, Prst. 7118); C. Basie: *Basie* (1957, Roul. 52003), incl. Fantail; *Chairman of the Board* (1959, Roul. 52032); L. Winchester: *Another Opus* (1960, NewJ 8244); New York Jazz Quartet: *The New York Jazz Quartet in Concert in Japan* (1975, Salvation 703); *Oasis* (1981, Enja 3083); B. Carter: *Over the Rainbow* (1988, Musicmasters 60196), incl. Atlanta; B. Clayton: *Live From Greenwich Village, NYC* (*c* late 1980s, Nagel-Heyer 030), incl. The One for Me

Dameronia: *Live at the Theatre Boulogne-Billancourt, Paris* (1989, SN 121202-2); C. Sloane: on *Sweet & Slow* (1993, Conc. 4564), One Morning in May, Sweet and Slow; H. Alden: *Your Story: the Music of Bill Evans* (1994, Conc. 4621); G. Harris: *It's the Real Soul* (1995, Conc. 4692); C. Sloane: *The Songs Sinatra Sang* (1996, Conc. 4725), incl. One for my Baby, Wee Small Hours; J. McGriff: *Straight up* (1998, Mlst. 9285); B. Stripling: *Stripling Now!* (1998, Nagel-Heyer 2002); F. Vignola: on *Off Broadway* (1999, Nagel-Heyer 2006), Cookin' at the Continental, It's all right with me

SELECTED FILMS AND VIDEOS

Rhythm in a Riff (1946); Newport Jazz Festival 1962 (1962); A Man Called Adam (1966); Jazz in America: Lincoln Center, New York (1982)

BIBLIOGRAPHY

SheridanCB
L. Feather: "Who's Who in the Basie Band," *MM*, xxx (27 March 1954), 9
D. Ioakimidis: "1 Frank + 1 Frank – 2 Franks," *Jh*, no.120 (1957), 10
S. Dance: "Wess Points," *DB*, xxxii/12 (1965), 28
M. Roman: "Frank Wess: the Modest Master," *JT* (Dec 1983), 7

BK

West, Cedric (Herbert) (*b* Rangoon, Burma, 9 Dec 1918). British guitarist and trombonist. He started playing guitar in the late 1930s with a college band in Burma. Following the Japanese invasion of the country in 1942 he was evacuated to India and played guitar and, later, trombone with Teddy Weatherford's band at the Grand Hotel, Calcutta (1942–5). After Weatherford's death he was a featured soloist with Reuben Solomon's Jive Boys, with whom he also made some recordings (including *My Gal Sal*, 1942, Col. FB40231), but later in 1945 he returned to Burma with his own band. He went to England in 1947, led several bands, and played and recorded with many others. From 1968 until his retirement in 1984 he concentrated on radio and television work.

BIBLIOGRAPHY

K. P. Darke: "Teddy Weatherford's Indian Recording Sessions 1941–45," *Matrix*, nos.107–8 (1975), 3
P. Darke and R. Gulliver: "Teddy Weatherford," *Sv*, no.65 (1976), 175
——: "Roy Butler's Story," *Sv*, no.71 (1977), 178
P. Darke and B. White: "Cedric West: the Jazzman from Burma," *Sv*, no.109 (1983), 20; addns and corrections to discography in *Sv*, no.115 (1984), 6

PETER DARKE

West, Doc [Hal, Harold] (*b* Wolford, ND, 12 Aug 1915; *d* Cleveland, 4 May 1951). Drummer. He played piano and cello before taking up drums, and first worked with Tiny Parham (1932) and in Chicago with Erskine Tate and Roy Eldridge. After deputizing for Chick Webb during the Webb orchestra's tour of Texas (late 1938) he played intermittently with Hot Lips Page (September 1939–1941), participated in jam sessions at Minton's Playhouse, New York, and deputized for Jo Jones in Count Basie's orchestra (early 1940). During the 1940s he was in demand for recordings with small swing groups, occasionally in those oriented towards the emergent bop style, and he took part in sessions with Sammy Price and Una Mae Carlisle (both 1941), Eldridge (1943), Slam Stewart and Joe Turner (ii) (both 1945), and Leo Watson and Wardell Gray (both 1946). West is chiefly remembered for his playing on a recording in a group led by Tiny Grimes which also included Charlie Parker (1944), on Parker's own recording with Erroll Garner's trio and Earl Coleman (1947), and on several excellent recordings with Garner's trio only (1945, 1950). He died while on tour with Eldridge.

For illustration *see* JAZZ (i), fig.5.

SELECTED RECORDINGS

As sideman: B. Holiday: Ghost of Yesterday/Falling in Love Again (1940, Voc. 5609); T. Grimes: Tiny's Tempo/I'll Always Love You Just the Same (1944, Savoy 526); Romance without Finance/Red Cross (1944, Savoy 532); D. Byas: Three o'Clock in the Morning/One o'Clock Jump (1945, Super Disc 1006); W. Gray: Easy Swing (1946, Jazz Selection 797); One for Prez (1946, Jazz Selection 803); The Great Lie (1946, Jazz Selection 805); C. Parker: Bird's Nest (1947, Dial 1014); Cool Blues (1947, Dial 1015); E. Garner: Tippin' out with Erroll/Lazy River (1950, Roost 614)

BIBLIOGRAPHY

ChiltonW; *FeatherE*

SCOTT YANOW

Westbrook [née Duckham]**, Kate** [Katherine Jane] (*b* Guildford, England, 18 Sept 1939). English singer and lyricist. While she was largely self-taught as a singer, she learned piano while at school. She then trained as a fine artist and from 1963 held shows of her paintings. In 1974 she joined the Brass Band of Mike Westbrook, whom she married in 1976, and commenced a dual career as a singer and artist. She has performed and recorded as a member of Westbrook's orchestra from 1979, his trio A Little Westbrook Music from 1982, and his dance band from 1986, doubling regularly on tenor horn. In 1985 she formed her own six-piece ensemble to perform *Revenge Suite*, a music and theater piece devised and scripted by her and incorporating songs, improvisations, and slide projections from her own paintings; songs from the suite are included on *Love for Sale* (1985). As a lyricist Westbrook collaborates closely with her husband and draws in particular on the influences of Berthold Brecht and Kurt Weill, English and American poetry, and the popular musical; she wrote and arranged the settings of poetry for such works as *The Cortège* (1982) and *London Bridge is Broken Down* (1987), as well as for *Westbrook – Rossini* (1986) and *Off Abbey Road* (1989). In 1992 she recorded her own album of songs exploring the myth of the actor Peter Lorre. A fluent singer in many European languages, Westbrook has a wide vocal range well suited to theatrical and dramatic works; she also plays piccolo and bamboo flute.

SELECTED RECORDINGS

As leader: *Good-bye Peter Lorre* (1992, Femme Music 9.01060)
As sideman with M. Westbrook: *The Cortège* (1982, Original 309); *Love for Sale* (1985, HA 2031); *Westbrook – Rossini* (1986, HA 2040); *London Bridge is Broken Down* (1987, Venture 13); *Off Abbey Road* (1989, Tiptoe 888805-2)

BIBLIOGRAPHY

K. Dallas: "Westbrook's Voices," *MM* (20 Feb 1982), 23
T. Quénum: "Le pop opéra de Westbrook," *Jm*, no.424 (1993), 47

SIMON ADAMS

Westbrook, Mike [Michael John David] (*b* High Wycombe, England, 21 March 1936). English composer, pianist, and bandleader. After working in an accountant's office and studying painting he took up music professionally; he was largely self-taught and has an empirical approach to composition. Around 1960 he organized a jazz workshop in Plymouth, where he wrote for a small ensemble that included John Surman, then early in 1963 he moved to London. From that time he has written pieces for a number of his own ensembles: the Mike Westbrook Band (1962–72), the Mike Westbrook Concert Band (1967–71), the multimedia group Cosmic Circus (1970–72), the jazz-rock band Solid Gold Cadillac (1971–4), the Mike Westbrook Brass Band (established in 1973 to perform in the theater and on television), the Mike Westbrook Orchestra (formed in 1974), A Little Westbrook Music, with his wife Kate Westbrook and Chris Biscoe (formed in 1982), Westbrook Music Theatre (formed in 1984 with Kate for mixed-media productions), the septet Westbrook Rossini (formed in 1984), Les Deux Trios (combining his own trio with that of Didier Levallet, Gérard Marais, and Dominique Pifarely, from 1985), and the Dance Band (formed in 1986). In 1992 the Westbrook Orchestra performed a BBC Promenade Concert.

Westbrook has worked with other groups, appearing as a conductor with many radio orchestras in Europe and he has collaborated with a number of theater companies, notably the National Theatre (1971), the Foco Novo Theatre Company (1985), and the Extemporary Dance Theatre (1986). In 1973, with John Jack, he founded the record company Cadillac (ii), which maintained a modest amount of activity through the 1990s, and in 1985 he began issuing a quarterly newsletter, the *Smith's Academy Informer*. He is the subject of a film documentary, *Mike Westbrook: Jazz Composer* (1978).

Westbrook is particularly adept at providing jazz improvisers with stimulating themes and settings and then enfolding their contributions within a wider context. He takes his inspiration from a wide variety of styles, many from outside jazz and drawing on European literary and classical music traditions, the visual arts, and theater; his work (often written in collaboration with Kate Westbrook) consists of highly personalized statements. Like Duke Ellington before him, he generally composes for specific musicians in his bands, notably Phil Minton and Biscoe; this results in highly colored music that is subject to few of the clichés of jazz composition. Among his best-known pieces are *Marching Song* (1969), *Metropolis* (1971), *Citadel/Room 315* (1975), *The Cortège* (1982), *Westbrook – Rossini* (1986), and *London Bridge is Broken Down* (1987).

Oral history material in *GBLnsa*.

Mike Westbrook at the 100 Club, London, 1993

RECORDED COMPOSITIONS

(selective list)

Marching Song (1969, Deram 1047–8); *Metropolis* (1971, RCA SF8396); *Citadel/Room 315* (1975, RCA SF8433); *Mama Chicago* (1979, RCA PL25252); *The Cortège* (1982, Original 309); *On Duke's Birthday* (1984, HA 2012); *Love for Sale* (1985, HA 2031); *Westbrook – Rossini* (1986, HA 2040); *London Bridge is Broken Down* (1987, Venture 13); *Off Abbey Road* (1989, TipToe 888805-2); *Bar Utopia* (1996, ASC 13)

BIBLIOGRAPHY

CarrJ; *ChiltonB*; *Feather '60s*; *Feather–Gitler '70s*; *GrayF*; *WickesIBJ*, i

P. Russell: "Plymouth Sound," *JM*, xi/7 (1965), 17 [incl. biographical footnote by D. Aldous]

B. Houston: "Westbrook: Wild Man from the West Country," *MM* (14 May 1966), 9

M. Shera: "Mike Westbrook and his Orchestra," *JJ*, xix/1 (1966), 10

C. Bird: "The Paradox of Westy," *MM* (17 May 1969), 8

L. Tomkins: "Mike Westbrook," *CI*, viii/1 (1969), 8

I. Carr: *Music Outside: Contemporary Jazz in Britain* (London, 1973), 15

K. Dallas: "Westbrook: Discipline of the 'Citadel'," *MM* (19 July 1975), 42

R. Cotterrell: "Mike Westbrook: Taking Music to the People," *JF* [intl edn], no.39 (1976), 38

A. Duncan: "Mike Westbrook," *Impetus* (1977), no.4, p.169; no.5, p.205

B. Case: "Warehouse of the Western World," *MM* (17 Feb 1979), 24

S. Loupien: "Mike Westbrook: 'j'ai oublié de m'enfermer dans un style'," *Jm*, no.275 (1979), 46

"Wagt sich in immer neue Gebiete vor Mike Westbrook," *JP*, xxviii/11 (1979), 6

C. Sheridan: "Multi-media Jazzman: Mike Westbrook," *JJI*, xxxiii/5 (1980), 30

K. Dallas: "Jazz: Present Use of the Past Tense," *MM* (13 June 1981), 28

——: "Westbrook's Voices," *MM* (20 Feb 1982), 23

R. Zabor: "Mike Westbrook Plays William Blake's Greatest Hits," *Musician*, no.58 (1983), 32

G. Lock: "Sweet Thunder," *The Wire*, no.14 (1985), 10

C. Parker: "Burning Bridges: Mike and Kate Westbrook Play Sad Songs for a Broken Europe," *Wire*, nos.46–7 (1987–8), 28

C. Emigholz: "Wander zwischen den Stilen: der Komponist, Arrangeur und Pianist Mike Westbrook," *Neue Zeitschrift für Musik*, cliii/12 (1992), 41

K. Mathieson: "On Mike's Birthday," *Wire*, no.103 (1992) 16

B. Morton: "Westbrook Ho!," *Wire*, no.104 (1992), 12

C. Parker: "With Mike and Kate in Catania," *Jazz the Magazine*, no.15 (1992), 36

"The Spirit of Difference," *The Guardian* (27 Aug 1992)

T. Quénum: "Le pop opéra de Westbrook," *Jm*, no.424 (1993), 47

<http://westbrookjazz.co.uk/> (2000)

CHARLES FOX/DIGBY FAIRWEATHER, SIMON ADAMS, BK

West Coast jazz. A style of jazz played by California musicians in the 1950s and related to Cool jazz. Many of the most prominent West Coast players during this era were associated with an approach built on the following characteristics: a preference for understatement and subtle shadings of sound; a focus on the melodic capabilities of all instruments, even the drums; an interest in counterpoint; an emphasis on tonal purity and clarity of expression; and a zeal for experimentation, especially in compositional forms and instrumental textures. This style was deeply influenced by several key predecessors, especially Miles Davis's "Birth of the Cool" band, Stan Kenton's orchestra, and the Kansas City jazz tradition of Count Basie and Lester Young.

Gerry Mulligan, who had both worked with Davis and written arrangements for Kenton, formed a Los Angeles-based pianoless quartet with Chet Baker in 1952 which exemplified the core virtues of this style in recordings such as *Bernie's Tune/Lullabye of the Leaves* (1952, PJ 601), *Line for Lyons* (1952, Fan. 522), and *Westwood Walk*, on the album *Gerry Mulligan and his Ten-tette* (1953, Cap. H439). Mulligan returned to New York in 1954 but left a lasting influence on West Coast jazz, while Baker went on to work with a wide range of other Los Angeles players and enjoyed an especially successful collaboration with the pianist Russ Freeman (i). Even before the Mulligan and Baker quartet was formed, Dave Brubeck and Paul Desmond had drawn on many of these same musical building blocks in shaping a cool-inflected, highly experimental style. Brubeck's success helped spur a Northern California offshoot of the West Coast sound, as reflected in the work of Cal Tjader, Vince Guaraldi, and others. The Lighthouse All Stars, a working band under the direction of Howard Rumsey which played at the Lighthouse in Hermosa Beach, California, was another influential force in shaping the West Coast sound in the 1950s. The movement drew heavily on alumni of the Kenton and Lighthouse bands, with Art Pepper, Shorty Rogers, Jimmy Giuffre, Shelly Manne, Bud Shank, Bill Perkins, Lennie Niehaus, Frank Rosolino, John Graas, Conte and Pete Candoli, and Bob Cooper emerging as some of the leading soloists and bandleaders of the day. Arrangers and composers also flourished, given the compositional formalism of much of the West Coast music, and Marty Paich, Bill Holman, and Gerald Wilson, among others, played a prominent role in the music. Other representative recordings of the West Coast sound include *You Go to my Head*, on the album *Dave Brubeck at Storyville: Trio and Quartet* (1952, Fan. 3-8), featuring Brubeck and Paul Desmond; *Bunny*, on *Shorty Rogers and his Giants* (1953, RCA LPM3137), with Pepper; Rogers's arrangement of *Mallets*, recorded by Manne (1953, Cont. 354); *The Train and the River*, on *Jimmy Giuffre Three* (1956, Atl. 1254); and *Cast your Fate to the Wind*, on Guaraldi's LP *Black Orpheus* (1962, Fan. 8089).

However, California jazz in this era was never as homogeneous as the term West Coast jazz might suggest. Bop and hard bop played an especially important if less well publicized role in West Coast jazz, as evidenced by the work of such players as Hampton Hawes, Sonny Criss, Carl Perkins, Curtis Counce, Harold Land, Dexter Gordon, Wardell Gray, Teddy Edwards, Frank Morgan, Dupree Bolton, Roy Porter, and Frank Butler. The formation of the Max Roach–Clifford Brown Quintet in Los Angeles in 1954 was a key event in the history of hard bop, and the influence of the West Coast sound on this band (and through it, on the emerging hard-bop style) is often overlooked in historical studies. The more intense currents of West Coast jazz may also be heard on recordings such as *Intermission Riff* by Sonny Criss (1951, Pablo 2310929), *Daddy Plays the Horn* by Dexter Gordon (1955, Beth. 36), *All Night Session* by Hampton Hawes (1956, Cont. 3545), *Carl's Blues* by Curtis Counce (1957, Cont. 3539), and *The Fox* by Harold Land (1959, Hi-Fi 612).

A strong trend towards experimental and avant-garde work was also evident among West Coast players, although many of the musicians involved (Eric Dolphy, Ornette Coleman, Don Cherry, Charles Mingus, Paul Bley) made their greatest strides after moving to the East Coast. At the opposite extreme, traditional jazz had long flourished in California, with many of the New Orleans pioneers, including Freddie Keppard, Jelly Roll Morton, and King Oliver, having made early visits to the state. During the years following World War II this tradition was revitalized under the impetus of musicians such as Lu Watters and Turk Murphy.

The burgeoning West Coast jazz movement during the 1950s was supported by a host of jazz record companies, most notably Fantasy, Pacific, and Contemporary, as well as a vibrant nightclub scene, which created economic opportunities for many jazz musicians. By the early 1960s, however, much of this support system had disappeared. The rise of rock-and-roll limited opportunities for jazz players, many of whom began focusing on work as studio musicians. Others moved east or overseas, where greater opportunities beckoned. Still others met an untimely death or were incarcerated through their use of drugs. Although a handful of players with new things to say, such as John Carter and Horace Tapscott, emerged on the West Coast during the 1960s, they struggled in a largely inhospitable environment. In sum, the West Coast jazz renaissance of the 1950s lasted little more than a decade before losing momentum, but many of the players who had taken part saw their careers revitalized in the 1970s and 1980s. Art Pepper, Chet Baker, and Frank Morgan returned to active performance, and recorded prolifically; much of their finer work dates from this later period. Studio regulars such as Bud Shank and Shorty Rogers began focusing again on jazz with excellent results. Dexter Gordon returned from Europe and garnered more fame than he had ever enjoyed during his California days. John Carter recorded a five-volume "Roots and Folklore" project to great critical acclaim. Hundreds of West Coast jazz recordings from the 1950s were reissued and sold well. Serious historical and critical scholarship of West Coast jazz began in earnest, and a number of important biographies were published. These events made it clear that West Coast jazz was not, as some had claimed in earlier years, a short-term fad in jazz fostered by the record industry, but was in fact a timeless body of music with nearly universal appeal.

BIBLIOGRAPHY

W. Claxton: *Jazz West Coast: a Portfolio of Photographs* (Hollywood, CA, 1954, 2/1980/R1996, as *Jazz*)
H. Hawes and D. Asher: *Raise up off me: a Portrait of Hampton Hawes* (New York and Toronto, 1974)
A. Pepper and L. Pepper: *Straight Life: the Story of Art Pepper* (New York and London, 1979, rev. 2/New York, 1994) [incl. discography by T. Selbert]
R. Gordon: *Jazz West Coast: the Los Angeles Jazz Scene of the 1950s* (London and New York, 1986)
A. Tercinet: *West Coast Jazz* (Marseilles, France, 1986)
T. Gioia: *West Coast Jazz: Modern Jazz in California, 1945–1960* (New York, and Oxford, England, 1992)
G. Marsh and G. Callingham, eds.: *California Cool: West Coast Cover Art* (Zurich, 1992)

TED GIOIA

West End. Nightclub in New York; *see* NIGHTCLUBS AND OTHER VENUES.

Western swing. A style of music originating largely in the fiddle and guitar bands in Texas during the 1920s. Such groups regularly played traditional frontier dance music at country dances, but they were more innovative than country bands in the Southeast; they were eclectic in their repertory and improvised like jazz bands, from whom they borrowed freely. An early group, the Light Crust Doughboys of Fort Worth, was of the fiddle and guitar tradition but also performed current popular songs, blues, and jazz. After 1934 two former members popularized western swing. The singer Milton Brown led one of the most popular country string bands in the Southwest, the Musical Brownies of Fort Worth. Bob Wills formed the Texas Playboys, which performed in Tulsa (1934–42) and later in California and elsewhere. A traditional country fiddler, Wills was receptive to innovative and jazz-oriented musicians; the Playboys began as a fiddle-dominated string band, but soon added drums, piano, electric guitars, and wind instruments and became very similar to the big popular swing bands of the 1930s.

The term "western swing" was not used widely until after World War II, when the bandleader Spade Cooley billed himself as the "King of Western Swing." Similar bands led by a former singer with Cooley's band, Tex Williams (*b* 1917), Hank Penny (*b* 1918), and to a lesser extent Ray Whitley (*b* 1901) made California the new center of the style in the 1940s. The western swing bands there, and elsewhere in the USA, influenced the mainstream of country music in the use of drums, walking bass patterns, and electric instruments. Western swing experienced a revival in the early 1970s, largely through the performances of such musicians as Merle Haggard, Red Steagall and his Coleman County Cowboys, and, above all, the bands Asleep at the Wheel (led by the guitarist Ray Benson) and Alvin Crow and the Pleasant Valley Boys.

BIBLIOGRAPHY

B. C. Malone: *Country Music, U.S.A.: a Fifty-year History* (Austin, TX, 1968, rev. and enlarged 2/1985 as *Country Music, U.S.A.*)
J. Zolten: "Western Swingtime Music: a Cool Breeze in the American Desert," *Sing Out!*, xxiii/2 (1972), 2
C. Wolfe: "Making Western Swing: an Interview with Johnnie Lee Wills," *Old Time Music*, no.15 (1974–5), 11
C. R. Townsend: *San Antonio Rose: the Life and Music of Bob Wills* (Urbana, IL, Chicago, and London, 1976)
G. Hunkel: *Western Swing & Country Jazz: eine Einführung mit Kurzporträts über Bob Wills und Milton Brown* (Menden, Germany, 1983)
M. Rowland: "Dance All Night, Stay a Little Longer: Fifty Years on, the Original Texas Playboys are Still the Kings of Western Swing," *Musician*, no.173 (1993), 58
C. Ginell and R. L. Brown: *Milton Brown and the Founding of Western Swing* (Urbana, IL, *c*1994)

BILL C. MALONE

Weston, Randy [Randolph Edward] (*b* New York, 6 April 1926). Pianist and composer. He received classical lessons on piano for a few years, but did not take these seriously, and at around the age of 14 he became interested in jazz. After serving in the army (1944–*c*1946), and while working outside of music, he received informal tuition from Thelonious Monk by visiting the latter's apartment to hear him play (late 1940s). In the early 1950s he toured the USA with rhythm-and-blues bands, including those of Bullmoose Jackson (1951) and Eddie "Cleanhead" Vinson, and then returned to New York and worked in bop groups with Kenny Dorham and Cecil Payne. In 1954 he became the first modern-jazz soloist to record for the Riverside label, and thereafter he worked as a leader, often with his boyhood friends Ahmed Abdul-Malik, Ray Copeland, and Payne, as well as with Booker Ervin and Melba Liston, who played trombone with and served as arranger for his groups from 1958 into the mid-1960s.

Weston performed in Lagos, Nigeria (1961, 1963), toured Africa and the Middle East with a sextet (1967), and toured Morocco with a trio consisting of Vishnu Wood and Ed Blackwell (1967). This trio worked in Rabat, Morocco, in 1968, and then went to Tangier, where Weston opened a nightclub, the African Rhythms Club. When Wood and Blackwell returned to the USA, Weston remained to run the club and played there until 1972, often accompanied by his son, the drummer Azzedin (Niles) Weston, and sometimes joined by Moroccan musicians; his collaborations with the Gnawa (traditional musicians of Morocco) began during this period.

From 1972 Weston toured extensively, living variously in New York, France (Paris and Annecy), and Tangier. In his

Randy Weston at the Pizza Express, Dean Street, London, 1978

early career he was occupied with small groups and, for special projects, large ensembles, but in 1974, when he appeared at a highly successful concert at the Montreux International Jazz Festival, Weston began performing (and occasionally recording) as an unaccompanied soloist. Talib Kibwe, Alex Blake, and the percussionist Neil Clarke are among those who served as sidemen in his groups for lengthy periods. In 1989 Weston was an artist-in-residence at the New England Conservatory, and in Paris in early June of that year he led a trio consisting of Jamil Nasser and Idris Muhammad for a series of recordings; three albums were produced: one of compositions associated with Duke Ellington's orchestra, one of compositions by Monk, and one of Weston's own works. He performed the following year in a trio with Azzedin Weston and Max Roach at the Brooklyn Museum. Early in 1993 he made a tour with a quintet (consisting of Benny Powell, Kibwe, Stafford James, and Clarke) and a trio of Gnawa musicians, in which the two groups combined for a finale at the end of each of their concerts. Weston's music was celebrated in a series of concerts at the Festival International de Jazz de Montréal in 1995.

Weston is one of the few major pianists to borrow directly from the style of Monk: *Sweet Sue* (1955) and the simple but dissonant thematic riff of *Kucheza Blues* (1960) provide clear examples. His interests extend far beyond Monk's, however, and such recordings as the suite *Uhuru Africa!* (1960, which makes use of lyrics by Langston Hughes and arrangements by Liston) and the popular jazz-funk album *Blue Moses* (1972) embrace African rhythms and romantic songs. Liston suffered a crippling stroke in 1985, but she was still able to write arrangements, and during the course of the 1990s (until shortly before her death in 1999) she collaborated with Weston on a series of pieces that were recorded by a big band in which he continued to celebrate connections between jazz and African musical traditions. A few of his early compositions, including *Berkshire Blues*, *Little Niles*, and *Hi-fly*, have become jazz standards.

Oral history material in *CtY, NjR, DSI* (JOHP), and *NN-Sc* (LAJOHP).

SELECTED RECORDINGS

* – composed by Weston

As unaccompanied soloist: *Informal Solo Piano* (1974, Hi-Fly 101); *Blues to Africa* (1974, Fre. 40153); *African Nite* (1975, Owl 01); *Marrakech in the Cool of the Evening* (1992, Verve 314-521588-2)

Duos: with Sam Gill: *Cole Porter in a Modern Mood* (1954, Riv. 2508); with David Murray: *The Healers* (1991, BS 0118)

As leader: *The Randy Weston Trio* (1955, Riv. 2515), incl. *Pam's Waltz, Sweet Sue; *With these Hands* (1956, Riv. 214), incl. *Little Niles; *Piano à la Mode* (1957, Jub. 1060), incl. *Saucer Eyes; on *New Faces at Newport* (1958, Metro. 1005), *Hi-fly; *Uhuru Africa!* (1960, Roul. 65001), incl. *Kucheza Blues; *Highlife* (1963, Colpix 456); *Randy!* (1964, Bak. 1001), incl. *Berkshire Blues; *Monterey '66* (1966, Verve 314-519698-2); *Blue Moses* (1972, CTI 6016); *Tanjah* (1973, Pol. 5055); *Portraits of Duke Ellington* (1989, Verve 841312); *Portraits of Thelonious Monk* (1989, Verve 841313); *Self-portraits* (1989, Verve 841314); *The Spirits of our Ancestors* (1991, Ant. 314-511896-2); *Volcano Blues* (1993, Ant. 314-519269-2); *Saga* (1995, Verve 314-529237-2); *Khepera* (1998, Verve 314-557821-2)

SELECTED FILMS AND VIDEOS

Jazz in Exile (1978); Randy Weston: a Legend in his own Time (1982); Jazz entre amigos (1987); Randy in Tangiers (1988); African Rhythms (1989); Thelonious Monk: American Composer (*c* early 1990s)

BIBLIOGRAPHY

F. P[ostif]: "Randy Weston," *Jh*, no.118 (1957), 14

I. Gitler: "Randy Weston," *DB*, xxxi/6 (1964), 16

M. Gardner: "Randy Weston," *JM*, xii/11 (1967), 2 [incl. discography and list of compositions]

V. Wilmer: "Back to the African Heartbeat," *Jazz People* (London, Indianapolis, and New York, 1970/*R*1985), 75

M. Cullaz and L. Goddet: "Randy Weston," *Jh*, no.336 (1977), 11; Eng. trans. in *Coda*, no.159 (1978), 4

L. Birnbaum: "Randy Weston: African-rooted Rhythm," *DB*, xlvi/15 (1979), 18 [incl. discography]

L. Lyons: *The Great Jazz Pianists, Speaking of their Lives and Music* (New York, 1983), 210

F. Bouchard: "Randy Weston's Pan-African Revival," *DB*, lvii/11 (1990), 22

S. L. Miller: "Randy Weston & Melba Liston: Together Again, Miraculously," *JT*, xxii/1 (1992), 24
B. Shoemaker: "Big Band Orchestral Visions," *JT*, xxii/10 (1992), 28
N. C. Weinstein: *A Night in Tunisia: Imaginings of Africa in Jazz* (Metuchen, NJ, and London, 1992)
B. Priestley: "Randy Weston," *Jazz: the Magazine*, no.17 (1993), 10
B. Blumenthal: "Time Works Positive Changes for Weston," *Boston Globe* (13 Aug 1995)
Z. Stewart: "Melba Liston & Randy Weston: the Spirit of Collaboration," *DB*, xlii/2 (1995), 22 [incl. discography]
K. L. Williams: "Keys to the Kingdom," *San Francisco Bay Guardian* (11 Oct 1995), 29
L. Birnbaum: "Caught: Randy Weston's Africa Revisited," *DB*, lxv/5 (1998), 70
G. Himes: "Weston's Passage from Africa," *Washington Post* (20 March 1998)
R. Mitchell: "Musical Storyteller: Pianist Shares Pride in Heritage through Language of Jazz," *Houston Chronicle* (18 Oct 1998)
T. Parker: "Randy Weston: African Soul," *DB*, lxv/10 (1998), 20
L. Andrews: "Randy Weston Celebrates his Gift of Music," *Amsterdam News* (5 Aug 1999)
B. Blumenthal: "Africa's Jazz Messenger," *Boston Globe* (16 April 1999)
B. Donaldson: "Randy Weston Interview," *Cadence*, xxvii (2001), no.2, p.5, no.3, p.15
<http://www.randyweston.myweb.nl/> (2001)

BK

Weston, Veryan (*b* Uckfield, England, 3 Sept 1950). English pianist. He was introduced to music as a child by his sisters. In 1972 he moved to London and began playing as a freelance and performing at the Little Theatre Club, and in 1975 he received a fellowship from the Digswell Arts Trust in Hertfordshire, enabling him to study and write about piano improvisation. While at Digswell he founded the group Stinky Winkles and collaborated with visual artists in London at the Victoria and Albert Museum (1979) and at the Hammersmith Jazz Festival (1980). He also wrote and performed soundtracks for films and documentaries, most notably Derek Jarman's *Carravaggio* (1985), in collaboration with Lol Coxhill. His interest in music and media collaboration led to a degree in performance art at Middlesex Polytechnic and a masters in music composition from Goldsmiths' College, University of London (1990). Weston has worked with numerous musicians, notably in a duo with Coxhill (from 1977), heard to best effect on *Boundless* (1998, Emanem 4021), and in a duo and quartet with Phil Minton (from 1991), for example, the duo album *Ways* (1992, ITM 1420). He was a member of Trevor Watts's Moiré Music from 1982 to 1989, joined Eddie Prévost's quartet in 1983, and established his own trio (with the double bass player John Edwards and the drummer Mark Sanders) in 1998. Weston has recorded two albums as an unaccompanied soloist, *Underwater Carol* (1986, Matchless 12) and *Playing Alone* (1996, Acta 9).

BIBLIOGRAPHY

H. Reich: "Leading the Charge," *Chicago Tribune* (16 May 1997)
M. Wastell: "Fingers on Keys: Veryan Weston," *Avant*, no.4 (1997), 43
<http://www.composer.co.uk/musicnow/composers/weston.html> (1999)
<http://www.shef.ac.uk/misc/rec/ps/efi/mweston.html> (1999) [incl. discography]

SIMON ADAMS

Westray, Ron(ald Kenneth, Jr.) (*b* Columbia, SC, 13 June 1970). Trombonist. He studied performance at South Carolina State University (BA) and Eastern Illinois University (MA). In 1991 he began working with Marcus Roberts, with whom he has performed around the USA and recorded; he plays the second trombone solo on *Early Rehearsal*, on Roberts's album *Blues for the New Millennium* (1996–7, Col. CK68637). In summer 1992 he toured with the group Jazz Futures II and the following year he became a member of the Lincoln Center Jazz Orchestra, in which he worked with Wycliffe Gordon. In the mid-1990s Westray and Gordon formed the quintet Bone Structure, with Roberts, Reginald Veal, and Herlin Riley as their sidemen; the group may be heard on *Bone Structure* (1996, Atl. 82936-2). Westray appeared as a soloist on the BBC Wales television show "Midnight Jazz: Brecon Jazz Festival 1992" (1993) and with Wynton Marsalis's ensemble in the video *Accent on the Offbeat* (*c*1994).

GK

Wethington, (Arthur) Crawford (*b* Chicago, 26 Jan 1904 or 1908; *d* 11 Sept 1994). Saxophonist. His year of birth has been published as 1908, but Wethington gave 1904 in his application for social security. He studied music in Chicago, and after playing there with the pianist Lottie E. Hightower (*c*1925) he performed and recorded as an alto saxophonist in Carroll Dickerson's band (1928), with which he worked under Louis Armstrong's leadership in New York (1929). Between 1930 and 1936 he made several recordings on clarinet and alto and baritone saxophones in the Mills Blue Rhythm Band (including *Black and Tan Fantasy*, 1931, Ban. 32199), and in 1937 he recorded as a tenor saxophonist with Edgar Hayes. He may be seen in the short film *Mills Blue Rhythm Band* (1934). Wethington also taught music, and although he ceased full-time performing after 1937 he continued to work as a teacher. The social security death index gives the date of his death and his last-known residence, White Plains, New York. (*McCarthyB*)

For illustration *see* MILLS BLUE RHYTHM BAND.

based on *ChiltonW*

Wettling, George (Godfrey) (*b* Topeka, KS, 28 Nov 1907; *d* New York, 6 June 1968). Drummer. From 1924 he worked in Chicago with a number of lesser-known bands, including that of Floyd Town, in which Muggsy Spanier and Jess Stacy were fellow sidemen in 1928. He played and recorded with Paul Mares (1935), toured with a band led in the USA by Jack Hylton, and performed with Wingy Manone in New York and Pittsburgh. After recording in Chicago with Jimmy McPartland (1936) and in New York with Manone, he worked with orchestras led by Artie Shaw (1936 – March 1937), Bunny Berigan (March–December 1937), Red Norvo (1938), and Paul Whiteman (December 1938 – March 1941). During the same time he was recording regularly as a freelance musician, often in dixieland groups with Eddie Condon, notably in sessions under the leadership of Berigan and Sharkey Bonano (both 1936), Max Kaminsky (1939), and Condon himself (from 1938).

In the early 1940s Wettling performed briefly with Bobby Hackett and Spanier (early 1941), then later with McPartland, Joe and Marty Marsala, the comedian Chico Marx, Benny Goodman (July 1943), and Miff Mole (1943–4). While working in New York as a studio musician for ABC (1943–52) he frequently appeared at Condon's club. He participated in Condon's first all-star concert at Town Hall (February 1942) and subsequent concerts there and at Carnegie Hall and the Ritz Theater in 1944–5, accompanied Wild Bill Davison, Hot Lips Page, Hackett, Louis Armstrong, and others in broadcasts from the club on several episodes of the television series "Eddie Condon Floor Show" (1949), and made radio broadcasts from the club with Condon's group in the early

1950s. He also rejoined Whiteman briefly (August 1945), gave a concert with Manone at Town Hall (947), and recorded with Wild Bill Davison and Georg Brunis (both 1943), Yank Lawson (1943–4), Kaminsky, Joe Marsala, Dick Cary, Billie Holiday, Pee Wee Russell, and Jack Teagarden (all 1944), Hackett (1944–5), Spanier (1944–6), Bud Freeman and Joe Sullivan (both 1945), Sidney Bechet (1949, 1950), and Ralph Sutton (1950, 1952).

In March and May 1951 Wettling organized a studio group, his Dixielanders, to record an early album for Columbia at the behest of *Collier's* magazine, which wanted to run an essay about his unusual dual talent as a drummer and painter; his original sidemen for this album were Davison, Jimmy Archey, Edmond Hall, Sullivan, and Bob Casey; Cutty Cutshall and Sutton replaced Archey and Sullivan in May. From 1953 he led his own dixieland bands in New York, but was associated intermittently with McPartland (1952–9), Condon (at whose club he again played regularly from 1954, and with whom he toured Britain in 1957), Freeman (1955, 1957–60), and Spanier (October 1959 – early 1960); he was a member of an all-star group that performed at the Central Plaza, New York, in the short film *Jazz Dance* (1954). In the 1960s he continued to play with Condon (including a performance on the television show "Salute to Eddie Condon" in March 1965), briefly rejoined Spanier again (August–September 1963), led a group at the Gaslight Club (from 1964), and worked with Clarence Hutchenrider. Wettling was influenced early in his career by Baby Dodds, but could adapt his playing to work in many different styles; he produced a crisp, clear sound and his inventive breaks make his recordings immediately identifiable. He also contributed as a writer to *Down Beat* magazine, and some of his work as an artist was used on album sleeves for recordings by Condon and Sullivan.

SELECTED RECORDINGS

Duos: with D. Cary: I thought about you/You took advantage of me (1944, Black and White 28); with R. Sutton: *Ralph Sutton at the Piano* (1952, Cir. [USA] 413)

As leader: Bugle Call Rag/I wish I could shimmy like my sister Kate (1940, Decca 18044); Home/Too marvelous for words (1944, Key. 1311); You brought a new kind of love to me/Somebody loves me (1944, Key. 1318); *George Wettling's Jazz Band* (1951, Col. CL6189), incl. After You've Gone, Collier's Clambake; *George Wettling's High Fidelity Rhythms* (1954, Weathers Industries 5501)

As sideman: B. Berigan: The Prisoner's Song (1937, Vic. 36208); Mamma, I wanna make rhythm (1937, Vic. 25677); Black Bottom (1937, Vic. 26138); E. Condon: Carnegie Drag/Carnegie Jump (1938, Com. 1500); Ja da (1938, Com. 500); B. Freeman: You took advantage of me (1938, Com. 501); I got rhythm (1938, Com. 502); My Honey's Lovin' Arms (1938, Com. 504); R. Norvo: Just You, Just Me (1938, Bruns. 8240); B. Freeman: Wingin' without Mezz (1938, Com. 514); The Blue Room/Exactly Like You (1938, Com. 513); E. Condon: I ain't gonna give nobody none of my jelly-roll/Ballin the Jack (1939, Com. 531); Strut Miss Lizzie (1939, Com. 530); W. B. Davison: That's a Plenty/Panama (1943, Com. 1511); Riverboat Shuffle/Muskrat Ramble (1943, Com. 518); Clarinet Marmalade/Original Dixieland One Step (1943, Com. 549); B. Hackett: Rose of the Rio Grande (1945, Melrose 1401); J. Sullivan: Got it and Gone (1945, Disc 6005); E. Condon: *Bixieland* (1955, Col. CL719), incl. Royal Garden Blues; *Condon's Treasury of Jazz* (1956, Col. CL 881); *The Roaring Twenties* (1957, Col. CL1089); *Tiger Rag & All That Jazz* (1958, WP 1292); P. W. Russell: *Pee Wee Russell Plays Pee Wee* (1958, Stere-o-Craft 105)

BIBLIOGRAPHY

ChiltonW; *ConnorBG*; *FeatherE*; *Feather '60s*; *Feather–Gitler '70s*
M. Jones: "George Wettling at the Brushes," *JM*, iii/3 (1957), 10
J. Simmen: "George Wettling," *BHcF*, no.193 (1969), 5
B. Spinney: "From the Past: George Wettling," *MD*, vii/6 (1983), 44
G. Lombardi: *Eddie Condon on Record, 1927–1971* (Milan, 1987)
M. Selchow: *Profoundly Blue: a Bio-discographical Scrapbook on Edmond Hall* (Lübbecke, Germany, 1988)
J. Litchfield and J. Showler: "The Keynote Recordings of George Wettling's New Yorkers," *Skivsamlaren*, no.23 (1989), 16
B. Korall: *Drummin' Men: the Heartbeat of Jazz: the Swing Years* (New York and Toronto, 1990), 310
B. Whyatt: *Muggsy Spanier: the Lonesome Road: a Biography and Discography* (New Orleans, 1995)

JOHNNY SIMMEN/BK

Wetzel [née Addleman], **Bonnie (Jean)** (*b* Vancouver, WA, 15 May 1926; *d* Vancouver, 12 Feb 1965). Double bass player. She received violin lessons but was self-taught on double bass. In the mid-1940s she played for two years in the all-female band led by Ada Leonard and was a member of the trio led by the guitarist Marian Gange. She married Ray Wetzel in 1949 and played alongside him in Tommy Dorsey's band two years later. Thereafter she worked in New York with Charlie Shavers, Roy Eldridge, and Herb Ellis's trio Soft Winds. In 1953–4 she toured Europe with Beryl Booker's trio; the group recorded under its own name (*Beryl Booker with Bonnie Wetzel and Elaine Leighton*, Dis. 3021) in 1953 and with Don Byas the following year. Wetzel was later active as a freelance in New York.

BIBLIOGRAPHY

FeatherE; *Feather '60s*
R. Gordon: *Jazz West Coast: the Los Angeles Jazz Scene of the 1950s* (London and New York, 1986), 115

Wetzel, Ray (*b* Parkersburg, WV, 1924; *d* Sedgwick, CO, 17 Aug 1951). Trumpeter. He performed and recorded as lead trumpeter in the bands of Woody Herman (late 1943 – summer 1945) and Stan Kenton (1945–8) and recorded with Vido Musso, Neal Hefti, and the Metronome All Stars (all 1947). In 1949 he married Bonnie Addleman. After touring and recording with Charlie Barnet (1949–50) he worked in Los Angeles with Tommy Dorsey (1950) and spent a brief period with Kenton (1951); his solo playing is well represented on *Over the Rainbow* (1949, Cap. 744), which he recorded with Barnet. Thereafter he and his wife toured and recorded with Dorsey for several months. Wetzel was killed in an automobile accident.

SELECTED FILMS AND VIDEOS

Stan Kenton and his Orchestra: Artistry in Rhythm (1945); Earl Carroll Vanities (1946); Talk about a Lady [Duchess of Broadway] (1946); Let's Make Rhythm (1947); Tommy Dorsey and his Orchestra (1951)

BIBLIOGRAPHY

FeatherE
W. D. Clancy with A. C. Kenton: *Woody Herman: Chronicles of the Herds* (New York and elsewhere, 1995)

Whalum, Kirk (Wendell) (*b* Memphis, 11 July 1958). Tenor saxophonist and leader. He began playing saxophone in his youth, working initially in church groups led by his father, a preacher. In his mid-teens he formed a rhythm-and-blues group and began to play jazz. At Texas Southern University in Houston he studied classical saxophone, flute, and French. After leading a local group, 150 Psalm (1977–9), he spent a year in Paris (1979–80), where he performed as a street musician and played Brazilian music. Having returned to Houston, he formed a group which performed regularly on the Texas club circuit; in February 1984 Bob James heard the group and asked him to travel to New York to record shortly thereafter. Whalum then toured with the keyboard player (1985–6), and he may be seen in the video *Bob James: at the Queen Mary Jazz Festival '85* (1985). He continued to work intermittently with James into the late 1990s, and in the mid-1990s the two men performed and recorded as co-leaders.

Whalum first recorded as a sole leader in the mid-1980s, after which he continued to lead his own groups; he also worked regularly with Larry Carlton from 1986 to 1990, and in 1987 he moved to Los Angeles. There he was active in recording studios accompanying pop musicians and contemporary-jazz and smooth-jazz musicians and groups. He toured and recorded with the pop singers Whitney Houston (from 1989) and Luther Vandross (1991) and with the pop group Everything But the Girl (1990), among others. Around 1993 he recorded with Joey DeFrancesco at the Five Spot in New York, and in 1995 he performed at a tribute to Arnett Cobb in Houston. In 1996 he settled in Nashville. He toured in the smooth-jazz group Guitar Saxes & More (1996), played with Joe Sample (late 1990s), and led the group the Staff (from 1998). In April 2000 he performed in South Africa at Johannesburg, Durban, and Cape Town. He doubles on soprano saxophone and flute.

SELECTED RECORDINGS

As leader: *Floppy Disk* (*c*1985, Col. FC40221); *Cache* (*c*1993, Col. CK46931); with B. James: *Joined at the Hip* (*c*1995, WB 46318-2)

As sideman: B. James: on *12* (1984, Col. FC39580), Ruby, Ruby; J. DeFrancesco: on *Live at the Five Spot* (*c*1993, Col. CK53805), Impressions

BIBLIOGRAPHY

F. Nemko: "Kirk Whalum: Another Tradition Bearer," *JT* (1989), Nov, 17

L. Hunter: "Kirk Whalum," *Saxophone Journal*, xv/2 (1990), 12 [incl. discography]

C. Perry: "Kirk Whalum Bids Adieu to America," *Houston Post* (29 April 1992)

J. Bradley: "Memphis Lifeblood of Whalum Album," *Denver Post* (19 Feb 1996)

P. Myers: "Kirk Whalum: Shades of Harmony," *JT*, xxvii/10 (1997), 102

A. Pryor: "Matters of Faith," *Jazziz*, xiv/11 (1997), 50

<http://www.wbjazz.com> (1999)

<http://www.kirkwhalum.com> (2001) [incl. discography]

GK

Wheeler, (Edward Burl) De Priest (*b* Kansas City, MO, 1 March 1903). Trombonist. After working in bands in Kansas City (from 1917) and St. Louis (1917) he performed with the saxophonist Dave Lewis and toured with a circus band (until 1922). In 1923 he joined the Syncopators, led by the violinist Wilson Robinson, which toured the Pantages circuit and was resident at the Cotton Club in New York as the Cotton Club Orchestra (from 1925); it was known as the Missourians before becoming Cab Calloway's orchestra. Wheeler played in the group until January 1940, and he may be seen in Calloway's films from this period. Although thereafter he ceased to work as a full-time musician, he continued to perform occasionally, including a period on baritone horn with the Senior Citizens Band, led by the saxophonist Charlie Frazier.

SELECTED RECORDINGS

As sideman: Cotton Club Orchestra: Everybody Stomp/Charleston Ball (1925, Col. 14113D); Missourians: Market Street Stomp (1929, Vic. 38067); Ozark Mountain Blues/You'll cry for me but I'll be gone (1929, Vic. 38071); Vine Street Drag (1929, Vic. 38103); Stoppin' the Traffic (1930, Vic. 38120); C. Calloway: Nobody's Sweetheart (1930, Bruns. 6105); Farewell Blues (1931, Ban. 32152)

BIBLIOGRAPHY

McCarthyB

based on *ChiltonW*/HOWARD RYE (recording-list)

Wheeler, Ian (Gordon) (*b* London, 13 Jan 1931). Clarinetist, alto saxophonist, and leader. In his teens he took up ukulele and then guitar, which he played in local groups after serving in the merchant navy (1949). Having changed to clarinet, in 1952 he formed the River City Jazzband. Late in 1954 he joined Ken Colyer's Jazzmen and Colyer's Omega Brass Band, and he remained with Colyer through the decade. In May 1960, with the trumpeter Ken Sims, he founded the Vintage Jazz Band, which recorded in Hamburg that year. From January 1961 to July 1968 Wheeler was a member of Chris Barber's band, with which he also played soprano saxophone and harmonica. After leaving Barber he led his own jazz band (1970–73), co-led another group with Rod Mason (October 1973–1976), and then, with Keith Smith, co-led the group Hefty Jazz (1976 – March 1979). In April 1979 he rejoined Barber, with whom he remained through the late 1990s.

SELECTED RECORDINGS

As leader: with K. Sims: *Sims–Wheeler Vintage Jazz Band* (1960, Pol. LPHM21598); *Introducing Ian* (1961, Col. SEG8110); with R. Mason: *Rod Mason–Ian Wheeler Band* (1974, WAM 5008); *Reed All About It* (1978, Hefty Jazz 104)

As sideman: C. Barber: *Chris Barber at the London Palladium* (1961, Col. 33SX1346); D. Wellstood: *Some Hefty Cats* (1977, Hefty Jazz 100)

GK

Wheeler, Kenny [Kenneth Vincent John] (*b* Toronto, 14 Jan 1930). Canadian trumpeter and flugelhorn player, composer, and leader. He grew up in a succession of towns in Ontario, including St. Catharines, where the family settled around 1945 and where his father played trombone in local bands. After studying harmony and trumpet at the Royal Conservatory in Toronto (1950–51) he moved briefly to Montreal (1952) and then went to London. By 1953 he was playing in English dance and jazz bands, including those of Carl Barriteau (January–April 1954), Tommy Whittle (autumn 1955), Buddy Featherstonaugh (October 1956–1957), and Vic Lewis (summer 1958 – early 1959). In April 1959 he toured as a member of Woody Herman's Anglo-American Herd.

While a member of John Dankworth's orchestra (1959–65) Wheeler studied composition with Richard Rodney Bennett (1962–3) and Bill Russo (1963–4); with Dankworth's group he made a recording in 1968 of his own composition *Windmill Tilter*, a suite inspired by Cervantes's *Don Quixote*. From the mid-1960s he toured and recorded with Friedrich Gulda's Euro-Jazz Orchestra (1965–6), played in small groups with Tubby Hayes (recording in 1966), Joe Harriott (recording in 1967), Ronnie Scott (recording in 1968), Alan Skidmore (1969–70, recording in 1969), and Tony Coe (in the group Coe, Wheeler, and Co., from April 1970), and recorded with Philly Joe Jones (1968), John Surman (1968, *c*1971), the Clarke–Boland Orchestra (1969), and John Taylor (1971). At the same time he took an interest in free jazz, which he played with many important musicians and groups: the Spontaneous Music Ensemble (1966–70), Mike Westbrook's orchestra (recording in 1969), Tony Oxley (1969–72), Anthony Braxton (at intervals, 1971–3; regularly, 1974–6), the Globe Unity Orchestra (from the early 1970s until it disbanded in 1989), and its successor, the Berlin Contemporary Jazz Orchestra (recording in 1989), which has performed some of his compositions. Wheeler has also played jazz-rock, in particular on recordings with Mike Gibbs (1969–75) and Bill Bruford (1977) and as a member of the United Jazz and Rock Ensemble (from 1978 into the new century).

Wheeler first led small groups and big bands whose recordings were devoted to his own compositions in the mid-1970s, and in 1976 he began working with Taylor and Norma Winstone as the trio Azimuth. He took part as a

Kenny Wheeler at the Queen Elizabeth Hall, London, 1999

freelance in recording sessions with Elton Dean (1977), Louis Moholo (1978), George Adams, Roscoe Mitchell, and Ralph Towner (all 1979), Arild Andersen, Rainer Brüninghaus, and the London Jazz Composers Orchestra (all 1980), Pepper Adams (1983), and Bill Frisell and Winstone (both 1984), among others. From 1982 to 1987 he was a member of Dave Holland's quintet, and from 1983 he made annual trips to Canada to teach at the jazz workshop in Banff, initially in association with Holland's group; he may be seen in the video *Dave Holland Quintet: Vortex* (*c*1994), filmed during this association. In 1987 Wheeler toured the USA and recorded at the Caravan of Dreams, Fort Worth, Texas, as a member of George Gruntz's Concert Jazz Band.

From the late 1980s Wheeler has been one of the musicians whom Jane Ira Bloom has drawn upon to form her small groups; he recorded with her in 1992 and again in 1995. From 1989 he performed and recorded with Klaus König's orchestra. He also recorded with Bobby Wellins (*c*1988), Claudio Fasoli (1988, 1994), the Dedication Orchestra (1992, 1994), Rabih Abou-Khalil (1992, 1994), Paolino Dalla Porta (1993), the European Music Orchestra (1994), Pierre Favre and Thomas Stabenow (both 1995), Michel Portal (1996), and John Abercrombie (1998). His quartet of Chris Laurence, Taylor, and Adam Nussbaum toured from 1997; another quartet, consisting of Lee Konitz, Frisell, and Holland, recorded in 1996 and then toured in 1999, but with Abercrombie in place of Frisell.

Wheeler's playing is clear, relaxed, and lyrical, and marked by a wide-ranging harmonic and rhythmic imagination. His compositions – heard on his albums as a leader – explore this same range of qualities, and it should be noted that, while lyricism nearly always comes to the fore in both his playing and his writing, it is invariably a peculiar, elliptical sort of lyricism which manages somehow to be odd and distinctive in a pretty way (and quite unlike the lyricism of catchy pop music). Together with *Windmill Tilter,* Wheeler's most ambitious composition is *The Sweet Time Suite*, recorded in 1990 and exemplifying some of the central ideals of modern big-band jazz: strong soloists, gorgeous ensemble writing, and a compelling sense of swing. An anthology of his compositions has been published as *Collected Works on ECM: Kenny Wheeler*, ed. F. Sturm (Vienna, *c*1997).

Oral history material in *GBLnsa*.

SELECTED RECORDINGS

(recorded for ECM unless otherwise indicated)

* – composed by Wheeler

Duos with P. Bley: *[Touché]* (1996, Justin Time 97-2)

As leader: **Windmill Tilter* (1968, Fon. 5494); *Song for Someone* (1973, Incus 10), incl. *Toot-toot; *Gnu High* (1975, 1069); *Deer Wan* (1977, 1102), incl. *Deer Wan, *3/4 in the Afternoon; of Azimuth (with J. Taylor and N. Winstone): *The Touchstone* (1978, 1130); *Around 6* (1979, 1156), incl. *Mai We Go Round; *Double, Double You* (1983, 1262); *Flutter by, Butterfly* (1987, SN 1146), incl. *Everybody's Song but my Own; *Music for Large & Small Ensembles* (1990, 1415–16), incl. *Sea Lady, *The Sweet Time Suite; *The Widow in the Window* (1990, 1417); *Angel Song* (1996, 1607), incl. *Kind Folk, *Nicolette

As sideman: Spontaneous Music Ensemble: *Karyöbin* (1968, Isl. 9079); T. Oxley: *The Baptised Traveller* (1969, CBS 52664); A. Braxton: *New York, Fall 1974* (1974, Ari. 4032); *Five Pieces 1975* (1975, Ari. 4064); E. Dean: *The Cheque is in the Mail* (1977, Ogun 610); B. Bruford: *Feels Good to Me* (1977, Pol. 6149); [no leader:] *Seven Steps to Evans* (1979, MPS 15553); United Jazz and Rock Ensemble: *Live in Berlin* (1981, Mood 28628); D. Holland: *Jumpin' In* (1983, 1269); *Seeds of Time* (1984, 1292); *The Razor's Edge* (1987, 1353); J. I. Bloom: *Art and Aviation* (1992, Arabesque 0107); C. Fasoli: *Ten Tributes* (1994, Ram 4517); J. I. Bloom: *The Nearness* (1995, Arabesque 0120)

For further recordings *see* GLOBE UNITY ORCHESTRA.

BIBLIOGRAPHY

ChiltonB; *EMC2*

R. Cotterrell: "Kenny Wheeler: Speaking Softly but Carrying a Big Horn," *JF* [intl edn], no.57 (1979), 38

M. Miller: "Kenny Wheeler's Many Vehicles," *DB*, xlvii/4 (1980), 22 [incl. discography]

P. Husby: "Kenny Wheeler: Interview," *Cadence*, vii/5 (1981), 12

P. Renaud: *La discographie du jazz anglais* (Chaumont, France, 1985)

B. Smith: "Kenny Wheeler: Windmill Tilter," *Coda*, no.207 (1986), 4

M. Miller: "Kenny Wheeler," *Boogie, Pete & the Senator: Canadian Musicians in Jazz: the Eighties* (Toronto, 1987), 290
J. Fordham: "Trumpet Voluntary," *The Guardian* (11 April 1997)
J. Hale: "Kenny Wheeler: in a Melancholy Tone," *DB*, lxiv/8 (1997), 34
J. D'Souza: "Windmill Tilter: Kenny Wheeler," *Coda*, no.282 (1998), 10
Fara C. and A. Dutilh: "Kenny Wheeler en confiance," *Jazzman*, no.33 (1998), 8
B. Blumenthal: "The Greatest Jazzman You Never Heard of," *Boston Globe* (23 May 1999)
<http://www.ejn.it/mus/wheeler.htm> (2000)

BK

Wheeler, Nedra (Jo) (*b* Los Angeles, 9 Oct 1961). Double bass player. She learned guitar, piano, and organ before taking up double bass at around the age of 13, and her first music teacher was her father, a singer. Later she had lessons with Red Callender (at the Wind College, run by John Carter and James Newton), and while a student at the California Institute for the Arts (BFA 1987, MFA 1989) she studied with Buell Neidlinger, John Clayton, Charlie Haden, and Larry Gales, as well as with Ghanaian percussionists. Active professionally from the mid-1970s, when she made her first recording with a gospel group, Wheeler worked extensively in recording, film, and television studios from the mid-1980s. She toured Bulgaria with Milcho Leviev in June 1990 and then stayed in Paris for a period before traveling to the Netherlands, where she met Winard and Philip Harper; later, after returning to Los Angeles, she toured and recorded with their group, the Harper Brothers (*c*1991). Around the same time she toured in a blues group led by the singer Pat Benatar. Wheeler worked regularly in Kenny Kirkland's various ensembles, including a trio with Jeff "Tain" Watts (1993–5). From the early 1990s she led her own small groups, and played with, among others, the violinists Karen Briggs (with whom she recorded in 1992), Lesa Terry, and Jan Cherry, the saxophonist Karl Denson (from December 1992, recording in 1993), the pianist John Wood, Eric Reed, Ann Patterson, Cedar Walton (1993), Herbie Hancock, and numerous others. In 1999 she toured Utah with Wycliffe Gordon. Wheeler has taught at the University of Southern California (in 1987 as an assistant to the reed player Harold Battiste), the Thelonious Monk Institute, and the Centennial High School in Compton, California (late 1990s).

Wheeler is a vigorous performer, whose hard-driving, rhythmically supple lines complement any ensemble in which she plays and consistently garner acclaim from reviewers (an honor not frequently accorded to bass players). A fine example of her style may be heard on the track *Down on Duncan*, recorded with the Harper Brothers around 1991. She has played electric bass guitar, albeit rarely, her most notable work on the instrument being a recording with Bob Dylan.

SELECTED RECORDINGS

As leader: *Gifts: Live at Birdland West* (1989, Splashing Sun 13009)
As sideman: Harper Brothers: *Artistry* (*c*1991, Verve 847956-2), incl. Down on Duncan; K. Briggs: *Karen* (1992, VTL 009); K. Denson: *Herbal Turkey Breast* (1993, Minor Music 801032)

BIBLIOGRAPHY

B. Kohlhaase: "Woman Bassist Walks in World of Men," *Los Angeles Times* (12 Sept 1993)
P. Crow: "Music School Focus Article: Nedra Wheeler," <http://indy1.calarts.edu/~alumni/musica.html> (1999)
<http://music2.csudh.edu/events/Nedra.htm> (1999)

GK

Whetsol, Artie [Arthur; Schiefe, Arthur Parker] (*b* Punta Gorda, FL, 1905; *d* New York, 5 Jan 1940). Trumpeter. He grew up in Washington, where he was a childhood friend of Duke Ellington and played in various local bands. In 1923, with Ellington, he moved to New York as a member of Elmer Snowden's band the Washingtonians, but returned to his home town the following year reportedly to study medicine at Howard University; Tucker (1991) discovered that no record of these studies exists, and thus Whetsol's activities over the next five years remain unknown. He re-joined the band, by then under Ellington's leadership, in 1928, remaining until autumn 1936, when ill-health forced him to retire; despite repeated efforts, he was never able to resume full-time playing. Whetsol was an outstanding lead trumpeter and a distinctive soloist whose highly melodic style of performance was gentle and often wistful.

SELECTED RECORDINGS

(all as sideman with D. Ellington)

Black Beauty (1928, Vic. 21580); The Dicty Glide/Stevedore Stomp (1929, Vic. 38053); Jungle Jamboree (1929, OK 8720); Rocky Mountain Blues (1930, OK 8836); Mood Indigo (1930, Bruns. 4952); Black and Tan Fantasy, first issued on unnamed LP (1932, Vic. L16007)

SELECTED FILMS AND VIDEOS

Black and Tan (1929); Check and Double Check (1930); Bundle of Blues (1933); Belle of the Nineties [It Ain't No Sin] (1934); Murder at the Vanities (1934); Symphony in Black (1934)

BIBLIOGRAPHY

ChiltonW; *McCarthyB*; *SchullerS*; *TuckerDE*
H. Pekar: "Arthur Whetsol," *JJ*, xvi/7 (1963), 19
G. E. Lambert: "The Ellingtonians, 1: Arthur Whetsol," *JM*, x/2 (1964), 16
G. Schuller: *Early Jazz: its Roots and Musical Development* (New York, 1968)
D. M. Bakker: *Duke Ellington on Microgroove: 1923–February 1940* (Alphen aan de Rijn, Netherlands, 1972; rev. 3/1977 as *Duke Ellington on Microgroove*, i: *1923–1936*) [incl. list of recorded solos]
D. Ellington: *Music is my Mistress* (Garden City, NJ, 1973, rev. 2/1982), 54
M. Tucker: *Ellington: the Early Years* (Oxford, England, Urbana, IL, and Chicago, 1991)

EDDIE LAMBERT/BK

Whigham, Jiggs [Oliver Haydn, III] (*b* Cleveland, 20 Aug 1943). Trombonist and educator. His nickname, Jiggs, was given to him by his grandfather, who was a fan of the children's comic characters Jiggs and Maggie. He took up trombone as a teenager, and after graduating from high school (1961) he worked in the Glenn Miller band under the direction of Ray McKinley (until 1962). In the latter part of 1963 he played in Stan Kenton's orchestra, with which he toured England, and a few months later he traveled to New York; there he met Richard Rogers, whose music he arranged for a new Broadway show. In 1964 he rejoined the Miller band, and the following year he returned to New York and worked as a freelance with Maynard Ferguson, Johnny Richards, and the bandleader Larry Elgart.

Having moved to Cologne, Germany, Whigham joined Kurt Edelhagen's orchestra (late 1965) at Westdeutscher Rundfunk, with which he toured Africa (1966), performed at the Berliner Jazztage (1967), and broadcast on German radio. The group disbanded in 1973, after which he performed as a freelance and as a member of Peter Herbolzheimer's Rhythm Combination & Brass, and in 1976 he joined the radio staff orchestra in Cologne. In addition he formed a trombone group with Albert Mangelsdorff, Bill Watrous, and Kai Winding (recording in 1980) and another with Watrous, Carl Fontana, and Ian McDougall (1987), and performed with Louie Bellson's big band, recorded with Klaus Weiss and the BBC Big Band (both 1984), and co-led a quintet with Lee Konitz on a tour of Britain (*c*1987). Whigham participated in numerous reunions of Kenton's orchestra from 1987, including the 50th anniversary tribute, "Back to Balboa," in Newport, California, in 1991, and in the mid-1990s he led the RIAS Big Band in Berlin. Whigham began teaching at the Musikhochschule in Cologne in the early 1970s, and in 1979 he was appointed head of its jazz department. He has also been a regular performer and a guest instructor at Bud Shank's annual jazz festival in Port Townsend, Washington. His playing may be heard to fine effect on an album by his small group, *The Jiggs Up* (1989, Capri 74024), and on a recording made in a duo with Gene Bertoncini, *Jiggs & Gene* (*c*1997, Azica 2204).

BIBLIOGRAPHY

CarrJ; *Feather'60s*; *ReclamsJ*
W. Panke: "Jazz-Professor in Köln," *Neue Musikzeitung*, xxviii/6 (1979), 12
D. von Szadowski: "Eine Professor für Jazz: kritische Anmerkungen zu einer neuen Einrichtung," *JP*, xxviii/12 (1979), 16
W. F. Lee: *Stan Kenton: Artistry in Rhythm* (Los Angeles, 1980/*R*1994) [incl. discography; *R* without discography]
"Jiggs Whigham," *ITA Journal*, xi/2 (1983), 15
L. Tomkins: "Sound, Range and the Trombone," *CI*, xv/7 (1988), 24
W. Englert: "Jiggs Whigham: Musik was soll's?," *JP*, xxxviii/10 (1989), 26
B. Reinhardt: "Jiggs Whigham," *JP*, xl/1 (1991), 45
G. Endress: "Survival: Jiggs Whigham," *JP*, xlii/9 (1993), 10
J. Maggs: "The Professor," *CJM*, xxxiii/3 (1996), 26
E. J. Ulman: "Jiggs," *ITA Journal*, xxiv/1 (1996), 34 [incl. discography]
D. Koch: "Jiggs Whigham und sein Plädoyer für die Jazzpädagogik," *JP*, xlvi/3 (1997), 6

GK

Whispa mute. *See* MUTE, §2(h).

Whistler [Threlkeld, Buford] (*b* Eminence, KY, 18 April 1893; *d* New York, *c*1934). Guitarist, nose-whistle player, and singer. After playing guitar around Henry and Shelby counties in Kentucky he moved to Louisville in 1914. Shortly afterwards he formed a string band, which he enlarged to a jug band around 1915. From then until 1932 this band played on the streets, for parties, and at the racetrack, and also toured widely through the North and Midwest. About 1919 Whistler took up the nose-whistle (sometimes called Humanophone). The band first recorded in 1924 with the pioneering jug blower B. D. Tite. On *The Jug Band Special/Pig Meat Blues* (1927, OK 8116) Whistler can be heard on both his instruments and also scat singing, with the juvenile prodigy Rudolph Thompson playing jug. In 1930 the band, augmented by two additional jug blowers, was filmed for a Fox-Movietone newsreel; the footage was not used but an edited version has been released on *Things Ain't What They Used to Be: Early Rural and Popular American Music from Rare Original Film Masters (1928–35)* (1992). In 1932, after being accused of a theft, Whistler was obliged to leave Louisville, and he worked in the New York area until his death.

BIBLIOGRAPHY

L. Wright, comp. [from material supplied by F. Cox, J. Randolph, and J. Harris]: *The Jug Bands of Louisville* (Chigwell, England, 1993 [*recte* 1994])
F. Cox, J. Randolph, and J. Harris: "The Jug Bands of Louisville," *Sv* (1993), no.155, p.164; no.156, p.204; (1994), no.157, p.4; no.158, p.43; no.159, p.83; no.160, p.145; (1995), no.161, p.188; no.162, p.203
B. Bogert: Liner notes, *Clifford Hayes & the Louisville Jug Bands*, i–iv (RST 1501-2, 1502-2, 1503-2, 1504-2, 1994)

HOWARD RYE

Whitaker, Rodney (Thomas) (*b* Detroit, 22 Feb 1968). Double bass player. He played violin from the age of eight and took up double bass when he was 13; his interest in jazz began after he heard Paul Chambers on a recording by John Coltrane. As a teenager he worked locally with various groups, notably Bird/Trane/Sko/Now!, led by the saxophonist Donald Washington. Whitaker replaced Robert Hurst in the quintet of Donald Harrison and Terence Blanchard (*c*1989), and after it disbanded he performed and recorded as a member of Blanchard's quintet (*c*1990–91). He then toured and recorded with Roy Hargrove's small group (into 1995) and toured with the Lincoln Center Jazz Orchestra's production of Wynton Marsalis's oratorio *Blood on the Fields* (1994). From 1995 he led his own groups and worked as a freelance. He toured with Junko Onishi and performed with, among others, Diana Krall, Branford Marsalis (with whom he appeared on television as a member of the house band for "The Tonight Show"), Joshua Redman, Stanley Turrentine, Antonio Hart, Harrison, Tommy Flanagan, Barry Harris, and John Hicks; with Kenny Garrett he recorded (*c*1996), toured (1997), and appeared in the video *Kenny Garrett: Pursuance, the Music of John Coltrane* (*c*1996). In addition Whitaker recorded as a freelance with Hart (1992), Eric Reed (1993–4), Onishi (1993, 1995), Mark Whitfield and Johnny Griffin (both 1994), Teodross Avery and Charles Sullivan (both 1995), Kevin Mahogany, Diane Reeves, and Clarence Penn (all 1996), and the pianist Orrin Evans (1996–8). In the late 1990s he was still living in Detroit; when not touring, he performed localy and worked as an adjunct professor at both the University of Michigan and Michigan State University. He owns a production company which is run by his wife, Monzola Whitaker.

SELECTED RECORDINGS

As leader: *Children of the Light* (1995, DIW 907); *Hidden Kingdom* (1996, DIW 929)
As sideman: E. Reed: *It's All Right to Swing* (1993, MoJazz 7006-2); J. Onishi: *Cruisin'* (1993, BN B21Z-28447); J. Griffin: on *Chicago, New York, Paris* (1994, Verve 314-527367-2), The Jamfs are Coming, Not Yet, To Love; K. Garrett: *Pursuance: the Music of John Coltrane* (*c*1996, WB 46209-2); C. Penn: *Penn's Landing* (1996, Criss Cross 1134)

BIBLIOGRAPHY

M. Stryker: "Bassist on the Brink," *Detroit News & Free Press* (12 May 1996)
G. Robinson: "Hearsay: Rodney Whitaker," *JT*, xxvii/3 (1997), 23
<http://www.jazz.detroit.net/focus/whitaker-r/review.html> (1999)

GK

White, Amos (Earl Mordechai) (*b* Kingstree, SC, 6 Nov 1889; *d* Oakland, CA, 2 July 1980). Cornetist. He entered Jenkins Orphanage in Charleston, South Carolina, at the age of nine. After learning cornet he toured with the orphanage band, performed with circus and minstrel groups (1913–18), and during World War I played in the 32-piece 816th Pioneer Regimental Brass Band in France. In August 1919, following his discharge, he settled in New Orleans, where he performed as a part-time musician with such leaders as Papa Celestin (for whom he deputized at times as leader of the Tuxedo Brass Band) and A. J. Piron and in the Excelsior Brass Band. He then led his own band and worked on the SS *Capitol* with Fate Marable, with whom he performed intermittently until 1924; his playing may be heard on Marable's *Frankie and Johnny* (1924, OK 40113). White left New Orleans around 1925, touring with several groups, including that of Mamie Smith (1927), and led the Georgia Minstrels (1928). Thereafter he worked as a sideman and leader in Phoenix, Arizona (after 1929), and settled in Oakland, California (1934), where he formed a band including the clarinetist Clem Raymond which toured locally. He later ceased full-time performing, but continued to play occasionally into the 1960s. Some examples of his work from 1960 may be found on *Frank "Big Boy" Goudie with Amos White* (1960–61, AM CD50). His death date is taken from the California death index.

Oral history material in *LNT*.

BIBLIOGRAPHY

ChartersJ; *ChiltonW*

G. Mills: "Amos White and his New Orleans Ragtime Band," *Eureka*, i/5 (1960), 5

J. Chilton: *A Jazz Nursery: the Story of the Jenkins' Orphanage Bands of Charleston, South Carolina* (London, 1980)

G. Mills: Liner notes, *Frank "Big Boy" Goudie with Amos White* (AM CD50, 1991)

R. H. Knowles: *Fallen Heroes: a History of New Orleans Brass Bands* (New Orleans, 1996), 52, 111

HOWARD RYE, BK

White, Andrew (Nathaniel, III) (*b* Washington, DC, 6 Sept 1942). Alto and tenor saxophonist. In 1947 his family moved to Nashville, where he remained through his high school years. He played soprano saxophone as a child, then changed to alto saxophone, and took up oboe in his early teens. From 1960 he studied oboe and theory at Howard University (BM 1964). During this period he led the JFK Quintet, which served as the house band at the Bohemian Caverns, then Washington's best jazz club; the quintet's members were the trumpeter Ray Codrington, the pianist Harry Killgo, Walter Booker, and the drummer Mickey Newman; Billy Hart also played drums in the group. From 1964 to 1968 White attended Dartmouth College, the conservatoire in Paris, and SUNY, Buffalo. He was the principal oboist with the orchestra of the American Ballet Theatre in New York (1968–70) and an electric bass guitarist for the soul singer Stevie Wonder and the pop group the Fifth Dimension (1969–73); in addition he played electric bass guitar on recordings by Weather Report (1971–*c*1973) and took a solo on english horn on the track *Unknown Soldier* on the group's album *I Sing the Body Electric* (1971–2). With McCoy Tyner he recorded as a saxophonist and, later, arranged and conducted music for a big-band tribute to John Coltrane at the Newport Jazz Festival in New York (1976). During the following decade he played alto and tenor saxophones as the leader of a quartet that included Mal Waldron and as a sideman with Elvin Jones (1980–81) and Beaver Harris (1983). In 1986 he performed in Washington with Tyner's trio at Blues Alley and in 1991 he performed regularly at the One Step Down. White joined the World Saxophone Quartet and Carl Grubbs to form a sextet which took part in the première in 1987 of Julius Hemphill's composition *Long Tongues: a Saxophone Opera*. When Hemphill left the World Saxophone Quartet in 1989 he formed his own saxophone sextet, and White became a permanent member. He thus participated in Hemphill's later large-scale works and recorded with the group in 1993 as a quintet, when the leader was too ill to play; he continued with the sextet after Hemphill's death in 1995. In October 1998, after a hiatus of 14 years, he again recorded as a leader, producing a four-volume set of CDs from performances at the One Step Down in a quartet which included Steve Novosel.

White is a tireless self-promoter, but unlike some others he goes about his work in a delightfully humorous and engaging way. In 1971 in Washington he formed Andrew's Music, which issues recordings of his own performances and publishes books, scores, and his own transcriptions of solos by Coltrane, Charlie Parker, and Eric Dolphy; the scope of his work on Coltrane (more than 600 transcriptions, many of demonic complexity) is unrivaled. Moreover, despite the devotion to Coltrane's music which necessarily went into the creation of these transcriptions, White has managed to avoid carrying over his devotion into his own playing; even in the setting most closely associated with Coltrane – as a member of Jones's quintet – he provided creative and personalized improvisations on a modal- and free-jazz repertory. He has also published his arrangements for jazz groups, a series of his chamber music, method books, and a jazz concerto; he has written and published numerous books, and he has issued the *Andrew Video-demo*, showing him in performance with a big band and quartet.

SELECTED RECORDINGS

(recorded for Andrew's Music unless otherwise indicated)

As leader: of JFK Quintet: *New Jazz Frontiers from Washington* (1961, Riv. 9396); *Passion Flower* (1974, 5); *Marathon '75*, iii (1975, 17); *Seven Giant Steps for Coltrane* (1976, 30); *Live in New York*, ii (1977, 31); *I Love Japan* (1979, 38)

As sideman with J. Hemphill: *Five Chord Stud* (1993, BS 120140-2)

WRITINGS

(selective list; all published in Washington)

Trane 'n Me: a Semi-autobiography: a Treatise on the Music of John Coltrane (1981)

Hey Kid! Wanna Buy a Record? A Treatise on Self Production in the Music Business (1982)

Andrew's X-rated Band Stories (1984)

I, Bassist!: Comedic Confessons of a Rock 'n' Roll Bass Player (*c*1990)

My Life in Paris and 25 Reflections (*c*1992)

I, Educator! (*c*1994)

I, Oboist! (*c*1994)

BIBLIOGRAPHY

GrayF

L. Goddet: "Interview: Andrew White," *Jh*, no.304 (1974), 14

C. Ingersoll: "Andrew White," *Different Drummer*, i/11 (1974), 13

J. Dreyfus: "'A Fine Musician of Many Dimensions'," *Washington Post* (30 Sept 1975)

S. Metalitz: "Andrew White: Working the Musical Mother Lode," *Washington Review of the Arts*, i/1 (1975), 9

C. Renninger: "'Andy's in the Basement'," *Radio Free Jazz* (1975), July, 10

B. Rusch: "Andrew White: Master Musician," *Cadence*, i/5 (1976), 5

——: "Andrew White: Interview," *Cadence*, iv/4 (1978), 10

D. E. McGinty: "Conversation with Andrew White: 'Keeper of the Trane'," *Black Perspective in Music*, xii/1 (1984), 80

M. Joyce: "Spotlight: Saxophone Sound of Surprise," *Washington Post* (24 Feb 1986)

H. McLeod: "Jazzman Spends Life Chasin' the Trane," *Richmond News Leader* [Virginia] (19 Sept 1991)

S. Baudot: "Andrew White: White Spirit," *Jh*, no.524 (1995), 17

ED HAZELL/BK

White, Bobby [Robert E.] (*b* Chicago, 28 June 1926). Drummer. In 1941 he moved to Los Angeles, where he won a talent contest at the Million Dollar Theater and began working in vaudeville shows. In 1948 he played locally with the trombonist Earle Spencer, and in May and June 1949 he appeared at Howard Rumsey's first Sunday afternoon concerts at the Lighthouse in Hermosa Beach. During the early 1950s he worked as a freelance with Ella Fitzgerald, Anita O'Day, Vido Musso (1951–2), the guitarist Alvino Rey, Gerry Mulligan, Art Pepper (recording in 1952–3), Chet Baker (he took part in the trumpeter's first recording session as a leader, 1953), Stan Getz, Harry James, and Charlie Barnet. In 1953 he replaced Art Blakey in Buddy DeFranco's quartet, which toured Europe the following year as part of Leonard Feather's Jazz Club USA troupe; he also recorded with Musso (1953–4), Benny Carter, DeFranco's pianist Sonny Clark, and Jimmy Raney (all 1954), and Cal Tjader (1955). After DeFranco's quartet disbanded in 1958, White worked as a freelance musician in the Los Angeles area, with the saxophonist Gil Bernal, the singers Don and Elisha

Cunningham, and others. From 1992 he led the house band at the Lighthouse on Sunday afternoons. At first influenced by Jo Jones, Buddy Rich, and Max Roach, White developed a style of bop drumming which made use of two bass drums.

SELECTED RECORDINGS

As leader: *Bobby White's Average Jazz Band* (1981, H.T. 1)

As sideman: A. Pepper: *Surf Ride* (1952, Savoy 12089); C. Baker: *The Chet Baker Quartet* (1953, PJ 3); B. DeFranco: *Buddy DeFranco and his Clarinet* (1954, Norg. 1012); *In a Mellow Mood* (1954, Norg. 1079); on [various artists]: *Alto Saxes* (1947–54, Norg. 1035), B. Carter: A Foggy Day, Poinciana; B. DeFranco: *Buddy DeFranco and Oscar Peterson Play George Gershwin* (1954, Norg. 1016); *The Buddy DeFranco Wailers* (1956, Norg. 1085)

BIBLIOGRAPHY

FeatherE

R. Gordon: *Jazz West Coast: the Los Angeles Jazz Scene of the 1950s* (London and New York, 1986)

THOMAS OWENS

White, Carla (Ruth) (*b* Oakland, CA, 15 Sept 1951). Singer. She grew up in Bellport, New York, and studied jazz dance, acting, and singing at high school. In 1969 she moved to London to attend the Webber–Douglas Academy of Dramatic Art; however, she did not enjoy the experience and left in 1971. Having traveled around Europe she moved in 1972 to New York, where she began working as an actress in off-Broadway performances. Shortly afterwards she decided to become a jazz singer and studied with Lennie Tristano; following his death she had lessons with Warne Marsh (1979–82) and various others, including the pianist Jill McManus (1987–9) and Armen Donelian (1994–6). From 1980 to 1985 she co-led a bop band with the trumpeter Manny Duran, in which she functioned mainly as another instrumentalist, persistently scat singing rather than delivering lyrics; their sidemen included Peter Madsen, Anthony Cox, Ed Howard, and Tim Horner. After hearing Joe Williams, White began working as a more conventional singer and formed her own quartet, in which from 1985 she has performed with Madsen, Dean Johnson, Tom Rainey, and Matt Wilson, among others.

SELECTED RECORDINGS

As leader: with M. Duran: *Andruline* (1983, Stash 237); *Orient Express* (1985–6, Mlst. 9147); *Listen Here* (1991, Evidence 22109); *Live at Vartan Jazz* (1996, Vartan Jazz 016)

BIBLIOGRAPHY

D. Kasrel: "Hearsay: Carla White," *JT*, xxv/5 (1995), 16

<http://www.jazzcorner.com/white/> (1999) [incl. discography]

GK

White, Chip [Alan] (*b* New York, *c*1948). Drummer. He began music studies at the age of nine and later attended Ithaca College and the Berklee School of Music; he studied orchestration with Frank Foster. In 1970 he settled in New York and worked with, among others, Carmen McRae, Jaki Byard, John Abercrombie, Johnny Coles, Tom Waits, Gary Bartz, and John Hicks, and recorded with James Moody (*c*1970), Enrico Rava (1972), and the saxophonist Ralph Simon (1981). He established his own group in 1984, and in 1990 he wrote and produced a jazz musical, *Manhattan Moments*. In the mid-1990s he joined ensembles led by Claudio Roditi (*c*1994) and Klaus Ignatzek (1995) and recorded as a sole leader (1994) and as a sideman with Teddy Edwards (1997), and in the late 1990s he worked regularly with Houston Person and Etta Jones. White has published a book of poetry about jazz musicians.

SELECTED RECORDINGS

As leader: *Harlem Sunset* (1994, Postcards 1006)

As sideman: E. Rava: *Il giro del giorno in 80 mondi* (1972, Cetra International 9021); R. Simon: *As* (1981, Postcards 1004); H. Person: *In a Sentimental Mood* (*c*2000, HighNote 7060)

BIBLIOGRAPHY

<http://www.view.com/white-bio.html> (2001)

GK

White, Chris(topher Westley) (*b* New York, 6 July 1936). Double bass player and educator. He studied piano before taking up double bass. After working intermittently with Cecil Taylor (1955–9) he performed and recorded with Bernard Peiffer (1960) and Nina Simone (1960–61). From 1962 to 1966 he was a member of Dizzy Gillespie's bop groups, and in 1963 he recorded with Gillespie's saxophonist James Moody; his playing as a sideman with Gillespie is well represented by *The Day After*, from the album *Something Old, Something New* (1963, Phi. 600091). White then collaborated with Billy Taylor (ii) (1966), worked as a freelance, gave private lessons, and studied at the Manhattan School of Music. In addition he played with Eubie Blake, Earl Hines, Moody, Teddy Wilson, and Willie "the Lion" Smith, and recorded with a quintet led by Jimmy Owens and Kenny Barron (1967), with Mary Lou Williams (*c*1969), and again with Owens (1970).

From the mid-1960s White was involved in numerous jazz education projects as a teacher, administrator, consultant, and writer, and until 1976 he was the director of the Institute of Jazz Studies at Rutgers. In the mid- to late 1970s he performed and recorded with Andrew Hill (1974, 1975, playing on the pianist's trio album *Invitation*, 1974, Ste. 1026), Kenny Barron (1975), and Kalaparusha Maurice McIntyre (1976), and recorded with Jimmy Ponder (1978). Later he recorded with Grachan Moncur III (1987), appeared with Gillespie in a televised tribute to the trumpeter (1988), and made his only album as a leader (1992). White taught in New Jersey at Newark Community School of the Arts (1980s) and Bloomfield College (1990s) and is the author of an essay on jazz as art and as entertainment ("Check Yourself!," *American Music: from Storyville to Woodstock*, ed. C. Nanry (New Brunswick, NJ, *c*1972), 189).

SELECTED FILMS AND VIDEOS

Dizzy Gillespie (1965); Dizzy Gillespie Quintet (1965); Great Performances: Wolf Trap Salutes Dizzy Gillespie: an All-star Tribute to the Jazz Master (1988)

BIBLIOGRAPHY

Feather '60s; *Feather–Gitler '70s*

V. Wilmer: "The Advantages of Gregariousness," *DB*, xxxiv/15 (1967), 22

E. Jost: *Jazzmusiker: Materialen zur Soziologie der afro-amerikanischen Musik* (Frankfurt am Main, Germany, Berlin, and Vienna, 1981), 175

BK

White, Georgia [Lawson, Georgia] (*b* Sandersville, GA, 9 March 1903). Pianist and singer. Her real or married name may have been Lawson, under which name she took part in one recording session. Little information is available about this artist, who worked and recorded with Jimmie Noone at the Apex Club, Chicago, in 1929–30. She is believed to have been working in the city's clubs during the years 1935–41, when she was a star singer in Decca's Race series, sometimes accompanying her own singing, sometimes with bands led by Richard M. Jones or Sammy Price, among others. In the late 1940s she led an all-female band in the area, and in

1949–50 was the pianist with Big Bill Broonzy's Laughing Trio. She worked in and around Chicago up to 1959, and is then thought to have retired.

SELECTED RECORDINGS

(all recorded for Decca)

As leader: [as singer]: Trouble in Mind (1936, 7192); Was I Drunk?/No Second-hand Woman (1936, 7216); [as singer and pianist]: Jazzin' Babies Blues/Late Hour Blues (1940, 7741); Papa Pleaser/Panama Limited Blues (1940, 7783)

BIBLIOGRAPHY

W. Broonzy and Y. Bruynoghe: *Big Bill: mes blues, ma guitare et moi* (Brussels, 1955, rev. and enlarged 2/1987, as *Big Bill Blues*; Eng. orig., London, 1955, as *Big Bill Blues*)
S. Harris: *Blues Who's Who: a Biographical Dictionary of Blues Singers* (New Rochelle, NY, 1979/*R*1994)
R. Reitz: Liner notes, *Georgia White Sings and Plays the Blues* (Rosetta 1307, 1982)

HOWARD RYE

White, Harry (Alexander) [Father] (*b* Bethlehem, PA, 1 June 1898; *d* New York, 14 Aug 1962). Composer, arranger, and trombonist. He played drums in show bands while still in his teens, but after moving to Washington, DC, around 1919 he concentrated on trombone. He worked with Duke Ellington, Elmer Snowden, and Claude Hopkins, among others, before forming the White Brothers Orchestra in 1925 with members of his family; Jimmy Mundy was a sideman in the band from 1926, and Shad Collins joined late in 1929. The group had a permanent engagement in Philadelphia, but White did not always work with it; instead he traveled regularly to New York, where he played with June Clark, Snowden (at the Bamville Club), and the drummer George Howe. From October 1927 to August 1928 he worked with Luis Russell, who had taken over Howe's band. He then formed another group of his own, which he led over the next few years in Newark, New Jersey, and at the Nest Club in New York, except for a brief period in summer 1929 when he was a member of Ellington's orchestra; while at the Nest, his big band included Russell Procope, Don Kirkpatrick, Joe Turner (i), Danny Barker, and Simon Marrero, among others. In 1931, after working with Cab Calloway, White and Edgar Hayes directed and wrote arrangements for the Mills Blue Rhythm Band. In June 1932 White rejoined Calloway as an arranger, composer, and player, and he is credited during this period with inventing the word "jitterbug." Early in 1935 he returned to Russell, whose band was then accompanying Louis Armstrong. He ceased full-time playing in 1936 for two years, then played with and wrote arrangements for Hot Lips Page (1938), Manzie Johnson (with whom he sometimes played alto saxophone as well as trombone, late 1938), and Hayes (late 1940); he also wrote arrangements for Bud Freeman (1940). Following a long illness he resumed part-time playing and writing in 1947 and worked at Small's with Happy Caldwell in 1953.

RECORDED COMPOSITIONS

(selective list; all with White as sideman)

C. Calloway: Evenin' (1933, Vic. 24414); Harlem Camp Meeting (1933, Vic. 24494); Zaz zuh zaz (1933, Vic. 24557); Chinese Rhythm (1933, Bruns. 6992)

SELECTED ARRANGEMENTS

(all with White as sideman)

Mills Blue Rhythm Band: Doin' the Shake/Wild Waves (1932, Ban. 32493); Rhythm Spasm (1932, Mlt. 12418); White Lightning (1932, Mlt. 12414); C. Calloway: Father's Got his Glasses On (1933, Vic. 24451); H. L. Page: Skull Duggery (1938, Bb 7583)

BIBLIOGRAPHY

ChiltonW; *FeatherE*; *McCarthyB*; *SchullerS*
J. Simmen: "Father's Got his Glasses On," *Sv*, no.129 (1987), 83
M. Tucker: *Ellington: the Early Years* (Oxford, England, Urbana, IL, and Chicago, 1991)

LAWRENCE KOCH/BK

White, Lenny [Leonard, III] (*b* New York, 19 Dec 1949). Drummer. He taught himself to play drums from the age of 14 and first worked with Jackie McLean (1968). Thereafter he recorded with Miles Davis (1969), Freddie Hubbard and Woody Shaw (1970), Gato Barbieri (1971), and Stanley Clarke (1972) and performed and recorded with Joe Henderson (1970–71) and Gil Evans (1971). After working with Stan Getz and the Latin rock group Azteca he toured as a member of Return to forever (1973–6), with which he played in an assertive style that incorporated elements of rock and Latin music. It was with this style that he became most closely identified, and he later led a group that was modeled after Return to Forever but which achieved far less critical success. White is also adept at playing hard bop, as he demonstrated in the 1970s and 1980s in his performances and recordings with Hubbard, Henderson, Clarke, Chick Corea, and (at different times) the singers Chaka Khan and Nancy Wilson in a group known variously as Echoes of an Era, the Griffith Park Band, and the Griffith Park Collection (1981–2).

In the 1990s White began performing and recording with Michal Urbaniak, and from the latter part of the decade he has been one of several drummers employed on an intermittent basis in groups led by Geri Allen and Wallace Roney. In New York he worked with Danilo Pérez at Sweet Basil and with Bob Berg at Birdland (where they recorded in 1998). In 1998 he formed a quartet, the Superband, with Jeff Lorber, Larry Carlton, and Stanley Clarke, and in 1999 he and Clarke co-led a quintet, Vertú, which included Rachel Z. White also recorded in an all-star group, Acoustic Masters II, consisting of Jerry Gonzalez, Craig Handy, Mulgrew Miller, Bobby Hutcherson, and Ron Carter (1993), and with Charles Fambrough and Ingrid Jensen (both 1994), George Garzone (1995), Tony Purrone (1996), and Buster Williams (1996, 1998). He has served as a producer for the Hip Bop label, for which he has taken part in a number of sessions, variously as leader, as a sideman, or in cooperative studio groups.

SELECTED RECORDINGS

As sideman: M. Davis: *Bitches Brew* (1969, Col. GP26); F. Hubbard: *Red Clay* (1970, CTI 6001); W. Shaw: *Blackstone Legacy* (1970, Cont. 7627–8); J. Henderson: *In Pursuit of Blackness* (1970–71, Mlst. 9034); C. Corea: *No Mystery* (1975, Pol. 6512); Echoes of an Era: *Echoes of an Era* (*c*1981, Elek. 60021); Acoustic Masters: *Acoustic Masters II* (1993, Atl. 82591); I. Jensen: *Vernal Fields* (1994, Enja 9013); G. Garzone: *Alone* (1995, NYC 6018); T. Purrone: *Set 'em Up* (1996, Ste. 31389); W. Roney: *Village* (1996, WB 46649)

SELECTED FILMS AND VIDEOS

Soundstage: New Jazz (1974); Soundstage: Downbeat Jazz Awards (1975); Chick Corea and Band: a Very Special Concert (1985 [filmed 1982]); Freddie Hubbard: Live at the Village Vanguard (1984); The Manhattan Project (*c*1990 [filmed 1989])

BIBLIOGRAPHY

Feather–Gitler '70s
M. Rozek: "A Matter of Values: a Conversation with Lenny White," *DB*, xlii/8 (1975), 15
A. Wald: "Beyond Forever: MD Talks with Lenny White," *MD*, i/4 (1977), 4
T. B. Wittet: "Lenny White: a New Brew," *MD*, xxi/6 (1997), 64
"Lenny White: Vertu is 21st Century Sound for the Millennium," *Los Angeles Sentinel* (10 June 1999)
K. Micallef: "(Return to) that F Word," *Jazziz*, xvi/10 (1999), 54

BK

White, Michael (Walter) (i) (*b* Houston, 24 May 1933). Electric violinist and composer. He was brought up in Oakland, California, and first came to public attention at the Monterey Jazz Festival in 1965 as a member of John Handy's quintet, with which he appeared that same year in the Canadian short film *John Handy at the Blue Horn*. In the late 1960s he was a member of the jazz-rock group Fourth Way. He recorded with Pharoah Sanders (1970–73), McCoy Tyner (1972), and Joe Henderson (1973). In 1971 White began leading his own groups, with which he has played principally his own compositions: among these are *The Sun and the Moon Have Come Together*; *Father Music, Mother Dance*; and the extended suite *The Land of Spirit and Light*. In the early 1980s he was a member of the stylistically wide-ranging trio Space Shuttle Omnibus, consisting of the reed player Russell Baba and Eddie Moore. In 1994, while living in Seattle, White returned to the San Francisco Bay area to participate in a brief reunion with Handy.

White possesses a formidable technique and performs with considerable emotional intensity. His style has been influenced more by such musicians as John Coltrane and Eric Dolphy than by earlier violinists: for example, he makes liberal use of multiple stopping, and his rocking of the bow between two notes produces an effect comparable with that of a wide-interval tremolo played by Coltrane or Dolphy.

SELECTED RECORDINGS

As leader: *The Land of Spirit and Light* (1973, Imp. 9241); *Father Music, Mother Dance* (1974, Imp. 9268); *X Factor* (1978, Elek. 138)

As sideman: J. Handy: *Live at the Monterey Jazz Festival* (1965, Col. CS9262); Fourth Way: *The Sun and Moon Have Come Together* (1969, Harvest 423); P. Sanders: *Thembi* (1970, Imp. 9206); M. Tyner: on *Song for my Lady* (1972, Mlst. 9044), Native Song; J. Handy: *Live at Yoshi's Nightspot* (1994, Boulevard 531)

BIBLIOGRAPHY

Feather '60s; *Feather–Gitler '70s*

R. Rouda: "The Fourth Way: Mike White," *Coda*, ix/12 (1971), 32

L. Feather: "Michael White: Blindfold Test," *DB*, xli/15 (1974), 31

DAVID FLANAGAN

White, Michael (G.) (ii) (*b* New Orleans, 29 Nov 1954). Clarinetist. He was an undergraduate at Xavier University, pursued graduate studies in Spanish at Tulane University (MA 1979, PhD 1984), and then joined the faculty at Xavier, where he was a professor of Spanish and also taught African-American music. He first played jazz with Doc Paulin's brass band in 1975, and was deeply inspired when in 1978 he first heard George Lewis (i) on record. He then joined the Young Tuxedo Brass Band (1979). In 1980 he performed with the show *One Mo' Time*, and the following year he played at Preservation Hall with Kid Sheik Cola and formed his own trio and band. From around 1984 he led the Original Liberty Jazz Band, whose members initially included the veterans Chester Zardis, Louis Nelson, Emanuel Sayles or Danny Barker, and Sadie Goodson (on piano), and two younger players, Gregg Stafford and the drummer Stanley Stephens. In 1985 he became a regular member of Kid Thomas Valentine's Preservation Hall Band, which has continued under the direction of Wendell Brunious. He recorded with Wynton Marsalis and in 1989 arranged the music for and performed in "A Tribute to Jelly Roll Morton" at Lincoln Center, New York. In 1990 White returned to Lincoln Center for another concert, performed at the Newport Jazz Festival, and appeared in the American Folk Masters series at Carnegie Hall. His Original Liberty Jazz Band changed significantly with the death of its veteran players and that of Stephens (in 1992); among the members in the early 1990s were Stafford or Brunious, and Freddie Lonzo. In the 1990s he worked in Stafford's quartet, performed at Preservation Hall, made two recordings with the Preservation Hall Jazz Band, organized and performed in further concerts at Lincoln Center, and toured Europe and Japan. White's full-bodied tone and imaginative improvisations reminiscent of Johnny Dodds established his reputation as one of the most exciting young African-American musicians in New Orleans in the late 1980s; he has since gone on to become one of the chief spokesmen for New Orleans jazz. He figures prominently in a Canadian film documentary on New Orleans jazz, *Liberty Street Blues* (1988).

SELECTED RECORDINGS

As leader: *Shake it & break it* (1981, Nola 22); *Crescent City Serenade* (1990, Ant. 422-848545-2); *New Year's at the Village Vanguard* (1991, Ant. 314-512168-2)

As sideman with W. Marsalis: *The Majesty of the Blues* (1988, Col. OC45091)

BIBLIOGRAPHY

M. Joly: "The Young Generation: Michael White," *SL*, xxxvii/4 (1985), 19

R. Spedale: "Keep Doin' What You're Doin'," *JF* [intl edn], no.107 (1987), 28

W. Carter: *Preservation Hall: Music from the Heart* (Wheatley, Oxford, England, and New York, 1991), 269

G. Wyckoff: "Michael White: Trad is Today," *JT*, xxi/4 (1991), 22

E. Mullener: "Journey into the Heart of Jazz," *New Orleans Times-Picayune* (2 May 1992)

C. Deffaa: "New Orleans Preservationist," *MR*, xx/10 (1993), 22

M. Laplace: "Dr. Michael White," *Jh*, no.505 (1993), 40

R. Reynard: "In the Tradition," *Jh Special 1996* (1996), 20

MARCEL JOLY/BK

White, Morris (Ellis) [Fruit] (*b* Nashville, 17 Jan 1908 or 1911; *d* Nov 1986). Guitarist and banjoist. His place of birth has been published as St. Louis, but in his application for social security he gave Nashville (and his full name and a birthday, but no year); the social security death index gives 1908, rather than 1911, the year found in the jazz literature. He grew up in Peoria, Illinois, and learned banjo as a child; by the 1920s he was doubling on guitar. After moving to St. Louis he performed with Charlie Creath on the Mississippi riverboat *St. Paul* (1926), with Dewey Jackson at the Chauffeur's Club (1927), and in a touring show with Ethel Waters. In 1928, on the death of his predecessor Charley Stamps, he joined the Missourians (with which he recorded in 1929–30), and he remained with the band when Cab Calloway assumed its leadership in 1930. White's banjo playing contributed a strong rhythmic drive to the orchestra's performances, and he occasionally contributed solos; he may be seen in Calloway's films from this period. After leaving Calloway in 1938 he worked briefly with Lionel Hampton (*c*1941) and then ceased full-time performing. The aforementioned index gives his last known residence as St. Louis. His brother, Baxter White, who played guitar and ukulele, had a musical act called the Pebbles, whose recordings of 1926–7 included the pairing *Hot Pebble Blues/Deep Henderson* (1927, Vic. 20774).

SELECTED RECORDINGS

As sideman: Missourians: Vine Street Drag (1929, Vic. 38103); Scotty Blues (1930, Vic. 38084); Two Hundred Squabble (1930, Vic. 38145); C. Calloway: Dixie Vagabond (1931, Ban. 32116); Mood Indigo (1931, Ban. 32152)

BIBLIOGRAPHY

ChiltonW; *McCarthyB*

HOWARD RYE

White, Rocky [Quentin] (*b* San Mares, TX, 3 Nov 1952). Drummer. He studied music at Texas Southern University from 1971 to 1973, and then joined Duke Ellington's orchestra, remaining until the leader's death in April 1974. Among the recordings he made during this period was the album *Duke Ellington's Third Sacred Concert* (1973, RCA APL1-0785). He continued to play intermittently with the band under the direction of Mercer Ellington. (B. Korall: "A Blast from the Past: the Great Drummers of Duke Ellington," *MD*, xxi/12 (1997), 82)

EDDIE LAMBERT

White, Sonny [Ellerton Oswald] (*b* Panama, 11 Nov 1917; *d* New York, 28 April 1971). Pianist. From the mid-1930s he worked with Jesse Stone (1936–7), Willie Bryant (1937–8), and Teddy Hill (1938), with Frankie Newton at Café Society, New York (1939), and with Billie Holiday (1939–40; for illustration *see* HOLIDAY, BILLIE). He was also a member of Sidney Bechet's band at the Long Cabin in Fonda, New York (*c* December 1939 – January 1940), and recorded with Bechet (February 1940). Except for a brief period with Artie Shaw (early 1941) he was a sideman in Benny Carter's orchestra (1940–41), and following his military service he rejoined Carter (1946) and worked with Hot Lips Page (1947). White then became a member of a band led by the trumpeter Harvey Davis, which was resident at the Cinderella Club, New York (1947–54), and at Jimmy Ryan's (1954). He performed and recorded with Wilbur De Paris (until the early 1960s), Louis Metcalf (1963–7), and Eddie Barefield's trio (1968). In 1969 he began playing with Jonah Jones, with whom he remained until his death. White recorded four tracks as an unaccompanied soloist (his sole recordings under his own name, 1969) and appeared in the film *L'aventure du jazz* (1970).

SELECTED RECORDINGS

As unaccompanied soloist: on [no leader]: *Master Jazz Piano*, iv (1969–72, MJR 8129), Blues for Betty C., I want a little girl, I got rhythm, Memories of You (1969)

As sideman: M. Mezzrow: That's How I Feel Today (1937, Vic. 25636); Hot Club Stomp (1937, Vic. 25612); B. Holiday: Strange Fruit/Fine and Mellow (1939, Com. 526); S. Bechet: Indian Summer/Preachin' Blues (1939, Bb 10623); One o'Clock Jump (1939, Vic. 27204); Sidney's Blues (1939, Bb 8509); B. Carter: Cocktails for Two/Takin' my Time (1940, Bb 10998)

BIBLIOGRAPHY

ChiltonW

J. Simmen: "Sonny White, 1917–1971," *BHcF*, no.212 (1971), 7

J. Chilton: *Billie's Blues: a Survey of Billie Holiday's Career, 1933–1959* (London, 1975)

——: *Sidney Bechet: the Wizard of Jazz* (London and New York, 1987/*R*1996)

N. Pierce: Liner notes, *The Complete Master Jazz Piano Series* (Mosaic 140, 1992)

D. Clarke: *Wishing on the Moon: the Life and Times of Billie Holiday* (London and New York, 1994)

JAMES M. DORAN/BK

Whitecage, Mark (*b* Litchfield, CT, 4 June 1937). Alto saxophonist. He took up soprano saxophone at the age of six and played the curved instrument in a family polka and wedding band with his father (a pianist), his elder brother (a trumpeter), and his sister (a singer); about two years later he changed to alto saxophone. When he was 12 he began learning classical clarinet, playing tenor saxophone in a local big band, and working professionally. Late in 1955 he joined the army, and while stationed in El Paso, Texas, he played bop in a local quintet (1959) and met Eric Dolphy, whose influence changed his approach to playing. In 1960 he moved to Boston to join Claude Thornhill's orchestra, but upon hearing Sam Rivers perform solos with the group he returned to Litchfield. From 1963 he lived in Waterbury, Connecticut, where he set up a piano-tuning business and began rehearsing with Mario Pavone, through whom he later worked with Bobby Naughton.

From the mid-1960s Whitecage lived and worked in New York, and around the years 1968–73 he led a trio with Pavone and the drummer Lawrence Cook – though it was sometimes augmented by the baritone saxophonist Trevor Koehler and Perry Robinson. During the same period he recorded with Naughton (1969–71), and from the early 1970s he worked regularly in Europe with Gunter Hampel's Galaxy Dream Band (recording from 1972), playing alto saxophone, alto flute, alto clarinet, and flute; in 1972 he began using clarinet in jazz contexts. In addition he collaborated with Jeanne Lee (recording in 1974 and *c*1992), John Fischer's Interface (mid-1970s), David Eyges (*c*1977), Saheb Sarbib's small and large ensembles (*c*1979 – early 1980s), and Robinson's Licorice Factory (early 1980s), and he recorded with Pavone (1979, 1985). Around 1980, after meeting François and Bernard Baschet in Paris, he began experimenting with sound sculptures and formed the Glass House Ensemble to perform works with them; unlike the Baschets, who used primarily steel, Whitecage employed copper and aluminum, among other metals, as well as non-metallic objects such as glass rods. He spent most of the remainder of the decade bringing up his children, although he performed in Europe as an unaccompanied soloist in 1986.

In the 1990s Whitecage formed duos with the pianist Michael Jefry Stevens (1993) and the double bass player Dominic Duval (1996), a trio, Double Duo, with Stevens and Herb Robertson (1994), and another trio, with Duval and the drummer Jay Rosen (1995); this last group appeared as a quartet with the cellist Tomas Ulrich, and as a quintet with Ulrich and the pianist Joseph Scianni. He also played in a dixieland band, the 9th Street Stompers, and from 1993 to 1995 he performed and recorded in the group Bottom's Out, which was co-led by the double bass player Joe Fonda and the composer Scott Miller. In 1995 he played with Hampel in a small group alongside Lee, Thurman Barker, and Ed Schuller, and became the alto saxophonist in a quartet led by Anthony Braxton (on piano) which performed standards; in 1996 he was a featured soloist in Braxton's opera *Trillium R.* From the following year he toured Europe and recorded in the group led by Fonda and Stevens, and performed and recorded with Duval's String Ensemble; in addition he recorded with Steve Swell and was a member of the Improviser's Collective, run by William Parker and his wife Patricia Nicholson-Parker (both 1997). Whitecage was the leader of the ensemble Liquid Time, with Dave Douglas, Stevens, and Fonda among his sidemen, and of the Other Quartet and the Other Other Quartet, both of which included the reed player Sabir Mateen. In the late 1990s he recorded as the co-leader of a small group with Marshall Allen.

SELECTED RECORDINGS

Duos with M. J. Stevens: *Short Stories* (1993, Red Toucan 9312)

As leader: *Mark Whitecage & Liquid Time* (1990, Acoustics 406); *Free for Once* (1996, CIMP 106); *Caged No More* (1996, CIMP 119); of Other Quartet: *Consensual Tension* (1997, CIMP 157); *Split Personality* (1998, GM 3038)

As sideman: S. Sarbib: *UFO* (1979, Cadence Jazz 1008); *Seasons* (1981, SN 1048); D. Duval and M. J. Stevens: *Elements* (1994, Leo 241); J. Fonda and M. J. Stevens: *Live from Brugge* (1997, DeWerf 10); S. Swell: *Moons of Jupiter* (1997, CIMP 149)

BIBLIOGRAPHY

B. Besecker: "The Mark Whitecage Interview," *Coda*, no.217 (1987–8), 8
B. Rusch: "Mark Whitecage: Interview," *Cadence*, xxiii/10 (1997), 5
<http://www.ejn.it/mus/whitebio.htm> (1999) [incl. discography]

GK

Whitehead, Annie [Lena Anne] (*b* Oldham, England, 16 July 1955). English trombonist and composer. After first performing in brass bands she joined Ivy Benson's band at the age of 16, then began playing Jamaican music. This early apprenticeship produced a raw style rooted in the more open characteristics of the instrument and a resourcefulness that she utilized for reggae sessions as well as for studio and touring work with such major popular artists as Joan Armatrading, Elvis Costello, Smiley Culture, and Dr. John. Whitehead also worked with John Stevens (first recording with his group Folkus in 1984), the Guest Stars, Toot Sweet, Working Week, the Lydia D'Ustebyn Swing Orchestra, the drummer Charlie Watts, Maggie Nicols, the singer Jan Ponsford, Carol Grimes, and the singer and keyboard player Robert Wyatt. In 1984 she began leading and writing material for her own groups, notably the Annie Whitehead Experience. In 1987 she toured Mozambique with Chris McGregor's Brotherhood of Breath. She then worked with Louis Moholo, Dudu Pukwana, Harry Beckett, James "Blood" Ulmer, Abdullah Ibrahim, Carla Bley, Jasper van 't Hof, Michal Urbaniak, Urszula Dudziak, and Ray Anderson's World Trombone Quartet. In the 1990s she composed extended works, played with the Penguin Café Orchestra and Gail Thompson's Jazz Afrika, and joined Roswell Rudd and Paul Rutherford in Elton Dean's group Newsense. Her directness and originality are as influenced by the timing of the Skatalites' trombonist Don Drummond as by the fluid style of J. J. Johnson. Whitehead sometimes plays trombone through a harmonizer (a type of synthesizer); *Platform One*, from her album *Naked* (1996), demonstrates her preferred use of this device, whereby her melody line is doubled in parallel motion at the interval of a whole tone below the pitch sounded, and, simultaneously, at a minor third above.

Oral history material in *GBLnsa*.

SELECTED RECORDINGS

As leader: *Mix up* (1985, Paladin 6); of Rude (with Ian Maidman): *This is Rude* (1996, Resurgence 115); *Naked* (1996, EFZ 1019), incl. Platform One; *Home* (1998, EFZ 1024)

As sideman: J. Stevens: *The Life of Riley* (1984, Affinity 130); Working Week: *Working Nights* (1985, Virgin 2345); R. Wyatt and Swapo Singers: *The Wind of Change* (1985, Rough Trade/Swapo 168); C. Watts: *Live at Fulham Town Hall* (1986, Col. FC40570); J. Stevens: *Free Bop: Live Tracks* (1986, Impetus 18610); C. McGregor: *Country Cooking* (1988, Virgin 17), incl. Country Cooking; Brotherhood of Breath: *The Memorial Concert* (1994, ITM Pacific 970086); R. Wyatt: *Schleep* (1997, Hannibal 1418); D. Cartwright: *Play* (1997, Blow the Fuse 9703); E. Dean: *Elton Dean's Newsense* (1998, Slam 229)

BIBLIOGRAPHY

CarrJ; *ChiltonB*
S. Britt, B. Case, and C. Murray: *The Illustrated Encyclopedia of Jazz* (London, 1978; rev. 2/1986), 189
V. Wilmer: "Woman on a Trombone," *City Limits* (6–12 Aug 1982), 40
G. Lock: "Bone Idol," *The Wire*, no.14 (1985), 18
I. Pye: "Style Warfare," *MM* (13 April 1985), 12
J. Fordham: "Women on the Jazz Beat," *The Guardian* (14 April 1989), 33
S. Marriott: "The Annie Whitehead Experience," *Jazz on CD*, i/1 (1993), 58
M. McGregor: *Chris McGregor and the Brotherhood of Breath: my Life with a South African Jazz Pioneer* (Flint, MI, 1995)
M. Zwerin: "'Cheerful Char' Finds Work with the Band," *International Herald Tribune* (7 Jan 1998)

VAL WILMER

Whitehead, Kevin (Francis) (*b* New York, 27 April 1952). Writer. He began listening to jazz while working towards a masters degree in American literature and culture at Syracuse University (MA 1978). Later he contributed to *Cadence* (1979–93), *Coda* (1980–95), *Musician* (1982–5, 1990–91), *Jazz Times* (1983–6), *Down Beat* (1985–95), *Ear* (late 1980s), *Pulse* (1989–95), the *Village Voice* (1991–5), and *CD Review* (1993–4), and also maintained an association with Baltimore's weekly *City Paper* (1981–92); in 1987 he became jazz critic for the NPR program "Fresh Air." In the early 1990s he compiled an American discography for Joachim-Ernst Berendt's *Das Jazzbuch: Entwicklung und Bedeutung der Jazzmusik* (Brooklyn, NY, rev. 6/1992; Eng. trans., by J. Berendt and G. Huesman, New York, 1992, as *The Jazz Book*), and for the *Village Voice* he wrote a notable essay in which he endeavored to provide a new descriptive framework for the various styles of jazz which have been lumped together under the rubric "avant garde." From 1995 to 1999 he divided his time between the Netherlands and the USA, and from 1996 he has been a regular contributor to the Dutch national daily *De Volkskrant*. He published a detailed look at the new music and improvisation milieu in Amsterdam (1998) and an edited collection of stories from the Dutch Bimhuis (1999). Whitehead settled in Chicago in June 2000 and began to write for *Schwann Inside* and the *Chicago Sun-Times*. In the course of his career he has also contributed essays to jazz collections and written liner notes to, and reviews of, numerous recordings.

Whitehead has a broad-minded perspective on the inherent qualities of jazz, and his profiles and reviews show a deep understanding of the music and its history. He is concerned with its social and cultural influences, and when writing about a recording or an artist's musical tendencies draws a highly focused picture.

WRITINGS

(selective list)

"It's Jazz, Stupid," *VV* (23 Nov 1993), jazz suppl., p.11
"Death to 'the Avant-garde'," *VV* (21 March 1995), 63
[untitled article], *Mixtery: a Festschrift for Anthony Braxton*, ed. G. Lock (Exeter, England, 1995), 155
New Dutch Swing (New York, 1998)
ed.: *Bimhuis 25: Stories of Twenty-five Years at the Bimhuis* (Amsterdam, 1999)
"Jazz Worldwide," *Jazz: the First Century*, ed. J. E. Hasse (New York, 2000), 168

GK

Whiteman, Paul (*b* Denver, 28 March 1890; *d* Doylestown, PA, 29 Dec 1967). Bandleader. He played viola in the Denver Symphony Orchestra from 1907 and in the San Francisco Symphony Orchestra from 1914. During World War I he led a 40-piece navy band, playing march tunes by day and show music by night. Sensing new dimensions for popular music in the transition from ragtime to jazz, he organized a dance band in San Francisco in 1918; he held an engagement there in 1919 and later moved to Los Angeles and Atlantic City, New Jersey, before settling in New York in 1920. There he soon became the best-known American bandleader, particularly with his recording of *Whispering* and *Japanese Sandman* (1920), which sold more than a million copies. By the early 1920s his lush orchestral style was widely copied on countless bandstands at home and abroad. He toured the British Isles in 1923 and Europe in 1926.

For his first extended concert tour of the USA Whiteman commissioned George Gershwin to write *Rhapsody in Blue*,

Paul Whiteman conducting his orchestra, 1938

which, as part of Whiteman's concert called "An Experiment in Modern Music," was performed with the composer as soloist in Aeolian Hall, New York, in 1924. Favorable publicity prompted Whiteman to stage seven performances of this kind between 1925 and 1938, thereby obtaining wide exposure for such American composers as Victor Herbert, William Grant Still, and Duke Ellington (*see* SYMPHONIC JAZZ). Between 1928 and 1952 Whiteman's orchestras were featured on many network radio shows and took part in several films, beginning with *King of Jazz* (1930) (*see* FILMS, §I, 2). He provided music for six Broadway shows and produced more than 600 phonograph recordings. Later he served as music director for ABC.

Whiteman was a key figure in American popular music. While jazz purists accused him of diluting the character of early jazz for commercial purposes, less biased observers applauded the high polish and versatility of his orchestras, which had to be as comfortable in the concert hall as at a college dance. He employed a number of talented musicians: in the original arrangement of *Rhapsody in Blue* three of his reed players were required to play a total of 17 instruments. Although his dance music tended to be sedate, there were occasional jazz solos from musicians such as Bix Beiderbecke, Frankie Trumbauer, Eddie Lang, Joe Venuti, Bunny Berigan, and Jack Teagarden, and the bass playing of Steve Brown added a jazzy punch to the orchestra's genteel rhythm section.

Whiteman's musical memorabilia, including his large library of more than 3000 arrangements, were bequeathed to Williams College in Williamstown, Massachusetts, where they now form the Whiteman Collection; *see* LIBRARIES AND ARCHIVES, §2.

See also JAZZ (i), §III, 4.

SELECTED RECORDINGS

Whispering/Japanese Sandman (1920, Vic. 18690); Whiteman Stomp (1927, Vic. 21119); Changes/Mary (1927, Vic. 21103); Concerto in F (Gershwin) (1928, Col. 50140D); Nobody's Sweetheart/After you've gone (1929, Col. 2098D); I'm coming Virginia/Aunt Hagar's Blues (1938, Decca 2145)

BIBLIOGRAPHY

P. Whiteman and M. M. McBride: *Jazz* (New York, 1926)
B. Rust: "Paul Whiteman: a Discography," *Recorded Sound*, no.27 (1967), 219; no.28 (1967), 255
M. Harrison: "Around Paul Whiteman," *JM*, no.185 (1970), 7
——: *A Jazz Retrospect* (Newton Abbot, England, 1976, rev. 2/1977/*R*1991), 184
C. Johnson: *Paul Whiteman: a Chronology* (Williamstown, MA, 1977, rev. 2/1979)
T. DeLong: *Pops: Paul Whiteman, King of Jazz* (Piscataway, nr New Brunswick, NJ, 1983)
B. Crowther: "Jean Goldkette & Paul Whiteman: Jazz Age Juggernauts," *JJI*, xliii/5 (1990), 14

CARL JOHNSON

Whitfield, Mark (Adrian) (*b* Syosset, NY, 6 Oct 1966). Electric guitarist. He grew up in Lindenhurst, New York, and played alto saxophone, double bass, and guitar as a child; he decided to concentrate on guitar after seeing George Benson on television. Whitfield rejected a full scholarship to begin studying medicine at Georgetown University in favor of attending the Berklee College of Music. After graduating in 1987 he moved to New York, where he worked on Wall Street by day and in the house band at the Blue Note at night. Recommendations from Benson brought jobs with Brother Jack McDuff and a recording contract, as well as work with, among others, Art Blakey, Roy Haynes, Carmen McRae, and Betty Carter. From August 1990 Whitfield lived in Baton Rouge, Louisiana, and began playing in New Orleans with Delfeayo Marsalis. In addition he recorded with Donald Harrison (1990), Cleo Laine (1992), Carl Allen and Nicholas Payton (both 1994), Teodross Avery, Courtney Pine, and Jimmy Smith (all 1995), Ernie Watts (1996), and McDuff (1998). He appeared in the jazz-based film *Kansas City* (1996) and performed on its soundtrack and on an associated album by the Kansas City Band (1995); he may also be seen in his *Instructional Video for Guitar* (1998).

SELECTED RECORDINGS

As leader: *Patrice* (1991, WB 26659-2); *True Blue* (1994, Verve 314-523591-2); *7th Avenue Stroll* (1995, Verve 314-529223-2); with C. McBride and N.

Payton: *Fingerpainting: the Music of Herbie Hancock* (1997, Verve314-537856-2)

As sideman: D. Harrison: *Full Circle* (1990, Sweet Basil 660.55.003); J. Smith: *Damn!* (1995, Verve 314-527631-2)

BIBLIOGRAPHY

P. Carles, A. Clergeat, and J.-L. Comolli: *Dictionnaire du jazz* (Paris, 1988, rev. and enlarged 2/1994)

L. Feather: "'Marksman' Mark Whitfield Keeps his Eye on the Target," *Los Angeles Times* (19 Dec 1990)

J. Nash: "Mark Whitfield: a Musical 'Marksman'," *JT*, xx/12 (1990), 51

L. Feather: "Mark Whitfield: Not Nostalgic – Natural," *DB*, lviii/5 (1991), 26

J. Ferguson: "Mark Whitfield: the New Wave of Old Jazz," *GP*, xxv/4 (1991), 51

G. Wyckoff: "Mark Whitfield: Developing his own Voice," *JT*, xxi/9 (1991), 50

T. Carman: "Guitarist Pays Blues their Due," *Houston Post* (22 Feb 1992)

S. Nicholson: "Mark Whitfield," *Jazz: the Magazine*, no.15 (1992), 14

S. Aiges: "Mark Whitfield: Hot Guitar and All that Jazz," *New Orleans Times-Picayune* (11 June 1993)

B. Milkowski: "Hearsay: Mark Whitfield," *JT*, xxiv/10 (1994), 11

S. Aiges: "Mark Whitfield: Uncuffed," *DB*, lxii/12 (1995), 46

R. Grosman: "Mark Whitfield: musicien de jazz," *Jh*, no.530 (1996), 32

——: "Mark Whitfield," *Jm*, no.469 (1997), 6

M. J. Summerfield: *The Jazz Guitar: its Evolution, Players and Personalities since 1900* (Blaydon on Tyne, England, 4/1998)

MARK GILBERT

Whitlock, Bob [Von Varlynn] (*b* Roosevelt, UT, 21 Jan 1931). Double bass player. He took up double bass at high school. During the 1950s he worked in Los Angeles, performing and recording with Gerry Mulligan (1952), Art Pepper and Chet Baker (both 1953), and Stan Getz (1954); he may be heard to advantage with Mulligan on *Walkin' Shoes/Soft Shoe* (1952, PJ 606). In addition he performed with Buddy DeFranco and recorded with Jack Sheldon (1956) and Joe Albany (1957), and towards the end of the decade he led his own quartet and undertook graduate study at the University of California. In the early 1960s he performed and recorded with Zoot Sims at the Blue Note in Paris (1961), recorded with Vi Redd and Curtis Amy (both 1962) and Victor Feldman (1962–3), and worked as a freelance; he appears with Sims in the French short film *Flash* (1962). Later he was associated with George Shearing, in whose group he toured (1965–8) and recorded (1968), and was a member of a trio led by Albany (1972).

BIBLIOGRAPHY

FeatherE; *Feather '60s*

R. Gordon: *Jazz West Coast: the Los Angeles Jazz Scene of the 1950s* (London and New York, 1986)

Whittaker, Sebastian (Charles) [Bash] (*b* Houston, 12 Sept 1966). Drummer. His full name is taken from the Texas birth summary index. He was left blind after suffering from retinal cancer when he was a year old and began playing drums at the age of three. Later he attended the High School for the Performing and Visual Arts in Houston and the University of Texas in Austin; while studying at William Patterson College in Wayne, New Jersey (1986–7), he worked briefly with Freddie Hubbard. Having returned to Houston in 1987, he formed his own group, the Creators, with which he recorded four albums and toured in the USA and Europe throughout the 1990s. In addition he recorded with the blues singer Kellye Gray (1990, 1997), the Creators' pianist Stefan Karlsson and Herb Ellis (both 1991), and the saxophonist Shelley Carrol (1996). In summer 1994 he toured Europe with Jesse Davis, and in the course of the next two years he performed on occasion with Ellis; in the same way he worked intermittently with Frank Lacy after recording with him in 1996. Whitaker's aggressive hard-bop style is strongly influenced by that of Art Blakey, and his band resembles Blakey's Jazz Messengers. His compositions may be heard on his albums *The Valley of the Kings* (1990) and *One for Bu!!* (1992).

SELECTED RECORDINGS

As leader: *First Outing* (1989, Justice 0201); *The Valley of the Kings* (1990, Justice 204); *Searchin' for the Truth* (1991, Justice 0202); *One for Bu!!* (1992, Justice 0203)

As sideman: S. Karlsson: *Room 292* (1991, Justice 0701); H. Ellis: *Down Home* (1991, Justice 1003); S. Carrol: *With Members of the Ellington Orchestra* (1996, Leaning House 003); K. Gray: *Tomato Kiss* (1997, Proteus 9701)

BIBLIOGRAPHY

T. Carman: "Whittaker Digs Deep into the Past for his Musical Inspiration," *Houston Post* (12 July 1990)

D. Kasrel: "Sebastian Whittaker: Lone Star Talent," *JT*, xxi/8 (1991), 8

T. Saccone: "Update: Sebastian Whittaker," *MD*, xvi/5 (1992), 8

T. Carman: "Jazz Musician Bashes Musical Message Home," *Houston Post* (21 May 1993)

R. Mitchell: "Three Generations of Jazz: Drummers Keep the Beat in Houston," *Houston Chronicle* (12 Sept 1993)

RICK MATTINGLY

Whittle, Tommy [Thomas] (*b* Grangemouth, Scotland, 13 Oct 1926). Scottish tenor saxophonist. He played with the trumpeter Johnny Claes, the bandleader Lew Stone (from August 1944), and Carl Barriteau (from June 1945), and performed and recorded with Harry Hayes (1946), Ted Heath (March 1947 – April 1952), and Tony Kinsey (1953–4). He appeared in the film *Dance Hall* (1950), and worked in London with the BBC Show Band (October 1952–1955), as the leader of his own quartet, which included Dill Jones (at the Flamingo club, 1954), and as leader of a quintet, with Jones and Harry Klein (at Studio 51, 1955). He then led a touring octet with Kenny Wheeler, Keith Christie, and Joe Temperley (1955–6), undertook solo engagements, and performed in France and the USA with his sextet, and again in the USA with his quartet. In 1956 he was a guest soloist with Stan Kenton in Britain. Whittle worked as a freelance musician from the late 1950s; he also led a quartet, as well as his own orchestra at the Dorchester Hotel, London (August 1958 – February 1961), and worked with the ATV orchestra under Jack Parnell (1960s – early 1970s). Later he ran a jazz club in Wembley, and recorded extensively as a freelance while appearing in the memorial Ted Heath orchestra under Don Lusher (1980s–1990s), the Jazz Journal All Stars at the Grande Parade du Jazz, Nice (1984), Bob Wilber's big band and octet (recording with the latter in 1994), and the Pizza Express All Stars, in which he took Danny Moss's place from February 1989, when Moss moved to Australia. Whittle performed in Australia in 1993 and formed a quintet with Colin Smith in 1996. He is married to the singer Barbara Jay (*b* Cardiff, Wales, 1937), with whom he recorded in 1982 and whom he later accompanied with his own quartet in the shows "Ella Fitzgerald Songbook" and "Ladies of Jazz."

SELECTED RECORDINGS

As leader: *Jigsaw* (1977, Alamo 4501); with A. Barnes: *Straight Eight* (1985, Miles Music 001); *Warm Glow* (1992, Tee Jay 193)

As sideman with B. Jay: *The Nearness of You* (1982, Tee Jay 101)

BIBLIOGRAPHY

CarrJ; *ChiltonB*; *Feather '60s*

R. Cotterrell, ed.: *Jazz Now: the Jazz Centre Society Guide* (London, 1976)

P. Vacher: "Best of British, No.5: Tommy Whittle, Jazz Refugee from the Mickey Mouse Bands," *JJI*, xxxi/7 (1978), 11

G. Copley: "Tommy Whittle," *JJI*, xxxviii/6 (1985), 16

DIGBY FAIRWEATHER

Whyte, Zack [Zach] (*b* Richmond, KY, 1898; *d* Kentucky, 10 March 1967). Bandleader and banjoist. He studied at Wilberforce College, Ohio, where he joined Horace Henderson's student band as an arranger and banjoist. He formed his own group around 1923, and in the late 1920s he began to lead the Chocolate Beau Brummels. Although the band was very successful it made only a small number of recordings, among them *Mandy* (1929, Gen. 6781; for illustration *see* Gennett) and *It's tight like that* (1929, Gen. 6798). Whyte's sidemen at various times included Eddie Barefield, Herman "Ivory" Chittison, Vic Dickenson, Roy Eldridge, Quentin Jackson, Sy Oliver, and Al Sears. He continued working as a leader into the 1930s.

BIBLIOGRAPHY

ChiltonB; *McCarthyB*
B. Demeusy and O. Flückiger: "The (Incomplete) Band Story of Zack Whyte," *Jazz-Statistics*, no.29 (1963), JS-6
T. Zwicky: "Zack is the Name, Whyte that is!," *Sv*, no.24 (1969), 214

Wick, Joe [Josef] (*b* Siegburg, Germany, 19 March 1916). German bandleader. He studied violin, drums, and piano at the conservatory in Bonn. At the age of 22 he played drums in the dance orchestras of Will Glahé and Bernard Etté, and in 1942 he was appointed director of the Universum Film Aktiengesellschaft dance orchestra. He entertained German and British troops during and after the war and also broadcast on the BBC. From 1948 he made a large number of recordings (including *Blue Skies*, 1948, Bruns. 82341, and *Torpedo Junction*, 1949, Bruns. 82380) and appeared in three films. When he retired from music in 1964, most of his sidemen joined Kurt Edelhagen's big band. ("Auf den Spuren vertrauter Töne," *Magazin der Bundeshauptstadt Bonn*, iii/1 (1981), 42)

RAINER E. LOTZ

Wickman, Putte [Hans-Olof] (*b* Borlänge, Sweden, 10 Sept 1924). Swedish clarinetist and bandleader. He became a professional musician in 1944, when he joined the violinist Hasse Kahn for a summer tour; he then worked in Stockholm in the quintet led by the double bass player Arthur Österwall at Nalen (1944–5) and in the band led by Miff Görling and Gösta Törner at La Visite (1945–6). After playing very briefly with Simon Brehm he rejoined Kahn's band in 1947, while it was at Nalen. In autumn 1948 Kahn was obliged to leave for military service, and Wickman took over the leadership of what was then a sextet; Kahn's long-standing sideman Reinhold Svensson remained in the group, serving as pianist and arranger for Wickman through its years at Nalen (to 1960).

Wickman was in the Swedish all-star band that appeared at the Paris Jazz Fair in 1949. He toured Europe with his band, appeared as a soloist in Germany and elsewhere, and in 1959 visited the USA, performing as a guest with several bands in New York, including an all-star group in concert in Carnegie Hall. From 1960 to 1961 he led another sextet (but without piano) in Sweden and then into the mid-1960s led a big band which played popular music (not jazz). Wickman also ran his own dance hall in Stockholm, Putte's, for a couple of years. He later performed with Svend Asmussen, the pianist Leif Asp, and others, though from the mid-1970s he has been active mainly as a freelance soloist, often with the pianist Claes Crona. In 1999 he toured and recorded in Sweden with his long-time friend and early source of inspiration, Buddy DeFranco. Wickman's playing has always been of the highest order and has grown more personal and intense over the years. In addition to his activities in jazz and popular music, he has performed Mozart's clarinet concerto and other classical pieces with symphony orchestras and chamber ensembles.

SELECTED RECORDINGS

Duos with Red Mitchell: *The Very Thought of You* (1987–8, Dra. 161)
As leader: *Happy New Year!* (1973, Odeon E06234822); *Putte Wickman Quartet Live in Stockholm* (1977, Out 7710); *Mr. Clarinet* (1985, Four Leaf Clover 5083)

BIBLIOGRAPHY

FeatherE
"Svenskt stjärnalbum" [Swedish star album], *Orkester journalen*, xiii/12 (1945), 5
"På omslaget" [On the cover], *Orkester journalen*, xxi/1 (1953), 6
A. von Konow: "Det måste finnas en grund att stå på" [There must be ground to stand on], *Orkester journalen*, xxxvii/3 (1969), 10
L. Collin: "60-årige Putte" [Putte at 60], *Orkester journalen*, lii/10 (1984), 13
J Bruér and L Westin: "Putte 75," [Putte at 75], *Orkester journalen*, lxvii/9 (1999), 2
<http://www.mic.stim.se/engelsk/11/facts/wickman.html> (2000)

ERIK KJELLBERG/LARS WESTIN

Widespread Depression Jazz Orchestra [Widespread Jazz Orchestra]. Nine-piece ensemble formed in 1972 at Marlboro College in southern Vermont. It was originally a 1950s-style rock-and-roll group with two guitars, piano, saxophone, electric bass guitar, drums, and singer, but later it evolved into a swing band that played dance music and jazz from the depression era – particularly the music associated with the big bands of Jimmie Lunceford, Count Basie, Duke Ellington, and Lionel Hampton (rather than that of the white swing bands). In 1978 the group moved to New York, and the following year it began recording; its members at that time were the trumpeter Jordan Sandke, the trombonist Tim Atherton, the saxophonists Michael Hashim (soprano and alto), Dean Nicyper (tenor), and David Lillie (baritone), the pianist Mike LeDonne, the double bass player James Wimpsheimer, the drummer John Ellis (who provided most of the group's arrangements), and the singer, leader, and vibraphonist Jon Holtzman. Around 1980 an offshoot of the band, which included Sandke, Hashim, and LeDonne, appeared as a bop quintet.

Holtzmann departed around 1982, after a number of creative differences had arisen within the group, and was replaced as the leader by Hashim; the ensemble was subsequently renamed the Widespread Jazz Orchestra, and its repertory was extended to incorporate elements of swing and bop. Among its later members were Dan Barrett, Tad Shull, and the singer Judy Niemack. In 1988 it performed regularly at Café Gianluca in New York.

SELECTED RECORDINGS

As Widespread Depression Jazz Orchestra: *Downtown Uproar* (1979, Stash 203); *Boogie in the Barnyard* (1980, Stash 206)
As Widespread Jazz Orchestra: *Swing is the Thing* (1982, Adelphi 5015); *Paris Blues* (1984, Col. FC40034)

BIBLIOGRAPHY

W. R. Stokes: "Uplifting Depression," *Washington Post* (19 April 1979)
——: "The Little Big Band," *Washington Post* (2 March 1980)
J. S. Wilson: "Jazz: Depression Quintet," *New York Times* (26 Dec 1980)
C. Cioe: "Backbeat: Widespread Jazz – No Longer Depressed!," *High Fidelity*, xxxiii/7 (1983), 84 [incl. discography]
J. S. Wilson: "A New Big Band Identity," *New York Times* (19 May 1988)
<http://www.retroactive.com/mar99/wdo.html> (1999)

GK

Widmann, Kutte [Kurt] (*b* Berlin, 2 March 1906; *d* Berlin, 27 Nov 1954). German bandleader. He began playing professionally with local bands in 1924. His own hot quintet was resident at the Imperator Diele in Berlin for ten years (1933–43), and he made his first recordings of dance music and jazz as the leader of a big band in 1938. Following military service (1943–4) he organized a new band, and he was the first German bandleader to resume recording commercially after the war (November 1946). On his numerous recordings (among them *St. Louis Blues*, 1939, Tempo 4284, and *Hey-ba-ba-re-bop*, 1947, Odeon 31761) he occasionally played drums, trombone, and accordion, and also sang. His life was the subject of a full-length film: *Die Kurt Widmann Story (Musik im Blut)* (1956).

RAINER E. LOTZ

Wierbos, Wolter (*b* Holten, Netherlands, 1 Sept 1957). Dutch trombonist. He played cornet and flugelhorn in a local brass band from the age of 11 and changed to trombone when he was 17. In 1979 he began playing with Ab Baars, the pianist Harry de Wit, and Larry Fishkind, among others, and the following year he joined Misha Mengelberg's ICP Orchestra and moved to Amsterdam. Soon he was working with such leaders as Harry Miller and Theo Loevendie, and he became a member of Maarten Altena's quartet (1981), octet (1982), and subsequent related groups. In the 1980s he played theater music written by the violist Maurice Horsthuis. Wierbos performed in Peter van Bergen's LOOS (1986–8), the Podium Trio (from 1986), Guus Janssen's octet (1987–91), and Sean Bergin's MOB (from 1987), and also as an unaccompanied soloist. He joined Gerry Hemingway's quintet in 1989 and the cooperative group Available Jelly in 1994. In the 1990s he worked with Michiel Braam's Bik Bent Braam, the group Sunchild, led by the guitarist Franky Douglas, and many other ensembles in and outside the Netherlands.

A prodigiously gifted trombonist, whose style shows the influence of Ray Anderson, George Lewis (ii), and Duke Ellington's trombonists of 1940 (Tricky Sam Nanton, Juan Tizol, and Lawrence Brown), Wierbos projects with an enormous open sound, usually delivered in terse bursts, but he is also capable of great subtlety and lyricism. Even when playing ensemble passages he has an uncanny ability to ignore the music in front of him and instead improvise a counterline that works even better than the written version. Early in his career he developed his own middle-of-the-lip pressure technique that allowed him to use varied embouchures with no physical damage.

SELECTED RECORDINGS

As unaccompanied soloist: *Wierbos* (1982, Data 824); *X Caliber* (1995, ICP 032)

As sideman: H. de Wit: *April '79* (1979, Bead 11); H. Miller: *"Down South"* (1983, Varajazz 4213); M. Mengelberg: *Bospaadje konijnehol*, i (1986, 1990, ICP 028); S. Bergin: *Kids Mysteries* (1987, Nimbus 502); C. Taylor: *Alms/Tiergarten (Spree)* (1988, FMP CD8–9); Podium Trio: *Take One* (1991, Disckus 04); G. Hemingway: *Down to the Wire* (1991, HA 6121); Available Jelly: *Happy Camp* (1996, Ramboy 10)

BIBLIOGRAPHY

K. Polling: "Misschien eindig ik nog wel eens als een nachtclubmuzikant" [Maybe someday I'll end up as a nightclub musician], *Jazzjaarboek*, ii (1983), 52

H. te Loo: "Wierbos/Van Kemenade/Kuiper: een democratisch trio," *Jazz nu*, no.148 (1991), 268

K. Whitehead, "The Edgar Winter of Wolter Wierbos," *Coda*, no.267 (1996), 22

——: *New Dutch Swing* (New York, 1998), 216

<http://netcetera.nl/jazzmarathon/95/jmwierbos.html> (1999)

KEVIN WHITEHEAD

Wieselman, Doug(las Joel) (*b* Los Angeles, 30 Nov 1954). Clarinetist, tenor saxophonist, and leader. He majored in music at the University of California, Santa Cruz (BA 1976). Having worked with Wayne Horvitz during his senior year (1975–6), he later joined other bands led by Horvitz (from 1982), including the jazz-rock band The President (1985–92). He worked briefly in the A.K.A. Orchestra led by the singer Robin Holcomb (1982), then later toured and recorded with her (1987–96). He recorded and performed with Bill Frisell (1987–8) and Guy Klucevsek (1988–90), and as a member of Anthony Coleman's bands By Night (1987–92) and Selfhaters (from 1993). In 1983 Wieselman formed a septet, the Kamikaze Ground Crew, which he co-leads with the saxophonist Gina Leishman. He was a founding member in 1986 of the New York Composer's Orchestra, with which he remained until 1996. He then joined John Lurie's Lounge Lizards, in which he doubles on electric guitar. He has been active in scoring original music for theatre and dance and in performances with the Flying Karamazov Brothers (from 1981) and various rock bands. He also plays baritone and soprano saxophone.

SELECTED RECORDINGS

Duos with B. Frisell: [no leader]: *Todos santos* (1988, Sound Aspects 019)

As leader with G. Leishman (of Kamikaze Ground Crew): *Madame Marie's Temple of Knowledge* (1991–2, New World 80438-2)

As sideman: New York Composer's Orchestra: *Music by Marty Ehrlich, Robin Holcomb, Wayne Horvitz, and Doug Wieselman* (1990, New World 397); *First Program in Standard Time* (1990, 1992, New World 80418-2)

GK

Wiggins, Gerry [Gerald Foster, Sr.; Wig] (*b* New York, 12 May 1922). Pianist and arranger, father of Hassan J. J. Wiggins. He had classical lessons from the age of four and was playing jazz by his early teens; while at high school he was inspired by hearing Art Tatum play in New York. After touring with the comedian Stepin Fetchit he worked in Les Hite's orchestra (1942–3) and with the De Paris brothers (at Ryan's), Louis Armstrong (on a tour of the South), and Benny Carter (1944). From 1944 to 1946 he served in the military in Fort Lewis, Washington, after which he spent periods in Seattle and San Francisco. He then moved to Los Angeles, where he served as accompanist to the singer Lena Horne (1950–51); thereafter he was associated with numerous singers, notably Kay Starr, Eartha Kitt, and Helen Humes (intermittently to 1974 and then regularly until Humes's death). Wiggins appeared in the short film *"King" Cole and his Trio* (with Carter's orchestra accompanying Cole, 1950) and in the television program "The Swingin' Singin' Years" (1960). In the 1960s he worked as a music director and vocal coach in film studios.

For several decades Wiggins led his own trios, with which he made a number of recordings; among his regular sidemen were Joe Comfort, Red Callender, Charles Drayton, and Andy Simpkins on double bass, and Bill Douglass (i), Lee Young, and Paul Humphrey on drums. He continued to perform as a trio leader and guest soloist around the Los Angeles area and was active with big bands, notably Gerald Wilson's orchestra and the Great American Jazz Orchestra. Later he worked occasionally with Scott Hamilton (from 1980s, recording in 1990–91) and Bill Berry (1990s) and accompanied dancers for the Jazz Tap Summit in San Francisco (1990). He appeared regularly at American jazz parties and festivals and occasionally at Japanese and European festivals and was in demand for recording sessions. His association with Concord resulted in a wide-ranging series of releases, all of which demonstrate his firm touch, all-round musicianship, and sense of swing.

Oral history material in *CLU*; video oral history material in *NCH* (HCJA).

SELECTED RECORDINGS

(recorded for Concord unless otherwise indicated)

As unaccompanied soloist: *Live at Maybeck Recital Hall*, viii (1990, 4450)

Duos with R. Callender: *Night Mist Blues* (1983, Hemisphere 1002)

As leader: *Reminiscin' with Wig* (1957, Motif 504); *Wig is Here* (1974, BB 33069); *Soulidarity* (1995, 4706)

As sideman: R. Eldridge: Easter Parade/Wild Driver (1950, Vogue 5044); Someone to watch over me (1950, Vogue 5046); O. Moore: *We'll Remember Nat* (1965, Surrey 1013); M. Holley: *Mule!* (1974, BB 33074); H. Edison: *Just Friends* (1977, BB 33106); E. Davis: *Light and Lovely* (1977, BB 33121); M. Holley: *Excuse me, Ludwig* (1977, BB 33156); H. Humes: *Muse All-Stars* (1979, Muse 5217); G. Wilson: *Love You Madly* (1982, Trend 531); Linda Hopkins: *How Blue Can You Get?* (1982, PAlt 8034), incl. Evil Gal Blues, Salty Papa Blues; Danny Turner: *First Time Out* (1983, Hemisphere 0001); M. Ellington: *Digital Duke* (*c*1986, GRP 1038); Red Holloway and C. Terry: *Locksmith Blues* (1989, 4390); S. Hamilton: *Radio City* (1990, 4428); F. Wess: *Live at the 1990 Concord Jazz Festival: Second Set* (1990, 4452); S. Hamilton, K. Peplowski, and Spike Robinson: *Groovin' High* (1991, 4509); S. Hamilton: *Race Point* (1991, 4492); F. Capp: *In a Hefti Bag* (1994–5, 4655)

BIBLIOGRAPHY

FeatherE; *Feather '60s*; *Feather–Gitler '70s*

J. P. Battestini: "Gerald Wiggins," *BHcF*, no.237 (1974), 5

R. Callender and E. Cohen: *Unfinished Dream: the Musical World of Red Callender* (London, 1985)

M. Richards: "Gerry Wiggins," *JJI*, xli/8 (1988), 6

B. Rusch: "Gerry Wiggins: Interview," *Cadence*, xix/3 (1993), 9

C. Bryant and others, eds.: *Central Avenue Sounds: Jazz in Los Angeles* (Berkeley, CA, Los Angeles, and London, 1998), 311

PETER VACHER

Wiggins, Hassan J. J. [Gerald Foster, Jr.; Ash-Shakur, Hassan Abdul] (*b* Los Angeles, 15 April 1956). Double bass player, son of Gerry Wiggins. He took up double bass at the age of four (when he had to stand on a chair to reach the neck of the instrument), and made his professional début when he was 12 as a member of the trio led by the young pianist Craig Hundley, performing on several major television shows and recording for Pacific Jazz; he also played in a trio led by his father. He studied at Los Angeles City College for two years and from 1974 into the 1990s worked with the Duke Ellington Orchestra under the direction of Mercer Ellington. He also accompanied, among others, Ella Fitzgerald, Dizzy Gillespie, Milt Jackson, Billy Eckstine, Sarah Vaughan, Joe Williams, and Herb Ellis, and played in pit orchestras for several Broadway shows. He toured the USA, Europe, and Japan with Monty Alexander (recording in 1980). Wiggins has appeared often at jazz festivals and on jazz cruises. He recorded with Bill Easley in 1990 and joined Pearl Bailey and Louie Bellson on a USO tour during the Gulf War (1991). In 1988 he became a member of Al Grey's group, and he continued to work with Alexander in the late 1990s.

SELECTED RECORDINGS

As sideman: M. Ellington: *Continuum* (1974–5, Fan. 9481); A. Grey: *Fab* (1990, Capri 74038); *Matzohs and Grits* (1996, Arbors 19167)

EDDIE LAMBERT/BK

Wiggs, Johnny [Hyman, John Wigginton] (*b* New Orleans, 25 July 1899; *d* New Orleans, 9 Oct 1977). Cornetist. He played mandolin and violin before taking up cornet. From the age of 12 he lived in Ocean Springs, Mississippi, where he played violin in a country band and cornet in a brass band. He moved with his family back to New Orleans when his father's health failed, and was inspired to become a musician after hearing King Oliver, but instead he studied journalism at Loyola University; after a brief attempt to become a newspaper reporter he began playing around 1920 with the drummer Earl Crumb, then worked with the pianist and double bass player Norman Brownlee (1924–5), the trombonist and guitarist Happy Schilling (1926), and other lesser-known players. In 1927 he toured with a vaudeville troupe and recorded, as John Hyman, with his Bayou Stompers (*Ain't love grand/Alligator Blues*, Vic. 20593); the following year he performed and recorded with Tony Parenti. After further affiliations with obscure bands, including that of Crumb once again, during the 1930s and 1940s he worked in the New Orleans public schools, first as a music teacher (his students included Pete Fountain and the trumpeter George Girard) and then, after a further period of study at Tulane University, as a teacher of architecture and mechanical drawing. He reinitiated his jazz career as the leader of band on WSMB radio in 1946–7; at this point he adopted the stage name Wiggs, so as not to offend the parish school board, which disapproved of jazz.

In 1948 Wiggs became a founder and the first president of the New Orleans Jazz Club. He sponsored concerts and parades, encouraged other and more significant retired musicians to restart their careers, established the New Orleans Jazz Museum (*see* LIBRARIES AND ARCHIVES), and created the Jazz Club Radio Show on station WWL. He also recommenced playing and, between 1948 and 1957, made several recordings with his own band. He retired from his teaching job in 1960 and continued to play until 1974, making numerous appearances at Preservation Hall from 1965 and further recordings between 1968 and 1974, notably at the Manassas Jazz Festival in Virginia.

Oral history material in *LNT*.

BIBLIOGRAPHY

A. Rose: "Both of ... Johnny Wiggs," *SL*, xi/9–10 (1961), 11

L. Borenstein and B. Russell: *Preservation Hall Portraits* (Baton Rouge, LA, 1968)

G. W. Kay: "The Johnny Wiggs Story," *JJ*, xxiii/6 (1970), 12

P. R. Haby: "Johnny Wiggs," *Fn*, ix/1 (1977), 4 [incl. discography]

Obituary, *New Orleans Times-Picayune* (14 Oct 1977)

J. Wiggs: "Wiggs Self-explained," *SL*, xxix (1977), spring, 3

W. Carter: *Preservation Hall: Music from the Heart* (Wheatley, Oxford, England, and New York, 1991)

BILL RUSSELL/BK

Wilber, Bob [Robert Sage] (*b* New York, 15 March 1928). Clarinetist, soprano and alto saxophonist, arranger, and composer. He took up piano at the age of ten and changed to clarinet three years later. In 1946–7 he studied with Sidney Bechet. With his first band, the Wildcats (including Dick Wellstood), he led the revival of traditional jazz on the East Coast after World War II. He played with Mezz Mezzrow at the Nice Jazz Festival in 1948. Until this point in his career he doubled on clarinet and the straight soprano saxophone, but upon being drafted during the Korean War, when he served in an army band (1952–4), he traded the latter instrument for a tenor saxophone. Following his discharge he was a member of a cooperative group, the Six, which combined elements of modern and traditional jazz. Later he worked with many important musicians, among them Bechet, Bobby Hackett (1957–8), Benny Goodman (with whom he toured in 1958 and 1959), Jack Teagarden, and

Eddie Condon. In the 1960s he acquired a curved soprano saxophone, which he immediately preferred to the straight instrument, because the curved bell yielded a comparatively fuller and sweeter tone in its lower register. Wilber was a founding member of the World's Greatest Jazz Band in 1969, and from 1974 to 1979 he led the group Soprano summit with Kenny Davern; he was also active with the New York Jazz Repertory Company, with which he toured the USSR in May 1975.

Many of Wilber's activities reflect his dedication to the preservation and dissemination of the traditions of jazz; in the late 1970s he began leading the Smithsonian Jazz Repertory Ensemble and founded his own record company, Bodeswell. From 1980 to early 1984 he led the Bechet legacy, and in 1982 he became the director of jazz studies at Wilkes College. He arranged the music for the film *The Cotton Club* (1984), and then toured as the leader of his own repertory group, giving concerts of music from the 1930s and 1940s, with Randy Sandke, Britt Woodman, Haywood Henry, and Chuck Riggs among the regulars in its changing pool of players. His work on *The Cotton Club* led to further commissions in film, television, and radio, and most notably he made an outstanding soundtrack for the film *Bix: an Interpretation of a Legend* (1990). From the late 1980s he worked with Davern in the revived Soprano Summit (as Soprano Reunion) and in the mid-1990s reactivated his Bechet Legacy band, and in 1996 he made a video and recording as the leader of a big band. He was also often heard at jazz festivals on cruise ships, and in 1992 he was the soloist at a classical concert in London, performing Mozart's Clarinet Concerto and concertos by Artie Shaw, with Shaw conducting. Wilber announced his "retirement" late in 1995, but this amounted to nothing more than a relaxation of his usually frenetic schedule, and he remained active, recording prolifically and touring internationally.

Wilber's many compositions include *Ode to Bechet*. In spite of his association with Bechet, he developed a highly distinctive individual voice, and his work is notable for its tastefulness and integrity. He published an autobiography, edited by D. Webster, *Music was not Enough* (London and New York, 1987), and contributed essays on Bechet to *Jazz Music* (1948) and to a Time-Life recorded anthology (1980).

Oral history material in *LNT*; video oral history material in *NCH* (HCJA).

SELECTED RECORDINGS

As leader: Wild Cat Blues (1947, Com. 584); *The Music of Hoagy Carmichael* (1969, MonE 6917); *Original Wilber* (1978, Phon. 7519); *The Music of King Oliver* (1981, Bodeswell 107); *Reflections* (1983, Bodeswell 106); *The Cotton Club* (1985, Geffen 70260); with A. Sarpila: *Moments like This* (1991, Phon. 8811); with D. Hyman: *A Perfect Match* (1997, Arbors 19193)

As sideman: S. Bechet: I'm through, goodbye (1949, Cir. [USA] 1059); World's Greatest Jazz Band: *Extra* (1968, Project 5039); Pug Horton: *Don't go Away* (1979, Bodeswell 102)

For further recordings *see* Bechet legacy and Soprano summit.

SELECTED FILMS AND VIDEOS

Bobby Hackett (1961); Jazz Scene USA: Ben Pollack and his Pick-a-Rib Boys (1962); The Great Rocky Mountain Jazz Party (1977); Jazz at the Smithsonian: Bob Wilber and the Smithsonian Jazz Repertory: a Tribute to Sidney Bechet (1982); Flip Phillips' 80th Birthday Party featuring the All-Stars (*c*1996 [filmed 1995]); The Bob Wilber Big Band: Bufadora Blow-up (*c*1997 [filmed 1996])

BIBLIOGRAPHY

O. Keepnews: "Wilber's Wildcats: Youthful Jazz Veterans are Giving Old Forms New Life," *Record Changer*, vii/5 (1948), 8
M. Williams: "Bob Wilber's Winnowed Ways," *DB*, xxxiii/25 (1966), 15
J. Norris: "Bob Wilber in Conversation," *Coda*, x/5 (1972), 3
M. Jones: "Wilber: I Do my own Thing," *MM* (5 Oct 1974), 64
——: "Alto? – I'm Still in the Woodshed," *MM* (8 Nov 1975), 49
W. Balliett: "The Westchester Kids," *New Yorker*, liii (9 May 1977), 77; repr. in *Improvising: Sixteen Jazz Musicians and their Art* (New York, 1977), 235; *BalliettA (1986)*; *BalliettA* (1996)
"Bob Wilber Today," *JJI*, xxxii/7 (1979), 7
E. Townley: "Specks and Spots and Other Things," *Sv*, no.81 (1979), 100
"Bob Wilber on Saxes: Some Questions Answered," *JJI*, xxxiii/2 (1980), 16
G. Endress: *Jazz Podium: Musiker über sich selbst* (Stuttgart, Germany, 1980), 40
B. Korall: "Bob Wilber: Personalizing the Trad Repertoire," *DB*, xlvii/9 (1980), 20
E. Cook: "Keepers of the Flame," *JJI*, xxxiv/11 (1981), 16
H. Duckham: "Bob Wilber: a Clarinetist for All Seasons," *The Clarinet*, ix/3 (1982), 17
A. Stevens: "Bob Wilber's Legacies," *CI*, xx/10 (1982), 8
P. Brodowski: "Bob Wilber: 'It Don't Mean a Thing if it Ain't Got that Swing'," *JF*, no.93 (1985), 24
J. Lucas: "The Jazz Baton: Bechet to Hodges to Wilber," *MR*, xii/3 (1985), 1
W. Royal Stokes: "Recreating the Golden Age," *JT* (1985), Nov, 14
B. Rusch: "Bob Wilber: Interview," *Cadence*, xii/8 (1986), 5
M. Jones: *Talking Jazz* (London, 1987), 12
K. Whitehead: "Bob Wilber: a Short Talk," *Cadence*, xiv/1 (1988), 23
J. Hamlin: "Bechet Disciple Heads Dixieland Jazz Festival," *San Francisco Chronicle Datebook* (21 May 1989)
E. Cook: "Bob Wilber," *JJI*, xlvi (1993), no.9, p.8; no.10, p.14
J. Bradley: "Bob Wilber's Long Gig Began with Bechet," *Denver Post* (18 Sept 1995)
C. Berg: "Bob Wilber: Life After Jazz," *JT*, xxvi/5 (1996), 44
A. Fell and P. Gaskell: "Bob Wilber Blows up a Storm on the Left Bank," *MR*, xxiii/4 (1996), 10
P. Carr: *Jimmy Archey: the Little Giant of the Trombone* (New Orleans, 1999)

DEREK WEBSTER/BK

Wilborn, Dave [David Buckley] (*b* Springfield, OH, 11 April 1904; *d* Detroit, 25 April 1982). Banjoist, guitarist, and singer. He played piano from the age of 12, but gave it up two years later to concentrate on banjo. In 1922 he began working with Cecil and Lloyd Scott. He then joined William McKinney's Synco Septet, which later became known as McKinney's Cotton Pickers. Wilborn was a regular member of the band until late 1934, recording with it between 1928 and 1931; *Zonky* (1930, Vic. 38118) provides a fine example of his singing and rhythm banjo playing, and he may be heard taking a brief solo in *Laughing at life* (1930, Vic. 23020). He continued to perform with the group from time to time until 1937. He also recorded with Louis Armstrong (1928). Thereafter he played guitar with his own sextet until 1950, when he ceased full-time performing. From September 1972 he was the featured singer with the New McKinney's Cotton Pickers; he recorded with the band that year and as a leader at the Manassas Jazz Festival the following year. He collapsed and died during a performance by the band.

For illustration *see* McKinney's cotton pickers.

BIBLIOGRAPHY

ChiltonW
T. Grove and M. Grove: "The Dave Wilbourne Story," *Music Mirror*, ii/6 (1955), 6
J. Chilton: *McKinney's Music: a Bio-discography of McKinney's Cotton Pickers* (London, 1978)
Obituary, J. Taylor, *MR*, ix/8 (1982), 7

HOWARD RYE

Wilcox, Eddie [Ed(win Felix)] (*b* Method, nr Raleigh, NC, 27 Dec 1907; *d* New York, 29 Sept 1968). Arranger and pianist. He was a pianist in bands during his high school years and played in a group led by Jimmie Lunceford while studying at Fisk University (1925–7). During the summers of 1927 and 1928 he performed in resorts in New Jersey, and in June 1929 he rejoined Lunceford, with whom he may be seen in the short film *Jimmie Lunceford and his Dance Orchestra* (1937). As an arranger Wilcox played an important part in developing the style of Lunceford's band, and his work is well represented by *Flaming Reeds and Screaming Brass/While Love Lasts* (1933, first issued on *Lunceford Special*, Col. CS9515). In the 1940s he helped the group to keep abreast of changing audience expectations, as may be heard on *I need a lift* (1945, V-disc 568) and *One o'Clock Jump* (1947, first issued on a British album of unknown title, Pol. 623272). His solo playing in the stride tradition is featured in Sy Oliver's arrangements for Lunceford of *Blue Blazes* (1939, Voc. 4667) and *Mandy* (1939, Voc. 4831); he performs in a less assertive mood in Lunceford's *Jeep Rhythm* (1944, Decca 18618) and *What to do* (1945, V-disc 586), arranged by Horace Henderson and Oliver respectively.

After Lunceford's death (1947) Wilcox shared the leadership of the band with Joe Thomas (iii) for two years and continued as its sole leader into the 1950s. He then worked in the New York area as an unaccompanied soloist and as the leader of small groups, one of which held a ten-year residency at Café Riviera. In addition he worked occasionally as a sideman and formed with Teddy McRae a record company, Raecox, for which Edmond Hall made a notable album (*Rumpus on Rampart Street*, 1959, Raecox 1120) with arrangements by Wilcox. In 1968 he performed in Canada with Big Chief Moore.

BIBLIOGRAPHY

ChiltonW; *FeatherE*; *Feather–GitlerBEJ*; *McCarthyB*; *SchullerS*
O. Flückiger: "Discography of Jimmie Lunceford – Eddie Wilcox Concerning with 1945 [*sic*]," *Jazz-Statistics*, no.15 (1960), [6]
I. Crosbie: "Jimmie Lunceford: Message from Memphis," *JJ*, xxv (1972), no.1, p.2; no.2, p.26
S. Dance: *The World of Swing* (New York, 1974), 110
B. Lyttkens: *The Jimmie Lunceford Legacy on Records* (Stockholm, 1996, loose-leaf suppl., 1997)

HOWARD RYE

Wilczewski, David (*b* Boston, 9 June 1952). Saxophonist. He played clarinet as a child, and when he was 15 he became interested in jazz and took up saxophone; later he studied the instrument at the Berklee College of Music (1968–70) and at the New England Conservatory (1970–75). In 1975 he toured the USA with the rock organist Al Kooper, and after visiting Los Angeles for the first time he persuaded his friend Steve Smith to move there with him. The pair returned to Boston once a year and met their former colleagues Tim Landers, Dean Brown, and Mike Stern, a relationship that eventually led to the formation of the group Vital Information in 1981. Although he moved to Sweden the following year, Wilczewski retained his links with America and played with Vital Information until 1989. In Sweden he performed regularly with the Swedish Radio Jazz Group, toured twice with Herbie Hancock and a Swedish rhythm section (1990–91), and worked with TIA-DIA under Lars Danielsson and Alex Acuña; he also played with Eje Thelin, Anders Jormin, the guitarist Goran Klinghagen, Bosse Broberg, the pianist Steve Dobrogosz, and the guitarist Rolf Jardemark.

SELECTED RECORDINGS

As leader: *I Don't Know Betty … but I Think You Can Dance to it* (1989, Caprice 21373); *Music Spoken Here/Brasso* (1998, Stunt 19812)
As sideman: S. Smith: *Vital Information* (1983, CBS FC38955); E. Thelin: *Raggruppamento* (1991, Phono Suecia 56); S. Dobrogosz: *Duckwalk* (1996, Dra. 300)

MARK GILBERT

Wilde, Laurent de (*b* Washington, DC, 19 Dec 1960). French pianist, composer, and leader. He moved to France with his family at the age of four and received his schooling there, eventually studying philosophy. In 1982 he returned to the USA to attend Long Island University, and while in New York he perfected his self-taught skills as a pianist through studies with Jim McNeely and Mulgrew Miller. In 1987 he made his first recording, as the leader of a trio comprising Ira Coleman and Jack DeJohnette. He then played with Greg Osby, Donald Harrison, Ernie Watts, Vincent Herring, Joshua Redman, and others. After returning to Paris in 1990 he collaborated with Barney Wilen, giving concerts in clubs and at summer festivals (including Nice, Marciac, and Toulouse in 1998) in trios, quartets, or quintets with such sidemen as Coleman, Eddie Henderson, Antonio Hart, and Billy Drummond. In the new century he has abandoned the acoustic piano to dedicate himself to computers and electronic music. Wilde is the author of *Monk* (Paris, 1996; Eng. trans., New York, 1997).

SELECTED RECORDINGS

As leader: *Off the Beat* (1989, Ida 015); *Open Changes* (1992, Ida 035); *The Back Burner* (1995, Col. 480784); *Spoon-a-rhythm* (1996, Col. CK68635); *Time 4 Change* (2000, Warner Music 8573843152)
As sideman with B. Wilen: *Talisman* (1993, Ida 037)

BIBLIOGRAPHY

J.-Y. Le Bec: "Gros plan: Laurent de Wilde," *Jm*, no.377 (1988), 46
P. Anquetil: "Laurent de Wilde," *Jazzman*, no.174 (1994), 4
G. Bourgadier: "La couleur de Wilde," *Jm*, no.451 (1995), 16
"La Baronne sortit autour de minuit … Laurent de Wilde," *Jm*, no.458 (1996), 20
F. Bergerot: "Groove and Spirit in New York," *Jazzman*, no.22 (1997), 16
F. W. Sportis: "Laurent de Wilde: atmosphère," *Jh*, no.539 (1997), 26
H. Mandel: "'No Cheaters in Jazz," *DB*, lxv/3 (1998), 44
B. Primack: "Hearsay: Laurent de Wilde," *JT*, xxviii/1 (1998), 26
M. Zwerin: "A French Jazzman's Quest for New Sounds," *International Herald Tribune* (16 Dec 1998)
F. Goaty: "Quand Laurent de Wilde se branche," *Jm*, no.508 (2000), 44

ANDRÉ CLERGEAT

Wilder, Joe [Joseph Benjamin] (*b* Colwyn, nr Philadelphia, 22 Feb 1922). Trumpeter. The son of a bandleader, he played cornet initially and studied music in Philadelphia, where Red Rodney and Buddy DeFranco were among his classmates. After working with Les Hite (from 1941) and Lionel Hampton he served for three years in the Marine Corps, first in special weapons and then as a bandmaster. He then re-joined Hampton (1946) and played with Jimmie Lunceford (continuing with the band for a period after the leader's death in mid-1947), Lucky Millinder, Erskine Hawkins, Dizzy Gillespie (*c*1948), Sam Donahue, Herbie Fields, and Noble Sissle (1951). While playing in pit orchestras on Broadway (to 1957) Wilder worked for six months with Count Basie (December 1953 – May 1954) and took part in a recording session led by Ernie Wilkins. In 1956 he recorded as a soloist on *Ballad for Joe* (a movement of J. J. Johnson's *Poem for Brass*), and four decades later he re-created this solo on a new recording with Johnson. In 1957 Wilder joined the music staff of ABC, with which he remained for 16 years; during the same period he toured the USSR with Benny Goodman (1962) and played on four occasions with the New York Philharmonic Orchestra. From 1973 he worked as a freelance in television, films, and recording studios. Throughout the 1980s he played in the pit orchestra for the Broadway show *42nd Street*; he recorded with Benny Carter in 1985 and as a guest soloist with John Colianni in 1986. Later he participated in the re-creation of Charles Mingus's symphony *Epitaph* (under Gunther Schuller), played in the Smithsonian Jazz Masterworks Orchestra, toured with the Lincoln Center Jazz Orchestra, and made new recordings as a leader. Wilder was a member of the Statesman of Jazz and appeared in its eponymous video (1994). He is also an accomplished photographer.

Oral history material in *DSI* (JOHP); video oral history material in *NCH* (HCJA).

SELECTED RECORDINGS

As leader: *Wilder 'n' Wilder* (1956, Savoy 12063); with J. Newman: *Hangin' Out* (1984, Conc. 262); *Alone with Just my Dreams* (1991, Evening Star 101); *No Greater Love* (1993, Evening Star 103)

As sideman: C. Basie: *Dance Session* (1953, Clef 626), incl. Softly with Feeling; Pete Brown: *Peter the Great* (1954, Beth. 1011); E. Wilkins: *Top Brass* (1955, Savoy 12044), incl. Trick or Treat, Willow Weep for Me; on [no leader]: *Music for Brass* (1956, Col. CL941), J. J. Johnson: Poem for Brass; B. Carter: *A Gentleman and his Music* (1985, Conc. 285)

SELECTED FILMS AND VIDEOS

The Great Rocky Mountain Jazz Party (1977); Jazz in America: Lincoln Center, New York (1982); Statesmen of Jazz (n.d. [filmed 1994])

BIBLIOGRAPHY

BalliettA (1986); *BalliettA (1996)*; *FeatherE*; *Feather '60s*; *Feather–Gitler '70s*

R. Horricks: *Count Basie and his Orchestra: its Music and its Musicians* (London and New York, 1957), 266

C. Deffaa: "Subtle Master," *MR*, xiii/10 (1986), 11; repr. in *In the Mainstream: 18 Portraits in Jazz* (Metuchen, NJ, and London, 1992), 248

"A Joe Wilder Photo Gallery," *ARJS*, v (1991), 181

"On the Phone with Joe Wilder," *The Note*, iii/3 (1991), 2

E. Berger: *Bassically Speaking: an Oral History of George Duvivier* (Metuchen, NJ, and London, 1993), 127

J. McDonough: "Riffs: Joe Wilder," *DB*, lx/12 (1993), 14

P. D. Atteberry: "Joe Wilder: where Music Begins," *Coda*, no.256 (1994), 12

S. Voce: "Joe Wilder," *JJI*, xlix (1996), no.2, p.6; no.3, p.12

CHRIS SHERIDAN/BK

Wildman, Joan (Marie) (*b* Milburn, NE, 1 Jan 1938). Pianist, keyboard player, and educator. She attended MacPhail College of Music in Minneapolis (BM and MM) and the University of Oregon (DMA 1977), and taught at Central Michigan University and the Fort Kent campus of the University of Maine. From 1977 she has taught at the University of Wisconsin, where she became chair of the jazz studies department in 1998. Between 1977 and 1980 she led a quartet that included the double bass player Joe Fonda. She then formed a trio, in which the double bass player Hans Sturm and Dane Richeson were her sidemen from 1985; it may be heard to excellent effect on her recording *Inside Out* (1992, Wild 1910). Wildman has also performed with the Duke Ellington Orchestra, the Milwaukee Symphony Orchestra, and Roscoe Mitchell, with whom she recorded the album *Four Compositions* (1988, Lovely Music 2021). With B. Benward, she published *Jazz Improvisation in Theory and Practice* (1984, Dubuque, IA).

GK

Wilen, Barney [Bernard Jean] (*b* Nice, France, 4 March 1937; *d* Paris, 25 May 1996). French tenor saxophonist. He grew up in the USA. His first recordings were with Roy Haynes (1954), and around 1955 he appeared at the Club Saint-Germain in Paris with Kenny Clarke, J. J. Johnson, Benny Golson, and Bud Powell. After recording with John Lewis (1956) he worked again with Powell (1957, 1959), took part with Miles Davis in the recording of the soundtrack to the film *L'ascenseur pour l'échafaud* (1957), and recorded with Milt Jackson (1958) and Kenny Dorham (1959). As a member of Art Blakey's Jazz Messengers he played on the soundtrack to the film *Les liaisons dangereuses 1960* (1959). In Europe he worked from 1967 as a leader in a style that incorporated elements of rock; in 1968 he recorded the album *Dear Prof. Leary*. Wilen lived in Africa from 1968 to 1973 and in 1977 returned to Nice. In 1982 he embraced jazz-rock and experimented with a fusion of jazz and African rhythms, though in his later work he has favored a bop style that recalls his playing in the late 1950s. In 1991 he worked in a duo with the pianist Alain Jeanmarie and in 1995 he appeared at the Jazz in Marciac festival.

SELECTED RECORDINGS

As leader: *Tilt* (1957, Swing 30058); with M. Jackson: *Jazz sur Seine* (1958, Phi. 771271); *Newport '59* (1959, Fresh Sound 165); *Dear Prof. Leary* (1968, MPS 15191); *French Ballads* (1987, Ida 014); *Sanctuary* (1991, Ida 029); *Modern Nostalgia* (*c*1991, Alfa Jazz 145); *Dream Time* (1992, Deux Z 84108); *Talisman* (1993, Ida 037)

BIBLIOGRAPHY

P. Carles and J.-L. Comolli: "Entretien avec Barney Wilen: portrait d'un fantôme," *Jm*, no.127 (1966), 30

M. LeBris: "Barney Wilen: ma direction c'est le rock," *Jh*, no.245 (1968), 28

M. Laplace: "Lexicon van Franse rietblazers," *Jazz Press*, no.12 (1977), 13

P. Lapijover: "Jazzman et Français," *Jh*, no.355 (1978), 30

P.-H. Ardonceau: "Wilen pour de vrai," *Jm*, no.357 (1987), 22

E. Lucas: "Le mythe Barney, le style Wilen," *Jm*, no.412 (1992), 29

J. R. Masson: "Le destin romantique de Barney Wilen," *Jm*, no.461 (1996), 21

MICHEL LAPLACE

Wiley [Willey], **Lee** (*b* Fort Gibson, OK, 9 Oct 1908; *d* New York, 11 Dec 1975). Singer. After her death the year of her birth was discovered to be 1908, not 1915, as widely published. Having modified the spelling of her name from Willey to Wiley, probably in the late 1920s, she went to New York around 1930 and soon began singing with Leo Reisman's society orchestra at the Central Park Casino. This led to regular exposure on radio, including broadcasts with Paul Whiteman, Willard Robison, Johnny Green, and other leaders, and, ultimately, her own program. In 1932 she began a professional and personal association with the arranger and composer Victor Young, with whom she broadcast, recorded, and collaborated in writing such songs as *Got the South in my Soul* and *Any time, any day, anywhere*. She sang in the short film *Woody Herman and his Orchestra* (1938) and beginning in 1939 made popular music history by recording the first four albums of jazz organized as tributes to composers: George Gershwin, Cole Porter, Harold Arlen, and the team of Rodgers and Hart. Her accompaniments on many of these performances were by musicians associated with Eddie Condon, among them Max Kaminsky, Bud Freeman, Pee Wee Russell, and Joe Bushkin. She was a regular and acclaimed guest at the guitarist's wartime concerts at Town Hall and the Ritz Theater in New York (1944–5), and she also appeared on the television series "Eddie Condon Floor Show" (1949).

Wiley was briefly married to Jess Stacy. She toured with his short-lived big band (July 1945 – May 1946) and remained closely identified with musicians of this style, as may be heard most notably on her album *Night in Manhattan* with Bushkin and Bobby Hackett (1950) and at an acclaimed performance with Hackett's band at the first Newport Jazz Festival in 1954. Thereafter she appeared and recorded irregularly, though she made one final LP in 1971 with an all-star septet of swing musicians. Her last major performance was with Hackett's quintet (Teddy Wilson, Bucky Pizzarelli, George Duvivier, Don Lamond) at Carnegie Hall during the Newport Jazz Festival New York of 1972.

With Ivie Anderson and a small number of others, Wiley was among the first generation of major singers to build on stylistic advances made in the late 1920s by Ethel Waters in developing a sophisticated, jazz-flavored approach to popular singing. Her husky, smoky contralto voice was made more expressive by a generous vibrato and the occasional use of a head register.

SELECTED RECORDINGS

Lee Wiley on the Air, i (1932–6, Totem 1021); Hands across the Table/I'll follow my secret heart (1935, Decca 322); What is Love?/I've got you under my skin (1937, Decca 15034); I've got a crush on you (1939, LMS 282); A little birdie told me/You took advantage of me (1940, Gala/ Rabson 3); *Lee Wiley on the Air*, ii (1944–5, Totem 1033); *Night in Manhattan* (1950, Col. CL6169), incl. Any time, any day, anywhere; *Lee Wiley Sings Rodgers and Hart* (1954, Sto. 312); *West of the Moon* (1956, RCA LPM1408); *Back Home Again* (1971, MonE 7041)

BIBLIOGRAPHY

ChiltonW; *FeatherE*
G. Frazier: "Lee," *Eddie Condon's Treasury of Jazz*, ed. E. Condon and R. Gehman (New York, 1956/*R*1975), 143
G. Kuhlman: "Lee Wiley," *Coda*, xi/6 (1974), 8
M. Jones: "Lee Wiley, Classy Chanteuse," *MM* (27 Dec 1975), 24
B. Goldblatt: *Newport Jazz Festival: the Illustrated History* (New York, 1977)
M. Pinfold: "Dead, but not … Remembered," *JJI*, xxx/12 (1977), 12
C. Schlouch: *Lee Wiley, Love-Lee: a Discography* (Marseilles, France, 1983)
L. Carr: Liner notes, *Lee Wiley Sings the Songs of George Gershwin and Cole Porter* (Audiophile AP1, 1985)
G. Lombardi: *Eddie Condon on Record, 1927–1971* (Milan, 1987)
L. Selk: "The LP Discography of Lee Wiley on Liberty Music Shop and Reissue Labels," *Record Research*, nos.233–4 (1988), 6
K. Keller: *Oh, Jess!: a Jazz Life: the Jess Stacy Story* (New York, 1989)
W. Friedwald: *Jazz Singing: America's Great Voices from Bessie Smith to Bebop and Beyond* (New York, 1992)
R. Hilbert: *Pee Wee Russell: the Life of a Jazzman* (New York, and Oxford, England, 1993)
G. Frazier: "On Lee Wiley, 1954," *Jazzbeat*, vii/2 (1995), 5
L. Selk and G. Kuhlman: *Lee Wiley: a Bio-discography* (Riverdale, NY, 1997)

RICHARD M. SUDHALTER/BK

Wilkerson, Don(ald A.) (*b* Moreauville, LA, 6 July 1932; *d* Houston, 18 July 1986). Tenor saxophonist. He grew up in Houston, played alto saxophone in high school there, and made his professional début on the instrument in Dayton, Texas; he also worked with Milt Larkin at the Eldorado Ballroom in Houston. Although he made one recording on alto saxophone with the blues singer and pianist Little Willie Littlefield, he soon changed to the tenor; however, he retained throughout his career a penchant for playing in the high register, as if he were trying to re-create the sound of an alto on the deeper instrument. In the late 1940s and early 1950s he played long one-nighter tours with Joe Turner (ii), T-Bone Walker, and the pianist and singer Amos Milburn, with whom he made his recording début on tenor saxophone in 1949. From 1950 he was again based in Houston. In 1952 he recorded with the pianist Danny Small in Miami, and the following year he performed and recorded with Charles Brown. By November 1954 Wilkerson had joined Ray Charles's band, with which he remained for about a year, and he contributed simple but effective statements to several of Charles's best-known recordings. About 1960 he moved to California, but he continued to return regularly to Houston. Over the next three years he recorded several soul-jazz albums. He recorded with Charles again in August 1960, and in September 1961 he joined the pianist's new big band, which toured Europe from autumn 1961 into spring 1962. This band played jazz big-band arrangements of some of the material Charles had recorded commercially only in pop-oriented presentations, and it may be seen in the film *Ballad in Blue* (1964); it also recorded with Louis Jordan under Charles's supervision. Wilkerson remained active into the 1980s and released a single on his own Tomel label in 1980.

SELECTED RECORDINGS

As leader: *Elder Don* (1962, BN 84121), incl. Drawin' a Tip, Lone Star Shuffle, Scrappy; *Preach Brother!* (1962, BN 84107); *Shoutin'!* (1963, BN 84145), incl. Blues for J, Easy living; Low Down Dirty Shame (1980, Tomel 101)

As sideman: L. W. Littlefield: Boogie Woogie Playgirl (*c*1948, Eddie's 1212) [a sax]; Calvin Boze: Baby, you're the tops with me (1950, Ala. 3086); Choo choo's bringing my baby home (1950, Ala. 3079); C. Brown: Don't leave poor me (1953, Ala. 3200); Lonesome feeling (1953, Ala. 3191); R. Charles: Hallelujah I love her so/What would I do without you (1955, Atl. 1096); *Berlin 1962* (1962, Pablo 5301-2), incl. Come rain or come shine

BIBLIOGRAPHY

Feather '60s; *Feather–GitlerBEJ*
D. Williams: Liner notes, *Preach Brother!* (BN 84107, 1962)
A. Govenar: *Meeting the Blues* (Dallas, TX, 1988), 184
J. Evensmo: *History of Jazz Tenor Saxophone: Black Artists*, iv: *1945–1949* (Oslo, 1999)

HOWARD RYE

Wilkerson, Ed(ward L.), Jr. (*b* Terre Haute, IN, *c*1953). Tenor saxophonist, clarinetist, pianist, composer, and leader. He grew up in Shaker Heights, a suburb of Cleveland, where he began playing clarinet at the age of 11 and took up baritone saxophone in his teens; later he changed to the tenor instrument. From 1971 he studied at the University of Chicago (BM 1975). After seeing a performance by the Art Ensemble of Chicago (in January 1972) Wilkerson began studies at the music school of the Association for the Advancement of Creative Musicians (AACM) (to 1975), and he performed with both the AACM big band and that of Muhal Richard Abrams (playing alto saxophone in the latter ensemble). In the mid-1970s he co-led, with the trumpeter Frank Walton, a hard-bop quintet and worked in the quartet Quadrisect, alongside George Lewis (ii), Douglas Ewart, and Mwata Bowden. In 1976 he was a founding member of the Ethnic Heritage Ensemble, and around the same time he joined Ewart's ensemble Clarinet Choir; he remained with both groups into the mid-1990s. In the early 1980s he continued his education, studying orchestration at Loop College (1981) and the American Conservatory of Music (1982), both in Chicago.

Wilkerson began to lead his own groups in the late 1970s. Initially he formed the ensemble Shadow Vignettes as a trio with Yosef Ben Israel on double bass and Reggie Nicholson on drums. Its membership continually expanded, and from the mid-1980s Shadow Vignettes operated as a large ensemble of up to 25 pieces, incorporating a string section and several percussionists; at this point Wilkerson served as its composer and conductor and did not play. The band may be seen performing in the video *Jazz Shorts* (*c*1986). In 1985 Wilkerson formed an octet, Eight Bold Souls, in which he played mainly tenor saxophone, and which has included among its members Bowden, the tuba player Aaron Dodd, the trumpeter Robert Griffin, the trombonist Isaiah Jackson, the cellist Naomi Millender, the double bass player Richard Brown, and Steve McCall; Brown and McCall were later replaced by Harrison Bankhead and Dushun Mosley respectively. From 1986 Wilkerson issued recordings by both groups on his record label Sessoms. In 1992 he recorded as the leader of a quartet consisting of the trumpeter Rod McGaha, Bankhead, and Nicholson. He has served as president of the AACM and taught at the AACM School of Music, and he has played tenor saxophone in bands accompanying the blues musicians Albert King and Bobby Blue Bland, as well as such popular music performers as Gene Chandler, Little Anthony and the Imperials, and the Temptations.

SELECTED RECORDINGS

As leader of Eight Bold Souls: *Eight Bold Souls* (c1986, Sessoms 0002); *Sideshow* (1991, Arabesque 0103); *Ant Farm* (1994, Arabesque 0114); *Last Option* (1999, Thrill Jockey 071)
As leader of other groups: of Shadow Vignettes: *Birth of a Notion* (c1985, Sessoms 0001); of quartet: *Light on the Path* (1992, Sound Aspects 050)
As sideman with Ethnic Heritage Ensemble: *Hang Tuff* (1990, Open Minds 2405); *Dance with the Ancestors* (1993, Chameleon 8088)

BIBLIOGRAPHY

GrayF
J. Litweiler: "Caught: Ed Wilkerson/Eight Bold Souls," *DB*, lii/6 (1985), 57
F. Davis: "Ed Wilkerson: Big Bands are Back ... with a Difference," *Musician*, no.95 (1986), 29
J. Litweiler: "Blowin' in from Chicago, 1986," *Wire*, no.33 (1986), 22
L. Kart: "The Edge of Stardom: Locale is Expanding for Edward Wilkerson Jr.," *Chicago Tribune* (18 Jan 1987)
M. Rimarchi: "The Leading Edge: Ed Wilkerson, Jr.," *Option*, no.22 (1988), 56
F. Davis: "Music: Blowing in from Chicago: Edward Wilkerson and his Two Jazz Bands are Set to Arrive Nationwide," *Atlantic*, cclxiii/2 (1989), 71; repr. in *Outcats: Jazz Composers, Instrumentalists, and Singers* (New York, and Oxford, England, 1990), 63
L. Sachs: "Bold Souls: a New Generation is Taking the Reins at One of the Country's Most Vital Centers for Jazz," *Chicago*, xxxviii/5 (1989), 146
N. Tesser: "Adventurous Jazz: Chicago's Ed Wilkerson Wows 'em in New York," *Chicago Tribune* (20 Nov 1989)
J. Corbett: "Ed Wilkerson: Togetherness is Everything," *DB*, lvii/4 (1990), 22 [incl. discography]
W. Jenkins: "Hearsay: Bold Soul," *JT*, xxii/4 (1992), 9
J. Litweiler: "Critics' Choice: Edward Wilkerson May be Poised for Jazz Stardom as CD Goes National," *Chicago Tribune* (6 Aug 1992)
J. Corbett: "Spencer Barefield/Don Moye/Ed Wilkerson Trio," *DB*, lx/5 (1993), 51
B. Frandzel: "Edward Wilkerson, Jr.: One Bold Soul," *Coda*, no.254 (1994), 30
F.-J. Hadley: "Profile: 8 Bold Souls," *Jazziz*, xii/8 (1995), 78
<http://aacmchicago.org/members/_wilkersonbio.html> (1999)
J. Corbett: "Bold Strokes," *DB*, lxvii/10 (2000), 52
<http://www.chireader.com/music/jazsfest/schedule98.html> (2000)
<http://www.8boldsouls.com/soulshistory.html> (2000)
<http://www.fred.net/jbowie/ehe.html> (2000)

GK

Wilkins, Dave [David Livingstone] (*b* Barbados, 25 Sept 1914; *d* London, 26 Nov 1990). Barbadian trumpeter. He learned to play trumpet in Salvation Army bands and first heard jazz on American recordings in Barbados and St. Vincent and through radio broadcasts in Trinidad, where he moved in 1935. There he was a member of the police band and the Blue Rhythm Orchestra, a group led by the double bass player John "Buddy" Williams. With three other musicians he traveled to London in 1937 to join Ken "Snake Hips" Johnson's West Indian Swing Band, with which he toured, recorded, and made radio broadcasts until Johnson's death in 1941. Wilkins then worked with British bandleaders, including Ted Heath, Harry Parry, and Joe Daniels; his playing may be heard to advantage on Parry's *I can't dance* (1942, Parl. R2851). He performed only sporadically for some years before ceasing to work in the 1970s.

Oral history material in *GBLnsa*.

BIBLIOGRAPHY

FeatherE
"Personal Points: Dave Wilkins," *MM* (17 May 1947), 4
"A Man and his Trumpet," *Checkers* (1948), Dec, 15
J. Green: "Bix in Barbados: Dave Wilkins, Trumpet," *Sv*, no.118 (1985), 136
Obituaries: V. Wilmer, *The Independent* (1 Dec 1990), 53; V. Wilmer, *Wire*, no.84 (1991), 5

JEFFREY P. GREEN

Wilkins, Ernie [Ernest Brooks, Jr.] (*b* St. Louis, 20 July 1919; *d* Copenhagen, 5 June 1999). Composer, arranger, and saxophonist. His year of birth has been published as 1922, but in his press kit Wilkins gave 1919, which he confirmed in a questionnaire for this dictionary. He learned piano and violin, and later studied music at Wilberforce University; he first played jazz in his teens in and around St. Louis. During his military service he was in a band led by Willie Smith, after which he worked with the Jeter–Pillars Orchestra and Earl Hines's last big band (1948). As an alto saxophonist he recorded with Dinah Washington (1949–50) and then joined Count Basie (May 1951). More importantly, while with Basie he gained widespread recognition as a composer; according to Sheridan (in *Count Basie: a Bio-discography*, 1986) Wilkins bore much of the burden for reviving Basie's fortunes during this period. He left the band early in 1955, but continued to write for it, and his scoring of *Every day I have the blues*, featuring Joe Williams (on the album *Count Basie Swings & Joe Williams Sings*, 1955, Clef MGC678) became one of Basie's biggest hits. Wilkins performed in and provided arrangements for the band led by Dizzy Gillespie that toured the Middle East and South America in 1956, then arranged for Tommy Dorsey and conducted studio orchestras and wrote for Washington; during these years he also wrote arrangements for small groups, notably those for Sarah Vaughan's album with Clifford Brown for EmArcy (1954), a number of recording dates for Savoy, variously under Kenny Clarke's leadership, as co-leader with Clarke, and under his own name (1955–7), and albums by Jimmy Cleveland for EmArcy and Mercury (1957–8). From 1958 to 1960 he was a staff composer for Harry James's orchestra, and made several contributions to its repertory.

During the 1960s Wilkins wrote for a band led by his brother, the trombonist Jimmy Wilkins (who had also played with Basie from 1951 to 1953), and in 1968 he joined Clark Terry's Big B-A-D Band as its music director and principal composer; he made three European tours with the band. After appearing with Terry at the Montreux International Jazz Festival Wilkins assembled his own band. He wrote further compositions for Basie, then served as head of the artists and repertory department of Mainstream Records (1971–3); he twice appeared at Carnegie Hall in Basie's reunion band (1973, 1976). Wilkins was active in jazz education, and spent periods as an instructor for Jazzmobile and in Joe Newman's Jazz Interactions program, as well as serving as chair of the Afro-American music department at the New England Conservatory of Music in Boston. From the mid-1970s he recorded with Art Farmer and the big band of the Österreichischer Rundfunk. In 1979 he toured Europe with Lionel Hampton and then settled in Copenhagen, where he worked with both local and visiting musicians. In 1980 he organized his own group, the 12-piece Almost Big Band, which performed and recorded into the 1990s; among its members were Richard Boone, Sahib Shihab, Jesper Thilo, Bent Jaedig, Kenny Drew, Mads Vinding, Jesper Lundgaard, Ed Thigpen, and Per Goldschmidt. He also toured as a soloist, contributed arrangements to a performance by Philip Catherine and Niels-Henning Ørsted Pederson with the Royal Copenhagen Chamber Orchestra (1989), arranged and conducted Jay McShann's Kansas City Big Band for a concert recorded in Paris (1989), and organized Ernie Wilkins's Orchestral Royal Tribute to Duke Ellington (1990), which involved a tour of Europe and the making of a video and a recording; the resulting album was by an all-star big band with Farmer, Benny Bailey, Alvin Batiste, and James Williams among its members. In 1991 Wilkins suffered a stroke which ended his career.

SELECTED RECORDINGS

As leader: with K. Clarke: *The Kenny Clarke–Ernie Wilkins Septet* (1955, Savoy 12007); *Ernie Wilkins and the Almost Big Band* (1980, Sto. 4051); *Ernie Wilkins' Almost Big Band Live* (1981, Matrix 29203); *Montreux* (1983, Ste. 1190); *On the Road* (1986, Ste. 1225); *K.a.l.e.i.d.o.d.u.k.e.* (1990, Birdology 519346-2)

As sideman: C. Basie: *Dance Session* (1953, Clef 626); *Blues Backstage* (1954, Clef 666); C. Terry: *Live on 57th Street* (1970, Etoile 1); *Clark Terry Live at the Wichita Jazz Festival 1974* (1974, Van. 79355); *Clark Terry Live at Buddy's Place* (1976, Van. 79373)

RECORDED COMPOSITIONS

* – with Wilkins as sideman

Recorded by others: C. Basie: *Bread (1952, Clef 89085); *Sixteen Men Swingin' (1954), on Basie: *Dance Session*, ii (1952, 1954, Clef 647); on Q. Jones: *The Great Wide World of Quincy Jones* (1959, Mer. 20561), Everybody's Blues, Ghana; on H. James: *The Spectacular Sound of Harry James* (1961, MGM 3897), Connectin' the Bones, The Jazz Connoisseurs

BIBLIOGRAPHY

CarrJ; *FeatherE*; *Feather '60s*; *Feather–Gitler '70s*; *SheridanCB*

R. Horricks: *Count Basie and his Orchestra: its Music and its Musicians* (London and New York, 1957), 247

I. Gitler: "Ernie Wilkins Returns," *DB*, xxxvi/7 (1969), 15

L. Tomkins: "The Ernie Wilkins Story," *CI*, xiv (1975), no.2, p.23; no.4, p.6

B. Rusch: "Ernie Wilkins: Oral History," *Cadence*, ii/6–7 (1977), 3

G. Engström: "Ernie Wilkins har blivit dansk," *Orkester journalen*, xlviii/3 (1980), 8

G. Holmberg: "Blommer till Sahib Shihab: och hela Wilkins Almost Big Band!," *Orkester journalen*, l/6 (1982), 8

S. Floyd: "An Oral History: the Great Lakes Experience," *Black Perspective in Music*, xi/1 (1983), 41

R. Baggenaes: "Ernie Wilkins: the Almost Big Band," *Coda*, no.194 (1984), 7

J. Armstrong: "Ernie Wilkins: the Orchestra is my Instrument," *JF* [intl edn], no.108 (1987), 42

"Ernie is Pleased to Lose his Title as Fastest Arranger in the West," *Inverness Courier* [Scotland] (8 Jan 1991)

Obituaries: [A. Shipton], *The Times* (7 June 1999); S. Voce, *The Independent* (8 June 1999); B. Ratliff, *New York Times* (8 June 1999); A. Morgan, *JJI*, lii/2 (1999), 16

STAN BRITT/BK

Wilkins, Jack (*b* New York, 3 June 1944). Guitarist. His father played tenor saxophone and his mother taught herself piano. He took up guitar when he was 14 and had lessons in jazz with John Mehegan from the age of 18. He then played vibraphone briefly, on which instrument he performed in a group that included the pianist Barry Manilow, and studied classical guitar. Wilkins worked for over a year in big bands, and in 1964 he was a member of a guitar group with Chuck Wayne; however, for much of this period he was occupied mainly with studio work and playing in pit orchestras for Broadway shows. Later he performed at Town Hall in New York with Earl Hines, with whom he recorded in 1973. After appearing in a duo with Michael Moore (i) and recording as the leader of a trio with Moore and Bill Goodwin (*c*1973) he toured for two years with Buddy Rich. In addition he worked with, among others, Stan Getz, Dizzy Gillespie, Mel Tormé, Sarah Vaughan, Morgana King (recording in 1978), and Benny Goodman; in November 1979 he took part in a performance with Goodman's septet which was broadcast on television early the following year. During the 1970s he led his own trio at Jimmy's on 52nd Street, performed regularly at Sweet Basil, often with Eddie Gomez (mid-1970s), and appeared at the Colorado Jazz Party (1974); as a sideman he recorded with Al Dailey (*c*1972), Sonny Fortune (1977), and Bob Brookmeyer and Charles Mingus (both 1978).

In the 1980s Wilkins toured internationally with Manhattan Transfer (1982) and with Claude Bolling and recorded in a duo with Nancy Harrow (1984), in Julius Hemphill's big band (1988), and with Mike Clark (1989). Later he was a member of the group Five Guitars Play Mingus and toured and recorded under Gunther Schuller with the orchestra that performed Charles Mingus's posthumously reconstructed symphony *Epitaph* (early 1990s). In 1992 he recorded in a group co-led by Britt Woodman, Joe Wilder, and John LaPorta, and as a member of the Mingus Epitaph Rhythm Section, alongside the double bass players Michael Formanek and Ed Schuller, the vibraphonist Joe Locke, and either Ronnie Burrage or George Schuller on drums. Wilkins has taught at the Manhattan School of Music (from 1984), the New England Conservatory, New York University, the New School for Social Research, Princeton University, and Long Island University, and he has made an instructional video, *Jack Wilkins Jazz Guitar Workshop* (*c*1997). He should not be confused with the tenor saxophonist and educator Jack Wilkins, who recorded in 1995.

SELECTED RECORDINGS

As leader: *Windows* (*c*1973, Mstr. 396); *Merge* (1977, Chi. 156); *Captain Blued* (*c*1980, Greenstreet 2004); *Call Him Reckless* (1989, Musicmasters 60211); *Alien Army* (1990, Musicmasters 5049-2); *Trio Art* (*c*1998, Arabesque 0135)

As sideman: B. Rich: *Very Live at Buddy's Place* (1974, GrM 3301); B. Brookmeyer: *The Bob Brookmeyer Small Band* (1978, Gryphon 785); J. Hemphill: on *Julius Hemphill Big Band* (1988, Elek. Mus. 9-68031-1), C-Saw; M. Clark: *Give the Drummer Some* (1989, Stash 22); Mingus Epitaph Rhythm Section: *Out of the Blue(s)* (1992, GM 3025); B. Woodman, J. Wilder, and J. LaPorta: *Playing for Keeps* (1992, GM 3026)

BIBLIOGRAPHY

Feather–Gitler'70s

A. Berle: "Jack Wilkins: from Big Bands to Small Clubs, a Jazz Jack of all Trades," *GP*, xii/5 (1978), 30

L. Jeske: "Stateside Scene – East Coast: Tiny, Jack and Chuck," *JJI*, xxxii/2 (1979), 19

T. Lathrop: "Private Lesson: Jack Wilkins Illuminates the Craft of Jazz Guitar," *GP*, xxii/1 (1988), 90 [incl. discography]

GK

Willebrandts, Dick (*b* 1911; *d* 1970). Dutch bandleader. He played piano with Kai Ewans in Copenhagen (1928), led a band with his brother, the pianist Philip Willebrandts (1929–34), and worked with the bass player Jack de Vries (1935–8) and under the bandleader Klaas Van Beeck (1938–40). In 1942 he formed his own band, which made recordings (including *Dick Willebrandts*, 1943, HEP 10) and eventually had as many as 19 members (1944). His career suffered after World War II owing to a belief that he had collaborated with the Nazis. In the late 1950s he led a string orchestra, worked as a piano soloist on radio, and was briefly with a dixieland band and with the OK Wobblers, led by the trombonist Pi Scheffer; he ceased playing in 1963.

WIM VAN EYLE

Willette, Baby Face [Roosevelt James] (*b* New Orleans or Little Rock, AR, 11 Sept 1933). Organist. He was probably born in New Orleans and grew up in Little Rock, but a conclusive source of information concerning this has yet to be found. His father was a minister of a church in Little Rock and his mother was a missionary and pianist. Willette's nickname, Baby Face, came from his youthful appearance and small physical stature. He studied piano from 1938 and in his youth played organ in his father's church. From the early 1950s he worked as a pianist and organist in gospel and rhythm-and-blues groups, touring with, among others, Joe Houston, King Kolax, and Johnny Otis. At some point during these years he made Chicago his home, and while there came to be influenced by local gospel organists; he was also attracted by the recordings of Charlie Parker.

Willette recorded on both piano and organ in a rhythm-and-blues style in 1952 and 1955, but by 1958 he had turned exclusively to jazz and made the organ his principal instrument. Late in January 1961, in New York, he recorded for Blue Note as a sideman with Lou Donaldson and Grant Green and then as a leader; he made another album for Blue Note under his own name in May of that same year. By 1963 he was again living and working in Chicago, where he recorded as a leader for Argo in 1964 and held a residency at the Pershing Hotel. Willette is known to have been performing in Chicago into 1971, but nothing else is known of his later career.

SELECTED RECORDINGS

As leader: *Face to Face* (1961, BN 84068); *Stop and Listen* (1961, BN 84084); *Mo' Rock* (1964, Argo 739); *Behind the 8 Ball* (1964, Argo 749)
As sideman: L. Donaldson: *Here 'Tis* (1961, BN 84066); G. Green: *Grant's First Stand* (1961, BN 84064)

BIBLIOGRAPHY

Feather '60s
<http://www.theatreorgans.com/grounds/doodlin/willette.html> (2001)

GK

William Ransom Hogan Jazz Archive. Archive in 1957 at Tulane University in New Orleans as the Archives of New Orleans Jazz; *see* LIBRARIES AND ARCHIVES, §2.

Williams, Al(fred) (*b* Memphis, 17 Dec 1919; *d* 15 Nov 1998). Pianist. He grew up in Chicago from 1922, studied piano from the age of seven, and worked professionally from the age of 16; when he was in his late teens he studied classical piano and organ at the Lincoln Conservatory in Chicago with Blanche Smith Walton. From 1936 to 1938 he led a 12-piece orchestra that played at dance halls in Chicago. He formed a trio, the Three Dudes (1942), joined Henry "Red" Allen's small group at the Down Beat Room (1943, 1944), and then played with Jimmie Noone and Erskine Tate. In 1945 he married the singer Audrey Hobbs, and in 1948–9 the two performed together as Alfred and Audrey. Williams wrote arrangements for many bands in Chicago, worked in the early 1950s at the Savoy Ballroom, and played in New York with Sam "the Man" Taylor (1956–7) and in dixieland groups at the Metropole (from 1957); one such group, including Allen, gave a jazz and poetry recital with the poet Langston Hughes (1958). He made tours of Europe with Buck Clayton (1959, when he recorded on the album *Copenhagen Concert*, Ste. 6006–7) and Johnny Hodges (1961). Later he recorded as the leader of a trio (1965), played for the satirical revue *The Establishment* (1968), and was the pianist, arranger, and music director for the Deep River Boys, led by Harry Douglas (1975). The social security death index gives his last known residence as Westbury, New York. Williams's style was essentially that of a blues pianist, but it also incorporated some elements of swing. He should not be confused with the New Orleans drummer Alfred Williams (1900–1963).

BIBLIOGRAPHY

FeatherE
A. J. McCarthy: "The Al Williams Story," *JM*, v/8 (1959), 12

JAMES M. DORAN

Williams, Bearcat. *See* WILLIAMS, JOHN (i).

Williams, (Ira) Buddy (*b* New York, 17 Dec 1952). Drummer. He is a nephew of the Adderley brothers' double bass player Walter Booker and consequently played in the band Natural Essence with the pianist and guitarist Nat Adderley, Jr.; while attending the High School of Music and Arts in New York, he recorded an album with the group that was produced by Cannonball Adderley. During his high school years Williams worked with Herbie Mann and the popular singers Roberta Flack (with whom he continued to tour and record through the 1990s) and Luther Vandross, and in 1971 he toured and recorded with the Voices of East Harlem. Throughout the 1970s he worked frequently with the popular singer Bette Midler, both touring and recording, and he appeared with her in the film *The Rose*. In the middle of the decade he was active in New York studios; he performed on albums by a variety of jazz and pop artists, among them Linda and Sonny Sharrock (1975), Eddie Daniels, Cedar Walton, and Hugh Masekela (all 1978), and Bob James and and Lee Ritenour (both 1979). From 1975 to 1986 he worked intermittently as house drummer for the NBC television program "Saturday Night Live."

In 1976 Williams began what became a long relationship with David Sanborn that involved recordings, tours, and an appearance in the video *Love & Happiness* (1986). He also toured frequently with Nat Adderley (1976–8), the singer Chaka Khan (1976–96), the trumpeter Herb Alpert (1978–9), and Sadao Watanabe (1979–90). From 1980 he maintained an enduring affiliation with Manhattan Transfer, during which he toured and recorded with the group. In addition he toured with Grover Washington, Jr. (1984), and continued to record with a variety of artists, notably Dizzy Gillespie and Ben Sidran (both 1981), Aretha Franklin (1982), Dave Grusin and Gerry Mulligan (both 1983), Washington (1984), Tania Maria (1985), Earl Klugh (1986), Carla Bley and Charles Earland (both 1988), and Joey DeFrancesco (1989). Later he toured with Maria (from 1991), George Benson (from 1992), and various pop singers (from 1994), and recorded with Jon Faddis (1991), Ryo Kawasaki (1997), Dave Valentin (1998), and many other jazz and pop artists.

SELECTED RECORDINGS

As sideman: Natural Essence: *In Search of Happiness* (1973, Fan. 9440); L. Sharrock and S. Sharrock: *Paradise* (1975, Atco 36121); N. Adderley: *Don't Look Back* (1976, Ste. 1059); B. Sidran: *Old Songs for the New Depression* (1981, Ant. 1004); D. Grusin: *Night-lines* (1983, GRP 9504); G. Mulligan: *Little Big Horn* (1983, GRP 9503); D. Sanborn: *Straight to the Heart* (1984, WB 25150); Manhattan Transfer: *Live '86* (1986, Atl. 81723); C. Bley: *Fleur Carnivore* (1988, Watt 21); C. Earland: *Front Burner* (1988, Mlst. 9165); J. DeFrancesco: *All of Me* (*c*1989, Col. CK44463); R. Kawasaki: *Live* (1997, One Voice 7)

BIBLIOGRAPHY

R. Tolleson: "Buddy Williams: Going for the Feeling," *MD*, x/3 (1986), 30

RICK MATTINGLY

Williams, Buster [Charles Anthony, Jr.] (*b* Camden, NJ, 17 April 1942). Double bass player. He was taught both double bass and drums by his father, a professional double bass player, but chose to concentrate on double bass after hearing a recording of Oscar Pettiford's solo playing. In 1959 he studied theory, harmony, and composition at Combs College of Music, Philadelphia. After working in the area of Camden (New Jersey) and in Philadelphia with Jimmy Heath (1960) he toured and recorded with a quintet led by Gene Ammons and Sonny Stitt (1960–61). From the early to mid-1960s he worked primarily as an accompanist to singers: Dakota Staton (1961–2), Betty Carter (1962–3), Sarah Vaughan

(1963) and Nancy Wilson (1964–8). During his years with Wilson he moved to Los Angeles, where he performed and recorded with the Jazz Crusaders (1967–9) and Miles Davis (1967) and recorded with Prince Lasha (1967) and the quintet led by Bobby Hutcherson and Harold Land (1967–8).

Late in 1968 Williams settled New York. There he worked with Herbie Mann and Art Blakey (both *c*1969–70), Herbie Hancock (1969–72), with whom he made several recordings, and, for nearly a decade, Mary Lou Williams (1969–78); in 1970 he participated in the premier of *Mary Lou's Mass* at St. Patricks Cathedral. He played in the musical *Company* on Broadway (1970) and recorded with Dexter Gordon (1969, 1972), Hank Jones and Tony Williams (1976), and many others. In a group led by Ron Carter (who functioned as a soloist on piccolo bass, while Williams held the double bass chair) he played in a rhythm section with Kenny Barron, rekindling an association that dated back to their youth in Philadelphia, and with Ben Riley (1976 – early 1980s). These three men performed and recorded independently as a trio from 1978, and, with the addition of Charlie Rouse in 1982, became known as Sphere, a cooperative quartet that performed and recorded to much critical acclaim until shortly before Rouse's death in 1988; the group's repertory included several of Williams's compositions. Williams also performed frequently in a duo with Barron (from around the mid-1970s), performed and recorded with Cedar Walton (from *c*1980) and the Timeless All-Stars (1982–3; *see* Timeless), and recorded a bass duo with Carter and the London Symphony Orchestra for the film *Les choix des armes* (1982). He may be seen with Abdullah Ibrahim in the video *The Cry of Reason: Beyers Naudé: an Afrikaaner Speaks Out* (made at a performance in San Francisco in 1987) and with Hancock's trio in the video *Newport Jazz '88* (1988); he recorded in Ibrahim's group Ekaya in 1989–90.

Williams led several recording sessions from 1976, and in 1989 he decided to focus on this aspect of his career. He formed a quintet, Something More, to perform a repertory comprised, in large part, of his own compositions and to provide a springboard for younger musicians performing in the tradition of the classic bands of Art Blakey and Miles Davis; among his sidemen at various times were Benny Green, Ralph Moore, Stephen Scott, Steve Wilson, Shunzo Ohno, Renee Rosnes, and Billy Drummond. In the late 1990s he also formed a trio with Billy Childs and Carl Allen. From 1997 he again played with Sphere, which re-formed with Gary Bartz as its fourth member. He has taught in the Jazz and Contemporary Music Program at the New School University.

Williams has one of the most distinctive sounds among double bass players in jazz – dark and woody, with a rich growl and a singing upper register. He commands a range of expressive techniques, among them voice-like inflections, slurs and glissandi that can be romantic, plaintive, or coarse, and bluesy, double-stops (which he at times strums, as if he were playing guitar), and hammer-ons and pull-offs that incorporate open strings in patterns of complex cross-rhythms.

SELECTED RECORDINGS

Duos with K. Barron: *Two as One* (1986, Red 214)

As leader: *Crystal Reflections* (1976, Muse 5101); *Heartbeat* (1978, Muse 5171); *Dreams Come True* (1981, Buddah 5728); *Tokudo* (1978, Denon YX7531); with K. Barron and B. Riley: *Green Chimneys* (1983, Criss Cross 1008) *Something More* (1989, In + Out 7004-2); *Somewhere Along the Way* (1996, TCB 97602); *Lost in a Memory* (1998, TCB 99252); with B. Childs and C. Allen: *Skim Coat* (1999, Metropolitan 1116)

As leader of Sphere: (with K. Barron, B. Riley, and C. Rouse): *Four in One* (1982, Elek. Mus. 60166); *Sphere on Tour* (1985, Red 191); *Four for All* (1987, Verve 831674), incl. Bittersweet; (with Barron, Riley, and G. Bartz): *Sphere* (1998, Verve 314-557796-2)

As sideman: G. Ammons and S. Stitt: *Boss Tenors* (1961, Verve 68426); S. Vaughan: *Sassy Swings the Tivoli* (1963, Mer. 60831); N. Wilson: *Lush Life* (1967, Cap. ST2757); H. Hancock: *The Prisoner* (1969, BN 84321); on *Fat Albert Rotunda* (1969, WB 1834), Tell me a bedtime story; M. L. Williams: *Free Spirits* (1975, Ste. 1043); Great Jazz Trio: *Love for Sale* (1976, EW 8046); R. Carter: *Piccolo* (1977, Mlst. 55004); L. Konitz: *Yes, Yes Nonet* (1979, Ste. 1119); James Williams: *The Arioso Touch* (1982, Conc. 192); F. Morgan: *Lament* (1986, Cont. 14021); B. Marsalis: on *Renaissance* (1986–7, Col. FC40711), The Peacocks (1986); R. Rosnes: *Without Words* (1992, BN B21Z-98168)

BIBLIOGRAPHY

Feather–Gitler '70s
D. C. Hunt: "Definitive Bass Artistry: Niels-Henning Ørsted Pedersen and Charles 'Buster' Williams," *J&P*, ix/10 (1970), 43
E. Meadow: "Buster Williams: About Time," *DB*, xxxvii/25 (1970), 20
R. Palmer: "Jazz Lives in New York," *RS*, no.248 (1977), 19
S. Miller: "Riffs: Buster Williams," *DB*, lviii/9 (1991), 12
S. Gribetz: "Buster Williams Counts his Blessings," *JT*, xxii/3 (1992), 37
A. Lewis and L. Lewis: "Buster Williams: Interview," *Cadence*, xxiv/6 (1998), 5
W. Jenkins: "Buster's Onion Theory," *DB*, lxvi/2 (1999), 48
<http://www.busterwilliams.com/busterwillbio.htm> (2000)

JOHN CURRY

Williams, Clarence (*b* Plaquemine, LA, 8 Oct ?1893; *d* New York, 6 Nov 1965). Pianist and composer. He moved to New Orleans in 1906 and traveled with a minstrel show as a singer and dancer in 1911. After returning to New Orleans he began a music publishing venture (*c*1915) with A. J. Piron. Later in the decade he moved briefly to Chicago and then permanently to New York, where he founded a music publishing firm and several music stores; he also organized many recording sessions, principally for OKeh (1923–30). The most important of Williams's groups was the Blue Five. Although it was noted more for its instrumental recordings made under Williams's name, this group was principally an accompanying band for such singers as Eva Taylor (Williams's wife from 1921), Sara Martin, and Sippie Wallace. It first recorded in 1923 with Thomas Morris (cornet), Charlie Irvis or John Mayfield (trombone), Sticky Elliott or Sidney Bechet (reeds), and Buddy Christian (banjo). From 1924 to 1925 the emerging genius of Louis Armstrong (who replaced Morris) rivaled Bechet's previous dominance in the group, and occasionally Buster Bailey, Aaron Thompson (replacing Bechet and Irvis), Coleman Hawkins, and Don Redman were added. This ensemble recorded a number of titles, notably fine versions of *Mandy, make up your mind* and *Cake-walking Babies from Home*. Following the departure of Armstrong and Bechet, the Blue Five, often including Bubber Miley, continued to record into 1927. Williams also made nearly one hundred recordings for OKeh (1927–30), Vocalion (1933–5), and Victor (1937–9) with his "washboard" bands, using such musicians as Ed Allen (cornet), Bailey or Cecil Scott (clarinet), and Floyd Casey (washboard).

Although he recorded more frequently than any other African-American musician of the 1920s (apart from Fletcher Henderson), Williams was a dependable rather than an exceptional pianist; his importance to early jazz lay instead in his gift for organization. He published and promoted the work of such composers as Fats Waller, James P. Johnson, Willie "the Lion" Smith, and, most notably, Spencer Williams. Among his many publications (in which he may have been involved as co-composer) were *Royal Garden Blues*, *Baby, won't you please come home*, *I ain't gonna give nobody none of my jelly roll, 'Tain't nobody's business if I do,* and *Squeeze Me*.

For illustrations *see* Bechet, sidney, and Okeh.

SELECTED RECORDINGS

Duos with Bessie Smith: Down-hearted Blues (1923, Col. 3844); Baby Won't You Please Come Home Blues (1923, Col. 3888); 'Tain't nobody's business if I do (1923, Col. 3898)

As leader of Blue Five: Wild Cat Blues/Kansas City Man Blues (1923, OK 4925); Mandy, make up your mind (1924, OK 40260); Cake-walking Babies from Home (1925, OK 40321)

As leader of other groups: Nobody but my baby is getting my love/Candy Lips (1927, OK 8440); Walk that Broad/Have you ever felt that way? (1928, OK 8629)

As sideman with Bessie Smith: Nobody knows you when you're down and out (1929, Col. 14451D)

BIBLIOGRAPHY

"Clarence Williams: a Specialist on Blues," *Metronome*, xxxix/9 (1923), 78
"Clarence Williams, the Man who Made the Blues Queens only Had Eight Lessons," *Afro-American* (9 Nov 1933), 18
C. E. Smith: "Clarence Williams: the Trail of an Unissued Album Led to the Most Fabulous Jazzman of Them All," *Record Changer*, vii/4 (1948), 6
L. Kunstadt and B. Colton: "Pioneer: Clarence Williams," *Record Research*, no.10 (1952), 8
S. B. Charters and L. Kunstadt: *Jazz: a History of the New York Scene* (Garden City, NY, 1962/*R*1981)
W. Smith and G. Hoefer: *Music on my Mind: the Memoirs of an American Pianist* (Garden City, NY, 1964/*R*1975)
E. Taylor: "My Husband Clarence Williams," *Sv*, no.13 (1967), 22
B. Rust: "Clarence Williams: an Appreciation," *Sv*, no.13 (1967), 25
M. Williams: *Jazz Masters of New Orleans* (New York and London, 1967/*R*1978)
"Looking Back with Eva," *Sv*, no.14 (1967–8), 17; no.15 (1968), 18; no.16 (1968), 19
D. M. Bakker: *Clarence Williams on Microgroove* (Alphen aan de Rijn, Netherlands, 1976)
T. Lord: *Clarence Williams* (Chigwell, England, 1976)

J. R. TAYLOR/R (with MIKE HAZELDINE)

Williams, Claude [Fiddler] (*b* Muskogee, OK, 22 Feb 1908). Violinist. He first played with a string band in local hotels, joined a roadshow, and worked in Oklahoma with the band of Oscar Pettiford and his brothers. In 1928 he joined Terrence Holder's important territory band, with which he remained after it became the Clouds of Joy under the leadership of Andy Kirk the following year. After a period with Alphonso Trent (1932) he performed in Chicago with Nat "King" Cole and Cole's brother, the double bass player Eddie Cole. Williams played guitar in Count Basie's orchestra from 1936 until March 1937, when he was replaced by Freddie Green. During the following decades he worked in obscurity as a guitarist in Michigan (1940s), as a member of the rhythm-and-blues band led by Roy Milton (early 1950s), and in Kansas City (from 1952), where he spent a period with Eddie "Cleanhead" Vinson (late 1950s). A recording as both violinist and guitarist with Jay McShann in 1972 revived his career, and Williams subsequently toured with McShann in the 1970s and appeared as a soloist at jazz festivals into the 1980s. He also toured as a soloist with the musical *Black and Blue* (1981) and the show *Masters of the Folk Violin* (1988). Williams remained active through the 1990s, working regularly in a swing string trio in Kansas City and in the Statesmen of Jazz in New York (from 1994). He served as a consultant for the film *Kansas City* (1996), toured Europe with Red Richards and Norris Turney (1997), and accompanied Etta Jones at the Charlie Parker Jazz Festival in Tompkins Square Park, New York (1998). His fluent style was influenced chiefly by the work of Joe Venuti.

Oral history material in *DSI* (JOHP); video oral history material in *NCH* (HCJA).

SELECTED RECORDINGS

As leader: *Call for the Fiddler* (1976, Ste. 1051); *Live at J's*, i–ii (1989, Arhoolie 405); *Swingtime in New York* (1994, Prog. 7093); *King of Kansas City* (1996, Prog. 7100)

As sideman: A. Kirk: Loose Ankles (1930, Bruns. 4803); C. Basie: St. Louis Blues, first issued on *The Count at the Chatterbox: 1937* (1937, Jazz Archives 16); J. McShann: *The Man from Muskogee* (1972, Sack. 3005)

SELECTED FILMS AND VIDEOS

The Last of the Blue Devils (1979); Confessin' the Blues: the Music of Jay McShann (1987); Fiddler's Dream (1987); Statesmen of Jazz (n.d. [filmed 1994])

BIBLIOGRAPHY

ChiltonW; *Feather–Gitler '70s*
B. Becker: "Claude Williams: Interview," *Cadence*, v/9 (1979), 8
S. Yanow: "Claude Williams: Interview," *Cadence*, v/10 (1979), 19
M. L. Hester: *Going to Kansas City* (Sherman, TX, 1980), 157
M. Glaser: "Williams on the Warpath: a Jazz Great Plays *Cherokee*," *Strings*, iv/2 (1989), 28 [incl. transcr.]
M. L. Hester: "The Fiddler will Play," *MR*, xvi/3 (1989), 8
J. L. Lieberman: "Claude Williams: Fiddling with Feeling," *Frets*, xi/1 (1989), 53 [incl. transcr.]
C. Battestini and J.-P. Battestini: "Claude Fiddler Williams," *BHcF*, no.435 (1995), 1
B. Donaldson: "An Interview with Claude 'Fiddler' Williams," *Marge Hofacre's Jazz News*, xiii (1997), Jan–Feb, 21 [incl. discography]
C. Haddix: "The Fiddler's Triumph: Claude Williams," *DB*, lxvi/3 (1999), 32

CHRIS SHERIDAN

Williams, Cootie [Charles Melvin] (*b* Mobile, AL, 10 July 1911; *d* New York, 15 Sept 1985). Trumpeter and bandleader. Most reference books give his birthdate as 24 July 1910. Without identifying a source, the *New York Times* obituary gives his age as 77, indicating 1908 as his year of birth; however, from his research for WKCR-FM, New York, Phil Schaap asserts that the correct date is 10 July 1911, and the social security death index confirms Schaap's research. Williams reportedly generated his nickname at the age of five in response to being asked what he had heard at a band concert: "Cootie, cootie, cootie," he replied. In school he played drums, trombone, and tuba before changing to trumpet, and he toured with the Young family band (which included Lester Young) when he was only 14. In 1928 he went to New York, where he made his first recordings (with James P. Johnson) and played briefly in the bands of Chick Webb and Fletcher Henderson. By February 1929 he had joined the Duke Ellington Orchestra as a replacement for Bubber Miley, beginning a long association which was to make him famous. In his first 11 years with Ellington his playing became an indispensable part of the band's sonority, and Ellington integrated solos for him into hundreds of compositions. Williams also took part in many excellent small-group recordings with Teddy Wilson, Billie Holiday, Lionel Hampton, Charlie Christian, and other leading jazz musicians of the swing period.

After leaving Ellington in November 1940, Williams played for a year in Benny Goodman's band and small groups, then formed his own successful big band, which was booked several times at the Savoy Ballroom, New York, and included some important aspiring bop musicians such as Bud Powell, Thelonious Monk, Eddie "Lockjaw" Davis, and Charlie Parker; Joe Guy, George Treadwell, Money Johnson, Louis Bacon, and Sam "the Man" Taylor also played in the band in its early years. Pearl Bailey and Eddie "Cleanhead" Vinson were Williams's singers, and from 1944 to early 1946 his band often accompanied Ella Fitzgerald. Gradually, though still at the height of his powers, Williams faded from public view. Forced to reduce his band to a smaller ensemble in 1948, and finally to discontinue it altogether, he became

Cootie Williams (left) with Harry James (trumpet) and Benny Goodman (clarinet), 1941

active as a rhythm-and-blues musician. From 1955 to 1962, until it closed, he once again led a band at the Savoy. Together with Rex Stewart he headed an all-star swing band for recording sessions in 1957–8. In late July 1962 he began a two-month tour with Goodman. He then rejoined Ellington's band, where he remained, with brief interruptions, until the late 1970s.

Williams was a master of swing-style jazz trumpet playing, and achieved a range of tone and shading on his instrument that was unsurpassed in his day. Having quickly mastered the growl and plunger effects of Bubber Miley, his predecessor in Ellington's band, Williams extended these techniques to encompass an unprecedented variety of moods and timbres, from gentle nostalgia to searing vehemence. Although he remained supreme in the use of the growl and plunger mutes, Williams was equally adept on the open instrument, particularly as an accompanist to jazz singers and as an interpreter of the blues. His playing inspired Ellington to one of his greatest masterpieces, the *Concerto for Cootie* (1940), where Williams may be heard using straight mute, plunger mute, and open trumpet. In later years his style lost some of its subtlety but none of its urgency and swing, as attested by his performance in the *New Concerto for Cootie* (1963), written by Ellington to celebrate his return to the band.

Williams was also an effective if reluctant jazz singer, and collaborated with Ellington on several pieces, such as *Echoes of the Jungle.* His big band made the first recording of Thelonious Monk's *'Round Midnight*; Williams is credited as a co-composer of this well-known ballad, evidently because he was the bandleader and because he contributed passages to this early arrangement that were later discarded from standard versions of the piece.

Oral history material in *NjR* (JOHP).

For further illustration *see* TRUMPET.

SELECTED RECORDINGS

As leader: Diga diga doo (1937, Var. 555); West End Blues (1941, OK 6370); 'Round Midnight (1944, Hit 7119); *Cootie in Hi-fi* (1958, RCA LPM1718)

As leader with R. Stewart: *The Big Challenge* (1957, Jzt. 1268); *Porgy and Bess Revisited* (1958, WB 1260)

As sideman with F. Henderson: The Wang-wang Blues (1929, Col. 1913D)

As sideman with D. Ellington: Ring dem bells (1930, Vic. 22528); Echoes of the Jungle (1931, Vic. 22743); Echoes of Harlem (Cootie's Concerto) (1936, Bruns. 7650); The New East St. Louis Toodle-oo (1937, Master 101); Concerto for Cootie (1940, Vic. 26598); Harlem Air Shaft (1940, Vic. 26731); *Suite Thursday* (1963, Atl. 2-304), incl. New Concerto for Cootie

SELECTED FILMS AND VIDEOS

Black and Tan (1929); Symphony in Black (1934); Cootie Williams and his Orchestra (1944); Duke Ellington and his Orchestra (1965); Duke Ellington in Europe: 1969 (1969)

BIBLIOGRAPHY

ConnorBG; *McCarthyB*; *SchullerS*; *TuckerDE*

A. Hodeir: *Hommes et problèmes du jazz, suivi de La religion du jazz* (Paris, 1954; Eng. trans., rev. Hodeir, as *Jazz: its Evolution and Essence*, New York, 1956/*R*1975)

H. P[anassié]: "Réflexions sur la récente tournée Cootie Williams," *BHcF*, no.86 (1959), 10

D. Hartmann: "Discography of Cootie Williams," *Jazz-Statistics* (1960), no.16, p.1; no. 17, [p.8]

J. Bradley and J. R. Failows: "Cootie Speaks," *Coda*, v/9 (1963), 2

W. Balliett: *Such Sweet Thunder* (Indianapolis, 1966), 108

V. Wilmer: "Cootie Williams," *JM*, xiii/6 (1967), 2

S. Dance: *The World of Duke Ellington* (London and New York, 1970/*R*1981), 102

V. Wilmer: "You Got to Keep Creating," *MM* (8 March 1975), 47

E. Townley: "Reminiscing with Cootie Williams," *Sv*, no.71 (1977), 170

C. Battestini and J.-P Battestini: "Cootie Williams parle de son grand orchestre (1942–1947)," *BHcF*, no.283 (1980), 9

E. Lambert: "Regal Cootie," *JJI*, xxxiv/2 (1981), 18

T. Burke and D. Penny: "The Cootie Williams Orchestra, 1942–1950," *Blues & Rhythm*, no.3 (1984), 12

Obituary, C. G. Fraser, *New York Times* (16 Sept 1985)

S. Nicholson: *Ella Fitzgerald, 1917–1996: a Biography of the First Lady of Jazz* (London, 1993)

B. Kernfeld: *What to Listen for in Jazz* (New Haven, CT, and London, 1995)

J. BRADFORD ROBINSON/BK

Williams, David [Happy] (*b* Port of Spain, Trinidad, West Indies, 17 Sept 1946). Double bass player. He studied violin at school and double bass with his father, a well-known player in the West Indies. Later he worked in New York with Beaver Harris (1969) and received tuition from Ron Carter. After playing with Chuck Mangione in Rochester, New York (1969–70), he performed and recorded with the popular singer Roberta Flack (1970–72). Thereafter he worked with Ornette Coleman, Donald Byrd, Charles McPherson, and Billy Taylor (ii), performed and recorded with Duke Jordan (1973), and recorded with Charles Davis and Kenny Barron (1974, playing both double bass and electric bass guitar). In 1975 Williams toured Europe with Elvin Jones and recorded in Rome with Don Pullen, George Adams, and Archie Shepp; following his return to the USA he continued to work with Jones (1975–6) and recorded with Sam Jones (1976), Art Pepper (1976, 1981), and Hadley Caliman (1977).

In 1983 Williams began performing and recording in various contexts with Cedar Walton: under the pianist's name, as a member of Walton's group Eastern Rebellion, and together at recording sessions led by Slide Hampton (1985), Steve Grossman (1985, 1993), Dave Pike (in the Netherlands, 1986), James Clay and Christopher Hollyday (both 1989), Terumasa Hino (1992–3), and Billy Higgins (1993). From the late 1980s he has performed and recorded further with Barron. Aside from these two affiliations Williams performed and recorded with small groups led by Woody Shaw (1986–7), Michael Carvin and David "Fathead"

Newman (both late 1980s), and Frank Morgan (1990–91), and with Clifford Jordan's big band (1991). In addition he worked with Stan Getz (1988) and again with Elvin Jones (1997) and recorded with Abdullah Ibrahim's group Ekaya (1985, 1988), Ronnie Mathews (1992), Larry Willis (1992–3), Ron Holloway (with Barron on piano, 1995), and Jackie McLean (2000).

SELECTED RECORDINGS

As sideman: E. Jones: *New Agenda* (1975, Van. 79362); C. Hollyday: *Christopher Hollyday* (1989, Novus 3055-2-N); K. Barron: *Invitation* (1990, Criss Cross 1044); B. Higgins: *Billy Higgins Quintet* (1993, Sweet Basil 8003), incl. The Vision; R. Holloway: *Struttin'* (1995, Mlst. 9238), incl. Amazon River, Come Rain or Come Shine, Dr. Free Zee/Mr. X

BIBLIOGRAPHY

Feather–Gitler '70s

K. Bennett: "The Bottom Line: Bob Cranshaw, George Mraz & David Williams Bare the Soul of Jazz Bass," *Musician*, no.211 (1996), 34

BK

Williams, Douglas (A.) (*b c* mid-1890s; *d* in or after 1942). Clarinetist. Nothing is known with certainty about the career of this artist before his arrival in Memphis to record for Victor in January 1928. At nine recording sessions (up to June 1930) he and his band, notably including the cornetist Nathaniel Williams, the pianist Edgar Brown, and the drummer Sam Sims, recorded some of the most passionate and blues-drenched jazz of the era. During this time Williams worked mainly at roadhouses and summer camps in country areas around Memphis. He left Memphis in 1935, and by 1937 was resident in St. Louis, where he organized another territory band, one of whose sidemen was the blues singer and guitarist J. D. Short. His name last appears in the city directory for 1942.

SELECTED RECORDINGS

(all recorded for Victor)

Duos with E. Brown: Buddy George/Neal's Blues (1928, 38518)

As leader: Roadhouse Stomp (1928, 21269); Far Away Texas Blues (1928, 21413); Memphis Gal (1929, 23362); Clarinet Jiggles (1929, 23337); Louisiana Hop/Three o'Clock Blues (1930, 38623)

BIBLIOGRAPHY

D. Raichelson: Liner notes, *Douglas Williams, 1928–1930* (Jazz Oracle 8012, 1999)

HOWARD RYE

Williams, Eddie [Edward] (*b* New York, *c*1910). Saxophonist. In the early 1930s he worked with Claude Hopkins and led his own band at the Savoy Ballroom, New York. He made recordings on clarinet with the Mills Blue Rhythm Band under Lucky Millinder (notably *Blue Rhythm Fantasy/Jungle Madness*, 1937, Var. 503) and with Billy Kyle (including *Margie*, 1937, Var. 531), on tenor saxophone with Don Redman (1939), and on alto saxophone with Jelly Roll Morton (1940); Morton's *Swinging the Elks* (General Tavern Tunes 1711) displays his unusual, "slippery" tone. After a further period with Millinder he played with Ella Fitzgerald (1941), Henry "Red" Allen and Chris Columbus (1942), and the De Paris brothers, Redman, Cliff Jackson, and James P. Johnson (all 1943–4) and performed and recorded on tenor saxophone on the West Coast with Garvin Bushell (late 1944). During his military service (1945–6) he played in Europe, and from the late 1940s he led his own small band. In the 1960s he was a regular member of Happy Caldwell's band. (*ChiltonW*)

HOWARD RYE

Williams, Elmer (A.) [Tone] (*b* Red Bank, NJ, 1905; *d* Red Bank, June 1962). Tenor saxophonist and clarinetist. He worked from 1926 to 1928 with Horace Henderson and from 1928 to 1935 with Chick Webb, with whom he appeared in the short film *After Seben* (1929); he also played briefly with McKinney's Cotton Pickers in summer 1931 and with Lucky Millinder early in 1932. Williams spent two lengthy periods in Fletcher Henderson's band (October 1935 – November 1936, February 1937 – spring 1939) and was then again with the latter's brother Horace (June 1939 – September 1940). He performed and recorded as a tenor saxophonist with Ella Fitzgerald (1942) and Millinder (1944–5) and worked with Claude Hopkins (1946) and once more with Fletcher Henderson (July 1950), this last just before a tour with the drummer Herbert Cowens. In the late 1950s he played in Milan with the tenor saxophonist Freddy Mitchell.

SELECTED RECORDINGS

As sideman with C. Webb: Stomping at the Savoy (1934, Col. 2926D); Lonesome Moments (1934, OK 41572); Don't be that way (1934, Decca 483)

BIBLIOGRAPHY

AllenH; ChiltonW

J. Evensmo: *The Tenor Saxophones of Budd Johnson, Cecil Scott, Elmer Williams, Dick Wilson, 1927–1942* (n.p. [Oslo], n.d. [?1977]) [discography]

J. Evensmo: *History of Jazz Tenor Saxophone: Black Artists*, i: *1917–1934* (Oslo, 1996); ii: *1935–1939* (Oslo, 1997); iii: *1940–1944* (Oslo, 1997)

HOWARD RYE, BK

Williams, Fess [Stanley R.] (*b* Danville, KY, 10 April 1894; *d* New York, 17 Dec 1975). Bandleader, clarinetist, and alto saxophonist. He began playing violin, but after 1909 concentrated on clarinet. In 1914 he moved to Cincinnati, where he later worked as a leader (1919–23). After settling in New York (1924) he led his own Royal Flush Orchestra (from 1925), which was resident at the Savoy Ballroom (1926 – January 1928); he made a number of recordings with the band as a singer, clarinetist, and alto saxophonist. Although Williams was capable of intense and effective blues playing, his style was marked by an extensive use of novelty effects. This has tended to obscure the quality of his bands, which recorded some of the finest examples of the Harlem style of the later 1920s, prominently featuring the trumpeter George Temple, the trombonist David "Jelly" James, and the pianist Hank Duncan, among other excellent soloists. Williams's vocal work includes "talking blues" in the manner of Bert Williams (*Gambler's Blues/I wasn't scared, but I just thought I had better go*, 1927). In 1928 he acted as the leader of Dave Peyton's band in Chicago. Having returned to New York (1929) he led his own bands there and on tour during the 1930s; among his sidemen in the early 1930s were Bob Shoffner, Rex Stewart, Albert Nicholas, Garvin Bushell, and Jerome Don Pasquall. He then ceased full-time playing but continued to lead a small group in the 1940s. In the 1960s he performed occasionally and managed a vocal group. Williams's brother was a musician, as were his children.

SELECTED RECORDINGS

As leader: Green River Blues (1925, Gen. 3182); Make me know it (1926, OK 8322); Atlanta Black Bottom (1926, Voc. 1058); White Ghost Shivers (1927, Voc. 1085); Gambler's Blues/I wasn't scared, but I just thought I had better go (1927, Voc. 1087); Variety Stomp/Phantom Blues (1927, Voc. 15550); Number Ten/Razor Edge (1927, Bruns. 3596); A Few Riffs/Do Shuffle (1929, Vic. 38064); Hot Town/Kentucky Blues (1929, Vic. 38077); Hot Mama (1930, Vic. 22864); All for Grits and Gravy (1930, Vic. 23025)

BIBLIOGRAPHY

ChiltonW; McCarthyB
H. Smith: "The Fess Williams Story," *Record Research*, iii/3 (1957), 3
F. Driggs: "Good-bye Fess," *Sv*, no.67 (1976), 14
D. Barker: *A Life in Jazz*, ed. A. Shipton (London and New York, 1986)

based on *ChiltonW*

Williams, Fiddler. *See* WILLIAMS, CLAUDE.

Williams, Franc(is) (*b* McConnell's Mills, PA, 20 Sept 1910; *d* Houston, PA, 2 Oct 1983). Trumpeter. He first performed with the reed player Marion Sears in Cleveland (1930) and the Chicago Nightingales, led by the trombonist Frank Terry (1930s), then in 1940 moved to New York and toured with the big band that Fats Waller directed for his stage shows. He continued to be associated with big bands, including those of Claude Hopkins, Edgar Hayes, Ella Fitzgerald (1941–2), Sabby Lewis (1943), and Machito (1944), before working with the Duke Ellington Orchestra (1945–9). An example of his solo playing may be heard on the third chorus of *Trumpet No End,* recorded with Ellington in 1946; he may be seen with the band in the short film *Symphony in Swing* (1949). During the 1950s and 1960s Williams played mainly with Latin bands and in theater orchestras, though he rejoined Ellington briefly in 1951. Thereafter he worked with Clyde Bernhardt, led his own quartet in New York, toured overseas as a solo artist, and from 1972 performed in the Harlem Blues and Jazz Band. From the late 1970s he was a member of Panama Francis's Savoy Sultans (ii).

Oral history material in *CtY.*

SELECTED RECORDINGS

As sideman: D. Ellington: Trumpet No End [Blue Skies] (1946, Musi. 484); Harlem Blues and Jazz Band: on *The Harlem Blues and Jazz Band: 1973–1980* (1973–80, Barron 403), Route 66 (1977); C. Bernhardt: *Clyde Bernhardt and the Harlem Blues and Jazz Band* (1977, Barron 7.402); P. Francis: *Grooving* (1982, Stash 218)

BIBLIOGRAPHY

ChiltonW; McCarthyB
E. Townley: "Franc Williams," *Sv*, no.70 (1977), 124
"Francis Williams," *BHcF*, no.267 (1978), 4
C. E. B. Bernhardt and S. Harris: *I Remember: Eighty Years of Black Entertainment, Big Bands, and the Blues* (Philadelphia, 1986), 159
L. Wright: *"Fats" in Fact* (Chigwell, England, 1992)
B. Kernfeld: *What to Listen for in Jazz* (New Haven, CT, and London, 1995)

EDDIE LAMBERT

Williams, Henry "Rubberlegs." *See* WILLIAMS, RUBBERLEGS.

Williams, Jackie (Arthur) (*b* New York, 2 Jan 1933). Drummer. He played piano before taking up drums, which he studied from 1949 to 1951. In the mid-1950s he worked as a freelance, and from the late 1950s he was with Buck Clayton, with whom he recorded in 1963. He first performed with the Saints and Sinners, co-led by Red Richards and Vic Dickenson, in summer 1961, and returned to the group intermittently from 1963 to 1966, recording with it in London in October 1965. In the 1960s he led his own trio and worked with Edmond Hall (spring 1961, early 1962, September 1963), Buster Bailey (September 1961), Earl Hines (autumn 1966), Joe Muranyi (late 1968), and Teddy Wilson (1969), and as well as with Roy Eldridge, Eddie Condon, Illinois Jacquet, Clark Terry, and the singer Odetta. In the early 1970s Williams began associations with Buddy Tate (with whom he recorded in 1973, 1975, and 1981) and Bobby Hackett, and he continued to appear with Dickenson, recording in a group co-led by Hackett and Dickenson in 1973 and under Dickenson's sole leadership in 1974 and 1976; he also recorded with Big Chief Moore (1973) and Billy Butler (1974). In March 1975 he performed in Paris in a quartet consisting of Johnny Guarnieri, Jimmy Shirley, and Slam Stewart. He recorded under the leadership of each of his three bandmates, and all four men recorded together as accompanists to Stephane Grappelli; another session was led by the pianist Pat Flowers, who took Guarnieri's place in the quartet for the occasion. In January 1976 Williams played in a group co-led by Doc Cheatham and Herb Hall. He recorded with Cliff Smalls (1976), Alberta Hunter (1977–*c*1979), and Zoot Sims (1978), appeared with Dickenson in Eddie "Lockjaw" Davis's group at the Grande Parade du Jazz in Nice (1978) and at a memorial tribute to Hackett (1979), and worked with Jay McShann (*c*1977 – mid-1980s); at the Kool Jazz Festival in 1982 he performed in both McShann's quartet and the group Jay McShann and his Kansas City Stompers, which included Buddy Tate and Al Grey.

Having worked with Cheatham again late in 1979, between 1980 and the trumpeter's death in 1997 Williams appeared regularly alongside Chuck Folds in Cheatham's quartet for Sunday brunch at Sweet Basil. He also often accompanied Maxine Sullivan (recording with her in 1984–6). In early 1985 he was a founding member of Howard Alden and Dan Barrett's quintet, and from the mid-1980s he performed with, among others, Milt Hinton, Ralph Sutton, Harold Ashby, Billy Mitchell, and Keith Ingham. At the JVC Jazz Festival New York in 1988 he participated in Ruby Braff's presentation *A Night for Lady Day.* Later he appeared at the Floating Jazz Festival, where he recorded with the pianist Jesse Green (1993) and performed (from 1994) and recorded (from 1995) in Junior Mance's trio. During the 1990s Williams recorded with Alain Bouchet (1990), Benny Waters (1993), the cabaret singer Bobby Short (from 1993), and Bob Barnard (1995).

Video oral history material in *NCH* (HCJA).

SELECTED RECORDINGS

Duos with C. Folds: *It's Rag Time* (1974, Jazzways 106/4)
As leader with J. Mance and K. Betts: *The Floating Jazz Festival Trio, 1995* (1995, Chi. 340)
As sideman: B. Tate: *The Texas Twister* (1975, MJR 8128); J. Guarnieri: *Walla Walla* (1975, BB 33078); J. McShann: *The Last of the Blue Devils* (1977, Atl. 8800); H. Alden and D. Barrett: *Swing Street* (1986, Conc. 349), incl. Fun City Swinger; *The A.B.Q. Salutes Buck Clayton* (1989, Conc. 4395); M. Hinton: on *Old Man Time* (1989–90, Chi. 310), Girl of my Dreams, This Time it's Up; D. Cheatham: *The Eighty-seven Years of Doc Cheatham* (1992, Col. CK53215); J. Mance: *Blue Mance* (1994, Chi. 331)

BIBLIOGRAPHY

Feather–GitlerBEJ
M. Selchow: *Profoundly Blue: a Bio-discographical Scrapbook on Edmond Hall* (Lübbecke, Germany, 1988)
——: *Ding! Ding!: a Bio-discographical Sketchbook on Vic Dickenson* (Westoverledingen, Germany, 1998)

BK, GK

Williams, James (Edward) (*b* Memphis, 8 March 1951). Pianist. He began learning piano at the age of 13 and at first played gospel music and rhythm-and-blues; he did not become interested in jazz until he began attending Memphis State University, where he majored in music education (BS 1974). After graduating he moved to Boston, where he taught at the Berklee College of Music (1974–7) and worked with many groups in the area, including those of Alan Dawson (1976–7), Joe Henderson, Woody Shaw, Milt Jackson, and Clark Terry. His most famous association was with Art

Blakey's Jazz Messengers (October 1977–1981), during which he matured as both a pianist and a composer. From the late 1970s Williams recorded as a leader, often with groups that involved Billy Pierce and Bill Easley; in 1982–3 he co-led a group with Pierce. He then led his own groups Progress Report (1985–93) and the Magical Trio (1988–90); among his sidemen on tour were Pierce, Kevin Eubanks, Rufus Reid, and Billy Higgins. In the mid-1980s he worked occasionally as a sideman with Sonny Stitt, Louis Hayes (1982), Slide Hampton, and Sadao Watanabe (in Tokyo, 1985), among others, and he taught at the Hartt School of Music in Hartford, Connecticut (1984–5). He twice toured in summer with a big band under Dizzy Gillespie's leadership (?1987, 1988), and he was a member of Art Farmer's American quintet (1987–91), Milt Jackson's quartet (from 1988), and Elvin Jones's Jazz Machine (1990–91).

In 1989 Williams formed the Contemporary piano ensemble in tribute to Phineas Newborn, and from 1994 he led ICU (Intensive Care Unit), a gospel, jazz, and blues group which has included Pierce or Steve Wilson, John Lockwood, Yoron Israel, and various singers. Through the 1980s and 1990s he recorded as an unaccompanied soloist and a leader, and as a sideman with Wynton Marsalis (1980), Emily Remler and Tal Farlow (both 1982), Frank Gordon and Watanabe (both 1985), Peter Leitch, Marvin "Smitty" Smith, and Tom Harrell (all 1989), Easley and Clifford Jordan (both 1990), Greg Abate, Javon Jackson, and Joe Wilder (all 1991), Eddie Gomez and Rickey Woodard (1992), Kenny Burrell (1993), Eubanks, Rick Margitza, and Ronald Muldrow (all 1994), Kevin Mahogany (1995), and Greg Osby (*c*1996). Williams is interviewed in the documentary film *Benny Carter: Symphony in Riffs* (1989) and performs with Jones's group in the video *Newport Jazz '90* (1990). In New York he heads Finas Sound Productions (named after Newborn), which produces recordings and concerts.

SELECTED RECORDINGS

As unaccompanied soloist: *James Williams at Maybeck: Maybeck Recital Hall Series*, xlii (1995, Conc. 4694)

Duos with D. Irwin: *Focus* (1977, Red 132)

As leader: *Everything I Love* (1979, Conc. 104); *Images* (1980, Conc. 140); *The Arioso Touch* (1982, Conc. 192); *Alter ego* (1984, Sunnyside 1007); *Progress Report* (1985, Sunnyside 1012); *Magical Trio*, i–ii (1987–8, EmA 832859-1, 834368-1); *Meet the Magical Trio* (1988, EmA 838653-2); *Talkin' Trash* (1993, DIW 887); *Truth, Justice & the Blues* (1994, Evidence 22142); *We've Got What You Need* (1996, Evidence 22207)

As sideman: A. Blakey: *In my Prime* (1977–8, Tim. 114, 118); C. Fuller: *Four on the Outside* (1978, Tim. 124); A. Blakey: *In this Korner* (1978, Conc. 68); *Live at Bubba's* (1980, Who's Who in Jazz 21019); *Album of the Year* (1981, Tim. 155); *Straight Ahead* (1981, Conc. 168); E. Remler: *Take Two* (1982, Conc. 195); T. Farlow: *Cookin' on all Burners* (1982, Conc. 204); J. Walrath: *Master of Suspense* (1986–7, BN 46095); A. Farmer: *Something to Live For* (1987, Cont. 14029); *Blame it on my Youth* (1988, Cont. 14042); M. Smith: *The Road Less Travelled* (1989, Conc. 4389); A. Farmer: *Ph.D.* (1989, Cont. 14055); T. Harrell: on *Visions* (1989, Cont. 14063), Visions of Gaudi; E. Gomez: *Next Future* (1992, Stretch 1106)

BIBLIOGRAPHY

F. Bouchard: "James Williams," *DB*, xlv/16 (1978), 48

J. Williams: "How to Write for the Jazz Messengers," *DB*, xlvi/17 (1979), 89

B. Rusch: "James Williams: Interview," *Cadence*, vii/10 (1981), 10

S. Vandermark: "James Williams," *Cadence*, x (1984), no.4, p.15; no.5, p.5

J. W. Poses: "Profile: James Williams," *DB*, lv/9 (1988), 47

E. Berger: *Bassically Speaking: an Oral History of George Duvivier* (Metuchen, NJ, and London, 1993), 185

E. Rideout: "Gospel: Caution: Tunes in your Hymnal May be Hipper than They Appear: a Private Lesson with James Williams," *Keyboard*, xxii/2 (1996), 56

J. Woodard: "James Williams: l'ambassadeur de Memphis," *Jh*, no.528 (1996), 21

W. Jenkins: "Spirits in Sound: James Williams," *JT*, xxviii/8 (1998), 44

SCOTT YANOW/BK

Williams, J. C. *See* Williams, johnny (ii).

Williams, Jeff(rey Lawrence) (*b* Mount Vernon, OH, 6 July 1950). Drummer. He grew up in Oberlin, Ohio; both of his parents were jazz fans, and his mother worked as a singer in New York during the 1960s. Williams began teaching himself drums around the age of seven and first played professionally in his mid-teens. Later he studied arranging and composition at the Berklee School of Music (from 1968) and had private drum lessons with Alan Dawson; around the 1980s he received further tuition from Dawson. In 1970 he returned to Ohio and worked mainly outside of music. After playing briefly in New York with Dave Liebman, Richard Beirach, Frank Tusa, and the drummer Bob Josbe (all late 1971) he joined the group led by Marc Cohen (who later became known as Marc Copland) and served as the house drummer in Cohen's loft. In 1972 he began what became a long-lasting association with Lee Konitz, with whom he worked intermittently into the 2000s. Following a period with Stan Getz (late 1972 – early 1973) he toured and recorded with Liebman and Beirach's group Lookout Farm (to 1976); together with Liebman, Beirach, Tusa, and Badal Roy, he published the instructional book *Lookout Farm: a Case Study of Improvisation for Small Jazz Groups* (New York, 1978). Williams also worked in Beirach's trio (recording in 1974–5) and recorded with Tusa (1976), David Eyges (1977), and the pianist Richard Sussman (1978).

In the 1980s Williams was a member of the cooperative trio Interplay with Peter Madsen and Anthony Cox (1984–6), toured with Getz (1988), and took part in the PBS program "Jazz Club" with the quintet led by Art Farmer and Clifford Jordan (1989). Later he worked regularly with Tim Hagans (1992), in Joe Lovano's quartet (1992, alongside Tom Harrell and Cox) and his sextet Universal Language (touring in 1993–4), with Peggy Stern (from the early 1990s), and in a quartet with Neal Kirkwood, Lindsey Horner, and Erwin Vann (from 1993). As a freelance he performed on recordings by the guitarist Ron Getz, Frank Kimbrough, and Rudy Linka (all 1988), Paul Bley, Kevin Hays, and Mike Richmond (all 1991), and Ron McClure (1996). Between 1991 and 1996 Williams led his own small group, Coalescence, with Hays and Doug Weiss as his sidemen, and in 1997 he formed the trio Circadian Rhythms with Tony Malaby and Michael Formanek. He also formed another trio, Left-handed Compliment, with the alto saxophonist John O'Gallagher and Madsen (on Hammond organ). In the late 1990s he joined groups led by the pianist Roberta Piket and the trumpeter Dave Ballou, and from 2000 he toured with McClure in Konitz's trio.

SELECTED RECORDINGS

As leader: *Coalescence* (1991, Ste. 31308); *Jazzblues* (1995, Willful 7695)

As sideman: D. Liebman: *Lookout Farm* (1973, ECM 1039); R. Beirach: *Eon* (1974, ECM 1054); *Methuselah* (1975, Trio [Jap.] PA7128); R. Getz: *Ego State* (1988, Alithea [unnumbered]); M. Richmond: *Blue in Green* (1991, Ste. 31296); P. Bley: *Paul Bley Plays Carla Bley* (1991, Ste. 31303); L. Konitz and P. Stern: *Lunasea* (1992, SN 121249-2); P. Stern: *Pleiades* (1993, Philology 82.2); R. McClure: *Pink Cloud* (1996, Naxos Jazz 86002)

BIBLIOGRAPHY

L. Nai: "Jeff Williams: Interview," *Cadence*, xxv/2 (1999), 8

<http://www.willfulmusic.com/> (2000) [incl. discography]

P. Madsen: "Jeff Williams – Drums in the House," <http://www.allaboutjazz.com/articles/wojb0500.htm> (2000)

GK

Williams, Jessica (Jennifer) (*b* Baltimore, 17 March 1948). Pianist. She took up piano at the age of seven and when she was nine enrolled at the Peabody Conservatory, where her first teacher, Richard Aitken, introduced her to jazz at an early stage and encouraged her to transcribe solos. She worked in the Baltimore area from the age of 14 and gave up lessons two years later, after Aitken had left the conservatory and her new teacher refused to let her improvise. While living in Philadelphia (from *c*1970) she worked with Lex Humphries and Philly Joe Jones and played in various Hammond organ groups. Later she moved to San Francisco (*c*1977), where she began performing as an unaccompanied soloist (1979); in addition she worked as the house pianist at the Keystone Korner and led a trio and an 11-piece ensemble, Liberation Army, which included Eddie Henderson. Although Williams used electronic keyboards during the 1970s, she later concentrated exclusively on acoustic piano. From October 1985 she lived briefly in Munich, but soon afterwards she returned to the San Francisco Bay area; she recorded there with Charlie Rouse in 1988. Around 1990 she began to gain more public prominence and to perform internationally. She moved around 1993 to the Pacific Northwest, where she has led a trio, and in 1995 she toured Europe as an unaccompanied soloist. At her best Williams is a powerful and brilliant pianist whose style is characterized by a swirl of broken rhythms, displaced fragments of melody, and hard-edged left-hand figures, which are delivered with a sense of wit and adventure. Her strongest influences are McCoy Tyner and Thelonious Monk.

SELECTED RECORDINGS

As unaccompanied soloist: *Jessica Williams at Maybeck: Maybeck Recital Series*, xxi (1992, Conc. 4525); *The Next Step* (1993, Hep 2054); *Arrival* (1993, Jazz Focus 001); *Gratitude* (1995, Can. 79721); *Intuition* (1995, Jazz Focus 010); *The Victoria Concert* (1995, Jazz Focus 015)

As leader: *Orgonomic Music* (1979, Clean Cuts 703); *Update* (1982, Clean Cuts 706); *Nothin' but the Truth* (1986, Black Hawk 51301); *...And Then, There's This* (1990, Tim. 345); *Momentum* (1994, Jazz Focus 003); *A Song that I Heard* (1994, Hep 2061); *Encounters* (1994, Jazz Focus 005); *Inventions* (1995, Jazz Focus 008); *Jessica's Blues* (1996, Jazz Focus 018); *Higher Standards* (1996, Can. 79736)

BIBLIOGRAPHY

CarrJ
J. N. Thomas: "Profile: Jessica Williams," *DB*, xlviii/6 (1981), 53
M. Unterbrink: *Jazz Women at the Keyboard* (Jefferson, NC, and London, 1983), 164
P. Elwood: "Jazz Composer Says *auf Wiedersehen*," *San Francisco Examiner* (1 Oct 1985)
P. Carles, A. Clergeat, and J.-L. Comolli: *Dictionnaire du jazz* (Paris, 1988, rev. and enlarged 2/1994)
P. Hawes: "Jessica Williams," *JJI*, xlviii/7 (1995), 6
H. Wong: "Jessica Williams: Art & Sorcery," *JT*, xxv/1 (1995), 63

GK

Williams, J. Mayo [Williams, Mayo Jay; Ink] (*b* Monmouth, IL, 26 July 1893; *d* Chicago, 2 Jan 1980). Record producer. His date of birth is taken from his application for social security, which he signed as J. Mayo Williams while stating that his given name was Mayo Jay Williams. After attending Brown University and working for a period as a professional football player, around 1924 he became a producer and talent scout for Paramount's race series in Chicago; he also ran the associated publishing company Chicago Music. In March 1927 he left Paramount to establish his own Chicago Record Company, but its Black Patti label survived only until around September of that year. He worked for the Vocalion and Brunswick race series, and again managed a related publishing operation, which remained in existence after he became head of the race department of the newly formed Decca company (1934). As one of the very few African-Americans employed in positions of responsibility in the recording business before World War II, he played an important role in recording many of the great jazz and blues musicians of the period. In the mid-1940s he worked as a freelance producer and ran a succession of small labels – Chicago, Southern, Harlem, and South Center – whose material was also leased to other companies, such as King and Decca. From the late 1940s his principal label was Ebony, on which he issued both newly recorded material and electronically modified reissues of prewar material. He retired owing to ill-health in the early 1970s.

BIBLIOGRAPHY

S. Dance: "Lightly and Politely 938: Back on the Scene," *JJ*, xvii/6 (1964), 24
R. M. W. Dixon and J. Godrich: *Recording the Blues* (London, 1970)
J. O'Neal and C. Baker: "Chicago Blues Label Guide," *Living Blues*, no.12 (1973), 8
Obituary, J. O'Neal, *Living Blues*, nos.45–6 (1980), 94

HOWARD RYE

Williams, Joe [Goreed, Joseph] (*b* Cordele, GA, 12 Dec 1918; *d* Las Vegas, 30 March 1999). Singer. He grew up in Chicago, where his primary musical influence was the gospel quartet in which he sang, and he began performing professionally in 1937 as a soloist in and around Chicago. Occasionally he sang with bands led by Jimmie Noone (1937), Coleman Hawkins (with whom he toured from Chicago to Memphis in the latter part of 1941), and Red Saunders (at the Club DeLisa in 1945; the detailed chronology in Harris (1979) places Williams regularly with Saunders at the club from 1945, but many other sources contradict this account). He also sang with Lionel Hampton in Boston (1943) and Andy Kirk in New York (1946). A period of ill-health greatly reduced his activities, but he had rejoined Saunders by October 1950, when Count Basie first heard him while both Basie's octet and Saunders's band were at the Club DeLisa. Williams continued with Saunders intermittently through 1953, then from 1954 to 1961 he was a member of Basie's big band, where his dramatic performance of ballads and powerful blues singing were an immediate success; among the many hit recordings he made with the group is *Every day I have the blues* (1955).

Thereafter Williams maintained a career as a soloist, appearing in clubs, on television, and at festivals. He toured and recorded with such musicians as Harry Edison (1961–2), Junior Mance (1962–4), George Shearing (1971), and Cannonball Adderley (1973–5) and frequently rejoined Basie. From the 1970s through the 1990s Norman Simmons usually served as the pianist in Williams's own groups, and Henry Johnson often appeared on guitar. In the course of these decades Williams was featured with Clark Terry's group on an extensive tour from Egypt to India in 1977, and he made a highly successful tour of the USA and Europe with the Count Basie Orchestra under the direction of Thad Jones in 1985; from time to time he took acting roles, and in 1985 he became Grandpa Al on the immensely popular television program, "The Cosby Show." While working frequently in the 1990s as a soloist on cruise ships, at festivals, and in hotels and clubs, especially in Las Vegas, he toured with the Basie Orchestra (under Frank Foster) and with Shearing (*c*1993–4), and in 1996–7 he sang with Louie Bellson's orchestra in a re-creation of Duke Ellington's suite *Black, Brown and Beige*. With his rich bass-baritone voice and passionate style of delivery, Williams reshaped the role of the big-band singer and brought it up to date without sacrificing his innate taste and musical imagination.

Video oral history material in *NCH* (HCJA).

SELECTED RECORDINGS

As leader: *Joe Williams Sings Everyday* (1950–51, Reg. 6002); *Together* (1961, Roul. 52069); *A Swingin' Night at Birdland: Joe Williams Live* (1962, Roul. 52085); *Joe Williams at Newport '63* (1963, RCA LSP2762); *Presenting Joe Williams* (1966, SolS 18008); *Joe Williams Live* (1973, Fan. 9441); with Prez Conference: *Prez and Joe* (1979, GNP Crescendo 2124); *Here's to Life* (1993, Telarc 83357)

As sideman: C. Basie: *Count Basie Swings & Joe Williams Sings* (1955, Clef MGC678), incl. Every day I have the blues; *Memories Ad-lib* (1958, Roul. 52021); C. Bolling: on *Jazz Gala 79* (1979, Amer. 015–16), Blues in my Heart

SELECTED FILMS AND VIDEOS

Newport Jazz Festival (1962); Duke Ellington at the White House (1969); Duke Ellington: We Love You Madly (1973); Monterey Jazz (1973); Jazz at the Smithsonian: Joe Williams (1982); Sarah Vaughan: Live from Monterey (1984); Jazz Profiles: Joe Williams (1985); The Monterey Jazz Festival 1985 (1985); Joe Williams: a Song is Born (*c*1992)

BIBLIOGRAPHY

SheridanCB

R. J. Gleason: "Every Day is a Good Day for Joe Williams," *DB*, xxiii/11 (1956), 11

R. Horricks: "Joe Williams," *JM*, ii/7 (1956), 7

L. Tomkins: "Frankly Speaking: Joe Williams," *Crescendo*, i/6 (1963), 10

B. Gardner: "Is Joe Williams Really Joe Williams?," *DB*, xxxi/32 (1964), 19

A. J. Smith: "Joe Williams: the Well Tempered Blaze of Vocal Excellence," *DB*, xliii/9 (1976), 11 [incl. discography]

S. Harris: *Blues Who's Who: a Biographical Dictionary of Blues Singers* (New Rochelle, NY, 1979/*R*1994)

S. Dance: *The World of Count Basie* (New York and London, 1980), 198

"Joe Williams: You and Me," *JP*, xxix/10 (1980), 12

J. E. Siegel: "Talking with Joe Williams," *Radio Free Jazz*, xxi (1980), Jan, 12

D. J. Travis: *An Autobiography of Black Jazz* (Chicago, 1983), 467

L. Gourse: *Every Day: the Story of Joe Williams* (London, Melbourne, Australia, and New York, 1985) [incl. discography]

D. Morgenstern: "Joe Williams: the Boy Singer," *JT* (1987), Oct, 36

W. Balliett: *American Singers: Twenty-seven Portraits in Song* (New York, and Oxford, England, rev. and enlarged 2/1988), 72

"Joe Williams," *JP*, xxxvii/7 (1988), 3

E. Calloway: "Defender Newsboy Joe Williams Grew up to be a Great Vocalist," *Chicago Defender* (28 April 1990), 33

R. Mitchell: "Joe Williams Saves a Few of his High Notes," *Houston Chronicle* (16 Feb 1994)

D. Zych: "Joe Williams: Celebrating Ev-e-ry-Day," *JT*, xxiv/2 (1994), 43

H. Gelb: "Blues Singer Joe Williams Has Seen Hard Times, but Takes Solace from his Saviour: Joyful Noise," *San Francisco Examiner Magazine* (5 Oct 1997), 10

Obituaries: D. Heckman, *Los Angeles Times* (31 March 1999); J. Pareles, *New York Times* (31 March 1999); B. Crowther, *JJI*, lii/5 (1999), 18

BOB WEIR/BK

Williams, John (Overton) [Bearcat] **(i)** (*b* Memphis, 13 April 1905; *d* Columbus, OH, 24 Nov 1996). Saxophonist and clarinetist. He studied piano briefly when he was eight, lived in Kansas City from around the age of 13, and took up the alto saxophone in January 1922. Self-taught, he began performing professionally in a band at a local ballroom that same year. Through 1925 he toured in the vaudeville show *Hits 'n Bits*, and soon afterwards he took over leadership of its band from Shirley Clay; the group's pianist was Mary Lou Burley, whom he married in 1926. Williams led the Synco Jazzers (including his wife) on tour and in Memphis; the group recorded in Chicago in 1927. Late in 1928 he joined Terrence Holder's orchestra in Oklahoma City, and he remained with the band when Andy Kirk assumed its leadership the following year (for illustration *see* WILLIAMS, MARY LOU). From 1933 Williams served as Kirk's music director. After leaving the band in 1939 he ceased playing and ran a restaurant; he and Mary Lou Williams divorced in 1940. In 1942 he briefly joined Cootie Williams's band as an alto and baritone saxophonist, and from 1942 to 1947 he held a lengthy engagement as baritone saxophonist in Earl Hines's big band. He then abandoned music and worked in a hotel and later in a factory in Chicago. Around 1971 he retired to Columbus.

Williams's alto saxophone playing may be heard with his Synco Jazzers on *Now Cut Loose* (1927, Gen. 6124) and his baritone playing on *Blue Clarinet Stomp* (1929, Bruns. 4694), one of the many recordings he made with Kirk (1929–38); as nominal leader of Kirk's band in 1929 (billed as John Williams and his Memphis Stompers) he recorded a version of his own composition *Lotta Sax Appeal* (Voc. 1453). He should not be confused with the alto saxophonist John Williams (*d* 1932), who performed and recorded with Lloyd and Cecil Scott.

Oral history material in *DSI* (JOHP).

BIBLIOGRAPHY

ChiltonW; *McCarthyB*

M. L. Williams: "My Friends the Kings of Jazz," *MM*, xxx (3–17 April 1954)

Obituary, *New York Times* (1 Dec 1996)

B. Donaldson: "An Interview with John Overton Williams of the Andy Kirk and Earl Hines Bands," *Marge Hofacre's Jazz News* (1997), April–June, 13

BK

Williams, John (ii) (*b* Windsor, VT, 28 Jan 1929). Pianist and leader. He took piano lessons from the age of eight and was playing in a local band by the time he was 12. After working as a church organist for four years he toured as a pianist in a big band from Boston led by Mal Hallett (March – September 1945). Williams finished high school in 1946 and then resumed his career in music; later he worked with Johnny Bothwell (1948) and Teddy Kotick before moving to New York (1949). On New Year's Eve 1950 he appeared with Charlie Parker at Revere Beach, near Boston. While serving in the army (from 1951) he spent periods playing baritone horn in military bands in the USA and Korea. Following his discharge early in 1953 he worked briefly with Charlie Barnet in February and then toured and recorded for six months with Stan Getz; that autumn he studied at the Manhattan School of Music, and towards the end of the year he recorded with Sal Salvador. In 1954 he worked with Don Elliott, Bob Brookmeyer, Nick Travis, and Bill De Arango, recorded as a leader, and rejoined Getz (October), with whom he remained until mid-1955. He then led his own trio and was active as a freelance, recording with Charlie Mariano, Cannonball Adderley, Jimmy Cleveland, and Phil Woods (all 1955), Al Cohn, Zoot Sims, and Jimmy Raney (all 1956), and the trombonist Lon Norman (*c*1957).

Williams became disillusioned by the harshness of a jazz musician's life in New York and consequently moved to Florida, where he spent a period playing in clubs in Miami Beach before abandoning music for a career as a city commissioner (1971–91) and bank executive (from 1978) in Hollywood, Florida. However, he continued to play on Friday nights and performed annually at the festival in Hollywood from the mid-1980s into the 1990s, appearing with Brookmeyer, Buddy DeFranco, Terry Gibbs, and Scott Hamilton; he also accompanied Spike Robinson in Clearwater, Florida (1987).

SELECTED RECORDINGS

As leader: *John Williams* (1954, EmA 26047); *John Williams Trio* (1955, EmA 36061)

As sideman: S. Getz: *Stan Getz at the Shrine Auditorium* (1954, Norg. 2000); P. Woods: *Woodlore* (1955, Prst. 7018)

BIBLIOGRAPHY

FeatherE

A. Morgan: "John Williams: the Pianist from Vermont," *JM*, viii (1962), no.8, p.3; no.9, p.13 [incl. discography]

R. Hart: "No Secret: Jazz Fest First-class: Hollywood Hopes for Future Fame," *Miami Herald* (5 Nov 1989)

"Interview with Johnny Williams," *The Note*, iii/3 (1991), 10

S. Voce: "John Williams," *JJI*, xlvii (1994), no.6, p.6; no.7, p.10; no.8, p.10

BK

Williams, John (Charles) (iii) (*b* London, 8 Feb 1941). English baritone saxophonist. His first professional work was as the leader of a resident big band at the Marquee Club, London (1961–3), where Neil Ardley and Phil Lee were among his sidemen. From the mid-1960s through the 1970s he worked with a number of leading pop musicians and played in orchestras for musical theater; although he was comparatively less involved in jazz during this period, he formed an octet (1969) and a big band (1973), led the saxophone quartet Changing Face (1976–8), and performed and recorded with Keith Tippett's Centipede (1970–75), Alan Cohen (1971–3), Joe Gallivan's Intercontinental Express (1977–8), and the Don Rendell Nine (1979–81). In the 1980s his octet included Dick Pearce, Pete Saberton, and Trevor Tomkins; Williams's playing is well represented by *Snow Palace*, from the group's album *The Year of the Buffalo* (1985, Spot. 532). Later he formed other ensembles, notably the trio Spectrum (1985), the Baritone Band (1985), which comprised four baritone saxophonists (among them Ronnie Ross and Chris Biscoe) and a rhythm player, and New Perspectives (1993), which combined a jazz septet (consisting of Pearce, the reed player Pete Hurt, Andy Panayi, Lee, Jeff Clyne, and Tomkins) and a classical wind quintet. Williams continued to lead his big band through the 1990s. He has composed music for all his groups, and in 1981 he instituted an annual summer music festival at his home in Shropshire. (R. Cotterrell, ed.: *Jazz Now: the Jazz Centre Society Guide*, London, 1976)

NEVIL SKRIMSHIRE/BK

Williams, John (B., Jr.) (iv) (*b* New York, 27 Feb 1941). Bass player. He played drums initially and took up double bass while in the army. After studying for two years with Ron Carter he performed, toured, and recorded with Horace Silver (1967–9) and worked with Kenny Burrell and Kai Winding (both 1969), Dizzy Gillespie and Hugh Masekela (both 1970), and Clark Terry and Zoot Sims. He recorded on double bass with Mose Allison (1970), on electric bass guitar with Count Basie (1970) and Leon Thomas (*c*1970), and on both instruments with Roy Ayers (1970–71) and the quintet led by Bobby Hutcherson and Harold Land (*c*1971). In 1972 he became a staff musician at NBC and played in the orchestra for "The Tonight Show." Later he performed and recorded on electric bass guitar with Billy Cobham and toured the Middle East as a member of Benny Carter's quintet (1975–6).

From 1978 to 1983 Williams was a member of Michael Wolff's trio. He also recorded with Louie Bellson (1975, 1976, 1978), Carl Burnett (1980), Gerald Wilson and Paul Humphrey (both 1981), and Jon Hendricks and the Art Farmer–Benny Golson Quintet (both 1982). As a leader he made the album *Let's Have Fun Together* (1982, New York Jazz 004), and he appears in a trio accompanying Nancy Wilson in the video *Newport Jazz '87* (1987). From 1989 to 1993 he performed on television with Wolff's band in "The Arsenio Hall Show"; after the program ended he toured and recorded as a member of the pianist's small groups, and he may be heard on Wolff's album *Portraiture: the Blues Period* (1997, Fuel 2000 1004). (*Feather–Gitler '70s*; *Feather–GitlerBEJ*)

Williams, John C. *See* Williams, Johnny (ii).

Williams, Johnny [John, Jr.] **(i)** (*b* Memphis, 13 March 1908; *d* New York, 23 Oct 1998). Double bass player. He first learned violin, but disliked the instrument and instead took up tuba while in high school. During the early 1930s he played tuba, then double bass, in southern territory bands. In 1936 he moved to New York, where he took part in several recording sessions with Henry "Red" Allen (1936–7), played with the Mills Blue Rhythm Band (1937–8), recorded with Buster Bailey (December 1938), and worked briefly with Benny Carter. In 1939 he made the first of several recordings with Billie Holiday (to 1942, under the leadership of Holiday or Teddy Wilson), played with Frankie Newton at the downtown location of Café Society, recorded with Harry James, James P. Johnson, J. C. Higginbotham, the Port of Harlem Jazzmen, the Port of Harlem Seven, Newton, and Sidney Bechet, and joined Coleman Hawkins's band. After leaving Hawkins the following year Williams played with Louis Armstrong until 1941. In summer 1941 he joined Wilson's sextet (for illustration *see* Wilson, Teddy), with which he appeared in the film short *Boogie Woogie Dream* (1941). He recorded with his fellow sideman Edmond Hall in January 1944 and remained at Café Society under Hall's leadership when Wilson disbanded in May 1944. During these years he was occasionally reunited with Armstrong, most notably at a concert involving Hall's band at Carnegie Hall in February 1947. When Hall disbanded in mid-June 1947, Williams joined Tab Smith at the Savoy Ballroom (to 1952) and Johnny Hodges (*c*1952–1955). He then ceased working as a full-time musician, but in 1968 he traveled to France with Buddy Tate, and in the 1970s he worked frequently with Red Richards. He also toured with Bob Greene's concert troupe, the World of Jelly Roll Morton, from 1978 to 1982, and with the Harlem Blues and Jazz Band from 1978 until June 1998, when a stroke ended his career.

SELECTED RECORDINGS

As sideman: Mills Blue Rhythm Band: Blue Rhythm Fantasy (1937, Var. 503); B. Holiday: Strange Fruit (1939, Com. 526); Port of Harlem Seven: Pounding Heart Blues (1939, BN 6); C. Hawkins: Bouncing with Bean (1940, Bb 10693); E. Hall: Rompin' in 44/Smooth Sailing (1944, BN 30); L. Armstrong: Rockin' Chair (1947, V-Disc 803); J. Hodges: *Used to be Duke* (1954, Norg. 1060); D. Cheatham and H. Hall: *Fessor's Nighthawks* (1979, Met. 627)

BIBLIOGRAPHY

J. Poinsot and L. Verdeaux: "Johnny Williams," *BHcF*, no.245 (1975), 5

J. Chilton: "Rhythm from Memphis," *Sv*, no.82 (1979), 132

P. Vacher: "Williams on Bass," *MR*, vii/12 (1980), 7

C. Hillman: "Johnny Williams," *JJI*, xxxvi/2 (1983), 25

C. Deffaa: "Still Counting his Blessings," *MR*, xiii/3 (1986), 8; repr. in *Swing Legacy* (Metuchen, NJ, and London, 1989), 103

J. Chilton: *Sidney Bechet: the Wizard of Jazz* (London and New York, 1987/*R*1996)

M. Selchow: *Profoundly Blue: a Bio-discographical Scrapbook on Edmond Hall* (Lübbecke, Germany, 1988)

A. Vollmer: "A Tribute to John Williams, Jr. (Tuba, String Bass, Vocal)," *IAJRC Journal*, xxxii/3 (1999), 28

CHIP DEFFAA/BK

Williams, Johnny [J(ohn) C.] **(ii)** (*b* Orangeburg, SC, 31 Oct 1936). Baritone saxophonist. There were many musicians in his family, though none before him made music their profession. He played piano from the age of four, took up alto saxophone just before his twelfth birthday, and began playing the baritone instrument while studying at South Carolina State College; after earning a degree in music education he began graduate studies in 1958 at Indiana University, but left after a year and a half because at that time the university did not offer a master's degree in saxophone performance. He then moved to Los Angeles, where he continued his music studies with Bill Green. Having been drafted into the armed forces in 1962, he attended the Navy School of Music and then served in military bands in California and Germany. Soon afterwards he undertook his last job as an alto saxophonist. He spent several years working with soul, blues, and rhythm-and-blues artists, including Ike and Tina Turner, Stevie Wonder, Gladys Knight, the Temptations, Marvin Gaye, and the Four Tops. Williams then joined Count Basie, twice replacing Cecil Payne (June–November 1970, June 1971 – June 1975) and later taking over from Charlie Fowlkes (from February 1980); after Basie's death he stayed with the band through the 1980s and 1990s under the leadership successively of Thad Jones, Frank Foster, and Grover Mitchell. He may be heard as a soloist on *Small Talk*, on the album *Have a Nice Day* (1971, Daybreak 2005). While with Basie he also doubled on bass clarinet.

For illustration *see* Recording, fig.6.

BIBLIOGRAPHY

SheridanCB
D. J. Gibson: "Count Basie Saxophone Section Celebrates 50th Anniversary," *Saxophone Journal*, xi/3 (1986), 40; xi/4 (1987), 39
B. Franklin: "Johnny Williams: Interview," *Cadence*, xvii/10 (1991), 9

GK, BK

Williams, Leroy (*b* Chicago, 3 Feb 1937). Drummer. He began playing drums at the age of 15 and was largely self-taught. From 1959 to 1964 he was a member of the trio led by the pianist Judy Roberts and then in 1967 he moved to New York, where he performed with Booker Ervin and began a longstanding affiliation with Barry Harris. In 1968 he played with Sonny Rollins and at the Newport Jazz Festival with Archie Shepp and joined Clifford Jordan's ensemble. A year later he made the first of his numerous albums with Harris, and also recorded with Big John Patton. After playing with Wilbur Ware, Williams worked with Hank Mobley (1970), Yusef Lateef (1971), and Ray Bryant (from 1971); while with Bryant he also recorded under Charles McPherson's leadership (1971–2). In 1973 he played with James Moody and Stan Getz, and in 1976 he toured Japan with Harris, McPherson, and Jimmy Raney, recording with all three men in Tokyo; the brilliant trio session under Raney's leadership includes an extended solo from Williams, on *Cherokee.* During the 1970s Williams also recorded with Andrew Hill (1975), Sonny Stitt (1975), Al Cohn (1976), Rein de Graaff (1976–7), Earl Coleman (1977), Jimmy Rowles, Buddy Tate, and Bob Wilber (all 1978), and Slide Hampton (1979). He appeared with Pepper Adams at the Kansas City Jazz Festival in 1979 and the following year recorded with Adams and with Stitt. In the early 1980s he played with Art Davis in a rhythm section that accompanied Tommy Flanagan and Harris. Having recorded with Junior Cook in 1977, Williams was later a member of groups led or co-led by Cook and Bill Hardman (1979 through the 1980s) and recorded with both leaders. He then recorded with the saxophonist Lewis Keel and Karl Berger (both 1990) and the pianist Bertha Hope (1991). In 1991 he renewed his association with Harris, recording with the pianist in a performance at Birdland under the leadership of Lee Konitz, and touring and recording in Europe as a member of Harris's trio. Later he recorded with Richard Wyands (1992), Ralph Lalama (1993), and Harris (1995, accompanying the guitarist Roni Ben-Hur). A versatile drummer, Williams provides strong support for the ensemble and produces a clean, crisp sound.

SELECTED RECORDINGS

As sideman: B. Harris: *Magnificent* (1969, Prst. 7733); *Barry Harris Plays Tadd Dameron* (1975, Xan. 113); *Tokyo 1976* (1976, Xan. 177), incl. Night in Tunisia; J. Raney: *Live in Tokyo* (1976, Xan. 132), incl. Cherokee; A. Cohn: *Al Cohn's America* (1976, Xan. 138); J. Cook: *Pressure Cooker* (1977, Affinity 53); P. Adams: *The Master* (1980, Muse 5213); J. Cook: *The Place to Be* (1988, Ste. 1240); B. Hardman: *What's Up* (1989, Ste. 1254)

BIBLIOGRAPHY

Feather–Gitler '70s

GARY CARNER/BK

Williams, Martin (Tudor Hansford) (*b* Richmond, VA, 9 Aug 1924; *d* Alexandria, VA, 11 or 12 April 1992). Writer. After studying English literature at the University of Virginia (BA 1948), the University of Pennsylvania (MA 1950), and Columbia University he held appointments as jazz critic for the *Saturday Review*, the *Evergreen Review*, and the *New York Times.* With Nat Hentoff, he founded the *Jazz Review* in 1958, and served as editor until 1961. He also contributed to *Down Beat* and other journals and wrote and edited several books. In 1970 Williams became director of the jazz and American culture programs in the division of performing arts of the Smithsonian Institution, and in 1983 he was appointed editor of special projects in books and recordings at the Smithsonian Press. In this capacity he regularly presented jazz concerts at the institution and selected and annotated recordings for the Smithsonian collections of Classic Jazz and (with Gunther Schuller) Big Band Jazz. Williams had been dead for at least a day before he was discovered in his home, hence the uncertain date of death. His papers are held at the Center for Black Music Research in Chicago (*see* Libraries and archives, §2).

Williams was one of the most powerful figures from the late 1950s in the history and dissemination of jazz. His presence and continuing influence have been complex and not easily summarized – with one crucial exception: until it was abruptly discontinued in 1997 his *Smithsonian Collection of Classic Jazz* served for over two decades as the centerpiece of jazz education in many institutions, either on its own, in lieu of a textbook, or in conjunction with other authors' textbooks, which were keyed to its recorded selections. These selections well mirror Williams's tastes and talents: he was scarcely interested in jazz styles extending from Coltrane's modal period onwards into the radical avant-garde, fusion, and later eclecticisms, and his offerings herein seemed somewhat reluctant and uninformed. Elsewhere, in performances extending from the music's origins in blues, ragtime, and popular music, through to bop and its various substyles, he was a passionate champion of the genre, with a nearly exhaustive and encyclopedic command of the recorded repertory and an uncanny sense of good taste.

See *also* Canon.

WRITINGS
(selective list)

ed.: *The Art of Jazz: Essays on the Nature and Development of Jazz* (New York, 1959/*R*1979)
King Oliver (London, 1960)
ed.: *Jazz Panorama* (New York and London, 1962/*R*1979)
Jelly Roll Morton (London, 1962)
Where's the Melody? A Listener's Introduction to Jazz (New York, 1966/*R*1983, rev. 2/1969)
Jazz Masters of New Orleans (New York and London, 1967/*R*1978)
Jazz Masters in Transition, 1957–69 (New York and London, 1970/*R*1980)
The Jazz Tradition (New York, 1970, rev. 2/1983)
Jazz Heritage (New York, and Oxford, England, 1985)

BIBLIOGRAPHY

Obituary, P. Elwood, *San Francisco Chronicle* (17 April 1992)

PAULA MORGAN/BK

Williams, Mary Lou [née Scruggs, Mary Elfrieda; Burley, Mary Lou] (*b* Atlanta, 8 May 1910; *d* Durham, NC, 28 May 1981). Pianist, composer, arranger, and leader. She grew up in Pittsburgh, where she was playing her mother's reed organ by the time she was four and worked professionally from a very early age; she had taken the surname Winn from a stepfather and the surname Burley from her next stepfather, and performed as Mary Lou Burley. In 1925 she joined the vaudeville show Hits 'n Bits, whose band was soon afterwards led by John Williams (i), whom she married in 1926; she toured extensively with Williams and recorded with his Synco Jazzers in 1927. While in New York (*c*1926) she worked briefly with Bubber Miley, Tricky Sam Nanton, and Sonny Greer, and she served as intermission pianist at Connie's Inn. When early in 1929 Andy Kirk took over Terrence Holder's band, of which John Williams was a member, Mary Lou served the group as deputy pianist and arranger. She participated in all of Kirk's recordings, and contributed *Mess-a-Stomp* and *Corky Stomp* to his first sessions of November 1929. In 1931 she became a regular member of the ensemble (see illustration). The fame of Kirk's band in the 1930s was due largely to Williams's distinctive arrangements, compositions, and solo performances on piano; she also provided noteworthy swing-band scores for Benny Goodman, Earl Hines, Tommy Dorsey, and others. John and Mary Lou Williams divorced in 1940. After leaving Kirk in 1942 Mary Lou formed a sextet in Pittsburgh which included Art Blakey and her second husband, Shorty Baker, on trumpet. Baker soon left to join Duke Ellington, and when the sextet failed Williams followed him and served for a short time as staff arranger for Ellington, for whom she scored *Blue Skies* (revised and popularized by Ellington in 1946 under its original title and also under the title *Trumpet No End*). Baker and Williams divorced around 1944.

From November 1944 Williams was resident at Café Society, working mainly in Manhattan at its downtown location for nearly four years. In 1946 three movements from her *Zodiac Suite* were performed at Carnegie Hall by the New York Philharmonic Orchestra, a very early instance of the recognition of jazz by a leading symphony orchestra. By now Williams had become an important figure in New York bop, contributing scores to Dizzy Gillespie's big band and advancing the careers of many younger musicians. After joining Slam Stewart's trio (with which she appeared in the film *Boy! What a Girl*) in 1947 and Benny Goodman's sextet in summer 1948, she worked in California and then returned to New York for an engagement at the Village Vanguard (until November 1949). In the early 1950s she led a group at Bop City. For a few months Oscar Pettiford and Kenny Clarke performed in a trio with Williams; the trio also accompanied prominent bop instrumentalists and the singer Billy Eckstine. From November 1952 through 1954 Williams was based in Europe. She retired from music in 1954 to pursue religious and charitable interests, but resumed her career in 1957. Throughout the 1960s and 1970s she led groups in New York clubs, including the Cookery, composed sacred works for jazz orchestra and voices, and devoted much of her time to teaching. She toured Europe in 1968–9, and in 1970, as a solo pianist and providing her own commentary, she recorded *The History of Jazz* (FW 2860). Towards the end of her life she received a number of honorary doctorates from American universities and taught on the staffs of the University of Massachusetts (1975–6) and

Mary Lou Williams with Andy Kirk and the Twelve Clouds of Joy at the Trianon Ballroom, Cleveland, 1937: (back row, left to right) Earl Miller, John Williams (i), Dick Wilson, and John Harrington (saxophones), Ben Thigpen (drums); (middle row) Harry Lawson, Paul King, and Earl Thomson (trumpets), Ted Donnelly (trombone), Kirk (director), Booker Collins (double bass); (front) Williams (piano)

Duke University (from 1977). Not fond of free jazz, she for some reason presented what, not surprisingly, proved to be an adversarial concert with Cecil Taylor in April 1977. She was a guest soloist in Goodman's 40th Anniversary Concert at Carnegie Hall, gave a concert as an unaccompanied soloist at the Montreux International Jazz Festival in Switzerland in 1978, and appeared on an episode of the television series "Oscar Peterson and Friends" in 1980. She also appeared posthumously in the film documentaries *Mary Lou Williams: Music on my Mind* (1990) and *A Great Day in Harlem* (1995).

Williams was long regarded as the only significant female musician in jazz, both as an instrumentalist and as a composer, but her achievement is remarkable by any standards. She was an important swing pianist, with a lightly rocking, legato manner based on subtly varied stride and boogie-woogie bass patterns. Yet by constantly exploring and extending her style she retained the status of a modernist for most of her career. She adapted easily in the 1940s to the new bop idiom, and in the 1960s her playing attained a level of complexity and dissonance that rivaled avant-garde jazz pianism of the time, but without losing an underlying blues feeling. A similar breadth may be seen in her work as a composer and arranger, from her expert swing-band scores for Kirk (*Walkin' and Swingin'*, *Mary's Idea*) to the large-scale sacred works of the 1960s and 1970s. Her *Waltz Boogie* of 1946 was one of the earliest attempts to adapt jazz to non-duple meters. Among her sacred works are a cantata, *Black Christ of the Andes* (1963), and three masses, of which the third, *Mary Lou's Mass* (1970), became well known in a version choreographed by Alvin Ailey. A tape recording of her jazz mass, as given in Wesleyan Chapel on 18 November 1973, is held at the World Music Archives at Wesleyan University, Middletown, Connecticut (*see* LIBRARIES AND ARCHIVES, §2).

Oral history material in *CtY*, *DSI* (JOHP) [P. O'Brien], *GBLnsa*, *NjR* (JOHP), and *NjR*.

SELECTED RECORDINGS

* – composed by Williams

As unaccompanied soloist: *From the Heart* (1971, Chi. 103); *Solo Recital: Montreux Jazz Festival 1978* (1978, PL 2308218)

As leader: *Little Joe from Chicago (1944, Asch 1002); *Roll 'em (1944, Asch 1003); **Zodiac Suite* (1945, Asch 620-21); *Waltz Boogie (1946, Vic. 20-2025); *In London* (1953, Vogue 22); **Black Christ of the Andes* (1963, Saba 15062); *Mary Lou Williams Presents* (1964, FW 32843); *From the Heart* (1970, Chi. 103); **Mary Lou's Mass* (1970–72, Mary 102); *Free Spirits* (1975, Ste. 1043); with C. Taylor: *Embraced* (1977, PL 2620108); *My Mama Pinned a Rose on Me* (1977, Pablo 2310819)

SELECTED ARRANGEMENTS

* – composed by Williams

Recorded by A. Kirk with Williams as sideman: *Mess-a-Stomp (1929, Bruns. 4694); *Corky Stomp (1929, Bruns. 4893); *Walkin' and Swingin' (1936, Decca 809); *Froggy Bottom (1936, Decca 729); *In the Groove (1937, Decca 1261); *Mary's Idea (1938, Decca 2326)

Recorded by J. Williams (i) with Williams as sideman: Lotta Sax Appeal (1929, Voc. 1453)

Recorded by B. Goodman: *Roll 'em (1937, Vic. 25627)

Recorded by D. Ellington: Blue Skies, first issued on *Duke Ellington and his Orchestra*, i (1943, Circle CLP101); Blue Skies [Trumpet No End] (1946, Musi. 484)

SELECTED FILMS AND VIDEOS

Boy! What a Girl (1947); A Great Day in Harlem (1995)

BIBLIOGRAPHY

ConnorBG; *McCarthyB*; *SchullerS*

D. Burley: "Miss Mary Lou Williams Swings for You," *New York Amsterdam News* (8 Oct 1938), 20

S. Pease: *Boogie-woogie Piano Styles* (Chicago, 1940, 1943) [incl. transcrs.]

M. Jones: "Mary Lou Williams: a Life Story," *MM*, xxx (3 April – 12 June 1954); repr. in *Talking Jazz* (London, 1987), 17

M. McPartland: "Mary Lou," *DB*, xxiv/21 (1957), 12

L. Tomkins: "The Mary Lou Williams Story," *CI*, ix/12 (1971), 6; x/1 (1971), 25

R. Baggenaes: "Mary Lou Williams: an Interview," *Coda*, xi/10 (1974), 2

N. Hentoff: *Jazz Is* (New York, 1976/R1991), 83

O. Coyle: "Mary Lou Williams & her Jazz Crusade," *MR*, iii/6 (1976), 5

W. Balliett: "Out Here Again," *Improvising: Sixteen Jazz Musicians and their Art* (New York, 1977), 59; repr. in *BallietA (1986)*, 96; *BallietA (1996)*, 103

C. Battestini and J.-P. Battestini: "Mary Lou Williams raconte sa vie," *BHcF*, no.266 (1978), 7

L. Feather, "Piano Giants of Jazz: Mary Lou Williams," *CK*, iv/6 (1978), 63

B. Rusch: "Cecil Taylor Interview," *Cadence*, iv/1 (1978), 3

D. A. Handy: "First Lady of the Jazz Keyboard," *Black Perspective in Music*, viii (1980), 195

E. Townley: "An Interview with Mary Lou," *MR*, vii/3 (1980), 4

S. Britt: "The First Lady of Jazz: Mary Lou Williams," *JJI*, xxxiv/9 (1981), 10

Obituary, J. P[escheux], *BhcF*, no. 291 (1981), 30

L. Lyons: *The Great Jazz Pianists, Speaking of their Lives and Music* (New York, 1983), 67

M. Unterbrink: *Jazz Women at the Keyboard* (Jefferson, NC, and London, 1983)

L. D. Holmes and J. W. Thomson: *Jazz Greats: Getting Better with Age* (New York, 1986)

C. J. Yampolsky: *The Solo Jazz Piano Music of Three American Composers: Armando "Chick" Corea, William "Billy" Taylor, Mary Lou Williams: a Performance Tape Project* (diss., U. of Maryland, 1986)

M. McPartland: "Into the Sun: an Affectionate Sketch of Mary Lou Williams," *All in Good Time* (New York, and Oxford, England, 1987), 69

A. Kirk, as told to A. Lee: *Twenty Years on Wheels* (Wheatley, Oxford, England, and Ann Arbor, MI, 1989)

J. BRADFORD ROBINSON/BK

Williams, Midge (*b* California, *c*1908; *d* ? after mid-1940s). Singer. She began singing professionally in 1927 and in the early 1930s she toured the Far East; she was resident at a club in Shanghai (1933) and then performed in Tokyo, where she made recordings in Japanese, including a version of *St. Louis Blues* (Col. 28213). After returning to the USA (1934) she presented her own radio series in Los Angeles (1934–6) and toured for a time with Fats Waller. In the late 1930s she made recordings with Frank Froeba and Teddy Wilson (both 1936), Miff Mole (1937), and in Chicago as a leader (1937–8, notably *I was born to swing*, 1937, Voc. 3838); at others of her own sessions she was accompanied by John Kirby's group. Williams sang with Louis Armstrong's big band for several years (1938–41) and recorded with Lil Armstrong (1940); after 1941 she worked as a solo singer. (L. Feather: "Harlem goes Japanese!," *MM* (28 May 1938), 2)

based on *ChiltonW*

Williams, Nelson [Cadillac] (*b* Birmingham, AL, 26 Sept 1917; *d* Voorburg, Netherlands, 15 Nov 1973). Trumpeter. He played piano before taking up trumpet. In the early 1930s he toured with the boogie-woogie pianist Cow Cow Davenport and with vaudeville shows. While based in Birmingham, Alabama (1938), he was music director of the Dixie Rhythm Girls on a tour of Florida. After working in Philadelphia he joined Tiny Bradshaw (1939), played in an army band for three years, and performed with Billy Eckstine, John Kirby, and Billy Kyle. From June 1949 to November 1951 he was a member of Duke Ellington's orchestra, with which he made several recordings and appeared in the film *Salute to Duke Ellington* (1950). Williams then moved to Paris and worked in Europe, performing and recording swing and mainstream jazz as a trumpeter, singer, and leader and playing with traditional revivalist groups. In April 1956 he rejoined Ellington's band to perform at Basin Street East in New York, after which he returned immediately to France; thereafter he appeared with the group on a number of occasions during Ellington's tours of Europe, in November 1958 and November 1969 and from June to August 1970. By

1963 he had settled in Voorburg in the Netherlands. His best European recordings were made in 1951 as the leader of a quintet that included Don Byas and Zutty Singleton; however, the uninspiring contexts in which he often worked in Europe in later years led to an *oeuvre* of variable quality. (*ChiltonW*; *FeatherE*; *Feather–GitlerBEJ*)

HOWARD RYE

Williams, Paul [Hucklebuck] (*b* Lewisberg, TN, 13 July 1915). Alto and baritone saxophonist and leader. He moved with his family to Bowling Green, Kentucky, at the age of two and thence to Detroit when he was 13; he started playing saxophone in junior high school. Along with the trumpeter Lloyd "Chainey" Henderson he joined the Boogie Band, which played for five years (to 1941) at the Morris Café on Michigan Avenue. During World War II he worked in defense plants and played in the Ford plant band, and in 1945 he became a member of Clarence Dorsey's band at the Sensation Club. He then joined King Porter's band, which was working at the Sportree in Detroit. Williams made his recording début with Porter around 1947, in which year he formed his own band from elements of Porter's. From September 1947 to 1951 on Savoy, then until 1956 on a succession of other labels, he produced a long series of recordings in the jump style, some under the name of one of his tenor saxophonists, Wild Bill Moore. These feature his strongly blues-based baritone saxophone, which Savoy favored for commercial reasons, and more rarely his lyrical playing on the alto instrument. The group, among whose other tenor saxophonists were Billy Mitchell (1949) and Noble Watts (1952–6), began touring outside Detroit in February 1948, when it appeared at the Royal Theater, Baltimore. However, it was the success of *The Huckle Buck* (1948) on the rhythm-and-blues charts that inaugurated the band's nationwide touring, often in package shows which placed increasing emphasis on singers and after about 1957 often presented the artists as rock-and-roll performers. An eight-piece nucleus was expanded as necessary for these engagements. Williams's group was the house band for the television series "Showtime at the Apollo" (1955) and may be seen in compilation films and videos derived from it, including *Rock 'n Roll Revue* (1955) and *Rhythm and Blues Revue* (1956). In mid-1958 Wiliams appeared at Smalls' Paradise, New York, accompanying the singer Ruth Brown. In the early 1960s he worked mainly with soul artists, notably directing James Brown's band, but in 1964 he gave up music to become a salesman. In 1968 he opened the Entertainment Bureau booking agency in New York. He recorded with Milt Larkin around 1976.

SELECTED RECORDINGS

(recorded for Savoy unless otherwise indicated)

As leader: Hastings Street Bounce (1947, 659); Paradise Valley Walk/Walkin' Around (1947, 680); Hoppin' John (1947, 683); first issued on *Paul Williams: the Complete Recordings*, i *(1947–1949)* (1947–9, Blue Moon 6020), Blues Swing (1947); first issued on *Honkers and Screamers* (1947–61, 2234), Boogie Mr. Williams, The Twister (1947), Back Bender, Jelly Roll Boogie (1949); The Huckle Buck (1948, 683); Juice Bug Boogie (1949, 721); Blues at Daybreak (1949, 773); Paul's Boogie/Jeep's Blues (1949–50, 758); Blowin' the Boogie (1951, 831); first issued on *The Hucklebuck* (1948–56, Saxophonograph 500), Alcohol, Huckle-Boogie (1952)

As sideman with W. B. Moore: Bubbles (1947, 662)

BIBLIOGRAPHY

K. Mohr: "Paul Williams Discography", *Jazz-Statistics*, nos.26–7 (1962), 3

P. Grendysa: Liner notes, *Paul Williams and his Orchestra: The Hucklebuck* (Saxophonograph 500, 1981)

J. Sasfy: "Blues from a Honker," *Washington Post* (7 Feb 1986); repr. in *Blues & Rhythm*, no.19 (1986), 14

A. Oess: Liner notes, *Paul Williams and his Hucklebuckers: Spider Sent Me* (Saxophonograph 510, 1988)

HOWARD RYE

Williams, Pearlis (*b* Gloucester, MS, 14 May 1909; *d* 11 March 1999). Drummer. His first job was with Albert Ammons. He then moved to Chicago, where from 1936 to 1938 he played and recorded with Herb Morand in the Harlem Hamfats. Later, in St. Louis, he joined Cootie Williams, with whom he toured to New York. Thereafter he settled permanently in Kansas City, where in the early 1950s he played with Miles Davis.

SELECTED RECORDINGS

(all recorded for Decca)

As sideman with Harlem Hamfats: You done tore your playhouse down (1936, 7206); Hamfat Swing (1936, 7262); Keep it swinging round and round (1936, 7266); Jam Jamboree (1937, 7312)

BIBLIOGRAPHY

P. Van Vorst: "The Harlem Hamfats," *MR*, iv/4 (1977), 5

MICHAEL TOVEY/HOWARD RYE (recording-list)

Williams, Richard (Gene) [Notes] (*b* Galveston, TX, 4 May 1931; *d* New York, 5 Nov 1985). Trumpeter. Having been inspired at an early age by the bop trumpet playing of Fats Navarro and the compositions of Charlie Parker, he took up tenor saxophone, then trumpet, while in his teens. He played in local bands on the Gulf coast of Texas, received a degree in music from Wiley College (1951), and served for four years in the air force; on his discharge in September 1956 he joined Lionel Hampton's big band, with which he toured Europe as a principal trumpeter. After returning to the USA he received a master's degree from the Manhattan School of Music (1961) and worked with Gigi Gryce (1959–62, recording in 1960–61), Charles Mingus (1959–64), Lou Donaldson (1960), Quincy Jones (1961), Slide Hampton (1961–3, performing and recording in Paris in 1962), Yusef Lateef (1963–4), Orchestra U. S. A. (1964), and Duke Ellington (1965, recording in 1965 and 1971); he also recorded in 1960 with the quintets of Leo Wright, Booker Ervin, and Red Garland, with Randy Weston's orchestra, and with his own quintet. Williams toured Europe and Japan and recorded with the Thad Jones–Mel Lewis Orchestra (1966–9), played with Gil Evans (1973), toured Europe (1973) and recorded (1974, 1976) with Clark Terry's big band, and then rejoined Hampton (1975); during this same period he performed in pit orchestras on Broadway. In the early 1970s in Europe he worked occasionally as a freelance with his own quartet; later he recorded with Duke Jordan (1975), Hilton Ruiz (1977), and Sam Jones (1979) and as a member of Mingus Dynasty (1982), and was co-leader of a quintet with Harold Vick (1980).

SELECTED RECORDINGS

As leader: *New Horn in Town* (1960, Can. 9003)

As sideman: G. Gryce: *Sayin' Something* (1960, NewJ 8230); L. Wright: *Blues Shout* (1960, Atl. 1358); O. Nelson: *Screamin' the Blues* (1960, NewJ 8243); B. Ervin: *Cookin'* (1960, Savoy 12154); C. Mingus: *The Black Saint and the Sinner Lady* (1963, Imp. 35); *Mingus, Mingus, Mingus, Mingus, Mingus* (1963, Imp. 54); Y. Lateef: *Live at Pep's* (1964, Imp. 69); *Club Date* (1964, Imp. 9310); G. Evans: *Svengali* (1973, Atl. 1643); Mingus Dynasty: *Reincarnation* (1982, SN 1042)

BIBLIOGRAPHY

Feather '60s; *Feather–Gitler '70s*

N. Hentoff: Liner notes, *New Horn in Town* (Can. 9003, 1961)

D. Ioakimidis: "Trois trompettistes de la nouvelle vague …," *Jh*, no.169 (1961), 20

H. Saunders: "Richard Williams: Graceful Notes," *JSN*, i/5 (1980), 34
B. Priestley: *Mingus: a Critical Biography* (London, Melbourne, Australia, and New York, 1982), 105

GARY THEROUX

Williams, Rod (*b* Detroit, 15 April 1954). Pianist and keyboard player. After studying at Eastern Michigan University and the University of Michigan he performed and recorded in David Murray's big band (1984), worked in Craig Harris's group Tailgaters Tales (recording in 1986), and performed in small groups led by, among others, Butch Morris, Henry Threadgill, and Warren Smith (ii). From 1987 into 1991 he was a member of Cassandra Wilson's group, in which he played both piano and synthesizer, and in 1991 he performed with Murray's quartet at the JVC Jazz Festival New York. Williams worked as a leader from the late 1980s, recording in 1988 and 1990, and led a small group at the What is Jazz? Festival in 1991. In addition he has written music for Japanese films and performed Japanese pop music, and in 1998–9 he toured in Nao Takeuchi's quartet.

SELECTED RECORDINGS

As leader: *Hanging in the Balance* (1989, Muse 5380); *Destiny Express* (1990, Muse 5412)
As sideman with C. Wilson: *She who Weeps* (1990, JMT 834443-2)

BIBLIOGRAPHY

H. Boyd and L. Sinclair: *Detroit Jazz Who's Who* (Detroit, 1984), 67

GK

Williams, Roy (*b* Salford, England, 7 March 1937). English trombonist. He first played piano, and took up trombone only at the age of 18. After military service he joined a band in London led by the trumpeter Mike Peters (1960), then performed and recorded with Terry Lightfoot (1961) and appeared in the film *It's Trad, Dad* (1962). With Alex Welsh's band, which he joined in April 1965, he toured and recorded with such visiting American musicians as Bud Freeman, Wild Bill Davison, and Ruby Braff. At this time Williams gained widespread recognition for his forceful ensemble playing and fluent, imaginative solos. While with Welsh he began to collaborate with his fellow sideman John Barnes; their band recorded in 1975. Shortly after leaving Welsh in February 1978 Williams joined Humphrey Lyttelton's band, with which he performed and recorded from May of that year to May 1983. Also in 1978 he toured Britain and Australia in the show "Salute to Satchmo" and made his first appearance at the Colorado Jazz Party. He was a founding member of the Pizza Express All Stars in 1980. That same year he recorded with Benny Waters and early in the 1980s he played with the trombone group Five-a-Slide, which recorded in 1981.

From 1983 Williams has worked as a freelance. He appeared at international festivals, performed and recorded in Switzerland and Canada with the sextet of Doc Cheatham and Jim Galloway (1983–5), recorded with Buddy Tate in the Netherlands (1986), toured Europe with the Harlem Blues and Jazz Band, the World's Greatest Jazz Band, Peanuts Hucko, and Bent Persson, and performed in New York with Bob Rosengarden. He was a guest soloist with Bob Wilber's big band, co-led a quartet with the pianist Stan Barker, and joined Digby Fairweather and the Welsh Reunion Band from 1994 for a revival of "Salute to Satchmo"; he also played with the Great British Jazz Band of Fairweather and Pete Strange (recording in 1994 and 1996), and with Keith Smith. In the 1990s he toured Germany annually with the band led by the drummer Peter York, recorded as a member of the European Jazz Giants (1994) and the cornetist Tom Saunders's Wild Bill Davison Band (1995), and worked in a trio with his son, the guitarist Andrew Williams, and the double bass player Leon Clayton. During his periods with Welsh and Lyttelton, Williams became an excellent sight reader, capable of playing in a variety of settings. His warm-toned, accurate, high-register playing alternates with roaring tailgate or an emphatic swing style.

SELECTED RECORDINGS

As leader: with J. Barnes: *Gruesome Twosome* (1980, BL 760507); with E. Thompson: *Something Wonderful* (1981, Hep 2015); *Royal Trombone* (1983, Phon. 7556); *Again! in Sweden* (1983, Phon. 7579); with B. Lemon and W. Vaché: *A Beautiful Friendship* (1995, Zephyr 4)
As sideman: A. Welsh: *Strike One* (1966, Strike One 102); [various artists:]: *The Melody Maker Tribute to Louis Armstrong* (1970, Pol. 2460123-5), incl. A. Welsh: Tea for Two; A. Welsh: *Alex Welsh in Concert* (1971, BL 12115–6); D. Cheatham and J. Galloway: *At the Bern Jazz Festival* (1983–5, Sack. 3045-2); European Jazz Giants: *Jazz Party with Peter "Banjo" Meyer* (1994, Nagel-Heyer 009); Great British Jazz Band: *Jubilee* (1994, Can. 79720); *A British Jazz Odyssey* (1996, Can. 79740); with R. Braff: *Braff Plays Wimbledon: the First Set* (1996, Zephyr 15)

BIBLIOGRAPHY

CarrJ; *ChiltonB*
M. Jones: "Roy Williams – Trombonist with Ambition," *MM* (17 Oct 1970), 12
E. Cook: "Roy Williams," *JJI*, xxxiii/10 (1980), 6
N. Simpson: *Roy Williams Discography* (Zwolle, Netherlands, 1991, rev. 2/1994)
"Doubletalk mit John Barnes & Roy Williams: the Gruesome Twosome," *JP*, xliv/6 (1995), 12

CLARRIE HENLEY/BK

Williams, Rubberlegs [Henry] (*b* Atlanta, 14 July 1907; *d* New York, 17 Oct 1962). Singer and dancer. He began his career in Atlanta at an early age and first worked on the Theater Owners' Booking Association circuit in 1920. During the 1920s and 1930s he toured the USA, performing in nightclubs and theaters for vaudeville and minstrel shows, and became particularly well known for his song *Bring it on home*. He also appeared in several revues, notably *Blackbirds of 1933–4*. Williams's nickname "Rubberlegs" describes his "legomania" dancing, which combined high kicks, wriggles, shimmies, and other steps; the short film *Smash your Baggage* (1933) clearly demonstrates his style of tap-dancing. Williams performed with Fletcher Henderson, Chick Webb, and Dicky Wells; he sang his own composition *That's the Blues* on a recording with Clyde Hart (1945, Contl 6013), and recorded under his own name accompanied by Herbie Fields's band (1945–6) and as a sideman with Oscar Pettiford and his 18 All Stars (including *Empty Bed Blues*, 1945, Manor 1002). From 1946 until his death he worked mainly away from the world of entertainment.

BIBLIOGRAPHY

M. Stearns and J. Stearns: *Jazz Dance: the story of American Vernacular Dance* (New York and London, 1968)
S. Harris: *Blues Who's Who: a Biographical Dictionary of Blues Singers* (New Rochelle, NY, 1979/*R*1994)

RAINER E. LOTZ

Williams, Rudy [Looney] (*b* Newark, NJ, 1909; *d* Cape Cod, MA, Sept 1954). Saxophonist and clarinetist. He began playing saxophone at the age of 12; although the alto saxophone became his chief instrument, he also played tenor and baritone. From 1937 to 1943 he was a prominent member of Al Cooper's Savoy Sultans (i), and in 1941 he took part in jam sessions at Minton's Playhouse, a fragment of which was preserved on a recording issued under the nominal leadership of Hot Lips Page. After leaving Cooper he worked with Page (June 1943), Luis Russell (September 1943), Eddie "Lockjaw" Davis (September 1943, mid-1945), Chris Columbus (December 1943), Dud Bascomb (1944), and John Kirby (summer 1945). From December 1945 into 1946 he toured the Far East with a USO show, and following his discharge he joined Babs Gonzales. Williams also led his own bands in 1944 (including engagements in Boston and, late that year, at the opening of the Spotlite, New York; Al Haig was his pianist in both locations), 1945 (at Minton's Playhouse, New York), and 1948 (again in New York). After performing with Tadd Dameron at the Royal Roost, New York (1948), he led his own band in Boston (1949–50, 1951), and he spent a brief period in Dizzy Gillespie's big band (September–October 1949). In 1951 he played in California with Illinois Jacquet and Gene Ammons, then toured the Far East in a band led by Oscar Pettiford, of which J. J. Johnson was also a member and which recorded under Howard McGhee's name. Back in the USA he led his own bands once again and worked as a freelance. Williams recorded with various musicians, among them Bascomb and Don Byas (both 1944), Gonzales (1947), Dameron and Davis (both 1948), Eddie "Cleanhead" Vinson (1950), Ammons and Bennie Green (both 1951), and Johnny Hodges (1952).

Williams's was a major talent in the last years of the swing era. His work presaged and incorporated many of the technical changes which marked bop, while remaining firmly wedded to the rhythmic concepts of the swing and jump styles.

SELECTED RECORDINGS

As sideman: A. Cooper: Jeep's Blues (1938, Decca 7502); Stitches (1939, Decca 2608); Little Sally Water (1939, Decca 2819); Jumpin' the Blues (1939, Decca 2930); Frenzy (1940, Decca 3142); H. L. Page: on *After Hours in Harlem* (1940–41, Onyx 207), Old Yazoo (1941); D. Byas: Bass C Jam (1944, Savoy 524); first issued on [no leader]: *Jam Session at Savoy* (1944–6, Savoy 9030), D. Byas: Savoy Jam Party (1944)

BIBLIOGRAPHY

ChiltonB; *McCarthyB*

D. Salemann, D. Hartmann, and M. Vogler: *Rudy Williams, 1936–1954: Solography, Discography, Band Routes, Engagements in Chronological Order* (Basel, Switzerland, 1987)

HOWARD RYE

Williams, Sandy [Alexander Balos] (*b* Summerville, SC, 24 Oct 1906; *d* New York, 25 March 1991). Trombonist. He grew up in Washington, DC, and first learned tuba; his early work included jobs in theater bands. In 1929 he played with Claude Hopkins, then from 1929 to 1931 he worked with Horace Henderson, during which time he spent brief periods with Hopkins, Fletcher Henderson, and Cliff Jackson. After a longer spell with Fletcher Henderson (*c* January 1932 – July 1933) he became a member of Chick Webb's band (1933), and remained with the group under Ella Fitzgerald's leadership (1939–40). He undertook further big-band engagements with Benny Carter (1940), Coleman Hawkins (1940–41), Lucky Millinder (1941), Fletcher Henderson (intermittently, 1941–2), and Cootie Williams (1942), and during the same period also worked with Sidney Bechet (intermittently, 1940–42), Wild Bill Davison, Mezz Mezzrow, and Pete Brown, successfully adapting his style to the needs of these small groups. Thereafter he played with Duke Ellington (summer 1943), Don Redman, Hot Lips Page, Roy Eldridge (summer 1944), Hopkins (1944–5), Bunk Johnson and Bechet (1945), Rex Stewart (1946, and in Europe, 1947–8), and Art Hodes (1946–7). Later he performed with various groups in New York at Jimmy Ryan's (1949–50). In the 1950s, on account of ill-health, he was obliged to abandon his career. He spent the remainder of his life working as an elevator operator, but performed occasionally at the Central Plaza in the late 1950s.

Williams played within a fairly narrow compass and seldom ventured into the lower register of the instrument. He produced a full, bright, even overripe, open tone, to which he sometimes added a burr (on longer notes especially); he employed a loose yet pushing staccato. In solos he often paraphrased the melody or built on a succession of different riff passages, working on each one for four bars; he increased the interest with varied fills between repetitions of riffs, by adroitly fusing riffs and fills, or by referring to a riff used earlier in the solo.

Oral history material in *NjR*.

For illustrations *see* HENDERSON, FLETCHER, and WEBB, CHICK.

SELECTED RECORDINGS

As leader: Gee, baby, ain't I good to you (1946, HRS 1029)

As sideman: C. Webb: If dreams come true (1934, Col. CB754); Stompin' at the Savoy (1934, Col. 2926D); That Rhythm Man (1934, Decca 173); Blue Minor (1934, Decca 172); Gotham Stompers: My Honey's Lovin' Arms (1937, Var. 629); C. Hawkins: Rocky Comfort (1940, OK 6284); S. Bechet: I know that you know (1940, Vic. 27574); I ain't gonna give nobody none o' this jelly-roll (1940, Vic. 27447); B. Johnson and S. Bechet: Up in Sidney's Flat (1945, BN 565)

BIBLIOGRAPHY

AllenH; *ChiltonW*; *McCarthyB*; *SchullerS*

S. Dance, "Sandy Williams: Trombone," *The World of Swing* (New York, 1974), 63

S. Traill and H. Whiston: "Sandy Williams: Confessions of a Trombonist," *JJ*, xxviii/2 (1975), 12

J. Simmen: "Sandy Williams," *BHcF* (1984), no.315, p.3; no.316, p.2; no.317, p.4; no.318, p.7; no.319, p.1; Eng. trans., abridged, in *Sv*, no.116 (1984–5), 48 [incl. discography]

J. Chilton: *Sidney Bechet: the Wizard of Jazz* (London and New York, 1987/*R*1996)

BOB ZIEFF

Williams, Spencer (*b* New Orleans, 14 Oct 1880 or 1889; *d* Flushing, NY, 14 July 1965). Composer and pianist. Williams himself gave conflicting birthdates to different interviewers. He grew up in Birmingham, Alabama, and played in Chicago before settling around 1916 in New York, where he worked with Clarence Williams and began to concentrate on composition. In 1923 he recorded one track as an accompanist to Lizzie Miles (*Black man (be on yo' way)*, Bruns. 2462). From the mid-1920s he worked mostly in Europe with Josephine Baker (1925–6, 1933), Fats Waller (1932, 1938), Lew Stone (1932), and several West Indian musicians. Williams returned briefly to the USA in 1929–30, during which period he recorded humorous vocal duets with both Teddy Bunn and Lonnie Johnson. From 1932 he lived in England and in the 1950s he moved to Stockholm. He gained fame and income from his many compositions, including *Basin Street Blues*, *Mahogany Hall Stomp*, *Royal Garden Blues*, *I've found a new baby*, *Papa de da-da*, *Tishomingo Blues*, *Shim-me-sha Wobble*, and *Careless Love*. In his book *Black Manhattan* (New York, 1930/*R*1968), the writer and lyricist James Weldon Johnson named Williams as one of the best African-American writers of popular songs.

BIBLIOGRAPHY

ChiltonW

J. Green: "Spencer Williams: Composer," *Sv*, no.123 (1986), 88

A. Rose: *I Remember Jazz: Six Decades among the Great Jazzmen* (Baton Rouge, LA, and London, 1987), 157

JEFFREY P. GREEN

Williams, Todd (Maxwell) (*b* St. Louis, 16 July 1967). Tenor and soprano saxophonist and clarinetist. He took up alto saxophone at the age of ten and changed to the tenor instrument in his teens. During high school he led a quintet that included the trumpeter Jeremy Davenport, Peter Martin, and the double bass player Christopher Thomas, and in 1983 he performed at the Montreux International Jazz Festival with the school's jazz band; he studied classical music at the Eastman School (1986–8). In 1988 he joined Wynton Marsalis. He performed in the trumpeter's sextet and septet through 1993 and also worked under Marsalis in the Lincoln Center Jazz Orchestra from 1989 to 1992; he may be seen in these settings in the videos *Accent on the Offbeat* (*c*1994) and *Garth Fagan's Griot New York* (*c*1995). Williams recorded with Marcus Roberts in 1988 and 1991 (the latter date in a duo), and in 1991 he took part in the recording project Tough Young Tenors. After leaving Marsalis he became a staff writer, band director, and teacher at the Times Square Church Musical Ministry. In 1997 he graduated from the Manhattan School of Music.

SELECTED RECORDINGS

As sideman: W. Marsalis: on *Standard Time*, ii: *Intimacy Calling* (1987–90, Col. CK47346), I'll Remember April (*c*1990); Tough Young Tenors: on *Alone Together* (1991, Ant. 422-848767-2), Blues on the Corner, Just you, just me, Stevie; W. Marsalis: *Levee Low Moan: Soul Gestures in Southern Blue*, iii (*c*1987–8, CK47975), incl. In the House of Williams; *Citi Movement (Griot New York)* (1992, Col. C2K53324); *In this House, on this Morning* (1992–3, Col. C2X53220), incl. Altar Call (Introspection)

BIBLIOGRAPHY

Feather–GitlerBEJ

H. Barnes: "Todd Williams: Ticket to the Top: Young U. City Saxophonist is Following in the Footsteps of Branford Marsalis," *St. Louis Post-Dispatch* (21 Oct 1990)

R. Orgill: "Young and Old in Jazz Collaboration," *Wall Street Journal* (14 Oct 1992)

N. Havouis: "Wynton & Co.: Jazz for the People," *Jm*, no.428 (1993), 36

GK

Williams, Tom(my) [Thomas Whitaker, Jr.] (*b* Baltimore, 4 Dec 1962). Trumpeter. He studied trumpet and drums privately while at high school and later attended Towson State University (1980–82). As a professional trumpeter he toured with Ray Charles in 1983 and was a member of the Ellington Orchestra under the direction of Mercer Ellington until 1987; in February 1987 he recorded with Jimmy Heath. During his army service he was a featured soloist in the groups Jazz Ambassadors and Army Blues. In 1991 Williams won second place in the Thelonious Monk Institute's Louis Armstrong International Trumpet Competition, and in the same year he made his first recording as a leader. Later he played with the Smithsonian Jazz Masterworks Orchestra (1992, from 1996), the Carnegie Hall Jazz Band (from 1995), the Vanguard Jazz Orchestra (1996), and Steve Turre (1997) and toured and recorded with Gary Bartz (1996–7). As a freelance he performed with Hank Jones, Philly Joe Jones, Woody Herman's orchestra, and Ben Riley, and accompanied various singers in show bands; he recorded with Antonio Hart and Steve Wilson (both 1991), Donald Brown and Rob Bargad (both 1992), Larry Willis (1993), the A la Carte Brass Ensemble (*c*1994), the saxophonist Mike Tomaro (1994), the Heath Brothers (1995), and the alto saxophonist Marty Nau (1996). Williams has also recorded as the leader and drummer of Interplay. He should not be confused with the double bass player Tommy Williams, who recorded with Stan Getz during the 1960s.

SELECTED RECORDINGS

As leader: *Introducing Tom Williams* (1991, Criss Cross 1064); *Straight Street* (1993, Criss Cross 1091)

As sideman: J. Heath: *Peer Pleasure* (1987, Landmark 1514); A. Hart: on *For the First Time* (1991, Novus 3120-2-N), Del sasser; S. Wilson: *New York Summit* (1991, Criss Cross 1062); Ron Holloway: on *Slanted* (1993, Mlst. 9219), Caravan, Pent-up House, Sneakin'; M. Nau: *Hemisphere* (1996, Nau's the Time 2)

BIBLIOGRAPHY

<http://www.tomwilliamsmusic.com> (1999)

GK

Williams, Tone. *See* WILLIAMS, ELMER.

Williams, Tony [Tillmon Anthony] (*b* Chicago, 12 Dec 1945; *d* Daly City, CA, 23 Feb 1997). Drummer. His forenames, Tillmon Anthony, appear in the California death index. His family moved to the Boston area when Williams was about two years old. His father, Tillmon Williams, a saxophonist, took him to sit in with musicians at various clubs, and by the age of 11 he was known well enough to visit the clubs on his own. He studied privately with Alan Dawson and, while still a child, played with Art Blakey and Max Roach; other influences were Philly Joe Jones, Jimmy Cobb, and Louis Hayes. By the time he was 15 he was active as a freelance musician in the Boston area.

In 1959–60 Williams began an important association with Sam Rivers, who became his informal mentor. In late 1962 he accompanied Jackie McLean, who invited him to join his group in New York. Here he was discovered by Miles Davis, and in May 1963 began to play in Davis's quintet. Williams stayed with Davis until mid-1969, earning an international

Tony Williams

reputation for the brilliance of his playing and for his interaction with other musicians. He frequently performed and recorded with other groups in New York and Boston, including those of Eric Dolphy, Herbie Hancock, and Rivers, and led his own studio groups. As Davis's quintet moved towards a fusion of jazz with rock, soul, and other elements, Williams became interested in forming a similar group of his own; the trio Lifetime, with Larry Young (organ) and John McLaughlin (electric guitar), issued its first recordings in 1969. But the group was not commercially successful, and its personnel changed over the next three years. In January 1972 Williams joined Stan Getz's group (Airto Moreira was transferred from the drum set to percussion), and he recorded with Getz in March. From 1973 to 1975 he was inactive as a performer, and a new group founded in 1975 had to disband again a year later. Williams then returned to jazz, touring and recording with Hank Jones in the Great Jazz Trio (1976–8) and with Hancock, Wayne Shorter, and other former associates under the name V.S.O.P. in 1976, 1977, 1979, and 1983 (*see also* V.S.O.P. (i)).

In 1977 Williams settled in the San Francisco Bay area, where he studied composition for some years with two professors from the University of California, Berkeley. In addition to his continuing work with V.S.O.P., he recorded with Sonny Rollins (1977–8, 1981) and in 1982 toured widely as a member of Hancock's quartet with Wynton Marsalis and Ron Carter. He began recording again as a leader for Blue Note in 1985 and in the spring of 1986 formed a quintet which toured America, Japan, and Europe. The group appeared in the video *New York Live* (*c*1993 [filmed 1989]). Its longstanding members included, from its inception, Wallace Roney, Billy Pierce, and Mulgrew Miller, and from 1989 the double bass player Ira Coleman; it disbanded early in 1993. Williams also performed with Hancock on television during the 1986 Grammy Award show and in a documentary from that same year, "Miles Ahead," from the PBS television series "Great Performances." His composition *Rituals: Music for String Quartet, Piano, Drums and Cymbals* was given its first performance with Hancock and the Kronos Quartet at the San Francisco Jazz Festival in 1991. In 1992 Williams spent six months traveling internationally in the Miles Davis Tribute Tour, which presented him in a quintet with Roney, Shorter, Hancock, and Carter; in the course of their tour the group appeared on television in the "Tonight Show."

Williams was a highly innovative drummer and a prime influence on jazz styles of the 1970s. From the 1960s he displayed astounding intuition in his accompaniment of soloists, often playing rhythmic figures together with the improviser. His own solos were dramatic essays composed of percussive effects without meter. Even at the fastest of tempos his playing was characteristically delicate and light and punctuated by surprising dynamic contrasts; he negotiated ritardandos and accelerandos with ease. He avoided the conventional accenting of alternate beats with the hi-hat, instead involving it in accents and drum patterns, and by 1966 he had introduced his trademark of closing the cymbal on every beat. His general approach to the drum set, in which he focused on the independence of the limbs, and his specific techniques with the hi-hat and other instruments were widely emulated by younger drummers. All recordings by Williams's own groups from 1969 contain heavily amplified guitar and driving rock rhythms, as well as experiments with dissonant sound effects. Williams played in a different style with these groups, using larger drums and thicker sticks. After his return to a jazz context in 1976, he played in a somewhat heavier manner than in his performances of the 1960s, but with equal brilliance and ingenuity.

SELECTED RECORDINGS

As leader: *Lifetime* (1964, BN 84180); *Spring* (1965, BN 84216); *Emergency* (1969, Pol. 24-4017-8); *Foreign Intrigue* (1985, BN 85119); *Native Heart* (1989, BN B21S-93170); *Tokyo Live* (1992, BN B22V-99031)

As sideman with M. Davis: *Seven Steps to Heaven* (1963, Col. CS8851); *Miles Davis in Europe* (1963, Col. CS8983); *My Funny Valentine* (1964, Col. CS9106); *Miles in Tokyo* (1964, CBS SOPL162); *Miles in Berlin* (1964, CBS BPG62976); *Miles Smiles* (1966, Col. CS9401), incl. Freedom Jazz Dance; *Miles in the Sky* (1968, Col. CS9628), incl. Black Comedy

As sideman with others: H. Hancock: *My Point of View* (1963, BN 84126); J. McLean: *One Step Beyond* (1963, BN 84137); E. Dolphy: *Out to Lunch* (1964, BN 84163); S. Rivers: *Fuchsia Swing Song* (1964, BN 84184); H. Hancock: *Maiden Voyage* (1965, BN 84195); S. Getz: *Captain Marvel* (1972, Col. KC32706); V.S.O.P.: *V.S.O.P.: The Quintet* (1977, Col. C2-34976); W. Marsalis: *Wynton Marsalis* (1981, Col. FC37574); G. Allen: *Twenty One* (1994, BN 30028-2)

BIBLIOGRAPHY

D. DeMicheal: "Tony Williams: Miles' Man," *DB*, xxxii/7 (1965), 19
P. Cox: "Tony Williams: an Interview Scenario," *DB*, xxxvii/11 (1970), 14
R. Williams: "Williams and his Electric Rhythms," *MM* (29 Aug 1970), 10
S. Woods: "Tony Williams," *J&P*, ix/1 (1972), 16
C. D. Woodson: *Solo Jazz Drumming: an Analytical Study of the Improvisational Techniques of Anthony Williams* (thesis, UCLA, 1973)
V. Gibbs: "Tony Williams: Report on a Musical Lifetime," *DB*, xliii/2 (1976), 16
J.-E. Berendt: *Ein Fenster aus Jazz: Essays, Portraits, Reflexionen* (Frankfurt am Main, Germany, 1977), 101
"Discography of Ron Carter and Tony Williams," *SJ*, xxxi/12 (1977), 290
A. Taylor: *Notes and Tones: Musician-to-musician Interviews* (Liège, Belgium, 1977, rev. and enlarged 2/1993)
S. Shaffer: "Tony Williams: Solo on 'Seven Steps to Heaven'," *MD*, iii/1 (1979), 48
L. Underwood: "Tony Williams: Aspiring to a Lifetime of Leadership," *DB*, xlvi/12 (1979), 20
I. Carr: *Miles Davis: a Critical Biography* (London and New York, 1982)
P. de Barros: "Tony Williams: Two Decades of Drum Innovation," *DB*, l/11 (1983), 14
R. Mattingly: "Tony Williams," *MD*, viii/6 (1984), 8
J. Chambers: *Milestones*, ii: *The Music and Times of Miles Davis since 1960* (Toronto, Buffalo, and London, 1985)
H. Wong: "World Class Drummer: Tony Williams," *JT* (1988), Sept, 18
B. Milkowski: "Tony Williams: a Master's Perspective," *MD*, xvi/7 (1992), 20
L. Hildebrand: "Walking Extra Miles with Davis," *San Francisco Chronicle Datebook* (13 Sept 1992)
T. Scherman: "Can't Stop Worrying, Can't Stop Growing: Tony Williams Reinvents Himself," *The Jazz Musician*, ed. M. Rowland and T. Scherman (New York, 1994), 247
B. Milkowski: "A Tribute to Tony Williams," *MD*, xxi/8 (1997), 50
——: "Tony Williams: the Final MD Interview," *MD*, xxi/8 (1997), 68
——: "Into the Wilderness: Driven by Stereotype and Prejudice as Much as by Artistic Ambition, Drummer Tony Williams Finds his own Road," *Jazziz*, xiv/1 (1997), 74
Obituaries: *San Francisco Examiner* (25 Feb 1997); *New York Times* (26 Feb 1997); *JT*, xxvii/5 (1997), 24
M. Point: "Tony Williams: the Final Interview," *DB*, lxiv/4 (1997), 22 [incl. discography]
B. Primack: "Tony Williams: into the Unknown," *JT*, xxvii/1 (1997), 40
R. Tolleson: "Hall of Fame: Tony Williams," *DB*, lxiv/8 (1997), 26

LEWIS PORTER/BK

Williams, Willie (*b* Wilmington, NC, 1 Nov 1958). Tenor and soprano saxophonist. He grew up in Philadelphia and took up clarinet when he was six; initially he had classical lessons, but from around the age of 12 he also received tuition from Odean Pope. A year later he began performing locally, working mostly in organ trios, including that of Don Patterson, and he made many studio recordings as a house musician for the pop music record label Philadelphia International. Having moved to New York (1982) he performed as a freelance with Rashied Ali, Sam Rivers, Art Blakey (deputizing for Jean Toussaint), Max Roach, Woody Shaw, Ronnie Mathews, and Bobby Watson and played in pit bands for Broadway shows. From 1989 to 1995 he was a member of Art Taylor's Wailers; during the same period he worked in Clifford Jordan's big band (recording in 1990–91), with T. S. Monk's sextet (from 1991) and tentet Monk on Monk (touring internationally in the late 1990s), and in an all-star group for Enja records (performing and recording at Sweet Basil, New York, in December 1992). In addition he recorded with an ensemble led by Cornell Rochester and Gerald Veasley (1985) and with Watson (1989), Gary Bartz (1991), and Kevin Mahogany (1994). Williams is a member of the Carnegie Hall Jazz Orchestra and has taught on the Jazzmobile and at the New School for Social Research, the Harlem School of the Arts, CUNY, and the Settlement Music School of Philadelphia.

SELECTED RECORDINGS

As leader: *House Calls* (1984–5, New Note 1005); *Spirit Willie* (1992, Enja 7045-2); *WW3* (1993, Enja 8060-2)

As sideman: T. S. Monk: *Take One* (1991, BN B21Z-99614); A. Taylor: *Mr. A. T.* (1991, Enja 7017-2); *Wailin' at the Vanguard* (1992, Verve 314-519677-2); Enja Band: *Live at Sweet Basil* (1992, Enja 8034-2)

BIBLIOGRAPHY

S. Gribetz: "Hearsay: Arrival Time: Willie Williams," *JT*, xxii/10 (1992), 12

G. Reynaud: "Rencontre: Willie Williams: Spirit Willie," *Jh*, no.525 (1995), 18

<http://www.jazzcorner.com/williams.html> (1998)

GK

Williamson, Bruce (*b* Portland, OR, 14 Sept 1951). Alto saxophonist. He grew up in Oakland, California, and performed in the San Francisco Bay area before studying studio music and jazz at the University of Miami (BM 1973). Later he studied composition at Hunter College, New York (MA 1990). He has played in a number of groups led by Art Lande, including Rubisa Patrol (1976–81), although Mark Isham rather than Williamson usually recorded with this group in the mid-1970s. From 1985 to 1986 Williamson worked with Brother Jack McDuff and in 1990 he joined the Manhattan New Music Project, with which he recorded the album *Mood Swing* (1992, SN 121207-2). He led a septet between 1989 and 1993, which included either Randy Brecker or Tim Hagans on trumpet; it may be heard on the album *Big City Magic* (1990, 1992, Tim. 413). Williamson has taught at SUNY (Purchase), Hunter College, Bennington College (Vermont), and Williams College (Massachusetts), and worked as an artist-in-residence in Osaka, Japan. He also plays clarinet, bass clarinet, and flute.

GK

Williamson, Claude (Berkeley, Jr.) (*b* Brattleboro, VT, 18 Nov 1926). Pianist, brother of Stu Williamson. His father played drums. He was classically trained and studied at the New England Conservatory in Boston (1944–7). In February 1947 he followed his piano teacher to southern California, and after obtaining his musicians' union card six months later began his first important engagement, with Charlie Barnet (until 1949), though he also worked briefly with Red Norvo (1948); he appeared with Barnet in several film shorts. He led his own trio in the 1950s, and from 1950 to September 1951 toured as arranger and accompanist for June Christy, with whom he made further film shorts. He was then drafted, and spent 16 months serving as a percussionist in Okinawa, Japan. Following his discharge in August 1953 he was a member of Howard Rumsey's All Stars from September 1953 through 1955, but was also away from Rumsey for three months, touring with Les Brown's big band. After performing in the Los Angeles area (initially at the Haig, January–June 1956) he toured and recorded with Bud Shank (visiting Europe and South Africa). Throughout the same period he also performed and recorded as the leader of a trio, and he recorded as a sideman with Charlie Mariano and Art Pepper (both 1953–4), Barney Kessel and Stan Levey (both 1954), Bob Cooper (1954–5), Tal Farlow (1955), his brother (1956), and Gerry Mulligan (1959, as co-leader with Johnny Hodges; 1960, under Mulligan's sole leadership).

For the next two decades Williamson worked sporadically in Hollywood, usually with a trio, but his principal activity was outside jazz, as a studio musician and arranger in films and television. His career took on a new impetus in the late 1970s, when he made a tour of Japan and recorded a series of fine albums in Hollywood and New York for Japanese labels; he made further recordings in Hollywood for Japanese labels in the 1980s and 1990s and performed and recorded for Fresh Sound in Barcelona in 1987. In August 1996 he appeared at the Jazz Showcase in Chicago in a duo with Kenny Burrell. Originally influenced by Teddy Wilson and Jess Stacy, Williamson was converted to a more modern approach, revising his style completely after hearing the work of Bud Powell. He brought to Powell's vocabulary a touch of elegance, and his playing has enlivened many West Coast recording sessions.

SELECTED RECORDINGS

As unaccompanied soloist: *Holography* (1977, Interplay 7708)

As leader: *Keys West* (1955, Cap. T6511); *'Round Midnight* (1957, Beth. 69); *Williamson Mulls the Mulligan Scene* (1958, Criterion 601); *Claude Williamson in Italy* (1958, Broadway International 3001); *All God's Chillun Got Rhythm* (1977, Sea Breeze 1003); *New Departure* (1978, Interplay 7717); *Tribute to Bud* (1981, Ewd 90009); *Claude Reigns* (1983, Bopland K26P-6310); *Blue Minor* (1985, Interplay 00280); *Live!: the Sermon* (1987, Fresh Sound 105); *Standards* (1988, DIW 22); *South of the Border, West of the Sun* (1992, Venus 79002); *Song for my Father* (1993, Venus 79034); *Hallucinations* (1995, V.S.O.P. 95)

As sideman: C. Barnet: Cu-ba (1949, Cap. 15417); Claude Reigns (1949, Cap. 1222); T. Farlow: *The Interpretations of Tal Farlow* (1955, Norg. 1027); S. Williamson: *Pee-Jay* (1956, Beth. 55); B. Shank: *The Bud Shank Quartet* (1956, PJ 1215)

SELECTED FILMS AND VIDEOS

Redskin Rhumba (1948); All God's Chillun Got Rhythm (1950); Cherokee (1950); He's Funny that Way (1950); Skyliner (1950); Record Hop (1957)

BIBLIOGRAPHY

FeatherE

"Claude Williamson," *SJ*, xxviii/7 (1974), 153 [discography]

M. Baillie: "Claude Williamson," *JJI*, xli/3 (1988), 14

T. Gioia: *West Coast Jazz: Modern Jazz in California, 1945–1960* (New York, and Oxford, England, 1992), 213

B. Rusch: "Claude Williamson: Interview," *Cadence*, xxiii/3 (1997), 11

MARK GARDNER/BK

Williamson, Steve (*b* London, 28 June 1964). English saxophonist. He began playing clarinet at the age of 13 and took up saxophone three years later. His early influences were funk artists such as Parliament and Grover Washington, Jr., and he also played reggae with various groups, including Misty in Roots. After discovering jazz he attended the jazz course at the Guildhall School of Music (1984–5). In 1986 he became a member of the Jazz Warriors, and in 1988 he and Courtney Pine accompanied the dance group IDJ at a concert in London which celebrated Nelson Mandela's 70th birthday. Williamson, one of a new crop of British jazz players that emerged around the mid-1980s, has also worked with Louis Moholo, Bheki Mseleku, the Brotherhood of Breath, and the Union Dance Company. His recordings as a leader show his admiration for the M-Base style associated with Steve Coleman and feature such American musicians as David Gilmore, Lonnie Plaxico, and Cassandra Wilson.

SELECTED RECORDINGS

As leader: *A Waltz for Grace* (*c*1989, Verve 843088-2); *Rhyme Time (That Fuss Was Us)* (1991, Pol. 511235-2)
As sideman: L. Moholo: *Exile* (1990–91, Ogun 003); B. Mseleku: *Celebration* (1991–2, World Circuit 028)

BIBLIOGRAPHY

CarrJ; *ChiltonB*
R. Cook and N. Coleman: "The New Men," *Wire*, no.36 (1987), 30
J. Fordham: "Horn of Plenty," *The Guardian* (7 March 1989)
S. S. Lwin: "Into the Light," *Jazz FM*, no.8 (1991), 18
T. Green: "Warrior's Journey," *Jazziz*, xiii/3 (1996), 53

MARK GILBERT

Williamson, Stu(art Lee) (*b* Brattleboro, VT, 14 May 1933; *d* Studio City, CA, 1 Oct 1991). Trumpeter and trombonist, brother of Claude Williamson. He lived from 1949 in Los Angeles, where he worked as a sideman with Stan Kenton (1951, 1954–5), Woody Herman (1952–3), Billy May, Charlie Barnet, and Shelly Manne (at intervals, 1954–8); he also played in several studio orchestras led by Marty Paich and performed and recorded in Terry Gibbs's Dream Band (1959–62). After taking up valve trombone in 1954 he made many recordings of jazz (until 1968) and popular music on both his instruments, notably with Howard Rumsey (1954–5), Lennie Niehaus (1954–6), Bill Perkins (1956), and Pepper Adams and Elmo Hope (both 1957). Thereafter the debilitating effects of narcotics addiction ended his musical career. Although Williamson often employed mutes his trumpet tone was consistently bright; this and his fluent valve trombone style made his playing strongly characteristic of West Coast jazz of the 1950s.

SELECTED RECORDINGS

As leader: *Sapphire* (1955, Beth. 1024); *Pee Jay* (1956, Beth. 55)
As sideman: W. Herman: Men from Mars (1953, Mars 800); S. Kenton: *Music of Bill Holman* (1954, Cap. H526), incl. King Fish; Z. Sims: *Zoot Sims Quintet* (1954, NewJ 1102); P. Adams: *Pepper Adams Quintet* (1957, Mode 112); M. Paich: *Broadway Bit* (1959, WB 1296)

BIBLIOGRAPHY

FeatherE
R. Gordon: *Jazz West Coast: the Los Angeles Jazz Scene of the 1950s* (London and New York, 1986)

SCOTT YANOW

Willis, Gary (Glen) (*b* Longview, TX, 28 March 1957). Electric bass guitarist. He first played white gospel music, accompanying his father, a pianist, in church. He attended Kilgore Junior College (1976), East Texas State University (1976–7), Eastfield Community College (1977–8), and North Texas State University (1978–80), where he played guitar before changing back to the bass instrument in 1979. After moving to the Los Angeles area in 1982 he began working at Donte's. He played with Phil Upchurch (1983–7), Hubert Laws (1984–7), Allan Holdsworth (1984), Wayne Shorter (1985–6), Robben Ford (1988), and others. However, he is best known as the co-leader, with the guitarist Scott Henderson, of Tribal Tech (from 1984), a group which built extensively on the style of Weather Report. He taught at the Musicians' Institute, Hollywood (1987–93), and the California Institute of the Arts, Valencia (1992–3), and from 1991 he has given workshops worldwide. He has made an instructional video, *Progressive Bassics* (1992), and he is the author of several books, including *Bass Lessons with the Greats* (1994), *Fingerboard Harmony for Bass* (Milwaukee, 1997), and *The Gary Willis Collection* (Milwaukee, 1998). The playing of Jaco Pastorius was a major formative influence on Willis's bass style, and his compositions owe a large debt to those of Joe Zawinul.

SELECTED RECORDINGS

As leader: *No Sweat* (1996, Alchemy 1009)
As sideman: W. Shorter: *Phantom Navigator* (*c*1986, Col. CK40373); J. Diorio and R. Ford: *Minor Elegance* (1990, MGR 1012); H. Laws: *My Time Will Come* (1990–92, MusicMasters 65100-2); A. Holdsworth: *None too Soon* (1996, Restless 72928)
For further recordings *see* Tribal tech.

BIBLIOGRAPHY

M. Resnicoff: "Gary Willis: Tribal Technician," *GP*, xxiii/10 (1989), 32
R. Garant: "Interview: Gary Willis," *Bassics*, ii/3 (1992), 8
K. Micallef: "Tribal Tech: a Graphic Tour," *JT*, xxii/6 (1992), 41
M. Resnicoff: "Guitar/Bass: Scott Henderson and Gary Willis," *Musician*, no.159 (1992), 73
C. Jisi: "The Big Groove of Gary Willis," *Bass Player*, iv/3 (1993), 51
C. Douse: "Ominous, Gary Willis," *Bassist*, no.8 (1995), 44
T. Wictor: "Gary Willis: No Sweat," *Bass Player*, vii/10 (1996), 14

MARK GILBERT

Willis, Larry [Lawrence Elliott] (*b* New York, 20 Dec 1940). Pianist, composer, and arranger. After graduating from the Manhattan School of Music he played with Jackie McLean (1963) and Hugh Masekela (1964) and recorded with McLean and Lee Morgan (both 1965). He then worked with Kai Winding (1965–7) and Stan Getz (1969) and recorded with Robin Kenyatta (1969). From the 1970s he played frequently on electric piano and sometimes on synthesizer, recording with Masekela (1970, 1972), Groove Holmes (*c*1972), and Joe Henderson (1973), and working with Cannonball Adderley (1971) and Earl May (1971–2). From 1972 to 1978 he was a member of Blood, Sweat and Tears. In addition he recorded as a sideman with Alphonse Mouzon (1972–3), Ryo Kawasaki (1977), and Sonny Fortune (*c*1978), and as a leader (*c*1973), and worked as a freelance in New York (1975).

Following a period with the pop trumpeter Herb Alpert, Willis recorded with David "Fathead" Newman and joined Nat Adderley (both 1982), with whom he may be seen in the video *Nat Adderley Quintet: Live at the Village Vanguard* (*c*1985). Later he worked with Carla Bley and Steve Swallow (1985–7), became a member of Woody Shaw's quintet (1986–7), and took part in sessions led by Chico Freeman (1985), Leni Stern (1985, 1987), Branford Marsalis (1986), and Cindy Blackman and Jimmy Heath (both 1987). From 1988 he toured and recorded with Jerry Gonzalez's Fort Apache Band. He also recorded with Carmen McRae (in performance in San Francisco, early 1988), Valery Ponomarev (1988), Bobby Battle and Datevik Hovanesian (both 1990), Louis Hayes and Eddie Henderson (both 1991), Dave Bargeron (1992), Norris Turney (1993), Gary Bartz and Attila Zoller (both 1994), Hamiet Bluiett, Roy Hargrove, and George Mraz (all 1995), and Ron Holloway (1997). In the 1990s he worked further with Joe Henderson and with Hargrove (1997) and recorded again with Heath (1998).

As well as playing piano Willis has served as an artists and repertory adviser for the Mapleshade label and has written numerous arrangements, notably for Holloway's album *Struttin'* (1995, Mlst. 9238); among his compositions is *To Wisdom, the Prize*, which has been recorded by Battle, Joey Calderazzo, Freeman, Gonzalez, Benny Green, and Tom Williams.

SELECTED RECORDINGS

As unaccompanied soloist: *Solo Spirit* (1992, Mapleshade 1432)

Duos with J. Walrath: *Portraits in Ivory & Brass* (1992, Mapleshade 02032)
As leader: *Heavy Blue* (1989, Ste. 31269); *How Do You Keep the Music Playing?* (1992, Ste. 31312); *A Tribute to Someone* (1993, Audioquest 1022)
As sideman: J. McLean: *Right Now!* (1965, BN 84215); J. Heath: *Peer Pleasure* (1987, Landmark 1514); C. McRae: on *Carmen Sings Monk* (1988, Novus 3086-2-N), Get it Straight, Suddenly; B. Battle: *The Offering* (1990, Mapleshade 01332), incl. To Wisdom, the Prize; A. Zoller: *When it's Time* (1994, Enja 9031-2)

BIBLIOGRAPHY

Feather–Gitler '70s
B. Shoemaker: "Hearsay: Larry Willis: Sound Quality," *JT*, xxiii/1 (1993), 12

BK

Wills, Bob [James Robert] (*b* nr Kosse, TX, 6 March 1905; *d* Fort Worth, 13 May 1975). Fiddler, singer, and bandleader. In 1931 he became one of the founding members of the seminal western-swing band the Light Crust Doughboys (named after the flour company that sponsored it on Fort Worth radio). Three years later he assembled the Texas Playboys, who played on radio station KVOO in Tulsa from 1934 to 1942. The group became very popular in the Southwest through broadcasts, recordings, personal appearances, and nightly dances at Cain's Ballroom; during the 1940s it took part in films, and throughout the 1950s and 1960s it toured and recorded extensively. As a fiddler Wills combined traditional hoedown music with blues inflections, but as a bandleader he was receptive to musicians who could play jazz or the hot dance tunes that he himself was incapable of producing. The Playboys consequently combined country music string instruments with drums and wind instruments and performed an eclectic repertory that included blues, jazz, popular standards, and country music. Along with Milton Brown, Wills was one of the chief popularizers of Western swing.

SELECTED RECORDINGS

Four or Five Times/St. Louis Blues (*c*1935, Voc. 03076); Steel Guitar Rag (1936, Voc. 03394); Rosetta (*c*1937, Voc. 03659); New San Antonio Rose (1940, OK 05694); Big Beaver (1940, OK 05905); *The Tiffany Transcriptions* (1945–8, Tishomingo 01)

BIBLIOGRAPHY

R. Sheldon: *Hubbin' it: the Life of Bob Wills* (Tulsa, OK, 1938)
C. R. Townsend: "Bob Wills," *Stars of Country Music*, ed. B. C. Malone and J. McCulloh (Urbana, IL, 1975), 157
——: *San Antonio Rose: the Life and Music of Bob Wills* (Urbana, IL, Chicago, and London, 1976) [incl. discography by B. Pinson]
R. Kienzle: Liner notes, *Bob Wills* (TL CW07, 1982)
G. Hunkel: *Western Swing & Country Jazz: eine Einführung mit Kurzporträts über Bob Wills und Milton Brown* (Menden, Germany, 1983)
R. Wills: "I Remember Daddy Bob," *Journal of Country Music*, xiv/2 (1992), 3
M. Rowland: "Dance All Night, Stay a Little Longer: Fifty Years on, the Original Texas Playboys are Still the Kings of Western Swing," *Musician*, no.173 (1993), 58

BILL C. MALONE

Wilmer, Val(erie (Sybil)) (*b* Harrogate, England, 7 Dec 1941). English writer and photographer. She wrote about jazz from the age of 18 and in 1959–60 studied photography in London. During the following decades she contributed hundreds of articles to *Melody Maker* (1960–1970s), *Down Beat* (of which she was the British correspondent from 1966 to 1970), *Jazz Journal*, *Jazz Monthly*, *Crescendo*, *Jazz magazine*, *Musica jazz*, *Swing Journal*, *Jazz Forum*, *The Wire*, and many other periodicals and national newspapers. She also provided the photographs used to illustrate several books as well as those used in John Jeremy's film *Jazz is our Religion* (1972). Wilmer has written extensively on the contribution of black British musicians, lectured and chaired forums in this area, and conducted interviews of numerous women and black British musicians for the oral history collection at the National Sound Archive of the British Library. Her own books include *Jazz People* (1970), an important collection of interviews with leading swing, bop, and free-jazz musicians; *The Face of Black Music* (New York, 1976), a book of photographs; *As Serious as your Life* (1977), a history of free jazz; and an autobiography (1989).

WRITINGS

(selective list)

Jazz People (London, Indianapolis, and New York, 1970/*R*1985)
C. Fox: *The Jazz Scene* (London, 1972) [photographs]
The Face of Black Music (New York, 1976) [photographs]
As Serious as your Life: the Story of the New Jazz (London, 1977, rev. [3]/1987)
B. Sidran: *Black Talk*: *schwarze Kultur: die andere Kultur im weissen Amerika* (Hofheim am Taunus, Germany, 1985) [photographs]
Mama Said There'd be Days Like This (London, 1989, rev. 2/1991)
H. Geerken and B. Hefele: *Omniverse Sun Ra* (Wartaweil, Germany, 1994) [photographs]
P. Trynka: *Portrait of the Blues* (London, 1996) [photographs]

ROBERT GANNON/BK

Wilson, Bert (*b* Evansville, IN, 15 Oct 1939). Reed player. He grew up in a family of vaudeville performers and from an early age appeared with his grandfather in a song and dance act; however, when he was four he was paralyzed by polio. By the time he was eight he had regained partial use of his arms and hands, and he learned piano and music theory. He played clarinet from the age of 13 and first heard recordings by Charlie Parker two years later. After moving from Chicago to Los Angeles when he was 18, he took up tenor saxophone and studied with Sonny Simmons and the drummer Smiley Winters. As the leader of his own groups he performed locally with George Morrow and Albert Stinson among his sidemen. In 1966 he sat in with John Coltrane at the It Club, and in the same year he moved to New York, where he performed and recorded with James Zitro and recorded with Simmons (1966). From 1969 he lived in Berkeley, California, and played with Eddie Marshall, Donald Garrett, and Barbara Donald, among others. Following a short period in Woodstock, New York, he settled in Olympia, Washington (1979), and formed the group Rebirth; his most regular sidemen were Chuck Stentz on tenor saxophone, Jack Perciful or Allen Youngblood on piano, Chuck Metcalf on double bass, Bob Meyer on drums, and Nancy Curtis on flute and soprano saxophone. Wilson plays clarinet, bass clarinet, and soprano, alto, C-melody, and tenor saxophones; his style reflects that of Eric Dolphy, though he is also highly regarded for his use of multiphonics and the saxophone's altissimo register.

SELECTED RECORDINGS

As leader: *Bebop Revisited* (1982–4, FMO [unnumbered]); *Live at the Zoo* (1988, Nine Winds 0138); *The Next Rebirth* (*c*1989, Nine Winds 0124); *Further Adventures in Jazz* (1992, FMO 004); *Endless Fingers* (1994, Arabesque 0123)
As sideman: S. Simmons: on *Music from the Spheres* (1966, ESP 1043), Dolphy's Days; J. Zitro: *James Zitro* (1967, ESP 1052)

BIBLIOGRAPHY

B. Rusch: "The Questionnaire," *Cadence*, xx/3 (1994), 33
G. Robinson: "Bert Wilson," *JT*, xxvii/5 (1997), 31
<http://www.halcyon.com/barchey/fmojazz> (1999) [incl. discography]

GK

Wilson, Buster [Albert Wesley] (*b* Atlanta, 18 Aug or 16 Dec 1897; *d* Los Angeles, 23 Oct 1949). Pianist. Levin (1996) gives his birthdate as 18 August, but California death records give

16 December; the latter also provide his full name. He grew up in Los Angeles, where he replaced Lil Hardin in King Oliver's band at Wayside Park in 1921. About 1922 he was with Dink Johnson, and from 1923 to 1926 he was a member of the cooperative Sunnyland Jazz Orchestra at the 15th and Main Ballroom. Later he was with Mutt Carey (1927), Jimmie Noone, Curtis Mosby, Paul Howard, Lionel Hampton (1935), and Les Hite. In 1941 he rehearsed with Jelly Roll Morton's band. He joined Kid Ory's band in 1944, and his contribution up to his departure in early 1948 was central to the band's style; *Dippermouth Blues/Savoy Blues* (1945, Exner 3) is typical. An album of private recordings, *Buster Wilson, 1947–49* (AM 89), reveals him also as a soloist and in a duo and a trio.

BIBLIOGRAPHY

ChiltonW
Obituary, J. T. Gipson, *Los Angeles Sentinel* (3 Nov 1949)
F. Levin: "I Remember Buster Wilson," *New Orleans Music*, vi/4 (1996), 6; repr. in *Jazzbeat*, viii/2 (1996), 6; *IAJRC Journal*, xxx/4 (1997), 1

HOWARD RYE

Cassandra Wilson at the New Orleans Jazz and Heritage Festival

Wilson, Cassandra (*b* Jackson, MS, 4 Dec 1955). Singer and leader. Her father, Herman Fowlkes, is an electric bass guitarist and a high school music teacher who recorded with her in 1990. She learned classical piano from around the age of seven into her early teens. When she was about 11 her father taught her some basic guitar chords and she began composing folk tunes; while at high school she briefly sang and played guitar in a folk trio. She read mass communications at Jackson State University, during which time she performed in a rhythm-and-blues band and worked as a folk singer in coffee houses; while singing with the local Black Arts Music Society she was introduced to bop by Alvin Fielder. After graduating she moved in 1981 to New Orleans, where she sat in with Kidd Jordan, Ellis Marsalis, and Earl Turbinton, Jr., with whom she also had lessons. In 1982 she studied ear training with Grachan Moncur III, in East Orange, New Jersey, and frequented jam sessions in New York; she moved to the city later that year and began working at the Galleon.

Wilson met Steve Coleman in 1983, after he had heard her singing *Cherokee* at a jam session, and he encouraged her to break away from the standard repertory and write her own material; she subsequently became associated with Coleman and others in the activities of the collective M-Base. Between 1985 and 1992 she recorded regularly with Coleman, often providing a wordless vocal accompaniment, and she appears in the video *M-BASE Jams at BAM* (*c*1989 [filmed 1988]). In 1986 she toured Europe and recorded in Milan with New Air, the avant-garde trio of Henry Threadgill, Fred Hopkins, and Pheeroan akLaff, and in the mid-1980s she performed with, among others, John Hicks, Al Dailey, Bob Cunningham, Dave Holland, Moncur, Jean-Paul Bourelly, and Geri Allen. Wilson was a member of the ensemble which gave the première of Wynton Marsalis's oratorio *Blood on the Fields* on National Public Radio in autumn 1994, and she recorded and toured with the group performing this work until around 1997. In addition she recorded with Chris White (1992), Bob Belden (1993–5), Courtney Pine (*c*1995), Holland (1995), Javon Jackson and Steve Turre (both 1996), Pat Martino (*c*1997), and Kurt Elling (1997), and sang on several film soundtracks.

Wilson's activities as a leader began around 1987; her principal sidemen were Rod Williams (until 1991), James Weidman (1991–*c*1993), and Kevin Bruce Harris and the drummer Mark Johnson (both until *c*1993). She made her first tour of Europe in 1988 and thereafter performed internationally. Between 1994 and 1997 Brandon Ross was her music director and her sidemen were Charles Burnham, Lonnie Plaxico, the drummer Lance Carter, and the percussionist Jeff Haynes, after which Onaje Allen Gumbs worked as her conductor and arranger, Plaxico as her music director, and Vincent Chancey joined the group. In 1999 she wrote and performed lyrics to songs associated with Miles Davis.

Wilson's voice varies from a full, rich, throaty contralto to a dark, husky whisper, and she is a master of rhythmic nuance. When singing jazz she incorporates elements from the styles of Sarah Vaughan, Carmen McRae, and, notably, Betty Carter; however, many of her recordings have been in more of a pop and folk-revivalist vein, in which she is indebted to Joni Mitchell and, in particular, Nina Simone. She is also a wonderful blues singer, as may be heard on her album *Blue Light 'til Dawn* (*c*1993).

SELECTED RECORDINGS

Duo with Ron Carter: on B. Belden: *Shades of Blue* (1994–5, BN B21Z-32166), Joshua Fit de Battle of Jericho (1994)

As leader: *Blue Skies* (1988, JMT 834419-1); *She who Weeps* (1990, JMT 834443-2); *Blue Light 'til Dawn* (*c*1993, BN B21Z-81357); *New Moon Daughter* (*c*1995, BN 32861-2); with J. Terrasson: *Rendezvous* (1997, BN 55484-2)

As sideman: New Air: *Air Show no.1* (1986, BS 0099), incl. Don't Drink that Corner, My Life is in the Bush; R. Williams: on *Destiny Express* (1990,

Muse 5412), False Face; D. Holland: on *Dreams of the Elders* (1995, ECM 1572), Equality; J. Jackson: on *A Look Within* (1996, BN 36496-2), Country Girl

BIBLIOGRAPHY

CarrJ; *GrayF*
I. Leymarie: "Gros plan: Cassandra Wilson," *Jm*, no.374 (1988), 23
K. Whitehead: "Cassandra Wilson: a New Kind of Singer, a New Kind of Song," *DB*, lv/2 (1988), 28
J. Macnie: "Beyond Interpretation," *Musician*, no.126 (1989), 10
H. Mandel: "Cassandra Wilson," *JT* (1989), Jan, 9
M. Smith: "Cassandra Wilson: the New Faces," *Coda*, no.227 (1989), 36
I. Leymarie and K. Akadiri-Soumaîla: "New York is Now: Cassandra Wilson," *Jm*, no.396 (1990), 37
J. Nash: "Cassandra Wilson," *JT* (1990), Aug, 17
D. Rubien: "Vocalist Leaps over Jazz Barriers," *San Francisco Chronicle Datebook* (29 July 1990)
K. Brodacki: "Cassandra Wilson: Vocal Prophetess," *JF* [intl edn], no.131 (1991), 27
R. Harrington: "Unchained Melody: Vocalist Cassandra Wilson Takes Liberties with her Jazz," *Washington Post* (26 June 1994)
T. Scherman: "Cassandra Wilson: Crossroads Blues," *Musician*, no.187 (1994), 44
J. Ephland: "Beyond the Dawn: Cassandra Wilson and Life after *Blue Light 'til Dawn*," *DB*, lxii/1 (1995), 22 [incl. discography]
K. Hammett-Vaughan: "Cassandra Wilson Finds the Groove," *Coda*, no.261 (1995), 8
L. Blumenfeld: "Cassandra Wilson: Anima Rising," *Jazziz*, xiii/5 (1996), 50
J. Ephland: "Joni Mitchell & Cassandra Wilson: Alternate Tunings," *DB*, lxiii/12 (1996), 18
F. Goaty: "Cassandra Wilson: 'pourquoi changer pour changer?'," *Jm*, no.458 (1996), 18
L. Jurgeit: "Cassandra Wilson," *JP*, xlv/6 (1996), 16
B. Milkowski: "Cassandra Wilson: Moonlight and Music," *JT*, xxvi/2 (1996), 34
M. Gayford: "The Magic of the Moment," *Daily Telegraph* (6 March 1999)
T. Pérémarti: "Cassandra Wilson: Travelling sur Miles," *Jazzman*, no.44 (1999), 18
J. Sullivan: "Cassandra Wilson Will Sing Songs of Trumpeter Davis her own Way," *San Francisco Chronicle Datebook* (2 May 1999)

GK

Wilson, Chuck [Charles Dee] (*b* Wichita Falls, TX, 31 July 1948). Alto saxophonist. He grew up near Corpus Christi, Texas, began on alto saxophone at the age of 11, and led a trio while in high school. Following his studies at North Texas State University he pursued a career primarily in big bands. He joined Jerry Gray at the Fairmont Hotel in Dallas (*c*1972), and after Gray's death (1976) he played lead alto saxophone with Buddy Rich, recording and touring internationally (1977–80). Having settled in New York he began to work extensively in the studios, doubling on clarinet and flute. He continued in big bands with Tito Puente (1980–81), Gerry Mulligan's Concert Orchestra (1981–9), Bob Wilber (*c*1983), Benny Goodman (his last band, August 1985 – June 1986), Buck Clayton (1986–90), and the clarinetist Walt Levinsky (late 1980s), and he also recorded with Loren Schoenberg's big band (1984). Wilson was a member of the quintet led by Howard Alden and Dan Barrett (1985–91), with which he may be heard as a soloist on *Swing Street* (1986, Conc. 4349) and *The A.B.Q. Salutes Buck Clayton* (1989, Con. 4395), playing in a style that somewhat incongruously intermingles the sound of a passionate, swing-era lead alto saxophone (after the manner of Johnny Hodges) with fleet bop lines (after the manner of Cannonball Adderley). In 1996 he formed the small group Chuck Wilson and Friends; his sidemen have included Alden, Murray Wall, and the trombonist Joel Helleny. (M. Bailie: "Chuck Wilson," *JJI*, xliii/6 (1990), 12)

GK

Wilson, Dennis (Edward) (*b* Greensboro, NC, 22 July 1952). Trombonist and arranger. He attended the Berklee College of Music (BM music education 1974) and was a member of Lionel Hampton's orchestra (1973–5), serving as its music director for 18 months. From 1974 he performed as a freelance with, among others, Stan Kenton and Clark Terry, and in March 1977 he joined Count Basie's orchestra, with which he made several recordings; he may be heard as the leader of Basie's orchestra on Manhattan Transfer's album *Vocalese* (1985, Atl. 81266), for which he also wrote arrangements. Wilson continued to work with the group, under the direction of first Thad Jones and then Frank Foster, until 1987, when he left to direct educational projects for Count Basie Enterprises and to play trombone and act in and arrange for the musical *Satchmo*. The following year he was lead trombonist in Dizzy Gillespie's big band, and in 1990 he worked in Frank Wess's big band, with which he toured and recorded in Japan both under Wess's name and accompanying Mel Tormé. Later he recorded with the American Jazz Orchestra (1991) and a big band under Benny Carter's leadership (1992) and performed with Robert Trowers at the JVC Jazz Festival New York (1995). From the 1970s he has been active as an educator, teaching privately and presenting workshops nationwide. (*Feather–GitlerBEJ*; *SheridanCB*)

For illustration *see* Recording, fig.6.

BK

Wilson, Dick [Richard] (*b* Mount Vernon, IL, 11 Nov 1911; *d* New York, 24 Nov 1941). Tenor saxophonist. He was brought up in Seattle, where he was taught alto saxophone by Joe Darensbourg. After changing to tenor saxophone he joined Don Anderson in Portland, Oregon, in 1929, but returned to Seattle the following year to play with Darensbourg's band at the Jungle Temple Inn. He later worked with Gene Coy's Happy Black Aces (1933–4), Zack Whyte (1934–5), and, finally, Andy Kirk's Clouds of Joy, with which he remained until his death (for illustration *see* Williams, mary lou).

Wilson developed a highly individual style on tenor saxophone which was influenced by Coleman Hawkins, Herschel Evans, and, possibly, Chu Berry, with a sinuous, slithery warmth of tone that suggests the later style of Paul Gonsalves. He is one of the rare musicians who is considered never to have recorded a bad solo.

SELECTED RECORDINGS

(recorded for Decca unless otherwise indicated)

As sideman: A. Kirk: Walkin' and Swingin' (1936, 809); Moten Swing (1936, 853); Lotta Sax Appeal/Bearcat Shuffle (1936, 1046); Froggy Bottom/Christopher Columbus (1936, 729); Corky (1936, 772); *Andy Kirk and his Clouds of Joy: 1937* (1937, Jazz Society 503); Wednesday Night Hop (1937, 1303); In the Groove (1937, 1261); Jump Jack Jump (1937, 2226); Six Men and a Girl: Tea for Two (1940, Var. 8193); Zonky (1940, Var. 8190); A. Kirk: Little Miss (1940, 3491); Ring dem Bells (1941, 3663); 47th Street Jive (1941, 4042)

BIBLIOGRAPHY

ChiltonW; *McCarthyB*; *SchullerS*
B. Niquet: "Dick Wilson," *BHcF*, no.62 (1956), 27
R. Russell: *Jazz Style in Kansas City and the Southwest* (Berkeley, CA, Los Angeles, and London, 1971, rev. 2/1973/*R*1997)
J. Evensmo: *The Tenor Saxophones of Budd Johnson, Cecil Scott, Elmer Williams, Dick Wilson, 1927–1942* (n.p. [Oslo], n.d. [?1977]) [discography]
——: *History of Jazz Tenor Saxophone: Black Artists*, i: *1917–1934* (Oslo, 1996); ii: *1935–1939* (Oslo, 1997)

FRANK DRIGGS

Wilson, Ed(ward John) [Milko] (*b* Sydney, 22 June 1944). Australian bandleader, trombonist, and arranger. He joined the Waratah Jazzmen in 1959 and during the late 1960s worked in nightclubs, as well as with the Sydney Symphony Orchestra and the dance band of the Australian Broadcasting Commission. With Warren Daly, he formed the Daly–Wilson Big Band, which was active from 1969 to 1971 and from 1973 to 1983; its recording *The Daly–Wilson Big Band* (1975, Rep. 60-0023) provides a good example of Wilson's playing. He then moved to Murwillumbah in New South Wales, where he formed another big band and small groups. In 1986 he became music director for the Jupiters Casino on the Gold Coast, Queensland. (B. Johnson: *The Oxford Companion to Australian Jazz*, Melbourne, Australia, 1987)

For further recordings and bibliography *see* Daly, warren.

BRUCE JOHNSON

Wilson, [née Goodall], **Edith** (*b* Louisville, KY, 2 Sept 1896; *d* Chicago, 30 March 1981). Singer. Her year of birth sometimes appears incorrectly as 1906 (in later years she trimmed ten years from her age for show-business purposes). After working in clubs and theaters in Louisville and Chicago she teamed up with Lena Wilson and the latter's pianist brother, Danny, whom she married. From late 1921 she worked with Johnny Dunn on tour and in Lew Leslie's revues at the Plantation Room, New York; she also recorded with Dunn's Original Jazz Hounds, including *Evil Blues/Pensacola Blues* (1922, Col. A3746). *Dixie Blues* (1922, Col. A3787) features a wordless passage, foreshadowing later use of this technique. Wilson appeared in London with the *Plantation Revue* company (May–September 1923), and was then resident at the Club Alabam, New York, with Fletcher Henderson (January–May 1924) and recorded with a small group from the band (*Daddy Change your Mind/I Don't Know and I Don't Care Blues*, 1924, Col. 14008D). In 1924–5 she toured widely with the entertainer Doc Straine before joining the revue *Blackbirds of 1926*, later presented in Paris and London. After mid-1927 she worked with the bands of Sammy Stewart, Duke Ellington, and Sam Wooding, and in summer 1928 toured Germany with Wooding. In 1929–30 she was in the musical *Connie's Hot Chocolates* in New York and on tour. She rejoined *Blackbirds* in 1933 and was in Britain with the show in 1934–5. During the period 1935 to 1939 she appeared with Cab Calloway, Lucky Millinder, Noble Sissle, and Fess Williams. After 1940 she worked mainly as an actress. Wilson retired in 1966, but began a musical comeback in 1971, often working with Little Brother Montgomery, with whom she appeared in the BBC television series "The Devil's Music" (1976). She visited Paris in March 1974 and appeared at festivals and concerts until shortly before her death.

BIBLIOGRAPHY

D. Stewart-Baxter: "Blues," *JJ*, xx/2 (1967), 14

——: *Ma Rainey and the Classic Blues Singers* (New York and London, 1970), 26

C. Ellis: Liner notes, *Edith Wilson, 1921–22, with Johnny Dunn's Original Jazz Hounds* (Fountain 302, 1974)

B. Koester: "He May be your Man: Biography of Edith Wilson," *Jazz Report*, ix/4 ([1978]), [21]

S. Harris: *Blues Who's Who: a Biographical Dictionary of Blues Singers* (New Rochelle, NY, 1979/*R*1994)

Obituaries: J. O'Neal, *Living Blues*, no.50 (1981), 44; *Chicago Tribune* (31 March 1981)

H. Rye: Liner notes, *Johnny Dunn & Edith Wilson*, i: *1921–1922* (RST 1522-2, 1995)

——: Liner notes, *Edith & Lena Wilson: Complete Recorded Works, 1924–1931*, ii (Document 5451, 1996)

HOWARD RYE

Wilson, Garland (Lorenzo) (*b* Martinsburg, WV, 13 June 1909; *d* Paris, 31 May 1954). Pianist. He spent a period in Washington, DC, then worked in a five-piece band in a beer garden in Atlantic City, New Jersey, before moving to New York, where he was resident at various clubs in Harlem (1929–32). While accompanying Monette Moore at Covan's Dew Drop Inn he was heard by John Hammond, and he subsequently achieved acclaim through recordings as an unaccompanied soloist (1931–2). In mid-1932 he performed on a weekly radio program in a trio with Frank Newton and Artie Bernstein, and the following November he appeared in France accompanying the singer Nina Mae McKinney, with whom he recorded and toured Europe (1933–4) and held a residency in Athens (April–May 1934); he may be seen as her accompanist performing *Dinah* in the film *BBC Voice of Britain* (1935) and in the film *On Velvet* (1938) performing *Swanee River*.

At the end of 1934 Garland began what became a long association with Le Boeuf sur le Toit in Paris; this was interrupted by a tour of Britain with the bandleader Jack Payne (1935–6) and an engagement at the Shim Sham Club in London (1936). In addition he recorded in Paris with the singer Jean Sablon (1936), as a soloist (1938), and with Danny Polo (1939). From 1939 he played in cabarets in Hollywood and New York, where he recorded with Cedric Wallace and performed with the singer Thelma Carpenter. Wilson worked again in London and Paris from 1951 until his death, at which time he was host in his own room at Le Boeuf sur le Toit.

SELECTED RECORDINGS

As unaccompanied soloist: Dear Old Southland/Limehouse Blues/St. James Infirmary/When your lover has gone (1931, Col. special pressing, first issued on *The Piano Album*, 1929–1940, Meritt 4); Memories of You/Rockin' Chair (1932, OK 41556); Blues en Si bémol (Blues in C Flat)/Get up, Bessie (1932, Bruns. A500220); The way I feel/You Rascal You (1933, Bruns. A500359); Shim Sham Drag (1936, Bruns. 02283); The Blues got Me (1938, Swing 19); The blues I love to play/Blue Morning [celesta] (1938, Swing 46)

As leader: Sweet Georgia Brown (1951, HMV B10413)

As sideman with D. Polo: You made me love you/Montmartre Moan (1939, Decca F7039)

BIBLIOGRAPHY

ChiltonW

J. Aldam: "A Study of Garland Wilson," *Piano Jazz*, i, ed. A. McCarthy and M. Jones (London, 1945), 13

M. Jones: "Garland Wilson: Self-portrait of a Jazz Pianist," *MM*, xxx (5 June 1954), 13

H. Rye: "Visiting Firemen, 11: Garland Wilson," *Sv*, no.119 (1985), 176; additional information in L. Wright, ed.: *Storyville 1998–9* (Chigwell, England, 1999), 128

HOWARD RYE

Wilson, Gerald (Stanley) (*b* Shelby, MS, 4 Sept 1918). Composer, arranger, bandleader, and trumpeter. When he was 14 his family moved to Detroit, and he studied music at high school. From August 1939 to April 1942 he worked with Jimmie Lunceford's band as a soloist, composer, and arranger (for illustration *see* Lunceford, jimmie). He then moved to Los Angeles, where he performed with Les Hite (1942–3) and Benny Carter (1943). After playing with Clark Terry and Ernie Royal in Willie Smith's navy band he organized his first big band, which he led from 1944 to 1947; it included such musicians as Snooky Young and Melba Liston and undertook a tour during which it played in New York. Wilson then worked with Count Basie, writing arrangements and performing with the band intermittently (1948–9), and Dizzy Gillespie (for six months, *c*1949) and wrote arrangements for Duke Ellington: "I'm happy to say that Duke Ellington liked my music so much he put his name on it," he recalled (Hildebrand, 1988). During the 1950s and 1960s he wrote for films and television and for such singers as Al Hibbler, Johnny Hartman, Sarah Vaughan, Nancy Wilson, and Ella Fitzgerald. He rarely played jazz during the 1950s, but recorded as a trumpeter with Buddy Collette (1956–9), Leroy Vinnegar (1957), Curtis Counce (1958), and Red Callender (*c*1958).

In 1961 Wilson formed a new band which recorded regularly until 1969 and gave many successful performances, most notably at the Monterey Jazz Festival in 1963. The orchestra was widely acclaimed, both for the caliber of its players (who included Harold Land, Elmo Hope, Charles Lloyd, Teddy Edwards, Bud Shank, Joe Maini, Mel Lewis, Joe Pass, Carmell Jones, Tony Ortega, and Jack Wilson) and for the quality of Wilson's compositions. He taught jazz courses at the University of Utah in the late 1960s and from 1969 to 1983 at San Fernando Valley State College (which in the 1970s became California State University, Northridge); from 1968 to 1973 he was a disc jockey on the jazz station in Los Angeles, KBCA. Later he taught at California State University, Los Angeles (1980–91). He led a new orchestra in the 1980s with such sidemen as Bobby Bryant, Land, Young, Oscar Brashear, Garnett Brown, Ernie Watts, Collette, Paul Humphrey, and his son, the guitarist Anthony Wilson (*b* Los Angeles, 9 May 1968); it performed at the Monterey Festival in 1987, and recorded.

In 1988 Wilson conducted the American Jazz Orchestra in a retrospective concert of his work. He received a Jazz Masters Fellowship from the National Endowment for the Arts in 1990 and in the following year joined the faculty of the University of California, Los Angeles, working in the jazz program headed by Kenny Burrell. He continued to lead his big band throughout the decade, giving performances mainly in the Los Angeles area, but also in Chicago, Washington, DC (spring 1996), and Europe (including a concert in Vienna in the late 1990s), and making new recordings. He also visited New York in November 1998 for a performance of his music by the Carnegie Hall Jazz Band. His autobiography (including photographs and biographical notes) appeared on compact disc as *Suite Memories: Reflections on a Jazz Journey* (MAMA Foundation 1014, 1996), and the score for his big-band composition *Nancy Jo* was published in *Down Beat* (xxx/10 (1963), 43). Materials relating to his career are at the Library of Congress in Washington, DC (*see* LIBRARIES AND ARCHIVES, §2).

Oral history material in *CLU* (CASOHP); video oral history material in *NCH* (HCJA).

SELECTED RECORDINGS

As leader: Moon Rise/Synthetic Joe (1945, Excelsior 122); *You Better Believe it!* (1961, PJ 34); *Portraits* (1963, PJ 80); *The Golden Sword* (1966, PJ 20111); *Lomelin* (1981, Dis. 833); *Jessica* (1982, Trend 531); *Jenna* (1989, Dis. 964); *State Street Sweet* (*c*1994, MAMA Foundation 1010)

As sideman with L. Vinnegar: *Leroy Walks* (1957, Cont. 3542)

RECORDED COMPOSITIONS

(selective list)

* – with Wilson as sideman

As leader: *The Moment of Truth* (1962, PJ 61), incl. Josefina, The Moment of Truth, Nancy Jo, Viva tirado

Recorded by J. Lunceford: *Yard Dog Mazurka (1941, Decca 4032)

SELECTED ARRANGEMENTS

Recorded by others: on D. Ellington: *Piano in the Background* (1960, Col. CS8346), Perdido; N. Wilson: *Yesterday's Love Songs, Today's Blues* (1963, Cap. ST2012)

SELECTED FILMS AND VIDEOS

An American in Paris (1951); The Swingin' Singin' Years (1960); Frankly Jazz: Gerald Wilson All-Star Orchestra (1962)

BIBLIOGRAPHY

FeatherE; *Feather '60s*; *Feather–Gitler '70s*; *SchullerS*

J. Tynan: "Facing Challenges: Gerald Wilson," *DB*, xxix/1 (1962), 18

L. Feather: "Gerald Wilson," *IM*, lxii/7 (1963), 18

L. Robinson: "Gerald Wilson," *Jazz*, iii/5 (1964), 12

J. Tynan: "Gerald Wilson," *BMI: the Many Worlds of Music* (1970), March, 20

L. Hildebrand: "50 Year Veteran: Another Big Band for Gerald Wilson," *San Francisco Chronicle Datebook* (17 Jan 1988)

G. G. Vercelli: "Gerald Wilson," *JJI*, xli/10 (1988), 12 [incl. discography]

S. Dance: "Gerald Wilson: Genius at Work," *JT* (1990), Feb, 6 [incl. discography]

J. Norris: "Gerald Wilson: Moment of Truth," *Coda*, no.248 (1993), 16 [incl. discography]

Z. Stewart: "Gerald Wilson's One-two Punch," *DB*, lxiv/1 (1997), 30 [incl. discography]

FREDERICK A. BECK/BK

Wilson, Herman (Herrington) (*b* Montego Bay, Jamaica, 10 Aug 1929). Jamaican trombonist, composer, and arranger. He started out playing light orchestral music, then joined Sonny Bradshaw's bop band. In 1951 he traveled to Britain with the pianist Ozzie Da Costa. He worked in Germany for 18 months for the US Special Services and played in London with Tubby Hayes, Jimmy Deuchar, Dizzy Reece, Sammy Walker, Jiver Hutchinson, and Cab Kaye. After moving to Paris he worked with George Johnson, Peanuts Holland, Don Byas, Pierre Michelot, and Kenny Clarke; he also toured with Bill Coleman (1953–4, 1956). Wilson toured Italy with the European All-Stars (a sextet including Reece, Guy Lafitte, and Wallace Bishop), and on the French Riviera he joined the opera orchestra of the dancer Katherine Dunham. Based in Germany from 1957 to 1959, he was featured on stage and radio there, in Belgium, and in the Netherlands. As a leader he played in Poland, and in Vienna he introduced cool jazz to the city's cafés and nightclubs. He wrote music for and performed in the film *The Jazz Bandits* (1958) and for a children's music book. In 1960 he returned to London, where he studied arranging, co-led a group with the trombonist Pete Myers, and wrote for nightclub acts. Having become involved in the jazz and poetry movement, he played and wrote for the New Departures big band, which accompanied poetry readings. In 1963 he took a group to Liberia, and the following year he toured the Caribbean and South America as a featured soloist on stage and radio. Wilson continued to play trombone, but by the end of the decade he was furthering his writing skills by working primarily as a music director in recording studios. Thereafter he concentrated on composition, scoring for films and creating large-scale works which have been performed in concert halls and on radio; he also worked as a university lecturer. His ten-piece Chamber Group, which recorded an album of his compositions, *At the Woodwinds' Ball*(1978, Spot. 512), involved Tony Coe and Don Rendell.

BIBLIOGRAPHY

V. Wilmer: "Musicians of the Caribbean, no.2: Herman Wilson," *Flamingo* [London], iii/3 (1963), 11

B. Green: Liner notes, *At the Woodwinds' Ball* (Spot. 512, 1979)

B. Coleman: *Trumpet Story: souvenirs d'un grand du jazz* (Paris, 1981; Eng. orig., London and Boston, 1990, as *Trumpet Story*)

VAL WILMER

Wilson, Jack(, Jr.) (*b* Chicago, 3 Aug 1936). Pianist. He grew up in Fort Wayne, Indiana, from the age of seven, took up piano when he was nine, studied formally, and began performing in local bands at the age of 14; while in high school he doubled on baritone saxophone, which he also played in working groups. After performing with James Moody for two weeks in 1953 he attended Indiana University for two years, then moved to Columbus, Ohio, where he played with Roland Kirk and led his own trio. In 1956–7 he worked with Dinah Washington; later he was active as a freelance in Chicago. Following his military service he rejoined Washington in 1961 and the following year settled in Los Angeles. From that time he worked with Roy Ayers (1963), Gerald Wilson, Harold Land, Shelly Manne, the quintet led by Clark Terry and Bill Brookmeyer, and Jimmy Witherspoon. As well as beng active as a studio musician he performed and recorded occasionally with his own groups. In the late 1970s and early 1980s he made further albums as a leader and also as a sideman, with Lorez Alexandria and Eddie Harris (both 1978, the latter in concert at Keystone Korner, San Francisco) and Terry (1980). Wilson has long been underrated; an accomplished bop pianist, he also plays soul jazz after the manner of Horace Silver.

SELECTED RECORDINGS

As leader: *The Jack Wilson Quartet* (1963, Atl. 1406); *The Two Sides of Jack Wilson* (1963, Atl. 1427); *Something Personal* (1967, BN 84251); *Easterly Winds* (1967, BN 84270); *Innovations* (1977, Dis. 777)

As sideman: Earl Anderza: *Outa Sight* (1962, PJ 65); C. Amy: *Katanga* (1963, PJ 70); R. Ayers: *West Coast Vibes* (1963, UA 6325); G. Wilson: *The Golden Sword* (1966, PJ 20111); C. Barnet: *Big Band 1967* (1966, Vault 9004); I. Isaacs (i): *Ike Isaacs at Freddie Jett's Pied Piper* (1967, RGB 2000)

BIBLIOGRAPHY

Feather '60s; *Feather–Gitler '70s*

G. G. Vercelli: "Jack Wilson: Ivory Innovator," *DB*, xlv/5 (1978), 18 [incl. discography]

SCOTT YANOW

Wilson, Joe [Joseph] **Lee** (*b* Bristow, OK, 22 Dec 1935). Singer and leader. He had classical singing lessons, attended Los Angeles City College, where he studied jazz, began his career as a jazz singer in Santa Monica, California (1958), and then toured the West Coast and Mexico. After moving to New York in 1962 he worked with Sonny Rollins, Lee Morgan, Miles Davis, Pharoah Sanders, and Jackie McLean. From 1971 to 1972 he sang with Archie Shepp, and his strong baritone voice may be heard to advantage on the title track of Shepp's album *Things Have Got to Change* (1971, Imp. 9212) and on *Steam*, from Shepp's album *Attica Blues* (1972, Imp. 9222). Wilson also worked with Sunny Murray and made recordings as a leader (1969, 1972, 1975), with the percussionist Mtume (*c*1972), and with the pianist Billy Gault (1974). From 1973 to 1978 he ran a loft, the Ladies Fort. During the same period he appeared at the Newport Festival New York (1973) and the Live Loft Festival (1975) and performed on radio and television. In 1977 he recorded with Clifford Jordan, and around 1978 he moved to England. Later, having settled in France, he toured Europe, performed at clubs in London, and sang periodically in New York. In 1996 he appeared with Charles Davis in Toulouse.

BIBLIOGRAPHY

Feather–Gitler '70s

V. Wilmer: "Joe Lee: 'Space' Singer," *MM* (28 Aug 1976), 28

D. Kastin: "Profile: Joe Lee Wilson," *DB*, xliv/4 (1977), 34

J. L. Wilson: "Joe Lee Wilson Travels Hopefully," *CI*, xvii/1 (1978), 15

P. Husby: "Joe Lee Wilson: Interview," *Cadence*, viii/3 (1982), 14

Wilson, Juice [Robert Edward] (*b* St. Louis, Jan 1904; *d* Chicago, July 1972). Violinist, pianist, clarinetist, and alto saxophonist. He grew up in Chicago, where he began playing with Jimmy Wade in 1916. In 1918–19 he was with Freddie Keppard at the city's Entertainers' Café, then from December 1919 he worked for three months in Toledo, Ohio, with a band including Jimmy Harrison. From 1921 to 1928 he was in Buffalo, New York, mainly with the band led by the drummer Gene Primus at the Paradise Ballroom. In September 1928 he joined Lloyd Scott at the Savoy Ballroom, New York. After short stints with Luckey Roberts and James P. Johnson (1929) he went to Europe in May 1929 with Noble Sissle's band. Wilson left Sissle in 1930 and played variously with Edwin Swayze, the pianist Tommy "Puss" Chase, Louis Douglas, and Leon Abbey, touring from Spain to Latvia. Around December 1931 he left Douglas in Barcelona and worked in Spain with the dancer, entertainer, and bandleader Harry Flemming and Chase until 1936, when he moved to Morocco. In December 1937 he joined the group of the singer, dancer, and entertainer Levy Wine and toured North Africa. In 1939 he settled in Malta and led trios at various clubs in Valetta and Sliema; in 1945 he had a big band at the Hotel Phoenicia, near Valetta. He remained in Malta until 1954, then toured American bars in Libya and Italy. By 1960 he was resident at the Safari Club, Tangier. He moved to Paris in 1962 and worked for several years as an alto saxophonist in the drummer Jean-Marie Masse's Hot Club de Limoges band before returning to the USA. The social security death index gives his last known residence as Chicago.

Although he was regarded by many contemporary musicians as among the greatest of jazz violinists, Wilson recorded only two solos commercially, both with Noble Sissle in 1929 (*Kansas City Kitty*, HMV B5731; *Miranda*, HMV B5723). No private recordings have yet come to light.

BIBLIOGRAPHY

ChiltonW

A. M. Boswell: "Juice Wilson," *Jazz Music*, iii/1 (1946), 13; repr. in *Sv*, no.75 (1978), 90; *Fable Bulletin: Violin Improvisation Studies*, no.5 (1995), 3

J. Mouyal and P. Bardin: "Un pionnier retrouvé à Tanger," *Jm*, no.56 (1960), 15; repr. in *Fable Bulletin: Violin Improvisation Studies*, no.5 (1995), 6

"Quelques propos de Juice Wilson," *BHcF*, no.121 (1962), 34; repr. in *Fable Bulletin: Violin Improvisation Studies*, no.5 (1995), 7

N. Skrimshire: "What's in a Name," *Sv*, no.35 (1971), 178; repr. in *Fable Bulletin: Violin Improvisation Studies*, no.5 (1995), 8

A. Barnett: "Juice Wilson: Collected Biographical Materials," *Fable Bulletin: Violin Improvisation Studies*, no.5 (1995) [issue devoted to Wilson]

HOWARD RYE

Wilson, Lena (*b* Charlotte, NC, *c*1898; *d* *c*1939). Singer. In 1918–20 she toured in a trio with her brother Danny, a pianist, and the singer Edith Goodall, who became her sister-in-law. She moved in 1921 to New York, where she worked in clubs and theaters. Between 1922 and 1924 she made recordings for nine companies, including *Here's your Opportunity/Memphis Tennessee* (1923, Para. 12042). Later she appeared in numerous revues, among them *Blackbirds of 1926* in London. From May 1929 into 1931 she was resident at the Lenox Club, New York, with Cliff Jackson, with whom she recorded *What's your Price?/My Man o'War* (1931, Col. 14618D). She continued to work in clubs and revues, often with her husband, the violinist Ralph "Shrimp" Jones, until her death from pneumonia.

BIBLIOGRAPHY

S. Harris: *Blues Who's Who: a Biographical Dictionary of Blues Singers* (New Rochelle, NY, 1979/*R*1994)

H. Rye: Liner notes, *Lena Wilson: Complete Recorded Works in Chronological Order*, i: *1922–1924* (Document 5443, 1996)

HOWARD RYE

Wilson, Matt(hew Edward) (*b* Knoxville, IL, 27 Sept 1964). Drummer and leader. He began playing drums professionally around the age of 13 and worked regularly during his high school years. He later studied percussion at Wichita State University (BM 1986) and with Ed Soph (1984). In 1987 he moved to Boston, where he performed and recorded with Charlie Kohlhase from 1989 and with the Either/orchestra between 1989 and 1994. During the same time he recorded with the Mandala Octet and Garrison Fewell. In 1992 Wilson moved to New York, where he has worked regularly with Cecil McBee and Dewey Redman (both from 1994) and Lee Konitz (from 1995); from 1996 he has toured and recorded with his own quartet (with Andrew D'Angelo, the tenor saxophonist Joel Frahm, and Yosuke Inoue). Wilson's interactive style is a blend of Max Roach's melodic approach and Ed Blackwell's sense of rhythmic freedom, and draws from genres other than jazz. His drumming always has a swing feeling and he is equally adept at both straight ahead and free playing. In addition to a conventional drum set and standard percussion he employs a number of unusual instruments, including a string of shells, a tube that whistles when swirled, duck calls, and a slide whistle; he incorporates these into his playing in a manner which is humorous and theatrical, yet consistently musical.

SELECTED RECORDINGS

As leader: *As Wave Follows Wave* (1996, Palmetto 2020); *Going Once, Going Twice* (1997, Palmetto 2032)

As sideman: Mandala Octet: *La spada di San Galgano* (1989–90, Accurate 3616); C. Kohlhase: *Research and Development* (1990, Accurate 3800); Either/Orchestra: *The Calculus of Pleasure* (1990, Accurate 3252); C. Kohlhase: *Good Deeds* (1992, Accurate 3801); G. Fewell: *A Blue Deeper than Blue* (1992, Accurate 4700); Either/Orchestra: *The Brunt* (1993, Accurate 3262); Don Friedman: *Almost Everything* (1995, Ste. 31368-2); D. Redman: *In London* (1996, Palmetto 2030)

BIBLIOGRAPHY

D. Kasrel: "Hearsay: Matt Wilson," *JT*, xxvii/9 (1996), 23
F.-J. Hadley: "Serious Kicks," *DB*, lxiv/11 (1997), 43
G. Santoro: "Different Drummer," *The Nation* (17 March 1997), 40
K. Micallef: "Profile: Matt Wilson: Young Matt Wilson has a Band (E-I-E-I-O)," *Jazziz*, xv/10 (1998), 74
B. Milkowski: "Matt Wilson," *MD*, xxii/11 (1998), 98

GK

Wilson, Nancy (Sue) (*b* Chillicothe, OH, 20 Feb 1937). Singer. She gained early experience in nightclubs and on television shows in Columbus, Ohio, and on a tour of the Midwest and Canada with Rusty Bryant's band (1956-8). In 1959 she sang in Columbus with the quintet led by Cannonball Adderley, who encouraged her to go to New York. She obtained a recording contract with Capitol Records and soon received national recognition; her singing drew immediate accolades from established jazz musicians and she was hailed as a major new artist. She appeared in concert halls, nightclubs, and jazz clubs in the USA and Europe, and made several recordings, notably with Adderley and George Shearing. After concentrating on a career in popular music, Wilson resumed her associations with leading jazz musicians, recording in Belgrade in 1978, and touring Japan and recording with Hank Jones's Great Jazz Trio (1981, 1982). She performed and recorded in San Francisco with the Griffith Park Band (an all-star group including Joe Henderson and Chick Corea) and at the Playboy Jazz Festival with the quintet led by Art Farmer and Benny Golson (both 1982); the Griffith Park Band may be seen in the video *Nancy Wilson* (*c*1985). A jazz trio incorporating John Williams (iv) and Roy McCurdy accompanied her on the PBS television show "Newport Jazz '87" (1987). Her extensive international touring and recording continued through the 1990s, and included performances at the New Orleans Jazz and Heritage Festival (1995) and the San Francisco Jazz Festival (1997). Wilson is a remarkably versatile interpreter of popular music; her singing, with its wide range of musical and emotional intensity, reflects the influence of Dinah Washington, and her voice is noted for its subtle variations in timbre.

Video oral history material in *NCH* (HCJA).

SELECTED RECORDINGS

As leader: with C. Adderley: *Nancy Wilson/Cannonball Adderley* (1962, Cap. ST1657); *Yesterday's Love Songs, Today's Blues* (1963, Cap. ST2012); *What's New* (1982, Ewd 90014); *Live in Europe* (1978, Jazz Door 1264)

As sideman with G. Shearing: *The Swingin's Mutual* (1960, Cap. ST1524)

BIBLIOGRAPHY

B. Gardner: "The Baby Grows up," *DB*, xxxi/30 (1964), 18
D. J. Travis: *An Autobiography of Black Jazz* (Chicago, 1983), 477
S. Holsey: "Nancy Wilson: 30 Years Later, She's Still Grateful, Says Talent is 'a Gift'," *Michigan Chronicle* (18 March 1989)
R. C. Whack: "Love Notes," *Chicago Tribune* (22 May 1994)
H. Reich: "It's Bonus Time," *Chicago Tribune* (5 Feb 1995)
L. Andrews: "Nancy Wilson Having her Way at 60," *Amsterdam News* (21 June 1997)

MICHAEL J. BUDDS/BK

Wilson, Phil(lips Elder, Jr.) (*b* Belmont, MA, 19 Jan 1937). Trombonist, educator, and arranger. He first learned piano and later took up trombone, which he studied at the New England Conservatory; while in Boston he played in Herb Pomeroy's big band (1955–7). After playing trombone and piano with Jimmy Dorsey intermittently from 1956 to 1958, in 1959 he led his own band until being drafted in December of that year. During his military service he briefly continued his studies at the Navy School of Music and played trombone in the North American Air Defense Command Band (1962). Wilson then became a regular soloist with Woody Herman, with whom he was associated from 1962 until 1965. The following year he was appointed to the faculty of the Berklee School of Music, where he became head of the trombone department and taught theory and arrangement; he also renewed his association with Pomeroy. Wilson wrote some arrangements for Buddy Rich (notably *Mercy, Mercy, Mercy*) during this period and later participated in Herman's fortieth anniversary concert (1976) and continued to make recordings sporadically (including the album *That's All* with Al Cohn). By the 1980s, however, he was known primarily as a teacher.

SELECTED RECORDINGS

As leader: *Prodigal Son* (1968, Freeform 101); with R. Matteson: *The Sound of the Wasp* (1975, ASI 203); *That's All* (1976, FaD 109); *Latin American Tour* (1985, Shiah 118); *The Wizard of Oz Suite* (1989, Capri 74040-2)

As sideman with W. Herman: *Woody Herman, 1963* (1962, Phi. 600065), incl. It's a Lonesome Old Town; *Encore: 1963* (1963, Phi. 600092); on *The 40th Anniversary Carnegie Hall Concert* (1976, RCA BGL2-2203), Bijou

SELECTED ARRANGEMENTS

(recorded by B. Rich)

Basically Blues, on *Swingin' New Big Band* (1966, PJ 20113); Mercy, Mercy, Mercy, on *Mercy, Mercy* (1968, PJ 20133)

BIBLIOGRAPHY

Feather '60s; *Feather–Gitler '70s*
L. Tomkins: "My Search for Freedom, by Phil Wilson," *CI*, xxi/12 (1983), 20; contd as "Phil Wilson: the Dues Band is Good News for us All," xxii/1 (1983), 6

S. Voce: "Phil Wilson," *JJI*, xxxvii (1984), no.10, p.6; no.11, p.12
L. Tomkins: "Talent Must be the Foundation, Insists Phil Wilson," *CI*, xxiv/4 (1987), 12
A. Lewis and L. Lewis: "Phil Wilson: Interview," *Cadence*, xviii/9 (1992), 7
W. D. Clancy with A. C. Kenton: *Woody Herman: Chronicles of the Herds* (New York and elsewhere, 1995)
G. Lees: *Leader of the Band: the Life of Woody Herman* (New York, and Oxford, England, 1995)

SCOTT YANOW

Wilson, Phillip (Sanford) (*b* St. Louis, 8 Sept 1941; *d* New York, 1 April 1992). Drummer. He took up violin when he was eight years old and changed to drums when he was nine; from the ages of ten to 15 he played in drum and bugle corps, and when he was 16 he made his début as a professional musician with the organist Don James. With the organist Sam Lazar he worked as a sideman in the bands of Gene Ammons and Sonny Stitt in Chicago, and in 1960 he performed at Minton's Playhouse in New York. From 1960 to 1964 he traveled widely with many groups, including the rock-and-roll group the Drifters and Chocolate Campbell's big band, which accompanied such soul singers as Martha Reeves; he also played in St. Louis with John Coltrane (1962) and in a quartet with Lester Bowie and Julius Hemphill (1962–3). After moving to Chicago in 1965 he joined the Association for the Advancement of Creative Musicians and played free jazz with Roscoe Mitchell's Art Ensemble; he left Chicago in 1968 to work with the Paul Butterfield Blues Band (to 1970) and the rock group Mother Load (1971). Wilson performed with Anthony Braxton at Town Hall, New York, in 1972 and in bands led by Bowie from 1974, and in 1975–6 he played soul and urban blues as a studio drummer for Stax Records in Memphis. In 1976 he moved to New York and worked principally in free jazz; he performed and recorded with David Murray (1976–7), played in Europe in a quartet alongside Olu Dara and Frank Lowe (1978), and was a member of a trio with Johnny Dyani and Wadada Leo Smith. In the mid-1980s he performed and recorded with Bill Laswell. He continued through the decade to perform and record as a sideman with Bowie's groups From the Root to the Source, Brass Fantasy, and, in 1990, New York Organ Ensemble. Wilson also worked with Lowe into the 1990s, recording as a sideman with the group Saxemple (1991) and in a duo (1992), the latter shortly before he was robbed, beaten, and then murdered in his apartment in New York.

SELECTED RECORDINGS

Duos with L. Bowie: *Duet* (1978, ImA 373854)
As leader: *Live at Moers Festival* (1978, Moers 01062); *Fruits* (1978, Cir. [Ger.] 10)
As sideman with L. Bowie: *Fast Last* (1974, Muse 5055); *The Great Pretender* (1981, ECM 1209); *All the Magic* (1982, ECM 1246–7)
As sideman with others: R. Mitchell: *Old/Quartet* (1967, Nessa 5); A. Braxton: *Town Hall 1972* (1972, Trio 3008–9); D. Murray: *David Murray Live at the Lower Manhattan Ocean Club* (1977, IndN 1032, 1044); F. Lowe: *Inappropriate Choices* (1991, ITM Pacific 970062)

BIBLIOGRAPHY

GrayF
B. Case: "New Far-outnesses at Changes Bar," *New Musical Express* (18 June 1977), 18
C. J. Safane: "Phillip Wilson," *DB*, xliv/15 (1977), 22
"Philip Wilson ou la batterie 'expressive'," *L'independant du jazz*, no.14 (1978), 8
B. Vuijsje: *De nieuwe jazz* (Baarn, Netherlands, 1978), 110
C. Stern: "Phillip Wilson: Beyond the Blues," *MD*, vii/10 (1983), 16

ED HAZELL

Wilson, Quinn (B.) (*b* Chicago, 26 Dec 1908; *d* Evanston, IL, 14 June 1978). Double bass and tuba player and arranger. He played violin as a child and later studied composition and arranging with Major N. Clark Smith in the *Chicago Defender* Boys Band. From 1925 he worked with various leaders, among them Tiny Parham (1927), Walter Barnes (1928), Dave Peyton, and Erskine Tate (late 1928 – early 1931), and as a freelance he recorded on tuba with Jelly Roll Morton (1927) and Richard M. Jones (1929). In the 1930s he played with Earl Hines (March 1931 – mid-1940; for illustration *see* HINES, EARL), with whom he recorded on tuba and double bass and for whom he wrote a number of arrangements, notably *Harlem Lament* (1933, Bruns. 6771) and *That's a-plenty* (1934, Decca 182). During this time he also recorded on double bass with Jimmie Noone (1931, 1933) and Jimmy Mundy (1937). After leaving Hines he was with Walter Fuller (until 1942). In the 1940s and 1950s he was active as a freelance in Chicago (sometimes playing electric bass guitar), played for 11 years with a rhythm-and-blues group led by Lefty Bates, and recorded with many blues singers (1953–61). Wilson worked with the clarinetist Bill Reinhardt at Jazz Ltd. in the 1960s and with the trumpeter Joe Kelly in the 1970s.

Oral history material in *NjR* (JOHP).

SELECTED RECORDINGS

As sideman on tuba: J. R. Morton: Beale Street Blues/The Pearls (1927, Vic. 20948); R. M. Jones: Novelty Blues (1929, Vic. 38040); T. Parham: Lucky "3-6-9" (1929, Vic. 38082); Fat Man Blues/Black Cat Moan (1929, Vic. 38126)
As sideman on double bass: E. Hines: Blue Drag (1932, Bruns. 6345); Swingin' Down (1934, Voc. 3392); G. T. Stomp (1939, Bb 10391); Riff Medley (1939, Bb 10531)

BIBLIOGRAPHY

McCarthyB
S. Dance: *The World of Earl Hines* (New York, 1977), 171
D. Hill: "Quinn Wilson: Autobiographical Note," *Cadence*, xiii/4 (1987), 16

based on *ChiltonW*/HOWARD RYE

Wilson, Shadow [Rossier(e) Van Donnel] (*b* Yonkers, NY, 25 Sept 1919; *d* New York, 11 July 1959). Drummer. His given name has appeared in reference sources as Rossiere Wilson, but Billy Eckstine (in Southern, 1979) gave it as Rossier Van Donnel Wilson. In 1935 in Philadelphia he joined the bandleader Jimmy Gorham; after moving to New York in 1938 the big band was taken over first by Bill Doggett and then, in May, by Lucky Millinder (to early 1939). From this time Wilson worked with some of the leading big bands of the period; his most important engagements were with Millinder (1939), Benny Carter, Tiny Bradshaw (1940), Lionel Hampton (1941, as a replacement for Lee Young), Earl Hines (1942–3), Eckstine (spring 1944), Georgie Auld (September 1944), Count Basie (November 1944–1946, replacing Jo Jones, who was drafted, and again briefly in 1948), and Woody Herman (1949). He also played in small groups led by Illinois Jacquet (1946–7, 1949–50, 1952–4), Erroll Garner (1950–52), Hines (1954), Ella Fitzgerald (1954–5), and Thelonious Monk (1957–8), and made important recordings with Tadd Dameron (1947) and Monk (1948). During the 1950s he performed frequently with Sonny Stitt and recorded with a variety of leaders, including Basie, Monk, and Lee Konitz. For the first decade of his career Wilson was noted as the driving rhythmic force behind large orchestras, and after 1950 he became highly regarded for his work in small groups. Equally proficient using sticks or brushes, he was one of the most flexible and accomplished drummers and an unfailingly sensitive player.

SELECTED RECORDINGS

As sideman: C. Basie: Taps Miller (1944, Col. 36831); L. Young: Indiana (1944), first issued on *The Master's Touch* (1944–9, Savoy 12071); C. Basie: Queer Street (1945, Col. 36889); I. Jacquet: Jivin' with Jack the Bellboy (1947, Ala. 179); T. Dameron: Our Delight (1947, BN 540); T. Monk: Evidence (1948, BN 549); E. Garner: Lover (1950, Col. 39111); T. Dameron: *Fontainebleau* (1956, Prst. 7037), incl. Delirium; P. Woods and G. Quill: *Phil and Quill* (1956, RCA LPM1284); T. Monk: *Thelonious Monk with John Coltrane* (1957, Jlnd 946)

BIBLIOGRAPHY

FeatherE; *McCarthyB*; *SheridanCB*
B. Eckstine: "When Sarah Vaughan Began to Sing," *MM*, xxx (21 Aug 1954), 5; contd as "Leading my Outfit" (28 Aug 1954), 13
Obituary, *Jm*, no.52 (1959), 15
I. Gitler: *Jazz Masters of the Forties* (New York, 1966/*R*1983 with discography), 190
S. Dance: *The World of Earl Hines* (New York, 1977)
D. Salemann: "Billy Eckstine Orchestra 1944–1947," *Pj*, no.14 (1978), 57
E. Southern: "Conversation with ... William Clarence 'Billy' Eckstine: 'Mr. B' of Ballad and Bop," *Black Perspective in Music*, vii (1979), 197
J. M. Doran: *Erroll Garner: the Most Happy Piano* (Metuchen, NJ, and London, 1985) [incl. discography]

MARK GARDNER/BK

Wilson, Steve(n Andre) (*b* Hampton, VA, 9 Feb 1961). Alto and soprano saxophonist. He began formal studies at the age of 12 and played in rhythm-and-blues and funk bands while at high school. At Virginia Commonwealth University, Richmond (1981–5), he studied with Ellis Marsalis, after which he worked with OTB (1986–9). In summer 1987 he moved to New York and around the same time he toured internationally with Lionel Hampton's orchestra. He then worked with Bruce Barth (from 1987), Michele Rosewoman and Ralph Peterson, Jr. (both from 1988), and Buster Williams and Loren Schoenberg (both from 1989); he was initially in Peterson's quintet V, and later replaced Don Byron in Peterson's Fo'tet. Later he joined groups led by Leon Parker, with whom he has also played in a duo, and Mulgrew Miller (both 1994), and Dave Holland (1997). At the end of 1997 he became a member of Chick Corea's sextet Origin, which the following spring toured South America, and in 1998 he led his own quartet at the Jazz Standard in New York, with Kevin Hays, Ed Howard, and Parker as his sidemen. Wilson has also worked with Renee Rosnes, the American Jazz Orchestra, the Smithsonian Jazz Masterworks Orchestra, and Louie Bellson's big band, among others. He has taught at William Paterson College (Wayne, New Jersey).

SELECTED RECORDINGS

As leader: *New York Summit* (1991, Criss Cross 1062); *Step Lively* (1993, Criss Cross 1096); *Four for Time* (1994, Criss Cross 1115)
As sideman: R. Peterson: *V* (1988, BN B21S-91730); O.T.B.: *Spiral Staircase* (1989, BN B21S-93006); R. Peterson: *Volition* (1989, BN B21S-93894); M. Rosewoman: *The Harvest* (1992, Enja 7069-2); K. B. Harris: *Folk Songs–Folk Tales* (1993, Tip Toe 888807-2); D. Braden: *After Dark* (1993, Criss Cross 1081); B. Barth: *Morning Call* (1994, Enja 8084-2); R. Peterson: *The Reclamation Project* (1994, Evidence 22113); James Williams: *Truth, Justice & the Blues* (1994, Evidence 22142); R. Peterson: *Fo'tet Plays Monk* (1995, Evidence 22174); D. Byron: *Bug Music* (1996, Nonesuch 79438-2); Bill Stewart: *Telepathy* (1996, BN 853210-2); L. Parker: *Belief* (*c*1996, Col. CK67457)

BIBLIOGRAPHY

R. Orgill: "A Sideman's Life: Whichever Way the Horns Blow," *New York Times* (1 Sept 1996)

GK

Wilson, Teddy [Theodore Shaw] (*b* Austin, TX, 24 Nov 1912; *d* New Britain, CT, 31 July 1986). Pianist. He grew up in Tuskegee, Alabama. At about the age of eight he began classical lessons on piano, and he also doubled as a violinist for several years. Having discovered jazz while in high school, he copied solos recorded by Earl Hines and Fats Waller; additionally during these years he played oboe and sopranino clarinet. He briefly studied music at Talladega College and began working professionally with the mid-western big band of Speed Webb, whose sidemen included Vic Dickenson and Roy Eldridge (1929 – early 1931). Wilson then replaced Art Tatum in Milton Senior's quartet in Toledo, Ohio; there he found many opportunities to listen to and play with Tatum, who exerted a strong influence on his developing personal style. He traveled with Senior to Chicago, then worked with Erskine Tate (1931) and lesser-known leaders, and recorded and toured with Louis Armstrong (January–March 1933). He returned to Chicago to play with Jimmie Noone (mid-1933).

At the instigation of John Hammond, Wilson moved in September 1933 to New York to join Benny Carter, with whom he recorded the following month in both the big band and a small group, the Chocolate Dandies. From 1934 to early 1935 he was a member of Willie Bryant's big band. Again through Hammond, he secured recording dates with Red Norvo and Benny Goodman. Hammond then introduced him to Billie Holiday and initiated the lengthy run of now classic recordings released variously under Wilson's or Holiday's name (1935–42). In this setting Wilson made crucial contributions to Holiday's career by selecting songs for her, and by organizing and rehearsing small recording groups which introduced her, in various combinations, to many of the greatest musicians of the swing era. Ironically, for all these accomplishments, Wilson underestimated Holiday's talent. When given the opportunity he chose other singers for his recordings, including Ella Fitzgerald, Lena Horne, and Helen Ward; he also recorded as a sideman with Mildred Bailey. His partnership with Holiday was almost exclusively in the studio, although in September 1935 they worked together for a week at the Famous Door on 52nd Street.

In this same year Wilson played informally with Goodman. He officially joined Goodman's trio the following year, thereby becoming one of the first black musicians to appear prominently with white artists. He remained with Goodman until February 1939, starring in the trio with Gene Krupa and the quartet with Krupa and Lionel Hampton. He then led his own big band for a year (May 1939 – April 1940); among his sidemen were Shorty Baker, Karl George, Doc Cheatham, Rudy Powell, Pete Clarke, Ben Webster, Al Casey, Al Hall, and J. C. Heard. The band had a fine reputation among musicians but made little impact, evidently because the leader's reserved personality did not satisfy his audiences' expectations.

In June 1940 Wilson founded a sextet with Bill Coleman, Benny Morton, Jimmy Hamilton, Al Hall, and Yank Porter. They first performed at Café Society in July and then in October opened the second Café Society, uptown. Wilson rejoined Goodman briefly from January to mid-February 1941, but continued with his own sextet. In the summer of 1941, after the group returned from performances in Chicago, Emmett Berry replaced Coleman and Israel Crosby succeeded Hall; soon wards Johnny Williams replaced Crosby, and by the end of the year Edmond Hall and Heard had joined. From this point until 1944, as Wilson continued his routine of alternating tours with long stands at the two Café Society venues, the sextet remained reasonably stable, comprising Berry or Joe Thomas (iv), Morton, Hamilton,

Teddy Wilson's sextet at Café Society, New York, June 1942: (left to right) Wilson (piano), Johnny Williams (double bass), Jack Parker (drums), Edmond Hall (clarinet), Emmett Berry (trumpet), and Benny Morton (trombone)

Wilson, Williams, and Heard, with Sid Catlett taking Heard's place from September 1942.

Wilson disbanded the sextet in May 1944 and worked with Goodman's sextet for just over a year. He was with CBS radio in New York from 1946 and led his own trios at WNEW, New York, from 1949 to 1952; concurrently during the summer from 1945 to 1952 he taught privately at the Metropolitan Music School and at the Juilliard School, an early instance of the recognition of jazz by an important conservatory. He made his first trip to Europe (autumn 1952 – early 1953) and then renewed his job at CBS, acting as host for a radio show as the leader of a trio with Milt Hinton and Jo Jones, various guest artists also took part, including Edmond Hall in 1955. Wilson left CBS soon afterwards to participate in the making of the film *The Benny Goodman Story.* He then began touring with his own trio and in 1958 performed at the World's Fair in Brussels before holding an engagement at the Embers in New York (summer 1958). He frequently rejoined Goodman for reunions, most notably for a tour of the USSR (1962) and for concerts at Carnegie Hall during the Newport Jazz Festival New York (1973) and its continuation as the Kool Jazz Festival (1982). He also appeared at a number of Dick Gibson's Colorado Jazz Parties from the mid-1960s into the 1970s, performed at Michael's Pub in New York during the 1970s, and made annual appearances at the Newport event. He toured regularly as a soloist, recorded numerous albums in Europe and Japan, and visited South America (where he gave concerts with Earl Hines, Ellis Larkins, and Marian McPartland in 1974) and Australia. He occasionally played with Benny Carter (1978–1981), mainly in the USA, but also in Japan (September 1980). In his final years he played on the television shows "Swing Reunion" (1985) and "Benny Goodman: Let's Dance: All-Star Swing Reunion" (1986).

Wilson was the most important pianist of the swing period. His early recordings reveal a percussive style, with single-note lines and bold staccatos, that was indebted to Earl Hines; but by the time of his first performances with Goodman he had fashioned a distinctive legato idiom that served him for the rest of his career. His style was based on the use of conjunct 10ths in the left hand; by emphasizing the tenor voice and frequently omitting the root of the chord until the end of the phrase he created great harmonic refinement and contrapuntal interest. For the right hand he adapted Hines's "trumpet" style, playing short melodic fragments in octaves, frequently separated by rests and varied with fleet, broken-chord passage-work. He used the full range of the piano, often changing register or texture to underscore formal divisions. His poised, restrained manner and transparent textures are especially evident on his solo recordings from the late 1930s, which served as models for countless pianists in the late swing period. From 1940 Wilson's playing became somewhat florid, with frequent pentatonic passage-work, but he retained his basic approach and prowess into the 1980s. A volume of transcriptions and simplified piano arrangements was published as *The Genius of Teddy Wilson* (Lyndhurst, NJ, n.d.).

Oral history material in *ATaT* and *NjR* (JOHP).

See also Improvisation, §4 (iii); and Piano, §3, and fig.2.

SELECTED RECORDINGS

As unaccompanied soloist: Liza/Rosetta (1935, Bruns. 7563); Don't Blame Me/Between the Devil and the Deep Blue Sea (1937, Bruns. 8025); Smoke Gets in your Eyes (1941, Col. 36631); Rosetta (1941, Col. 36632); Body and Soul (1941, Col. 36634); I can't get started (1941, Col. 36633); *With Billie in Mind* (1972, Chi. 111); *Striding after Fats* (1974, BL 308); *Cole Porter Classics* (1977, BL 51505)

As leader: I wished on the moon (1935, Bruns. 7501); Mean to me (1937, Bruns. 7903); Just a Mood (1937, Bruns. 7973); What shall I say? (1939, Bruns. 8314); Liza (1939, Col. 35711); I know that you know (1941, Col. 36633); with L. Young: *Pres and Teddy* (1956, Verve 8205); *Teddy Wilson and his All Stars* (1976, Chi. 150); *Three Little Words* (1976, BB 33094)

As sideman: L. Armstrong: I've got the world on a string (1933, Vic. 24245); Chocolate Dandies: I Never Knew (1933, Col. 2897D); Krazy Kapers (1933, OK 41568); B. Carter: Symphony in Riffs (1933, Col. 2898D); Blue

Lou (1933, OK 41567); R. Norvo: Old Fashioned Love (1934, Col. 3059D); I Surrender, Dear (1934, Col. 2977D): B. Goodman: After You've Gone/Body and Soul (1935, Vic. 25115); Nobody's Sweetheart (1936, Vic. 25345); Sweet Sue, Just You (1936, Vic. 25473); The Man I Love (1937, Vic. 25644); The Blues in my Flat (1938, Vic. 26044); B. Holiday: Jim (1941, OK 6369); B. Carter: on *3, 4, 5: the Verve Small Group Sessions* (1954–5, Verve 849395-2), Rosetta, The moon is low (1954)

SELECTED FILMS AND VIDEOS

Hollywood Hotel (1937); Harlem Hotshots (1940); Boogie Woogie Dream (1941); Something to Shout About (1943); Make Mine Music [Swing Street] (1945); The Benny Goodman Story (1955); Steve Allen in Movieland (1955); Swing into Spring (1958); Playback (1963); Jazz Circle (1971)

BIBLIOGRAPHY

ConnorBG; McCarthyB; SchullerS
S. F. Dance: "Theodore Wilson," *Jh*, 1st ser., no.1 (1935), 29
J. Hammond: "Theodore Wilson," *Swing Music*, i/7 (1935), 85
T. Wilson: "How to Relax on Wax," *MM* (21 Dec 1946), 9
A. Hodeir: "Teddy Wilson," *Jh*, no.42 (1950), 21
L. Feather: *The Book of Jazz: a Guide to the Entire Field* (New York, 1957, rev. 2/1965)
J. Mehegan: *Jazz Improvisation*, ii: *Jazz Rhythm and the Improvised Line* (New York, 1962), 80
——: *Jazz Improvisation*, iii: *Swing and Early Progressive Piano Styles* (New York, 1964), 15
J. Simmen: "Le grand orchestre de Teddy Wilson, 1939–1940," *BHcF*, no.201 (1970), 10; no.202 (1970), 10
D. M. Bakker: *Billie & Teddy on Microgroove, 1932–1944* (Alphen aan de Rijn, Netherlands, 1975)
S. Dance: *The World of Earl Hines* (New York, 1977), 183
J. McDonough: "Teddy Wilson: History in the Flesh," *DB*, xliv/4 (1977), 17
G. Gelles and J. McDonough: Liner notes, *Giants of Jazz: Teddy Wilson* (TL 20, 1981)
M. Berger, E. Berger, and J. Patrick: *Benny Carter: a Life in American Music* (Metuchen, NJ, and London, 1982)
D. Hyman: "Thinking about Teddy Wilson," *Keyboard*, viii/9 (1982), 59 [incl. transcr.]
L. Lyons: *The Great Jazz Pianists, Speaking of their Lives and Music* (New York, 1983), 59
Obituaries: B. Doerschuk, *Keyboard*, xii/10 (1986), 29; J. Simmen, *BHcF*, no.341 (1986), 5
M. Selchow: *Profoundly Blue: a Bio-discographical Scrapbook on Edmond Hall* (Lübbecke, Germany, 1988)
D. Clarke: *Wishing on the Moon: the Life and Times of Billie Holiday* (London and New York, 1994)
F. Krieger: "Jazz-Solopiano: zum Stilwandel am Beispiel ausgewählter *Body and Soul*: Aufnehmen von 1938–1992," *Jf*, xxvii (1995), 5 [incl. transcrs.]
S. Nicholson: *Billie Holiday* (Boston, 1995, London, 1996)
T. Wilson, A. Ligthart, and H. van Loo: *Teddy Wilson Talks Jazz* (London and New York, 1996) [incl. discography by H. Rye]

J. BRADFORD ROBINSON/BK

Winburn [?née Darden; Pilgrim]**, Anna Mae** [Door, Anita] (*b* Port Royal, TN). Singer and bandleader. She grew up in Indiana. Having first sung with the studio band of Radio WOW, Fort Wayne, and worked at various clubs, including the Chateau Lido in Indianapolis (where she appeared under the pseudonym Anita Door), she embarked on a career fronting territory bands, starting with Lloyd Hunter's Serenaders (1936–7). In 1938 she took over the Oklahoma-based Kansas City Blue Devils, and she toured with them into 1939 as Anna Mae Winburn and her Cotton Club Boys. From 1940 to 1941 she fronted Red Perkins's band, operating out of Omaha, Nebraska, then from early 1942 she fronted the International Sweethearts of Rhythm; she participated in a USO tour of Europe in 1945 and remained with the group until June 1948, when she left to marry Eustace "Duke" Pilgrim. In 1950 she re-formed the Sweethearts of Rhythm with Pilgrim as manager. The orchestra toured extensively, though by 1953 it had been reduced to a small group. The trade press notes some recordings for the Unique label in 1951, but these have not been found. The Sweethearts disbanded in 1956, ending Winburn's musical career. However, she attended the reunion of the International Sweethearts of Rhythm at the Women's Jazz Festival in Kansas City in 1980, and she was interviewed in the film *International Sweethearts of Rhythm* (1986). An effective singer, she may be heard to good effect with the International Sweethearts performing *Central Avenue Boogie* (first issued on the album *A Date with Lena Horne featuring Fletcher Henderson and his Orchestra*, 1944, Sunbeam 212) and *Jump Children* (1945, Guild 141), but she is presented at her best in the Sweethearts' short films, where her stage presence and skills when fronting a band can be appreciated.

SELECTED FILMS AND VIDEOS

International Sweethearts of Rhythm (1946); How about that Jive (1946); Harlem Jam Session (1946)

BIBLIOGRAPHY

"Why Girl Bands Don't Click," *Jet* (1954), Feb, 60
S. Placksin: *American Women in Jazz, 1900 to the Present: their Words, Lives, and Music* (New York, 1982, London, 1985, as *Jazzwomen, 1900 to the Present: their Words, Lives, and Music*)
D. A. Handy: *The International Sweethearts of Rhythm* (Metuchen, NJ, and London, 1983, rev. 2/1996)
L. Dahl: *Stormy Weather: the Music and Lives of a Century of Jazzwomen* (London, Melbourne, Australia, and New York, 1984)
S. Tucker: *Swing Shift: "All-girl" Bands of the 1940s* (Durham, NC, and London, 2000)

HOWARD RYE

Winchester, Lem(uel Davis) (*b* Philadelphia, 19 March 1928; *d* Indianapolis, 13 Jan 1961). Vibraphonist. His grandfather was a drummer. He attended high school in Wilmington, Delaware, where he played flute and then tenor and baritone saxophone; he took up vibraphone in 1947, after experimenting with a two-finger piano style. During the 1950s he worked in Wilmington as a policeman and moonlighted as a vibraphonist. In 1958 he performed and recorded at the Newport Jazz Festival as a protégé of Leonard Feather, and in the same year he recorded as a leader, accompanied by Ramsey Lewis's trio. Having resigned from the police force early in 1960 to work full-time as a musician, Winchester led a quintet and recorded with Oliver Nelson, Shirley Scott, Brother Jack McDuff, Etta Jones, and Johnny Hammond. Feather, in *The Encyclopedia of Jazz in the Sixties*, reports that "he was demonstrating a trick with a revolver and accidently killed himself."

SELECTED RECORDINGS

As leader: *Lem Winchester and the Ramsey Lewis Trio* (1958, Argo 642); *Winchester Special* (1959, NewJ 8223); *Lem's Beat* (1960, NewJ 8239); *Another Opus* (1960, NewJ 8244)
As sideman: O. Nelson: *Nocturne* (1960, Mdsv. 13); on E. Jones: *Hollar* (1960, Prst. 7284), I've Got it Bad, The more I see you, They can't take that away from me; J. Hammond: *Gettin' the Message* (1960, Prst. 7217)

BIBLIOGRAPHY

FeatherE; Feather'60s
"The End of a Perfect Cop," *DB*, xxvii/20 (1960), 17
"'Russian Roulette' Gun Death," *MM* (21 Jan 1961), 11
"A Gun with an Empty Chamber," *DB*, xxviii/4 (1961), 11

GK

Windhurst, Johnny [John Henry] (*b* New York, 5 Nov 1926; *d* Poughkeepsie, NY, 2 Oct 1981). Trumpeter. A self-taught musician who never learned to read music, he made his professional début in spring 1944 at one of Eddie Condon's concerts at Town Hall, New York. The following year he performed and recorded with Sidney Bechet at the Savoy in Boston, and in September 1946 he returned to Town Hall with Art Hodes and James P. Johnson. Following a period in Chicago he appeared again at the Savoy as a member of

Edmond Hall's band (April–May 1949). Windhurst also played with Louis Armstrong and Nappy Lamare before leading his own band in Ohio and Boston. In the early 1950s he worked with Eddie Condon (1950) and recorded in Boston alongside Ruby Braff in one of the groups known as Jazz at Storyville (1951). In New York he performed at Condon's club (1952–3) and made recordings with Jack Teagarden (1955), the singer Barbara Lea (1955–7), and his own swing quartet (*Jazz at Columbus Avenue*, 1956, Tran. 2), in which Buell Neidlinger was a sideman.

In 1956 Windhurst played in a stage band and worked for a week with Vic Dickenson at Storyville (December). Later he spent another period in Ohio, toured as a leader (1957–9), and performed again at Condon's club. In 1961 at Nick's, New York, he led his Sheridan Squares, which included Cutty Cutshall and Cliff Leeman, and from at least 1964 to 1969 he was a member of Joe Muranyi's group. Having deputized for Wild Bill Davison at Condon's in the early 1950s, he filled the same role for an engagement at Jimmy Ryan's in 1965. He appeared as a freelance elsewhere in the city before moving upstate to Poughkeepsie, where he finished his career playing in a dixieland band at Frivolous Sal's Last Chance Saloon.

BIBLIOGRAPHY

FeatherE; *Feather–GitlerBEJ*
J. Chilton: *Sidney Bechet: the Wizard of Jazz* (London and New York, 1987/*R*1996), 170
M. Selchow: *Profoundly Blue: a Bio-discographical Scrapbook on Edmond Hall* (Lübbecke Germany, 1988)
J. Sohmer: Liner notes, E. Condon: *Eddie Condon's Band Featuring Johnny Windhurst*, ii (Sto. 6048, 1994)
M. Selchow: *Ding! Ding!: a Bio-discographical Sketchbook on Vic Dickenson* (Westoverledingen, Germany, 1998)

BK

Winding, Kai (Chresten) (*b* Århus, Denmark, 18 May 1922; *d* Yonkers, NY, 6 May 1983). Trombonist. He moved with his family to the USA when he was 12 and took up trombone while in his teens; he was largely self-taught. He played in the big bands of Sonny Dunham and Alvino Rey and for three years belonged to a service band while he was a member of the US Coast Guard (from 1942); he also took part in early bop jam sessions at Minton's Playhouse and Monroe's Uptown House in New York and was a member of big bands led by Benny Goodman (November 1945 – January 1946), Stan Kenton (1946 – mid-1947), and Charlie Ventura (autumn 1947–1948); in 1947 he appeared with Kenton's band in the short film *Let's Make Rhythm*). At the end of the 1940s he led his own group (including Brew Moore and George Wallington), performed as a sideman with Moore and Gerry Mulligan, and worked at the Royal Roost, Birdland, and Bop City with Tadd Dameron, Charlie Parker, Miles Davis, and Allen Eager; during this period he recorded with J. J. Johnson, as a member of the Metronome All Stars and in Davis's "Birth of the Cool" nonet (both 1949).

Winding then worked as a studio musician, and in 1954 he formed a quintet with Johnson that was known as Jay and Kai ("my name is pronounced *Kai* as in *fly*, *Wind*ing as in wood*wind*," he told *Crescendo International*, though not unreasonably many people mispronounced Kai to rhyme with Jay). Among their sidemen were Dick Katz, Charles Mingus, Milt Hinton, Peck Morrison, Paul Chambers, Al Harewood, and Osie Johnson. After the quintet disbanded in July 1956 Winding led a septet consisting of four trombones and a rhythm section, which included at various times Carl Fontana, Wayne Andre, Bill Watrous, Ross Tompkins, and Eddie de Haas; he also toured briefly with Johnson in 1958. Late in 1962 he reduced his group to a quartet and began working as music director for the Playboy clubs in New York. He also appeared in the film *A Man Called Adam* (1966).

In 1969 Winding moved to California and resumed his career as a studio musician, but he toured with the Giants of Jazz (1971–2) and briefly replaced Fontana in the World's Greatest Jazz Band. In 1977 he ceased his studio work and settled in Spain. He was a member of Lionel Hampton's band in 1978, together with Curtis Fuller toured again as a guest soloist with Hampton in 1979, and then with Fuller led the group Giant Bones (1979–80). He also played in Mel Lewis's quintet and joined Albert Mangelsdorff, Jiggs Whigham, and Watrous in another group featuring four trombones. In 1982 he appeared at the Aurex Jazz Festival in Japan with Johnson and at the Kool Jazz Festival in New York.

Winding was one of the first bop trombonists and one of the most important. The distinct sound he brought to Kenton's trombone section was achieved partly by his persuading the players to produce a vibrato with the lip rather than with the slide (van Engelen, 1985). His solo work was characterized initially by a rough, exuberant, biting tone, recalling earlier trombone styles (a fine example may be heard on Kenton's recording of *Lover*, 1947), though a more restrained manner is evident in the brief solos he contributed to the first of Davis's "Birth of the Cool" sessions (1949). On forming the group Jay and Kai, Winding began to produce a delicate sound; he improvised in a manner so close to that of Johnson that it is sometimes difficult to distinguish between the two musicians. A number of Winding's arrangements have been published by H. Leonard and a collection of lead sheets and transcribed solos was issued as *Kai Winding Jazz Trombone Solos* (Pacific, MO, n.d. [?1970s]). He prepared a method book: *Mel Bay's Mr. Trombone: the Kai Winding Method of Jazz Trombone Improvisation* (Pacific, MO, 1979).

For illustrations *see* Jazz (i), fig.6, and Navarro, fats.

SELECTED RECORDINGS

As leader: Sid's Bounce/A Night on Bop Mountain (1949, NewJ 809); *Incredible Trombones* (1961, Imp. 3); *The Kai Winding Trombones* (1963, Jazz Vault 107); *Danish Blue* (1977, Glendale 6003)

As leader with others: J. J. Johnson: *Jay and Kay: December 3, 1954* (1954, Prst. 195); *The Great Kai and J. J.* (1960, Imp. 1); Giants of Jazz: *Giants of Jazz* (1971, Atl. 2-905); C. Fuller: *Giant Bones at Nice* (1980, Ahead 757)

As sideman: S. Kenton: Ain't no misery in me/Artistry in Percussion (1946, Cap. 289); Willow Weep for Me (1946, Cap. 287); Machito (1947, Cap. 900); Lover (1947, Cap. 904); M. Davis: Godchild (1949, Cap. 60005); Budo (1949, Cap. 15404); Brew Moore: Mud Bug (1949, Savoy 968); Z. Sims: Tangerine/Zootcase (1952, Prst. 1348) [EP]

BIBLIOGRAPHY

FeatherE; *Feather '60s*; *Feather–Gitler '70s*
J. Burns: "Bopping Bones," *J&B*, ii/7 (1972), 16
K. Winding: "Still Multiplying the Trombones," *CI*, xi/5 (1972), 26
N. Catalano: "His Long and Winding Road," *DB*, xlv/15 (1978), 27
S. Woolley: "Meandering with Kai," *JJI*, xxxii/9 (1979), 14
"The Primary Purpose of Kai Winding," *CI*, xix/3 (1980), 12; contd as L. Tomkins: "Trombone Topics," xix/4 (1980), 23
Obituary, *New York Times* (8 May 1983)
P. van Engelen: *Where's the Music? The Discography of Kai Winding* (Amsterdam, 1985)

LEE JESKE/BK

Winstone, Norma (Ann) (*b* London, 23 Sept 1941). English singer. She trained as a pianist and organist and began singing in the 1950s. By the age of 17 she was working semiprofessionally with a dance band led by Al Dukardo (who taught her voice control); she was influenced especially by the interpretations of jazz standards by such singers as Frank Sinatra, Lena Horne, and Ella Fitzgerald. Through the first half of the 1960s she performed with the drummer Ted Humphrey, whom she married in 1962, and during this period she came under the influences of Miles Davis, Eric Dolphy, and John Coltrane. She met their challenge to find a greater freedom of performance with a singularly expressive brand of wordless improvisation; this instrumental style emerged in her work with Michael Garrick's sextet, in which she replaced a saxophonist in 1968. In the mid-1960s she worked with John Stevens, Mike Carr, and Neil Ardley's New Jazz Orchestra and made her first appearance at Ronnie Scott's club (late 1966).

Winstone became known internationally as the partner of John Taylor (whom she married in 1972), notably in the trio Azimuth, in which they collaborated with Kenny Wheeler; the three continued to work together in various contexts through the 1990s. Winstone also toured with John Dankworth's orchestra as a substitute for Cleo Laine (November–December 1972) and recorded with Mike Westbrook (1970) and Eberhard Weber (1979). In 1989 she recorded as a guest soloist with the duo of Urs Leimgruber and John Wolf Brennan and toured with Ian Carr's Orchestra UK.

In 1994 Winstone worked with Tony Coe and appeared with the London Jazz Orchestra, and the following year she formed the quartet New Friends, with Anthony Kerr and John Parricelli among her sidemen; in 1996 she led another quartet that included Don Thompson. While continuing to work with Taylor, both in a duo and in Azimuth, and in the group with Kerr and Parricelli (which by this time had become a quintet with the addition of Paul Clarvis) she sang in a trio with the pianist Steve Gray and the double bass player Chris Laurence, in a quartet (no longer with Thompson), and alongside Jay Clayton, Urszula Dudziak, and Jon Hendricks's daughter Michelle Hendricks in the group Vocal Summit. In the late 1990s she appeared with, among others, Lee Konitz and Tony Coe in a tribute to Duke Ellington at the Jersey Jazz Festival (1996), sang at the Monterey Jazz Festival (1997), and performed with Taylor and David Murray in London (1999). As well as using her voice instrumentally, Winstone remains a fine interpreter of popular songs; she has set lyrics to instrumental compositions by Ralph Towner, Egberto Gismonti, and Steve Swallow.

Oral history material in *GBLnsa*.

SELECTED RECORDINGS

As leader: *Edge of Time* (1971, Argo 148); of Azimuth (with J. Taylor and K. Wheeler): *Azimuth* (1977, ECM 1099), *Azimuth '85* (1985, ECM 1298); *Somewhere Called Home* (1987, ECM 1337); *Well Kept Secret* (1993, Koch 7836)

As sideman: M. Westbrook: *Love Songs* (1970, Deram 1069); M. Garrick: *The Heart is a Lotus* (1970, Argo 135); *Home Stretch Blues* (1972, Argo 154); K. Wheeler: *Music for Large & Small Ensembles* (1990, ECM 1415–16)

BIBLIOGRAPHY

CarrJ; *ChiltonB*; *Feather–Gitler '70s*; *GrayF*; *WickesIBJ*, i

B. Dawbarn: "Norma: New Voice from the Pubs of London," *MM* (5 March 1966), 6

M. Jones: "Norma," *MM* (5 Nov 1966), 8

B. Dawbarn: "Norma's Wisdom," *MM* (7 Feb 1970), 12

L. Henshaw: "Triumph for a Jazz Cinderella," *MM* (13 March 1971), 18

V. Wilmer: "Norma Winstone: the Human Voice," *JF* [intl edn], no.11 (1971), 54

C. Bird: "Not Enough of Norma," *MM* (15 April 1972), 57

S. Woolley: "Norma Winstone," *JJ*, xxviii/7 (1975), 4

A. Macintosh: "John Taylor & Norma Winstone: a Jazz Partnership," *JF* [intl edn], no.59 (1979), 38

S. Gore-Humphries and P. Hanson: "Avant Courier: Norma Winstone," *JJI*, xxxvi/8 (1983), 10

G. Lock: "The Singing is the Song," *The Wire*, no.15 (1985), 40

P. Renaud: *La discographie du jazz anglais* (Chaumont, France, 1985)

J. Fordham: "Honesty & Integrity," *Boz*, no.28 [incorporating *Jazz Express*, no.188] (1996), 28

<http://www.normawinstone.com> (1999)

CHRIS SHERIDAN/BK

Winter, Horst (*b* Beuthen, Germany [now Bytom, Poland], 24 Sept 1914). Austrian clarinetist, singer, and bandleader. He began to play jazz in Berlin in the 1930s. During World War II he made recordings for the German record label Tempo with Willi Berking, Meg Tevelian, and others. He moved to Vienna in 1945 and became an Austrian citizen the following year. Also in 1946 he formed the Wiener Tanz Orchester, with which he made many recordings, including *Gin Fizzes* (1947, ES 8225). A gifted swing clarinetist, Winter played in the style of Artie Shaw. He ceased to perform jazz in the mid-1950s.

BIBLIOGRAPHY

McCarthyB

D. H. Kraner and K. Schulz: *Jazz in Austria: historische Entwicklung und Diskographie des Jazz in Österreich* (Vienna, rev. 2/1972) [text in Eng. and Ger.]

KLAUS SCHULZ

Winter, Paul (Theodore, Jr.) (*b* Altoona, PA, 31 Aug 1939). Soprano and alto saxophonist and bandleader. While at Northwestern University he formed the Paul Winter Sextet, with which he played alto saxophone. In 1961 this group won the Intercollegiate Jazz Festival, at which Dizzy Gillespie and John Hammond were among the judges; the latter engaged the group to record for Columbia. In the 1960s Winter's performances and recordings brought him to national and international prominence, and in 1962, sponsored by the US State Department, he undertook an extensive tour of Latin America. At this time he considered establishing a group that departed from the conventional instrumentation of jazz; he performed works inspired by his visit in "Paul Winter Sextet" (1964), an episode of the television series "Jazz Casual." In 1967 he formed the Paul Winter Consort, which combined Latin American, African, and Western instruments; in the early 1970s the group included the guitarist Ralph Towner, the double bass player Glen Moore, the sitarist and percussionist Collin Walcott, the reed player Paul McCandless, and the cellist David Darling; after Towner, Moore, Walcott, and McCandless formed the cooperative group Oregon in 1970, all five sidemen successively left the Winter consort, though McCandless remained until 1973. *Icarus*, composed by Towner, became Winter's theme tune.

During the same period Winter became concerned with conservation and the problem of endangered species. He joined expeditions led by the organization Greenpeace and, in often successful attempts to communicate with animals in the wild, played to whales off the Canadian coast and to wolves in the mountains of California and Minnesota. Tapes of these experiments formed the basis for the album *Common Ground* (1977). In 1980 he formed a nonprofit organization dedicated to fostering general participation in music and a new awareness of the potential of harmony and rhythm. Winter and his group continue to perform and record on the organization's behalf, often in natural environments such as the Grand Canyon.

SELECTED RECORDINGS

Jazz Premiere: Washington (1961–2, Col. CS8797); *Jazz Meets the Bossa Nova* (1962, Col. CS8725); *New Jazz on Campus* (1963, Col. CS8864); *Rio* (1964, Col. CS9115); *Something in the Wind* (1969, A&M 4207); *Icarus* (*c*1971, Epic 31643); *Earthdance* (1977, A&M 4653); *Common Ground* (1977, A&M 4698)

BIBLIOGRAPHY

Feather '60s; *Feather–Gitler '70s*

D. DeMicheal: "The Paul Winter Sextet from the Campus to the White House," *DB*, xxx/1 (1963), 17

M. Bourne: "Paul Winter: One World Music," *DB*, liii/5 (1986), 26 [incl. discography]

J. Dulzo: "Environmentalist Musician Sings of Humanity," *Detroit News* (12 May 1989)

P. Harris: "Music of the 'Whole Earth'," *St. Louis Post-Dispatch* (14 Oct 1990)

C. McGowan and R. Pessanha: *The Brazilian Sound: Samba, Bossa Nova and the Popular Music of Brazil* (New York, 1991, 3/1998)

L. Tabor: "Paul Winter: Celebrating the Creatures and Cultures of the Earth through Music," *IM*, xci (1992), Nov, 14

BILL MILKOWSKI

Winters, Tiny [Gittens, Frederick] (*b* London, 24 Jan 1909; *d* London, 7 Feb 1996). English double bass player and singer. After taking up trumpet, violin, and clarinet, he taught himself to play double bass. He began playing professionally in the 1930s and performed with the bandleaders Roy Fox and Bert Ambrose (both 1932) and Lew Stone (1932–7). From 1932 he played in the Georgians, Nat Gonella's band within Stone's band, with which he made many recordings, continuing from 1935 after Gonella led the group independent of Stone; he may be seen in the short film *Pity the Poor Rich* (*Nat Gonella and his Georgians*) (1935). At the same time he took part in several recording sessions with Ray Noble (1932–4), performed again with Ambrose (March 1937–1938, late 1939–1940), and joined the Heralds of Swing (1939). He also made recordings with Coleman Hawkins (including *Lady Be Good*, 1934, Parl. R2007) and under his own name (*How many times/Frankie and Johnnie*, 1936, Decca F6031). During military service Winters played with Billy Amstell's quintet, which became the RAF Rhythm Five. After his demobilization he rejoined Stone, was resident at Hatchett's Club, London (1948–55), worked as a session musician, and played regularly in theater orchestras. From 1962 to 1972 he performed for the "Black and White Minstrel Show," and for three and a half years during this period was a member of George Chisholm's Jazzers. He retired briefly in the mid-1970s, but resumed working as a freelance and led the Palm Court Trio and a big band, the Café Society Orchestra. From 1982 he toured with Digby Fairweather in a tribute to Nat Gonella and in 1984, with Fairweather, established the Kettner's Five. He finally retired in the early 1990s, after receiving the freedom of the City of London and writing his memoirs (which perhaps remain unpublished).

BIBLIOGRAPHY

CarrJ; *ChiltonB*

Obituaries: A. Shipton, *The Guardian* (2 March 1996); B. Amstell, *JJI*, xlix/4 (1996), 19

J. Stone: "A Profile of Tiny Winters," *Memory Lane*, no.109 (1996), 45

DIGBY FAIRWEATHER/SIMON ADAMS, BK

Winterschladen, Reiner (*b* Bergisch Gladbach, Germany, 30 June 1956). German trumpeter and flugelhorn player. He was self-taught and began to work as a professional musician in the late 1970s. In 1983 he was a founder of the group Pension Winnetou and in the following year of the trio Blue Box (with the double bass player Alois Kott and the drummer Peter Eisold). Thereafter he was a central figure in numerous groups in the Cologne area and from Hamburg, including the trio Winterschladen, Krämer, Manderscheid (1989, with Achim Krämer and Dieter Manderscheid), his duo with the percussionist Manos Tsangaris (1990), the quartet DRAFT (with Frank Gratkowski, saxophone, Kai Kanthak, double bass, and Klaus Kugel, drums), the band Trance Groove (1992), and the duo Nighthawks (1998, with the bass player, guitarist, and keyboard player Dal Martino). From 1995 Winterschladen was a member of the NDR Big Band, and in 1998 he began to collaborate with the string quartet Indigo. He frequently played in the groups of Ekkehard Jost and Klaus König as well as with the Pata Masters, led by the reed player Norbert Stein, in Manfred Schoof's big band, and in the European Jazz Ensemble. He has toured for the Goethe-Institut in Brazil, Eastern Europe, Southeast Asia, and India. Winterschladen frequently seeks to unite jazz and recent developments in popular music in his work.

SELECTED RECORDINGS

Duos with M. Tsangaris: *King Gong* (1992, Jazz Haus Musik 56); with D. Martino (as Nighthawks): *Citizen Wayne* (1998, Call it Anything 4004)

As sideman with Blue Box: *Sweet Machine* (1985, Enja 5001); *10* (1985–6, 1994, Tiptoe 888818-2); *Stambul Boogie* (1986, Enja 5025); *Captured Dance Floor* (1989, Tiptoe 888801-2); *Time We Sign* (1991, Tiptoe 888813-2)

As sideman with E. Jost: *Weimarer Balladen* (1991, Fish Music 004); *Von Zeit zu Zeit* (1993, Fish Music 005); *Out of Jost's Songbook* (1994; Fish Music 006); *Deep* (1997, Fish Music 007); *Wintertango* (1997, Fish Music 008)

As sideman with N. Stein: *Ritual Life* (1991, Pata 5); *The Secret Act of Painting* (1993, Pata 7); *Blue Silt* (1994, Pata 8); *Pata Bahia* (1997, Pata 11)

As sideman with others: K. König: *Times of Devastation/Poco a poco* (1989, Enja 6014-2); *Hommage à Douglas Adams* (1991, Enja 6078-2); Ulla Oster: *Beyond Janis* (1992, Jazz Haus Musik 52); Hugo Read: *Songs of a Wayfarer* (1992, Nabel 4653); K. König: *The Song of Songs* (1992, Enja 7057-2); Draft: *Travelling Birds* (1993, Jazz Haus Musik 68); H. Lüdemann: *FutuRISM* (1997, Jazz Haus Musik 92–93)

MARCUS GAMMEL

Winther, Jens (*b* Næstved, Denmark, 29 Oct 1960). Danish trumpeter, composer, and arranger. He took up trumpet at the age of ten and became a professional jazz musician in 1978, playing with Pierre Dørge, Erling Kroner (recording in 1986), and the group Cadentia Nova Danica. In 1980 he represented Denmark in the European Youth Jazz Orchestra. He joined Ernie Wilkins's Almost Big Band in 1981 and the Radioens Big Band in 1982, when he also formed a quintet with Tomas Franck as co-leader. In 1989 he went to New York, where he joined the Jazz Composer's Workshop under the direction of Bob Brookmeyer and played with Toshiko Akioshi, Kenny Barron, Max Roach, Mario Bauzá, and George Mraz, among others. He returned to Denmark in 1991 to work as a composer, soloist, and bandleader. Winther has written for symphony orchestras, choirs, small groups, and big bands throughout Europe and has toured and performed with such musicians as Carla Bley (with whom he recorded in 1988), Brookmeyer, Michel Camilo, Miles Davis, Al Foster, Dizzy Gillespie, Joe Henderson, Abdullah Ibrahim, Thad Jones, Hermeto Pascoal, Steve Swallow, and Clark Terry.

SELECTED RECORDINGS

As leader: *Jens Winther Quintet* (1986, Stunt 8603); *Jens Winther – the Danish Radio Big Band* (1990–91, Olufsen 5167); *Scorpio Dance* (1991, Sto. 4179); *The Planets* (1994, Stunt 19502); *The Four Elements* (1996, Stunt 19802)

BIBLIOGRAPHY

K. Frandsen: *Politikens jazzleksikon* (Copenhagen, 1987)

J. R. K. Keller: "Himlen over Winther" [The sky above Winther], *Jazz Special*, no.31 (1996), 14
L. Tømming: "Skorpionens dans" [Scorpio dance], *Musikeren*, no.3 (1997), 8

FRANK BÜCHMANN-MØLLER

Wis. Nickname of WARREN SMITH (ii).

Wissels, Diederik (*b* Rotterdam, Netherlands, 6 Dec 1960). Dutch pianist and composer. He learned classical piano from the age of five; later he received lessons from Kenny Drew and John Lewis and studied at the Berklee College of Music (1982). After returning to Europe he settled in Brussels and quickly gained work as an accompanist to such musicians as Slide Hampton, Chet Baker, Joe Henderson, Junior Cook, and Kenny Wheeler. In the course of widespread touring he gave numerous concerts in which his piano playing evoked the delicacy and virtuosity of Bill Evans (ii). In 1992 Wissels began collaborating with David Linx in a duo and as the co-leader of small groups.

SELECTED RECORDINGS

As leader: with L. Schneider: *Milanka* (1987, Tim. 254); *Tender is the Night* (1990, B Sharp 75); *The Hillock Songstress* (1994, Igloo 110)
As leader with D. Linx: *Kamook* (1992, B Sharp 83); *If One More Day* (1993, Crépuscule 970-2); *Up Close* (1995, Label Bleu 6582); *Bandarkâh* (1998, Label Bleu 6606)
As sideman: P. Catherine: *Transparence* (1986, Inak 8701); James Baldwin and D. Linx: *A Lover's Question* (1986–7, Crépuscule 928-2); S. Houben: *Blue Circumstances* (1993, Igloo 102)

BIBLIOGRAPHY

F. Bergerot: "David Linx, Diederik: le quarte plus," *Jazzman*, no.34 (1998), 20

ANDRÉ CLERGEAT

Witherspoon, Jimmy [James; Spoon] (*b* Gurdon, AR, 18 Aug 1921; *d* Los Angeles, 18 Sept 1997). Singer. According to his son, Witherspoon's previously published birthdate of 8 August 1923 is incorrect. He first sang in his local Baptist church choir and began listening to recordings by blues singers at an early age. While in the Merchant Marine (1941–3) he performed in Calcutta with Teddy Weatherford's band. From 1944 to 1948 he was a member of Jay McShann's group, but in 1947 he achieved great success on the rhythm-and-blues chart with his own recording of *Ain't nobody's business*. In 1949 he formed a six-piece band, and he soon became a leading singer. However, the loss of his popularity after the advent of rock-and-roll, together with the bad management of his finances, resulted in Witherspoon being declared bankrupt in 1953, and he worked infrequently until 1958. He made a big impact at the Monterey Jazz Festival in 1959 and thereafter began recording albums with major jazz musicians. Having established a second career as a soloist, he made tours of Europe (with Buck Clayton, 1961) and Japan (with Count Basie, 1963) and appeared frequently on television and at festivals. In 1971 he reached a new and wider audience when he toured with the rock singer Eric Burdon, and from 1972 he hosted a blues and rhythm-and-blues radio show in Los Angeles. He returned frequently to Monterey in the 1960s and 1970s and toured Europe on a regular basis into the early 1980s; he also appeared occasionally in the Far East. After overcoming a battle with cancer in 1983 he resumed work and remained active internationally until mid-1997, often with Bross Townsend as his accompanist. Witherspoon was one of the first singers who managed to adapt his classic and extrovert style of blues shouting to the harmonic and rhythmic demands of modern jazz styles without sacrificing its essential qualities (*see* BLUES, §9).

Oral history material in *GBLnsa*; video oral history material in *NCH* (HCJA).

SELECTED RECORDINGS

As leader: Wandering Gal Blues (1947, Supreme 1500); Hey Mr. Landlord (1947, Supreme 1508); Money's Getting Cheaper (1947, Supreme 1501); Ain't nobody's business (1947, Supreme 1506); In the evening when the sun goes down/Six Foot Two Blues (1947, Supreme 1533); Thelma Lee Blues (1948, Modern 20-604); Big Fine Girl/No Rollin' Blues (1949, Modern 20-721); I'm just a country boy (1950, Modern 20-782); *Jimmy Witherspoon at Monterey* (1959, HiFi 421); *Roots* (1962, Rep. 96057); *Spoonful* (1975, BN LA534G); with P. Francis: *Jimmy Witherspoon & Panama Francis' Savoy Sultans* (1980, BB 33177)
As sideman: J. McShann: Hard Working Man's Blues (1945, Philo 109); Ernestine/Roll on, Katy (1946, Mer. 8018); Voodoo Woman Blues (1946, Mer. 8020); I want a little girl (1946, Mer. 8026); B. Clayton: *Olympia Concert* (1961, Vogue 546)

SELECTED FILMS AND VIDEOS

Buck Clayton and his All Stars (1961); Paul Horn Quintet (1962); Jazz Casual: Jimmy Witherspoon – Ben Webster and the Vince Guaraldi Trio (1963); L. A. Jazz, no.1 (1981)

BIBLIOGRAPHY

P. Welding: "Spoon: an Informal Portrait," *DB*, xxix/29 (1962), 22
A. Rotante: "Jimmy Witherspoon Discography," *Record Research*, no.62 (1964), 5; no.63 (1964), 7; no.64 (1964), 4; no.65 (1964), 2; no.66 (1965), 8; no.67 (1965), 10; no.68 (1965), 7; no.71 (1965), 10
V. Wilmer: "Jimmy Witherspoon: There'll Always be Blues," *DB*, xxxiv/14 (1967), 23
L. Feather: "Spoon Gets the Sugar," *MM* (13 Nov 1971), 24
M. Jones: "Laughing Spoonful," *MM* (18 Aug 1973), 56
T. Cummings: "The Seven Ages of Spoon," *Black Music* (1974), May, 39
M. Jones: "The Lovin' Spoonful," *MM* (2 March 1974), 65
——: "Spoon Puts the Bulldog Record Straight," *MM* (18 Sept 1976), 41
A. Navarro and F. Joseph: "Living Blues Interview: Jimmy Witherspoon," *Living Blues*, no.33 (1977), 15
A. Shaw: *Honkers and Shouters: the Golden Years of Rhythm and Blues* (New York, 1978), 211
S. Harris: *Blues Who's Who: a Biographical Dictionary of Blues Singers* (New Rochelle, NY, 1979/*R*1994)
S. Dance: *The World of Count Basie* (New York and London, 1980), 306
C. Deffaa: "The Blues is Nothing but Personal: Jimmy Witherspoon," *Living Blues*, no.93 (1990), 17
R. Astbury: "Jimmy Witherspoon on Crown and Kent," *Blues & Rhythm*, no.101 (1995), 14
C. Deffaa: *Blue Rhythms: Six Lives in Rhythm and Blues* (Urbana, IL, and Chicago, 1996), 207
A. Hobus: "Jimmy Witherspoon: an Interview," *Blues Gazette*, no.3 (1996), 15
Obituaries: J. Pareles, *New York Times* (22 Sept 1997); T. Russell, *The Guardian* (24 Sept 1997); D. Clarke, *Juke Blues*, no.39 (1997), 34; B. Crowther, *JJI*, l/11 (1997), 16; B. Dahl, *Living Blues*, no.136 (1997), 48; D. Penny, *Blues & Rhythm*, no.124 (1997), 19; M. Redenac, *Soul Bag*, no.149 (1998), 36; B. Powell, *Blues Access*, no.32 (1998), 48
A. Hobus: "Un point de vue 'jeune' sur Jimmy Witherspoon," *Soul Bag*, no.149 (1998), 32
A. Vasset: "Jimmy Witherspoon," *BHcF*, no.467 (1998), 8

BOB WEIR/HOWARD RYE, BK

Wittwer, Stephan (*b* Zurich, 1 March 1953). Swiss guitarist and electronic sound designer. He took piano lessons as a child but taught himself to play electric guitar. Later he gained a teacher's diploma in classical guitar at the Musikakademie in Zurich and studied electronic music informally at the Musikakademie in Basel. From 1976 to 1979 he worked with Radu Malfatti in a duo; they recorded two albums, including *Und?* (1977, FMP 0470). Wittwer gave electronic music performances in the quartet Polyphonie Zürich (1980–84) and often participated in Werner Lüdi's projects (1981–99). In addition he worked with Christy Doran and Fredy Studer in the trio Red Twist and Tuned Arrow (1985–6, recording in 1985) and was a member of Rüdiger Carl's quintet COWWS (1987–97). After recording an album in performance at the Susan Wyss Gallery in Zurich as an unaccompanied soloist (*World of Strings*, 1989, Intakt 017) he led the Trio Sludge 5–0 (1989–90), which played improvisations influenced by heavy metal. From 1991 he worked sporadically in a duo with Han Bennink and in a trio with Martin Schütz and Paul Lovens, and between 1994 and 2000 he was associated with another trio, Sludge 2/3000, which toured the USA in 1996. He also played in Dueling Guitars, a duo with the guitarist Donald Miller (1995), and led the Stephan Wittwer Guitar Sound System (1999). His principal activity from 1997 has been the duo Werther/Wittwer in collaboration with the drummer and composer Michael Wertmüller, with whom he recorded the album *Werther/Wittwer* (1998, Grob 204). Much of Wittwer's music is based on noise and electronic "errors," and, despite numerous concert performances, the majority of his work has been in studio settings.

ARMIN BÜTTNER

Wofford, Mike [Michael Riley] (*b* San Antonio, TX, 25 Feb 1938). Pianist. He was brought up in San Diego, where he began playing piano at the age of seven and was introduced to jazz when he was 16. He worked with Howard Rumsey's Lighthouse All Stars (1962), Shorty Rogers (1963), Red Norvo (1964), Shelly Manne (1966–83), Sarah Vaughan (1979, 1983), Benny Carter (1988–9), and Ella Fitzgerald (1990–94). From 1967 he led a number of small groups, with Brian Lynch, J. R. Monterose, Rufus Reid, Andy Simpkins, John Guerin, Joe LaBarbera, Akira Tana, Monty Budwig, and others as sidemen. As a studio musician (1968–78) he played with Kenny Burrell (1973), Tom Scott (1973), Oliver Nelson (1975), and Bud Shank (*c*1976); later he recorded with Russ Garcia (on electric piano, 1980), Lorez Alexandria (1980, 1987), the flutist Holly Hoffman (1989–92), Pete Christlieb (1990), Harry Edison and Shank (both 1991), and the singer Kenny Rankin (*c*1994).

Video oral history material in *NCH* (HCJA).

SELECTED RECORDINGS

As unaccompanied soloist: *Afterthoughts* (1978, Dis. 784); *Mike Wofford at Maybeck: Maybeck Recital Hall Series*, xviii (1991, Conc. 4514)

Duos with M. Lowe: on *Souvenirs* (1977, 1992, Jazz Alliance 10011), Body and Soul, Wofford's Blues Bernardo (1992)

As leader: *Summer Night* (1967, Mlst. 9012); *Mike Wofford Plays Jerome Kern*, ii (1980, Dis. 816); *Funkallero* (1987, Trend 552)

As sideman: J. Pass: *Joy Spring* (1964, BN LT1103); S. Manne: *Alive in London* (1970, Cont. 7629); B. Bryant and J. Richardson: *The Drum Session* (1974, Phi. [Jap.] 32JD87); C. McPherson: *The Prophet* (1983, Dis. 882); Z. Sims: *Quietly There: Zoot Sims Plays Johnny Mandel* (1984, Pablo 2310903); H. Hoffman: *Further Adventures* (1989, Capri 74022); H. Edison: *How Long, How Long Blues* (1991, Village 1004); B. Shank: *The Doctor is in* (1991, Can. 79520)

BIBLIOGRAPHY

P. Carles, A. Clergeat, and J.-L. Comolli: *Dictionnaire du jazz* (Paris, 1988, rev. and enlarged 2/1994)

GK

Wojtasik, Piotr (*b* Wrocław, Poland, 10 June 1964). Polish trumpeter and flugelhorn player. He studied jazz at the academy of music in Katowice and joined its faculty after graduating in 1987; from that same year into the mid-1990s he made many recordings as a member of Krzysztof Popek's ensemble Young Power. In 1988 Wojtasik gave a successful performance at the Jazz Jamboree in Warsaw as a member of the group New Presentation. From 1992 to 1995 he was a member of Jan Wróblewski's group Made in Poland, and in 1994 he formed the Traveling Birds Quintet, with Piotr Baron, Kuba Stankiewicz, Darek Oleszkiewicz, and the drummer Cezary Konrad. From 1996 he has led his own quintet, of which Maciej Sikała is a member. He has organized special groups for tours and recordings with Gary Bartz, Billy Harper, Buster Williams, Ben Riley, and Ed Schuller, among others; the sidemen on his album *Quest* (*c*1996) include Leszek Możdżer, Harper, and Williams.

SELECTED RECORDINGS

As leader: *Piortr Wojtasik* (1993, Polonia 012); *Lonely Town* (1995, Power Bros. 00137); *Quest* (1995, Power Bros. 00147); *Escape* (1998, Power Bros. 00177)

As sideman: Young Power: *Young Power* (1987, Muza 2525); New Presentation: *Lonesome Dancer* (1989, Polskie Nagrania 2840); Young Power: *The Man of Tra* (1990, Power Bros. 00111); New Presentation: *You've Changed* (1992, Power Bros. 00117); J. Śmietana: *Ballads and other Songs* (1993, Starling 0004); K. Popek and Volker Greve: *Places* (1993, Power Bros. 00115); Traveling Birds Quintet: *Traveling Birds Quintet* (1994, Polonia 030); Leszek Kułakowski: *Black and Blue* (1994, Polonia 031); K. Popek: *Letters and Leaves* (*c*1995, Power Bros. 00139); Traveling Birds Quintet: *Return to the Nest* (1995, Polonia 041)

BIBLIOGRAPHY

A. Chodkowski, ed.: *Encyklopedia muzyki* (Warsaw, 1995)
P. Brodowski: "Magiczna Trąbka" [Magic trumpet], *JF*, no.164 (1995), 32
<http://www.powerbros.com.pl/woj-info.html> (2001)

ADAM CEGIELSKI, BK

Wolf, Thilo (*b* Nuremberg, Germany, 8 Sept 1967). German pianist, drummer, arranger, and bandleader. He studied accordion for eight years, then took up piano, double bass, and saxophone before studying drums with Charly Antolini. He began working professionally at the age of 15, and wrote his first arrangement the following year. After winning a prize at the Forum junger Deutscher Komponisten für Orchestermusik in 1984, he founded his own big band, which accompanied such guest soloists as Max Greger, the singer Etta Cameron, and Toots Thielemanns. He also led a trio. In 1990 he began working in a television series, "Swing It!." Influenced by Count Basie, Wolf has written many compositions for films and television and arrangements for other bands. His recordings include *Thilo Wolf Big Band Live: Swing It!* (1993, MDL 1915) and *Mr. Grooverix* (1995, MDL 1925). (G. Conrad: "Thilo Wolf," *Der Jazzfreund*, no. 159 (1995), 4)

GERHARD CONRAD

Wolfe, Ben(jamin Jonah) (*b* Baltimore, 3 Aug 1962). Double bass player. He grew up in Portland, Oregon, where he played tuba and trombone in school bands and electric bass guitar in funk and pop groups; while he was at college he took up double bass, on which he is primarily self-taught, although he had some lessons with Ray Brown. Having moved to New York (*c*1985) he played with Dakota Staton, Duke Jordan, and Junior Cook, and then worked with Harry Connick, Jr., initially in a duo (1988) and later in a trio and a big band (until 1993). Wolfe joined Wynton Marsalis's septet in January 1994 and toured and recorded with the group until it disbanded later that year; he may be seen in the video *Garth Fagan's Griot New York* (*c*1995). In 1995 he worked again with Marsalis in the Lincoln Center Jazz Orchestra and began leading his own groups. Wolfe also performed with Branford Marsalis and Marcus Roberts, and recorded with Frank Kimbrough (1988), Carl Allen (as a leader, 1993, and in Allen's Manhattan Projects, 1994), the tenor saxophonist David Schumacher (*c*1995), the singer Mary Stallings (1996), Branford Marsalis's group Buckshot LeFonque (1996), Mark Turner and James Moody (1997), and the tenor saxophonist

Ned Goold (*c*1998), who is a regular member of his groups. In 1997 he toured with Diana Krall and Benny Green.

SELECTED RECORDINGS

As leader: *13 Sketches* (1996, Mons 874791); *Bagdad Theater* (1997, Mons 874827)

As sideman: F. Kimbrough: *Lonely Woman* (1988, Mapleshade 512628-2); H. Connick, Jr.: *Lofty's Roach Soufflé* (1990, Col. CK46223); E. Reed: *Musicale* (1996, Imp. 196)

BIBLIOGRAPHY

D. Kasrel: "Hearsay: Ben Wolfe," *JT*, xxvii/5 (1997), 28

<http://www.raba.com/jazz/ben/ben.html> (1999) [incl. discography]

GK

Wolff, Michael (Blieden) [Mike] (*b* Victorville, CA, 31 July 1952). Pianist, keyboard player, and leader. He grew up in Memphis and then in Berkeley, California (from 1961), and took up piano at the age of eight. Later he studied music at the University of California in Los Angeles and Berkeley (1970–71) and at the Manhattan School of Music. After working with Cal Tjader (1972–4) he was a member for several months of Airto Moreira's group Fingers (1974–5) and performed briefly with Cannonball Adderley's quintet (1975). Wolff then recorded with Tom Harrell (1976, on piano and electric piano) and worked with Sonny Rollins (1976–8) and Nancy Wilson (1978–83), for whom he wrote a number of arrangements. From the mid-1970s into the early 1980s he led trios with John Williams (iv), John Heard, or Rufus Reid on double bass and either Dick Berk or Roy McCurdy on drums; during the same period he was joint leader with Alex Foster of the fusion quintet Answering Service (1978–80), in which, at various times, John Abercrombie, John Scofield, Barry Finnerty, Lincoln Goines, Charles Fambrough, Ron McClure, Andy Narrell, and Billy Hart served as sidemen. In 1982 he performed with Art Farmer and Benny Golson at the Playboy Jazz Festival in Los Angeles.

During the mid-1980s Wolff worked as a jazz comedian, and from 1989 to 1993 he was music director for the television program "The Arsenio Hall Show." Thereafter he led a trio (1994–6) with Christian McBride and Tony Williams, Kenny Davis and Clarence Penn, and John Williams (iv) and McCurdy among his sidemen. In 1997 he renewed his association with Foster, with whom he recorded in a duo and co-led a quartet. Two years later he performed at Jazzfest Berlin. By the late 1990s Wolff was dividing his year between the coasts, living alternately in Los Angeles and New York. He has also been involved in television and film music and wrote the music for the film *The Tic Code* (1998), which he produced in collaboration with his wife, the actress Polly Draper; the subject of the film is Tourette's syndrome, from which Wolff suffers.

SELECTED RECORDINGS

As leader: *2AM* (*c*1995, Cabana Boy 9605); *Portraiture: the Blues Period* (1997, Fuel 2000 1004)

As sideman with C. Adderley: *Phenix* (1975, Fan. 79004)

BIBLIOGRAPHY

Feather–Gitler '70s

H. Wong: "Profile: Mike Wolff," *DB*, xli/21 (1974), 32

D. Kasrel: "Different Channel: Mike Wolff," *JT*, xxv/10 (1995), 27

M. Drexler: "'Posse' Boss to Hit City with Jazzed-up Act," *Plain Dealer* [Cleveland] (31 May 1996)

M. Droney: "At Pollywood with Michael Wolff," *Mix* (1996), Dec, 175

J. Lloyd: "After Time Out for TV, He's a Bandleader Now," *Philadelphia Inquirer* (19 July 1996)

Z. Stewart: "Inspired by Picasso," *DB*, lxv/5 (1998), 55

C. Deffaa: "Out & About in New York, USA: Jazz Pianist Michael Wolff ... and Tourette's Syndrome," *CJM*, xxvi/5 (1999), 6

BK

Wollesen, Kenny [Kenneth George] (*b* Farmington, NM, 9 April 1966). Drummer. He grew up in Santa Cruz, California, and at the age of 12 he began playing drums at school and in a jazz group with the saxophonist Donny McCaslin; later he studied music at Cabrillo Junior College in Santa Cruz (1984), where he played with his fellow student Ben Goldberg. After performing with Jessica Williams (1987–93) Wollesen moved to New York and worked with John Zorn (from 1993), Drew Gress's group Jagged Sky (from 1994), Wayne Horvitz's quartet (from winter 1994), Steven Bernstein's Sex Mob and Andy Laster's Interpretations of Lessness (both from 1996), and Bill Frisell and John Scofield (both from 1999). He also played with Dominique Eade's trio (1994), Steve Beresford (recording in 1994), Ellery Eskelin's ensemble devoted to the music of Gene Ammons (from the mid-1990s), Jim Hall (touring in 1999), the group Lan Xang (alongside McCaslin, the saxophonist Dave Binney, and Scott Colley), the tenor saxophonist Ilhan Ersahin, Myra Melford, Tom Waits, the New Klezmer Trio (with Goldberg), Marty Ehrlich, Brad Shepik, and Wolfgang Muthspiel. During the 1990s he performed on more than 30 recordings. In 1997 he formed his own group, the Wollesens. He doubles on vibraphone and percussion.

SELECTED RECORDINGS

As sideman: E. Eskelin: *The Sun Died* (1996, SN 121282-2); I. Ersahin *Our Song* (1998, Golden Horn 007); J. Scofield: *Bump* (1999, Verve 314-543430-2); Lan Xang: *Hidden Gardens* (1999, Naxos Jazz 86046-2); Sex Mob: *Solid Sender* (1999, Knitting Factory 244)

MARK GILBERT

Wolverines [Wolverine Orchestra]. Band formed in 1923 in the Chicago area. After appearing at the Stockton Club in Hamilton, Ohio, and early the following year at Doyle's Dance Hall in Cincinnati, it recorded in Richmond, Indiana, for Gennett (for illustration *see* Recording, fig.3), when its members were Dick Voynow (piano and leader), Bix Beiderbecke (cornet), Al Gandee (trombone), Jimmy Hartwell (clarinet and alto saxophone), George Johnson (tenor saxophone), Bob Gillette (banjo), Min Leibrook (brass bass), and Vic Moore (drums; later replaced temporarily by Vic Berton). After Gandee left the band it played on weekends with Hoagy Carmichael and during the week at the Rainbow Casino Gardens in Indianapolis, and in May 1924 it again recorded for Gennett. Later that year in New York it performed at the Cinderella Ballroom and recorded several tracks (on some of which Georg Brunis was a guest trombonist and on others of which Jimmy McPartland replaced Beiderbecke), then disbanded. The Wolverines were most strongly influenced by the New Orleans Rhythm Kings.

SELECTED RECORDINGS

(all recorded in 1924 for Gennett)

Fidgety Feet/Jazz Me Blues (5408); Oh Baby/Copenhagen (5453); Riverboat Shuffle/Susie (5454); Sensation/Lazy Daddy (5542); When my Sugar Walks Down the Street/Prince of Wails (5620)

BIBLIOGRAPHY

G. Johnson: "The Wolverines and Bix," *Frontiers of Jazz*, ed. R. de Toledano (New York, 1947, rev. 2/1962), 123

B. James: *Bix Beiderbecke* (London, 1959); repr. in *Kings of Jazz*, ed. S. Green (South Brunswick, NJ, and New York, 1978)

R. M. Sudhalter, P. R. Evans, and W. Dean-Myatt: *Bix: Man and Legend* (New Rochelle, NY, and London, 1974), 92–122

WARREN VACHÉ, SR.

The Wolverines, 1924: (left to right) Vic Moore (drums), George Johnson (tenor saxophone), Jimmy Hartwell (clarinet and alto saxophone), Dick Voynow (piano, standing), Bix Beiderbecke (cornet), Al Gandee (trombone), Min Leibrook (sousaphone), and Bob Gillette (banjo)

Women. Women have participated on every instrument, in every style, and in every era of jazz history. Yet, with the notable exception of singers and a number of pianists, female jazz musicians have been continuously overlooked in the most prestigious areas of jazz practice, marketing, and documentation. These include the recording and broadcasting industries, major performance venues, trade magazines, and jazz history books. Also impeding the acceptance of women in venerated jazz roles and on jazz circuits are prevailing definitions of gender that made it appear unfeminine for women to play the most highly valued jazz instruments and styles, to perform in the venues where jazz was heard and where jazz skills were shared and developed, to appear on the stage, or to compete with men. Women's jazz musicianship throughout the history of the music has persevered despite such obstacles.

In addition to the persistent, if marginalized, presence of women in jazz generally, evidence exists of separate spheres of participation where female players found work opportunities and relative acceptance. These spheres – which constituted different things at different times – have included family bands, all-woman bands, local venues, music education, novelty acts, singing, and playing so-called feminine instruments (harp, for instance, rather than trumpet). Women jazz musicians whose careers followed these paths paid a price of omission, however, as such activities were routinely ignored, trivialized, or considered "not real jazz" by historians, journalists, bookers, agents, audiences, and/or fellow musicians. In a sense, these feminized, devalued spheres simultaneously enabled women's participation in jazz and guaranteed their erasure from its history. The appearance of a special entry on women in this dictionary is both testimony and corrective to this history.

1. Gender and music. 2. Historical overview. 3. History and criticism.

1. Gender and music. In assessing women's activities in jazz history it is important to distinguish between sex as a biological category and gender as a social category, and to recognize that the omission of female musicians from certain jazz activities, instruments, genres, markets, and historical consideration stems not from inherent physical, mental, or emotional differences between men and women but from culturally produced ideas about masculinity and femininity at particular times and places. Many feminist theorists have pointed out that, even in a single time and place, definitions of gender do not apply in the same ways to all women and men across class, race, ethnicity, and other social categories. Although ideas about gender norms and their effects on music-making vary from culture to culture and are ever-changing, several generalizations can be made that span the course of jazz history.

(i) Gender-coding of instruments. The division of instruments into those associated with femininity and those identified with masculinity is found in many musics of the world, and jazz is no exception. Throughout jazz history singing has been understood as relatively feminine, or an activity in which women could participate without appearing "abnormal," compared with the playing of brass, reeds, bass, and drums – instruments typically associated with men. Indeed, singing is the area in which women have received the greatest acceptance and historical acknowledgement in jazz,

as evidenced by the large number of recordings by women jazz singers and the not uncommon inclusion of female singers in jazz history books. In addition, the piano, flute, and harp are among those instruments which have been variously associated with women in the USA since the emergence of jazz. Historians of women in jazz have traced this particular gender-coding of instruments to both European and West African musical traditions.

Despite the historical prominence of "piano men" throughout jazz history, there is evidence that men sometimes worried about the ramifications that playing the piano might have on their masculine reputations. The popularity of the piano as a treasured item of furniture and for entertainment in 19th- and early 20th-century homes of white and African-American families who could afford them contributed to the instrument's domestic connotations. Not only did girls and women in such households have access to the instrument, they were encouraged to play it, though this acceptance did not generally encompass their professional aspirations, particularly in middle- or upper-class families. The Victorian "cult of true womanhood," a definition of appropriate femaleness available to middle and upper-class white women, included a positive equation of girls' and women's musical training with the social status of their fathers and husbands. Although male professional pianists have not historically been perceived as "abnormal" in the same way as have female professional reed and brass players, the acceptability of the piano as "appropriate" for women in an amateur sense did result in a relative public acceptance of the professional musicianship of female pianists when compared with female players of other instruments. The power of gender-coding of instruments is palpable in the numbers of women who have worked as professional jazz pianists throughout the history of the music, despite enduring biases against jazz as an appropriate genre. Indeed, many upper- and middle-class, aspiring middle-class, and religious families historically, both white and African-American, have discouraged jazz as a genre for musical daughters. These biases have not held universal sway, however. For many poor and working-class families, particularly African-American families, musical careers in any genre represented a far preferable livelihood to sharecropping, domestic work, and other gruelling and limited labor options.

Other instruments generally considered "appropriate" for women during the span of jazz history have included harp, violin, and flute. However, because these have been less accepted as appropriate jazz instruments, such players as the harpists Adele Girard and Dorothy Ashby and the violinist Ginger Smock have been marginalized in jazz history, despite their acknowledged achievements on these instruments. In addition, African-American men and women who played instruments and repertory associated with Western classical music have been subject to a history of discrimination for crossing what Jon Michael Spencer has called the "essentialist color line," or for daring to enter the musical terrain of European "high culture" constructed and protected as "inherently" white and upper-class. What gender- and race-coding has meant in terms of jazz history is not that musicians have unilaterally steered clear of instruments considered outside the narrow confines of current gender and race definitions (though for these reasons many, undoubtedly, did), but that when musicians did cross these lines they were often perceived not just as making aesthetic choices but as disturbing social norms, either in threatening, ludicrous, or titillating ways. When women chose careers playing instruments associated with men, their "novelty" potential often overshadowed the likelihood of their being heard as skilled players.

(ii) Effects of gender stereotypes on labor practices, marketing, and audience reception. Ethnomusicologists studying the musical participation of women in various cultural contexts have noted several trends that may occur when women cross musical gender boundaries by playing instruments, repertory, or styles associated with men. Sometimes the "normal" sexuality of women musicians is called into question; sometimes the music they produce is considered "inauthentic"; and in some cases their participation is perceived as a threat to the social order. Indeed, in many jazz contexts, women who played instruments or styles associated with men were stigmatized, with stunning polarity, as hypersexual or asexual; they were perceived as feminine sex-spectacles directed at titillating men, as ludicrous displays of unexpected behavior (akin to dancing dogs), or as masculine women "trying to be men." Female jazz musicians and all-woman jazz bands have been historically marketed and consumed as novelty acts, even when they played the same instruments in the same styles and cultivated the same skills as male musicians of the same periods. Women jazz musicians who played instruments associated with men have often been billed as though they were cross-dressers of sorts: "the female Louis Armstrong," "Gene Krupa with a skirt." A comparison of reviews in the mainstream trades and black press indicates that this has been especially true within white cultural circuits. In the entertainment pages of national weekly black newspapers during the 1920s, 1930s, and 1940s, African-American women musicians received a level of respect that was generally not paralleled in the white-owned trades.

Notions of appropriate and inappropriate roles for women and men, depending upon race and class, have not only affected how jazz musicians were perceived, but have also shaped their working conditions, the marketing strategies that would be deployed to draw audiences, and the very impressions that audiences formed of the sights and sounds emanating from the bandstand or stage. Both black and white female instrumentalists have frequently been expected to sing and dance, as well as play, and, in some cases, to circulate among patrons during breaks and double as "B"-girls (i.e. mingling and encouraging patrons to buy drinks). Even women musicians who were able to focus on their playing were expected to exhibit popular representations of female glamor while on the bandstand. This stipulation often caused difficulties; for example, costumes with low necklines were uncomfortable for women wearing saxophone neck straps, the embouchures of brass and reed players were impeded by their lipstick, and high heels complicated the leverage of bass drum pedals for drummers. All of these practices added to the workload of female musicians, but, ironically, also added to the impression that they were not "really working," and, therefore, not "real professional musicians."

Historically there has been a tendency for women instrumentalists and all-woman bands to be marketed and consumed as visual rather than auditory attractions. While the femininity of female singers could be captured on a recording, gender difference eluded the microphone when it came to all-girl bands that strove to play in styles undifferentiated from men. Combined with the fact that, as with other industry prizes, opportunities to record carried prestige and benefits more likely to be bestowed upon men than upon women, this must be considered as part of the context for examining the shortage of such opportunities for women jazz musicians. Because jazz historians have traditionally relied on recordings for evidence of historical significance, the dearth of recordings by women who played instruments other than piano, as well as the abundance of recordings of women singers, has contributed profoundly to a historical memory that embraces the pantheon of great female singers and forgets the women who played band instruments. Those female instrumentalists fortunate enough to record were often required to sing as well as play. All-female bands that received the widest broadcasting and industry support were those whose performances emphasized popular styles of "femininity" as well as musicality. Clearly, historical or musical "significance" is not the only factor that determined who was recorded.

Because gender difference could be more easily communicated visually than aurally, women musicians were involved in a higher percentage of short jazz films than recordings, including a number of soundies made between 1940 and 1946. White all-girl bands, particularly those offering a version of femininity popular in other forms of mainstream entertainment, received far more opportunities to appear in such films than their African-American counterparts. This is no doubt partly a result of the ambivalence of white circuit owners concerning how to represent many black women on the stage together playing band instruments, amid Hollywood's narrow repertory of degrading images of maids, mammies, and exotic sex objects. In addition, if such a film's entertainment value depended on mainstream audience perceptions that women did not or could not play jazz, then the preference of the white-owned film companies for presenting white women's bands may be also stem from white cultural ambivalence about whether black women played "authentic jazz" because they were black, or "unauthentic jazz" because they were women. Again, the results of these gender- and race-specific marketing considerations – the emphasis on visual media, the lack of recordings, and the privileging of performances by those women musicians who least challenged dominant stereotypes about jazz and "pretty girls" as nonoverlapping categories – have all been used as justification for the marginalization of women in jazz history. One of the important points raised by historians in the 1980s and 1990s is that the criteria for the inclusion of women in jazz history must be examined and reconfigured if we are to recognize their participation in and contributions to jazz.

(iii) Spheres historically considered "appropriate" for women. While there has been a relative acceptance of women who played instruments considered "appropriate" for their sex, women musicians have also found more acceptance in some jazz activities than others. As with all notions of gender, the jazz practices that have been considered acceptable realms for women's participation have constituted different things at different times and places for different people. Three general examples that can be traced throughout jazz history are family bands and musical families, music education, and "all-girl" or all-woman bands.

Family bands represent one area in which the need to maximize the talent pool has historically outweighed dominant gender expectations regarding women and music. Many women musicians began in ensembles with both male and female relatives, and many famous musical families included female reed and brass players and drummers, as well as pianists, singers, and dancers. While they are often portrayed in jazz histories merely as the homely settings for the "humble beginnings" of famous male musicians, family bands deserve further study as unique historical settings for mixed-gender musical collaboration conducive to the encouragement of women's musical development. The saxophonist Irma Young played alongside her brothers Lester (tenor saxophone) and Lee (drums) in the Young family band. Marjorie Pettiford is another saxophonist who thrived in a family band together with her brother Oscar (double bass). The pianist Norma Teagarden received her music education from her mother, Helen, a ragtime pianist, as did her brothers, Jack (trombone), Charlie (trumpet), and Cub (drums). At various times Jack Teagarden hired all of his siblings, male and female, for his band.

If the spectrum of what counts as jazz history included music educators, women would constitute a formidable presence. Sources such as the black press and oral histories of both male and female jazz musicians contain much evidence that music education was a field in which women historically found acceptance, work opportunities, and respect in jazz circles. The privileging of recordings and performances, as well as primitivist stereotypes of jazz musicians as untutored geniuses playing from their hearts, has promoted the production of jazz histories that overlooked education as an important aspect of jazz practice. New trends in academic jazz studies indicate growing interest in how jazz musicians learned their skills historically, but whether this will result in acknowledgement of female jazz educators is not yet clear. The mothers of many well-known male musicians, such as Milt Hinton's mother, Hilda Robinson, and Serge Chaloff's mother, Margaret Chaloff, were highly regarded music teachers, as was Ray Bryant's sister, Vera. Many Los Angeles jazz musicians, among them Dexter Gordon, Melba Liston, Clora Bryant, and Charles Mingus, received training in the children's band led by drummer and music teacher Alma Hightower. Historians of women in jazz have found that many women musicians turned from performing to teaching during periods when female players met with most resistance, for instance in the years after World War II.

Known as "all-girl" bands before the 1970s, jazz and swing bands consisting entirely of women have existed from the turn of the century through the present day. As early as the 1880s both white and African-American women's concert bands, marching bands, orchestras, and minstrel bands offered opportunities to women brass and reed players, drummers, and double bass players who had difficulty obtaining work in men's bands. In the early 20th century all-girl bands found work in circuses, carnivals, and tent shows. Black and white all-female big bands were popular on vaudeville stages in the 1920s and 1930s; some broke into the lucrative sphere of ballroom employment during the swing era, and some African-American women's bands became popular attractions on the black theater circuit. During World War II all-girl big bands entertained the troops on racially segregated USO circuits. A number of all-female groups survived the postwar years playing in nightclubs, and some white women found work in all-woman television bands in the 1950s. The tradition of all-female big bands was renewed in the 1970s, during the second-wave women's movement, with the emergence of new audiences for women performers, new strategies for women's equality, and new interest in women's cultural and historical contributions. The reasons for this enduring tradition of all-woman bands vary according to historical context, and range from impresarios cashing in on an abiding American fascination with acts perceived as "novelty" entertainment to feminist agendas of some women musicians to provide career opportunities and skill development for themselves and female colleagues.

2. Historical overview. Although it is true that women have participated in all historical periods of jazz history, it is also true that historical events have affected women differently from the ways in which they have affected men. Historians have not only painstakingly located historical information on female jazz musicians that was omitted from mainstream jazz histories, but they have also located jazz in a socio-historical context that incorporates changing perceptions of gender (as it intersects with such other categories as race and class) in order to understand women's participation in jazz. It should be clear from the following sketch that this vast and complex history deserves further study and incorporation in more complete and gender-conscious narratives of jazz history.

(i) History through the 1920s. African-American women were active innovators and participants in the musical forms that formed the roots of jazz, including work songs, spirituals, gospel, and blues. In the early 19th century, in New Orleans' famed Congo Square, African-American women participated in the musical traditions that accompanied *vodun* (voodoo) ceremonies, sometimes serving in prestigious roles as chant-leaders and drummers. The historical predominance of women in black Christian musical traditions takes into account the central participation of African-American women in spirituals from slavery onwards, including the arranged concert spirituals associated with musical messengers from historically black colleges, such as the Fisk Jubilee Singers, as well as in gospel and hymnody. In the late 19th century black female pianists could be found playing in African-American minstrel bands, and in the early 20th century it was not uncommon to find female pianists in ragtime and vaudeville bands. The ragtime piano craze of the early 1900s involved numerous female performers and composers, both black and white. The Kansas City pianist Julia Lee played ragtime early in her career. Among other women who played and/or composed piano rags were Ragtime Kate Beckham and May Aufderheide. The early 1900s saw female participation, usually on piano, but sometimes on brass, reeds, and rhythm, in circus, carnival, tent shows, and family bands, in both black and white entertainment circuits. Several women served as pianists and directors of orchestras in black theaters in the 1910s and 1920s.

African-American female singers were the primary artists of the earliest blues recordings during what is known as the classic blues era of the 1920s. Historians have noted that the "blues queens," such as Mamie Smith, Bessie Smith, and Ma Rainey, starred on the recordings that launched the blues recording industry, thus providing settings for many of the earliest recorded jazz solos by such instrumentalists as Coleman Hawkins, Louis Armstrong, and Sidney Bechet.

The extent to which women held down the piano chairs in early jazz bands in cities such as New Orleans and Chicago is significant. Jazz band pianists in New Orleans included Dolly Adams, Sweet Emma Barrett, Jeanette Kimball, and Olivia Cook, whereas in Chicago the long list of highly regarded early jazz pianists includes Lil Armstrong and Lovie Austin. Women's training and professional participation on instruments other than piano (or voice) was less visible, but a number of female cornetists, trumpet players, and saxophonists were celebrated in the black press in the 1920s, among them the trumpet playing mother and daughter Dyer and Dolly Jones (also known as Dolly Armenra or Dolly Hutchinson). Frequently the women who played instruments other than piano in jazz bands of the 1920s did so in the contexts of all-woman bands, usually on vaudeville circuits, but they sometimes performed for dancing. Dolly Jones was a member of Bobbie Howell's American Syncopators in 1929. Other all-woman bands of the 1920s include Bobbie Grice and the Fourteen Bricktops, the Pollyanna Syncopators, and the Gibson Navigators.

(ii) The Great Depression. The high unemployment and dire economics of the Great Depression made its impact in all industries and often resulted in the firing of women workers to provide jobs for unemployed men. However, the powerful need of people for diversion in the face of these difficult times, as well as the alternative economic system provided by prohibition-era nightclubs run by gangsters, meant that some facets of the entertainment industry were uniquely stable employers during the 1930s. Indeed the Great Depression was a period during which women musicians participated as pianists in men's jazz bands, as instrumentalists in all-girl bands, and as featured players of instruments associated with men, especially if such players provide the services of several entertainers for the price of one – perhaps singing and dancing as well as playing an instrument, as did the "Queen of the Trumpet," Valaida Snow. Some women, among them the singer Blanche Calloway and the clarinetist Ann Dupont, led male bands.

The tradition of relative acceptance of women pianists continued in the 1930s, most notably, perhaps, in Kansas City, where Mary Lou Williams and Margaret "Countess" Johnson exerted their influence on that wide-open city's swinging sound. In addition to the two all-female ensembles led by Lil Armstrong, African-American all-girl bands of the 1930s included the popular Harlem Playgirls, the Dixie Rhythm Girls, and the Dixie Sweethearts, out of which emerged many of the great jazz soloists and lead players of the 1940s all-girl bands, such as the International Sweethearts of Rhythm, Eddie Durham's All-Stars, and the Darlings of Rhythm. Several white all-girl bands of the 1930s gained access to the lucrative circuits of the growing mass entertainment industry, particularly those that communicated visual and musical messages that they weren't "really" jazz bands. This was especially true in the case of Phil Spitalny's "Hour of Charm" orchestra, which played primarily light classical music and emphasized a Victorian image of talented "angels of the hearth," despite a roster of highly trained and experienced professional musicians. Spitalny's orchestra received unprecedented network radio sponsorships and recording opportunities between 1934 and 1954. While Ina Rae Hutton's 1930s band played jazz pieces and included improvising soloists, the image of the blond bombshell, popularized by the screen actress Jean Harlow, encouraged an overall presentation of sex-spectacle.

(iii) World War II. Gender roles drastically shifted during World War II, affecting all fields of labor in the USA, including jazz and swing musicianship. The draft, enlistment, and new flexible definitions for "what is a worker" and "what is a woman," which accompanied the production boom and labor crisis, all resulted in a transformation of the presence of women in male-dominated civilian occupations as acceptable and even patriotic. As male big bands suffered personnel crises amid an enormous demand for dance music, female big bands acquired a new patriotic image and were even popular entertainers on USO camp show units sent out to entertain military troops. The celebrated International Sweethearts of Rhythm traveled to Germany under the aegis of the USO after black troops launched letter-writing campaigns specially requesting this famous African-American all-woman band. Other black women's bands which, like the Sweethearts, sometimes covertly broke the color line by engaging white women included Eddie Durham's All-Stars and the Darlings of Rhythm. The Prairie View Co-eds was a popular black all-female band, composed of college students at the historically black Prairie View Argicultural and Mechanical College of Texas, which spent its summers traveling on road tours that culminated with performances at the Apollo Theatre. Among white all-woman bands of the 1940s were Ada Leonard's "All-American" Girls, a band that made several USO tours of America, and groups led by the trumpet player Joy Cayler and the double bass player Sharon Rogers, both of which traveled on USO tours to the Philippines, Korea, and Japan. In addition to taking advantage of the expanding opportunities and acceptance women found in wartime all-girl bands, women musicians were sometimes employed in men's bands. Male leaders responded to war-induced personnel crises by supplementing their ranks with an unprecedented number of teenage boys, male musicians over the age of 35, and women. Woody Herman hired the trumpet player Billie Rogers and the vibraphonist Marjorie Hyams, Gerald Wilson took on the trombonist Melba Liston, and Lionel Hampton engaged the saxophonist Elsie Smith, to name only a few.

(iv) The postwar years. A side-effect of the wartime acceptance of women workers as "pitching in for the war effort" was that, after the war was over, it seemed natural that returning GIs should reclaim their roles and women should "go back home." The fact that most women workers had not come from home, but had worked before the war, did not hinder this perception. As with women workers in other fields, women musicians were inundated with messages that they should become full-time housewives and mothers, whether or not it was economically feasible or desirable to do so. In fact, the presence of women in the labor force grew rather than dwindled in the postwar years, and, rather than "going home," many women welders and riveters moved into "pink-collar" occupations (jobs such as beautician, teacher, and nurse, which had traditionally been thought of as "women's work"). Accordingly, many women musicians moved into musical fields traditionally considered "appropriate" for women, such as education. Some put down their brass or reed instruments and changed to piano or Hammond organ to take advantage of the historic acceptance of women at the keyboard; such moves were also a response to a postwar musical trend towards smaller groups playing in nightclubs instead of ballrooms, and to the concomitant money-saving maneuver of the clubowners, such as replacing bands with unaccompanied solo, duo, or trio acts that revolved around piano or organ.

Some women from the all-girl big bands of the 1940s formed groups that remained active through the postwar years, including Tiny Davis's Hell Divers (comprised of members of the International Sweethearts of Rhythm, the Darlings of Rhythm, and the Prairie View Co-eds), and the Vadel Quintet (which emerged from Virgil Whyte's big band). Some women, such as the trumpet player Clora Bryant, worked as freelance soloists in nightclubs. The emergence of television brought employment for some, in particular those who found work in the white all-girl television bands led by Hutton and Leonard.

Significant women instrumentalists who participated in jazz activities associated with the civil rights movement include the pianist, harpist, percussionist, and composer Alice McLeod Coltrane, who replaced McCoy Tyner in John Coltrane's group in 1966, and the pianist and organist Amina Claudine Myers, one of the few women associated with the Association for the Advancement of Creative Musicians in Chicago in the 1960s and 1970s.

(v) The second-wave women's movement. The emergence of the second-wave women's movement in the 1960s and 1970s raised public consciousness about issues such as sex discrimination in the workforce. It also raised the consciousness of women about the importance of documenting their lost history and cultural activities, and of creating new theories and practices conducive to women's liberation from limiting gender stereotypes. Much of this work unconsciously reflected the desires and assumptions of white middle-class women about gender. While the creation of a genre of "women's music" consisted nearly exclusively of acoustic folk-revivalist music with feminist lyrics, there were, however, effects pertinent to jazz. One was the emergence of a new audience for women's jazz performances, as well as for recordings of and information about historical women in jazz. Another was the adaption of the success and popularity of "women's music" festivals to the development in the late 1970s of women's jazz festivals. The chronology of "women's music" usually begins with coffeehouse performers in the 1960s, the emergence of recordings and record companies in the early 1970s, the first National Women's Music Festival in 1974, and the first Michigan Womyn's Music Festival in 1976.

1978 was a pivotal year for the effects of these events on women in jazz. The first Women's Jazz Festival was held in Kansas City in March 1978 and was followed that June by the Universal Jazz Coalition's Salute to Women in Jazz, the first of 14 annual New York women's jazz festivals produced by Cobi Narita. In the same year Stash Records released an anthology of historical recordings and radio broadcasts featuring women in jazz. These recordings were accompanied by Frank Driggs's informative booklet with its explicit call for more research in the field of women's historical participation in jazz. In the early to mid-1980s four books on women in jazz were published by D. Antoinette Handy, Linda Dahl, and Sally Placksin. Rosetta Reitz founded a record company (Rosetta Records) dedicated to reissuing historical jazz and blues recordings by women. Two documentary films, by Greta Schiller (1986) and Andrea

Weiss (1988), focused attention on the International Sweethearts of Rhythm.

All-woman groups and big bands returned to popularity in the 1970s, this time with the support of a new type of audience that was enthusiastic about the nontraditional accomplishments of women and critical about modes of representation that objectified women's bodies or trivialized their labor. Notable all-woman groups founded in this decade included Sisters in Jazz (based in New York, 1974–7) and Maiden Voyage (Los Angeles, 1979–).

(vi) Women and jazz in the early 21st century. While women continued to play jazz in all styles and on all instruments available to men, it would be naive to suggest at the end of the 20th century that women were simply accepted for their musical abilities. While many well-respected female musicians keep on blazing the trail on brass, reeds, and drums, as well as on instruments traditionally considered "feminine," they also persist in raising eyebrows when they mount the bandstand. Women musicians continue to experience different kinds of expectations than do their male colleagues, from their employers, from male co-workers, and from audiences. These range from a disproportionate interest in what they will wear, rather than what they will play, to assumptions that they will not play aggressively enough and a resentment that their presence may disrupt established social patterns of rehearsals, performance, and travel. The press continues to respond to the existence of female musicians as though they were just now appearing on the scene. Although recording opportunities are common for such women pianists as JoAnne Brackeen, Marilyn Crispell, and Geri Allen, and appear to have significantly improved for other instrumentalists (as evidenced by multiple releases by such contemporary jazzwomen as the drummer Cindy Blackman, the saxophonists Jane Bunnett and Jane Ira Bloom, and the trumpet players Rebecca Coupe Franks and Ingrid Jensen), there is still overwhelming evidence that women jazz musicians do not receive the same encouragement or opportunities as do men of comparative skill. Contemporary efforts to correct these persistent inequalities include programs such as the Sisters in Jazz mentorship program of the International Association of Jazz Educators. In 1995 the need for organizations that would support and promote women's jazz musicianship was still great enough for Cobi Narita in New York to found International Women in Jazz, Inc. In 1996 the Smithsonian Institution and 651, An Arts Center produced a symposium on women in jazz, and the Kennedy Center presented the first Mary Lou Williams three-day jazz festival.

3. History and criticism. On the steam of the second-wave women's movement and the accompanying interest in documenting and celebrating the nontraditional accomplishments of women in the past, book-length histories of women in jazz began to be published in the 1980s. Among these, D. Antoinette Handy documented hidden histories of black women musicians and located her findings in an African-American social-historical context in two important works: *Black Women in American Bands and Orchestras* (1981) and *The International Sweethearts of Rhythm* (1983). Handy's volumes, along with Sally Placksin's *American Women in Jazz, 1900 to the Present* (1982), and Linda Dahl's *Stormy Weather: the Music and Lives of a Century of Jazzwomen* (1984), and other histories of women-in-jazz provide indispensable groundwork for studying women's participation on all instruments and in all eras of jazz (not exclusively as singers).

The fact that "universal" jazz histories (in which women exist exclusively as singers) continued to appear subsequent to the publication of these distinguished volumes indicates that dominant assumptions about gender not only affect jazz practice, but permeate the ideological frameworks through which information is circulated and filtered, affecting the practices of writing, reading, and thinking about jazz history as well. Though the histories of women in jazz are increasingly included in footnotes and bibliographies of supposedly "gender-free" jazz histories, the reconfigurations of what counts as jazz history developed and utilized by Handy, Dahl, and Placksin have been all but ignored in these works.

The emergence of academic jazz studies, influenced by contemporaneous trends in cultural studies, musicology, and ethnomusicology, has produced new work that focuses on interrelationships between historically specific ideas about masculinity and race in jazz. Although these works have tended to ignore all over again the participation of women in jazz, this interest in jazz masculinity, ironically, may actually bode well for the development of approaches to jazz studies that acknowledge gender as an active ingredient of jazz history.

SELECTED RECORDINGS

(all anthologies by various artists)

The Women: Classic Female Jazz Artists 1939–1952 (1939–52, Bb 6755-2-RB); *Jazzwomen: a Feminist Retrospective* (1923–57, Stash 109); *Women in Jazz: All-women Groups* (1945–54, Stash 111); *Women in Jazz: Pianists* (1924–61, Stash 112); *Women in Jazz: Swingtime to Modern* (1935–59, Stash 113); *Forty Years of Women in Jazz* (1926–59, Jass 9–10)

BIBLIOGRAPHY

L. Gillenson, ed.: *Esquire's World of Jazz* (New York, rev. 1975)
F. Driggs: *Women in Jazz: a Survey* (New York, 1977)
V. Wilmer: *As Serious as your Life: the Story of the New Jazz* (London, 1977, rev. [3]/1987)
D. A. Handy: *Black Women in American Bands and Orchestras* (Metuchen, NJ, and London, 1981, rev. 2/1998)
S. Placksin: *American Women in Jazz, 1900 to the Present: their Words, Lives, and Music* (New York, 1982, London, 1985, as *Jazzwomen, 1900 to the Present: their Words, Lives, and Music*)
D. A. Handy: *The International Sweethearts of Rhythm* (Metuchen, NJ, and London, 1983, rev. 2/1996)
M. Unterbrink: *Jazz Women at the Keyboard* (Jefferson, NC, and London, 1983)
L. Dahl: *Stormy Weather: the Music and Lives of a Century of Jazzwomen* (London, Melbourne, Australia, and New York, 1984)
S. Fry: *The Story of the All Women's Orchestras in California, 1893–1955* (Northridge, CA, 1985)
J. Leder: *Women in Jazz: a Discography of Instrumentalists, 1913–1968* (Westport, CT, 1985)
L. Feather: *The Jazz Years: Earwitness to an Era* (London and New York, 1986)
M. McPartland: *All in Good Time* (New York, and Oxford, England, 1987)
D. D. Harrison: *Black Pearls: Blues Queens of the 1920s* (New Brunswick, NJ, 1988)
E. Koskoff: *Women and Music in Cross-cultural Perspective* (Urbana, IL, and Chicago, 1989)
P. Sunderland: *Cultural Meanings and Identity: Women of the African-American Art World of Jazz* (diss., U. of Vermont State Agricultural College, 1992)
D. S. Hunt: *Women who Play Jazz: a Study of the Experiences of Three Los Angeles Musicians* (diss., U. of California, Los Angeles, 1994)
L. Gourse: *Madame Jazz: Contemporary Women Instrumentalists* (New York, and Oxford, England, 1995)
S. Tucker: "Telling Performances: Jazz History Remembered and Remade by the Women in the Band," *Sung/Unsung: Jazzwomen* (Washington, DC, 1996); repr. in *Women and Music: a Journal of Gender and Culture*, i (1997), 12, and *Oral History Review*, xxvi/1 (1999), 67
A. Y. Davis: *Blues Legacies and Black Feminism: Gertrude "Ma" Rainey, Bessie Smith, and Billie Holiday* (New York, 1997)
H. Rye: "What the Papers said: the Harlem Play-Girls and Dixie Rhythm

Girls (and Dixie Sweethearts)," *Storyville 1996/7*, ed. L. Wright (Chigwell, England, 1997), 173
D. W. Middlebrook: *Suits Me: the Double Life of Billy Tipton* (Boston and New York, 1998)
B. Johnson: *The Inaudible Music: Jazz, Gender and Australian Modernity* (Strawberry Hills, New South Wales, Australia, 1999)
L. Wright: "Pieces of the Jigsaw: Harlem Playgirls," *Storyville 1998/9* (Chigwell, England, 1999), 178
S. Tucker: *Swing Shift: "All-girl" Bands of the 1940s* (Durham, NC, 2000)

SHERRIE TUCKER

Wong, Francis [Ming] (*b* ?San Francisco, 1957). Tenor saxophonist, violinist, record producer, and leader. He first played violin but took up alto saxophone after hearing recordings by Charlie Parker. From 1975 he attended Stanford University, where he initially studied chemistry; while there he met future collaborators in Jon Jang and Glenn Horiuchi and changed to the tenor instrument, on which he was influenced by the music of John Coltrane and Sonny Rollins. He then studied jazz at San Jose State University, and later he graduated from Stanford with a degree in economics (1985). From around 1983 Wong worked in Jang's ensembles 4-in-One and the Pan-Asian Arkestra. He also held a lasting association with Horiuchi and worked in Fred Ho's Afro-Asian Music Ensemble and Asian American Art Ensemble. In 1987 Wong and Jang established Asian improv, and in 1988 they formed Asian Improv Arts, a nonprofit arts organization in which Wong served as artistic director from 1992. Later he worked with Tatsu Aoki's trio Urban Reception and in Spirit Complex, led by the pianist Vijay Iyer, recording with both in 1995. His own groups have included the Great Wall, Asian Improv Arts Composers Workshop (an octet), and Ming Light (a trio). Having studied the traditional musics of both China and Japan, Wong was a founding member of the San Francisco Gagaku Society. He doubles on flute, clarinet, *dizi*, *yokobue*, *erhu*, and *shinobue*, and has collaborated with poets, dance troupes, and other various multimedia performers. He has taught at San Francisco State University and the University of California in Santa Cruz.

SELECTED RECORDINGS

Duos: with T. Aoki: *Chicago Time Code* (1994, Asian Improv 0019); with Elliot Humberto Kavee: *Duets I* (1996, Asian Improv 0028)
As leader: *Ming* (1994, Asian Improv 0020), incl. Autumn Moon Revisited [violin]; *Pilgrimage* (1994, Music & Arts 974); with T. Aoki and Dave Pavkovic: *Urban Reception* (1995, Southport 0039)
As sideman: J. Jang: *Are You Chinese or Charlie Chan?* (*c*1983, RPM 5); *Never Give Up!* (1989, Asian Improv 0007); G. Horiuchi: *Oxnard Beat* (1989, SN 121228-2); J. Jang: *Self Defense!* (1991, SN 121203-2); *Tiananmen!* (1993, SN 121223-2); V. Iyer: on *Memorophilia* (1995, Asian Improv 0023), March & Epilogue

BIBLIOGRAPHY

D. Richardson: "Francis Wong: Creating a Musical Community," *Bay Area Guardian* (18 Sept 1986)
D. Ouellette: "East and West," *DB*, lvi/8 (1989), 61
N. Provizer: "Outside in: Do You Hear the Struggle?," *Jazziz*, xii/2 (1995), 68
<http://www.inmotionmagazine.com/jjfw1.html> (1999)
<http://www.kzy.com/caajf/wong.htm> (1999)
<http://www.wp.com/horiuchi/wong.html> (1999)
<http://www.asianimprov.com/artists_one.asp?artistid=26> (2000)

GK

Wonsey, Anthony(, Jr.) (*b* Chicago, 21 Sept 1971). Pianist. He received his first lessons from his mother, who was trained as a classical pianist, and later studied with Zilner Randolph and Mulgrew Miller. As a member of a student jazz band he appeared at the Chicago Jazz Festival. In autumn 1989 he moved to Boston, where he studied composition for films at the Berklee College of Music (BA 1994) and performed locally with Roy Hargrove, Antonio Hart, and others; during the same period he led a trio at jam sessions in Chicago (summer 1990) and toured with Christopher Hollyday, Kenny Garrett, and Nnenna Freelon. Wonsey has worked with Carl Allen from around 1993 and with Nicholas Payton from around 1996, as well as with Christian McBride.

SELECTED RECORDINGS

As leader: *Anthonyology* (1995, Evidence 22151); *Another Perspective* (1996, Evidence 22188)
As sideman: C. Allen: *The Pursuer* (1993, Atl. 82572-2); Eddie Allen: *R 'n' B* (1995, Enja 9033-2); N. Payton: *Payton's Place* (1997, Verve 314-557327-2)

BIBLIOGRAPHY

"Auditions: Anthony Wonsey, Jr.," *DB*, lvii/12 (1990), 70

GK

Wood, Bill. *See* WOOD, VISHNU.

Wood, Booty [Bootie, Mitchell W.] (*b* Dayton, OH, 27 Dec 1919; *d* Dayton, 10 June 1987). Trombonist. His professional career began in the late 1930s, and in the early 1940s he played with Tiny Bradshaw (1942–3) and Lionel Hampton (1943–4). During his navy service in World War II he performed in a band that included Clark Terry, Willie Smith, and Gerald Wilson. When he left the navy (1945) he again worked with Hampton before playing with Arnett Cobb's small band (1947–8), Erskine Hawkins (1948–50), and Count Basie (spring 1951). While his daughters were growing up he stayed for eight years in Dayton, working as a postman and performing nightly in a local group with Snooky Young. In September 1959 he joined Duke Ellington for a European tour. He worked with Ellington until October 1960, again for a recording session in January 1962, and briefly for the musical *My People* in August 1963, but otherwise returned to Dayton to care for his children after his wife was incapacitated by illness. He toured Europe with Earl Hines in 1968, and after his wife's death was again with Ellington, from December 1969 to October 1972. Later he played with various leaders, among them Mercer Ellington. He performed and recorded with Basie from 1979 until the leader's death in 1984. During his time with Ellington, Wood became a skilled specialist in playing with the plunger mute; in his unmuted solos his style resembled that of Trummy Young.

SELECTED RECORDINGS

As sideman: A. Cobb: Cobb's Boogie (1947, Apollo 781); E. Hawkins: Beale Street Blues (1950, Vic. 20-3668); D. Ellington: *Blues in Orbit* (1959, Col. CS8241), incl. Sweet and Pungent; *Nutcracker Suite* (1960, Koala 14117), incl. Black and Tan Fantasy, Creole Love Call, The Mooche; C. Anderson: *Plays W. C. Handy* (1978, BB 33163); C. Basie: *On the Road* (1979, PT 2312112), incl. Booty's Blues; *Me and You* (1983, Pablo 2310891), incl. Me & You, Crip

BIBLIOGRAPHY

SheridanCB
S. Dance: *The World of Duke Ellington* (London and New York, 1970/*R*1981), 199
B. Rusch: "Booty Wood," *Cadence*, x/9 (1984), 5
S. Floyd: "An Oral History: the Great Lakes Experience," *Black Perspective in Music*, xi/1 (1983), 41
J. Simmen: Ceux qui s'en vont: Michael [*sic*] 'Bootie' Wood," *BHcF*, no.361 (1988), 22

EDDIE LAMBERT/BK

Wood, Chris. Bass player in the group Medeski, Martin & Wood; *see* MEDESKI, JOHN.

Wood, Vishnu [Bill; William Clifford] (*b* Wilkesboro, NC, 7 Nov 1937). Double bass player and educator. His father was a reed player. Around the age of ten he moved to Detroit, where he played trumpet and, in his teens, took up double bass; he studied at the Detroit Institute of Musical Arts and had private lessons with John Matthews of the Detroit Symphony Orchestra. He worked with Dorothy Ashby in 1957 and then with Yusef Lateef and Joe Henderson. After moving to New York in 1962 he performed as a freelance with, among others, Kenny Dorham, Carmen McRae, Terry Gibbs, Leo Wright, the singer Gloria Lynne, Roy Haynes, and Archie Shepp; with Gibbs's group he recorded in 1963 alongside Alice McLeod (who later married John Coltrane). From that year Wood's primary association was with Randy Weston, with whom he toured Africa, spent an extended period in Morocco, and recorded into the 1970s; in addition he played *'ūd* in a recorded performance with Alice Coltrane in 1970. Later he worked with Sathima Bea Benjamin (1979) and in a duo with Walter Bishop, Jr. (mid-1980s), and he performed extensively as a member of the Harlem Blues and Jazz Band. In the mid-1990s he was involved in jam sessions in New York, and in 1998 he played with Shepp in New Hampshire. Wood founded Safari East Cultural Presentations, Inc., with which he led workshop ensembles that explored the instruments and musics of various cultures; he also taught at Hampshire College in Massachusetts and at SUNY-Purchase.

SELECTED RECORDINGS

Duos with R. Weston: *Perspective* (1976, Denon YX7564ND)
As sideman: R. Weston: *Randy!* (1964, Bakton 1001); *Alone . . . and Together* (1965, Ari. 1026); A. Coltrane: on *Journey to Satchidananda* (1970, Imp. 9203), Isis and Osiris

BIBLIOGRAPHY

Feather '60s ("Wood, William Clifford (Bill)")
V. Wilmer: *As Serious as your Life: the Story of the New Jazz* (London, 1977, rev. [3]1987)
<http://www.knightongale.com/vwood2.htm> (1999)

GK

Woodard, Rickey (D.) (*b* Nashville, 5 Aug 1950). Tenor saxophonist. He started on clarinet but soon changed to saxophone, and first played rhythm-and-blues in his family's band in and around Nashville. Gene Ammons was his early role model. After attending Tennessee State University, in 1980 he joined Ray Charles's big band, with which he toured for six and a half years; he also toured with Jimmy Smith and Horace Silver. Having settled in the Los Angeles area in the late 1980s, he joined Jimmy and Jeannie Cheatham's Sweet Baby Blues Band, the Clayton–Hamilton big band, and Frank Capp's Juggernaut, worked as a freelance (including recordings with Silver, 1995, Nnenna Freelon, 1996, and John Leitham, 1996–7, among others) and led his own small groups. Woodard is a powerful player with a rich, warm tone and a strong sense of swing; he plays the soprano and alto instruments as well as clarinet and flute.

SELECTED RECORDINGS

As leader: *California Cooking!* (1991, Can. 79509); *Night Mist* (1991, Fresh Sound 0190); *The Frank Capp Trio Presents Rickey Woodard* (1991, Conc. 4469); *The Tokyo Express* (1992, Can. 79527); *Yazoo* (1994, Conc. 4629); *The Silver Strut* (1995, Conc. 4716)
As sideman with Clayton–Hamilton Jazz Orchestra: *Groove Shop* (1989, Capri 74021-2), incl. Brush This, Georgia, Night Train, Raincheck; *Heart and Soul* (1991, Capri 74028-2), incl. I be serious 'bout dem blues; *Absolutely!* (1994, Lake Street 52002), incl. Blues for Stephanie, Jazz Party, Max
As sideman with others: J. Smith: *Prime Time* (1989, Mlst. 9176); J. Cheatham and J. Cheatham: *Basket Full of Blues* (1991, Conc. 4501); *Blues and the Boogie Masters* (1993, Conc. 4579); F. Capp: *Quality Time* (1993–4, Conc. 4677); J. Cheatham and J. Cheatham: *Gud Nuz Bluz* (1995, Conc. 4690); J. Leitham: *Lefty Leaps In* (1996, USA 940); *Live!* (1997, USA 0020)

BIBLIOGRAPHY

Feather–GitlerBEJ
T. Gieske: "Rickey Woodard," *Windplayer*, vi/5 (1989), 14
P. Vacher: "Rickey Woodard," *Wire*, no.102 (1992), 10
M. Rylance: "Stepping in: Rickey Woodard," *Jazz: the Magazine*, no.20 (1993), 6
S. Yanow: "Hearsay: Rickey Woodard: Jazz Matters," *JT*, xxiii/4 (1993), 9
B. Kohlhasse: "You'll Be Hearing More of Saxman Woodard," *Los Angeles Times* (30 Aug 1996)

THOMAS OWENS

Woodblock. A wooden slit-drum with a resonant and penetrating tone; *see* DRUM SET, §I, 7(i).

Woode, Jimmy [James Bryant] (*b* Philadelphia, 23 Sept 1926/1927). Double bass player. His father, the music teacher and pianist Jimmy (James Moseby) Woode, traveled to Europe with Hot Lips Page in 1947 and soon afterwards settled in Sweden, where he played into the 1990s; in the first edition of this dictionary one of his recordings was mistakenly attributed to his son: it was in fact the elder Jimmy Woode who recorded with Zoot Sims in Stockholm in 1950.

The younger Jimmy Woode told Matthews (1997) that he never had a birth certificate, and his older sisters disagree on whether his year of birth was 1926 or 1927; 1928 has appeared, incorrectly, in many sources. In his teens, while living alternately in Camden, New Jersey, and Boston, he studied piano and double bass. He then served in the US Navy (1945 – May 1946) and formed a small group in which he played piano, but shortly afterwards he began to concentrate on double bass in his professional work; however, in the late 1940s he occasionally held jobs as a pianist. As a double bass player he toured with Flip Phillips (1949), recorded with Toots Thielemans in Stockholm (1950), and worked with Sarah Vaughan and Ella Fitzgerald (both 1950) and Nat Pierce (at intervals, 1951–2). For two years he was a house double bass player in Boston at Storyville and its companion club, Mahogany Hall, where he recorded with Sidney Bechet and Billie Holiday (both 1953). After forming a duo with Jaki Byard and recording with Miles Davis at the Hi Hat in Boston, he toured from late 1955 in Duke Ellington's orchestra (for illustration *see* ELLINGTON, DUKE, fig.2). He also recorded as a leader (1957) and as a sideman with, among others, Johnny Hodges (1955–8) and Clark Terry (1956–9); in 1959 he first worked in a group (at this point, a quartet) co-led by Kenny Clarke and Francy Boland.

Woode left Ellington in April 1960 and moved to Sweden. He recorded with Eric Dolphy the following year and played in the ensembles which evolved into the Clarke–Boland Big Band. In the 1960s and 1970s he lived successively in Cologne, Germany (from 1964), where the Clarke–Boland Big Band was based and where he managed his own publishing firm, and then in the Netherlands (from 1966) and Munich (by 1975). During this period he was associated with the Clarke–Boland group (until it disbanded in 1973), worked frequently in radio, television, and films, appeared at many festivals, and recorded with such musicians as Don Byas and Albert Nicholas (both 1963), Johnny Griffin and Sahib Shihab (1964–8), the quartet led by Ted Curson and Booker Ervin (1966), Milt Buckner (1966–9), Benny Bailey and Hampton Hawes (both 1968), Mal Waldron (1968–77), and Helen Humes (1974); he toured with Hawes and frequently with Waldron.

Following a period in the early 1980s in Vienna, Woode settled in 1984 in Berne, Switzerland, and from 1985 to 1988 was a member of the Paris Reunion Band. He continued to work throughout Europe, appearing as a freelance at festivals and clubs and in concerts; in addition he recorded with Nathan Davis's small groups and Dusko Goykovich's quartet (both 1987), as a member of Jay McShann's big band in Paris (1989), in the Super Trio (1994, alongside the pianist Dirk Raufeisen and Charly Antolini), and in Junior Mance's trio (1994). In spring 1995 he worked with Allan Clare. Although Woode rarely performed in the USA after emigrating, he toured there in 1995 as a member of Lionel Hampton's Golden Men of Jazz. In 1998 he celebrated his "70th" (actually his 71st or 72nd) birthday by touring Europe for a few weeks in September and October as the leader of a quintet that consisted of his daughter, the singer Shawnn Monteiro, Andy McKee, Dado Moroni, and Keith Copeland.

SELECTED RECORDINGS

As leader: *The Colorful Strings of Jimmy Woode* (1957, Argo 630)

As sideman: C. Parker: *New Bird: Hi Hat Broadcasts, 1953* (1953, Phoenix Jazz 10), incl. Ornithology; S. Chaloff and B. Mussulli: *Serge and Boots* (1954, Sto. 310), incl. All I do is dream of you, You brought a new kind of love, Zdot; J. Hodges: *Creamy* (1955, Norg. 1045); D. Ellington: *Ellington at Newport* (1956, Col. CL934), incl. Diminuendo and Crescendo in Blue; *Such Sweet Thunder* (1956–7, Col. CL1033), incl. Sonnet in Search of a Moor; [no leader:] *Americans in Europe*, ii (1963, Imp. 37), incl. A. Nicholas: Why daughter, how are you?; N. Davis: *Happy Girl* (1965, Saba 15025); *The Hip Walk* (1965, Saba 15063); M. Waldron: *Oneupmanship* (1977, Enja 2092); D. Goykovich: *Celebration* (1987, Hot House 1003); J. Mance: *Softly as in a Morning Sunrise* (1994, Enja 8080-2)

SELECTED FILMS AND VIDEOS

Jazz Made in America (1960); Coleman Hawkins Quartet (1962); Jazz 625: Coleman Hawkins Quintet (1964); Clark Terry Quartet (1985)

BIBLIOGRAPHY

FeatherE; *Feather '60s*; *Feather–Gitler '70s*

J.-L. Ginibre: "Woode: de Duke à Klook," *Jm*, no.121 (1965), 26

P. B. Matthews: "Jimmy Woode Interview," *Cadence*, xxiii (1997), no.8, p.10; no.9, p.5; no.10, p.12

M. Hennessey: "Jimmy Woode Celebrates his 70th Birthday with Jazz-a-plenty," *CJM*, xxxv/4 (1998), 10

Wooding, Sam(uel David) (*b* Philadelphia, 17 June 1895; *d* New York, 1 Aug 1985). Pianist, arranger, and bandleader. He organized his first band, the Society Syncopators, in 1919 to work at Scott's Hotel in Atlantic City, New Jersey, and later played in clubs in New York, among them the Club Alabam (1924–5). The band then accompanied the touring revue *Chocolate Kiddies* to Europe, where Wooding remained; he also toured South America with his all-star group, which included Tommy Ladnier, Herb Flemming, Garvin Bushell, and Gene Sedric. The orchestra presented a mixture of comedy routines and outstanding jazz performances and achieved great eminence in Europe; it was unable, however, to duplicate its success in the USA on its return there in 1927, and the following year Wooding again traveled to Europe, taking additional soloists – Doc Cheatham, Albert Wynn, and Jerry Blake. Having disbanded this group late in 1931 he organized another that played in the New York area until 1935. He then studied music at the University of Pennsylvania and later became a full-time music teacher. He led the Southland Spiritual Choir (1937–41) and then another vocal group (from the mid-1940s), and in the 1950s founded his own record label, Ding Dong. In the 1960s he made a world tour with the singer Rae Harrison. Wooding also wrote a number of arrangements, notably *Shanghai Shuffle*. Materials relating to his career are at the Schomburg Center for Research in Black Culture, New York Public Library (*see* LIBRARIES AND ARCHIVES, §2).

Oral history material in *NjR* (JOHP).

SELECTED RECORDINGS

Shanghai Shuffle/Alabamy Bound (1925, Vox 01890); Bull Foot Stomp (1929, Parl. 25424); Carrie (1929, Parl. 25420); Sweet Back Blues (1929, Parl. 25421); Downcast Blues (1929, Pathé X8684)

BIBLIOGRAPHY

ChiltonW; *McCarthyB*

H. Panassié: *Douze années de jazz (1927–1938): souvenirs* (Paris, 1946), 39

A. Napoleon: "A Pioneer Looks Back: Sam Wooding, 1967," *Sv* (1967), no.9, p.3; no.10, p.4

H. Flemming: "Old Sam: the Man who Brought Jazz to Europe," *JJ*, xxi/5 (1968), 8

M. Jones: "Sam Wooding: Bandleader from the Past," *MM* (7 Dec 1968), 8; (14 Dec 1968), 10

A. Batashev: *Sovietski dzaz* (Moscow, 1972), 18; Eng. trans., *Sv*, no.53 (1974), 165

B. H. Behncke: "Sam Wooding and the Chocolate Kiddies at the Thalia-Theater in Hamburg, 28th July 1925 to 24th August 1925," *Sv*, no.60 (1974), 214

B. Englund: "Chocolate Kiddies: the Show that Brought Jazz to Europe and Russia in 1925," *Sv*, no.62 (1975), 44

H. J. P. Bergmeir: "Sam Wooding Recapitulated," *Sv*, no.74 (1977–8), 44

C. Goddard: *Jazz away from Home* (London and New York, 1979)

A. Papo: *El jazz a Catalunya* (Barcelona, 1985), 15

G. Bushell and M. Tucker: "On the Road with the Chocolate Kiddies in Europe and South America, 1925–1927," *Sv*, no.131 (1987), 182; no.132 (1987), 213

C. Deffaa: *Voices of the Jazz Age: Portraits of Eight Vintage Jazzmen* (Wheatley, Oxford, England, Urbana, IL, and Chicago, 1990), 1

FRANK DRIGGS/BK

Woodman, Britt (Bingham) (*b* Los Angeles, 4 June 1920; *d* Hawthorne, CA, 13 Oct 2000). Trombonist. His father, William B. Woodman, Sr. (*b* Mississippi, 14 Nov 1896; *d* Los Angeles, 27 April 1972), played trombone with Sonny Clay in the mid-1920s and may be heard on Clay's *Plantation Blues* (1926, Voc. 1000); he was a member of Teddy Buckner's band in the 1940s and 1950s. Britt Woodman learned piano from the age of five before taking up the trombone. From his early teens he worked steadily as a trombonist, tenor saxophonist, and clarinetist in the Woodman Brothers, which he co-led with Coney Woodman (*b* Jackson, MS, 7 June 1917; *d* Los Angeles, 20 June 2001) (piano, banjo, and guitar) and William "Brother" Woodman, Jr. (*b* Los Angeles, 22 April 1919) (trumpet, alto saxophone, and clarinet); they initially worked as a quartet with the drummer George Reed (who later joined Horace Henderson). Jessie Sailes replaced Reed, and Joe Comfort (doubling on cornet) added his double bass to the band of the multi-instrumentalist Woodmans, as did Britt's boyhood friend Charles Mingus; the brothers Ernie and Marshal Royal were members of the group around 1938. Woodman continued playing on the West Coast with Phil Moore (1939) and Floyd Turnham, whose band was taken over by Les Hite in autumn 1939. Britt and Coney then toured with Hite until enlisting in the army (1942 – January 1946), during which time, according to Roy Porter, Woodman, Collette, and Mingus recorded in Porter's band (late 1944 or early 1945), although the recording was never issued.

Immediately after army service Woodman played in the Stars of Swing, a cooperative septet comprising John Anderson, Woodman, Collette, Lucky Thompson, the pianist Spaulding Givens, Mingus, and the drummer Oscar Bradley. He worked with Boyd Raeburn's big band and for three months with Eddie Heywood's sextet, then joined Lionel

Hampton in late 1946. Between 1948 and 1950 he studied music at Westlake College, Los Angeles, after which he replaced Lawrence Brown in Duke Ellington's band (March 1951), where he played brilliantly as the leader of the trombone section. His performances as a soloist covered a wide range of styles, and Ellington captured an aspect of his musical personality in the miniature concerto *Sonnet to Hank Cinq* (from *Such Sweet Thunder*). In July 1954 Woodman was a member of Mingus's Jazz Composers' Workshop for a performance at the first Newport Jazz Festival, and in 1955 he recorded, with Mingus, in a quintet led by Miles Davis; later he played in three sessions under Mingus's leadership (1960–63). After leaving Ellington in 1961 he worked in a number of Broadway shows and briefly in September 1966 played in Mingus's band at the Village Gate; he also played in big bands under Quincy Jones, Oliver Nelson, Dizzy Gillespie, Mercer Ellington, and Clark Terry.

In 1970 Woodman returned to California, where he performed as a freelance and recorded with his own octet (1977) and as a member of the Akiyoshi-Tabackin (1974–6) and Capp-Pierce (1976, 1978) big bands; he also was a member of Bill Berry's big band (1974–7), but recorded with Berry only in a small group devoted to Ellington's music. During this same period, with Benny Carter, he performed in a tribute to Fletcher Henderson at the Monterey Jazz Festival in 1976 and toured Japan twice (1977–8). After returning to New York, in the late 1970s to early 1980s Woodman played intermittently with Harry Edison, Buddy Tate, Budd Johnson, James Moody, Teddy Wilson, Ray Brown, and Benny Goodman. In 1983 he performed in Europe with Al Grey and Curtis Fuller. Later he was a member of Terry's Spacemen (from 1987, recording in 1989), and he continued to work with all-star swing and bop groups, including an orchestra that gave performances of Mingus's reconstructed symphony, *Epitaph* (1989 – early 1990s), an orchestra formed under Louie Bellson's leadership for a re-creation of Ellington's suite *Black, Brown and Beige* (1992), and the Lincoln Center Jazz Orchestra (1990s).

Oral history material in *CLU* (CASOHP) and*CtY*.

SELECTED RECORDINGS

As leader: *In L.A.* (1977, Falcon 100); with J. Wilder and J. LaPorta: *Playing for Keeps* (1992, GM 3026)

As sideman with D. Ellington: *Seattle Concert* (1952, RCA LJM1002), incl. Sultry Serenade; *Dance to the Duke* (1953–4, Cap. T637), incl. Things ain't what they used to be; *Ellington Showcase* (1953–5, Cap. T679), incl. Theme for Trambeam; *Such Sweet Thunder* (1956–7, Col. CL1033), incl. Sonnet to Hank Cinq; *Jazz at the Plaza*, ii (1958, Col. C32471), incl. Red Garter

As sideman with others: C. Mingus: on *Mingus!* (1960, Can. 9021), MDM; J. Hamilton: *It's About Time* (1961, Swingville 2022); B. Carter: *Live and Well in Japan* (1977, PT 2308216); B. Berry: *For Duke* (1978, RT 101), incl. Perdido

SELECTED FILMS AND VIDEOS

"King" Cole and his Trio (1950); Sarah Vaughan and Herb Jeffries/Kid Ory and his Creole Jazz Band/Mahagony Magic (1950); Caravan (1952); The Hawk Talks (1952); The Mooche (1952); Mood Indigo (1952); Solitude (1952); Sophisticated Lady (1952); V.I.P.'s Boogie (1952)

BIBLIOGRAPHY

R. Horricks: "An Interview with Britt Woodman," *JM*, v (1959), no.5, p.9; no.7, p.10; no.9, p.13; rev. as "From the Sidelines: Britt Woodman," *CI*, xxi (1983), no.8, p.24; no.9, p. 24; addns and corrections in no.12, p.25

C. Mingus: *Beneath the Underdog*, ed. N. King (New York and London, 1971/*R*1991)

R. Sinclair: "Britt Woodman Today," *JJI*, xxxiii/3 (1980), 7 [incl. discography]

M. Berger, E. Berger, and J. Patrick: *Benny Carter: a Life in American Music* (Metuchen, NJ, and London, 1982)

B. Priestley: *Mingus: a Critical Biography* (London, Melbourne, Australia, and New York, 1982)

C. Hofmann: *Man of Many Parts: a Discography of Buddy Collette* (Amsterdam, 1985)

M. Royal and C. P. Gordon: *Marshal Royal: Jazz Survivor* (London and New York, 1996), 56

C. Bryant and others, eds.: *Central Avenue Sounds: Jazz in Los Angeles* (Berkeley, CA, Los Angeles, and London, 1998)

Obituaries: J. Thurber, *Los Angeles Times* (15 Oct 2000); S. Voce, *The Independent* (17 Oct 2000)

EDDIE LAMBERT/BK

Woods, Chris(topher Columbus) (*b* Memphis, 25 Dec 1925; *d* New York, 4 July 1985). Alto saxophonist. He first played professionally in Memphis and then moved to St. Louis, where he worked with the Jeter–Pillars Orchestra and the trumpeter George Hudson and recorded as a leader (1952–62). From 1962 he lived in New York and performed, toured, and recorded with Dizzy Gillespie and Clark Terry. After playing with Sy Oliver from 1970 to 1973 he worked as a freelance musician. He collaborated further with Terry in the late 1970s, touring with the trumpeter from Egypt to India in 1978. In 1983 he joined Count Basie. Besides his principal instrument he played flute and baritone saxophone, and he may be heard on all of his instruments on an album that he recorded with Oliver. Equally at home in small groups or big bands, Woods was a compelling soloist; his style was influenced by Charlie Parker but had a fierce edge derived from his own roots in rhythm-and-blues. He was also active as a composer, and his work in this capacity is well represented by *Rhode Island Red*, which may be heard on Brew Moore's eponymous album (1957, Fan. 3264).

SELECTED RECORDINGS

As leader: Brazil/Blues for Lou (1953, Del. 151); *Somebody Done Stole my Blues* (1953, Del. 434); *Chris Meets Paris* (1973, Futura 2007); *From Here to Eternity* (1974, BB 33100); *Modus operandi* (1978, Del. 437)

As sideman: T. Curson: *Cattin' Curson* (1973, Marge 01); S. Oliver: *Yes, Indeed* (1973, BB 33048), incl. Move, Pennies from Heaven, Rumble, Undecided; C. Terry: *Lucerne 1978* (1978, TCB 0208-2); *Ain't Misbehavin'* (1979, PT 2312105); C. Basie: *Me and You* (1983, Pablo 2310891), incl. Bridge Work

BIBLIOGRAPHY

Feather–Gitler '70s; *SheridanCB*

K. Harris: "Chris Woods – TDWR," *JSN*, ii/1 (1980), 22

B. Rusch: "Chris Woods: Interview," *Cadence*, x/6 (1984), 5

Obituary, *New York Times* (6 July 1985)

PETER VACHER

Woods, Jimmy [James H.] (*b* St. Louis, 29 Oct 1934). Alto saxophonist. He grew up in Seattle and took up clarinet in his early teens. When he was 15 he joined a local big band, and in 1951 he played rhythm-and-blues with Homer Carter. After serving in the air force (1952–6) he settled in Los Angeles and worked in various rhythm-and-blues bands, including that of Roy Milton. In 1959 he began playing in other styles while studying for a degree in sociology at Los Angeles State College, and the following year he replaced Walter Benton in Horace Tapscott's orchestra. That December he made his first recording, as a sideman with Teddy Edwards, and began working regularly with Joe Gordon, with whom he recorded in July 1961. From 1963 Woods performed intermittently as a freelance with Gerald Wilson's orchestra, appearing at the Monterey Jazz Festival in that year and recording in 1966, and between January 1964 and April 1965 he played tenor saxophone and flute in Chico Hamilton's group, with which he appeared on television, spent eight weeks in London accompanying the singer Lena Horne (1964), toured Japan, and recorded (March 1965). Nothing is known of his later activities.

SELECTED RECORDINGS

(recorded for Contemporary unless otherwise indicated)

As leader: *Awakening!* (1961–2, 7605); *Conflict* (1963, 7612)

As sideman: T. Edwards: *Back to Avalon* (1960, 14074-2); J. Gordon: *Lookin' Good* (1961, 7597); G. Wilson: *Portraits* (1963, PJ 80); *The Golden Sword* (1966, PJ 20111), incl. The Feather

BIBLIOGRAPHY

Feather '60s

L. Tomkins: "Close-up on Jimmy Woods," *Crescendo*, iii/5 (1964), 19

P. Carles, A. Clergeat, and J.-L. Comolli: *Dictionnaire du jazz* (Paris, 1988, rev. and enlarged 2/1994)

GK

Woods, Phil(ip Wells) (*b* Springfield, MA, 2 Nov 1931). Alto saxophonist and leader. He devoted himself to the saxophone from the age of 12 and briefly took private lessons in improvisation from Lennie Tristano when he was about 15. In summer 1948 he went to New York to study at the Manhattan School of Music, then in the autumn he enrolled at the Juilliard School (where he was obliged to major in clarinet); while completing his studies (BM 1952) he briefly played in Charlie Barnet's dance band. In 1955–6 he worked with George Wallington (in whose band he replaced Jackie McLean), Kenny Dorham, and Friedrich Gulda and traveled to the Near East and South America with Dizzy Gillespie. For the next decade he led a number of small jazz groups, among them a quintet with Gene Quill as co-leader, known as Phil and Quill (intermittently, 1957–8), one with Teddy Kotick and Nick Stabulas in the rhythm section, and another whose rhythm section included Herbie Hancock and Ron Carter. Woods also performed in Buddy Rich's quintet alongside Willie Dennis and John Bunch (April 1959), toured Europe with Quincy Jones (1959–60) and the USSR with Benny Goodman (May–July 1962), and worked as a studio musician, playing various reed instruments for recording sessions, television, films, and advertising jingles. During the summers from 1964 to 1967 he taught at the Ramblerny performing arts camp in New Hope, Pennsylvania. In 1967 he performed in New York as the leader of a quartet consisting of Hal Galper, Richard Davis, and Dottie Dodgion and played in Clark Terry's big band.

In March 1968 Woods moved to France, which marked his return to playing small-group jazz. In Paris that same year he formed the quartet the European Rhythm Machine, with George Gruntz (later Gordon Beck) on keyboards, Henri Texier on double bass, and Daniel Humair on drums; he also wrote for Danish and Belgian radio, and he composed a ballet for French television. The European Rhythm Machine remained intact until 1972, when Woods organized an experimental electronic quartet in Los Angeles; this was given a cold reception and soon disbanded. Woods then moved to the East Coast and settled in Delaware Water Gap, Pennsylvania. In October 1973 he formed an outstanding acoustic jazz group with Mike Melillo, Steve Gilmore, and Bill Goodwin. With this ensemble he won acclaim during this period as the finest alto saxophonist in mainstream jazz, a reputation confirmed by his performances on *Images* (1975, with Michel Legrand), *Live from the Showboat* (1976, recorded with an expanded group including the guitarist Harry Leahey and a percussionist), and *I love you just the way you are* (1977, with the popular singer Billy Joel), all of which received Grammy awards; the last named introduced Woods's sound (albeit anonymously) to an audience far larger than the normal reach of jazz.

Phil Woods, New York, 1977

For about 18 months in the mid-1970s Leahey stayed with the group, but he preferred not to tour on a regular basis; otherwise the quartet remained intact for nearly eight years, achieving a level of cohesion and group interplay that the typically ever-changing circumstances of the jazz life rarely allows. This stability has continued into the new century, with Gilmore and Goodwin surviving as permanent members, although the piano chair passed successively from Melillo to Hal Galper (1980 – July 1990), Jim McNeely (August 1990 – late 1994), and Bill Charlap (from April 1995). In 1983 the group once again became a quintet when Tom Harrell joined; at this point Woods began to play clarinet on a regular basis, especially in combination with Harrell's muted trumpet. Since that time he has continued to work with a brass instrument, with Hal Crook (on trombone) replacing Harrell in 1989, and then Brian Lynch (on trumpet) succeeding Crook in 1992. The group continues to tour internationally and to record.

In 1978 Woods was the key figure in the founding of an annual festival, the Delaware Water Gap Celebration of the Arts, which has continued into the new century. At the Chicago Jazz Festival in 1989 he participated in Benny Carter's re-creation of his famous album of 1961, *Further Definitions* (on which Woods had played); that same year he initiated a permanent autobiographical column, "Phil in the Gap," in *The Note*.

Woods acknowledged a profound debt to Charlie Parker, and his effortless virtuosity, bright tone, witty quotations, gruff ballad style, and frequent references to the blues invited comparison between the two musicians, as did Woods's renditions of tunes associated with Parker (*Patterns of Jazz*, 1957). His melodic lines, however, like those of Cannonball Adderley, were more continuous and chromatic than Parker's (*Cottontail, Body and Soul*, 1961), and he often repeated ideas, sometimes displacing them within the meter or developing them sequentially (*A Bit of Blues*, 1956). In later years these features remained central to his style of improvisation. His repertory expanded to include not only bop (*Airegin*, 1974), but also, with the European Rhythm Machine, funk (*The Meeting*) and occasional passages of free jazz (*Riot*) (both 1970), and, with his new group, Latin jazz (*Brazilian Affair*, 1976). In the 1970s Woods began to make his instrument sound like a tenor saxophone, developing a larger and brighter tone and adding a carefully controlled, many-shaded growl reminiscent of Coleman Hawkins (*A Sleepin' Bee*, 1976). He has written large-scale suites such as *Rights of Swing* (1961) and *I Remember* (1978) which, like his shorter jazz pieces, serve as vigorous frameworks for improvisation; a volume of transcriptions of his performances, *Phil Woods: Improvised Saxophone Solos*, has been published (Hialeah, FL, 1981). In 1984 he recorded an album with Chris Swansen on which the latter attempted to achieve the sound of a big band on a synthesizer, but it was poorly received. On his other, highly successful, recordings of the 1980s (above all the album *Integrity*), Woods continued to play in an unamplified but fiery hard-bop style.

Video oral history material in *NCH* (HCJA).

SELECTED RECORDINGS

As leader: *Woodlore* (1955, Prst. 7018); with D. Byrd: *The Young Bloods* (1956, Prst. 7080); *Warm Woods* (1957, Epic 3436); *Rights of Swing* (1961, Can. 9016); *Greek Cooking* (*c*1966, Imp. 9143); *Round Trip* (1969, Verve 68791); *Phil Woods and his European Rhythm Machine at the Montreux Jazz Festival* (1970, MGM 4695), incl. Riot; *Phil Woods and his European Rhythm Machine at the Frankfurt Jazz Festival* (1970, Embryo 530), incl. The Meeting; *Musique du bois* (1974, Muse 5037), incl. Airegin; *"Live" from the Showboat* (1976, RCA BGL2-2202), incl. Brazilian Affair, A Sleepin' Bee; *Songs for Sisyphus* (1977, Gryphon 782)

I Remember (1978, Gryphon 788); *Quartet* (1979, Clean Cuts 702); *Birds of a Feather* (1981, Ant. 1006); *At the Vanguard* (1982, Ant. 1013); with Budd Johnson: *The Ole Dude and the Fundance Kid* (1984, Upt. 2719); *Integrity* (1984, Red 177); *Heaven* (1984, Black Hawk 50401); *Gratitude* (1986, Denon 33CY1316); *Evolution* (1988, Conc. 361); *All Bird's Children* (1990, Conc. 4441); *Real Life* (1990, Chesky 47); *The Phil Woods Quintet Plays the Music of Jim McNeely* (1995, TCB 95402); with B. Carter: *Another Time, Another Place* (1996, Evening Star 104)

As sideman: J. Raney: *Jimmy Raney Quintet* (1955, NewJ 1103); G. Wallington: *Jazz for the Carriage Trade* (1956, Prst. 7032); [no leader:] *The Birdland Stars on Tour* (1956, RCA LPM1327–8), incl. A Bit of Blues; C. Payne: *Patterns of Jazz* (1957, Signal 1204); T. Monk: *The Thelonious Monk Orchestra at Town Hall* (1959, Riv. 1138); Q. Jones: *Live at Newport '61* (1961, Mer. 60653); B. Carter: *Further Definitions* (1961, Imp. 12), incl. Body and Soul, Cottontail; T. Monk: *Big Band and Quartet in Concert* (1963, Col. CS8964); M. Legrand: *Images* (1975, RCA BGL1-1027); B. Joel: on *The Stranger* (1977, Col. PC34987), I love you just the way you are

SELECTED FILMS AND VIDEOS

The Hustler (1961); The Great Rocky Mountain Jazz Party (1977); Jazz in Exile (1978); Gibson Jazz Concert (*c*1982); Celebration: Music in the Gap (*c*1984); Ben Sidran: on the Live Side (1986); Phil Woods in Concert (n.d. [filmed *c*1988]); Phil Woods Quartet (early 1990s [filmed 1979]); Birdmen & Birdsongs: a Tribute to Charlie Parker, ii (n.d. [filmed 1990]); Flip Phillips' 80th Birthday Party featuring the All-Stars (*c*1996 [filmed 1995]); Dexter Gordon: More than You Know (*c*1996)

BIBLIOGRAPHY

N. Hentoff: "Phil is Now out of the Woods," *DB*, xxiv/2 (1957), 13
I. Gitler: "This is Phil Woods," *DB*, xxviii/9 (1961), 20
M. Gardner: "Phil Woods," *JM*, no.184 (1970), 2; no.185 (1970), 2
A. J. Smith: "Out of the Forest into the Woods," *DB*, xlii/21 (1975), 22 [incl. discography]
Z. Knauss: *Conversations with Jazz Musicians* (Detroit, 1977), 226–61
J. DeMuth: "Phil Woods: Working More and Enjoying it no Less," *DB*, xlvi/1 (1979), 14
L. Tomkins: "Phil Woods Today," *CI*, xix (1981), no.6, p.20; no.7, p.12
D. Morgenstern: "Phil Woods: Chief Alto of the Jazz Tribe," *DB*, xlix/1 (1982), 16 [incl. discography]
"Phil Woods," *SJ*, xxxvii/10 (1983), 212 [discography]
L. Tomkins: "Phil Woods: Update," *CI*, xxiv/3 (1987), 8
J. Levenson: "Phil Woods Quintet: Woodshedding with Phil," *DB*, lv/11 (1988), 20
F. Bouchard: "Altos on the Adriatic," *DB*, lviii/10 (1991), 16
C. Deffaa: "Phil Woods: Speaking out," *JT*, xxi/5 (1991), 28
J. Bradley: "Phil in Peak Form at 60," *Denver Post* (8 May 1992)
B. Moody: *The Jazz Exiles: American Musicians Abroad* (Reno, NV, 1992), 105
Chan Parker: *Ma vie en si bémol* (Paris, 1993; Eng. trans., Columbia, SC, 1999, as *My Life in E-flat*)
M. Bourne: "Phil Woods: Jazz Soldier," *DB*, lxiii/12 (1996), 42
S. Voce: "Phil Woods," *JJI*, xlix/10 (1996), 8
G. Jack: "Phil Woods," *JJI*, li/9 (1998), 6
<http://www.upbeat.com/philwoods/> (2000) [incl. discography]

BK

Woodyard, Sam(uel) (*b* Elizabeth, NJ, 7 Jan 1925; *d* Paris, 20 Sept 1988). Drummer. He was a self-taught musician. After playing with local groups in and around Newark, New Jersey, he joined Paul Gayten's rhythm-and-blues group (1950), then worked with the tenor saxophonist Joe Holiday (1951) and Roy Eldridge (1952). He played briefly with Holiday again in 1953 before performing and recording with Milt Buckner's trio (1953–5). In July 1955 he joined the Duke Ellington Orchestra, with which he remained (with occasional breaks) until November 1966. Thereafter he became a member of the trio that accompanied Ella Fitzgerald, and settled in Los Angeles, but during the early 1970s he suffered from ill-health. Later Woodyard performed occasionally with Bill Berry and played conga with Ellington and Buddy Rich. From the mid-1970s he worked in New York and Europe, where he appeared with Claude Bolling's band, performed at many jazz festivals, recorded (in Paris) and gave concerts with Milt Buckner (1976–7), toured with Harold Ashby, Norris Turney, Booty Wood, and Aaron Bell (1978), and recorded with Teddy Wilson, Buddy Tate, Slam Stewart, and others as the Great Eight (1983). Having settled in Paris, he recorded with Steve Lacy's group one month before his death. Woodyard was a temperamental musician, but at his best was one of the greatest jazz drummers. His work with Ellington was frequently of the highest quality, combining an understanding of the leader's requirements with an individual, earthy kind of swing.

SELECTED RECORDINGS

As sideman with D. Ellington: *Ellington at Newport* (1956, Col. CL934); *Such Sweet Thunder* (1956–7, Col. CL1033); *Newport '58* (1958, Col. CL1245); *Duke Ellington Meets Coleman Hawkins* (1962, Imp. 26), incl. Wanderlust; *Duke Ellington and John Coltrane* (1962, Imp. 30); *The Symphonic Ellington* (1963, Rep. 6097); *Duke Ellington's Jazz Violin Session* (1963, Atl. 1688); *Duke Ellington Plays Mary Poppins* (1964, Rep. 6141), incl. Step in Time; *Soul Call* (1966, Verve 68701), incl. La plus belle Africaine; *Far East Suite* (1966, RCA LSP3872)

As sideman with others: B. Strayhorn: *Billy Strayhorn: Live!* (1958, Roul. 52119), incl. Mr. Gentle and Mr. Cool; M. Buckner: *A Night at the Popcorn* (1975, Riverboat 900281); C. Anderson: *Plays W. C. Handy* (1978, BB 33163); Great Eight: *Swingin' the Forties with the Great Eight* (1983, Tim. 185–6); S. Lacy: on *The Door* (1988, Novus 3049-1), Virgin Jungle

SELECTED FILMS AND VIDEOS

Duke Ellington and his Orchestra (1962); Newport Jazz Festival 1962 (1962); Playback: Duke Ellington (1963); Duke Ellington and his Orchestra (1965); Duke Ellington at the Côte d'Azur with Ella Fitzgerald (1966); Norman Granz présente improvisation: documents exceptionnels et inédits des plus grands noms de jazz (n.d.)

BIBLIOGRAPHY

TuckerDE
"Interviews with the Men besides [*sic*] Duke Ellington: Sam Woodyard," *Jazz Statistics*, no.8 (1959), 9
M. Jones: "To a Drummer it's the Tone that Counts," *MM*, xxxix (7 March 1964), 16
S. Dance: *The World of Duke Ellington* (London and New York, 1970/*R*1981), 189
D. Ellington: *Music is my Mistress* (Garden City, NJ, 1973, rev. 2/1982), 227

C. Carrière: "Jam with Sam," *Jh*, no.318 (1975), 17
Obituaries: *New York Times* (23 Sept 1988); *JJI*, xli/11 (1988), 16
J. Pescheux: "Sam Woodyard," *BHcF*, no.365 (1989), 1
B. Korall: "A Blast from the Past: the Great Drummers of Duke Ellington," *MD*, xxi/12 (1997), 82

EDDIE LAMBERT/BK

Wookie. Nickname of BYRON LANDHAM.

Wooldridge, Gaby. *See* LINCOLN, ABBEY.

Wootten, Red [Lawrence Bernard] (*b* Social Circle, GA, 5 Nov 1921). Double bass player. After playing with the bandleaders Jan Savitt (1945) and Tony Pastor (1947) he performed and recorded in Los Angeles with Tommy Dorsey (1949), Woody Herman (February–December 1951), and Charlie Barnet (1956). In 1957 he worked in rhythm sections alongside Red Norvo for recordings by Harry Babasin's Jazzpickers and Jack Montrose; he is heard to advantage with the Jazzpickers on *Command Performance* (1957, EmA 36123). In addition he performed and recorded with Norvo (1957–8) and toured Europe (1959) and recorded (1959, 1960) with Benny Goodman. Thereafter he was less active as a jazz musician and concentrated instead on studio work; he also composed and arranged film scores. In the mid-1970s he recorded with Anita O'Day. His name has occasionally been spelled Wootton.

BIBLIOGRAPHY

FeatherE
W. D. Clancy with A. C. Kenton: *Woody Herman: Chronicles of the Herds* (New York and elsewhere, 1995), 166

BK

Workman, Reggie [Reginald] (*b* Philadelphia, 26 June 1937). Double bass player. He played piano, tuba, and euphonium before taking up double bass with rhythm-and-blues groups in 1955. Around this time he joined a quartet which included Odean Pope and Hasaan and, with McCoy Tyner and the drummer Eddie Campbell, formed a trio in Philadelphia that accompanied such guest soloists as John Coltrane, Benny Golson, and Jackie McLean. As the house bass player at a local club he worked with Phineas Newborn, Aretha Franklin, Yusef Lateef, Lee Morgan, and others. His first important association after moving to New York (1957) was with Gigi Gryce (1958). Thereafter he worked with Red Garland and Roy Haynes (both 1959) and Coltrane; he toured internationally and recorded extensively with the saxophonist's small groups (1961), in which he sometimes shared the bass duties with Art Davis or Jimmy Garrison (who replaced him at the end of the year). He then played with James Moody (1962), Art Blakey's Jazz Messengers (1962–4), and Tommy Flanagan, and in 1964 spent a month at the Five Spot in New York in a house rhythm section with Cedar Walton and Albert "Tootie" Heath; at this time he became active in the Jazz Composer's Guild. He joined Lateef's band (1964–5), toured Japan with McLean (1965), deputized for Ron Carter in Miles Davis's quintet (November 1965), and worked with Herbie Mann (on tour in Japan, 1966) and Thelonious Monk (1967). He also recorded with Donald Byrd, Duke Jordan, and Richard Williams (all 1960), Booker Little (1961), Grant Green (1962), Freddie Hubbard (1962–3, 1969), Wayne Shorter (1964–6), Archie Shepp (1964, 1967), Morgan (1964–5, 1968, 1971), Booker Ervin (1965), Hank Mobley (1966), Bobby Hutcherson and the Jazz Composer's Orchestra (both 1968), and Walton (1969).

In the late 1960s Workman became active in music education; he first taught at the New Muse Community Museum of Brooklyn, where in 1975 he was appointed director of the music workshop. In 1973–4 he joined Max Roach and Shepp on the faculty of the University of Massachusetts, Amherst, and he taught at Long Island University. He worked with Roach (1968–78), Alice Coltrane (recording in 1971), and Charles Tolliver's group Music, Inc., with which he toured Brazil and Europe (1972, recording in the Netherlands), and recorded with Billy Harper and Mal Waldron (both 1973), Sonny Fortune and Makanda Ken McIntyre (both 1975), Shepp and Sonny Stitt (both 1977), and Art Farmer (in Tokyo, 1979).

From around 1984 Workman has been active creating theatrical performances in collaboration with the dancer and choreographer Maya Milanovic; they married in 1986. In 1985 he participated in concerts and recordings celebrating the revival of the Blue Note label, for which he had made many of his recordings in the 1960s. He continued his affiliation with Waldron: the two men recorded in New York and on tour in Japan in 1983, recorded two albums in 1986, and made the video *Mal Waldron and Friends: Live at the Village Vanguard* (filmed 1986]), and worked together again from 1989 into the 1990s. In 1985 Workman formed the Black Swan Quartet, whose unusual instrumention comprises violin (played by Akbar Ali), two cellos (Eileen Folson and Abdul Wadud), and double bass; the quartet improvises on European classical structures. In 1987 he joined the faculty of the New School for Social Research in New York, where he was later appointed professor of music and curriculum coordinator of the Jazz and Contemporary Music Program (which continued from 1996 at the Mannes/New School and from autumn 1999 at the New School University). He was a member of Trio Transition with Mulgrew Miller and Freddie Waits from 1987 to 1989, and during the same period he toured Europe with Fortune.

From the late 1980s through the 1990s Workman and Andrew Cyrille were members of each other's groups, and in 1989 they toured under Workman's leadership in a quartet with Oliver Lake and Marilyn Crispell. Workman also joined Paul Motian, Gerry Hemingway, and others for international tours with Crispell (1989–90), led his own quartet with Hemingway in place of Cyrille, and formed the cooperative Trio 3 with Lake and Cyrille. He has led other formations with such sidemen as Don Byron, Jeanne Lee, Jason Hwang, and, for two acclaimed recordings in the mid-1990s, Julian Priester and Sam Rivers. He recorded with Byron (1990 or 1991), in Berlin in Aki Takase's trio (with Sunny Murray, 1993), and with Ernie Watts (1996), and in 1995 he held an engagement with Sonny Simmons at the Iridium in New York and performed with Priester, Rivers, Andrew Hill, and Pheeroan akLaff in the group Summit Conference.

Workman is one of several outstanding double bass players who came to prominence in the 1960s. He is equally comfortable with hard bop or free jazz, and his playing is strongly rhythmic and melodic. His unflagging bass lines and inventive solos were particularly appreciated by Coltrane and Blakey.

SELECTED RECORDINGS

As leader: *Images* (1989, Music & Arts 634); *Summit Conference* (1993, Postcards 1003); *Cerebral Caverns* (1995, Postcards 1010)
As sideman: G. Gryce: *Sayin' Something* (1960, NewJ 8230); D. Jordan: *Flight to Jordan* (1960, BN 4046); J. Coltrane: *Africa/Brass* (1961, Imp. 6); *Olé Coltrane* (1961, Atl. 1373); *Live at the Village Vanguard* (1961, Imp. 10); A. Blakey: *Free for All* (1964, BN 84170); *Indestructible* (1964, BN

84193); W. Shorter: *Juju* (1964, BN 84182); A. Shepp: *Four for Trane* (1964, Imp. 71); Y. Lateef: *Psychicemotus* (1965, Imp. 92); B. Ervin: *The Trance* (1965, Prst. 7462); W. Shorter: *Adam's Apple* (1966, BN 84232); L. Morgan: *Taru* (1968, BN LT1031); M. Waldron: *Up Popped the Devil* (1973, Enja 2034); D. Murray: *Morning Song* (1983, BS 0075); M. Waldron: *The Git Go* (1986, SN 1118); *The Seagulls of Kristiansund* (1986, SN 1148); Trio Transition: *Trio Transition with Special Guest Oliver Lake* (1988, DIW 829); M. Crispell: *Live in Zurich* (1989, Leo 122); *Circles* (1990, Victo 012); A. Cyrille: *My Friend Louis* (1991, DIW 858); A. Takase: *Clapping Music* (1993, Enja 8090-2)

BIBLIOGRAPHY

Feather '60s; *Feather–Gitler '70s*
H. Smith: "Black Swan Quartet: in the Tradition of Originality and Artistic Achievement," *Strings*, iii/3 (1989), 46
G. P. Chapin: "Reggie Workman: Educator on the Edge," *Option*, no.34 (1990), 40
——: "Reggie Workman: the Spirit behind the Music," *Strings*, vii/2 (1992), 22
N. Dadoun: "Speak Low: Reggie Workman Finds his own Voice," *Coda*, no.241 (1992), 16
S. Stein: "Reggie Workman's Sound Sculptures," *JT*, xxiii/3 (1993), 38
B. Rusch: "Reggie Workman: Interview," *Cadence*, xxi/7 (1995), 5
L. Birnbaum: "Low End Theory: Reggie Workman," *Jazziz*, xiii/7 (1996), 72
——: "Reggie Workman: Keep Moving!," *DB*, lxiii/3 (1996), 36 [incl. discography]
L. Andrews: "Workman's New Project Brings Him to the 'Executive Suite'," *Amsterdam News* (11 Sept 1997)
J. Rosenbaum: "Reggie Workman: Continuing Coltrane's Quest," *Bass Player*, viii/4 (1997), 34

MARK GARDNER/BK

Workshop de Lyon [Free Jazz Workshop]. French avant-garde group. It was founded in Lyons in 1967 as Free Jazz Workshop by the saxophonists Jean Bolcato and Maurice Merle and the double bass player Jean Mereu, and in 1976 it took the name Workshop de Lyon. Christian Rollet played drums in the group from 1968, Merle was replaced by Louis Sclavis in 1975, and the saxophonist Jean Paul Austin joined in 1987; Sclavis left two years later. The band played concerts which involved guests from the fields of free jazz and contemporary improvised music. Workshop de Lyon was influenced by African-American free jazz of the 1960s but soon embraced a broader aesthetic leading to the establishment of an "imaginary folklore" as propagated by Arfi, the musicians' initiative founded by workshop members and other musicians in 1977. Workshop de Lyon's characteristic reliance on musical communication among its members is evident on *Telie* (from its album *La chasse de Shirah Sharibad*, 1975, Palm 8) and *Moulin noir* and *Chant bien fatal* (both on *Musique basalt*, 1981, ARFI Move 005).

BIBLIOGRAPHY

A.-R. Hardy: "Le Workshop de Lyon: interview aléatoire," *Jm*, no.256 (1977), 16

WOLFRAM KNAUER

World Pacific. Record label founded in 1958 by Richard Bock as a subsidiary of his company PACIFIC JAZZ.

World Saxophone Quartet [WSQ]. It was founded in 1976 by David Murray (tenor saxophone) and three members of the Black Artists Group of St. Louis: Oliver Lake (alto), Julius Hemphill (alto), and Hamiet Bluiett (baritone). For many years John Purcell (alto and saxello) deputized for its regular members on an ad hoc basis. Although the players concentrate on saxophones, they also occasionally play flute, alto clarinet, and bass clarinet. Their style is fundamentally original, though they have drawn extensively on rhythmic, melodic, and timbral traditions of blues-flavored African-American popular music, and the jazz approaches of Ornette Coleman and Albert Ayler. Their compositions sometimes recall the saxophone writing of Duke Ellington, Thad Jones, and Oliver Nelson. Although the quartet occasionally plays passages of free jazz, by deftly interweaving composed parts with improvised solos and ensembles the musicians achieve a greater balance of contrasts than Coleman. Also significant are their broad spectrum of earthy tone-colors, their light-hearted manner, and their unique amalgam of compositional approaches, ranging from 20th-century concert music to rhythm-and-blues and free jazz.

In 1986–7 the World Saxophone Quartet devoted considerable attention to performing and recording each member's arrangements of songs by Ellington and Billy Strayhorn. In 1989 the group appeared on the television shows "Night Music" and "VH-1 Jazz," and in the autumn of that year it initiated a collaboration with three African percussionists, Mor Thiam, Chief Bey, and Mar Gueye, for a concert at the Brooklyn Academy of Music; this led to one of its most successful recordings, *Metamorphosis*, made in 1990, after Arthur Blythe had replaced Hemphill. During the 1990s the quartet was working together for three or four months of each year. In the mid-1990s Blythe was replaced by Eric Person and then by James Spaulding (by an alternative account, Spaulding also preceded Blythe). Eventually Purcell joined Lake, Murray, and Bluiett as a regular member of the group, which recorded again with the three African percussionists on *Four Now* (*c*1995).

SELECTED RECORDINGS

Point of No Return (1977, Moers 01034); *Steppin' with the World Saxophone Quartet* (1978, BS 0027); *World Saxophone Quartet* (1980, BS 0046); *Revue* (1980, BS 0056); *The World Saxophone Quartet Plays Duke Ellington* (1986, Nonesuch 79137-1); *Rhythm and Blues* (1989, Elek. Mus. 60864-2); *Metamorphosis* (1990, Elek. Nonesuch 9-79258-2); *Four Now* (*c*1995, Justin Time 83)

BIBLIOGRAPHY

C. J. Safane: "The World Saxophone Quartet," *DB*, xlvi/16 (1979), 26
K. R. Bachmann: "World Saxophone Quartet," *JP*, xxxiv/5 (1985), 23
F. Davis: *In the Moment: Jazz in the 1980s* (New York, and Oxford, England, 1986/*R*1996), 243
P. Elwood: "Saxophone Quartet Digs Deep into Duke Ellington," *San Francisco Examiner* (8 Nov 1986)
B. Primack: "The World Saxophone Quartet's Metamorphosis," *JT*, xxi/5 (1991), 30
B. Bernatos: "The World Saxophone Quartet," *Windplayer*, x/1 (1993), 15
H. Boyd: "World Saxophone Quartet: New Life after Julius," *DB*, lxiii/9 (1996), 22 [incl. discography]
J. Ephland: "Setting the Record Straight: Julius & the World Sax Quartet," *DB*, lxiii/12 (1996), 15
W. Jenkins: "World Saxophone Quartet: High Ground," *JT*, xxvii/3 (1997), 38

BK

World's Greatest Jazz Band (of Yank Lawson and Bob Haggart). Ensemble founded in 1968 by the trumpeter Yank Lawson and the double bass player Bob Haggart. Its original sidemen were the trumpeter and flugelhorn player Billy Butterfield, the trombonists Lou McGarity and Carl Fontana, the clarinetist and soprano saxophonist Bob Wilber, the tenor saxophonist Bud Freeman, the pianist Ralph Sutton, the drummer Morey Feld, and the banjoist, guitarist, and singer Clancy Hayes. It grew from a band that played from the early 1960s at engagements organized by the businessman Dick Gibson and which worked from 1965 at the Trocadero Ballroom in Denver, using variously the names the Eight, Nine, or Ten Greats of Jazz. It was to have included Cutty Cutshall, who not only participated in recordings by the Greats of Jazz but also recorded the group's first album under the name the World's Greatest Jazz

Band; however, Cutshall died before its first public performance, and Fontana took his place.

Gibson encouraged the members of the ensemble to work together full-time; he also suggested the band's new name, under which it first performed in New York in November 1968. After this Hayes and Feld left, and the latter was replaced by Gus Johnson. With Maxine Sullivan, the group undertook several long residencies in New York. Haggart's arrangements of jazz classics and contemporary pop songs, spiced with the powerful solo work of the musicians, were an important aspect of the band's appeal to a younger audience. In 1971 Barker Hickox replaced Gibson as the group's impresario and organized its record label, World Jazz. By this time the trombonists were Ed Hubble and Vic Dickenson. Butterfield left in 1972 and Bobby Hackett took his place at concerts recorded in 1973 and 1974; by 1975 the group had seven members, with Benny Morton as the sole trombonist, but it was augmented for special events. Butterfield returned on numerous occasions, touring Europe with the band in 1974 and recording in 1975–7; as the group took on more of an ad hoc nature in the mid-1970s its personnel included Bucky Pizzarelli, Johnny Best, George Masso, Peanuts Hucko, Tommy Newsom, Al Klink, Urbie Green, Hank Jones, Johnny Mince, Sonny Russo, Bobby Donaldson, Bill Stegmeyer, Lou Stein, Cliff Leeman, Phil Bodner, John Bunch, Bob Rosengarden, Roger Kellaway, and Nick Fatool. In 1978 Lawson and Haggart abandoned the band's title, but they used it again on occasions in the mid-1980s.

SELECTED RECORDINGS

World's Greatest Jazz Band (1968, Project 5033), incl. Ode to Billy Joe, Up, up, and away; *Extra* (1969, Project 5039), incl. Alfie; *Jazz in the Troc* (1969, WCS 3330); *World's Greatest Jazz Band Live at the Roosevelt Grill* (1970, Atl. 1570); *What's New?* (1970, Atl. 1582); *Century Plaza* (1972, World Jazz 1); *World's Greatest Jazz Band in Concert*, ii: *At Carnegie Hall* (1973, World Jazz 4); *World's Greatest Jazz Band of Yank Lawson and Bob Haggart on Tour* (1975, World Jazz 8); *World's Greatest Jazz Band of Yank Lawson and Bob Haggart Plays Duke Ellington* (1976, World Jazz 9); *World's Greatest Jazz Band of Yank Lawson and Bob Haggart Plays George Gershwin* (1977, World Jazz 11)

BIBLIOGRAPHY

I. Gitler: "'Now is the Renaissance': the World's Greatest Jazz Band," *DB*, xxxvi/9 (1969), 16
G. W. Kay: "The World's Greatest (and Happiest) Jazz Band," *SL*, xxii (1969), Sept–Oct, 221
K. Gallacher: "The World's Greatest Jazz Band," *JM*, no.182 (1970), 9
J. S. Wilson: "The World's Greatest Jazz Band," *IM*, lxviii/12 (1970), 11
K. Gallacher: "The World's Greatest Jazz Band," *J&B*, i/8 (1971), 9
M. Jones: "The Band's All Here," *MM* (4 Dec 1971), 24
J. Klee: "The World's Greatest Jazz Band of Yank Lawson and Bob Haggart," *DB*, l/16 (1973), 18
B. Korall: *The World's Greatest Jazz Band of Yank Lawson and Bob Haggart* (n.p. [Phoenix, AZ], 1973)
F. Levin: "The World's Greatest Jazz Band," *JJI*, li/1 (1998), 10

BRIAN PEERLESS

World Wide. Record label. A subsidiary of Savoy (ii), it was established by Herman Lubinsky in Newark, New Jersey, in 1958. It was intended that the repertory should exploit to best advantage the innovations of stereo recording techniques, but only two such albums were issued; both, by all-star bands that included Bobby Jaspar, Frank Rehak, Frank Wess, Bill Harris (i), Joe Wilder, and Pepper Adams, were arranged by Billy Ver Planck and produced by Ozzie Cadena. World Wide also issued recordings by Coleman Hawkins, Bobby Donaldson, and Sammy Price. A separate series of World Wide singles was devoted to gospel music. (M. Ruppli and B. Porter: *The Savoy Label: a Discography*, Westport, CT, and London, 1980)

MARK GARDNER/BK

World Wide Jazz. Subsidiary record label founded in the 1990s by Timeless.

Worrell, Lewis (James) (*b* Charlotte, NC, 10 Sept or 7 Nov 1934). Double bass player. Carles, Clergeat, and Comolli (1994) give his birthdate as 10 September, but Schreiber and Klatt (*c*1992) give 7 November; it is unknown which is correct. Worrell played tuba from the age of 11 and changed to double bass when he was 17. He worked in Orchestra USA, and with Bud Powell and Elmo Hope, and first recorded with Hank Crawford in October 1963. The following year he performed and recorded (September) with Steve Lacy and replaced Don Moore in and recorded with (November) the New York Art Quartet; however, by December he had left the group. He performed and recorded with Albert Ayler from early 1965 through 1966. During the same period he recorded with Sonny Murray (November 1965), performed and recorded with Archie Shepp in San Francisco (February 1966), and recorded with Roswell Rudd (September 1966). In February 1967 he recorded with Robin Kenyatta in a trio with Walter Booker, but thereafter nothing is known of his life. Worrell is heard to advantage on *New York Art Quartet* (1964, ESP 1004), but perhaps his best work, undertaken in a small group which included two double bass players (himself and Charlie Haden) is on Rudd's recording *Everywhere* (1966, Imp. 9126).

BIBLIOGRAPHY

GrayF
J. Cooke: "New York Nouvelle Vague, 5: The New York Art Quartet," *JM*, xxi/9 (1966), 2
V. Wilmer: *As Serious as your Life: the Story of the New Jazz* (London, 1977, rev. [3]/1987)
P. Carles, A. Clergeat, and J.-L. Comolli: *Dictionnaire du jazz* (Paris, 1988, rev. and enlarged 2/1994)
H. Schreiber and T. Klatt: Liner Notes, *New York Art Quartet* (ESP 1004-2, *c*1992)
<http://www.gslis.utexas.edu/~jeffs/ayler.html> (2000)

GK

Worth, Bobby [Robert Charles Dodsworth] (*b* London, 8 Jan 1949). English drummer. He took up drums at the age of 11 and was one of the first to play them in Bill Ashton's National Youth Jazz Orchestra (1965–7). Worth held a West End residency with the trumpeter Grischa Farfel (1966–8), toured with the singer Frankie Vaughan (1969–73), and spent nine years in the Bert Rhodes Orchestra at the Talk of the Town (1973–82). As a jazz musician he worked widely as a freelance, playing in concerts and recording with Brian Dee, Kenny Baker, Humphrey Lyttelton, Spike Robinson, the singer Barbara Jay and Tommy Whittle, Digby Fairweather, Keith Smith, and Bob Wilber, among others. He also accompanied many visiting Americans, notably Jessica Williams, Charlie Byrd, Scott Hamilton, and Warren Vaché, and led his own quartet.

SELECTED RECORDINGS

As sideman: B. Dee: *Homeing In* (1988–9, Spot. 539); Perfect Pitch: *Tippin' the Scales* (1989, Spot. 540); E. Delmar: *'S Wonderful* (1992, Ronnie Scott's Jazz House 027); H. Lyttelton and A. Bilk: *Humph & Acker: Together for the Very First Time!* (1992, Calligraph 027); S. Robinson: *Tenor Madness* (1997, Essential Jazz 600)

BIBLIOGRAPHY

ChiltonB

MARK GILBERT

Wright. Family of musicians.

(1) Lammar Wright(, Sr.) (i) (*b* Texarkana, TX, 20 June 1905 or 1907; *d* New York, 13 April 1973). Trumpeter. His year of birth has been published as 1907, but his application for social security gives 1905. He grew up in Kansas City, and in 1923 became a member of Bennie Moten's band, which was playing at the Panama Club. In 1927 he went to New York to join the Missourians, and he remained with the group when it was taken over by Cab Calloway; Wright, a high-note specialist and a soloist, worked as Calloway's lead trumpeter regularly until 1942 (for illustration *see* CALLOWAY, CAB), then intermittently for the rest of the decade. He also played with Don Redman (1943), Claude Hopkins (1944–6), Cootie Williams (1944), Lucky Millinder (periodically, 1946–52), Sy Oliver (1947), and Louis Armstrong. Occasionally Wright led his own band, and in the 1950s and 1960s, while also working as a teacher, he became active as a studio musician. He recorded with Arnett Cobb and Count Basie (both 1951) and the Sauter–Finegan Orchestra (1957), among others, and performed and recorded with George Shearing's big band (1959). In 1968 he appeared in the film *The Night They Raided Minsky's*.

SELECTED RECORDINGS

As sideman: B. Moten: Elephant's Wobble (1923, OK 8100); Thick Lips Stomp/Harmony Blues (1926, Vic. 20406); Muscle Shoals Blues (1926, Vic. 20811); Midnight Mama (1926, Vic. 20422); Missourians: Market Street Stomp (1929, Vic. 38067); C. Calloway: Gotta darn good reason now (1930, Bruns. 4936); S. Oliver: Lammar's Boogie (1947, MGM 10133); G. Shearing: *Satin Brass* (1959, Cap. ST1326)

SELECTED FILMS AND VIDEOS

Hi-de-ho (1937); Blues in the Night (1942); Minnie the Moocher (1942); The Night They Raided Minsky's (1968)

BIBLIOGRAPHY

ChiltonW; *FeatherE*; *McCarthyB*
R. Russell: *Jazz Style in Kansas City and the Southwest* (Berkeley, CA, Los Angeles, and London, 1971, rev. 2/1973/*R*1997), 93
Obituary, *DB*, 1/11 (1973), 41

(2) Lammar [Lamar] **Wright(, Jr) (ii)** (*b* Kansas City, MO, 26 Sept 1924; *d* Los Angeles, 8 July 1983). Trumpeter, son of (1) Lammar Wright. A birthdate of 28 September 1927 appears in Feather (1960), but social security and California death indexes give 26 September 1924, and both give his forename as Lamar, rather than Lammar. He played with Lionel Hampton (1943–6) and Dizzy Gillespie (1947), then worked as a principal soloist in Charlie Barnet's band (1948–9).

SELECTED RECORDINGS

As sideman: L. Hampton: Million Dollar Smile (1944, Decca 18719); D. Gillespie: Algo bueno (1947, Vic. 20-3186); C. Barnet: Redskin Rhumba (1948, Cap. 10174)

BIBLIOGRAPHY

FeatherE
Obituary, *Coda*, no.192 (1983), 35

(3) Elmon Wright (*b* Kansas City, MO, 27 Oct 1929; *d* 1984). Trumpeter, son of (1) Lammar Wright. He worked with Don Redman, toured with Dizzy Gillespie's first big band (1945), joined Roy Eldridge for about six months, and then returned to Gillespie, with whom he performed and recorded from 1946 to 1950. After touring with Earl Bostic (1954–5) he became active as a freelance musician in New York and played with rhythm-and-blues groups at the Apollo Theatre and with rock-and-roll bands. In 1959 he performed with Buddy Rich and Earle Warren, and in 1963 he recorded with Milt Jackson.

SELECTED RECORDINGS

As sideman: D. Gillespie: One Bass Hit (1946, Musi. 404); R. Eldridge: Tippin' out (1946, Decca 23637); E. Bostic: Cocktails for Two (1955, King 4790)

BIBLIOGRAPHY

FeatherE
D. Gillespie and A. Fraser: *To be, or not ... to Bop: Memoirs* (Garden City, NY, 1979, London, 1980, as *Dizzy: the Autobiography of Dizzy Gillespie*)
Obituary, *Orkester journalen*, lii/6 (1984), 26

FREDERICK A. BECK/BK

Wright, Frank (*b* Grenada, MS, 9 July 1935; *d* Wuppertal, Germany, 17 June 1990). Tenor saxophonist and leader. While growing up he played electric bass guitar in rhythm-and-blues groups in Memphis and in Cleveland, where he met Albert Ayler; it was Ayler's example that inspired him to take up tenor saxophone. After moving to New York (early 1960s) he played free jazz with Larry Young, Noah Howard, and Sunny Murray, worked briefly with Cecil Taylor and John Coltrane, and recorded as a leader (1965, 1967). In 1969 he appeared alongside Howard, Bobby Few, and Muhammad Ali at a festival of jazz, rock, and new music organized by BYG near Amougies in Belgium, and towards the end of that year he and Ali moved to Paris; there the same quartet made several recordings under the leadership of both Howard and Wright, although Art Taylor sometimes played drums in place of Ali.

In addition Wright led a quartet that consisted of Few, Alan Silva, and Ali; in 1972 the members of this group founded the cooperative publishing and production company Center of the World Productions, which they used to release their own recordings and those licensed from others (for further information on its recordings *see* ALI (2), MUHAMMAD). With Few and Silva, Wright recorded in a cooperative trio in 1975. He spent a brief period in the USA in 1971, but later led an itinerant life; in the late 1970s he recorded in Paris (1977), New York (with Hannibal Peterson and as a leader, both 1978), and Munich (1979), and in the early 1980s he performed with Harry Miller and Louis Moholo at the 100 Club in London (1981) and made further recordings in Hamburg (with Peter Brötzmann, 1981) and New York (with Saheb Sarbib, 1981, and as a leader, 1982). During a period as a sideman with Cecil Taylor (mid-1980s) he took part in sessions in Milan (1984) and Berlin (1986). His month of death appeared erroneously in some obituaries as May or July.

SELECTED RECORDINGS

Duos with M. Ali: *Adieu Little Man* (1974, Center of the World 004)
As leader: *Your Prayer* (1967, ESP 1053), incl. No End; *One for John* (1969, BYG 529336); *Center of the World* (1972, Center of the World 001); *Last Polka in Nancy* (1973, Center of the World 002)

BIBLIOGRAPHY

GrayF
P. Carles: "Wright is Right," *Jm*, no.173 (1969), 13
F. Postif: "The Noah Howard–Frank Wright Quartet," *Jh*, no.257 (1970), 18
V. Wilmer: "Superman of the Tenor," *MM* (11 April 1970), 14
V. Heibel: "Meine Musik ist universell gültig: Frank Wright," *JP*, xxiv/6 (1975), 10
B. McRae: "Avant Courier: Frank Wright: Working On," *JJ*, xxviii/8 (1975), 12

J. Eigo: "Frank Wright," *Coda*, no.151 (1976), 33
V. Wilmer: *As Serious as your Life: the Story of the New Jazz* (London, 1977, rev. [3]/1987)
Obituaries: J. Fordham, *The Guardian* (28 June 1990); B. McRae, *JJI*, xliii/8 (1990), 21; V. Wilmer, *The Independent* (21 June 1990)
<http://www.mindspring.com/~scala/wright.html> (1999) [discography]

BK

Wright, Gene [Eugene Joseph; Senator] (*b* Chicago, 29 May 1923). Double bass player. He studied cornet in school, then took up double bass. He worked with his own group, the Dukes of Swing (1943–6), before performing and recording with Gene Ammons (1946–51), Count Basie (1948–9), Arnett Cobb (1951–2), Buddy DeFranco (1953–5), Red Norvo (1955–6), and Cal Tjader (1955–8). Late in 1957 he became a member of the Dave Brubeck Quartet, in which his solid timekeeping provided the foundation for Brubeck's experiments with polyrhythms; in the course of his international travels with the group he acquired his nickname, Senator. After the quartet disbanded in 1967 Wright presented concerts at colleges (1969–70) and played in Monty Alexander's trio (1971–4). From 1974 he became involved in television and film work and was active as a teacher and composer; for a time he served as chairman of the jazz department at the University of Cincinnati and as a member of the advisory board of the jazz division of the International Society of Bassists (1974–6). Wright continued to play for reunions of Brubeck's quartet, notably at the Kool Jazz Festival in 1985 and in Moscow in 1988. He is married to an actress and director, and he has made numerous appearances on television shows. He performed at the Sacramento Dixieland Jubilee in 1990. From 1996 he has recorded with Hadda Brooks. Wright has been teaching privately from 1969 and is the author of an instruction book, *Modern Music for Bass* (Miami Beach, *c*1980s).

See also Brubeck, dave.

SELECTED RECORDINGS

As leader: *The Wright Groove* (1962, Phi. 8755)
As sideman: G. Ammons: on *"Jug" Sessions* (1947–9, EmA 2-400), Going for the okey doak (1947); B. DeFranco: *In a Mellow Mood* (1954, Norg. 1079); C. Tjader: *Jazz at the Blackhawk* (1957, Fan. 3241), incl. Thinking of You, MJQ; D. Brubeck: *Dave Brubeck in Europe* (1958, Col. CL1168); *Countdown Time in Outer Space* (1961–2, Col. CS8575), incl. Why Phillis; M. Alexander: *Here Comes the Sun* (1971, MPS 15324)

SELECTED FILMS AND VIDEOS

Theology and Jazz (*c*1960); Jazz Casual: Dave Brubeck Quartet (1963); Jazz the intimate Art (1968); Dave Brubeck (1970)

BIBLIOGRAPHY

Feather–Gitler '70s
M. Jones: "This World of Jazz," *MM*, xxxiii (22 Feb 1958), 13
A. J. Smith: "A Quarter of a Century Young: the Dave Brubeck Quartet," *DB*, xliii/6 (1976), 18
E. Tiegel: "Eugene Wright: Acoustic Bassist Eager to Resume Brubeck Touring," *Billboard*, lxxxix (12 March 1977), 141
F. M. Hall: *It's About Time: the Dave Brubeck Story* (Fayetteville, AR, 1996), 85

BRENDA PENNELL/BK

Wright, Lammar (i). *See* Wright family, (1) Lammar.

Wright, Lammar (ii). *See* Wright family, (2) Lammar.

Wright, Leo (Nash) (*b* Wichita Falls, TX, 14 Dec 1933; *d* Vienna, 4 Jan 1991). Alto saxophonist, flutist, and clarinetist. He learned saxophone with his father Mel Wright (who played with Booker Ervin in Texas) and John Hardee, and studied flute at colleges in Austin and San Francisco. While stationed in Germany he led an army band that included Don Ellis, Eddie Harris, Lex Humphries, and Cedar Walton (*c*1957). He performed with Charles Mingus at the Newport Jazz Festival in July 1959. From August 1959 to 1962 he played in Dizzy Gillespie's quintet and big band, appearing at the Monterey, Newport, and Antibes–Juan-les-Pins festivals, recording several albums, and taking part in the "Dizzy Gillespie Quintet" episode of the television series "Jazz Casual" (1962). He also recorded with Richard Williams (1960), Eldee Young (1961), and Dave Pike (1962), and in New York as the leader of bop quartets and quintets (1960–63); among his sidemen were Junior Mance, Art Davis, Charli Persip, Williams, Kenny Burrell, and Ron Carter. After leaving Gillespie, Wright recorded with Lalo Schifrin and Brother Jack McDuff (both 1962) and Antonio Carlos Jobim, Jimmy Witherspoon, and Johnny Coles (all 1963).

Late in 1963 Wright permanently left the USA for Europe, where following a period spent mainly in Scandinavia, he worked as a freelance and recorded with George Gruntz (1965) and with Lee Konitz in the all-star group Alto Summit (1968). He then settled in Berlin and played with the studio band of Sender Freies Berlin (1965–81) and other groups, and appeared at jazz festivals in Germany, Switzerland, Hungary (where he recorded with Aladár Pege in 1976), and Finland. On a visit to America in 1978 he appeared as a guest soloist with Red Garland's trio at the Keystone Korner in San Francisco. He later lived in Vienna and retired from music for a period from 1981; he first played again in 1986, recording an album of duets with his wife and performing with Nat Adderley, Grachan Moncur III, and Kenny Drew in the Paris Reunion Band. Gardner's obituary reports that he then finished his autobiography, *God is my Booking Agent*, which remains unpublished. A versatile instrumentalist, Wright was strongly influenced as a saxophone player by Johnny Hodges; his timbre on the alto instrument and the bluesy character of his solos show evidence of this. His flute sound, supported by a superb technique, is airy and resonant.

SELECTED RECORDINGS

As leader: *Blues Shout* (1960, Atl. 1358); *Modern Jazz Studio Nr.4* (1965, Amiga 855056); *It's All-Wright* (1972, MPS 20-21375-7)
As sideman: R. Williams: *New Horn in Town* (1960, Can. 9003); D. Gillespie: *A Musical Safari* (1961, Booman 1001); *New Wave* (1962, Phi. 600070); J. Coles: *Little Johnny C.* (1963, BN 84144); Alto Summit: *Alto Summit* (1968, MPS 15192); R. Garland: *I Left my Heart* (1978, Muse 5311)

BIBLIOGRAPHY

FeatherE; *Feather '60s*; *Feather–Gitler '70s*
Obituaries: M. Gardner: *JJI*, xliv/3 (1991), 19; J. Simmen, *BHcF*, no.392 (1991), 38

GARY CARNER/BK

Wright, Specs [Charles] (*b* Philadelphia, 8 Sept 1927; *d* Philadelphia, 6 Feb 1963). Drummer. After service in an army band (to 1947) he played bop with Jimmy Heath, toured France and recorded with Howard McGhee (1948), and performed and recorded with Dizzy Gillespie (1949–51). In the first half of the 1950s he took part in sessions led by Earl Bostic (1952), with whom he also toured, and Kenny Drew (1953) and worked as a freelance in Philadelphia (to 1955). During the following years he performed and recorded with Cannonball Adderley (1955–6) and Carmen McRae (1957–8) and made recordings with Nat Adderley (1956) and Art Blakey and Ray Bryant (both 1957). In 1958 he recorded with Monday Night at Birdland (an all-star bop group that included Hank Mobley, Curtis Fuller, and Lee

Morgan), Sonny Rollins, and Betty Carter; later he played and recorded with Red Garland (1959) and worked with Lambert, Hendricks, and Ross (1960–61). He is heard to advantage on *Red Garland at the Prelude* (1959, Prst. 7170). (*FeatherE*; *Feather '60s*; *ReclamsJ*)

Wrightsman, Stan(ley A.) (*b* Gotebo, OK, 15 June 1910; *d* Palm Springs, CA, 17 or 18 Dec 1975). Pianist. He first played at a hotel in Gulfport, Mississippi, in territory bands in Oklahoma, and in New Orleans under the bandleader Ray Miller (1930). Thereafter he worked for a period in California and was a member of Ben Pollack's group in Chicago (1935–6), then settled in Los Angeles and recorded in Hollywood with Santo Pecora (1937). From the late 1930s he was active as a freelance and played frequently in film studios; he may be seen performing in the film *The Man I Love* (1946). In addition he recorded with Artie Shaw (1940), performed and recorded dixieland at intervals with Wingy Manone (1940–49) and Eddie Miller (1944–50), and played and recorded with Nappy Lamare (1945, 1946) and Bob Crosby (1950–51) and recorded with the Rampart Street Paraders (1953–7), Matty Matlock (1954–60), and Pete Fountain (1956); in 1958 he took part in sessions led by Bob Scobey, Ray Bauduc, and Wild Bill Davison and played on the soundtrack to the film *The Five Pennies*. Later he performed and recorded again with Fountain (1959–67), recorded with Muggsy Spanier (1962), and worked in television and films. He is heard to advantage on *Pete Fountain on Tour* (1961, Coral 57337). (*ChiltonW*; *FeatherE*; *Feather–Gitler '70s*)

Wrobel, Engelbert (*b* Dormagen, Germany, 19 Nov 1959). German clarinetist and soprano, alto, and tenor saxophonist. He learned clarinet from his father, played in local dance bands as a teenager, and studied at the music school in Düren. At the age of 16 he founded his own band, the Happy Jazzmen. During military service he played in an army band. Thereafter he was a member of various groups, including Rod Mason's Hot Five and Savannah Orchestra. Having learned to play saxophone, he founded his group Swing Society in 1990, though he also played in Peter Fleischhauer's big band.

SELECTED RECORDINGS

As leader: *Live at Sägewerk* (1994, Tim. 588); *A Heartful of Swing* (1995, NCC 8502)

As sideman: R. Mason: *Rod Mason's Hot Music* (1988, Tim. 550–51); O. Klein: *Moonglow* (1995, Nagel-Heyer 021); P. Fleischhauer: *King of Swing Orchestra directed by Peter Fleischhauer Performing the Famous Benny Goodman Sound* (*c*1996, NCC 8505)

BIBLIOGRAPHY

G. Conrad: "Ein bemerkenswerter deutscher Swing-Klarinettist: Engelbert Wrobel," *Der Jazzfreund*, no. 166 (1997), 7

GERHARD CONRAD

Wróblewski, Jan [Ptaszyn, Ptak] (*b* Kalisz, Poland, 27 March 1936). Polish tenor saxophonist and composer. He is known among his colleagues and on stage as Ptaszyn or Ptak (Bird). While studying agricultural mechanics at the polytechnic in Poznań he played clarinet, tenor and baritone saxophone, and piano, after which he took courses in music theory at the high school of music in Kraków (from 1958). His professional début was in 1956, when he performed and recorded with Krzysztof Komeda at the first jazz festival in Sopot. He was chosen to play in Marshall Brown's International Youth Band at the Newport Jazz Festival in 1958 and thereafter was invited to perform with many Polish groups. Wróblewski led the Jazz Believers (1958–9), a quintet (1959–61), the Jazz Outsiders (1961–3), and the Polish Jazz Quartet (1963–6) and also played with Andrzej Kurylewicz (1962–3). In the second half of the 1960s he worked mainly as a freelance musician, then in 1968 he formed the orchestra of the Studio Jazzowe Polskiego Radia (Polish Radio Jazz Studio), which he led until 1977; most of the important Polish jazz musicians of the era played in this group at one time or another. During the same period he worked for radio and served as vice-president and later president of the Polish Jazz Society.

From 1973 to 1977, with Wojciech Karolak as co-leader, Wróblewski led the group Mainstream; the group performed in France in 1975 and in Poland at the Jazz Jamboree in 1975 and 1976, and Ewa Bem sang with it in 1975. He then formed Chałturnik, an orchestra that played mainly musical persiflages, his Grand Standard Orchestra, in which he played jazz standards with a string section included, and a quartet, with which he appeared at the Jazz Jamboree (1978, 1980), at Jazz Yatra in India (1980, again with Bem), and in the USA (1981). From 1982 to 1984 he led the sextet New Presentation, which promoted the careers of such emerging young musicians as the trumpeter Robert Majewski, and from 1984 to 1992 he led other such groups under his own name, with Majewski, Kuba Stankiewicz, Bogdan Hołownia, Darek Oleszkiewicz, and the double bass player Adam Cegielski appearing among his sidemen at various times. From 1992 to 1995 he led a ten-piece group, Made in Poland, whose members included Andrzej Jagodziński, Piotr Wojtasik, Henryk Miśkiewicz, Krzysztof Herdzin, and Cegielski; he also formed a sextet and his Czwartet (quartet) (1993).

Wróblewski was one of the first Polish musicians to play in a free-jazz style, and, although later he used a more traditional approach, he remained open to musical experimentation. Some of his compositions are influenced by Polish folk music, such as *Bandoska in Blue*; another major composition, *Wariant Warszawski* (Warsaw variant), was performed by his jazz quartet with a symphony orchestra in 1975. His later works for jazz soloist and symphony orchestra include *Czytanki muzyczne* (Musical readers; 1982), *Maestoso combinato* (1983), and *Altissimonica* (2000). From 1970 he has presented the weekly radio show "Trzy kwadranse jazzu" (Three quarters of jazz), and from the year 2000 he has been one of the hosts of the weekly television show "Jazz nocą" (Jazz by night).

SELECTED RECORDINGS

As leader: *Jazz Outsiders* (1962, Muza 0197); *Polish Jazz Quartet* (1964, Muza 0246); with W. Karolak: *Mainstream* (1973, Muza 1139); *S.P.P.T. Chałturnik* (early 1970s, Muza 1079); *Czwartet: Live in Hades* (1993, Polonia 017); *Made in Poland* (1995, Gowi 20); *Henryk Wars Songs* (1998, CD Sound 103)

As sideman: A. Kurylewicz: *Go Right* (1963, Muza 0186); E. Bem: *Bright Ella's Memorial* (1997, Koch Jazz 3957)

BIBLIOGRAPHY

Feather–Gitler '70s

J. Byrczek: "Eurojazz Personalities: Poland," *JF* [intl edn], no.18 (1972), 87

K. Czyż: "Jan Ptaszyn Wróblewski: the Sole Survivor," *JF* [intl edn], no.73 (1981), 24 [incl. discography]

WOLFRAM KNAUER/ADAM CEGIELSKI

WSQ. *See* WORLD SAXOPHONE QUARTET.

Wulf, Joe (*b* Mayen, Germany, 19 June 1961). German trombonist, arranger, and bandleader. He began his music studies in 1980 with Jiggs Whigham in Cologne. From 1983 to 1984 he was a member of the band led by the clarinetist and saxophonist Pierre Paquette, then joined Rod Mason. While with Mason (until 1991) he wrote his first arrangements and also worked as a studio musician and as a teacher at the Musikhochschule Cologne and at the university in Bonn. From 1992 he led his own band, Joe Wulf and his Gentlemen of Swing, and changed his style from traditional jazz to swing of the 1930s and 1940s. From October to December 1998 he toured with Buddy DeFranco and Terry Gibbs.

SELECTED RECORDINGS

As leader: *That's why I Like New Orleans* (1993, TTM 7011); *Live at the Stellwerk* (1995, Skywalk 190661); with B. Barnard: *Shades of Duke* (1995, Roughtrade 190662)

As sideman: R. Mason: *The Pearls* (1986, BL 51114); *Rod Mason's Hot Music* (1988, Tim. 550-51)

<http://www.joe-wulf.de/index.shtml> (2000)

GERHARD CONRAD

Wyands, Richard (Francis) (*b* Oakland, CA, 2 July 1928). Pianist. His full name is taken from California birth records. He took classical piano lessons, but also learned about jazz piano playing from Wilbur Baranco; while in junior high school, high school, and college he doubled as a drummer. He began his professional career in 1944 and worked with local groups from around 1950. As a member of Vernon Alley's group, which formed the house rhythm section at the Blackhawk in San Francisco, he accompanied many leading soloists (to 1954). After serving as the intermission pianist at the Downbeat Club (1955) he left San Francisco for a brief tour of the West Coast with Ella Fitzgerald (three months in 1956). Around 1957 he accompanied popular singers for ten months at a club in Ottawa, Canada, working with Wyatt Ruther, and then toured for three months with Carmen McRae, with whom he went to New York in 1958. There he played with Roy Haynes, Charles Mingus (1959), Jerome Richardson (1959), and Gigi Gryce. Wyands was at his most prolific in 1960–61, when his tidy solos enlivened recordings by musicians as diverse as Gryce, Oliver Nelson, Etta Jones, Eddie "Lockjaw" Davis, Lem Winchester, Gene Ammons, Willis "Gator" Jackson, Roland Kirk, and Taft Jordan. In the 1960s he was a member of Illinois Jacquet's group.

From 1965 to 1974 Wyands toured with Kenny Burrell's group, traveling to England in 1969 and Japan in 1971. He was also active as a freelance, and recorded with Freddie Hubbard in 1971. In 1974 he became a member of Budd Johnson's JPJ Quartet, replacing Dill Jones. He also undertook extensive work in pit bands for Broadway and off-Broadway musicals during the 1970s and played in various clubs in piano and bass duos; around 1979 he led a trio at Windows on the World, a restaurant in the World Trade Center. He recorded with Benny Bailey (1978), Zoot Sims (1982), Al Grey and Buddy Tate (1984), Eric Alexander (1992), and Frank Wess and Warren Vaché (both 1993), and as the leader of trios consisting of Peter Washington and Kenny Washington (1986) and Lisle Atkinson and Leroy Williams (1992). In the 1980s and 1990s he performed as a sideman with countless groups in New York, including Jacquet's big band (late 1980s) and Benny Carter (1988, at Carlos I). In 1990 he formed a rhythm section with Reggie Johnson and Alvin Queen for numerous performances at the JVC Grande Parade du Jazz in Nice, where they accompanied Vaché and André Villéger and recorded as a quintet under Villéger's nominal leadership. In the early 1990s he returned to Europe to perform with Teddy Edwards and Art Farmer, and in 1996 he toured as a member of Cecil Payne's group Bebop Generation. He continues to be in demand as an accompanist and ensemble player, but his worth as a soloist has inexplicably been undervalued. His sensitive and effective playing of ballads is reminiscent of the work of Hank Jones.

SELECTED RECORDINGS

As leader: *Then, Here and Now* (1979, Jazzcraft 6); *Reunited* (1986, Criss Cross 1105); *The Arrival* (1992, DIW 611); *Get out of Town* (1996, Ste. 31401)

As sideman: J. Richardson: *Roamin' with Jerome Richardson* (1959, NewJ 8226); G. Gryce: *Sayin' Something* (1960, NewJ 8230); O. Nelson: *Screamin' the Blues* (1960, NewJ 8243); Etta Jones: *Don't Go to Strangers* (1960, Prst. 7186); R. Haynes: *Just Us* (1960, NewJ 8245); G. Ammons: *Jug* (1961, Prst. 7192); K. Burrell: *The Tender Gender* (1966, Cadet 722); A. Grey and B. Tate: *Just Jazz* (1984, Upt. 2721); C. Payne: *Casbah* (1985, Empathy E-1005); B. Carter: *The Benny Carter All-star Sax Ensemble: Over the Rainbow* (1988, MusicMasters 60196); *Cookin' at Carlos I* (1988, MusicMasters 60230); E. Alexander: *New York Calling* (1992, Criss Cross 1077); W. Vaché: *Horn of Plenty* (1993, Muse 5524)

BIBLIOGRAPHY

FeatherE; *Feather–Gitler '70s*

M. Richards: "Richard Wyands," *JJI*, xliii/12 (1990), 6

"Interview with Richard Wyands," *The Note*, iv/2 (1992), 2

R. Rusch: "Richard Wyands: Interview," *Cadence*, xxii/5 (1996), 5

MARK GARDNER/BK

Wyble, Jimmy [James Otis] (*b* Port Arthur, TX, 25 Jan 1922). Guitarist. He worked in Houston with local bands, including that of Peck Kelley, and was a staff musician for a radio station (1941–2). After completing his military service he moved around 1946 to Los Angeles as a member of Bob Wills's Texas Playboys. During the following years he worked in television and films, recorded with Shorty Rogers (1952) and Barney Kessel (1953), studied privately with Laurindo Almeida (1953–4), and performed and recorded with Red Norvo (1957–64); he is heard to advantage with Norvo on *Hi-five* (1957, RCA LPM1420) and may be seen playing with the vibraphonist's group in the film *Kings Go Forth* (1958). With Benny Goodman he toured abroad in autumn 1959 and performed and recorded in the USA in 1960–61 and 1963, and alongside Norvo he toured in the backup group of Frank Sinatra in 1964. Later he studied with George Van Eps (1968–9) and worked as a freelance musician in studios in Los Angeles (1965–75); as a member of Five Guitars (from mid-1970s) he performed five-part harmonizations of compositions by Charlie Christian under the leadership of the guitarist Tony Rizzi. In 1975 and 1977 he recorded an album of West Coast jazz as a leader (*Jimmy Wyble and Love Bros.*, Jazz Chronicles 773–4).

From the 1970s Wyble incorporated elements of classical guitar style into his playing; this preoccupation and his activities as a teacher in Los Angeles have led him to publish texts on guitar techniques (notably *The Art of Two Line Improvisation*, 1978) and to contribute to *Guitar Player* and *Songwriter Magazine* (1979–80).

BIBLIOGRAPHY

ConnorBG; *FeatherE*; *Feather–Gitler '70s*

F. R. Nemko: "Whether with Spade Cooley, Benny Goodman, or in L.A.'s Studios ... He's Always Been Jimmy Wyble," *GP*, xi/6 (1977), 22 [incl. discography]

BK

Wynn, Al(bert (L.)) (*b* New Orleans, 29 July 1907; *d* Chicago, May 1973). Trombonist. After touring with Ma Rainey (for illustration *see* Blues, fig.1) he led his own band in Chicago

(1926–8) and performed and recorded with Charlie Creath in St. Louis (1927); his style is represented particularly well on *Down by the Levee/Parkway Stomp* (1928, Voc. 1220). He then moved to Europe (1928), where he became a freelance musician before working with Sam Wooding (from summer 1929) and the pianist Harry Flemming; he may be heard to advantage on Wooding's *Hallelujah!* (1929, Pathé X8696). In 1930 he recorded in Paris with a group led by the Anglo-Sierra Leonian violinist James Boucher. Having returned to the USA (September 1932) he played in New York with the New Orleans Feetwarmers and in Chicago with Albert Ammons, Jesse Stone, Jimmie Noone, Richard M. Jones, and Earl Hines. He performed with Fletcher Henderson between May 1937 and spring 1939 and then joined Noone's big band. In the 1940s and early 1950s Wynn played as a freelance in Chicago with various musicians, among them the drummer Floyd Campbell, Baby Dodds, and Lil Armstrong. Later he worked with Franz Jackson (1956–60) and the Gold Coast Jazz Band (1960–64) and made recordings with Armstrong (1961) and as a leader (1961, notably *Al Wynn's Gutbucket Seven*, Riv. 9426) as part of Riverside's Living Legends series. Ill-health restricted his musical activities from the mid-1960s.

Oral history material in *LNT*.

BIBLIOGRAPHY

ChiltonW; *FeatherE*

H. Panassié: "Albert Wynn," *Jh*, no.16 (1937), 16

——: "Albert Wynn," *Jazz Forum: Quarterly Review of Jazz and Literature*, no.3 (1947), 13

HOWARD RYE

Wynn, Big Jim [James A.; Jimmy] (*b* El Paso, TX, 21 June 1908; *d* Los Angeles, 19 July 1977). Tenor and baritone saxophonist. He moved to Los Angeles as a child and took up saxophone before the age of ten. In the early 1930s he was a member of the band led by the trumpeter Charlie Echols at Young Papke's dance hall on 18th Street, and in 1936 he formed his own band to play at the Harlem Club, where he accompanied the dancing of T-Bone Walker. He first recorded in 1946 as a tenor saxophonist, using the name Jimmy Wynn's Bobalibans. Wynn led a jump band until at least 1960; the group recorded, and it accompanied such artists as T-Bone Walker (for whose tours Wynn was regularly engaged) and Jimmy Witherspoon. From 1947 onwards he concentrated increasingly on baritone saxophone. In the 1960s, when jump bands were no longer fashionable, he became a session musician in West Coast studios, but he re-emerged in 1970 to join Johnny Otis's new band, which may be seen performing at the Monterey Jazz Festival in the film *Play Misty for Me* (1971); he toured Europe with Otis in 1972 and worked regularly with the Johnny Otis Show until at least 1975.

SELECTED RECORDINGS

As leader: Ee-Babalibu (1945, 4-Star 1026) [t sax]; A Rhapsody in Minor/Jelly Kelly Blues (1945, Gilt Edge 531) [t sax]; Fat Meat (1947, Specialty 312) [t sax]; Blow, Wynn, Blow (1949, Supreme 1509) [bar sax]; Goofin' off (1949, Supreme 1522) [bar sax]

BIBLIOGRAPHY

B. Millar: "Big Jim Wynn: Sax Man," *Blues Unlimited*, no.115 (1975), 18

Obituary, B. Millar, *Living Blues*, no.35 (1977), 41

J. Evensmo: *History of Jazz Tenor Saxophone: Black Artists*, iv: *1945–1949* (Oslo, 1999)

HOWARD RYE

Xanadu. Record company and label. The company was founded in New York in 1975 by Don Schlitten. It quickly became a highly respected enterprise, and it issued more than 200 albums. The repertory is divided into two parts. The Silver Series contains newly made recordings by such leaders as Al Cohn, Barry Harris, Dolo Coker, Jimmy Raney, Sonny Criss, Dexter Gordon, Bob Mover, Frank Butler, and others and a sequence of albums made at the Montreux International Jazz Festival of 1978. The Gold Series is devoted to reissues, chiefly of swing and bop. Among these are Billy Eckstine's first recordings, many historically important items from the early 1930s, and material produced by Bob Shad after World War II. As well as producing all new sessions himself, Schlitten designs the album liners, takes the photographs, and in some instances has written the accompanying notes. He has also been concerned to ensure that musicians or their families are paid the appropriate royalties for reissues. To mark the tenth anniversary of its inception the company issued a sampler of representative material from its catalogues.

In 1976 Xanadu sponsored several of its musicians to undertake a tour of Japan, where it holds leasing agreements. A similar visit was organized in 1980 to West Africa, where the company was one of the first to record American jazz in Africa for distribution elsewhere. Following the settlement of a protracted legal dispute in 1988, Schlitten brought into the Xanadu catalogue a number of masters secured from Muse and Onyx, including previously unissued recordings by Terry Gibbs. Xanadu remained active in the 1990s, licensing its material for distribution internationally on CDs.

BIBLIOGRAPHY

M. Segell: "Once More, Jazz is Big Business," *RS*, no.282 (1978–9), 78
L.-V. Mialy: "Don Schlitten: Xanadu Records," *Jh*, no.556 (1998–9), 25

MARK GARDNER/BK

Xiques, Ed(ward F., Jr.) (*b* New York, 9 Oct 1939). Saxophonist. While studying music at Boston University (BM 1962) he performed with Jaki Byard and Herb Pomeroy. He then moved to New York and worked as a schoolteacher (1962–8), played as a freelance with Buddy Morrow, the trumpeter Les Elgart and the alto saxophonist Larry Elgart, and Duke Pearson, and toured briefly and recorded with Woody Herman (1970). From 1971 to the late 1970s he performed, recorded, and toured Europe with the Thad Jones–Mel Lewis Orchestra, in which he played flute and clarinet as well as saxophone (for illustration *see* Jones, fig.1*b*). In addition he was active as a freelance, performing and recording with Bill Watrous's groups Manhattan Wildlife Refuge and Ten Wheel Drive (both mid-1970s) and with Frank Foster (in Tokyo, 1975) and McCoy Tyner (1977); he is heard to advantage with Watrous on *The Tiger of San Pedro* (1975, Col. PC33701).

Although Xiques performed and recorded with Toshiko Akiyoshi between 1983 and 1986, his principal association from 1983 has been with Liza Minnelli's backup bands. From the late 1980s he has been involved in the activities of the BMI Jazz Composers Workshop as both a writer and a player; he also continued his education, studying composition with fellow workshop members Manny Albam, Bob Brookmeyer, and Jim McNeely, and as an outgrowth of this study he recorded his own compositions as the principal saxophone and flute soloist in and the leader of small groups (the albums *Little Bear*, 1987–8, Edex 48, and *Spacewalk*, 1995, Edex 54). In the 1990s he deputized occasionally in Mario Bauzá's big band, Maria Schneider's orchestra, the Vanguard Jazz Orchestra, and McNeely's tentet. Xiques teaches woodwind privately and, when not touring, at Vassar College in Poughkeepsie, New York. (*Feather–Gitler '70s*)

BK

XtraWatt. Subsidiary record label formed by Watt.

Xylophone. A tuned percussion instrument probably of African or Asian origin, known in Europe from the early 16th century. The modern orchestral instrument consists of a set of wooden bars arranged in two ranks similar to a keyboard configuration, each bar suspended over a tube resonator. The xylophone has a compass of four octaves ascending from *c′* or three and a half octaves from *f′* or *g′*. When struck with hard-headed mallets it produces a bright, penetrating sound; softer mallets, giving a less distinct sound, are occasionally used. It has been used infrequently in jazz. Red Norvo began his career as a xylophone player and recorded on the instrument both as a leader (*Hole in the Wall*, 1933, Bruns. 6562) and as a sideman with Hoagy Carmichael (*Moon*

Country, 1934, Vic. 24627); he continued to play xylophone regularly until 1944. The xylophone was the second instrument of the washboard player Jimmy Bertrand, who in 1928 played it during a recording session led by the blues singer Blind Blake, in which Johnny Dodds also took part.

BIBLIOGRAPHY

L. Feather: *The Book of Jazz: a Guide to the Entire Field* (New York, 1957, 2/1965 as *The Book of Jazz from Then till Now: a Guide to the Entire Field*)

J. Blades: *Percussion Instruments and their History* (London, 1970, rev. [3]/1984)

CLIFFORD BEVAN

Yaged, Sol(omon) (*b* New York, 8 Dec 1922). Clarinetist. He was inspired to take up the clarinet by Benny Goodman's broadcasts for the National Biscuit Company (1935) and studied for several years with Simeon Bellison of the New York Philharmonic Orchestra; he declined the offer of a chair in the Buffalo Philharmonic Orchestra. In 1942 he played at the Swing Club, New York, and after army service, for a year beginning in 1945, worked at Jimmy Ryan's. He continued to work mainly in New York: after playing with various renowned musicians, notably Phil Napoleon's Memphis Five and Henry "Red" Allen, from the mid-1950s he usually led his own trios, quartets, and quintets. He was technical adviser for the film *The Benny Goodman Story* (1955) and taught Steve Allen to play clarinet. Among the numerous clubs at which he played were the Metropole (1954–61), the Gaslight (from 1966), and Jimmy Weston's (1970s); in 1977 he was said to be New York's busiest musician, and he was still playing swing in the city in the late 1990s. Yaged established a reputation as Goodman's most fanatical admirer, and an unabashed imitator of the style that Goodman perfected in the 1930s and early 1940s; this reputation has tended to overshadow his own proficiency as a performer as well as his leaning towards a dixieland idiom. He is heard to advantage on his album *It Might as Well be Swing* (*c*1956, Herald 0103).

Video oral history material in *NCH* (HCJA).

BIBLIOGRAPHY

FeatherE

L. Feather: "Meet Mr. Yaged: He's all for Benny Goodman, Body and Sol," *DB*, xxiii/3 (1956), 16

J. S. Wilson: "No.1 Benny Goodman Fan Takes his Work Seriously," *New York Times* (19 March 1972)

——: "Sol Yaged," *IM*, lxxi/4 (1972), 6

Z. Knauss: *Conversations with Jazz Musicians* (Detroit, 1977), 262

JEFFREY COOPER

Yagi, Masao (*b* Tokyo, 14 Nov 1932). Japanese pianist, composer, and arranger. He began his career performing Hawaiian music on steel guitar, and then, while still in high school, played jazz piano with the Ichiban Octet, led by the tenor saxophonist Shin Matsumoto. In 1956 he joined the Cozy Quartet when Toshiko Akiyoshi left the band and Sadao Watanabe took over its leadership. In 1959 he formed his own group, which the following year recorded music by Thelonious Monk, in whose work he had taken a keen interest. He recorded with Charlie Mariano and Hidehiko Matsumoto (1964) and then began working as a composer and arranger; he also recorded with Helen Merrill (1969). Later he led a jazz-rock ensemble, continued to lead a bop group, and recorded as a leader (1976). Yagi's best-known composition is *Oniwa soto, fukuwa uchi* (Demons go away, happiness come in); his others include *Grow*, *Etude*, and *Jinku* (all 1964). He wrote arrangements for Nobuo Hara's Sharps and Flats (*Little Giant* and *Flute Salad*, both 1969), the female singing group Eve, and the singer Yoshiko Goto, and provided scores for more than 250 Japanese films.

SELECTED RECORDINGS

(all recorded for King)

As leader: *Masao Yagi Plays Thelonious Monk* (1960, 3014); *Inga* (1976, SKA3021)

As sideman: C. Mariano and H. Matsumoto: *Jazz Interaction* (1964, K20P-6155); A. Miyazawa: *Round Midnight* (1985, K28P-6358)

YOZO IWANAMI/KAZUNORI SUGIYAMA

Yamada, Joh [Yamajoh] (*b* Kyoto, Japan, 27 Oct 1968). Japanese alto and soprano saxophonist and leader. He took lessons on piano from the age of five and trombone from the age of ten and changed to alto saxophone when he was 12; two years later he began to play jazz. His first work was in Yutaka Shiina's group, Yoichi Kobayashi's Good Fellas, and a band led by Motohiko Hino and Terumasa Hino. In 1992 he led a quartet consisting of Shiina, Shigeo Aramaki, and Dairiki Hara. Yamada also co-led the group Alto Nakayoshi Koyoshi with Seiji Tada (from 1993) and worked with Keiji Matsushima's quintet and with Aramaki's group. His name has been misspelled in music literature as Joe Yamada, and he has thereby been confused with a Japanese-born American pianist and composer of the same name.

SELECTED RECORDINGS

As leader: *Blue Stone* (1997, Alfa Jazz 3914); *In the Pleasant Shade* (1999, Alfa Jazz 3937)

As sideman with M. Osaka: *Twelve Colors* (1994, King KIJC371); *Club Toko*, ii (1998, East Works 0007)

KAZUNORI SUGIYAMA

Yamaguchi, Mabumi (*b* Karatsu, Japan, 1 Sept 1946). Japanese tenor saxophonist and leader. He started on alto saxophone in the big band at Keio University (Tokyo) at the age of 18 and first played professionally with Ryo Kawasaki's quintet in 1970. Having changed to the tenor instrument, he was a member of George Otsuka's quintet from 1971 through 1974. Thereafter he worked with Hiromasa Suzuki's group The Players (1975–81), Otsuka again (1978–85), Masahiko Sato (from 1989), and Shigeharu Mukai's J Quintet (from 1990). From 1969 to 1974, and again from 1985 into the new century, Yamaguchi led his own quartet.

SELECTED RECORDINGS

As leader: *After the Rain* (1976, Union GU5001); *Leeward* (1978, Union GU5007); *Mabumi* (1981, Trio PAP25004); *Squad* (1987, Tei. 30CP-131); *Regalo* (1997, East Works MAB001)
As sideman with M. Hino: *Ryuhyo/Sailing Ice* (1976, Three Blind Mice 61)

KAZUNORI SUGIYAMA

Yamamoto, Tsuyoshi (*b* Niigata, Japan, 23 March 1948). Japanese pianist. He received some piano lessons as a child, but taught himself to play in his high school years after listening to recordings by Art Blakey's Jazz Messengers. While at Nippon University he began working professionally, initially accompanying the Japanese pop singer Micky Curtis, with whom he toured Europe in 1967. From 1974 he was the house pianist at Misty, a popular jazz club in Tokyo, and later that same year he made his first recordings as a leader. Later he performed at the festivals in Monterey (1977) and Montreux (1979) and lived in New York for a year, when he performed with Dizzy Gillespie, Carmen McRae, Sam Jones, Billy Higgins, Elvin Jones, and Sonny Stitt, among others. Yamamoto continued to play at Misty into the 1990s and recorded on a regular basis.

SELECTED RECORDINGS

(recorded for Three Blind Mice unless otherwise indicated)

Midnight Sugar (1974, 23); *Misty* (1974, 30); *Live at Misty* (1974, 37); *Blues for Tee* (1974, 41); *The In Crowd* (1974, 74); *Summertime* (1976, 69); *Star Dust* (1977, 3009); *Midnight Sun* (1978, 5009); *Live in Montreux* (1979, 5019); *Speak Low* (1999, Venus 35083)

BIBLIOGRAPHY

<http://main.tvz.com/TBM/cat_e/yamamoto.htm> (2000) [discography]

KAZUNORI SUGIYAMA

Yamashita, Yosuke (*b* Tokyo, 26 Feb 1942). Japanese pianist. He worked professionally from the age of 17, attended the Kunitachi College of Music in Tokyo (1962–7), and was a member of quartets led by Masahiko Togashi and Sadao Watanabe. His early style, which owed something to the work of Bill Evans (ii), gave way to one considerably more adventurous around 1969, and he played free jazz as the leader of groups that included the tenor saxophonist Kazunori Takeda, the tenor and soprano saxophonist Seiichi Nakamura, and Akira Sakata. From 1974 he worked principally in Europe, and he recorded in Germany as the leader of a trio (1974–6), as a sideman with Manfred Schoof (1975), as an unaccompanied soloist (1975–6), and in a duo with Adelhard Roidinger (1977); he also appeared at festivals in Germany and Yugoslavia and at the Newport Jazz Festival in New York. From 1988 he led his New York trio, consisting of Cecil McBee and Pheeroan akLaff, which appeared annually at Sweet Basil and toured Japan and Europe regularly, sometimes with Joe Lovano or Ravi Coltrane added as a guest soloist. Yamashita continues to tour worldwide with various groups. He was the only Japanese musician featured at the concert held at Carnegie Hall in 1994 to celebrate the fiftieth anniversary of the Verve label, and he appears in the resulting video, *Carnegie Hall Salutes the Jazz Masters* (1994). He is well known in Japan for his numerous published essays, the majority of which are surrealistic diaries of his tours.

SELECTED RECORDINGS

As unaccompanied soloist: *Sentimental* (1985, Kitty H33K20018)
As leader: *Concert in New Jazz* (1969, Union JUP4); *Clay* (1974, Enja 2052); *Frozen Days* (1974, Crown GGP6); *Chiasma* (1975, MPS 15458); *Arashi* (Storm; 1976, Frasco 7019–20); *First Time* (1979, Frasco 7029); *Jyugemu* (1981, Frasco 28PJ1005); *Live and then Picasso* (1982, Panja YF7070); *In Europe 1983* (1983, Panja YF7079); *Breath* (1984, Denon YF7091); *Crescendo* (1988, Kitty 20011); *Yosuke Yamashita Plays Gershwin* (1989, Kitty 20013); *Sakura* (1990, Pol. 1035); *Kurdish Dance* (1992, Pol. 1135); *Ways of Time* (1994, Pol. 1250); *Me wo miharu Canvas* (1997, Pol. 1360); *Fragments 1999* (1999, Pol. 1455)

BIBLIOGRAPHY

Feather–Gitler '70s
A.-R. Hardy: "Le piano terrible de Yamashita," *Jm*, no.253 (1977), 18 [incl. discography]
B. Doerschuk: "Conflict and Harmony at the Fringes of Jazz: Avant-garde Pianist Yosuke Yamashita," *Keyboard*, xi/8 (1985), 42

YOZO IWANAMI/KAZUNORI SUGIYAMA

Yancey, Jimmy [James Edwards] (*b* Chicago, 20 Feb 1898; *d* Chicago, 17 Sept 1951). Pianist. From the age of six he toured the USA and Europe as a singer and tap-dancer in vaudeville shows. He gave this up in 1915 to settle in Chicago, where he took up piano. From around 1919 he performed in public but also played baseball in the professional African-American leagues, and from 1925 until just before his death he was groundskeeper at Comiskey Park for the Chicago White Sox baseball team. He played informally at clubs and rent parties, helping to establish the style known as Boogie-woogie and influencing Meade "Lux" Lewis and Albert Ammons. He received some attention as a result of Lewis's recording of *Yancey Special* in 1936, and subsequently won a court battle over royalites to the piece, which Lewis had claimed as his own. In 1939–40 he issued a series of his own recordings, including many works composed by him years earlier. These highly regarded performances reveal a remarkable balance and expressivity despite Yancey's unassuming technique and limited harmonic and melodic resources. Unlike other boogie pianists, Yancey frequently altered his bass patterns in response to the right hand, producing shifting polyrhythms and varied bass lines. He suffered a stroke in 1941 but continued to play, even though the use of his left hand was restricted. In later years he continued to record, sometimes accompanying his own singing or that of his wife Mama [Estella] Yancey (*b* Cairo, IL, 1 Jan 1896; *d* Chicago, 4 May 1986), with whom, in 1948, he appeared at Carnegie Hall. He played at the Bee Hive Club in Chicago from *c*1948 to 1950. Transcriptions of his solos are included in the volume *Six Blues-root Pianists* by E. Kriss (New York and London, 1973).

See also Piano, §3.

SELECTED RECORDINGS

Yancey Stomp/State Street Special (1939, Vic. 26589); Slow and Easy Blues/The Mellow Blues (1939, Vic. 26591); Cryin' in my Sleep/Death Letter Blues (1940, Bb 8630); Yancey's Bugle Call/35th and Dearborn (1940, Vic. 27238); At the Window (1943, Session 10-005)

BIBLIOGRAPHY

G. Hoefer: "Yancey Had Three Loves: his Piano, Wife, White Sox," *DB*, xviii/22 (1951), 4 [incl. discography]
D. Stewart-Baxter: "Mama and Jimmy Yancey," *JJ*, viii/10 (1954), 3
F. S. Driggs: "Jimmy Yancey: a Permanent Requiem," *Record Research*, ii/1 (1956), 3
M. Harrison: "Boogie-woogie," *Jazz: New Perspectives on the History of Jazz*, ed. N. Hentoff and A. J. McCarthy (New York and Toronto, 1959/ *R*1974), 105-35

W. Russell: "Jimmy Yancey," *The Art of Jazz: Essays on the Nature and Development of Jazz*, ed. M. Williams (New York, 1959/*R*1979 as *The Art of Jazz: Ragtime to Bebop*), 98
M. Harrison: "*State Street Special*: an Analysis," *JR*, iii/3 (1960), 41
Y. Bruynoghe: "Jimmy Yancey," *Jazz Era: the 'Forties*, ed. S. Dance and others (London, 1961/*R*1985), 249
J. Holley: "Jimmy Yancey: a Discography," *Matrix*, no.95 (1971), 3; addns and corrections in no.105 (1974), 6
B. Rusch: "Mama Yancey: Interview," *Cadence*, iv/11 (1978), 3
S. Harris: *Blues Who's Who: a Biographical Dictionary of Blues Singers* (New Rochelle, NY, 1979/*R*1994)
K. Nowakowski: Liner notes, *Jimmy Yancey: Complete Recorded Works 1939–50 in Chronological Order* (Document 5041/42/43, 1991)
J. Bowers and W. Westcott: "Mama Yancey and the Revival Blues Tradition," *Black Music Research Journal*, xii/2 (1992), 171

J. BRADFORD ROBINSON/BK

Yancy, Youseff [Sidi ibn Mohammed Yusef el-Rashied] (*b* New Orleans, 19 Feb 1937). Trumpeter, flugelhorn player, percussionist, and composer of Muslim parentage. He played tuba and french horn in Kansas City and studied with Charlie Parker's teacher, Leo H. Davis, before winning a scholarship to Central Missouri State College; at after-hours sessions he learned advanced technique from older musicians. Following graduation he worked with Jay McShann and accompanied visiting artists, including Eddie "Cleanhead" Vinson and T-Bone Walker. He then worked with rhythm-and-blues singers and joined the touring bands of Fats Dennis, Chuck Jackson, Johnny Houston, and (from 1963) James Brown, accompanied Johnnie Taylor and Etta James, and settled in Florida as music director for Little Willie John. In 1965 Yancy moved to Boston and began a long association with Byard Lancaster. In New York he became involved in free-jazz circles and played with Noah Howard, Sun Ra, Sam Rivers, and Ted Daniel. He studied composition and electronic music and experimented with playing acoustic instruments through electronic manipulators. In the 1970s, with Archie Shepp, he accompanied his own electronically produced trumpet line, an early manifestation of this procedure in jazz. Yancy also revived the theremin, and in 1979 he played this instrument with Sunny Murray and in Ronald Shannon Jackson's first electric band.

SELECTED RECORDINGS

As sideman: S. Murray: *Apple Cores* (1978–9, Philly Jazz 1004); B. Lancaster: on *Documentation: the End of a Decade* (1979, Bellows 801), Blue Nature [theremin, trumpet], Rib Crib [flugelhorn], Sweetness [theremin]; James Baldwin, D. Linx, and Pierre van Dormael: on *A Lover's Question* (1986–7, Label Bleu 6607), A Lover's Question, pts i–ii [theremin, trumpet]

BIBLIOGRAPHY

V. Wilmer: *As Serious as your Life: the Story of the New Jazz* (London, 1977, rev. [3]/1987)

VAL WILMER

Yardbird. Nickname of CHARLIE PARKER.

Yarra Yarra Jazz Band. Australian New Orleans revival band. The trumpeter Maurie Garbutt (*b* Melbourne, 29 May 1941) formed a band in Melbourne in 1958 which took the name Yarra Yarra Jazz Band the following year, and, with numerous changes in membership, continued throughout the 1990s. The band toured Europe in 1969 and the USA in 1971, when guest soloists included Alvin Alcorn, Don Ewell, Wild Bill Davison, and Ken Colyer. From 1989 (and notably on a tour of Japan in 1994) Garbutt occasionally led an all-star lineup combining past and present members, some based in Sydney. The album *Yarra Yarra Reunion Band* (1994, Newmarket 1041) exemplifies the band's enduring qualities.

BIBLIOGRAPHY

B. Johnson: *The Oxford Companion to Australian Jazz* (Melbourne, Australia, 1987)
E. Brown: "25 Years of the Yarra Yarra Jazz Band, 1958–84" *Jazzline*, xvii/3 (1984), 21; xviii/1 (1985), 24

ADRIAN JACKSON

Yaw, Ralph (Percy) (*b* Enosburg Falls, VT, 22 Oct 1898; *d* California, 25 Apr 1963). Composer and arranger. After moving in 1919 to Los Angeles he played piano in bands that toured California and Arizona. From 1927 to 1934 he worked as a pianist and manager at the Coconut Grove in Bakersfield, California. During the following years he contributed arrangements to the bands led by Eddie Barefield (1934–5) and Cab Calloway (1935–9) and occasionally to those of Chick Webb, Isham Jones, Count Basie, and Les Brown. For Stan Kenton in the early 1940s he wrote arrangements and about 40 original compositions, including *Two Moods* (recorded in 1940 and first issued on *The Kenton Era, 1940–54*, Cap. WDX569); he also provided arrangements for Red Nichols and Johnny Richards. Yaw ended his career in jazz in 1947, when he began to play and write country music. His death date comes from the California death index, which does not give a last known residence or place of death. (*FeatherE*)

Yellin, Pete(r Michael) (*b* New York, 18 July 1939). Alto saxophonist and educator. His year of birth appears as 1941 in Feather and Gitler's *Encyclopedia of Jazz in the Seventies*, but in his questionnaire for this dictionary he gives 1939. His father, a staff pianist with NBC, played classical violin, and during his childhood Yellin unwillingly took lessons on this instrument for several years. Around 1957, while attending Denver University on a basketball scholarship, he heard a recording by Art Pepper and decided to pursue a career as a saxophonist. After returning to New York he studied music with his father, and shortly afterwards he had private clarinet lessons and attended the Juilliard School, where he learned saxophone; he also received private tuition on the instrument from John La Porta. In the 1960s he worked in the big bands of Lionel Hampton (1961–5) and Buddy Rich, with whom he recorded (1966) and performed at the Monterey Jazz Festival (1968). From 1965 to 1972 Yellin was a member of Tito Puente's large ensemble, and around 1970 he joined Joe Henderson's small group, with which he recorded the following year. At the Newport Jazz Festival New York he led his own small group in 1973 and performed with Puente in 1974. Later he worked with Jaki Byard (1975), Sam Jones's big band (recording in 1979), Bob Mintzer's big band (recording from 1980), Mario Bauzá (recording in 1993), Henderson's big band (recording in 1992, performing in 1994–5), and Puente again (1998), and appeared as a guest soloist with the Klüvers Big Band of Denmark. In addition he recorded as a leader in the early 1970s and the mid-1990s. Having gained an MFA from Brooklyn College he founded a jazz program at Long Island University in 1984, from which time his principal activities have been in conjunction with the university's programs. Yellin has published the instructional books *Jazz Saxophone*, i–iii (?New York, n.d.) and *Improvising Rock Sax* (New York, *c*1978). He also plays flute and clarinet.

SELECTED RECORDINGS

As leader: *It's the Right Thing* (1973, Mstr. 397); *Pete Yellin's European Explosion: Live!* (1994, Jazz4ever 4722)
As sideman with S. Jones: *Something New* (1979, Interplay 7726)

BIBLIOGRAPHY

Feather–Gitler '70s
W. R. Stokes: "Yellin's Improvisin'," *Washington Post* (7 March 1982)
<http://www.jazzcorner.com/yellin/index.html> (1999) [incl. discography]

GK

Yellowjackets. Jazz-fusion group. It was formed in 1980 from the ensemble which had accompanied the guitarist Robben Ford on his début album the previous year. After the group's eponymous first recording Ford left to pursue a solo career, although he continued to feature as a guest until the mid-1980s. The Yellowjackets' founding members, the pianist and synthesizer player Russell Ferrante and the electric bass guitarist Jimmy Haslip, have played alongside various drummers, initially Ricky Lawson, then from 1986 William Kennedy (*b* Oakland, CA, 9 May 1960), and from 1999 Peter Erskine. Following the departure of Ford the soloists were the alto saxophonist Marc Russo (1984–90) and the saxophonist and bass clarinetist Bob Mintzer, whose arrival (1990) coincided with an increase in the jazz content of the group's music. Its blend of jazz, pop, rhythm-and-blues, and world music attracted considerable commercial success.

SELECTED RECORDINGS

Mirage à trois (1983, WB 23813); *Samurai Samba* (*c*1984, WB 25204), incl. Samurai Samba; *Four Corners* (*c*1986, MCA 5994); *Politics* (*c*1988, MCA 6236); *Like a River* (1992, GRP 9689); *Club Nocturne* (1998, WB 9362-47031-2)

BIBLIOGRAPHY

S. Yanow: "The Yellowjackets' New Attitude," *DB*, liv/2 (1987), 23
J. Potter: "Up & Coming: the Yellowjackets' William Kennedy," *MD*, xiii/2 (1989), 100
R. Tolleson: "The Yellowjackets: Yellowjackets' New Buzz," *DB*, lvi/11 (1989), 20
D. Heckman: "Yellowjackets: a New Attitude," *JT*, xx/4 (1992), 26
F. Gonzalez: "From Pop-fusion to Jazz," *Boston Globe* (28 May 1993)
P. Myers: "Hearsay: Marc Russo," *JT*, xxiv/5 (1994), 14
S. Berg: "*P & K* Interview: Polish and Fusion," *Piano & Keyboard*, no.186 (1997), 26
P. Cole: "Yellowjackets: 'We Gave Up Writing for Airplay'," *DB*, lxiv/6 (1997), 27
L. Jurgeit: "Yellowjackets," *JP*, xlvi/6 (1997), 32
<http://www.yellowjackets.com> (1999) [incl. discography]

MARK GILBERT

Yerba Buena Jazz Band. Traditional jazz band formed in 1940 in Oakland, California, by LU WATTERS.

Yoder, Walt(er Eli) (*b* Hutchinson, KS, 21 April 1914; *d* California, 2 or 3 Dec 1978). Double bass player. He began playing piano at the age of ten but changed to double bass in his teens. After working with Joe Haymes and Tommy and Jimmy Dorsey he joined Isham Jones, with whom he also recorded between 1934 and 1936. When Jones's group disbanded Yoder became a member of the band formed from its members by Woody Herman; a fine example of his playing may be heard on Herman's *Yardbird Shuffle* (1941, Decca 4353). He was drafted into the army in 1943. Having moved to California he became a founding member of Herman's Second Herd, working with the band from mid-October 1947 to mid-March 1948, when he yielded the bass chair to Harry Babasin and took over as the group's road manager. Yoder performed regularly with Ben Pollack in the late 1940s and early 1950s and made three recordings with his group in 1949; he also worked with Bob Crosby and Russ Morgan and recorded later with Red Nichols (1963). In the 1970s he settled in Studio City, California, where he worked as a freelance musician. Chilton gives his death date as 2 December; the California death index, where his middle name is found, gives 3 December. (W. D. Clancy with A. C. Kenton: *Woody Herman: Chronicles of the Herds*, New York and elsewhere, 1995)

based on *ChiltonW*/BK

Yoshioka, Hideaki (*b* Nobeoka, Japan, 1 Feb 1960). Japanese pianist and leader. He started piano lessons at the age of eight, learned violin from the age of ten, and took up drums when he was 13. Having made his début at a hotel lounge in Miyazaki in 1978, he moved to Tokyo in 1981 and joined Isao Suzuki's group Soul Family. He then played in the bands led by the guitarist Yoshiyuki Miyanoue (from 1983), the tenor saxophonist Masato Imazu (from 1988), the trumpeter Hiroshi Murata and Yoichi Kobayashi (both 1986–9), and Eiji Kitamura (from 1997). In 1990 Yoshioka, who is known for his funky swing style, formed a trio, which was sometimes expanded to a quintet.

SELECTED RECORDINGS

(recorded for Fun House unless otherwise indicated)

As leader: *Here We Go* (1990, 1076); *Any Time, Any Way* (1991, 1131); *Always* (1992, 2021); *Strong Man* (1994, 2191); *Live at Browny* (1999, Browny 4001)
As sideman with M. Imazu: *Masato* (1989, 7126)

KAZUNORI SUGIYAMA

Yoshizawa, Motoharu (*b* Tokyo, 30 April 1931; *d* Tokyo, 12 Sept 1998). Japanese double bass player. A professional musician from 1959, he performed with the alto saxophonist Keiichiro Ebihara, Eiji Kitamura, and Shungo Sawada before joining Yosuke Yamashita's trio in 1965; in this last year he began to accompany poets, actors, and dancers. In 1968 he formed his own trio, with saxophone (Mototeru Takagi) and drums (Tatsuya Nakamura, replaced by Yoshisaburo Toyozumi), and in the late 1960s to early 1970s he worked with Masahiko Togashi, in whose quartet (alongside Takagi and Masayuki Takayanagi) he recorded in 1969. In 1970 he began to appear as an unaccompanied soloist, though he continued to work as a sideman and leader, playing, for example, with Takayanagi (in whose trio he recorded in that same year) and in a duo or trio with Kaoru Abe (recording in 1975), and appearing as a guest soloist with Toshinori Kondo and others in the cooperative group Evolution Ensemble Unity (*c*1976). Having recorded in Tokyo in groups led by Steve Lacy (1975), Milford Graves (1977), and Derek Bailey (1978), Yoshizawa became associated with a number of leading American and European avant-garde musicians; he appeared with Bailey, George Lewis (ii), Fred Frith, Julie Tippetts, Keith Tippett, Phil Wachsmann, and others during the Company week of late June to early July 1982, and he performed at other times with Lacy, Bailey, and Peter Brötzmann. He spent a year on a mountain, in meditation, in 1985, and then resumed a busy schedule; in 1989 he gave 95 concerts. Yoshizawa appeared in New York, organized Butch Morris's concerts in Japan in 1995, and, though seriously ill with cancer, toured the USA with Morris in March 1998.

SELECTED RECORDINGS

(recorded for PSF unless otherwise indicated)

As unaccompanied soloist: *Wareta kagami matawa kaseki no tori* (A cracked mirror or a fossilized bird) (1975, ALM 6); *Outfit: Bass Solo 2½ (1975, Trio PA7133); N.Y. Live (1990, 8); From the Faraway Near (1992, 21); Empty Hats (1994, 54)*

Duos: with M. Takagi: *Shinkai* (Abyss; 1969, 47); with Dave Burrell: *Dreams* (1973, Trio PA9010); with Y. Toyozumi: *Inland Fish* (1974, Trio PAP9020); with K. Abe: *Nord* (1975, ALM URCD5); with B. Phillips: *Uzu* (1996, 75)

As leader: *Live* (1992, 22)

As sideman: M. Togashi: *We Now Create* (1969, Vic. [Jap.] SMJX10065); M. Takayanagi: *Independence* (1970, Tei.–Union JUP3); M. Graves: *Meditation among Us* (1977, Kitty 1021); D. Bailey: *Duo and Trio Improvisations* (1978, Kitty 1034); B. Morris: *Conduction no.50: Environment* (1995, New World 80488-2)

BIBLIOGRAPHY

B. Rusch: "The Questionnaire," *Cadence*, xvi/3 (1990), 87

KAZUNORI SUGIYAMA

Young, Dave [David Anthony] (*b* Winnipeg, Canada, 29 Jan 1940). Canadian double bass player. He worked with Lenny Breau in Winnipeg, then studied at the Berklee School of Music, Boston (1962), and the Royal Conservatory of Music, Toronto (1967–9). He later played in both jazz and classical music settings, the latter including symphony orchestras during the mid-1970s in Edmonton, Hamilton, and Winnipeg. Based in Toronto from 1975, Young has been a favored accompanist of several pianists; he toured intermittently with Oscar Peterson (from 1975) and Oliver Jones (1988–99) and enjoyed lengthy associations with Gene DiNovi and Wray Downes. He has worked in clubs in Toronto with visiting musicians and has led his own small bands both locally and on several tours of Canada. His duo recordings in 1995 with 11 Canadian and American pianists (including Peterson, Kenny Barron, and Tommy Flanagan) reveal his impeccable technique and measured sense of swing, as well as a deft and uncommonly accurate arco style.

SELECTED RECORDINGS

Duos: with L. Breau: *Live at Bourbon St.* (1983, Guitarchives 0001); with K. Barron, C. Chestnut, T. Flanagan, Barry Harris, J. Hicks, O. Jones, E. Marsalis, Mulgrew Miller, O. Peterson, R. Rosnes, and C. Walton: *Piano–Bass Duets: The Complete Sessions* (1995, Justin Time 106–08)

As leader: *Fables and Dreams* (1993, Justin Time 53); *Inner Urge* (1997, Justin Time 110)

As sideman: O. Peterson: *Oscar Peterson Live* (1986, Pablo 2310940); O. Jones: *Cookin' at Sweet Basil* (1987, Justin Time 25); G. DiNovi: *The Gene DiNovi Trio Live at the Montreal Bistro* (1993, Can. 79726); W. Downes: *For You ... E* (1995, Justin Time 79)

BIBLIOGRAPHY

EMC2

B. King: "Dave Young: the Pursuit of Excellence," *Jazz Report*, ii/2 (1988), 1

B. Milkowski: "Hearsay: Dave Young: Northern Composure," *JT*, xxvi/3 (1996), 23

G. Sutherland: "Strings Attached," *Jazz Report*, ix/4 (1996), 16

M. Point: "Tradin' Fours: Art of the Duet," *DB*, lxiv/3 (1997), 41

MARK MILLER

Young, David A. [Dave] (*b* Nashville, 14 Jan 1912; *d* 25 Dec 1992). Tenor saxophonist. As a child he moved with his family to Chicago, where he studied music as a member of the *Chicago Defender* Newsboy Band under the direction of Major N. Clark-Smith. He played with various leaders from 1932, among them Frankie "Half Pint" Jaxon (1933), Carroll Dickerson (1936), and Roy Eldridge (1936–8). After working with Fletcher Henderson (*c* November 1938 – June 1939) he was a member of Horace Henderson's band (June 1939 – August 1940). In the early 1940s he played with Walter Fuller and Eldridge and recorded with Lucky Millinder and Sammy Price (1942). In 1944–5 he was in a navy band, and after his military service he led his own band in Chicago; it recorded with Dinah Washington (1947) and accompanied her at the Ritz Lounge. Young then ceased full-time performing and became an advertising executive for *The Defender*. The date of his death is taken from the social security death index, which gives his last-known residence as Chicago.

SELECTED RECORDINGS

As sideman: F. Jaxon: My Baby's Hot (1933, Voc. 2553); R. Eldridge: first issued on *Roy Eldridge Live! at the Three Deuces Club 1937* (1937, Jazz Archives 24), I never knew, Little Jazz, Swing is here; H. Henderson: Shufflin' Joe (1940, Voc. 5518); S. Price: Blow, Katy, Blow (1942, Decca 8624); D. Washington: There's got to be a change (1947, Mer. 8061)

BIBLIOGRAPHY

AllenH; *ChiltonW*

D. J. Travis: *An Autobiography of Black Jazz* (Chicago, 1983), 486

J. Evensmo: *History of Jazz Tenor Saxophone: Black Artists*, i: *1917–1934* (Oslo, 1996); ii: *1935–1939* (Oslo, 1997); iii: *1940–1944* (Oslo, 1997)

HOWARD RYE

Young, Eldee (*b* Chicago, 7 Jan 1936). Bass player and singer. He learned double bass at high school and later studied at the Chicago Conservatory. After working with King Kolax (1951) and with various blues singers, including Joe Turner (ii), T-Bone Walker, and Joe Williams (mid-1950s), from 1956 he played cello and double bass in Ramsey Lewis's trio, which made many recordings for Argo. Young also recorded as a sideman with Lorez Alexandria (1957) and James Moody (*Hey! It's Moody*, 1959, Argo 666) and as a leader (1961). In 1966 he and Redd Holt (Lewis's drummer) left Lewis and formed the soul band Young–Holt Unlimited, with which Young played both double bass and electric bass guitar. In 1990 Young–Holt Unlimited was a trio with the pianist Jeremy Monteiro. Young and Holt also appeared together in April 1984 in a reunion with Lewis at Blues Alley in Washington, DC. Although he often performed in Singapore and Hong Kong in the 1990s, Young remained based in Chicago, where he recorded as a singer accompanied by groups led by the drummer Ruben DeAndrea and the pianist Marshall Vente. (*FeatherE*; *Feather '60s*)

HOWARD RYE, BK

Young, John (Merritt) (*b* Little Rock, AR, 16 March 1922). Pianist. He grew up in Chicago and studied piano from the age of nine. After working with Andy Kirk (1942–5, 1946–7), the rhythm-and-blues tenor saxophonist Dick Davis (1947–50), and Eddie Chamblee (1951–5) he led his own trio in Chicago (from 1955). In addition he accompanied many important visiting musicians and recorded with, among others, T-Bone Walker (1955), Lorez Alexandria (1962–3), and Gene Ammons and Dexter Gordon (1970). In 1969 he began a long association with Von Freeman, with whom he recorded (1972, 1975, 1977) and toured Europe (1977). Young continued to perform as a leader into the 1990s, and in 1992 he recorded with Freeman and Yusef Lateef. He should not be confused with the more prominent blues musician Johnny (John O.) Young (1918–1974), who was based in Chicago from the 1940s.

SELECTED RECORDINGS

As leader: *Opus de funk* (1957, VJ 3060); *Serenata* (1959, Del. 403); *Themes and Things* (1961, Argo 692); *Think Young* (1987, Major Label 3707)

As sideman with V. Freeman: *Doin' it Right Now* (1972, Atl. 1628); *Serenade and Blues* (1975, Nessa 11); *Young and Foolish* (1977, Daybreak 002)

BIBLIOGRAPHY

Feather '60s

GK

Young, Larry(, Jr.) [Aziz, Khalid Yasin Abdul] (*b* Newark, NJ, 7 Oct 1940; *d* New York, 30 March 1978). Organist. Although his father was an organist, Young never took formal organ instruction and instead studied piano. He began his career in 1957 in Elizabeth, New Jersey, as a member of rhythm-and-blues groups, and in 1960 he recorded with Jimmy Forrest and as a leader. After recording the album *Groove Street* (1962) he played hard bop with Grant Green (recording in 1964–5), Joe Henderson, Lee Morgan, Donald Byrd, and Tommy Turrentine, and in 1964 toured Europe; the following year he won critical recognition for his album *Into Somethin'*. He performed with John Coltrane, recorded as the leader of a group that included Woody Shaw and Elvin Jones (1965) and as a sideman with Shaw (1966) and Buddy Tate (1967), toured in a trio with Byard Lancaster (1968), and played jazz-rock with Miles Davis (1969), John McLaughlin (1970), and Tony Williams's Lifetime (1969–71). Young is best known for his jazz playing, which combined aspects of hard bop, modal jazz, and free jazz after the style of Coltrane; his jazz-rock work became increasingly disappointing and unsuccessful. As a jazz organist he utilized a deep and dry sound, achieved by favoring the instrument's lowest drawbars (i.e., producing notes made of a greater than usual proportion of fundamental pitch in relation to their overtones) and also by turning off the rotation of the organ's Leslie speaker (which ordinarily produces a mechanical vibrato).

SELECTED RECORDINGS

As leader: *Groove Street* (1962, Prst. 7237); *Into Somethin'* (1964, BN 84187); *Unity* (1965, BN 84221); *Of Love and Peace* (1966, BN 84242); *Contrasts* (1967, BN 84266); *Mother Ship* (1969, BN LT1038)

As sideman: G. Green: *Talkin' About* (1964, BN 84183); *Street of Dreams* (1964, BN 84253); *I Want to Hold your Hand* (1964, BN 84202); M. Davis: *Bitches Brew* (1969, Col. GP26); J. McLaughlin: *Devotion* (1970, Douglas 4); T. Williams: *Turn it Over* (1970, Pol. 4021); *Ego* (1971, Pol. 4065)

BIBLIOGRAPHY

Feather '60s; *Feather–Gitler '70s*

A. Frenier: "Portrait de Larry Y," *Jm*, no.178 (1970), 18

L. K. McMillan, Jr.: "Larry Young: a Sound Apart," *JF* [intl edn], no.25 (1973), 43

M. Cuscuna: Liner notes, *The Complete Blue Note Recordings of Larry Young* (Mosaic 137, 1991)

GARY THEROUX/BK

Young, Lee [Leonidas Raymond] (*b* New Orleans, 7 March 1917). Drummer and leader, brother of Lester Young. With his older brother Lester and his sister Irma, he appeared with an orchestra led by his father, the pianist Willis Handy Young, performing for minstrel shows, at carnivals, and on the Theater Owners' Booking Association circuit; even before he was old enough to play in the band he participated as its "conductor," all the while studying soprano saxophone, trumpet, trombone, and piano. At some point (?1925) the family formed a short-lived band of seven saxophonists, comprising his father, his stepmother, his sister, himself and his brother, and two cousins. During this period of extensive touring, while Young was still a child, the family spent its winters in Memphis, in Warren, Arkansas (1923–4), and several times in Minneapolis, where he attended grammar school (mid-1920s). He became the drummer in his father's band around 1929, when it was based in Albuquerque, Phoenix, and from the end of the year, Los Angeles, where soon afterwards he began working as a singer at the Apex Club. Later he sang with the pianist Walter Johnson (1934) and played drums with Mutt Carey (1934), Buck Clayton (1936), Eddie Barefield (1936–7), and Fats Waller (at the Famous Door, 1937), with whom he also recorded.

Young was briefly the drummer in Nat "King" Cole's small group before leaving to join Les Hite (both *c*1937). He then worked for the Paramount and Metro–Goldwyn–Mayer studios and performed and recorded as a singer and drummer with Lionel Hampton (September 1940 – January 1941). In 1941 he recorded with Cole, and at Billy Berg's Club Capri in Hollywood he formed a group, the Esquires of Rhythm, which played material written by Billy Strayhorn and Gerald Wilson and which included Bumps Myers, Red Callender, and, from May of that year, his brother Lester; in December 1941 Lester, having finally obtained his local musicians' union card, became co-leader of the group, which broadcast from the club two nights per week on radio station KHJ. The following year Jimmie Rowles joined the Esquires of Rhythm, which in April, when Club Capri closed, transferred to Berg's Trouville Club; there the band accompanied Billie Holiday. Bumps Myers temporarily left in mid-year, but he returned in September when the group traveled east to perform in New York at the downtown location of Café Society, with Sir Charles Thompson replacing Rowles. Clyde Hart took Thompson's place in January 1943, but the following month the Esquires of Rhythm disbanded when the Youngs learned of their father's death and returned to Los Angeles.

In March 1943 Young led a group consisting of George Treadwell, Floyd Turnham, Myers, Irving Ashby, and Charles Mingus at Billy Berg's Swing Club, and in 1944 he recorded with Bunk Johnson's group in Los Angeles. While working for Columbia Pictures (1944–8) he made recordings with Dinah Washington (1945), Ivie Anderson (1946), and Mel Powell (1947, including *Anything Goes*, Cap. 15056), performed and recorded with Jazz at the Philharmonic (1944, 1946), Hampton (1947), and Benny Goodman (briefly in 1947), and continued to lead groups in Los Angeles; one such band, at the Downbeat, involved Russell Jacquet, Joe Liggins, Marshal Royal, and Lucky Thompson; another consisted of Art Pepper, Dexter Gordon, and Gerry Wiggins, with either Mingus or Joe Mondragon on double bass.

From June 1953 to March 1962 Young was a member of Cole's trio. Thereafter he worked as a producer and executive for Vee-Jay Records (1964–5), the Sunset label of United Artists, ABC and Dunhill Records (1969–77), and Motown Records (1979–83). Young's position in most of the bands with which he played was principally that of a timekeeper; he may be heard in this role on many albums, though most are unfortunately poorly recorded. His work is better represented on *Jazz at the Philharmonic*, ii, iii, xi (1946, Mer./Clef 35003, 35004, 35011).

Oral history material in *CLU, DSI* (JOHP), and *NjR* (JOHP).

SELECTED FILMS AND VIDEOS

I Dood It [By Hook and by Crook] (1943); Sarah Vaughan and Herb Jeffries/Kid Ory and his Creole Jazz Band/Mahogany Magic (1950); St. Louis Blues (1958)

BIBLIOGRAPHY

ChiltonW; *FeatherE*; *Feather '60s*

V. Wilmer: "The Lee Young Story," *JJ*, xiv/1 (1961), 3

L. Porter: *Lester Young* (Boston and London, 1985)

F. Büchmann-Møller: *You Just Fight for your Life: the Story of Lester Young* (New York, Westport, CT, and London, 1990)

J. L. Anderson: "Lee and Lester, pt 1: Marching to a Different Drummer," *MR*, xx/2 (1992), 1

C. Bryant and others, eds.: *Central Avenue Sounds: Jazz in Los Angeles* (Berkeley, CA, Los Angeles, and London, 1998), 51

BK

Lester Young

Young, Lester (Willis) [Pres, Prez] (*b* Woodville, MS, 27 Aug 1909; *d* New York, 15 March 1959). Tenor saxophonist and leader, brother of Lee Young.

1. Life 2. Music.

1. Life. Young was the oldest of three children and grew up in the vicinity of New Orleans. His father, Willis Handy Young, was a versatile musician who taught all his children instruments and eventually formed a family band. In 1919 his parents separated. The children stayed with their father, and from about 1920 they toured with carnivals and other shows, and spent the winters in Minneapolis. Young studied violin, trumpet, and drums, settling on alto saxophone by about the age of 13. After one of many disputes with his father he left the family band at the end of 1927. He spent the following year touring with Art Bronson's Bostonians. Remembrances of his switching to tenor saxophone during these years are inconsistent; he doubled on this instrument, as well as soprano, C-melody, and baritone saxophones at various times during the 1920s, but evidently he made the alto his principal instrument until late in the decade.

Young rejoined his family in New Mexico during 1929, but when they moved to California he returned to Minneapolis, where during 1930 he played briefly with Walter Page's Blue Devils and again with Bronson, and during 1931 with Eddie Barefield and various leaders at the Nest Club. Early in 1932 he joined the Thirteen Original Blue Devils, and while on tour in Oklahoma City met Charlie Christian. He probably also worked briefly with King Oliver in 1932. When the Blue Devils disbanded in the middle of 1933, Young made Kansas City his base, and played with Oliver, the tenor saxophonist Clarence Love, the Bennie Moten–George E. Lee Band, and, on one night in December, Fletcher Henderson, then on tour with his star saxophonist, Coleman Hawkins; that night, and into the next morning, he reportedly outplayed Hawkins at a legendary jam session involving Ben Webster, Dick Wilson, Herschel Evans, and other tenor saxophonists based in Kansas City.

Early in 1934 Young joined Count Basie, beginning an association that eventually led to national recognition. He left Basie at the end of March as a provisional replacement for Hawkins in Henderson's band. Henderson's musicians rejected Young's very different approach to the saxophone, however, and he left after a few months. He joined Andy Kirk en route back to Kansas City, then Boyd Atkins and the trumpet player Rook Ganz in Minnesota, and for the next year performed mostly in these two areas on a freelance basis. By 1936 Young had resumed his association with Basie, whose band was at the Reno Club in Kansas City. He temporarily left to play with Louis Metcalf at the Renaissance Casino in New York in October of that year, but then rejoined Basie in Kansas City. They departed immediately. On the way to New York, in the course of a month-long stand at the Grand Terrace, Chicago, in November 1936, Young made his first recordings with a small group from Basie's band. His solos on *Lady be Good* and *Shoe Shine Boy* were immediately regarded by musicians, many of whom learned them note for note. During the next few years, as Basie's band became more famous, Young was prominently featured on its recordings and broadcasts. Although he received mixed reviews from the critical establishment, the younger generation of musicians, including Dexter Gordon, Illinois Jacquet, and others, were enthusiastic about his music. His small-group performances, particularly *Lester leaps in* (1939) and his many recordings with Billie Holiday, were especially influential.

Young left Basie in December 1940 to form his own sextet with Shad Collins, Clyde Hart, John Collins, the double bass player Nick Fenton, and Doc West; they performed at Kelly's Stable, New York, early in 1941. In May he moved to Los Angeles to lead a band with his brother Lee, which went to New York's Café Society in September 1942; among their notable sidemen were Bumps Myers, Red Callender, and a number of pianists: Jimmie Rowles, Charles Thompson (whom at this point Young nicknamed "Sir"), and Hart. The group disbanded early the next year when the Youngs' father died; Lee returned to Los Angeles and Lester to New York, where he played as a freelance and then left to tour with Al Sears's USO big band (April – 1 October 1943). Back in New York once again, he deputized for Don Byas in Basie's band for a week and preceded Byas in the incipient bop band led by Dizzy Gillespie and Oscar Pettiford at the Onyx. By December 1943 he had rejoined Basie, and it was during this second tenure with the band that Young came to the notice of the general public. In 1944 he won first place in the *Down Beat* poll for tenor saxophonists, the first of many such honors. He also became the favorite of a new generation of jazz musicians, among them John Coltrane, Sonny Rollins, and Stan Getz. He was prominently featured in the short film *Jammin' the Blues*.

On 30 September 1944 Young was drafted into the army, which he found a nightmarish experience. Cut off from his musical outlets, he was discovered using drugs and was court-martialed the following February. After serving several months in detention barracks in Georgia he was released at the end of 1945 and resumed recording and performing in Los Angeles. At his first recording session he produced a masterpiece, *These Foolish Things*.

Beginning in 1946 Young spent part of almost every year playing with Jazz at the Philharmonic, touring the rest of the time with his own small groups. From 1947 to 1949 his style showed the influence of some of the young bop musicians in his groups (including Sadik Hakim – then still known as Argonne Thornton – and Roy Haynes) in the occasional use of double-time and in the selection of repertory. The trumpeters Jesse Drakes and Tony Fruscella, the pianists Junior Mance, Kenny Drew, John Lewis, Wynton Kelly, Gil Coggins, Horace Silver, and Gildo Mahones, the double bass players Joe Shulman, Aaron Bell, and Gene Ramey, and the drummers Haynes, Jo Jones, Connie Kay, and Lee Abrams were among the members of his small groups between 1949 and 1955; during these years he routinely rejoined JATP, with which he made his first European tours. He continued to develop and modify his approach successfully except when he was drinking, but by this time his reliance on alcohol was becoming a health problem. From about 1953 until his death Young's recordings were noticeably less consistent, yet he was still able to produce some of his best work on concert recordings such as *Prez in Europe* (1956). He made guest appearances with Basie's band in 1952–4 and again at the Newport Jazz Festival in 1957, but he never rejoined as a regular member. He became increasingly dependent on alcohol, and on several occasions he was hospitalized. During his final years he usually led groups on an ad hoc basis, drawing from a large pool of leading swing and bop musicians, although Willie Jones served as his regular drummer from December 1956 until his death. In January 1959 he began an engagement at the Blue Note club in Paris. He made his last recordings there in March, then became severely ill and returned to New York, where he died shortly afterwards.

2. Music. Young was one of the most influential musicians in jazz. His style was viewed as revolutionary when he was first recorded during the late 1930s, and it was a primary force in the development of modern jazz in general and the music of Charlie Parker in particular (*see* Saxophone, §2). The only influences Young ever admitted to were two white saxophonists of the 1920s, Jimmy Dorsey and Frankie Trumbauer, especially the latter. Both possessed exceptional classical technique and a light, dry sound. Dorsey was fond of timbral effects achieved through low honks and alternative fingerings, and Young carried these further. From Trumbauer he

Ex.1 From *Lady be Good* (1936, Voc. 3459); transcr. L. Porter

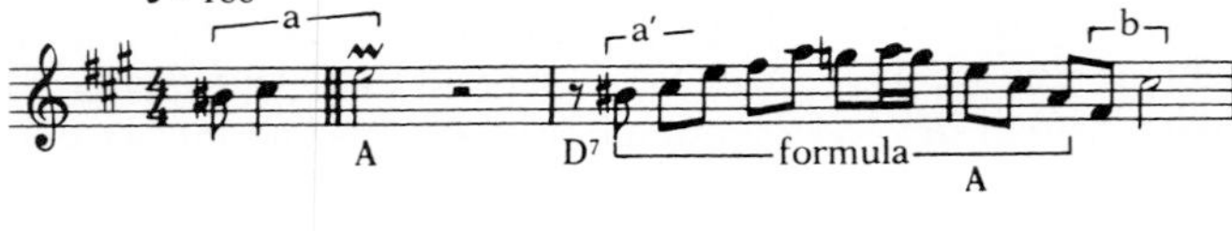

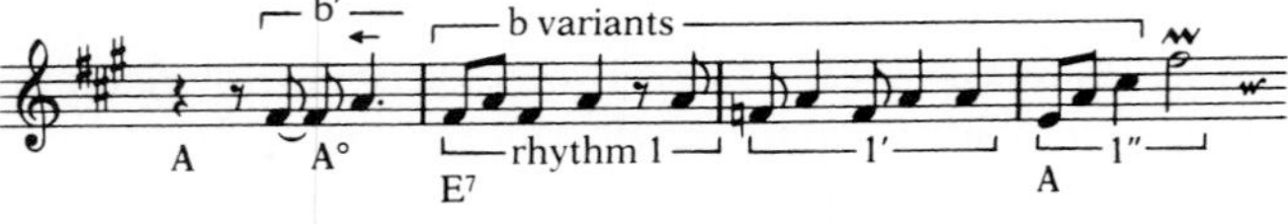

← = note slightly anticipated

= pronounced vibrato

adopted a strong sense of musical form, which was apparent even in his earliest recordings, such as *Lady be Good* (ex.1) with its short motivic and rhythmic constructions, each building upon its predecessor. Young's beautiful and delicate sound must be heard in order to appreciate fully the impact of this solo.

Young's work of the 1940s and 1950s was different in style from that of his early years, but not necessarily inferior, as many critics have claimed. His tone was much heavier and his vibrato wider. He was more overtly emotional and filled his solos with wails, honks, and blue notes. He drew more heavily on a small repertory of formulas, especially simple ones such as the arpeggiation of the tonic triad in first inversion at phrase endings. His solos also contained astonishing leaps and bold contrasts (ex.2), relying more

Ex.2 From *After Theatre Jump* (1944, Key. 1302); transcr. L. Porter

→ = note slightly delayed

on the alternation of repetition and surprise than on motivic development. Significantly, musicians have praised his recordings of the 1940s alongside his early ones, indicating a clear appreciation of their musical value.

Young's impact on the course of jazz was profound. His superb melodic gift and logical phrasing were the envy of musicians on all instruments, and his long, flowing lines set the standard for all modern jazz. His personal formulas are now the common property of all jazz musicians, and recur in countless jazz compositions and improvisations. Sadly, the public, while familiar with Young's name, has little awareness of his music and its role in jazz history. The feature film *Round Midnight* (1986), which was dedicated to Young and Bud Powell, was largely based on Young's life story.

Oral history material in *NjR*.

SELECTED RECORDINGS

As leader: with N. Cole: Indiana/Body and Soul (1942, Philo 1000); Sometimes I'm Happy (1943, Key. 604); These Foolish Things (1945, Philo/Ala. 124); with B. Rich: I cover the waterfront/Somebody loves me (1945, Clef 11048), I found a new baby (1945, Clef 11049); Jumpin' with Symphony Sid (1947, Ala. 163); *The Lester Young Story* (1949–56, Verve 8308), incl. [with T. Wilson:] Pres Returns; *Prez in Europe* (1956, Onyx 218), incl. Lester leaps in

As sideman: Jones–Smith, Inc. [C. Basie]: Shoe Shine Boy (1936, Voc. 3441); Lady be Good (1936, Voc. 3459); C. Basie: *Count Basie and his Orchestra, 1938* (1938, Fanfare 18), incl. Flat Foot Floogie, Lady be Good; Jumpin' at the Woodside (1938, Decca 2212); Kansas City Six: Them There Eyes (1938, Com. 511); C. Basie: Taxi War Dance (1939, Voc. 4748); Clap hands, here comes Charlie (1939, Voc. 5085); Lester leaps in (1939, Voc. 5118); Tickle Toe (1940, Col. 35521); Easy does it (1940, Col. 35448); B. Goodman: Ad-lib Blues, Lester's Dream (both 1940), first issued on C. Christian and L. Young: *Together Again* (1940–41, Jazz Archives 6); B. Holiday: All of me (1941, OK 6214); Kansas City Seven: After Theatre Jump (1944, Key. 1302)

SELECTED FILMS AND VIDEOS

Jammin' the Blues (1944); The Sound of Jazz (1957); Song of the Spirit: the Story of Lester Young (1988); Norman Granz présente improvisation: documents exceptionnels et inédits des plus grands noms de jazz (n.d.)

TRANSCRIPTIONS

B. Cash: *Prez: 25 of Prez's Famous Tenor Saxophone Recordings* (Carnaby, England, n.d.)

R. Luckey: *Lester Young Solos* (Lafayette, LA, 1994)

F. Hess: *Prez: Lester Young's Greatest Transcribed Solos* (Lebanon, IN, *c*1995)

BIBLIOGRAPHY

AllenH; McCarthyB; SchullerS; SheridanCB; WrightK
P. Harris: "Pres Talks about Himself, Copycats," *DB*, xvi/8 (1949), 15
R. Russell: "Be-Bop Reed Instrumentation, 1: the Parent Style, Lester Young," *Record Changer*, viii/4 (1949), 6
L. Feather: "Here's Pres!," *MM* (15 July 1950), 3
——: "Pres Digs Every Kind of Music," *DB*, xviii/22 (1951), 13
N. Hentoff: "Pres," *DB*, xxiii/5 (1956), 9
JM, ii/10 (1956) [special issue]
N. Hentoff: "Lester Young," *The Jazz Makers*, ed. N. Shapiro and N. Hentoff (New York, 1957/*R*1979 as *The Jazz Makers: Essays on the Greats of Jazz*), 243–75
D. Morgenstern: "Lester Leaps In," *JJ*, xi/8 (1958), 1
W. Burckhardt and J. Gerth: *Lester Young: ein Porträt* (Wetzlar, Germany, 1959)
L. Gottlieb: "Why so Sad, Pres?," *Jazz: a Quarterly of American Music*, no.3 (1959), 185
H. P[anassié]: "Lester Young," *BHcF*, no.87 (1959), 4
F. Postif: "Lester: Paris, 1959," *JR*, ii/8 (1959), 6; repr. in *Jazz Panorama*, ed. M. Williams (New York and London, 1962/*R*1979), 139; new transcr., *Jh*, no.362 (1979), 18; no.363 (1979), 34
V. Franchini: *Lester Young* (Milan, 1961)
B. James: *Essays on Jazz* (London, 1961/*R*1990), 61
B. Green: *The Reluctant Art: Five Studies in the Growth of Jazz* (London, 1962, enlarged 2/1991)
D. Heckman: "Pres and Hawk: Saxophone Fountainheads," *DB*, xxx/1 (1963), 20
J. G. Jepsen: *A Discography of Lester Young* (Copenhagen, 1968)
M. Williams: *The Jazz Tradition* (New York, 1970, rev. 2/1983)
R. Blesh: *Combo, USA: Eight Lives in Jazz* (Philadelphia and London, 1971), 85
J. Burns: "Lester Young: the Postwar Years," *J&B*, i/4 (1971), 4
L. Feather: *From Satchmo to Miles* (New York, 1972/*R*1987), 115
J. Hammond and H. Woodfin: "Two Views of Lester Young: Recollections and Analysis," *J&B*, iii/5 (1973), 8
E. Lambert: "The Alternative Lester Young," *JJ*, xxvi/2 (1973), 22
G. Colombé: "Time and the Tenor: Lester Young in the Fifties," *Into Jazz*, i/3 (1974), 32
H. Schröder: [discography], *Micrography*, no.41 (1976), 21; no.42 (1976), 21; no.44 (1977), 19; no.48 (1977), 16
J. Evensmo: *The Tenor Saxophone and Clarinet of Lester Young, 1936–1942* (n.p. [Oslo], n.d. [?1977], rev. [2]/n.d. [?1983] as *The Tenor Saxophone and Clarinet of Lester Young, 1936–1949*) [discography]
S. Dance: *The World of Count Basie* (New York and London, 1980)
J. McDonough: Liner notes, *Lester Young* (TL J13, 1980)
L. Gushee: "Lester Young's 'Shoeshine Boy'," *IMSCR*, xii *Berkeley 1977*, ed. D. Heartz and B. Wade (Basel, 1981), 151
R. A. Luckey: *A Study of Lester Young and his Influence on his Contemporaries* (diss., U. of Pittsburgh, 1981)
H. Lyttelton: *The Best of Jazz*, ii: *Enter the Giants, 1931–1944* (London, 1981), 171
L. Porter: "Lester Leaps In: the Early Style of Lester Young," *Black Perspective in Music*, ix (1981), 3
B. Cash: *An Analysis of the Improvisation Technique of Lester Willis Young, 1936–1942* (thesis, U. of Hull, England, 1982)
W. Balliett: "Pres," *Jelly Roll, Jabbo and Fats* (New York, and Oxford, England, 1983), 119
D. H. Daniels: "History, Racism, and Jazz: the Case of Lester Young," *Jf*, xvi (1984), 87
D. Gelly: *Lester Young* (Tunbridge Wells, England, 1984)
D. H. Daniels: "Lester Young: Master of Jive," *American Music*, iii (1985), 313
L. Porter: *Lester Young* (Boston and London, 1985)
D. H. Daniels: "Big Top Blues: Jazz-minstrel Bands and the Young Family Tradition," *Jf*, xviii (1986), 133
L. Delannoy: *Lester Young, profession: président* (Paris, 1987; Eng. trans., 1993, as *Pres: the Story of Lester Young*) [incl. discography by D. Richard]
D. H. Daniels: "Goodbye Pork Pie Hat: Lester Young as a Spiritual Figure," *ARJS*, iv (1988), 161
F. Postif: *Les grandes interviews de Jazz hot* (Paris, 1989)
F. Büchmann-Møller: *You Just Fight for your Life: the Story of Lester Young* (New York, Westport, CT, and London, 1990)
——: *You Got to Be Original Man!: the Music of Lester Young* (New York, Westport, CT, and London, 1990)
L. Porter, ed.: *A Lester Young Reader* (Washington, DC, and London, 1991)
A. Knight: "*Jammin' the Blues*, or the Sight of Jazz, 1944," *Representing Jazz*, ed K. Gabbard (Durham, NC, and London, 1995), 11
P. Benkimoun: *Lester Young* (Paris, 1997)
J. Evensmo: *History of Jazz Tenor Saxophone: Black Artists*, i: *1917–1934* (Oslo, 1996); ii: *1935–1939* (Oslo, 1997)

LEWIS PORTER/BK

Young, Snooky [Snookie; Eugene Edward] (*b* Dayton, OH, 3 Feb 1919). Trumpeter. He first played zither, and after receiving lessons on trumpet (from around the age of six) he toured the South with his parents and four siblings as a member of a family band. While in high school he played with the Wilberforce Collegians band, and later he worked with the bandleader Chick Carter, whose group included Gerald Wilson. From 1939 to 1942 Young was lead trumpeter and soloist in Jimmie Lunceford's orchestra (for illustration *see* Lunceford, jimmie), and he was featured with the band on the soundtrack for the short film *Blues in the Night* (1941). He deputized for Buck Clayton (who was ill) in Count Basie's orchestra in Dayton and on tour (June 1942), then toured with Lionel Hampton (1942–3) and played in California with the bands of Les Hite and Benny Carter (in both of which Wilson was again among his fellow sidemen). From June to December 1943 he spent another period with Basie (appearing in the film *Choo Choo Swing* [*Band Parade*], 1943) before joining Wilson's own big band, but then returned to Hampton. He worked with Basie again from June 1945 to January 1948, during which period he recorded as a soloist in a small group alongside Lester Young accompanying Helen Humes (1945), and from September 1957 to May 1962, when, with Wendell Culley and Thad Jones, he was a member of a notable trumpet section; during the intervening years he led his own group in Dayton, with Booty Wood and Slam Stewart among his sidemen.

In 1962 Young became a studio trumpeter for NBC. He was a founding member in 1966 of the Thad Jones–Mel Lewis Orchestra and remained with that band until 1972, when he moved to Los Angeles with "The Tonight Show" orchestra. On the West Coast he played with the Capp–Pierce Juggernaut and the orchestras of Wilson and Louie Bellson, toured with the Basie Alumni (1981), and later began working with the Clayton–Hamilton Orchestra and with Jeannie and Jimmy Cheatham; he also co-led a quintet with Bob Cooper which recorded in 1985. In 1992 the comedian Johnny Carson left "The Tonight Show," and its house orchestra, under Doc Severinsen, disbanded, ending Young's lengthy engagement; later that same year he performed at the Colorado Jazz Party. Thereafter, despite his advancing age, Young retained the strength to play high-pitched trumpet melodies, and he remained busy in the Los Angeles area, mainly playing in big bands, including those of Clayton and Hamilton and Wilson, and in Frank Capp's continuation (following Nat Pierce's death) of the Juggernaut, but also with the Cheathams' small group.

Although he has usually been employed as a lead trumpeter, Young is an accomplished improviser, whether playing a full-bodied, relaxed, plunger-muted melody or scampering around in the high register. Highlights from early in his career include a gorgeous blues solo recorded immediately upon joining Lunceford, *Uptown Blues* (1939), and the retrospectively titled *Riffin' without Helen* (1945), perhaps a one-off performance, on which he showed a considerable fondness for the newly emerging bop trumpet style – rather surprising in light of his otherwise strong allegiance to swing. From the mid-1980s his affiliation with the Cheathams has afforded him consistent opportunities to show off his talents as a soloist in the recording studios.

Video oral history material in *NCH* (HCJA).

SELECTED RECORDINGS

As leader: on *The Boys from Dayton* (1971, MJR 8130), L'il Darlin', Hard Boiled Rock; with M. Royal: *Snooky's and Marshall's Album* (1978, Conc.

55); *Horn of Plenty* (1979, Conc. 91); with B. Cooper: *In a Mellotone* (1985, Cont. 14017)

As sideman with J. and J. Cheatham (all recorded for Concord): *Sweet Baby Blues* (1984, 258); *Midnight Mama* (1986, 297); *Homeward Bound* (1987, 4321); *Back to the Neighborhood* (1988, 4373); *Luv in the Afternoon* (1990, 4429); *Basket Full of Blues* (1991, 4501); *Blues and the Boogie Masters* (1993, 4579); on *Gud Nuz Blues* (1995, 4690), Coal Yard and Ice House Blues, Fine and Mellow, Gud Nuz Bluz

As sideman with others: J. Lunceford: Uptown Blues (1939, Voc. 5362); Lunceford Special (1939, Voc. 5326); H. Humes: Voo-it (1945, Philo 121); [no leader:] first issued on *The Complete Aladdin Recordings of Lester Young* (1942, 1945–7, BN 32787-2), Riffin' without Helen; H. Humes: Pleasing Man Blues (1945, Philo 125); See See Rider (1945, Philo 126); C. Basie: *Chairman of the Board* (1959, Roul. 52032), incl. Who Me?; L. Bellson: *The Louie Bellson Explosion* (1975, Pablo 2310755), incl. Movin' on; T. Newsom: *Tommy Newsom & His T.V. Jazz Stars* (1990, Laserlight 15331); G. Wilson: on *State Street Sweet* (*c*1994, MAMA Foundation 1010), Jammin' in C

BIBLIOGRAPHY

ChiltonW; *McCarthyB*; *SheridanCB*; *SchullerS*

S. Dance: "Snooky Young," *JJ*, xv/4 (1962), 8; repr. in *The World of Count Basie* (New York and London, 1980), 137

E. Townley: "Horn of Plenty: Snooky Young," *JJI*, xxxv/11 (1982), 19

B. Rusch: "Snooky Young: Interview," *Cadence*, xii/7 (1986), 5

J. Bradley: "Snooky Young Plays Gibson Gig," *Denver Post* (20 Nov 1992)

BK

Young, Trummy [James Osborne] (*b* Savannah, GA, 12 Jan 1912; *d* San Jose, CA, 10 Sept 1984). Trombonist and singer. He first played trumpet but soon took up trombone; he made his professional début in Washington, DC, where he played from 1928 with the pianist Booker Coleman and his Hot Chocolates. He acquired his nickname while in a band led by the drummer Tommy Myles. In late 1933 he followed Myles's arranger, Jimmy Mundy, into Earl Hines's orchestra. Although he played on some 40 commercial recordings with Hines's band, Young contributed solos to only a small number; his style was in the process of formulation at this period, and his work displays an indication of his relaxed and individual approach to timing as well as his formidable command of the trombone's upper register. When Hines was not working, Young played with Albert Ammons, Roy Eldridge, and others. He finally left Hines in August 1937 and developed his talents fully while a member of Jimmie Lunceford's orchestra (September 1937 – March 1943); he obtained a full and rounded tone throughout the range of the instrument and perfected his "trumpet style," which owed something to the influence of Jimmy Harrison and Louis Armstrong. Lunceford's arranger, Sy Oliver, wrote several pieces to display his gifts as a soloist. Young was also one of the band's singers; he had a rather high-pitched and distinctive voice and was frequently called on to perform "jive" and somewhat comic songs, such as *Margie*.

After leaving Lunceford, Young spent a brief period with Charlie Barnet (March 1943). He led his own band (with Lester Young as co-leader in spring 1943) and worked with Boyd Raeburn, Tiny Grimes, Eldridge, and Claude Hopkins (all 1944), as well as with Johnny Bothwell (January 1945) and Benny Goodman (February–August 1945). In 1945 he made recordings with Dizzy Gillespie's sextet, including *Good Bait*. Having played further with Grimes (May 1946) and Hopkins (briefly in 1947), he toured with Jazz at the Philharmonic (1946, 1947) and then moved to Hawaii. In September 1952 he joined Armstrong's All Stars, a step that was seen as controversial at the time, since the dixieland-oriented repertory of the group was regarded by some as too restrictive for his improvisational and harmonic ideas. Young used the affiliation as an opportunity to develop the role of the trombone in traditional jazz, and his range and power made him an ideal partner for Armstrong. His contribution to the ensemble (which represented a considerable simplification of his earlier style) was less of a solo line and more a modification of the tailgate style with a sophisticated harmonic and rhythmic content, and was far more balanced than that of his predecessor, Jack Teagarden. On opening statements of a theme Young often played in parallel harmony to Armstrong's melody, throwing the clarinet part into relief against the brass, before adopting a mobile contrapuntal line and syncopated eighth-notes for subsequent choruses. His own solos were characterized by a biting attack and great power as well as the use of vocal tones. Young left Armstrong on 1 January 1964 and returned to Hawaii, though he continued to tour as a soloist and work with a number of bandleaders in the last two decades of his life, notably with Hines in 1971, with Chris Barber in Europe and, in the early 1980s, at the Grande Parade du Jazz in Nice, France.

Oral history material in *NjR* (JOHP).

For illustrations *see* Lunceford, Jimmie, and Pettiford, Oscar.

SELECTED RECORDINGS

As sideman: J. Lunceford: Margie (1938, Decca 1617); Tain't what you do (1939, Voc. 4582); I got it (1940, Col. 35510); D. Gillespie: Good Bait (1945, Manor 1042); L. Armstrong: on *The Best of Louis Armstrong's All Stars in Concert* (1953, Rarities 18–19), Margie; *Louis Armstrong Plays W. C. Handy* (1954, Col. CL591); *Satch Plays Fats* (1955, Col. CL708); on *Louis Armstrong at Pasadena* (1956, GNP 11001), My bucket's got a hole in it; L. Armstrong and D. Ellington: *The Great Reunion* (1961, Roul. 52103), incl. The Beautiful Americans

SELECTED FILMS AND VIDEOS

Blues in the Night [Hot Nocturne] (1941); Jam Session (1944); Satchmo the Great [Saga of Satchmo] (1956); The Beat Generation (1958); Die Nacht vor der Premiere (1959); Jazz on a Summer's Day (1960); Louis Armstrong and the All Stars (1961); Black Music in America: From Then Til Now (1971); Louis Armstrong (1971); The Great Rocky Mountain Jazz Party (1977)

BIBLIOGRAPHY

ChiltonW; *ConnorBG*; *McCarthyB*; *SchullerS*

A. J. McCarthy: "Trummy Young," *JM*, i/3 (1955), 10

M. Jones: "Young Man with an Axe," *MM*, xxxi (5 May 1956), 3; (12 May 1956), 6; (19 May 1956), 6

B. Esposito: "Trummy Young, Trombonist," *JJ*, xxiii/7 (1970), 20

L. Feather: "Trummy's Happy in Honolulu," *MM* (19 Dec 1970), 12

S. Dance: *The World of Earl Hines* (New York, 1977), 220

C. E. Martin: "Trummy Young: an Unfinished Story," *SL*, xxx (1978), summer, 30

M. A. Bloom: "Trummy Young: Interview," *Cadence*, vii/5 (1981), 5

J. Reldy: "En bavardant avec Trummy," *BHcF*, no.288 (1981), 5

M. L. Hester: "Trummy," *MR*, xv/2 (1987), 1

A. Shipton: *Groovin' High: the Life of Dizzy Gillespie* (New York, and Oxford, England, 1999)

ALYN SHIPTON

Young Tuxedo Brass Band. New Orleans group. It was founded in 1938 by John Casimir, who served as leader until his death early in 1963, and became one of the most important groups in the resuscitation of the brass-band tradition in New Orleans after World War II. Numbering between nine and 11 players, and consisting typically of two trumpets, two trombones, two reed players, sousaphone, snare drum, and bass drum, it performed in the film *Cinerama Holiday* (1953) and recorded in 1958 (*New Orleans Joys*, Atl. 1297), the latter involving such musicians as the trumpeters Andy Anderson (i) and John Brunious, the trombonists Clement Tervalon, Eddie Pierson, and Jim Robinson, Herman Sherman, Andrew Morgan, Paul Barbarin, and the bass drummer Emile Knox. Casimir's cousin, the alto saxophonist Wilbert Tilman, a founding member of the band, changed from saxophone to sousaphone around 1945 and took over the group's leadership in 1963, but ill-health forced his retirement in August the following year; leadership then transferred to Morgan, until his death in 1972, to Sherman, until his death in 1984, and to Gregg Stafford. Under Sherman's leadership the band recorded *Jazz Continues* (1983, 504 10), with Stafford, Michael White (ii), and the drummer Charles Barbarin. The band may be seen in the Canadian film documentary *Liberty Street Blues* (1988).

BIBLIOGRAPHY

G. Giddins: *Rhythm-a-ning: Jazz Tradition and Innovation in the '80s* (New York, and Oxford, England, 1985), 183

C. Stafford: "Gang Meeting at the Mediterannean Café," *SL*, xlii (1990), winter, 18

R. H. Knowles: *Fallen Heroes: a History of New Orleans Brass Bands* (New Orleans, 1996), 242

WILLIAM J. SCHAFER/BK

Ysaguirre, Bob [Robert; Clarence (Fitzroy)] (*b* Belize, British Honduras [now Belize City, Belize], 22 Feb 1897; *d* New York, 27 March 1982). Double bass and tuba player. He began playing tuba at the age of 18, and after performing in a military band (1917–19) he moved to New Orleans, where he worked with Amos White (1922). He made a number of recordings as a tuba player with A. J. Piron's orchestra in New York (1923–5), then was a member of Elmer Snowden's band (1925–6) and the Plantation Orchestra, led by the violinist Alex Jackson (1926–9). In 1927 he recorded with Snowden's band under the leadership of the trombonist Te Roy Williams. He also performed briefly with Fletcher Henderson (from September 1929 until about March 1930) and Horace Henderson (from late 1930 into 1931). In 1931 he began a long association with Don Redman, with whom he made many recordings on tuba and double bass; he may be seen with Redman's band in the short film *Don Redman and his Orchestra* (1934). In the late 1930s he used the name Clarence Fitzroy Ysaguirre. He left Redman in 1940 and continued to play in and around New York until the late 1960s, but worked mainly outside music. His strong sense of rhythm is clearly displayed in his performances on both tuba and double bass.

SELECTED RECORDINGS

As sideman on tuba: A. J. Piron: Lou'siana Swing/Sittin' on the Curbstone Blues (1924, OK 40189); A. Jackson: I call you sugar/Missouri Squabble (1927, Gen. 6296); T. R. Williams: Oh Malinda/Lindbergh Hop (1927, Har. 439)

As sideman on double bass with D. Redman: Shakin' the African (1931, Bruns. 6211); I heard (1931, Bruns. 6233); I got rhythm (1932, Bruns. 6354); Got the Jitters (1934, Bruns. 6745)

BIBLIOGRAPHY

AllenH

HOWARD RYE

Yukl, Joe [Joseph William] (*b* New York, 5 March 1909; *d* Los Angeles, 16 March 1981). Trombonist and leader. He began on violin, taking lessons from his father, and concentrated on trombone only later, in the mid-1920s. After moving to New York (1927) he played with Red Nichols, worked as a staff musician for CBS, and recorded with the orchestra of Jimmy and Tommy Dorsey (1930). In the early 1930s he worked in Baltimore, then returned to New York to perform and record under the bandleader Joe Haymes (1934). In 1934–5 he performed and again recorded with the Dorseys, and in 1935 he went to the Los Angeles area with Jimmy Dorsey, in whose band he remained until January 1937. He also worked with Louis Armstrong (1936), made recordings with Bing Crosby (1935–7) and as a member of Ray McKinley's sextet (*New Orleans Parade*, 1936, Decca 1019), performed and recorded with Ben Pollack (1937–8), and worked with Frankie Trumbauer (1938) and the orchestra of the songwriter Ted Fio Rito (1939). Later he was active as a freelance and worked in studios in Hollywood; he recorded dixieland with Wingy Manone (1944–6), with Charlie LaVere (1944, 1949), and as a leader (1945), acted and performed in Pete Daily's band in the film *Rhythm Inn* (1951), and played some of the trombone solos in *The Glenn Miller Story* (1953). His full name and details of his death are taken from the California death index. (*ChiltonW*; *FeatherE*)

Z

Z, Bojan. *See* Zulfikarpasic, bojan.

Z, Rachel [Nicolazzo, Rachel Carmel] (*b* New York, 28 Dec 1962). Pianist and keyboard player. She grew up in Manhattan, where she was directed by her mother towards a career in opera; she began singing lessons when she was two and learned piano from the age of seven. However, a visit to the Berklee College of Music in summer 1979 sparked her interest in jazz, and the following year she began studying at the New England Conservatory. After graduating in 1984 she worked in the Boston area with, among others, George Garzone, Miroslav Vitous, and Bob Moses. In September 1988 she returned to New York and in February 1989 she toured with the saxophonist Najee; she joined Mike Mainieri's group Steps Ahead that same year and played with it intermittently until 1996. In addition Z recorded and toured with Al Di Meola (1988, 1998), Wayne Shorter (1995), the jazz-influenced Italian singer Pino Daniele (1997–8), and under Stanley Clarke and Lenny White in the group Vertú (1999). From 1992 she made several recordings as a leader, and in 1999 she recorded a program as part of Marian McPartland's series "Piano Jazz" for NPR radio. As R. Z. she wrote "True Confessions of a Girl Gone Smooth," which was published in *Jazziz* (xvi/2 (1999), 40).

SELECTED RECORDINGS

As leader: *Trust the Universe* (1992, Col. CK53216); *Room of One's Own* (1996, NYC 6023-2)

As sideman: A. Di Meola: *Kiss my Axe* (1988, 1991, Tomato R279751); Steps Ahead: *Yin-yang* (1992, NYC 6001-2); W. Shorter: *High Life* (1995, Verve 314-529224-2); S. Weinert: *The Bottom Line* (1996, VeraBra 2177-2)

BIBLIOGRAPHY

B. Milkowski: "Hearsay: Rachel Z: under Ze Spell," *JT*, xxiii/4 (1993), 11

L. Gourse: *Madame Jazz: Contemporary Women Instrumentalists* (New York, and Oxford, England, 1995), 43

R.L. Doerschuk: "Rachel Z and Adam Holzman: Wayne Shorter Four Hands," *Keyboard*, xxii/3 (1996), 14

B. Primack: "Hearsay: Rachel Z," *JT*, xxvi/8 (1996), 23

<http://www.jazzateria.com/artists/rachelz-old.html> (1999)

L. Jurgeit: "Rachel Z: 'Ich bin nur ein Werkzeug'," *JP*, xlviii/4 (1999), 26

MARK GILBERT

Zabiegliński, Janusz [His] (*b* Pabianice, Poland, 5 April 1934; *d* Warsaw, 17 March 2001). Polish clarinetist, alto and tenor saxophonist, and leader. His nickname, "His," may seem odd to English speakers; it derives from the appearance of this word in the album title *Janusz Zabiegliński and his Swingtet* (1966). Self-taught in music, Zabiegliński led a dixieland band (1956–68), performed in the Stodoła Big-Band (1968–71), and then worked in Orkiestra Rozrywkowa Polskiego Radia (the Light Music Orchestra of Polish Radio; 1971–3). He also played with Krzysztof Komeda, Henryk Majewski, and Andrzej Jagodziński. His Swingtet (formed in 1958) and the dixieland group the Old Timers, led by Henryk Majewski (which he joined in 1982), both remained active into the new century. From the 1950s until his retirement in the 1990s Zabiegliński maintained a separate career as a civil engineer, in which his speciality was bridge-building.

SELECTED RECORDINGS

As leader: on [various artists]: *Spotkanie z Conoverem w Polace* (Meeting with Conover in Poland) (1959, Muza 0291), Flyin' Home; *Janusz Zabiegliński and his Swingtet* (1966, Muza 0357)

As sideman: Stodoła Big-Band: *Let's Swing Again* (1971, Muza 0826); Marianna Wróblewska: *Meeting* (1975, Muza 1220); Wojciech Kamiński: *Open Piano* (1981, Muza 2402); Old Timers: *Old Timers* (1983, Poljazz 124), *Jubileum* (1987, Poljazz 192); K. Jonkisz: *Tribute to Duke* (1996, Polonia 087); Blues Fellows: *Live in Akwarium* (1999, Polonia 196–7)

BIBLIOGRAPHY

"Janusz 'His' Zabiegliński: ten stary dobry swing" [Janusz 'His' Zabiegliński: that good old swing]," *JF*, no.187 (1998), 46

ADAM CEGIELSKI, BK

Zacharias, Helmut (*b* Berlin, 27 Jan 1920). German violinist. He grew up in a musical family and received his first lessons from his father, a concert violinist; at the age of six he performed professionally, playing classical music for radio and in concert. In the 1930s he joined the Berlin Chamber Orchestra, and at the same time he discovered jazz. He recorded with his own group from 1941, playing in a style modeled after that of the Quintette du Hot Club de France. Zacharias is important for having made, in 1948, some of the first German bop recordings (*Be-bop nr.2*, Amiga 1150; *Be-bop nr.1*, Amiga 1151). His playing style was fluent and he often used German hit songs as a basis for his arrangements; however, in the so-called bop recordings he sounds mannered and ill at ease. In the 1950s Zacharias became involved in popular dance music.

WOLFRAM KNAUER

Zadeh, Aziza Mustafa. *See* Mustafa zadeh, aziza.

Żądło, Leszek (*b* Kraków, Poland, 1 April 1945). Polish tenor and soprano saxophonist, clarinetist, and flutist. He first played clarinet in local bands, then, after winning a scholarship in a competition in Vienna, moved to Austria to study at the Hochschule für Musik in Graz (1966). During his three years there he played with Eje Thelin, and in 1970 he joined the newly formed big band of Österreichischer Rundfunk, led from 1972 by Erich Kleinschuster. Later he played with Kleinschuster's sextet, and from around 1970 he led his own groups. In 1974 he moved to Munich. He performed with the European Jazz Quintet (1977–82) and recorded with Michael Naura and the poet Peter Rühmkorff (1978, 1987) and with the group Springtime, led by Günter Lenz (1979). In the 1980s he toured with George Russell and Elvin Jones and recorded with Bireli Lagrene (1982). After martial law was declared in his home country he organized a touring band, the Polski Jazz Ensemble, which gave concerts in aid of the Polish trade union Solidarność (1983–6). From the late 1980s he led small groups involving the pianist Chris Beier and the bass player Rainer Glas; they recorded as a quartet, with Billy Elgart on drums, in 1989 and as a cooperative trio without drums in 1994. In 1996 Żądło recorded as co-leader with the organist Chris Bantzer. He teaches in Munich and Würzburg and also composes music for films and the theater.

SELECTED RECORDINGS

As leader: *Sting* (1980, Fusion 8001); *Breath!* (1989, Enja 6026-2); with C. Beier and R. Glas: *Space* (1994, Clearaudio 181)

BIBLIOGRAPHY

J. Borkowski: "Leszek Żądło: Inner Silence," *JF* [intl edn], no.24 (1973), 41
M. A. Wölfle: "Leszek Żądło," *Jazz in Bayern*, ed. W. Kraus (Regensburg, Germany, 1997), 262

WOLFRAM KNAUER/BK

Zappa, Frank [Francis Vincent, Jr.] (*b* Baltimore, 21 Dec 1940; *d* Los Angeles, 4 Dec 1993). Electric guitarist and composer. He moved with his family to California at the age of ten, began playing drums when he was 12, and took up the guitar soon afterwards. While in his teens he sang blues and rock, and for six months he studied theory at Chaffey College, Alta Loma, California. Although he is best known as a rock songwriter and guitarist, his work often included elements of jazz. His group the Mothers of Invention, which he led from the mid-1960s to the mid-1970s, involved such jazz-rock musicians as the saxophonist Ian Underwood (on a regular basis) and George Duke and Bruce Fowler (both periodically during the early 1970s). In 1969 Jean-Luc Ponty recorded an album of Zappa's compositions (*King Kong*, PJ 20172), and in 1972 Zappa led the Grand Wazoo, a jazz-rock big band of which Jay Migliori, Charles Owens, and David Parlato were members. Around 1973 he recorded the album *A-pos-tro-phe* (Discreet 2175), with Ponty, Duke, Fowler, and Jack Bruce among his sidemen. Among later members of his groups were Vinnie Colaiuta (1978–82) and Chad Wackerman (1981–8). Always a highly eclectic musician, as a soloist Zappa incorporated blues, rock, raga, and jazz licks into his improvised lines. From the mid-1970s his work was much more closely related to rock and to contemporary classical music than to jazz, but connections with the jazz aesthetic remained on, for example, the albums *Jazz from Hell* (*c*1986, Barking Pumpkin 74205) and *Make a Jazz Noise Here* (*c*1990, Barking Pumpkin D2AS74234).

BIBLIOGRAPHY

Feather–Gitler '70s
L. Kart: "Frank Zappa: the Mother of Us All," *DB*, xxxvi/22 (1969), 14
H. Siders: "Meet the Grand Wazoo," *DB*, xxix/18 (1972), 13
D. Walley: *No Commercial Potential: the Saga of Frank Zappa and the Mothers of Invention* (New York, 1972, 2/1980) [incl. discography]
J. Schaffer: "The Perspective of Frank Zappa," *DB*, l/15 (1973), 14
R. Denyer, I. Guillory, and A. M. Crawford: *The Guitar Handbook* (London and Sydney, 1982), 28
M. Davis: "Frank Zappa Makes a Jazz Noise," *DB*, lviii/7 (1991), 29
Obituaries: J. Pareles, *New York Times* (6 Dec 1993); D. Ouellette, *DB*, lxi/3 (1994), 20

BK

Zarchy, Zeke [Rubin] (*b* New York, 12 June 1915). Trumpeter. After recording under the bandleader Joe Haymes (1935–6) he toured and recorded with Benny Goodman (1936) and Artie Shaw (1936–7), by turns with Bob Crosby and Red Norvo (1937–9), and with Tommy Dorsey (1939–40) and Glenn Miller (1940); he continued to play in Miller's bands while working as a staff musician at NBC (recording in 1941 and 1942) and while serving in the US Army (touring and recording from October 1942 to 1945). Having settled in Los Angeles, he worked in studios and as a freelance; he made recordings with Boyd Raeburn (1945), Goodman and Woody Herman (1947), Crosby (1950–51), Jerry Gray (1950, *c*1959), Sarah Vaughan (1951), Ray Anthony (1955), and Frank Capp (1960), and appeared in the film *The Glenn Miller Story* and the television show "The Swingin' Singin' Years" (1960). Zarchy retired from studio work in 1980. Although he re-created solos by Louis Armstrong, Bix Beiderbecke, and others as a member of the Great Pacific Jazz Band in the 1980s and 1990s, he is not an improviser. In 1995–6 he recorded in Hungary as a guest leader with Tamás Ittzés's Bohém Ragtime Jazz Band (*Zeke Zarchy with the BRJB: Some of these Days*, Pannon Jazz 1020).

BIBLIOGRAPHY

FeatherE
R. Gulliver: "Zeke Zarchy," *JJI*, xxxvi/12 (1983), 14
J. Chilton: *Stomp Off, Let's Go! The Story of Bob Crosby's Bob Cats & Big Band* (London, 1983), 46

BK

Zardis, Chester [Little Bear] (*b* New Orleans, 27 May 1900; *d* New Orleans, 14 Aug 1990). Double bass player. He learned double bass in 1916, taking lessons from Billy Marrero, and performed locally (*c*1919) and in California with Buddy Petit. In the 1920s he played in New Orleans with Chris Kelly, Kid Rena, and A. J. Piron, among others, and in the early 1930s he was on the Mississippi riverboats with Sidney Desvigne (on double bass and tuba) and Fats Pichon, with whom he also played in Memphis (late 1934 – early 1935). He then worked with Harold Dejan (1936–7), Kid Howard (*c*1937), as a leader (with Polo Barnes among his sidemen), and again with Pichon on the SS *Capitol* (1939), and recorded with Bunk Johnson (1942) and George Lewis (i) (1943). After his military service he held a long residency in Denver during which he was a member of the band led by the violinist George Morrison, and in 1951 he returned to New Orleans and joined the band led by Andy Anderson (i). In 1954 he abandoned music, and he spent the next decade as a farmer. Zardis began working again as a musician in New Orleans in 1965, playing regularly at Preservation Hall and performing and recording with the Preservation Hall Jazz Band in New Orleans (1966) and Europe (1967). In 1967 he toured Japan with Kid Sheik Cola. Following a period of ill-health he led his own band in the 1980s and performed with the Legends

Weather Report playing at the Montreux International Jazz Festival, 1976: (left to right) Joe Zawinul (keyboards), Wayne Shorter (tenor saxophone), Manolo Badrena (percussion), Alex Acuña (drums), and Jaco Pastorius (electric bass guitar)

of Jazz (from 1983) and in Europe with Kid Thomas Valentine (1983). Zardis was a founding member around 1984 of the Original Liberty Jazz Band, led by Michael White (ii), and he remained active through the decade; he gave his last performance at Preservation Hall only a month before his death. His life is celebrated in the documentary film *Chester Zardis: the Spirit of New Orleans* (1989), which includes performances with Danny Barker, Louis Nelson, Wendell Brunious, and others.

Oral history material in *LNT*.

SELECTED RECORDINGS

As sideman: first issued on *Dance New Orleans Style* (1937–41, MONO 12), K. Howard: Song of the Wanderer, Sweet Georgia Brown (*c*1937); G. Lewis: Milenberg Joys (1943, Climax 102); B. Pierce and D. D. Pierce: *Billie and De De* (1966, Preservation Hall 3)

BIBLIOGRAPHY

B. Turnock: "'Little Bear' Chester Zardis," *Sv*, no.26 (1969), 60
A. Shipton: "Styles of New Orleans Bass Playing," *Fn*, vii/1 (1976), 18
Obituaries: *New York Times* (17 Aug 1990); M. Hazeldine, *New Orleans Music*, ii/1 (1990), 21
W. Carter: *Preservation Hall: Music from the Heart* (Wheatley, Oxford, England, and New York, 1991)
D. Meyer: "Chester Zardis" <http://www.geocities.com/BourbonStreet/5135/Zardis.html> (1997)

HOWARD RYE

Zawadi, Kiane. *See* Mckinney family, (2) Kiane Zawadi.

Zawinul, Joe [Josef Erich] (*b* Vienna, 7 July 1932). Keyboard player, composer, and bandleader. He played accordion as a child and then began classical piano lessons; later he studied music at the Vienna Conservatory. In the early 1950s he performed with leading Austrian dance and radio orchestras and worked as house pianist for Polydor; he also played with Hans Koller (1952), Friedrich Gulda (including a period in 1955 when he played bass trumpet), and Karl Drewo and Fatty George (both from 1956). In 1959 he emigrated to the USA. After touring with Maynard Ferguson (1959) and serving as accompanist to Dinah Washington (October 1959 – March 1961) he spent a month with Harry Edison's quintet accompanying Joe Williams. In April 1961 he joined Cannonball Adderley, with whom he performed and recorded until 1970. He also played with Miles Davis in the late 1960s and early 1970s. In December 1970, with Wayne Shorter, Zawinul founded Weather report (see illustration), which he led until 1985. Following a brief attempt to continue Weather Report in 1986 as Weather Update (with Steve Khan replacing Shorter) he gave concerts on acoustic piano in Europe in a duo with Gulda and then returned to the USA to found a fusion band, the Zawinul Syndicate, which toured internationally; his sidemen have included Scott Henderson, Gerald Veasley, Cornell Rochester, and, in the late 1990s, former members of Weather Report Manolo Badrena and Victor Bailey, together with the guitarist Gary Poulson and the drummer, dancer, and lamellophone player Paco Sery. Also, in Vienna in 1995 he led the Austrian All Stars–Fatty George reunion band.

Zawinul was one of the most original and prolific jazz composers and arrangers to emerge in the 1970s: *Mercy, mercy, mercy* achieved considerable popular success in its recording by Adderley; *In a Silent Way* served as the title track of an album on which Davis made an early attempt, with strong impressionist overtones, to fuse jazz and rock; and *Birdland* became a disco hit in a recording by Weather Report as well as receiving much exposure in versions by Maynard Ferguson and Manhattan Transfer. Zawinul's performances in Adderley's group on Wurlitzer and Fender-Rhodes electric pianos influenced other jazz musicians to adopt these instruments in place of the standard piano, thus drastically altering the tone color of an entire branch of jazz music. His use of the Oberheim, ARP, and Prophet synthesizers and the ring modulator was also masterful. In Weather Report, where the role of the individual soloists was subservient to that of the ensemble, which produced rich and varied tone colors and fresh and exotic rhythmic textures, he created one of the first musically successful vehicles for collective improvisation since the early New Orleans bands. Manuscript scores of his works are in the holdings of the BMI Archives in New York.

See also HARMONY (i), §2, and ex.27; and PIANO, §6.

SELECTED RECORDINGS

As leader: *Money in the Pocket* (1966, Atl. 3004); *The Rise and Fall of the Third Stream* (1967, Vortex 2002); *Zawinul* (1970, Atl. 1579); *Lost Tribes* (*c*1992, Col. CK46057)

As sideman: C. Adderley: *Nippon Soul* (1963, Riv. 9477); B. Webster: *Soul Mates* (1963, Riv. 9476); C. Adderley: *Mercy, Mercy, Mercy* (1966, Cap. ST2663); *Country Preacher* (1969, Cap. SKAO404); M. Davis: *In a Silent Way* (1969, Col. CS9875); *Bitches Brew* (1969, Col. GP26)

For further recordings *see* WEATHER REPORT.

SELECTED FILMS AND VIDEOS

Jazz Scene USA: Cannonball Adderley Sextet (1962); Jazz Casual: the Julian "Cannonball" Adderley Quintet (1963); Jazz 625 (1964); Play Misty for Me (1971); Weather Report: in Concert (*c* mid-1980s); Newport Jazz '90 (1990)

BIBLIOGRAPHY

CarrJ

P. Welding: "From Vienna with Love: Joe Zawinul," *DB*, xxxiii/23 (1966), 23

S. Lake: "Our Music ... it's So Simple," *MM* (20 Dec 1975), 33

R. Townley: "The Mysterious Travellings of an Austrian Mogul," *DB*, xlii/2 (1975), 15

L. Lyons: "Josef Zawinul: Multiple Keyboard Magician," *CK*, iii/9 (1977), 26

J. Coryell and L. Friedman: *Jazz-rock Fusion* (New York and London, 1978)

M. C. Gridley: *Jazz Styles* (Englewood Cliffs, NJ, 1978, rev. 6/1997)

C. Silvert: "Joe Zawinul: Wayfaring Genius," *DB*, xlv (1978), no.11, p.13; no.12, p.21

L. Feather: "Piano Giants of Jazz: Joe Zawinul," *CK*, vi/5 (1980), 48

L. Lyons: *The Great Jazz Pianists, Speaking of their Lives and Music* (New York, 1983), 284

G. Armbruster: "Zawinul Continued Hot, Chance of Record Highs," *Keyboard*, x/3 (1984), 44 [incl. discography]

J. Diliberto: "The Siren Song of Synths: Zawinul," *DB*, li/8 (1984), 16

J. Chambers: *Milestones*, ii: *The Music and Times of Miles Davis since 1960* (Toronto, Buffalo, and London, 1985)

T. Schnabel: *Stolen Moments: Conversations with Contemporary Musicians* (Los Angeles, 1988), 211

J. Woodard: "Joe Zawinul: the Dialects of Jazz," *DB*, lv/4 (1988), 16

F. Shuster: "Groove Gangster: Joe Zawinul," *DB*, lix/6 (1992), 21 [incl. discography]

J. Abbott: "Brother Joe," *Jazz Express*, no.186 (1996), 32 [suppl. to *Boz*, no.26]

Z. Stewart: "Riffs: Weather Report to Re-form," *DB*, lxii/4 (1996), 14

L. Birnbaum: "Zawinul's Small World," *DB*, lxiv/1 (1997), 40

B. Milkowski: "A Few Rounds with Joe Zawinul," *JT*, xxvii/1 (1997), 46

J. Woodard: "[Return of the Mysterious Traveller]," *Jazziz*, xiv/1 (1997), 44

G. Endress: "Joe Zawinul," *JP*, xlvii/7–8 (1998), 18

M. Gilbert: "Joe Zawinul," *JJI*, li/5 (1998), 12

<http://www.freeweb.org/musica/zawinul/index.htm> (2000)

BK

Zbořil, Pavel [Buddy] (*b* Rokycany, Czechoslovakia [now Czech Republic], 16 Sept 1964). Czech drummer. His parents were amateur musicians. From the age of 12 he played clarinet, saxophone, and drums and performed in a local brass band. He studied drums and percussion at the conservatory in Plzeň (1979–85), where he played in different rock bands and began to concentrate on jazz. In 1987 he became a member of the Czech Radio Jazz Orchestra (known from the early 1990s as Big Band Radio Prague), and he also performed with a variety of small jazz and funk groups in Prague, in the course of which he had opportunities to work as a sideman with George Mraz, Benny Golson, and Benny Bailey.

SELECTED RECORDINGS

As sideman: on [no leader]: *Tribute: 60th Anniversary of Karel Velebný* (1991, Arta 0019-2), Velaband: Breakdown Household; Jazz Face: *Resolution* (1992–3, Arta 0039-2); Jaromír Honzák: *Getting There Together* (1994, P&J 011-2); Spring Rolls Quartet: *Spring Rolls Quartet* (1998, Cube & Metier 9803); R. Pokorný: *Blue Point* (1999, Arta 0097-2)

JAROSLAV PAŠMIK

Zeitlin, Denny [Dennis Jay] (*b* Chicago, 10 April 1938). Keyboard player. He grew up in a musical family and received extensive training in classical music, though he was always interested in improvisation. While in high school and at the University of Illinois he frequently spent time in Chicago jazz clubs, playing with such notable musicians as Joe Farrell, Wes Montgomery, Ira Sullivan, Wilbur Ware, Bob Cranshaw, and Johnny Griffin. As a medical student at Johns Hopkins University he performed frequently, concentrating on bop, and while studying at Columbia University in 1963 he took part in an audition for John Hammond, who subsequently produced four albums by Zeitlin's trio. Later in 1963 Zeitlin moved to the San Francisco area, where he pursued two careers – one in psychiatry and one as a jazz musician. He formed a trio, which from 1964 to 1967 included Charlie Haden. In the late 1960s his experiments with prepared piano led him to use electronic keyboard instruments, but he was again concentrating on piano in the late 1980s, when his trio (consisting of the double bass player Joel DiBartolo and the drummer Peter Donald) moved into the area of lighter mood music known as new age. In the 1990s Zeitlin gave performances as an unaccompanied soloist, with his trio, and in an acclaimed duo with David Friesen; these displayed his thorough grasp of jazz theory, a sense of structure, and mastery of free improvisation. He has written some film scores (notably that for Philip Kaufman's *Invasion of the Body Snatchers*, 1978), and his composition *Quiet Now* was often performed and recorded by Bill Evans (ii).

SELECTED RECORDINGS

As unaccompanied soloist: *Soundings* (1978, 1750 Arch 1770); *Homecoming* (1986, Living Music 998) *Denny Zeitlin at Maybeck: Maybeck Recital Hall Series*, xxvii (1992, Conc. 4572)

Duos: with C. Haden: *Time Remembers One Time Once* (1981, ECM 1239); with D. Friesen: *Concord Duo Series*, viii (1994, Conc. 4639)

As leader: *Cathexis* (1964, Col. CS8982); *Zeitgeist* (1966–7, Col. CS9548); *Expansion* (1973, Double Helix 1); *Syzygy* (1977, 1750 Arch 1759)

BIBLIOGRAPHY

R. B. Hadlock: "The Combined Careers of Denny Zeitlin: Analyst's Couch and Piano Bench," *DB*, xxxii/22 (1965), 14

S. Toomajian: "Body & Soul: the Total Experience of Denny Zeitlin," *DB*, xxxiv/21 (1967), 19

M. Zipkin: "Denny Zeitlin: Keyboard Patching for Body Snatching," *DB*, xlvi/10 (1979), 16

G. Endress: "Denny Zeitlin," *JP*, xxxiii/5 (1984), 12

D. Milano: "The Psychology of Improvisation," *Keyboard*, viii/10 (1984), 25

L. Hildebrand: "From Couch to Bench, He Meshes Two Careers," *San Francisco Chronicle Datebook* (14 June 1987)

B. Doerschuk: "New Age Hits Middle Age: Denny Zeitlin: New Age by Experiment," *Keyboard*, xiv/10 (1988), 47

H. Wong: "The Dual Life of Denny Zeitlin," *JT* (1988), Oct, 44

M. Bourne: "Riffs: Denny Zeitlin," *DB*, lvi/2 (1989), 14

Z. Stewart: "Pianist Denny Zeitlin's Alter Ego: Psychiatrist," *Los Angeles Times* (4 Jan 1991)

ROBERT L. DOERSCHUK/BK

Zentner, Si(mon H.) (*b* New York, 13 June 1917; *d* Las Vegas, 31 Jan 2000). Trombonist and bandleader. He played with Les Brown (1940–42), Harry James (1943), Jimmy Dorsey (1944), and various groups in Los Angeles (1944–9); during this period he appeared in the films *Seven Days Leave* (1942), with Brown, and *Lost in a Harem* (1944), with Dorsey. He then worked as a studio musician for MGM from 1949 to 1957, when he formed his own band; in the early 1960s Zentner's was the only newly formed jazz-oriented big band to achieve success. *Up a Lazy River* (1960, Lib. 55374), an arrangement by Bob Florence of the standard by Hoagy Carmichael and Sidney Arodin, was his biggest hit. The group toured the USA, accompanying such popular singers as Johnny Mathis and Nancy Wilson, and played frequently in Las Vegas. In 1965 it appeared in "Si Zentner and his Orchestra," an episode of the television series "The Big Bands." Zentner was firmly committed to the concept of big bands and campaigned vigorously to promote them. Early in 1998, at the age of 80, he was still touring as a bandleader; he played his last engagement in Las Vegas in July 1999.

BIBLIOGRAPHY

FeatherE; *Feather '60s*

J. Tynan: "The Struggles of Si," *DB*, xxviii/9 (1961), 18

D. Cerulli: "Si Zentner: 'The Disappointments are Many, but so are the Discoveries'," *IM*, lxi/5 (1962), 13

J. Wölfer: *Si Zentner and his Orchestra, also Including Bob Florence and his Orchestra: a Discography* (Langenhagen, Germany, 1981)

Obituary, E. Koch, *Las Vegas Sun* (4 Feb 2000)

WAYNE SCHNEIDER

Zerbe, Hannes (*b* Lodz, Poland, 17 Dec 1941). German pianist and keyboard player. He took private piano lessons (1948–60) and studied piano and composition in Dresden and Berlin. From the early 1970s he worked as a jazz musician in the East German bands FEZ (1974–7) and Osiris (1977–9), with musicians such as Manfred Hering, Helmut "Joe" Sachse, and Manfred Schulze, and with his own groups; among these are an ensemble of electronics and voice (from 1989), duos with the tuba player Dietrich Unkrodt (from 1980; *Duo Unkrodt/Zerbe*, 1987, Amiga 856336) and the clarinetist Jürgen Kupke (from 1996), and the Hannes Zerbe Blechband (from 1979), an ensemble consisting of jazz and classical musicians. From the mid-1980s Zerbe has worked extensively with synthesizers and computers, which he has used to further his aim of mediating between the worlds of contemporary composition and free improvisation. He also likes to involve poetry in his performances, as was heard, for example, in concerts given in 1990 ("Merz Jazz," based on texts by Kurt Schwitters) and 1996 ("Die Hydra," after texts by Heiner Müller); different aspects of his work have been documented on the recording *Metamorphosen I* (after texts by Hanns Eisler; 1984, Pläne 88416).

BIBLIOGRAPHY

J. Senkpeil: "Hannes Zerbe: 'Der zeitgenössische Jazz ist die wichtigste und aussagekräftigste Spielform in der DDR'," *JP*, xxxvi/10 (1987), 24

B. Noglik: "Hannes Zerbe – Heiner Müller: Die Hydra," *Wespennest*, no.1 (1996), 60

WOLFRAM KNAUER

Zes Winden, de [the Six Winds]. Dutch saxophone sextet. It was founded in 1984 by the baritone saxophonist Ad Peijnenburg, who added bass and sopranino instruments to the standard saxophone quartet he had established in 1976. After an early version of the group, with Bill Smith (ii) on sopranino saxophone and Paul Termos on the alto instrument (*c*1986), Peijnenburg kept a stable personnel together for more than a decade. Frans Vermeerssen (alto), Klaas Hekman (bass), John Tchicai (tenor), and the other members contributed to the repertory of the band, which encompassed a colorful range, from big-band and free-jazz traditions to world music and European compositions, as heard on *Elephants Can Dance* (1988, Sack. 3042) and *Manestraal* (1998, BVHaast 9706). In 1999 a new version of the group included Andrew White on tenor and Kazutoki Umezu on alto saxophone.

BIBLIOGRAPHY

S. Vickery: "The Six Winds," *Coda*, no.222 (1988), 16

ERIK VAN DEN BERG

Zetterlund, Monica (*b* Hagfors, Sweden, 20 Sept 1938). Swedish singer. In 1957 she sang with Ib Glindemann's band in Copenhagen and performed with Arne Domnérus's orchestra in Stockholm; she made several recordings with Domnérus (from 1958) and also recorded with studio bands of various sizes. In 1959–60 she appeared in Great Britain and the USA. Notable among her recordings are *Waltz for Debby* (1964, Phi. 08222PL), made with a trio led by Bill Evans (ii); *Hej man* (1975, Odeon 06235171), recorded under her own name; and *It Only Happens Every Time* (1977, EMI 06235454), with Thad Jones as leader. Zetterlund's style is cool but sensitive and shows a genuine sympathy with the jazz idiom, though her repertory includes Swedish classical songs and folksongs. She is also an actress, and has worked in films, television, and the theater, both in drama and comedy. She published *Hågkomster ur ett dåligt minne* [Reminiscenses from a faulty memory] (Stockholm, 1992).

Oral history material in *SSsv*.

BIBLIOGRAPHY

C.-E. Lindgren: "Babs är bäst!" [Babs is best!], *Estrad*, xix/4 (1958), 7

A. von Konow: "Monica Z. i våra hjärtan!" [Monica Z. in our hearts!], *Orkester journalen*, li/7–8 (1983), 11

J. Strand: "Z: 40 år på scenen" [Z: 40 years on the stage], *Orkester journalen*, lxiiii/12 (1997), 2

<http://www.mic.stim.se/engelsk/11/facts/zetterlund.html> (2000)

ERIK KJELLBERG

Zgraja, Krzysztof (*b* Gliwice, Poland, 20 Feb 1950). Polish flutist and composer. He played violin and piano from the age of six, then studied at the high school of music in Katowice, where he gained diplomas in flute (1972) and composition (1977). Although he was educated in classical music he was also interested in rock, and around 1970 he started to play jazz; he began with experiments in free jazz and only later acquired a knowledge of earlier styles. Having formed a duo with the double bass player Czesław Gladowski, he continued to explore this instrumental combination into the 1980s. Zgraja performed and recorded with Barre Phillips (1975) and with the double bass player Jacek Bednarek (from 1976); he is heard to advantage on *La concha* (1981, JG 052), recorded in a duo with Bednarek. After the proclamation of martial law in Poland in 1981 both Zgraja and Bednarek settled in Hannover, Germany. Thereafter Zgraja began to focus on other activities; he has given flute recitals, composed for film and theater, and contributed to multi-media creations.

BIBLIOGRAPHY

B. Noglik: "Krzysztof Zgraja," *Jazzwerkstatt international* (Berlin, 1981), 414 [incl. discography]

<http://www.zgraja.de> (2001)

WOLFRAM KNAUER/BK

Zigmund, Eliot (*b* New York, 14 April 1945). Drummer. He began playing drums while at school and later studied theory at the Mannes College of Music. After graduation from CCNY in 1969 he moved to California, where from 1970 he appeared as a freelance with, among others, Ron McClure, Steve Swallow, Art Lande, Mike Nock, and Mel Martin, and worked regularly with Vince Guaraldi. In 1974 he returned to New York and performed in the Persian Room at the Plaza Hotel. Zigmund played drums with Bill Evans (ii) from

January 1975 through 1977, and occasionally afterwards until November 1978. During his tenure with Evans he worked in a short-lived trio with Eddie Gomez and Bennie Wallace and recorded under Gomez's leadership (1976). He then joined Richard Beirach's trio Eon and worked as a freelance in Jim Hall's trio (alongside Harvie Swartz), as well as with Chet Baker, Stan Getz, and others. He toured Japan in Fred Hersch's trio with Red Mitchell in 1979, and worked with Don Friedman from that year into the mid-1980s, recording in 1979. In 1984 he joined Michel Petrucciani's trio, which may be seen performing, with Hall, in the video *Live at the Village Vanguard*, ii (*c*1989 [filmed 1986]). He left Petrucciani in the late 1980s, and from that time he has led his own small groups while continuing to work extensively as a freelance. Zigmund recorded with Gary Peacock (1980), the guitarist Carl Barry (1982), the pianist Keith Greko (*c*1985), the double bass player Eiji Makayama (1988, in a trio with Friedman), the pianist Stefan Karlsson (1995), and many others. He performs regularly in Italy, and he has taught at William Paterson College in Wayne, New Jersey, and at New York University.

SELECTED RECORDINGS

As leader with David Berkman and M. Richmond: *Dark Street* (1993, Freelance 022)

As sideman: B. Evans: *Crosscurrents* (1977, Fan. 9568); *You Must Believe in Spring* (1977, WB HS3504Y); G. Peacock: *Shift in the Wind* (1980, ECM 1165); M. Petrucciani: *Pianism* (1985, BN 85124); K. Greko: on *Last Train outta Flagstaff* (*c*1985, Concept 4), All the things you are, Come rain or come shine, Sophisticated Lady, Stella by Starlight; S. Karlsson: *Live at Vartan Jazz*, i (1995, Vartan Jazz 010)

BIBLIOGRAPHY

J. Potter: "Portraits: Eliot Zigmund," *MD*, xi/4 (1987), 34

P. Pettinger: *Bill Evans: How my Heart Sings* (New Haven, CT, and London, 1998)

GK

Zingaro, Carlos [Corujo de Magalhàes Alves, Carlos] (*b* Lisbon, 15 Dec 1948). Portugese violinist. He studied classical music at a conservatory in Lisbon (*c*1953–1965) and learned organ at a school of sacred music (1967–8). During the 1960s he was a member of a chamber orchestra at Lisbon University, and in 1967 he founded the group Plexus, which explored a fusion of rock, contemporary classical music, and improvisation. Following a period in the Portugese Army, in 1975 he studied graphic art and stage design at a theater school in Lisbon, and from 1974 to 1980 he served as the music director for a theater company, Comicos; later he founded an art gallery of the same name in which he displayed his own works. He also wrote for the theater, and in 1988 he collaborated on an Italian production of a trilogy by Franz Kafka.

Zingaro performed free jazz and improvised music throughout Europe with Daunik Lazro (from 1975), Kent Carter (from 1977, recording in 1979), and Richard Teitelbaum (from the late 1970s); in the 1980s he worked with, among others, Radu Malfatti and the percussionist Andrea Centazzo (both 1980), the Mitteleuropa Orchestra (1981), Tristan Honsinger and Tony Oxley (both 1982), Raymond Boni and Albert Mangelsdorff (both 1983), Evan Parker, Steve Lacy, and Jon Rose. In 1979, under a Fulbright Scholarship, he was invited by the Creative Music Foundation in Woodstock, New York, to participate in meetings, classes, and performances with Anthony Braxton, Roscoe Mitchell, George Lewis (ii), Leo Smith, Tom Cora, Karl Berger, and Teitelbaum. Later he performed and recorded at Company Week in London (1987) with Lee Konitz, Derek Bailey, Honsinger, Barre Phillips, Teitelbaum, and the percussionist Steve Noble. From 1990 Zingaro worked with Rüdiger Carl in Joëlle Léandre's Canvas Trio, which appeared the following year at the Taktlos Festival in Zurich. As a member of the group Periferia he recorded in 1993 alongside Lazro, Sakis Papadimitriou, and the double bass player Jean Bolcato. In 1994 he returned to the Taktlos Festival in a trio with Teitelbaum and Barre Phillips, and in 1996 he recorded in duos with the cellist Peggy Lee and with Dominique Pifarély.

In his improvisations Zingaro draws heavily on his classical background. Although he has worked in many jazz and jazz-related contexts, he has never considered himself a jazz musician; indeed, in the 1990s he renounced his association with jazz.

SELECTED RECORDINGS

As unaccompanied soloist: *Solo* (1989, Adda 590076)

Duos: with P. Lee: *Western Front* (1996, Hatology 513); with D. Pifarély: on [various artists]: *Icis* (1996, In Situ 167–9), *Pifarély/Zingaro* (In Situ 167)

As leader with D. Lazro, J. Bolcato, and S. Papadimitriou: *Periferia* (1993, In Situ 164)

As sideman: D. Lazro: on *Sweet Zee* (1983–4, HA 2010), Empire (1983); Company: on *Once* (1987, Incus CD04), Sextet, Trio II; J. Léandre: *L'histoire de Mme. Tasco* (1992, HA 6122); Canvas Trio: *Moments* (1996, Music & Arts 999)

BIBLIOGRAPHY

C. Aguetaï: "Voix nouvelle: Carlos Zingaro," *Jm*, no.335 (1985), 56

P. Carles, A. Clergeat, and J.-L. Comolli: *Dictionnaire du jazz* (Paris, 1988, rev. and enlarged 2/1994)

<http://www.shef.ac.uk/misc/rec/ps/efi/mzingaro.html> (1999) [incl. discography]

GK

Zinger cymbal. A Turkish cymbal clamped to a bass drum and activated by a small striker attached to the bass-drum beater; *see* Drum set, §I, 5.

Zoller, Attila (Cornelius) (*b* Visegrad, nr Budapest, 13 June 1927; *d* Townshend, VT, 26 Jan 1998). Hungarian guitarist. He grew up in a musical family and first studied violin and trumpet; he changed to guitar when he decided to make music his career. After playing in Budapest with Mihály Tabányi's Pinocchio Ensemble (1946–8) he performed and recorded in Vienna, where he had spent a brief period as a double bass player in a pit orchestra, with Vera Auer (1948–54). In Frankfurt he played bop with Jutta Hipp (1954–5), whose group also included Auer. He followed Hipp to the USA early in 1956, but soon returned to Germany, where he worked with Hans Koller (April 1956–1959) and visiting American musicians, notably Oscar Pettiford (he occasionally played double bass while Pettiford played cello). In 1959 he was awarded a scholarship to the Lenox School of Jazz and moved to the USA. Following a short period with Chico Hamilton (1960) he performed with Herbie Mann (1962–5), then served as leader, with Don Friedman, of a modal-jazz quartet (1964–6).

From the mid-1960s Zoller worked regularly in the USA and Europe: he played swing with Red Norvo (1966) and Benny Goodman (1967), recorded in a trio with Koller (1965) and as co-leader of a group with Lee Konitz and Albert Mangelsdorff (1968), and in the course of the decade contributed original jazz soundtracks to a number of American and German films. He toured Japan with Astrud Gilberto in 1970 and with Jim Hall and Kenny Burrell in 1971 and made frequent tours of Europe. In 1974 he appeared at the Half Note in New York as an unaccompanied soloist and in duos with the bass player Bill Takas, and in 1979 he recorded in a trio with Koller and George Mraz. Having given workshops at the Vermont Jazz Center for seven years from 1974, in 1981 he became a founder of the Center of Creative Jazz Study and Performance (also in Vermont), where he continued to teach into the 1990s. He performed and recorded in New York and Germany in a duo with Jimmy Raney (1979–80), and again in Germany in a trio (with Michael Formanek and Daniel Humair) and quartet (with Kirk Lightsey added to the group) (1986). In the 1990s he worked in duos with Wolfgang Lackerschmid and the Russian guitarist Andrei Ryabov, and in a trio (1994–5) with Lackerschmid and Konitz. Zoller toured Europe with Friedman in March 1995 and recorded in a trio with Tommy Flanagan and Mraz shortly before his death. He also worked as a designer of electronic instruments, and in 1971 patented a bidirectional pickup for guitars.

SELECTED RECORDINGS

As unaccompanied soloist: *Conjunction* (1979, Enja 3051); *Lasting Love* (1997, Acoustic Music 319-1131-2)
Duos: with J. Raney: *Jim and I: Live in Frankfurt* (1980, L+R 40013); with W. Lackerschmid: *Live Highlights '92* (1991–2, Bhakti 28)
As leader: *Heinrich Heine: Lyrik and Jazz* (1964, Phi. 840479); with H. Koller and M. Solal: *Zoller–Koller–Solal* (1965, Saba 15061); *The Horizon Beyond* (1966, EmA 66013); with L. Konitz and A. Mangelsdorff: *Zo-ko-ma* (1968, MPS 15170); *Gypsy Cry* (1969, Embryo 523); *Dream Bells* (1976, Enja 2078); *Overcome* (1979, 1986, Enja 5053); *Memories of Pannonia* (1986, Enja 5027); *When it's Time* (1994, Enja 9031-2); with L. Konitz and D. Friedman: *Thingin'* (1995, HA 6174)
As sideman: O. Pettiford: *Das Oscar Pettiford Quartet* (1959, DSC 24); H. Mann: *Live at Newport* (1963, Atl. 1413); D. Friedman: *Dreams and Explorations* (1964, Riv. 9485); *Metamorphosis* (1966, Prst. 7488); with L. Dudás: *Monte Carlo* (1982, Rayna 1005)

BIBLIOGRAPHY

FeatherE; *Feather '60s*; *Feather–Gitler '70s*
A. Zoller: "Die beste Jazzlehre: die USA," *JP*, x/2 (1961), 37
D. Morgenstern: "The Odyssey of Attila Zoller," *DB*, xxxii/14 (1965), 25
E. T. Vogel: "Attila Zoller: können allein genügt nicht," *JP*, xx/2 (1971), 56
J.-E. Berendt: *Ein Fenster aus Jazz: Essays, Portraits, Reflexionen* (Frankfurt am Main, Germany, 1977)
A. Berle: "Attila Zoller," *GP*, xiii/12 (1979), 61
B. Paulot: *Albert Mangelsdorff: Gespräche* (Waakirchen, Germany, 1993)
G. G. Simon: *Magyar jazzdiszkografia, 1905–1994* (Budapest, 1994)
G. Endress: "Atilla Zoller," *JP*, xliv/3 (1995), 22
K. Zipernovszky: "Zoller Attila és a Konitz-stílus" [Attila Zoller and the Konitz style], *Magyar hírlap* [Budapest] (22 June 1996)
Obituary, M. Gilbert, *JJI*, li/3 (1998), 18
G. G. Simon: "Archív interjú Zoller Attilával" [Archival interview with Attila Zoller], *Gramofon* [Budapest] (1998), March, 27
B. Donaldson: "Attila Zoller Interview," *Cadence*, xxv/3 (1999), 5

DAVID FLANAGAN/GÉZA GÁBOR SIMON, BK

Zonophone. Record label. It was founded in 1899 by Frank Seamon and was continued by Victor after that company took over Seamon's National Gramophone Corporation. After 1910 the name was not used in the USA, but it remained in use in Britain (and was later also adopted in Australia) as the Gramophone Company's cheap label. Much of the repertory was recorded in Britain and includes some of the most highly regarded British hot dance music of the 1920s; the catalogue also contained American material recorded by Victor. Following the setting up of EMI, Zonophone was merged in January 1933 with British Columbia's label Regal to form Regal-zonophone.

BIBLIOGRAPHY

B. Rust: *The American Record Label Book* (New Rochelle, NY, 1978), 332
A. Sutton and K. Nauck: *American Record Labels and Companies: an Encyclopedia (1891–1943)* (Denver, 2000), 231

HOWARD RYE

Zorn, John [Hajime, Dekoboko; Tzizit, Rav] (*b* New York, 2 Sept 1953). Alto saxophonist, composer, and leader. He studied piano, flute, and guitar initially and learned contemporary art music through a program of self-study. In additon he was interested in doo-wop and other pop music, film music, and the cartoon music of Carl Stallings, and as a teenager he played electric bass guitar in a surf-rock group. By this time he had already begun to write after the manner of such 20th-century composers as Igor Stravinsky, Anton Webern, Charles Ives, Edgar Varèse, Karlheinz Stockhausen, John Cage, and Mauricio Kagel; the influence of the last two men figures strongly in Zorn's later works, in which he incorporates aspects of chance (after Cage) and game pieces (after Kagel).

Zorn attended Webster College in St. Louis, and through Oliver Lake (a teacher at the college) he came under the influence of the Black Artists Group and, later, the Association for the Advancement of Creative Musicians; inspired by the energy and structural clarity of Anthony Braxton's unaccompanied solo recording *For Alto*, he took up alto saxophone at the age of 20 and began to study jazz. In 1974 he left college, and early the following year he settled in New York. From that time he worked in and led his own free-improvisation groups, collaborating with, among others, Fred Frith, Eugene Chadbourne, Tom Cora (at that time known as Corra), and the synthesizer player Bob Ostertag. By the late 1970s he was performing regularly on alto saxophone, disassembled parts of saxophones and clarinets, and various instruments that imitated bird and duck calls; the last of these he sometimes played in buckets of water. In addition, through the mid- to late 1970s, he developed his "game" theory of composition, in which the roles of the performers are mediated through a series of flash cards and gestures; at an early stage he both conducted and played in these pieces. In 1978 he recorded his first such work, *Lacrosse*, playing alto and soprano saxophones and clarinet; later works in this idiom include *Pool* and *Hockey* (both 1980) and *Archery* (1981). Among the regular participants in these recordings were George Lewis (ii), Robert Dick, the violinist Polly Bradfield, Anthony Coleman, Wayne Horvitz, Chadbourne (on guitar and dobro), Cora, Bill Laswell, and the drummer and percussionist David Moss. From the late 1980s Zorn's principal game piece was *Cobra*, during performances of which he served mainly as a conductor.

Zorn also performed in a trio with Phillip Johnston and Joel Forrester (*c*1977) and recorded with Frank Lowe (1977), the drummer Andrea Centazzo (1978), Chadbourne (1979 – early 1980s), and Horvitz (1980). With Horvitz he collaborated regularly into the 1990s: they co-led the Sonny Clark Memorial Quartet from the mid-1970s, recording with Bobby Previte and Ray Drummond as sidemen in the mid-1980s; the group's album *Voodoo* (1985) provides a fine example of both leaders' skills within the bop vernacular and helped to establish each as an orthodox jazz player. Zorn appears with Horvitz in the documentary *Rising Tones Cross* (1984). As the leader of his own groups he performed at various clubs in New York, notably 8BC, Roulette, Chandelier, and his own tiny venue, the Saint, and conducted performances of his game pieces. As a freelance in other improvisational settings he formed duos with the bass trombonist Jim Staley (1983), the *shamisen* player Michihiro Sato (mid-1980s, recording in 1984–5), Frith (late 1980s), Sergey Kuryokhin (1988), and Ostertag (1989), and trios with Staley and Dick (1984), René Lussier and the vocalist Tenko

John Zorn at the Outside In festival, Crawley, England, 1990

(1988), and Greg Osby and Ned Rothenberg (1988). In 1984 he performed and recorded at Jazzfest Berlin as a member of Peter Brötzmann's Clarinet Project.

In the mid-1980s Zorn began recording for Nonesuch, and he received high praise for his arrangements and performances of film music by Ennio Morricone on his first album, *The Big Gundown* (1984–5). Following its release he began to achieve recognition beyond the realm of free improvisation, and at the Next Wave Festival at the Brooklyn Academy of Music he made the video *Once upon a Time in the East Village: John Zorn Arranges and Conducts the Music of Ennio Morricone* (1986). Around 1987 Zorn, Bill Frisell, and Lewis formed the jazz trio News for Lulu; it recorded in the same year and in performance at the Stadttheater Basel in 1989. In 1987 Zorn also appeared in a group with Guus Janssen, Mark Dresser, and Martin van Duynhoven at the October Meeting in the Netherlands.

Around this time Zorn began to divide his time equally between New York and Tokyo, where he performed variously with Japanese folk, pop, jazz, and classical musicians. In the late 1980s he formed a quintet which was known under a number of names – Spy vs Spy, W.R.U., and C & D – and which performed brief, aggressive interpretations of Ornette Coleman's compositions; in 1988 the group performed in Germany and recorded in New York. Between 1989 and 1993 Zorn led the group Naked City, with Frisell, Frith (on electric bass guitar), Horvitz, and Joey Baron as his sidemen. In addition he worked in an avant-garde soul-jazz group with Big John Patton, Frisell, and Previte, took part in an informal project in tribute to Dorothy Ashby, and was a member of the trios Slan (early 1990s, with the avant-garde guitarist Elliott Sharp and the heavy-metal drummer Ted Epstein) and Painkiller (early 1990s, with Laswell and the drummer Mick Harris). Around 1990 he organized three separate ensembles that were known collectively as the New Traditions in East Asian Bar Bands and in which actresses read texts while two or more instrumentalists improvised. Each group was named in honor of a film actress: Hwang Chine-ee (two drummers with a Korean narrator); Qu Tran (two keyboard players with a Vietnamese narrator); and Hu Die (two guitarists with a Chinese narrator). From 1992 Zorn served as an executive producer for the record label Avant.

In 1992 Zorn embraced his Jewish heritage when he composed an episodic work, *Kristallnacht*, on the subject of the Holocaust. The following year he initiated Masada (named after a hilltop fortress where Jewish rebels committed suicide rather than surrender to Roman conquerers), which has operated primarily as a jazz quartet. The first manifestation of Masada was the Thieves Quartet (with Dave Douglas, Greg Cohen, and Baron as its sidemen), which performed in September 1993 during Zorn's month-long birthday celebration at the Knitting Factory; thereafter the group performed under the name Masada. Other components of this project are the Masada String Trio, which consists of Mark Feldman, Erik Friedlander, and Cohen, and Bar Kokhba, a sextet that comprises Marc Ribot, Feldman, Friedlander, Cohen, Baron, and the percussionist Cyro Baptista; the latter group gave Zorn's Masada compositions a gentler sound. Zorn also established the series "Radical Jewish Culture," under which heading he produced recordings, organized concerts in tribute to Jewish performers and composers, and composed song cycles based on the writings of Franz Kafka. In 1995 he founded the recording company and label Tzadik.

By the mid-1990s Zorn had ended his annual trips to Tokyo and was living full-time in New York. Apart from his activities with Masada he participated in improvisational groups in San Francisco (January 1994), performed and recorded with Ostertag, Frith, Phil Minton, Guy Klucevsek, Dresser, and Gerry Hemingway at the Festivale Internazionale di Musica in Bologna, Italy (May 1994), and in a trio with Derek Bailey and William Parker (*c*1995). In addition he recorded under the pseudonyms Rav Tzizit and Dekoboko Hajime (1995), appeared in duos with Sharp (1996) and Susie Ibarra (at the Vision Festival in 1997), performed and recorded with Milford Graves (summer 1997 and at the Festival International Musique Actuelle Victoriaville in 1999), and recorded in a duo with Previte (1997) and as leader of a quartet that consisted of Sharp, Horvitz, and Previte (1998). In the late 1990s, after years of working at the Knitting Factory, he terminated this association in protest against Internet broadcasts that were made from the venue without artists' permission; thereafter he organized and presented performances at a new club in New York, Tonic.

Zorn is a prominent composer, conceptualizer, and conductor of the avant-garde movement, and jazz is but one of the many genres from which he draws. Nonetheless he is a brilliant jazz musician, both as an instrumentalist and as a composer and organizer. As an alto saxophonist he is equally adept at performing a soulful, beautifully rendered melodic line or playing outrageous sonic outbursts which recall vividly the best free-jazz saxophonists. His own works are highly structured pieces in which compositional elements dictate the performers' roles without necessarily inhibiting their creative output; even the game pieces, for all their cut-and-paste spontaneity, are painstakingly set forth through his conducting. Zorn's episodic works deal in block composing and recall consistently the jump-cut mentality of the finest cartoon music; these pieces are landmarks in the late 20th-century deconstruction of genre and style, and their jazz elements have contributed significantly to the emerging notion of jazz as a process rather than as a collection of styles. A jazz style *per se* is more apparent in Zorn's compositions for Masada, particularly in his incorporation of the 1960s free-jazz style of Ornette Coleman and in his use of prolonged improvisations on simple chordal ostinatos (which contrast sharply to the jump-cut approach); however, these ostinatos may be understood as belonging to traditional Jewish music, an interpretation which is reinforced by Zorn's practice of basing Masada songs on "Jewish" scales (either a major scale with a flatted second or a minor scale with a raised fourth).

SELECTED RECORDINGS

As unaccompanied soloist: *A Classic Guide to Strategy*, i–ii (1983, 1985, Lumina 004, 010)

Duos: with J. Staley: on Staley: *OTB* (*c*1984, Lumino 008), Craps; with N. Rothenberg: on Rothenberg: *Trespass* (1985, Lumina 011), Kakei; with A. Harth: on Harth: *Plan Eden* (1986–7, Creative World 1008), Atom-sex-kino (1986); with F. Frith: *The Art of Memory* (*c*1995, Incus 20); with B. Previte: *Euclid's Nightmare* (1997, Depth of Field 1-2)

As leader: with E. Chadbourne: *School* (1977–8, Parachute 004/006), incl. Lacrosse (1978); *Pool* (1980, Parachute 0011/0012); *Archery* (1981, Parachute 017/018); with D. Bailey and G. Lewis: *Yankees* (*c*1982, Celluloid 5006); *The Big Gundown* (1984–5, Elektra/Nonesuch 79139-2); on [no leader]: *Godard, ça vous chante?* (1985, Nato 634), Godard; *Cobra* (1985–6, HA 2034); *Spillane* (1986–7, Elektra/Nonesuch 79172-2); with G. Lewis and B. Frisell: *News for Lulu* (1987, HA 6005); with G. Janssen, Christian Marclay, and L. Sclavis: *October Meeting '87*, i (1987, Bimhuis 001); *Spy vs Spy* (1988, Elek. Mus. 60844-2); with G. Lewis and B. Frisell: *More News from Lulu* (1989, HA 6055); with D. Bailey and W. Parker: *Harras* (1995, Avant 056); with W. Horvitz, E. Sharp, and B. Previte: *Downtown Lullaby* (1998, Depth of Field 2-2)

As leader of Naked City: *Naked City* (1989, Elektra/Nonesuch 79238-2); *Grand Guignol* (*c*1989–90, Avant 002); *Heretic* (1991, Avant 001); *Radio* (1992, Avant 003); *Absinthe* (1992–3, Avant 004)

As leader of Masada [quartet]: *Alef* (1994, DIW 888); *Beit* (1994, DIW 889); *Gimel* (1994, DIW 890); *Het* (1996, DIW 925); *Tet* (1997, DIW 933); *Live in Middleheim* (1999, Tzadik 7326)

As sideman: F. Lowe: *Lowe & Behold* (1977, Musicworks 3002); A. Centazzo: *Environment for Sextet* (1978, Ictus 0017); E. Chadbourne: on *There'll be No Tears Tonight* (1980, Parachute 013), Dang Me [duo], Honey don't, The last word in lonesome is me, Swingin' Doors; W. Horvitz: on *Simple Facts* (1980, Theatre for your Mother 004), Art Thieves, No Place Fast; Sonny Clark Memorial Quartet: *Voodoo* (1985, BS 0109); J. Staley: on *Mumbo Jumbo* (1986, Rift 12), [untitled]; [no leader]: *Company 91*, iii (1991, Incus CD18); on [no leader]: *Sax Legends*, i–ii (1992, PW KICJ139, KICJ140), Blues from 52nd Street, Devil's Island, Promptus; S. Beresford: *Signals for Tea* (1994, Avant 039); B. J. Patton: *Minor Swing* (1994, DIW 896)

BIBLIOGRAPHY

CBY 1999
B. Milkowski: "Profile: John Zorn," *DB*, li/2 (1984), 44
J. Solothurnmann: "New Sounds from the Lower East Side," *JF* [intl edn], no.95 (1985), 30
P. Watrous: "John Zorn," *Musician*, no.81 (1985), 17
B. Chant: "John Zorn: Game Plan," *Coda*, no.221 (1988), 24
J. Rockwell: "As Important as Anyone in his Generation," *New York Times* (21 Feb 1988)
G. Santoro: "John Zorn: *Quick-change Artist* Makes Good," *DB*, lv/4 (1988), 23
——: "Music: John Zorn," *The Nation* (30 Jan 1988), 138; repr. in *Dancing in your Head: Jazz, Blues, Rock and Beyond* (New York, 1994), 281
E. Strickland: "Spillane, the Works … Looking for Zorn," *Fanfare*, xi/5 (1988), 344
J.-Y. Le Bec: "Les aides de Zorn," *Jm*, no.378 (1989), 18
H. Reich: "Music: Waves of Sound: John Zorn Serves up his Music Layer by Layer," *Chicago Tribune* (11 June 1989)
P. Watrous: "Pop/Jazz: John Zorn Takes Over the Town," *New York Times* (24 Feb 1989)
B. Barthelmes: "Der beschleunigte Blick: von John Zorn zu Arthur Lourie," *Musica*, xliv/4 (1990), 231
H. Mandel: "John Zorn: I Have a Lot of Little Tricks," *Ear*, xv/5 (1990), 13
J. Pareles: "There are 8 Million Stories in John Zorn's Naked City," *New York Times* (8 April 1990)
D. Rubien: "John Zorn: Explosive Sounds are a Clash of Genres," *San Francisco Chronicle Datebook* (13 May 1990)
A. Lange: "Komponieren heute: der Architekt der Spiele: Gespräch mit John Zorn über seine musikalischen Regalsysteme," *Neue Zeitschrift für Musik*, no.152 (1991), 33
J. Pareles: "Pop/Jazz: 3 Veterans of No-name Music Return," *New York Times* (7 June 1991)
P. N. Wilson: "Klangmomente: Früchte des (John) Zorn: improvisierte Musik im Zeitalter der Simulation," *Neue Zeitschrift für Musik*, no.152 (1991), 40
E. M. Hisama: "Postcolonialism on the Make: the Music of John Mellencamp, David Bowie and John Zorn," *Popular Music*, xxii/2 (1993), 91
S. Drury: "A View from the Piano Bench, or, Playing John Zorn's *Carny* for Fun and Profit," *Perspectives of New Music*, xxxii/1 (1994), 194
D. Hamilton: "Zorn's 'Garden' Sprouts Discontent," *Los Angeles Times* (15 Aug 1994)
A. Pierrepont: "Un mois à la Knitting Factory," *Jm*, no.436 (1994), 28
M. Bäumel: "John Zorn," *JP*, xliv/5 (1995), 6
F. Davis: *Bebop and Nothingness: Jazz and Pop at the End of the Century* (New York, 1996), 182
E. Amrofel: "PS Zornien," *Jm*, no.466 (1997), 5
D. Yaffe: "Zorn Meets Bacharach," *DB*, lxiv/12 (1997), 99
J. Pareles: "Klezmer Keeps Growing: Was that Beethoven?" *New York Times* (7 March 1998)
L. Blumenfeld: "John Zorn: Scene by Scene," *Jazziz*, xvi/8 (1999), 42
B. Blumenthal: "The Age of Masada: John Zorn's Quartet Brings Jazz to New Levels," *Boston Globe* (28 May 1999)
<http://members.tripod.com/%7EJFGraves/zorn-index.html> (1999)
<http://utenti.tripod.it/RADIOHERETIC/HOME.htm> (1999)
<http://www.wnur.org/jazz/artists/zorn.john/> (1999) [incl. discography, bibliography]
F. Kaplan: "Musical Events: Horn of Plenty: the Composer who Knows No Boundaries," *New Yorker* (14 June 1999), 84
A. Schatz: "Crossing Music's Borders in Search of Identity: Downtown, a Reach for Ethnicity," *New York Times* (3 Oct 1999)
K. McNeilly: "Ugly Beauty: John Zorn and the Politics of Postmodern Music," <http://muse.jhu.edu/journals/postmodern_culture/v005/5.2mcneilly.html> (2000)
B. Milkowski: "One Future, Two Views: Conversation with John Zorn," *JT*, xxx/2 (2000), 29
S. Nicholson: "Arresting Originality," *TheSpectator* (12 Feb 2000), 46

GK

Zubov, Aleksey (Nikolayevich) (*b* Moscow, 15 Nov 1936). Russian saxophonist and composer. Self-taught as a musician, he played clarinet in the brass band of the Moscow M. V. Lomonosov State University, where he studied physics (graduating in 1958), and tenor saxophone in the big band of the Tsentral'ny Dom Rabotnikov Iskusstva (Central house of artists; 1954–7). In 1956 he joined the octet Vosmoyrka, at that time the best jazz group in Moscow. Later he was a member of Oleg Lundstrem's orchestra (1960–65) and the Kontsertny Estradny Orkestr Tsentral'novo TV i Vsesoyuznovo Radio (Concert variety orchestra of central TV and all-union radio). In 1967–8 he led two groups known by the name Crescendo – a quintet in which the vibraphonist Leonid Garin played in 1968 and a quartet. From 1974 to 1979 he worked with the ensemble Melodiya, and in the 1980s he was active as a freelance and wrote film music. In 1985 he moved to the USA. Zubov's playing is well represented by the album *Barometr* (1983, Mel. C60 19675001). In addition to his principal instrument he plays flute and synthesizer. (S. F. Starr: *Red and Hot: the Fate of Jazz in the Soviet Union, 1917–1980*, New York, and Oxford,

England, 1983, rev. 2/1994, as *Red and Hot: the Fate of Jazz in the Soviet Union, 1917–1990*)

WALTER OJAKÄÄR

Zuccheri, Luciano (*b* Spilimbergo, Italy, 1911; *d* Asti, Italy, *c*1977). Italian guitarist and leader. He played guitar from the age of six. In 1934 he recorded as an unaccompanied soloist and in 1938 formed a group that later became the Quintetto Ritmico di Milano; this was modeled after the Quintette du Hot Club de France and included three guitars (of which Zuccheri played the lead), a violin (from 1947 a clarinet), and a double bass. Zuccheri's style is exemplified by the recording *Programma BBC* (1947, Fonit 12593).

ADRIANO MAZZOLETTI

Zudekoff, Moe. See MORROW, BUDDY.

Zulfikarpasic, Bojan [Z, Bojan] (*b* Belgrade, 2 Feb 1968). Serbian pianist and composer. He discovered jazz in 1984 and quickly became one of the busiest pianists in Belgrade. After gaining a scholarship to the University of Michigan (1986) he spent time with Clare Fischer, under whose influence he renewed his approach to the piano. In the course of his service in the Serbian army (1987) he directed an ethnic music orchestra, and this supplied further inspiration for his music making. In 1988 he settled in Paris, where in the early 1990s he played in Noël Akchoté's groups Trash Corporation and Unit and in 1992 founded Quartet Z. He joined Henri Texier's Azur Quartet (1992) and Sonjal Septet (1996), played in Sylvain Beuf's quartet, formed an international group including, most notably, Julien Lourau, and appeared at the festival Banlieues Bleues (1997), where he presented *Koréni*, a work which makes use of the repertory of Balkan folk music. He performed with Texier in 1997–8 and recorded with Michel Portal in 1997.

SELECTED RECORDINGS

As leader: *Bojan Z Quartet* (1993, Label Bleu 6565); *Yopla!* (Label Bleu 6590); *Koreni* (1998, Label Bleu 6614)

As sideman: Annette Lowman: *Movies Memories* (1992, Le Chante du Monde 274941); H. Texier: *An Indian's Week* (1993, Label Bleu 6558); *Mad Nomads* (1995, Label Bleu 6568); Simon Sprang-Hanssen: *Instant Blue* (1997, Sto. 4217); M. Portal: *Dockings* (1997, Label Bleu 6604); H. Texier: *Mosaic Man* (1998, Label Bleu 6608)

BIBLIOGRAPHY

"Petit dictionnaire illustré des monstres," *Jm*, no.426 (1993), 39

F. Garat: "Le premier jet est toujours le mieux," *Jm*, no.438 (1994), 35

S. Loupien: "Z comme Zulfikarpasic," *Libération* (1 June 1994), 32

F. Médioni: "Bojan Zulfikarpasic: my Favorite Things," *Jm*, no.459 (1996), 26

P. Anquetil: "Du beau monde aux Balkans: Z comme Zulfikarpasic," *Jazzman*, no.23 (1997), 11

F. Cruz: "Bojan Z: bacchanales balkaniques," *Jazzman*, no.44 (1999), 22

A. Merlin: "Bojan: zoom sur Z," *Jazzman*, no.56 (2000), 12

JACQUES ABOUCAYA

Zurke, Bob [Robert Albert; Zukowski, Bogusław Albert] (*b* Detroit, 17 Jan 1912; *d* Los Angeles, 16 Feb 1944). Pianist and composer. At an early age he displayed a precocious talent for playing piano in an assertive, confident style influenced by the blues. He worked in Philadelphia as a member of an orchestra led by the pianist Oliver Naylor, recording in 1925 and appearing at the Palace d'Or and the Orient restaurant in the late 1920s and early 1930s; he also spent a period with the Playboys, led by the double bass player Thelma Terry (recording in 1928). After performing with the singer Seymour Simons and at Smokey's Club in Detroit he came to prominence as a member of Bob Crosby's band (late 1936 – mid-1939), in which he was Joe Sullivan's replacement; while with Crosby he gained recognition as a leading exponent of the boogie-woogie style, and in 1939 he was named "best pianist" by *Down Beat*. In the same year he published transcriptions of music by Count Basie, among others, and three of his own compositions, *Hobson Street Blues*, *Eye Opener*, and *Southern Exposure*. Following a brief and unsuccessful period as a bandleader (1939) Zurke worked in Chicago, Detroit, and St. Paul as an unaccompanied soloist. From summer 1942 until his death he was resident at the Hangover Club in Los Angeles, and in January 1944 he recorded the music for the cartoon film *Jungle Jive*.

SELECTED RECORDINGS

(recorded for Decca unless otherwise indicated)

As sideman: B. Crosby: Gin Mill Blues (1937, 1170); Little Rock Getaway (1937, 1552); Squeeze Me (1937, 1960); Stumbling (1937, 1593); Who's Sorry Now (1937, 1865); Grand Terrace Rhythm (1938, 1725); Milk Cow Blues (1938, 1962); Big Foot Jump (1938, 2108); Call Me a Taxi (1938, 2207); Honky Tonk Train (1938, 2208); Diga diga doo (1938, 2275); Eye Opener (1939, 2282); All Star Band: Blue Lou/The Blues (1939, Vic. 26144)

BIBLIOGRAPHY

ChiltonW; *FeatherE*

P. Pitt: "Bob Zurke," *JJ*, xxii/2 (1969), 6

Obituary, R. Spencer," *JJI*, xxxiv/4 (1981), 17

J. Chilton: *Stomp Off, let's Go! The Story of Bob Crosby's Bob Cats & Big Band* (London, 1983), 41

KEN RATTENBURY/BK

Zwerin, Mike [Michael] (*b* New York, 18 May 1930). Writer, trombonist, and bass trumpeter. He initially learned violin, piano, and accordion, and took up trombone at the age of 13 when he began studying at the High School of Music and Art. In his late teens he led a group briefly at a hotel in the Catskills with Kenny Drew, Nick Stabulas, and Marty Flax among his sidemen. Later he attended the University of Miami, and while on summer vacation in 1948 he played trombone with Miles Davis's nonet at the Royal Roost in New York. After graduating he gave up music and worked in his father's steel business. He resumed playing in Paris in 1957, and later that year he returned to New York, where he worked with Billy May (1957), Urbie Green (1958), Sonny Dunham (1958), Claude Thornhill (1958–9), and Maynard Ferguson (1959–60). Following his father's death in 1960 Zwerin became president of the Capitol Steel Corporation, although he continued to work as a musician. He played bass trumpet and trombone with Orchestra USA (1962–5, recording in 1962) and served as the music director and arranger for a sextet drawn from this large group, which recorded the album *Mack the Knife* (1964, RCA 3498); he also performed in the Upper Bohemia Six (1962–4) and worked in Bill Russo's rehearsal band.

In 1964 Zwerin began working as a writer for the *Village Voice*, and he served as its jazz columnist through 1969. During this period he toured the USSR with Earl Hines (July – August 1966) and accompanied Ella Fitzgerald at the Riverboat as a member of Hines's big band (November 1966). From 1969 he lived in London, where he served as the European editor of the *Village Voice* until he moved to Paris in 1972; in the late 1960s he also contributed articles to *Down Beat* and *Sounds and Fury*. Between 1973 and 1975 he wrote for the periodicals *Rolling Stone* and *Penthouse*, as well as for the *Village Voice*, and in 1977 he was appointed music critic for the *International Herald Tribune*. Around this time he began playing again, and he worked with Alexis Korner (recording in 1978), Steve Potts, Hal Singer, Christian Escoudé, Hans Dulfer, and Alan Silva's Celestrial Communication Orchestra (recording 1978–82). In 1978 he performed and recorded the album *Not Much Noise* (Spot. 19) as the leader of a trio, Not Much Noise, with Escoudé and the baritone saxophonist Gus Nemeth as his sidemen. He continued to work sporadically with the group into the early 1980s and then formed a quartet of varying personnel. In addition Zwerin recorded with Michel Petrucciani (1980) and George Gruntz's Concert Jazz Band (1982), performed and recorded in Paris as a member of Big Band Charlie Mingus (1988), and published *Close Enough for Jazz* (London, 1983), his autobiography, and *La tristesse de Saint Louis: Swing under the Nazis* (London, Melbourne, Australia, and New York, 1985).

BIBLIOGRAPHY

Feather '60s; *Feather–Gitler '70s*; *ReclamsJ*

P. Sullivan: "Mike Zwerin: the Man with Two Hats," *JF* [intl edn], no.72 (1981), 49

J. Weiss: "Michael Zwerin," *Coda*, no.186 (1982), 10

P. Carles, A. Clergeat, and J.-L. Comolli: *Dictionnaire du jazz* (Paris, 1988, rev. and enlarged 2/1994)

GK

Zwingenberger, Axel (*b* Hamburg, Germany, 7 May 1955). German pianist, brother of Torsten Zwingenberger. He studied classical piano from the age of six and adopted the boogie-woogie style in 1973. From 1974 he performed at numerous boogie-woogie, blues, and jazz festivals and broadcast frequently on television and radio throughout Europe, and between 1983 and 1991 he made regular appearances on the television program "ZDF-Teleillustrierte." In addition he toured with Monty Sunshine and Max Collie (both 1978) and Alexis Korner (March 1979), recorded in Los Angeles with Joe Turner (ii) (May 1978, 1981), and toured and recorded with Lionel Hampton (April–May 1980, 1982, 1983) and the blues singer Champion Jack Dupree (October 1980, 1988, 1990). From the early 1980s Zwingenberger toured in the shows *Stars of Boogie Woogie* and *Hot Jazz Meeting*, and he made tours of East Asia (1981), Indonesia and Malaysia (1982), North Africa (1983), and West and Central Africa (early 1996) under the sponsorship of the Goethe-Institut. He recorded with Joe Newman (1982), the singer Mama Yancey (1982–3), with whom he appeared in the US television documentary "Chicago Melodie" (1983), and Sippie Wallace (1983, 1984, the latter during a tour of Europe); most of these albums have been issued under Zwingenberger's name by his own record company and label, Vagabond. In January 1986 he appeared in the English televison program "Southbank Show: a Left Hand Like God," and from April 1996 he performed at Carnegie Hall in a series of boogie-woogie festivals. He has also collaborated extensively with the pianist Vince Weber, and recorded with his brother Torsten Zwingenberger (1988) and with Jay McShann (1990).

SELECTED RECORDINGS

As unaccompanied soloist: *Boogie Woogie Classics* (1991, Vagabond 8.92023)

Duos with S. Wallace: *Axel Zwingenberger and the Friends of Boogie Woogie*, iii: *An Evening with Sippie Wallace* (1984, Vagabond 8.86006)

As leader: *Axel Zwingenberger and the Friends of Boogie Woogie*, ii: *Between Hamburg and Hollywood* (1978, 1981–2, Vagabond 8.85005); with J. Turner (ii): *Boogie Woogie Jubilee* (1981, Telefunken 6.28572); with J. McShann: *Blue Pianos* (1990, Vagabond 891017)

BIBLIOGRAPHY

CarrJ

"Boogie Woogie über alles ... Axel Zwingenberger," *JP*, xxix/11 (1980), 12

K. Mümpfer: "Play, Maestro, Blues und Boogie: Sippie Wallace und Axel Zwingenberger," *JP*, xxxv/5 (1986), 23

<http://www.boogie-woogie.net/a_zwingenberger/facts_az.html> (1999)

<http://www.boogie-woogie.net/books_notes_books_note.html> (1999) [incl. discography]

GK

Zwingenberger, Torsten (*b* Hamburg, Germany, 12 Jan 1959). German drummer, brother of Axel Zwingenberger. From the mid-1970s he led his own groups and performed and recorded regularly with his brother; in 1978 the two recorded in Los Angeles as accompanists to Joe Turner (ii). In 1983 Zwingenberger made the album *Buddy Tate Meets Torsten Zwingenberger* (Moustache Music 120159) and formed the Swingburger Quintet, and in the 1990s he led a quartet. He recorded again as a leader in 1989 (with Plas Johnson as his guest soloist) and in 1993 (the album *Open Sunroof*, Blackbird 41012) and as an unaccompanied soloist in 1991. In November 1992 he played in New York in a hard-bop trio with Peter Bernstein and the double bass player Ari Roland.

BIBLIOGRAPHY

ReclamsJ

"Jazz News," *JP*, xxxii/7 (1983), 37

A. Geyer: "Buddy Tate und Torsten Zwingenberger Band," *JP*, xxxvii/1 (1988), 35

C. Hasenmaile: "Moderner geworden: Torsten Zwingenberger," *JP*, xxxi/6 (1990), 6 [incl. discography]

H. H. Joehnk: "Mainstream im besten Sinn: Torsten Zwingenberger," *JP*, xxxix/5 (1990), 36

P. Watrous: "Jack Kleinsinger's Highlights in Jazz," *New York Times* (12 Nov 1992)

GK

Illustration Acknowledgments

We are grateful to those listed below, who have supplied illustrative material, or given permission for it to be reproduced, or both: where two or more names are given, separated by a spaced slash (/), the name given first is usually that of the supplier of the illustration, who may or may not be the copyright holder; names of photographers are given wherever possible, preceded by "photo." Every effort has been made to contact copyright holders and we apologize to anyone whose name may have been omitted from this list.

The majority of photographs have been supplied from his own collection by Frank Driggs (New York); only where the photographer of one of these is known is the item listed below, following the abbreviation FD /. Alan Forster prepared the drawings (except where otherwise stated).

Nightclubs and other venues *1* photo David Redfern, London; *2* FD / photo Ruysdal, Paris; *3* FD / photo A. P. Bedou, New Orleans; *4, 6* David Redfern Photography, London / photo William Gottlieb; *5* FD / photo © Popsie Randolph
Norvo, Red FD / photo © Timme Rosenkrantz

O'Day, Anita FD / photo © Leo Arsene
Oliver, King FD / photo Daguerre, Chicago
Organ *1* FD / photo Robert Steinau, Louisville, KY
Original Dixieland Jazz Band FD / photo Apeda Studios, New York
Ørsted Pedersen, Niels-Henning photo David Redfern, London
Oxley Tony, photo Peter Symes, London
Parker, Charlie *1* FD / photo Ray Whitten, Los Angeles
Pass, Joe photo Tim Motion, London
Pastorius, Jaco photo David Redfern, London
Patitucci, John photo Tim Motion, London
Peterson, Oscar photo © Chuck Stewart, Teaneck, NJ
Petrucciani, Michel photo Tim Motion, London
Piano *3* David Redfern Photography, London / photo Andrew Putler
Ponty, Jean-Luc photo David Redfern, London
Potter, Chris (Quartet) photo Peter Symes, London
Powell, Bud FD / photo © Duncan P. Schiedt, Pittsboro, IN
Pukwana, Dudu photo Peter Symes, London
Pullen, Don photo Tim Motion, London

Raeburn, Boyd FD / photo Rube Lewis, Chicago
Recording *1* Trustees of the Science Museum, London; *2* EMI Records Ltd., London; *4b* Alan Forster, London; *6* photo Nancy Miller Elliott, New York
Redman, Joshua photo David Redfern, London
Reid, Rufus photo Peter Symes, London
Reinhardt FD / photo Jack Albers, Bad Nauheim, Germany
Rivers, Sam photo Tim Motion, London
Roditi, Claudia photo Tim Motion, London
Rogers, Shorty photo © Chuck Stewart, Teaneck, NJ
Rollins, Sonny photo © Chuck Stewart, Teaneck, NJ
Rudd, Roswell photo Peter Symes, London
Russell, George photo Peter Symes, London
Russell, Pee Wee FD / photo Otto Hess

Sanchez, David photo Tim Motion, London
Sanders, Pharoah photo Peter Symes, London
Saxophone *1* Brian and Constance Dear; *2* Popperfoto, London; *3* FD / photo Joe Alper; *4* photo © Chuck Stewart, Teaneck, NJ
Scofield, John photo Tim Motion, London
Shaw, Artie FD / photo © Leo Arsene
Shepp, Archie photo Peter Symes, London
Sheppard, Andy photo Tim Motion, London
Shorter, Wayne photo David Redfern, London
Singing *1* Paul Oliver Collection, Woodstock, England
Singleton, Zutty FD / photo ZOG, New York
Smith, Bessie FD / photo Edward F. Elcha, New York
Smith, Jimmy photo © Chuck Stewart, Teaneck, NJ
Solal, Martial photo Peter Symes, London
Stern, Mike photo Peter Symes, London
Stewart, Bill photo Tim Motion, London
Stitt, Sonny FD / photo © Popsie Randolph
Strayhorn, Bill photo Tim Motion, London
Sullivan, Joe FD / photo Jack Masters
Sun Ra photo David Redfern, London
Surman, John photo Paul Wood, London
Sutton, Ralph photo David Redfern, London
Swallow, Steve photo Peter Symes, London

Tabackin, Lew photo © Chuck Stewart, Teaneck, NJ
Tatum, Art FD / photo © Dunc Butler
Taylor, Billy (ii) FD / photo © Charles Nadell
Tchicai, John photo Val Wilmer, London
Terry, Clark photo Tim Motion, London
Threadgill, Henry photo Peter Symes, London
Tracey, Stan photo David Redfern, London
Tristano, Lennie FD / photo © Duncan P. Schiedt, Pittsboro, IN
Tyner, McCoy photo Peter Symes, London

Vasconcelos, Nana photo Peter Symes, London
Vaughan, Sarah FD / photo © Popsie Randolph
Vibraphone *1a* Macmillan Publishers Ltd., London; *1b* Brian and Constance Dear

Waldron, Mal photo David Redfern, London
Waller, Fats FD / photo Metropolitan photo Service, New York
Watters, Lu FD / photo © Duncan P. Schiedt, Pittsboro, IN
Webb, Chick FD / photo Apeda Studios, New York
Weber, Eberhard photo David Redfern, London
Wells, Dicky FD / photo © Timme Rosenkrantz
Westbrook, Mike photo Peter Symes, London
Weston, Randy photo Tim Motion, London
Wheeler, Kenny photo Peter Symes, London
Williams, Mary Lou FD / photo Gordon Conner Studio, Cleveland
Wilson, Cassandra photo David Redfern, London
Woods, Phil photo David Redfern, London

Young, Lester FD / Don Peterson, Chevy Chase, MD / photo Charles Peterson

Zawinul, Joe David Redfern Photography, London / photo Andrew Putler
Zorn, John photo Peter Symes, London

Music Example Acknowledgments

We are grateful to music publishers, and others, as listed below, for permission to reproduce copyrighted material. Every effort has been made to trace copyright holders and we apologize to anyone whose name may have been omitted from this list.

Notation *2a* Aisha Music Co., Alpine, NJ; *2b* by permission of Ecaroh, Inc., Malibu, CA; *3* Woodrow Music, Newington, CT

Piano *4* from H. Martin: *Enjoying Jazz,* © 1986 Schirmer Books, a division of Macmillan, Inc., New York, reprinted by permission; *13* © 1966 Unit Core (BM1), worldwide administration rights controlled by Celestial Harmonies, div. of Mayflower Music Corp.; *12a, 12d* by permission of *Annual Review of Jazz Studies,* New Brunswick, NJ, © Paul Rinzler; *8* by permission of Leonard Feather

Rollins, Sonny by permission of Twayne Publishers, a division of G. K. Hall & Co., Boston

Singing reproduced by permission of Columbia Pictures Publications, Miami, FL, and EMI Music Publishing Ltd. and International Music Publications, London

Tatum, Art *1a* © Morley Co., New York; *1b* and *2* from *The Art Tatum Collection*, transcribed by Brent Edstrom and Ronny S. Schiff © Hal Leonard Corporation, WI

Young, Lester *1, 2* by permission of Twayne Publishers, a division of G. K. Hall & Co., Boston

Poem Extracts Acknowledgments

We are grateful to the publishers, and others, as listed below, for permission to reproduce copyrighted material. Every effort has been made to trace copyright holders and we apologize to anyone whose name may have been omitted from this list.

1. "Jazz Fantasia" by Carl Sandburg, from *Smoke and Steel*. Copyright ©1920 by Harcourt Brace & Co. Copyright renewed 1948 by Carl Sandburg. Reprinted by permission of Harcourt Brace & Co.

2. "Jazzonia" by Langston Hughes, from *The Weary Blues*. Copyright ©1926 by Alfred A. Knopf, Inc/Harold Ober Associates Inc. Copyright renewed 1954 by Langston Hughes.

3. Excerpt from "Ma Rainey" by Sterling A. Brown, from *The Collected Poems of Sterling A. Brown* edited by Michael S. Harper. Copyright ©1932 by Harcourt Brace & Co. Copyright renewed 1960 by Sterling A. Brown. Reprinted by permission of HarperCollins Publishers Inc.

4. "Walking Parker Home" by Bob Kaufman, from *Solitudes Crowded with Loneliness*. Copyright ©1965 by Bob Kaufman. Reprinted by permission of New Directions Publishing Corp.

5. Excerpt from "The Day Lady Died" by Frank O'Hara, from *Lunch Poems*. Copyright ©1965 by Frank O' Hara. Reprinted by permission of City Lights Books.

6. Excerpt from "Here Where Coltraine Is" by Michael S. Harper, from *Images of Kin: New and Selected Poems*. Copyright ©1977 by Michael S. Harper. Reprinted by permission of the poet and the University of Illinois Press.

7. Excerpt from "Healing Animal" by Joy Harjo, from *In Mad Love and War*. Copyright ©1990 by Joy Harjo and Wesleyan University Press.

8. "Mingus in Shadow" by William Matthews, from *After All: Last Poems*. Copyright ©1998 by Houghton Mifflin.

Appendix 1

BIBLIOGRAPHY

This bibliography is based on items cited at the ends of individual articles in the dictionary; further items have been added to make a comprehensive (though not exhaustive) listing of resources on jazz. In general only items concerning jazz are cited, though some on related styles (such as ragtime and blues) have been included because they contain substantial amounts of relevant information. The following kinds of publication are not generally included here: the catalogues of libraries and sound archives (*see* the individual entries on such collections in the article Libraries and archives), anthologies of transcriptions, pedagogical texts, and booklets published in conjunction with recordings. Exceptionally, a small number of important articles in journals are included.

The list is divided into the following categories: Bibliographies and reference materials; Discographies (General, Name discographies, Record label listings, Other listings); Other books; and Periodicals (bio-discographies are listed under "Other books"). Within each category, except the last, entries are ordered alphabetically by name(s) of author(s), then by title (ignoring the definite and indefinite articles). For an explanation of periodicals listings, see below. Cross-references are included throughout the list where they are helpful (from the names of second authors, and alternative titles of journals, for example); unless otherwise indicated these references should be understood to lead to entries within the same category or subcategory.

The bibliography was prepared for this second edition by Howard Rye.

BIBLIOGRAPHIES AND REFERENCE MATERIALS

A. J. Agostinelli: *The Newport Jazz Festival, Rhode Island, 1954–1971: a Bibliography, Discography, and Filmography* (Providence, RI, 1977)

R. N. Albert: *An Annotated Bibliography of Jazz Fiction and Jazz Fiction Criticism* (Westport, CT, and London, 1996)

M. K. Aldin: *Blues Magazine Selective Index by Artist and Subject* (Hollywood, CA, 1996, rev. 2/1997, rev. 3/1998, rev. 4/1999)

D. Allen: *Bibliography of Discographies,* ii: *Jazz* (New York and London, 1981)

W. C. Allen: *Allen's Poop Sheet* (Belleville, NJ, 1958–74) [catalogue of books on jazz, issued irregularly]

P. Anquetil, ed.: *Euro Jazz Book: International Jazz Directory 96/97* (Paris, 1996 [*recte* 1997])

Australian Music Centre, see *Jazz: Australian Compositions*

S. C. Barr: *The (Almost) Complete 78 rpm Record Dating Guide* (Toronto, 1980, rev. Huntington Beach, CA, 2/1992, as *The Almost Complete 78 rpm Record Dating Guide (II)*)

R. J. Benford, see A. P. Merriam

Bibliothèques de la ville de Paris: *Jazz: bibliographie et guide de l'amateur Parisien* (Paris, 1984)

C. Bird: *The Jazz and Blues Lover's Guide to the US* (Reading, MS, and elsewhere, 1991, rev. 2/1994; Ger. trans., Berlin, 1994, as *Jazz & Blues Führer durch die USA*)

C. Bohländer and K. H. Holler: *Reclams Jazzführer* (Stuttgart, Germany, 1970, rev. and enlarged 2/1977, rev. and enlarged 3/1989 by C. Bohländer, K. H. Holler, and C. Pfarr, rev. and enlarged 4/2000) [*ReclamsJ*]

M. W. Booth: *American Popular Music: a Reference Guide* (Westport, CT, and London, 1983)

T. Bourke: *Index of Record Label Listings* (Ongar, England, 1988)

J. Bradley, see D. Morgenstern

P. Carles, A. Clergeat, and J.-L. Comolli: *Dictionnaire du jazz* (Paris, 1988, rev. and enlarged 2/1994)

P. Carls [*sic*], see also F. Ténot

G. Carner: *Jazz Performers: an Annotated Bibliography of Biographical Materials* (New York, 1991)

I. Carr, D. Fairweather, and B. Priestley: *Jazz: the Essential Companion* (London, 1987)

——: *Jazz: the Rough Guide* (London, 1995, rev. and enlarged 2/2000; Ger. trans., Stuttgart, Germany, 1999, as *Jazz*) [*CarrJ*]

Centre Nationale d'Action Musicale: *Jazz de France, portraits-contacts* (Paris, 1989)

S. B. Charters: *Jazz: New Orleans, 1885–1957: an Index to the Negro Musicians of New Orleans* (Belleville, NJ, 1958, rev. New York, 2/1963/*R*1983, as *Jazz: New Orleans, 1885–1963: an Index to the Negro Musicians of New Orleans*) [*ChartersJ*]

J. Chilton: *Who's Who of British Jazz* (London and New York, 1997) [*ChiltonB*]

——: *Who's Who of Jazz: Storyville to Swing Street* (London, 1970, rev. and enlarged Philadelphia, 2/1972, rev. and enlarged n.p. [?New York], 3/1978, rev. and enlarged London, 4/1985, rev. 5/1989) [*ChiltonW*]

C. Clark: *Jazz* (Penzance, England, 1982)

P. Clayton and P. Gammond: *Jazz: A–Z* (Enfield, England, 1986; Sp. trans., Madrid, 1990, Buenos Aires, 1991, as *Jazz: A–Z*)

R. D. Clear: *Jazz on Film and Video in the Library of Congress* (Washington, DC, 1993; updated at <http://lcweb.loc.gov/rr/mopic/jazz>)

A. Clergeat: *Dictionnaire du jazz* (Paris, 1966)

A. Clergeat, see also P. Carles

J.-L. Comolli, see P. Carles

D. E. Cooper: *International Bibliography of Discographies: Classical Music and Jazz & Blues, 1962–1972* (Littleton, CO, 1975)

R. Cotterrell, ed.: *Jazz Now: the Jazz Centre Society Guide* (London, 1976)

M. Cotto: *Enciclopedia del blues e della musica nera* (Milan, 1994)

R. Crawford and J. Magee: *Jazz Standards on Record, 1900–1942: a Core Repertory* (Chicago, 1992)

A. M. Dauer, see S. Longstreet

[P. Donisch:] *Who's Dead in Blues, Jazz, Rock, e.e.* (Berlin, 1982)

B. M. Eagle, see M. L. Hart

K. O. Eckland: *Jazz West, 1945–1985: the A–Z Guide to West Coast Jazz Music* (Carmel, CA, 1986, rev. San Rafael, CA, 2/1995) [biographical dictionary]

H.-G. Ehmke, see J. Jørgensen

A. Elings: *Bibliografie van de nederlandse jazz* (Nijmegen, Netherlands, 1966)

T. G. Everett: "An Annotated List of Englishlanguage Jazz Periodicals," *JJS*, iii/2 (1976), 47 [addns and corrections in *JJS*, iv/1 (1977), 110; iv/2 (1977), 94; v/2 (1978), 99; *ARJS*, i (1982), 167; *ARJS*, iii (1984), 205]

D. Fairweather, see I. Carr

L. Feather: *The Encyclopedia of Jazz* (New York, 1955, rev. and enlarged 2/1960/*R*1984) [*FeatherE*]

——: *The Encyclopedia of Jazz in the Sixties* (New York, 1966/*R*1986) [*Feather '60s*]

——: *The Encyclopedia Yearbook of Jazz* (New York, 1956/*R*1993, with *The New Yearbook of Jazz*, as *The Encyclopedia Yearbooks of Jazz*)

——: *The New Yearbook of Jazz* (New York, 1958/*R*1993, with *The Encyclopedia Yearbook of Jazz*, as *The Encyclopedia Yearbooks of Jazz*)

L. Feather and I. Gitler, eds.: *The Biographical Encyclopedia of Jazz* (New York, and Oxford, England, 1999) [*Feather–GitlerBEJ*]

——: *The Encyclopedia of Jazz in the Seventies* (New York, 1976/*R*1987) [*Feather–Gitler '70s*]

S. A. Floyd, Jr., and M. J. Reisser: *Black Music in the United States: an Annotated Bibliography of Selected Reference and Research Materials* (Millwood, nr Ossining, NY, 1983)

R. Ford: *A Blues Bibliography: the International Literature of an African-American Music Genre* (Bromley, England, 1999)

K. Frandsen: *Politikens jazzleksikon* (Copenhagen, 1987)

P. Gammond: *A Guide to Popular Music* (London, 1960)

——: *The Oxford Companion to Popular Music* (Oxford, England, and New York, 1991)

P. Gammond, see also P. Clayton

J. Ganfield: *Books and Periodical Articles on Jazz in America from 1926–1932* (New York, 1933)

G. Gart: *ARLD: the American Record Label Directory and Dating Guide, 1940–1959* (Milford, NH, 1990)

M. Gautier: *Jazz au cinéma* (Paris, 1961)

M. Gautier, see also H. Panassié

G. J. Gibson, see P. R. Klotman

I. Gitler, see L. Feather; D. Morgenstern

J. Gonda, ed: *Who's Who in Hungarian Jazz* (Budapest, 1974)

R. S. Gold: *A Jazz Lexicon: an A–Z Directory of Jazz Terms* (New York, 1964, rev. Indianapolis, 2/1975, as *Jazz Talk*) [*GoldJL*]

J. Gray: *Fire Music: a Bibliography of the New Jazz, 1959–1990* (New York, 1991) [*GrayF*]

A. A. Gurwitch [*sic*], see H. Panassié

S. Harris: *Blues Who's Who: a Biographical Dictionary of Blues Singers* (New Rochelle, NY, 1979/——1994)

M. L. Hart, B. M. Eagle, and L. N. Howarth: *The Blues: a Bibliographic Guide* (New York, 1989)

M. Hayes, R. Scribner, and P. Magee: *The Encyclopedia of Australian Jazz* (Brisbane, Australia, 1976)

A. Heerkens: *Jazz* (Alkmaar, Netherlands, n.d. [?1956]) [pictorial encyclopedia; parallel texts in Dutch, Fr., Eng., and Ger.]

B. Hefele: *Bibliographie Jazz Rock Pop, 1990* (Pullach, nr Munich, 1993)

——: *Jazz Bibliography: International Literature on Jazz, Blues, Spirituals, Gospel and Ragtime Music with a Selected List of Works on the Social and Cultural Background from the Beginning to the Present/Jazz-Bibliographie: Verzeichnis des internationalen Schrifttums über Jazz, Blues, Spirituals, Gospel und Ragtime, mit einer Auswahlbibliographie über den sozialen und kulturellen Hintergrund von den Anfängen bis zur Gegenwart* (Munich and elsewhere, 1981) [texts in Eng. and Ger.]

——: *Jazz – Rock – Pop: eine Bibliographie der deutschsprachigen Literatur, 1988 bis 1989* (Munich, 1991)

G. Herzhaft: *Encyclopédie du blues: étude bio-discographique d'une musique populaire négro-américaine* (Lyons, France, 1979, rev. Paris, [2]/1990, as *Encyclopédie du blues*, rev. n.p. [France], [3]/1997, as *La Grande Encyclopédie du blues*; Eng. trans., Fayetteville, AR, 1992, rev. 2/1997, as *Encyclopedia of the Blues*; Ger. trans., St. Andrä-Wördern, Germany, 1992, rev. [2]/1998, as *Enzyklopädie des Blues*)

J.-R. Hippenmeyer: *Jazz sur films, ou 55 années de rapports jazzcinéma vus à travers plus de 800 films tournés entre 1917 et 1972: filmographie critique* (Yverdon, Switzerland, 1973)

K. H. Holler, see C. Bohländer

D. Horn: *The Literature of American Music in Books and Folk Music Collections: a Fully Annotated Bibliography* (Metuchen, NJ, 1977)

L. N. Howarth, see M. L. Hart

Jazz: Australian Compositions (Sydney, 1978) [pubn of Australian Music Centre]

B. Johnson: *The Oxford Companion to Australian Jazz* (Melbourne, Australia, 1987)

J. Jørgensen and E. Wiedemann, eds.: *Jazzens hvemhvadhvor* (Copenhagen, 1962; rev. Ger. trans., by H.G. Ehmke, Hamburg, Germany, 1966, as *Mosaik Jazzlexikon*)

H. Kallmann, G. Potvin, and K. Winters, eds.: *Encyclopedia of Music in Canada* (Toronto, Buffalo, and London, 1981, rev. 2/1992, ed. H. Kallmann, G. Potvin, K. Winters, and M. Miller) [*EMC1, EMC2*]

R. Kane, see J. Voigt

B. Kellner, ed.: *The Harlem Renaissance: a Historical Dictionary for the Era* (New York and London, 1987)

D. Kennington: *The Literature of Jazz: a Critical Guide* (London, 1970, rev. 2/1980 with D. L. Read)

R. D. Kinkle: *The Complete Encyclopedia of Popular Music and Jazz, 1900–1950*, i: *Music Year by Year, 1900–1950*; ii: *Biographies A through K*; iii: *Biographies L through Z*; iv: *Indexes and Appendices* (New Rochelle, NY, and Westport, CT, 1974; ii and iii repr. Mt. Vernon, IN, 1998, as vols. i and ii of *Leading Musical Performers (Popular Music and Jazz) 1900–1950*, with new vol. iii of addns and corrections) [iv incl. discography and full listings for a number of major labels during a portion of the 78 era]

——: *Leading Musical Performers (Popular Music and Jazz) 1900–1950: 2150 biographies updated to 1996 with additions and corrections*, iii: *Extension of The Complete Encyclopedia of Popular Music and Jazz, 1900–1950 Published 1974* (Mt. Vernon, IN, 1998)

P. R. Klotman: *Frame by Frame: a Black Filmography* (Bloomington, IN, and London, 1979)

P. R. Klotman and G. J. Gibson: *Frame by Frame II: a Filmography of the African-American Image 1978–1994* (Bloomington, IN, and Indianapolis, 1997)

Knaurs Jazz Lexikon, see S. Longstreet

M. Kunzler: *Jazz-Lexicon* (Reinbek, nr Hamburg, Germany, 1988)

W. Laade, W. Ziefle, and D. Zimmerle: *Jazz-Lexikon* (Stuttgart, Germany, and elsewhere, 1953)

C. Larkin, ed.: *The Guinness Who's Who of Blues* (London, 1993, rev. Enfield, England, 2/1995)

——: *The Guinness Who's Who of Jazz* (London, 1992, rev. Enfield, England, 2/1995; Hung. trans., Budapest, 1993, as *Guinness jazz-zenészek lexikona, ki kicsoda a jazzben?*)

——: *The Virgin Encyclopaedia of the Blues* (London, 1998)

D.-R. de Lerma: *Bibliography of Black Music* (Westport, CT, and London, 1981–4)

J.-P. Levet: *Talkin' that Talk: le langage du blues et du jazz* (Paris, 1992)

S. Longstreet and A. M. Dauer: *Knaurs Jazz Lexikon* (Munich and Zurich, 1957)

L. Lowe: *Music Master Directory of Popular Music* (London, 1975, rev. Hastings, England, 2/1986, rev. 3/1992)

D. Luciano: *Jazz: Yesterday, Today and Tomorrow: an Encyclopedia of People, Places, Venues and the Media Chronicling 100 Years of Jazz* (Upland, PA, 1996)

P. Magee, see M. Hayes

C. Major: *Dictionary of Afro-American Slang* (New York, 1970, London, 1971, as *Black Slang: a Dictionary of Afro-American Talk*)

——: *Juba to Jive: a Dictionary of African-American Slang* (New York and London, 1994)

R. Markewich: *Bibliography of Jazz and Pop Tunes Sharing the Chord Progressions of Other Compositions* (New York, 1970, rev. 2/1974 [privately pubd])

A. Matzner, I. Poledňák, and I. Wasserberger, eds.: *Encyklopedie jazzu a moderní populární hudby* (Prague, 1990)

A. Mazzoletti, ed.: *Grande enciclopedia del jazz* (Rome, 1980; Sp. trans., Madrid, 1980, as *Gran enciclopedia del jazz*)

E. S. Meadows: *Jazz Reference and Research Materials: a Bibliography* (New York and London, 1981)

C. G. Herzog zu Mecklenburg: *International Bibliography of Jazz Books*, i: *1921–1949* (Baden-Baden, Germany, 1983); ii: *1950–1959* (Baden-Baden, 1988)

——: *International Jazz Bibliography: Jazz Books from 1919 to 1968* (Strasbourg, France, and Baden-Baden, Germany, 1969; suppls. 1971, 1975)

D. Meeker: *Jazz in the Movies: a Tentative Index to the Work of Jazz Musicians for the Cinema* (London, 1972)

——: *Jazz in the Movies: a Guide to Jazz Musicians, 1917–1977* (London, 1977, rev. 2/1981, as *Jazz in the Movies*)

B. Meier: *Literatur und Studienmaterialen zur Jazzimprovisation: eine annotierte Bibliographie zu den theoretischen und technischen Grundlagen der Jazzimprovisation einschlägig ihren pädagogischen sowie stilistichen Aspekten* (Stuttgart, Germany, 1988)

A. P. Merriam and R. J. Benford: *A Bibliography of Jazz* (Philadelphia, 1954/*R*1970)

P. Moon, comp.: *A Bibliography of Jazz Discographies Published since 1960* (South Harrow, England, 1969, rev.2/1972)

D. Morgenstern, I. Gitler, and J. Bradley, eds.: *Bird & Diz: a Bibliography* (New York, 1973)

J. J. Mulder: *Jazz op schrift, een biografie van Nederlandstalige jazzliteratur*, i: *Boeken en platen* (Amsterdam, 2000)

L. Mustazza: *Sinatra: an Annotated Bibliography* (Westport, CT, and London, 1999)

E. Myers, ed.: *Australian Jazz Directory 1998* (Sydney, 1998)

K. Nauck, see A. Sutton

N. R. Ortiz Oderigo: *Diccionario del jazz* (Buenos Aires, 1959)

H. Panassié and M. Gautier: *Dictionnaire du jazz* (Paris, 1954, rev. and enlarged 1971, enlarged 2/1980, rev. and enlarged 3/1987 by A. Vasset and J. Pescheux; Eng. trans., London, 1956, rev. A. A. Gurwitch [*sic*], Boston, 1956/*R*1973, as *Guide to Jazz*)
R. Pernet, J.-P. Schroeder, and others: *Dictionnaire du jazz à Bruxelles et en Wallonie* (Liège, Belgium, 1991)
J. Pescheux, see H. Panassié
B. L. Peterson, Jr.: *A Century of Musicals in Black and White: an Encyclopedia of Musical Stage Works by, about, or involving African-Americans* (Westport, CT, and London, 1993)
I. Poledňák, see A. Matzner
G. Poole: *Enciclopedia de swing* (Buenos Aires, 1939)
G. Potvin, see H. Kallmann
N. Powell: *The Language of Jazz* (Manchester, England, 1997)
B. Priestley, see I. Carr
D. L. Read, see D. Kennington
Reclams Jazzführer, see C. Bohländer
C. Reggentin-Scheidt, see N. Ruecker
R. G. Reisner: *The Literature of Jazz: a Preliminary Bibliography* (New York, 1954, rev. and enlarged 2/1959, as *The Literature of Jazz: a Selective Bibliography*)
M. J. Reisser, see S. A. Floyd, Jr.
P. Renaud: *Simply not Cricket: British Jazz Discography, 1964–94* (Blois, France, 1994)
A. Rose and E. Souchon: *New Orleans Jazz: a Family Album* (Baton Rouge, LA, 1967, rev. 2/1978, rev. and enlarged 3/1984)
N. Ruecker: *Jazz Literature* (Frankfurt am Main, Germany, 1981–4; Schmitten, Germany, 1985–) [nos.1, 2, untitled; nos.3–5 as *Jazz Blues Literature*; nos.7– as *Jazz Literature, Jazz Videos*] [annual catalogue, with annual suppl. from no.5]
N. Ruecker and C. Reggentin-Scheidt: *Jazz Index: Bibliographie unselbständiger Jazzliteratur/Bibliography of Jazz Literature in Periodicals* (Frankfurt am Main, Germany, 1977–87) [7 vols.]
N. Ruecker, see also C. G. Herzog zu Mecklenburg
B. Rust: *The American Record Label Book* (New Rochelle, NY, 1978)
R. Santelli: *The Big Book of Blues: a Biographical Encyclopedia* (New York, 1993)
H. R. Schleman: *Rhythm on Record: a Complete Survey and Register of all the Principal Recorded Dance Music from 1906 to 1936, and a Who's Who of the Artists Concerned in the Making* (London, 1936/*R*1978)
J.-P. Schroeder, see R. Pernet
R. Scribner, see M. Hayes
J. Shepherd and others: *Popular Music Studies: a Select International Bibliography* (London and Washington, DC, 1997)
G. G. Simon and W. Hirschenberger: *The Chronological Ragtime Discography of the Austro-Hungarian Monarchy* (Budapest, 1992, rev. 2/1999)
J. Skowronski: *Black Music in America: a Bibliography* (Metuchen, NJ, and London, 1981)
J. Slawe: *Wörterbuch zur Jazzmusik* (Zurich, 1953)
E. Souchon, see A. Rose
E. Southern: *Biographical Dictionary of Afro-American and African Musicians* (Westport, CT, 1982)
S. Stanton: *The Tombstone Tourist: Musicians* (Portland, OR, 1998)
A. Sutton: *Directory of American Disc Record Brands and Manufacturers, 1891–1943* (Westport, CT, and London, 1994)
A. Sutton and K. Nauck: *American Record Labels and Companies: an Encyclopedia (1891–1943)* (Denver, 2000)
F. Ténot and P. Carls [*sic*]: *Dictionnaire du jazz* (Paris, 1967)
G. C. Testoni and others: *Enciclopedia del jazz* (Milan, 1953, rev. and enlarged 2/1954)
E. Townley: *Tell your Story: a Dictionary of Jazz and Blues Recordings, 1917–1950* (Chigwell, England, 1976)
——: *Tell your Story: a Dictionary of Mainstream Jazz and Blues Recordings*, ii: *1951–1975* (Chigwell, England, 1987)
D. Tudor and others, eds.: *Popular Music Periodicals Index, 1973[–6]* (Metuchen, NJ, 1974–7)
W. van Eyle, ed.: *Jazz geimproviseerde muziek en Nederland* (Utrecht, Netherlands, and Antwerp, Belgium, 1978)
K. R. Vann: *Black Music in Ebony: an Annotated Guide to the Articles on Music in Ebony Magazine, 1945–1985* (Chicago, 1990)
A. Vasset, see H. Panassié
J. Voigt and R. Kane: *Jazz Music in Print* (Winthrop, ME, 1975, rev. and enlarged 3/1982, as *Jazz Music in Print and Jazz Books in Print*)
I. Wasserberger, see A. Matzner
M. White: *"You Must Remember This . . . ": Popular Songwriters, 1900–1980* (London, 1983)
E. Wiedemann, see J. Jørgensen
S. D. Winick: *Rhythm: an Annotated Bibliography* (Metuchen, NJ, 1974)
K. Winters, see H. Kallmann
J. Woelfer: *Lexicon des Jazz* (Munich, 1993)
M. Woelfle: *Das kleine Jazzlexicon* (Munich, 1995)
B. Wood: *The Song for Me: a Glossary of New Orleans Musicians (and Others of that Ilk)* (Walmer, England, 1999)
W. Ziefle, see W. Laade
D. Zimmerle, see W. Laade

DISCOGRAPHIES

General

A. J. Agostinelli, see BIBLIOGRAPHIES AND REFERENCE MATERIALS
G. Avakian, see C. Delaunay
J. Bergh: *Norwegian Jazz Discography, 1905–1998* (Oslo, 1999)
J. Bergh, see also OTHER BOOKS, B. Stendahl
Bielefelder Katalog, see M. Scheffner
O. Blackstone: *Index to Jazz: Jazz Recordings, 1917–1944*, i–iv (Fairfax, VA, 1945–8/*R*1978)
R. Boretti: *Collector's Catalog* (Cosenza, 1969, rev. 2/1977); see also PERIODICALS, Collector
O. Brard and D. Nevers: *Le jazz en France: Jazz and Hot Music Discography, Selection 1* (Paris, 1989); *Selection 2* (Paris, 1989); *Selection 3* (Paris, 1991)
D. Brigaud: *Liste alphabétique des disques chroniqués dans Le bulletin du Hot Club de France (3ème série, no.1 à 243)* (Paris, 1979)
D. Brigaud, see also M.-F. Hernequet
W. Bruyninckx: *50 Years of Recorded Jazz, 1917–1967* (n.p. [Mechelen, Belgium], n.d. [1968–?1975]; rev. and enlarged 2/n.d. [1978–80], as *60 Years of Recorded Jazz, 1917–1977*; suppls. 1985; rev. and enlarged 3/n.d. [1987–99], as *70 Years of Recorded Jazz, 1917–1987*; rev. and enlarged 4/n.d. [2000–], by W. Bruyninckx and D. Truffandier, as *85 Years of Recorded Jazz, (1897) 1917–2002*) [CD-ROM]
——: *Jazz: Swing, 1920–1985: Swing Dance Bands & Combos* (n.p. [Mechelen, Belgium], n.d. [1986–90])
——: *Jazz: Traditional Jazz, 1897–1985: Origins, New Orleans, Dixieland, Chicago Styles* (n.p. [Mechelen, Belgium], n.d. [1987–90])
——: *Jazz: The Vocalists, 1917–1988: Singers & Crooners* (n.p. [Mechelen, Belgium], n.d. [1988–90])
——: *Modern Jazz: Bebop, Hard Bop, West Coast* (n.p. [Mechelen, Belgium], n.d. [1984–7])
——: *Modern Jazz: Modern Big Band* (n.p. [Mechelen, Belgium], n.d. [1985–9])
——: *Progressive Jazz: Free, Third Stream, Fusion* (n.p. [Mechelen, Belgium], n.d. [1984–9])
M. Cabanowski and H. Choliński: *Polska dyskografia jazzowa, 1955–1972* (Warsaw, 1974)
D. Carey and A. J. McCarthy: *The Directory of Recorded Jazz and Swing Music* [cover title *Jazz Directory*], i–iv (Fordingbridge, England, 1949–51; ii–iv rev. London, 2/1955–7); v, vi (London, 1954–7)
Catalogue des 33 tours de jazz de la communaute française de Belgique (Brussels, 1984)
G. Cherrington and others: *Jazz Catalogue 1960[–1971]*, i–viii (London, n.d.); ix–xi (Sevenoaks, England, n.d.) [periodical discography]
H. Choliński, see M. Cabanowski
G. Conrad: *Discographie der Jazz und Semijazzaufnahmen im Bereich der heutigen Volksdemokratien*, i–xi (Menden, Germany, 1983–91)
C. Crump, see T. Stagg
W. R. Daniels: *The American 45 and 78 rpm Record Dating Guide, 1940–1959* (Westport, CT, and London, 1985)
A. G. Debus, see B. Rust
J. de Donder: *"On Tour": a Disco and Tapeography of the Recordings Made by New Orleans Musicians with Local Bands* (Dilbeek, Belgium, 1983)
C. Delaunay: *Hot Discography* (Paris, 1936, rev. 4/1943 as *Hot discographie*, rev. and enlarged, by W. E. Schaap and G. Avakian, New York, 5/1948/*R*1982, as *New Hot Discography: the Standard Directory of Recorded Jazz*)
C. Delaunay and K. Mohr: *Hot discographie encyclopédique* (Paris, 1951) [inc., A–Hefti, Neal only]
D. Diehl: *The Blue Pages: a Guide to 78 rpm Party Records* (Harlingen, TX, 1996, rev. 2/1997, rev. 3/1998, as *The Blue Pages: the Encyclopedic Guide to 78 rpm Party Records*, updated at <http://www.hensteeth.com/>)
R. M. W. Dixon and J. Godrich: *Blues & Gospel Records, 1902–1942* (Hatch End, nr London, 1964, rev. and enlarged London, 2/1969, as J. Godrich and R. M. W. Dixon: *Blues & Gospel Records, 1902–1942*, rev. and enlarged Chigwell, England, 3/1982, as R. M. W. Dixon and J. Godrich: *Blues & Gospel Records, 1902–1943*, rev. and enlarged Oxford, England, 4/1997, as R. M. W. Dixon, J. Godrich, and H. Rye: *Blues & Gospel Records, 1890–1943*)
E. Edwards, Jr., G. Hall, and B. Korst: *Modern Jazz Piano* (Whittier, CA, 1965)
B. Englund, see H. Nicolausson
J. Evensmo: *History of Jazz Tenor Saxophone: Black Artists*, i: *1917–1934* (Oslo, 1996); ii: *1935–1939* (Oslo, 1997); iii: *1940–1944* (Oslo, 1997); iv: *1945–1949* (Oslo, 1999)
L. Fancourt, see M. Leadbitter
S. Forbes, see B. Rust
A. Gainsbury, see J. Rowe
J. Godrich, see R. M. W. Dixon

U. Goeman, see OTHER BOOKS, P. Klaasse
R. Grandorge, see B. Rust
J. Grunnet Jepsen, see J. G. Jepsen
G. Hall, see E. Edwards, Jr.
D. Hamilton-Smith, see J. Rowe
L. H. Harrison, see M. R. Pitts
C. Hayes: *A Discography of Gospel Records, 1937–1971* (n.p. [Copenhagen], 1973) [covers 14 musicians and groups]
C. J. Hayes and R. Laughton: *Gospel Records, 1943–1969: a Black Music Discography*, i: *A to K* (London, 1992); ii: *L to Z* (London, 1992)
U. Heier and R. E. Lotz: *The Banjo on Record: a Bio-discography* (Westport, CT, and London, 1993)
M.-F. Hernequet and D. Brigaud: *Liste alphabétique des disques chroniqués dans Le bulletin du Hot Club de France (3ème série, no. 244 à 343)* (n.p. [Paris], 1989)
J.-R. Hippenmeyer: *Swiss Jazz Disco* (Yverdon, Switzerland, 1977)
Y. Hori, see N. Susuki
D. O. Huggard: *Jazz Recordings of New Zealand* (Auckland, 1996, rev. 2/1996)
IJS Jazz Register (Newark, NJ, 1979–) [incl. indexes; on microfiche; issued irregularly]
T. Ikegami: *New Orleans Renaissance on Record* (Tokyo, 1980)
D. A. Jasen: *Recorded Ragtime, 1897–1958* (Hamden, CT, 1973) [incl. listings of 78 r.p.m. recordings of jazz versions of ragtime pieces]
Jazz Hero's Data Bank (Tokyo, 1991)
J. G. Jepsen: *Jazz Records, 1942–[1969]: a Discography*, v, vi (Copenhagen, 1963); vii, viii, i–iva (Holte, Denmark, 1964–8); iv*b–d* (Copenhagen, 1969–70)
R. Jewson, see J. Rowe
B. Korst, see E. Edwards, Jr.
J. Lacomme, comp.: *Jazz Organ: a Discography* (Paris, 1997)
R. D. Laing and C. Sheridan: *Jazz Records: the Specialist Labels* (Copenhagen, 1981)
R. Laird: *Tantalizing Tingles: a Discography of early Ragtime, Jazz, and Novelty Syncopated Piano Recordings, 1889–1934* (Westport, CT, and London, 1995)
H. H. Lange: *Die deutsche "78er": Discographie der Jazz und Hot-Dance-Musik, 1903–1958* (Berlin, 1966, rev. and enlarged 2/1978, rev. and enlarged 3/1992)
——: *Die deutsche Jazz-Discographie: eine Geschichte des Jazz auf Schallplatten von 1902 bis 1955* (Berlin, 1955)
R. Laughton, see C. J. Hayes
M. Leadbitter and N. Slaven: *Blues Records, January, 1943 to December, 1966* (London, 1968)
——: *Blues Records, 1943–1970: a Selective Discography*, i: *A to K* (London, 1987)
M. Leadbitter, L. Fancourt, and P. Pelletier: *Blues Records, 1943–1970: "the Bible of the Blues,"* ii: *L to Z* (London, 1994)
J. Leder: *Women in Jazz: a Discography of Instrumentalists, 1913–1968* (Westport, CT, 1985)
J. Litchfield: *The Canadian Jazz Discography, 1916–1980* (Toronto, Buffalo, and London, 1982)
——: *This is Jazz* (Montreal, 1985) [index to a radio program]
R. E. Lotz: *Discographie der deutschen Tanzmusik* (Bonn, 1993–)
——: *German Ragtime and the Prehistory of Jazz*, i: *The Sound Documents* (Chigwell, England, 1985) [lists discs, cylinders, piano rolls, music boxes, and films]
A. McCarthy: *Jazz Discography*, i: *An International Discography of Recorded Jazz, Including Blues, Gospel and Rhythm-and-blues for the Year January–December 1958* (London, 1960)
A. McCarthy, see also D. Carey
T. Middleton: *BBC Radio Rhythm Club, 1940–1946* (London, 1997)
W. H. Miller, see J. Mitchell
J. Mitchell: *Australian Discography*, ed. W. H. Miller (Melbourne, Australia, 1950, 2/1960)
K. Mohr: *Discographie du jazz: tous les disques actuellement dans le commerce en Suisse* (Geneva, 1945)
K. Mohr, see also C. Delaunay
D. Nevers, see O. Brard
H. Nicolausson: *Svensk jazzdiskografi* (Stockholm, 1953, rev. and enlarged 2/1983, with B. Englund, as *Swedish Jazz Discography*)
K. Pensoneault and C. Sarles: *Jazz Discography Additions and Corrections* (Jackson Heights, NY, 1944)
R. Pernet: *Belgian Jazz Discography (1897–1999)* (Brussels, 1999)
G. Pétard: *The Black Female LPs Catalogue & Price Guide* (Boulogne, France, 1987)
M. R. Pitts and L. H. Harrison: *Hollywood on Record: the Film Stars' Discography* (Metuchen, NJ, 1978)
E. Raben: *A Discography of Free Jazz* (Copenhagen, 1969)
E. Raben, ed.: *Jazz Records, 1942–80: a Discography* (Copenhagen, 1990–)
P. Renaud: *La discographie du jazz anglais* (Chaumont, France, 1985)
The Rigler and Deutsch Record Index: a National Union Catalog of Sound Recordings (Syracuse, NY, 1985) [pt i: 78 r.p.m. recordings in the holdings of members of the ARSC; in microform]
A. Rogers: *Dance Bands and Big Bands* (Tempe, AZ, 1986) [discography and price guide]
J. Rowe and T. Watson: *Junkshopper's Discography* (London, 1945, rev. and enlarged by A. Gainsbury, 2/1956, as *Guide to Junkshoppers*; rev. by D. Hamilton-Smith, R. Jewson, and R. Webb as *Arthur Gainsbury's Guide to Junkshoppers*, *Sv*, no.1 (1965) to no.55 (1974))
B. Rust: *The American Dance Band Discography, 1917–1942* (New Rochelle, NY, 1975)
——: *The HMV Studio House Bands, 1912–1939* (Chigwell, England, 1976)
——: *Jazz Records*, i: *1897–1931* (Hatch End, nr London, 1961, 2/1962 with index by R. Grandorge); ii: *1932–1942* (Hatch End, 1965); i, ii, as *Jazz Records: A–Z, 1897–1942* (rev. London, [3]/1969, rev. and enlarged New Rochelle, NY, 4/1978, rev. Chigwell, England, 5/n.d. [1983])
——: *The Zonophone Studio House Bands, 1924–1932* (Chigwell, England, 1976)
B. Rust and A. G. Debus: *The Complete Entertainment Discography, from the mid-1890s to 1942* (New Rochelle, NY, 1973, rev. New York, 2/1989)
B. Rust and E. S. Walker: *British Dance Bands, 1912–1939* (London, 1973, rev. and enlarged Harrow, England, 2/1986, by Rust and S. Forbes as *British Dance Bands on Record, 1911–1945*; suppl., 1989)
H. Rye, see R. M. W. Dixon
C. Sarles, see K. Pensoneault
W. E. Schaap, see C. Delaunay
M. Scheffner and others, eds.: *Katalog der Jazzschallplatten* [from 1974 *Bielefelder Katalog: Verzeichnis der Jazz-schallplatten*, from 1981 *G. Braun–Bielefelder Katalog Jazz: Verzeichnis der JazzSchallplatten*, from 1984 *Bielefelder Katalog, Schallplatten, Compact Discs: Jazz*, from 1986 *Bielefelder Katalog, Schallplatten, Compact Discs, MusiCassetten: Jazz*, in 1996 *Bielefelder Katalog, Compact Discs, Schallplatten, MusiCassetten: Jazz*, from 1997 *Bielefelder Katalog Jazz: Compact Discs, MusiCassetten, Schallplatten*] (Bielefeld, Germany, 1959–80; Karlsruhe, Germany, 1981–3; Stuttgart, Germany, 1984–) [periodical catalogue, yearly]
M. Scheffner, see OTHER BOOKS, C. G. Herzog zu Mecklenburg
A. Schwaninger and A. Gurwitsch: *Swing discographie* (Geneva, 1945)
L. Seel: *Deutsches Jazz-Festival Frankfurt, 1953–1992* (Frankfurt am Main, Germany, 1994) [discography of recordings from the festival in the archives of Hessischer Rundfunk]
C. Sheridan, see R. D. Laing
G. G. Simon: *Magyar jazzdiszkografia, 1905–1994* (Budapest, 1994)
——: *Magyar jazzlemezek/Hungarian Jazz Records, 1912–1984* (Pécs, Hungary, 1985)
N. Slaven, see M. Leadbitter
J. R. Smart: *Radio Broadcasts in the Library of Congress, 1924–1941: a Catalog of Recordings* (Washington, DC, 1982)
T. Stagg and C. Crump: *New Orleans, the Revival: a Tape and Discography of Negro Traditional Jazz Recorded in New Orleans or by New Orleans Bands, 1937–1972* (n.p. [London], 1973)
K. Stratemann: *Jazz Ball & Feather on Jazz* (Menden, Germany, 1981) [index to two television programs]
——: *Negro Bands on Film*, i: *Big Bands, 1928–1950: an Exploratory Filmo-discography* (Lübbecke, Germany, 1981)
N. Susuki: *Jazz on Japanese TV, Jan–Dec 1990* (Shizuoka, Japan, 1991)
N. Susuki and Y. Hori: *Jazz on Japanese TV, Jan–Dec 1991* (Shizuoka, Japan, 1992)
——: *Jazz on Japanese TV, Jan–Dec 1992* (Shizuoka, Japan, 1993)
E. Towler: *British Dance Bands (1920–1949) on 12-inch Long-playing Records* (Harrow, England, 1985; suppl., 1987)
E. Townley, see OTHER BOOKS, S. Traill
D. Truffandier, see W. Bruyninckx
K. Tsuchiyama: *Blues Albums in Japan, 1960–1964, plus Supplement '85: a Guide to 25 Years of Blues LPs* (Tokyo, 1986)
W. van Eyle, see H. Zwartenkot
P. Vernon: *African-American Blues, Rhythm and Blues, Gospel and Zydeco on Film and Video, 1926–1997* (Aldershot, England, and Brookfield, VT, 1999)
E. S. Walker, see B. Rust
T. Watson, see J. Rowe
R. Webb, see J. Rowe
H. Westerberg: *Suomalaiset jazzlevytykset, 1932–1976/A Finnish Jazz Discography, 1932–1976: 45 Americans, 92 Europeans, and Hundreds of Finns* (Helsinki, 1977)
H. Zwartenkot and others: *The Dutch Jazz and Blues Discography, 1916–1980*, ed. W. van Eyle (Amsterdam, 1981)

Name discographies

B. H. Aasland: *The "Wax Works" of Duke Ellington* (Stockholm, 1954); part rev. and enlarged as *The "Wax Works" of Duke Ellington*, i: *6 March 1940–30 July 1942: RCA Victor Period* (Järfälla, nr Sollentuna, Sweden, 1978); ii: *31 July 1942–11 Nov 1944: the Recording Ban Period* (Järfälla, 1979) [contd in *DEMS* [Duke Ellington Music Society] *Bulletin*]

R. W. Ackelson: *Frank Sinatra: a Complete Recording History of Techniques, Songs, Composers, Lyrics, Arrangers, Sessions and First-issue Albums, 1939–1984* (Jefferson, NC, 1992)
A. Astrup: *A Discography of Brew Moore* (Søborg, Denmark, 1992)
——: *The Gerry Mulligan Discography* (Søborg, Denmark, 1989)
——: *The John Haley Sims Discography* (Lyngby, Denmark, 1980; suppl., Karlslunde, Denmark, 1983; suppl., Søborg, Denmark, 1990)
——: *The Stan Getz Discography* (Texarkana, TX, 1978, rev. and enlarged Karlslunde, Denmark, 2/1984, as *The Revised Stan Getz Discography*, rev. and enlarged Søborg, Denmark, 3/1991, as *The New Revised Stan Getz Discography*)
S. Bailey: *Greatest Slideman Ever Born* (Southwick, England, n.d. [1998], rev. 2/n.d. [1999], suppl. to 1st edn, Southwick, England, 1999) [discography of Kid Ory]
D. M. Bakker: *Billie & Teddy on Microgroove, 1932–1944* (Alphen aan de Rijn, Netherlands, 1975) [Billie Holiday and Teddy Wilson]
——: *Clarence Williams on Microgroove* (Alphen aan de Rijn, Netherlands, 1976)
——: *Duke Ellington on Microgroove: 1923–February 1940* (Alphen aan de Rijn, Netherlands, 1972, rev. 2/1974, as *Duke Ellington on Microgroove, 1923–1942*, rev. 3/1977 as *Duke Ellington on Microgroove*, i: *1923–1936*)
D. M. Bakker, see also P. Koster
E. M. Bakker, see C. Hofmann
B. H. Behncke: *The Recordings of Joe "King" Oliver* (Hamburg, Germany, 1997)
B. H. Behncke and K.-U. Dürr: *Jimmie Noone* (Hamburg, Germany, 1996)
R. Bergerone: *Company, 1976–1983: Radio Broadcasts, Records, Concerts* (Sierre, Switzerland, 1983)
R. Bergerone, see also G. Cerutti
G. Bielderman: *Acker Bilk Discography* (Zwolle, Netherlands, 1988, rev. 2/1992, rev. 3/1995, rev. 4/1996, rev. 5/2000)
——: *Alain Marquet Discography* (Zwolle, Netherlands, 2000)
——: *Alan Elsdon Discography* (Zwolle, Netherlands, 1994, rev. 2/1996)
——: *Alex Welsh Discography* (Zwolle, Netherlands, 1990, rev. 2/1993, rev. 3/1997, rev. 4/2000)
——: *Axel Zwingenberger Discography* (Zwolle, Netherlands, 2000)
——: *Beryl Bryden: Discography, Biography* (Zwolle, Netherlands, 1972, rev. and enlarged 2/1979, rev. 3/1983, rev. 4/1985, rev. 5/1988, rev. 6/1995, rev. 7/1998, rev. 8/2000)
——: *Bob Wallis Discography* (Zwolle, Netherlands, 1992, rev. 2/1995, rev. 3/1996)
——: *Brian White Discography* (Zwolle, Netherlands, 1996)
——: *Charly Antolini Discography* (Zwolle, Netherlands, 1996, rev. 2/2000)
——: *Chris Barber Discography, 1949–1975* (Zwolle, Netherlands, 1976; loose-leaf suppl., *c*1978, rev. and enlarged Vlaardingen, Netherlands, 1991, by Bielderman and J. Purser, as *Chris Barber: 40 Years in Music: Discography, 1949–1989*, rev. and enlarged 2/1992)
——: *Cy Laurie Discography* (Zwolle, Netherlands, 1986, rev. 2/1987, rev. 3/1993. rev. 4/1995, rev. 5/2000)
——: *Daniel Barda Discography* (Zwolle, Netherlands, 1999)
——: *Dave Brennan Discography* (Zwolle, Netherlands, 1998)
——: *Dick Hawdon Discography* (Zwolle, Netherlands, 1998)
——: *Discography of British Traditional Jazz Bands*, i (Zwolle, Netherlands, 1996, rev. 2/1999); ii (Zwolle, 1997); iii (Zwolle, 1998); iv (Zwolle, 1998); v (Zwolle, 2000); vi (Zwolle, 2001)
——: *A Discography of Bud Freeman in Europe* (Zwolle, Netherlands, 2000)
——: *Discography of Dutch Traditional Jazz Bands*, i (Zwolle, Netherlands, 1998, rev. 2/2000); ii (Zwolle, 1999), iii (Zwolle, 2001)
——: *Discography of Mike Durham and West Jesmond Rhythm Kings* (Zwolle, Netherlands, 1997)
——: *Discography of the Down Town Jazz Band* (Zwolle, Netherlands, 1997)
——: *Discography of the Temperance Seven* (Zwolle, Netherlands, 2000)
——: *Dutch Swing College Band Discography* (Zwolle, Netherlands, 1984, rev. 1990, rev. 2/1995, rev. 3/1997, rev. 4/2000)
——: *Eggy Ley Discography* (Zwolle, Netherlands, 1987, rev. 2/1995, rev. 3/2000)
——: *Frank Brooker Discography* (Zwolle, Netherlands, 2000)
——: *Frank Roberscheuten Discography* (Zwolle, Netherlands, 1998)
——: *Frits Kaatee Discography* (Zwolle, Netherlands, 1991, rev. 2/1993, rev. 3/1994, rev. 4/1996)
——: *Geoff Cole Discography* (Zwolle, Netherlands, 1998)
——: *George Kaatee Discography incorporating the New Orleans Syncopators* (Zwolle, Netherlands, 1998)
——: *George Melly Discography, 1950–1993, including Mick Mulligan's Jazz Band* (Zwolle, Netherlands, 1993, rev. 2/1997)
——: *Harlem Ramblers Discography* (Zwolle, Netherlands, 1997)
——: *Isla Eckinger Discography* (Zwolle, Netherlands, 2000)
——: *Jack Fallon Discography* (Zwolle, Netherlands, 1998)
——: *Jan Morks Discography* (Zwolle, Netherlands, 1986, rev. 2/1990, rev. 3/1996)
——: *Joep Peeters Discography* (Zwolle, Netherlands, 2000)
——: *John Petters Discography* (Zwolle, Netherlands, 1997, rev. 2/1999)
——: *John R. T. Davies Discography* (Zwolle, Netherlands, 1998)
——: *Johnny Parker Discography* (Zwolle, Netherlands, 1987, rev. 2/1994, rev. 3/2000)
——: *Jon Marks Discography* (Zwolle, Netherlands, 2000)
——: *Keith Smith Discography* (Zwolle, Netherlands, 1995, rev. 2/2000)
——: *Ken Colyer Discography, incorporating the Crane River Jazz Band* (Zwolle, Netherlands, 1983, rev. 2/1983, rev. 3/1984, rev. 4/1986, rev. 5/1986, rev. 6/1989, rev. 7/1994, rev. 8/1996, rev. 9/1999)
——: *Ken Sims Discography* (Zwolle, Netherlands, 1999)
——: *Kenny Ball Discography* (Zwolle, Netherlands, 1989, rev. 2/1989, rev. 3/1994, rev. 4/1996, rev. 5/2000)
——: *Lars Erstrand Discography* (Zwolle, Netherlands, 1999)
——: *Laurie Chescoe Discography* (Zwolle, Netherlands, 1999)
——: *Martin Litton Discography* (Zwolle, Netherlands, 1996, rev. 2/1999)
——: *Max Collie Discography* (Zwolle, Netherlands, 1987, rev. 2/1990, rev. 3/1994, rev. 4/1999)
——: *Merseysippi Jazz Band Discography* (Zwolle, Netherlands, 1997)
——: *Mickey Ashman Discography* (Zwolle, Netherlands, 1984, rev. 2/1986, rev. 3/1992, rev. 4/1995, rev. 5/2000)
——: *Mike Pointon Discography* (Zwolle, Netherlands, 1999)
——: *Monty Sunshine Discography* (Zwolle, Netherlands, 1994, rev. 2/1995, rev. 3/2000)
——: *Nevil Skrimshire Discography* (Zwolle, Netherlands, 2000)
——: *Neville Dickie Discography* (Zwolle, Netherlands, 1995, rev. 2/1999)
——: *Paul Strandberg Discography* (Zwolle, Netherlands, 1997)
——: *Pete Allen Discography* (Zwolle, Netherlands, 1998)
——: *Pete Lay Discography* (Zwolle, Netherlands, 1999)
——: *Peter "Banjo" Meyer Discography* (Zwolle, Netherlands, 1997, rev. 2/1998)
——: *Phil Mason Discography* (Zwolle, Netherlands, 1999)
——: *Ray Smith Discography* (Zwolle, Netherlands, 1992, rev. 2/1995, rev. 3/1996)
——: *Rob Agerbeek Discography* (Zwolle, Netherlands, 2000)
——: *Rod Mason Discography* (Zwolle, Netherlands, 1986, rev. 2/1986, rev. 3/1986, rev. 4/1987, rev. 5/1991, rev. 6/1995, rev. 7/1996)
——: *Roger Marks Discography* (Zwolle, Netherlands, 1997, rev. 2/1999, rev. 3/2000)
——: *Sammy Rimington Discography, Nov. 1959–Jan. 1981* (Zwolle, Netherlands, 1981, rev. 2/1981, rev. 3/1982, as *Sammy Rimington Discography, 1959–1982*, rev. 4/1986, by G. Bielderman and L. Fält, as *Sammy Rimington Discography*, rev. 5/1988, rev. and enlarged 6/1998, by G. Bielderman)
——: *Sandy Brown Discography* (Zwolle, Netherlands, 1985, rev. 2/1990, rev. 3/1995, rev. 4/1997 by G. Bielderman and J. Latham)
——: *Swiss Dixie Stompers* (Zwolle, Netherlands, 1997)
——: *Ted Easton Discography* (Zwolle, Netherlands, 2000)
——: *Terry Lightfoot Discography* (Zwolle, Netherlands, 1991, rev. 2/1991, rev. 3/1996)
G. Bielderman and G. Elliott: *Scott Hamilton Discography* (Zwolle, Netherlands, 2001)
G. Bielderman and E. Elvers: *Abbi Hübner Discography* (Zwolle, Netherlands, 1988)
——: *Danish traditional jazz bands*, i (Zwolle, Netherlands, 1999); ii (Zwolle, Netherlands, 2000)
G. Bielderman, E. Elvers, and S. Gruyters: *Papa Bue Discography* (Zwolle, Netherlands, 1989, rev. 2/1994, by G. Bielderman, E. Elvers, L Fält, and S. Gruyters, rev. 3/1994, rev. 4/1999, by G. Bielderman, E. Elvers, and S. Gruyters)
G. Bielderman and R. Lee: *Annie Hawkins Discography* (Zwolle, Netherlands, 1999)
G. Bielderman and A. van de Munt: *Charquet & Co. Discography* (Zwolle, Netherlands, 1987, rev. 2/1990, rev. 3/1995)
——: *Discography: Peruna Jazzmen* (Zwolle, Netherlands, 1997)
——: *Tomas Örnberg, Bent Persson Discography* (Zwolle, Netherlands, 1996)
G. Bielderman and R. Stansby: *Freddy Randall Discography* (Zwolle, Netherlands, and Hornchurch, England, 1987, rev. Zwolle, 2/1990, rev. 3/ 1995)
G. Bielderman and A. Wideröe: *Henri Chaix Discography* (Zwolle, Netherlands, 1997)
G. Bielderman and Y. Yanagisawa: *Peter Ecklund Discography* (Zwolle, Netherlands, 2000)
G. Bielderman, see also M. N. Clutten; E. Elvers; S. Gruyters; R. Hubbard; J. Latham; J. Purser; N. Simpson; R. Stansby
L. Bijl and F. Canté: *Monk on Records: a Discography of Thelonious Monk* (Amsterdam, 1982, enlarged 2/1985)
R. Boenzli: *Discography of Howard McGhee* (Basel, Switzerland, 1961)
P. Borthen, see J. Evensmo
R. Bregman, L. Bukowski, and N. Saks: *The Charlie Parker Discography* (Redwood, NY, 1993)
R. Brethour: *A Rose Murphy Discography* (Aurora, Ontario, n.d. [1996])
D. C. Brigaud: *Art Tatum: essai pour une discographie des enregistrements hors commerce* (Paris, 1980) [incl. listings of radio broadcasts, film music, and V-discs]

D. Brown: *Sarah Vaughan: a Discography* (New York, 1991)
E. Bryce, see M. Hill
L. Bukowski, see R. Bregman; N. Saks
J. Callis: *Charlie Christian, 1939–1941: a Discography* (London, 1958)
R. L. Campbell: *The Earthly Recordings of Sun Ra* (Redwood, NY, 1994, rev. 2/2000, by R. L. Campbell and C. Trent)
F. Canté, see L. Bijl
J. S. Capes: *Steve Lane Discography* (Zwolle, Netherlands, 1994, rev. 2/1999)
G. Cerutti: *Discographie de John Tchicai* (Sierre, Switzerland, n.d. [?1980], rev. and enlarged 2/n.d. [?1982] as *Guidebook John Tchicai*, rev. and enlarged 3/n.d. [?1986] as *John Tchicai Discography (on Records), 1962–1985*)
——: *Fred van Hove Discography, 1968–1983 (on Records)* (Sierre, Switzerland, 1984)
——: *Joe McPhee Discography* (Sierre, Switzerland, 1983)
G. Cerutti and R. Bergerone: *Discographie: Evan Parker* (Sierre, Switzerland, n.d. [?1981], rev. and enlarged 2/n.d. [1985], as *Evan Parker Discography (on Records and Cassettes), 1968–1983*)
G. Cerutti and G. Maertens: *Discographie Archie Shepp, 1960–1980* (Sierre, Switzerland, 1982)
J. Chilton: *Bill Coleman on Record* (London, 1966)
M. N. Clutten: *A Bruce Turner Discography* (South Harrow and Leicester, England, n.d. [1972], rev. and enlarged Zwolle, Netherlands, 2/2000, by J. Purser and G. Bielderman)
——: *A George Chisholm Discography* (Leicester, England, 1977; suppl. i, 1980, suppl. ii by S. R. Gallichan, 1984, rev. and enlarged Zwolle, Netherlands, 2/1996, by M. Clutten and S. Gallichan)
M. Clutten, see also OTHER BOOKS, B. Turner
The Complete Django Reinhardt Discography (New York, 1988)
H. de Craen and E. Janssens: *Anthony Braxton Discography* (Brussels, 1982)
——: *Marion Brown Discography* (Brussels, 1985)
H. de Craen, see also E. Janssens
M. Cuscuna, see D. Wild
J. R. T. Davies: *The Music of Thomas "Fats" Waller* (London, 1953, rev. in *Sv*, nos.2–12, 1965–7)
M. Davis, see R. Hunter
Y. Delmarche and I. Fresart: *A Discography of Ben Webster, 1931–1973* (n.p. [Surhout, Belgium], n.d. [1983])
——: *A Discography of Coleman Hawkins, 1922–1969* (n.p., n.d. [?1983])
E. De Voghelaere: *Bobby Jaspar: a Biography, Appreciation, Record Survey and Complete Discography* (Antwerp, Belgium, 1967); addns and corrections in *Swingtime*, no.24 (1977), 10
A. Dupuy-Raufaste: *Strange Serenade: the Andrew Hill Discography* (Mirande, France, 1998)
K.-U. Dürr: *Johnny Dodds* (Hamburg, Germany, 1996, rev. 2/1997, as *The Recordings of Johnny Dodds*, rev. 3/2000)
——: *Louis Armstrong, 1923–1932* (Hamburg, Germany, 1996)
——: *The Recordings of Albert Nicholas* (Hamburg, Germany, 1994, rev. 2/2000)
——: *The Recordings of Jabbo Smith and Bob Shoffner* (Hamburg, Germany, 1995)
——: *The Recordings of Omer Simeon* (Hamburg, Germany, 1996)
——: *The Recordings of Preston Jackson* (Hamburg, Germany, 1999)
——: *The Recordings of Tommy Ladnier* (Hamburg, Germany, 1998)
K.-U. Dürr, see also B. H. Behncke
E. Edwards, Jr.: *Bill Harris (Trombone): a Complete Discography* (n.p. [?Whittier, CA], 1966)
——: *Woody Herman and his Orchestra: a Discography*, i, ii (Brande, Denmark, 1961); iii: *1959–1965* (Whittier, CA, 1965)
E. Edwards, Jr., G. Hall, and B. Korst: *Charlie Barnet and his Orchestra* (Whittier, CA, 1965, rev. 2/1970)
——: *Jimmie Lunceford* (Whittier, CA, 1965)
——: *Jimmy Dorsey and his Orchestra* (Whittier, CA, 1966)
G. Elliott: *Kenny Davern Discography* (Zwolle, Netherlands, 2001)
G. Elliott, see also G. Bielderman
E. Elvers and G. Bielderman: *Abbi Hübner Discography* (Zwolle, Netherlands, 1988, rev. 2/1995)
——: *Barrelhouse Jazzband Discography* (Zwolle, Netherlands, 1994, rev. 2/1995, rev. 3/1996)
——: *Claude Luter Discography* (Zwolle, Netherlands, 1997)
——: *A Discography of Wild Bill Davison in Europe* (Zwolle, Netherlands, 2001)
——: *Ole "Fessor" Lindgreen Discography* (Zwolle, Netherlands, 1993, rev. 2/1993, rev. 3/1994, rev. 4/1997)
——: *Keith Ingham Discography* (Zwolle, Netherlands, 1997)
——: *Marc Laferrière Discography* (Zwolle, Netherlands, 2000)
——: *Oscar Klein Discography* (Zwolle, Netherlands, 1986, rev. 2/1986, rev. 3/1987, rev. 4/1994, rev. 5/1991, rev. 6/1994, rev. 7/1999)
——: *Werner Keller – Tremble Kids Discography* (Zwolle, Netherlands, 1997, rev. 2/1998)
E. Elvers, see also G. Bielderman
J. Evensmo: *The Flute of Wayman Carver, the Trombone of Dickie Wells, 1927–1942, the Tenor Saxophone of Illinois Jacquet* (n.p. [Oslo], n.d. [?1983])
——: *The Guitars of Charlie Christian, Robert Normann, Oscar Alemán (in Europe)* (n.p. [Oslo], n.d. [?1976])
——: *The Tenor Saxophone and Clarinet of Lester Young, 1936–1942* (n.p. [Oslo], n.d. [?1977], rev. [2]/n.d. [?1983], as *The Tenor Saxophone and Clarinet of Lester Young, 1936–1949*)
——: *The Tenor Saxophone of Ben Webster, 1931–1943* (n.p. [Oslo], n.d. [?1978])
——: *The Tenor Saxophone of Coleman Hawkins, 1929–1942* (n.p. [Oslo], n.d. [?1976])
——: *The Tenor Saxophone of Leon Chu Berry* (n.p. [Oslo], n.d. [?1976])
——: *The Tenor Saxophones of Budd Johnson, Cecil Scott, Elmer Williams, Dick Wilson, 1927–1942* (n.p. [Oslo], n.d. [?1977])
——: *The Tenor Saxophones of Henry Bridges, Robert Carroll, Herschal [sic] Evans, Johnny Russell* (n.p. [Oslo], n.d. [?1976])
——: *The Trumpet of Roy Eldridge, 1929–1944* (n.p. [Oslo], n.d. [?1979])
——: *The Trumpets of Bill Coleman, 1929–1945, Frankie Newton* (n.p. [Oslo], n.d. [?1978])
——: *The Trumpets of Dizzy Gillespie, 1937–1943, Irving Randolph, Joe Thomas* (n.p. [Oslo], n.d. [?1982])
J. Evensmo and P. Borthen: *The Trumpet and Vocal of Henry Red Allen, 1927–1942* (n.p. [Oslo], n.d. [?1977])
J. Evensmo, P. Borthen, and I. S. Thomsen: *The Alto Saxophone, Trumpet and Clarinet of Benny Carter, 1927–1946* (n.p. [Oslo], n.d. [?1982])
L. Fält: *Sammy Rimington Discography* (Malmö, Sweden, 1997)
L. Fält and H. B. Håkånsson: *Hymn to George: George Lewis on Record and Tape* (n.p. [Malmö, Sweden, and Stockholm], 1985)
L. Fält, see also G. Bielderman
F. Fini and L. Rigazio: *The Oscar Peterson Discography* (Imola, Italy, 1992)
K. G. Fischer, see OTHER BOOKS, I. Storb
O. Flückiger: *Discography and Solography of Cab Calloway* (Reinach, nr Basel, Switzerland, 1960, repr. in *JJ*, xiv (1961), no.5, p.1; no.6, p.13; no.7, p.11)
——: *Lionel Hampton: Selected Discography, 1966–1978* (Reinach, nr Basel, Switzerland, 1978, rev. and enlarged 2/1980, as *Lionel Hampton: Porträt mit Discography, 1966–79*)
I. Fresart, see Y. Delmarche
M. Frohne: *Bright Moments: the Rahsaan Roland Kirk Discography, 1956–77* (Freiberg, Germany, 1989, rev. and enlarged 2/1992, rev. and enlarged 3/1997, rev. and enlarged 4/1998)
——: *Cannonball Adderley Discography* (Freiberg, Germany, 1998)
——: *Subconscious-Lee: 35 Years of Records and Tapes: the Lee Konitz Discography, 1947–1982* (Freiburg, Germany, 1983)
R. Fuehrer: *Paul Desmond Discography* (Essen, Germany, 1996)
Y. Fujioka with L. Porter and Y. Hamada: *John Coltrane: a Discography and Musical Biography* (Metuchen, NJ, and London, 1995)
S. R. Gallichan, see M. N. Clutten
D. Garçon, see J. Lubin
C. Garrod: *Bob Crosby and his Orchestra*, i: *1935–1945* (Zephyrhills, FL, 1996); ii: *1946–1985* (Zephyrhills, 1993, rev. 2/1996)
——: *Buddy Morrow and his Orchestra* (Zephyrhills, FL, 1995)
——: *Charlie Barnet and his Orchestra* (Spotswood, NJ, and Zephyrhills, FL, 1973, rev. 2/1984, rev. 3/1996, as *Charlie Barnet and his Orchestra, 1933–1973*; rev. Portland, OR, 4/1999)
——: *Charlie Spivak and his Orchestra* (Spotswood, NJ, and Zephyrhills, FL, 1974, rev. 2/1986, rev. 3/1996)
——: *Chick Webb and his Orchestra, including Ella Fitzgerald and her Orchestra* (Zephyrhills, FL, 1992)
——: *Claude Thornhill and his Orchestra* (Spotswood, NJ, and Zephyrhills, FL, 1971, rev. 2/1975, rev. 3/1985, rev. 4/1996)
——: *Count Basie and his Orchestra*, [i]: *1936–1945* (Zephyrhills, FL, 1987); ii: *1946–1957* (Zephyrhills, 1988); iii: *1958–1967* (Zephyrhills, 1989)
——: *The Dorsey Brothers and their Orchestra* (Zephyrhills, FL, 1992)
——: *Elliot Lawrence and his Orchestra* (Spotswood, NJ, and Zephyrhills, FL, 1974, rev. Zephyrhills, 2/1987, rev. 3/1996)
——: *Erskine Hawkins and his Orchestra* (Zephyrhills, FL, 1992)
——: *Frank Sinatra*, i: *1935–1951* (Zephyrhills, FL, 1989); ii: *1952–1981* (Zephyrhills, 1990)
——: *Glenn Miller and his Orchestra*, i: *1935–1940* (Zephyrhills, FL, 1995); ii: *1941–1942* (Zephyrhills, 1995); iii: *1943–1944 (The Air Force Band)* (Zephyrhills, 1995)
——: *Hal Kemp and his Orchestra; plus: Art Jarrett and his Orchestra* (Zephyrhills, FL, 1990)
——: *Hal McIntyre and his Orchestra* (Spotswood, NJ, and Zephyrhills, FL, 1974, rev. 2/1988, rev.3/1997; rev. Portland, OR, 4/1999)
——: *Helen Forrest* (Zephyrhills, FL, 1993)
——: *Isham Jones and his Orchestra* (Zephyrhills, FL, 1992)
——: *Jack Teagarden and his Orchestra* (Zephyrhills, FL, 1993)
——: *Jimmie Lunceford and his Orchestra* (Zephyrhills, FL, 1990)
——: *Jimmy Dorsey and his Orchestra* (Zephyrhills, FL, 1980, rev. 2/1988)
——: *Joe Venuti and his Orchestra* (Zephyrhills, FL, 1993)

——: *John Kirby and his Orchestra; Andy Kirk and his Orchestra* (Zephyrhills, FL, 1991)
——: *Les Brown and his Orchestra, 1936–1952* (Spotswood, NJ, 1974, rev. and enlarged Zephyrhills, FL, 2/1986, as *Les Brown and his Orchestra, 1936–1960*)
——: *Louis Jordan and his Orchestra* (Zephyrhills, FL, 1994)
——: *Louis Prima and his Orchestra* (Zephyrhills, FL, 1991)
——: *Ray Noble and his Orchestra* (Zephyrhills, FL, 1991)
——: *Raymond Scott and his Orchestra* (Portland, OR, 2000)
——: *Russ Morgan and his Orchestra* (Zephyrhills, FL, 1993)
——: *Stan Kenton and his Orchestra*, i: *1940–1951* (Zephyrhills, FL, 1984; rev. Portland, OR, 2/1999); ii: *1952–1959* (Zephyrhills, 1984; rev. Portland, 2/2000); iii: *1960–1979* (Zephyrhills, 1991; rev. Portland, 2/2000)
——: *Sy Oliver and his Orchestra* (Zephyrhills, FL, 1993)
——: *Tex Beneke and his Orchestra* (Spotswood, NJ, 1973, rev. 2/1986, rev. 3/1997)
——: *Tiny Bradshaw and his Orchestra, plus Lucky Millinder and his Orchestra* (Zephyrhills, FL, 1994)
——: *Tony Pastor and his Orchestra* (Zephyrhills, FL, 1973, rev. 2/1986, rev. 3/1997)
——: *Wingy Manone and his Orchestra* (Zephyrhills, FL, 1994)
——: *Woody Herman and his Orchestra*, i: *1936–1947* (Zephyrhills, FL, 1985, rev. 2/1997); ii: *1948–1957* (Zephyrhills, 1986, rev. 2/1997); iii: *1958–1987* (Zephyrhills, 1988, rev. 2/1997)
C. Garrod and B. Gottlieb: *Buddy Clark and his Orchestra* (Zephyrhills, FL, 1991)
C. Garrod and P. Johnston: *Harry James and his Orchestra*, i: *1937–1946* (Zephyrhills, FL, 1975, rev. 2/1995, as *1937–1945*); ii: *1946–1954* (Zephyrhills, 1975, rev. 2/1995, as *1946–1957*); iii: *1955–1982* (Zephyrhills, 1985, rev. 2/1995, as *1958–1987*)
C. Garrod and B. Korst: *Bob Crosby and his Orchestra* (Zephyrhills, FL, 1987; rev. Portland, OR, 2/1999)
——: *Boyd Raeburn and his Orchestra plus Johnny Bothwell and George Handy* (Zephyrhills, FL, 1985, rev. 2/1997)
——: *Gene Krupa and his Orchestra*, i: *1935–1946* (Zephyrhills, FL, 1984, rev. Portland, OR, 2/2000, by Garrod only); ii: *1947–1973* (Zephyrhills, 1984, rev. 2/1996, by Garrod only; rev. Portland, 3/2000)
——: *Georgie Auld and his Orchestra* (Zephyrhills, FL, 1992, rev. Portland, OR, 2/1999)
——: *Glen Gray and the Casa Loma Orchestra* (Zephyrhills, FL, 1987, rev. 2/1993)
——: *Les Brown and his Orchestra, 1936–1960* (Zephyrhills, FL, 1986)
——: *Nat "King" Cole: his Voice and his Piano* (Zephyrhills, FL, 1987)
——: *Raymond Scott and his Orchestra* (Zephyrhills, FL, 1988)
——: *Sam Donahue and his Orchestra* (Zephyrhills, FL, 1992)
——: *Sonny Dunham and his Orchestra; Ziggy Elman and his Orchestra* (Zephyrhills, FL, 1990)
——: *Will Bradley and his Orchestra; Freddie Slack and his Orchestra* (Zephyrhills, FL, 1986, rev. 2/1997)
C. Garrod, W. Scott, and F. Green: *Tommy Dorsey and his Orchestra* (Zephyrhills, FL, n.d. [?1980–82], rev. 2/1988, as i: *1928–1945*, ii: *1946–1956*)
C. Garrod, see also B. Korst
C. Gazdar: *First Bass: the Oscar Pettiford Discography* (Bangalore, India, 1991)
H. Geerken: *Chronological Discography of the Acoustic Works of Sun Ra, 1956–1981* (Athens, 1982)
J. Gicking: *Charlie Haden's Discography* (New York, 1979)
A. V. Gillet: *The European Recordings by Louis A. Mitchell* (Brussels, 1957, rev. 2/1957)
——: *The Mitchell's Jazz Kings (discographie critique)* (Brussels, 1957)
B. Goldberg: *WKCR Miles Davis Festival Handbook* (New York, 1979)
E. Goldman: *Clarence Williams Discography* (London, n.d. [?1945])
K. Gottwald: *The Recordings of Tom Harrell: Discography and Beyond, 1969–1999* (Kelsterbach, nr Frankfurt am Main, Germany, 2000)
F. Green, see C. Garrod
D. Griffiths: *Dill Jones Discography* (Zwolle, Netherlands, 1996, rev. 2/2000)
——: *Duncan Swift Discography* (Zwolle, Netherlands, 1998)
K. Grosen: *In the Key of Oscar: Oscar Peterson on LP/CD* (Lunderskov, Denmark, 1996)
——: *On Bass, Ray Brown: a Discography* (Lunderskov, Denmark, 1996)
D. Groslier, see OTHER BOOKS, H. O. Dance
J. Grunnet Jepsen, see J. G. Jepsen
S. Gruyters and G. Bielderman: *Doc Houlind Discography* (Zwolle, Netherlands, 1998)
S. Gruyters, see also G. Bielderman
M. Haggerty with M. Annenberg: *A Flower for Kenny* (n.p., 1985) [discography of Kenny Clarke]
H. B. Håkånsson, see L. Fält
G. Hall: *Boyd Raeburn and his Orchestra: a Complete Discography* (Laurel, MD, 1972)
——: *Harry James and his Orchestra* (Laurel, MD, 1971)
——: *Nat "King" Cole: a Jazz Discography* (Laurel, MD, 1965)
——: *The Ruby Braff Discography* (Laurel, MD, 1965)
G. Hall and S. Kramer: *Gene Krupa and his Orchestra* (Laurel, MD, 1975)
G. Hall, see also E. Edwards, Jr.
C. Hallstrom, see B. Scherman
Y. Hamada, see Y. Fujioka
M. Hames: *Albert Ayler, Sunny Murray, Cecil Taylor, Byard Lancaster, and Kenneth Terroade on Disc and Tape* (Ferndown, England, 1983)
——: *John Tchicai on Disc and Tape* (Ferndown, England, 1979)
M. Hames and R. Wilbraham: *Don Cherry on Disc and Tape* (Ferndown, England, 1980)
D. HamiltonSmith, see H. H. Lange
E. Harkins: *Maynard Ferguson: a Discography* (n.p. [Solana Beach, nr Del Mar, CA], 1976)
J. Hartley, see M. Sparke
F. Hedman, K. Liliedahl, and L. Zackrisson: *Alice Babs* (Stockholm, 1973)
R. Hilbert with D. Niven: *Pee Wee Speaks: a Discography of Pee Wee Russell* (Metuchen, NJ, and London, 1992)
R. Hilbert, Jr., see OTHER BOOKS, S. E. Brown
M. Hill and E. Bryce: *Jelly Roll Morton: a Microgroove Discography and Musical Analysis* (Salisbury East, South Australia, 1977)
C. C. Hintze, see OTHER BOOKS, D. Meriwether
C. Hofmann: *Man of Many Parts: a Discography of Buddy Collette* (Amsterdam, 1985) [incl. interview and list of compositions]
C. Hofmann and E. M. Bakker: *Shorty Rogers: a Discography* (Amsterdam, 1983)
F. Hoffman: *Henry "Red" Allen (Jan. 7th 1908 – Apr. 17th 1967)/J. C. Higginbotham (May 11th 1906 – May 26th 1973): Discography, 1927–1968: Excerpt out a Future "Red Allen Biodisco"* (MS, Berlin, 1982; rev. 2/1994, as *Henry "Red" Allen (Jan. 7th 1908 – Apr. 17th 1967)/J. C. Higginbotham (May 11th 1906 – May 26th 1973): Discography, 1927–1969*) [unpubd typescripts]
——: *Henry "Red" Allen (Jan. 7th 1908 – Apr. 17th 1967)/J. C. Higginbotham (May 11th 1906 – May 26th 1973): a Bio-disco Working Book part 2: 1940–1953* (Berlin, 1998)
H. Hollenstein: *Lennie Tristano on LPs [sic] Records* (Sierre, Switzerland, 1984)
G. J. Hoogeveen: *Meet Mr. Gordon: a Discography of Bob Gordon* (Amsterdam, 1987)
R. Hubbard and G. Bielderman: *Zenith Hot Stompers* (Zwolle, Netherlands, 1997, rev. 2/1998)
G. Hulme: *Mel Tormé: a Chronicle of his Recordings, Books and Films* (Jefferson, NC, 2000)
R. Hunter and M. Davis: *Hampton Hawes Discography* (Manchester, England, 1986) [incl. biography and list of compositions]
S. Iwamato: *Have You Met Mister Jones* (Tokyo, 1987) [discography of Hank Jones]
——: *Ralph Sutton: a Discography* (Tokyo, 1987)
E. Janssens and H. de Craen: *Art Ensemble of Chicago Discography: Unit and Members* (Brussels, 1983) [incl. list of compositions]
E. Janssens, see also H. de Craen
G. von Jena: *Discografie [sic] of Serge Chaloff* (Berlin, 1986)
J. G. Jepsen: *A Discography of Charlie Parker* (Copenhagen, 1968)
——: *A Discography of Dizzy Gillespie* (Copenhagen, 1969)
——: *A Discography of Fats Navarro, Clifford Brown* (Brande, Denmark, 1960)
——: *A Discography of Lester Young* (Copenhagen, 1968)
——: *A Discography of Louis Armstrong, 1923–1971* (Copenhagen, 1973)
——: *A Discography of Thelonious Monk & Bud Powell* (Copenhagen, 1969)
——: *Kid Ory* (Copenhagen, 1957)
J. G. Jepsen and K. Mohr: *Hot Lips Page* (Basel, Switzerland, 1961)
J. G. Jepsen, see also B. Scherman
R. Jewson, see H. H. Lange
P. Johnston, see C. Garrod
H. Jones: *Bobby Hackett: a Bio-discography* (Westport, CT, and London, 1999)
E. "T". Kaleveld and L. Coleman: *Bill Coleman Discography* (n.p., n.d. [1987])
I. Kanth: *A Discography of Jimmy Blanton* (Stockholm, 1970)
H. Kluck: *The Paul Bley Recordings* (Emmen, Netherlands, 1996)
D. Koechlin: *50 ans de jazz avec Barney Bigard* (n.p. [Darnetal, France], n.d. [1979], rev. 2/n.d. [1989])
——: *Liste des enregistrements réalisés avec Jay McShann* (n.p., n.d.)
E. M. Komara: *The Dial Recordings of Charlie Parker: a Discography* (Westport, CT, and London, 1998)
B. Korst and C. Garrod: *Artie Shaw and his Orchestra* (Spotswood, NJ, and Zephyrhills, FL, 1974, rev. 2/1986)
B. Korst, see also E. Edwards, Jr.; C. Garrod
P. Koster: *Barry Harris: a Discography* (Amsterdam, 1988)
P. Koster and D. M. Bakker: *Charlie Parker*, i: *1940–1947* (Alphen aan de Rijn, Netherlands, 1974); ii: *1948–1950* (Alphen aan de Rijn, 1975); iii:

1951–1954 (Alphen aan de Rijn, 1975); iv: *1940–1955* (Alphen aan de Rijn, 1976) [addns and corrections]
P. Koster and H. Mobach: *Lestorian Notes: a Discography and Bibliography of Lester Young* (Amsterdam, 1998)
P. Koster and C. Sellers: *Dizzy Gillespie*, i: *1937–1953* (Amsterdam, 1985); ii: *1953–1987* (Amsterdam, 1988)
S. Kramer, see G. Hall
D. H. Kraner: *Die Hans Koller Discographie, 1947–1966* (Graz, Austria, *c*1967)
H. H. Lange: *The Fabulous Fives* (Lübbecke, Germany, 1959, rev. Chigwell, England, 2/1978, by R. Jewson, D. HamiltonSmith, and R. Webb) [discography of Original Dixieland Jazz Band, Louisiana Five, New Orleans Jazz Band, Original Indiana Five, Original Georgia Five, Original Memphis Five]
——: *Stan Kenton: Discography* (Berlin, 1959) [bound with H. J. Dietzel: *Stan Kenton:* Biography; see other books]
P. Langhorn and T. Sjøgren: *Ben: the Music of Ben Webster: a Discography* (Copenhagen, 1996)
J. Latham and G. Bielderman: *Al Fairweather Discography* (Zwolle, Netherlands, 1994)
J. Latham, R. Lee, and G. Bielderman: *Stan Greig Discography* (Zwolle, Netherlands, 1995, rev. 2/2001)
R. Lee: *Big Jim: a Discography of Jim Robinson* (Zwolle, Netherlands, 1998)
——: *Brian Turnock Discography* (Zwolle, Netherlands, 1999)
——: *Chris Blount Discography* (Zwolle, Netherlands, 1992, rev. 2/1994, rev. 3/1995, rev. 4/1996, rev. 5/1999)
——: *Colin Bowden Discography* (Zwolle, Netherlands, 1993, rev. 2/1994, rev. 3/1999)
——: *Cuff Billett Discography* (Zwolle, Netherlands, 1994, rev. 2/1999)
——: *Dan Pawson Discography* (Zwolle, Netherlands, 2000)
——: *Discography of Gerhard "Doggy" Hund and the Maryland Jazz Band of Cologne* (Zwolle, Netherlands, 1996)
——: *A Discography of Harold Dejan incorporating the Olympia Brass Band* (Zwolle, Netherlands, 2001)
——: *Lars Edegran Discography* (Zwolle, Netherlands, 2000)
——: *Love Songs of the Nile: a Discography of Billie and Dede Pierce* (Zwolle, Netherlands, 1999, rev. 2/2000)
——: *New Orleans Clarinet: a Discography of Willie Humphrey* (Zwolle, Netherlands, 1996)
——: *Orange Kellin Discography* (Zwolle, Netherlands, 1996)
——: *Over the Waves: a Discography of Capt. John Handy* (Zwolle, Netherlands, 1995)
——: *Ray Foxley Discography* (Zwolle, Netherlands, 1992, rev. 2/1995, rev. 3/2000)
——: *Sheik's Blues: a Discography of Kid Sheik Cola* (Zwolle, Netherlands, 1998)
——: *Sonny Morris Discography* (Zwolle, Netherlands, 1999)
——: *Tony Pringle Discography, incorporating the New Black Eagle Jazz Band* (Zwolle, Netherlands, 1993, rev. 2/1993, rev. 3/1999)
R. Lee and G. Smits: *Clarinet Wizard: a Discography of Albert Burbank* (Zwolle, Netherlands, 1997)
R. Lee, see also G. Bielderman
H. H. Lerfeldt and T. Sjøgren: *Chet: the Discography of Chesney Henry Baker* (Copenhagen, 1985, rev. 1993, by Sjøgren, as *Chet: the Music of Chesney Henry Baker: a Discography*)
K. Liliedahl, see F. Hedman
H. L. Lindenmaier: *25 Years of Fish Horn Recording: the Steve Lacy Discography, 1954–1979* (Freiburg, Germany, 1982) [incl. list of compositions]
H. L. Lindenmaier and H. Salewski: *The Man who Never Sleeps: the Charles Mingus Discography, 1945–1978* (Freiburg, Germany, 1983)
J. Lohman: *The Sound of Miles Davis: the Discography: a Listing of Records and Tapes, 1945–1991* (Copenhagen, 1992)
K. Lohmann, see M. Selchow
G. Lombardi: *Eddie Condon on Record, 1927–1971* (Milan, 1987)
A. I. Lonstein and V. R. Marino: *The Compleat Sinatra: Discography, Filmography, Television Appearances, Motion Picture Appearances, Radio Appearances, Concert Appearances, Stage Appearances* (Ellenville, NY, 1970, 2/1979, as *The Revised Compleat Sinatra: Discography, Filmography, Television Appearances, Motion Picture Appearances, Radio Appearances, Concert Appearances, Stage Appearances*, suppl. 1991)
J. Lubin and D. Garçon: *Louis Jordan Discography, 1929–1974* (Levallois-Perret, France, 1987)
B. Lyttkens: *The Jimmie Lunceford Legacy on Records* (Stockholm, 1996, loose-leaf suppl., 1997)
A. J. McCarthy, see other books, B. Holiday
H. MacKenzie: *The Johnny Mercer Chesterfield Music Shop* (Glasgow, 1986) [catalogue of radio broadcasts]
W. K. McNeil and L. Hatchett: *Stuff Smith Discography* (Portland, OR, 1999)
G. Maertens, see G. Cerutti
V. R. Marino, see A. I. Lonstein
F. Martinelli: *Anthony Braxton Discography* (Pontedera, Italy, 2000)
——: *Evan Parker Discography* (Pontedera, Italy, 1994)
L. Massagli, L. Pusateri, and G. M. Volonté: *Duke Ellington's Story on Records* (Milan, 1966–83, rev. 2/1999, by Massagli and G. M. Volonté, as *The New DESOR: an Updated Edition of Duke Ellington's Story on Records, 1924–1974*)
A. Mathiesen: *Mal Waldron: a Black Artist: a Discography* (Copenhagen, 1989)
H. J. Mauerer: *A Discography of Sidney Bechet* (Copenhagen, 1969)
T. Middleton: *Buddy Featherstonhaugh* (London, 1995)
——: *Caspar Reardon* (London, 1994)
——: *Don Rendell* (London, 1993)
——: *Harry Parry* (London, 1995)
——: *Jane Froman Discography* (London, 1998)
——: *The Jazz Couriers* (London, 1996)
——: *Joe Daniels* (London, 1982)
——: *Joe Harriott* (London, 1996)
——: *Johnny Claes* (London, 1994)
——: *The Kirchin Band, 1952–1957* (London, 1996)
——: *Ronnie Scott Discography* (London, 1997)
——: *Sid Phillips Discography* (London, 1997)
——: *The Skyrockets* (London, 1995)
——: *The Squadronaires R.A.F. Dance Orchestra: an Exploratory Discography, 1940–1945* (London, 1976)
——: *The Squadronaires*, i: *1940–1946* (London, 1996)
——: *Steve Conway Discography* (London, 1996)
——: *Tony Sampson and his Orchestra, 1946–1949* (London, 1992)
——: *Vic Lewis: a Discography* (Amsterdam, 1985)
T. Middleton, see also other books, R. Horricks
J. Millar: *Born to Sing: a Discography of Billie Holiday* (Copenhagen, n.d. [?1979])
——: *Fine and Mellow: a Discography of Billie Holiday* (Ramsgate, England, 1992–) [loose-leaf suppls.]
——: *The Billie Holiday Extension*, i: *The 78s* (Ramsgate, England, 1995)
J. Mitchell, see other books, G. Bell
H. Mobach, see P. Koster
K. Mohr, see J. G. Jepsen
M. Montgomery, see F. H. Trolle
P.A. Monti: *Booker Little Discography* (Sierre, Switzerland, 1983)
——: *Discographie de Phineas Newborn* (Sierre, Switzerland, n.d. [?1980])
T. A. Morgereth: *Bing Crosby: a Discography, Radio Program List, and Filmography* (Jefferson, NC, 1987)
D. Morrill: *Woody Herman: a Guide to the Big Band Recordings, 1936–1987* (New York, 1990)
F.-X. Moulé: *A Guide to the Duke Ellington Recorded Legacy on LP and CD*, i: *Concerts, Radio Broadcasts, Television Shows, Radio Transcriptions, V-discs, Film Soundtracks* (Le Mans, France, 1992)
L. Moxhet: *A Discography of Earl Hines, 1923–1977* (Sannois, France, 1978)
P. Murphy: *Chick Bullock: a Discography of his Recordings* (Melbourne, Australia, 1983)
G. Nelson: *Take No Prisoners: a Drumography of Buddy Rich* (Berlin, 1996, rev. 2/1997)
R. Nieus: *A Discography of Dexter Gordon* (n.p. [Jambes, Belgium], n.d. [1986])
C. Popa: *Jerry Gray and his Orchestra* (Zephyrhills, FL, 1984)
——: *Ray McKinley and his Orchestra* (Zephyrhills, FL, 1979, rev. 2/1988)
J. Popa: *Cab Calloway and his Orchestra* (Zephyrhills, FL, 1976, rev. 2/1987)
L. Porter, see Y. Fujioka
B. Priestley, see other books, I. Carr
J. Purser and G. Bielderman: *Keith Nichols Discography* (Zwolle, Netherlands, 1993, rev. 2/1996, rev. 3/2000)
——: *Wally Fawkes Discography* (Zwolle, Netherlands, 1999, rev. 2/2000)
J. Purser, J. Wilyman, and P. Schwalm: *Humph: a Discography of Humphrey Lyttelton, 1945–1983* (WaltononThames, England, 1985)
J. Purser, see also G. Bielderman; M. N. Clutten
L. Pusateri, see L. Massagli
C. de Radzitsky: *A 1960–1967 Clark Terry Discography with Biographical Notes* (n.p. [Brasschaat, Belgium], 1968)
B. Räftegård: *The Kenny Dorham Discography* (Karlstad, Sweden, 1982)
L. Rasmussen: *Abdullah Ibrahim: a Discography* (Copenhagen, 1999)
U. Reichardt: *Like a Human Voice: the Eric Dolphy Discography* (Schmitten, Germany, 1986)
J. Remaud: *Discographie de Tommy Ladnier* (n.p. [France], 1994)
D. Richard, see other books, L. Delannoy
E. Ronowski: *Gene Krupa: LP- und FS-Liste* (Dassel, Germany, 1987)
M. Ruppli: *Charles Mingus Discography* (Frankfurt am Main, Germany, 1982)
B. Rust, see other books, P. Foster
H. Rye: *"Fats" in Fact: the Reissues* (Chigwell, England, 1993)
H. Rye, see also other books, A. Cheatham; A. Kirk; M. Royal; T. Wilson
N. Saks and L. Bukowski: *Yardbird Inc.: the Charlie Parker Discography* (Port Jefferson, NY, 1989)
N. Saks, see also R. Bregman
D. Salemann: *A Discography of Page Cavanaugh* (Berlin, 2000)

H. Salewski, see H. L. Lindenmaier
L. Sanfilippo: *General Catalogue of Duke Ellington's Recorded Music* (Palermo, Sicily, 1964)
B. Scherman, C. Hallstrom, and J. G. Jepsen: *A Discography of Count Basie* (Copenhagen, 1969)
C. Schlouch: *Bobby Timmons: a Discography* (Marseilles, France, 1999)
——: *Charlie Parker: a Discography* (Marseilles, France, 1999)
——: *Come Back! Hank Mobley: a Discography* (n.p. [Marseilles, France], 1983)
——: *Grant Green: a Discography* (Marseilles, France, 1999)
——: *Hank Mobley: a Discography* (Marseilles, France, 1999)
——: *In Memory of Ike Quebec: a Discography* (Marseilles, France, 1983, rev. 2/n.d., rev. 3/1985, as *Ike Quebec: a Discography*, rev. 4/1999)
——: *In Memory of Wardell Gray: a Discography* (Marseilles, France, 1983)
——: *Lee Morgan: a Discography* (Marseilles, France, 1999)
——: *Lee Wiley, LoveLee: a Discography* (Marseilles, France, 1983, rev. 2/1999)
——: *Once upon a Time: Bud Powell: a Discography* (Marseilles, France, 1983, rev. 2/1993, rev. 3/1999)
——: *Sonny Clark: a Discography* (Marseilles, France, 1999)
——: *The Unforgettable Kenny Dorham* (Marseilles, France, 1977, rev. 1983, rev. 1993, rev. 1996, rev. 1999, as *Kenny Dorham: a Discography*)
——: *Wardell Gray: a Discography* (Marseilles, France, 1999)
——: *Wynton Kelly: a Discography* (Marseilles, France, 1992, rev. 2/1993, rev.3/1999)
J. Schütte: *Discographie des RBT-Orchesters und der anderen Formationen des Berliner Rundfunks* (Menden, Germany, 1977)
J. Schütte and A. Stöcklin: *Teddy Stauffer: Discographie der Original Teddies (Teddy Stauffer und Eddie Brunner) und der kleinen Formationen mit Musikern der Teddies* (Menden, Germany, 1983)
P. Schwalm, see J. Purser
W. Scott, see C. Garrod
T. Selbert, see OTHER BOOKS, A. Pepper
M. Selchow and K. Lohmann: *Edmond Hall: a Discography* (Westoverledingen and Göttingen, Germany, 1981)
C. Sellers, see P. Koster
T. Shoppee, see OTHER BOOKS, S. Voce
G. G. Simon: *Benkó Dixieland Band: bibliográfia és cikkgy axujtemény* [The Benkó Dixieland Band: bibliography and selected articles] (Budapest, 1988)
——: *Benko Dixieland Band Discography* (Zwolle, Netherlands, 1991, rev. 2/1997)
R. Simonds: *King Curtis: a Discography* (Edgware, England, 1983, rev. 2/1984)
N. Simpson and G. Bielderman: *Archie Semple Discography* (Zwolle, Netherlands, 1997)
——: *Brian Lemon Discography* (Zwolle, Netherlands, 1997)
——: *Digby Fairweather Discography* (Zwolle, Netherlands, 1997)
——: *Fred Hunt Discography* (Zwolle, Netherlands, 1998)
——: *John Barnes Discography* (Zwolle, Netherlands, 1995, rev. 2/2000)
——: *Lennie Felix Discography* (Zwolle, Netherlands, 1998)
——: *Lennie Hastings Discography* (Zwolle, Netherlands, 1996)
——: *Pete Strange Discography* (Zwolle, Netherlands, 1998)
——: *Roy Williams Discography* (Zwolle, Netherlands, 1991, rev. 2/1994, rev. 3/1996)
T. Sjøgren: *The Duke Jordan Discography* (Copenhagen, 1982, rev. and enlarged 2/1984, rev. and enlarged Søborg, Denmark, 3/1992)
——: *Long Tall Dexter: the Discography of Dexter Gordon* (Copenhagen, 1986)
——: *The Sonny Rollins Discography* (Copenhagen, 1983, rev. Søborg, Denmark, 2/1993, as *The Discography of Sonny Rollins*)
T. Sjøgren, see also P. Langhorn; H. H. Lerfeldt
I. Skovgaard and E. Traberg: *Some Clark Bars: Sonny Clark: a Discography* (Copenhagen and Madrid, 1984) [incl. biography]
O. S. Sousisha: *Discography of Anthony Braxton* (Tokyo, c1997)
M. Sparke and P. Venudor: *Stan Kenton: the Studio Sessions* (Lake Geneva, WI, 1998)
M. Sparke and P. Venudor, with J. Hartley: *Kenton on Capitol and Creative World: a Discography* (Lake Geneva, WI, 1994)
M. Sparke, P. Venudor, and J. Hartley: *Kenton on Capitol: a Discography* (Hounslow, England, 1966, 2/1967)
R. Stansby and G. Bielderman: *Dave Shepherd Discography* (Zwolle, Netherlands, 1996)
R. Stansby, see also G. Bielderman
R. L. Stockdale: *Tommy Dorsey: on the Side* (Metuchen, NJ, and London, 1995)
A. Stöcklin, see J. Schütte
K. Stratemann: *Buddy Rich and Gene Krupa: a Filmodiscography* (Lübbecke, Germany, 1980)
J. Ström: *Jimmy Lyons Sessionography: a Listing of Record and Tapes, 1961–1985* (Gusum, Sweden, 2000)
J. W. Susat: *Discography of the "Uncompromising Lennie Tristano"* (Menden, Germany, 1986)
N. Suzuki: *Herbie Hancock, 1961–1969* (Shizuoka, Japan, 1988)
T. Tajiri: *Gil Evans Discography, 1941–1982* (Tokyo, 1983)
K. Teubig: *Straighten up and Fly Right: a Chronology and Discography of Nat "King" Cole* (Westport, CT, and London, 1994)
H. Takahashi: *Satoh Masahiko Discography* (Tokyo, 1998) [discography of Masahiko Sato]
I. S. Thomsen, see J. Evensmo
W. E. Timner: *Ellingtonia: the Recorded Music of Duke Ellington and his Sidemen* (Montreal, 1976, rev. and updated 2/1979, rev. and enlarged Metuchen, NJ, and London, 3/1988, rev. and enlarged Lanham, MD, New Brunswick, NJ, and London, 4/1996)
E. Traberg, see I. Skovgaard
F. H. Trolle: *James P. Johnson: Father of the Stride Piano* (Alphen aan de Rijn, Netherlands, 1981) [incl. rollography by M. Montgomery]
B. Ulanov: *The Incredible Crosby* (New York, 1949)
J. Valburn: *The Directory of Duke Ellington's Recordings* (Hicksville, NY, 1986)
——: *Duke Ellington on Compact Disc: an Index and Text of the Recorded Work of Duke Ellington on Compact Disc* (Hicksville, NY, 1993)
P. van Engelen: *Where's the Music? The Discography of Kai Winding* (Amsterdam, 1985)
W. F. van Eyle: *Don Byas Discography* (Zaandam, Netherlands, 1967)
R. Venables and C. White: *A Complete Discography of Red Nichols and his Five Pennies* (Melbourne, Australia, 1946, 2/1947)
P. Venudor, see M. Sparke
J.-F. Villetard: *Coleman Hawkins*, i: *1922–1944* (Amsterdam, 1984); ii: *1945–1957* (Amsterdam, 1985)
G. M. Volonté, see L. Massagli
H. Wachtmeister: *A Discography & Bibliography of Anthony Braxton* (Stocksund, nr Stockholm, 1982)
H. Watanabe: *Helen Ward Discography* (Nara, Japan, 1998)
G. Wattiau: *Book's Book: a Discography of Booker Ervin* (Amsterdam, 1987)
R. Webb, see H. H. Lange
B. Weir: *Art Ford's TV Jazz Party 1958: TV & Radio Broadcasts* (Cardiff, 1987, rev. 2/1991)
——: *Buck Clayton Discography* (Chigwell, England, 1989; addns and corrections in *Names & Numbers*, no.7 (1998), 21; no.8 (1999), 27)
——: *Clarence Gene Shaw Discography* (Cardiff, 1986, rev. and enlarged 2/1986)
——: *Clifford Brown Discography* (Cardiff, 1982, rev. and enlarged 2/1983, rev. and enlarged 3/1984, rev. and enlarged 3[*recte* 4]/1986, rev. and enlarged 5/1990)
——: *Dupree Bolton Discography* (Cardiff, 1986, rev. and enlarged 2/1986, rev. and enlarged 3/1990)
——: *Helen Merrill Discography* (Amsterdam, 1987)
——: *The L. A. Four Discography* (Cardiff, 1985, rev. and enlarged 2/1986)
B. Weir, see also OTHER BOOKS, B. Clayton; S. Price
R. Wernboe: *A Blue Time: a Blue Mitchell Discography* (Amsterdam, 1989)
——: *Lee Morgan Discography* (Saltsjöbaden, Sweden, 1985)
——: *Leeway: Lee Morgan Discography* (Redwood, NY, 1998)
H. Westerberg: *Boy from New Orleans: Louis "Satchmo" Armstrong, on Records, Films, Radio and Television* (Copenhagen, 1981) [incl. discography]
B. White: *The Eddie Condon "Town Hall Broadcasts," 1944–1945: a Discography* (Oakland, CA, 1980)
C. White, see R. Venables
A. Wideröe, see G. Bielderman
R. J. Wilbraham: *Jackie McLean: a Discography with Biography* (London, 1968)
——: *Milt Jackson: a Discography and Bibliography* (London, 1968)
R. Wilbraham, see also M. Hames
D. Wild and M. Cuscuna: *Ornette Coleman, 1958–1979: a Discography* (Ann Arbor, MI, 1980)
J. Wilyman, see J. Purser
J. Wolfer: *Anita O'Day: an Exploratory Discography* (Zephyrhills, FL, 1990)
——: *Si Zentner and his Orchestra, also Including Bob Florence and his Orchestra: a Discography* (Langenhagen, Germany, 1981)
E. Woodward and A. Hobson: *The Boswell Sisters and Connee Boswell: a Discography* (Oldbury, England, 1998)
Y. Yanigisawa: *Peter Ecklund Jazz Discography* (Matsudo City, Japan, 1996)
Y. Yanigisawa, see also G. Bielderman
L. Zackrisson, see F. Hedman

Record label listings

AFR&TS Gold Label transcriptions catalogue, see R. E. Lotz
AFRS catalogues, see C. Garrod; R. E. Lotz; L. F. Kiner; H. Mackenzie; B. White
W. Agenant: *Columbia 78 rpm Record Listing 20001 thru 21571: plus OKeh Records 18001 thru 18059* (Zephyrhills, FL, 1996)
Aladdin catalogue, see M. Ruppli
R. C. Ames, see C. Garrod
F. Andrews: *Columbia 10" Records, 1904–30* (London, 1985) [pubn of City of London Phonograph and Gramophone Society]

F. Andrews, A. Badrock, and E. S. Walker: *World Records, Vocalion "W", Fetherflex and Penny Phono Recordings: a Listing* (Spalding, England, 1992)

F. Andrews, see also A. Badrock

Apple catalogue, see P. M. Pelletier

Associated Transcription catalogue, see C. Garrod

Atlantic catalogues, see P. A. Grendysa; M. Ruppli

A. Badrock: *English Pathé Perfect: a Catalogue and History* (Hayes, England, 1983)

——: *The Parlophone Red Label Popular Series E5000–E6428* (Cupar, Scotland, 1994)

A. Badrock and F. Andrews: *Complete Regal Catalogue* (Malvern, England, 1991)

A. Badrock, see also F. Andrews

R. Baum, see C. Garrod

Beltone catalogue, see P. M. Pelletier

B. Bennett: *Capitol Record Listing 101–3031* (Zephyrhills, FL, 1987)

M. Berresford, see H. Thygesen

R. Bidwell and others: *Columbia 78 rpm Record Listing 37000 thru 41963: Working Draft* (Zephyrhills, FL, 1989)

Black and Blue catalogue, see M. Ruppli

G. Blacker, see B. Korst

Black Swan catalogue, see H. Thygesen

Bluebird catalogues, see H. Panassié; BIBLIOGRAPHIES AND REFERENCE MATERIALS, R. D. Kinkle

Blue Note catalog, see M. Cuscuna

Blue Star catalogue, see M. Ruppli

R. Brandt, see C. Garrod

T. Brooks, see B. Rust

W. Brown: *The Columbia Records 35000/40000 Series Popular Singles Discography, 1939–1974* (Zephyrhills, FL, 1995)

Brunswick catalogues, see J. G. Hayes; E. Jackson; *Jazz on LP's*; P. Pelletier; BIBLIOGRAPHIES AND REFERENCE MATERIALS, R. D. Kinkle

Capitol catalogues, see B. Bennett; C. Garrod; *Jazz on LP's*; M. Montgomery; P. Pelletier

G. Cerutti: *Five British Independent Labels, 1968–1987* (Sierre, Switzerland, 1988) [Bead, Incus, Matchless, Leo, Ogun]

Challenge catalogue, see M. Montgomery

Chess catalogue, see L. Fancourt; M. Ruppli

Clef/Verve catalogue, see M. Ruppli

Columbia catalogues, see W. Agenant; R. Bidwell; W. Brown; C. Garrod; D. Mahony; M. Montgomery; P. Pelletier; B. Randle; B. Rust; *Other listings*, G. Avakian; BIBLIOGRAPHIES AND REFERENCE MATERIALS, R. D. Kinkle

Command Performance, USA! catalogue, see H. Mackenzie

Coral catalogues, see C. Garrod; *Jazz on LP's*; P. Pelletier

K. Crawford, see C. Garrod

Crown catalogue, see R. R. Olsen

Cupol catalogue, see B. Englund

M. Cuscuna and M. Ruppli: *The Blue Note Label: a Discography* (New York, Westport, CT, and London, 1988)

B. Daniels, see M. Ruppli

W. DeBlock, see S. Wante

Debut catalogue, see V. Weiler

Decca catalogues, see C. Garrod; J. G. Hayes; E. Jackson; *Jazz on LP's*; *Jazz on 78s*; P. Pelletier; M. Ruppli; BIBLIOGRAPHIES AND REFERENCE MATERIALS, R. D. Kinkle

R. Dethlefson, see R. R. Wile

Deutsche Grammophon catalogue, see J. Grundmann

Dream catalogue, see P. M. Pelletier

Ducretet-Thompson catalogue, see *Jazz on LP's*

Duke catalogue, see C. Garrod

Durium catalogue, see *Jazz on LP's*

Edison catalogues, see R. R. Wile

Edison Bell Winner catalogue, see J. G. Hayes

Elite catalogue, see B. Korst

B. Englund: *Jazz på Cupol* (Stockholm, 1982)

——: *Metronome, 1949–1956* (Stockholm, 1992)

——: *Sonora II: Swingserien* (Stockholm, 1974)

L. Fancourt: *Chess R&B Discography* (Faversham, England, 1984, rev. 2/1991, as *Chess R&B: a Discography of the R&B Artists on the Chess Labels, 1947–1975*)

Felsted catalogues, see *Jazz on LP's*; P. Pelletier

Fetherflex catalogue, see F. Andrews

F. Fini: *Soul Note: a Label Discography* (Imola, Italy, 1997)

Four Star catalogue, see C. Garrod

S. Furusho: *Riverside Jazz Records* (Chiba, Japan, 1984)

C. Garrod: *AFRS One Night Stands 1001 thru 2000: Working Draft* (Zephyrhills, FL, 1996)

——: *AFRS One Night Stands 2001 thru 3000: Working Draft* (Portland, OR, 1999)

——: *AFRS One Night Stands 3001 thru 4000: Working Draft* (Portland, OR, 1999)

——: *Columbia Chicago 78 rpm Master Listing: Chicago: 501–4999, January 12, 1933 to February 2, 1949* (Zephyrhills, FL, n.d.)

——: *Columbia 78 rpm Master Listing: Los Angeles, plus Hollywood thru 7/30/45* (Zephyrhills, FL, 1989)

——: *Columbia 78 rpm Master Listing: New York: 20000–22999, October 5, 1936 thru March 24, 1938* (Zephyrhills, FL, 1995)

——: *Coral Records 60000 and 61000 Series* (Zephyrhills, FL, 1995)

——: *Coral Records 62000 and 69000 Series* (Zephyrhills, FL, 1995)

——: *Decca 8500, 11000, 12000, 14000, 15000, 16000 Record Series* (Zephyrhills, FL, 1993)

——: *Decca 10000 Record Series: 10000–10530* (Zephyrhills, FL, 1993)

——: *Decca 23000 and 24000 Record Series* (Zephyrhills, FL, 1993)

——: *Decca 25000 and 27000 Record Series* (Zephyrhills, FL, 1993)

——: *Decca 28000 and 29000 Record Series* (Zephyrhills, FL, 1993)

——: *Decca 30000 and 31000 Record Series* (Zephyrhills, FL, 1994)

——: *Decca Chicago Master Numbers* (Zephyrhills, FL, 1992)

——: *Decca Los Angeles Master Numbers*, i: *1–5000* (Zephyrhills, FL, 1992); ii: *5001–8999* (Zephyrhills, 1993); iii: *9000–11999* (Zephyrhills, 1994)

——: *Decca New York Master Numbers*, i: *38277–62999* (Zephyrhills, FL, 1992); ii: *63000–67999* (Zephyrhills, 1992); iii: *68000–71999* (Zephyrhills, 1992); iv: *72000–75999* (Zephyrhills, 1992); v: *76000–82999* (Zephyrhills, 1993); vi: *83000–86999* (Zephyrhills, 1993); vii: *87000–89999* (Zephyrhills, 1993); viii: *100000–103999* (Zephyrhills, 1994); ix: *104000–107999* (Zephyrhills, 1994)

——: *Decca Record Listing*, i: *100–2225* (Zephyrhills, FL, 1991); ii: *2226–4455* (Zephyrhills, 1992)

——: *Decca Records 5000 and 7000 Series* (Zephyrhills, FL, 1993)

——: *Decca Records 18000 Series* (Zephyrhills, FL, 1993)

——: *Four Star and Gilt Edge Records* (Zephyrhills, FL, 1993)

——: *Keystone Transcriptions* (Portland, OR, 1999)

——: *Macgregor Radio Transcriptions 1 to 920* (Zephyrhills, FL, 1990)

——: *MGM Record Listing 10001 thru 13506* (Zephyrhills, FL, 1989)

——: *World Radio Transcriptions 100 to 758: Working Draft* (Zephyrhills, FL, 1990)

C. Garrod and R. Baum: *Associated Transcription Listing: Original and A Series* (Zephyrhills, FL, 1991)

——: *Associated Transcription Listing: 60,000 Series, 60,000–60,099* (Zephyrhills, FL, 1992)

——: *Associated Transcription Master Numbers, October 2, 1934 – July 12, 1942* (Zephyrhills, FL, 1991)

C. Garrod and R. Brandt: *Capitol Transcription Listing* (Zephyrhills, FL, 1995)

C. Garrod, K. Crawford, and D. Kressley: *World Transcriptions Original Series, 1–11268* (Zephyrhills, FL, 1992)

C. Garrod, D. Kressley, and K. Crawford: *Musak Transcriptions: Working Draft* (Zephyrhills, FL, 1995)

——: *Standard Transcription Listing*, i: *Series A–T* (Zephyrhills, FL, 1993); ii: *Series U–Z* (Zephyrhills, 1993)

——: *Thesaurus Transcription Listing: Working Draft*, 2 vols. (Zephyrhills, FL, 1992)

C. Garrod and E. Novitsky: *Columbia 78 rpm Record Listing*, i: *35000 thru 36999* (Zephyrhills, FL, 1995); ii: *37000 thru 38999* (Zephyrhills, 1995); iii: *39000 thru 41000* (Zephyrhills, 1995); iv: *41001 thru 42930* (Zephyrhills, 1995) [iii & iv by Garrod only]

——: *Columbia Dallas Master Numbers* (Zephyrhills, FL, 1995)

——: *MGM 78 rpm Master Numbers Listing*, i: *1946 thru 1952: Working Draft*, ii: *1953 thru 1956* (Zephyrhills, FL, 1990)

C. Garrod, see also B. Korst; E. Novitsky

G. Gart and R. C. Ames: *Duke/Peacock Records: an Illustrated History with Discography* (Milford, NH, 1990)

Gilt Edge catalogue, see C. Garrod

P. A. Grendysa: *Atlantic Master Book #1* (Milwaukee, 1975)

J. Grundmann: *Jazz aus den Trummern: Discographie der Eigenaufnahmen der Deutschen Grammophon, 1945–48* (Menden, Germany, 1982)

Harvest catalogue, see P. M. Pelletier

J. G. Hayes: *Edison Bell Winner: the W1 Series, 1933–1935* (Liverpool, England, 1984)

——: *The F1000 Series, Decca, 1929–1934*, Disc Research England (Liverpool, England, 1970/*R*1984)

J. G. Hayes, B. Luxton, and D. Luxton: *English Brunswick 78/45 r.p.m. (0)1000 Series*, i: *Issues 1001 to 02000 (Dec 1930 to May 1935)*, Numerical Catalogue Listings, no.E1 (n.p., n.d.)

His Master's Voice catalogues, see E. Jackson; P. Pelletier; M. Smith

Hit catalogue, see B. Korst

Imperial catalogue, see M. Ruppli

Infinity catalogue, see P. M. Pelletier

E. Jackson: *"His Master's Voice" Swing Music and Hot Rhythm Records* (Hayes, England, n.d. [1940], rev. and enlarged 2/n.d. [1942], rev. and enlarged 3/1944, rev. and enlarged 4/1946, rev. and enlarged 5/n.d. [1948], with various titles)

——: *The Parlophone "Rhythm-Style" Series: the Complete List of Records up to and Including December, 1935, Arranged Alphabetically and Numerically Together with the Personnels of the Orchestras and Index to Artistes*

(London, n.d. [?1936], rev. and enlarged 2/n.d. [1941], rev. and enlarged 3/n.d. [1942], rev. and enlarged 4/n.d. [1944], rev. and enlarged 5/n.d. [1946], rev. and enlarged 6/n.d. [1948], with various titles)
E. Jackson and L. Hibbs: *Decca, Brunswick, Vocalion Encyclopedia of Swing* (London, 1941)
Jazz on LP's: a Collectors' Guide to Jazz on Decca, Brunswick, Capitol, London and Felsted Long Playing Records (London, 1955, rev. 2/1956, as *Jazz on LP's: a Collectors' Guide to Jazz on Decca, Brunswick, London, Felsted, Ducretet-Thompson, Vogue, Coral, Telefunken and Durium Long Playing Records*)
Jazz on 78s: a Guide to the Many Examples of Classic Jazz (London, 1954) [pubn of Decca Record Co.]
F. J. Karlin: *Edison Diamond Discs, 50001–52651, 1912–1929* (Santa Monica, CA, 1972)
Keystone catalogue, see C. Garrod
L. F. Kiner and H. Mackenzie: *[AFRS] Basic Music Library, "P" Series, 1–1000* (New York, Westport, CT, and London, 1990)
King catalogue, see M. Ruppli
B. Korst: *RCA Victor Record Listing, 20-1500 thru 20-7300*, ed. C. Garrod (Zephyrhills, FL, n.d. [1986])
B. Korst, G. Blacker, and B. Porter: *Elite, Hit and Majestic Master Listing* (Zephyrhills, FL, 1989)
B. Korst, see also R. R. Olsen
D. Kressley, see C. Garrod
J. Lacomme, comp.: *The Muse Label: a Discography* (Paris, 1998)
London catalogues, see *Jazz on LP's*; P. Pelletier
R. E. Lotz: *The AFR&TS (Gold Label) Transcription Library: a Label Listing* (Menden, Germany, 1978)
R. E. Lotz and U. Neuert: *The AFRS "Jubilee" Transcription Programs: an Exploratory Discography* (Frankfurt am Main, Germany, 1985)
J. Lubin, see M. Ruppli
B. Luxton and D. Luxton, see J. G. Hayes
S. MacGillivray, see M. Terenzio
B. McGrath: *The R & B Indies* (West Vancouver, BC, 2000)
Macgregor catalogue, see C. Garrod
H. Mackenzie: *AFRS Downbeat Series: a Working Draft* (Zephyrhills, FL, 1986)
——: *Command Performance, USA!: a Discography* (Westport, CT, and London, 1996)
——: *The Directory of Armed Forces Radio Service Series* (Westport, CT, and London, 1999)
H. Mackenzie and L. Polanski: *One Night Stand Series, 1–1001* (Westport, CT, and London, 1996)
H. Mackenzie, see also L. F. Kiner
D. Mahony: *The Columbia 13/14000D Series: a Numerical Listing* (Stanhope, NJ, 1961, rev. Highland Park, NJ, 2/1966/R1973 with addns)
Majestic catalogue, see B. Korst
MCA catalogue, see P. M. Pelletier
Melotone catalogue, see BIBLIOGRAPHIES AND REFERENCE MATERIALS, R. D. Kinkle
Mercury catalogue, see M. Ruppli
Metronome catalogue, see B. Englund
MGM catalogues, see C. Garrod; E. Novitsky; M. Ruppli
M. Montgomery: *Columbia, Capitol, Supertone, and Challenge Word Roll Catalog* (n.p. [Southfield, MI], n.d. [?1984])
Musak catalogue, see C. Garrod
Muse catalogue, see J. Lacomme
U. Neuert, see R. E. Lotz
E. Novitsky and C. Garrod: *MGM Record Listings: 30000, 20000, 50000, 55000 and 60000* (Zephyrhills, FL, 1994)
E. Novitsky, see also C. Garrod; M. Ruppli
T. Okajima, ed.: *Jazz Critique 1997*, no. 3: *The Riverside Book: Discography of All Series* (Tokyo, 1997)
OKeh catalogues, see F. Andrews; BIBLIOGRAPHIES AND REFERENCE MATERIALS, R. D. Kinkle
Okeh Race Records (New York, n.d. [?1924]/R1976) [R1976 is a facs. of Clarence Williams's annotated copy]
Okeh Race Records: the Blue Book of Blues (New York, n.d. [?1927]/R)
T. Okuda, see M. Terenzio
R. R. Olsen and B. Korst: *"Two Hits for Two Bits": Crown Record and Master Listing* (Zephyrhills, FL, 1993)
Palette catalogue, see P. Pelletier
H. Panassié: *144 Hot Jazz Bluebird and Victor Records* (Camden, NJ, 1939)
Paramount catalogue, see M. E. Vreede
Parlophone catalogues, see A. Badrock; E. Jackson; P. M. Pelletier
Pathé catalogue, see A. Badrock
Peacock catalogue, see C. Garrod
[P. Pelletier]: *British Brunswick Complete Singles Listing* (London, ?1977; suppl. 1980) [Record Information Services pubn]
——: *British Capitol Singles & E.P.s*, i: *1948–1955* (London, 1977) [Record Information Services pubn]
——: *British London Jazz Complete L.P. Listing* (London, 1976) [Record Information Services pubn]
——: *British London Label L.P./E.P. Listing* (London, 1974) [pt i of *British London Label Complete Listing*; Record Information Services pubn]
——: *British London Complete Listing, Part Two* (London, 1974) [Record Information Services pubn]
——: *London – American 78/45 r.p.m. Singles from 1949 to December 1974* (London, 1975) [pt iii of *British London Label Complete Listing*; Record Information Services pubn]
——: *British London Label Complete Listing, Part Four, plus Felsted & (Vogue-)Coral* (London, 1975) [Record Information Services pubn]
——: *British London, London Jazz E.P. Listing* (London, 1976) [Record Information Services pubn]
——: *British London Singles, Felsted Popular Singles & EPs Listing* (London, 1976) [Record Information Services pubn]
——: *British Sue Complete Singles, E.P.s & L.P.s Listing* (London, 1976) [Record Information Services pubn]
——: *British Top Rank, Stateside Long-play Listing* (London, 1975) [Record Information Services pubn]
——: *British Top Rank, Stateside, Triumph, Palette Singles/E.P. Listing* (London, 1975) [Record Information Services pubn]
P. M. Pelletier: *British Capitol 45 r.p.m. Singles Catalogue: 1954–1981* (Chessington, England, 1982) [Record Information Services pubn]
——: *Complete British Directory of Popular 78/45 rpm Singles, 1950–1980*, i: *Columbia, Decca, H.M.V.* (London, 1986); ii: *Apple, Beltona, Brunswick, Capitol, Coral, Deram, EMI, Harvest, Infinity, MCA, Parlophone, Purple, Regal-Zonophone, Rhino, Sidewalk, T. Rex, Threshold, Uni* (London, 1987) [Record Information Services pubn]
——: *Decca 78 r.p.m. Ten-inch and 45 r.p.m. Seven-inch Complete Singles Catalogue, 1954–1983* (Chessington, England, 1984) [Record Information Services pubn]
——: *London 78 r.p.m. Ten-inch and 45 r.p.m. Seven-inch Complete Singles Catalogue: 1949–1982* (Chessington, England, 1982) [Record Information Services pubn]
Penny Phono catalogue, see F. Andrews
Perfect catalogues, see A. Badrock; BIBLIOGRAPHIES AND REFERENCE MATERIALS, R. D. Kinkle
B. Porter: *Signature Record Company Master Listing* (Zephyrhills, FL, 1989)
B. Porter, see also B. Korst; M. Ruppli
Prestige catalogue, see M. Ruppli
Purple catalogue, see P. M. Pelletier
B. Randle: *The Columbia 1-D Series, 1923–1929* (Bowling Green, OH, 1974)
RCA Victor catalogue, see B. Korst
Record Information Services, see P. Pelletier
Regal catalogue, see A. Badrock
Regal-Zonophone catalogue, see P. M. Pelletier
Rhino catalogue, see P. M. Pelletier
Riverside catalogues, see S. Furusho; T. Okajima
M. Ruppli: *The Aladdin/Imperial Labels: a Discography* (New York, Westport, CT, and London, 1991)
——: *Atlantic Records: a Discography* (Westport, CT, and London, 1979)
——: *The Chess Labels: a Discography* (Westport, CT, and London, 1983)
——: *The Decca Labels*, i: *The California Sessions*; ii: *The Eastern and Southern Sessions (1934–1942)*; iii: *The Eastern Sessions (1943–1956)*; iv: *The Eastern Sessions (1956–1973)*; v: *Country Recordings, Classical Recordings, and Reissues*; vi: *Record Numerical Listings and General Artist Index* (Westport, CT, and London, 1996)
——: *The Mercury Labels*, i: *The 1945–1956 Era*; ii: *The 1956–1964 Era*; iii: *The 1964–1969 Era*; iv: *The 1969–1991 Era and Classical Recordings*; v: *Record & Artist Indexes* (Westport, CT, and London, 1993)
——: *Prestige Jazz Records, 1949–1969 [recte 1971]: a Discography* (n.p. [Copenhagen], 1972; rev. and enlarged Westport, CT, and London, 2/1980, with B. Porter, as *The Prestige Label: a Discography*)
——: *Swing* (Paris, 1989)
——: *Vogue*, i (Paris, 1992)
M. Ruppli and B. Daniels: *The King Labels: a Discography* (Westport, CT, and London, 1985) [country music, rhythm-and-blues, some jazz]
M. Ruppli and J. Lubin: *Blue Star* (Paris, 1992)
M. Ruppli and E. Novitsky: *The MGM Labels: a Discography* (Westport, CT and London, 1998)
M. Ruppli and B. Porter: *The Clef/Verve Labels: a Discography*, i: *The Norman Granz Era*; ii: *The MGM Era* (New York, Westport, CT, and London, 1986)
——: *The Savoy Label: a Discography* (Westport, CT, and London, 1980)
M. Ruppli and J.-P. Tahmazian: *Black and Blue* (Paris, 1995)
M. Ruppli, see also M. Cuscuna
B. Rust: *The Victor Master Book*, ii: *1925–1936* (Stanhope, NJ, 1970) [projected vol. i: 1903–25, and vol. iii: 1936–42, not pubd]
B. Rust and T. Brooks: *The Columbia Master Book Discography* (Westport, CT, and London, 1999) [covers 1901–34]
M. J. Savada: *V-disc Title Listing* (Harrison, NY, 1989)
Savoy catalogue, see M. Ruppli
R. S. Sears: *V-discs: a History and Discography* (Westport, CT, and London, 1980; suppl., 1986)
R. Shor, see H. Thygesen

Sidewalk catalogue, see P. M. Pelletier
Signature catalogue, see B. Porter
M. Smith: *H.M.V. Recordings: "BD" Series: Magenta Label: a Discography* (Hastings, England, 1992)
Sonora catalogue, see B. Englund
Soul Note catalogue, see F. Fini
Soundies catalogue, see M. Terenzio
Standard catalogue, see C. Garrod
Stateside catalogues, see P. Pelletier
Sue catalogue, see P. Pelletier
Supertone catalogue, see M. Montgomery
Swing catalogue, see M. Ruppli
J.-P. Tahmazian, see M. Ruppli
Telefunken catalogue, see *Jazz on LP's*
M. Terenzio, S. MacGillivray, and T. Okuda: *The Soundies Distributing Corporation of America: a History and Filmography of their "Jukebox" Musical Films of the 1940s* (Jefferson, NC, and London, 1991)
K. Teubig: *V-disc Catalogue*, ii (Berlin, 1976)
Thesaurus catalogue, see C. Garrod
Threshold catalogue, see P. M. Pelletier
H. Thygesen, M. Berresford, and R. Shor: *Black Swan: the Record Label of the Harlem Renaissance* (Nottingham, England, 1996)
Top Rank catalogues, see P. Pelletier
T. Rex catalogue, see P. M. Pelletier
Triumph catalogue, see P. Pelletier
Uni catalogue, see P. M. Pelletier
V-disc catalogues, see M. J. Sawada; R. S. Sears; K. Teubig; S. Wante
Verve catalogue, see M. Ruppli
Victor catalogues, see B. Korst; H. Panassié; B. Rust; BIBLIOGRAPHIES AND REFERENCE MATERIALS, R. D. Kinkle
Vocalion catalogues, see F. Andrews; E. Jackson; BIBLIOGRAPHIES AND REFERENCE MATERIALS, R. D. Kinkle
Vogue catalogues, see *Jazz on LP's*; M. Ruppli
M. E. Vreede: *Paramount 12/13000 Series* (London, 1971)
E. S. Walker, see F. Andrews
S. Wante and W. DeBlock: *V-disc Catalogue*, i (Antwerp, Belgium, 1954)
U. Weiler: *The Debut Label: a Discography* (Norderstedt, Germany, 1994)
B. White: *AFRS Basic Music Library*, i: *P-1 to P-1200* (Zephyrhills, FL, 1988); ii: *P-1200 to P-2400* (Zephyrhills, 1988); iii: *P-2401 to P-3602* (Zephyrhills, 1988)
R. R. Wile: *Edison Disc Artists & Records, 1910–1929*, ed. R. Dethlefson (New York, 1985) [incl. dating guide]
——: *Edison Disc Recordings* (Philadelphia, 1977) [pubn of Eastern National Park and Monument Assn]
World catalogues, see F. Andrews; C. Garrod

Other listings

P. Adler and P. de Chocqueuse: *Passeport pour le jazz: les grands CD des grands de jazz* (Paris, 1995, rev. 2/1997, as *Passeport pour le jazz: les grands CD des grands de jazz, 1994–1997*)
Angelicum Santandrea catalogo generale, see *Santandrea catalogo generale*
G. Avakian: *Jazz from Columbia: a Complete Jazz Catalog* (New York, 1956) [listeners' guide]
Bielefelder Katalog, see *General*, M. Scheffner
H. J. Blumenthal: *The Blues CD Listener's Guide* (New York, 1998)
——: *The Jazz CD Listener's Guide* (New York, 1998)
P. Bonetta: *Jazz: discografia essenziale* (Reggio Emilia, Italy, 1978)
Catalogo: discos – long play (Buenos Aires, 1962–?); annual cumulative indexes [periodical catalogue, quarterly]
G. Cherrington, see OTHER BOOKS, S. Traill
P. de Chocqueuse, see P. Adler
D. Coller, see OTHER BOOKS, S. Traill
R. Cook and B. Morton: *The Penguin Guide to Jazz on CD, LP & Cassette* (London, 1991, rev. 2/1994, rev. 3/1996, as *The Penguin Guide to Jazz on CD*, rev. 4/1998, as *The Penguin Guide to Jazz on Compact Disc*, rev.5/2000)
Le courrier du disque microsillon (Paris, ?1952–1958), new ser. (Paris, 1959–?) [periodical catalogue, weekly, from nos.64–5 (6 Feb 1959) fortnightly]
J. Cowley and P. Oliver, eds.: *The New Blackwell Guide to Recorded Blues* (Oxford, England, 1996)
M. Cullaz: *Guide des disques de jazz: les 1000 meilleurs disques de spirituals, gospel songs, blues, rhytm* [*sic*] *and blues, jazz, et leur histoire* (Paris, 1971)
Diapason: la revue du disque microsillon, new ser. (Angers, France, Oct–Dec 1955–Nov 1956; Paris, Dec 1956–?); monthly suppl. *La discographie de la France* (1955–64), contd independently (see PERIODICALS) [periodical catalogue, 11 issues yearly]
La discographie française: revue bimensuelle du disque [by no.12 (15 May 1957) *La discographie française: la seule revue complète d'actualité du disque*; from no.121 (15 Sept 1962) *La discographie française et L'édition musicale française*] (Paris, 1 Dec 1956–) [periodical catalogue, fortnightly]
Discopop '77: tous les disques de pop, blues, folk, free-jazz, rock (Paris, 1977) [catalogue]
Disques de longue durée (Paris, autumn 1953–?); various suppls. [periodical catalogue, bimonthly, from no.12 (1957) yearly]
F. Dutton, see OTHER BOOKS, S. Traill
M. Erlewine, ed.: *All Music Guide to the Blues: the Expert's Guide to the Best Blues Recordings* (San Francisco, 1996, rev. 2/1999)
M. Erlewine, see also R. Wynn
L. Federighi: *Le grandi voci della musica americana: guida ai CD dei grandi cantanti USA tra jazz, soul, blues, gospel, country e pop* (Milan, 1997)
C. Ferguson and M. Johnson: *Mainstream Jazz Reference and Price Guide, 1949–1965* (Phoenix, AZ, 1984) [price guide]
J. Fordham: *Jazz on CD: the Essential Guide* (London, 1991, rev. [2]/1993, rev. 3/1995)
Forty-fiver (New York, Sept 1951–? Dec 1957) [periodical catalogue, monthly]
C. Fox, P. Gammond, and A. Morgan: *Jazz on Record: a Critical Guide* (London, 1960) [listeners' guide]
C. Fox, see also M. Harrison
P. Gammond and R. Horricks: *Big Bands*, Music on Record, ii (Cambridge, England, 1981)
M. Gayford: *The Best of Jazz: the Essential CD Guide* (San Francisco, 1993)
P. Gammond, see also C. Fox
G. Graff, ed.: *MusicHound R&B: the Essential Album Guide* (Detroit, MI, 1998 [*recte* 1997])
P. Guralnick: *The Listener's Guide to the Blues* (Poole, England, 1982)
L. Hanousek, ed.: *CD World Reference Guide Popular Music Edition* [from 1998 *CD World Reference Guide Popular Music Edition "Major Markets"*] (Milwaukie, OR, and Backnang, Germany, 1990; Milwaukie, 1991–) [periodical catalogue, twice yearly]
R. Harris and B. Rust: *Recorded Jazz: a Critical Guide* (Harmondsworth, England, 1958) [listeners' guide]
S. Harris: *Jazz on Compact Disc: a Critical Guide to the Best Recordings* (New York, 1987)
M. Harrison and others: *Modern Jazz: the Essential Records: a Critical Selection* (London, 1975) [listeners' guide]
M. Harrison, C. Fox, and E. Thacker: *The Essential Jazz Records*, i: *Ragtime to Swing* (London, and Westport, CT, 1984) [listeners' guide]
M. Harrison, E. Thacker, and S. Nicholson: *The Essential Jazz Records*, ii: *Modernism to Postmodernism* (London, 2000)
L. Hibbs: *21 Years of Swing Music on Brunswick Records* (London, 1937)
R. Horricks, see P. Gammond
A. Jackson, see E. Jackson
E. Jackson, A. McCarthy, A. Jackson, and R. Seeley, eds.: *The Gramophone Long Playing Popular Record Catalogue* [from July 1955 *The Gramophone Popular Record Catalogue*; from ?1973 *Gramophone Popular Catalogue*; from March 1985 *The Pop Cat*] (Harrow, England, July 1954–Sept 1987); annual cumulative indexes (1955–84) [periodical catalogue, quarterly]
Jazz Catalogue, see *General*, G. Cherrington
Jazz 'n Pops: a Comprehensive Catalog of Jazz and Popular Longplay Records, see *The Long Player*
M. Johnson, see C. Ferguson
Morley Jones: *Jazz*, Simon and Schuster's Listener's Guides, ed. A. Rich (New York, 1980)
B. Kernfeld: *The Blackwell Guide to Recorded Jazz* (Oxford, England, and Cambridge, MA, 1991, rev. 2/1995)
S. Knopper, ed.: *MusicHound Swing: the Essential Album Guide* (Detroit, MI, 1999)
G. Langley: *The Official Music Master Jazz Catalogue* (Hastings, England, 1990, rev. and enlarged London, 2/1994, as *Music Master Jazz and Blues Catalogue*)
G. Lascelles, see OTHER BOOKS, S. Traill
The Long Player [from v/7 (July–Aug 1956) *The Long Player: a Complete Catalog of Long-playing Records*] (New York, 1952–summer 1959); separate catalogue of jazz and popular music as *The Long Player: a Complete Catalog of Popular & Jazz Longplay Records* (New York, Jan 1957–summer 1959) [from i/2 (March 1957) *Jazz 'n Pops: a Comprehensive Catalog of Jazz and Popular Longplay Records*] [periodical catalogue]
L. Lyons: *The 101 Best Jazz Albums: a History of Jazz on Records* (New York, 1980) [listeners' guide]
J. McCalla: *Jazz: a Listener's Guide* (Englewood Cliffs, NJ, 1982, rev. 2/1994)
A. McCarthy and others: *Jazz on Record: a Critical Guide to the First 50 Years: 1917–1967* (London, 1968) [listeners' guide]
A. McCarthy, see also E. Jackson
D. Marsh, see J. Swenson
Micro surco: catálogo completo de discos larga duracion: 331/3 y 45 r.p.m. (Buenos Aires, 1955–?) [periodical catalogue]
A. Morgan, see C. Fox
B. Morton, see R. Cook
Music Master [*1974*] [from 1984 *Music Master: the World's Greatest Record Catalogue*, by 1991 *The Official Music Master Albums Catalogue*]

(London, 1974–?1978; Hastings, England, ?1979–1991) [periodical catalogue, yearly]
Music Master CD Index [in 1989 *Music Master CD Catalogue*, from 1990 *The Official Music Master CD Catalogue*, from 1992 *Music Master CD Catalogue*, from 1996 *RED Compact Disc Catalogue*, from 1997 *RED CD Catalogue*] (Hastings, England, 1986–90; London, 1991–) [periodical catalogue, quarterly, 1986–8; yearly from 1989]
Music Master Labels List [1991 *The Official Music Master Labels Catalogue*] (Hastings, England, 1980–86, 1988–90; London, 1991) [periodical catalogue, yearly]
S. Nicholson, see M. Harrison
P. Oliver, ed.: *The Blackwell Guide to Blues Records* (Oxford, England, 1989, rev. 1991, as *The Blackwell Guide to Recorded Blues*)
P. Oliver, see also J. Crowley
H. Panassié: *Discographie critique des meilleurs disques de jazz* (Paris, 1958)
——: *Petit guide pour une discothèque de jazz* (Paris, 1955)
T. Piazza: *The Guide to Classic Recorded Jazz* (Iowa City, IA, 1995)
F. Ramsey, Jr.: *A Guide to Longplay Jazz Records* (New York, n.d. [1954]/ *R*1977) [listeners' guide]
Revista "Long-playing" (n.p., ?1957–1960; São Paulo, 1960–?) [periodical catalogue, bimonthly, from no.27 (Nov/Dec 1960) quarterly]
A. Rich, see Morley Jones
The Rolling Stone Jazz Record Guide, see J. Swenson
L. Rucker, ed.: *MusicHound Blues: the Essential Album Guide* (Detroit, MI, 1998 [*recte* 1997])
B. Rust, see R. Harris
Santandrea catalogo generale dischi microsolio 331/3 e 45 e.p. [from xv/2 (March/April 1968) *Angelicum Santandrea catalogo generale dischi microsolio 331/3 e 45 e.p.*] (Milan, Jan/Feb 1955–?) [periodical catalogue, bimonthly]
[W. Schwann]: *Long Playing Record Catalog* [from March 1953 *Schwann: Long Playing Record Catalog*, from Jan 1971 *Schwann Record & Tape Guide*, from Jan 1972 *Schwann-1: Record & Tape Guide*, from Dec 1983 *The New Schwann*, from June 1986 *Schwann*, from spring 1990 *Spectrum*, from *c* fall 1992 *Schwann Spectrum*, from 2001 annual pubns *Schwann Spectrum* (incl. jazz), *Schwann Popular* (incl. blues)] (Cambridge, MA, 1949–53; Boston, 1953–92; Santa Fe, NM, 1992–7; Woodland, CA, 1999–); from fall 1964, half-yearly suppl. *The Schwann Catalog of Imported Records* [from 1966 *The Schwann Supplementary Catalog*, from 1971 *The Schwann Supplementary Record Guide*, from 1972 *Schwann-2: Record & Tape Guide*] (1964–83); monthly suppl. *Schwann Compact Disc* (1986–Dec 1989); also *CD Review Digest* (jazz, popular, etc.), from 1995 as *Schwann CD Review Digest*, viii/4 (rock, pop, jazz, etc.) [viii/1–3 not pubd]; concurrently from 15 Jan – 15 Feb 1990 to 15 March – 15 April 1991, *InMusic* (Chatsworth, CA), formed by the union of, and partially continuing, *Schwann* and *Schwann Compact Disc* [6 issues annually]
R. Seeley, see E. Jackson
K. Shadwick, ed.: *The Gramophone Jazz Good CD Guide* (Harrow, England, 1995, rev. 2/n.d. [1997])
C. E. Smith and others: *The Jazz Record Book* (New York, 1942/*R*1978) [listeners' guide with discography]
J. Swenson, ed.: *The Rolling Stone Jazz Record Guide* (New York and Toronto, 1985) [listeners' guide; incl. material previously pubd in D. Marsh and J. Swenson, eds.: *The Rolling Stone Record Guide* (New York, 1979)]
N. Tesser: *Playboy Guide to Jazz* (New York, 1998)
E. Thacker, see M. Harrison
S. Traill, see OTHER BOOKS
N. Umphred: *Goldmine's Guide to Collectable Jazz Albums, 1949–1969* (Iola, WI, 1992, rev. 2/1994)
J. S. Wilson: *The Collector's Jazz: Modern* (Philadelphia, 1959) [listeners' guide]
——: *The Collector's Jazz: Traditional and Swing* (Philadelphia, 1958) [listeners' guide]
——: *Jazz: the Transition Years, 1940–1960* (New York, 1966) [listeners' guide]
R. Wynn, ed.: *All Music Guide to Jazz* (San Francisco, 1994, rev. 2/1996, ed. M. Erlewine, rev. 3/1998, ed. M. Erlewine and others)
S. Yanow: *Afro-Cuban jazz* (San Francisco, 2000)

OTHER BOOKS

K. Abé: *50 Jazz Greats "from Heaven"* (Tokyo, 1995) [photo album]
——: *Jazz Giants: a Visual Retrospective* (Tokyo, 1986, Columbus, OH, and London, 1988)
M. Abrams: *The Book of Django* (Los Angeles, 1973) [bio-discography]
R. W. Ackelson: *Frank Sinatra: a Complete Recording History of Techniques, Songs, Composers, Lyrics, Arrangers, Sessions, and First-issue Albums, 1939–1984* (Jefferson, NC, 1992)
G. Adamo, S. G. Biamonte, and L. Bonifazi: *Jazz e cultura mediterranea* (Rome, 1985)
A. J. Agostinelli: *Don Ellis: a Man for our Time (1934–1978)* (Providence, RI, 1986) [bio-discography]
——: *Stan Kenton: the Many Musical Moods of his Orchestras* (Providence, RI, 1986) [bio-discography]
B. Aimé, see J.-L. Poisier
Y. M. Ajchenbaum, see S. Grappelli
C. Albertson: *Bessie: Empress of the Blues* (New York, 1972)
G. Albus: *Paris Pittsburgh: a Story in Jazz: the Life of Nathan Davis* (Munich, Germany, 1991)
C. Alexander, ed.: *Masters of Jazz Guitar: the Story of the Players and their Music* (London, 1999)
F. Alkyer, ed.: *Down Beat: Sixty Years of Jazz* (Milwaukee, 1995) [colln of previously pubd articles]
R. B. Allen, see W. J. Schafer
W. C. Allen: *Hendersonia: the Music of Fletcher Henderson and his Musicians: a Biodiscography* (Highland Park, NJ, 1973) [*AllenH*]
W. C. Allen, ed.: *Studies in Jazz Discography*, i (New Brunswick, NJ, 1971) [proceedings of *Discographical Research, i New Brunswick, NJ, 1968*; *Discographical Research, ii New Brunswick, NJ, 1969*; *Preservation and Extension of the Jazz Heritage: New Brunswick, NJ, 1969*]
W. C. Allen and B. A. L. Rust: *King Joe Oliver* (Belleville, NJ, 1955) [completely rev. version by L. Wright (Chigwell, England, 1987)]
O. Alvarenga: *Música popular brasileña* (Buenos Aires, 1947)
R. Ambor: *Ella: ein Bildband* (Hamburg, Germany, 1961)
R. Ameen, see L. Gourse
American Folklife Center, Library of Congress, see *Ethnic Recordings in America*
B. Amstell and R. T. Deal: *Don't Fuss, Mr. Ambrose: Memoirs of a Life Spent in Popular Music* (Tunbridge Wells, England, 1986) [autobiography of Billy Amstell]
E. Anderson, ed.: *Esquire's 1947 Jazz Book: Year Book of the Jazz Scene* (New York, 1947); see also P. E. Miller
J. Anderson: *This was Harlem: a Cultural Portrait, 1900–1950* (New York, 1982)
M. Anderson: *Music in the Mix: the Story of South African Popular Music* (Johannesburg, 1981)
U. Andresen: *Keith Jarrett: sein Leben, seine Musik, seine Schallplatten* (Gauting, Germany, n.d. [1985])
B. Andriessen: *Tetterettet* (Ubbergen, Netherlands, 1996)
O. Angell, J. E. Vold, and G. Økland, eds.: *Jazz i Norge* (Oslo, 1975)
F. J. Angstmann: *Jazz* (Zurich, 1979; Fr. trans., Zurich, 1979, as *Jazz*; It. trans., Zurich, 1979, as *Jazz*)
A. Antonietto, see F. Billard
L. Araque: *Defensa de la música del jazz* (Barcelona, 1946)
L. Arganian: *Stan Kenton: the Man and his Music* (East Lansing, MI, 1989)
D. Armstrong: *Wild Bill Davison: a Celebration* (Ottawa, 1991)
L. Armstrong: *Ma Nouvelle-Orléans* (Paris, 1952; Eng. orig. pubd New York, 1954/*R*1986, as *Satchmo: my Life in New Orleans*; Dutch trans., Zeist, Netherlands, 1958, as *Mein jeugd in New Orleans*; Ger. trans., Zurich, 1977, as *Mein Leben in New Orleans*; It. trans., Milan, 1956, as *Satchmo: la mia vita a New* Orleans; Polish trans., Kraków, 1974, as *Moje życie w Nowym Orleanie*)
[L. Armstrong] *Satchmo: Collector's Copy* (Hollywood, CA, 1971) [iconography]
——: *Swing that Music* (London, New York, and Toronto, 1936/*R*1993) [incl. transcrs.]
G. Arnaud, see J. Chesnel
L. M. G. Arntzenius: *Amerikaansche kunstindrukken* (Amsterdam, 1927)
P. Arzano: *Jazz Live in Bergamo* (Bergamo, Italy, 1983)
H. Asbury: *The French Quarter: an Informal History of the New Orleans Underworld* (London, 1937)
D. Asher, see H. Hawes
J. Asman, see S. F. Dance
J. Asman and B. Kinnell, eds.: *American Jazz*, i (London, n.d. [1945]); ii (London, 1946)
A. Asriel: *Jazz: Analysen und Aspekte* (Berlin, 1966)
Association St. Louis Jazz and H. Lenormand: *St. Louis Jazz* (Nantes, France, 1996) [concerned with jazz in St. Louis, Senegal]
A. Astrup, see J. Kuehn
R. Atkins: *Jazz: the Ultimate Guide, from New Orleans to the New Jazz Age* (London, 1996)
M. Audibert: *Fletcher Henderson et son orchestre, 1924–1951: sa place dans l'histoire du jazz* (Bayonne, France, 1983)
M. Ausserbauer, see G. Filtgen
J. Back: *Triumph des Jazz* (Vienna, 1946/*R*1992)
R. Badger: *A Life in Ragtime: a Biography of James Reese Europe* (New York, and Oxford, England, 1995)
V. Bagneris, see L. Touchet
D. Bailey: *Improvisation: its Nature and Practice in Music* (Ashbourne, England, 1980, Englewood Cliffs, NJ, 1980, as *Musical Improvisation: its Nature and Practice in Music*, rev. London, 2/1992; Ger. trans., Hofheim am Taunus, Germany, 1986, as *Musikalische Improvisation: Kunst ohne Werk*)
C. Baker: *As Though I Had Wings: the Lost Memoir* (New York, 1997; Ger. trans., St.-Andrä-Wördern, Germany, 1998, as *Als hätte ich Flügel:*

verlorene Erinnerungen; Sp. trans., Barcelona, 1999, as *Como si tuviera alas: las memorias perdidas*)
D. Baker: *Advanced Improvisation* (Chicago, 1971, rev. 1979)
——: *Arranging and Composing for the Small Ensemble: Jazz, R & B, Jazz-rock* (Chicago, 1970)
——: *Jazz Improvisation: a Comprehensive Method for all Players* (Chicago, 1969, rev. 2/1983; Ger. trans., Rottenburg, Germany, 1984, as *Jazz Improvisation: eine umfassende Methode für alle Instrumente*)
——: *Jazz Pedagogy: a Comprehensive Method of Jazz Education for Teacher and Student* (Van Nuys, CA, 1998)
——: *The Jazz Style of Cannonball Adderley: a Musical and Historical Perspective* (Lebanon, IN, 1980) [incl. transcrs.]
——: *The Jazz Style of Clifford Brown: a Musical and Historical Perspective* (Hialeah, FL, 1982) [incl. transcrs.]
——: *The Jazz Style of Fats Navarro: a Musical and Historical Perspective* (Hialeah, FL, 1982) [incl. transcrs.]
——: *The Jazz Style of John Coltrane: a Musical and Historical Perspective* (Lebanon, IN, 1980) [incl. transcrs.]
——: *The Jazz Style of Miles Davis: a Musical and Historical Perspective* (Lebanon, IN, 1980) [incl. transcrs.]
——: *The Jazz Style of Sonny Rollins: a Musical and Historical Perspective* (Lebanon, IN, 1980) [incl. transcrs.]
——: *Jazz Styles & Analysis: Trombone: a History of the Jazz Trombone via Recorded Solos, Transcribed and Annotated* (Chicago, 1973)
——: *J. J. Johnson, Trombone* (New York, 1979) [transcrs.; incl. discography and list of compositions]
D. Baker, ed.: *New Perspectives on Jazz: Report on a National Conference held at Wingspread, Racine, Wisconsin, September 8–10, 1986* (Washington, DC, n.d. [c1990])
D. Baker, see also P. Coker
D. N. Baker, L. M. Belt, and H. C. Hudson, eds.: *The Black Composer Speaks* (Metuchen, NJ, and London, 1978)
M. Baldin, see W. E. Studwell
N. Balen: *Billie Holiday: corps et âme* (Paris, 2000)
——: *L'odyssée du jazz: des origines à nos jours* (Paris, 1993)
C. Ballantine: *Marabi Nights: Early South African Jazz and Vaudeville* (Johannesburg, and Athens, OH, 1993)
W. Balliett: *Alec Wilder and his Friends* (Boston, 1974) [colln of previously pubd articles]
——: *American Musicians: Fifty-six Portraits in Jazz* (New York, and Oxford, England, 1986) [*BallietA (1986)*]
——: *American Musicians, II: Seventy-two Portraits in Jazz* (New York, and Oxford, England, 1996) [*BallietA (1996)*]
——: *American Singers* (New York, 1979, rev. and enlarged New York, and Oxford, England, 2/1988, as *American Singers: Twenty-seven Portraits in Song*)
——: *Barney, Bradley, and Max: 16 Portraits in Jazz* (New York, 1989)
——: *Collected Works: a Journal of Jazz, 1954–2000* (New York, 2000) [colln of previously pubd articles]
——: *Dinosaurs in the Morning* (Philadelphia, 1962/*R*1978) [colln of previously pubd articles and reviews]
——: *Ecstasy at the Onion* (New York and Indianapolis, 1971) [colln of previously pubd articles and reviews]
——: *Goodbyes and other Messages: a Journal of Jazz, 1981–1990* (New York, 1991)
——: *Improvising: Sixteen Jazz Musicians and their Art* (New York, 1977) [colln of previously pubd articles]
——: *Jelly Roll, Jabbo and Fats* (New York, and Oxford, England, 1983) [colln of previously pubd articles]
——: *New York Notes: a Journal of Jazz, 1972–1975* (Boston, 1976) [colln of previously pubd reviews]
——: *Night Creature: a Journal of Jazz, 1975–1980* (New York, 1981) [colln of previously pubd reviews]
——: *The Sound of Surprise* (New York, 1959/*R*1978) [colln of previously pubd articles and reviews]
——: *Such Sweet Thunder* (Indianapolis, 1966) [colln of previously pubd articles and reviews]
——: *Super Drummer: a Profile of Buddy Rich* (Indianapolis, 1968)
Amiri Baraka: *The Autobiography of Leroi Jones* (New York, 1984/*R*1996, complete orig. text, New York, 1997)
Amiri Baraka and Amina Baraka: *The Music: Reflections on Jazz and Blues* (New York, 1987)
Amiri Baraka, see other works listed under alternative name, L. Jones
A. Baresel: *Das Jazz-Buch: Anleitung zum Spielen, Improvisieren und Komponieren moderner Tanzstücke mit besonderer Berücksichtigung des Klaviers* (Leipzig, Germany, 1926, rev. 1929, as *Das neue Jazzbuch: ein praktisches Handbuch für Musiker, Komponisten, Arrangeure, Tänzer und Freunde der Jazzmusik*)
——: *Jazz in der Krise: Jazz in Umbruch* (Trossingen, Germany, 1959)
D. Barker: *A Life in Jazz*, ed. A. Shipton (London and New York, 1986) [autobiography of Danny Barker; incl. discography]
D. Barker, see also J. V. Buerkle
O. Barletta: *100 immagini di jazz* (Turin, Italy, 1992)
W. Barlow and C. Finley: *From Swing to Soul: an Illustrated History of African American Popular Music from 1930 to 1960* (Washington, DC, 1994)
W. Barlow, see also T. L. Morgan
K. Barnes: *Sinatra and the Great Song Stylists* (London, 1972)
C. Barnet and S. Dance: *Those Swinging Years: the Autobiography of Charlie Barnet* (Baton Rouge, LA, and London, 1984/*R*1992) [incl. discography]
A. Barnett: *Black Gypsy: the Recordings of Eddie South: an Annotated Discography and Itinerary* (Lewes, England, 1999)
——: *Desert Sands: the Recordings and Performances of Stuff Smith: an Annotated Discography and Biographical Source Book* (Lewes, England, 1995; suppl., 1998, as *Up Jumped the Devil*)
A. Barnett and E. Løgager: *Stuff Smith: Pure at Heart* (Lewes, England, 1991)
S. Baron, ed.: *Benny, King of Swing: a Pictorial Biography Based on Benny Goodman's Personal Archives* (London and New York, 1979/*R*1987; Ger. trans., Wilhelmshaven, Germany, 1984, as *Benny Goodman–King of Swing: ein Bildbibliographie mit Fotogr. aus Benny Goodmans eigenem Archiv*)
K. Barron, see Y. Lateef
L. Barron: *Odyssey of the Mid-nite Flyer: a History of Midwest Bands* (Omaha, NE, 1987)
T. Barrow, see V. Lewis
J. Barthiel, see R. Clooney
E. Bartsch: *Neger, Jazz und tiefer Süden* (Leipzig, Germany, 1956)
L. Bash, see J. Kuzmich, Jr.
C. Basie and A. Murray: *Good Morning Blues: the Autobiography of Count Basie* (New York, 1985/*R*1995; Ger. trans., Düsseldorf and elsewhere, 1987, as *Good Morning Blues: ein Autobiographie*; Fr. trans., Paris, 1988, as *Good Morning Blues, Count Basie*)
P. Bas-Rabérin: *Les incontournables du blues* (Paris, 1994)
B. Bastin: *Never Sell a Copyright: Joe Davis and his Role in the New York Music Scene, 1916–1978* (Chigwell, England, 1990)
A. Batashev: *Sovietski dzaz* (Moscow, 1972)
C. Batchelor: *This Thing Called Swing: a Study of Swing Music and the Lindy Hop, the Original Swing Dance* (London, 1997)
B. Bauer with T. Luba: *Sideman: the Autobiography of Billy Bauer* (New York, 1997)
H. Baumgartner: *"Jazz" in den zwanziger Jahren in Zürich: zur Enstehung und Wervendung einer populärkulturellen Bezeichnung* (Zurich, 1989)
A. Bausch: *Jazz in Europa* (Echternach, Luxembourg, 1985)
J. Bauzá Doria: *Jazz: grabaciones maestras*, i: *Los inicios y los años 20* (Alicante, Spain, 1986)
M. Bayles: *Hole in our Soul: the Loss of Beauty and Meaning in American Popular Music* (New York and Toronto, 1994)
G. Beall: *Frontiers of Jazz* (New York, 1947, rev. 2/1962)
L. T. Beauchamp, Jr.: *Art Ensemble of Chicago: Great Black Music, Ancient to the Future* (Chicago, 1998)
S. Bechet: *Treat it Gentle: an Autobiography*, ed. D. Flower (New York and London, 1960/*R*1975; Fr. trans., Paris, 1977, as *La musique c'est ma vie*; Ger. trans., Zurich, 1961, as *Alle Kinder Gottes tragen eine Krone: eine Autobiographie*, *R*/1992, as *Petite fleur: Errinerungen eines begnadeten Jazzmusikers*)
M. Becker: *Chormusik im Jazz* (Idstein, Germany, 1992)
S. F. Bedwell: *A Glenn Miller Discography and Biography* (London, 1955)
K. Behounek: *Má láska je jazz* (Toronto, 1986)
P. O. E. Bekker, Jr.: *The Story of the Blues* (New York, 1994)
R. Belcher: *Maynard Ferguson File* (Caversham, England, 1975–6) [colln of articles and printed ephemera]
L. B. Belker: *Seems Like Old Times: a Story of the Midwest's "Big Bands"* (Lincoln, NE, 1992)
G. Bell: *Australian Jazzman: his Autobiography* (French's Forest, Australia, 1988) [incl. discography by J. Mitchell]
C. Bellest, see L. Malson
L. M. Belt, see D. N. Baker
O. Bender: *Swing unterm Hakenkreuz in Hamburg, 1933–1943* (Hamburg, Germany, 1993)
P. Benkimoun: *Lester Young* (Paris, 1997)
B. Bennett: *The Ladies who Sing with the Band* (Lanham, MD, and elsewhere, 2000)
T. Bennett with W. Friedwald: *The Good Life: the Autobiography of Tony Bennett* (New York, 1998)
E. Benson, ed.: *Barney Kessel* (Atlanta, 1997) [incl. discography]
K. Benson, see J. Haskins
K. W. Benston: *Baraka: the Renegade and the Mask* (New Haven, CT, and London, 1976)
K. W. Benston, ed.: *Imamu Amiri Baraka (Leroi Jones): a Collection of Critical Essays* (Englewood Cliffs, NJ, 1978)
B. Benward and J. Wildman: *Jazz Improvisation in Theory and Practice* (Dubuque, IA, 1984)
J.-E. Berendt: *Ein Fenster aus Jazz: Essays, Portraits, Reflexionen* (Frankfurt am Main, Germany, 1977)
——: *Der Jazz: eine zeitkritische Studie* (Stuttgart, Germany, 1950)

——: *Das Jazzbuch: Entwicklung und Bedeutung der Jazzmusik* (Frankfurt am Main, Germany, 1953; Dutch trans., Utrecht, Netherlands, 1956, as *Jazz van New Orleans tot cool*; rev. 2/1959 as *Das neue Jazzbuch: Entwicklung und Bedeutung der Jazzmusik*; It. trans., Florence, 1960, as *Il nuove libro del jazz: evoluzione e significato della musica jazz*; Eng. trans., New York, 1962, London, 1964, as *The New Jazz Book*; Fr. trans., Paris, 1962, as *Le jazz*; Sp. trans., Mexico City, *c*1962, as *El jazz: su origen y desarollo*; rev. and enlarged Stuttgart, Germany, 3/1968, as *Das Jazzbuch: von Rag bis Rock: Entwicklung, Elemente, Definition d. Jazz, Musiker, Sänger, Combos, Big Band, Electric Jazz, Jazz-Rock der siebziger Jahre*; Sp. trans., Mexico City, 1973, as *Jazz: del rag el rock*; Port. trans., São Paulo, Brazil, 1975, as *O jazz: do rag ao rock*; rev. and enlarged Frankfurt am Main, Germany, 4/1975, as *Das Jazzbuch: von Rag bis Rock: Entwicklung, Elemente, Musiker, Sänger, Combos, Big Bands*; Eng. trans., St. Albans, England, 1976, as *The Jazz Book*; rev. and enlarged 5/1981, as *Das grosse Jazzbuch: von New Orleans bis Jazz Rock*; Eng. trans., Westport, CT, 1982, as *The Jazz Book: from New Orleans to Fusion and Beyond*, London, 1983, as *The Jazz Book: from New Orleans to Jazz Rock and Beyond*; It. trans., Milan, 1986, as *Nuovo libro del jazz: dal New Orleans al jazz rock*; rev. Brooklyn, NY, 6/1992; Fr. trans., Monaco, 1986, as *Le grand livre de jazz*, rev. 1994; rev. and enlarged by G. Huesman, 1989, as *Das Jazzbuch*; Eng. trans., by J. Berendt and G. Huesman, New York, 1992, as *The Jazz Book*)
——: *Jazz-optisch* (Munich, Germany, 1954, rev. 2/1956; Dutch trans., The Hague, 1956, as *Jazz in foto's*)
——: *Das Leben-ein Klang: Wege zwischen Jazz und Nada Brahma* (Munich, 1996)
——: *Nada Brahma: die Welt ist Klang* (Frankfurt am Main, Germany, 1983)
——: *Photo-Story des Jazz* (Frankfurt am Main, Germany, 1978; Eng. trans., New York and London, 1979, as *Jazz: a Photo-history*; It. trans., Milan, 1979, as *Fotostoria del jazz*)
——: *Die Story des Jazz vom New Orleans zum Rock Jazz* (Stuttgart, Germany, and elsewhere, 1976)
——: *Variationen über Jazz* (Munich, 1956)
——: *William Claxton: Jazz Life: auf d. Spuren d. Jazz* (Offenburg, Germany, 1961)
D. Berg and B. Liebscher: *Ein Vierteljahrhundert Dixieland Dresden* (Dresden, Germany, 1995)
I. Berg, I. Yeomans, and N. Brittan: *Trad: an A to Z Who's Who of the British Traditional Jazz Scene* (London and elsewhere, 1962)
D. G. Berger, see M. Hinton
E. Berger: *Bassically Speaking: an Oral History of George Duvivier* (Metuchen, NJ, and London, 1993) [incl. musical analysis by D. Chevan]
E. Berger, see also M. Berger; C. Nanry; T. Reig
H. M. Berger: *Metal, Rock and Jazz: Perception and the Phenomenology of Musical Experience* (Hanover, NH, 1999)
M. Berger, E. Berger, and J. Patrick: *Benny Carter: a Life in American Music* (Metuchen, NJ, and London, 1982)
F. Bergerot: *Miles Davis: introduction à l'écoute du jazz moderne* (Paris, 1996)
F. Bergerot and A. Merlin: *L'épopée du jazz*, i: *Du blues au bop* (Paris, 1991)
——: *L'épopée du jazz*, ii: *Au-delà du bop* (Paris, 1991, Eng. trans., New York, 1993, as *The Story of Jazz: Bop and Beyond*)
J. Bergh and J. Evensmo: *Jazz Tenor Saxophone in Norway, 1917–1959* (Oslo, 1996)
J. Bergh, see also B. Stendahl
H. J. P. Bergmeier: *The Weintraub Story: Incorporating the Ady Rosner Story* (Menden, Germany, 1982) [incl. discography]
H. J. P. Bergmeier and R. E. Lotz: *Alex Hyde Biodiscography* (Menden, Germany, 1985)
——: *Bernard Etté: a Bio-discography* (Dietramzell, Germany, 1995)
——: *Billy Bartholomew Bio-discography* (Menden, Germany, 1985)
——: *Eric Borchard Story* (Menden, Germany, 1988)
——: *Hitler's Airwaves: the Inside Story of Nazi Radio Broadcasting and Propaganda Swing* (New Haven, CT, and London, 1997)
——: *Lud Gluskin: a Bio-discography* (Dietramzell, Germany, 1995)
L. Bergreen: *Louis Armstrong: an Extravagant Life* (New York and London, 1997; Ger. trans., Zurich, 2000, as *Louis Armstrong: ein extravagantes Leben*)
E. A. Berlin: *King of Ragtime: Scott Joplin and his Era* (New York, and Oxford, England, 1994)
——: *Ragtime: a Musical and Cultural History* (Berkeley, CA, Los Angeles, and London, 1980/*R*1984 with addns)
P. F. Berliner: *Thinking in Jazz: the Infinite Art of Improvisation* (Chicago and London, 1994)
E. Bernhard and J. de Vergnies: *Apologie du jazz* (Brussels, 1945)
P. Bernhard: *Jazz: eine musikalische Zeitfrage* (Munich, 1927/*R*1987)
C. E. B. Bernhardt and S. Harris: *I Remember: Eighty Years of Black Entertainment, Big Bands, and the Blues* (Philadelphia, 1986) [autobiography of Clyde Bernhardt; incl. discography]
J. Bernlef, see P. Klaasse
L. Bernstein, see R. Carver
J. Berrett, ed.: *The Louis Armstrong Companion: Eight Decades of Commentary* (New York, 1999) [colln of previously pubd articles]
J. Berrett and L. G. Bourgeois III: *The Musical World of J. J. Johnson* (Lanham, MD, 1999)
J. Berry, J. Foose, and T. Jones: *Up from the Cradle of Jazz: New Orleans Music since World War II* (Athens, GA, and London, 1986)
R. Berton: *Remembering Bix: a Memoir of the Jazz Age* (New York and elsewhere, 1974/*R*2000)
T. Bethell: *George Lewis: a Jazzman from New Orleans* (Berkeley, CA, and London, 1977)
C. Béthune: *Charles Mingus* (Montpellier, France, 1988)
——: *Sidney Bechet* (Marseilles, France, 1997) [incl. discography]
C. Béthune, see also F. Hofstein
A. Bettex and others: *Montreux Jazz* (Lausanne, Switzerland, 1976)
F. Biagi, see L. Patruno
E. Biagioni: *Herb Flemming: a Jazz Pioneer around the World* (Alphen aan de Rijn, Netherlands, n.d. [?1977])
S. G. Biamonte, see G. Adamo
D. Bied: *Dan Bied's Jazz Reader* (West Burlington, IA, 1994)
——: *Jazz Memories* (Burlington, IA, 1994)
A. Bienville: *Encyclopédie Jazz Hot: New Orleans* (Paris, 1990)
B. Bigard: *With Louis and the Duke*, ed. B. Martyn (London, 1985) [autobiography of Barney Bigard]
F. Billard: *Ella Fitzgerald* (Paris, 1996)
——: *Jazz Anthology* (Castellina-in-Chianti, Italy, 1991)
——: *La vie quotidienne des jazzmen américains jusqu'aux années 50* (Paris, 1989)
——: *Lennie Tristano* (Montpellier, France, 1988)
——: *Les chanteuses de jazz* (Paris, 1990)
F. Billard and A. Antonietto: *Django Reinhardt: un géant sur son nuage* (Paris, 1993)
F. Billard and G. Tordjman: *Duke Ellington* (Paris, 1994)
C. J. Binkowski: *Musical New York: an Informal Guide to its History and Legends and a Walking Guide of its Sites and Landmarks* (Philadelphia, 1999)
Bird: the Chan Parker Collection (London, 1996) [auction catalogue, Christie's South Kensington]
J. Bisceglia: *Black & White Fantasy* (Troense, Denmark, 1984)
A. Bisset: *Black Roots, White Flowers: a History of Jazz in Australia* (Sydney, 1979, rev. 2/1987)
B. Bissonette: *The Jazz Crusade: the Inside Story of the Great New Orleans Jazz Revival of the 1960s* (Bridgeport, CT, 1992) [incl. discography]
D. C. Black: *Matrix Numbers: their Meaning and History* (Melbourne, Australia, n.d. [1940s])
J. Blades: *Percussion Instruments and their History* (London, 1970, rev. [3]/1984)
C. Blancq: *Melodic Improvisation in American Jazz: the Style of Theodore "Sonny" Rollins, 1951–1962* (diss., Tulane U., 1977); rev. as *Sonny Rollins: the Journey of a Jazzman* (Boston, 1983)
E. L. Blandford: *Artie Shaw* (Hastings, England, 1974) [bio-discography]
A. Blatter: *Instrumentation/Orchestration* (New York and London, 1980)
R. Blesh: *Combo, USA: Eight Lives in Jazz* (Philadelphia and London, 1971)
——: *Shining Trumpets: a History of Jazz* (New York, 1946, London, 1949, rev. and enlarged New York and London, 2/1958/*R*1975)
——: *This Is Jazz* (London, 1945)
R. Blesh and H. Janis: *They all Played Ragtime* (New York, 1950, rev. 2/1959, rev. 3/1966, rev. 4/1971)
P. Bley with D. Lee: *Stopping Time: Paul Bley and the Transformation of Jazz* (n.p. [Montreal], 1999)
G. Boas: *Rudi Anhang: ein Musiker im Hintergrund* (Menden, Germany, n.d. [*c*1986])
E. Bockemuehl [G. Bockey]: *On the Road with the Jimmy Dorsey Aggregation, 1947–1949* (San Diego, 1996)
P. Boggio: *Boris Vian* (Paris, 1993)
D. Bogle: *Brown Sugar: Eighty Years of America's Black Female Superstars* (New York, 1980/*R*1990)
——: *Dorothy Dandridge: a Biography* (New York, 1997)
——: *Toms, Coons, Mulattoes, Mammies & Bucks: an Interpretative History of Blacks in American Films* (New York, 1973, rev. 2/1989, rev. New York and Oxford, England, 3/1994)
C. Bohländer: *Die Anatomie des Swing* (Frankfurt am Main, Germany, 1986)
——: *Das Wesen der Jazzmusik* (Frankfurt am Main, Germany, 1954)
E.-M. Bolay: *Jazzmusikerinnen: Improvisation als Leben: eine empirische Untersuchung zu Laufbahnen und Lebenswelten von Jazzinstrumentistinnen in der 90er Jahren* (Kassel, Germany, 1995)
W. Bolcom, see R. Kimball; P. Oliver
P. Boncompagni and A. Lastella, eds.: *Chet Baker in Italia: storie di vita e di musica* (Rome, 1991)
L. Bonifazi, see G. Adamo
E. Bonini: *La véritable Joséphine Baker* (Paris, 2000)
A. Bontemps, see W. C. Handy

M. Bookspan and R. Yockey: *André Previn: a Biography* (Garden City, NY, 1981)
L. Borenstein and B. Russell: *Preservation Hall Portraits* (Baton Rouge, LA, 1968) [photographs by N. Rockmore]
B. Borgström and C. Landergren: *Chet Baker* (Stockholm, 1990)
B. Borgström, see also C. Landergren
E. Borneman: *A Critic Looks at Jazz* (London, 1946) [orig. pubd in *Record Changer*]
F. Bosshard, see P. Landolt
L. Bouffé: *Aventure jazz ...!: Souvenirs de Lionel Bouffé* (n.p. [Neuilly-sur-Seine, France], n.d. [1994])
G. Boulard: *"Just a Gigolo": the Life and Times of Louis Prima* (Lafayette, LA, 1989)
D. Boulton: *Jazz in Britain* (London, 1958)
A. S. Bourgeois: *Blueswomen: Profiles of Thirty-seven Early Performers, with an Anthology of Lyrics, 1920–1945* (Jefferson, NC, and elsewhere, 1996)
L. G. Bourgois III: *Jazz Trombonist J. J. Johnson: a Comprehensive Discography and Study of the Early Evolution of his Style* (diss., Ohio State U., 1986)
L. G. Bourgois III, see also J. Berrett
S. Bourne: *Black in the British Frame: Black People in British Film and Television, 1896–1996* (London and Washington, DC, 1998)
M. Bouvier-Ajam: *Connaissance du jazz* (Paris, 1952)
H. Boyd and L. Sinclair: *Detroit Jazz Who's Who* (Detroit, 1984)
B. Boyer and J. Boyer, see S. Davis, Jr.
P. Bradford: *Born with the Blues: . . . the True Story of the Pioneering Blues Singers and Musicians in the Early Days of Jazz* (New York, 1963)
A. G. Bragaglia: *Jazz Band* (Milan, 1929)
J. Bramy, see S. Grappelli
J. Brand and B. Korst: *Shelly Manne: the Different Percussionist* (Rockford, IL, 1997) [bio-discography]
C. Brandt and C. Roemer: *Standardized Chord Symbol Notation: a Uniform System for the Music Profession* (Sherman Oaks, CA, 1976)
O. Brask: *Photographs Jazz* (Kiel, Germany, 1994) [text in Ger. and Eng.]
O. Brask, see also D. Morgenstern
G. Braunschweig and others: *Jazz et photographie* (Paris, 1983) [exhibition catalogue of the Musée d'Art Moderne, Paris]
B. Breakey and S. Gordon: *Beyond the Blues: Township Jazz in the '60s and '70s* (Cape Town and elsewhere, 1997)
G. Brennan, see J. Clare
M. Breslow and D. Guaraldi: *Jazzography: Profiles of Regional Jazz Musicians who Perform in San Francisco* (Glenview, IL, 2000)
Bricktop and J. Haskins: *Bricktop* (New York, 1983) [autobiography of Bricktop (Ada Smith)]
B. Bridges, see L. Merian
J.-D. Brierre: *Le jazz français de 1900 à aujourd'hui* (Paris, 2000)
R. Brinkmann, ed.: *Avantgarde, Jazz, Pop: Tendenzen zwischen Tonalität und Atonalität* (Mainz, Germany, and London, 1978)
S. Britt: *Frank Sinatra: a Celebration* (New York, 1995)
——: *The Jazz Guitarists* (Poole, England, 1984)
——: *Long Tall Dexter: a Critical Musical Biography of Dexter Gordon* (London, 1989, New York, 1989, as *Dexter Gordon: a Musical Biography*; Ger. trans., Vienna, 1990, as *Round Midnight: Dexter Gordon: nicht nur um Mitternacht*)
S. Britt, see also B. Case
N. Brittan, see I. Berg
P. Broadbent: *Charlie Christian* (Winona, MO, and Newcastle upon Tyne, England, 1996)
X. Brocker: *Le roman vrai du jazz en Lorraine, 1917–1991* (Jarville, France, 1992)
C. Broecking: *Der Marsalis-Faktor: Gesprache über afroamerikanische Kultur in den neunziger Jahren* (Waakirchen, Germany, 1995)
C. Broecking, ed.: *Jazz in Berlin: wo man Jazz hören, spielen und kaufen kann* (Berlin, 1998)
G. Brom, with J. Zapletal and J. Majer: *Gustav: muj zivot s kapelu* (Prague, 1994)
E. Brooks: *The Bessie Smith Companion: a Critical and Detailed Appreciation of the Recordings* (Wheathampstead, nr St. Albans, England, and New York, 1982/*R*1989)
W. Broonzy and Y. Bruynoghe: *Big Bill: mes blues, ma guitare et moi* (Brussels, 1955, rev. and enlarged Paris, 2/1987, as *Big Bill Blues*; Eng. orig., London, 1955, as *Big Bill Blues*) [autobiography of Big Bill Broonzy]
T. Brothers, ed.: *Louis Armstrong in his own Words: Selected Writings* (New York and Oxford, England, 1999)
M. Brouwer, see B. Raaymakers
J. Broven: *South to Louisiana: the Music of the Cajun Bayous* (Gretna, LA, 1983) [incl. discography]
——: *Walking to New Orleans: the Story of New Orleans Rhythm and Blues* (Bexhill-on-Sea, England, 1974, Gretna, LA, 1983, as *Rhythm & Blues in New Orleans*) [incl. discography]
C. Brown, see R. Brown
L. W. Brown: *Amiri Baraka* (Boston, 1980)
M. Brown: *Recollections: Essays, Drawings, Miscellanea* (Frankfurt am Main, Germany, 1984)
R. Brown and C. Brown: *Georgia on my Mind: the Nat Gonella Story* (Horndean, England, 1985)
R. Brown and A. Yule: *Miss Rhythm: the Autobiography of Ruth Brown, Rhythm and Blues Legend* (New York, 1996)
S. E. Brown: *A Case of Mistaken Identity: the Life and Music of James P. Johnson* (diss., Yale U., 1982); rev. and enlarged as *James P. Johnson: a Case of Mistaken Identity* (Metuchen, NJ, and London, 1986) [incl. R. Hilbert, Jr.: *A James P. Johnson Discography, 1917–1950*]
T. D. Brown: *A History and Analysis of Jazz Drumming to 1942* (diss., U. of Michigan, 1976)
[D. Brubeck] *Biography of Dave Brubeck* (New York, 1972)
H. Brubeck: *Dave Brubeck* (New York, 1961) [BMI pubn; incl. discography]
H. O. Brunn: *The Story of the Original Dixieland Jazz Band* (Baton Rouge, LA, 1960/*R*1977)
P. Brunner and J. Kunz: *Jazz! Swinging Portraits* (Vienna, 1992)
P. Brunner, see also J. Kunz
Y. Bruynoghe, see W. Broonzy
C. Bryant and others, eds.: *Central Avenue Sounds: Jazz in Los Angeles* (Berkeley, CA, Los Angeles, and London, 1998)
E. Bubley and H. O'Neal: *Charlie Parker, Ray Brown, Benny Carter, J. C. Heard, Johnny Hodges, Barney Kessel, Oscar Peterson, Flip Phillips, Charlie Shavers, Ben Webster (Norman Granz Jam Sessions)* (Levallois-Perret, France, 1995) [album of photos of 1952 jam session]
J. Buchanan: *Emperor Norton's Hunch: the Story of Lu Watters' Yerba Buena Jazz Band* (Sausalito, CA, 1996)
F. Büchmann-Møller: *Is This to be my Souvenir? Jazz Photos from the Timme Rosencrantz Collection, 1918–1969* (Odense, Denmark, 2000)
——: *You Got to be Original Man!: the Music of Lester Young* (New York, Westport, CT, and London, 1990)
——: *You Just Fight for your Life: the Story of Lester Young* (New York, Westport, CT, and London, 1990)
R. T. Buckner and S. Weiland, eds.: *Jazz in Mind: Essays on the History and Meanings of Jazz* (Detroit, *c*1991)
M. J. Budds: *Jazz in the Sixties: the Expansion of Musical Resources and Techniques* (Iowa City, IA, 1978, rev. and enlarged 2/1990)
U. Buechter-Roemer: *New Vocal Jazz: Untersuchungen zur zeitgenössischen improvisierten Musik mit der Stimme anhand ausgewählter Beispiele* (Frankfurt am Main, Germany, 1991)
J. V. Buerkle and D. Barker: *Bourbon Street Black: the New Orleans Black Jazzman* (New York, 1973)
M. Buholzer, A. Schmitt-Rosenthal, and V. Wilmer: *Auf der Suche nach Cecil Taylor* (Hofheim am Taunus, Germany, 1990)
Y. Buin: *Thelonious Monk* (Paris, 1988)
J. Bulterman: *The Ramblers Story* (Bussum, Netherlands, 1973)
E. Bunker, see F. Purim
W. Burckhardt and J. Gerth: *Lester Young: ein Porträt* (Wetzlar, Germany, 1959)
E. W. Buser: *Swinging Basel: Basler Big- und Swingbands, 1924–1950* (Basel, Switzerland, 1988)
G. Bushell and M. Tucker: *Jazz from the Beginning* (Wheatley, Oxford, England, 1988, Ann Arbor, MI, 1990)
P. Bussy: *Coltrane* (Paris, 1999)
G. Butcher: *Next to a Letter from Home: Major Glenn Miller's Wartime Band* (Edinburgh, 1986, rev. London, 2/1994) [incl. discography]
A. Büttner and O. Flückiger: *Die Lanigiro Story*, i: *1924–1939* (Basel, Switzerland, 2000)
J. Buzelin and F. Buzelin: *William Breuker* (Paris, 1992)
V. Byrd, ed.: *Jump for Joy: Jazz at Lincoln Center Celebrates the Ellington Centennial, 1899–1999* (New York, 1999)
R. Byrnside, see C. Hamm
A. Calabrese, see M. Waller
E. Calderon, see P. De Barrios
R. Callender and E. Cohen: *Unfinished Dream: the Musical World of Red Callender* (London, 1985) [autobiography of Red Callender]
G. Callingham, see G. Marsh
C. Calloway and B. Rollins: *Of Minnie the Moocher and Me* (New York, 1976) [autobiography of Cab Calloway]
J. Campbell, ed.: *The Picador Book of Blues and Jazz* (London, 1995) [colln of previously pubd articles]
G. Cane: *Canto nero: il free jazz degli anni sessanti* (Bologna, Italy, 1993)
——: *Facciamo che eravamo negri: il jazz e il suo blackground* (Bologna, Italy, 1988)
G. Cane and P. M. Morgante: *Introduzione al jazz, alla storia e alle opera* (Bologna, Italy, 1994)
B. Cannon, ed.: *Tutti Legends*, i: *Louis Armstrong* (Coconut Grove, FL, 1995)
——: *Tutti Legends*: *Billie Holiday* (Coconut Grove, FL, 1996)
S. von Canon, see B. Raaymakers
L. Cantor: *Wheelin' on Beale: How WDIA-Memphis Became the Nation's First All-black Radio Station* (New York, 1992)

D. B. Caplan: *In Township Tonight! South Africa's Black City Music and Theatre* (London and New York, 1985)
A. Caraceni: *Il jazz dalle origini ad oggi* (Milan, 1937, rev. 2/1945)
P. Carles: *Jazzmen, 1979–1991* (Paris, 1991)
P. Carles and A. Clergeat, eds.: *Jazz: les incontournables* (Paris, 1990, enlarged 2/1992)
P. Carles and J.-L. Comolli: *Free Jazz, Black Power* (Paris, 1971/*R*2000; Sp. trans., Barcelona, 1973; It. trans., Turin, Italy, 1974)
P. Carles, see also F. Ténot
[H. Carmichael] *An Exhibition Honoring the 75th Birthday of Hoagland Howard Carmichael, Ll.B., 1926, D.M., 1972, Indiana University* (Bloomington, IN, 1972) [catalogue]
H. Carmichael: *The Stardust Road* (New York and Toronto, 1946/*R*1999 with Carmichael and S. Longstreet: *Sometimes I Wonder: the Story of Hoagy Carmichael*) [autobiography]
H. Carmichael and S. Longstreet: *Sometimes I Wonder: the Story of Hoagy Carmichael* (New York, 1965/*R*1999 with Carmichael: *The Stardust Road*)
G. Carner, ed.: *The Miles Davis Companion: Four Decades of Commentary* (New York, 1996)
N. Carnovale: *Gunther Schuller: a Bio-bibliography* (New York, 1987)
I. Carr: *Keith Jarrett: the Man and his Music* (New York, 1991) [incl. discography]
——: *Miles Davis: a Critical Biography* (London and New York, 1982, rev. and enlarged 2/1998; Fr. trans., Marseilles, France, 1991, as *Miles Davis*; Ger. trans., Baden-Baden, Germany, 1985, as *Miles Davis, eine kritische biographie*) [incl. discography by B. Priestley]
——: *Music Outside: Contemporary Jazz in Britain* (London, 1973)
P. Carr: *Jimmy Archey: the Little Giant of the Trombone* (New Orleans, 1999)
R. Carr: *A Century of Jazz* (London and New York, 1997)
R. Carr, B. Case, and F. Dellar: *The Hip: Hipsters, Jazz and the Beat Generation* (London and Boston, 1986; Ger. trans., Kiel, Germany, 1989, as *The Hip: Hipsters, Jazz und die Beat Generation*)
H. Carruth: *Sitting in: Selected Writings on Jazz, Blues, and Related Topics* (Iowa City, IA, 1986, rev. and enlarged 2/1993)
——: *Suicides and Jazzers* (Ann Arbor, MI, 1992)
L. T. Carter: *Eubie Blake: Keys of Memory* (Detroit, 1979)
M. E. Carter: *Shades of Jazz: Desire, Difference, and the Politics of Culture* (diss., U. of Wisconsin, 1992)
W. Carter: *Preservation Hall: Music from the Heart* (Wheatley, Oxford, England, and New York, 1991, rev. New York and London, 2/1999)
R. Carver and L. Bernstein: *Jazz Profiles: the Spirit of the Nineties* (New York, 1998)
B. Case and S. Britt: *The Illustrated Encyclopedia of Jazz* (London, 1978; It. trans., Milan, 1981, as *Enciclopedia illustrata del jazz*; Sp. trans., Madrid, 1983, as *Enciclopedia illustrada del jazz*)
B. Case, see also R. Carr
B. Cash: *An Analysis of the Improvisation Technique of Lester Willis Young, 1936–1942* (thesis, U. of Hull, England, 1982)
V. Castelli and others: *The Bix Bands: a Bix Beiderbecke Discobiography* (Milan, 1972)
N. Catalano: *Clifford Brown: the Life and Art of the Legendary Jazz Trumpeter* (New York, 2000)
L. Cerchiari: *Il jazz: una civilità musicale afro-americana ed europea* (Milan, 1997)
L. Cerri: *Antologia del jazz* (Pisa, Italy, 1955)
——: *Jazz in microsolco* (Pisa, Italy, 1962)
——: *Jazz: musica d'oggi* (Milan, 1948)
——: *Mezzo secolo di jazz* (Pisa, Italy, 1981)
D. Cerulli, B. Korall, and M. Nasatir, eds.: *The Jazz Word* (New York, 1960/*R*1987) [incl. previously pubd articles]
D. Chamberlain and R. Wilson, eds.: *The Otis Ferguson Reader* (Highland Park, IL, 1982) [colln of previously pubd articles]
S. Chamberlain: *An Unsung Cat: the Life and Music of Warne Marsh* (Lanham, MD, 2000)
J. Chambers: *Milestones*, i: *The Music and Times of Miles Davis to 1960* (Toronto, Buffalo, and London, 1983); ii: *The Music and Times of Miles Davis since 1960* (Toronto, Buffalo, and London, 1985); i and ii repr. 1989, as *Milestones: the Music and Times of Miles Davis*)
R. Charles and D. Ritz: *Brother Ray: Ray Charles' own Story* (New York, 1978, rev. 2/1992; Ger. trans., St. Andrä-Wördern, Germany, 1994, as *Ray Charles: What I Say*)
S. B. Charters: *The Country Blues* (New York and Toronto, 1959/*R*1975; Ger. trans., Reinbek, nr Hamburg, Germany, 1962/*R*1994, as *Der Country Blues: Songs und Geschichten*)
——: *The Roots of the Blues: an African Search* (Boston and London, 1981)
S. B. Charters and L. Kunstadt: *Jazz: a History of the New York Scene* (Garden City, NY, 1962/*R*1981)
A. S. Chase: *Sun Ra: Musical Change and Musical Meaning in the Life and Work of a Jazz Composer* (thesis, Tufts U., 1992)
G. Chase, ed.: *The American Composer Speaks: a Historical Anthology, 1770–1965* (n.p. [Baton Rouge, LA], 1966)
M. P. Chase: *Improvisation: Music from the Inside Out* (Berkeley, CA, 1988)
J.-L. Chautemps, see C. Gauffre
M. Chauvard, see J. Demêtre
A. Cheatham: *I Guess I'll Get the Papers and Go Home: the Life of Doc Cheatham*, ed. A. Shipton (London and New York, 1995) [incl. discography by H. Rye]
T. Cherrett, comp.: *The Genius that was Django* (Addlestone, England, 1998)
G. Cherrington, see S. Traill
J. Chesnel: *Le jazz en quarantaine, 1940–1946: Occupation–Liberation* (Cherbourg, France, 1994)
J. Chesnel and G. Arnaud: *Les grands créateurs de jazz* (Paris, 1989, rev. 2/1993)
D. Chevan, see E. Berger
P. Chevigny: *Gigs: Jazz and the Cabaret Laws in New York City* (New York and London, 1991)
J. Chilton: *Billie's Blues: a Survey of Billie Holiday's Career, 1933–1959* (London, 1975) [incl. discography]
——: *Jazz* (Sevenoaks, England, 1979)
——: *A Jazz Nursery: the Story of the Jenkins' Orphanage Bands of Charleston, South Carolina* (London, 1980)
——: *Let the Good Times Roll: the Story of Louis Jordan and his Music* (London and New York, 1992)
——: *McKinney's Music: a Bio-discography of McKinney's Cotton Pickers* (London, 1978)
——: *Ride, Red, Ride: the Life of Henry "Red" Allen* (London, 1999)
——: *Sidney Bechet: the Wizard of Jazz* (London and New York, 1987/*R*1996)
——: *The Song of the Hawk: the Life and Recordings of Coleman Hawkins* (London and New York, 1990)
——: *Stomp Off, Let's Go! The Story of Bob Crosby's Bob Cats & Big Band* (London, 1983)
J. Chilton, see also Max Jones
F. Chisenhall, see M. McKee
L. Chiswick: *Milestones of Jazz: a Chronological Survey of Jazz Music in Photographs* (Godalming, England, 1997)
C. Chitti, see W. Rovere
A. Cichero: *Guia del jazz* (Buenos Aires, 1976)
W. D. Clancy with A. C. Kenton: *Woody Herman: Chronicles of the Herds* (New York and elsewhere, 1995)
J. Clare [G. Brennan, pseud.]: *Bodgie Dada and the Cult of Cool* (Sydney, 1995)
D. Clarke: *All or Nothing at all: a Life of Frank Sinatra* (London, 1997)
——: *The Rise and Fall of Popular Music* (London, 1995)
——: *Wishing on the Moon: the Life and Times of Billie Holiday* (London and New York, 1994; Ger. trans., Munich and elsewhere, 1995, as *Billie Holiday – Wishing on the Moon: eine Biographie*)
J. H. Clarke, ed.: *Harlem, U.S.A.* (Berlin, 1964)
L. Clarke and F. Verdun: *Dizzy Atmosphere: conversations avec Dizzy Gillespie* (Arles, France, 1990)
W. Claxton: *Claxography* (Kiel, Germany, 1995) [photo album; text in Eng. and Ger.]
——: *Jazz Seen* (Cologne, Germany, 1999) [photo album; text in Eng., Fr., and Ger.]
——: *Jazz West Coast: a Portfolio of Photographs* (Hollywood, CA, 1954, Pasadena, CA, 2/1980/*R*1996, as *Jazz*)
——: *Young Chet: the Young Chet Baker* (Munich, 1993; Fr. trans., Munich, 1993, as *Young Chet: photographies à la mémoire du légendaire musicien de jazz*; Ger. trans., Munich, 1993, as *Young Chet: der junge Chet Baker*)
W. Claxton and H. Namekata: *Jazz West Coast: Artwork of Pacific Jazz Records* (Tokyo, 1992)
B. Clayton and N. M. Elliott: *Buck Clayton's Jazz World* (London and New York, 1986) [incl. discography by B. Weir]
P. Clayton, see P. Gammond
A. Clergeat, see P. Carles; Siné
R. Clooney with J. Barthiel: *Girl Singer: an Autobiography* (New York, 1999)
P. Clute, see J. O. Goggin
M. Clutten, see B. Turner
A. Coeuroy and A. Schaeffner: *Le jazz* (Paris, 1926/*R*1988, by A. Schaeffner, as *Le Jazz*, with addns by L. Malson and J. B. Hess)
J. Cohassey, see S. Wilson
M. T. Cohen: *The Police Card Discord* (Metuchen, NJ, and London, 1993)
L. Cohn, ed.: *Nothing but the Blues* (New York, London, and Paris, 1993; Fr. trans., Paris, 1994, as *Le Blues, sa musique et ses musiciens*)
J. Coker: *Improvising Jazz* (Englewood Cliffs, NJ, 1964/*R*1986; It. trans., Padova, Italy, 1982, as *Improvisazione jazz*)
——: *The Jazz Idiom* (Englewood Cliffs, NJ, and London, 1975; Sp. trans., Buenos Aires, 1976, as *El lenguaje del jazz*)
——: *Listening to Jazz* (Englewood Cliffs, NJ, 1978; rev. as *How to Listen to Jazz*)
——: *The Teaching of Jazz* (Rottenburg, Germany, 1989)
J. Coker and others: *Patterns for Jazz* (Lebanon, IN, 1970)

P. Coker and D. Baker: *Vocal Improvisation: an Instrumental Approach* (Lebanon, IN, 1981) [incl. discography]
M. Cole: *Nat King Cole* (New York, 1991)
B. Coleman: *Trumpet Story: souvenirs d'un grand du jazz* (Paris, 1981; Eng. orig., London and Boston, 1990, as *Trumpet Story*) [autobiography]
J. Coleman and A. Young: *Mingus/Mingus: Two Memoirs* (Berkeley, CA, 1991)
S. Colin: *And the Bands Played On* (London, 1980)
——: *Ella: the Life and Times of Ella Fitzgerald* (London, 1986; Hung. trans., Budapest, 1991, as *Ella Fitzgerald élete és kora*)
D. Coller, see S. Traill
B. Collette with S. Isoardi: *Jazz Generations: a Life in American Music and Society* (London, 2000)
G. Collier: *Inside Jazz* (London, 1973)
——: *Jazz: a Student's and Teacher's Guide* (London, 1975; Ger. trans., Wilhelmshaven, Germany, 1982, as *Jazz: ein Führer für Lehrer und Schüler*; It. trans, Milan, 1989, as *Jazz: conoscere e suonare il jazz*)
G. Collier, comp. and ed.: *Cleo and John: a Biography of the Dankworths* (London, 1976)
J. L. Collier: *Benny Goodman and the Swing Era* (New York, and Oxford, England, 1989; Ger. trans., St. Andrä Wördern, Germany, 1992, as *Benny Goodman, King of Swing: virtuoses Spiegelbild einer Epoche*)
——: *Duke Ellington* (New York and London, 1987; Ger. trans., Vienna, 1989, Berlin, 1999, as *Duke Ellington, Genius des Jazz*)
——: *Jazz: the American Theme Song* (New York, 1993) [colln of previously pubd articles]
——: *Louis Armstrong: an American Genius* (New York, 1983, London, 1984, as *Louis Armstrong: a Biography*; Fr. trans., Paris, 1986, as *Louis Armstrong*; Ger. trans., Bergisch-Gladbach, Germany, 1987, as *Louis Armstrong*)
——: *The Making of Jazz: a Comprehensive History* (New York and London, 1978; Fr. trans., Paris, 1981, as *L'aventure du jazz*)
——: *The Reception of Jazz in America: a New View* (New York, 1988)
L. Collins (autobiography), see F. J. Gillis
R. Collins: *New Orleans Jazz: the Development of American Music from the Origin to the Big Bands* (New York, 1996)
T. Collins: *Rock Mr. Blues: the Life and Music of Wynonie Harris* (Milford, NH, 1995) [incl. discography]
J. Collinson and E. Kramer: *The Jazz Legacy of Don Ewell* (Chigwell, England, 1991) [incl. discography]
J. Collis: *The Complete Guide to the Music of Frank Sinatra* (London, 1998)
K. Colyer: *When Dreams are in the Dust (Going Down Easy, Going Down Slow)* (Ryarsh, England, 1989)
S. Combe: *Anleitung zur Improvisation für Schlagzeug* (Mainz, Germany, 1974)
J.-L. Comolli, see P. Carles
E. Condon and R. Gehman, eds.: *Eddie Condon's Treasury of Jazz* (New York, 1956/*R*1975)
E. Condon and H. O'Neal: *The Eddie Condon Scrapbook of Jazz* (New York, 1973)
E. Condon and T. Sugrue: *We Called it Music: a Generation of Jazz* (New York, 1947/*R*1988; Ger. trans., Munich, Germany, 1960/*R*1988, as *Jazz: wir nannten's Musik*)
D. R. Connor: *BG off the Record: a Bio-discography of Benny Goodman* (Fairless Hills, PA, 1958, rev. and enlarged New Rochelle, NY, [2]/1969, as D. R. Connor and W. W. Hicks: *BG on the Record: a Bio-discography of Benny Goodman*, rev. and enlarged New York, [3]/1984, as *The Record of a Legend: a Bio-discography of Benny Goodman*, rev. and enlarged Metuchen, NJ, and London, [4]/1988, as D. R. Connor: *Benny Goodman: Listen to his Legacy*, addns and corrections Lanham, MD, New Brunswick, NJ, and London, 1996, as *Benny Goodman: Wrappin' it up*) [*ConnorBG*]
G. Conrad: *Heinz Wehner: eine Bio-Discographie* (Menden, Germany, c1989)
——: *Posaunen-Dob: kleine Biographie Walter Dobschinskis* (Menden, Germany, 1983)
——: *Trevor Mac: an Investigation* (Menden, Germany, 1998)
C. Cons and G. Von Physter: *Destiny: a Sketch-book from the Lives of Swing Musicians* (Chicago, 1938)
B. Cook: *Listen to the Blues* (New York, 1973, New York and London, 1975/*R*1995)
G. Cook, see F. C. Taylor
M. Cooke: *The Chronicle of Jazz* (London, 1997)
T. Coolman: *The Bass Tradition: Past, Present, Future* (New Albany, IN, 1987)
D. Cooper with J. Titsworth: *Buddy Rich: a Lifetime of Music* (n.p. [England], 1974, rev. Blackpool, England, 2/1991)
R. Cooper with S. Dougherty: *Amateur Night at the Apollo: Ralph Cooper Presents Five Decades of Great Entertainment* (New York, 1990)
R. Copeland: *The Ray Copeland Method and Approach to the Creative Art of Jazz Improvisation* (St. Albans, NY, 1974)
J. Corbett: *Extended Play: Sounding off from John Cage to Dr. Funkenstein* (Durham, NC, and London, 1994)
J. Coryell and L. Friedman: *Jazz-rock Fusion* (New York and London, 1978)
C. Cosmetto: *La vraie musique de jazz: les échos du jazz* (Lausanne, Switzerland, 1945)
B. Coss: *Charles Mingus* (New York, 1961) [incl. annotated list of compositions]
R. Cotterrell, ed.: *Orbit: a Jazz Anthology of Articles and Features* (Leicester, England, 1973) [colln of previously pubd articles]
P. Cotto: *Chantes libres: le free jazz en France, 1960–1975* (Paris, 1999)
P. Coulangeon, ed.: *Les musiciens de jazz en France* (Paris, 1999)
H. Courlander: *Negro Folk Music U.S.A.* (New York and London, 1963/*R*1992)
B. Y. Cox: *Central Avenue: its Rise and Fall, 1890–c.1955* (Los Angeles, 1997)
B. Cox, see also P. Tanner
G. Crane: *Jazz Elements and Formal Compositional Techniques in Third Stream Music* (thesis, Indiana U., 1970)
A. M. Crawford, see R. Denyer
R. Crawford: *Music in the Street* (New Orleans, 1983) [exhibition catalogue]
M. Creutziger: *Jazzphotographie* (Hofheim am Taunus, Germany, 1996) [photo album]
F. Cromey, see G. Marsh
B. Crosby and P. Martin: *Call Me Lucky* (New York, 1953/R1993) [autobiography of Bing Crosby]
G. Crosby and R. Firestone: *Going my own Way* (New York, 1983)
R. R. Crosby: *Kenny Baker: the Life and Times of a Jazz Musician: the Authorised Biography* (Chalkwell-on-Sea, England, 1999)
H. Crothers, see J. Haskins
B. Crow: *From Birdland to Broadway: Scenes from a Jazz Life* (New York, and Oxford, England, 1992)
——: *Jazz Anecdotes* (New York, and Oxford, England, 1990)
H. Crowder with H. Speck: *As Wonderful as All That: Henry Crowder's Memoir of his Affair with Nancy Cunard, 1928–1935* (Navarro, CA, 1987)
B. Crowther: *Benny Goodman* (London, 1988)
——: *Gene Krupa* (Tunbridge Wells, England, and New York, 1987) [incl. discography]
B. Crowther and M. Pinfold: *The Big Band Years* (Newton Abbot, England, and London, 1988)
——: *The Jazz Singers: from Ragtime to the New Wave* (Poole, England, 1986)
——: *Singing Jazz: the Singers and their Styles* (London, 1997)
I. Cruickshank: *The Guitar Style of Django Reinhardt and the Gypsies* (Woodcote, nr Reading, England, 1982, rev. and enlarged 2/1985)
I. Cruickshank, ed.: *Django's Gypsies: the Mystique of Django Reinhardt and his People* (Newcastle upon Tyne, England, 1994)
C. Crumpacker and B. Crumpacker: *Jazz Legends* (Layton, UT, 1995)
L. Cugny: *Electrique: Miles Davis, 1968–1975* (Marseilles, France, 1993)
——: *Las Vegas tango: une vie de Gil Evans* (Paris, 1989) [incl. discography]
M. Cullaz and F. W. Sportis: *Encyclopédie Jazz Hot: Gospel* (Paris, 1990)
M. Cuney-Hare: *Negro Musicians and their Music* (Washington, DC, 1936/*R*1996)
L. D. Cunningham and J. Jones: *Sweet, Hot and Blue: St. Louis' Musical Heritage* (Jefferson, NC, and London, 1989)
S. Curtis: *Dancing to a Black Man's Tune: a Life of Scott Joplin* (Columbia, MO, and elsewhere, 1994)
M. Cuscuna, see F. Wolff
P. Czada and G. Grosse: *Comedian Harmonists: ein Vokalensemble erobert die Welt* (Berlin, 1993)
D. da Fonseca and B. Weiner: *Brazilian Rhythms for Drumset* (New York, 1991) [incl. discography, bibliography, transcrs.]
L. Dahl: *Morning Glory: a Biography of Mary Lou Williams* (New York, 2000)
——: *Stormy Weather: the Music and Lives of a Century of Jazzwomen* (London, Melbourne, Australia, and New York, 1984)
R. Dale: *Teach Yourself Jazz* (London and New York, 1989)
——: *The World of Jazz* (Oxford, England, 1980, rev. 2/1986, rev. Edison, NJ, 3/1996; Fr. trans., Paris, 1980, as *Le monde du jazz*, 2/1994, as *Le monde du jazz: spirituals, ragtime, New-Orleans, blues, swing, bop, free*)
V. Danca: *Bunny: a Bio-discography of Jazz Trumpeter Bunny Berigan* (Rockford, IL, 1978)
H. O. Dance: *Stormy Monday: the T-Bone Walker Story* (Baton Rouge, LA, and London, 1987) [incl. discography by D. Groslier and others]
S. Dance: *The World of Count Basie* (New York and London, 1980) [colln of previously pubd interviews]
S. Dance: *The World of Duke Ellington* (London and New York, 1970/*R*1981; Fr. trans., Paris, 1976, as *Duke Ellington par lui-même et ses musiciens*) [colln of previously pubd articles and interviews]
——: *The World of Earl Hines* (New York, 1977)
——: *The World of Swing* (New York, 1974; Sp. trans., Buenos Aires, 1977, as *El mundo del swing*) [colln of previously pubd interviews]
S. Dance and others: *Jazz Era: the 'Forties* (London, 1961/*R*1985)
S. F. Dance, J. Asman, and B. Kinnell, eds.: *Jazz Notebook* (Chilwell, nr Newark-on-Trent, England, n.d. [?1945])

S. Dance, see also C. Barnet; M. Ellington; D. Wells
L. Dankner, see G. Lichtenstein
A. Dankworth: *Jazz: an Introduction to its Musical Basis* (London, New York, and Toronto, 1968)
J. Dankworth: *Jazz in Revolution* (London, 1998)
M. Danzi and R. E. Lotz: *American Musician in Germany, 1924–1939* (Schmitten, Germany, 1986) [autobiography of Mike Danzi]
J. Darensbourg: *Telling it Like it is*, ed. P. Vacher (London, 1987, Baton Rouge, LA, 1987, as *Jazz Odyssey: the Autobiography of Joe Darensbourg*)
R. Daschkey, A. Erlewein, and P. E. Weisenborn, eds.: *1969–1984: 15 Jahre Jazz in Dortmund* (Dortmund, Germany, 1984)
A. M. Dauer: *Jazz, die magische Musik: ein Leitfaden durch den Jazz* (Bremen, Germany, 1961)
——: *Der Jazz: seine Ursprünge und seine Entwicklung* (Kassel, Germany, 1958, 3/1977)
——: *Tradition afrikanischer Blasorchester und Entstehung des Jazz* (Graz, Austria, 1985)
M. Daver: *Jazz Album Covers: the Rare and the Beautiful* (Tokyo, 1994)
X. Daverat: *John Coltrane* (Paris, 1995)
J. David: *Le jazz et les hommes d'aujourd'hui* (Brussels, 1946)
J. R. T. Davies and L. Wright: *Morton's Music* (London, 1968)
A. Y. Davis: *Blues Legacies and Black Feminism: Gertrude "Ma" Rainey, Bessie Smith, and Billie Holiday* (New York, 1998)
F. Davis: *Bebop and Nothingness: Jazz and Pop at the End of the Century* (New York, 1996)
——: *History of the Blues* (New York, 1995)
——: *In the Moment: Jazz in the 1980s* (New York, and Oxford, England, 1986/*R*1996; Ger. trans., Vienna, 1988, as *In the Moment: Jazz der 80er Jahre*) [colln of previously pubd articles]
——: *Outcats: Jazz Composers, Instrumentalists, and Singers* (New York, and Oxford, England, 1990)
M. Davis with Q. Troupe: *Miles: the Autobiography* (New York, 1989; Ger. trans., Hamburg, Germany, 1990, as *Die Autobiographie*)
M. Davis, see also K. Satoh
N. Davis: *Writings in Jazz* (Dubuque, IA, 2/1978, 3/1985)
N. T. Davis: *Charlie Parker's Kansas City Environment and its Effects on his Later Life* (diss., Wesleyan U., 1974)
S. Davis, Jr., with J. Boyer and B. Boyer: *Why Me? The Autobiography of Sammy Davis, Jr.* (London, 1989; Ger. trans., Gütersloh, Germany, 1989, as *Warum ich? Eine Legende in Swing und Step*)
U. B. Davis: *The Afro-American Musician and Writer in Paris during the 1950s and 1960s: a Study of Kenny Clarke, Donald Byrd, Chester Himes, and James Baldwin* (diss., U. of Pittsburgh, 1983) [incl. oral history material]
J. Dawson: *Nervous Man Nervous: Big Jay McNeely and the Rise of the Honking Tenor Sax!* (Milford, NH, 1994) [incl. discography]
S. Day: *Two Full Ears: Listening to Improvised Music* (Chelmsford, England, 1998)
D. D. Deakins: *Cylinder Records* (Bombay, 1956, 2/1958)
R. T. Deal, see B. Amstell
R. T. Dean: *New Structures in Jazz and Improvised Music since 1960* (Buckingham, England, and Bristol, PA, 1992)
W. Dean-Myatt, see R. M. Sudhalter
P. De Barros and E. Calderon: *Jackson Street After Hours: the Roots of Jazz in Seattle* (Seattle, 1993)
C. Deffaa: *Blue Rhythms: Six Lives in Rhythm and Blues* (Urbana, IL, and Chicago, 1996)
——: *In the Mainstream: 18 Portraits in Jazz* (Metuchen, NJ, and London, 1992)
——: *Jazz Veterans: a Portrait Gallery* (Fort Bragg, CA, 1996)
——: *Swing Legacy* (Metuchen, NJ, and London, 1989)
——: *Traditionalists and Revivalists in Jazz* (Metuchen, NJ, and London, 1993)
——: *Voices of the Jazz Age: Portraits of Eight Vintage Jazzmen* (Wheatley, Oxford, England, Urbana, IL, and Chicago, 1990)
H. Dejan: *Everything is Lovely: a Family Portrait* (Pijnacker, Netherlands, 1989)
L. Delannoy: *Billie Holiday* (Paris, 2000)
——: *Lester Young, profession: président* (Paris, 1987; Eng. trans., Fayetteville, AR, 1993, as *Pres: the Story of Lester Young*) [incl. discography by D. Richard]
C. Delaunay: *Delaunay's Dilemma: de la peinture au jazz* (Mâcon, France, 1985)
——: *De la vie et du jazz* (Paris, 1940, Lausanne, Switzerland, 2/1945)
——: *Django, mon frère* (Paris, 1968)
——: *Django Reinhardt: souvenirs* (Paris, 1954; Eng. trans., London, 1961/*R*1982, rev. Gateshead, England, 2/1981/*R*1993) [incl. discography]
——: *L'histoire de Sidney Bechet* (Paris, 1960)
——: *Hot Iconography* (Paris, 1939)
C. Delaunay and P. du Peuty: *Noirs au blanc: images de jazzmen* (Paris, 1986) [portraits]
T. S. DeLay, Jr.: *An Historical Study of the Armed Forces Radio Service to 1946* (diss., U. of Southern California, 1951)
F. Dellar, see R. Carr
T. DeLong: *Pops: Paul Whiteman, King of Jazz* (Piscataway, nr New Brunswick, NJ, 1983)
J. Demêtre and M. Chauvard: *Voyage au pays du blues/Land of the Blues* (Levallois-Perret, France, 1994) [text in Eng. and Fr.]
D. DeMicheal, see G. Lees
G. Demole: *Sidney Bechet: his Musical Activities from 1907 to 1959* (Geneva, 1996, rev. 2/1998)
R. S. Demory, see D. D. Megill
R. Denyer, I. Guillory, and A. M. Crawford: *The Guitar Handbook* (London and Sydney, 1982)
E. De Pascale: *Bessie's Blues: la su vita e i suoi blues* (Viterbo, Italy, 1992)
E. Determeyer: *Ruige dagen: 70 jaar jazz in Groningen* (Groningen, Netherlands, 1988)
J. de Valk: *Ben Webster: his Life and Music* (Berkeley, CA, 2001)
——: *Chet Baker* (Schaftlach, Germany, 1991)
——: *Chet Baker: herrinerungen aan een lyrisch trompettist* (Amsterdam, 1989)
S. DeVeaux: *The Birth of Bebop: a Social and Musical History* (Berkeley, Los Angeles, and London, 1997)
——: *Jazz in Transition: Coleman Hawkins and Howard McGhee, 1935–1945* (diss., U. of California, Berkeley, 1985)
S. N. DeVeaux: *Jazz in America: Who's Listening?* (Carson, CA, 1995) [National Endowment for the Arts Research Division Report, no.31]
M. Dewe: *The Skiffle Craze* (Aberystwyth, Wales, 1998) [incl. discography]
D. Dexter, Jr.: *Jazz Cavalcade: the Inside Story of Jazz* (New York, 1946/*R*1977)
——: *The Jazz Story: from the '90s to the '60s* (Englewood Cliffs, NJ, 1964)
H. Dial: *All this Jazz about Jazz: the Autobiography of Harry Dial* (Chigwell, England, 1984)
C. Díaz Ayala: *Musica cubana del areyto a la nueva trova* (San Juan, PR, 1981)
M. Dibango with D. Rouard: *Three Kilos of Coffee: an Autobiography* (Chicago, 1995)
D. Dicaire: *Blues Singers: Biographies of Fifty Legendary Artists of the Early 20th Century* (Jefferson, NC, and elsewhere, 1999)
L. H. Dickert, Jr.: *An Analysis of Freddie Green's Style and his Importance in the History of Jazz Guitar* (diss., U. of Memphis, 1994)
K. Dietrich: *Duke's Bones: Ellington's Great Trombonists* (Rottenburg, Germany, 1995)
K. R. Dietrich: *Joe "Tricky Sam" Nanton, Juan Tizol and Lawrence Brown: Duke Ellington's Great Trombonists, 1926–1951* (diss., U. of Wisconsin, 1989)
H. J. Dietzel and H. H. Lange: *Stan Kenton* (Berlin, 1959) [H. J. Dietzel: *Stan Kenton: Biography* and H. H. Lange: *Stan Kenton: Discography* bound together]
J. Distler: *Art Tatum* (New York, 1981)
Dixon, see Giltrap
B. Dixon: *L'opéra: a Collection of Letters, Writings, Musical Scores, Drawings, and Photographs*, i: *1967–1986* (North Bennington, VT, 1986)
R. M. W. Dixon and J. Godrich: *Recording the Blues* (London, 1970)
R. M. W. Dixon, see also P. Oliver
B. Dixon-Gottschild: *Waltzing in the Dark: African-American Vaudeville and Race Politics in the Swing Era* (New York, 2000)
J. C. DjeDje and E. S. Meadows, eds.: *California Soul: Music of African-Americans in the West* (Berkeley, CA, Los Angeles, and London, 1998)
B. Dobbins: *The Contemporary Jazz Pianist: a Comprehensive Approach to Keyboard Improvisation* (Jamestown, RI, 1978, 2/1984)
G. L. Doctor: *The Sinatra Scrapbook* (New York, 1991)
W. Dodds and L. Gara: *The Baby Dodds Story* (Los Angeles, 1959, rev. Baton Rouge, LA, and elsewhere, 2/1992)
P. Dodge, ed.: *Hot Jazz and Jazz Dance: Roger Pryor Dodge Collected Writings, 1929–1964* (New York, and Oxford, England, 1995)
R. Dollase, M. Rusenberg, and H. J. Stollenwerk: *Das Jazzpublikum: zur Sozialpsychologie einer kulturellen Minderheit* (Mainz, Germany, and London, 1978)
T. Domentat: *Coca-Cola, Jazz & AFN: Berlin und die Amerikaner* (Berlin, 1995)
J. M. Doran: *Erroll Garner: the Most Happy Piano* (Metuchen, NJ, and London, 1985) [incl. discography]
——: *Herman Chittison: a Bio-discography* (Bel Air, MD, 1993)
M. Dorf: *Knitting Music: a Five-year History of the Knitting Factory* (New York, 1992)
M. Dorigné: *La guerre du jazz* (Paris, 1948)
——: *Jazz*, i: *Les origines du jazz: le style Nouvelle-Orléans et ses prolongements* (Paris, 1968)
——: *M.J.C. valise culturelle sur le jazz* (Paris, 1967) [pubn of Fédération des Maisons de Jeunes et de la Culture]
L. Dorůžka and I. Poledňák: *Československý jazz: minulost a přítomnost* [Czech jazz, past and present] (Prague, 1967) [with Eng. summary]
S. Dougherty, see R. Cooper
Down Beat Jazz Record Reviews, see G. Lees
Down Beat's Yearbook of Swing, see P. E. Miller

E. Dreyer, see L. Saxon
F. Driggs: *Women in Jazz: a Survey* (New York, 1997) [liner notes, Stash ST109, *Jazzwomen: a Feminist Retrospective*]
F. Driggs and H. Lewine: *Black Beauty, White Heat: a Pictorial History of Classic Jazz, 1920–1950* (New York, 1982/*R*1996 [omits 16 pages of color illustrations])
R. D'Rozario: *North Sea Jazz Festival, 1976–1985* (The Hague, 1985) [photographs]
J. Duclos-Arkilovitch: *Jazzin' Riviera: 70 ans de jazz sur la Côte-d'Azur* (Nice, France, 1997)
W. Dufty, see B. Holiday
H. Dulfer: *Jazz in China: en andere perikels uit de geïmproviseerde muziek* (Amsterdam, 1980)
P. du Petit and J. Ody: *Django Reinhardt* (Paris, 1997)
R. Dupuis: *Bunny Berigan: Elusive Legend of Jazz* (Baton Rouge, LA, 1993)
J. Durante and J. Kofoed: *Nightclubs* (New York, London, and Toronto, 1931)
F. Dutton, see S. Traill
T. Dybo: *Jan Garbarek: det aapne roms estetikk* (Oslo, 1996)
G. Dyer: *But Beautiful: a Book about Jazz* (London, 1991, New York, 2/1996, London, 2/1998; It. trans., Turin, Italy, 1996, as *Natura morta con custodia di sax: storie di jazz*)
C. Easton: *Straight Ahead: the Story of Stan Kenton* (New York, 1973)
ECM [Editions of Contemporary Music]: *Sleeves of Desire: a Cover Story* (Baden, Germany, 1996)
V. Edelhagen and J. Holzt-Edelhagen: *Die Big Band Story: die Big-Bands nach 1945 in der BRD* (Frankfurt am Main, Germany, 1988)
G. Eder, W. Gratzer, and A. Smudits, eds.: *Jazz, neue Musik und Medien: Dokumentation Saalfeldener Musiktage 1994 und 1995* (Saalfelden, Austria, 1996)
G. Eells, see A. O'Day
B. Egan: *Florence Mills: Remembering the Little Blackbird* (Canberra, 1997)
M. Ehlers, see J. Stoll
H. Eklund and L. Lindström: *Jazzen i Stockholm, 1920–1960* (Stockholm, 1983)
D. Ellington: *Music is my Mistress* (Garden City, NY, 1973; Ger. trans., Munich, 1974/*R*1992, as *Autobiographie: Duke Ellington*; Hung. trans., Budapest, 1979, as *Mindenem a musika*); index by H. F. Huon separately pubd, Melbourne, Australia, n.d. [?1977], rev. 2/1982) [autobiography of Duke Ellington]
M. Ellington and S. Dance: *Duke Ellington in Person: an Intimate Memoir* (Boston and London, 1978; Ger. trans., Stuttgart, Germany, Zurich, and Vienna, 1980, as *Duke Ellington: eine Biographie*)
N. M. Elliott, see B. Clayton
M. Ellison: *Lyrical Protest: Black Music's Struggle against Discrimination* (New York, 1989)
R. Ellison: *Shadow and Act* (New York, 1964)
E. van der Elsken: *Jazz, fotos 1955–1961* (Amsterdam, 1991; It. trans., S. Oreste, Italy, 1991, as *Jazz 1955–1959–1961*) [photo album]
L. F. Emery: *Black Dance in the United States from 1619 to 1970* (Palo Alto, CA, 1972)
G. Endress: *Jazz Podium: Musiker über sich selbst* (Stuttgart, Germany, 1980)
W. Enstice and P. Rubin: *Jazz Spoken Here: Conversations with Twenty-two Musicians* (Baton Rouge, LA, and London, 1992)
D. M. Epstein: *Nat King Cole* (New York, 1999)
L. A. Erenberg: *Swingin' the Dream: Big Band Jazz and the Rebirth of American Culture* (Chicago, 1998)
A. Erlewein, see R. Daschkey
K. Eshun: *More Brilliant than the Sun* (London, 1998)
Esquire's Jazz Book, see E. Anderson; P. E. Miller
Esquire's World of Jazz, see J. Poling
Ethnic Recordings in America: a Neglected Heritage: Washington 1977 (Washington, 1982) [pubn of the American Folklife Center, Library of Congress]
L. Evans, see S. Hester; P. R. Evans
P. R. Evans and L. K. Evans: *The Leon Bix Beiderbecke Story* (Bakersfield, CA, 1998)
P. R. Evans and L. F. Kiner, with W. Trumbauer: *Tram: the Frank Trumbauer Story* (Metuchen, NJ, and London, 1994)
P. R. Evans and others: *The Red Nichols Story: After Intermission, 1942–1965* (Lanham, MD, and elsewhere, 1997)
P. R. Evans, see also S. Hester; R. M. Sudhalter
J. Evensmo, see J. Bergh
D. Ewen: *All the Years of American Popular Music* (Englewood Cliffs, NJ, 1977)
M. Fabre: *Way Back There: a Street Guide to African-Americans in Paris* (New York, 1992, rev. Paris, 2/1996, by Fabre and J. A. Williams, as *A Street Guide to African-Americans in Paris*)
A. Fanelli: *Encyclopédie Jazz Hot: Blues* (Paris, 1990)
——: *Encyclopédie Jazz Hot: Rhythm and Blues* (Paris, 1990)
R. Fark: *Die missachtete Botschaft: publizistische Aspekte des Jazz im soziokulturellen Wandel* (Berlin, 1971)
J. W. Farrell, see W. L. Grossman
M. Fauré, see B. Vian
F. Fayenz: *Anatomia elementaire del jazz* (Rome, 1992)
——: *Il jazz dal mito all' avanguardia* (Milan, 1970)
——: *La musica jazz* (Milan, 1996)
F. Fayenz, see also R. Sierra
L. Feather: *The Book of Jazz: a Guide to the Entire Field* (New York, 1957, 2/1965, as *The Book of Jazz from Then till Now: a Guide to the Entire Field*)
——: *From Satchmo to Miles* (New York, 1972/*R*1987)
——: *Inside Be-bop* (New York, 1949/*R*1977 as *Inside Jazz*)
——: *The Jazz Years: Earwitness to an Era* (London and New York, 1986)
——: *Modern Jazz: an Exciting Story of the Past 20 Years* (Los Angeles, 1958)
——: *The Passion for Jazz* (New York, 1980/*R*1990)
——: *The Pleasures of Jazz: Leading Performers on their Lives, their Music, their Contemporaries* (New York, 1976)
L. Feather and J. Tracy: *Laughter from the Hip* (New York, 1963/*R*1979 as *Laughter from the Hip: the Lighter Side of Jazz*)
L. Feather, see also Max Jones
E. Fechner: *Die Comedian Harmonists: sechs Lebensläufe* (Weinheim, Germany, 1988)
L. Federighi: *Blues nel mio animo: temi e poesia del blues* (Milan, 1981)
——: *Cantare il jazz: l'universale vocale afroamericano* (Rome, 1986)
——: *Ella Fitzgerald: swing, genio e candori della jazz lady* (Viterbo, Italy, 1994)
L. Feigin, ed.: *Russian Jazz: New Identity* (London, 1985)
J. Feldmann-Buergers: *Tango und Jazz: kulturelle Wechselbeziehungen?* (Münster, Germany, 1996)
A. Felix: *Wild about Harry: the Illustrated Biography of Harry Connick, Jr.* (Dallas, 1995)
J. L. Fell and T. Vinding: *Stride! Fats, Jimmy, Lion, Lamb, and all the other Ticklers* (Lanham, MD, 1999)
E. Ferand: *Die Improvisation in der Jazzmusik: eine entwicklungsgeschichtliche und psychologische Untersuchung* (Zurich, 1938)
O. Ferguson, see D. Chamberlain
G. Fernett: *Swing Out: Great Negro Jazz Bands* (Midland, MI, 1970/*R*1993)
G. M. Fidelman: *First Lady of Song: Ella Fitzgerald for the Record* (New York, 1994)
D. Filipacchi, ed.: *Les années jazz magazine: 40 ans de passion* (Paris, 1994, rev. Levallois-Perret, France, 2/2000)
G. Filtgen and M. Ausserbauer: *John Coltrane: sein Leben, seine Musik, seine Schallplatten* (Gauting, Germany, 1983, rev. and enlarged Schaftlach, Germany, 2/1989)
G. Filtgen, see also H. Weber
S. W. Finkelstein: *Jazz: a People's Music* (New York, 1948/*R*1975)
C. Finley, see W. Barlow
R. Firestone: *Swing, Swing, Swing: the Life and Times of Benny Goodman* (New York, 1993)
R. Firestone, see also G. Crosby
K.-G. Fischer: *Jazzin' the Black Forest: Discography und Geschichte des Saba/MPS-Labels* (Berlin, 1999)
L. Fisher and D. Liebman: *Miles Davis and David Liebman: Jazz Connection* (Lewiston, NY, 1997)
T. Fitterling: *Thelonious Monk: sein Leben, seine Musik, seine Schallplatten* (Waakirchen, nr Bad Tölz, Germany, 1987; rev. Eng. trans., Berkeley, CA, 1997, as *Thelonious Monk: his Life and Music*)
T. Fletcher: *100 Years of the Negro in Show Business* (New York, 1954/*R*1984)
H. N. Flint, see M. A. Hood
D. Flower, see S. Bechet
J. Flower: *Moonlight Serenade: a Bio-discography of the Glenn Miller Civilian Band* (New Rochelle, NY, 1972)
S. A. Floyd, Jr.: *The Power of Black Music: Interpreting its History from Africa to the United States* (New York, and Oxford, England, 1995)
S. A. Floyd, Jr., ed.: *Black Music in the Harlem Renaissance: a Collection of Essays* (Knoxville, TN, 1993)
O. Flückiger: *John Gordon: Trombone Master* (Reinach, nr Basel, Switzerland, 1982)
O. Flückiger, see also A. O. Büttner
M. Fontanes: *Billie Holiday et Paris: chronique de la vie de Billie Holiday à Paris en 1954 et 1958* (Paris, 1999)
J. Foose, see J. Berry
A. Ford: *Anthony Braxton: Creative Music Continuums* (Exeter, England, 1997)
J. Fordham: *Jazz* (London, 1993; Ger. trans., Munich, 1994, as *Das grosse Buch vom Jazz: Musiker, Instrumente, Geschichte, Aufnahmen*; It. trans., Rimini, Italy, 1994, as *Jazz, la storia, gli strumenti, gli interpreti, i dischi*; Fr. trans., Paris, 1995, as *Jazz, les instruments, les musiciens, les enregistrements*)
——: *Jazz Heroes* (London, 1998)
——: *Let's Join Hands and Contact the Living: Ronnie Scott and his Club* (London, 1986, rev. 2/1995, as *Jazz Man: the Amazing Story of Ronnie Scott and his Club*)

——: *Shooting from the Hip: Changing Tunes in Jazz* (London, 1996) [colln of previously pubd articles]
——: *The Sound of Jazz* (London, 1989; Fr. trans., adapted by J.-L. Houdebine, Paris, 1990, as *Les sons du jazz*)
R. C. Foreman, Jr.: *Jazz and Race Records, 1920–32: their Origins and their Significance for the Record Industry and Society* (diss., U. of Illinois, 1968)
B. Foskett: *A Jazz Pictorial: a Collection of Photographs Capturing Some of the Greats of the Jazz and Blues World* (Cambridge, England, 1997)
F. Fossati, see M. Mannucci
P. Foster, T. Stoddard, and R. Russell: *Pops Foster: the Autobiography of a New Orleans Jazzman* (Berkeley, CA, Los Angeles, and London, 1971) [incl. discography by B. Rust]
P. Fountain and B. Neely: *A Closer Walk: the Pete Fountain Story* (Chicago, 1972)
C. Fox: *Fats Waller* (London, 1960); repr. in *Kings of Jazz*, ed. S. Green (South Brunswick, NJ, and New York, 1978)
——: *Jazz in Perspective* (London, 1969)
——: *The Jazz Scene* (London, 1972)
J. L. Fox and J. B. Fox: *The Melody Lives On: Scenes from the Golden Years of West Coast Jazz* (Santa Barbara, CA, 1996)
T. Fox: *In the Groove: the People Behind the Music* (New York, 1988)
——: *Showtime at the Apollo* (New York, 1983/*R*1993)
J. Fraim: *Spirit Catcher: the Life and Art of John Coltrane* (West Liberty, OH, 1996)
V. Franchini: *Lester Young* (Milan, 1961)
A. Francis: *Jazz* (Paris, 1958; rev. Eng. trans., by M. Williams, New York and London, 1960/*R*1976; Sp. trans., Caracas, 1972, as *Panorama del jazz*; It. trans., Verona, Italy, 1981)
——: *Jazz: l'histoire, les musiciens, les styles, les disques* (Paris, 1991)
R. E. Frank: *Tap! The Greatest Tap Dance Stars and their Stories, 1900–1955* (New York, 1990, rev. and enlarged 2/1994)
A. V. Frankenstein: *Syncopating Saxophones* (Chicago, 1925)
A. Franklin and D. Ritz: *Aretha: from these Roots* (New York, 1999)
A. Fraser, see D. Gillespie
W. A. Fraser: *Jazzology: a Study of the Tradition in which Jazz Musicians Learn to Improvise* (diss., U. of Pennsylvania, 1983)
Fred Böhler Kuratorium: *Fred Böhler: sein Leben, seine Music* (Dübendorf, Switzerland, 1996)
M. Freedland: *André Previn* (London, 1991)
B. Freeman: *If you Know of a Better Life, Please Tell Me* (Dublin, 1976) [autobiography of Bud Freeman]
——: *You don't Look like a Musician* (Detroit, 1974) [autobiography of Bud Freeman]
B. Freeman and R. Wolf: *Crazeology: the Autobiography of a Chicago Jazzman* (Wheatley, Oxford, England, and Urbana, IL, 1989)
P. Fresu: *Paolo Fresu si racconta: i protagonisti del jazz italiano* (Milan, 1996) [text in Eng. and It.]
T. Frew: *Scott Joplin and the Age of Ragtime* (New York, 1996)
L. Friedlander: *The Jazz People of New Orleans* (New York and London, 1992)
C. Friedman: *The Jazz Pictures* (Santa Fe, NM, 1999) [photo album]
C. Friedman and G. Giddins: *A Moment's Notice: Portraits of American Jazz Musicians* (New York and London, 1983)
L. Friedman, see J. Coryell
W. Friedwald: *Jazz Singing: America's Great Voices from Bessie Smith to Bebop and Beyond* (New York, 1992; Ger. trans., St. Andrä-Wordern, Germany, 1992, as *Singing Voices of America: ein Kompendium grosser Stimmen*)
——: *Sinatra! The Song is You: a Singer's Art* (New York, 1995; Ger. trans., St. Andrä-Wördern, Germany, 1996, as *Frank Sinatra: ein Mann und seine Musik*)
W. Friedwald, see also T. Bennett
H. Fruehauf: *Lester Bowie's Brass Fantasy: European Tour, Oct/Nov 86: eine Tournee-Dokumentation* (Burghausen, Germany, 1988)
Y. Fujioka, with L. Porter and Y. Hamada: *John Coltrane: a Discography and Musical Biography* (Metuchen, NJ, and London, 1995)
K. Gabbard: *Jammin' at the Margins: Jazz and the American Cinema* (Chicago, 1996)
K. Gabbard, ed.: *Jazz among the Discourses* (Durham, NC, and London, 1995)
——: *Representing Jazz* (Durham, NC, and London, 1995)
E. F. Gabel: *Stan Kenton: the Early Years, 1941–1947* (Lake Geneva, WI, 1993)
P. Gamble and P. Symes: *Focus on Jazz* (London, 1988) [photo album]
P. Gammond: *Duke Ellington* (London, 1987) [incl. discography]
P. Gammond, ed.: *The Decca Book of Jazz* (London, 1958)
——: *Duke Ellington: his Life and Music* (London and New York, 1958/*R*1977)
P. Gammond and P. Clayton: *Fourteen Miles on a Clear Night* (London, 1966)
L. Gara, see W. Dodds
J. Garcia, ed.: *Jazz grafico: diseño y fotografia en al disco de jazz, 1940–1968* (Valencia, Spain, 1999) [exhibition catalogue]
J. M. García Martínez: *Del fox-trot al jazz flamenco: el jazz en España, 1919–1996* (Madrid, 1996)
M. Gardner, see P. Klaasse
G. Garlick, see C. Wareing
G. Gart, ed.: *First Pressings: the History of Rhythm & Blues, Special 1950 Volume* (Milford, NH, 1993)
——: *First Pressings: the History of Rhythm & Blues*, i: *1951* (Milford, NH, 1991); ii: *1952* (Milford, 1992); iii: *1953* (Milford, 1989); iv: *1954* (Milford, 1990); v: *1955* (Milford, 1990); vi: *1956* (Milford, 1991); vii: *1957* (Milford, 1993); viii: *1958* (Milford, 1995)
G. Gaslini: *Tecnica e arti del jazz: il ritmo, le scale, gli accordi, la composizione, l'improvvizatione, le nuove strade* (Milan, 1982)
C. Gauffre: *Billie Holiday* (Paris, 1995)
C. Gauffre and J.-L. Chautemps: *Charlie Parker* (Paris, 1997)
M. Gayford: *The Best of Jazz* (San Francisco, 1993)
F. Gazzara: *Acid jazz: i gruppi, gli ambienti e gli stili del movimento che ha cambiato l'immaginario musicale del nostro tempo* (Rome, 1996)
H. R. Gee: *Saxophone Soloists and their Music, 1844–1985* (Bloomington, IN, 1986)
H. Geerken and B. Hefele: *Omniverse Sun Ra* (Wartaweil, Germany, 1994) [incl. discography, comprehensive bibliography]
R. Gehman, see E. Condon
H. Geller, see B. Willoughby
D. Gelly: *Icons of jazz* (London, 2000) [photo album]
——: *Lester Young* (Tunbridge Wells, England, 1984)
D. Gelly, ed.: *Masters of Jazz Saxophone* (London, 2000)
D. George: *The Real Duke Ellington* (London, 1982)
N. George: *The Death of Rhythm and Blues* (New York, London, Sydney, and Cologne, Germany, 1988)
C. D. Gerard: *Jazz in Black and White: Race, Culture, and Identity in the Jazz Community* (Westport, CT, and London, 1998)
A. Gerber: *Le cas Coltrane* (Marseilles, France, 1985)
——: *Fiesta in Blue: textes de jazz*, i (Paris, 1998); ii (Paris, 1999)
——: *Lester Young* (Paris, 2000)
U. Germinale: *La luce nell'ombra: jazz portraits on stage* (Genoa, Italy, 1998) [photo album]
M. Gerow, see P. O. W. Tanner
J. Gerth, see W. Burckhardt
E. Gétaz, see *Montreux Jazz Festival, 1967–1996*
H. N. Giardina: *La città del jazz* (Casalecchio di Reno, Italy, 1992)
W. Gibson: *The Internal Dialogue of the Jazz Musician* (Manchester, England, 1999)
G. Giddins: *Celebrating Bird: the Triumph of Charlie Parker* (New York, 1987/*R*1999)
——: *Faces in the Crowd: Players and Writers* (New York, and Oxford, England, 1992)
——: *Rhythm-a-ning: Jazz Tradition and Innovation in the '80s* (New York, and Oxford, England, 1985) [colln of previously pubd articles]
——: *Riding on a Blue Note: Jazz and American Pop* (New York, and Oxford, England, 1981/*R*2000) [colln of previously pubd articles]
——: *Satchmo* (New York and elsewhere, 1988; Fr. trans., Paris, 1991, as *Satchmo*; Ger. trans., Stuttgart, Germany, 1991, as *Louis Armstrong: sein Leben und sein Zeit*)
——: *Visions of jazz: the First Century* (New York, and Oxford, England, 1998)
G. Giddins, see also C. Friedman
H. Giese: *Art Blakey: sein Leben, seine Musik, seine Schallplatten* (Schaftlach, Germany, 1990)
D. Gignoux: *Dizzy Gillespie* (Kiel, Germany, 1993; Fr. trans., Thones, France, 1995) [photo album; text in Ger. and Eng.; Fr. trans. has additional material]
W. G. Gilbert: *Rumbamuziek: volksmuziek van de midden-amerikaansche negers* (The Hague, n.d. [?1947])
W. G. Gilbert and C. Poustochkine: *Jazzmuziek: inleiding tot de volksmuziek der noord-amerikaansche negers* (The Hague, 1939, rev. 2/1948)
R. Gili: *El jazz* (Barcelona, 1978, rev. 2/1984)
J. Gill: *Queer Noises: Male and Female Homosexuality in Twentieth-century Music* (London, 1995)
D. Gillespie and A. Fraser: *To be, or not . . . to Bop: Memoirs* (Garden City, NY, 1979, London, 1980, as *Dizzy: the Autobiography of Dizzy Gillespie*; Fr. trans., Paris, 1981, as *To be or not to Bop*; Ger. trans., Vienna, 1984/*R*1994, as *Dizzy: to be or not to Bop*)
A. V. Gillet: *Louis A. Mitchell: bio-disco-bibliographie* (Brussels, 1966)
C. Gillett: *Making Tracks: Atlantic Records and the Growth of a Multi-billion-dollar Industry* (London, 1975)
——: *The Sound of the City: the Rise of Rock and Roll* (New York, 1970, rev. and enlarged London, 2/1983, rev. and enlarged 3/1996; Fr. trans., Paris, 1986, as *Histoire du rock 'n' roll: the Sound of the City*)
F. J. Gillis and J. W. Miner, eds.: *Oh, didn't he Ramble: the Life Story of Lee Collins* (Urbana, IL, Chicago, and London, 1974/*R*1989) [incl. discography]
O. Gillissen and J.-P. Leloir: *Ray Charles* (Paris, 1989)
Giltrap and Dixon: *Kid Ory* (London, n.d. [?1958])

T. Gioia: *The History of Jazz* (New York, 1997)
——: *The Imperfect Art: Reflections on Jazz and Modern Culture* (New York, and Oxford, England, 1988)
——: *West Coast Jazz: Modern Jazz in California, 1945–1960* (New York, and Oxford, England, 1992)
I. Gitler: *Jazz Masters of the Forties* (New York, 1966/*R*1983 with discography)
——: *Masters of Bebop: a Listener's Guide* (New York, 2001)
——: *Swing to Bop: an Oral History of the Transition in Jazz in the 1940s* (New York, and Oxford, England, 1985)
J. Giuffre: *Jazz Phrasing and Interpretation: Aspects of Jazz Performance, Analyzed for the Player . . . a Personal Approach* (New York, 1969)
J. J. Gjedsted: *Montmartre gennem 10 år* [The Montmartre club over ten years] (Copenhagen, 1986)
M. Glaser and S. Grappelli: *Jazz Violin* (New York and elsewhere, 1981) [incl. transcrs.]
S. Gläss: *Die Rolle der Geige im Jazz* (Berne, 1991 [*recte* 1992])
R. J. Gleason: *Celebrating the Duke, and Louis, Bessie, Billie, Bird, Carmen, Miles, Dizzy, and other Heroes* (Boston and Toronto, 1975/*R*1995)
R. J. Gleason, ed.: *Jam Session: an Anthology of Jazz* (New York and London, 1958)
S. Glover and B. Weber: *Savion: my Life in Tap* (New York, 2000)
F. Goaty: *Miles Davis* (Paris, 1995)
J. Godbolt: *All this and Many a Dog: Memoirs of a Loser/Pessimist* (London, 1987)
——: *All this and 10%* (London, 1976)
——: *A History of Jazz in Britain, 1919–50* (London, Melbourne, Australia, and New York, 1984)
——: *A History of Jazz in Britain, 1950–1970* (London, 1989)
C. Goddard: *Jazz away from Home* (London and New York, 1979)
J. Godrich, see R. M. W. Dixon; P. Oliver
U. Goeman, see P. Klaasse; P. N. Wilson
R. Goffin: *Aux frontières du jazz* (Paris, 1932)
——: *Jazz: from the Congo to the Metropolitan* (Garden City, NY, 1944/*R*1975, rev. [2]/1946, as *Jazz: from Congo to Swing*; Fr. orig., Montreal, 1945, as *Histoire du jazz*, rev. Paris, [2]/1948, as *Nouvelle histoire du jazz: du Congo au bebop*)
——: *Louis Armstrong: le roi du jazz* (Paris, 1947; Eng. trans., New York, 1947/*R*1977, as *Horn of Plenty: the Story of Louis Armstrong; Hung. trans., Budapest, 1974, as Armstrong: a dzsessz királya*)
——: *La Nouvelle-Orléans: capitale du jazz* (New York, 1946)
J. Goggin: *Turk Murphy: Just for the Record* (San Leandro, CA, 1982) [incl. discography]
J. O. Goggin and P. Clute: *The Great Jazz Revival: a Pictorial Celebration of Traditional Jazz* (San Rafael, CA, 1994)
J. Goggin, see also D. Oxtot
L. Goines and R. Ameen: *Funkifying the Clavé: Afro-Cuban Grooves for Bass and Drums* (New York, 1990)
H. Gold: *Gold, Doubloons and Pieces of Eight: the Autobiography of Harry Gold* (London, 2000)
J. Goldberg: *Jazz Masters of the Fifties* (New York and London, 1965/*R*1980)
B. Goldblatt: *Newport Jazz Festival: the Illustrated History* (New York, 1977)
B. Golden, see B. Thiele
J. Goldsby: *Bowing Techniques for the Improvising Bassist* (New York, 1989)
P. D. Goldsmith: *Making People's Music: Moe Asch and Folkways Records* (Washington, DC, and London, 1998)
E. Goldson, ed.: *Seeing Jazz: Artists and Writers on Jazz* (San Francisco, 1997) [exhibition catalogue]
M. Goldstein, see V. Skaarup
J. Gonda: *Jazz: tortenet-elmélet-gyakorlat* [Jazz: history, theory, practice] (Budapest, 1965, rev. 2/1979; Bulgarian trans., Sofia, 1975, as *Dzsazi isztoriája, teorijá, praktiká*)
——: *Mi a jazz?* [What is jazz?] (Budapest, 1983)
J. Gonda, ed.: *Jazz School Directory* (Budapest, 1980)
B. Gonzales: *I Paid my Dues: Good Times . . . No Bread* (New York, 1967)
——: *Movin' on Down de Line* (Newark, NJ, 1975)
B. Gonzales and P. Weston: *Boptionary: What is Bop?* (Hollywood, CA, 1949)
B. Goodman and I. Kolodin: *The Kingdom of Swing* (New York, 1939; Ger. trans., Zurich, 1961/*R*1993, as *Mein Weg zum Jazz: eine Autobiographie*)
C. P. Gordon, see M. Royal
M. Gordon: *Live at the Village Vanguard* (New York, 1980)
R. Gordon: *Jazz West Coast: the Los Angeles Jazz Scene of the 1950s* (London and New York, 1986)
S. Gordon, see B. Breakey
R. Gottlieb, ed.: *Reading Jazz: a Gathering of Autobiography, Reportage & Criticism from 1900 to Now* (New York, 1996) [colln of previously pubd articles]
W. P. Gottlieb: *The Golden Age of Jazz* (London, Melbourne, Australia, and New York, 1979, rev. San Francisco, 2/1995)
L. Gourse: *Every Day: the Story of Joe Williams* (London, Melbourne, Australia, and New York, 1985) [incl. discography]
——: *Louis' Children: American Jazz Singers* (New York, 1984)
——: *Madame Jazz: Contemporary Women Instrumentalists* (New York, and Oxford, England, 1995)
——: *Sassy: the Life of Sarah Vaughan* (New York and Toronto, 1993)
——: *Straight no Chaser: the Life and Genius of Thelonious Monk* (New York, 1997)
——: *Unforgettable: the Life and Mystique of Nat King Cole* (New York, 1991; Ger. trans., St. Andrä-Wördern, Germany, 1993, as *Nat King Cole: Leben und Geheimnis des Nat King Cole*)
——: *Wynton Marsalis: Skain's Domain: a Biography* (New York, 1999)
L. Gourse, ed.: *The Billie Holiday Companion: Seven Decades of Commentary* (New York, 1997) [colln of previously pubd articles]
——: *The Ella Fitzgerald Companion: Seven Decades of Commentary* (New York, 1998) [colln of previously pubd articles]
A. Govenar: *Meeting the Blues* (Dallas, TX, 1988)
A. Govenar and B. Joseph: *The Early Years of Rhythm & Blues: Focus on Houston* (Houston, 1990)
A. B. Govenar: *Deep Ellum and Central Track: Where the Black and White Worlds of Dallas Converged* (Denton, TX, 1998)
J. de Graef: *Jazz in Belgie: de swingperiode (1935–1947)* (Antwerp, Belgium, 1980)
C. Graham and D. Morgenstern: *Jazz Day in Harlem* (Emeryville, CA, 1999) [photo album]
C. L. Granata: *Sessions with Sinatra: Frank Sinatra and the Art of Recording* (Chicago, 1999)
Les grandes signatures: album photo (Paris, 1987) [special pubn by *Jazz hot*]
A. Granholm: *Finnish Jazz* (Helsinki, 1974, rev. and enlarged 2/1982, by M. Konttinen, rev. and enlarged 3/1986, by J.-P. Vuorela, rev. and enlarged 5/1997, by M. Huuskonen, J. Muikku, and T. Vähäsilta)
N. Granz: *The Jazz Scene* (New York, 1949)
S. Grappelli and Y. M. Ajchenbaum: *Stéphane Grappelli* (Paris, 1996) [incl. Eng. trans. and transcrs.]
S. Grappelli, J. Oldenhove, and J.-M. Bramy: *Mon violon pour tout bagage: mémoires* (Paris, 1992)
S. Grappelli, see also M. Glaser
H. Grässer: *Der Jazzgeiger Stéphane Grappelli: Untersuchungen zur Entwicklung seines Personalstils und zu seiner Violintechnik* (Regensburg, Germany, 1996)
W. Gratzer, see G. Eder
B. Grauer, Jr., see O. Keepnews
J. Graves: *Könige des Blues* (Zurich, 1961)
H. Gray: *Producing Jazz: the Experience of an Independent Record Company* (Philadelphia, 1988) [history of Theresa Records]
B. Green: *Drums in my Ears* (New York and London, 1973)
——: *The Reluctant Art: Five Studies in the Growth of Jazz* (London, 1962, enlarged New York, 2/1991)
——: *Swingtime in Tottenham* (London, 1976)
J. Green: *Glenn Miller and the Age of Swing* (London, 1976)
J. P. Green: *Edmund Thornton Jenkins: the Life and Times of an American Black Composer, 1894–1926* (Westport, CT, and London, 1982)
J. P. Green, see also L. Thompson
S. Green, ed.: *Kings of Jazz* (South Brunswick, NJ, and New York, 1978)
S. A. Green: *Grant Green: Rediscovering the Forgotten Genius of Guitar* (San Francisco, 1999)
R. Greene: *Duke Ellington* (Zurich, 1961)
A. Grey and M. Grey: *Plunger Techniques: the Al Grey Plunger Method for Trombones and Trumpets* (New York, 1987)
M. C. Gridley: *Concise Guide to Jazz* (Englewood Cliffs, NJ, and London, 1992, rev. Upper Saddle River, NJ, 2/1998)
——: *Jazz Styles* (Englewood Cliffs, NJ, 1978, rev. 2/1985, as *Jazz Styles: History and Analysis*, with suppl. *Instructor's Manual and Discography*, rev. 3/*c*1988, rev. 4/1990, rev. 5/1994, rev. Upper Saddle River, NJ, 6/1997 [*recte* 1996])
W. Grieder: *Hazy Osterwald Story: Musik ist ein Trumpf* (Zurich, 1961)
N. Griffin: *To be or not to Bop* (New York, 1948)
D. Griffiths: *Hot Jazz from Harlem to Storyville* (Lanham, MD, New Brunswick, NJ, and London, 1998)
K. Grime: *Jazz at Ronnie Scott's* (London, 1979)
——: *Jazz Voices* (London, 1983)
C. Groom: *Rockin' and around Croydon: Rock, Folk, Blues & Jazz in and around the Croydon Area, 1960–1980* (Purley, England, 1999)
G. Grosse, see P. Czada
W. L. Grossman and J. W. Farrell: *The Heart of Jazz* (New York, 1956/*R*1976)
E. Grossmann: *Tiny Parham's Victor Recordings and Toad's Krazy Kats' Golden Lily* (Menden, Germany, 1989)
A. Groves and A. Shipton: *The Glass Enclosure: the Life of Bud Powell* (Tunbridge Wells, England, 1993)
R. Grudens: *The Best Damn Trumpet Player: Memories of the Big Band Era and Beyond* (Stony Brook, NY, 1996)

——: *Jukebox Saturday Night: More Memories of the Big Band Era and Beyond* (Stony Brook, NY, 1999)
——: *The Music Men: the Guys who Sang with the Bands and their Styles* (Stony Brook, NY, 1998)
D. Guaraldi, see M. Breslow
J. P. Guckin, see F. Kaufman
I. Guillory, see R. Denyer
J. Guinle: *Jazz panorama* (Rio de Janeiro, 1953)
The Guitar Player Book (Saratoga, nr Los Gatos, CA, and New York, 1978, 2/1979) [colln of previously pubd articles]
F. Gulda: *Worte zur Musik* (Munich, 1971)
L. Gullo and A. Leonardi: ... *Visintin: Gato Barbieri* (Milan, 1979)
L. Guttridge, see J. D. Smith
R. Haarmann and I. Wulff, eds.: *Jazzbaltica '91: eine Dokumentation* (Kiel, Germany, 1991) [exhibition catalogue]
R. Hadlock: *Jazz Masters of the Twenties* (New York, 1965/*R*1985)
A. G. Hager: *Satin Dolls: the Women of Jazz* (New York, 1996)
D. Hajdu: *Lush Life: a Biography of Billy Strayhorn* (New York, 1996)
G. Halász: *Jazz Kanizsán* [Jazz in Kanisza] (Nagykanisza, Hungary, 1996)
F. Hall: *Dialogues in Swing: Intimate Conversations with the Stars of the Big Band Era* (Ventura, CA, 1989)
——: *More Dialogues in Swing* (Ventura, CA, 1991)
F. M. Hall: *It's About Time: the Dave Brubeck Story* (Fayetteville, AR, 1996)
Y. Hamada, see Y. Fujioka
O. Häme: *Rytmin voittokulku* [The triumph of rhythm] (Helsinki, 1949)
C. Hamm, B. Nettl, and R. Byrnside: *Contemporary Music and Music Cultures* (Englewood Cliffs, NJ, 1975)
B. Hammond, comp., and P. O'Connor: *Josephine Baker* (Boston, Toronto, and London, 1988). [incl. discography]
J. Hammond and I. Townsend: *John Hammond on Record: an Autobiography* (New York, 1977)
L. Hampton with J. Haskins: *Hamp: an Autobiography* (New York, 1989) [incl. discography]
D. A. Handy: *Black Women in American Bands and Orchestras* (Metuchen, NJ, 1981, rev. and enlarged Lanham, MD, 2/1998)
——: *The International Sweethearts of Rhythm* (Metuchen, NJ, and London, 1983, rev. Lanham, MD, New Brunswick, NJ, and London, 2/1996)
——: *Jazz Man's Journey: a Biography of Ellis Louis Marsalis, Jr.* (Lanham, MD, 1999)
W. C. Handy: *Father of the Blues: an Autobiography*, ed. A. Bontemps (New York, 1941/*R*1991)
L. Haney: *Naked at the Feast: a Biography of Josephine Baker* (London, 1981)
J. Hannusch: *I Hear You Knockin': the Sound of New Orleans Rhythm and Blues* (Ville Platte, LA, 1985)
C. Hansen, see A. Hodes
D. Hardie: *The Loudest Trumpet: Buddy Bolden and the Early History of Jazz* (San Jose, CA, 2000)
J. Harris, see Laurie Wright
K. Harris: *First Call Drummer: Don Lamond* (Brandon, Suffolk, England, 1997)
——: *Geraldo's Navy* (Brandon, Suffolk, England, 1998)
M. W. Harris: *The Rise of Gospel Blues: the Music of Thomas Andrew Dorsey in the Urban Church* (New York, and Oxford, England, 1992)
R. Harris: *Jazz* (London, 1952, 5/1957)
Sheldon Harris, see C. E. B. Bernhardt
Steve Harris: *Kenton Kronicles: a Biography of Modern America's Man of Music* (Pasadena, CA, 2000)
D. D. Harrison: *Black Pearls: Blues Queens of the 1920s* (New Brunswick, NJ, 1988)
M. Harrison: *Charlie Parker* (London, 1960); repr. in *Kings of Jazz*, ed. S. Green (South Brunswick, NJ, and New York, 1978)
——: *A Jazz Retrospect* (Newton Abbot, England, 1976, rev. 2/1977/*R*1991)
M. Harrison, see also P. Oliver
P. C. Harrison, see C. Stewart
J. Hartley and J. Woelfer: *Johnny Richards: the Definitive Bio-discography* (Lake Geneva, WI, 1999)
D. Hartmann, see D. Salemann
J. Haskins: *The Cotton Club* (New York, 1977/*R*1994)
——: *Ella Fitzgerald: a Life through Jazz* (Sevenoaks, England, and London, 1991; Fr. trans., Paris, 1992, as *Ella Fitzgerald: une vie à travers le jazz*; Ger. trans., St. Andrä-Wördern, Germany, 1992, as *Sing Me a Swing Song and Let Me Dance: Ella Fitzgerald: die First Lady des Jazz*)
——: *Mabel Mercer: a Life* (New York, 1987)
——: *Queen of the Blues: a Biography of Dinah Washington* (New York, 1987) [incl. discography]
J. Haskins and K. Benson: *Nat King Cole* (New York, 1984, rev. Chelsea, MI, 1990, as *Nat King Cole: a Personal and Professional Biography*)
J. Haskins with H. Crothers: *Scatman: an Authorized Biography of Scatman Crothers* (New York, 1991)
J. Haskins and N. R. Mitgang: *Mr. Bojangles: the Biography of Bill Robinson* (New York, 1988/*R*2000)
J. Haskins, see also Bricktop; L. Hampton
J. E. Hasse: *Beyond Category: the Life and Genius of Duke Ellington* (New York, 1993)
——: *The Creation and Dissemination of Indianapolis Ragtime, 1897–1930* (diss., Indiana U., 1981)
——: *The Works of Hoagy Carmichael* (Cincinnati, 1983)
J. E. Hasse, ed.: *Jazz: the First Century* (New York, 2000)
——: *Ragtime: its History, Composers, and Music* (New York and London, 1985)
H. Hawes and D. Asher: *Raise up off Me: a Portrait of Hampton Hawes* (New York and Toronto, 1974; Ger. trans., Frankfurt am Main, Germany, 1983, as *Ganz tief Luft holen: Autobiographie eines Jazzmusikers*)
M. Hawkins: *A Shot in the Dark: Nashville Jumps, Blues and Rhythm on Nashville's Independent Labels, 1945–1955* (Vollersode, Germany, 2000) [liner notes, Bear Family BCD15864HL]
G. Haydon and D. Marks, eds.: *Repercussions: a Celebration of Afro-American Music* (London, 1985)
C. Hayes: *The Dance Band Diary* (Ventnor, England, 1985–)
M. Hazeldine: *Bill Russell's American Music* (New Orleans, 1993)
M. Hazeldine, see also B. Russell
E. Hazell, see L. Porter
K. Hazzard-Gordon: *Jookin': the Rise of Social Dance Formations in African-American Culture* (Philadelphia, 1990)
M. Heath: *I Haven't Said Thanks: the Story of Ted and Moira Heath* (Oldham, England, 1999)
T. Heath: *Listen to my Music: an Autobiography* (London, 1957)
T. Heath and others: *Ted Heath Pictorial Souvenir* (London, 1948)
A. Heble: *Landing on the Wrong Note: Jazz, Dissonance and Critical Practice* (New York, 2000)
F. Hedman: *Alice Babs: berättelsen om artisten Alice "Babs" Nilson* [Alice Babs: the story of the artist Alice "Babs" Nilson] (Stockholm, 1975)
A. Heerkens: *Jazz* (Baarn, Netherlands, 1956)
B. Hefele, see H. Geerken
M. Heffley: *The Music of Anthony Braxton* (New York, 1996)
K. Gert zur Heide: *Deep South Piano: the Story of Little Brother Montgomery* (London, 1970)
K. Heidkamp: *It's All Over Now: Musik einer Generation: 40 Jahre Rock und Jazz* (Berlin, 1999)
K. Heidkamp, ed.: *In the Mood: Jazz-Geschichten* (Hamburg, Germany, 1991)
F. Heinrich: *Swing-Generation: Selbsterlebtes* (Menden, Germany, 1988)
J. Hélian: *Les grands orchestres de music hall en France* (Paris, 1984)
H. Hellhund: *Cool Jazz: Grundzüge seiner Entstehung und Entwicklung* (Mainz, Germany, 1985)
N. Hellström, ed.: *Jazz: historia, teknik, utövare* (Stockholm, 1940)
D. Hendrikse: *Twintig reuzen van de jazz* (Haarlem, Netherlands, 1960)
B. Henius: *Svend Asmussen* (Copenhagen, 1963)
M. Hennessey: *Klook: the Story of Kenny Clarke* (London, 1990)
T. J. Hennessey: *From Jazz to Swing: Afro-American Jazz Musicians and their Music, 1890–1935* (Detroit, 1994)
——: *From Jazz to Swing: Black Jazz Musicians and their Music, 1917–1935* (diss., Northwestern U., 1973)
J. Henriksson: *Chasing the Bird: Functional Harmony in Charlie Parker's Bebop Themes* (Helsinki, 1998)
N. Hentoff: *Jazz Is* (New York, 1976/*R*1991)
——: *The Jazz Life* (New York and London, 1961/*R*1975) [incl. previously pubd articles]
——: *John Lewis* (New York, 1960)
——: *Listen to the Stories: Nat Hentoff on Jazz and Country Music* (New York, 1995) [incl. previously pubd articles]
——: *Speaking Freely: a Memoir* (New York, 1997)
N. Hentoff and A. J. McCarthy, eds.: *Jazz: New Perspectives on the History of Jazz by Twelve of the World's Foremost Jazz Critics and Scholars* (New York and Toronto, 1959/*R*1974; Sp. trans., Buenos Aires, 1982, as *Jazz: psicología y sociologíe*)
N. Hentoff and R. Sanjek: *Charlie Parker* (New York, 1960) [list of compositions]
N. Hentoff, see also N. Shapiro; D. Stock
D. A. Herfort: *A History of the National Association of Jazz Educators and a Description of its Role in American Music Education, 1968–1978* (diss., U. of Houston, 1979)
H. Herling: *Capt. John Handy: kleine Studie über Leben und Werk sowie seinen Einfluss auf die heutige "New Orleans Revival Jazz"-scene* (Menden, Germany, 1978) [incl. discography]
W. Herman and S. Troup: *The Woodchopper's Ball: the Autobiography of Woody Herman* (New York, 1990; Ger. trans., St. Andrä-Wördern, Germany, 1992, as *Woodchopper's Ball: der König der Big Band-Ära erzählt*)
T. Hershorn, comp.: *Make Freedom Swing: Norman Granz and Jazz at the Philharmonic, 1944–1957: an Itinerary and Bibliography* (Fairfax, VA, 1996)
C. Herwig: *Fond Memories of Frank Rosolino: Historical Notes and Solo Transcriptions* (New Albany, IN, 1996)
J. Hess: *Encyclopédie Jazz Hot: Bebop* (Paris, 1990)

J. B. Hess, see also A. Coueroy
K. E. Hester: *The Melodic and Polyrhythmic Development of John Coltrane's Spontaneous Composition in a Racist Society* (Lewiston, NY, Queenston, Ontario, and Lampeter, Wales, 1997)
M. L. Hester: *Going to Kansas City* (Sherman, TX, 1980)
Stanley Hester, Stephen Hester, P. Evans, and L. Evans: *The Red Nichols Story: After Intermission, 1942–1965* (Lanham, MD, and London, 1996)
B. Heuvelmans: *De la bamboula au be-bop: esquisse de l'évolution de la musique de jazz* (Paris, 1951)
W. W. Hicks, see D. R. Connor
R. Hilbert: *Pee Wee Russell: the Life of a Jazzman* (New York, and Oxford, England, 1993)
R. Hilbert, Jr., see S. E. Brown
L. Hildebrand: *Stars of Soul and R&B* (New York, 1994)
C. V. Hill: *Brotherhood in Rhythm: the Jazz Tap Dancing of the Nicholas Brothers* (New York, and Oxford, England, 2000)
D. Hill: *Sylvester Ahola: the Gloucester Gabriel* (Metuchen, NJ, and London, 1993)
S. Hill: *Tal Farlow: Jazz Guitarist* (Wheatley, Oxford, England, 1987)
C. Hillman: *Bunk Johnson: his Life and Times* (Tunbridge Wells, England, 1988)
C. Hillman and R. Middleton, with H. van Veelo: *Richard M. Jones: Forgotten Man of Jazz* (Tavistock, England, 1997 [*recte* 1998]) [incl. discography]
R. Himsel: *Bilder av jazz* (Växjö, Sweden, 1983)
M. Hinton and D. G. Berger: *Bass Line: the Stories and Photographs of Milt Hinton* (Philadelphia, 1988)
M. Hinton, D. G. Berger, and H. Manson: *Over Time: the Jazz Photographs of Milt Hinton* (San Francisco, 1991)
J.-R. Hippenmeyer: *Le jazz en Suisse, 1930–1970* (Yverdon, Switzerland, 1971)
——: *Sidney Bechet* (Geneva, 1980)
A. Z. Hirsch, Jr.: *Black and Tan Fantasy: the Sociology of Jazz Music* (MS, 1946, *NNSc*)
T. Hirschmann: *Charlie Parker: kritische Beiträge zur Bibliographie sowie zu Leben und Werk* (Tutzing, Germany, 1994)
——: *Untersuchungen zu den Kompositionen von Charlie Parker* (diss., U. of Mainz, Germany, 1982)
E. Hobsbawm: *Uncommon People: Resistance, Rebellion and Jazz* (New York, 1998)
E. J. E. Hobsbawm, see also F. Newton
W. Hobson: *American Jazz Music* (New York, 1939/*R*1976, rev. London, 2/1941/*R*1956)
A. Hodeir: *Hommes et problèmes du jazz, suivi de La religion du jazz* (Paris, 1954/*R*1981, Marseilles, 2/1985; Eng. trans., rev. Hodeir, as *Jazz: its Evolution and Essence*, New York, 1956/*R*1975)
——: *Introduction à la musique de jazz* (Paris, 1948)
——: *Le jazz, cet inconnu* (Paris, 1945)
——: *Jazzistiques* (Marseilles, France, 1984)
——: *Les mondes du jazz* (Paris, 1970/*R*1993; Eng. trans., New York, 1972)
——: *Toward Jazz* (New York, 1962/*R*1976) [in Eng. trans.]
A. Hodes and C. Hansen: *Hot Man: the Life of Art Hodes* (Oxford, England, and Chicago, 1992) [incl. discography by H. Rye]
A. Hodes and C. Hansen, eds.: *Selections from the Gutter: Jazz Portraits from "The Jazz Record"* (Berkeley, CA, Los Angeles, and London, 1977)
G. Hoefer, see W. Smith
B. Hoehne: *Jazz in der DDR* (Frankfurt am Main, Germany, 1991)
F. Hoffman: *Henry "Red" Allen in England, 1964, 1966, 1967: an Excerpt out a Future Henry "Red" Allen Biodisco, 1908–1967* (MS, Berlin, n.d.) [unpubd typescript]
——: *Henry "Red" Allen (Jan. 7th 1980–Apr. 17th 1967)/J. C. Higginbotham (May 11th 1906–May 26th 1973): Compiled Negro-press Material about Bands with Henry Red Allen, 1927–1940* (MS, Berlin, 1979, rev. 1982) [unpubd typescript]
F. Hoffmann and I. Buckley, comp.: *Jazz Advertised, 1910–1967: a Documentation*, i–iii: *The Negro Newspapers of New England, 1910–1967*; iv–vi: *The Chicago Defender, 1910–1967*; vii: *The New York Times, 1929–1950*; viii: *Index* (Berlin, [1997])
M. Hoffman: *Tony Bennett* (New York, 1997)
F. Hofstein: *Le rhythm and blues* (Paris, 1991)
F. Hofstein and C. Béthune, eds.: *Revue d'esthétique*, no.19: *Jazz* (Paris, 1991)
D. Holder: *Completely Frank: Life of Frank Sinatra* (London, 1995; Ger. trans., Munich, 1995, as *Frank Sinatra: I Did it my Way*)
B. Holiday and W. Dufty: *Lady Sings the Blues* (Garden City, NY, 1956/*R*1984 with discography by A. J. McCarthy; Fr. trans., Marseilles, France, 1984/*R*1992, as *Lady Sings the Blues*; Ger. trans., Hamburg, Germany, 1983/*R*1992, as *Lady Sings the Blues*) [autobiography of Billie Holiday]
L. D. Holmes and J. W. Thomson: *Jazz Greats: Getting Better with Age* (New York, 1986)
F. Holt: *ECM-musik: en undersøgelse af pladeselskabet ECM's jazzudgivelser med særlig henblik på – gennem historiske, æstetiske og værkanalytiske betragtninger – at belyse deres specifikke musikalske fællestræk* [ECM music: a study of the jazz recordings on the record label ECM with special reference, through historical, aesthetic, and analytical reflections, to an understanding of their specific common musical characteristics] (thesis, U. of Copenhagen, 1997)
J. Holzt-Edelhagen: *Jazz-Geschichte(n)* (Frankfurt am Main, Germany, 1989)
——: *Das Orchester Kurt Edelhagen* (Frankfurt am Main, Germany, 1990)
M. A. Hood and H. N. Flint, eds.: *"Jelly Roll" Morton: the Original Mr. Jazz* (New York, 1975)
R. J. Hopf: *Sidekicks of the Swing Era* (Menden, Germany, 1981)
P. Horn with L. Underwood: *Paul Horn: the Spiritual Odyssey of a Universal Traveler* (San Francisco, 1990)
J. Hornsby, see G. Martin
R. Horricks: *Count Basie and his Orchestra: its Music and its Musicians* (London and New York, 1957)
——: *Dizzy Gillespie and the Be-bop Revolution* (Tunbridge Wells, England, and New York, 1984) [incl. discography by T. Middleton]
——: *Gerry Mulligan's Ark* (London, 1986) [incl. discography by T. Middleton]
——: *The Importance of Being Eric Dolphy* (Tunbridge Wells, England, 1988)
——: *Profiles in Jazz: from Sidney Bechet to John Coltrane* (New Brunswick, NJ, 1991)
——: *Quincy Jones* (Tunbridge Wells, England, and New York, 1985) [incl. discography by T. Middleton]
——: *Stephane Grappelli, or The Violin with Wings: a Profile* (Tunbridge Wells, England, and New York, 1983) [incl. discography]
——: *Svengali, or The Orchestra Called Gil Evans* (Tunbridge Wells, England, and New York, 1984) [incl. discography by T. Middleton]
R. Horricks and others: *These Jazzmen of our Time* (London, 1959)
R. Horricks, see also A. Morgan
R. Hoskins: *Louis Armstrong: Biography of a Musician* (Los Angeles, 1979) [incl. discography and list of films]
B. Hoskyns: *Waiting for the Sun: the Story of the Los Angeles Music Scene* (London, 1995)
J. A. Howard: *The Improvisational Techniques of Art Tatum* (diss., Case Western Reserve U., 1978)
M. Howe: *Blue Jazz* (Bristol, England, 1934)
F. A. Howlett: *An Introduction to Art Tatum's Performance Approaches: Composition, Improvisation, and Melodic Variation* (diss., Cornell U., 1983)
J. Howlett: *Frank Sinatra* (New York, 1994)
P. Hucker: *Jazz* (Paris, 1996; Ger. trans., Bergisch-Gladbach, Germany, 1999, as *Jazz*)
H. C. Hudson, see D. N. Baker
A. Huebner: *Louis Armstrong: sein Leben, seine Musik, seine Schallplatten* (Waakirchen, Germany, 1994)
L. Hughes: *The Big Sea: an Autobiography* (New York, 1945; It. trans., Turin, 1948, as *Nel mare della vita*)
——: *Famous Negro Music Makers* (New York, 1955)
——: *The First Book of Jazz* (New York, 1954, rev. 2/1962)
——: *I Wonder as I Wander* (New York, 1964)
L. Hughes and M. Meltzer: *Black Magic: a Pictorial History of the Negro in American Entertainment* (Englewood Cliffs, NJ, 1967/*R*1990)
R. Hughes, ed.: *The Jazz Family Album* (East Stroudsburg, PA, 1992); ii (East Stroudsburg, 1993); iii (East Stroudsburg, 1995); iv (East Stroudsburg, 1995); v (East Stroudsburg, 1997)
S. Hughes: *Opening Bars* (London, 1946) [autobiography]
——: *Second Movement* (London, 1951) [autobiography]
V. E. Hughes, see M. Kaminsky
R. Hultin: *Jazzens tegn* (Oslo, 1991; Eng. trans., London, 1998, as *Born under the Sign of Jazz*) [autobiography]
G. Hunkel: *Western Swing and Country Jazz: eine Einführung mit Kurzporträts über Bob Wills und Milton Brown* (Menden, Germany, 1983)
H. F. Huon, see D. Ellington
M. Huuskonen, see A. Granholm
In a Silent Way: Miles Davis (Zurich, 1989)
A. Ingram: *Wes Montgomery* (Gateshead, England, 1985/*R*1993) [bio-discography]
S. Isoardi, see B. Collette
A. Jackson: *The World of Big Bands: the Sweet and Swinging Years* (New York, 1977)
M. Jacobs: *All that Jazz: die Geschichte einer Musik* (Stuttgart, Germany, 1996; Hung. trans., Budapest, 1999, as *Fejezetek a jazz történetéből*)
A. Jaffe: *Jazz Theory* (Dubuque, IA, 1983)
M.-C. Jalard: *Le jazz, est-il encore possible* (Marseilles, France, 1986)
P. Jalkanen: *Ravintola: ja tanssiorkesterilaitoksen murros Helsingissä 1920-luvulla* [Changes in the dance orchestra in Helsinki in the 1920s] (diss., U. of Helsinki, 1975); rev. as *Alaska, Bombay ja Billy Boy* (Helsinki, 1989)
B. James: *Billie Holiday* (Tunbridge Wells, England, 1984)
——: *Bix Beiderbecke* (London, 1959); repr. in *Kings of Jazz*, ed. S. Green (South Brunswick, NJ, and New York, 1978)

——: *Coleman Hawkins* (Tunbridge Wells, England, 1984)
——: *Essays on Jazz* (London, 1961/*R*1985/*R*1990, with new foreword and index)
E. James and D. Ritz: *The Etta James Story: Rage to Survive* (New York, 1995)
M. James: *Dizzy Gillespie* (London, 1959); repr. in *Kings of Jazz*, ed. S. Green (South Brunswick, NJ, and New York, 1978)
——: *Miles Davis* (London, 1961); repr. in *Kings of Jazz*, ed. S. Green (South Brunswick, NJ, and New York, 1978)
——: *Ten Modern Jazzmen: an Appraisal of the Recorded Work of Ten Modern Jazzmen* (London, 1960)
H. Janis, see R. Blesh
D. A. Jasen and G. Jones: *Spreadin' Rhythm Around: Black Popular Songwriters, 1880–1930* (New York, 1998)
——: *That American Rag! The Story of Ragtime from Coast to Coast* (New York, 2000)
D. A. Jasen and T. J. Tichenor: *Rags and Ragtime: a Musical History* (New York, 1978)
Jazz à Vienne: 20 ans, l'album anniversaire (Veurey, France, 2000)
Jazz hot: *Les grandes signatures: album photo* (Paris, 1987)
——: *Les grandes voix du jazz: album photo* (Paris, 1989) [text in Fr. and Eng.]
——: *Un demi-siècle de swing et de jazz: album photo du cinquantenaire de Jazz hot* (Paris, 1986) [text in Fr. and Eng.]
Jazz magazine: *Les années Jazz magazine: 40 ans de passion* (Paris, 1994) [colln of previously pubd articles]
——: *Les années Jazz magazine: 1954–2000* (Levallois-Perret, France, 2000) [colln of previously pubd articles]
Jazzman: *Jazz et world: la belle histoire* (Paris, 1999)
Jazz on Television (New York, 1985) [exhibition catalogue of the Museum of Broadcasting]
Jazz op 3: die heimliche Liebe des Jazz zur europäischen Moderne (Vienna and Munich, 1986)
Jazz sous les pommiers, 83–84: festivals de Coutances (Coutances, France, n.d. [?1985])
E. Jensen, see N. Miller
D. Jewell: *Duke: a Portrait of Duke Ellington* (London and New York, 1977, 2/1978)
H.-H. Joehnk: *Baltic Swing: neue Beiträge zu 4 Jahrzehnten Kieler Jazz- und Tanzmusikgeschichte, 1928–1970* (Kiel, Germany, 2000)
——: *Jazz in Kiel: die Kieler Jazzchronik, 1947 bis 1964* (Kiel, Germany, 1994)
——: *Jazz in Kiel: die Kieler Jazzchronik, 1965 bis 1980* (Kiel, Germany, 1996)
B. Johnson: *The Inaudible Music: Jazz, Gender and Australian Modernity* (Sydney, 2000)
C. Johnson: *Paul Whiteman: a Chronology* (Williamstown, MA, 1977, rev. 2/1979)
J. W. Johnson: *Black Manhattan* (New York, 1930)
M. Johnson, see J. Lowe
N. Johnstone, ed.: *The Melody Maker History of 20th Century Popular Music* (London, 1999)
A. Jones: *Plunderphonics, Pataphysics and Pop Mechanics: an Introduction to Musique Actuelle* (London, 1995)
C. Jones: *The Bob Crosby Band* (London, 1946)
——: *Jazz in New York* (London, 1944)
——: *J. C. Higginbotham* (London, 1944)
——: *New Orleans and Chicago Jazz* (London, 1944)
C. Jones, ed.: *Black and White*, i (London, n.d.); ii, ed. R. Venables and C. Jones (London, 1946)
——: *Eye Witness Jazz*, i (London, n.d.); ii (London, 1946)
C. Jones, see also R. Venables
G. Jones, see D. A. Jasen
G. W. Jones: *Black Cinema Treasures Lost and Found* (Denton, TX, 1991)
J. Jones, see L. D. Cunningham
L. Jones: *Black Music* (New York, 1967/*R*1998; Fr. trans., Paris, 1970, as *Musique noire*; Ger. trans., Frankfurt am Main, Germany, 1970/*R*1994, as *Schwarze Musik*)
——: *Blues People: Negro Music in White America* (New York, 1963; Sp. trans., Mexico City, 1966, as *Los grandes del jazz*; Fr. trans., Paris, 1968, as *La peuple du blues: la musique noire dans l'Amérique blanche*; It. trans., Turin, 1968, as *Il popolo del blues: sociologia dei negri americani attraverso l'evoluzione del jazz*; Hung. trans., Budapest, 1970, *as A blues népe: néger zene a fehér Amerikában*; Ger. trans., Darmstadt, Germany, 1979, as *Blues People: Schwarze und ihre Musik in weissen Amerika*)
L. Jones, see also other works listed under alternative name, Amiri Baraka
Max Jones: *Jazz Photo Album: a History of Jazz in Pictures* (London, 1947)
——: *Talking Jazz* (London, 1987/*R*2000) [colln of previously pubd interviews]
Max Jones and J. Chilton: *Louis: the Louis Armstrong Story, 1900–1971* (London, 1971/*R*1988)
Max Jones and A. McCarthy: *A Tribute to Huddie Ledbetter* (London, 1946)
Max Jones and A. McCarthy, eds.: *Jazz Review* (London, 1945)
Max Jones, J. Chilton, and L. Feather: *Salute to Satchmo* (London, 1970)
Max Jones, see also A. McCarthy
P. Jones: *The Analysis of the Music and Evolution of Style of Composer/Singer/Pianist Mose Allison* (thesis, U. of Missouri, 1985)
——: *One Man's Blues: the Life and Times of Mose Allison* (London, 1995)
T. Jones, see J. Berry
S. Jordan: *Rhythm Man: Fifty Years in Jazz* (Ann Arbor, MI, 1991)
B. Jørgensen: *Leo Mathisen* (Copenhagen, 1962)
E. José: *Jazz: musica y musicos* (Barcelona, 1984)
B. Joseph, see A. Govenar
P. Joseph and H. J. Ottenheimer: *Cousin Joe: Blues from New Orleans* (Chicago and London, 1987) [incl. discography]
E. Jost: *Europas Jazz, 1960–1980* (Frankfurt am Main, Germany, 1987)
——: *Free Jazz* (Graz, Austria, 1974/*R*1994; Ger. trans., Mainz, Germany, 1975, as *Free Jazz: stilkrit Untersuchungen z. Jazz d. 60er Jahre*)
——: *Jazzmusiker: Materialen zur Soziologie der afro-amerikanischen Musik* (Frankfurt am Main, Germany, Berlin, and Vienna, 1981)
——: *Sozialgeschichte des Jazz in den USA* (Frankfurt am Main, Germany, 1982/*R*1991)
E. Jost, ed.: *Darmstadter Jazz Forum 89: Beiträge zur Jazzforschung* (Hofheim am Taunas, Germany, 1990)
M. Jouan: *Notoriéte et légitimation en jazz: l'exemple de Rahsaan Roland Kirk* (Paris, 1999)
J. R. Jové: *Vidas de jazz* (Lleida, Spain, 1995)
J.-P. Julien: *Escale au New Morning* (Paris, 1993) [photos of artists performing at New Morning club, Paris]
J. Jungermann: *Ella Fitzgerald: ein Porträt* (Wetzlar, Germany, 1960)
A. Kahn: *Kind of Blue: the Making of the Miles Davis Masterpiece* (New York, 2000)
E. J. Kahn: *The Voice* (New York, 1947)
K. Kaisla, see T. Kärki
I. Kamin, see J. Lyons
M. Kaminsky and V. E. Hughes: *My Life in Jazz* (New York, 1963/*R*1981) [autobiography of Max Kaminsky]
Kansas City Jazz Museum: *Kansas City and All that Jazz* (Kansas City, MO, 1999)
T. Kärki and K. Kaisla: *Rytmimusiikki* (Turku, Finland, 1946)
T. Kärki, see also M. Niiniluoto
I. Karl, ed.: *Franz Koglmann Pipetet* (Vienna, 1994) [text in Ger. and Eng.]
——: *Hans Koller: the Man who Plays Jazz* (Vienna, 1993) [text in Ger. and Eng.]
——: *24 Mai 1994: Reminiscin' Duke: zum 20 Todestag von Duke Ellington* (Vienna, 1994) [text in Ger. and Eng.]
W. Karten: *Anthologie du jazz classique: la synthèse d'un demi-siècle de swing* (Sierre, Switzerland, 2000)
M. H. Kater: *Different Drummers: Jazz in the Culture of Nazi Germany* (New York, 1992; Ger. trans., Cologne, Germany, 1995, as *Gewagtes Spiel: Jazz im Nationalsocialismus*)
P. Kauffmann: *Jazz Szenen: ethnographisches Solo über einen städtischen Groove* (Wuppertal, Germany, 1997)
F. Kaufman and J. P. Guckin: *The African Roots of Jazz* (Los Angeles, 1979)
O. Keepnews: *The View from Within: Jazz Writings, 1948–1987* (New York, and Oxford, England, 1988) [colln of previously pubd articles]
O. Keepnews and B. Grauer, Jr.: *A Pictorial History of Jazz: People and Places from New Orleans to Modern Jazz* (New York and London, 1956, rev. London, 1959, rev. New York, 2/1966, London, 1968/*R*1981)
D. Keller, see R. Porter
K. Keller: *Oh, Jess!: a Jazz Life: the Jess Stacy Story* (New York, 1989)
C. Kellersmann: *Jazz in Deutschland, 1933–1945* (Menden, Germany, 1990)
D. Kennedy: *Big Band Jump Personality Interviews* (Atlanta, 1993)
R. Kennedy: *Jelly Roll, Bix, and Hoagy: Gennett Studios and the Birth of Recorded Jazz* (Bloomington, IN, and Indianapolis, 1994)
R. Kennedy and R. McNutt: *Little Labels – Big Sound: Small Record Companies and the Rise of American Music* (Bloomington, IN, and Indianapolis, 1999)
W. H. Kenney: *Chicago Jazz: a Cultural History, 1904–1930* (New York, and Oxford, England, 1993)
A. C. Kenton, see W. D. Clancy
B. Kernfeld: *What to Listen for in Jazz* (New Haven, CT, and London, 1995)
B. D. Kernfeld: *Adderley, Coltrane, and Davis at the Twilight of Bebop: the Search for Melodic Coherence (1958–59)* (diss., Cornell U., 1981)
F. Kerschbaumer: *Miles Davis: stilkritische Untersuchungen zur musikalischen Entwicklung seines Personalstils* (Graz, Austria, 1978) [incl. discography]
E. E. Khair: *Passion's Piano: the Eddie Heywood Story* (Atlanta, 1997)
R. Kimball and W. Bolcom: *Reminiscing with Sissle and Blake* (New York, 1973/*R*2000)
L. F. Kiner, see P. R. Evans
I. King and J. Richard: *60 years of Jazz in Croydon and Beyond* (London, 1995)
J. King: *What Jazz Is: an Insider's Guide to Understanding and Listening to Jazz* (New York, 1997)
N. King, see C. Mingus

M. Kington, ed.: *The Jazz Anthology* (London, 1992) [colln of previously pubd articles]
B. Kinnell, ed.: *Jazz Orchestras no.1* (Chilwell, England, 1946)
B. Kinnell and J. Asman, eds.: *Jazz Writings* (Chilwell, England, 1946)
B. Kinnell, see also J. Asman; S. F. Dance
C. E. Kinzer: *The Tio Family: Four Generations of New Orleans Musicians, 1814–1922* (diss., Louisiana State U., 1993)
B. Kirchner, ed.: *A Miles Davis Reader* (Washington, DC, and elsewhere, 1997)
A. Kirili: *Célébrations: l'invitation faite au jazz* (Paris, 1997) [photo album]
A. Kirk, as told to A. Lee: *Twenty Years on Wheels* (Wheatley, Oxford, England, and Ann Arbor, MI, 1989) [incl. discography by H. Rye]
E. Kirkeby, D. P. Schiedt, and S. Traill: *Ain't Misbehavin': the Story of Fats Waller* (London and New York, 1966/*R*1978; Ger. trans., Ravensburg, Germany, 1981) [incl. discography by the Storyville Team]
R. Kirkpatrick: *Stan Getz: an Appreciation of his Recorded Work* (Bath, England, 1992)
J. Kisch and E. Mapp: *A Separate Cinema: Fifty Years of Black Cast Posters* (New York, 1992)
C. Kitzinger, see M. Laverdure
E. Kjellberg: *Svensk jazzhistoria: en översikt* [Swedish jazz history: an overview] (Stockholm, 1985)
P. Klaasse, M. Gardner, and J. Bernlef: *Jamsession: Portraits of Jazz and Blues Musicians Drawn on the Scene* (Weesp, Netherlands, 1984; Ger. trans., with discography by U. Goeman, Königstein, Germany, 1984)
M. Klapholz and M. Laverdure: *New York Jazz, 1964* (Toulouse, France, 1993)
B. H. Klauber: *World of Gene Krupa: that Legendary Drummin' Man* (Ventura, CA, 1990)
H. Kleinhout and W. van Eyle: *The Wallace Bishop Story* (Alphen aan de Rijn, Netherlands, 1981)
J. Klinkowitz: *Listen: Gerry Mulligan: an Aural Narrative in Jazz* (New York, 1991)
C. de Kloet and G. de Wagt: *Mooi Holland: de woelige jaren van de Ramblers* (Hilversum, Netherlands, 1981)
J. van de Klomp: *One Night Stand: Jazzconcerten in Nederland, 1947–1967* (Amsterdam, 1999)
G. Klussmeier: *Benny Goodman und Deutschland* (Frankfurt am Main, Germany, 1989)
H. A. Kmen: *Music in New Orleans: the Formative Years, 1791–1841* (Baton Rouge, LA, 1966)
W. Knauer: *Zwischen Bebop und Free Jazz: Komposition und Improvisation des Modern Jazz Quartet* (Mainz, Germany, 1990 [*recte* 1991])
W. Knauer, ed.: *Duke Ellington und die Folgen* (Hofheim am Taunus, Germany, 2000)
——: *Jazz in Deutschland* (Hofheim am Taunus, Germany, 1996)
——: *Jazz in Europa* (Hofheim am Taunus, Germany, 1994)
——: *Jazz und Komposition* (Hofheim am Taunus, Germany, 1992)
——: *Jazz und Sprache, Sprache und Jazz* (Hofheim am Taunus, Germany, 1998)
Z. Knauss: *Conversations with Jazz Musicians* (Detroit, 1977)
J. Knowles: *Lennie Breau Fingerstyle Jazz* (Pacific, MO, *c*1985)
R. H. Knowles: *Fallen Heroes: a History of New Orleans Brass Bands* (New Orleans, 1996)
K. Knox and G. Lindkvist: *Jazz amour affair: en bok om Lars Gullin* (Stockholm, 1986) [incl. discography]
L. O. Koch: *Yardbird Suite: a Compendium of the Music and Work of Charlie Parker* (Bowling Green, OH, 1988, rev. Boston, 2/1999)
F. W. Koebner: *Jazz und Shimmy: Brevier der neuesten Tänze* (Berlin, 1921)
R. Koechl, P. Tippelt, and R. Wiedamann: *Dusko Gojkovic: Jazz ist Freiheit* (Regensburg, Germany, 1995) [incl. discography]
D. Koechlin: *50 ans de jazz avec Barney Bigard* (n.p. [Darnetal, France], n.d. [1979])
S. Koechlin: *Le blues* (Paris, 2000)
J. Koemer: *Big Bands* (New York, 1992)
——: *Swing Kings* (New York, 1994)
K. Koenig: *Jazz Map of New Orleans* (New Orleans, 1985) [annotated map]
——: *"Just a Closer Walk": the Walker's Guide to Jazz's History in the French Quarter* (New Orleans, 1988)
——: *Sonic Boom: Drums, Drummers and Drumming in Early Jazz* (Covington, LA, 1990)
——: *Under the Influence: Four Great New Orleans Cornetists* (n.p. [Abita Springs, LA], n.d. [1996])
——: *Words of Mouth: Jazz Oral History Interviewing* (Covington, LA, n.d. [*c*1990])
J. Kofoed, see J. Durante
F. J. Kofsky: *Black Music, White Business: Illuminating the Historical and Political Economy of Jazz* (New York, 1998)
——: *Black Nationalism and the Revolution in Music* (New York, 1970, rev. and enlarged as *Black Nationalism and the Revolution in Music: Social Change and Stylistic Development in the Art of John Coltrane and Others, 1954–1967*, diss., U. of Pittsburgh, 1973/*R*1991, rev. and enlarged 2/1998, as *John Coltrane and the Jazz Revolution of the 1960s*)
P. Kohler and K. Schacht: *Die Jazzmusiker: zur Soziolologie einer kreativen Randgruppe* (Freiburg, Germany, 1983)
P. Köhler and M. Schubert, eds.: *Vom Ragtime endlich auch dem Swing: zur frühen Geschichte des Jazz in Deutschland* (Neu-Isenberg, Germany, 1991)
E. Kolleritsch: *Jazz in Graz: von den Anfängen nach dem 2. Weltkrieg bis zu seiner akademischen Etablierung: ein zeitgeschichtlicher Beitrag zur Entwicklung des Jazz in Europa* (Graz, Austria, 1995)
I. Kolodin, see B. Goodman
G. Koltay: *Benkó Dixieland Band Story* (Budapest, 1982)
B. König, ed.: *Jazzrock: Tendenzen einer modernen Musik* (Reinbek, Germany, 1983)
M. Konttinen, see A. Granholm
B. Korall: *Drummin' Men: the Heartbeat of Jazz: the Swing Years* (New York and Toronto, 1990)
——: *The World's Greatest Jazz Band of Yank Lawson and Bob Haggart* (n.p. [Phoenix, AZ], 1973)
B. Korall, see D. Cerulli
B. Korst, see J. Brand
R. Koster: *Texas Music* (New York, 1998)
P. Kowald: *Almanach der '365 Tage am Ort', Luisenstrasse Wuppertal* (Köln, Germany, 1998)
P. Krähenbühl: *Der Jazz und seine Menschen: eine soziologische Studie* (Berne and Munich, 1968)
E. Kramer, see J. Collinson
D. H. Kraner: *Jazz in Austria: a Brief History and Discography of all Jazz and Jazz-like Recordings Made in Austria* (Graz, Austria, 1969, rev. Vienna, 2/1972, by D. H. Kraner and K. Schulz, as *Jazz in Austria: historische Entwicklung und Diskographie des Jazz in Österreich*) [text in Eng. and Ger.]
W. Kraus, ed.: *Jazz in Bayern* (Regensburg, Germany, 1997)
——: *Jazz in Bayern, Band 2* (Regensburg, Germany, 2000)
E. Kraut: *George Lewis: Streifzug durch ein Musiker-Leben* (Menden, Germany, 1980) [incl. discography]
——: *The Revival: Documents of the American Music Sessions, 1940–45* (Arcegno, nr Ascona, Switzerland, 1986) [exhibition catalogue, Festa New Orleans Music, Ascona; text in Ger. and It.]
S. Kravetz: *Ethel Ennis: the Reluctant Jazz Star* (Baltimore, 1984)
T. J. Krebs: *Momente des Jazz* (Hamburg, Germany, 1991) [photo album]
R. C. Kriebel: *Blue Flame: Woody Herman's Life in Music* (Lafayette, IN, 1995)
F. Krieger: *Jazz-Solopiano: zum Stilwandel am Beispeiel ausgewählter "Body and Soul": Aufnahmen von 1938–1992* (Graz, Austria, 1995 [*recte* 1996])
E. Kriss: *Barrelhouse and Boogie Piano* (New York and London, 1974) [incl. discography and transcrs.]
S. M. Kristensen: *Hvad jazz* (Copenhagen, 1938)
——: *Jazz og dens problemer* (Copenhagen, 1946)
J. Kruth: *Bright Moments: the Life and Legacy of Rahsaan Roland Kirk* (New York, 2000)
A. Kű, ed.: *Benkó Dixieland Band* (Budapest, 1983, rev. 3/1987)
G. Kubik: *Africa and the Blues* (Jackson, MS, 1999)
L. Kuehl and E. Schokert: *Billie Holiday Remembered* (New York, 1973)
J. Kuehn and A. Astrup: *Buddy DeFranco: a Biographical Portrait and Discography* (Metuchen, NJ, and London, 1993)
G. Kuhlmann, see L. Selk
B. J. Kukla: *Swing City: Newark Nightlife, 1925–50* (Philadelphia, 1991)
H. Kumpf: *Postserielle Musik und Free Jazz: Wechselwirkungen und Parallelen* (Herrenberg, Germany, 1975, rev. 2/1981)
L. Kunstadt, see S. B. Charters
J. Kunz: *Back to the Roots: 100 Jahre Jazz* (Vienna, 1996) [with photos by P. Brunner]
J. Kunz, see also P. Brunner
J. Kuzmich, Jr., and L. Bash: *Complete Guide to Instrumental Jazz Instruction: Techniques for Developing a Successful School Jazz Program* (West Nyack, NY, 1984)
A. Lacombe: *Ella Fitzgerald* (Montpellier, France, 1988)
S. Lacy: *Findings: my Experience with the Soprano Saxophone* (Paris, 1994) [text in Eng. and Fr.]
J. Lahr: *Sinatra: the Music and the Man* (New York, 1997)
C. Laine: *Cleo: an Autobiography* (London, 1994)
T. Lalo: *John Lewis* (Paris, 1991) [incl. discography]
E. Lambert: *Duke Ellington: a Listener's Guide* (Lanham, MD, and London, 1999)
G. E. Lambert: *Duke Ellington* (London, 1959); repr. in *Kings of Jazz*, ed. S. Green (South Brunswick, NJ, and New York, 1978)
——: *Johnny Dodds* (London, 1961); repr. in *Kings of Jazz*, ed. S. Green (South Brunswick, NJ, and New York, 1978)
C. Landergren: *Body & Soul: en jazzbok i bild och text* (Stockholm, 1987 [*recte* 1988]) (text in Swed. and Eng.]
P. Landolt and R. Wyss, eds.: *Die lachenden Aussenseiter: Musikerinnen und Musiker zwischen Jazz, Rock und Neuer Musik: die 80er und 90er Jahre* (Zurich, 1993)

P. Landolt, R. A. Meier, and F. Bosshard, eds.: *Portrait Irene Schweizer* (Zurich, 1991)
I. Lang: *Jazz in Perspective: the Background of the Blues* (London and elsewhere, 1947/*R*1976)
H. H. Lange: *Als der Jazz begann, 1916–1923: von der Original Dixieland Jazz Band bis zu King Olivers Creole Jazz Band* (Berlin, 1991, rev. and enlarged Hildesheim, Germany, 2/2000)
——: *Jazz in Deutschland: die deutsche Jazz-Chronik, 1900–1960* (Berlin, 1966, rev. and enlarged Hildesheim, Germany, 2/1996, as *Jazz in Deutschland: die deutsche Jazz-Chronik bis 1960*)
——: *Loring "Red" Nichols: ein Porträt* (Wetzlar, Germany, 1960)
——: *Nick LaRocca: ein Porträt* (Wetzlar, Germany, 1960)
H. H. Lange, see also H. J. Dietzel
P. Lapijover: *Jazz à Nice: photo-parade* (Nice, France, n.d. [1987])
M. Laplace: *Jabbo Smith: the Misunderstood and the "Modernistic"* (Menden, Germany, 1988)
——: *Portraits of French Jazz Musicians* (Menden, Germany, 1985)
——: *Roger Guerin or The Jazz Trumpet, 1946–1988* (Menden, Germany, 1992)
J. LaPorta: *Developing the School Jazz Ensemble* (Boston, 1965)
——: *A Guide to Improvisation* (Boston, 1968)
P. Larkin: *All what Jazz: a Record Diary, 1961–68* (London and New York, 1970) [colln of previously pubd articles]
——: *Reference Back: Philip Larkin's Uncollected Jazz Writings, 1940–1984* (Hull, England, 1999) [colln of previously pubd articles]
S. Larson: *Some Aspects of the Album "Out of the Woods" by the Chamber Ensemble "Oregon"* (thesis, U. of Oregon, 1981)
S. L. Larson: *Schenkerian Analysis of modern Jazz*, i–iii (diss., U. of Michigan, 1987) [incl. transcrs.]
G. Lascelles, see S. Traill
A. Lastella, see P. Boncompagni
Y. Lateef, K. Barron, and others: *Something Else: Writings of the Yusef Lateef Quartet* (New York, 1973)
R. Latxague: *Jazz: la photographie* (Chambéry, France, 1996)
A. Laubich and R. Spencer: *Art Tatum: a Guide to his Recorded Music* (Metuchen, NJ, 1982) [bio-discography]
W. Lauth: *These Foolish Things: Jazztime in Deutschland, ein swingender Rückblick* (Mannheim, Germany, 1999)
M. Laverdure: *Louis Armstrong* (Paris, 1996)
——: *New York Jazz 1964* (Toulouse, France, 1994)
M. Laverdure and C. Kitzinger: *Jazz in Marciac: la belle aventure jazziste* (Bordeaux, France, 1987)
M. Laverdure, see also M. Klapholz
J.-M. Leduc and C. Mulard: *Louis Armstrong* (Paris, 1995)
A. Lee, see A. Kirk
D. Lee, see R. Blesh
P. Lee: *Miss Peggy Lee: an Autobiography* (New York, 1989)
W. Lee: *MF Horn: Maynard Ferguson's Life in Music* (Ojai, CA, 1997)
W. F. Lee: *Stan Kenton: Artistry in Rhythm* (Los Angeles, 1980/*R*1994) [incl. discography; *R* without discography]
——: *People in Jazz: Jazz Keyboard Improvisors of the 19th and 20th Centuries* (Hialeah, FL, 1984)
G. Lees: *Arranging the Score: Portraits of the Great Arrangers* (London and New York, 2000)
——: *Cats of any Color: Jazz Black & White* (New York, 1994)
——: *Leader of the Band: the Life of Woody Herman* (New York, and Oxford, England, 1995)
——: *Meet Me at Jim & Andy's: Jazz Musicians and their World* (New York, and Oxford, England, 1988)
——: *Oscar Peterson: the Will to Swing* (Toronto, 1988, rev. and enlarged New York, 2/2000; Ger. trans., Vienna, 1990, as *The Will to Swing: Oscar Peterson*)
——: *Singers and the Song* (New York, and Oxford, England, 1987, rev. and enlarged 2/1998, as *Singers and the Song II*)
——: *Waiting for Dizzy* (New York, and Oxford, England, 1991/*R*2000)
G. Lees and D. DeMicheal, eds.: *Down Beat Jazz Record Reviews* (Chicago, 1957–64) [annual colln of reviews pubd in *DB*, 1956–63]
G. Lees and J. Reeves: *Jazz Lives: 100 Portraits in Jazz* (Toronto, 1992)
G. Lees, see also L. Tanner
G. Legrand: *Puissances du jazz* (Paris, 1953)
J.-P. Leloir: *Du jazz plein les yeux* (CagnessurMer, France, 1983)
J.-P. Leloir, see also O. Gillissen
C. Lems-Dworkin: *Africa in Scott Joplin's Music* (Evanston, IL, 1991)
H. Lenormand, see Association St. Louis Jazz
H. Leonard: *Jazz Memories* (Levallois-Perret, France, 1995) [photo album]
——: *L'oeil du jazz* (Paris, 1985, 2/1996; Eng. trans., New York and London, 1989, as *The Eye of Jazz*)
N. Leonard: *Jazz and the White Americans: the Acceptance of a New Art Form* (Chicago, London, and Toronto, 1962)
——: *Jazz: Myth and Religion* (New York, and Oxford, England, 1987)
A. Leonardi, see L. Gullo
G. Le Querrec: *Jazz comme une image* (Paris, 1993)
——: *JazzFotos* (Bonn, 1991) [exhibition catalogue]
——: *Photographe de jazz de J à ZZ* (Paris, 1996)
J. Lester: *Too Marvelous for Words: the Life and Genius of Art Tatum* (New York, and Oxford, England, 1994)
D. Levallet and D. C. Martin: *L'Amérique de Mingus: musique et politique: les "Fables of Faubus" de Charles Mingus* (Paris, 1991)
J. Levey: *Basic Jazz Improvisation* (Delaware Water Gap, PA, 1971)
E. Levi and G. C. Testoni: *Introduzione alla vera musica di jazz* (Milan, 1938) [incl. discography]
F. Levin: *Classic Jazz: a Personal View of the Music and Musicians* (Berkeley, CA, and elsewhere, 2000) [colln of previously pubd articles]
R. Levin, see P. Rivelli
L. Levine: *Black Culture and Black Consciousness: Afro-American Folk Thought from Slavery to Freedom* (London, Oxford, England, and New York, 1977)
P. Levinson: *Trumpet Blues: the Life of Harry James* (New York, 1999)
L. H. Levy: *The Formalization of New Orleans Jazz Musicians: a Case Study of Organizational Change* (diss., Virginia Polytechnic Institute and State U., 1976)
L. Lewien: *Charlie Mariano: Tears of Sound: Wanderer zwischen den Musikwelten* (St.-Andrä-Wördern, Germany, 1993) [incl. discography]
——: *Chet Baker: Blue Notes* (Vienna, 1991)
H. Lewine, see F. Driggs
V. Lewis and T. Barrow: *Music and Maiden Overs: my Showbusiness Life* (London, 1987) [autobiography of Vic Lewis]
R. Leydi: *Sarah Vaughan* (Milan, 1961)
I. Leymarie: *La salsa et le latin jazz* (Paris, 1993)
——: *Latin jazz* (Paris, 1998)
W. T. Lhamon, Jr.: *Deliberate Speed: the Origins of a Cultural Style in the American 1950s* (Washington, DC, 1990)
K. Libisch: *Feketére festve: Szabó Gábor gitárművész bio-diszkográfiája* [Painted black: bio-discography of the guitar artist Gábor Szabó] (Budapest, 1993, 4/1998)
K. Libisch and G.G. Simon: *Dudás Lajos* (Sikonda, Hungary, 1988) [biography of Lajos Dudás]
G. Lichtenstein and L. Dankner: *Musical Gumbo: the Music of New Orleans* (New York, 1993)
S. R. Lieb: *Mother of the Blues: a Study of Ma Rainey* (Amherst, MA, 1981) [incl. discography]
J. L. Lieberman: *Blues Fiddle* (New York and elsewhere, 1986) [incl. transcrs.]
D. Liebman: *Self-portrait of a Jazz Artist: Musical Thoughts and Realities* (Rottenberg, Germany, 1988, rev. 2/1996)
D. Liebman and others: *Lookout Farm: a Case Study of Improvisation for Small Jazz Group* (n.p., 1978)
D. Liebman, see also L. Fisher
B. Liebscher, see D. Berg
A. Ligthart, see T. Wilson
G. Lindkvist, see K. Knox
H.-J. Lindner, see B. Noglik
L. Lindström, see H. Eklund
N. Linehan: *Norm Linehan's Australian Jazz Picture Book* (Salisbury, Australia, 1980)
N. Linehan, ed.: *Bob Barnard, Graeme Bell, Bill Haesler, John Sangster, on the Australian Jazz Convention* (?Melbourne, Australia, 1981)
N. Linehan, see also T. McCardell
O. Lington: *Jazz skal der til* [Jazz is what we need] (Copenhagen, 1941)
K. Lippegaus, see I. Wulff
H. Lippmann, ed.: *Das Barrelhouse-Buch: 40 Jahre Jazz* (Frankfurt am Main, Germany, 1993) [incl. discography of Barrelhouse Jazz Band]
A. Little: *From Harlem to the Rhine* (New York, 1936)
J. Litweiler: *The Freedom Principle: Jazz after 1958* (New York, 1984/*R*1990; Ger. trans., Schaftlach, Germany, 1988, as *Das Prinzip Freiheit: Jazz nach 1958*)
——: *Ornette Coleman: a Harmolodic Life* (London, 1992, New York, 1994)
G. Lock: *Blutopia: Visions of the Future and Revisions of the Past in the Works of Sun Ra, Duke Ellington, and Anthony Braxton* (Durham, NC, 1999)
——: *Chasing the Vibration: Meetings with Creative Musicians* (Exeter, England, 1994)
——: *Forces in Motion: Anthony Braxton and the Meta-reality of Creative Music: Interviews and Tour Notes, England, 1985* (London, 1988, New York, 1989) [incl. work-list, discography, and bibliography]
——: *Mixtery: a Festschrift for Anthony Braxton* (Exeter, England, 1995)
A. Lodetti: *Jazz e jazzmen: le radici e i protagonisti della musica afro-americana* (Milan, Italy, 1992)
E. Løgager, see A. Barnett
A. Lomax: *Mister Jelly Roll: the Fortunes of Jelly Roll Morton, New Orleans Creole and "Inventor of Jazz"* (New York, 1950, London, 1952, Berkeley, CA, 2/1973/*R*1993; Fr. trans., Paris, 1964/*R*1980, as *Mister Jelly Roll: les aventures de Jelly Roll Morton, créole de la Nouvelle Orléans et inventeur de jazz*)
G. Lombardi: *New Orleans–Chicago–New York: retrospectiva sul jazz tradizionale alla ricerca di un patrimonio de salvare* (Anzio, Italy, 1993)

R. A. Long: *The Black Tradition in American Dance* (London, 1989)
S. Longstreet: *Jazz from A to Z: a Graphic Dictionary* (Highland Park, NJ, 1989)
——: *The Real Jazz, Old and New* (Baton Rouge, LA, 1956/*R*1969)
——: *Sportin' House: a History of the New Orleans Sinners, and the Birth of Jazz* (Los Angeles, 1965)
——: *Storyville to Harlem: 50 Years in the Jazz Scene* (New Brunswick, NJ, and London, 1986) [drawings]
S. Longstreet, see also H. Carmichael
T. Lord: *Clarence Williams* (Chigwell, England, 1976) [bio-discography]
M. Lorrai and R. Masotti, eds.: *Italian Instabile Orchestra: jazz come ricerca colettiva negli anni '90* (Milan, Italy, 1997) [text in Eng. and It.]
R. E. Lotz: *Black People: Entertainers of African Descent in Europe, and Germany* (Bonn, 1997)
——: *Carlo Minari* (Menden, Germany, 1979) [incl. discography]
——: *Eddie Dittke and his Boys* (Menden, Germany, 1979) [incl. discography]
——: *George F. Hirst* (Menden, Germany, 1982) [incl. discography]
——: *Hot Dance Bands in Germany: a Photo Album*, i: *The Prehistory* (Menden, Germany, 1987); ii: *The 1920s* (Menden, 1982)
——: *Tony Morello* (Menden, Germany, 1981) [incl. discography]
R. E. Lotz and I. Pegg, eds.: *Under the Imperial Carpet: Essays in Black History, 1780–1950* (Crawley, England, 1986)
R. E. Lotz, see also H. J. P. Bergmeier; M. Danzi
S. Loupien: *Miles Davis* (Paris, 1999)
C. Lourie, see F. Wolff
P. Love: *A Thousand Honey Creeks Later: my Life in Music from Basie to Motown – and Beyond* (Hanover, NH, and London, 1997)
J. Lowe, C. Preiss, and M. Johnson: *Jazz: Photographs of the Masters* (New York, 1994; Fr. trans., Paris, 1995, as *Jazz: portraits des maîtres*)
G. Lowinger: *Jazz Violin: Roots and Branches* (New York and London, 1981) [incl. transcrs.]
Y. Lucas: *Chet Baker* (Paris, 1998)
R. A. Luckey: *A Study of Lester Young and his Influence on his Contemporaries* (diss., U. of Pittsburgh, 1981)
R. A. Luckey, ed. and transcr.: *West Coast Jazz Saxophone Solos: Fifteen Recorded Solos from 1952–1961* (Lafayette, LA, *c*1996) [incl. transcrs.]
V. Lupo: *Vocal Groups in Modern Jazz, Vocalese: storia, discografia, biografie* (Ferrara, Italy, 1986)
G. Lust: *"The Flat Foot Floogie ... treudeutsch, treudeutsch": Erlebnisse eines Hamburger Swingheinis* (Hamburg, Germany, 1992)
M. Luzzi: *Charlie Mingus* (Rome, 1983)
——: *Uomini e avanguardie jazz* (Milan, 1980)
M. Lydon: *Ray Charles: Man and Music* (New York, 1999; Fr. trans., Clichy, France, 1999, as *Ray Charles*)
J. Lyons and I. Kamin: *Dizzy, Duke, the Count, and Me: the Story of the Monterey Jazz Festival* (San Francisco, 1978)
L. Lyons: *The Great Jazz Pianists, Speaking of their Lives and Music* (New York, 1983) [incl. discographies]
L. Lyons and D. Perlo: *Jazz Portraits: the Lives and Music of the Jazz Masters* (New York, 1989)
L. Lystedt: *Swinging Umeå* (Umeå, 1998)
H. Lyttelton: *The Best of Jazz*, i: *Basin Street to Harlem: Jazz Masters and Masterpieces, 1917–1930* (London, 1978); ii: *Enter the Giants, 1931–1944* (London, 1981)
——: *I Play as I Please: the Memoirs of an Old Etonian Trumpeter* (London, 1954)
——: *Second Chorus* (London, 1958) [autobiography]
——: *Take it from the Top: an Autobiographical Scrapbook* (London, 1975)
——: *Why No Beethoven?* (London, 1984)
M. M. McBride, see P. Whiteman
T. McCardell: *Jazz Speaks All Languages*, ed. N. Linehan (?Melbourne, Australia, 1985)
A. McCarthy: *Big Band Jazz* (New York and London, 1974) [*McCarthyB*]
——: *Coleman Hawkins* (London, 1963); repr. in *Kings of Jazz*, ed. S. Green (South Brunswick, NJ, and New York, 1978)
——: *The Dance Band Era: the Dancing Decades from Ragtime to Swing, 1910–1950* (London, 1971/*R*1982)
——: *Louis Armstrong* (London, 1960); repr. in *Kings of Jazz*, ed. S. Green (South Brunswick, NJ, and New York, 1978)
——: *The Trumpet in Jazz* (London, 1945)
A. McCarthy, ed.: *Jazzbook, 1947* (London, 1947)
——: *Jazzbook, 1955* (London, 1955)
——: *The PL Jazzbook* (London, 1946)
——: *The PL Yearbook of Jazz, 1946* (London, 1946)
A. McCarthy and Max Jones, eds.: *Jazz Folio* (London, 1944)
——: *Piano Jazz*, i (London, 1945); ii (London, 1945)
A. McCarthy, see also N. Hentoff; B. Holiday; Max Jones
C. McDevitt: *Skiffle: the Definitive Inside Story* (London, 1997)
M. McGregor: *Chris McGregor and the Brotherhood of Breath: my Life with a South African Jazz Pioneer* (Flint, MI, 1995)
P. S. Machlin: *Stride: the Music of Fats Waller* (Boston and London, 1985)
M. McKee and F. Chisenhall: *Beale Street Black and Blue: Life and Music on Black America's Main Street* (Baton Rouge, LA, and London, 1981/*R*1993)
J. F. McKinney: *The Pedagogy of Lennie Tristano* (diss., Fairleigh Dickinson U., 1978)
R. Mackintosh, see B. Short
R. McNutt, see R. Kennedy
M. McPartland: *All in Good Time* (New York, and Oxford, England, 1987) [colln of previously pubd articles; incl. autobiography]
B. McRae: *Dizzy Gillespie: his Life & Times* (Tunbridge Wells, England, 1988) [incl. discography]
——: *The Jazz Cataclysm* (London, South Brunswick, NJ, and New York, 1967/*R*1985)
——: *The Jazz Handbook* (Harlow, England, 1987)
——: *Miles Davis* (London, 1988) [incl. discography]
——: *Ornette Coleman* (London, 1988)
T. Maeusli: *Jazz und geistige Landesverteidigung* (Zurich, 1995)
——: *Jazz und Sozialgeschichte* (Zurich, 1994)
P. Maffei: *Benny Goodman* (Milan, 1961)
D. L. Maggin: *Stan Getz: a Life in Jazz* (New York, 1996)
P. Maier, see A. Schmitz
J. Majer, see G. Brom
F. Malabe and B. Weiner: *Afro-Cuban Rhythms for Drumset* (New York, 1990) [incl. discography, bibliography]
L. Malson: *Des musiques de jazz* (Roquevaire, France, 1983, rev. Marseilles, France, 2/1989)
——: *Histoire du jazz* (Paris, 1967; Ger. trans., Lausanne and Zurich, 1967, as *Geschichte des Jazz*)
——: *Histoire du jazz et de la musique afro-américaine* (Paris, 1976, rev. and enlarged 2/1994)
——: *Histoire du jazz moderne* (Paris, 1961)
——: *Les maîtres du jazz* (Paris, 1952, rev. 2/n.d., rev. 3/n.d., rev. 4/1962, rev. 5/1966, rev. 6/1972, rev. 7/1979, as *Les maîtres du jazz d'Oliver à Coltrane*, rev. 8/1985, as *Les maîtres du jazz*, rev. 10/1993; Ger trans., Hamburg, *c* early 1950s, as *Die Meister des Jazz*; It. trans., Milan, 1954, as *I maestri del jazz*)
L. Malson and C. Bellest: *Le jazz* (Paris, 1987, rev. 2/1989, rev. 3/1992)
L. Malson, see also A. Coueroy; B. Vian
J. Mance: *How to Play Blues Piano* (New York, 1967)
H. Mandel: *Future Jazz* (New York, and Oxford, England, 1999)
M. Mannucci and F. Fossati: *I grandi della musica jazz* (Milan, 1979)
W. Manone and P. Vandervoort: *Trumpet on the Wing* (Garden City, NY, 1948) [autobiography of Wingy Manone]
H. Manson, see M. Hinton
E. Mapp, see J. Kisch
F. Marchand: *Jazz: manies et collections* (Toulouse, France, 1997)
D. Margolick: *Strange Fruit: Billie Holiday, Cafe Society, and an Early Cry for Civil Rights* (Philadelphia, 2000)
M. L. Mark: *Contemporary Music Education* (New York and London, 1978, rev. 2/1986)
R. Markewich: *The New Expanded Bibliography of Jazz Compositions Based on the Chord Progressions of Standard Tunes* (New York, 1974)
D. Marks, see G. Haydon
D. Marquis: *In Search of Buddy Bolden, First Man of Jazz* (Baton Rouge, LA, and London, 1978/*R*1993; Fr. trans., Paris, 1989, as *Buddy Bolden, le premier musicien de jazz*)
D. M. Marquis: *Finding Buddy Bolden, First Man of Jazz: the Journal of a Search* (Goshen, IN, 1978, rev. 2/1990, as *Finding Buddy Bolden: the Journal of a Search for the First Man of Jazz*)
G. Marri: *Un mare di facce: 10 anni di Umbria jazz* (Rome, 1984) [photo album]
W. Marsalis: *Marsalis on Music* (New York, 1995)
W. Marsalis and F. Stewart: *Sweet Swing Blues on the Road* (New York, 1994; Ger. trans., Hamburg, Germany, 1995)
G. Marsh and G. Callingham, eds.: *California Cool: West Coast Cover Art* (Zurich, 1992)
——: *The Cover Art of Blue Note Records*, ii (Zurich, 1997)
——: *East Coasting: the Cover Art of New York's Prestige, Riverside and Atlantic Records* (Zurich, 1993)
G. Marsh, G. Callingham, and F. Cromey, eds.: *The Cover Art of Blue Note Records* (Zurich, 1992)
D. C. Martin, see D. Levallet
F. Martin: *Bessie Smith* (Paris, 1994)
G. Martin and J. Hornsby: *All you Need is Ears* (London, 1979)
H. Martin: *Charlie Parker and Thematic Improvisation* (Lanham, MD, and London, 1996)
——: *Enjoying Jazz* (New York, 1986)
——: *Jazz Harmony* (diss., Princeton U., 1980)
P. Martin, see B. Crosby
F. Martinelli: *Mario Schiano: discografia* (Pontedera, Italy, 1996)
R. J. Martinez, ed.: *Portraits of New Orleans Jazz: its People and Places* (Jefferson, LA, 1971)
B. Martyn: *New Orleans Jazz: the End of the Beginning* (New Orleans, 1998)

B. Martyn, see also B. Bigard
R. Masotti: *You Turned the Tables on Me* (Milan, 1994) [photo album; text in It. and Fr.]
R. Masotti, see also M. Lorrau
K. Mathieson: *Giant Steps: Bebop and the Creators of Modern Jazz, 1945–65* (Edinburgh, 1999)
B. Matthew: *Trad Mad* (London, 1962)
R. Mattingley: *The Drummer's Time: Conversations with the Great Drummers of Jazz* (Cedar Grove, NJ, 1998)
G. Maty: *Johnny Hess* (Paris, 1997)
A. Matzner and I. Wasserberger: *Jazzové profily* (Prague and Bratislava, 1969)
H. J. Mauerer: *The Pete Johnson Story* (New York, and Frankfurt am Main, Germany, 1965) [incl. discography]
W. Mauro: *Louis Armstrong: il re del jazz* (Milan, 1979)
——: *La storia del jazz* (Rome, 1994)
A. Mazzoletti: *Il jazz in Italia: dalle origini al dopoguerra* (Rome, 1983) [incl. discography]
——: *Stringin' the Blues* (Rome, 1997) [bio-discography of Eddie Lang]
D. Mead, see M. Taylor
E. S. Meadows, see J. C. DjeDje
C. G. Herzog zu Mecklenburg: *Stilformen des Jazz*, i: *Vom Ragtime zum Chicago-Stil* (Vienna, 1973) [incl. discography by M. Scheffner]
——: *Stilformen des modernen Jazz*[, ii]: *Vom Swing zum Free Jazz* (Baden-Baden, Germany, 1979) [incl. discography by M. Scheffner]
C. G. Herzog zu Mecklenburg and W. Scheck: *Die Theorie des Blues in modernen Jazz* (Strasbourg, France, and Baden-Baden, Germany, 1963)
D. D. Megill and R. S. Demory: *Introduction to Jazz History* (Englewood Cliffs, NJ, 1984)
D. W. Megill and P. O. W. Tanner: *Jazz Issues: a Critical History* (Madison, WI, 1995)
J. F. Mehegan: *Contemporary Styles for the Jazz Pianist* (New York, n.d. [?1964–70], 2/n.d. [?1980])
——: *Jazz Improvisation*, i: *Tonal and Rhythmic Principles* (New York, 1959); ii: *Jazz Rhythm and the Improvised Line* (New York, 1962); iii: *Swing and Early Progressive Piano Styles* (New York, 1964); iv: *Contemporary Piano Styles* (New York, 1965)
——: *The Jazz Pianist: Studies in the Art and Practice of Jazz Improvisation* (New York, n.d. [?1960–61])
——: *Styles for the Jazz Pianist* (New York, n.d. [?1962–3])
R. A. Meier, see P. Landolt
A. Melhardt: *Geschichte und G'schictln: 20 Jahre Jazzland* (Vienna, 1992) [history of Vienna jazzclub]
W. F. Mellers: *Music in a New Found Land: Themes and Developments in the History of American Music* (London, 1964/*R*1975)
M. Melloni: *50 anni di jazz a Savona* (Savona, Italy, 1999)
G. Melly: *Mellymobile, 1970–1982* (London, 1982) [autobiography]
——: *Owning up* (London, 1965/*R*2000 with Melly: *Rum, Bum, and Concertina* [autobiography]) [autobiography]
——: *Revolt into Style: the Pop Arts in Britain* (London, 1970)
——: *Rum, Bum, and Concertina* (London, 1977/*R*2000 with Melly: *Owning Up* [autobiography]) [autobiography]
D. Meltzer, ed.: *Reading Jazz* (San Francisco, 1993) [colln of previously pubd articles]
——: *Writing Jazz* (San Francisco, 1999) [colln of previously pubd articles]
M. Meltzer, see L. Hughes
R. W. S. Mendl: *The Appeal of Jazz* (London, 1927)
L. Merian with B. Bridges: *Leon Merian: the Man behind the Horn* (n.p., 2000)
D. Meriwether, Jr.: *The Buddy Rich Orchestra and Small Groups* (Spotswood, NJ, 1974, rev. Chicago, 2/1984, as *We Don't Play Requests: a Musical Biography/Discography of Buddy Rich*)
D. Meriwether: *Mister, I am the Band!: Buddy Rich: his Life and Travels* (North Bellmore, NY, 1998) [incl. discography by Meriwether and C. C. Hintze]
A. Merlin, see F. Bergerot
J. Merod, ed.: *Jazz as a Cultural Archive* (Durham, NC, 1995)
R. Meryman: *Louis Armstrong: a Self-Portrait* (New York, 1971)
E. N. Meyer: *Giant Strides: the Legacy of Dick Wellstood* (Lanham, MD, and London, 1999)
R. F. Meyer: *Backwoods Jazz in the Twenties* (Cape Girardeau, MI, 1989)
M. Mezzrow and B. Wolfe: *Really the Blues* (New York, 1946/*R*1999; It. trans., Milan, 1949, as *Ecco i blues*; Fr. trans., Paris, 1950/*R*1982, as *La rage de vivre*; Ger. trans, Zurich, 1956/*R*1986, as *Jazz-Fieber*) [autobiography of Mezz Mezzrow]
G. Michelone: *Jazz-film: rapporti tra cinema e musica afro-americana* (Bologna, Italy, 1997)
R. Middleton: *The Rise of Jazz* (Milton Keynes, England, 1979)
R. Middleton, see also C. Hillman
T. Middleton, see R. Horricks
H. Miedema: *Jazz Styles and Analysis: Alto Sax* (Chicago, 1975) [125 transcrs. of performances by 103 players]
T. Miessgang, ed.: *Semantics: neue Musik im Gespräch* (Hofheim am Taunus, Germany, 1991)
B. Milkowski: *Jaco: the Extraordinary and Tragic Life of Jaco Pastorius, "the World's Greatest Bass Player"* (San Francisco, 1995)
G. Miller: *Glenn Miller's Method for Orchestral Arranging* (New York, 1943)
M. Miller: *Boogie, Pete & the Senator: Canadian Musicians in Jazz: the Eighties* (Toronto, 1987)
——: *Cool Blues: Charlie Parker in Canada, 1953* (London, Ontario, 1989)
——: *Jazz in Canada: Fourteen Lives* (Toronto, Buffalo, and London, 1982)
——: *Such Melodious Racket: the Lost History of Jazz in Canada, 1914–1949* (Toronto, 1997)
M. Miller, ed.: *Louis Armstrong: a Cultural Legacy* (Seattle, 1994; Ger. trans, Munich, 1996, as *Louis Armstrong: King of Jazz*) [catalogue of exhibition at the Queens Museum of Art]
N. Miller with E. Jensen: *Swingin' at the Savoy: the Memoir of a Jazz Dancer* (Philadelphia, 1996) [autobiography of Norma Miller]
P. E. Miller: *Down Beat's Yearbook of Swing* (Chicago, 1939/*R*1978, repr. 1943 as *Miller's Yearbook of Popular Music*)
P. E. Miller, ed.: *Esquire's Jazz Book* (New York, 1944–6) [three vols., pubd annually; abridged P. Miller and R. Venables (London, 1947)]; see also E. Anderson
W. Miller: *Three Brass: Floyd O'Brien, Maxie Kaminsky, Shorty Sherock* (Melbourne, Australia, 1945)
J. W. Miner, see F. J. Gillis
C. Mingus: *Beneath the Underdog*, ed. N. King (New York and London, 1971/*R*1991; Fr. trans., Marseilles, France, 1982, as *Moins qu'un chien*; Ger. trans., Hamburg, Germany, 1980, 2/1986, as *Autobiographie*)
——: *More than a Fake Book* (New York, 1991) [scores with commentary]
W. Minor: *Unzipped Souls: a Jazz Journey through the Soviet Union* (Philadelphia, 1995)
W. Minor and B. Wishner: *Monterey Jazz Festival: Forty Legendary Years* (Santa Monica, CA, 1997)
J. Mitchell: *Back Together Again: the Story of the Port Jackson Jazz Band* (Sydney, 1995)
N. R. Mitgang, see J. Haskins
A. Moller: *Arthur Briggs* (Menden, Germany, 1981)
N. Mongan: *The History of the Guitar in Jazz* (New York, London, and Sydney, 1983; Fr. trans., Paris, 1986, as *Histoire de la guitare dans le jazz*) [incl. transcrs. and discography]
I. Monson, ed.: *The African Diaspora: a Musical Perspective* (New York and elsewhere, 2000)
I. T. Monson: *Saying Something: Jazz Improvisation and Interaction* (Chicago and elsewhere, 1996)
Montreux Jazz Festival, 1967–1996 (Paris, 1996, Zurich, 1996, as *Montreux Jazz Festival, 1967–1996: 30 Jahre Musikgeschichte*) [photo album; preface by F. Ténot (Fr. edn), E. Gétaz (Swiss edn)]
B. Moody: *The Jazz Exiles: American Musicians Abroad* (Reno, NV, 1992)
E. B. Moogk: *Roll Back the Years: History of Recorded Sound and its Legacy: Genesis to 1930* (Ottawa, 1975)
M. S. Moore: *Yankee Blues: Musical Culture and American Identity* (Bloomington, IN, 1985)
D. L. Moorman: *An Analytic Study of Jazz Improvisation, with Suggestions for Performance* (diss., New York U., 1984)
A. Moré, see Alfredo Papo
F. Morey: *Jazz indépendant: cinq labels d'aujourd-hui: Chabada, ECM, Hat-Hut, Nato, Steeplechase* (Paris, 1988)
A. Morgan: *Count Basie* (Tunbridge Wells, England, 1984)
A. Morgan and R. Horricks: *Gerry Mulligan: a Biography, Appreciation, Record Survey and Discography* (London, 1958)
——: *Modern Jazz: a Survey of Developments since 1939* (London, 1956/*R*1977)
T. L. Morgan and W. Barlow: *From Cakewalks to Concert Halls: an Illustrated History of African-American Popular Music from 1895–1930* (Washington, DC, 1993)
P. M. Morgante, see G. Cane
D. Morgenstern: *Jazz People* (New York, 1976/*R*1993) [with photographs by O. Brask]
D. Morgenstern, see also C. Graham
R. L. Morris: *Wait until Dark: Jazz and the Underworld, 1880–1940* (Bowling Green, OH, 1980; Fr. trans., Paris, 1997, as *Le jazz et les gangsters*)
T. Mortensen: *Miles Davis: den ny jazz* (Copenhagen, 1977)
T. Mosnes: *Jazz i Molde* (Ålesund, Norway, 1980)
T. Motion: *Jazz Portraits: an Eye for the Sound: Images of Jazz and Jazz Musicians* (London, 1995)
G. Mouëllic: *Jazz et cinema* (Paris, 2000)
——: *Le jazz: une esthétique du XXe siècle* (Paris, 2000)
R. Mouly: *Sidney Bechet, notre ami* (Paris, 1959)
J.-P. Moussaron: *Feu le free? et autres écrits sur le jazz* (Morangis, France, 1990) [colln of previously pubd articles]
J. Muccioli, ed.: *The Gil Evans Collection: 15 Study and Sketch Scores from Gil's Manuscripts* (Milwaukee, n.d. [?1997])

H. Mückenberger: *Meet Me Where They Play the Blues: Jack Teagarden und seine Musik* (Gauting, Germany, 1986)
J. Muikku, see A. Granholm
N. Mukoda, ed.: *Jazzical Moods: Artwork of Excellent Jazz Labels* (Tokyo, 1993)
C. Mulard, see J.-M. Leduc
T. Mulhern, ed.: *Bass Heroes* (San Francisco, 1993)
A. Muller: *Blue Burton, 1933–1989* (Schoorl, Netherlands, 1999)
S. Muller, see C. A. Pirie
A. Murray: *Stomping the Blues* (London and New York, 1976/*R*1989)
A. Murray, see also C. Basie
L. Mustazza: *Ol' Blue Eyes: a Frank Sinatra Encyclopedia* (Westport, CT, and London, 1998)
L. Mustazza, see also S. Petkov
W. Muth: *Ernst Höllerhagen: ein deutscher Jazzmusiker* (Magdeburg, Germany, n.d. [1964])
M. E. Nabe: *Nuage* (Paris, 1993)
T. Naitho: *Miles* (Pyworthy, nr Holsworthy, England, 1981) [photographs]
H. Nakadaira: *Jazz Giants of the 60's* (Tokyo, 1981)
H. Namekata, see W. Claxton
C. Nanry, ed.: *American Music: from Storyville to Woodstock* (New Brunswick, NJ, 1972)
C. Nanry and E. Berger: *The Jazz Text* (New York and elsewhere, 1979)
C. A. Nanry: *The Occupational Subculture of the Jazz Musician: Myth and Reality* (diss., Rutgers U., 1970)
M. Nasatir, see D. Cerulli
K. R. Nauck III, see M. W. Sherman
M. Naura: *Jazz-Toccata: Ansichten und Attacken* (Reinbek, nr Hamburg, Germany, 1991)
B. Neely, see P. Fountain
D. Nelson: *Jimmy Giuffre: a List of Compositions Licensed by BMI* (New York, 1961)
J. Nesbitt: *Inside Buddy Rich: a Study of the Master Drummer's Style and Technique* (Delevan, NY, 1984)
S. Nestico: *The Complete Arranger* (Delevan, NY, 1994)
B. Nettl, see C. Hamm
K. Neumeister: *And our Hearts in New Orleans: die Geschichte des Hot-Jazz im Hamburg* (Schacht-Audorf, Germany, 1998)
F. Newton [E. J. E. Hobsbawm]: *The Jazz Scene* (London, 1959, New York, 1960/*R*1989 as by E. Hobsbawm; Fr. trans., Paris, 1966, as *Sociologie du jazz*; It. trans., Rome, 1982, by E. J. Hobsbawm, as *Storia sociale del jazz*)
S. Nicholson: *Billie Holiday* (Boston, 1995, London, 1996)
——: *Ella Fitzgerald: a Biography of the First Lady of Jazz* (London, 1993, New York, 1994; Ger. trans., Munich, 1993, as *Ella: die Stimme des Jazz*; addns, 1996, as *Ella Fitzgerald, 1917–1996: a Biography of the First Lady of Jazz*) [incl. discography]
——: *Jazz-rock: a History* (Edinburgh, 1998)
——: *Jazz: the Modern Resurgence* (London, 1990, New York, 1995, as *Jazz: the 1980s Resurgence*)
——: *Reminiscing in Tempo: a Portrait of Duke Ellington* (London, 1999)
M. Niiniluoto: *Toivo Kärki: siks oon ma suruinen* [Toivo Kärki: the reason why I am sad] (Helsinki, 1982)
E. Nisenson: *Ascension: John Coltrane and his Quest* (New York, 1993)
——: *The Making of 'Kind of Blue': Miles Davis and his Masterpiece* (New York, 2000)
——: *Open Sky: Sonny Rollins and his World of Improvisation* (New York, 2000)
——: *'Round about Midnight: a Portrait of Miles Davis* (New York, 1982, rev. and enlarged 2/1996; Fr. trans., Paris, 1983, as *'Round about Midnight: un portrait de Miles Davis*; Ger. trans., Vienna, 1985, as *'Round about Midnight: ein Porträt von Miles Davis*)
B. Noglik: *Jazzwerkstatt international* (Berlin, 1981, 2/1983)
——: *Klangspuren: Wege improvisierter Musik* (Berlin, 1990)
B. Noglik and H.-J. Lindner: *Jazz im Gespräch* (Berlin, 1978)
R. Nolden: *Count Basie: sein Leben, seine Musik, seine Schallplatten* (Schaftlach, Germany, 1990)
——: *Ella Fitzgerald: ihr Leben, ihre Musik, ihre Schallplatten* (Gauting, Germany, 1986)
D. J. Noll: *Zur Improvisation im deutschen Free Jazz: Untersuchungen zur Ästhetik frei improvisierter Klangflächen* (Hamburg, Germany, 1977)
C. Norman: *Musikant med brutet gehör* [Musician with broken ear] (Stockholm, 1980)
G. Oakley: *The Devil's Music: a History of the Blues* (London, 1976; Fr. trans., Paris, 1985, as *Devil's Music: une histoire du blues*; Ger. trans., Bergisch-Gladbach, Germany, 1981, as *Blues: die schwarze Musik: die Geschichte des Blues*)
R. O'Brien: *Louis Armstrong* (Zurich, 1960)
P. Occhiuto, ed.: *Umbria & jazz: 25 anni de musica* (Milan, 1998) [photo album]
S. J. O'Connell: *Bing: a Voice for All Seasons* (Tralee, Ireland, 1984) [incl. discography]
P. O'Connor, see B. Hammond
A. O'Day and G. Eells: *High Times, Hard Times* (New York, 1981, rev. 2/1989) [incl. discography] [autobiography of Anita O'Day]
J. Ody, see P. du Petit
J. Oehlmann, ed.: *Jazzaz: Texte zur Jazzmusik* (Giessen, Germany, 1982)
K. J. Ogren: *The Jazz Revolution: Twenties America and the Meaning of Jazz* (New York, and Oxford, England, 1989)
W. Ojakäär: *Continuity of National Tradition in Estonian Jazz* (Menden, Germany, 1989)
G. Økland, see O. Angell
J. Oldenhove, see S. Grappelli
D. Oliphant: *Texan Jazz* (Austin, TX, 1996)
D. Oliphant, ed.: *The Bebop Revolution in Words and Music* (Austin, TX, 1994)
P. Oliver: *Bessie Smith* (London, 1959); repr. in *Kings of Jazz*, ed. S. Green (South Brunswick, NJ, and New York, 1978)
——: *Blues Fell this Morning: the Meaning of the Blues* (London, 1960, New York, 1961, as *The Meaning of the Blues*; Fr. trans., Paris, 1962, as *Le monde du blues*; rev. Cambridge, England, 2/1990; Ger trans., Vienna, 1991, as *Blues Fell this Morning*)
——: *Blues off the Record: Thirty Years of Blues Commentary* (Tunbridge Wells, England, and New York, 1984) [colln of previously pubd items]
——: *Conversation with the Blues* (London, 1965, rev. Cambridge, England, 2/1997)
——: *Savannah Syncopators: African Retentions in the Blues* (London, 1970)
——: *Screening the Blues* (London, 1968, New York, 1970/*R*1989, as *Aspects of the Blues Tradition*)
——: *Songsters and Saints: Vocal Traditions on Race Records* (Cambridge, England, and elsewhere, 1984)
——: *The Story of the Blues* (London, 1969/*R*1982, rev. 2/1997; Sp. trans., Madrid, 1977, as *Historia del blues*; Ger. trans., St. Andrä-Wördern, Germany, 1978/*R*1994, as *Die Story des Blues*)
P. Oliver, ed.: *Black Music in Britain: Essays on the Afro-Asian Contribution to Popular Music* (Milton Keynes, England, and Philadelphia, 1990)
P. Oliver, M. Harrison, and W. Bolcom: *The New Grove Gospel, Blues and Jazz* (London and New York, 1986 [*recte* 1987])
P. Oliver and others: *Yonder Come the Blues* (Cambridge, England, 2001) [rev. repr. of P. Oliver: *Savannah Syncopators: African Retentions in the Blues* (London, 1970); R. M. W. Dixon and J. Godrich: *Recording the Blues* (London, 1970); T. Russell: *Blacks, Whites and Blues* (London, 1970); with additional material by P. Oliver, T. Russell, and H. Rye]
S. Ollivier: *Charles Mingus* (Paris, 1997)
B. Olsson: *Memphis Blues and Jug Bands* (London, 1970)
R. O'Meally: *Lady Day: the Many Faces of Billie Holiday* (New York, 1991; Ger. trans., St. Andrä-Wördern, 1995, as *Billie Holiday: Lady Day*)
R. G. O'Meally, ed.: *The Jazz Cadence of American Culture* (New York, 1998)
H. O'Neal: *Charlie Parker: Norman Granz Jam Session Series* (Paris, 1995)
——: *Les fantômes de Harlem: l'histoire du quartier mythique de jazz* (Levallois-Perret, France, 1997)
H. O'Neal, see also E. Bubley; E. Condon
L. Onori: *Jazz e Africa* (Anzio, Italy, 1996)
On Stage, Backstage: Montreux Jazz Festival (Lausanne, Switzerland, 1986) [photographs]
J. Orlay: *Jazzdobbal a világ körül* [Around the world with jazz drums] (Budapest, 1943) [autobiography of Chappy]
W. Ortiz: *Music: Black, White & Blue* (New York, 1972)
N. R. Ortiz Oderigo: *Estética del jazz* (Buenos Aires, 1951)
——: *História del jazz* (Buenos Aires, 1952)
——: *Panorama de la música afroamericana* (Buenos Aires, 1944)
——: *Perfiles del jazz* (Buenos Aires, 1955)
H. D. Osgood: *So This is Jazz* (Boston, 1926/*R*1978)
J. R. Osterholm: *Bing Crosby: a Bio-bibliography* (Westport, CT, 1994)
H. Osterwald: *Kriminaltango: die Geschichte meines Leben* (Berne, 1999)
L. Ostransky: *The Anatomy of Jazz* (Seattle, 1960)
——: *Jazz City: the Impact of our Cities on the Development of Jazz* (Englewood Cliffs, NJ, and London, 1978)
——: *Understanding Jazz* (Englewood Cliffs, NJ, 1977)
J. Otis: *Listen to the Lambs* (New York, 1968)
——: *Upside your Head! Rhythm and Blues on Central Avenue* (Hanover, NH, and London, 1993)
H. J. Ottenheimer, see P. Joseph
T. Owens: *Bebop: the Music and its Players* (New York, and Oxford, England, 1995)
——: *Charlie Parker: Techniques of Improvisation* (diss., UCLA, 1974)
——: *Improvisation Techniques of the Modern Jazz Quartet* (thesis, UCLA, 1965)
D. Oxtot and J. Goggin: *Jazz Scrapbook: Dick Oxtot: Me and other Stuff* (Berkeley, CA, 1999)
G. Paczynski: *Une histoire de la batterie de jazz*, i: *Des origines aux années swing* (Paris, 1997); ii: *Les années bebop: la voie royal et les chemins de traverse* (Paris, 2000)
C. I. Page: *Boogie Woogie Stomp: Albert Ammons and his Music* (Cleveland, 1997) [incl. discography]

D. Page: *Drew's Blues: a Sideman's Life with the Big Bands* (Baton Rouge, LA, and London, 1980)
A. Pailler: *Plaisir d'Ellington: Le Duke et ses hommes, 1940–1942* (Paris, 1998)
S. Pál: *A hazai jazz-történet emlékei*, I rész: *Csányi Attila tanulmánya és lemezei Alapján* [Relics of Hungarian jazz history, vol. i: After Attila Csányi' s essay and recordings] (Budapest, 1983)
J. Palau: *Los grandes del jazz* (Madrid, 1980)
Richard Palmer: *Oscar Peterson* (Tunbridge Wells, England, 1984) [incl. discography]
——: *Sonny Rollins: the Cutting Edge* (Hull, England, 1998)
——: *Stan Getz* (London, 1988)
Robert Palmer: *Deep Blues* (New York and London, 1981)
H. Panassié: *La bataille du jazz* (Paris, 1965)
——: *Cinq mois à New-York* (Paris, 1947)
——: *Douze années de jazz (1927–1938): souvenirs* (Paris, 1946)
——: *Histoire du vrai jazz* (Paris, 1959; Sp. trans., Barcelona, 1961, as *Historia del verdadero jazz*)
——: *Le jazz hot* (Paris, 1934; Eng. trans., rev. Panassié, London and New York, 1936/*R*1970, as *Hot Jazz*; Sp. trans., Santiago de Chile, 1939, as *Hot jazz: guia de la musica swing*)
——: *Jazz panorama* (Paris, 1950)
——: *Louis Armstrong* (Paris, 1947)
——: *Louis Armstrong* (Paris, 1969; Eng. trans., New York, 1971/*R*1980)
——: *Monsieur Jazz* (Paris, 1975)
——: *La musique de jazz et le swing* (Paris, 1943, [2]/1945; Dan. trans., Copenhagen, 1944, as *Jazzmusik og swing*; Swed. trans., Stockholm, 1945, as *Jazzmusik och swing*)
——: *The Real Jazz* (New York and Toronto, 1942 [in Eng. trans.], rev. and enlarged 2/1960/*R*1973 by Panassié; Fr. orig. pubd as *La véritable musique de jazz*, Paris, 1945, rev. and enlarged 2/1952; Sp. trans., Buenos Aires, unknown date, as *El autentico jazz*)
——: *Quand Mezzrow enregistre* (Paris, 1952)
W. Panek, ed.: *Z Polskiej krytyki jazzoweg: eseje, dyskasje, reportaze, recenzje, felietony, wywiady, 1956–1976* (Kraków, Poland, 1978)
J. Panish: *The Color of Jazz: Race and Representation in Postwar American Culture* (Jackson, MI, 1997)
Alfredo Papo: *El jazz a Catalunya* (Barcelona, 1985)
——: *Jazz para cinco instrumentos* (Barcelona, 1975) [with photographs by A. Turbau; text in Sp., Eng., and Fr.]
Alfredo Papo and J. Suñol: *30 anos de jazz: vistos por Aguilar Moré* (Barcelona, 1987) [portraits by A. Moré, with photographs by Anna Papo and J. Suñol; text in Sp., Eng., and Fr.]
C. Parker: *Ma vie en si bémol* (Paris, 1993; Eng. trans., Columbia, SC, 1999, as *My Life in E-flat*)
C. Parker and F. Paudras: *To Bird with Love* (Antigny, France, 1981) [photographs]
C. Parker, see also R. Russell
E. Parker: *A Flat Tire on my Ass: the Autobiography of Errol Parker* (Redwood, NY, 1995; Fr. trans., Paris, 1996, as *De bohème en galère: les pérégrinations d'un musicien de jazz à New York*)
T. Parker: *The Greatest Swing Band in the World: the Ted Heath Story* (Oldham, England, 1993)
C. Partsch: *Schräge Töne: Jazz und Unterhaltungsmusik in der Kultur der Weimarer Republik* (Stuttgart, Germany, 2000)
J. M. Pasternak: *Dixieland: the Birth of Jazz* (New York, 1995)
G. Patane: *Be-bop ou pas be-bop? ou A la découverte du jazz* (Geneva, 1951)
J. Patrick, see M. Berger
L. Patruno and F. Biagi: *Una vita in jazz e non solo* (Rome, 2000)
F. Paudras: *La danse des infidèles: Bud Powell* (Paris, 1986; Eng. trans., New York, 1998, as *Dance of the Infidels: a Portrait of Bud Powell*)
F. Paudras, see also C. Parker
B. Paulot: *Albert Mangelsdorff: Gespräche* (Waakirchen, Germany, 1993)
A. Pavlow: *The R&B Book: a Disc-history of Rhythm and Blues* (Providence, RI, 1983) [covers the period 1920–*c*1980]
N. W. Pearson, Jr.: *Goin' to Kansas City* (Urbana, IL, and London, 1988)
S. Pease: *Boogie-woogie Piano Styles* (Chicago, 1940, 1943) [incl. transcrs.]
C. Pecoraro, ed.: *Giovanni Tommaso: quarnt'anni di jazz* (Salerno, Italy, 1998)
I. Pegg, see R. E. Lotz
D. Pener: *The Swing Book* (Boston, New York, and London, 1999)
A. Pepper and L. Pepper: *Straight Life: the Story of Art Pepper* (New York and London, 1979, rev. New York, 2/1994; Fr. trans., Marseilles, France, 1989, as *Straight Life*) [incl. discography by T. Selbert]
B. W. Peretti: *The Creation of Jazz: Music, Race, and Culture in Urban America* (Urbana, IL, 1992)
——: *Jazz in American Culture* (Chicago, 1997)
J. P. Perhonis: *The Bix Beiderbecke Story: the Jazz Musician in Legend, Fiction, and Fact* (diss., U. of Minnesota, 1978)
D. Perlo, see L. Lyons
R. Pernet: *Jazz in Little Belgium, 1881–1966* (Brussels, 1967)
A. Pernye: *A jazz* (Budapest, 1964, rev. 2/1966)
M. Perrin: *All that Jazz* (Paris, 1995) [colln of previously pubd articles]
D. Perry: *Jazz Greats* (London, 1996)
C. Persip: *How Not to Play Drums (Not for Drummers Only)* (New York, 1987)
G. Pestureau, see B. Vian
S. Petkov and L. Mustazza, eds.: *The Frank Sinatra Reader* (New York, and Oxford, England, 1995) [colln of previously pubd articles]
H. Petrik: *Bill Evans: sein Leben, seine Musik, seine Schallplatten* (Schaftlach, Germany, 1989)
L. T. Petruzzi: *Lead Trumpet Performance in the Thad Jones–Mel Lewis Jazz Orchestra: an Analysis of Style and Performance Practices* (diss., New York U., 1993)
P. Pettinger: *Bill Evans: How my Heart Sings* (New Haven, CT, and London, 1998)
P. du Peuty, see C. Delaunay
T. Piazza: *Blues Up and Down: Jazz in our Time* (New York, 1997) [colln of previously pubd articles]
T. Piazza, ed.: *Setting the Tempo: 50 Years of Great Jazz Liner Notes* (New York and elsewhere, 1996)
J. Picardi, see D. Wade
A. Pierraci, see K. Tocchi
M. Pinfold: *Louis Armstrong* (Tunbridge Wells, England, and New York, 1987) [incl. discography]
M. Pinfold, see also B. Crowther
C. A. Pirie and S. Muller: *Artistry in Kenton: the Bio-discography of Stan Kenton and his Music*, i (Vienna, 1969, rev. 1995, as C. Pirie: *Artistry in Rhythm*, i); ii (Vienna, 1973)
S. Placksin: *American Women in Jazz, 1900 to the Present: their Words, Lives, and Music* (New York, 1982, London, 1985, as *Jazzwomen, 1900 to the Present: their Words, Lives, and Music*; Ger. trans., Vienna, 1989)
H. Pleasants: *Death of a Music? The Decline of the European Tradition and the Rise of Jazz* (London, 1961)
——: *The Great American Popular Singers* (New York, 1974)
——: *Serious Music, and All that Jazz* (London, 1969)
W. Poehlert: *Jazz: 100 Jahre: die Geschichte des authentischen Jazz vom Blues der schwarzen Sklaven bis zum Free-Jazz der 60er Jahre* (Schwetzingen, Germany, 1989)
U. G. Poiger: *Jazz, Rock and Rebels: Cold-war Politics and American Culture in a Divided Germany* (Berkeley, CA, 2000)
N. Poindexter: *The Pony Express: Memoirs of a Jazz Musician* (Frankfurt am Main, Germany, 1985)
J.-L. Poirier and B. Aimé: *Blues graphimes* (Saint-Contest, France, 1989)
I. Poledňák: *Mne všechno dvakrát, aneb, O Jiřím Stivinovi* [Twice as much for me, or, On Jiří Stivín] (Prague, 1989)
I. Poledňák, see also L. Dorůžka
E. F. Polic: *The Glenn Miller Army Air Force Band: Sustineo alas – I Sustain the Wings* (Metuchen, NJ, and London, 1989)
A. Polillo: *Jazz* (Segrate, Italy, 1998)
——: *Jazz: la vicenda e i protagonisti della musica afroamericana* (Milan, n.d [?1977]; Ger. trans., Munich and Berlin, 1978, rev. Munich, 2/1981, rev. 3/1987, as *Jazz: Geschichte und Persönlichkeiten der afro-amerikan Musik*)
——: *Stasera jazz* (Milan, 1978)
J. Poling: *Esquire's World of Jazz* (New York, 1962, rev. 2/1975)
B. Polster: *"Swing Heil": Jazz im Nationalsozialismus* (Berlin, 1989)
A. Pomerance: *Repeal of the Blues* (Secaucus, NJ, 1988)
J. Ponzio and F. Postif: *Blue Monk: un portrait de Thelonious: essai* (Arles, France, 1995; Ger. trans., St. Andrä-Wördern, Germany, 1997, as *Blue Monk: Prophet der Moderne in Jazz*)
F. Porret and H. Porret: *Les années folles et le jazz band* (Le Chaffaut, France, 1994) [biography of Julien Porret]
L. Porter: *Jazz, a Century of Change: Readings and New Essays* (New York and elsewhere, 1997)
——: *John Coltrane: his Life and Music* (Ann Arbor, MI, 1998)
——: *John Coltrane's Music of 1960 through 1967: Jazz Improvisation as Composition* (diss., Brandeis U., 1983)
——: *Lester Young* (Boston and London, 1985)
L. Porter, ed.: *A Lester Young Reader* (Washington, DC, and London, 1991)
L. Porter, M. Ullman, and E. Hazell: *Jazz: from its Origins to the Present* (Englewood Cliffs, NJ, 1993)
L. Porter, see also Y. Fujioka
R. Porter: *There and Back*, ed. D. Keller (Wheatley, Oxford, England, and Baton Rouge, LA, 1993) [incl. discography]
S. Porto: *Pequeña história do jazz* (Rio de Janeiro, 1953)
K. Porzelt: *Die Swingstars: Chronik einer Band aus Frankfurt am Main* (Dreieich, Germany, 1987)
F. Postif: *Jazz Me Blues: interviews et portraits de musiciens de jazz et de blues* (Paris, 1998)
——: *Les grandes interviews de Jazz hot* (Paris, 1989)
F. Postif, see also J. Ponzio
C. Poustochkine, see W. G. Gilbert
C. Preiss: *The Steve Lacy Festival Handbook* (New York, 1982) [incl. discography]
C. Preiss, see also J. Lowe

D. Preston: *Mood Indigo* (Egham, England, 1946)
A. Previn: *No Minor Chords: my Days in Hollywood* (New York, 1991)
E. Prévost: *No Sound is Innocent: AMM and the Practice of Self-invention, Meta-musical Narratives, Essays* (Matching Tye, England, 1996)
S. Price and C. Richmond: *What do They Want? A Jazz Autobiography* (Oxford, England, and Chicago, 1989) [autobiography of Sammy Price; incl. discography by B. Weir]
B. Priestley: *Charlie Parker* (Tunbridge Wells, England, and New York, 1984) [incl. discography]
——: *Jazz on Record: a History* (London, 1988; Ger. trans., Vienna, 1990, as *Jazz on Record: die Geschichte des Jazz auf Schallplatte*)
——: *John Coltrane* (London, 1987) [incl. discography]
——: *Mingus: a Critical Biography* (London, Melbourne, Australia, and New York, 1982)
B. Priestley, see also I. Carr
G. Prinssen: *Hannover: Momente in einer Weltstadt des Jazz* (Dudenhausen, Germany, 1999) [photo album]
S. Pujol: *Jazz el sur: la música negra en la Argentina* (Buenos Aires, 1992)
F. Purim with E. Bunker: *Freedom Song: the Story of Flora Purim* (New York, 1982)
J. Putfarcken: *Jazz Portraits* (Kiel, Germany, 1994)
G. Putschoegl: *John Coltrane und die afroamerikanische Oraltradition* (Graz, Austria, 1993)
L. A. Pyke: *Jazz, 1920 to 1927: an Analytical Study* (diss., U. of Iowa, 1962)
R. Quincke: *Jazz + More* (Kiel, Germany, 1992)
B. Raaymakers, M. Brouwer, S. von Canon, and others: *Celebrating Willem Breuker Kollektief 25 Years on the Road* (Amsterdam, 1999) [incl. discography]
R. Radano: *Anthony Braxton and his Two Musical Traditions: the Meeting of Concert Music and Jazz* (diss., U. of Michigan, 1985)
R. M. Radano: *New Musical Figurations: Anthony Braxton's Cultural Critique* (Chicago and London, 1993) [incl. discography]
B. B. Raeburn: *New Orleans Style: the Awakening of American Jazz Scholarship and its Cultural Implications* (diss., Tulane U., 1991)
A. Raggenbass and others: *Jazz in Willisau* (Lucerne, Switzerland, 1978)
D. K. Ramsey: *Jazz Matters: Reflections on the Music and Some of its Makers* (Fayetteville, AR, 1989)
F. Ramsey, Jr.: *Been Here and Gone* (New Brunswick, NJ, and London, 1960)
——: *Chicago Documentary: Portrait of a Jazz Era* (London, 1944)
——: *Where the Music Started: a Photographic Essay* (New Brunswick, NJ, 1970)
F. Ramsey, Jr., and C. E. Smith, eds.: *Jazzmen: the Story of Hot Jazz Told in the Lives of the Men who Created it* (New York, 1939/*R*1977)
J. Randolph, see Laurie Wright
L. Rasmussen: *Sathima Bea Benjamin: Embracing Jazz* (Copenhagen, 2000) [incl. discography]
K. Rattenbury: *Duke Ellington: Jazz Composer* (London and New Haven, CT, 1990)
A. Raymond: *Swinging Big Bands ... into the 90's* (Broomall, PA, 1992)
——: *Swinging Big Bands ... into the Millennium* (Broomall, PA, 1999)
O. Read and W. L. Welch: *From Tin Foil to Stereo: Evolution of the Phonograph* (Indianapolis and New York, 1959/*R*1971, rev. 2/1976)
J. Réda: *Anthologie des musiciens de jazz* (Paris, 1981)
——: *L'improviste: une lecture de jazz* (Paris, 1980)
D. Redfern: *David Redfern's Jazz Album* (London, 1980/*R*1982 as *Jazz Portraits*) [photographs]
——: *The Unclosed Eye: the Music Photography of David Redfern* (London, 1999)
B. Reed: *Hot from Harlem: Profiles in Classic African-American Entertainment* (Los Angeles, 1998)
T. Reed: *The Black Music History of Los Angeles: its Roots: a Classical Pictorial History of Black Music in Los Angeles from 1920–1970* (Los Angeles, 1992)
J. Reeves, see G. Lees
G. Régnier: *Jazz au Havre and Caux, depuis les années 20 ... et ça continue* (Luneray, France, 1997)
S. Reich Ullán: *El jazz y sus criticas: criterio básico de crítica artistica* (Barcelona, 1958)
C. Reiff: *Nights in Birdland: Jazz Photographs, 1954–1960* (New York, 1987; Ger. trans., Vienna, 1988, as *Nights in Birdland: Jazz Photographien aus 1954–1960*)
T. Reig and E. Berger: *Reminiscing in Tempo: the Life and Times of a Jazz Hustler* (Metuchen, NJ, and London, 1990) [autobiography of Teddy Reig]
J. Reilly: *The Harmony of Bill Evans* (New York, 1992)
T. L. Reis: *Just Before Jazz: Black Musical Theatre in New York, 1890–1915* (Washington, DC, 1989)
R. G. Reisner: *Bird: the Legend of Charlie Parker* (New York, 1962/*R*1975)
——: *The Jazz Titans* (Garden City, NY, 1960/*R*1977)
C. Rentsch, ed.: *25 Years George Gruntz Concert Band: "Breaking Walls"* (Basel, Switzerland, 1996) [text in Ger. and Eng.]
Repedések: valami jazz Győrött [Crackings: something jazz in Győr] (Győr, Hungary, 1997)
G. Reynard: *Encyclopédie Jazz Hot: Fusion* (Paris, 1990)
J. Richard, see I. King
C. Richmond, ed.: *Duke Ellington and New Orleans* (Ascona, Switzerland, 1989)
C. Richmond, see also S. Price
S. Richter: *Zu einer Ästhetik des Jazz* (Frankfurt am Main, Germany, 1995)
J. Ridgway: *The Sinatra File* (Birmingham, England, 1977–80)
J. Riedel, see W. J. Schafer
W. Riefler: *Jazz, eine improvisierte Musik: dargestellt an vergleichenden Analysen des St. Louis Blues* (Menden, Germany, 1984)
J. F. Riesco: *El jazz clasico y Johnny Dodds, su rey sin corona* (Santiago, 1972)
T. Riis: *Black Musical Theatre in New York, 1890–1915* (diss., U. of Michigan, 1981)
T. Ripmaster: *Bucky Pizzarelli: a Life in Music* (Pacific, MO, 1998)
U. Risak, ed.: *Drittes Jazz im Film Festival: Programmheft zur Veranstaltung* (Vienna, 1985)
G. Riskó: *Bingó, Benkó!* (Budapest, 1985)
——: *Pege Aladár* (Budapest, 1985)
F. Ritter, ed.: *Heinrich Himmler und der Liebe zum Swing: Erinnerungen und Dokumente* (Leipzig, Germany, 1994)
D. Ritz, see R. Charles; A. Franklin; J. Wexler
P. Rivelli and R. Levin, eds.: *Black Giants* (New York and Cleveland, 1970/*R*1980 as *Giants of Black Music*) [colln of previously pubd articles]
J. S. Roberts: *Black Music of Two Worlds* (New York, Washington, DC, and London, 1972/*R*[?1990])
——: *Latin Jazz: the First of the Fusions, 1880s to Today* (New York, 1999)
——: *The Latin Tinge: the Impact of Latin American Music on the United States* (New York, and Oxford, England, 1979)
E. Rocco: *The Great Lost Photographs of Eddie Rocco* (New York, 1997) [photo album]
N. Rockmore, see L. Borenstein
J. Rockwell: *All American Music: Composition in the Late Twentieth Century* (New York, 1983/*R*1997)
——: *Sinatra: an American Classic* (New York, 1984)
J.-L. S. Rodriguez: *Jazz, flamenco, tango: las orillas de un ancho rió* (Madrid, 1994)
C. Roemer, see C. Brandt
W. Roggeman: *Free en andere jazz-essays* (The Hague, 1969)
A. Roidinger: *Der Elektrobass im Jazz* (Vienna, 1981)
——: *Jazzimprovisation und Pentatonik* (Rottenburg, Baden-Württemberg, Germany, 1984)
——: *Der Kontrabass im Jazz* (Vienna, 1980)
P. Roland, ed.: *Jazz Singers* (London, 1999; Ger. trans., Berlin, 2000)
A. Rollini: *Thirty Years with the Big Bands* (London, Urbana, IL, and Chicago, 1987) [autobiography]
B. Rollins, see C. Calloway
G. C. Roncaglia: *Italia jazz oggi* (Anzio, Italy, 1995)
——: *Jazz e il suo mondo* (Turin, Italy, 1979)
E. Ronowski: *Gene Krupa: seine Musik auf Schallplatten, 1927–1973: Biographie und Diskographie* (Dassel, Germany, 1985)
A. Rose: *Eubie Blake* (New York, 1979)
——: *I Remember Jazz: Six Decades among the Great Jazzmen* (Baton Rouge, LA, and London, 1987)
——: *Storyville, New Orleans: being an Authentic, Illustrated Account of the Notorious Red-light District* (Tuscaloosa, AL, and London, 1974/*R*1989)
C. Rose: *Instants de jazz* (Paris, 1996) [photo album]
P. Rose: *Jazz Cleopatra: Josephine Baker in her Time* (New York, 1989; Ger. trans., Vienna and Darmstadt, Germany, 1990, as *Josephine Baker, oder Wie eine Frau der Welt erobert*)
T. Rosenkrantz: *Swing Photo Album* (Copenhagen and London, 1939, rev. Lowestoft, England, and London, 2/1964, as *A Revised Reissue of Photographs based on Timme Rosenkrantz's Swing Photo Album, 1939: Incorporating a Selection of Photographs from other Rosenkrantz Publications including "Jazzrevy and Swing Music"*)
D. H. Rosenthal: *Hard Bop: Jazz and Black Music, 1955–1965* (New York, 1992)
G. S. Rosenthal, ed.: *Jazzways: a Year Book of Hot Music* (Cincinnati, 1946)
A. Ross, see B. Semeonoff
D. Rouard, see M. Dibango
E. R. Routley: *Is Jazz Music Christian?* (London, 1964)
G. Rouy: *Chet Baker* (Paris, 1992) [bio-discography]
W. Rovere and C. Chitti, eds.: *John Zorn* (Milan, Italy, 1998)
J. Rowe, ed.: *Vocal Jazz* (London, n.d. [1945])
M. Rowland and T. Scherman, eds.: *The Jazz Musician* (New York, 1994) [colln of previously pubd articles]
M. Royal and C. P. Gordon: *Marshal Royal: Jazz Survivor* (London and New York, 1996) [incl. discography by H. Rye]
P. Rubin, see W. Enstice
H.-J. Rüdiger, ed.: *ReFlexion über/an/in Jazz* (Essen, Germany, 1993)
R. Rudorf: *Jazz in der Zone* (Cologne, Germany, and Berlin, 1964)

M. Rüegg: *Vienna Art Orchestra, 1977–1997* (Vienna, 1997)
W. Ruff: *A Call to Assembly: the Autobiography of a Musical Storyteller* (New York, 1991)
H. Ruland: *Duke Ellington: sein Leben, seine Musik, seine Schallplatten* (Gauting, Germany, 1983)
R. D. Rusch: *Jazztalk: the Cadence Interviews* (Secaucus, NJ, 1984) [colln of previously pubd interviews]
M. Rusenberg, see R. Dollase
B. Russell: *New Orleans Style*, comp. and ed. B. Martyn and M. Hazeldine (New Orleans, 1994)
B. Russell, see also L. Borenstein
G. Russell: *The Lydian Chromatic Concept of Tonal Organization for Improvisation* (New York, 1959)
R. Russell: *Bird Lives: the High Life and Hard Times of Charlie "Yardbird" Parker* (New York, 1973/*R*1994; Ger. trans., Vienna, 1985, as *Bird lebt: die Geschichte von Charlie "Yardbird" Parker*; Fr. trans., Paris, 1995, as *Bird Lives* [preface by Chan Parker])
——: *Jazz Style in Kansas City and the Southwest* (Berkeley, CA, Los Angeles, and London, 1971/*R*1983, rev. 2/1973/*R*1997)
R. Russell, see also P. Foster
T. Russell: *Blacks, Whites and Blues* (London, 1970)
T. Russell, see also P. Oliver
W. Russell, comp.: *"Oh, Mister Jelly": a Jelly Roll Morton Scrapbook* (Copenhagen, 1999)
W. Russell, see also B. Russell
W. Russo: *Composing for the Jazz Orchestra* (Chicago and London, 1961)
——: *Jazz Composition and Orchestration* (Chicago and London, 1968, rev. 2/1975)
B. Rust: *Brian Rust's Guide to Discography* (Westport, CT, and London, 1980)
——: *The Dance Bands* (London, 1972)
——: *My Kind of Jazz* (London, 1990)
B. Rust, see also W. C. Allen; P. Foster
J. Rychlik: *A jazz világában (povéry a problému jazzu)* [In the world of jazz] (Budapest, 1963)
H. Rye, see P. Oliver
K. Rysavy: *Jazzimpressionem im Foto* (Menden, Germany, 1988)
D. Salemann: *Five Tenors: Ray Abrams, 1944–1949; Yusef Lateef, 1938–1949; Billy Mitchell, 1941–1950; Sonny Rollins, 1949; Charlie Rouse, 1944–1950: Solography, Discography, Bandroutes, Engagements* (Berlin, 1999)
——: *James Moody, 1946–1951: Solography, Discography, Bandroutes, Engagements* (Berlin, 1999)
——: *Joe Mooney, 1911–1975, a Sunshine Boy? The Story of an Under-rated Jazzman* (n.p. [Berlin], n.d. [*c*1998]) [bio-discography]
D. Salemann, D. Hartmann, and M. Vogler: *Aaron Sachs: Discography, Solography, Bandroutes, Engagements* (Basel, Switzerland, 1989)
——: *Åke "Stan" Hasselgård, 1922–1948: Discography, Solography, Bandroutes, Engagements* (Basel, Switzerland, 1988)
——: *Don Byas, 1912–1950* (Basel, Switzerland, 1992)
——: *Edmund Gregory, Sahib Shihab: Solography, Discography, Band Routes, Engagements, in Chronological Order* (Basel, Switzerland, 1986)
——: *Ernie Henry: Discography, Solography, Bandroutes, Engagements* (Basel, Switzerland, 1988)
——: *Jimmy Heath: Solography, Discography, Band Routes, Engagements, in Chronological Order* (Basel, Switzerland, 1986)
——: *John Brown: Discography, Solography, Bandroutes, Engagements* (Basel, Switzerland, 1989)
——: *Rudy Williams, 1936–1954: Solography, Discography, Band Routes, Engagements in Chronological Order* (Basel, Switzerland, 1987)
——: *Sonny Criss, 1943–1952: Solography, Discography, Band Routes, Engagements in Chronological Order* (Basel, Switzerland, 1987)
——: *Sonny Stitt: Solography, Discography, Band Routes, Engagements, in Chronological Order* (Basel, Switzerland, 1986)
——: *Wardell Gray: Discography, Solography, Bandroutes, Engagements* (Basel, Switzerland, 1986)
G. Sales: *Jazz: America's Classical Music* (Englewood Cliffs, NJ, 1984/*R*1992)
J. Sallis: *The Guitar Players: One Instrument and its Masters in American Music* (New York, 1982, rev. Lincoln, NE, and London, 2/1994)
J. Sallis, ed.: *The Guitar in Jazz: an Anthology* (Lincoln, NE, 1996)
——: *Jazz Guitars: an Anthology* (New York, 1984)
H. T. Sampson: *Blacks in Black and White: a Source Book on Black Films* (Metuchen, NJ, 1977, rev. 2/1995)
——: *Blacks in Blackface: a Source Book on Early Black Musical Shows* (Metuchen, NJ, 1980)
C. Samuels, see E. Waters
K. Sandegren and others: *Boken om jazz* (Oslo, 1954)
W. Sandner: *Jazz: zur Geschichte und stilistischen Entwicklung afroamerikanischer Musik* (Laaber, Germany, 1982)
W. Sandner, ed.: *Jazz in Frankfurt: Geschichten, Bilder, Lebensläufe* (Frankfurt am Main, Germany, 1990)
H. Sanford: *Tommy and Jimmy: the Dorsey Years* (New Rochelle, NY, 1972)
R. Sanjek, see N. Hentoff
R. Santelli, see M. Weinberg
A. Santi, ed.: *Jazz: immagini e note: i concerti de Centro d'Arte* (Padova, Italy, 1997) [exhibition catalogue]
G. Santoro: *Dancing in your Head: Jazz, Blues, Rock and Beyond* (New York, 1994)
——: *Myself when I am Real: the Life and Music of Charles Mingus* (New York, 2000)
——: *Stir it Up: Musical Mixes from Roots to Jazz* (New York, and Oxford, England, 1997) [colln of previously pubd articles]
W. Sargeant: *Jazz, Hot & Hybrid* (New York, 1938, rev. and enlarged 2/1946, rev. and enlarged 3/1964/*R*1975, as *Jazz: a History*)
K. Satoh and M. Davis: *Kohshin the Best to Best Miles* (Kamakura, Japan, 1992)
M. Savage: *Les mémoires de Joséphine Baker* (Paris, 1949)
L. Saxon, E. Dreyer, and R. Tallant, eds.: *Gumbo Ya-ya* (Boston, 1945/*R*)
T. Scanlan: *The Joy of Jazz: Swing Era, 1935–1947* (Golden, CO, 1996)
H.-J. Schaal: *Stan Getz: sein Leben, seine Musik, seine Schallplatten* (Waakirchen, Germany, 1994)
K. Schacht, see P. Kohler
J. Schadeburg, ed.: *The Fifties People of South Africa* (n.p. [South Africa], 1987)
A. Schaeffner, see A. Coeuroy
W. J. Schafer and R. B. Allen: *Brass Bands and New Orleans Jazz* (Baton Rouge, LA, and London, 1977)
W. J. Schafer and J. Riedel: *The Art of Ragtime* (Baton Rouge, LA, 1973)
W. Schätzlein, ed.: *Vierzig Jahre Jazz Studio Nürnberg: ein Kellerloch als Tor zur Welt* (Regensburg, Germany, 1994)
W. Scheck, see C. G. Herzog zu Mecklenburg
M. Scheffner, see C. G. Herzog zu Mecklenburg
T. Scherman: *Backbeat: Earl Palmer's Story* (Washington, DC, 1999)
T. Scherman, see also M. Rowland
R. Schestag and W. Stiefele: *Jazz in Stuttgart* (Esslingen, Germany, 2000)
K. Scheuer: *Bix Beiderbecke: sein Leben, seine Musik, seine Schallplatten* (Waakirchen, Germany, 1995)
D. Schiedt: *The Jazz State of Indiana* (Pittsboro, nr Lebanon, IN, 1977)
D. Schiedt, see also E. Kirkeby
D. P. Schiedt: *Twelve Lives in Jazz* (Parma, OH, 1996)
R. S. Schiff, ed.: *The Jazz Vocalists: a Tribute to the Singers and the Songs of the Jazz and Swing Eras* (New York, 1997)
J. Schiffman: *Harlem Heyday: a Pictorial History of Modern Black Show Business and the Apollo Theatre* (Buffalo, 1984)
——: *Uptown: the Story of Harlem's Apollo Theatre* (New York, 1971)
B. Schiozzi: *Count Basie* (Milan, 1961)
U. Schlicht: *"It's Gotta be Music First": zur Bedeutung, Rezeption und Arbeitssituation von Musikerinnen* (Karben, Germany, 2001)
K. Schmitt: *Pieces of Jazz in Black and Colour* (Kiel, Germany, 2000) [photo album]
A. Schmitt-Rosenthal, see M. Buholzer
A. Schmitz: *Jazzgitarristen* (Schaftlach, Germany, 1992)
A. Schmitz and P. Maier: *Django Reinhardt: sein Leben, seine Musik, seine Schallplatten* (Gauting, Germany, 1985)
F. Schmuecker: *Das Jazzkonzertpublikum: das Profil einer kulturellen Minderheit im Zeitvergleich* (Munster and Hamburg, Germany, 1993)
H. Schneider: *... und Abends Swing: ein Buch voll Jazz, nicht nur für Fans* (Hinterzarten, Germany, 1985)
O. Schnider, see F. Wolff
E. Schokert, see L. Kuehl
J. Schoustrup Thomsen: *Erik Moseholm* (Copenhagen, 1962) [incl. discography]
C. Schreiner, ed.: *Jazz aktuell* (Mainz, Germany, 1968)
H. Schroeder: *Tanz- und Unterhaltungsmusik in Deutschland, 1918–1933* (Bonn, 1990)
J.-P. Schroeder: *Bobby Jaspar: itinéraires d'un jazzman européen (1926–1963)* (Sprimont, Belgium, 1998)
——: *Histoire du jazz à Liège de 1900 à 1980* (Liège, Belgium, 1985)
M. Schubert, see P. Köhler
G. Schuller: *Early Jazz: its Roots and Musical Development* (New York, 1968; Fr. trans., Paris, 1997, as *L'histoire du jazz 1: le premier jazz des origines à 1930*; It. trans., Turin, Italy, n.d./*R*1996, as *Il Jazz: il periodo classico*)
——: *J. J. Johnson: a List of Compositions Licensed by B.M.I.* (New York, 1961)
——: *Musings: the Musical Worlds of Gunther Schuller* (New York, and Oxford, England, 1986) [incl. previously pubd items]
——: *The Swing Era: the Development of Jazz, 1930–1945* (New York and Oxford, England, 1989) [*SchullerS*]
K. Schulz, see D. H. Kraner
D. Schulz-Köhn: *Django Reinhardt: ein Porträt* (Wetzlar, Germany, 1960)
——: *Kleine Geschichte des Jazz* (Gütersloh, Germany, 1963)
——: *Stan Kenton: ein Porträt* (Wetzlar, Germany, 1961)
——: *Wesen und Gestalten der JazzMusik* (Kevelaer, Germany, 1951)
S. Schulz-Köhn: *Die Evergreen Story: 40 x Jazz* (Weinheim, Germany, 1990)

J. Schwab: *Die Gitarre im Jazz: zur stilistischen Entwicklung von der Anfängen bis 1960* (Regensburg, Germany, 1998)
I. Schwerké: *Kings Jazz and David/Jazz et David rois* (Paris, 1927, 3/1936, as *Views and Interviews*) [text in Eng. and Fr.]
W. Schwoerer: *Jazzszene Frankfurt: eine musiksoziologische Untersuchung zur Situation anfangs der achtziger Jahre* (Mainz, Germany, 1989)
R. Scivales: *The Right Hand According to Tatum* (Bedford Hills, NY, 1998) [incl. transcrs.]
J. Scobey: *He Rambled! 'Til Cancer Cut Him Down* (Northridge, CA, 1976) [biography of Bob Scobey]
Rebecca Scott with M. Scott: *A Kind of Madness: Ronnie Scott Remembered* (London, 1999)
Ronnie Scott: *Some of my Best Friends are the Blues* (London, 1979) [autobiography of Ronnie Scott]
L. Seel: *Deutsches Jazz-Festival Frankfurt, 1953–1992* (Frankfurt am Main, Germany, 1994)
T. Selbert, ed.: *The Art Pepper Companion: Writings on a Jazz Original* (New York, 2000)
M. Selchow: *Ding! Ding!: a Bio-discographical Sketchbook on Vic Dickenson* (Westoverledingen, Germany, 1998)
——: *Profoundly Blue: a Bio-discographical Scrapbook on Edmond Hall* (Lübbecke, Germany, 1988) [incl. discography by M. Selchow and K. Lohmann]
L. Selk and G. Kuhlmann: *Lee Wiley: a Bio-discography* (Riverdale, NY, 1997)
B. Semeonoff: *Record Collecting: a Guide for Beginners* (Chislehurst, England, 1949, rev. Lingfield, England, 2/1951) [incl. A. Ross: "Collecting Jazz Records"]
C. A. Sengstock: *Jazz Music in Chicago's Early South-side Theaters* (Northbrook, IL, 2000)
C. Senn: *Hugues Panassié* (Lutry, Switzerland, 1996)
R. Serra and F. Fayenz: *Nottetempo: storie di jazz per immagini e ricordi* (Bolgna, Italy, 1992) [photo album]
J. D. Shacter: *Piano Man: the Story of Ralph Sutton* (Chicago, 1975, rev. and enlarged Chicago, [2]/1994, as *Loose Shoes: the Story of Ralph Sutton*) [incl. discography]
K. Shadwick: *The Illustrated Story of Jazz* (New York, 1992)
——: *Jazz: Legends of Style* (London, 1998)
N. Shapiro and N. Hentoff, eds.: *Hear Me Talkin' to Ya: the Story of Jazz by the Men who Made it* (New York and London, 1955/*R*1966; Ger. trans., Munich, 1959/*R*1984, as *Jazz erzählt*)
——: *The Jazz Makers* (New York, 1957/*R*1975, 1979, as *The Jazz Makers: Essays on the Greats of Jazz*)
M. A. Shaughnessy: *Les Paul: an American Original* (New York, 1993)
Arnold Shaw: *Honkers and Shouters: the Golden Years of Rhythm and Blues* (New York, 1978)
——: *The Jazz Age: Popular Music in the 1920s* (New York, and Oxford, England, 1987)
——: *Sinatra: Twentieth-century Romantic* (New York, 1965)
——: *The Street that Never Slept: New York's Fabled 52nd Street* (New York, 1971/*R*1977 as *52nd Street: the Street of Jazz*)
Artie Shaw: *The Trouble with Cinderella: an Outline of Identity* (New York, 1952/*R*1992) [autobiography]
A. Shay: *What it's Like to be a Musician* (Chicago, 1972)
D. Shepherd and R. F. Slatzer: *Bing Crosby: the Hollow Man* (New York, 1981)
C. Sheridan: *Count Basie: a Bio-discography* (Westport, CT, and London, 1986) [*SheridanCB*]
——: *Dis Here: a Bio-discography of Julian "Cannonball" Adderley* (Westport, CT, and London, 2000)
M. W. Sherman and K. R. Nauck III: *Note the Notes: an Illustrated History of the Columbia 78 r.p.m. Record Label, 1901–1958* (New Orleans, 1998)
A. Shipton: *Fats Waller: his Life & Times* (Tunbridge Wells, England, and New York, 1988)
——: *Groovin' High: the Life of Dizzy Gillespie* (New York, and Oxford, England, 1999)
A. Shipton, see also D. Barker; A. Groves
T. Shoppee, see S. Voce
B. Short with R. Mackintosh: *Bobby Short: the Life and Times of a Salon Singer* (New York, 1995) [autobiography]
D. Sickler: *The Artistry of John Coltrane* (New York, 1979)
B. Sidran: *Black Talk* (New York, 1971/*R*1981; Ger. trans., Hofheim am Taunus, Germany, 1985, as *Black Talk: schwarze Kultur: die andere Kultur im weissen Amerika*)
——: *Talking Jazz: an Illustrated Oral History* (Petaluma, CA, 1992, rev. and enlarged New York, 2/1995)
P. J. Silvester: *A Left Hand Like God: a Study of Boogie Woogie* (London, 1988, New York, 1989)
F.-R. Simon: *John Coltrane* (Paris, 1996)
G. G. Simon: *The Book of Hungarian Jazz* (Budapest, 1992)
——: *John Coltrane öröksege: életrajzi mozaikok* [The John Coltrane Legacy] (Budapest, 1981)
——: *A klarinét dimenziói: portré Dudás Lajosról* [Dimensions of the clarinet: a portrait of Lajos Dudás] (Pécs, Hungary, 1990)
——: *A magyar jazz 1945–1990* [Hungarian jazz 1945–1990] (Pécs, Hungary, 1987, Budapest, rev. 2/1999)
——: *Magyar jazztőrténet* (Budapest, 1999)
——: *A Szegedi Molnár Dixieland története* [History of Molnár Dixieland from Szeged] (Szeged, Hungary, 1984)
G. T. Simon: *The Big Bands* (New York and London, 1967, rev. and enlarged New York, 2/1971, rev. New York and London, 3/1974, 4/1981)
——: *The Feeling of Jazz* (New York, 1961)
——: *Glenn Miller and his Orchestra* (New York, 1974/*R*1980; Ger. trans., Vienna, 1987, as *Glenn Miller: sein Leben – seine Musik*)
——: *Simon Says: the Sights and Sounds of the Swing Era, 1935–1955* (New Rochelle, NY, 1971)
G. T. Simon and others: *The Best of the Music Makers* (Garden City, NY, 1979)
V. Simosko: *Artie Shaw: a Musical Biography and Discography* (Lanham, MD, New Brunswick, NJ, and London, 2000)
——: *Serge Chaloff: a Musical Biography and Discography* (Lanham, MD, New Brunswick, NJ, and London, 1998)
——: *Serge Chaloff: an Appreciation and Discography* (Montreal, 1989, rev. 3/1991)
V. Simosko and B. Tepperman: *Eric Dolphy: a Musical Biography and Discography* (Washington, DC, 1974, rev. New York, 2/1996)
C. O. Simpkins: *Coltrane* (New York, 1975/*R*1989)
N. Sinatra: *Frank Sinatra: an American Legend* (London, 1995)
L. Sinclair, see H. Boyd
Siné and A. Clergeat: *Sinéclopédie du jazz* (Paris, 1996)
A. Singer and H. Singer: *Hal Singer: Jazz Roads* (Paris, 1990) [autobiography of Hal Singer]
B. Singer: *Black and Blue: the Life and Lyrics of Andy Razaf* (New York and Toronto, 1992)
A. Siragusa: *Portrait in jazz* (Alcamo, Italy, 1996) [photo album]
J. Siron: *La partition intérieure: jazz, musiques improvisées* (Paris, 1992)
V. Skaarup and M. Goldstein: *Jazz: dens udvikling, former og udøvere* [Jazz: its development, forms, and creators] (Copenhagen, 1934)
J. Skvorecky: *Talkin' Moscow Blues* (New York, 1990)
R. F. Slatzer, see D. Shepherd
N. Slaven: *Electric Don Quixote: the Story of Frank Zappa* (London, 1997)
J. Slawe: *Einführung in die Jazzmusik* (Basel, Switzerland, 1948)
——: *Louis Armstrong: zehn monographische Studien* (Basel, Switzerland, 1953)
M. Small and Andrew Taylor: *Masters of Music: Conversations with Berklee Greats* (Boston, 1999)
A. Smith, see Bricktop
C. Smith: *Hit the Right Lick: the Recordings of Big Bill Broonzy* (Bedford, England, n.d. [1996])
C. E. Smith, see F. Ramsey, Jr.
G. Smith: *Stéphane Grappelli: a Biography* (London, 1987, Fr. trans., Paris, 1989, as *Stéphane Grappelli)*
G. E. Smith: *Homer, Gregory, and Bill Evans? The Theory of Formulaic Composition in the Context of Jazz Piano Improvisation* (diss., Harvard U., 1983)
J. Smith: *Off the Record: an Oral History of Popular Music* (New York, 1988)
J. D. Smith and L. Guttridge: *Jack Teagarden: the Story of a Jazz Maverick* (London, 1960/*R*1988)
M. P. Smith: *New Orleans Jazz Fest: a Pictorial History* (Gretna, LA, 1991)
W. Smith and G. Hoefer: *Music on my Mind: the Memoirs of an American Pianist* (Garden City, NY, 1964/*R*1975) [autobiography of Willie "the Lion" Smith]
W. O. Smith: *Sideman: the Long Gig of W. O. Smith: a Memoir* (Nashville, 1991)
A. Smudits and H. Steinert, eds.: *Jazz aus Ereignis und Conserve* (Vienna, 1997)
A. Smudits, see also G. Eder
H. Snitzer: *Jazz: a Visual Journey* (Clearwater, FL, 1999) [photo album]
O. Søby: *Jazz kontra europaeisk musikkultur* (Copenhagen, 1935)
Y. Sol: *Faces of Jazz: Polaroid Portraits* (Kiel, Germany, 1991) [photo album]
M. T. Solomon: *Let's Go See Some Jazz* (Sacramento, CA, 2000) [photo album]
A. Sonnier, Jr.: *Second Linin': Jazzmen of Southwest Louisiana, 1900–1950* (Lafayette, LA, 1989)
A. M. Sonnier, Jr.: *Willie Geary "Bunk" Johnson: the New Iberia Years* (New York, 1977) [incl. discography]
E. Southern: *The Music of Black Americans: a History* (New York and London, 1971, rev. 2/1983, rev. 3/1997; Fr. trans., Paris, 1976/*R*1992, as *Histoire de la musique noire americaine*)
E. Southern, ed.: *Readings in Black American Music* (New York and Toronto, 1971, rev. 2/1983)
F. Sovilla: *Jazz bianco e nero: volti e strumenti* (Udine, Italy, 1993) [photo album]
R. Spagnardi: *The Great Jazz Drummers* (Cedar Grove, NJ, 1992)

M. Sparke, ed.: *The Great Kenton Arrangers* (Whittier, CA, 1968) [incl. discography]
M. Sparke, see also P. Venudor
R. Spautz: *Django Reinhardt: Mythos und Realität* (Luxembourg, 1983; Fr. trans., Paris, 1984) [incl. discography]
——: *Luxemburgs Pioniere der leichten Muse: eine Porträtsammlung* (Luxembourg, 1983)
H. Speck, see H. Crowder
R. Spedale, Jr.: *A Guide to Jazz in New Orleans* (New Orleans, 1984)
A. B. Spellman: *Four Lives in the Bebop Business* (New York, 1966/*R*1970 as *Black Music: Four Lives*)
R. Spencer, see A. Laubich
D. Spitzer: *Jazz* (San Francisco, 1994) [photo album]
D. D. Spitzer: *Jazzshots: a Photographic Essay* (Miami, 1979)
D. Spivey: *Union and the Black Musician: the Narrative of William Everett Samuels and Chicago Local 208* (Lanham, MD, New York, and London, 1984)
F. W. Sportis: *Encyclopédie Jazz Hot: Swing* (Paris, 1990)
F. W. Sportis, see also M. Cullaz
Y. Sportis: *Encyclopédie Jazz Hot: Free Jazz* (Paris, 1990)
F. Stacy: *Harry James Pin-up Life Story* (New York, 1944)
T. Stahl: *Sun Ra Materialen/Sun Ra Materials* (Freudenberg, nr Siegen, Germany, 1983, rev. and enlarged 2/1987) [text in Ger. and Eng.; incl. discography]
B. Starr: *I'm in the Groove Man* (Inglewood, CA, 1986)
S. F. Starr: *Red and Hot: the Fate of Jazz in the Soviet Union, 1917–1980* (New York, and Oxford, England, 1983, rev. 2/1994, as *Red and Hot: the Fate of Jazz in the Soviet Union, 1917–1991*; Ger. trans., with additional material, Vienna, 1990, as *Red and Hot: Jazz in Russland von 1917–1990*)
T. Stauffer: *Es war und ist ein herrliches Leben* (Berlin, Frankfurt am Main, Germany, and Vienna, 1968) [autobiography of Teddy Stauffer]
M. Stearns and J. Stearns: *Jazz Dance: the Story of American Vernacular Dance* (New York and London, 1968/*R*1979)
M. W. Stearns: *The Story of Jazz* (New York, 1956, London, 1957, rev. and enlarged New York and London, 2/1958, enlarged 1970; Ger. trans., Munich, 1959, as *Die Story vom Jazz*; Dutch trans., Utrecht, 1961, as *Jazz: verleden, heden en toekomst*; Dan. trans., Copenhagen, 1962, as *Historien om jazzen*; It. trans., Milan, 1957, as *Storia del jazz*; Port. trans., São Paulo, Brazil, 1964, as *A história do jazz*)
R. A. Stebbins: *The Jazz Community: the Sociology of a Musical Subculture* (diss., U. of Minnesota, 1964)
J. T. Steed: *Duke Ellington: a Spiritual Biography* (New York, 1999)
H. Steinert: *Die Entdeckung der Kulturindustrie, oder Warum Professor Adorno Jazz-Musik nicht ausstehen konnte* (Vienna, 1992)
H. Steinert, see also A. Smudits
B. Stenczer, ed.: *"Egy könyv visszhangja": Simon Géza Gábor: magyar jazzlemezek, 1912–1984/Hungarian Jazz Records, 1912–1984* ["Echo of a book": Géza Gábor Simon: magyar jazzlemezek, 1912–1984/Hungarian Jazz Records, 1912–1984] (Pécs, Hungary, 1987)
B. Stendahl: *Jazz, Hot & Swing: jazz i Norge, 1920–1940* (n.p. [Oslo], 1987) [incl. discography]
B. Stendahl and J. Bergh: *Cool, Kløver and Dixie: jazz i Norge, 1950–1960* (Oslo, 1997) [incl. discography]
——: *Sigarett Stomp: jazz i Norge, 1940–1950* (Oslo, 1991) [incl. discography]
C. Stewart and P. C. Harrison: *Chuck Stewart's Jazz Files* (Boston, 1985/*R*1991) [photographs]
F. Stewart, see W. Marsalis
M. L. Stewart: *Structural Development in the Jazz Improvisational Technique of Clifford Brown* (diss., U. of Michigan, 1973; pubd in *Jf*, vi–vii (1974–5), 141–273)
R. Stewart: *Jazz Masters of the Thirties* (New York and London, n.d. [1972])
R. Stewart and C. P. Gordon: *Boy Meets Horn* (Wheatley, Oxford, England, and Ann Arbor, MI, 1991)
D. Stewart-Baxter: *Ma Rainey and the Classic Blues Singers* (New York and London, 1970)
W. Stiefele, see R. Schestag
D. Stock and N. Hentoff: *Jazz Street* (Garden City, NY, and London, 1960)
R. L. Stockdale: *Jimmy Dorsey: a Study in Contrasts* (Lanham, MD, and London, 1999)
——: *Tommy Dorsey on the Side* (Metuchen, NJ, 1995)
T. Stoddard: *Jazz on the Barbary Coast* (Chigwell, England, 1982, rev. Berkeley, CA, 2/1998)
T. Stoddard, see also P. Foster
W. R. Stokes: *The Jazz Scene: an Informal History from New Orleans to 1990* (New York, 1991)
——: *Living the Jazz Life: Conversations with Forty Musicians about their Careers in Jazz* (New York, and Oxford, England, 2000)
——: *Swing Era New York: the Jazz Photographs of Charles Peterson* (Philadelphia, 1994)
J. Stoll and M. Ehlers: *Jazz Memories: a Book of Days* (Corte Madera, CA, 1987)
H. J. Stollenwerk, see R. Dollase
I. Storb: *Dave Brubeck: Improvisation und Kompositionen: die Idee der kulturellen Wechselbesiehungen* (Frankfurt am Main, Germany, 1991; Eng. trans., New York, 1994, as *Dave Brubeck: Improvisation and Compositions: the Idea of Cultural Exchange*) [Eng. trans. incl. rev. and updated discography by K. G. Fischer]
——: *Jazz Meets the World – the World Meets Jazz* (Münster, Germany, 1999)
——: *Louis Armstrong, mit Selbstzeugnissen und Bilddokumenten* (Reinbek, nr Hamburg, Germany, 1989; Eng. trans., New York, 1996, as *Louis Armstrong: the Definitive Biography*)
T. Stovall: *Paris noir: African-Americans in the City of Light* (New York, 1996)
D. W. Stowe: *Swing Changes: Big Band Jazz in New Deal America* (Cambridge, MA, and London, 1994)
K. Stratemann: *Duke Ellington Day by Day and Film by Film* (Copenhagen, 1992)
——: *Louis Armstrong on the Screen* (Copenhagen, 1996)
E. Strickland: *American Composers: Dialogues on Contemporary Music* (Bloomington, IN, 1991)
S. M. Stroff: *Red Head: a Chronological Survey of "Red" Nichols and his Five Pennies* (Lanham, MD, and London, 1996)
J. A. Stuart [pseud. of D. Tait]: *Call Him George* (London, 1961) [biography of George Lewis (i)]
W. E. Studwell and M. Baldin: *The Big Band Reader: Songs Favored by Swing Era Orchestras and other Popular Ensembles* (New York and elsewhere, 2000)
C. J. Stuessy, Jr.: *The Confluence of Jazz and Classical Music from 1950 to 1970* (diss., Eastman School, 1970)
P. Stump: *Go Ahead John: the Music of John McLaughlin* (Wembley, England, 1999)
F. Sturm: *Changes over Time: the Evolution of Jazz Arranging* (n.p., 1995)
D. G. Such: *Avant-garde Jazz Musicians: Performing "Out There"* (Iowa City, IA, 1993)
——: *Music, Metaphor, and Values among Avant-garde Musicians Living in New York City* (diss., UCLA, 1985)
R. Sudhalter: *Lost Chords: White Musicians and their Contribution to Jazz, 1915–1945* (New York and Oxford, England, 1999)
R. M. Sudhalter, P. R. Evans, and W. Dean-Myatt: *Bix: Man & Legend* (New Rochelle, NY, and London, 1974) [incl. chronology and discography]
T. Sugrue, see E. Condon
M. J. Summerfield: *The Jazz Guitar: its Evolution and its Players* (Gateshead, England, 1978, 2/1979, Newcastle upon Tyne, England, 3/1993, as *The Jazz Guitar: its Evolution, its Players and Personalities since 1900*; Blaydon on Tyne, England, 4/1998, as *The Jazz Guitar: its Evolution, Players and Personalities since 1900*)
J. Suñol, see Alfredo Papo
D. Sutro: *Jazz for Dummies* (Foster City, CA, 1998; Ger. trans., Bonn, 1999, as *Jazz für Dummies*)
R. E. Sweet: *Music Universe, Music Mind: Revisiting the Creative Music Studio, Woodstock, New York* (Ann Arbor, MI, 1996)
P. Symes, see P. Gamble
J. Sypniewski: *Ein Problem der Gegenwartsmusik: Jazz, unter besonderer Berücksichtigung des symphonisches Jazz (George Gershwin)* (diss., U. of Zurich, 1949)
G. Szabados and T. Váczi: *A zene kettős természetű fénye* [Double-natured light of the music] (Budapest, 1990)
D. von Szadkowski: *Auf schwarzweissen Flügeln: Jazz-Musik, europäische Perspektiven* (Giessen, Germany, 1983)
J. F. Szwed: *Jazz 101: a Complete Guide to Learning and Loving Jazz* (New York, 2000)
——: *Space is the Place: the Lives and Times of Sun Ra* (New York, 1997)
D. Tait, see J. A. Stuart
R. Tallant, see L. Saxon
L. Tanner: *Images of Jazz* (New York, 1996) [photo album]
L. Tanner, comp.: *Dizzy: John Birks Gillespie in his 75th Year* (San Francisco, n.d. [?1992]) [with an essay by G. Lees]
P. Tanner and B. Cox: *Every Night was New Year's Eve: ... on the Road with Glenn Miller* (Tokyo, 1992)
P. O. W. Tanner and M. Gerow: *A Study of Jazz* (Dubuque, IA, 1964, rev. 2/1973, rev. 3/1977, rev. 4/1981, rev. 5/1983, rev. 6/1987, with D. W. Megill, rev. 7/1992, as *Jazz*, rev. 8/Madison, WI, 1997)
P. O. W. Tanner, see also D. W. Megill
M. Tarabelli: *Il gomito de jazzista: vent' anni di Ancona Jazz* (Ancona, Italy, 1998)
Andrew Taylor, see M. Small
Arthur Taylor: *Notes and Tones: Musician-to-musician Interviews* (Liège, Belgium, 1977, rev. and enlarged New York, 2/1993)
B. Taylor: *Jazz Piano: History and Development* (Dubuque, IA, 1982)
F. C. Taylor and G. Cook: *Alberta Hunter: a Celebration in Blues* (New York and elsewhere, 1987)
M. Taylor and D. Mead: *Kiss and Tell: Autobiography of a Travelling Musician* (London, 2000)

T. Tedesco: *Confessions of a Guitar Player: an Autobiography* (Fullerton, CA, 1993)
F. Ténot: *Boris Vian, le jazz à Saint-Germain* (Paris, 1999)
——: *Boris Vian, le jazz et Saint-Germain* (Paris, 1993)
——: *Je voulais en savoir davantage* (Paris, 1997) [autobiographical sketches]
F. Ténot and P. Carles: *Le jazz* (Paris, 1978)
F. Ténot, see also *Montreux Jazz Festival 1967–1996*
B. Tepperman, see V. Simosko
A. Tercinet: *Be-bop* (Paris, 1991)
——: *Charlie Parker* (Marseilles, France, 1997)
——: *Parker's Mood* (Marseilles, France, 1998)
——: *Stan Getz* (Montpellier, France, 1989)
——: *West Coast Jazz* (Marseilles, France, 1986)
G. C. Testoni, see E. Levi
B. Thiele and B. Golden: *What a Wonderful World: a Lifetime of Recordings* (New York, and Oxford, England, 1995)
W. Thiers: *El jazz ciolla y otra yerbas* (Buenos Aires, 1999)
B. Thomas: *The One and Only Bing* (New York, 1977)
J. C. Thomas: *Chasin' the Trane: the Music and Mystique of John Coltrane* (Garden City, NY, 1975; Ger. trans., St. Andrä-Wördern, Germany, 1993, as *Chasin' the Trane: Musik und Mystik von John Coltrane*)
L. Thompson and J. P. Green: *An Autobiography* (Crawley, England, 1985) [autobiography of Leslie Thompson]
J. W. Thomson, see L. D. Holmes
V. Thomson: *The Musical Scene* (New York, 1945)
L. Thoorens: *Essai sur le jazz* (Liège, Belgium, 1942)
E. Thorpe: *Black Dance* (London, 1989)
T. J. Tichenor, see D. A. Jasen
P. Tippett, see R. Koechl
F. Tirro: *Jazz: a History* (New York, 1977, rev. 2/1993)
J. Titon: *Early Downhome Blues: a Musical and Cultural Analysis* (Urbana, IL, Chicago, and London, 1977, rev. Chapel Hill, NC, 2/1995)
J. Titsworth, see D. Cooper
K. Tocchi and A. Pierraci: *Jazz e la canzone* (Genoa, Italy, 1994)
R. de Toledano, ed.: *Frontiers of Jazz* (New York, 1947, rev. 2/1962, rev. Gretna, LA, 3/1994) [colln of previously pubd articles]
D. Toop: *Ocean of Sound: Aether Talk, Ambient Sound and Imaginary Worlds* (London, 1995)
G. Tordjman, see F. Billard
M. Tormé: *It Wasn't All Velvet: an Autobiography* (New York, 1990)
——: *My Singing Teachers: Reflections on Singing Popular Music* (New York, 1994)
——: *Traps, the Drum Wonder: the Life of Buddy Rich* (New York, and Oxford, England, 1991)
L. Touchet and V. Bagneris: *Rejoice When You Die: the New Orleans Jazz Funerals* (Baton Rouge, LA, 1998) [photo album]
L. Tournès: *New Orleans sur Seine: histoire du jazz en France* (Paris, 1999)
E. Townley, see S. Traill
I. Townsend, see J. Hammond
P. Townsend: *Jazz in American Culture* (Edinburgh, 2000)
W. Tozzi: *Jazz-Drumming: Studien zum Spiel von Jack DeJohnette* (Graz, Austria, 1994)
J. Tracy, see L. Feather
S. Tracy: *Bands, Booze and Broads* (Edinburgh, 1995)
S. Traill, ed.: *Concerning Jazz* (London, 1957)
——: *Play that Music: a Guide to Playing Jazz* (London, 1956)
S. Traill and G. Lascelles, eds.: *Just Jazz* (London, 1957–60) [four annual vols.: incl. D. Coller and E. Townley: *Jazz Discography, 1956[–1957]*; F. Dutton and E. Townley: *Jazz Discography, 1958*; G. Cherrington: *Jazz Discography, 1959/60*]
S. Traill, see also E. Kirkeby
D. J. Travis: *An Autobiography of Black Chicago* (Chicago, 1981)
——: *An Autobiography of Black Jazz* (Chicago, 1983)
——: *The Duke Ellington Primer* (Chicago, 1996)
J. de Trazegnies: *Duke Ellington: Harlem Aristocrat of Jazz* (Brussels, 1946)
J. A. Treichel: *Keeper of the Flame: Woody Herman and the Second Herd, 1947–1949* (n.p. [Zephyrhills, FL], 1978) [biodiscography]
C. Trent: *Another Shade of Blue: Sun Ra on Record* (Exeter, England, 1997)
W. W. Triggs: *The Great Harry Reser* (London, 1978) [bio-discography]
S. Troup, see W. Herman
Q. Troupe: *Miles and Me* (Berkeley, CA, 2000)
Q. Troupe, see also M. Davis
N. Troxler: *Jazz Blvd: Niklaus Troxler Posters* (Baden, Germany, 1999)
——: *Jazz Plakate = Jazz Posters = Affiches de jazz* (Schaftlach, Germany, 1991)
A. Trulls: *Blues: vieja musica, nueva musica* (Madrid, 1996)
A. Tsumura and H. Umeda: *Louis Armstrong: Tsumura Collection* (n.p. [Japan], 1989)
Mark Tucker: *Ellington: the Early Years* (Oxford, England, Urbana, IL, and Chicago, 1991)
Mark Tucker, ed.: *The Duke Ellington Reader* (New York, and Oxford, England, 1993) [colln of previously pubd articles] [*TuckerDE*]
Mark Tucker, see also G. Bushell
Michael Tucker: *Jan Garbarek: Deep Song* (Hull, England, 1998)
S. Tucker: *Swing Shift: "All-girl" Bands of the 1940s* (Durham, NC, and London, 2000)
A. Turbau, see Alfredo Papo
G. Turi: *Art mondom: Jazz: interjúk magyar jazzmuzsikusokkal* [I say that: jazz: interviews with Hungarian jazz musicians] (Budapest, 1983)
——: *Jazz from Hungary: History, Musicians, Contacts* (Budapest, 1987)
——: *A jazz ideje* [Jazztime] (Budapest, 1998)
B. Turner: *Hot Air, Cool Music* (London, Melbourne, Australia, and New York, 1984) [autobiography; incl. discography by M. Clutten]
F. Turner: *Remembering Song: Encounters with the New Orleans Jazz Tradition* (New York, 1982, rev. and enlarged 2/1994)
D. Turrell, see G. Valentin
W. Twittenhoff: *Jugend und Jazz: ein Beitrag zur Klärung* (Mainz, Germany, 1953)
L. Tyrmand: *U brzegów jazzu* [On the side of jazz] (Kraków, Poland, 1957)
B. Ulanov: *Duke Ellington* (New York, 1946/*R*1975)
——: *A Handbook of Jazz* (New York, n.d. [?1957]/*R*1975)
——: *A History of Jazz in America* (New York, 1952/*R*1972; Fr. trans., Paris, 1955, as *Histoire du jazz*)
M. Ullman: *Jazz Lives: Portraits in Words and Pictures* (Washington, DC, 1980)
M. Ullman, see also L. Porter
H. Umeda, see A. Tsumura
L. Underwood, see P. Horn
Union des Musiciens de Jazz: *Le livre de jazz en France* (Paris, 1997)
M. Unterbrink: *Jazz Women at the Keyboard* (Jefferson, NC, and London, 1983)
F. Usinger: *Kleine Biographie des Jazz* (Offenbach am Main, Germany, 1953)
W. W. Vaché: *Back Beats and Rim Shots: the Johnny Blowers Story* (Lanham, MD, New Brunswick, NJ, and London, 1996)
——: *Crazy Fingers: Claude Hopkins' Life in Jazz* (Washington, DC, and London, 1992)
——: *Jazz Gentry: Aristocrats of the Music World* (Lanham, MD, and London, 1999)
W. W. Vaché, Sr.: *Pee Wee Erwin: this Horn for Hire* (Metuchen, New Jersey, 1987) [incl. discography]
P. Vacher, see J. Darensbourg
K. Vail: *Bird's Diary: the Life of Charlie Parker, 1945–1955* (Chessington, England, 1996)
——: *Dizzy Gillespie: The Bebop Years, 1937–1952* (Cottenham, England, 2000)
——: *Jazz Milestones: a Pictorial Chronicle of Jazz, 1900–90* (Chessington, England, 1993)
——: *Lady Day's Diary: the Life of Billie Holiday, 1937–1959* (Chessington, England, 1996)
——: *The Life of Duke Ellington*, i: *1927–1950* (Cambridge, England, 1999)
——: *Miles' Diary: the Life of Miles Davis, 1947–1961* (Chessington, England, 1996)
V. Vale and M. Wallace, eds.: *Swing! The New Retro Renaissance* (San Francisco, 1998)
G. Valentin and D. Turrell: *And all that Jazz: Copenhagen Jazz Festival* (Copenhagen, 1983) [text in Dan. and Eng.]
J. Vance: *Fats Waller: his Life and Times* (Chicago, 1977/*R*1992)
P. Van der Merwe: *Origins of the Popular Style: the Antecedents of Twentieth-century Popular Music* (Oxford, England, 1989)
P. Vandervoort, see W. Manone
W. van Eyle, see H. Kleinhout
H. van Loo, see T. Wilson
G. Van Rijn: *Roosevelt's Blues: African-American Blues and Gospel Songs on FDR* (Jackson, MS, 1997)
H. van Veelo, see C. Hillman
E. A. Vare, ed.: *Legend: Frank Sinatra and the American Dream* (New York, 1995) [colln of previously pubd articles]
T. Vähäsilta, see A. Granholm
A. Vasset: *Black Brother: la vie et l'oeuvre de Big Bill Broonzy* (Gerzat, France, 1996) [incl. discography]
J. Vedey: *Band Leaders* (London, 1950)
H. Vemane: *Swing et moeurs* (Lille, France, 1943)
R. Venables and C. Jones, eds.: *Eye Witness Jazz*, i (London, n.d. [1946]); ii (London, 1946)
R. Venables, see also P. E. Miller
P. Venudor and M. Sparke: *The Standard Stan Kenton Directory*, i: *1937–1949* (Amsterdam, 1968)
F. Verdun, see L. Clarke
J. de Vergnies, see E. Bernhard
B. Vian: *Autres écrits sur le jazz*, i and ii (Paris, 1981; i and ii repr. in 1 vol. 1994; Ger. trans., Vienna, 1990, as *Schriften, Glossen und Kritiken über Jazz*, i: *Rundherum um Mitternacht*, ii: *Stolz und Vorurteile*) [colln of previously pubd articles]

——: *Chroniques de jazz* (Paris, 1967) [colln of previously pubd articles, ed. L. Malson]
——: *Derrière la zizique* (Paris, 1976) [colln of previously pubd articles, ed. M. Fauré]
——: *En avant la zizique* (Paris, 1958/R1971)
——: *Jazz in Paris: chroniques de jazz pour la station de radio WNEW, New York (1948–1949)* (n.p. [Paris], 1997) [text in Fr. and Eng., ed. G. Pestureau]
——: *Manual de Saint-Germain-des-Prés* (Paris, 1974)
J. Viera: *Der Free Jazz: Formen und Modelle* (Vienna, 1974)
——: *Jazz: Musik unserer Zeit* (Schaftlach, Germany, 1992)
——: *20 Jahre Jazz in Burghausen* (Burghausen, Germany, 1989)
——: *Das Saxophon im Jazz* (Vienna, 1977)
J. Viera and others: *Reihe Jazz*, ii: *Grundlagen der Jazzharmonik* (Vienna, 1970)
G. Vigna: *Jazz e la sua storia* (Milan, Italy, 1998)
T. Vincent: *Keep Cool: the Black Activists who Built the Jazz Age* (London and East Haven, CT, 1995)
T. Vinding, see J. L. Fell
I. Vitkovics: *Mister dob* [Mister Drums] (Budapest, 1989) [biography of Gyula Kovács]
S. Voce: *Woody Herman* (London, 1986) [incl. discography by T. Shoppee]
M. Vogler, see D. Salemann
J. E. Vold, see O. Angell
G. Von Physter, see C. Cons
B. Vuijsje: *De nieuwe jazz* (Baarn, Netherlands, 1978)
——: *Jazzportretten: van Ben Webster to Wynton Marsalis* (Amsterdam, 1983)
J.-P. Vuorela, see A. Granholm
I. Wachler: *Benny Goodman: ein Porträt* (Wetzlar, Germany, 1961)
D. Wade and J. Picardie: *Music Man: Ahmet Ertegun, Atlantic Records and the Triumph of Rock and Roll* (New York and London, 1990, rev. London, 2/1993, as J. Picardie and D. Wade: *Atlantic and the Godfathers of Rock and Roll*)
G. de Wagt, see C. de Kloet
T. Waldo: *This is Ragtime* (New York, 1976) [incl. discography]
E. S. Walker: *Don't Jazz, it's Music, or Some Notes on Popular Syncopated Music in England during the 20th Century* (Walsall, England, 1978)
L. Walker: *The Big Band Almanac* (Hollywood, CA, 1978, rev. New York, 2/1989)
——: *The Wonderful Era of the Great Dance Bands* (Berkeley, CA, 1964/R1990)
V. G. Walker: *Hubert Laws: Observations on his Life, Philosophy, and Jazz Improvisational Techniques* (thesis, Bowling Green State U., 1980)
M. Wallace, see V. Vale
G. A. Waller: *Main Street Amusements: Movies and Commercial Entertainment in a Southern City, 1896–1930* (Washington, DC, 1995)
M. Waller and A. Calabrese: *Fats Waller* (New York and London, 1977/R1997) [incl. discography and list of compositions]
E. Walles: *Jazzen anfaller* (Stockholm, 1946)
D. Walley: *No Commercial Potential: the Saga of Frank Zappa and the Mothers of Invention* (New York, 1972, 2/1980) [incl. discography]
R. Walser: *Keeping Time: Readings in Jazz History* (New York and Oxford, England, 1999) [colln of previously pubd articles]
O. M. Walton: *Music: Black, White and Blue: a Sociological Survey of the Use and Misuse of Afro-American Music* (New York, 1972)
C. Wareing and G. Garlick: *Bugles for Beiderbecke* (London, 1958) [incl. discography]
I. Wasserberger, see A. Matzner
B. Waters: *The Key to a Jazzy Life* (n.p. [Toulouse, France], n.d. [1985]) [autobiography of Benny Waters]
E. Waters [and C. Samuels]: *To Me it's Wonderful* (New York and elsewhere, 1972) [autobiography of Ethel Waters]
E. Waters and C. Samuels: *His Eye is on the Sparrow* (New York and London, 1951/R1992) [autobiography]
H. J. Waters, Jr.: *Jack Teagarden's Music: his Career and Recordings* (Stanhope, NJ, 1960)
C. Way: *The Big Bands Go to War* (Edinburgh and London, 1991)
——: *Glenn Miller in Britain Then and Now* (London, 1996)
B. Weber, see S. Glover
H. Weber and G. Filtgen: *Charles Mingus: sein Leben, seine Musik, seine Schallplatten* (Gauting, Germany, 1984)
D. Webster, see B. Wilber
S. Weiland, see R. T. Buckner
A. Weill, ed.: *Jazz, Pop, Rock* (Paris, 1993) [album of poster reproductions]
M. Weinberg and R. Santelli: *The Big Beat: Conversations with Rock's Great Drummers* (Chicago, 1984)
B. Weiner, see D. da Fonseca; F. Malabe
N. C. Weinstein: *A Night in Tunisia: Imaginings of Africa in Jazz* (Metuchen, NJ, and London, 1992)
B. Weir, see B. Clayton; S. Price
P. E. Weisenborn, see R. Daschkey
M. Weiss: *Jazz Styles and Analysis: Piano* (Chicago, c1982)
W. L. Welch, see O. Read
D. Wells and S. Dance: *The Night People: Reminiscences of a Jazzman* (Boston and London, 1971, rev. Washington, DC, 2/1992) [autobiography of Dicky Wells]
G. Wendt, ed.: *Die Jazz Frauen* (Hamburg, Germany, 1992)
C. H. Werner: *Playing the Changes: from Afro-modernism to the Jazz Impulse* (Urbana, IL, 1995)
I. Werther: *Bebop: die Geschichte einer musikalischen Revolution und ihrer Interpreten* (Frankfurt am Main, Germany, 1988)
B. Westin: *Sag det med musik: Thore Ehrling och hans orkester* [Say it with music: Thore Ehrling and his orchestra] (Stockholm, 1987) [incl. discography]
P. Weston, see B. Gonzales
H. Wetzelsdorfer: *Follow the Rhythm: Impressionen aus Wiesen* (Pottendorf, Austria, 1991) [photo album]
J. Wexler and D. Ritz: *Rhythm and Blues: a Life in American Music* (New York, 1993, London, 1994) [autobiography of Jerry Wexler]
J. Wheaton: *All that Jazz* (New York, 1994)
G. Wheeler: *Jazz by Mail: Record Clubs and Record Labels 1936 to 1958, including Complete Discographies for Jazztone and Dial Records* (Manassas, VA, 1999)
I. Whitcomb: *After the Ball* (Harmondsworth, nr London, 1972)
A. White: *Jazz Party: a Photo Gallery of Great Jazz Musicians* (Little Rock, AR, 2000) [photo album]
A. N. White III: *Andrew's X-rated Band Stories* (Washington, DC, 1984)
——: *Hey Kid! Wanna Buy a Record? A Treatise on Self Production in the Music Business* (Washington, DC, 1982)
——: *Trane 'n Me: a Semi-autobiography: a Treatise on the Music of John Coltrane* (Washington, DC, 1981; Ger. trans., Frankfurt am Main, Germany, 1982, as *Trane 'n Me: eine Abhandlung über die Musik von John Coltrane*)
J. White: *Artie Shaw: Non-stop Flight* (Hull, England, 1998)
——: *Billie Holiday* (Tunbridge Wells, England, and New York, 1987) [incl. discography]
K. Whitehead: *New Dutch Swing* (New York, 1998)
K. Whitehead, ed.: *Bimhuis 25: Stories of Twenty-five Years at the Bimhuis* (Amsterdam, 1999)
P. Whiteman and M. M. McBride: *Jazz* (New York, 1926)
J. Whiteoak: *Early Modern Jazz in Australia: the Introduction of Bop* (diss., LaTrobe U., Australia, 1986)
B. Whyatt: *Muggsy Spanier: the Lonesome Road: a Biography and Discography* (New Orleans, 1995)
J. Wickes: *Innovations in British Jazz*, i: *1900–1980* (Chelmsford, England, 1999) [*WickesIBJ*]
R. Wiedamann, ed.: *Bavarian First Herd: 10 Jahre Landes-Jugend-jazz-orchester* (Regensburg, Germany, 1998)
R. Wiedamann, see also R. Koechl
E. Wiedemann: *Jazz i Danmark i tyverne, trediverne og fyrrerne: en musikkulturel undersøgelse* [Jazz in Denmark in the twenties, thirties, and forties: a study of musical culture] (Copenhagen, 1982) [incl. discography]
K. Wiernicki: *Dal divertimento dei nobili alla propaganda: storia del jazz in Russia* (Naples, Italy, 1991)
P. Wiessmüller: *Miles Davis: sein Leben, seine Musik, seine Schallplatten* (Gauting, Germany, 1984, rev. and enlarged Schaftlach, Germany, 2/1988)
L. Wigh, ed.: *Jazz på fotografiska: Fotografiska Museet i Moderna Museet 12 april–3 augusti 1986* (Stockholm, 1986) [catalogue of exhibition at the Fotografiska Museet]
B. Wilber with D. Webster: *Music Was Not Enough* (London and New York, 1987)
R. J. Wilbraham: *Charles Mingus: a Biography and Discography* (London, 1967) [incl. list of compositions]
D. Wild: *The Recordings of John Coltrane* (Ann Arbor, MI, 1979)
L. de Wilde: *Monk* (Paris, 1996; Eng. trans., New York, 1997)
A. Wilder: *American Popular Song: the Great Innovators, 1900–1950* (London and New York, 1972)
J. Wildman, see B. Benward
M. W. Wilkes: *Swinging 21: 100 Jahre Jazz in New Orleans Today* (Frankfurt am Main, Germany, 2000)
H. Willard: *The Wildest One: the Life of Wild Bill Davison* (Monkton, MD, 1996)
E. Willems: *Le jazz et l'oreille musicale: étude psychologique* (Geneva, 1945)
A. Williams: *Fall from Grace: the John Kirby Story* (Pensacola, FL, 1993)
J. K. Williams: *Themes Composed by Jazz Musicians of the Bebop Era: a Study of Harmony, Rhythm, and Melody* (diss., Indiana U., 1982)
Martin Williams: *Jazz Changes* (New York, 1992)
——: *Jazz Heritage* (New York, and Oxford, England, 1985) [colln of previously pubd articles]
——: *Jazz in its Time* (New York and Oxford, England, 1989)
——: *Jazz Masters in Transition, 1957–69* (New York and London, 1970/R1980) [colln of previously pubd reviews]
——: *Jazz Masters of New Orleans* (New York and London, 1967/R1978)

——: *The Jazz Tradition* (New York, 1970, rev. New York, and Oxford, England, 2/1983)
——: *Jelly Roll Morton* (London, 1962); repr. in *Kings of Jazz*, ed. S. Green (South Brunswick, NJ, and New York, 1978)
——: *King Oliver* (London, 1960); repr. in *Kings of Jazz*, ed. S. Green (South Brunswick, NJ, and New York, 1978)
Martin Williams, ed.: *The Art of Jazz: Essays on the Nature and Development of Jazz* (New York, 1959/*R*1979 as *The Art of Jazz: Ragtime to Bebop*)
——: *Jazz Panorama* (New York and London, 1962/*R*1979) [colln of previously pubd articles]
Martin Williams, see also A. Francis
Mike Williams: *The Australian Jazz Explosion* (London and elsewhere, 1981)
P. Williams: *Django* (Montpellier, France, 1991, rev. and enlarged Marseilles, France, 2/1998, as *Django Reinhardt*) [incl. discography]
R. Williams: *Die Legenden des Jazz: eine Hommage in Bildern* (Königswinter, Germany, 1994; Eng. orig., New York, 1994, as *Jazz: a Photographic Documentary*)
——: *Long Distance Call: Writings on Music* (London, 2000)
——: *Miles Davis: the Man in the Green Shirt* (London, 1993; Fr. trans., Paris, 1993, as *Miles Davis: l'homme à la chemise verte*; Ger. trans., Munich, 1993, as *Miles Davis: Perfectly Cool: die Bildbiographie*)
K. Williamson, ed.: *This is Jazz* (London, 1960)
B. Willoughby: *Jazz in L.A.* (Kiel, Germany, 1990) [photo album; text by H. Geller and M. Zwerin]
V. Wilmer: *As Serious as your Life: the Story of the New Jazz* (London, 1977, rev. [2]/1980, rev. [3]/1987/*R*2000)
——: *The Face of Black Music* (New York, 1976)
——: *Jazz People* (London, Indianapolis, and New York, 1970/*R*1985; Sp. trans., Buenos Aires, 1973, as *Gente del jazz*)
——: *Mama Said There'd be Days Like This* (London, 1989, rev. 2/1991)
V. Wilmer, see also M. Buholzer
E. Wilson: *Sinatra: an Unauthorized Biography* (New York, 1976)
J. S. Wilson: *Jazz* (Budapest, 1972)
P. N. Wilson: *Anthony Braxton: sein Leben, seine Musik, seine Schallplatten* (Waakirchen, Germany, 1993)
——: *Hear and Now: Gedanken zur improvisierten Musik* (Hofheim am Taunus, Germany, 1999)
——: *Ornette Coleman: sein Leben, seine Musik, seine Schallplatten* (Schaftlach, Germany, 1989; Eng. trans., Berkeley, CA, 1999, as *Ornette Coleman: his Life and Music*)
——: *Sonny Rollins: sein Leben, seine Musik, seine Schallplatten* (Schaftlach, Germany, 1991)
——: *Spirits Rejoice! Albert Ayler und seine Botschaft* (Hofheim am Taunus, Germany, 1996)
P. N. Wilson and U. Goeman: *Charlie Parker: sein Leben, seine Musik, seine Schallplatten* (Schaftlach, Germany, 1988)
R. Wilson, see D. Chamberlain
S. Wilson with J. Cohassey: *Toast of the Town: the Life and Times of Sunnie Wilson* (Detroit, MI, 1998)
T. Wilson, A. Ligthart, and H. van Loo: *Teddy Wilson Talks Jazz* (London and New York, 1996) [incl. discography by H. Rye]
E. Withers, see W. S. Worley
J. Woelfer: *Dizzy Gillespie: sein Leben, seine Musik, seine Schallplatten* (Waakirchen, nr Bad Tölz, Germany, 1987)
——: *Lexicon des Jazz* (Munich, 1993)
C. Woideck, ed.: *The Charlie Parker Companion: Six Decades of Commentary* (New York, 1998) [incl. previously pubd articles]
——: *The John Coltrane Companion: Five Decades of Commentary* (New York, 1998) [incl. previously pubd articles]
K. Woideck: *Charlie Parker: his Music and Life* (Ann Arbor, MI, 1996)
R. Wolf: *Story Jazz: a History of Chicago Jazz Styles* (Lansing, IA, 1995)
R. Wolf, see also B. Freeman
B. Wolfe, see M. Mezzrow
F. Wolff: *The Blue Note Years: the Jazz Photography of Francis Wolff*, ed. M. Cuscuna, C. Lourie, and O. Schnider (New York, 1995; Ger. trans., Kilchberg, Switzerland, 1995, as *The Blue Note Years: die Jazz-Fotographie von Francis Wolff*; Fr. trans., Paris, 1996, as *Les années Blue Note*)
——: *Blue Note: Jazz Photography of Francis Wolff*, ed. M. Cuscuna, C. Lourie, and O. Schnider (New York, 2000)
A. Woll: *Black Musical Theatre: from Coontown to Dreamgirls* (Baton Rouge, LA, 1989)
E. Wood: *Born to Swing* (London, 1996)
——: *The Josephine Baker Story* (London, 2000)
B. Woods: *When the Music Stopped: the Big Band Era Remembered* (New York, 1994)
C. D. Woodson: *Solo Jazz Drumming: an Analytical Study of the Improvisational Techniques of Anthony Williams* (thesis, UCLA, 1973)
W. S. Worley and E. Withers: *Beale Street: Crossroads of American Music* (Leneka, KS, 1998)
D. G. Wright: *Millergate: the Final Solution* (Southampton, England, 1998)
J. Wright, ed.: *New Perspectives on Music: Essays in Honour of Eileen Southern* (Warren, MI, 1992)
Laurie Wright: *"Fats" in Fact* (Chigwell, England, 1992)
——: *Mr. Jelly Lord* (Chigwell, England, 1980) [bio-discography of Jelly Roll Morton]
Laurie Wright, comp. [from material supplied by F. Cox, J. Randolph, and J. Harris]: *The Jug Bands of Louisville* (Chigwell, England, 1993 [*recte* 1994])
Laurie Wright, ed.: *Storyville 1996/7* (Chigwell, England, 1997) [colln of essays]
——: *Storyville 1998–9* (Chigwell, England, 1999) [colln of essays]
——: *Storyville 2000–1* (Chigwell, England, 2001) [colln of essays]
Laurie Wright and others: *Walter C. Allen & Brian A. L. Rust's "King" Oliver* (Chigwell, England, 1987) [bio-discography; completely rev. version of Allen and Rust: *King Joe Oliver* (Belleville, NJ, 1955)]
Laurie Wright, see also J. R. T. Davies
Leo Wright: *God is my Booking Agent* (London, 1996) [autobiography]
W. Wright: *The Glenn Miller Burial File* (Southampton, England, 1990)
——: *Millergate: the Real Glenn Miller Story* (Southampton, England, 1993)
I. Wulff: *Chet Baker in Europe, 1975–1988* (Kiel, Germany, 1993)
——: *Diary: a Perpetual Jazz Calendar* (Kiel, Germany, 1996) [incl. interviews by K. Lippegaus]
I. Wulff, see also R. Haarman
M. Wyler: *A Glimpse of the Past: an Illustrated History of some Early Record Companies that Made Jazz History* (West Moors, England, 1957)
T. Wyndham: *Texas Shout: How Dixieland Jazz Works* (Seattle, WA, 1997) [colln of previously pubd articles]
R. Wyss, see P. Landolt
S. Yanow: *Bebop* (San Francisco, 2000)
——: *Duke Ellington* (New York, 1999)
——: *Swing* (San Francisco, 2000)
I. Yeomans, see I. Berg
R. Yockey, see M. Bookspan
A. Young: *Bodies and Souls: Musical Memoirs* (Berkeley, CA, 1981)
——: *Drowning in the Sea of Love: Musical Memoirs* (Hopwell, NJ, 1995) [incl. previously pubd articles]
——: *Kinds of Blue: Musical Memoirs* (San Francisco, 1984)
——: *Things Ain't What They Used to Be: Musical Memoirs* (Berkeley, CA, 1987)
A. Young, see also J. Coleman
B. Young: *Dixonia: a Bio-discography of Bill Dixon* (Westport, CT, and London, 1998)
A. Yule, see R. Brown
M. Yves-Bonnet: *Jazz 'n' jazz: une histoire de jazz* (Montrouge, France, 1987)
R. Zahn: *Jazz in Köln seit 1945: Kellerkunst und Konsertkultur* (Cologne, Germany, 1997)
——: *Jazz in Nordrhein-Westfalen seit 1946* (Cologne, Germany, 1999)
F. Zammarchi: *Sidney Bechet* (Paris, 1989) [incl. discography]
J. Zapletal, see G. Brom
D. Zinn: *The Structure & Analysis of the Modern Improvised Line*, i: *Theory* (New York, and Bryn Mawr, PA, 1981)
C. Zinner Frühbeis: *Wie waren ja die Grossten: deutsche Jazz- und Unterhaltungs-Musiker zwischen 1920 und 1950* (Frankfurt am Main, Germany, 1991 [*recte* 1992])
W. Zinsser: *Willie and Dwike: an American Profile* (New York and Toronto, 1984/*R* 2000) [biographies of Willie Ruff and Dwike Mitchell]
K. Zipernovszky, ed.: *Jazz Guide to Hungary '98* (Budapest, 1998)
A. Zoli: *...Fortissimamente jazz! Incontro con Franco D'Andrea* (Rome, n.d. [1983])
M. Zufferey: *Jazz als sozio-politisches Selbstverständnis der Schwarzen in Amerika* (Zurich, 1980; Fr. trans., Sierre, Switzerland, 1980)
M. Zwerin: *Close Enough for Jazz* (London, 1983) [autobiography]
——: *La tristesse de Saint Louis: Swing under the Nazis* (London, Melbourne, Australia, and New York, 1985/*R*2000; Ger. trans., Vienna, 1988, as *Swing unter den Nazis*; It. trans., Turin, Italy, 1993, as *Musica degenerata: il jazz sotto il nazismo*)
M. Zwerin, see also H. Willoughby
J. Zylber: "40 Jahren Jazz in Polen," *Radar* [Ger. edn], no.3 (Warsaw, 1966), 7

PERIODICALS

In the following list entries are ordered alphabetically by title. Periodicals of the same name are ordered chronologically by date of first issue, and those with the same title but no subtitle precede those with a subtitle (this is pertinent chiefly to those periodicals named *Jazz* and *Jazz: . . .*). Cross-references are incorporated for alternative titles of journals where helpful. In respect of periodicals not devoted entirely to jazz, selection has been made on the basis of the quantity, quality, and, in some cases, historical importance of their jazz coverage. Included, for example, are a large number of specialist periodicals devoted to blues, since virtually all have regular coverage of artists who are also associated with jazz, but there are obviously many more general music periodicals with occasional significant articles on jazz than we will have discovered or have space to enumerate. Part works are not included. Coverage of the new field of web magazines is inevitably fitful, and it has proved impossible to establish a hard and fast line between websites which are regularly updated and those whose function is genuinely analogous to that of a periodical. Dates of publication and publication intervals for printed periodicals are given where known; in general, publication intervals are given for webzines only when they are stated by the webmasters. The listing of a web edition of a print magazine may imply anything from the posting of the entire content of the current or past issues to the posting of supplementary material often of an ephemeral character – or even in some cases a separate edition of unrelated material. However, its inclusion always implies that material to be found at the website was of a periodical character at the time our research was undertaken.

c.i. – cumulative index(es)
incorp. – incorporated, incorporating
irreg. – irregular
s.i. – special issue(s)

AAMOA Reports [Afro-American Music Opportunities Association] (Minneapolis, 1969–75), quarterly (7 vols.)
Absolute Jazz (London, 1995–?), bimonthly, <http://www.abjazz.com> [web only]
Absolute Music (Sea Cliff, NY, ?–), irreg., from Feb 1999 bimonthly
Accordion Times & Musical Express [from no.70 (6 Feb 1948) *Musical Express*; from no.269 (7 March 1952) *New Musical Express*] (London, 4 Oct 1946–), weekly; suppl.: *New Musical Express Annual* [sometimes *New Musical Express Xmas Annual*] (1953–), annually [no significant jazz content from *c*1970]
Acid Jazz (Vimercate, Italy, 1987–), monthly
Acoustic Guitar (San Rafael, CA, July/Aug 1990–), bimonthly; contd from *Frets: the Magazine of Acoustic String Instruments*; web edn at <www.acousticguitar.com>
Actualité musicale (Brussels, 1944–57), 10 or 11 issues a year, from mid-1951 bimonthly
Actuel: jazz, musique contemporaine, théatre, poésie (Paris, Oct 1968–1975; Nov 1979–), monthly (58 nos. 1968–75)
Ad Lib (Toronto, 1944–7), monthly
Aktuality melodie, see *Melodie* (Prague)
All About Jazz (Philadelphia, 1996–), monthly, <http://www.allaboutjazz.-com> [web only]
Alley Music (Chadstone Centre, Victoria, Australia, ?1967–?), irreg.
All-jazz Clearinghouse (Clovis, CA, April 1996–?), monthly, <http://www.alljazz.com> [web only]
Allmusic Zine (Ann Arbor, MI, Aug 1999–?), daily, <http://allmusic.com/zine> [web only]
Amateur and Semi-pro Musician [from ii/3 (March/April [1962] *Dance Band and Jazz Musician* (Ponders End, England, 1961–late 1960s), 7 issues a year
American Jazz, see OTHER BOOKS, J. Asman and B. Kinnell
American Jazz Monthly [from Nov 1944 *American Jazz Review*] (New York, 1944 – March 1947), monthly (?3 vols.)
American Music (Urbana, IL, spring 1983–), quarterly
American Musician (Cincinnati, Jan 1897 – July 1901), monthly (55 nos.); contd as *International Musician*
American Rag (Fresno, CA, 1995–), 11 issues a year; contd from *West Coast Rag*
And All that Jazz (Kerrville, TX, 1974–), 4 issues a year
Angry Penguins (Melbourne, Australia, autumn 1946–), quarterly
Annual Review of Jazz Studies (New Brunswick, NJ, 1982–), irreg.; contd from *Journal of Jazz Studies*
Anschläge: Zeitschrift des Archivs für Populäre Musik (Bremen, Germany, 1978–81), quarterly (7 nos.)
Archtop: the Journal of Jazz Guitar (Doncaster, England, May/June 1987–?1989), quarterly
Arts Midwest Jazzletter (Minneapolis, 1982 – Sept 1997), quarterly
ASCAP Jazz Notes (New York, Feb 1962 – June 1965), monthly (39 nos.)
Atlanta Jazz Report (Decatur, GA, 1984–)
Auditorium (Milan, Jan 1989–), quarterly
AustralAsian Jazz and Blues, see *Australian Jazz and Blues*
Australian Jazz and Blues [from 1995 *AustralAsian Jazz and Blues*] (Bondi Junction, New South Wales, 1993–4; Crows Nest, New South Wales, 1994–), bimonthly
Australian Jazz Quarterly: a Magazine for the Connoisseur of Hot Music (Melbourne, Australia, May 1946 – April 1957), irreg. (31 nos.)
Avant (Chelmsford, England, 1997–), quarterly
BAD, see *Black Arts & Dance*
Ballroom and Band (England, Nov 1934 – March 1935), monthly (1 vol. = 5 nos.)
Band (London, July 1947-?), monthly
Band Leaders (New York, Aug 1943 – June 1946), quarterly, from Nov 1943 bimonthly, from March 1946 monthly; contd from *All-American Band Leaders* [details unknown]; contd by *Band Leaders and Record Review* (New York, Aug 1946–1947), monthly except July and Sept
Band Wagon (London, 14 Oct 1939 – 6 Sept 1940, June 1945 – June 1953), fortnightly (36 nos. 1939–40), from June 1945 monthly
Band Yearbook, see *Billboard Advertising*
Basin Street (New Orleans, March 1945–), monthly
Bass Frontiers (Nashville, 1995–), bimonthly
Bassist (Bath, England, Nov 1994–), every 4 weeks, 13 issues a year
Bass Player (San Mateo, CA, autumn 1988–), monthly, from autumn 1988 irreg., from spring 1990 quarterly, from Nov 1995 monthly; web edn at <http://www.bassplayer.com>
Bass World: Annual Journal [*Bass World: Journal of International Society of Bassists*], see *International Society of Bassists*
The Beat (London, 1947–9), 3 vols.; contd as *New Beat*
The Beat (Sydney, Sept–Nov 1949), monthly (3 nos.)
Beat: the Heart of the Music Scene [from ii/7 (July 1958) *Jazz Beat: the Heart of the Music Scene*] (London, n.d. [1956]/1957 – July 1958), monthly (2 vols.)
Be-bop and Beyond (Los Angeles, Jan/Feb 1983–), bimonthly, from v/1 (spring 1987) quarterly
Berklee Today [from xi/1 (summer 1999) *BT*] (Boston, summer 1989–), 3 issues a year; web edn at <http://www.berklee.edu/bt/default.html>
Berlin-Jazz: Miteilungsblatt des Jazz Club Berlin (Berlin, Oct 1955 – April/May 1958), 4 vols.
Best Rated CDs, Jazz, Popular, etc. (Voorheesville, NY, 1992–), annually
Bielefelder Katalog Jazz, see DISCOGRAPHIES, *General*, M. Scheffner
Big Apple Jazz (New York, winter 1997–), quarterly
Big Bands International Newsletter [from no.20 (Aug 1982) *Big Bands International Magazine*] (Reading, England, *c*1980–), bimonthly
Big City Blues (Detroit, ?1995–), bimonthly
Billboard Advertising [from 1 Nov 1896 *The Billboard*; from 9 Jan 1961 *Billboard: the International Music-record Newsweekly*; from 7 June 1969 *Billboard: the International Music-record-tape Newsweekly*] (Cincinnati, later New York, 1894/5–1971; Los Angeles, 1971–), weekly; song charts; c.i. 1972–3; suppls.: *Billboard: Index of the New York Legitimate Stage* (1931/2–1938/9), annually; *Band Yearbook* (1939–42), annually; *Talent and Tunes on Music Machines* (1939–41), annually; *Who's Who in the World of Music* (1961–), annually
Bird Lives! (Northern Westchester, NY, May 1998–), fortnightly, <http://www.birdlives.com> [web only]
Black Arts & Dance [from Jan 1992 *BAD*] (Bonn, Germany, 1990 – Dec 1993), 11 issues a year (37 nos.)
Blackfolk: Journal of Afro-American Folklore (Los Angeles, spring 1972–), ?quarterly
Black Lines: a Journal of Black Studies (Pittsburgh, autumn 1970 – winter 1972), quarterly
Black Music (London, 1973–8), monthly (5 vols. = 52 nos.); contd as *Black Music and Jazz Review*
Black Music and Jazz Review (London, April 1978–1984), monthly (7 vols.); contd from *Black Music*; incorp. into *Blues and Soul* [no significant jazz content after 1979]
Black Music Research Bulletin, see *Black Music Research Newsletter*
Black Music Research Journal (Nashville, 1980–82; Nashville and Chicago, 1983–4; Chicago, 1985–), annually; from viii/1 (1988) 2 issues a year; c.i. (with *Black Music Research Newsletter*) 1980–85 pubd separately
Black Music Research Newsletter [from x/1 (spring 1998) *Black Music Research Bulletin*] (Carbondale, IL, summer 1977/8; Nashville, 1978/9–1981/2; Nashville and Chicago, 1983/4–1984; Chicago, 1985 – fall 1990), quarterly, from 1980 half-yearly (12 vols.); c.i. (with *Black Music Research Journal*) 1980–85 pubd separately
Black Perspective in Music (New York, spring 1973–1990), annually; from xi/1 (spring 1983) 2 issues a year, in 1989 and 1990 annual combined vol. (18 vols); c.i. 1973–82
Black Stars (Chicago, 1971–81), monthly
Bleu banane (Stavelot, Belgium, autumn 1997 – spring 2000), irreg. (4 nos.)
Block (Almelo, Netherlands, March/April 1975–), quarterly
Blue Light: the DESUK Newsletter/the Newsletter of the Duke Ellington Society, see *DESUK* [Duke Ellington Society (UK)] *Newsletter*
Blue Rhythm (Dortmund, Germany, 1995–); web edn at <http://www.jazzthing.de/blue/bluerhythm.html>
Blue Rhythm, see *Jazz Notes* (Melbourne)

Blues: bimestrial internationale (Brussels, Belgium, 1970–?), bimonthly

Il blues: blues & dintorni (Milan, 1983–), quarterly

Blues Access (Boulder, CO, spring 1990–), quarterly

Blues & Rhythm: the Gospel Truth (London, July 1984 – Sept 1986; Cheadle, Greater Manchester, England, Oct 1986 – Nov 1992; Morley, Yorkshire, England, Jan 1993 – Jan 1994; Bromham, Bedfordshire, England, Feb 1994–), 10 issues a year; index of record reviews in nos.1–10 pubd separately (1985); c.i. nos.1–120 pubd separately (1997)

Blues and Swing Magazine (Marseilles, 1970–*c*1975), irreg.

Blues Art Studio Journal (Vienna, 2000–), 11 issues a year, <http://www.bluesartstudio.at/NeueSeiten/page50.html> [web only]

Blues Bytes ... a Monthly On-line Magazine of Blues CD Reviews (Phoenix, AZ, Dec 1996–), monthly, <http://www.bluenight.com/BluesBytes/>; archived at <http://www.bluenight.com/BluesBytes/backissu.html> [web only]

Blues, etc (Paris, 1996–), quarterly

Blues et jazz (Sint Stevens Woluwe, Belgium, *fl.* 1970s), irreg.

Blues gazette (Sinaai, Belgium, Dec 1995 – fall 1996), quarterly (4 nos.)

Blues Life (Vienna, 1978–), quarterly

Blues-link (Barnet, England, Aug/Sept 1973–1974; Hitchin, England, 1975 (no.5); Barnet, England, no.6 (July [1975]), bimonthly; from no.4, irreg.; incorp. *Blues World* from no.4 (1974)

Blues Magazine (Toronto, 1975–9), bimonthly (5 vols.)

Blues News (Altena, Germany, 1995–), quarterly

Blues Notes: erstes deutschsprachiges Blues- & Jazzmagazin (Linz, Austria, 1969–79), irreg. (11 vols. = 37 nos.)

Blues Research, see *Record Research*

Blues Revue, see *Blues Revue Quarterly*

Blues Revue Quarterly [from no.12 (spring 1994) *Blues Revue*] (West Union, WV, July 1991 – Feb 1998; Salem, WV, April 1998–), quarterly, from no.16 (March/April 1995) bimonthly, from no.31 (Oct 1997) 10 issues a year; web edn at <http://www.bluesrevue.com>

Blues-Statistics, see *Jazz-Statistics*

Blues To-do's (Seattle, 1993–), monthly

Blues Unlimited: the Journal of the Blues Appreciation Society [from no.5 (1963) *Blues Unlimited*] (Bexhill-on-Sea, England, April 1963 – Dec 1974/ Jan 1975; London, March/April 1975 – winter 1987), 10 issues a year, from no.102 (June 1973) bimonthly, from no.134 (March/June 1979) half-yearly, from no.146 (autumn/winter 1984) irreg. (149 nos.); *Free Discographical Supplement, Additions to Discographies featured in "Blues Unlimited" nos.1–6*, incl. c.i. nos.1–5, pubd separately (1963)

Blues World (Knutsford, England, 1965–74), bimonthly, from no.22 (Dec 1968) quarterly, from no.26 (Jan 1970) monthly (50 nos.); nos.46–9 combined issue (1973); c.i. nos.1–12 pubd in no.17 (Nov 1967); contd by *Blues-link*

Blu Jazz (Rome, 1989–), 11 issues a year

BMI: the Many Worlds of Music, see *News about BMI Music & Writers*

Boogie Woogie & Blues Collector (Amsterdam, 1967–?), irreg. [very limited editorial content]

Boss, see *The Sound*

Bossa: Brazilian Jazz World Guide (Boston, June 1995–), monthly, from 1998 10 issues a year

Boz (London, March 1994–), 10 issues a year; incorp. *Jazz Express* (retaining independent numeration)

Brass Bulletin (Moudon, Switzerland, 1971–80; from no.30 (1980) Bulle, Switzerland), 3 issues a year, from no.13 (1976) quarterly [in Eng., Fr., and Ger.]

Brass Player (New York, ?1975–), quarterly

Break Bulletin (Tampere, Finland, 1977–81), quarterly

Bremen Radio Jazzbrief [*Jazzbrief*] (Bremen, Germany, 1966–), monthly

Brilliant Corners: a Journal of Jazz and Literature (Williamsport, PA, winter 1996–), biennially

Browbeat (Oakland, CA, Jan 1993–), half-yearly; web edn at <http://www.meer.net/~browbeat>

BT, see *Berklee Today*

Buddy DeFranco Newsletter (Lucememines, PA, 1984–93)

Buffalo Jazz Report (Buffalo, NY, 1974–?)

Le Bulletin (Montreuil, France, 1995–), bimonthly

Bulletin du Hot Club de France, [1st ser.] (Paris, Dec 1940 – June 1945 [from late 1941 – Oct 1944 as *Circulaire du Hot Club de France*]), 43 nos.; [2nd ser.] (Paris, Oct 1945 – n.d.), 3 nos.; 3rd ser. (Montauban, France, Oct 1950 – Sept/Oct 1977; St.-Vrain, nr Corbeil-Essonnes, France, April 1978 – Jan 1999; Nogent-sur-Marne, France, Feb 1999–), 10 issues a year; c.i. 3rd ser. nos.1–243, excluding record reviews, pubd separately (St.-Vrain, n.d.); for c.i. to record reviews, 3rd ser. nos.1–243, see DISCOGRAPHIES, *General*, D. Brigaud; for c.i. to record reviews, 3rd ser. nos.244–343, see DISCOGRAPHIES, *General*, M.-F. Hernequet and D. Brigaud

Bulletin du Hot Club de Genève (Geneva, 1950–), 8 issues a year

Bulletin/Montreal Vintage Music Society (Montreal, 1968–83), monthly

Bulletin of the/de l'International Jazz Club (Brussels, Dec 1953; Milan, Italy, 1954–?), irreg.

Bulletin Panassié (Paris, ?–Nov 1947), 4 nos.

Buttrag (Chicago, Aug 1993–), irreg.

Cadence: the American Review of Jazz & Blues [from xv/1 (Jan 1989) *Cadence: the Review of Jazz & Blues: Creative Improvised Music*] (Redwood, nr Watertown, NY, Jan 1976–), monthly

Cahiers du jazz: revue musicale (Paris, *c*Nov 1959–1968; 1994–?1997; 2001–), irreg. (17 nos. 1959–68; nos.18 and 19 bound with *Jazz Magazine* (Paris), Nov 1970 and Oct 1971); 1994–?1997 3 issues a year; new ser. Jan 2001–

California Jazz Now (Oakland, CA, 1991–), 11 issues a year

Canadian Musician Magazine (Toronto, March/April 1979–), bimonthly

Catalogo: discos–long play, see DISCOGRAPHIES, *Other listings*

CBMR [Center for Black Music Research] *Digest* (Chicago, summer 1988–), 2 to 3 issues a year

Charlotte Jazz News & Notes (Charlotte, NC, 1993–), monthly

Chet's Choice (Raleigh, NC, 1991–6)

Chicago Jazz & Blues News (Chicago, March 1988–)

Chicago Jazz Bulletin (Chicago), irreg.

Christensen's Ragtime Review [from ii/6 (May 1916) *Ragtime Review*] (Chicago, Dec 1914 – Jan 1918), monthly (4 vols. = 33 nos.)

Circulaire du Hot Club de France, see *Bulletin du Hot Club de France*

Clarevoyonce (Torrance, CA, 1989–), annually

Citizen Jazz (Paray-Vieille-Poste, France, early 2001–), <http://www.citizenjazz.com>; contd from *Le Jazz* [web only]

Classic Rag (Cincinnati, 197?–), irreg.

Clef (Santa Monica, CA, March–Sept 1946), monthly (1 vol. = 7 nos.)

Climax (New Orleans, 1955–6), 2 nos.

Club de ritmo (Granollers, Spain, 1946–), monthly

Coda [from Jan 1981 *Coda Magazine*] (Toronto, May 1958–), monthly, from vi/6 (Feb 1964) bimonthly, from no.136 (March 1975) irreg., from no.151 (Oct 1976) bimonthly

Collana di musica jazz [*Collezione di musica jazz*] (Milan, 1960–?)

Collector (Cosenza, Italy, ?1960–? [after 1985]), irreg. [some issues in Eng. and It.]; s.i. (in place of nos.29–35) pubd as *Collector's Catalog*, ii (Cosenza, 1972)

Collectors Items (Walton-on-Thames, England, Aug 1980 – March 1992; Taunton, England, June 1992 – spring 1995), bimonthly, from no.42 (June 1987) irreg. (69 nos.); c.i. nos.1–12 pubd separately (1983)

Combo (Munich, April 1949–), fortnightly

Compact Disc Magazine: édition jazz blues (Bagneux, France, *c*April 1993–), 11 issues a year

Connchord (Elkhart, IN, 1958–), 3 issues a year

Consolidated Artist Newsletter (New York, 1976–)

Contemporary Jazz (Kansas City, 27 Jan 1996–), updated *c* daily, <http://www.contemporaryjazz.com> [web only]

Contemporary Keyboard [from vii/7 (July 1981) *Keyboard*] (Saratoga, nr Los Gatos, CA, later Cupertino, nr Santa Clara, CA, Sept 1975 – Sept 1993; San Mateo, CA, Oct 1993–), bimonthly, from iii/1 (Jan 1977) monthly; web edn at <www.keyboardmag.com>

Le courrier du disque microsillon, see DISCOGRAPHIES, *Other listings*

Crazy Music: the Journal of the Australian Blues Society ([Canberra], Australia, 1974–?), irreg.

CRC [Collector's Record Club] *Newsletter* [from v/2 (Aug 1979) to v/3 (Sept/ Dec 1979) *Jazzology Newsletter*] (Decatur, GA, ?1975–) half-yearly, from v (1979) 3 or 4 issues a year

Creative World: *the Creative World of Stan Kenton* (Los Angeles, *fl.* 1970s)

Crescendo [from v/9 (April 1967) *Crescendo International*; from May 1991 *Crescendo and Jazz Music*] (London, July 1962 – June/July 1986; from xxiv/1 (Jan 1987) Kent, England; from xxv/11 (Nov/Dec 1988) London; from xxviii/1 (June/July 1991) Ilford, England; from xxix/5 (Oct/Nov 1992) London), monthly, from xxii/1 (Oct/Nov 1983) irreg., from xxiv/1 (Jan 1987) monthly, from xxv/11 (Nov/Dec 1988) irreg., from xxx/3 (Aug/ Sept 1993) bimonthly

The Cricket: Black Music in Evolution (Newark, NJ, 1969–)

Le criquette: bulletin de l'Association Français des Amateurs du Jazz N.O. (Paris, early 1970s–1972), bimonthly; contd by *Jazz o'Maniac*

Cuadernos de jazz (Madrid, Nov 1990–), bimonthly

Dallas Jazz News Letter [from i/8 (Dec 1977) *Dallas Jazz News*; from ii/11 (Nov 1978) *Texas Jazz*] (Dallas, May 1977 – Dec 1982), monthly (6 vols. = ?68 nos.); contd as *Texas Ragg*

Dance Band and Jazz Musician, see *Amateur and Semi-pro Musician*

Delta Snake Blues News (California, 1981– late 1980s), ?irreg.; contd by *Delta Snake Blues News: the Online Blues 'Zine* (California, Jan 1994 – Feb 1999), monthly, from no.23 (Dec 1997) irreg. (27 nos.), <http://www.island.net/~blues/snake.html>, archived [web only]

Delta Snake Daily Blues (California, May 1998–), <http://www.netmagic.net/~snake/index.html> [web only]

DEMS [Duke Ellington Music Society] *Bulletin* [from no.1988/1 *International DEMS Bulletin*] (Järfälla, Sweden, 1979 – Oct–Dec 1995 (no.1995/ 3); Meerle, Belgium, Sept–Nov 1996–), irreg.

Denver Jazz Club News (Denver), bimonthly

DESUK [Duke Ellington Society (UK)] *Newsletter* [from 1996 *Blue Light: the DESUK Newsletter*; from v/2 (April–June 1998) *Blue Light: the Newsletter of the Duke Ellington Society (UK)*] (London, Dec 1994–), quarterly

Detroit Jazz (Detroit, Aug 1995–), bimonthly

Diapason, see discographies, *Other listings*

Different Drummer: the Magazine for Jazz Listeners (Rochester, NY, Sept 1973 – Jan 1975), monthly (1 vol. = 15 nos.)

Discographical and Micrographical Basics (Amsterdam, Sept 1988 – Feb 1990), irreg. (4 nos.) [in Eng.]

Discographical Forum (London, 1960 – summer 1985), bimonthly, from 1972 irreg. (50 nos.)

La discographie de la France: tous les disques de la quinzaine [by no.88 (15 April 1970) *La discographie de la France: bandes et disques de la quinzaine*] (Paris, March 1966–?), fortnightly [contd from suppl. to *Diapason*, see discographies, *Other listings*]

La discographie française, see discographies, *Other listings*

Discography: for the Jazz Student (London, Oct 1942–1944), monthly, from April 1944 irreg.; incorp. into *Jazz Music* (1947)

The Discophile: the Magazine for Record Information (London, Aug 1948 – Dec 1958), irreg. (61 nos.); incorp. into *Matrix* (1959)

Discopop '77, see discographies, *Other listings*

Discounter [from ii/1 (Jan 1949) *Jazz Discounter*] (Evansville, IN, Jan 1948–?), monthly

Disc'ribe (Ann Arbor, MI, 1980–?), irreg.

Disk in the World (Tokyo, July 1980–)

Disques de longue durée, see discographies, *Other listings*

Doctor jazz: contactblad voor liefhebbers en versamelaars van classic jazz, blues, en verwante volksmuziek [from no.42 (June/July 1970) *Doctor Jazz Magazine*] (Eindhoven, Netherlands, Jan 1963 – Sept/Oct 1964; Utrecht, Netherlands, Nov 1964 – July 1992; Santpoort, Netherlands, Sept 1992–), bimonthly, from no.82 (1977) quarterly; c.i. nos.11–16 (1965)

Down Beat: the Contemporary Music Magazine [from l/9 (July 1983) *Down Beat: for Contemporary Musicians*; from lvii/4 (April 1990) *Down Beat: Jazz, Blues and Beyond*] (Chicago, 1934–), monthly, from vi/10 (Oct 1939) semimonthly, from xiii/1 (1 Jan 1946) fortnightly, from xxxvii/11 (28 May 1970) monthly or fortnightly, from xlvi/13 (July 1979) monthly; incorp. *Tempo: the Modern Musical Newsmagazine* (?1940); suppl.: *Down Beat Music* [1960–62 *Down Beat's Music*] (1956–80), annually

Der Drummer (Germany, 1953–7)

Drums & Percussion (Unterschleissheim, Munich, Germany, 1982–), bimonthly

Dynaflow: Official Organ of the Stan Kenton Society (Bloxwich, England, Dec 1953–?), irreg.

Ear (New York, ?1977–?), irreg.; from 1989 10 issues a year

Earshot [*Earshot Jazz*] (Seattle, 1984–), monthly

L'écho des sociétés musicales, harmonies, fanfares, symphonies, chorales, jazz, accordéons (Brussels, 1946–8), monthly

Edge Jazz Newsletter [from 10 April 2001 *Jazz Matters: About Jazz*] (New York, 1998–), irreg.; web edn at <http://jazz.miningco.com> [from 10 April 2001 web only, weekly]

Ekrano: Film: Jazz (Seattle, and State College, PA, Jan 1997 – Feb 1999), irreg., <http://www.ekrano.org/index.htm>; archived at <http://www.ekrano.com> [web only]

Ella: the Journal of the Ella Fitzgerald Music Appreciation Society (Tours, France, May 1991–), 3 to 4 issues a year [in Eng. and Fr.]

Encore (New York, 1986–), quarterly

Erroll Garner Gems (Stockport, Cheshire, England, 1991–), quarterly; from iii/4 (Oct 1993) annually

Estrad (Stockholm, 1929–), monthly

Eureka: the Bi-monthly Magazine of New Orleans Jazz (London, Jan/Feb 1960 – Jan/Feb 1961), bimonthly (2 vols. = 7 nos.)

European Jazz Directory (New York, *fl.* 1980s)

Extra Jazz (Bordeaux, France, winter 1993–)

Fable Bulletin: Violin Improvisation Studies (Lewes, England, 1993–), irreg.

Fanfare (London, 1943–?1946), monthly (?4 vols.)

Fanfare (Tenafly, NJ, 1977–), bimonthly

Federation Jazz (Rahway, NJ, Oct 1985 – [early] 1994; from spring 1994 West Sacramento, CA), irreg., from spring 1994 quarterly

Federation Jazz (Savannah, GA, Oct 1985 – April 1986), bimonthly

Federation Jazz (Colorado Springs, CO, 1987–), quarterly

Federazione Italiana del Jazz New Jazz Society bolletino d'informazioni (Milan, 1952–3), monthly; contd by *New Jazz Record*

Fi (North Hollywood, CA, Jan 1996–), bimonthly

5/4 Magazine (northwestern USA, Feb 1995–), monthly

Fly: Dope Music Magazine (London, 1995–), irreg., <http://www.fly.co.uk/index.html> [web only]

Fongi: der wilder Jazzgeist (Germany, March 1958–1962)

Footnote: Dedicated to New Orleans Music (Cambridge, England, n.d. [Dec 1969] – Feb 1976; Meldreth, nr Cambridge, March 1976 – Oct 1983; Melbourn, nr Cambridge, Nov 1983 – Aug/Sept 1989), monthly, from ii/4 (April 1971) bimonthly (20 vols.); c.i. 1969–1984/5 (vols.i–xvi) pubd separately (1986); contd by *New Orleans Music*

Forty-fiver, see discographies, *Other listings*

The Forum (Reno, NV), quarterly

Fox auf 78 (Fox auf Achtundziebzig) (Dietramszell, Germany, 1986–), irreg.

Free sons (Montrouge, France, 1975–), quarterly

Freiburger Jazzhaus Journal (Freiburg, Germany, 1987–), monthly

French Guitar (Paris, March 1997–), bimonthly

Frets: the Magazine of Acoustic String Instruments (Cupertino, CA, 1979–90), monthly; contd by *Acoustic Guitar*

Frisco Cricket (San Francisco, July 1997–), quarterly

Gazette du jazz (France, June 1949–1951), bimonthly (3 vols.)

Gene Lees Jazzletter [*Jazzletter*] (Ojai, CA, 15 Aug 1981 – Dec 1986; Oak View, CA, Jan 1987–), monthly; c.i. 1981–6 annually, 1987– biennially

German Blues Circle Info. (Frankfurt am Main, Germany, Aug 1976–), monthly

Gift of Jazz Connection Magazine (Denver, Aug 1995–), monthly

Golden Age (Corby, England, 1986–?), monthly; c.i. nos.1–30 pubd separately (1990)

La gouttière: bulletin of the International Jazz Club (Paris, Dec 1953–1957), irreg.

The Grackle: Improvised [*Improvisational*] *Music in Transition* (New York, n.d. [1975]–1979), irreg. (5 nos.)

Gramofon: the Hungarian CD Review (Budapest, May 1996–), monthly

Gramophone Long Playing Popular Record Catalogue, see discographies, *Other listings*, E. Jackson

Gränslöst (Haverdal, Sweden, Jan 1995–), quarterly; web edn at <http://www.granslost.com>

Great Lakes Jazz Letter (Cleveland, 1984–)

Green Mountain Jazz Messenger (Brattleboro, VT, Aug/Sept 1997–), bimonthly

Groovin' the Vibes [from 1998 *Vibes Net*] (Milan, Sept 1996–), bimonthly, <http://www.thevibes.net> [web only]

Guía de jazz (Buenos Aires, Nov 1984–), bimonthly

Guide AKAI du disque: jazz, blues, pop, rock (Paris, 1979–), annually

Guitarist (Bath, England, 1984–), monthly

Guitar Player: the Magazine for Professional and Amateur Guitarists [from xv/7 (July 1981)*Guitar Player*] (San Jose, CA, later Saratoga, nr Los Gatos, CA, 1967–71; Los Gatos, 1971–), 4 issues a year, from ii (1968) 6 issues a year, from iv (1970) 8 issues a year, from viii (1974) monthly; web edn at <http://www.guitarplayer.com>

Guitar World (New York, July 1980–), bimonthly; from 1987 9 issues a year; from 1988 11 issues a year; from 1990 monthly

Gunn Report (Hadleigh, Essex, England, ?1967–1989), bimonthly; from 1980 quarterly (112 nos.)

Haagse Jazz Club (Voorburg, Netherlands, 1951–?)

Halana (Ardmore, PA, 1996–), irreg.; web edn (Narberth, PA) at <http://www.halana.com>

HCD [Hot Club Dortmund]*-Bulletin* [from 1956 *Westjazz: Jazz-Nachrichten aus Westdeutschland*] (Dortmund, Germany, 1955; Wanne-Eickel, Germany, 1956–?)

Heritage Music Review (Seattle, *fl.* 1980s)

Hip: the Jazz Record Digest (Sterling, nr Reston, VA, later McLean, VA, March 1967 – Dec 1971), 12 issues a year in 2 vols. (10 vols.); contd from *Hip: the Milwaukee Jazz Letter*; contd as *Jazz Digest*

Hip: the Milwaukee Jazz Letter (Milwaukee, Sept 1962 – Jan 1967), 5 vols.; contd as *Hip: the Jazz Record Digest*

Horizon-line: situs comunitas and informasi jazz Indonesia (Jakarta, Indonesia, 4 Nov 1998–) <http://www.horizon-line.com> [web only]

H.o.t.: tidsskrift for moderne musik (Copenhagen, 1934/5), monthly (1 vol. = 12 nos.)

Hot Club de Belgique, see *Jazz* (Brussels, 1945)

Hot Club Journal (Stuttgart, Germany, 1947/8–1949), bimonthly (2 vols.)

Hot Club magazine: revue internationale de jazz (Brussels, Jan 1946 – Aug 1948), monthly (29 nos.); contd from *Jazz* (Brussels, 1945); incorp. into *Jazz hot: la revue internationale de la musique de jazz* (Nov 1948)

Hot Club News (Nuremberg, Germany, ?1991–), quarterly

Hot House (New York, ?1982–), monthly

Hot Jazz Club (Sastre, Argentina, 1944–? [after 1950]), quarterly

Hot Jazz Info (Offenbach, Germany, 1972 – after 1983), monthly

Hot Jazz Today (Stevenage, England, June/July 1990–1991 or later), bimonthly, from no.3 (Nov/Dec 1990) quarterly

Hot News and Rhythm Record Review (London, April–Sept/Oct 1935), monthly (1 vol. = 6 nos.); incorp. into *Jazz Music* (1942)

Hot Notes (Waterford, Ireland, March 1946 – spring 1948), bimonthly

Hot Notes (New York, Jan 1969 – ?March 1975), monthly (7 vols.)

Hot Record Society Rag, see *H.R.S. Rag*

Hot-revue: revue mensuelle de jazz-hot (Lausanne, Switzerland, Dec 1945 – May 1947), monthly (2 vols.); incorp. into *Jazz-hot*

H.R.S. [Hot Record Society] *Rag* (New York, July 1938 – March 1941), irreg. (?11 nos.), from no.4 (Aug 1940) monthly

IAJRC [International Association of Jazz Record Collectors] *Record* [from ii/1 (Jan 1969) *IAJRC Journal*] (New York, later Indianapolis, 1967 – summer 1997; Sterling Heights, MI, fall 1997; Jamaica, NY, winter 1998 – fall 1998; Bel Air, MD, winter 1999 – summer 1999; Manassas, VA, fall 1999; Bel Air, MD, winter 2000–), quarterly, except 1982–3; c.i

Ifiúsági jazz klub híradója [Youth jazz club news] (Budapest, Jan–April 1964), monthly (4 nos.)

Images musicales (Paris, Dec 1945–), weekly

Impetus: New Music [from no.7 (1978) *Impetus*] (London, [April/May] 1976–1979), irreg. (9 nos.)
Improjazz (Savenay, France, Dec 1993–), 10 issues a year; web edn at <http://perso.wanadoo.fr/improjazz>
The Improvisor: International Journal of Free Improvisation (Birmingham, AL, 1982–), irreg.
L'indépendant du jazz (Paris, Oct 1974 – May 1980), monthly, 1 issue in 1976, from 1977 quarterly (21 nos.)
Infojazz (Bois-Guillaume, France, 1994–), quarterly
InJazz (London, Sept 1992–), irreg. [edns in Eng. and Fr.]
Innerviews: Music without Borders (San Francisco, 1995–), <http://www.innerviews.org> [web only]
Instante Musicale (Argentina, 1946–), monthly
The Instrumentalist (Glen Ellyn, IL, Sept/Oct 1946–1954; Evanston, IL, 1954 – Sept 1984; Northfield IL, Oct 1984–), 5 issues a year, from v/1 (Sept 1950) 6 issues a year, from vii/1 (Sept 1953) 9 issues a year, from x/1 (Sept 1955) 10 issues a year, from xi/11 (Aug 1957) 11 issues a year, from xxxiii/1 (Aug 1978) monthly
Interjazz: the Internet Jazz Plaza (New York, 1994–), <http://interjazz.com> [web only]
Intermission (Buena Park, CA, 1968–), monthly
International Arts of Jazz Newsletter (Stony Brook, NY, 1974–), monthly
International Association of Jazz Record Collectors Journal, see *IAJRC Record*
International DEMS Bulletin, see *DEMS* [Duke Ellington Music Society] *Bulletin*
International Discophile (Fresno, CA, summer 1955–*c*1960), irreg.
Das internationale Podium [iii/4 (April 1954) *Jazz-Podium*; from iii/5 (May 1954) *Das internationale Jazz-Podium*; from iv/1 (Jan 1955) *Jazz Podium*] (Vienna and Munich, 1947 or 1948 – ?Aug 1952; Stuttgart, Munich, and Vienna, ?Sept 1952 – June 1965; Stuttgart and Munich, July 1965 – Feb 1966; Stuttgart, March 1966–), monthly; incorp. *Jazz-Spiegel der Deutschen Jazz-Föderation* (?Sept 1952)
International Jazz Archives Journal (Pittsburgh, autumn 1993–), annually
International Musician [from xviii (1919/20) *International Musician: Official Journal of the American Federation of Musicians of the United States & Canada*] (St. Louis, July 1901–1922; Newark, NJ, and elsewhere, 1922–75; New York, 1975–), monthly; contd from *American Musician*
International Record News (Imola, Italy, May 1982–?), ?irreg. [in Eng.]
International Society of Bassists: Newsletter [each 4th issue *Bass World: Annual Journal*; from ix/1 (autumn 1982) *International Society of Bassists: Journal*; from xxi/1 (1996) *Bass World: Journal of International Society of Bassists*] (Cincinnati, autumn 1974–), quarterly, from ix/1 (autumn 1982) 3 issues a year
Into Jazz (London, Feb–Aug 1974), monthly (1 vol. = 7 nos.)
Intra musiques (Strasbourg, France, Oct 1981–?), quarterly
ITA [*International Trombone Association*] *Journal* (Denton, TX, 1972–), quarterly
ITG [*International Trumpet Guild*] *Journal* (Clearwater, FL, Oct 1976–), quarterly; web edn at <http://www.itg.dana.edu/~itg>, later <http://www.trumpetguild.org/journal/journal.htm>; c.i. 1976–99 at <http://www.trumpetguild.org/journal/journal.htm>
Jahrbuch für improvisierte Musik, see *Jazz Container*
Jam Session: le bulletin de l'Association de Jazz de Montréal (Montreal, Jan–Feb 1990–), bimonthly
Jazz (Stockholm, 1934–6), 3 vols.
Jazz (New York, June 1942 – Dec 1943), irreg. (1 vol. = 10 nos.); new ser. (Dec 1944 – Jan 1945), monthly (1 vol. = 2 nos.)
Jazz (Antwerp, Brussels, and Breda, 1945), monthly (6 nos.)
Jazz [*Hot Club de Belgique*] (Brussels, March 1945 – Nov 1945), bimonthly (6 nos.); contd as *Hot Club magazine: revue internationale de jazz*
Jazz (Reykjavík, March–Nov 1947), monthly
Jazz (Gothenburg, Sweden, Oct 1948–1949), monthly (2 vols.)
Jazz (Frankfurt am Main, Germany, Dec 1949), "monthly" (1 no.)
Jazz (Warsaw, 1956–81), see *Magazyn muzyczny* [*MM*]
Jazz (Lisbon, 1958–?) 9 or 10 issues a year
Jazz [*Jazz Magazine*] [from vi/8 (Aug 1967) *Jazz & Pop*] (New York, Oct 1962 – Sept 1971), monthly (10 vols. = 95 nos.)
Jazz (Aneby, Sweden, 1965–?), 6 issues a year
Jazz (Thessaloniki, Greece, 1977–)
Jazz (Hellerup, Denmark, 1979-81), 3 issues a year
Jazz (Washington, DC, 1979 – *c*1981), annually; merged with *Composers/National Endowment for the Arts* and *Solo Recitalists* to form *Music Fellowships*
Jazz (Minneapolis, 1980–?), monthly
Jazz (Sydney, 1981–6), quarterly
Jazz (Basel, Switzerland, 1982–?), bimonthly
Jazz (Budapest, 1982–8), 3 issues a year (24 nos.)
Jazz (North Hollywood, CA, 1987–), bimonthly
Jazz (Belgrade, 1990–), monthly
Jazz (Lyons, France, 1992–), annually
Jazz (Warsaw, 1994), bimonthly
Le Jazz (Paray-Vieille-Poste, France, March 1997 – early 2001), <http://lejazz.simplenet.com> [in Fr. and Eng.]; contd as *Citizen Jazz* [web only]
Jazz (Prague, 1997–), irreg.
Jazz (Copenhagen), see *Jazzavisen*
Jazz (Chilwell, nr Newark-on-Trent, England), see *Jazz Record*
Jazz (London), see *Jazz fm*
Jazz (Northport, NY), see *Jazz Magazine* (1976)
Jazz: l'actualité intellectuelle (Paris, Dec 1928 – 30 March 1931), monthly (15 nos.)
Jazz: the Australasian Contemporary Music Magazine (Sydney, Jan/Feb 1981–1986), bimonthly, from iv (1984) quarterly
Jazz: list věnovaný jazzu a moderní hudbě [Jazz: jazz and modern music journal] (Prague, 1947–8), 2 vols.
Jazz: the Magazine (London), see *Jazz fm*
Jazz: metodiká publicace určená členum jaazové sekce [from 1979 *Jazz: bulletin současné hudbe*] (Prague, *fl.* 1970s–1980s), irreg.
Jazz: miesięcznik ilustrowany (Gdańsk, Poland, 1956–8; Warsaw, 1959–)
Jazz: nouvelle revue de jazz et de pop music (Nîmes, France, Oct–Dec 1970–?), quarterly
Jazz: a Quarterly of American Music (Berkeley, CA, Oct 1958 – winter 1960), irreg. (5 nos.)
Jazz: revue d'information (Marseilles, France, 1957–61); contd by *Jazz hip*
Jazz: Unterhaltungs- und Informationszeitschrift für Jazz, Blues, Gospel and Spirituals, Rhythm 'n' Blues, Soul [from ?v/1 (Jan/Feb 1978) *Jazz & Classic*] (Muttenz, Switzerland, ?1974–1979), bimonthly (6 vols. = ?36 nos.)
Jazz actuel (Tours, Jan 1995–), quarterly
Jazz Age Chronicles, see *Ted Slampyak's Jazz Age Chronicles*
Jazz Agenda (Nijmegen, Netherlands, 1989–), annually
Jazz a go-go [*Jazz Klub Akwarium*] (Warsaw, Jan 1994–), every 6 weeks
Jazz & Blues (London, April 1971 – Dec 1973), monthly (3 vols. = 32 nos.); contd from *Jazz Monthly*; incorp. into *Jazz Journal* (Jan 1974)
Jazz and Bluesletter (Oklahoma City, ?1984–)
Jazz & Blues Radio Listings, see *Jazz Vine*
Jazz & Blues Report, see *Jazz Report* (Buffalo)
Jazz & Classic, see *Jazz: Unterhaltungs- und Informationszeitschrift . . .*
Jazz & Culture (Zurich, March 1999–), monthly
Jazz & Keyboard [*Jazz and Keyboard Workshop*] (Katonah, NY, 1986 – Aug/Sept 1988), 9 issues a year; contd by *Piano Stylist & Jazz Workshop*
Jazz & Pop, see *Jazz* (New York, 1962)
Jazz & Tzaz (Athens, 1993–), monthly
Jazz à Paris (Paris, 1988), monthly
Jazz Archivist: a Newsletter of the William Ransom Hogan Jazz Archive (New Orleans, May 1986–), half-yearly
Jazz Around (Brussels, Jan 1995 – Nov 1998), 5 issues a year (17 nos.)
Jazz at the Pizza Express [from no.29 (Feb 1982) *Jazz Express Incorporating Jazz at the Pizza Express*; from no.50 (March 1984) *Jazz Express*] (London, 1978 – Dec 1993/Jan 1994), 11 issues a year (161 nos.); from no.162 (March 1994) incorp. into *Boz* (retaining independent numeration)
Jazz at Ronnie Scott's (London, Aug/Sept [1979]–), bimonthly
Jazz aus Stuttgart: Mitteilungsblatt (Stuttgart, 1956–?)
Jazz Australia (Sydney, 1976–), monthly
Jazz Australia Magazine (Brisbane, 1980–81), monthly
Jazzavisen [from i/5 (1934) *Jazz*; from v/1 (1938) *Jazz og film*; from v/7 (1938) *Musik og film*] (Copenhagen, 1934–8), monthly (5 vols.)
Jazzband (Buenos Aires, March/April 1972 – Feb 1974), irreg. (6 nos.)
Jazzbarátok kiskönyvtára (Pécs, Hungary, 1990–), irreg.
Jazz Bazaar (Rotterheide, Germany, April 1969 – June 1971; Neustadt Rotterheide, Germany, Sept 1971 – Dec 1971/Jan 1972), irreg. (12 nos.)
Jazz Beat (New Orleans, 1989–), quarterly
Jazz Beat: the Heart of the Music Scene, see *Beat*
Jazz Beat: the Lively Jazz Magazine [from ii/1 (Jan 1965) *Jazzbeat: the Official Publication of the Jazzbeat Association*] (London, Jan 1964 – Dec 1966), monthly (3 vols.); contd from *Jazz News & Review*, see *Jazz News* (London)
Jazzbladid (Reykjavík)
Jazz Blast (Mt. Ephraim, NJ, ? – Dec 1973), monthly
Jazz, Blues and Co. (Paris, 1975–83), irreg. (7 vols. = 64 nos.)
Jazz, Blues Soul (Novara, Italy, 1993–), weekly
Jazzbrief auf der Jazz-Institut Darmstadt (Darmstadt, 1997–), irreg.
Jazz bulletin [from no.81 (Aug 1960) *Jazz Scene*; from no.93 (May 1961) *Swiss Jazz Notes*] (Basel, Switzerland, Oct 1952–1960; Birsfelden, nr Basel, 1960–61; Reinach, nr Basel, 1961–3), 3 issues a year, from 1953 monthly, later 10 issues a year, then irreg. (97 nos.); suppl.: *Who's Who: Discograph* (1952–6), annually; c.i. nos.1–54 pubd separately as *Who's Where in our Jazz-bulletin* (1957)
Jazz-bulletin (Pilzen, Czechoslovakia [now Czech Republic], 1967), 6 issues a year
Jazz bulletin du Hot Club de Marseille [from no.3 (Jan 1957) *Jazz bulletin*] (Marseilles, France, Oct 1956–1963), monthly, from no.2 (*c*Nov 1956) 9 issues a year (33 nos.)

Jazz butlletí (Barcelona), bimonthly

Jazz Canadiana (Markham, Canada, Aug 1996–), <http://www.jazzcanadiana.on.ca> [web only]

Jazz Cassette, see *Jazz CD*

Jazz Catalogue, see DISCOGRAPHIES, *General*, G. Cherrington

Jazz CD [also *Jazz Cassette*] (Saffron Walden, England, 1992, from i/2 Bishop's Stortford, England), monthly (3 nos.)

Jazz CD, Record, Video [1986], see *Swing Journal*

Jazz Changes: the Magazine of the International Association of Schools of Jazz (London, spring 1994–), 3 issues a year; web edn at <http://www.jazzcontinuum.com> [after vii/3 (autumn 2000) web only]

JazzChord (Sydney, 1993–), irreg.; web edn at <http://www.magna.com.au/georhgeh/ozjazzjc.html#jazzchord>

Jazz Circle News (Manchester, England, Feb 1978 – Oct 1979), monthly (18 nos.)

Jazz classique (Corneville, France, June 1998–), 5 issues a year

Jazz Club Bulletin, see *Second Line*

Jazz Club Karlsruhe eV (Rastatt, Germany), bimonthly

Jazz Club News (Frankfurt am Main, Germany, Aug 1945 – Feb 1948), monthly

Jazz Commentary (Dalbeattie, Scotland, 1944–5)

Jazz Communicator [*Jazz Communicator Newsletter*] (Jenison, MI, Feb–April 1995–), quarterly

Jazz Composers Collective Newsletter (New York, 1992–), 5 issues a year; web edn at <http://www.jazzcollective.com/newsletters.html>

Jazz Container [*Jahrbuch für improvisierte Musik*] (Hofheim am Taunus, Germany, 1986–7), annually (2 nos.)

Jazz.co.nz (Auckland, New Zealand, 1996–), <http://www.jazz.co.nz> [web only]

Der Jazz-Courier, see *Vier Viertel*

Jazz diffusion magazine (Lille, France, Sept 1994–), bimonthly

Jazz Digest (New Orleans, Jan–March 1966), monthly (3 nos.)

Jazz Digest (McLean, VA, Jan/Feb 1972 – June 1974), irreg. (3 vols. = 18 nos.); suppl.: *Jersey Jazz* (1973); contd from *Hip: the Jazz Record Digest*

Jazz di ieri e di oggi (Milan, 1959–), quarterly, then annually

Jazz-disco (Malmö, Sweden, April 1960–?), quarterly

Jazz Disco & Video [1984–5], see *Swing Journal*

Jazz Discounter, see *Discounter*

Jazz Dixie/Swing: du Ragtime au Big Band (Saint-Leu La Forêt, France, cNov 1993 – Aug 1995; Chéronvilliers, France, Nov 1995–), quarterly

Jazz Down Under (Camden, Australia, 1974–), bimonthly

Jazz Down Under (Sydney, 1975–7), monthly (20 nos.)

Jazz Echo: Publication of the International Jazz Federation, see *Swinging Newsletter*

Jazz-Echo: ständige Gondel-Beilage für die Jazzfreunde (Hamburg, Germany, 1949–?1968), monthly; suppl. to *Gondel Magazine*

Jazz Education, Jazz Animation (Budapest, 1979–80), half-yearly (2 nos.)

Jazz Educators Journal, see *National Association of Jazz Educators: Newsletter*

Jazz ensuite (Paris, Oct 1983 – summer 1984), bimonthly (5 nos.)

Der Jazzer (Germany, March 1960 – April 1962)

Jazzette (Boston, 1944–5)

Jazz Express, see *Jazz at the Pizza Express*

Jazz Facts (Amsterdam, 1997–), weekly, <http://www.netcetera.nl/jazzfacts> [web only]

Jazz Festivals International Directory, see World Jazz Calendar of Festivals & Events

Jazz 57 [from ii/1 (Dec 1957) *Jazz 58*] (Brussels, Dec 1956–1958), 10 issues a year

Jazzfinder [from ii/1 (Jan 1949) *Playback*] (New Orleans, Jan 1948 – March 1950, Jan–March/April 1952), irreg. (4 vols. = 29 nos.)

Jazz fm [from no.12 (1992), *Jazz: the Magazine*; from no.22 (1993), *Jazz/a Guardian Magazine*, from no.23 (March 1994), *Jazz: the Magazine*; from no.24 (May/June 1994) *Jazz Magazine*, from no.28 (Jan/Feb 1993) *Jazz Magazine International*] (London, 1990 – May/June 1995), bimonthly (30 nos.)

Jazz, Folk & Blues: a Monthly Discographical Listing of Current Record Releases, see *Jazz Monthly*

Jazzforschung/Jazz Research (Graz, Austria, 1969–), annually

Jazzforum (Vienna, 1955), 1 vol.

Jazz Forum (Stockholm, 1966–), 6 issues a year

Jazz Forum (Warsaw and Vienna, 1967–), bimonthly [2 edns, Eng. (intl edn) and Pol., to no.136–7 (1992); thereafter Pol. edn only]

Jazz Forum: Quarterly Review of Jazz and Literature (Fordingbridge, England, May 1946 – July 1947), quarterly (5 nos.)

Jazz Freak (Breda, Netherlands, Sept 1973–1995), bimonthly

Der Jazzfreund (Itzehoe, Germany, 1953–5), 3 vols.; contd as *Mitteilungsblatt der Arbeitsgemeinschaft norddeutscher Jazz-Clubs*

Der Jazzfreund: Mitteilungsblatt für Jazzfreunde in Ost und West (Goseck, nr Halle, Germany, March 1958 – April 1960; Wanne-Eickel, Germany, Sept 1962 – March 1965; Menden, Germany, June 1965–), monthly, from Sept 1962 quarterly

Jazz Friends Review (Chatham, NY, Dec 1995–?), irreg., <http://tri-millenia.net/jfr/about.htm> [web only]

Jazzgram (Chicago, 1969–), monthly

Jazz Guide (London, 1964/5–1965/6), monthly (3 vols.)

Jazz Guitar International: String Jazz (Doncaster, England, 1997–), <http://www.musicweb-uk.com> [web only]

Jazz Guitar Online (Orlando, FL, July 1995–), <http://www.jazzguitar.com> [web only]

Jazz halo (Torhout, Belgium, 1997–), quarterly

Jazz Happenings (Vancouver, Canada, 1978–), monthly

Jazz Heritage Foundation (Los Angeles, 1980–c1988), bimonthly, from 1988 quarterly

Jazz hihyo (Tokyo, 1972–), quarterly

Jazz hip (Marseilles, France, Oct 1961 – Sept 1965), *c* monthly (38 nos.); contd from *Jazz: revue d'information*

Jazzhíradó: a Benkó Dixieland Club tájékoztatója [Jazz news: bulletin of the Benkó Dixieland Club] (Budapest, 1971 – Sept 1975), irreg. (17 nos.)

Jazzhíradó: a Szegedi ifiúsági jazz klub híradója [Jazz news: newsletter of the Szeged youth jazz club] (Szeged, Hungary, March, April 1964), 2 nos.

Jazz Home (Frankfurt am Main, Germany, April–Aug 1949), monthly (1 vol.)

Jazz-hot: revue internationale de la musique de jazz, [1st ser.] (Paris, March 1935 – July/Aug 1939), 11 issues a year [in Fr. and Eng.] (32 nos.); new ser. as *Jazz hot* (Paris, March 1945–), to Dec 1947 irreg., 1948–76 11 issues a year, 1977 – Jan 1991, 9 or 10 issues a year, Jan 1991 – Aug 1991 irreg., from 1991 11 issues a year; main title index to [1st ser.] and new ser. nos.1–500 pubd in no.500 (1993), 501 (1993), 502 (1993); c.i. at <http://www.jazzhot.net/fr/documentation.html>; suppl.: *Annuaire de jazz*; incorp. *Jazz hot: la revue internationale de la musique de jazz* (Brussels) and *Hot-revue: revue mensuelle de jazz-hot* (Lausanne, Switzerland)

Jazz hot: la revue internationale de la musique de jazz (Brussels, 1948–9), monthly (2 vols.); incorp. *Hot Club magazine* (Nov 1948); incorp. into *Jazz-hot*

Jazz House (Silver Spring, MD, spring 1997–), <http://www.jazzhouse.org> [web only]

Jazzig (Bergisch Gladbach, Germany, May 1991 – Nov 1991), monthly

Jazz Illustrated (London, 1949/50), monthly (1 vol. = 8 nos.)

Jazz Improv (Jenkintown, PA, 1997–2000; Grafton, VT, 2000–), quarterly

Jazz Index: Bibliographie unselbständiger Jazzliteratur/Bibliography of Jazz Literature in Periodicals, see BIBLIOGRAPHIES AND REFERENCE MATERIALS, N. Ruecker

The Jazzine (n.p., 1999–), <http://www.jazzine.com> [web only]

Jazz Information (New York, 8 Sept 1939 – Nov 1941), weekly, from ii/1 (26 July 1940) fortnightly, later irreg. (2 vols. = 51 nos.)

Jazz information (Paris, May 1949 – late 1949), 5 nos.

Jazzinformation (Copenhagen, Feb 1950 – June/July 1950), monthly (5 nos.)

Jazzinformation: tribune, see Tribune

Jazz in Japan (Tokyo, June 2000–), weekly

Jazz Institute of Chicago (Chicago, 1997–), monthly, <http://www.jazzinstituteofchicago.org> [web only]

Jazz Interactions (Glen Oaks, NY, ?–), semimonthly

Jazz International (Germany, Feb 1960)

Jazz in the Midlands (Brighton, England, 1987–), bimonthly

Jazz in the North West (Brighton, England, 1987–), bimonthly

Jazz in the South (Brighton, England, 1987–), bimonthly

Jazz in the South West (Brighton, England, 1987–), bimonthly

Jazz in Time (Neuville, Belgium, Feb 1989–1995), 10 issues a year

Jazz in Wales (Brighton, England, 1987–), bimonthly

Jazz in Yorkshire & the North (Brighton, England, 1987–), bimonthly

Jazzit (Helsinki, 1987–94), bimonthly; contd by *Jazzrytmit*

Jazz It: Italian jazz magazine (Terni, Italy, Sept/Oct 1999–), bimonthly

Jazziz (Gainesville, FL, Jan/Feb 1984–), bimonthly, from Nov 1994 monthly

Jazzjaarboek (Amsterdam, 1982–8), annually (7 nos.)

Jazz Journal [from vi/2 (Feb 1953) to vi/11 (Nov 1953) *Jazz Journal and Popular Music Review*; incorp. *Jazz & Blues* in xxvii/1 (Jan 1974) to form *Jazz Journal and Jazz and Blues*; from xxvii/11 (Nov 1974) to xxviii/8 (Aug 1975) *Jazz Journal: Incorporating "Jazz and Blues"*; from xxx/5 (May 1977) *Jazz Journal International*] (London, 1948 – July 1999; from lii/8 (Aug 1999) Loughton, England), monthly

Jazz Journal (Heemstede, Netherlands, Feb 1955 – July 1956), monthly (11 nos.)

Jazz Journal (Halle, Germany, 1955–6), 2 vols.

Jazz-journalen (Tønsberg, Norway, 1959–60), 2 nos.

Jazz, Jump & Jive (London, spring 1988; March 1995 – May/June 1996), irreg. (5 nos.)

Jazz Junction Jive (England, 1943–5), annually

Jazz Kalendar (Munich, 1956–?)

Jazzklarinétos [Jazz clarinetist] (Dunakeszi, Hungary, May 1995 – Aug 1996), irreg. (3 nos.)

Jazz Klub Akwarium, see *Jazz a go-go*

Jazzkutatás [Jazz research] (Budapest, Jan – June 1995, March 1999–), irreg. (3 nos.); from March 1999 quarterly CD-ROM

Jazz Letter (New York, 1960–), monthly

Jazzletter (Minneapolis, *fl.* 1980s)

Jazzletter, see *Gene Lees Jazzletter*

JazzLife (Tokyo, ?1978–), monthly

Jazzline (Glen Oaks, NY), weekly

Jazzline (Melbourne, Australia, June 1968–?), quarterly

Jazz Line (Rosslyn, NY, 1980 – 27 April 1981; Mineola, NY, 1981–), fortnightly, from 1981 monthly

Jazzline: the Journal of Traditional and Mainstream Music (Hull, England, 1992), monthly (2 nos.)

Jazzlink (San Diego, May 1988–?), monthly

Jazz Listener (Perth, Australia, 1994–8), irreg.

Jazzlive (Vienna, 1983–), quarterly; web edn at <http://www.onstage.at/jazzlive/INDEX.HTM>

Jazz magasinet, see *Jazz Society: månedsblad for jazz*

Jazz Magazine (Barcelona, Aug 1935 – June 1936), 8 nos.

Jazz Magazine (Buenos Aires, Sept 1945 – Oct 1946), monthly, later 4 to 7 issues a year

Jazz magazine (Paris, Dec 1954–), monthly; web edn at <http://www.jazzmagazine.com>

Jazz Magazine (Northport, NY, summer 1976 – spring 1980), quarterly (3 vols. = 14 nos.)

Jazz Magazine (Amsterdam, 1993–), bimonthly [Dutch edn of *Jazz magazine* (Paris)]

Jazz Magazine [*Jazzi magazine*] (Warsaw, 1995–), bimonthly; contd from *Jazz* (Warsaw)

Jazz magazine (Vimerate, Italy, 1998–), monthly [CD-ROM]

Jazz Magazine (Chilwell, nr Newark-on-Trent, England), see *Jazz Record*

Jazz Magazine (New York) see *Jazz* [*Jazz & Pop*] (1962)

Jazz Magazine (London), see *Jazz fm*

Jazz Magazine International, see *Jazz fm*

Jazzman (Paris, March 1995–), 11 issues a year; contd from *Jazzman: supplément du monde de la musique*

Jazzman: supplément du monde de la musique (Paris, Oct 1992 – Feb 1995), 11 issues a year (27 nos.); contd by *Jazzman*

Jazzmanía (Buenos Aires, 1957–), irreg.

Jazz Matters: About Jazz, see *Edge Jazz Newsletter*

Jazzmen News (England, 1945–), monthly

Jazz Moderne (Vienna, 1953/4), 1 vol.

Jazz Monthly (London, March–May 1955; St. Austell, England, June 1955 – Feb 1971), monthly (192 nos.); suppl.: *Jazz Records: a Monthly Discographical Listing of Current Jazz Releases* [from at latest Nov 1965 *Jazz, Folk & Blues: a Monthly Discographical Listing of Current Record Releases*] (England, ? Oct 1962 – Feb 1966); contd as *Jazz & Blues*

Jazz Music [from 1954 *Jazz Music: the International Jazz Magazine*] (London, Oct 1942 – March/April 1944; *c*July 1946 – April 1960), monthly (2 vols. = 18 nos. 1942–4), from 1946 bimonthly (11 vols.); incorp. *Hot News and Rhythm Record Review*; incorp. *Jazz Tempo* (London) (1946); incorp. *Discography* (1947); contd as *Jazz Times* (London); nos.1–3 repr. in 1 vol. (1943)

Jazz Music Mirror, see *Music Mirror*

Jazz Music News (London, April–July 1982), monthly, from no.5 semimonthly (5 nos.)

Jazz Music U.S.A., see *Metronome*

Jazzmusik (Germany, Dec 1958–?)

Jazz, musique, ailleurs (Dijon, France, 1989–), quarterly

Jazznet (Paris, Jan 1996–), <http://www.culturekiosque.com/jazz/index.htm> [web only]

Jazz New England (Andover, MA, Oct 1974 – ?Nov 1975), irreg. (?8 nos.)

Jazz New England Journal (West Upton, MA, autumn 1983–), quarterly

Jazz News (Liège, Belgium, May 1945 – ?June 1946), bimonthly

Jazz News [from vi/44 (7 Nov 1962) *Jazz News & Review*] (London, Nov 1956 – Dec 1963), monthly, from 5 Dec 1958 fortnightly, from iv/7 (25 March 1960) weekly; contd as *Jazz Beat*

Jazz News (Idyllwild, CA, 1974–), quarterly

Jazz News (Auckland, New Zealand, 1983), monthly

Jazz News (Netherlands, Sept 1996–), monthly

Jazz News (Dublin), see *Jazz News: Ireland's Jazz & Blues Magazine*

Jazz N.E.W.S., see *No Name Jazz News*

Jazz News: Blue Star Revue (Paris, Dec 1948 – June 1950), 10 issues a year (11 nos.)

Jazz News: Ireland's Jazz & Blues Magazine [from no.3 (May/June 1987) *Jazz News*; from ii/3 (July/Aug 1988) *Jazz News International*] (Dublin, Dec 1986–), bimonthly

Jazz News: offizielles Organ des Hot Club Zürich (Zurich, Nov 1940 – Jan/Feb 1942), 9 nos. [variously in Eng., Fr., and Ger.]

Jazz News Bluesletter (Lincoln, NE)

Jazz News des Jazzring Austria (Vienna, 1971–)

Jazz News International, see *Jazz News: Ireland's Jazz & Blues Magazine*

Jazz Newsletter (Kerrville, TX, Jan 1984 – April 1986), monthly; contd from *The Jazzologist*

Jazz Newsletter, see *NOJC News*

Jazz-Newsletter (Darmstadt, Germany), see *JID Newsletter*

Jazz New York (New York, 195?–)

Jazznocracy (Liverpool, England, n.d. [1973]; Wavendon, England, n.d. [1974]), irreg. (5 nos.)

Jazz-note (Lyons, France, 1953), bimonthly (2 nos.)

Jazz Notes [from no.37 (Feb 1944) *Jazz Notes and Blue Rhythm*; from no.60 (Jan 1946) *Jazz Notes*; no.96 (Sept 1949) and no.97 (Oct 1949) *Jazz Notes, Incorporating Hot Notes*] (Melbourne, Australia, Jan 1941 – Oct 1950; July 1960 – Dec 1962) three-weekly, from i/4 (March 1941) monthly [ceased pubn 1950–60] (113 nos.); incorp. *Blue Rhythm* (Feb 1944)

Jazz Notes (New Orleans, Sept 1951–?), quarterly

Jazz Notes (Indianapolis, *fl.*1959–68), irreg.

Jazz Notes (Harwich Post, nr Boston, 1978–), quarterly

Jazz Notes (Minneapolis, 1978–), monthly

Jazz Notes (Littleton, CO, 198?–), quarterly

Jazz Notes (Dennisport, MA, ?1983–), irreg.

Jazz Notes (Kewdale, Western Australia, 1984–), monthly

Jazz Notes (Las Vegas, NV, April 1992–), bimonthly

Jazz Notes (Calgary, Canada)

Jazz Notes (Gainesville, FL)

Jazz Notes: a Newsletter of the Jazz Journalists Association (Silver Spring, MD, spring 1989–), quarterly

Jazz Notes: la revue du jazz Rhône-Alpes (Lyons, France, Jan 1989–), bimonthly

Jazz Not Jazz (Palermo, Sicily, Dec 1993–), quarterly

Jazz Now Interactive, see *Jazz Now Magazine*

Jazz Now Magazine (Oakland, CA, May 1991–), 11 issues a year; web edn, entitled *Jazz Now Interactive* (1994–), at <http://www.jazznow.com>

Jazz nu: maandblad voor aktuele geïmproviseerde muziek (Tilburg, Netherlands, Oct 1978 – summer 1980; Amsterdam, Sept 1980 – autumn 1985; Groningen, Netherlands, Nov 1985–), monthly; contd from *Jazz press*; c.i. annually

Jazznytt [from May 1969 *Jazz-nytt*, from 1973 to 1976 *Jazz nytt*] (Bergen, Norway, 1960–65; Molde, Norway, 1965–1975/6; Oslo, 1976–), 5 issues a year, from 1983 (new ser.) 6 issues a year

Jazznytt [from 1967 *Jazznytt från SJR* [Svenska Jazzklubbarnas Riksforbund]] (Stockholm, 1965–), 5 issues a year, from 1982 bimonthly; contd from *Jazz Times* (Stockholm)

Jazz NZ (Wellington, New Zealand, 1981–), quarterly

Jazz og film, see *Jazzavisen*

Jazzogie journal (Champagne-au-Mont-d'Or, France, 1991–), quarterly

The Jazzologist (Orange, nr Santa Ana, CA, May 1963 – Oct 1972; Kerrville, TX, Nov 1972 – Dec 1983), monthly, from July 1968 5 issues a year; contd as *Jazz Newsletter*

Jazzology (London, 1944); new ser. (London, Jan 1946 – Feb 1947), monthly (14 nos.)

Jazzology (Lleida, Spain, 1992–), half-yearly

Jazzology Newsletter, see *CRC Newsletter*

Jazz on Cassette, see *Jazz on CD*

Jazz on CD [also *Jazz on Cassette*] (London, May 1993 – Jan 1996), monthly, from no.16 (May 1995) irreg. (19 nos.)

Jazz One: the Jazz Magazine You Can Play (USA, April 1999–)

Jazz Online (San Francisco, 1991–), daily, <http://www.jazzonln.com> [web only]

Jazz o'Maniac (Paris, Feb 1972 – after 1976), *c* monthly; contd from *Le criquette: bulletin de l'Association Français des Amateurs du Jazz N.O.*

Le Jazzophone (Paris, autumn 1978–), quarterly

Jazzosphère (Blagnac, France, Feb–April 1997–), quarterly

Jazz Ottawa (Ottawa, March 1975–) [some issues are reportedly titled *Jazz Messenger* or *Jazz Notes* but no details are available]

JazzOwl Weekly Jazz Classic, weekly, <http://www.chameleonprod.com/jazzowl> [web only]

Jazz Page (Tokyo, Nov 1995–), <http://www.impr.com> [web only]

Jazz panorama (Marseilles, France, July 1960 – Sept 1960), 2 nos.

Jazz Panorama: the Canadian Music Scene (Toronto, Dec 1946 – May 1948), irreg.

Jazzpapír [Jazz paper] (Budapest, Sept 1995), 1 no.

Jazz Parade (Adelaide, Australia, Jan 1957–?), monthly

Jazz Parade (Copenhagen), irreg.

Jazz passion (Lussy-sur-Morges, Switzerland, Jan 1989–?), monthly

Jazz Player (Medfield, MA, 1993–); web edn at <http://www.dornpub.com>

Jazz Podium, see *Das internationale Podium*

Jazz press (Almelo, Netherlands, 17 Sept 1975 – 1 Sept 1978), fortnightly, from no.43 (Sept 1977) monthly (54 nos.); contd as *Jazz nu: maandblad voor aktuele geïmproviseerde muziek*

Jazzpress (Budapest, 1990), irreg. (4 nos.)

Jazz Publications (Basel, Switzerland, 1957–61, Berne, 1961–2), irreg.

Jazz Quarterly (Chicago, spring 1942 – autumn 1946), irreg. (?2 vols. = ?7 nos.)

Jazz Quarterly (Kingsville, TX, summer 1942–1945)

Jazz Rag (Berkeley, CA, ?1979–), monthly

Jazz Rag (Birmingham, England, 1987–), bimonthly

Jazz Rag (Wellington, New Zealand, May 1989–1995), quarterly
Jazz Rambler (San Diego, ?1983–), bimonthly
Jazz Rapporter (Copenhagen, July/Aug 1943–1946), 11 issues a year
Jazzrealities Magazine (Freiburg, Germany, Aug 1982–), irreg.
Jazz Record (New York, Feb 1943 – Nov 1947), monthly (60 nos.)
Jazz Record [from Sept 1946, *Jazz incorporating Jazz Record* (cover title *Jazz Magazine*)] (Chilwell, nr Newark-on-Trent, England, 1943 – April 1944; Sept 1946–1947), monthly, from Sept 1946 irreg. (12 nos., 1943–4); incorp. in *Vox Pop* (1945), then *Keynote* (1945–6); independent pubn resumed at iii/1 (Sept 1946)
Jazz Record Review [from ii/10 (Nov 1971) *Jazz Review*] (Adelaide, Australia, 1970–?), irreg.
Jazz Records: a Monthly Discographical Listing of Current Jazz Releases, see *Jazz Monthly*
Jazz Records [1975–83], see *Swing Journal*
Jazz Register (San Diego, Jan–March 1965 – ?Jan–March 1966), quarterly (2 vols. = 5 nos.)
Jazz Report (St. Louis, 1953 – mid-1958; Chicago, mid-1958 – May 1960), irreg. (8 vols.); contd as *Jazz Report* (Ventura, CA)
Jazz Report [from ii/5 (Jan 1962) *Jazz Report: the Record Collector's Magazine*] [*Jazz Report U.S.A.*] (Ventura, CA, Sept 1960 – April 1982), monthly, from iii/3–4 (Jan–Feb 1963) bimonthly, from iv/6 (Nov–Dec 1965) irreg. (10 vols.); contd from *Jazz Report* (St. Louis, later Chicago)
Jazz Report [later *Jazz & Blues Report*] (Buffalo, March 1974–?; Cleveland, April 1978–), monthly
Jazz Report (Toronto, Aug/Sept 1987–), quarterly
Jazz Report (San Diego, 1996–), monthly
Jazzreports: organ for "swing fans" i Danmark (Copenhagen, 1941–3), 3 vols.
Jazz Reprints (Portsmouth, England, 1962/3), 1 vol. (3 nos.)
Jazz Research, see *Jazzforschung/Jazz Research*
Jazz Research News (Graz, Austria, Nov 2000–), quarterly
Jazz Research Papers, see *Proceedings of NAJE Research*
Jazz Research Proceedings, see *Proceedings of NAJE Research*
Jazz Review (New York, Nov 1958 – Jan 1961), irreg. (4 vols. = 23 nos.)
Jazz Review [*Jazz Review and Collector's Discography*] (Long Beach, CA, Jan 1991–), monthly
Jazz Review (Milwaukee, March 1997–), weekly, <http://www.jazzreview.com> [web only]
Jazz Review (Edinburgh, Oct 1999–), monthly; c.i. to record reviews, nos.1–12, pubd separately
Jazz Review, see *Jazz Record Review*
Jazz revista (Barcelona, 1980), 2 nos.
Jazz Revue (Berlin, July 1950 – Dec 1953), monthly (5 vols.); v (1954) incorp. as suppl. in *Vier Viertel*
Jazzrevy (Copenhagen, 1935–6), 2 vols.
Jazzrevy, see *Musikrevue*
Jazz, Rhythm & Blues: schweizerische Jazz-Zeitschrift/Revue suisse de jazz (Zurich, 1968), monthly (1 vol.)
Jazz Riffs (Antwerp, Belgium, 1940, 1946–8), monthly (30 nos.)
Jazzring Austria, see *Jazz News* (Vienna, 1971)
Jazz rytm i piosenka (Warsaw), monthly
Jazzrytmit (Helsinki, 1994–), bimonthly; contd from *Jazzit*
Jazz Scene (London, June 1962– later in 1962), monthly [first issue numbered i/2]
Jazz Scene (Portland, OR, 197?–), monthly
Jazz Scene, see *Jazz-bulletin*
Jazzscope (Chapel Hill, NC), ?quarterly
Jazz Session (Chicago, Sept 1944 – July 1946), variously monthly and bimonthly (13 nos.)
Jazz Society: månedsblad for jazz [from ii/5 (1958) *Jazz Society: organ for Norsk jazzforbund*, from iii/1 (1959) *Jazz magasinet* (Oslo, 1957–9), monthly (3 vols. = 20 nos.)
Jazz Society of Baton Rouge [*Jazz Society*] (Baton Rouge, LA, 1980–), monthly
Jazz Society of Pensacola (Pensacola, FL, 1983–), irreg., from Feb 1995 monthly
Jazz South (Atlanta, autumn 1989–), quarterly
Jazz Special (Copenhagen, 1991–), bimonthly
JazzSpiegel der Deutschen Jazz-Föderation, see *Das internationale Podium*
Jazz Spotlite News (New York, June 1979 – summer 1982), half-yearly (2 vols. = 10 nos.)
Jazz Stage (Gothenburg, Sweden, 1995–), quarterly
Jazz-Statistics (Basel, Switzerland, April 1956 – Oct 1957; Reinach, Switzerland, *c*1958 (no.7) – Sept 1961; Basel, Dec 1961 – Oct 1963), irreg. (29 nos.); suppl.: *Blues-Statistics* (1963), irreg. (3 nos.)
Jazz String Newsletter (Milwaukee, 1982 – July–Sept 1983), quarterly
Jazz Studies (High Wycombe, England, autumn 1964 – autumn 1965; Chinnor, England, autumn 1966), irreg. (4 nos.); [new ser.] Chinnor, England, 1967; London, 1968, Nov 1970), 3 to 4 issues a year, 1 no. in 1970 (3 vols. = 8 nos.); incorp. into *Pieces of Jazz* (1969)
Jazz Studium (Győr-Budapest, 1979–90), irreg. (19 nos.) [incl. 8 music cassette suppls, 1983–8]
Jazz Swing Journal (Paris, Nov–Dec 1986–?), bimonthly
Jazz tajekoztato, see *A Magyar zenemfűvészek szövetsége jazz szakosztalyanak tájékoztatója*
Jazz Talk (Coventry, England, 1991–2), 4 nos. (3 issues)
Jazz tango [Dec 1931–1940 *Jazz tango dancing*]: *revue internationale de la musique de danse* (Paris, 1930–40), monthly (66 nos.); incorp. into *L'orchestre: organe d'informations musicales* to form *L'orchestre et Jazz tango réunis* (1963–8), bimonthly; contd from *La revue du jazz: tout ce qui concerne la musique de danse et le disque*
Jazz Tempo (London, March 1943 – March 1944), irreg. (19 nos.); incorp. into *Jazz Music* (1944)
Jazz Tempo (Hollywood, CA, Dec 1945–), irreg.
Jazz Tempo: Zeitschrift für die Freunde des Jazz (Kassel, Germany, April/May 1951), 1 vol.
Jazzthetik: Zeitschrift für Jazz und Anderes (Münster, Germany, May 1987–), monthly; web edn at <http://www.jazzthetik.de>
Jazz Thing (Cologne, Oct 1993–), 5 issues a year; web edn at <http://www.jazzthing.de> (Oct 1996–)
Jazz 360° (Sierre, Switzerland, Oct 1977 – April 1986), monthly (88 nos.)
Jazztime (Italy, 1952), 3 nos.
Jazz Time (Schneisingen, Switzerland, 1983–), bimonthly
Jazz Time (Frankfurt am Main, Germany, 1991-2)
Jazz Times (Stockholm, 1955–1961/2), irreg. (?18 nos.); contd as *Jazznytt*
Jazz Times (London, Sept 1964 – Dec 1971/Jan 1972), monthly; contd from *Jazz Music*
Jazz Times (Altrincham, England, 1986–94), monthly
Jazz Times (Washington, DC), see *Sound Exposure*
Jazz Today (New York, Oct 1956–1957), monthly
Jazz Trumpet Journal (Bassett, CA, April 1991–), monthly
Jazz UK (Cardiff, 1995–), bimonthly
Jazz Up! (Buenos Aires, June 1965–)
Jazz USA (Portland, OR, Jan 1997–), monthly, <http://jazzusa.com> [web only]
Jazz View (Toronto, 1993–), irreg., <http://www.music.mcgill.ca/~jazz/JazzView/Overview.html> [web only]
Jazz Vine, see *Montreal jazz grapevine*
Jazz Wax (Birmingham, England, Aug–Oct 1948), monthly (3 nos.)
Jazzways [*Jazzways: a Yearbook of Hot Music*] (Cincinnati, 1946–7), 2 vols.
De jazzwereld (The Hague, 1931 – Nov/Dec 1940), monthly (10 vols.)
Jazz wereld (Hilversum, Netherlands, July 1965 – May/June 1973), bimonthly (43 nos.); c.i. nos.1–24 pubd in no.25 (Aug/Sept 1969)
Jazz West (Oakland, CA, June 1999–), daily, <http://www.jazzwest.com> [web only]
Jazz West Newsletter (Oakland, CA), monthly by e-mail from <http://www.jazzwest.com>
Jazzwise (London, 1997–), 10 issues a year
Jazz World (New York, March 1957–), bimonthly
Jazz World (New York, 1984–), bimonthly
Jazz World (Manchester, England, Feb 1991–), monthly; contd from *Juzz Jazz*
Jazz World, see *Swinging Newsletter*
Jazz World Index, see *Swinging Newsletter*
Jazz Writings, see OTHER BOOKS, B. Kinnell and J. Asman
Jazz-Zeitung (Munich, 1982–), monthly; web edn at <http://www.jazzzeitung.de>
Jazz Zine (Sun City, CA, Dec 1997–), irreg., <http://members.aol.com/plabjazz> [web only]
Jefferson Blues Magazine from no.7 (1969), *Jefferson*] (Sundsvall, Sweden, no.1–6 (1968–9), Vallentura, Sweden, ?1969–? [after 1983], Stockholm, ? [after 1983]–), quarterly
Jelly Music Magazine (Seattle, 1995–), quarterly; archived at <http://www. roll.com>
Jerry's Rhythm Rag (Uppsala, Sweden, winter 1993–1994), irreg. (5 nos.)
Jersey Jazz (Pluckemin, nr Plainfield, NJ, later Rahway, NJ, later Verona, NJ, 1973–) mostly 10 or 11 issues a year; i (1973) (= 11 nos.) as suppl. to *Jazz Digest*
JID [Jazz-Instituts Darmstadt] *Newsletter* [from 1993 *Jazz-Newsletter*] (Darmstadt, Germany, Sept 1992), irreg., suppl.: *Wegweiser Jazz* (1993–), every other year
Joslin's Jazz Journal (Parsons, KS, Feb 1982–), quarterly
Journal of Jazz Discography (Newport, Monmouthshire, Wales, Nov 1976 – Sept 1979), irreg. (5 nos.)
Journal of Jazz Studies: Incorporating Studies in Jazz Discography [from iii/2 (spring 1976) *Journal of Jazz Studies*] (New Brunswick, NJ, 1973/4–1980/81), half-yearly; contd as *Annual Review of Jazz Studies* (1982–), irreg.
Juke (Tokyo, summer 1982–?), irreg.
Juke Blues (London, July 1985–), quarterly; c.i. nos.1–26 pubd separately (1992)
Jukebox (Auckland, New Zealand, Aug 1946 – April 1947), monthly
Just Jass (Birmingham, England, April 1962–?) irreg., from Jan 1963 bimonthly
Just Jazz (Moorhead, MN, 1992–), quarterly
Just Jazz (New York), irreg.

Just Jazz (Houston)

Just Jazz (London), see OTHER BOOKS, S. Traill and G. Lascelles

Just Jazz Aquitane (Bordeaux, France, 1982–4), bimonthly

Just Jazz: the Traditional Jazz Magazine (Sidcup, England, May 1998 – Aug 1996; London, Sept 1996–), monthly

Just Jazz Guitar (Atlanta, 1994–), quarterly

Juzz Jazz (Manchester, England, June 1990 – Oct 1990), monthly (5 nos.); contd by *Jazz World* (Manchester, England)

Kansas City JAM: Jazz Ambassador Magazine (Kansas City, MO, 1995–?), daily, <http://www.kansascity.com/kcjazz> [web only]

KC Jazz Ambassador (Kansas City, MO, May 1986–), bimonthly

Keskidee: a Journal of Black Musical Traditions (Rochford, Essex, England, autumn 1986 – summer 1993), irreg. (3 nos.)

Keyboard, see *Contemporary Keyboard*

Keyboard Classics (Paramus, NJ, 1980 – Jan–Feb 1993; from April–May 1993 Katonah, NY), bimonthly; from April–May 1993 merged with *Piano Stylist* to become *Keyboard Classics & Piano Stylist*

Keynote (Beverly Hills, CA, March 1941–), bimonthly

Keynote [from ii/1 (Jan 1947) *Keynote: the Music Magazine*] (London, autumn 1945 – Oct/Nov 1947), quarterly, from Jan 1947 irreg.; incorp. *Jazz Record* [until autumn 1946], *LLCU Newsletter*, and *Vox Pop*

Keynote: a Magazine for the Musical Arts (New York, 1977–), monthly

Keynote: the Music Magazine for Moderns (Birmingham, England, Nov 1956–?)

Killer Diller (London, autumn 1996–), irreg.

Klacto: Hawaii's Jazz Newsletter (Honolulu, Feb 1980 – April 1981), monthly except July, from i/9 (Nov 1980) bimonthly (2 vols. = ?15 nos.)

Label jazz (Boulazac, France, *c*1990–), irreg.

L.A. Jazz Scene (North Hollywood, CA), monthly

Latin Beat Magazine (Gardena, CA, 1991–), 10 issues a year

Letter from Evans (Winter Park, FL, Sept–Oct 1989–), bimonthly, from winter 1994 quarterly

Liner Notes: Music News & Reviews for Music People (Washington, DC, 1972–)

Living Blues [from no.21 (1975) *Living Blues: a Journal of the Black American Blues Tradition*] (Chicago, 1970 – spring 1983; University, MS, autumn 1983–) quarterly, from no.19 (Jan–Feb 1975) bimonthly, from no.43 (summer 1979) quarterly, from no.67 (1985) 5 issues a year, from no.78 (Jan–Feb 1988) bimonthly; suppl.: *Living Blues Letter* (Jan 1983 – Dec 1984), monthly; c.i. nos.1–39 pubd in no.40 (1978)

The Long Player, see DISCOGRAPHIES, *Other listings*

Looking Ahead (Vancouver, Canada, Feb–March 1991–), bimonthly

Magazyn muzyczny [*MM*] [from before 1963 *Jazz*] (Warsaw, 1956–81) monthly except July–Aug; contd by *Jazz Magazine* [*Jazzi magazine*]

A Magyar zenemfűvészek szövetsége jazz szakosztalyanak tájékoztatója [Bulletin of the Hungarian musicians' soviets jazz section] [from no.7 (Dec 1976) *Jazz tajekoztat* [Jazz bulletin]] (Budapest, Dec 1975 – Sept 1981), irreg. (21 nos.)

Mainstream (Richmond, Surrey, England, summer 1974), 1 no.

MaJazz (Budapest, Oct 1995–?Dec 1996), monthly

Making Music (Swanley, England, April 1986–), monthly

Marge Hofacre's Jazz News, see *No Name Jazz News*

Margen (Lugo, Spain, 1994–), quarterly

Matrix: Jazz Record Research Magazine (Victoria, Australia, July 1954 – Dec 1958; Stoke on Trent, later Madeley, nr Crewe, England, Jan 1959 – Dec 1975), bimonthly, from no.93 (July 1971) irreg. (108 nos.); c.i. 1954–63; incorp. *The Discophile* (1959)

Mecca: the Magazine of Traditional Jazz (New Orleans, 1974), monthly (3 nos.)

Melbourne Jazz News (Melbourne, Australia, March 1959–?)

Melodie (Berlin, June 1946 – June 1949), monthly

Melodie (Prague, 1962–), monthly; suppl. *Aktuality melodie* (1969–70), fortnightly

Melodie und Rhythmus (Berlin, 1957–), semimonthly, from April 1971 monthly

Melody Maker and British Metronome [from no.70 (Oct 1931) *Melody Maker*] (London, Jan 1926 – May 1933), monthly; new ser. as *Melody Maker* [from no.330 (Oct 1939) to no.965 (15 March 1952) *Melody Maker Incorporating "Rhythm"*; from no.966 (22 March 1952) *Melody Maker*] (London, 27 May 1933–2000), weekly [no significant jazz content after 1982]

Memory Lane [from ii/1 (Nov 1969) *Memory Lane International*; from v/1 (winter 1972–3) *Memory Lane*] (Whitley Bay, England, Nov 1968–1972; Leigh-on-Sea, England, 1972–), quarterly

Meritt Rag (Hicksville, NY, autumn 1980 – summer 1987), irreg. (8 nos.)

Metronome: Modern Music and its Makers [from lxxvi/1 (Jan 1959) to lxxvii/4 (April 1960) *Music USA*] (New York, 1885 – Dec 1961), monthly (77 vols.); suppl.: *Metronome Yearbook* [*Jazz Music U.S.A.*] (1950–51, 1953–9), annually

Micrography: Jazz and Blues on Microgroove (Deventer, Netherlands, n.d. [Dec 1968] – Feb 1971; Alphen aan de Rijn, Netherlands, May 1971 – June 1982; Amsterdam, Feb 1983 – Oct 1988), irreg. (76 nos.) [in Eng.]; c.i.

Micro surco, see DISCOGRAPHIES, *Other listings*

Midwest Jazz (Minneapolis, spring 1994–), quarterly

Mississippi Coast Jazz Society (Biloxi, MS, 1994–), monthly

Mississippi Rag: the Voice of Traditional Jazz and Ragtime (Minneapolis, Nov 1973–), monthly

Mister Lucky (San Francisco, Dec 1993 – after 1995), monthly; web edn, as *Mr. Lucky: Music for Grown-ups* (1995–), at <http://www.mrlucky.com> [later web only]

Mitteilungen für Jazz-Interessen (Berlin, 1943), 3 nos.

Mitteilungsblatt der Arbeitsgemeinschaft norddeutscher Jazz-Clubs (Hamburg, Germany, 1956–?); contd from *Der Jazzfreund* (Itzehoe, Germany)

MM, see *Magazyn muzyczny*

MM: tidsskrift for rytmisk musik m.m. [from xvii/1 (Jan 1985) *MM: månedsblad for rock og jazz m.m.*; from xvii/9 (Sept 1985) *MM: månedsblad for rock & jazz*] (Copenhagen, 1967–), 9 issues a year

Modern Drummer (Clifton, NJ, 1977–), quarterly, from 1979 6 issues a year, from 1980 9 issues a year, from 1983 monthly; web edn at <http://www.moderndrummer.com>

Modern jazz (Bologna, Italy, 1967–), annually

Modern Percussionist (Cedar Grove, NJ, Dec–Feb 1985 – Sept–Nov 1987), quarterly

Montreal Jazz Grapevine [from Sept/Oct 1993 – 1996 *Jazz Vine* [*Jazzvine*]; from spring 1997 *Planet Jazz*] (Montreal, 1993–), irreg; suppl.: *Jazz and Blues Radio Listings* (Jan ?1996–)

Mumbles (Flushing, NY), quarterly

Münchner Jazznachrichten (Germany, *fl.* 1974–6)

Music (Brussels, 1924 – Dec 1939), monthly

Music (London, 1951/2–1953/4), monthly (3 vols.); contd as *Music Mirror*

Music (New York, 1997–)

Musica disques: lyrique, danse, variétés, jazz (Paris, 1954–?), monthly

Musica jazz (Milan, 1945–), monthly

Musical America Magazine (Boulder, CO, Oct 1976 – March–April 1982), bimonthly

Musical Express, see *Accordion Times & Musical Express*

Musical News [from June 1936 *Musical News & Dance Band*] (London, Oct 1935 – May 1938), monthly

Music and Rhythm (Chicago, Nov 1940 – Aug 1942), irreg. (3 vols.)

Music Box (Cincinnati, 1991–), irreg.

Music Educators Journal (Reston, VA, 1934–), monthly except June–Aug, from July 1994 6 issues a year

Musiche (La Spezia, Italy, 1988–), quarterly

Musician, Player and Listener [from no.43 (April 1983) *Musician* [*Musician Magazine*]] (Gloucester, MA, Sept/Oct 1977–), 8 issues a year

Music in Sweden (Stockholm, 1978–), half-yearly

Music Life (Tokyo, 1950–?), monthly [in Jap.]

Music Maker [from Dec 1971 *Musicmaker*] (Sydney, ?1906–1954, new ser. 1955–), monthly

Music Maker (London, Oct 1966–?), monthly

Music Maker: Official Magazine of the Harry James Appreciation Society [from no.21 (Nov 1990) *Music Maker International*] (London, 1977–), quarterly

Music Master, see DISCOGRAPHIES, *Other listings*

Music Memories [from iii/2 (April 1963) *Music Memories Monthly*; from iii/5 (autumn 1963) *Music Memories Quarterly*; from iii/6 (winter 1963) *Music Memories and Jazz Report*] (Birmingham, AL, July 1961 – spring 1965), 6 issues a year, from iii/2 (April 1963) monthly, from iii/5 (autumn 1963) quarterly (4 vols.); incorp. *Jazz Report* (1961)

Music Mirror [from iv/11 (Dec 1957) alternate issues entitled *Jazz Music Mirror* and *Pop Music Mirror*] (London, May 1954 – July 1958), monthly, from iv/11 (Dec 1957) fortnightly (5 vols.); contd from *Music* (London)

Music Publishers Journal (Jan 1943 – July–Aug 1946), bimonthly

Music Scene (Toronto, 1967–89), irreg.

Music Scene (Dietikon, Switzerland, 1979–93), monthly except July–Aug

Music Scene (Baden, Germany, 1995–), 11 issues a year, from 1996 10 issues a year

Music USA (Heemstede, Netherlands, Feb–May 1954), monthly (4 nos.)

Music USA, see *Metronome*

Musigram (Covina, CA, Jan 1963–), monthly except June–Aug

Musik-Echo: Zeitschrift für Melodie und Rhythmus (Berlin, June 1930 – March 1934), bimonthly

Musik Fokus (Norway)

Musik für dich (Germany, July–Aug 1948)

Musikjournalen: blad for moderne dansemusikk, see *Norsk jazz*

Musik og film, see *Jazzavisen*

Musik Parade (Copenhagen, July 1949–), monthly

Musikrevue [subtitle varies: *tidsskrift for jazzmusik*; *Jazz, pop, klassik*; from 1961, no.5, to 1970 *Jazzrevy*] (Copenhagen, Sept 1954–1972), 4 issues a year (19 vols.)

NAJE Educator, see *National Association of Jazz Educators: Newsletter*

Names & Numbers (Amsterdam, April 1985 – Jan 1987, Oct 1998–), irreg., (6 nos.) 1985–7, from no.7 (Oct 1998) quarterly [in Eng.]

NARAS Journal (Burbank, CA, April 1990–), half-yearly

National Association of Jazz Educators: Newsletter [from ii/2 (Dec 1969/Jan 1970) *NAJE Educator*; from xiii/2 (Dec 1980/Jan 1981) *Jazz Educators Journal*] (Manhattan, KS, 1968/9–), irreg., from ii/2 (Dec 1969/Jan 1970) 5 issues a year, from iv/1 (Oct/Nov 1971) quarterly, from xxviii/1 (July 1995) 6 issues a year; web edn at <http://jazzcentralstation.com/iaje>
National Jazz Foundation Archive Newsletter (Loughton, Essex, England, spring 1996–), annually
National Society for Jazz Study, see *Organ of the Northern Society for Jazz Study*
Nederlands Jazz Archief Bulletin (Amsterdam, Sept 1991–), quarterly; c.i. nos.1–12 pubd separately (1994), c.i. nos.13–16 pubd separately (1995), c.i. nos.17–20 pubd separately (1996); for web edn see *Jazz Facts*
The Needle: Record Collectors' Guide (New York, June 1944 – summer 1945), irreg. (2 vols. = 6 or 7 nos.)
Needle Time (Swanage, England, Nov–Dec 1985 – Nov 90), bimonthly (31 nos.)
Nerosubianco (Rome, 1994–?)
The Network: Stan Kenton Newsletter (Providence, RI, 1985–), half-yearly
New Beat (London, July 1949 – July 1950), monthly (13 nos.); contd from *The Beat*
New Jazz Record (Vigevano, Italy, May 1954–?), bimonthly; contd from *Federazione Italiana del Jazz New Jazz Society bolletino d'informazioni*
New Jazz Tempo (Hollywood, CA)
New Musical Express, see *Accordion Times & Musical Express*
New Orleans Jazz & Heritage Foundation Quarterly (New Orleans, 1989–), quarterly
New Orleans Jazz Club of California (San Francisco, 1963–71), monthly; contd as *New Orleans Jazz Club of Northern California* (San Francisco, 1972–)
New Orleans Jazz Study Newsletter (Denver, Aug 1991–), irreg.
New Orleans Music (Wheatley, Oxford, England, Oct–Nov 1989 – June 1991; Urmston, England, Aug 1991 – June 1995; Bishop's Stortford, England, Sept 1995–), bimonthly, from iii/2 (Dec 1991) quarterly; contd from *Footnote*
News: Mitteilungsblatt der BFN Rhythm Clubs, see *News Sheet*
News about BMI Music & Writers [from Nov 1964 *BMI: the Many Worlds of Music*] (New York, 1963–), 10 issues a year, from 1972 7 issues a year, from 1973 3 or 4 issues a year; suppl.: *Rhythm and Blues* [1943–68] (1969)
News from NYJO [National Youth Jazz Orchestra] (Harrow, England, April 1988–), quarterly
News of the Muse: the Newsletter of the Creative Opportunity Orchestra (Austin, TX, ?–), irreg.
News Sheet: Mitteilungsblatt der Anglo-German Swing-Clubs [from 1950/51 *News: Mitteilungsblatt der BFN* [British Forces Network] *Rhythm Clubs*] (Hamburg, Germany, 1949/50–1950/51), 2 vols.
New York Jazz Gazette (New York, 1976–?1977), irreg.
Nights at the Turntable (Yaxley, Suffolk, England, 1998–), quarterly
NJSO Journal: the Quarterly Publication of the National Jazz Service Organization (Washington, DC, 1989–), quarterly
NOJC [New Orleans Jazz Club] *News* [*Jazz Newsletter*] (Tiburon, CA, 1971–), monthly
No Name Jazz News [*Jazz N.E.W.S.*] [from 1994 *Marge Hofacre's Jazz News*] (Cincinnati, 1985–93; San Diego, 1994–), bimonthly
Norsk jazz: ukeavis for jazz og moderne dansemusikk [from iii/4 (1957) *Musikjournalen: blad for moderne dansemusikk*] (Bergen, Norway, 1955–7), irreg. (3 vols.)
Northeast Ohio Jazz Society Update (Cleveland), monthly
Northern Society for Jazz Study, see *Organ of the Northern Society for Jazz Study*
Nostalgia (London, May 1975–1977; New Barnet, England, 1978–1991 or later), quarterly
The Note (East Stroudsburg, PA, Sept 1989–), irreg.
Note, Hollywood (Hollywood, CA, March–July 1946), monthly
Notes: le magazine des autres musiques (Nantes, France, 1990–), irreg.
Not Just Jazz (New York, 1980–), 8 issues a year, later quarterly
N.S.J.S., see *Organ of the Northern Society for Jazz Study*
Nuovo musica (Turin, Italy, ?1979–)
NYC/Jazz (New York)
Offbeat (New Orleans, 1993–), monthly; web edn at <http://www.offbeat.com>
Offbeat Jazz (Scarsdale, NY, 1983–)
Oh, Play that Thing (San Francisco, 1948–?), irreg.
On the One (San Francisco, May 1994–1998), quarterly
O papel do jazz (Lisbon, July–Sept 1997 – April–June 1998), quarterly
Option (Santa Monica, CA, March–April 1985 – July–Aug 1998), bimonthly (91 nos.)
Orchestra World (New York, 1925–?1954), irreg., from iv (1928) 10 issues a year (29 vols.)
L'orchestre et Jazz tango réunis, see *Jazz tango*
Organ of the Northern Society for Jazz Study [from no.9 (1944) *N.S.J.S.* (cover title *Northern Society for Jazz Study*); from no.17 (1945) *N.S.J.S.* (cover title *National Society for Jazz Study*)] (Dewsbury, England, 1943–6), 8 issues a year, in 1945 4 issues, in 1946 2 issues (22 nos.)
Original Chicago Blues Annual (Chicago, 1989–92), annually (4 nos.)
Orkester journalen: aktuella nyheter för dansorkestrar [from iv/1 (Jan 1936) *Orkester journalen: tidskrift för modern dansmusik*; from xxi/1 (Jan 1953) *Orkester journalen: tidskrift för jazzmusik*; from li/4 (April 1983) *Orkester journalen: om jazz*] (Stockholm, Nov 1933–), monthly
Panoramade: le magazine des fans de John Zorn (Paris, 1993–), irreg.
Percussionist (Terre Haute, IN, 1963–80), quarterly
Percussive Notes (Urbana, IL, 1962–) irreg.; suppl.: *Percussive Notes Research Edition*, 2 issues a year
Perfectly Frank: the Journal of the Sinatra Music Society (London, later elsewhere in England, 1955–), 6 issues a year
Performing Arts in Canada [from xxvi/3 (spring 1991) *Performing Arts & Entertainment in Canada*] (Toronto, 1961–), quarterly
pfMentum (Ventura, CA, autumn 1997–), ?quarterly
Philharmonic (Heemstede, Netherlands, Jan 1950 – Dec 1953), monthly (32 nos.)
Piano and Keyboard (San Anselmo, CA, 1993–), bimonthly; contd from *Piano Quarterly*
Piano Quarterly [*Piano Quarterly Newsletter*; *Essential Piano Quarterly*] (Wilmington, VT, autumn 1958–1992), quarterly; contd as *Piano & Keyboard*
Piano Stylist & Jazz Workshop [*Piano Stylist*] (Paramus, NJ, Oct–Nov 1988–), bimonthly; contd from *Jazz & Keyboard*; contd by *Keyboard Classics & Piano Stylist*
Piano Today (Katonah, NY, autumn 1995–), quarterly
Pickin' the Blues (East Calder, Scotland, n.d. [Jan 1982] – June 1983), 10 issues a year (15 nos.)
Pickup (London, Jan 1946 – Dec 1947), monthly (2 vols.)
Pieces of Jazz (Canterbury, England, winter 1967–1971), irreg. (9 nos.); no.7 (1969) incorp. *Jazz Studies*
Pittsburgh Jazz Notes (Pittsburgh, 1996–), quarterly
Planet Jazz, see *Montreal Jazz Grapevine*
Platter Chatter (Seattle, Sept 1945–1948), ?monthly
Playback, see *Jazzfinder*
Playback: the Bulletin of the National Sound Archive (London, spring 1992–), quarterly
Le point du jazz (Brussels, 1969 – May 1986), irreg. (20 nos.)
Pop, Jazz & Show Choir Magazine (Greeley, CA, 198?–), quarterly
Pop Music Mirror, see *Music Mirror*
Popular Music (Rockville, ME, April 1958–)
Popular Music (Cambridge, England, 1981–), annually, from 1987 3 issues a year; web edn at <http://www.cup.org> or <http://www.cup.cam.ac.uk>
Prehled rozhlasu (Prague, March 1932 – 14 Jan 1939), monthly
Pretty Obscure: Jazz Notes and Unpopular Culture in Review (Arlington, VA), monthly
Proceedings of NAJE Research [from 1984 *Jazz Research Papers*; from 1997 *Jazz Research Proceedings*] (Manhattan, KS, 1981–), annually
The Professional (Holland-on-Sea, England, Jan 1974–?), monthly
Quarterly Rag, [1st ser.] (Sydney, Oct 1955 – June 1967), 3 or 4 issues a year (39 nos.); 2nd ser. (Sydney, April 1976–), quarterly
Quartette (USA, Jan–March 1970), 2 nos.; incorp. into *R and B Collector*
Quartica jazz (Barcelona, April 1981 – May 1984; May 1985 – Oct 1987), monthly
Radio Free Jazz, see *Sound Exposure*
Ragtimer, see *Ragtime Society Bulletin*
Ragtime Review, see *Christensen's Ragtime Review*
Rag Times (Los Angeles, May 1967–), bimonthly, quarterly
Ragtime Society Bulletin [from vi (1967) *Ragtimer*] (Weston, Canada, 1962–), bimonthly
R and B Collector [from July 1970 *R and B Magazine*] (Northridge, CA, 1970–), bimonthly, from July 1970 monthly; incorp. *Quartette*
R & B Monthly (Kenley, Surrey, England, Feb 1964 – Jan/Feb 1966), monthly (24 nos.); c.i. nos.1–20 pubd separately [1965]
R & B Scene (Manchester, England, 1964–? [1965 or later]), monthly
Rate (Pismo Beach, CA, ?1983–)
Raunchy Records (Wembley, England, Sept 1971–1972), monthly, from i/3 (Nov 1971), irreg. (6 nos.)
Real Blues (Victoria, Canada, 1996–), bimonthly
Record Advertiser (Northolt, England, Jan 1948–), monthly, then bimonthly
Record Changer (Fairfax, VA, Aug 1942 – Dec 1947; New York, Jan 1948 – 1957), monthly, from xiv/1 (Jan 1955) bimonthly, from xiv/7 (Jan 1956) irreg. (15 vols. = 152 nos.)
Record Exchange (Toronto, March 1948–1952), monthly
Record Exchanger (Anaheim, CA, ?1971–)
Record Finder (San Diego, 1956–?)
Record Finder (Newport News, VA, June 1981 – Nov 1988), monthly, from July 1986 10 issues a year
Recordiana (Norwich, CT, May–Oct 1944), irreg.
Record Memory Club Magazine (Brussels, 1983 – April 2001), quarterly (19 vols. = 52 nos.)

Record Research (New York, Feb 1955 – Jan 1995), irreg. (254 nos., many double issues); suppl.: *Blues Research* (June 1955 – Aug 1965), irreg. (18 nos.)

Record Review (Los Angeles, 1976 – Jan 1995), bimonthly [trial issue i/A (1976), regular issues from i/1 (1977)]

Record Sales Various Prices [from no.17 (Oct 1966) *RSVP*; from no.19 (Dec 1966) *RSVP Monthly*; from no.25 (June 1967) *RSVP: the Record Collectors' Journal*] (London, May 1965–? [1974 or later]), monthly, from no.59 (Feb–March 1971), irreg., from no.66 (Jan–Feb 1972) bimonthly

Red Bank Special: Official Journal of the Count Basie Society (Crawley, England, 1981 – Oct 1999; Totnes and Old Basing, England, Feb 2000–), quarterly

Resonance (London, 1992–), irreg.

Revista "Long-playing", see DISCOGRAPHIES, *Other listings*

La revue du jazz (Paris, Jan 1949 – March/April 1950, 1952), 11 nos.

La revue du jazz: revue trimestrielle d'éducation musicale des orchestres de jazz (Paris, 1937), quarterly (1 vol.)

La revue du jazz: tout ce qui concerne la musique de danse et le disque (Paris, July 1929 – March 1930), monthly (9 nos. = 8 issues); contd by *Jazz tango*

Revue & corigée (Grenoble, France, *c*1989–), *c* quarterly

Revue suisse de jazz, see *Jazz, Rhythm & Blues*

Rhythm (London, Sept 1927 – Sept 1939), monthly (13 vols. = 144 nos.); incorp. into *Melody Maker* (Oct 1939)

Rhythm and Blues, see *News about BMI Music & Writers*

Rhythm and Blues: Covering the Blues and Jazz Scene (Derby, CN, 1960–?), quarterly

Rhythm and Blues Gazette (Petersfield, England, June 1963 – Sept 1963), *c* monthly (3 nos.)

Rhythm and Blues Panorama (Brussels, *c*1960–1966), 7 vols. (45 nos., some double issues)

Rhythm & News (Old Saybrook, CN, 1980), 1 no.

Rhythm & News (Chicago); web edn at <http://www.jazzmart.com/rhythm.htm> (*c*June 1998–)

Rhythme (Eindhoven, Netherlands, Oct 1949 – Sept 1961), monthly (144 nos.)

Rhythm Review: Hot Record Collectors Monthly Guide (London, April 1947–?)

Right On (Hollywood, 1971–), monthly

Ritmo (Madrid, 1929–), monthly, from March 1982 fortnightly

Ritmo (Milan, Italy, ?1995–), monthly

Ritmo y melodia (Barcelona, 1943–52), monthly

Roaring Jazz Crooner Chronicle (Breda, Netherlands, 1969–), bimonthly

Rock & Blues News (Sacramento, CA, Dec 1998–), bimonthly

Rock & Folk: pop music, rhythm and blues, jazz, chanson (Paris)

Rolling Stone (San Francisco, 9 Nov 1967–1977; New York, 22 Sept 1977–), fortnightly

Rondo (Munich, 1992–), bimonthly; web edn at <http://www.rondomagazin.de>

Route (Münster, Germany, 1956–8), quarterly

RSVP: the Record Collectors' Journal, see *Record Sales Various Prices*

Rubberneck (Birmingham, England, 1985–9; Basingstoke, England, Nov 1989 – Dec 1999), quarterly (30 nos.); from April 2000 web only at <http://www.btinternet.com/~rubberneck>, monthly

Ruch muzyczny (Kraków, Poland, 1945–56; Warsaw, 1957–), fortnightly, from 1949 semimonthly, from 1974 fortnightly

Rythmer (Copenhagen, 1936–42), monthly

Rytmi (Helsinki, April 1934 – Dec 1937, Jan 1949 – Dec 1981; Tampere, Finland, Jan 1982–), 3 to 6 issues a year, later 10 issues a year

Sabin's Happenings, see *Sound Exposure*

Sabin's Radio Free Jazz, USA, see *Sound Exposure*

Santandrea catalogo generale, see DISCOGRAPHIES, *Other listings*

Saxophone Journal, see Saxophone Sheet

Saxophone Sheet [from 1980 *Saxophone Journal*] (Medfield, MA, 1976/7–), 3 issues a year, from no.26 (summer 1981) quarterly, from xiii/2 (Sept–Oct 1988) bimonthly; web edn at <http://www.dornpub.com>

The Scene (Brighton, England, ?1987–), bimonthly

SCHJS Fanfare, see *Southern California Hot Jazz Society Fanfare*

Schlagzeug: das Jazz-Magazin (Berlin, July 1956 – Feb 1960), monthly (5 vols.)

Schwann: Long Playing Record Catalog, see DISCOGRAPHIES, *Other listings*

SEAC [South East Asia Command] *Jazz News* (Colombo, Ceylon [now Sri Lanka], Nov 1946 – July 1947), irreg.

Second Line [*Jazz Club Bulletin*] (New Orleans, April 1950–), 12 paired issues a year, from xxv/[1] (Jan 1971) quarterly

SEMJA [South East Michigan Jazz Association] *Newsletter* (Ann Arbor, MI, 1987–8)

SEMJA [South East Michigan Jazz Association] *Update* (Ann Arbor, MI, Jan 1999–), <http://www.semja.org>, archived [web only]

78 Quarterly (New York, 1967; 1988–) irreg. [nos.1–2 combined *R*1992]

Shout, see *Soul Music*

Signal to Noise, see *SoundBoard*

Skivsamlaren (Gothenburg, Sweden, Nov 1975–), irreg.

Slagwerkkrant (Amsterdam, 1984–?); web edn at <http://valley.interact.nl/av/musweb/k18/slagwerk.html>

Solid and Raunchy (Wembley, England, 1972–74, Hitchin, England, Dec 1974), monthly (13 nos.)

Solid Ground: a New World Journal (Detroit, autumn 1981–?1982), irreg.

Solid Set (St. Joseph, MO, 1943 – Aug 1945), monthly

Solo Blues (Madrid, 1985–?), 13 nos.

Song Hits (Dunellen, NJ, May 1937–), monthly

Sonora (Florence, Italy, 1990–), quarterly

Soul: the Magazine for the R & B Collector [from Jan 1967 *Soul Music Monthly*] (Plymouth, England, Jan 1966 – Sept 1967), bimonthly; contd from *Soul Music*

Soul and Jazz Record (Hollywood, CA)

Soul Bag (Levallois-Perret, France, 1968–), irreg., from no.86 (Dec 1981) bimonthly, from no.105 (1986) quarterly

Soul Music [from no.34 (19 Oct 1968) *Shout formerly Soul Music*; from no.53 *Shout*] (London, [Nov] 1967 – July 1977), bimonthly, from no.3 (3 Feb 1968) *c* weekly, from no.34 (19 Oct 1968) irreg. (112 nos.); contd from *Soul Music Monthly*; repr. of articles from nos.2–40 as *Shout-Soul Music Reprint*, i (London, 1976)

Soul Music Monthly, see *Soul: the Magazine for the R & B Collector*

The Sound [from no.8 (March 1986) *Boss*] (Edgware, England, 1984–8), bimonthly, from no.12 (Nov 1986) irreg. (19 nos.); contd in *Pipeline Instrumental Review* (Thames Ditton, England) from no.5 (spring 1990)

Sound-Board [from Oct 1998 *Signal to Noise*] (South Burlington, VT, Sept 1997–?), bimonthly; web edn at <http://www.sover.net/~asp/signaltonoise>

Sound Exposure [from x/? (Oct 1970) *Sabin's Happenings*; from xii/? (May 1972) *Sabin's Radio Free Jazz, USA*; from xv/6 (June 1975) *Radio Free Jazz*; from June 1980 *Jazz Times*] (Washington, DC, ?1961–), irreg., from 1973 monthly, from xx/12 (Dec 1990) 10 issues a year

Sounds: die Zeitschrift für Musik von heute (Cologne, Germany, 1967–?)

Sounds & Fury (Utica, NY, July 1965 – Aug 1966), bimonthly (6 nos.)

Sounds Magazine (New York, 1976–)

Southern California Hot Jazz Society Fanfare [*SCHJS Fanfare*] (Los Angeles)

So What (Paris, Oct 1995–), monthly; web edn at <http://sowhat.telecorporate.com>

Spinner (Norwich, England, Feb 1992 – June 1997; autumn 1997–), irreg., from no.46 (autumn 1997) quarterly

Stars of Jazzette (Versailles, France, Jan 1976–1978), irreg. (9 nos.) [in Eng. and Fr.]

State of the Art (Lakewood, CO, 1985–)

Step Jazz, see *Stylus*

Sternberg híradó jazzalbum [Sternberg news jazz album] (Budapest, Jan 1935), 1 no.

Storyville (London, Oct/Nov 1965 – Oct/Nov 1973; Chigwell, England, Dec 1973/Jan 1974 – June 1995), bimonthly, from no.128 (Dec 1986/Jan 1987) quarterly (162 nos.); main title index to nos.1–150 pubd in no.150 (16 June 1992); c.i. nos.1–6; 7–12, etc., to 157–62 pubd separately and incl. in bound vols. of 6 issues; contd by biannual vols., see OTHER BOOKS, Laurie Wright

Straight No Chaser (London, summer 1988–) [latterly with little significant jazz content]

Strings (San Anselmo, CA, 1986–), quarterly, from 1989 bimonthly

Stuttgarter Brief: Mitteilungsblatt des Clubs der Schlüssel (Stuttgart, Germany, 1951), 1 vol.

Stylus [later *Step Jazz*] (San Diego, CA, 1990–?), bimonthly; web edn at <http://www.stylusmag.com>

Sun Ra Research (Millbrae, CA, 1995–), 5 issues a year

Supersonic Jazz (Marseilles, France, 1996–)

Swing (Buenos Aires, Oct 1936–), irreg.

Swing (Detroit, May 1938–1940), monthly

Swing (Auckland, New Zealand, Oct 1941 – Aug 1942), monthly

Swing: the Guide to Modern Music (New York, April 1938–1940), monthly

Swing: officeel orgaan van the Batavia Rhythm Club (Batavia [now Jakarta], Java, 1937–8), monthly

Swing: tidskrift för ungdom, modern musik, sport och dans (Stockholm, Oct 1944 – ?Dec 1945), monthly (?15 nos.)

Swing and Sound (Le Tour-de-Peilz, Switzerland, ?1998–), annually

Swing & Sweet from Hollywood and 52nd Street (Amsterdam, Jan–May 1950), monthly (5 nos.)

The Swinger (Hartford, CT, 1960–?)

Swingin' Down the Lane (Little Rock, AR, 1994–), quarterly, from 1 Jan 2000 web only, at <http://www.bigband-era.com/Newsletter/main.html>, monthly

Swinging Newsletter [from no.5 (June 1973) *Swinging Newsletter: Bulletin of the European Jazz Federation*; from ?no.32 (?April 1977) *Swinging Newsletter: Publication of the International Jazz Federation*; from no.39 (Jan 1979) *Jazz Echo: Publication of the International Jazz Federation*; from no.46 (Aug 1981) *Jazz World Index*; from no.59 (1984) *Jazz World*] (Vienna, 1972–7; New York, Dec 1977–), monthly, from ?nos.16–17 (?1975) bimonthly, from ?no.32 (?April 1977) irreg., from no.59 (1984) bimonthly

Swing Jazz Journal (Paris, 1968–?), 11 issues a year
Swing Journal (Tokyo, 1947–), monthly; s.i. irreg.; discographical suppls.: *[?1974] Swing Journal* (1975), annually; *Jazz Records [1975–83]* (?1976–1983), annually; *Jazz Disco & Video [1984–5]* (1984–5), annually; *Jazz CD, Record, Video [1986]* (1987–), annually [in Jap.]
Swing Music (London, March 1935 – autumn 1936), monthly, from i/8 (1935) bimonthly, from no.14 (1936) quarterly (2 vols. = 14 nos.)
Swing Session (Wellington, New Zealand, Jan 1947 – Oct 1948), monthly
Swing Shop Mag-list [*Swing Shop Magazine*] (London, 1952–5), bimonthly; suppl. to *Directory of Recorded Jazz and Swing Music*
Swing Time (London, 1997–9), <http://www.jivenet.org/jive/st_current/swingtime.html> [web only]
Swingtime: maandblad voor jazz en blues (Ruiselede, Belgium, 1950 – Nov 1981), 10 issues a year (53 nos.)
Swing Time: revue mensuelle de jazz (Verviers, Belgium, 1950 – Nov 1981), 10 issues a year (53 nos.)
Swing Time Magazine (San Francisco, summer 1995 – summer 1999), quarterly (14 nos.)
Swiss Jazz Notes, see *Jazzbulletin* (Basel)
Syncopation (Sydney, Dec 1946 – June 1947), irreg. (5 nos.)
Syncopa y ritmo: revista de jazz (Buenos Aires, Aug 1934 – Aug 1944), monthly (*c*75 nos.)
Die Synkope (Hannover, Germany, May 1948 – Jan 1949), monthly
Takephivejazz.com (Miami, Oct 1998–), <http://www.rpi.edu/~papep>, later <http://www. takephivejazz.com> [web only]
Takephivejazz.com Newsletter, irreg., by e-mail from <http://www. takephivejazz.com>
Talent and Tunes on Music Machines, see *Billboard Advertising*
Talking Blues (London, April–June 1976–1979), quarterly, from no.8 (Jan–March 1978), irreg. (9 nos.)
Taneční hudba a jazz [Dance music and jazz] (Prague, 1960–)
Ted Slampyak's Jazz Age Chronicles [from 1990 *Jazz Age Chronicles*] (Walworth, NY, Jan 1988–1989, from 1990 Westland, MI), monthly
Tempo [later *Tempo and Television*] (Sydney, Sept 1937 – Jan 1960), irreg. (22 vols.)
Tempo: the Modern Musical Newsmagazine (Los Angeles, 15 June 1933 – 10 May 1940), 8 to 10 issues a year, from viii/1 (Oct 1939) fortnightly (8 vols.); incorp. into *Down Beat* (?1940)
Texas Jazz, see *Dallas Jazz News Letter*
Texas Ragg (Dallas, Jan–Nov 1983), monthly (11 nos.); contd from *Texas Jazz*, see *Dallas Jazz News Letter*
Theme (North Hollywood, CA, 1933–40)
Theme (North Hollywood, CA, July 1953 – autumn 1957), irreg.
Think Jazz Newsletter (Las Vegas, NV, May 1975 – May 1982), monthly
Third Line (Frankfurt am Main, Germany, *fl.* 1965–7)
TJ Today (Watsonville, CA, spring 1981–1992), quarterly
Tone Clusters (New York, *fl.* 1990s)
Tonesetter (Torhout, Belgium, 1994–5), monthly
Tracking Angle (San Jose, CA, 1995 – Oct 1998), quarterly
Tradjazz-nytt: organ för trad jazz (Stockholm, 1973–), 6 issues a year
Tribune: tidsskrift for moderne dansemusik [from no.8 (1946) *Jazzinformation: tribune*] (Copenhagen, 1945–6), 11 nos.
Tunesmith (Concord, NH, 1937–), monthly
Tune Times (London, Sept 1933 – May 1935), monthly (2 vols. = 21 nos.)
The Turntable (Holland-on-Sea, England, 1986–?), irreg.
Twisted (London, July–Nov 1995), 2 nos.
Ungdomens jazzkalendar (?Stockholm, 1955–)
United Jazz Society (Bochum, Germany, 1987–), bimonthly; web edn (updated *c* weekly) at <http://www.ujs.de>
Universal Jazz (Reading, England, May 1946–?), monthly
Unterhaltungskunst: Journal art and action (Berlin, 1969–90), monthly
Vancouver Jazz (Vancouver, Canada, Sept 1999–), updated *c* weekly, <www.vancouverjazz.com> [web only]
Variety: a Variety Paper for Variety People [from xviii/12 (1910) *Variety*] (New York, 16 Dec 1905–), weekly
Vibes Net, see *Grooving' the Vibes*
Vibrations (New York, 1967–), monthly
Vibrations (Lausanne, Switzerland, 1991–), monthly
Vibrations: le magazine world jazz rap (Paris, 1992–), bimonthly [Fr. edn of *Vibrations* (Lausanne, Switzerland)]
Victory Music Folk & Jazz Review [from x/5 (May 1985)*Victory Music Review* , later *Victory Review*] (Bonney Lake, WA, Sept 1976–), monthly
Vier Viertel: MusikMagazin für Schlager-, Film-, Jazz-, und Schallplattenfreunde [subtitle varies: also *Halbmonatsschrift für Musik und Tanz*] (Berlin, Nov 1947–1956), 24 issues a year (10 vols.); suppls.: *Jazz Revue* (1954), monthly (1 vol.); *Der JazzCourier* (1955–6)
Vintage Jazz Mart [from Feb 1961 *VJM Palaver* (12 nos.); in 1962 reverted to *Vintage Jazz Mart*; from summer 1994 *VJM's Jazz and Blues Mart*] (London, Dec 1953–1990; Nottingham, England, Oct/Nov 1990–), irreg., from no.80 (Oct/Nov 1990) quarterly; incorp. *Jazz Times* (London); web edn at <http://www.vjmuk.demon.co.uk>
Viva la musica (Geneva, 1975–), monthly
VJM's Jazz and Blues Mart, see *Vintage Jazz Mart*
VJM Palaver, see *Vintage Jazz Mart*
Vox Pop (London, 1944 – June 1945), monthly (2 vols.); incorp. *Jazz Record and LLCU Newsletter: Journal of the Workers' Music Association*; incorp. by *Keynote*
Wavelength (New Orleans, Nov 1980 – Nov 1991), monthly (133 nos.)
West Coast Rag ; contd by *American Rag*
Western Australia's Music Maker (Perth, Australia, Jan 1983–)
Westjazz: Jazz-Nachrichten aus Westdeutschland, see *HCD-Bulletin*
The Wheel (Kannapolis, NC, May–Sept 1948), monthly
Whiskey, Women, and . . . (Haverhill, MA, ?1971–1989), irreg. (17 nos., incl. 2 double issues)
Who's Who: Discograph, see *Jazzbulletin*
Who's Who in the World of Music, see *Billboard Advertising*
Wild Bill's Legacy (Dover, NJ, spring 1992–)
Windplayer (Northridge, CA, 1985–), bimonthly
The Wire [from no.24 (Feb 1986) *Wire*] (London, summer 1982–), quarterly, from no.8 (Oct 1984) monthly; c.i. nos.1–22 pubd separately; web edn at <http://www.dfuse.com/the-wire>, later <http://www.the-wire.co.uk>
World Jazz Calendar of Festivals & Events [later (1980s) *Jazz Festivals International Directory*] (New York, June 1980–), 2 issues a year, then annually
Yam: tidskrift för dansmusik och film (Helsinki, 15 Jan 1942 – 15 May 1944), monthly (3 vols.) [in Swed.]
Yardbird Newsletter (Edmonton, Canada, September 1995–), 5 issues a year
Zene: a QAP zenei melléklete [Music: musical supplement of the QAP] (Budapest, Dec 1978 – Feb 1979), 2 nos.
Le zine (Reims, France, 1994–), monthly

Appendix 2

Calendar of Births and Deaths

JANUARY

1

born

1884 Celestin, Papa
1894 Taylor, Jasper
1908 Johnson, Howard (i)
1916 Gaillard, Slim [date uncertain]
1919 McKibbon, Al
1923 Jackson, Milt
1930 Van Rooyen, Ack
1931 Brandt, Helmut
1932 Reilly, Jack
1936 Greenwich, Sonny
1938 Wildman, Joan
1942 Ikeda, Yoshio
1946 McCorkle, Susannah
1947 Chizhik, Leonid
1950 Hayashi, Eiichi
1951 Gonzalez, Andy
1951 Murakami, Shuichi
1952 Leimgruber, Urs
1971 Potter, Chris

died

1942 Ježek, Jaroslav
1958 McGrath, Fulton
1984 Korner, Alexis
1998 Schildkraut, Dave

2

born

1910 Goodwin, Henry
1914 Clarke, Kenny [or 9 Jan]
1915 Fatool, Nick
1927 McLevy, John
1932 Weil, Kurt
1933 Williams, Jackie
1944 Brown, Ari
1946 Suzuki, Isao

died

1973 Harriott, Joe
1977 Garner, Erroll
1980 Williams, J. Mayo
1981 Schiöpffe, William
1989 Heywood, Eddie
1997 Rose, Wally
2000 Adderley, Nat

3

born

1890 Teagarden, Helen
1898 Rich, Fred
1902 Jackson, Preston [date uncertain]
1922 Minerve, Geezil
1931 Jenkins, John
1936 Haider, Joe
1938 Hunter-Randall, Ian
1946 Hino, Motohiko
1966 McAll, Barney
1969 Carter, James

died

1948 Marshall, Kaiser
1959 Cuffee, Ed
1968 Swope, Earl
1973 De Paris, Wilbur
1975 Thomas, René
1982 Bryant, Tommy

4

born

1905 Robeson, Orlando
1906 Newton, Frankie
1907 Marsala, Joe
1918 Rose, Boris
1919 Bell, Roger
1922 Wess, Frank
1929 Dreares, Al
1940 Smetaček, Pavel
1941 Lee, David
1942 McLaughlin, John
1950 Dick, Robert
1954 Chadbourne, Eugene
1956 Cline, Alex
1956 Cline, Nels
1971 Hitchcock, Nigel

died

1964 Bernstein, Artie
1969 Chambers, Paul
1991 Barefield, Eddie
1991 Wright, Leo
1992 Grace, Teddy
2000 Frampton, Roger
2001 Brown, Les

5

born

1906 Davison, Wild Bill
1924 Moriyasu, Shotaro
1925 Fohrenbach, Jean-Claude
1925 Hastings, Lennie
1926 Brokensha, Jack
1930 Klein, Oscar
1931 Reece, Dizzy
1934 See, Cees
1935 Flores, Chuck
1942 Mori, Kenji
1944 Stewart, Louis
1946 Ceccarelli, André
1950 Baron, Art
1953 Wertico, Paul
1957 Melford, Myra
1961 Baron, Piotr

died

1940 Whetsol, Artie
1964 Teagarden, Jack
1964 Scott, Cecil
1979 Mingus, Charles
1981 Paquinet, Guy
1985 Assunto, Papa Jac
1996 Bivona, Gus
1999 Petrucciani, Michel

6

born

1905 De Vries, Louis
1906 Stark, Bobby
1907 Brown, Vernon
1910 Henriksen, Bruno
1925 Abrams, Lee
1931 Christie, Keith
1932 Burch, John
1941 Moore, Danny
1943 Altschul, Barry
1944 Sickler, Don
1947 Bolognesi, Jacques
1949 Laurence, Chris
1951 Céléa, Jean-Paul

died

1969 Moore, Johnny
1993 Gillespie, Dizzy
1995 Clay, James

7

born

1908 Allen, Henry "Red"
1913 Henry, Haywood [or 10 Jan]
1915 Pozo, Chano
1915 Purnell, Keg
1925 Schildkraut, Dave
1925 Woodyard, Sam
1933 Payne, Don
1935 Davern, Kenny
1936 Young, Eldee
1943 Harper, Billy
1946 Tropea, John
1957 Seay, Clarence
1963 Colianni, John

died

1981 Martin, Chink
1985 Guarnieri, Johnny
1999 Hopkins, Fred

JANUARY

8

born

1906 Culley, Wendell
1923 Tucker, Bobby
1932 Charlesworth, Dick
1942 Goodwin, Bill
1942 Mbambisa, Tete
1944 Battle, Bobby
1948 Barker, Thurman
1948 Szukalski, Tomasz
1949 Worth, Bobby
1953 Laka Daisical
1955 Mazur, Marilyn
1960 Weckl, Dave

died

1988 Bauduc, Ray
1990 Auld, Georgie
1992 Meyer, Johnny
1992 Niebergall, Buschi
1997 Handy, George
1998 Butts, Jimmy

9

born

?1885 Garland, Ed
1902 Stitzel, Mel
1914 Clarke, Kenny [or 2 Jan]
1916 Harris, Charlie
1917 Maxwell, Jimmy
1920 Roche, Betty
1926 Guérin, Roger
1926 Pizzarelli, Bucky
1931 Smith, Carson
1937 Cecil, Malcolm
1952 Rassinfosse, Jean-Louis

died

1956 Stuart, Rory
1964 Goudie, Frank "Big Boy"
1967 Swope, Rob
1982 Musso, Vido

10

born

1913 Henry, Haywood [or 7 Jan]
1915 Johnson, Buddy
1918 Bridgers, Aaron
1924 Roach, Max
1926 Dennis, Willie
1927 Eager, Allen
1940 Reed, Waymon
1944 Trovesi, Gianluigi
1952 Parker, William
1953 Stern, Mike
1974 McKinney, Carlos

died

1971 Caceres, Ernie
1974 Safranski, Eddie
1977 Evans, Doc
1981 Traill, Sinclair
1984 Jederby, Thore
1985 Frazier, Cié
1986 Farrell, Joe
1995 Böhler, Fred

11

born

?1890 Scott, Budd
1900 De Paris, Wilbur
1901 Dyett, Capt. Walter
1909 Smith, Tab
1911 Jones, Betty Hall
1912 Bertschy, René
1923 Johnson, Osie
1927 Gaynair, Wilton "Bogey"
1927 Massey, Cal
1930 Nimitz, Jack
1930 Varro, Johnny
1934 Johansen, Egil
1952 Ritenour, Lee
1955 Schuller, Ed
1959 Nabatov, Simon

died

1952 Allen, Henry, Sr.
1984 Beamter, Jenő
1985 Clare, Kenny
1994 Ramirez, Ram
1996 Isaacs, Ike (ii)

12

born

1900 Roy, Harry
1912 Young, Trummy
1916 McShann, Jay
1927 Lafitte, Guy
1929 Matteson, Rich
1931 Alphonso, Roland
1932 Caliman, Hadley
1936 Pauls, Raimonds
1940 Jackson, Ronald Shannon
1941 Olu Dara
1946 Duke, George
1948 Etheridge, John
1955 Bloom, Jane Ira
1961 Perelman, Ivo
1964 Malaby, Tony
1966 Jensen, Ingrid
1966 Lake, Gene

died

1963 Casimir, John
1971 Handy, Capt. John
1988 Albany, Joe
1998 Sellin, Pierre
1890 Brown, Steve

13

born

1902 Dandridge, Putney
1905 Humphrey, Percy
1908 or 1910 Johnson, Otis
1909 Barker, Danny
1909 Burke, Ed
1909 Jackson, Quentin
1925 Peck, Nat
1926 Liston, Melba
1929 Pass, Joe
1931 Wheeler, Ian
1941 Koivistoinen, Eero
1946 Easley, Bill
1952 Pohjola, Pekka
1961 Winchester, Lem

died

1963 Clark, Sonny
1971 Lewis, Willie
1979 Martinez, Sabu
1983 Galbraith, Barry
1983 Ouwerx, John
1996 Corb, Morty

14

born

1910 Crawford, Jimmy
1912 Young, David A.
1916 Davis, Maxwell
1917 Butterfield, Billy
1928 Muranyi, Joe
1930 Gerhard, Siggi
1930 Wheeler, Kenny
1931 Downes, Wray
1932 Tate, Grady
1938 Inzalaco, Tony
1941 Bellonzi, Charles
1942 Hunter, Jerome
1946 Hines, Gregory
1951 Egan, Mark
1955 Maltese, Stefano
1957 Jordan, Steve (ii)
1959 Lê, Nguyên

died

1949 Baquet, George
1987 Purnell, Alton

JANUARY

15

born

1909 Krupa, Gene
1909 Lammi, Dick
1916 Shapiro, Artie
1919 Jordan, Steve (i)
1927 Banks, Buddy (ii)
1928 Dies, Werner
1930 Matthews, Onzy
1945 Maize, Bob
1947 Carroll, Baikida
1952 Termos, Paul

died

1966 Smith, Charlie
1994 Brun, Philippe

16

born

1866 Robichaux, John
1894 Mills, Irving
1913 Musso, Vido
1917 Block, Sandy
1920 Abadie, Claude
1926 Guilbeau, Phil
1929 Hogan, G. T.
1930 Robinson, Spike
1941 Romano, Aldo
1946 Wells, Spike
1954 Tabbal, Tani
1956 Johansson, Ulf
1965 Van Bavel, Rob

died

1947 Berman, Sonny
1947 Marable, Fate
1963 Quebec, Ike
1970 Davis, Lem
1973 Sampson, Edgar
1977 Archia, Tom
1979 Elizalde, Fred
1981 Delamont, Gordon
1987 De Kers, Robert
1990 Brocksieper, Freddie
1991 Smith, Jabbo
1995 Dillard, Bill
1997 Galbraith, Charlie
1997 Peer, Beverly
2000 Harris, Gene

17

born

1896 Reser, Harry
1897 Holder, Terrence
1908 or 1911 White, Morris
1910 Catlett, Sid
1912 Zurke, Bob
1920 Handy, George
1922 Costa, John
1931 Solomon, Clifford
1934 Walton, Cedar
1937 Dunbar, Ted
1953 Berlin, Jeff
1955 Akiyama, Kazumasa
1958 Robert, Yves
1963 Chestnut, Cyrus
1965 Igarashi, Issei

died

1955 Engstrøm, Kalle
1962 Jones, Claude
1965 Robichaux, Joseph
1992 Ventura, Charlie
1994 Chiboust, Noël
2001 Turney, Norris

18

born

1903 Leibrook, Min
1911 Delaunay, Charles
1912 Red Mack
1915 Gunther, Paul
1921 Sims, Ray
1925 Kellens, Christian
1932 Kral, Irene
1940 Thompson, Don
1944 Foster, Al
1951 Grossman, Steve
1952 Ferrante, Russell
1954 Marsh, Tina
1957 Schwaller, Roman
1961 Broom, Bobby
1961 Landesbergen, Frits
1964 Panayi, Andy
1967 Epstein, Peter

died

1960 Bentley, Gladys
1971 Shields, Harry
1988 Hall, Al
1994 Hultcrantz, Torbjörn

19

born

1900 Brunies, Abbie
1917 Ewing, John
1917 Shepherd, Shep
1919 Crosby, Israel
1927 Monterose, J. R.
1931 Parlan, Horace
1936 O'Brien, Hod
1937 Wilson, Phil
1939 Brown, Sam
1943 Pizzi, Ray
1953 Micus, Stephan
1960 Magnarelli, Joe
1969 Moreira, Pedro
1970 Rantala, Iiro

died

1969 Pavageau, Alcide "Slow Drag"
1995 Fol, Hubert
1996 Mulligan, Gerry

20

born

1922 Anthony, Ray
1927 Le Sage, Bill
1929 Cobb, Jimmy
1930 Johnson, Jimmie
1940 Navarro, Jorge
1941 Tommaso, Giovanni
1943 Ponomarev, Valery
1944 Domanico, Chuck
1957 Sheppard, Andy
1959 Hervé, Antoine
1960 Andrews, Jeff
1960 Watts, Jeff "Tain"
1966 Genus, James

died

2001 Assumpção, Nico

21

born

1899 Blesh, Rudi
1902 Ballew, Smith
1906 Wayland, Hank
1910 Squires, Bruce
1917 Maxted, Billy
1931 Whitlock, Bob
1943 Gilmore, Steve
1945 Potts, Steve
1949 Mukai, Shigeharu
1972 Van Ruller, Jesse
1975 Moran, Jason

died

1951 Dickerson, R. Q.
1978 Peterson, Chuck
1981 Procope, Russell
1999 Brown, Charles

JANUARY

22

born

1895 Taylor, Eva
1900 Tizol, Juan
1908 McRae, Teddy
1908 Weersma, Melle
1909 Lewis, Ed
1909 Randolph, Irving "Mouse"
1912 Parry, Harry
1917 Brown, Pud
1921 Hodeir, André
1924 Johnson, J. J.
1932 Smith, Teddy
1933 Viale, Jean-Louis
1938 Jost, Ekkehard
1939 Silva, Alan
1940 Weber, Eberhard
1943 Altena, Maarten
1943 Urbaniak, Michal
1945 Selden, Fred
1950 Lee, Scott
1952 Fine, Milo
1955 Johnston, Phillip
1957 Denley, Jim

died

1975 Rediske, Johannes
1980 Garland, Ed "Montudi"
1993 Greenlee, Charles
2001 Schmidli, Peter

23

born

1902 Waters, Benny
1908 Blake, Jerry
1909 Turnham, Floyd
1910 Reinhardt, Django
1911 Warlop, Michel
1912 Kluger, Jack
1914 Napoleon, Teddy
1915 Carry, Scoops
1917 Beckett, Fred
1920 Abrams, Ray
1925 Paich, Marty
1926 Counce, Curtis [or 27 Jan]
1928 Black, Dave
1929 Ousley, Harold
1930 Kleinschuster, Erich
1931 Coscia, Gianni
1943 Burton, Gary
1944 Jones, Randy
1949 Stahl, Dave
1955 Droz, Raymond

died

1973 Ory, Kid
1980 Gonzales, Babs
1989 Lovett, Baby
2001 Levy, Lou
2001 McDuff, Brother Jack

24

born

1902 Kok, James
1909 Winters, Tiny
1917 Parrish, Avery
1920 Forrest, Jimmy
1924 Albany, Joe
1928 Mulligan, Mick
1933 McBrowne, Lennie
1936 Wellins, Bobby
1938 Hemphill, Julius
1944 Degen, Bob
1956 Forman, Mitchel
1967 Printup, Marcus
1970 Pierończyk, Adam

died

1965 Peyton, Benny
1974 Fagerquist, Don
1976 Theselius, Gösta
1989 Spann, Les
1998 Bishop, Walter, Jr.
2001 Parker, Frank

25

born

1891 Braud, Wellman
1911 Parham, Truck
1917 Smith, Floyd
1922 Wyble, Jimmy
1925 Carroll, Barbara
1927 Jobim, Antonio Carlos
1929 Golson, Benny
1938 Golstain, Gennady
1938 James, Etta
1942 Lyall, Graeme
1947 Nakagawa, Masami
1957 Domancich, Sophia
1967 Jackson, D. D.
1980 Dorůžka, David

died

1987 Bergh, Øivind
1987 Dial, Harry
1997 Powell, Seldon
1998 Porter, Roy
2000 Halliday, Lin

26

born

1904 or 1908 Wethington, Crawford
1908 Grappelli, Stephane
1924 Babs, Alice
1928 Nash, Dick
1937 Stephenson, Ronnie
1945 Gumpert, Ulrich
1948 Takase, Aki
1955 Crosby, Gary

died

1971 Perrilliat, Nat
1974 Benjamin, Joe
1974 Semple, Archie
1985 Clarke, Kenny
1998 James, Michael
1998 Zoller, Attila

27

born

1869 Cook, Will Marion
1908 Page, Hot Lips
1910 Aaron, Abe
1910 Holmes, Charlie
1916 Raskin, Milt
1920 Zacharias, Helmut
1926 Counce, Curtis [or 23 Jan]
1930 Meldonian, Dick
1933 Bond, Jimmy
1938 Smith, Jimmie
1938 Tusques, François
1941 Hutcherson, Bobby
1945 Moriyama, Takeo
1945 Texier, Henri
1946 Castleman, Jeff
1953 Mintzer, Bob
1955 akLaff, Pheeroan
1957 Popek, Krzysztof

died

1965 Masman, Theo Uden
1986 Moule, Ken
1994 Calhoun, Eddie
2000 Abney, Don
2000 Gulda, Friedrich

28

born

1880 or 1885 Nelson, Big Eye Louis
1899 Randolph, Zilner T.
1907 Sands, Bobby
1916 Foss, Niels
1918 Larsson, Rolf
1927 Scott, Ronnie
1929 Bilk, Acker
1929 Williams, John (ii)
1948 Moses, Bob
1954 Johnson, Henry
1959 Ware, Bill
1963 Haque, Fareed
1966 Argüelles, Julian

died

1974 Allen, Ed
1976 Nance, Ray
1980 Crawford, Jimmy
1981 Biondi, Ray
1983 Barrett, Sweet Emma
1990 Sharpe, C.

JANUARY

29

born

1899 Hall, Robert
1902 Snaer, Albert
1912 Livingston, Ulysses
1915 Ramsey, Fred
1920 Watkins, Earl
1921 Ross, Arnold
1922 Sels, Jack
1926 Cerri, Franco
1929 Shaughnessy, Ed
1932 Bailey, Derek
1932 Assunto, Frank
1933 Distel, Sacha
1937 Clyne, Jeff
1939 Lee, Jeanne
1940 Young, Dave
1967 Cary, Marc
1967 Milne, Andy

died

1965 Hylton, Jack
1979 Payne, Sonny
1981 Cole, Cozy
1986 Barksdale, Everett
1993 Moore, Gerry

30

born

1902 Lanigan, Jim
1909 Allen, Sam
1911 Eldridge, Roy
1919 Suter, Robert
1921 Leighton, Bernie
1927 Abdul-Malik, Ahmed
1930 Montgomery, Buddy
1935 Hayes, Tubby
1935 Hoffmann, Ingfried
1936 Jankowski, Horst
1937 Johansson, Åke
1940 Levin, Tony
1944 Humphries, Roger
1951 Lalama, Ralph

died

1946 Beckett, Fred
1959 Brown, Boyce
1994 Davis, Tiny
1995 James, George
1996 Thiele, Bob

31

born

1894 Jones, Isham
1902 Blue, William Thornton
1907 Morton, Benny
1907 Sayles, Emanuel
1915 Hackett, Bobby
1921 Anderson, John
1932 Patterson, Ottilie
1936 Brown, Garnett
1942 Mann, Tony
1947 Kako, Takashi
1949 Ricotti, Frank

died

1935 Swayze, Edwin
1947 Jones, Snags
1955 Washington, Buck
1978 Herbert, Gregory
1979 Green, Grant
2000 Russell, Ross
2000 Zentner, Si

January (the date unknown)

born

1904 Wilson, Juice

died

1936 Washington, Steve [month uncertain]
1970 Dixon, Lawrence
1980 Albert, Don
1985 Collins, Booker
1986 Watts, Grady
1992 France, Percy
1996 Haynes, Cyril

FEBRUARY

1

born

1894 Johnson, James P.
1902 Josephson, Barney
1904 Nanton, Tricky Sam
1921 Tabányi, Mihály
1931 McFall, Reuben
1933 Watanabe, Sadao
1939 Sample, Joe
1940 Black, James
1940 Brown, Tyrone
1940 Irakli
1960 Yoshioka, Hideaki
1969 Redman, Joshua

died

1937 Hill, Alex
1950 Stewart, Buddy
1971 Roy, Harry
1981 Carroll, Joe "Bebop"

2

born

1888 Keppard, Louis
1900 Brown, Andrew
1904 Paul, Emanuel
1910 Laine, Bob
1920 Mondragon, Joe
1924 Stitt, Sonny
1925 Prysock, Red
1926 Perrin, Mimi
1927 Getz, Stan
1929 Bas, Vlady
1932 Christian, Jodie
1940 Gould, Tony
1942 Ulmer, James "Blood"
1944 Coetzee, Basil
1951 Johnson, Alphonso
1953 Longnon, Jean-Loup
1953 Sclavis, Louis
1956 Muldrow, Ronald
1956 Padovani, Jean-Marc
1958 Newton, David
1965 King, Jonny
1966 Gisbert, Greg
1968 Zulfikarpasic, Bojan

died

1935 Smith, Clara
1983 Allen, Moses
1986 Walker, Sammy
1987 Hughes, Spike
1987 Lion, Alfred
1990 Lewis, Mel
1992 Blakeney, Andy
1994 Randolph, Zilner T.

3

born

1895 Jaxon, Frankie "Half Pint"
1896 Valentine, Kid Thomas
1898 or 1902 Armstrong, Lil
1906 Firman, Bert
1919 Young, Snooky
1920 Alvarez, Chico
1933 Handy, John
1937 Durham, Bobby
1937 Williams, Leroy
1941 Ranger, Claude
1945 Stewart, Bob
1966 Tardy, Greg
1970 Hollyday, Christopher

died

1956 Claes, Johnny
1992 Werner, Lasse
1994 Stephenson, Louis

4

born

1862 Tio, Papa
1908 Klein, Manny
1909 Bernstein, Artie
1925 Hipp, Jutta
1927 Cirillo, Wally
1927 Fruscella, Tony
1931 Dubin, Larry
1934 Legge, Wade
1943 Baker, Newman Taylor
1945 Stubblefield, John
1950 Chancey, Vincent
1953 Rapson, John

died

1961 Picou, Alphonse
1970 Alexander, Charlie
1975 Jordan, Louis
1982 DeMicheal, Don
1992 Cook, Junior
2000 Berendt, Joachim-Ernst
2001 Johnson, J. J.

5

born

1890 Smith, Russell
1913 Claxton, Rozelle
1915 Schroeder, Gene
1918 Volonté, Eraldo
1923 Ruther, Wyatt
1926 Simmons, Art
1930 Goldie, Don
1935 Kessler, Siegfried
1941 Laird, Rick
1942 Ingham, Keith
1943 Bass, Mickey
1944 Mays, Bill
1947 Biscoe, Chris
1956 Colaiuta, Vinnie
1959 Cárdenas, Steve
1961 Tracey, Clark
1963 Dankworth, Jacqui
1964 Gilmore, David

died

1962 Watkins, Doug
1964 Steele, Joe
1968 Roberts, Luckey
1971 Remue, Chas
1973 Brunies, Merritt
1975 Persson, Åke
1990 Perry, King
1999 Purbrook, Colin

6

born

1902 Brunis, Georg
1922 Gozzo, Conrad
1924 Nestico, Sammy
1926 Glow, Bernie
1926 Schiöpffe, William
1927 Fagerquist, Don
1927 McIntosh, Tom
1928 Boyd, Nelson
1931 Pisano, John
1936 Inomata, Takeshi
1941 Nørregaard, Svend-Erik
1944 Mine, Kosuke
1945 Krivda, Ernie
1954 Lejeune, Philippe
1966 Grenadier, Larry

died

1948 Arodin, Sidney
1962 Hite, Les
1963 Wright, Specs
1973 Stabulas, Nick
1976 Guaraldi, Vince
1977 Battle, Edgar
1978 Wayne, Frances
1988 Bock, Richard
1995 Taylor, Art
2000 Johnson, Gus

7

born

1882 Sweatman, Wilbur
1883 Blake, Eubie
1886 Borchard, Eric
1907 Colignon, Raymond "Coco"
1914 Barriteau, Carl
1924 Crawford, Ray
1927 Hausser, Michel
1929 Shepherd, Dave
1933 Brodie, Hugh
1934 Curtis, King
1953 Kibwe, Talib
1958 Bak, Frans
1969 Doky, Christian Minh

died

1948 McKenzie, Red
1951 Clay, Shirley
1957 Parker, Sonny
1979 Holland, Peanuts
1993 Gabriel, Percy
1996 Winters, Tiny
1999 Boone, Richard
1999 Troup, Bobby

FEBRUARY

8

born

1889 Johnson, Lonnie
1905 Metcalf, Louis
1916 Skidmore, Jimmy
1919 Morrow, Buddy
1926 Poindexter, Pony
1928 Lees, Gene
1930 Locke, Eddie
1930 Maini, Joe
1941 Dudás, Lajos
1941 Williams, John (iii)
1945 Rundqvist, Gösta
1947 Biddell, Kerrie
1968 Perko, Jukka

died

1982 Edelhagen, Kurt
1994 Scott, Raymond
1996 Ellington, Mercer
1998 Cullaz, Alby

9

born

1900 Page, Walter
1910 Holland, Peanuts
1922 Dodge, Joe
?1928 Carr, Bruno
1958 Evans, Bill (iii)
1961 Wilson, Steve
1963 Storaas, Vigleik

died

1939 Evans, Herschel
1964 Bryant, Willie
1977 Johnson, Buddy
1980 Fowlkes, Charlie
1981 Frye, Don
1999 Caton, Lauderic

10

born

1907 Haymes, Joe
1907 Thomas, Foots
1909 Niosi, Bert
1909 Webb, Chick
1914 Adler, Larry
1930 Sawada, Shungo
1932 Hanna, Sir Roland
1932 Perkins, Walter
1934 Burton, Rahn
1937 Polcer, Ed
1944 Reid, Rufus
1947 Morris, Butch
1958 Weiss, Michael
1961 Fresu, Paolo

died

1961 Gibson, Andy
1961 Middleton, Velma
1966 Johnson, Osie
1974 Binyon, Larry
1987 Colignon, Raymond "Coco"
1988 Patterson, Don
1992 Pepper, Jim
2001 Tate, Buddy

11

born

1901 Jones, Claude
1909 Casey, Bob
1914 Dennis, Matt
1922 Carter, Bob
1928 Janis, Conrad
1931 Lamb, Bobby
1932 Hnilička, Jaromír
1934 Sewing, Jack
1937 Lemon, Brian
1939 Temiz, Okay
1944 Drew, Martin
1945 Fishkind, Larry
1947 Haverhoek, Henk
1956 Björkenheim, Raoul
1956 Lockwood, Didier
1960 Freeman, Russ (ii)

died

1962 Parker, Leo
1967 Brehm, Simon
1967 Hall, Edmond
1971 Arnold, Harry
1975 Harris, Little Benny
1987 Malachi, John
1988 Hall, René
1999 Byard, Jaki

12

born

1904 Lambert, Donald
1909 Ware, Munn
1912 Bascomb, Paul
1913 Gaines, Bubba
1914 Beneke, Tex
1914 Landl, Ernst
1916 Harris, Le Roy (ii)
1919 Privin, Bernie
1920 Shad, Bob
1921 Koller, Hans
1923 Mardigan, Art
1923 Powell, Mel
1926 Childers, Buddy
1948 Booth, Jiunie
1949 Herr, Michel
1955 Laswell, Bill
1960 Horton, Ron
1963 Keogh, Stephen
1967 Speed, Chris

died

1955 Brunies, Little Abbie
1965 Wetzel, Bonnie
1967 Spanier, Muggsy
1980 Keenan, Norman
1983 Blake, Eubie

13

born

1900 Manone, Wingy
1903 Hite, Les
1908 Hayton, Lennie
1912 Rollini, Art
1913 Dance, Helen Oakley
1921 Gray, Wardell
1926 Jefferson, Ron
1933 Ndlazilwana, Victor
1936 Furuya, Takashi
1940 Pirchner, Werner
1945 Nichols, Keith
1947 Povel, Ferdinand
1954 Brennan, John Wolf
1966 Shepik, Brad
1970 Cruz, Adam

died

1986 Danzi, Mike
1992 Kovács, Gyula
1995 Gaynair, Wilton "Bogey"
1997 Frank, Edward
1998 Chapin, Thomas
2001 Simon, George T.

14

born

1893 Bradford, Perry
1909 Tolbert, Skeets
1920 Lesberg, Jack
1925 Lawrence, Elliot
1930 Mitchell, Dwike
1935 McConnell, Rob
1939 Pyne, Chris
1941 Baudoin, Philippe
1943 Parker, Maceo
1947 Spearman, Glenn
1957 Campbell, Tommy
1957 Riley, Herlin
1969 Di Battista, Stefano

died

1959 Dodds, Baby
1963 McCord, Cass
1987 Sete, Bola
1996 Deniz, Laurie
1997 Moffett, Charles

FEBRUARY

15

born

1910 Fuller, Walter
1914 or 1915 Jordan, Taft
1920 Boas, Günter
1924 Horrox, Frank
1937 Davis, Nathan
1937 Lightsey, Kirk
1939 Deseő, Csaba
1944 Morell, Marty
1944 Threadgill, Henry
1945 Sarmanto, Pekka
1945 Vesala, Edward
1953 Penland, Ralph
1956 Landgren, Nils
1958 Holzman, Adam

died

1946 Dandridge, Putney
1965 Cole, Nat "King"
1969 Russell, Pee Wee
1979 Seifert, Zbigniew
1987 Barclay, Bob
1988 Cohn, Al
1999 Roche, Betty

16

born

1907 Malmstén, Eugen
1908 or 1909 Machito
1916 Doggett, Bill
1916 Fowlkes, Charlie
1929 Barth, Benny
1931 Segal, Jerry
1936 Deppenschmidt, Buddy
1943 Riley, Howard
1945 Christlieb, Pete
1955 Clayton, Jeff

died

1944 Zurke, Bob
1963 Reynolds, Jimmy
1975 Schroeder, Gene
1988 Delaunay, Charles
1994 Powell, Jimmie
1996 Dobschinski, Walter

17

born

1898 Hyde, Alex
1899 Brooks, Harvey
1906 Bishop, Wallace
1907 Dial, Harry
1907 Spivak, Charlie
1917 Monsbourgh, Ade
1920 Garros, Christian
1923 DeFranco, Buddy
1924 Jones, Buddy
1926 Gill, Elmer
1926 Watts, Noble
1933 Heatley, Spike
1934 Björksten, Hacke
1938 Coates, John
1939 Cale, Bruce
1940 Novosel, Steve
1941 Lewis, Herbie
1942 Weiss, Klaus
1944 Jenkins, Karl
1947 Madison, Jimmy
1949 Frith, Fred
1960 Mazetier, Louis
1965 Lee, Keiko

died

1943 Piron, A. J.
1964 Mettome, Doug
1969 Barbarin, Paul
1982 Monk, Thelonious
1993 Lowe, Sammy
1997 Graham, Kenny

18

born

1892 Barnes, Emile
1904 Johnson, Walter
1904 Pierce, De De
1922 Lombardi, Clyde
1922 Osterwald, Hazy
1926 Burrowes, Roy
1928 Butler, Frank
1928 Land, Harold
1935 Petrovic, Boško
1949 Almario, Justo
1949 Peeters, Joep

died

1919 Ragas, Henry
1974 Smith, Frank
1980 Howard, Paul
1981 Froeba, Frank
1981 Thomas, Joe (i)
1986 Keppard, Louis
1995 Lawson, Yank

19

born

1897 Dunn, Johnny
1902 Bubbles, John
1903 Hall, Clarence
1937 Van Hove, Fred
1937 Yancy, Youseff
1944 Mathewson, Ron
1951 Rose, Jon
1955 Murray, David
1963 Ikeda, Atsushi
1968 Rosenberg, Stochelo

died

1972 Morgan, Lee
1980 Sherock, Shorty
1984 Hopkins, Claude
1984 Hutton, Ina Ray
1993 Norman, Fred

20

born

1898 Yancey, Jimmy
1901 Robinson, Fred
1908 Österwall, Seymour
1909 Alemán, Oscar
1922 Stenfalt, Norman
1925 Isola, Frank
1926 Jaspar, Bobby
1929 Lee, William F.
1933 Kynard, Charles
1937 Wilson, Nancy
1941 Burnett, Carl
1944 Soloff, Lew
1949 Lockwood, John
1950 Zgraja, Krzysztof
1951 Davis, Anthony
1952 Kropinski, Uwe
1956 Del Fra, Riccardo
1958 Jones, Leroy
1963 Oleszkiewicz, Darek
1964 Ballamy, Iain
1970 Legnini, Eric
1970 Taborn, Craig

died

1963 Farmer, Addison
1971 Tsfasman, Aleksandr
1992 Friley, Vern
1997 Breaux, Zachary
1998 Mairants, Ivor

21

born

1907 Pletcher, Stew
1910 Sears, Al
1917 Dameron, Tadd
1925 Chaix, Henri
1925 Oida, Toshio
1930 Haas, Eddie de
1931 Collie, Max
1932 Higgins, Eddie
1935 Wallgren, Jan
1937 Collier, Graham
1943 Swift, Duncan
1945 Sakata, Akira
1949 Fuchs, Wolfgang
1949 Fukumura, Hiroshi
1951 Robertson, Herb
1951 Vaché, Warren
1957 Hunter, Chris
1964 Bentzon, Nikolaj
1968 Farnsworth, Joe

died

1972 Horrox, Frank

FEBRUARY

22

born

1881 Europe, James Reese
1897 Ysaguirre, Bob
1898 Edwards, Bass
1902 Tarto, Joe
1907 Stewart, Rex
1908 Williams, Claude
1912 Tate, Buddy
1922 Wilder, Joe
1925 Bonal, Jean
1926 Bailey, Dave
1928 Bowden, Ron
1932 Mitchell, Whitey
1938 Dyląg, Roman
1939 Haslam, George
1944 Charig, Marc
1947 Mason, Harvey
1948 LaBarbera, Joe
1950 Moeckel, Thomas
1968 Whitaker, Rodney

died

1961 LaRocca, Nick
1971 Humble, Derek
1979 Hulan, Ludek
1985 Traynor, Frank

23

born

1893 Elliott, Sticky
1904 Frazier, Cié
1906 Bose, Stirling
1918 Johnson, Money
1919 Lim, Harry
1920 Overton, Hall
1921 Laurence, Baby
1922 Carisi, Johnny
1930 Boone, Richard
1930 Condon, Les
1935 Frommer, Gary
1941 Martyn, Barry
1951 Bem, Ewa

died

1952 Morand, Herb
1963 Clark, June
1966 Kyle, Billy
1993 Landers, Wes
1996 Dawson, Alan
1997 Williams, Tony
1999 Dance, Stanley

24

born

1900 Bertrand, Jimmy
1915 Miller, Johnny
1920 Chamblee, Eddie
1927 Peña, Ralph
1928 Morgan, Alun
1932 Legrand, Michel
1933 Newman, David "Fathead"
1945 Berrios, Steve
1947 Chekasin, Vladimir
1947 Magnusson, Bob
1948 Nicols, Maggie
1957 Manndorff, Andy
1940 Kelly, Guy

died

1989 Brannon, Teddy
1998 Görling, Miff

25

born

1896 Cox, Ida
1900 Parham, Tiny
1915 Perry, Ray
1919 Katz, Fred
1927 Thomas, René
1928 Gay, Al
1929 Brown, Sandy
1929 Newsom, Tommy
1931 Gushee, Lawrence
1932 Persson, Åke
1935 McRae, Barry
1937 Skeat, Len
1938 Wofford, Mike
1947 Kawasaki, Ryo
1951 Jansson, Lars
1957 Tanggaard, Aage

died

1936 Morgan, Sam
1974 Dash, Julian
1974 Assunto, Frank
1981 Malneck, Matty
1988 Morrison, Peck
1997 Queener, Charlie

26

born

1905 Russell, Bill
1907 Gold, Harry
1909 Haughton, Chauncey
1925 Pell, Dave
1936 Purbrook, Colin
1939 Watts, Trevor
1942 Åberg, Lennart
1942 Yamashita, Yosuke
1947 Horler, John
1947 Klucevsek, Guy
1947 Maslak, Keshavan
1948 Richmond, Mike
1958 Hammer, Tardo
1960 Hayasaka, Sachi

died

1967 Pichon, Fats
1982 Szabó, Gábor
1986 Vlach, Karel
1989 Eldridge, Roy
1989 Jones, Reunald
1991 Gaillard, Slim

27

born

1890 Keppard, Freddie
1898 Watson, Leo
1907 Bailey, Mildred
1912 Panassié, Hugues
1920 Most, Abe
1922 Kelso, Jackie
1923 Gordon, Dexter
1923 Wayne, Chuck
1924 Powell, Jesse
1928 Saury, Maxim
1928 Shimizu, Jun
1940 Hooper, Les
1940 Jones, Harold
1941 Williams, John (iv)
1955 Horiuchi, Glenn
1962 Brown, Rob
1965 Calderazzo, Joey

died

1978 Combelle, Alix
1981 Isaacs, Ike (i)
1981 Johnson, J. C.
1984 Henriksen, Bruno
1985 Ellington, Ray
1989 Moore, Mel
1999 Tapscott, Horace

28

born

1898 Gregor
1905 Cohanier, Edmond
1915 Castle, Lee
1916 Asmussen, Svend
1917 Jones, Max
1921 Gwaltney, Tommy
1923 Douglass, Bill (i)
1925 Green, Bill
1930 Grosz, Marty
1932 Garrett, Donald
1934 Bobo, Willie
1939 Gayle, Charles
1944 Dikker, Loek
1946 Dørge, Pierre
1950 Salis, Antonello
1951 Vitro, Roseanna

died

1981 Robert, Jean
1989 Moore, Billy
1994 Johnson, Otis

29

born

1904 Dorsey, Jimmy
1932 Bowden, Colin
1940 Rutherford, Paul
1948 Cole, Richie
1964 France, Martin

died

1972 Philburn, Al
2000 Matsumoto, Hidehiko

February (the date unknown)

died

1936 Green, Charlie
1958 Johnson, Gene
1973 Godley, A. G.
1973 Washington, Leon
1976 Hall, Skip
1977 Elliott, Sticky
1982 Reinhardt, Joseph

MARCH

1

born

1897 Rena, Joseph [or 11 March]
1903 Wheeler, De Priest
1904 Miller, Glenn
1905 Smith, Ben
1912 Reinhardt, Joseph
?1915 Deems, Barrett
1932 Teschemacher, Frank
1917 Barelli, Aimé
1917 Gleason, Ralph J.
1921 Baker, Kenny
1928 Hardaway, Bob
1929 Jones, Eddie
1930 Powell, Benny
1940 Perla, Gene
1940 Towner, Ralph
1946 Golia, Vinny
1947 Connors, Norman
1949 Matta, Nilson
1953 Wittwer, Stephan
1954 Benavent, Carles
1956 Dennard, Kenwood

died

1932 Teschemacher, Frank
1937 Holiday, Clarence
1957 Laine, Alfred "Baby"
1970 Hegamin, Lucille
1974 Timmons, Bobby
1982 Spivak, Charlie
1987 Green, Freddie

2

born

1897 Hall, Minor
1906 Widmann, Kutte
1912 Saunders, Red
1914 Strittmatter, Mac
1922 Davis, Eddie "Lockjaw"
1923 Keepnews, Orrin
1934 Watkins, Doug
1936 Neidlinger, Buell
1942 Neloms, Bob
1945 Watkins, Derek
1946 Rachabane, Barney
1948 Bowler, Phil
1948 Carlton, Larry
1960 Bailey, Craig
1960 Ginman, Lennart
1965 Muthspiel, Wolfgang
1968 Penn, Clarence
1970 Lourau, Julien

died

1942 Christian, Charlie
1964 Rushton, Joe
1970 Barnes, Emile
1973 De Brest, Spanky
2000 Lewis, Jimmy

3

born

1905 Coppieters, Fernand
1906 Bigard, Barney
1918 Smalls, Cliff
1928 Michelot, Pierre
1929 Bolton, Dupree
1934 Garrison, Jimmy
1940 Gasca, Luis
1942 Nakamura, Teruo
1944 Bingert, Hector
1950 Arnesen, Dag
1951 Cooper, Lindsay
1955 Mseleku, Bheki
1957 Trowers, Robert

died

1978 Marsala, Joe
1984 Roane, Kenneth
1991 Nistico, Sal (ii)

4

born

1917 Kavka, Arnošt
1926 Rendell, Don
1927 Touff, Cy
1932 Schlitten, Don
1933 Burton, Ann
1937 Wilen, Barney
1941 Darling, David
1941 Shew, Bobby
1944 McMurdo, Dave
1947 Brüning, Uschi
1947 Garbarek, Jan
1947 Nichols, Jim
1954 Ford, Ricky
1955 Bisio, Michael
1956 Driscoll, Kermit
1977 Marsalis, Jason

died

1963 Jaspar, Bobby
1989 Grimes, Tiny
1992 Osborne, Mary
1993 Hall, Gene
1993 Hodes, Art
1995 Blöchlinger, Urs
1999 McRae, Teddy

5

born

1909 Yukl, Joe
1910 Rodgers, Gene
1918 Pemberton, Bill
1924 Burns, Dave
1927 Probert, George
1928 Levy, Lou
1928 Little, Wilbur
1928 Moore, Pee Wee
1935 Fischer, William
1937 Sloane, Carol
1942 Green, Dave
1944 Toyama, Yoshio
1964 Fiuczynski, David

died

1952 Eldridge, Joe
1968 Hazel, Monk
1981 Saunders, Red
1983 Shoffner, Bob
1996 Hall, Herb

6

born

1905 Wills, Bob
1915 De Weille, Benny
1916 Callender, Red
1918 McGhee, Howard
1923 Montgomery, Wes
1934 Root, Billy
1939 Bertles, Bob
1941 Brötzmann, Peter
1941 Mikkelborg, Palle
1942 Kenyatta, Robin
1942 Purim, Flora
1942 Tolliver, Charles
1943 Davis, Spanky
1950 Beresford, Steve
1951 Unt, Toivo

died

1980 Jones, Bobby
1983 McFarlane, Howard [date uncertain]
1987 Durham, Eddie
1994 Ford, Jimmy
1997 Green, Chuck

7

born

1888 Pavageau, Alcide "Slow Drag"
1891 Robertson, Zue
1903 Smith, Cal
1908 Gonella, Nat
1911 Cottrell, Louis, Jr
1917 Young, Lee
1923 Clark, Mahlon
1926 Vasseur, Benny
1933 Naude, Jean-Claude
1937 Williams, Roy
1938 Glawischnig, Dieter
1939 Bushler, Herb
1947 Brunet, Alain
1955 Christi, Ellen

died

1967 Smith, Willie
1971 McNair, Harold
1973 Templin, Lutz
1989 Velebný, Karel
1990 Jacquet, Russell
1991 Klink, Al
1995 Fields, Kansas
1997 Green, Chuck

MARCH

8

born

1899 Mitchell, George
1900 Robichaux, Joseph
1903 Ouwerx, John
1908 Hudson, Will
1911 Hamilton, John "Bugs"
1915 Hall, Al
1920 Turner, Danny
1921 Pitterson, Pete
1927 Hyman, Dick
1930 Sellin, Pierre
1935 Coleman, George
1936 Szabó, Gábor
1941 D'Andrea, Franco
1947 Lytton, Paul
1949 Itabashi, Fumio
1951 Williams, James
1957 Childs, Billy

died

1941 Johnson, Ken "Snake Hips"
1965 Dameron, Tadd
1967 Chittison, Herman "Ivory"
1988 Colyer, Ken
1992 Callender, Red
1993 Eckstine, Billy
1993 Palmer, Singleton

9

born

1903 White, Georgia
1906 Christensen, Bernhard
1930 Ash, Vic
1930 Coleman, Ornette
1938 Watts, Marzette
1940 Rigby, Joe
1943 Correa, Mayuto
1944 Hess, Fred
1948 Karashima, Fumio
1957 Chapin, Thomas

died

1941 Reardon, Casper
1961 Sweatman, Wilbur
1965 Douglas, Tommy
1974 Bean, Floyd
1992 Budwig, Monty
1993 Crosby, Bob
1994 Purtill, Moe

10

born

1903 Beiderbecke, Bix
1911 Clarke, Pete
1920 Vian, Boris
1923 Abney, Don
1927 Trenner, Donn
1940 Moholo, Louis
1944 Friedman, David
1950 Hartog, Jim
1953 Marcotulli, Rita
1957 Cinélu, Mino
1958 Bryson, Jeanie

died

1967 Whyte, Zack
1982 Utyosov, Leonid
1987 Jaffe, Allan (i)
1993 Howard, Camille

11

born

1897 Rena, Joseph [or 1 March]
1898 Mole, Miff
1902 Morehouse, Chauncey
1914 Krahmer, Carlo
1919 Ellington, Mercer
1920 Carpenter, Ike
1920 Scott, Calo
1922 Mills, Jackie
1931 Ganley, Allan
1932 Jenkins, Leroy
1945 Clark, Charles
1950 McFerrin, Bobby
1952 Giordano, Vince
1954 Jang, Jon
1954 Niemack, Judy
1957 Namtchylak, Sainkho

died

1954 Newton, Frankie
1997 Coetzee, Basil
1997 Lawson, Hugh
1999 Williams, Pearlis

12

born

1904 Johnson, Freddy
1924 Combe, Stuff
1928 Maiden, Willie
1935 Lawson, Hugh
1940 Jarreau, Al
1944 Davis, Quin
1948 Koch, Hans

died

1955 Parker, Charlie
1957 Graettinger, Bob
1960 Ellboj, Lulle
1980 Strittmatter, Mac
1990 South, Harry
1998 Richards, Red

13

born

1901 Morgan, Andrew
1906 Brown, John
1906 Teschemacher, Frank
1908 Williams, Johnny (i)
1909 Dutrey, Sam [or 29 May]
1909 King, Saunders
1914 Haggart, Bob
1916 Hutton, Ina Ray
1924 Katz, Dick
1925 Haynes, Roy
1930 Mitchell, Blue
1938 Bahula, Julian
1939 Eckert, John
1940 Brackeen, Charles
1942 Sandström, Nisse
1957 Van Bergen, Peter
1962 Blanchard, Terence
1969 Scott, Stephen

died

1957 Billings, Josh
1964 Long, Slats
1972 Hayes, Clancy
1984 Fierstone, George
1985 Shad, Bob
1991 McPartland, Jimmy
1994 Barker, Danny
2000 Kaye, Cab

14

born

1900 Hill, Ernest
1904 De Faut, Volly
1911 Mooney, Joe
1912 Brown, Les
1921 Ottersen, Frank
1925 Cohn, Sonny
1932 Murphy, Mark
1933 Jones, Quincy
1934 Scott, Shirley
1940 Schwindt, Christian
1944 Bouchet, Alain
1945 D'Imperio, Danny
1948 Murakami, Hiroshi
1952 Sasajima, Akio
1952 Tana, Akira
1957 Rubin, Vanessa
1961 Ascione, Joe
1966 Aramaki, Shigeo

MARCH

15

born

1901 Masman, Theo Uden
1905 Hill, Chippie
1907 McPartland, Jimmy
1916 James, Harry
1919 Avakian, George
1921 Burke, Vinnie
1928 Wilber, Bob
1929 Taylor, Cecil
1933 Nakamure, Sadanori
1938 Lloyd, Charles
1944 Kühn, Joachim
1947 Boni, Raymond
1962 Okegwo, Ugonna

died

1929 Smith, Pine Top
1937 Pinkett, Ward
1959 Young, Lester
1975 Brown, Sandy
1988 Potter, Tommy
1991 Freeman, Bud

16

born

1902 Roppolo, Leon
1906 Hemphill, Shelton
1906 Hutchinson, Jiver
1910 Lessey, Bob
1917 Raglin, Junior
1922 Young, John
1923 Walker, Sammy
1927 Braff, Ruby
1930 Flanagan, Tommy
1940 Mustafa-Zade, Vagif
1947 Belichenko, Sergey
1953 Akagi, Kei
1953 Plimley, Paul
1954 Torff, Brian
1957 Sellin, Hervé
1959 Lindberg, John

died

1974 Lubinsky, Herman
1975 Walker, T-Bone
1981 Yukl, Joe
1983 Royal, Ernie
1988 Richmond, Dannie
1994 Harrington, John

17

born

1884 Nunez, Alcide "Yellow"
1916 Ellington, Ray
1917 Cole, Nat "King"
1919 Lovett, Leroy
1930 Horn, Paul
1930 Mitchell, Grover
1931 Velebný, Karel
1948 Williams, Jessica
1952 Badrena, Manolo
1971 Burton, Abraham

died

1958 Perkins, Carl
1963 Miles, Lizzie
1983 Gryce, Gigi
1989 Biziński, Marek
1990 Noren, Jack
1995 Braceful, Fred
2001 Zabiegliński, Janusz

18

born

1893 Goldkette, Jean
1899 Curl, Langston
1906 Orendorff, George
1909 Russell, Ross
1911 Kincaide, Deane
1918 Donahue, Sam
1924 Gerard, Fred
1930 Halcox, Pat
1951 Frisell, Bill
1951 Naissoo, Tõnu
1954 Narell, Andy
1954 Sokal, Harry
1956 Kirkwood, Neal
1959 Locke, Joe
1964 Pine, Courtney

died

1983 Lucas, Buddy
1988 Butterfield, Billy
1995 Ramsey, Fred

19

born

1913 De Souza, Yorke
1914 Bennett, Buster
1916 Wick, Joe
1917 Harding, Buster
1917 Russell, Curly
1919 Tristano, Lennie
1921 Babasin, Harry
1922 Rust, Brian
1925 Mettome, Doug
1928 Winchester, Lem
1929 Taylor, Gene
1930 Henderson, Bill
1940 Longo, Mike
1940 Smith, Keith
1948 Schnitter, David
1950 Fowlkes, Curtis
1950 Houben, Steve
*c*1952 Brown, Jeri
1960 Elias, Eliane

died

1945 Hart, Clyde
1977 Hug, Armand

20

born

1914 Caiazza, Nick
1915 Tharpe, Sister Rosetta
1916 Bales, Burt
1918 McPartland, Marian
1921 Coe, Jimmy
1926 Koíróssy, János
1927 Davies, John R. T.
1929 Russo, Sonny
1936 Mabern, Harold
1943 Christensen, Jon
1960 Gontsana, Lulu

died

1947 Warlop, Michel
1949 Fazola, Irving
1981 Red, Sonny
1988 Evans, Gil
1991 Butler, Billy
1996 Margolis, Sam

21

born

1895 Utyosov, Leonid
1909 Görling, Miff
1915 D'Amico, Hank
1918 Thompson, Sir Charles
1927 Lane, Joe
1932 Imada, Masaru
1936 Dee, Brian
1936 Westbrook, Mike
1940 Joos, Herbert
*c*1942 Myers, Amina Claudine
1945 Soph, Ed
1946 Suzuki, Yoshio
1948 Giddins, Gary
1950 Okoshi, Tiger
1952 Actis Dato, Carlo
1956 Szabó, Sándor
1968 Courtois, Vincent

died

1970 Sels, Jack
1978 Cottrell, Louis, Jr
1981 Pleasure, King
1986 Burke, Raymond

MARCH

22

born

1914 Burke, Sonny
1929 Anderson, Fred
1933 Houston, John
1940 Hassell, Jon
1940 Togashi, Masahiko
1941 Rasmussen, Hugo
1943 Benson, George
1946 Sparks, Melvin
1947 Bliziński, Marek
1948 Huck, Daniel
1949 Johansson, Markku
1949 Ohno, Shunzo
1952 Mover, Bob
1965 Linx, David
1966 Lundgren, Jan

died

1944 Porter, Yank
1974 Donahue, Sam
1977 Shertzer, Hymie
1999 Fay, Rick

23

born

1909 Hayes, Harry
1917 Guarnieri, Johnny
1932 Aarons, Al
1933 Frishberg, Dave
1933 Trzaskowski, Andrzej
1940 Kikuchi, Masabumi
1943 Gannon, Oliver
1947 Rozenbergs, Gunārs
1948 McNeil, John
1948 Yamamoto, Tsuyoshi
1955 Hemingway, Gerry
1971 Możdżer, Leszek
1973 Harris, Stefon

died

1967 Johnson, Pete
1977 Green, Bennie
1982 Greer, Sonny
1983 Jones, Wallace
1985 Sims, Zoot
1990 Sears, Al

24

born

1900 Clark, June
1922 Pleasure, King
1932 Mackay, Dave
1936 McIntyre, Kalaparusha Maurice
1938 Kuhn, Steve
1947 McCandless, Paul
1954 Jones, Vince
1954 LaSpina, Steve
1954 Roberts, Hank
1962 Rosnes, Renee
1963 Douglas, Dave
1963 Vloeimans, Eric
1965 Overwater, Tony
1968 Irby, Sherman

died

1961 Johnson, Freddy
1962 Goldkette, Jean
1989 Cobb, Arnett
1994 Benford, Tommy
1998 Charles, Dennis [or 26 March]

25

born

1897 Barrett, Sweet Emma
1902 Burbank, Albert
1904 Johnson, Pete
1915 Garner, Linton
1923 Brice, Percy
1931 Motian, Paul
1936 Gales, Larry
1940 Hillyer, Lonnie
1942 Franklin, Aretha
1950 Militello, Bobby
1960 Wackerman, Chad
1961 Catingub, Matt
1961 Ozone, Makoto

died

1951 Catlett, Sid
1957 Livingston, Fud
1958 Brown, Tom
1979 Manzecchi, Franco
1991 Bryant, Rusty
1991 Williams, Sandy
1993 Porter, Jake

26

born

1908 Bolar, Abe
1915 Phillips, Flip
1918 Hamilton, Andy
1924 Moore, Brew
1925 Moody, James
1929 Simon, Maurice
1933 Bailey, Donald
1940 Tabackin, Lew
1950 Ino, Nobuyoshi
1952 Damiani, Paolo
1953 Scherer, Uli

died

1933 Lang, Eddie
1975 Esbensen, Egon
1996 Gunther, Paul
1998 Charles, Dennis [or 24 March]

27

born

1892 Grofé, Ferde
1905 Kemp, Hal
1906 Russell, Pee Wee
1909 Webster, Ben
1920 Norin, Carl-Henrik
1924 Vaughan, Sarah
1925 Ashby, Harold
1927 Barron, Bill
1931 Collins, Burt
1936 Wróblewski, Jan
1937 Klein, Miriam
1943 Morel, Jean-Pierre
1960 Bailey, Victor

died

1952 Simpson, Cassino
1966 Smith, Russell
1972 Bonano, Sharkey
1975 Clarke, Pete
1977 Moten, Benny
1982 Ysaguirre, Bob
1983 Wayland, Hank
1993 Jordan, Clifford

28

born

1890 Whiteman, Paul
1907 Hall, Herb
1923 Isaacs, Ike (i)
1923 Jones, Thad
1926 Bradshaw, Sonny
1930 Anthony, Bill
1930 Dixon, Eric
1930 Hughes, Bill
1933 Montoliu, Tete
1941 D'Ambrosio, Meredith
1947 Miles, Barry
1954 Brown, Donald
1957 Willis, Gary
1959 Abarius, Gintautas
1965 Hoogendijk, Jarmo

died

1958 Handy, W. C.
1966 Howard, Kid
1971 Feld, Morey
1973 Chappy
1978 Johnson, Money
1985 Cavalli, Pierre
2001 Koffman, Moe

MARCH

29

born

1901 Arodin, Sidney
1907 Lincoln, Abe
1914 Howard, Camille
1915 Chisholm, George
1916 Behounek, Kamil
1918 Bailey, Pearl
1923 Palmier, Remo
1938 Déczi, Ladislav
1940 Botschinsky, Allan
1949 Brecker, Michael
1951 Śmietana, Jarosaw
1953 Emborg, Jørgen
1953 Hauser, Fritz
1953 Rosewoman, Michele
1969 Rebello, Jason

died

1982 George, Fatty
1982 Smith, Floyd
1991 Noone, Jimmy, Jr.
1994 Weiss, Sid
1995 Flores, Luca
2001 Lewis, John

30

born

1900 Heath, Ted
1926 Kretzschmar, Heinz
1934 Morgan, Lanny
1935 Berger, Karl
1944 Barda, Daniel
1947 Crispell, Marilyn
1949 Berger, David
1950 D'Earth, John
1957 Stryker, Dave
1961 May, Tina
1963 Milanta, Philippe
1963 Tebar, Ximo

died

1962 Purvis, Jack
1976 Bloom, Rube
1978 Young, Larry
1979 Ventura, Ray
1981 Wilson, Edith
1995 Claxton, Rozelle
1999 Williams, Joe

31

born

1895 Miles, Lizzie,
1902 Pecora, Santo
1908 Norvo, Red
1911 Green, Freddie
1922 Acheson, Merv
1928 Semple, Archie
1938 Holloway, Laurie
1951 Fonseca, Duduka da
1961 Lockheart, Mark
1965 Moriya, Junko

died

1981 Mastren, Carmen
1991 Carter, John
1995 Rutherford, Rudy

March (the date unknown)

died

1942 Adde, Leo
1959 Fields, Ted
1974 Mavounzy, Robert
1974 Ware, Leonard
1975 Nichols, Bobby
1979 Pozo, Chino
1983 Martin, Bobby
1991 Eardley, Jon
1998 Watts, Marzette

APRIL

1

born

1910 Carney, Harry
1910 Harris, Ace
1920 LaPorta, John
1921 Agostini, Dante
1921 Race, Steve
1922 Jordan, Duke
1923 Butterfield, Don
1925 Stobart, Kathy
1935 López Ruiz, Jorge
1944 Gebert, Bobby
1945 Żądło, Leszek
1947 Ineke, Eric
1947 Tusa, Frank
1949 Scott-Heron, Gil
1949 Vintskevich, Leonid
1963 Roney, Antoine

died

1947 Webster, Freddie
1964 Von Eichwald, Håkan
1982 Richards, Ann [date uncertain]
1983 Kersey, Kenny
1989 Johnson, Lem
1991 Miller, Eddie
1991 Nerem, Bjarne
1992 Wilson, Phillip
1999 Stone, Jesse

2

born

?1892 Palmer, Roy
1908 Von Eichwald, Håkan
1909 Marsala, Marty
1911 Cagnolatti, Cag
1911 Coles, Honi
1916 Lundstrem, Oleg
1921 Richman, Boomie
1926 Greger, Max
1938 Little, Booker
1940 MacRae, Dave
1943 Coryell, Larry
1945 Lazro, Daunik
1947 Sharrock, Linda
1953 Oatts, Dick
1956 Binder, Károly
1963 Oishi, Manabu
1966 Cain, Michael
1966 Pokorný, Roman

died

1935 Moten, Bennie
1978 Noble, Ray
1987 Rich, Buddy
1994 Greenberg, Rowland
1995 Hemphill, Julius

3

born

1903 Miley, Bubber
1906 Taylor, Billy (i)
1916 Kersey, Kenny
1917 Finegan, Bill
1920 Mitchell, Bob (i)
1928 Potts, Bill
1936 LaFaro, Scott
1936 McGriff, Jimmy
1936 Vick, Harold
1949 Kloss, Eric
1958 Speake, Martin
1962 Mackrel, Dennis

died

1963 Sedric, Gene
1972 Grofé, Ferde
1984 Mehegan, John
1986 Skjoldborg, Anker
1990 Vaughan, Sarah
1998 Tyler, Alvin "Red"

4

born

1904 Hülphers, Arne
1913 Ramey, Gene
1929 Cooper, Buster
1931 Hanna, Jake
1939 Masekela, Hugh
1939 Thompson, Danny
1941 Leroux, Gilbert
1945 Hansen, Ole Kock
1946 Okoun, Mikhail
1954 Camilo, Michel
1956 Smulyan, Gary
1963 Green, Benny

died

1943 Parham, Tiny
1976 Short, Bob
1988 Ewans, Kai

5

born

1900 Flemming, Herb [date uncertain]
1926 Levey, Stan
1930 Totah, Nobby
1932 Baldock, Kenny
1934 Turrentine, Stanley
1934 Zabiegliński, Janusz
1939 Fuller, Jerry
1944 Parker, Evan
1952 Sheppard, Bob
1953 Harris, Jerome
1954 Lowe, Allen
1959 Parricelli, John

died

1964 Hagemann, Henry
1971 Carruthers, Earl
1988 Shorter, Alan
1990 Nelson, Louis

6

born

1902 Filu
1902 McHargue, Rosy
1914 Ricci, Paul
1922 Donegan, Dorothy
1924 Rouse, Charlie
1926 Weston, Randy
1927 Mulligan, Gerry
1928 Efford, Bob
1928 Gaines, Will
1928 Hubble, Ed
1929 Previn, André
1929 Taylor, Art
1933 Hardman, Bill
1934 Tapscott, Horace
1936 Schoof, Manfred
1937 Bertoncini, Gene
1937 Otsuka, George
1943 Howard, Noah
1943 Niewood, Gerry
1960 Pizzarelli, John
1964 Beuf, Sylvain

died

1968 Henderson, Rosa
1977 Featherstone, Benny
1979 Coughlan, Frank [or 7 April]
1994 Cary, Dick
1999 Norvo, Red

7

born

1897 Morgan, Isaiah
1915 Holiday, Billie
1918 Hucko, Peanuts
1918 Simmen, Johnny
1921 Fox, Charles
1921 Hayse, Al
1922 Santamaria, Mongo
1934 Feldman, Victor
1938 Hubbard, Freddie
1938 La Roca, Pete
1938 Schlippenbach, Alex
1944 Grimes, Carol
1944 LaBarbera, Pat
1951 Berg, Bob
1963 Lundin, Fredrik
1966 Pastre, Michel

died

1946 Nelson, Dave
1976 Garrison, Jimmy
1977 Mullens, Moon
1979 Coughlan, Frank [or 6 April]
1983 Cagnolatti, Cag
1987 Sullivan, Maxine

APRIL

8

born

1909 Dixon, George
1920 McRae, Carmen
1922 Bellest, Christian
1928 Hogg, Derek
1928 Sunshine, Monty
1929 Kitamura, Eiji
1933 Jeffrey, Paul
1938 Brimfield, Bill
1943 Lee, Phil
1951 Schaap, Phil
1962 Leloup, Denis

died

1938 Oliver, King [or 10 April]

9

born

1894 Doucet, Clément [date uncertain]
1894 Jenkins, Edmund Thornton
1899 Briggs, Arthur
1902 Bonano, Sharkey
1905 Roy, Teddy
1916 Dash, Julian
1941 Gafa, Al
1945 Gadd, Steve
1951 Ragin, Hugh
1956 Hashim, Michael
1957 Honda, Toshiyuki
1960 Howard, Ed
1961 Abrahams, Chris
1963 Clarvis, Paul
1966 Wollesen, Kenny

died

1963 Edwards, Eddie
1968 Myers, Bumps
1971 Johnson, Manzie
1983 Garcia, King
1983 Lanigan, Jim
1986 Casey, Bob
1998 Cora, Tom
1999 Firman, Bert

10

born

1894 Williams, Fess
1906 Ewans, Kai
1906 Livingston, Fud
1917 Corb, Morty
1918 Ulanov, Barry
1927 Freeman, George
1928 MacPherson, Fraser
1928 Matuszkiewicz, Jerzy
1930 Bolling, Claude
1938 Zeitlin, Denny
1949 Rudolph, Steve
1951 Lodder, Steve
1971 DeFrancesco, Joey

died

1938 Oliver, King [or 8 April]
1970 Escudero, Ralph
1979 Clark, Gus
1994 Lyons, Jimmy (i)

11

born

1889 LaRocca, Nick
1904 Wilborn, Dave
1912 Levy, John
1918 Lewis, Jimmy
1925 Mangelsdorff, Emil
1943 Samson, Jacky
1947 Mantooth, Frank
1964 Nagórski, Grzegorz

died

1949 Haymer, Herbie
1960 Görling, Zilas
1974 Candrix, Fud
1982 Minor, Dan
1984 Robinson, Fred
1992 Williams, Martin [or 12 April]

12

born

1892 Dodds, Johnny
1911 Mobiglia, Tullio
1915 Borneman, Ernest
1916 Garcia, Russ
1939 Giger, Peter
1940 Hancock, Herbie
1940 Nistico, Sal (ii)
1951 Krystall, Marty
1965 De Bethmann, Pierre
1973 Kisor, Ryan

died

1963 Nichols, Herbie
1967 Bailey, Buster
1971 Kelly, Wynton
1976 Buckner, Ted
1992 Williams, Martin [or 11 April]

13

born

1905 Williams, John (i)
1906 Freeman, Bud
1907 Jones, Slick
1928 Charles, Teddy
1934 Stuart, Kirk
1936 Majewski, Henryk
1938 Marshall, Eddie
1940 Mitchell, J. R.
1942 Jones, Rusty
1961 Croft, Monte
1961 Perkiömäki, Jari

died

1962 Graas, John
1973 Clay, Sonny
1973 Wright, Lammar (i)
1981 Barnes, Polo
1983 Coker, Dolo
1986 Ashby, Dorothy

14

born

1915 or 1919 Namaro, Jimmy
1920 Fuller, Gil
1924 Rogers, Shorty
1925 Ammons, Gene
1925 Harris, Bill (ii)
1938 Waters, Monty
1945 Zigmund, Eliot
1955 Cugny, Laurent
1956 Tsilis, Gust William
1967 Davis, Steve (iii)

died

1954 Green, Lil
1974 Morgan, Al
1978 Douglas, Billy
1988 Poindexter, Pony
1992 Price, Sammy
1995 Turner, Danny

APRIL

15

born

1894 Smith, Bessie
1905 Addison, Bernard
1907 Reardon, Casper
1909 Baranco, Wilbert
1927 Smith, Charlie
1930 Davis, Richard
1930 Pomeroy, Herb
1935 Cherico, Gene
1954 Williams, Rod
1956 Wiggins, Hassan J. J.
1957 Lussier, René

died

1969 Clark, Charles
1984 Machito
1991 Culley, Frank
1995 Brown, Cleo

16

born

1908 Ventura, Ray
1910 Brown, Boyce
1911 Purnell, Alton
1916 Farreras, Joe
1923 Daly, Geo
1923 Green, Bennie
1930 Mann, Herbie
1931 Badini, Gérard
1943 Kroner, Erling
1947 Uematsu, Takao
1952 Tolonen, Jukka
1958 Wakenius, Ulf
1964 Svensson, Esbjörn
1967 Onishi, Junko

died

1991 Lind, Ove

17

born

1890 St. Cyr, Johnny
1907 or 1909 Bowles, Russell
1920 McCarthy, Albert
1922 Smith, Paul
1926 Balliett, Whitney
1930 Barber, Chris
1930 Noto, Sam
1934 Chiasson, Warren
1942 Bennink, Han
1942 Williams, Buster
1948 Hammer, Jan
1953 Gumede, Sipho
1956 Hobbs, Steve

died

1943 Thompkins, Eddie
1967 Allen, Henry "Red"
1972 Parenti, Tony
1986 Kotick, Teddy
1992 Herfurt, Skeets

18

born

1893 Whistler
1906 Montgomery, Little Brother
1925 Parker, Leo
1926 Rowser, Jimmy
1928 Colyer, Ken
1931 Pickens, Willie
1937 Rivers, James
1938 Galper, Hal
1939 Galbraith, Gus
1945 Adåker, Ulf
1946 Copeland, Keith
1953 Gottlieb, Danny
1955 Takeuchi, Nao
1957 Hasler, Gabriele
1960 Schubert, Matthias

died

1973 Smith, Willie "the Lion"
2001 Mitchell, Billy

19

born

1905 Benford, Tommy
1906 Hill, Alex
1915 Burnside, Vi
1922 Masetti, Glauco
1928 Korner, Alexis
1935 Moore, Dudley
1943 Bartkowski, Czesław
1951 Pearce, Dick
1956 Coleman, Denardo

died

1944 Noone, Jimmie
1974 Pâques, Jean
1974 Price, Jesse
1988 Burke, Ed
1991 Curl, Langston
1993 Scott, Clifford

20

born

1895 Christian, Emile
1908 Hampton, Lionel
1919 Auer, Vera
1923 Puente, Tito
1925 Renaud, Henri
1926 Laurie, Cy
1935 Blake, Ran
1936 Brown, Sonny
1936 Harris, Beaver
1936 James, Billy
1939 Kennel, Hans
1948 Bonner, Joe
1955 Glerum, Ernst
1956 Raja, Mario
1956 Rogers, Paul
1958 Schlott, Volker
1961 Stripling, Byron
1970 Cohen, Avishai

died

1921 Jackson, Tony
1970 Bradford, Perry
1976 Krahmer, Carlo
1977 Robeson, Orlando
1980 Boykins, Ronnie
1992 Abrams, Lee
1992 Phillips, Gene

21

born

1893 Tio, Lorenzo, Jr.
1904 Adde, Leo
1908 Lion, Alfred
1911 Blowers, Johnny
1911 Görling, Zilas
1914 Yoder, Walt
1917 Dixon, Joe
1922 Lowe, Mundell
1925 Berman, Sonny
1925 Ray, Carline
1932 Hampton, Slide
1933 Carr, Ian
1935 Rebillot, Pat
1938 Noone, Jimmy, Jr.
1942 Skidmore, Alan
1944 Kowald, Peter
1948 Jarzębski, Paweł
1962 Rojas, Marcus

died

1966 Assunto, Freddie
1974 Crump, Jesse
1977 Garland, Joe
1981 Sauter, Eddie
1985 Mills, Irving
1998 Ward, Helen

APRIL

22

born

1908 Howard, Kid
1909 Shertzer, Hymie
*c*1910 Drootin, Buzzy
1919 Jackson, Bullmoose
1921 Camero, Candido
1922 Mingus, Charles
1922 Stein, Lou
1928 Turrentine, Tommy
1935 Chambers, Paul
1936 Bunink, Floris Nico
1936 Lüdi, Werner
1936 Menza, Don
1941 Grusin, Don
1947 Guy, Barry
1948 Kaspersen, Jan
1956 Bijma, Greetje
1961 Calderazzo, Gene

died

1983 Hines, Earl
1987 Ashby, Irving
1995 Pullen, Don

23

born

1895 Noone, Jimmie
1919 Harris, Little Benny
1924 Rosengarden, Bob
1929 Barnard, Len
1930 Flagstad, Michael
1935 Green, Bunky
1940 Courbois, Pierre
1947 Broadbent, Alan
1950 Clark, Curtis
1959 Berg, Thilo
1959 Carrott, Bryan
1960 Talbot, Jamie

died

1940 Barnes, Walter
1969 Komeda, Krzysztof
1984 Garland, Red
1984 Tizol, Juan
1998 Skidmore, Jimmy
1999 Liston, Melba

24

born

1902 Bloom, Rube
1922 Bell, Aaron
1927 George, Fatty
1928 Griffin, Johnny
1930 Strazzeri, Frank
1935 Jaffe, Allan (i)
1937 De Brest, Spanky
1937 Henderson, Joe
1945 Walcott, Collin
1946 James, Stafford
1951 Ferré, Boulou

died

1967 Margulis, Charlie
1969 Compère, René
1971 Hayton, Lennie
1983 Mundy, Jimmy
1988 Attenoux, Michel
1994 Deniz, Joe
1998 Powell, Mel
2001 Hibbler, Al

25

born

1913 Bostic, Earl
1913 Johnson, George
1913 Sturgis, Ted
1917 Fitzgerald, Ella
1928 Henderson, Rick
1928 Jackson, Willis "Gator"
1930 Schneider, Hawe
1941 Miller, Harry
1946 Fairweather, Digby
1947 Dobbins, Bill
1960 Laginha, Mário
1961 Allen, Carl
1966 Mantler, Karen

died

1945 Weatherford, Teddy
1949 Rena, Kid
1962 South, Eddie
1963 Yaw, Ralph
1978 Dubin, Larry
1982 Wilborn, Dave
1986 Hunt, Fred
1990 Gordon, Dexter
1990 Jones, Rufus
1991 Vauchant, Léo
1998 Namaro, Jimmy

26

born

1886 Rainey, Ma
1907 Tough, Dave
1913 George, Karl
1921 Giuffre, Jimmy
1924 Edwards, Teddy
1928 Foster, Herman
1942 Byrne, Bill
1944 Carl, Rüdiger
1950 Artero, Patrick
1962 Swana, John

died

1952 Cohn, Zinky
1977 Johnson, Walter
1984 Basie, Count
1986 Leeman, Cliff

27

born

1907 Matlock, Matty
1917 Best, Denzil
1925 Brooke, Eric
1927 Kay, Connie
1927 Mosca, Sal
1931 Komeda, Krzysztof
1933 Newborn, Calvin
1943 Waits, Freddie
1952 Whitehead, Kevin
1959 Robinson, Scott
1967 Smith, Tommy

died

1975 Marsala, Marty
1999 Hirt, Al

28

born

1896 Lee, George E.
1907 or 1910 Barksdale, Everett
1911 Bauzá, Mario
1922 Boucaya, William
1926 Dearie, Blossom
1928 Fol, Raymond
1933 Jackson, Oliver
1936 Tchicai, John
1941 Tucker, Mickey
1947 Khan, Steve
1950 Alvim, Cesarius
1952 Stern, Leni
1965 Newsome, Sam

died

1949 McDonald, Earl
1971 White, Sonny
1982 McEachern, Murray
1983 LaVere, Charlie
1993 Saudrais, Charles

29

born

1899 Ellington, Duke
1904 Morgan, Russ
1906 Pinkett, Ward
1908 Brun, Philippe
1909 Butler, Jacques
1911 Teagarden, Norma
1922 Thielemans, Toots
1927 McNeely, Big Jay
1928 Buddle, Errol
1929 Barretto, Ray
1930 Ogerman, Claus
1931 Donegan, Lonnie
1932 Simpkins, Andy
1940 Adams, George
1942 Rimington, Sammy
1952 Valentin, Dave
1956 Coleman, Ira

died

1961 Mole, Miff
1981 Anderson, Cat
1982 Jones, Jimmy

30

born

1887 Duhé, Lawrence
1900 Shoffner, Bob
1906 Pillars, Hayes
1914 Weiss, Sid
1915 Scott, Mabel
1923 Heath, Percy
1931 Twardzik, Dick
1931 Yoshizawa, Motoharu
1946 Futterman, Joel
1947 Wadud, Abdul
1960 Kendrick, Rodney

died

1981 Socolow, Frank
1992 Kärki, Toivo
2000 Jones, Jonah
2000 Ulanov, Barry

April (the date unknown)

born

1921 Love, Preston
1942 Christmann, Günter

died

1962 Marsh, George
1968 Blue, William Thornton
1973 Aiken, Gus
1976 Jones, Al
1977 Strong, Jimmy
1981 Brown, Olive
1991 Jones, Willie

MAY

1

born

1907 Alvis, Hayes
1908 Chambers, Henderson
1909 Price, Jesse
1927 Byers, Billy
1931 Lidström, Jack
1931 Sullivan, Ira
1934 Horn, Shirley
1940 Papadimitriou, Sakis
1940 Ward, Carlos
1941 Denis, Michel
1953 Bottlang, René
1953 Newton, James
1961 Gebbia, Gianni
1967 Terai, Naoko
1968 Hays, Kevin

died

1979 Fol, Raymond
1996 Byers, Billy
1999 Chamblee, Eddie

2

born

1904 Crosby, Bing
1909 Stauffer, Teddy
1923 Smythe, Pat
1931 Holmes, Groove
1937 Hultcrantz, Torbjörn
1938 Braceful, Fred
1941 Crothers, Connie
1945 Rockwell, Bob
1946 Forrester, Joel
1953 Chirillo, James
1957 Stockhausen, Markus
1963 Person, Eric

died

1950 Watson, Leo
1978 Davidson, Trump
1984 Ballew, Smith
1985 Clinton, Larry
1986 Bishop, Wallace
1994 Kavka, Arnošt
2000 Munn, Billy
2000 Thornton, Teri

3

born

1911 Lawson, Yank
1920 Lewis, John
1926 Cleveland, Jimmy
1926 Merritt, Jymie
1930 Fischer, Johnny
1930 Havens, Bob
1939 Hübner, Ralf
1949 Abe, Kaoru
1951 Andersson, Krister
1952 Elmes, Barry

died

1935 Irwin, Cecil
1972 Flax, Marty
1990 Remler, Emily [or 4 May]
2001 Higgins, Billy

4

born

1916 Purtill, Moe
1919 McCall, Mary Ann
1926 Payne, Sonny
1928 Ferguson, Maynard
1928 Gullin, Lars
1931 Williams, Richard
1932 Smith, Warren (ii)
1935 Friedman, Don
1937 Carter, Ron
1938 Folds, Chuck
1939 Owens, Charles
1945 Stapleton, Bill
1953 Di Pasqua, Michael
1956 Ali, Amin
1969 Ambarchi, Oren

died

1951 West, Doc
1976 Robinson, Jim
1987 Little, Wilbur
1990 Remler, Emily [or 3 May]

5

born

1899 Barbarin, Paul
1911 Daily, Pete
1914 Carlson, Frank
1931 Sharpe, C.
1933 Collins, Cal
1941 Cowell, Stanley
1946 Walrath, Jack
1947 Cook, Marty
1953 Beier, Chris
1959 Barret, Eric
1971 McBride, Nate

died

1959 McIntyre, Hal
1977 Cirillo, Wally
1982 Tjader, Cal
1991 Larsson, Rolf
1991 Turnham, Floyd

6

born

1921 Randall, Freddy
1931 Hasaan
1939 Eckinger, Isla
1942 Friesen, David
1944 Schönenberg, Detlef
1953 Dunmall, Paul
1971 Brönner, Till

died

1950 Quealey, Chelsea
1966 Webster, Paul
1967 Carver, Wayman
1968 Guesnon, George
1969 Drummond, Don
1983 Smythe, Pat
1983 Winding, Kai
1995 Calabrese, Bucky
1998 McCook, Tommy

7

born

1899 Jacobs, Pete
1900 Abbey, Leon
1904 O'Brien, Floyd
1906 Inge, Edward
1910 Bunn, Teddy
1913 Murphy, Rose
1926 Steward, Herbie
1931 Brewer, Teresa
1941 Sjösten, Lars
1947 Ford, Joe
1952 McLaurine, Marcus
1955 Zwingenberger, Axel
1958 Formanek, Michael
1963 Dolphin, Dwayne

died

1950 Hill, Chippie
1995 McKinley, Ray
1998 Barker, Blue Lu

MAY

8

born

1899 Bland, Jack
1905 Nichols, Red
1910 Williams, Mary Lou
1915 Haynes, Cyril
1927 Cohran, Phil
1930 Papa Bue
1941 Smoker, Paul
1945 Jarrett, Keith
1948 Orszaczky, Jackie
1949 Turner, Dave
1951 Silvano, Judi
1952 Purcell, John
1957 Urbani, Massimo
1958 Jacob, Christian
1964 Kellso, Jon-Erik

died

1958 Donnelly, Ted
1962 Lambert, Donald
1964 Maini, Joe
1974 Deloof, Gus
1981 Squires, Bruce
1982 Glow, Bernie
1988 Lamare, Nappy
1995 Royal, Marshal
1999 Thomas, Leon

9

born

1912 Simon, George T.
1940 Morrissey, Dick
1948 Maria, Tania
1956 Grencsó, István
1959 Chambers, Dennis
1963 Miles, Ron

died

1979 Jefferson, Eddie
1989 Shaw, Woody
1991 Fox, Charles
1995 Raney, Jimmy

10

born

1907 Hunt, Pee Wee
1920 Hendrickson, Al
1929 Lewis, Mel
1934 Nay, Joe
1935 Golla, George
1936 Cortez, Jayne
1937 Melvoin, Mike
1946 Ponder, Jimmy
1947 Abdullah, Ahmed
1949 Reichel, Hans
1953 Foster, Alex
1954 Lofsky, Lorne
1957 Brechtlein, Tom
1958 Deppa, Claude
1960 Tada, Seiji
1965 Harper, Philip

died

1919 Europe, James Reese
1984 Viale, Jean-Louis
1995 Drewo, Karl

11

born

1885 Oliver, King
1906 Higginbotham, J. C.
1916 Mullens, Moon
1920 Bryden, Beryl
1924 Valdambrini, Oscar
1931 Garcia, Dick
1938 Bley, Carla
1944 Humphrey, Ralph
1946 Arnström, Kenneth
1955 Joode, Wilbert de
1962 Balzar, Robert
1966 Joseph, Julian

died

1966 Morgan, Isaiah
1970 Hodges, Johnny
1989 Gordon, Max
1997 Fields, Ernie

12

born

1910 Jenney, Jack
1911 Munn, Billy
1916 Murray, Albert
1922 Wiggins, Gerry
1928 DeMicheal, Don
1935 Peacock, Gary
1936 Doldinger, Klaus
1936 Rhyne, Mel
1938 Smith, Bill (ii)
1941 Tomkins, Trevor
1957 Hwang, Jason
1966 Perowsky, Ben

died

1972 Greer, Big John
1975 Mooney, Joe
1976 Bishop, Joe
1987 Feldman, Victor
1997 Barbarin, Louis

13

born

1911 Sullivan, Maxine
1912 Evans, Gil
1913 Gersh, Squire
1914 Plater, Bobby
1923 Garland, Red
1928 Dahlander, Bert
1929 Taylor, Creed
1930 Moseholm, Erik
1933 Miyake, Martha
1935 Engels, John
1938 Tompkins, Ross
1941 Von Ohlen, John
1942 Douglas, Jim
1951 Janssen, Guus

died

1946 Hall, Tubby
1956 Kirkpatrick, Don
1975 Wills, Bob
1988 Baker, Chet
1997 Turrentine, Tommy
1999 Hino, Motohiko

14

born

1889 Douglas, Louis
1897 Bechet, Sidney
1898 Singleton, Zutty
1909 Williams, Pearlis
1916 Martin, Skip
1918 Lowe, Sammy
1925 Porcino, Al
1933 Williamson, Stu
1943 Bruce, Jack
1951 Beckenstein, Jay
1951 Porter, Lewis
1956 Forman, Bruce
1959 Mayhew, Virginia
1960 Dankworth, Alec

died

1959 Bechet, Sidney
1965 Sanders, Joe
1967 Treadwell, George
1973 Snowden, Elmer
1974 Gonsalves, Paul
1998 Sinatra, Frank

MAY

15

born

1898 Abriani, John
1901 Hall, Edmond
1902 Barzizza, Pippo
1903 Martin, Bobby
1923 Larkins, Ellis
1926 Wetzel, Bonnie
1928 Gordon, Joe
1932 Barnes, John
1937 Krog, Karin
1940 Castro-Neves, Oscar
1945 Donald, Peter
1950 Jackson, Chip
1960 Petrin, Umberto

died

1956 Rollini, Adrian

16

born

1913 Herman, Woody
1915 Morris, Marlowe
1916 Bascomb, Dud
1922 Bert, Eddie
1929 Carter, Betty
1930 Gulda, Friedrich
1932 Holt, Redd
1938 Hemmeler, Marc
1944 Cobham, Billy
1945 Moore, Michael (i)
1950 Jacobsen, Pete

died

1953 Reinhardt, Django

17

born

1907 McCord, Cass
1907 McCord, Ted
1908 Smith, Warren (i)
1915 Viseur, Gus
1916 Quinichette, Paul
1920 Roland, Joe
1925 Badie, Peter
1928 Katzman, Lee
1929 Drewo, Karl
1931 Kanai, Hideto
1931 McLean, Jackie
1931 Redman, Dewey
1932 Izenzon, David
1934 Picard, John
1936 Trunk, Peter
1938 Pethman, Esa
1949 Bruford, Bill
1949 Fosset, Marc
1951 Nathanson, Roy
1957 Van Kemenade, Paul
1961 Paulo, João
1964 Braam, Michiel

died

1955 Van 't Hoff, Ernst
1975 Trappier, Art
1976 Gullin, Lars
1996 Conover, Willis

18

born

1892 Foster, Pops
1894 Hooper, Lou
1905 McPartland, Dick
1911 Turner, Joe (ii)
1922 Winding, Kai
1930 Zwerin, Mike
1933 Novak, Larry
1937 Fourie, Johnny
1938 Guin, François
1949 McNeely, Jim
1951 Deffaa, Chip
1958 Fioravanti, Ettore
1963 Théberge, François

died

1974 Glenn, Tyree
1979 Brown, Vernon
1984 Copeland, Ray
1984 Hardee, John
1986 Bubbles, John
1990 Miller, Sing
1990 Thelin, Eje
1999 Randall, Freddy

19

born

1902 Moore, Monette
1919 Auld, Georgie
1924 Häme, Olli
1929 Slinger, Cees
1934 Bryant, Bobby
1935 McBee, Cecil
1939 Fortune, Sonny
1939 Teitelbaum, Richard
1947 Herbert, Gregory
1948 Scott, Tom
1961 Farnham, Allen

died

1939 Douglas, Louis
1967 Hope, Elmo
1969 Hawkins, Coleman
1978 Hill, Teddy
1980 Moro, Joe
1986 Lyons, Jimmy (ii)
1998 Donegan, Dorothy
2001 McCorkle, Susannah

20

born

1907 Cless, Rod
1911 Gabler, Milt
1931 Gumina, Tommy
1931 Smith, Louis
1932 Florence, Bob
1933 Davis, Charles
1935 Saluzzi, Dino
1936 Harley, Rufus
1939 Shy, Robert
1943 Enriquez, Bobby
1948 Frampton, Roger
1950 Lewis, Victor
1952 Petersen, Edward
1958 Gallon, Ray
1962 Peterson, Ralph, Jr
1963 Jones, Brad

died

1932 Miley, Bubber
1969 Peña, Ralph
1979 Rank, Bill
1982 Montgomery, Monk
1986 Bernhardt, Clyde
1998 Normann, Robert

21

born

1898 Goffin, Robert
1904 Waller, Fats
1920 Barber, Bill
1921 Johnson, Floyd "Candy"
1927 Holman, Bill
1929 Marable, Larance
1930 Bryant, Tommy
1935 Lightfoot, Terry
1950 Méchali, François
1953 Hofstra, David
1954 Ribot, Marc
1956 Puschnig, Wolfgang
1959 Jackson, Ed
1960 Droste, Silvia
1961 Ferrell, Rachelle
1970 Herdzin, Krzysztof
1972 McBride, Christian

died

1979 Berking, Willy
1979 Mitchell, Blue
1988 Babasin, Harry
1990 Moore, Eddie
2000 Drootin, Buzzy

MAY

22

born

1891 Edwards, Eddie
1905 Segure, Roger
1914 Sun Ra
1916 Springer, Joe
1917 Munro, Charlie
1921 Brom, Gustav
1926 Bacsik, Elek
1927 Johnson, Frank
1930 Ball, Kenny
1934 Werner, Lasse
1935 Logan, Giuseppi
1939 Berk, Dick
1941 Louiss, Eddy
1946 Francioli, Léon
1947 Koglmann, Franz
1953 Burr, Jon
1959 Hara, Dairiki
1961 Taylor, Mark (i)

died

1971 Ottersen, Frank
1977 Hawes, Hampton
1987 De Gregori, Rio
2001 Alexandria, Lorez

23

born

1897 Guy, Fred
1904 Hayes, Edgar
1910 Harrington, John
1910 Shaw, Artie
1919 Bothwell, Johnny
1921 Lyttelton, Humphrey
1928 Clooney, Rosemary
1929 Euell, Julian
1932 Spann, Les
1933 Masuda, Ichiro
1935 Mitchell, Bob (ii)
1938 Humair, Daniel
1939 Stamm, Marvin
1940 Johansen, Bjørn
1942 Colville, Randy
1946 Moye, Don
1947 Beirach, Richard
1949 Sandke, Randy
1957 Skowron, Janusz
1959 Peplowski, Ken
1967 Hunter, Charlie

died

1967 Norin, Carl-Henrik
1985 Glenn, Lloyd
1988 Paul, Emanuel
1994 Pass, Joe
1995 Pyne, Mick

24

born

1901 Moraweck, Lucien
1901 Signorelli, Frank
1902 Ahola, Sylvester
1919 Fields, Herbie
1926 Lobligeois, Roland
1927 Greenlee, Charles
1928 Bennett, Max
1931 Basso, Gianni
1933 White, Michael (i)
1937 Antolini, Charly
1937 Shepp, Archie
1941 Earland, Charles
1960 Schaphorst, Ken
1961 Savolainen, Jarmo
1962 Monder, Ben

died

1955 Martin, Sara
1965 Best, Denzil
1970 Jackson, Cliff
1973 Phillips, Sid
1974 Ellington, Duke
1985 Darensbourg, Joe
1989 McCall, Steve
1998 Kelly, George

25

born

1878 Robinson, Bill
1907 Guesnon, George
1910 Terrell, Pha
1915 Phillips, Gene
1917 Hamilton, Jimmy
1923 Trotman, Lloyd
1924 Allen, Marshall
1926 Bernhart, Milt
1926 Davis, Miles
1927 Oliver, Paul
1932 Noordijk, Piet
1936 Foster, Gary
1953 Lauer, Christof
1960 Roney, Wallace
1961 Laster, Andy

died

1938 McDonough, Dick
1955 Gray, Wardell
1983 Quinichette, Paul
1994 Gale, Eric
1996 Wilen, Barney

26

born

1883 Smith, Mamie
1910 Rosner, Ady
1914 Baker, Shorty
1914 Elman, Ziggy
1915 Alley, Vernon
1919 Jackson, Calvin
1928 DiNovi, Gene
1931 Gant, Frank
1934 Vitet, Bernard
1937 Ardley, Neil
1940 Suzuki, Hiromasa
1942 Bull, Geoff
1953 Torn, David

died

1963 Kluger, Jack
1973 Higginbotham, J. C.
1989 Newborn, Phineas
1990 McGregor, Chris
1992 Morrow, George
1994 Fuller, Gil
1994 Sharrock, Sonny

27

born

1900 Nicholas, Albert
1900 Zardis, Chester
1910 Carruthers, Earl
1920 Lee, Peggy
1926 Shank, Bud
1930 Dennis, Kenny
1931 Disley, Diz
1935 Lewis, Ramsey
1936 Jones, Rufus
1946 Ørsted Pedersen, Niels-Henning
1946 Jaremko, Zbigniew
1948 Copland, Marc
1950 Bridgewater, Dee Dee
1953 Barefield, Spencer
1955 Reeves, Nat
1963 Rubalcaba, Gonzalo
1967 Roseman, Josh

died

1972 Mitchell, George
1985 Best, Skeeter
1988 Oliver, Sy
1994 Rodney, Red
1996 Brown, Pud
2001 Dance, Helen Oakley

28

born

1898 Kirk, Andy
1900 Ladnier, Tommy
1907 Foresythe, Reginald
1907 Herbert, Arthur
1910 Trappier, Art
1910 Walker, T-Bone
1911 Herfurt, Skeets
1912 Barbour, Dave
1921 Tinney, Al
1926 Freeman, Russ (i)
1928 Marsh, Arno
1930 Lofton, Tricky
1939 Karolak, Wojciech
1939 Raubiško, Raimonds
1940 Dulfer, Hans
1946 Roditi, Claudio
1954 Dickey, Whit

died

1981 Williams, Mary Lou
1996 Rowles, Jimmie
1998 Dixon, Joe

MAY

29

born

1890 Alexander, Charlie
1909 Dutrey, Sam [or 13 March]
1912 Saucier, Edgar
1920 Mac Kac
1922 Brooks, Bubba
1922 Lindström, Erik
1923 Wright, Gene
1927 Hafer, Dick
1927 Schwartz, Thornal
1928 Redd, Freddie
1929 Mosse, Sandy
1932 Shorter, Alan
1934 Eaton, John
1952 Ruiz, Hilton
1955 Schärli, Peter
1957 Arriale, Lynne
1958 Snidero, Jim
1958 Washington, Kenny
1960 Linka, Rudy
1967 Gordon, Wycliffe
1967 Nightingale, Mark

died

1973 De Faut, Volly
1976 Maiden, Willie
1984 Pecora, Santo
1994 Jackson, Oliver
1998 Dunbar, Ted

30

born

1901 Trumbauer, Frankie
1905 De Paris, Sidney
1907 Arbello, Fernando
1909 Goodman, Benny
1913 Erwin, Pee Wee
1924 Peraza, Armando
1927 Bryant, Clora
1927 Keane, Shake
1930 McKenna, Dave
1933 Garrick, Michael
1935 Beckett, Harry
1939 Gordon, John
1941 Popkin, Lenny
1959 Tonolo, Pietro
1962 Grant, Darrell

died

1956 Snow, Valaida
1967 Lane, Morris
1977 Desmond, Paul
1986 Mobley, Hank
1987 Murphy, Turk
1993 Sun Ra
1994 Omer, Jean
2000 Beneke, Tex

31

born

1904 Brenders, Stan
1904 Hardwick, Otto
1908 Gifford, Gene
1913 Shirley, Jimmy
1921 Clare, Alan
1922 Rose, Denis
1925 Thompson, Eddie
1927 Holloway, Red
1935 Heath, Albert "Tootie"
1937 Hayes, Louis
1947 Abate, Greg
1948 Da Costa, Paulinho
1955 Ehrlich, Marty

died

1954 Wilson, Garland
1967 Strayhorn, Billy
1980 Burke, Sonny
1992 Quersin, Benoit
1994 Klein, Manny
1997 Jones, Eddie
1998 Motley, Frank
2000 Puente, Tito
2000 Puma, Joe

May (the date unknown)

died

1942 Poston, Joe
1955 Thomas, Millard G.
1955 Peyton, Dave
1973 Wynn, Al
1974 Laurence, Baby
1974 Lewis, Sylvester
1978 Collins, Shad [or June]
1978 George, Karl
1978 Morris, Marlowe
1981 Nelson, George
1982 Fowler, T. J.
1982 Hayse, Al
1982 Pace, Sal

JUNE

1

born

1898 White, Harry
1921 Riddle, Nelson
1924 Lovelle, Herbie
1924 McKusick, Hal
1929 Niehaus, Lennie
1935 Steckar, Marc
1940 Bavan, Yolande
1948 Palmer, Jeff
1959 Mrubata, McCoy

died

1949 Jones, Clarence M.
1966 Laine, Papa Jack
1969 Brenders, Stan
1992 Marshall, Joe
1996 Grolnick, Don
1999 Daly, Geo

2

born

1904 Snow, Valaida
1907 Stephenson, Louis
1921 Napoleon, Marty
1921 Peacock, Burnie
1921 Royal, Ernie
1923 Hood, Ernie
1929 Mahones, Gildo
1932 Igarashi, Akitoshi
1937 Favre, Pierre
1941 Schweizer, Irène
1946 Morell, John
1951 Miškiewicz, Henryk
1970 Garrison, Matthew

died

1929 Murray, Don
1942 Berigan, Bunny
1969 Stinson, Albert
1990 Davis, Walter
1996 Wallgren, Jan
1997 Cheatham, Doc
1999 Simpkins, Andy

3

born

1888 Brown, Tom
1904 Howard, Earle "Nappy"
1918 Pruitt, Carl
1920 Smock, Ginger
1923 Harewood, Al
1923 Nimmons, Phil
1931 Staton, Dakota
1935 Curson, Ted
1937 Moncur, Grachan, III
1939 Hering, Manfred
1942 Backer, Steve
1944 Wilkins, Jack
1948 Franzetti, Carlos
1955 Hovanesian, Datevik

died

1944 Gandee, Al
1975 Gleason, Ralph J.
2000 Horiuchi, Glenn

4

born

1909 Russell, Johnny
1920 Woodman, Britt
1926 Thompson, Chuck
1928 Kotick, Teddy
1929 Kovács, Andor
1930 King, Morgana
1932 Nelson, Oliver
1936 Branscombe, Alan
1937 Whitecage, Mark
1943 Daniel, Ted
1945 Braxton, Anthony
1948 D'Rivera, Paquito
1953 Elson, Steve
1954 Blöchlinger, Urs
1962 Harper, Winard

died

1939 Ladnier, Tommy
1949 Leary, Ford
1965 Rhodes, Todd
1988 Reuss, Allan
1989 Boone, Lester
1992 Minerve, Geezil
1994 Warren, Earle
1997 Hammond, Johnny

5

born

1876 Jackson, Tony
1920 Edelhagen, Kurt
1922 Powell, Specs
1932 Jolly, Pete
1935 Mengelberg, Misha
1949 Gonzalez, Jerry
1952 Sudler, Monnette
1954 Erskine, Peter
1956 Hutton, Mick

died

1983 Herbert, Mort
1993 Bolton, Dupree
1996 Teagarden, Norma
1999 Tormé, Mel
1999 Wilkins, Ernie
2000 Ross, Arnold

6

born

1890 Lewis, Ted
1902 Lunceford, Jimmie
1904 Burke, Raymond
1904 Maxey, Leroy
1911 Matthews, Dave
1916 Mehegan, John
1924 Cuppini, Gil
1925 Grey, Al
1926 Bergheim, Kristian
1927 Bush, Lennie
1935 Green, Grant
1944 Alexander, Monty
1944 Taylor, Dave
1946 Sadykhov, Vagif
1946 Seifert, Zbigniew
1949 Lovens, Paul
1959 Bollenback, Paul
1962 Faku, Feya
1966 Delbecq, Benoît

died

1953 Mosiello, Mike
1959 Marrero, Lawrence
1960 Davis, Martha
1968 Wettling, George
1990 Blackburn, Lou [or 7 June]
1991 Getz, Stan

7

born

1902 Cuffee, Ed
1902 Robinson, Prince
1904 Murray, Don
1906 Gray, Glen
1906 Hirst, George F.
1910 Porter, Gene
1921 Farlow, Tal
1922 Booker, Beryl
1928 Ortega, Anthony
1931 Acquaye, Speedy
1932 Brooks, Tina
1941 Galeta, Hotep Idris
1942 Martin, Mel
1947 Barbaro, Clifford
1955 Balke, Jon
1956 Johnson, Jimmy
1958 Hellborg, Jonas

died

1964 Lewis, Meade "Lux"
1968 Duncan, Hank
1971 Pollack, Ben
1976 Hackett, Bobby
1990 Blackburn, Lou [or 6 June]
1994 Humphrey, Willie
1999 McHargue, Rosy

JUNE

8

born

1901 Black, Lou
1904 Rank, Bill
1904 Smith, Charles Edward
1907 Pierce, Billie
1916 Holmes, Johnny
1919 Lehn, Erwin
1927 Calabrese, Bucky
1929 Clare, Kenny
1931 Aldebert, Louis
1939 Watrous, Bill
1944 Reinhardt, Babik
1947 Tippetts, Julie
1956 Caine, Uri
1959 Bex, Emmanuel
1960 Gewelt, Terje
1968 Jones, Willie, III

died

1943 Leibrook, Min
1972 Rushing, Jimmy
1973 Hayes, Tubby

9

born

1860 Hall, Edward
1911 Gold, Sanford
1922 Theselius, Gösta
1926 Gourley, Jimmy
1938 Thelin, Eje
1939 Melillo, Mike
1940 Boyd, Curtis
1943 Barron, Kenny
1944 Bril, Igor
1945 Goodrick, Mick
1952 Hirsch, Shelley
1952 Wilczewski, David

died

2000 Jones, Buddy
2000 Lincoln, Abe

10

born

1886 Martin, Chink
1894 Miller, Punch [or 24 Dec 1897]
1898 Blakeney, Andy
1905 Lewis, Willie
1907 Wells, Dicky
1921 Kilbert, Porter
1925 Hentoff, Nat
1930 Pedersen, Guy
1940 Stevens, John
1944 Goloshchokin, David
1953 Sargent, Gray
1961 Thomas, Gary
1964 Wojtasik, Piotr
1967 Moffett, Charnett
1970 Burno, Dwayne

died

1908 Tio, Lorenzo, Sr.
1965 Kress, Carl
1990 Rostaing, Hubert
1992 Pierce, Nat

11

born

1899 or 1902 Marshall, Kaiser
1904 Smith, Pine Top
1912 Martiny, Lajos
1920 Manne, Shelly
1920 Scott, Hazel
1928 Gordon, Bob
1929 Vander, Maurice
1933 Lindberg, Nils
1939 Purdie, Bernard
1944 Mauro, Turk
1953 Nauseef, Mark
1954 Riley, John
1956 Tacuma, Jamaaladeen
1957 Vyšniauskas, Petras
1964 Sarpila, Antti
1967 Parson, Dion

died

1956 Trumbauer, Frankie
1964 Christian, Charles
1964 Harris, Ace
1976 Eriksberg, Folke
1980 Martin, Stu
1984 Häme, Olli
1989 Holmes, Johnny
1999 Chaix, Henri

12

born

1913 Hall, Gene
1915 Zarchy, Zeke
1927 Fairweather, Al
1936 Belgrave, Marcus
1939 Carter, Kent
1939 Gauthé, Jacques
1941 Corea, Chick
1946 Bronson, Eddie
1954 Higgins, Patience
1954 Lundgaard, Jesper
1954 Peet, Wayne
1957 Allen, Geri

died

1957 Dorsey, Jimmy
1960 Barbarin, Isidore
1963 Scobey, Bob
1971 Ambrose, Bert
1997 Andrus, Chuck

13

born

1879 Elgar, Charlie
1892 Jones, Richard M.
1905 Cheatham, Doc
1906 Swayze, Edwin
1908 Hutchenrider, Clarence
1909 Wilson, Garland
1910 Beal, Eddie
1917 Zentner, Si
1918 Moore, Wild Bill
1919 Bodner, Phil
1927 Zoller, Attila
1930 Sehring, Rudi
1931 Arvanitas, Georges
1933 Catlett, Buddy
1937 Strozier, Frank
1938 Murphy, Allen
1942 Van Duynhoven, Martin
1947 Danko, Harold
1967 Stringle, Julian
1970 Westray, Ron

died

1986 Goodman, Benny
1995 Smock, Ginger
2001 McIntyre, Makanda Ken

14

born

1905 Lamare, Nappy
1907 Phillips, Sid
1918 Simmons, John
1928 Auer, Pepsi
1930 Attenoux, Michel
1932 Frank, Edward
1937 Berghofer, Chuck
1937 Greene, Burton
1938 McDougall, Ian
1942 Lemer, Pete
1945 Paulus, Tiit
1946 Stefański, Janusz
1947 Brubeck, Darius
1958 Drew, Kenny, Jr.
1959 Miller, Marcus

died

1952 Kirby, John
1969 Harris, Wynonie
1978 Matlock, Matty
1978 Wilson, Quinn
1980 Autrey, Herman
1993 Red Mack

JUNE

15

born

1891 or 1895 Stein, Johnny
1900 Mares, Paul
1910 Wrightsman, Stan
1912 Combelle, Alix
1913 Tyndale, George
1914 Bruder, Rudy
1915 Reuss, Allan
1918 Van Lake, Turk
1921 Garner, Erroll
1922 Byard, Jaki
1923 Moore, Mel
1927 Kawaguchi, George
1935 Jeanneau, François
1938 Oxley, Tony
1940 King, Nancy
1958 Thompson, Gail
1961 Hart, John
1961 Haynes, Phil

died

1968 Montgomery, Wes
1974 Jefferson, Maceo
1982 Pepper, Art
1996 Fitzgerald, Ella

16

born

1919 Viola, Al
1924 Thompson, Lucky
1926 Shaw, Clarence
1927 Ford, Jimmy
1933 Thomas, Joe (v)
1936 Halliday, Lin
1938 Dailey, Al
1939 Gare, Lou
1946 Harrell, Tom
1947 Malone, Tom
1948 Avenel, Jean-Jacques
1948 Studer, Fredy
1954 Kuryokhin, Sergey
1958 Eade, Dominique
1965 Jackson, Javon
1970 Hutchinson, Gregory

died

1939 Webb, Chick
1970 Johnson, Lonnie
1987 Valentine, Kid Thomas
1996 Cuppini, Gil
1997 Ericson, Rolf

17

born

1895 Wooding, Sam
1902 Columbus, Chris
1905 Kirkpatrick, Don
1907 Sedric, Gene
1914 Miller, Sing
1921 Scott, Tony
1940 Rainey, Chuck
1941 Pepper, Jim
1951 Tolkachev, Vladimir
1957 Varner, Tom

died

1964 Moore, Bill
1966 St. Cyr, Johnny
1968 Brooks, Harvey
1974 Rodin, Gil
1982 Sutton, Mynie
1988 Oliva, Hernán
1990 Wright, Frank
1994 Austin, Claire

18

born

1884 Martin, Sara
1901 Templin, Lutz
1907 Payne, Bennie
1909 Bauduc, Ray
1910 McKinley, Ray
1911 Russin, Babe
1919 Swanerud, Thore
1924 Cheatham, Jimmy
1924 Mathews, Mat
1924 Rutherford, Rudy
1928 Havlik, Ferdinand
1946 Hooker, William
1949 Erquiaga, Steve

19

born

1907 Laakko, Bruno
1909 Thomas, Joe (iii)
1912 Jerome, Jerry
1912 King, Bertie
1917 Lambert, Dave
1932 Ranglin, Ernest
1945 Palmer, Robert
1947 Gayvoronsky, Vyacheslav
1952 Endresen, Sidsel
1956 Bell, Kelvyn
1956 Scott, Aaron
1957 Riessler, Michael
1959 Drummond, Billy
1961 Wulf, Joe
1967 Barrett, Darren

died

1982 Butler, Joe
1983 Lucas, Al
1997 Green, Thurman

20

born

1905 or 1907 Wright, Lammar (i)
1906 Howard, Bob
1906 Stevenson, George
1907 Evans, Doc
1922 Van Vliet, Toon
1928 Dolphy, Eric
1929 Venuto, Joe
1934 Regoli, Enrique
1938 Budimir, Dennis
1938 Martin, Stu

died

1981 Erwin, Pee Wee
1983 Hakim, Sadik
2000 Lüdi, Werner
2001 McKinney, Harold

21

born

1900 Jackson, Dewey
1906 Goodman, Harry
1908 Wynn, Big Jim
1914 Collins, Booker
1924 Fawkes, Wally
1928 Scott, Clifford
1932 Nasser, Jamil
1932 Schifrin, Lalo
1936 Dean, Donald
1943 Mankunku, Winston
1944 Hiseman, Jon
1947 Ntoni, Victor
1948 Dvoskin, Victor
1949 Doran, Christy
1952 Theus, Sonship
1957 Schneiderman, Rob
1964 Aerts, Philippe
1970 Reed, Eric

died

1931 Blythe, Jimmy
1945 Jackson, Mike
1990 Christy, June
1993 Fairweather, Al

JUNE

22

born

1903 Pollack, Ben
1910 Berking, Willy
1914 Davis, Lem
1934 Mantilla, Ray
1936 Pascoal, Hermeto
1937 McGann, Bernie
1939 Sarmanto, Heikki
1942 Deodato, Eumir
1942 Prévost, Eddie
1944 Wilson, Ed
1950 Mosca, John
1951 Maruyama, Shigeo
1956 Chase, Allan

died

1959 Vian, Boris
1960 Rand, Odell
1979 Hunt, Pee Wee
1984 Jones, Dill
1993 Berry, Emmett

23

born

1909 Humes, Helen
1910 Hinton, Milt
1911 Miller, Eddie
1920 Harrison, Lance
1923 Russell, George
1925 Shihab, Sahib
1926 Shaw, Hank
1928 Badgley, Bob
1952 Jackson, Anthony
1954 Mahlangu, Khaya
1960 Harrison, Donald
1961 Machado, Jean-Marie

died

1991 Takayanagi, Masayuki
2000 Richardson, Jerome

24

born

1900 Handy, Capt. John
1903 Margulis, Charlie
1922 Albam, Manny
1924 Pelzer, Jacques
1925 Landers, Wes
1927 Christie, Ian
1928 Grah, Bill
1932 Gruntz, George
1943 Lowe, Frank
1944 Beck, Jeff
1946 Houston, Clint
1954 Saussois, Patrick
1961 Smith, Marvin "Smitty"
1964 Eliez, Thierry
1965 Weinert, Susan
1970 Sassetti, Bernardo

died

1928 O'Bryant, Jimmy
1993 Matteson, Rich
1993 Urbani, Massimo
2000 Houston, Clint

25

born

1908 Robert, Jean
1913 Girard, Adele
1922 Smith, Johnny
1928 Russo, Bill
1941 Cullaz, Alby
1942 Chambers, Joe
1944 Cliff, Dave
1944 Naughton, Bobby
1952 Toneff, Radka
1960 Cudzich, Andrzej
1960 Hunter, Steve
1961 Tangerding, Götz

died

1957 Mosby, Curtis
1965 Purnell, Keg
1976 Mercer, Johnny
1982 Welsh, Alex

26

born

1905 Grace, Teddy
1908 McLin, Jimmy
1912 Profit, Clarence
1914 Habart, Ladislav
1925 Moule, Ken
1928 Lanphere, Don
1928 Speers, Stewie
1930 Deuchar, Jimmy
1934 Grusin, Dave
1937 Workman, Reggie
1940 Cicero, Eugen
1944 Doyle, Arthur
1947 Abrahams, Brian
1953 Valente, Gary
1954 Gray, Larry
1955 Baron, Joey
1956 Cunliffe, Bill
1960 Breaux, Zachary
1965 Knutsson, Jonas

died

1956 Brown, Clifford
1956 Powell, Richie
1962 Snaer, Albert
1968 Elman, Ziggy
1971 Humphrey, Earl
1984 Dailey, Al
1987 Rehak, Frank

27

born

1897 Sbarbaro, Tony
1908 McFay, Monk
1909 Washington, Leon
1909 or 1910 Collins, Shad
1916 Normann, Robert
1923 Hope, Elmo
1928 Collier, James Lincoln
1939 Braith, George
1945 Hill, Calvin
1949 Vidacovich, John
1950 Ferris, Glenn
1954 Eastman, Madeline
1955 Debriano, Santi
1956 João, Maria
1973 Růžička, Karel, Jr.

died

1978 Bigard, Alex
1980 Bigard, Barney
1984 Goffin, Robert
1992 Tyler, Charles
2001 O'Farrill, Chico

28

born

1902 Smith, Joe
1903 Rollini, Adrian
1903 or 1904 Turner, Henry
1907 Mundy, Jimmy
1909 Shaw, Arnold
1913 Traxler, Gene
1923 Candoli, Pete
1923 Sherman, Herman
1926 White, Bobby
1952 Lee, John
1956 Flanigan, Phil
1956 Gräwe, Georg
1964 Williamson, Steve
1965 Medeski, John

died

1965 Nichols, Red
1979 Hayes, Edgar
1982 Matthews, George
1984 Orendorff, George
1992 Roberts, Howard

29

born

1922 Alexander, Mousey
1922 Burns, Ralph
1926 Lind, Ove
1935 Priester, Julian
1936 Van Breedam, Camiel
1941 Gordon, Bobby
1946 Hyder, Ken
1947 Tarasov, Vladimir
1955 Derome, Jean
1960 Evans, Sandy

died

1964 Dolphy, Eric
1984 Nosov, Konstantin
1991 Holmes, Groove
2000 Droz, Raymond

30

born

1899 Shields, Harry
1908 Watts, Grady
1925 Davenport, Wallace
1925 Herbert, Mort
1926 Reilly, Dean
1937 Hill, Andrew
1938 Hinze, Chris
1947 Van 't Hof, Jasper
1951 Clarke, Stanley
1954 von Essen, Eric
1956 Winterschladen, Reiner

died

1990 Pukwana, Dudu
1995 Braslavsky, Pierre
1997 Gaines, Bubba
2001 Henderson, Joe

June (the date unknown)

born

1931 Gilberto, João
1941 Muniak, Janusz

died

1958 Bose, Stirling
1962 Williams, Elmer
1969 Harden, Wilbur
1969 Teagarden, Cub
1977 Mardigan, Art
1977 Pruitt, Carl
1978 Collins, Shad [or May]
1981 Johnson, Floyd "Candy"
1993 Jenkins, John [month uncertain]

JULY

1

born

1910 Anderson, Ed
1914 Warren, Earle
1935 Rashied Ali
1952 Chancler, Ndugu
1960 Friedlander, Erik

died

1965 Thornhill, Claude
1983 Mosse, Sandy
1985 Hillyer, Lonnie
1989 Haughton, Chauncey
1995 Stacy, Jess

2

born

1892 Hylton, Jack
1905 Leonard, Harlan
1920 Harper, Herbie
1926 Allen, Lee
1926 Usselton, Billy
1927 Kennedy, Charlie
1928 Wyands, Richard
1930 Jamal, Ahmad
1942 Abene, Mike
1952 Haddad, Jamey
1954 Dial, Garry
1965 Warfield, Tim
1966 Mullins, Riley
1973 Avery, Teodross

died

1949 Scott, Bud
1971 Donaldson, Bobby
1979 Goodwin, Henry
1980 White, Amos
1988 Vinson, Eddie "Cleanhead"
1998 Parker, Errol

3

born

1915 Gray, Jerry
1926 Coles, Johnny
1930 Bright, Ronnell
1930 Collier, Ron
1930 Fountain, Pete
1930 Piana, Dino
1934 Ruppli, Michel
1935 Intra, Enrico
1938 Heard, John
1942 Smith, Lonnie
1946 Klemmer, John
1947 Blake, John
1953 Jackson, Duffy
1956 Gardony, Laszlo
1964 Fuhler, Cor

died

1950 Lindsay, John
1960 Collins, Lee
1980 Bennett, Buster
1986 Russell, Curly
1996 Jacobs, Pim

4

born

1902 Tuxen, Erik
1905 Davis, Leonard
1913 Oliva, Hernán
1921 Esbensen, Egon
1923 Sachs, Aaron
1928 McKinney, Harold
1938 Mainieri, Mike
1943 Bauer, Conrad
1943 Wesley, Fred
1944 Miles, Butch
1950 Ratzer, Karl
1961 Froman, Ian

died

1931 Petit, Buddy
1972 McCracken, Bob
1985 Woods, Chris
1986 Shu, Eddie
1992 Newman, Joe
1999 Skeat, Bill

5

born

1896 Berton, Vic
1905 Biondi, Ray
1922 Turner, Bruce
1924 Friley, Vern
1940 Blythe, Arthur
1949 Okuchi, Junichiro
1955 Watson, Eric
1956 Jenkins, Billy
1969 Fryland, Thomas

died

1945 Mougin, Stéphane
1960 Johnson, Bill (iii)
1964 Napoleon, Teddy
1983 James, Harry
1984 Elliott, Don
1989 Alston, Ovie
1991 Bowles, Russell

6

born

1920 Kenney, Dick
1924 Bellson, Louie
1927 Kiffe, Karl
1929 Smith, Betty
1932 Wilkerson, Don
1934 Urtreger, René
1936 White, Chris
1950 Williams, Jeff
1953 Stafford, Gregg
1965 Honing, Yuri

died

1961 LaFaro, Scott
1971 Armstrong, Louis
2000 Miyazawa, Akira

7

born

1888 Mosby, Curtis
1911 Redland, Charles
1916 Grimes, Tiny [date uncertain]
1926 Rehak, Frank
1927 Severinsen, Doc
1930 Mobley, Hank
1930 Trujillo, Bill
1932 Zawinul, Joe
1948 Dalto, Jorge
1951 Evans, Sue
1951 Henderson, Michael
1955 Campbell, John
1956 Bickford, Bill

died

1949 Johnson, Bunk
1950 Navarro, Fats
1956 Hyde, Alex

JULY

8

born

1892 Robinson, J. Russel
1904 Challis, Bill
1905 Barnes, Walter
1908 Jordan, Louis
1912 Mince, Johnny
1914 Eckstine, Billy
1921 Hanna, Ken
1940 Babbington, Roy
1942 Duggan, Barry
1943 Szakcsi Lakatos, Béla
1948 Saarsalu, Lembit
1953 Berroa, Ignacio
1953 Kukko, Sakari
1958 Tunnell, Jimi
1967 Belmondo, Stéphane

died

1933 Hall, Edward
1965 Dennis, Willie
1971 Shavers, Charlie
1979 Kynard, Charles
1983 Wright, Lammar (ii)

9

born

1906 Darensbourg, Joe
1915 Richmond, June
1916 Liggins, Joe
1920 Burrell, Duke
1921 Kluger, Irv
1929 Welsh, Alex
1934 Bailey, Colin
1935 Wright, Frank
1950 Saberton, Pete

died

1982 Manone, Wingy
1994 Lewis, Sabby

10

born

1889 Sissle, Noble
1905 Anderson, Ivie
1911 Barclay, Bob
1911 Williams, Cootie
1915 Buckner, Milt
1916 Cary, Dick
1924 Holley, Major
1929 Clark, Buddy
1938 Lawrence, Arnie
1938 Morgan, Lee
1939 Seffer, Yoch'ko
1946 Priestley, Brian
1947 Fowler, Bruce
1955 Dresch, Mihály
1958 Fleck, Béla

died

1922 Tio, Papa
1941 Morton, Jelly Roll
1964 Haymes, Joe
1972 Austin, Lovie
1986 Villegas, Enrique
1987 Hammond, John
1987 Salmi, Klaus
1992 Myers, Wilson

11

born

1905 Bernhardt, Clyde
1915 Gabriel, Percy
1941 Lowther, Henry
1942 Stańko, Tomasz
1946 Caratini, Patrice
1946 Itoh, Kimiko
1955 Einarsdotter, Elise
1956 Brady, Tim
1958 Bica, Carlos
1958 Whalum, Kirk
1961 Koonse, Larry

died

1949 Polo, Danny
1956 Höllerhagen, Ernst
1959 Wilson, Shadow
1985 Duvivier, George
1989 Kovács, Andor
1993 Bauzá, Mario
1993 Tee, Richard
1994 Humphries, Lex
1995 Coleman, Earl
1998 Lafitte, Guy

12

born

1895 Laine, Alfred "Baby"
1912 Bradley, Will
1916 Taylor, Sam "the Man"
1918 Dedrick, Rusty
1920 Gonsalves, Paul
1927 Candoli, Conte
1927 Houston, Joe
1928 Cavalli, Pierre
1935 Patton, Big John
1944 Jenny-Clark, Jean-François
1945 Lubat, Bernard
1951 Bourde, Hervé
1953 Soskin, Mark
1957 Allen, Eddie
1958 Haerter, Harald
1962 Walker, Mike
1965 Hasselbring, Curtis

died

1947 Lunceford, Jimmie
1976 Featherstonhaugh, Buddy
1978 Jenkins, Freddie
1986 Henkels, Kurt
1988 Smith, Howard

13

born

1900 Lewis, George (i)
1908 Van 't Hoff, Ernst
1915 Williams, Paul
1918 Parker, Erik
1920 Cesàri, Umberto
1923 Hartman, Johnny
1926 De Villers, Michel
1926 Wallin, Bengt-Arne
1928 Vinnegar, Leroy
1929 Iturralde, Pedro
1936 Ayler, Albert
1939 Szabados, György
1949 Ranier, Tom
1953 Cohen, Greg

died

1957 Ilcken, Wessel
1982 Finch, Candy
1995 Barelli, Aimé

14

born

1898 Jefferson, Maceo
1907 Williams, Rubberlegs
1914 Kyle, Billy
1929 Dawson, Alan
1930 Martinez, Sabu
1933 Napper, Kenny
1933 Rubin, Stan
1939 Archer, Tony
1952 Lewis, George (ii)
1954 Coolman, Todd

died

1965 Eiberg, Valdemar
1965 Williams, Spencer
1969 Farrow, Ernie
1975 Singleton, Zutty
1978 Hastings, Lennie
1984 Stapleton, Bill
1998 Bryden, Beryl

JULY

15

born

1904 Reeves, Talcott
1919 Hakim, Sadik
1923 Jones, Philly Joe
1928 Harriott, Joe
1964 Delius, Tobias

died

1933 Keppard, Freddie
1979 Hohenberger, Kurt
1989 Bradley, Will
1989 Ertegun, Nesuhi
1991 Briggs, Arthur

16

born

1898 Escudero, Ralph
1909 Buckner, Teddy
1923 Sete, Bola
1924 Longnon, Guy
1925 Pierce, Nat
1925 Tjader, Cal
1932 Chilton, John
1955 Whitehead, Annie
1957 Previte, Bobby
1964 Inoue, Yosuke
1967 Williams, Todd

died

1957 Chaloff, Serge

17

born

1899 Krueger, Benny
1907 or 1910 Washington, Jack
1908 Candrix, Fud
1915 Dougherty, Eddie
1920 Lloyd, Jerry
1921 Barnes, George
1921 Osborne, Mary [or 18 July]
1922 Bank, Danny
1925 Scott, Little Jimmy
1926 Copeland, Ray
1928 Guaraldi, Vince
1928 Morello, Joe
1933 Middlebrooks, Wilfred
1933 Riley, Ben
1936 Brignola, Nick
1936 Morgan, Sonny
1946 Wallin, Per Henrik
1947 Laboriel, Abe
1949 Freeman, Chico
1955 Feldman, Mark
1957 Nicholson, Reggie
1957 Richeson, Dane
1962 Sepulveda, Charlie
1969 Wallen, Byron
1970 Garnett, Alvester

died

1959 Holiday, Billie
1967 Coltrane, John
1987 McGhee, Howard
1992 Letman, Johnny

18

born

1900 Crawley, Wilton
1906 Webb, Speed
1908 Mairants, Ivor
1910 LaVere, Charlie
1914 Helm, Bob
1917 Comfort, Joe
1921 Osborne, Mary [or 17 July]
1927 Bagley, Don
1928 Fontana, Carl
1938 Niebergall, Buschi
1938 Pukwana, Dudu
1939 Landrum, Richard
1939 Yellin, Pete
1943 Tate, Frank
1956 Van de Geyn, Hein
1957 Barretto, Carlos
1957 Seaton, Lynn

died

1960 Brunner, Eddie
1979 Gee, Matthew
1983 Liggins, Jimmy
1986 Wilkerson, Don
1991 Traxler, Gene

19

born

1902 Bailey, Buster
1902 Jackson, Cliff
1912 Brunner, Eddie
1913 Teagarden, Charlie
1916 Shepard, Ernie
1922 Haig, Al [or 22 July]
1923 Allyn, David
1924 Collins, Dick
1924 Graham, Kenny
1934 Bradford, Bobby
1936 Jones, Carmell
1941 Upchurch, Phil
1944 Levallet, Didier
1950 Jaffe, Allan (ii)
1955 Madsen, Peter
1955 Spendel, Christoph
1956 Higashihara, Rikiya
1960 Bradford, Carmen

died

1944 Cook, Will Marion
1977 Wynn, Big Jim
1988 Miller, Johnny
1993 Prysock, Red
2000 Scott, Mabel

20

born

1888 Peyton, Benny
1911 Dillard, Bill
1914 Kleindin, Teddy
1919 Fishkin, Arnold
1919 Wilkins, Ernie
1922 Berendt, Joachim-Ernst
1922 Krautgartner, Karel
1928 Ind, Peter
1941 Tyler, Charles
1950 Guri, Lucky
1955 Lubambo, Romero

died

1946 Nanton, Tricky Sam
1978 Bunn, Teddy
1989 Roger Henrichsen, Børge
2001 Gabler, Milt

21

born

1902 Simeon, Omer
1922 Starr, Kay
1926 Edghill, Arthur
1929 or 1930 Merrill, Helen
1931 Clark, Sonny
1931 Johnson, Plas
1932 Hedges, Chuck
1935 Cullaz, Pierre
1939 Aebersold, Jamey
1944 Kellin, Orange
1951 Minafra, Pino
1953 Ponce, Daniel
1955 Linkola, Jukka
1956 Kiermyer, Franklin
1959 Simmonds, Mark
1965 Wendholt, Scott

died

1935 Dutrey, Honore
1942 Guarente, Frank
1981 Mosley, Snub
1990 Turner, Joe (i)
1995 McLin, Claude

JULY

22

born

1909 Simpson, Cassino
1913 Gorni, Kramer
1915 Miller, Taps
1916 Moer, Paul
1917 McGarity, Lou
1922 Haig, Al [or 19 July]
1924 Perkins, Bill
1928 Betts, Keter
1933 Schiano, Mario
1934 Cook, Junior
1936 Patterson, Don
1937 Downes, Bob
1939 Rivera, Mario
1949 Fine, Grigory
1952 Wilson, Dennis
1954 Bauer, Johannes
1954 Di Meola, Al
1955 Breakstone, Joshua
1955 Perry, Rich

died

1977 Kamuca, Richie
1982 Stitt, Sonny
1995 Humphrey, Percy

23

born

1898 Holiday, Clarence
1915 Berry, Emmett
1923 Luter, Claude
1928 Lee, Bill (i)
1930 Kamuca, Richie
1934 Lacy, Steve
1934 Lee, Tony
1946 Jamal, Khan
1947 Subramaniam, L.
1949 Edwards, Marc
1953 Weidman, James
1958 Schoenberg, Loren
1959 Barnes, Alan
1962 Sambeat, Perico
1964 Rocheman, Manuel
1965 Moreira, Bernardo

died

1931 Harrison, Jimmy
1960 Robinson, Prince

24

born

1904 Vauchant, Léo
1909 Thomas, Joe (iv)
1915 Haymer, Herbie
1921 Taylor, Billy (ii)
1927 Lang, Ronnie
1927 Quersin, Benoit
1933 Savery, Finn
1934 Collins, Rudy
1938 Nosov, Konstantin
1939 McPherson, Charles
1940 Richmond, Kim
1942 Lyons, Len
1953 Faddis, Jon
1956 Horner, Tim
1960 Szafran, Lora

died

1944 Spencer, O'Neill
1978 Hülphers, Arne
1984 Butler, Frank
1987 Maxey, Leroy
1987 Wellstood, Dick

25

born

1885 Christian, Charles
1899 Wiggs, Johnny
1901 Moore, Bill
*c*1901 Howard, Darnell
1903 Caldwell, Happy
1904 Robinson, Ikey
1905 Allen, Fletcher
1907 Hodges, Johnny
1926 Gilson, Jef
1928 Skeat, Bill
1930 Ross, Annie
1934 Ellis, Don
1938 Lenz, Günter
1955 Harris, Ratzo
1956 Dalla Porta, Paolino
1963 Murata, Yoichi
1970 Blade, Brian

died

1954 James, Elmer
1998 Farlow, Tal

26

born

1893 Williams, J. Mayo
1902 or 1903 Aiken, Gus
1912 Böhler, Fred
1914 Hawkins, Erskine
1929 Persip, Charli
1930 Six, Jack
1931 Bown, Patti
1932 Mosca, Ray
1937 López Fürst, Rubén
1938 Brackeen, JoAnne
1941 Ellington, Steve
1956 Krantz, Wayne
1961 Slocum, Melissa

died

1952 Harris, Joe (i)
1970 Arbello, Fernando
1980 Turner, Henry
1990 Lim, Harry [or 27 July]
1991 Russell, Johnny
1995 Almeida, Laurindo

27

born

1921 Queener, Charlie
1922 Thiele, Bob
1925 Moeketsi, Kippie
1930 Iversen, Einar
1937 Shoemake, Charlie
1944 Thompson, Barbara
1956 Cartwright, Deirdre
1957 Freelon, Nnenna
1957 Toussaint, Jean
1959 Sagmeister, Michael
1969 Simon, Edward

died

1977 Buckner, Milt
1986 Bridges, Henry
1990 Lim, Harry [or 26 July]
1999 Edison, Harry
1999 Hemmeler, Marc
2001 Land, Harold

28

born

1907 Prima, Leon
1924 Corcoran, Corky
1936 Galloway, Jim
1936 Hughart, Jim
1944 Browne, Allan
1950 Crook, Hal
1955 Veasley, Gerald
1958 Jones, David (ii)
1962 Sänger, Christof
1962 Washington, Reggie
1965 Marsalis, Delfeayo

died

1962 Costa, Eddie

JULY

29

born

1900 Redman, Don
1907 Wynn, Al
1916 Christian, Charlie
1919 Lewis, Vic
1924 Hirt, Gerald
1928 Hawes, Pat
1936 Capon, Jean-Charles
1936 Lee, Alan
1942 Horowitz, David
1945 Beck, Joe
1954 Benita, Michel

died

1967 Krueger, Benny
1991 Tangerding, Götz
1996 Green, Bill
1997 Wayne, Chuck

30

born

1903 Jefferson, Hilton
1906 Allen, Moses
1912 Featherstone, Benny
1923 Porter, Roy
1926 Campbell, Wilbur
1927 Smith, Frank
1928 Fournier, Vernel
1937 Spaulding, James
1945 Sanborn, David
1946 Patterson, Ann
1949 Baker, Duck
1950 Jankeje, Jan
1950 Stowell, John
1958 Mahogany, Kevin
1959 Weiskopf, Walt

died

1934 Borchard, Eric
1942 Blanton, Jimmy
1960 Garrison, Arv
1986 Clark, Bill

31

born

1887 Bocage, Peter
1907 Milton, Roy
1912 Deniz, Frank
1915 Kelly, George
1923 Ertegun, Ahmet
1923 Nerem, Bjarne
1925 Clark, Bill
1931 Burrell, Kenny
1936 Lewis, Art “Shaki”
1938 Mangione, Gap
1948 Wilson, Chuck
1949 Bagneris, Vernal
1952 Wolff, Michael
1954 Rodowicz, Piotr
1955 Stewart, Michael
1959 Jordan, Stanley

died

1963 Counce, Curtis
1986 Wilson, Teddy
1987 Liggins, Joe
1989 Jackson, Bullmoose
1991 Beal, Charlie

July (the date unknown)

born

1907 Craig, Al

died

1972 Wilson, Juice
1978 Madison, Bingie
1980 Lattimore, Harlan
1981 Hudson, Will
1985 Vance, Dick [or August]
1995 Rodriguez, Rod

AUGUST

1

born

1908 Crumbley, Elmer
1929 Charters, Samuel B.
1931 Hála, Kamil
1952 Watkins, Mitch
1954 Thornton, Steve

died

1950 Burroughs, Alvin
1966 Powell, Bud
1985 Wooding, Sam
1992 Alvarez, Chico
1993 Jones, Max

2

born

1894 or 1896 Dominique, Natty
1920 Müller, Werner
1922 Nicholas, Big Nick
1929 Crimmins, Roy
1944 Stinson, Albert
1945 Vasconcelos, Nana
1962 Kilson, Billy

died

1957 Shulman, Joe
1966 Raeburn, Boyd
1996 Auer, Vera

3

born

1903 Hopkins, Claude [or 12 Aug 1898, or 24 Aug 1903]
1904 or 1909 Wallace, Cedric
1907 Brown, Lawrence
1913 Villegas, Enrique
1916 Porter, Jake
1917 Shavers, Charlie
1918 Jefferson, Eddie
1925 Romão, Dom Um
1926 Bennett, Tony
1928 Christie, Lyn
1935 Vogel, Vic
1936 Wilson, Jack
1940 Draper, Ray
1940 Mitchell, Roscoe
1941 Balliu, Rudy
1955 Drake, Hamid
1960 Osby, Greg
1961 Porter, Art
1962 Wolfe, Ben

died

1943 Cornelius, Corky
1981 Österwall, Seymour
1984 Burnet, Bob
1986 Thomas, Joe (iii)
1987 Niosi, Bert
1999 Vinnegar, Leroy

4

born

1901 Armstrong, Louis
1904 Coleman, Bill
1910 Brady, Stumpy
1921 Ellis, Herb
1922 Swope, Earl
1924 Talbert, Thomas
1933 Simmons, Sonny
1944 Stenson, Bobo
1953 Hamilton, Jeff
1953 Jagodziński, Andrzej
1957 Tuncboyaçiyan, Arto
1962 Bonafede, Salvatore
1965 Carrington, Terri Lyne
1968 Alexander, Eric

died

1970 Carry, Scoops
1973 Condon, Eddie
1975 Nanri, Fumio
1980 Pöyry, Pekka
1984 Russin, Babe
1993 Drew, Kenny

5

born

1903 Hazel, Monk
1903 Lington, Otto
1904 Reynolds, Jimmy
1908 Albert, Don
1909 or 1910 Davis, Tiny
1940 Schwab, Sigi
1941 Breau, Lenny
1941 Moreira, Airto
1944 Wachsmann, Phil
1949 Jansen, Robbie
1950 Woodard, Rickey
1951 Riggs, Chuck
1965 Webber, John
1966 Borstlap, Michiel
1968 Grey, Carola

died

1945 Jaffe, Nat
1970 Hardwick, Otto
1972 Mezzrow, Mezz
1993 Burrell, Duke
1993 Cooper, Bob

6

born

1900 Parenti, Tony
1902 Russell, Luis
1906 Dickenson, Vic
1907 Froeba, Frank
1909 Johnson, Lem
1918 Granz, Norman
1921 Collette, Buddy
1923 Parnell, Jack
1928 Gossez, Pierre
1928 McFadden, Eddie
1930 Lincoln, Abbey
1931 Chautemps, Jean-Louis
1932 Ashby, Dorothy
1936 Diorio, Joe
1937 Baden Powell
1937 Haden, Charlie
1940 Kapstad, Egil
1942 Lancaster, Byard
1942 Levin, Marc
1946 Holdsworth, Allan
1949 Boutté, Lillian
1949 Deschepper, Philippe
1957 Meurkens, Hendrik
1961 Goines, Victor
1965 Coltrane, Ravi
1966 Carter, Regina

died

1931 Beiderbecke, Bix
1974 Ammons, Gene
1984 Thomas, Joe (iv)
1994 Pelzer, Jacques
1996 Enriquez, Bobby

7

born

1893 Roberts, Luckey
1910 Slack, Freddie
1912 Beamter, Jenoí
1913 Van Eps, George
1917 or 1918 Culley, Frank
1920 Arnold, Harry
1921 Covington, Warren
1923 Sulieman, Idrees
1935 Kirk, Roland
1937 Bohanon, George
1941 Johnson, Howard (ii)
1963 Roberts, Marcus

died

1969 Morgan, Russ
1998 Gonella, Nat

AUGUST

8

born

1900 Gaines, Charlie
1900 Millinder, Lucky
1904 Packay, Peter
1904 Story, Nat
1907 Carter, Benny
1909 Cole, Rupert
1918 Parker, Knocky
1921 Pickering, Tom
1926 Green, Urbie
1927 Traynor, Frank
1928 Burrows, Don
1929 Dean, Vinnie
1951 Frink, Laurie
1959 Goldberg, Ben

died

1940 Dodds, Johnny
1975 Adderley, Cannonball
1976 Rosner, Ady
1983 Moore, Wild Bill
1991 Mares, Joe
1997 Swift, Duncan

9

born

1913 Bryan, Mike
1924 Williams, Martin
1942 DeJohnette, Jack
1962 Gomez, Edsel
1966 Kawashima, Tetsuro

died

1970 Ware, Munn
1972 Ekyan, André
1974 Chase, Bill
1983 Ewell, Don
1992 Russell, Bill
1998 Scott, Calo

10

born

1872 or 1874 Johnson, Bill (i)
1906 De Kers, Robert
1906 Pace, Sal
1909 Minor, Dan
1909 Thornhill, Claude
1918 Cobb, Arnett
1929 Wilson, Herman
1936 Israels, Chuck
1943 Mantler, Mike
1953 Leitham, John
1957 Gallant, Joe
1957 Ho, Fred

died

1965 Slack, Freddie
1976 Gray, Jerry
1991 Smith, Buster

11

born

1904 Stacy, Jess
1908 Procope, Russell
1921 Freeman, Bruz
1926 Rediske, Johannes
1930 Fischer, John
1934 Rae, Johnny
1940 King, Peter
1954 Nelson, Steve
1959 Gershon, Russ
1966 Okudaira, Shingo

died

1962 Crosby, Israel
1982 Roland, Gene
1985 Ceroli, Nick
1987 Acheson, Merv
1989 Thompson, Sonny
1992 Pillars, Hayes
1998 Waters, Benny

12

born

1898 Hopkins, Claude [or 3 or 24 Aug 1903]
1904 Boone, Lester
1905 Anderson, Andy (i)
1907 Bentley, Gladys
1912 Douglas, Billy
1915 West, Doc
1925 Axen, Bent
1930 Greig, Stan
1939 Cotton, Mike
1940 Green, Thurman
1945 Villéger, André
1954 Metheny, Pat
1958 Levy, Jed

died

1959 Watson, Gilbert
1984 Breau, Lenny
1987 Brown, John
1994 Cherico, Gene
1995 Paich, Marty

13

born

1903 Paquinet, Guy
1909 Smith, Stuff
1912 Kazebier, Nate
1912 Moore, Big Chief
1914 De Bie, Ivon
1919 Shearing, George
1920 Galbraith, Charlie
1925 Bailey, Benny
1927 Puma, Joe
1938 Smith, Michael
1940 Blairman, Allen
1945 Mekoa, Johnny
1950 Bacqueville, Patrick
1954 Assumpção, Nico
1955 Miller, Mulgrew
1958 D'Agaro, Daniele

died

1955 Johnson, Bill (ii)
1971 Curtis, King
1974 Brooks, Tina

14

born

1903 Gardner, Jack
1911 Mondello, Toots
1914 Naret, Bobby
1923 Beckenstein, Ray
1929 Alexandria, Lorez
1930 Costa, Eddie
c early 1930s Cheatham, Jeannie
1943 Sidran, Ben
1949 Masuda, Mikio
1960 Swanton, Lloyd
1963 Catoul, Jean-Pierre
1968 Robinson, Justin
1971 Blanding, Walter

died

1962 Richmond, June
1969 Fruscella, Tony
1978 Venuti, Joe
1989 Garrett, Donald
1990 Zardis, Chester
1992 Kincaide, Deane
1997 Von Essen, Eric

15

born

1883 Smith, Crickett
1903 Garland, Joe
1915 Feld, Morey
1925 Morrow, George
1925 Peterson, Oscar
1927 Castro, Joe
1928 France, Percy
1931 Pollard, Terry
1933 Dowdy, Bill
1934 Garanian, Georgy
1938 Hooper, Stix
1941 Gale, Eddie
1954 Gonzalez, Dennis
1956 Desmarais, Lorraine

died

1947 Hamilton, John "Bugs"
1963 Legge, Wade
1976 Burbank, Albert
1978 Kral, Irene
1988 Collins, Rudy

16

born

1888 Piron, A. J.
1914 Lucas, Buddy
1915 Hibbler, Al
1915 McEachern, Murray
1917 Ludvik, Emil
1920 Felix, Lennie
1925 Waldron, Mal
1927 Moss, Danny
1928 Perkins, Carl
1929 Evans, Bill (ii)
1932 Suzuki, Shoji
1935 Spoerri, Bruno
1943 Ermoll, Serge
1950 Queen, Alvin
*c*1956 Dixon, Fastina
1959 Brooks, Cecil, III
1959 Eskelin, Ellery

died

1925 Hicks, Edna
1968 Cutshall, Cutty

17

born

1908 Sherman, Jimmy
1909 Clinton, Larry
1918 Quebec, Ike
1920 Duvivier, George
1922 Garrison, Arv
1922 Sperling, Jack
1924 Deniz, Laurie
1926 Melly, George
1931 Smith, Derek
1932 Pearson, Duke
1933 Camicas, Michel
1934 Schulze, Manfred
1955 Auguščik, Grażyna
1957 Abou-Khalil, Rabih
1959 Strzelczyk, Maciej
1960 De Vito, Maria Pia
1961 Houle, François
1970 Martin, Peter

died

1951 Wetzel, Ray
1966 Billberg, Rolf
1971 Smith, Tab
1973 Shaw, Clarence
1987 Mac Kac
1990 Bailey, Pearl
1995 Davis, Wild Bill

18

born

1897 Wilson, Buster [or 16 Dec]
1908 Cohn, Zinky
1918 Shu, Eddie
1919 Parker, Frank
1920 Lamond, Don
1921 Witherspoon, Jimmy
1930 Connors, Chuck
1940 Makowicz, Adam
1944 Brashear, Oscar
1953 Benoit, David

died

1949 Mares, Paul
1974 Anderson, John
1991 Hutchenrider, Clarence
1991 Naret, Bobby
1994 Redland, Charles

19

born

1906 Durham, Eddie
1906 Johnson, Manzie
1908 Morgan, Al
1908 Murphy, Spud
1918 Rowles, Jimmie
1922 Brown, Olive [or 30 Aug]
1923 Jones, Dill
1930 Sharpe, Jack
1934 Naura, Michael
1944 Leitch, Peter
1948 Escheté, Ron
1949 Mixon, Danny
1954 Hagans, Tim
1955 Brown, Dean
1957 Ducret, Marc
1963 Belmondo, Lionel
1965 Maseli, Bernard

died

1929 Kelly, Chris
1953 Kahn, Tiny
1968 Stegmeyer, Bill
1973 Moore, Brew
1985 Wallace, Cedric

20

born

1900 Moore, Freddie
1908 Mares, Joe
1911 Amstell, Billy
1916 Drelinger, Art
1926 Rosolino, Frank
1927 Raney, Jimmy
1927 Sherrill, Joya
1931 Capp, Frank
1941 Graves, Milford
1943 Rava, Enrico
1943 Whigham, Jiggs
1944 Clarke, Terry
1951 Houmark, Karsten
1952 Clayton, John
1953 Weber, Reto

died

1937 Dunn, Johnny
1949 Nelson, Big Eye Louis
1972 Bryan, Mike
1979 Maycock, George
1986 Jones, Thad
1995 Gilmore, John

21

born

1902 Scott, Lloyd
1904 Basie, Count
1917 Richardson, Rodney
1928 Farmer, Addison
1928 Farmer, Art
1930 Legrand, Christiane
1941 Coster, Tom
1941 Vukán, George
1945 Honda, Takehiro
1949 Thompson, Malachi
1954 Smith, Steve
1960 Apfelbaum, Peter
1964 Rossy, Jorge
1965 Parker, Leon
1970 Jordan, Marlon

died

1973 Harris, Bill (i)
1987 Davis, Steve (i)

AUGUST

22

born

1901 Starr, Henry
1906 Fleagle, Brick
1912 Myers, Bumps
1916 Thompson, Sonny
1930 Billberg, Rolf
1930 Kirkwood, Johnny
1936 Humphries, Lex
1937 Favors, Malachi
1937 Vining, Ted
1943 Daly, Warren
1946 Parker, Kim
1955 Hirshfield, Jeff
1956 Barthélémy, Claude
1959 Boeren, Eric

died

1965 Edwards, Bass

23

born

1892 Eiberg, Valdemar
1894 Lindsay, John
1918 Bonfils, Kjeld
1927 Solal, Martial
1928 Coggins, Gil
1929 Barcelona, Danny
1934 De Souza, Raul
1936 Luk'yanov, German
1937 Page, Nathen
1953 Watson, Bobby
1954 Malach, Bob
1954 Sharpe, Avery
1960 Uotila, Jukka-Pekka
1970 Mehldau, Brad

died

1963 Gray, Glen
1986 Daily, Pete
1988 Garros, Christian

24

born

1902 Philburn, Al
1903 Hopkins, Claude [or 12 Aug 1898, or 3 Aug 1903]
1904 Smith, Buster
1905 Trent, Alphonso
1909 Webster, Paul
1912 Brocksieper, Freddie
1913 Harris, Wynonie
1934 Caunedo, Jesús
1943 Sedergreen, Bob
1945 Spring, Bryan
1953 Holloway, Ron
1954 Ścierański, Krzysztof
1957 Berry, Steve
1959 Creese, Malcolm

died

1968 Souchon, Edmond
1972 Byas, Don
1978 Prima, Louis
1981 Coleman, Bill
1981 Jepsen, Jørgen Grunnet
1986 Tarto, Joe
1997 Montoliu, Tete
1998 Barriteau, Carl

25

born

1905 Garcia, King
1912 Roberts, Caughey
1913 Crosby, Bob
1918 Kohlman, Freddie
1920 Gaskin, Leonard
1931 Southall, Henry
1933 Gustafsson, Rune
1933 Shorter, Wayne
1940 Benkó, Sándor
1941 Smith, Carrie
1942 Donato, Michel
1943 Sommer, Günter
1944 Martino, Pat
1947 Tippett, Keith
1950 Fambrough, Charles
1952 Brown, Ben
1952 Marcus, Michael
1954 Ngcukana, Ezra
1960 Saunders, Keith
1975 Riggins, Karriem

died

1971 Lewis, Ted
1974 Viseur, Gus
1979 Kenton, Stan
1985 Blesh, Rudi

26

born

1902 or 1903 Rushing, Jimmy
1904 Lee, Sonny
1911 or 1913 Short, Bob
1924 Wayne, Frances
1927 Bates, Norman
1928 Appleyard, Peter
1939 Jones, Virgil
1941 Jarvis, Clifford
1950 Lonzo, Freddie
1954 Henderson, Scott
1958 Finck, David
1960 Beard, Jim
1960 Marsalis, Branford

died

1980 Forrest, Jimmy
1981 Thomas, Foots
1987 Socarras, Alberto
1992 Benskin, Sammy

27

born

1909 Young, Lester
1925 Crombie, Tony
1925 English, Bill
1926 Flory, Med
1927 Hawdon, Dickie
1930 Delaney, Jack
1937 Coltrane, Alice
1940 Sharrock, Sonny
1946 Prince, Roland

died

1971 Armstrong, Lil
1971 Dutrey, Sam
1991 Stauffer, Teddy

28

born

1867 Tio, Lorenzo, Sr.
1904 Fields, Ernie
1911 Clarke, George
1920 Greenberg, Rowland
1921 Aless, Tony
1926 Russell, Hal
1926 Seamen, Phil
1941 Marshall, John
1953 Jackson, Michael Gregory
1962 Rotondi, Jim
1964 Washington, Peter
1968 Goldings, Larry

died

1955 Gordon, Bob
1957 Tuxen, Erik
1971 McGarity, Lou
1975 Smith, Warren (i)
1984 Weiss, René

AUGUST

29

born

1905 Teagarden, Jack
1906 Strong, Jimmy
1907 Paque, Glyn
1920 Parker, Charlie
1922 Ericson, Rolf
1924 Washington, Dinah
1927 Kelly, Red
1932 Dodgion, Jerry
1937 Rucker, Ellyn
1939 Rovère, Gilbert
1940 Maupin, Bennie
1945 Richards, Trevor
1956 Raney, Doug

died

1928 Evans, Stump
1953 Paque, Glyn
1986 Mallard, Oett
1988 Henderson, Horace

30

born

1896 Lubinsky, Herman
1898 Rena, Kid
1904 Bean, Floyd
1908 Bryant, Willie
1922 Brown, Olive [or 20 Aug]
1924 Dorham, Kenny
1930 Falay, Maffy
1931 Jackel, Conny
1937 Brown, Jewel
1944 Surman, John
1945 Panov, Nikolay
1946 Davis, Francis
1948 Suchanek, Bronisław
1955 Coleman, Anthony
1956 Jones, Rodney
1957 Beier, Detlev
1966 Gunther, John

died

1982 Dominique, Natty
1985 Jones, Philly Joe
1988 Black, James

31

born

1900 Rhodes, Todd
1904 Alix, May (ii)
1907 Sampson, Edgar
1910 Caton, Lauderic
1918 Jones, Hank
1928 Cooper, Leroy
1928 Prina, Curt
1933 Riley, Herman
1937 Hampel, Gunter
1939 Winter, Paul
1940 Felder, Wilton
1953 Fujiwara, Kiyoto
1965 Battaglia, Stefano

died

1966 Roy, Teddy
1970 Ervin, Booker
1996 Larkin, Milt
2000 King, Saunders

August (the date unknown)

born

1927 Jepsen, Jørgen Grunnet
1951 Moondoc, Jemeel

died

1960 Abriani, John
1960 Bertrand, Jimmy
1960 Brown, Andrew
1969 Foster, Willie
1973 Elgar, Charlie
1974 Segal, Jerry
1977 Moses, J. C.
1979 Smith, Teddy
1985 Prima, Leon
1985 Vance, Dick [or July]

SEPTEMBER

1

born

1898 Danzi, Mike
1904 Mertz, Paul
1910 Weiss, Sammy
1917 Middleton, Velma
1923 Bates, Bob
1925 Pepper, Art
1931 Ruff, Willie
1933 Harris, Gene
1934 Thornton, Teri
1946 Yamaguchi, Mabumi
1955 Horvitz, Wayne
1956 Essiet Essiet
1957 Wierbos, Wolter
1964 O'Higgins, Dave

died

1941 Melrose, Frank
1977 Waters, Ethel
1993 Malmstén, Eugen
1994 Dixon, George

2

born

1896 Wilson, Edith
1901 Napoleon, Phil
1915 Moncur, Grachan
1917 Almeida, Laurindo
1917 Trovajoli, Armando
1918 De Boeck, Jeff
1925 Nilson, Gunnar
1928 Silver, Horace
1929 Guilhot, Claude
1931 Jordan, Clifford
1932 Davis, Walter
1932 Richards, Emil
1936 Koch, Klaus
1940 Pyne, Mick
1942 Donald, Barbara
1953 Zorn, John
1954 Masakowski, Steve
1963 Maricle, Sherrie

died

1934 Nunez, Alcide "Yellow"
1966 Howard, Darnell
1981 King, Bertie
1986 Payne, Bennie
1986 Taylor, Billy (i)

3

born

1891 Cook, Doc
1897 Christian, Frank
1916 Alpert, Trigger
1916 Hurley, Clyde
1921 Kaye, Cab
1926 Henry, Ernie
1932 Roker, Mickey
1937 Ridley, Larry
1938 Brooks, Roy
1940 Dapogny, James
1940 van Manen, Willem
1949 Gumbs, Onaje Allen
1950 Feldman, Lawrence
1950 Weston, Veryan
1951 Bayeté
1967 Bernstein, Peter
1968 Sanchez, David

died

1948 Carey, Mutt
1973 Nicholas, Albert
1985 Jones, Jo
1986 Parker, Knocky

4

born

1905 Lewis, Meade "Lux"
1908 Norris, Al
1914 McQuater, Tommy
1918 Wilson, Gerald
1922 Greene, Bob
1932 Viera, Joe
1935 Sardaby, Michel
1942 Stadler, Heiner
1946 Liebman, Dave
1948 Cochrane, Michael
1960 Plaxico, Lonnie
1961 Davis, Kenny
1966 Lagrene, Bireli

died

1984 Morks, Jan
1991 Barnet, Charlie
1993 Rae, Johnny

5

born

1892 Salnave, Bertin
1894 Dixon, Lawrence
1925 Preston, Eddie
1926 Freund, Joki
1928 Mangelsdorff, Albert
1931 Gonsalves, Virgil
1931 Powell, Richie
1933 Finch, Candy
1947 Shaw, Charles "Bobo"
1948 Borca, Karen
1958 Danielsson, Lars

died

1935 De Vries, Louis
1977 Barnes, George
1980 Banks, Don
1988 Brown, Lawrence
1992 Russell, Hal
1994 Usselton, Billy

6

born

1877 Bolden, Buddy
1910 Hagemann, Henry
1917 Letman, Johnny
1919 Malachi, John
1925 Duran, Eddie
1926 Schlinger, Sol
1936 Thornton, Clifford
1937 Broberg, Bosse
1941 Kuznetsov, Aleksey
1942 Bargeron, Dave
1942 White, Andrew
1947 Persson, Bent
1948 Dean, Roger
1952 Markowitz, Phil
1962 Filipe, Laurent
1967 Martin, Claire
1968 Kreusch, Cornelius Claudio

died

1985 Montgomery, Little Brother
1994 Kaminsky, Max
1999 Fishkin, Arnold

7

born

1908 Kaminsky, Max
1912 Alcorn, Alvin
1914 Bell, Graeme
1921 or 1922 Newman, Joe
1929 South, Harry
1930 Coppieters, Francis
1931 McIntyre, Makanda Ken
1938 Saudrais, Charles
1941 Doriz, Dany
1951 Isham, Mark
1952 Rayner, Alison
1953 Wall, Dan
1957 Jormin, Anders
1958 Barth, Bruce
1961 Sikała, Maciej
1962 Bargad, Rob
1965 Blake, Ron

died

1957 Sanchez Reinoso, Raúl
1967 Stewart, Rex
1976 Peiffer, Bernard
1991 Banks, Buddy (i)
1993 Girard, Adele

SEPTEMBER

8

born

1896 Schoebel, Elmer
1912 Grasso, Alfio
1914 Bowman, Dave
1921 Turney, Norris
1923 Ware, Wilbur
1924 Cole, Gracie
1926 Anton, Artie
1927 Wright, Specs
1935 Brown, Marion
1935 Clay, James
1937 Gallivan, Joe
1939 Warren, Butch
1941 Wilson, Phillip
1952 Lee, Will
1962 Preissac, Ludovic de
1967 Wolf, Thilo

died

1954 Gowans, Brad
1956 Rich, Fred
1960 Pettiford, Oscar

9

born

1902 Humphrey, Earl
1912 Omer, Jean
1917 Maycock, George
1927 Jones, Elvin
1930 Benton, Walter
1930 Rollins, Sonny
1935 Stone, Fred
1939 Namysłowski, Zbigniew
1944 Mraz, George
1952 Eduardo, Zé
1954 Parker-Sparrow, Bradley
1964 Norby, Cæcilie

died

1950 Doucet, Clément
1969 Haywood, Cedric
1973 Aerts, Jos
1978 Abe, Kaoru
1979 Ware, Wilbur
1981 Coppieters, Fernand
1993 Deuchar, Jimmy

10

born

1904 Coughlan, Frank
1906 Rodriguez, Rod
1908 Scott, Raymond
1913 Deniz, Joe
1913 Leeman, Cliff
1914 Johnson, Ken "Snake Hips"
1924 Wickman, Putte
1929 Lasha, Prince
1931 Manzecchi, Franco
1934 Worrell, Lewis [or 7 Nov]
1939 Burnap, Campbell
1940 Ayers, Roy
1940 Burrell, Dave
1941 Oki, Itaru
1943 Horler, David
1953 Harris, Craig
1957 Ayado, Chie
1958 Davis, Steve (ii)
1958 Redd, Chuck

died

1984 Sherman, Herman
1984 Young, Trummy
1986 Adams, Pepper
1995 Suzuki, Shoji

11

born

1893 Desvigne, Sidney
1917 Acea, John
1919 Morrison, Peck
1920 Enevoldsen, Bob
1928 Geller, Lorraine
1929 Moffett, Charles
1933 Willette, Baby Face
1934 Jones, Oliver
1939 Kwela, Allen
1952 Stabenow, Thomas
1955 Bullock, Hiram
1955 Rowles, Stacy
1955 Shahid, Jaribu
1964 Vandermark, Ken
1967 Connick, Harry, Jr

died

1994 Wethington, Crawford

12

born

1916 Anderson, Cat
1923 Rohde, Bryce
1923 Shulman, Joe
1925 Coleman, Earl
1942 Christianson, Denny
1948 Turre, Steve
1951 Léandre, Joëlle
1954 Hamilton, Scott
1955 Di Castri, Furio
1956 Johnson, Dean
1956 Lynch, Brian
1966 Whittaker, Sebastian
1972 Presencer, Gerard

died

1926 Jenkins, Edmund Thornton
1957 Mitchell, Louis
1962 Starr, Henry
1985 Holmes, Charlie
1987 Pastorius, Jaco
1995 Gales, Larry
1998 Yoshizawa, Motoharu
2000 Turrentine, Stanley

13

born

1893 Shields, Larry
1898 Etté, Bernard
1898 Goudie, Frank "Big Boy"
1908 Berry, Chu
1914 Feather, Leonard
1914 Valentine, Jerry
1922 Brown, Charles
1925 Tormé, Mel
1932 Hallberg, Bengt
1932 James, Michael
1940 Riel, Alex
1946 Ewart, Douglas
1955 Morris, Joe (ii)

died

1967 De Paris, Sidney
1969 Watkins, Joe
1981 Bates, Bob
1981 Humes, Helen
1990 Napoleon, Phil [or 30 Sept]
1993 Jordan, Steve (i)

14

born

1896 Johnson, J. C.
1908 Beal, Charlie
1918 Cachao
1928 Cameron, Jay
1930 Berry, Bill
1937 Jarman, Joseph
1938 Moore, Eddie
1942 Lake, Oliver
1948 Koyake, Tamami
1951 Williamson, Bruce
1961 Lüdemann, Hans
1962 Bonnet, Michel
1962 Kondakov, Andrei

died

1985 Martiny, Lajos
1988 Weersma, Melle

SEPTEMBER

15

born

1896 Ambrose, Bert
1908 Cola, Kid Sheik
1910 Dance, Stanley
1913 Ramirez, Ram
1915 Casey, Al
1921 Roland, Gene
1923 Shaw, Arvell
1924 Nichols, Bobby
1928 Adderley, Cannonball
1951 White, Carla
1956 Rothenberg, Ned
1960 Robert, George
1964 Schröder, John

died

1944 Voynow, Dick
1965 Brown, Steve
1975 Abbey, Leon
1980 Evans, Bill (ii)
1981 Bullock, Chick
1983 Bobo, Willie
1983 Hartman, Johnny
1985 Williams, Cootie
1993 Acquaye, Speedy
1994 Henry, Haywood
1998 Deems, Barrett

16

born

1898 or 1908 Bullock, Chick
1901 Pâques, Jean
1903 Venuti, Joe
1908 Binyon, Larry
1921 Hendricks, Jon
1925 Byrd, Charlie
1929 Levitt, Rod
1931 Johansson, Jan
1938 Beck, Gordon
1939 Rettenbacher, J. A.
1940 Atkinson, Lisle
1940 Bluiett, Hamiet
1952 Szabo, Frank
1954 Klugh, Earl
1960 Haynes, Graham
1964 Zbořil, Pavel
1968 Cheek, Chris

died

1964 Hill, Ernest
1986 Speers, Stewie
1994 Leighton, Bernie
1998 Trzaskowski, Andrzej

17

born

1902 Nelson, Louis
1918 Rostaing, Hubert
1923 Sharon, Ralph
1926 McDuff, Brother Jack
1927 May, Earl
1930 Loevendie, Theo
1934 Peagler, Curtis
1938 Robinson, Perry
1946 Miranda, Roberto Miguel
1946 Williams, David
1957 Rainey, Tom
1966 Møller, Lars

died

1951 Yancey, Jimmy
1958 Fields, Herbie
1959 Simeon, Omer
1977 Hooper, Lou
1993 Crumbley, Elmer
1996 Grah, Bill

18

born

1902 Thomas, John
1910 Fowler, T. J.
1918 Graham, Bill
1923 Socolow, Frank
1925 Beck, Pia
1939 Marcus, Steve
1939 Westbrook, Kate
1951 Slagle, Steve
1957 Fedchock, John
1957 Remler, Emily
1959 Bründl, Manfred
1960 Molvaer, Nils Petter
1962 Johansen, Jonas
1964 Felten, Eric
1965 Bramerie, Thomas

died

1970 Davis, Maxwell
1978 Kronberg, Günter
1983 Milton, Roy
1985 Lewis, Ed
1997 Witherspoon, Jimmy

19

born

1887 Austin, Lovie
1901 Socarras, Alberto
1916 Ward, Helen
1928 Hounslow, Keith
1930 Abrams, Muhal Richard
1932 Coxhill, Lol
1945 Marais, Gérard
1952 Kaiser, Henry
1952 Markussen, Uffe
1956 Lackerschmid, Wolfgang
1957 Aoki, Tatsu
1959 Cox, Bruce

died

1972 Morgan, Andrew
1979 Simmons, John

20

born

1895 Howard, Paul
1902 Pasquall, Jerome Don
1910 Williams, Franc
1913 Collins, John
1920 Guy, Joe
1921 De Arango, Bill
1927 Dankworth, John
1927 Mitchell, Red
1927 Paris, Jackie
1928 Redd, Vi
1929 Temperley, Joe
1937 Schmidli, Peter
1938 Gale, Eric
1938 Zetterlund, Monica
1941 Cullum, Jim, Jr.
1947 Bang, Billy
1956 Coleman, Steve
1965 Sarin, Michael

died

1956 Thompson, Rudolph
1963 Brown, Pete
1973 Webster, Ben
1982 Krautgartner, Karel
1988 Woodyard, Sam
1994 Hamilton, Jimmy

21

born

1873 Laine, Papa Jack
1914 Orchard, Frank
1914 Stewart, Slam
1918 Potter, Tommy
1921 Hamilton, Chico
1923 Hunt, Fred
1927 Swingle, Ward
1929 Hadi, Shafi
1932 Preston, Don
1940 Hahn, Jerry
1940 Pochée, John
1940 Shearer, Dick
1944 Clark, John
1947 Nix, Bern
1949 Butler, Henry
1971 Wonsey, Anthony

died

1943 Smith, Trixie
1970 Stevenson, George
1989 Barron, Bill

SEPTEMBER

22

born

1919 De Gregori, Rio
1926 Smith, Bill (i)
1939 Gallardo, Joe
1940 Mumford, John
1946 Stern, Peggy
1952 Dagradi, Tony
1959 Reedus, Tony

died

1975 Delaney, Jack
1994 Buckner, Teddy
1994 Feather, Leonard
1999 Salvador, Sal
2000 Cook, Willie

23

born

1883 Nicholas, Wooden Joe
1894 Lovett, Baby
1905 Bradshaw, Tiny
1907 Ammons, Albert
1912 Matthews, George
1926 Coltrane, John
1926 or 1927 Woode, Jimmy
1928 Foster, Frank
1928 Gaudry, Michel
1929 Dodgion, Dottie
1930 Charles, Ray
1935 McCann, Les
1938 Dudek, Gerd
1938 Warren, John
1941 Turbinton, Earl
1941 Winstone, Norma
1943 Steig, Jeremy
1947 Escoudé, Christian
1947 Grolnick, Don
1950 Garzone, George
1964 Shiina, Yutaka

died

1967 Mussulli, Boots

24

born

1872 Barbarin, Isidore
1905 Ratip, Ahmed
1914 Winter, Horst
1916 Jeffries, Herb
1917 Butts, Jimmy
1922 Costanzo, Jack
1923 Navarro, Fats
1929 Carter, John
1933 Symonds, Nelson
1939 Henderson, Wayne
1949 Connors, Bill
1965 Milder, Joakim

died

1983 Porter, King

25

born

1899 Bigard, Alex
1902 Bushell, Garvin
1906 Ježek, Jaroslav
1908 Allen, Charlie
1914 Wilkins, Dave
1919 Bohländer, Carlo
1919 Wilson, Shadow
1923 Rivers, Sam
1935 Alexander, Roland
1937 Arnold, Horacee
1937 Gibbs, Mike
1942 Taylor, John
1948 Pierce, Billy
1954 Jones, Victor
1962 Handy, Craig
1964 Dennerlein, Barbara

died

1967 Smith, Stuff

26

born

1909 Deloof, Gus
1911 Hall, René
1917 Williams, Nelson
1924 Wright, Lammar (ii)
1926 Kronberg, Günter
1926 London, Julie
1927 Mussolini, Romano
1934 Heckstall-Smith, Dick
1940 Bartz, Gary
1973 Payton, Nicholas

died

1937 Smith, Bessie
1973 Etté, Bernard
1984 Manne, Shelly
1989 Shaw, Arnold
1993 Monterose, J. R.
1998 Carter, Betty
2000 Fatool, Nick

27

born

1907 Harris, Joe (i)
1909 Hall, Skip
1912 Bauschke, Erhard
1916 Brannon, Teddy
1922 Benskin, Sammy
1922 Shapiro, Nat
1924 Powell, Bud
1927 Levy, Hank
1927 Oda, Satoru
1927 Rodney, Red
1931 Klaasen, Tandie
1934 Glindemann, Ib
1936 Erstrand, Lars
1938 Gordon, Frank
1940 Nock, Mike
1945 Ecklund, Peter
1952 Weldon, Jerry
1958 Grabowsky, Paul
1964 Wilson, Matt

died

1965 Reser, Harry
1988 Heard, J. C.
1992 Rasmussen, Peter
2000 Raubiško, Raimonds

28

born

1930 Thigpen, Ed
1931 Gilmore, John
1938 Warleigh, Ray
1940 Mason, Rod
1940 Sirone
1941 Osborne, Mike
1945 Biensan, François
1945 Wall, Murray
1949 Harth, Alfred
1954 Hoggard, Jay
1955 Kirkland, Kenny
1966 Osaka, Masahiko

died

1955 Moriyasu, Shotaro
1966 Millinder, Lucky
1991 Davis, Miles
1993 MacPherson, Fraser

SEPTEMBER

	29	**30**	**September** (the date unknown)
born	1929 Kühn, Rolf	1912 Johnson, Bill (iii)	
	1941 Griffiths, Malcolm	1913 Atkins, Cholly	
	1942 Ponty, Jean-Luc	1917 Rich, Buddy	
	1948 Jörgensmann, Theo	1922 Pettiford, Oscar	
	1952 Campbell, Roy	1927 Leggio, Carmen	
	1953 Juris, Vic	1928 Eardley, Jon	
	1961 Kikoski, Dave	1933 McCall, Steve	
		1954 Rushen, Patrice	
		1956 Murphy, Tim	
		1961 Ilg, Dieter	
		1968 Hart, Antonio	
died	1968 Wilcox, Eddie	1962 Stein, Johnny	1954 Williams, Rudy
	1969 Hall, Clarence	1963 Robinson, J. Russel	1963 Allen, Sam
	1974 Pierce, Billie	1978 Booker, Beryl	1963 Hurley, Clyde
	1984 Reig, Teddy	1990 Napoleon, Phil [or 13 Sept]	1975 Reeves, Reuben
	1988 Josephson, Barney		1980 Reeves, Talcott
	1990 Kohlman, Freddie		1983 Holder, Terrence
			1985 Aless, Tony

OCTOBER

1

born

1912 Meyer, Johnny
1920 Goyens, Al
1926 Paquinet, André
1935 Richards, Ann
1940 Franklin, Henry
1942 Braugham, Charlie
1942 Harrison, Wendell
1946 Holland, Dave
1950 Helias, Mark
1952 Tissendier, Claude
1955 Dumas, Tony
1955 Larsen, Morten Gunnar
1955 Lundy, Curtis
1956 Kassap, Sylvain
1960 Chéron, Paul

died

1938 Washington, Mack
1991 Williamson, Stu

2

born

1885 McDonald, Earl
1906 Myers, Wilson
1913 Rose, Wally
1915 Mallard, Oett
1925 Urso, Phil
1927 Slyde, Jimmy
1929 Roberts, Howard
1933 Ross, Ronnie
1953 Goines, Lincoln
1960 Bates, Django
1965 Powell, Roy
1965 Tinkler, Scott

died

1958 Lee, George E.
1976 Jackson, Quentin
1978 Brunies, Abbie
1981 Scott, Hazel
1981 Windhurst, Johnny
1983 Williams, Franc
1992 Grossman, Richard
1993 Abdul-Malik, Ahmed

3

born

1889 Manetta, Manuel
1907 Battle, Edgar
1909 Banks, Buddy (i)
1909 Pitman, Booker
1922 Freeman, Von
1925 Wein, George
1930 Harrow, Nancy
1935 Bailey, Judy
1943 Bakr, Rashid
1946 Clark, Mike
1950 Laws, Ronnie
1954 Tibbetts, Steve
1956 Tonooka, Sumi
1957 Hołownia, Bogdan
1960 Godard, Michel
1961 Bowie, Michael
1963 Doky, Niels Lan
1967 Dahl, Carsten

died

1966 Lambert, Dave
1976 Flemming, Herb
1976 Spivey, Victoria
1979 Corcoran, Corky
1987 McCarthy, Albert
1992 Carisi, Johnny
1994 Browne, Scoville

4

born

1904 Walton, Greely
1909 Chiboust, Noël
1909 Featherstonhaugh, Buddy
1910 Norman, Charlie
1915 Pozo, Chino
1915 Roger Henrichsen, Børge
1922 Hasselgård, Stan
1927 Bishop, Walter, Jr.
1937 Thomas, Leon
1938 Levine, Mark
1940 Swallow, Steve
1944 Gomez, Eddie
1958 Pawlik, Włodek
1960 Horner, Lindsey
1964 Hurst, Robert

died

1986 De Souza, Yorke
1994 Challis, Bill
1999 Farmer, Art

5

born

1893 Guarente, Frank
1908 Engstrøm, Kalle
1910 Norman, Fred
1912 Höllerhagen, Ernst
1925 Dixon, Bill
1942 Ayler, Donald
1949 Clausen, Thomas
1957 Anderson, Clifton

died

1943 Roppolo, Leon
1961 Little, Booker
1971 Thigpen, Ben
1981 Cooper, Al
1986 Sayles, Emanuel
1990 Taylor, Sam "the Man"

6

born

1903 Dean, Demas
1908 Price, Sammy
1913 Mastren, Carmen
1929 Antritter, Dieter
1929 Simmons, Norman
1941 Sato, Masahiko
1958 Gatto, Roberto
1966 Whitfield, Mark

died

1985 Riddle, Nelson
1998 Jenny-Clark, Jean-François
2000 Flowers, Pat

7

born

1908 Moore, Alton
1911 Jones, Jo
1912 Peer, Beverly
1924 Flax, Marty
1925 Stoller, Alvin
1934 Baraka, Amiri
1940 Jaume, André
1940 Young, Larry
1947 Jarczyk, Jan
1958 Mitchell, Tyler
1975 Nakagawa, Eijiro

died

1945 Bauschke, Erhard
1964 Travis, Nick
1968 Richards, Johnny
1988 Livingston, Ulysses
1992 Blackwell, Ed

OCTOBER

8

born

?1893 Williams, Clarence
1903 Moore, Gerry
1911 Vlach, Karel
1916 Stegmeyer, Bill
1917 Heard, J. C.
1917 Webb, George
1919 Ambrosetti, Flavio
1919 Singer, Hal
1923 Igoe, Sonny
1930 Adams, Pepper
1939 Pege, Aladár
1945 Betsch, John
1961 Bernstein, Steven
1963 Ballantyne, Jon

died

1964 Gozzo, Conrad
1974 Carney, Harry
1979 Izenzon, David
1981 Moore, Oscar
1988 Inge, Edward
1998 Spearman, Glenn
1999 Privin, Bernie

9

born

1900 Snowden, Elmer
1903 Sutton, Mynie
1908 Wiley, Lee
1920 Lateef, Yusef
1931 Ishikawa, Hisao
1934 Ibrahim, Abdullah
1939 Xiques, Ed
1941 Valdés, Chucho
1946 Thollot, Jacques
1948 Samuels, Dave
1957 Boiarsky, Andrés
1960 Garrett, Kenny
1961 Wheeler, Nedra

died

1973 Tharpe, Sister Rosetta
1977 Wiggs, Johnny
1988 Alexander, Mousey
1993 Walton, Greely
1999 Jackson, Milt

10

born

1903 Blair, Lee
1905 Towles, Nat
1906 Jenkins, Freddie
1906 Mathisen, Leo
1910 Larkin, Milt
1914 Perry, King
1915 Edison, Harry
1917 Monk, Thelonious
1918 Byrne, Bobby
1921 Kral, Roy
1921 Montgomery, Monk
1926 Brown, Oscar, Jr.
1929 Blackwell, Ed
1935 Humphrey, Paul
1942 Bridgewater, Cecil
1942 Sides, Doug
1956 O'Neal, Johnny
1963 Goode, Brad

died

1960 Cole, June
1965 Tucker, George
1969 Manetta, Manuel
1980 Alemán, Oscar

11

born

1903 Weatherford, Teddy
1919 Blakey, Art
1920 Choquart, Loys
1927 Amy, Curtis
1927 Kinsey, Tony
1929 Hulan, Ludek
1936 Higgins, Billy
1941 Bowie, Lester
1947 Bowden, Mwata
1947 Hopkins, Fred
1955 Sprague, Peter
1956 Lawrence, Doug

died

1975 Sherman, Jimmy
1976 Boswell, Connee

12

born

1895 Hall, Tubby
1901 Madison, Bingie
1902 Archey, Jimmy
1926 Matsumoto, Hidehiko
1936 Tolley, David
1946 Masuo, Yoshiaki
1954 Cherry, Ed
1959 Mossman, Michael Philip
1966 Allen, Harry

died

1933 Wade, Jimmy
1992 Cesàri, Umberto
1992 Schwindt, Christian

13

born

1902 Lee, Julia [or 31 Oct]
1909 Tatum, Art
1915 Browne, Scoville
1915 Fallon, Jack
1924 Gibbs, Terry
1926 Brown, Ray
1926 Whittle, Tommy
1927 Konitz, Lee
1932 Lytle, Johnny
1935 Kozlov, Aleksey
1940 Sanders, Pharoah
1960 Robinson, Orphy

died

1958 Geller, Lorraine
1969 Pitman, Booker
1971 Sullivan, Joe
1972 Seamen, Phil
1984 Bonfils, Kjeld
2000 Woodman, Britt

14

born

1880 or 1889 Williams, Spencer
1895 Hicks, Edna
1899 McKenzie, Red
1917 Graas, John
1922 Liggins, Jimmy
1925 Morks, Jan
1931 Goykovich, Dusko
1943 Pauer, Fritz
1953 Fewell, Garrison
1953 Watanabe, Kazumi
1958 Franck, Tomas

died

1945 Terrell, Pha
1959 Trent, Alphonso
1977 Crosby, Bing

OCTOBER

15

born

1896 Sanders, Joe
1903 Remue, Chas
1906 Spivey, Victoria
1908 Chittison, Herman "Ivory"
1913 Jederby, Thore
1916 Killian, Al
1917 Tanner, Paul
1925 Baker, Mickey
1934 Elsdon, Alan
1939 Roccisano, Joe
1946 Danielsson, Palle
1946 Stief, Bo
1952 Clausen, Bent
1955 Neville, Chris
1955 Shull, Tad
1960 Bolberg Pedersen, Henrik
1966 Charlap, Bill
1967 Hopkins, Tim

died

1966 Blair, Lee
1972 Lanoue, Conrad

16

born

1903 Lewis, Charlie
1903 Washington, Buck
1917 Flowers, Pat
1923 Hambro, Lenny
1932 Aronov, Ben
1952 Anderson, Ray
1954 Berne, Tim
1961 Jackson, Gene
1965 Kerr, Anthony
1969 Hargrove, Roy

died

1959 Hall, Minor
1973 Krupa, Gene
1977 Raskin, Milt
1990 Blakey, Art

17

born

1900 Harrison, Jimmy
1901 Collins, Lee
1901 Thompson, Leslie
1903 Bee, David
1903 Godley, A. G.
1906 Cole, Cozy
1911 Šima, Jan
1923 Kessel, Barney
1936 Benjamin, Sathima Bea
1949 Umezu, Kazutoki
1952 Giammarco, Maurizio
1953 Bowie, Joseph
1956 Shilkloper, Arkady
1958 Alden, Howard
1961 Moffett, Cody

died

1927 Cottrell, Louis, Sr.
1962 Williams, Rubberlegs
1984 Hunter, Alberta
1989 Gluskin, Lud

18

born

1885, 1890, or 1891 Kelly, Chris
1904 Evans, Stump
1906 Quinn, Snoozer
1907 Washington, George
1908 Lanoue, Conrad
1908 Stearns, Marshall W.
1918 Troup, Bobby
1919 O'Day, Anita
1933 Townsend, Bross
1935 Jædig, Bent
1936 Moses, J. C.
1946 Graillier, Michel
1950 Afrika, Mervyn
1951 Vincent, Ron
1954 Purrone, Tony
1955 Rek, Vitold
1961 Marsalis, Wynton
1966 Stewart, Bill
1967 Pyysalo, Severi

died

1956 Parry, Harry
1971 Pasquall, Jerome Don
1976 Kok, James
1977 Hauger, Kristian
1991 Sønstevold, Gunnar
1994 Allen, Lee
1995 Sturgis, Ted
1999 Crombie, Tony
2000 London, Julie

19

born

1878 Picou, Alphonse
1908 Hughes, Spike
1908 Lewis, Sylvester
1910 Smith, Howard
1912 Richards, Red
1922 Sash, Leon
1929 Noren, Jack
1937 Gwangwa, Jonas
1941 Daniels, Eddie
1959 Burrage, Ronnie
1960 Pilc, Jean-Michel
1962 Hofseth, Bendik
1966 Garland, Tim

died

1956 Jones, Isham
1967 Chambers, Henderson
1982 Powell, Jesse
1989 Dixon, Eric
1992 Stoller, Alvin
1995 Cherry, Don

20

born

1890 Morton, Jelly Roll
?1901 Hall, Adelaide
1906 Moore, Johnny
1907 Kress, Carl
1913 Best, Johnny
1920 Linn, Ray
1929 Jones, Willie
1934 Harris, Eddie
1956 Flores, Luca
1956 Taylor, Martin
1957 Noriki, Soichi
1962 Moroni, Dado
1971 Gunn, Russell

died

1973 Moraweck, Lucien
1984 Johnson, Budd

21

born

1899 Voynow, Dick
1912 Byas, Don
1913 Clark, Gus
1913 Di Ceglie, Cosimo
1917 Gillespie, Dizzy
1926 Elliott, Don
1935 Few, Bobby
1935 Rader, Don
1936 Hermann, Heinz von
1947 Bergonzi, Jerry
1952 Ryerson, Ali
1953 Johnson, Marc
1955 Hersch, Fred
1957 Gioia, Ted
1966 Hara, Tomonao
1967 Mateen, Tarus

died

1955 Twardzik, Dick
1962 Moore, Monette
1982 Toneff, Radka
1994 Ehrling, Thore

OCTOBER

22

born

1897 Blake, Cyril
1898 Yaw, Ralph
1900 Nelson, George
1926 Drakes, Jesse
1928 Fischer, Clare
1929 Gaslini, Giorgio
1943 Dudziak, Urszula
1955 Bunnett, Jane

died

1944 Profit, Clarence
1969 Kazebier, Nate
1986 Stubø, Thorgeir
1994 McFay, Monk [or 23 Oct]
1997 Goodman, Harry

23

born

1921 Bennett, Betty
1922 Peiffer, Bernard
1926 Warland, Jean
1927 Criss, Sonny
1927 Sadi, Fats
1933 McFarland, Gary
1942 Schiaffini, Giancarlo
1945 Watts, Ernie
1949 Honsinger, Tristan
1953 Grainger, Gary
1956 Helleny, Joel
1956 Reeves, Dianne
1963 Labarrière, Hélène
1965 Goodman, Gabrielle

died

1949 Wilson, Buster
1951 Creath, Charlie
1960 Kilbert, Porter
1976 Tevelian, Meg
1987 Rodgers, Gene
1994 McFay, Monk [or 22 Oct]
1998 Williams, Johnny (i)

24

born

1900 Marrero, Lawrence
1900 Watkins, Joe
1902 Barbarin, Louis
1905 Hauger, Kristian
1906 Williams, Sandy
1907 Ekyan, André
1914 Powell, Jimmie
1920 Marshall, Wendell
1929 Morgenstern, Dan
1938 Pope, Odean
1942 De Graaff, Rein
1943 Paakkunainen, Seppo
1954 Cox, Anthony
1955 Anderson, Jay
1955 Montier, Nicolas
1960 Osamu, Koichi
1961 Margitza, Rick

died

1986 Dyani, Johnny
1989 Shihab, Sahib
2000 Lee, Jeanne

25

born

1897 Souchon, Edmond
1902 Lang, Eddie
1905 Reeves, Reuben
1914 Dallwitz, Dave
1918 Jackson, Chubby
1923 Banks, Don
1924 Palmer, Earl
1926 Heath, Jimmy
1935 Hing, Kenny
1936 Goldberg, Morris
1942 Hino, Terumasa
1947 Koyama, Shota
1955 Eubanks, Robin
1956 Ghiglioni, Tiziana
1961 Amsallem, Franck

died

1941 Lind, Nisse “Bagarn”
1972 Massey, Cal
1981 Craig, Al
1987 Jackson, Willis “Gator”
1990 Holley, Major
1990 Robinson, Ikey
1992 De Villers, Michel
1993 Carr, Bruno

26

born

1896 Duncan, Hank
1900 Conaway, Sterling
1907 Pastor, Tony
1913 Barnet, Charlie
1927 Marsh, Warne
1934 Loussier, Jacques
1940 Henderson, Eddie
1942 Lee, Ranee
1956 LeDonne, Mike
1958 Fraser, Hugh

died

1989 Bales, Burt
1995 Sangster, John

27

born

1904 Lind, Nisse “Bagarn”
1910 Eriksberg, Folke
1912 Törner, Gösta
1913 Raeburn, Boyd
1916 or 1919 Gonzales, Babs
1917 Warwick, Carl
1918 Delamont, Gordon
1929 Elmon Wright
1931 Dallas, Sonny
1934 Jullien, Ivan
1934 Phillips, Barre
1942 Catherine, Philip
1945 Andersen, Arild
1952 Filiano, Ken
1954 Brunious, Wendell
1956 Besiakov, Ben
1958 Hazeltine, David
1961 Butman, Igor
1968 Yamada, Joh
1969 Galland, Stéphane

died

1964 Turner, Charlie
1966 Braud, Wellman
1975 Nelson, Oliver
1981 Metcalf, Louis
1986 Branscombe, Alan
1987 Dalto, Jorge

28

born

1892 Johnson, Dink
1907 Powell, Rudy
1916 Harris, Bill (i)
1921 O’Farrill, Chico
1927 Laine, Cleo
1939 Bey, Andy
1941 Clayton, Jay
1941 Moore, Glen
1945 Dean, Elton
1945 Pilz, Michel
1948 Sachse, Helmut “Joe”
1952 Andress, Tuck
1958 Jordan, Kent
1970 Rosenwinkel, Kurt

died

1965 Bostic, Earl

OCTOBER

29

born

1908 Culver, Rollie
1908 Dobschinski, Walter
1916 Brooks, Hadda
1922 Hefti, Neal
1925 Sims, Zoot
1934 Jacobs, Pim
1934 Woods, Jimmy
1939 Ntshoko, Makaya
1941 Errisson, King
1943 Busch, Sigi
1945 Jean-Marie, Alain
1960 Van den Dungen, Ben
1960 Winther, Jens
1964 Gustafsson, Mats

died

1987 Herman, Woody
1988 Comfort, Joe
1997 Nicholas, Big Nick

30

born

1925 Macero, Teo
1928 Jones, Bobby
1930 Brown, Clifford
1930 Parker, Errol
1951 Gurtu, Trilok

died

1941 Berry, Chu
1946 Smith, Mamie [date uncertain]
1953 Quicksell, Howdy
1969 Foster, Pops
1969 Sbarbaro, Tony
1976 Powell, Rudy
2000 Allen, Steve

31

born

1896 Waters, Ethel
1896 Watson, Gilbert
1902 Lee, Julia [or 13 Oct]
1905 Chappy
1915 Griffin, Chris
1915 Jarvis, Jane
1921 Miyama, Toshiyuki
1922 Jacquet, Illinois
1922 Nash, Ted (i)
1923 Graettinger, Bob
1930 Ervin, Booker
1930 Tomkins, Les
1936 Williams, Johnny (ii)
1939 Guerin, John
1940 Essen, Reimer von
1944 Ferguson, Sherman
1945 Parlato, David
1950 Santoro, Gene
1956 Belden, Bob

died

1969 Pastor, Tony
1977 Taylor, Eva
1980 Morehouse, Chauncey
1991 Bushell, Garvin
1999 Ruther, Wyatt

October (the date unknown)

born

1889 Hightower, Willie
1918 Blanton, Jimmy

died

1944 Stevenson, Tommy
1957 Dickerson, Carroll
1976 Morgan, Sonny
1982 Teagarden, Helen
1983 Baranco, Victor
1983 Valentine, Jerry
1984 Ball, Ronnie
1985 Block, Sandy
1985 Boyd, Nelson

NOVEMBER

1

born

1898 Wallace, Sippie
1904 Bacon, Louis
1905 Assunto, Papa Jac
1907 Rushton, Joe
1912 Jackson, Franz
1914 Lewis, Sabby
1923 Margolis, Sam
1926 Donaldson, Lou
1926 Markham, John
1929 Baltazar, Gabe
1939 Kellaway, Roger
1948 Malik, Raphé
1954 Lundy, Carmen
1956 Landers, Tim
1958 Williams, Willie
1959 Herwig, Conrad

died

1982 Draper, Ray
1986 Wallace, Sippie

2

born

1908 Berigan, Bunny
1911 Richards, Johnny
1920 Allen, Walter C.
1928 Geller, Herb
1931 Woods, Phil
1940 Minton, Phil
1945 Mullen, Jim
1953 Dawkins, Ernest
1956 Kimbrough, Frank
1957 Ullmann, Gebhard
1965 D'Angelo, Andrew
1967 Elling, Kurt

died

1969 Jones, Slick
1994 Pitterson, Pete
1997 Smith, Carson

3

born

1907 Turner, Joe (i)
1911 Ellboj, Lulle
1926 Mitchell, Billy
1927 McGhee, Andy
1935 Grimes, Henry
1939 McPhee, Joe
1939 Shibuya, Takeshi
1946 Miklin, Karlheinz
1952 White, Rocky
1953 Lawrence, Azar

died

1971 McFarland, Gary
1986 Davis, Eddie "Lockjaw"
1992 Moore, Freddie
1996 Moncur, Grachan

4

born

1906 Sullivan, Joe
1919 Benjamin, Joe
1919 Schilperoort, Peter
1922 Sutton, Ralph
1926 Valdez, Carlos "Patato"
1928 Bunker, Larry
1944 Breuker, Willem
1952 Lorber, Jeff
1954 Demierre, Jacques
1954 Ignatzek, Klaus
1957 Le Lann, Eric

died

1931 Bolden, Buddy
1963 Gordon, Joe
1994 Sharpe, Jack
1994 Webb, Speed
1996 Linn, Ray
2000 Fournier, Vernel

5

born

1914 McVea, Jack
1917 Fierstone, George
1921 Wootten, Red
1926 Windhurst, Johnny
1929 Shannon, Terry
1931 McNair, Harold
1941 Nahorny, Włodzimierz
1956 Jannah, Denise
1957 Marino, Tony
1963 Veal, Reginald

died

1954 Page, Hot Lips
1956 Tatum, Art
1975 Van Vliet, Toon
1985 Williams, Richard
1989 Watters, Lu
1996 Harris, Eddie

6

born

1889 White, Amos
1912 or 1913 Kolax, King
1913 Gibson, Andy
1916 Conniff, Ray
1918 Green, Chuck
1923 Lusher, Don
1924 Cathcart, Dick
1929 Boland, Francy
1929 Parker, Johnny
1937 Brisker, Gordon
1939 Johnson, Dewey
1940 Dalseth, Laila
1949 Sandoval, Arturo
1950 Eyges, David
1950 Goldstein, Gil
1951 Miller, Mark
1958 Rodriguez, E. J.

died

1965 Williams, Clarence
1986 Thompson, Eddie

7

born

1916 Bushkin, Joe
1917 Rumsey, Howard
1922 Hirt, Al
1932 Batiste, Alvin
1934 Allan, Jan
1934 Worrell, Lewis [or 10 Sept]
1937 Wood, Vishnu
1949 Ware, David S.
1952 Faber, Johannes
1955 Margolis, Kitty
1959 Suonsaari, Klaus
1962 Taylor, Mark (ii)

died

1956 Carlisle, Una Mae
1964 Taylor, Jasper
1971 Thomas, John
1993 Hall, Adelaide
1994 Rogers, Shorty
1996 Cola, Kid Sheik
1996 Jones, Carmell

NOVEMBER

8

born

1927 Connor, Chris
1934 Riedel, Georg
1940 Quaye, Terri
1944 Sullivan, Charles
1955 Barber, Patricia
1958 Byron, Don
1963 Malone, Russell

died

1966 Baker, Shorty
1967 Johnson, Keg
1984 Walcott, Collin
1992 Mitchell, Red
1993 Cathcart, Dick
1999 Bowie, Lester
2000 Morrissey, Dick

9

born

1899 Mezzrow, Mezz
1901 Spanier, Muggsy
1906 Brown, Pete
?1906 Douglas, Tommy
1925 Hopkins, Linda
1938 Remus, Alfredo
1948 Jonkisz, Kazimierz
1965 Davis, Jesse

died

1968 Johansson, Jan
1997 Roccisano, Joe

10

born

1916 May, Billy
1932 Bley, Paul
1934 Person, Houston
1938 Matshikiza, Pat
1939 Cyrille, Andrew
1939 Laws, Hubert
1945 Davis, Stanton
1945 LaBarbera, John
1965 Turner, Mark

died

1955 Raglin, Junior
1967 Cox, Ida
1983 Leonard, Harlan
1994 McRae, Carmen
1997 Keane, Shake

11

born

1903 Aerts, Jos
1911 Wilson, Dick
1917 White, Sonny
1923 Cook, Willie
1925 Fol, Hubert
1926 Stokes, Irvin
1927 Allison, Mose
1928 Anderson, Ernestine
1929 Mayers, Lloyd
1932 Levitt, Al
1940 Pavone, Mario
1948 Peterson, Hannibal
1953 El'Zabar, Kahil
1953 McKee, Andy
1958 Laudet, François
1962 Morrison, James
1975 Wasilewski, Marcin

died

1982 Törner, Gösta
1986 Markowitz, Marky
1993 Hawkins, Erskine
1998 Kirkland, Kenny [date uncertain]

12

born

1911 Clayton, Buck
1922 Blackburn, Lou
1923 Mariano, Charlie
1924 Jones, Sam
1925 Silva, Michael
1930 Braslavsky, Pierre
1933 Schlüter, Wolfgang
1938 Artin, Tom
1943 Stubø, Thorgeir
1950 Pugh, Jim
1952 Boussaguet, Pierre
1954 Hutman, Olivier
1954 Vatcher, Michael

died

1970 Gifford, Gene
1983 Jackson, Preston
1985 Wells, Dicky
1992 Coles, Honi

13

born

1894 McFarlane, Howard
1894 Moten, Bennie
1912 Donnelly, Ted
1912 Palmer, Singleton
1913 Barker, Blue Lu
1921 Calhoun, Eddie
1928 Farrow, Ernie
1928 Hawes, Hampton
1931 Roda, Ricard
1939 Muhammad, Idris
1940 Lawson, Janet
1943 Gary, Shelton
1945 Douglass, Bill (ii)
1945 Riisnæs, Knut
1953 Coke, Alex
1953 Flory, Chris
1954 Reijseger, Ernst
1958 Lakatos, Tony

died

1987 Vick, Harold
1996 Doggett, Bill
2000 Kirkwood, Johnny

14

born

?1904 Hodes, Art
1908 Hayes, Clancy
1915 Bauer, Billy
1916 Ewell, Don
1930 Migliori, Jay
1932 Yagi, Masao
1934 Marsalis, Ellis
1937 Grossman, Richard
1944 Cables, George

died

1965 Harding, Buster
1968 Jefferson, Hilton
1980 Guérin, Beb
1989 Davison, Wild Bill
1992 Adams, George

NOVEMBER

15

born

1885 Baquet, Achille
1913 Johnson, Gus
1919 Lowe, Curtis
1920 Richardson, Jerome
1925 Harvey, Eddie
1928 Powell, Seldon
1936 Zubov, Aleksey
1943 Haurand, Ali
1955 Swainson, Neil
1957 Eubanks, Kevin
1959 Rosenthal, Ted
1970 Ibarra, Susie
1974 Rogers, Reuben

died

1973 Williams, Nelson
1992 Mondello, Toots
1997 Matthews, Onzy [date uncertain]
1998 Williams, Al

16

born

1873 Handy, W. C.
1901 Stone, Jesse
1905 Condon, Eddie
1906 Jones, Wallace
1908 Thigpen, Ben
1914 Dunham, Sonny
1914 Nicolosi, Roberto
1916 Lucas, Al
1925 Travis, Nick
1927 Coker, Dolo
1930 Bates, Jim
1939 Donner, Otto
1948 Figueroa, Sammy
1951 Conte, Luis
1952 Newton, Lauren
1963 Argüelles, Steve
1964 Krall, Diana

died

1967 Archey, Jimmy
1978 Nottingham, Jimmy
1982 Haig, Al
1984 Dickenson, Vic
1989 Murphy, Rose
1990 Castle, Lee
1992 Hood, Bill

17

born

1915 Sherock, Shorty
1926 Masso, George
1927 Drasnin, Bob
1928 Andrus, Chuck
1928 Sangster, John
1930 Amram, David
1931 Andre, Wayne
1934 Montgomery, Marian
1935 Rudd, Roswell
1944 Bachträgl, Erich
1951 Ellis, Lisle
1966 Allison, Ben
1967 Matsushima, Keiji

died

1955 Johnson, James P.
1957 Nicholas, Wooden Joe
1962 Fulbright, Dick
1969 Dyett, Capt. Walter
1990 Schilperoort, Peter
1998 Carpenter, Ike

18

born

1909 Mercer, Johnny
1915 Peterson, Chuck
1916 Lyons, Jimmy (i)
1917 Mussulli, Boots
1926 Williamson, Claude
1927 Sproles, Victor
1928 Jordan, Sheila
1930 Lastie, Melvin
1936 Cherry, Don
1946 Wallace, Bennie
1956 Tononi, Tiziano
1959 Blackman, Cindy

died

1965 Black, Lou
1969 Heath, Ted
1978 Tristano, Lennie
1989 Waits, Freddie
1994 Calloway, Cab
1994 Levitt, Al

19

born

1926 Hara, Nobuo
1927 Persiany, André
1951 Werner, Kenny
1959 Wrobel, Engelbert
1961 Lockett, Mornington
1964 Herring, Vincent
1973 Glover, Savion

died

1949 King, Stan
1964 Burnside, Vi
1967 Hoefer, George
1972 Allen, Charlie
1974 Brunis, Georg
1977 Criss, Sonny
1995 Goldie, Don

20

born

1891 Fuhs, Julian
1914 Best, Skeeter
1921 Price, Ray
1925 Blevins, Leo
1925 Christy, June
1934 Smith, Colin
1946 Tommaso, Bruno
1950 Lafertin, Fapy
1959 Gress, Drew
1963 Braden, Don
1963 Tafenau, Raivo

died

1956 Baquet, Achille
1970 Stovall, Don
1982 Plater, Bobby
1995 Breyre, Jos
1997 Palmer, Robert
1998 Alphonso, Roland

21

born

1891 Johnson, Charlie
1904 Hawkins, Coleman
1909 Glenn, Lloyd
1911 Burroughs, Alvin
1918 Austin, Claire
1923 Greer, Big John
1925 Salvador, Sal
1929 Gousset, Claude
1935 Warren, Peter
1941 Makasi, Duke
1948 Mouzon, Alphonse
1949 Brüninghaus, Rainer
1953 Kobayashi, Yoichi
1954 Doneda, Michel
1955 Baars, Ab
1957 Tanksley, Francesca
1970 Keezer, Geoff
1973 Shim, Mark

died

1953 Shields, Larry
1958 Morris, Joe (i)
1968 Story, Nat

NOVEMBER

22

born

1899 Carmichael, Hoagy
1901 Barnes, Polo
1904 Henderson, Horace
1905 Scott, Cecil
1906 Kelly, Guy
1911 Caceres, Ernie
1925 Schuller, Gunther
1927 Knepper, Jimmy
1930 Wanzo, Mel
1941 McClure, Ron
1946 Richard, Marc
1967 Kataoka, Yuzo
1969 Faulk, Dan

died

1959 Hutchinson, Jiver
1971 Guy, Fred
1983 Behounek, Kamil
1984 Rose, Denis

23

born

1904 McCracken, Bob
1912 Glenn, Tyree
1916 Keenan, Norman
1916 Porter, King
1918 Reig, Teddy
1925 Mandel, Johnny
1929 Patrick, Pat
1934 Gaskin, Vic
1935 Fielder, Alvin
1942 Stivín, Jiří
1943 Turnbull, Alan
1944 Rabold, Frederic
1946 Drummond, Ray
1947 Mustafa, Melton
1950 Burnham, Charles
1960 Bourelly, Jean-Paul

died

1948 Hasselgård, Stan
1965 Shepard, Ernie
1968 Svensson, Reinhold
1973 Pierce, De De
1979 Coker, Henry
1996 Porter, Art

24

born

1896 Henderson, Rosa
1912 Wilson, Teddy
1918 Davis, Wild Bill
1923 Chaloff, Serge
1925 Cohn, Al
1932 Kurylewicz, Andrzej
1933 Barnard, Bob
1943 Tee, Richard
1947 Vapirov, Anatoly
1949 Dmitriev, Igor
1963 Colley, Scott
1963 Israel, Yoron

died

1941 Wilson, Dick
1972 Overton, Hall
1985 Turner, Joe (ii)
1991 Stenfalt, Norman
1996 Williams, John (i)

25

born

1897 Smith, Willie "the Lion"
1902 Breyre, Jos
1908 Lattimore, Harlan
1909 Spencer, O'Neill
1910 Smith, Willie
1915 Bivona, Gus
1919 Carroll, Joe "Bebop"
1924 Desmond, Paul
1925 Gee, Matthew
1927 Wellstood, Dick
1928 Jones, Etta
1929 Bryant, Rusty
1931 Adderley, Nat
1931 Crosby, Charles
1934 Cohen, Alan
1946 Franco, Guilherme
1957 Caumont, Elisabeth
1960 Johns, Steve
1966 Stafford, Terrell
1969 Honda, Tamaya

died

1949 Robinson, Bill
1965 Wells, Johnny
1979 Sash, Leon
1983 Reed, Waymon
1993 Makasi, Duke

26

born

1907 Melrose, Frank
1908 Davidson, Trump
1912 Sønstevold, Gunnar
1919 Archia, Tom
1925 Perciful, Jack
1932 Zawadi, Kiane
1939 Themen, Art
1952 Dresser, Mark
1953 Sayama, Masahiro

died

1956 Dorsey, Tommy
1957 Gardner, Jack
1958 Bradshaw, Tiny
1968 O'Brien, Floyd
1978 Rosolino, Frank
1990 Wilkins, Dave
1999 Jarvis, Clifford

27

born

1904 South, Eddie
1905 Dorsey, Tommy
1907 Bishop, Joe
1908 Smith, John
1917 Ertegun, Nesuhi
1930 Fonsèque, Raymond
1935 Portal, Michel
1937 Morris, Wilber
1941 Van Dijk, Louis
1944 Furniss, Paul
1945 Brecker, Randy
1953 Mays, Lyle
1960 Schneider, Maria
1961 Franks, Rebecca Coupe
1962 Teepe, Joris
1964 Anderson, Wessell
1966 Terrasson, Jacky

died

1954 Widmann, Kutte
1973 Christian, Frank

28

born

1907 Wettling, George
1914 or 1915 Vance, Dick
1924 Pring, Bobby
1925 Gryce, Gigi
1932 Coker, Jerry
1934 Barbieri, Gato
1936 McCurdy, Roy
1941 Roidinger, Adelhard
1941 Thilo, Jesper
1943 Thompson, Butch
1951 Irwin, Dennis
1956 Kohlhase, Charlie

died

1964 Washington, Jack
1972 Lytell, Jimmy
1985 Jackson, Calvin
1993 Turner, Bruce
1999 Bertschy, René

NOVEMBER

29

born

1894 Hegamin, Lucille
1902 Alvin, Danny
1912 Smith, Viola
1914 Goode, Coleridge
1914 McIntyre, Hal
1915 Strayhorn, Billy
1917 Gershman, Nat
1922 Donaldson, Bobby
1932 Bickert, Ed
1934 Coe, Tony
1936 Perrilliat, Nat
1939 Fasoli, Claudio
1940 Hart, Billy
1940 Mangione, Chuck
1954 White, Michael (ii)
1955 Nussbaum, Adam
1962 Jordan, Ronny
1965 Davis, Troy

died

1954 Johnson, Dink
1962 Towles, Nat
1978 Pletcher, Stew
1989 Burton, Ann
1993 Clare, Alan
1998 Van Eps, George

30

born

1914 Hadnott, Billy
1916 Moten, Benny
1931 Sheldon, Jack
1935 Burns, Roy
1945 Dyani, Johnny
1945 Jefferson, Carter
1948 Sulzmann, Stan
1949 Reichenbach, Bill (ii)
1954 Wieselman, Doug
1965 Weiss, Doug
1968 Courvoisier, Sylvie

died

1957 McPartland, Dick
1964 Redman, Don
1965 Haynes, Frank
1988 Rouse, Charlie
1994 Kay, Connie
2000 Tolbert, Skeets

November (the date unknown)

born

1938 Bernhardt, Warren

died

1930 Thomas, Fathead
1967 Crawley, Wilton
1970 Aaron, Abe
1970 Ayler, Albert
1973 Conaway, Sterling
1977 Moore, Alton
1980 Hall, Skip

DECEMBER

1

born

1904 Lytell, Jimmy
1919 Isaacs, Ike (ii)
1921 Bunch, John
1923 Ilcken, Wessel
1925 Johnson, Dick
1927 Brown, Ted
1931 Lyons, Jimmy (ii)
1935 Rawls, Lou
1938 Garnett, Carlos
1940 Van den Broeck, Rob
1947 Cuypers, Leo
1950 Donelian, Armen
1950 Tavaglione, Steve
1951 Pastorius, Jaco
1963 Nakaji, Hideaki

died

1981 Jordan, Taft
1997 Grappelli, Stephane
1999 Hadnott, Billy

2

born

1890 Marable, Fate
1896 Mosiello, Mike
1914 Sauter, Eddie
1915 Bridges, Henry
1916 Ventura, Charlie
1926 Swope, Rob
1931 Kelly, Wynton
1932 Court, Raymond
1935 Mathews, Ronnie
1941 Perry, P. J.

died

1937 Smith, Joe
1949 Ammons, Albert [or 3 Dec]
1959 Desvigne, Sidney
1971 Miller, Punch
1978 Yoder, Walt [or 3 Dec]
1986 Bascomb, Paul
1998 Burrowes, Roy
1999 Byrd, Charlie

3

born

1902 Thomas, Joe (i)
1903 Gowans, Brad
1907 Boswell, Connee
1908 Salmi, Klaus
1909 Bergh, Øivind
1914 Cornelius, Corky
1915 Kärki, Toivo
1919 Nichols, Herbie
1929 Assunto, Freddie
1935 Manusardi, Guido
1951 Finnerty, Barry

died

1949 Ammons, Albert [or 2 Dec]
1951 Blake, Cyril
1965 D'Amico, Hank
1967 Bocage, Peter
1972 Johnson, Bill (i)
1973 Christian, Emile
1978 Yoder, Walt [or 2 Dec]
1986 Howard, Bob
1989 Shirley, Jimmy
1998 Haggart, Bob

4

born

1904 Autrey, Herman
1915 Heywood, Eddie
1917 Jacquet, Russell
1928 Tiberi, Frank
1930 Hall, Jim
1933 Charles, Dennis
1933 Lamb, John
1940 Carlsson, Rune
1947 LaVerne, Andy
1950 Kjellemyr, Bjørn
1953 Houtkamp, Luc
1954 Moore, Michael (ii)
1955 Wilson, Cassandra
1962 Williams, Tom
1965 Ovesen, Thomas

died

1972 Lastie, Melvin
1983 Landl, Ernst
1991 Tyndale, George
1993 Zappa, Frank
1998 Johansen, Egil
1999 Vesala, Edward

5

born

1906 Johnson, Archie
1912 Royal, Marshal
1915 Fields, Kansas
1920 Davis, Kay
1925 Tyler, Alvin "Red"
1927 Bhumibol Adulyadej
1928 Allen, Gene
1934 Davis, Art
1944 Bukovsky, Mike
1944 Johnson, Oliver
1947 Gismonti, Egberto
1949 Pieranunzi, Enrico
1958 Kitagawa, Kiyoshi
1960 Bromberg, Brian
1960 Labutis, Vytautas
1961 Bergcrantz, Anders

died

1972 Dorham, Kenny
1977 Kirk, Roland
1985 Jackson, Calvin
1990 Hardman, Bill

6

born

1906 Long, Slats
1907 McGrath, Fulton
1910 Hug, Armand
1920 Brubeck, Dave
1925 Cooper, Bob
1927 Miyazawa, Akira
1928 Dunlop, Frankie
1934 Maeda, Norio
1936 Ashton, Bill
1937 Gladden, Eddie
1940 Leonhart, Jay
1947 Beckerhoff, Uli
1947 Vitous, Miroslav
1948 Swartz, Harvie
1954 Swell, Steve
1960 Wissels, Diederik

died

1940 Dixon, Charlie
1958 Alvin, Danny
1988 Harris, Bill (ii)

7

born

1902 Irwin, Cecil
1906 James, George
1909 Hill, Teddy
1911 Prima, Louis
1913 Marshall, Joe
1917 Moore, Billy
1924 Fabricius-Bjerre, Bent
1932 Boykins, Ronnie
1936 Phillips, Sonny
1937 Carr, Mike
1941 Wilmer, Val
1946 Treloar, Phil
1948 Vinding, Mads
1949 Waits, Tom
1955 Loeb, Chuck
1960 Ameen, Robby
1960 Shipp, Matthew
1963 Stankiewicz, Kuba
1965 Haffner, Wolfgang
1968 Akchoté, Noël

died

1967 Casey, Floyd
1999 Baker, Kenny

DECEMBER

8

born

- 1907 or 1909 Brown, Cleo
- 1922 Yaged, Sol
- 1925 Smith, Jimmy
- 1933 Cross, Earl
- 1936 Vuckovich, Larry
- 1952 Rüegg, Mathias
- 1970 Blake, Seamus

died

- 1944 Cless, Rod
- 1945 Jones, Richard M.
- 1958 Lee, Julia
- 1967 Bacon, Louis
- 1974 Panassié, Hugues
- 1984 Culver, Rollie
- 1984 Ramey, Gene
- 1988 Quill, Gene
- 1988 Swanerud, Thore
- 1991 Clayton, Buck
- 1994 Jobim, Antonio Carlos
- 1997 Chisholm, George

9

born

- 1903 Malneck, Matty
- 1906 Rodin, Gil
- 1916 Scobey, Bob
- 1918 West, Cedric
- 1931 Hammond, Johnny [or 16 Dec 1933]
- 1932 Byrd, Donald
- 1939 Allen, Byron
- 1943 Owens, Jimmy
- 1952 Blakeslee, Rob
- 1954 Hanrahan, Kip
- 1954 Rodby, Steve
- 1957 O'Mara, Peter

died

- 1948 Tough, Dave
- 1975 Signorelli, Frank
- 1985 Munro, Charlie
- 1985 See, Cees
- 1993 Jefferson, Carter

10

born

- 1912 Fazola, Irving
- 1913 Nance, Ray
- 1918 Aho, Erkki
- 1927 Tucker, George
- 1932 Cranshaw, Bob
- 1933 Petrowsky, Ernst-Ludwig
- 1936 Boudreaux, John, Jr.
- 1937 Sebesky, Don
- 1937 Trippel, Fritz
- 1939 Pöyry, Pekka
- 1941 Ambrosetti, Franco
- 1941 Lang, Mike
- 1951 Svoboda, Milan
- 1953 Colombo, Eugenio
- 1953 Schuur, Diane
- 1958 Goldsby, John

died

- 1959 Parrish, Avery
- 1984 Teagarden, Charlie
- 1986 Stone, Fred
- 1987 Stewart, Slam

11

born

- 1903 Skjoldborg, Anker
- 1906 Purvis, Jack
- 1920 Johnson, Eddie
- 1923 Markowitz, Marky
- 1938 Tyner, McCoy
- 1961 Jones, Darryl
- 1961 Nolet, Jim
- 1967 Fischer, Jacob
- 1970 McPherson, Eric

died

- 1963 Russell, Luis
- 1965 Barbour, Dave
- 1975 Wiley, Lee
- 1992 Kirk, Andy
- 1994 Connors, Chuck
- 1999 Earland, Charles

12

born

- 1903 Davis, Bert Etta
- 1907 Elizalde, Fred
- 1909 Barefield, Eddie
- 1913 Stovall, Don
- 1915 Sinatra, Frank
- 1918 Williams, Joe
- 1923 Dorough, Bob
- 1925 Lystedt, Lars
- 1925 Marmarosa, Dodo
- 1929 Akiyoshi, Toshiko
- 1935 Aaltonen, Juhani
- 1941 Barone, Gary
- 1943 Washington, Grover, Jr.
- 1944 Acuña, Alex
- 1944 Carvin, Michael
- 1945 Williams, Tony
- 1946 Ditmas, Bruce
- 1950 Galliano, Richard
- 1956 Pardo, Jorge
- 1960 Tramontana, Sebi
- 1961 Murley, Mike
- 1962 Kristiansen, Søren
- 1964 Mondesir, Mark

died

- 1951 Bailey, Mildred
- 1989 Nilson, Gunnar
- 1990 Roberts, Caughey
- 1991 Ross, Ronnie

13

born

- *c*1895 Greer, Sonny
- 1909 Mucci, Lou
- 1913 Thompson, Rudolph
- 1924 Hood, Bill
- 1926 Bergman, Borah
- 1930 Tucker, Ben
- 1940 Johnson, Reggie
- 1947 Findley, Chuck
- 1949 Elf, Mark

died

- 1959 Johnson, Charlie
- 1983 Brown, Marshall
- 1984 Pemberton, Bill

14

born

- 1905 Alston, Ovie
- 1906 Tsfasman, Aleksandr
- 1910 Johnson, Budd
- 1911 Gentry, Chuck
- 1913 Buckner, Ted
- 1917 Davis, Martha
- 1920 Terry, Clark
- 1922 Payne, Cecil
- 1931 Newborn, Phineas
- 1933 Wright, Leo
- 1940 Bergalli, Gustavo
- 1944 Levinovsky, Nikolay
- 1945 Crouch, Stanley
- 1946 Cooper, Jerome
- 1946 Rully, Aura
- 1952 Lurie, John
- 1955 Barrett, Dan
- 1956 Bauer, Stefan

died

- 1963 Washington, Dinah
- 1970 Schoebel, Elmer
- 1975 Feza, Mongezi
- 1981 Jones, Sam [or 15 Dec]
- 1993 Boas, Günter
- 1994 Dougherty, Eddie
- 1994 McCall, Mary Ann

DECEMBER

15

born

1897 Allen, Ed
1910 Hammond, John
1911 Kenton, Stan
1924 Butler, Billy
1925 Nottingham, Jimmy
1927 Quill, Gene
1929 Harris, Barry
1931 Richmond, Dannie
1934 Fuller, Curtis
1936 Palmieri, Eddie
1936 Sadowski, Krzysztof
1948 Kondo, Toshinori
1948 Zingaro, Carlos
1952 Gertz, Bruce

died

1943 Waller, Fats
1944 Miller, Glenn [date uncertain]
1954 Celestin, Papa
1981 Jones, Sam [or 14 Dec]
1982 Hanna, Ken
1983 McLin, Jimmy
1983 Moore, Big Chief
1983 Shapiro, Nat
1984 Beal, Eddie
1990 Guilhot, Claude
1992 Lington, Otto
1995 Lytle, Johnny

16

born

1897 Wilson, Buster [or 18 Aug]
1906 Rasmussen, Peter
1907 Flood, Bernard
1915 Teagarden, Cub
1915 Murphy, Turk
1921 Allen, Steve
1925 Piliso, Ntemi
1930 Most, Sam
1933 Hammond, Johnny [or 9 Dec 1931]
1937 Farrell, Joe
1943 Malfatti, Radu
1944 Abercrombie, John
1946 McLean, Rene
1947 Parran, J. D.
1948 Dvorak, Jim
1951 Ford, Robben
1960 Fahn, Mike
1961 Cottle, Laurence

died

1945 Jenney, Jack
1956 Fulford, Tommy
1969 Mathisen, Leo
1970 Smith, Charles Edward
1978 Calloway, Blanche
1980 Christie, Keith
1983 Miller, Harry

17

born

1885 Mitchell, Louis
1898 Casimir, John
1899 Steele, Joe
1903 Noble, Ray
1910 Henkels, Kurt
1910 Oliver, Sy
1919 Williams, Al
1925 Bolden, Walter
1932 Red, Sonny
1933 Booker, Walter
1933 Ore, John
1941 Zerbe, Hannes
1942 Smith, Sonelius
1944 Ganelin, Vyacheslav
1952 Williams, Buddy
1960 Katori, Yoshihiko
1963 Vann, Erwin

died

1975 Sissle, Noble
1975 Williams, Fess
1975 Wrightsman, Stan [or 18 Dec]
1977 De Weille, Benny
1978 Ellis, Don
1978 Tate, Erskine
1979 Mustafa-Zade, Vagif
1982 Stuart, Kirk
1999 Washington, Grover, Jr.

18

born

1887 Morgan, Sam
1897 Henderson, Fletcher
1907 Lucie, Lawrence
1908 Sanchez Reinoso, Raúl
1917 Vinson, Eddie "Cleanhead"
1919 Galbraith, Barry
1920 Conover, Willis
1923 Reichenbach, Bill (i)
1927 Grove, Dick
1928 Gitler, Ira
1929 Stabulas, Nick
1930 Jones, Al
1932 Heckman, Don
1941 Smith, Wadada Leo
1955 Kochan, Jacek
1956 Ferré, Elios

died

1966 Stearns, Marshall W.
1975 Wrightsman, Stan [or 17 Dec]
1977 Weiss, Sammy
1987 Marsh, Warne
1990 Addison, Bernard
1991 Kolax, King
2000 Piliso, Ntemi

19

born

1895 Tate, Erskine
1911 Watters, Lu
1929 Brookmeyer, Bob
1935 Timmons, Bobby
1937 Leviev, Milcho
1938 Blank, Roger
1938 Strange, Pete
1940 Weller, Don
1949 White, Lenny
1957 Marienthal, Eric
1960 Wilde, Laurent de
1969 Mustafa Zadeh, Aziza

died

1989 Rettenbacher, J. A.
1992 Peagler, Curtis
1994 Douglass, Bill (i)
2000 Hinton, Milt

20

born

1918 Hardee, John
1919 Svensson, Reinhold
1922 Eichenberg, Walter
1924 Domnérus, Arne
1933 Falzone, Sam
1940 Willis, Larry
1942 Levin, Pete
1944 Columby, Bobby

died

1957 Page, Walter

21

born

1918 Francis, Panama
1918 or 1919 Treadwell, George [or 23 Dec]
1920 Brown, Marshall
1920 Diéval, Jack
1921 Freichel, Louis
1924 Reys, Rita
1931 Baker, David
1934 Crawford, Hank
1940 Zappa, Frank
1941 Hicks, John
1945 Brown, Cameron
1951 Blake, Alex
1951 Emery, James
1957 Ottaviano, Roberto

died

1940 Kemp, Hal
1958 Norris, Ray
1989 Laakko, Bruno
1997 Coles, Johnny

DECEMBER

22

born

1901 Polo, Danny
1910 Jones, Reunald
1919 Green, Lil
1927 Ball, Ronnie
1929 Balaban, Red
1932 Takayanagi, Masayuki
1935 Wilson, Joe Lee
1939 Ceroli, Nick
1941 Guérin, Beb
1951 Benbow, Warren
1958 Gambale, Frank
1959 Patitucci, John
1961 Verploegen, Angelo

died

1939 Rainey, Ma
1963 Palmer, Roy
1990 Nay, Joe
1991 Harris, Beaver

23

born

1888 Jackson, Mike
1908 Thomas, Joe (ii)
1918 or 1919 Treadwell, George [or 21 Dec]
1926 Harris, Joe (ii)
1927 Drew, John
1927 James, Pinocchio
1929 Baker, Chet
1933 Morgan, Frank
1936 Ali, Muhammad
1954 Senba, Kiyohiko
1959 Hobgood, Laurence
1961 Bowen, Ralph
1961 Martins, Carlos
1966 Gordon, Jon

died

1958 Foresythe, Reginald
1974 Allen, Walter C.
1994 Mince, Johnny
1996 Scott, Ronnie

24

born

1897 Miller, Punch [or 10 June 1894]
1898 Dodds, Baby
1908 Smith, Jabbo
1910 Nanri, Fumio
1916 Drootin, Al
1919 Coker, Henry
1920 Bartholomew, Dave
1928 Campbell, Jimmy
1931 Bryant, Ray
1931 Takahashi, Tatsuya
1934 Critchinson, John
1936 McGregor, Chris
1937 Rosengren, Bernt
1943 Kriegel, Volker
1944 Shaw, Woody
1952 Ray, Michael
1956 Moore, Ralph

died

1933 Tio, Lorenzo, Jr.

25

born

1878 Cottrell, Louis, Sr.
1886 Ory, Kid
1890 Robinson, Jim
1895 Brunies, Merritt
1903 Friedman, Izzy
1904 Lawson, Harry
1905 Carver, Wayman
1907 Butler, Joe
1907 Calloway, Cab
1908 Gibbs, Eddie
1912 or 1916 Moore, Oscar
1914 Jenkins, Pat
?1914 Safranski, Eddie
1915 Rugolo, Pete
1925 Woods, Chris
1926 Fay, Rick
1927 Andrews, Ernie
1928 Klein, Harry
1932 Sauer, Heinz
1934 Dixon, Ben
1939 Alias, Don
1939 James, Bob
1941 Cuber, Ronnie
1941 Pullen, Don
1959 Barlow, Dale
1959 Ngqawana, Zim

died

1958 Cook, Doc
1972 Bascomb, Dud
1992 Young, David A.
1995 Brom, Gustav

26

born

1900 Roane, Kenneth
1908 Wilson, Quinn
1915 Carlisle, Una Mae
1917 Ballard, Butch
1929 Budwig, Monty
1933 Bean, Billy
1933 De la Rosa, Frank
1942 Hammond, Doug
1944 Dickerson, Dwight
1950 Mandel, Howard
1951 Kerr, Brooks
1951 Scofield, John
1957 Barker, Guy
1957 Bullock, Belden
1957 Fields, Brandon
1957 Pifarély, Dominique
1962 Buck, Tony

died

1951 Berton, Vic
1965 Packay, Peter
1973 Rena, Joseph
1974 Norris, Al
1980 Kelley, Peck
1987 Thompson, Leslie
1996 Valdambrini, Oscar
1998 Grove, Dick

27

born

1888 Foster, Willie
?1889 Johnson, Bunk
1907 Wilcox, Eddie
1916 Frigo, Johnny
1919 Wood, Booty
1925 McLin, Claude
1927 Crow, Bill
1929 Kovács, Gyula
1931 Norris, Walter
1936 Barone, Mike
1945 Altschul, Mike
1949 Monk, T. S.

died

1949 Anderson, Ivie [or 28 Dec]
1962 Saucier, Edgar
1981 Carmichael, Hoagy
1983 Orchard, Frank
1986 Combe, Stuff
2000 McVea, Jack

28

born

1878 Perez, Manuel
1903 Hines, Earl
1906 Compère, René
1909 Ware, Leonard
1912 Mackel, Billy
1915 Klink, Al
1921 Otis, Johnny
1928 Koffman, Moe
1930 Conners, Gene
1934 Cunningham, Bob
1938 Sudhalter, Dick
1940 Smith, Lonnie Liston
1945 Carter, Daniel
1951 Robinson, Janice
1956 Cohn, Joe
1959 Nash, Ted (ii)
1962 Kellock, Brian
1962 Petrucciani, Michel
1962 Z, Rachel

died

1949 Anderson, Ivie [or 27 Dec]
1964 Bowman, Dave
1977 Brown, Sam
1985 Morton, Benny
1991 Johnson, Howard (i)

DECEMBER

29

born

1900 Humphrey, Willie
1905 Mosley, Snub
1911 Cutshall, Cutty
1912 Ehrling, Thore
1931 Konopasek, Jan
1933 Brown, Brian
1938 Watanabe, Fumio
1952 Lovano, Joe
1958 Schuller, George
1965 Pérez, Danilo

died

1945 Stark, Bobby
1952 Henderson, Fletcher
1957 Henry, Ernie
1967 Whiteman, Paul
1972 Alvis, Hayes
1978 Caldwell, Happy
1980 Felix, Lennie

30

born

1890 Creath, Charlie
1909 Mougin, Stéphane
1918 Jones, Jimmy
1923 Motley, Frank
1926 Tracey, Stan
1928 Mayl, Gene
1928 Montrose, Jack
1935 Dauner, Wolfgang
1940 Granelli, Jerry
1958 Nash, Lewis
1965 Vignola, Frank
1966 Affif, Ron
1966 Turner, Matt
1971 Mácha, Stanislav

died

1977 Schwartz, Thornal
1987 Laine, Bob
1993 Rollini, Art
1997 Crawford, Ray
1999 Campbell, Wilbur

31

born

1908 Kirby, John
1909 Jones, Jonah
1914 Haywood, Cedric
1921 Brehm, Simon
1924 Harden, Wilbur
1931 Melle, Gil
1935 Herbolzheimer, Peter
1944 Senensky, Bernie
1951 Haslip, Jimmy
1959 König, Klaus

died

1952 Stitzel, Mel
1968 Lewis, George (i)
1973 Trunk, Peter
1978 Howard, Earle "Nappy"
1991 Patrick, Pat

December (the date unknown)

born

1904 Traill, Sinclair

died

1959 Hemphill, Shelton
1959 Hightower, Willie
1963 Burns, Billy
1981 Filu
1985 Springer, Joe

Appendix 3

LIST OF CONTRIBUTORS

Below are listed all signatories of articles in this dictionary. The entries by each are listed after his/her name; where a title is preceded by an asterisk (*), the contributor concerned is a co-author. The signature "BK" is the dictionary's editor, Barry Kernfeld, and "GK," its associate editor, Gary Kennedy.

Aboucaya, Jacques: Alvim, Cesarius; Amsallem, Franck; Barthélémy, Claude; Cugny, Laurent; De Bethmann, Pierre; Domancich, Sophia; *Galliano, Richard; Graillier, Michel; Labarrière, Hélène; Lourau, Julien; Machado, Jean-Marie; Marais, Gérard; Padovani, Jean-Marc; Pilc, Jean-Michel; Robert, Yves; Théberge, François; Thollot, Jacques; Zulfikarpasic, Bojan

Adams, Simon: Acid jazz; Alperin, Mikhail; *Ambrosetti, Franco; AMM; Ardley, Neil; *Ash, Vic; *Ashton, Bill; *Bahula, Julian; *Bailey, Derek; *Ballamy, Iain; Bates, Django; *Beckett, Harry; *Bennink, Han; Bergman, Borah; Berlin Contemporary Jazz Orchestra; Biscoe, Chris; Brennan, John Wolf; *Brötzmann, Peter; Brüninghaus, Rainer; Burr, Jon; Cadillac (ii); Charig, Marc; *Chilton, John; *Christmann, Günter; *Clare, Alan; *Coe, Tony; *Cohen, Alan; Collier, Graham; Company; Cortez, Jayne; Crombie, Tony; *Dickerson, Walt; Doran, Christy; *Dudek, Gerd; *Elsdon, Alan; *Favre, Pierre; Frith, Fred; Gare, Lou; Gayle, Charles; *Gibbs, Mike; *Globe Unity Orchestra; Golia, Vinny; Goode, Coleridge; *Guy, Barry; *Hampel, Gunter; *hat Hut; *Hawdon, Dickie; *Heckstall-Smith, Dick; Hooker, William; Hunter, Chris; Hyder, Ken; Incus; Ind, Peter; *Jacobsen, Pete; Jazz Centre Society; Jazz Services; Jenkins, Karl; Kaiser, Henry; *Klein, Oscar; *Kowald, Peter; *Kühn, Joachim; Last Exit; Laurence, Chris; Leimgruber, Urs; Lemer, Pete; Leo (ii); Le Sage, Bill; London Jazz Composers Orchestra; *Loose Tubes; *Lovens, Paul; *Lowther, Henry; Lytton, Paul; Maneri, Mat; Marshall, John; Maslak, Keshavan; Material; Mathewson, Ron; Melford, Myra; *Moore, Gerry; Mosaic (i); Music Revelation Ensemble; *Nightclubs and other venues: England (London); Ogun; Peacock, Annette; Perelman, Ivo; *Picard, John; Pine, Courtney; *Priestley, Brian; Reichel, Hans; Ricotti, Frank; *Riley, Howard; ROVA; Russell, Hal; Rutherford, Paul; *Schoof, Manfred; *Scott, Ronnie; *South, Harry; Spontaneous Music Ensemble; *Spring, Bryan; *Stevens, John; Surman, John; *Themen, Art; Tippetts, Julie; *Tracey, Stan; Unit; *Van Hove, Fred; Wachsmann, Phil; Warleigh, Ray; Watts, Trevor; Westbrook, Kate; *Westbrook, Mike; Weston, Veryan; *Winters, Tiny

Allen, Richard B.: Jackson, Preston

Anderson, William E.: *Nightclubs and other venues: USA (Cleveland)

Ashforth, Alden: Barrett, Sweet Emma; *Bigard family; Cagnolatti, Cag; Desvigne, Sidney; *Frazier, Cié; Handy, Capt. John; Howard, Kid; Johnson, Bill (i); Lewis, George (i); Pavageau, Alcide "Slow Drag"; *Pichon, Fats; *Piron, A. J.; Rena, Kid; Robinson, Jim; *Tio family

Ayala, Cristóbal Díaz: Caunedo, Jesús; *Bauzá, Mario; *Irakere; *O'Farrill, Chico; *Sandoval, Arturo; *Valdés, Chucho

Bacon, Tony: *Electric bass guitar; *Guitar

Baggenaes, Roland: *Bailey, Benny; Blackburn, Lou; Clarke–Boland Big Band; *Hampton, Slide; Jaspar, Bobby; Lundgaard, Jesper; Martinez, Sabu; *Shihab, Sahib; *Spaulding, James; *Sulieman, Idrees

Ballantine, Christopher: Jazz Maniacs; Manhattan Brothers; Merry Blackbirds

Barbera, André: *Albany, Joe; Burns, Dave; *Christy, June; *Coles, Johnny; Connor, Chris; *Copeland, Ray; *Drew, Kenny; *Freeman, Russ (i); *Hardman, Bill; *Levy, Lou

Barker, Danny: Hamfat

Barnett, Anthony: *Asmussen, Svend; *Cello; Crouch, Stanley; Smock, Ginger; *South, Eddie; *Violin

Barrell, Alan: *Alcorn, Alvin; Baquet, Achille; Baquet, George; *Collins, Lee

Bash, Lee: *International Association of Jazz Educators

Beck, Frederick A.: Battle, Edgar; *Brashear, Oscar; *Bridgewater, Cecil; *Candoli, Conte; *Candoli, Pete; Collins, Burt; Dedrick, Rusty; Eardley, Jon; Fagerquist, Don; Harden, Wilbur; *Henderson, Eddie; Hillyer, Lonnie; *Johnson, Money; Moore, Danny; *Owens, Jimmy; *Porcino, Al; *Rader, Don; Travis, Nick; *Wilson, Gerald; *Wright family

Belichenko, Sergey: Butman, Igor; Dmitriev, Igor; Dvoskin, Victor; Fine, Grigory; Gayvoronsky, Vyacheslav; *Goloshchokin, David; Kondakov, Andrei; Labutis, Vytautas; Molokoedov, Oleg; Okoun, Mikhail; Panov, Nikolay; Sadykhov, Vagif; Shilkloper, Arkady; Tolkachev, Vladimir; Vintskevich, Leonid

Bemis, Ed *Dearie, Blossom; *McRae, Carmen

Bennett, Bill: *Davis, Richard; *Dawson, Alan; *Taylor, Billy (ii)

Berendt, Joachim E.: *Dauner, Wolfgang; *Kühn, Rolf

Berger, Edward: Carter, Benny; *Discography; *Edison, Harry; Hammond, John; Institute of Jazz Studies

Bergh, Johs: Arnesen, Dag; Balke, Jon; Brazz Brothers; Dalseth, Laila; Endresen, Sidsel; *Johansen, Bjørn; Johansen, Egil; Kjellemyr, Bjørn; Larsen, Morten Gunnar; Nerem, Bjarne; *Nightclubs and other venues: Norway; Norsk Jazzforum (i); Norsk Jazzforum (ii); Riisnæs, Knut; Storaas, Vigleik; Toneff, Radka

Bernardo, Leonard: Belichenko, Sergey

Berresford, Mark: Arnold, Billy; *Sweatman, Wilbur

Bevan, Clifford: *Cornet; Flugelhorn; Horn; Marimba; Mellophone; Multiphonics; *Mute; Saxhorn; Trombone; Trumpet; Tuba; Vibraphone; Xylophone

Blake, Ran: *Monk, Thelonious

Blumenthal, Bob: *Nightclubs and other venues: USA (Boston metropolitan area)

Bonoff, Edward L.: *Grimes, Tiny

Boulton, Heidi: *Beckerhoff, Uli; *Doldinger, Klaus; Freund, Joki; Greger, Max; *Kriegel, Volker; Mangelsdorff, Emil; *Naura, Michael; Rediske, Johannes

Boyd, Herb: *Nightclubs and other venues: USA (Detroit)

Boyer, H. C.: *Gospel

Boziwick, George: *Libraries and archives

Braman, Chuck: *Chancler, Ndugu; *Erskine, Peter; *Gadd, Steve; *Motian, Paul; *Muhammad, Idris; *Washington, Kenny

Britt, Stan: *Beck, Gordon; *Carr, Ian; *Carr, Mike; *Clyne, Jeff; *Dillard, Bill; *Drew, Martin; *Gaillard, Slim; *Hiseman, Jon; *King, Peter; *Morgan, Lanny; *Morrissey, Dick; *Mullen, Jim; Rose, Denis; *Thompson, Barbara; *Wilkins, Ernie

Brockman, William S.: *Domanico, Chuck;*Friesen, David; *Gaskin, Vic; *Hughart, Jim; Lee, John; Magnusson, Bob; *Moore, Michael (i); *Richmond, Mike; *Sproles, Victor; *Swartz, Harvie; *Warren, Peter

Brodowski, Pawel: *Matuszkiewicz, Jerzy; *Śmietana, Jarosław

Brown, T. Dennis: *Alvin, Danny; Barcelona, Danny; *Bauduc, Ray; Berton, Vic; *Crawford, Jimmy; *Drootin, Buzzy; Drum set; *Fatool, Nick; *Feld, Morey; *Fields, Kansas; *Francis, Panama; *Hall, Minor; *Hall, Tubby; *Johnson, Manzie; *Johnson, Walter; *Marshall, Kaiser; *Morehouse, Chauncey; Rudiments; *Sbarbaro, Tony; *Spencer, O'Neill; *Trappier, Traps

Brubeck, Darius: Galeta, Hotep Idris; Gwangwa, Jonas; Kwela, Allen; Mahlangu, Khaya; Makasi, Duke; Mbambisa, Tete; Mekoa, Johnny; Mrubata, McCoy; Ndlazilwana, Victor; Ngcukana, Ezra; Ngqawana, Zim; Nkosi, Zacks; Ntoni, Victor; Rachabane, Barney; Tabane, Philip

Brunner, Gerhard: *Gulda, Friedrich

Brylawski, Samuel S.: *Mercer, Johnny; Robinson, Bill

Büchmann-Møller, Frank: Bak, Frans; Bentzon, Nikolaj; Besiakov, Ben; Bolberg Pedersen, Henrik; *Botschinsky, Allan; *Clausen, Thomas; Dahl, Carsten; Debut (ii); *Dørge, Pierre; *Emborg, Jørgen; Fischer, Jacob; Franck, Tomas; Fryland, Thomas; Ginman, Lennart; *Glindemann, Ib; *Jaedig, Bent; Johansen, Jonas; Kaspersen, Jan; Kristiansen, Søren; *Kroner, Erling; Lundin, Fredrik; Markussen, Uffe; *Mazur, Marilyn; *Mikkelborg, Palle; Møller, Lars; *Nightclubs and other venues: Denmark; Norby, Cæcilie; Nørregaard, Svend-Erik; *Ørsted Pedersen, Niels-Henning; Ovesen, Thomas; *Radioens Big Band; Raney, Doug; *Riel, Alex; Rockwell, Bob; *Savery, Finn; Schiöpffe, William; *Stief, Bo; Tanggaard, Aage; *Tchicai, John; Thilo, Jesper; *Vinding, Mads; Winther, Jens

Budds, Michael J.: *Hirt, Al; *Schifrin, Lalo; *Tormé, Mel; *Wilson, Nancy

Bushard, Anthony: *Nightclubs and other venues: USA (Kansas City)

Büttner, Armin: Alpine Jazz Herd; *Archia, Tom; Blöchlinger, Urs; *Coe, Jimmy; Kennel, Hans; Koch, Hans; *Johnson, Eddie; Lüdi, Werner; McLin, Claude; *Mallard, Oett; OM; *Schärli, Peter; Washington, Leon; Wittwer, Stephan

Campbell, Robert L.: *Archia, Tom; *Bennett, Bustere; *Coe, Jimmy; *Johnson, Eddie; *Mallard, Oett

Carner, Gary: *Alemán, Oscar; *Ashby, Irving; *Beck, Joe; *Brignola, Nick; *Cook, Junior; Davis, Steve (i); *Gales, Larry; *Puma, Joe; *Williams, Leroy; *Wright, Leo

Cegielski, Adam: *Auguścik, Grażyna; *Bartkowski, Czesław; *Bem, Ewa; *Cudzich, Andrzej; *Herdzin, Krzysztof; *Hołownia, Bogdan; *Jagodziński, Andrej; *Jaremko, Zbigniew; *Jonkisz, Kazimierz; *Karolak, Wojciech; *Kochan, Jacek; *Kurylewicz, Andrzej; *Majewski, Henryk; *Maseli, Bernhard; *Matuszkiewicz, Jerzy; *Miśkiewicz, Henryk; *Możdżer, Leszek; *Nagórski, Grzegorz; *Nahorny, Włodzimierz; *Namysłowski, Zbigniew; *Pawlik, Włodek; *Popek, Krzystof; *Rodowicz, Piotr; *Sadowski, Krzysztof; *Ścierański, Krzysztof; *Sikala, Maciej; *Skowron, Janusz; *Stankiewicz, Kuba; *Strzelczyk, Maciej; *Suchanek, Bronisław; *Szafran, Lora; *Szukalski, Tomasz; *Trzaskowski, Andrzej; *Walk Away; *Wasilewski, Marcin; *Wojtasik, Piotr; *Wróblewski, Jan; *Zabiegliński, Janusz

Chilton, John: *Bailey, Buster; *Bostic, Earl; Boswell, Connee; *Bradford, Perry; *Brown, Pete; *Celestin, Papa; *Cheatham, Doc; *Clayton, Buck; *Cole, Cozy; *Crosby, Bob; *Davison, Wild Bill; *Dickenson, Vic; Dutrey, Honore; *Foster, Pops; *Greer, Sonny; *Hackett, Bobby; *Hamilton, Jimmy; *Harris, Bill (i); Harrison, Jimmy; *Hinton, Milt; Jackson, Tony; James, Harry; Laine, Papa Jack; McKinney's Cotton Pickers; *Marable, Fate; *Mezzrow, Mezz; *Morton, Benny; *Murphy, Turk; New Orleans Rhythm Kings; Original Dixieland Jazz Band; *Page, Hot Lips; *Petit, Buddy; *Picou, Alphonse; *Rollini, Adrian; *Shavers, Charlie; Simmen, Johnny; *Smith, Joe; *Tio family; *Trumbauer, Frankie

Clergeat, André: Aebi, Irene; Akchoté, Noël; Artero, Patrick; Attenoux, Michel; Avenel, Jean-Jacques; *Badini, Gérard; Baudoin, Philippe; Belmondo, Lionel; Belmondo, Stéphane; Benita, Michel; Beuf, Sylvain; Bex, Emmanuel; Bolling, Claude; Bolognesi, Jacques; Bottlang, René; Bourde, Hervé; Boussaguet, Pierre; Bramerie, Thomas; Caratini, Patrice; Caumont, Elisabeth; Ceccarelli, André; Céléa, Jean-Paul; Courtois, Vincent; Delaunay, Charles; Del Fra, Riccardo; Deschepper, Philippe; Ducret, Marc; Eliez, Thierry; Few, Bobby; *Fol, Hubert; *Fol, Raymond; Fosset, Marc; Garros, Christian; *Gilson, Jef; Godard, Michel; Hemmeler, Marc; Herr, Michel; Hervé, Antoine; Hodeir, André; *Humair, Daniel; Hutman, Olivier; Irakli; Jean-Marie, Alain; *Jenny-Clark, Jean-François; Johnson, Oliver; Kassap, Sylvain; *Lafitte, Guy; Lazro, Daunik; Legrand, Michel; Leloup, Denis; Linx, David; *Lockwood, Didier; *Louiss, Eddy; Loussier, Jacques; *Michelot, Pierre; *Nightclubs and other venues: France; Orchestre National de Jazz; Panassié, Hugues; Pedersen, Guy; Potts, Steve; Quintette du Hot Club de France; *Reinhardt family; *Renaud, Henri; Rocheman, Manuel; *Romano, Aldo; Saury, Maxim; Seffer, Yoch'ko; *Silva, Alan; *Solal, Martial; Tissendier, Claude; Tuxedo Big Band; Urban Sax; *Urtreger, René; Vasseur, Benny; *Viale, Jean-Louis; Villéger, André; Wilde, Laurent de; Wissels, Diederik

Cogswell, Michael: Armstrong, Louis

Coller, Derek: Collie, Max; Donegan, Lonnie; Fairweather, Al; *Halcox, Pat; *Lightfoot, Terry; *Rimington, Sammy; *Smith, Keith; Webb, George

Collier, James Lincoln: Bands; *Barnet, Charlie; *Bechet, Sidney; Dixieland; *Dorsey, Jimmy; *Dorsey, Tommy; Grofé, Ferde; *Hall family; *Henderson, Fletcher; *Higginbotham, J. C.; *Holiday, Billie; Jazz (i).; Mainstream jazz; *Miller, Glenn; *Raeburn, Boyd; Tailgate; *Teagarden family; *Wells, Dicky

Collins, Catherine: *Acuña, Alex; *Barbieri, Gato; Camero, Candido; *Castro-Neves, Oscar; *Clarke, Stanley; *D'Rivera, Paquito; *Farrell, Joe; *Gismonti, Egberto; MacDonald, Ralph; Valdez, Carlos "Patato"

Collinson, John: Blythe, Jimmy; Ewell, Don

Conrad, Gerhard: Antritter, Dieter; Barrelhouse Jazzband; Behounek, Kamil; Boas, Günter; Brom, Gustav; Déczi, Ladislav; Dobschinski, Walter; Droste, Silvia; Eichenberg, Walter; Essen, Reimer von; Gerhard, Siggi; Habart, Ladislav; Hála, Kamil; Havlik, Ferdinand; Hnilička, Jaromír; Hulan, Ludek; Ježek, Jaroslav; Kavka, Arnošt; *Konopasek, Jan; Krautgartner, Karel; Kretzschmar, Heinz; Ludvik, Emil; Nagel-Heyer; RBT-Orchester; *Richards, Trevor; Schneider, Hawe; Šima, Jan; Smetaček, Pavel; Velebný, Karel; Vlach, Karel; Wolf, Thilo; Wrobel, Engelbert; Wulf, Joe

Cook, Eddie: *Cobb, Arnett; *Hucko, Peanuts; *Jacquet, Illinois; *Jacquet, Russell; *Johnson, Budd; *Klink, Al; *Person, Houston; *Tate, Buddy

Cooper, Jeffrey: Caceres, Ernie; *Douglas, Tommy; *Fazola, Irving; Hutchenrider, Clarence; Mince, Johnny; Yaged, Sol

Cooper, Reg: *Chisholm, George; Kral, Irene; *Kral, Roy; *McCall, Mary Ann; Roche, Betty; *Ross, Annie; Sherrill, Joya; *Turner, Bruce; *Waters, Benny

Cowley, John: *Appleton, Joe; *Blake, Cyril; *Hutchinson, Jiver; *King, Bertie; *Johnson, Ken "Snake Hips"

Cox, Kenn: *Nightclubs and other venues: USA (Detroit)

Crawford, Richard: *McKenna, Dave

Curry, John: Abdul-Malik, Ahmed; Booker, Walter; Brown, Cameron; Hammer-on; Houston, Clint; Lombardi, Clyde; Lucas, Al; Maize, Bob; May, Earl; Merritt, Jymie; Mitchell, Red; Mitchell, Whitey; Parham, Truck; Pemberton, Bill; Pull-off; Raglin, Junior; Ruther, Wyatt; Warren, Butch; *Ware, Wilbur; Williams, Buster

Daniel, Oliver: Overton, Hall

Dapogny, James: *Beiderbecke, Bix; *Berigan, Bunny; *Freeman, Bud; *Hines, Earl; *Lang, Eddie; Livingston, Fud; *Mole, Miff; *Nichols, Red; *Rushing, Jimmy; *Russell, Pee Wee; Schoebel, Elmer; Wallace, Sippie

Darke, Peter: Solomon, Reuben; West, Cedric

Davies, Hugh: *Synthesizer

Dean, Roger T.: Ambarchi, Oren; *Bailey, Derek; *Bailey, Judy; *Banks, Don; *Beckett, Harry; *Bell, Graeme; *Brokensha, Jack; Bronson, Eddie; Buck, Tony; *Buddle, Errol; Bukovsky, Mike; Bull, Geoff; *Burrows, Don; Cale, Bruce; Computers; *Dallwitz, Dave; Denley, Jim; *Dickerson, Walt; Ermoll, Serge; Evans, Sandy; Frampton, Roger; Furniss, Paul; *Golla, George; Grabowsky, Paul; *Guy, Barry; *Hampel, Gunter; Hopkins, Tim; Hounslow, Keith; *Kühn, Joachim; Lane, Joe; MacRae, Dave; *Munro, Charlie; Naughton, Bobby; *Nock, Mike; Pochee, John; *Price, Ray; *Rohde, Bryce; *Sangster, John; Simmonds, Mark; *Speers, Stewie; Tinkler, Scott; Tolley, David; *Turnbull, Alan

Deffaa, Chip: Beckett, Fred; Coker, Henry; Gee, Matthew; *Hamilton, Scott; *Igoe, Sonny; Johnson, Charlie; *Napoleon family; Tarto, Joe; *Vaché, Warren; Williams, *Johnny (i)

de Ledesma, Charles: *Bahula, Julian; *Dyani, Johnny; *Feza, Mongezi; *McGregor, Chris; *Masekela, Hugh; *Miller, Harry; *Moholo, Louis; *Pukwana, Dudu

DeVeaux, Scott: *Adderley, Nat; *Best, Skeeter; *Boyd, Nelson; *Collins, Rudy; Farmer, Addison; *Foster, Frank; *Gaskin, Leonard; *Green(e), Freddie; *Greenlee, Charles; *Guy, Joe; *Harris, Joe (ii); *McGhee, Howard; *Mills, Jackie; Parker, Leo; *Potter, Tommy; *Rumsey, Howard; *Russell, Curly; *Sears, Al; *Thompson, Sir Charles; *Wayne, Chuck

Dibussolo, Frank A.: *Bertoncini, Gene; *Szabó, Gábor

Dickow, Robert: Barone, Gary; *Barone, Mike; *Blanchard, Terence; *Bryant, Bobby; *Ellis, Don; *Faddis, Jon; *Ferris, Glenn; *Harrell, Tom; *Henderson, Wayne; Noto, Sam

Dobbins, Bill: *Brackeen, JoAnne; *Cole, Nat "King"; *Corea, Chick; *Flanagan, Tommy; *Garland, Red; *Hancock, Herbie; *Hanna, Sir Roland; *Harris, Barry; *Hart, Clyde; *Hopkins, Claude; *Jarrett, Keith; *Jones family; *Kelly, Wynton; *Peterson, Oscar; *Rivers, Sam; *Shearing, George; *Silver, Horace; *Smith, Jimmy; *Smith, Willie "the Lion"; *Stacy, Jess; *Taylor, Cecil; *Tyner, McCoy; *Waller, Fats

Doerschuk, Robert L.: *Kirkland, Kenny; *Mance, Junior; *Marmarosa, Dodo; Miles, Barry; *Nock, Mike; *Ozone, Makoto; *Petrucciani, Michel; *Rowles, Jimmie; *Strazzeri, Frank; *Waldron, Mal; *Zeitlin, Denny

Donozo, Leandro: *Navarro, Jorge

Donzallaz, Jacques: *Combe, Stuff

Doran, James M.: Bowman, Dave; *Bushkin, Joe; Calhoun, Eddie; Chittison, Herman "Ivory"; *Duncan, Hank; Hill, Alex; *Jackson, Cliff; Jaffe, Nat; *Johnson, Pete; *Jones, Jimmy; *Jones, Richard M.; *Kerr, Brooks; *Richards, Red; Ross, Arnold; *Schroeder, Gene; *Signorelli, Frank; *Simmons, Norman; Weatherford, Teddy; *Wein, George; *White, Sonny; Williams, Al

Driggs, Frank: Bascomb, Dud; Bascomb, Paul; *Blakeney, Andy; Cab Jivers; Chocolate Dandies; Dash, Julian; Douglas, Billy; Gibson, Andy; Holland, Peanuts; *Howard, Paul; Jeter–Pillars Orchestra; Jones–Smith, Inc.; *Jordan, Louis; Kansas City Rockets; Kansas City Six; *Lee, George E.; *Lee, Julia; *Leonard, Harlan; Lewis, Ed; *Lewis, Willie; Little Chicks; *McShann, Jay; *Millinder, Lucky; Missourians; Palmer, Singleton; *Randolph, Irving "Mouse"; *Robinson, Prince; Sampson, Edgar; *Smith, Tab; Spirits of Rhythm; Stovall, Don; *Thomas, Joe (iii); *Thomas, Joe (iv); Washington, Jack; Wilson, Dick; *Wooding, Sam

Duarte, José: Barretto, Carlos; Bica, Carlos; Eduardo, Zé; Filipe, Laurent; João, Maria; Laginha, Mário; Martins, Carlos; Moreira, Bernardo; Moreira, Pedro; *Nightclubs and other venues: Portugal; Paulo, João; Sassetti, Bernardo

Edfeldt, Åke: *Nightclubs and other venues: Sweden

Fairweather, Digby: *Ambrose, Bert; *Ash, Vic; *Ashton, Bill; *Ballamy, Iain; *Barber, Chris; *Chilton, John; *Clare, Alan; *Coe, Tony; *Cohen, Alan; *Cotton, Mike; *Dankworth family; *Davies, John R. T.; Downes, Bob; *Ellington, Ray; *Elsdon, Alan; *Fallon, Jack; *Fierstone, George; *Galbraith, Charlie; Galbraith, Gus; *Gay, Al; *Gibbs, Mike; *Graham, Kenny; *Greig, Stan; *Hawdon, Dickie; *Heckstall-Smith, Dick; Heralds of Swing; *Hogg, Derek; *Hughes, Spike; Hylton, Jack; *Ingham, Keith; *Jacobsen, Pete; *Klein, Harry; *Korner, Alexis; Lee, Tony; *Lemon, Brian; *Loose Tubes; *Lowther, Henry; *Lyttelton, Humphrey; *Montgomery, Marian; *Moore, Gerry; Mulligan, Mick; Munn, Billy; *Picard, John; *Priestley, Brian; *Seamen, Phil; *Scott, Ronnie; *Smith, Brian; *South, Harry; *Spring, Bryan; *Temperley, Joe; *Themen, Art; *Thompson, Eddie; *Tracey, Stan; Warren, John; *Westbrook, Mike; Whittle, Tommy; *Winters, Tiny

Feather, Leonard: *Singing

Feinstein, Sascha: Poetry

Ferguson, Jim: *Bauer, Billy; *Breau, Lenny; *Collins, John; *Diorio, Joe; *Electric bass guitar; *Ellis, Herb; Galbraith, Barry; *Guitar; *Hall, Jim; *Holdsworth, Allan; *Jordan, Stanley; *Lagrene, Bireli; Nichols, Jim; *Palmier, Remo; Quinn, Snoozer; *Remler, Emily; *Reuss, Allan; *Roberts, Howard

Ferko, Josh: *Films; *Hammond, Johnny; *Jackson, Willis "Gator"; *Kynard, Charles; *Landers, Wes; *McGriff, Jimmy; *Patterson, Don; *Red, Sonny; *Scott, Shirley; *Sparks, Melvin

Fernández, Laureano: *Boiarsky, Andrés; *Franzetti, Carlos; *López Fürst, Rubén; *López Ruiz, Jorge; *Navarro, Jorge; *Oliva, Hernán; *Porteña Jazz Band; *Remus, Alfredo; *Saluzzi, Dino; *Sanchez Reinoso, Raúl; *Santa Paula Serenaders; *Trío Argentina; *Villegas, Enrique

Finlay, Rick: *Berimbau; *Cuíca; Darabukka; Ganzá; *Notation; Salsa; Straight; Time (i)

Flanagan, David: *Asmussen, Svend; *Bang, Billy; Byers, Billy; *Byrd, Charlie; Carver, Wayman; Dennis, Matt; *Finegan, Bill; *Garland, Joe; *Jackson, Chubby; *Jobim, Antonio Carlos; *Kincaide, Deane; Lamare, Nappy; *Lucie, Lawrence; *Mastren, Carmen; McIntosh, Tom; Marrero, Lawrence; *Scott, Bud; *Steig, Jeremy; White, Michael (i); *Zoller, Attila

Flückiger, Otto: *Ambrosetti, Flavio; Bertschy, René; Brooke, Eric; Cavalli, Pierre; *Combe, Stuff; Droz, Raymond; Gill, Elmer; Klein, Miriam; *Moeckel, Thomas; *Paque, Glyn; Prina, Curt; Spörri, Bruno; Strittmatter, Mac; Suter, Robert; Townsend, Bross; Weber, Reto; Weil, Kurt

Fox, Charles: *Barber, Chris; *Dankworth family; *Foresythe, Reginald; *Gibbs, Mike; *Lyttelton, Humphrey; *Scott, Ronnie; *Tracey, Stan; *Westbrook, Mike

Franklin, David: *Wallace, Bennie

Frederickson, Scott: *Anderson, Ivie; *Bey, Andy; Boone, Richard; *Bridgewater, Dee Dee; *Bryson, Jeanie; *Christi, Ellen; Franks, Michael; *Freelon, Nnenna; Goodman, Gabrielle; *Hall, Adelaide; *Harrow, Nancy; Hibbler, Al; *Hirsch, Shelley; *Lee, Peggy; *McCorkle, Susannah; *Marsh, Tina; *Newton, Lauren; *Rawls, Lou; *Reeves, Diane; *Rubin, Vanessa; *Schuur, Diane; *Troup, Bobby; *Vitro, Roseanna; Ward, Helen

Freeland, Tom: *Newborn, Calvin

Gabbard, Krin: Canon; *Films; "Jazz": etymology

Gagnon, Yves: *Boland, Francy

Gammel, Marcus: Bauer, Johannes; *Beckerhoff, Uli; Delbecq, Benoît; *Doldinger, Klaus; Fuchs, Wolfgang; Jörgensmann, Theo; Kölner Saxophon Mafia; Kreusch, Cornelius Claudio; *Kriegel, Volker; Micus,Stephan; Nabatov, Simon; Namtchylak, Sainkho; Schnyder, Daniel; Winterschladen, Reiner

Gannon, Robert: James, Michael; *McRae, Barry; Morgan, Alun; Oliver, Paul; Rust, Brian; Traill, Sinclair; *Wilmer, Val

García-Brunelli, Omar: *Boiarsky, Andrés; *Franzetti, Carlos; *López Fürst, Rubén; *López Ruiz, Jorge; *Navarro, Jorge; *Oliva, Hernán; *Porteña Jazz Band; *Remus, Alfredo; *Saluzzi, Dino; *Sanchez Reinoso, Raúl; *Santa Paula Serenaders; *Trío Argentina; *Villegas, Enrique

Gardner, Mark: Argo; Atco; Ava; Bakton; Bee Hive; Bethlehem; Black Jazz; Charlie Parker Records; *Christlieb, Pete; *Cleveland, Jimmy; Cobblestone; Contact; *Contemporary; *Criss Cross Jazz; Dauntless; *Davis, Charles; Dial; *DiNovi, Gene; *Discovery; East: West; Epic; *Ervin, Booker; *ESP-disk; *Foster, Gary; *Fresh Sound; Galaxy; *GNP-Crescendo; Green, Bennie; Guild; *Hayes, Tubby; Hep; Hifijazz; *Hogan, G. T.; IAJRC (i); Imperial; *Impulse!; Jaro; Jazzline (i); Jazz West; *Jones, Carmell; *Jordan, Clifford; Judson; Kahn, Tiny; Klacto; *Knepper, Jimmy; *Kotick, Teddy; *Land, Harold; *Little, Wilbur; Macero, Teo; *Mariano, Charlie; Metrojazz; Mettome, Doug; Mole; *Moody, James; Morrow, George; Musicraft; *Onyx (ii); *Pacific Jazz; Peacock's Progressive Jazz; Phoenix Jazz; Pleasure, King; Progressive; Regina; *Reprise; Revelation; *Richardson, Jerome; *Rosolino, Frank; *Sackville; Scepter; 77; *Signal; *Spotlite (ii); Storyville (ii); Time (ii); Transition; *Turrentine, Tommy; United Artists; Vault; Warwick; Wave; *Williamson, Claude; *Wilson, Shadow; *Workman, Reggie; *World Wide; *Wyands, Richard; *Xanadu

Gariglio, Raymond J.: Arodin, Sidney; *Bilk, Acker; *Bivona, Gus; Browne, Scoville; *Bushell, Garvin; Caldwell, Happy; *Cless, Rod; D'Amico, Hank; *De Faut, Volly; *Dixon, Joe; *Fountain, Pete; Inge, Edward; Jackson, Rudy; *Lytell, Jimmy; McCracken, Bob; *Muranyi, Joe; *Nelson, Big Eye; *Parenti, Tony; *Polo, Danny; Rodin, Gil

Gelly, Dave: *Auld, Georgie; *Coker, Jerry; *Hafer, Dick; *Lanphere, Don; Marsh, Arno; Mosse, Sandy; *Steward, Herbie

Gentieu, Norman P.: *Sullivan, Joe; *Sutton, Ralph

Gilbert, Mark: Akagi, Kei; *Allen, Geri; Andrews, Jeff; Argüelles, Julian; Argüelles, Steve; Bailey, Victor; Barker, Guy; Barlow, Dale; Barnes, Alan; Beard, Jim; Belden, Bob; Benoit, David; Berg, Bob; *Berg, Thilo; Bergonzi, Jerry; Berlin, Jeff; Bickford, Bill; Bollenback, Paul; Bourelly, Jean-Paul; Breakstone, Joshua; Breaux, Zachary; Brechtlein, Tom; Brisker, Gordon; Brooks, Cecil, III; Broom, Bobby; Brown, Dean; Brown, Norman; Bruce, Jack; Bruno, Jimmy; Bullock, Hiram; Burnap, Campbell; Byron, Don; Caine, Uri; Calderazzo, Gene; Calderazzo, Joey; Cárdenas, Steve; Carlsson, Rune; Carrington, Terri Lyne; Chambers, Dennis; Clarvis, Paul; Clausen, Bent; Cliff, Dave; *Coltrane family; Coster, Tom; Cottle, Laurence; Cox, Anthony; Coxhill, Lol; Crawford, Hank; Creese, Malcolm; Critchinson, John; *Dankworth family; Dean, Elton; Dee, Brian; DeFrancesco, Joey; Dennard, Kenwood; Dennerlein, Barbara; *Digital delay; Disco; Doky, Christian Minh; Doky, Niels Lan; Drew, Kenny, Jr.; Dulfer, Hans; Dunmall, Paul; *Dvorak, Jim; Epstein, Peter; Erquiaga, Steve; Escoudé, Christian; Etheridge, John; *Evans, Bill (iii); Feldman, Lawrence; Ferrante, Russell; Ferré, Boulou; Ferré, Elios; Ferrell, Rachelle; *Findley, Chuck; Finnerty, Barry; Fiuczynski, David; Fleck, Béla; Ford, Robben; France, Martin; Froman, Ian; Gambale, Frank; Garland, Tim; *Garrett, Kenny; Garrick, Michael; Garrison, Matthew; Garzone, George; Genus, James; Gewelt, Terje; Gilmore, David; Goines, Lincoln; Goldings, Larry; Goldstein, Gil; Grainger, Gary; Grey, Carola; Grolnick, Don; Grusin, Don; Haerter, Harald; Hammond, Doug; Haque, Fareed; Hargrove, Roy; Harris, Eddie; Hart, John; Haslam, George; Haslip, Jimmy; Hassell, Jon; Hawes, Pat; Haynes, Graham; Hellborg, Jonas; Henderson, Scott; Herwig, Conrad; Hip hop; Hitchcock, Nigel; Hofseth, Bendik; Holloway, Laurie; Holzman, Adam; Honing, Yuri; *Honsinger, Tristan; Horler, David; Horler, John; Houmark, Karsten; Howard, Ed; Hutton, Mick; Ilg, Dieter; Isham, Mark; Itchy Fingers; Jackson, Anthony; Jacob, Christian; Jansson, Lars; Jazz-rock; Jenkins, Billy; Johnson, Jimmy; Johnson, Marc; Jones, Darryl; Jones, Leroy; Jordan, Ronny; Jordan, Steve (ii); Jormin, Anders; Joseph, Julian; Kellock, Brian; Keogh, Stephen; Kerr, Anthony; Kikoski, Dave; Kilson, Billy; Krantz, Wayne; Lamb, Bobby; Landers, Tim; Laswell, Bill; Lê, Nguyên; Lee, Phil; Levin, Pete; Levin, Tony; Ligado; Locke, Joe; Lockett, Mornington; Lockheart, Mark; Loeb, Chuck; Lusher, Don; *Lynch, Brian; Mairants, Ivor; Malach, Bob; Margitza, Rick; Marienthal, Eric; Masqualero; *M-Base; Meurkens, Hendrik; Milder, Joakim; Minton, Phil; Mintzer, Bob; *Moffett family; Molvaer, Nils Petter; Morrison, James; Mseleku, Bheki; Mustafa Zadeh, Aziza; Muthspiel, Wolfgang; Mwendo Dawa; Newton, David; Nicols, Maggie; Nightingale, Mark; Novak, Gary; O'Higgins, Dave; Osborne, Mike; Osby,Greg; Oxley, Tony; *Ozone, Makoto; Parker, Evan; Parker, Leon; Parricelli, John; Patitucci, John; Paz; Pearce, Dick; Pifarély, Dominique; Porter, Art; Powell, Roy; Presencer, Gerard; Prévost, Eddie; Race, Steve; Rap; Rasmussen, Hugo; Ratzer, Karl; Rebello, Jason; Reggae; Rendell, Don; Robinson, Orphy; Robinson, Spike; Rogers, Paul; Rosenberg, Stochelo; Rosenwinkel, Kurt; Ross, Ronnie; Saberton, Pete; Sclavis, Louis; Scofield, John; Sewing, Jack; Sharpe, Jack; Shepherd, Dave; Shepik, Brad; Sheppard, Bob; Ska; Skidmore, Alan; Slinger, Cees; Smith, Tommy; Smooth jazz; Soft Machine; Speake, Martin; *Spotlite (ii); Stenfalt, Norman; Stephenson, Ronnie; Stern, Leni; Stewart, Louis; Stewart, Michael "Patches"; Stockhausen, Markus; Stryker, Dave; Sulzmann, Stan; Swift, Duncan; *Synthesizer; Talbot, Jamie; Tavaglione, Steve; Taylor, Martin; Thomas, Gary; Thompson, Danny; Thompson, Gail; Tippett, Keith; Torn, David; Tracey, Clark; Tribal Tech; Tropea, John; Tunnell, Jimi; Van de Geyn, Hein; van den Broeck, Rob; Wakenius, Ulf; Walker, Mike; Wall, Dan; Watkins, Derek; Watkins, Mitch; Weckl, Dave; Weinert, Susan; Weller, Don; Wells, Spike; Whitfield, Mark; Wilczewski, David; Williamson, Steve; Willis, Gary; Wollesen, Kenny; Worth, Bobby; Yellowjackets; Z, Rachel

Gillaspie, Deborah: Braugham, Charlie; Campbell, Wilbur; Frigo, Johnny; Gray, Larry; *Holt, Redd; *Jackson, Franz; *Jones, Rusty; *Nightclubs and other venues: USA (Chicago); Novak, Larry; Pickens, Willie; Scott, Aaron; Shy, Robert

Gioia, Ted: West Coast jazz

Girsberger, Russ: *Alias, Don; Conte, Luis; Figueroa, Sammy; Nauseef, Mark; Ponce, Daniel; Thornton, Steve

Glaser, Matt: *South, Eddie; *Smith, Stuff; *Violin

Gould, Tony: Barnard, Bob; Barnard, Len; Biddell, Kerrie; Brown, Brian; Lee, Alan; Monsbourgh, Ade; Sedergreen, Bob; Smith, Frank; Traynor, Frank

Graziano, John: *Sissle, Noble

Green, Jeffrey P.: *Briggs, Arthur; Jenkins, Edmund Thornton; Jenkins Orphanage bands; *Johnson, Ken "Snake Hips"; Thompson, Leslie; Wilkins, Dave; Williams, Spencer

Greene, Philip: *Allison, Mose; Bavan, Yolande; *Bishop, Walter, Jr.; Hammer, Jan; *Hendricks, Jon; *Lambert, Dave; Lambert, Hendricks, and Ross; *Mahones, Gildo; Mitchell, Dwike; Ruff, Willie

Gridley, Mark C.: Cool jazz; Hard bop

Gronow, Pekka: Aaltonen, Juhani; Aho, Erkki; Ahola, Sylvester; Björkenheim, Raoul; *Danielsson, Palle; Donner, Otto; Häme, Olli; Hansen, Ole Kock; Johansson, Markku; Kärki, Toivo; Koivistoinen, Eero; Kukko, Sakari; Laakko, Bruno; Lindström, Erik; Linkola, Jukka; Malmstén, Eugen; *Nightclubs and other venues: Finland; Paakkunainen, Seppo; Perkiömäki, Jari; Perko, Jukka; Persson, Bent; Pethman, Esa; Pohjola, Pekka; Pöyry, Pekka; Pyysalo, Severi; Radiojazzgruppen (ii); Rantala, Iiro; Salmi, Klaus; Sarmanto, Heikki; Sarmanto, Pekka; Sarpila, Antti; Savolainen, Jarmo; Schwindt, Christian; Stenson, Bobo; Suomen Jazzliitto; Tolonen, Jukka; UMO; Uotila, Jukka-Pekka; Vesala, Edward

Gushee, Lawrence: New Orleans jazz; *Oliver, King; Traditional jazz

Haefliger, Kathleen: Charters, Samuel B

Hall, Marjorie Lynn: *Hall, Gene

Harrison, Andrew: Artisans Workshop; Rose, Jon; Swanton, Lloyd

Harrison, Max: *Chaloff, Serge; *Charles, Teddy; *Dameron, Tadd; *Desmond, Paul; *Haig, Al; Progressive jazz; *Russell, Luis; *Solal, Martial; Symphonic jazz

Hasse, John Edward: *Blesh, Rudi; Carmichael, Hoagy; Parker, Knocky; Robinson, J. Russel; *Rose, Wally; *Scobey, Bob

Hatch, Marty: Alexandria, Lorez; Brewer, Teresa; Carroll, Joe "Bebop"; *Dorough, Bob; *Gilberto, Astrud; Gilberto, João; Hartman, Johnny; *Jordan, Sheila; *Lincoln, Abbey; *McFerrin, Bobby

Hazeldine, Mike: Adde, Leo; *Armstrong, Lil; Bean, Floyd; Big Four; Black Bottom Stompers; Blair, Lee; Bland, Jack; *Bocage, Peter; Brown, Boyce; *Cary, Dick; Chicago Footwarmers; Christian family; Cottrell, Louis, Jr.; Cottrell, Louis, Sr.; Dixie Syncopators; *Gowans, Brad; Guesnon, George; *Harlem Blues and Jazz Band; Hayton, Lennie; *Hodes, Art; Hot Five; *Jackson, Franz; Jazz Cardinals; Johnson, Bunk; Jones and Collins Astoria Hot Eight; Legends of Jazz; Louisiana Five; New Orleans Feetwarmers; New Orleans Wanderers; *Nightclubs and other venues: USA (New Orleans); Original Creole Band; Original New Orleans Jazz Band (i); Original New Orleans Jazz Band (ii); *Preservation Hall Jazz Band; Prima, Leon; Prima, Louis; Ragas, Henry; Red Hot Peppers; *Red Onion Jazz Babies; Rhythmakers; Robichaux, John; Robichaux, Joseph; *Robinson, Fred; *Russell, Bill; Spikes' Seven Pods of Pepper; State Street Ramblers; Washboard Rhythm Kings; *Williams, Clarence

Hazell, Ed: Arnold, Horacee; Black Artists Group; *Blake, Ran; *Blythe, Arthur; *Bradford, Bobby; *Burrell, Dave; *Carter, John; *Coltrane family; Cooper, Jerome; *Cowell, Stanley; *Freeman family; *Greene, Burton; Harris, Beaver; *Hill, Andrew; *Holland, Dave; *Ibrahim, Abdullah; Jackson, Ronald Shannon; Jazz Composer's Orchestra Association; *Lyons, Jimmy (ii); *McBee, Cecil; *McIntyre, Kalaparusha Maurice; *Moffett family; Moncur, Grachan, III; *Patrick, Pat; *Riley, Howard; *Smith, Warren (ii); *Stevens, John; *Stewart, Bob; *Wadud, Abdul; *White, Andrew; Wilson, Phillip

Henley, Clarrie: *Barnes, John; *Bryden, Beryl; Christie, Ian; *Christie, Keith; Crimmins, Roy; *Disley, Diz; *Fairweather, Digby; Felix, Lennie; *Gold, Harry; *Hastings, Lennie; *Hunt, Fred; Melly, George; Moule, Ken; *Moss, Danny; Parry, Harry; Semple, Archie; *Welsh, Alex; *Williams, Roy

Hodeir, André: *Ellington, Duke

Holden, Stephen: Bennett, Tony; Blood, Sweat and Tears

Homzy, Andrew: *Boland, Francy

Hosiasson, José: *Calloway, Cab; *Carney, Harry; Ory, Kid; *Rich, Buddy; Strayhorn, Billy

Howlett, Felicity: Tatum, Art

Huesmann, Günther: Auer, Pepsi; Berking, Willy; *Brocksieper, Freddie; De Weille, Benny; Edelhagen, Kurt; *Lenz, Günter; *Weber, Eberhard; Wehner, Heinz; Weintraub Syncopators

Hultin, Randi: Andersen, Arild; Christensen, Jon; Garbarek, Jan; Krog, Karin; Rypdal, Terje; Stubø, Thorgeir

Iannapollo, Robert J.: *Bennink, Han; *Brötzmann, Peter; *Christmann, Günter; *Dudek, Gerd; *Favre, Pierre; *Globe Unity Orchestra; *Harris, Craig; Jamal, Khan; *Kowald, Peter; *Lovens, Paul; Niebergall, Buschi; *Schoof, Manfred; *Sharrock, Sonny; *Van Hove, Fred

Innes, Brian: Temperance Seven

Isoardi, Steven L.: *Caliman, Hadley; *Collette, Buddy; Green, Bill; Kelso, Jackie; Matthews, Onzy; Morris, Wilber; Tapscott, Horace; Theus, Sonship

Iwanami, Yozo: Hara, Nobuo; *Hino, Motohiko; *Hino, Terumasa; *Honda, Toshiyuki; Ishikawa, Hisao; Kawaguchi, George; *Karashima, Fumio; *Kawasaki, Ryo; *Kikuchi, Masabumi; *Kitamura, Eiji; *Maeda, Norio; *Masuda, Ichiro; *Masuo, Yoshiaki; *Matsumoto, Hidehiko; *Miyama, Toshiyuki; *Miyazawa, Akira; *Mukai, Shigeharu; Nakamura, Teruo; *Ohno, Shunzo; *Sakata, Akira; *Sato, Masahiko; *Shimizu, Jun; *Suzuki, Yoshio; *Takahashi, Tatsuya; *Togashi, Masahiko; *Watanabe, Kazumi; *Yagi, Masao; *Yamashita, Yosuke

Jackson, Adrian: Browne, Allan; Duggan, Barry; *Gould, Tony; Jones, Vince; *Lyall, Graeme; McAll, Barney; Vining, Ted; Yarra Yarra Jazz Band

Jaffe, Andrew: *Abney, Don; *Broadbent, Alan; *Byard, Jaki; *Costa, Eddie; *Davis, Wild Bill; *Earland, Charles; *Fuller, Gil; Guaraldi, Vince; *Guarnieri, Johnny; *Heywood, Eddie; *Holmes, Groove; *Jolly, Pete; *Katz, Dick; *Kersey, Kenny; *Lang, Mike; *Lytle, Johnny; *McDuff, Brother Jack; Massey, Cal; *Mathews, Ronnie; Morris, Marlowe

James, Michael: *Giuffre, Jimmy; *Herman, Woody; *McPherson, Charles; *Marsh, Warne; *Mobley, Hank; *Morgan, Lee; *Reinhardt family; *Wellins, Bobby

Jeske, Lee: *Abrams, Muhal Richard; *Adams, Pepper; *Benson, George; *Bowie, Lester; *Farmer, Art; *Hutcherson, Bobby; *Lateef, Yusef; *Laws, Hubert; *McLean, Jackie; *Marsalis family; *Rudd, Roswell; *Thomas, Leon; *Winding, Kai

Johnson, Bruce: Acheson, Merv; *Bell, Graeme; Bell, Roger; *Brokensha, Jack; Coughlan, Frank; *Dallwitz, Dave; Daly, Warren; Featherstone, Benny; *Munro, Charlie; *Nightclubs and other venues: Australia; Pickering, Tom; *Price, Ray; Wilson, Ed

Johnson, Carl: Whiteman, Paul

Joly, Marcel: Allen, Henry, Sr.; Balliu, Rudy; Barnes, Emile; *Barnes, Polo; *Boutté, Lillian; *Dirty Dozen Brass Band; Foster, Willie; Laine, Alfred "Baby"; McCord, Ted; Mares, Joe; Nelson, George; Parker, Frank; Petit, Joseph; Purnell, Alton; Rena, Joseph; Sayles, George; Van Breedam, Camiel; *White, Michael (ii)

Jones, Kevin: Port Jackson Jazz Band

Kaye, Harold S.: *New Yorkers (i)

Kennedy, Gary: A (i); Abate, Greg; Abdullah, Ahmed; Abou-Khalil, Rabih; Accurate; ACT; *Aebersold, Jamey; Affif, Ron; Aladdin; Alden, Howard; Alexander, Eric; Alexander, Roland; *Ali family; Allen, Byron; Allen, Carl; *Allen, Geri; Allen, Harry; Allison, Ben; Almario, Justo; Anderson, Clifton; Anderson, Jay; Anderson, Wessell; Andress, Tuck; Antilles; Anton, Artie; Aoki, Tatsu; *Apfelbaum, Peter; Apollo; Arabesque; Arbors; Arcado; *Arista; Arkadia; Aronov, Ben; *Arriale, Lynne; Artin, Tom; Artists' Jazz Band; Ascione, Joe; Asian Improv; Assumpção, Nico; Audioquest Music; Avant; Avery, Teodross; Backer, Steve; Badgley, Bob; Bailey, Craig; Baker, Duck; Baker, Newman Taylor; Bakr, Rashid; Ballantyne, Jon; Barbaro, Cliff; Barber, Patricia; Barefield, Spencer; Bargad, Rob; Bargeron, Dave; Baron, Art; Baron, Joey; Barrett, Dan; Barrett, Darren; Barth, Bruce; Bass, Mickey; Bassic Sound; Battle, Bobby; Bauer, Stefan; Bebop and Beyond; Beckenstein, Jay; *Beier, Chris; Beier, Detlev; Belgrave, Marcus; *Bell, Kelvyn; Benbow, Warren; Benjamin, Sathima Bea; Beresford, Steve; Bergalli, Gustavo; Berger, David; *Berklee College of Music; Berne, Tim; Bernstein, Peter; Bernstein, Steve; Berrios, Steve; Berroa, Ignacio; Berry, Steve; Betsch, John; Billy Tipton Memorial Saxophone Quartet; Bisio, Michael; Black, Jim; Black Hawk; Blackman, Cindy; Blade, Brian; *Blairman, Allen; Blake, Alex; Blake, John; Blake, Ron; Blakeslee, Rob; Blanding, Walter; *Bley, Paul; Bloom, Jane Ira; BMG; Bolden, Walter; Bonafede, Salvatore; Boni, Raymond; Bonilla, Luis; Booth, Jiunie; Borca, Karen; Bowden, Colin; Bowden, Mwata; Bowden, Ron; Bowie, Michael; Bowler, Phil; Boyd, Curtis; Braceful, Fred; Brackeen, Charles; Braden, Don; Bradford, Carmen; Braith, George; Brannon, Teddy; Brimfield, Bill; Brodie, Hugh; Brown, Ari; Brown, Ben; Brown, Donald; Brown, Jeri; Brown, Rob; Brown, Tyrone; Brownstone; Brubeck, Darius; *Bryson, Jeanie; Bullock, Belden; Burno, Dwayne; Burrage, Ronnie; Burton, Abraham; Butler, Henry; BYG; Cachao; Cadence Jazz; Cain, Michael; Calabrese, Bucky; Camilo, Michel; Campbell, John; Campbell, Roy; Capri; Caribbean Jazz Project; Carnegie Hall

Jazz Band; Carr, Bruno; Carrott, Bryan; Carter, James; Carter, Regina; Cary, Marc; Catingub, Matt; Chadbourne, Eugene; Challenge; Chancey, Vincent; Chapin, Thomas; Charlap, Bill; Charlesworth, Dick; Chase, Allan; Cheek, Chris; Cherry, Ed; Chesky; Chestnut, Cyrus; Childs, Billy; Chirillo, James; *Christi, Ellen; Christian, Jodie; CIMP; Clark, Curtis; Clark, John; Clark, Mahlon; Clark, Mike; Classics; Clay, James; Clayton, Jay; Cline, Alex; Cline, Nels; Clusone 3; CMP; Cochrane, Michael; Cohelmec; Cohen, Avishai; Cohen, Greg; Cohn, Joe; Cohran, Phil; Coke, Alex; Coleman, Denardo; Coleman, Ira; *Coleman, Steve; Colianni, John; Colley, Scott; Colville, Randy; Connick, Harry, Jr.; Conover, Willis; Contemporary jazz; Contemporary Piano Ensemble; Cook, Marty; Coolman, Todd; *Cooper, Lindsay; Copland, Marc; Cora, Tom; Costa, John; Courvoisier, Sylvie; Cox, Bruce; Creative Construction Company; Crispell, Marilyn; Croft, Monte; Crook, Hal; Crosby, Charles; *Crosby, Gary; Crothers, Connie; Cruz, Adam; CTI; Cuscuna, Michael; Dagradi, Tony; Dallas, Sonny; Dalto, Jorge; D'Ambrosio, Meredith; Dance, Helen Oakley; Daniel, Ted; Danko, Harold; Davis, Francis; Davis, Jesse; Davis, Kenny; Davis, Spanky; Davis, Stanton; Davis, Steve (ii); Davis, Steve (iii); Davis, Troy; Davis, Xavier; Dawkins, Ernest; Dawn; D'Earth, John; Debriano, Santi; Debut (i); Dee Gee; Deffaa, Chip; Demierre, Jacques; *Deppa, Claude; Dial, Garry; Di Battista, Stefano; Dick, Robert; D'Imperio, Danny; Diva (ii); *DIW; Dixon, Ben; Dixon, Fostina; Dobbins, Bill; Doctor Jazz; Dolphin, Dwayne; Doneda, Michel; Donelian, Armen; Double-Time (ii); Douglas, Dave; Douglas, Jim; Douglass, Bill (ii); Drake, Hamid; Dreamstreet; Dreyfus Jazz; Drummond, Billy; Drummond, Ray; Dubin, Larry; Durham, Bobby; Dyett, Capt. Walter; Eade, Dominique; Easley, Bill; Eastman, Madeline; Eaton, John; Eckert, John; Ecklund, Peter; Edwards, Marc; Efford, Bob; Ehrlich, Marty; Either/Orchestra; Elf, Mark; Elgart, Billy; Elling, Kurt; Elson, Steve; El'Zabar, Kahil; Emanem; Emery, James; Enriquez, Bobby; Eskelin, Ellery; *Esquire All Stars; Ethnic Heritage Ensemble; Eubanks, Robin; Evidence (ii); EWI; Eyges, David; Fahn, Mike; Fambrough, Charles; Farnham, Allen; Farnsworth, Joe; Fat Cat's Jazz; Faulk, Dan; Fay, Rick; Fedchock, John; Feldman, Mark; Felten, Eric; Fewell, Garrison; Fields, Brandon; Filiano, Ken; Finck, David; *Findley, Chuck; Fine, Milo; Flory, Chris; Folds, Chuck; Fonseca, Duduka da; Ford, Jimmy; Ford, Joe; Forman, Mitchel; Forrester, Joel; Foster, Alex; Fowler, Bruce; Francioli, Léon; Franklin, Henry; Franks, Rebecca Coupe; *Freelon, Nnenna; *Freeman family; Freeman, Russ (ii); Friedlander, Erik; Fringe, The; Frink, Laurie; Futterman, Joel; Gale, Eddie; Gallant, Joe; Gallardo, Joe; *Galliano, Richard; Gallivan, Joe; Gallon, Ray; Gant, Frank; Garnett, Alvester; *Garrett, Kenny; Gazell (ii); Gershon, Russ; Gertz, Bruce; Gibbs, Melvin; Gioia, Ted; *Giordano, Vince; Gisbert, Greg; GM; Goines, Victor; Goldsby, John; Gomez, Edsel; Gonsalves, Virgil; Gonzalez, Andy; Gonzalez, Dennis; Gonzalez, Jerry; Goode, Brad; Gordon, Frank; Gordon, John; Gordon, Jon; Gordon, Max; Gordon, Wycliffe; Grant, Darrell; Green, Benny; Green, Bunky; Grenadier, Larry; Gress, Drew; GRIM; Grossman, Richard; Gunn, Russell; Gunther, John; Haffner, Wolfgang; Hagans, Tim; Halliday, Lin; Hammer, Tardo; Handy, Craig; Hanrahan, Kip; Harper, Philip; Harper, Winard; Harris, Jerome; Harris, Ratzo; Harris, Stefon; Harrison, Wendell; *Harrow, Nancy; Hart, Antonio; Hartog, Jim; Hasaan; Hashim, Michael; Hasselbring, Curtis; Hauser, Fritz; Haynes, Frank; Haynes, Phil; Hays, Kevin; Hazeltine, David; Heckman, Don; Hedges, Chuck; Helleny, Joel; Hemingway, Gerry; Hering, Manfred; Herring, Vincent; Hersch, Fred; Hess, Fred; Higgins, Eddie; HighNote; Hill, Calvin; Hing, Kenny; *Hirsch, Shelley; Hirshfield, Jeff; Ho, Fred; Hobbs, Steve; Hofstra, David; Holloway, Ron; Hollyday, Christopher; *Honsinger, Tristan; Horiuchi, Glenn; Horner, Lindsey; Horner, Tim; Horton, Ron; Horvitz, Wayne; Howard, Earle "Nappy"; Human Feel; Hunter, Charlie; Hunter, Jerome; Hunter-Randall, Ian; Hutchinson, Gregory; Hwang, Jason; Ignatzek, Klaus; In + Out; India Navigation; Ineke, Eric; Intakt; International Association of Schools of Jazz; Irby, Sherman; Israel, Yoron; Jackson, Chip; Jackson, Ed; Jackson, Gene; Jackson, Javon; Jaffe, Allan (ii); James, Etta; Jang, Jon; Jankeje, Jan; Japo; Jarvis, Jane; Jazz at Lincoln Center; Jazz Composers Collective; Jazz education; Jazz Focus; Jazz4ever; Jazz Haus Musik; Jazz Passengers; Jazzpoint; J Curve; Jefferson, Carter; Johansson, Sven-Åke; Johns, Steve; Johnson, Archie; Johnson, Dean; Johnson, Dewey; Johnson, Henry; Johnston, Phillip; Johnston, Randy; Joint Venture; Jones, Brad; Jones, Randy; Jones, Virgil; Jordan family; Josephson, Barney; Kamikaze Ground Crew; Keezer, Geoff; Kellin, Orange; Ken Music; Kendrick, Rodney; Kessler, Siegfried; Kibwe, Talib; Kiermyer, Franklin; Kilbert, Porter; Kimbrough, Frank; King, Jonny; King, Nancy; Kirkwood, Neal; Kisor, Ryan; Klucevsek, Guy; Knitting Factory; Koch, Klaus; Koch Jazz; Kohlhase, Charlie; *Kondo, Toshinori; Konnex; Koonse, Larry; Krivda, Ernie; Kropinski, Uwe; Krystall, Marty; *Kynard, Charles; Label Bleu; Lacy, Frank; Lake, Gene; Lalama, Ralph; Landham, Byron; LaSpina, Steve; Laster, Andy; Lauer, Christof; Lawrence, Doug; Léandre, Joëlle; LeDonne, Mike; *Lee, Peggy; Lee, Scott; Lee, William F.; Legacy; Leitham, John; Levy, Jed; Lewis, Victor; Lincoln Center Jazz Orchestra; Lindsay, Erica; Linka, Rudy; Lipstick; Lockwood, John; Lodder, Steve; London, Julie; Lonzo, Freddie; Lovano, Joe; Lowe, Allen; Lubambo, Romero; Lundy, Carmen; Lundy, Curtis; Lurie, John; *Lynch, Brian; McBride, Christian; McBride, Nate; *McCorkle, Susannah; McKee, Andy; *McKinney family; McLaurine, Marcus; McLevy, John; McNeil, John; McPherson, Eric; Madison, Jimmy; Madsen, Peter; Magnarelli, Joe; Mahogany, Kevin; Mainstream; Malaby, Tony; Malfatti, Radu; Malik, Raphé; Malone, Russell; MAMA Foundation; Mandala Octet; Manderscheid, Dieter; Maneri, Joe; Manhattan; Manhattan Jazz Quintet; Mantler, Karen; Mapleshade; Marcus, Michael; Margolis, Kitty; Maricle, Sherrie; Marino, Tony; Markowitz, Phil; *Marsalis family; *Marsh, Tina; Martin, Claire; Martin, Mel; Martin, Peter; Martin, Stu; Masakowski, Steve; Massey, Zane; Mateen, Tarus; Matta, Nilson; Mauro, Turk; May, Tina; Mayhew, Virginia; *M-Base; MCA; Méchali, François; Medeski, John; Mehldau, Brad; Melle, Gil; Melody Four; Merseysippi Jazz Band; Messidor; Microscopic Septet; Miles, Ron; Militello, Bobby; Miller, Mark; Mingus Big Band; Mingus Orchestra; Minor Music; Miranda, Roberto Miguel; Mitchell, J. R.; Mitchell, Tyler; Mobley, Bill; Monder, Ben; Mondesir, Mark; Monk, T. S.; Mons; Moondoc, Jemeel; Moore, Michael (ii); Moore, Ralph; Moran, Jason; Moroni, Dado; Morris, Joe (ii); Mosca, John; Mosca, Ray; Moscow Composers Orchestra; Mossman, Michael Philip; Muldrow, Ronald; Mullins, Riley; Murphy, Tim; Murray, Diedre; Music & Arts; Music Improvisation Company; Musicmasters; Mustafa, Melton; Nabel; *Nash family; Nash, Lewis; Nathanson, Roy; Nato; Naxos Jazz; Nelson, Steve; Neville, Chris; New and Used; New Orchestra Workshop; *Newton, Lauren; New Winds; New World; New York Composers Orchestra; New York Voices; Nicholson, Reggie; Niemack, Judy; *Nightclubs and other venues: USA (New York); Nippon Columbia; Nix, Bern; Nonesuch; Noren, Jack; Normaphone; Novosel, Steve; Novus; NOW; *Ntshoko, Makaya; Nueva Manteca; N.Y. Hardbop Quintet; Oatts, Dick; O'Brien, Hod; Okegwo, Ugonna; Okka Disk; O'Mara, Peter; O'Neal, Johnny; One for All; Orange then Blue; OTB; Page, Nathen; Palmer, Jeff; Palmetto; Palmieri, Eddie; Panayi, Andy; Papadimitriou, Sakis; Paris Reunion Band; Parker, Errol; Parker, Kim; Parker, Maceo; Parker, William; Parker-Sparrow, Bradley; Parran, J. D.; Parson, Dion; Pascoal, Hermeto; Payton, Nicholas; Penland, Ralph; Penn, Clarence; Peplowski, Ken; Pepper, Jim; Pérez, Danilo; Perowsky, Ben; Perry, Rich; Person, Eric; Petersen, Edward; Peterson, Ralph, Jr.; Petrovic, Boško; *Petrowsky, Ernst-Ludwig; Phalanx; Pieces of Time; Popkin, Lenny; Porter, Lewis; Postcards; Potter, Chris; Previte, Bobby; Prima Materia; Pring, Bobby; Printup, Marcus; Puente, Tito; Purcell, John; Purrone, Tony; Quest; Ragin, Hugh; Rainey, Tom; RAM; Ranier, Tom; Rapson, John; *Rawls, Lou; Ray, Michael; Re-Birth Brass Band; Red Baron; Redd, Chuck; Redman,

Joshua; Reedus, Tony; *Reeves, Diane; Reeves, Nat; Reig, Teddy; Reijseger, Ernst; Reilly, Jack; *Repertory band; Reservoir; Rhyne, Mel; Ribot, Marc; Richeson, Dane; Riggs, Chuck; Riley, Herlin; Rivera, Mario; Riverside Reunion Band; Robert, George; Roberts, Hank; Roberts, Marcus; Robertson, Herb; Robinson, Justin; Rochester, Cornell; Rodby, Steve; Roditi, Claudio; Rogers, Billie; Rogers, Reuben; Rojas, Marcus; Roney, Antoine; Roney, Wallace; Roseman, Josh; Rosenthal, Ted; Rosetta; Rosewoman, Michele; Ross, Brandon; Rossy, Jorge; Rothenberg, Ned; Rotondi, Jim; Rubalcaba, Gonzalo; Rubin, Stan; *Rubin, Vanessa; Rucker, Ellyn; Rudolph, Steve; Ruffins, Kermit; Ryerson, Ali; Rykodisc; Sachse, Helmut "Joe"; *Sanchez, David; Sandke, Randy; Santoro, Gene; Sarbib, Saheb; Sargent, Gray; Sasajima, Akio; Sash, Leon; Saunders, Keith; Savant; Schaap, Phil; Schaphorst, Ken; *Schärli, Peter; *Schlippenbach, Alex; Schneider, Larry; Schneider, Maria; Schneiderman, Rob; Schoenberg, Loren; Schönfeld, Friedhelm; Schröder, John; *Schuller family; Schulze, Manfred; Schütz, Martin; *Schuur, Diane; Schwartz, Thornal; *Schweizer, Irène; Scott, Calo; Scott, Stephen; Seaton, Lynn; Seay, Clarence; Sendecki, Władysław; Sepulveda, Charlie; *Shad, Bob; Shahid, Jaribu; Sharpe, Avery; Sharpe, C; Sharp Nine; Sharrock, Linda; Shaw, Clarence; Sheppard, Andy; Shim, Mark; Shipp, Matthew; Shook, Travis; Shorter, Alan; Shull, Tad; Sickler, Don; Siddik, Rasul; Sides, Doug; Sidran, Ben; Signature; Silkheart; Silvano, Judi; Simon, Edward; *Singing; Skeat, Bill; Skeat, Len; Slagle, Steve; Slickaphonics; Sloane, Carol; Smith, Colin; Smith, Lonnie; Smith, Sonelius; Smithsonian Institution; Smoker, Paul; Smulyan, Gary; Snidero, Jim; *Sommer, Günter; *Sonet; Songlines; Sony; *SOS; Soskin, Mark; Space Jazz Trio; *Sparks, Melvin; Spearman, Glenn; Speed, Chris; Sprague, Peter; *Spyro Gyra; Stabenow, Thomas; Stadler, Heiner; Stafford, Gregg; Stafford, Terrell; *Stańko, Tomasz; Stern, Peggy; Stewart, Bill; *Stivín, Jiří; Stomp Off; Stowell, John; Strange, Pete; Strata Institute; Stretch; Stringle, Julian; Stuart, Rory; Sudhalter, Dick; Sudler, Monette; Suonsaari, Klaus; Swana, John; Swell, Steve; Tabbal, Tani; Taborn, Craig; *Takase, Aki; Talbert, Thomas; Tangerding, Götz; Tanksley, Francesca; Tardy, Greg; Tate, Frank; Taylor, Creed; Taylor, Dave; Taylor, Mark (i); TCB; Teepe, Joris; Telarc; Temiz, Okay; Terrasson, Jacky; Texier, Henri; *Thelin, Eje; Thelonious Monk Institute; Thiam, Mor; Thiele, Bob; Thompson, Malachi; Thornton, Teri; Three Blind Mice; Three of a Kind; Tibbetts, Steve; T. J. Kirk; Ton-Art; Tonooka, Sumi; Tremble Kids; Tribe; Trio da Paz; Trio Transition; *Troup, Bobby; Trowers, Robert; Tsilis, Gust William; Tuck & Patti; Tuncboyaçiyan, Arto; Turbinton, Earl; Turner, Mark; Turner, Matt; Tusques, François; Tutu; *29th Street Saxophone Quartet; Ulanov, Barry; Unity; Uptown; Valente, Gary; Valentin, Dave; *Vandermark, Ken; Vanguard Jazz Orchestra; Varner, Tom; Varro, Johnny; Vatcher, Michael; Veal, Reginald; Veasley, Gerald; Vee-Jay; Via; Victo; Vidacovich, John; Vignola, Frank; Vincent, Ron; Vinyl; Vitet, Bernard; *Vitro, Roseanna; von Essen, Eric; V.S.O.P. (iii); Vuckovich, Larry; Waits, Nasheet; Wall, Murray; Wallen, Byron; Ware, Bill; Warfield, Tim; Warner Bros.; Washington, Peter; Washington, Reggie; Watson, Eric; Watt; Watts, Jeff "Tain"; Watts, Marzette; WDR Big Band; Webber, John; Weidman, James; Weiskopf, Walt; Weiss, Doug; Weiss, Michael; Weldon, Jerry; Wendholt, Scott; Werner, Kenny; Wertico, Paul; Wesley, Fred; Westray, Ron; Whalum, Kirk; Wheeler, Ian; Wheeler, Nedra; Whigham, Jiggs; Whitaker, Rodney; White, Carla; White, Chip; Whitecage, Mark; Whitehead, Kevin; Widespread Depression Jazz Orchestra; Wieselman, Doug; Wildman, Joan; Wilkerson, Ed; Wilkins, Jack; Willette, Baby Face; *Williams, Jackie; Williams, Jeff; Williams, Jessica; *Williams, Johnny (ii); Williams, Rod; Williams, Todd; Williams, Tom; Williams, Willie; Williamson, Bruce; Wilson, Bert; Wilson, Cassandra; Wilson, Chuck; Wilson, John S.; Wilson, Matt; Wilson, Steve; Winchester, Lem; Wofford, Mike; Wolfe, Ben; Wong, Francis; Wonsey, Anthony; Wood, Vishnu; Woods, Jimmy; Worrell, Lewis; Yellin, Pete; Young, John; Zigmund, Eliot; Zingaro, Carlos; Zorn, John; Zwerin, Mike; Zwingenberger, Axel; Zwingenberger, Torsten

Kenney, William H., III: *Condon, Eddie; *De Paris, Sidney; De Paris, Wilbur

Kenselaar, Robert: *Redman, Don

Kernfeld, Barry: *Abene, Mike; *Abercrombie, John; *Abney, Don; Abraham, Phil; *Abrams, Muhal Richard; *Accordion; *Acoustic bass guitar; *Acuña, Alex; *Adams, George; *Adams, Pepper; Adderley, Cannonball; *Adderley, Nat; *Aebersold, Jamey; Aerts, Philippe; *Afro-Cuban jazz; *Akiyoshi, Toshiko; akLaff, Pheeroan; *Albam, Manny; *Albany, Joe; *Albert, Don; *Alemán, Oscar; *Alexander, Monty; *Ali family; *Alias, Don; *Allen, Henry ""Red""; Allen, Marshall; *Allen, Steve; *Allen, Walter C.; Alley, Vernon; *Allison, Mose; *Almeida, Laurindo; *Altschul, Barry; *Alvin, Danny; *Alvis, Hayes; *Ambrose, Bert; *Ambrosetti, Franco; *Ammons, Albert; Ammons, Gene; *Amram, David; Amy, Curtis; Anderson, Andy (i); *Anderson, Cat; *Anderson, Ernestine; *Anderson, Fred; *Anderson, Ivie; *Anderson, Ray; Andre, Wayne; Andrus, Chuck; *Anthony, Ray; *Antolini, Charly; *Apfelbaum, Peter; *Archey, Jimmy; *Arista; *Armstrong, Lil; *Arriale, Lynne; Art Ensemble of Chicago; Artists House; *Ash, Vic; *Ashby, Harold; *Ashby, Irving; Association for the Advancement of Creative Musicians; *Atlantic; *Auguścik, Grażyna; *Auld, Georgie; Australian Jazz Quartet; *Autrey, Herman; *Ayers, Roy; Ayler, Albert; *Babasin, Harry; *Babbington, Roy; Baden Powell; *Badini, Gérard; Badrena, Manolo; Bagley, Don; *Bailey, Benny; *Bailey, Buster; Bailey, Colin; *Bailey, Dave; *Bailey, Donald; *Bailey, Mildred; *Baker, Chet; *Baker, Kenny; Bałata, Marek; *Baldock, Kenny; Bales, Burt; *Ballamy, Iain; Balliett, Whitney; *Bang, Billy; *Barbarin family; *Barber, Bill; *Barber, Chris; *Barbieri, Gato; *Barbour, Dave; *Barksdale, Everett; *Barnes, George; *Barnes, John; *Barnes, Polo; *Barnet, Charlie; *Barone, Mike; *Barretto, Ray; *Barron, Bill; *Barron, Kenny; Barth, Benny; *Bartkowski, Czesław; *Bartz, Gary; *Basie, Count; Batiste, Alvin; *Bauduc, Ray; *Bauer, Billy; *Bauer, Conrad; *Bauzá, Mario; Beal, Charlie; Beat; *Bechet, Sidney; *Bechet Legacy; *Beck, Gordon; *Beck, Joe; Beckenstein, Ray; Bedford, Ronnie; *Beiderbecke, Bix; *Beier, Chris; *Beirach, Richard; *Bell, Aaron; *Bellson, Louie; *Bem, Ewa; *Benjamin, Joe; Bennett, Lou; *Benson, George; *Berg, Thilo; Berger, Karl; Berghofer, Chuck; *Berigan, Bunny; *Berimbau; *Berklee College of Music; *Bernhardt, Warren; *Bernstein, Artie; *Berry, Bill; *Berry, Chu; *Berry, Emmett; *Bert, Eddie; *Bertoncini, Gene; *Best, Skeeter; *Betts, Keter; *Bey, Andy; Bickert, Ed; *Bigard family; *Bilk, Acker; *Biondi, Ray; *Bishop, Wallace; *Bishop, Walter, Jr.; *Bivona, Gus; Black, Dave; *Black Lion; Black Saint; *Blackwell, Ed; *Blairman, Allen; *Blake, Ran; *Blakey, Art; *Blanchard, Terence; *Blesh, Rudi; *Bley, Carla; *Bley, Paul; *Bliziński, Marek; Blowers, Johnny; *Bluebird; *Blue note (i); *Blue Note (ii); *Blues; Blues progression; *Bluiett, Hamiet; *Blythe, Arthur; *Bocage, Peter; *Boiarsky, Andrés; Bongos; Bossa nova; *Bostic, Earl; *Boutté, Lillian; Bowie, Joseph; *Bowie, Lester; *Boyd, Nelson; Boykins, Ronnie; *Brackeen, JoAnne; *Bradford, Bobby; *Bradford, Perry; *Braff, Ruby; *Branscombe, Alan; *Brashear, Oscar; *Braud, Wellman; *Braxton, Anthony; Break; *Breau, Lenny; Brecker, Michael; *Brecker, Randy; *Breuker, Willem; *Bridgewater, Cecil; *Bridgewater, Dee Dee; Briggs, Bunny; *Bright, Ronnell; *Brignola, Nick; *Broadbent, Alan; *Brookmeyer, Bob; *Brooks, Roy; Brown, Cleo; *Brown, Clifford; *Brown, Lawrence; *Brown, Marion; *Brown, Marshall; Brown, Oscar, Jr.; *Brown, Pete; *Brown, Ray; *Brubeck, Dave; *Bruford, Bill; *Brunies family; *Bryant, Bobby; *Bryant, Ray; *Bryden, Beryl; *Buckner, Teddy; *Budwig, Monty; *Bunch, John; *Bunker, Larry; *Bunn, Teddy; *Burbank, Albert; *Burch, John; *Burrell, Dave; Burton, Gary; Bush, Lennie; *Bushell, Garvin; *Bushkin, Joe; *Butler, Frank; *Butts, Jimmy; *Byard, Jaki; *Byrd, Charlie; Byrd, Donald; Cabay, Guy; *Cables, George; *Caiazza, Nick; Call and response; *Calloway, Cab; *Camelia Brass Band; *Cameron, Jay; Candid; *Candoli, Conte; *Candoli,

Pete; *Carey, Mutt; *Carisi, Johnny; *Carlton, Larry; *Carney, Harry; Carpenter, Ike; *Carr, Ian; *Carr, Mike; Carroll, Baikida; Carroll, Barbara; Carter, Betty; *Carter, John; Carter, Kent; Carter, Ron; *Carvin, Michael; *Cary, Dick; *Casa Loma Orchestra; *Casey, Bob; *Castellucci, Bruno; *Castro-Neves, Oscar; Catalyst; *Catherine, Philip; Catoul, Jean-Pierre; CBS; Cecil, Malcolm; *Celestin, Papa; *Cello; *Challis, Bill; *Chaloff, Serge; Chambers, Paul; *Chancler, Ndugu; Charles, Dennis; *Charles, Teddy; Chase; Chase, Bill; *Cheatham, Doc; *Cherico, Gene; Cherry, Don; Chiaroscuro; Chiasson, Warren; *Childers, Buddy; *Chilton, John; *Chisholm, George; *Christie, Keith; *Christlieb, Pete; *Christy, June; Cinélu, Mino; Circular breathing; *Clare, Alan; *Clark, Sonny; *Clarke, Kenny; *Clarke, Stanley; Clavichord; *Clayton, Buck; Clef; *Cless, Rod; *Cleveland, Jimmy; *Clooney, Rosemary; *Clyne, Jeff; Coates, John; *Cobb, Arnett; *Cobb, Jimmy; *Cobham, Billy; *Coe, Tony; Coggins, Gil; *Cohn, Al; *Coker, Jerry; *Cole, Cozy; *Cole, Nat "King"; *Coleman, George; *Coleman, Ornette; *Coleman, Steve; *Coles, Johnny; *Collette, Buddy; Collier, James Lincoln; *Collins, Cal; Collins, Dick; *Collins, John; *Collins, Lee; *Collins, Rudy; *Coltrane family; *Columbia; Comfort, Joe; Concord; *Condon, Eddie; *Condon, Les; Conga; Conniff, Ray; Connors, Norman; *Contemporary; *Cook, Junior; *Cook, Willie; *Cooper, Bob; *Cooper, Buster; *Copeland, Ray; *Corb, Morty; *Corea, Chick; Coryell, Larry; *Costa, Eddie; *Cotton, Mike; *Cowell, Stanley; *Cranshaw, Bob; *Crawford, Jimmy; Crawford, Ray; Crawley, Wilton; Creative World; *Criss, Sonny; *Criss Cross Jazz; *Crosby, Bing; *Crosby, Bob; *Crow, Bill; *Crumbley, Elmer; Cuber, Ronnie; *Cudzich, Andrzej; *Cuíca; *Cyrille, Andrew; *Dailey, Al; *Dameron, Tadd; *Daniels, Eddie; *Danielsson, Palle; *Dankworth family; *Dapogny, James; Darling, David; Davenport, Wallace; *Davies, John R. T.; Davis, Anthony; *Davis, Art; *Davis, Charles; *Davis, Eddie "Lockjaw"; *Davis, Lem; Davis, Miles; *Davis, Nathan; *Davis, Richard; *Davis, Walter; *Davis, Wild Bill; *Davison, Wild Bill; *Dawson, Alan; Dean, Donald; Dean, Vinnie; *De Arango, Bill; *Dearie, Blossom; *Dębski, Krzesimir; *Deems, Barrett; *De Faut, Volly; DeFranco, Buddy; Degen, Bob; *Dejan, Harold; *DeJohnette, Jack; Delmark; *De Paris, Sidney; Deppenschmidt, Buddy; *Desmond, Paul; *Dickenson, Vic; *Dickerson, Carroll; *Digital delay; *Dillard, Bill; *Di Meola, Al; *DiNovi, Gene; *Diorio, Joe; *Dirty Dozen Brass Band; *Discography; *Discovery; *Disley, Diz; Distel, Sacha; Ditmas, Bruce; Dixon, Bill; *Dixon, Eric; *Dixon, George; *Dixon, Joe; *Dodds, Baby; Dodge, Joe; *Dodgion, Dottie; *Dodgion, Jerry; Dolphy, Eric; *Domanico, Chuck; *Donahue, Sam; Donald, Peter; *Donaldson, Lou; Donato, Michel; Dorham, Kenny; *Dorough, Bob; *Dorsey, Jimmy; *Dorsey, Tommy; *Douglas, Tommy; Douglass, Bill (i); Drakes, Jesse; Dresser, Mark; *Drew, Kenny; *Drew, Martin; *D'Rivera, Paquito; Drootin, Al; *Drootin, Buzzy; *Dudziak, Urszula; *Duhé, Lawrence; *Dukes of Dixieland; *Dunbar, Ted; *Duncan, Hank; Duran, Eddie; *Duvivier, George; Du wah; *Dyani, Johnny; Dyląg, Roman; *Eagle Band; *Earland, Charles; *Eckinger, Isla; Eckstine, Billy; ECM; *Edison, Harry; *Egan, Mark; *Eldridge, Roy; Elektra Musician; *Elgar, Charlie; *Elias, Eliane; *Ellington, Duke; *Ellington, Mercer; *Ellington, Ray; *Elliott, Don; *Ellis, Don; *Ellis, Herb; *Elsdon, Alan; *EMI; *Enevoldsen, Bob; English, Bill; Enja; *Ericson, Rolf; *Erskine, Peter; *Ervin, Booker; *Erwin, Pee Wee; *ESP-disk; *Esquire All Stars; Eubanks, Kevin; *Eureka Brass Band; *Evans, Bill (ii); *Evans, Bill (iii); *Evans, Doc; *Evans, Gil; *Ewart, Douglas; *Faddis, Jon; *Fairweather, Digby; *Fake book; Falay, Maffy; *Fallon, Jack; False fingering; Famous Door (ii); Fantasy; *Farlow, Tal; *Farmer, Art; *Farrell, Joe; *Fatool, Nick; Favors, Malachi; *Favre, Pierre; *Fawkes, Wally; *Fazola, Irving; *Feather, Leonard; *Feld, Morey; *Felder, Wilton; *Feldman, Victor; Ferguson, Maynard; *Ferris, Glenn; *Festivals; *Feza, Mongezi; *Fields, Kansas; *Fierstone, George; *Films; *Finegan, Bill; *Fischer, Clare; Fischer, John; Fishkin, Arnold; *Fitzgerald, Ella; *Flanagan, Tommy; *Flanigan, Phil; *Flory, Med; Flying Dutchman; FMP; *Fol, Hubert; *Fol, Raymond; *Fontana, Carl; *Ford, Ricky; Forman, Bruce; Formanek, Michael; *Forrest, Jimmy; *Fortune, Sonny; *Foster, Al; *Foster, Frank; *Foster, Gary; *Foster, Pops; *Fountain, Pete; Fournier, Vernel; *Francis, Panama; Franklin, Aretha; *Franzetti, Carlos; *Frazier, Cié; *Freeman family; *Freeman, Bud; *Freeman, Russ (i); *Fresh Sound; *Friedman, David; *Friedman, Don; *Friesen, David; *Frisell, Bill; *Frishberg, Dave; *Fujiwara, Kiyoto; *Fuller, Curtis; *Fuller, Gil; *Gadd, Steve; *Gaillard, Slim; *Galbraith, Charlie; *Gale, Eric; *Gales, Larry; Galland, Stéphane; *Galper, Hal; Ganley, Allan; *Garland, Joe; *Garland, Red; *Garner, Erroll; Garrison, Jimmy; *Gaskin, Leonard; *Gaskin, Vic; *Gay, Al; *Geller, Herb; *Geller, Lorraine; *Getz, Stan; Ghost note; *Gibbs, Terry; Giddins, Gary; *Gilberto, Astrud; *Gillespie, Dizzy; Gilmore, John; *Gilson, Jef; *Gismonti, Egberto; *Giuffre, Jimmy; *Gladden, Eddie; *Glenn, Tyree; Gliss; *GNP-Crescendo; *Gold, Harry; Gold, Sanford; *Golson, Benny; *Gomez, Eddie; Gonella, Nat; *Gonsalves, Paul; *Gonzales, Babs; Goodrick, Mick; Good Time Jazz; *Goodwin, Bill; Gordon, Bobby; *Gordon, Dexter; *Gospel; *Gottlieb, Danny; *Gourley, Jimmy; *Gowans, Brad; *Graham, Kenny; Gramavision; Granelli, Jerry; *Grappelli, Stephane; *Graves, Milford; *Gray, Wardell; *Green, Dave; *Green, Freddie; *Green, Grant; *Green, Urbie; *Greene, Burton; *Greenlee, Charles; Greenwich, Sonny; *Greer, Sonny; *Greig, Stan; *Grey, Al; Griffin, Chris; Griffin, Johnny; *Griffiths, Malcolm; *Grimes, Henry; *Grimes, Tiny; Groove (i); *Grossman, Steve; Grosz, Marty; Growl; GRP; *Gruntz, George; *Grusin, Dave; *Guarnieri, Johnny; *Gumbs, Onaje Allen; *Gumpert, Ulrich; Gurtu, Trilok; *Guy, Joe; Gwaltney, Tommy; *Hackett, Bobby; Haden, Charlie; Hadi, Shafi; *Hafer, Dick; Hahn, Jerry; *Haig, Al; Hakim, Omar; *Hakim, Sadik; *Halcox, Pat; Half-valve; *Hall family; *Hall, Adelaide; *Hall, Al; *Hall, Jim; *Hall, Minor; Hall, Skip; *Hall, Tubby; Hamilton, Chico; *Hamilton, Jeff; *Hamilton, Jimmy; *Hamilton, Scott; *Hammond, Johnny; *Hampton, Lionel; *Hampton, Slide; *Hancock, Herbie; *Hanna, Jake; *Hanna, Sir Roland; Hardaway, Bob; Hardee, John; *Hardman, Bill; *Hardwick, Otto; Harley, Rufus; Harmolodic theory; *Harmonica; Harp (i); *Harper, Billy; Harper, Herbie; *Harrell, Tom; *Harris, Barry; *Harris, Bill (i); *Harris, Bill (ii); *Harris, Craig; *Harris, Gene; *Harris, Joe (ii); *Harris, Little Benny; Harrison, Donald; *Hart, Billy; *Hart, Clyde; *Hastings, Lennie; *hat Hut; Havens, Bob; *Hawdon, Dickie; *Hawes, Hampton; *Hawkins, Coleman; Hayes, Edgar; *Hayes, Louis; *Hayes, Tubby; Haynes, Roy; *Hazel, Monk; *Heard, J. C.; *Heard, John; *Heatley, Spike; Hegamin, Lucille; Helias, Mark; Helm, Bob; *Hemphill, Julius; *Henderson, Eddie; *Henderson, Fletcher; *Henderson, Horace; Henderson, Joe; *Henderson, Wayne; *Hendricks, Jon; *Henry, Ernie; *Henry, Haywood; Hentoff, Nat; *Herdzin, Krzysztof; *Herman, Woody; *Heywood, Eddie; *Hicks, John; *Higginbotham, J. C.; *Higgins, Billy; *Hill, Andrew; Hill, Buck; *Hill, Chippie; *Hill, Teddy; *Hines, Earl; *Hino, Terumasa; *Hinton, Milt; *Hirt, Al; *Hiseman, Jon; *Hite, Les; *Hodes, Art; *Hodges, Johnny; *Hogan, G. T.; *Hogg, Derek; *Hoggard, Jay; *Holder, Terrence; *Holdsworth, Allan; *Holiday, Billie; Holiday, Clarence; *Holland, Dave; *Holley, Major; *Holman, Bill; Holmes, Charlie; *Holmes, Groove; *Hołownia, Bogdan; *Holt, Redd; *Hooper, Les; *Hope, Elmo; *Hopkins, Claude; Hopkins, Fred; Horizon; *Horn, Paul; Houben, Steve; *Howard, Darnell; *Howard, Noah; Hubbard, Freddie; Hübner, Ralf; *Hucko, Peanuts; Hudson, Will; *Hughart, Jim; *Hughes, Spike; *Hultcrantz, Torbjörn; *Humair, Daniel; Humble, Derek; *Humes, Helen; Humphrey, Paul; Humphrey, Ralph; *Hunt, Fred; Hunt, Pee Wee; *Hutcherson, Bobby; *Hyman, Dick; *Ibrahim, Abdullah; *Igoe, Sonny; Improvisation; Improvised music; *Impulse!; *Ingham, Keith; Inner City; *Ino, Nobuyoshi; Inzalaco, Tony; *Irakere; Irwin, Dennis; Isaacs, Ike (ii); Isola, Frank; *Israels, Chuck; Issue number; *Itoh , Kimiko; *Jackson, Chubby; *Jackson, Cliff; *Jackson, Franz; *Jackson, Willis "Gator"; *Jacobsen, Pete; *Jacquet, Illinois; *Jagodziński, Andrej; *Jamal, Ahmad; *James,

Bob; Jarczyk, Jan; *Jaremko, Zbigniew; Jarman, Joseph; *Jarrett, Keith; Jarvis, Clifford; Jazz Band Ball Orchestra; Jazzline (ii); Jazz Workshop; Jefferson, Eddie; *Jefferson, Hilton; *Jenkins, Freddie; Jenkins, Leroy; *Jenny-Clark, Jean-François; *Jerome, Jerry; *Jobim, Antonio Carlos; Johnson, Alphonso; *Johnson, Budd; Johnson, Dick; *Johnson, Dink; *Johnson, Gus; *Johnson, Howard (ii); *Johnson, J. J.; *Johnson, Keg; *Johnson, Manzie; *Johnson, Money; *Johnson, Osie; *Johnson, Pete; *Johnson, Reggie; *Johnson, Walter; *Jolly, Pete; *Jones family; *Jones, Carmell; Jones, Etta; *Jones, Jimmy; *Jones, Jo; *Jones, Philly Joe; *Jones, Quincy; *Jones, Richard M.; Jones, Rodney; *Jones, Rusty; *Jones, Sam; Jones, Willie; *Jonkisz, Kazimierz; *Jordan, Clifford; *Jordan, Duke; *Jordan, Sheila; *Jordan, Stanley; Jordan, Steve (i); Jost, Ekkehard; *Jump; Juris, Vic; *Kaminsky, Max; *Kamuca, Richie; *Karolak, Wojciech; *Katz, Dick; *Kawasaki, Ryo; Keepnews, Orrin; *Kellaway, Roger; *Kelly, George; Kelly, Red; *Kelly, Wynton; *Kenton, Stan; Kenyatta, Robin; *Keppard, Freddie; *Kerr, Brooks; *Kersey, Kenny; Kessel, Barney; Keynote; *Khan, Steve; *Kincaide, Deane; King , Morgana; *King, Peter; *Kinsey, Tony; *Kirby, John; *Kirk, Andy; Kirk, Roland; *Kirkland, Kenny; *Klein, Harry; Klein, Oscar; *Klemmer, John; *Klink, Al; *Kloss, Eric; *Kluger, Irv; *Knepper, Jimmy; *Kochan, Jacek; *Kondo, Toshinori; *Konitz, Lee; *Konopasek, Jan; *Korner, Alexis; *Kotick, Teddy; Koto; *Krahmer, Carlo; *Kral, Roy; *Kress, Carl; *Kriegel, Volker; *Krupa, Gene; *Kuhn, Steve; *Kurylewicz, Andrzej; *Kyle, Billy; *LaBarbera family; Laboriel, Abe; *Lacy, Steve; LaFaro, Scott; *Lafitte, Guy; *Lagrene, Bireli; Lake, Oliver; *Lambert, Dave; *Lamond, Don; *Lancaster, Byard; *Land, Harold; Lande, Art; *Landers, Wes; Landmark; *Lang, Eddie; *Lang, Mike; Lang, Ronnie; *Lanphere, Don; *Larkins, Ellis; *La Roca, Pete; *Lateef, Yusef; Latin jazz; LaVerne, Andy; *Lawrence, Arnie; Lawrence, Elliot; *Laws, Hubert; *Lawson, Hugh; Leaders; Lee, Bill (i); *Lee, George E.; *Lee, Jeanne; *Lee, Julia; Lee, Will; *Leeman, Cliff; Leggio, Carmen; Legnini, Eric; Lehn, Erwin; Leighton, Bernie; *Lemon, Brian; *Lenz, Günter; *Leonard, Harlan; Leonhart, Jay; Lesberg, Jack; *Levey, Stan; *Leviev, Milcho; Levine, Mark; Levitt, Al; Levy, John; *Levy, Lou; *Lewis, George (ii); Lewis, Herbie; *Lewis, Meade "Lux"; *Lewis, Mel; *Lewis, Ramsey; *Lewis, Sabby; Lewis, Vic; *Liebman, Dave; *Lightfoot, Terry; *Lightsey, Kirk; Lim, Harry; Limelight; *Lincoln, Abbey; Lincoln, Abe; Lindberg, John; *Liston, Melba; *Little, Wilbur; *Lloyd, Charles; Lloyd, Jerry; Locke, Eddie; *Lockwood, Didier; *Longo, Mike; Loos, Charles; *Lorber, Jeff; *Louiss, Eddy; Love, Preston; *Lowe, Frank; *Lowe, Mundell; *Lowther, Henry; *Lucie, Lawrence; *Lunceford, Jimmie; *Lyons, Jimmy (ii); *Lytell, Jimmy; *Lytle, Johnny; *Lyttelton, Humphrey; *Mabern, Harold; *McBee, Cecil; *McCall, Mary Ann; *McCandless, Paul; *McCann, Les; *McClure, Ron; *McCurdy, Roy; McDonough, Dick; *McDuff, Brother Jack; *McFerrin, Bobby; *McGarity, Lou; *McGhee, Howard; *McGregor, Chris; *McGriff, Jimmy; *Machito; McIntyre, Hal; *McIntyre, Kalaparusha Maurice; *Mackel, Billy; *McKenna, Dave; *McKibbon, Al; *McKinney family; *McKusick, Hal; McLaughlin, John; *McLean, Jackie; McLean, Rene; *McNair, Harold; McNeely, Jim; *McPartland, Marian; McPhee, Joe; *McPherson, Charles; *McRae, Barry; *McRae, Carmen; *McShann, Jay; *Madison, Bingie; Mahavishnu Orchestra; *Mahones, Gildo; *Mainieri, Mike; *Majewski, Henryk; *Malachi, John; Malone, Tom; *Mance, Junior; *Mandolin; Mangione, Chuck; *Mann, Herbie; *Mann, Tony; Manne, Shelly; *Manone, Wingy; *Mantler, Mike; *Marable, Fate; Marable, Larance; Marcus, Steve; Margolis, Sam; Margulis, Charlie; *Maria, Tania; *Mariano, Charlie; *Marmarosa, Dodo; *Marsala, Joe; *Marsalis family; *Marsh, Warne; Marshall, Eddie; *Marshall, Kaiser; *Marshall, Wendell; *Martin, Sara; Martin, Skip; Martino Pat; *Masekela, Hugh; *Maseli, Bernhard; *Mason, Harvey; Masso, George; Master (i); Master Jazz Recordings; Mastersounds; *Mastren, Carmen; *Mathews, Ronnie; Matrix number; *Matuszkiewicz, Jerzy; *Maupin, Bennie; Mays, Bill; *Mays, Lyle; *M-Base; Mehegan, John; Meldonian, Dick; *Melillo, Mike; *Mengelberg, Misha; Menza, Don; Mercury; Merrill, Helen; Metcalf, Louis; Metheny, Pat; *Mezzrow, Mezz; *Michelot, Pierre; Migliori, Jay; *Miles, Lizzie; *Miller, Glenn; *Miller, Harry; *Miller, Marcus; Miller, Mulgrew; *Miller, Punch; *Millinder, Lucky; *Mills, Jackie; Mingus, Charles; *Mingus Dynasty; *Minor, Dan; *Miśkiewicz, Henryk; Mitchell, Billy; Mitchell, Blue; *Mitchell, George; *Mitchell, Grover; Mitchell, Roscoe; Mixon, Danny; *Mobley, Hank; Modal jazz; Moers Music; *Moffett family; *Moholo, Louis; *Mole, Miff; *Mondragon, Joe; *Monk, Thelonious; MONO; Monterose, J. R.; *Montgomery family; *Montgomery, Marian; Montoliu, Tete; *Moody, James; Mooney, Joe; Moore, Billy; Moore, Brew; *Moore, Eddie; *Moore, Freddie; *Moore, Glen; *Moore, Michael (i); Moore, Oscar; Moore, Pee Wee; *Morehouse, Chauncey; *Moreira, Airto; Morell, Marty; Morello, Joe; *Morgan family; *Morgan, Frank; *Morgan, Lanny; *Morgan, Lee; *Morgenstern, Dan; Morrison, Peck; *Morrissey, Dick; *Morton, Benny; Mosaic (ii); Mosca, Sal; Mosley, Snub; *Moss, Danny; *Most, Abe; *Moten, Bennie; *Motian, Paul; Mover, Bob; Moye, Don; *Możdżer, Leszek; MPS; Mraz, George; *Muhammad, Idris; *Mullen, Jim; *Mulligan, Gerry; *Mumford, John; Mundy, Jimmy; *Muniak, Janusz; *Muranyi, Joe; Murphy, Mark; Murphy, Spud; *Murphy, Turk; Murray, David; *Murray, Sunny; Muse (ii); Musette; Musso, Vido; Mussulli, Boots; Myers, Amina Claudine; *Nagórski, Grzegorz; *Nahorny, Włodzimierz; *Namysłowski, Zbigniew; Nance, Ray; *Nanton, Tricky Sam; *Napoleon family; *Napper, Kenny; *Narell, Andy; Nascimento, Milton; *Nasser, Jamil; Neidlinger, Buell; Neloms, Bob; *Nelson, Big Eye; Nelson, Louis; Nelson, Oliver; *Nesbitt, John; *Newborn, Calvin; *Newborn, Phineas; *Newman, Joe; Newsom, Tommy; Newton, James; New York Art Quartet; New York Contemporary Five; New York Saxophone Quartet; *Nicholas, Albert; Nicholas, Big Nick; *Nichols, Keith; *Nichols, Red; Niewood, Gerry; *Nightclubs and other venues: Chile, China, India, Morocco, Singapore, Sri Lanka, Switzerland, USA (Atlanta, Baltimore, Boston metropolitan area, Chicago, Cincinnati, Dallas, Houston, Indianapolis, Kansas City, Minneapolis, Newark, New York, Philadelphia, Pittsburgh, Portland, St. Paul, San Antonio, San Francisco Bay area, Seattle, Washington); *Nimitz, Jack; *Nistico, Sal (ii); *Nock, Mike; Nocturne; *Noone, Jimmie; Norman, Fred; *Norris, Al; *Norris, Walter; Norvo, Red; Nussbaum, Adam; O'Day, Anita; *O'Farrill, Chico; *Ohno, Shunzo; *Oki, Itaru; *Okoshi, Tiger; Old and New Dreams; Oleszkiewicz, Darek; *Oliver, King; *Oliver, Sy; *Olu Dara; *Olympia Brass Band; *Onyx (ii); *Oregon; *Ørsted Pedersen, Niels-Henning; *Ortega, Anthony Robert; Osborne, Mary; *Ousley, Harold; *Owens, Jimmy; Owl; *Ozone, Makoto; Pablo; Pace, Sal; *Pacific Jazz; *Page, Hot Lips; *Page, Walter; *Paich, Marty; Pallemaerts, Dré; *Palmer, Earl; *Palmer, Roy; *Palmier, Remo; Palo Alto; *Parenti, Tony; Paris, Jackie; *Parker, Johnny; *Parlan, Horace; *Parnell, Jack; *Pass, Joe; *Pastorius, Jaco; *Patrick, Pat; *Patton, Big John; *Paul, Emanuel; *Pawlik, Włodek; Payne, Cecil; *Payne, Sonny; *Peacock, Gary; Pearson, Duke; *Peer, Beverly; *Pege, Aladár; *Peiffer, Bernard; Pell, Dave; Pepper, Art; *Peraza, Armando; *Perez, Manuel; *Perkins, Bill; Perkins, Carl; *Perkins, Walter; Perla, Gene; Persip, Charli; *Person, Houston; Peterson, Hannibal; *Peterson, Oscar; *Petit, Buddy; *Petrucciani, Michel; *Pettiford, Oscar; *Phillips, Barre; Phillips, Flip; *Picard, John; *Picou, Alphonse; Pierce, Billie; Pierce, Billy; *Pierce, De De; *Pierce, Nat; Pierończyk, Adam; *Pike, Dave; *Pillars, Hayes; Pinkett, Ward; *Pisano, John; *Pizzarelli, Bucky; *Pizzarelli, John; *Pizzi, Ray; Plaxico, Lonnie; Polcer, Ed; *Polo, Danny; Pomeroy, Herb; *Ponder, Jimmy; Ponomarev, Valery; Ponty, Jean-Luc; Pope, Odean; *Popek, Krzystof; *Porcino, Al; Porter, Roy; Post-bop; *Potter, Tommy; *Powell, Benny; *Powell, Bud; Powell, Mel; *Powell, Seldon; *Preservation Hall Jazz Band; *Prestige; Preston, Don; Preston, Eddie; *Priester, Julian; Procope, Russell; Prowizorka Jazz Band; *Pruitt, Carl; Pugh, Jim; *Pukwana, Dudu; Pullen,

Don; *Puma, Joe; *Purbrook, Colin; Purim, Flora; Purtill, Moe; *Pyne, Chris; *Pyne, Mick; *Quebec, Ike; *Queen, Alvin; Queener, Charlie; *Quinichette, Paul; *Rader, Don; *Rae, Johnny; *Raeburn, Boyd; *Rainey, Chuck; Ramey, Gene; *Randall, Freddy; *Randolph, Irving "Mouse"; Randolph, Zilner T.; *Raney, Jimmy; Rassinfosse, Jean-Louis; *Rava, Enrico; *RCA Victor; *Recording; *Red, Sonny; *Redd, Freddie; *Redd, Vi; Redman, Dewey; *Redman, Don; *Red Onion Jazz Babies; *Reece, Dizzy; Reed, Waymon; Rehak, Frank; Reid, Rufus; *Reinhardt family; *Remler, Emily; *Renaud, Henri; *Repertory band; *Reprise; *Reuss, Allan; Revolutionary Ensemble; *Rich, Buddy; *Richards, Emil; *Richards, Red; *Richards, Trevor; *Richardson, Jerome; *Richardson, Rodney; Richman, Boomie; *Richmond, Dannie; *Richmond, Mike; Ridley, Larry; *Riley, Ben; Riley, Herman; *Rimington, Sammy; Ritenour, Lee; *Rivers, Sam; Riverside; *Roach, Max; *Roberts, Howard; *Roberts, Luckey; *Robinson, Fred; *Robinson, Ikey; Robinson, Janice; *Robinson, Perry; *Robinson, Prince; Roccisano, Joe; *Rodney, Red; *Rodowicz, Piotr; *Rogers, Shorty; *Roker, Mickey; Roland, Gene; *Rollini, Adrian; Rollins, Sonny; *Romano, Aldo; Romano, Joe; Romão, Dom Um; Root, Billy; Rose, Boris; *Rose, Wally; *Rosengren, Bernt; *Rosolino, Frank; *Ross, Annie; Roulette; Rouse, Charlie; Rousselet, Richard; *Rowles, Jimmie; Rowser, Jimmy; Roy, Badal; *Royal, Ernie; *Royal, Marshal; Royal Roost (ii); *Rudd, Roswell; *Rumsey, Howard; Ruppli, Michel; *Rusch, Bob; Rushen, Patrice; *Rushing, Jimmy; *Russell, Bill; *Russell, Curly; *Russell, George; *Russell, Luis; *Russell, Pee Wee; *Russo, Bill; Saba; Sachs, Aaron; *Sackville; *Sadowski, Krzysztof; *Safranski, Eddie; *St. Cyr, Johnny; *Sakata, Akira; *Saluzzi, Dino; *Salvador, Sal; Sample, Joe; Samuels, Dave; Sanborn, David; *Sanchez, David; Sanders, Pharoah; *Sandoval, Arturo; *Santamaria, Mongo; *Savoy (ii); *Sbarbaro, Tony; *Schifrin, Lalo; Schlitten, Don; *Schnitter, David; *Schroeder, Gene; *Schwaller, Roman; *Ścierański, Krzysztof; *Scobey, Bob; *Scott, Bud; *Scott, Cecil; Scott, Raymond; *Scott, Ronnie; Scott, Shirley; Scott, Tom; Scott, Tony; Scott-Heron, Gil; *Seamen, Phil; *Sears, Al; *Sebesky, Don; Seifert, Zbigniew; Selden, Fred; *Severinsen, Doc; Shake; Shakti; *Shank, Bud; *Shannon, Terry; Shapiro, Artie; *Sharrock, Sonny; *Shaughnessy, Ed; *Shavers, Charlie; *Shaw, Arvell; *Shaw, Hank; Shaw, Woody; Shearer, Dick; *Shearing, George; *Sheldon, Jack; Shepp, Archie; Shertzer, Hymie; *Shew, Bobby; *Shihab, Sahib; Shoemake, Charlie; Shoffner, Bob; Short, Bob; Shorter, Wayne; Shulman, Joe; *Signal; *Signorelli, Frank; *Sikala, Maciej; *Silva, Alan; *Silver, Horace; *Simeon, Omer; *Simmons, John; *Simmons, Norman; *Simmons, Sonny; *Simpkins, Andy; Sims, Zoot; Simtaine, Félix; *Sinatra, Frank; *Singing; *Singleton, Zutty; Sirone; *Sissle, Noble; Sitar; *Sjösten, Lars; *Skidmore, Jimmy; *Skowron, Janusz; *Śmietana, Jarosław; Smith, Bill (i); *Smith, Brian; Smith, Carson; Smith, Derek; *Smith, Floyd; *Smith, Jimmy; *Smith, Joe; *Smith, John; Smith, Johnny; *Smith, Keith; Smith Lonnie Liston; Smith, Louis; Smith, Michael; *Smith, Russell; *Smith, Stuff; *Smith, Tab; Smith, Trixie; Smith, Wadada Leo; *Smith, Warren (ii); *Smith, Willie "the Lion"; *Snowden, Elmer; *Solal, Martial; Soloff, Lew; Soph, Ed; *Soprano Summit; *SOS; Soul jazz; *Soul Note; *South, Harry; *Spanier, Muggsy; *Spaulding, James; *Spencer, O'Neill; *Spring, Bryan; *Sproles, Victor; *Stacy, Jess; Stahl, Dave; *Stamm, Marvin; *Stankiewicz, Kuba; Staton, Dakota; *Stearns, Marshall W.; Steel drum; Steeplechase; *Steig, Jeremy; Stein, Lou; *Steps Ahead; *Stern, Mike; *Steward, Herbie; *Stewart, Bob; *Stewart, Rex; Stewart, Slam; *Stitt, Sonny; *Stobart, Kathy; Stop-time; *Strazzeri, Frank; String Trio of New York; *Strzelczyk, Maciej; Stubblefield, John; Studer, Fredy; Subtone; *Suchanek, Bronisław; *Sulieman, Idrees; Sullivan, Charles; *Sullivan, Joe; *Sullivan, Maxine; Sun (ii); Sunnyside; Sun Ra; *Sunshine, Monty; *Sutton, Ralph; *Suzuki, Isao; *Suzuki, Shoji; *Swallow, Steve; *Swartz, Harvie; *Swing (i); *Szabo, Frank; *Szafran, Lora; *Szukalski, Tomasz; Tablā; *Tacuma, Jamaaladeen; *Take; *Tate, Buddy; *Tate, Grady; *Taylor, Art; *Taylor, Billy (i); *Taylor, Billy (ii); *Taylor, Cecil; *Taylor, Gene; *Taylor, John; Taylor, Mark (ii); *Teagarden family; *Tee, Richard; *Teitelbaum, Richard; *Temperley, Joe; Terminal vibrato; *Terry, Clark; *Teschemacher, Frank; *Themen, Art; Theresa; Thielemans, Toots; *Thigpen, Ed; *Thomas, Foots; *Thomas, Joe (iii); *Thomas, Joe (iv); *Thomas, Leon; *Thomas, René; *Thompson, Barbara; *Thompson, Eddie; *Thompson, Lucky; *Thompson, Sir Charles; *Thornhill, Claude; *Threadgill, Henry; Tiberi, Frank; Timeless; Timmons, Bobby; *Tio family; *Tizol, Juan; *Tjader, Cal; Tolliver, Charles; Tomkins, Les; *Tomkins, Trevor; *Tompkins, Ross; Torff, Brian; *Tormé Mel; Tough, Dave; Toussaint, Jean; *Towner, Ralph; *Tracey, Stan; *Transcription (i); *Trappier, Traps; Traxler, Gene; *Trent, Alphonso; Trip; *Tristano, Lennie; Trujillo, Bill; *Trumbauer, Frankie; Tucker, Ben; *Tucker, Bobby; *Tucker, George; *Tucker, Mickey; *Turner, Bruce; Turner, Danny; *Turner, Joe (ii); Turre, Steve; Turrentine, Stanley; *Turrentine, Tommy; Twardzik, Dick; *29th Street Saxophone Quartet; *Tyler, Charles; *Tyner, McCoy; ūd; Ulmer, James "Blood"; *Umezu, Kazutoki; Urbaniak, Michal; Urso, Phil; *Urtreger, René; *Vaché, Warren; *Valdés, Chucho; *Valentine, Kid Thomas; *Vamp; *Vandermark, Ken; Vanguard; Vann, Erwin; *Van 't Hof, Jasper; Vasconcelos, Nana; Vaughan, Sarah; Ventura, Charlie; Venuti, Joe; Verve; *Viale, Jean-Louis; *Vinnegar, Leroy; Vinson, Eddie "Cleanhead"; Viola, Al; Vitous, Miroslav; *Vocalese; Von Ohlen, John; *Wadud, Abdul; Waits, Freddie; Waits, Tom; Walcott, Collin; *Waldron, Mal; *Walk Away; Wallington, George; *Walrath, Jack; Walton, Cedar; *Wanzo, Mel; *Ward, Carlos; Ware, David S.; Ware, Munn; *Ware, Wilbur; Warland Jean; Warren, Earle; *Warren, Peter; Warwick, Carl; Washington, Dinah; Washington, Grover, Jr.; *Washington, Kenny; *Wasilewski, Marcin; *Watanabe, Kazumi; *Watanabe, Sadao; *Waters, Benny; *Waters, Ethel; Waters, Monty; *Watkins, Doug; Watkins, Julius; *Watrous, Bill; Watson, Bobby; *Watters, Lu; Watts, Ernie; Wa-wa; *Wayne, Chuck; Wayne, Frances; Weather Report; *Webb, Chick; *Weber, Eberhard; Webster, Ben; *Wein, George; *Weiss, Klaus; *Wellins, Bobby; *Wells, Dicky; Wellstood, Dick; *Welsh, Alex; Wess, Frank; *Westbrook, Mike; Weston, Randy; *Wettling, George; Wheeler, Kenny; *Whetsol, Artie; *White, Amos; *White, Andrew; White, Chris; *White, Harry; White, Lenny; *White, Michael (ii); *White, Sonny; *Wiggs, Johnny; *Wilber, Bob; *Wilder, Joe; *Wiley, Lee; *Wilkins, Ernie; *Williams, Cootie; Williams, David; *Williams, Elmer; *Williams, Jackie; *Williams, James; *Williams, Joe; Williams, John (i); Williams, John (ii); *Williams, John (iii); *Williams, Johnny (i); *Williams, Johnny (ii); *Williams, Leroy; *Williams, Martin; *Williams, Mary Lou; *Williams, Roy; *Williams, Tony; *Williamson, Claude; Willis, Larry; *Wilmer, Val; Wilson, Dennis; *Wilson, Gerald; *Wilson, Nancy; *Wilson, Shadow; *Wilson, Teddy; Windhurst, Johnny; *Winding, Kai; *Winstone, Norma; *Winters, Tiny; *Witherspoon, Jimmy; *Wojtasik, Piotr; Wolff, Michael; *Wood, Booty; *Wooding, Sam; *Woodman, Britt; Woods, Phil; *Woodyard, Sam; Wootten, Red; *Workman, Reggie; World Saxophone Quartet; *World Wide; *Wright family; Wright, Frank; *Wright, Gene; *Wright, Leo; *Wyands, Richard; Wyble, Jimmy; *Xanadu; Xiques, Ed; *Yancey, Jimmy; *Yoder, Walt; *Young, Eldee; *Young, Larry; Young, Lee; *Young, Lester; Young, Snooky; *Young Tuxedo Brass Band; *Zabiegliński, Janusz; *Żądło, Leszek; Zappa, Frank; Zarchy, Zeke; Zawinul, Joe; *Zeitlin, Denny; *Zgraja, Krysztof; *Zoller, Attila; *Zurke, Bob

Kimbrough, Frank: Nichols, Herbie

Kinzer, Charles: *Elgar, Charlie; *Onward Brass Band (i)

Kjellberg, Erik: *Allan, Jan; *Arnold, Harry; *Babs, Alice; *Billberg, Rolf; *Björksten, Hacke; *Cook, Willie; *Domnérus, Arne; *Ehrling, Thore; *Ellboj, Lulle; *Eriksberg, Folke; Görling, Miff; Görling, Zilas; *Gullin, Lars; *Gustafsson, Rune; *Hallberg, Bengt; *Hasselgård, Stan; *Hedrenius, Gugge; Hülphers, Arne; Jederby, Thore; *Johansson, Jan; Kustbandet; *Laine, Bob; *Larsson, Rolf; Lidström, Jack; Lind, Nisse "Bagarn"; Lind,

Ove; *Metronome; *Nilson, Gunnar; *Norin, Carl-Henrik; *Norman, Charlie; *Österwall, Seymour; Paramountorkestern; *Persson, Åke; Redland, Charles; *Rena Rama; *Riedel, Georg; *Rosengren, Bernt; *Sandström, Nisse; *Sonet; *Svenska Hotkvintetten; Svensson, Reinhold; *Swanerud, Thore; *Thelin, Eje; *Theselius, Gösta; *Törner, Gösta; *von Eichwald, Håkan; Wallin, Bengt-Arne; *Werner, Lasse; *Wickman, Putte; Zetterlund, Monica

Knauer, Wolfram: ARFI; *Bartkowski, Czesław; *Bliziński, Marek; Bohländer, Carlo; Borneman, Ernest; Brönner, Till; Bründl, Manfred; Brüning, Uschi; Busch, Sigi; Carl, Rüdiger; *Dauner, Wolfgang; *Dębski, Krzesimir; Faber, Johannes; Giger, Peter; Glawischnig, Dieter; Goykovich, Dusko; Gräwe, Georg; Haider, Joe; Harth, Alfred; Hasler, Gabriele; Haurand, Ali; Herbolzheimer, Peter; *Jaremko, Zbigniew; Joos, Herbert; *Karolak, Wojciech; Kay, Connie; König, Klaus; *Kühn, Rolf; Kulpowicz, Sławomir; *Kurylewicz, Andrzej; Lackerschmid, Wolfgang; Lakatos, Tony; Lüdemann, Hans; *Majewski, Henryk; Makowicz, Adam; Mangelsdorff, Albert; *Muniak, Janusz; *Namysłowski, Zbigniew; *Naura, Michael; Nay, Joe; *Nightclubs and other venues: Germany; Novi Singers; Orchestra U. S. A.; Passport; Pilz, Michel; Rabold, Frederic; Rek, Vitold; Rettenbacher, J. A.; Riessler, Michael; Roidinger, Adelhard; *Sadowski, Krzysztof; Sagmeister, Michael; Sänger, Christof; Sauer, Heinz; Schlott, Volker; Schlüter, Wolfgang; Schönenberg, Detlef; Schubert, Matthias; Schwab, Sigi; Sehring, Rudi; Spendel, Christoph; Stefański, Janusz; *Suchanek, Bronisław; *Szukalski, Tomasz; *Trzaskowski, Andrzej; Ullmann, Gebhard; United Jazz and Rock Ensemble; Viera, Joe; *Weiss, Klaus; Workshop de Lyon; *Wróblewski, Jan; Zacharias, Helmut; *Żądło, Leszek; Zerbe, Hannes; *Zgraja, Krysztof

Koch, Lawrence: *Albert, Don; *Anderson, Ernestine; *Archey, Jimmy; *Babasin, Harry; Bates family; *Bernstein, Artie; *Bert, Eddie; *Carisi, Johnny; Catlett, Buddy; Chambers, Henderson; Clark, Buddy; Cole, June; Coleman, Earl; *Collette, Buddy; *Cranshaw, Bob; Creath, Charlie; *Crow, Bill; *Davis, Eddie "Lockjaw"; Dominique, Natty; *Donaldson, Lou; Drew, John; *Duvivier, George; Eager, Allen; *Enevoldsen, Bob; *Fontana, Carl; Fowlkes, Charlie; *Gonzales, Babs; *Gray, Wardell; Hayes, Clancy; *Henry, Ernie; *Holley, Major; *Howard, Darnell; Hughes, Bill; Jackson, Quentin; Jazztet; *Johnson, Keg; *Jones, Sam; McEachern, Murray; McFarland, Gary; McRae, Teddy; Mares, Paul; *Marshall, Wendell; Matthews, George; *Minor, Dan; Morrow, Buddy; Nelson, Dave; *Nicholas, Albert; Nicholas, Wooden Joe; *Nimitz, Jack; Nunez, Alcide "Yellow"; Pecora, Santo; Peña, Ralph; Piano; *Powell, Seldon; Six, Jack; Stewart, Buddy; Swope, Earl; *Taylor, Billy (i); *Vinnegar, Leroy; Watson, Leo; *White, Harry

Koenig, Karl: Assunto family; Brown, Tom; *Dejan, Harold; *Dukes of Dixieland; *Johnson, Dink; Kelly, Chris; *Perez, Manuel; Stein, Johnny

Kolleritsch, Elisabeth: Institut für Jazzforschung

Kramlich, Raymonde S.: *Bailey, Mildred; Swingle Singers

La Barbara, Joan: *Teitelbaum, Richard

Laird, Paul R.: Berliner Jazztage; Colorado Jazz Party; *Festivals; Festival International de Jazz de Montréal; Festival Mondial du Jazz Antibes–Juan-les-Pins; Grande Parade du Jazz; International Jazz Jamboree Festival; International New Jazz Festival Moers; Molde International Jazz Festival; Monterey Jazz Festival; Montreax International Jazz Festival; New Orleans Jazz & Heritage Festival; Newport Jazz Festival; North Sea Jazz Festival; Pori Jazz; Sacramento Dixieland Jubilee; Umbria Jazz

Lamb, Andrew: Noble, Ray

Lambert, Eddie: *Ashby, Harold; *Bell, Aaron; *Brown, Lawrence; Carruthers, Earl; Carry, Scoops; *Cook, Willie; *Cooper, Buster; Davis, Kay; *Davis, Lem; *Dixon, Eric; *Ellington, Mercer; Goodwin, Henry; *Glenn, Tyree; Guy, Fred; *Hardwick, Otto; *Holder, Terrence; Irvis, Charlie; *Jefferson, Hilton; *Jenkins, Freddie; Johnson, Jimmie; Lamb, John; Maxwell, Jimmy; Mills, Irving; Minerve, Geezil; *Oliver, Sy; Powell, Specs; *Quebec, Ike; *Quinichette, Paul; *Scott, Cecil; *Smith, John; *Stone, Fred; *Sweatman, Wilbur; *Thomas, Foots; *Tizol, Juan; Webb, Speed; Webster, Paul; *Whetsol, Artie; White, Rocky; Wiggins, Hassan J. J.; Williams, Franc; *Wood, Booty; *Woodman, Britt; *Woodyard, Sam

Laplace, Michel: Abadie, Claude; Agostini, Dante; Anachronic Jazz Band; *Arvanitas, Georges; Bacqueville, Patrick; *Bailey, Benny; Barda, Daniel; Barelli, Aimé; Barret, Eric; Bellest, Christian; Bellonzi, Charles; Biensan, François; Bonal, Jean; Bonnet, Michel; Boucaya, William; Bouchet, Alain; Braslavsky, Pierre; Brun, Philippe; Brunet, Alain; Camicas, Michel; Capon, Jean-Charles; Chautemps, Jean-Louis; Chéron, Paul; Chiboust, Noël; Cohanier, Edmond; Combelle, Alix; Cullaz, Alby; Cullaz, Pierre; Daly, Geo; Denis, Michel; De Villers, Michel; Diéval, Jack; Doriz, Dany; Double Six; Dumoustier Stompers; Ekyan, André; *Ferris, Glenn; Fohrenbach, Jean-Claude; Fonsèque, Raymond; Gaudry, Michel; Gauthé, Jacques; Gerard, Fred; Gossez, Pierre; Gousset, Claude; Gregor; Guérin, Beb; Guérin, Roger; Guilhot, Claude; Guin, François; Hausser, Michel; Hot Antic Jazz Band; Jaume, André; Jeanneau, François; Jullien, Ivan; Laudet, François; Legrand, Christiane; Lejeune, Philippe; Le Lann, Eric; Leroux, Gilbert; Levallet, Didier; Longnon, Jean-Loup; Lubat, Bernard; Luter, Claude; Mac Kac; Manzecchi, Franco; Mazetier, Louis; Milanta, Philippe; Montier, Nicholas; Moraweck, Lucien; Mougin, Stéphane; Naude, Jean-Claude; Paquinet, André; Paquinet, Guy; Paris Washboard; Pastre, Michel; *Peiffer, Bernard; Perrin, Mimi; Persiany, André; Portal, Michel; Preissac, Ludovic de; Richard, Marc; Rostaing, Hubert; Rovère, Gilbert; Samson, Jacky; Sardaby, Michel; Saudrais, Charles; Saussois, Patrick; Sellin, Hervé; Sellin, Pierre; Steckar, Marc; Vander, Maurice; Vauchant, Léo; Ventura, Ray; Vian, Boris; Warlop, Michel; Weiss, René; Wilen, Barney

Larson, Steve: *Bryant, Ray; Bryant, Tommy; *Feldman, Victor; *Frishberg, Dave; *Grusin, Dave; *Hawes, Hampton; *Lewis, Ramsey; *Oregon

LeBlanc, Eric: *Bennett, Buster

Lee, William F., III: *Almeida, Laurindo; Alvarez, Chico; Bernhart, Milt; *Childers, Buddy; *Cooper, Bob; *Holman, Bill; Levy, Hank; Maiden, Willie; *Salvador, Sal; *Shank, Bud

Levin, Floyd: Austin, Claire; Burrell, Duke; Cathcart, Dick; *Corb, Morty; Cullum, Jim, Jr.; Daily, Pete; Gabler, Milt; *Giordano, Vince; Girard, Adele; Goldie, Don; Jaffe, Allan (i); Janis, Conrad; Jazz Man; McHargue, Rosy; Robinson, Scott; Spikes brothers

Lindenmaier, H. L.: Berendt, Joachim-Ernst; *Lacy, Steve

Listavičiūtė, Aušra: Abarius, Gintautas; Vyšniauskas, Petras

Litchfield, Jack: *Davidson, Trump; Harrison, Lance; *Holmes, Johnny; Hooper, Lou; Jackson, Calvin; *McKay, Cliff; Namaro, Jimmy; *Niosi, Bert; *Sutton, Mynie; *Thomas, Millard; *Watson, Gilbert

Lotz, Rainer E.: Abbey, Leon; Abriani, John; Andreozzi, Eduardo; *Bacsik, Elek; Barriteau, Carl; Barton, Billy; Bauschke, Erhard; *Beamter, Jenő; *Benkó, Sándor; Berlin, Ben; Berry's; Bhumibol Adulyadej; Böhler, Fred; Borchard, Eric; Brandt, Helmut; *Brocksieper, Freddie; Brunner, Eddie; Bubbles, John; *Buttola, Ede; Castandet, Sam; *Chaix, Henri; *Chappy; Choquart, Loys; Danzi, Mike; De Gregori, Rio; Dies, Werner; Douglas, Louis; Etté, Bernard; *Filu; Flemming, Herb; Freichel, Louis; Fuhs, Julian; Gluskin, Lud; Goldene Sieben; Guarente, Frank; Henkels, Kurt; Heymans, Phyllis; Hirst, George F.; Hohenberger, Kurt; Höllerhagen, Ernst; Hyde, Alex; Kaye, Cab; Kleindin, Teddy; Kok, James; *Kőrössy, János; *Kovács, Andor; *Kovács, Gyula; Lanigiros; Laurence, Baby; McFarlane, Howard; McKenzie, Red; *Martiny, Lajos; Mavounzy, Robert; Maycock, George; Müller, Werner; New Hot Players; *New Yorkers (i); Nicholas Brothers; Notte, Flavius; Osterwald, Hazy; Pitman, Booker; *Ratip, Ahmed; Rosner, Ady; Salnave, Bertin; Siobud, André; Smith, Crickett; Stauffer, Teddy; *Szabados, György; *Tabányi, Mihály; Templin, Lutz; Tevelian, Meg; Wick, Joe; Widmann, Kutte; Williams, Rubberlegs

McCord, Kimberly: *Dodgion, Dottie; *Dodgion, Jerry; *Dudziak, Urszula; *Elias, Eliane; *Geller, Herb; *Geller, Lorraine; International Sweethearts of Rhythm; Rully, Aura

Machlin, Paul S.: *Larkins, Ellis

Madson, Brad: *American Federation of Jazz Societies; *Hall, Gene; *International Association of Jazz Educators; *Mantooth, Frank; *Matteson, Rich

Malone, Bill C.: Western swing; Wills, Bob

Mandel, Howard: Air; McCall, Steve; *Olu Dara; *Threadgill, Henry

Mantooth, Frank: *Mantooth, Frank

Marsh, Dave: Charles, Ray

Mathieson, Kenny: *Nightclubs and other venues: Scotland

Matteson, Mikki: *Matteson, Rich

Matthiessen, Ole: *Tchicai, John

Mattingly, Rick: Alexander, Mousey; Ameen, Robby; Brice, Percy; Burns, Roy; Campbell, Jimmy; Campbell, Tommy; Capp, Frank; Chambers, Joe; Clark, Bill; Colaiuta, Vinnie; Copeland, Keith; Ellington, Steve; Ferguson, Sherman; Franco, Guilherme; Haddad, Jamey; Harewood, Al; Hooper, Stix; Humphries, Lex; Jackson, Duffy; Jackson, Oliver; Mackrel, Dennis; *Marsalis family; Miles, Butch; *Moore, Eddie; Moses, Bob; Mouzon, Alphonse; *Peraza, Armando; Purdie, Bernard; *Rae, Johnny; Riley, John; Smith, Charlie; Smith, Marvin “Smitty”; Smith, Steve; Tana, Akira; Wackerman, Chad; Whittaker, Sebastian; Williams, Buddy

Mazzoletti, Adriano: Alvaro, Romero; Barzizza, Pippo; *Basso, Gianni; *Cerri, Franco; Cottiglieri, Piero; *Cuppini, Gil; Di Ceglie, Cosimo; Galli, Cesare; *Gaslini, Giorgio; Gorni, Kramer; Grasso, Alfio; Masetti, Glauco; Mobiglia, Tullio; Mojoli, Franco; Mussolini, Romano; Nicolosi, Roberto; Roman New Orleans Jazz Band; Rossi, Aldo; *Rotondo, Nunzio; Trovajoli, Armando; *Valdambrini, Oscar; Volonté, Eraldo; Zuccheri, Luciano

Milkowski, Bill: Beck, Jeff; *Bruford, Bill; *Carlton, Larry; *Catherine, Philip; *Di Meola, Al; *Evans, Bill (iii); *Frisell, Bill; Guerin, John; *James, Bob; *Liebman, Dave; *Miller, Marcus; *Rainey, Chuck; *Stern, Mike; *Tacuma, Jamaaladeen; Winter, Paul

Miller, Mark: Appleyard, Peter; Blake, Seamus; Bowen, Ralph; Brady, Tim; Bunnett, Jane; Christianson, Denny; Clarke, Terry; Collier, Ron; *Davidson, Trump; Delamont, Gordon; Derome, Jean; Desmarais, Lorraine; Downes, Wray; Ellis, Lisle; Elmes, Barry; Fraser, Hugh; Fuller, Jerry; Galloway, Jim; Gannon, Oliver; *Holmes, Johnny; Houle, François; Jackson, D. D.; Jensen, Ingrid; Jones, Oliver; Justin Time; Koffman, Moe; Krall, Diana; Lee, Ranee; Leitch, Peter; Lofsky, Lorne; Lussier, René; McConnell, Rob; McDougall, Ian; *McKay, Cliff; McMurdo, Dave; MacPherson, Fraser; Milne, Andy; Murley, Mike; *Nightclubs and other venues: Canada; Nimmons, Phil; *Niosi, Bert; Norris, Ray; Perry, P. J.; Plimley, Paul; Ranger, Claude; Rosnes, Renee; Senensky, Bernie; Smith, Bill (ii); *Stone, Fred; *Sutton, Mynie; Swainson, Neil; Symonds, Nelson; *Thomas, Millard G.; Thompson, Don; Turner, Dave; Vogel, Vic; *Watson, Gilbert; Young, Dave

Mongan, Norman: *Barbour, Dave; *Barksdale, Everett; *Barnes, George; Bean, Bill; Budimir, Dennis; *Collins, Cal; *Gourley, Jimmy; Hendrickson, Al; *Kress, Carl; *Lowe, Mundell; *Pisano, John; *Raney, Jimmy; Sete, Bola; *Shirley, Jimmy; *Thomas, René

Monson, Karen: *McPartland, Marian

Moore, Carman: *Russell, George

Morgan, Paula: Gushee, Lawrence; *Morgenstern, Dan; Shaw, Arnold; *Williams, Martin

Morgenstern, Dan: *Berry, Chu; *Challis, Bill; Gifford, Gene; *Nightclubs and other venues: USA (New York)

Mumma, Gordon: *Recording

Murray, Edward: *Evans, Bill (ii)

Nemko, Frankie: *Feather, Leonard

Newton, Peter: *Nightclubs and other venues: Australia

Noglik, Bert: *Bauer, Conrad; *Dašek, Rudolf; *Gumpert, Ulrich; *Petrowsky, Ernst-Ludwig; *Schlippenbach, Alex; *Schweizer, Irène; *Sommer, Günter; *Stańko, Tomasz; *Stivín, Jiří; *Szabados, György; *Union Deutscher Jazzmusiker

Nyquist, Bengt: *Nightclubs and other venues: Sweden

Ojakäär, Walter: Bril, Igor; Chekasin, Vladimir; Chizhik, Leonid; Ganelin, Vyacheslav; Garanian, Georgy; *Goloshchokin, David; Golstain, Gennady; Hovanesian, Datevik; Kozlov, Aleksey; Kuryokhin, Sergey; Kuznetsov, Aleksey; Levinovsky, Nikolay; Luk'yanov, German; Lundstrem, Oleg; Mustafa-Zade, Vagif; Naissoo, Tõnu; Nosov, Konstantin; Pauls, Raimond; Paulus, Tiit; Raubiško, Raimond; Rozenbergs, Gunārs; Saarsalu, Lembit; Tafenau, Raivo; Tarasov, Vladimir; Tsfasman, Aleksandr; Unt, Toivo; Utyosov, Leonid; Vapirov, Anatoly; Zubov, Aleksey

Oliver, Paul: Barrelhouse; *Blues; Boogie-woogie; Cox, Ida; Hokum; Johnson, Lonnie; Jug band; Race record; Rainey, Ma; Smith, Bessie; Smith, Mamie; Smith, Pine Top; Spivey, Victoria; *Tharpe, Sister Rosetta; *Turner, Joe (ii); Washboard band

Olliver, Guillermo I.: *Ratip, Ahmed

Ostransky, Leroy: *Barber, Bill; Brown, Garnett; Butterfield, Don; *Cohn, Al; De la Rosa, Frank; *Elliott, Don; *Grey, Al; *Harris, Bill (ii); *Horn, Paul; *Jones, Quincy; *Mann, Herbie; *Newman, Joe; *Payne, Sonny; *Powell, Benny; *Redd, Vi; *Richards, Emil; *Royal, Ernie; *Royal, Marshal; *Safranski, Eddie; Three Sounds

Owens, Thomas: Aarons, Al; Andrews, Ernie; American Jazz Orchestra; Baltazar, Gabe; Berk, Dick; Black/Note; Blevins, Leo; Bohanon, George; Bop; Bromberg, Brian; B Sharp; Burnett, Carl; Burrell, Kenny; Byas, Don; *Calypso; Ceroli, Nick; Christian, Charlie; Clayton, Jeff; Clayton, John; Cole, Richie; *Criss, Sonny; Crusaders; Cunliffe, Bill; Dickerson, Dwight; Dumas, Tony; Escheté, Ron; *Felder, Wilton; Florence, Bob; Forms; Frommer, Gary; *Gillespie, Dizzy; *Granz, Norman; Grove, Dick; Gryce, Gigi; Gumina, Tommy; Handy, John; Heath family; Hillery, Art; Horn, Shirley; Hurst, Robert; International Association of Jazz Appreciation; Jackson, Milt; Jazz at the Philharmonic; Johnson, Plas; Jones, Willie, III; Kirkwood, Johnny; L. A. Four; Lewis, John; Mackay, Dave; *Marsalis family; Mathews, Mat; *Middlebrooks, Wilfred; Modern Jazz Quartet; Navarro, Fats; Niehaus, Lennie; *Nightclubs and other venues: USA (Los Angeles metropolitan area); Patterson, Ann; Poindexter, Pony; Quill, Gene; Reed, Eric; Richmond, Kim; Rowles, Stacy; Samba; Smith, Paul; Sperling, Jack; *Stitt, Sonny: Supersax; Tanner, Paul; Upchurch, Phil; Van Gelder, Rudy; V.S.O.P. (i); White, Bobby; Woodard, Rickey

Papo, Alfredo: Albalat, Sebastià; Bas, Vlady; Benavent, Carles; Farrás, Josep-María; Farreras, Joe; Guri, Lucky; Iturralde, Pedro; Moro, Joe; *Nightclubs and other venues: Spain; Pardo, Jorge; Puertas, Josep; Regoli, Enrique; Roda, Ricard; Sambeat, Perico; Tebar, Ximo

Pasmik, Jaroslav: Balzar, Robert; Baron, Piotr; Dorůžka, David; Mácha, Stanislav; *Nightclubs and other venues: Czech Republic; Pokorný, Roman; Růžička, Karel, Jr.; Svoboda, Milan; Zbořil, Pavel

Passy, Charles: *Lewis, George (ii)

Patrick, James: *Nightclubs and other venues: USA (Buffalo); Parker, Charlie; Tinney, Al

Peerless, Brian: Beneke, Tex; Benford, Bill; Benford, Tommy; Bernhardt, Clyde; Best, Johnny; Bob Cats; Bonano, Sharkey; Brown, Vernon; Butterfield, Billy; Clambake Seven; Cutshall, Cutty; Elman, Ziggy; *Erwin, Pee Wee; Gramercy Five; Haggart, Bob; Hubble, Ed; Humphrey family; Lawson, Yank; *McGarity, Lou; Miller, Eddie; *Miller, Punch; O'Brien, Floyd; Privin, Bernie; Rosengarden, Bob; Shu, Eddie; Van Eps, George; World's Greatest Jazz Band

Pellegrinelli, Lara: Atkinson, Lisle; Essiet Essiet; Higgins, Patience; Hobgood, Laurence; Jones, Victor; Newsome, Sam; Riggins, Kariem; Slocum, Melissa

Pennell, Brenda: *Brecker, Randy; *Budwig, Monty; De Brest, Spanky; *Flory, Med; *Kloss, Eric; *Mondragon, Joe; *Ortega, Anthony Robert; *Tucker, George; *Wright, Gene

Pernet, Robert: Aerts, Jos; Bay, Francis; Bee, David; Bistrouille ADO; Bob Shots; Brenders, Stan; Breyre, Jos; Bruder, Rudy; Candrix, Fud; Claes, Johnny; Clark, Gus; Colignon, Raymond "Coco"; Compère, René; Coppieters, Fernand; Coppieters, Francis; Cotton City Jazz Band; De Bie, Ivon; De Boeck, Jeff; De Kers, Robert; Deloof, Gus; Dixie Stompers; Doucet, Clément; Excellos Five; Hot (ii); Hot Club de Belgique; Jazz Club de Belgique; Kluger, Jack; Naret, Bobby; *Nightclubs and other venues: Belgium; Omer, Jean; Ouwerx, John; Packay, Peter; Pâques, Jean; Pelzer, Jacques; Quersin, Benoit; Remue, Chas; Robert, Jean; Sadi, Fats; Sels, Jack; Van Ha Trio; Viseur, Gus

Phillips, David C.: *Ukulele

Pleasants, Henry: *Bailey, Mildred; *Crosby, Bing; *Laine, Cleo; *Sinatra, Frank; *Waters, Ethel

Porter, Lewis: Bassoon; *Bigard family; *Blakey, Art; Clarinet; *DeJohnette, Jack; Flute; *Gordon, Dexter; *Hawkins, Coleman; *Hodges, Johnny; *Johnson, J. J.; *Montgomery family; Oboe; Saxophone; *Williams, Tony; *Young, Lester

Potter, Jeff: Best, Denzil; Bobo, Willie; Correa, Mayuto; Da Costa, Paulinho; *Dahlander, Bert; *Deems, Barrett; Dunlop, Frankie; *Goodwin, Bill; *Johnson, Osie; *Kluger, Irv; Landrum, Richard; *Levey, Stan; *McCurdy, Roy; *Mason, Harvey; *Narell, Andy; *Richmond, Dannie; *Riley, Ben; *Roker, Mickey; *Shaughnessy, Ed; *Taylor, Art

Pressing, Jeff: *Bailey, Judy; *Banks, Don; *Buddle, Errol; *Burrows, Don; *Golla, George; *Gould, Tony; *Johnson, Frank; *Lyall, Graeme; *Rohde, Bryce; *Sangster, John; *Speers, Stewie; *Turnbull, Alan

Priestley, Brian: *Adams, George; *Amram, David; Burns, Ralph; Cirillo, Wally; Dennis, Willie; Heath, Ted; Hefti, Neal; *Henderson, Horace; Jazz Artists Guild; *Johnson, Howard (ii); Jones, Bobby; LaPorta, John; McCarthy, Albert; *Mingus Dynasty; *Morgan, Frank; New York Jazz Repertory Company; Rugolo, Pete; Sauter, Eddie; Strozier, Frank; *Walrath, Jack

Radano, Ronald M.: *Casa Loma Orchestra; Gray, Glen; Hunter, Alberta; *Thornhill, Claude

Ramana, Nishlyn: Coetzee, Basil; Faku, Feya; Fourie, Johnny; Goldberg, Morris; Gontsana, Lulu; Gumede, Sipho; Jansen, Robbie; Klaasen, Tandie; Mankunku, Winston; Matshikiza, Pat; Moeketsi, Kippie; Piliso, Ntemi

Rasmussen, Lars: *Ntshoko, Makaya

Rattenbury, Ken: *Allan, Jan; *Baker, Kenny; Baker, Shorty; Ball, Kenny; California Ramblers; Collins, Shad; Donaldson, Bobby; *Ericson, Rolf; Jordan, Taft; *Kaminsky, Max; McKinley, Ray; *Martin, Sara; Moore, Big Chief; Original Memphis Five; *Randall, Freddy; *Reece, Dizzy; Roy, Harry; *South, Harry; *Zurke, Bob

Rechniewski, Peter: SIMA

Rhyan, Dianna: *Caliman, Hadley; *Cherico, Gene; Herbert, Gregory; Isaacs, Ike (i); *Khan, Steve; *Lorber, Jeff; *McKusick, Hal; Ore, John; *Simpkins, Andy; *Watkins, Doug

Richards, Martin: Turney, Norris

Ridley, Harrison, Jr.: *Nightclubs and other venues: USA (Philadelphia)

Riis, Thomas: *Theater Owners' Booking Association

Rinzler, Paul: *Alexander, Monty; *Arvanitas, Georges; Baker, David; *Barron, Bill; *Barron, Kenny; *Beirach, Richard; Bonner, Joe; *Bright, Ronnell; *Bunch, John; *Cables, George; *Cameron, Jay; Coker, Dolo; *Davis, Walter; *De Arango, Bill; *Dunbar, Ted; *Friedman, Don; *Galper, Hal; *Gumbs, Onaje Allen; *Hakim, Sadik; *Hammond, Johnny; *Hyman, Dick; Jackson, Michael Gregory; *Jordan, Duke; *Kuhn, Steve; *Laine, Cleo; Legge, Wade; *Longo, Mike; *Mabern, Harold; *McCandless, Paul; *Mainieri, Mike; *Malachi, John; Manhattan Transfer; *Maria, Tania; Melvoin, Mike; *Moore, Glen; *Newborn, Calvin; *Newborn, Phineas; *Parlan, Horace; *Patterson, Don; *Pizzi, Ray; Powell, Richie; Previn, André; Rare Silk; *Schnitter, David; *Tompkins, Ross; *Tucker, Mickey

Roberts, David Thomas: Bloom, Rube; Schutt, Arthur

Roberts, John Storm: *Barretto, Ray; *Machito; Pozo, Chano; *Santamaria, Mongo; *Tjader, Cal

Robinson, J. Bradford: *Abercrombie, John; *Akiyoshi, Toshiko; *Allen, Henry ""Red"; *Anderson, Cat; *Baker, Chet; *Basie, Count; *Bellson, Louie; *Beiderbecke, Bix; Blanton, Jimmy; *Bley, Carla; *Blue note (i); Bolden, Buddy; *Brookmeyer, Bob; *Brown, Ray; Catlett, Sid; Chicago jazz; *Cobham, Billy; *Dodds, Baby; Dodds, Johnny; *Eldridge, Roy; Evans, Herschel; *Farlow, Tal; *Fitzgerald, Ella; Free jazz; *Garner, Erroll; *Getz, Stan; *Gonsalves, Paul; *Granz, Norman; *Grappelli, Stephane; *Hampton, Lionel; *Humes, Helen; Jarreau, Al; *Jones, Jo; Kansas City jazz; *Kenton, Stan; *Kirby, John; Komeda, Krysztof; *Konitz, Lee; *Lunceford, Jimmie; *Mulligan, Gerry; *Nanton, Tricky Sam; *Page, Walter; *Pass, Joe; *Pastorius, Jaco; *Pettiford, Oscar; Pollack, Ben; *Powell, Bud; Riff; *Rogers, Shorty; Scat singing; *Singleton, Zutty; Smith, Willie; *Stewart, Rex; *Sullivan, Maxine; *Swallow, Steve; *Swing (i); Territory band; *Terry, Clark; *Towner, Ralph; *Trent, Alphonso; *Tristano, Lennie; *Vocalese; *Webb, Chick; *Williams, Cootie; *Williams, Mary Lou; *Wilson, Teddy; *Yancey, Jimmy

Rockwell, John: Palmer, Robert

Rolland, Michel: *Nightclubs and other venues: Spain

Root, Deane L.: *Vamp

Rouder, Willa: Johnson, James P.

Rowe, Monk: Kellso, Jon-Erik; Murray, Albert; Stripling, Byron

Roy, James G., Jr.: *Russell, George

Russell, Bill: *Barbarin family; *Braud, Wellman; *Brunies family; Butler, Joe; Dutrey, Sam; Hug, Armand; Manetta, Manuel; *Morgan family; *Nightclubs and other venues: USA (Mississippi River, New Orleans); *Palmer, Roy; *Pierce, De De; *St. Cyr, Johnny; *Simeon, Omer; *Thomas, Joe (i); Thompson, Butch; Watkins, Joe; *Wiggs, Johnny

Rye, Howard: Ace of Hearts; AFRS; *Aiken, Gus; Ajax; *Alcorn, Alvin; Alexander, Charlie; *Allen, Ed; Allen, Lee; Allen, Moses; *Allen, Sam; American Music; American Record Corporation; *Ammons, Albert; Anderson, Ed; *Appleton, Joe; Arco; Arto; Atkins, Cholly; *Atlantic; Audiophile; Aurora; Autograph; Bagneris, Vernal; Baker, Mickey; Banks, Buddy (i); Banks, Buddy (ii); Banner; Baranco, Wilbert; Barclay; Barnes, Walter; Bartholomew, Dave; *Bechet, Sidney; Bennett, Buster; Bentley, Gladys; Berry Brothers; *Bishop, Wallace; Black and Blue; Black & White; *Black Lion; Black Patti; Black Swan; *Blake, Cyril; *Blake, Jerry; *Blakeney, Andy; Blu-disc; Blue, William Thornton; *Bluebird; *Blue Note (ii); Blue Star; Booker, Beryl; *Boone, Lester; Braddy, Pauline; *Bradford, Perry; *Brady, Stumpy; Bridgeport Die & Machine Co.; Bridges, Henry; *Briggs, Arthur; British Rhythm Society; Broadway; Brooks, Bubba; Brooks, Hadda; Brown, Charles; Brown, Olive; Brunious, Wendell; Brunswick; Bryant, Rusty; Buddy; *Bunn, Teddy; Burnside, Violet; *Burroughs, Alvin; Butler, Billy; *Butler, Jacques; *Butts, Jimmy; Calloway, Blanche; *Calypso; Cameo; Capitol; Cardinal; *Carey, Mutt; *Carlisle, Una Mae; Carroll, Bob; Carson, Norma; *Casey, Floyd; *Casimir, John; *Chambers, Elmer; Chamblee, Eddie; Champion; Cheatham, Jeannie; Cheatham, Jimmy; *Christian, Buddy; Circle (i); Clark, Garnet; Clark, June; Clarke, George; *Clarke, Pete; Claxtonola; Clay, Shirley; Clay, Sonny; Climax; Cobb, Junie; Cohn, Zinky; Cole, Rupert; *Coleman, Bill; Coles, Honi; Collectors Items; *Collins, Lee; *Columbia; Columbus, Chris; Commodore; Conaway, Sterling; Conners, Gene; Conqueror; Continental; Cooper, Ann; Cooper, Harry; Craig, Al; Crown; *Cuffee, Ed; Culley, Frank; Cupol; *Curtis, King; *Davies, John R. T.; Davis, Bert Etta "Birdie"; *Davis, Leonard; Davis, Martha; Davis, Maxwell; Davis, Tiny; *Dean, Demas; Decca; Delta; De Luxe; Derby (ii); Deutsche Grammophon; Dial, Harry; *Dickerson, Carroll; *Dickerson, R. Q.; *Dillard, Bill; *Dixon, Charlie; *Dixon, George; Donegan, Dorothy; *Dougherty, Eddie; DuConge, Peter; Edison; Edison-Bell; *Eldridge, Joe;

Electrola; *Elgar, Charlie; *Elliott, Sticky; Emerson; *EMI; Ertegun, Ahmet; Ertegun, Nesuhi; *Escudero, Ralph; *Evans, Stump; Everybody's; Exclusive; Famous; Felsted; Fields, Ernie; Fields, Geechie; Fowler, Lemuel; Fowler, T. J.; France, Percy; François, Ryan; *Frank, Edward; *Frazier, Cié; *Freeman family; Fulbright, Dick; Fuller, Bob; Gabriel, Percy; Gaines, Bubba; Gaines, Will; Gant, Cecil; Gary, Shelton; General; Gennett; *George, Karl; Gilt-edge; Glenn, Lloyd; Glover, Savion; Godley, A. G.; Goffin, Robert; *Gospel; Goudie, Frank "Big Boy"; Grace, Teddy; Grainger, Porter; Gramophone Company; Green, Chuck; Green, Lil; Greer, Big John; Grey Gull; Griffin Brothers; *Grimes, Tiny; Groove (ii); Guardsman; Guesnon, George; Gunther, Paul; Hadnott, Billy; Hall, René; *Hamilton, Jimmy; Handy, W. C.; Handy Record Company; *Harlem Hamfats; Harlequin; Harmograph; *Harmonica; Harmony (ii); Harris family; Harris, Ace; Harris, Wynonie; *Haughton, Chauncey; Hayes, Clifford; Haymes, Joe; *Hazel, Monk; Henderson, Rosa; *Henry, Haywood; *Herbert, Arthur; Herwin (i); Herwin (ii); Hicks, Edna; Hill, Ernest; Hines, Gregory; His Master's Voice; Hit of the Week; Holloway, Red; Hollywood; Hopkins, Linda; Hot Club de France; Hot Jazz Club of America; Hot Record Society; Houston, Joe; Howard, Camille; *Howard, Paul; Howard, Rosetta; Huck, Daniel; *Hutchinson, Jiver; Irwin, Cecil; Jackson, Bullmoose; Jackson, Mike; *Jacquet, Russell; James, George; *Jam session; Jazz (ii); Jazzology; Jazz Record; Jazz Society (i); Jazztone; Jefferson, Maceo; Jewel; Johnson, Buddy; Johnson, Cee Pee; Johnson, Floyd "Candy"; Johnson, Freddy; *Johnson, George; Johnson, Howard (i); Johnson, J. C.; *Johnson, Ken "Snake Hips"; *Johnson, Lem; Johnson, Otis; Jones, Betty Hall; Jones, Clarence M.; Jones, David; Jones, Dolly; Jones, Luke; *Jones, Snags; *Jones, Wallace; *Jones, Wardell; *Jordan, Louis; Jumbo, Freddie; *Jump; King; *King, Bertie; King, Saunders; King Jazz; King Porter; Kolax, King; *Kyle, Billy; Lambert, Donald; Lane, Morris; Lang-Worth; Lattimore, Harlan; Lee, Sonny; Letman, Johnny; Lewis, Charlie; *Lewis, Sabby; *Lewis, Willie; Liberty Music Shop; Liggins, Jimmy; Liggins, Joe; Lincoln; Lindström; Lobligeois, Roland; London; Longnon, Guy; Longshaw, Fred; Lonzo, Freddy; Lovett, Baby; Lowe, Sammy; Lucas, Buddy; McCoy, Viola; McDonald, Earl; McFay, Monk; McNeely, Big Jay; *McVea, Jack; *Mackel, Billy; *Madison, Bingie; Manor; Marathon; Marshall, Joe; Marsh Laboratories; *Martin, Chink; *Martin, Sara; Master (ii); Maxey, Leroy; Medallion; Melotone; Melrose, Frank; Meritt (i); Meritt (ii); Miller, Johnny; Miller, Taps; Milton, Roy; Mitchell, Freddie; Mitchell, Louis; Modern; *Montgomery, Little Brother; Montgomery Ward; *Moore, Alton; *Moore, Freddie; Moore, Johnny; Moore, Monette; Moore, Wild Bill; *Morand, Herb; Morris, Joe (i); Morris, Thomas; Mosby, Curtis; Mosely, Bob; Mosiello, Mike; Motley, Frank; Murphy, Rose; Muse (i); Myers, Bumps; Myers, Wilson; National (i); National (ii); National (iii); *Nesbitt, John; New York Recording Laboratories; *Nightclubs and other venues: Belgium, Egypt, England (London), France, Greece, Hungary, Malta, Morocco, Singapore, Sri Lanka, Spain, Switzerland, USA (Atlanta, Baltimore, Boston metropolitan area, Chicago, Cincinnati, Dallas, Indianapolis, Kansas City, New York, Philadelphia, Pittsburgh), Noone, Jimmy, Jr.; Nordskog; *Norris, Al; *O'Bryant, Jimmy; Odeon; Okeh; *Oliver, King; Oriole (i); Oriole (ii); Otis, Johnny; *Ousley, Harold; *Palmer, Earl; Panachord; *Paque, Glyn; Paradox; Paramount; Parham, Tiny; Parker, Sonny; Parlophone; Parrish, Avery; Pasquall, Jerome Don; Pathé; *Patton, Big John; *Peer, Beverly; Perfect; Perry, King; *Perry, Ray; Peyton, Benny; Phillips, Gene; *Pichon, Fats; *Pillars, Hayes; *Piron, A. J.; Plaza Music Company; *Porter, Gene; Porter, Jake; Porter, James; Porter, King; *Poston, Joe; Powell, Jesse; *Prestige; *Price, Jesse; *Price, Sammy; Profit, Clarence; *Pruitt, Carl; Prysock, Red; Puretone; Puritan; QRS; *Queen, Alvin; Rampart; *Rand, Odell; Ray, Carline; *RCA Victor; *Recording; Red Mack; Reeves, Reuben; *Reeves, Talcott; Regal (i); Regal (ii); Regal (iii); Regal-Zonophone; Regis; *Reinhardt family; Rex; Reynolds, Jimmy; Rhodes, Todd; Rhythm-and-blues; Rialto; *Richardson, Rodney; Richmond, June; Ricketts, Bob; Roane, Kenneth; Robinson, Eli; *Robinson, Ikey; Rodgers, Gene; *Rodriguez, Rod; Romeo; *Royal, Marshal; Russell, Johnny; St. Clair, Cyrus; Sampson, Deryck; Saucier, Edgar; Saunders, Red; Savoy (i); *Savoy (ii); Sayles, Emanuel; Scala; Scott, Clifford; Scott, Lloyd; Scott, Mabel; SESAC; Session (ii); *Shad, Bob; *Shepherd, Shep; *Sherman, Jimmy; *Shirley, Jimmy; Silva, Michael; Silvertone; Simon, Stafford; Simpson, Cassino; Singer, Hal; Sittin' in With; Slyde, Jimmy; Smith, Ben; Smith, Cal; Smith, Carrie; Smith, Clara; *Smith, Floyd; *Smith, Tab; Snow, Valaida; *Snowden, Elmer; Solo Art; Soloman, Clifford; Sonora; *Springer, Joe; *Stafford, George; Starr; Starr, Henry; Stevenson, George; Stevenson, Tommy; Stokes, Irvin; *Stone, Jesse; *Strong, Jimmy; Sturgis, Ted; Sun (i); Sunrise; Sunset; Sunset (ii); Sunshine; Super Disc; Superior; Supertone (i); Supertone (ii); Supertone (iii); Supreme; Swaggie; *Swayze, Edwin; *Sweatman, Wilbur; Swing (ii); Symphonola; *Take; Taylor, Sam "the Man"; Teddy Wilson School for Pianists; Tempo (ii); *Tharpe, Sister Rosetta; *Theater Owners' booking Association; *Thomas, Joe (i); Thomas, Joe (ii); *Thomas, Joe (iii); Thompson, Rudolph; Thompson, Sonny; Three Eddies; Timely Tunes; Tite, B. D.; Tolbert, Skeets; Towles, Nat; Transcription (ii); Transcription (iii); Treadwell, George; Triangle; Trotman, Lloyd; *Tucker, Bobby; Turner, Charlie; *Turner, Henry; *Turner, Joe (i); Tyler, Alvin "Red"; UHCA; *Ukulele; United; Variety (i); Variety (ii); Varsity; V-disc; Victor; Vocalion; Vogue; Walker, T-Bone; *Wallace, Cedric; Ware, Leonard; Washington, Buck; Washington, George; Washington, Mack; Washington, Steve; Watkins, Earl; Watts, Noble; *Wells, Johnny; *Wheeler, De Priest; Whistler; *White, Amos; White, Georgia; White, Morris; Wilborn, Dave; Wilcox, Eddie; Wilkerson, Don; Williams, Douglas; Williams, Eddie; *Williams, Elmer; Williams, J. Mayo; Williams, Nelson; Williams, Paul; *Williams, Pearlis; Williams, Rudy; Wilson, Buster; Wilson, Edith; Wilson, Garland; Wilson, Juice; Wilson, Lena; *Wilson, Quinn; Winburn, Anna Mae; *Witherspoon, Jimmy; Wynn, Al; Wynn, Big Jim; *Young, David A.; *Young, Eldee; Ysaguirre, Bob; Zardis, Chester; Zonophone

Sandmeyer, Aldo: *Ambrosetti, Flavio

Santi, Piero: *Gaslini, Giorgio

Schafer, William J.: Brass band; *Camelia Brass Band; *Eagle Band; *Eureka Brass Band; Excelsior Brass Band; Imperial Orchestra; *Olympia Brass Band; Olympia Orchestra; *Onward Brass Band (i); Onward Brass Band (ii); Original Tuxedo Orchestra; Ragtime; *Young Tuxedo Brass Band

Scheinin, Richard: *Lee, Jeanne

Schneider, Wayne: *Anthony, Ray; Bradley, Will; Castle, Lee; Clinton, Larry; *Donahue, Sam; Gray, Jerry; *Hite, Les; Jones, Isham; May, Billy; Zentner, Si

Schuller, Gunther: *Afro-Cuban jazz; Arrangement; *Coleman, Ornette; *Ellington, Duke; *Evans, Gil; *Jam session; *Krupa, Gene; Morton, Jelly Roll; *Moten, Bennie; Smith, Buster; Stomp; Third stream; Walking bass

Schulz, Klaus: Auer, Vera; Austrian All Stars; Bachträgl, Erich; Cech, Christoph; Drewo, Karl; George, Fatty; Grah, Bill; *Gulda, Friedrich; Hermann, Heinz von; Kleinschuster, Erich; Koglmann, Franz; Koller, Hans; Landl, Ernst; Manndorff, Andy; Miklin, Karlheinz; *Nightclubs and other venues: Austria; Pauer, Fritz; Pirchner, Werner; Puschnig, Wolfgang; Reform Art Unit; Scherer, Uli; Sokal, Harry; Upper Austrian Jazz Orchestra; Vienna Art Orchestra; Winter, Horst

Schwab, Erik: *Nightclubs and other venues: USA (Seattle)

Schwalm, Peter: *Ambrosetti, Franco; *Antolini, Charly; Court, Raymond; *Eckinger, Isla; *Gruntz, George; *Klein, Oscar; *Moeckel, Thomas; Schmidli, Peter; *Schwaller, Roman; Trippel, Fritz

Scott, Andrew: *Nightclubs and other venues: USA (Boston metropolitan area)

Shand, John: Abrahams, Chris; Bertles, Bob; Dean, Roger; Gebert, Bobby; Hunter, Steve; Jones, David (ii); McGann, Bernie; Orszaczky, Jackie; Treloar, Phil

Shaw, Arnold: Bailey, Pearl

Shaw, Lew: *American Federation of Jazz Societies

Sheridan, Chris: *Bolton, Dupree; Brooks, Tina; Deuchar, Jimmy; *Elizalde, Fred; *Green, Urbie; Harding, Buster; Harriott, Joe; Henderson, Bill; *Johnson, Gus; Jones, Eddie; Jones, Harold; Jones, Rufus; Keane, Shake; Keenan, Norman; Killian, Al; *Mitchell, Grover; Most, Sam; Plater, Bobby; *Recording; Rutherford, Rudy; Smith, Jimmie; *Taylor, John; *Wilder, Joe; Williams, Claude; *Winstone, Norma

Shipton, Alyn: *Accordion; *Acoustic bass guitar; Banjo; Barker, Blue Lu; Barker, Danny; Battle of bands; Celesta; Cola, Kid Sheik; *Cornet; Double bass; Firehouse Five Plus Two; Firman, Bert; Garland, Ed "Montudi"; *Goodman, Benny; *Hall family; *Hall, Al; Harpsichord; Jones, Dill; Kelley, Peck; Keppard, Louis; Kohlman, Freddie; Lafertin, Fapy; *Landers, Wes; Lindsay, John; *Mandolin; *Martin, Chink; Martyn, Barry; *Mitchell, George; Miller, Sing; *Morgan family; Morris, Butch; *Mute; New Black Eagle Jazz Band; *Nightclubs and other venues: England (London), Netherlands; Organ; *Paul, Emanuel; Piccolo bass; Reed organ; Sherman, Herman; Skiffle; Slap-bass; Slap-tonguing; Smith, Jabbo; *Stone, Jesse; String band; *Teagarden family; Tiple; Trad; *Violin; *Waller, Fats; Waso; Young, Trummy

Simmen, Johnny: *Alvis, Hayes; *Autrey, Herman; *Berry, Emmett; *Buckner, Teddy; *Bunn, Teddy; *Carlisle, Una Mae; *Coleman, Bill; *Kelly, George; *Kyle, Billy; *Leeman, Cliff; Mills Blue Rhythm Band; Newton, Frankie; Savoy Sultans (i); Savoy Sultans (ii); *Shaw, Arvell; *Simmons, John; *Smith, Russell; *Turner, Joe (i); *Wettling, George

Simon, Géza Gábor: *Bacsik, Elek; *Beamter, Jenő; *Benkó, Sándor; Binder, Károly; *Buttola, Ede; *Chappy; Deseő, Csaba; Dresch, Mihály; Dudás, Lajos; *Filu; Gardony, Laszlo; Grencsó, István; Ittzés, Tamás; *Kőrössy, János; *Kovács, Andor; *Kovács, Gyula; Magyar Jazzkutatási Társaság; *Martiny, Lajos; Pannon Jazz; *Pege, Aladár; Szabó, Sándor; *Szabados, György; *Szabo, Frank; *Szabó, Gábor; Szakcsi Lakatos, Béla; *Tabányi, Mihály; Trio Midnight; Vukán, George; *Zoller, Attila

Skrimshire, Nevil: Amstell, Billy; Archer, Tony; *Babbington, Roy; *Baldock, Kenny; *Branscombe, Alan; Clare, Kenny; Colyer, Ken; *Condon, Les; *Dvorak, Jim; Featherstonhaugh, Buddy; *Green, Dave; *Griffiths, Malcolm; Harvey, Eddie; Hayes, Harry; *Heatley, Spike; *Kinsey, Tony; *Krahmer, Carlo; Laurie, Cy; McQuater, Tommy; *Mann, Tony; *Mumford, John; *Parnell, Jack; Phillips, Sid; *Purbrook, Colin; *Pyne, Chris; *Pyne, Mick; *Shaw, Hank; *Skidmore, Jimmy; Smith, Betty; Smythe, Pat; Squadronaires; *Sunshine, Monty; *Williams, John (iii)

Smith, Ernie: *Films

Smith, Gregory E.: *Abene, Mike; *Clark, Sonny; *Dailey, Al; *Harris, Gene; *Hope, Elmo; *Kellaway, Roger; *Lawson, Hugh; Mayers, Lloyd; *Norris, Walter; *Redd, Freddie

Smith, Steve: *Ali family; *Bell, Kelvyn; Burnham, Charles; Carter, Daniel; Coleman, Anthony; D'Angelo, Andrew; Dickey, Whit; Driscoll, Kermit; Fowlkes, Curtis; Goldberg, Ben; Ibarra, Susie; Mandel, Howard; Nolet, Jim; Pavone, Mario; Peet, Wayne; Rodriguez, E. J.; Sarin, Michael

Southern, Eileen: Blake, Eubie; Cook, Will Marion; Europe, James Reese

Spring, Howard: Dance

Starkie, Walter: *Elizalde, Fred

Strunk, Steven: *Albam, Manny; Altered scale; *Berry, Bill; *Brown, Marshall; *Fischer, Clare; *Golson, Benny; Graas, John; Handy, George; Harmony (i); *Harris, Little Benny; *Hill, Teddy; *Hooper, Les; *LaBarbera family; Mandel, Johnny; *Melillo, Mike; Nestico, Sammy; Ogerman, Claus; *Paich, Marty; Phillips, Sonny; Richards, Johnny

Such, David G.: *Anderson, Fred; *Brown, Marion; *Ewart, Douglas; Garnett, Carlos; *Hemphill, Julius; *Howard, Noah; *Lancaster, Byard; *Lowe, Frank; McIntyre, Makanda Ken; *Tyler, Charles

Sudhalter, Richard: Bose, Stirling; Edwards, Eddie; Goldkette, Jean; Klein, Manny; LaRocca, Nick; McPartland, Dick; McPartland, Jimmy; Rollini, Art; Shields family; *Wiley, Lee

Sugiyama, Kazunori: Abe, Kaoru; Akiyama, Kazumasa; Aramaki, Shigeo; Ayado, Chie; *DIW; *Fujiwara, Kiyoto; Furuya, Takashi; Hara, Dairiki; Hara, Tomonao; Hayasaka, Sachi; Hayashi, Eiichi; Higashihara, Rikiya; *Hino, Motohiko; *Hino, Terumasa; Honda, Takehiro; Honda, Tamaya; *Honda, Toshiyuki; Igarashi, Akitoshi; Igarashi, Issei; Ikeda, Atsushi; Ikeda, Yoshio; Imada, Masaru; *Ino, Nobuyoshi; Inomata, Takeshi; Inoue, Yosuke; Itabashi, Fumio; *Itoh, Kimiko; Kako, Takashi; Kanai, Hideto; *Karashima, Fumio; Kataoka, Yuzo; Katori, Yoshihiko; Kawashima, Tetsuro; *Kikuchi, Masabumi; Kitagawa, Kyoshi; *Kitamura, Eiji; Kobayashi, Yoichi; *Kondo, Toshinori; Koyake, Tamami; Koyama, Shota; Lee, Keiko; *Maeda, Norio; Maruyama, Shigeo; *Masuda, Ichiro; Masuda, Mikio; *Masuo, Yoshiaki; *Matsumoto, Hidehiko; Matsushima, Keiji; Mine, Kosuke; Miyake, Martha; *Miyama, Toshiyuki; *Miyazawa, Akira; Mori, Kenji; Moriya, Junko; Moriyama, Takeo; Moriyasu, Shotaro; *Mukai, Shigeharu; Murakami, Hiroshi; Murakami, Shuichi; Murata, Yoichi; Nakagawa, Eijiro; Nakagawa, Masami; Nakaji, Hideaki; Nakamure, Sadanori; Nanri, Fumio; Noriki, Soichi; Oda, Satoru; Oida, Toshio; Oishi, Manabu; *Oki, Itaru; *Okoshi, Tiger; Okuchi, Junichiro; Okudaira, Shingo; Onishi, Junko; Osaka, Masahiko; Osamu, Koichi; Otsuka, George; *Sakata, Akira; *Sato, Masahiko; Sawada, Shungo; Sayama, Masahiro; Senba, Kiyohiko; Shibuya, Takeshi; *Shimizu, Jun; Shiina, Yutaka; Suzuki, Hiromasa; *Suzuki, Isao; *Suzuki, Shoji; *Suzuki, Yoshio; Tada, Seiji; *Takahashi, Tatsuya; *Takase, Aki; Takayanagi, Masayuki; Takeuchi, Nao; Terai, Naoko; *Togashi, Masahiko; Toyama, Yoshio; Uematsu, Takao; *Umezu, Kazutoki; Watanabe, Fumio; *Watanabe, Kazumi; *Watanabe, Sadao; *Yagi, Masao; Yamada, Joh; Yamaguchi, Mabumi; Yamamoto, Tsuyoshi; *Yamashita, Yosuke; Yoshioka, Hideaki; Yoshizawa, Motoharu

Tallmadge, William H.: *Watters, Lu

Taylor, J. R.: *Keppard, Freddie; *Kirk, Andy; Miley, Bubber; *Roberts, Luckey; *Spanier, Muggsy; *Teschemacher, Frank

Taylor, J. R.: *Williams, Clarence

Thacker, Eric: Allyn, David; Arnet, Jan; Hot (i); *McVea, Jack

Theroux, Gary: *Ayers, Roy; *Curtis, King; *Friedman, David; *Gibbs, Terry; Gordon, Joe; *Mantler, Mike; *Pike, Dave; *Sheldon, Jack; Williams, Richard; *Young, Larry

Tovey, Michael: Barrelhouse jazz; *Burbank, Albert; *Casimir, John; *Duhé, Lawrence; Hightower, Willie; *Hill, Chippie; *Jones, Snags; *Manone, Wingy; *Miles, Lizzie; *Montgomery, Little Brother; *O'Bryant, Jimmy; *Price, Sammy; Roppolo, Leon; Tate, Erskine; Taylor, Jasper; *Valentine, Kid Thomas; *Williams, Pearlis

Tucker, Mark: *Allen, Steve; Brown, Les; Jungle music; Lewis, Ted; Mills Brothers; Pastor, Tony; Riddle, Nelson; *Schuller family; Scott, Hazel; *Severinsen, Doc; *Transcription (i); Washingtonians

Tucker, Sherrie: Bryant, Clora; Historiography; Sager, Jane; Smith, Viola; Women

Ullman, Michael: *Ali family; *Benjamin, Joe; *Blackwell, Ed; *Cyrille, Andrew; *Daniels, Eddie; *Davis, Art; Fields, Herbie; *Gomez, Eddie; *Graves, Milford; *Higgins, Billy; *Jones, Philly Joe; *Kamuca, Richie; *Moreira, Airto; *Murray, Sunny; *Peacock, Gary; *Perkins, Bill

Vaché, Warren, Sr.: Addison, Bernard; *Braff, Ruby; Casey, Al; *Clooney, Rosemary; Corcoran, Corky; *Evans, Doc; *Flanigan, Phil; Haymer, Herbie; *Jerome, Jerry; *Marsala, Joe; Marsala, Marty; Matlock, Matty; *Mercer, Johnny; *Most, Abe; *Nash family; Pettis, Jack; *Pizzarelli, Bucky; *Pizzarelli, John; Powell, Rudy; Sedric, Gene; Wolverines

Vacher, Peter: Buckner, Milt; Buckner, Ted; Callender, Red; Claxton, Rozelle; Darensbourg, Joe; Davern, Kenny; Durham, Eddie; Edwards, Teddy; *Forrest, Jimmy; Green, Thurman; *Heard, J. C.; *Middlebrooks, Wilfred; Peagler, Curtis; Roberts, Caughey; Smalls, Cliff; Turnham, Floyd; Wiggins, Gerry; Woods, Chris

Vanberg, Vidar: Bergh, Øivind; Bergheim, Kristian; Big Chief Jazzband; Engstrøm, Kalle; Flagstad, Michael; Greenberg, Rowland; Hauger, Kristian; Iversen, Einar; *Johansen, Bjørn; Kapstad, Egil; Normann, Robert; Ottersen, Frank; Sønstevold, Gunnar

Van den Berg, Erik: Bijma, Greetje; BIM; Cuypers, Leo; Dikker, Loek; Jannah, Denise; *Nightclubs and other venues: Netherlands; van Manen, Willem; Zes Winden, De

Van Eyle, Wim: Altena, Maarten; Beck, Pia; *Bishop, Wallace; Boeren, Eric; Borstlap, Michiel; *Breuker, Willem; Bunink, Floris Nico; Burton, Ann; Courbois, Pierre; De Graaff, Rein; De Vries, Louis; Dutch Swing College Band; Engels, John; Haverhoek, Henk; Hinze, Chris; Hoogendijk, Jarmo; Houdini's; Houtkamp, Luc; Ilcken, Wessel; Jacobs, Pim; Janssen, Guus; Landesbergen, Frits; Loevendie, Theo; Masman, Theo Uden; *Mengelberg, Misha; Meyer, Johnny; Morks, Jan; Muziek en Theater Netwerk; *Nightclubs and other venues: Netherlands; Noordijk, Piet; Overwater, Tony; Peeters, Joep; Povel, Ferdinand; Ramblers; Reys, Rita; Schilperoort, Peter; See, Cees; Stichting Jazz en Geïmproviseerde Muziek in Nederland; Van Bavel, Rob; van den Dungen, Ben; Van Dijk, Louis; van Kemenade, Paul; Van Roon, Mark; Van Rooyen, Ack; Van Ruller, Jesse; *Van 't Hof, Jasper; Van 't Hoff, Ernst; Van Vliet, Toon; Vloeimans, Eric; Weersma, Melle; Willebrandts, Dick

Van Vorst, Paige: Chicago Rhythm Kings; *Harlem Hamfats

Vaughan, Sheila M.: *Kersey, Kenny

Vaughn, Genevieve: *Russo, Bill

Vincent, Julian F. V.: Banjulele; *Ukulele

Voigt, John: Bennett, Max; *Betts, Keter; Bond, Jimmy; Counce, Curtis; Crosby, Israel; *Egan, Mark; Gilmore, Steve; *Grimes, Henry; Haas, Eddie; *Heard, John; Izenzon, David; James, Stafford; *Johnson, Reggie; Laird, Rick; *McClure, Ron; *Nasser, Jamil; *Phillips, Barre; Stinson, Albert; *Taylor, Gene; Totah, Nobby

Vollmer, Albert: Barefield, Eddie; *Harlem Blues and Jazz Band; Purnell, Keg; Ramirez, Ram

Waggoner, Andrew: Brown, Sam; Brown, Sonny; *Carvin, Michael; *Fuller, Curtis; *Green, Grant; *Ponder, Jimmy; Vick, Harold

Wang, Richard: *Brubeck, Dave; *Cole, Nat "King"; *Jamal, Ahmad; *Noone, Jimmie; *Goodman, Benny; Shaw, Artie

Wasserberger, Igor: *Dašek, Rudolf

Webster, Derek: *Bechet Legacy; *Soprano Summit; *Wilber, Bob

Weir, Bob: Cohn, Sonny; Countsmen; Larkin, Milt; Metronome All Stars; *Price, Jesse; Saints and Sinners; *Williams, Joe; *Witherspoon, Jimmy

Westin, Lars: Åberg, Lennart; Adåker, Ulf; *Allan, Jan; Andersson, Krister; *Arnold, Harry; Arnström, Kenneth; *Babs, Alice; Bergcrantz, Anders; *Billberg, Rolf; Bingert, Hector; *Björksten, Hacke; Brehm, Simon; Broberg, Bosse; *Dahlander, Bert; Danielsson, Lars; *Danielsson, Palle; *Domnérus, Arne; Dragon; *Ehrling, Thore; Einarsdotter, Elise; *Ellboj, Lulle; *Ericson, Rolf; *Eriksberg, Folke; Erstrand, Lars; *Gullin, Lars; Gustafsson, Mats; *Gustafsson, Rune; *Hallberg, Bengt; *Hasselgård, Stan; *Hedrenius, Gugge; *Hultcrantz, Torbjörn; Johansson, Åke; *Johansson, Jan; Johansson, Ulf; Kenneth; Knutsson, Jonas; *Laine, Bob; Landgren, Nils; *Larsson, Rolf; Lindberg, Nils; Lundgren, Jan; *Metronome; *Nilson, Gunnar; *Norin, Carl-Henrik; *Norman, Charlie; *Österwall, Seymour; *Persson, Åke; Phontastic; *Rena Rama; *Riedel, Georg; *Rosengren, Bernt; Rundqvist, Gösta; *Sandström, Nisse; *Sjösten, Lars; *Sonet; *Svenska Hotkvintetten; Svensson, Esbjörn; *Swanerud, Thore; *Theselius, Gösta; *Törner, Gösta; *von Eichwald, Håkan; Wallgren, Jan; Wallin, Per Henrik; *Werner, Lasse; *Wickman, Putte

Whitehead, Kevin: Allen, Eddie; Baars, Ab; Bergin, Sean; Braam, Michiel; D'Agaro, Daniele; Delius, Tobias; Fishkind, Larry; Fuhler, Cor; Glerum, Ernst; ICP; Joode, Wilbert de; Termos, Paul; van Bergen, Peter; Van Duynhoven, Martin; Verploegen, Angelo; Wierbos, Wolter

Whiteoak, John: *Bailey, Judy; *Banks, Don; *Buddle, Errol; *Burrows, Don; *Golla, George; *Gould, Tony; *Johnson, Frank; *Lyall, Graeme; *Rohde, Bryce; *Sangster, John; *Speers, Stewie; *Turnbull, Alan

Wideröe, Arild: *Chaix, Henri

Wiedemann, Erik: Axen, Bent; Bonfils, Kjeld; *Botschinsky, Allan; Christensen, Bernhard; *Clausen, Thomas; *Dørge, Pierre; Eiberg, Valdemar; *Emborg, Jørgen; Esbensen, Egon; Ewans, Kai; Fabricius-Bjerre, Bent; Foss, Niels; *Glindemann, Ib; Hagemann, Henry; Harlem Kiddies; Henriksen, Bruno; *Jaedig, Bent; *Kroner, Erling; Lington, Otto; Mathisen, Leo; *Mazur, Marilyn; *Mikkelborg, Palle; Moseholm, Erik; Parker, Erik; *Radioens Big Band; Radiojazzgruppen (i); Rasmussen, Peter; *Riel, Alex; Roger Henrichsen, Børge; *Savery, Finn; Skjoldborg, Anker; *Stief, Bo; *Tchicai, John; Tuxen, Erik; *Vinding, Mads

Wild, David: *Altschul, Barry; *Anderson, Ray; *Bartz, Gary; *Bluiett, Hamiet; *Coleman, George; Curson, Ted; *Davis, Nathan; Draper, Ray; *Ford, Ricky; *Fortune, Sonny; *Grossman, Steve; *Harper, Billy; *Hoggard, Jay; *Klemmer, John; *Lawrence, Arnie; Lawrence, Azar; *Lewis, George (ii); Little, Booker; *Lloyd, Charles; *Marsalis family; *Maupin, Bennie; Newman, David "Fathead"; Owens, Charles; *Priester, Julian; *Robinson, Perry; *Simmons, Sonny; Tabackin, Lew; *Ward, Carlos

Will, Patrick T.: *Bernhardt, Warren; *Gale, Eric; *Gottlieb, Danny; Klugh, Earl; Lee, David; *Mays, Lyle; Return to Forever; *Sebesky, Don; *Steps Ahead; *Spyro Gyra

Williams, J. Kent: *Bailey, Dave; *Bailey, Donald; *Brooks, Roy; *Bunker, Larry; *Butler, Frank; *Cobb, Jimmy; *Foster, Al; *Gladden, Eddie; *Hamilton, Jeff; *Hanna, Jake; *Hart, Billy; *Hayes, Louis; *La Roca, Pete; *Lewis, Mel; McBrowne, Lennie; Morgan, Sonny; *Perkins, Walter; *Tate, Grady; Thigpen, Ben; *Thigpen, Ed

Williams, Martin: *Lewis, Meade "Lux"

Wilmer, Val: Abrahams, Brian; Acquaye, Speedy; A.F.O.; Afrika, Mervyn; Alpha Cottage School; Alphonso, Roland; Badie, Peter; Barclay, Bob; Black, James; Blank, Roger; *Bolton, Dupree; Boudreaux, John, Jr.; Bradshaw, Sonny; Bridgers, Aaron; Burrowes, Roy; Cartwright, Deirdre; Caton, Lauderic; Cobbs, Call; Cole, Gracie; Cooper, Leroy; *Cooper, Lindsay; *Crosby, Gary; Cross, Earl; Deniz family; *Deppa, Claude; De Souza, Yorke; Doyle, Arthur; Drummond, Don; *Ellington, Ray; Falana, Mike; Fielder, Alvin; *Frank, Edward; Gaynair, Wilton "Bogey"; Grimes, Carol; Guest Stars; Hamilton, Andy; Jazz and People's Movement; Jazz Jamaica; Jazz Warriors; Laka Daisical; Lastie, Melvin; Lewis, Art ""Shaki""; McCook, Tommy; Murphy, Allen; *Nightclubs and other venues: England (London); Perrilliatt, Nat; Pitterson, Pete; Quaye, Terri; Ranglin, Ernest; Rayner, Alison; Rigby, Joe; Rivers, James; Scott, Little Jimmy; Simmons, Art; Skatalites; Smith, Ruthie; Stephenson, Louis; Terroade, Kenneth; Tyndale, George; Walker, Sammy; Whitehead, Annie; Wilson, Herman; Yancy, Youseff

Wilson, Clive: *Hall family

Wilson, Olly: *Brown, Clifford; *Clarke, Kenny; *Jones family; *Roach, Max

Witmer, Robert: Ax; Back; Ballad; Bend; Blow; Bomb; Book; Chops; Comp; *Fake book; Fill; Honk; Lead; Lead sheet; Lick; Lip; *Notation; Standard

Woolley, Stan: *Israels, Chuck; *Liston, Melba; *McKibbon, Al; *Stamm, Marvin; *Wallace, Bennie

Worsfold, Sally-Ann: *Burch, John; *Fawkes, Wally; *McNair, Harold; *Napper, Kenny; *Nichols, Keith; *Parker, Johnny;

Patterson, Ottilie; *Shannon, Terry; *Stobart, Kathy; *Tomkins, Trevor; Taylor, Mike

Yanow, Scott: Berman, Sonny; Castro, Joe; Doggett, Bill; Duke, George; Fuller, Walter; Hawkins, Erskine; *Hicks, John; Hurley, Clyde; Jones, Jonah; Jones, Reunald; Lawson, Janet; *Lamond, Don; *Leviev, Milcho; *Lightsey, Kirk; *McCann, Les; Maini, Joe; Matthews, Dave; Montrose, Jack; Mullens, Moon; New York Jazz Quartet; *Nistico, Sal (ii); Nottingham, Jimmy; *Pierce, Nat; Rebillot, Pat; *Rodney, Red; Ruiz, Hilton; Sherock, Shorty; *Shew, Bobby; Spivak, Charlie; Stoller, Alvin; Sullivan, Ira; *Thompson, Lucky; Vance, Dick; *Watrous, Bill; Webster, Freddie; West, Doc; *Williams, James; Williamson, Stu; Wilson, Jack; Wilson, Phil

Zager, Daniel: *Allen, Walter C.; Baraka, Amiri; Dance, Stanley; *Dapogny, James; DeMicheal, Don; Gitler, Ira; Gleason, Ralph J.; Hoefer, George; Lyons, Len; Ramsey, Fred; *Rusch, Bob; Shapiro, Nat; Simon, George T.; Smith, Charles Edward; *Stearns, Marshall W.; *Wanzo, Mel

Zenni, Stefano: Actis Dato, Carlo; *Basso, Gianni; Battaglia, Stefano; *Cerri, Franco; Cesàri, Umberto; Colombo, Eugenio; Coscia, Gianni; *Cuppini, Gil; Dalla Porta, Paolino; Damiani, Paolo; D'Andrea, Franco; DeVito, Maria Pia; *Di Battista, Stefano; Di Castri, Furio; Egea; Fasoli, Claudio; Fioravanti, Ettore; Flores, Luca; Fresu, Paolo; *Gaslini, Giorgio; Gatto, Roberto; Gebbia, Gianni; Ghiglioni, Tiziana; Giammarco, Maurizio; Intra, Enrico; Italian Instabile Orchestra; Maltese, Stefano; Manusardi, Guido; Marcotulli, Rita; Minafra, Pino; *Nightclubs and other venues: Italy; Ottaviano, Roberto; Petrin, Umberto; Philology; Piana, Dino; Pieranunzi, Enrico; Raja, Mario; *Rava, Enrico; Red; *Rotondo, Nunzio; Salis, Antonello; Schiaffini, Giancarlo; Schiano, Mario; *Soul Note; Splasc; Tommaso, Bruno; Tommaso, Giovanni; Tonolo, Pietro; Tononi, Tiziano; Tramontana, Sebi; Trovesi, Gianluigi; Urbani, Massimo; *Valdambrini, Oscar

Zieff, Bob: *Allen, Ed; Austin, Lovie; *Carey, Mutt; *Dickerson, Carroll; Dunn, Johnny; Green, Charlie; Jones, Claude; Ladnier, Tommy; Stark, Bobby; Williams, Sandy